THE DICTIONARY OF

Drink

A Guide to Every Type of Beverage

D1625462

THE DICTIONARY OF
Drink
A Guide to Every Type of Beverage

Graham & Susan Edwards

SUTTON PUBLISHING

This book was first published in 1988 under the title
The Language of Drink

This new revised edition first published in 2007 by
Sutton Publishing Limited · Phoenix Mill
Thrupp · Stroud · Gloucestershire · GL5 2BU

Copyright © Graham and Susan Edwards, 2007

All rights reserved. No part of this publication may be reproduced, stored in a retrieval system, or transmitted, in any form, or by any means, electronic, mechanical, photocopying, recording or otherwise, without the prior permission of the publisher and copyright holders.

Whilst every care has been taken to ensure that all measurements and details given in the recipes are correct, the publisher cannot accept any responsibility for any inaccuracies.

British Library Cataloguing in Publication Data
A catalogue record for this book is available from the British Library

ISBN 978-0-7509-4245-4

Typeset in 9/10pt Joanna.
Typesetting and origination by
Sutton Publishing Limited.
Printed and bound in India by Imago.

KU-023-199

CONTENTS

PREFACE

Thank you for purchasing this new edition and we hope you get as much pleasure and information from it as we have had researching and consulting it.

It is now almost 20 years since this book was first published and many things have happened within the drinks industry.

Keeping up with these 'changes' has been a mammoth task and there is always a risk that some data may have been missed or over-looked.

We have seen a great surge in 'new world' wines and also wines from less well-known wine-producing countries appearing onto the market. Also the interest in soft drinks and mineral waters is very much in all our minds.

With more of these wines and soft drinks becoming available and with label terms that can be very confusing, the up-date has tried to address these issues making for quick reference.

The book has become a kind of 'album' to us as we find more and more entries. Like stamp collectors we find better examples of existing entries, find many new entries and of course have many entries that are now no longer available and whilst it would be logical to remove them the information will still of interest to some readers who may still wish to know about a particular beverage past or present and would not have a previous edition of the dictionary or other source of reference.

We have included mineral waters in this up-date. The interest in bottled waters has increased immensely and the contents of these waters is important for those on special diets, etc. We have only included the main minerals in the listing (where available) and only included additional minerals if over 1mg/l.

This edition has started to see the inclusion of internet addresses (www and 'e'mail) and were correct as of June 2006. The internet is a great source of information – but searching through it can be both time consuming and not always accurate (and you need a computer at hand which is not always convenient). Log on to Château and you will see our point with over four and a half million sites!

Graham Edwards
Guernsey

E MAIL ENTRY

If readers have any items/corrections/up-dates that are not included in this edition, they are welcome to send the details to the author's 'e'mail address below.

Senders are requested to put the information in the 'e' mail itself and NOT as an attachment as any attachments will NOT be opened on any account!

Information can also be sent to the publishers for re-direction to the authors.

Thank you for your future assistance.

'e'mail address: gnsycdps@guernsey.net

ACKNOWLEDGEMENTS

If we were to mention everyone who had assisted us in the compilation of this work then another book would be required to include them all. Over the last eighteen years we have solicited the help of countless in our quest for the correct information. So to all the thousands of trade and individual friends our deepest thanks.

We would, though, like to say a very special thanks to our families, our colleagues at work and the Tastevins de Guernesey, for their original encouragement in seeing the work through, especially when our enthusiasm was flagging.

How This Book Works

This book is not meant to provide a *complete* answer to a question and was never designed to be an encyclopaedia (there are many excellent examples on the market to fill that role). It is as a comprehensive, single volume point of reference for a word, saying, name, etc., required quickly and sought alphabetically (regardless of subject area or word structure), that it serves its main purpose.

To this end 'Château X' or 'Clos X' appear under 'C' and not 'X' – the principle being that these are known and used in this form, the 'Château' or 'Clos' being a part of the name. Many entries starting with 'Le', 'La' or 'Les', however, are not given under 'L' as many readers may be uncertain as to which form applies, or indeed as to whether or not the definite article is considered a part of the name.

Many of the words originating in the Eastern Bloc, Arabian and Asian countries have gained a variety of spellings derived during their phonetic transcription into anglicised or western forms. These variants have been included wherever possible.

In most instances information is very concise. The names of the vineyards, wineries and châteaux are entered principally for spelling and location purposes; further information can be obtained easily, either elsewhere in this book or in other specialist books on the relevant region, once this has been identified. For example, looking up 'Château Musar' will quickly identify it as a wine from the Lebanon. Similarly, once 'Château Tahbilk' is known to be Australian, a book on Australian wines can be consulted for further information. There are also a number of entries for products which are no longer in production. These have been included because it is often difficult to find definitions in other reference books.

There are around 7,500 German vineyards listed, each having an individual entry giving its location. The entries are laid out as follows: first the *anbaugebiet* (one of the thirteen German wine regions); then its *bereich* (a subdivision of this region); the *grosslage* (a grouping of villages within the *bereich*); and the village itself (the einzellage). The abbreviations used are (Anb), (Ber), (Gro), (Vil), (Vin). These entries are cross-referenced so that any one detail can help lead to a specific identification.

Cocktails are entered under the names by which they were given to the authors. Recipes vary greatly from barman to barman and where possible they have been averaged but, as the reader will see, some cocktail names embrace many different recipes. For the beer entries the original gravity (O.G.) and/or alcohol by volume is given.

Finally it is worth noting that entries can be deceptive in their brevity. In order not to waste space, maintain comprehensiveness and cater for all levels of expertise, entries are cross-referenced for beverage-related words and are not simplified where the additional information can be gleaned by following these up. In this way there is virtually no limit to the reading which could result from looking up one initial word, and a vast amount of knowledge can be gained from a start anywhere among the 57,000 or so entries.

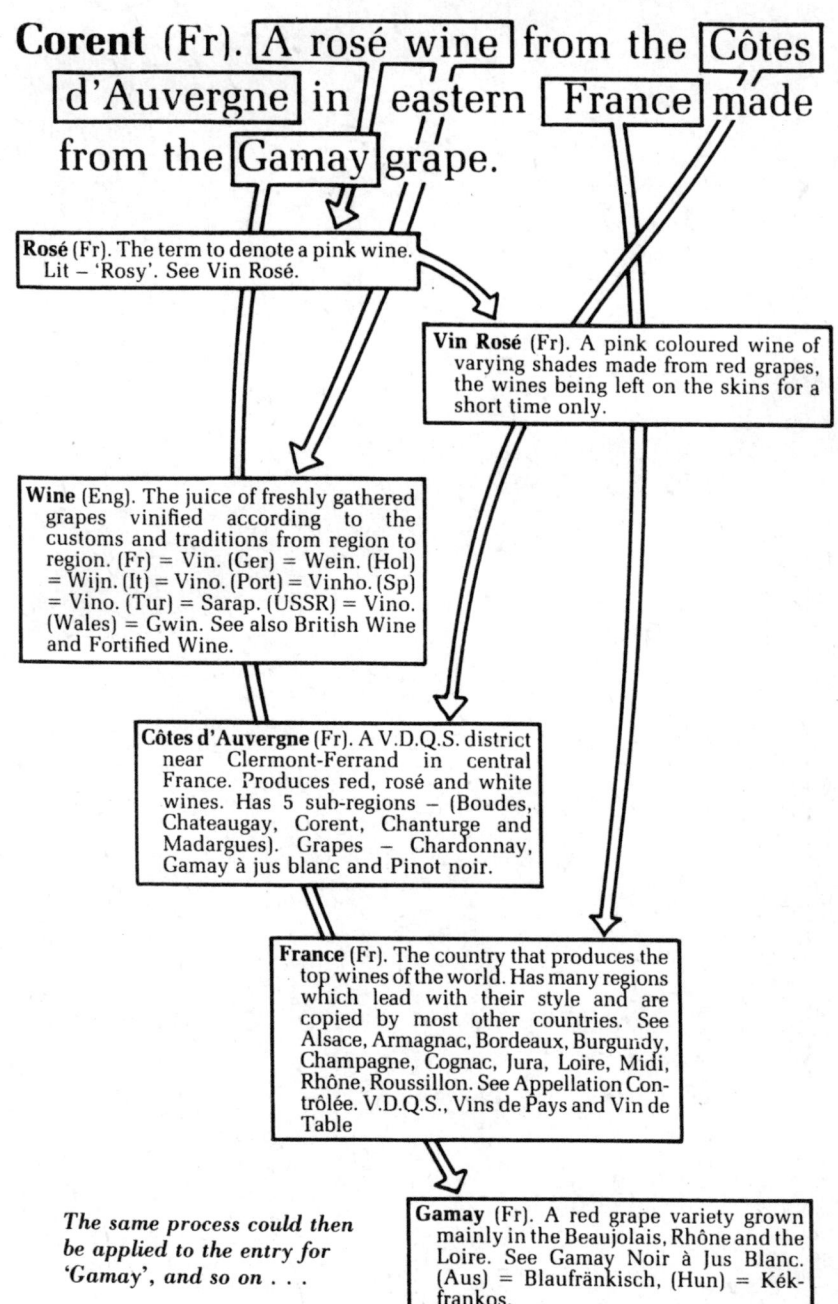

Corent (Fr). A rosé wine from the Côtes d'Auvergne in eastern France made from the Gamay grape.

Rosé (Fr). The term to denote a pink wine. Lit – 'Rosy'. See Vin Rosé.

Vin Rosé (Fr). A pink coloured wine of varying shades made from red grapes, the wines being left on the skins for a short time only.

Wine (Eng). The juice of freshly gathered grapes vinified according to the customs and traditions from region to region. (Fr) = Vin. (Ger) = Wein. (Hol) = Wijn. (It) = Vino. (Port) = Vinho. (Sp) = Vino. (Tur) = Sarap. (USSR) = Vino. (Wales) = Gwin. See also British Wine and Fortified Wine.

Côtes d'Auvergne (Fr). A V.D.Q.S. district near Clermont-Ferrand in central France. Produces red, rosé and white wines. Has 5 sub-regions – (Boudes, Chateaugay, Corent, Chanturge and Madargues). Grapes – Chardonnay, Gamay à jus blanc and Pinot noir.

France (Fr). The country that produces the top wines of the world. Has many regions which lead with their style and are copied by most other countries. See Alsace, Armagnac, Bordeaux, Burgundy, Champagne, Cognac, Jura, Loire, Midi, Rhône, Roussillon. See Appellation Contrôlée. V.D.Q.S., Vins de Pays and Vin de Table

The same process could then be applied to the entry for 'Gamay', and so on . . .

Gamay (Fr). A red grape variety grown mainly in the Beaujolais, Rhône and the Loire. See Gamay Noir à Jus Blanc. (Aus) = Blaufränkisch, (Hun) = Kékfrankos.

ABBREVIATIONS

(Add)	Address	(Ger)	Germany
(Afr)	Africa	(Gre)	Greece
(Am)	Americas	(Gro)	Grosslagen
(Anb)	Anbaugebiet	(Hol)	Holland
(Arg)	Argentina	(Ind)	India
(Arm)	Armenia	(Indo)	Indonesia
(Asia)	Asia	(Iran)	(Iran)
(Aus)	Austria	(Ire)	Ireland
(Austr)	Australia	(Isr)	Israel
(Ban)	Bangladesh	(It)	Italy
(Bel)	Belgium	(Jor)	Jordan
(Ber)	Bereich	(Kor)	Korea (S.N)
(Bio)	Biological	(Lat)	Latin
(Bos)	Bosnia Herzogovina	(Latv)	Latvia
(Bot)	Botanical	(Leb)	Lebanon
(Bul)	Bulgaria	(Lit)	Lithuania
(C.Am)	Central America	(Mac)	Macedonia
(Can)	Canada	(Mal)	Malaysia
(Chi)	China	(M.East)	Middle East
(Chile)	Chile	(Mex)	Mexico
(Ch.Isles)	Channel Islands	(Mol)	Moldovia
(Com)	Commune	(Mor)	Morocco
(Cro)	Croatia	(N.Am)	North America
(Cub)	Cuba	(N.Kor)	North Korea
(Cyp)	Cyprus	(Nor)	Norway
(Czec)	Czechoslovakia	(N.Z)	New Zealand
(Den)	Denmark	(Pak)	Pakistan
(Egy)	Egypt	(Par)	Paraguay
(Eng)	England	(Peru)	Peru
(Esp)	Esperanto	(Phil)	Philippines
(Est)	Estonia	(Pol)	Poland
(Eth)	Ethiopia	(Rus)	Russia
(Euro)	Europe	(Rwa)	Rwanda
(Fin)	Finland	(S.Afr)	South Africa
(Geo)	Georgia	(S.Am)	South America

(S.Arabia)	Saudi Arabia	(Thai)	Thailand
(Scot)	Scotland	(Tib)	Tibet
(S.E.Asia)	South East Asia	(Tun)	Tunisia
(Ser)	Serbia	(Tur)	Turkey
(Sey)	Seychelles	(UAE)	United Arab Emirates
(Sing)	Singapore	(Ukr)	Ukraine
(S.Kor)	South Korea	(USA)	United States of America
(Slo)	Slovenia	(Ven)	Venezuela
(Slov)	Slovakia	(Viet)	Vietnam
(Sri.L)	Sri Lanka	(Vil)	Village
(Swe)	Sweden	(Vin)	Vineyard
(Switz)	Switzerland	(Wal)	Wales
(Syria)	Syria	(W.Ind)	West Indies
(Tai)	Taiwan		

THE DICTIONARY OF

Drink

A Guide to Every Type of Beverage

A

A.A. (Eng) *abbr:* **A**lcoholics **A**nonymous, an international body to help those people who have a 'drink' problem.

A.A.A. (Eng) *abbr:* **A**ction on **A**lcohol **A**buse, a body who wish to raise the price on alcohol in a bid to cut consumption, based in London, advocates everything in moderation and more education regarding alcohol abuse.

Aachener Kaiserbrunnen (Ger) a natural mineral water (established 1884) from Kaiserquelle, Bad Aachen, north-western Germany. Mineral contents (milligrammes per litre): Sodium 1295mg/l, Calcium 62mg/l, Magnesium 9mg/l, Potassium 69mg/l, Bicarbonates 876mg/l, Chlorides 1486mg/l, Sulphates 277mg/l.

Aachener Quelle (Ger) a natural mineral water. Mineral contents (milligrammes per litre): Sodium 176mg/l, Calcium 151mg/l, Magnesium 19mg/l, Potassium 15mg/l, Bicarbonates 442mg/l, Chlorides 231mg/l, Sulphates 165mg/l.

Aachener Sprudel (Ger) a natural mineral water from Granusquelle, Bad Aachen, north-western Germany.

Aalborg (Den) the town where akvavit was first produced.

Aalborg Akeleje Snaps (Den) an akvavit flavoured with herbs. 40% alc by vol.

Aalborg Brewery (Den) a major brewery based in North Jutland.

Aalborg EsksPort Akvavit (Den) an akvavit with a slightly burnt taste due to the addition of Madeira wine. 45% alc by vol.

Aalborg Fuselfri Akvavit (Den) a low strength akvavit flavoured with caraway.

Aalborg Jubiloeums Akvavit (Den) a dill-flavoured akvavit produced by DDS. 45% alc by vol.

Aalborg Porse Snaps (Den) an akvavit flavoured with bog myrtle 45% alc by vol.

Aalborg Taffel Akvavit (Den) a caraway-flavoured akvavit produced by DDS.

Aalto (Sp) a Vino de la Tierra wine from Burgos, Castilla-Léon. See also Mauro, San Román.

Aan de Doorns Co-operative (S.Afr) a co-operative winery based in Worcester. (Add): Box 235, Worcester 6850. Produces varietal wines.

Aan-de-Drift (S.Afr) a small vineyard that sells its grapes to the Mooiuitsig Wynkelders.

Aangeschoten (Hol) drunken / tipsy.

Aardvark Estate (USA) a winery based in the Carneros district of northern California. Grape variety: Pinot noir.

Aargau (Switz) a minor north wine producing district, produces mainly white wines.

Aarp West Virginia (USA) a natural mineral water from Virginia.

Aass Brewery (Nor) based in Drammen, south-east Norway. Is noted for Bayer, Bok and Jule Ales.

A.B. (Port) *abbr:* an **A**guardente **B**randy produced by Caves São João. 43% alc by vol.

Abadal (Sp) a winery based in the D.O. region of Pla de Bages, north-eastern Spain. Grape variety: Picapoll.

Abadía Retuerta (Sp) a winery based either side of the banks of the Ribera del Duero. Produces 7 wines: Primicia, Rivola, Abadía Retuerta, Cuvée El Palomar, Cuvée El Campanario, Pago Valdebellón, Pago La Negralada. Part of vineyards fall in D.O. Ribera del Duero. 600ha. in total of which 214ha. are not entitled to D.O.

Abadía Retuerta (Sp) a winery (and name of wine) based in the D.O. Castilla y Léon from 65% Tempranillo, 30% Cabernet, 5% Merlot. Matured for 1 year in cask. Label: Cuvée Palomar.

Abadir-Dukem (Afr) one of the three main wine-producing regions in Ethiopia. See also Eritire and Guder.

Abafado (Mad) pure grape juice fortified with up to 20% alc by vol, used in the final blending of rich Bual (Boal) and Malmsey Madeiras.

Ábalos (Sp) a Zona de Crianza in the Rioja Alta, north-western Spain.

Abanico (Sp) a straw-coloured, Fino Sherry with a tang of salt and flor produced by Bobadilla in Jerez de la Frontera.

Abanilla (Sp) a Vino de la Tierra of Murcia in south-eastern Spain (2000ha) planted with Monastrell, Garnacha tinta, Merseguera and Airén.

Abarchage Traditionnel (Fr) an old method of stacking oak casks in the Cognac region whilst the spirit matures.

Abatilles (Fr) a natural mineral water. Mineral contents (milligrammes per litre): Sodium 74.5mg/l, Calcium 16.4mg/l, Magnesium 8mg/l, Potassium 2.8mg/l, Bicarbonates 112mg/l, Chlorides 95mg/l, Sulphates 7.8mg/l.

Abbaye (Bel) a strong, naturally-conditioned, bottled beer, brewed by five Trappist abbayes.

Abbaye d'Aulne (Bel) an abbaye-produced beer from south-east Belgium.

Abbaye de Bonne Espérance (Bel) an 8% alc by vol. special beer brewed by Lefèbvre at Quenast.

Abbaye de Fontfroide (Fr) a vineyard in the A.C. Corbières, south-western France. Label: De Gratias.

Abbaye de la Grâce de Dieu (Fr) a noted liqueur producer based in Doubs. Noted for Trappistine liqueur.

Abbaye de la Moinette (Bel) an abbaye beer brewed by the Dupont Brasserie in Tourpes.

Abbaye de Leffe Radieuse (Bel) an abbaye-style beer brewed by the Stella Artois Brasserie in Lourain.

Abbaye de Leffe Triple (Bel) was once an abbaye brewery, now a golden beer brewed by the Stella Artois Brasserie.

Abbaye-de-Morgeot (Fr) see Morgeot (a Premier Cru A.C. Chassagne-Montrachet), Côte de Beaune, Burgundy 10.92ha. Also spelt L'Abbaye de Morgeot.

Abbaye de St. Amand (Fr) a 7% alc by vol. top-fermented, bottle-conditioned, dark straw coloured special beer brewed by S.A.R.L. Forest, Haussy.

Abbaye de Thélème (Bel) an abbaye brewery produced beer.

Abbaye Notre Dame de St. Remy (Bel) a brewery in Belgium that brews Trappistes Rochefort 8 and Trappistes Rochfort 10.

Abbazia dell'Annunziata (It) a winery based at La Morra (a district of Barolo), Piemonte.

Abbey Ale (Eng) a strong cask-conditioned bitter ale brewed by the Cirencester Brewery in Gloucestershire.

Abbey Brewery (Eng) a small brewery (established 1981) near Retford, Nottinghamshire that produces cask-conditioned beers.

Abbey Ales Brewery (Eng) a brewery (established 1997) based in Camden Row, Bath, Avon BA1 5LB. Brews a variety of ales including: Bath Star 4.5% alc by vol., Bellringer 4.2% alc by vol., Best Bitter 4.2% alc by vol., Black Friar 5.3% alc by vol., Cardinal Sin 4.8% alc by vol., Chorister 4.5% alc by vol., Three Strikes 4.5% alc by vol., Twelfth Night 5% alc by vol., White Friar 5% alc by vol. Website: http://www.abbeyales.co.uk 'E'mail: am@abbeyales.co.uk

Abbey Brewery (Scot) the name for the head office of the Scottish & Newcastle Brewery, Edinburgh, Midlothian.

Abbey Cocktail [1] (Cktl) 35mls (1½fl.ozs) gin, juice ¼ lemon, dash orange bitters. Shake well over ice, strain into a cocktail glass and top with a cherry.

Abbey Cocktail [2] (Cktl) ½ measure dry gin, ¼ measure Lillet, ¼ measure orange juice, dash Angostura. Shake well over ice and strain into a cocktail glass.

Abbey Cocktail [3] (Cktl) 25mls (1fl.oz) dry gin, 10mls (½fl.oz) sweet vermouth, 10mls (½fl.oz) orange juice, dash Angostura. Shake well over ice, strain into cocktail glass and dress with a cherry.

Abbeydale Brewery (Eng) a micro-brewery (established 1996). (Add): Unit 8, Aizlewood Road, Sheffield South Yorkshire S8 0YX. Brews a variety of ales including: Absolution 5.3% alc by vol., Advent 4.7% alc by vol., Archangel 4.7% alc by vol., Moonshine 4.3% alc by vol. Website: http://www.abbeydalebrewery.co.uk

Abbey Export (Eng) a standard keg bitter beer produced by Shepherd Neame, Faversham, Kent.

Abbey Knight (Eng) a dry, white wine made from the Müller-Thurgau grape by the Macrae Farms (Highwayman Vineyard), Bury St. Edmunds, Suffolk.

Abbey Well Water (Eng) a still and sparkling natural mineral water (established 1910) produced by Waters and Robson, Morpeth, Northumberland, NE61 6JE. Green glass denotes sparkling, clear glass bottle denotes still water. Mineral contents (milligrammes per litre): Sodium 62mg/l, Calcium 60mg/l, Magnesium 28mg/l, Potassium 4.8mg/l, Bicarbonates 350mg/l, Chlorides 75mg/l, Sulphates 25mg/l, Fluoride 0.16mg/l, Nitrates 0.3mg/l. pH 7.9 Website: http://www.abbey-well.co.uk 'E'mail: enquiries@abbey-well.co.uk

Abboc (It) abbr: for abbocato.

Abbocado (Sp) medium sweet.

Abboccato (It) lit: 'soft caressing', describes wines as either sweet or semi-sweet.

Abbot Ale (Eng) a strong bitter ale brewed by the Greene King Brewery in either of their breweries at Biggleswade, Bedfordshire or at Bury St. Edmunds, Suffolk. 5% alc by vol.

Abbot's Aged Bitters (USA) aromatic bitters produced in Baltimore since 1865.

Abbot's Choice (Scot) a blended Scotch whisky created by McEwan in Perthshire. (Part of the DCL group). 40% alc by vol.

Abbots Lager (Austr) a lager beer brewed by the Carlton and United Brewery in Victoria. 3.9% alc by vol.

A.B.C. (Eng) abbr: Aylesbury Brewery Company. Based in Buckinghamshire. Has now merged with Halls of Oxford but the public houses still run under the A.B.C. name but as part of the Ind Coope empire.

ABC (E.Asia) medium stout brewed by the Archipelago Brewery in Kuala Lumpur, Malaya.

ABC (Eng) abbr: a modern slang term for Anything But Chardonnay.

ABC (Eng) a 4% alc by vol. beer brewed by the Bartrams Brewery, Suffolk.

A.B.C. (USA) abbr: Alcoholic Beverage Control. (Board).

ABC Bitter (Eng) a 4.1% alc by vol. bitter beer brewed by the Belvoir Brewery, Leicestershire.

A.B.C.C. (USA) abbr: Alcoholic Beverage Control Commission.

A.B.D. (Eng) abbr: Arthur Bell Distillers.

AB Blonde (Scot) a 5% alc by vol. ale brewed by the Arran Brewery C°. Ltd, Isle of Arran.

Abdijbieren (Hol) a trappiste-produced abbaye beer.

Abeille (Fr) bee. See also Bees.

Abeille de Fieuzal [L'] (Fr) second wine of Château de Fieuzal.

A

Abel and C°. (N.Z) a small winery based at Ponoma Road, Kumeu. Produces red and white wines including Beaunois and Ponoma Valley Claret.

Abele [Henri] (Fr) a Champagne producer. (Add): 50, Rue de Sillery, 51051 Reims Cedex. Produces vintage and non-vintage wines. Vintages: 1975, 1976, 1982, 1983, 1986, 1989, 1990. Labels include Grande Marque Impériale and Sourire de Reims.

Abel Jobart (Fr) a Champagne producer. (Add): 4, Rue de la Sous-Préfecture, 51170 Sarcy. Produces vintage and non-vintage Champagnes. Produces: Brut Millésime, Brut Réserve, Brut Rosé, Brut Selection, Demi-Sec. Website: http://www.Champagne-abeljobart.com 'E'mail: contact@Champagne-abeljobart.com

Abel Lepitre (Fr) a Champagne producer. (Add): B.P.124, Ave. du General Giraud, 51055 Reims. Produces vintage and non-vintage wines. Vintages: 1926, 1928, 1934, 1937, 1941, 1943, 1945, 1947, 1949, 1952, 1953, 1955, 1959, 1961, 1962, 1964, 1966, 1969, 1970, 1971, 1973, 1974, 1975, 1976, 1978, 1979, 1980, 1981, 1982, 1983, 1985, 1990, 1996. De Luxe Cuvée: Prince A. de Bourbon-Parme.

Abel-Musk (Ind) an aromatic plant, its seeds are often mixed with coffee as a stimulant and for flavour. It has a musk aroma.

Abelsberg (Ger) vineyard (Anb): Württemberg. (Ber): Remstal- Stuttgart. (Gro): Weinsteige. (Vil): Stuttgart (ortsteil Gaisburg).

Abenakis (Can) a natural mineral water from St. François du Lac. Mineral contents (milligrammes per litre): Sodium 4300mg/l, Calcium 542mg/l, Magnesium 320mg/l, Potassium 50mg/l, Bicarbonates 406mg/l, Chlorides 8180mg/l, Sulphates 745mg/l.

Abenbury (Wal) a natural mineral water from Abenbury Spring, Wrexham.

Abendroth (Aus) an ancient red vine variety, rarely grown nowadays.

Abenstaler Quelle (Ger) a natural mineral water from Abenstaler Quelle, Elsendorf-Hornegg, BY.

Abercorn Wines (Austr) a winery based in Mudgee, Australia. Website: http://www.abercornwine.com.au

Aberbares (Ken) a natural mineral water from the Aberdare National Park.

Aberdeen Ale Ltd. (Scot) formed in 1982 at the Devanha Brewery, Alford in Aberdeen. Brews Devanha XB 1036 O.G. and Triple 1043 O.G. See Devanha Brewery.

Aberdeen Angus (Arg) the brand-name of a red wine produced by the Bodegas Goyenechea.

Aberdeen Angus (Cktl) ⅔ measure Scotch whisky, ⅓ measure Drambuie, 35mls (1½fl.ozs) honey, juice ½ lime. Stir whisky, honey and lime juice in a warmed mug, add flaming liqueur, stir and serve.

Aberdeen Cows (USA) a cream-based liqueur made with Scotch whisky.

Aberfeldy (Scot) a single highland malt whisky distillery based in Perthshire. Produces a 12 y.o. single malt 40% alc by vol. Owned by John Dewars & Sons. Website: http://www.dewarsworldofwhisky.com

Aberfoyle (Can) a still natural mineral water (established 1992) based in Ontario (also British Columbia). Mineral contents (milligrammes per litre): Sodium 33mg/l, Calcium 100mg/l, Magnesium 37mg/l, Potassium 2mg/l, Bicarbonates 240mg/l, Chlorides 68mg/l, Sulphates 61mg/l, Nitrates 0.2 5mg/l.

Aberlour (Scot) a 12 year old highland malt whisky produced by the Aberlour-Glenlivet Distillery in Morayshire. 43% alc by vol. Also as a 10 year old, plus a 22 year old version distilled in 1969, bottled in 1991.

Aberlour-Glenlivet (Scot) a single malt whisky distillery based south of Rothes, Morayshire (on the river Spey). A highland malt whisky. 40% alc by vol. Owned by Pernod-Ricard. See Campbell and Son.

Abf. (Ger) abbr: for Abfüllung.

Abfüller (Aus)(Ger) bottler.

Abfüllung (Ger) abbr: Abf. bottling.

Abgebaut (Ger) a term used to describe a wine that has lost its acidity.

Abghan Toos Mashhad (Iran) a natural mineral water brand.

Abîmes (Fr) a wine village in the Savoie, produces dry white wine of same name. Also spelt Abymes.

Abington Bitter (Eng) a bitter ale brewed by Charles Wells in Bedford for the supermarkets. Sold in cans and PET bottles.

Abington Park Brewery (Eng) a home-brew pub in Northampton, Northamptonshire. Owned by Clifton Inns. Produces Cobblers Ale 1037 O.G. Extra 1047 O.G. Becket, Supreme.

A.B.I. Permit (USA) abbr: Alcoholic Beverage Import Permit.

Abir Brewery (Isr) a famous Israeli brewery. Produces a lager beer of same name at 11° Balling.

Abisante (USA) aniseed flavoured spirit. 40% alc by vol.

Abkari (Asia) the manufacture or sale of alcoholic liquors and the excise duty levied upon them.

ABK6 (Fr) a Cognac brand. Label: VS Premium. Website: http://www.Abk6-cognac.com

ABN Agua Mineral (Arg) a natural mineral water. Mineral contents (milligrammes per litre): Sodium 9mg/l, Magnesium 0.1mg/l, Bicarbonates 377mg/l, Chlorides 14mg/l, Sulphates 5mg/l, Nitrates 13mg/l, Manganese 0.1mg/l. pH 7.8

Abocado (Sp) see Abbocado.

Abolengo (Sp) a 3 year old solera brandy produced by Romate.

Abona (Sp) a D.O. wine zone of Tenerife, Canarias.

Abondance (Eng) a name given to wine that has been well diluted with water. The term can apply to the practice of adulterating the wine, or for the consumption by children by lowering the alcohol content (also makes it go further!).

Abonnement (Fr) the practice of forming a contract

5

on a fixed term basis to buy the complete harvest (vintage) of a château for a number of years, at an agreed price in Bordeaux. A deal between the négociant and the grower (château).

Abouriou (Fr) an aromatic red grape variety grown in the Côtes du Marmandais, Lot-et-Garonne, south-west France.

Abran (Rus) a medium dry white wine from the Crimea.

Abrastol (Eng) an illegal additive to wine, used as a preservative, which also gives the wine a reddish colour.

Abrau-Dursso (Rus) a large wine-producing collective in southern Russia. Produces mainly sparkling wines.

Abre à Liqueur (Fr) see Toddy Palm.

Abreu Estate (USA) a winery based in the Napa Valley, California. Grape varieties include: Cabernet sauvingnon. Label: Madrona Ranch.

Abricot d'Anjou (Fr) a brandy-based liqueur, flavoured with apricots. Produced in Angers, Loire. 31% alc by vol.

Abricotine (Fr) an almond and apricot liqueur, yellow coloured. Has a slight taste of almonds acquired from the apricot stones used. Produced by Garnier at Enghien-lès-Bains. 31.5% alc by vol.

Åbro Bryggeri (Swe) a small brewery based in south-east Sweden. (Add): 598 89 Vimmerby, Sweden. Brews bitter ales and lagers. Is one of the country's smallest. Website: http://wwwabro.se 'E'mail: info@abro.se

Abrotonite (It) a wine consumed by the Romans. It was flavoured with artesimia (wormwood).

Abruzzi (It) see Abruzzo.

Abruzzo (It) a region to the east of Latium on the east coast. Capital is L'Aquila. Main wines include Montepulciano d'Abruzzo and Trebbiano d'Abruzzo. Home to I.G.T.'s Colline Teatine, Valle Peligna.

Abruzzo Bianco (It) a white grape variety grown in Abruzzo. Known in Tuscany as the Trebbiano.

Abs. (Eng) abbr: Acrylonitrile-butadiene-styrene.

Absdorf (Aus) a vineyard site based on the banks of the River Kamp in the Kamptal region.

Absinth (Fr) an alternative spelling of absinthe.

Absinthe (Fr) Artemisia absinthium (wormwood).

Absinthe (Fr) a liqueur flavoured with wormwood (Artimisia absinthium), aniseed, angelica, cloves etc, coloured yellow-green. Invented by a Frenchman (Dr. Ordiniare) in Couvet, Switzerland. The recipe was sold to a Mr. Pernod in 1797, was banned as absinthe in 1914 because of toxic nature. Now known as pastis at a reduced strength. 40%–43% alc by vol. Is produced at original high strengths in eastern European countries (see Absinthe-Hapsburg). To drink (classic method): place an absinthe spoon over a small stemmed glass and put a cube of sugar in the centre of the spoon. Pour a measure of absinthe over the sugar and set the cube alight. The molten sugar and absinthe will drip into the glass (setting fire to the absinthe in the glass), when all sugar has melted,

douse with a little iced water and drink. See also Green Fairy, Le Fée and Wormwood. (It) = assenzio, (Mor) = chiba, (Sp) = ajenjo.

Absinthe-American Style (Cktl) 1 dash Angostura, 4 dashes syrup, 25mls (1fl.oz) pastis, 25mls (1fl.oz) water. Shake over ice until frozen, strain into cocktail glass. Add a twist of lemon peel.

Absinthe Cocktail [1] (Cktl) 1 part Pernod, 1 part water, 1 dash sugar syrup, 1 dash Angostura. Shake over ice and strain into a cocktail glass.

Absinthe Cocktail [2] (Cktl) 25mls (1fl.oz) pastis, 2 dashes Angostura, dash orgeat syrup, dash anisette. Stir well over ice and strain into a cocktail glass.

Absinthe Cocktail [3] (cktl) shake 35mls (1½fl.ozs) absinthe, 15mls (½fl.oz) water, dash anis, 1tspn egg white and 10mls (¼fl.oz) gomme syrup over crushed ice, strain into a cocktail glass and dress with a twist of lime.

Absinthe Cooler (Cktl) 3 dashes Pernod, 60mls (½ gill) whisky, 30mls (⅛ gill) lemon juice, 2 dashes Angostura, 250mls (½ pint) ginger ale. Stir in a tall glass with ice cube, serve with Pernod on top.

Absinthe Drip (Cktl) made with a special drip glass. A cube of sugar and a cube of ice are placed in the dripper and a measure of absinthe (pastis) is placed in the glass. Ice cold water is poured over the sugar and ice to drip into the absinthe (a tea-strainer can be substituted for the dripper).

Absinthe-French Style (Cktl) see Absinthe Drip.

Absinthe-Hapsburg (Bul) a 72.5% alc by vol. absinthe. Also available as a Super De-Luxe Extra version at 85% alc by vol.

Absinthe Special (Cktl) ½ measure absinthe, ½ measure dry gin, dash Angostura, dash grenadine. Shake over ice and strain into a cocktail glass.

Absinthe Suissesse (Cktl) 25mls (1fl.oz) Pernod, 3 dashes anisette, 3 dashes orange flower water, 4 dashes crème de menthe, 1 egg white. Shake over ice and strain into a cocktail glass.

Absinthe-Swiss Style (Cktl) also known as Mominette. 75mls (3fl.ozs) absinthe in a tumbler, add syrup to taste, then top up with iced water. Grenadine may be used in lieu of syrup (see Une Tomate, Une Purée).

Absinthe-Trenet (Fr) 60% alc by vol. absinthe, also available as a Premium Trenet version.

Absinthism (Eng) a disease condition caused by the over-drinking of absinthe.

Absolut (Swe) the brand-name of a vodka 37.5% alc by vol. produced by Absolut Vodka and distributed by A.B.D. in Perth, Scotland. Also available in citron, blackcurrant and peach flavours. Also produce Alsolut Vanilla and Level.

Absolute Alcohol (Eng) 99% pure alcohol (ethanol).

Absolute Deco (Cktl) ⅓ vodka, ⅓ peach schnapps, ⅓ cranberry juice, shake over ice and strain into a cocktail glass.

Absolution (Eng) a 5.3% alc by vol. ale brewed by the Abbeydale Brewery Ltd., South Yorkshire.

Absolut Star (Cktl) 40mls Absolut Vodka, 20 mls fresh lime juice, 20 mls crème de cassis, dash gomme syrup. Shak over ice and strain into iced cocktail glass.

Absolut Vanilla (Swe) a vanilla-flavoured vodka produced by Absolut Vodka.

Abson (USA) an aniseed flavoured liqueur.

Absopure (USA) a distilled and natural mineral water.

Abstatt (Ger) village (Anb): Württemberg. (Ber): Württembergisch Unterland. (Gro): Schozachtal. (Vins): Burgberg, Burg Wildeck, Sommerberg.

Abstemius (Eng) to drink only moderately.

Abstention (Eng) to refrain from drinking, to give up drinking any alcohol temporarily for some reason.

Abstich (Ger) racking.

Abstinence (Eng) the carrying out of abstention.

Abstinente (Fr) teetotaller.

Abt (Bel) *abbr:* **Abb**ot, the strongest trappist-style ale from St. Sixtus Abbaye, Westvleteren. Also Prior and Pater ales produced.

Abtei (Ger) vineyard (Anb): Nahe. (Ber): Schloss Böckelheim. (Gro): Rosengarten. (Vil): Sponheim.

Abtei (Ger) vineyard (Anb): Mosel-Saar-Ruwer. (Ber): Zell/Mosel. (Gro): Rosenhang. (Vil): Bremm.

Abteiberg (Ger) vineyard (Anb): Mosel-Saar-Ruwer. (Ber): Zell/Mosel. (Gro): Rosenhang. (Vil): Mesenich.

Abteilikoer (Ger) lit: 'abbot's liqueur', a herb-based liqueur which is popular as a digestive.

Abtei Ruppertsberg (Ger) vineyard (Anb): Nahe. (Ber): Kreuznach. (Gro): Schlosskapelle. (Vil): Weiler.

Abtei Ruppertsberg (Ger) vineyard (Anb): Nahe. (Ber): Kreuznach. (Gro): Schlosskapelle. (Vil): Bingen-Bingenbrück.

Abtel (Ger) grosslage (Anb): Rheinhessen. (Ber): Bingen. (Vils): Appenheim, Gau-Algesheim, Nieder-Hilbersheim, Ober-Hilbersheim, Partenheim, Sankt Johann, Sprendlingen, Wolfsheim. (*See also* Orbel, Abtey).

Abtey (Ger) grosslage (Anb): Rheinhessen. (Ber): Bingen. (Vils): Appenheim, Gau-Algesheim, Nieder-Hilbersheim, Ober-Hilbersheim, Partenheim, Sankt Johann, Sprendlingen, Wolfsheim. (*See also* Orbel, Abtel).

Abtsberg (Ger) vineyard (Anb): Baden. (Ber): Ortenau. (Gro): Fürsteneck. (Vil): Offenburg (ortsteil Zell-Weierbach).

Abtsberg (Ger) vineyard (Anb): Franken. (Ber): Mainviereck. (Gro): Reuschberg. (Vil): Hörstein.

Abtsberg (Ger) vineyard (Anb): Mosel-Saar-Ruwer. (Ber): Bernkastel. (Gro): Munzlay. (Vil): Graach.

Abtsberg (Ger) vineyard (Anb): Mosel-Saar-Ruwer. (Ber): Saar-Ruwer. (Gro): Römerlay. (Vil): Mertesdorf (ortsteil Maximin Grünhaus).

Abtsberg (Ger) vineyard (Anb): Pfalz. (Ber): Südliche Weinstrasse. (Gro): Herrlich. (Vil): Impflingen.

Abtsfronhof (Ger) vineyard (Anb): Pfalz. (Ber): Mittelhaardt-Deutsche Weinstrasse. (Gro): Schenkenböhl. (Vil): Bad Dürkheim.

Abtsleite (Ger) vineyard (Anb): Franken. (Ber): Maindreieck. (Gro): not yet assigned. (Vil): Würzburg.

Abtswind (Ger) village (Anb): Franken. (Ber): Steigerwald. (Gro): Schild. (Vin): Altenberg.

Abtwingert (Euro) the famous vineyard of Rotes Haus (Red House) in Liechtenstein. Noted for white wines.

A'bunadh (Scot) bottled single malt whisky from Campbell Distillers. Matured in Oloroso Sherry casks. 59.6% alc by vol.

Abundance Vineyard (USA) a label for a red wine (Pinot noir) produced by Namasté Vineyards, Oregon.

ABV (Eng) *abbr:* Alcohol by Volume. Also written as abv.

Abymes (Fr) *see* Abîmes.

Abyssinian Coffee (Eng) the old name for Ethiopian coffee.

A.C. (Fr) *abbr:* Appellation Contrôlée. *See also* A.O.C.

Acacia (Eng) a gum used to prevent the premature depositing of red wine colouring matter.

Acacia Cocktail (Cktl) 1 measure dry gin, ½ measure Bénédictine. Shake over ice and strain into a cocktail glass.

Acacia Winery (USA) a winery (established 1979) based in the Napa Valley, California. 21ha. Grape varieties: Chardonnay and Pinot noir. Noted for single vineyard Pinot noir wines. Labels: Beckstoffer, Las Amigas Vineyard, St. Clair Vineyard.

Académie du Vin de Bordeaux (Fr) the world famous Bordeaux wine school based in the town of Bordeaux, western France.

Academy Ale (Eng) a 4.2% alc by vol. ale brewed by the Tirril brewery, Cumbria.

Academy of Food and Wine Service (Eng) an organisation (established 1988). (Add): Burgoine House, 8 Lower Teddington Road, Kingston, Surrey Kt1 4ER. Website: http://www.acfws.org 'E'mail: acfws@acfws.org

Acadian Distillery (Can) a whisky distillery that produces a 100% rye whisky. 40% alc by vol.

Acampo Winery and Distilleries (USA) the former name for the Barengo Vineyards in Sacramento Valley, California.

Acanage (Fr) the process of tying up the vines in the spring as they start to shoot.

Acapulco (Cktl) 35mls (1¼fl.ozs) white rum, 5mls (¼fl.oz) Triple Sec, 1 barspoon sugar syrup, dash egg white. Shake well over ice, strain into an ice-filled old-fashioned glass and top with a sprig of mint.

Acapulco Cocktail (Cktl) ½ measure tequila, ½ measure white rum, 125mls (5fl.ozs) pineapple juice, juice ½ lime. Shake well over ice, strain into an ice-filled collins glass, top with a pineapple cube.

Acapulco Gold Cocktail (Cktl) 25mls (1fl.oz) each of golden tequila, golden rum, coconut cream, grapefruit juice, 60mls (2½fl.ozs) pineapple juice. Shake well over ice and strain into an ice-filled highball glass.

Acariose (Eng) a vine pest, a species of mite that feeds on the leaves and fruit. Various species such as the Grape Rust mite (*Calepitrimerus vitis*) and the Grape Bud Mite (*Eriophyes vitis*). Is treated with copper sulphite spray.

Acariosis (Eng) a vine condition due to attack from the vine mite. Symptoms are stunted growth and withered foliage.

Accademia dei Racemi (It) an association in Puglia that brings together small-scale, fine wine makers to pool knowledge and improve the quality of wine making in the area.

Accademia Torregiorgi (It) wine merchant and grower based at Neive, Piemonte.

Accolage (Fr) the tying of the vine branches to horizontal wires.

Accra Brewery (Afr) a brewery based in Accra, Ghana which is noted for Club Beer.

Ace Lager (Eng) federation of Newcastle keg lager-beer.

Acenscency (Eng) describes a wine affected by acetic bacteria. Detected by a sharp vinegary taste and a film on the surface.

Ace of Clubs (Eng) a brown ale brewed by Federation, Lancaster Road, Dunston, Newcastle.

Acerbe (Fr) lit: 'bitter / sharp', denotes immature, acid wine.

Acerbitas (Lat) bitterness.

Acerbité (Fr) bitterness / sharpness.

Acerbity (Eng) astringency / sharpness.

Acerbo (Port) bitter / sharp.

Acérrimo (Port) very bitter.

Acescence (Fr) to make the wine smell and taste like vinegar.

Acetaldehyde (Eng) found in wine, it is formed during fermentation. The enzyme zymase turns the acetaldehyde to alcohol. Has an apple taste and aroma.

Acetamide (Eng) a malady found in wine caused by spoilage bacteria. Produces an unpleasant, mousy flavour.

Acetic Acid (Eng) CH$_3$COOH vinegar. Caused by Acetic fermentation.(Fr) = acide acétique.

Acetic Fermentation (Eng) is caused generally by an infection with *Acetobacter aceti*, but several other species of organisms and certain types of film yeasts may initiate the process. Is detectable by smell and an oily sheen on top of the wine / beer.

Acetification (Eng) turning into vinegar.

Acetify (Eng) turn to vinegar.

Acétimètre (Fr) acetimeter, an implement used to measure vinegar concentration.

Acétique (Fr) acetic acid / vinegar.

Aceto (It) vinegar.

Acetobacter aceti (Lat) a mould which after fermentation will break down the alcohol in the wine and produce vinegar in the presence of air (acetic acid).

Acetoin (Eng) a wine malady, caused by *Lactobacilli*. Produces an off-flavour in the wine, can be prevented by cleanliness.

Acetometer (Eng) an instrument for measuring the acetic acid content in vinegar etc.

Acetosella (It) a sparkling mineral water from Fonti Acidule, Plinio. Mineral contents (milligrammes per litre): Sodium 50.7mg/l, Calcium 276mg/l, Magnesium 58mg/l, Potassium 9.9mg/l, Bicarbonates 1086mg/l, Chlorides 106mg/l, Sulphates 20mg/l, Fluoride 0.25mg/l, Silicates 26.5mg/l. pH 6.33

Acetous (Eng) having a taste of vinegar, vinegar tasting.

Acetum (Lat) vinegar.

Acetylmethyl-Carbinol (Eng) a glycerine-related compound found in wine in small quantities.

Achaea (Gre) a province in the southern Peloponnese which produces mainly red and white wines.

Achaia Clauss (Gre) famous winery built in the 1860's by a Bavarian, Gustav Clauss on a hillside above Patras, Peloponnese.

Achaia-Clauss Wine Company (Gre) a company which makes Mavrodaphne (a dessert wine of Greece) and brandy. *see* Clauss (Gustav).

Achemeta (Geo) a sweet, white, dessert wine produced in Georgia.

Achentoul Spring Water Company (Scot) produce a range of Caithness natural spring mineral waters.

Acheria Rouge (Fr) a red grape variety grown in the Madiran district of south-western France.

Achern [ortsteil Oberachem] (Ger) village (Anb): Baden. (Ber): Ortenau. (Gro): Schloss Rodeck. (Vins): Alter Gott, Bienenberg

Achkarren (Ger) village (Anb): Baden. (Ber): Kaiserstuhl-Tuniberg. (Gro): Vulkanfelsen. (Vins): Castellberg, Schlossberg.

Achleiten (Aus) a vineyard site on the banks of the River Danube situated in the Wachau region, Niederösterreich.

Achromatous (Eng) used to describe a white wine with little or no colour. (achromic = colourless).

Achs [Paul] (Aus) vineyard-producer (18 ha) based in Gols, Neusiedlersee. (Add): Neubaugasse 13, 7122 Gols. Grape varieties: Blaufränkisch, Cabernet sauvignon, Chardonnay, Muskat-Ottenel, Pinot blanc, Pinot noir, Saint-Laurent, Traminer, Welschreisling, Zweigel. Produces a Pannobile cuvée.

Achspoint (Aus) a vineyard site on the banks of the River Danube situated in the Wachau region, Niederösterreich.

Achtarak (Rus) a wine-producing centre in Armenia, southern Russia. Produces most styles of wines.

Achtaraque (Rus) a white, Sherry-style wine produced in Armenia, southern Russia.

Acid (Eng) imparts lasting qualities, adds bouquet and flavour. Too much acid makes wines sharp or sour. Too little makes wine flat. Gives wines freshness. (Den) = syre, (Fr) = acide, (Ger) = saüre, (Hol) = zuur, (Ire) = aigédach, (It) = acido, (Lat) = acidus, (Port) = acido, (Sp) = acido, (Tur) = ekşi, (Wal) = asid.

Acide (Fr) acid.

Acide Acétique (Fr) acetic acid.

Acide Citrique (Fr) citric acid.

Acide Lactique (Fr) lactic acid.

A

Acide Malique (Fr) malic acid.

Acide Tartrique (Fr) tartaric acid.

Acidez (Port)(Sp) sourness / acidity.

Acidic (Eng) having an overpowering acid taste. (Fr) = acidité, (It) = acidulo.

Acidification (Eng) the name given to the addition of acid (usually citric or tartaric) to a must to correct a deficiency of acid or from infection from spoilage micro-organisms which increase the acidity.

Acidimetric Outfit (Eng) equipment used to check the acid content of a liquid solution.

Acidità (It) acidity.

Acidité (Fr) acidity.

Acidity (Eng) in coffee gives a sharp, plumey taste that is necessary for a balanced style.

Acidity (Eng) the intensity of acid in a must or wine. Is measured on the pH scale. Also fixed or total acidity of combined acids measured by an acidimetric outfit. In wine the acidity contributes to the bouquet, freshness, etc. (Fr) = acidité, (Ire) = aigéadacht, (It) = acidità.

Acido (It) acid.

Ácido (Port)(Sp) acid / tart / sour.

Acid Rain (Eng) a limited edition beer (2005–2006) brewed by the Ash Vine Brewery in Trudoxhill, near Frome, Somerset to raise money for the pressure group – *'surfers against sewage'*. *See also* Toxic Waste.

Acidulé (Fr) the term used for mineral waters that have been charged with carbonic gas (CO_2).

Acidulo (It) acidic.

Acidus (Lat) acid.

Acilik (Tur) bitterness in wine or coffee.

Acinum (Lat) grape / berry. *See also* Baca.

Acitité (Fr) acidic taste in wines.

ACJ Wines (S.Afr) a winery (established 2004) based in Tyger Valley, Durbanville, Western Cape. Grape varieties: Chenin blanc, Colombard, Sauvignon blanc, Shiraz. Label: Bryde.

Acker Leithen (Aus) a vineyard area on the banks of the River Danube in the Kremstal region.

Ackerman 1811 Rosé (Fr) sparkling rosé wine produced by Ackerman-Laurance using the méthode traditionelle. 1811 was the date of the house's foundation.

Ackerman-Laurance (Fr) a wine-producer (established 1811) based in the Saumur, Anjou-Saumur, Loire. Noted for Crémant de Loire produced by the méthode traditionelle.

Ackerman Winery (USA) a winery based in Iowa. Produces mainly French hybrid wines.

Acme (Can) a purified drinking water.

Acme Pale Ale (USA) a 4.1% alc by vol. top-fermented, bottled pale ale brewed by the North Coast Brewing C°., Fort Bragg, Mendocino County, California.

Aconcagua Valley (Chile) a wine region of central Chile. Produces good quality red wines from the Cabernet and Malbec grapes.

Açores (Port) the Azores islands (Graciosa, Pico and Terceira) that have DOC status.

Acorn Coffee (Eng) a coffee made from acorns by removing the cups, chopping the flesh and roasting in oven. Cool, grind and infuse in boiling water for 10 minutes. Use same quantities as for ground coffee. *see* Ballota Oak.

Acorn Brewery (Eng) a brewery (established 2003). (Add): Unit 11, Mitchells Enterprise Centre, Bradberry Balk Lane, Barnsley, South yorkshire, S73 8HR. Brews a variety of ales including: 3rd Noel 4.9% alc by vol., Barnsley Bitter 3.8% alc by vol., Barnsley Gold 4.3% alc by vol., Darkness 4.2% alc by vol., Forester 4.1% alc by vol., Old Manor Porter 4.4% alc by vol. 'E'mail: acornbrewery@tiscali.co.uk

Acorn Lager (Eng) a 3.8% alc by vol. lager brewed by the Oakwell Brewery, Barnsley.

Acqua (It) drinking water.

Acqua (Lat) water.

Acqua Amerino (It) a natural mineral water from San Francesco. Mineral contents (milligrammes per litre): Sodium 11mg/l, Calcium 139mg/l, Magnesium 8.2mg/l, Bicarbonates 396mg/l, Chlorides 21mg/l, Sulphates 77mg/l, Fluoride 0.95mg/l, Nitrates 4mg/l, Silicates 13mg/l.

Acqua Arve (It) a natural mineral water from Salsomaggiore Terme, Parma. Mineral contents (milligrammes per litre): Sodium 310mg/l, Calcium 694mg/l, Magnesium 124mg/l, Potassium 13mg/l, Bicarbonates 550mg/l, Chlorides 310mg/l, Sulphates 1918mg/l, Fluorides 0.5mg/l, Silicate 70mg/l. pH 6.45

Acquabaida (It) a natural mineral water from Sicilia. Mineral contents (milligrammes per litre): Sodium 9mg/l, Calcium 99.8mg/l, Magnesium 33.8mg/l, Potassium 3mg/l, Bicarbonates 183mg/l, Chlorides 24.9mg/l, Sulphates 19.3mg/l, Nitrates 7mg/l. pH 6.9

Acquachiara (It) a sparkling natural mineral water from the Valle del Pasubio. (Add): Norda S.p.A. Milano. Mineral contents (milligrammes per litre): Sodium 1.5mg/l, Calcium 23.6mg/l, Magnesium 8.7mg/l, Potassium 0.85mg/l, Bicarbonates 85mg/l, Chlorides 0.8mg/l, Sulphates 24.4mg/l, Nitrates 2.8mg/l, Silicate 7.2mg/l. pH 8.09

Acquachiara (It) a sparkling natural mineral water from Cortiane. Mineral contents (milligrammes per litre): Sodium 1.3mg/l, Calcium 29.2mg/l, Magnesium 16.1mg/l, Potassium 0.6mg/l, Bicarbonates 156.1mg/l, Chlorides 1.5mg/l, Sulphates 10.1mg/l, Nitrates 4.3mg/l, Silicate 5.7mg/l. pH 7.8

Acqua Claudia (It) an acidic sparkling natural mineral water from Anguillara Sabazia, Rome. Mineral contents (milligrammes per litre): Sodium 63mg/l, Calcium 96mg/l, Magnesium 24.3mg/l, Potassium 81mg/l, Bicarbonates 543mg/l, Chlorides 57mg/l, Sulphates 48mg/l, Nitrates 4.4mg/l, Silicate 103mg/l, Fluorides 1.6mg/l. pH 5.75

Acqua Corse (Fr) a natural mineral water from Bianca, Corsica.

A

Acqua del Cardinale (It) a sparkling natural mineral water. Mineral contents (milligrammes per litre): Sodium 0.81mg/l, Calcium 39.3mg/l, Magnesium 0.51mg/l, Potassium 0.3mg/l, Bicarbonates 122mg/l, Chlorides 3.7mg/l, Sulphates 0.6mg/l, Nitrates 0.8mg/l. pH 7.7

Acqua dell'Imperatore (It) a natural mineral water from the Fonti San Candido.

Acqua della Grotta (It) a natural mineral water from Bari, Puglia.

Acqua della Madonna (It) a sparkling mineral water from Castellamarre di Stabia, Naples. Mineral contents (milligrammes per litre): Sodium 73mg/l, Calcium 304mg/l, Magnesium 62mg/l, Potassium 15mg/l, Bicarbonates 1135mg/l, Chlorides 170mg/l, Sulphates 28mg/l, Fluorides 0.28mg/l, Silicate 37mg/l, Nitrates 6.2mg/l. pH 6.0

Acqua di Nepi (It) a slightly acidic sparkling natural mineral water from the Antiche Terme die Gracchi, Nepi. Mineral contents (milligrammes per litre): Sodium 26mg/l, Calcium 84mg/l, Magnesium 27mg/l, Potassium 44mg/l, Bicarbonates 459mg/l, Chlorides 18mg/l, Sulphates 36mg/l, Fluorides 1.4mg/l, Silicate 94mg/l, Nitrates 8mg/l. pH 5.68

Acqua di Seltz (It) soda water.

Acqua di Sorgente (It) spring water.

Acqua di Tempia (It) a sparkling natural mineral water from Sardegna. Mineral contents (milligrammes per litre): Sodium 37mg/l, Calcium 13.5mg/l, Magnesium 7.6mg/l, Potassium 2.07mg/l, Chlorides 54.71mg/l, Sulphates 18mg/l, Fluorides 0.53mg/l, Silicate 25.8mg/l, Nitrates 0.79mg/l. pH 6.69

Acqua Diva (It) a natural mineral water.

Acquae Vite (Lat) lit: 'water of life', applied to spirits.

Acquafine (Bra) an acidic sparkling natural mineral water. Mineral contents (milligrammes per litre): Sodium 14mg/l, Calcium 6.6mg/l, Magnesium 2.3mg/l, Potassium 4.4mg/l, Bicarbonates 459mg/l, Chlorides 0.7mg/l, Sulphates 0.9mg/l, Fluorides 0.08mg/l, Nitrates 8.8mg/l. pH 4.87

Acqua Fucoli (It) a sparkling natural mineral water from Siena, Tuscany. Mineral contents (milligrammes per litre): Sodium 23.2mg/l, Calcium 615mg/l, Magnesium 89mg/l, Potassium 2.9mg/l, Bicarbonates 492mg/l, Chlorides 30.2mg/l, Sulphates 1450mg/l, Fluorides 1.1mg/l, Silicate 12.5mg/l, Nitrates 1.5mg/l. pH 6.7

Acqua Gassosa (It) soda water.

Acqua Lilia (It) a sparkling natural mineral water from Lilia, Potenza. Mineral contents (milligrammes per litre): Calcium 35mg/l, Magnesium 10.5mg/l, Potassium 26.5mg/l, Bicarbonates 265.5mg/l, Fluorides 0.7mg/l, Nitrates 5.3mg/l. pH 5.9

Acqua Madonna delle Grazie (It) a natural mineral water from Sorgente, Acquaruolo.

Acqua Minerale (It) mineral water.

Acqua Panna (It) a sparkling natural mineral water (established 1927) from Panna, Tuscan Appennine. Mineral contents (milligrammes per litre): Sodium 6.5mg/l, Calcium 30.2mg/l, Magnesium 6.9mg/l, Potassium 0.9mg/l, Bicarbonates 100mg/l, Chlorides 7.1mg/l, Sulphates 21.4mg/l, Fluorides <0.1mg/l, Silicate 8.2mg/l, Nitrates 5.7mg/l. pH 8.2

Acqua Paradiso (It) a still and sparkling natural mineral water from Bergstrakterna (blue label: carbonated / green label: light carbonation / red label: still). Mineral contents (milligrammes per litre): Sodium 3.2mg/l, Calcium 71mg/l, Magnesium 26mg/l, Potassium 0.7mg/l, Bicarbonates 274mg/l, Chlorides 3.3mg/l, Sulphates 51mg/l, Silicate 9.8mg/l, Nitrates 12mg/l. pH 6.7

Acqua Perla (It) a sparkling natural mineral water from Santa Fiora. Mineral contents (milligrammes per litre): Sodium 108.5mg/l, Calcium 75.8mg/l, Magnesium 30mg/l, Potassium 3.2mg/l, Bicarbonates 390.4mg/l, Chlorides 121.8mg/l, Sulphates 51mg/l, Silicate 20.6mg/l, Nitrates 13mg/l. pH 7.7

Acqua Regina (It) a natural mineral water. Mineral contents (milligrammes per litre): Sodium 5570mg/l, Calcium 657.3mg/l, Magnesium 119.16mg/l, Potassium 129.5mg/l, Bicarbonates 619.15mg/l, Chlorides 8792mg/l, Sulphates 1506mg/l, Fluorides 0.8mg/l. pH 6.4

Acquarossa (It) a sparkling natural mineral water from Belpasso, Cantania, Sicily. Mineral contents (milligrammes per litre): Sodium 158.5mg/l, Calcium 120.2mg/l, Magnesium 150.9mg/l, Potassium 13.5mg/l, Bicarbonates 1108.4mg/l, Chlorides 70.8mg/l, Nitrates 11.3mg/l. pH 6.5

Acqua Sacra (It) a sparkling natural mineral water. Mineral contents (milligrammes per litre): Sodium 51.9mg/l, Calcium 189mg/l, Magnesium 16.6mg/l, Potassium 41.9mg/l, Bicarbonates 768.6mg/l, Chlorides 42.6mg/l, Sulphates 64mg/l, Fluorides 2.4mg/l, Silicate 47mg/l, Nitrates 15mg/l. pH 6.56

Acqua Sadia (Bra) a natural mineral water.

Acquasana (It) a natural mineral water from Aquila, Abruzzo.

Acqua San Bernardo (It) a still or sparkling mineral water bottled at source in Garession.

Acqua Santa di Chianciano (It) a natural mineral water. Mineral contents (milligrammes per litre): Sodium 40.5mg/l, Calcium 714mg/l, Magnesium 172mg/l, Potassium 6.1mg/l, Bicarbonates 829.6mg/l, Chlorides 18.7mg/l, Sulphates 1810mg/l, Fluorides 2mg/l, Silicate 48mg/l, Nitrates 2.2mg/l. pH 6.8

Acqua Silva (It) a still natural mineral water. Mineral contents (milligrammes per litre): Sodium 4.9mg/l, Calcium 31.5mg/l, Magnesium 9.5mg/l, Potassium 0.7mg/l, Bicarbonates 107mg/l, Chlorides 4.7mg/l, Sulphates 9.5mg/l, Fluorides <0.1mg/l, Silicate 33.3mg/l, Nitrates 0.8mg/l. pH 7.8

Acqua Terziana (It) a natural mineral water.

Acqua Tettuccio (It) a natural mineral water from Pistoia. Mineral contents (milligrammes per litre): Sodium 2622mg/l, Calcium 392.8mg/l,

Magnesium 64.44mg/l, Potassium 77.6mg/l, Bicarbonates 488mg/l, Chlorides 4212mg/l, Sulphates 732mg/l. pH 6.9

Acqua Vitae (Lat) as for Acquae Vite.

Acquavite (It) brandy.

Acquaviva delle Fonti (It) a natural mineral water from Acquaviva, Bari.

Acquette (Fr) a liqueur with gold or silver leaf added. Has a spicey aroma (from angelica, cinnamon, cloves and nutmeg) together with lemon peel. Resembles the Goldwasser and Silberwasser of Germany.

Acquette d'Argent (Fr) acquette with silver leaf.

Acquette d'Or (Fr) acquette with gold leaf.

Acquevive (It) a natural mineral water from Capo Volturno, Rocchetta al Volturno, Isernia.

Acquit-à-Caution (Fr) a document that accompanies all shipments of wines and spirits for which French duties have not been paid.

Acquit Jaune d'Or (Fr) a yellow-gold coloured certificate that accompanies every shipment of Armagnac and Cognac that is exported.

Acquit Régional Jaune d'Or (Fr) the French Government's certificate of authenticity of Cognac in Cognac.

Acquits Verts (Fr) accompanying documents of wines.

Acre (Eng) 4840 square yards. 4046.86 square metres. 2.41 acres = 1 hectare.

Âcre (Fr) denotes a harsh, acid or bitter wine.

Acre of Stone (S.Afr) the label for a red wine (Shiraz) produced by the Goedevertrouw Estate winery, Walker Bay, Western Cape.

Acrolein (Eng) an aldehyde found in wine which contributes to the bouquet.

Acrylonitrile-butadiene-styrene (Eng) *abbr*: Abs. a material often used for valves, pipework and containers used for wine. Is low in cost and easy to sterilise.

Action on Alcohol Abuse (Eng) *see* A.A.A.

Activ (Fr) a natural mineral water.

Activated Carbon (USA) a method of purifying contaminated water or sewage by passing it through the activated carbon so that after chlorination it is fit to drink.

Activated Charcoal (Eng) used in vodka production, a highly absorptive, porous form of carbon used to remove the colour and any impurities.

Activated Sludge (USA) the method of treating sewage water with bacteria to make it fit for drinking after it has been chlorinated.

ActivO2 (Ger) a natural mineral water from Bad Adelholzen, Siegsdorf. Mineral contents (milligrammes per litre): Sodium 10mg/l, Calcium 69.8mg/l, Magnesium 31mg/l, Potassium 1.1mg/l, Bicarbonates 330mg/l, Chlorides 22.5mg/l, Sulphates 23.1mg/l, Fluorides 0.22mg/l, Nitrates 0.11mg/l.

Actual Alcohol (Eng) *abbr*: alc by vol. the amount of ethanol present in the wine, spirit or liqueur measured as a percentage of the total volume at 20°C. *see* Potential Alcohol, Total Alcohol.

Acuático (Sp) water.

Acuoso (Sp) watery.

Adabag (Tur) a medium dry red wine.

Adakarasi (Tur) a white grape variety grown in western Turkey.

Adalsan (N.Kor) a natural mineral water. Mineral contents (milligrammes per litre): Sodium 0.93mg/l, Calcium 4mg/l, Magnesium 1.2mg/l, Potassium 0.48mg/l, Bicarbonates 2.5mg/l, Sulphates 0.005mg/l, Fluorides 0.013mg/l. pH 7.0

Adam [Edouard] (Fr) invented the process of redistillation in the seventeenth century at the University of Montpellier. *See* Alambic Armagnaçais, Verdier.

Adamado (Port) sweet.

Adam and Eve (Cktl)(1) ½ measure gin, ⅛ measure Amaretto di Saronno, ⅛ measure Drambuie, 1 dash grenadine, 1 dash gomme syrup. Shake over ice, strain and decorate with a cherry and lemon slice.

Adam and Eve (Cktl)(2) 25mls (1fl.oz) each of brandy, Forbidden Fruit, dry gin, 1 dash lemon juice. Shake over ice and strain into cocktail glass.

Adam and Eve Cocktail (Cktl) ⅓ measure Plymouth gin, ½ measure orange Curaçao, ⅙ measure Yellow Chartreuse. Stir with ice and strain into a cocktail glass.

Adam Cocktail (Cktl) ½ measure Jamaican rum, ¼ measure grenadine, ¼ measure lemon juice. Shake over ice and strain into a cocktail glass.

Adam-Garnotel (Fr) a Champagne producer. (Add): 15 Rue de Chigny, 51500 Rilly-la-Montagne. Récoltants-Manipulants. Produce vintage and non-vintage wines. Vintages: 1973, 1975, 1976, 1979, 1982, 1985, 1989. Prestige cuvee: Louis Adam.

Adams (Port) Vintage Port Shippers. Vintages: 1935, 1945, 1947, 1948, 1950, 1955, 1960, 1963, 1966, 1967, 1970.

Adams [Leon] (USA) the founder of the Wine Institute in San Francisco in 1934.

Adam's Ale (Austr) a mineral water. Mineral contents (milligrammes per litre): Sodium 1.1mg/l, Calcium 6mg/l, Potassium 0.6mg/l.

Adam's Ale (Eng) the nickname for water.

Adam's Apple Cocktail (Cktl) 35mls (1½fl.ozs) Calvados, 25mls (1fl.oz) dry gin, 25mls (1fl.oz) Italian vermouth, 2 dashes yellow Chartreuse. Stir all ingredients over broken ice. Strain into a cocktail glass, decorate with cherry and add a twist lemon peel.

Adams County Winery (USA) a winery based in Orrtanna, Pennsylvania. Produces both European and hybrid wines.

Adams Fairacre Farms (Can) a natural mineral water from Grey and Wellington Counties, Ontario.

Adam's Wine (Eng) a nickname for water.

Adana-Hatay (Tur) a vineyard based in southern Turkey which is noted for medium-dry, white wines.

Adanti (It) a winery in the DOCG Sagrantino di Montefalco, Umbria region. Also produces Passito.

A

Addington Cocktail (Cktl) ½ measure sweet vermouth, ½ measure dry vermouth. Stir over ice, strain into an ice-filled highball glass and top with soda water.

Addlestones Draught Cider (Eng) a 5% alc by vol. cask-conditioned traditional cider produced by Gaymers (Showerings) of Somerset. Also a bottled version produced.

Adega (Port) a warehouse for storing wine, a wine cellar.

Adega Cooperativa (Port) describes a co-operative winery.

Adega Cooperativa de Redondo (Port) a co-operative winery based in Alentejo. Labels include Porta da Ravessa, Real Lavrados.

Adega Cooperativa Regional de Monção (Port) one of three commercial producers of Alvarinho. Labels: Deu la Deu (Alvarinho), Muralhas de Monção (Alvarinho & Trajadura).

Adega Cooperative de Palmela (Port) a large producer of Setúbal. Makes 10% of region's total production.

Adega Cooperative de Ponte da Barca (Port) a co-operative winery that produces the Aguardente Ponte da Barca.

Adega Cooperative de Ponte de Lima (Port) a co-operative winery in Peñafiel (a sub-region of Vinho Verde). Noted for red Vinho Verde.

Adegas Exportadores de Vinhos de Madeira (Mad) a large firm that ships Madeira wines to the U.K.

Adega Velha (Port) a double distilled, oak aged brandy produced by the Sociedade Agrícola da Quinta de Avelada.

Adelaida Cellars (USA) a winery based in the Paso Robles, California. (Add): 5805 Adelaida Road, Paso Robles, CA 93446. Grape varieties: Cabernet sauvignon, Counoise, Grenache noir, Mourvedre, Syrah. Label: Viking Vineyard. Website: http://www.adelaida.com

Adelaide Hills (Austr) wine area 3338ha in South Australia where vines were first planted 1839 Districts: Lenswood, Picadilly Valley. Wineries include Ashton Hills, Bird in Hand, Chain of Ponds, Heggies, Leabrook Estate, Longview Vineyard, Nepenthe, Mountadam, Petaluma, Pike & Joyce, Setana, Shaw and Smith, Starvedog Lane, The Lane. Many vineyards have been recently replanted.

Adelaide Plains (Austr) a hot region that starts in the city suburbs and stretches north and west. Wineries include the Primo Estate.

Adelberg (Ger) Grosslagen. (Anb): Rheinhessen. (Ber): Bingen. (Vils): Armsheim, Bermersheim v.d.H., Bornheim, Ensheim, Erbes-Bürdesheim, Flonheim, Lonsheim, Nack, Nieder-Weisen, Sulzheim, Wendelsheim, Wörrstadt.

Adelberg (S.Afr) a blended red wine made from the Cabernet, Pinotage and Shiraz grapes. From the Simonsig Estate, Stellenbosch.

Adelbodner (Switz) a sparkling natural mineral water (established 1559) from Adelboden (red label: high carbonation / blue label: slight carbonation /

green label: still). Mineral contents (milligrammes per litre): Sodium 5.5mg/l, Calcium 520mg/l, Magnesium 35mg/l, Potassium 1.4mg/l, Bicarbonates 291mg/l, Chlorides 5.6mg/l, Sulphates 1160mg/l, Fluoride 0.2mg/l, Nitrates 3mg/l.

Adelgaçar (Port) to dilute, thin down.

Adelheidquelle (Ger) a sparkling natural mineral water from Heilwasser, Bad Überkingen, BW. Mineral contents (milligrammes per litre): Sodium 966mg/l, Calcium 132mg/l, Magnesium 102mg/l, Potassium 43,5mg/l, Chlorides 131mg/l, Sulphates 317mg/l, Fluoride 0.7mg/l, Nitrates <0.1mg/l. Website: http://www.mineralbrunnen-ag.de

Adelholzener (Ger) a natural mineral water from Bad Adelholzen, Siegsdorf. Mineral contents (milligrammes per litre): Sodium 10mg/l, Calcium 69.8mg/l, Magnesium 31mg/l, Potassium 1.1mg/l, Bicarbonates 330mg/l, Chlorides 22.5mg/l, Sulphates 23.1mg/l, Fluoride 0.22mg/l, Nitrates 0.11mg/l.

Adelholzener Heilwasser (Ger) a sparkling natural mineral water from Bad Adelholzen, Siegsdorf. Mineral contents (milligrammes per litre): Sodium 4.6mg/l, Calcium 94mg/l, Magnesium 31mg/l, Potassium 0.5mg/l, Bicarbonates 430mg/l, Chlorides 3.6mg/l, Sulphates 10mg/l, Fluoride 0.08mg/l, Nitrates 4mg/l, Silicates 9.4mg/l.

Adelindis-Quelle (Ger) a natural mineral water from Bad Buchau, BW.

Adello (Ger) a still and sparkling natural mineral water from Bad Liebenwerda, BB. Mineral contents (milligrammes per litre): Sodium 7.9mg/l, Calcium 16.7mg/l, Magnesium 2.7mg/l, Potassium 1.6mg/l, Bicarbonates 16.5mg/l, Chlorides 5mg/l, Sulphates 55.4mg/l, Nitrates <0.5mg/l.

Adello (Switz) a natural mineral water from Oeybad, Adelboden. Mineral contents (milligrammes per litre): Sodium 5.6mg/l, Calcium 505mg/l, Magnesium 37mg/l, Bicarbonates 297mg/l, Chlorides 4.3mg/l, Sulphates 1140mg/l, Fluoride 0.23mg/l, Nitrates <0.1mg/l.

Adelpfad (Ger) vineyard (Anb): Rheinhessen. (Ber): Bingen. (Gro): Kaiserpfalz. (Vil): Engelstadt.

Adelpracht (S.Afr) the label for a late harvest white wine (Chenin blanc) produced by the Drostdy Wine Cellar winery (under their Drostdy-Hof range), Tulbagh, Western Cape.

Adelsberg (Ger) vineyard (Anb): Nahe. (Ber): Schloss Böckelheim. (Gro): Paradiesgarten. (Vil): Bayerfeld-Steckweiler.

Adelscott (Fr) a 6.6% alc by vol. light amber, novelty, smoked beer brewed from malt kilned with peat by the Adelshoffen Brasserie, Schiltigheim.

Adelscott Noir (Fr) a 6.6% alc by vol. dark novelty, smoked beer brewed from malt kilned with peat by the Adelshoffen Brasserie, Schiltigheim.

Adelscott (Fr) a novelty beer brewed from peat kiln malt by the Fischer / Pêcheur Brasserie in Strasbourg, Alsace.

A

Adel Seward S.A. (Fr) a Cognac producer. (Add): 45, Rue Grande, 16100 Cognac. Produces a range of Cognacs under the Adel label (***, V.S.O.P. and Napoléon).

Adelsheim Vineyard (USA) a vineyard (established 1971) based near Dundee, Willamette Valley, Oregon. Grape varieties: Chardonnay, Merlot, Pinot blanc, Pinot gris, Pinot noir. Labels: Bryan Creek Vineyard (Pinot noir), Caitlin's Reserve. 8ha.

Adelshoffen (Fr) a pilsener lager beer brewed in Alsace by the Schiltigheim Brasserie.

Adelshoffen Brasserie (Fr) a brewery based in Alsace. Brews Adelscott.

Adena (Fr) a natural mineral water from the island of Réunion. Mineral contents (milligrammes per litre): Sodium 7.5mg/l, Calcium 10mg/l, Magnesium 6.8mg/l, Potassium 1.3mg/l, Bicarbonates 84.2mg/l, Chlorides 6.3mg/l, Sulphates 3mg/l, Fluoride 0.08mg/l, Nitrates 3.4mg/l.

Ades (Indo) a natural mineral water from Bogor. Mineral contents (milligrammes per litre): Sodium 8.5mg/l, Calcium 36mg/l, Magnesium 16mg/l, Bicarbonates 80mg/l, Chlorides 12mg/l, Sulphates 5mg/l. pH 7.0

Adgestone Vineyard (Eng) a vineyard (established 1968) based on the Isle of Wight. (Add): Upper Road, Adgestone, Sandown, Isle of Wight. 10.5ha. Soil: calcareous flinty loam. Grape varieties: Müller-Thurgau, Reichensteiner and Seyval blanc.

Adige [River] (It) a river that flows from the Alps (in the north), south-east to the Adriatic sea. Flows through the Trentino-Alto-Adige (Süd-Tirol) from which it gets its name.

Adios Amigos (Cktl) 35mls (1½fl.ozs) white rum, 25mls (1fl.oz) each of Cognac, gin, dry vermouth, lime juice. Shake well over ice, strain into an ice-filled highball glass.

Adissan (Fr) a wine-producing commune in the Clairette du Languedoc, southern France.

Adjuncts (Eng) the name given to the fermentable materials (other cereal starches, caramel, invert sugar) found in the wort other than the water, barley malt, yeast and hops.

Adldorfer (Ger) a natural mineral water from the Dreibogenquelle, Adldorf. Mineral contents (milligrammes per litre): Sodium 3.8mg/l, Calcium 87mg/l, Magnesium 29mg/l, Potassium 1mg/l, Bicarbonates 383mg/l, Chlorides 5.5mg/l, Sulphates 23mg/l, Fluoride 0.2mg/l, Nitrates 0.1mg/l, Silicates 21mg/l.

Adler (Ger) vineyard (Anb): Mosel-Saar-Ruwer. (Ber): Zell/Mosel. (Gro): Schwarze Katz. (Vil): Zell-Merl.

Adler (S.Afr) a winery (established 2004) based in Wellington, Western Cape. Grape varieties: Cabernet sauvignon, Merlot, Petit verdot, Sauvignon blanc, Viognier. Labels: Cap Classique, Modus M. Website: http://www.olimeck.co.za/adler

Adler Brauerei (Switz) an independent brewery based in Schwanden.

Administracion Geral de Alcool (Port) abbr: A.G.E. a body that receives grape spirit from the Comissão and disposes it to Port companies for brandying their wines or to firms for elaboration as brandy.

Admiral (Aus) the label for a red wine (Zweigelt, Cabernet and Merlot blend) produced by the Pöckl winery, Burgenland.

Admirable [L'] (USA) an 'altar wine' (angelica) produced by Novitiate in Los Gatos, California.

Admiral Cocktail [1] (Cktl) ⅓ measure Bourbon whiskey, ⅓ measure French vermouth, juice ½ lemon. Shake well over ice, strain into an ice-filled old-fashioned glass and add twist of lemon peel juice.

Admiral Cocktail [2] (Cktl) 1 measure gin, ½ measure cherry brandy, ½ measure lemon juice. Shake over ice and strain into a cocktail glass.

Admiral Dewey Waters (USA) a distilled drinking water and spring water range.

Admiral's Ale (Eng) a cask-conditioned premium bitter ale 1048 O.G. brewed by the Southsea Brewery, Portsmouth, Hampshire.

Admirals Ale (Eng) a 4% alc by vol. ale brewed by the Ventnor Brewery Ltd. Isle of Wight.

Admiral's Reserve (Eng) a 5% alc by vol. ale brewed by Woodforde's Ltd., Norfolk.

Admiral's Sherry-Drake's Fino (Sp) a brand of Fino Sherry produced by Lustau.

Admiralty House (S.Afr) the label for a range of wines produced by the Cape Bay winery, Walker Bay, Western Cape.

Admiral Vernon (Eng) see Old Rummy.

Adnams Brewery (Eng) a brewery and wine merchant. (Add): Sole Bay Brewery, Southwald, Suffolk. Produces Smooth Bitter, Broadside, Mild Ale, MM, Olde Ale, Regatta Ale, Explorer and Tally Ho Barley Wine. Also major wine merchants of note dealing in fine wines.

Adobe (Mex) the name used for the oven that the piñas (part of the agave cactus) are cooked in prior to the production of tequila.

Adobe Springs (USA) a natural mineral water based in California. Mineral contents (milligrammes per litre): Sodium 6.2mg/l, Calcium 4.4mg/l, Magnesium 110mg/l, Chlorides 6mg/l, Sulphates 13mg/l, Nitrates 3.1mg/l. pH 8.4

Adoc (Fr) old term for sour milk.

Adolf Coors Brewery (USA) see Coors Brewery (Adolf).

Adoli Ghis (Gre) a white wine produced from 90% Lagorthi and 10% Chardonnay grapes by Antonopoulos Vineyards, Vassiliko, Peloponnese.

Adolzfurt (Ger) village (Anb): Württemberg. (Ber): Württembergisch Unterland. (Gro): Lindelberg. (Vin): Schneckenhof.

Adomado (Port) sweet.

Adom Atic (Isr) a semi-dry, red wine for the USA market made from French grape varieties. Produced by Carmel.

Adonis (Cktl) ⅔ measure dry Sherry, ⅓ measure sweet vermouth, 1 dash orange bitters. Stir over ice, strain into a cocktail glass and add a twist of orange peel.

13

Adonis Heilwasser (Ger) a natural mineral water from the Adonis Quelle, Birrisborn. Mineral contents (milligrammes per litre): Sodium 516mg/l, Calcium 105mg/l, Magnesium 80mg/l, Potassium 29mg/l, Bicarbonates 2041mg/l, Chlorides 40.4mg/l, Sulphates 18mg/l, Fluoride 0.19mg/l, Nitrates 4.1mg/l.

Adria (Pol) a natural mineral water from Torun-Czerniewice. Mineral contents (milligrammes per litre): Sodium 5mg/l, Calcium 50.3mg/l, Magnesium 6.6mg/l, Potassium 1.1mg/l, Bicarbonates 146.4mg/l, Chlorides 10.6mg/l, Sulphates 22.5mg/l.

Adrianum (It) a white wine produced in Roman times in north-eastern Italy.

Adrianus and Fiona (S.Afr) the label for a red wine produced by the Saxenberg winery, Stellenbosch, Western Cape.

Adriatica (Euro) the brand-name for a co-operative association which markets wines in the USA.

Adrumenitanum (It) a full red wine which was produced in Sicily in Roman times.

Adry Cocktail (Cktl) 25mls (1fl.oz) Bourbon whiskey, 4 dashes Cointreau. Shake over ice, strain into a cocktail glass with crushed ice. Dress with a cherry.

Adulterate (Eng) denotes the addition of one (foreign) liquid into another liquid. e.g. water into spirits, beer, wine, etc. to illegally increase bulk. *see* Cut.

Ad Valorem Tax (Eng) a tax introduced for a year in 1924 that stated that the wealthy had to pay more for finer Champagne than the cheaper sparkling wines.

Advent (Eng) seasonal cask ale brewed by the Morrell Brewery, Oxford.

Advent (Eng) a 4.7% alc by vol. ale brewed by the Abbeydale Brewery Ltd., South Yorkshire.

Advent Ale (Eng) a 4.4% alc by vol. ale brewed by the Hogs Back brewery Ltd., Surrey.

Advocaat (Hol) a liqueur of egg yolks, sugar, vanilla and brandy. 15% –18% alc by vol.

Advocaat (Hol) egg-nog.

Advocate Ale (Eng) a cask-conditioned ale 1032 O.G. brewed by the Crouch Vale Brewery, Essex.

Advocatenborrel (Hol) a brand of advocaat drink. 17% alc by vol.

Ad-vo-tizer (Cktl) 50mls (2fl.ozs) dry vermouth, 25mls (1fl.oz) advocaat and Tizer. Build advocaat and vermouth into an ice-filled highball glass. Stir in Tizer, add slice of orange.

ADZs (Eng) *abbr:* Alcohol Disorder Zones.

Æblemost (Den) apple juice.

Æbleræendevin (Den) apple jack.

Aecht Schenkerla Rauchbier (Ger) a 4.8% bottled dark smoked beer brewed by the Heller Brauerei, Bamberg.

Aegean Islands (Gre) a group of islands in eastern Greece. Samos, Lemnos, Lesbos and Khios. Produce mainly sweet dessert wines from the Muscat grape.

Aegean Lager (Gre) a bottled lager beer 5% alc by vol. brewed by Henniger Hellas SA, Atlanti, near Athens.

Aegean Wines (Gre) wines that were popular in ancient Greece.

Aegidius Brunnen (Ger) a natural mineral water from Bad Honnef, north-western Germany. Mineral contents (milligrammes per litre): Sodium 290mg/l, Calcium 40mg/l, Magnesium 40mg/l, Potassium 10mg/l, Bicarbonates 760mg/l, Chlorides 140mg/l, Sulphates 120mg/l.

Aemilia (It) a sparkling natural mineral water from Aemilia. Mineral contents (milligrammes per litre): Sodium 48.3mg/l, Calcium 76.1mg/l, Magnesium 71.4mg/l, Potassium 3.3mg/l, Bicarbonates 542.7mg/l, Chlorides 23.7mg/l, Sulphates 102.6mg/l, Silicates 17mg/l, Nitrates 29.8mg/l. pH 7.2

Aeolian Islands (It) also known as the Lipari Islands. Situated in the north of Sicily, within the jurisdiction of the province of Messina.

Aequicum (It) a red wine produced in central-eastern Italy in Roman times.

Aerate (Eng) to charge with gas i.e. CO_2 in beer and wines. *See also* Carbonation.

Aerobausqueador (Sp) an electric pump that helps to redistribute the cap and solids in the fermenting vat.

Aerobic (Eng) when applied to organisms denotes that they need air to respire and therefore reproduce (see Binary Fission). Wild yeasts in the grape musts are '*aerobic*' and are prevented from reproducing by the addition of SO_2. *See also* Anaerobic.

Aerts 1900 (Bel) 7.5% alc by vol. special beer brewed by Palm Brasserie, Steenhuffel. Fermented three times (once in bottle).

Aesculap Water (Hun) an aperient mineral water from the Aesculap spring in Kelenföld, Budapest. High in Sodium and Magnesium sulphates.

Afames (Cyp) a deep red wine produced from the Mavron grape in the Troodos mountains around Platres, south-eastern Cyprus.

Aferrin (Eng) the alternative name for **Calcium phytate** (a fining agent) that removes excess iron, copper and zinc from wines.

A Few Good Men (S.Afr) the label for a range of wines produced by the Riebeek Cellars winery, Swartland, Western Cape.

Affalterbach (Ger) village (Anb): Württemberg. (Ber): Württembergisch Unterland. (Gro): Schalkstein. (Vin): Neckarhälde.

Affaltrach (Ger) village (Anb): Württemberg. (Ber): Württembergisch Unterland. (Gro): Salzberg. (Vins): Dieblesberg, Zeilberg.

Affchen (Ger) vineyard (Anb): Rheinhessen. (Ber): Bingen. (Gro): Rheingrafenstein. (Vil): Wöllstein.

Affecionados (Sp) lovers of fine Sherries or wines.

Affenberg (Ger) vineyard (Anb): Rheinhessen. (Ber): Wonnegau. (Gro): Liebfrauenmorgen. (Vil): Worms.

Affenflasche (Ger) lit: 'monkey bottle', bottle used for the Affenthal wines (affe means monkey).

Affenthaler Spätburgunder (Ger) a red wine produced in the bereich of Ortenau in Baden from Blauer spätburgunder grape variety and bottled in a monkey embossed bottle. Produced in a valley called Ave Thal.

Affile (It) *see* Cesanese di Affile.

Affinage (Fr) a term used to describe the long ageing of Banyuls Grand Cru wines in underground cellars at a constant temperature for a minimum of 30 months.

Affinity [1] (Cktl) ⅓ measure sweet vermouth, ⅔ measure Scotch whisky, 2 dashes Angostura. Stir over ice and strain into a cocktail glass.

Affinity [2] (Cktl) ⅓ measure Scotch whisky, ⅓ measure Port, ⅓ measure dry Sherry, 2 dashes Angostura. Shake well over ice and strain into an ice-filled old-fashioned glass.

Affinity (S.Afr) the label for a red wine (Cabernet sauvignon 86% Merlot 14%) produced by the La Bri winery, Franschhoek, Western Cape.

Affinity Cocktail (Cktl) ⅔ measure French vermouth, ⅓ measure Italian vermouth, ½ measure crème de violette. Shake well over ice and strain into a cocktail glass.

Affligem Blond (Bel) 7% alc by vol. straw-coloured, bottle-conditioned, special abbaye beer brewed at Afflingem Abbaye by De Smedt Brouwerij, Opwijk.

Affligem Dubbel (Bel) 7% alc by vol. brown-coloured, bottle-conditioned, special abbaye beer brewed at Afflingem Abbaye by De Smedt Brouwerij, Opwijk.

Affligem Tripel (Bel) 8.5% alc by vol. bottle-conditioned, special straw triple abbaye beer brewed at Afflingem Abbaye by De Smedt Brouwerij, Opwijk.

Aficionado (Port) lover of Port.

Aficionado (Sp) a supporter of a particular wine.

Afonso III (Port) a brand of dry white wine produced in Lagoa, Algarve.

Afreeka (S.Afr) 5% alc by vol. sparkling drink produced from the African marula berry.

African Collection (S.Afr) the export label for a range of wines produced by the Rooiberg Winery, Robertson, Western Cape.

African Dawn (S.Afr) the export label for a range of wines produced by the Rooiberg Winery, Robertson, Western Cape.

African Gin (Afr) a fairly bland, dry gin.

African Gold (S.Afr) the label for a range of wines (for export) produced by the Dominion Wine Company, Stellenbosch, Western Cape.

African Gold Collection (S.Afr) the label for a range of red and white wines marketed by the Old Bridge Wines company, Western Cape.

African Lager (Eng)(slang) an old nickname for Guinness stout.

African Pride Wines (S.Afr) a winery (established 2002) based in Winmeul, Paarl, Western Cape. Grape varieties: Cabernet sauvignon, Chardonnay, Sauvignon blanc, Shiraz. Labels: Cape MacLear, Footprint, Lady Anne Barnard. Website: http://www.africanpridewines.co.za

African Sky (S.Afr) the label for a range of wines for export produced by the Drostdy Wine Cellar winery, Tulbagh, Western Cape.

African Tea (Afr) *see* Khat.

African Teas (Afr) main countries of production are Kenya, Uganda, Malawi, Tanzania and Mozambique.

African Terroir (S.Afr) a winery (established 1991) based in Windmeul, Paarl, Western Cape. Grape varieties: Cabernet sauvignon, Chardonnay, Merlot, Pinotage, Sauvignon blanc, Shiraz. Labels: Diemersdal, Elixer, Harmony, Milton Grove, Out of Africa, Sonop Organic, Tribal Winemakers Collection, Winds of Change. 75ha. Website: http://www.african-terroir.co.za

African Wine Adventure (S.Afr) the label for a range of red and white wines produced by the Mooiuitsig Wine Cellars winery, Robertson, Western Cape.

Afrothes (Gre) term for sparkling wine.

Afrutado (Sp) a white Montilla-Moriles wine bottled and sold in the year of production. *see* Vinos Generosos.

After Dark (Eng) a special ale brewed by the Arundel Brewery, West Sussex for Hallowe'en.

After Dinner (Cktl) ⅓ measure lemon juice, ⅓ measure cherry brandy, ⅓ measure Prunelle. Shake over ice and strain.

After Dinner Cocktail [1] (Cktl) 25mls (1fl.oz) Triple Sec, 25mls (1fl.oz) apricot brandy, juice of a lime. Shake over ice, strain into a cocktail glass and add a slice of lime.

After Dinner Cocktail [2] (Cktl) 1 measure maraschino, 1 measure kirsch, 3 dashes curaçao, 3 dashes Angostura. Stir over ice, strain into a balloon glass, top with 2 measures pineapple juice and a twist of lemon peel juice.

After Dinner Coffee (Eng) the name given to dark roasted, strong coffees.

After Eight (Cktl) ⅓ measure J&B Scotch whisky, ⅓ measure Royal Mint Chocolate liqueur, ⅓ measure cream. Shake well over ice and strain and top with grated chocolate.

After Five (S.Afr) the label for a range of wines produced by the McGregor Wines winery, Robertson, Western Cape.

Afternoon (Cktl) ⅓ measure Cognac, ⅓ measure Fernet Branca, ⅓ measure maraschino. Stir over crushed ice, pour into a Champagne saucer, top with a dash of soda water, orange slice and serve with straws.

Afternoon Tea (Eng) tea (usually China) and light refreshments served in the middle afternoon. Was started in the late eighteenth century by Anna Duchess of Bedford.

After One (Cktl) ¼ measure Campari, ¼ measure gin, ¼ measure sweet vermouth, ¼ measure Galliano. Shake over ice, strain, with a twist of orange peel and a cocktail cherry.

Afters (Eng) an illegal request for a drink after 'permitted hours'.

After Shock (Eng) 40% alc by vol. hot and cool cinnamon-flavoured liqueur produced by Jim Beam Brands.

After Supper Cocktail (Cktl) 1 measure Triple Sec, 1 measure apricot brandy, juice ¼ lemon. Shake over ice and strain into a cocktail glass.

After-taste (Eng) the taste left in the mouth after the wine has been spat out or swallowed. (Fr) = arrière-goût.

Afuera (Sp) denotes a wine produced from grapes grown on Albariza soil in south-western Spain.

Agabuna (It) a natural mineral water from Agabuna.

Agave Cactus (Mex) *Agave tequilana* a plant of which the root is used for making pulque from which tequila is distilled (blue in colour), thought to be a succulent not a cactus. Takes 8–10 years to mature. *see* Blanco Tequila, Reposado, Añejo Tequila, Gusano. Also known as the Blue Maguey, Century Plant and Maguey.

Agave Tequilana (Mex) a sub-species of agave cactus which is grown on Sierra Madre slopes by tequila shippers.

Agave Tequilana (Mex) *see* Agave Cactus

Agave Worm (Mex) added to bottles of tequila to show quality and potency. If alcohol content was weak, worm would rot in the bottle. Often now substituted with slivers of maguey or sugar cane (because of the expense of the worms). Also known as the Gusano and Maguey Worm.

Agawam (Can) a white grape variety grown in Niagara. Originates from the *Vitis labrusca*.

A.G. Brandy (USA) a gecht brandy produced and bottled by White Manor Liquor House.

Age (Eng) refers to the maturing of wine.

A.G.E. Bodegas Unidas, S.A. (Sp) vineyard. Alta region, Rioja, north-eastern Spain. 50ha. (Add): Barrio Estracion 21, Fuenmayor, (La Rioja). Produces red, rosé and white wines from grape varieties Tempranillo, Garnacha and Viura.

Aged Coffee (Eng) the name given to green coffee beans that have been held for 6–7 years to mature in warehouses.

Âge des Épices [L'] (Fr) a 15 year old Cognac produced by Gourmel (L). Has a subtle flavour of cocoa and vanilla.

Âge des Fleurs [L'] (Fr) a 12 year old Cognac produced by Gourmel (L). Has a subtle aroma of vine flowers.

Aged in Wood (Eng) denotes the maturation of the wine in wooden casks for a given period. *See also* LBV Port. (Fr) = vieilli au tonneau.

Âge Inconnu (Fr) a grading for old brandies.

Âge Inconnu (Fr) an old Cognac brandy produced by Croizet.

Agenais (Fr) a Vin de Pays area in the Lot-et-Garonne département in south-western France.

Agglomerate (Eng) *see* Aggloméré.

Agglomerated Cork (Eng) a cork built up from small pieces of cork glued and pressed together. Used for stoppering cheap table wines or as a firm base on sparkling wine corks to resist the wire cage and cap cutting into the cork. (Fr) = aggloméré.

Aggloméré (Fr) lit: 'compressed dust', a cork made from cork pieces glued together. In sparkling wines discs of cork are glued to the base of the

agglomerated top. *see* Miroir. (Eng) = agglomerated cork.

Aggressività (It) astringency or sharpness, word used by Italian connoisseurs to describe sharp red wines.

Aghiorghitico (Gre) a red grape variety found especially in the Peloponnese islands.

Agias Marinas (Gre) a natural mineral water from Asterousia, Kreta. Mineral contents (milligrammes per litre): Sodium 17.9mg/l, Calcium 56.1mg/l, Magnesium 19mg/l, Potassium 0.8mg/l, Bicarbonates 219.6mg/l, Chlorides 37.2mg/l, Sulphates 21.6mg/l, Nitrates 0.6mg/l.

Agiorgitiko (Gre) a red grape variety, also known as Saint Georges. Produces dry red wines.

Agioritikos (Gre) the name given to white, rosé and red wines. The white made from the Assirtico and Athiri grapes, the rosé from the Grenache grape and the red from 40% Cabernet sauvignon and 60% Limnio grapes.

Agitated Wine (USA) a term used in California for Sherry-style wines where flor is added to the wine and stirred through it to give a 'flor taste'.

Agker (Hun) the State Wine Organisation.

Aglianico (It) a thick skinned and tannic red grape variety of the Basilicata region of southern Italy. Has aromas and flavours of herbs, liquorice and minerals. Is also known as the Aglianico de Cassano and the Gaglioppo.

Aglianico del Vulture (It) a D.O.C. red wine (awarded 1971) from the Basilicata region. Aglianico grape. Cannot be sold before November 1st of year following the vintage. If total alcohol content is 12% by vol. and aged for 3 years (2 in wood) then it is graded 'vecchio'. If 5 years (2 in wood) then graded 'riserva'. The D.O.C. also applies to the natural sparkling wines.

Aglianico di Cassano (It) the local (Pollino, Calabria) name for the red Gaglioppo grape. *See also* Aglianico.

Agliano (It) an alternative name for Aleatico.

Agly [River] (Fr) a river in the Pyrénées Orientales within the Languedoc-Roussillon.

Agnesienberg (Ger) vineyard (Anb): Nahe. (Ber): Kreuznach. (Gro): Kronenberg. (Vil): Bad Kreuznach.

Ag. Nikolaos (Cyp) a natural mineral water from Stegis, Nicosia.

Agos Oro (Sp) white wine produced by Bodegas Lopez-Agos. Made from 100% Viura grapes, matured for 1 year in oak and 2 years in bottle.

Agostado (Sp) a method of pulling up the old vines in the Sherry region by digging up to ¼ metre deep. This removes the old roots and brings the lower earth to the surface.

Agostinelli (S.Afr) the label for a range of Italian-style wines produced by the Fairview winery, Suider-Paarl, Western Cape.

Agraço (Port) unripe grape juice, juice from unripe grapes.

Agrafe (Fr) a clamp which holds down the cork on a Champagne bottle during the second fermentation. Usually made of iron or steel. (Sp) = grapa.

Agraffe (Fr) *see* Agrafe.

Agramont (Sp) the label used by Bodegas Cenalsa-Pamplona in the Navarra region for their red, rosé and white wines.

Agras (Alg) sweet, almond-flavoured, unripe grape juice which is drunk ice cold.

Agraz (Sp) unripe grape.

Agrazo (Sp) unripe grape juice, the juice from unripe grapes.

Agreeable (Eng) a term which denotes that a wine, beer, cocktail, etc., has a pleasant, acceptable taste, aroma, etc.

Agrément (Fr) official approval for any French wine for its own A.C. (based on tasting and analysis). Usually between November and April immediately after the harvest.

Agressif (Fr) a term to denote a wine that is unharmonious, or made from unripe grapes.

Agresto (It) unripe grape juice, the juice from unripe grapes.

Agricola [La] (Arg) a winery based east of Mendoza. Produces Santa Julia and Q ranges of wines. Grape varieties: Sangiovese, Bonarda, Zinfandel, Syrah, Viognier, Tempranillo.

Agricola Alimentare (It) a Chianti Putto producer in Tuscany.

Agrícola Castellana S. Cooperativa (Sp) a noted winery based in La Seca, Valladolid, north-western Spain.

Agricola Monterinaldi Srl (It) a winery. Website: http://www.monterinaldi.it

Agricola Querciabella (It) a 25ha. winery. (Add): Via Carducci 16, 20123 Milano. Produces Chianti Classico Riserva and I.G.T. Batàr.

Agricola Tedeschi (It) (Add): Via G Verdi 4/A, 37010 Pedemonte di S. Pietro Incariano (Verona). Famous producer of Valpolicella wines.

Agricole Vallone (It) winery. (Add): Via XXV Luglio 7, 73100 Lecce. 660 ha winery. Produce D.O.C. Salice Salentino Rosso. Brindisi Rosso, Brindisi Rosato. I.G.T. Salento Bianco.

Agricole (Fr) the name given to rum made from cane juice.

Agricoltori del Chianti Geografico (It) a vineyard in the D.O.C.G. Chianti Classico, Tuscany. Produces: Monte-giachi. Website:http://www.chiantigeografico.it

Agricoltura Biologica (It) organic cutivation.

Agridulce (Sp) bitter sweet.

Agrio (Sp) sour / bitter / tart / rough.

Agritiusberg (Ger) vineyard (Anb): Mosel-Saar-Ruwer. (Ber): Saar-Ruwer. (Gro): Scharzberg. (Vil): Oberemmel.

Agro de Bazán (Sp) a winery with vineyards in Val do Salnés, Rías Baixas, D.O. Galicia. Produces three wines: Granbazán Verde, Granbazán Amba, Crianza Granbazán Limousin.

Agrokombinat (Slov) co-operative.

Agronavarra (Sp) *see* CENALSA.

Agros Sport (Cyp) a natural mineral water from Agros. Mineral contents (milligrammes per litre):

Sodium 14.9mg/l, Calcium 28.9mg/l, Magnesium 13.1mg/l, Potassium 0.4mg/l, Bicarbonates 134.2mg/l, Chlorides 14.2mg/l, Sulphates 20.2mg/l.

Agterkliphoogte Wynkelder Koöp (S.Afr) a co-operative winery based in Robertson. (Add): Box 267, Robertson 6705. Produces varietal wines.

Agterplaas Wines (S.Afr) a winery (established 2003) based in Stellenbosch, Western Cape. Grape varieties: Cabernet sauvignon, Chardonnay, Cinsaut, Merlot. Labels: Bordeaux Blend, Mike's Red.

Agua (Sp) water.

Água (Port) water.

Água Castello (Port) a natural mineral water. Mineral contents (milligrammes per litre): Sodium 39mg/l, Calcium 103mg/l, Magnesium 30.7mg/l, Bicarbonates 377mg/l, Chlorides 87mg/l, Sulphates 17.7mg/l. pH 7.2

Aguaceiro (Port) water carrier.

Água Cristalina de Anapolis (Bra) a natural mineral water high in acidity. Mineral contents (milligrammes per litre): Sodium 0.36mg/l, Calcium 0.05mg/l, Magnesium 0.03mg/l, Potassium 0.05mg/l, Bicarbonates 0.63mg/l, Chlorides 0.17mg/l, Fluoride 0.13mg/l. pH 4.2

Agua de Albarcin (Sp) a still natural mineral water from Guadix, Granada. Mineral contents (milligrammes per litre): Sodium 20mg/l, Calcium 42mg/l, Magnesium 15mg/l, Potassium 0.3mg/l, Bicarbonates 157mg/l, Chlorides 36mg/l, Sulphates 42mg/l, Fluoride 0.1mg/l, Nitrates 8mg/l.

Agua de Cañizar (Sp) a still natural mineral water from Fuen-Mayor, Cañizar del Olivar, Teruel. Mineral contents (milligrammes per litre): Sodium 1.4mg/l, Calcium 71.3mg/l, Magnesium 18mg/l, Potassium 0.5mg/l, Bicarbonates 293mg/l, Chlorides 2.6mg/l, Sulphates 12.8mg/l, Fluoride 0.1mg/l, Nitrates 1.7mg/l.

Agua de Carabaña (Sp) a natural mineral water (established 1885) from Carabaña. Mineral contents (milligrammes per litre): Sodium 26882mg/l, Calcium 504.7mg/l, Magnesium 552.1mg/l, Potassium 27.1mg/l, Bicarbonates 341.6mg/l, Chlorides 2493mg/l, Sulphates 54980mg/l, Fluoride 0.9mg/l.

Agua de Cuevas (Sp) a natural mineral water from Puerto de San Isidoro, Asturia. Mineral contents (milligrammes per litre): Sodium 1.4mg/l, Calcium 47.3mg/l, Magnesium 25.3mg/l, Potassium 0.4mg/l, Bicarbonates 238.3mg/l, Chlorides 2.6mg/l, Sulphates 12.9mg/l, Fluoride 0.1mg/l, Nitrates 1.7mg/l.

Agua de Fuente (Sp) spring water (f).

Agua del Rosal (Sp) a still natual mineral water from Calera y Chozas, Toledo. Mineral contents (milligrammes per litre): Sodium 48.8mg/l, Calcium 63.3mg/l, Magnesium 12.2mg/l, Potassium 1.8mg/l, Bicarbonates 282.9mg/l, Chlorides 49.8mg/l, Sulphates 7mg/l, Fluoride 0.5mg/l, Nitrates 17.5mg/l.

Agua de Manatial (Sp) spring water (m).

Agua de Mondariz (Sp) a natural mineral water from Mondariz IV, Mondariz Baln, Pontevedra. Mineral contents (milligrammes per litre): Sodium 50.5mg/l, Calcium 9.2mg/l, Magnesium 4.9mg/l, Potassium 5.1mg/l, Bicarbonates 163.4mg/l, Chlorides 17.9mg/l, Sulphates 1.5mg/l, Fluoride 0.4mg/l, Nitrates 1.9mg/l, Silicates 16.8mg/l, Iron 0.23mg/l. pH 6.48

Agua de Quess (Sp) a still natural mineral water from Manatial de Quess, Quess-Piloña, Asturias. Mineral contents (milligrammes per litre): Sodium 4.1mg/l, Calcium 0.5mg/l, Magnesium 0.7mg/l, Bicarbonates 4.5mg/l, Chlorides 7mg/l, Sulphates 1.2mg/l, Fluoride 0.1mg/l.

Agua de Sierra (Sp) a still natural mineral water from the Fuente la Higuera, Cariñena, Zaragoza. Mineral contents (milligrammes per litre): Calcium 118mg/l, Magnesium 51mg/l, Potassium 2.9mg/l, Bicarbonates 2000mg/l, Sulphates 239mg/l.

Agua Destilada (Sp) distilled water.

Água Doce (Port) fresh water.

Água do Fastio (Port) a natural mineral water high in acidity. Mineral contents (milligrammes per litre): Sodium 4.95mg/l, Calcium 1.5mg/l, Silicates 13.5mg/l, Potassium 0.65mg/l, Bicarbonates 9.4mg/l, Chlorides 4.8mg/l, Sulphates 0.85mg/l. pH 5.78

Água do Marao (Port) a natural mineral water. Mineral contents (milligrammes per litre): Sodium 3mg/l, Calcium 2.2mg/l, Silicates 5.9mg/l, Bicarbonates 9mg/l, Chlorides 4.5mg/l. pH 5.7

Agua Helada (Sp) iced water.

Água Magnesiana do Campestre (Bra) a natural mineral water. Mineral contents (milligrammes per litre): Sodium 102.24mg/l, Calcium 2.4mg/l, Magnesium 121.77mg/l, Potassium 7.12mg/l, Bicarbonates 553.69mg/l, Chlorides 152.74mg/l, Sulphates 32.34mg/l, Nitrates 41.9mg/l. pH 7.4

Agua Manatial (Mex) a natural spring mineral water from Acapulco. Mineral contents (milligrammes per litre): Sodium 2mg/l, Calcium 36mg/l, Magnesium 17mg/l, Bicarbonates 10mg/l, Chlorides 42mg/l, Sulphates 9mg/l. pH 8.0

Aguamanil (Sp) ewer / water jug.

Aguamiel (Mex) lit: 'honey water', the sap of the agave cactus used in the making of pulque and tequila.

Água Mineral (Port) mineral water.

Agua Mineral (Sp) mineral water.

Água Mineral Kaiary (Bra) a natural mineral water high in acidity. Mineral contents (milligrammes per litre): Sodium 0.01mg/l, Calcium 0.11mg/l, Magnesium 0.11mg/l, Potassium 0.47mg/l, Bicarbonates 0.4mg/l, Sulphates 0.1mg/l, Fluoride 0.07mg/l, Nitrates 0.001mg/l, Silicates 1.94mg/l. pH 4.8 Website: http://www.aguakaiary.com

Agua Mineral Prata do Vale (Bra) an acidic sparkling natual mineral water (established 1995) from the Fonte Lêda. Mineral contents (milligrammes per litre): Sodium 15.25mg/l, Calcium 3.4mg/l, Magnesium 0.24mg/l, Potassium 1.09mg/l, Bicarbonates 1.46mg/l, Silicates 9.6mg/l, Nitrates 0.24mg/l. pH 4.5

Agua Mineral San Felipe (Ecu) a natural mineral water from Eloy Alfaro in the Cotopaxi province. Mineral contents (milligrammes per litre): Sodium 276mg/l, Calcium 130.3mg/l, Magnesium 417.7mg/l, Potassium 19mg/l, Chlorides 141.9mg/l. pH 6.4

Água Pe (Port) lit: 'foot water', a light red wine produced by adding water to the grape skins and refermenting. Produced in the Douro region. 4%–5% alc by vol.

Aguapié (Sp) second pressing of the grapes which produces the juice after the Yema (1st pressing) when gypsum is added.

Agua Potable (Sp) drinking water.

Água Potavel (Port) drinking water.

Agua Purificada Aquasystem (Mex) a bottled still, purified drinking water from Iztapalata-Tlahuac, Coyoacan. pH 7.5

Águar (Port) to water / to dilute.

Aguar (Sp) to dilute.

Aguardente (Port) a spirit (brandy) distilled from wine made from grape pressings (pulp).

Aguardente de Cana (Bra) a spirit made from fermented sugar cane, known as cachaça – the national drink of Brazil.

Aguardente de Cana-de-Acucar (Bra) the name used for white rum in the nineteenth century.

Aguardente Medrohono (Port) an eau-de-vie popular in the Algarve.

Aguardiente (Sp) brandy, usually made by distilling the wine made from the grape pressings (pulp).

Aguardiente (W.Ind) in the distillation of rum refers to the heart of the distillation. (*See also* Madilla).

Aguardiente de Orujo (Sp) a term for the French equivalent of marc. Made in Galicia, it often reaches 48% alc by vol.

Agua Ropador (Sp) a natural mineral water from the Canary Islands.

Agua Salus (Ury) a natural mineral water from the Sierra de Minas. Mineral contents (milligrammes per litre): Sodium 7.2mg/l, Calcium 36mg/l, Magnesium 8.9mg/l, Potassium 0.71mg/l, Chlorides 7.1mg/l, Sulphates 5.7mg/l, Nitrates 0.7mg/l.

Agua Sana (Sp) a still natural mineral water from A Granxa, Belesar, Baiona, Galicia. Mineral contents (milligrammes per litre): Sodium 5.8mg/l, Calcium 1.1mg/l, Magnesium 0.6mg/l, Bicarbonates 6.7mg/l, Chlorides 8.7mg/l, Fluoride 0.4mg/l.

Agua Santa Ines (Bra) an acidic natural mineral water. Mineral contents (milligrammes per litre): Sodium 1.09mg/l, Calcium 0.88mg/l, Magnesium 0.63mg/l, Potassium 4.64mg/l, Bicarbonates 5.7mg/l, Chlorides 1.2mg/l, Sulphates 0.3mg/l, Fluoride 0.01mg/l, Nitrates 8mg/l. pH 4.81 Website: http://www.aguasantaines.com.br

A

Água Sao Silvestre (Port) a natural mineral water. Mineral contents (milligrammes per litre): Sodium 30.4mg/l, Calcium 31.5mg/l, Bicarbonates 115mg/l, Chlorides 34.1mg/l. pH 7.1

Aguas Belnature (Sp) a still natural mineral water from Bel-Nature, Artetz-Valle de Ollo, Navarra. Mineral contents (milligrammes per litre): Sodium 6.5mg/l, Calcium 75.4mg/l, Bicarbonates 213.5mg/l, Sulphates 11mg/l, Nitrates 9mg/l.

Aguascalientes (Mex) a top wine-producing district in central Mexico.

Águas da Mata Atlântica (Bra) a naturally sparkling mineral water of high acidity. Mineral contents (milligrammes per litre): Sodium 1.41mg/l, Calcium 0.54mg/l, Magnesium 0.33mg/l, Potassium 1.1mg/l, Bicarbonates 3.79mg/l, Chlorides 1.29mg/l, Sulphates 0.37mg/l, Fluoride <0.001mg/l, Nitrates 2.35mg/l, Silicates 4.12mg/l. pH 5.33 Website: http://www.aguasdamata.com.br

Aguas de Cañazar (Sp) a natural mineral water from Cañizar de Olivar.

Águas de Carvalhelhos [1] (Port) a natural mineral water. (Add): Fonte Estela.

Águas de Carvalhelhos [2] (Port) a natural mineral water. (Add): Fonte Lucy.

Aguas del Plata (Arg) a still natural mineral water (established 1987) from Vista Flores, Mendoza. Mineral contents (milligrammes per litre): Sodium 3.2mg/l, Calcium 20mg/l, Magnesium 3.5mg/l, Potassium 0.5mg/l, Bicarbonates 70mg/l, Chlorides 4.8mg/l, Sulphates 21mg/l. pH 7.58

Aguas de Manzanera (Sp) a natural mineral water from El Salvador, Manzanera, Teruel. Mineral contents (milligrammes per litre): Sodium 2690mg/l, Calcium 672mg/l, Chlorides 4770mg/l.

Aguas de Mijas (Sp) a natural mineral water from La Ermitica, Mijas, Malaga.

Aguas de Ribagorza (Sp) a still natural mineral water from Ribagorza, Graus, Huesca. Mineral contents (milligrammes per litre): Sodium 23.8mg/l, Calcium 71.3mg/l, Magnesium 25.8mg/l, Potassium 3.2mg/l, Bicarbonates 332.6mg/l, Chlorides 26.7mg/l, Sulphates 18.1mg/l, Fluoride 0.3mg/l, Nitrates 1mg/l.

Aguas de São Pedro (Bra) an alkaline natural mineral water. Mineral contents (milligrammes per litre): Sodium 793.96mg/l, Calcium 1.49mg/l, Magnesium 0.18mg/l, Potassium 1.79mg/l, Bicarbonates 288.5mg/l, Chlorides 778.53mg/l, Sulphates 214.2mg/l, Fluoride 7.68mg/l, Nitrates 0.1mg/l, Silicates 8.68mg/l. pH 9.21

Aguas de Sousas (Sp) a natural mineral water (established 1859) from Verin. Mineral contents (milligrammes per litre): Sodium 118mg/l, Bicarbonates 355mg/l, Fluoride 2mg/l, Silicates 61mg/l.

Agua Sem Gas (Port) sparkling mineral water.

Aguasol (Sp) a sparkling natural mineral water (established 2002) from Lugo-Saria. Mineral contents (milligrammes per litre): Sodium 89.5mg/l, Calcium 26.5mg/l, Potassium 4.3mg/l, Bicarbonates 288.3mg/l, Chlorides 27.2mg/l, Sulphates 27.2mg/l, Fluoride 1mg/l.

Aguas Verdes (Sp) a natural mineral water from Fuerteventura. Mineral contents (milligrammes per litre): Sodium 2720mg/l, Calcium 208mg/l, Magnesium 256mg/l, Potassium 72mg/l, Bicarbonates 409mg/l, Chlorides 4500mg/l, Sulphates 880mg/l, Fluoride 151mg/l, Nitrates 13mg/l. pH 7.4

Aguavida (Sp) a natural mineral water from the Fuente Mina, Casarabonela, Malaga.

Agua Vila del Turbon (Sp) a still natural mineral water from Virgin de la Pena. Mineral contents (milligrammes per litre): Sodium 0.6mg/l, Calcium 47.7mg/l, Magnesium 1.5mg/l, Bicarbonates 145.5mg/l, Chlorides 0.6mg/l, Sulphates 3.7mg/l, Silicates 3.6mg/l. pH 7.2

Agua Vital de Fournier (Sp) a natural mineral water from La Garriga. Mineral contents (milligrammes per litre): Sodium 15.2mg/l, Calcium 75.4mg/l, Magnesium 20.9mg/l, Bicarbonates 300mg/l, Chlorides 11.7mg/l, Sulphates 47.2mg/l, Silicates 18.6mg/l.

Água Viva (Port) a natural mineral water. pH 6.8

Agueda (Port) small region on the river Mondego. Produces wines similar to Dão wines and sparkling wines.

Aguila (S.Am) a 4% alc by vol. pale straw, bottled lager beer brewed by Aguia Brewery, Barranquilla, Colombia.

Agulha (Port) a fine, dry D.O. Vinho Verde which is slightly pétillant. Sold in stone bottles.

Agulhas (S.Afr) the label for a white wine (Chenin blanc, Colombard and Sauvignon blanc blend) produced by the Merwespont Winery, Robertson, Western Cape.

Agulhas Wines (S.Afr) a winery (established 2002) based in Elim, Bredasdorp, Southern Cape. 65ha. Grape varieties: Chardonnay, Sauvignon blanc, Shiraz. Label: First Sighting.

Agusta Winery (S.Afr) the old name for the Grand Provence winery, Franschhoek, Western Cape.

Agwa (Hol) a spirit distilled in Amsterdam. made from Bolivian coco leaves, contains guarana, ginseng and several herbs 30% alc by vol.

Ahachéni (Geo) a red grape variety grown in Georgia. Used in the making of dessert wines.

Ahlafors Bryggerier (Swe) a brewery. (Add): Box 3060 449 15 Alafors, Sweden. Brews a variety of beers and lagers.

Ahlgren Vineyard (USA) a winery based at Boulder Creek, Santa Cruz, California. Produces varietal wines from Cabernet sauvignon, Petite syrah and Zinfandel grapes.

Ahméta (Gor) a white grape variety grown in Georgia. Used in the making of dessert wines.

Ahn (Lux) a village on the river Moselle. Vineyard sites are Palmberg and Vogelsang.

Ahr [River] (Ger) a tributary of the river Rhine. Flows through the Ahr wine anbaugebiete.

A

Ahr (Ger) anbaugebiet (Ber): Walporzheim/Ahrtal. (Gro): Klosterberg. (Vils): Ahrweiler, Altenahr, Bachem, Bad Neuenahr, Dernau, Heimersheim, Heppingen, Marienthal, Mayschoss, Rech, Walporzheim. Soil: slate and volcanic rock. 85% of the grape producton is Spätburgunder.

Ahrbleichert (Ger) lit: 'bleached wine', an old name for rosé wine made in the Ahr from the Spätburgunder (Pinot noir) grape. The skins were removed very quickly from the must.

Ahrenberg (Ger) vineyard (Anb): Rheinhessen. (Ber): Bingen. (Gro): Adelberg. (Vil): Nach.

Ahr Information Service (Ger) Gebietsweinwerbung Ahr.e.V. Elligstr 14, 5483 Bad Neuenahr-Ahrweiler, West Germany.

Ahrtaler Landwein (Ger) one of 15 Deutsche tafelwein zones.

Artalquelle (Ger) a natural mineral water from Sinzig, RP.

Ahrweiler (Ger) village (Anb): Ahr. (Ber): Walporzheim/Ahrtal. (Gro): Klosterberg. (Vins): Daubhaus, Forstberg, Riegelfeld, Rosenthal, Silberberg, Ursulinengarten.

Ahr Wine Festivals (Ger) see Gebietsweinmark. Winzerfest.

Ahsis (Isr) an aromatic wine often mentioned in the Bible, described as having a perfumed bouquet.

Ahtanum Gold (Eng) a 4.3% alc by vol. beer brewed by the Oldershaw Brewery, Lincolnshire.

Åhusaquavit (Swe) a cumin-flavoured akvavit.

Ahus Taffel (Swe) a caraway-flavoured aquavit. 40% alc by vol.

Aichelberg (Ger) village (Anb): Württemberg. (Ber): Remstal-Stuttgart. (Gro): Wartbühl. (Vin): Luginsland.

Aichinger [Josef] (Aus) a winery based in the Kamptal region. (Add): Hauptstrasse 15, 3562 Schönberg am Kamp. Grape varieties: Grüner veltliner, Pinot blanc, Zweigelt. Produces a range of wines and is a noted Heurige.

Aidani (Gre) a white grape variety grown mainly in southern Greece in the Cyclades Islands. Used to make a straw wine called Santorini on the Isle of Thira. See also Assyrtiko, Athiri.

Ai Danil (Rus) a full-bodied red wine from the Crimea.

Aidarinis (Gre) a 5ha. winery based in Goumenissa. Grape varieties: Xinomavro, Negoska, Rhoditis, Sauvignon blanc.

Aigéadacht (Ire) acidity.

Aigéchate (Arm) a red, Port-style wine produced in the Armenia region.

Aigédach (Ire) acid.

Aigillières [Les] (Fr) a Premier Cru vineyard in the A.C. commune of Pommard, Côte de Beaune, Burgundy. 3.64ha.

Aigle (Switz) a white, medium-dry, table wine produced in the Chablais region.

Aigle Noir (S.Afr) the label for a red wine (Cabernet sauvignon, Merlot and Pinotage blend) produced by the Remhoogte Estate winery, Stellenbosch, Western Cape.

Aiglon [L.] (Cktl) ½ measure Mandarine Napoleon, ¼ measure Champagne. Serve 'on the rocks', and garnish with a slice of orange.

Aigre (Fr) sour wine. i.e. (vinaigre = vinegar).

Aigrots [Les] (Fr) a Premier Cru vineyard in the A.C. commune of Beaune, Côte de Beaune, Burgundy. 22ha.

Aigua d'Andorra (And) see Arinsal.

Aiguebelle (Fr) a green liqueur made by white monks (Cistercian) near Valence, from 35 different herbs, roots, flowers seeds and neutral spirit. There is also a sweeter yellow version. Also known as Liqueur de Frère Jean.

Aiguière (Fr) lit: 'ewer', the name for a claret jug with metal fittings. Also name for a water jug.

Aile d'Argent (Fr) an A.C. Bordeaux blanc wine produced from Mouton vineyards. see Baron Philippe de Rothschild SA.

Ailenberg (Ger) vineyard (Anb): Württemberg. (Ber): Remstal-Stuttgart. (Gro): Weinsteige. (Vil): Esslingen.

Ailenberg (Ger) vineyard (Anb): Württemberg. (Ber): Remstal-Stuttgart. (Gro): Weinsteige. (Vil): Stuttgart (ortsteil Obertürkheim).

Ailric's Ale (Eng) a cask-conditioned old ale 1045 O.G. Brewed by Phillips Brewery, Marsh Gibbon, Bicester, Buckinghamshire.

Aimé Boucher S.A. (Fr) a noted négociant in the Loire. (Add): 279, Route de Chambourd, 41350, Husseau-sur-Casson.

Aïn [River] (Fr) a tributary of the river Rhône which flows through the Jura region in the département of Ain.

Ain-Bessem-Bouira (Alg) a wine-producing area in Alger that produces full-bodied red and dry white wines.

Aîné (Fr) senior partner.

Ainslie and Heilbron (Scot) whisky producer (part of DCL). Most of its whisky is exported. Distillery based at Clynelish (Highland). Whiskies include Ainslie's Royal Edinburgh and Clynelish (12 year old).

Ainslie's Royal Edinburgh (Scot) a blended Scotch whisky produced by Ainslie and Heilbron for export.

Aiola [L'] (It) a Chianti Classico producer based in Tuscany.

Aiou-Dag (Rus) a red muscat dessert wine from southern Crimea.

Air (Indo) water.

Aird [L'] (Cktl) 8/10 measure Scotch whisky, 1/10 measure Kahlúa, 1/10 measure Bols maraschino, 1/10 measure ginger wine. Shake with ice and strain into a goblet.

Air Dried (Eng) the process of laying grape on trays to partially dry (30% to 40% of moisture) to concentrate the sugar content. Process is either practiced using the sun (Sherry grapes) or using hot air (Italian wineries such as Valpolicella, Soave). Wine is either then made from the crushed grapes or the dried grapes added to the fermenting must. See Amarone, Appassimento,

Commandaria, Governo, Passito, Schilfwein, Strohwein, Vin de Paille, Vin Santi.

Airén (Sp) a white grape variety of the central regions of Spain. The most widely planted grape in the world (most is planted in Spain). Very productive with a fine light bouquet and colour and 12%–14% by vol. of alcohol. Is the principal variety in the regions of La Mancha and Valdepenãs. Most wine is distilled into brandy.

Airlie (USA) a winery (established 1986) based in Willamette Valley, Oregon. Grape varieties: Chardonnay, Gewürztraminer, Maréchal foch, Müller-Thurgau, Pinot noir, Riesling, late-harvest Gewürztraminer. Labels: Dunn Forest Vineyard, 2 Vineyard Old Vines.

Airlock (Eng) a device used by Home wine-makers to prevent air, bacteria or insects from contaminating the fermenting must. Made of glass or plastic and filled with water it allows the CO_2 gas to escape. see Bubbler.

Air Mineral (Mal) a still (blue label) natural mineral water from Jalan. (Add): Off Jalan Air Kuning, 34000 Taiping, Perak. Mineral contents (milligrammes per litre): Sodium 6mg/l, Calcium 12mg/l, Magnesium 1.6mg/l, Potassium 1.6mg/l, Bicarbonates 83mg/l, Chlorides <1mg/l, Sulphates 7.7mg/l, Nitrates 9.5mg/l, Silicates 48mg/l. pH 7.4

Air Pressure (Eng) a system of dispensing beer that is used mainly in Scotland.

Aisling (Eng) a 4% alc by vol. beer brewed by the Potbelly Brewery Ltd., Northamptonshire.

Aisne (Fr) a département of which part is in the Champagne region that adjoins Marne.

Aït Souala (Afr) a red wine from the Aït Souala cellars at Aït Yazem in the Mekries region of Morocco. Produced from the Carignan and Cinsault grapes and bottled by CVM. Also a rosé of same name produced.

Aiud (Rum) a wine-producing area noted for medium-dry white wines.

Aiven (Asia) a spirit made from fermented mare's milk by the Tartars in Mongolia.

Aix-en-Provence (Fr) a red, white and rosé A.C. wine centre of Provence in south-eastern France.

Aix-la-Chapelle (Fr) an alkaline mineral water centre.

Aix-les-Bains (Fr) an alkaline mineral water centre.

Aix-les-Bains (Fr) a still (blue label) natural mineral water from Raphy Saint Simon Est., Savoie. Mineral contents (milligrammes per litre): Sodium 14mg/l, Calcium 72mg/l, Magnesium 38mg/l, Potassium 2mg/l, Bicarbonates 329mg/l, Chlorides 6mg/l, Sulphates 81mg/l, Fluoride 0.3mg/l, Nitrates <1mg/l. pH 7.4

A.J. (Cktl) 35mls (1½fl.ozs) apple jack, 25mls (1fl.oz) grapefruit juice. Shake well over ice and strain into a cocktail glass.

Ajaccio (Fr) the capital of Corsica and A.C. name given to a range of vintage and non-vintage red, rosé and white wines. 250ha. Soil: granite. Grape varieties: Carignan, Cinsault, Grenache, Sciacarello, Ugni blanc, Vermentino.

Ajenjo (Sp) wormwood (absinthe).

Ajudhia Distillery (Ind) a large rum distillery based at Raja-Ka-Sahaspur, Distt Moradabad. Is owned by the National Industrial Corporation Ltd. (known as Nicol's), New Delhi. Produces Black Bull XXX (5 year old), Field Marshal XXX, Himalayan XXX and Nicol's Standard XXX Rums.

Aka (Eng) a super premium lager 7.5% alc by vol. from Courage. Made using the Champagne yeast.

Akadama (Jap) lit: 'symbol of the rising sun', the first sweet white wine to be launched in 1907 by Shinjiro Torii. Made from Ume Shu plums.

Akamina (Tur) a natural mineral water. Mineral contents (milligrammes per litre): Sodium 20mg/l, Calcium 400mg/l, Magnesium 29mg/l, Bicarbonates 1403mg/l, Chlorides 7.3mg/l, Nitrates 4mg/l. pH 6.17

Akarangi Wines (N.Z) a 5ha. winery at River Road, Havelock North.

Akavitte (Scan) Scandinavian gin, is stronger than Dutch gin. 40% alc by vol.

Akba Minerale (Rus) see Baikal.

AK Bitter (Eng) a light bitter ale brewed by the Simpkiss Brewery, Brierley Hill, Staffs in the West Midlands (Black Country).

Ak-Boulak (Rus) a sparkling, white wine produced in Kazakhstania.

Akeleje Akvavit (Den) an akvavit flavoured with many herbs. 43% alc by vol.

Akevit (Scan) the name for rectified spirit distilled from grain or potatoes and flavoured with certain aromatic seeds, especially caraway seeds. 45% alc by vol. see Aquavit and Akvavit.

Akhaïa (Gre) a red wine produced in Peloponnese.

Akhameta (Geo) a white wine from Rioni Gorge in Georgia using the Mtzvane grape.

Akhasheni (Geo) a semi-sweet red wine produced in Georgia from the Saperavi grape.

Akira (S.Afr) the label for a red wine (Cabernet sauvignon 49% plus Pinotage and Petit verdot blend) produced by the Umkhulu Wines winery, Stellenbosch, Western Cape.

Akkerbos (S.Afr) the label for a white wine (Chardonnay) produced by the Fairview winery, Suider-Paarl, Western Cape.

Akkerdal Estate (S.Afr) a winery (established 2000) based in Franschhoek, Western Cape. Grape varieties: Barbera, Chardonnay, Malbec, Merlot, Mourvèdre, Petit verdot, Pinotage, Roobernet, Sauvignon blanc, Sémillon, Syrah, Tempranillo, Viognier. Labels: Kallie's Dream, Passion Red and White, Wild Boar. 18ha.

Akkerman (Mol) a wine-producing district of Moldavia (was formally part of Rumania known as Bessarabia).

AK Mild (Eng) a cask-conditioned mild brewed by McCullen Brewery of Hertford, Hertfordshire.

Aksinia (Rus) a sparkling natural mineral water (established 1996). Mineral contents (milligrammes per litre): Sodium 171.8mg/l, Calcium 177.3mg/l, Magnesium 41.6mg/l, Potassium 1.9mg/l, Bicarbonates 459.3mg/l,

Chlorides 76.5mg/l, Sulphates 485.2mg/l, Fluoride 1.5mg/l, Silicates 8mg/l. pH 7.6

Akstafa (Rus) a dessert wine produced near Baku.

Aksu (Rus) a natural mineral water. Mineral contents (milligrammes per litre): Magnesium 65mg/l, Potassium 299mg/l, Bicarbonates 435mg/l, Chlorides 264mg/l, Sulphates 792mg/l. Website: http://www.akso.ru

Akt. Ges. (Ger) *abbr:* **Akt**iengesellschaft (denotes a German Corporation).

Aktiebolaget Vin & Spritcentralem (Swe) state monopoly that makes 19 types of brannvin including Explorer and Renat.

Akitienbrauerei Kaufbeuren AG (Ger) a brewery. (Add): Hohe Buchleuthe 3, Kaufbeuren D-87600 Germany. Brews avariety of beers and lagers. Website: http://www.aktien-brauerei.de

Akva (Ice) a natural mineral water from Akva-lindir, Glerardalur, Akureyri.

Akvaviittee (Scan) aquavit.

Akvavit (Den) the name for a rectified spirit distilled from grain or potatoes and flavoured with certain aromatic seeds, especially caraway, cumin, coriander and fennel seeds. *see* Aquavit, Akevit or Aalborg.

Akvavit Clam Cocktail (Cktl) ½ measure akvavit, ¼ measure clam juice, ¼ measure tomato juice, 4 dashes lemon juice, 2 dashes Worcester sauce, salt, pepper, cayenne. Stir well over ice and strain into an ice-filled old fashioned glass.

A.K.W. Wines (S.Afr) *abbr: see* Ashton Koöperatiewe Wynkelders.

Ala (It) a fortified wine made from herbs infused in alcohol and wine produced by the Corvo Winery in Sicily.

Alabama (USA) a wine-producing state in southern USA. Produces French and Muscat-style wines.

Alabama Cocktail (Cktl) 35mls (1½fl.ozs) brandy, 10mls (½fl.oz) lemon juice, 5mls (¼fl.oz) Triple Sec, dash gomme syrup. Shake over ice and strain into a cocktail glass.

Alabama Fizz (Cktl) 50mls (2fl.ozs) gin, juice ½ lemon, teaspoon powdered sugar. Shake over ice, strain into ice-filled highball glass, top with soda and fresh mint.

Alabamie Wine C°. (Austr) a winery (established 1975) at Campbell Ave., Irymple, Victoria. Grape varieties: Chardonnay, Sauvignon blanc, Sémillon, Cabernet sauvignon, Riesling.

À la Castellana (Sp) the term used to describe a low and unsupported vine-training method.

À la Ciega (Sp) a similar to En vaso method of vine training. Fist-shaped fruiting top with buds at each end. Used in Montilla-Moriles.

Al Ain (UAE) a natural mineral water (established 1990) from Al-Khattam.

Alain Siret (Fr) a récoltant-manipulant Champagne producer. (Add): 11, Rue de la Marie, 51130 Gionges. Produces Blanc de Blancs. Website: http://www.Champagnesiret.com 'E'mail: as@Champagnesiret.com

Alaki (Chi) a type of raki made from rice beer before 800 BC.

À la Manchega (Sp) a term used to denote 'spur or head' pruning. Is similar to 'en vaso' pruning method. Used in La Mancha.

Alamas Ridge (Arg) the second label of Bodegas Esmeralda. *See also* Catena.

Alambic (Fr) lit: 'still', a type of pot-still. *See also* Alembic (an alternative spelling) and Alambique. (Arab) = al-anbïq, (Ire) = leamóg.

Alambicar (Port) to distill.

Alambic (Fr) still (spirits).

Alambic Armagnaçais (Fr) a specially modified continuous still used in the Armagnac region, invented by Edouard Adam. *See also* Verdier. Also spelt Alembic Armagnaçais.

Alambic Charentais (Fr) a special pot-still used in the production of Cognac.

Alambics (Fr) denotes Pot-stills.

Alambie Wine C°. (Austr) a winery (estabvlished 1975). (Add): Campbell Avenue, Irymple, Victoria. Grape varieties: Chardonnay, Riesling, Sauvignon blanc, Sémillon, Cabernet sauvignon.

Alambique (Fr)(Port)(Sp) still. *see* Alambic.

Alambrado (Sp) the wrapping of fine wire mesh around some Spanish bottles with a lead seal to guarantee the contents. *see* Alambre.

Alambre (Sp) the light wire netting that is wrapped around some bottles of wine as an added seal to guarantee the authenticity of the contents. *See also* Alambrado.

Alameda (USA) a wine-producing region in central California.

Alamos Ridge (Arg) the second label of Bodegas Esmeralda. *See also* Catena.

Alana Estate (N.Z) a vineyard based in the Martinborough region of the North Island.

Al-Anbïq (Arab) the still (distillation).

Alanine (Eng) an amino acid found in wines. Is formed by the yeasts.

Alardo (Port) a natural mineral water from Castelo Novo, Castelo Branco. Mineral contents (milligrammes per litre): Sodium 3.4mg/l, Calcium 0.8mg/l, Bicarbonates 6.7mg/l, Chlorides 2mg/l, Silcates 12mg/l, Nitrates 2mg/l.

Alarije (Sp) *see* Alarijen.

Alarijen (Sp) a white grape variety grown in Cáceres, south-western Spain and in the Extremadura. Also spelt Alarije.

Alasch Kümmel (Ger) an alternative spelling of Allasch Kümmel.

Alasia (Cyp) the brand-name of a Commandaria produced by Loël Ltd. in Limassol.

Alasia Brut (It) a spumante wine produced by Araldici Vini Piemontesi, 14040 Castel Boglione from Chardonnay and Pinot noir grapes. Part of the Poderi Alasia range.

Alaska (Cktl) ⅔ measure dry gin, ⅓ measure Yellow Chartreuse. Shake well over ice, strain into a cocktail glass.

Alaska (Ger) a sparkling (blue label) natural mineral water from Bad Liebenwerda-Dobra, BB; Ebersburg-Weyhers, HE. Mineral contents (milligrammes per litre): Sodium 4.2mg/l, Calcium 12.3mg/l, Magnesium 2.2mg/l, Potassium 1.1mg/l, Bicarbonates 49.7mg/l, Chlorides 4.8mg/l, Sulphates 3mg/l, Fluoride <0.2mg/l, Nitrates <0.5mg/l.

Alaska Chill (USA) a natural mineral water from Misty Fjords, National Monument, Alaska. Mineral contents (milligrammes per litre): Calcium 35mg/l, Magnesium 0.93mg/l. pH 8.5

Alaska Glacier Cup (USA) a natural mineral water from Anchrage, Alaska.

Alaskan Amber (USA) 5% alc by vol. alt beer brewed and bottled in Juneau, Alaska by the Alaskan Brewing & Bottling C°.

Alaskan Brewing & Bottling C°. (USA) based (established 1986) in Juneau, Alaska. Brews Alaskan Amber, Alaskan Seasonal Smoked Porter.

Alaskan Seasonal Smoked Porter (USA) a 5.9% alc by vol. smoked porter brewed and bottled in Juneau, Alaska by the Alaskan Brewing & Bottling C°. Bottled with the year of production on the label.

Alateen (Eng)(USA) a group (established 1957 in the USA) to help young people whose parents have a 'drink' problem.

Alatera Vineyards (USA) a winery based in the Napa Valley, California. Grape varieties: Cabernet sauvignon, Chardonnay, Gewürztraminer, Johannisberg riesling and Pinot noir. Produces varietal wines and Paradis (a white wine from the Pinot noir).

Ala-Too (Rus) a red grape variety grown in the Kirghizian district. Produces Port-style red wines.

Alava (Sp) a wine-producing district in Chacolí, near Rioja, north-eastern Spain.

Alavesas S.A. (Sp) see Bodegas Alavesas.

Alayor (Sp) a wine-producer based on Minorca, Balearic Islands.

Alba (It) a sparkling natural mineral water from Alba, Vicenza, Veneto. Mineral contents (milligrammes per litre): Sodium 1.8mg/l, Calcium 7mg/l, Magnesium 3mg/l, Potassium 0.2mg/l, Bicarbonates 30.5mg/l, Chlorides 1mg/l, Sulphates 7.7mg/l, Silicates 7mg/l, Nitrates 2.5mg/l. pH 7.3

Alba (Scot) a 7.5% alc by vol. beer brewed by Heather Ale Ltd., Lanarkshire.

Albacete (Sp) a wine-producing province of upper La Mancha, central Spain.

Albachtaler (Ger) vineyard (Anb): Mosel-Saar-Ruwer. (Ber): Ober-Mosel. (Gro): Gipfel. (Vil): Wasserliesch.

Alba de Bretón (Sp) see Bodegas Bretón.

Alba Flora (Sp) a medium-dry white wine produced on the island of Majorca.

Alba Iulia (Rum) a wine district in the Tîrnave, Transylvania. Noted for medium-dry white wines produced from the Fetească, Italian riesling and Muskat-Ottonel grapes. Also spelt Alba Julia.

Alba Julia (Rum) an alternative spelling of Alba Iulia.

Albalonga (Ger) an early ripening white grape variety. A cross between the Riesling and Silvaner, it produces high must sugars.

Albán (Sp) the alternative name used for the Palomino grape.

Albana (It) a white grape variety from Emilia-Romagna.

Albana di Romagna (It) a D.O.C.G. white wine from Emilia-Romagna region. Produced from the Albana grape, it is either Secco (dry) or Amabile (semi-sweet). The D.O.C. applies to sparkling wines according to regulations within the provinces of Forlí, Bologna and Ravenna.

Albania (Alb) a small wine-producing country producing average quality wines that are consumed locally.

Albanibräu (Switz) a strong bier brewed by the Haldengut Brauerei.

Albani Brewery (Swe) a brewery based in Odense. Produces Giraf Beer 5.7% alc by vol. Julebryg Christmas Beer 5.3% alc by vol. Jule ØL (a low-alc, tax-free beer) and Påske Bryg.

Albano (It) a white wine from the Emilia-Romagna region.

Albanum (It) an ancient red wine produced in Roman times in central western Italy.

Alban Wine (It) the name for the wine of Alba in Roman times.

Albany Surprise (N.Z) the most widely planted black table grape in New Zealand. Is a clonal selection of the American Isabella variety. Being very acidic, the wines are almost undrinkable.

Albarello (Sp) a red grape variety grown in western Spain.

Albariño (Sp) a white grape variety grown in the Rías Baixas and Ribeiro areas of north-western Spain. Has peach and jasmine aromas and lemon zest flavours.

Albariño del Palacio (Sp) the name given to a dry, pétillant, white wine produced in the Galicia region by Marqués de Figueroa.

Albariño Santiago Ruíz (Sp) a winery with vineyards in Sotomayor, Rías Baixas, D.O. Galicia. (Add): San Miguel de Tobagón, 36770 O Rosal. Produces O Rosal.

Albariza (Sp) the chalky soil found in the heart of the Sherry region between Jerez and the Guadalquivir river.

Albarizona (Sp) in the Sherry area a cross between the Barros and Albariza soils. Has 25% chalk. Found near Trebujena.

Albarizones (Sp) same as Albarizona.

Albarolo (It) a white grape variety grown in northern Italy that produces light dry wines. Also known as the Erbarola in Liguria.

Albaviva (It) a natural mineral water from Albaviva.

Alben (Ger) an alternative name for the Elbling grape.

Albenet (S.Afr) the label for a red wine (Cinsaut, Merlot and Ruby cabernet blend) from the Nelson's Creek range produced by the Nelson Estate winery, Paarl, Western Cape.

Alberello (It) the name given to the traditional low-yield, vine-training system on a single pole, pruned low with three stems and two buds per stem. Also known as the bush system. see Spalliera.

A

Alberese (It) the name for limestone, marl and schistous clay soil in Chianti, Tuscany.

Alberga (Fr) an old mediaeval word for inn or tavern. *See also* Auberge.

Albergue (Port) inn.

Albermarle Fancy Free (Pousse Café) in a liqueur glass pour in order: ⅓ measure cherry brandy, ⅓ measure Cointreau, ⅓ measure apricotine.

Albermarle Fizz (Cktl) 25mls (1fl.oz) dry gin, 2 dashes raspberry syrup, juice ½ lemon, dash gomme syrup. Stir over ice, strain into an ice-filled highball, top with soda and 2 cherries and serve with straws.

Albermarle Thirst Chaser (Cktl) the juice of ½ of orange and lemon, ⅓ of an egg white. Shake over ice, strain into a tumbler and top with lemonade.

Alberndorf (Aus) a wine village in the district of Retz, northern Austria. Produces mainly white wines. Is also known as Europadorf.

Alberos (Sp) the chalky soil found in Montilla-Moriles. *See also* Ruedos.

Albersweiler (Ger) village (Anb): Pfalz. (Ber): Südliche Weinstrasse. (Gro): Königsgarten. (Vins): Kirchberg, Latt.

Alberta (Can) a small wine producing region.

Alberta Distillery (Can) a distillery based in Alberta which is noted for a 100% rye whisky.

Albert Ale (Eng) a 4.4% alc by vol. ale brewed by the Earl Soham Brewery, Suffolk.

Albert Egger AG (Switz) a brewery. (Add): Brauereiweg 3, 3076 Worb, Switzerland. Brews a variety of beers and lagers.

Albert Grivault (Fr) a cuvée based in the Premier Cru vineyard of Meursault-Charmes in the A.C. Meursault, Côte de Beaune, Burgundy. Is owned by the Hospices de Beaune 0.5ha.

Albert Mann (Fr) a winery based in Alsace that produces a range of Alsace wines including Grand Cru wines.

Alberto (It) a D.O.C. Valpolicella Classico from Zenato in Verona. 70% Cabernet sauvignon, 15% Merlot, 15% Corvina veronese grapes.

Albertusquelle (Ger) a natural mineral water from Danzig, BY.

Albig (Ger) village (Anb): Rheinhessen. (Ber): Nierstein. (Gro): Petersberg. (Vins): Homberg, Hundskopf, Schloss Hammerstein.

Albilla (S.Am) a white grape variety grown in Peru.

Albillo (Sp) a white grape variety grown Galicia and in the central-southern regions of Spain. Also known as the Calgalon.

Albillo Castellano (Sp) *see* Abillo.

Albion Bitter (Eng) the name given to a bitter ale brewed by Marston's Brewery, Burton-on-Trent, Staffordshire.

Albion Distillery (S.Am) a small rum distillery based in Guyana. Owned by the Guyana Distillers. (Government owned).

Albion Keg Mild (Eng) a mild ale brewed by the Marston's Brewery, in Burton-on-Trent, Staffordshire.

Albion Porter (Eng) a porter brewed by Marston's Brewery at Burton-on-Trent under the Head Brewers Choice banner. 4.8% alc by vol. *see* Regimental Ale, Union Mild.

Albion Water (USA) a natural mineral water (established 1913) from San Francisco, CA.

Albis (Chile) the label for a red wine (Cabernet sauvignon 70%–85% and Carmenère 15%–30%) produced by the Haras de Pirque winery, Maipo Valley.

Albisheim (Ger) village (Anb): Pfalz. (Ber): Mittelhaardt-Deutsche Weinstrasse. (Gro): Schnepfenflug vom Zellartal. (Vin): Heiligenbrom.

Albling (Ger) an alternative name for the Elbling grape.

Albor (Sp) a rosé wine produced by the Bodegas Cavedi, Tierra de Castilla.

Alborz (Iran) a natural mineral water from the Alborz mountains. Mineral contents (milligrammes per litre): Sodium 17mg/l, Calcium 78mg/l, Magnesium 22mg/l, Potassium 1.9mg/l, Bicarbonates 320mg/l, Chlorides 19mg/l, Sulphates 83mg/l, Fluoride 0.46mg/l, Nitrates 5.5mg/l. pH 6.9

Albra Brauerei (Fr) the name derived from the merger of 4 breweries taken over by Heineken. Uses Ancre and Mutzig brand-names. Based in Alsace.

Albrecht Dürer Pils (Ger) a premium lager beer brewed by Patrizier Bräu AG, Nurnberg.

Albright (Eng) a standard draught bitter produced by Bass.

Albumen (Eng) a protein found in egg white, blood, etc. (egg whites and blood are used for fining wines). *See also* Albumin and Albuminous protein.

Albumin (Eng) another spelling of Albumen.

Albuminous Protein (Eng) the protein found in blood and egg white, used to fine wines. The protein reacts with the tannin in the wine, leaving the wine clear. The particles fall to the bottom of the cask by gravitation.

Alc. (Eng) *abbr*: **alc**ohol.

Alcaeus (Gre) a poet who wrote many songs and poems relating to wine and love in Ancient Greece.

Alcamo (It) a D.O.C. white wine produced from 80%–100% Catarratto bianco, Damaschino, Grecanico, Trebbiano toscano grapes in the provinces of Palermo and Trapani in Sicily.

Alcanadro (Sp) a Zona de Crianza in the Rioja Baja, north-eastern Spain.

Alcañol (Sp) the alternative name for the Alcañon, Macabeo and Viura grape.

Alcañon (Sp) the alternative name for the Alcañol, Macabeo and Viura grape. Is popular in Somontano.

Alcantud (Sp) a natural mineral water from Finca Baños de Alcantud, Alcantud, Cuena.

Alcatraz (USA) a brand of natural mineral water.

Alcayata (Sp) a black grape variety. Also known as the Monastrell.

Alcazar Ale (Eng) an ale brewed by the Alcazar Brewery, Nottinghamshire.

Alcazar Amontillado (Sp) the brand-name for an Amontillado Sherry produced by Bobadilla in Jerez de la Frontera.

Alcazar Brewery (Eng) a pub micro-brewery. (Add): Fax & Crown, Church Street, Old Basford, Nottingham, Nottinghamshire. NG6 0GA. Brews a variety of ales including: Alcazar Ale, Bowman Bounty, Devout Stout, Gaolers Ale, Little John Myth, Maiden's Magic and Scarlet Fever. Website: http://www.alcazarbrewingco.com 'E'mail: alcazarbrewery@tiscali.co.uk

Alcazar Cocktail (Cktl) 35mls (1½fl.ozs) Canadian Club whisky, 10mls (½fl.oz) Bénédictine. Stir ingredients over broken ice, strain into a cocktail glass. Decorate with a cherry and dash of orange peel juice (a small dash of orange bitters may be included).

alc by vol. (Eng) *abbr:* **Alc**ohol **by vol**ume. 0% (pure water) and 100% (pure alcohol). *see* OMIL. *See also* Original Gravity.

Al-Chark Brewery (Arab) a brewery which produces pilsener-style beers in Syria.

Alchemist (Eng) the name for a chemist during the middle ages. *see* Jeber.

Alchemy (Eng) a 4.2% alc by vol. beer brewed by the Burrington Brewery, Devon.

Alchemy (S.Afr) the label for a red wine (Cabernet franc, Cabernet sauvignon, Merlot, Pinotage and Shiraz blend) produced by the Mont Rochelle Mountain Vineyards winery, Franschhoek, Western Cape.

Alchemy Gold (Eng) a 4.4% alc by vol. golden, cask wheat ale brewed by Wychwood Brewery, Eagle Maltings, Witney, Oxfordshire.

Alchermes (It) a red liqueur made from rose and jasmine flower extract added to nutmeg, cinnamon and coriander distillation.

Alcobaça (Port) a DOC district within the region of Estremadura. Sited in 'The Ocean' of the river Tejo. Produces red and white wines from the Ramisco vine.

Alco–Cola [Mac 'n Ernie's] (Eng) a 4% alc by vol. micro-brewed cola drink with a real head.

Alcohol (Eng) *abbr:* alc. alcohol. *See also* alc by vol, Alcohol [Ethyl], Alcohol [Methyl]. (Cro) = alkohol, (Den) = alkohol, (Fr) = alcool, (Ire) = alcól, (It) = alcool, (Hol) = alcohol, (Port) = alcohol, (Sp) = alcohol, (Tur) = alkol, (Wal) = alcohol.

Alcohol Content (Eng) the amount of alcohol as a percentage of the total content of the bottle of beer, spirit, wine, etc. Is presented as Gay Lussac, Alc by vol. or as OIML. *See also* Sykes, Proof, and U.S. Proof.

Alcohol Destillado de Vino (Sp) a spirit produced in a continuous still from wine. 95% alc by vol.

Alcohol Disorder Zones (Eng) *abbr:* ADZs. a category of licensed premises within a defined troublesome area (caused by drink-related incidents) that are levied a charge for policing until the area is deemed free of trouble. Introduced in 2005.

Alcohol [Ethyl] (Eng). C_2H_5OH obtained by the action of yeast on sugar during fermentation (1 millilitre of alcohol weighs 0.788 gramme at 20°C). Its strength can be further increased by distillation. Harmful only in large quantities.

Alcohol Free (Eng) defined as 0% - 0.05% alc by vol. (Den) = alkoholfri.

Alcohol-Free Beer (Eng) low-alcohol beers brewed for the motorist that are mainly lager-style beers. *see* Barbican, Birrell, Danish Lite, Gerstal, Hunter, Kaliber, St. Christopher, Swan Lite.

Alcoholfreier Wein (Ger) alcohol-free wine.

Alcoholic (Eng) a person who depends on alcohol, one who is addicted to alcoholic liquor. (Cro) = alkoholni, (Den) = alkoholholdig, (Hol) = alcoholisch, (Ire) = alcólach, (It) = alcoolico, (Sp) = alcohólico, (Tur) = alkolik.

Alcoholicity (Eng) refers to the strength of an alcoholic liquor.

Alcohólico (Sp) alcoholic.

Alcoholics Anonymous (Eng) *abbr:* A.A. Group to help alcoholics.

Alcoholic Strength (Eng) the measurement of alcohol by volume in a given quantity of an alcoholic beverage. *see* Gay Lussac, Sykes, OIML. US. Proof and Alcohol Content.

Alcoholic Yoghurt (Ire) a nickname for the cream liqueur Carolans.

Alcoholisation (Eng) fermentation. *See also* Alcoholization.

Alcoholisch (Hol) alcoholic.

Alcoholise (Eng) to turn into an alcoholic liquor, to ferment. *see* Alcoholize.

Alcoholism (Eng) a condition of a person who relies on acohol to exist and is in a permenant intoxicated condition. *See also* Cirrhosis and Nephritis. (Fr) = alcoolisme, (Ire) = alcólacht.

Alcoholization (Eng) fermentation. *See also* Alcoholisation.

Alcoholize (Eng) *see* Alcoholise.

Alcoholmeter (Eng) a calibrated instrument for measuring alcohol in a liquid.

Alcohol [Methyl] (Eng) CH_3OH. a wood alcohol, obtained from the distillation of wood sugar by yeast. Is poisonous.

Alcoholometry (Eng) measuring or calculating alcoholic strengths.

Alcól (Ire) alcohol.

Alcola (Eng) a 4% alc by vol. bottled cola from Brothers Drinks.

Alcólach (Ire) alcoholic.

Alcólacht (Ire) alcoholic.

Alcool (Fr) the name given to a Cognac brandy that is over 84% alc by vol.

Alcool (Fr)(It) alcohol.

Alcool (Port) alcohol.

Alcool Blanc (Fr) white alcohol, defines clear liqueurs that have been matured in glass not wood so that no colour is gained. Usually distilled from fruit.

Alcool Denaturé (W.Ind) the local name used in Mauritius for de-naturalised rum.

Alcoolico (It) alcoholic.
Alcoolique (Fr) spirituous.
Alcoolisme (Fr) alcoholism.
Alcools de Cœur (Fr) a name given to the middle part of the distillation. *see* Brouillis.
Alcool Vinico (Mad) denotes brandy distilled from wine.
Alcopop (Eng) a slang (circa 1995) term to describe many of the brand-named alcoholic drinks available that were originally non-alcoholic. E.G. lemonade, orangeade, cola, soda water. Now no longer used as it was linked to under-age drinking. This style of drink is now known as RTD's.
Alcudia (Cktl) ⅖ measure dry gin, ⅕ measure crème de banane, ⅕ measure Galliano, ⅕ measure grapefruit juice. Shake well over ice, strain and add twist of grapefruit peel.
Aldeanueva (Sp) a Zona de Crianza in the Rioja Baja, north-eastern Spain.
Aldehydes (Eng) flavour elements, the result of alcoholic distillation.
Alderbro (Hun) a wine-producing village in the Debrö region. Noted for Debrö Hárslevelü.
Alder Brook (USA) a winery based in the Russian River Valley, Sonoma County, California. Grape variety: Pinot noir.
Alderic (Fr) the name of an A.C. Blanquette de Limoux produced by Producteurs de Blanquette de Limoux.
Aldermoor Vineyard (Eng) a vineyard (established 1975). (Add): Poulner Hill, Ringwood, Hampshire. 2.5ha. Grape varieties include Müller-Thurgau and Reichensteiner.
Alderney Ale (Ch.Isles) a malt-extract brew 1035 O.G. from the Braye Brewery, St. Annes, Alderney. Brewery now no longer in existence.
Aldersbach Freiher von Aretin (Ger) a brewery. (Add): GmbH & Co. KG., Freiherr von Aretin Platz 1, Aldersbach D-94501, Germany. Brews a variety of beers and lagers. Website: http://www.aldersbacher.de 'E'mail: info@aldersbacher.de
Aldo Conterno (It) a wine-producer based in Monforte d'Alba (a district of Barolo), Piemonte.
Ale (Eng) an aromatic malt beer (originally un-hopped but now flavoured with hops). Types are: Bitter ale, Pale ale, Brown ale, India Pale ale (IPA), Export ale, Strong ale. (Den) = øl, (Ire) = leann.
Aleatico (It) a red grape variety of the Muscat family. Produces sweet dessert red wines. Also known as Agliano or Leatico. *See also* Aleatico-Nero.
Aleatico (USA) *see* California Aleatico.
Aleatico di Gradoli (It) a D.O.C. sweet red wine from Latium produced from Aleatico grape.
Aleatico di Gradoli Liquoroso (It) a D.O.C. fortified wine made from slightly dried Aleatico grapes with a minimum alc. content of 12% by vol. Fortified to 17.5% by vol. then aged for six months from date of fortification. From Latium.
Aleatico di Portoferraio (It) a sweet, deep-coloured red wine from Elba in Tuscany, Aleatico grape, 14%–5% alc by vol.
Aleatico di Puglia (It) a D.O.C. red wine produced from the Aleatico, Negro amaro, Malvasia nero and Primitivo grapes which are partially dried. Two styles: Dolce Naturale and Liquoroso Dolcenaturale (fortified). From Puglia. If graded Riserva then must be aged for 3 years.
Aleatico-Nero (It) *see* Aleatico.
Aléatiko (Rus) a white grape variety grown in Uzbekistania. Produces white dessert wines.
Aleberry (Punch) add 2 tablespoons of fine oatmeal to 500mls (1pint) mild ale. Stand for four hours, strain and boil 5 minutes. Add 1 bottle claret, juice of lemon and grated nutmeg. Serve hot in mugs with thin slices of toast.
Ale Carafe (Eng) a large glass carafe used in the eighteenth century for carrying ale from the cellar to the table of the gentry. Usually of ¼ gallon (1 litre) capacity.
Alec's Angel (Cktl) ¾ liqueur glass of crème de cacao, top with fresh cream.
Ale Flip [New Recipe] (Eng) 1200mls (2pints) ale, 100mls (4fl.ozs) brandy, 3 eggs, grated rind of 1 lemon, ½ barspoon ground ginger, 200gms. (8ozs) brown sugar. Heat the rind and ale, beat rest of ingredients, pour heated ale into egg mixture, blend, return to pan until mix is creamy. Top with grated nutmeg.
Ale Flip [Old Recipe] (Eng) old ale whisked up with egg yolk and sugar and serve hot or cold with grated nutmeg on top.
Alefons Giovanett-Weinkellerei Castelfeder (It) a large winery based in Neumarkt, Südtirol (Alto-Adige).
Ale Force (Eng) a 4.2% alc by vol. cask ale brewed by Storm Brewing, Macclesfield, Cheshire.
Ale for Nigel (Eng) a 4.7% alc by vol. ale brewed by Kelham Brewery in Sheffield to commemorate the death of one of their staff. Limited edition (10 x 36 gallon barrels only).
Ale Fresco (Eng) a 4.5% alc by vol. ale brewed by the Tisbury Brewery, Tisbury, Wiltshire by the Sussex Leisure C°.
Alegar (Eng) malt vinegar.
Alegret [José] (Sp) a wine producer based in Penedés. (Add): Calle Sol 22, Vilafranca del Penedés, Barcelona. Produces fine red wines.
Ale House (Eng) a sixteenth century establishment that sells ales only (a public-house). (Ire) = teach leanna.
Alella (Sp) a Denominación de Origen of the Cataluña region of south eastern Spain. 50ha. Produces mostly dry white wines but some red and rosé also produced. Grape varieties: Pansá blanca, Garnacha blanca, Chardonnay, Pansá rosado, Chenin blanc, Macabeo, Garnacha tinta, Ull de llebre (Tempranillo), Garnacha peluda. Plus experimantal plantings of Cabernet sauvignon, Cabernet franc, Pinot noir.
Alella Cooperative Winery (Sp) a co-operative based in the Alella region. Has 153 members. Produces wines sold under the Marfil label.
Ale Malt (Eng) a biscuit-tasting malt used in traditional ales.

A

Alemannenbuck (Ger) vineyard (Anb): Baden. (Ber): Markgräflerland. (Gro): Lorettoberg. (Vil): Mengen.

Ale Marie (Eng) an ale 6% alc by vol brewed by the RCH Brewery, Avon.

Alembic (Fr) an alternative spelling of Alambic.

Alembic Armagnaçais (Fr) see Alambic Armagnaçais.

Alembics (Fr) see Alambics.

Aleno (Sp) the brand-name of a Cream Sherry shipped to the U.K. by John Buccleugh of Warrington, Lancashire.

Alenouer (Port) a DOC wine region located in Oeste, Estremadura. Produces red and white wines.

Alentejano (Port) a large wine region based in south-eastern Portugal which contains the DOC of Alentejo.

Alentejo (Port) a DOC wine-producing region in southern Portugal. 40000ha. Has 5 D.O.C. areas (Borba, Portalegre, Redondo, Reguengos, Vidigueira) and 3 I.P.R. areas (Évora, Moura, Granja-Amareleja). Produces 80% red and 20% white wines. Cooperatives account for 85% of production. Grape varieties: Aragonez, Alicanté bouschet, Trincadeira, Periquita, Touriga nacional, Roupeiro, Fernão Pires, Perrum, Arinto.

Ale of Wight (Eng) a 4% alc by vol. ale brewed by the Goddards Brewery, Isle of Wight.

Ale Posset (Eng) heat 500mls ale (½ pint) and 500mls milk (½ pint) with sugar, ginger and nutmeg to taste. Is served hot.

Alepou (Gre) lit: 'fox', a clone of the Rhoditis grape, *See also* Migdali.

Alep Pine (Gre) see Aleppo Pine.

Aleppo (Arab) a hilly wine-producing region in northern Syria.

Aleppo Pine (Gre) *Calitris quadrivalvis* a pine species from which the resin is used exclusively for the making of Retsina. Also known as the Alep pine.

Ale Sangaree (Cktl) dissolve 10gms (½oz.) of sugar into 125mls (5fl.ozs) water. Place in a large tumbler, fill up with ale and top with grated nutmeg.

Alesman (Eng) a 3.7% alc. by vol. bitter ale brewed by Green Bottle Ltd., Worth Brewery, Keighley, Yorkshire.

Ales of Scilly (U.K) a brewery (established 2001) based in Higher Trenoeth, St. Mary's, Scilly Isles. TR21 0NS. Brews a variety of ales including: 3 Sheets 4.3% alc by vol., Maiden Voyage 4% alc by vol., Natural Beauty 4.2% alc by vol., Scuppered Ale 4.6% alc by vol. 'E'mail: mark@alesofscilly.co.uk

Alessano (It) a white grape variety of the Puglia region.

Alet (Fr) a sparkling natural mineral water from the Pyrénées Atlantiques. Mineral contents (milligrammes per litre): Sodium 13mg/l, Calcium 63mg/l, Magnesium 23mg/l, Potassium 1.8mg/l, Bicarbonates 300mg/l, Chlorides 11mg/l, Sulphates 14mg/l, Fluoride <0.02mg/l, Nitrates 2mg/l. pH 7.4

Alete Mineralquelle (Ger) a natural mineral water from Polling-Weiding/Kreis, Mühldorf am Inn, BY.

Ale Trail Mild (Eng) a 3.5% alc by vol. mild ale brewed by the Dark Star Brewery, Brighton under the Skinners brand label.

Alexander [1] (Cktl) 2 parts dry gin, 1 part crème de cacao, 1 part double cream. Shake over ice and strain into a cocktail glass.

Alexander [2] (Cktl) ¾ measure rye whiskey, ¼ measure Bénédictine. Stir over ice, strain into a cocktail glass and add a twist of orange peel on top.

Alexander (It) a natural mineral water from Alexander, Bologna.

Alexander Baby (Cktl) ⅓ measure navy rum, ⅓ measure crème de cacao, ⅓ measure cream. Shake over ice, strain into a cocktail glass and top with grated nutmeg.

Alexander Cocktail (Cktl) 25mls (1fl.oz) brandy, 25mls (1fl.oz) white crème de cacao, 25mls (1fl.oz) cream. Shake over ice, strain into cocktail glass and top with grated nutmeg.

Alexanderfontein (S.Afr) the label for a range of wines produced by the Ormonde Vineyards winery, Swartland, Western Cape.

Alexander Quelle (Ger) a natural mineral water from Eppelborn-Weisbach, SL.

Alexander Rodenbach (Bel) 6% alc by vol. top-fermented, bottled fruity kriek beer brewed by Brouwerij Rodenbach N.V., Roeslare.

Alexander's Brother (Cktl) ⅓ measure dry gin, ⅓ measure crème de menthe, ⅓ measure cream. Shake over ice and strain into a cocktail glass.

Alexander's Crown (USA) a vineyard based in the Alexander Valley, California. 25ha. Grape variety: Cabernet sauvignon. Is owned by Sonoma Vineyards.

Alexander's Downfall (Scot) a 4.3% alc by vol (1045 O.G.) ale brewed by Burntlisland Brewery, Fife.

Alexander's Sister [1] (Cktl) ⅓ measure dry gin, ⅓ measure (white) crème de menthe, ⅓ measure cream. Shake over ice and strain into a cocktail glass.

Alexander's Sister [2] (Cktl) ⅓ measure Kahlúa, ⅓ measure Cognac, ⅓ measure cream. Shake well over ice, strain into a cocktail glass and top with grated nutmeg.

Alexander Valley (USA) an A.V.A. region in Sonoma County, north of Napa Valley, California. Home to the wineries of Clos du Bois, Château Souverain, Château St. Jean, Field Stone, Simi. Grape varieties include Cabernet sauvignon, Chardonnay, Merlot, Sauvignon blanc, Zinfandel

Alexander Valley Vineyards (USA) a winery based in Alexander Valley, Sonoma County, California. 100ha. Grape varieties: Cabernet sauvignon, Chardonnay, Chenin blanc, Gewürztraminer, Johannisberg riesling and Pinot noir. Produces varietal wines.

Alexander Vineyard (N.Z) a vineyard based in Dublin St. Extension, Martinborough. 2ha. Grape varieties: Cabernet franc, Cabernet sauvignon, Merlot.

Alexandra Brewery (Eng) a brewery (established 1982) based in Brighton, Sussex. Trades under the name of Becket's Bars and Ales. Produces beers and 'Old Snowy' 1054 O.G.

Alexandra Kingsley (Austr) a full-bodied white wine (Chardonnay) produced by the Red Bank Winery, Victoria, Australia.

Alexandrakis (Afr) a winery based in northern Ethiopia. Produces medium-quality wine.

Alexandre [Serge] (Fr) a Cognac producer. (Add): Rue de Cagouillet, 16100 Cognac. Owns vineyards in the Fins Bois. Produces Vieux Cognac from Premier Cru (average age 12 years).

Alexandre d'Almeida (Port) a family-owned winery based near Lameira. Produces fine red, rosé and white wines.

Alexandria (Fr) a name for the Portuguese Moscatel do Setúbal grape.

Alexis Bailly Vineyard (USA) a bonded winery based in Minnesota. 4ha. Produces hybrid wines.

Alexis Heck Cocktail (Cktl) ⅔ measure Cognac, ⅙ measure Grand Marnier, ⅙ measure golden rum, ⅙ measure dry vermouth. Stir over ice and strain into a Champagne saucer.

Ale Yeasts (Eng) top-fermenting yeasts that stick together as they multiply so that they form a surface on top of the ferment. The ale results from top-fermentation.

Aleyor (Sp) a dark red table wine produced on the island of Mallorca.

Alezio (It) a D.O.C. red wine from Salento, Apulia. Made from the Negroamaro grape.

Alf (Ger) village (Anb): Mosel-Saar-Ruwer. (Ber): Zell/Mosel. (Gro): Grafschaft. (Vins): Arrasburg-Schlossberg, Herrenberg, Hölle, Kapellenberg, Katzenkopf, Kronenberg.

Alfa Blue (Ind) a natural mineral water (established 2002) from Rudrapur, Uttaranchal. Mineral contents (milligrammes per litre): Sodium 11.69mg/l, Calcium 33.45mg/l, Magnesium 9.74mg/l, Chlorides 6.95mg/l, Sulphates 12.73mg/l, Fluoride 0.34mg/l, Nitrates 2.17mg/l. pH 7.77

Alfa Bokbier (Hol) 6.5% alc by vol. bottled ruby-red bock beer brewed by Alfa Bier Brouwerij, Schinnen.

Alfa Brouwerij (Hol) a brewery. (Add): Thull 15-19, 6365 AC Schinnen, South Limburg, Netherlands. Noted for Super Dortmunder 7.5% alc by vol. (the strongest beer in the Netherlands) and Alfa Edel (an all-malt pilsener 5% alc. by vol). Alfa Oud Bruin, Alfa Bokbier, Alfa Lentebock, Mid-zomerbier.

Alfa Edel (Hol) a 5% alc by vol. pils beer brewed by Alfa Brouwerij, Schinnen, South Limburg from Czec. and German hops, French and Dutch malt.

Alfaro (Sp) a Zona de Crianza in the Rioja Baja, north-eastern Spain.

Alfie Cocktail (Cktl) 35mls (1½ fl.ozs) lemon vodka, dash pineapple juice, dash triple sec. Shake over ice and strain into a cocktail glass.

Alfie Cocktail (Cktl)(Non-alc) ⅓ measure lemon juice, ⅓ measure pineapple juice, ⅓ measure orange juice. Shake over ice, strain into cocktail glass and dress with cube of fresh pineapple.

Alfiero Boffa (It) a winery based at San Marzano Oliveto, Piemonte. Produce D.O.C. Barbera wines. Labels include Collina della Vedova, Velo di Maya, La Riva.

Alföld (Hun) one of fifteen wine-producing regions situated on the 'Great Plain'.

Alfons Giovanett-Weinkellerei Castelfeder (It) a large winery based in Neumarkt, Südtirol (Alto-Adige).

Alfonso (Cktl) 25mls (1fl.oz) Dubonnet, 1 lump sugar, 2 dashes Angostura. Place sugar in a Champagne glass, shake bitters onto sugar cube. Add Dubonnet, fill a glass with iced Champagne, stir slightly and add a twist of lemon.

Alfonso (Sp) a dry Oloroso Sherry produced by Gonzalez Byass in Jerez de la Frontera, Cadiz.

Alfonso del Sordo [d'] (It) a 100ha. winery based in San Severo, Puglia. Produces white and rosé D.O.C. Posta Arignano, plus I.G.T. Casteldrione., Contrado del Santo..

Alfonso El Sabio (Sp) a top quality brandy from Valdespino, Jerez de la Frontera.

Alfonso Maldonado (Sp) a noted wine-producer based in Rueda. see Viña Rebelde.

Alfonso Special (Cktl) ½ measure Grand Marnier, ¼ measure gin, ¼ measure French vermouth, 2 dashes Italian vermouth, 1 dash Angostura. Stir over ice and strain into a cocktail glass.

Alford Arms (Eng) a home-brew pub in Frithsden, Herts, England that is owned by Whitbreads. Products include: Cherrypicker's, Rudolf's Revenge and Strong Amber ales.

Alforra (Port) mildew.

Alfresco (Eng) the brand-name of a soft fruit drink produced from mineral water, apple, lemon, elderflower and lime water from Hall and Woodhouse Brewery, Dorset.

Alfrocheiro Preto (Port) the main red grape variety grown in Alentejo and Dão, provides colour and structure.

Algarve (Port) a wine region based in the south of Portugal. Has the DOC areas of: Lacos, Lagoa, Portimao and Tavira. Produces mainly red wines from Periquita and Tinta Negra Mole grapes.

Alger (Alg) one of the three wine-producing regions of Algeria. The main areas within the region are Ain-Bessem-Bouira, Coteaux du Zaccar and Médéa.

Algeria (Alg) a Mediterranean wine producing country. 3 regions are Alger, Constantine and Oran. Produces mainly red, fat, soft and alcoholic wines 11%–15% alc by vol. Has an even climate with consistant vintages.

Al-Ghadir (S.Arabia) a natural mineral water from Riyadh, Saudi Arabia.

Algonquin Cocktail (Cktl) ½ measure rye whiskey, ¼ measure French vermouth, ¼ measure pineapple juice. Shake over ice, strain into an ice-filled old-fashioned glass.

A

Alhama (Sp) a still natural mineral water from Sondeo no 14, Alhama de Almeria, Almeria. Mineral contents (milligrammes per litre): Sodium 21.2mg/l, Calcium 122mg/l, Magnesium 51mg/l, Potassium 4mg/l, Bicarbonates 384mg/l, Chlorides 23mg/l, Sulphates 224mg/l, Fluoride 1.5mg/l, Nitrates 0.5mg/l.

Alhambra Cervezas (Sp) a brewery. (Add): Grupa Cervezas, Alhambra S.L. Granada 18012 Spain. Brews a variety of beers and lagers. Website: http://www.cervezasalhambra.es

Alhambra (USA) a natural mineral water (established 1902). Mineral contents (milligrammes per litre): Sodium 3.8mg/l, Calcium 0.7mg/l, Magnesium 0.8mg/l, Chlorides 3.5mg/l, Sulphates 3.4mg/l. pH 7.2

Aliança Seco (Port) a dry white wine from Caves Aliança. Website: http://www.caves-alianca.pt

Alicante (Sp) a Denominación de Origen wine region of southern Spain. Produces red, rosé and white wines sometimes sold under the appellation 'Montana'. Most of the vineyards are in the province of Alicante but some are in the district of Albanilla, in the province of Murcia. Grape varieties: Bobal, Granacha, Monastrell, Moscatel romano and Tintorera.

Alicante (Sp) a red grape variety grown in north-western Spain where it is also known as the Garnacha tintorera.

Alicanté Bouschet (USA) a red grape variety producing red and dessert wines. A cross of Petit bouschet x Grenache. Has red flesh.

Alicanté Ganzin (USA) a red grape variety, produces dessert wines.

Alicanté Grenache (Afr) a red grape variety, producing full-bodied, soft, alcoholic (14% by vol) wines. Grown in Tunisia.

Alicantina (Sp) another name for the Grenache grape.

Alice Brewery (Scot) a brewery in Inverness which produces: Alice Ale 1040 O.G. Sixty 1060 O.G. Keg-Longman Lager 1040 O.G. and 80/- Export 1040 O.G. (a bottled beer).

Alice Extraordinary Vodka (Eng) a vodka and 'energy' drink from The Active Vodka Company 41.25% alc by vol. Distilled 5 times it is produced in two styles Alice Red and Alice Blue (flavoured with chamomile, elderflowers and hops).

Aligate (Rus) a medium dry white wine from the Moldavia region.

Aligoté (Fr) a prolific white grape variety grown mainly in the Burgundy region, it produces mainly dry, acidic wines with a green unripe apple and pear flavour. see Kir and Sparkling Burgundies. Also known as the Blanc de Troyes, Chaudenet gras and Giboudot blanc.

Aligoté Ay-Danil (Rus) a dry white wine from the Crimean Peninsular.

Aligoté des Hautes-Côtes (Fr) a light, dry, fruity wine from the vineyards of the A.C. Hautes-Côtes in Burgundy.

Alijo (Port) a small wine area in the Douro, north-east of Pinhão.

Alión (Sp) a new style of wine produced by Bodegas Vega Sicilia at their Bodega Almez. 100% Tinto fino that is fermented in stainless steel. Aged in French oak barriques.

Alios (Fr) ironstone soil (red sandstone, rich in iron).

Ali-Pasha (Yug) a still natural mineral water. Mineral contents (milligrammes per litre): Sodium 0.3mg/l, Calcium 18.4mg/l, Magnesium 11.18mg/l, Potassium 0.07mg/l, Bicarbonates 100.04mg/l, Chlorides 6.03mg/l, Sulphates 3mg/l. pH 7.29

Alises (Fr) an Alsace eau-de-vie produced from sorb-apples.

Alisea (It) a natural mineral water from Sorgente, Leonardo. Mineral contents (milligrammes per litre): Sodium 2.5mg/l, Calcium 12.3mg/l, Magnesium 2.6mg/l, Potassium 0.6mg/l, Bicarbonates 41.6mg/l, Chlorides 0.9mg/l, Sulphates 10.1mg/l, Silicates 8.7mg/l, Nitrates 2.5mg/l. pH 7.9

Alive (Eng) still fruit drinks of 'orange cascade' and 'tropical torrent' flavours from C.C.G.B. Sold in plastic bottles.

Alizé (Fr) a pastis produced by Pernod-Ricard 40% alc by vol. Also produces a V.S. and VSOP version plus flavoured varieties including: Alizé Gold (passion fruit) and Alizé Red (passion fruit and cranberry).

Aliziergeist (Fr) an eau-de-vie (fruit brandy) made from the berries of the wild service tree 45% alc by vol.

Aljarafe (Sp) a Vino Comarcal of Sevilla in Andalucía.

Alkaline Water (Eng) waters (natural spring) that are rich in minerals. Aix-la-Chapelle, Aix-les-Bains, Evian, Malvern, Perrier, Selters, St. Galmier, Vichy.

Al Kastal (Jor) a natural mineral water from Qasr al Mushatta. Mineral contents (milligrammes per litre): Sodium 23mg/l, Calcium 44mg/l, Magnesium 12mg/l, Potassium 5.1mg/l, Bicarbonates 149mg/l, Chlorides 43mg/l, Sulphates 19mg/l, Nitrates 1.5mg/l. pH 7.3

Alken (Ger) village (Anb): Mosel-Saar-Ruwer. (Ber): Zell/Mosel. (Gro): Weinhex. (Vins): Bleidenberg, Burgberg, Hunnenstein.

Alken-Maes Brasserie (Bel) a brewery (established 1881) based in Alken. Owned by Watney, Mann and Truman. Noted for Maes Cool, Pils, Grimbergen (an abbaye style beer), Tourtel Malt (alcohol-free).

Alkermès (Fr) a red-coloured cordial, the dye is obtained from insects found in Mediterranean Kermes oak. Spirit is flavoured with cinnamon, cloves, mace, rose water and sugar. Popular in the eighteenth and nineteenth centuries.

Alkie (Austr)(Eng)(USA) see Alky.

Alkimya (Fr) the name of an A.C. white botrytised wine produced from Menu Pineau grapes by Domaine les Cailloux du Paradis, Loire.

Alko (Fin) the Finnish state company which controls

all drink production and sales in the country. Has a basic brief to limit the detrimental effects of alcohol consumption. Limits consumption by pricing with lower tax on weaker drinks, limiting licences to sell alcohol, enforcing age limits (18 years for weaker products, 20 years for all products).

Al Kohl (Arab) alcohol.

Alkohol (Cro)(Den) alcohol.

Alkoholfri (Den) non-alcoholic/alcohol free.

Alkoholholdig (Den) alcoholic.

Alkoholni (Cro) alcoholic.

Alkol (Tur) alcohol.

Alkolik (Tur) alcoholic.

Alkollü (Tur) alcoholic liquor.

Alkoomi (Austr) a winery based in the Frankland River region of Western Australia. Grape varieties include: Cabernet sauvignon. Riesling, Sauvignon blanc, Shiraz.

Alky (Austr)(Eng)(USA) a slang term for an alcoholic.

Allandale Winery (Austr) a winery. (Add): Allandale Road, Pokolbin, via Maitland, New South Wales, 23210. 7ha. Grape varieties: Chardonnay, Pinot noir and Sémillon.

Allan's Special (Cktl) ½ measure crème de banane, 1 measure gin, ½ measure lemon juice, dash egg white. Shake over ice, strain into a cocktail glass and add dash of grenadine.

Alla Ruta (It) a green-coloured grappa that has a herb plant in every bottle.

Allas-Champagne (Fr) a commune in the Charente-Maritime département whose grapes are classed Petite Champagne (Cognac).

Allasch Kümmel (Ger) a style of kümmel made in Stettin on the Polish / German border. 41% alc by vol.

Alla Sua (It) lit: 'your health'.

All Black Port (N.Z) a Port-type wine produced by Mother's Cellar Winery in Henderson, North Island.

Allbright (Eng) a draught bitter beer brewed by the Coors Brewers Ltd.

Allbright Brewery (Eng) a brewery that produces Welsh Brewer's keg bitter plus Mitchells and Butlers bottled beer 1040 O.G.

Allée Bleu (S.Afr) a winery (established 2000) based in Franschhoek, Western Cape. Grape varieties: Cabernet sauvignon, Chardonnay, Grenache, Merlot, Pinotage, Sémillon, Shiraz. Labels: Isabeau, L'Amour Toujours, Starlette Rouge. 30ha. Website: http://www.alleebleu.com

Allegheny Cocktail (Cktl) 1 measure Bourbon whiskey, 1 measure French vermouth, ¼ measure lemon juice, ¼ measure blackberry liqueur. Shake over ice, strain into a cocktail glass and add a twist of lemon peel.

Allegra (Switz) a still natural mineral water from Malix. Mineral contents (milligrammes per litre): Sodium 1.5mg/l, Calcium 90mg/l, Magnesium 23.1mg/l, Potassium 0.5mg/l, Bicarbonates 335.6mg/l, Chlorides 1.2mg/l, Sulphates 42.2mg/l, Fluoride 0.05mg/l, Nitrates 1.8mg/l.

Allegrini (It) a famous winery based in Verona, Veneto region north-eastern Italy. Produces Valpolicella and other wines. Also owns La Poja vineyard.

Allegro (Port) a red wine produced in Lafões.

Allegro (USA) a winery (established 1973) based in York County, west of Susquehanna River, Pennsylvania. Produces Cadenza from Bordeaux varieties.

Alleinbesitz (Ger) a wine-producers monoply.

Alleluia (Cktl) 10mls (½ fl.oz) maraschino, 10mls (½ fl.oz) blue curaçao, 10mls (½ fl.oz) lemon juice, 35mls (1½ fl.ozs) tequila. Shake over ice into an ice-filled highball glass. Top with bitter lemon and decorate with a slice of lemon, sprig of mint and a cherry.

Allen Cocktail (Cktl) 1 measure dry gin, ½ measure maraschino, juice ¼ lemon. Shake over ice, strain into a cocktail glass.

Allerfeinste (Ger) lit: 'first of all', the pre 1971 labelling term found on casks.

Allesverloren Estate (S.Afr) a winery (established 1704) based in Swartland. (Add): Allesverloren, Riebeck-Wes 6800. Grape varieties include: Cabernet sauvignon, Shirz, Tinta barocca, Touriga nacional. Produces varietal wines and an LBV Port-style wine. Website: http://www.allesverloren.co.za

Allgäu-Quelle (Ger) a natural mineral water from Oberstaufen-Thalkirchdorf, BY.

Allgäuer Brauhaus AG (Ger) a brewery. (Add): Postfach 1109, Kempten D-87401 Germany. Brews a variety of beers and lagers.

Allied Breweries (Eng) major brewers: Ansell's, Ind Coope and Tetley's have five breweries producing a large variety of beers.

Allied Brewery Traders Association (Eng) a brewers organization. (Add): 85 Tattenhall Road, Wolverhampton, West Midlands WV3 9NE. 'E'mail: info@abta-online.org.uk

Allied Distillers (Scot) a distillery group (formed in January 1988) by Allied Lyons to manage the Scotch whisky companies it owns i.e. George Ballantine, Hiram Walker. see Allied-Domecq.

Allied-Domecq (Eng) the new name for Allied-Lyons in 1994. Now one of the top 100 companies in Europe. Brands include Ballantine's, Ballygowan, Beefeater Gin, Bodegas Domecq, Bodegas y Bebidas, Campo Viejo, Canadian Club, Cockburns Port, Corvoisier Cognac, Harveys Sherry, Kahlúa, La Ina Sherry, Lanson Champagne, Laphroaig, Montana Vineyards, Siglo, Teachers Whisky, Tia Maria, Viña Alcorta. Hiram Walker is now known as Allied-Domecq Spirits and Wine. (Add): Prewetts Mill, Worthing Road, Horsham, West Sussex. RH12 1ST. Website: http://www.allieddomecqplc.com

Allied-Domecq Spirits and Wine (Eng) the new name for Hiram Walker.

Allied-Lyons (Eng) a major company which owned many brand-name beverages both alcoholic and non-alcoholic. These include: Allied Breweries, Grants of St.James', Showerings. Now part of Allied-Domecq.

Allies Cocktail (Cktl) 1 part dry gin, 1 part French vermouth, 3 dashes kümmel. Stir over ice and strain into a cocktail glass.

All in Cocktail (Eng) the nickname for a lethal mixture of glass 'slops' left in the bar that is often drunk by alcoholics.

All Malt (Jap) a whiskey produced by the Nikka company from vatted malts produced from both pot and Coffey stills spirits

Allmersbach a.W. (Ger) village (Anb): Württemberg. (Ber): Württembergisch Unterland. (Gro): Schalkstein. (Vin): Alter Berg.

All Nations (Eng) a pub which brews its own traditional ale, a light mild. (Add): Coalport Road, Madeley (now part of Telford New Town), Shropshire.

All Niter (Eng) a 3.8% alc by vol. beer brewed by Northern Brewing, Cheshire.

Alloa Brewery (Scot) part of Allied Breweries. Based in Alloa, Clackmannanshire. Amongst its brews are Arrol's 70/- Ale, Diamond Heavy and Skol.

Allobrogia (Fr) a white grape variety grown in Roman times, noted for a resin flavour.

Allogrogie (Fr) a Vin de Pays area in the Savoie département in south-eastern France.

All-Party Parlimentary Beer Group (Eng) an organization (established 1993). (Add): Pentre Farm, Pentre, Bucknell, Shropshire SY7 0BU. 'E'mail: humphreysr@parliment.uk

Allsach (Ger) a kümmel flavoured liqueur with aniseed, almonds and spices. 40% alc by vol.

All Saints Winery (Austr) a large winery based at Wahgunyah in north-east Victoria.

All Seasons (Eng) a 4.2% alc by vol. ale brewed by Hanby Ales Ltd., Shropshire.

Allsopp Brewery (Eng) the revived name (1985) for Allied Breweries East Midland East Anglia C°.

Allsopps (W.Ind) a lager beer brewed by the Carib C°. in Trinidad under licence from Allied Breweries of England.

Allsopp's Pilsener (Afr) a pilsner lager beer 1042 O.G. brewed by the East African Breweries of Tanzania under licence from the Allied Breweries in England.

Allt-a-Bhainne (Scot) a new single malt distillery (established 1974) in Speyside under Ben Rinnes in Banffshire. A highland malt whisky 40% alc by vol. (part of Seagram).

Alluvia (S.Afr) a winery (established 2002) based in Stellenbosch, Western Cape. Grape varieties: Cabernet sauvignon, Sauvignon blanc. 8ha. Website: http://www.alluvia.co.za

Alluvial (Eng) (Fr) rich soil found on river banks that is not suitable for wine grape cultivation because it is too rich. Produces flabby wines.

Allwedd Costrell (Wal) corkscrew.

All-White Frappé (Cktl) ¼ measure peppermint schnapps, ¼ measure (white) crème de cacao, ¼ measure anisette, ¼ measure lemon juice. Shake over ice, strain into a cocktail glass with a teaspoon of crushed ice.

Alma (Cktl) ³⁄₁₀ measure Mandarine Napoléon, ³⁄₁₀ measure vodka, ¹⁄₁₀ measure Campari, ³⁄₁₀ measure grapefruit juice. Shake well over ice, strain into a cocktail glass.

Almacenista (Sp) the name given to a high-quality, old, unblended Sherry. Usually purchased by aficioñados who mature the sherries then sell them back to the shippers.

Almaden (USA) a wine-producing region in central California.

Almaden Vineyards (USA) a large winery based in California. 2810ha. Has vineyards in Alameda, Benito and Monterey with 5 wineries. Produces all styles of wines sold under Alamaden and Charles Lefranc labels. Owned by National Distillers.

Almaha (Leb) a natural mineral water (established in 1998) from El Maten. Mineral contents (milligrammes per litre): Sodium 13.12mg/l, Calcium 65.24mg/l, Magnesium 6.085mg/l, Potassium 3.204mg/l, Bicarbonates 90mg/l, Chlorides 22.5mg/l, Sulphates 22mg/l, Nitrates 7.4mg/l. pH 7.5

Almansa (Sp) a Denominación de Origen in the province of Albacete in La Mancha, central Spain. 7,600ha. Grape varieties: 45% Monastrell plus Cencibel, Garnacha tintorera, Airén, Merseguera. Noted for red and rosado wines.

Almansar (Sp) a D.O. of Levante in southern Spain.

Almarla Vineyards (USA) a small winery based in Matherville, Mississippi. Produces wines from French and American hybrid vines.

Al-Marraei (Syr) a natural mineral water from Qunaitra.

Almasif (S.Arabia) a natural mineral water from Saudi Arabia. Mineral contents (milligrammes per litre): Sodium 22mg/l, Calcium 22mg/l, Magnesium 14mg/l, Potassium 2mg/l, Bicarbonates 98mg/l, Chlorides 39mg/l, Sulphates 18mg/l, Fluoride 0.66mg/l, Nitrates 8mg/l. pH 7.6

Almaviva (Chile) a red wine produced by Viña Almaviva, Puento Alto, Maipo from 75% Cabernet sauvignon, 19% Merlot, 6% Cabernet franc (a joint venture between Concha y Toro and Baron Philippe de Rothschild of Bordeaux). Matured in Bordeaux barriques for 16 months.

Almaza Brewery (Leb) a small brewery based in eastern Beirut.

Almedijar (Sp) a natural mineral water. Mineral contents (milligrammes per litre): Sodium 7.1mg/l, Calcium 22mg/l, Magnesium 26.5mg/l, Potassium 1.2mg/l, Bicarbonates 210mg/l, Chlorides 8.8mg/l, Sulphates 6mg/l, Fluoride 0.2mg/l, Nitrates 3.5mg/l.

Almeirim (Port) an I.P.R. wine area which produces red and white wines in I.P.R. region of Ribatejo on the plains of the river Tejo.

Almendralejo (Sp) a red grape variety grown in the Estremadura and Léon districts. Produces good red wines.

Almendralejo (Sp) a wine-producing region in Estremadura.

Almeria (Cktl) ⅗ measure dark rum, ⅖ measure Tia

Maria, white of egg. Shake over ice and strain into a cocktail glass.

Almería (Sp) a province of the D.O. Andalucía, home to the Vino Comarcal area Laujar.

Almíbar (Sp) invert sugar solution used, mixed with wine, to sweeten pale sherries.

Almíjar (Sp) a yard in Jerez, where the grapes are placed on mats to dry in the sun. *see* Esparto Grass and Esparto Mats.

Almizcate (Sp) the name for the space between two bodega buildings.

Almog (Isr) a sweet red wine in the style of a Málaga. Produced for the USA market.

Almond Blossom (Cktl) ⅔ measure Perisco, ⅓ measure cherry brandy, shake over ice, strain into a cocktail glass and dress with a cherry.

Almond Brewery (Eng) a former brewery in Wigan. Name revived by the Burtonwood Breweries in 1984. Used for a few pubs plus Almond's Bitter 1036.5 O.G.

Almond Eye Cocktail (Cktl) ⅓ measure marsala, ⅓ measure crème de cacao, ⅓ measure cream. Shake over ice and strain into a cocktail glass.

Almond Grove (S.Afr) the label for a noble late harvest white wine (Weisser riesling) produced by the Robertson Co-operative Winery, Robertson, Western Cape.

Almondocato (Cktl) fill a liqueur glass ⅔ full of advocaat and top with a dash of crème de noyaux.

Almude (Port) a measure of 25 litres used for blending Port wine.

Almuneco (Sp) a red grape variety grown in D.O. Hoyo de Mazo on La Palma, Canary Islands.

Al Nabek (Jor) a natural mineral water from Qasr al Mushatta: Mineral contents (milligrammes per litre): Sodium 23mg/l, Calcium 44mg/l, Magnesium 12mg/l, Potassium 5.1mg/l, Bicarbonates 149mg/l, Chlorides 43mg/l, Sulphates 19mg/l. pH 7.3

Alofat (Eng) a mediaeval (Saxon) word for ale. *See also* Alu and Ealu.

Aloha Coffee Liqueur (Scot) a whisky-based coffee liqueur 29% alc by vol.

Aloisius Quelle (Ger) a still and sparkling natural mineral water from Schwäbische Alb. Mineral contents (milligrammes per litre): Sodium 2.4mg/l, Calcium 77mg/l, Magnesium 27mg/l, Potassium 1.9mg/l, Bicarbonates 368mg/l, Chlorides 3.2mg/l, Sulphates 11.7mg/l, Fluoride 0.1mg/l.

Alois Gangl (Aus) vineyard owner-producer. (Add): Obere Hauptstrasse 32, 7142 Illmitz. Produces white and sweet white wines.

Alois Lageder (It) a noted winery based in Bozen, Südtirol (Alto-Adige).

Along the Shelf (Eng) the term used in drinking parties (usually 'stag parties') where only spirits are consumed. Normally starting from one side of the bar and drinking a measure from each of the bottles 'on optic' along the shelf.

Aloque (Sp) red wines of the Valdepeñas region of Spain. Made from the Cencibel grape variety.

Alosa (Ger) a natural mineral water from the Tieflandquelle, Stralsund, MV.

Alouchta (Rus) a red Port-style wine produced in the Crimea, in southern Russia.

Aloxe Corton (Fr) an A.C. commune within the Côte de Beaune in Burgundy. 130ha. Produces fine red and white wines. Soil: chalk and marl. Vineyards: **Grand Crus**: Corton plus the name of vineyard (En Paulaud [part], Clos du Roi, La Vigne au Saint, Le Corton, Les Bressandes, Les Charlemagne [part], Les Chaumes [part], Les Combes [part], Les Fietres, Les Grèves, Les Languettes [part], Les Maréchaudes [part], Les Meix [part], Les Meix-Lallemant [part], Les Perrières, Les Pougets [part], Les Renardes, Voirosses). **Premier Crus**: En Pauland [part], La Coutière, La Maréchaude, La Toppe-au-Vert, Les Chaillots, Les Fournières, Les Grandes-Lolières, Les Guérets, Les Maréchaudes [part], Les Meix [part], Les Petites-Lolières, Les Valozières [part], Les Vercots. *See also* vineyards of Ladoix-Serrigny and Château Corton Grancey. Grape varieties: Chardonnay and Pinot noir.

Alpenbräu (Switz) a bier brewed by the Hürlimann Brauerei in Zürich, northern Switzerland.

Alpenkraeuter-Likoer (Ger) a liqueur based on alpine herbs and roots, also with wormwood.

Alpenrose (Switz) a natural mineral water from Adelboden. Mineral contents (milligrammes per litre): Sodium 5.4mg/l, Calcium 569mg/l, Magnesium 37mg/l, Bicarbonates 281mg/l, Chlorides 4.9mg/l, Sulphates 1290mg/l, Fluoride 0.4mg/l, Nitrates 1.6mg/l.

Alpes-Maritimes (Fr) a département of Provence in south-eastern France that produces red, rosé and white wines.

Alpestre Alpina (Costa Rica) a natural mineral water from San José. Mineral contents (milligrammes per litre): Sodium 6.7mg/l, Calcium 11.1mg/l, Magnesium 11mg/l, Potassium 0.4mg/l, Bicarbonates 33mg/l, Chlorides 19.4mg/l, Sulphates 29.8mg/l, Fluoride 0.29mg/l, Nitrates 2.4mg/l. pH 6.6

Alpha (Chi) a natural mineral water. Mineral contents (milligrammes per litre): Calcium 17.4mg/l, Magnesium 16.4mg/l, Fluoride 2.8mg/l. pH 7.8

Alpha (Fr) a white wine made from Sauvignon, Sémillon and Muscadelle grapes in Pomerol. The grapes are grown in Entre-deux-Mers, Graves de Vayres. The second wine is known as Athos.

Alpha (USA) a red hybrid grape variety. Produces high acidity and can withstand low temperatures.

Alpha Acid (Eng) found in the hop flower in the alpha resin that causes the bitterness in the beer.

Alphart [Karl] (Aus) a winery based in Traiskirchen, Thermenregion. (Add): Wiener Strasse 46, 2514 Traiskirchen. Grape varieties: Rotgipfler, Riesling, Pinot blanc, Zierfandler.

Alpha Zeta (It) a winery based in the Veneto region. Produces DOC Valpolicella and Amarone wines.

Alphen Hill (S.Afr) the label for a range of wines produced Cru Wines marketing company, Western Cape.

Alphen Wines (S.Afr) the label for varietal wines made by Gilbeys Ltd. with grapes grown by the Bairnsfather-Cloete Estate in Stellenbosch.

Alphonse Lavalee (N.Z) a sweet red wine produced by the Fino Valley Winery in Henderson, North Island.

Alpia (It) a natural mineral water. Mineral contents (milligrammes per litre): Sodium 3.5mg/l, Calcium 5.7mg/l, Magnesium 3.4mg/l, Potassium 1.2mg/l, Bicarbonates 33.7mg/l, Chlorides 1.1mg/l, Sulphates 4.7mg/l, Fluoride 0.2mg/l, Nitrates 3.4mg/l, Silicates 16.7mg/l. pH 8.1

Alpi Bianche (It) a still and sparkling natural mineral water from Alta Montagna, Piedmonte. Mineral contents (milligrammes per litre): Sodium 1.2mg/l, Calcium 14mg/l, Bicarbonates 39mg/l, Sulphates 9mg/l, Silicates 2.5mg/l. pH 7.5

Alpi Cozie (It) a still natural mineral water. Mineral contents (milligrammes per litre): Sodium 1.7mg/l, Magnesium 1mg/l, Potassium 0.6mg/l, Chlorides 0.6mg/l, Sulphates 3.4mg/l. pH 7.2

Alpina (It) *see* Fior d'Alpi.

Alpine (Mal) a still natural mineral water from Kota Tinggi. Mineral contents (milligrammes per litre): Sodium 5mg/l, Calcium 20mg/l, Magnesium 16mg/l, Potassium 4.2mg/l, Bicarbonates 335.6mg/l, Chlorides 12mg/l, Sulphates <5mg/l. pH 7.2

Alpine (Rwa) a still natural mineral water from Kilgali. Mineral contents (milligrammes per litre): Sodium 27.8mg/l, Calcium 18.9mg/l, Magnesium 7.3mg/l, Potassium 3.8mg/l, Chlorides 43mg/l, Sulphates 11mg/l, Nitrates 4.3mg/l. pH 7.37

Alpine [The] (Cktl) 1 measure extra dry Cinzano, 1 dash fresh lemon juice. Serve in an ice-filled highball glass and top with tonic water.

Alpineb (Mal) a natural mineral water. Mineral contents (milligrammes per litre): Sodium 6.9mg/l, Calcium 66mg/l, Magnesium 4mg/l, Potassium 5mg/l, Bicarbonates 89mg/l, Chlorides 6mg/l, Sulphates 4.6mg/l. pH 7.2

Alpine Lager Beer (Can) a local brand of lager beer produced by the Moosehead Brewery.

Alpine Punch (Punch) 1 bottle elderberry wine, the peel and juice of 2 oranges, 8 cloves, ½ cinnamon stick. Stand for 2 hours, heat until near boiling, strain and serve with orange slices.

Alpine Vineyards (USA) a winery (established 1976) based in Willamette Valley, Oregon. 12.7ha. Grape varieties: Chardonnay, Pinot noir, Pinot gris, Riesling, Gewürztraminer, Cabernet sauvignon, White cabernet.

Alpirsbacher Abbaye Brauerei (Ger) a brewery (established 1880) based at C. Glauner (also known as the Alpirsbacher Klosterbräu). (Add): Marktplatz 1, Alpirsbach, D-72275, Germany. Brews Alpirsbacher Kloster-Hefeweissbier. Website: http://www.alpirsbacher.de 'E'mail: info@alpirsbacher.de

Alpirsbacher Kloster-Hefeweissbier (Ger) a 5.2% alc by vol. bottle-conditioned wheat beer brewed by Alpirsbacher Abbaye Brauerei, C. Glauner.

Alpquell (Aus) a carbonated natural mineral water (established 1611) from Münster, Tirol. Mineral contents (milligrammes per litre): Sodium 3.8mg/l, Calcium 242.9mg/l, Magnesium 41.1mg/l, Potassium 1.9mg/l, Bicarbonates 256.8mg/l, Chlorides 3.4mg/l, Sulphates 548.7mg/l, Fluoride <0.2mg/l, Nitrates 2.2mg/l.

Alp's (Aus) a natural mineral water from Frankenmarkt, Salzkammergut. Mineral contents (milligrammes per litre): Sodium 4.6mg/l, Calcium 37.9mg/l, Magnesium 15.2mg/l, Bicarbonates 165mg/l, Chlorides <1mg/l, Sulphates 10.1mg/l, Fluoride 4mg/l, Nitrates 0.6mg/l, Iodine 24mg/l. pH 7.85 Website: http://www.alpswater.net

Alps Water (USA) a brand of natural mineral water pH 7.0.

Al-Qassim (S.Arabia) a natural mineral water. Mineral contents (milligrammes per litre): Sodium 31.2mg/l, Calcium 7.6mg/l, Magnesium 1.2mg/l, Potassium 0.54mg/l, Bicarbonates 18.2mg/l, Chlorides 34.8mg/l, Sulphates 19.3mg/l, Fluoride 0.75mg/l, Nitrates 13.3mg/l. pH 7.5

Alquitara (Sp) a pot-stilled spirit at 60%–65% alc by vol.

Alsace (Fr) a wine region in north-east France that gained it's A.O.C. status in 1962. 12000ha. Lies in the foothills of the Vosges mountains between Mulhouse in the south and Strasbourg in the north. Noted for fine '*noble grape*' dry white wines from the Gewurztraminer, Muscat, Riesling, Sylvaner and Tokay-Pinot Gris. Small percentage of Pinot noir for red wine. *see* Alsace Grand Cru, Alsatia, Lieux-dits, Sélection des Grains Nobles, Réserve Personnelle, Vendange Tardive. Websites: http://www.alsacewine.com / http://www.vinsalsace.com

Alsace Grand Cru (Fr) a new A.C. white wines introduced in 1975. 1600ha. Soil: has a variety of soils including granite, gravel, slate, schist, sandstone, chalk and marl. Wines must be from named sites (lieux-dits) and from the following grapes only: Gewurztraminer, Muscat, Tokay-Pinot Gris, Riesling. Min alc. 10% by vol. for Riesling and Muscat, 12% by vol. for the other two. Reduced yields and the wines have to be passed by a tasting committee. 15% of Alsace wine is entitled to Grand Cru status. **Sites:** Altenberg de Bergbieten /Altenberg de Bergheim / Altenberg de Woixheim / Brand (Turckheim) / Bruderthal (Molsheim) / Eichberg (Eguisheim) / Engelberg (Dahlenheim) / Florimont (Ingersheim) / Frankstein (Dambach-la-Ville) / Froehn (Zellenberg) / Furstentum (Kientzheim et Sigolsheim) / Geisberg (Ribeauvillé) / Gloeckelberg (Rodern et Saint-Hippolyte) / Goldert (Gueberschwihr) / Hatschbourg (Hattstatt et Voegtlinshoffen) / Hengst (Wintzenheim) / Kazlerberg (Bergheim) / Kastelbrg (Andlau) /

Kessler (Guebwiller) / Kirchberg de Barr / Kirchberg de Ribeauvillé / Kitterlé (Guebwiller) / Mambourg (Sigolsheim) / Mandelberg (Mittelwihr) / Marckrain (Bennwihr) / Moenchberg (Andlau et Eichhoffen) / Muenchberg (Nothalten) / Ollwiller (Wuenheim) / Osterberg (Ribeauvillé) / Pfersigberg (Eguisheim) / Pfingstberg (Orschwihr) / Praelatenberg (Orschwiller et Kintzheim) / Rangen (Thann) / Rosaker (Hunawihr) / Saering (Guebwiller) / Schlossberg (Kaysersberg et Kientzheim) / Schoenenbourg (Riquewihr) / Sommerberg (Niedermorschwihr et Katzenthal) / Sonnenglanz (Beblenheim) / Spiegel (Berbholtz et Guebwiller) / Sporen (Riquewihr) / Steinert (Pfaffenheim) / Steingrubler (Wettolsheim) / Steinklotz (Marlenheim) / Vorbourg (Westhalten et Rouffach) / Wiebelsberg (Andlau) / Wineck-Schlossberg (Katzenthal) / Winzenberg (Blinschwiller) / Zinnkoepflé (Soultzmatt et Westhalten) / Zotzenberg (Mittelbergheim).

Alsace Grand Vin (Fr) a term used when the wine has a minimum natural alcohol content of 11% by vol. Also called Alsace Réserve.

Alsace Réserve (Fr) see Alsace Grand Vin.

Alsace Willm (Fr) a noted wine-producer based in Alsace. (Add): 67140 Barr. 12ha.

Alsatia (Eng) the mediaeval name for Alsace, France.

Alsator (Fr) a low-alc. lager 0.8% alc by vol. brewed and packaged in Strasbourg. Sold in cans and bottles.

Alsenz (Ger) village (Anb): Nahe. (Ber): Schloss Böckelheim. (Gro): Paradiesgarten. (Vins): Elkersberg, Falkenberg, Hölle, Pfaffenpfad.

Alsheim (Ger) village (Anb): Rheinhessen. (Ber): Nierstein. (Gro): Krötenbrunnen. (Vin): Goldberg.

Alsheim (Ger) village (Anb): Rheinhessen. (Ber): Nierstein. (Gro): Rheinblick. (Vins): Fischerpfad, Frühmesse, Römerberg, Sonnenberg.

Al Shouli (Syr) a natural mineral water from Jabal Al-Sheikh.

Alsina & Sardán (Sp) a noted Cava producer. (Add): Cosechero, 08733 Pla del Penedés, Barcelona. 40ha.

Alsterwasser (Ger) a 'Hamburg shandy', consists of lemonade and lager beer.

Alt (Ger) old.

Alta (Can) a beer brewed by the Carling O'Keefe Brewery, Toronto.

Alta Alella (Sp) a winery based in Alella region. 70ha. Produces Marqués de Alella (a white wine produced from 60% Pansa and 40% Xarel-lo grapes).

Altai (Rus) a 40% alc by vol. wheat vodka produced in Siberia.

Altaïr Sideral (Chile) a winery based in the Cachapoal Valley, Central Chile.

Altamura Vineyards (USA) a 35ha. vineyard based in the foothills of the Napa Valley. Grape varieties: Cabernet sauvignon, Sangiovese.

Altarberg (Ger) vineyard (Anb): Mosel-Saar-Ruwer. (Ber): Zell/Mosel. (Gro): Goldbaumchen. (Vil): Ellenz-Poltersdorf.

Altärchen (Ger) vineyard (Anb): Mosel-Saar-Ruwer. (Ber): Bernkastel. (Gro): Michelsberg. (Vil): Trittenheim.

Altare [Elio] (It) a winery based in the DOCG Barolo, Piemonte.

Altar Wine (Eng) the fermented juice of fresh grapes used for sacramental purposes.

Altau (Aus) a vineyard site on the banks of the River Danube situated in the Wachau region, Niederösterreich.

Altavilla (Afr) a winery based in northern Ethiopia. Produces average table wines.

Alta Vineyard (USA) a small winery based in the Napa Valley, California. 3ha. Grape variety: Chardonnay.

Alta Vista (Arg) a winery (61ha in 4 vineyards) based in the Mendoza region, eastern Argentina. (part of the Edonia Group). Grape varieties include: Cabernet sauvignon, Chardonnay, Malbec, Torrontés. Label: Alto (Malbec). Has vineyard holdings in Bordeaux (Fr), Cafayate (Arg) and Tokaj (Hun). Website: http://www.altavistawines.com 'E'mail: altavista@altavistawines.com

Altbier (Ger) a locally consumed, over-fermented bier of Dusseldorf. Equivalent of an English ale 4.3% –4.5% alc by vol. with a strong hop flavour. Name derives from the old style of brewing. i.e. Top fermentation as opposed to lager which is bottom fermented.

Alt-Bürgerbrunn (Ger) a natural mineral water.

Altdorf (Ger) village (Anb): Baden. (Ber): Breisgau. (Gro): Burg Lichteneck. (Vin): Kaiserberg.

Altdorf (Ger) village (Anb): Pfalz. (Ber): Südliche Weinstrasse. (Gro): Trappenberg. (Vins): Gottesacker, Hochgericht.

Altdörr (Ger) vineyard (Anb): Rheinhessen. (Ber): Nierstein. (Gro): Gutes Domtal. (Vil): Dalheim.

Altdörr (Ger) vineyard (Anb): Rheinhessen. (Ber): Nierstein. (Gro): Gutes Domtal. (Vil): Friesenheim.

Alte Burg (Ger) vineyard (Anb): Baden. (Ber): Breisgau. (Gro): Burg Lichteneck. (Vil): Mundingen.

Alte Burg (Ger) vineyard (Anb): Baden. (Ber): Breisgau. (Gro): Burg Lichteneck. (Vil): Köndringen.

Alte Burg (Ger) vineyard (Anb): Hessiche Bergstrasse. (Ber): Starkenberg. (Gro): Rott. (Vil): Zwingenberg.

Alteburg (Ger) vineyard (Anb): Nahe. (Ber): Kreuznach. (Gro): Schlosskapelle. (Vil): Waldlaubersheim.

Alte Ernte (Ger) a kornbranntwein produced by Schlichte.

Alte Lay (Ger) vineyard (Anb): Ahr. (Ber): Walporzheim/Ahrtal. (Gro): Klosterberg. (Vil): Walporzheim.

Altenahr (Ger) village (Anb): Ahr. (Ber): Walporzheim/Ahrtal. (Gro): Klosterberg. (Vins): Eck, Übigberg.

Altenbamberg (Ger) village (Anb): Nahe. (Ber):

A

Schloss Böckelheim. (Gro): Burgweg. (Vins): Kehrenberg, Laurentiusberg, Rotenberg, Schlossberg, Treuenfels.

Altenberg (Aus) a vineyard area on the banks of the River Danube in the Kremstal region.

Altenberg (Aus) a vineyard area based in the Kitzeck district of Süd-Steiermark.

Altenberg (Ger) lit: 'old hill', a common vineyard name used in the German regions. There are 38 individual vineyard sites with the name in Germany.

Altenberg (Ger) vineyard (Anb): Baden. (Ber): Badische Bergstrasse/Kraichgau. (Gro): Mannaberg. (Vil): Heidelsheim.

Altenberg (Ger) vineyard (Anb): Baden. (Ber): Badische Frankenland. (Gro): Tauberklinge. (Vil): Lauda.

Altenberg (Ger) vineyard (Anb): Baden. (Ber): Badische Frankenland. (Gro): Tauberklinge. (Vil): Oberlauda.

Altenberg (Ger) vineyard (Anb): Baden. (Ber): Badische Frankenland. (Gro): Tauberklinge. (Vil): Oberschüpf.

Altenberg (Ger) vineyard (Anb): Baden. (Ber): Markgräflerland. (Gro): Burg Neuenfels. (Vil): Ballrechten-Dottingen.

Altenberg (Ger) vineyard (Anb): Baden. (Ber): Markgräflerland. (Gro): Burg Neuenfels. (Vil): Britzingen.

Altenberg (Ger) vineyard (Anb): Baden. (Ber): Markgräflerland. (Gro): Burg Neuenfels. (Vil): Britzingen (ortsteil-Dattingen).

Altenberg (Ger) vineyard (Anb): Baden. (Ber): Markgräflerland. (Gro): Burg Neuenfels. (Vil): Laufen.

Altenberg (Ger) vineyard (Anb): Baden. (Ber): Markgräflerland. (Gro): Burg Neuenfels. (Vil): Sulzburg.

Altenberg (Ger) vineyard (Anb): Baden. (Ber): Markgräflerland. (Gro): Lorettoberg. (Vil): Grunern.

Altenberg (Ger) vineyard (Anb): Baden. (Ber): Ortenau. (Gro): Schloss Rodeck. (Vil): Neuweier.

Altenberg (Ger) vineyard (Anb): Franken. (Ber): Steigerwald. (Gro): Schild. (Vil): Abtswind.

Altenberg (Ger) vineyard (Anb): Franken. (Ber): Steigerwald. (Gro): Schlosstück. (Vil): Ergersheim.

Altenberg (Ger) vineyard (Anb): Mosel-Saar-Ruwer. (Ber): Obermosel. (Gro): Gipfel. (Vil): Wellen.

Altenberg (Ger) vineyard (Anb): Mosel-Saar-Ruwer. (Ber): Saar-Ruwer. (Gro): Römerlay. (Vil): Trier.

Altenberg (Ger) vineyard (Anb): Mosel-Saar-Ruwer. (Ber): Saar-Ruwer. (Gro): Scharzberg. (Vil): Filzen.

Altenberg (Ger) vineyard (Anb): Mosel-Saar-Ruwer. (Ber): Saar-Ruwer. (Gro): Scharzberg. (Vil): Hamm.

Altenberg (Ger) vineyard (Anb): Mosel-Saar-Ruwer. (Ber): Saar-Ruwer. (Gro): Scharzberg. (Vil): Kanzem.

Altenberg (Ger) vineyard (Anb): Mosel-Saar-Ruwer.

Altenberg (Ger) vineyard (Anb): Mosel-Saar-Ruwer. (Ber): Saar-Ruwer. (Gro): Scharzberg. (Vil): Mennig.

Altenberg (Ger) vineyard (Anb): Mosel-Saar-Ruwer. (Ber): Saar-Ruwer. (Gro): Scharzberg. (Vil): Oberemmel.

Altenberg (Ger) vineyard (Anb): Nahe. (Ber): Schloss Böckelheim. (Gro): Paradiesgarten. (Vil): Meddersheim.

Altenberg (Ger) vineyard (Anb): Rheinhessen. (Ber): Nierstein. (Gro): Krötenbrunnen. (Vil): Hillesheim.

Altenberg (Ger) vineyard (Anb): Pfalz. (Ber): Mittelhaardt-Deutsche Weinstrasse. (Gro): Mariengarten. (Vil): Wachenheim.

Altenberg (Ger) vineyard (Anb): Pfalz. (Ber): Mittelhaardt-Deutsche Weinstrasse. (Gro): Rosenbühl. (Vil): Weisenheim/Sand.

Altenberg (Ger) vineyard (Anb): Pfalz. (Ber): Südliche Weinstrasse. (Gro): Kloster Liebfrauenberg. (Vil): Bad Bergzabern.

Altenberg (Ger) vineyard (Anb): Württemberg. (Ber): Kocher-Jagst-Tauber. (Gro): Kocherberg. (Vil): Dörzbach.

Altenberg (Ger) vineyard (Anb): Württemberg. (Ber): Kocher-Jagst-Tauber. (Gro): Kocherberg. (Vil): Weissbach.

Altenberg (Ger) vineyard (Anb): Württemberg. (Ber): Remstal-Stuttgart. (Gro): Sonnenbühl. (Vil): Weinstadt (ortsteil Strümpfelbach).

Altenberg (Ger) vineyard (Anb): Württemberg. (Ber): Remstal-Stuttgart. (Gro): Wartbühl. (Vil): Beutelsbach.

Altenberg (Ger) vineyard (Anb): Württemberg. (Ber): Remstal-Stuttgart. (Gro): Wartbühl. (Vil): Schnait i.R.

Altenberg (Ger) vineyard (Anb): Württemberg. (Ber): Remstal-Stuttgart. (Gro): Weinsteige. (Vil): Stuttgart (ortsteil Untertürkheim).

Altenberg (Ger) vineyard (Anb): Württemberg. (Ber): Württembergisch Unterland. (Gro): Heuchelberg. (Vil): Stockheim.

Altenberg (Ger) vineyard (Anb): Württemberg. (Ber): Württembergisch Unterland. (Gro): Kirchenweinberg. (Vil): Flein.

Altenberg (Ger) vineyard (Anb): Württemberg. (Ber): Württembergisch Unterland. (Gro): Kirchenweinberg. (Vil): Heilbronn.

Altenberg (Ger) vineyard (Anb): Württemberg. (Ber): Württembergisch Unterland. (Gro): Salzberg. (Vil): Ellhofen.

Altenberg (Ger) vineyard (Anb): Württemberg. (Ber): Württembergisch Unterland. (Gro): Salzberg. (Vil): Löwenstein.

Altenberg (Ger) vineyard (Anb): Württemberg. (Ber): Württembergisch Unterland. (Gro): Salzberg. (Vil): Sülzbach.

Altenberg (Ger) vineyard (Anb): Württemberg. (Ber): Württembergisch Unterland. (Gro): Salzberg. (Vil): Wimmental.

Altenberg de Bergbieten (Fr) an A.C. Alsace Grand Cru vineyard in Bergbieten, Bas-Rhin. 29ha.

Altenberg de Bergheim (Fr) an A.C. Alsace Grand Cru vineyard at Bergheim, Haut-Rhin. 35.06ha.

A

Altenberg de Wolxheim (Fr) an A.C. Alsace Grand Cru vineyard at Wolxheim, Haut-Rhin. 28ha.

Altendorf Pilsener (Eng) a pilsener lager beer 1034 O.G. brewed by the Watney Mann Brewery in London. Sold in cans.

Altenforst (Ger) vineyard (Anb): Pfalz. (Ber): Südliche Weinstrasse. (Gro): Bischofskreuz. (Vil): Burrweiler.

Altenmünster (Ger) a naturally fermented Bavarian lager beer 4.5% alc by vol. from Franz Joseph Sailer Brauerei. Sold in a clamp-stoppered bottle.

Alte Point (Aus) a vineyard site on the banks of the River Danube situated in the Wachau region, Niederösterreich.

Alter (Aus) in a heurigen inn denotes last years wine.

Alter Berg (Ger) vineyard (Anb): Franken. (Ber): Maindreieck. (Gro): Not yet assigned. (Vil): Lengfurt.

Alter Berg (Ger) vineyard (Anb): Pfalz. (Ber): Südliche Weinstrasse. (Gro): Trappenberg. (Vil): Römerberg.

Alter Berg (Ger) vineyard (Anb): Württemberg. (Ber): Württembergisch Unterland. (Gro): Schalkstein. (Vil): Allmersbach a.W.

Alte Reben (AUS)(Ger) old vines. (Fr) = vieilles vignes, (Sp) = viñas viejas.

Alter Ego de Palmer (Fr) the second wine of Château Palmer. Was originally known as Réserve du Général.

Alter Ego Wines (S.Afr) a winery (established 2001) based in Tulbagh, Western Cape. Grape varieties: Cabernet sauvignon, Merlot, Sémillon. Labels: Asher, Elroy's Pawt. 4ha. Website: http://www.kloofzichtwines.co.za

Alter Gott (Ger) vineyard (Anb): Baden. (Ber): Ortenau. (Gro): Schloss Rodeck. (Vil): Achern (ortsteil Oberachem).

Alter Gott (Ger) vineyard (Anb): Baden. (Ber): Ortenau. (Gro): Schloss Rodeck. (Vil): Lauf.

Alter Gott (Ger) vineyard (Anb): Baden. (Ber): Ortenau. (Gro): Schloss Rodeck. (Vil): Obersasbach.

Alter Gott (Ger) vineyard (Anb): Baden. (Ber): Ortenau. (Gro): Schloss Rodeck. (Vil): Sasbachwalden.

Alternative Wines (Eng) a term used for Bordeaux wines sold instead of the well-known 'Great Wines'. e.g. Wines from the Côtes de Blaye and Côtes de Bourg instead of the Haut-Médoc.

Alte Römerstrasse (Ger) vineyard (Anb): Nahe. (Ber): Schloss Böckelheim. (Gro): Rosengarten. (Vil): Mandel.

Alte Römerstrasse (Ger) vineyard (Anb): Rheinhessen. (Ber): Bingen. (Gro): Rheingrafenstein. (Vil): Volxheim.

Alteserre Monferrato (It) a D.O.C. white wine from Cantine Bava, Azienda Vitivincola, Cocconato.

Altes Löhl (Ger) vineyard (Anb): Pfalz. (Ber): Südliche Weinstrasse. (Gro): Königsgarten. (Vil): Landau.

Altesse (Fr) a white grape variety grown in the Bugey and Seyssel regions of eastern France. Also known as the Roussette.

Altes Tramdepot (Switz) a brewery. (Add): Brauerei Restaurant AG, Grosser Muristalden 6, Bern CH-3006, Switzerland. Brews a variety of beers and lager. Website: http://www.altestramdepot.ch 'E'mail: info@altestramdepot.ch

Alte Vette (It) a still natural mineral water from Cuneo, Piedmonte. Mineral contents (milligrammes per litre): Sodium 1.2mg/l, Calcium 14mg/l, Bicarbonates 39mg/l, Sulphates 9mg/l, Silicates 2.5mg/l. pH 7.75

Althälde (Ger) vineyard (Anb): Württemberg. (Ber): Württembergisch Unterland. (Gro): Salzberg. (Vil): Ellhofen.

Althälde (Ger) vineyard (Anb): Württemberg. (Ber): Württembergisch Unterland. (Gro): Salzberg. (Vil): Lehreusteinsfeld.

Althälde (Ger) vineyard (Anb): Württemberg. (Ber): Württembergisch Unterland. (Gro): Salzberg. (Vil): Weinsberg.

Althof (Ger) vineyard (Anb): Baden. (Ber): Ortenau. (Gro): Schloss Rodeck. (Vil): Ottersweier.

Alt-Höflein (Aus) a wine village in the Falkenstein-Matzen district of north-eastern Austria. Produces mainly white wines.

Al Tiempo (Mex) at room temperature. (Fr) = chambre.

Altin Cam Su (Tur) a natural mineral water (established 1994) from Kocaeli.

Altise (Eng) a beetle pest that feeds on the vine leaves leaving them looking like lace. Treated by spraying with insecticide.

Altl (Aus) denotes a taste of age in wines.

Altlichtenwarth (Aus) a wine village in the Falkenstein-Matzen district of north-eastern Austria. Produces mainly white wines.

Altmannsdorf (Ger) village (Anb): Franken. (Ber): Steigerwald. (Gro): Not yet assigned. (Vin): Sonnenwinkel.

Altmühltaler (Ger) a natural mineral water from Treuchtlingen, BY. Mineral contents (milligrammes per litre): Sodium 45.9mg/l, Calcium 46.8mg/l, Magnesium 11.2mg/l, Potassium 29.1mg/l, Bicarbonates 291mg/l, Chlorides 1mg/l, Sulphates 64mg/l, Fluoride 0.5mg/l.

Alt Münchener Dunkelgold (Ger) a 5.5% alc by vol. bottled lager brewed by Hofbräu München.

Alto (Gre) a 100% Sauvignon blanc wine produced by Gentilini, Cephalonia

Alto (Indo) a natural mineral water (established 1998) from Babakan Pari-Sukabumi. Mineral contents (milligrammes per litre): Sulphates 2.46mg/l, Fluoride 0.35mg/l, Nitrates 8mg/l. pH 6.95

Alto (S.Afr) a red wine estate in the region of Stellenbosch.

Alto-Adige (It) a part of the region of Trentino-Alto-Adige. Also known as the Südtirol (South Tyrol).

Alto-Adige Cabernet (It) a D.O.C. red wine from the Cabernet grape produced in the Trentino-Alto-

Adige region. If aged for 2 years then can be called Riserva.

Alto-Adige Lagrein Rosato (It) a D.O.C. ruby red and rosé wine from the Trentino-Alto-Adige. Made from the Lagrein kretzer grape. If produced from grapes from the Bolzano then entitled to the additional specification Lagrein di Gries.

Alto-Adige Lagrein Scuro (It) a D.O.C. red wine from the Trentino-Alto-Adige. Made from the Lagrein dunkel (also known as the Lagrein Scuro) grape. If aged for 2 years then called Riserva. If grapes grown in Bolzano commune then entitled to the additional specification of Lagrein di Gries.

Alto-Adige Malvasia (It) a D.O.C. red wine from Trentino-Alto-Adige. Made from the Malvasier (Malvasia) grape.

Alto-Adige Merlot (It) a D.O.C. red wine from the Trentino-Alto-Adige. Made from the Merlot grape. If aged minimum 2 years then classed Riserva.

Alto-Adige Moscato Giallo (It) a D.O.C. white wine from the Trentino-Alto-Adige. Made from the Golden muskateller (Moscato giallo) grape.

Alto-Adige Moscato Rosa (It) a D.O.C. rosé wine from the Trentino-Alto-Adige. Made from the Rosenmuskateller (Moscato rosa) grape.

Alto-Adige Pinot Bianco (It) a D.O.C. white wine from the Trentino-Alto-Adige. Made from the Weissburgunder (Pinot bianco) grape. D.O.C. also applies to sparkling wines.

Alto-Adige Pinot Grigio (It) a D.O.C. white wine from the Trentino-Alto-Adige. Made from the Ruländer (Pinot grigio) grape. D.O.C. also applies to sparkling wines.

Alto-Adige Pinot Nero (It) a D.O.C. red wine from the Trentino-Alto-Adige. Made from the Blauburgunder (Pinot nero) grape. If aged 1 year minimum then classed Riserva. D.O.C. also applies to sparkling wines.

Alto-Adige Riesling Italico (It) a D.O.C. white wine from the Trentino-Alto-Adige. Made from the Welschriesling (Riesling italico) grape.

Alto-Adige Riesling Renano (It) a D.O.C. white wine from the Trentino-Alto-Adige. Made from the Rhein riesling (Riesling renano) grape.

Alto-Adige Riesling x Sylvaner (It) a D.O.C. white wine from the Trentino-Alto-Adige. Made from the Müller-Thurgau (Riesling x Sylvaner) grape.

Alto-Adige Sauvignon (It) a D.O.C. white wine from the Trentino-Alto-Adige. Made from the Sauvignon grape.

Alto-Adige Schiave (It) a D.O.C. red wine from the Trentino-Alto-Adige. Made from the Vernatsch (Schiave) grape.

Alto-Adige Sylvaner (It) a D.O.C. white wine from the Trentino-Alto-Adige. Made from the Sylvaner grape.

Alto-Adige Traminer Aromatico (It) a D.O.C. white wine from the Trentino-Alto-Adige. Made from the Gewürztraminer (Traminer aromatico) grape.

Alto Corgo (Port) a part of the Upper Douro where Port originates from.

Alto Couro (Port) a part of the Upper Douro where Port originates from.

Alt Oberurseler Brauhaus (Ger) a brewery. (Add): Ackergasse 13, Aberursel D-61440, Germany. Brews a variety of beers and lagers. Website: http://www.alt-oberursler-brauhaus.st-designs.com 'E'mail: brauhaus@hochtaunusnet.net

Alt Oder Firn (Ger) a term used to describe a wine that has lost its freshness.

Alto Douro (Port) the upper valley of river Douro. Vineyards produce the only wine entitled to use the name Port.

Alto Ebro (Sp) a Vino de Mesa wine from the province of Álava in País Vasco, northern Spain.

Alto Estate (S.Afr) a winery (established 1906) based in Stellenbosch, Western Cape. (Add): Alto Wynlandgoed, Box 184, Stellenbosch 7600. Grape varieties include: Cabernet franbc, Cabernet sauvignon, Merlot, Shiraz. Produces varietal wines. Website: http://www.alto.co.za

Alto Jiloca (Sp) a Vino Comarcal of Teruel in Aragón.

Altons Pride (Eng) a 3.8% alc by vol. beer brewed by the Triple FFF Brewing C°, Hampshire.

Alto Predicato (It) the generic name for both red and white wines produced from vineyards in the Chianti Classico zone.

Altos de Andelia (Arg) a winery based in the Mendoza region, eastern Argentina. Website: http://www.andelia.com

Altosur (Arg) the label for a red wine (Malbec) produced by the Finca Sophenia winery in the Mendoza region.

Altöttingen (Ger) a brewery that brews Golden Weissbier (a wheat beer at 5.3% alc by vol).

Alto Turia (Sp) a blanco seco wine produced in D.O. Valencia from 100% Merseguera grapes (10% alc by vol).

Alto Wynlandgoed (S.Afr) *see* Alto Estate.

Altrheingauer Landwein (Ger) one of the 15 Deutsche Landwein zones.

Altrincham Brewing Company [The] (Eng) a micro-brewery based in Altrincham, Greater Manchester.

Altschweier (Ger) village (Anb): Baden. (Ber): Ortenau. (Gro): Schloss Rodeck. (Vin): Sterenberg.

Altus (USA) a wine-producing area. The wineries of Mount Bethel, Post Sax and Wiederkehr are based here.

Altydgedacht Estate (S.Afr) a winery (158ha) based in Tygerberg, Durbanville. Grape varieties: Barbera, Cabernet sauvignon, Chardonnay, Chenin blanc, Gewürztraminer, Merlot, Riesling, Viognier. Produces: Chatelaine and varietal wines. Website: http://www.altydgedacht.co.za

Alu (Eng) the mediaeval word for ale (non-hopped beer).

Aluntinum (It) a red wine produced in Roman times in Sicily.

Alupka (Rus) a grape (red and white) variety grown in the Crimea. Produces Port-style wines.

Alupka (Rus) a pink dessert wine from the southern Crimea.

A

Alushita (Rus) a dry red wine from the Crimean Peninsular.

Alushta (Rus) the alternative spelling of Alushita.

Alva (Port) a white grape variety grown in Beiras. Known as Roupeiro in the Alentejo.

Alvarelhão (Port) a red grape variety used in the Dão region. Also called the Pilongo.

Alvarez Camp y Cº (W.Ind) one of the main rum producers in Cuba. Now state owned.

Alvarez y Díez (Sp) a noted winery based in Nava del Rey, Valladolid, north-western Spain.

Alvarinho (Port) a white grape variety used for making D.O. Vinho Verdes. Only variety allowed to be used in the Monção region.

Alvarinho Cepa Velha (Port) one of the best Vinhos Verdes. *see* Vinhos de Monção and Adega Cooperativa Regional de Monção.

Alvaro Palacios l'Ermita (Sp) a full-bodied red wine produced in Priorato, Catalonia.

Alvear (Arg) the brand-name of a sparkling wine.

Alvear (Sp) a brandy and wine producer in Montilla-Moriles.

Alvear Palace (Cktl) ⅜ measure vodka, ⅛ measure apricot brandy, ¼ measure pineapple juice. Shake over ice and strain into a cocktail glass.

Alves [João Camillo] Lda. (Port) a noted wine producer based in Bucelas.

Alvinne Picobrouweij (Bel) a micro-brewery. (Add): oostrozebekestraat 114, 8770 Ingelmunster, Belgium. Website: http://www.alvinne.be 'E'mail: info@alvinne.be

Alvi's Drift (S.Afr) a winery (established 2002) based in Worcester, Western Cape. Grape varieties: Chenin blanc, Muscat de frontignan.

Alwa (Ger) a still natural mineral water from the Alwaris-Quelle, Sachsenheim-Spielberg, BW. Mineral contents (milligrammes per litre): Sodium 16.5mg/l, Calcium 485mg/l, Magnesium 65.6mg/l, Bicarbonates 403mg/l, Chlorides 28.1mg/l, Sulphates 1107mg/l, Fluoride 0.31mg/l.

Alwadi (S. Arabia) a natural mineral water. Mineral contents (milligrammes per litre): Sodium 35mg/l, Calcium 60mg/l, Magnesium 8mg/l, Potassium 0.8mg/l, Bicarbonates 140mg/l, Chlorides 45mg/l, Sulphates 14mg/l. pH 7.4

Al'Wheat Pet (Eng) a 4.1% alc by vol. ale brewed by the Mordue Brewery Ltd., Tyne & Wear.

Alzey (Ger) village (Anb): Rheinhessen. (Ber): Wonnegau. (Gro): Sybillenstein. (Vins): Kapellenberg, Pfaffenhalde, Römerberg, Rotenfels, Wartberg.

Alzeyer Scheurebe (Ger) a white grape variety used mainly in the Rheinhessen.

Alzinger (Aus) a winery (7ha) based in the Wachau. (Add): Unterloiben 11, 3601 Dürnstein. Grape varieties: Chardonnay, Grüner veltliner, Riesling. Produces a range of dry and sweet (botrytised) wines.

Alzola (Sp) a still natural mineral water from Alzola-Elgoibar, Gipuzcoa. Mineral contents (milligrammes per litre): Sodium 45.7mg/l, Calcium 59.3mg/l, Magnesium 5.4mg/l, Potassium 0.9mg/l, Bicarbonates 180mg/l, Chlorides 65.5mg/l, Sulphates 22.8mg/l, Fluoride 0.2mg/l, Nitrates 1.5mg/l.

a/M (USA) *abbr:* **am M**oselle, found on a Moselle (Mosel) bottle label.

Amabile (It) medium sweet.

Amabile Beone (Cktl) ⅔ measure (green) crème de menthe, ½ measure Drambuie, dash Pernod, 2 dashes gomme syrup. Shake over ice and strain into a sugar-rimmed (Pernod) cocktail glass.

Amadalia (S.Afr) the export label for a range of wines produced by the Rooiberg Winery, Robertson, Western Cape.

Amadé (S.Afr) a red wine from the Welgemeend Estate, Suider-Paarl, Western Cape blended from Grenache 30%, Pinotage 30% and Shiraz 40% grapes.

Amadeo I (Sp) a V.S.O.P. brandy produced by Campeny in Barcelona.

Amadeu (Bra) a vineyard based in the Gaúcha Mountains that produces a range of wines (white, red and sparkling).

Amador (USA) a sub A.V.A. area within the Sierra Foothills, north Californian county. Grows mainly Zinfandel grapes.

Amalie (S.Afr) the label for a red wine (Grenache and Viognier blend) produced by the Solms-Delta winery, Franschhoek, Western Cape.

Amalienstein (S.Afr) the label for a white wine (Muscadel) produced by the Southern Cape Vineyards winery, Barrydale, Little Karoo.

Amalgamated Distilled Products (Scot) the drinks division of the Argyll Group. Produce a wide range of whiskies including Burberry's, Glen Scotia, Littlemill, Royal Culrose and Scotia Royale.

Amalia (It) a producer of sparkling wines (made by the cuve close method) based in Emilia-Romagna region.

Amalienbrunnen (Ger) a natural mineral water from Berlin, BE.

Amalienstein (S.Afr) a vineyard based in the Ladismith area. (Add): Box 70 Ladismith 6885. Grapes are vinified in the local co-operative.

Amance [Marcel] (Fr) a Burgundy négociant based at Santenay. An associate company of Prosper Maufoux q.v.

Amanda (Fr) a natural mineral water from St. Amand les Eaux. Mineral contents (milligrammes per litre): Sodium 45mg/l, Calcium 243mg/l, Magnesium 77mg/l, Potassium 8mg/l, Bicarbonates 295mg/l, Sulphates 675mg/l, Fluoride 2.1mg/l, Nitrates 0.5mg/l.

Amanda (Gre) a Dutch cream and Metaxa brandy-based liqueur produced by Metaxa. 17.5% alc by vol.

Amandi (Sp) a wine-producing area based in Galicia. Produces red and white wines.

Amandiers [Les] (Fr) a vineyard of Dopff & Irion in Alsace. Named because of the almond trees that grow in the vineyard. Produces Muscat wines.

Amandusquelle (Ger) a natural mineral water from

Mönchengladbach, NW. Mineral contents (milligrammes per litre): Sodium 226mg/l, Calcium 126mg/l, Magnesium 60mg/l, Potassium 6mg/l, Bicarbonates 278mg/l, Chlorides 390mg/l, Sulphates 271mg/l.

Amani Vineyards (S.Afr) a winery (established 1997) based in Stellenbosch, Western Cape. Grape varieties: Cabernet sauvignon, Chardonnay, Merlot, Sauvignon blanc. Label: Atkinson Ridge, I am I, plus varietal wines. 32ha. Website: http://www.amani.co.za

Aman n'Rasrou (Alg) a natural mineral water. Mineral contents (milligrammes per litre): Sodium 12.8mg/l, Calcium 58.4mg/l, Magnesium 42.5mg/l, Potassium 3.1mg/l, Bicarbonates 372.7mg/l, Chlorides 17.7mg/l, Sulphates 28.5mg/l, Silicates 8.2mg/l.

Amanzanillado (Sp) a style of aged Manzanilla Sherry from Sanlúcar.

Amara (S.Am) see Amargo.

Amarante (Port) a wine region of the Entre Minho e Douro district. Produces both red and white pétillant wines.

Amarava Wines (S.Afr) a winery (established 1999) based in Somerset West, Stellenbosch, Western Cape. Grape varieties: Cabernet franc, Cabernet sauvignon, Merlot, Sauvignon blanc, Shiraz. 17ha. Website: http://www.amaravawines.com

Amarela (Port) a red grape variety grown in the Upper Douro district to produce Barca Velha. Also produces an I.P.R. wine of the sama name.

Amaretto Coffee (Liq.Coffee) see Café Amaretto.

Amaretto Comforter (Cktl) ½ measure amaretto, ½ measure Southern Comfort. Shake well together over ice, strain into a small wine goblet, float 25mls (1fl.oz) whipped cream on top. Sprinkle with grated chocolate.

Amaretto di Amore (It) a well-known brand of amaretto.

Amaretto di Saronno (It) a bitter amaretto liqueur with an apricot brandy base, flavoured with almonds 28% alc by vol.

Amaretto Florio (It) a bitter-sweet Sicilian almond liqueur produced near Trapini. 26% alc by vol.

Amaretto Heartwarmer (Cktl) ½ measure Southern Comfort, ¼ measure French vermouth, ¼ measure amaretto, 2 blanched almonds, 1 crushed peach stone, 2 dashes gomme syrup. Warm the Southern Comfort, add nuts and syrup, stir and cool. Add amaretto and vermouth, stir, strain into an ice-filled old-fashioned glass.

Amaretto Sour (Cktl) 2 measures Amaretto di Saronno, 1 measure lemon juice. Stir with ice, strain over ice in an old-fashioned glass.

Amargo (Port) (Sp) bitterness / bitter.

Amargo (S.Am) a style of apéritif produced in Uruguay. Is also known as Amara.

Amarit (E.Asia) a lager beer brewed by the Thai Amarit Brewery in Bangkok, Thailand.

Amarit Brewery (E.Asia) a brewery based in Bangkok, noted for a beer with same name and Krating.

Amaro (Can) a still, natural spring water from Berthier County, Quebec. Mineral contents (milligrammes per litre): Sodium 12mg/l, Calcium 17mg/l, Magnesium 4mg/l, Potassium 1mg/l, Bicarbonates 98mg/l, Chlorides 2mg/l, Sulphates 6mg/l.

Amaro (It) bitter, used to describe very dry wines.

Amaro (It) a dark brown bitters made from tree barks, herbs and other botanicals either with or without alcohol.

Amaro (S.Afr) a red wine made from vine-dried grapes and produced by the Asara Estate winery, Stellenbosch, Western Cape.

Amaro Cora (It) an Italian bitter apéritif.

Amarognolo (It) denotes a bitter, almond-like flavour.

Amarone (It) bitter or very dry.

Amarone della Valpolicella (It) a D.O.C. red wine from Veneto. Made using Recioto grapes that are fully fermented. 14%–15% alc by vol. Grape varieties: Corvina, Rondinella, Molinara. See also Recioto della Valpolicella.

Amaro Ramazzotti (It) a bitter apéritif wine produced in Milan. 30% alc by vol.

Amarula (S.Afr) a fruit liqueur produced by the Southern Liqueur C°. from the fruit of the Marula tree.

Amasimi Cellars (S.Afr) a winery based in the Western Cape. Grape varieties include: Sauvignon blanc.

Amata (It) a natural mineral water from Castello. Mineral contents (milligrammes per litre): Sodium 20mg/l, Calcium 99mg/l, Magnesium 42mg/l, Potassium 2.3mg/l, Bicarbonates 496mg/l, Chlorides 29mg/l, Sulphates 5.7mg/l, Silicates 18mg/l. pH 6.8

Amateur Winemaker (Eng) the name given to anyone who makes wine for their own personal use. Not for sale.

Amateur Winemaker (Eng) the monthly magazine produced for amateur wine-makers.

Amathus (Cyp) the brand-name used by Loël of Limassol for a range of their wines.

Amatitan (Mex) the brand-name of a popular tequila.

Amayna (Chile) a winery based in the Leyda Valley that produces a variety of wines.

Amazens (Port) a name for the wine lodges in Vila Nova de Gaia.

Ambar (Sp) the name for a range of lager beers brewed at La Zaragozana Bewery, Aragón. Range includes Ambar Sin (export strong extra), Ambar Green (low alcohol), Ambar Premium, Ambar 1900, Ambar Especial, Marlen.

Ambassadeur (Fr) the brand-name of an aromatised wine flavoured with quinine and orange peel. 16% alc by vol.

Ambassador (Cktl) 25mls (1fl.oz) tequila, juice of an orange, 2 dashes gomme syrup. Stir over ice, strain into an ice-filled old-fashioned glass and top with a slice of orange.

Ambassador (Ger) a natural mineral water from Berlin, BE.

Ambassador (USA) the brand-name used by the Perelli-Minetti Winery in California for a range of their wines.

Ambassador Royal (Scot) the name of a 12 year old blended Scotch whisky. 43% alc by vol.

Ambelakia (Gre) a dry red table wine produced in eastern Greece.

Ambelitis Winery (Cyp) produces Ayia Moni (a dry red wine) and Avacas (a dry white wine).

Ambel Lager (Eng) a lager beer brewed by Courage.

Amber (Eng) a bottled beer 1033 O.G. brewed by Newcastle breweries in Newcastle, Northumberland.

Amber (Eng) a 4.2% alc by vol. ale brewed by the Pitfield Brewery, Shoreditch, London.

Amber (Eng) a keg ale 1033 O.G. brewed by Whitbread Brewery.

Amber (Eng) a term used as a description for the colour of old (especially sweet) white wines.

Amber (Hol) a 5% alc by vol. dark-straw, unpasteurised bottled beer brewed by Grolsch Bier Brouwerij, Enschede-Groenlo.

Amber (Rus) a beer at 19° brewed by the Yantar Brewery. Matured for 82 days.

Amber (Wal) a bottled ale 1033 O.G. brewed by Crown Brewery Mid-Glamorgan.

Amber Ale (Eng) a 4% alc by vol. beer brewed by a micro-brewery in Hull to celebrate their 1st year of ownership.

Amber Ale (Wal) the name given to an ale once brewed by Hancock's (now part of Welsh Brewers).

Amber Beers (Euro) the name used for light-coloured beers (bock beers) that have a smooth, creamy texture and full hop flavour.

Amberdown (Eng) a 6% alc by vol. medium-dry cider from Cellars International, London.

Amber Dry (Eng) the brand-name for a Clairette du Languedoc sold in the U.K.

Amber Fizz (Punch) 450mls (15fl.oz) dry cider, 200mls (7fl.ozs) soda water, 100mls (4fl.ozs) Cognac, 75mls (3fl.ozs) Cointreau. Mix altogether and chill well in a refrigerator. Serve in punch cups with apple slices.

Amber Forever (S.Afr) the label for a fortified wine (Muscat d'Alsace) produced by the Muratie Estate winery, Stellenbosch, Western Cape.

Ambler Gambler (Eng) a 3.9% alc by vol. beer brewed by the Cheriton Brewhouse, Hampshire.

Amber Gold (Fr) a 3–4 year old *** Cognac from unblended, estate-bottled, premier Fins Bois. Produced by Roullet et Fils.

Amber Green Cocktail (Cktl) ⅔ measure dry gin, ⅓ measure sweet vermouth, 2 dashes Yellow Chartreuse, dash Angostura. Shake over ice and strain into a cocktail glass.

Amberley Estate (Austr) a winery based in the Margaret River region of Western Australia. Grape varieties include: Cabernet sauvignon, Merlot.

Amber Malt (Eng) malted barley added to the kiln and cooled slowly to obtain the required colour.

Amber Moon (Cktl) a mixture of Tobasco, raw egg and whisky blended together. Used as a 'pick me up'.

Amber Road (Euro) the name given to the old Roman trade route from Italy to northern Europe. Was the main wine route from Italy to the Roman legions.

Amberton (Austr) a winery. (Add): Henry Lawson Drive, Mudgee, New South Wales 2850. 24ha. Grape varieties: Cabernet sauvignon, Shiraz, Chardonnay, Rhine riesling, Sauvignon blanc, Sémillon and Traminer.

Ambix (Gre) cup.

Ambleville (Fr) a commune in the Charente département whose grapes are classed Grande Champagne (Cognac).

Ambo (Eth) a still natural mineral water from Ambo. Mineral contents (milligrammes per litre): Sodium 252mg/l, Calcium 22mg/l, Magnesium 46mg/l, Potassium 39mg/l, Bicarbonates 1126mg/l, Chlorides 32.5mg/l, Sulphates 0.77mg/l.

Amboina Exotica (Cktl) 25mls (1fl.oz) Pisang Ambon Henkes, 25mls (1fl.oz) gin, 25mls (1fl.oz) lemon juice. Build into an ice-filled highball glass. Top up with an apricot-orange drink.

Amboise (Fr) a commune in the Touraine district of the Loire. Allowed to use its name in the Touraine A.C.

Ambonnay (Fr) a Grand Cru Champagne village in the Canton d'Aÿ. District: Reims.

Amboss Lager (Eng) a keg lager 1036 O.G. brewed by Hydes brewery in Manchester.

Ambra (It) a sparkling natural mineral water from Pozzo 3, Torrenova, Messina. Mineral contents (milligrammes per litre): Sodium 48.6mg/l, Calcium 92.8mg/l, Magnesium 51.84mg/l, Potassium 4.3mg/l, Bicarbonates 454.45mg/l, Chlorides 67.35mg/l. pH 7.1

Ambra (It) a style of marsala from Sicily. See also Oro and Rubino.

Ambrato (It) an amber hue noted in many dessert wines.

Ambré des Flandres (Fr) a 6.4% alc by vol. amber coloured, top-fermented, bottled bière de garde brewed by the Jeanne d'Arc Brasserie, Ronchin.

Ambria (It) a natural mineral water from Pracastello.

Ambrosette (Port) a 30 y.o. tawny Port from the Sandeman Port shippers.

Ambrosia (Cyp) a red wine produced by the Keo C°. in Limassol.

Ambrosia (Eng) lit: 'nectar of the gods', used to describe sweet drinks.

Ambrosia Cocktail (Cktl) ½ measure Calvados, ½ measure brandy, juice of a small lemon, 1 dash triple sec. Shake over ice, strain into an ice-filled highball glass and top with iced Champagne.

Ambush (Eng) a 5% alc by vol. cider produced by Nadder Valley Cider in Downton.

Amé (Eng) a lightly sparkling, non-alcoholic red, rosé or white drink containing jasmine, gentian, limeflower, schisandra (eastern herbs), vitamins and fruit juices. Produced by Britvic.

Ameis (Aus) a wine village in the Falkenstein-Matzen district of north-eastern Austria that produces mainly white wines.

Ameisenberg (Ger) vineyard (Anb): Mittelrhein. (Ber): Rheinburgengau. (Gro): Burg Rheinfels. (Vil): St. Goar-Werlau.

Amelbergabronnen (Bel) a natural mineral water from Amelberga, Mater.

Améléon (Fr) a style of cider (scrumpy) from the Normandy region.

Amelho (S.Afr) the label for a white (Sauvignon blanc 60% and Sémillon 40%) and red (Cabernet sauvignon 46% plus Malbec, Merlot, Petit verdot and Shiraz blend wines produced by the Ingwe winery, Stellenbosch, Western Cape.

Amelia Springs (USA) a natural spring water from Amelia.

Amelioration (Eng) the name given to any treatment grape must has before fermentation (e.g. Chaptalisation, SO_2, etc.) which will improve the quality of the finished wine. (Fr) = amélioré.

Amélie la Reine (Fr) a natural mineral water (established 1639) from Cornillon en Trièves, Les Alpes du Dauphiné. Mineral contents (milligrammes per litre): Sodium 45mg/l, Calcium 390mg/l, Magnesium 27.5mg/l, Potassium 2.8mg/l, Bicarbonates 1376.61mg/l, Chlorides 19mg/l, Sulphates 36mg/l, Fluoride 0mg/l, Nitrates 2mg/l.

Amélioré (Fr) to improve by the addition of grape must or sugar before fermentation.

Amen (Eng) a 5.4% alc by vol. beer brewed by Lastingham Brewery, Lastingham, near Pickering, North Yorkshire.

Amer (Fr) lit: 'bitter', bitters.

Amer Campari (It) a bitter liqueur produced by the Campari C°.

Amer. Gal. (USA) *abbr*: **Amer**ican **Gal**lon.

America (USA) a large wine producing country in the northern hemisphere. Has two distinct regions: the East Coast (New York State) which produces mainly wines made from native grape species and the West Coast (California, Oregon and Washington States) where European grapes are used. Also has other small wine producing regions.

American Absinthe (Cktl) 60mls (2½ fl.ozs) Pernod, 175mls (6fl.ozs) water, dash gomme syrup to taste. Shake over ice and strain. Soda water may be added.

American Aloe (USA) the name for Mezcal Cacti. *See also* Century Plant and Agave Cactus.

American Beauty (Cktl) ⅓ measure brandy, ⅓ measure French vermouth, ⅓ measure orange juice, 2 dashes (white) crème de menthe. Shake over ice, strain into an old-fashioned glass and float 10mls (½ fl.oz) of Port on top.

American Beauty Cocktail (Cktl) ¼ measure dry vermouth, ¼ measure brandy, ¼ measure grenadine, ¼ measure orange juice, dash (white) crème de menthe, Port wine. Shake all together except Port wine and strain into a 125mls (5fl.oz) goblet and top with Port wine.

American Beauty Special (Cktl) ⅓ measure Cognac, ⅓ measure Cointreau, ⅓ measure golden rum. Shake over ice, strain into a Champagne saucer and dress with a twist of lemon peel juice.

American Blended Light Whiskey (USA) a new category of whiskey consisting of less than 20% of straight whiskies at 100° U.S. Proof (50% alc by vol.) and more than 80% of American Light whiskey.

American Blight (USA) *see* Apple Blight.

American Coffee (USA) the coffee-producing region between Mexico and Uruguay. Most coffee produced is used for blending and includes both Arabica and Robustas.

American Cream Ale (USA) an ale 4.75% alc by vol. brewed by the Genesee Brewery in Rochester, New York.

American Distilling Company Inc. (USA) a major Bourbon whiskey distillery based in Pekin, Illinois. Produces Bourbon Supreme 40% alc by vol.

American Fizz (Cktl) ⅓ measure gin, ⅓ measure brandy, ⅓ measure lemon juice, dash grenadine, dash gomme syrup. Shake well over ice, strain into an ice-filled collins glass and dress with a slice of lemon.

American Flyer Cocktail (Cktl) 40mls (⅓ gill) white rum, juice of a lime, ½ teaspoon sugar. Shake well over ice, strain into a Champagne flute. Top with iced Champagne.

American Gallon (USA) 128 American fl.ozs (1 American fl.oz = 0.960 U.K.fl.oz / 1 U.K.fl.oz = 1.0416 American fl.ozs).

American Glory (Cktl) place the juice of half an orange in a tumbler, add 2 ice cubes, fill with equal parts of Champagne and soda water, stir and serve.

American Grog (Cktl) 35mls (1½ fl.ozs) dark rum, 5mls (¼ fl.oz) lemon juice, cube of sugar. Place all into a warmed goblet, top with very hot water and stir.

American Legion Margarita (Cktl) ½ measure tequila, ⅙ measure Cointreau, ⅙ measure lime juice, ⅙ measure lemon juice. Shake over ice and strain into a salt-rimmed (lime juice) cocktail glass.

American Lemonade (USA) lemon squash with 30mls (¼ gill) of Port wine poured on top.

American Light Whiskey (USA) *see* Light Whiskey.

American Market (Mad) the old-style name used for Rainwater Madeira.

Americano (It) a wine-based apéritif produced by Gancia.

Americano [The] (Cktl) place 1 measure Italian vermouth into an ice-filled highball glass. Top with soda water and a twist of lemon peel juice.

American Oak (USA) the wood used in the making of wine and spirit casks. Mainly from the forests in Kentucky and Ohio. Imparts sharp, dry flavours into the wines. *see* Oak.

Americano Cocktail (Cktl) 1 jigger Campari, 1 jigger sweet vermouth. Pour over ice into a

A

highball glass, fill with soda and add a twist of lemon.

American Rose Cocktail (Cktl) 1 measure Cognac, dash grenadine, dash Pernod. Shake well over ice, strain into a balloon glass, top with iced Champagne and a cherry.

American Viticultural Area (USA) *abbr*: A.V.A. Originally known as Approved Viticultural Area. Introduced in 1978 by the Bureau of Alcohol, Tobacco and Firearms. To be labelled as a varietal, the wine must contain a minimum of 75% of named grape. If geographical source is named, 75% of wine must come from there. If the vintage or property are mentioned, 95% of wine must come from that vintage or property.

American Vodka (USA) a style of spirit that is totally neutral in taste 40% alc by vol.

Amerino (It) a sparkling natural mineral water from Terni, Umbria. Mineral contents (milligrammes per litre): Sodium 11mg/l, Calcium 139mg/l, Magnesium 8.2mg/l, Potassium 1.8mg/l, Bicarbonates 396mg/l, Chlorides 21mg/l, Sulphates 77mg/l, Fluoride 0.95mg/l, Silicates 13mg/l, Nitrates 4mg/l. pH 7.1

Amerino Sorgenti di San Francesco (It) a natural mineral water from Sorgenti di San Francesco.

Amer Picon (Fr) a bitters, an apéritif 21% alc by vol. flavoured with orange and gentian.

Amer Picon Cocktail [1] (Cktl) 35mls (1½ fl.ozs) Amer Picon, teaspoon grenadine, juice of a lime. Shake over ice, strain into a cocktail glass.

Amer Picon Cocktail [2] (Cktl) ½ measure Amer Picon, ½ measure Italian vermouth. Shake over ice, strain into a well-chilled cocktail glass.

Amer Picon Cooler (Cktl) ⅓ measure Amer Picon, ⅓ measure dry gin, dash gomme syrup, dash lemon juice. Shake over ice, strain into an ice-filled highball glass, top with soda water.

Amer Picon Highball (Cktl) ⅔ measure Amer Picon, ⅓ measure grenadine. Stir over ice, strain into an ice-filled collins glass, top with soda water.

Amertume (Fr) a term that describes bitterness and a loss of colour in wine when it throws a deposit and turns acid. *See also* Mannitol.

Amery Vineyards (Austr) a winery. (Add): McLaren Vale, South Australia. 5171. 25ha. Grape varieties: Cabernet sauvignon, Muscat à petit grains blanc, Pinot noir, Riesling, Shiraz and Traminer.

Amethustos (Gre) sober, not intoxicated.

Amethystos (Gre) a cava wine produced by Kostas Lazaridis from old vine Cabernet sauvignon grapes. Aged for 18 months plus 2 years in bottle.

Ameztoi (Sp) the label for a txakoli wine produced in the D.O. region of Getariako Txakolina, north-eastern Spain.

Am Gaisberg (Ger) vineyard (Anb): Pfalz. (Ber): Südliche Weinstrasse. (Gro): Herrlich. (Vil): Herxheimweyher.

Am Heiligen Häuschen (Ger) vineyard (Anb): Rheinhessen. (Ber): Wonnegau. (Gro): Liebfrauenmorgen. (Vil): Worms.

Am Hohen Stein (Ger) vineyard (Anb): Pfalz. (Ber):

Mittelhaardt-Deutsche Weinstrasse. (Gro): Schnepfenflug vom Zellertal. (Vil): Rittersheim.

Amica (It) a natural mineral water from San Lorenzo, Perugia, Umbria.

Amigne (Switz) a white grape variety of old Valais and Vaud stock. It produces wines which are smooth, generous and well robed.

Amigo (Cktl) 10mls (½ fl.oz) apricot brandy, 25mls (1fl.oz) vodka, 75mls (3fl.ozs) lemon juice, 3 dashes grenadine, 3 dashes Angostura. Shake over ice, strain into an ice-filled highball glass. Stir in pineapple juice.

Amigo Hnos & Cia (Sp) a wine-producer based in Reus, Tarragona.

Amilcar (Afr) a co-operative-produced wine from Tunisia.

A Millers Ale (Eng) a 3.8% alc by vol. ale brewed by the Millstone Brewery, Lancashire.

Amindeo (Gre) an A.O.Q.S wine area of Macedonia. Grape variety: Xynomavro. Red and sparkling rosé wines produced.

Aminean Grape (It) a grape variety that was popular in Roman times. Had many species both red and white.

Aminean Wine (It) a wine favoured in ancient times. Made from the Aminean grapes. *See also* Amminean Wine.

Amines (Eng) a name for the chemicals produced by spoilage organisms in beer and wines (especially home-made). Are identified by their fishy smell. This can be prevented by good hygiene.

Amiot (Fr) a winery based in Chassagne-Montrachet, Côte de Beaune, Burgundy. Label: Premier Cru Caillerets.

Amira (S.Afr) a red wine (Cabernet franc and Merlot blend) produced by the Avondale winery, Paarl, Western Cape.

Amiral de Beychevelle (Fr) an A.C. Saint Julien. The second wine of Château Beychevelle.

Amis de la Chartreuse [Les] (Fr) a liqueur society. (Add): Club Les Amis de la Chartreuse, 4 Boulevard Edgar Kofler, B.P. 102, 38503 Voiron, France.

Amity Vineyards (USA) a small vineyard based in Willamette Valley, Oregon. 3.5ha. Produces vinifera-based wines. Specialises in Pinot noir. Label: Schouten Single Vineyard, Winemaker's Reserve.

Ammerlanden (Ger) vineyard (Anb): Württemberg. (Ber): Kocher-Jagst-Tauber. (Gro): Kocherberg. (Vil): Möckmühl.

Ammerschwihr (Fr) a wine-producing commune of the Haut-Rhin in Alsace.

Amminean Wine (It) a famous wine from the eastern half of the Roman Empire favoured by the Romans. *See also* Aminean Wine.

Ammostatoio (It) wine press.

Amn Carbonica Insalus (Sp) a sparkling natural mineral water. Mineral contents (milligrammes per litre): Sodium 11.2mg/l, Calcium 367.4mg/l, Magnesium 0.2mg/l, Potassium 1.7mg/l, Chlorides 15mg/l, Sulphates 161.9mg/l, Fluoride 0.2mg/l, Nitrates 3mg/l.

A

Amnesia (Wal) a 4.9% alc by vol. ale brewed by the Bragdy Ynys Mon brewery, Gwynedd.

Amolo (Iran) a sparkling natural mineral water from Parasm Spring, Alborz Mountain. Mineral contents (milligrammes per litre): Sodium 37mg/l, Calcium 227.2mg/l, Magnesium 56.64mg/l, Potassium 4mg/l, Bicarbonates 620mg/l, Chlorides 34mg/l, Sulphates 130mg/l, Fluoride 1mg/l, Silicates 17mg/l. pH 6.83

Amoltern (Ger) village (Anb): Baden. (Ber): Kaiserstuhl-Tuniberg. (Gro): Vulkanfelsen. (Vin): Steinhalde.

Amont (Sp) *abbr*: **Amont**illado Sherry.

Amontillado (Sp) are Fino Sherries that have lost, due to age, the delicate character of finos, but develop a nutty flavour of their own.

Amontillado Abolengo (Sp) a brand of Amontillado Sherry produced by the Marqués de Misa.

Amontillado Cocktail (Cktl) ½ measure Amontillado Sherry, ½ measure Dubonnet. Stir in an ice-filled highball glass, top with a twist of lemon peel juice.

Amontillado 51–1a (Sp) a bone dry Amontillado Sherry with a walnut flavour. Average age of 60 years. Produced by Domecq.

Amontillado Viejo (Sp) a very old, rare, mature Amontillado Sherry.

Amorgiano (Gre) a red grape variety grown mainly in the southern regions. Produces medium bodied red wines.

Amoricano (Cktl) 1 measure Campari, 1 measure dry Martini. Stir with ice, strain into a highball glass, top with soda and decorate with a twist of lemon.

Amorosa (Cyp) a dry rosé wine from Loël Ltd. in Limassol.

Amorosa (It) a slightly acidic sparkling natural mineral water from Commune di Massa Carrara. Mineral contents (milligrammes per litre): Sodium 4.03mg/l, Calcium 0.97mg/l, Magnesium 0.6mg/l, Potassium 0.13mg/l, Bicarbonates 4.3mg/l, Chlorides 6.73mg/l, Sulphates 0.85mg/l, Fluoride 0.02mg/l, Silicates 4.25mg/l, Oxygen 10.45mg/l, Nitrates 0.42mg/l. pH 5.7

Amorosa (S.Afr) a popular medium sweet rosé wine from Kellerprinz Wines S.F.W. Made from Cinsault and Pinotage grapes.

Amoroso (Sp) sweetened Oloroso Sherry, prepared for the British market (unknown in Spain).

Amouille (Fr) the first milk of a cow after giving birth. *see* Beestings.

Amour Cocktail (Cktl) ½ measure cream Sherry, ½ measure French vermouth, dash Angostura. Shake over ice, strain into a cocktail glass. Top with a squeeze of orange peel juice and spiral of orange peel.

Amourette (Fr) a violet-coloured liqueur.

Amoureuses [Les] (Fr) a Premier Cru vineyard in the A.C. commune of Chambolle-Musigny, Côte de Nuits, Burgundy. 5.4ha.

Ampainen Cocktail (Cktl) ½ measure crème de banane, ½ measure vodka. Stir over ice in a highball glass. Top with ginger ale. Dress with a slice of orange.

Ampeau [Robert] (Fr) a leading wine producer in Meursault, Côte de Beaune, Burgundy.

Ampelidaceae (Lat) the botanical family of which the vine *Vitis vinifera* is a member.

Ampelographic (Eng) vine growing and vine classification.

Ampélographie (Fr) ampelography.

Ampelography (Eng) the study of the vine. (Fr) = ampélographie.

Ampelopsis (Gre) the study of the vine.

Ampelos (Gre) grapevine.

Ampelotherapy (Eng) the treatment of illness with wines or with grapes as part of the medicine. Mainly in mediaeval times.

Amphora (Gre) a two-handled vessel, jar or pitcher used in ancient times for holding wine or oil. *See also* Ampulla.

Amphora Bottle (It) an amphora-shaped bottle first introduced by producer Fazi Battaglia in 1953 and used for bottling Verdicchio dei Castelli di Jesi.

Ampulla (It) a two-handled bottle used for wine etc. in Roman times. *See also* Amphora.

Ampulla (Lat) a vessel in early Christianity for holding the wine and water for the Eucharist.

Ampurdán Costa Brava (Sp) a Denominación de Origen of the Cataluña region of south-eastern Spain on the French border. 2977ha. Most of the wine produced is rosé. Some red, white and Garnatxa also produced. Grape varieties: 67% Cariñena, 26% Garnacha tinta, plus Garnacha blanca, Macabeo. *see* Garnatxa.

Amrat Jal (Pak) a natural mineral water from Gurudwarra, Hassan Abdal. Mineral contents (milligrammes per litre): Sodium 24.72mg/l, Calcium 40mg/l, Magnesium 20.5mg/l, Potassium 254mg/l, Bicarbonates 2.8mg/l, Chlorides 32.5mg/l, Nitrates 24.3mg/l.

Am Sand (Aus) a vineyard area on the banks of the River Danube in the Kremstal region.

Amselberg (Ger) vineyard (Anb): Baden. (Ber): Ortenau. (Gro): Fürsteneck. (Vil): Reichenbach.

Amselfelder Spätburgunder (Euro) a sweet red Burgundac wine from the 'Kosovo Pilje' vineyards. Also called by that name. *See also* Burgomer Burgundec.

Amstel Beer (Hol) a 4% alc by vol. draught special beer brewed by Heineken Netherlands Brouwerij, Zoeterwoude.

Amstel Brouwerij (Hol) a famous Dutch brewery in Amsterdam. (Add): Burg Smeetsweg 1, Postbus, 2380 BD, Zoeterwoude, Netherlands. Taken over by Heineken. Website: http://www.amstel.nl

Amstel Gold (Hol) a 7% alc by vol. bottled special beer brewed by Heineken Netherlands Brouwerij, Zoeterwoude.

Amstel Lentebock (Hol) a 7% alc by vol. bottled bock beer brewed by Heineken Netherlands Brouwerij, Zoeterwoude.

Amstel Malt (Hol) a 0.1% alc by vol. bottled, alcohol-free beer brewed by Heineken Netherlands Brouwerij, Zoeterwoude.

Amstel Pilsener Bier (Hol) a 5% alc by vol. bottled pilsener brewed by Heineken Netherlands Brouwerij, Zoeterwoude.

Amstel Pilsener 1870 (Hol) a 5% alc by vol. bottled pilsener brewed by Heineken Netherlands Brouwerij, Zoeterwoude.

Amsterdam Amber Beer (USA) a hand-made lager beer made from crystal and roasted malt, fresh hops and lager yeast. Brewed and bottled in New York, sold in long necked bottles.

Amsterdam Brewing C° Ltd (Can) a brewery. (Add): 600 King Street West, Toronto, Ontario. Brews lager beers. 'E'mail: info@amsterdambeer.com

Amsterdam Cocktail (Cktl) ½ measure Hollands gin, ¼ measure orange juice, ¼ measure Cointreau, dash Angostura. Shake over ice and strain into a cocktail glass.

Amtliche Prüfungsnummer (Ger) the official German Government testing number given to the wines that have passed the most stringent examinations by tasting. Found on all quality wine labels. e.g. 3-533-094-03-97. 3 (testing station N°), 533 (village N°), 094 (producers N°), 03 (N° of samples passed), 97 (year wine was bottled).

Amtliche Weinkostkommission (Aus) abbr: WKK. the name given to the official wine tasting commission who check the quality seal (Weingütesiegel).

Amtsgarten (Ger) vineyard (Anb): Mosel-Saar-Ruwer. (Ber): Bernkastel. (Gro): Kurfürstlay. (Vil): Mülheim.

Am Wagram (Aus) a wine-producing area on the eastern side of the Kamp Valley.

Amyl Acetate (Eng) an ester found in wine that has an aroma of pear drops. Formed from Acetic acid and Amyl alcohol.

Amyl Alcohol (Eng) $C_5H_{11}OH$ a higher alcohol, part of the fusel oils.

Amylolysis (Eng) the conversion of starch into sugar in barley malting.

Amylozyme 100 (Eng) the name for the amylase enzyme which is used to convert starch into fermentable sugars.

Amynteon (Gre) a red wine made from the red Xynomavro grape. Grown mainly in the northern regions.

Amy's Ale (Eng) a 4.8% alc by vol. limited edition strong hoppy ale brewed by the Teignworthy Brewery, Newton Abbot, Devon.

Amy's Blend [The] (Austr) the label for a red (Cabernet sauvignon) wine produced by the Moss Wood Estate, Western Australia.

Anacreon (Gre) a poet (572–488 BC) who wrote many songs / poems on wine and love.

Añada (Sp) single year, a vintage wine.

Añadas (Sp) the place where brandy matures before blending.

Añadas (Sp) denotes Sherry of a single year before it goes into the criaderas.

Anaerobic (Eng) respiration without oxygen, applies to wine yeasts that can multiply without oxygen. *See also* Aerobic.

Anaerobic Respiration (Eng) a term denoting the conversion of carbohydrate into alcohol and CO_2 by yeast fermentation.

Anaga (Sp) a Vino de Mesa area of Tenerife, Canary Islands.

Anagrus Epos (Bio) a wasp species which feeds on the eggs of the Grape Leafhopper. Is encouraged by the Vignerons.

Anagrus Wasp (USA) *see Anagrus epos.*

Anakena (Chile) a winery based in the Cachapoal Valley, Central Chile. Grape varieties include: Carmenère, Viognier. Label: Single Vineyard.

Anakie Cabernet (Austr) a red wine produced from the Cabernet sauvignon and Cabernet franc grapes. A well-balanced and well-flavoured wine, soft and with no bitterness. Produced by the Hickinbotham family vineyard, Victoria.

Analyser (Eng) the name given to the part of a continuous still that vaporises the fermented brew so that the alcohol can be extracted in the rectifier.

Anapa (Rus) the chief wine centre of the Crimea Peninsular.

Anapa Riesling (Rus) a medium dry white wine from the Crimea. Made from the Welschriesling.

Anapsiktiko (Gre) beverage / drink.

Añares (Sp) the brand label for red and white Rioja wines from Boedega Olarra.

Anarkali (Ind) a still wine produced mainly from a blend of Cabernet sauvignon with Bangalore purple (an Indian red grape variety). Grown on east facing slopes in a 42ha. vineyard in the Sahyadri Valley.

Anatolia (Tur) a natural mineral water (established 1982) from Yenicaga Bolu. Mineral contents (milligrammes per litre): Sodium 22mg/l, Calcium 249mg/l, Magnesium 20mg/l, Chlorides 17mg/l, Sulphates 76mg/l, Nitrates 0.016mg/l. pH 6.5

Anatolia (Tur) the best Turkish wine producing area which has the districts of Ankara, Elazig and Gaziantep.

Anatu Wines (S.Afr) a winery based in Stellenbosch, Western Cape. Grape variety: Shiraz. Website: http://www.anatu.com

Anav (Isr) grape.

Ana Vie (Rom) a natural mineral water.

Ana Vineyard (USA) the label for a red wine (Pinot noir) produced by the Lachini Vineyard winery, Dundee Hills, Oregon.

Anb. (Ger) abbr: **Anb**augebiete.

Anbaugebiet (Ger) a cultivated territory or region for wines in Germany. 13 regions: Ahr, Mosel-Saar-Ruwer, Nahe, Rheingau, Mittelrhein, Pfalz (Palatinate or Rheinpfalz), Baden, Württemberg, Franken (Franconia), Rheinhessen, Hessische Bergstrasse, Saale-Unstrut, Sachsen (each is divided into a number of bereich).

Anbaugebiete (Ger) see Anbaugebiet (pl).

A

Ancellotta (It) a red grape variety grown in Emilia-Romagna.

Ancestor (Scot) a de luxe blended Scotch whisky from John Dewar & Sons Ltd., Perth, Perthshire.

Ancestor Ale (Eng) a bitter ale brewed by the Tetley Brewery in Leeds to celebrate the 175th anniversary of the brewery. Part of the Carlsberg-Tetley Tapster's Choice range.

Ancestral (Scot) a 14 year old malt whisky from Inverarity Vaults Ltd., Balmenach. 40% alc by vol.

Anchialos (Gre) a white wine produced in the Thessaly region in northern Greece. Is made from the Rhoditis and Savatiano grapes.

Anchor Beer (Eng) a keg and canned beer brewed by North Country Brewery, Hull, Yorkshire.

Anchor Beer (E.Asia) a pilsener-type beer brewed by the Archipelago Brewery in Kuala Lumpur, Malaya.

Anchor Beer (E.Asia) a beer brewed by the Burgess and Maugham's in Brewery, Singapore.

Anchor Bitter (Eng) a keg bitter brewed by the Anchor Brewery, Salisbury Wiltshire.

Anchor Bitter (Eng) a pale brew made from malt and hops but no sugar. Brewed by Godson's Brewery, Clapton, East London.

Anchor Brewery (Eng) the name for Gibbs Mew's brewery based in Salisbury, Wiltshire.

Anchor Keg (Eng) see Chairman's Choice.

Anchor Steam Brewery (USA) a San Francisco brewery producing Anchor Steam Beer and Porter using clarifiers (long shallow pans) for fermentation.

Ancien Estate (USA) a winery based in the Russian River Valley, Sonoma County, California. Grape varieties include: Pinot noir.

Ancienne Méthode (Fr) an old method of making wine without the aid of any chemicals etc.

Ancient Age Distillery (USA) a Bourbon whiskey producer based at Leestown, Frankfort. Labels include: Ancient Age 107 10 year old, Ancient Age 10 Star (90° proof), Blanton's Bourbon, Elmer T. Lee, Rock Hill Farm, Hancock's Reserve.

Ancient Druids (Eng) a pub brewery (established 1984) in Cambridge by Charles Wells Brewery of Bedford, Bedfordshire. The beer is brewed at the pub. Produces Kite Bitter 1038 O.G. and Druids Special 1045 O.G.

Ancient Proverb Port (USA) the brand-name used by the Llords and Elwood Winery in California for a range of their Port-style wines.

Ancla (S.Am) a 4.8% alc by vol. bottled premium lager beer brewed by the Ancla Brewery, Bogotá, Colombia.

Ancre (Fr) the brand-name used by the Albra Breweries for their beers.

Andalucía (Sp) a region in south-west Spain. Contains the provinces of Almería, Cádiz, Córdoba, Granada, Huelva, Jaén, Málaga, Sevilla. Home to the D.O.'s of Condado de Huelva, Málaga, Montilla-Moriles. The D.E. zone of brandy de Jerez. Vino de la Tierra areas of Cádiz, Contraviesa-Alpujarra (Granada). Vino Comarcal areas of Laujar (Almería), Villaviciosa (Córdoba), Lopera (Jaén), Aljarafe, Lebrija, Los Palacios (Sevilla). Vino de Mesa areas of Bailén and Torreperogil (Jaén).

Andalusia Cocktail (Cktl) ⅓ measure dry Sherry, ⅓ measure Bacardi White Label, ⅓ measure brandy. Stir over ice and strain into a cocktail glass.

Andalusia Wines (S.Afr) see Vaalharts Co-operative.

Andean Vineyards (Arg) a major wine producer based in the central region.

Andechs Brauerei (Ger) a brewery in Erling-Andechs, Bavaria noted for its malty bock beers. Produces: Andechser Weissbier, Bergbock Hell, Bergbock Dunkel, Doppelbock Hell and Doppelbock Dunkel.

Andechser Weissbier (Ger) a 5.1% alc by vol. bottle-conditioned wheat beer brewed by Andechs Brauerei, Erling-Andechs, Bavaria.

Andeker (USA) the name for a beer brewed by the Pabst Brewery in Los Angeles.

Andel (Ger) village (Anb): Mosel-Saar-Ruwer. (Ber): Bernkastel. (Gro): Kurfürstlay. (Vin): Schlossberg.

Anderida (Eng) see Horam Manor from where it originates. A wine made from mainly Müller-Thurgau with some Seyval blanc. Bottled by Merrydown Wine C°. Ltd.

Anderson Cocktail (Cktl) ¼ measure dry gin, ¼ measure Italian vermouth. Stir well over ice, strain into a cocktail glass and top with twist of orange peel.

Anderson Valley (USA) an A.V.A. a wine-producing area in the Mendocino County, northern California. Grape varieties include Gewürztraminer, Pinot noir, Chardonnay. Noted for still and sparkling wines.

Anderson Valley Brewing Company (USA) a brewery. (Add): P.O. Box 505, 17700 Hwy 253, Boonwille, 95415 California. Brews beers and lager. Website: http://www.avbc.com

Anderson Valley Vineyards (USA) a winery based in A.V.A. Northern Rio Grande Valley, New Mexico.

Anderson Vineyards (USA) a winery based in the Napa Valley, California. 9.5ha. Grape variety: Chardonnay.

Andosilla (Sp) a Zona de Crianza in the Rioja Baja region of north-eastern Spain.

Andover Ale (Eng) a cask-conditioned ale 1040 O.G. brewed by the Bourne Valley Brewery, Hampshire.

Andrac Vineyards (Wal) a winery. (Add): Llanvahes, Gwent. Produces the sparkling wine Vintners Choice from predominantly Chardonnay grapes (made by the traditional method).

Andraitx (Sp) a Vino de Mesa area of the island Mallorca, Balearic Islands.

Andrea da Ponte (It) a well-known brand of grappa.

André Delaunois (Fr) a Premier Cru Champagne producer. (Add): 17, Rue Roger Salengro, 51500 Rilly-la-Montagne. Produces both vintage and non-vintages Champagnes. Label: Cuvée Royale.

Andrea Oberto (It) a vineyard. (Add): Via G. Marconi 25, 12064 La Morra (CN). Produces D.O.C. Barbera d'Alba from 1.2ha. vineyard. Aged 15 months in oak barriques.

Andreasberg (Ger) vineyard (Anb): Baden. (Ber): Ortenau. (Gro): Fürsteneck. (Vil): Ortenberg.

Andreasberg (Ger) vineyard (Anb): Mosel-Saar-Ruwer. (Ber): Saar-Ruwer. (Gro): Römerlay. (Vil): Trier.

Andreas Bock (Ger) a fine, malty bock beer from the Aying Brauerei in Bavaria.

Andreasquelle (Ger) a natural mineral water from Sulzbach am Main-Soden, BY.

André Diligent (Fr) a Champagne producer (10ha). (Add): 23 Grande Rue, 10110 Buxeuil. Produces vintage and non-vintage Champagnes. Vintages: 1995, 1996, 1997, 1998, 1999, 2000.

Andresen [J.H.] Sucrs. Lda. (Port) a Port producer. (Add): Apartado 1510, 4401-901 Vila Nova de Gaia. Noted for range of Colheita Ports.

Andres Winery (Can) a winery based in Winona, Niagara. Produces hybrid wines.

Andrew Bain (S.Afr) the label for a range of wines produced by the Cape Vineyards winery, Rawsonville, Western Cape. Also an Andrew Bain Reserve.

Andros (Gre) an island in the northern Cyclades, Aegean sea. Long history of fame for the wines especially in ancient Greece.

Andy Mitchell Wines (S.Afr) a winery (established 2003) based in Greyton, Southern Cape. Grape variety: Syrah. Website: http://www.andymitchellwines.com

Añejado (Port)(Sp) a term meaning 'aged by'.

Añejo (Sp) old.

Anejo Cacique (S.Am) a rum aged for 2 years in cask from Venuezuela.

Añejo Tequila (Mex) a tequila that has spent 1 year in oak. *See also* Reposado, Blanco Tequila.

Ané Rouge (S.Afr) the label for a red wine (Cabernet sauvignon, Cinsaut and Merlot blend) produced by the Mostertsdrift Noble Wines winery, Stellenbosch, Western Cape.

Anesone (It)(USA) an anis-liquorice flavoured liqueur. 45% alc by vol.

Anesone Troduo (It) an absinthe-based spirit apéritif. 40% alc by vol.

Anfiteatro (It) a red I.G.T. wine produced from 100% Sangiovese grapes by Tenuta Vecchie Terre di Montefili in Tuscany.

Anfora (It) amphora or jar.

Anfora (Port) a large clay vessel used to ferment and store wine.

Anfora (Port) a red wine produced by Fonseca in Estremadura.

Angad (Afr) an A.O.G. area in the wine-producing region of eastern Morocco.

Angeac-Champagne (Fr) a commune in the Charente-Maritime département whose grapes are classed Petite Champagne (Cognac).

Angeac-Charente (Fr) a commune in the Charente-Maritime département whose grapes are classed Petite Champagne (Cognac).

Angel (Eng) a mineral water from Wenlock Edge, Shropshire. Mineral contents (milligrammes per litre): Sodium 32mg/l, Calcium 45mg/l, Magnesium 22mg/l, Potassium 2.3mg/l,

Chlorides 34mg/l, Sulphates 17mg/l, Fluoride 0.091mg/l, Nitrates <1mg/l.

Angel Face Cocktail (Cktl) ⅓ measure Calvados, ⅓ measure dry gin, ⅓ measure apricot brandy. Shake over ice and strain into a cocktail glass.

Angel Fire (USA) a natural mineral water.

Angel Hill (Eng) a 4.2% alc by vol. beer brewed by the Boggart Hole Clough Brewery, Greater Manchester.

Angelica (It) a natural mineral water from Perugia, Umbria. Mineral contents (milligrammes per litre): Sodium 3.2mg/l, Calcium 95mg/l, Magnesium 1.2mg/l, Potassium 0.65mg/l, Bicarbonates 289mg/l, Chlorides 5.1mg/l, Sulphates 2.3mg/l, Fluoride 0.05mg/l, Silicates 7.2mg/l, Nitrates 7.7mg/l. pH 7.38

Angelica (Sp) a sweet yellow liqueur somewhat similar to Chartreuse. Made in the Basque country.

Angelica (USA) a fortified 'altar wine', tawny in colour. Produced in California. *see* California Angelica.

Angelica Antigua (USA) a fortified 'altar wine' produced by the East-Side Winery, Lodi, California.

Angelicant (Fr) an alternative name for the Muscadelle grape.

Angelikalikoer (Ger) an angelica-based liqueur.

Angelo (Cktl) 10mls (½ fl.oz) Galliano, 10mls (½ fl.oz) Southern Comfort, 25mls (1fl.oz) Smirnoff vodka, dash egg white. Shake over ice, strain into an ice-filled highball glass. Top with orange and pineapple juice.

Angel Organic (Scot) a 5% alc by vol. organic ale brewed by Broughton Ales Brewery, Lanarkshire.

Angel's Delight (Pousse Café) pour into an elgin glass in order equal quantities of grenadine, crème d'Yvette and cream.

Angel's Dream (Pousse Café) pour into an elgin glass in order equal quantities of maraschino, crème d'Yvette and Cognac.

Angel's Kiss (Cktl) 30mls (¼ gill) Bénédictine, 30mls (¼ gill) cream. Put liqueur into a large elgin glass, float cream on top.

Angel's Kiss [1] (Pousse Café) ¼ measure crème de cacao, ¼ measure prunelle brandy, ¼ measure crème de violette, ¼ measure cream. Pour each carefully into a narrow (elgin) glass in order.

Angel's Kiss [2] (Pousse Café) equal measures poured in order into an elgin glass: crème de cacao, crème d'Yvette, Cognac and cream.

Angel Special (Cktl)(Non-alc) 1 egg yolk, 2 dashes grenadine, 2 dashes Angostura, 200mls (⅓ pint) orange juice. Blend with a scoop of crushed ice in a blender, pour in a Champagne flute and dress with a cherry.

Angel's Share (Eng) the term given to the spirit evaporation which occurs whilst it is maturing in cask. (brandy, whisky etc). Up to 25% of the total may be lost. (Fr) = la part des anges.

Angel's Smile Cocktail (Cktl) ⅓ measure kirsch, ⅓ measure Cointreau, ⅓ measure vodka, dash grenadine. Shake over ice, strain into cocktail glass and dress with a cherry.

Angels Tears (S.Afr) the label for a range of wines Pink (Chenin blanc and Pinotage blend), Red (Cabernet sauvignon and Merlot blend) and White (Chenin blanc and Hanepoot blend) produced by the Grand Provence winery, Franschhoek, Western Cape.

Angel's Tip (Cktl) ¾ measure brown crème de cacao, ¼ measure cream. Float cream on top of liqueur in a large elgin glass.

Angel's Tit (Pousse Café) pour into an elgin glass in order, equal quantities of maraschino and cream. Top with a cherry.

Angel's Wing (Pousse Café) 1 part crème de cacao, 1 part brandy, 1 part cream. Pour in order into an elgin glass.

Angel's Wing (Pousse Café) another name for Angel's Kiss.

Angelus [L'] (Fr) a 7% alc by vol. bottom-fermented, unpasteurised wheat beer brewed by the Annoeullin Brasserie, Annoeullin.

Angeou (Eng) the sixteenth century spelling of Anjou.

Angereichert (Ger) sugared. (Fr) = chaptalisatise.

Angern (Aus) a vineyard site on the banks of the River Danube situated in the Wachau region, Niederösterreich.

Angern (Aus) a wine village in the Falkenstein-Matzen district in north-eastern Austria that produces mainly white wines.

Angers Rose (Cktl) ⅓ measure Cointreau, ⅓ measure Bourbon, ⅓ measure pineapple juice, dash egg white, dash Campari, shake over ice, strain into a cocktail glass, decorate with a small slice of orange and cherry.

Angevine (Fr) a white grape variety, See also Madeleine Angevine.

Anggur (Indo) grape.

Anghelu Ruju (It) lit: 'red angel', a rich, red, ruby wine similar to Port, produced in Sardinia, it has a pronounced bouquet and sweet, aromatic taste. Made from selected grapes partially dried in the sun.

Anglada-Deleger (Fr) a propriétaire-récoltant based in Chassagne-Montrachet that produces A.C. Premier Cru Blanchot-Dessus.

Anglade (Fr) a commune in the A.C. Côtes de Blaye in north-eastern Bordeaux.

Angled Racks (USA) the name for pupître-styled racks used for storing sparkling wines in a cellar.

Angler Cocktail (Cktl) 20mls (⅙ gill) Vantogrio, 40mls (⅓ gill) gin, 2 dashes orange bitters, 2 dashes Angostura. Stir over ice, strain into a cocktail glass. Add squeeze of lemon peel juice on top.

Angler Lager (Eng) a strong, bottled lager 1054 O.G. brewed by the Charles Wells Brewery, Bedford, for export.

Angler's Cocktail (Cktl) 1 measure dry gin, 3 dashes orange bitters, 2 dashes Angostura, 1 dash grenadine. Shake well over ice and strain into an ice-filled old-fashioned glass.

Anglerwein (Ger) a brand of white tafelwein produced by Deinhard in Koblenz.

Angles [Les] (Fr) a Premier Cru vineyard in the A.C. commune of Volnay, Côte de Beaune, Burgundy. 3.5ha.

Anglet (Fr) a town near Bayonne that is noted for Vin de Sable.

Anglian Ale (Eng) a strong, keg and bottled ale 1048 O.G. brewed by the Anglian brewery, Norwich, Norfolk.

Anglias (Cyp) a brandy produced by Haggipavlu, both domestic and export brands produced.

Anglo-Australian Wine Company (Eng) an importer of Australian wines. Range available at 9, Greenways, Sandhurst, Camberley, Surrey. Also at Will Logan Wine Agencies, Church Street, Hayfield, Stockport, Cheshire.

Anglo Dutch Brewery (Eng) a brewery. (Add): Unit 12, Savile Bridge Mills, Mill st. East, Dewsbury, West Yorkshire. WF12 6QQ. Brews a bitter and other ales including: Anglo Dutch Best Bitter 3.8% alc by vol., At t'Ghoul & Ghost 5.2% alc by vol., Ghost on the Rim 4.5% alc by vol., Imperial Pint 4% alc by vol., Kletswater 4% alc by vol., Spike's on t'way 4.2% alc by vol., Tabatha the Knackered 6% alc by vol. Website: http://www.anglo-dutch-brewery.co.uk 'E'mail: mike@anglo-dutch-brewery.co.uk

Anglo German Bewery (Eng) a brewery. (Add): 227–247 Gascoigne Road, Barking, Essex. IG11 7LN Brews lager beer. Website: http://www.anglogermanbreweries.co.uk 'E'mail: sales@anglogermanbreweries.co.uk

Anglo Vino de Sankta Georgo (Eng) a wine created to celebrate the 100th anniversary of the Esperanto Society. From St. George's Vineyard, Waldron, East Sussex.

Angola (Afr) a wine made from palm sap in West Africa.

Angora (S.Afr) a winery (established 2002) based in Bonnievale, Robertson, Western Cape. Grape variety: Shiraz. 16ha.

Angoris (It) a producer of sparkling wines (all methods) based in the Friuli-Venezia Giulia region. Labels include Modelet Brut.

Angosto (Sp) a still natural mineral water from Angosto, Albacete. Mineral contents (milligrammes per litre): Sodium 21mg/l, Calcium 64mg/l, Magnesium 32mg/l, Bicarbonates 255mg/l.

Angostura (S.Am) a famous rum-based bitters (created 1824), flavoured with bark and gentian, originally produced in Venezuela, now produced in Trinidad 23% alc by vol.

Angostura (S.Am) a Venezuelan town where Dr. J.G.B. Siegert created the famous bitters of the same name. The town is now called Ciudad Bolivar.

Angostura Aquavit (Swe) a flavoured aquavit, flavoured with Angostura.

Angostura Bark (S.Am) a tree of the genus **Cusparia** or **Galipea** which is the principal flavour of Angostura bitters.

Angostura Bitters (S.Am) see Angostura.

Angostura Fizz [1] (Cktl)(Non-alc) 30mls (¼ gill)

Angostura bitters, 15mls (⅛ gill) plain syrup, 60mls (½ gill) lemon juice, white of egg. Shake well over ice, strain into a tumbler. Top with soda water.

Angostura Fizz [2] (Cktl)(Non-alc) 25mls (1fl.oz) Angostura, 1 egg white, dash grenadine, dash cream. Shake over ice, strain into an ice-filled highball glass. Top with soda and spiral of lemon peel.

Angoumois (Fr) a famous town in the north-east of the Cognac region whose wines are distilled into Cognac.

Angoves' St. Agnes Old Liqueur (Austr) a 14–40 y.o. brandy aged in French oak casks for 7 years before blending from Angoves Vineyard.

Angoves Vineyard (Austr) a winery. (Add): Bookmark Avenue, South Australia, 5341. 393ha. Grape varieties: Cabernet sauvignon, Chardonnay, Chenin blanc, French colombard, Malbec, Rhine riesling, Sauvignon blanc, Shiraz, Sylvaner, Traminer.

Anguillula aceti (Lat) see Vinegar Eel.

Angus Dundee Distillers (Eng) a whisky and spirits distillery. (Add): Hillman House, 79, Marylebone Lane, London W1U 2PU. Website: http://www.angusdundee.co.uk 'E'mail: sales@angusdundee.co.uk

Anhaltiner Berquelle (Ger) a natural mineral water from Hecklingen-Gänsefurth, ST.

Anhaltiner Felsenquelle (Ger) a natural mineral water from Hecklingen-Gänsefurth, ST.

Anheuser-Busch (USA) the world's largest brewery (established 1860) based in St. Louis, Missouri. Produces Budweiser and Michelob beers. See also Bud Ice, 180. Has U.K. base (Add): Anheuser-Busch Europe Ltd., Thames Link house, 1 Church Road, Richmond, Surrey TW9 2QW Website: http://www.budweiser.co.uk

Anhialos (Gre) an A.O.Q.S. dry white wine produced near Thessaly from Rhoditis grape (plus small amount of Savatiano). Also spelt Ankialos.

Anhydride Sulfureux (Fr) sulphur-dioxide.

Anice Forte (It) an absinthe-based spirit apéritif 41% alc by vol.

Animador (Cktl) ⅓ measure gin, ⅓ measure sweet vermouth, ⅓ measure Apérital Delor. Shake over ice and strain into a cocktail glass.

Animator (Ger) a doppelbock beer brewed by the Hacker-Pschorr Brauerei of Munich, West Germany.

Animus (Gre) a 100% Robola wine from Gentilini, Cephalonia.

Añina (Sp) an area within the Andalusia region with mainly chalk soil, grapes grown here make the best sherries.

Anis (Fr)(Sp) a popular liqueur and apéritif, flavoured with star anis seeds. Was substituted for the banned absinthe (Pernod is an example 43% alc by vol).

Anis (Port) aniseed.

Anisado (Sp) aniseed brandy.

Anis del Mono (Sp) an aniseed liqueur from Barcelona. Available in a sweet or dry form. 38% alc by vol.

Anise (Eng) *Pimpinella anisum* an umbelliferous plant of the Mediterranean. Used in the making of aniseed-flavoured beverages.

Anise Chinchón (Sp) an anise-flavoured liqueur in Chinchón 38% alc by vol.

Anisetta Stillata (It) an aniseed liqueur from the Aurum Distillery in Pescara.

Anisette (Fr) an aniseed-flavoured liqueur with coriander and various other herbs etc. 25% alc by vol.

Anisette Classique (Swe) an anisette liqueur produced by Aktiebolaget Vin and Spritcentralem.

Anjou (Fr) an A.C. region of the Loire (western) producing white, red and rosé wines. 3500ha, the soil is mainly schale and chalky. Noted mainly for rosé and sweet whites wines. (Bonnezeaux, Coteaux du Layon, Quarts de Chaume). see Anjou-Saumur.

Anjou Coteaux de la Loire (Fr) an A.C. district (60ha) and white wine from the Anjou region of the river Loire produced from the Chenin blanc grape on shale and chalk soils.

Anjou Coteaux de la Loire Rosé de Cabernet (Fr) an A.C. rosé wine no longer produced. see Cabernet Rosé.

Anjou Coteaux de Saumur (Fr) an old A.C. wine classification no longer used for white, red and rosé wines.

Anjou Fillette (Fr) a 35 cls. bottle from the central Loire, a cross between a Champagne bottle and a languedoc bottle, also used in the Touraine, Loire.

Anjou Mousseux (Fr) an A.C. white sparkling wine from the Anjou region of the river Loire.

Anjou Rosé (Fr) a highly popular A.C. rosé wine from the Anjou region of the river Loire. Slightly sweet and often pétillant. Produced from Grolleau, Cabernet franc and / or Gamay.

Anjou Rosé de Cabernet (Fr) an A.C. rosé from Anjou region on the river Loire. see Cabernet Rosé.

Anjou-Saumur (Fr) an A.C. district within the Anjou region of the river Loire. Produces white, red and rosé wines. Grape varieties: Cabernet Franc (Breton), Cabernet sauvignon, Chenin blanc (Pineau de la Loire), Gamay, Grolleau (Groslot) and Malbec (Cot). Main A.C. wines: Anjou (rouge, blanc, mousseux), Bonnezeaux, Cabernet d'Anjou, Coteaux du Layon, Quarts de Chaume, Saumur (rouge, blanc, mousseux), Saumur Champigny, Savennières.

Anjou-Saumur Rosé de Cabernet (Fr) an A.C. rosé wine produced in the Saumur district of Anjou region.

Anjou-Villages (Fr) an A.C. red wine district (250ha) within the Anjou-Samur region of the Loire, wines produced from Cabernet sauvignon and Cabernet franc grapes on clay and schale soils. See also Anjou-Villages-Brissac.

Anjou-Villages-Brissac (Fr) a new A.C. 110ha. within the A.C. Anjou-Villages.

Anjoux S.A. (Fr) a négociant-éleveur based at Saint-Georges de Reneins, Burgundy.

A

Ankara (Tur) a vineyard based in the middle Anatolia region. Produces red and white wines.

Anker (Eng) 10 gallon cask.

Anker (Scot) an old whisky cask of approximately 8 gallons capacity.

Anker Brasserie (Bel) a brewery that is noted for abbaye-style beers. *see* Het Anker Brasserie, Floreffe.

Ankialos (Gre) *see* Anhialos.

Ankola Coffee (E.Ind) coffee beans from Sumatra, produces a mellow flavour with a good strong aroma.

Anl'eau (Hol) a natural mineral water from Bronput 3, Annen.

Annaba (Alg) a red wine-producing region in eastern Algeria.

Annaberg (Aus) a vineyard area based in the Kitzeck district of Süd-Steirmark.

Annaberg (Ger) vineyard (Anb): Mosel-Saar-Ruwer. (Ber): Bernkastel. (Gro): Probstberg. (Vil): Schweich.

Annaberg (Ger) vineyard (Anb): Pfalz. (Ber): Mittelhaardt-Deutsche Weinstrasse. (Gro): Feuerberg. (Vil): Kallstadt.

Annacquare (It) to dilute with water, watered-down wine.

Anna de Cordorníu (Sp) the name of a 90% Chardonnay, 10% Parellada método tradicional sparkling wine produced by Cordorníu.

Anna Maria Old Stage Merlot (USA) a red wine produced by Valley View Vineyards in Applegate Valley, south-western Oregon.

Anna Maria's Vintners Reserve (USA) a red wine produced by Valley View Vineyards in Applegate Valley, south-western Oregon from a blend of Cabernet sauvignon, Cabernet franc, Merlot and 52% Zinfandel grapes.

Annandale Wine Estate (S.Afr) a winery (established 1996) based in Annandale, Stellenbosch. Grape varieties include: Cabernet franc, Cabernet sauvignon, Merlot, Shiraz. Labels: Cavalier, CVP-2001. 45ha. Website: http://www.annandale.co.za

Anna-Quelle (Ger) a natural mineral water from Bad Peterstal-Griesbach, BW.

Annata (It) year / vintage.

Année Jalouse (Fr) a term used to denote a year of greatly varying quality of wine production in Bordeaux.

Annie Green Springs (USA) the brand-name used by United Vintners.

Annie's Lane (Austr) a winery based in the Clare Valley, South Australia. Grape varieties include: Riesling.

Annie's Wine (S.Afr) the label for a noble late harvest wine (Sauvignon blanc and Sémillon blend) produced by the Stony Brook winery, Franschhoek, Western Cape.

Anninger Perle (Aus) a white wine.

Anniversaire Très Ancienne Sélection (Fr) a Cognac produced by Monnet.

Anniversary Ale (Eng) a 4.5% alc by vol. ale brewed by Enville Ales Ltd., West Midlands.

Anniversary Ale (Eng) a 4% alc by vol. seasonal beer brewed by Gale's Brewery, Horndean, Hampshire.

Anniversary Porter (Eng) a 500mls bottled porter brewed by McMullen Brewery, Hertfordshire.

Annoeullin Brasserie [D'] (Fr) a brewery (established 1905) based at Annaoeullin. Brews L'Angelus, Pastor Ale.

Ann Street Brewery (Ch.Isles) a Jersey-based brewery now known as Jersey Brewery, produces beers under the Mary Ann label. Brews Hurlimann Sternbräu and Skol lagers under licence. Took over Bucktrout and C°. including the Guernsey Brewery in Guernsey. *see* Jersey Brewery.

Annual Yield (Fr) a part of the A.C. laws. *see* 'Plafond Limité de Classement'.

Annular-Knopped Glass (Eng) an eighteenth century glass consisting of a flat round based, swollen stem and trumpet bowl.

Año (Sp) year, when seen on wine labels as 4°Año = 4 years before bottled.

Anogydd (Wal) apéritif / cocktail.

Anoia (Sp) a Vino Comarcal wine from the province Barcelona in Cataluña.

Anosmia (Lat) loss of the sense of smell.

Anreichern (Ger) chaptalisation, the improvement of musts by addition of sugar, also known as Anreicherung.

Anreicherung (Ger) *see* Anreichern.

Ansella (S.Afr) the label for a red wine (Cabernet sauvignon 40% and Merlot 60%) produced by the Muratie Estate winery, Stellenbosch, Western Cape.

Ansell's Brewery (Eng) a brewery based in Birmingham with 5 subsidiary companies.

Anselmi (It) a winery based in Monteforte, near Soave, Veneto.

Ansonica (It) a white grape variety used in Sicily and Tuscany. Also known as Inzolia.

Ansprechend (Ger) denotes an attractive engaging wine.

Antabuse (Eng) a drug (registered trade-mark) used to treat alcoholism, induces nausea if alcohol is consumed, contains **Tetraethylthiuram disulphide**.

Antão Vaz (Port) a white grape variety grown in the Alentejo.

Antarctica Paulista Cerveceria (Bra) a brewery based in São Paulo, south-eastern Brazil.

A.N.T.A.V. (Fr) *abbr*: Association Nationale Technique pour l'Amélioration de la Viticulture. A research institute for the improvement of the vine. Based at the Domaine de l'Espiguette, Le Grau du Roi, Gard.

Antea (Sp) a barrel-fermented white wine made from Viura grapes by Marqués de Cáceres, Rioja. *see* Satinela.

Antech [Edmund] (Fr) a producer of A.C. Blanquette de Limoux based at Limoux in southern France.

Ante Cocktail (Cktl) ⅓ measure Calvados, ⅓ measure red Dubonnet, ⅓ measure triple sec. Stir over ice and strain into a cocktail glass.

Antenau (Aus) a vineyard site based on the banks of the River Kamp in the Kamptal region.

A

Ante Prandium (Lat) lit: 'before a meal', an apéritif / cocktail.

Antequera (Sp) a wine-producing district based in north-western Málaga. Grows Pedro Ximénez grapes.

Anthem (Eng) a 3.9% alc by vol. ale brewed by the Facers Brewery, Greater Manchester.

Anthemis (Gre) a natural mineral water from Ira.

AntHill Wines (S.Afr) a winery (established 2000) based in Somerset West, Western Cape. Grape varieties: Chardonnay, Sauvignon blanc. Label: Letermago.

Anthocyanes (Fr) anthocyanins.

Anthocyanins (Eng) blue, red or orange flower or fruit pigments. Water soluble they are extracted during wine and liqueur production. In black grapes it is found in the skins and gives wine its red colour. (Fr) = anthocyanes.

Anthocyanols (Eng) a group of pigments that give the red colour that is extracted from the grape skins by the action of alcohol.

Anthony de Jager Wines (S.Afr) a winery (established 2000) based in the Suider-Paarl, Western Cape. Grape varieties: Shiraz, Viognier. Label: Homtini.

Anthony Smook Wines (S.Afr) a winery (established 2001) based in the Noorder-Paarl, Western Cape. Grape varieties: Cabernet sauvignon, Chardonnay, Merlot, Pinotage, Shiraz. Produces varietal wines. Website: http://www.smookwines.co.za

Anthony's Yard (S.Afr) the label for a red wine (Cabernet sauvignon, Merlot, Cabernet franc blend) produced by the Graham Beck winery, Coastal Region.

Anthoxanthins (Eng) important plant pigments for home-made wine production, responsible for the yellow and orange colour in certain wines. Also known as Flavones.

Anthracnose (Eng) the fungus that appears as stains on vine leaves, shoots and fruit, holes then appear where the stains were. Treated with Bordeaux / Burgundy mixture.

Antialcoolique (Fr) teetotal, See also Tempérance (De).

Antica Casa Vinicola Scarpa (It) a winery based at Nizza Monferrato, Piemonte.

Antica Confraria de Saint-Andu de la Galiniera (Fr) a wine society based in the Hérault département, southern France.

Antica Fonte (It) a natural mineral water from Antica Fonte.

Antica Fonte Rabbi (It) a sparkling natural mineral water from Rabbi, Trento. Mineral contents (milligrammes per litre): Sodium 510mg/l, Calcium 123.4mg/l, Magnesium 44.9mg/l, Potassium 26mg/l, Bicarbonates 1670mg/l, Chlorides 232mg/l, Sulphates 6.8mg/l, Silicates 30.5mg/l. pH 6.1

Antica Fonte Tartaville (It) a natural mineral water from Taceno, Lake Como.

Antica MM (S.Afr) the label for a red wine (Cabernet sauvignon) produced by the Signal Hill winery, Cape Town, Western Cape.

Antica Querica (It) a producer of sparkling (metodo tradizionale) wines based in the Veneto region north-eastern Italy.

Anticipation Cocktail (Cktl) 40mls (⅓ gill) Irish Velvet, scoop vanilla ice cream, blend together in a blender with a little crushed ice, pour in a Champagne flute and top with grated chocolate.

Antico Borgo di Sugame (It) an IGT organic winery based in Greve, Tuscany. Label: Bosco Grosso

Anticuario (Sp) a solera reserva brandy produced in Jerez de la Frontera by Blazquez.

Antier (Fr) an old, established Cognac house who united with Pomeral in 1949 to form the house of Gaston de Lagrange.

Antifogmatic (USA) an early colonial term for a cider or beer consumed early in the morning. See also Phlegm Cutter, Fog Cutter and Eye Opener.

Antigua Coffee (W.Ind) a smooth, mellow and somewhat spicy coffee with a smokey taste and aroma.

Antigua Distillery Ltd (W.Ind) a large rum distillery based in Antigua. Produces light-bodied rums. Is noted for Cavalier Antigua Rum.

Antika (Gre) a dry white wine from Patras, Peloponnese.

Antillano (Cktl) 20mls (⅙ gill) light rum, 20mls (⅙ gill) golden rum, 20mls (⅙ gill) grapefruit juice, 20mls (⅙ gill) pineapple juice, dash Angostura, 1 barspoon of grenadine. Shake over ice, strain into a highball glass with crushed ice. Decorate with pineapple, orange and a glacé cherry and serve with straws.

Antilles Cocktail (Cktl) ⅔ measure Bacardi White Label, ⅓ measure white Dubonnet. Shake well over ice, strain into a cocktail glass and dress with twist of orange peel juice.

Antinori (It) a noted Florence wine family who produce Chianti and Orvieto.

Anti-Oxidant (Eng) the name given to any chemical that stops wine musts from oxidising. see Ascorbic Acid.

Antipodean [The] (Austr) a winery at Tongue Farm Road, P.O. Box 5, Mata Kana. 1.8ha. Grape varieties: Cabernet sauvignon, Malbec, Merlot, Shiraz, Sauvignon blanc, Sémillon.

Antipodes Mineral Water (N.Z) a natural mineral water from the Rotoma Hills.

Antiqua (Sp) a brandy produced by the Caves Alicança.

Antiquary [The] (Scot) a blended de luxe Scotch whisky first produced by J. And W. Blackworth Hardie. Marketed by William Sanderson and Son Ltd. 12 year old at 40% alc by vol. and a 21 year old 43% alc by vol.

Antique (Fr) a class for fine old Cognac. see Hine Antique.

Antique (Scot) a brand of de luxe blended Scotch whisky from Hiram Walker. 40% alc by vol.

Antique (USA) the brand-name of a 6 y.o. Kentucky Bourbon whiskey. Distilled by Frankfort Distilling C°., Athertonville, Kentucky 40% alc by vol.

Antiquíssima (Port) on a label denotes 'very old'.

Antis Wines (Arg) a winery based in the Mendoza region, eastern Argentina. Website: http://www.antiswines.com 'E'mail: info@antiswines.com

Antler Bitter (Eng) a cask-conditioned and keg bitter brewed by Watney Mann.

Antonin (Fr) a natural mineral water. Mineral contents (milligrammes per litre): Sodium 350mg/l, Calcium 220mg/l, Magnesium 70mg/l, Potassium 46mg/l, Bicarbonates 2000mg/l, Chlorides 21mg/l, Sulphates 6mg/l, Fluoride 2.45mg/l. pH 6.5

Antoine Cocktail (Cktl) ⅔ measure vodka, ⅓ measure lime juice, 2 dashes crème de cassis. Stir over ice, strain into an ice-filled highball. Top with orange juice and slice of orange.

Antoine Special (Cktl) ½ measure Dubonnet, ½ measure French vermouth, float vermouth on the top of the iced Dubonnet in a 125mls (5fl.oz) paris goblet.

Antoine's Smile (Cktl) 35mls (1½ fl.ozs) Calvados, 10mls (½ fl.oz) lemon juice, 10mls (½ fl.oz) gomme syrup. Shake over ice and strain into a cocktail glass.

Antoinette (Fr) a dry cider apple grown in the Normandy region, used to produce dry French ciders.

Antonello San Marco (It) a winery in the DOCG Sagrantino di Montefalco, Umbria region.

Antonio (Cktl) ⅓ measure brandy, ⅓ measure dry gin, ⅙ measure maraschino, ⅙ measure (white) crème de menthe, shake well over ice and strain into a cocktail glass.

Antonio Barbadillo (Sp) a noted Sherry bodega based in Sanlúcar de Barrameda, Andalusia.

Antoniolo (It) a major producer of Gattinara wine in northern Piemonte.

Antonius Abt (Ger) a 6% alc by vol. straw, bottle-conditioned, special beer from Liempds Gildenbier. Brewed by De 3 Horne Bier Brouwerij, Kaatsheuvel.

Antoniusberg (Ger) vineyard (Anb): Mosel-Saar-Ruwer. (Ber): Saar-Ruwer. (Gro): Scharzberg. (Vil): Serrig.

Antoniusbrunnen (Ger) vineyard (Anb): Mosel-Saar-Ruwer. (Ber): Saar-Ruwer. (Gro): Scharzberg. (Vil): Saarburg.

Antonius-Quelle (Ger) a natural mineral water from Warburg-Germete, NW.

Anton Lindner (It) a small, private winery based in Eppan, Südtirol (South Tyrol).

Antonopoulos Vineyards (Gre) a winery based at Vassiliko, Peloponneses. Grape varieties: Lagorthi, Chardonnay. Produces Adoli Ghis (a dry white table wine).

Antrim Hills (Ire) a natural mineral water from Ballyclare, Northern Ireland. Mineral contents (milligrammes per litre): Sodium 12mg/l.

Ants in the Pants (Cktl) ½ measure gin, ¼ measure sweet vermouth, ¼ measure Grand Marnier, dash lemon juice. Shake over ice, strain into a cocktail glass and dress with a lemon peel spiral.

Antunes [Luiz] & Cia (Bra) one of brazil's leading wine-producing companies.

Antuzzi's Winery (USA) a large winery based in Delran, New Jersey.

Antwerp Brasserie (Bel) a brewery based in northern Belgium. Noted for top-fermented draught Ales.

Anubis (Arg) the label for a range of wines (white, rosé and red) produced by the Dominio del Plata winery in the Mendoza region.

Anura Vineyards (S.Afr) a winery (established 2001) based in the Klapmuts, Paarl, Western Cape. Grape varieties: Cabernet sauvignon, Chardonnay, Chenin blanc, Malbec, Merlot, Mourvèdre, Pinotage, Sangiovese, Shiraz, Syrah, Viognier. Labels: Frog Hill and varietal wines. 118ha. Website: http://www.anura.co.za

Anvil (S.Afr) the label (discontinued) for a range of wines for the Franschhoek Vineyards, Western Cape.

Anvil Smooth (Eng) a 4% alc by vol. beer brewed by Hydes Brewery.

Anvil Strong Ale (Eng) a dark winter beer brewed by Hyde's Brewery of Manchester.

Anwilka (S.Afr) a winery (established 1997) based in the Helderberg, Stellenbosch, Western Cape. Grape varieties: Cabernet sauvignon, Merlot, Shiraz. A joint venture between Château l'Angelus (Saint-Émilion) and Bruno Prats. 40ha.

A° (Sp) *abbr*: Año (year).

A.O.C. (Fr) *abbr*: Appellation d'Origine Contrôlée. *see* Appellation Contrôlée.

A.O.G. (Afr) *abbr*: Appellation d'Origin Garantie. The Moroccan wine quality grade which is only given to a wine if it meets very high standards (12% alc by vol. recognised vines, etc).

A.1 (Cktl) ⅔ measure dry gin, ⅓ measure Grand Marnier, 1 dash lemon juice, 1 dash grenadine. Shake well over ice, strain into a cocktail glass and dress with a spiral of lemon peel.

A1 Amber Ale (Eng) a 4% alc by vol. ale brewed by Rockingham Ales, Cambridgeshire.

A.O.Q.S. (Gre) *abbr*: Appellation d'Origine de Qualité Supérieur. Designation used for light wines.

A.O.V.D.Q.S. (Fr) *abbr*: Appellation d'Origine de Vins Délimité Qualité Supérieur. The full designation for V.D.Q.S.

Apagado (Sp) a term used to describe a Sherry with a weak bouquet.

Apaleador (Sp) the name given to the pole used to stir the wine during the fining process.

Apalta Vineyard (Chile) a vineyard in the DO Colchagua Valley, a part of the Montes Estates. Grape variety: Syrah.

Apani (USA) a mineral water (established 1997) from the state of Texas.

A.P.B. (Eng) *abbr*: A Pint of Bitter 3.5 % alc by vol. canned bitter from Hogs Back Brewery, Tongham, Surrey.

APCOR (Port) *abbr*: Association Portuguese Cork.

Apczer (Hun) the brand-name of a white table wine.

Apeach (Swe) a peach-flavoured vodka produced by Absolut Spirits.

Apennines (It) a mountain range (volcanic) separating the regions of Emilia-Romagna in the east and Toscana in the west.

Apenta (Hun) a sparkling natural mineral water from Budapest. Mineral contents (milligrammes per litre): Sodium 280mg/l, Calcium 197mg/l, Magnesium 55mg/l, Bicarbonates 600mg/l, Chlorides 250mg/l, Sulphates 440mg/l, Fluorides 2.2mg/l.

Aperient Waters (Eng) mineral waters that have high saline constituents mainly sulphate of magnesia and sulphate of soda. e.g. Cheltenham, Leamington Spa, Montmirail, Seidlity.

Aperire (Lat) lit: 'to open', where the term apéritif originates from.

Aperital Delor (Fr) a fortified apéritif wine from Delor.

Apéritif (Fr) a pre-meal drink / cocktail to encourage the gastric juices to flow, can be a commercially made product or a mixed drink. e.g. Fino Sherry or a dry martini. (It) = aperitivo, (Rus) = apyereeteef, (Wal) = anogydd.

Apéritif Grill (Cktl) ⅓ measure (white) crème de menthe, ⅓ measure Fernet Branca, ⅓ measure sweet vermouth, pour gently into a cocktail glass in order, do not stir. A '*pick-me-up*'.

Apéritif Perrier (Cktl) 20mls (⅙ gill) gin, 20mls (⅙ gill) Noilly Prat, 2 dashes Rose's lime juice. Shake over ice, strain into a large goblet with 2 ice cubes, add Perrier water and decorate with cucumber peel.

Apéritif Port (Port) a white Port in which the sugar has been fermented out, it is the driest Port possible.

Aperitivo (Fr) a low-alcohol bitters and herb flavoured drink, is less than 1% alc by vol. *see* Kattell Roc.

Aperitivo (It) aperitif.

Aperitivo (Port) a wine used as an apéritif.

Aperitivo Rosso (It) the brand-name of an apéritif.

Aperol Aperitivo (It) a bitter apéritif, orange coloured and flavoured, based on fruits and herbs 11% alc by vol.

Apestoso (Sp) a term used to describe a Sherry that has an unpleasant smell and taste.

Apetlon (Aus) a wine village in Burgenland, noted for medium-sweet and sweet white wines which are produced on sandy soils.

A.P.E.V.V. (Port) *abbr:* **A**ssociacão dos **P**rodutores-**E**ngarrafadores de **V**inho **V**erde.

Apfelsaft (Ger) a non-alcoholic apple juice.

Apfelsinlikoer (Ger) a brandy-based orange liqueur.

Apfelwein (Ger) cider.

Aphrodes (Gre) sparkling.

Aphrodis (Fr) the brand-name of an A.C. Muscat de Rivesaltes, a V.d.N. in Roussillon, south-western France. (Add): SIVIR Route des Crêtes, 66650 Banyuls-sur-Mer.

Aphrodisiac (Cktl) heat 125mls (5fl.ozs) Port wine with a dash of curaçao until nearly boiling. Pour into a warmed, heat-proof glass. Dress with grated nutmeg and a slice of lemon.

Aphrodite (Cyp) a dry white wine produced by Keo in Limassol.

Apiarist's Delight (Eng) a 4.6% alc by vol. cask-conditioned honey ale brewed by Flounder and Firkin.

Apiculate (Eng) lemon-shaped, the word is used to describe the shape of wild yeasts found in the bloom on grape skins.

A Pint of Bitter (Eng) *see* A.P.B.

Apitiv (Port) the brand-name of a dry white Port and Sherry from Sandeman.

Aplostra (Cyp) the name for the mats used to dry the grapes for the production of fortified wines.

A.P. N° (Ger) *abbr:* **A**mtliche **P**rüfungsnummer.

Apoferment (Eng) the start of fermentation.

À Point (Fr) lit: 'just right', a term when used for wines denotes that they have reached perfection and are ready to drink.

Apollinaris (Ger) a naturally sparkling spring water (established 1853) from the Ahr Valley at Bad Neuerahr-Ahrweiler, RP. (high gas: yellow label / low gas: blue label / still: whijte label). Mineral contents (milligrammes per litre): Sodium 410mg/l, Calcium 100mg/l, Magnesium 130mg/l, Potassium 20mg/l, Bicarbonates 1810mg/l, Chlorides 100mg/l, Sulphates 80mg/l. Website: http://www.apollinaris.de

Apoplexy (Eng) a vine disease known as Esca (a cryptogamic disease). The name derives from the way the vine dies.

Apostelberg (Ger) vineyard (Anb): Nahe. (Ber): Kreuznach. (Gro): Schlosskapelle. (Vil): Guldental.

Apostelgarten (Ger) vineyard (Anb): Franken. (Ber): Mainviereck. (Gro): Not yet assigned. (Vil): Michelbach.

Apostelhoeve (Hol) a vineyard owner and merchant based at Louwberg, Maastricht produces white wine from the Riesling grape variety. Website: http://www.apostelhoeve.nl

Apostles (Ger) the name for twelve large casks of old Rhine wine kept in cellars in Bremen.

Apostles Falls Vineyard (S.Afr) a vineyard based in Stellenbosch. Grape variety: Chardonnay.

Apostoles (Sp) a Palo Cortado Sherry produced by Gonzales Byass in Jerez de la Frontera, Cadiz. Aged for 30 years. Part of their Rare Old Solera range.

Apostrophe Special 2000 (Cktl) $^{2}/_{10}$ measure Mandarine Napoléon, $^{2}/_{10}$ measure curaçao (orange), $^{3}/_{10}$ measure gin, $^{3}/_{10}$ measure dry vermouth. Shake well over ice, strain into a cocktail glass.

Apotheca (Lat) wine-cellar.

Apothecary Brandy (USA) the name given to a brandy sold in an apothecary-style jar that is produced by Paul Masson, California.

Apotheke (Ger) vineyard (Anb): Mosel-Saar-Ruwer. (Ber): Bernkastel. (Gro): Michelsberg. (Vil): Trittenheim.

Appalachian Spring Water (USA) a natural spring water from Suches, Georgia.

A

Appassimento (It) lit: 'air-drying', a term given to describe the fermentation of the air-dried grapes (30% to 35% water loss) used in Valpolicella Amarone and Recioto.

Appassire (It) the hanging of bunches of grapes to dry over the winter in the Abruzzi region to make dessert wines.

Appeal (Eng) a 4.5% alc by vol. beer brewed by the Edale Brewery C°. Derbyshire.

Appelsinjuice (Den) orange juice.

Appelsinvand (Den) orangeade.

Appella (Den) a peach and apple drink that is unsweetened.

Appellation (Fr) the identifying name or title. see A.C.

Appellation Calvados Contrôlée (Fr) the top classification of Calvados produced within the Pays d'Auge in Normandy. See also Appellation Calvados Réglementée, Appellation Réglementée.

Appellation Calvados Réglementée (Fr) a classification of Calvados in Normandy other than the top A.C. Calvados of the Pays d'Auge.

Appellation Communale (Fr) top appellations of the Premier and Grand Crus of Burgundy.

Appellation Complète (Lux) fine wine category. Label must indicate the grape variety, locality, vineyard site, name of grower and his domicile, vintage year and must complete a testing. See also Marque Nationale.

Appellation Contrôlée (Fr) a French law to protect names, improve the quality (rules on grape types, viticultural, vinicultural, harvesting, etc.) and limit production of wines from demarcated districts. Guarantees the name on label and the contents of container.

Appellation d'Origine (Fr) see Appellation Contrôlée.

Appellation d'Origine Contrôlée (Fr) abbr: A.O.C. see Appellation Contrôlée.

Appellation d'Origine Contrôlée (Gre) abbr: A.O.C. Used for liqueur wines. A.O.Q.S. is used for light wines. T.A. is used for Retsina.

Appellation d'Origine de Qualité Supérieur (Gre) abbr: A.O.Q.S. A designation used for light wines. A.O.C. is used for liqueur wines, T.A. for Retsina.

Appellation Régionale (Fr) a lesser appellation which often produces cheap, poor quality wines.

Appellation Réglementée (Fr) abbr: A.R. Spirituous equivalent of V.D.Q.S. See Appellation Calvados Réglementée.

Appellation Simple (Fr) pre 1935 designation for wine of quality. See also A.C.

Appeltofftska Brewery (Swe) a brewery based in Halmstead, southern Sweden. One of the country's smallest.

Appelwijn (Hol) cider.

Äppelwoi (Ger) the name used in the Frankfurt area for applewine.

Appendicitis (Cktl) ⅔ measure dry gin, ⅙ measure lemon juice, ⅙ measure Cointreau, 1 egg. Shake well over ice, strain into a cocktail glass.

Appenheim (Ger) village (Anb): Rheinhessen. (Ber): Bingen. (Gro): Abtel. (Vins): Daubhaus, Drosselborn, Eselpfad, Hundertgulden.

A.P.P.E.R.A.M. (W.Ind) abbr: Association Professionnelle des Producteurs Embouteilleurs de Rhum Agricole de la Martinique. An organisation formed to represent the interests of bottled rum producers on the island of Martinique.

Appetiser (USA) see Appetizer.

Appetizer (Eng) a small amount of drink (or food) consumed to stimulate the appetite. See Apéritif. Also spelt Appetiser.

Appetizer Wines (USA) apéritif wines, vermouths, etc.

Appia (It) a sparkling natural mineral water from Appia. Mineral contents (milligrammes per litre): Sodium 52.2mg/l, Calcium 110.2mg/l, Magnesium 21.65mg/l, Potassium 66.3mg/l, Bicarbonates 802mg/l, Chlorides 33.75mg/l, Sulphates 43.9mg/l, Fluorides 1.05mg/l, Nitrates 33.7mg/l, Silicates 96.2mg/l.

Appleade (Eng) pour 500mls (1 pint) of boiling water over 3 sliced apples, stand for 15 minutes, strain, add sugar to taste. Serve hot or cold.

Appleback (Eng) a vodka, apple juice and ginger ale bottled drink produced by Smirnoff Vodka.

Apple Blight (Eng) Eriosoma lanigera an insect (aphid) that infests apple trees with a waxy, powdery secretion, also called American blight.

Apple Blossom Cocktail (Cktl) ½ measure Calvados, ½ measure Italian vermouth. Shake over ice and strain into a cocktail glass.

Apple Blow Fizz (Cktl) 60mls (½ gill) Calvados, juice ½ lemon, 1 egg white, 1 teaspoon powdered sugar. Shake well over ice, strain into an ice-filled highball glass and top with soda water.

Apple Brandy (Eng) spirit distilled from cider. (Fr) = calvados, (Ire) = biotáille úll, (USA) = applejack.

Apple Brandy Cocktail (Cktl) 1 measure applejack brandy, 1 teaspoon lemon juice, 4 dashes grenadine. Shake over ice and strain into a cocktail glass.

Apple Brandy Highball (Cktl) place 25mls (⅛ gill) of Calvados into an ice-filled highball glass. Top with soda water, stir and dress with a spiral of lemon peel.

Applecar Cocktail (Cktl) ⅓ measure apple brandy, ⅓ measure Triple Sec, ⅓ measure lemon juice. Shake over ice and strain into a cocktail glass.

Apple Cocktail (Cktl) ⅓ measure Calvados, ⅓ measure sweet cider, ⅙ measure dry gin, ⅙ measure brandy. Shake over plenty of ice and strain into a large glass.

Apple Cooler (Cktl)(Non-alc) place 300mls (½ pint) apple tea, juice of a lemon, 300mls (½ pint) lemonade and 25mls (1fl.oz) gomme syrup into an ice-filled jug. Stir, dress with apple slices and serve in ice-filled highball glasses.

Appledore (Eng) a white cider produced by Inch's, Winkleigh, Devon

Apple Gin (Scot) a colourless liqueur compounded in Leith. 40% alc by vol.

Apple Jack (USA) the American (New England) name for apple brandy, the distillation from cider. (Fr) = calvados, (Den) = æblebrændevin.

Apple Jack Cocktail (Cktl) 60mls (½ gill) apple jack brandy, 2 dashes gum syrup, 2 dashes Angostura. Stir over ice, strain into a cocktail glass, add an olive and squeeze of lemon peel juice.

Apple Jack Highball (Cktl) 1 measure apple brandy placed into an ice-filled highball glass. Top with ginger ale and a twist of lemon peel juice, stir.

Apple Jack Punch (Cktl) 1 bottle apple brandy, 75mls (3fl.ozs) grenadine, 500mls (1 pint) orange juice. Mix all well together in a punch bowl with ice. Add 800mls (1½ pints) ginger ale and apple slices.

Apple Jack Rabbit [1] (Cktl) 35mls (1½ fl.ozs) Calvados, juice ½ lemon, juice ½ orange, teaspoon grenadine. Shake over ice and strain into a cocktail glass.

Apple Jack Rabbit [2] (Cktl) ⅗ measure applejack brandy, ⅕ measure lemon juice, ⅕ measure orange juice, 10mls (½ fl.oz) maple syrup. Shake well over ice, strain into a sugared old-fashioned glass (with the maple syrup), add 2 ice cubes.

Apple Jack Rickey (Cktl) 1 measure apple brandy, juice ½ lime. Place together in an ice-filled highball glass, top with soda, stir and add a slice of lime.

Apple Jack Sling (Cktl) *see* Hot Apple Jack Sling.

Apple Jack Sour (Cktl) 1 measure apple brandy, ½ teaspoon powdered sugar, juice ½ lemon. Shake over ice, strain into sour glass, dress with a cherry and a slice of lemon.

Applejack Trading Company (Eng) a drinks manufacturer. (Add): Diplomat House, 3, High Road, Eastcote, Pinner, Middlesex HA5 2EW. Produces avariety of alcoholic beverages including cider, liqueurs, spirits and wines. Website: http://www.applejacktradingcompany.co.uk 'E'mail: sales@applejacktradingcompany.co.uk

Apple Juice (Eng) a non-alcoholic drink produced from crushed, sweet dessert apples. (Den) = æblemost.

Apple Marc (Fr) apple pomace pulp after the juice has been extracted.

Apple Mill (Eng) used to cut up the apples before pressing for cider.

Applemony (W.Ind) the nickname for a blend of Appleton Estate Rum and Monymusk Rum in Jamaica.

Apple of Paradise (W.Ind) a liqueur made from local fruit on the island of Cuba.

Apple Pie Cocktail (Cktl) ½ measure white rum, ½ measure sweet vermouth, 2 dashes grenadine, 4 dashes brandy, 4 dashes lemon juice. Shake over ice and strain into a cocktail glass.

Apple Rum Punch (Punch) 6 oranges studded with cloves, bake in hot oven until brown. Add to a Punch bowl containing 1 bottle rum, ½ bottle brandy, 4 tablespoons sugar, stir and then flame. Extinguish with 3 bottles apple juice. Sprinkle with ground cinnamon and nutmeg. Serve warm.

Apple Rum Rickey (Cktl) 1 part apple brandy, 1 part rum, 4 dashes lime juice, place rum and brandy into an ice-filled highball glass, top with soda water, stir and add lime juice on top.

Apple Schnapps (Sp) an apple-flavoured liqueur produced by Larios.

Apple Spark (Eng) the original name for a sparkling apple drink from the Merrydown C°. Now known as Sparkling Apple Juice.

Apple Splitz (USA) a sparkling cooler made from white wine and apple juice. 1.2% alc by vol.

Appletini (Cktl) 40mls Wyborowa Apple, 20mls dry vermouth, stir over ice, strain into a chilled martini glass with a twist of green apple peel.

Appletise (Eng) a non-alcoholic, carbonated apple drink from Schweppes.

Apple Toddy (Cktl) bake an apple, peel, place piece of apple in an old-fashioned glass (or toddy glass), add a cube of sugar, slice of lemon, 40mls (⅓ gill) Calvados, top with boiling water and stir with stick of cinnamon.

Appleton (W.Ind) the brand-name of a white rum produced in Jamaica. Is produced by Wray & Nephew. Sold in the U.K. by the United Rum Merchants. 40% alc by vol. Brands include Appleton Estate Special (5 y.o.), Appleton Estate V/X, Appleton White Overproof, Appleton Gold and Appleton White Classic.

Appleton Estate Distillery (W.Ind) a large rum distillery based in the Black River Valley, Jamaica. Produces white and dark rums.

Appleton Estate Special (W.Ind) a 40% alc by vol. rum produced by Wray & Nephew. *See also* Appleton Estate V/X, Appleton White Overproof.

Appleton Estate V/X (W.Ind) an 80% alc by vol. rum produced by Wray & Nephew. *See also* Appleton Estate Special, Appleton White Overproof.

Appleton White Overproof (W.Ind) a 62% alc by vol. rum produced by Wray & Nephew. *See also* Appleton Estate Special, Appleton Estate V/X.

Applewood (Eng) a 3% alc by vol. bottled cider produced by the Taunton Cider C°. Ltd., North Fitzwarren, Somerset.

Appley (Eng) the term to describe young white wines where the malic acidity evokes a raw apple smell and tart flavour.

Appollonia (S.Afr) the label for a white wine produced by the Saxenberg winery, Stellenbosch, Western Cape.

Approved Viticultural Area (USA) *see* American Viticultural Area, A.V.A.

Apre (Fr) harsh or sharp, excess tannin.

Apremont (Fr) a white wine of Savoie, eastern France.

Apprentice (Eng) a 3.8% alc by vol. beer brewed by the Wizard Brewery, Warwickshire.

Après Ski Cocktail (Cktl) ⅓ measure pastis, ⅓ measure (white) crème de menthe, ⅓ measure vodka. Shake over ice, strain into an ice-filled highball glass. Top with soda water and dress with mint and a lemon slice and serve with straws.

Apricot Anise Collins (Cktl) 1 measure dry gin, 1 measure anisette, ⅓ measure apricot brandy, 4 dashes lemon juice. Shake over ice, strain into a collins glass, top with soda, add 2 ice cubes and a slice of lemon.

Apricot Brandy (Eng) a liqueur made by maceration of fruit in base spirit, then re-distilling. 20%–35% alc by vol. *see* Barack Pàlinka.

Apricot Brandy Cooler (Cktl) place 2 skinned fresh apricots, 40mls (⅓ gill) apricot brandy, 20mls (⅙ gill) gomme syrup and juice of a lemon into a blender with a scoop of crushed ice and pour into a flute glass.

Apricot Cocktail (Cktl) 1 part apricot brandy, 2–3 parts dry gin, 4 dashes orange juice, 4 dashes lemon juice. Shake over ice and strain into a cocktail glass.

Apricot Cooler (Cktl) 1 liqueur glass apricot brandy, 2 dashes of grenadine, dash Angostura, juice of lemon or lime. Shake over ice (except bitters). Strain into a highball glass, top up with soda water add bitters and a spiral of lemon peel.

Apricot Daiquiri (Cktl) ½ measure white rum, ½ measure lemon juice, ¼ measure apricot brandy, 2 skinned and stoned apricots, scoop of crushed ice. Blend well together in a blender, pour into a Champagne saucer, dress with an apricot slice and mint sprig.

Apricot d'Anjou (Fr) an apricot brandy produced by Jacques Giffard in Angers, Loire.

Apricot Fizz (Cktl) 1 measure apricot brandy, 1 teaspoon powdered sugar, juice ½ lemon and ½ lime. Shake over ice, strain into an ice-filled highball glass and top with soda.

Apricot Flavoured Brandy (USA) a brandy-based liqueur infused with apricots.

Apricot Gin (Eng) a liqueur gin produced by Hawker's of Plymouth, Devon.

Apricot Lady (Cktl) 25mls (1fl.oz) apricot brandy, 25mls (1fl.oz) golden rum, 10mls (½fl.oz) lime juice, 3 dashes orange Curaçao, 2 dashes egg white. Blend with ½ scoop crushed ice and pour into small wine glass.

Apricot Liqueur (USA) also known as Apry, Abricotine, a liqueur made by the maceration technique.

Apricot Nog (Cktl) ⅓ measure Bacardi White Label, ⅙ measure apricot brandy, ⅙ measure apricot juice, 3 dashes cream. Blend with scoop of crushed ice, pour into a collins glass.

Apricot Sour (Cktl) 25mls (1fl.oz) apricot brandy, 50mls (2fl.ozs) lemon juice, dash Angostura, dash gomme syrup, dash egg white. Shake over ice, strain into a Champagne flute and add a wedge of apricot.

Aprikose mit Whisky (Ger) *see* Kirsch mit Whisky.

Aprikosengeist (Ger) a brandy-based liqueur flavoured with apricots.

Aprilia (It) a D.O.C. red and white wines from Lazio. Red wines produced from Merlot, Montepulciano and Sangiovese grapes. White wines from Trebbiano grapes.

Aprilskloof (S.Afr) the label for a wine range (red, rosé and white) produced by the Lammershoek Winery, Swartland, Western Cape.

Aproz (Switz) a still and sparkling natural mineral water from Aproz (high gas: blue label / low gas:

green label / still: red label). Mineral contents (milligrammes per litre): Sodium 5mg/l, Calcium 365mg/l, Magnesium 65mg/l, Potassium 2.5mg/l, Bicarbonates 255mg/l, Chlorides 14mg/l, Sulphates 910mg/l, Nitrates 2mg/l, Silicates 3mg/l.

Apry (Fr) a tawny-coloured liqueur made of apricots soaked in sweetened brandy.

Apsinthion (Gre) wormwood, from which absinthe derives.

Apulia (It) the heel of Italy's '*boot*', the region produces such wines as Bombino, Barletta, D.O.C. Castel del Monte, Guilia, D.O.C. Locorotondo, Martina Franca, Santo Stefano, D.O.C. San Severo, D.O.C. Squinzano. Region is also known as Puglia.

Apyelseenaviy Sok (Rus) orange juice.

Apyereeteef (Rus) apéritif.

AQA (Switz) a still mineral water from St. Erhard, LU. Mineral contents (milligrammes per litre): Sodium 7.3mg/l, Calcium 130mg/l, Magnesium 25mg/l, Potassium 2.1mg/l, Bicarbonates 470mg/l, Chlorides 12mg/l, Sulphates 18mg/l, Fluorides <0.1mg/l, Silicates 3mg/l. Website: http://www.aqa.ch

Aqua (Can) a 5.5% alc by vol. range of flavoured bottled schnapps produced by Archers. Flavours include lime, cranberry, peach and orange. *See also* Peach County Schnapps.

Aqua (Egy) a natural mineral water from El Sadat City. Mineral contents (milligrammes per litre): Sodium 38mg/l, Calcium 30.4mg/l, Magnesium 12.96mg/l, Potassium 3.5mg/l, Bicarbonates 195.2mg/l, Chlorides 24mg/l, Sulphates 15mg/l, Silicates 28mg/l.

Aqua (Indo) a natural mineral water from Pandaan. Mineral contents (milligrammes per litre): Sodium 18.9mg/l, Calcium 35mg/l, Magnesium 14.6mg/l, Bicarbonates 140mg/l, Chlorides 23mg/l, Sulphates 40mg/l. pH 7.1

Aqua Africa (S.Afr) a natural mineral water. Mineral contents (milligrammes per litre): Sodium 17mg/l, Calcium 7mg/l, Magnesium 2mg/l, Potassium 1mg/l, Chlorides 5mg/l, Sulphates <5mg/l, Fluorides 0.5mg/l, Nitrates 2mg/l. pH 7.6

Aqua Antonia (Czec) a natural mineral water (established 1856) from Marienbad. Mineral contents (milligrammes per litre): Sodium 5mg/l, Calcium 36.69mg/l, Magnesium 236.3mg/l, Potassium 2.04mg/l, Bicarbonates 1292mg/l, Chlorides 3.95mg/l, Sulphates 25mg/l, Fluorides 0.134mg/l, Silicates 71.1mg/l.

Aqua Ardens (Lat) fiery spirit, raw spirit.

Aqua Austria (Aus) a natural mineral water.

Aqua Bella (Czec) a still natural mineral water from Trebonska. Mineral contents (milligrammes per litre): Sodium 5.65mg/l, Calcium 21.2mg/l, Magnesium 1.96mg/l, Chlorides 12mg/l, Sulphates 16mg/l, Nitrates 10.1mg/l.

Aqua Bella (S.Afr) a sparkling mineral water from Paarl, Western Cape. Mineral contents (milligrammes per litre): Sodium 0.14mg/l,

Calcium 2mg/l, Magnesium 0.8mg/l, Chlorides 12.7mg/l, Sulphates 1.4mg/l, Nitrates 2.7mg/l. pH 4.8

Aqua Bianca (It) an acquette using silver leaf. *see* Silver Acquette. (Fr) = acquette d'argent.

Aqua Bros (Pol) a natural mineral water from Szczecin.

Aqua Clara (Jap) a natural mineral water. Mineral contents (milligrammes per litre): Sodium 5mg/l, Calcium 9.8mg/l, Magnesium 1.2mg/l, Potassium 1.7mg/l. pH 7.3

Aqua Classique (S.Afr) a still bottled natural mineral water. (Add): Witkoppen Road, Midrand, P.O.Box 328 Saxonwold 2131. Mineral contents (milligrammes per litre): Sodium 36mg/l, Calcium 2mg/l, Magnesium o.8mg/l, Chlorides 12.7mg/l, Sulphates 32mg/l, Nitrates 0.5mg/l, Fluoride 0.28mg/l. pH 7.2 Website: http://www.minerale.co.za

Aqua de Teror (Sp) a natural mineral water (established 1916).

Aqua de Valtorre (Sp) a natural mineral water. Mineral contents (milligrammes per litre): Sodium 30.5mg/l, Calcium 25.6mg/l, Magnesium 23.6mg/l, Bicarbonates 191mg/l, Chlorides 39.7mg/l, Nitrates 4mg/l.

Aqua Diamant (Czec) a natural mineral water from K'r'ny. Mineral contents (milligrammes per litre): Sodium 23.5mg/l, Calcium 42.1mg/l, Magnesium 10.9mg/l, Chlorides 21.5mg/l, Sulphates 52.2mg/l, Nitrates 1.2mg/l.

Aquadiente (Mex) a liqueur made from the Maquey aloe. Distilled from Pulque.

Aqua d'Or (Den) a still natural mineral water from Kilden. Mineral contents (milligrammes per litre): Sodium 14.9mg/l, Magnesium 6mg/l, Potassium 1.2mg/l, Bicarbonates 71mg/l, Chlorides 16.5mg/l, Sulphates 11mg/l, Nitrates <2.2mg/l. pH 7.6

Aqua d'Or (S.Afr) a slightly acidic natural mineral water from Paarl, Winelands. Mineral contents (milligrammes per litre): Sodium 8mg/l, Calcium 0.6mg/l, Magnesium 0.8mg/l, Potassium 0.3mg/l, Chlorides 12.7mg/l, Sulphates 1.4mg/l, Fluorides 0.06mg/l. pH 4.8

Aqua d'Oro (It) a version of the German Goldwasser. *see* Gold Acquette. (Fr) = acquette d'or.

Aquae Arnementiae (Eng) the Roman name for the Buxton Spring Water spring in the Peak district, Derbyshire.

Aqua Fennica (Fin) a natural mineral water from Tuomijoja. Mineral contents (milligrammes per litre): Sodium 3.7mg/l, Calcium 3.5mg/l, Magnesium 1.4mg/l, Potassium 0.4mg/l, Bicarbonates 23.5mg/l, Chlorides 1mg/l, Sulphates 1.1mg/l, Fluorides 0.04mg/l, Nitrates 0.1mg/l. pH 6.7

Aquafina (Can) a natural mineral water from the Lac St. Charles, Québec. Mineral contents (milligrammes per litre): Sodium 11mg/l, Calcium 35mg/l, Magnesium 22mg/l, Potassium 4mg/l, Bicarbonates 46mg/l, Chlorides 71mg/l, Sulphates 8mg/l. pH 7.0

Aqua Fontis (It) a natural mineral water from Montegrosso. Mineral contents (milligrammes per litre): Sodium 2.1mg/l, Calcium 56mg/l, Magnesium 8mg/l, Potassium 0.4mg/l, Bicarbonates 185mg/l, Chlorides 1mg/l, Sulphates 22mg/l, Nitrates 2.5mg/l, Silicates 4.5mg/l. ph 7.99

Aqua Hundred (Austr) a natural mineral water. Mineral contents (milligrammes per litre): Calcium 25mg/l, Magnesium 10mg/l, Chlorides 5mg/l. pH 7.4

Aqua Laura (It) a still natural mineral water from San Francesco, Casino al Piano. Mineral contents (milligrammes per litre): Sodium 3.8mg/l, Calcium 35.6mg/l, Magnesium 4.9mg/l, Potassium 0.8mg/l, Bicarbonates 135.5mg/l, Chlorides 1.4mg/l, Sulphates 1.2mg/l, Nitrates 4.8mg/l, Silicates 14.3mg/l. pH 8.0

Aqua Leggera (Rom) a slightly sparkling mineral water from the F8 Spring, Biborteni. Mineral contents (milligrammes per litre): Sodium 102mg/l, Calcium 270.7mg/l, Magnesium 84mg/l, Potassium 7.2mg/l, Chlorides 95mg/l, Sulphates 12.34mg/l. pH 6.0

Aqua Libra (Eng) a brand-name for a natural herbal fruit drink made from a Swiss recipe. Contains alkaline forming ingredients to help balance the body's acidity. Low in calories.

Aqualine (Aus) a natural mineral water. Mineral contents (milligrammes per litre): Calcium 243.69mg/l, Magnesium 37.21mg/l, Nitrates 2mg/l, Fluorides 0.16mg/l.

Aqualite (Ken) a natural mineral water.

Aqua Luna (Ger) a natural mineral water from Bad Leonhardspfunzen, Rosenheim. Mineral contents (milligrammes per litre): Sodium 7.3mg/l, Calcium 109mg/l, Magnesium 27mg/l, Potassium 1.6mg/l, Bicarbonates 435mg/l, Chlorides 18.1mg/l, Sulphates 14.8mg/l, Nitrates <0.05mg/l, Silicates 14.2mg/l. pH 7.44

Aqua Maria (Czec) a still and sparkling natural mineral water from BJ6 Mariánské Láznì. Mineral contents (milligrammes per litre): Sodium 22.!6mg/l, Calcium 25.49mg/l, Magnesium 15.64mg/l, Potassium 2.827mg/l, Bicarbonates 99.42mg/l, Chlorides 36.8mg/l, Sulphates 47.92mg/l, Fluorides 0.115mg/l, Nitrates 1.21mg/l, Silicates 34.5mg/l.

Aqua Mater (Ven) a natural mineral water from Los Teques.

Aqua Mathias (Hun) a natural mineral water from Székesfehérvár. Mineral contents (milligrammes per litre): Sodium 79mg/l, Calcium 228mg/l, Magnesium 58mg/l, Potassium 4.4mg/l, Bicarbonates 1160mg/l, Chlorides 5mg/l, Sulphates 29mg/l, Fluorides 0.1mg/l, Silicates 46mg/l.

Aquamine (S.Afr) a still (blue label) and sparkling (green label) natural mineral water (established 1988) from the Cradle of Humankind. Mineral contents (milligrammes per litre): Sodium 3.91mg/l,

Calcium 43.9mg/l, Magnesium 37.9mg/l, Potassium 3.13mg/l, Bicarbonates 218mg/l, Chlorides 8.64mg/l, Sulphates 8mg/l, Nitrates 1.47mg/l, Silicates 9.36mg/l, Fluorides 0.1mg/l. pH 7.1 Website: http://www.aquamine.com

Aqua Mineral Imperial (Equ) a natural mineral water from the Fuente del Cotopaxi. Mineral contents (milligrammes per litre): Sodium 175mg/l, Calcium 47.05mg/l, Magnesium 145mg/l, Potassium 175mg/l, Bicarbonates 1130mg/l, Chlorides 143mg/l, Sulphates 28mg/l.

Aqua Minerale (Den) a natural mineral water from Faxe.

Aqua Minerale (Pol) a sparkling natural mineral water from Pniewy. Mineral contents (milligrammes per litre): Sodium 30mg/l, Calcium 88mg/l, Magnesium 19mg/l, Potassium 6mg/l, Bicarbonates 425mg/l, Chlorides 16mg/l, Sulphates 2.9mg/l, Fluorides 0.4mg/l. pH 7.1

Aqua Minerale (Rus) a natural mineral water from St. Petersburg. Mineral contents (milligrammes per litre): Calcium 30mg/l, Magnesium 20mg/l, Potassium 40mg/l, Bicarbonates 200mg/l, Chlorides 150mg/l, Sulphates 250mg/l.

Aqua Montana (It) a still (green label) and sparkling (red label) natural mineral water from Sorgente, Sovrana. Mineral contents (milligrammes per litre): Sodium 6.4mg/l, Magnesium 37mg/l, Potassium 0.6mg/l, Bicarbonates 400mg/l, Sulphates 17mg/l, Fluorides 0.2mg/l, Nitrates 6.7mg/l, Silicates 23mg/l. pH 7.7

Aquanate (Austr) a natural mineral water (established 2003) from Peats Ridge, NSW.

Aqua Nori (It) a natural mineral water. Mineral contents (milligrammes per litre): Sodium 8.9mg/l, Calcium 91.2mg/l, Magnesium 32.1mg/l, Potassium 0.76mg/l, Bicarbonates 353.9mg/l, Chlorides 3.9mg/l, Sulphates 77.1mg/l, Fluorides 0.35mg/l, Nitrates 2.7mg/l, Silicates 9.3mg/l. pH 7.38

Aqua Nova (Czec) a natural mineral water from Radimer 88.

Aqua Pannonia (Aus) a natural mineral water from Johannisbrunen, Bad Gleichenberg. Mineral contents (milligrammes per litre): Sodium 1020mg/l, Calcium 187mg/l, Magnesium 107.7mg/l, Potassium 44mg/l, Bicarbonates 3420mg/l, Chlorides 279mg/l, Iron 6.32mg/l.

Aqua Parmalat (It) a natural mineral water. Mineral contents (milligrammes per litre): Sodium 1.5mg/l, Calcium 40mg/l, Magnesium 21mg/l, Potassium 36mg/l, Bicarbonates 57mg/l.

Aqua Perla (It) a natural mineral water.

Aquaplus (Bra) an acidic natural mineral water from the Fonte Paredao, Vermelho. Mineral contents (milligrammes per litre): Sodium 1.41mg/l, Calcium 1.81mg/l, Magnesium 5.18mg/l, Potassium 3.7mg/l, Chlorides 4.71mg/l, Sulphates 0.36mg/l, Nitrates 33.46mg/l, Fluorides 0.061mg/l. pH 4.0

Aqua Prima (Phil) a natural mountain spring water from Palsahingin Springs, Brgy. Kaytapos, Indang Cavite. Mineral contents (milligrammes per litre): Sodium 15.97mg/l, Calcium 18.56mg/l, Magnesium 14.34mg/l, Potassium 2.14mg/l, Bicarbonates 97.78mg/l, Chlorides 7.8mg/l, Sulphates 4.45mg/l. pH 6.61

Aqua Pura (Eng) a natural mineral water from Low Plains, Armathwaite, Cumbria. Mineral contents (milligrammes per litre): Sodium 8mg/l, Calcium 7mg/l, Magnesium 2.3mg/l, Potassium 2mg/l, Bicarbonates 18mg/l, Chlorides 11mg/l, Sulphates 8mg/l, Fluorides <0.1mg/l, Nitrates 6mg/l. pH 6.4

Aqua Pura (Eng) a low mineral spring water (still or sparkling) bottled at Church Stretton in Shropshire.

Aqua Pure British Natural Spring Water (Eng) the name of a bottled still spring water from the Cwm Dale Spring in Shropshire.

Aqua Quell (Slo) a natural mineral water (established 2000) from Novo Selo, Vrnjacka Banja. Mineral contents (milligrammes per litre): Sodium 26.1mg/l, Calcium 7.2mg/l, Magnesium 43.98mg/l, Potassium 1mg/l, Bicarbonates 287mg/l, Chlorides 4.82mg/l, Sulphates 5.63mg/l, Nitrates <0.05mg/l, Silicates 43.17mg/l, Fluorides 0.19mg/l. pH 7.97

Aquarein (Hol) a natural mineral water from Maresca-2, Maarheeze.

Aquarel (Switz) the brand name for a natural spring mineral water produced by the Nestlé company.

Aquarel (Bel) a natural mineral water. Mineral contents (milligrammes per litre): Sodium 2mg/l, Calcium 70mg/l, Bicarbonates 210mg/l.

Aquarel (Cro) a natural mineral water (established 2003) from Bjelovar.

Aquarel (Fr) the natural spring mineral water brand of the Nestlé company. Mineral contents (milligrammes per litre): Sodium 2mg/l, Calcium 70mg/l, Magnesium 2.1mg/l, Bicarbonates 210mg/l, Chlorides mg/l, Sulphates mg/l, Fluorides mg/l, Nitrates 4mg/l. Website: http://www.nestle-aquarel.com

Aquarel (Sp) a natural spring mineral water from Abrucies, Girona. Mineral contents (milligrammes per litre): Sodium 7mg/l, Calcium 47.5mg/l, Magnesium 4.5mg/l, Bicarbonates 160mg/l, Nitrates 3mg/l. pH 7.51

Aquarius Cocktail (Cktl) ½ measure Bourbon whiskey, ½ measure cherry brandy, ¼ measure cranberry juice. Shake over ice, strain into an ice-filled old-fashioned glass.

Aqua Römer (Ger) a sparkling mineral water from the Römerquelle, Mainhardt-Baad, BW. Mineral contents (milligrammes per litre): Sodium 19.4mg/l, Calcium 572mg/l, Magnesium 41.8mg/l, Bicarbonates 190mg/l, Chlorides 9.7mg/l, Sulphates 1.45mg/l.

Aqua Safe (Pak) a natural mineral water.

Aquasana (Cro) a still natural mineral water from

Vukovica Vrilo. Mineral contents (milligrammes per litre): Sodium 1.5mg/l, Calcium 62.2mg/l, Magnesium 6.6mg/l, Potassium 0.3mg/l, Bicarbonates 219mg/l, Chlorides 2.5mg/l, Sulphates 6mg/l, Fluorides 0.02mg/l.

Aqua Siwa (Egy) the brand name for a natural mineral water.

Aqua Star (Ger) a sparkling mineral water from Brunnen, Reichelsheim Beienheim, Friedberg-Dorheim, HE. Mineral contents (milligrammes per litre): Sodium 8.4mg/l, Calcium 66mg/l, Magnesium 16.1mg/l, Potassium 1.5mg/l, Bicarbonates 285mg/l, Chlorides 7.2mg/l.

Aqua Styria (Aus) a natural mineral water from Styria.

Aqua Terrena (Swe) a natural mineral water from Morarp. Mineral contents (milligrammes per litre): Sodium 9.8mg/l, Calcium 3.3mg/l, Magnesium 0.95mg/l, Potassium 0.8mg/l Fluorides 0.06mg/l. pH 8.7

Aqua Trakia (Bul) a natural mineral water from Vojvodinovo, Gemiende Mariza, Plovdiv Region. Mineral contents (milligrammes per litre): Sodium 111mg/l, Calcium 18.1mg/l, Magnesium 1.7mg/l, Potassium 1.2mg/l, Bicarbonates 160mg/l, Chlorides 24.8mg/l, Sulphates 121mg/l, Nitrates <0.3mg/l, Fluorides 0.53mg/l. pH 8.09

Aqua Una (Slov) a still natural mineral water (established 2002) from Belosavac, Zagubica. Mineral contents (milligrammes per litre): Sodium 2.12mg/l, Calcium 88.89mg/l, Magnesium 3.65mg/l, Potassium 0.72mg/l, Bicarbonates 256mg/l, Chlorides 3.79mg/l, Sulphates 27.58mg/l, Fluorides 0.2mg/l, Nitrates 5mg/l. pH 7.3

Aqua V (Eng) the brand-name of an alcohol-base and soft drink.

Aquavit (Scan) the name for a spirit distilled from grain or potatoes (rectified spirit) and flavoured with certain aromatic seeds, especially caraway seeds.

Aqua Vita (Mac) a natural mineral water (established 2000) from Geoterma, Kocani, Macedonia. Mineral contents (milligrammes per litre): Sodium 150.5mg/l, Calcium 38.5mg/l, Magnesium 15.76mg/l, Potassium 148mg/l, Bicarbonates 537mg/l, Chlorides 16.9mg/l, Sulphates 46mg/l, Fluorides 1.5mg/l. pH 6.8

Aqua Vitae (Lat) lit: 'water of life', early name given to brandy and other distillates.

Aquavit Fizz (Cktl) 25mls (⅛ gill) aquavit, 2 dashes cherry brandy, 2 dashes lemon juice, 4 dashes gomme syrup, 1 egg white. Shake well over ice, strain into an ice-filled collins glass and top with soda.

Aqua Viva (Hol) a natural mineral water from Moorees, Lieshout. Mineral contents (milligrammes per litre): Sodium 8.5mg/l, Calcium 8mg/l, Magnesium 0.4mg/l, Potassium 0.7mg/l, Bicarbonates 28mg/l, Chlorides 11mg/l, Sulphates 1.5mg/l, Nitrates 0.9mg/l.

Aqua Viva (Yug) a natural mineral water from the Vencac Mountain. Mineral contents (milligrammes per litre): Sodium 9.17mg/l, Calcium 88.09mg/l, Magnesium 12.88mg/l, Potassium 2.01mg/l, Bicarbonates 305mg/l, Chlorides 13.51mg/l, Sulphates 17.77mg/l, Fluorides 0.2mg/l.

Aqueduct Cocktail (Cktl) ⅓ measure vodka, ⅓ measure brandy, ⅓ measure Curaçao, 4 dashes lime juice. Shake over ice, strain into a cocktail glass and top with a twist of orange peel.

Aquella (Ger) a still and sparkling natural mineral water from Bochum, NW. (sprudelnde: sparkling / stille mineralquelle: light gas / extra stille mineralquelle: still). Mineral contents (milligrammes per litre): Sodium 88mg/l, Calcium 165mg/l, Magnesium 22mg/l, Potassium 2.3mg/l, Bicarbonates 506mg/l, Chlorides 48mg/l, Sulphates 192mg/l, Silicates 34.1mg/l, Fluorides 0.14mg/l.

Aquella (Switz) a still and sparkling mineral water from Valais (blue label: sparkling / green label: light gas / red label: still). Mineral contents (milligrammes per litre): Sodium 3mg/l, Calcium 310mg/l, Magnesium 75mg/l, Potassium 2mg/l, Bicarbonates 245mg/l, Chlorides 9mg/l, Sulphates 830mg/l, Nitrates 1mg/l, Silicates 3mg/l.

aQuellé (S.Afr) a natural mineral water from Kwa-Zulu, Natal. Mineral contents (milligrammes per litre): Sodium 8mg/l, Calcium 3mg/l, Magnesium 2mg/l, Potassium 4mg/l, Chlorides 11mg/l, Sulphates <5mg/l, Fluorides 0.06mg/l. pH 6.4

Aqueous (Eng) water-like.

Aqui (Switz) a sparkling natural mineral water from Zürich. Mineral contents (milligrammes per litre): Sodium 320mg/l, Calcium 2.5mg/l, Magnesium 0.8mg/l, Potassium 1.8mg/l, Bicarbonates 239mg/l, Chlorides 160mg/l, Sulphates 130mg/l, Nitrates 0.3mg/l, Fluorides 3.2mg/l.

Aquifer (Mal) a still natural mineral water (established 2001) from Jalan Tasoh. Mineral contents (milligrammes per litre): Sodium 26.25mg/l, Calcium 81mg/l, Magnesium 19.6mg/l, Potassium 8mg/l, Chlorides 23.8mg/l. pH 7.09

Aquila (Czec) a natural mineral water from Karlovy Vary. Mineral contents (milligrammes per litre): Calcium 37.6mg/l, Magnesium 11.1mg/l, Bicarbonates 186mg/l, Chlorides 3mg/l, Sulphates 42.4mg/l, Nitrates 2.98mg/l, Fluorides 0.18mg/l.

Aquila (S.Afr) the label for a red wine (Cabernet sauvignon 80% and Merlot 20%) produced by the Eldorado Wines winery, Paarl, Western Cape.

Aquila Ross (Sp) a noted wine-producer based in the Penedés region of south-eastern Spain. Also produces vermouths.

A

Aquileia (It) a D.O.C. red and white wines from Friuli-Venezia Giulia. Wines named after main grape varieties. **Reds**: Aquileia Merlot, Cabernet, Reposco. **Whites**: Aquileia tocai, Friulano, Pinot bianco, Pinot grigio.

Aquintéll (Ger) a natural mineral water from Duisburg, NW.

Aquintus (Ger) a sparkling mineral water from Duisburg-Walsum, NW. (white label: sparkling / blue label: light gas). Mineral contents (milligrammes per litre): Sodium 254mg/l, Calcium 1.4mg/l, Magnesium 0.6mg/l, Potassium 4.9mg/l, Bicarbonates 393mg/l, Chlorides 119mg/l

Aquitani (Lat) the Roman name for Bordeaux.

AquOForce (USA) a mineral water brand.

A.R. (Fr) *abbr*: Appellation Réglementée.

a/R. (Ger) *abbr*: am Rhein (on the Rhine).

Arabian Tea (Afr) an alternative name for Khat.

Arabica (Afr) *see* Coffee Arabica.

Arabinose (Eng) a monosaccharide found in wine that is unfermentable by yeast.

Arack (M.East) *see* Arak.

Arac Punsch (Nor) an akvavit-based drink produced by A/S Vinmonopolet.

Arad (Rum) a wine producing district in the Siebenbürgen region of western Rumania.

Aragnan (Fr) a white grape variety grown in Palette, Provence.

Aragón (Sp) a wine producing area in the Upper Ebro. Home to the D.O.'s of Cava, Cariñena, Campo de Borja, Calatayud, Somontano. Vino de la Tierra areas of Bajo Aragón (Teruel), Tierra Baja de Aragón, Valdejalón (Zaragoza). Vino Comarcal areas of Alto Jiloca, Muniesa (Teruel), Belchite, Daroca (Zaragoza).

Aragón Cocktail (Cktl) ⅓ measure Cognac, ⅓ measure crème de banane, ⅓ measure cream. Shake well over ice, strain into a cocktail glass.

Aragonês (Port) *see* Aragonez (alternative spelling of).

Aragonez (Port) a red grape variety grown in Alentejo. Also known as the Tinta Roriz in the Douro. Known as the Tempranillo in Spain.

Aragón y Cía (Sp) a wine-producer based in Lucena, Montilla-Moriles.

Araignan (Fr) a white grape variety grown in Palette, Provence.

Arak (M.East) any type of spirit made in the middle eastern countries from a variety of ingredients. *see* Arack, Arrack.

Arak Cooler (Cktl) 25mls (⅛ gill) arak, 15mls (⅛ gill) white rum, dash gomme syrup, dash lemon juice. Shake over ice, strain into an ice-filled highball glass and top with iced Champagne.

Araki (M.East) a liqueur made from the juice of dates.

Aral (Tur) a noted large winery that produces red and white wines.

Araldici Vini Piemontesi (It) a co-operative wine estate. (Add): 14040 Castel Boglione (AT). Made up of 3 co-operatives with 1,000 members, 2,000ha. of vines. Grape varieties include:

Barbera, Dolcetto, Cortese, Nebbiolo, Pinot noir, Arneis, Chardonnay, Moscato. Produces a range of wines under the Poderi Alasia label including Riveand Sorilaria. Also Araldica Revello (DOCG Barolo). Website: http://www.araldicavini.com

Arame (Port) the fine wire mesh found on old Reserva bottles.

Aramon (Fr) a red grape variety grown in the south of France and USA. Has a high fruit level and produces average quality wines.

Aramonte (It) a winery based on the island of Sicily. Grape varieties include: Catarratto.

Arana (Sp) a 6 year old, light, red wine produced by Bodegas La Rioja Alta, Rioja.

Aranciata (It) orangeade.

Aranzada (Sp) a land (and vineyard) measure. 1 Aranzada = 0.475ha.

Arapri [d'] (It) a winery based in San Severo, Puglia. Produces sparkling Pas Dosé Bombino bianco and Pinot noir grapes), a Brut rosé (100% Montepulciano grapes) and Riserva Nobile (100% Bombino bianco grapes).

Ararat-Ani (Arm) a 5 and 6 year old eau-de-vie from Armenia (from the Ararat distillery in Yerevan). Used as a base for 2 brandies from Muscadine, Saperavi, Chilar, Sercial, Voskeat and Verdelho grapes.

Ararimu (N.Z) the label of a Matua Valley Winery for their Gisborne Chardonnay wine.

Arataki (N.Z) an area in Hawkes Bay where the second government vineyard was established in 1903.

Araujo Estate (USA) a 16.5ha winery in Calistoga. Grape varieties: Cabernet, Sauvignon blanc, Syrah, Viognier. Label: Eisele Vineyard.

Arawatta (Austr) a wine-producing area in Victoria.

Arbanats (Fr) a commune in the A.C. Graves region in south-western Bordeaux. Le Basque is the main vineyard.

Arbanne (Fr) a lesser white grape variety used in the production of some Champagne wines.

Arbin (Fr) a deep-coloured, red A.C. wine made from the Mondeuse grape in the Savoie region.

Arbois (Fr) a white grape variety grown in Touraine, Loire. Also known as Petit pineau, Pineau menu.

Arbois (Fr) the best known A.C. wine district (950ha) of the Jura in south eastern France, produces red, rosé, white and vin jaune wines on clay-chalk soils. Grape varieties: Chardonnay, Pinot noir, Poulsard, Savagnin, Trousseau.

Arbois Pupillin (Fr) an A.C. commune in the Jura region. Produces red, rosé and white wines.

Arboleda (Chile) a range of wines produced in Caliterra. Named after the 1,000ha. wine estate. Grape varieties include Cabernet sauvignon, Merlot, Carmenère. Aged in French and American oak.

Arborea (It) a D.O.C. dry white, red and rosé wine produced in Sardinia.

Arbor Mist (Eng) a 5.5% alc by vol. wine based cocktail containing Chardonnay wine and peach flavours. Produced by Matthew Clark.

A

Arbour Light (Eng) a 3.6% alc by vol. ale brewed by Whim Ales Ltd., Derbyshire.

Arbre à Thé (Fr) tea plant / tea bush.

Arbuissonnas (Fr) a commune in the Beaujolais. Has A.C. Beaujolais-Villages or Beaujolais-Arbuissonnas status.

Arbutus (USA) a mineral water from Long Island, New York.

Arc (Eng) a beer brewed by the Coors Brewers Ltd.

Arcen Brouwerij (Hol) a brewery based in Arcen, Limburg. Noted for top-fermented beers. Arcen Triple 7.5% alc by vol. Magnus 6.5% alc by vol. and Oud Limburgs 5.5% alc by vol.

Arcens [1] (Fr) a natural mineral water from the Ardèche. Mineral contents (milligrammes per litre): Sodium 290mg/l, Calcium 88mg/l, Magnesium 66mg/l, Potassium 7mg/l, Bicarbonates 1280mg/l, Chlorides 52mg/l, Sulphates 3.77mg/l, Silicates 49mg/l. pH 6.4

Arcens [2] (Fr) a natural mineral water from the Ardèche. Mineral contents (milligrammes per litre): Sodium 438.9mg/l, Calcium 14.5mg/l, Magnesium 23.7mg/l, Potassium 10.7mg/l, Bicarbonates 1213mg/l, Chlorides 43mg/l, Sulphates 11mg/l, Silicates 37.7mg/l, Fluorides 1.3mg/l, Nitrates 0.14mg/l. pH 6.35

Arcens [3] (Fr) a natural mineral water from the Ardèche. Mineral contents (milligrammes per litre): Sodium 520mg/l, Calcium 25mg/l, Magnesium 33mg/l, Potassium 10mg/l, Bicarbonates 1455mg/l, Chlorides 52mg/l, Sulphates 11mg/l, Silicates 49mg/l, Fluorides 1.2mg/l, Nitrates <1mg/l. pH 6.5

Archanes (Gre) an A.O.Q.S. wine region of the isle of Crete that is noted for dry red wine of same name made from Kotsifeli and Mandilari grapes.

Archanes (Gre) a wine made in Crete from the Athiri, Kotsifali, Nandilari and Vilana grapes.

Archangel (Eng) a 4.7% alc by vol. ale brewed by the Abbeydale Brewery Ltd., South Yorkshire.

Archbishop (Eng) mulled claret. The wine is heated together with sugar, oranges studded with cloves, then set alight before it is served.

Archer Daniels Midland Co. (USA) a large distillery based in Peoria, Illinois. Is noted for Cane Rums.

Archer's Brewery (Eng) a brewery (established 1979) based in Swindon, Wiltshire. Brews Headbanger, Village, Best, Golden, Swindon Pride, Dragon's Teeth and commemorative ale Triple Tun. Took over Tom Hoskins Beaumanor Brewery in Leicester. Now known as the Swindon Brewing C° Ltd. Website: http://www.archersbrewery.co.uk 'E'mail: sales@archersbrewery.co.uk

Archer's Schnapps C°. (Eng) a schnapps producer. Produces: Archer's Peach Schnapps 21% alc. by vol., Archer's Schnapps Aqua in a variety of flavours (cranberry / lime / orange / peach / raspberry) at 5.5% alc by vol. and Archer's Schnapps Vea which has a lower sugar content (apple / wildberry / tropical [pineapple and passion fruit]) 4% alc by vol. Owned by Diago.

Archer Stout (Eng) a 4.8% alc by vol. cask-conditioned stout brewed by Lees (J.W.) in Middelton, Manchester using roasted barley.

Archetto Toscano (It) a pruning method used in the Chianti district of Tuscany. Involves a hard pruning of the vines to give a small but high quality crop.

Archiac (Fr) a commune in the Charente-Maritime département whose grapes are classed Petite Champagne (Cognac).

Archibald Arrow 70/- (Scot) a 70/- ale brewed by Allied's Alloa Brewery, Clackmannanshire.

Archibald Beckett (Eng) a 4.3% alc by vol. beer brewed by Tisbury Brewery, Tisbury, Wiltshire.

Archimedean Screw (Eng) a style of corkscrew where the cork-penetrating part of the corkscrew is shaped on the Archimedean screw (spiral blade) principle to aid the grip on the cork.

Archipelago Brewery (E.Asia) a brewery based in Kuala Lumpur, Malaya which produces ABC stout and Anchor beer.

Archway Bitter (Eng) a bitter ale brewed by the Tooley Street Brewery in London.

Arcins (Fr) a lesser commune of the Haut-Médoc, Bordeaux.

Arcobräu (Ger) a leading private Bavarian brewery. Brews Coronator Doppelbock, Dunkel Weisse, Mooser Dunkel, Mooser Hell, Pilsener, 4.9% alc by vol. Urfass, Urweisse.

Arcs [Les] (Fr) a wine-producing village in the Côtes de Provence.

Arctic Ale (Eng) a rich warming ale brewed by Carlsberg-Tetley using fuggles and golding hops. 5.2% alc by vol. One of fifteen ales in the Tapster's Choice range.

Arctic Lite (Eng) a low carbohydrate lager 1032 O.G. from Burton-on-Trent in Staffordshire.

Ardaillon (Fr) a Vin de Pays area in the Hérault département of southern France. Red and rosé wines.

Ardanza (Sp) a 5 year old red wine produced by Bodegas La Rioja Alta, Rioja.

Ardbeg Malt (Scot) a single malt whisky from the Ardbeg distillery Ltd, Isle of Islay, Argyll. An Islay malt whisky. 40% alc by vol. 9 and 10 year old (both 46% alc by vol.) plus a 17 year old, 1974, 1975 and 1978 vintage produced. Also produces an Oloroso Finish Cask Malt 46% alc by vol.

Ardeas (It) a red wine produced by the Romans in central-western Italy.

Ardèche (Fr) a département of the Côtes du Rhône, the river Loire rises here.

Ardein Estate (S.Afr) a small vineyard in Robertson. Produces a medium sweet white wine from Clairette and Raisin blanc grapes. Also sells its grapes to the Mooiuitsig Wynkelders.

Arden House (Scot) the brand-name of a 37.5% alc by vol. Scotch whisky that is sold by the Co-operative Society.

Ardent Spirits (Eng) brandy, rum and whisky, denotes flavoured spirits with a burning sensation as well as flavour.

Ardey-Quelle (Ger) a sparkling mineral water from

Dortmund (blue label: sparkling / green label: low gas). Mineral contents (milligrammes per litre): Sodium 52.6mg/l, Calcium 76.5mg/l, Magnesium 16.7mg/l, Potassium 6.3mg/l, Bicarbonates 330mg/l, Chlorides 36.3mg/l, Sulphates 72.6mg/l.

Ardillats [Les] (Fr) a commune in the Beaujolais district. Has the A.C. Beaujolais-Villages or Beaujolais-Ardillats status. Also known as Beaujolais-les-Ardillats.

Ardine (Fr) an apricot brandy liqueur made by the firm of Bardinet.

Ardmore (Scot) a single malt whisky distillery based east of Dufftown, Banffshire. A Highland malt whisky. (Speyside). 40% alc by vol. Also a 1981 version.

Ardoise (Fr) slate (soil).

Ardon (Switz) a wine-producing village based near Sion in the Valais Canton. Noted for Fendant wines.

Ardsley Cocktail (Cktl) ½ measure sloe gin, ½ measure Calisaya. Shake well over ice and strain into a cocktail glass.

Ardsley Cooler (Cktl) 1 measure dry gin stirred over ice in a highball glass, top with ginger ale and decorate with sprig of mint.

Arealva (Port) a winery based in Lisbon, produces red and white wines.

Arechabaia (W.Ind) a major rum producer in Cuba. Now owned by the State.

Arecibo Distillery (W.Ind) a distillery based in Puerto Rico. Owned by the Puerto Rico Distillers Inc. (part of Seagram). Produces most styles of rum.

Arela (It) the name given to the bamboo racks that are used to dry some of the grapes for passiti in the production of D.O.C. Recioto della Valpolicella.

Arena (Eng) the brand-name of a 4% alc by vol. sparkling white wine and tropical fruits drink.

Arenaceous Soil (Eng) sandy soil / sandstone.

Arenas (Sp) sandy soil found in the Sherry region (Andalusia), contains 10% chalk plus a proportion of iron-oxide.

Arendal Brewery (Nor) a brewery based in Arendal, southern Norway. Brews Heineken under licence.

Arendsig Hand-Crafted Wines (S.Afr) a winery (established 2004) based in Robertson, Western Cape. Grape varieties: Chardonnay, Shiraz. Produces varietal wines. 15ha. Website: http://www.arendsig.co.za

Aréni (Arm) a red grape variety grown in Armenia.

Arens (Lat) thirsty.

Areometer (Eng) a device for measuring the S.G. of grape must. Other names include Oechsle, Baumé, Mustimeter.

Arequipa (Peru) an ancient Inca city where vineyards are planted. Produces mainly white wines.

Ares (Fr) an old measure of land.

Aretuza (Pol) a natural mineral water from Opacz. Mineral contents (milligrammes per litre): Sodium 95mg/l, Calcium 44mg/l, Magnesium 26mg/l, Bicarbonates 379mg/l, Chlorides 75mg/l, Sulphates 20mg/l, Nitrates 0.4mg/l. pH 7.2

Arévchate (Arm) a red, fortified wine produced in Armenia.

Arf an' Arf (Eng) equal quantities of pale ale and porter. See also Half and Half.

Argal (Eng) see Argol and Argoil.

Argarth Plant (Mex) another name for the Mezcal cactus. See also Century Plant.

Argens (Fr) a Vin de Pays area in Provence, Var département, south-eastern France.

Argentina (S.Am) one of the largest producers (fifth) of wine in the world, 90% of the wine is produced in the Cuyo region. (Add): Güemes 4464 C1425BLF Buenos Aires. Regions: Cuyo (central), North and Patagonia (south). Main wine areas: Catamarca, La Rioja, Mendoza, Neuquén, Northern Vineyards, Rio Negro, Salta, San Juan, San Raphael and Tucumán. Grape varieties: Barbera, Bonarda, Cabernet sauvignon, Carmenère, Criolla, Malbec, Syrah, Tempranillo for red / rosé wine, Chenin blanc, Pedro Ximénez, Sémillon and Torrontés for whites. see Juan Cedron. Website: http://www.winesofargentina.org 'E'mail: info@winesofargentina.org

Argento Wine Company (Arg) a winery (established 1999) and range of wines produced by Nicolas Catena wines, Mendoza. Grape varieties include: Bonarda, Carmenère, Chardonnay, Malbec, Pinot grigio. Website: http://www.argentowine.com 'E'mail: info@argentowine.com

Argile (Fr) clay (soil).

Argile Rouge (S.Afr) the label for a red wine (Merlot) produced by the Signal Hill winery, Cape Town, Western Cape.

Argile Rouge Bruyère (Fr) a sweet cider apple grown in the Normandy region. Used in the production of sweet ciders.

Argillaceous Soil (Eng) sedimentary soil of fine ground material e.g. clay.

Argillats [Les] (Fr) a Premier Cru vineyard [part] in the A.C. commune of Nuits-Saint-Georges, Côte de Nuits, Burgundy. Also a vineyard in A.C. Nuits-Saint-Georges.

Argillières [Les] (Fr) a Premier Cru vineyard in the A.C. commune of Pommard, Côte de Beaune, Burgundy 3.64ha.

Argilo-Calcaires (Fr) clay and chalk soil.

Arginine (Eng) an amino acid found in wine, formed by the yeast.

Argoil (Eng) see Argol.

Argol (Eng) Potassium hydrogen tartrate tartaric deposit thrown as the wine matures in cask.

Argonaut Winery (USA) a small winery based in the Sierra Foothills, Amador, California. Grape varieties: Barbera and Zinfandel. Produces varietal wines.

Argonne Oak (Fr) an oak tree from the Ardenne forest, used for Champagne casks.

Argyle Brewery (Scot) an Edinburgh brewery (established 1982), originally established as the Leith Brewery, noted for 80/- ale 1043 O.G.

A

Argyle (USA) a winery (established 1987) based in Willamette Valley, Oregon. Noted for its sparkling wines. Grape varieties: Chardonnay, Pinot gris, Pinot noir for still wines. Label: Nuthouse.

Aria (Sp) a cava wine produced by Segura Viudas from 20% Parellada, 20% Xarel-lo, 60% Macabeo grapes. Spends 36 months on the lees.

Aricinum (It) a red wine produced in Roman times in central Italy.

Ariégoise (Fr) a natural mineral water from La Prime, Seem. Mineral contents (milligrammes per litre): Sodium 1.8mg/l, Calcium 3.7mg/l, Magnesium 0.58mg/l, Potassium 0.5mg/l, Bicarbonates 6.7mg/l, Chlorides 0.8mg/l, Sulphates 8mg/l, Nitrates <1mg/l, Silicates 6.9mg/l, Iron 2mg/l. pH 6.5

Ariel Four Square (Eng) a 5.3% alc by vol. ale brewed by The Concertina Brewery, South Yorkshire.

Arienheller (Ger) a natural mineral water (established 1897) from Westerwald. Mineral contents (milligrammes per litre): Sodium 228mg/l, Calcium 44mg/l, Magnesium 55mg/l, Potassium 16mg/l, Bicarbonates 616mg/l, Chlorides 164mg/l, Sulphates 118mg/l.

Arienheller-Brunnen (Ger) a natural mineral water from Rheinbrohl, RP.

Arilli (Lat) grape pips / raisins.

Arinsal (And) a natural mineral water (established 2005) from the Font d'Arinsal. Mineral contents (milligrammes per litre): Sodium 3.7mg/l, Calcium 26.9mg/l, Magnesium 1.2mg/l, Potassium 0.5mg/l, Bicarbonates 54.3mg/l, Chlorides 5.6mg/l, Sulphates 26.9mg/l, Nitrates 2.5mg/l, Silicates 6.5mg/l, Fluorides <0.2mg/l. pH 7.56. Also sold as Aigua d'Andorra.

Arinto (Port) a white grape variety believed to be derived from the Riesling of Germany. Used in the making of Bucelas wines. Also known as Padernã. Known as the Pedernã in the Vinho Verde.

Arinto Cachudo (Port) a sub-variety of Arinto.

Arinto do Dão (Port) a white grape variety grown in the Dão region. Also known as the Assario Branco and Malvasia Fino.

Arinto Miudo (Port) a sub-variety of Arinto.

Aris (Ger) a white grape variety, a cross between (Riparia x Gamay) and Riesling. Is early ripening and has a high sugar output.

Arise my Love (Cktl) iced Champagne with 4 dashes of crème de menthe. Served in a Champagne flute.

Aristocrat Brandy (USA) the brand-name of a brandy produced by the California Wine Association, Delano, California. 40% alc by vol.

Ariston-Sprudel (Ger) a natural mineral water from Mendig, RP.

Aristophanes (Gre) a poet and playwright who wrote about wine and wine drinking in ancient Greece.

Arius Neuf (USA) a winery in Healdsburg. Grape varieties: Grenache, Mourvèdre, Syrah, Zinfandel.

Ariwa (Ger) a mineral water from the David-Quelle, Bad Peterstal, BW.

Arizu (Arg) the brand-name of a noted sparkling wine.

Arjan (Asia) another name for koumiss (fermented mare's milk), made by the Tartars.

Arjoado (Port) a system of vine training using wires stretched between trees.

Arkangel (Eng) the brand-name of a lager and vodka mixed drink produced by Whitbread.

Arkansas (USA) a small wine-producing region with vineyards mainly in the north of the state in the Ozark mountains.

Arkell's Brewery (Eng) a large brewery (established 1843). (Add): Kingsdown Brewery, Swindon, Wilts. SN2 7RU. Noted for cask-conditioned beers and 2Bs 3.2% alc by vol., 3Bs (premium draught bitter) 4% alc by vol., Arkell's Smooth Bitter 4% alc by vol., Bees Organic 4.5% alc by vol., Chocolate Stout 4.8% alc by vol., JRA 3.6% alc by vol., Kingsdown Ale 5% alc by vol., Mash Tum Mild 3.5% alc by vol., Peter's Porter 4.8% alc by vol., Summer Ale 4.2% alc by vol. Website: http://www.arkells.com 'E'mail: arkells@arkells.com

Arkell's Bitter (Eng) a 3.2% alc by vol. bitter ale from Arkell's of Swindon, Wilts.

Arkia Mineralwasser (Ger) a natural mineral water from the Ried-Quelle, Bad Vilbel, HE.

Arkina Yverdon (Switz) a still and sparkling mineral water from Yverdon les Bains (green label: sparkling / blue label: still). Mineral contents (milligrammes per litre): Sodium 7.1mg/l, Calcium 37mg/l, Magnesium 22mg/l, Bicarbonates 239mg/l, Chlorides 2.9mg/l, Sulphates 8.8mg/l, Nitrates <0.1mg/l, Fluorides 1.2mg/l.

Arlaux (Fr) a Champagne producer. Vintages: 1995, 2000.

Arlewood Estate (Austr) a winery (established 1988) based in Wilyabrup Valley, Margaret River, Western Australia. Grape varieties include: Cabernet sauvignon, Merlot.

Arline (Fr) a natural mineral water from Franconville. Mineral contents (milligrammes per litre): Sodium 8mg/l, Calcium 165mg/l, Magnesium 36mg/l, Potassium 2.3mg/l, Bicarbonates 393mg/l, Chlorides 14mg/l, Sulphates 220mg/l, Nitrates <2mg/l.

Arlit & Cie (Fr) a Champagne producer. (Add): 93 Ave. de Champagne, BP 204, 51009, Chalons-sur-Marne. 5ha.

Armada Ale (Eng) a cask / bottled premium bitter produced by Harvey's Brewery in Lewes, Sussex to mark the 400th anniversary of the Spanish Armada.

Armada Cream (Sp) a brand of Cream Sherry produced by Sandeman.

Armadillo (Eng) a draught British Sherry distributed by Vine Products.

Armagnac (Fr) an A.O.C. brandy region in the département of Gers in south-eastern France. A.C. is second only to Cognac, its brandies are more fiery than Cognac. Districts are Bas Armagnac 2%,

A

Haut Armagnac 65% and Ténarèze 23%. Grape
varieties: Baco 22, Colombard, Folle blanche,
Ugni blanc (also Clairette de gascogne, Graisse,
Jurançon blanc, Mauzac and Meslier St-François).
Distilled in an Alambic Armagnacais (between
52% and 72%) and aged mainly in Montlezun
oak. Grades: *** (Trois Etoiles): 2 years old,
VSOP: fives years old, XO: over six years old, Hors
d'Age: minimum 10 years old. *See also* Angel's
Share, Blanche d'Armagnac and Trou Gascon.

Armagnaçais (Fr) a form of continuous still used for
the making of Armagnac. *see* Alambic
Armagnaçais.

Armagnac Blanc (Fr) a nickname for the Haut
Armagnac. Derives from the chalk and limestone
outcrops.

Armagnac Information (Fr) the Armagnac
information centre. (Add): Maison du Tourisme,
32000 Auch, Haut Armagnac, Gers.

Armagnac Lafontan (Fr) an Armagnac producer.
(Add): Castelnau d'Auzan, 32800 Eauze, Bas
Armagnac. Produces a range of Armagnac
brandies.

Armagnac Marquis de Terraube (Fr) an Armagnac
producer. (Add): Terraube, 32700-Lectoure, Haut
Armagnac. Produces a range of Armagnac
brandies.

Armagnac Noir (Fr) a nickname for the Bas
Armagnac. Derived from the local dark oak and
pine woods.

Armagnac Samalens St, V.E.V.A. (Fr) distillers of
Armagnac. (Add): Laujuzan, 32110, Nogoro.
Produces ***, V.S.O.P, Vintage 1930, 1939, Vieille
Rélique 15 y.o. Cuvée Anniversaire (consists of
certain Bas Armagnacs which are almost 100 y.o.).

Armagnac Sour (Cktl) ⅓ measure Armagnac, ⅔
measure fresh lemon juice, 1 teaspoon castor
sugar, 1 teaspoon egg white, dash Angostura.
Shake over ice, strain into a Champagne flute, top
with a slice of orange.

Armagnac Vve Goudoulin (Fr) an Armagnac
producer. (Add): Domaine de Bigor Courrensan,
32330-Gondrin. Produces a range of Armagnac
brandies.

Armazem (Port) a warehouse or wine store.

Armenia (Arm) an important wine region of south-
eastern Europe producing mainly dessert wines.

Armenias (S.Am) a noted coffee-producing region in
Colombia.

Armentia y Madrazo (Sp) a red wine from the Haro
district of Rioja.

Armillaria Mellea (Lat) a fungus that attacks the
vine roots. *see* Armillaria Root-Rot.

Armillaria Root-Rot (Eng) a fungal disease which
attacks the roots of the vines especially in sandy
soils. Family: **Pourridié**. *See also* **Armillaria mellea**,
Dermatophora necatrix and **Rosellinia necatrix**.

Arminius-Quelle (Ger) a natural mineral water from
Gütersloh, NW.

Armistic Ale (Eng) a 4.2% alc by vol. ale brewed by
the 1648 Brewery Company, East Sussex.

Armit (Fr) a Champagne producer noted for a non-

vintage blanc de blancs. Part of the group of semi-
independent firms of the Paillard Chanoine
group.

Armorial (Sp) the name of a Rioja wine produced by
Maese Joan, Sdad. Coop. Ltda., Oyon, Alava.

A.R. Morrow Brandy (USA) the brand-name of a
brandy produced by the California Wine
Association, Delano, California. Is Oak matured
for 10 years.

Armsheim (Ger) village (Anb): Rheinhessen. (Ber):
Bingen. (Gro): Adelberg. (Vins): Geiersberg,
Goldstückchen, Leckerberg.

Arnaldo-Caprai (It) a winery (150ha) in the DOCG
Sagrantino di Montefalco, Umbria region. (Add):
Località Torre 06036 Montefalco (Pg) Umbria.
Website: http://www.arnaldocaprai.it 'E'mail:
info@arnaldocaprai.it

Arnberg (Ger) vineyard (Anb): Franken. (Ber):
Maindreieck. (Gro): Rosstal. (Vil): Gössenheim.

Arnedo (Sp) a Zona de Crianza in the Rioja Baja
region of north-eastern Spain.

Arneis (It) a white grape variety grown in Piemonte.

Arnes Journal (Ger) a wine and food monthly
magazine. (Add): Arne-Verlag, Postfach 1247,
6203 Hochheim, western Germany.

Arnesque [L'] (Fr) the label of a Châteauneuf-du-
Pape produced by Laget (Marie), 3 Rue des
Cigales, 84230 Châteauneuf-du-Pape, southern
Rhône.

Arnevels [Les] (Fr) the label of a Châteauneuf-du-
Pape produced by Quiot at Ave. Baron le Roy,
84230 Châteauneuf-du-Pape, southern Rhône.
Other labels include Couversets (les), Domaine
du Vieux Lazeret.

Arngoon (Thai) grape.

Arnim Sauvignon Rouge (S.Afr) the label for red
wine (Cabernet sauvignon 60%, Sauvignon blanc
40%) produced by the Cabrière Estate winery,
Franschhoek, Western Cape.

Arniston Bay (S.Afr) a winery based in the Western
Cape. Noted for Chardonnay, Chenin blanc wines.

Arnoa (Fr) a vineyard in the A.C. Corbières, south-
western France. Label: Grande Réserve.

Arnoison (Fr) an alternative name for the
Chardonnay grape.

Arnould [Michel] (Fr) a Champagne producer.
(Add): 28 Rue de Mailly, 51360 Verzenay. 12ha.
Produces both vintage and non-vintage
Champagnes.

Arnoult [Jean] (Fr) a Champagne négociant-
manipulant. (Add): Celles-sur-Ource, 10110 Bar-
sur-Seine. Produces both vintage and non-vintage
Champagnes.

Arnstein (Ger) village (Anb): Franken. (Ber):
Maindreieck. (Gro): Rosstal. (Vins): Assorted parts
of vineyards.

Aroka (Asia) a fiery potent spirit made from mare's
milk by the Tartar tribesmen with added grape
juice.

Arolser Schlossbrunnen (Ger) a natural mineral
water from Arolsen, HE.

Aroma (Eng) a distinctive fresh fragrance which is

given off by the wine after being exposed to the air. Part of the bouquet.

Aroma (Eng) the smell/bouquet that the coffee grounds release when they are brewed.

Aromatic Geneva (Hol) a liqueur made with old Geneva which has been flavoured with aromatic herbs.

Aromatised Wines (Eng) wines flavoured with herbs and other substances, often fortified.

Arome (Fr) the odour or bouquet of wines or spirits.

Around the World Cocktail (Cktl) ⅓ measure white rum, ⅓ measure orange juice, ⅓ measure lemon juice, 4 dashes orgeat syrup, 2 dashes Cognac. Blend altogether in a blender with a scoop of crushed ice. Pour into a flute glass and serve with straws.

Arpa (Tur) barley.

Arpu (Egy) the old Egyptian word for wine.

Arquebuse (Fr) a white herb digestive liqueur. *See also* Eau d'Arquebuse.

Arrábida (Port) an I.P.R. region found in the Setúbal peninsula planted with French grapes as well as Moscatel and Periquita.

Arraca (Fr) the old word to denote the removal of the wine off the lees. *see* Racking.

Arrack (M.East) the name derived from the Arabic for juice or sweet and designates native spirits (distilled from rice, palm juice, maize, etc.). There are many types of arrack, but they all have a spicy flavour. Other names are Arraki, Arak, Aruk, Raki.

Arrack Punsch (Scan) another name for Swedish Punsch. *See also* Caloric Punsch.

Arrack-Verschnitt (Ger) verschnitt containing at least 10% arrack.

Arraki (M.East) *see* Arrack.

Arrakverschnitt (Ger) a rum and arrack blend (10% arrack).

Arran Ale (Scot) a 3.8% alc by vol. bitter ale brewed by the Arran brewery C°. Ltd. Isle of Arran.

Arran Blonde (Scot) a 5% alc by vol. blonde ale brewed by the Arran brewery C°. Ltd. Isle of Arran.

Arran Brewery (Scot) a brewery. (Add): Cladach, Brodick, Isle of Arran KA27 8DE. Brews beers, ales and lager including: AB Blonde 5% alc by vol., Arran Ale 3.8% alc by vol., Arran Blonde 5% alc by vol., Arran Dark 4.3% alc by vol., Arran Fireside 4.7% alc by vol., Arran Sunset 4.4% alc by vol. Website: http://www.arranbrewery.co.uk 'E'mail: Richard@arranbrewery.co.uk

Arran Dark (Scot) a 4.3% alc by vol. dark ale brewed by the Arran brewery C°. Ltd. Isle of Arran.

Arran Fireside (Scot) a 4.7% alc by vol. bitter ale brewed by the Arran brewery C°. Ltd. Isle of Arran.

Arran Sunset (Scot) a 4.4% alc by vol. light ale brewed by the Arran brewery C°. Ltd. Isle of Arran.

Arras (Austr) a winery based in Tasmania and owned by Hardys.

Arrasburg-Schlossberg (Ger) vineyard (Anb): Mosel-Saar-Ruwer. (Ber): Zell/Mosel. (Gro): Grafschaft. (Vil): Alf.

Arrata's Vineyard (USA) a small vineyard based in Santa Clara County, California. Grape variety: Cabernet sauvignon.

Arraubo (Mad) boiled down grape must, also spelt Arrobe.

Areet (Ger) a natural mineral water from Bad Hönningen, RP.

Arriba Kettle (Sp) a noted bodega based in the Penedés region. Produces Mont Marcel (a dry white wine).

Arribes (Sp) a D.O. region based on the north-eastern border with Portugal.

Arrière Côtes (Fr) communes in Burgundy region that are to the west of the Côte d'Or, consisting of the Hautes Côtes de Nuits and the Hautes Côtes de Beaune. *see* Dijon.

Arrière-Goût (Fr) after-taste.

Arroba (Sp) a wine measure holding 16⅔ litres which can vary in other Spanish speaking countries.

Arrobe (Mad) *see* Arraubo.

Arrobe (Port) fruit syrup.

Arrogant Frog [The] (Fr) a brand name for a French wine for the American market. The name designed to appeal to the Americans in place of the complicated French label names!

Arrol's 80/- (Scot) a 4.4% alc by vol. ale.

Arrol's 90/- (Scot) a 4.9% alc by vol. ale.

Arrope (Sp) boiling down the wine to sweeten and add colour to sherries. First made by the Moors. Boiled down to ⅕ quantity in Jerez and ⅓ in Málaga.

Arrosé (Fr) watered.

Arrouart-Haumont (Fr) a Champagne producer. (Add): 17, Rue des Falloises, 51130 Vertus. Produces vintage and non-vintage wines. Website: http://www.champagne-arrouart.com 'E'mail: info@champagne-arrouart.com

Arrowfield (Austr) a winery based in the Hunter Valley, New South Wales.

Arrow Head (Cktl) 25mls (⅙ gill) Bourbon whiskey, 2 dashes dry vermouth, 2 dashes sweet vermouth, 2 dashes lemon juice, dash egg white. Shake over ice and strain into a cocktail glass.

Arrowhead Bitter (Eng) a 3.9% alc by vol. bitter beer brewed by the Cannon Royall Brewery, Worcestershire.

Arrowhead (USA) a natural mineral water (established 1894) from San Bernardino Mountains, California. Mineral contents (milligrammes per litre): Sodium 12.1mg/l, Calcium 20mg/l, Magnesium 3.5mg/l, Potassium 1.4mg/l, Bicarbonates 239mg/l, Chlorides 13.2mg/l, Sulphates 4.6mg/l, Nitrates 1.2mg/l, Silicates 30.6mg/l. pH 7.8

Arrowood (USA) a winery based in Sonoma Valley, California that is noted for Chardonnay wines.

Arroyo [Rafael] (W.Ind) a chemist who greatly improved the rum distilling and ageing process in the early twentieth century in Puerto Rico.

Arroyo Seco (USA) lit: 'dry wash', on a wine label denotes that the wine originates from a river-bottom area in Salinas Valley, Monterey County, California.

Arroyo Seco (USA) the label for a red wine (Pinot noir) produced by the Carmel Rond winery, Monterey County, California.

Arroyo Seco Vineyard (USA) a large vineyard based in Salinas Valley, Monterey County, California. 150ha. Grape varieties: Cabernet sauvignon, Chardonnay, Merlot and Petite syrah. Produces varietal wines.

Arruda (Port) a DOC wine area within the region of Estremadura.

Arrufiat (Fr) a white grape grown in Madiran, south-west France. Also spelt Arrufiac.

Arrumbador (Sp) the name for a bodega employee.

Ars (Fr) a commune in the Charente-Maritime département whose grapes are classed Petite Champagne (Cognac).

Arsac (Fr) a commune within the district of the Médoc, Bordeaux. Château du Terre is the top wine. Red wines can use A.C. Margaux designation.

Arsinoe (Cyp) a very dry white wine produced by Sodap.

Arsos Winery (Cyp) a winery that produces a range of wines under the Laona label.

Art (Ger) a term to denote character in a wine.

Art and Science of Brewing (USA) *see* Zymurgy.

Artardi Winery (Sp) a winery in the Rioja Alavasa. Produces: Viña el Pisón. Also has vineyards in the D.O. Navarra. Label: Artazuri (rosé).

Artemisia absinthium (Lat) wormwood.

Artes (Czec) a natural mineral water from K'r'ny.

Artesa Winery (USA) a winery based in the Carneros district of northern California. Grape variety: Pinot noir.

Artesia (USA) a natural mineral water from Texas.

Artesian Well (Eng) a water well sunk through impermeable strata into water bearing strata from an area at a higher altitude than that of the well. This allows sufficient pressure to force the water to flow upwards. (Tur) = artezyen.

Artesia-Quelle (Ger) a still and sparkling mineral water from Reuth bei Erbendorf, BY. Mineral contents (milligrammes per litre): Sodium 16.3mg/l, Calcium 25mg/l, Magnesium 9.2mg/l, Potassium 1.9mg/l, Bicarbonates 118mg/l, Chlorides 16.3mg/l, Sulphates 16mg/l, Nitrates <0.5mg/l, Fluorides 1.02mg/l.

Artezyen (Tur) an artesian well.

Arthenac (Fr) a commune in the Charente-Maritime département whose grapes are classed Petite Champagne (Cognac).

Arthur (USA) a white (Chardonnay) wine produced by Domaine Drouhin winery, Oregon.

Arthur Bell and Sons (Scot) *see* Bell's.

Arthur Bells Distillers (Eng) *abbr*: A.B.D. (established 1987) by the Guinness take-over of Bells and then the Distillers Company. A.B.D. was formed by a merger of these two.

Arthur Cooper (Eng) the trading name used by Imperial Retail Shops Ltd. (a division of Courage Ltd). Over 200 wine shops.

Arthur Girard (Fr) a cuvée (part of Marconnets) in the A.C. commune of Savigny-lès-Beaune, Côte de Beaune, Burgundy. Is owned by the Hospices de Beaune.

Arthur Narf (Eng) the slang term for a drink consisting of ½ bottled Guinness and ½ draught Guinness mixed together.

Arthur Rackham (Eng) a chain of specialist wine shops in London's Thames Valley area. Runs the Vintner wine club. *see* Vintner (The).

Artic Blue (Fin) a still natural mineral water from Lapland. pH 6.8

Artic Chiller (Can) a natural mineral water from Valemount BC. Mineral contents (milligrammes per litre): Calcium 23.4mg/l, Magnesium 6.4mg/l, Potassium 10.9mg/l, Bicarbonates 89.8mg/l, Chlorides 0.4mg/l, Sulphates 30mg/l, Fluorides 0.1mg/l.

Artic Glacier (Can) a natural mineral water from Toba Inlet BC. Mineral contents (milligrammes per litre): Calcium 0.8mg/l, Magnesium 0.2mg/l, Potassium 0.2mg/l, Bicarbonates 1mg/l, Chlorides 1mg/l, Sulphates 1mg/l, Fluorides 0.1mg/l.

Artichoke Brandy (Fr) a distillation of Jerusalem artichokes. *see* Eau-de-vie-de-Topinambours.

Artic Ice (Austr) a natural mineral water from Victoria. Mineral contents (milligrammes per litre): Sodium 9.6mg/l, Calcium 17mg/l, Magnesium 14.1mg/l, Potassium 0.9mg/l, Bicarbonates 162mg/l, Chlorides 22mg/l, Sulphates 5.2mg/l, Silicates 0.8mg/l.

Artic Mist (USA) a natural mineral water from Palmerton PA.

Artificiel (Fr) a term applied to a kirsch made from a neutral alcohol which is diluted to normal strength and flavoured with essences.

Artig (Ger) smooth rounded wine.

Artillery Cocktail (Cktl) ½ measure gin, ½ measure Italian vermouth, 2 dashes Angostura. Stir over ice and strain into cocktail glass.

Artillery Punch (Punch) juice of 2 pineapples, and 8 oranges, 300mls (¾ pint) light rum, 300mls (¾ pint) Bourbon whiskey, 1400mls (2½ pints) dry cider. Stir altogether and chill, add 3 pints iced Champagne (or sparkling wine).

Artimisia absinthium (Lat) *see* Wormwood.

Artimino (It) a Chianti Putto wine producer in Tuscany.

Artis (Fr) *abbr*: a Cru **Artis**ans. Bordeaux classification, now no longer used.

Artist (Eng) a slang term used to describe an experienced drinker.

Artisans & Estates (USA) a group that has formed together a collection of top Californian wine properties and wines. Estates include: Jackson Park Vineyard, Kendall-Jackson Estate, Matanzas Creek.

Artist Bitter (Eng) a light keg bitter 1032 O.G. from Morland's Abingdon, Brewery, Abingdon, Berkshire.

Artist's Ale (Eng) a premium cask-conditioned bitter

A

1055 O.G. from Paradise Brewery, Hayle, Cornwall.

Artist's Cocktail (Cktl) ⅓ measure whisky, ⅓ measure Sherry, ⅙ measure groseille (gooseberry) syrup, ⅙ measure lemon juice. Shake over ice and strain into a cocktail glass.

Artois Bock (Bel) a bock beer 6.2% alc by vol. relaunched (2005) by Interbrew in 275mls bottles (created 1895 and last sold by the Artois Brasserie in 1960).

Artois Brasserie (Bel) a brewery (established 1966) based in Louvain. Noted for Abbaye De Leffe, Artois Bock, Chevalier Marin, Ginder, Hertog Jan Pilsener, Ketje, Loburg, Radieuse, Vieux Temps and Wielemans beers. *See also* Stella Artois Brasserie.

Arts Déco Noces de Perle (Fr) a Grande Champagne Cognac produced by Hardy.

Artus Dreikönigsquelle (Ger) a natural mineral water from Bad Hönningen, Westerwald. Mineral contents (milligrammes per litre): Sodium 13mg/l, Calcium 67mg/l, Magnesium 21mg/l, Potassium 2mg/l, Bicarbonates 226mg/l, Chlorides 22mg/l, Sulphates 44mg/l, Fluorides 0.3mg/l.

Artus Hubertus Sprudel (Ger) a natural mineral water from Bad Hönningen, Westerwald. Mineral contents (milligrammes per litre): Sodium 740mg/l, Calcium 80mg/l, Magnesium 100mg/l, Potassium 40mg/l, Bicarbonates 1850mg/l, Chlorides 370mg/l, Sulphates 170mg/l.

Aruba (W.Ind) a small island off the coast of Venezuela. Produces light rums.

Aruk (M.East) *see* Arrack.

Arukari (Jap) a natural mineral water. Mineral contents (milligrammes per litre): Sodium 24mg/l, Calcium 18mg/l, Magnesium 0.04mg/l, Potassium 0.4mg/l. pH 8.2

Arumdale (S.Afr) the label for a red wine (Shiraz) produced by the Thelma Mountain Vineyards winery, Stellenbosch, Western Cape.

Arunda Sektkellerei (It) a noted sparkling wine producer (by the metodo tradizionale) based in Môlten, Südtirol (South Tyrol).

Arundel Brewery (Eng) a brewery (established 1992). (Add): Unit C7, Ford Airfield Ind. Estate, Ford, Arundel, West Sussex BN18 0HY. Beers include: Arundel Castle 3.8% alc by vol., Arundel Gauntlet 3.5% alc by vol., Arundel Gold 4.2% alc by vol., Arundel Special Bitter 4.5% alc by vol., ASB 4.5% alc by vol., Old Knucker 5.5% alc by vol., Stronghold 4.7% alc by vol., Sussex Mild 3.7% alc by vol., After Dark., Plod 4.5% alc by vol. 'E'mail: arundelbrewery@dsl.pipex.com

Arundel Special Bitter (Eng) a 4.5% alc by vol. bitter beer brewed by the Arundel Brewery, West Sussex. Also known as ASB.

Arva (E.Ind) a fermented liquor produced in Polynesia. *see* Ava and Ava Ava.

Arvelets [Les] (Fr) a Premier Cru vineyard in the A.C. commune of Fixin, Côte de Nuits, Burgundy. 3.36ha.

Arvelets [Les] (Fr) a Premier Cru vineyard in the A.C. commune of Pommard, Côte de Beaune, Burgundy. 8.5ha.

Arvenis (It) a natural mineral water from Arvenis, Ovara, Udine.

Arvèze (Fr) a gentian liqueur apéritif from Auvergne.

Arvie (Fr) a sparkling natural mineral water (established 1884) from the Puy de Dôme. (Add): Arvie à Augnat 63340. Mineral contents (milligrammes per litre): Sodium 650mg/l, Calcium 170mg/l, Magnesium 92mg/l, Potassium 130mg/l, Bicarbonates 2195mg/l, Chlorides 387mg/l, Sulphates 31mg/l, Silicates 77mg/l, Fluorides 0.9mg/l. pH 6.3

Arvine (Switz) a white grape variety. Old Valais and Vaud stock, giving a wine that is dry and full-bodied. Also dessert wines.

Arvino (It) a local name for the Gaglioppo grape in Savuto and Pollino, Calabria.

Arzelle (Fr) decomposed mica soil found in the Condrieu and Château Grillet estates, northern Rhône.

Arzheim (Ger) village (Anb): Pfalz. (Ber): Südliche Weinstrasse. (Gro): Königsgarten. (Vins): Rosenberg, Seligmacher.

Arzlay (Ger) vineyard (Anb): Mosel-Saar-Ruwer. (Ber): Zell/Mosel. (Gro): Rosenhang. (Vil): Cochem.

Arzni (Arm) a natural mineral water (established 1925).

Asagiri Heights Super-Vanadium (Jap) a natural mineral water from Mount Fugi. Mineral contents (milligrammes per litre): Sodium 40mg/l, Calcium 10mg/l, Magnesium 15mg/l.

Asahi Mineral Water (Jap) a naturel mineral water. Mineral contents (milligrammes per litre): Sodium 4.6mg/l, Calcium 6.4mg/l, Magnesium 2.6mg/l, Potassium 0.7mg/l.

Asahi Brewery (Jap) a brewery based in Hokkaido. Has 6 divisions and produces light and dark beers including bottled Super Dry 5% alc by vol. and Black Lager 5% alc by vol. *See also* Wakamusha. Website: http://www.asahibeer.co.uk

Asali (Afr) an East African beverage fermented from honey.

Asara Estate (S.Afr) a winery (established 1691) based in the Stellenbosch region, Western Cape. Grape varieties include: Cabernet franc, Cabernet sauvignon, Chardonnay, Chenin blanc, Malbec, Merlot, Petit verdot, Sauvignon blanc, Shiraz. Labels: Bell Tower Collection Estate Wine, Cape Fusion, Ebony. 120ha. Website: http://www.AsaraWine.com

ASB (Eng) *abbr: see* Arundel Special Bitter.

Asbach Uralt (Ger) a famous German brandy matured in Limousin oak. 40% alc by vol.

Asbestos Pulp (Eng) originally used for filtering wines and beers. Now succeeded by cellulose pads and membrane filters.

Aschaffenburg (Ger) village (Anb): Franken. (Ber): Mainviereck. (Gro): Not yet assigned. (Vin): Pompejaner.

A

Asciutto (It) dry wine.

Ascorbic Acid (Eng) vitamin C, an additive to wines, acts as an anti-oxidant. SO_2 must be present. Used with caution.

Ascot (Eng) the label of a sparkling wine from the Thames Valley Vineyard, Stanlake Park, Twyford, Berkshire.

Ascot Vineyards (Eng) vineyards (established 1979) 1.7ha. (Add): Ascot Farm, Ascot, Royal Berkshire. Grape varieties: Madeleine angevine, Madeleine sylvaner, (3% each), Müller-Thurgau 50%, Pinot noir 3%, Reichensteiner 35%, Siegerrebe 3% and Zweigeitrebe 3%.

Asda Farm Stores (Eng) a branded mineral water.

A.S.E. (USA) *abbr*: American Society of Enologists.

Asensio Carcelen (Sp) a small winery and wine museum based in Jumilla. Produces mainly Monastrell wines.

Aserpiado (Sp) the process of 'trenching' between the vines in the Sherry vineyards to trap any rainwater and feed it to the vines.

Asescence (Eng) a wine malady, has a strong smell of nail varnish and tastes vinegary. Attacked by acetobacter, requires presence of air. Caused mainly by bad storage in vat or a faulty cork. *See also* Piqûre.

Ashanti Gold (Den) a chocolate liqueur produced by Peter Heering near Copenhagen.

Ashanti Wines (S.Afr) a winery (established 1997) based in the Paarl, Western Cape. Grape varieties: Cabernet sauvignon, Chardonnay, Chenin blanc, Malbec, Merlot, Pinotage, Shiraz. Labels: Chiwara, Concept Wines, French Kiss, Joseph's Hat, Nicole's Hat, Sunset Hat. Website: http://www.ashantiwines.com

Ashbourne (Eng) a still and sparkling natural spring water from Dovedale, Derbyshire. (Add): Nestlé & C°., St. Georges House, Croydon, Surrey. Mineral contents (milligrammes per litre): Sodium 11mg/l, Calcium 90mg/l, Magnesium 15mg/l, Potassium 3mg/l, Chlorides 25mg/l, Sulphates 35mg/l, Fluorides 0.1mg/l.

Ashbourne (S.Afr) the label for a red wine (Pinotage) produced by the Southern Right winery, Hemel-en-Aarde Valley, Western Cape (formerly known as Bastenburg).

Ashbrook Estate (Austr) a vineyard based in the Margaret River region. (Add): P.O. Box 263, West Perth, Western Australia. 6005. Grape varieties: Cabernet franc, Cabernet sauvignon, Chardonnay, Merlot, Sauvignon blanc, Verdelho. Winery address: South Harmans Road, Willyabrup, W. Australia.

Ashbrook Mountain Spring (Eng) a natural spring water from Church Stretton, Shropshire. Mineral contents (milligrammes per litre): Sodium 13mg/l, Calcium 14mg/l, Magnesium 5.1mg/l, Potassium 1.4mg/l, Chlorides 22.7mg/l, Sulphates 24.5mg/l, Nitrates 13mg/l.

Ashdon Spring (Eng) a natural spring water from Ashe Park Estate, Steventon, Hampshire.

Ash Drink (Eng) *see* Frénette.

Ashe Park Water (Eng) a mineral water from source in Ashe Park Estate, Steventon, Hampshire (still and carbonated varieties).

Asher (S.Afr) the label for a red wine (Cabernet sauvignon 60% and Merlot 40%) from Alter Ego Wines, Tulbagh, Western Cape.

Ashes Ale (Eng) a 4.3% alc by vol. ale brewed by the York Brewery Company, North Yorkshire.

Ashford Brewery (Eng) a brewery (established 1983) based in Ashford, Kent. Produces Challenger 1039 O.G. Kentish Gold 1035 O.G. Old Gold 1047 O.G.

Ash Hollow (USA) a winery based near Walla Walla Valley, Washington. Grape varieties include: Merlot.

Ashkelon (Isr) a Palestinian wine written about by the Romans.

Ashland Vineyards (USA) a winery based in Rogue Valley. Noted for Bordeaux-style wines. Grape varieties: Cabernet sauvignon, Merlot, Chardonnay, Sauvignon blanc, Pinot gris, Müller-Thurgau.

Ashley's Vineyard (USA) the label for a red wine (Pinot noir) produced by Consillience winery, Santa Barbara County, California.

Ashman's Winery (Austr) a part of Tyrell's, New South Wales.

Ashridge (Wal) a mineral water. Mineral contents (milligrammes per litre): Sodium 8.9mg/l, Calcium 101mg/l, Magnesium 1.8mg/l, Potassium 0.9mg/l, Chlorides 18mg/l, Sulphates 3mg/l, Nitrates 4.6mg/l, Fluorides 0.05mg/l. pH 7.4

Ashtarak (Arm) a dessert wine produced in Armenia.

Ashton Hills (Austr) a vineyard 3ha. Based at the Piccadilly Valley in the Adelaide Hills, South Australia. Grape varieties: Chardonnay, Pinot noir and Riesling.

Ashton Koôperatiewe Wynkelder (S.Afr) a co-operative winery (established 1962) based in Ashton, Robertson, Western Cape. (Add): Box 40, Ashton 6715. Grape varieties: Cabernet sauvignon, Chardonnay, Colombard, Pinotage, Pinot noir, Red Muscadel, Sauvignon blanc, Shiraz, White Muscadel. Produces: Satyn Rooi and a range of varietals (known as A.K.W) 1200ha.

Ash Vine Brewery (Eng) a brewery. (Add): Trudoxhill, near Frome, Somerset. Brews Acid Rain, Toxic Waste (both limited edition beers). Also Hop and Glory, Ash Vine Bitter 3.5% alc by vol. Black Bess 4.2% alc by vol. Challenger 4.1% alc by vol. Penguin Porter 4.2% alc by vol. Hell For Leather 5.2% alc by vol.

Asia (Tur) a mineral water from Alaattin, Keykubat.

Asia Pacific Breweries Ltd. (S.E.Asia) based in Singapore. Brews: Tiger Lager Beer.

Asid (Wal) acid.

Asidig (Wal) acidic.

Asifansons (Pak) a natural mineral water from the Great Springs. Mineral contents (milligrammes per litre): Sodium 2150mg/l, Calcium 119mg/l, Magnesium 106mg/l, Potassium 10mg/l, Bicarbonates 316mg/l, Chlorides 1850mg/l, Sulphates 1200mg/l, Nitrates 5mg/l. pH 8.17

Asindirmak (Tur) vine grafting.

Asit (Tur) acid.

Askalon (Isr) a noted wine co-operative that produces red and white table wines.

Askeri (Iran) a small sweet white grape variety.

Askos (Gre) wineskin / skin bottle (bag) for holding wine, used in ancient Greece.

Asma (Tur) a word used to describe a hanging vine (trellised).

Aso (Jap) a natural mineral water.

Asociacíon de Criadores Exportadores de Vino de Jerez (Sp) the Sherry growers and exporters association. Replaces the disbanded Grupo de Exportadores.

Aspacher Klosterquelle (Ger) a natural mineral water from the Klosterquelle, Aspach-Rietenau, BW.

Aspall Cyder House (Eng) a traditional family cider-producing firm based in Debenham, Stourmarket, Suffolk. Four styles produced – organic dry 7% alc. by vol, extra dry, medium and lightly sparkling at 7% alc by vol. alsp Premier Cru dry 7% alc. by vol and Suffolk Cyder 5.5% alc by vol. Produced using a blend of dessert, culinary and bittersweet apples including Kingston Black, Yarlington Mill, Médaille d'Or, Blenheim Orange, Chivers Delight.

Aspartic Acid (Eng) an amino acid found in wines. Is formed by the yeast.

Aspenberg (Ger) vineyard (Anb): Nahe. (Ber): Schloss Böckelheim. (Gro): Paradiesgarten. (Vil): Bayerfeld-Steckweiler.

Aspenberg (Ger) vineyard (Anb): Nahe. (Ber): Schloss Böckelheim. (Gro): Paradiesgarten. (Vil): Oberndorf.

Aspen Ridge Winery (N.Z) a small winery at Waerenga Road, Te Kauwhata in the North Island. 6ha.

Asperg (Ger) village (Anb): Württemberg. (Ber): Württembergisch Unterland. (Gro): Schalkstein. (Vin): Berg.

Aspergillus oryzae (Jap) a special fungus called 'malted rice fungus' used in the brewing of saké. Also known as koji mould.

Aspersion (Fr) a frost precaution used in the Burgundy and Champagne regions. The vines are sprayed with water to form a protective coating of ice.

Aspinall Cambrinus Craft (Eng) a brewery based in Knowsley, Merseyside. Brews Celebrance 6.5% alc by vol. Deliverance 4.2% alc by vol. Dominance 5.5% alc by vol. Lamp Oil 5% alc by vol. Renaissance 3.3% alc by vol.

Aspiran (Fr) a wine-producing commune in the A.C. Clairette du Languedoc, southern France.

Aspirating Valve (Eng) a valve which maintains the condition of beers which remain in cask for several days. Allows the beer to be drawn from cask and for CO₂ to replace it. Also called a 'cask breather' or 'demand valve'.

Aspisheim (Ger) village (Anb): Rheinhessen. (Ber): Bingen. (Gro): Sankt Rochuskapelle. (Vins): Johannisberg, Sonnenberg.

Asprinio (It) a white grape variety used to produce a wine of same name.

Asprinio (It) a white wine produced in Basilicata from the grape of same name.

Aspro (Gre) the name given to lesser table wines produced by Tsantali.

Asprolithi (Gre) lit: 'white stone', a V.Q.P.R.D. white wine of Patras made from Rhoditis grapes. Produced by Oenoforos S.A.

Assaggiatore (It) wine taster.

Assam (Ind) a major Indian tea-growing and producing region.

Assam (Ind) a variety of single-stemmed tea bush, has light leaved and dark leaved varieties.

Assario (Port) a white grape variety grown in Alentejo.

Assario Branco (Port) another name for the Arinto do Dão. Also known as the Malvasia Fina.

Asseer Burtuqal (Arab) orange juice.

Assemat [J.C.] (Fr) a propriétaire-récoltant based at Rocquemaure, 30150 Gard. Produces A.C. Lirac. see Rouge d'Été, Lirac Rouge Classique, Domaine des Causses et Saint-Eynes.

Assemblage (Fr) the blending of wines of the same age, region, district, commune or vineyard of origin. See also Coupage.

Assenovgrad (Bul) a D.G.O. wine-producing area based in the Southern Basic Region. Noted for Mavrud wines.

Assenzio (It) absinthe.

Asseer (Arab) juice / fruit juice.

Assetato (It) thirsty.

Assindia (Ger) a natural mineral water from the Assindia Quelle, Essen-Kray, NW. Mineral contents (milligrammes per litre): Sodium 30.2mg/l, Calcium 18.1mg/l, Magnesium 47.6mg/l, Potassium 18.1mg/l, Bicarbonates 528mg/l, Chlorides 75.3mg/l, Sulphates 193mg/l, Fluorides 0.11mg/l.

Assirtico (Gre) a white grape variety used in the production of the white wine Agioritikos.

ASSIVIP (It) abbr: Associazione Interprovinciale Produttori Vini Pregiati. (established 19091) a regional association of fine wine producers in the Marche area.

Assmannshausen (Ger) a village on the north west of the Rheingau region noted for red wines made from the Spätburgunder grape.

Assmannshausen (Ger) village (Anb): Rheingau. (Ber): Johannisberg. (Gro): Steil. (Vin): Frankentha.

Assmannshausen-Aulhausen (Ger) village (Anb): Rheingau. (Ber): Johannisberg. (Gro): Burgweg. (Vin): Berg Kaisersteinfels.

Assmannshausen-Aulhausen (Ger) village (Anb): Rheingau. (Ber): Johannisberg. (Gro): Steil. (Vins): Hinterkirch, Höllenberg.

Associacao dos Produtores-Engarrafadores de Vinho Verde (Port) abbr: A.P.E.V.V. (established January 1985) an association of the single quinta estates in the Vinhos Verdes to protect and improve Vinhos Verdes wines.

Associado (Port) denotes a partner in a co-operative winery.

Associated Tavern Owners of America (USA) *abbr*: A.T.O.A. the USA equivalent of the Licensed House Managers Association in the U.K.

Associated Vintners (USA) the main wine producer in Yakima Valley, Washington, Pacific North-West. Produces wines from a 13ha. vineyard based in Redwood.

Association de Proprietaires de Grands Crus Classés de Saint-Émilion (Fr) (Add): Les Templiers, Rue Guadet. BP 46, 33330 Saint-Émilion.

Association des Viticulteurs de la Côte d'Or (Fr) a body which advises the growers in the Côte d'Or, Burgundy.

Association Nationale Technique pour l'Amélioration de la Viticulture (Fr) *see* A.N.T.A.V.

Association Professionelle des Producteurs Embouteilleurs de Rhum Agricole de la Martinique (W.Ind) *see* A.P.P.E.R.A.M.

Association Technique Viticole de Bourgogne (Fr) a body whose aim is to improve vine growing and wine making in Burgundy.

Assoiffé (Fr) thirsty.

Assumption Abbey (USA) the brand-name for Brookside Cellar wines in San Bernardino, California.

Assyrtiko (Gre) a white grape variety grown mainly in southern Greek islands of Cyclades. Produces the straw wine Santorini. *See also* Aidani, Athiri.

Astenbecker [Der] (Ger) a wheat-based branntwein produced by Fürstlich Münster von Derneburgische Brennerei, Astenbeck.

Astheim (Ger) village (Anb): Franken. (Ber): Maindreieck. (Gro): Kirchberg. (Vin): Karthäuser.

Asti (It) the new name for Asti Spumante since upgraded to D.O.C.G. A white sparkling wine produced in the Piemonte region by natural fermentation using the Moscato naturale d'Asti grape. Has an aromatic taste which is characteristic of the Muscat grape. *See also* Moscato d'Asti.

Asti (USA) a red wine-producing area based in the Italian Swiss Colony, California.

Astica (Bul) a Bulgarian State lager produced by Bulgarsko Pivo (Bulgarian State Brewery).

Astinenza (It) abstinence.

Asti Spumante (It) a D.O.C.G. white sparkling wine. Now known as Asti. *See also* Moscato d'Asti Spumante.

Astley Gold (Eng) a 3.8% alc by vol. beer brewed by the Merlin Brewery, Lancashire.

Astley Vineyards (Eng) a winery. (Add): The Crundels, Astley, Stourport-on-Severn, Worcestershire DY13 0RU. 1.7ha. Grape varieties: Huxelrebe, Kerner, Madeleine angevine, Müller-Thurgau. Produces white, rosé and sparkling wines. Website: http://www.heff.co.uk 'E'mail: office@heff.co.uk

Aston Manor Brewery (Eng) a brewery (established 1983). (Add): 173, Thimblemill Lane, Aston, Birmingham, West Midlands B7 5HS. Brews Black Adder 5.3% alc by vol (a blackcurrant-flavoured cider and lager)., Snake Bite 5.5% alc by vol (a cider and lager mix). Also Billy's Pooch, Chillin, Green Mamba, Old Deadly's White Cider. Website: http://www.astonmanor.co.uk 'E'mail: sales@astonmanor.co.uk

Aston Manor Malvern Spring (Eng) a mineral spring water from the Malvern Hills. Mineral contents (milligrammes per litre): Sodium 9mg/l, Calcium 76mg/l, Magnesium 32mg/l, Potassium 3mg/l, Bicarbonates 310mg/l, Chlorides 16mg/l, Sulphates 41mg/l, Nitrates 31mg/l, Fluorides 0.1mg/l. pH 7.1

Astoria Cocktail (Cktl) 25mls (⅛ gill) Calvados, dash Amer Picon. Shake over ice, strain into a cocktail glass and add a squeeze of lemon peel juice on top.

Astra Beer (Ger) the principal beer of the Bavarian St. Pauli Brauerei of Hamburg.

Astra Quelle (Ger) a natural spring water from Bad Vilbel, HE. Mineral contents (milligrammes per litre): Sodium 292mg/l, Calcium 13.6mg/l, Magnesium 4.2mg/l, Potassium 7.3mg/l, Chlorides 43mg/l, Fluorides 3.4mg/l.

Astringency (Eng) having an excess of tannin. *see* Astringent. (It) = aggressività.

Astringent (Eng) a term used by a wine taster and applied to wines with an excess of tannin. Many red wines are astringent when young, but mellow and soften with age. (Fr) = rude.

Astronaut Cocktail (Cktl) ⅓ measure vodka, ⅓ measure white rum, ⅓ measure lemon juice, dash passion fruit juice. Shake over ice, strain into an ice-filled highball glass and top with a slice of lemon.

Asugar (Sp) *see* Muscavado.

A/S Vinmonopolet (Nor) the State wine and spirits monopoly. *see* Jorgen B. Lysholm Distillery.

Asyla (Scot) a vatted malt whisky. 70% grain / 30% malt. Includes a 12 y.o. Linkwood (Speyside) and 10–21 y.o. malts from Cameronbridge. From Compass Box, Edinburgh.

Aszar-Neszmely (Hun) one of the fifteen wine regions. Situated in northern Transdanubia, it is noted for fine white wines.

Asztali Bor (Hun) table wine. Not permitted on wine imported into the E.C. *see* Minöségi Bor.

Aszú (Hun) a term found on the labels of Tokaji wines. Indicates a sweet, luscious wine made with botrytis-attacked grapes. *see* Puttonyos.

Aszúbor (Hun) denotes a sweeter type of Tokaji wine. *see* Aszú.

Atacama (Chile) noted vineyards based in northern Chile.

Ata Rangi Vineyard (N.Z) a winery. (Add): Puruatanga Road, Martinborough. 5ha. Grape varieties: Cabernet sauvignon, Chardonnay, Merlot, Pinot gris, Pinot noir, Sauvignon blanc, Syrah. Produce: Célèbre from a blend of Cabernet, Merlot and Syrah grapes, Craighall, Kahu Botrytised Riesling, . *See also* Family of Twelve.

Ataraxia (S.Afr) a winery (29ha) based in Walker Bay, Hermanus, Western Cape. Grape variety: Sauvignon blanc.

A

Ataturk Farm Administration (Tur) a co-operative winery that produces fine, full wines.

Atatürk [Kemal] (Tur) a statesman who built a winery in 1925 in the hope of encouraging more wine production amongst the muslim people in Turkey.

Atel (Rum) an important wine-producing area. Is part of the Tîrnave vineyard.

Athenaeus (Gre) a wine lover and gourmet of Ancient Greece. He wrote much on the art of wine making, wine drinking etc.

Athenaeus (Egy) a writer who lived in ancient Egypt and produced works on wine and gastronomy, notably the Deipnosophistae. Lived in the third century AD.

Athiri (Gre) a white grape variety grown mainly in southern Greece in the Cyclades Islands. Used to make a straw wine called Santorini on the Isle of Thira. *See also* Assyrtiko, Aidani.

Athol Brose (Scot) a liqueur based on whisky mixed with honey and / or oatmeal and cream.

Athol Brose Number One (Cktl) 1 measure Athol Brose, 1 dessertspoon clear honey, 1 Sherry glass cream, mix well, warm slightly and allow to cool before drinking.

Athol Brose Number Two (Cktl) 1 teaspoon clear honey into a tumbler containing 2 measures of Athol Brose. Top with heated milk, allow to cool before drinking.

Athos (Gre) a monastery that produces palatable local wines.

Athos (Fr) *see* Alpha.

Ativa (It) a natural mineral water from Valle della Vecchia, Trento.

Atkinson Ridge (S.Afr) an oak-aged Chardonnay produced by the Amani Vineyards, Stellenbosch, Western Cape.

Atlantica (Cktl) 2 measures dark rum, 1 measure amaretto, 1 measure blue Curaçao, mix with ice, strain into martini glass, top with apple juice and serve with a straw.

Atlantic Cognac Cocktail (Cktl) ⅔ measure Cognac, ⅓ measure crème de café, shake over ice, strain into a collins glass, top with orange juice, stir and decorate with a cherry and orange slice.

Atlantic Distillers (Can) a subsidiary of Seagram. Produces a range of Canadian whiskies.

Atlantis-Quelle (Ger) a natural spring water from Bocholt, NW.

Atlas Brewery (Scot) a brewery based in Lab Road, Kinlochleven, Argyll PH50 4SG. Brews a variety of beers (bitter / cask-conditioned / mild ale / bottled beers): Blizzard 4.7% alc by vol., Dark Island 4.6% alc by vol., Latitude 3.6% alc by vol., Nimbus 5% alc by vol., Tempest 4.9% alc by vol., Three Sisters 4.2% alc by vol., Wayfarer 4.4% alc by vol. Part of the Highlands and Islands Breweries Ltd. Website: http://www.atlasbrewery.co.uk 'E'mail: info@atlasbrewery.com

Atlas Peak Winery (USA) an A.V.A. of Napa Valley, California since 1992. Sole winery of same name. 40ha. Grape varieties: Cabernet sauvignon, Sangiovese, Consenso (a varietal of Sangiovese).

Atlas Premium (Ind) a natural spring water from New Dehli. Mineral contents (milligrammes per litre): Calcium 16mg/l, Magnesium 6.8mg/l, Potassium 1.6mg/l, Chlorides 16mg/l, Nitrates 1mg/l. pH 7.5

Atlas Really Strong Export (Eng) a 6.5% alc by vol. beer brewed by the Preston Brewing Company based in Lancashire.

A.T.O.A. (USA) *abbr*: Associated Tavern Owners of America.

Atomic Cocktail (Eng) an aqueous solution of a radioactive substance such as sodium iodine which is drunk as part of the treatment for cancer.

Atta Boy Cocktail (Cktl) ⅔ measure dry gin, ⅔ measure French vermouth, 4 dashes grenadine. Shake well over ice and strain into a cocktail glass.

Attemporators (Fr) spiral-shaped metal coils which are immersed in the fermentation vats and through which hot or cold water is passed. This regulates the temperature of the fermenting must.

Attenuate (Eng) a term used for the amount of sugar which has been used up by the yeast during fermentation.

At t'Ghoul & Ghost (Eng) a 5.2% alc by vol. ale brewed by the Anglo Dutch Brewery, West Yorkshire.

At The Limiet (S.Afr) the label for a naturally sweet white wine (Hárslevelü, Sémillon and Chenin blanc blend) produced by the Nabygelegen Private Cellar winery, Wellington, Western Cape.

Attica (Gre) a wine-producing area of the Kephesia district in central Greece where most of the Retsina is produced.

Atticus (S.Afr) the label for a red wine (Cabernet sauvignon, Petit verdot and Pinotage blend) produced by the Bellevue Estate winery, Stellenbosch, Western Cape.

Attic Wine (Gre) the collective name which is used for the wines from the Attica region.

Attila Cocktail (Cktl) ⅔ measure Banyuls, ⅓ measure vodka. Stir over ice, strain into a cocktail glass. Add soda water and dress with a spiral of lemon peel.

Attilafelsen (Ger) grosslage (Anb): Baden. (Ber): Kaiserstuhl-Tuniberg. (Vils): Gottenheim, Merdingen, Munzingen, Niederrimsingen, Oberrimsingen, Opfingen, Tiengen, Waltershofen.

Atzberg (Aus) a vineyard site on the banks of the River Danube situated in the Wachau region, Niederösterreich.

Atzmauth (Isr) a sweet dessert wine.

Atzmon (Isr) a medium-dry, red, table wine.

Aua Alva (Switz) a natural mineral water from Rothenbrunnen.

Aubad-Quelle (Aus) a natural spring water from the Tirol. Mineral contents (milligrammes per litre): Sodium 4.4mg/l, Calcium 431.26mg/l, Magnesium 47.2mg/l, Potassium 2.05mg/l, Bicarbonates 246.52mg/l, Chlorides 3.83mg/l, Sulphates 1027.86mg/l, Nitrates 0.6mg/l, Silicates 7.8mg/l.

Aubaine (Fr) an alternative name for the Chardonnay grape.

A

Aube (Fr) a département that adjoins Marne in the south of the Champagne region. District: Château Thierry. *see* Canton de l'Aube.

Aubel (Bel) a 6.9% alc by vol. unpasteurised, bottle-conditioned special beer brewed by D'Aubel Brasserie, Aubel.

Aubel [D'] Brasserie (Bel) a brewery based in Aubel. Brews: Aubel Beer.

Auberge (Fr) inn or tavern. *see* Alberga.

Auberge (Fr) part of a range of Vin de Pays wines from the Languedoc and Gascony region through Grants of St. James.

Aubergiste (Fr) innkeeper.

Aubin Blanc (Fr) a white wine produced in the Côtes de Toul, Lorraine.

Au Bon Climat (USA) a winery based in California. (Add): Mind Behind, Santa Maria, California B.W. 5107. Has vineyards in Santa Barbara (Santa Maria Valley). Grape variety: Pinot noir. Labels include: Isabelle Morgan, Knox Alexander. Website: http://www.aubonclimat.com

Aubry Fils (Fr) a Champagne producer. (Add): 4-6 Grande Rue, 51390 Jouët-lès-Reims.

Aubun (Fr) a red grape variety grown in the Rhône. Also known as Counoise.

Auburg Quelle (Ger) a natural spring water (established 1984) from Wagenfeld, NI. Mineral contents (milligrammes per litre): Sodium 19.8mg/l, Calcium 110mg/l, Magnesium 10.4mg/l, Potassium 2.5mg/l, Bicarbonates 431mg/l, Chlorides 28.9mg/l, Sulphates 8.5mg/l, Nitrates 0.28mg/l, Silicates 32.3mg/l, Fluorides 0.12mg/l.

Aucerot (Austr) a minor white grape used for blending, grown in the Hunter Valley, New South Wales.

Auch (Fr) a town in the Armagnac brandy region. Gers department.

Auchan (Sp) a natural mineral water from Cuenca. Mineral contents (milligrammes per litre): Sodium 0.8mg/l, Calcium 64.9mg/l, Magnesium 18.5mg/l, Potassium <0.5mg/l, Bicarbonates 255.1mg/l, Chlorides 2mg/l, Sulphates 23.8mg/l.

Auchentoshan (Scot) a lowland malt distillery noted for its triple distilled whisky. (Add): Dalmuir, near Glasgow, Dunbartonshire. 40% alc by vol. Owned by Bowmore Distillers. Produces 10 and 18 years old malts and a Three Wood Malt (American Bourbon / Spanish Oloroso / Pedro Ximinez casks). *see* Weaks and Strongs.

Auchere [Jacques et Fils] (Fr) a noted producer of A.C. Sancerre wines (white, rosé and red). (Add): Le Bois de l'Abbaye, Bué, 18300 Sancerre, Loire.

Auchroisk (Scot) a single highland malt whisky distillery north of Dufftown, Banffshire. 40% alc by vol.

Auchterturra (Scot) a special malt whisky that is not for general sale. Name derived from a mythical highland village, bottled for professional entertainers to use on special occasions.

Auckland (N.Z) a wine-producing area on the north west coast of the North Island. Produces mainly red wines on clay soil.

Au Closeau (Fr) a Premier Cru vineyard of the commune A.C. Gevrey-Chambertin, Côte de Nuits, Burgundy. 0.5ha.

Auction (Eng) *see* Wine Auctions.

Audacia Estate (S.Afr) a winery (established 1930) based in Stellenbosch, Western Cape. (Add): Audacia Langoed, P.O. Box 50, Lynedoch 7603. Grape varieties: Cabernet franc, Cabernet sauvignon, Merlot, Roobernet, Shiraz. Produces: Coeur de Rouge, Rouge Noble and varietal wines. 20ha. Website: http://www.audacia.co.za

Aude (Fr) a département of the Languedoc-Roussillon in the Plaine de l'Aude.

Audit Barley Wine (Eng) a barley wine brewed by the Greene King Brewery Biggleswade, Bedfordshire.

Auen (Ger) village (Anb): Nahe. (Ber): Schloss Böckelheim. (Gro): Paradiesgarten. (Vins): Kaulenberg, Römerstich.

Auenstein (Ger) village (Anb): Württemberg. (Ber): Württembergisch Unterland. (Gro): Schozachtal. (Vins): Burgberg, Schlossberg.

Auersthal (Aus) a wine village in the Falkenstein-Matzen district of north-eastern Austria. Produces mainly white wines.

Aufbesserung (Aus) the sugaring of the grape must to increase the alcohol content. (Fr) = chaptalisation, (Ger) = anreicherung.

Auf Dem Zimmerberg (Ger) vineyard (Anb): Nahe. (Ber): Schloss Böckelheim. (Gro): Paradiesgarten. (Vil): Oberstreit.

Auf der Hald (Aus) a vineyard area on the banks of the River Danube in the Kremstal region.

Auf Der Heide (Ger) vineyard (Anb): Mosel-Saar-Ruwer. (Ber): Bernkastel. (Gro): Schwarzlay. (Vil): Traben-Trarbach (ortsteil Wolf).

Auf der Höhe (Aus) a vineyard area on the banks of the River Danube in the Kremstal region.

Auf Der Kupp (Ger) vineyard (Anb): Mosel-Saar-Ruwer. (Ber): Saar-Ruwer. (Gro): Scharzberg. (Vil): Konz.

Auf der Setz (Aus) a vineyard site based on the banks of the River Kamp in the Kamptal region.

Aufgesetzter (Ger) the name used for kornbranntwein or pure alcohol that is flavoured with blackcurrant juice.

Auflangen (Ger) grosslage (Anb): Rheinhessen. (Ber): Nierstein. (Vil): Nierstein.

Aufwaerts Koöperatiewe Wynkelder (S.Afr) vineyards based in Goudini. (Add): Bpk. Box 51, Rawsonville 6845. Produces Sherry-type and white wines.

Augarant (Fr) a vineyard in the A.C. Fleurie Cru Beaujolais-Villages, Burgundy.

Auge (Fr) a region of Normandy awarded A.O.C. for cider in 1996. *See also* Cornouaille.

Augenscheiner (Ger) vineyard (Anb): Mosel-Saar-Ruwer. (Ber): Saar-Ruwer. (Gro): Römerlay. (Vil): Trier.

Auggen (Ger) village (Anb): Baden. (Ber):

Markgräflerland. (Gro): Burg Neuenfels. (Vins): Letten, Schäf.

Auggener Winzerfest (Ger) an annual wine festival held in the village of Auggen, Markgräferland, southern Baden on the third weekend in September.

Augier et Frères (Fr) the oldest Cognac house (established 1643). Now owned by Seagram.

Augina (It) a natural mineral water from Augina, Venezia.

Augsburger (USA) a premium beer 5.5% alc by vol. brewed by the Huber Brewery in Monroe, Wisconsin.

Augusta (It) a natural mineral water from Feja, Arcore. Mineral contents (milligrammes per litre): Sodium 38.5mg/l, Calcium 67mg/l, Magnesium 40.5mg/l, Potassium 0.8mg/l, Bicarbonates 378.5mg/l, Chlorides 79.6mg/l, Sulphates 39.3mg/l, Nitrates 4.9mg/l, Silicates 18mg/l, Fluorides 0.3mg/l. pH 7.3

Augusta (USA) an American grape variety, has both red and white varieties.

Augusta (USA) a small community based on the Missouri river, has its own appellation, wines given this appellation must contain 85% of Augusta grape.

Augusta Sorgente Fornace (It) a sparkling natural mineral water from Feja, Alessandria, Piedmonte. Mineral contents (milligrammes per litre): Sodium 52mg/l, Magnesium 43mg/l, Potassium 1.8mg/l, Bicarbonates 390mg/l, Sulphates 45mg/l, Nitrates 6.3mg/l, Silicates 17.8mg/l. pH 7.5

Augusta Victoria (Ger) a natural mineral water from Löhnberg-Selters, HE. Mineral contents (milligrammes per litre): Sodium 315mg/l, Calcium 173mg/l, Magnesium 68mg/l, Potassium 15.6mg/l, Chlorides 388mg/l, Fluorides 0.54mg/l.

Augustinian Ale (Eng) a 4.5% alc by vol. ale brewed by Nethergate Holdings Ltd., Suffolk.

Augustrebe (Aus) a white grape variety now no longer grown.

Augustijn Grand Cru (Bel) a 9% alc by vol. top-fermneted, bottle-conditioned, straw-coloured special beer brewed by Bios-Van Steenberge Brewery, Ertvelde.

Augustiner (Ger) a famous old brewery of München. Noted for Bock beers. *see* Augustiner Dunkel and Maximator.

Augustinerberg (Ger) vineyard (Anb): Baden. (Ber): Kaiserstuhl-Tuniberg. (Gro): Vulkanfelsen. (Vil): Breisach a. Rh.

Augustiner Dunkel (Ger) a dark rich malty beer from the Augustiner Brauerei of München.

Augustowianka (Pol) a natural mineral water from Augustow. Mineral contents (milligrammes per litre): Sodium 150mg/l, Calcium 67.3mg/l, Magnesium 24.3mg/l, Potassium 10mg/l, Bicarbonates 440mg/l, Chlorides 175mg/l, Sulphates 10mg/l, Fluorides 1.2mg/l.

August Schmidt (Ger) a distillery. (Add): 3000 Hannover, Hainholz. Distiller of Kornbranntweins and Weizenkorns.

Augustus Barnett (Eng) a specialist wine retail chain of shops owned by Bass.

Aujoux et Cie (Fr) a Burgundy négociant-éleveur. (Add): 20 Bld. Emile-Guyot, Saint-Georges-de-Reneins. Deals mainly in Beaujolais and Côte d'Or wines.

Aul (Scan) the name for the viking beer brewed from barley. (Eng) = ale, (Den) = öl, (Nor)= øl, (Swe) = öl.

Auld Alliance (Cktl) ⅓ measure French vermouth, ⅓ measure Glayva, ⅓ measure Cognac. Stir over ice and strain into an old-fashioned glass.

Auld Alliance (Scot) a 4% alc by vol. ale brewed by the Fyfe Brewery, Fife.

Auld Ginger (Ch.Isles) a 5% alc by vol. ale with a hint of ginger from Guernsey Brewery, St. Peter Port, Guernsey (now no longer produced).

Auld Hemp (Eng) a 3.8% alc by vol. beer brewed by the High House Farm brewery, Tyne & Wear.

Auld Man's Milk (Cktl) ½ measure Jamaican rum, ½ measure Cognac, 1 teaspoon sugar, 1 egg, 2 measures boiling milk. Shake in a heated shaker, pour into a goblet and top with grated nutmeg.

Auld Man's Milk (Scot) a slang term for whisky.

Auld Man's Milk (Punch) heat a bottle of strong ale in pan. Add ¼ teaspoon cinnamon, ¼ teaspoon nutmeg, ¼ teaspoon ginger. Stir in 2 beaten egg yolks and 2 teaspoons brown sugar when ale has almost boiled. Mix slowly and well. Add 2 measures of Scotch whisky and serve as hot as possible.

Auld Reekie (Scot) a cask-conditioned ale 1037 O.G. brewed by the Rose Street Brewery. An Alloa home-brew public house in Edinburgh.

Auldstone Cellars (Austr) a winery (established 1987). (Add): Booth's Road, Taminick, via Glenrowan, Victoria. Grape varieties: Cabernet, Muscat, Riesling.

Aulenberg (Ger) vineyard (Anb): Rheinhessen. (Ber): Nierstein. (Gro): Krötenbrunnen. (Vil): Ülversheim.

Aulerde (Ger) vineyard (Anb): Rheinhessen. (Ber): Wonnegau. (Gro): Bergkloster. (Vil): Westhofen.

Aultmore (Scot) a single highland malt whisky distillery based near Keith, Banffshire. 40% alc by vol.

Aum (Ger) a wine cask usually about 160litres.

Aumann (Aus) a winery based in Tribuswinkel, Thermenregion. (Add): Oberwaltersdorfer Strasse 105, 2512 Tribuswinkel. Grape varieties: Blauer portugieser, Cabernet sauvignon, Pinot blanc, Zweigelt.

Aume (Fr) an Alsace cask of 114litres (25.1 gallons).

Aunt Jemima (Pousse Café) ⅓ measure each in order brandy, (white) crème de menthe and Bénédictine.

Aupy [Henri] (Fr) a wine producer based at Le-Puy-Notre-Dame, Saumur, Anjou-Saumur, Loire. Noted for Saumur Mousseux.

Aura (Thai) a natural mineral water from Mae Rim, Chian Mai Provence. Mineral contents (milligrammes per litre): Sodium 4.8mg/l,

A

Calcium 69mg/l, Magnesium 8.1mg/l, Potassium 1.3mg/l, Bicarbonates 237.37mg/l, Chlorides 0.6mg/l, Sulphates 4.6mg/l, Nitrates 1.9mg/l, Silicates 47mg/l, Fluorides 0.33mg/l. pH 7.1

Aurélie (Lux) a natural mineral water from Mölleschbour.

Aurelius (Fr) a Grand Cru A.C. Saint-Émilion produced by the Unions des Producteurs de St. Émilion, Bordeaux. Grape varieties: Cabernet franc 15%, Merlot 85%.

Auret Cape Blend (S.Afr) the label for red wine (Cabernet sauvignon, Merlot and Pinotage blend) produced by the Clos Malverne winery, Stellenbosch, Western Cape.

Aurora (Port) a still natural mineral water from Aurora. Mineral contents (milligrammes per litre): Sodium 1mg/l, Calcium 0.5mg/l, Magnesium 0.1mg/l, Potassium 0.1mg/l, Chlorides 1mg/l, Sulphates 0.5mg/l, Nitrates 0.05mg/l, Fluorides 0.05mg/l. pH 6.0

Aurora (USA) a white hybrid grape variety, also known as Siebel 5279.

Aurore Cocktail (Cktl) ⅔ measure Bacardi White Label, ⅙ measure Mandarine Napoléon, ⅙ measure crème de framboise. Shake over ice, strain into a cocktail glass and top with a spiral of orange and lemon peel.

Aurum (It) a pale gold brandy-based liqueur with a flavour of oranges. 40% alc by vol.

Aurum Cocktail (Cktl) ¼ measure aurum, ¼ measure gin, ½ measure sweet vermouth. Stir over ice and strain into a cocktail glass.

Aus (Aus)(Ger) abbr: **Aus**sle. A wine from selected grapes.

Ausbau (Aus) the process of cask aging wines in a winery. See also Klassischer Ausbau.

Ausberger (S.Afr) a sweet white wine made from a blend of Steen and other grape varieties from the SFW produced under the Autumn Harvest label.

Ausbruch (Aus) a wine category, wines are made from over-ripe, naturally shrivelled grapes attacked by Botrytis. (Min. must weight 27°KMW, 138° Oechsle) fresh grape must (auslese or beerenauslese from the same Cru may be added for harmony). Wine must be bottled in Austria and cannot be sold before 1st May of year following the harvest. see Prädikatsweine.

Ausbruchwein (Aus) see Ausbruch.

Ausdruckslos (Ger) a term used to describe an undistinctive wine.

Aus Eigenem Lesegut (Ger) lit: 'from producer's own estate'.

Ausejo (Sp) a Zona de Crianza in the Rioja Baja region of north-eastern Spain.

Ausg'stecktist (Aus) a Viennese daily paper from which can be found the list of the Heurigen open that day.

Aus Ländern Der E.W.G. (E.C.) a table wine blended and bottled in Germany from wines produced by E.C. member countries.

Auslese (Aus) a wine category, must be produced from fully ripe grapes, separated from any semi-ripe, imperfect or unhealthy grapes. (Minimum must weight 21° KMW. 105° Oechsle). Wine must be bottled in Austria and cannot be sold before 1st May of year following the harvest. see Prädikatsweine.

Auslese (Ger) lit: 'late picked', a wine quality category, produced from late picked, selected ripe bunches of grapes. Makes a sweet white wine. 83°–105° Oe. See also Beerenauslese and Trokenbeerenauslese. (It) = scelto.

Ausleseweine (Ger) an old term for wine of Auslese quality. Pre 1971.

Ausone (Fr) a Premier Grand Cru Classé of Saint-Émilion. see Château Ausone.

Ausonia (It) a sparkling, slightly acidic natural mineral water from Ausonia, Verbiana, Piedmonte. Mineral contents (milligrammes per litre): Sodium 28.4mg/l, Calcium 53.5mg/l, Magnesium 63.6mg/l, Potassium 5.9mg/l, Bicarbonates 460mg/l, Chlorides 9.6mg/l, Sulphates 70mg/l, Nitrates 1.1mg/l, Silicates 29mg/l, Fluorides 0.27mg/l. pH 5.85

Ausonius (Lat) a fourth century Roman poet from Bordeaux. Château Ausone was named after him.

Ausoniusstein (Ger) vineyard (Anb): Mosel-Saar-Ruwer. (Ber): Zell/Mosel. (Gro): Weinhex. (Vil): Lehmen.

Aussay (Eng) the old English name for the wines of Alsace. See also Osey.

Aussichtsterrasse der Deutschen Weinstrasse (Ger) lit: 'Viewpoint of the German wine route' seen at the Schloss Ludwigshöhe near Edenkoben in the Pfalz.

Aussle (Ger)(Aus) a wine from selected grapes.

Ausstich (Aus) a selection of the best finished auslese wines, blended, can be red or white.

Aussy [Les] (Fr) a Premier Cru vineyard [part] in the A.C. commune of Volnay, Côte de Beaune, Burgundy.

Austere (Eng) a tasting term to describe red wines that have excessive acidity and tannins (grape and cask) that when thin in body are usually from poor vintages.

Austin Nichols Distilling C°. (USA) a noted distillery based in Kentucky. Noted for 8 year old Wild Turkey Bourbon. 53% alc by vol.

Australia (Austr) a wine-producing country in the southern hemisphere, has been producing wines for over 200 years (first vines planted 1788 and replantings 1791 by Captain Arthur Phillip). Wine regions predominantly in southern part of country. New South Wales, South Australia, Victoria and Western Australia. Main districts are Adelaide Hills, Barossa Valley, Clare Watervale, Coonawarra, Great Western, Hunter Valley, Keppoch, Margaret River, McLaren Vale, Mudgee, Murray Valley, Southern Vales, Swan Valley, Tasmania and Yarra Valley. Website: http://www.australianwinebureau.com

Australian Rum (Austr) production commenced in the late nineteenth century, both white and dark rums produced. see Beenleigh and Bundaberg.

Australian Sherry (Austr) the name given to wines

made in the style of true Spanish Sherry, most is of the cream and medium styles.

Australian Spring (Austr) a natural spring water.

Australian Whiskey (Austr) a grain whiskey distilled in a style which is a cross between Scottish and Irish whiskies.

Australian Wine and brandy Corporation (Austr) *abbr*: AWBC. a regulatory body that controls wine and spirits in Australia.

Australian Wine Board (Austr) the governing body of the Australian wine industry, government controlled.

Australian Wine Research Institute (Austr) an organisation based at Glen Osmond, near Adelaide, South Australia. Helps raise standards and promotes Australian wines.

Austria (Aus) a major wine producing country in central Europe 51,000 hectares / approx. 31000 growers (3500 full-time and 28,000 part-time). Wines are produced to the same style as the German wines. Regions: Burgenland, Carnuntum, Donauland, Kamptal, Kremstal, Mittelburgenland, Neusiedlersee, Neusiedlersee-Hügelland, Niederösterreich, Styria (Steiermark), Sud-Bergenland, Sud-Oststeiermark, Sud-Steiermark, Thermenregion, Traisental, Vienna (Wien), Wachau, Weinviertel, Weststeiermark (also included are Bergland Österreich and Weinland Österreich). In 1985 the country had a major wine scandal with adulterated wines (anti-freeze added to wines to increase sweetness). New wine laws introduced 1995 in line with Austria's entry into the European Union. Websites: http://www.weinausoesterreich.at / http://www.winesfromaustria.com

Austrian Rum (Aus) a blend of spirits and rum similar to rumverschnitt. (2% rum), known as inländerrum.

Austrian Wine Marketing Board (Aus) the promotional body for Austrian wines. (Add): Gumpendorferstr. 5, A-1060 Vienna. Website: http://www.austrian.wine.co.at/wine 'E'mail: austrian.wine@inmedias.at

Austried (Ger) a term to denote the first signs that the growers have of the condition of the vines after the winter and spring frosts.

Autenrieder Schlossgartenquelle (Ger) a natural spring mineral water from Ichenhausen-Autenried, BY. Mineral contents (milligrammes per litre): Sodium 5mg/l, Calcium 82.4mg/l, Magnesium 20.9mg/l, Potassium 0.6mg/l, Bicarbonates 283.7mg/l, Chlorides 18mg/l, Sulphates 33.3mg/l, Fluorides 0.1mg/l.

Auténtico (Sp) a fresh, fruity, young red wine produced in Binisalem, Majorca. Made from the Montenegro grape.

Authental (Ger) vineyard (Anb): Rheinhessen. (Ber): Nierstein. (Gro): Vogelsgärten. (Vil): Guntersblum.

Authentication of Origin (Austr) a scheme established so that if a geographical origin is named on a label at least 80% of the wine must come from that source. This rises to 85% if the wine is exported to E.C. countries.

Authentique Rosé (Fr) a Grand Cru rosé brut (6 grammes dosage) Champagne from the house of E. Barnaut matured for 3–4 years before release (10% to 15% Chardonnay) with the remainder Pinot noir.

Autleithen (Aus) a vineyard site on the banks of the River Danube situated in the Wachau region, Niederösterreich.

Autoclave (It) the name given to the 'tank method' of sparkling wine production. The second fermentation occurs in pressurised tanks.

Autol (Sp) a Zona de Crianza in the Rioja Baja region, north-eastern Spain.

Autolysis (Eng) describes yeast decomposition in wine that is prevented by regular racking.

Automatic Red Wine Vinificators (Eng) stainless steel vats specially made to encourage extraction of colour by a continuous juice sprinkler in rotating horizontal vats.

Autovac (Eng) an old style of beer engine. Beer which has over-flowed into the drip-tray is recycled through the pump. Also known as an Economiser.

Autovinification (Port) a method of vinification in which the mantle is moved to the bottom of the vat continuously. Also permits hygiene and temperature control. Uses pressure from the CO_2.

Autovinificator (Port) the name given to the special vat used in the production of Port. An automatic fermentation process using CO_2 pressure to syphon and circulate the must and extract the maximum colour and tannin quickly.

Autreau [G.E.] Père et Fils (Fr) a Champagne producer. (Add): 15 Rue René Baudet, Champillon, 51160 Ay. Récoltants-manipulants, produce vintage and non-vintage wines.

Autrichen (Fr) the French name for the red grape Portugieser.

Autumn Ale (Eng) a 5% alc by vol. ale brewed by the Coach House Brewing C°. based in Cheshire.

Autumn Ale (Eng) a 4.7% alc by vol. brewed by the Hesket Newmarket Brewery, Cumbria.

Autumn Ale (Eng) a 4.5% alc by vol. ale from the Wye Valley Brewery, Hereford.

Autumnale [S] (Eng) a 4.6% alc by vol. ale brewed by the Wickwar Brewing C°. Gloucestershire.

Autumn Frenzy (Eng) a smooth full-bodied ale brewed with rye by Ushers of Trowbridge. 4% alc by vol. Brewed with rye and nutmeg.

Autumn Glory (Eng) a rich hoppy 4.5% alc by vol. seasonal beer from the Exe Valley Brewery, Silverton, Devon (September–November).

Autumn Gold Cider (Eng) the original name for the draught / bottled cider from Matthew Clark in Somerset. Renamed Blackthorn Sweet Cider.

Autumn Harvest (Eng) a perry cider produced using pears from Continental Wine and Food.

Autumn Harvest Wines (S.Afr) the brand-name wines from the S.F.W.

Autumn Knights (Eng) a 4.7% alc by vol. seasonal beer brewed by Castle Eden Brewery in County Durham.

Autumn Leaves (Eng) a 4.3% alc by vol. ale brewed by the Millstone Brewery, Lancashire.

Autumn Riesling Sylvaner (N.Z) a dry white, blended wine from the Penfolds Winery, Henderson, North Island.

Autumn Seer (Eng) a 4.8% alc by vol. beer brewed by the Hogs Back Brewery, Ltd., Surrey.

Autumn Tyne (Eng) a 4% alc by vol. beer brewed by the Mordue Brewery Ltd., Tyne & Wear.

Autumn Wind Vineyard (USA) a vineyard based in Oregon, noted for Chardonnay varietal wines.

Auvergnac Gris (Fr) lit: 'wine of the grey friar', the French name for the Hungarian wine Szürkebaràt.

Auvergne (Fr) a V.D.Q.S. wine-producing region. *see* Fronton.

Auvernat Blanc (Fr) an alternative name for the Chardonnay grape.

Auvernat Gris (Fr) an alternative name for the Pinot meunier grape grown in the eastern Loire and Champagne.

Auvernier (Switz) a Neuchâtel village noted for Oeil de Perdrix.

Auvigue, Burrier, Revel et Cie (Fr) a small négociant-éleveur company based at Charney-lès-Mâcon, Côte Mâconnais, Burgundy.

Aux Argillats (Fr) a Premier Cru vineyard [part only] of the A.C. commune of Nuits-Saint-Georges, Côte de Nuits, Burgundy. 2.5ha.

Aux Beaux-Bruns (Fr) a Premier Cru vineyard of the commune A.C. Chambolle-Musigny, Côte de Nuits, Burgundy. 2.4ha.

Aux Boudots (Fr) a Premier Cru vineyard in the A.C. Nuits-Saint-Georges, Côte de Nuits, Burgundy. 6.4ha.

Aux Bousselots (Fr) a Premier Cru vineyard in the A.C. commune of Nuits-Saint-Georges, Côte de Nuits, Burgundy. 4.5ha.

Aux Brûlées (Fr) a Premier Cru vineyard of the commune A.C. Vosne-Romanée, Côte de Nuits, Burgundy. 3.8ha.

Aux Chaignots (Fr) a Premier Cru vineyard in the A.C. commune of Nuits-Saint-Georges, Côte de Nuits, Burgundy. 5.6ha.

Aux Champs-Perdrix (Fr) a Premier Cru vineyard [part only] in the A.C. commune of Nuits-Saint-Georges, Côte de Nuits, Burgundy. 2.1ha.

Aux Charmes (Fr) a Premier Cru vineyard of the commune A.C. Morey-Saint-Denis, Côte de Nuits, Burgundy. 1.2ha.

Aux Cheusots (Fr) *see* Clos Napoléon.

Aux Clous (Fr) a Premier Cru vineyard [part] of the A.C. commune of Savigny-lès-Beaune, Côte de Beaune, Burgundy.

Aux Combottes (Fr) a Premier Cru vineyard of the commune A.C. Chambolle-Musigny, Côte de Nuits, Burgundy. 2.27ha.

Aux Combottes (Fr) a Premier Cru vineyard of the commune A.C. Gevrey-Chambertin, Côte de Nuits, Burgundy. 4.9ha.

Aux Coucherias (Fr) a Premier Cru vineyard [part] of the A.C. commune of Beaune, Côte de Beaune, Burgundy. 9.27ha.

Aux Cras (Fr) a Premier Cru vineyard in the A.C. commune of Beaune, Côte de Beaune, Burgundy. 5.02ha.

Aux Cras (Fr) a Premier Cru vineyard in the A.C. commune of Nuits-Saint-Georges, Côte de Nuits, Burgundy. 3ha.

Aux Crots (Fr) a Premier Cru vineyard [part only, including Château Gris] in the A.C. Nuits-Saint-Georges, Côte de Nuits, Burgundy. 8.9ha.

Aux Échanges (Fr) a Premier Cru vineyard in the A.C. commune of Chambolle-Musigny, Côte de Nuits, Burgundy. 1ha.

Auxerre (Fr) a city in the Yonne département. Produces mainly red wines. Noted vineyards are Le Clos de la Chaînette, Côteau de Migraine and Trancy.

Auxerrois (Fr) a red grape variety grown in Cahors. Also known as the Malbec and Côt.

Auxerrois Blanc (Fr) a white grape variety also known as the Pinot auxerrois. At one time grown as a lesser variety in Alsace but now no longer used.

Auxerrois Gris (Fr) an alternative name for the Pinot gris grape. *See also* Fauvet, Malvoisie, Pinot beurot and Ruländer.

Auxerroix (Fr) a red grape variety grown in the Lorraine district to produce the light pink Vin gris. Also known as Malbec.

Auxey-Duresses (Fr) a famous red and white wine-producing village 140ha. in the Côte de Beaune, Burgundy. 1er Crus: Bas des Duresses, Climat du Val known as Clos du Val [part], Les Bréterins, Les Duresses, Les Ecusseaux [part], Les Grands-Champs, Reugne.

Auxey-le-Grand (Fr) a small wine-producing district in the Côte d'Or. Red wines only.

Aux Fourneaux (Fr) a Premier Cru vineyard [part] in the A.C. commune of Savigny-lès-Beaune, Côte de Beaune, Burgundy.

Aux Grand-Liards (Fr) a Premier Cru vineyard [part] in the A.C. commune of Savigny-lès-Beaune, Côte de Beaune, Burgundy.

Aux Gravains (Fr) a Premier Cru vineyard in the A.C. commune of Savigny-lès-Beaune, Côte de Beaune, Burgundy.

Aux Guettes (Fr) a Premier Cru vineyard [part] in the A.C. commune of Savigny-lès-Beaune, Côte de Beaune, Burgundy.

Auxiliary (Eng) the Association of Publican's Wives, devoted to charitable activities.

Auxillaries (Eng) *see* Auxillary.

Aux Malconsorts (Fr) a Premier Cru vineyard of the commune A.C. Vosne-Romanée, Côte de Nuits, Burgundy. 5.9ha. Also known as Les Malconsorts.

Aux Murgers (Fr) a Premier Cru vineyard in the A.C. commune of Nuits-Saint-Georges, Côte de Nuits, Burgundy. 5ha.

Auxois (Fr) an alternative name for the Pinot gris grape.

Aux Perdrix (Fr) a Premier Cru vineyard of the commune A.C. Nuits-Saint-Georges, Côte de Nuits, Burgundy. 3.4ha.

Aux Petits-Liards (Fr) a Premier Cru vineyard [part] in the A.C. commune of Savigny-lès-Beaune, Côte de Beaune, Burgundy.

Aux Petits-Mons (Fr) a Premier Cru vineyard in the A.C. commune of Vosne-Romanée, Côte de Nuits, Burgundy. 3.7ha.

Aux Reignots (Fr) a Premier Cru vineyard in the A.C. commune of Vosne-Romanée, Côte de Nuits, Burgundy. 1.7ha.

Aux Serpentières (Fr) a Premier Cru vineyard [part] in the A.C. commune of Savigny-lès-Beaune, Côte de Beaune, Burgundy.

Aux Thorey (Fr) a Premier Cru vineyard in the A.C. commune of Nuits-Saint-Georges, Côte de Nuits, Burgundy. 6.2ha.

Aux Vergelesses (Fr) a Premier Cru vineyard (including Bataillière) in the A.C. commune of Savigny-lès-Beaune, Côte de Beaune, Burgundy.

Aux Vignes-Rondes (Fr) a Premier Cru vineyard in the A.C. commune of Nuits-Saint-Georges, Côte de Nuits, Burgundy. 3.4ha.

Auzat (Fr) a natural mineral water from Montcalm, Vallée d'Auzat, Ariège. Mineral contents (milligrammes per litre): Sodium 1.5mg/l, Calcium 3mg/l, Magnesium 0.6mg/l, Potassium 0.4mg/l, Bicarbonates 5.2mg/l, Chlorides 0.6mg/l, Sulphates 8.7mg/l, Nitrates <1mg/l, Silicates 7.5mg/l. pH 6.8

Auzonnet (Fr) a lemon and mint flavoured liqueur produced by the Germain company in southern France.

A.V.A. (USA) *abbr*: American Viticultural Area. Originally known as Approved Viticultural Area.

Ava (E.Ind) a fermented liquor made from the roots of a local pepper plant (**Macropiper methysticum**). High in alcohol is also known as Kava or Yava. *See also* Arva and Ava Ava. Produced in Polynesia.

Av-02 (USA) a natural spring mineral water from Florida.

Ava Ava (E.Ind) *see* Ava and Arva.

Ava-Ava (USA) an alternative name for Kava.

Avacas (Cyp) a dry white wine from the Ambelitis Winery. *see* Ayia Moni.

Avahy (Bra) a slightly acidic natural mineral water. Mineral contents (milligrammes per litre): Sodium 34.4mg/l, Calcium 26.1mg/l, Magnesium 57.3mg/l, Potassium 10.8mg/l, Chlorides 14.9mg/l, Sulphates 30.8mg/l. pH 5.6

Avallon (Fr) a town in the Yonne département. Produces red and white wines. *see* Côte Rouvre (La), Montcherin and Vézelay.

Avalon (Can) a natural mineral water from Guelph, Ontario. Mineral contents (milligrammes per litre): Sodium 9mg/l, Calcium 73mg/l, Magnesium 36mg/l, Potassium 1mg/l, Bicarbonates 260mg/l, Chlorides 16mg/l, Sulphates 57mg/l.

Avalon Springtime (Eng) a 4% alc by vol. beer brewed by the Moor Beer Company, Somerset.

Avalon Vineyard (Austr) a winery (established 1986) based near Whitfield, Victoria. Grape varieties: Cabernet sauvignon, Pinot noir, Chardonnay, Sémillon.

Avalon Vineyard (Eng) a vineyard based in East Pennard, Shepton Mallet, Somerset. Grape variety: Seyval blanc.

Avani (Can) a natural spring mineral water.

Avanus (Ger) a natural mineral water (established 1985) from Belm, NI. Mineral contents (milligrammes per litre): Sodium 8mg/l, Calcium 52mg/l, Magnesium 25mg/l, Potassium 1.2mg/l, Bicarbonates 269mg/l, Chlorides 13mg/l, Sulphates 21mg/l, Fluorides 0.2mg/l.

Avaux [Les] (Fr) a Premier Cru vineyard in the A.C. commune of Beaune, Côte de Beaune, Burgundy. 13.4ha.

Avdat (Isr) a dry, light red and white wines produced by Carmel for sale in the USA.

Avec les Bons Voeux de la Brasserie Dupont (Bel) a strong winter ale 9.5% alc by vol. from the Brasserie Dupont.

Aveleda (Port) a Vinho Verde from near Penafiel in northern Portugal. The largest selling of the Vinhos Verdes.

Avelsbach (Ger) a fine wine area between the rivers Mosel and Ruwer in the Mosel-Saar-Ruwer.

Avelsbacher Hammerstein (Ger) a white medium dry table wine from Avelsbach on the Mosel.

Avena (Can) a natural spring water from Northampton, New Brunswick.

Avenay (Fr) a Premier Cru Champagne village in the Canton d'Aÿ. District: Reims.

Avenir Estate [L'] (S.Afr) a winery. (Add): P.O. Box 1135, Stellenbosch. Main grape varieties: Chardonnay, Chenin blanc, Merlot, Pinotage, Sauvignon blanc.

Avensan (Fr) a lesser Haut-Médoc commune in Bordeaux.

Aventinus (Ger) a dark, strong wheat beer brewed by the Schneider Brauerei in Münich. 8% alc by vol.

Aveq (Eng) a drink produced from a blend of French white wine, herbal extracts, fruit juices and spring water from the Gaymer Group.

Avery's of Bristol (Eng) a large old established and famous firm of wine merchants based in Bristol. (Add): 7, Part Street, Bristol BS1 5NG.

Avesso (Port) a white grape variety used in the making of Vinhos Verdes.

Avesta Bryggeri (Swe) a brewery. (Add): Garpenbergsvagen 41, Fors 77497, Sweden. Brews bitter ales and lagers. Website: http://www.avestabryggeri.se

Aveta Celtic Goddess of Healing Waters (Ire) a still natural mineral water from County Cork. Mineral contents (milligrammes per litre): Sodium 67.25mg/l, Calcium 1.51mg/l, Magnesium 16.6mg/l, Potassium 1.45mg/l, Chlorides 89mg/l, Sulphates 30.2mg/l, Nitrates <4.4mg/l, Fluorides 0.13mg/l, Iron 39.4mg/l. pH 7.5

Avian (Ind) a natural spring mineral water.

Aviator Ale (Eng) a 4% alc by vol. ale brewed by the Dent Brewery, Cumbria.

Aviation Cocktail [1] (Cktl) ⅔ measure gin, ⅓ measure lemon juice, 2 dashes maraschino. Shake over ice and strain into cocktail glass.

Aviation Cocktail [1] (Cktl) ½ measure sweet Sherry, ½ measure red Dubonnet. Stir over ice, strain into cocktail glass and dress with a spiral of orange peel.

Avicenna (Arab) an Arab alchemist who wrote about alcohol strengths and distillation.

Aviemore Brewery (Scot) a brewery based in Aviemore, north-east Scotland. Brews: Ruthven Brew 3.8% alc by vol.

Avignon (Fr) a wine town which is in centre of southern Rhône vineyards including A.C. Côtes du Rhône and A.C. Châteauneuf-du-Pape.

Avignonesi (It) a winery (86ha) based at Montepulciano, Tuscany. Noted for Vino Nobile di Montepulciano.

Avillo (Sp) an alternative name for the Folle blanche grape.

Avinagrado (Port) a taste of vinegar, sour.

Aviner (Fr) lit: 'to season', the process of seasoning new oak casks for some wines so that they lose their 'wood' taste. Usually done with old wine. Is also applied to new oak vats.

Avita (USA) a still natural mineral water (established 1948). Mineral contents (milligrammes per litre): Sodium 1mg/l, Calcium 45.9mg/l, Magnesium 10.3mg/l, Potassium 0.32mg/l, Bicarbonates 151mg/l, Sulphates 6mg/l, Fluorides 0.1mg/l.

Aviva (Isr) a leading wine-producing company in northern Israel.

Avize (Fr) a Grand Cru Champagne village in the Canton d'Avize. District: Épernay.

Avize (Fr) see Canton d'Avize.

Avo (Port) a sparkling wine made by the traditional method from Sociedade Agrícola dos Vinhos Messias.

Avoca (Austr) see Pyrenees.

Avoccata [L'] (It) a D.O.C. Barbera d'Asti wine aged in large oak casks by Coppo (Luigi) in Piemonte.

Avoir Soif (Fr) thirsty.

Avondale (S.Afr) a winery (established 1997) based in the Suider-Paarl, Western Cape. Grape varieties include: Cabernet sauvignon, Chardonnay, Chenin blanc, Merlot, Muscat blanc, Muscat rouge, Sauvignon blanc, Shiraz, Syrah. Labels: Amira, Graham Reserve, Julia, Les Pleurs, Propietor's Shiraz.

Avonside (Scot) a de luxe Scotch whisky, blended and sold by Gordon and Macphail of Elgin, Morayshire.

Avontuur Estate (S.Afr) a winery (established 1850) based in Somerset West, Stellenbosch, Western Cape. Grape varieties: Cabernet franc, Cabernet sauvignon, Chardonnay, Chenin blanc, Merlot, Sauvignon blanc. Labels: Baccarat, Luna de Miel and varietal wines. Website: http://www.avontuurestate.co.za

Avra (Gre) a natural mineral water from Aiyion. Mineral contents (milligrammes per litre): Sodium 9.7mg/l, Calcium 68.1mg/l, Magnesium 6.7mg/l, Potassium 1.2mg/l, Bicarbonates 223.3mg/l, Chlorides 10.7mg/l, Sulphates 16.1mg/l, Nitrates 4.4mg/l pH 7.4

Awa (Afr) a slightly acidic natural spring mineral water from Abidjan, Ivory Coast. Mineral contents (milligrammes per litre): Sodium 21.5mg/l, Calcium 56.7mg/l, Magnesium 2.7mg/l, Potassium 4.3mg/l, Bicarbonates 216mg/l, Chlorides 8.7mg/l, Sulphates 8.6mg/l.

Awatea Cabernet Merlot (N.Z) a full-flavoured, deep coloured red wine from the Te Mata vineyards, Hawkes Bay, North Island.

A.W.B.C. (Austr) abbr: Australian Wine and Brandy Corporation.

Awein (Rus) a milk-based, alcoholic spirit produced by the Tartars.

AWK (S.Afr) a producer of a range of sparkling wines produced by the cuve close method.

Axarquía (Sp) a wine-producing district in south-eastern Málaga. Grows Pedro ximénez grapes.

Axas (Port) a lesser white grape variety grown in the Minho province.

Axbridge (Eng) see Cheddar Valley Vineyard.

Axe Hill (S.Afr) a vineyard (established 1993) based in Calitzdorp, Little Karoo. Grape varieties: Souzão, Tinta barocca, Touriga nacional. Produces Cape Vintage Port.

Axemans Block (Eng) a 3.6% alc by vol. beer brewed by the TigerTops Brewery, West Yorkshire.

Axemans Light (Eng) 3.6% alc by vol. ale brewed by the TigerTops Brewery, West Yorkshire.

Axeman's Wheat Mild (Eng) a wheat-based mild ale brewed by micro-brewery Prince of Wales, Foxfields, near Broughton, Cumbria. See also Lock 47.

Axe Vale Brewery (Eng) a small brewery (established 1983). (Add): Colyton, Devon. Produces Battleaxe 1053 O.G. and Conqueror 1066 O.G.

Axios (USA) a red wine (Cabernet sauvignon) produced in the Napa Valley, California.

Aÿ (Fr) a wine commune in the Marne département. Noted for fine Champagnes. see Canton d'Aÿ and Aÿ-Champagne.

Ayala (Fr) a Champagne producer. (Add): 2 Boulevard du Nord, 51160 Aÿ. Grande Marque. 33ha. Produces vintage and non-vintage wines. Vintages: 1906, 1911, 1919, 1921, 1926, 1928, 1929, 1934, 1937, 1941, 1942, 1943, 1945, 1947, 1949, 1952, 1953, 1955, 1959, 1961, 1962, 1964, 1966, 1969, 1970, 1975, 1976, 1979, 1982, 1983, 1985, 1988, 1989, 1990, 1995, 1996. Now owned by Bollinger. See also Montebello.

Aÿ-Champagne (Fr) a Grand Cru Champagne town in the Canton of Aÿ. District: Reims.

Ay-Danil (Rus) a very sweet wine from the Crimean Peninsular from the Pinot gris grape.

Ayguemortes (Fr) a commune in the A.C. Graves region of south-western Bordeaux.

Ayia Moni (Cyp) a dry red wine from the Ambelitis Winery. see Avacas.

Ayias Mamas (Cyp) a village on the south east end of the island that produces grapes for Commandaria dessert wine.

A

Ayilmak (Tur) to sober up, become sober after a heavy drinking bout.

Aying Brauerei (Ger) a small brewery based in Aying, Bavaria. Noted for clean tasting, malty beers. *see* Platzl Special and Andreas Bock.

Ayios Georghios (Cyp) a village in the south eastern end of the island that produces the grapes for Commandaria dessert wine.

Ayl (Ger) village (Anb): Mosel-Saar-Ruwer. (Ber): Saar-Ruwer. (Gro): Scharzberg. (Vins): Herrenberger, Kupp, Scheidterberger.

Aylesbury Brewery (Eng) *see* A.B.C.

Ayran (Tur) buttermilk.

Aysu (Asia) a slightly acidic natural mineral water from Azerbaijan. Mineral contents (milligrammes per litre): Sodium 3.2mg/l, Calcium 51.5mg/l, Magnesium 9.2mg/l, Potassium 3.2mg/l, Bicarbonates 187mg/l, Chlorides 7mg/l, Sulphates 26mg/l. pH 5.4

Aysu (Tur) a natural mineral water from the Taurus Mountains. Mineral contents (milligrammes per litre): Calcium 27mg/l, Magnesium 4.6mg/l. pH 7.66

Aytac (Tur) a natural spring mineral water. Mineral contents (milligrammes per litre): Sodium 2.8mg/l, Calcium 21mg/l Chlorides 6.3mg/l, Fluorides 0.08mg/l. pH 7.8

Ayyas (Tur) denotes a drunkard, an alcoholic.

Ayze (Fr) an A.C. Vin de Savoie white wine, pétillant, it is made from 75% Gringet and 25% Roussette grapes.

Azal (Port) a white grape variety used in the production of Vinhos Verdes.

Azal Branco (Port) a white grape variety of the Entre Minho e Douro. Used to produce Vinhos Verdes.

Azal Tinto (Port) a black grape variety grown in the Entre Minho e Douro. Produces deep red wines.

Azay-le-Rideau (Fr) a commune in the Touraine, Loire, which can add its name to A.C. Touraine.

Azbuka (Bul) a premium red wine produced by the B.V.C. *See also* Musika.

Azedo (Port) bitter / acidic.

Azedume (Port) acid taste / acidic / bitter taste.

Azeitao (Port) vineyards sited between Lisbon and Setúbal in southern Portugal.

Azerbaijan (Rus) a wine region that produces mainly dessert wines. Also part in Iran.

Azienda (It) denotes a firm or business.

Azienda Agricola (It) when preceeding producer's name, guarantees that the wine is made from his own grapes.

Azienda Agricola Antonelli San Marco (It) a 140ha winery based at Loc. San Marco 59, 06036 Montefalco (PG). Noted for D.O.C. Montefalco range of wines.

Azienda Agricola Attilio Simonini (It) a winery based at Donadoni in Puglia. Produces red, rosé and white wines.

Azienda Agricola Cà dei Frati (It) a vineyard (established 1782) based in Lugana di Sirmione. (Add): Viticoltori in Lugana di Sirmione, Italy. Produces Tre Filer. Website: http://www.cadeifrati.it

Azienda Agricola Camigliano (It) a noted producer in Siena, Tuscany of Brunello di Montalcino.

Azienda Agricola Carobbio s.r.l. (It) a winery (8ha). (Add): Via San Martino e Cecione 26, 50022 Panzano, Chianti. Produces Chianti Classico Riserva, Pietraforte del Carobbio, Leone del Carobbio, Vin Santo.

Azienda Agricola Cascina Garitina (It) a winery. (Add): Via Giancola 20, 14040 Castel Boglione (AT). 13ha. vineyard that produces 70% Barbera plus Dolcetto, Pinot noir, Brachetto and Cabernet sauvignon grapes.

Azienda Agricola Cennatoio (It) a winery. (Add): Via San Leolino 35, 50020 Panzano in Chianti (FI). Grape varieties include Sangiovese, Cabernet sauvignon, Merlot, Chardonnay.

Azienda Agricola Cesani Vincenzo (It) a winery based in the DOCG Vernaccia di San Gimignano in the Tuscany region. Website: http://www.agriturismo-cesani.com

Azienda Agricola Ceuso (It) a winery based on the island of Sicily. Label: Scurati. Website: http://www.ceuso.it 'E'mail: sales@ceuso.it

Azienda Agricola Concadora (It) a 18ha. winery. (Add): Loc. Concadora 67, 53011 Castellini in Chianti, (SI). Noted for Chianti Classico Riserva.

Azienda Agricola Conte Loredan Gasparini (It) a winery. (Add): Via Martignano Alto, 24/A, I-31040 Venegazzù di Volpago del Montello. Has 80ha. of vineyards in Veneto. Produces Capo di Stato, Venegazzù della Casa wines.

Azienda Agricola di Angelo Gaja (It) a winery based in Barbaresco, Piemonte. 55ha.

Azienda Agricola F.lli Tedeschi (It) a winery based in the DOC Valpolicella Classico region of Veneto. (Add): Via Verdi 4-37020 Pedemonte, Verona. Produces a variety of local wines. Labels: Capital di Nicalo, La Fabriseria, Monte Olmi. Website: http://www.tedeschiwines.com

Azienda Agricola Greppo (It) *see* Biondi-Santi.

Azienda Agricola Italo Mattei (It) a winery and principal producer of Verdicchio di Matelica.

Azienda Agricola Lanciola II (It) a winery (34ha). (Add): Via Imprunetana 210, 50023 Impruneta (FI). Noted for Le Masse di Greve Chianti Classico Riserva, Vin Santo and Grappa. Also I.G.T. Terricci (from 80% Sangiovese grosso, 15% Cabernet sauvignon, 5% Cabernet franc grapes that are barrique-aged), I.G.T. Terricci Chardonnay, Bianco della Lanciola.

Azienda Agricola Livernano (It) a wine estate (5.5ha) based in Radda, Tuscany. Grape varieties: Cabernet franc, Carmenère, Sangiovese, Merlot, Cabernet sauvignon, Chardonnay, Sauvignon blanc, Gewurztraminer,. Produces Purosangue and Livernana wines.

Azienda Agricola M. &. G. Fugazza (It) a winery (40ha) based in Luzzano, Romito and Luzzano. Wines bottled at Castello di Luzzano. Labels include: Merloblú.

Azienda Agricola Masciarelli (It) a winery (250ha) based in San Martino sulla Marrucina in the province of Chieti (Abruzzo region). Grape varieties include: Chardonnay, Cococciola, Trebbiano. Labels: Marina Cvetic, Villa Gemma. Website: http://www.masciarelli.it

Azienda Agricola Moletto (It) winery. Website: http://www.moletto.com 'E'mail: moletto@moletto.com

Azienda Agricola Monte del Frá (It) a winery based in the Lombardy region. Grape varieties include: Cortese, Garganega, Trebbiano. Lombardy region. Produces DOC Bianco di Custoze. Label: Cà del Magro.

Azienda Agricola Piazzo Armando (It) a winery. (Add): Fraz. S. Rocco Seno d'Elvio 31, 12053 Alba. Produces D.O.C.G. Barolo, Asti, Barbaresco, D.O.C. Barbera d'Alba, Dolcetto d'Alba, Nebbiolo d'Alba, Langhe Chardonnay.

Azienda Agricola Poderi Marcarini (It) a winery based in the DOCG Barolo, Piemonte. Produces Barolo Brunate. Website: http://www.marcarini.it

Azienda Agricola Vigna Rionda (It) a winery based in the DOCG Barolo. Website: http://www.massolino.it 'E'mail: massolino@massolino.it

Azienda de La Mea di Marco Maci (It) a winery based at Brindisi, Puglia. Produces Sire, Vitu plus D.O.C. Salice Salentino, Squinzano and Copertino. I.G.T. wines from Chardonnay sauvignon, Negroamaro and Malvasia grapes.

Azienda Masciarelli (It) a vineyard (194.5ha) Based in the Abruzzo region. (Add): Villa Gemma, San Martino Sulla Marrucina (CH), Abruzzo. Produces: Marina Cvetic, Masciarelli Classico, Villa Gemma.

Azienda Santa Barbara (It) a winery based in the DOC Verdicchio dei Castelli di Jesi, Marches region. (Add): Borgo Mazzini 35-60010 Barbara (Acncona). Label: Le Vaglie. Website: http://www.vinisantabarbara.it

Azienda Agricola Spadafora (It) a winery based on the island of Sicily. Label: Monreale (Syrah). Website: http://www.spadafora.com

Azienda Vinicola (It) when preceeding the producer's name, guarantees that the wine is made from the producer's own grapes and bought in grapes.

Azienda Vinicola Benanti (It) a winery based on the island of Sicily. Label: Serra della Contessa. Website: http://www.novumwines.com 'E'mail: info@novumwines.com

Azienda Vinicola Bosco Nestore (It) a winery (established 1897) based in Nocciano (PE). Produces D.O.C. Montepulciano d'Abruzzo. Label: Cerasulo. Website: http://www.nestorebosco.com 'E'mail: info@nestorebosco.com

Azienda Vinicola Rivera (It) a winery based in Puglia that produces DOC Castel del Monte Rosso (from Nero di troia grapes). Label: Puer Apuliae. Website: http://www.rivera.it

Azijn (Hol) vinegar.

Azores (Port) islands in the North Atlantic that produced wines of note until vineyards were destroyed by Oidium and Phylloxera. see Açores. See also Fayal and Pico.

Aztali (Hun) see Tokaji Aztali.

Azteca Cocktail (Cktl) 25mls (⅙ gill) tequila, juice ½ lime, 2 dashes gomme syrup, slice of fresh mango. Blend with a scoop of crushed ice in a blender. Pour into a Champagne saucer and dress with 2 lime slices and serve with straws.

Aztecato (Ch.Isles) the rand-name of a commercially produced tomato wine. Medium sweet and dry versions. (Add): Guernsey Tomato Centre, Kings Mills, Câtel, Guernsey. Re-named Vin de Câtel before being discontinued (circa 1992).

Aztec Punch (Cktl) 1 part tequila, 5 parts grapefruit juice, ⅛ part strong tea, 1 part lemon juice, sugar syrup to taste. Stir all together, chill and serve.

Azuaga (Sp) a vino comarcal wine from the province of Badajoz in the Extremadura.

Azur (Ger) a still natural mineral water from Lichtenau, SN. Mineral contents (milligrammes per litre): Sodium 176mg/l, Calcium 177mg/l, Magnesium 29.9mg/l, Potassium 16.3mg/l, Bicarbonates 784mg/l, Chlorides 214mg/l, Sulphates 23mg/l.

Azza Newt (Eng) a 4% alc by vol. bitter ale brewed by the Burrington Brewery, devon.

Azzurra (It) a sparkling natural mineral water from Camonda. Mineral contents (milligrammes per litre): Sodium 1.1mg/l, Calcium 88mg/l, Magnesium 34mg/l, Potassium 0.9mg/l, Bicarbonates 227mg/l, Chlorides 1.3mg/l, Sulphates 167mg/l, Nitrates 5mg/l. pH 7.65

Azzurrina (It) a natural mineral water (established 1996) from Betulla. Mineral contents (milligrammes per litre): Sodium 4mg/l, Calcium 12.2mg/l, Magnesium 1mg/l, Potassium 1.7mg/l, Bicarbonates 42.7mg/l, Chlorides 4.7mg/l, Sulphates 2.6mg/l, Nitrates 1.3mg/l, Silicates 7mg/l. pH 8.1

B

Baa (Jap) bar.

Baach (Ger) village (Anb): Württemberg. (Ber): Remstal-Stuttgart. (Gro): Wartbühl. (Vin): Himmelreich.

Baadog (Mon) a 4.6% alc by vol. ale brewed by Utan Bator Breweries Ltd.

Baar (Fr) a commune in the Bas-Rhin, Alsace, grows mainly Riesling and Sylvaner grapes.

Baar Brauerei (Switz) an independent brewery based in Baar.

Baaten (Jap) bartender.

Bab (Eng) a 4.6% alc by vol. ale brewed by The Branscombe Vale brewery, Devon.

Baba Budan (Ind) the nickname for coffee. So called after the Muslim merchant who first introduced coffee to India in the seventeenth century.

Babbie's Special (Cktl) 1 measure apricot brandy, 1 dash gin, 1 dessertspoon cream, 1 dash sugar syrup. Shake over ice, strain into a cocktail glass.

Babeasca (Rum) a pleasant red, acidic wine with a taste of cloves from the Nicoresti region. Made from grape of same name.

Babeasca (Rum) a red grape variety from Focsani, produces acidic wines with a slight taste of cloves, also known as Babeasca Neagra.

Babeasca Neagra (Rum) see Babeasca.

Babe Chardonnay (Fr) a brand name for a French rosé-coloured Chardonnay wine produced for the American market, the name designed to appeal to the Americans in place of the complicated French label names!

Babeurre (Fr) buttermilk.

Babic (Slo) an ordinary red table wine produced on the Dalmatian coast.

Babich Family Vineyard (N.Z) a winery. (Add): Babich Road, Henderson, Auckland. 64ha. Grape varieties: Cabernet sauvignon, Merlot, Chardonnay, Gewürztraminer, Müller-Thurgau, Palomino, Pinotage, Pinot noir, Sauvignon blanc, Syrah. Labels include: Family Reserve.

Babilafuente (Sp) a still natural mineral water from the Antigua Fuente del Caño Babilafuente, Salamanca. Mineral contents (milligrammes per litre): Sodium 13.3mg/l, Calcium 45.7mg/l, Magnesium 5.1mg/l, Bicarbonates 164.7mg/l, Chlorides 4.4mg/l, Sulphates 8.3mg/l, Nitrates 15.8mg/l.

Babo (It) a mustimetre used in Italy, has the same scale as the Baumé system.

Babsi (Cktl) 25mls (1fl.oz) Grand Marnier, 20mls (¼ fl.oz) Bourbon whiskey, 2 dashes lemon juice, 2 dashes orange juice, build into a Champagne glass, top with iced sekt.

Babu (Eng) the Esquire Premium Draught Lager 4.6% alc by vol. a double fermented lager brewed by McMullen & Sons Ltd., Hertfordshire. Served through a portable keg system that does not require a gas cylinder, pipes or valves to dispense its lager. 12.5 litre capacity.

Baby (Eng) split / nip / quarter bottle.

Babycham (Eng) a sparkling white or pink perry drink produced by Showerings. Both dry and sweet styles, sold in 100mls and 75 cls bottles.

Baby Duck (Can) an ordinary sparkling wine, CO_2 injected.

Babylon (S.Afr) a red wine (Cbernet, Merlot and Pinotage blend) produced by the Babylon's Peak winery, Swartland, Western Cape.

Babylon Banks (Eng) a 4.1% alc by vol. ale brewed by the Fenlands Brewery Ltd, cambridgeshire.

Babylonians (M.East) the first real recorded wine-makers of any note, although wine was made long before them.

Babylon's Peak (S.Afr) a winery (established 2003) based in Swartland, Western Cape. Grape varieties: Cabernet sauvignon, Merlot, Pinotage, Syrah. Label: Babylon.

Babylon Toren (S.Afr) the label for a range of wines produced by the Backsberg Cellars, Suider-Paarl, Western Cape.

Baby Polly (Eng) the name given to a small 'split' Apollinaris mineral water.

Baby Whisk (Scot) a sparkling pink mix of Scotch whisky and carbonated water. Launched by Argyll Whiskade C°. in Glasgow, created on Isle of Mull.

Baca (Lat) small round berried fruit. i.e. Grapes. See Bacciferous and Acinum.

Bacarat (Fr) Kattell-Roc, low alcohol red vermouth. Is less than 1% alc by vol.

Bacardi (W.Ind) a well-known brand (established in Cuba 1862) of Bahamian, Brazilian, Cuban, Mexican and Puerto Rican white rums. See also Metz, Still Metz, Black Metz. Website: http://www.brown-forman.com

Bacardi Anejo (W.Ind) a cask-aged white rum produced by Bacardi. Is aged for six years.

Bacardi Apple (W.Ind) a 32% alc by vol apple-flavoured Bacardi rum (using Bacardi Carta Blanca rum). See also Bacardi Berry.

Bacardi Berry (W.Ind) a 32% alc by vol berried fruits-flavoured Bacardi rum (using Bacardi Carta Blanca rum). See also Bacardi Apple.

Bacardi Blossom Cocktail (Cktl) ½ measure Bacardi, ½ measure orange juice, dash maraschino. Shake over ice, strain into a cocktail glass.

Bacardi Breezer (W.Ind) the label of a 5.4% alc by vol. RDT drink produced from white Bacardi rum mixed with lime, lemon, orange, pineapple, cranberry or tropical watermelon. Sold in 275mls bottles. Also half-sugar versions (Bursting Blueberry / Crisp Apple / Refreshing Raspberry / Zesty Lemon) at 4% alc by vol. Website: http://www.bacardi-breezer.co.uk

Bacardi Cocktail (Cktl) 35mls (1½ fl.ozs) Bacardi White Label, juice of ½ lime, 1 teaspoon grenadine. Shake well together over ice, strain into a cocktail glass. Decorate with a cherry.

Bacardi Collins (Cktl) 35mls (1½ fl.ozs) Bacardi White Label, juice of ½ lime, 1 teaspoon sugar. Combine sugar with juice, add 2 or 3 ice cubes and Bacardi then fill glass with soda. Garnish with a cherry and a slice of orange.

Bacardi Crusta (Cktl) 40mls (⅓ gill) Bacardi, 1 teaspoon Pernod, 20mls (⅙ gill) lemon juice, 2 dashes Angostura bitters. Shake over broken ice. Moisten inside of a wine glass with lemon juice and sprinkle with ½ teaspoon powdered sugar. Put in lemon peel cut in a spiral then strain in mixture and add some sliced fruit.

Bacardi Cuba Libre (Cktl) place some ice into a highball glass, add 50mls (2fl.ozs) Bacardi and top with Cola.

Bacardi 8 Anos (W.Ind) a premium aged rum matured for 8 years in small oak casks in the tropics.

Bacardi Elixir Pousse (Pousse Café) in a liqueur Elgin pour Bacardi Elixir until the glass is ½ full. Fill the glass slowly with cream. Cross with a cherry on cocktail stick.

Bacardi Highball (Cktl) fill a highball glass with ice, add 50mls (2fl.ozs) of Bacardi Anejo. Top with soda water.

Bacardi Mojito (Cktl) 50mls (2fl.ozs) Bacardi White Label, 1 teaspoon sugar, juice ½ lime, 2 dashes Angostura, 3 mint leaves. Combine sugar and juice, crush with mint leaves. Add 2 ice cubes, stir again. Add Bacardi and bitters. Top with soda water, add a slice of lime.

Bacardi Old Fashioned (Cktl) 50mls (2fl.ozs) Bacardi Gold Label, 3 dashes Angostura, 1 teaspoon sugar, 1 teaspoon water. Muddle the sugar, bitters and water, add ice and Bacardi. Mix well and garnish with a cherry, slice of orange, pineapple and rind of lime. Serve with straws.

Bacardi Pineapple Fizz (Cktl) 35mls (1½ fl.ozs) Bacardi White Label, 25mls (1fl.oz) pineapple juice, 1 teaspoon sugar. Shake well with ice, strain into 200 ml. (8fl.oz) glass, fill with soda water.

Bacardi Rigo (W.Ind) a 5.4% alc by vol. ready mixed drink flavoured with lime and soda.

Bacardi Sour (Cktl) 50mls (2fl.ozs) Bacardi White Label, juice ½ lime, 1 teaspoon sugar. Combine juice with sugar, put rum in a shaker, add ice, shake well. Strain into a cocktail glass. Decorate with slice of pineapple, orange and a cherry.

Bacardi Special (Cktl) ⅔ measure Bacardi White Label, ½ measure gin, juice of a lime, 1 dash grenadine, 2 dashes gomme syrup. Shake together over ice except the rum, add rum, shake again, then strain into a cocktail glass.

Bacardi Spice (W.Ind.) a 40% alc by vol. rum with rich Caribbean spices from Bacardi & C°. Ltd.

Baccarat (Eng) a style of glass of plain thin lead crystal of various sizes.

Baccarat (Fr) the trade-mark name of famous French crystal glass manufacturer.

Baccarat (S.Afr) a red wine (Cabernet franc, Cabernet sauvignon and Merlot blend) produced by the Avontuur Estate, Stellenbosch, Western Cape.

Bacchai (Lat) a priestess of Bacchus. Female devotees of Bacchus. *see* Bakkhe.

Bacchanal (Eng) drunken or riotous celebration.

Bacchanal (Eng) follower of Bacchus, relating to Bacchus.

Bacchanalia (Eng) denotes drunken revelry. e.g: A Bacchanalian party (rites associated with Bacchus).

Bacchanalis (Lat) relating to Bacchus. *see* Bacchanal.

Bacchans (Lat) devotees of Bacchus.

Bacchant (Eng) priest of Bacchus. Male devotee of Bacchus.

Bacchante (Eng) priestess of Bacchus. Female devotee of Bacchus.

Bacchanté (S.Afr) the label for a white wine (Chenin blanc and Colombard blend) produced by the Brandvlei Cellar winery, Worcester, Western Cape.

Bacchari (Lat) to celebrate the Bacchanalia.

Bacchic (Eng) relating to Bacchus.

Bacchic (Eng) riotously drunk.

Bacchos (Gre) the name sometimes given to Dionysos (from which Bacchus derives). *See also* Bakkhos.

Bacchus (Ger) a white grape variety, a cross between the Silvaner, Riesling and Müller-Thurgau. Early ripening, gives fruity wines.

Bacchus (Lat) the Roman god of wine. Jupiter (father) and Semele (mother). (It) = bacco.

Bacchus (USA) a small, black hybrid grape variety that produces good quality, full-bodied wines.

Bacchus Wines (S.Afr) the brand-name white wines from the S.F.W.

Bacciferous (Eng) berry-bearing (applied to grape vines) from the Latin '*Baca*'.

Baccio Punch (Punch) ½ bottle dry gin, ½ bottle grapefruit juice, ½ bottle Champagne, ¼ bottle anisette, ½ syphon soda water in a large bowl (not the Champagne) with ice. Add fruit in season and lastly the Champagne.

Bacco (It) Bacchus.

Bacco d'Oro (It) a sparkling (metodo tradizionale) wine produced by Contratto in the Piemonte region.

Bacelo (Port) denotes a newly planted vine.

Bacharach (Ger) bereich (Anb): Mittelrhein. (Gros): Schloss Reichenstein, Schloss Stahleck.

Bacharach (Ger) a Rhine port from which together

with Hockheim, was where most wines were shipped in the Middle Ages. *see* Bachrag, Backrag.

Bacharach (Ger) village (Anb): Mittelrhein. (Ber): Bacharach. (Gro): Schloss Stahleck. (Vins): Hahn, Insel Heylessern Wert, Kloster Fürsteutal, Postern, Mathias Weingarten, Wolfshöhle.

Bacharach/Steeg (Ger) village (Anb): Mittelrhein. (Ber): Bacharach. (Gro): Schloss Stahleck. (Vins): Hambusch, Lennenborn, St.Jost, Schloss Stahlberg.

Bachelor's Bait Cocktail (Cktl) 1 measure dry gin, 1 dash Amer Picon, 2 dashes grenadine, 1 egg white. Shake over ice, strain into cocktail glass.

Bachem (Ger) village (Anb): Ahr. (Ber): Walporzheim/Ahrtal. (Gro): Klosterberg. (Vins): Karlskopf, Sonnenschein, Steinkaul.

Bacheroy-Josselin (Fr) wine négociants based at Chablis, Burgundy.

Bachfischfest (Ger) a Rheinhessen wine festival held in Worms in August.

Bachrag (Eng) an old English pronunciation of Bacharach the wine port which together with Hockheim shipped most of the German wines associated with Mosel wines. *See also* Bachray.

Bachsatz (Aus) a vineyard site on the banks of the River Danube situated in the Wachau region, Niederösterreich.

Bachtobel (N.Z) a clone of the Pinot noir grape. Suitable for sparkling wine production as it does not have much colour.

Bacigalupi Vineyard (USA) an independent vineyard based in the west of Sonoma County, California.

Bacio Divino (USA) a red wine produced by Caymus Vineyards, Napa Valley, California. First vintage in 1993. 1995 vintage produced from 66% Cabernet sauvignon, 22% Sangiovese and 12% Petite Sirah grapes.

Back-Blending (N.Z) the addition of concentrated or unfermented grape juice to wine before bottling.

Backöfchen (Ger) vineyard (Anb): Nahe. (Ber): Kreuznach. (Gro): Pfarrgarten. (Vil): Wallhausen.

Backofen (Ger) vineyard (Anb): Mittelrhein. (Ber): Rheinburgengau. (Gro): Herrenberg. (Vil): Kaub.

Backrag (Eng) an old English pronunciation of Bacharach. *see* Bachrag.

Backsberg Estate Cellars (S.Afr) a wine estate (established 1916) in Suider-Paarl, Western Cape. (Add): P.O. Box 1, Klapmuts 7625. Grape varieties: Cabernet sauvignon, Chardonnay, Chenin blanc, Malbec, Merlot, Pinotage, Sauvignon blanc, Shiraz, Viognier. Produces a range of varietal wines. Labels include: Babylons Toren, Black Label, Camp, Elba, Klein Babylonstoren, Kosher, Pinneau, Pumphouse. Website: http://www.backsberg.co.za

Back 2 Basics (Eng) a still spring water from the Global Beer Company in Chesterfield, Derbyshire.

Backus Vineyard (USA) a small vineyard based in the western part of the Napa Valley, California. Grape variety: Cabernet sauvignon. Owned by the Joseph Phelps Estate.

Backus Y. Johnson Brewery (Peru) a brewery based in Lima. Brews: Cristal Lager.

Backwoods (Eng) a 5.1% alc by vol. ale brewed by the Cropton Brewery, Pickering.

Baco I (USA) the alternative name for the Baco noir.

Baco [Maurice] (Fr) a noted French grape hybridiser who has produced many varieties for both the USA and France.

Baco Noir (USA) a red hybrid grape variety. Also known as Baco I.

Baco 22A (USA) a white hybrid grape variety (established 1898), a cross between the Noah and Folle blanche. Is grown in USA, New Zealand and in Armagnac, France where it is known as the Plant de Grèce and Piquepouls de Pays.

Bacteria (Eng) microscopic, single-celled organisms that generally cause spoilage in beer, wines and foodstuffs. Prevented by good hygiene.

Bacterial Haze (Eng) a condition in wine caused by bacteria. Wine turns cloudy after being originally clear. Caused through poor hygiene and is found especially in home-made wines.

Bacterium (Lat) the singular of Bacteria.

Bacterium gracile (Lat) the bacteria responsible for the malo-lactic fermentation.

Bacterium mannitopoem (Lat) a bacteria that ferments Fructose into Mannitol, Ethanoic acid, CO_2 and Lactic acid.

Bacterium tartarophtorum (Lat) *see* Tourne.

Bad (Aus)(Ger) spa.

Badacsonki Rizling (Hun) a pale, dry, white full-bodied wine from Badacsony.

Badacsony (Hun) a district within the region of Lake Balatòn, North Transdanubia. Produces full-bodied white wines. Badacsonyi Szürkebaràt. Also spelt Badacsonyi.

Badacsonyer Burgunder (Hun) a red wine produced from Pinot gris grapes.

Badacsonyi (Hun) *see* Badacsony.

Badacsonyi Auvergnac Gris (Fr) the French spelling of the Hungarian Badacsonyi Szürkebaràt.

Badacsonyi Kéknyelü (Hun) a wine from the Lake Balatòn region known popularly as 'Blue Stalk'.

Badacsonyi Szürkebaràt (Hun) a wine made from the Pinot Gris grape in the Lake Balatòn region. Considered to be the best of the region, it is an aromatic, yellow-gold, fruity wine. *See also* Badacsonyi Auvergnac Gris.

Badacsonytomaj (Hun) a wine-producing town in the south-west are of Lake Balatòn.

Badajoz (Sp) a large wine-producing region on the river Guadiana in south-western Spain. A province of Extremadura. Home to the Vino de la Tierra areas of Matanegra, Ribera Alta de Guadiana, Ribera Baja de Guadiana, Tierra de Barros (D.O). Vino Comarcal areas of Azuaga, La Serena. Grape varieties are still in debate until the full D.O. is awarded but include (white) 60% Pardina, 20% Cayetana plus Montúa (Mantúa), Macabeo, Alarije, (red) Cencibel, Garnacha tinta. Red, white and rosado wines are produced.

Bad Altprags (It) a natural mineral water from Bad Altprags, Bozen. Mineral contents (milligrammes per litre): Sodium 1.85mg/l, Calcium 158mg/l,

Magnesium 57.9mg/l, Potassium 1.12mg/l, Bicarbonates 205mg/l, Sulphates 510mg/l, Silicates 5.5mg/l, Fluorides 0.6mg/l.

Badamli (Azer) a natural spring mineral water from Badamili, Azerbaijan.

Badarijan (Mac) a sparkling natural mineral water (established 2001) from Badar, Skopje, Macedonia. Mineral contents (milligrammes per litre): Calcium 234mg/l, Magnesium 159mg/l, Bicarbonates 888.5mg/l, Chlorides 99mg/l, Sulphates 152mg/l, Fluoride 1mg/l, Nitrates 0.9mg/l. pH 6.3

Bad Bellingen (Ger) village (Anb): Baden. (Ber): Markgräflerland. (Gro): Burg Neuenfels. (Vin): Sonnenstück.

Bad Bergfall (It) a natural mineral water from Bad Bergfall, Geiselberg, Bozen. Mineral contents (milligrammes per litre): Sodium 9.9mg/l, Calcium 571mg/l, Magnesium 82.4mg/l, Potassium 1.9mg/l, Bicarbonates 200mg/l, Chlorides 4mg/l, Sulphates 1545mg/l, Silicates 5mg/l, Fluorides 0.45mg/l, Strontium 7.4mg/l.

Bad Bergzabern (Ger) village (Anb): Pfalz. (Ber): Südliche Weinstrasse. (Gro): Guttenberg. (Vin): Wonneberg.

Bad Bergzabern (Ger) village (Anb): Pfalz. (Ber): Südliche Weinstrasse. (Gro): Kloster Liebfrauenberg. (Vin): Altenberg.

Bad Brambacher (Ger) a natural mineral water (established 1800) from Bad Brambach, SN. Mineral contents (milligrammes per litre): Sodium 15mg/l, Calcium 65mg/l, Magnesium 17mg/l, Potassium 2mg/l, Bicarbonates 232mg/l, Chlorides 13mg/l, Sulphates 53mg/l.

Bad Camberger Taunusquelle (Ger) a still and sparkling natural mineral water (established 1994) from Taunus. Mineral contents (milligrammes per litre): Sodium 130mg/l, Calcium 70mg/l, Magnesium 20mg/l, Potassium 5mg/l, Bicarbonates 420mg/l, Chlorides 123mg/l, Sulphates 33mg/l.

Bad Cannstatt (Ger) village (Anb): Württemberg. (Ber): Remstal Stuttgart. (Gro): Weinsteige. (Vins): The following are near and are classified under the village of Stuttgart. Berg, Halde, Herzogenberg, Mönchberg, Steinhalde, Zuckerle.

Bad Cortina (It) a natural mineral water from Bad Cortina, Enneberg, Bozen. Mineral contents (milligrammes per litre): Sodium 3mg/l, Calcium 158mg/l, Magnesium 48mg/l, Potassium 1.6mg/l, Bicarbonates 247mg/l, Sulphates 415mg/l, Fluorides 1.6mg/l, Strontium 6.5mg/l.

Bad Driburger (Ger) a natural mineral water from Bad Driburg, NW, Eggegebirge. Mineral contents (milligrammes per litre): Sodium 14mg/l, Calcium 171mg/l, Magnesium 37mg/l, Potassium 4mg/l, Bicarbonates 333mg/l, Chlorides 9mg/l, Sulphates 313mg/l.

Bad Driburger Bitterwasser (Ger) a natural mineral water from the Marcus-Quelle, Bad Driburg, NW, Eggegebirge. Mineral contents (milligrammes per litre): Sodium 14mg/l, Calcium 180mg/l,

Magnesium 117mg/l, Potassium 5mg/l, Bicarbonates 14·.5mg/l, Chlorides 103mg/l, Sulphates 1340mg/l.

Bad Driburger Caspar Heinrich Quelle (Ger) a natural spring mineral water from Bad Driburg. Mineral contents (milligrammes per litre): Sodium 29mg/l, Calcium 283mg/l, Magnesium 67mg/l, Potassium 3.4mg/l, Bicarbonates 1144mg/l, Chlorides 35.4mg/l, Sulphates 104.4mg/l, Nitrates 5.8mg/l, Silicates 22.8mg/l.

Bad Dürkheim (Ger) village (Anb): Pfalz. (Ber): Mittelhaardt-Deutsche Weinstrasse. (Gro): Feuerberg. (Vins): Herrenmorgen, Nonnengarten, Steinberg.

Bad Dürkheim (Ger) village (Anb): Pfalz. (Ber): Mittelhaardt Deutsche Weinstrasse. (Gro): Hochmess. (Vins): Hochbenn, Michelsberg, Rittergarten, Spielberg.

Bad Dürkheim (Ger) village (Anb): Pfalz. (Ber): Mittelhaardt Deutsche Weinstrasse. (Gro): Schenkenböhl. (Vins): Abstfronhof, Fronhof, Fuchsmantel.

Bad Dürrheimer (Ger) a sparkling natural mineral water (established 1958) from the Johannisquelle. Mineral contents (milligrammes per litre): Sodium 14.4mg/l, Calcium 340mg/l, Magnesium 50mg/l, Bicarbonates 365mg/l, Chlorides 928mg/l, Sulphates 735mg/l, Nitrates <0.3mg/l, Fluorides 0.53mg/l.

Bad Egard (It) a natural mineral water (established circa 1500) from Partschins, Töll, Bozen. Mineral contents (milligrammes per litre): Sodium 6.6mg/l, Calcium 82.6mg/l, Magnesium 23.4mg/l, Potassium 7.2mg/l, Bicarbonates 257mg/l, Chlorides 4mg/l, Sulphates 100mg/l, Silicates 13.3mg/l, Fluorides 0.3mg/l.

Bad Elf (Eng) a 6% alc by vol. ale brewed by Ridgeway Brewing, Berkshire.

Badel 70 (Cktl) ⅓ measure cherry brandy, ⅓ measure Vinjak Cezar, ⅓ measure dry vermouth. Stir over ice. Strain into cocktail glass.

Badel-Vinoprodukt (Aus) a noted rum-producer based at Zagreb. Brands include Rum Domaci.

Bad Ems (Ger) village (Anb): Mittelrhein. (Ber): Rheinburgengau. (Gro): Lahntal. (Vin): Hasenberg.

Baden (Aus) a wine town south of Vienna. Produces mainly white wines from the Zierfändler and Rotgipfler grape varieties.

Baden (Ger) anbaugebiete (Bers): Badische Bergstrasse/Kraichgau, Badisches Frankenland, Breisgau, Bodensee, Kaiserstuhl-Tuniberg, Markgräflerland, Ortenau. Wine region in the south-west of Germany on the French / Swiss borders. Main Grape varieties: Müller-Thurgau, Riesling, Ruländer and Spätburgunder. Produces 79% white wine and 21% red / rosé (weissherbst) wines. 15,300ha.

Baden-Baden (Ger) a lithiated mineral water from the Baden region.

Baden-Baden (Ger) village (Anb): Baden. (Ber): Ortenau. (Gro): Schloss Rodeck. (Vins): Eckberg, Sätzler.

Badenheim (Ger) village (Anb): Rheinhessen. (Ber): Bingen. (Gro): Sankt Rochuskapelle. (Vins): Galgenberg, Römerberg.

Baden Information Service (Ger) Weinwerbezentrale Badische Winzergenossenschaften. (Add): Ettlinger Strasse 12 7500 Karlsruhe, Western Germany.

Badenweiler (Ger) village (Anb): Baden. (Ber): Markgräflerland. (Gro): Burg Neuenfels. (Vin): Römerberg.

Baden Wine Festivals (Ger) Freiburger Weintage, Kurpfälzisches Winzerfest, Kaiserstuhl-Tuniberg-Weinfest.

Baden Wine Route (Ger) Badische Weinstrasse.

Badestädter Mineralquelle (Ger) a natural spring mineral water from Bad Driburg, NW.

Badewasserquelle (It) a natural spring mineral water from Tisens, Bozen. Mineral contents (milligrammes per litre): Sodium 2.9mg/l, Calcium 108.5mg/l, Magnesium 24.6mg/l, Potassium 1.4mg/l, Bicarbonates 129mg/l, Chlorides 1mg/l, Sulphates 245mg/l, Fluoride 0.4mg/l, Silicates 8mg/l.

Badfeld (Aus) a vineyard site based on the banks of the River Kamp in the Kamptal region.

Badger Beers (Eng) the name for beers brewed by the Hall and Woodhouse Brewery based in Blanford St. Marys, Dorset DT11 9LS. Brews: Best Cask Bitter 1041 O.G., Brock Lager 1033 O.G., Champion Ale 4.6% alc by vol., IPA 3.6% alc by vol., LA Bitter, Robert's Pride. Website: http://www.badgerales.com 'E'mail: info@badgerales.com

Badger Best Bitter (Eng) the new name for Dorset Best. 4% alc by vol.

Badger Brewery Dorset Best (Eng) a bitter ale brewed by the Hall and Woodhouse Brewery, Dorset. see Badger Best Bitter, Blandford Fly.

Badger IPA (Eng) a 3.6% alc by vol. India pale ale brewed by Hall and Woodhouse in Dorset.

Badger LA Bitter (Eng) a low alcohol bitter 0.9% alc by vol. from Hall and Woodhouse Brewery, Dorset.

Bad Griesbacher Natürliches Heilwasser (Ger) a sparkling natural mineral water from the Schwarzwald. Mineral contents (milligrammes per litre): Sodium 83mg/l, Calcium 292.8mg/l, Magnesium 31.2mg/l, Potassium 8.67mg/l, Bicarbonates 1183mg/l, Chlorides 6.88mg/l, Sulphates 77mg/l, Nitrates 0.42mg/l, Silicates 40.6mg/l, Fluorides 0.82mg/l, Strontium 3.73mg/l.

Bad Harzburger (Ger) a natural mineral water from Bad Harzburg. Mineral contents (milligrammes per litre): Sodium 8mg/l, Calcium 38mg/l, Magnesium 8mg/l, Bicarbonates 98mg/l, Chlorides 10mg/l, Sulphates 48mg/l.

Bad Harzburger Juliushaller (Ger) a natural mineral water from Bad Harzburg. Mineral contents (milligrammes per litre): Sodium 307mg/l, Calcium 69mg/l, Magnesium 19mg/l, Bicarbonates 117mg/l, Chlorides 465mg/l, Sulphates 152mg/l.

Bad Hersfelder Naturquell (Ger) a natural spring mineral water from Bad Hersfeld, HE.

Bad Honnefer (Ger) a natural spring mineral water (established 1898) from the Fürstenquelle, Bad Honnef, NW. Mineral contents (milligrammes per litre): Sodium 340mg/l, Calcium 50mg/l, Magnesium 50mg/l, Potassium 10mg/l, Bicarbonates 880mg/l, Chlorides 180mg/l, Sulphates 130mg/l.

Bad Honnefer Drachenquelle (Ger) a natural spring mineral water (established 1898) from Bad Honnef.

Bad Hönningen (Ger) village (Anb): Mittelrhein. (Ber): Rheinbergengau. (Gro): Burg Hammerstein. (Vin): Schlossberg.

Badia a Coltibuono (It) a D.O.C.G. Chianti Classico producer based in Gaiole, Tuscany.

Badiane (Fr) *Illicium anisatum* a form of anise from originating from China, used in the making of Pastis.

Badische Bergstrasse/Kraichgau (Ger) bereich (Anb): Baden. (Gros): Hohenberg, Mannaberg, Rittersberg, Stiftsberg.

Badische Rotgold (Ger) a quality rosé wine from Baden. Is usually designated 'rotling', made from grapes, juice or mash from the Grauburgunder and Spätburgunder grape varieties.

Badisches Frankenland (Ger) bereich (Anb): Baden. (Gro): Tauberklinge.

Badische Weinstrasse (Ger) Baden wine route.

Bad Kissinger (Ger) a natural spring mineral water from Bad Kissinger, BY.

Bad Kochenmoos (It) a natural mineral water from Naturns, Staben, Bozen. Mineral contents (milligrammes per litre): Sodium 11.8mg/l, Calcium 59.5mg/l, Magnesium 15.4mg/l, Potassium 5.2mg/l, Bicarbonates 160mg/l, Chlorides 4mg/l, Sulphates 100mg/l, Fluoride 1mg/l, Silicates 13mg/l.

Bad Kreuznach (Ger) the principle town in the Nahe anbaugebiet.

Bad Kreuznach (Ger) village (Anb): Nahe. (Ber): Kreuznach. (Gro): Kronenberg. (Vins): Agnesienberg, Berg, Breitenweg, Brückes, Forst, Galgenberg, Gutental, Himmelgarten, Hinkelstein, Hirtenhain, Hofgarten, Höllenbrand, Honigberg, Hungriger Wolf, In den Mauern, In den 17 Morgen, Junker, Kahlenberg, Kapellenpfad, Katzenhölle, Krötenpfuhl, Mollenbrunnen, Mönchberg, Monhard, Narrenkappe, Nonnengarten, Osterhöll, Paradies, Römerhalde, Rosenberg, Rosenheck, Rosenhügel, St. Martin, Schloss Kauzenberg, Steinberg, Steinweg, Tilgesbrunnen, Vogelsang.

Bad Krotzingen (Ger) village (Anb): Baden. (Ber): Markgräflerland. (Gro): Lorettoberg. (Vin): Steingrüble.

Bad Lad (It) a natural mineral water from Bad Lad, St. Pankraz, Bozen. Mineral contents (milligrammes per litre): Sodium 6.3mg/l, Calcium 46.7mg/l, Magnesium 10.7mg/l, Potassium 4.05mg/l, Bicarbonates 154mg/l, Chlorides 2mg/l, Sulphates 44mg/l, Fluorides 0.45mg/l, Silicates 15.4mg/l.

Bad Lauchstäter Heilbrunnen (Ger) a natural

B

mineral water. Mineral contents (milligrammes per litre): Sodium 58.2mg/l, Calcium 112mg/l, Magnesium 44.2mg/l, Potassium 22.3mg/l, Bicarbonates 325mg/l, Chlorides 37mg/l, Sulphates 287mg/l, Silicates 13.8mg/l, Nitrates 0.71mg/l.

Bad Liebenwerda (Ger) a still and sparkling natural mineral water from Niederlausitzer, Heidelandschaft. Mineral contents (milligrammes per litre): Sodium 7.3mg/l, Calcium 16.9mg/l, Magnesium 2.9mg/l, Potassium 1.6mg/l, Bicarbonates <3mg/l, Chlorides 5.7mg/l, Sulphates 58.9mg/l, Fluoride <0.2mg/l, Nitrates <0.5mg/l.

Bad Liebenzeller (Ger) a natural mineral water (established 1926) from Paracelsus-Quelle. Mineral contents (milligrammes per litre): Sodium 278mg/l, Calcium 44mg/l, Magnesium 7mg/l, Potassium 17mg/l, Bicarbonates 337mg/l, Chlorides 312mg/l, Sulphates 59mg/l.

Bad Mergentheimer Albertquelle (Ger) a natural spring mineral water. Mineral contents (milligrammes per litre): Sodium 12870mg/l, Calcium 794mg/l, Magnesium 783mg/l, Potassium 268mg/l, Bicarbonates 3111mg/l, Chlorides 16590mg/l, Sulphates 7370mg/l, Fluoride 0.52mg/l, Silicates 32mg/l, Nitrates <0.1mg/l, Iron 9.73mg/l, Lithium 13.3mg/l.

Bad Mergentheimer Karlsquelle (Ger) a natural spring water.

Badminton Cup (Cup) 1 bottle claret, 90mls (½ gill) brown curaçao, 2 bottles soda water, 75gms (3ozs) icing sugar, juice, rind of 1 lemon. Place all the ingredients (except soda) into a bowl with some ice chips. Leave ½ hour. Strain, add soda, serve with lemon rind and slices of cucumber on top.

Bad Moos (It) a natural mineral water (established circa 1800) from Sexten, Bozen. Mineral contents (milligrammes per litre): Sodium 2.5mg/l, Calcium 560mg/l, Magnesium 59mg/l, Potassium 0.7mg/l, Bicarbonates 219mg/l, Chlorides 1mg/l, Sulphates 1430mg/l, Fluoride 1.1mg/l, Strontium 5.9mg/l.

Bad Münster a. St-Ebernburg (Ger) village (Anb): Nahe. (Ber): Schloss Böckelheim. (Gro): Burgweg. (Vins): Erzgrupe, Felseneck, Feuerberg, Götzenfels, Höll, Köhler-Köpfchen, Königsgarten, Luisengarten, Rotenfelser im Winkel, Schlossberg, Steigerdell, Stephansberg.

Bad Nauheimer (Ger) a sparkling natural mineral water from Friedberg-Dorheim, HE. Mineral contents (milligrammes per litre): Sodium 15mg/l, Calcium 64mg/l, Magnesium 15.5mg/l, Potassium 2.6mg/l, Bicarbonates 289mg/l, Chlorides 6.5mg/l.

Bad Nauheimer Urquelle (Ger) a natural mineral water from Friedberg-Dorheim, HE.

Badnerland-Quell (Ger) a natural spring mineral water from Bad Peterstal-Griesbach, BW.

Bad Neuenahr (Ger) village (Anb): Ahr. (Ber): Walporzheim/Ahrtal. (Gro): Klosterberg. (Vins): Kirchtürmchen, Schieferley, Sonnenberg.

Bad Neuenahrer Heilwasser (Ger) a natural mineral water from the Ahr. Mineral contents (milligrammes per litre): Sodium 295mg/l, Calcium 77.6mg/l, Magnesium 84.3mg/l, Potassium 22mg/l, Chlorides 67.7mg/l, Sulphates 63mg/l, Fluoride 0.95mg/l.

Bad Niedernauer Römer-Sprudel (Ger) a natural mineral water from Rottenburg am Necker-Bad Niedernau, BW.

Bad Nieratz-Quelle (Ger) a natural spring mineral water from Wangen im Allgäu, BW.

Badoit (Fr) a natural sparkling water from Saint Galmier, Loire Valley. (Add): S.A. Evian – B.P.87, 74503 Evian. Mineral contents (milligrammes per litre): Sodium 165mg/l, Calcium 190mg/l, Magnesium 85mg/l, Potassium 10mg/l, Bicarbonates 1300mg/l, Chlorides 44mg/l, Sulphates 38mg/l, Silcate 35mg/l, Fluride 1.2mg/l. pH 6.0

Bad Pedraces (It) a natural mineral water from Abtei, Bozen. Mineral contents (milligrammes per litre): Sodium 78mg/l, Calcium 3.2mg/l, Magnesium 2.2mg/l, Potassium 0.98mg/l, Bicarbonates 185mg/l, Chlorides 3mg/l, Sulphates 48mg/l, Fluoride 1.1mg/l, Silicates 10.4mg/l.

Badplaats (Hol) spa.

Bad Pyrmonter (Ger) a natural mineral water (established 1985) from Bad Pyrmont. Mineral contents (milligrammes per litre): Sodium 5.2mg/l, Calcium 53mg/l, Magnesium 24.5mg/l, Potassium 0.9mg/l, Bicarbonates 251mg/l, Chlorides 14.1mg/l, Sulphates 9mg/l, Fluoride 0.05mg/l, Nitrates <1mg/l.

Bad Pyrmonter Heilwasser (Ger) a natural spring mineral water from Bad Pyrmont. Mineral contents (milligrammes per litre): Sodium 374mg/l, Calcium 184mg/l, Magnesium 45.5mg/l, Potassium 7.69mg/l, Chlorides 14.1mg/l, Sulphates 653mg/l, Fluoride 0.54mg/l.

Badquelle (Ger) a natural spring mineral water from Göppingen, BW.

Bad Rappenauer Urquelle (Ger) a natural spring mineral water. Mineral contents (milligrammes per litre): Sodium 79mg/l, Calcium 373mg/l, Magnesium 83mg/l, Potassium 2.5mg/l, Chlorides 66mg/l.

Bad Salomonsbrunn (It) a natural mineral water from Rasen Antholz, Bosen. Mineral contents (milligrammes per litre): Sodium 3.7mg/l, Calcium 13.7mg/l, Magnesium 2.7mg/l, Potassium 1.5mg/l, Bicarbonates 37mg/l, Chlorides 1.4mg/l, Sulphates 18mg/l, Fluoride 0.55mg/l.

Bad Salt (It) a natural mineral water from Martell, Bozen. Mineral contents (milligrammes per litre): Sodium 1.85mg/l, Calcium 36.4mg/l, Magnesium 7.8mg/l, Potassium 2.25mg/l, Bicarbonates 99mg/l, Sulphates 45mg/l, Fluoride 0.4mg/l, Silicates 7.8mg/l.

Bad Salzschlirfer Mineralwasser (Ger) a natural mineral water from Retzmann-Brunnen, Bad Salzschlirf, HE.

B

Badsberg Koöperatiewe Wynkelder (S.Afr) a co-operative winery (established 1951) based in Goudini, Worcester, Western Cape. (Add): Grootvlakte, Box 72, Rawsonville 6845. Grape varieties: Chardonnay, Chenin blanc, Hanepoot, Hanepoot jerepigo, Red jeripigo, Red muscadel, Sauvignon blanc. Produces varietal, late (and noble late) harvest and sparkling wines. (1000ha). Website: http://www.badsberg.co.za

Badstube (Ger) grosslage (Anb): Mosel-Saar-Ruwer. (Ber): Bernkastel. (Vil): Bernkastel-Kues.

Bad Suderoder (Ger) a natural mineral water from Bad Suderoder. Mineral contents (milligrammes per litre): Sodium 12.4mg/l, Calcium 224mg/l, Magnesium 29mg/l, Potassium 1.4mg/l, Bicarbonates 281mg/l, Chlorides 20.9mg/l, Sulphates 575mg/l.

Bad Valdander (It) a natural mineral water from S. Martin, Bozen. Mineral contents (milligrammes per litre): Sodium 3.05mg/l, Calcium 525mg/l, Magnesium 43.7mg/l, Potassium 1.51mg/l, Bicarbonates 232mg/l, Chlorides 1mg/l, Sulphates 1220mg/l, Fluoride 0.5mg/l, Silicates 3.7mg/l, Strontium 5.05mg/l.

Bad Vilbeler Elisabethen Quelle (Ger) a sparkling natural spring mineral water from Bad Vilbel, HE. (spritzig: sparkling / sanfte quelle: light gas / stille quelle: still). Mineral contents (milligrammes per litre): Sodium 6.3mg/l, Calcium 110mg/l, Magnesium 20.2mg/l, Potassium 5.4mg/l, Bicarbonates 397mg/l, Chlorides 6.3mg/l, Sulphates 43mg/l. Website: http://www.hassia.com

Bad Vilbeler Hermanns Quelle (Ger) a natural spring mineral water from Bad Vilbel, HE.

Bad Vilbeler Riedquelle (Ger) a natural spring mineral water from Bad Vilbel, HE. Mineral contents (milligrammes per litre): Sodium 99.6mg/l, Calcium 171mg/l, Magnesium 23.1mg/l, Potassium 12.9mg/l, Bicarbonates 714mg/l, Chlorides 112mg/l, Sulphates 30mg/l.

Bad Vilbeler Urquelle (Ger) a sparkling natural spring mineral water from Bad Vilbel, HE. Mineral contents (milligrammes per litre): Sodium 90mg/l, Calcium 174mg/l, Magnesium 25.8mg/l, Potassium 13.6mg/l, Bicarbonates 702mg/l, Chlorides 93.6mg/l, Sulphates 36mg/l.

Bad Wildunger Georg-Viktor-Quelle (Ger) a natural spring mineral water (established 1378). Mineral contents (milligrammes per litre): Sodium 38.5 mg/l, Calcium 184mg/l, Magnesium 94.6mg/l, Potassium 4mg/l, Bicarbonates 1064mg/l, Chlorides 16.5mg/l, Sulphates 58.9mg/l, Fluoride 0.26mg/l, Silicates 22.6mg/l, Iron 6.9mg/l.

Bad Wildunger Helenenquelle (Ger) a natural spring mineral water (established 1378). Mineral contents (milligrammes per litre): Sodium 605mg/l, Calcium 240mg/l, Magnesium 239mg/l, Potassium 15.6mg/l, Bicarbonates 2897mg/l, Chlorides 560mg/l, Sulphates 28mg/l, Fluoride 0.13mg/l, Silicates 36.4mg/l, Iron 4.4mg/l.

Bad Wildunger Reinhardquelle (Ger) a natural spring mineral water (established 1378). Mineral contents (milligrammes per litre): Sodium 16.9mg/l, Calcium 142.2mg/l, Magnesium 58.2mg/l, Potassium 2.2mg/l, Bicarbonates 703mg/l, Chlorides 20.2mg/l, Sulphates 35mg/l, Fluoride 0.18mg/l, Silicates 9.4mg/l, Iron 3.2mg/l.

Bad Windsheimer Urquelle (Ger) a natural spring mineral water from Bad Windsheim, BY.

Baere (Eng) an anglo-saxon word for barley from which beer originated.

Baerenfang (Ger) a honey-based liqueur from Prussia. Flavoured with lime and mullein flowers.

Baerlic (Eng) an old English word denoting 'made from barley'.

Baffo d'Oro (It) a 4.6% alc by vol. full-malt, bottled lager brewed by Birra Moretti, San Giorgo Di Nogaro, Udine.

Bag (Tur) vineyard.

Baga (Port) the name for the elderberry juice that was once used to colour Port wine.

Baga (Port) a red grape variety grown in Bairrada region.

Bagaceira (Port) a brandy made from the residue of wine pulp. (Fr) = marc, (It) = grappa, (Sp) = aguardiente.

Bagaço (Port) grape brandy.

Baga de Louro (Port) a red grape variety grown in the Dão region.

Bagasse (W.Ind) the name given to residual sugar cane pulp after the juice has been removed in rum production.

Bagatelle (Fr) a natural spring mineral water from Source Blanche, La Réunion. Mineral contents (milligrammes per litre): Sodium 7.8mg/l, Calcium 14.4mg/l, Magnesium 13.1mg/l, Potassium 1.6mg/l, Bicarbonates 61mg/l, Chlorides 8.9mg/l, Sulphates 1.2mg/l, Nitrates 2.4mg/l.

Bagborough Vineyard (Eng) a vineyard based in Somerset. Produces dry table wines.

Bagbozumu (Tur) vintage, grape harvest.

Bag [Coffee] (Eng) used for the transportation of the beans (60 kilos).

Bages (Sp) a Vino de la Tierra wine of Barcelona in Cataluña.

Bag in the Box (Austr) the term given to the wines sold in polythene bags in cardboard box containers. Usually in litre or (multiples of) packs. See also Convenience Cask.

Baglio di Pianetto (It) a winery based on the island of Sicily. Label: Ramione.

Bago (Port) a single grape.

Bagpiper (Ind) a popular brand of local whiskey.

Bagrina (Slo) a noted red wine produced in eastern Serbia.

Baguette (Fr) the name given to the main fruiting canes that remain after pruning.

Bahamas Cocktail (Cktl) ½ measure Southern Comfort, ½ measure light rum, ½ measure lemon juice, dash crème de banana, shake over ice and strain into a cocktail glass.

Bahama Sunrise (Cktl) 1 measure Galliano, 2

measures Mount Gay Eclipse Barbados Rum, 6 measures grapefruit juice. Stir over ice, strain into an ice-filled highball glass on top of ½ measure Galliano. Dress with mint sprig and serve with straws.

Bahamian Delight (Cktl) ½ measure Campari, ½ measure pineapple juice. Stir over ice, strain into an ice-filled club goblet. Top with a cherry.

BAH Humbug (Eng) a 4.9% alc by vol. ale brewed by Mauldon's Ltd., Suffolk.

BAH Humbug (Eng) a 4.9% alc by vol. ale brewed by the Wizard Brewery, Warwickshire.

Bahia (Bra) a liqueur that is a blend of grain spirit and coffee.

Bahia Cocktail (Cktl) ½ measure golden rum, ⅙ measure coconut cream, ⅙ measure pineapple juice, ⅙ measure grapefruit juice. Blend in a blender with a scoop of crushed ice. Pour into a highball glass. Top with a cherry and pineapple cube and serve with straws.

Bahia Cristal (Arg) a natural mineral water from Concepcion del Uruguay. Mineral contents (milligrammes per litre): Calcium 55mg/l, Magnesium 17mg/l, Chlorides 42mg/l, Sulphates 113mg/l, Nitrates 4.4mg/l, Fluorides 1.1mg/l. pH 7.4

Bahlingen (Ger) village (Anb): Baden. (Ber): Kaiserstuhl-Tuniberg. (Gro): Vulkanfelsen. (Vin): Silberberg.

Bahnbrücken (Ger) village (Anb): Baden. (Ber): Badische Bergstrasse/Kraichgau. (Gro): Stiftsberg. (Vin): Lerchenberg (ortsteil).

Baie de Houx (Fr) a brandy-based liqueur flavoured with holly berries.

Baier (Nor) a Bavarian-style beer which is a dark copper-brown in colour.

Baikal (Rus) a natural spring mineral water from lake Baikal. Mineral contents (milligrammes per litre): Sodium 4mg/l, Calcium 17mg/l, Magnesium 4mg/l, Potassium 2mg/l, Bicarbonates 70mg/l, Chlorides 1.5mg/l, Sulphates 7.5mg/l.

Baiken (Ger) vineyard (Anb): Rheingau. (Ber): Johannisberg. (Gro): Steinmacher. (Vil): Rauenthal.

Baiken (Ger) a vineyard within the village of Rauenthal 14ha. (67.9%) of which is proposed to be classified as Erstes Gewächs.

Bailén (Sp) a Vino de Mesa of Jaén, Andalucía.

Baileyana Winery (USA) a winery based in the Edna Valley, San Luis Obispo County, California. (Add): 5828 Orcutt Road, San Luis Obispo, CA 93401. Grape variety: Pinot noir. Label: Grand Firepeak Cuvée. Website: http://www.baileyana.com

Bailey Classification (USA) a scientist who produced alternate names for the American native vine species. *see* **Vitis argentifolia, Vitis sola, Vitis tiloefolia** and **Vitis vulpina.**

Baileys Brewery (Eng) a new brewery (established 1983) in Malvern, Worcestershire. Produces Best Bitter 1040 O.G. Super Brew 1047 O.G.

Bailey's Cream (Ire) a cream liqueur created in 1975

and made in Dublin from Irish whiskey, cream, chocolate and neutral spirits. 15% alc by vol.

Bailey's Irish Cream (Ire) *see* Bailey's Cream.

Baileys of Glenrowan (Austr) a vineyard 102ha. (Add): Taminick Gap Road, Glenrowan, Victoria 3675. Grape varieties: Aucerot, Brown muscat, Cabernet sauvignon, Hermitage, Muscadelle, Rhine riesling.

Bailhot (Fr) a basket used for harvesting grapes.

Bailie Nicol Jarvie (Scot) the name of a blended Scotch whisky. 40% alc by vol.

Bai Lin Tea (Chi) the brand-name of a China tea which, if drunk soon after a meal (it was claimed), will help to burn up the calories and so reduce weight.

Bailiwick (Ch.Isles) a medium-bodied red wine (Pinot noir) produced (2005) by the La Mare Vineyards, Jersey to celebrate the 60th anniversary of the liberation of the Channel Islands.

Bailley (Ind) a natural spring mineral water from Mumbai.

Bain-de-Pied (Fr) lit: 'footbath', a term used to describe the overflow of coffee (or tea) into the saucer. Denotes the over-filling of a vessel.

Bainskloof (S.Afr) the label for a red wine (Merlot) from the Isabela range produced by the Thirtytwo [32] South Ltd winery, Stellenbosch, Western Cape.

Bain's Way (S.Afr) the label for a range of wines produced by the Wamakersvallei Winery, Wellington, Western Cape.

Baira Interior (Port) a DOC region based in central Portugal in the Beiras region.

Bairoque (Fr) a white grape variety grown in Tursan, Landes département, south-western France.

Bairrada (Port) a small DOC region on the river Mondego that produces wines similar to red Dão from the Baga grape and sparkling wines.

Baitz (Austr) a major spirit and liqueur producer of the country.

Baixo Corgo (Port) a district of the Alto Douro downstream of the Corgo river in the lowlands.

Baiyu (Chi) a local name for the white Rkatsiteli grape.

Baja California (Mex) a wine-producing area in northern Mexico. Home to the regions of Guadalupe, Santo Tomás, Tañama and Valle Redondo.

Baja de Aragón (Sp) situated in the province of Zaragoza. A Vino de la Tierra Aragón. Classified for red, rosé and white wines from Garnacha tinta, Garnacha blanca, Macabeo, Mazuelo, Cabernet sauvignon, Tempranillo grape varieities. Not to be confused with Bajo Aragón.

Baja Montana (Sp) one of five D.O. wine-producing regions based in the Navarra region.

Bajan Beer (W.Ind) a pilsner lager beer 4.8% alc by vol. brewed in Barbados by Bank's Brewery and now in Sussex by King and Barnes.

Bajo Aragón (Sp) 10,000ha of vines in the province of Teruel, Aragón. Vino de la Tierra Aragón. Divided into three sub-zones: Medio (largest), plus Occidental and Oriental. Grape varieties: 60% Garnacha tinta, 30% Garnacha blanca, Macabeo, Mazuelo, Cabernet sauvignon.

Bajo Ebre-Montsiá (Sp) a Vino Comarcal wine from the province Tarragona in Cataluña.

Bajulos Palos (Sp) a method of vine training on low stakes.

Bak (Tur) drunk (consumed).

Bakano (N.Z) a light, acidic, red, hybrid wine that is produced by the McWilliams Winery in Hawkes Bay.

Bakaver (N.Z) a red wine produced by the Balic Winery, Sturges Road, Henderson, North Island. Produced from Baco and Seibel grapes.

Bak Beer (Hun) a strong dark beer brewed by the Kobànya Brewery.

Bakbuk (Isr) bottle.

Baked (Eng) a term used to describe wines with a high alcoholic content giving a taste of grapes gathered during very hot weather.

Bake House Ales (Eng) a brewery. (Add): C/o Margaret Hall, Scar Bank, Millers Road, Warwick, Warwickshire CV34 5DB. Brews bitter ales. Website: http://www.bakehouseales.co.uk 'E'mail: jonathan@bakehouseales.co.uk

Bakenskop (S.Afr) the label for a range of red wines produced by the Jonkeer winery, Robertson, Western Cape.

Bakermat (S.Afr) the label for a red wine (Cabernet sauvignon, Merlot and Shiraz blend) produced by the Joostenberg Wines winery, Paarl, Western Cape.

Baker's (USA) a 7 year old Bourbon whiskey from the James Beam Distilling C°., Clermont-Beam, Kentucky. Bottled at 107° US proof (53.5% alc by vol.)

Bakersfield (USA) a noted wine town in the wine districts of Kern County and San Joaquin Valley, California.

Bakewell Best (Eng) a 4.2% alc by vol. bitter beer brewed by the Barn Brewery, Derbyshire.

Bakkhe (Gre) a priestess of Bacchus. Plural Bakkhai.

Bakkhos (Gre) Bacchus. *See also* Bacchos.

Baksmalla (Swe) a slang term used for a hangover.

Baku (Rus) a wine-producing region based in southern Russia. Produces mainly dessert wines.

Balaclava (Eng) a strong ale brewed and bottled by Gilmour and C°. Ltd. Sheffield.

Balaclava (Punch) 1 bottle Champagne, 1 bottle claret, juice 2 lemons, 1 bottle soda water. Stir gently over ice, dress with sliced cucumber. Serve in Champagne flutes.

Balaclava Punch (Punch) 1½ litres (3 pints) tea, 1 bottle dry white wine, 300mls (½ pint) vodka, stick of cinnamon, 2 measures grapefruit juice, 1 measure crème de menthe. Heat all the ingredients together, strain, serve with slice of orange.

Baladí (Sp) a white grape variety grown in the Montilla-Moriles region.

Balagne (Fr) a wine-producing region in north-western Corsica.

Balalaika (Cktl) ⅓ measure Cointreau, ⅓ measure vodka, ⅓ measure lemon juice. Shake over ice, strain into cocktail glass.

Balalaika (Eng) a proprietary brand of vodka 40% alc by vol.

Balance (Eng) a term used to describe a wine which has all the good qualities expected combined in a wine. It has no deficiencies in its bouquet, flavour or character. A well-balanced wine is always a good wine, often a great wine.

Balance (S.Afr) the export label for a range of wines produced by the Overhex Private Cellar winery, Worcester, Western Cape.

Balatòn (Hun) Lake Balatòn, an area that produces mainly dry white wines.

Balatònboglár Winery (Hun) a winery that has 400ha. vineyards and produces wines from Chardonnay and Irsai olivér grapes on Lake Balatòn.

Balatònfüred (Hun) a town on Lake Balatòn shore that is noted for soft, white wines (sweet and dry styles).

Balatònfüred-Csopak (Hun) a wine-producing region in northern Transdanubia around Lake Balatòn.

Balatòni Furmint (Hun) a medium dry white wine with a fresh bouquet, from the Lake Balatòn region. Made with the Furmint grape.

Balatòni Riesling (Hun) a medium sweet white wine from the Lake Balatòn region. Made with the Welschriesling grape.

Balatònmellek (Hun) a wine-producing region based in northern Transdanubia around Lake Balatòn. Noted for fine white wines.

Balatònudvari (Hun) a wine-producing town sited in the south-eastern area of Lake Balatòn.

Balavaud (Switz) a white wine produced in the Johannisberg district of the Valais canton.

Balbach [Anton] (Ger) a noted Rheinhessen wine estate, vineyards are based in Nierstein.

Balbaina (Sp) a district within the Sherry region, has chalk soil and produces the best wines.

Balbi Vineyard (Arg) a winery based in Mendoza. Grape varieties: Chardonnay, Chenin blanc, Cabernet sauvignon, Malbec, Syrah.

Balbino d'Altromonte (It) a sweet white wine from Calabria. 15%–16% alc by vol.

Balbi Vineyard (Arg) a vineyard based in the Andean Mountains.

Balblair (Scot) a single highland malt whisky distillery. (Add): Edderton, Ross-Shire. 16 year old at 40% alc by vol.

Balda (It) a sparkling natural mineral water from Balda, Verona, Veneto. Mineral contents (milligrammes per litre): Sodium 9.6mg/l, Calcium 56mg/l, Magnesium 29mg/l, Potassium 2.4mg/l, Bicarbonates 323mg/l, Chlorides 4mg/l, Sulphates 19mg/l, Fluorides 0.15mg/l. pH 7.6

Baldassare (It) an oak aged red wine produced by Tenuta Torciano in Tuscany from 34% Sangiovese grosso, 33% Cabernet sauvignon, 33% Merlot grapes.

Baldear (Port) to decant.

Balderdash (Ire) a mixture of drinks which are generally unrelated. i.e. wine and milk (it is also an Irish term for illogical conversation).

Baldinelli-Shenandoah Valley Winery (USA) a winery based in Amador, California. Produces red, rosé and white wines from Cabernet sauvignon and Zinfandel grapes.

Baldovska (Slo) a sparkling natural mineral water (established 1780) from Baldovske Kupele, District of Levoca, Eastern Slovakia. Mineral contents (milligrammes per litre): Sodium 90mg/l, Calcium 378.9mg/l, Magnesium 93.7mg/l, Potassium 0.6mg/l, Bicarbonates 1557mg/l, Chlorides 78mg/l, Sulphates 215mg/l, Nitrates 0.1mg/l, Fluorides 0.2mg/l, Iron 1.34mg/l.

Balduin Quelle (Ger) a natural spring mineral water from Dreis, Vulkaneifel. Mineral contents (milligrammes per litre): Sodium 7.2mg/l, Calcium 16.3mg/l, Magnesium 10mg/l, Potassium 4.9mg/l, Bicarbonates 82mg/l, Chlorides 5.7mg/l, Sulphates 20mg/l.

Baldus-Quelle (Ger) a natural spring mineral water from Neuenburg-Steinenstadt, BW.

Balduzzi Vineyards & Winery (Chile) a winery based in San Javier, Maule Valley. 100ha. Grape varieties: Chardonnay, Sauvignon blanc, Cabernet sauvignon.

Balearic Islands (Sp) a group of islands in the Mediterranean off the Levante coast of Spain. Islands are Formentera, Ibiza, Majorca and Minorca. Home to the D.O. zone Binissalem the Vino de la Tierra area of Pla í Llevant de Mallorca and the Vino de Mesa area of Andraitx. Grape varieties include Manto negro, Callet, Monastrell, Tempranillo, Moll, Macabeo, Parellada.

Bale Mill Cellars (USA) the brand-name used by the Shaw winery in California for their varietal wines.

Balfi (Hun) a natural mineral water from Balf. Mineral contents (milligrammes per litre): Sodium 240mg/l, Calcium 222mg/l, Magnesium 23.3mg/l, Bicarbonates 1320mg/l.

Balgarske Slantse (Bul) lit: 'Bulgarian sun', basic dry white wine made from the Furmint grape.

Balgownie Vineyard (Austr) a winery. (Add): Hermitage Road, Maiden Gully, via Bendigo, Victoria 3551. 13ha. Grape varieties: Cabernet sauvignon, Chardonnay, Pinot noir, Syrah.

Bali Coffee (E.Ind) a coffee of the arabica category, produces a mellow but strong aroma. Produced in Indonesia.

Balic Vineyard (N.Z) a winery. (Add): Sturges Road, Henderson, North Island. 15ha. Grape varieties: Baco 22A, Müller-Thurgau, Palomino, Pinotage. Noted for Bakaver and Vin Ché.

Balic Winery (USA) a winery based in Mays Landing, New Jersey. Produces mainly hybrid wines.

Balifico (It) a red vino da tavola wine produced from 65% Sangiovese and 35% Cabernet sauvignon grapes by Castello di Volpaia in Tuscany.

Bali Hai (USA) a popular 'pop wine' produced by the Swiss Colony Cº. (Part of United Vintners).

Balikesir (Tur) a noted vineyard based in the Thrace and Marmara regions. Produces white wines.

Balkan Gin (Rus) a light neutral gin.

Ballabio [Angelo] (It) a producer of sparkling wines (by the metodo tradizionale) based in Lombardy. Produces both white and rosé wines from the Pinot noir grape.

Ballantine [George and Son] (Scot) the main Scotch whisky brand of Hiram Walker (Canada) - now part of Allied-Domecq. See also Ballantine's Whisky.

Ballantine Ale (USA) a style of ale brewed by Falstaff's Narrangansett Brewery, Cranston, Rhode Island.

Ballantine Brewery (USA) a brewery that was based in Newark, New Jersey. Closed in 1972, beers are now brewed by the Falstaff's Narrangansett Brewery in Cranston, Rhode Island.

Ballantine's Whisky (Scot) a blended Scotch whisky produced by George Ballantine and Sons Ltd. in Dumbarton and in Elgin. Also 12, 17, and 30 year old de luxe varieties. Sold in a square bottle. 40% alc by vol.

Ballarat Bitter (Austr) the brand-name of bitter ales brewed by the Carlton and United Breweries in Ballarat, Victoria.

Ballard Canyon Winery (USA) a small winery in Santa Barbera, Santa Cruz Valley, California. Grape varieties: Cabernet sauvignon, Chardonnay and Johannisberg riesling. Produces varietal wines.

Ballards (Eng) an annual limited edition bottled beer (1095 O.G. 9.6% alc by vol. in 1995).

Ballard's Brewery (Eng) a brewery (established 1980). (Add): Unit C, The Old Sawmill, Nyewood, Rogate, Petersfield, Hampshire. GU31 5HA. Produces Ballard's Best Bitter, Ballard's Nyewood Gold, Ballard's Trotton Bitter, Ballard's Wild, Cunning Stunts, Divine, Duakademon, Gone Fishing 1091 O.G. Midhurst Mild, NMD, On the Hop, Wassail Ale 1060 O.G., Wheatsheaf. Website: http://www.ballardsbrewery.org.uk 'E'mail: info@ballardsbrewery.org.uk

Balle (Ger) a brand of rum produced by Hansen in Hensburg.

Baller Lager (Ind) a lager beer 1040 O.G. brewed by the Mohan Meakin Brewery, Simla Hills, Solan.

Balling (USA) a scale of sugar density in grape musts. Invented by a Czech scientist. Operated at 60°F (15.55°C). See also Brix and Sykes.

Ball of Malt (Ire) a request for a straight malt whiskey.

Ballon (Fr) a Paris goblet, plain round-bowled, stemmed glass.

Ballonge (Fr) an oval-shaped tub which can hold up to a ton of grapes which is used to carry them from the vineyard to the winery.

Balloon (Eng) a type of glass with a large bowl and narrow rim, used for brandy in the U.K. and as a sampling (nosing) glass for immature wines in France.

Ballota Oak (Sp) a species of oak tree who's acorns are roasted and used as a coffee substitute. see Acorn Coffee.

Ballrechten-Dottingen (Ger) village (Anb): Baden. (Ber): Markgräflerland. (Gro): Burg Neuenfels. (Vins): Altenberg, Castellberg.

Bally (W.Ind) the name of a rum from Martinique. Two versions produced 1979 and a 1987 both at 45% alc by vol.

Ballygowan (Ire) a still and sparkling natural mineral water (established 1981), bottled by the Ballygowan Spring Water Company, Newcastle West, County Limerick (from source at County Limerick and Kilkenny). Mineral contents (milligrammes per litre): Sodium 15mg/l, Calcium 114mg/l, Magnesium 16mg/l, Potassium 3mg/l, Bicarbonates 400mg/l, Chlorides 28mg/l, Sulphates 15mg/l, Nitrates 9mg/l. pH 7.2. Also produce flavoured low-calorie sparkling natural mineral waters. Website: http://www.ballygowanmineralwater.com

Balmenach-Glenlivet (Scot) a single highland malt whisky, owned by Haig & Haig. 43% alc by vol.

Balmes Dauphinoises (Fr) a Vin de Pays area in the Isère département in central France. Produces red, rosé and white wines.

Balm Wines (Eng) a fermented brew produced from balm leaves infused in boiling water with sugar, strained and allowed to cool. Yeast is added, fermented and fined with egg white.

Balnarring Vineyard (Austr) a winery (established 1982). (Add): Bittern-Dromana Road, Balnarring, Victoria. Grape varieties: Chardonnay, Gewürztraminer, Riesling, Cabernet, Merlot, Pinot noir.

Balnaves (Austr) a winery based in the Coonawarra, South Australia. Grape varieties include: Cabernet sauvignon, Shiraz. Label: The Tally Reserve.

Balnot-sur-Laignes (Fr) a Cru Champagne village in the Canton de l'Aude. District: Château Thierry.

Baloes (Port) pomegranate-shaped tanks of white concrete found in the Douro region. See also Igloos.

Balouzet (Fr) a local name for the Malbec grape in southern France.

Balsamina (S.Am) a local name for the Syrah grape in Argentina.

Balsam of Herbs (Ger) an aromatic bitters from Wolfschmidt in Riga.

Balseiros (Port) huge upstanding vats used for blending Port. See also Toneis.

Balthasar (Eng) an alternative spelling of Balthazar.

Balthazar [1] (Fr) a bottle notably of Champagne with a capacity of 16 standard bottles.

Balthazar [2] (Fr) a large bottle of (12 litres) 16 standard bottles capacity used in the Champagne region. see Champagne Bottle Sizes.

Balthazar Classic (S.Afr) the label for a red wine (Cabernet sauvignon) produced by the Roodezandt Wines & Vineyards winery, Robertson, Western Cape.

Balti Beer (Eng) a keg beer brewed by the Highgate & Walsall Brewing Company.

Baltika Brewery (Rus) a brewery. (Add): 3, 6th Verkhny Pereulok, St. Petersburg 194292 Russia. Brews a variety of beers including a bottled '3' lager beer 5% alc by vol. Website: http://www.baltika.ru

Baltimore Bracer (Cktl) ½ measure Anisette, ½ measure brandy, 1 egg white. Shake over ice, strain into a cocktail glass.

Baltimore Egg Nogg (Cktl) 1 egg, 1 teaspoon sugar, 125mls (1 gill) Madeira, 30mls (¼ gill) brandy, 30mls (¼ gill) dark rum. Shake well with a little fresh milk over ice, strain into a large tumbler with grated nutmeg on top.

Baltzinger [Robert] (Fr) a wine producer based in Alsace. (Add): 68, Rue de l'Eau, Gertwiller, 67140 Barr.

Baluster Stem (Eng) a style of lead crystal glass with bubbles in the form of 'tear drops' in the stem.

Balvenie (Scot) a single highland malt whisky distillery. (Add): Dufftown, Banffshire. Owned by William Grant & Sons. Produce a 10 and 12 year old at 40% alc by vol. Also a 15 year old single barrel at 50.4% alc by vol. (also produces a range of different cask maturings Bourbon, Port, Sherry, etc.). Also known as The Balvenie.

Balverne Vineyards (USA) a winery based in Sonoma Valley, California. Grape varieties: Cabernet sauvignon, Chardonnay, Gewürztraminer, Johannisberg riesling, Sauvignon blanc, Zinfandel. Produces varietal wines.

Balzner (Euro) the name for the wines produced from Balzers in the state of Liechtenstein.

Bamako Beer (Afr) a light beer brewed in Mali.

Bamberg (Ger) dark 'smoked' beer from Bavaria. Also known as 'Rauchbier', it is brewed from malt that has been fire-dried over beechwood logs. Brewed in Kaiserdom Brauerei and Schlenkerla home-brew house.

Bamboo Cocktail [1] (Cktl) also known as a 'Reform Cocktail'. 1 dash orange bitters, 30mls (¼ gill) dry Sherry, 30mls (¼ gill) French vermouth. Stir over ice, strain into cocktail glass. Squeeze of lemon peel on top.

Bamboo Cocktail [2] (Cktl) ½ measure dry Sherry, ¼ measure dry vermouth, ¼ measure sweet vermouth. Stir well over ice, strain into a cocktail glass.

Bamboo Leafgreen Chiew (Chi) a speciality white wine.

Bamboozle (Eng) a 4.8% alc by vol. beer brewed by the Loddon Brewery, Berkshire.

Bamlach (Ger) village (Anb): Baden. (Ber): Markgräflerland. (Gro): Vogtei Rötteln. (Vin): Kapellenberg.

Banadry (Fr) a banana-flavoured liqueur produced by Bardinet of Bordeaux. 26% alc by vol.

Banana (Eng) a term used to describe the bouquet of a wine produced from frost attacked grapes. Also used to describe a wine that is in poor condition. See also Banana Skin.

Banana Bird (Cktl) ½ measure Bourbon whiskey, ½ measure cream, 2 dashes crème de banane, 1 dash Triple Sec. Shake over ice, strain into a cocktail glass.

Banana Bliss (Cktl) ½ measure banana liqueur, ½

measure brandy. Stir over ice, strain into a cocktail glass.

Banana Cocktail (Cktl) ½ measure crème de banane, ¼ measure gin, ¼ measure white rum. Shake well over ice, strain into a cocktail glass.

Banana Cow Cocktail (Cktl) 100mls (4fl.ozs) coconut milk, 35mls (1½fl.ozs) golden rum, 1 banana. Blend altogether in a blender with a scoop of crushed ice. Pour into a highball glass. Serve with straws.

Banana Daiquiri (Cktl) 10mls (½fl.oz) crème de banane, 35mls (1½fl.ozs) white rum, juice ½ lime, ½ peeled banana, 2 scoops crushed ice. Blend on high speed in blender, pour into a glass unstrained. Serve with short, thick straws.

Banana Daktari (Cktl) *see* Daktari.

Banana Liqueur (Fr) a crème de banane 25%–30% alc by vol. *see* Banadry.

Banana Mint Cocktail (Cktl) ⅓ measure crème de banane, ⅓ measure (white) crème de menthe, ⅓ measure cream. Shake well over ice, strain into a cocktail glass.

Banana Punch (Cktl) 1 measure vodka, ⅔ measure apricot brandy, juice ½ lime. Pour ingredients into a highball glass over crushed ice, top with soda. Dress with sliced banana and mint sprig.

Banana Royal Cocktail (Cktl) ½ measure golden rum, ½ measure coconut milk, 2 measures pineapple juice, 2 dashes cream, 1 banana. Blend altogether with a scoop of crushed ice in a blender. Pour into an old-fashioned glass. Top with toasted dessicated coconut.

Banana's Breeze (Cktl) 5mls (¼fl.oz) apricot brandy, 20mls (¾fl.oz) crème de banane, 25mls (1fl.oz) brandy, 35mls (1½fl.ozs) orange juice, 10mls (½fl.oz) sweet and sour lemon juice, 3 drops Prothee. Shake over ice, strain into cocktail glass.

Banana Skin (Eng) an aroma often produced during maceration carbonique fermentation e.g. Beaujolais Nouveau.

Banat (Rum) the largest wine-producing region. The best red wine is from the Kadarka grape.

Banater Riesling (Rum) an erroneous varietal name for the grape Creaca, Kreaca, Kriacza, Zakkelweiss. Known as the Grüzer in Austria.

Banatski Rizling Kreaca (Ser) a Riesling-style white grape variety grown in the Banat region Vojvodina.

Ban Bourguignone (Fr) a song sung at wine fraternities of Burgundy.

Bancha (Jap) the coarsest grade of green tea that has been 'roasted', contains twigs and stems as well as the leaves. Is usually served free in restaurants with a meal.

Banco Brewery (Swe) a co-operative brewery based in Skruv in south-east Sweden.

Bancroft Ranch (USA) the label for a fine red wine (Cabernet sauvignon) from the Beringer Vineyards, Napa Valley, California.

Banda Azul (Sp) a red wine produced by Federico Paternina of Rioja. Produced from the Tempranillo, Mazuelo and Garnacha grapes, it is matured for 1 year in oak and 1-2 years in bottle.

Banda Dorada (Sp) a white wine produced by Federico Paternina of Rioja from 70% Viura and 30% Malvasia.

B and B (Cktl) ½ measure brandy and ½ measure Bénédictine mixed together.

B and B (Fr) a liqueur produced by Bénédictine near Fécamp. A blend of Bénédictine and old Cognac. Is drier than the Bénédictine liqueur. 43% alc by vol.

B and B Vineyards (USA) a winery based in Stockton, New Jersey. Produces mainly hybrid wines.

Bande à Côté (Fr) turning the cask on its side so that the bung is also on the side.

Bande Dessous (Fr) a term used to describe a full cask with the bung uppermost.

Bandeira (Sp) a wine similar in style to Port, produced in north-western Spain.

Ban des Vendanges (Fr) official opening ceremony of the Graves and Médoc vintage. Allows the Confrères Vignerons to set a date for the harvest.

Ban de Vendange (Fr) lit: 'prohibition of the harvest', is actually a proclamation of the date when the harvest may start in A.O.C. regions (declared by the local INAO committee). *See also* Banvin.

Bandiera Winery (USA) a winery. (Add): Cloverdale, Sonoma Valley, California. Grape varieties: Cabernet sauvignon, Chenin blanc, Gamay, Petit syrah and Zinfandel. Produces varietal wines.

Bandol (Fr) an A.C. controlled place name for certain wines of Provence on the south coast of Aix. 1430ha. (49 domaines 5 co-operatives), soil: clay-limestone, maximum yield 40hl/ha. Produces A.C. red 35%, rosé 60% and white 5% wines. Communes- Bandol, Beausset [part], Evenos [part], La Cadière d'Azur, Le Castellet, Ollioules [part], Saint-Cyr-sur-Mer [part] and Sanary. Main grape varieties: Bourboulenc, Clairette, Ugni blanc and Sauvignon blanc (40% maximum) for the white wines and Cinsault, Grenache, Mourvaison and Mourvèdre (minumum 50%) for the red wines. Minimum alcohol by vol. 11%. Red wines must spend 18 months in cask.

B & T Brewery (Eng) a brewery. (Add): The Brewery, Shefford, Bedfordshire SG17 5DZ. Brews a variety of ales and beers including: Dragonslayer 4.5% alc by vol., Edwin Taylor's Extra Stout 4.5% alc by vol., Shefford Bitter 3.8% alc by vol., Shefford Mild 3.8% alc by vol., Shefford Old Dark 5% alc by vol., Shefford Old Strong 5% alc by vol., Shefford Pale Ale 4.5% alc by vol., Two Brewers Bitter 3.6% alc by vol. Website: http://www.banksandtaylor.com 'E'mail: brewery@banksandtaylor.com

Banff (Scot) a 15 year old single highland malt whisky produced by Slater Rodger and C°, part of the DCL. group. 45% alc by vol.

Bang (Cktl) half warmed ale, half dry cider, 1 wine glass whisky, stir well and sprinkle with ginger or nutmeg. Note that gin may be substituted in place of the whisky.

Bang (Ind) *see* Bhang.

Bangalore Purple (Ind) a local red grape variety.

Bangla Beer (Eng) the name of a beer brewed by Refresh UK Ltd., Oxfordshire.

Banham Single Varietal Cox (Eng) an 8.2% alc by vol. cider from Banham Cider, The Appleyard, Banham, Norfolk.

Bankia (Bul) an alkaline still and sparkling natural mineral water from Sofia. Mineral contents (milligrammes per litre): Sodium 61.9mg/l, Calcium 3.2mg/l, Potassium 0.65mg/l, Bicarbonates 61mg/l, Chlorides 4.3mg/l, Sulphates 52.7mg/l, Fluorides 0.6mg/l. pH 9.3

Banks and Taylor Brewery (Eng) a new brewery (established 1981) based in Shefford, Bedfordshire. Noted for Shefford Bitter 1038 O.G. Eastcote Ale 1041 O.G. SOS 1050 O.G. and Dragon Slayer.

Bank's Beer (W.Ind) a light beer 5% alc by vol. brewed by the Banks Brewery in Barbados.

Bank's Belter (Eng) a cask-conditioned ale brewed by Bank's Brewery.

Bank's Brewery (Eng) one of the remaining two breweries in the West Midlands belonging to the Wolverhampton & Dudley Breweries Ltd. Produces many fine beers. *See also* Hanson's Brewery.

Banks (Barbados) Brewery (W.Ind) a brewery. (Add): Wildey, St. Michael, Barbados. Brews Bank's beers, Ebony Lager (a dark lager beer), Bajan Beer and Stallion Stout. Website: http://www.banksbeer.com 'E'mail: info@banksbeer.com

Banks DIH Ltd. (S.Am) a rum producer based in Guyana. Produces Gold Medal, Royal Liquid Gold, Super White and XM Standard.

Banks's Draught (Eng) a canned version of the famous mild ale from Bank's Brewery with a widget in the can.

Banks's Number Nine [N°9] (Eng) *see* Number Nine.

Banks's Passion (Eng) a cask-conditioned ale brewed by Bank's Brewery.

Bank Top Brewery (Eng) a brewery (established 1995). (Add): The Pavillion, Ashworth Lane, Bank Top, Bolton, Lancashire BL1 8RA. Brews a variety of ales and beers including: Brydge Bitter 3.8% alc by vol., Dark Mild 3.5% alc by vol., Flat Cap 4% alc by vol., Game Set and Match 3.8% alc by vol., Gold Digger 4% alc by vol., Old Slapper 4.2% alc by vol., Pavillion Pale Ale 4.5% alc by vol., Samual Cromptom Ale 4.2% alc by vol., Santa Claus 5% alc by vol., Smoke Stack Lightnin 5% alc by vol., Volunteer Bitter 4.2% alc by vol. Website: http://www.banktopbrewery.co.uk 'E'mail: john@banktopbrewery.co.uk

Banner Bitter (Eng) a bitter ale launched in summer 1994 to commemorate County Durhams links with mining industry. From micro-brewery John Constable, Butterknowle Brewery, Lynesack, County Durham. 4% alc by vol.

Bannockburn (Scot) a beer brewed by the Bridge of Allan Brewery, Stirlingshire.

Bannockburn Vineyard (Austr) a winery. (Add): Midland Highway, Bannockburn, Victoria 3331.

16ha. Grape varieties: Cabernet sauvignon, Chardonnay, Pinot noir, Sauvignon blanc and Shiraz.

Baños de Ebro (Sp) a noted wine-producing village based in the Rioja Alavesa, north-eastern Spain.

Banrock Station Sparkling Shiraz (Austr) a tank-fermented sparkling Shiraz at 14.5% alc by vol. from Hardy's.

Banshee Cocktail (Cktl) ⅓ measure crème de cacao, ⅓ measure crème de banane, ⅓ measure cream, dash gomme syrup. Blend altogether in a blender with a scoop of crushed ice. Pour into a cocktail glass.

Banskà Bystrica Brewery (Czec) a brewery (established 1971) in eastern Czec. Noted for light pilsener beers.

Banvin (Fr) an old law which allowed the lord of the manor to sell his wines first before his tenants (over a set period of time). Also the old custom of fixing the date of the harvest. The fore-runner of the Ban de Vendange.

Banyuls (Fr) an A.C. vin doux naturel from the Roussillon district 1900ha. of the Midi region, made with the Grenache and Carignan grapes, brown in colour, consumed as an apéritif in France. Soil: shale. Communes: Banyuls-sur-Mer, Cerbère and Port-Vendres. Must have a minimum alc by vol. of 21.5% and maximum 7% unfermented sugar. *see* Banyuls Grand Cru and Banyuls Rancio.

Banyuls-Citron (Cktl) 60mls (½ gill) Banyuls, 20mls (⅙ gill) irop de citron, soda water. Stir over ice, strain into a highball glass and top with soda water.

Banyuls Grand Cru (Fr) an A.C. Banyuls that must be aged for a minimum of 30 months in wood in under-ground cellars. *see* Affinage and Banyuls.

Banyuls Rancio (Fr) a term applied to those A.C. Banyuls wines whose containers are left out in the sun unsealed and who develop a slightly sour, strongly oxidised character.

Banyuls-sur-Mer (Fr) a commune in the A.C. Banyuls region of south-western France.

Baobab (Afr) a North African drink produced from the fruit of the tree of same name.

Baobab (S.Afr) the export label for a range of wines produced by the Stettyn Winery, Worcester, Western Cape.

Baptizer (Port) to water down wine (or milk) etc.

Bar [1] (Eng) *abbr:* **bar**-counter where drinks are served or a barrier between staff and the customer. Also applied to room where the bar is. *see* 'Cocktail Bar', 'Public Bar' and 'Lounge Bar'. *See also* Gantry.

Bar [2] (Eng) *abbr:* **bar**red. To prevent entry into a Public house to undesirables.

Bar (Tur) a café serving alcoholic drinks. A drinking bar (place). *See also* Birahane. (Arab) = hana, (Aus) = kneipe, (Chi) = jiuba, (Cro) = bife, (Den) = bar, (Fr) = bistro / bar, (Ger) = kneipe, (Gre) = bar, (Hol) = bar, (Indo) = bar, (Ire) = barra, (Isr) = bar, (It) = bar, (Jap) = baa, (Kor) = suljip, (Port) = bar, (Rus) = bar, (Sp) = bar, (Thai) = bar.

B

Barack Pàlinka (Hun) a dry unsweetened brandy made from the distilled juice of apricots. Sold in a short squat bottle with a long, fairly wide neck. Has a slight taste of almonds.

Barad (S.Arabia) a natural mineral water. Mineral contents (milligrammes per litre): Sodium 35mg/l, Calcium 2.4mg/l, Magnesium 1mg/l, Potassium 0.7mg/l, Bicarbonates 20mg/l, Chlorides 35mg/l, Sulphates 8.5mg/l. pH 7.2

Baraka (Egy) a still and sparkling natural mineral water from Kafir El Arbein Region (blue label: sparkling / green label: still). Mineral contents (milligrammes per litre): Sodium 62mg/l, Calcium 60mg/l, Magnesium 26mg/l, Potassium 5mg/l, Bicarbonates 325mg/l, Chlorides 50mg/l, Sulphates 45mg/l, Silicates 40.6mg/l.

Barancourt-Brice, Martin, Tritant (Fr) Champagne Récoltants-Manipulants. (Add): Place Tritant, BP 3, Bouzy 51150, Tours-sur-Marne. 160ha. Produces vintage and non-vintage wines. Vintages: 1969, 1970, 1971, 1973, 1975, 1976, 1979, 1982, 1983, 1985, 1988.

Baratke (Rum) a wine-producing area, is part of the Banat Vineyard.

Barbacarlo (It) a dry or semi-sweet red wine from Oltrepó Pavese, Lombardy.

Barbadillo (Sp) a noted Sherry and brandy producer of Jerez de la Frontera. Also in Sanlúcar de Barrameda. Owns many vineyards and a 415ha. vineyard and winery with Harveys. Sherry labels include Luis de Eguilas II, Pedro Rodriguez, Solera Manzanilla Pasada and a 60 year old Manzanilla. Solera brandy: Fanez de Minaya, Solera gran reserva: Crequi Eva, Extra, Fanez de Minaya, Gran Capitan.

Barbados Cream (Fr) see Crème des Barbades.

Barbados Distilleries (W.Ind) a major rum distillers in the West Indies.

Barbados Rum (W.Ind) a medium coloured rum with a light, slightly sweet flavour.

Barbados Water (W.Ind) an old seventeenth century nickname for rum.

Barbancourt (W.Ind) a famous Haitian rum distillery.

Barbantane (Fr) a vin doux naturel produced in the commune of Barbantane in the Bouches-du-Rhône, southern France.

Bårbar (Bel) a honey-flavoured beer brewed by the Lefebvre Brasserie.

Barbara Cocktail (Cktl) 1 measure vodka, ½ measure crème de cacao, ½ measure cream. Shake well over ice, strain into a cocktail glass.

Barbarella Cocktail (Cktl)(Non-alc) ½ measure Angostura, ½ measure syrop de fraises. Stir over ice in a highball glass. Top with grape juice.

Barbaresco (It) a famous D.O.C.G. red wine from Piemonte. Made from the Nebbiolo grape, aged 2 years (1 year in oak/chestnut casks). If aged 3 years: Riserva. 4 years or more: Riserva Speciale.

Barbarian (Eng) a 5.2% alc by vol. bitter ale from Worldham Brewery, Worldham, near Alton, Hampshire. See also Old Dray.

Barbarian Beer (Eng) a cask-conditioned bitter ale 1045 O.G. brewed by the Pheasant and Firkin home-brew public house in London.

Barbarossa (It) a black grape variety grown in central eastern Italy.

Barbarossa-Brunnen (Ger) a natural spring mineral water from Löhnberg-Selters, HE.

Barbary Coast Cocktail (Cktl) ⅕ measure each of gin, Scotch whisky, crème de cacao, rum and cream, 1 dash gomme syrup. Shake well over ice, strain into a cocktail glass.

Barbeillon [J.C.] (Fr) a producer of sparkling wines based at Oisly, Touraine, Loire.

Barbeito (Mad) a noted Madeira wine shipper.

Barbelroth (Ger) village (Anb): Pfalz. (Ber): Südliche Weinstrasse. (Gro): Kloster Liebfrauenberg. (Vin): Kirchberg.

Barbera (It) a red wine grape grown principally in Piemonte, also to a small extent in California. The wine produced is deep-coloured, full-bodied and full flavoured.

Barbera (USA) see California Barbera.

Barbera Amabile (It) a slightly sparkling, sweet red wine from the Barbera grape.

Barbera Bianca (It) a white grape variety grown in northern Italy.

Barbera d'Alba (It) a D.O.C. red wine made from the Barbera grape in the commune of Alba in the province of Cuneo, Piemonte. Aged for 2 years (1 year in wood). 13% alc by vol. If aged 3 years then classed Superiore.

Barbera d'Asti (It) a D.O.C. red wine made from the Barbera grape in the commune of Asti, Piemonte. Aged for 2 years (1 year in wood). 13% alc by vol. If aged 3 years then classed Superiore.

Barbera del Monferrato (It) a D.O.C. red wine made from 75%–90% Barbera and 10%–25% Freisa, Grignolino and Dolcetto. Under D.O.C. rules are allowed to add a % of non-Piedmontese grapes. If alc. content not less than 12.5% by vol. and aged not less than 2 years then classed Superiore.

Barberino (It) a commune of Chianti Classico Riserva.

Barbère (S.Afr) the label for a rosé wine (Cinsaut) part of the Jacques de Savoy range produced by the Vrede en Lust Wine Farm winery, Paarl, Western Cape.

Barbero (It) a leading bitters and vermouth producer based in the Piemonte. Noted for Diesus bitter apéritif. Also produce Moscato d'Asti.

Barberone (USA) see California Barberone.

Barberoux (Fr) a red grape variety grown in south-eastern France. Known as Barbarossa in Italy.

Barbezieux (Fr) a noted town in the Charente département in the Petite Champagne, Cognac whose grapes are distilled into Cognac des Bois.

Barbican (Eng) a popular, alcohol-free lager brewed by Bass Charrington.

Barbican Cocktail (Cktl) ⁷⁄₁₀ measure Drambuie, ²⁄₁₀ measure passion fruit juice, ¹⁄₁₀ measure Scotch whisky. Shake over ice, strain into a cocktail glass.

Barbier [René] (Sp) a wine producer based in

Penedés. Grape varieties: Cabernet sauvignon, Cariñena, Garnacha, Monastrell, Parellada, Tempranillo, Xarello.

Bar Blender/Liquidiser (Eng) used for making drinks that require puréed fruits.

Barbonne Fayel (Fr) a Cru Champagne village in the Canton de Sézanne. District: Épernay.

Barbosa [Joao T.] Lda. (Port) a noted shipper of fine Dão wines.

Barbotage (Fr) process of bubbling the vapour through the arriving wine. Adds to the final flavour and aroma of the spirit in Armagnac.

Barbotage (Cktl) ½ measure orange juice, ½ measure lemon juice, dash grenadine. Shake over ice, strain into a flute glass and top with iced Champagne.

Barboteo (Sp) the name given to the art of 'chewing' the wine, i.e. retaining the wine in the mouth to warm it and improve the bouquet and flavour.

Barbotine (Fr) *see* Mugwort.

Barboursville Vineyard (USA) a winery based in Barboursville, Virginia in A.V.A. of Monticello. 100ha. Produces vinifera wines. Grape varieties include Cabernet franc, Pinot grigio, Sangiovese, Chardonnay, Nebbiolo, Traminer aromatico.

Barbour Estate (USA) a winery based in the Napa Valley, California. Grape varieties include: Cabernet sauvingnon.

Barbus Barbus (Eng) a 4.6% alc by vol. beer brewed by the Butts Brewery Ltd., Berkshire.

Barca Velha (Port) a red wine (first vintage 1952 only 14 vintages produced to 2005) produced by Ferreira from 15% Amarela, 60% Roriz and 20% Touriga francesa grapes grown at Meao in the upper Douro. Is matured at Vila Nova de Gaia. Vintages: 1952, 1953, 1954, 1957, 1964, 1965, 1966, 1978, 1981, 1982, 1983, 1985, 1991, 1995 (alc by vol: 12%–12.5%). Owned by SOGRAPE.

Barcelo (Port) a lesser white grape variety grown in the Dão region.

Barcelo [Luis] (Sp) a producer and exporter of Málaga.

Barcelona (Sp) a province of Cataluña, north-eastern Spain. Home to the D.O. wines of Alella and Penedés, the Vino de la Tierra wine of Bages, the Vino Comarcal wine of Anoia, the Vinos de Mesa wines of Hospitalet de Llobregat and Ullastrell.

Barclays [Jas] & Cº. (Can) a distiller of a range of Canadian whiskies. Subsidiary of Allied-Domecq.

Barclay Square (Can) a blended Canadian whisky produced by Jas Barclay and Cº. 40% alc by vol.

Barco [El] (Sp) a large cooperative based in Galicia.

Barco Reale (It) a D.O.C. red wine produced in Carmignano. Produced from the same grapes as Carmignano D.O.C.G. it receives only 1 year of ageing.

Barcos Rabelos (Port) the boats used to take down the casks of new Port wine from Pinhão to Oporto along the river Douro. Not used so much now as road and railway has been built. Mainly used now for promotional purposes. On the 24th June a regatta and race (using the barco rabelos)

is held in honour of St. John (the patron saint of Oporto).

Bardenheim Wine Cellars (USA) a winery based in St. Louis, Missouri. Produces vinifera and hybrid wines.

Bardinet (Fr) a liqueur and rum producers based in Bordeaux. Produces Ardine, Kümmel, Manzana Verde, Negrita (a brand of rum), Parfait Amour and Triple Sec.

Bardinet (W.Ind) a noted rum distillery based on the island of Martinique.

Bardo (Port) a system of vine training using wires stretched between granite pillars or wooden posts.

Bardolino (It) a D.O.C. red wine from the Corvina veronese, Rondinella, Molinara, Negrara, Rossignola, Barbera and Sangiovese grapes. *See also* Bardolino Classico. If minimum alc. content 11.5% by vol. and aged minimum 1 year then classed Superiore.

Bardolino Chiaretto (It) a D.O.C. rosé wine from grape varieties used in the making of Bardolino. *See also* Bardolino Chiaretto Classico.

Bardolino Chiaretto Classico (It) a wine from the central and best part of the region of production.

Bardolino Classico (It) a wine from the central and best part of the region of production.

Barebones (Eng) a 4.7% alc by vol. ale brewed by the Springhead Brewery, Nottinghamshire.

Bärenblut (USA) a red wine produced by the Beringer Brothers Winery in the Napa Valley, California. Made from the Grignolino and Pinot noir grapes.

Bärenfang (Ger) a honey-flavoured lime and mullein flower liqueur, made using neutral spirit.

Barengo Winery (USA) a large winery based in the northern part of the San Joaquin Valley, California. Owns vineyards in Fresno, Lodi and Modesto (also buys in grapes). Produces most styles of wines. *See also* Cremocha.

Bärentrank (Ger) lit: 'bear's drink', a strong spirit from eastern Prussia, distilled from potatoes and flavoured with honey.

Barfly (Eng) a slang term for a 'bar-hogger', a person who sits at the bar counter of licensed premises all the time, thus making it difficult for other customers to get served.

Bar Fly (USA) the nickname for a person who frequents bars (licensed premises).

Barge & Barrel Brewing Company (Eng) a micro-brewery based at Elland, near Halifax, West Yorkshire. Brews: Nettlethrasher 4.4% alc by vol. Bargee, TJ's 5K, Black Stump and Best Bitter 4% alc by vol. Now known as Eastwood & Sanders Ltd (Fine Ales).

Bargee (Eng) an ale brewed by the Barge & Barrel Brewing Company, Elland, near Halifax, West Yorkshire.

Bargee (Eng) a 3.8% alc by vol. ale brewed by Eastwood & Sanders Ltd (Fine Ales), West Yorkshire.

Bargetto Winery (USA) a winery based in Soquel,

B

Santa Cruz, California. Grape varieties: Barbera, Cabernet sauvignon, Chardonnay, French colombard, Johannisberg riesling and Zinfandel. Produces varietal wines.

Bar Glass (Cktl) a mixing glass for mixing cocktails, also known as a Jigger.

Baril (Fr) barrel, cask, 72 litres (16 gals) capacity, used for spirits, wine, etc.

Baril (Wal) cask barrel.

Barile (It) barrel/cask.

Barillet (Fr) keg.

Barista (It) bartender.

Barkham Manor (Eng) a vineyard based at Piltdown, Uckfield, East Sussex.

Barking Frog (Eng) a 5.5% alc by vol drink produced by Allied-Domecq from a mix of purple tequila and citrus. Sold in a purple 275 ml. bottle.

Barking Owl Winery (Austr) a winery based in Western Australia. Grape varieties include: Cabernet sauvignon, Malbec, Merlot.

Bar-le-Duc (Fr) a red wine (vin de table) producing town based in the Lorraine region.

Bar-le-Duc (Hol) a natural mineral water from Baarle-Nassau. Mineral contents (milligrammes per litre): Sodium 11.5mg/l, Calcium 75mg/l, Magnesium 6.5mg/l, Potassium 2.6mg/l, Bicarbonates 220mg/l, Chlorides 23mg/l, Sulphates 28mg/l.

Bärleiten (Aus) a vineyard site on the banks of the River Danube situated in the Wachau region, Niederösterreich.

Barley (Eng) the main grain used in the production of beer and whisky. Ideal because of its high sugar, low starch content. see Two Row, Four Row and Six Row Barley.

Barley Corn (Eng) a single grain of barley.

Barleycorn Ale (Eng) a pale keg ale 1033 O.G. brewed by Hall's Brewery, Burton-on-Trent, Staffs.

Barley Malt (Eng) the name for maltose (malt sugar) used in the beer and malt whisky brewing processes.

Barleymead (Eng) a 4.8% alc by vol. premium draught ale from the Elgood Brewery Cambridgeshire.

Barleymole (Eng) a 4.2% alc by vol. ale brewed by the Moles Brewery, Wiltshire.

Barley Tea (Kor) see Porich'a.

Barley Water (Eng) wash 2 tablespoons of barley and boil for 2 hours in 2 quarts of water. Strain, add sugar to taste and allow to cool. Is beneficial to the kidneys. (Ire) = uisce eorna.

Barley Water (Eng) see Robinson's Barley Water.

Barley Wine (Eng) a dark, fruity beer with a very high alcohol content of over 1060 O.G. The strongest of ales, it is normally sold in nips.

Barlinka (Alg) a red wine grape introduced to the Cape in the mid 1920's

Bar Liquidiser/Blender (Eng) used for making drinks that require puréed fruits.

Barlys (Wal) barley.

Barm (Eng) in brewing the frothy head seen on the top of the fermenting vessel.

Barm (Eng) an old English name for yeast. see Barmr from which it derives.

Barmaid (Eng) a female who serves and operates behind a bar or counter to dispense drinks. See also Bartender. (Ire) = cailim tabhairne.

Barman (Eng)(Fr)(Gre)(Hol)(Port) a man who serves and operates behind a bar or counter to dispense drinks. See also Bartender, Trayer. (Ire) = buachaill tabhairne.

Barmaster Cocktail (Cktl) ⅓ measure Mandarine Napoléon, ⅔ measure orange juice, dash Campari, dash vodka, dash egg white. Shake well over ice, strain into a cocktail glass, dress with slice of orange and a cherry.

Barmen (Tur) barman/bartender.

Barmera (Eng) a range of Australian wines from Shaftesbury Vintners. Imported from Consolidated Co-operative Wineries.

Barm Pot (Eng) a 3.8% alc by vol. ale brewed by the Goose Eye Brewery, West Yorkshire.

Barmr (Scan) the old Norse name for yeast. see Barm.

Barms (Ger) an old gothic name for yeast.

Bar-myen (Rus) bartender.

Barna (Hun) a malty, dark beer 4% alc by vol.

Barn Ale Bitter (Eng) a 4% alc by vol. cask-conditioned bitter beer, also a 5.4% alc by vol. bottled version brewed by the Old luxters Brewery, Oxfordshire.

Barnard Griffin (USA) a wine producer based in the Columbia Valley, Washington State. Grape varieties include Syrah.

Barnaut [Edmond] (Fr) a Champagne producer (established 1874). (Add): 2, Rue Gambetta, 51150 Bouzy. Grand Cru vineyards of Pinot noir 100%. Produces: Authentique Rosé, Grand Cru Blanc de Noir Brut 100% Pinot noir, La Cuvée Edmond 40% Chardonnay, 40% Pinot noir, 20% Pinot meunier, Cuvée Douceur and a variety of Grand Cru white and rosé Champagnes. Also produces Bouzy Rouge, Fine Marc de Champagne, Vieux Marc de Champagne and Ratafia. Vintages: 1996, 1999. Website: http://www.Champagne-barnaut.com 'E'mail: contact@Champagne-barnaut.com

Barn Brewery (Eng) a brewery (established 2005). (Add): Chatsworth, Bakewell, Derbyshire DE45 1EX. Brews: Bakewell Best 4.2% alc by vol., Swift Nick 3.8% alc by vol. 'E'mail: peakales.barnbrewery@virgin.net

Barnes Winery (Can) a major wine producer based in Ontario.

Barnett (Fr) a Cognac producer.

Barnett Vineyards (USA) a 5.6ha. steeply terraced vineyard (established 1984) at Spring Mountain, Napa Valley, California. Also has vineyards in Monterey County. Grape varieties: Chardonnay, Cabernet franc, Cabernet sauvignon, Merlot, Pinot noir. Labels: Rattlesnake Hill, Sleepy Hollow Vineyard.

Barnfield Brewery (Eng) a micro-brewery based at Huddersfield, West Yorkshire.

Barngates Brewery (Eng) a brewery. (Add):

Barngate, Ambleside, Cumbria LA22 0NG. Brews: Cat Nap Ale 3.6% alc by vol., Chesters Strong Ale 5.2% alc by vol., Cracker Ale 3.9% alc by vol., Tag Lag 4.4% alc by vol. Website: http://www.drunkenduckinn.co.uk 'E'mail: info@drunkenduckinn.co.uk

Barningham Vineyard (Eng) a vineyard (established 1972), 1.75ha. Soil: sandy loam over gravel. Grape variety: 95% Riesling x Sylvaner.

Barn Owl Bitter (Eng) a 4.5% alc by vol. bitter ale from the Cotleigh Brewery, Wiveliscombe, Somerset.

Barnsgate Manor Vineyards (Eng) a small winery based in Herons-Ghyll, near Uckfield, East Sussex. 8.25ha. Grape varieties: Chardonnay, Kerner, Müller-Thurgau, Pinot noir, Reichensteiner, Seyval blanc. Is owned by Pieroth of Germany.

Barnsley Bitter (Eng) a 3.8% alc by vol. bitter beer brewed by the Acorn Brewery, South Yorkshire.

Barnsley Bitter (Eng) a 3.8% alc by vol. bitter ale from the Barnsley Brewing Company, Elsecar, near Barnsley.

Barnsley Brewery Company (Eng) a brewery based in Elsecar, South Yorkshire. Brews: Barnsley Bitter, Barnsley Glory, Eh-up! It's Christmas.

Barnsley's Glory (Eng) a 4.8% alc by vol. ale brewed by Barnsley Brewery Company, Elsecar. Brewed to mark the football club's promotion.

Bansley Gold (Eng) a 4.3% alc by vol. ale brewed by the Acorn Brewery, South Yorkshire.

Barnstablasta (Eng) a 6.6% alc by vol. ale brewed by the Barum Brewery, Devon,

Barnstormer (Eng) a 4.7% alc by vol. ale brewed by Bath Ales Ltd., Avon.

Barnstormer Ale (Eng) a strong ale 1048 O.G. brewed by Stallion Brewery in Chippenham, Berkshire.

Barnyard Fermented (Eng) a term used by coffee tasters to denote a poor coffee.

Barocco (It) a red I.G.T. wine produced from 50% each of Cabernet and Montepulciano grapes by Terre Cortesi Moncaro in the Marche.

Barochan (Scot) a 4.1% alc by vol. ale brewed by the Houston Brewing C°., Renfrewshire.

Barolo (It) a D.O.C.G. red wine produced from the Nebbiolo grape in the Piemonte region. Aged for minimum of 1 year in oak/chestnut casks. Can be released after 3 years of age. Min. alc. 12.5% by vol. (originally 13% alc by vol). If aged not less than 4 years then classified Riserva, if aged not less than 5 years then classified Riserva speciale.

Barolo Bianco (It) an alternative name for the white Arneis grape.

Barolo Chinato (It) an apéritif of Barolo wine flavoured with quinine.

Baron (Ger) vineyard (Anb): Pfalz. (Ber): Südliche Weinstrasse. (Gro): Schloss Ludwigshöhe. (Vil): St. Martin.

Baron Albert (Fr) a Champagne producer. (Add): Porteron, 02310 Charly-sur-Marne. A négociant-manipulant. Vintages include 1987, 1989. Labels: Cuvée Jean de la Fontaine, Cuvée La Préférence

Barona Vermouth (Eng) the brand-name of a vermouth from Linfood Cash and Carry, Northamptonshire.

Baron B (Arg) a sparkling wine produced by the Bodegas Proviar.

Baron Cocktail (Cktl) 1 measure gin, 1 measure Triple Sec, ¼ measure Italian vermouth, ¼ measure French vermouth. Stir over ice, strain into a cocktail glass, add a twist of lemon peel.

Baron d'Arques (Fr) a red wine produced as a joint venture between Baron Philippe de Rothschild SA and Les Vignerons du Sieur d'Arques, Limoux.

Baron de L' (Fr) *see* Baron de Ladoucette.

Baron de Ladoucette (Fr) the owner of Château du Nozet, who produces a fine Pouilly Fumé, under the name of Baron de L'.

Baron de Ley (Sp) a 90ha vineyard. (Add): Ctra. Mendavia-Lodosa km 5, 31587 Mendavia, Navarra. Grape varieties: Tempranillo, Viura. Produces: Reserva and Gran Reserva wines.

Baron de Lustrac (Fr) an Armagnac producer. Produces a range of Armagnacs including vintage brandies.

Baron de Pibrac (Fr) the label of a 10 year old and V.S. Armagnac.

Baron de Rio Negro (Arg) the brand-name of a sparkling white wine.

Baron de Sigognac (Fr) an Armagnac producer based in Armagnac, Gers.

Baron Edmond (S.Afr) the label for a red wine (Chardonnay) produced by the Rupert & Rothschild Vignerons winery, Paarl, Western Cape.

Baronesse Nadine (S.Afr) the label for a white wine (Cabernet sauvignon and Merlot blend) produced by the Rupert & Rothschild Vignerons winery, Paarl, Western Cape.

Baron et Fils (Fr) a Champagne producer based in Épernay.

Baron-Fuenté (Fr) a Champagne producer. (Add): Charly-sur-Marne. Produces vintage and non-vintage wines. Produces: Grand Millésime. Vintages: 1998.

Barongavale Winery (Austr) a winery (established 1981). (Add): East West Road, Barongarook, Victoria. Grape varieties: Cabernet sauvignon, Pinot noir, Shiraz, Chardonnay, Colombard, Riesling, Traminer.

Baronial (Cktl) ⁷⁄₁₀ measure Lillet, ³⁄₁₀ measure lemon gin, 2 dashes Angostura, 2 dashes Cointreau. Stir over ice, strain into a cocktail glass.

Baroni di San Lorenzo (It) a winery based on the island of Sicily. Label: Blu dei Baroni Eloro.

Baron le Roy de Boiseaumarie (Fr) in 1920's was responsible for pioneering A.C. laws in Châteauneuf-du-Pape, Rhône. Owned Château Fortia.

Baronne (S.Afr) the label for a soft, red wine made from (Cabernet sauvignon 40% and Shiraz 60%) produced by the Nederburg Estate, Wellington, Western Cape.

Baronne du Chatelârd (Fr) a winery based in the A.C. Beaujolais Cru Morgon, southern Burgundy.

Also produces: A.C. Beaujolais Cru's Brouilly and Moulin-à-Vent.

Baronnie d'Estourard (Fr) the label of a Châteauneuf-du-Pape produced by M.T. Jean in Châteauneuf-du-Pape, southern Rhône.

Baronoff (Eng) a proprietary brand of vodka. 40% alc by vol.

Baron Otard (Fr) an 8 year old V.S.O.P. Cognac produced by the Otard C°. in Cognac.

Baron Philippe Collection (Fr) a range of wines from Baron Philippe de Rothschild SA, Bordeaux. Includes wines from Pauillac, Médoc, Saint-Estèphe, Saint-Émilion, Pomerol, Graves, Entre-Deux-Mers.

Baron Philippe de Rothschild (Fr) a range of Vin de Pays d'Oc wines produced by Baron Philippe de Rothschild SA. Includes Cabernet sauvignon, Merlot, Chardonnay, Sauvignon blanc.

Baron Philippe de Rothschild SA (Fr) a large famous company based in Bordeaux that encompasses Châteaux: Mouton de Rothschild, d'Armailhaçq, Clerc-Milon, Coutet, plus Aile d'Argent, Heritage, Mouton Cadet, Baron Philippe Collection, Agneau Rosé, Berger Baron, Bordeaux Baron, Escudo Rojo, La Belière, Mapa, Mise de la Baronnie Pauillac, Domaine de Lambert. Also joint ventures Almaviva, Baron d'Arques, Opus One.

Barons Dark (Eng) a 4.1% alc by vol. mild ale brewed by the Exe Valley brewery, Devon.

Barons Hopsit (Eng) a 4.1% alc by vol. ale brewed by the Exe Valley Brewery, Devon.

Baron Villeneuve de Cantemerle (Fr) the second wine of Château Cantemerle, A.C. Haut-Médoc. (Com): Macau. *See also* Château Royal Médoc.

Baron Vineyard [Le] (USA) a vineyard (6ha) based in Sonoma County, California. Grape variety: Rhine riesling. Owned by Sonoma Vineyards.

Baron von Holt (S.Afr) the label for a red wine (Cabernet sauvignon 70%, Merlot 15% and Petit verdot 15% blend) produced by the Old Vine Cellars winery, Cape Town, Western Cape.

Baroosh (Eng) a beer brewed by McMullen & Sons Ltd. Brewery, Hertfordshire.

Baroque (USA) a red hybrid grape variety developed by the University of California and grown in the Paul Masson Vineyards.

Baroque (Fr) a white grape used in Côtes du Brulhois wines.

Barossa Co-operative (Austr) an estate in the Barossa Valley, South Australia. Uses the Kaiser Stuhl label for its wines.

Barossa Pearl (Austr) a sparkling wine of Barossa Valley from the Gramp Winery, South Australia.

Barossa Valley (Austr) a famous wine region near Adelaide, South Australia. Mainly planted with ungrafted vines. Has a warm climate and red-brown alluvial loam soil over clay. Sub-Regions: Greenock (sandy soil), Kalimna (sandy soil).

Barouche Cape Blend (S.Afr) the label for a red wine (Cabernet sauvignon, Cinsaut, Pinotage and Shiraz blend) produced by the Blaauwklippen Agricultural Estate winery, Stellenbosch, Western Cape.

Bar Person (Eng) the designation given to barmen and women to comply with the Sex Discrimination Act of 1975.

Barquero (Sp) an extra dry Montilla produced by Pérez Barquero in Montilla-Moriles, southern Spain.

Barr (Fr) a famous old wine town in Alsace, north-eastern France.

Barr (Scan) an old Norse name for barley from which the word derives.

Barr [A.G.] (Scot) a soft drinks producer (established 1830) and based in Glasgow. Brands include Irn-bru, Dandilion and Burdock, Jusoda Orange, Orangina, Strike Cola, Tizer. Website: http://www.agbarr.co.uk 'E'mail: info@agbarr.co.uk

Barra (Ire) bar.

Barra (Port) single spur pruned cordon. *see* Cruzeta.

Barracas (Cktl) ⅔ measure sweet vermouth, ⅓ measure Angostura. Shake well over ice, strain into an ice-filled cocktail glass.

Barracheiros (Port) stalwarts who carry up to 75 kilo loads of grape bunches on their shoulders in baskets.

Barracuda (Cktl) 25mls (1fl.oz) light rum, 10mls (½ fl.oz) grenadine, 25mls (1fl.oz) pineapple juice, 5mls (¼ fl.oz) lime juice, 2 dashes gomme syrup. Shake over ice, strain into a pineapple shell. Top with Champagne. Decorate with a slice of pineapple and lime.

Barracuda Cocktail (Cktl) ½ measure golden rum, ¼ measure Galliano, ½ measure pineapple juice, 1 dash lime juice, 1 dash gomme syrup. Shake over ice, strain into an old-fashioned glass. Top with iced Champagne and a slice of lime.

Barraque (S.Afr) a dry, blended, white wine from Alpha Wines (part of Gilbeys).

Barre [La] (Fr) a Premier Cru vineyard in the A.C. commune of Volnay, Côte de Beaune, Burgundy. 2ha. Also known as Clos de la Barre.

Barred (Eng) a term to denote that a person may not use certain licensed premises because they may have caused a disturbance (or other reason).

Barrelage (Eng) the term used to denote the number of barrels per week/year that are bought/sold.

Barrelage Agreement (Eng) a term by which a public house is obliged to purchase a certain annual barrelage from a brewery in return for a reduced interest loan.

Barrel (Eng) a wooden (mainly oak) container for holding alcoholic beverages. Many different sizes world-wide. (Fr) = tonneau, (Ger) fass, (Ire) = cuirim, (Sp) = barril.

Barrel [Beer] (Eng) holds 36 gallons/288 pints (163.6 litres). (USA). 31.5 US. gallons.

Barrel Fermented (Eng)(USA) a term used when the fermentation process occurs in barrels as opposed to tanks, vats or in the bottle.

Barrelhouse (USA) a cheap drinking establishment which usually has unsavoury characteristics.

Barrel [Rum] (W.Ind) holds 40 gallons approximately (175litres–200 litres).

Barrel Select (S.Afr) the label for a range of wines

produced by the Graham Beck Wines winery, Franschhoek, Western Cape.

Barrel Select (USA) the label for a red wine (Pinot noir) produced by the Cottonwood Canyon winery, Santa Maria Valley, santa Barbara County, California.

Barrel Select (USA) the label for a red wine (Pinot noir) produced by the Henry Estate winery, Umpqua Valley, Oregon.

Barrel [Wine] (Fr) holds 26½ gallons (119.5 litres), but can vary from country to country and from region to region.

Barret (Fr) a commune in the Charente département whose grapes are classed Petite Champagne (Cognac).

Barretts Wines (Austr) a winery (established 1983) based in Victoria. Grape varieties: Riesling, Traminer, Cabernet sauvignon, Pinot noir.

Barriasson (Fr) a Cognac producer.

Barrica (Sp) a 225 litre oak cask. (Fr) = barrique.

Barrier Reef (Cktl) 1 scoop ice cream, 20mls (¾ fl.oz) Cointreau, 25mls (1fl.oz) gin, dash Angostura. Stir together with ice and add a few drops of blue Curaçao.

Barril (Sp) barrel.

Barril del Gasto (Sp) denotes a barrel of cheap wine from which the vineyard workers drink.

Barrique (Fr) hogshead, a large barrel/cask. Bordeaux = 225 litres, Burgundy = 228 litres, Cognac = 205 litres, Loire = 213 litres and Mâcon = 210 litres. (Sp) = barrica

Barrique à Vin (Ch.Isles) wine cask.

Barrique Bordelaise (Fr) cask, holds 49½ gallons (225litres). Made of Limousin oak. 4 barriques equal 1 tonneau, 1 barrique equals 288 standard (75cls) bottles.

Barrique de Transport (Fr) a specially strengthened cask which is suitable for dispatching wine. Has metal rims at both ends.

Barriques Nouveau (S.Afr) the label for a white wine (Chardonnay) produced by the Stellen Hills Wines winery, Stellenbosch, Western Cape.

Barriquot (Fr) the eighteenth century name for a small cask or barrel.

Barristers Bitter (Eng) a 4.3% alc by vol. bitter ale brewed by the Judges Brewery, Rugby, Warwickshire.

Barrocão (Port) a winery (established 1920) that produces red and white Garrafeiras in Bairrada.

Barron Brewery (Eng) a brewery (established 1984) based in Silverton, Devon. Noted for Barron's Draught 1040 O.G.

Bar Room (Eng) a room in a building where alcoholic drinks are permitted to be served (sold) for consumption on the premises. Must be licensed.

Barros (Port) vintage Port shippers. Vintages: 1948, 1955, 1957, 1958, 1960, 1963, 1965, 1966, 1970, 1974, 1975, 1977, 1978, 1979, 1980, 1982, 1983, 1985, 1987, 1989, 1991, 1994, 1995, 1997, 1998.

Barros (Sp) the clay soil found in the Andalusia region. Also spelt Barrosa.

Barrosa (Sp) see Barros.

Barros Almeida (Port) vintage Port shippers (established 1919). Company brands include Feist, Feuerheerd, Hutcheson, Kopke.

Barrosa Valley (Austr) mis-spelling of Barossa Valley.

Barry & Nephew (S.Afr) a 5 year old Cape brandy distllied by the Barrydale Koöperatiewe Wynmakery, Little Karoo.

Barrydale (S.Afr) a wine-producing area in the Klein Karoo region. Noted for brandy and Burgundy-style table wines.

Barrydale Koöperatiewe Wynmakery (S.Afr) a co-operative winery based in Klein Karoo. (Add): Box 59, Barrydale 6750. Produces varietals and Barry & Nephew a 3 y.o. Cape brandy, Joseph a 5 y.o. pot-stilled brandy. (The only co-operative brandy distillery in South Africa).

Barrys Brewery (Wal) a pub brewery at Bryn Arms, Gellilydan, near Trawsfynydd. Brews: Mel y Moelwyn bitter 1038 O.G.

Barry Wine Company (USA) a winery based on the west bank of the Hemlock Lake, Finger Lakes, New York. 60ha. Produces vinifera and hybrid wines.

Barsac (Fr) a famous A.C. commune 650ha of Sauternes in south-western Bordeaux on the west bank of the river Garonne, which can use the Sauternes A.C. or its own. Soil: red sandstone and chalk. Grape varieties: Sémillon, Sauvignon blanc, Muscadelle. Produces sweet white wines attacked by botrytis cinerea.

Bársonyos-Császár (Hun) a northerly wine area. The town of Mór is noted for Ezerjó (one of the finest dry white wines of Hungary).

Bar Spoon (Eng) a long handled spoon with a disk base (muddler) on top, made of stainless steel, silver or E.P.N.S.

Bar sur Aube (Fr) a commune within the Côte des Bar, Champagne. (Add): Place de l'Hotel de Ville, 10200 Bar sur Aube. Website: http://www.barsuraube.net 'E'mail: ot-bar@barsuraube.net

Bar sur Seine (Fr) a commune within the Côte des Bar, Champagne. (Add): 33, Rue Gambetta, 10110 Bar sur Seine. Website: http://www.champagne-multimedia.com 'E'mail: ot-bar@wanadoo.fr

Bar Syrup (Eng) sugar and water mixture ratio 3-1, used to sweeten cocktails.

Bart [André] (Fr) a Burgundy négociant based at 24, Rue de Mazy, 21160 Marsannay-la-Côte.

Bartels (USA) the brand-name used by the Lion Brewery in Wilkes-Barre, Pennsylvania for their range of beers.

Bartels Winery (USA) a winery based in Pensacola, Florida. Produces Muscadine wines.

Bartender (USA) see Barman/Barmaid/Barperson. (Arab) = saki, (Aus) = wirt/wirtin, (Chi) = jiubajian zhaodaiyuan, (Den) = bartender, (Fr) = barman, (Ger) = wirt/wirtin, (Gre) = barman, (Hol) = barman, (Indo) = bartender, (Ire) = buachaill tabhairne, (Isr) = mozeg, (It) = barista, (Jap) = baaten, (Kor) = batenduh, (Port) =

barman, (Rus) = bar-myen, (Sp) = cantinero/cantinera, (Thai) = konpasomkruangdum.

Bartender Cocktail (Cktl) ¼ measure dry vermouth, ¼ measure gin, ¼ measure Dubonnet, ¼ measure dry Sherry, dash Grand Marnier. Stir over ice, strain into a cocktail glass.

Bartho Eksteen Family Wines (S.Afr) a winery (established 1998) based in Walker Bay, Western Cape. Grape varieties: Sauvignon blanc, Syrah. Label: Classified.

Bartholomew Sykes (Eng) *see* Sykes Hydrometer, Sykes.

Bath Star (Eng) a cask-conditioned seasonal golden brown bitter brewed by Abbey Ales, Lansdown, Bath.

Bartlett Beers (Eng) a home-brew public house beers from the Tavern in Newnham Bridge, Worcestershire. Produces Bartlett Mild 1040 O.G. Bartlett Bitter 1042 O.G.

Barton (S.Afr) the label for range of wines produced by the Luddite Wines winery, Walker Bay, Western Cape.

Barton and Guestier (Fr) wine négociants in Bordeaux who deal in fine Bordeaux wines. Wines are distributed by Seagram.

Barton Best (Eng) an ale brewed by Bridgewater Ales in Salford.

Barton Distillery (USA) a Bourbon whiskey based south-west of Frankfort in Kentucky.

Barton Farm (S.Afr) a winery (established 2001) based in Walker Bay, Western Cape. Grape varieties: Cabernet sauvignon, Chenin blanc, Sauvignon blanc, Syrah.

Barton Manor Vineyard (Eng) a vineyard (established 1977) 2.5ha. (Add): Whippingham, East Cowes, Isle of Wight. Grape varieties: Gewürztraminer, Huxelrebe, Müller-Thurgau, Reichensteiner and Seyval blanc.

Barton Special (Cktl) 1 measure applejack, ½ measure Scotch whisky, ½ measure gin. Shake well over ice, strain into an ice-filled old-fashioned glass.

Bartrams Brewery (Eng) a brewery (established 1999). (Add): Rougham Estate, Ipswich Road, Rougham, Bury St. Edmunds, Suffolk IP30 9LZ. Brews: ABC 4% alc by vol., Bees Knees 4.2% alc by vol., Captain Bill Bartrams Bitter 4.5% alc by vol., Captains Stout 4.8% alc by vol., Coal Porter 4.5% alc by vol., Green Man 4% alc by vol. Website: http://www.captainbill.co.uk 'E'mail: marc@captainbill007.plus.com

Bartzch (Asia) a spirit made from hogsweed, produced mainly in northern Asia. Made from a variety of 'weed' plants.

Barum Brewery (Eng) a brewery (established 1996). (Add): C/o The Reform Inn, Pilton High Street, Pilton, Barnstaple, Devon EX31 1PD. Brews: Barnstablasta 6.6% alc by vol., Barumburg 4.6% alc by vol., Breakfast 5% alc by vol., BSE 3.7% alc by vol., Challenger 5.6% alc by vol., Dark Star 5.8% alc by vol., Gold 5% alc by vol., Liquid Lunch 4.6% alc by vol., Original 4.4% alc by vol., Technical Hitch 5.3% alc by vol., XTC 3.9% alc by vol. Website: http://www.barumbrewery.co.uk 'E'mail: lord.basil@barumbrewery.co.uk

Barumburg (Eng) a 4.6% alc by vol. ale brewed by the Barum Brewery, Devon.

Baruther Johannesbrunnen (Ger) a natural spring mineral water from Baruth/Mrk, BB. Mineral contents (milligrammes per litre): Sodium 4.4mg/l, Calcium 57.8mg/l, Magnesium 5.5mg/l, Potassium 0.6mg/l, Bicarbonates 186mg/l, Chlorides 8mg/l, Fluorides 0.13mg/l.

Barwell and Jones (Eng) a division of Tollemache and Cobbold Breweries. Has eight retail wine outlets in East Anglia.

Barzy-sur-Marne (Fr) a Cru Champagne village in the Canton de Condé-en-Brie. District: Château Thierry.

Basaltic (It) a basalt rich soil found in central Italy.

Bas-Armagnac (Fr) a sub-region of Armagnac in the Gers département, where Armagnac brandy is made.

Bas-Beaujolais (Fr) the southern region of the Beaujolais. South of the Nizerand river. Also known as Bâtard-Beaujolais. Has chalky top-soil with manganese subsoil. *See also* Haut-Beaujolais.

Bas-des-Duresses [Les] (Fr) a Premier Cru vineyard in the A.C. commune of Auxey-Duresses, Côte de Beaune, Burgundy. 5.9ha.

Bas-des-Teurons [Le] (Fr) a Premier Cru vineyard in the A.C. commune of Beaune, Côte de Beaune, Burgundy. 7.32ha.

Base (Eng) another name for the wash in gin production.

Basedow Winery (Austr) a winery based in Murray Street, Tanunda, Barossa Valley, South Australia. Buys in grapes to make table wine. Grape varieties: Chardonnay, Sémillon, Cabernet sauvignon, Shiraz.

Bashas' Artesian Spring Water (USA) a natural spring mineral water from Oak Creek Canyon, Sedona, Arizona.

Basi (E.Ind) a spirit fermented from sugar cane, berries and bark in the Ilocos region of the Phillipines.

Basic Wine (Eng) the name given to vermouth after blending the wine with mistelle and before infusion with herbs.

Basic Yield (Fr) the '*Rendement de Base*', the amount of wine that can be produced under the A.C. laws.

Basil Cocktail (Cktl) ¼ measure Grand Marnier, ¼ measure Tia Maria, ¼ measure Irish whiskey. Stir over ice, strain into a cocktail glass. Float ¼ measure of cream on top and add zest of lemon.

Basil Hayden's (USA) an 8 year old Kentucky Bourbon whiskey bottled at 80° proof (40% alc by vol.) distilled by James Beam Distilling C°., Clermont-Beam, Kentucky.

Basilicata (It) a mountainous region, surrounded by Puglia, Campania and Calabria and reaching the Ionian and Tyrrhenian seas. The garnet red wine Aglianico de Vulture from the Monte Vulture vineyard is the most noted. Muscat and Malvasia grape varieties are the most predominant, and the '*passito*' treatment is used.

B

Basilisco (It) a winery based in Rionero in Vulture, Basilicata region. Produces: D.O.C. Aglianico del Vulture.

Basilium (It) a co-operative winery in Basilicata. 150 members have 300ha. of vines. Produce D.O.C. Aglianico del Vulture and I.G.T. Valle del Trono, an Aglianico white called I Portali, plus I.G.T. Greco and Pipoli (an aged Aglianico).

Basinus Bonaris Quelle (Ger) a natural spring mineral water from Neustadt an der Aisch, BY.

Basinus Quelle (Ger) a sparkling natural spring mineral water from the Florianquelle, Bad Windsheim, BY. (blue label: sparkling/green label: low gas). Mineral contents (milligrammes per litre): Sodium 129mg/l, Calcium 230mg/l, Magnesium 60mg/l, Potassium 12mg/l, Bicarbonates 548mg/l, Chlorides 146mg/l, Sulphates 418mg/l, Nitrates 0.4mg/l, Fluorides 0.43mg/l.

Basinus Sinus-Quelle (Ger) a sparkling natural spring mineral water from Eilenbuhrg, SN. (blue label: sparkling/green label: low gas). Mineral contents (milligrammes per litre): Sodium 11mg/l, Calcium 72.2mg/l, Magnesium 10.4mg/l, Potassium 1.9mg/l, Bicarbonates 262mg/l, Chlorides 15mg/l, Sulphates 15mg/l, Nitrates <0.3mg/l, Fluorides 0.38mg/l.

Baska (Fr) a coffee liqueur from Angers.

Bäska Dropper (Swe) lit: 'bitter drops', a bitters flavoured with wormwood.

Basket Press (Fr) an old type of press now mainly out of date except for Champagne and other sparkling wines.

Basler Kirschwasser (Switz) a clear spirit-liqueur made from cherry stones 40% alc by vol.

Basler Trinkwasser (Switz) a natural spring mineral water from Basle. Mineral contents (milligrammes per litre): Sodium 1.2mg/l, Calcium 123mg/l, Magnesium 0.9mg/l, Potassium <0.2mg/l, Bicarbonates 343mg/l, Chlorides 2mg/l, Sulphates 14.8mg/l, Nitrates 10.2mg/l, Fluorides <0.02mg/l.

Baslieux (Fr) a Cru Champagne village in the Canton de Châtillon-sur-Marne. District: Reims.

Bas-Médoc (Fr) the northern region of the Médoc, Bordeaux. Produces middle quality red wines.

Basquaise (Fr) a flat, fat, long necked flagon used for Armagnac brandy. Also called 'Pot Gascon'.

Basqueador (Sp) see Mecedor

Bas-Rhin (Fr) lit: 'Lower Rhine', a wine-producing region of Alsace.

Bass Ale (Ire) a keg bitter 1036 O.G. brewed by the Bass Ulster branch in Ireland.

Bassareus (Lat) a word used for Bacchus. See also Dionysus, Eleleus, Euhan, Euan, Euhius, Euius, Lacchus, Lyaeus, Thyoneus and Bromius.

Bass Brewers (Eng) the biggest English brewers who have merged with Worthington, Mitchells and Butlers, Charringtons and acquired Carlsberg-Tetley. Now known as Coors Brewers. (Add): 137, High Street, Burton-on-Trent, DE14 1JZ. Produces: Allbright, Arc, Bass Blue, Breaker Malt Lager, Breaker Super Lager, Brew XI, Caffrey's, Carling, Carling Premier, Coors Fine Light Beer, Export Light (bottled ales), Grolsch, Gulpener Korenwolf, Hancocks HB, LA (low alcohol bitter), Lamot Pils, M&B Mild, Nº1 (bottled barley wine), Best Scotch, Light 5 (draught ales), Reef, Screamers,Special Bitter (premium draught bitter), Special (canned or draught ale), Stone's Bitter, Toby Bitter, Toby Light, Worthington's Ale, Worthington's Cask, Worthington's Classic, Worthington's Cream Flow, Worthington's White Shield. Also Fat Apple, Kasteel Cru, Mojo, Twisted Vine. Based at Burton-on-Trent, runs several breweries and owns many public houses. See also Charrington. Website: http://www.coorsbrewers.com 'E'mail: rose.holden@coorsbrewers.com

Basse Normande (Fr) a straight sided, dumpy bottle, used especially in the Rhône.

Basses-Alpes (Fr) a noted wine-producing département which has the Provence region within its boundaries.

Basses-Mourettes (Fr) a Premier Cru vineyard in the commune of Ladoix-Serrigny, A.C. Aloxe-Corton, Côte de Beaune, Burgundy. Produces red wines only.

Basses Tiges (Fr) in Calvados denotes a half standard system of apple tree pruning resulting in a crop occurring in the 3rd year rather than after 10 or 15 years. A much higher density than Haut Tiges.

Basses-Vergelesses (Fr) a Premier Cru vineyard in the A.C. commune of Savigny-lès-Beaune, Côte de Beaune, Burgundy.

Basses-Vergelesses [Les] (Fr) a Premier Cru vineyard in the A.C. commune of Savigny-lès-Beaune, Côte de Beaune, Burgundy. 17.5ha.

Bassets [Les] (Fr) a vineyard in the A.C. commune of Montagny, Côte Chalonnaise, Burgundy.

Bassgeige (Ger) vineyard (Anb): Baden. (Ber): Kaiserstuhl-Tuniberg. (Gro): Vulkanfelsen. (Vil): Oberbergen.

Bassin de Vichy (Fr) a natural sparkling mineral water from Bassin de Vichy, Saint-Yorre. Royal French Spring.

Bass LA (Eng) a low alcohol bitter beer 1% alc by vol. brewed by Bass.

Bass Museum [The] (Eng) a unique brewing museum. (Add): Horninglow Street, Burton-on-Trent. Offers a fascinating insight into the history of brewing in Burton-on-Trent. Has a micro brewery on site. 'E'mail: brewery@museum.brewers.bass.com

Bass North (Eng) part of Bass breweries, northern division. Includes Stone's Brewery, and breweries at Runcorn, Tadcaster and Sheffield.

Bass Nº1 (Eng) a barley wine cask-conditioned for 6 months, on sale in December and January. Brewed by Bass in Burton-on-Trent.

Bass Phillip (Austr) a winery (established 1979) at Tosch's Road, Leongatha South, Victoria. Grape varieties: Chardonnay, Pinot noir.

Bass Special (Scot) a keg ale 1035 O.G. brewed by Tennent Caledonian Brewery in Edinburgh and Glasgow.

Bass Worthington (Eng) a part of the Bass group, has

100

breweries all over Great Britain producing a large range of ales and lagers.

Bastard (Eng) a white to tawny-coloured wine produced in the seventeenth century.

Bastard Bottle (Eng) another name for the bladder bottle, named so after the name of a family that first used them.

Bastard Lager (Eng) a term used in the brewing industry for the top-fermented beer called lager.

Bastardo (Mad) a rare type of Madeira which is light and has a sweet taste.

Bastardo (Port) a red grape variety used in the making of red Dão.

Bastasiolo (It) a winery based in the DOCG Barolo. Label: La Corda della Briccolina.

Bastei (Ger) vineyard (Anb): Nahe. (Ber): Schloss Böckelheim. (Gro): Burgweg. (Vil): Traisen.

Bastel (Ger) vineyard (Anb): Franken. (Ber): Steigerwald. (Gro): Schild. (Vil): Greuth.

Bastia (Fr) the chief northern wine producing area of Corsica. Produces A.C. Patrimonio rosé.

Bastida (Sp) a still natural mineral water from Sa Bastida, Alaro, Baleares. Mineral contents (milligrammes per litre): Sodium 33.7mg/l, Calcium 104.2mg/l, Magnesium 25.3mg/l, Potassium 1.5mg/l, Bicarbonates 362.3mg/l, Chlorides 76.3mg/l, Sulphates 24.8mg/l, Nitrates 0.5mg/l, Fluorides 0.1mg/l.

Bastide la Verrerie (Fr) an A.C. Côtes du Luberon. The second wine of Château la Verrerie.

Bastide Saint Dominique [La] (Fr) the name for a red and white Châteauneuf-du-Pape produced by Bonnet (M.C. et G.), 84350 Courthèzon, southern Rhône.

Basto (Port) a region of the Entre Minho e Douro that produces both red and white Vinhos Verdes.

Basuqueadores (Sp) *see* Mecadores.

Batalla del Vino (Sp) lit: 'wine battle', an annual wine fight held in Haro in late June each year where participants (the public) throw, squirt, etc. the local red wine at each other! Website: http://www.haro.org

Batàr (It) an I.G.T. Chardonnay wine produced by Agrícola Querciabella, Via Carducci 16, 20123 Milano.

Bâtard-Beaujolais (Fr) other name for the Bas-Beaujolais.

Bâtard-Montrachet (Fr) a Grand Cru A.C. vineyards in Chassagne-Montrachet, Côte de Beaune, Burgundy. Produces some of the finest white wines in the world.

Batavia (E.Ind) a noted coffee-producing region of Java.

Batavian Arak (E.Ind) a rum made on the island of Java (dry and aromatic).

Bateel (Arab) an alcohol-free, sparkling drink produced from the juice of dates.

Bateleur (S.Afr) a barrel-selected Chardonnay wine produced by the De Wetshof Estate in Robertson. *See also* Bon Vallon.

Bateman [George] & Son Ltd (Eng) a brewery (established 1874). (Add): Salem Bridge Brewery, Wainfleet, Skegness, Lincolnshire PE24 4JE. A family-owned brewery. Produces many brews. Noted for Combined Harvest 4.4% alc by vol., Dark Lord 5% alc by vol., Dark Mild 3% alc by vol., Hooker 4.5% alc by vol., Miss Saucy 4.3% alc by vol., Rosey Nosey 4.9% alc by vol., Salem Porter 4.7% alc by vol., Spring Breeze 4.2% alc by vol., Spring Goddess 4.2% alc by vol., Summer Swallow 3.9% alc by vol., Victory Ale 5.9% alc by vol., XB Bitter 3.7% alc by vol., XXXB Bitter 4.8% alc by vol. Also Nut Brown 1033 O.G. Double Brown 1037 O.G. Ploughman's Ale 1049 O.G. Lincolnshire Hot Stuff, 'Yella' Belly, Valiant Bitter 4.2% alc by vol., Jolly's Dome, Miss Whiplash, Winter Wellie. Website: http://www.bateman.co.uk 'E'mail: sales@bateman.co.uk

Bateman's XXXB (Eng) a 4.8% alc by vol. classic bitter ale brewed by Bateman's, Lincolnshire. Part of the Tapster's Choice range.

Batenduh (Kor) bartender.

Bates Brewery (Eng) a brewery (established 1983) based in Bovey Tracey, South Devon. Produces Bates Bitter 1045 O.G.

Bates Ranch (USA) a small independent vineyard based in the Santa Cruz mountains, Santa Clara, California. Grape variety is mainly Cabernet sauvignon.

B.A.T.F. (USA) *abbr*: **B**ureau of **A**lcohol, **T**obacco and **F**irearms. (Department).

Bath Ales (Eng) a brewery (established 1995). (Add): Unit 3–7 Plot A2, Caxton Industrial Estate, Tower Road North, Warmley, Bristol, Avon BS30 8XN. Brews Barnstormer 4.7% alc by vol., Gem 4.1% alc by vol., Organic Lager 5% alc by vol., White Friar 5% alc by vol. Website: http://www.bathales.com 'E'mail: hare@bathales.co.uk

Batham & Son [Daniel] (Eng) a brewery. (Add): Delph Brewery, Brierly Hill, West Midlands. Brew Best Bitter (draught and bottled), Mild Ale (draught), Delph Strong Ale (draught winter warmer).

Bath Natural Mineral Water (Eng) a spa mineral water from Bath, Avon. (Add): Stall Street, Bath.

Bath Star (Eng) a 4.5% alc by vol. beer brewed by Abbey Ales Ltd., Avon.

Bath-Tub Gin (USA) an illegal spirit distilled during the prohibition era, also called Rotgut.

Batida (Eng) the label of a Brazilian alcoholic fruit cocktail drink produced by Spilt Drinks, Exeter.

Batida (Cktl) a mixture of cachaça, passion fruit juice, lemon juice, tamarind and sugar shaken over ice, strained into an ice-filled highball.

Batida Abaci (Cktl) 1 measure cachaça, 2 teaspoons sugar, slice of fresh pineapple, blend with crushed ice, serve unstrained in a club goblet.

Batida Caju (Cktl) 1 measure cachaça, 2 teaspoons sugar, dessertspoon cashew nuts, blend with crushed ice, serve unstrained in a club goblet.

Batida de Côco (It) coconut liqueur with milk. 16% alc by vol. Produced by G. Burton & C.S.p.A. Trieste, under supervision of Mangaroca Liquores do Brazil Ltda, São Paulo. *see* Batida.

Batida Goiaba (Cktl) 1 measure cachaça, 2 teaspoons sugar, slice of fresh guava. Blend with crushed ice, serve unstrained in a club goblet.

Batida Limão (Cktl) 1 measure cachaça, 2 teaspoons sugar, juice of fresh lime, blend with crushed ice, serve unstrained in a club goblet.

Batida Mango (Cktl) 1 measure cachaça, 2 teaspoons sugar, slice of fresh mango, blend with crushed ice, serve unstrained in a club goblet.

Batida Maracuja (Cktl) 1 measure cachaça, 2 teaspoons sugar, 50mls (2fl.ozs) Fruit of Brazil, blend with crushed ice, serve unstrained in a club goblet.

Batida Morango (Cktl) 1 measure cachaça, 2 teaspoons sugar, 3 fresh strawberries, blend with crushed ice, serve unstrained in a club goblet.

Batna (Alg) a natural mineral water. Mineral contents (milligrammes per litre): Sodium 12.8mg/l, Calcium 58.4mg/l, Magnesium 42.5mg/l, Potassium 3.1mg/l, Bicarbonates 372.7mg/l, Chlorides 17.7mg/l, Sulphates 28.5mg/l, Silicates 8.2mg/l.

Bâtonnage (Fr) the term used for the stirring up of the wine on its lees during fermentation (at a low temperature).

Batoque (Port) the cask bung-hole.

Bat's Rock (S.Afr) the label for a range of wines produced by the Lutzville Cape Diamond Vineyards winery, Oliphants River, Western Cape.

Batte (Fr) a wooden implement used to hammer home the corks into the necks of the wine bottle.

Battenburg (Ger) village (Anb): Pfalz. (Ber): Mittelhaardt-Deutche Weinstrasse. (Gro): Höllenphad. (Vin): Schlossberg.

Batterieberg (Ger) vineyard (Anb): Mosel-Saar-Ruwer. (Ber): Bernkastel. (Gro): Schwarzlay. (Vil): Enkirch.

Battersea Bitter (Eng) a 4% alc by vol. bitter beer brewed by the Battersea Brewery C°., London.

Battersea Brewery (Eng) a pub brewery (established 2001). (Add): Prince of Wales, 43 Glycena Road, Battersea, London SW11 5TP. Owned by Watney Mann. Brews: Battersea Bitter 4% alc by vol., Pogada 3.8% alc by vol., Power House 1050 O.G., Power Station Porter 4.9% alc by vol. Website: http://www.batterseabrewery.co.uk 'E'mail: enquiries@batterseabrewery.co.uk

Battleaxe (Eng) a 4.2% alc by vol. ale brewed by the Rudgate Brewery, North Yorkshire.

Battleaxe Ale (Eng) a strong cask-conditioned ale 1053 O.G. brewed by Axe Vale Brewery in Devon.

Battleaxe Best (Eng) a 4.2% alc by vol. bitter ale brewed by Rudgate Brewery, Tockwith, North Yorkshire.

Battle of Bosworth (Austr) a winery based in the McLaren Vale, South Australia. Grape varieties: Cabernet sauvignon, Shriaz.

Battlin Brauerei (Ger) a small brewery based in Esch.

Batto Vineyard (USA) a small vineyard based in the southern part of the Sonoma Valley, Sonoma County, California. Grape variety is mainly Cabernet sauvignon.

Bauchet Père et Fils (Fr) a Champagne producer. (Add): 51159 Bisseuil, Marne. Produces Premier Cru Champagnes.

Baudes [Les] (Fr) a Premier Cru vineyard in the A.C. commune of Chambolle-Musigny, Côte de Nuits, Burgundy. 3.5ha.

Baudin (Austr) a red wine produced by Capel Vale in West Australia from a blend of Bordeaux grape varieties.

Baudot (Fr) cuvées in the A.C. Meursault-Genevrières, Côte de Beaune, Burgundy. Les Genevrières Dessous 0.75ha. and Les Genevrières Dessus 0.2ha. Are owned by the Hospices de Beaune.

Bauer (Aus) a winery based in Feuersbrunn am Wagram, Donauland. (Add): Neufang 52, 3483 Feuersbrunn am Wagram. Grape varieties: Chardonnay, Pinot blanc, Riesling, Sauvignon blanc, Zweigelt.

Bauerbach (Ger) village (Anb): Baden. (Ber): Badische Bergstrasse/Kraichgau. (Gro): Stiftsberg. (Vin): Lerchenberg.

Bäuerl [Wolfgang] (Aus) a winery based in the Wachau. (Add): Loiben 28, 3601 Dürnstein. Grape varieties: Grüner veltliner, Müller-Thurgau, Riesling. Produces a range of dry and sweet (botrytised) wines.

Bauget-Jouette (Fr) a Champagne producer. Produces vintage and non-vintage wines.

Baulne-en-Brie (Fr) a Cru Champagne village in the Canton of Condé-en-Brie. District: Château Thierry.

Baumann-Zirgel (Fr) a small (5ha) wine estate based in Alsace.

Baumé [Antoine] (Fr) 1728-1804. Invented the hydrometer. see Baumé Scale.

Baumé Scale (Fr) a hydrometer for measuring sugar in grape must. Invented by Antoine Baumé (1728-1804). 1° Baumé = 144.3 ([s-1]/s). 1° Baumé is approximately 1.8° Brix.

Baury (Fr) a vineyard in the commune of Arsac. A.C. Médoc, Bordeaux. Cru Bourgeois Supérieur.

Bausch (Ger) vineyard (Anb): Franken. (Ber): Steigerwald. (Gro): Schild. (Vil): Castell.

Bausch (Ger) vineyard (Anb): Franken. (Ber): Steigerwald. (Gro): Herrenberg. (Vil): Castell.

Bausendorf (Ger) village (Anb): Mosel-Saar-Ruwer. (Ber): Bernkastel. (Gro): Schwarzlay. (Vins): Herzlay, Hubertuslay.

Baux (Ger) a 5% alc by vol. light beer brewed by Scherdel, sold in an aluminium bottle.

Bava [Roberto] (It) a noted producer of Barbera d'Asti and sparkling wines (by the cuve close method) based in Piemonte, north-western Italy. Labels include Arbest, Pianoalto and Stradivarius. Website: http://www.bava.com

Bavaisienne [La] (Fr) a 7% alc by vol. amber coloured, top-fermented, bottled bière de garde brewed by the Theillier Brasserie, Bavay.

Bavaria Brouwerij (Hol) a brewery (established 1719) based in Lieshout, North Brabant. Is noted for Bavaria 8.6, Bavaria Malt, Bavaria Pilsner Bier and Dortmunder 5% alc by vol.

Bavaria 8.6 (Hol) an 8.6% alc by vol. deep gold, bottled special beer brewed by the Bavaria Brouwerij, Lieshout.

Bavaria Malt Bier (Ger) an alcohol-free beer brewed by the Bavaria Brouwerij, Lieshout. 0.1% alc by vol.

Bavarian (N.Z) a sweet, copper-coloured beer 1036 O.G. brewed by the Christchurch branch of the New Zealand Breweries.

Bavarian Beer (USA) a lager beer brewed by the Duquesne Brewing Cº., Cleveland, Ohio.

Bavarian Brewers Association (Ger) *abbr*: B.B.A. equivalent to the English Brewers' Society. Protects and promotes the Rheinheitsgebot.

Bavarian Glass (Eng) a patent design for a beer glass. 500mls (1 pint) capacity, is slim, thick-based and waisted in centre. Produced by the Dema Glass Cº.

Bavaria Pilsner Bier (Ger) a 5% alc by vol. pilsner brewed by the Bavaria Brouwerij, Lieshout.

Bavaria Quelle (Ger) a natural spring mineral water from Utting am Ammersee, BY.

Bavaria-St. Pauli (Ger) a brewery of Hamburg. Nothing to do with Bavaria (name only adopted). Produces fine beers such as Grenzquell and Astra, also has subsidiary breweries, notably Jever's in Friesland. There is no connection with St. Pauli beer in USA.

Bavaria Weitz (Ger) a 5.3% alc by vol. bottled wheat beer brewed by Eders Brauerei, Grossostheim.

Bavaroise (Fr) an old nineteenth century drink of egg yolk, sugar, milk, tea, with spirit, served hot and frothing, chocolate was often substituted for the tea and citrus juices were also added.

Bavaroise aux Choux (Fr) a nineteenth century mixed drink of absinthe and orgeat.

Bavik Brasserie (Bel) a brewery (established 1894). (Add): NV Rijksweg 33, 8531 Bavikhove. Brews Petrus Triple. Website: http://www.bavik.be 'E'mail: info@bavik.be

Baya (Sp) berry (grape).

Bayard Fizz (Cktl) 35mls (1½ fl.ozs) gin, juice of a lemon, 1 barspoon sugar, 1 dash maraschino, 1 dash grenadine. Shake over ice, strain into a highball glass and top with soda water.

Baycovin (Eng) *Diethylprocarbonate* a preservative for wine.

Baye (Fr) a Cru Champagne village in the Canton de Montmort. District: Épernay.

Bayel (Fr) a commune within the Côte des Bar, Champagne. (Add): 2, Rue Belle Verrière, 10310 Bayel. Website: http://www.bayel-cristal.com 'E'mail: o.tbayel@bayel-cristal.com

Bayer (Nor) a dark, Bavarian ale 4.5% alc by vol. brewed by the Aass Brewery in Drammen.

Bayer Bodensee (Ger) bereich (Anb): Franken. (Gro): Lindauer Seegarten. (Vil): Nonnenhorn. (Vins): Seehalde, Sonnenbüchel. *See also* Bayerischer Bodensee.

Bayerfeld-Steckweiler (Ger) village (Anb): Nahe. (Ber): Schloss Böckelheim. (Gro): Paradiesgarten. (Vins): Adelsberg, Aspenberg, Mittelberg, Schloss Stolzenberg.

Bayerischer Bodensee (Ger) a bereich (same as Bayer Bodensee).

Bayerischer Bodensee Landwein (Ger) one of the Deutsche tafelwein zones.

Bayern (Ger) a region which has 3 Untergebiete (table-wine sub-areas), Donau, Lindau and Main.

Bay of Fires (Austr) a winery based in Tasmania. Label: Tigress Riesling.

Bay of Plenty (N.Z) a wine-producing area in the North Island.

Bayon (Fr) a commune based in the A.C. Côtes de Bourg in north-eastern Bordeaux.

Bayonet (Eng) a 5% alc by vol. ale brewed by the Filament and Firkin, Tyneside.

Bayou Cocktail (Cktl) 25mls (⅛ gill) Cognac, juice ¼ lime, 4 dashes peach juice. Shake well over ice, strain into a cocktail glass and top with a squeeze of lime peel juice.

Bay Rum (W.Ind) a seventeenth century rum produced from bay leaves on the island of St. Thomas as an ingredient of a hair tonic.

Bay View (S.Afr) the label for a range of wines produced by the Longridge Winery, Stellenbosch, Western Cape.

Bay View Vineyard (N.Z) a vineyard (20ha). Part of Glenvale Winery.

Bazas (Fr) a vineyard in the Gironde that produces mainly red wines.

Bazens Brewery (Eng) a brewery (established 2002). (Add): Unit 6, Knoll Sr. Ind Park, Knoll Street, Salford, Manchester, Greater Manchester M7 2BL. Brews: Black Pig Mild 3.6% alc by vol., Blue Bullet 4.5% alc by vol., eXSB 5.5% alc by vol., Flatbac 4.2% alc by vol., Freshers Special 5.5% alc by vol., Knoll Street Porter 5.2% alc by vol., Pacific Bitter 3.8% alc by vol., Red Shed 3.8% alc by vol., Santas Reindeer 4.6% alc by vol., Wass Ale 4.5% alc by vol., Zebra Best Bitter 4.3% alc by vol. Website: http://www.bazensbrewery.co.uk 'E'mail: enquiries@bazensbrewery.co.uk

Baz's Super Brew (Eng) a ruby coloured ale brewed by the Parish Brewery, Somerby, Leicestershire.

Bazzard Estate (N.Z) a 4ha winery. (Add): 74 Awa Road, Huapai. Grape varieties: Cabernet franc, Merlot, Pinot noir, Chardonnay.

B.B. (Eng) *abbr*: West Country's Boys Bitter.

B.B.A. (Ger) *abbr*: Bavarian Brewers Association.

BBB [Three B's] (Eng) *abbr*: Best Bitter Beer. Produced by Arkell's Brewery, Stratton St. Margaret, near Swindon. 1038 O.G.

BBB [Three B's] (Eng) *abbr*: Buster Brew Bitter. Produced by Gales of Hampshire. 1037 O.G.

BBBB [Four B's] (Eng) *abbr*: Berrow Brewery Best Bitter. Produced by the Berrow Brewery, Somerset.

BBC1 (Eng) a light bitter ale 5.2% alc by vol. from the Blackburn Brewing Company.

BBC2 (Eng) a dark bitter ale 3.8% alc by vol. from the Blackburn Brewing Company.

B.B.I. (Eng) *abbr*: British Bottler's Institute.

B.B. Martine (Fr) a 5 year old V.S.O.P. Armagnac produced by Ducastaing.

BBN (Eng) *abbr*: see Best Bar None.

BBPA (Eng) *abbr*: **B**ritish **B**eer and **P**ub **A**ssociation.

BC (S.Afr) *abbr*: **B**randvlei **C**ellar the label for a range of wines from winery of same name. Website: http://www.bcwines.co.za

B Cruz (Arg) the label for a red wine produced by the Bodegas y Viñedos O. Fournier, Mendoza region.

BDS (Eng) a cask-conditioned ale 1055 O.G. brewed by the Pig and Whistle home-brew public house in London. A Hampshire home-brew public house.

Bé (Fr) *abbr*: **Baumé**. i.e. °Bé.

BE (USA) a new (2005) a fruit-flavoured variety of Budweiser at 5% alc by vol. sold in 355cls black bottles produced by the Anheuser-Busch company.

Beach Boys (Eng) a 4.5% alc by vol. ale brewed by the Blencowe Brewing C°. Rutland.

Beach Break Vineyard (USA) the label for a red wine (Pinot noir) from the Cambria winery, Santa Barbara County, California.

Beachcomber (Cktl) a mixture of 3 parts mineral water and 1 part crème de menthe. Serve in a highball glass over ice. Dress with a mint sprig.

Beachcomber (Eng) a 4.5% alc by vol. beer brewed by the Teignworthy Brewery, Devon.

Beachcomber (Eng) a liqueur of British wine, Jamaican rum and coconut produced by the Goldwell C°.

Beachcomber Belle (Cktl) 35mls (1½ fl.ozs) Jamaican rum, 75mls (3fl.ozs) grapefruit juice. Shake well with ice, strain into a highball glass. Top up with 75mls (3fl.ozs) ginger beer. Serve with straws and dress with sprig of fresh mint.

Beachcomber Cocktail (Cktl) ⅗ measure white rum, ⅕ measure Triple Sec, ⅕ measure lime juice, dash maraschino. Shake over ice, strain into a sugar rimmed (with lime juice) cocktail glass.

Beach's Borough Bitter (Eng) a cask-conditioned bitter 1038 O.G. brewed by the Market Brewery, Southwark, London.

Beacon Bitter (Eng) *see* Everards Beacon Bitter.

Beacon Block (S.Afr) the label for a red wine (Shiraz) produced by the Fairview winery, Suider-Paarl, Western Cape.

Beacon Valley Winery (Eng) a winery. (Add): Hamstead Brewing Centre, 37 Newton Road, Great Barr, Birmingham, West Midlands B43 6AD. Produces a range of wines. 'E'mail: chris@hampstead-brewing-centre.co.uk

Bead (Eng) a term used to describe the stream of bubbles in sparkling drinks, especially wines. The smaller the bead, the better the quality of the wine.

Beadlestone (Cktl) ½ measure Scotch whisky, ½ measure French vermouth. Stir over ice, strain into cocktail glass.

Beaker (Eng) a cup with a wide mouth, made of china, clay, glass or plastic. Also of waxed paper or wood.

Beals Cocktail (Cktl) ⅗ measure Scotch whisky, ⅕ measure French vermouth, ⅕ measure Italian vermouth. Stir over ice, strain into a cocktail glass.

Beam (USA) *see* James Beam Distilling C°.

Beamish and Crawford Brewery (Ire) a famous brewery of Cork. (Add): South Main Street, Cork. Noted for Stout, but also brews Bass beers and Carling Black Label Lager under licence. Website: http://www.beamish.ie 'E'mail: customer.service@beamish.ie

Beamish Irish Stout (Ire) a 4.2% alc by vol. stout brewed by Beamish and Crawford Brewery, Cork.

Beamish Red (Ire) a 4.5% alc by vol. nitrokeg premium Irish ale from Scottish Courage in Cork.

Bear Ale (Scot) a 5% alc by vol (1050 O.G) strong draught ale brewed by the Traquair House Brewery, Scotland.

Beard Family (Eng) a public house chain in Sussex. Ceased brewing at their Star Lane brewery in 1950's. Sell beers from the Harvey Brewery, Lewes.

Beard's Best Bitter (Eng) a 1040 O.G. bitter ale brewed to an independent recipe by Arundel Brewery, Sussex.

Bear Island (Eng) a 4.6% alc by vol. ale brewed by the Newby Wyke Brewery, Lincolnshire.

Bearly Literate (Eng) a 4.5% alc by vol. ale brewed by the Beartown Brewery, Cheshire.

Bearm (Eng) an old mediaeval name for yeast.

Bear Mountain Winery (USA) the former name of the Lamont Winery Delano, Kern County, California.

Béarn (Fr) an A.C. region 300ha. of south west France. Province covers Iroulégy, Jurançon, Madiran and Pacherenc du Vic Bihl. Produces white, rosé and red wines, noted for Rosé de Béarn. Tannat is main grape for red and rosé wines with Cabernet franc (Bouchy), Cabernet sauvignon, Courbu noir, Fer servadou (Pinenc) and Manseng noir. Gros and Petit manseng are the main grapes for the whites with Courbu, Raffiat and Sauvignon blanc.

Bear's Drink (Ger) a name given to the Prussian '*bärentrank*', a beverage distilled from potatoes and flavoured with honey.

Bearskinful (Eng) a 4.2% alc by vol. beer brewed by the Beartown brewery, Cheshire.

Bearsted Vineyard (Eng) a vineyard based in Kent, grape varieties include Bacchus.

Beartown Brewery (Eng) a brewery. (Add): Bromley House, Spindle Street, Congleton, Cheshire CW12 1QN Brews: Bearly Literate 4.5% alc by vol., Bearskinful 4.2% alc by vol., Black Bear 5% alc by vol., Bruins Ruin 5% alc by vol., Kodiak Gold 4% alc by vol., Polar Eclipse 4.8% alc by vol. Website: http://www.beartownbrewery.co.uk 'E'mail: headbrewer@beartownbrewery.co.uk

Beatnik (Cktl) place a cube of sugar in goblet. Add 1 measure of fresh orange juice, 2 dashes Pernod, 1 measure vodka. Stir and serve with a slice of orange.

Beatrix Selection (S.Afr) the label for a red wine (60% Shiraz plus Cabernet sauvignon and Pinotage blend) produced by the Klein Parys Vineyards winery, Suider-Paarl, Western Cape.

Beatty Ranch (USA) a vineyard based east of St. Helena, Napa Valley, California. Grape varieties: Cabernet sauvignon and Zinfandel.

B

Beaufort [Herbert et Fils] (Fr) Champagne producers. (Add): 32 Rue de Tours, 51150 Tours-sur-Marne. 16.5ha. Récoltants-manipulants. Produces vintage and non-vintage wines. Vintages: 1973, 1975, 1976, 1979, 1982, 1983, 1985, 1989.

Beauforts Ale (Eng) a 3.8% alc by vol. ale brewed by the Storm Brewing C°., Cheshire.

Beaujeu (Fr) a commune in the Beaujolais. Has A.C. Beaujolais-Villages or A.C. Beaujolais-Beaujeu status.

Beaujolais (Fr) a large district (22700ha.) in the south of burgundy. A.C. red wines produced from the Gamay (au jus blanc) grape are fruity, light and early drinking, A.C. white wines from the Chardonnay. Soil: clay-chalk and granite. Has three classifications [1] A.C. Crus Villages: Brouilly, Côte de Brouilly, Chénas, Chiroubles, Fleurie, Juliénas, Morgon, Moulin à Vent, Regnié, Saint-Amour and Cru Beaujolais-Villages 6,400ha. [2] A.C. Beaujolais Villages 6100ha and [3] A.C. Beaujolais. Produces mainly red wines with a small amount rosé and white wines. Websites: http://www.rendez-vous-beaujolais.com/http://www.beaujolais.net

Beaujolais (Fr) the base A.C. of the Beaujolais region. The maximum permitted yield is 66 hl/ha. See also Beaujolais.

Beaujolais-Arbuissonnas (Fr) see Arbuissonnas.

Beaujolais-Ardillats (Fr) see Ardillats (Les).

Beaujolais-Beaujeu (Fr) see Beaujeu.

Beaujolais-Blacé (Fr) see Blacé.

Beaujolais-Cercié (Fr) see Cercié.

Beaujolais-Chânes (Fr) see Chânes.

Beaujolais-Charentay (Fr) see Charentay.

Beaujolais Cru Villages (Fr) are: 6400ha Brouilly, Côte de Brouilly, Chénas, Chiroubles, Fleurie, Juliénas, Morgon, Moulin à Vent, Regnié, Saint-Amour and Cru Beaujolais-Villages. The maximum permitted yield is 58 hl/ha. See also Beaujolais.

Beaujolais de l'Année (Fr) the latest Beaujolais vintage until next one.

Beaujolais-Denice (Fr) see Denice.

Beaujolais-Durette (Fr) see Durette.

Beaujolais-Émeringes (Fr) see Emeringes.

Beaujolais-Jullié (Fr) see Jullié.

Beaujolais-la Chapelle-de-Guinchay (Fr) see Chapelle-de-Guinchay (La).

Beaujolais-Lancié (Fr) see Lancié.

Beaujolais-Lantigné (Fr) see Lantigné.

Beaujolais-le Perréon (Fr) see Perréon (Le).

Beaujolais-les Ardillats (Fr) see Ardillats (Les).

Beaujolais-Leynes (Fr) see Leynes.

Beaujolais-Marchampt (Fr) see Marchampt.

Beaujolais-Montmélas-Saint-Sorlin (Fr) see Montmélas-Saint-Sorlin.

Beaujolais Nouveau (Fr) wine from the latest vintage, produced by the Macération Carbonique fermentation. Used to be released on the night of 14th/15th November but now at midnight on 3rd Thursday in November (from 1985). see Beaujolais Nouveau Race.

Beaujolais Nouveau Race (Eng) a race first held in 1972 (created by Allan Hall of the Sunday Times) from Beaujolais to Central London. Competition to get the first case of new wine to London. £1,000 prize. Ceased because of danger on roads through fast driving. Now held for charity – (unofficially).

Beaujolais-Odenas (Fr) see Odenas.

Beaujolais Pot (Fr) a 500mls mug or half bottle from which the locals drink their wine.

Beaujolais Primeur (Fr) the name given to wines that are released before the general Beaujolais release date of December 15th following harvest. Only wines of Beaujolais and Beaujolais Villages can be released.

Beaujolais-Quincié (Fr) see Quincié.

Beaujolais Regnié (Fr) a new Cru Beaujolais-Villages A.C. created 1985. see Regnié.

Beaujolais-Rivolet (Fr) see Rivolet.

Beaujolais-Romanèche-Thorins (Fr) see Romanèche-Thorins.

Beaujolais-Saint-Amour-de-Bellevue (Fr) see Saint-Amour-de-Bellevue.

Beaujolais-Saint-Étienne-des-Ouillières (Fr) see Saint-Étienne-des-Ouillières.

Beaujolais-Saint-Étienne-la-Varenne (Fr) see Saint-Étienne-la-Varenne.

Beaujolais-Saint-Julien-en-Montmélas (Fr) see Saint-Julien-en-Montmélas.

Beaujolais-Saint-Leger (Fr) see Saint-Leger.

Beaujolais-Saint-Symphorien-d'Ancelles (Fr) see Saint-Symphorien-d'Ancelles.

Beaujolais-Saint-Véran (Fr) see Saint-Véran.

Beaujolais-Salles (Fr) see Salles.

Beaujolais Supérieur (Fr) any wine from the communes of Beaujolais that has reached a minimum of 10% alc by vol.

Beaujolais-Vaux-en-Beaujolais (Fr) see Vaux-en-Beaujolais.

Beaujolais-Vauxrenard (Fr) see Vauxrenard.

Beaujolais-Villages (Fr) individual A.C. wines from within Beaujolais 6100ha. soil is mainly shale and granite. Wines can be sold as their A.C. as Villages or as Beaujolais plus the commune name (e.g. Beaujolais-Blacé). Communes are: Arbuissonas, Beaujeu, Blacé, Cercié, Chânes, Charentay, Denice, Emeringes, Jullié, Lancié, La Chapelle-de-Guinchay, Lantigné, Le Perréon, Leynes, Marchampt, Montmélas-Saint-Sorlin, Odenas, Pruzilly, Quincié, Regnié, Rivolet, Romanèche-Thorins, Saint-Amour-de-Bellevue, Saint-Étienne-des-Ouillières, Saint-Étienne-la-Varenne, Saint-Julien-en-Montmélas, Saint-Lager, Saint-Symphorien-d'Ancelles, Saint-Véran, Salles, Vaux-en-Beaujolais, Vauxrenard and Villié-Morgon. 5,300ha. under vine. The maximum permitted yield is 60 hl/ha. see Beaujolais and Beaujolais Nouveau.

Beaujolais-Villié-Morgon (Fr) see Villié-Morgon.

Beaukett (S.Afr) the label for a white wine (Chenin blanc and Muscat blend) produced by the Bovlei Winery, Wellington, Western Cape.

Beaukett (S.Afr) the label for a range of white wines produced by the Robertson Co-operative Winery, Robertson, Western Cape.

Beaulieu-sur-Layon (Fr) an A.C. commune in the

Coteaux du Layon district of the Anjou-Saumur region in the Loire.

Beaulieu Vineyard (Eng) a vineyard (planted 1958–1961), 2.25ha. (Add): Brockenhurst, Hampshire. Grape varieties: 90% Müller-Thurgau with Huxelrebe, Seyve villard and Seibel. Soil: gravel over loam. Labels: Private Cellars, Coastal Estates.

Beaulieu Vineyard (USA) vineyards of Rutherford, Napa Valley, California, noted for full-bodied red wines from Cabernet sauvignon and Pinot noir grapes. Also produces dessert and sparkling wines. Label: Georges de Latour Private Reserve. Website: http://www.bvwines.com

Beaumé (Fr) an alternative spelling of Baumé. *see* Baumé (Antoine).

Beaumes (Fr) a vineyard in the A.C. Hermitage, central Rhône, southern France.

Beaumes-de-Venise (Fr) a Côtes-du-Rhône-Villages A.C. famous for it's A.C. vin doux naturel white wine Muscat de Beaumes-de-Venise, now also produces an A.C. red wine awarded its A.O.C. in 2005.

Beaumet (Fr) a Champagne producer. (Add): 3 Rue Malakoff 51207 Épernay. 16.5ha. Produces vintage and non-vintage wines. De luxe vintage cuvée is Cuvée Malakoff.

Beau Monde (Fr) a bottled sparkling wine cocktail made by the méthode traditionelle.

Beaumont des Crayères (Fr) a Champagne co-opèrative. (Add): 64 Rue de la Liberté, BP 1030, Mardeuil. 210 growers own 80ha. Produces vintage and non-vintage wines. Vintages : 1995, 1996, 1997, 1998, 1999, 2000, 2001. Website: http://www.champagne-beaumont.com 'E'mail: contact@champagne-beaumont.com

Beaumonts-Bas [Les] (Fr) *see* Beaux-Monts (Les).

Beaumonts-Hauts [Les] (Fr) *see* Beaux-Monts (Les).

Beaumont-sur-Vesle (Fr) a Grand Cru Champagne village in the Canton de Verzy. District: Reims.

Beaumont Wines (S.Afr) a winery (established 1750) based in Walker Bay, Western Cape. (Add): P.O. Box 3, Bot River 7185, Elgin, Overberg (34ha). Grape varieties: Chardonnay, Chenin blanc, Mouvrvèdre, Pinotage, Sauvignon blanc, Shiraz. Labels: Cape Vintage, Goutte d'Or, Hope Marguerite, Jack's River, Raoul's Old Basket Press Rustic Red. Website: http://www.beaumont.co.za

Beaunay (Fr) a Cru Champagne village in the Canton de Montmort. District: Épernay.

Beaune (Fr) a wine town in the Côte d'Or, Burgundy. Also A.C. red wine commune around the town. Premier Cru vineyards: À l'Écu, Aus Coucherais [part], Aux Cras [or Les Cras], Bélissaud, Champ Pimont [or Champimonts], Clos du Roi [part], En Genêt, En l'Orme, La Mignotte, Le Bas des Teurons, Le Clos de la Mousse, Les Aigrots, Les Avaux, Les Blanches Fleurs [part], Les Boucherottes, Les Bressandes, Les Cent Vignes, Les Chouacheux, Les Clos des Mouches, Les Epenottes [part], Les Fèves, Les Grèves, Les Marconnets, Les Montrevenots [part], Les Perrières, Les Reversées, Les Seurey, Les Sizies, Les Teurons, Les Toussaints, Les Tuvilains, Les Vignes Franches, Pertuisots, Sur-lès-Grèves and Tiélandry. 305.52ha.

Beaunois (Fr) the local name in Chablis, northern Burgundy for the Chardonnay grape.

Beaunois (N.Z) a Pinot chardonnay red wine produced by Abel and C°. of Kumeu.

Beaupré (Fr) a natural mineral water from Montagne de Provence. Mineral contents (milligrammes per litre): Sodium 3mg/l, Calcium 58mg/l, Magnesium 24mg/l, Potassium <1mg/l, Bicarbonates 280mg/l, Chlorides 5mg/l, Sulphates 8mg/l, Fluorides <0.1mg/l, Nitrates <1mg/l. pH 7.6

Beauregard (Fr) a Premier Cru vineyard [part] in the A.C. commune of Santenay, Côte de Beaune, Burgundy.

Beauregard Brasserie (Switz) a brewery based in Fribourg. Part of the Sibra Group (Cardinal) Breweries.

Beauregard Ranch (USA) a small vineyard in Santa Cruz County, California Grape varieties: Johannisberg riesling and Zinfandel.

Beauregard Vineyard (USA) *see* Felton-Empire.

Beau-Rivage (Fr) the label for an A.C. Bordeaux wine (white and red) from the Borie Manoux stable.

Beauroy (Fr) a Premier Cru vineyard in the A.C. Chablis, Burgundy.

Beau Sea Viognier (Austr) a fine Viognier wine produced by the Longview Vineyard, Adelaide Hills, South Australia.

Beausset (Fr) a commune [part] in the A.C. Bandol, southern France.

Beautiran (Fr) a commune in the A.C. Graves region of south-west Bordeaux.

Beauty Spot Cocktail (Cktl) 1 measure dry gin, ½ measure French vermouth, ½ measure Italian vermouth, 4 dashes orange bitters. Shake over ice, strain into a cocktail glass with a dash of grenadine in the bottom.

Beau Val Wines (USA) a winery based in the Shenandoah Valley, Amador, California. Grape variety: Zinfandel.

Beauvoisin (Fr) an area of vinification for V.D.Q.S. wines of Costières du Gard, Languedoc, southern France.

Beaux-Champs [Les] (Fr) a vineyard in the A.C. commune of Montagny, Côte Chalonnaise, Burgundy.

Beaux Frères (USA) a vineyard based in the Willamette Valley, Oregon. Part owned by Robert Parker. Produces Pinot noir.

Beaux-Monts [Les] (Fr) a Premier Cru vineyard in the A.C. commune of Vosne-Romanée, Côte de Nuits, Burgundy. 2.4ha. Consists of Les Beaumonts Hauts and Bas.

Beaux Vins [Les] (Fr) the fine (noble) wines label. i.e. Les beaux vins de Bordeaux. (The best wines of Bordeaux).

Beaver Bitter (Eng) a 4.3% alc by vol. bitter beer brewed by the Belvoir Brewery, Leicestershire.

Beaver Bottle (Can) a brand of Canadian whisky produced by the Hudson's Bay C°. (a subsidiary of Seagrams).

B

Beaver Lager (Eng) an export lager 1045 O.G. brewed by Greenhall Whitley, Warrington, Cheshire.

Beba (Sp) a red grape variety, produces poor quality wines, usually turned into raisins.

Bebedeira (Port) a drunken spree, a booze up.

Bebedero (Sp) a drinking vessel.

Bebedice (Port) drunkeness.

Bêbedo (Port) drunk/intoxicated.

Beber (It) a natural mineral water from Sorgente, Doppio. Mineral contents (milligrammes per litre): Sodium 0.7mg/l, Calcium 28mg/l, Magnesium 16mg/l, Potassium 0.3mg/l, Bicarbonates 168mg/l, Chlorides 1mg/l, Sulphates 4.55mg/l.

Beber (Port)(Sp) to drink/swallow.

Bebida (Port)(Sp) beverage/drink.

Bebida de Moderación (Mex) seen on beer labels, denotes that the alcoholic strength has been kept within the 5% alc by vol. limit, satisfying the 1931 law that it is not an intoxicating drink.

Bechenheim (Ger) village (Anb): Rheinhessen. (Ber): Wonnegau. (Gro): Sybillenstein. (Vin): Fröhlich.

Becherbrunnen (Ger) vineyard (Anb): Nahe. (Ber): Schloss Böckelheim. (Gro): Rosengarten. (Vil): Mandel.

Becherovka (Czec) a herb-flavoured yellow liqueur produced in the Karlovanska factory at Karlsbad.

Bech-Kleinmacher (Lux) a wine village on the river Moselle. Sites: Roetschelt, Fousslach.

Bechtau (Rus) a white grape variety grown in Stavropol to produce dry white wines.

Bechtheim (Ger) village (Anb): Rheinhessen. (Ber): Wonnegau. (Gro): Gotteshilfe. (Vins): Geyersberg, Rosengarten, Stein.

Bechtheim (Ger) village (Anb): Rheinhessen. (Ber): Wonnegau. (Gro): Pilgerpfad. (Vins): Hasensprung, Heiligkreuz.

Bechtolsheim (Ger) village (Anb): Rheinhessen. (Ber): Nierstein. (Gro): Petersberg. (Vins): Homberg, Klosterberg, Sonnenberg, Wingertstor.

Beckerich (Lux) a natural mineral water from Ophélie, Beckerich. Mineral contents (milligrammes per litre): Sodium 2.8mg/l, Calcium 96.5mg/l, Magnesium 5mg/l, Potassium 0.6mg/l, Bicarbonates 274mg/l, Chlorides 6.3mg/l, Sulphates 29.6mg/l, Nitrates 6.5mg/l. pH 7.4

Becker [J.] (Fr) a noted producer of Crémant d'Alsace in Zellenberg, Alsace.

Becker's Premium Pils (Ger) a 4.9% alc by vol. lager from the Becker Brauerei.

Becket Beer (Eng) the brand-name of cask-conditioned beers from the Alexandra Brewery, Brighton.

Beckett's Gold (Ire) a 4.7% alc by vol. light ale, amber in colour brewed by Dublin Brewing Company in Dublin.

Beckett's Winterine (Eng) a non-alcoholic 'brandy' produced in the north of England in Victorian times for the Temperance movement.

Beckon (Chi) a natural mineral water. Mineral contents (milligrammes per litre): Sodium 130.5mg/l, Calcium 42.42mg/l, Magnesium 17.79mg/l, Potassium 4.84mg/l, Silicates 15.3mg/l.

Beck's (Ger) the biggest exporter of German beers brewed in Bremen. Top of range are Beck's Bier, Beck's Vier and St. Pauli brands. *See also* Haake-Beck.

Beck's Bier (Afr) a beer brewed under licence by the Intercontinental Breweries.

Beck's Bier (Ger) a popular bier produced by Beck's of Bremen. 1045 O.G. 5% alc by vol. It is a malty full beer.

Beckstein (Ger) village (Anb): Baden. (Ber): Badische Frankenland. (Gro): Tauberklinge. (Vins): Kirchberg. Nonnenberg.

Beckstoffer (USA) the label for a red wine (Pinot noir) from the Las Amigas Vineyard and produced by the Acacia winery, Napa Valley, California.

Beckstoffer-Tokalon (USA) a quality red wine (Cabernet sauvignon) produced by the Schrader Estate, Napa Valley, California.

Beckstones Brewery (Eng) a brewery (established 2002). (Add): Upper Beckstones Mill, The Green, Millom, Cumbria LA18 5HL. Brews: Beer Olock 3.9% alc by vol., Bit Of That 4.6% alc by vol., Bitter Clout 4.6% alc by vol., Black Beck Strong 4.9% alc by vol., High Road 7.3% alc by vol., Iron Town 3.8% alc by vol. 'E'mail: david@beckstonebrewery.com

Beck's Vier (Ger) a draught lager 4% alc by vol. brewed by the Beck's Brewery, Bremen.

Beclan (USA) a red grape variety.

Bedafse Vreugde (Hol) a 5.5% alc by vol. bottle-conditioned special beer brewed by Jantjes Bier Brouwerij, Uden.

Bédarrides (Fr) a noted wine village and commune of Châteauneuf-du-Pape, southern Rhône.

Bedes Gold (Eng) a 4.2% alc by vol. ale brewed by The Durham Brewery Ltd., County Durham.

Bedford [Anna Duchess of] (Eng) started the fashion of afternoon teas in the late eighteenth century to relieve the boredom between lunch and dinner.

Bedfordshire Clanger (Eng) a 3.8% alc by vol. beer from Banks & Taylor, Shefford, Bedfordshire. Named due to an experiment with a traditional recipe that resulted in a new beer.

Bedrock (Eng) a 4.2% alc by vol. cask-conditioned ale brewed by Poole Brewery, Poole.

Bedrock Black (S.Afr) the label for a red wine (Syrah) produced by the Weltevrede Estate winery, Robertson Western Cape.

Bed Tea (Afr) the name given to early morning tea in African hotels.

Bed Tea (Pak) tea served to a house guest in bed in the morning.

Beech Nut (Eng) a 4% alc by vol. seasonal fruity ale from Morland, Abingdon, Oxfordshire.

Beechwood Beer (Eng) a top cask-conditioned bitter ale 4.3% alc. by vol (1043 O.G.) brewed by the Chiltern Brewery, Buckinghamshire.

Beefeater (Eng) the famous brand-name of a dry gin 40% alc by vol. produced by Burrough of London.

107

B

Beefeater Cocktail (Cktl) ¼ measure Royal Irish Coffee liqueur, ¼ measure Royal Irish Mint chocolate liqueur, ½ measure Irish whiskey. Stir together and float cream on top.

Beefeater Crown Jewel (Eng) a 50% alc by vol. gin produced by Burrough of London.

Beef Tea (Eng) a stock made from minced lean beef, usually with nothing added to it. Is cooked in a Champagne (or stoppered cider) bottle with a cork in a bain-marie (hot water bath). Used for invalids.

Beehive Beer (Eng) a keg bitter 1032 O.G. brewed by Brakspear's Brewery, Henley-on-Thames.

Beelbangera Winery (Austr) a part of the McWilliams Winery, New South Wales.

Beenleigh (Austr) a noted rum producer based in Queensland.

Beenleigh Manor Vineyard (Eng) a vineyard based in Devon. Grapes include Cabernet sauvignon, Merlot.

Beer (Eng) fermentation (average 4% alc by vol) of malted barley 4%, liquor 95% (water – which may be burtonised) and hops. Can also have other cereals, caramel and invert sugar (adjuncts) added. *see* Ale and Lager. *See also* Gambrinus, Wallop. (Arab) = beera, (Aus) = bier, (Bel) = bière, (Chi) = pijiu, (Ch.Isles) = bièthe, (Den) = øl, (Fr) = bière, (Ger) = bier, (Gre) = bira, (Hol) = bier, (Indo) = bir, (Ire) = beoir, (Isr) = beera, (It) = birra, (Jap) = biiru, (Kor) = maekjoo, (Lat) = cervisa, (Port) = cerveja, (Rus) = peeva, (Sp) = cerveza, (Thai) = beer, (Tur) = bira, (Wal) = cwrw.

Beer (Eng) a 5% alc by vol. beer brewed by the Milk Street Brewery, Somerset.

Beer (USA)(Can) the name given to the brew after fermentation and before distillation for whiskey.

Beera (Arab)(Isr) beer.

Beer Belly (Eng) a slang term given to a large, extended stomach on a man. Also spelt Beerbelly.

Beer Box (Eng) a disposable, air-sealed container (square) used to store up to 22½ litres (5 gallons) of beer. Keeps it fresh for up to 1 month. Is easy to store.

Beer Buffet (Eng) a slang term for a pub (or bar) that has ten or more beers on sale.

Beer Buster Cocktail (Cktl) 1 measure vodka, 1 bottle malt liquor beer, 2 dashes Tabasco sauce. Place vodka and Tobasco in a 300mls (12fl.oz) beer glass, add iced beer and stir gently.

Beer Can (Eng) *see* Drinks Can.

Beer Cask (Eng) *see* cask. *See also* Gantry.

Beer Cask Tap (Eng) a brass, stainless steel or modern plastic tap with a perforated filter at the rear which is driven into the keystone in a beer cask. (Fr) = mettre en perce.

Beer Crate (Eng) a container for holding beer bottles, made of either wood or moulded plastic. 12 x 500 ml. (1pint) or 24 x 250 / 300 ml. (½ pint) sizes.

Beerenauslese (Aus) must be made from over-ripe grapes which have been affected by botrytis, and which have been picked from the best parts of the vineyard. Minimum must weight of 25° KMW. (127° Oechsle). Wine must be bottled in Austria and connot be sold before the 1st May of the year following the harvest. *see* Prädikatsweine.

Beerenauslese (Ger) late picked selected over-ripe grapes which have been attacked by botrytis (edelfäule). Produces luscious sweet Qmp wines. 110°Oe–128°Oe.

Beerenberg (Hol) *see* Beerenburg.

Beerenburg (Hol) a herb bitters of angelica, bay leaves, gentian, etc. Known as Friesengeist in Germany. 30% alc by vol. Also spelt Beerenberg.

Beer Engine (Eng) a method of drawing cask-conditioned ales from the cask in the cellar by suction. Each pull of the pump handle will deliver a full half pint. *see* Fobbing.

Beer Engine Brewery (Eng) a pub brewery (established 1984). (Add): Newtown St. Cyes, Exeter, Devon EX5 5AX. Brews its own cask-conditioned ales. Produces; Rail Ale 3.8% alc by vol. (1037 O.G.)., Piston Bitter 4.8% alc by vol. (1044 O.G.)., Sleeping Heavy 5.4% alc by vol., Whistlemas. Website: http://www.thebeerengine.co.uk 'E'mail: peter@thebeerengine.co.uk

Beerenlay (Ger) grosslagen (Anb): Mosel-Saar-Ruwer. (Ber): Bernkastel. (Vil): Lieser. (Vins): Niederberg-Helden, Rosenlay, Süssenberg.

Beerens [Albert] (Fr) a Champagne producer. (Add): Chemin de la Creuse, 10200 Bar-sur-Aube.

Beer Festival (Eng) a CAMRA sponsored festival where British traditional cask-conditioned ales (from 20 plus varieties) are available to try over a short period (2–3 days).

Beer Garden (Eng) a garden area outside of licenced premises set aside for drinking in the summer months.

Beermat (Eng) originally made of cork, now made of thin card, a mat used for soaking up spilt drinks, they are collected by enthusiasts (breweries etc. use them as an advertising medium). *See also* Dripmat, Coaster

Beer Muller (Eng) a copper conical container with a handle, used to heat (mull) the beer over an open fire.

Beer O'Clock (Eng) a 3.9% alc by vol. ale brewed by the Beckstones Brewery, Cumbria.

Beer Octasphere (Eng) *see* Beer Sphere.

Beer on Tap (Eng) draught beer. (Fr) = bière en fût.

Beer Pressure (Eng) a slang term used to describe a peron being encourage to drink the same drinks as your peers during a social gathering.

Beer Sangaree (Cktl) in a long glass dissolve a teaspoon of sugar in a little water, top with chilled beer and add grated nutmeg.

Beer Scraper (USA) a bone implement for removing dried beer slops off the bar top.

Beer Seidl (USA) a 450 ml. (16fl.oz) beer glass.

Beer Shell (USA) a 250 ml. (8fl.oz–10fl.oz) beer glass.

Bees Organic (Eng) a 4.5% alc by vol. organic ale brewed by Arkell's Brewery Ltd., Wiltshire.

Beer Sphere (Eng) a round container holding 20, 30

108

or 40 litres of beer or lager, made airtight with a rubber seal and metal cap which is crimped over the neck. Will keep beer for seven days when opened. *See also* Beer Octashpere (an eight-sided beer sphere).

Beer Station [The] (Eng) the brand label of the Hepworth & C°. Brewery.

Beer Tankard (Eng) a pewter or silver-plate beer mug of either a half pint or pint capacity for drinking draught ales. (Fr) = pot à bière, (Ger) = stein.

Beer-Up (Austr) a slang term for a heavy drinking bout.

Beery (Eng) a bad smell in the bottle caused by a secondary fermentation, resulting in an unsound wine.

Beery (Eng) a slang term for a heavy smell of beer on the breath, or having a taste of beer.

Bees (Eng) a type of yeast which has the unique property of rising and falling in lumps during fermentation (like a bee) hence bee(s) wine.

Beesengenever (Hol) a blackcurrant-flavoured genever (gin).

Bee's Knees (Cktl) ⅓ measure dry gin, ⅓ measure fresh lemon juice, ⅓ measure (clear) honey, shake well over ice and strain into a cocktail glass.

Bees Knees (Eng) a 4.5% alc by vol. ale brewed by the Hampshire Brewery, Hampshire.

Bees Knees (Eng) a 4.2% alc by vol. ale brewed by the Bartrams Brewery, Suffolk.

Bee Sting (Eng) a 4.7% alc by vol. cask-conditioned ale brewed by Brakspear, Henley-on-Thames.

Beestings (Eng) the name given to the first milk from a cow after parturition (giving birth). (Fr) = amouille.

Bees Wine (Eng) *see* Bee Wine and Fliers.

Beeswing (Eng) another name for the sediment thrown after maturation in red wines.

Beeswing (Port) the floating sediment that has not settled with the crust in vintage Port.

Bee Wine (Eng) made from the gingerplant, a fungus which possesses peculiar properties. (See Bees). Brewed by adding bees to water with sugar, after fermentation it is ready in six weeks for drinking.

Beezone Honey Beer (Eng) a 3.8% alc by vol. beer brewed by the Highgate Brewery, West Midlands.

Bégadan (Fr) a commune in the Bas Médoc north-west Bordeaux.

Begg [John] (Scot) a Scotch whisky and malt whisky producer owned by DCL. Brands include John Begg's Bluecap and Lochnager.

Beggars Brew (Eng) a 1.2% alc by vol. brew with herbal extracts including capsicum, juniper, lemon, speedwell, yarrow. Sold under the Fentimans name by Gaymer.

Bègles (Fr) a commune in the A.C. Graves in south-western Bordeaux.

Begnins (Switz) a wine-producing area in La Côte on the western bank of Lake Geneva.

Behhari (Ger) an old name for a beaker, jug.

Behind the Wall (Cktl) 35mls (1½ fl.ozs) vodka, 25mls (1fl.oz) Mandarine Napoléon, 25mls (1fl.oz) Galliano, 35mls (1½ fl.ozs) orange juice, shake with ice, strain into a tall glass, add ice and top with ginger ale.

Behind the Wall (Scot) a brewery. (Add): 14, Melville Street, Falkirk, Stirlingshire FK1 1HZ. Brews ales and lager.

Behrens & Hitchcock (USA) a winery based in the Napa Valley Cardinale, Napa-Sonama Counties, California. Grape varieties include: Cabernet sauvignon. Label: Kenefick Ranch.

Beihingen (Ger) village (Anb): Württemberg. (Ber): Württembergisch Unterland. (Gro): Schalkstein. (Vin): Neckarhälde.

Beijian (Chi) a natural mineral spring water from Beijing. Mineral contents (milligrammes per litre): Sodium 28.1mg/l, Calcium 56.3mg/l, Magnesium 17.4mg/l, Potassium 2.43mg/l, Chlorides 10.1mg/l, Sulphates 38.6mg/l, Silicates 18.9mg/l. pH 7.66

Beilberg (Ger) vineyard (Anb): Baden. (Ber): Badische Frankenland. (Gro): Tauberklinge. (Vil): Grossrinderfeld.

Beilberg (Ger) vineyard (Anb): Baden. (Ber): Badische Frankenland. (Gro): Tauberklinge. (Vil): Werbach.

Beilstein (Ger) village (Anb): Mosel-Saar-Ruwer. (Ber): Zell/Mosel. (Gro): Rosenhang. (Vin): Schlossberg.

Beilstein (Ger) village (Anb): Württemberg. (Ber): Württembergisch Unterland. (Gro): Wunnenstein. (Vins): Schlosswengert, Steinberg, Wartberg.

Beilstein (Ger) village (Anb): Württemberg. (Ber): Remstal-Stuttgart. (Gro): Kopf. (Vin): Grossmulde.

Beine (Fr) a canton in the Reims district in Champagne. Has the Cru villages of Berru, Cernay-lès-Reims and Nogent-l'Abbesse.

Beines (Fr) a commune in the A.C. Chablis, Burgundy.

Bein Wine (S.Afr) a winery (established 2002) based in Maitieland, Stellenbosch, Western Cape. Grape variety: Merlot. 2.2ha. Website: http://www.beinwine.com

Beira Alta (Port) a region between Dão and the Spanish border, produces red and white wines.

Beira Interior (Port) a D.O.C. formed by combining the I.P.R. Cova de Beira and Pinhel. Based in the Beiras region.

Beiras (Port) a wine region in the north of Portugal. Has the DOC regions of: Baira Interior, Bairrada, Dão, Lafoes and Tavora-Varosa.

Beirbrouwerij De Leeuw BV (Hol) a brewery. (Add): Prinses Beatrixsingel 2, Postbus, 6300 AV, Valkenburg A/D Geul Netherlands. Brews beers and lagers. Website: http://www.leuwbier.nl 'E'mail: info@leeuwbier.nl

Beisl (Aus) a city inn that operates like a heurige (new local wines can be purchased by the glass).

Beivre (Fr) a thirteenth century word meaning 'to drink'. *see* Bevrage.

Beizi (Chi) cup.

Bejaoua (Tun) a co-operative winery based in Tunisia. Belongs to the UCCVT.

Beker (Hol) cup/beaker.

Bekka Valley (Leb) a noted wine-producing region in Lebanon. *see* Château Musar.

B

Bekond (Ger) village (Anb): Mosel-Saar-Ruwer. (Ber): Bernkastel. (Gro): Sankt Michael. (Vins): Brauneberg, Schlossberg.

Bel-Air (Fr) a Premier Cru vineyard in the A.C. commune of Gevrey-Chambertin, Côte de Nuits, Burgundy. 3.72ha.

Belan (Euro) a wine-producing region based in southern Macedonia.

Bel Arbors (USA) a new name for Bel Arbres, second label of the Fetzer Vineyards.

Bel Arbres (USA) the brand-name formally used by the Fetzer Vineyards for their second label table wines. Based in Redwood Valley, California. see Bel Arbors.

Bela Rex (Aus) the label for a red wine (Cabernet sauvignon and Merlot blend) produced by the Gesellmann winery, Mittel-Burgenland.

Belbourie (Austr) a winery based in the Hunter Valley in New South Wales.

Bel Canto (S.Afr) the label for a red wine (60% Cabernet sauvignon, 13% Merlot, 27% Shiraz) produced by the Kleinvallei Winery, Paarl, Western Cape.

Belcher's Best (Eng) an ale brewed by a micro-brewery in Sutton. see Belcher's Original.

Belcher's Original (Eng) an ale brewed by a micro-brewery in Sutton. see Belcher's Best.

Belchite (Sp) a Vino Comarcal of Zaragoza in Aragón. Produces red and white wines that are high in alcohol.

Beldi (Tun) a white grape variety.

Belemnitic (Fr) the chalk soil in Champagne.

Belezos (Sp) the label of a Riojan wine produced by Zugobes, S.A. Both joven and crianza styles.

Belfast Glass (Ire) a top Irish glass making centre in Northern Ireland.

Belfield (S.Afr) a winery (established 2000) based in Elgin, Western Cape. 1.64ha. Grape varieties: Cabernet sauvignon, Merlot. Produces varietal wines.

Belgian Coffee (Liq.Coffee) using a measure of Elixir d'Anvers.

Belhaven Brewery (Scot) a brewery based in Spott Road, Dunbar, East Lothian. Is a major exporter to the USA and Italy. Brews a large selection of beers including Fowler's Wee Heavy 1070 O.G. Monkscroft House Ale 1070 O.G. Premium Scottish Export 3.9% alc by vol. Texas Ale 1056 O.G. Winston's Stout 1053 O.G.

Beli Burgundec (Slo) a local name for the Pinot blanc grape.

Belin [J.] (Fr) a négociant-éleveur based at Prémeaux, Côte de Nuits, Burgundy.

Belina (Euro) a white grape variety grown in Serbia and Slovenia. Known as Stajerska Belina in Croatia, Hunnentraube and Weisser Heunisch in Germany.

Beli-Pinot (Euro) a version of the Pinot blanc grape.

Beli Plavac (Euro) a white grape variety.

Belisario (It) a co-operative winery. (Add): Matelica e Cerreto D'Esi scarl, Via A. Merloni 12, 62024 Mateica. 220ha. vineyard established in 1971. Produces five different Verdicchio di Matelica wines from different vineyards: I Ritratti, L'Anfora, Vigneti del Cerro, Vigneti Belisario, Riserva Cambrugiano.

Bélissauds [Les] (Fr) a Premier Cru vineyard in the A.C. commune Beaune, Côte de Beaune, Burgundy. 4.88ha.

Belji (Cro) a noted wine-producing town based in northern Croatia.

Bell (USA) a winery based in the Napa Valley, California. Grape varieties include: Cabernet sauvignon.

Bella (Euro) a natural spring mineral water from Qormi. Mineral contents (milligrammes per litre): Sodium 64mg/l, Calcium 53mg/l, Magnesium 11mg/l, Potassium 3mg/l, Bicarbonates 130mg/l, Chlorides 80mg/l. pH 7.4

Belladonna Cocktail (Cktl) ⅓ measure vodka, ⅓ measure crème de noyaux, ⅓ measure cream. Shake over ice, strain into a cocktail glass.

Bell'Agio (It) the brand-name of a sweet, white wine produced by Banfi from Moscato grapes.

Bella Napoli (USA) a winery in San Joaquin Valley, California. Produces wines under the Bella Napoli and Vine Flow brand labels.

Belland [Adrien] (Fr) a Burgundy négociant-éleveur. (Add): Place du Jet d'Eau, 21590 Santenay.

Bellapais (Cyp) a slightly sparkling white wine produced by the Keo Company based in Limassol.

Bellaqua (Ger) a a slightly sparkling natural spring mineral water from the Franzisquelle, Mineralquellen Huber GmbH, 77740 Bad peterstal. Mineral contents (milligrammes per litre): Sodium 14.8mg/l, Calcium 14.1mg/l, Magnesium 5.2mg/l, Bicarbonates 93mg/l, Chlorides 6.1mg/l, Nitrates 4.8mg/l.

Bellaqua (Ger) a sparkling natural spring mineral water from the Wilhelmquelle, Mineralbrunnen Huber GmbH, 77776 Bad Rippoldsau. Mineral contents (milligrammes per litre): Calcium 6.4mg/l, Magnesium 2mg/l, Bicarbonates 17.7mg/l, Sulphates 6mg/l.

Bellaris-Quelle (Ger) a natural spring mineral water from Bad Liebenzell, BW: Bellheim/Pfalz, RP.

Bellarmine Bottle Jug (Eng) a glazed jug of the seventeenth century in many sizes, with a bearded mask at the neck of the bottle to represent bishop Bellarmine's (a temperance man) face as a joke to ridicule him.

Bellaterra (Chile) the name of a white wine made from the Sauvignon blanc grape by Torres (of Spain).

Bell Canyon (USA) the brand-name used by the Burgess Cellars for their range of varietal wines.

Belle Epoque (Fr) see Perrier-Jouët Belle Epoque, Fleur de Champagne.

Bellegarde (Fr) a commune in the A.C. Languedoc in the Midi, southern France. Noted for dry white wine Clairette de Bellegarde made from the Clairette grape.

Belle Glos (USA) a winery based in the Santa Maria Valley, Santa Barbara County, California. Also has vineyards in Monterey County. Grape variety:

B

Pinot noir. Labels: Clark & Telephone Vineyard, Las Alturas Vineyard.

Belle Idée de Champagne [La] (Fr) a special cuvée Champagne produced by Vranken Lafitte in Vertus.

Belle Isle (Ire) a cream liqueur flavoured with butterscotch.

Belle Poule [La] (Cktl) 10mls (½ fl.oz) Mandarine Napoléon, 100mls (4fl.ozs) dry white wine, 25mls (1fl.oz) sweet vermouth, stir over ice, serve in a wine goblet with ice and a twist of tangerine peel.

Belle Sandrine [La] (Fr) a liqueur produced from passion fruit and Armagnac brandy.

Belles Soeurs (USA) a wine label of the Shea Vineyards, Oregon.

Belles Roches (Fr) a natural mineral water from the Ardèche. Mineral contents (milligrammes per litre): Sodium 14mg/l, Calcium 6.6mg/l, Magnesium 3.2mg/l, Potassium 2.9mg/l, Bicarbonates 71.7mg/l, Chlorides 5.2mg/l, Sulphates 1.09mg/l, Nitrates 0.8mg/l.

Belle Strasbourgeoise (Fr) a beer from the Fischer/Pêcheur Brasserie in Schiltigheim.

Bellet (Fr) an A.C. wine area 50ha. (soil of silcon and chalk) in Nice, Riviera, Southern France. Produces dry red, rosé and white wines. Districts: Candau, Cappan, Crémat, Golfan, Gros-Pin, La Tour, Le Grand-Bois, Le Pilon, Les Séoules, Lingestière, Mont-Bellet, Puncia, Saint-Romain-de-Bellet, Saint-Sauveur, Saquier and Serre-Long. The region is noted for pebbly *'pudding stone'* soil. Main Grape varieties: **(red)**: Folle, Braquet and Cinsault. **(white)**: Chardonnay, Clairette, Rolle and Rousanne,

Bellet de Nice (Fr) another name for the Bellet area in south-eastern France.

Belle Terre Vineyard (USA) a vineyard in Alexander Valley, Sonoma County, California. Grape varieties: Cabernet sauvignon, Chardonnay and Johannisberg riesling. Produces varietal wines. *See also* Château St. Jean.

Belle Vallée Cellars (USA) a winery based in the Willamette Valley, Oregon. Grape variety: Pinot noir. Label: Grand Cuvée.

Belle Vue Beer (Bel) a gueuze beer.

Belle-Vue Framboise (Bel) a lambic bier 5.7% alc by vol. flavoured with raspberries and cherries.

Belle-Vue Kriek (Bel) a lambic bier 5.1% alc by vol. flavoured morello cherries and elderberries.

Bellevue Estate (Austr) a winery based in Hunter Valley, New South Wales. Owned by Drayton. Produces varietal and table wines.

Bellevue Vineyards (S.Afr) a winery (established 1701) based in Koelenhof, Stellenbosch, Western cape. 193ha. Grape varieties: Cabernet franc, Cabernet sauvignon, Malbec, Merlot, Petit verdot, Pinotage, Shiraz. Labels: Atticus, Morkel, PK Morkel, Rozanne, Tumara. Website: http://www.bellevue.co.za

Bellheim (Ger) village (Anb): Pfalz. (Ber): Südliche Weinstrasse. (Gro): Trappenberg. (Vin): Gollenberg.

Bellheimer Weiz'n Bräu Hefe-Weizen (Ger) a 5.4% alc by vol. bottle-conditioned wheat beer brewed by K. Silbernagel Brauerei, Bellheim.

Bellheimer Weiz'n Bräu Kristall (Ger) a 4.9% alc by vol. clear wheat beer brewed by K. Silbernagel Brauerei, Bellheim.

Bell Hill Vineyard (USA) a small vineyard based in Lake County, California. Grape variety: Cabernet sauvignon.

Bellingham (S.Afr) a winery (established 1693) based in Wellington, Western Cape. Grape varieties: Cabernet sauvignon, Chardonnay, Chenin blanc, Colombard, Johannisberger riesling, Merlot, Pinotage, Sauvignon blanc, Shiraz. Labels: Maverick, Our Founders, Premier Grand Cru, Spitz, The Blends. Website: http://www.bellingham.co.za

Bellingham Wines (S.Afr) a winery based in Franschhoek, Western Cape. Noted for Pinotage, Merlot, Cabernet sauvignon, Shiraz and Chardonnay wines.

Bellini (Cktl) Champagne and peach juice. Fill a Champagne flute ⅓ full with peach juice, top with iced Champagne.

Bellinzonese (Switz) a noted vineyard based in the Sopra Ceneri area of Ticino.

Bell Mountain Vineyards (USA) a winery. (Add): Hill County Winery, Fredenicksberg, Texas. 52 acres. Noted for Cabernet sauvignon wines.

Bellone (It) a white grape variety grown in the Latium region.

Bellonie, Bourdillon et Cie (W.Ind) a rum distillery based on the island of Martinique. Produces La Mauny Rum.

Belloe Vino (Rus) white wine.

Bellow & C° (Eng) a coffee producer (established 1954). (Add): 5–7, Hope Way, Liverpool, Merseyside L8 7PH. 'E'mail: info@bellowcoffee.co.uk

Bellows Partners Choice (USA) the brand-name of a blended whiskey.

Bellringer (Eng) a 4.2% alc by vol. cask bitter brewed by the Abbey Ales Brewery, Avon.

Bells Brewery (Eng) a brewery (established 2004). (Add): Unit E3, Elms Farm, Ullesthorpe Road, Lutterworth, Leicestershire LE17 4SD. Brews: Bells Bitter 3.7% alc by vol., Cosbys 3.7% alc by vol., Dreamcatcher 4.7% alc by vol., IPA 4.1% alc by vol., Rainmaker 4.1% alc by vol. Website: http://www.bellsbrewery.co.uk 'E'mail: jon@bellsbrewery.co.uk

Bell's (Scot) Arthur Bell & Sons Ltd. Distillers of malt whisky (Blair Athol, Dufftown, Inchgower and Pittyvaich distilleries) and blenders of Scotch whisky (Bells, C & J. McDonald and The Real Mackenzie). Owned by Guinness.

Bell Tower Collection Estate Wine (S.Afr) a red wine (Cabernet sauvignon 90% plus Cabernet franc, Malbec, Merlot and Petit verdot) produced by the Asara Estate winery, Stellenbosch, Western Cape.

Bell Wine Cellars (USA) a winery based in Rutherford, Napa Valley, California. Grape variety: Cabernet sauvignon. Label: Clone 6 Baritelle Vineyards.

Bellydancer (Eng) a 5.2% alc by vol. ale brewed by the Brewster Brewing C°. Ltd., Leicestershire.

Bellyfull (Eng) a slang term that denotes having had sufficient to drink or eat (full up).

Belly Rumbler (Eng) the label of a 5% alc by vol. ale.

Belmont Cocktail (Cktl) 1 measure dry gin, 4 dashes raspberry cordial, ⅔ measure cream. Shake well over ice, strain into a cocktail glass.

Belmont Light (Ger) a low alcohol drink with a taste of grapes. 2.8% alc by vol. bottled by Langguth Erben in Traben-Trabach for Booker Cash & Carry.

Belmont Springs (USA) a natural spring water.

Bel Normande (Eng) a sparkling non-alcoholic apple juice drink from Copak Drinks Ltd.

Belon (Tur) a sweet coffee, also known as Sukar Ziada.

Belpaïs (Cyp) a white wine produced in the middle ages in eastern Cyprus by the Premonstratensian (white Canons) monks.

Belsenberg (Ger) village (Anb): Württemberg. (Ber): Kocher-Jagst-Tauber. (Gro): Kocherberg. (Vin): Heilig Kreuz.

Beltane Vineyard (USA) a vineyard based in the south-east of Sonoma County California. Grape varieties: Cabernet sauvignon and Chardonnay. Produces varietal wines.

Belter (Eng) a 5% alc by vol. seasonal winter ale brewed by Banks in Wolverhampton.

Belval-Sous-Châtellon (Fr) a Cru Champagne village in the Canton de Châtillon-sur-Marne. District: Reims.

Belvedere (Pol) a brand of rye-based vodka.

Belvedere (It) a 300ha. wine estate in Bolgheri. Produces Vermentino and Guado al Tasso.

Belvedere Cellars (Austr) a winery (established 1986) based in Victoria. (Add): 399 High Street, Nagambie, Victoria. Grape varieties: Cabernet sauvignon, Shiraz, Riesling. Also produce Port and Sherry-style wines.

Belvinta Supreme (Cyp) the brand-name of a medium-sweet Cyprus Sherry.

Belvoir Brewery (Eng) a brewery (established 1995). (Add): Woodhill, Nottingham Lane, Old Dalby, Melton Mowbray, Leicestershire LE14 3LX. Brews: ABC Bitter 4.1% alc by vol., Beaver Bitter 4.3% alc by vol., Gordon Bennett 4.1% alc by vol., Lilibet's Best 4.5% alc by vol., Meloncholly 4.1% alc by vol., Mild Ale 3.4% alc by vol., Old Dalby Ale 5.1% alc by vol., Peacock's Glory 4.7% alc by vol., Scrumdown 4.5% alc by vol., Spirit of Freedom 4.3% alc by vol., Star Bitter 3.9% alc by vol., Whippling Golden Bitter 3.6% alc by vol., Virgin Beaver, Liquid Gold. Website: http://www.belvoirbrewery.co.uk

Belvoir Pressé (Eng) a selection of bottled, flavoured sparkling spring water from Belvoir Fruit Farms. 'E'mail: info@belvoircordials.co.uk

Belz (Ger) vineyard (Anb): Pfalz. (Ber): Mittelhaardt-Deutsche Weinstrasse. (Gro): Mariengarten. (Vil): Wachenheim.

Belzebuth (Fr) a 15% alc by vol. amber coloured, top-fermented, bottled special beer brewed by Jeanne d'Arc Brasserie, Ronchin.

Bem Saúde (Port) a natural mineral water from Bem Saúde.

Benaglia (It) a natural mineral water from Benaglia, Lazise, Verona.

Benais (Fr) the top wine-producing commune in Bourgueil, Touraine, Loire.

Ben-Ami (Isr) the brand-name of a range of red and white table wines.

Bénard-Pitois (Fr) a Champagne producer. (Add): 21, Rue Duval, 51160 Mareuil-sur-Aÿ. Propriétaire-Récoltant. Produces vintage and non-vintage wines. 'E'mail: BERNARD-PITOIS@wanadoo.fr

Bénard Roland (Fr) a Champagne producer. (Add): 21, Rue Corbier, 51160 Mareuil-sur-Aÿ. Propriétaire-Récoltant. Produces vintage and non-vintage wines. Vintages: 1991, 1995. 'E'mail: champagnebenard.roland@wanadoo.fr

Benavente (Sp) a Vino Comarcal wine of the province Zamora in Castilla-León.

Benavides (Sp) a noted vineyard based in the Montilla-Moriles region.

Bench Grafting (Eng) the grafting of *Vitis vinifera* scions onto American root stock in nurseries and allowing them to set before planting in the vineyard. *See also* Field Grafting and Omega Grafting.

Benchmark (USA) the brand-name of a 6 y.o. and 7 y.o. Kentucky Bourbon whiskey produced by Sazerac (part of Seagram). Also an XO single barrel.

Benchmark (Eng) a 3.5% alc by vol. beer brewed by Bunce's Brewery in Wiltshire. *See also* Famous Pigswill, Old Smokey.

Bender (Eng) a slang term for a heavy drinking bout. i.e. '*To go on a bender*'.

Ben du Toit (S.Afr) the label for a red wines (Merlot, Pinotage and Shiraz blend) and (Cabernet sauvignon 50% plus Merlot and Petit verdot blend) produced by the Helderkruin Wine Cellar winery, Stellenbosch, Western Cape.

Bendigo/Ballarat (Austr) small vineyards based in Victoria.

Beneagles (Scot) a blended Scotch whisky, noted for its ceramic '*eagle*' bottles. (Add): Peter Thompson (Perth) Ltd., Box 22, Crieff road, Perth, Scotland. PH1 2SC.

Ben Ean (Austr) a light, dry white wine from Lindemans 'Ben Ean' vineyard New South Wales.

Benedict (Bel) an abbaye-style beer brewed by the De Kluis Brasserie in Hoegaarden.

Benedict Cocktail (Cktl) ½ measure Bénédictine, ½ measure Scotch whisky. Stir over ice in an old-fashioned glass and top with ginger ale.

Bénédictine (Fr) a distillery based in Fécamp, Normandy, produces liqueur of same name. *See also* B and B. Also owns the Garnier liqueur distillery.

Bénédictine (Fr) a herb-flavoured, brandy-based liqueur, 43% alc by vol. distilled in Fécamp, Normandy. *see* D.O.M. and B and B. Also produced in Madrid, Spain.

Bénédictine Cocktail (Cktl) ½ measure Cognac, ¼ measure Bénédictine, ¼ measure lemon juice. Shake well over ice, strain into a cocktail glass.

Bénédictine Scaffa Cocktail (Cktl) ¼ measure Bénédictine, ¼ measure rum, ¼ measure gin, ¼ measure Scotch whisky, dash Angostura. Stir over ice, strain into a cocktail glass.

Benedictus (Eng) an 8.4% alc by vol. barley wine brewed by The Durham Brewery Ltd., County Durham.

Benediktinerberg (Ger) vineyard (Anb): Mosel-Saar-Ruwer. (Ber): Saar-Ruwer. (Gro): Römerlay. (Vil): Trier.

Benediktusberg (Ger) vineyard (Anb): Franken. (Ber): Maindreieck. (Gro): Ravensburg. (Vil): Retzbach.

Beneficio (Port) a rule in the Douro Port wine region that allows wineries to use a maximum of three hectolitres of Port wine must (juice) to be used for still red Douro wines.

Bénefontaine Brasserie (Fr) a brewery (established 1926) based in Bénefontaine. Brews Korma.

Benesov Brewery (Czec) a brewery (established 1897) based in north-west Czec. Noted for fine clean beers.

Beneventanum (It) a red wine produced in central Italy in Roman times.

Benfield & Delamare (N.Z) a 2.5ha. winery at Cambridge Road, Martinborough. Grapes include Cabernet franc, Merlot.

Benfro (Wal) the name given to a range of beers: Bitter 1036–1038 O.G. Benfro Extra (premium bitter) 1041–1043 O.G. brewed at a micro-brewery in Llanteg, Dyfed.

Bengal (S.Afr) a leading brand of double-distilled cane spirit.

Bengal Cocktail (Cktl) ½ measure brandy, ⅛ measure maraschino, ⅛ measure Curaçao, ¼ measure pineapple juice, 6 dashes Angostura. Stir over ice, strain into a cocktail glass.

Bengal Lancers Punch (Punch) ½ cup Cointreau, 100mls (2 pints) lime juice, sugar to taste, 300mls (½ pint) claret, ½ cup Jamaican rum, ½ cup pineapple and orange juice, ice, mix altogether, top with a magnum of Champagne and garnish with lime slices.

Bengal Tiger (Eng) a 4.5% alc by vol. ale brewed by The Concertina Brewery, South Yorkshire.

Bengel (Ger) vineyard (Anb): Baden. (Ber): Bodensee. (Gro): Sonnenufer. (Vil): Meersburg.

Bengel (Ger) village (Anb): Mosel-Saar-Ruwer. (Ber): Bernkastel. (Gro): Schwarzlay. (Vin): sites not yet chosen.

Ben Haroun (Alg) a sparkling natural spring mineral water. Mineral contents (milligrammes per litre): Sodium 52.8mg/l, Calcium 38.8mg/l, Magnesium 6.8mg/l, Potassium 1.35mg/l, Bicarbonates 157mg/l, Chlorides 41.6mg/l, Sulphates 50mg/l, Silicates 2.5mg/l, Fluorides 0.5mg/l.

Benicarló (Sp) a red grape variety grown in Valencia. Is known as the Mourvèdre in France.

Benicarló (Sp) a red wine from Valencia from the grape of same name.

Benicasim (Sp) a vino de mesa wine from the province of Castellón in Valencia.

Beni di Batasiolo (It) wine producer in Barolo.

(Add): Frazione Annunziata, 87-1-12064 La Morra (CN). Produces Vigneto Corda della Briccolina. Website: http://www.batasiolo.com

Benificio (Port) denotes the amount of wine permitted to be made into Port in the Douro.

Beni M'Tir (Afr) an A.O.G. area in the wine-producing region of Meknès-Fez, Morocco.

Benin (Afr) a Nigerian palm wine made from fermented palm sap.

Beninoise [La] (Afr) a lager beer 10.5° Plato brewed in Benin.

Beni Sadden (Afr) an A.O.G. area in the wine-producing region of Meknès-Fez, Morocco.

Benisalem (Sp) a wine-producing area on the island of Majorca, noted for full red wines.

BenMarco (Arg) the label for a range of wines (Cabernet sauvignon/Malbec) produced by the Dominio del Plata winery in the Mendoza region. Also Expresivo.

Benmarl Vineyard (USA) a small estate winery based at Marlboro in the Hudson River Valley in eastern America. Produces mainly French-American hybrid grape wines.

Benmorven Müller-Thurgau (N.Z) a light, fruity white wine from the Montana Wines.

Benmorven Riesling-Sylvaner (N.Z) a slightly sweet white wine produced by Montana Wines. Was originally known as Bernkaizler.

Benn (Ger) vineyard (Anb): Rheinhessen. (Ber): Wonnegau. (Gro): Bergkloster. (Vil): Westhofen.

Benn (Ger) vineyard (Anb): Pfalz. (Ber): Mittelhaardt-Deutsche Weinstrasse. (Gro): Grafenstück. (Vil): Obrigheim.

Bennachie Scotch Whisky Company [The] (Scot) produces a range of malt whiskies including 10, 17 and 21 year olds, Formidable Jock plus 3 and 8 year old blended whiskies.

Bennets Strong Ale (Eng) a strong ale 1057 O.G. brewed by the Five Towns Brewery, Stoke-on-Trent, Staffs.

Bennett Cocktail (Cktl) 40mls (⅓ gill) Old Tom gin, 20mls (⅙ gill) fresh lime juice, 2 dashes Angostura. Shake well over ice, strain into a cocktail glass.

Bennett Valley (USA) a new A.V.A. in the Sonoma County, California.

Ben Nevis (Scot) the name for a beer brewed by the Bridge of Allan Brewery, Stirlingshire.

Ben Nevis (Scot) a single highland malt whisky distillery. (Add): Ben Nevis Distillery (Fort William) Ltd., Lochy Bridge, Fort William PH33 6TJ. 40% alc by vol., a 26 year old version 40% alc by vol. and a 40 year old 'Dew of Ben Nevis 40% alc by vol. are available. Also produce a grain whisky.

Benniarés (Sp) a Vino Comarcal from the province of Alicante in Valencia.

Benningen (Ger) village (Anb): Württemberg. (Ber): Württembergisch Unterland. (Gro): Schalkstein. (Vin): Neckarhälde.

Benoist (Wal) a still/sparkling mineral water from Prysg Spring.

B

Benoit Serres (Fr) a distillery. (Add): 46, Rue à Viadieu, Toulouse. Producer of Donjon (a liqueur with a brandy and almond base), Liqueur de Violette 25% alc by vol. Eau de Noix Serres (160 year old French liqueur made with green walnuts) at 30% alc by vol.

Bénovie (Fr) a Vin de Pays area in the Hérault département, southern France. Produces red and rosé wines.

Benriach-Glenlivet (Scot) a single highland malt whisky produced by The Longmorn-Glenlivet Distilleries Ltd. 40% alc by vol. Also a 10 year old 43% alc by vol. and a 1982 version at 60.6% alc by vol. (cask strength).

Benrinnes (Scot) a single highland malt whisky distillery. 43% alc by vol. (part of the DCL Group).

Benromach (Scot) a single highland (Speyside) malt whisky distillery (established 1898) based in Forres. 40% alc by vol. Also a 1976 vintage at 43% alc by vol. Owned by Gordon & McPhail. Website: http://www.benromach.com

Ben Ryé (It) a dessert wine made from passito-dried Moscato grapes grown on the island of Pantelleria (off the coast of Sicily) by Donnafugata.

Bensheim (Ger) village (Anb): Hessische Bergstrasse. (Ber): Starkenburg. (Gro): Wolfsmagen. (Vins): Kalkgasse, Kirchberg, Steichling, Hernsberg, Paulus.

Bensheim-Auerbach (Ger) village (Anb): Hessische Bergstrasse. (Ber): Starkenburg. (Gro): Rott. (Vins): Höllberg, Fürstenlager.

Bensheim-Schönberg (Ger) village (Anb): Hessische Bergstrasse. (Ber): Starkenburg. (Gro): Rott. (Vin): Herrnwingert.

Benskins Brewery (Eng) a brewery belonging to Ind Coope. Beers brewed at Romford, Essex and bottled in Burton. Produces all types of ales.

Bentley (Cktl) ½ measure applejack brandy, ½ measure Dubonnet, stir over ice and strain into a cocktail glass.

Bentleys Yorkshire Breweries (Eng) abbr: B.Y.B.

Benton Harbor (USA) a wine district in the region of Michigan State. Main grape varieties are Catawba, Concord and Delaware.

Bentonite (Eng) a diatomaceous earth. see Bentonite Clay.

Bentonite Clay (USA) a fine clay from Wyoming, used to clear wine as a fining, a diatomaceous earth (hydrated silicate of aluminium). see Louisiana Clay.

Benton Lane (USA) a winery based in Monroe, Oregon. Grape variety: Pinot noir. Label: First Class.

Ben Truman (Eng) the brand-name of Watney's keg bitter 1038 O.G. and Export 1045 O.G.

Ben Wyvis (Scot) a single highland malt whisky distillery sited north of Inverness. 40% alc by vol.

Benzaldehyde (Eng) an aldehyde found in wine which contributes to the bouquet and flavour of the wine.

Benziger (USA) a winery based in the Sonoma County, California. Grape varieties include: Cabernet sauvignon.

Benzoic Acid (Eng) a chemical which may be added to stop fermentation and prevent all the sugar from being fermented out to produce a sweetish wine. Used mainly in home-made wines.

Beoir (Ire) beer.

Beone (It) a drunkard.

Beor (Eng) a mediaeval word for beer.

Beotia (Gre) a wine region of Central Greece.

Beowulf Brewery (Eng) a micro-brewery based in Yardley, Birmingham. Brews: Crackling, Dragons Smoke Stout, Grendals, Heroes, Noble Bitter, Squires, Wergild.

Béquignol (Fr) a rare red Bordeaux grape variety, now mainly grown in south-western France.

Ber (Ger) abbr: Bereich.

Bérange (Fr) a Vin de Pays area in the Hérault département, southern France.

Bérard [Victor] (Fr) a Burgundy négociant-éleveur based in Varennes-lès-Mâcon, Burgundy. Produces Burgundy and Beaujolais.

Berat [J. et Jacques] (Fr) a Champagne producer. (Add): 8 Rue St. Roch, Boursault, 51200 Épernay. Récoltants-manipulants. Produces vintage and non-vintage wines. Vintages: 1971, 1973, 1975, 1976, 1979, 1982, 1983, 1985, 1989, 1990, 1995, 1998, 1999, 2000.

Berberana. S.A. (Sp) see Bodegas Berberana. S.A.

Bercy (Fr) also known as Quai de Bercy, a part of Paris on the river Seine where most of the city's wines arrive and are distributed.

Bère (Ch.Isles) to drink.

Bere (Eng) the mediaeval name for barley from which beer derived.

Bere (It) drink.

Bereich (Ger) an area within an anbaugebiete, chosen for its similar soil and terrain type. e.g. Bernkastel in the Mosel-Saar-Ruwer.

Berem (Wal) yeast.

Berenberg (Hol) see Beerenburg.

Berenburg (Hol) a bitters from Holland.

Berentzen Appel (Eng) a light apple and spirit drink 21% alc by vol. from Merrydown.

Berentzen Appel (Ger) an apple and whiskey-based liqueur produced by Berentzen. 25% alc by vol.

Beresan Winery (USA) a winery based near Walla Walla Valley, Washington. Grape variety: Merlot.

Berg (Ger) lit: 'hill or mountain', a popular name used for vineyards in Germany, 23 individual sites have the name.

Berg (Ger) vineyard (Anb): Ahr. (Ber): Walporzheim/Ahrtal. (Gro): Klosterberg. (Vil): Heppingen.

Berg (Ger) vineyard (Anb): Baden. (Ber): Badische Bergstrasse/Kraichgau. (Gro): Stiftsberg. (Vil): Herbolzheim.

Berg (Ger) vineyard (Anb): Baden. (Ber): Badische Bergstrasse/Kraichgau. (Gro): Stiftsberg. (Vil): Neudenau.

Berg (Ger) vineyard (Anb): Franken. (Ber): Maindreieck. (Gro): Kirchberg. (Vil): Escherndorf.

Berg (Ger) vineyard (Anb): Mittelrhein. (Ber): Rheinburgengau. (Gro): Burg Hammerstein. (Vil): Unkel.

114

B

Berg (Ger) vineyard (Anb): Nahe. (Ber): Kreuznach. (Gro): Kronenberg. (Vil): Bad Kreuznach (ortsteil Winzenheim).

Berg (Ger) vineyard (Anb): Nahe. (Ber): Schloss Böckelheim. (Gro): Rosengarten. (Vil): Roxheim.

Berg (Ger) vineyard (Anb): Pfalz. (Ber): Mittelhaardt-Deutsche Weinstrasse. (Gro): Pfaffengrund. (Vil): Diedesfeld.

Berg (Ger) vineyard (Anb): Rheingau. (Ber): Johannisberg. (Gro): Daubhaus. (Vil): Hochheim.

Berg (Ger) vineyard (Anb): Rheingau. (Ber): Johannisberg. (Gro): Daubhaus. (Vil): Kostheim.

Berg (Ger) vineyard (Anb): Rheingau. (Ber): Johannisberg. (Gro): Landkreis Melsungen. (Vil): Böddiger.

Berg (Ger) vineyard (Anb): Württemberg. (Ber): Württembergisch Unterland. (Gro): Schalkstein. (Vil): Aspreg.

Berg (Ger) vineyard (Anb): Württemberg. (Ber): Württembergisch Unterland. (Gro): Schalkstein. (Vil): Markgröningen.

Berg (Ger) vineyard (Anb): Württemberg. (Ber): Württembergisch Unterland. (Gro): Staufenberg. (Vil): Brettach.

Berg (Ger) vineyard (Anb): Württemberg. (Ber): Württembergisch Unterland. (Gro): Staufenberg. (Vil): Cleversulzbach.

Berg (Ger) vineyard (Anb): Württemberg. (Ber): Remstal-Stuttgart. (Gro): Kopf. (Vil): Hanweiler.

Berg (Ger) vineyard (Anb): Württemberg. (Ber): Remstal-Stuttgart. (Gro): Kopf. (Vil): Korb.

Berg (Ger) vineyard (Anb): Württemberg. (Ber): Remstal-Stuttgart. (Gro): Kopf. (Vil): Winnenden.

Berg (Ger) vineyard (Anb): Württemberg. (Ber): Remstal-Stuttgart. (Gro): Weinsteige. (Vil): Stuttgart (ortsteil Cannstatt).

Berg (Ger) vineyard (Anb): Württemberg. (Ber): Remstal-Stuttgart. (Gro): Weinsteige. (Vil): Stuttgart (ortsteil Feuerbach).

Berg (Ger) vineyard (Anb): Württemberg. (Ber): Remstal-Stuttgart. (Gro): Weinsteige. (Vil): Stuttgart (ortsteil Münster).

Berg (Ger) vineyard (Anb): Württemberg. (Ber): Remstal-Stuttgart. (Gro): Weinsteige. (Vil): Stuttgart (ortsteil Wangen).

Berg (Ger) vineyard (Anb): Württemberg. (Ber): Remstal-Stuttgart. (Gro): Weinsteige. (Vil): Stuttgart (ortsteil Zuffenhausen).

Bergamot Liqueur (Fr) a fruit liqueur made from a variety of Mediterranean oranges.

Bergamottelikoer (Ger) a liqueur based on bergamot, an aromatic herb.

Berg Bildstock (Ger) vineyard (Anb): Rheingau. (Ber): Johannisberg. (Gro): Steinmacher. (Vil): Niederwalluf.

Bergbock Dunkel (Ger) a dark bock bier from the Andechs Brauerei in Erling-Andechs, Bavaria.

Bergbock Hell (Ger) a malty bock bier from the Andechs Brauerei in Erling-Andechs, Bavaria.

Bergborn (Ger) vineyard (Anb): Nahe. (Ber): Kreuznach. (Gro): Sonnenborn. (Vil): Langenlonsheim.

Bergel (Ger) vineyard (Anb): Pfalz. (Ber):

Mittelhaardt-Deutsche Weinstrasse. (Gro): Höllenpfad. (Vil): Grünstadt.

Bergel (Ger) vineyard (Anb): Pfalz. (Ber): Südliche Weinstrasse. (Gro): Schloss Ludwigshöhe. (Vil): Edenkoben.

Berger (Aus) a winery based (established 1818) in the Kremstal region. (Add): Wiener Strasse 3, 3494 Gedersdorf. Grape varieties: Grüner veltliner, Riesling, Neuberger, Zweigelt. Produces a range of wine styles.

Berger (Fr) a pastis and anisette producer who market under the Fournier label and Le Crystal.

Bergerac (Fr) a wine region 8000ha. of south-west France, 80 miles from the town of Bordeaux and having a variety of soil types including: sand, clay, chalk, gravel. Produces red, rosé, white and sweet white wines. Grape varieties: Cabernet franc, Cabernet sauvignon, Malbec, Merlot, Muscadelle, Sauvignon blanc, Sémillon,, Ugni blanc. A.C.'s of Bergerac, Côtes de Bergerac, Côtes de Montravel, Côtes de Saussignac, Haut-Montravel, Monbazillac, Montravel, Pécharmant and Rosette.

Berger Baron [Le] (Fr) a non-vintage wine from the Mouton Rothschild stable under the La Bergerie label.

Bergerbier (Bel) a pilsner beer brewed in Mons.

Bergerdorf Brauerei (Ger) a subsidiary brewery of Holstein, based in Hamburg.

Bergères-lès-Vertus (Fr) a Premier Cru Champagne village in the Canton de Vertus. District: Châlons.

Bergerie de l'Hortus (Fr) a rosé wine from the Domaine de l'Hortus in the Coteaux du Languedoc.

Bergeron (Fr) a white grape variety grown in the Savoie region, south-eastern France. Also known as Roussanne.

Berghalde (Ger) vineyard (Anb): Württemberg. (Ber): Remstal-Stuttgart. (Gro): Kopf. (Vil): Grunbach.

Berghaupten (Ger) village (Anb): Baden. (Ber): Ortenau. (Gro): Fürsteneck. (Vin): Kinzigtäler.

Berghausen (Ger) village (Anb): Baden. (Ber): Badische Bergstrasse/Kraichgau. (Gro): Hohenberg. (Vin): Sonnenberg.

Bergheim (Fr) a commune of the Haut-Rhin in Alsace.

Bergheim (S.Afr) a winery (established 2000) based in Paarl, Western Cape. Grape variety: Pinotage.

Berghof (Switz) a noted producer of eau-de-vie.

Bergier [Jean] (Fr) a Cognac producer. (Add): Brives S/Charente, 17800 Pons. 12ha. in the Petite Champagne.

Bergische Waldquelle (Ger) a still and sparkling natural spring mineral water from Haan, NW. (red label: sparkling/green label: light gas/blue label: still). Mineral contents (milligrammes per litre): Sodium 6.7mg/l, Calcium 34mg/l, Magnesium 5.1mg/l, Potassium 1mg/l, Bicarbonates 83mg/l, Chlorides 22mg/l, Sulphates 28mg/l. Website: http://www.haanerfelsenquelle.de

Berg Kaisersteinfels (Ger) vineyard (Anb): Rheingau. (Ber): Johannisberg. (Gro): Burgweg. (Vil): Assmannshausen-Aulhausen.

Bergkelder (S.Afr) a wine and spirit merchant of Stellenbosch, the wine arm of Oude Meester

B

Group. 4,800ha. Brand-names include Two Oceans, Fleur du Cap, Stellenryck Collection, Drostdy-Hof and Grünberger.

Bergkirche (Ger) vineyard (Anb): Rheinhessen. (Ber): Nierstein. (Gro): Auflangen. (Vil): Nierstein.

Bergkirchweih (Ger) a beer festival held at Erlanger in Franconia.

Bergkloster (Ger) grosslagen (Anb): Rheinhessen. (Ber): Wonnegau. (Vils): Bermersheim, Eppelsheim, Esselborn, Flomborn, Gundersheim, Gundheim, Hangen-Weisheim, Westhofen.

Bergland Österreich (Aus) a new wine region comprising of all the remaining wine-producing regions except Styria and those in the Weinland Österreich.

Bergle (Ger) vineyard (Anb): Baden. (Ber): Breisgau. (Gro): Burg Zähringen. (Vil): Lehen.

Bergle (Ger) vineyard (Anb): Baden. (Ber): Ortenau. (Gro): Fürsteneck. (Vil): Offenburg (ortsteil Fessenbach).

Bergman's Lager (Wal) a lager beer 1033 O.G. brewed by Peter Walker Brewery, Wrexham, North Wales.

Bergpfad (Ger) vineyard (Anb). Rheinhessen. (Ber). Nierstein. (Gro): Gutes Domtal. (Vil): Dexheim.

Berg-Quelle (Ger) a natural spring mineral water from Schwollen, RP.

Berg Rondell (Ger) vineyard (Anb): Franken. (Ber): Maindreieck. (Gro): Honigberg. (Vil): Dettelbach.

Berg Roseneck (Ger) vineyard (Anb): Rheingau. (Ber): Johannisberg. (Gro): Burgweg. (Vil): Rüdesheim.

Berg Roseneck (Ger) a vineyard within the village of Rüdesheim, 26.7ha. (60.7%) of which is proposed to be classified as Erstes Gewächs.

Berg Rottland (Ger) vineyard (Anb): Rheingau. (Ber): Johannisberg. (Gro): Burgweg. (Vil): Rüdesheim.

Berg Rottland (Ger) a vineyard within the village of Rüdesheim, 36.2ha. (89.2%) of which is proposed to be classified as Erstes Gewächs.

Berg Schlossberg (Ger) vineyard (Anb): Rheingau. (Ber): Johannisberg. (Gro): Burgweg. (Vil): Rüdesheim.

Berg Schlossberg (Ger) a vineyard within the village of Rüdesheim, 25.5ha. (91%) of which is proposed to be classified as Erstes Gewächs.

Bergschlösschen (Ger) vineyard (Anb): Mosel-Saar-Ruwer. (Ber): Saar-Ruwer. (Gro): Scharzberg. (Vil): Saarburg.

Bergsig Estate (S.Afr) a winery (established 1843) based at Breede River, Worcester, Western Cape. 253ha. (Add): Bergsig, Box 15, Breërivier 6858. Grape varieties: Cabernet sauvignon, Chardonnay, Chenin blanc, Gewürztraminer, Merlot, Shiraz, Weisser riesling. Produces a range varietal wines. Website: http://www.bergsig.co.za

Bergsträsser Weinmarkt (Ger) a Hessische Bergstrasse wine festival held in Heppenheim in June.

Bergsträsser Winzerfest (Ger) a Hessische Bergstrasse wine festival held at Bensheim in September.

Bergstrom (Austr) the name given to a pot-still designed by a coppersmith with same name.

Bergstrom Vineyard (USA) the Ranchita Oaks

Winery in California. Grape varieties: mainly Cabernet sauvignon.

Bergwäldle (Ger) vineyard (Anb): Baden. (Ber): Badische Bergstrasse/Kraichgau. (Gro): Mannaberg. (Vil): Wiesloch.

Bergwein (Aus) describes a wine produced from grapes grown on slopes exceeding 26° steep.

Beringer Group (USA) owners of Beringer, Château St. Jean, Château Souverain and Meridian vineyards. Recently 2001 purchased by Mildara Blass.

Beringer Vineyard (USA) a large winery in the St. Helena district of the northern Napa Valley, California. Also has vineyards in Knights Valley, Sonoma County, California. Produces table and dessert wines from a variety of grape varieties. *see* Lemon Ranch. Labels: Bancroft Ranch, Founder's Estate, Stone Cellars..

Beriolo (It) a producer of Moscato d'Asti in the Piemonte region.

Berisford Solera (Sp) a 1914 manzanilla pasada Sherry produced by José Pemartin in Jerez de la Frontera.

Berkane (Mor) an A.O.G. wine-producing area based in eastern Morocco.

Berkeley Wine Cellar (USA) the brand-name used by Wine and the People, California.

Berkshire Best Bitter (Eng) a name used during its trial by Morland Brewery, Oxfordshire. Now known as Tanner's Jack.

Berkshire Centenary Ale (Eng) a bottled centenary ale brewed by Courage's Reading Brewery to mark Berkshire Council's centenary. 200 individually numbered bottles.

Berliner Kümmel (USA) a very dry kümmel.

Berliner Pilsner (Ger) a 5% alc by vol. bottled pilsner brewed by the Berliner Pilsner Brauerei, Berlin.

Berliner Pilsner Brauerei (Ger) a brewery (established 1842) based in Berlin. Brews Berliner Pilsner.

Berliner Weisse (Ger) a light coloured wheat beer brewed in Berlin. It is known locally as 'The Cool Blonde'. The beer is bottle conditioned, low in alcohol (3%) and is often flavoured with raspberry juice or woodruff when consumed. *see* Kindl and Schultheiss.

Bermatingen (Ger) village (Anb): Baden. (Ber): Bodensee. (Gro): Sonnenufer. (Vin): Leopoldsberg.

Bermersbach (Ger) village (Anb): Baden. (Ber): Ortenau. (Gro): Fürsteneck. (Vin): Kinzigtäler.

Bermersheim (Ger) village (Anb): Rheinhessen. (Ber): Wonnegau. (Gro): Bergkloster. (Vin): Hasenlauf.

Bermersheim v.d.H. (Ger) village (Anb): Rheinhessen. (Ber): Bingen. (Gro): Adelberg. (Vins): Hildegardisberg, Klosterberg.

Bermersheim/Worms (Ger) village (Anb): Rheinhessen. (Ber): Wonnegau. (Gro): Burg Rodenstein. (Vin): Seilgarten.

Bermester (Port) a vintage Port shipper.

Bermet (Ser) a locally made red vermouth produced in the Vojvodina area. Also a white version.

Bermondsey Beer (Eng) a cask-conditioned ale brewed by Bridge House Brewery.

Bermuda Bouquet (Cktl) 1 measure gin, ⅔ measure apricot brandy, ⅔ measure grenadine, ⅓ measure Triple Sec, 1 teaspoon powdered sugar, juice ½ lemon, 4 dashes orange juice. Shake well over ice, strain into an ice-filled highball glass.

Bermuda Gold Liqueur (W.Ind) a liqueur produced by Somers Distilleries in Bermuda. 40% alc by vol.

Bermuda Highball (Cktl) ⅓ measure gin, ⅓ measure brandy, ⅓ measure French vermouth. Stir over ice, strain into an ice-filled highball glass. Top with ginger ale and a twist of lemon peel.

Bermuda Rose (Cktl) 1 measure gin, ¼ measure apricot brandy, ¼ measure grenadine. Shake over ice, strain into a cocktail glass.

Bermudiana Rose (Cktl) ⅗ measure dry gin, ⅕ measure apricot brandy, ⅕ measure lemon juice. Shake well over ice, strain into a cocktail glass.

Bernache (Fr) the name given to alcoholic (fortified) grape juice in the Loire.

Bernadett-Brunnen (Ger) a natural spring mineral water from Ingolstadt, BY.

Bernadino Spumante (N.Z) a fruity, sparkling white wine produced by Montana Wines from Dr. Hogg Muscat grapes.

Bernard (It) a producer of Prosecco di Conegliano-Valdobbiadene in the Veneto region.

Bernard Brewery (Czec) a brewery (established 1597) based in Humpolec. Brews: Bernard Svetly Pivo 10%, Bernard Polotmavé Pivo 11%, Bernard Svetly Lezák 12%.

Bernard Hatté et Fils (Fr) a Champagne producer (established 1954). (Add): 1, Rue Petite Fontaine, 51360 Verzenay. 8ha. Récoltant-Manipulant. Produces vintage and non-vintage wines. Vintages: 1995, 1996, 1997, 1999. A member of the Club Tresors de Champagne. Labels: Cuvée Benjamin, Cuvée 'Special Club' Millésimée (50% Chardonnay, 50% Pinot noir).

Bernardine [La] (Fr) the label of a Châteauneuf-du-Pape produced by Charpoutier in Tain l'Hermitage, northern Rhône.

Bernard Lancelot Brasserie (Fr) a brewery based in St. Servant-sur-Oust. Brews: Telenn Du.

Bernardo Winery (USA) a small winery based in San Diego, California. Produces varietal and dessert wines.

Bernard Polotmavé Pivo 11% (Czec) a 4.9% Polotmavé (light brown), bottled lager brewed by the Bernard Brewery, Humpolec.

Bernard V11 XO (Fr) a 10 year old Armagnac brandy produced by the Ducastaing C°.

Bernard Svetly Lezák 12% (Czec) a 5.1% straw coloured, bottled lager brewed by the Bernard Brewery, Humpolec.

Bernard Svetly Pivo 10% (Czec) a 4.5% straw coloured, bottled lager brewed by the Bernard Brewery, Humpolec.

Bernardus Pater (Bel) *see* St. Bernardus.

Bernardus Vineyards and Winery (USA) a winery (15.25ha) based in Carmel Valley, California. Grape varieties: Cabernet sauvignon, Chardonnay, Malbec, Merlot.

Berneroy Calvados (Fr) the brand-name of a Calvados produced by UNGC.

Bernet (Ser) *see* Bermet.

Bernheim Wines (S.Afr) a winery (established 2004) based in Nooder-Paarl, Western Cape. 11ha. Grape varieties: Cabernet sauvignon, Chardonnay, Chenin blanc, Colombard, Merlot, Pinotage, Shiraz. Label: JH Pacas & C°. Also produces varietal wines. Website: http://www.bernheimwines.com

Bernhoffen (N.Z) a medium-dry, white wine produced by the Pacific Vineyards, Mcleod Road, Henderson, North Island. Made from the Müller-Thurgau grape variety.

Bernice Cocktail (Cktl) ½ measure vodka, ½ measure Galliano, juice of ½ lime, 2 dashes Angostura. Shake over ice, strain into cocktail glass.

Bernie's LXIV (Eng) a 4.5% alc by vol. ale brewed by the Rudgate Brewery, North Yorkshire.

Bernina (It) a natural mineral water from Piuro (SO), Sondrio, Lombardi. Mineral contents (milligrammes per litre): Sodium 1.05mg/l, Calcium 8.6mg/l, Magnesium 0.75mg/l, Potassium 0.85mg/l, Bicarbonates 22.6mg/l, Chlorides 0.8mg/l, Sulphates 8.05mg/l, Nitrates 3.5mg/l, Silicates 6.5mg/l. pH 7.25

Bernina Frizzante (It) a naturally sparkling mineral water, bottled at the spring at Piuro, Sondrio, in the Alps.

Bernina Naturale (It) a still mineral water from Piuro, Sondrio, Lombardy.

Bernkaizler Riesling (N.Z) *see* Benmorven Riesling.

Bernkastel (Ger) bereich (Anb): Mosel-Saar-Ruwer. (Gros): Badstube, Beerenlay, Kurfürslay. Michelsberg, Munzlay, Nachtarsch, Probstberg, Sankt Michael, Schwarzlay, Von Hessen Stein.

Bernkasteler Docktor (Ger) the greatest German vineyard. So named because of Archbishop Bomund 2nd, Elector of Trier (1351–1362) who was so ill that, on his death-bed, he was given wine from this vineyard and so recovered. He bestowed the appellation on the vineyard. *See also* Doctor.

Bernkasteler Docktor und Badstube (Ger) a pre 1971 designation of the Docktor wines in which grapes from the adjoining vineyard were used. Now no longer allowed.

Bernkasteler Docktor und Bratenhöfchen (Ger) a pre 1971 designation of the Docktor wines in which grapes from the adjoining vineyard were used. Now no longer allowed.

Bernkasteler Docktor und Graben (Ger) a pre 1971 designation of the Docktor wines in which grapes from the adjoining vineyard were used. Now no longer allowed.

Bernkasteler-Kues (Ger) village (Anb): Mosel-Saar-Ruwer. (Ber): Bernkastel. (Gro): Kurfurstlay. (Vins): Johannisbrünnchen, Kardinalsberg, Rosenberg, Schlossberg, Stephanus-Rosengärtchen, Weissenstein.

Bernkasteler-Kues (Ger) village (Anb): Mosel-Saar-Ruwer. (Ber): Bernkastel. (Gro): Badstube. (Vins): Bratenhöfchen, Docktor, Graben, Lay, Matheisbildchen.

Bernreiter (Aus) a winery based in the Wien region. (Add): Amtsstrasse 24-26, 1210 Wien-Jedlersdorf. Grape varieties: Grüner veltliner, Müller-Thurgau, Pinot gris, Welschriesling, Zweigelt. Produces a range of wine styles.

Bernstein (Ger) vineyard (Anb): Mittelrhein. (Ber): Rheinburgengau. (Gro): Schloss Schönburg. (Vil): Oberwessel.

Bernstein Vineyards (USA) a winery based at Mount Veeder, California.

Berntal (Aus) a vineyard site based on the banks of the River Kamp in the Kamptal region.

Berolina (Eng) a low alcohol lager 0.5% alc by vol. from Christopher Longman.

Berón (Sp) a red wine produced by Bodegas Beronia, S.A. Rioja. Oak-matured and bottle-aged. 70%–80% Tempranillo and 20%–30% Viura.

Beronia (Sp) red wines produced in Bodegas Beronia, S.A. Rioja. Oak-matured and bottle-aged.

Beroun Brewery (Czec) a brewery (established 1872) based in north-west Czec. Noted for fine beers.

Berri (Austr) a district of New South Wales that produces fine quality wines.

Berrie (Fr) a commune in the Vienne département. Wines are under the A.C. Saumur, Anjou-Saumur, Loire.

Berri Estates (Austr) vineyards in South Australia, part of Berri Remano. (Add): Sturt Highway, Glossop, S. Australia, 5344. Grape varieties: Cabernet sauvignon, Gordo, Riesling and Shiraz. Produces varietal wines, a carbonated Passion wine and liqueurs.

Berrington (Eng) a natural spring mineral water.

Berri Renmano (Austr) a large vineyard estate (3000ha). in South Australia. see Berri Estates. 34 varieties of grapes grown. (Add): P.O. Box 238 Berri, South Australia, 5343.

Berri Rouge (Eng) a red berry and spring water drink from Panda Drinks, Blandford Forum, Dorset.

Berrow Brewery (Eng) a brewey (established 1982). (Add): Coast Road, Berrow, Burnham-on-Sea, Somerset TA8 2QU. Brews: cask-conditioned Berrow Brewery Best Bitter 4% alc by vol. (1038 O.G.)., Berrow Brewery Porter 4.6% alc by vol., Carnivale 4.5% alc by vol., E.S.B. 4.7% alc by vol., Topsy Turvy 6% alc by vol. (1055 O.G.)., Xmas Ale 4.8% alc by vol. 'E'mail: david@beckstonebrewery.com

Berru (Fr) a Cru Champagne village in the Canton de Beine. District: Reims.

Berry (Eng) another name for the grape. Plural: Berries.

Berry Brothers & Rudd (Scot) Scotch whisky producers (Cutty Sark is one of their noted brands) and famous wine merchants (established 1698). (Add): 3, St. Jame's Street, London SW1A 1EG. Website: http://www.bbr.com 'E'mail: orders@bbr.com

Berry Good Ale (Eng) a 4.5% alc by vol. ale brewed in September by Hydes Anvil, Manchester for Hallowe'en using natural seasonal berry juice.

Berry Shatter (USA) the name given to the poor spring time setting of the fruit, caused by inclement weather during and just after flowering.

Berrywine Plantation (USA) a small vineyard (2.5ha) based in Mount Airy, Maryland. Produces French hybrid wines.

Bersano (It) a noted producer of Moscato d'Asti And Barbera d'Asti wines based at Nizza Monferrato, Piemonte, north-western Italy. see Generali.

Berserker Export Pale Ale (Scot) a 7.5% alc by vol. strong pale ale brewed by the Hebridean Brewery C°. Isle of Lewis.

Berson (Fr) a commune in the A.C. Côtes de Blaye in north-east Bordeaux.

Bertani (It) a well-known Veneto wine producer. Noted for cuve close sparkling wines.

Bertemati (Sp) a Spanish brandy producer.

Bertero Winery (USA) a winery based in southern Santa Clara, California. Grape varieties: Barbera and Zinfandel. Produces varietal wines.

Berthelot [Paul] (Fr) a Champagne producer. (Add): 889 Ave. du Général-Leclerc, Dizy, 51200 Épernay. 20ha.

Bertier-Bichot (Fr) a producer of sparkling A.C. Vouvray based at Rochecorbon, Loire.

Bertie's Rocket Fuel (Eng) a cask-conditioned ale brewed by the Six Bells Brewery, Bishop's Castle, Shropshire.

Bertins [Les] (Fr) a Premier Cru vineyard [part] in the A.C. commune of Beaune, Côte de Beaune, Burgundy.

Bertins [Les] (Fr) a Premier Cru vineyard [part] in the A.C. commune of Pommard, Côte de Beaune, Burgundy. 3.7ha.

Bertola (Sp) a brandy and Sherry producer based in Jerez de la Frontera. Part of Bodegas Internacionales.

Bertoldsquelle (Ger) a natural spring mineral water from Bad Dürrheim. Mineral contents (milligrammes per litre): Sodium 8mg/l, Calcium 325mg/l, Magnesium 55mg/l, Bicarbonates 342mg/l, Sulphates 737mg/l.

Bertolli (It) a famous Chianti Classico producer in Sienna, Tuscany.

Bertolli Fizzano (It) a Chianti Classico producer based in Tuscany.

Bertams VO (S.Afr) a 43% alc by vol. VO brandy produced by Distell. (Add): P.O. Box 184 Stellenbosch 7599, West Cape.

Bertram Wines (S.Afr) a winery based in Stellenbosch. (Add): Box 199, Stellenbosch 7600. Produces varietal wines.

Bertran [José López] (Sp) a large bodega based in Tarragona. 50ha. Produces mainly white wines and Corrida table wines.

Bertrand (Fr) a distiller of Marc d'Alsace. (Add): Wernach 67350, Pfaffenhoffen and Uberach.

Béru (Fr) a commune in the A.C. Chablis, Burgundy.

Berwangen (Ger) village see Kirchardt.

Berwick Glebe (Eng) a small vineyard based in Sussex. 1ha. (Add): Frensham College, Berwick, near Polegate, East Sussex. Grape varieties: Müller-Thurgau, Reichensteiner.

Berzamino (It) a variety of the red grape variety Marzemino.

Beserka (Wal) a special porter 4.5% alc by vol. from the Dyfrryn Clwyd Brewery, Denbigh, Clwyd (the official ale of the 1995 Llandudno Beer Festival).

Besigheim (Ger) village (Anb): Württemberg. (Ber): Württembergisch Unterland. (Gro): Schalkstein. (Vins): Felsengarten, Katzenöhrle, Neckarberg, Wurmberg.

Besitz (Ger) the sole owner of a vineyard.

Besnard-Pitos [L] (Fr) a Champagne producer. Vintages: 1995, 1999, 2001.

Beso (Gre) a noted wine merchant based near Patras in Peloponnese.

Besotted (Eng) intoxicated, incapable through alcoholic drink, stupefied through alcohol.

Bessans (Fr) a Vin de Pays area in the Hérault département in southern France. Produces red, rosé and dry white wines.

Bessarabia (Rus) now known as Moldavia, was part of Bulgaria until 1940. Produces fine table and dessert wines such as Negri de Purkar, Fetjaska, Romanesti, Trifesti and Gratasti.

Bessards [Les] (Fr) a vineyard in the Coteaux de l'Hermitage, northern Rhône (red).

Bessa Valley Wines (Bul) a winery based in the Bessay Valley, Pazarjik. Labels include: Enira (20% Cabernet, 80% Merlot). 266ha.

Bessay (Fr) a vineyard in the A.C. Juliénas Cru Beaujolais-Villages.

Bessen (Hol) a blackcurrant liqueur produced by De Kuyper. 20% alc by vol.

Besserat de Bellefon (Fr) a Champagne house. (Add): BP 301, Allée du Vignoble, 51061 Reims. 10ha. Produces vintage and non-vintage wines. Vintages: 1971, 1973, 1975, 1977, 1978, 1979, 1982, 1985, 1988, 1989, 1990, 1995, 1998, 2000. Owned by Pernod-Ricard.

Bessi (It) a producer of Chianti (Rufina district) who uses neither the D.O.C.G. or Classico designation but his own Chianti Superiore which is only used as a personal guarantee.

Bessin [Jean-Claude] (Fr) a winery based in the A.C. Chablis, Burgundy. Produces a range of Chablis wines including Premier Cru Montmains.

Best (Eng) the designation for top quality ales. see Best Bitter, Best Mild.

Best Bar None (Eng) abbr: BBN an accreditation scheme for pubs that can show that they have taken steps to be responsible by having a proactive drugs search policy, well-trained staff, preventing under-age sales and drinking, etc.

Best Barrique (S.Afr) the label for a red wine (Merlot) produced by the Raka winery, Walker Bay, Western Cape.

Best Before Date (Eng) the date (month and year) that is required by law to be printed on the label of drinks that have a limited shelf life. The date is the manufacturer's forcast as to when the product will start to lose it's quality.

Best Bitter (Eng) the designation of the top ale in a brewery's Portfolio.

Best Bristol Bitter (Eng) a cask-conditioned bitter 1045 O.G. from a Bristol-based home-brew public house.

Beste (Ger) best.

Bestimmtes Anbaugebiet (Ger) a designated region. see Anbaugebiete.

Best Mild (Eng) the designation of the top mild ale in a brewery's Portfolio.

Best Pale Ale (Eng) abbr: BPA, a 5% alc by vol. young beer brewed by Greene King at the Westgate Brewery, Bury St. Edmunds, Suffolk. Used in the production of Suffolk Strong.

Best Scotch (Scot) see Lorimer and Clark.

Bests Great Western (Austr) vineyards. (Add): Concongello Vineyards, Great Western, Victoria 3377. 24ha. Grape varieties: Cabernet sauvignon, Chardonnay, Chasselas, Pinot meunier, Riesling and Shiraz. Noted for sparkling wines.

Best Spingo (Eng) a cask-conditioned ale 5.3% alc by vol. from the Blue Anchor Brewery.

Bestué de Otto Bestué (Sp) a rosé wine (Cabernet sauvignon and Tempranillo blend) produced by Bodegas Otto Bestué, Aragón.

Beta Centauri (S.Afr) the label for a red wine (Cabernet franc 44%, Cabernet sauvignon 44% and Petit verdot 12% blend) produced by the Mulderbosch Vineyards winery, Stellenbosch, Western Cape.

Betanzos (Sp) a Vino Comarcal wine from the province A Coruña in Galicia.

Betelu (Sp) a still natural mineral water from Ama-Iturri, Betelu, Navarra. Mineral contents (milligrammes per litre): Sodium 157mg/l, Calcium 100.8mg/l, Magnesium 23.3mg/l, Potassium 6.5mg/l, Chlorides 265.5mg/l, Sulphates 111.1mg/l, Nitrates 0.8mg/l, Fluorides 0.8mg/l.

Bethany (Austr) a winery in Bethany Road, Barossa Valley, South Australia. Produces late-harvest Riesling plus Grenache and Shiraz wines.

Bethel Heights Vineyard (USA) a winery (established 1977) based in Willamette Valley, Oregon. (51acres). Grape varieties: Pinot noir, Chardonnay, Chenin blanc, Pinot blanc, Pinot gris, Gewürztraminer. Label: Southeast Block Reserve.

Bethon (Fr) a Cru Champagne village in the Canton d'Esternay. District: Épernay.

Betol (Viet) a natural spring water.

Betrunken (Ger) drunk.

Betschgräbler (Ger) vineyard (Anb): Baden. (Ber): Ortenau. (Gro): Schloss Rodeck. (Vil): Eisental.

Betsy Flanagan (USA) an Irish lady (landlady) who is purported to have invented the cocktail using the trimed tail feathers of a cockerel to stir the drinks. see Cocktail.

Betsy Ross (Cktl) 25mls (1fl.oz) Port, 25mls (1fl.oz) brandy, ¼ teaspoon Cointreau, dash Angostura. Shake over ice, strain into a cocktail glass.

Bettelhaus (Ger) vineyard (Anb): Pfalz. (Ber): Mittelhaardt-Deutsche Weinstrasse. (Gro): Kobnert. (Vil): Ungstein.

Béttola (It) public house/tavern.

Betty James (Cktl) ½ measure gin, ½ measure maraschino, ¼ measure lemon juice, dash

Angostura. Shake with ice, strain into a cocktail glass.

Betty Stogs (Eng) a 4% alc by vol. pale amber ale brewed by Skinner's Brewery, Truro, Cornwall.

Between the Sheets (Cktl) ⅓ measure white rum, ⅓ measure brandy, ⅓ measure Cointreau, dash lemon juice. Shake over ice, strain into a cocktail glass.

Betz (USA) a winery based in the Columbia Valley, Washington State. Grape varieties include: Syrah. Label: La Serenne.

Beugnons (Fr) an A.C. Premier Cru Chablis, often reclassified as the Premier Cru Vaillons.

Beuicarlo (Sp) a strong red wine from the region of Castellón de la Plana in Valencia.

Beulsberg (Ger) vineyard (Anb): Mittelrhein. (Ber): Rheinburgengau. (Gro): Schloss Schönburg. (Vil): Urbar by St. Goar.

Beuren (Ger) village (Anb): Mosel-Saar-Ruwer. (Ber): Zell/Mosel. (Gro): Grafschaft. (Vin): Pelzerberger.

Beuren (Ger) village (Anb): Württemberg. (Ber): Remstal-Stuttgart. (Gro): Hohennefffen. (Vin): Schlossteige.

Beurot (Fr) a local Burgundy name for the white grape Pinot gris. See also Burot.

Beutelsbach (Ger) village (Anb): Württemberg. (Ber): Remstal-Stuttgart. (Gro): Wartbühl. (Vins): Altenberg, Käppele, Sonnenberg. see Feuerwant.

Beutelsbach (Ger) village (Anb): Württemberg. (Ber): Remstal-Stuttgart. see Weinstadt and Feuerwant.

Beutelsstein (Ger) vineyard (Anb): Nahe. (Ber): Schloss Böckelheim. (Gro): Paradiesgarten. (Vil): Oberndorf.

Beuv'rie (Ch.Isles) alcoholic liquor. See also Bev'rie and Litcheur.

Bévaeux (Ch.Isles) a boozer or drinker. See also Béveux.

Beva Fresca (It) a term for a very young wine or describing fresh grape juice which may be added to older wine before drinking.

Bevanda (It) beverage/drink.

Bevano (It) a natural spring mineral water from Carignano, Terme, Pesaro.

Bevans Bitter (Wal) a 4.2% alc by vol. bitter beer brewed by The Rhymney Brewery Ltd., Mid-Glamorgan.

Bevee (Fr) an old word for a drink.

Beverage (Eng) collective name for any drink (other than water) both alcoholic and non-alcoholic. (Arab) = sharab, (Aus) = getränk, (Chi) = yinliao, (Cro) = piće, (Den) = drik, (Fr) = boisson, (Ger) = getränk, (Gre) = anapsiktiko, (Hol) = drank, (Indo) = minuman, (Isr) = mashke, (It) = bevanda, (Jap) = nominono, (Kor) = eumryosu, (Port) = bebida, (Rus) = napitki, (Sp) = bebida, (Thai) = kruangdeum, (Wal) = diod.

Beverage Brands (UK) Ltd (Eng) distillers (established 1989). (Add): Rockwood House, Parkhill Road, Torquay, Devon TQ1 2DU. Produces vodka and liqueurs. Website: http:///www.wkd.co.uk 'E'mail: info@beverage-brands.co.uk

Beverage Testing Institute (USA) abbr: B.T.I. A body

based in New York that promotes and develops the tastes in wines. see Hendonic Scale.

Beverage Wine (USA) denotes an ordinary table wine.

Beveraggio (It) beverage/drink.

Beveridge (Eng) a drink produced from white sugar, spring water and orange juice.

Beverly Hills Cocktail (Cktl) 60mls (½ gill) Calvados, 2 dashes Angostura. Stir over broken ice, strain into a cocktail glass. Serve with a cherry and dash of lemon peel juice on top.

Bevernagie Brasserie (Bel) a brewery based in Lichtervelde in west Flanders. Brews: Oud Piro (a red beer).

Béveux (Ch.Isles) see Bévaeux.

Bevibile (It) drinkable.

Bevin Boys (Eng) a 4.5% alc by vol. ale brewed by the Blencowe Brewing C°., Rutland.

Bevitore (It) drinker.

Bévottaïr (Ch.Isles) booze/alcoholic drink.

Bévounnaïr (Ch.Isles) tipple. See also Grogier.

Bevrage (Fr) an old word for drink other than water.

Bév'rie (Ch.Isles) alcoholic liquor. See also Beuv'rie and Litcheur.

Bevvies (Eng) the plural of Bevvy. i.e. "A few bevvies" (a few drinks).

Bevvy (Eng) abbr: beverage, a slang term for a drink, term mainly used in and around Liverpool in north-western England.

Bévy (Fr) old village not far from the Nuits-Saint-Georges, dating from tenth century. Produces red and white wines from the Pinot noir and Chardonnay vines. see Hautes Côtes de Nuits.

Bewl Valley Vineyards (Eng) a vineyard based in Wadhurst, Kent. Noted producers of organic wines.

Beyaz (Tur) a semi-dry white wine.

Beyer [Léon] (Fr) a family wine business in Eguisheim, Alsace.

Beyerskloof (S.Afr) a winery (established 1998) based in the Koelenhof, Stellenbosch, Western Cape. (Add): P.O. Box 107, Koelenhof 7605, Stellenbosch. Grape varieties: Cabernet sauvignon, Merlot, Pinotage, Shiraz, Touriga. Labels: Lagare Cape Vintage, Synergy.

Beylerce (Tur) a red grape variety.

Beyond the Pale (Eng) a 4% alc by vol. ale brewed by Eastwood & Sanders Ltd (Fine Ales), West Yorkshire.

Beypazari (Tur) a natural spring mineral water (established 1967) from Karakoca.

Bézique (W.Ind) the brand-name of a lemon-flavoured Bacardi rum.

Bezirkswinzergenossenschaft (Ger) a district co-operative. See also Gebietswinzergenossenschaft.

Bezoya (Sp) a still natural natural mineral water from Ortigosa del Monte, Sierra de Guagarrama. Mineral contents (milligrammes per litre): Sodium 2.5mg/l, Calcium 2.1mg/l, Magnesium 0.3mg/l, Bicarbonates 10.4mg/l, Chlorides 0.7mg/l, Nitrates 2.8mg/l, Silicates 11.2mg/l. pH 6.36

Bezzants Bitter (Eng) a 4% alc by vol. bitter beer brewed by the Spectrum Brewery, Norfolk.

B4 (Eng) a 4% alc by vol. ale brewed by the Milk Street Brewery, Somerset.

B-52 (Pousse Café) 30mls Baileys Irish Cream Liqueur, 30mls Kahula, 30mls Grand Marnier carefully layered in a pousse café glass.

B.Fuggled (Eng) a 6% alc by vol. strong ale brewed by the Highgate Brewery, West Midlands.

BGI Beer (Viet) a 4.5% alc by vol. golden straw coloured, bottled lager brewed with malt and rice by BGI, My Tho, Vietnam.

Bhang (Ind) a beverage made from a fermentation of hemp leaves and twigs infused with water. *See also* Bang.

Bia (It) a natural spring mineral water from Abrau 2. pH 7.9

Biale [Aldo] (USA) a vineyard in the Sonoma Valley, California. Noted for Zinfandel wines.

Bianca Fernanda (It) a white grape variety grown in the Lombardy region. Also known as the Cortese.

Biancame (It) a white grape variety grown in the Abruzzi region. Also known as the Passenna in the Marches and Bianchello in northern Italy.

Bianca Neve (It) a natural mineral water from Zogno (BG). Lombardi. Mineral contents (milligrammes per litre): Sodium 0.64mg/l, Calcium 59.6mg/l, Magnesium 26.5mg/l, Potassium 0.24mg/l, Bicarbonates 271.5mg/l, Chlorides 0.51mg/l, Sulphates 28.5mg/l, Nitrates 3.3mg/l, Silicates 3.5mg/l.

Bianchello (It) a white grape variety grown in the Marches (where it is also known as the Passenna). *See also* Biancame.

Bianchello del Metauro (It) a D.O.C. white wine from the Marches. Produced from the Bianchello and Malvasia grapes. Metauro is a river which flows to the Adriatic.

Bianchetta (It) the name used in Verona and Treviso in northern Italy for Prosecco wine. *See also* Ombretta.

Bianchetta Trevigiana (It) a white grape variety grown in the Trentino-Alto-Adige.

Bianchet Winery (Austr) a winery (established 1976). (Add): Victoria Road, Lilydale, Yarra Valley. Grapes include Merlot, Verduzzo.

Bianchi (Arg) the brand-name of the Hudson, Ciovini, Buenos Aires. Produced in the San Rafael district of Mendoza.

Bianchi Borgogna (Arg) a red wine produced by Bodegas Bianchi.

Bianco (It) a golden white-coloured, medium-sweet vermouth.

Bianco (It) the term used to describe a white wine.

Bianco [In] (It) a term which denotes that the juice is taken quickly from the skins.

Bianco Alcamo (It) *see* Alcamo.

Bianco Capena (It) a D.O.C. white wine from Latium. Produced from the Malvasia di candia, Malvasia del lazio, Toscano, Trebbiano toscano, Romagnolo, Giallo, Bellone and Bombino grape varieties.

Bianco d'Alessano (It) a white grape variety grown in Puglia. *See also* Alessano.

Bianco d'Arquata (It) a dry white wine from near Perugia in the Umbria.

Bianco dei Colli Maceratesi (It) a D.O.C. white wine from the Marches. Produced from the Trebbiano toscano and Maceratino 50%, plus Malvasia toscano and Verdicchio grape varieties. Produced in the commune of Loreto in the province of Macerata.

Bianco di Alcamo (It) a D.O.C. white wine from western Sicily in the Trapani province based mainly on the Cataratto grape.

Bianco di Alessano (It) a white grape variety grown in Puglia region.

Bianco di Custoza (It) a D.O.C. white wine from the Lombardy region. Produced from the Trebbiano 5%–15%, Garganega 20%–30%, Trebbianello 5%–15% and Cortese 20%–30% grapes. The D.O.C. also describes the naturally sparkling wine produced from musts and wines according to regulations.

Bianco di Ostuni (It) a D.O.C. white wine from the Puglia region. Produced from the Impigno, Francavilla, Bianco di Alessano and Verdeca grapes.

Bianco di Pitigliano (It) a D.O.C. white wine from the Tuscany region. Produced from Trebbiano toscano, Greco, Malvasia bianca toscano and Verdelho grapes. The wine is produced 'vinificato in bianco'.

Bianco Fine Wines (S.Afr) a winery (established 1997) based in Tulbagh, Western Cape. 16ha. Grape varieties: Cabernet sauvignon, Nebbiolo, Pinotage, Shiraz. Label: Boulder Red. Website: http://www.bianco.co.za

Biancolella (It) a white grape variety grown on the island of Ischia on the southern tip of Italy.

Biancolella (It) a white wine from the grape of the same name produced on the island of Ischia.

Biancone (It) a white grape variety grown in Tuscany.

Biancosarti (It) the brand-name for an apéritif wine produced in northern Italy.

Bianco Vergine Valdichiana (It) a D.O.C. white wine from the Tuscany region. Produced from the Trebbiano toscano and Malvasia del chianti grapes. Vinification takes place without the skins.

Bianco Vermouth (It) a sweet, white vermouth 16% alc by vol.

Biane (USA) a brand-name used by the Brookside Winery of California.

Biar (Ger) an old local (Frisian) word for beer.

Biassa (It) one of the five towns in the Cinque Terre, Liguria, north-western Italy.

Biba (Rus) a natural spring mineral water (established 1997) from Cherkessk.

Bibber (Eng) drinker, tippler, someone who likes alcoholic drink. *see* Wine Bibber and Bibbers.

Bibbers (Eng) an old name for heavy drinkers. *see* Bibber.

Bibbiano (It) a noted Chianti Classico producer.

Biberacher Mineralwasser (Ger) a natural spring mineral water from Biberacher Mineralquelle, Heilbronn am Neckar, BW.

Bibere (Lat) to drink. *see* Imbibe.

Bibita (It) drink/beverage.

Bible Wines (Eng) a collective name used for the

B

many wines mentioned in the Holy Bible. Ahsis, Khemer, Khometz, Mesech, Mimsach, Schechar, Soveh, Tirosh and Yayin.

Biblioteca (Sp) wine cellars which are similar to libraries with samples of all vintages for reference tastings.

Biborteni Aqua Magnesia (Rom) a sparkling natural spring mineral water (established 1897) from the F9 Spring, Biborteni, Transylvania. Mineral contents (milligrammes per litre): Sodium 257.1mg/l, Calcium 264.5mg/l, Magnesium 87.6mg/l, Potassium 38mg/l, Chlorides 90mg/l, Sulphates 15.2mg/l. pH 6.3

Bibulus (Lat) to be fond of drink.

Bica (Port) a small black coffee, Portuguese espresso coffee.

Bica Aberta (Port) a method of keeping the must from the skins in the making of white Port.

Bical (Port) a white grape variety grown in the Bairrada and Dão regions. Known as Borrado das Moscas in Dão.

Bical da Bairrada (Port) another name for the Borrado das moscas grape.

Bicane Chasselas (Fr) a species of the white Chasselas grape. Is also known as the Napoléon.

Bicchiere (It) drinking glass.

Bicentenary Brew (Eng) a 5.5% alc by vol. strong pale ale from Harvey and Son, Bridge Wharf Brewery, Lewes.

Bicentenary Pageant Ale (Eng) see Pageant Ale.

Bicentenary Pale Cream (Sp) a brand of cream Sherry from Garveys of Jerez.

Bichot [Maison Albert] (Fr) a négociant-éleveur based in Beaune. Owns 100ha. Of vineyards in Chambertin, Clos de Vougeot and Richbourg. Owns: Domaine Long-Depaquit (Chablis), Domaine du Clos Frantin (Vosne-Romanée), Domaine de Pavillon (Pommard). Website: http://www.albertbichot.com 'E'mail: bourgogne@albert-bichot.com

Bickensohl (Ger) village (Anb): Baden. (Ber): Kaiserstuhl-Tuniberg. (Gro): Vulkanfelsen. (Vins): Herrenstück, Steinfelsen.

Biddenden (Eng) a vineyard (established 1969 – 1970) 7.5ha. Soil: loam over clay. (Add): Little Whatmans, Gribble Bridge Lane, Biddenden, Ashford, Kent TN27 8DF. Grape varieties: Müller-Thurgau 75%, Huxelrebe, Ortega, Pinot noir, Reichensteiner, Scheurebe and Seyval. Produces a variety of still and sparkling wines and ciders. Website: http://www.biddendenvineyards.com 'E'mail: info@biddendenvineyards.co.uk

Biddy Early Brewery (Ire) a brewery. (Add): Inagh, Ennis, County Clare. Brews beers and lager. Website: http://www.beb.ie 'E'mail: info@beb.ie

Bidon (Fr) an eighteenth century wooden jug of approximately 5 litres capacity. Now made of metal.

Bidon (Fr) can.

Bidon à Bière (Fr) can of beer/beer can.

Biebelnheim (Ger) village (Anb). Rheinhessen. (Ber): Nierstein. (Gro): Petersberg. (Vins): Pilgerstein, Rosenberg.

Biebelsheim (Ger) village (Anb): Rheinhessen. (Ber): Bingen. (Gro): Sankt Rochuskapelle. (Vins): Honigberg, Kieselberg.

Biegler[Manfred] (Aus) a winery based in Gumpoldkirchen, Thermenregion. (Add): Wiener Strasse, 2352 Gumpoldkirchen. Grape varieties: Chardonnay, Pinot blanc, Riesling, Rotgipfler, Zierfandler, Zweigelt. Label:

Biela Sladka Grasica (Slo) a regional name for the white Welschriesling.

Bienenberg (Ger) vineyard (Anb): Baden. (Ber): Breisgau. (Gro): Burg Lichteneck. (Vil): Malterdingen.

Bienenberg (Ger) vineyard (Anb): Baden. (Ber): Ortenau. (Gro): Schloss Rodeck. (Vil): Achern (ortsteil Oberachem).

Bienenberg (Ger) vineyard (Anb): Mittelrhein. (Ber): Rheinburgengau. (Gro): Schloss Schönburg. (Vil): Niederburg.

Bienenberg (Ger) vineyard (Anb): Mittelrhein. (Ber): Rheinburgengau. (Gro): Schloss Schönburg. (Vil): Oberwessel.

Bienengarten (Ger) vineyard (Anb): Baden. (Ber): Ortenau. (Gro): Fürsteneck. (Vil): Durbach.

Bienengarten (Ger) vineyard (Anb): Mosel-Saar-Ruwer. (Ber): Zell/Mosel. (Gro): Rosenhang. (Vil): Sonheim.

Bienengarten (Ger) vineyard (Anb): Mosel-Saar-Ruwer. (Ber): Zell/Mosel. (Gro): Weinhex. (Vil): Güls.

Bienengarten (Ger) vineyard (Anb): Rheingau. (Ber): Johannisberg. (Gro): Honigberg. (Vil): Winkel.

Bienenlay (Ger) vineyard (Anb): Mosel-Saar-Ruwer. (Ber): Zell/Mosel. (Gro): Grafschaft. (Vil): Ediger-Eller.

Biengarten (Ger) vineyard (Anb): Pfalz. (Ber): Mittelhaardt-Deutsche Weinstrasse. (Gro): Meerspinne. (Vil): Gimmeldingen.

Biengarten (Ger) vineyard (Anb): Pfalz. (Ber): Südliche Weinstrasse. (Gro): Königsgarten. (Vil): Frankweiler.

Biengen (Ger) village (Anb): Baden. (Ber): Markgräflerland. (Gro): Lorettoberg. (Vin): Maltesergarten.

Bieninberg (Ger) vineyard (Anb): Baden. (Ber): Breisgau. (Gro): Burg Lichteneck. (Vil): Heimbach.

Bien Nacido Vineyard (USA) based in the Santa Maria Valley, Santa Barbara County, California. Noted for Pinot noir. Owned by the Foxen Estate.

Bienteveo (Sp) a look-out post that is temporarily situated in the vineyard prior to the vintage (harvest).

Bienvenues-Bâtard-Montrachet (Fr) a Grand Cru vineyard in the A.C. commune of Puligny-Montrachet, Côte de Beaune, Burgundy. 2.3ha.

Bier (Aus) (Ger) (Hol) beer/ale.

Bierbrouwerij de Drie Hoefijzers (Hol) the Three Horseshoes Brewery. Brews Breda and Skol lagers. See also Drie Hoefijzers and Breda.

Bierbrouwerij De Koningshoeven (Hol) a brewery. (Add): Eindhovensweg 3, Berkel Enschot, Postbus 394, 5000 AJ Tilburg, Netherlands. Brews a range of beers and lagers. Website: http://www.latrappe.nl

Bier d'Alsace (Fr) a beer brewed in Alsace.

Bière (Fr) beer/ale.

Bière Ambrée (Fr) the name for George Killan's Irish Red Ale brewed by the Pelforth Brewery under licence from Letts of Eire. *See also* Bière Rousse.

Bière Blanche (Fr) the name for the pale brown abbaye-style beers.

Bière Blonde (Fr) the name for the light brown abbaye-style beers.

Bière Brune (Fr) the name for the dark brown abbaye-style beers.

Bière de Garance (Fr) a local home-made bier brewed from the madder plant.

Bière de Garde (Fr) lit: 'laying down beer', produced in wine-shaped bottles with a cork. Made with a mixture of Pilsen and Munich malt beers. 5½–6% alc by vol. *See also* Jenlain and St. Leonard.

Bière de Garde de Saint Léonard (Fr) a high-strength bière de garde brewed by the St. Léonard Brasserie, 62200 St. Martin/Bologne. 6% alc by vol.

Bière de Gingembre (Fr) ginger beer.

Bière de Malt (Fr) malt beer.

Bière de Ménage (Fr) home-brewed beer.

Bière des Druids (Ger) the name of a 1045 O.G. beer sold in silver swing top bottles.

Bière du Démon [La] (Fr) a strong lager 12% alc by vol. from Enfants de Gayant, Douai.

Bière du Désert (Fr) a 7% alc by vol. pale straw coloured, bottled lager brewed by Enfants de Gayant, Douai.

Bière en Fût (Fr) beer on tap/draught beer.

Bière Panachée (Fr) lit: 'mixed beers', can also denote a Shandy.

Bière Rousse (Fr) the name for George Killan's Irish Red Ale brewed by the Pelforth Brewery under licence from Letts of Eire. *See also* Killan.

Bière Saint Omer (Fr) a pilsener lager 1046 O.G. brewed by Groupe Saint Arnould. Breweries at Lille, Boulogne, Saint Omer.

Bières De Chimay SA (Bel) a trappiste brewery. (Add): Route Charlmagne 8, 6464 Baileux, Chimay, Belgium. Brews a range of beers and lagers. Website: http://www.chimay.com

Bières de l'Abbaye (Bel) abbey beers and trappiste beers.

Bieringen (Ger) village (Anb): Württemberg. (Ber): Kocher-Jagst-Tauber. (Gro): Kocherberg. (Vin): Schlüsselberg.

Bierkan (Hol) beer can.

Bierkeller (Eng) a public house that is decorated in the German style and specialises in German beers (especially lager) and served in stein glasses.

Biern (Aus) a vineyard site on the banks of the River Danube situated in the Wachau region, Niederösterreich.

Bierritz (Eng) the brand-name for malt liquor and orange wine drink 7% alc by vol.

Biersuppe (Ger) a beer eggnog. 500mls (1pint) ale, 100gms (4ozs.) sugar, cinnamon and lemon zest. Heat, whisk into 4 egg yolks with a little milk. Strain and cool, serve with soaked raisins.

Bierzo (Sp) a D.O. region in Castilla-Léon. Region is known as El Bierzo. 7,500ha. of vineyards of which 3,300ha. are D.O. Produces red, rosé and white wines. Grape varieties: Mencía (62%), Garnacha tintorera, Doña blanca, Godello, Malvasía, Palomino.

Bies Brewery (Den) a brewery based in Hobro in northern Jutland.

Biesjes Craal (S.Afr) the label for a white wine (Sauvignon blanc) produced by the Durbanville Hills winery, Durbanville, Western Cape.

Bièthe (Ch.Isles) beer.

Bietigheim (Ger) village (Anb): Württemberg. (Ber): Württembergisch Unterland. (Gro): Schalkstein. (Vin): Neckarberg.

Bietzener Wiesen (Ger) a natural mineral water from Merzig, SL.

Biferno (It) a D.O.C. red wine from Molise. Produced mainly from the Montepulciano grape.

Biferno (It) a D.O.C. white wine from Molise. Produced mainly from the Malvasia and Trebbiano grape varieties.

Biffy (Cktl) 1 measure gin, ¼ measure Swedish Punsch, juice ½ lemon. Shake over ice, strain into a cocktail glass.

Big Apple (Eng) a 5.3% alc by vol. bottled cider drink produced by Thatcher's of Somerset.

Big Apple (Cktl) a ⅓ measure Scotch Apple, ⅓ measure Amaretto di Saronno, ⅓ measure Drambuie, dash grenadine, dash lemon juice. Shake over ice, strain into an ice-filled highball glass. Dress with apple slice.

Big Apple Cocktail (Cktl) hollow out the centre of an eating apple to form a glass. Chill well after firstly rubbing the inside with lemon juice. Blend pulp with 25mls (⅕ gill) Cognac, 40mls (⅓ gill) orange juice, 20mls (⅙ gill) lemon juice and ½ scoop crushed ice. Strain into apple, serve with straws.

Big Bamboo Cocktail (Cktl) ⅓ measure golden rum, ⅓ measure orange juice, ⅓ measure pineapple juice, ¼ measure grenadine, 2 dashes lemon juice. Shake well over ice, strain into highball glass filled with ice. Dress with a mint sprig and orange slice.

Big Bang (Eng) a beer brewed with the addition of ginger by the Wye Valley Brewery, Hertfordshire.

Big Barrel Lager (Austr) a sweetish copper-coloured lager brewed in 1974 by the Cooper's Brewery in South Australia for the Schützenfest.

Big Ben (Eng) a bottled strong ale 1050 O.G. brewed by Thwaites Brewery, Blackburn.

Big Boy Cocktail (Cktl) 30mls (¼ gill) dry gin, 30mls (¼ gill) Italian vermouth, 30mls (¼ gill) French vermouth, dash Pernod, dash Angostura. Stir over broken ice, strain into a cocktail glass. Decorate with cherry and dash of lemon peel juice.

Bigbury Beer (Eng) a cask-conditioned best bitter 1044 O.G. from the Summerskill Brewery, Devon.

Big Fat Santa (Eng) a 4.2% alc by vol. seasonal ale brewed by the Brewery On Sea, Lancing, West Sussex.

Big Finish (Eng) a 9% alc by vol. strong ale brewed by Hobdens Wessex Brewery, Wiltshire.

Biggles Finale (Eng) the last high gravity cask beer brewed by Greene King at Biggelswade in Bedfordshire before a change over to lager production.

Bigi [Luigi and Figlio] (It) noted wine-producers in Tuscany and Umbria.

Big Indian (USA) a natural spring mineral water.

Big John's Chocolate Flavoured American Soda Pop (USA) a chocolate-flavoured, non-alcoholic drink produced by Vimto.

Big Lamp Bitter (Eng) a 1038–1040 O.G. hoppy bitter beer brewed by the Big Lamp Brewery, Tyneside.

Big Lamp Brewery (Eng) a brewery (established 1982) (Add): Grange Road, Newburn, Newcastle-upon-Tyne, Tyne & Wear NE15 8NL. Produces: Best Bitter 1040 O.G. Big Lamp Bitter 1038-1040 O.G., Extra Special 1052 O.G. Old Genie 1070 O.G. Blackout 11% alc by vol., Prince Bishop Ale and Summerhill Stout. Website: http://www.biglampbrewers.co.uk 'E'mail: admin@biglampbrewers.co.uk

Big Nev (Eng) a 3.8% alc by vol. cask-conditioned ale brewed by the Six Bells Brewery, Bishop's Castle, Shropshire.

Bigny (Fr) an alternative name for the Merlot grape.

Bigot (Fr) a vineyard worker's two pronged hoe.

Big Ranch Road Vineyard (USA) part of the Beringer Vineyards based in California.

Big Red (Eng) a 4.5% alc by vol. ale brewed by the Wolf Brewery, Norfolk.

Big Six Collection (S.Afr) the label for a range of red and white wines marketed by the Old Bridge Wines company, Western Cape.

Big 'T' (Scot) the brand-name of a blended Scotch whisky produced by the Tomatin Distillery C°.

Big Tackle (Eng) a 4.1% alc by vol. dark seasonal ale brewed by Ridleys of Essex. Available in October for the 1999 Rugby World Cup.

Big Time Soft Drinks Ltd (Eng) a still and carbonated, non-alcoholic drinks manufacturer (established 1988). (Add): Unit 20, Culwell Trading Estate, Woden Road, Wolverhampton, West Midlands WV10 0PG. Website: http://www.bigtimesoftdrinks.co.uk 'E'mail: info@bigtimesoftdrinks.co.uk

Big Tom (Eng) a bottled spicy tomato drink that contains 22 ingredients including celery, lemon, Worcestershire sauce and spices.

Biguine (Cktl) ½ measure mango jus, ¼ pineapple juice, ⅛ schrubb, ⅛ Cognac. Shake over ice and strain into a highball glass.

Bihosteleagd (Rum) a wine-producing district in the Siebenbürgen region.

BII (Eng) abbr: The British Institue of Innkeeping.

Biiru (Jap) beer.

Bijeli Klikun (Cro) a white wine produced near Vukovar in south-eastern Croatia.

Bijeli Pinot (Cro) the local name for the Pinot blanc grape.

Bijelo (Cro) white.

Bijou Cocktail (Cktl) 20mls (⅙ gill) Plymouth dry gin, 20mls (⅙ gill) Italian vermouth, 20mls (⅙ gill) Green Chartreuse, dash orange bitters. Stir over ice, strain into cocktail glass, add an olive and a cherry. Squeeze of lemon peel on top.

Bikarr (Scan) an old Norse word for beaker or jug.

Bikavér (Hun) see Egri Bikavér.

Bikers' Coolant (USA) a natural spring mineral water from Ashcamp, Kentucky.

Bikos (Gre) beaker/jug.

Bilbainas (Sp) see Bodegas Bilbainas.

Bilberry Grog (Cktl) 75mls (3fl.ozs) Scotch whisky, 75mls (3fl.ozs) bilberry juice, 75mls (3fl.ozs) water. Heat gently, stirring constantly. When nearly boiling pour into a mug containing 10gms (½ oz.) poached bilberries. Serve with a cinnamon stick and slice of orange.

Bildberg (Ger) vineyard (Anb): Pfalz. (Ber): Südliche Weinstrasse. (Gro):Trappenberg. (Vil): Freimersheim.

Bildstock (Ger) vineyard (Anb): Rheinhessen. (Ber): Nierstein. (Gro): Spiegelberg. (Vil): Nierstein.

Bildstock (Ger) vineyard (Anb): Rheinhessen. (Ber): Wonnegau. (Gro): Liebfrauenmorgen. (Vil): Worms.

Bilecik (Tur) a vineyard based in the Thrace and Marmara region. Produces red wines.

Bilfingen (Ger) village (Anb): Baden (Ber): Badische Bergstrasse/Kraichgau. (Gro): Hohenberg. (Vin): Klepberg.

Bilge (Eng) the bottom of a beer cask where the sediment is retained as the beer is drawn off.

Bilge Beer Brewery (Eng) a brewery based at West Byfleet, Surrey. Promotes the Hacker Pschorr Premium beer range.

Bilina Brewery (Czec) a brewery (established 1674) in north-west Czec.

Bilinska Kyselka (Czec) a sparkling natural mineral water (established 1664) from Bilina. Mineral contents (milligrammes per litre): Sodium 1743mg/l, Calcium 133.8mg/l, Magnesium 45.14mg/l, Potassium 90.76mg/l, Bicarbonates 4471mg/l, Chlorides 230.1mg/l, Sulphates 574mg/l, Silicates 52.1mg/l, Fluorides 4.48mg/l, Lithium 3.67mg/l.

Billabong Brewery (Austr) a brewery. (Add): 72a McCoy, St. Myaree, Perth 6154. Brews a variety of beers and lager. Website: http://www.billabongbrewing.com.au 'E'mail: sales@billabongbrewery.com.au

Billardet (Fr) a cuvée in the Les Arvelets 0.4ha. Les Noizons 0.5ha. Les Rugiens 0.33ha. and Petits-Epenots 0.66ha. Premier Cru vineyards in the A.C. Pommard, Côte de Beaune, Burgundy. Owned by the Hospices de Beaune.

Bill Brewer (Eng) a low alcohol mild ale, less than 1% alc by vol. from the Harvey Brewery in Lewes, East Sussex.

Billecart-Salmon (Fr) a Champagne producer. (Add): 40, Rue Carnot, Mareuil-sur-Aÿ, 51160, Aÿ. A Grande Marque. Produces vintage and non-vintage wines. Vintages: 1971, 1973, 1975, 1976, 1978, 1979, 1982, 1983, 1985, 1986, 1987, 1988, 1989, 1990, 1996, 1998, 2001. Brand labels include Crémant des Moines, Rosé Millésimé, Cuvée Nicolas François Billecart, Cuvée Elisabeth Salmon (a prestige cuvée).

Billes (Fr) small balls made of neutral alginate used

B

in the Champagne region. Are porous and trap the yeasts, deposits and any cloudiness in the Champagne bottle. Help to shorten the length of time of the remuage. Still under trial.

Billetal Quelle (Ger) a natural mineral water from Reinbek bei Hamburg. Mineral contents (milligrammes per litre): Sodium 14mg/l, Calcium 85.6mg/l, Magnesium 5.7mg/l, Bicarbonates 217mg/l, Chlorides 23.3mg/l, Sulphates 6mg/l.

Bill Gibb (Cktl) 50mls (2fl.ozs) Beefeater gin, 100mls (4fl.ozs) fresh orange juice, dash egg white. Shake with ice, strain into a highball glass, add 25mls (1fl.oz) Mandarine Napoléon, decorate with slice of orange and a cherry. Do not stir and serve with straws.

Billigheim-Ingenheim (Ger) village (Anb): Pfalz. (Ber): Südliche Weinstrasse. (Gro): Kloster Liebfrauenberg. (Vins): Mandelpfad, Pfaffenberg, Rosenberg, Sauschwänzel, Steingebiss, Venusbuckel.

Billiot Fils [H.] (Fr) a Champagne producer. (Add):1 Place de la Fontaine, Ambonnay, Marne. 100% Grand Cru.

Bill's Bevy (Eng) a cask-conditioned beer 1037 O.G. brewed by the Finnesko and Firkin, a home-brew public house in Dereham Road, Norwich. (Formerly known as the Reindeer Brewery).

Bill's Spring Brew (Eng) a strong seasonal ale from the Morland Brewery in Oxfordshire. Named after a retiring brewman in 1996.

Billur Su (Tur) a still natural spring mineral water (established 1967) from Mount Aydin. Mineral contents (milligrammes per litre): Sodium 0.5mg/l, Calcium 1.2mg/l, Magnesium 0.2mg/l, Chlorides 6.37mg/l, Nitrates 7.4mg/l, Fluorides 0.07mg/l. pH 7.1

Billy Hamilton (Cktl) ⅓ measure (brown) crème de cacao, ⅓ measure brandy, ⅓ measure orange curaçao, dash egg white. Shake over ice and strain into a cocktail glass.

Billy-le-Grand (Fr) a Premier Cru Champagne village in the Canton de Suippes. District: Châlons.

Billy's Pooch (Eng) alcoholic lemonade produced by Aston Manor, Birmingham.

Billy Taylor Cocktail (Cktl) 1 measure gin, juice ½ lime. Stir over ice, strain into an ice-filled highball glass and top with soda water.

Biltmore Company (USA) a winery based in Ashville, North Carolina. Produces French-American hybrid wines.

Bilton Estate (S.Afr) a winery (established 1998) based in Lynedoc, Stellenbosch region, Western Cape. 80ha. Grape varieties: Cabernet sauvignon. Merlot, Shiraz. Website: http://www.biltonwines.com

Bilyara Vineyards (Austr) a winery. (Add): P.O. Box. 396, Nuriootpa, South Australia 5355. 45ha. Produces varietal wines.

Bin (Austr) a name often used for a special 'cuvée' of wine (not a blend) usually given a number or name.

Bin (Eng) a slot for holding a bottle of wine horizontally in a cellar. see Bin Label and Bin Number.

Bin (Jap) bottle.

Binary Fission (Eng) the term given to the method of reproduction which yeast may use to multiply. One cell divides into two, those two into four and so on. Needs warmth, food, moisture and time (20 minutes per division (approximately) depending on temperature) to reproduce.

Binau (Ger) village (Anb): Baden. (Ber): Badische Bergstrasse/Kraichgau. (Gro): Stiftsberg. (Vin): Herzogsberg.

Binaymina (Isr) a dry rosé wine produced mainly for the USA market.

Binding Brauerei (Ger) a brewery (established 1870) based in Frankfurt, Germany. Noted for Binding Lager 4.5% alc by vol., Clausthaler and Birell beers.

Bine (Eng) the hop plant climbing stem made of twine.

Binelli-Mesthé (Fr) an Armagnac producer. (Add): 29 Rue Thierry Cazes, 32500-Fleurance.

Bin Ends (Eng) small lots of wines sold off by wine merchants at a reduced cost because the lot is too small to include on new list.

Bin Eng (Ger) small storage place for bottles of wine in a cellar.

Bin Fifty 50 (S.Afr) the label for a range of wines produced by the Swartland Wine Cellar winery, Swartland, Western Cape.

Bing (Chi) ice.

Bing (Eng) a 4.8% alc by vol. ale brewed by the Engineer Arms Brewery, Bedfordshire.

Binge Drinking (Eng) a modern slang term to denote heavy drinking bouts especially amongst the late teenage to mid-twenties age group.

Bingen (Ger) bereich (Anb): Rheinhessen. (Gros): Abtel (Abtey), Adelsberg, Kaiserpfalz, Kurfürstenstück, Rheingrafenstein, Sankt Rochuskapelle.

Bingen (Ger) village (Anb): Rheinhessen. (Ber): Bingen. (Gro): Sankt Rochuskapelle. (Vins): Bubenstück, Kapellenberg, Kirchberg, Osterberg, Pfarrgarten, Rosengarten, Scharlachberg, Schelmenstück, Schlossberg-Schwätzerchen.

Bingen-Bingerbrück (Ger) village (Anb): Nahe. (Ber): Kreuznach. (Gro): Schlosskapelle. (Vins): Abtei Ruppertsberg, Hildegardisbrünnchen, Klostergarten, Römerberg.

Bingen Pencil (Ger) the name for a corkscrew in the Rheinhessen. Derived from when the Burgermeister of Bingen asked for a pencil at a council meeting but no one offered one. When later he produced some wine and asked for a corkscrew, everyone present offered him one!

Bingen Wine Cellars (USA) see Mount Elise Vineyards.

Bingerberg (Ger) vineyard (Anb): Rheinhessen. (Ber): Bingen. (Gro): Adelberg. (Vil): Flonheim.

Binger Rochusberg (Ger) a fine white wine produced in Bingen Rheinhessen.

Bingerweg (Ger) vineyard (Anb): Nahe. (Ber): Kreuznach. (Gro): Schlosskapelle. (Vil): Waldlaubersheim.

Bibifaldo (Sp) a still natural spring mineral water from the Font des Pedregaret y Binifaldo, Escorca, Balearic Islands. Mineral contents (milligrammes per litre): Sodium 10.8mg/l, Calcium 53.7mg/l, Magnesium 3.4mg/l, Potassium 0.7mg/l, Chlorides 22.1mg/l, Sulphates 22mg/l, Nitrates 1.6mg/l.

Binissalem-Mallorca (Sp) a D.O. wine-producing region on Majorca, Balearic Isles. 305ha. Grape varieties: Manto negro (min. 50%), plus Callet, Monastrell, Tempranillo (red), Moll (min. 70%) plus Macabeo, Parellada (white). Red, rosé and white wines are produced.

Bin Label (Eng) a label used to denote what wine is in a particular 'bin' to save disturbing the bottle. Has the name of wine, vintage, shipper, etc.

Binning (Eng) the storing of wines in a cellar for development.

Bin Number (Eng) the number found on wine lists to denote which 'bin' the wine is held in. Also helps customers in that they do not have to pronounce the name.

Binson-Orquigny (Fr) a Cru Champagne village in the Canton de Châtillon-sur-Marne. District: Reims.

Bintang Brewery (E.Ind) a brewery based in Surabaja, Java which brews a pilsener-style beer 5% alc by vol.

Bin-3 (S.Afr) the label for a red wine (Cabernet sauvignon, Merlot and Pinotage blend) produced by the Kaapzicht Estate winery, Stellenbosch, Western Cape.

Binzen (Ger) village (Anb): Baden. (Ber): Markgräflerland. (Gro): Vogtei Rötteln. (Vin): Sonnhohle.

Bio Beer (Ind) see Lady Bird Bio Beer.

Bío-Bío (Chile) a noted wine-producing province and river based in the Southern Zone.

Biodynamic (Fr) a system of cultivation from an idea created by Rudolf Steiner in 1924 in which the lunar and other cosmic events influence vineyard and wine-making activities. The main aim is to enable a vineyard to express its personality through the grapes it produces without chemical intervention with herbicides or artificial fertilisers.

Bioethanol (Euro) the name given by the EC to the alcohol distilled from the EC 'wine lake' to be used as fuel for cars.

Biography (S.Afr) the label for a red wine (Shiraz) produced by the Raka winery, Walker Bay, Western Cape.

Biokovka (Cro) a sparkling natural mineral water from Makarska. Mineral contents (milligrammes per litre): Sodium 141mg/l, Calcium 14.2mg/l, Magnesium 7.8mg/l, Potassium 1.53mg/l, Chlorides 200mg/l, Sulphates 33mg/l, Nitrates 0.428mg/l.

Bioleve (Bra) a natural spring mineral water (established 1994). Mineral contents (milligrammes per litre): Sodium 4.59mg/l, Calcium 36.72mg/l, Magnesium 33.33mg/l, Potassium 6.66mg/l, Chlorides 0.44mg/l, Nitrates 2.22mg/l, Fluorides 0.02mg/l. pH 7.0

Biologique (Fr) organic. see Latte Intégrée.

Biondi (It) a winery based on the island of Sicily. Label: Outis.

Biondi-Santi (It) a winery house on the Greppo estate at Montalcino in Tuscany. Noted for Brunello wines. Also 100% Sangiovese red Vino da Tavola called Sassoalloro.

Bior (Ger) the high German word for beer.

Biotáille Úll (Ire) apple brandy.

Biotin (Eng) a vitamin found in minute traces in wine.

Biou (Fr) the name given to the gigantic bunch of grapes that is carried during the procession of the Fête du Biou held annually in Arbois, Jura, eastern France.

Bio Vive (Fr) a natural spring mineral water from Dax. Mineral contents (milligrammes per litre): Sodium 3mg/l, Calcium 172mg/l, Magnesium 32mg/l, Potassium 22mg/l, Bicarbonates 2mg/l, Chlorides 15mg/l, Sulphates 8mg/l, Nitrates 126mg/l. pH 7.7

Bir (Indo) beer.

Bira (Gre)(Tur) beer/ale.

Birac (Fr) a commune in the Charente département whose grapes are classed Petite Champagne (Cognac).

Bira Fabrikasi (Tur) brewery.

Birahane (Tur) public house/bar. See also Bar.

Birbaum (Aus) a vineyard area on the banks of the River Danube in the Kremstal region.

Bir Bintang (E.Ind) a lager beer brewed in the Dutch-style in Jakarta, Indonesia.

Birch Wine (Eng) a fermented wine produced from birch sap, sugar, water, yeast and dry white wine in Sussex.

Birdfield (S.Afr) a range of wines produced by the Klawer Wine Cellar in Olifantsriver. Noted for Pinotage wine which is aged in small American oak barrels.

Bird Goldings (Eng) a variety of hop. see Mathon Goldings.

Bird in Hand (Austr) a vineyard 30ha (established 1997) based in the Adelaide Hills. Grape varieties: Cabernet sauvignon, Merlot, Pinot noir, Sauvignon blanc, Sémillon. Labels: Two in the Bush, Nest Egg. Website: http://www.OlivesOilWine.com

Bird of Paradise Fizz (Cktl) 1 measure gin, juice ½ lemon, 1 teaspoon powdered sugar, 4 dashes grenadine, 1 egg white. Shake over ice, strain into an ice-filled highball glass. Top with soda water.

Bir Drassen (Afr) a wine co-operative based in Tunisia. Owned by the UCCVT.

Birdwood Vineyards (N.Z) old established vineyards based in Birdwood, Henderson, Auckland.

Bire (Ch.Isles) beer/ale.

Birell Lager (Ger) a low alcohol lager 0.5% alc by vol. brewed by Binding Brauerei in Frankfurt, west Germany.

Birell Lager (Switz) a low-alcohol lager 0.8% alc by vol. brewed by Hurlimann Brauerei.

Bir'er (Ch.Isles) brewer.

Birgy (Ger) a natural mineral water from Bielefeld, NW. Mineral contents (milligrammes per litre): Sodium 117mg/l, Calcium 59.8mg/l, Magnesium 4.3mg/l, Potassium 5.4mg/l, Bicarbonates

348mg/l, Chlorides 70.5mg/l, Sulphates 42mg/l, Fluorides 1.9mg/l.

Birkenberg (Ger) vineyard (Anb): Nahe. (Ber): Kreuznach. (Gro): Pfarrgarten. (Vil): Sommerloch.

Birkenberg (Ger) vineyard (Anb): Nahe. (Ber): Schloss Böckelheim. (Gro): Rosengarten. (Vil): Roxheim.

Birkenhead (S.Afr) a brewery. (Add): P.O. Box 530, Stanford 7210 South Africa. Brews a variety of beers and lager. Website: http://www.birkenhead.co.za 'E'mail: chrisg@birkenhead.co.za

Birkmyer Vineyard (USA) a small vineyard in the Napa Valley, California. Grape variety is mainly Johannisberg riesling.

Birkweiler (Ger) village (Anb): Pfalz. (Ber): Südliche Weinstrasse. (Gro): Königsgarten. (Vins): Kastanienbusch, Mandelberg, Rosenberg.

Birkwoods (Eng) *see* WF6 Brewing C°., West Yorkshire. Beers include: Birkwoods Boulevard, Festive Fuel, January Ales, Original, St. Georges Day and Time.

Birl (Eng) a sixteenth century word for applying a person with drink.

Birnengeist (Ger) a pear liqueur (an eau-de-vie).

Birnenwasser (Ger) an eau-de-vie de poire.

Biron (Fr) a commune in the Charente-Maritime département whose grapes are classed Petite Champagne (Cognac).

Birra (It) beer/ale.

Birra Bellinzona Brewery (Switz) an independent brewery based in Bellinzona. Produces fine beers. *see* Chic.

Birra di Marzo (It) a bock beer.

Birra Doppio Malto (Eng) an all-malt, strong, pale ale brewed by the Gales Brewery in Horndean, Hampshire for the Italian market.

Birra Friulana (It) a 4.5 % alc by vol. pilsener lager from Moretti.

Birraio (It) a brewer who brews ales and lager beers.

Birra Menabrea (It) a brewery (established 1846) based in Biella, producers of Menabrea Birra Lager 4.8% alc by vol.

Birra Moretti (It) a brewery (established 1859) based in San Giorgo Di Nogaro, Udine. Brews Birri Moretti 4.6% alc by vol. and Baffo d'Oro. Owned by Heineken. Website: http://www.birramoretti.co.uk

Birra Stelvio Sri (It) a brewery. (Add): Via Roma 27, 23100 Bormio SO. Brews a variety of beers and lager. Website: http://www.birrastelvio.it 'E'mail: info@birrastelvio.it

Birrell (Eng) a low-alcohol lager brewed by the Watney Brewery.

Birreria (It) brewery. *See also* Fabbrica di Biarra.

Birresborner (Ger) a natural spring mineral water from Birresborn, R.P. Mineral contents (milligrammes per litre): Sodium 530mg/l, Calcium 110mg/l, Magnesium 80mg/l, Potassium 30mg/l, Bicarbonates 2080mg/l, Chlorides 40mg/l, Sulphates 20mg/l.

Birrificio Cittavecchia (It) a brewery. (Add): Via Stazione di Prosecco, 5/c 34010 Sgonico, Trieste. Brews a variety of beers and lager. Website: http://www.cittavecchia.com

Birrificio Italiano (It) a brewery. (Add): Nuovo Birrificio Italiano, Srl Via Castello 51, 22070 Lurago Marionone. Brews a variety of beers and lager. Website: http://www.birrificio.it 'E'mail: birrificio@birrificio.it

Birrificio Starbess (It) a brewery. (Add): Via Passaglia N° 1, Roma. Brews a variety of beers and lager. Website: http://www.starbess.it

Birrifico Torino (It) a brewery. (Add): via Parma 30, 10152bTorino. Brews a variety of beers and lager. 'E'mail: info@birrificio.com

Birr'rie (Ch.Isles) brewery.

Birstono Versme (Lit) a natural spring mineral water from Birstonas.

Birthday Brew (Eng) a premium ale brewed by Caythorpe Brewery, Hoveringham.

Birute (Lit) a natural spring mineral water from Birstonas. Mineral contents (milligrammes per litre): Sodium 736mg/l, Calcium 290mg/l, Magnesium 128mg/l, Bicarbonates 245mg/l, Chlorides 1988mg/l, Sulphates 460mg/l.

Bisamberg (Aus) a wine-producing area based with noted vineyards on the left bank of the river Danube in the Wien region.

Biscal (Port) a white grape variety grown in Bairrada.

Biscardo (It) a noted wine producer of Bardolino. (Add): 37010, Calmasino di Bardolino, Verona.

Bisceglia (It) a wine estate (30ha) based in the district of Lavello in the Basilicata region. (Add): Azienda Agricola Bisceglia S.R.L. Basilicata, Italy. Produces D.O.C. Aglianico del Vulture, IGT Chardonnay, IGT Armille, IGT Tréje, IGT Vulcano.. Website: http://www.agricloabisceglia.com 'E'mail: info@agricolabisceglia.com

Bisceglia Bros (USA) a winery based in San Joaquin, California.

Bischof (Fr) *see* Bishop (cocktail).

Bischoff (Scan) *see* Bishop (cocktail).

Bischoffingen (Ger) village (Anb): Baden. (Ber): Kaiserstuhl-Tuniberg. (Gro): Vulkanfelsen. (Vins): Enselberg, Rosenkranz, Steinbuck.

Bischof Frappé (Fr) *see* Iced Bishop.

Bischöfliches Weingut (Ger) a Mosel-Saar-Ruwer estate based at Trier. 94.5ha. of vineyards at Ayl, Eitelsbach, Kasel, Piesport, Scharzhofberg, Trittenheim, Ürzig and Wiltingen.

Bischofsberg (Ger) vineyard (Anb): Franken. (Ber): Mainviereck. (Gro): Not yet assigned. (Vil): Grossheubach.

Bischofsberg (Ger) vineyard (Anb): Rheingau. (Ber): Johannisberg. (Gro): Burgweg. (Vil): Rüdesheim.

Bischofsgarten (Ger) vineyard (Anb): Pfalz. (Ber): Mittelhaardt-Deutsche Weinstrasse. (Gro): Schepfenflug an der Weinstrasse. (Vil): Forst.

Bischofsgarten (Ger) vineyard (Anb): Pfalz. (Ber): Mittelhaardt-Deutsche Weinstrasse. (Gro): Schnepfenflug an der Weinstrasse. (Vil): Friedelsheim.

Bischofsgarten (Ger) vineyard (Anb): Pfalz. (Ber): Mittelhaardt-Deutsche Weinstrasse. (Gro): Schnepfenflug an der Weinstrasse. (Vil): Wachenheim.

Bischofshub (Ger) vineyard (Anb): Mittelrhein. (Ber): Bacharach. (Gro): Schloss Stahleck. (Vil): Oberdiebach.

Bischofskreuz (Ger) grosslagen (Anb): Pfalz. (Ber): Südliche Weinstrasse. (Vils): Böchingen, Burrweiler, Dammheim, Flemlingen, Gleisweiler, Knöringen, Nussdorf, Roschbach, Walsheim.

Bischofsquelle (Ger) a natural spring mineral water from Dodow, MV.

Bischofstein (Ger) vineyard (Anb): Mosel-Saar-Ruwer. (Ber): Zell/Mosel. (Gro): Weinhex. (Vil): Burgen.

Bischofstuhl (Ger) vineyard (Anb): Mosel-Saar-Ruwer. (Ber): Zell/Mosel. (Gro): Goldbäumchen. (Vil): Cochem.

Bischofsweg (Ger) vineyard (Anb): Pfalz. (Ber): Mittelhaardt-Deutsche Weinstrasse. (Gro): Meerspinne. (Vil): Mussbach.

Bisci (It) a winery in the D.O.C. Verdicchio di Matelica, Marches region. Label: Vigneto Fogliano.

Biscoitos (Port) a DOC region on the island of Terceira in the Azores.

Biscuity (Eng) a term used to describe the bouquet in some sparkling wines. Derived from acetaldehydes owing to age in bottle or vinification method. Term can also apply to pasteurised beers.

Biser (Slov) sparkling.

Bishop (Cktl) juice ½ an orange, 2 dashes lemon juice, tablespoon powdered sugar, 1 wine-glass soda water. Dissolve together in a tall glass, half fill with ice, and top with red Burgundy. Stir, add a little dark rum. Garnish with fruits in season and serve with drinking straws.

Bishop (Eng) mulled Port, the Port is heated up with sugar, oranges, cloves and set alight before it is served. See also Archbishop. (Scan) = bischoff.

Bishop Brewery (Eng) a brewery (established 1984) based in Somerset. Produces Bishop's PA. 1037 O.G. and Bishop's Best Bitter 1041 O.G.

Bishop Fugger (It) see Fugger [Bishop].

Bishop of Riesling Moselle (Ger) a medium-dry, white, QbA wine produced by Rudolph Müller.

Bishop Potter Cocktail (Cktl) ¼ measure vermouth, ¼ measure sweet vermouth, ½ measure dry gin, 2 dashes orange bitters, 2 dashes Calisaya. Shake well over ice, strain into a cocktail glass.

Bishop's Ale (Eng) a strong barley wine 1080 O.G. from Ridley's Brewery, Essex.

Bishop's Anger (Eng) a strong bottled ale 1053 O.G. brewed by Shepherd Neame Brewery, Kent.

Bishop's Brewery (Eng) a brewery based in London. Brews: Thirsty Willy 3.7% alc by vol. Willy's Revenge 4.7% alc by vol.

Bishop's Cream (Eng) a nitrokeg beer brewed by Shepherd Neame, Kent. see Master Brew Smooth, Casey's Cream.

Bishop's Farewell (Eng) a 4.6% alc by vol. ale brewed by Oakham Ales, cambridgeshire.

Bishop's Finger (Eng) a 4.5% alc by vol. (1053 O.G.) bottled or draught beer from Shepherd Neame Brewery, Kent.

Bishop's Formula (Eng) the name given to a way of predicting the extracts from a brew in brewing. Named after the inventor Dr. Laurence Bishop.

Bishops Gold (Eng) a 4.5% alc by vol. ale brewed by The Durham Brewery Ltd., County Durham.

Bishop's Tipple [The] (Eng) a sweet barley wine 6.5% alc by vol. (1066 O.G.) brewed by Gibbs Mews Brewery, Salisbury.

Bishop's Tipple [The] (Eng) a 5.2% alc by vol. ale brewed by the Usher Brewery.

Bishop's Tipple [The] (Eng) a 5.5% alc by vol. draught bitter brewed by the Wadworth Brewery.

Bishopswood Bitter (Wal) a 4.3% alc by vol. bitter beer brewed by the Swansea Brewing C°., West Glamorgan.

Bisingar et Cie (Fr) a Champagne producer. (Add): Aÿ, Marne. Produces non-vintage wines.

Biskirchener Karlssprudel (Ger) a natural spring mineral water from Leun-Biskirchen, HE. Mineral contents (milligrammes per litre): Sodium 569mg/l, Calcium 169mg/l, Magnesium 62mg/l, Potassium 26.1mg/l, Bicarbonates 1340mg/l, Chlorides 592mg/l, Sulphates 32.3mg/l, Silicates 9.2mg/l, Fluorides 0.6mg/l.

Bisleri (Ind) a still natural spring mineral water. Mineral contents (milligrammes per litre): Calcium 13.6mg/l, Magnesium 7.77mg/l, Bicarbonates 58mg/l, Chlorides 22mg/l, Sulphates 19.34mg/l, Nitrates 2mg/l. pH 7.2

Bismarck (USA) see Bismark.

Bismark (Eng) a mixture of equal quantities of chilled Champagne and Guinness. Also known as Black Velvet.

Bisol [Desiderio & Figli] (It) a producer of sparkling wines including DOC Prosecco di Valdobbiadene (metodo tradizionale) based in Veneto. Label: Cartizze.

Bisquit Dubouch (Fr) a Cognac producer. (Add): Ste. Ricard, Domaine de Ligneres, 16170 Rouillac. 200ha. in Fins Bois. Produce Extra Vieille Or. 40 year old.

Bisquit No1 (Fr) a long drink based on Cognac with lemon and guarana extract plus sparkling water.

Bisse (Switz) an aqueduct used for irrigating the vineyards in Valais.

Bisserheim (Ger) village (Anb): Pfalz. (Ber): Mittelhaardt-Deutsche Weinstrasse. (Gro): Schwarzerde. (Vins): Goldberg, Held, Orlenberg, Steig.

Bisseuil (Fr) a Premier Cru Champagne village in the Canton d'Aÿ. District: Reims.

Bissig (Ger) describes a wine with a strong tannin content, or a biting taste of acid.

Bissingen (Ger) village (Anb): Württemberg. (Ber): Württembergisch Unterland. (Gro): Schalkstein. (Vin): Neckarberg.

Bissinger Auerquelle (Ger) a natural spring mineral water from Auerquelle Tiefbrunnen 1, Bissingen/Schwaben, BY.

Bisson [Colonel] (Fr) an eighteenth century Colonel who made any of his troops 'present arms' when they passed the Clos de Vougeot vineyard in the Côte d'Or. The practice is still carried out today.

Bistra (Cro) a still natural spring mineral water. Mineral contents (milligrammes per litre): Sodium 1.8mg/l, Calcium 81.8mg/l, Magnesium 10.4mg/l, Potassium 0.8mg/l, Bicarbonates 298.9mg/l, Chlorides 1.6mg/l, Sulphates 2.5mg/l, Fluorides 0.06mg/l.

Bistra (Slo) a still natural spring mineral water. Mineral contents (milligrammes per litre): Sodium 9.5mg/l, Calcium 58.7mg/l, Magnesium 11.9mg/l, Potassium 0.9mg/l, Bicarbonates 252mg/l, Chlorides 1.5mg/l, Sulphates 2.3mg/l, Nitrates 2.2mg/l, Silicates 19.5mg/l. pH 7.5

Bistria (Rum) a wine-producing area noted for medium-dry, white wines.

Bistro (Fr) pub/café/tavern.

Bitartrates (Sp) found in Sherry, gypsum is added to convert insoluble tartrates which will settle out. They make the wine go cloudy.

Bitburger Brauerei Th. Simon GmbH (Ger) a brewery. (Add): Roemermauer 3, D-54634 Bitburg. Brews a variety of lager beers. Website: http://www.bitburger.de 'E'mail: info@bitburger.de

Bitburger Brewery (Eng) a brewery (established 1817). (Add): 114a Knighton Church Road, Leicester, Leicestershire LE2 3JH. Is a subsidiary of the Bitburger Brauerei Th. Simon GmbH. Brews a beers variety of lager beers. Website: http://www.bitburger.de

Bitburger Pils (Ger) a 4.6% alc by vol. premium pilsener lager brewed by the Simon Brauerei in Bitburg, Rhineland Palatinate.

Bite (Eng) a term given to the tannin taste of some red wines which are heavy in tannins.

Biter Cocktail (Cktl) 1 measure gin, ½ measure Green Chartreuse, ½ measure lemon juice, dash Absinthe, sugar syrup to taste. Shake over ice, strain into a cocktail glass.

Bite IPA (Eng) a 4.6% alc by vol. India pale ale brewed by the Newmans Brewery, Avon.

Bit O' Black (Eng) a dark ale brewed by the Steampacket Brewery in West Yorkshire. *See also* Bitter Blow.

Bit Of That (Eng) a 4.6% alc by vol. ale brewed by the Beckstones Brewery, Cumbria.

Bitola (Mac) a wine-producing district in Macedonia.

Bittall (Eng) the brand-name of a Port-based apéritif.

Bitter (Den) bitters.

Bitter (Eng) bad taste/unpleasant taste. (Fr) = amer, (It) = amaro/amarone, (Port) = acerbo/amargo, (Sp) = amargo.

Bitter (Ger)(Hol) bitter (beer).

Bitter Ale (Eng) a copper-coloured beer that has a high proportion of hops to give a bitter taste. O.G. between 1030 - 1055. The most popular of beers in Britain. (Ger) = bitter, (Hol) = bitter.

Bitter & Twisted (Scot) a 3.8% alc by vol. bottled bitter beer brewed by the Haviestoun Brewery, Clackmannanshire.

Bitter Blow (Eng) a 3.7% alc by vol. session ale from the Steampacket Brewery, Knottingley, West Yorkshire. Also known as Blow Job.

Bitter Chilled Cask (Eng) a chilled beer brewed by Brakspear, Henley-on-Thames.

Bitter Clout (Eng) a 4.6% alc by vol. bitter beer brewed by the Beckstones Brewery, Cumbria.

Bitter Curaçao (Fr) an apéritif made from Bitter Français, curaçao and soda water. Stir over ice, strain into a tall glass containing ice.

Bitter Disease (Eng) also known as Tourne. Occurs in low-alcohol, sweet wines. Is caused by lactic acid producing bacteria and leaves the wine tasting bitter. Prevented by using sulphite.

Bitter End [The] (Eng) a 5% alc by vol. cask-conditioned beer brewed to celebrate the end of the Century and the Millennium by Elgood's North Brink Brewery.

Bitter Experience (Eng) a 4% alc by vol. bitter beer brewed by the Storm Brewing C°., Cheshire.

Bitter Français (Fr) a noted French bitters.

Bitter Highball (Cktl) put 25mls (¼ gill) Angostura into an ice-filled highball glass. Top with soda water (or ginger ale). Dress with a spiral of lemon peel.

Bitter Hour (Hol) cocktail (apéritif) hour.

Bitterkeit (Ger) bitterness/sharpness.

Bitterl (Aus) lit: 'little bitter one', denotes a very sharp, bitter wine.

Bitter Lemon (Eng) a non-alcoholic sparkling 'mixer' that contains quinine.

Bitter Melon (Cktl) 1 part Midori, 4 parts bitter lemon, stir over ice in a highball glass.

Bitterness (Eng) an acrid taste, like the taste of aspirin or quinine. (Fr) = acerbité, (Lat) = acerbitas, (Port) = amargo, (Sp) = amargo, (Tur) = acilik.

Bitter Pineapple (Cktl)(Non-alc) 1 measure pineapple juice, juice ½ lemon, 3 dashes Angostura. Shake over ice, strain into a highball glass. Top with ginger ale.

Bitter Rosso (It) a dry apéritif from Martini and Rosso. Pink in colour. 25% alc by vol.

Bitters (Eng) spirits of varying alcoholic strengths, flavoured with roots and herbs. Having in common only their bitterness and their claim to medicinal powers. Used in cocktails. Abbot's Aged Bitters, Amer Picon, Angostura, Beerenburg, Boonkamp's, Campari, Catz Bitters, Champion Bitters, Fernet Branca, Law's Peach Bitters, Orange Bitters, Pommeranzen, Sécrestat, Toni Kola, Underberg, Unicum and Welling's are examples. (Den) = bitter.

Bitter Sécrestat (Fr) bitters.

Bitter Sharp (Eng) a cider apple species similar to the Bitter Sweet, but higher in acidity.

Bitters Highball (Cktl) place 10mls of selected bitters (½ fl.oz) into an ice-filled highball glass. Top with ginger ale or soda and twist of lemon peel.

Bitter Smooth (Eng) a 3.7% alc by vol. chilled bitter ale from Burtonwood Brewery, Warrington, Cheshire.

Bitter Smooth Brewed (Eng) a 4% alc by vol. nitrokeg bitter brewed by Marston Brewery, Burton-on-Trent.

Bitters Shaker (Eng) a glass decanter-shaped unit

with a hole in the base (used for re-filling). Is used for mixing bitters and spirits (mainly whisky).

Bitter Stout (Ire) a style of stout of which the Irish now produce the most. Beamish, Guinness and Murphy's are main breweries. Has between 4%–7.5% alc by vol.

Bitter Sweet [1] (Cktl) ½ measure gin, ¼ measure apricot brandy, ¼ measure Cerasella liqueur, ½ measure orange juice (sweet) or ¼ measure lemon juice (dry). Shake over ice and strain into a cocktail glass.

Bitter Sweet [2] (Cktl) ½ measure French vermouth, ½ measure Italian vermouth, dash orange bitters, dash Angostura. Stir over ice, strain into a cocktail glass. Add a twist of orange peel.

Bitter Sweet (Eng) a cider apple species of the West Country and West Midlands with a high acidity and plenty of sugar.

Bitter Sweet Orange (Cktl) 1 measure Yellow Izarra, 1 measure Campari, juice of orange. Shake over ice, strain into a cocktail glass.

Bitter-Sweet Punch (Punch) heat 1200mls (2pts) cider, 1 cinnamon stick, pinch grated nutmeg and 100gms (4ozs) cranberries until the berries burst. Add 450mls (¾ pt) red wine, bring almost to the boil, strain and serve.

Bittertropfen (Ger) lit: 'bitter drops', a herb liqueur used to season mixed drinks.

Bitzingen (Ger) village (Anb): Mosel-Saar-Ruwer. (Ber): Obermosel. (Gro): Gipfel. (Vin): Sites not yet chosen.

B.I.V.B. (Fr) *abbr*: **B**ureau **I**nterprofessionnel des **V**ins de **B**ourgogne.

Biyundong (Chi) a natural spring mineral water. Mineral contents (milligrammes per litre): Calcium 68mg/l, Magnesium 18.6mg/l, Bicarbonates 306.8mg/l, Chlorides 28.7mg/l. pH 7.5

Bizkaiko Txakolina (Sp) a 56ha. D.O. vineyard area in the province of Vizcaya in the zone of País Vasco. Grape variety used to produce white Txakoli is Ondarrabí Zurí. Ondarribí Beltza is used for red and rosé production. 80% of wine produced is white. All Txakoli wines are Jóvenes in style. Also known as Chacolí de Vizkaya.

Bizanet (Fr) a wine-producing village based in the Corbières district of the Languedoc.

Bizerta (Tun) a town around which is produced most of the wines of the country. *see* Cap Bon.

Bizzl Mineralwasser (Ger) a natural spring mineral water. Mineral contents (milligrammes per litre): Sodium 13.2mg/l, Calcium 62mg/l, Magnesium 10.8mg/l, Potassium 1.5mg/l, Bicarbonates 103mg/l, Chlorides 25.8mg/l, Sulphates 102mg/l. Website: http://www.hassia.com

Bizzy Izzy Highball (Cktl) 30mls (¼ gill) rye whiskey, 30mls (¼ gill) pale Sherry, dash lemon juice, sugar to taste. Mix well together, top up with ice cold soda water.

Bjalo Vino (Bul) white wine.

Björnbärslikör (Nor) blackberry liqueur.

Bjorr (Scan) an old norse word for beer.

Bjor-Reir (Ice) pleasantly intoxicated.

Blaauwklippen Agricultural Estate (S.Afr) a winery (established 1690) based in Stellenbosch, Western Cape. 80ha. (Add): Box 54, Stellenbosch 7600. Grape varieties: Cabernet franc, Cabernet sauvignon, Chenin blanc, Cinsaut, Gewürztraminer, Merlot, Muscat ottonel, Pinotage, Sauvignon blanc, Sémillon, Shiraz, Zinfandel. Labels: Barouche, Blaauwklippen, Landau, Vineyard Selection. Website: http://www.blaauklippen.com

Blacé (Fr) a commune in the Beaujolais. Has A.C. Beaujolais-Villages or A.C. Beaujolais-Blacé status.

Black Abbot (Eng) a 5.3% alc by vol. beer brewed by The Durham Brewery Ltd., County Durham.

Black Adder (Eng) a pilsner-style lager and cider mix that is blackcurrant-flavoured. 5.3% alc by vol. From the Aston Manor Brewery. *See also* Snake Bite.

Black Adder (Eng) a 5.3% alc by vol. ale brewed by Mauldon's Ltd., Suffolk.

Blackamoor Stout (Eng) a sweet stout 1044 O.G. brewed by Hardys and Hansons, Kimberley Brewery, Nottingham.

Black and Black (Eng) a mixture of Guinness and blackcurrant.

Black and Tan (Cktl) ½ measure sweet vermouth, ¼ measure pastis, ¼ measure crème de cassis. Shake over ice, strain into a cocktail glass. Top with a lemon slice.

Black and Tan (Eng) 300mls (½ pint) bitter ale, 300mls (½ pint) stout. Pour slowly together into glass (a dry stout such as Guinness is best). *See also* Black Dash.

Black and White (Scot) a blended Scotch whisky created by James Buchanan. Produced at their Glentauchers Distillery, Mulben, Speyside. 40% alc by vol.

Blackawton Brewery (Eng) a brewery (established 1977). (Add): Unit 7, Peninsular Park, Moorlands Trading Estate, Saltash, Cornwall PL12 6LX. Brews: Devon Best 1036 O.G. Blackawton Bitter 4.5% alc by vol. (1037 O.G.)., Dark Mild, Devon Gold 4.1% alc by vol., Headstrong 5.2% alc by vol. (1048 O.G.)., Original Bitter 3.8% alc by vol., Shepherd's Delight 4.6% alc by vol., Squires 1044 O.G., VE Commemorative Ale, West Country Gold 4.1% alc by vol., Winter Fuel 5% alc by vol. 'E'mail: info@blackawtonbrewery.com

Blackawton Bitter (Eng) a 4.5% alc by vol. bitter beer brewed by the Blackawton Brewery, Cornwall.

Black Baron (Eng) a 4.3% alc by vol. winter warmer beer produced by Greene King, East Anglia. Part of the Carlsberg-Tetley Tapster's Choice range.

Black Bear (Eng) a 5% alc by vol. porter brewed by the Beartown Brewery, Cheshire.

Black Beard (Ind) a lager beer 1044 O.G. brewed by the Vinedale Brewery, Hyderabad.

Black Beauty Eng) a 4.3% alc by vol. porter brewed by Vale Brewery, Buckinghamshire.

Black Beauty Stout (Eng) a 4.4% alc by vol. stout brewed by by the Old Stables Brewing Company, Bedfordshire.

Black Beck Strong (Eng) a 4.9% alc by vol. strong ale

B

brewed by the Beckstones Brewery, Cumbria.

Black Beer (Eng) a heavy malt beer from the Mather Brewery, Leeds. A bottled beer 7% alc by vol. If mixed with lemonade then called Sheffield Stout.

Blackberry Brandy (Eng) a liqueur made with blackberries, sugar and brandy. 20%–30% alc by vol.

Blackberry Flavoured Brandy (USA) a brandy-based liqueur infused with blackberries.

Blackberry Julep (It) an apéritif wine made for the USA market.

Blackberry Liqueur (USA)(Pol)(Ger) produced from blackberries by the maceration technique. Occasionally has a small amount of red wine added. 23% alc by vol.

Blackberry Nip (N.Z) a fortified wine produced by Mayfair Vineyards, Henderson, North Island.

Black Bess (Eng) a 4.2% alc by vol. dark porter from the Ash Vine Brewery, Trudoxhill, near Frome, Somerset.

Black Bess Stout (Eng) a bottled stout 1043 O.G. brewed by Timothy Taylor's Brewery, Yorkshire.

Black Bottle Scotch Whisky (Scot) a blended Scotch whisky produced by Gordon Graham and C°. Ltd., Westhorn, 1780 London Road, Glasgow G32. 8XA. Sold in a black glass bottle. Now part of Long John International.

Black Brandy (USA) a liqueur (grape) brandy.

Black Buffle Stout (Eng) a 4.5% alc by vol. stout brewed by the Spectrum Brewery, Norfolk.

Black Bull (Ind) a wood-aged, 5 year old rum distilled by the Ajudhia Distillery.

Black Bull Bitter (Eng) a 3.9% alc by vol. bitter beer brewed by the Ossett Brewing C°. Ltd., West Yorkshire.

Black Bull Bitter (Eng) a keg bitter 1035 O.G. brewed by Theakston, Masham, Ripon, Yorkshire.

Black Bull Cider (Eng) the brand-name of a cider produced by the Saffron Cider Company, Radwinter, Essex.

Black Bull Mild (Eng) a 3.6% alc by vol. mild ale brewed by the Blanchfield Brewery, Essex.

Blackburn Beer Company (Eng) a brewery (Add): Hornby Hotel, Blackburn, East Lancashire. The original Blackburn Beer Company was bought by Duttons of Blackburn in 1928. Duttons taken over by Whitbread in 1960's. (Whitbread never used the name).

Blackburn Brewing Company (Eng) a brewery that brews BBC1 light bitter 5.2% alc by vol., BBC2 darker bitter 3.8% alc by vol.

Black Bush (Ire) a soft de luxe Irish whiskey from the Bushmills Distillery. 8 years old. 40% alc by vol.

Black Cap (Eng) a 4.4% alc by vol. dry hopped ale brewed by HB Clark, Wakefield.

Black Cat (Eng) a 3.4% alc by vol. dark-style mild brewed by Moorhouse Brewery in Burnley, Lancashire.

Black Christmas (Eng) a 5.8% alc by vol. beer brewed by Whim Ales, Hartington, near Buxton, Derbyshire.

Black Cider (Eng) a 4.1% alc by vol. ale made from a blend of malt, hops and apples. Has a stout-like creamy head. Produced by Bulmers.

Black Cockerel (It) the D.O.C.G. seal logo for the Chianti Classico wines in Tuscany. see Gallo Nero.

Black Coffee (Eng) a hot coffee served without milk or cream. (Den) = kaffe uden fløde, (Rus) = chorni kofyeh.

Black Coral (Eng) a blackcurrant-flavoured rum produced by Lamb and Watt of Liverpool, Lancashire.

Black Country Ale (Eng) a bottled old ale 1052 O.G. brewed by the Simpkiss Brewery, West Midlands.

Black Country Bitter (Eng) a cask-conditioned bitter 1039 O.G. brewed by Holden Brewery.

Black Country Wobble (Eng) a 4.5% alc by vol. ale brewed by the Malvern Hills Brewery, Worcestershire.

Blackcurrant Liqueur (Fr) see Crème de Cassis.

Blackcurrant Stout (Wal) a 4% alc by vol. stout brewed by the Cwmbran Brewery, Gwent.

Blackcurrant Tea Cup (Cup) place into a punch bowl 300mls (½ pint) sparkling apple juice, 300mls (½ pint) white wine, 500mls (1pint) blackcurrant tea and the juice of 2 lemons. Stir with ice, dress with apple slices.

Black Dash (Austr) a mixed drink similar to a Black and Tan but with 350mls (⅗ pint) stout and 200mls (⅓ pint) beer. Popular in South Australia.

Black Death (Eng) the popular nickname for aquavit on the rocks.

Black Death (Ice) a schnapps presented in a wooden coffin. Launched by The Luxembourg Wine C°. The coffins are made by inmates of an Icelandic prison.

Black Death (Pol) a 40% alc by vol. vodka produced by the Sigurdsson family.

Black Devil Cocktail (Cktl) 1 measure dark rum, ¼ measure Italian vermouth. Stir over ice, strain into a cocktail glass. Dress with a black olive.

Black Diamond Porter (Eng) a 4.8% alc by vol. porter brewed by the Butterknowle Brewery, Lynesack, near Bishop Auckland, County Durham.

Black Dog (Eng) a 3.6% alc by vol. cask-conditioned classic dark mild from the Elgood North Brink Brewery, Wisbech, Cambs.

Black Dog Brewery (Eng) a brewery. (Add): St. Hilda's Business Centre, The Ropery, Whitby, North Yorkshire YO22 4EU. Brews a range of ales and beers. Website: http://www.synthesys.co.uk 'E'mail: blackdog@synthesys.co.uk

Black Douglas (Scot) a 5.2% alc by vol. dark, ruby red bottled ale brewed by Broughton Ales Brewery, Lanarkshire.

Blackdown Porter (Eng) a cask-conditioned dark beer from Eldridge Pope. 4% alc by vol.

Black Dragon (Wal) the brand-name of an own label strong dry cider sold in 1 and 2 litre PET bottles from Symonds (based in Cardiff). See also Gold Dragon, Red Dragon and Silver Dragon.

Black Eagle (Eng) a 5% alc by vol. bark ale brewed by the Pitfield Brewery (London) Ltd., London.

Black Eagle (S.Afr) the label for an organic white wine (Chenin blanc) produced by the Porterville Cellars winery, Swartland, Western Cape.

131

Black Eagle (S.Afr) a winery (established 2000) based in Piketberg, Western Cape. 40ha. Grape varieties: Chenin blanc, Colombard, Shiraz.

Black Eagle Brewery (Eng) a brewery based in Westerham, Kent that closed 1n 1965. Was owned by Friary Coope, Ind Coope and eventually by Allied Breweries.

Black Eagle Special Pale Ale (Eng) a 3.8% alc by vol. special pale ale brewed by the Westerham Brewery, C°., Kent.

Black Forest Cocktail (Cktl) ⅔ measure cherry brandy, ⅓ measure gin, dash maraschino. Shake over ice, strain into a cocktail glass.

Black Forest Girl (Ger) a well-known brand of fruity, white wine made from the Müller-Thurgau grape by the ZBW in Baden.

Black Forest Pearl (Ger) a natural spring mineral water from Hansjakobquelle, Bad Rippoldsau. Mineral contents (milligrammes per litre): Sodium 0.3mg/l, Calcium 3.2mg/l, Magnesium 3.8mg/l, Potassium 1.5mg/l, Bicarbonates 23.2mg/l, Chlorides 0.8mg/l, Sulphates 3mg/l.

Black Fox (Wal) a cask-conditioned bitter 1038 O.G. brewed by The Globe, a home-brew public house in Fishgard using malt extract.

Black Friar (Eng) a 5.3% alc by vol. beer brewed by Abbey Ales Brewery, Avon.

Blackfriars Distillery (Eng) produces Plymouth gin. The original Plymouth gin '*Coates*' infused with Italian juniper. The name is protected by law from injunctions in the 1880's.

Black Frost [The] (Bra) the name given to the devastating frost that occurred on 17th July 1975 (Black July) which almost destroyed the Brazilian Coffee industry and raised the World coffee prices. Also known as '*The Great Frost*'.

Black Glass (Eng) an expression that refers to the glass of the early bottles which were in fact olive green. Helped to hide the impurities the wine.

Black Gold (Eng) a 3.5% alc by vol. ale brewed by the Castle Rock Brewery, Nottinghamshire.

Black Gold (Eng) a 3.7% alc by vol. ale brewed by the Copper Dragon Skipton Brewery, North Yorkshire.

Black Gold (Fr) the name given to the volcanic cinder found in the soil of the Champagne region.

Black Gold (Scot) a 4.4% alc by vol. dark ale brewed by The Cairngorm Brewery C°. Ltd., Inverness.

Black Goo (USA) vine decline, vines are diseased during propagation. Sap darkens and development is stunted reducing crop yields.

Black Granite (S.Afr) the label for a red wine (Shiraz) produced by the Darling Cellars winery, Swartland.

Black Guard Porter (Eng) a 4.5% alc by vol. porter brewed by Butts Brewery Ltd., Berkshire.

Black Half Hour (Eng) the name given in the eighteenth century to the half hour before dinner when guests arrived. No drinks were served and so the '*apéritif*' was invented to break the ice.

Black Hamburg (Ger) an alternative name for the Trollinger grape.

Black Hawk (Cktl) ½ measure Bourbon whiskey, ½ measure sloe gin. Stir over ice, strain into cocktail glass. Top with a cherry.

Black Heart (Eng) a stout 4.6% alc by vol. from South Yorkshire Brewing Company, Elsecar, near Barnsley.

Black Heart (W.Ind) a dark Jamaican rum matured in England by United Rum Merchants.

Black Hermitage (Austr) a red claret-style wine made from the Syrah grape.

Black Hole (Eng) a 6% alc by vol. ale from the Star Brewery, Brighton (under the Dark Star brand). *see* Dark Star, Solstice.

Black Horse Ale (USA) an ale brewed by the Champale Brewery in Trenton.

Black Horse Ale (USA) an ale brewed by the Koch Brewery in Dunkirk.

Black Horse Bitter (Eng) a cask-conditioned bitter 1048 O.G. brewed by Godson's Brewery, London.

Black Isle Brewing Ltd (Scot) a brewery (established 1998). (Add): Old Allangrange, Munlochy, Ross-shire IV8 8NZ. Brews organic beers including: Black Isle Organic B C Scotch Ale 4.5% alc by vol., Black Isle Organic B C Wheat Beer 4.5% alc by vol., Black Isle Organic Blonde 4.5% alc by vol., Black Isle Organic Porter 4.5% alc by vol., Black Isle Organic Red Kite Ale 4.5% alc by vol., Black Isle Organic Yellow Hammer 4% alc by vol. Website: http://www.blackislebrewery.com 'E'mail: greatbeers@blackislebrewery.com

Black Jack (Cktl) ⅓ measure Cointreau, ⅓ measure Kahlúa, ⅓ measure Scotch whisky, dash lemon juice. Shake over ice, Strain into a cocktail glass.

Black Jack [1] (Eng) the name given to an eighteenth century leather drinking mug of 1pint (500mls) capacity used for cider or ale. Tarred to make it water tight.

Black Jack [2] (Eng) a bottle made of leather used in Tudor times for carrying and storing wine.

Black Jack (Eng) a 5% alc by vol. cider made from specially selected ciders with fermented hops and yeast by Bulmers in Hereford.

Blackjack Cocktail (Cktl) ⅜ measure kirsch, ⅜ measure strong black coffee, ⅛ measure brandy. Shake over ice, strain into an ice-filled old-fashioned glass.

Black John (Eng) a stout brewed by the Ledbury Brewery Company in Herefordshire.

Black Jock (Scot) a seasonal cask oat malt stout brewed by Maclay Brewery based in Alloa.

Black July (Bra) a black grape variety.

Black July (Bra) *see* Black Frost (The).

Black Knight (Eng) a classic winter porter, dark ruby-red in colour brewed by Goff's Brewery, Winchcombe, Gloucestershire.

Black Label (Austr) a red wine from the Seppelts Vineyard in South Australia.

Black Label (Scot) a top brand de luxe blended whisky 43% alc by vol. from Johnnie Walker.

Black Label-John Martin (S.Afr) the label for an oak-fermented, white wine (Sauvignon blanc) produced by the Backsberg Cellars, Suider-Paarl,

Western Cape.

Black Label Reserve (S.Afr) the label for a red wine (Cabernet sauvignon 30%, Pinotage 35% plus Cabernet franc and Merlot blend) produced by the L'Avenir Estate winery, Stellenbosch, Western Cape.

Black Magic (Cktl) 2 dashes Mandarine Napoléon, juice 2–3 grapes, dry sparkling wine. Pour grape juice and liqueur into Champagne flute. Top up with wine, decorate with 2 black grapes on side of rim.

Black Magic Cocktail (Cktl) 1 measure vodka, ½ measure Kahlúa, dash lemon juice. Stir over ice, strain into an ice-filled old-fashioned glass and top with a twist of lemon peel.

Black Magic (Eng) a 4.3% alc by vol. ale brewed by the Wizard Brewery, Warwickshire.

Blackmagic Mild (Eng) a 4% alc by vol. mild ale brewed by Hanby Ales Ltd., Shropshire.

Black Malt (Eng) a special dark roasted malted barley used to add colour to beer.

Black Malvoisie (Austr) an alternative name for the Cinsault grape.

Black Mammy (Cktl) 30mls (¼ gill) brandy, juice of a small grapefruit, juice of a lemon, 90mls (¾ gill) dark rum, 2 cloves, 3 dashes sugar syrup. Shake over ice, strain into a highball glass and decorate with orange and lemon peel.

Black Maria (Cktl) ¼ measure coffee liqueur, ½ measure dark rum, ¼ measure strong black coffee, sugar to taste, stir over ice and strain into a large balloon glass over ice.

Black Martini (Cktl) as for a Dry Martini but using a black olive in place of a green olive.

Bläck Mäx (Ger) a 4.9% alc by vol. schwarzbier (black beer) brewed by the Moritz Fiege Brauerei, Bochum.

Black Metz (W.Ind) a mixed bottled drink containing Bacardi and schnapps. *See also* Metz, Still Metz.

Black Monukka (USA) a white grape variety related to the Muscat grape. Used in the making of sweet fortified wines in California.

Black Moon Stout (Eng) a 4.8% alc by vol. stout brewed by the Three Rivers Brewing C°., Cheshire.

Black Mountain Liqueur (Wal) a 20% alc by vol. liqueur produced by the Celtic Spirit C°. based at Grove Farm, Abergavenny, Monmouthshire. Also known as Mynydd Da.

Black Mountain Spring Water (USA) a natural spring mineral water (established 1937). Mineral contents (milligrammes per litre): Sodium 8.3mg/l, Calcium 25mg/l, Magnesium 0.73mg/l, Potassium 0.67mg/l, Chlorides 10mg/l. pH 7.2

Black Mountain Vineyard (USA) a winery based in Alexander Valley, Sonoma County, California. Grape varieties: Chardonnay, Sauvignon blanc and Zinfandel. Produces varietal wines.

Black Mud (Eng) the nineteenth century nickname for Turkish Coffee.

Black Muscat (USA) a black grape variety grown in California. Also known as the Muscat Hamburg.

Black Muscat (USA) a red wine produced in California from the Black muscat grape.

Black Nikka (Jap) a brand of whiskey produced by the Nikka Distilleries.

Black Noble (Austr) a dessert wine produced by De Bortoli, New South Wales.

Black of Alexandria (S.Afr) an alternative name for the Muscat Hamburg grape.

Black Out (Eng) a 11% alc by vol. beer from the Big Lamp Brewery in Newcastle.

Black Oystercatcher (S.Afr) a winery (established 1998) based in Elim, Southern Cape. 14.5ha. Grape varieties: Cabernet sauvignon, Merlot, Sauvignon blanc, Sémillon, Shiraz.

Blackout Winter Warmer (Eng) a 5.5% alc by vol. dark ale brewed in December by the Cain Brewery, Stanhope Street, Liverpool.

Black Panther (Eng) a dark ale brewed by the Moorhouses Brewery (Burnley) Ltd., Lancashire.

Black Pear Premium Bitter (Eng) a 4.4% alc by vol. bitter beer brewed by the Malvern Hills Brewery, Worcestershire.

Black Pearl (Eng) a 4.3% alc by vol. dark ale brewed by the Milestone Brewery C°., Nottinghamshire.

Black Pearl (Eng) 5% alc by vol. ale brewed by the Port Mahon Brewery, South Yorkshire.

Black Pearl Cocktail (Cktl) ½ measure Cognac, ½ measure Tia Maria. Stir together over crushed ice in a tulip glass. Top with iced Champagne and dress with a black cherry.

Black Pearl Wines (S.Afr) a winery (established 1998) based in Suider-Paarl, Western Cape. 16ha. Grape varieties: Cabernet sauvignon, Shiraz. Website: http://wwwblackpearlwines.com

Black Pig Mild (Eng) a 3.6% alc by vol. mild ale brewed by the Bazens Brewery, Greater Manchester.

Blackpool Best Mild (Eng) a cask-conditioned mild 1036 O.G. brewed by Bass.

Black Porter (Eng) a 4.4% alc by vol. porter brewed by the Captain Cook Brewery, Cleveland.

Black Porter (Eng) a 5.3% alc by vol. porter from micro-brew pub Mash and Air, Manchester.

Black Prince (Eng) a 4% alc by vol. beer brewed by the St. Austell Brewery C° Ltd., Cornwall.

Black Prince (Scot) a blended Scotch whisky produced by the Burn Stewart Group under the Bols brand name.

Black Prince (USA) a white grape variety used in the making of dessert wines in California.

Black Prince Mild (Wal) a ruby-coloured cask dark mild beer 5% alc by vol. brewed by S.A. Brain & C°. Ltd. in Cardiff, South Wales.

Black Rat Cider (Eng) a 6.5% alc by vol. draught cider or 8.4% alc by vol. bottled cider produced by Moles Brewery, Melksham, Wiltshire. Also a traditional Black Rat (like a scrumpy).

Black Regent (Czec) a black lager 4.8% alc by vol. from Trebon.

Black Ridge Winery (N.Z) a winery. (Add): Conroys Road, P.O.Box 54, Alexandra. 8ha. Grape varieties: Cabernet sauvignon, Pinot noir, Chardonnay, Gewurztraminer, Riesling.

B

Black Rock (S.Afr) the label for a red wine (Shiraz 76% plus Carignan and Grenache blend) produced by The Winery, Stellenbosch, Western Cape.

Black Rock Ale (Scot) a 4.2% alc by vol. ale brewed by Islay Ales, Argyll.

Black Rock Stout (Eng) a 4.7% alc by vol. organic stout brewed by the Organic Brewery, Cornwall.

Black Rot (USA) a vine disease (fungal) of American origin. Causes the grapes to shrivel. Treated with Copper sulphate.

Black Russian (Cktl) place some ice into a tall glass, pour in 25mls (1fl.oz) coffee liqueur, 50mls (2fl.ozs) vodka, stirred together.

Black Sanglain Cabernet Sauvignon (Austr) a full-bodied red wine produced by the Setanta Vineyard, Adelaide Hills, South Australia.

Blacksberg (S.Afr) a winery based in the Paarl region. Grape varieties include: Cabernet sauvignon.

Black Sea (Eng) a vodka-based mixer drink from Berentzen Distillers, Hailsham, Sussex. See also Puschkin Red.

Black Seal (W.Ind) a noted brand of dark rum produced by the Wray and Nephew Group on the island of Jamaica.

Black Sheep (Cktl) 50mls (2fl.ozs) dry stout, 25mls (1fl.oz) Kahlúa, 25mls (1fl.oz) Glayva. Stir over ice, strain into an old-fashioned glass and float double cream on top.

Black Sheep Brewery [The] (Eng) a brewery (established 1992). (Add): Wellgarth, Masham, North Yorkshire HG4 4EN. Brews: Preview Ale 5.6% alc by vol. Best Bitter 3.8% alc by vol. Emmerdale Ale 4.2% alc by vol., Black Sheep Special 4.4% alc by vol. Riggwelter 5.9% alc by vol. Yorkshire Square Ale 5% alc by vol. and Holy Grail. Website: http://www.blacksheepbrewery.com 'E'mail: Patrick.green@blacksheep.co.uk

Black Sheep Best Bitter (Eng) a 3.8% alc by vol. cask ale brewed by Black Sheep Brewery, Masham, North Yorkshire.

Black Sheep Special (Eng) a 4.4% alc by vol. cask ale brewed by Black Sheep Brewery, Masham, North Yorkshire.

Blacksmith (Eng) 300mls (½ pint) Guinness and 200mls (⅓ pint) barley wine.

Blacksmith (S.Afr) the label for a non-vintage red wine produced by the Van Scoor Wines winery, Robertson, Western Cape.

Blacksmith Ale (Eng) a 5% alc by vol. ale brewed by the Coniston Brewing Company Ltd., Cumbria.

Blacksmith Cocktail (Cktl) ⅓ measure Drambuie, ⅓ measure crème de café, ⅓ measure Cognac. Stir over ice in an old-fashioned glass.

Black Soil (Fr) the soil from the floor of the Montagne de Reims forest, used to replace topsoil washed away in Champagne. see Black Gold.

Black Sombrero (Cktl) 1 measure Tia Maria placed into a narrow liqueur glass and float 1 measure of cream on top.

Black Spot (Euro) a vine disease of the leaf (fungal).

Black Stallion (Slo) a sweet red wine produced from the Vranac grape in the southern Titov Veles area.

Blackstone Cocktail (Cktl) 1 measure gin, ½ measure Italian vermouth, ½ measure French vermouth. Shake over ice, strain into a cocktail glass. Decorate with orange peel.

Blackstone Cooler (Cktl) 35mls (1½fl.ozs) Jamaican rum poured into an ice-filled highball, top soda water and decorate with lemon peel.

Blackstone Vineyards (USA) a winery based in the Dry Creek Valley, Sonoma County. Grape varieties include: Merlot, Petite sirah, Syrah.

Black Strap Stout (USA) a stout brewed by the Bridgeport Brewing Company, Portland, Oregon.

Blackstrap (W.Ind) the local name given to molasses mixed with rum.

Black Stripe (Cktl) dissolve 1 tablespoon of honey in a little hot water in a tumbler. When cool add 2 ice cubes, 90mls (¾ gill) dark rum and top with iced water. Stir, top with grated nutmeg and add a twist of lemon. Can also be served hot.

Black Stump (Eng) an ale brewed by the Barge & Barrel Brewing Company, Elland, near Halifax, West Yorkshire.

Black Swan (Eng) a 3.3% alc by vol. dark mild brewed by Vale Brewery, Buckinghamshire.

Black Tea (Eng) the designation for fully fermented teas, is the main and most popular tea style. Graded into: Broken Orange Pekoe, Fine Leaf Fannings, Flowery Orange Pekoe, Orange Pekoe, and Tippy Golden Flowery Orange Pekoe. Produces the darkest colour and flavoured teas.

Blackthorn Cidermaster (Eng) a premium strong cider from Matthew Clark in Somerset.

Blackthorn Cocktail [1] (Cktl) 20mls (⅙ gill) sloe gin, 20mls (⅙ gill) French vermouth, 20mls (⅙ gill) Italian vermouth, 1 dash orange bitters, 1 dash Angostura. Stir over ice, strain into a cocktail glass, add a squeeze of lemon peel juice on top.

Blackthorn Cocktail [2] (Cktl) 30mls (¼ gill) Irish whiskey, 30mls (¼ gill) French vermouth, 3 dashes absinthe, 3 dashes Angostura. Stir over ice, strain into a cocktail glass, squeeze of lemon peel juice on top.

Blackthorn Cocktail [3] (Cktl) 20mls (⅙ gill) Italian vermouth, 20mls (⅙ gill) French vermouth, 20mls (⅙ gill) Scotch whisky, ½ teaspoon orange bitters, dash Angostura. Stir over broken ice, strain into a wine glass. Decorate with a cherry and dash lemon peel juice.

Blackthorn Gold Smooth Cider (Eng) a 4.8% alc by vol. smoothflow draught cider produced by Matthew Clark in Somerset.

Blackthorn LA (Eng) a low alcohol cider 0.9% alc by vol. sold in cans from Matthew Clark in Somerset.

Blackthorn Super (Eng) a 8.2% alc by vol. cider from Matthew Clark in Somerset.

Blackthorn Sweet Cider (Eng) the new name in 1994 for Autumn Gold Cider 4.5% alc by vol.

Black Thursday Sauvignon Blanc (Austr) a dry white wine named after the 1990 bush fires in the region by the Chain of Ponds vineyard, Adelaide Hills.

Black Tot Day (Eng) the British naval seamens' name

for July 31st 1970 when the traditional daily tot of rum was abolished!

Black Tower (Ger) the brand-name for a Liebfraumilch QbA. from H. Kendermann of Bingen in the Rheinhessen, sold in a black glass (stone-shaped) bottle. Bought by European Cellars in February 1987.

Black Velvet (Can) a Canadian rye whisky produced by Gilbey Canada Ltd.

Black Velvet (Cktl) a mixture of chilled Champagne and stout. Also known as Bismarck and Bismark.

Black Velvet (Eng) a 4% alc by vol. stout brewed by The Durham brewery, County Durham.

Black Vintners' Alliance (S.Afr) *see* South African Black Vintners' Alliance.

Black Watch Cocktail (Cktl) ⅓ measure Scotch whisky, ⅓ measure Kahlúa, stir over ice in an old-fashioned glass, top with a dash of soda water and lemon peel spiral.

Black Water Mild (Eng) a 3.7% alc by vol. mild ale brewed by the Crouch Vale Brewery, Essex.

Black Widow Cocktail (Cktl) ⅔ measure Jamaican rum, ⅓ measure Southern Comfort, juice ½ lime, dash gomme syrup. Shake over ice and strain into a cocktail glass.

Black Wine of Cahors (Fr) the name given to the wine made with the Auxerrois (Malbec/Côt) grape in which the skins were left for a long period during fermentation, producing an astringent and tannic wine.

Blackwood Distillers (Scot) a distillery (established 2002). (Add): 159, Commercial Street, Lerwick, Shetland Isles. Produces a range of spirits including: Premium Nordic vodka (triple distilled and ice-filtered over Nordic birch charcoal), Jago's Love Cream Liqueur, Jago's Vanilla Cream liqueur, (plus gin and including Shetland Whisky) and iced cider under license. Website: http://www.blackwooddistillers.com 'E'mail: info@blackwooddistillers.com

Blackwood Valley (Austr) one of five sub-regions of the south-eastern corner of Western Australia.

Black Zak (Eng) a 4.6% alc by vol. ale brewed by the Wentworth Brewery, South Yorkshire.

Bladder Shape (Eng) an early glass bottle (1715–1730) developed from the onion shape. Also known as the '*bastard bottle*'.

Blades Wembley Brew (Eng) an ale brewed by Ward's in Sheffield.

Bladnoch (Scot) a single malt whisky distillery in southern Scotland. Produces an 8 y.o. Lowland malt whisky. 43% alc by vol. Produced by Bells.

Bladen (N.Z) a vineyard at Conders Bend Road Wairau River, Renwick, Marlborough. Grape varieties include Riesling, Sauvignon blanc.

Blagny (Fr) the only Burgundian communal place-name that has no accompanying commune. Blagny is a hamlet divided between Meursault and Puligny-Montrachet on the Côte de Beaune. Premier Crus are: Hameau de Blagny, La Garenne, La Jeunelotte, La Pièce sous le Bois and Sous-le-Dos-d'Ane. 20ha.

Blaignan (Fr) a commune in the Bas Médoc, north-western Bordeaux.

Blain-Gagnard (Fr) a négociant-éleveur based in Chassagne-Montrachet, Burgundy. 7.5ha in Grand Crus : Criots, Bâtards and Motrachet. Premier Crus: Boudriotte and Caillerets.

Blair Athol (Scot) a single malt whisky distillery of Arthur Bell and Sons Ltd., based in Pitlochry, Perthshire PH16 5LY. An 8 year old highland malt whisky. 40% alc by vol.

Blairmhor (Scot) a single highland malt whisky distillery. Owned by R. Carmichael and Sons. 40% alc by vol. Also an 8 year old special vatted malt.

Blaison d'Or (Fr) an Armagnac produced by Chabot-Marquis de Puységur.

Blaj (Rum) a noted wine-producing area, part of the Tîrnave Vineyard.

Blak's Gosport Bitter (Eng) a 5.2% alc by vol. bitter beer brewed by the Oakleaf Brewing C°. Ltd., Hampshire.

Blake's Heaven (Eng) a 7% alc by vol. strong ale brewed by the Oakleaf Brewing C°. Ltd., Hampshire.

Blanc (Fr) white.

Blanc [En] (Port) *see* Bica Alberta.

Blanc [Le] (USA) the label used by the Californian growers for their generic and varietal wines and brandies.

Blanca-Roja (Sp) the alternative name for the white grape variety known as the Blancquirroja, Malvasia and Tobía.

Blancart Pastis (Fr) a low calorie, alcohol-free aniseed based drink. Has no colouring and has 1.8 calories per 100 ml. before dilution.

Blanc-Black Cocktail (Cktl) place 25mls (⅙ gill) blackberry brandy into a flute glass and top with chilled dry white wine.

Blanc d'Anjou (Fr) a local (Anjou-Saumur) name for the Chenin blanc grape variety.

Blanc de Blancs (Fr) white wines (still and sparkling) made with white grapes only.

Blanc de Cabernet Sauvignon (USA) a Californian white wine made from the Cabernet sauvignon grape (a blanc de noirs), must have at least 51% of named grape.

Blanc de la Bri (S.Afr) a white wine made from 40% Sauvignon blanc and 60% Sémillon grapes by the La Bri Vineyard.

Blanc de Marbonne (S.Afr) a dry Chenin blanc-based wine produced by the Koopmanskloof Estate in Stellenbosch.

Blanc de Mer (S.Afr) the label for white wine (Chardonnay, Pinot blanc, Riesling and Sauvignon blanc blend) produced by the Bouchard Findlayson winery, Walker Bay, Western Cape.

Blanc de Millenaires (Fr) a Champagne prestige cuvée of Heidsieck-Henriot (Charles). Produced from 5 Crus: Avize, Cramant, Le Mesnil-sur-Oger, Oger, Vertus.

Blanc de Morgex (It) a white grape variety grown in the Valle d'Aosta.

Blanc de Morgex (It) a D.O.C. white wine from the

Valle d'Aosta. Made from the Blanc de morgex grape.

Blanc de Noir (S.Afr) the label for a rosé wine produced by the Groot Constantia estate, Constantia, Western Cape.

Blanc de Noir (S.Afr) a dry, bottle-fermented, sparkling rosé wine from the KWV. Made from Cabernet and Pinotage grapes.

Blanc de Noirs (Fr) a white wine made with black or red grapes. e.g. Champagne.

Blanc de Pinot Noir (USA) a Californian white wine made from the Pinot noir grape (a blanc de noirs), must have at least 51% of the named grape.

Blanc de Savoie (Fr) a white grape variety of south eastern France.

Blanc des Millénaires (Fr) the label of a blanc de Blancs vintage Champagne produced by Charles Heidsieck.

Blanc de Troynes (Fr) a lesser name for the Aligoté grape.

Blanc d'Euvézin (Fr) a dry white wine produced in the Côtes de Toul in the Lorraine region, north-eastern France.

Blanc de Wet (S.Afr) the label for a white wine (Sauvignon blanc and Sémillon blend) produced by the De Westshof Estate winery, Robertson, Western Cape.

Blanc Doux (Fr) an alternative name for the Sémillon grape.

Blanc Foussy (Fr) a wine producer based in Touraine, Loire. Noted for Vin Vif de Touraine and Blanc Foussy (a sparkling méthode traditionelle from the Chenin blanc grape).

Blanc Fumé (Fr) lit: 'white smoke', a white grape variety also known as the Sauvignon. Used in the Pouilly region of the Loire.

Blanc Fumé (S.Afr) a superb dry white wine from the Sauvignon blanc grape produced by the Le Bonheur estate in Stellenbosch, Western Cape.

Blanc Fumé (S.Afr) the label for a dry white wine (Sauvignon blanc) produced by The Stables winery, Kwa-Zulu, Natal.

Blanc Fumé de Pouilly (Fr) an A.C. dry white wine from the Sauvignon grape in the Pouilly-sur-Loire, Central Vineyards, Loire.

Blanche Barkly (Austr) a winery (established 1972) at Rheola Road, Kingower, Victoria. Grape varieties: Cabernet sauvignon, Shiraz.

Blanche Cocktail (Cktl) ⅓ measure Cointreau, ⅓ measure anisette, ⅓ measure white Curaçao, shake over ice and strain into a cocktail glass.

Blanche d'Armagnac (Fr) a new name for Eau-de-Vie Blanche from 2003. It is a colourless Armagnac made exclusively from the Folle blanche grape and has a floral bouquet. Is now replacing Armagnac for the traditional Trou Gascon.

Blanche de Louvain (Bel) a white wheat beer.

Blanche de Naumur (Bel) an aromatic wheat malt beer 4.5% alc by vol. from Du Bocq. See also Gauloise (la), Saison, Triple Moine, St. Benoit Blonde, St. Benoit Brune.

Blanche De Newland (Eng) a 4.5% alc by vol. ale brewed by the TigerTops Brewery, West Yorkshire.

Blanche Feuille (Fr) an alternative name for the Pinot meunier.

Blanches-Fleurs [Les] (Fr) a Premier Cru vineyard [part] in the A.C. commune of Beaune, Burgundy. 1.16ha.

Blanchfield Brewery (Eng) a brewery (established 1997). (Add): 3 Fleet Hall Road, Rochford, Essex SS4 1NF. Brews: Black Bull Mild 3.6% alc by vol., Bull Best Bitter 3.9% alc by vol., Golden Bull 4.2% alc by vol., IPA Twist 3.6% alc by vol., Killer Bull 6% alc by vol., Raging Bull Bitter 4.9% alc by vol. Website: http://www.blanchfields-brewing.com 'E'mail: richlunn@btinternet.com

Blanchots (Fr) an A.C. Grand Cru of Chablis, Burgundy. Produces supple, fragrant wines which are often quite heady.

Blanck [Marcel] (Fr) an Alsace négociant-éleveur based in Kientzheim.

Blanck [Paul et Fils] (Fr) an Alsace wine producer. (Add): Domaine des Comtes de Lupfen, 32, Grand-Rue, BP.1, 68240 Kientzheim.

Blanco (Sp) white.

Blanco Abbocado (Sp) a medium-sweet white wine from Alella, Cataluña.

Blanco Añada (Sp) a full-bodied, dry white wine produced by Mont-Marcal in the Penedés region.

Blanco Reciente (Sp) a white wine produced by the Bodegas Olarra, S.A. from 100% Viura grapes.

Blanco Selecto (Sp) a brand-label used by the Bodegas Bosch-Guell in the Penedés region.

Blanco Tequila (Mex) a term used when tequila has no ageing. See also Reposado, Añejo Tequila.

Blanc Ramé (Fr) a white grape variety used in the making of Cognac.

Blanc Sur Lie (Fr) lit: 'off the lees', see Muscadet and Sur Lie.

Bland (Eng) a tasting term that denotes a characterless wine.

Blando (Sp) a term used to describe a soft Sherry.

Blandy Brothers (Mad) a company that produces Duke of Sussex Sercial, Duke of Cambridge Verdelho, Duke of Cumberland Bual, Duke of Clarence Malmsey (all Madeira wines).

Blaner (Eng) a slang term for Blanquette de Limoux.

Blandford Fly (Eng) a bottled ale 5.2% alc by vol. produced by the Badger Brewery in Dorset, the beer is said counteract the effects of the Blandford fly's (an insect that lives in the river Stour) bites!

Blankenburger Wiesenquell (Ger) a natural spring mineral water from Blankenburg/Harz, ST. Mineral contents (milligrammes per litre): Sodium 7.8mg/l, Calcium 109mg/l, Magnesium 16.9mg/l, Bicarbonates 307mg/l.

Blankenhornsberg (Ger) see Ihringen, Baden.

Blanket Pressure (Eng) low pressure Carbon-dioxide (CO_2) applied to beer casks to prevent contact with the air.

Blankiet Estate (USA) a winery based in the Napa Valley, California. Grape varieties include: Cabernet sauvignnon. Label: Paradise Hill.

Blanquefort (Fr) a commune of the A.C. Haut-Médoc, north-eastern Bordeaux.

Blanquette (Fr) an alternative local name for the white Colombard grape variety in the Dauphiné region. Also known as the Bon blanc, Bourboulenc, Clairette, Mauzac, Ondenc and Pied-tendre.

Blanquette de Limoux (Fr) an A.C. sparkling wine of the Languedoc 1000ha. Soils of chalk-clay, chalk, pudding stones. Made by the méthode traditionelle from white Mauzac, Chardonnay and Chenin blanc grapes. Has associated A.C.'s of Crémant de Limoux, Blanquette Méthode Ancestrale and Limoux (dry white).

Blanquette Méthode Ancestrale (Fr) a sparkling wine made from Mauzac grapes. Wine is left to ferment a second time in bottle without disgorging the sediment. 6% alc by vol.

Blanquirroja (Sp) the alternative name for the Blanca-Roja white grape variety. Also known as the Malvasia and Tobía.

Blansingen (Ger) village (Anb): Baden. (Ber): Markgräflerland. (Gro): Vogtei Rötteln. (Vin): Wolfer.

Blanton's (USA) a Bourbon whiskey bottled at 93° US proof (46.5% alc by vol.) Sold in a decanter. Produced by the Ancient Age Distillery, Leestown, Frankfort.

Blanzac [Comte de] (Fr) a Champagne producer based in Épernay.

Blarney Stone (Cktl) ⅓ measure Irish whiskey, ⅓ measure green Curaçao, ⅓ measure dry vermouth, 3 dashes orange bitters. Shake with ice, strain into a cocktail glass.

Blarney Stone Cocktail (Cktl) 1 measure Irish whiskey, 2 dashes Pernod, 2 dashes Cointreau, 1 dash maraschino, 1 dash Angostura, shake over ice, strain into a cocktail glass, add an olive and a twist of orange peel.

Blason de France Rosé (Fr) a non-vintage rosé Champagne produced by Perrier-Jouët.

Blason des Papes (Fr) a Châteauneuf-du-Pape produced by Le Caveau des Disciples, 84230 Châteauneuf-du-Pape, southern Rhône.

Blason d'Or (Fr) a 15 year old Cognac produced by Château de la Grange.

Blason Fine Champagne (Fr) a V.S.O.P. 10 year old Cognac produced by Gilles Cosson.

Blasson Timberlay (Fr) an oak-aged, red and white Bordeaux wines produced by Robert Giraud at Saint-André-de-Cuzac to celebrate the anniversary of Château Timberlay.

Blassfarbig (Ger) a term used to describe a schillerwein that is pale pink in colour.

Bláthach (Ire) buttermilk.

Blatina (Slo) a red grape variety, produces a wine of the same name in Mostar.

Blatn Brewery (Czec) a brewery (established 1896) based in Blatn in western Czec. Produces fine light beers.

Blattenberg (Ger) vineyard (Anb): Mosel-Saar-Ruwer. (Ber): Bernkastel. (Gro): Sankt Michael. (Vil): Mehring.

Blau Arbst (Ger) a variety of the Blauburgunder

grape grown in the Baden region. Used in the production of Affenthaler.

Blauburgunder (Aus) an alternative name for the Pinot noir.

Blauburger (Aust) a red grape variety, a cross between Portugieser x Blaufränkisch (in 1920 by Dr. Zweigelt at Klosterneuburg).

Blauer Burgunder (Aus) a cross red grape variety (Blauer Portugieser x Blaufränisch) created in 1922 by Professor Zweigelt, also a local name for the Pinot Noir.

Blauer Burgunder (Ger) see Blauburgunder.

Blauer Malvasier (Aus) an alternative name for the Trollinger grape.

Blauer Portugieser (Aus)(Ger) a red grape variety. see Portugieser.(Cro) = Portugizac crni/Portugaljka, (Fr) = Portugais bleu, (Hun) = Kékoporto, (Rom) = Kékoporto,

Blauer Spätburgunder (Aus)(Ger) a red grape variety, also known as the Pinot noir.

Blauer Trollinger (Ger) see Trollinger.

Blauer Wildbacher (Aus) an old (4th century) red grape variety only planted in Styria, produces Krätzer or Schilcher wines, also known as the Kracher, Krätzer and Schilcher. See also Heckenklescher.

Blauer Zierfandler (Aus) a red grape variety now no longer grown.

Blauer Zweigelt (Aus) see Zweigelt.

Blauer Zweigelt Rebe (Aus) a dry red wine, high in alcohol (11.5%–12% alc by vol.) from the Mailberg Vineyards in the Weinvertal. Owned by the Order of Malta and administered by the Lenz Moser C°.

Blaufränkisch (Aus) an old (10th century), established red grape variety grown in Burgenland. (Bul) = gamé, (Fr) = gamay noir à jus blanc, (Ger) = lemberger/limburger, (Hun) = kékfrankos/nagyburgundi, (It) = franconia, (N.Am) = lemberger, (Slo) = frankovka.

Blaulack (Ger) a kabinett wine from the Herrgottströpfchen range of wines from Jakob Gerhardt.

Blaurock (Switz) a noted wine produced in Stein-am-Rhein.

Blavod (Eng) the name of a 40% alc by vol. black vodka from the Original Black Vodka Company. The black colour is obtained by distilling the vodka with the flavourless herb catechu (a herb found in southern Asia).

Blaxland [Gregory] (Austr) the first vine grower in Australia to export wine to London, England.

Blayais (Fr) the name given to the wines of the Côtes de Blaye district in north-eastern Bordeaux.

Blaye (Fr) a commune in the A.C. Premières Côtes de Blaye in north-east Bordeaux. Created as an A.C. in 2000 (50 hl/ha).

Blaye (Fr) a district within Bordeaux on right bank of river Gironde. see Côtes de Blaye.

Blaye-Plassac (Fr) a commune in the A.C. Côtes de Blaye in north-east Bordeaux.

Blayney Vineyards (Ch.Isles) a vineyard and winery (established 1972). (Add): St. Mary, Jersey,

Channel Islands. 2ha. Grape varieties: Müller-Thurgau, Reichensteiner and Huxelrebe. Wines sold under 'Clos de la Mare' label.

Blayney Wines (Eng) the trading name used by James Bell and C°. for their Off-Licenses.

Blazing Hill (S.Afr) the label for a red wine (Shiraz) produced by the Pax Verbatim Vineyards winery, Stellenbosch, Western Cape.

Blazquez [Agustin] (Sp) a Sherry bodega based at Carretera de Jerez-Algeciras, Km 2, 300 , P.O. Box 540, 11406 Jerez de la Frontera. Noted for Carta Blanca and Carta Oro sherries. Also produces Anticuario, Don Agustin, Felipe II, Toison de Oro, Très Medallas brandies.

Blean Vineyard (Eng) a winery based in Kent. Noted for dry Müller-Thurgau wines.

Bleasdale Winery (Austr) a family winery at Langhorne Creek and Clare-Watervale, Southern Vales.

Bleckenweg (Aus) a vineyard site based on the banks of the River Kamp in the Kamptal region.

Bleeding Heart (Cktl) in a liqueur glass pour in order ½ measure advocaat and ½ measure cherry brandy. The cherry brandy will pursue a vein-like course (hence the name).

Bleichert (Ger) a word used for rosé wines, denotes a pale rosé wine.

Bleichheim (Ger) village (Anb): Baden. (Ber): Breisgau. (Gro): Burg Lichteneck. (Vin): Kaiserberg.

Bleidenberg (Ger) vineyard (Anb): Mosel-Saar-Ruwer. (Ber): Zell/Mosel. (Gro): Weinhex. (Vil): Alken.

Blémond [De] (Fr) a Champagne coopérative in Côte des Blancs. (Add): Rte. de Cramant, 51530 Cuis. Produces 1er Cru Blanc de blancs.

Blencathra Bitter (Eng) a 3.4% alc by vol. bitter ale (named after a local hill) brewed at the Old Crown Inn, Hesket, Newmarket, Cumbria.

Blencowe Brewing C° (Eng) a brewery. (Add): Barrowden, Oakham, Rutland LE15 6EQ. Brews: Beach Boys 4.5% alc by vol., Bevin Boys 4.5% alc by vol., Farmer Boys 3.6% alc by vol., Naughty Boys Bitter 4.8% alc by vol., Water Boys Bitter 4.1% alc by vol., Young Boys Bitter 4.1% alc by vol. Website: http://www.exterarms.com 'E'mail: info@exterarms.com

Blend (Eng) mixing together. e.g. wines in assemblage, drinks, fruit and ice in cocktails.

Blend (S.Afr) the label for a red wine (Cabernet sauvignon, Pinotage and Shiraz blend) produced by the De Meye Wines winery, Stellenbosch, Western Cape.

Blended Bourbon (USA) a mixture of Bourbon whiskey with a straight whiskey or neutral spirit.

Blended Comfort (Cktl) blend together 50mls (2fl.ozs) Bourbon whiskey, 25mls (1fl.oz) Southern Comfort, 25mls (1fl.oz) orange juice, juice ½ lemon, 2 dashes French vermouth, ½ a fresh peach and a small scoop of crushed ice. strain over ice into a highball glass decorated with a slice of peach and orange.

Blended Light Whiskey (USA) a light whiskey which is mixed with less than 20% of straight whiskey on a proof gallon (USA) basis.

Blended Malt (Scot) the new name 2005 (by law) for Vatted Malt.

Blended Straight Whiskey (USA) a mixture of two or more straight whiskies.

Blended Whiskey (USA) an inexpensive whiskey being a blend of straight whiskey and Neutral spirits. It is lighter in character and is especially useful as a cocktail ingredient.

Blender (Cktl) a machine with rotating blades that mixes and blends ingredients for cocktails. Mainly fresh fruit cocktails.

Blender (Eng) a person who uses their nose to judge the qualities of the wines or spirits to be used in the final product.

Blending [1] (Eng) the mixing together of different wines or spirits to produce a final product of best quality. see Assemblage.

Blending [2] (Eng) the mixing of more than one type of green coffee bean or grades of roasted beans to obtain a particular flavour.

Blending [3] (Eng) the mixing of teas of different grades and countries to obtain a standard taste.

Blending Materials (USA) permitted materials such as Sherry, peach juice, prune juice etc. added to whiskey up to 2.5% by volume.

Blend 37 (Eng) the brand-name of a dark, continental instant coffee produced by Nestlé C°.

Blenheim (Cktl) ½ measure vodka, ¼ measure Tia Maria, ¼ measure fresh orange juice, shake over ice and strain into cocktail glass.

Blenheimer (N.Z) the brand-name used by Montana Wines for a dry white wine.

Blenheim Vineyards (N.Z) noted vineyards and a winery owned by Montana Wines.

Blenheim Water (Eng) a natural spring mineral water (established 1992). (Add): The Estate Office, Blenheim Palace, Woodstock, Oxfordshire OX20 1PP. Website: http://www.blenheimpalace.com 'E'mail: estate@blenheimpalace.com

Blénod-les-Toul (Fr) a commune in the Côtes de Toul, Lorraine region, north-eastern France. Produces Vins gris.

Blenton Cocktail (Cktl) 30mls (¼ gill) Plymouth gin, 30mls (¼ gill) French vermouth, dash Angostura. Stir over ice, strain into a cocktail glass. Also known as the Naval Cocktail.

Bleu (Mal) a natural spring mineral water. Mineral contents (milligrammes per litre): Sodium 30mg/l, Calcium 23mg/l, Magnesium 3mg/l, Potassium 0.8mg/l, Bicarbonates 116mg/l, Chlorides 4mg/l, Sulphates 4mg/l, Nitrates 0.02mg/l. pH 7.1

Bleucua (Sp) a D.O. Somontano red wine produced by Viñas del Vero, Somontano from a blend of Cabernet sauvignon, Merlot, Tempranillo, Garnacha. Grapes are hand picked, the wine aged in new oak.

Bleu de Brasserie (Eng) a (1041 O.G.) French-style lager produced by Allied Breweries.

Bleu-Do-It (Cktl) 10mls (½ fl.oz) vodka, 10mls (½

fl.oz) gin, 10mls (½ fl.oz) tequila, 10mls (½ fl.oz) blue Curaçao, 25mls (1fl.oz) lemon juice, dash egg white. Shake over ice, strain into an ice-filled highball glass and top with a splash of soda water.

Blew Cap Pilsner (Eng) a 4.8% alc by vol. pilsner beer brewed by the Darwin Brewery, Tyne & Wear.

Blezards Bitter (Eng) a cask-conditioned bitter 1039 O.G. brewed by the New Fermor Arms, a home-brew public house in Lancashire.

Bligny (Fr) a Cru Champagne village in the Canton de Ville-en-Tardenois. District: Reims.

Blin-Laurent [Guy] (Fr) a Champagne producer. (Add): 6, Rue de la Chapelle, 51140 Trigny. Produces vintage and non-vintage wines. Website: http://www.champagne-guy-blin-laurent.com 'E'mail: info@champagne-guy-blin-laurent.com

Blin [H.] (Fr) a Champagne producer. (Add): 5 Rue de Verdun, BP 35, 51700 Vincelles. 85 growers own 100ha. Produces vintage and non-vintage wines. Vintages include 1988, 1989, 1990, 1995, 1998, 1999.

Blind Drunk (Eng) a term used to describe a person who has blurred vision through intoxication. Extremely intoxicated.

Blindmans Brewery (Eng) a brewery (established 2002). (Add): Talbot Farm, Leighton, Frome, Somerset BA11 4PN. Brews: Conquest 3.8% alc by vol., Eclipse 4.2% alc by vol., Golden Spring 4% alc by vol., Icarus 4.5% alc by vol., Mine Beer 4.2% alc by vol., Siberia 4.7% alc by vol. Website: http://www.blindmansbrewery.co.uk 'E'mail: info@blindmansbrewery.co.uk

Blind Tasting (Eng) a method of testing wines without an identification label so as not to be guided by the fame of the label, does not mean with the eyes covered!

Blitz-Weinhard Brewery (USA) producers of America's strongest beer, The 'Olde English 800' 7.5% alc by vol. Also a lager 'Henry Weinhard's Private Reserve'. (Add): Portland, Oregon.

Bliz's Royal Rickey (Cktl) into a tumbler place 2 ice cubes, add juice of ½ a lime, juice of ¼ lemon, 1 teaspoon raspberry syrup, 60mls (½ gill) French vermouth, 30mls (¼ gill) gin. Top up with ginger ale, stir, top with fruit and serve with spoon.

Blizzard (Eng) a 4.5% alc by vol. event ale brewed by Ridleys of Essex. Available in January.

Blizzard (Scot) a 4.7% alc by vol. ale brewed by the Atlas Brewery, Argyll.

Block (Austr) the name often given to a wine made from a parcel of particular vines within a vineyard area. The wine is often given a number or name.

Block (S.Afr) the label (Block 3 and Block 5) for a range of wines (Sauvignon blanc) produced by the Lomond winery, Cape Agulhas, Southern Cape.

Block and Fall (Cktl) ⅓ measure Cointreau, ⅓ measure apricot brandy, ⅙ measure anisette, ⅙ measure applejack brandy. Stir over ice, strain into a cocktail glass.

Blockesberg (Hun) a red table wine from Alderberg.

Bloemdal Wines (S.Afr) a winery (established 1902) based in Durbanville, Western Cape. 140ha. Grape varieties: Cabernet sauvignon, Merlot, Sauvignon blanc, Sémillon, Shiraz. Labels: Blosend Rooi, Suider Terras. Also known as Jacobsdal Wynkelder.

Blonde (Bel) a beer style of medium to strong alcohol content (6% alc by vol. to 8.5% alc by vol.) with a sweet, malty flavour.

Blonde (It) a sweet white vermouth also known as Bianco. Flavoured with vanilla and cinnamon.

Blondeau (Fr) a cuvée of the vineyards of En Champans, En l'Ormeau, Ronceret and Taille-Pieds in A.C. Volnay, Côte de Beaune, Burgundy. Owned by the Hospices de Beaune.

Blonde Dubonnet Thirst Quencher (Cktl) in a highball glass place 2 measures of Dubonnet blonde and top with chilled ginger ale. Dress with a lemon peel spiral.

Blonde Lady (Cyp) a brand of semi-sweet white wine produced by Etko.

Blondwich (Eng) the name for an ale brewed by the Moorhouses Brewery (Burnley) Ltd., Lancashire.

Blondy Cocktail (Cktl) ½ measure anisette, ½ measure Cointreau. Shake over ice and strain into a cocktail glass.

Blood (Eng) used as a fining agent, is an albuminous protein which coagulates in the wine and as it sinks takes any fine particles down with it. Also helps to reduce the acidity and astringency of the wine. *See also* Ox Blood.

Blood Alcohol (Eng) the alcohol in the blood produced by the body in the action of the gastric juices on the sugars and starches consumed (on average .003% to .005% alc by vol). This is raised with the consumption of alcoholic beverages.

Blood Alcohol Level (Eng) the level of alcohol that has been absorbed by the body into the blood stream. Measured by many methods.

Blood and Sand (Cktl) ½ measure Scotch whisky, ½ measure sweet vermouth, ½ measure cherry brandy, ½ measure orange juice. Shake over ice, strain into a cocktail glass.

Blood Bronx (Cktl) ½ measure gin, ½ measure French vermouth, juice of ¼ blood orange. Shake over ice, strain into a cocktail glass.

Bloodhound (Cktl) 20mls (⅙ gill) dry gin, 20mls (⅙ gill) French vermouth, 20mls (⅙ gill) Italian vermouth, ½ teaspoon sugar, 6 raspberries. Shake well over ice, strain well into a cocktail glass.

Bloodiest Mary (Cktl) 40mls (⅓ gill) Nicholoff Red vodka, 80mls (⅔ gill) tomato juice, juice of ½ lemon, 2 dashes Angostura. Shake over ice, strain into a highball glass, add salt and pepper if required.

Bloodshot (Cktl) 25mls (1fl.oz) vodka, 50mls (2fl.ozs) tomato juice, 50mls (2fl.ozs) beef bouillon, dash lemon juice, 2 dashes Worcester sauce, celery salt. Shake over ice, strain into a cocktail glass.

Bloodstone (Austr) the label for a red wine (Shiraz) produced by the Gemtree winery, McLaren Vale, South Australia.

Blood Tub (Eng) 34 litre cask.

B

Bloody Bull Cocktail (Cktl) 25mls (1fl.oz) tequila, 50mls (2fl.ozs) tomato juice, 50mls (2fl.ozs) cold beef bouillon, dash lemon juice. Stir over ice in an old-fashioned glass. Dress with celery leaves and lemon slice.

Bloody Bullshot (Cktl) a combination of 2 cocktails: Bloody Mary and Bullshot.

Bloody Caesar (Cktl) 100mls (4fl.ozs) Clamato juice, 25mls (1fl.oz) vodka, dash lemon juice, 2 dashes Worcester sauce. Shake over ice, strain into a cocktail glass.

Bloody Maria (Cktl) as for a Bloody Mary but using tequila in place of vodka.

Bloody Marie (Cktl) ⅔ measure vodka, ⅓ measure blackberry brandy. Shake over ice, strain into a cocktail glass.

Bloody Mary (Cktl) 1 measure vodka, 4 measures tomato juice, dash lemon juice, dash Worcester sauce, salt, pepper and celery salt. Place in old-fashioned glass, stir with stick of celery. Add ice if required. Named after Queen Mary First of England by a French barman called Fernand Petiot in the 19th century.

Bloody Tonic (Cktl) place 4cls. vodka and 4cls. cranberry juice over ice in a highball glass and top with 5cls. Schweppes Indian tonic water.

Bloom (Eng) a term used to describe the wine yeasts that settle on the grape skins together with wild yeasts and acetobacters. Used in a natural fermentation or destroyed with SO_2 in a controlled fermentation.

Bloomfield Vineyards (N.Z) a winery. (Add): 119 Solway Crescent, Masterton, Wellington. 8ha. Grape varieties: Cabernet sauvignon, Cabernet franc, Merlot, Pinot noir, Sauvignon blanc.

Bloomin' Ale (Eng) a 4% alc by vol. cask-conditioned ale. Part of the Tapster's Choice range from Carlsberg-Tetley. Available in June.

Blosend Rooi (S.Afr) the label for a red wine (70% Shiraz) produced by the Bloemendal estate winery, Durbanville, Western Cape.

Blossom (Cktl) ½ measure Bacardi White Label, ½ measure orange juice, dash grenadine. Shake over ice, strain into a cocktail glass.

Blossom Hill (USA) the brand-name given to a collection of varietal wines: Cabernet sauvignon, Chardonnay, Sauvignon blanc, Zinfandel from Mendoza, California.

Blotto (Eng) a slang term that denotes a person who is unconscious (or semi-conscious) through alcohol. Very drunk.

Blotto (Eng) a seasonal ale brewed by Franklin's Brewery, Harrogate, North Yorkshire.

Blouvlei Wines (S.Afr) a winery based in Wellington, Western Cape. Grape varieties: Cabernet franc, Cabernet sauvignon, Merlot.

Blow Job (Eng) see Bitter Blow.

Blowsy (Eng) a term used to describe an overblown, exaggerated, fruity bouquet on some wines.

B.L.R.A. (Eng) abbr: Brewers and Licensed Retailers Association.

Blu (It) a sparkling natural nineral water from Crodo.

Mineral contents (milligrammes per litre): Sodium 5.5mg/l, Calcium 60.3mg/l, Magnesium 7.3mg/l, Potassium 3.2mg/l, Bicarbonates 103.2mg/l, Chlorides 1.8mg/l, Sulphates 102.5mg/l, Nitrates 3.9mg/l, Silicates 8.6mg/l. pH 7.64

Blücherhöhe (Ger) vineyard (Anb): Pfalz. (Ber): Südliche Weinstrasse. (Gro): Schloss Ludwigshöhe. (Vil): Edenkoben.

Blücherpfad (Ger) vineyard (Anb): Rheinhessen. (Ber): Wonnegau. (Gro): Burg Rodenstein. (Vil): Ober-Flörsheim.

Blüchertal (Ger) vineyard (Anb): Mittelrhein. (Ber): Rheinburgengau. (Gro): Herrenberg. (Vil): Kaub.

Blue (Austr) a low alcohol beer (2.7% alc by vol) brewed by the Toohey's Brewery.

Blue (Eng) a 5% alc by vol. vodka-based, bottled drink produced by Bass. Contains herbal extracts. Also a Red version.

Blue (Can) the name used for a top lager brewed by Labatt Brewery. 5% alc by vol.

Blue (Eng) the name used for Ruddles Breweries' Rutland Bitter 1032 O.G.

Blue Agave (Mex) an alternative name for the Agave Cactus.

Blue Anchor Brewery (Eng) a public house brewery (established 1850). (Add): 50 Coinagehall Street, Helston, Cornwall TR13 8EL. Noted for cask-conditioned ales. Brews: Bragget 6% alc by vol., Christmas Special Ale 7.6% alc by vol., Easter Special 7.6% alc by vol., IPA 4.2% alc by vol., Mild 1040 O.G. Medium 1050 O.G. BB 1053 O.G. Special 1066 O.G. Extra Special 1070 O.G., Spingo (Middle Spingo 5% alc by vol., Best Spingo 5.3% alc by vol. and Special Spingo 6.6% alc by vol.). Website: http://www.spinoales.com 'E'mail: theblueanchor@btconnect.com

Blue Bell Brewery (Eng) a brewery (established 1998). (Add): Sycamore House, Lapwater Lane, Holbeach St. Marks, Spalding, Lincolnshire PE12 8EX. Brews a variety of beers. Website: http://www.bluebellbrewery.co.uk 'E'mail: enquiries@bluebellbrewery.co.uk

Blueberry Hill (S.Afr) a winery (established 1998) based in Franschhoek, Western Cape. 0.6ha. Grape varieties include: Merlot.

Blueberry Tea (Cktl) in a heatproof glass place 15mls (⅛ gill) amaretto. Top with freshly brewed Ceylon tea, stir, add 15mls (⅛ gill) Grand Marnier.

Blue Bird (S.Afr) the label for a red wine (Cabernet sauvignon, Merlot, Pinotage blend) produced by the Devon Hill Winery, Stellenbosch, Western Cape.

Bluebird Bitter (Eng) a 3.6% alc. by vol bitter ale brewed by Coniston Brewery, Lake District.

Blue Bird Cocktail (Cktl) ¾ measure gin, ¼ measure Cointreau, dash orange bitters. Stir over ice, strain into a cocktail glass, add cherry and lemon peel twist.

Bluebird Exp (Eng) a 4.2% alc by vol. ale brewed by the Coniston Brewing Company Ltd., Cumbria.

Blue Blazer (Cktl) 50mls (2fl.ozs) Scotch whisky (heated), 50mls (2fl.ozs) boiling water, barspoon

140

powdered sugar. Place whisky in a silver 1gill (125mls) jigger, and the water into another silver 1gill (125 mls) jigger. Ignite the whisky and mix both ingredients by pouring from one measure to the other. Sweeten and serve in an old-fashioned glass.

Blue Blazer Coffee (Eng) stir 2 sugar cubes into a cup of hot, strong, black, freshly brewed coffee. Top with grated orange zest, then pour 25mls (⅕ gill) of heated and ignited Irish whiskey on top.

Blue Bottle (Cktl) ½ measure gin, ¼ measure blue curaçao, ¼ measure passion fruit liqueur. Stir over ice and strain into a cocktail glass.

Blue Bottle (Ger) a flute shaped bottle made with blue glass used in the nineteenth century in the Nahe region. Used now by some wine shippers as a gimmick.

Blue Bottle (Wal) *see* Ty-Nant Spring Water.

Blue Boy (Gre) the name given to a medium-sweet, white table wine made by Tsantali.

Blue Bullet (Eng) a 4.5% alc by vol. ale brewed by the Bazens Brewery, Greater Manchester

Blue Cool (Austr) a natural spring mineral water.

Blue Crane Vineyards (S.Afr) a winery based in Tulbagh, Western Cape. 6ha. Grape varieties: Cabernet sauvignon, Merlot, Sauvignon blanc, Shiraz. Website: http://www.bluecrane.co.za

Blue Creek Wines (S.Afr) a winery (established 1995) based in Piet Retief Street, Stellenbosch, Western Cape. 7.5ha. Grape varieties: Cabernet sauvignon, Merlot, Pinotage.

Blue Curaçao (Fr) a liqueur made from Curaçao and natural blue colouring. Used mainly for cocktails.

Blue Danube (Aus) a dry, white wine produced by Lenz Moser from a blend of Gewürztraminer and Wälschriesling grapes.

Blue Danube (Cktl) ¼ measure blue Curaçao, ¾ measure dry gin, dash absinthe. Shake over ice, strain into a cocktail glass.

Blue Danube (Eng) the brand-name of a Viennese coffee produced by the Walter Williams Co.

Blue Devil (Cktl) 1 measure gin, ½ measure blue Curaçao, 2 dashes lemon juice, 2 dashes lime cordial. Stir well over ice, strain into cocktail glass with crushed ice. Serve with straws.

Blue Devil Cocktail (Cktl) 1 measure gin, juice ¼ lemon, juice ¼ lime, ¼ measure maraschino, 2 dashes crème yvette. Shake over ice, strain into a cocktail glass.

Blue Fining (Eng) ***Potassium ferrocyanide*** used to clear excess metallic (iron & copper) salts from the wine. If left these salts would tend to oxidise with air leaving the wine cloudy and bitter tasting. *see* Ferric Casse. Is poisonous if used in excess. (Ger) = möslinger fining.

Blue Grove Hill (S.Afr) the label for a range of wines (Cabernet sauvignon-Merlot and a Sauvignon blanc) produced by the Capaia Wines winery, Philadelphia, Western Cape.

Blue Hanger (Scot) a de luxe blended Scotch whisky produced by Berry Brothers and Rudd. 40% alc by vol.

Blue Hawaiian (Cktl) 10mls (½ fl.oz) blue Curaçao, 25mls (1fl.oz) coconut cream, 25mls (1fl.oz) white rum, 50mls (2fl.ozs) pineapple juice, 1 scoop crushed ice. Blend, pour into a 125 ml. (5fl.oz) wine goblet.

Blue Heron (USA) a pale ale brewed by the Bridgeport Brewing Company, Portland, Oregan.

Blue Imperial (Austr) an alternative name for the Cinsaut.

Blue Jacket (Cktl) ¼ measure blue Curaçao, ½ measure gin, ¼ measure orange bitters. Stir over ice, strain into a cocktail glass.

Blue Keld Springs (Eng) a sparkling natural spring mineral water (established 1993) from the Yorkshire Wolds. (Add): Throstle Nest, Cranswick, Driffield, East Yorkshire YO25 9RE. Mineral contents (milligrammes per litre): Sodium 8mg/l, Calcium 88mg/l, Magnesium 3mg/l, Potassium 3.5mg/l, Bicarbonates 203mg/l, Chlorides 17mg/l, Sulphates 6.8mg/l, Fluorides 0.08mg/l, Nitrates 20.24mg/l. pH 7.6 Website: http://www.bluekeld.co.uk 'E'mail: bluekeld@ukf.net

Blue Label (Euro) a keg ale brewed by the Farsons Brewery in Malta.

Blue Label (Eng) a bottled beer brewed by the Harveys Brewery, Sussex. 1033 O.G.

Blue Label (Eng) a bottled beer brewed by the Timothy Taylor Brewery, West Yorkshire. 1043 O.G.

Blue Lady (Cktl) ½ measure blue Curaçao, ¼ measure gin, ¼ measure fresh orange juice, dash egg white. Shake over ice, strain into a cocktail glass.

Blue Lagoon (Cktl) 10mls (½ fl.oz) blue Curaçao, 10mls (½ fl.oz) vodka, lemonade. Pour vodka and curaçao over ice in a highball glass. Top up with ice-cold lemonade.

Blue Maguey (Mex) a cactus from which mezcal is made. Also known as the Mezcal Azul.

Blue Margarita (Cktl) ⅗ measure tequila, ⅕ measure blue Curaçao, ⅕ measure lime juice. Shake over ice, strain into a salt-rimmed cocktail glass.

Blue Mezcal (Mex) the name for the agave (cactus) plant.

Blue Monday (Cktl) ¾ measure vodka, ¼ measure blue Curaçao. Stir over ice, strain into cocktail glass.

Blue Moon (Cktl) ¼ measure crème yvette, ½ measure gin, ¼ measure lemon juice. Shake over ice, strain into a cocktail glass.

Blue Moon Cocktail (Cktl) ½ measure dry gin, ½ measure parfait amour, shake over ice, strain into a cocktail glass.

Blue Mountain Coffee (W.Ind) the finest of all the Jamaican coffees, an Arabica strain, the beans are a dull blue and give a rich full-bodied and full nutty flavour.

Blue Mountain Vineyard (USA) a vineyard based in western Texas (south of Fort Dans). 16ha. Produces hybrid wines.

Blue Negligée (Cktl) ⅓ measure Green Chartreuse, ⅓ measure parfait amour, ⅓ measure ouzo. Stir over ice, strain into a cocktail glass. Add a cherry.

Blue Nile Brewery (Afr) a brewery based in

Kharthoum, Sudan. Owned by the State of Sudan, brews Carmel Beer 1044 O.G.

Blue Nun (Ger) a top selling QbA Liebfraumilch from H. Sichel and Sons. A sparkling version is also available together with a Rosé, Riesling and Merlot.

Blue Nun Gold (Ger) a QmP version of Blue Nun.

Blueprint (S.Afr) the label for a red wine (Shiraz) produced by the De Trafford Wines winery, Stellenbosch, Western Cape.

Blue Pyrenees Estate (Austr) a winery based in Avoca, Victoria. Grape varieties: Cabernet sauvignon, Merlot, Shiraz.

Bluer Burgunder (Aus) an alternative spelling for the Blauer burgunder.

Blue Riband (Cktl) ⅓ measure blue Curaçao, ⅓ measure white Curaçao, ⅓ measure gin. Stir over ice, strain into a cocktail glass.

Blue Ribbon (USA) a sweetish beer brewed by the Pabst Brewery, Newark, Peoria, Milwaukee.

Blue Rocket (Eng) a 4.5% alc by vol. cask-conditioned ale brewed by the Steampacket Brewery, Knottingley, Yorkshire.

Blue Rock Vineyard (N.Z) a vineyard. (Add): Dry River Road, P.O. Box 55, Martinborough. 18ha. Produces unfiltered red wines.

Blue Ruin (USA) a slang term for gin (so named because of its blue hue).

Blue Sea (Cktl) ¾ measure Bacardi White Label rum, ½ measure blue Curaçao, 1 egg white, dash lemon juice, dash Pernod. Shake over ice, strain into a highball glass, top with lemonade and dress with sprig of mint and lemon slice.

Blue Seal (S.Am) the brand-name of demerara rum produced in Guyana by the Guyana Distilleries.

Blue Stalk (Hun) a popular name given to the Badacsonyi Kéknyelü of the Balatòn region.

Blue Star (Cktl) ⅓ measure blue Curaçao, ⅓ measure gin, ⅙ measure Lillet, ⅙ measure orange juice. Shake over ice, strain into a cocktail glass.

Blue Star (Eng) the logo of the Newcastle Brewery, Newcastle.

Blue Stripe White Burgundy Supreme (Austr) a full-bodied, rich and fruity white wine made with the Chardonnay grape by the Houghton Vineyard, Western Australia.

Blue Tasting Glass (Fr) a glass used by professional Cognac tasters. Is coloured blue so that they do not influence their judgement by looking at the colour.

Blue Tea (Tai) a light-brown coloured tea that has a medium caffeine and anti-oxidant content (less than black tea and higher than green teas) which is drunk without milk or sugar.

Bluetongue Brewery Pty Ltd (Austr) a brewery. (Add): 42 Stenhouse Drive, Cameron Park, NSW 2285. Brews beers and lagers. Website: http://www.bluetonguebrewery.com.au 'E'mail: info@bluetonguebrewery.com.au

Blue Train Special (Cktl) 1 measure brandy, 1 measure pineapple syrup. Shake over ice, strain into a highball glass, top with iced, dry Champagne.

Blue Triangle Ale (Eng) a top bottled pale ale 1041 O.G. from Bass.

Blue White (S.Afr) the label for a white wine (Chenin blanc) sold in a blue bottle and produced by the Old Vine Cellars winery, Cape Town, Western Cape.

Blümchen (Ger) vineyard (Anb): Mosel-Saar-Ruwer. (Ber): Obermosel. (Gro): Gipfel. (Vil): Nittel.

Blümchen (S.Afr) the label for a white naturally sweet wine (Colombard and Hanepoot blend) produced by the Landzicht GWK Eines winery, Jacobsdal, Northern Cape.

Blume (Ger) bouquet/aroma.

Blume (Ger) vineyard (Anb): Ahr. (Ber): Walporzheim/ Ahrtal. (Gro): Klosterberg. (Vil): Rech.

Blume (Ger) vineyard (Anb): Rheinhessen. (Ber): Nierstein. (Gro): Domherr. (Vil): Stadecken-Elsheim.

Blumig (Ger) denotes a wine with a good bouquet.

Blunderbus Old Porter (Eng) a porter produced by the Coach House Brewery.

Blushing Barmaid (Cktl) 25mls (1fl.oz) Campari, 25mls (1fl.oz) Amaretto di Saronno, dash egg white. Shake together over ice, strain into large ice-filled goblet. Stir in bitter lemon. Decorate with apricot wedge.

Blushing Bride (Cktl) ¼ measure vodka, ¼ measure cherry brandy, ¼ measure orange Curaçao, dash orange bitters, dash egg white. Shake well over ice, strain into a cocktail glass.

Blushing Princess (Eng) a brand-name cider cocktail from Symonds of Hereford. Contains cider, gin and damson wine.

Blush Wines (USA) a term used for rosé wines with a light pink colour.

Blyde Wines (S.Afr) a winery based in Paarl, Western Cape. Grape varieties include: Cabernet sauvignon, Merlot, Shiraz. Label: Bona Dea, Jacobus Petrus.

Blythe Bitter (Eng) a 4% alc by vol. bitter beer brewed by the Blythe Brewery, Staffordshire.

Blythe Brewery (Eng) a brewery (established 2003). (Add): Blythe House Farm, Hamstall Ridware, Stafford, Staffordshire WS15 3QQ. Brews: Blythe Bitter 4% alc by vol., Chase Bitter 4.4% alc by vol., Palmers Poison 4.5% alc by vol. 'E'mail: info@blythebrewery.plus.com

Blythe Vineyards (USA) a small winery based in La Plata, Maryland. Produces hybrid wines.

B.N.I.A. (Fr) abbr: **B**ureau **N**ational **I**nterprofessionnel d'**A**rmagnac.

B.N.I.C. (Fr) abbr: **B**ureau **N**ational **I**nterprofessionnel du **C**ognac.

B.N.I.C.E. (Fr) abbr: **B**ureau **N**ational **I**nterprofessionnel des **C**alvados et de-Vie-de-Cidre-et-de-Poire.

B.N.M.W.A. (Eng) abbr: **B**ritish **N**ational **M**ineral **W**aters **A**ssociation.

Boadicea Ale (Eng) a 4.6% alc by vol. ale brewed by the Rother Valley Brewing C°., East Sussex.

Boag Brewery (Austr) a brewery based in Launceston.

Boais (Port) a white grape variety used in the making of Setúbal wine.

Boal (Mad) a deep, golden-coloured, sweet, full-bodied Madeira. Has a fine balance of sugar, acid and tannin with a somewhat smokey taste. Also spelt Bual. Made from the Boal Cachudo grape.

Boal Cachudo (Mad) the most commonly planted white Boal grape variety grown on Madeira.

Boal di Madeira (USA) a white grape variety used in the production of dessert wines in California.

Boal do Porto Santo (Mad) a white grape variety used in the production of Madeira wine.

Boardroom Port (Port) a fine, tawny Port from the Dow Port Shipping C°.

Boario (It) a natural mineral water from Boario. Mineral contents (milligrammes per litre): Sodium 5mg/l, Calcium 133mg/l, Magnesium 40mg/l, Potassium 2mg/l, Bicarbonates 300mg/l, Chlorides 5mg/l, Sulphates 246mg/l, Fluorides 0.3mg/l, Nitrates 6mg/l, Silicates 10mg/l. pH 7.3

Boat Brewery (Eng) a brewery. (Add): Boat Inn, Boat Lane, Allerton Bywater, Castleford, West Yorkshire WF10 2BX. Brews a range of beers and lager. Website: http://www.boatbrewery.co.uk 'E'mail: ron@boatbrewery.co.uk

Boa Vista (Port) a Port wine estate in the Alto Douro. Owned by Offley. *see* Offley Forrester Boa Vista.

B.O.B. (Eng) *abbr*: **B**uyer's **O**wn **B**rand. Champagne sold under a retailer's own brand name.

B.O.B. (Eng) *abbr*: **B**uyers **O**wn **B**ottling.

Bob (Eng) a 3.6% alc by vol. ale brewed by the Butlers Brewery C° Ltd., Berkshire.

Bob (Eng) a % alc by vol.4% alc by vol. ale brewed by the Wickwar Brewing C°. Ltd., Gloucestershire.

Bobadilla (Sp) the brand-name for '103' brandy made in Andalusia (Etiquetta Blanca, Etiquetta Amarilla, Etiquetta Negra), Ragel and 'Gran Capitán'. Also major Sherry producers, producing Alcazar Amontillado, Banico Fino, Capitán Oloroso, La Merced and Sadana.

Bobal (Sp) a black grape variety grown in south-eastern Spain. Is also known as the Tinto de requena and Requeno.

Bobal Blanco (Sp) an alternative name for the Tortosí grape.

Bobbie Burns Shiraz (Austr) a red wine produced by Campbells of Rutherglen, north east Victoria.

Bobbin-Knopped Glass (Eng) an eighteenth century wine glass whose stem is a series of balls of glass on a round flat base, with a trumpet bowl.

Bobby Ale (Eng) a 5% alc by vol. ale brewed by Felon & Firkin, Great George Street, Leeds, West Yorkshire. *see* Felon Bitter.

Bobby Ales (Ch.Isles) the brand-name for beers brewed by Randalls Vauxlaurens Brewery St. Peter Port, Guernsey (now no longer produced).

Bobby Burns (Cktl) 1½ measures Scotch whisky, ½ measure sweet vermouth, 2 dashes Bénédictine. Shake over ice, strain into a cocktail glass.

Bobby Burns Cocktail (Cktl) 1 measure malt whisky placed into a liqueur glass and top with double cream.

Bobby Mild (Ch.Isles) a mild ale brewed by Randalls Vauxlaurens Brewery, St. Peter Port, Guernsey. 1036 O.G (now no longer produced).

Bobenheim am Berg (Ger) village (Anb): Pfalz. (Ber): Mittelhaardt-Deutsche Weinstrasse. (Gro): Feuerberg. (Vins): Kieselberg, Ohligpfad.

Boberg (S.Afr) a wine district that produces Sherry-type fino wines noted for their natural flor.

Böbingen (Ger) village (Anb): Pfalz. (Ber): Südliche Weinstrasse. (Gro): Trappenberg. (Vin): Ortelberg.

Bobs Brewing Company (Eng) a brewery (established 2002). (Add): The Red Lion, 73 Dewsbury Road, Ossett, West Yorkshire WF5 9NQ. Brews: Chardonnayle 5.1% alc by vol., Golden Lion 4.5% alc by vol., Lion Cub 4.1% alc by vol., Silver Bullet 4.7% alc by vol., White Lion 4.3% alc by vol., Yakima Pale Ale 4.5% alc by vol.

Bob's Gold (Eng) a 4.7% alc by vol. bottled beer brewed using the dwarf hop First Gold by Ruddles Brewery, Leicester. Part of their Ruddles Character Ale range. *See also* Laxton's Honey Beer, Parry's Porter, Ebeneezer's Surprise.

Boca (Cro) bottle. D.O.C.

Boca (It) a D.O.C. red wine from the Piemonte region. Produced from the Nebbiolo 45%–70%, Vespolina 20%–40% and Bonarda novarese 20%. Aged 3 years (2 years in chestnut/oak casks). A dry wine with an aftertaste of pomegranates.

Boca Chica Carioca (W.Ind) a brand of rum produced in Puerto Rico for export.

Bocal (Fr) jar/bottle.

Boccale (It) mug/jar.

Bocchino (It) a brand-name of a grappa.

Boccie Ball (Cktl) 50mls (2fl.ozs) Amaretto di Saronno, 50mls (2fl.ozs) orange juice. Mix in a highball glass, add ice and top up with soda.

Böchingen (Ger) village (Anb): Pfalz. (Ber): Südliche Weinstrasse. (Gro): Bischofskreuz. (Vin): Rosenkranz.

Bock (Eng) a 6.4% alc by vol. bock beer brewed by the TigerTops Brewery, West Yorkshire.

Bock (Fr) a beer tankard made of glass which holds about a ½ pint (285mls), used for drinking draught beer.

Bock (Fr) a glass of beer.

Bock (Ger) lit: 'buck beer', a special brew of heavy, dark and sweetened beer. 6.25% alc by vol. *see* Einbeck. Belgian Bock is less alcoholic.

Bockaar Triple Bock (Hol) a 9% alc by vol. bottle-conditioned, dark, triple bock beer brewed by De 3 Horne Bier Brouwerij, Kaatsheuvel.

Bock Beer Day (Ger) a day when winter brews of bock beers are consumed (when these beers are ready for drinking). It is supposed to herald the arrival of Spring.

Bockbieres (Ger) denotes beers with an original gravity of 16%–18%.

Bock-Damm (Sp) the label of a dark beer brewed by Estrella-Damm in Barcelona.

Bockel (Fr) an Alsace wine producer. (Add): 2, Rue de la Montagne, BP. 53, 67140 Mittelbergheim.

Bockenau (Ger) village (Anb): Nahe. (Ber): Schloss Böckelheim. (Gro): Rosengarten. (Vins): Geisberg, Im Felsneck, Im Neuberg, Stromberg.

Bockenheim (Ger) village (Anb): Pfalz. (Ber): Mittelhaardt-Deutsche Weinstrasse. (Gro): Grafenstück. (Vins): Burggarten, Goldgrube, Hassmannsberg, Heiligenkirche, Klosterschaffnerei, Schlossberg, Sonnenberg, Vogelsang.

Bockfüssl (Aus) a vineyard site on the banks of the River Danube situated in the Wachau region, Niederösterreich.

Bockor (Bel) a natural spring mineral water from Bockor, Bellegem.

Bockrus (Nor) a slang term for a hangover.

Bocksbeeren (Euro) an East European name for blackcurrant Liqueur.

Bocksberg (Ger) vineyard (Anb): Nahe. (Ber): Schloss Böckelheim. (Gro): Paradiesgarten. (Vil): Feilbingert.

Bocksberg (Lux) a vineyard site in the village of Wasserbillig.

Bocksbeutel (Ger) an attractively shaped bottle for holding Franconian steinwein. Now used extensively in Portugal, South Africa and Chile. see Boxbeutel and Brévaire.

Bocksbeutelstrasse (Ger) the Franken wine route.

Böckser (Aus) a wine with a foul smell or taste. See also Seniffeln.

Bockshaut (Ger) vineyard (Anb): Rheinhessen. (Ber): Bingen. (Gro): Kurfürstenstück. (Vil): Gau-Bickelheim.

Bockshoden (Ger) lit: 'male goat's testicles', an erroneous varietal name for the red Trollinger grape.

Bockstein (Ger) vineyard (Anb): Mosel-Saar-Ruwer. (Ber): Saar-Ruwer. (Gro): Scharzberg. (Vil): Ockfen.

Bockstein (Ger) vineyard (Anb): Rheinhessen. (Ber): Bingen. (Gro): Kaiserpfalz. (Vil): Gross-Winternheim.

Bockstein (Ger) vineyard (Anb): Rheinhessen. (Ber): Nierstein. (Gro): Domherr. (Vil): Stadecken-Elsheim.

Bockwingert (Euro) a single domaine in Liechtenstein which makes up approximately half the vineyard area in Vaduz the capital.

Bocoy (Sp) a large cask used in the north of Spain of approximately 600litres (132 Imp.gallons) in capacity.

Bodagfährtle (Ger) a term used to describe the taste of the red wines whose grapes are grown on shell limestone soil. e.g. in Württemberg Anbaugebiete.

Böddiger (Ger) village (Anb): Rheingau. (Ber): Johannisberg. (Gro): Landkreis Melsungen. (Vin): Berg.

Boddington's Brewery (Eng) an independent brewery in Manchester. Brews cask-conditioned Mild 1033 O.G., Bitter 1035 O.G. cask beers are now brewed by Hydes Brewery at Moss Side, Manchester.

Boddington's Draught (Eng) a 3.8% alc by vol. draught bitter packed in cans. Brewed by Boddington, Whitbread Beer Company, Manchester.

Boddington's Export Draught (Eng) a draught ale in a bottle. 4.8% alc by vol. brewed by Boddington, Whitbread Beer Company, Manchester.

Boddington's Manchester Gold (Eng) a 4.8% alc by vol. draught nitrokeg beer from Whitbread Strangeways Brewery.

Bodega (Port) a wine shop, usually of a poor grade, selling cheap table wine.

Bodega [1] (Sp) lit: 'wine cellar/storeroom', a Spanish winery, warehouse for wine storage or bar.

Bodega [2] (Sp) a wine shop, shop selling wine.

Bodega Alanís, S.A. (Sp) a winery in Ribeiro. Produces Gran Alanís and San Trocado.

Bodega Antucura (Arg) a winery based in the Mendoza region, eastern Argentina. Website: http://www.antucura.com 'E'mail: info@antucura.com

Bodega Balbi (Arg) a winery based in the Mendoza region, eastern Argentina.

Bodega Benvenuto de la Serna (Arg) a winery based in the Mendoza region, eastern Argentina. Website: http://www.benvenutodelaserna.com

Bodega Biurko Gorri (Sp) organic winery in Rioja that is noted for old vine Garnacha wine, plus a Tempranillo/Garnacha blend.

Bodega Catena Zapata (Arg) a winery (established 1902) based in the Mendoza region, eastern Argentina. Grape variety: Malbec. Website: http://www.catenawines.com 'E'mail: info@catenawines.com

Bodega Clos de los Siete (Arg) a winery based in the Uco Valley, Mendoza region, eastern Argentina. Website: http://www.monteviejo.com 'E'mail: closdelossiete@clos7.com.ar

Bodega Colomé (Arg) see Colomé.

Bodega Coop. del Campo Nuestra Señora de Manjavacas (Sp) co-operative wine-producers based in La Mancha. Labels include Zarragon.

Bodega Coop. del Valle de Ocón (Sp) a major co-operative winery based in the Rioja region.

Bodega Coop. de Ribeiro (Sp) the largest co-operative winery based in Galicia. Produces seven types of wine: Granel, Lar, Pazo (red, rosé and white) and Xeito (rosé and white).

Bodega Coop. la Bastida (Sp) a large wine co-operative based in Rioja.

Bodega Coop. Nuestra Señora de la Anunciación (Sp) a wine co-operative based in Rioja.

Bodega Coop. Nuestra Señora de Valvanera de Cuzcurrita, Tirjo y Sajazarra (Sp) a major wine co-operative based in Rioja.

Bodega Coop. Nuestra Señora de Vico (Sp) a wine co-operative based in the Rioja region.

Bodega Coop. San Isidro (Sp) a major wine co-operative based in the Rioja region.

Bodega Coop. San Miguel (Sp) a wine co-operative based in the Rioja region.

Bodega Coop. San Pedro Apóstol (Sp) a major wine co-operative based in the Rioja region.

Bodega Coop. Santa Daria (Sp) a wine co-operative based in the Rioja region.

Bodega Coop. Sonsierra (Sp) a major wine co-operative based in the Rioja region.

Bodega Coop. Virgen de la Vega (Sp) a wine co-operative based in the Rioja region.

B

Bodega del Fin del Mundo (Arg) a winery (established 1999) based in Neuquén, Rio Negro, Pategonia. Grape varieties include: Cabernet sauvignon, Chardonnay, Malbec, Merlot, Pinot noir, Sauvignon blanc, Sémillon, Syrah. Label: Newen. Website: http://www.bodegadelfindelmundo.com 'E'mail: info@bdfm.com.ar

Bodega Don Cristobel (Arg) a winery 150ha on 3 estates: Finca La Niña (Junin)/Finca La Pinta (Rivadavia)/Finca La Santa Maria (Luján de Cuyo) based in the Mendoza region, eastern Argentina. Grape varieties: Bonarda, Cabernet sauvignon, Malbec, Merlot, Sangiovese, Sauvignon blanc, Shiraz, Verdelho, Viognier. Website: http://www.doncristobal.com.ar 'E'mail: exportaciones@doncristobal.com.ar

Bodega Eral Bravo (Arg) a winery based in the Mendoza region, eastern Argentina. Website: http://www.eralbravo.com 'E'mail: info@eralbravo.com

Bodega Fabre Montmayou (Arg) a winery based in the Mendoza region, eastern Argentina. Website: http://www.fabremontmayou.com 'E'mail: export@bodegasdomvistalba.com.ar

Bodega Familia Schroeder (Arg) a winery (established 1859) based in San Patricio del Chañar in the Patagonia region, southern Argentina. Grape varieties: Chardonnay, Malbec, Merlot, Pinot noir, Sauvignon blanc. Labels: Saurus, Saurus Select. Website: http://www.familiaschroeder.com 'E'mail: info@familiaschroeder.com

Bodega Filus (Arg) a winery based in the Mendoza region, eastern Argentina. Website: http://www.filuswine.com 'E'mail: info@filuswine.com

Bodega Finca La Chamiza (Arg) a winery based in the Mendoza region, eastern Argentina. Website: http://www.lachamiza.com 'E'mail: lunaluntasa@tisoluciones.net

Bodega Goyenechea (Arg) a winery based in the Mendoza region, eastern Argentina. Website: http://www.goyenechea.com 'E'mail: export@goyenechea.com

Bodega Humberto Canale (Arg) a winery based in the Patagonia region, southern Argentina. Website: http://www.bodegahcanale.com 'E'mail: comex@bodegahcanale.com

Bodega Infinitus (Arg) a winery based in the Patagonia region, southern Argentina. Website: http://www.bodegainfinitus.com 'E'mail: export@bodegasdomvistalba.com.ar

Bodega Jacques & François Lurton (Arg) a winery based in the Mendoza region, eastern Argentina. Website: http://www.bodegalurton.com

Bodega Jean Bousquet (Arg) a winery based in the Mendoza region, eastern Argentina. Website: http://www.jeanbousquet.com 'E'mail: info@jeanbousquet.com

Bodega Lagarde (Arg) a winery based in the Mendoza region, eastern Argentina. Website: http://www.lagarde.com.ar 'E'mail: info@lagarde.com.ar

Bodega Los Haroldcs (Arg) a winery based in the Mendoza region, eastern Argentina. Website: http://www.familiafalasco.com.ar 'E'mail: comexterior@bodegaslosharoldos.com

Bodega Millás Hnos. S.A (Arg) a winery based in the San Juan district, Cuyo region, eastern Argentina. Website: http://www.bodegasmillashnos.com.ar 'E'mail: analiamillas@bodegasmillashnos.com.ar

Bodega Navarro Correas (Arg) a winery (established 1798) based in the Mendoza region, eastern Argentina. Website: http://www.ncorreas.com

Bodega Nieto Senetiner (Arg) a winery based in the Mendoza region, eastern Argentina. Website: http://www.nietosenetiner.com.ar 'E'mail: fruiz@nietosenetiner.com.ar

Bodega Norton (Arg) a winery (established 1895) based in the Mendoza region, eastern Argentina. 680ha. (Add): Lujan de Guyo, Mendoza. Produces Privada (a red wine from Merlot, Cabernet sauvignon, Malbec grapes). Website: http://www.norton.com.ar 'E'mail: info@norton.com.ar

Bodega NQN Viñedos de la Patagonia (Arg) a winery based in the Patagonia region, southern Argentina. Website: http://www.bodeganqn.com.ar 'E'mail: bodeganqn{@bodeganqn.com.ar

Bodega Noemia de Patagonia S.A (Arg) a winery based in the Patagonia region, southern Argentina. Website: http://www.bodeganoemia.com 'E'mail: bodeganoemia@anylink.com.ar

Bodega RJ Viñedos (Arg) a winery based in the Mendoza region, eastern Argentina. Website: http://www.rjvinedos.com 'E'mail: rjvinedos@rjvinedos.com

Bodega Terrazas de los Andes (Arg) a winery based in the Mendoza region, eastern Argentina. Website: http://www.bodegaterrazasdelosandes.com 'E'mail: info@bodegaterrazasdelosandes.com

Bodegas Abeica SDAD. Coop. (Sp) a winery. (Add): El Calvario, 26339 Abalos (La Rioja). 25ha. Main wines are Chulato, Longrande.

Bodegas Afersa S.A. (Sp) a winery. (Add): Ctra. Logroño, s/n 26340 San Asensio, La Rioja. 10ha. Produces Riojan wines.

Bodegas Alavesas S.A. (Sp) a winery. (Add): Carretera de Elciego, s/n Laguardia, Alva. Founded in 1972. Grape varieties: Tempranillo 80% and Viura 20%. Produces Solar de Samaniego: red and white wine of Vintage, Reserva and Gran Reserva quality Rioja.

Bodegas Altanza (Sp) a winery based in Le Altanza in the D.O.Ca Rioja region. Grape varieties include: Tempranillo. Label: Le Altanza (rosé).

Bodegas Alvarez (Sp) a modern winery based in La Rueda. 100ha. (also buys in grapes). Produces cask matured white wines under the Mantel label.

Bodegas Amezola de la Mora (Sp) a winery. (Add): Paraje Viña Vieja, s/n 26359 Torremontralbo, Rioja. 70ha. Produces Viña Amezola from Tempranillo and Mazuelo grapes and Señorio Amezola.

Bodegas Antigua Usanza S.A. (Sp) a winery. (Add): Cmno. Garugele, 26338 San Vincente de la Sonsierra, La Rioja. 15ha. Main wines: Viña Azai, Peña Bajenza, Antigua Usanza.

Bodegas Arias (Sp) a winery based in Nava del Rey, Valladolid region, north-western Spain.

Bodegas Arzuaga (Sp) a winery based at Navarro in the D.O. Ribera del Duero. Produces Arzuaga from 90% Tinto fino plus Cabernet sauvignon and Merlot grapes.

Bodegas Ayuso (Sp) a winery based in La Mancha. Labels include Mirlo and Viña Q.

Bodegas Bardón (Sp) a winery based in Corella, Ribera Baja. Produces Togal: (a red wine from mainly Garnacha grapes) Don Luis and Zarums.

Bodegas Baron de Ley S.A. (Sp) a winery. (Add): Ctra. de Lodosa, Km 5, 31587 Mendavia, Navarra. 90ha. Main wine is Baron de Ley.

Bodegas Benegas (Arg) a winery based in Mendoza. Grape varieties: Cabernet franc, Cabernet sauvignon, Carmenère, Malbec, Merlot. Label: Lynch Meritage.

Bodegas Berberana S.A. (Sp) a winery. (Add): Ctra. Eloego, s/n Cenicero, La Rioja. 130ha. in Alta region of Rioja. Grape varieties: Tempranillo 65%, Viura 20%, Garnacha, Mazuelo and Graciano 5% each. Produces red, rosé and white wines. *see* Carta de Plata, Carta de Oro, Preferido and Viña Maria.

Bodegas Beronia S.A. (Sp) a winery. (Add): Ollauri Najera, La Rioja. 10ha. in Alta region of Rioja. Grape varieties: Tempranillo 85%, Viura, Garnacha and Mazuelo 15%. Produces red 90% and white 10% wines. Owned by Gonzalez Byass. *see* Berón. Labels include: III aC. Website: http://www.gonzalezbyass.com

Bodegas Bianchi (Arg) a wine producer at San Rafael. Owned by Seagram. Produces Cabernet wines under the labels of Don Valentin and Particular.

Bodegas Bilbaínas S.A. (Sp) a winery. (Add): Apartado 124, Particular del Norte 2, Bilbao 3. Alta region of Rioja. 240ha. Grape varieties: Tempranillo, Garnacha, Viura and Malvasia. Produces red 60%, rosé 15%, white 25% wines. 250ha. *see* Royal Carlton, Vendimia Especial (red and white), Viña Ederra, Viña Paceta, Viña Pomal, Viña Zaco.

Bodegas Bosch-Guell (Sp) a noted winery based in the Penedés region.

Bodegas Bretón Y Cia S.A. (Sp) a winery. (Add): Avda. Lope de Vega 20, 26006, Logroño, La Rioja. 100ha. Produces Crianza, Reserva and Gran Reserva wines. Labels include Dominio de Conte (90% Tempranillo, 10% Graciano grapes), aged for 30 months in American oak, Alba de Bretón Reserva from 80 year old Tempranillo vines. Aged 24 months in new American and Allier oak, then 2 months in Virginian oak.

Bodegas Buten (Sp) a winery based on the island of Tenerife. Label: Crater.

Bodegas Callia (Arg) a winery (241ha) based in the San Juan district, Cuyo region, eastern Argentina. Grape varieties include: Malbec, Syrah. Website: http://www.bodegascallia.com 'E'mail: info@bodegascallia.com

Bodegas Camacho (Sp) producers of fine Montilla wines (amontillado and fino) in the Montilla-Moriles, south-eastern Spain under the Sombra label.

Bodegas Campillo (Sp) a winery. (Add): Carretera de Logroño, s/n Oyon, Alava Alavesa region of Rioja. Grape varieties: Tempranillo, Viura and Malvasia. 100ha. in the Rioja Alavesa.

Bodegas Campo Blanco (Sp) a winery. (Add): Avdo. Estación s/n Cenicero, Rioja. Do not own vineyards. 100% red wines bought in from Rioja Alta and Alavesa.

Bodegas Campo Burgo S.A. (Sp) a winery. (Add): Avda. del Ebro, s/n 26540 Alfaro, Rioja. 35ha. Produces Crianza, Reserva and Gran Reserva wines.

Bodegas Campo Viejo (Sp) a winery. (Add): c/Gustavo Adolfo Bécquer 3, 26006 Logroño, La Rioja. Grape varieties: Tempranillo 80%, Garnacha 15%, Mazuelo 5%. 350ha. (275ha. in the Rioja Alta and Rioja Baja). Produces Marqués de Villamanga.

Bodegas Canale (Arg) a winery in Rio Negro. Produces quality wines from Cabernet sauvignon, Sémillon.

Bodegas Cantabria (Sp) a winery based in Laguardia, Rioja Alavesa.

Bodegas Carballo (Sp) a wine producer on La Palma, Canary Islands.

Bodegas Carlos Serres S.A. (Sp) a winery. (Add): P.O. Box 4, Haro, La Rioja. Alta region of Rioja. Own no vineyards. Produce red 70%, rosé 10% and white 20% wines. *see* Carlomango and Tercher Ano.

Bodegas Castro Martin (Sp) a winery with vineyards in Val do Salnés, Rías Baixas, D.O. Galicia. (Add): Puxafeita 3, Barrantes 36636, Ribadumia. Produces Casal Caeiro from Albariño grapes.

Bodegas Cadevi (Sp) a winery based in the Tierra de Castilla, Castilla. Label: Albor (rosé).

Bodegas Cenalsa-Pamplona (Sp) a new winery based in Navarra. Owned by the shareholders and Department of Agriculture in Navarra. Promotes the image of Navarra wines. Labels include: Agramont and Campo Nuevo.

Bodegas Concavins (Sp) a winery based in Conca de Barberà, Cataluña. Label: Castillo d'Mont-Blanc (rosé).

Bodegas Cooperativas el Barco (Sp) a wine co-operative in Galicia in north-western Spain. Produces Valdeorras Tinto.

Bodegas Cooperativas Sta. María la Real (Sp) a noted co-operative based in Nájera in the Rioja Alta.

Bodegas Cooperativas Vinícola de Labastida (Sp) a wine co-operative based in Labastida, Rioja Alavesa.

Bodegas Corral S.A. (Sp) a winery. (Add): D. Florencio Corral Daroca, Presidente Carretera de Logroño, KM 10, 26370 Navarrete, La Rioja. Grape varieties: Tempranillo, Garnacha, Viura and Malvasia. Produces red 90%, rosé 5% and white 5% wines under the Don Jacoba label. 40ha. in the Rioja Alta.

Bodegas Crillon (Arg) a winery owned by Seagram that produces sparkling wines by the Tank method.

Bodegas de Crianza (Sp) bodegas that are registered with the Consejo Regulador in Rioja that must age their wines in oak.

Bodegas de la Real Divisa S.A. (Sp) a winery. (Add):

Barrio del Montalvo, s/n 26339 Abalos, Rioja. 35ha. Main wines are Real Divisa, Marqués de Legarda.

Bodegas de la Torre y Lapuerta (Sp) a winery based in Alfaro, La Rioja. Produces red and white wines under the Campo Burgo label.

Bodegas del Delfin (Mex) a winery based in Parras de la Fuente, Coahuila.

Bodegas Delicia (Sp) a noted winery based in Ollauri, Rioja Alta.

Bodegas del Romerol (Sp) a winery based in Fuenmayor, Logroño. Produces red and white wines.

Bodegas del Rosario (Mex) a winery based in Parras de la Fuente, Coahuila.

Bodegas del Vesubio (Mex) a winery based at Parras de la Fuente, Coahuila.

Bodegas de Monte Casino (Mex) a winery based in Saltillo, Coahuila.

Bodegas de Perote (Mex) a winery based in Parras de la Fuente, Coahuila.

Bodegas de San Lorenzo (Mex) Casa Madero's winery based in Parras de la Fuente, Coahuila.

Bodegas de Santo Tomàs (Mex) a large winery (established 1888) and based at Ensenda.

Bodegas de San Ygnacio (Mex) a winery based in Saltillo, Coahuila.

Bodegas de Vilariño-Cambados (Sp) a winery with vineyards in Val do Salnés, Rías Baixas, D.O. Galicia. (Add): Burgans 91, Vilariño, 36630 Cambados. Biggest producer in Rías Baixas. Produces three wines: Martín Codax, Burgans, Organistrum.

Bodegas Domecq S.A. (Sp) a winery. (Add): Carretera Villabuena 9, 01340 Elciego, Alava. Grape varieties: Tempranillo and Viura. 320ha. in the Rioja Alavesa. Produces Privilegio del Rey Sancho and Viña Eguia. Owned by Allied Domecq.

Bodegas Don Ramos (Sp) a Sherry producer based in Jerez de la Frontera. Noted for Don Ramos (a fine Fino Sherry).

Bodegas El Coto S.A. (Sp) a winery. (Add): Oyón, Alava. 123ha. in Alavesa region of Rioja. Grape varieties: Tempranillo 85% and Viura 15%. Produces Cotode Imaz.

Bodegas El Hoyo (Sp) a wine producer on La Palma, Canary Islands.

Bodegas El Montecillo (Sp) a winery. (Add): San Cristobal, 34 Fuenmayor, La Rioja. Alta region of Rioja. Owns no vineyards. Produces red 85%, rosé 2.5% and white 12.5% wines. Cumbrero Viña Monty is their brand label.

Bodegas Escorihuela Gascón (Arg) a winery based in the Mendoza region. Grape varieties include: Malbec. Label: Candela. Website: http://www.escorihuela.com 'E'mail: exports@escorihuela.com

Bodegas Esmeralda (Arg) a winery based in Mendoza. The second label is Alamos Ridge. Produces wines from Cabernet sauvignon and Chardonnay. Labels also include Cantena. Website: http://www.cantenawines.com

Bodegas Etchart (Arg) a winery (450ha) based in Cafayate in the Salta region, northern Argentina.

(owned by Pernod-Ricard). Grape varieties: Cabernet franc, Cabernet sauvignon, Chardonnay, Merlot, Pinot noir, Syrah, Tannat. Website: http://www.vinosetchart.com

Bodegas Familia Saviron (Sp) a noted winery based in La Mancha. Produces red and white wines.

Bodegas Fariña (Sp) a fine winery based in the D.O of Toro. (Add): Camino de Palo, s/n 49800 Toro (Zamora), Spain. Label: Gran Colegiata Campus. Website: http://www.bodegasfarina.com 'E'mail: comercial@bodegasfarina.com

Bodegas Faustino Martinez S.A. (Sp) a winery. (Add): Carretera de Logroño, s/n 01320 Oyón, Alava. 350ha. in Alavesa region of Rioja. Grape varieties: Viura 10%, Tempranillo 80%, Mazuelo 5% and Graciano 5% wines. Faustino de Autor Reserva is a Rioja from 88% Tempranillo and 12% Graciano grapes. Aged 29 months in new French oak.

Bodegas Federico Paternina (Sp) a large winery based in Rioja. (Add): Avenida Santo Domingo II, Haro, La Rioja. 480ha. Produces a range of fine red, rosé and white wines.

Bodegas Felix Solis (Sp) a large winery based in Valdepeñas. Produces Valdoro (a cold fermented white wine), Viña Albali (an oak matured red wine) and a 100% Cencible red wine.

Bodegas Fernando Remirez de Ganuza (Sp) a winery based in Samaniego, Rioja. Website: http://www.remirezdeganuza.com 'E'mail: remirez@eniac.es

Bodegas 501 (Sp) producers of Mary Cruz, Soberbio, 501 Etiquetta Amarilla, Grana, Tercios Oro brandies in Jerez de la Frontera.

Bodegas Flichman (Arg) a winery based in Mendoza. Produces Caballero de la Cepa (red and white) and sparkling wines. Grape varieties: Merlot and Syrah.

Bodegas Francisco Viguera (Sp) a winery based in Haro, Rioja Alta.

Bodegas Franco-Españolas S.A. (Sp) a winery. (Add): Cabo Noval 2, 26006 Logroño, Rioja. 350ha. Produces red 65%, rosé 10% and white 25%. Part of the Rumasa Group. *see* Damante, Rioja Bordon and Viña Soledad.

Bodegas F. Rivero Ulecia (Sp) a noted winery based in Arnedo, Rioja. Produces Señorío de Prayla.

Bodegas García Carrión (Sp) a winery based in Jumilla. Produces Chiquito, Covanegra, Don García, Fiesta, Puente Viejo and San Simón.

Bodegas Gómez Cruzado (Sp) a major wine co-operative based in Rioja.

Bodegas Gonzales Videla (Arg) a small winery that sells its wines under the Panquehua and Tromel labels.

Bodegas Goyenechea (Arg) a winery noted for red Aberdeen Angus wine.

Bodegas Gracia (Sp) a winery based in the Montilla-Moriles region.

Bodegas Gurpegui (Sp) a winery. (Add): Avda, Celso Muerza, 8 San Adrian, y Cuevas, 32/34/36, Haro. 200ha. in Baja and Alta regions of Rioja. Grape varieties: Tempranillo 40% and Viura 60%. Produces red 50%, rosé 30% and white 20%. *see* Viña Berceo.

Bodegas Heredad de Baroja (Sp) a winery. (Add): Cercas Altas 6, 01309 Elvillar, Alava. Produces Rioja Reserva wines that are aged for 36 months in American and French oak.

Bodegas Hispano Argentinas (Arg) a winery based in the Mendoza region, eastern Argentina. Website: http://www.bodegasha.com.ar 'E'mail: enriquec@bha.com

Bodegas Ijalba (Sp) a 100% Graciano Rioja wine produced from a 18ha. vineyard. Label: Dionoslo Ruiz. Website: http://www.ijalba.com

Bodegas Insulares (Sp) a top wine producer on island of Tenerife, Canary Islands.

Bodegas Internacionales (Sp) a winery that produces a range of Sherries under the Duke of Wellington label. Also brandies under labels Baron de Brodzia, Mayorazgo, Pomartin, Royal Misa (all Solera brandies), Duke of Wellington, Samora (Solera Reserva) brandy 1810 (Solera gran reserva).

Bodegas Irache (Sp) a winery based in Estella, Navarra. Produces both Crianza and Reserva red wines.

Bodegas J. Freixedes (Sp) a winery based in Vilafranca del Penedés. Produces Viña Santa Marta range of red and white wines.

Bodegas José Palacios (Sp) a winery. (Add): Apartado 1152, Poligono de Cantabria, Logroño, La Rioja. Grape varieties: Tempranillo 40% and Garnacha 60%. Produces red, rosé and white wines. 350ha. in a co-operative system in the Alta and Baja regions. Dos Viñedos (lit: two vineyards) is a red Rioja made from selected grapes from selected vineyards that are vinified separately, then aged for 10 months in new French and USA oak. *See also* Eral, Herencia Remondo and Utero.

Bodegas Julián Chivite (Sp) a winery based in Navarra. Produces fine red, rosé and dry/sweet white wines.

Bodegas la Cuesta (Sp) *see* Cuesta.

Bodegas Lafuente (Sp) a winery based in Fuenmayor, Rioja Alta.

Bodegas Lagunilla S.A. (Sp) a winery. (Add): Carretera de Victoria kms. 182/183, Fuenmayor, La Rioja. Alta region of Rioja. Owns no vineyards. Produces red 80%, rosé 14% and white 6% wines.

Bodegas Lan (Sp) *see* Bodegas Landalan.

Bodegas Landalan (Sp) a winery. (Add): Paraje de Buicio, s/n 26360 Fuenmayor, Rioja. 70ha. in Alta region of Rioja. Grape varieties: Tempranillo, Mazuelo and Viura. Produces red, rosé and white wines under the Lancorta and Viña Lanciano labels. Culmen Reserva is produced from a single vineyard. Also known as Bodegas Lan.

Bodagas Larchago (Sp) a winery. (Add): c/Camino de la Poveda s/n, 01306 Lapuebla de Labarca, Alava. Produces Reserva Rioja wines from 80% Tempranillo, 20% Mazuelo grapes.

Bodegas la Rioja Alta (Sp) a winery based in the Rioja Alta. Produces red, rosé and dry/sweet white wines.

Bodegas la Rural (Arg) a winery based at Coquimbito. Grape varieties: Riesling and Traminer.

Bodegas la Seca (Sp) a large winery based in León.

Produces mainly red wines from the Prieto picudo grape.

Bodegas Latorre y Lapuerta (Sp) a winery based in Alfaro, Rioja Baja.

Bodegas Laturce (Sp) a 123ha. winery based in the Rioja Alta and Alavesa. (Add): Logroño, La Rioja. Produces red wines.

Bodegas Lavaque (Arg) a winery (established 1889) based in Cafayate Valley, in the Salta region, northern Argentina. 330ha. Grape varieties include: Bonarda, Cabernet sauvignon, Malbec, Syrah. Website: http://www.lavaque.com 'E'mail: info@lavaque.com

Bodegas Lonje (Sp) a top wine producer on the island of Tenerife, Canary Islands.

Bodegas Lopez (Arg) a small winery noted for Cabernet sauvignon wines.

Bodegas Lopez-Agos (Sp) a winery. (Add): Carretera de Logroño s/n. Fuenmayor, La Rioja. 45ha. in Alta region of Rioja. Grape varieties: Tempranillo 90% and Viura 10%. Produces red 90%, rosé 5% and white 5% wines.

Bodegas los Curros (Sp) a winery based in Fuente del Sol and Rueda, Valladolid. *see* Queen Isabella.

Bodegas Luis Cañas (Sp) a winery. (Add): Ctra. de Samaniego 10, 01307 Villabuena, Alava. Produces Reserva Rioja wines from 95% Tempranillo plus 5% Graciano, Mazuelo and Garnacha grapes.

Bodegas Magical (Sp) a Sherry producer based in Jerez de la Frontera. Labels include: Cream Game Fair, Hiru 3 Racimos, Magical and Selección de la Familia..

Bodegas Marco Real (Sp) a winery based in Navarra that produces Gran Feudo Rosado.

Bodegas Marqués de Cáceres (Sp) a noted winery. (Add): Ctra. de Logroño s/n, Cenicero, La Rioja. Alta region of Rioja. Grape varieties: Tempranillo 80%, Mazuelo 5%, Graciano 3%, Garnacha 6% and Viura 6%. Produces white, rosé and red wines. Labels include: Gaudium, MC, Riojas and Satinela. Website: http://www.marquesdecaceres.com

Bodegas Marqués de Ciria (Sp) a winery based in the Rioja Alta. (Add): Calle Gustavo Adolpho Becquer 3, Logroño, La Rioja. Produces red and white wines under the Marqués de Ciria label.

Bodegas Marqués del Puerto (Sp) a 40ha. winery based in the Rioja Alta. (Add): Carretera de Logroño s/n, 26360 Fuenmayor, La Rioja. Produces a range of red, rosé and white wines including Señorío Agos.

Bodegas Marqués de Monistrol (Sp) a winery based in Catalonia. Owned by Martini and Rossi. Produces dry/sweet red and sparkling wines.

Bodegas Marqués de Murríeta (Sp) a winery. (Add): Finca Ygay, Carretera de Zaragoza Km 5, Apartado, 109, 26006 Logroño. Alavesa region of Rioja. Grape varieties: Tempranillo 60%, Garnacha 10%, Viura 25%, Mazuelo, Malvasia and Graciano 5%. Produces red 20% and white 20%. 160ha. in the Rioja Alta. *See also* Castillo Ygay.

Bodegas Martinez Bujanda (Sp) a 200ha. winery based in the Rioja region. (Add): Camino Viejo de

Logroño s/n, 01320 Oyǿn, Alava. Produces red and white wines under the Conde Valdemar and Valdemar labels. Finca de Valpiedra is a Rioja produced from 90% Tempranillo, 6% Graciano and 4% Merlot grapes. Matured in American and French oak for 18 months.

Bodegas Martinez Lacuesta (Sp) a winery based in the Rioja region. (Add): Calle la Ventilla 71, 26200 Haro, La Rioja. Owns no vineyards but buys in grapes mainly from the Rioja Alta. Produces red and white wines.

Bodegas Megía e Hijos [J.A.] (Sp) a winery based in Valdepeñas. Produces Corcova Crianza from 100% Tempranillo. Also has 40ha. of Cabernet sauvignon.

Bodegas Miguel Calatayud (Sp) a winery based in Valdepeñas. Produces Vegaval Plata Reserva, Gran Reserva And Caberent sauvignon Reserva. Also Avalon Merlot Reserva.

Bodegas Monje (Sp) a winery based on the island of Tenerife. Grape varieties: Listán blanco, Listán negro and Negramoll. Label: Monje de Autor.

Bodegas Montecillo (Sp) a winery based at Ctra. Fuenmayor-Navarrete Km 3, 26370 Navarrete, Rioja Alta. Owns no vineyards.

Bodegas Montecristo (Sp) the brand-name of wines from Montilla-Moriles.

Bodegas Monteleiva S.A. (Sp) a winery. (Add): Ctra. de Cenicero, s/n 26360 Fuenmayor, Rioja. Owns no vineyards. Produces red, white and rosé wines.

Bodegas Morenito (Sp) an old established winery based in Valdepeñas, central Spain.

Bodegas Muerza S.A. (Sp) a winery. (Add): Vera Magallon Square 1, Apartado 44, San Adrián, Navarra. Baja region of Rioja. Owns no vineyards. Produces red 75%, rosé 15% and white 10% wines sold under the Rioja Vega label.

Bodegas Muga S.A. (Sp) a winery. (Add): Barrio de la Estación, s/n Haro, Rioja. 22ha. in Alta region of Rioja. Grape varieties: Tempranillo, Garnacha, Mazuela and Viura. Produces red 95% and white 5%. see Prado Enea and Muga (red, rosé and white). Also Conde de Haro (a sparkling wine). Website: http://www.bodegasmuga.com 'E'mail: informacion@bodegasmuga.com

Bodegas Murua Entrena S.A. (Sp) a winery. (Add): Ctra. Laguardia, s/n 01340 Elciego, Alava. 110ha. Wines include Crianza, Reserva and Gran Reserva.

Bodegas Nacari (Arg) a small co-operative in La Rioja. Noted for Torrontes wines.

Bodegas Navarro S.A. (Sp) a winery based in the Montilla-Moriles region that produces Montilla wine.

Bodegas Navarro Correas (Arg) see Correas.

Bodegas Norton (Arg) a well-established winery based in Luján de Cuyo, Mendoza. Noted for sparkling wines sold under the Consecha Especial and Norton labels. Also produces table wines under the Perdriel label.

Bodegas Ocha (Sp) a winery based in Olite, Navarra. Produces mainly light red and rosé wines.

Bodegas Olarra (Sp) a winery. (Add): Polígono de Cantabria, s/n Logroño. Alta region of Rioja. Owns no vineyards. Produces red 65%, rosé 5% and white 30%. Summa Añares – a Rioja from 40 year old vines (60% Tempranillo, 25% Mazuelo, 15% Graciano grapes). Also grows Malbec. See also Cerro Añon.

Bodegas Ondarre S.A. (Sp) a winery. (Add): Ctra. de Aras, s/n 31230 Viana, Navarra.

Bodegas Ontañon S.A. (Sp) a winery. (Add): Ctra. de Arrudo, 1 26570 Quel, Rioja. 10ha. Produces Crianza, Reserva and Gran Reserva wines.

Bodegas Otero (Sp) a winery based in Benavente, Zamora.

Bodegas Otto Bestué (Sp) a winery based in Somontano, Aragón. Grape varieties include: Cabernet sauvignon, Tempranillo. Label: Bestué de Otto Bestué (rosé).

Bodegas Palacio (Sp) a winery based at San Lázaron 1, 01300 Laguardia, Alava. Produces red, rosé and white wines. Owned by Seagram.

Bodegas Palacio de Fefiñanes (Sp) a winery (established 1904) with vineyards in Val do Salnés, Rías Baixas, D.O. Galicia. (Add): Pza. Fefiñanes s/n, 36630 Cambados. Oldest producer. Produces two styles of wine: Fefiñanes, and an oak-aged 1583. Website: http://www.habarcelo.es

Bodegas Palacios Remondo (Sp) see Bodegas José Palacios.

Bodegas Paternina S.A. (Sp) a Bodegas based at Ollauri in the Rioja Alta. Produces fine red and dry white wines.

Bodegas Penaflor (Arg) a large old winery in Mendoza. Produces most styles of wines.

Bodegas Peñalba López (Sp) a winery based in Ribera del Duero. Uses the Torremilanos label.

Bodegas Perez de Albaniz (Sp) the Bodegas where Faustino 1 is produced. see Bodegas Faustino Martinez. S.A.

Bodegas Pinord (Sp) a winery based in Vilafranca del Penedés. Produces Chateldon from 100% Cabernet sauvignon.

Bodegas Pintia (Sp) a winery based in the DO Toro, Ribera del Duero. Noted for its Pintia. Owned by Vega Sicilia.

Bodegas Piqueras (Sp) a winery based in the D.O. Almansa. Produces Palacio de Ciral. Grape varieties: Garnacha and Tempranillo.

Bodegas Prestige (Sp) a modern winery based in Villena, Alicante.

Bodegas Primicia (Sp) a winery based at Camino de la Hoya 1, 01300 Laguardia, Alava. Grape varieties: Cabernet sauvignon, Garnacha, Tempranillo.

Bodegas Princesa (Sp) a noted winery based in Valdepeñas. Produces Viña del Calar.

Bodegas Protos (Sp) a winery based in Ribera del Duero. Produces Crianza, Reserva and Gran Reserva wines.

Bodegas Proviar (Arg) a winery noted for sparkling wines sold under the labels of Baron B and M. Chandon (produced with the help of Moët et Chandon of France). Also produces fine red and white wines.

Bodegas Ramírez (Sp) a winery based at 3a Travesia

de San Roque, 26338 San Vincente de la Sonsierra. Produces Ramirez de la Piscina.

Bodegas Ramón Bilbao S.A. (Sp) a winery. (Add): Apartado Postal N°.15, 26200 Haro, La Rioja. Produces red 85%, rosé 5% and white 10% wines. 10ha.

Bodegas Real (Sp) a 300ha. wine estate in Valdepeñas. 90% Tempranillo, 10% of Cabernet sauvignon and Merlot. Produce Vega Ibor Crianza, Bonal Tempranillo, Viñaluz Blanco, Viña Vita.

Bodegas Real Divisa (Sp) a winery based in Abalos, Rioja Alavesa.

Bodegas Ribera Duero (Sp) a winery based in Peñafiel. Noted for red wines.

Bodegas Riojanas S.A. (Sp) a winery. (Add): Estación 1-21, 26350 Cenicero, Rioja Alta. 200ha. in Alta region of Rioja. Grape varieties: Tempranillo, Mazuelo, Graciano, Garnacha and Viura. Produces red 80%, rosé 6% and white 14% wines. *see* Canachales 2°Ano, Monte Real and Viña Albina.

Bodegas Rioja Santiago (Sp) a winery. (Add): Barrio Estación s/n, 26200 Haro. 27ha. in Alta region of Rioja. Grape varieties: Tempranillo 65% and Garnacha 35%. Produces red 50%, rosé 12% and white 38% wines. Owned by Pepsi Cola.

Bodegas Rivero (Sp) a winery based in Arnedo, Rioja Baja.

Bodegas Roda (Sp) a winery based in Haro, Rioja. Label: Cirsión. Website: http://www.roda.es

Bodegas Rojas y Cía (Sp) a winery based in Laguardia, Rioja Alavesa.

Bodegas Salentein (Arg) a winery based in Tupungato, Valle de Uco, south-west of Mendoza. Grape varieties: Cabernet sauvignon, Merlot, Pinot noir, Chardonnay, Sauvignon blanc, Malbec, Syrah. Website: http://www.bodegasalentein.com 'E'mail: info@bodegasalentein.com

Bodegas Salnesur (Sp) a co-operative with 350 members and 150ha. of vineyards in Val do Salnés, Rías Baixas, D.O. Galicia. (Add): Bouza 1, Castrelo, 36630 Cambados. Produces three wines from Albariño Grapes varieties: Clásico, Enxebre and Carballo Galego.

Bodegas San Huberto (Arg) a winery (established 1905) based in the La Rioja district, Cuyo r egion, central Argentina. 400ha. Has holdings in the Peoples' Republic of China. (Website: http://www.bodegassanhuberto.com.ar 'E'mail: info@bodegassanhuberto.com.ar

Bodegas San Miguel (Sp) a winery. (Add): Ctra. Zaragoza, 7 26513, Ausejo, Rioja. 550ha. Wines include Cambolosa, Peña Vieja.

Bodegas Santa Ana (Arg) a noted winery based in Guaymallen, Mendoza. Produces red, rosé, sparkling and white wines. Website: http://www.bodegas-santa-ana.com.ar 'E'mail: avivas@bodegas-santa-ana.com.ar

Bodegas Schenk (Sp) a winery based in Valencia. Produces both red and white wines.

Bodegas Señorío de Nava S.A. (Sp) a winery based in Ribera del Duero. Produce Crianza and Reserva wines.

Bodegas Sierra Cantabria S.A. (Sp) a winery. (Add): C/Amorebieta, 3 26338 San Vincente de la Sonsierra, Rioja. Produces mainly Vino Joven. 100ha. of Tempranillo, Garnacha, Viura, Malvasia.

Bodegas Sonsierra, SDAD. Coop. (Sp) a winery. (Add): El Remedio, s/n 26338 San Vincente de la Sonsierra, Rioja. 640ha.

Bodegas Suter (Arg) a winery owned by Seagram. Noted for Etiquette Blanca (white) and Marron (red) wines.

Bodeags Torre de Oña S.A. (Sp) a winery. (Add): Finca San Martín, 01307 Paganos-Laguardia, Alava. 50ha.

Bodegas Torres (Sp). *see* Torres.

Bodegas Trapiche (Arg) a winery. (Add): 5513 Coquimbito Maipu, Mendoza. Grape varieties: Cabernet sauvignon, Malbec, Chardonnay, Chenin blanc.

Bodegas Valcarlos (Sp) a winery based in the D.O. Navarra, north-eastern Spain. Grape varieties include: Cabernet sauvignon, Merlot, Tempranillo. Label: Fortius (rosé), Fortius Selección (rosé).

Bodegas Valdemar (Sp) a winery based in the Rioja.

Bodegas Valduero (Sp) a winery based at Doctor Esquerdo, 165 28007, Ribera del Duero.

Bodegas Vega Sicilia (Sp) a noted fine wine producer of the Valladolid region. 900ha. Grape varieties: Albillo, Cabernet sauvignon, Garnacho tinto, Malbec, Merlot and Tinto aragonés. Produces Valbuena and Vega Sicilia (red wines only).

Bodegas Velazquez S.A. (Sp) a winery. (Add): Azcarraga 27-29, Cenicero, La Rioja Alta region of Rioja. 50ha. Grape varieties: Tempranillo 80% and Garnacha 20%. Produces 100% red wine under the Monte Velaz label.

Bodegas Viña Salceda S.A. (Sp) a winery based in Elciego, Rioja Alavesa. Produces fine red wines.

Bodegas Virgen del Valle S.A. (Sp) a winery. (Add): Ctra. a Villabuena, s/n 01307 Samaniego, Alava. Owns no vineyards.

Bodegas Vista Alegre (Sp) a winery based in Haro, Rioja Alta.

Bodegas Weinert (Arg) a small winery noted for fine wines.

Bodegas Ysios (Sp) a winery owned by Allied Domecq and based in Rioja. Website: http://www.allieddomecqbodegas.com

Bodegas y Viñedos Alvarez S.A (Arg) a winery based in the Mendoza region, eastern Argentina. 'E'mail: jlpinares@infovia.com.ar

Bodegas y Viñedos de Gomez Cruzada S.A. (Sp) a winery. (Add): Avda. Vizcaya, Rioja. 100ha.

Bodegas y Viñedos Maza Tonconogy (Arg) a winery based in the Mendoza region, eastern Argentina. Website: http://www.mazatonconogy.com.ar 'E'mail: info@mazatonconogy.com.ar

Bodegas y Viñedos O. Fournier (Arg) a winery (94ha) based in the Mendoza region, eastern Argentina. Grape varieties: Cabernet sauvignon, Malbec, Merlot, Sauvignon blanc, Syrah, Tempranillo. Labels: Alfa Crux and B Crux. Website: http://www.ofournier.com 'E'mail: info@ofournier.com

Bodegas y Vinedos Pascal Toso S.A (Arg) a winery

B

(established 1890) based in the Mendoza region. Grape varieties include: Malbec, Merlot, Tempranillo. Produces a range of wine styles including sparkling wines. Labels: Magdalena Toso, Toso Brut. Website: http://www.bodegastoso.com.ar 'E'mail: tosowines@bodegastoso.com.ar

Bodegas y Viñedos San Polo S.A.I.C.A (Arg) a winery based in the Mendoza region, eastern Argentina. Website: http://www.sanpolo.com.ar 'E'mail: administracion@sanpolo.com.ar

Bodegas y Viñedos Santiago Graffigna (Arg) a winery (established 1876) based in the Tulum Valley, San Juan district, Cuyo region, eastern Argentina (owned by Pernod-Ricard). Website: http://www.pernod-ricard-argentina.com/http://www.graffignawines.com

Bodeguero (Sp) a bodega owner/wine maker.

Bodello (Sp) a white grape variety grown in north-western Spain.

Bodengeschmack (Ger) a term used to describe a wine that has an earthy taste.

Bodenham English Wines (Eng) a winery (established 1972). (Add): Broadfield Court Estate, Bodenham, Hereford, Herefordshire HR1 3LG. Produces a variety of wines and liqueurs. Also known as Broadfield Vineyard. Website: http://www.broadfieldcourt.co.uk 'E'mail: alex@broadfieldcourt.co.uk

Bodenham Reichensteiner (Eng) a dry white wine produced by the Broadfield Vineyard, Hereford.

Bodenheim (Ger) village (Anb): Rheinhessen. (Ber): Nierstein. (Gro): Sankt Alban. (Vins): Burgweg, Ebersberg, Heitersbrünnnchen, Hoch, Kapelle, Kreuzberg, Leidhecke, Monchspfad, Reichsritterstift, Silberberg, Westrum.

Bodensee (Ger) bereich (Anb): Baden. (Gro): Sonnenufer.

Bodensee (Ger) alternative name for Lake Constance. Bereich of Baden.

Bodental-Steinberg (Ger) vineyard (Anb): Rheingau. (Ber): Johannisberg. (Gro): Burgweg. (Vil): Lorch.

Bodental-Steinberg (Ger) a vineyard within the village of Lorch, 28.1ha. (43.8%) of which is proposed to be classified as Erstes Gewächs.

Bodenton (Ger) the taste of the soil, term is used for some of the Württemberg wines.

Bodgers Barley Wine (Eng) a 8.5% alc by vol. barley wine brewed by The Chiltern Brewery, Buckinghamshire.

Bodicote Brewery (Eng) a brewery. (Add): Plough, Bodicote, Banbury, Oxfordshire OX15 4BZ. Brews a variety of beers and lager including cask-conditioned Jim's Brew 1036 O.G. and Nø 9 1043 O.G. Website: http://www.banbury-cross.co.uk

Bodman (Ger) village (Anb): Baden. (Ber): Bodensee. (Gro): Sonnenfer. (Vin): Königsweingarten.

Bodmin Boar (Eng) a 4.3% alc by vol. ale brewed by the Ring 'O' Bells Brewery, Cornwall.

Bodo Brewery (Nor) a brewery based in Bodo in north Norway.

Bodraai Private Cellar (S.Afr) a winery (established

1999) based in Stellenbosch, Western Cape. 4ha. Grape varieties: Cabernet sauvignon, Shiraz

Bodrum (Tur) cellar.

Body (Eng) a description of strength and fullness in a wine from a high degree of alcohol and fruit.

Bodyline (Eng) a 4.3% alc by vol. ale brewed by Stonehenge Ales [Bunces Brewery], Wiltshire.

Boeckel [E.] (Fr) an Alsace wine producer. (Add): 67140 Mittelbergheim. 21ha.

Boeckser (Ger) a term used to describe a wine with a smell and taste of bad eggs.

Boeger Winery (USA) a winery based in Placerville, Eldorado, California. 8.5ha. Grape varieties: Cabernet sauvignon and Chenin blanc. Produces varietal and house wine under the Hangtown label.

Boekenhoutskloof (S.Afr) a winery based in Franschhoek, Western Cape. Grape varieties: Cabernet sauvignon, Cinsaut, Grenache, Merlot, Sauvignon blanc, Sémillon, Syrah, Viognier. Labels: The Chocolate Box, Porcupine Ridge, Wolftrap.

Boerenjongens (Hol) lit: 'farmer boys', a raisin-flavoured brandewijn.

Boerenmeisjes (Hol) lit: 'farmer girls', an apricot-flavoured brandewijn.

Boero Schnapps (Hol) the name given to a range of fruit schnapps: peach, melon, apple, water melon, lemon, tangerine.

Boffa (It) see Alfiero Boffa.

Bofferding (Lux) the label of a lager beer brewed by the Bofferding Brasserie.

Bofferding Brasserie (Lux) see Brasserie Nationale.

Bogazkarasi (Tur) a fine red wine produced in Anatolia from the Bogazkere grape.

Bogazkere (Tur) a red grape variety.

Bogbolter (Eng) a commemorative beer 1043 – 1050 O.G. brewed by the Frog & Firkin pub for the opening of the new public conveniences in West London.

Bogdanusa (Euro) a Dalmation white grape variety.

Bogen (Ger) the guyot system of vine training. see Einzelbogen and Doppelbogen.

Bogey (Cktl) in a 500mls (1pint) tankard containing ice cubes add 50mls (2fl.ozs) vodka, 25mls (1fl.oz) lime juice cordial. Top up with ginger beer and decorate with slice of lemon.

Boggart Hole Clough Brewery (Eng) a brewery (established 2000). (Add): Unit 13, Brookside Works, Clough Road, Manchester, Greater Manchester M9 4SP. Brews: Angel Hill 4.2% alc by vol., Bog Standard Pioneer 4% alc by vol., Boggart Bitter 3.8% alc by vol., Boggart Dark Mild 4% alc by vol., Boggart Light Mild 3.8% alc by vol., Boggart's Brew 4.3% alc by vol., Steaming Boggart 9% alc by vol., Sun Dial 4.7% alc by vol., The Dark Side 4.4% alc by vol. Website: http://www.boggart-brewery.co.uk 'E'mail: boggart@btinternet.com

Boggs Cranberry Liqueur (USA) a cranberry-flavoured liqueur produced by the Heublein Cº. in Hartford, Connecticut. 40° US proof.

Bogle Vineyards (USA) a winery based in Clarksburg, Yolo, California. Grape varieties:

151

Chenin blanc and Petit syrah. Produces varietal wines.

Bogota (S.Am) a fine grade of coffee beans from Colombia.

Bogotas (S.Am) a noted coffee-producing region in Colombia. *see* Bogota.

Bog Standard Pioneer (Eng) a 4% alc by vol. ale brewed by the Boggart Hole Clough Brewery, Greater Manchester.

Boguzkere (Tur) a red grape variety used in the making of Buzbag.

Bohea (Chi) a black tea from the Wu-i Shan hills, much favoured in the eighteenth century. Now of little quality.

Bohemia (Czec) an old wine region that now produces only a little wine. Both red and white is made from the Blauer Burgunder, St. Laurent, Blaufränkirscher for the reds and Pinot, Traminer and Sylvaner for the whites.

Bohemia (S.Am) a 4.8% alc by vol. straw coloured, bottled lager brewed by the Cuauhtémoc Brewery, Monterrey, Mexico.

Bohemia Beer House (Eng) a distillery (established 1996). (Add): P.O. Box 97, Hertford, Hertfordshire SG13 8UD. Produces a range of spirits. Website: http://www.eabsinthe.com 'E'mail: info@eabsinthe.com

Bohemian Maid (Can) the brand-name of a malt beer.

Bohemian Rhapsody (Eng) 5% alc by vol. ale brewed by the Hampshire Brewery, Hampshire.

Bohemia Regal (Czec) a range of sparkling red and white wines produced by Bohemia Sekt, Staky Pizenec.

Bohemia Regent a.s. (Czec) a brewery. (Add): Trocnovské namesti 124, 379 01 Trebon, Czec Republic. Brews: Bohemia Regent Ale 4.8% alc by vol. and other ales and lagers.

Böhlig (Ger) vineyard (Anb): Pfalz. (Ber): Mittelhaardt-Deutsche Weinstrasse. (Gro): Mariengarten. (Vil): Wachenheim.

Boil (Eng) also known as 'the boil' is the term used in brewing when the wort and hops are boiled together in the copper.

Boileau [Etienne] (Fr) a winery based in the A.C. Chablis, Burgundy. Produces a range of Chablis wines including Premier Crus Mont de Milieu and Vaillons.

Boiled (USA) a slang term for intoxicated/very drunk.

Boilermaker (Eng) ½ pint (300mls) brown ale and ½ pint (300mls) mild ale mixed.

Boilermaker (USA) a neat whiskey with a beer chaser.

Boiling Water (Eng) the condition to which water must be heated 100°C (212°F) for the brewing of tea. Must be at a rapid, rolling boil to produce the best infusion.

Boillot (Fr) a cuvée in the A.C. vineyard of Les Duresses in the commune of Auxey-Duresses, Côte de Beaune, Burgundy. Is owned by the Hospices de Beaune. 0.75ha.

Boillot [Henri] (Fr) a Burgundy négociant-éleveur based at Volnay, 21190 Meursault.

Boire (Fr) to drink.

Boire à la Santé de (Fr) a toast. "*Lets drink to the health of*".

Bois (Fr) the name given to the wood chips added to wine to replace cask aging but still give the wine a flavour of wood.

Bois (Fr) wood/woody taste, *See also* Gout de Bois.

Boisage (Fr) the addition of concentrated tannin extracts sometimes used in Cognac production.

Bois à Terroir (Fr) *see* 'Bois Communs Dits à Terrior'.

Bois Communs Dits à Terroir (Fr) the seven grades of Cognac.

Boiscin Tae (Ire) tea caddy.

Bois d'Arcon [Le] (Fr) a Cru A.C. Chinon wine produced by Domaine de Bel Air in Touraine from 60 year old vines. *See also* La Fosse aux Loups.

Bois Dur (Fr) a lesser name for the red Carignan grape variety in south- western France.

Boisé (Fr) the addition of oak shavings, liquid or extract of powdered oak to eau-de-vie as it is aging to help speed the process up. Also addition of a solution in which wood chips have been boiled to extract tannins (or hot water into new casks).

Bois Lauzun (Fr) a red Châteauneuf-du-Pape produced by Tézier (Henri), Rte. de Ste. Cécile, 64830 Sérignan.

Bois Ordinaires et Bois Communs (Fr) the sixth Cru of Cognac which covers 6% of area.

Bois Rosé (Cktl) ⅓ measure B and B, ⅓ measure Noilly Prat, ⅓ measure blackcurrant. Shake over ice, strain into a cocktail glass and add a slice of lemon.

Boisseaux Estivant (Fr) a Burgundy négociant based at Beaune. A small company who ship fine wines.

Boisset [Jean Claude] (Fr) a large négociant-éleveur of Nuits-Saint-Georges, Côtes de Nuits, Burgundy. (Add): 2 Rue Frères Montgolfier, 21700 Nuits-Saint-Georges. Owns : Bassot, Bouchard Aîné, Celliers de Samson, Chauvenat, Delaunay, Domaines Michel Bernard, Drouhin, Jaffelin Frères, L'Héritier-Guyot, Moreau & Fils (J.), Morin, SNJ Pellerin, Pierre Ponnelle, Ropiteau Frères, Thorin, Vienot, Violland (Louis). Has a joint venture with Vincor International of Canada to develop the vineyard Le Clos Jordan in Ontario on the Niagara Peninsula. *See also* French Rabbit.

Boissière (Fr) a noted producer of Chambéry in south-eastern France Created Domaine de la Vougeraie in 1999

Boissières [Les] (Fr) a red wine produced mainly from Grenache grapes by Domaine Font-Caude in Montpeyroux.

Boissin (Ch.Isles) public bar.

Boisson (Fr) drink/beverage/booze.

Boisson Alcoolique (Fr) liquor/alcoholic beverages.

Boisson de Sureau (Fr) elderberry cordial.

Boissons d'Orge (Fr) a non-alcoholic barley cordial (liquorice flavoured).

Boissons Fermentées (Fr) fermented drinks (beverages).

Boîte (Fr) cannister. e.g. Boîte à Biere.

Boîte à Biere (Fr) beer can.

Boîte à Thé (Fr) tea caddy.

Boizel (Fr) a Champagne house. (Add): 16 Rue de Bernon, 51200 Épernay. Produces vintage and non-vintage Champagne. Vintages: 1900, 1904, 1906, 1909, 1911, 1914, 1915, 1919, 1921, 1926, 1928, 1929, 1934, 1937, 1941, 1943, 1945, 1947, 1949, 1952, 1953, 1955, 1959, 1961, 1962, 1964, 1966, 1969, 1970, 1971, 1973, 1975, 1976, 1978, 1979, 1980, 1982, 1983, 1985, 1988, 1990, 1995, 1998, 1999. Labels include the De luxe cuvée : Joyau de France.

Bok (Hol) a seasonal beer, available between October and December. Is reddish-black in colour with a strong malty taste and aroma.

Bokbier (Hol) a 6.5% alc by vol. bottle-conditioned, dark, autumn bock beer brewed by De Drie Ringen Amersfoort Bier Brouwerij, Amersfoort.

Bokma (Hol) a distillery based in Leeuwarden. Owned by Heineken. Produces Jenevers and fine range of liqueurs.

Bok Ol (Nor) bock beer.

Bol (Euro) a wine-producing region in Dalmatia.

Bolaffi Guide (It) an Italian wine guide compiled by Luigi Veronelli.

Boland Cellar (S.Afr) see Bolandse Koöperatiewe Wyndkelders.

Bolanden (Ger) village (Anb): Pfalz. (Ber): Mittelhaardt-Deutsche Weinstrasse. (Gro): Schnepfenflug vom Zellertal. (Vin): Schlossberg.

Bolandse Koöperatiewe Wynkelders (S.Afr) a co-operative winery (2400ha) based in Nooder-Paarl, Western Cape. (Add): Box 2, Hugenot 7645. Grape varieties: Cabernet sauvignon, Chardonnay, Chenin blanc, Merlot, Nouvelle, Pinotage, Red Muscadel, Riesling, Sémillon, Shiraz, White Muscadel. Merged with the Paarl-Valle Wynkoöperasie Beperk to form this large winery. Label: Boland Cellar (Boland Kelder), Bon Vino, Reserve. Website: http://www.bolandkelder.co.za

Bolay Tea (Chi) a mandarin tea with a distinctive 'mouldy' taste, also known as Pu'er.

Bold Forester (Eng) a spring ale 4.2% alc by vol. brewed by the Ringwood Brewery, Hampshire, England.

Bolée (Fr). An earthenware bowl used in Normandy for the drinking of cider.

Bolée de Cidre (Fr) cider bowl. See also Boulée and Bolée.

Bolero Cocktail (Cktl) 1 measure dark rum, ½ measure Calvados, 2 dashes Italian vermouth. Stir over ice, strain into a cocktail glass.

Bolgheri (It) a D.O.C. rosé wine from Livorno, Tuscany. Made from Cabernet, Montepulciano and Sangiovese grapes.

Bolgheri D.O.C. Sassicaia (It) the official name for Sassicaia from 1994. Produced from 85% Cabernet sauvignon and 15% Cabernet franc grapes.

Bolivar (Sp) a dry Amontillado Sherry produced by Domecq (dating from 1898).

Bolivia (S.Am) a country that has some of the highest vineyards in the world in the Chuqisaca province. Has been producing wine since the sixteenth century. Most wine drunk locally.

Bölkstoff (Ger) a 4.9% alc by vol. bottled pilsner brewed by the Gilde Brauerei, Hanover.

Bolla (It) a well-known Veneto wine producer, including cuve close sparkling wines.

Bollbier Hell (Ger) produced in Bavaria. see Graf Arco.

Bollène (Fr) a commune of the Principauté d'Orange département in the southern Rhône.

Bolleponge (W.Ind) a word used for a drink made of spirit, lemon juice, sugar, mace and toast.

Bollinger (Fr) a grande marque Champagne house (established 1829). (Add): 4 Bld. du Marechal de Lattre de Tassigny, 51160 Aÿ. 140ha. Produces vintage, non-vintage and a vieilles vignes (blanc de noirs) wines. Vintages: 1904, 1906, 1914, 1919, 1921, 1924, 1926, 1928, 1929, 1934, 1937, 1941, 1943, 1945, 1947, 1949, 1952, 1953, 1955, 1959, 1961, 1962, 1966, 1969, 1970, 1973, 1975, 1976, 1979, 1982, 1983, 1985, 1986, 1988, 1989, 1990. Recent R.D. Vintages: 1953, 1959, 1961, 1964, 1966, 1970, 1973, 1975, 1976, 1979, 1982, 1983, 1985, 1986, 1988, 1990, 1995. See also R.D.

Bollschweil (Ger) village (Anb): Baden. (Ber): Markgräflerland. (Gro): Lorettoberg. (Vin): Steinberg.

Bolo (Eng) a mixture of spirit (usually rum), fresh fruit juices and spices drunk in the eighteenth century.

Bologna [Giacomo] (It) a winery based in Braida, Piemonte. Is noted for Brachetto d'Acqui and Grignolino d'Asti.

Bologne (W.Ind) a rum distillery based in Guadeloupe.

Bols (Hol) a famous Dutch firm of liqueurs and spirit producers. see Bols (Lucas).

Bols [Lucas] (Hol) a Dutchman who was one of the first makers of liqueurs. The modern firm of Erven Lucas Bols are descendants of the original firm started in the sixteenth century.

Bolsberry (USA) a mild pleasant liqueur made from blackcurrants and other fruits. In Holland it is classed as an apéritif.

Bolscherwhisk (Hol) a cherry brandy and Scotch whisky liqueur produced by the Bols Cº.

Bolshoi Vodka (USA) a vodka brand imported by Park Ave. Imports, New York. 40% alc by vol.

Bolskaya (Can) a brand of vodka produced by Hiram Walker. 40% alc by vol.

Bolskümmel (Hol) the original kümmel first produced in 1575 by Erven Lucas Bols.

Bolten Alt (Ger) a 4.7% alc by vol. alt beer brewed by the Bolten Brauerei, Korschenbroich.

Bolten Brauerei (Ger) a brewery (established 1266) based at Korschenbroich. Brews Bolten Alt.

Bolzano (It) a wine province of the Trentino-Alto-Adige. Produces red and white wines. The best being Santa Maddalene.

B

Bomas (Eng) the seventeenth century spelling used for Bommes (commune in the A.C. Sauternes).

Boma's 10/4 (Eng) a 15% alc by vol. fortified wine drinks from the Global Beer Company. 4 flavours- banana, blue strawberry, red banana, tangerine.

Bomba (Sp) the name for the siphon used for racking in the bodegas.

Bombach (Ger) village (Anb): Baden. (Ber): Breisgau. (Gro): Burg Lichteneck. (Vin): Sommerhalde.

Bombard (Eng) a large leather jug used for carrying ale etc. up from the cellar to the bar. Up to 8 gallons capacity.

Bombardier Bitter (Eng) a cask-conditioned bitter 4.3% alc by vol. (1042 O.G.) brewed by the Charles Wells Brewery, Bedford.

Bombay (Cktl) ½ measure brandy, ¼ measure dry vermouth, ¼ measure sweet vermouth, dash pastis, 2 dashes orange Curaçao. Stir over ice, strain into a cocktail glass.

Bombay (Eng) a brand of gin produced by Greenall Whitley at Warrington. 40% alc by vol.

Bombay Cooler (Cktl) 2 measures dry gin, ½ measure Curaçao, juice of ½ orange, dash Angostura. Shake over ice, strain into a highball glass. Top up with tonic water.

Bombay Punch (Punch) 2¼ litres (2quarts) Champagne, 1.1ltrs. (1quart) soda water, 60mls (½gill) orange Curaçao, 60mls (½gill) maraschino, 500mls (1pint) Sherry, 500mls (1pint) brandy. Stir together gently in a chilled punch bowl. Decorate with nuts and fruits in season.

Bombay Sapphire (Eng) a 40% alc by vol. London dry gin sold in a blue bottle. Contains 10 herbs and spices and is distilled by passing the vapour from the grain spirits through spiles.

Bombay Sherry Punch (Punch) 1 bottle each of brandy and Sherry, 1 tablespoon each of maraschino and Cointreau, 2 bottles dry sparkling wine, syphon of soda water. Mix with large ice cubes in a punch bowl. Decorate with fruit in season. Add wine and soda last.

Bomber (Eng) a 4.4% alc by vol. bitter ale brewed by Mitchell's, Lancaster.

Bomber County (Eng) a 4.8% alc by vol. ale brewed by the Highwood Brewery, Lincolnshire.

Bombilla (S.Am) a silver tube with a strainer at the lower end which is used to drink Yerba Maté tea through. (The lower end being inserted into the gourd the tea is served in).

Bombino (It) a red grape variety grown in Puglia and Latium.

Bombino Bianco (It) a white grape variety grown in Latium. Also called the Ottonese or Trebbiano d'Abruzzo. see Bombino.

Bombino Nero (It) a black grape variety grown in Latium.

Bombo [El] (Sp) a noted vineyard based in the Moriles area of Montilla-Moriles, southern Spain.

Bombom Crema (W.Ind) a honey-flavoured liqueur produced in Cuba.

Bombonas (Sp) a pear-shaped glass bottle that some

Priorato wines are aged in called Vino Rancios (they have a Sherry-style taste).

Bombshell Bitter (Eng) a bitter ale brewed by the Quay Brewery, Hope Square, Weymouth.

Bom Fim (Port) a noted quinta belonging to Dow's Port shippers.

Bomita (Sp) a white grape variety grown in Cáceres, south-western Spain.

Bommerlunder (Ger) a brand of aquavit.

Bommes (Fr) a commune in Sauternes in Bordeaux. Wines sold under the A.C. Sauternes. A sweet white wine, the grapes are attacked by *Botrytis cinerea*. *See also* Bomas.

Bömund II [Archbishop] (Ger) 1351–1362. Elector of Trier. Recovered from serious illness by drinking the wines of the 'Doktor' vineyard in Bernkastel, Mosel-Saar-Ruwer.

Bona Dea (S.Afr) the label for a red wine (Cabernet sauvignon, Merlot and Shiraz blend) produced by Blyde Wines, Paarl, Western Cape.

Bonafort (Mex) a natural spring mineral water from Toluca.

Bonaparte (Fr) a Champagne producer. (Add): 2 Rue Villiers-aux-Bois, BP 41, 51130 Vertus.

Bonaqa (Pol) a sparkling natural spring mineral water from Radzymin. Mineral contents (milligrammes per litre): Sodium 30mg/l, Calcium 95mg/l, Magnesium 75mg/l, Bicarbonates 357mg/l, Chlorides 300mg/l, Sulphates 2.3mg/l.

Bonaqa (USA) a natural spring mineral water brand.

Bonaqua (Ger) a natural spring mineral water brand.

Bonaqua (Chi) a mineralised (includes: magnesium sulphate, potassium chloride, sodium chloride and water) water brand. Website: http://www.bonaqua.com.hk

Bonaqua (Hun) a sparkling natural mineral water. Mineral contents (milligrammes per litre): Sodium 13.1mg/l, Magnesium 46.4mg/l, Potassium 17.8mg/l, Bicarbonates 649mg/l, Chlorides 16.2mg/l, Sulphates 215.6mg/l.

Bonaqua (Rus) a natural spring mineral water from Nishnij, Nowgorod. Mineral contents (milligrammes per litre): Calcium 32.4mg/l, Magnesium 32mg/l, Bicarbonates 60mg/l, Chlorides 200mg/l, Sulphates 60mg/l.

Bonarda (It) a red grape variety grown in Piemonte. Also known as Croatina, Uva rara.

Bonarda (S.Am) a red grape variety grown in Argentina and Brazil.

Bonarda di Gattinara (It) a red grape variety used in the making of Gattinara wine in Piemonte.

Bonarda Novarese (It) a red grape variety also known as the Uva rara.

Bonarda Oltrepo Pavese (It) a D.O.C. red wine from Piemonte. Made from the Bonarda grape.

Bonardi (It) a producer of Moscato d'Asti in the Piemonte region.

Bonaterra Vineyards (USA) the label used by Fetzer for their organically grown wines produced from Cabernet sauvignon and Chardonnay grapes.

BoNatura (Mex) a natural spring mineral water (established 1990). pH 6.8

Bon Blanc (Fr) the local Bugey and Seyssel area name for the Chasselas grape in south-eastern France. Also known as the Colombar and the Pied-tendre.

Bonbonne (Fr) carboy.

Bon Cap (S.Afr) an organic winery (established 2001) based in Robertson, Western Cape. 45ha. Grape varieties: Cabernet sauvignon, Chardonnay, Merlot, Pinotage, Sauvignon blanc, Syrah, Viognier. Labels; Organic, Ruins. Website: http://www.boncaporganic.co.za

Bonci (It) a winery in the D.O.C. Verdicchio dei Castelli di Jesi, Marches region. Label: San Michele Superiore.

Boncompagni Ludovisi (It) a winery based in the Latium region. Is noted for red wines including Fiorana.

Bon Courage Wine Estate (S.Afr) a winery (established 1927) based in Robertson, Western Cape. 150ha. (Add): P.O. Box 589, Robertson 6705. Grape varieties: Chardonnay, Colombard, Gewürztraminer, Merlot, Sauvignon blanc, Shiraz, White muscadel. Labels: Cap Classique Jacques Bruére, Inkará, Prestige Cuvée. Also produces: sparkling, noble late harvest and Port-style wines. Website: http://www.boncourage.co.za

Bond (Eng) the storage of excisable liquor on which duty and taxes have not been paid.

Bonde (Fr) a word used for a bung or stopper.

Bonde Bordelaise de Sûreté (Fr) an unbroachable stopper used to seal wine that is maturing in barrels.

Bonded (Eng) wines and spirits are bonded in a 'Bonded Warehouse' under Government supervision until Customs and Excise duties are paid by the owner.

Bonded (S.Am) a brand of rum produced in Guyana by the Guyana Distilleries.

Bonded Warehouse (Eng) the premises where liquor is kept in bond until duty is paid.

Bond Vecina Estate (USA) a winery based in the Napa Valley, California. Grape varieties include: Cabernet sauvignon. Label: Vecina.

Bonde sur le Côte (Fr) the practice of storing the casks with their bungs on their sides so as to exclude the air from the wine.

Bondola (Switz) a red wine from the Ticino region, a smooth and fruity wine.

Bond 7 (Austr) a popular brand of whiskey produced by Gilbeys. Part of International Distillers and Vintners.

Bond Stacking (Eng) a method breweries adopt for stacking beer crates to distribute the weight. Is similar to brick building.

Bone Dry (Eng) a light, dry, fino Sherry from Avery's of Bristol.

Bone-Dry (Eng) the term to describe a wine with no sugar and plenty of acidity.

Bone Idyll (Austr) a light red wine produced by the Idyll Vineyard in Moorabool, Victoria.

Boneparte Shandy (Eng) brandy and lemonade.

Bonesio Winery (USA) a winery based in Santa Clara, California. Produces varietal wines.

Bone Structure (Eng) a description used to indicate the body in a red wine.

Bonfoi Estate (S.Afr) a winery (established 1699) based at Vlottenburg, Stellenbosch, Western Cape. 98ha. (Add): Bonfoi Box 9, Vlottenburg 7580. Grape varieties: Cabernet sauvignon, Chardonnay, Merlot, Sauvignon blanc, Shiraz. Label: Overture. Website: http://www.bonfoiwines.co.za

Bon Goût (Fr) good taste/good flavour (applicable to wines or spirits).

Bonhams Wine Auctions (Eng) specialist wine auctioneers. (Add): Montpelier Galleries, Montpelier Street, Knightsbridge, London SW1 1HH.

Bonheur Estate [Le] (S.Afr) a vineyard based in Stellenbosch. (Add): P.O. Klapmuts 7625. Produces a fine Blanc Fumé from the Sauvignon blanc grape.

Bonhomme [Le] (Fr) a wine village in Alsace. (Ger) = Dieboldshausen.

Bonillo [El] (Sp) a Vino de Mesa area in the province of Albacete, Castilla-La Mancha.

Bonita (Yug) a natural spring mineral water from Lypian, Kosovo.

Bonito (Sp) a term used to describe an elegant Sherry.

Bonnaire (Fr) récoltants-manipulants of Champagne. (Add): 51200 Épernay. Produces vintage and non-vintage wines. Member of the C.V.C. Vintages include 1934, 1947, 1949, 1952, 1955, 1959, 1961, 1964, 1966, 1969, 1971, 1973, 1975, 1976, 1990, 1995, 1996, 1998, 1999, 2000. *see* Cramant Bonnaire.

Bonnaire-Bouquemont (Fr) a Champagne producer and grower. Produces a 100% blanc de blancs Cramant Grand Cru.

Bonne Bouche (Fr) good mouthful.

Bonne Chauffe (Fr) lit: 'good fire', in Cognac production the heart of the distillate, was supposedly invented by Chevalier de la Croix Maron in the sixteenth century.

Bonne Esperance (S.Afr) a red wine of the Bordeaux-style produced mainly for the USA market by KWV. Also a rosé and white wine are sold under this label.

Bonne Nouvelle (S.Afr) the label for a red wine (Cabernet sauvignon and Merlot blend) produced by the Remhoogte Estate winery, Stellenbosch, Western Cape.

Bonnes-Mares (Fr) an A.C. Grand Cru vineyard of the commune Morey-Saint-Denis in the Côte de Nuits. The smallest of the Grand Crus it is shared with the Chambolle-Musigny commune. 1.8ha. of marl and chalk soils.

Bonnes-Mares (Fr) an A.C. Grand Cru vineyard of the commune Chambolle- Musigny in the Côte de Nuits. Also in the grand Cru Morey-Saint-Denis commune. 13.7ha. of marl and chalk soils.

Bonnet [F. et Fils] (Fr) a Champagne producer. (Add): 12 Allé du Vignoble, BP 129, 51055 Reims. 10ha. Produces vintage and non-vintage wines. Vintages: 1973, 1976, 1979, 1980, 1986, 1988, 1989, 1990, 1995, 1998, 1999.

Bonnet-Gilmert (Fr) a Champagne producer. (Add):

Rue des Gouttes d'Or, 51190 Oger. Propriétaire-récoltant. Produces 100% Grand Cru Blanc de Blancs, Grande Réserve d'Amboise, Blanc de Blancs Cuvée Réserve.

Bonneuil (Fr) a commune in the Charente département whose grapes are classed Grande Champagne (Cognac).

Bonnevaux [Les] (Fr) a vineyard in the A.C. commune of Montagny, Côte Chalonnaise, Burgundy.

Bonnezeaux (Fr) a site on the commune of Thouarcé, Coteaux du Layon. Produces sweet white wines from Chenin blanc grapes attacked by botrytis. A.C. from Pineau de la Loire. 125ha. 13%–16% alc by vol. (soil: shale, sand and sandstone). *see* Syndicat du Cru de Bonnezeaux.

Bonnie Prince Charlie (Cktl) 10mls (½ fl.oz) Drambuie, 25mls (1fl.oz) brandy, 25mls (1fl.oz) lemon juice. Shake over ice and strain into a cocktail glass.

Bonnievale (S.Afr) a district within the Klein Karoo region. Noted for brandy.

Bonnievale Co-operative Winery (S.Afr) a co-operative winery (established 1694) based in Bonnievale, Breede River, Robertson, Western Cape. 800ha. (Add): Box 206, Bonnievale 6730. Grape varieties: Cabernet franc, Cabernet sauvignon, Chardonnay, Chenin blanc, Cinsaut, Colombard, Ruby cabernet, Sauvignon blanc, Shiraz. Labels: Bonnievale, Kelkerooi, Kelkiewit, Pich'n'Wyntjie, Vertex Reserve. Also produces varietal, late harvest and Port-style wines. Website: http://www.bonnievalecellar.co.za

Bönnigheim (Ger) village (Anb): Württemberg. (Ber): Württembergisch Unterland. (Gro): Stromberg. (Vins): Kirchberg, Sonnenberg.

Bonnonee Winery (Austr) a winery. (Add): Box 145, Campbell Avenue, Irymple, Victoria. Grape varieties: Barbera, Chardonnay, Crouchen, Gewürztraminer, Rhine riesling, Ruby cabernet, Shiraz. Produces varietal and table wines.

Bonny Doon (USA) a winery based near Santa Cruz. (Add): 2485 Highway 46 West, Paso Robles. CA 93446. Concentrates on producing red Bordeaux, Rhône and Italian grape varieties: Barbera, Dolcetto, Grenache, Pinot gris, Riesling, Roussanne, Sangiovese. Produces Old Telegram, Cigare Voltant (le). Website: http://www.bonnydoonvineyard.com

Bonny Lass (Eng) a 3.9% alc by vol. bitter ale brewed by The Durham Brewery Ltd., County Durham.

Bonora (It) a natural spring mineral water from Bonora, Rimini.

Bon Père William [Le] (Switz) an eau-de-vie-de-poire.

Bons Bois (Fr) the fifth Cru of Cognac. Covers 24.7% of area.

Bons Bourgeois (Fr) *see* Cru Bourgeois.

Bon Spuronza Vineyards (USA) a small winery based in Westminster, Maryland. Produces French/American hybrid wines.

Bontemps (Fr) a scoop or wooden pail used to hold the finings (egg whites).

Bonterra Vineyards (N.Am) a winery based in North Coast Region, California. Owned by Fetzer, it produces a variety of wines and organic wines. Website: http://www.bonterra.com

Bon-Val (Bel) a natural spring mineral water from Bon-Val, Bavikhove.

Bon Valaisan (Switz) a 27% alc by vol. gin and gentian-based elixir from Morand Distillerie, Martigny, Valais

Bon Vallon (S.Afr) an unoaked Chardonnay wine matured on the lees produced by the De Wetshof Estate in Robertson. *See also* Bateleur.

Bonvedro (Austr) a red grape variety.

Bonvillars (Switz) a wine-producing area in northern Vaud. Produces both red and white wines.

Bonville [F. et Fils] (Fr) a Champagne producer. (Add): 9 Rue Pasteur, 51190 Avize. Récoltants-manipulants. Produce vintage and non-vintage wines.

Bonvin (Switz) a grower and merchant based in Sion, south-west Switz.

Bonvino (It) a red grape variety grown in Latium.

Bon Vino (S.Afr) the name for a series of wines produced by the Boland Kelder, Paarl, Western Cape.

Bon Vivant (Can) a Canadian rye whisky produced by the Canadian Gibson Distilleries.

Bonwa Mineralwasser (Ger) a natural spring mineral water from Bad Rappenau-Bonfeld, BW.

Bonwin Wines (S.Afr) wines made and sold by Mooiuitsig Wynkelders.

Booarra Estate (Austr) a winery based in Western Australia. Grape varieties include: Cabernet sauvignon, Merlot.

Booby Cocktail (Cktl) 1 measure gin, ½ measure lime juice, dash grenadine. Shake over ice, strain into a cocktail glass.

Boodles (Eng) the brand-name of a gin produced by Seagram. 40% alc by vol.

Booker's (USA) a Bourbon whiskey over 120° US proof, bottled between 6–8 years by Jim Beam without filtration or reduction. 63% alc by vol.

Bookers Vineyard (Eng) a winery (established 1972). (Add): Foxhole Lane, Bolney, Haywards Heath, West Sussex RH17 5NB. Produces a large range of wines (white, rosé and sparkling). Website: http://www.bookersvineyard.co.uk 'E'mail: sam@bookersvineyard.co.uk

Boom Boom Punch (Punch) 1 bottle dark rum, 500mls (1pint) orange juice, 1 bottle Italian vermouth, ½ bottle iced Champagne. Pour all (except the Champagne) into a large punchbowl. Chill down, add the wine, stir gently and decorate with banana slices.

Boomerang Cocktail (Cktl) 20mls (⅙ gill) gin, 25mls (⅕ gill) French vermouth, 20mls (⅙ gill) Italian vermouth, dash Angostura, 2 dashes maraschino. Stir over ice, strain into a cocktail glass, add a cherry and squeeze of lemon peel on top.

Boomsma (Hol) a distillery based in Leeuwarden that produces Genever and Beerenburg aromatic bitters.

Boon Brasserie (Bel) a brewery based in Lembeck, noted for Kriek beers.

Boondoggle (Eng) a 3.9% alc by vol. light-coloured ale brewed by Ringwood Brewery.

Boonekamp (Hol) a brand of aromatic bitters 35% alc by vol.

Boon Rawd Brewery (E.Asia) a brewery (established 1903) based in Bangkok, Thailand. Produces Singha Lager beer.

Boon Spa (Austr) a sparkling natural spring mineral water (established 1890) from Sailor Falls. Mineral contents (milligrammes per litre): Sodium 110mg/l, Calcium 68mg/l, Magnesium 50mg/l, Potassium 4.5mg/l, Bicarbonates 620mg/l, Chlorides 12mg/l, Sulphates <1mg/l, Nitrates 0.06mg/l, Silicates 21mg/l, Iron 6.4mg/l. pH 7.3

Booranga Vineyard (Austr) a part of the College Winery, New South Wales. 13ha. Grow mainly the Cabernet sauvignon grape.

Boor Brandy (S.Afr) the name used by English settlers to describe the brandy that the Boer farmers drank.

Boordy Vineyard (USA) vineyards in Ryderwood, Maryland and New York State on the south shore of Lake Erie. Produces fine wines.

Boos (Ger) village (Anb): Nahe. (Ber): Schloss Böckelheim. (Gro): Paradiesgarten. (Vin): Herrenberg, Kastell.

Booster Cocktail (Cktl) 50mls (2fl.ozs) brandy, 1 teaspoon Cointreau, 1 egg white. Shake well with ice, strain into a medium-sized glass and grate nutmeg on top.

Boot (Eng) a part of the corking procedure, a cylindrical leather container. see Boot and Flogger.

Boot and Flogger (Eng) an old English method of corking bottles. The Boot was a cylindrical leather container to hold the bottle and the wooden Flogger used to drive home the cork. Still used in some small cellars.

Booth Brothers (Austr) a winery based in north-east Victoria.

Booth's Dry Gin (Eng) a famous London dry gin produced by the Booths Distillery (part of The Distiller Co. Ltd). 40% alc by vol.

Booth's Party Punch (Punch) 3 wine glasses Booth's gin, ½ wine glass Cointreau, ¼ wine glass brandy, juice of 1½ lemons, ½ teaspoon powdered sugar. Mix well with ice in a punch bowl. Add ½ flagon of lemonade. Decorate with sliced cucumber.

Booth's Taminick Cellars (Austr) a winery. (Add): Booth's Road, Taminick via Glenrowan, Victoria. Grape varieties: Cabernet franc, Cabernet sauvignon, Chardonnay, Merlot, Shiraz, Trebbiano, late-harvested Trebbiano.

Bootilka (Rus) bottle.

Bootlace Beer (Eng) a cask-conditioned ale 1038 O.G. brewed by a home-brew public house in Bristol.

Bootlegger (USA) a person who smuggled alcoholic liquor into America during the Prohibition.

Bootlegging (USA) the term used during Prohibition for the practice of carrying a flask of illegal whiskey in the top of the boot.

Booze (USA) a slang term for alcoholic drink.

Booze Artist (Eng) a slang term for a consistant drinker of alcoholic liquor.

Booze Compass (Austr) a slang term used to describe the instinct of a person finding their way when they are blind drunk.

Booze Cruise (Eng) a new term for people who travel over to France by ferry in order to purchase cheaper alcoholic drinks.

Boozer (Eng) a slang term for a public house/also for a reputed drinker.

Booze-Up (Eng) a slang term for a heavy drinking bout.

Boozy (Eng) a slang term used to describe a person, place, etc. that is associated with above the normal consumption of alcoholic liquor. i.e. 'a boozy place'.

B.O.P. (Eng) abbr: Broken Orange Pekoe a grade of black tea.

Boplaas Estate (S.Afr) a winery (established 1880) based at Klein Karoo, Western Cape. 70ha. (Add): Boplaas Langoed, P.O. Box 156, Calizdorp 6660. Grape varieties: Cabernet sauvignon, Chardonnay, Merlot, Pinotage, Red muscadel, Sauvignon blanc, Shiraz, Touriga. Labels include: Kuip & Clay. Website: http://www.boplaas.co.za

Boppard (Ger) village (Anb): Mittelrhein. (Ber): Rheinburgengau. (Gro): Gedeonseck. (Vins): Elfenlay, Engelstein, Fässerlay, Feuerlay, Mandelelstein, Ohlenberg, Weingrube.

Bopser (Ger) vineyard (Anb): Württemberg. (Ber): Remstal-Stuttgart. (Gro): Weinsteige. (Vil): Gerlingen.

Bór (Hun) wine. see Borok.

Bora (It) a katabatic wind of northern Italy and western Slav.

Bora Sambuca (It) a sambuca produced by Stock in Trieste, 40% alc by vol.

Borba (Port) a D.O.C. district near the Spanish border in Alentejo. Noted for full-bodied red wines.

Borba Cooperativo (Port) a co-operative based in Alentejo. Produces mainly red wines.

Borbecker Helles Dampfbier (Ger) a 4.8% alc by vol. steam beer brewed by the Stern Dampfbier Brauerei, Essen-Borbeck.

Bord de Mer (S.Afr) the label for a red wine (Merlot and Cabernet sauvignon blend) produced by the Whalehaven Wines, Walker Bay, Western Cape.

Bordeaux (Fr) considered to be the most famous of all wine regions. Is situated in south-western France. Produces fine red wines (see Graves, Médoc, Pomerol and Saint-Émilion), dry white (see Graves) and the finest sweet white (see Barsac and Sauternes). Also produces rosé and sparkling wines. A.C.'s are Barsac, Bordeaux, Bordeaux Clairet, Côtes de Bordeaux, Côtes de Castillon, Bordeaux Supérieur Côtes de Castillon, Bordeaux Côtes de Franc, Bordeaux Mousseux, Bordeaux Rosé, Bordeaux Supérieur, Cadillac, Cérons, Côtes Canon Fronsac, Côtes de Blaye, Côtes de Bordeaux Sainte-Macaire, Côtes de Bourg, Côtes de Fronsac, Entre-Deux-Mers, Graves, Graves Supérieures, Graves de Vayres, Haut-Médoc, Lalande de Pomerol, Listrac,

Loupiac, Lussac-Saint-Émilion, Margaux, Médoc, Montagne-Saint-Émilion, Moulis, Pauillac, Pessac-Léognan, Pomerol, Premières Côtes de Bordeaux, Puisseguin-Saint-Émilion, Sainte-Croix-du-Mont, Saint- Émilion, Saint-Estèphe, Sainte-Foy-Bordeaux, Saint-Georges-Saint-Émilion, Saint-Julien and Sauternes. *See also* Talbot [John]. Website: http://www.bordeaux.com

Bordeaux (Fr) an A.C. designation for basic wines of the region (red and white). i.e. Bordeaux rouge and Bordeaux blanc. Minimum alcohol content **red**: 10% and **white**: 10.5% by vol.

Bordeaux Blend (S.Afr) the label for a red wine (Cabernet franc 18%, Cabernet sauvignon 58% and Merlot 24%) produced by the Idiom winery, Sir Lowry's Pass, Western Cape.

Bordeaux Blend (S.Afr) the label for a red wine (Cabernet sauvignon 58% Merlot 21% and Petit verdot 21% blend) produced by the Miles Mossop Wines winery, Stellenbosch, Western Cape.

Bordeaux Bottle (Fr) a tall bottle with full shoulders used in Bordeaux and most other wine producing countries. Green coloured for red wines and clear for white.

Bordeaux Bottles (Fr) Magnum: 2 bottles, Marie-Jeanne: 3 bottles, Double Magnum: 4 bottles, Jeroboam: 6 bottles, Impériale: 8 bottles. *See also* Tappit Hen.

Bordeaux Buttermilk (Cktl) mix of frozen lime juice and tequila.

Bordeaux Clairet (Fr) an A.C. designation for rosé wines from the region.

Bordeaux Cooler (Cktl) 50mls (2fl.ozs) claret, 5mls (¼ fl.oz) Cognac, juice of ⅓ lemon, 25mls (1fl.oz) orange juice, 10mls (½ fl.oz) gomme syrup. Stir well over ice, strain into a club goblet. Dress with a spiral of lemon peel.

Bordeaux Côtes de Castillon (Fr) an A.C. designation for red wines. The district is sited south-east of Bordeaux. Most wines are sold as A.C. Bordeaux Supérieur.

Bordeaux Côtes de Franc (Fr) an A.C. designation for red wines. District on the south-east of Bordeaux. Wines often sold as A.C. Bordeaux Supérieur.

Bordeaux Fête le Vin (Fr) a wine festival held in Bordeaux during the end of June and beginning of July. Website: http://www.bordeaux-fete-le-vin.com

Bordeaux Mixture (Fr) a mixture of copper sulphate, quicklime and water used to prevent mildew and other fungal diseases.

Bordeaux Mousseux (Fr) an A.C. designation for the sparkling wines of the region. Produced mainly by the méthode traditionelle. Grape varieties: (red) Cabernet franc, Cabernet sauvignon, Carmenère, Colombard, Malbec, Mauzac, Merlot, Petit verdot and Ugni blanc. (white) Sauvignon blanc, Sémillon and Muscadelle. Minimum alcohol content before second fermentation in bottle of 11% by vol.

Bordeaux Rosé (Fr) an A.C. dry rosé wine produced from permitted grapes and must have a minimum alcohol content of 11% by vol.

Bordeaux Supérieur (Fr) an A.C. designation for red wines from the region. Has a higher alcohol content than A.C. Bordeaux. Minimum 11% alc by vol. Also rosé and dry sweet white wines.

Bordeaux Supérieur Côtes de Castillon (Fr) an A.C. designation, higher in alcohol than A.C. Bordeaux Côtes de Castillon. Often sold as A.C. Bordeaux Supérieur. A.C. covers red wines from permitted grapes with a minimum alcohol content of 11% by vol.

Bordeaux Supérieur Côtes de Francs (Fr) an A.C. red and white sweet or dry wines from the region. Minimum alcohol content of red 11% and white 11.5% by vol.

Bordeaux Supérieur Haut-Bénauge (Fr) an A.C. sweet white wines from the Haut-Bénauge region (in the Entre-Deux-Mers). Produced from permitted grapes and a minimum alc. content of 11.5% by vol.

Bordeauxwijn (Hol) claret.

Bordelaise Lourde (Fr) another name for the Bouteille Bordelaise.

Bordeleau (Isr) a red grape variety.

Bordelesas (Sp) the name for the standard Bordeaux wine cask.

Bordeleza Belch (Euro) an alternative name for the Tannat grape in eastern Europe.

Border Brewery (Wal) closed down in 1984 by Marstons in Burton. All their beers now brewed by Marstons in Burton.

Border Gold (Eng) a 6% alc by vol. organic beer brewed by Broughton Ales Ltd, Lanarkshire.

Borderies (Fr) the third Cru of Cognac. Regarded as good as Petite Champagne. Covers 4.7% of the Cognac region. In the communes of Burie, Chérac, Chevres, Cognac, Javrezac, Louzac, Saint-André, Saint-Laurent-de-Cognac, Saint-Sulpice and Richemont.

Border Scotch Beer (Eng) a keg beer 1035 O.G. brewed by Theakston's Brewery.

Bordes [Les] (Fr) a vineyard in the A.C. commune of Montagny, Côte Chalonnaise, Burgundy.

Bordo (Bra) a red grape variety. Also known as Ives noir.

Bordo (Tur) the name for French red wine (usually from Bordeaux).

Bordo (Rus) a red grape variety grown in Bessarabia Combine.

Bordo Ay-Danil (Rus) a dry red wine from the Crimean Peninsular.

Bordón (Sp) the brand-name for the red Rioja wines from Bodegas Franco Españolas.

Bordvin (Den) table wine.

Boreale (Can) a brewery. (Add): 875 Michele-Bohec, Blainville, Quebec J7C 5J6. Brews a variety of beers. Website: http://www.boreale.com 'E'mail: info@boreale.com

Borealis Brut (S.Afr) the label for a methode cap classique sparkling wine (Chardonnay 50% Pinot noir 50%) produced by the Twee Jongegezellen Estate winery, Tulbagh, Western Cape.

Boared Doe (S.Afr) a Bordeaux-style red wine

produced by the Fairview Estate from a blend of Cabernet sauvignon 28%, Malbec 13%, Merlot 48% and Petit verdot 11%.

Borelli Winery (USA) a winery based in San Joaquin County, California. Grape varieties: Chenin blanc and Zinfandel. Produces varietal wines.

Borga (Swe) a natural spring mineral water. Mineral contents (milligrammes per litre): Sodium 14mg/l, Calcium 2.3mg/l, Magnesium 0.7mg/l, Potassium 9mg/l, Chlorides 4.5mg/l, Sulphates 2.1mg/l, Fluorides <0.1mg/l.

Borg Brewery (Nor) a brewery based in Sarpsborg, south-east Norway.

Borges (Port) vintage Port shippers. Vintages: 1914, 1922, 1924, 1963.

Borges and Irmao (Port) a producer of Gatao and Gamba brands of vinhos verdes and Trovador.

Borges Iglio (It) a winery based in Cormons in the Friuli-Venezia-Guilia region. Produces a range of wines in the Collio district.

Borghese Winery (USA) a winery based in the North Fork of Long Island, New York State. Grape variety: Pinot noir.

Borgogna Crna (Slo) a local name for the Gamay noir à jus blanc.

Borgogno [Giacomo] (It) a noted winery based in Barolo, Piemonte.

Borgoña (Chile) the name for a Burgundy style wine.

Borgonja (Slo) a red wine produced in Porec, north-western Slovenia.

Borgo San Daniele (It) a winery based in the Friuli-Venezia-Guilia region.

Borg Special (Cktl) ⅓ measure cherry brandy, ⅓ measure Drambuie, ⅓ measure Bacardi rum. Shake over ice, strain into a cocktail glass.

Borie [La] (S.Afr) a wine estate in Paarl owned by the KWV. Produces red, white and sparkling wines under La Borie label.

Borie-Manoux (Fr) a négociant-éleveur of Châteaux Batailley, Beau-Site, Haut Bages-Monpelou and Trottevielle and Domaine de l'Église. Also produces Beau-Rivage (white and Red A.C. Bordeaux wines). 'E'mail: borie-manoux@dial.oleane.com

Borines (Sp) a still natural mineral water from Manantial de Borines, Borines-Piloña, Asturias. Mineral contents (milligrammes per litre): Sodium 31.9mg/l, Calcium 5.4mg/l, Magnesium 2mg/l, Potassium 0.9mg/l, Bicarbonates 93.3mg/l, Chlorides 7.5mg/l, Sulphates 4.6mg/l, Fluorides 0.6mg/l, Nitrates 2.7mg/l.

Borinquen Cocktail (Cktl) 1 measure dark rum, ½ measure passion fruit syrup, 4 dashes high proof navy rum, ½ measure lime juice, ½ measure orange juice. Blend all the ingredients together with a scoop of crushed ice and pour into an old-fashioned glass.

Borja (Sp) a demarcated area in the Aragón region. Produces wines that are high in alcohol.

Borj el Amrl (Afr) a noted co-operative based in Tunisia. Belongs to the UCCVT.

Borjomi (Geo) a sparkling natural spring mineral water (established 1829) from the Bojormi Valley. Mineral contents (milligrammes per litre): Sodium 1500mg/l, Calcium <100mg/l, Magnesium <50mg/l, Potassium 0.9mg/l, Bicarbonates 4005mg/l, Chlorides 380mg/l, Sulphates <10mg/l pH 7.5

Borkülönlegességeszölögazdasàgànak (Hun) a speciality from the vineyards of the regions named.

Borlido (Port) a winery in Bairrada. Produces Garrafeira red and white wines.

Borna (Ger) a natural spring mineral water from Bochum, NW.

Bornava Misketi (Tur) a red grape variety grown in the Aegean region.

Bornchen (Ger) village (Anb): Rheinhessen. (Ber): Baden. (Gro): Adelberg. (Vins): Hähnchen, Hütte-Terrassen, Kirchenstück, Schönberg.

Börnchen (Ger) vineyard (Anb): Rheinhessen. (Ber): Nierstein. (Gro): Sankt Alban. (Vil): Harxheim.

Bornchen (Ger) village (Anb): Pfalz. (Ber): Südliche Weinstrasse. (Gro): Trappenberg. (Vin): Neuberg.

Borneo (Mal) a natural spring mineral water from Mount Serapi, Kuching. Mineral contents (milligrammes per litre): Sodium 12.2mg/l, Calcium 37mg/l, Magnesium 1.76mg/l, Potassium 0.8mg/l, Bicarbonates 116mg/l, Chlorides 3.27mg/l, Sulphates 8.57mg/l, Fluorides 0.2mg/l. pH 7.5

Borneret (Fr) a vineyard in the A.C. commune of Savigny-lès-Beaune, Côte de Beaune, Burgundy. Is owned by the Hospices de Beaune.

Bornich (Ger) village (Anb): Mittelrhein. (Ber): Rheinburgengau. (Gro): Loreleyfelsen. (Vin): Rothenack.

Borniques [Les] (Fr) a Premier Cru vineyard in the A.C. commune of Chambolle-Musigny, Côte de Nuits, Burgundy. 1.5ha.

Bornóva (Tur) a wine-producing area at Izmir in western Turkey. Noted for red and white wines.

Bornpfad (Ger) vineyard (Anb): Rheinhessen. (Ber): Nierstein. (Gro): Vogelsgärten. (Vil): Guntersblum.

Borok (Hun) wines. *see* Bor.

Boroka Vineyard (Austr) a vineyard (established 1976). (Add): RMB 2072 via Stawell, Victoria 3380 (Pomonal Road, Halls Gap, Victoria). 10ha. Grape varieties: Cabernet sauvignon, Chardonnay, Colombard and Shiraz.

Borough Beer (Eng) a cask-conditioned bitter 1045 O.G. brewed by The Goose and Firkin home-brew public house, London.

Borough Brown Ale (Eng) a bottled brown ale 1034 O.G. brewed by Shepherd Neame Brewery, Faversham, Kent.

Borovicka (Czec) a water-coloured spirit similar to gin. Also spelt Borovivka. 35% alc by vol.

Borovivka (Czec) the alternative spelling of Borovicka.

Borraçal (Port) a black grape variety grown in the Entre Minho e Douro to produce dark red wines. Known as Caiño tinto in Vinho Verde.

Borraccia (It) water-bottle.

B

Borracheiros (Mad) men who carry the goat-skin containers (Borrachos).

Borracho (Port) a drunkard.

Borracho (Sp) drunk/intoxicated.

Borrachos (Mad) a goat-skin back-sacks for carrying the grape juice to the wineries.

Borrachos (Port) drunkard.

Borrado das Moscas (Port) lit: 'fly droppings' a white grape variety grown in the Dão. Also known as the Bical/Bical da Bairrada.

Borra Winery (USA) a winery based near Lodi, San Joaquin Valley in California. 9ha. Grape varieties: Barbera, Carignane and Zinfandel. Produces varietal wines.

Borrel (Hol) a small glass of liquor.

Borreluur (Hol) apéritif hour.

Borret (Fr) the name given to the new wine of Armagnac prior to when it is placed in the still for distilling.

Boru Vodka (Ire) a 37.5% and 40% alc. by vodka, quadruple distilled at Carbery Disitillery in Ballineen, County Cork. Made from Irish barely and spring water. Filtered through ten feet of Irish oak charcoal. Produces a variety of flavoured vodkas. Also sold as 3 x 20 cl. bottles containing grain, citrus and orange flavours.

Borve House Brewery (Scot) a brewery based on the Isle of Lewis. Produces cask-conditioned Pale Ale 1038 O.G. Heavy 1043 O.G. and Extra 1085 O.G.

Borzoi (Eng) a British gin and a vodka distilled by Burroughs.

Bosador (Sp) the name given to a funnel that is inserted into a fermenting barrel of must. The must can rise in this during fermentation.

Bosca (It) a noted wine producer in Asti. Produces spumanti and vermouth. *see* Bosca (Giovanni).

Bosca [Giovanni] (It) a noted producer of a fine range of wines and vermouths based in Canelli, Piemonte. Sold under the names of Gibó, Sereno and Tosti.

Bosca y Figli [Luigi] (It) a sparkling wine producer (metodo tradizionale) based in Piemonte.

Boschendal Estate (S.Afr) a winery (established 1685) that has vineyards in the Drakenstein Valley and Franschhoek Valley. 200ha. (Add): Groot Drakenstein 7680. Produces Lanoy and varietal wines including Le Barquet, Le Mirador and Le Pavillon. Grapes varieties include: Cabernet sauvignon, Chardonnay, Chenin blanc, Merlot, Pinotage, Sauvignon blanc, Shiraz, Viognier. Website: http://www.boschendal.com

Boschenmeer (S.Afr) the export label for a range of wines from Oaklands Wine Exporters, Western Cape.

Boschetto Rosso (S.Afr) the label for a red wine (Cabernet sauvignon, Merlot Sangiovese and Shiraz blend) produced by the Stellekaya Winery, Stellenbosch, Western Cape.

Bosché Vineyard (USA) a vineyard based in Rutherford, Napa Valley in California. 6.6ha. Grape variety: Cabernet sauvignon.

Bosch Guell (Sp) a winery based near Vilafranca, Penedés region. Noted for table wines.

Boschheim (S.Afr) a winery based in Maitieland, Stellenbosch, Western Cape. Grape varieties include: Cabernet sauvignon, Shiraz, Viognier. Label: Elemental.

Boschkloof (S.Afr) a winery (established 1996) based in Stellenbosch, Western Cape. 19ha. Grape varieties: Cabernet sauvignon, Chardonnay, Merlot, Syrah. Website: http://www.boschkloof.co.za

Boschrivier (S.Afr) a winery (established 1997) based in Caledon, Stanford. 14ha. Grape varieties: Cabernet sauvignon, Chardonnay, Shiraz. Website: http://www.boschrivier.co.za

Bosco (It) a white grape variety of northern Italy.

Bosco Eliceo (It) a D.O.C. wine area of Emilia-Romagna.

Bosco Grande Merlot (It) a soft, vevelty red wine produced from a 7ha. plot by the Cantina Beato Bartolomeo co-operative, Breganze, Veneto.

Borsec (Rum) a sparkling natural spring mineral water (established circa 1600) from Borsec Spa, Transylvania. Mineral contents (milligrammes per litre): Sodium 53mg/l, Calcium 310mg/l, Magnesium 97mg/l, Potassium 12mg/l, Bicarbonates 1800mg/l, Chlorides 29mg/l, Sulphates 24mg/l. pH 6.45

Bosham Brewery (Eng) a brewery (established 1984) in Sussex. Produces cask-conditioned Old Bosham 1044 O.G. and FSB 1058 O.G.

Boskydel Vineyards (USA) a small winery based in north Michigan that produces generic and hybrid wines.

Bosley Cloud (Eng) a 4.1% alc by vol. beer brewed by the Storm Brewing C°., Cheshire.

Bosman and C°. (S.Afr) a producer of Buchu brandy.

Bosman Brower Szczecin SA (Pol) a brewery. (Add): ul Chemlelewskiego 16, 70-028 Szczecin. Brews lager beers. Website: http://www.bosman.byss.pl 'E'mail: browar@bosman.pl

Bosman's Hill (S.Afr) the export label for a range of wines produced by the Saxenberg winery, Stellenbosch, Western Cape.

Bosmere (Eng) a vineyard (established 1976) based in West Tytherton, Chippenham, Wiltshire. 0.8ha. Grape varieties: Madeleine angevine, Müller-Thurgau, Pinot noir, Seyval plus others.

Bosmere Vineyard (Eng) a vineyard. (Add): Saxmundham, Suffolk. 4.5ha. Grape variety is Müller-Thurgau.

Bosnia-Herzegovina (Bos) a lesser wine-producing State. Home to the Zilavka grape that produces a dry white wine called Zilavka Mostar. Other wine is Blatina Mostar (dry red). Hepok is main wine producer.

Bosom Caresser (Cktl) 1 egg yolk, 30mls (¼ gill) each of brandy, Curaçao, Madeira and grenadine. Shake well over ice, strain into a wine glass.

Bosquet des Papes (Fr) a red or white Châteauneuf-du-Pape produced by Boiron (Maurice), Route d'Orange, 84230 southern Rhône.

Bossa Nova Special (Cktl) 25mls (1fl.oz) white rum, 25mls (1fl.oz) Galliano, 5mls (¼fl.oz) apricot brandy, 50mls (2fl.ozs) pineapple juice, 5mls (¼

B

fl.oz) lemon juice, dash egg white. Shake over ice, strain into highball with ice and decorate with fruit in season.

Bosso (It) Distilleria Bosso Luigi and C°. (a distiller of grappa).

Bostandschi-Oglu-Kakour (Rus) a red wine from the Crimea region.

Bosteels Brasserie (Bel) a brewery (established 1791) based in Buggenhout. Brews: Pauwel Kwak, Tripel Karmeliet.

Boston Beer (Eng) a nitrokeg beer from Whitbread, County Durham at their Castle Eden Brewery under the Samuel Adams' label. 4.6% alc by vol.

Boston Beer C°. (USA) a brewery in Massachusetts. Produces a German-style bock lager using Champagne yeast. 17.5% alc by vol (a barley wine).

Boston Bullet (Cktl) as for Dry Martini but served with an olive stuffed with an almond.

Boston Cocktail [1] (Cktl) 25mls (1fl.oz) Bourbon, 25mls (1fl.oz) dry Madeira, 1 egg yolk, 1 teaspoon powdered sugar. Shake well with ice, strain into a wine goblet and top with grated nutmeg.

Boston Cocktail [2] (Cktl) ½ measure gin, ½ measure apricot brandy, juice ¼ lemon, 4 dashes grenadine. Shake over ice, strain into a cocktail glass.

Boston Cooler [1] (Cktl) put into a highball glass the peel of a lemon and an ice cube. Add equal parts of ginger ale and sarsaparilla.

Boston Cooler [2] (Cktl) place juice of ¼ lemon, 1 teaspoon powdered sugar, 50mls (2fl.ozs) soda water into a collins glass. Stir, top with 50mls (2fl.ozs) each of rum and ginger ale. Decorate with a spiral of orange peel over rim of glass.

Boston Eggnog (Cktl) 25mls (⅕ gill) each of sweet Madeira and milk, dash Cognac, dash Jamaican rum, 4 dashes gomme syrup. Blend altogether in a blender with a scoop of crushed ice. Strain into a cocktail glass and top with grated nutmeg.

Boston Flip (Cktl) 30mls (¼ gill) Madeira, 30mls (¼ gill) rye whiskey, 1 egg yolk. Shake well over ice, strain into a cocktail glass.

Boston Gold (Cktl) 1 measure vodka, ½ measure crème de banane. Shake over ice, strain into an ice-filled highball glass and top with orange juice.

Boston Shaker (USA) a cocktail shaker comprising of two cones, one made of glass the other stainless steel or silver.

Boston Sidecar (Cktl) ⅓ measure Jamaican rum, ⅓ measure brandy, ⅓ measure Cointreau, juice ½ lime. Shake over ice and strain into a cocktail glass.

Boston Sour (Cktl) 1 measure whiskey, juice ½ lemon, 1 teaspoon powdered sugar, 1 egg white. Shake over ice, strain into a sour glass, add a slice of lemon and a cherry.

Boston Tea Party (USA) an event that took place in Boston when 342 chests of tea were dumped into the harbour after the Tea Act was passed (1773).

Bosun Beer (Eng) a top grade bitter ale 1048 O.G. Brewed by the Brewhouse Brewery, Poole, Dorset.

Bosun Beer (Eng) a cask-conditioned dark mild ale 1032 O.G. brewed by Southsea Brewery, Portsmouth.

Bosun Bitter (I.O.M.) a 3.8% alc by vol. bitter ale brewed by Old Laxey Brewing Company at the Shore Inn.

Bosun Premium (Eng) a 4.6% alc by vol. cask-conditioned ale brewed by Poole Brewery, Poole.

Bota (Fr) an old provincial name for a cask.

Bota (Sp) butt or cask, holds 108 gallons (490 litres).

Bota (Sp) a leather wine bag made of goats-skin, pitch lined.

Bota Bodeguera (Sp) the name given to a very old butt now no longer in use.

Bota Chica (Sp) a shipping butt of 110 Imp. Gallons, also known as a Bota de Embarque.

Bota de Embarque (Sp) the alternative name for the Bota Chica.

Bota de Recibo (Sp) a butt of 111.63 Imp. gallons.

Bota Gordo (Sp) a storage butt of 132–146 Imp. gallons used in the wine bodegas.

Botaina (Sp) a brand of old Amontillado Sherry produced by Domecq in Jerez.

Botanical Beer (Eng) non-alcoholic beers brewed in the days of the temperance movement.

Botanicals (Eng) herbs and peels used to flavour wines and spirits (liqueurs).

Botelha (Port) bottle.

Botella (Sp) bottle.

Botequim (Port) a bar/café bar.

Botenheim (Ger) village (Anb): Württemberg. (Ber): Württembergisch Unterland. (Gro): Heuchelberg. *see* Brackenheim.

Botha Wine Cellar (S.Afr) a co-operative winery (established 1949) based in Rawsonville, Worcester, Western Cape. 1775ha. (Add): Botha Co-operative Wine Cellar, P.O. Botha 6857. Grape varieties: Cabernet sauvignon, Chardonnay, Chenin blanc, Colombard, Honepoot jerepigo, Merlot, Pinotage, Red jerepigo, Syrah. Produces: Dassie's, Port-style and varietal wines.

Bothy (Scot) distillery.

Bothy Vineyard [The] (Eng) a vineyard based at Bothy Cottage, Frilford Heath, Abingdon, Oxfordshire. 1.35ha. Grape varieties: Huxelrebe, Optima, Ortega, Perle.

Botija (Port) a stone bottle, jar.

Botmaskop (S.Afr) the label for a red wine (Cabernet sauvignon) produced by the Delaire Winery, Stellenbosch, Western Cape.

Botobolar Vineyards (Austr) a vineyard. (Add): Botobolar Lane, Mudgee, New South Wales. 23ha. Grape varieties: Cabernet sauvignon, Chardonnay, Couchen, Marsanne, Rhine riesling, Shiraz and Traminer.

Botol (Indo) bottle.

Botromagno (It) a co-operative in Gravina, Puglia that is noted for producing D.O.C. Gravina wines made from Greco and Malvasia grapes.

Botrus (Lat) a bunch of grapes.

Botrys (Gre) a producer of brandy and table wines (red and white).

161

Botrytis (Lat) a grey mould. *see* **Pourriture gris**.

Botrytis cinerea (Lat) noble rot, the mould which in certain districts forms on the skins of grapes and penetrates the skin, so causing the water in the juice to evaporate. This concentrates the sugar to give high sugar musts. These produce luscious, sweet wines. e.g. the Sauternes of France and Trockenbeerenauslese of Germany. *See also* Passerillage and Marciume Nobile. (Eng) = noble rot, (Fr) = pourriture noble, (Ger) = edelfäule, (Hun) = aszú, (It) = muffa nobile, (S.Afr) = edelkeur, (Switz) = flétri, (USA) = noble mould.

Bottaio (It) cooper/cask maker.

Bottchen (Ger) vineyard (Anb): Mosel-Saar-Ruwer. (Ber): Bernkastel. (Gro): Schwarzlay. (Vil): Wittlich.

Botte (Fr) an old word for butt, barrel.

Botte (It) barrel/cask.

Bottelary Hills (S.Afr) a winery (established 2003) based in Stellenbosch, Western Cape. Formed by 6 wineries: Bellevue, Goede Hoop, Groenland, Kaapzicht, Mooiplaas and Sterhuis. Grape varieties include: Cabernet sauvignon, Chardonnay, Cinsaut, Merlot, Pinotage, Sauvignon blanc, Syrah. Labels: Limerick, M23, Rhapsody. Website: http://www.bottelaryhills.coza

Bottelary Koöperatiewe Wynkelder (S.Afr) a co-operative winery based in Stellenbosch. (Add): Box 16, Koelenhof 7605. Produces varietal wines.

Bottelary Wine International (S.Afr) a winery based in Stellenbosch, Western Cape. Grape varieties: Cabernet sauvignon, Cinsaut, Hanepoot jerepigo, Merlot, Pinotage, Sauvignon blanc, Shiraz. Label: Rocco Bay (red, rosé and white wines).

Bottenau (Ger) village (Anb): Baden. (Ber): Ortenau. (Gro): Fürsteneck. (Vin): Renchtäler.

Bott-Geyl (Fr) an Alsace wine producer. (Add): 68980 Beblenheim.

Botti (It) oak wine casks.

Botticino (It) a small commune in the Garda district of Lombardy. Derives its name from botte (barrel). Their logo is also a small barrel.

Botticino (It) a red wine from the Garda district of Lombardy. Grapes used are Barbera 30%–40%, Schiava gentile 20%–30%, Marzemino 15%–25% and Sangiovese 10%–20%. D.O.C.

Böttigheim (Ger) village (Anb): Franken. (Ber): Maindreick. (Gro): Not yet assigned. (Vin): Wurmberg.

Bottiglia (It) bottle.

Bottiglieria (It) a wine-shop.

Bottigua (It) bottle.

Bottle (Eng) a glass container for holding liquids, many shapes, sizes and colours, standard wine bottle holds 75 cls. or 750mls (Arab) = qenena, (Aus) = flasche, (Chi) = ping, (Cro) = boca, (Den) = flaske, (Fr) = bouteille, (Ger) = flasche, (Gre) = boukali, (Hol) = fles, (Indo) = botol, (Ire) = cuirim, (Isr) = bakbuk, (It) = bottiglia, (Jap) = bin, (Kor) = byung, (Port) = garrafa, (Rus) = bootilka, (Sp) = botella, (Thai) = kuad, (Wal) = potel.

Bottle Age (Eng) the time the wine has spent in bottle.

Bottle and Basket (Eng) retail off-licenses owned by the Virani hotel and property group.

Bottle Bank (Eng) organised points of collection where used, empty bottles can be deposited for recycling. Usually charity-organised and run.

Bottle Bib (Eng) an absorbent crepe paper ring that encircles around the bottle neck to catch any drips that occur whilst pouring.

Bottle Brush (Eng) a thin wire handle with bristles intertwined with the wire at the one end. Used to remove stains and debris from used bottles (and decanters) before re-use. Used mainly by home-made wine makers.

Bottle Bursts (Fr) a term used in Champagne and other sparkling wine regions for bottles that have weakened glass and that burst during second fermentation when the pressure is increased.

Bottle Collar (Eng) a silver or other metal ring which fits over the neck of the wine bottle and rests on the shoulder. Has the name and the bottle contents engraved on it.

Bottle Conditioned (Eng) applies to ales that have a second fermentation in the bottle which leaves a sediment.

Bottle Cradle (Eng) *see* Cradle.

Bottled Beer (Eng) pasteurised (or fine filtered) and carbonated beers (all styles) sold in sealed bottles (crown cork or screw cap). (Den) = på flaske.

Bottled-in-Bond Stamp (USA) the government's treasury department's decision N°1299 reads "Is no guarantee as to purity or quality of the spirits, and the Government assumes no responsibility with respect to claims by dealers in this connection in advertising Bottled-in-Bond spirits".

Bottled-in-Bond Whiskey (USA) these are straight whiskies bottled at 100° USA proof. Matured in cask for at least 4 years in warehouses controlled by the government. Hence the name.

Bottle Fermented (USA) Méthode Traditionelle.

Bottle Fever (Eng) *see* Bottle Sickness.

Bottle Green Drinks Cº. (Eng) a soft drinks company (established 1989) based in the Cotswold. (Add): Frogmarsh Mills, South Woodchester, Stroud, Gloucestershire GL5 5ET. Produce a pressé range of sparkling mineral drinks (cordials) – elderflower, ginger, cranberry, limeflower, citrus. Website: http://www.bottlegreen.co.uk 'E'mail: info@bottlegreen.co.uk

Bottle Label (Eng) *see* Decanter Label.

Bottle-O (Austr) a dealer who specialises in empty bottles.

Bottle Party (Eng) a drinks party where each guest brings a bottle of alcoholic liquor.

Bottle Ripe (Eng) a term used for a wine that has been stored in bottle and gained bottle age and maturity and is ready for drinking. After it has reached this stage it will then slowly start to deteriorate.

Bottler's Code (Eng) a code of letters and numbers

found on the capsule or cork to guarantee authenticity of the wine.

Bottle Safe (Eng) a device to put over the neck and cork of bottles of wines or spirits in the early twentieth century. This is locked in position to prevent any pilferage.

Bottle'scape (Eng) a wall-mounted cabinet which when closed appears to be a picture. Stores bottles and glasses. Popular in the nineteenth century.

Bottle Scent (Eng) describes saké that has deteriorated usually due to poor storage (i.e. in direct sunlight).

Bottlescrew (Eng) the name given to the first corkscrew.

Bottleship (Eng) a bookcase, magazine rack, cocktail cabinet and occasional table all-in-one. Held 6 bottles and several glasses, popular in the nineteenth century.

Bottle Sickness (Eng) a condition that happens to some newly bottled wines. Disappears after some months. Result of oxygen absorption and the formation of acetaldehyde. Causes loss of bouquet. (Fr) = malade de mise, (Ger) = flaschentrank.

Bottle Stink (Eng) **Hydrogen sulphide** a smell that sometimes exudes from newly opened wines. Mainly due to the air between the cork and the wine, treated by decanting and aerating.

Bottle Ticket (Eng) also called decanter labels, used to indicate the contents of the bottle or decanter. Made of parchment, pewter, silver, wood, ivory or bone.

Bottling (Eng) the placing of beverages into clean, sterile bottles of various capacities. Mainly done automatically but some wines still bottled by hand (e.g. home-made wines).

Bottom Fermentation (Eng) applied to those beers where the yeast falls to the bottom of the vat during fermentation. e.g. lager, bock, pilsner, etc. Yeast: **Saccharomyces uvarum**.

Bottom Rose (Cktl) ⅛ measure Cinzano Rossi, ⅛ measure apricot brandy, ¾ measure genever gin. Shake over ice and strain into a cocktail glass.

Bottoms (Eng) the lees or dregs left after racking or decanting. In a 36 gallon (163.6 litres) barrel of beer the natural sediment (yeasts and hops debris) amounts to about 1 gallon (4.5 litres).

Bottoms Up (Eng) a chain of off-licenses taken over by Peter Dominic in 1985, now taken over by IDV.

Bottoms Up (Eng) an informal toast, a request to drain the glass of its contents.

Bottwar [River] (Ger) a tributary of the river Neckar in the Württemberg anbaugebiete. Soil: red marl.

Bötzingen (Ger) village (Anb): Baden. (Ber): Kaiserstuhl-Tuniberg. (Gro): Vulkanfelsen. (Vins): Eckberg, Lansenberg.

Bouaki (Rus) a white grape variety used mainly as a table grape and for some dessert wines in Uzbekistania.

Boual (Mad) another spelling of the Boal grape variety of Madeira.

Bou A-Rkoub (Afr) a co-operative based in Tunisia. Belongs to the UCCVT.

Bouaye (Fr) a town in the Muscadet, Nantais region of the Loire.

Bouchalès (Fr) a red grape variety grown in parts of Bordeaux.

Bouchaon (Ch.Isles) cork.

Bouchard Aîné et Fils (Fr) a Burgundy négociant (established 1750) based at Beaune. Ships many fine wines. (Add): 36 Rue Ste-Marguerite, 21203 Beaune. Has large holdings in the Côte d'Or including Beaune Grêves Vigne de l'Enfant Jesus and Beaune Marconnets. Owned by Boisset.

Bouchard Finlayson (S.Afr) a winery (established 1989) based in Kaaimansgat, Overberg, Western Cape. 15ha. (Add): P.O. Box 303, Hermanus 7200. Grape varieties: Barbera, Chardonnay, Mourvèdre, Nebbiolo, Pinot blanc, Pinot noir, Riesling, Sangiovese, Sauvignon blanc. Labels: Blanc de Mer, Galpin Peak, Hannibal, Kaaimansgat, Missionvale, Sans Barrique. Website: http://www.bouchardfinlayson.co.za 'E' mail: info@bouchardfinlayson.co.za

Bouchard [Pascal] (Fr) a winery based in the A.C. Chablis, Burgundy. Produces a range of Chablis wines including Premier Crus Beauroy and Fourchame.

Bouchard Père et Fils (Fr) a Burgundy négociant (established 1731). Acquired by the Champagne house Henriot (Joseph). Has a large holding of Burgundy vineyards.

Bouchard-Philippe (Fr) a Burgundy négociant-éleveur based at Saint Jean des Vignes. Owns a small domaine at Savigny-lès-Beaune and one at Beaune.

Bouché (Fr) a term to denote that the bottle is closed with a cork.

Bouchemaine (Fr) a commune in the A.C. Savennières, Anjou-Saumur, Loire.

Bouche Père et Fils (Fr) a Champagne producer. (Add): Rue Général-de-Galle, Pierry, 51200 Épernay. 35ha. Vintages include 1986, 1988.

Boucher [Aimé S.A.] (Fr) a noted négociant in the Loire. (Add): 279 Route de Chambourd, 41350, Husseau-sur-Casson.

Bouchères [Les] (Fr) a Premier Cru vineyard in the A.C. commune of Meursault, Côte de Beaune, Burgundy. 4.25ha.

Boucheron (Fr) a Champagne producer. (Add): Rue Georges Legros, BP 1, 51500 Chigny-lès-Roses.

Boucherottes [Les] (Fr) a Premier Cru vineyard [part] in the A.C. commune of Beaune, Côte de Beaune, Burgundy. 8.6ha.

Boucherottes [Les] (Fr) a Premier Cru vineyard [part] in the A.C. commune of Pommard, Côte de Beaune, Burgundy. 1.7ha.

Boucher Père et Fils (Fr) a Champagne producer, produces vintage and non-vintage wines.

Bouches du Rhône (Fr) a Vin de Pays area in the Languedoc-Roussillon region.

Bouchet (Fr) a red grape variety used in Saint-Émilion. Local name for the Cabernet franc. *see*

Château St. Georges. Is known in the Loire as the Breton, Bouchy or Véron.

Boucheur (Fr) the name given to the person who inserts and hammers the cork into the neck of a Champagne bottle.

Bouchon (Fr) stopper/cork.

Bouchon Couronne (Fr) the name for the crown cork, used in some Champagne houses during the second fermentation.

Bouchon de Tirage (Fr) in Champagne, the temporary cork used during the second fermentation in the bottle and up to dégorgement, many of the houses have now replaced it with a Crown Cork.

Bouchonné (Fr) denotes a corked wine, from a defective cork.

Bouchots [Les] (Fr) a vineyard in the A.C. commune of Montagny, Côte Chalonnaise, Burgundy.

Bouchots [Les] (Fr) a Premier Cru vineyard in the A.C. commune of Morey-Saint-Denis, Côte de Nuits, Burgundy. 2ha.

Bouchy (Fr) the local Loire (and Madiran) name for the Cabernet franc grape. See also Breton, Bouchet and Véron.

Bouchy (Fr) a red wine produced in the Jurançon region.

Boudalés (Fr) an alternative name for the Cinsault grape.

Boude (Fr) bung.

Boudes (Fr) a sub-appellation of the V.D.Q.S. district Côtes d'Auvergne, southern France.

Boudriottes [La] (Fr) a Premier Cru vineyard [part] in the A.C. commune of Chassagne-Montrachet, Côte de Beaune, Burgundy. 17.81ha. (red and white).

Bouéchage (Fr) a term that describes the manual digging around the vine where the plough cannot reach.

Bougneau (Fr) a commune in the Charente-Maritime département whose grapes are classed Petite Champagne (Cognac).

Bougros (Fr) an A.C. Grand Cru of Chablis, Burgundy. Produces a full wine with a long aftertaste.

Bougy (Switz) a wine-producing area in La Côte on the western bank of Lake Geneva.

Bouillage (Fr) the first fermentation in Champagne when the must literally foams and hisses (imitates boiling).

Bouille (Fr) a milk churn.

Bouilleurs de Cru (Fr) farmers in Cognac who only distill the wine from the grapes they grow.

Bouilleurs de Profession (Fr) professional distillers in Cognac, those who sell their distillates to the Cognac houses.

Bouillie Bordelaise (Fr) see Bordeaux Mixture.

Bouilloire (Fr) kettle/copper.

Bouilly (Fr) a Cru Champagne village in the Canton de Ville-en-Tardenois. District: Reims.

Boukali (Gre) bottle.

Boukha (M.East) an eau-de-vie made from figs. Also called Mahia.

Boukha Soleil (M.East) a fig flavoured eau-de-vie from Tunisia.

Boulaouane (Mor) a wine-producing area in Morocco based south of Rabat. Produces red and rosé wines.

Boulard [Raymond] (Fr) a Champagne producer. (Add): 51480 La Neuville aux Larris. A négociant-manipulant. 10ha. Labels include Cuvée l'Année de la Cornète.

Boulard Mist (Cktl) 40mls (⅓ gill) Calvados, juice of ½ lemon, 1 teaspoon sugar, shake well over ice and strain into an old-fashioned glass.

Boulbène (Fr) the name given to the fine clay and sandy soils of the Armagnac region.

Boulder Brewery (USA) a brewery based in Boulder, Colorado. Noted for top-fermented, bottle-conditioned beers.

Boulder Hill Vineyard (USA) a winery based in Laporte, Indiana. Produces hybrid wines.

Boulder Red (S.Afr) the label for a non-vintage red wine (Cabernet sauvignon, Pinotage and Shiraz blend) from Bianco Fine Wines, Tulbagh, Western Cape.

Boule à Thé (Fr) tea ball. See also Infuseur à Thé.

Bouleuse (Fr) a Cru Champagne village in the Canton de Ville-en-Tardenois. District: Reims.

Bound SO₂ (Eng) **Sulphur-dioxide** added to wine which has combined with sugar or aldehydes, or has converted to **Sulphuric acid** (H_2SO_3).

Bounty (USA) the brand-name used by California Growers for a range of wines.

Bounty (W.Ind) the brand-name of a rum produced on Saint Lucia by the St. Lucia Distillers Ltd.

Bououillaon (Ch.Isles) beef tea/consommé.

Bouquet (Fr) aromas, a collection of smells and aromas given off by wines which, in the right type of glass, can be concentrated at the top of the glass (at the rim) to give the scent of the grape, soil grown in, age and class (type) of wine. (Sp) = ramillete.

Bouquet [Le] (S.Afr) a late harvest wine produced from Bukettraube, Gewürztraminer and Muscat grapes by the Boschendal Estate.

Bouquet Blanc (S.Afr) a fruity white wine made with the Steen grape by the Landskroon Estate in Paarl, Western Cape.

Bouquet Blanc (S.Afr) the label for a white wine (Chenin blanc) produced by the Rhebokskloof Private Cellar winery, Noorder-Paarl, Western Cape.

Bouquet Blanc (S.Afr) the label for a white wine (Chenin blanc and Hanepoot blend) produced by the Villiersdorp Cellar winery, Worcester, Western Cape.

Bouquet de Cissus (Fr) a co-operative in the Médoc. A.C. Haut-Médoc. (Add): 33250 Cissac, Médoc. (Com): Cissac. 30ha. Grape varieties: Cabernet sauvignon 50% and Merlot 50%.

Bouqueté (Fr) fragrant.

Bouquet Rouge (S.Afr) a red wine from the Landskroon Estate.

Bourbon Cocktail (Cktl) 25mls (⅛ gill) Bourbon whiskey, juice ½ lemon, 4 dashes Triple Sec, 4 dashes Bénédictine, dash Angostura, shake over ice and strain into a cocktail glass. Top with twist of lemon peel juice.

Bourbon Coffee (E.Afr) coffee beans from the island of Bourbon (also known as Réunion Island). Are oblong in shape and yellow in colour.

Bourbon Coffee (Afr) the alternative name for **Coffea arabica.**

Bourbon Coffee (Liq.Coffee) using a measure of Bourbon whiskey.

Bourbon Collins (Cktl) 25mls (⅕ gill) Bourbon whiskey, 15mls (⅛ gill) lemon juice, 1 teaspoon sugar. Stir over ice in a collins glass, top with soda water, dress with a lemon slice and serve with straws.

Bourbon Cooler (Cktl) fill a tall glass with cracked ice, fill half with lime juice, add 25mls (1fl.oz) Bourbon, top up with pineapple juice, stir and serve with straws.

Bourbon Créole Coffee (Fr) see Café Créole Bourbon.

Bourbon de Luxe (USA) the brand-name of a Bourbon whiskey produced in Kentucky.

Bourbonella (Cktl) ½ measure Bourbon whiskey, ¼ measure orange Curaçao, ¼ measure vermouth, dash grenadine. Stir over ice, strain into a cocktail glass.

Bourbon Fog (Cktl) 1100mls (1quart) each of vanilla ice cream, Bourbon whiskey, cold strong black coffee. Stir altogether in a punch bowl until well blended and serve in Champagne flutes.

Bourbon Highball (Cktl) pour 25mls (⅕ gill) Bourbon whiskey into an ice-filled highball glass. Top with soda water and dress with a lemon peel spiral.

Bourbon Mist (Cktl) 25mls (⅕ gill) Bourbon whiskey into an old-fashioned glass filled with crushed ice and dress with a lemon peel spiral.

Bourbon Santos (Bra) a top quality coffee bean from the Santos region. Produces fine coffees with good flavour and acidity.

Bourbon Sour (Cktl) 25mls (1fl.oz) Bourbon whiskey, juice ½ lemon, teaspoon of powdered sugar. Shake over ice and strain into a small tumbler.

Bourbon Straight Up (USA) a request for a neat whiskey with no ice.

Bourbon Supreme (USA) the brand-name of a Bourbon whiskey produced by the American Distilling Company Inc. in Pekin, Illinois.

Bourbon Whiskey (USA) originally made in Bourbon County, Kentucky. Must have not less than 51% maize spirit. Matured in new charred oak casks for at least two years. see Craig (Reverend Elijah).

Bourbouenc (Fr) an alternative spelling of Bourboulenc.

Bourboulenc (Fr) a red grape variety used in the southern Rhône. Gives finesse to the wines. See also Bourbouenc.

Bourdin [Jean-Claude] (Fr) a wine-producer based at Jurquant, Saumur, Anjou-Saumur, Loire. Noted for sparkling Saumur wines.

Bourdon (W.Ind) a noted rum distillery based in Guadeloupe.

Bourée Fils (Fr) Burgundy négociants based in Gevrey-Chambertin, Côte de Nuits, Burgundy.

Bourg (Fr) a commune in the A.C. Côtes de Bourg in north-east Bordeaux.

Bourg (Fr) an A.C. district within Bordeaux on the right bank of the river Gironde in the north-east of the region. see Côtes de Bourg.

Bourg-Bourgeais (Fr) an A.C. for red, demi-sec, sweet and dry white wines from the right bank of the Gironde (opposite the Haut-Médoc).

Bourg-Charente (Fr) a commune in the Charente département whose grapes are classed Petite Champagne (Cognac).

Bourgeais (Fr) the name given to the wines from the Côtes de Bourg.

Bourgeois (Fr) a term used in the Médoc. see Cru Bourgeois. Denotes that the wines are of medium quality.

Bourgeonnage (Fr) the thinning of surplus florets in May prior to flowering.

Bourgignon Noir (Fr) an alternative name for the Gamay noir à jus blanc in south-western France.

Bourgneuf-Val d'Or (Fr) a noted wine commune in the A.C. Mercurey, Côte Chalonnaise, Burgundy.

Bourgogne (Fr). Burgundy.

Bourgogne (Fr) a canton in the Reims district of Champagne, has the Cru villages of Brimont, Cauroy-les-Hermonville, Cormicy, Merfy, Pouillon, Saint-Thierry, Thil and Villers-Franqueux.

Bourgogne Aligoté (Fr) a dry white wine of Burgundy made with the Aligoté grape. Minimum alc. content 9.5% by vol.

Bourgogne Aligoté de Bouzeron (Fr) an A.C. dry white wine produced from the Aligoté grape in the commune of Bouzeron. 50ha. planted.

Bourgogne Blanc (Fr) a dry white wine of Appellation Regionale category, minimum alcohol content 10.5% by vol.

Bourgogne Chitry (Fr) a local appellation found in the Yonne. Covers wines from the village of Chitry le Fort, made from César, Chardonnay, Pinot noir, Sacy or Tressot grapes.

Bourgogne Clairet de Marsannay (Fr) the A.C. of the light rosé produced in the commune of Marsannay-la-Côte in the Burgundy region. See also Rosé de Marsannay.

Bourgogne Côte d'Auxerre (Fr) a local appellation found in the Yonne. Covers wines from the villages of Auxerre, St. Bris le Vineux and Vaux made from César, Chardonnay, Pinot noir, Sacy or Tressot grapes.

Bourgogne Côtes du Couchois (Fr) the new appellation for red wines from the vineyards of the Couchois district in the north of the department of Saône-et-Loire. 200ha. divided between the communes Couches, Dracy-les-Couches, Saint-Maurice-les-Couches, Saint-Sernin-du-Plain, Saint-Jean-de-Trézy. (yields are 48 hl/ha.).

Bourgogne Côte St. Jacques (Fr) a local appellation found in the Yonne. Covers 10ha. area of vineyards overlooking town of Joigny. Red and vin gris wines made from Pinot gris and Pinot noir grapes.

Bourgogne Coulanges (Fr) a local appellation found in the Yonne. Covers wines from the villages of Coulanges la Vineuse, Escolives, Jussy and Migé made from César, Chardonnay, Pinot noir, Sacy or Tressot grapes.

Bourgogne Epineuil (Fr) a local appellation found in the Yonne. Red and rosé wines made from Pinot noir grapes grown in the Armancon valley.

Bourgogne et Est (Fr) a Vin de Pays region in central-eastern France which contains the Vin de Pays districts of: de Franche-Comté/de Franche-Comté 'Coteaux de Champlitte'/de Sainte-Marie-la-Blanche/des Coteaux de Coiffy/des Coteaux de l'Auxois.

Bourgogne Grand Ordinaire (Fr) an Appellation Regionale which includes red, rosé and white wines. see Bourgogne Passe-Tout-Grains.

Bourgogne Hautes-Côtes de Beaune (Fr) an A.C. designation granted on 4th August 1961. Red and rosé wines made from Pinot noir, white wines made from Chardonnay and Pinot blanc.

Bourgogne Hautes-Côtes de Nuits (Fr) an A.C. designation granted on 4th August 1961. Red wines made from Pinot noir, white wines made from Chardonnay and Pinot blanc.

Bourgogne Irancy (Fr) an A.C. red and rosé wines produced south-west of Chablis from the César, Pinot noir and Tressot grapes. Now granted a Village Appellation for red wines produced from Pinot noir grapes.

Bourgogne Marsannay (Fr) the A.C. of the red wines of the commune of Marsannay-la-Côte and Couchey.

Bourgogne Mousseux (Fr) sparkling Burgundy, applies to white and rosé wines, reds excluded (since December 1985). Minimum alcohol content 9.5% by vol. which must be natural.

Bourgogne Ordinaire (Fr) a rare Appellation Regionale of Burgundy which produces red, rosé and white wines.

Bourgogne Passe-Tout-Grains (Fr) a red or rosé wine which is made from ⅔ Gamay and ⅓ Pinot noir. Often has the A.C. Bourgogne Grand Ordinaire. Minimum alc. content of above 9.5% by vol.

Bourgogne Rosé (Fr) an A.C. rosé wine produced in the Yonne département in the Burgundy region from César, Pinot noir and Tressot grapes.

Bourgogne Rosé de Marsannay (Fr) a rosé (the only one in the Côte d'Or) produced in the commune of Marsannay-la-Côte. Also known as Bourgogne Clairet de Marsannay.

Bourgogne Rouge (Fr) an Appellation Regionale wine which varies with each region its produced in. Often of high quality for its price. Made with most of the red grape varieties grown in Burgundy.

Bourgogne Rouge de Marsannay (Fr) an A.C. red wine produced from the Pinot noir grape in Marsannay-la-Côte.

Bourgueil (Fr) a wine district of the Touraine in the middle Loire. Produces red and rosé A.C. wines from the Cabernet sauvignon and the Cabernet franc grapes. Minimum alc. content of 9.5% by vol.

Bourguignonnes (Fr) the name given to the 75cls bottles with a long sloping shoulder and short necks used in Burgundy.

Bourne Valley Brewery (Eng) a brewery (established 1978) based in Andover, Hampshire. Brews cask-conditioned Weaver's Bitter 1037 O.G. Andover Ale 1040 O.G. Henchard Bitter 1045 O.G. and Wallop 1056 O.G.

Bournvita (Eng) a commercially prepared, powdered, malted chocolate drink™. Usually reconstituted with hot milk. Produced by Cadburys. (Part of Kenco-Typhoo). See also Maltivita.

Bourret (Fr) a white grape variety used in the making of vermouth.

Bourro (Fr) a spiced wine. See also Vin Bourro.

Bourru (Fr) a term to denote a rough, crude wine.

Boursault (Fr) a Cru Champagne village in the Canton of Dormans. District: Épernay.

Bousa (Afr) a beer made from millet.

Bouscaut (Fr) an estate in the commune of Cadaujac in the A.C. Graves, Bordeaux.

Bouschet Sauvignon (Fr) another name for the Cabernet sauvignon grape.

Bousse d'Or (Fr) a Premier Cru vineyard in the A.C. commune of Volnay, Côte de Beaune, Burgundy. 1.9ha. Also known as La Bousse d'Or.

Boutari (Gre) the name of a major wine merchant based in Thessaloniki who deals in Macedonian wines. Produces: Kretikos, Naoussa.

Boute (Fr) the name given to a barrel that is bigger than a carrique but smaller than a foudre, used in Provence.

Bouteille (Fr) bottle.

Bouteille à Vin (Ch.Isles) wine bottle.

Bouteille Consignée (Fr) a returnable bottle.

Bouteille Fantaisie (Fr) an unusually shaped bottle used for a special event or market.

Bouteille Nantaise (Fr) a long necked, dumpy bottle used in the Nantais region for Muscadets.

Bouteillerie (Fr) bottle store.

Bouteille Sur-Lie (Fr) a flute-shaped green bottle with a 'sur-lie' logo at the point of the bottle's neck taper, used for Muscadet and Gros-plant 'sur-lie-bottled' wines.

Bouteille Tradition (Fr) an old Cognac bottle, clear glass bottle used by the Hennessey's (Cognac) to sell their brandies.

Bouteville (Fr) a commune in the Charente département whose grapes are classed Grande Champagne (Cognac).

Boutière [La] (Fr) a Premier Cru vineyard in the A.C. commune of Cheilly-lès-Maranges, Santenay, Côte de Beaune, Burgundy.

Boutières [Les] (Fr) a vineyard in the commune of Solutré-Pouilly, A.C. Pouilly-Fuissé, Mâcon, Burgundy.

Boutinet [Bernard] (Fr) a Cognac producer with 26ha. in the Fins Bois. (Add): La Brissonneau, 16360 Breville.

Boutinot Wines (Eng) a wine importer (established

1981). (Add): Brook House, Northenden Road, Gatley, Cheadle, Cheshire SK8 4DN. Agents and importers of a wide range of wines. Website: http://www.boutinot.com 'E'mail: sales@boutinot.com

Boutique Winery (USA) a small winery that only produces one or two styles of wine.

Bouton Blanc (Fr) an alternative name for the Carmenère grape. *See also* Carbonet, Carbouet, Cabernelle, Carmenelle, Grande Vidure, Grand Carmenet.

Bouvet-Ladubay (Fr) an A.C. sparkling Saumur, made by the méthode traditionelle at St. Hilaire St. Florent, from the Chenin blanc, Cabernet franc and Cabernet sauvignon grapes. Owned by Taittinger.

Bouveur (Fr) drinker.

Bouvier (Aus) a white grape (table) variety. Is used to produce Auslese, Spätlese and Prädikat wines due to its low acidity and early maturation. Is also used in the making of sturm. Also known as Bouviertraube.

Bouvier (Euro) a red grape variety used to make Plemenka, a wine from the Vojuodina region. Also grown in Hungary and Austria where it is often used for sweet wines. Known also as Bouviertraube and Ranina.

Bouviertraube (Aus) *see* Bouvier.

Bouvrage (Eng) a raspberry drink from Scottish raspberries prduced by Ella Drinks. Sold in bottles and cans.

Bouwland (S.Afr) a winery (established 1996) based in Koelenhof, Stellenbosch, Western Cape. 40ha. Grape varieties: Cabernet sauvignon, Chenin blanc, Merlot, Pinotage.

Bouwland Wines (S.Afr) *see* Kanonkop Estate.

Bouzeron (Fr) a small village in the Chalonnaise near Chagny. Produces fine A.C. Bourgogne Aligoté.

Bouzouki (Gre) the name given to a medium-sweet, red table wine made by Tsantali.

Bouzy (Fr) a Grand Cru Champagne village in the Canton d'Aÿ. District: Reims. Is famous for still red wines of same name.

Bouzy Brut (Fr) a 100% grand Cru Champagne produced in Bouzy by the local vineyard of Barancourt.

Bouzy Rouge (Fr) an A.C. red wine made in the district of Bouzy in Champagne, mainly used for the families of the proprietors of Champagne and also for mixing to make rosé Champagne.

Bovale Grande (It) a red grape variety grown in Sardinia, also known as the Girone.

Bovale Sardo (It) a red grape variety grown in Sardinia, also known as the Muristellu.

Bovlei Co-operative (S.Afr) a co-operative winery (established 1907) based in Wellington, Western Cape. 560ha. (Add): Box 82, Wellington 7655. Has 66 members. Grape varieties: Cabernet franc, Cabernet sauvignon, Chardonnay, Chenin blanc, Merlot, Pinotage, Pinotage rosé, Sauvignon blanc, Shiraz. Labels: Beaukett, Grand Rouge, Reserve. Website: http://www.bovlei.co.za

Bovril (Eng) the famous™ brand-name for a concentrated beef extract drink, is diluted with boiling water.

Bowen (Arg) a wine-producing area based in southern Argentina.

Bowen Estate (Austr) a winery. (Add): P.O. Box 4B, Coonawarra, South Australia 5263. 30ha. Grape varieties: Cabernet sauvignon, Rhine riesling and Shiraz. (Add): Naracoote Road, 2 miles north of Penola.

Bowl (Eng) an old English term to denote a drink of intoxicating liquor. i.e. 'To partake in a bowl of brandy'.

Bowland Beer Company (Eng) a brewery (established 2003). (Add): Bashall Barn, Twitter Lane, Bashall Town, Clitheroe, Lancashire BB7 3LQ. Brews: Headless Pig 4.5% alc by vol., Hen Harrier 4% alc by vol., Hunters Moon 3.9% alc by vol., Oak 4% alc by vol., Sawley Tempted 4.7% alc by vol. Website: http://www.bowlandbrewery.com 'E'mail: Richard@bowlandbeer.fsnet.co.uk

Bow Lane Reserve Fino (Eng) a light, dry Fino Sherry from the Balls Brothers of London.

Bowle (Ger) a wine cup prepared with wine, herbs, fruit, liqueurs or brandy.

Bowlewein (Ger) a slang term for wines that are only suitable for cups and punches as a base.

Bowman Beer (Eng) a brown ale 1030 O.G. and strong ale 1054 O.G. brewed by Charles Wells, Bedford.

Bowman Bounty (Eng) a beer brewed by the Alcazar Brewery, Nottinghamshire.

Bowman Vineyard (USA) a vineyard based in Amador County, California. Grape variety: Zinfandel.

Bowman Wine Cellars (USA) a winery based in Weston, Missouri. Produces hybrid wines.

Bowmore (Scot) a single Islay malt whisky distilled at the Bowmore distillery on the Isle of Islay by Bowmore Distillers. 10, 12, 15, 17, 21, 25 year old. Also the 12 y.o. as a 1965 bi-centenary version (a limited edition). Cask Strength at 56% alc by vol. Bowmore Legend 40% alc by vol., Bowmore Darkest 43% alc by vol. aged for two years in Oloroso Sherry casks. Website: http://www.bowmore.com

Bowwood (S.Afr) the label for a red wine (Cabernet sauvignon and Merlot blend) produced by the Flagstone Winery, Somerset West, Western Cape.

Bow Wow (Eng) a 5% alc by vol. ale brewed by The Dog House Brewery C°, Cornwall.

Boxberg [stadtteil Unterschüpf] (Ger) village (Anb): Baden. (Ber): Badische Frankenland. (Gro): Tauberklinge. (Vin): Mühlberg.

Boxbeutel (Ger) *see* Bocksbeutel.

Boxer Brewery (Switz) an independent brewery based in Lausanne.

Boxing Hare (Eng) the label of a seasonal ale brewed by Vaux Breweries.

Box Steam Brewery (Eng) a brewery. (Add): Oaks Farm, Rode Hill, Colerne, Chippenham, Wiltshire SN14 8AR. Brews a variety of beers and lager. Website: http://www.boxsteambrewery.com

Boxton Vineyards (Eng) a vineyard based in Boyton End, Stoke-by-Clare, Suffolk. 2ha. Grape varieties: Huxelrebe and Müller-Thurgau.

Boy (Eng) a slang term used for a bottle of Champagne in the Victorian/Edwardian eras.

Boyer (Fr) a commune in the Mâconnais where Mâcon Supérieur is produced.

Boynton's of Bright (Austr) a vineyard (established 1987). (Add): Ovens Valley Hwy., Porepunkah, Victoria. Grape varieties: Cabernet sauvignon, Chardonnay, Mataro, Riesling, Sauvignon blanc, Shiraz.

Boy's Bitter (Eng) the other name for the pale ale brewed by the Hall and Woodhouse Brewery at Blandford Forum, Dorset.

Boyton Vineyard (Eng) a vineyard based in Suffolk. Grape variety: Huxelrebe.

Boza (Slo) a Turkish-style, non-alcoholic brew made from corn.

Bozcaada (Tur) a wine-producing area. Growers make their own wine.

Boze Down (Eng) a vineyard based in Berkshire. Produces dry table wines.

Bozner Leiten (It) *see* Colli di Bolzano.

B.P. (Eng) *abbr:* Broken Pekoe, a tea grade.

B.P.A. (Eng) *abbr:* Best Pale Ale, a general stock beer 5% alc by vol. brewed by the Greene King at the Westgate Brewery, Bury St. Edmunds, Suffolk. Often used for bottled brand beers and in their Winter Ale. *see* Suffolk Strong.

Braastad (Fr) an Cognac producer. Produces a range of Cognacs including VSOP 40% alc by vol., V.S. 40% alc by vol., V.O.40% alc by vol. and X.O 40% alc by vol. Label: Château de Triac, Réserve de Famille 41.3% alc by vol.

Brabrux Brasserie (Bel) a brewery based in Wolvertem in northern Belgium.

Brac (Slo) a wine-producing island off the Dalmatian coast.

Bracca (It) a sparkling natural mineral water from Bracca. Mineral contents (milligrammes per litre): Sodium 19.8mg/l, Calcium 132mg/l, Magnesium 41.3mg/l, Potassium 1.5mg/l, Bicarbonates 256.3mg/l, Chlorides 32.2mg/l, Sulphates 277.9mg/l, Fluorides 0.43mg/l, Nitrates 0.93mg/l, Silicates 6.6mg/l, Strontium 1.6mg/l. pH 7.32

Bracer (Eng) a slang term for a stiff drink e.g. gin, rum, whisky, etc. to give a person courage to do a task. Or as a tonic.

Brace Up (Cktl) 60mls (½ gill) brandy, juice of small lime, 2 dashes white anisette, 2 dashes Angostura, fresh egg. Shake well over ice, strain into a tumbler and top up with Vichy water.

Brachetto (It) a red grape variety grown in the Piemonte region. Produces brilliant red, light wines. Known as Braquet in France.

Brachetto d'Acqui (It) a red pétillant wine produced from the Brachetto grape in Piemonte. D.O.C.

Brachetto d'Acqui (It) a term under the D.O.C. regulations used to describe the naturally sparkling wines obtained from the musts and

wines produced in the region of Acqui Terme in Piemonte.

Brackenheim (Ger) village (Anb): Württemberg. (Ber): Württembergisch Unterland. (Gro): Heuchelberg. (Vins): Dachsberg, Mönchsberg, Schlossberg, Wolfsaugen, Zweifelberg.

Brackenheim [ortsteil Botenheim] (Ger) village (Anb): Württemberg. (Ber): Württembergisch Unterland. (Gro): Heuchelberg. (Vin): Ochsenberg.

Bradfield Brewery (Eng) a brewery (established 2004). (Add): Watt House Farm, High Bradfield, Sheffield, South Yorkshire S6 6LG. Brews a variety of beers. Website: http://www.bradfieldbrewery.com 'E'mail: info@bradfieldbrewery.com

Bradgate (S.Afr) a label for a range of wines (Chenin blanc & Sauvignon blanc/Cabernet sauvignon & Merlot/Syrah) from the Jordan Vineyards, Stellenbosch.

Brador (Can) a hopped ale that has been top-fermented. Produced by the Molson Brewery in Quebec. 6.25% alc by vol.

Bradshaw Estate Winery (N.Z) a winery. (Add): 291 Te Mata Road, Havelock North. 4ha. Grape varieties: Chardonnay, Cabernet sauvignon, Merlot.

Braes of Glenlivet (Scot) a single highland malt whisky distillery in north-east Scotland. Owned by Seagram. 40% alc by vol.

Braeuisge Spring (Scot) a carbonated natural mineral water.

Braga (Port) a wine district in the region of Entre Minho e Douro. Produces red and white Vinhos Verdes.

Bragdy (Wal) brewery.

Bragdy Dyffryn Clwyd (Wal) a micro-brewery based in Denbigh. Sold to Flannery's of Aberystwyth, Wales. Produces Castle Bitter 4.2% alc by vol. Cwrw Denwydd 3.9% alc by vol. Cwrw Cysur Bitter 3.6% alc by vol. Pedwar Bawd 4.8% alc by vol.

Bragdy Ynys Mon (Wal) a brewery (established 1999). (Add): Cae Cwta Mawr, Talwrn, Llangefni, Gwynedd LL77 7SD. Brews: Amnesia 4.9% alc by vol., Medra 4% alc by vol., Sosban Fach 4.3% alc by vol., Tarw Du 4.5% alc by vol., Wennol 4.1% alc by vol. Website: http://www.angleseyales.co.uk 'E'mail: martyn@angleseyales.co.uk

Bragget (Eng) a 6% alc by vol. ale brewed by the Blue Anchor Brewery, Cornwall.

Braggot (Eng) an old-fashioned beverage of spices, honey and ale wort.

Bragi (Ch.Isles) intoxicated/tipsy/drunk.

Brahma Beer (Bra) a pilsener beer 5% alc by vol. (1048 O.G.) brewed in Brazil by the Brahma Brewery in Rio and exported for sale in USA.

Brahma Brewery (Bra) a brewery based in Rio de Janerio. Noted for Brahma Chopp beer.

Brahma Chopp (Bra) a pilsener-type beer 1048 O.G. brewed by the Brahma Brewery in Rio.

Brahms and Liszt (Eng) a bottle-conditioned sediment beer brewed by the Selby Brewery, Selby, North Yorkshire.

Brahms and Liszt (Eng) a Cockney rhyming slang to

B

denote a drunken person. Someone under the influence of alcohol.

Brain & C°. Ltd. [S.A.] (Wal) an old (established 1882) well-known brewery. (Add): The Cardiff Brewery, P.O. Box 53, Crawshay Street, Cardiff, South Glamorgan CF10 1SP. Produces many fine beers including Red Dragon 1035 O.G. Red Dragon Dark 1035 O.G. Red Dragon Bitter 1035 O.G. Black Prince Ale, Easter Ale, Rev. James (The), St. David's Day Ale, (S.A.) Summer Ale, Victory Ale, at Trick, keg Capital 1033 O.G. I.P.A. 4.5% alc by vol. Merged with Crown Buckley in 1997. Website: http://www.sabrain.com 'E'mail: brains@sabrain.com

Brain Crown Buckley (Wal) see Brain & C°. Ltd., Crown Buckley.

Braine (Fr) a canton in the Soissons district of Champagne. Has the Cru village of Cersauil.

Brainstorm (Cktl) 50mls (2fl.ozs) Irish whiskey, 2 dashes Bénédictine, 2 dashes dry vermouth. Serve in an old-fashioned glass with ice, twist of orange peel. Stir.

Brain-sur-Allonnes (Fr) a commune in the A.C. Saumur, Anjou-Saumur, Loire. Produces red and white wines.

Brakspear (Eng) a 2.5% ac. by vol. cask-conditioned bitter from the Brakspear Brewery, Henley-on-Thames, Oxon.

Brakspear's Brewery (Eng) also known as the Henley Brewery, Henley-on-Thames, Oxon. Produces Strong Ale 5% alc by vol. XXX Mild 1030 O.G. XXXX Old 1043 O.G. Beehive Keg Bitter 1035 O.G. and Special 1043 O.G. Bee Sting, Brakspear, Hooray Henry, Henry on Thames, Brooklyn Bridge, 2.5 and Downpour. Also a Brewers Selection- Resolution, Three Sheets, Ted & Bens, 'O' Be Joyful, Hooray Henley, Leaf Fall, Live Organic.

Bramaterra (It) a D.O.C. red wine from Piemonte. Made mainly from the Nebbiolo grape.

Brambledown (Eng) a 5% alc by vol. traditional strong dry cider from Lanchester of Durham.

Bramley & Gage (Eng) distillers (established 1996). (Add): Unit 4, Longmeadow, South Brent, Devon TQ10 9YT. Produces a variety of spirits and liqueurs. Website: http://www.bramleyandgage.co.uk 'E'mail: bramleygage@fsbdial.co.uk

Bramlin Cross (Eng) an English hop variety which has a good aroma.

Brammie (Scot) a 23% alc by vol. bramble flavoured Scotch whisky liqueur.

Brampton Vineyard (S.Afr) a vineyard based in Stellenbosch. Grape varieties include: Cabernet sauvignon, Chardonnay. Website: http://www.rustenberg.co.za

Brancaia (It) an 18ha. wine estate in Castellina. Produces a Chianti Classico and a red I.G.T. (super Tuscan) wine from Merlot, Sangiovese and Cabernet sauvignon grapes. Website: http://www.brancaia.com

Branca Menta (Fr) a green, mint digestif produced by Fernet Branca (uses many herbs), aged for 1 year in Slovenian oak. Softer than Fernet Branca.

Brancelho (Port) a white grape variety used in the production of Vinhos Verdes.

Brancellao (Sp) a red grape variety grown on the Ribera area of north western Spain. Produces deep-coloured acidic wines.

Branco (Port) white.

Branco Extra Seco (Port) a white Port produced by Quinta do Noval. The sugar is fermented out before the spirit (brandy) is added.

Branco Lameiro (Port) a white grape variety grown in Lima for Vinhos Verdes.

Branco Seco (Bra) dry white wine.

Branco Suave (Bra) mellow white wine.

Brand (Fr) an A.C. Alsace Grand Cru based in Turckheim, Haut-Rhin. 57ha.

Brand [Lucien] (Fr) an Alsace wine producer. (Add): 67120 Ergersheim.

Branda (Ire) brandy.

Branda (It) an old Piemontese name for acqua vitae.

Brand Brouwerij (Hol) see Brand's Brouwerij.

Brandcott Estate (N.Z) the label used by Montana Wines, Marlborough for a Sauvignon blanc wine. See also Ormond Estate, Renwick Estate.

Brande Conde (Sp) a famous brandy produced by Osborne.

Branded Glassware (Eng) glassware of a particular shape (many exclusive to the drink's manufacturer) having the brand logo engraved on the glass.

Branded Wines (Eng) wines sold on their brand name instead of the area or regional name. e.g. Blue Nun, Mateus Rosé, Piat d'Or, etc.

Brandeln (Ger) a term used to describe a wine with a taste of caramel or brandy.

Brandenburger Kurfürst Quelle (Ger) a natural spring mineral water from Natupark Hoher Fläming, Brandenburg. Mineral contents (milligrammes per litre): Sodium 6.5mg/l, Calcium 49.7mg/l, Magnesium 6.4mg/l, Potassium 1mg/l, Bicarbonates 145mg/l, Chlorides 13.7mg/l, Sulphates 27mg/l, Nitrates <0.3mg/l.

Brandenburger Urquell (Ger) a sparkling natural spring mineral water from Diedersdorf bei Zossen, BB. Mineral contents (milligrammes per litre): Sodium 8.1mg/l, Calcium 72.1mg/l, Bicarbonates 192mg/l, Chlorides 23.6mg/l.

Brandenburger Urstromquelle (Ger) a natural spring mineral water from Baruth. Mineral contents (milligrammes per litre): Sodium 4.5mg/l, Calcium 60.9mg/l, Magnesium 6.5mg/l, Potassium 0.6mg/l, Bicarbonates 204mg/l, Chlorides 8.5mg/l, Fluorides 0.16mg/l, Silicates 23mg/l.

Brandenburger Waldquelle (Ger) a natural spring mineral water from Wiesenburg, Naturpark 'Hoher Fläming'. Mineral contents (milligrammes per litre): Sodium 5.3mg/l, Calcium 64.4mg/l, Magnesium 5.2mg/l, Potassium 1.2mg/l, Bicarbonates 216mg/l, Chlorides 6.6mg/l, Sulphates 13mg/l, Fluorides 0.11mg/l, Nitrates <0.3mg/l.

Branderij and Gistfabriek 'Hollandia 11' BV (Hol) a large moutwijn producer. Part of Grist-Brocades NV group.

Brander Winery (USA) a small winery based in the Santa Ynes Valley, Santa Barbara County, California.

Grape varieties: Cabernet sauvignon, Sauvignon blanc.

Brandeston Priory (Eng) a vineyard (established 1975) based in Woodbridge, Suffolk. 2.5ha closed in December 1988. Grape varieties Müller-Thurgau 90% plus small parcels of other varieties.

Brandevin (Fr) brandy (unmatured clear wine spirit).

Brandevinier (Fr) a travelling distiller of brandy or eau-de-vie.

Brandewijn (Hol) lit: 'burnt wine', brandy. (Fr) = vin brûlé.

Brandewyn (Hol) the same as Brandewijn.

Brandied Ginger (Cktl) ⅔ measure Cognac, ⅓ measure Stones Ginger Wine, 2 dashes lime juice, 2 dashes orange juice. Shake over ice, strain into a cocktail glass. Serve with a piece of preserved ginger and grated chocolate.

Brandied Madeira (Cktl) ⅙ measure brandy, ⅙ measure Boal Madeira, 4 dashes French vermouth. Stir over ice, strain into an ice-filled old-fashioned glass and add twist of lemon.

Brandied Port (Cktl) ¼ measure brandy, ¼ measure tawny Port, 4 dashes lemon juice, 4 dashes maraschino. Shake over ice, strain into an ice-filled old-fashioned glass and add slice of orange.

Brandig (Ger) the term used to describe a wine with a spirity, brandy taste.

Branding (Eng) a method of placing a mark with hot iron on the cork to give authenticity to the bottles contents.

Brandl (Aus) a winery based in the Kamptal region. (Add): Heiligensteinstrasse 13, 3561 Zöbing. Grape varieties: Grüner veltliner, Pinot blanc, Riesling, Zweigelt.

Brand Labelling (Eng) the names on wine labels that are to do with the producer and have no actual name of wine. e.g. 'Mateus Rosé', 'Piat d'Or', etc.

Brand Name (Eng) see Branded Wines.

Brand's Brouwerij (Hol) a brewery based in Wijke, Limburg. Noted for a wide range of unpasteurised beers including Imperator and Brand Up '52. Granted the title Koninklijke (Royal) by the Queen of the Netherlands.

Brandstatt (Aus) a vineyard site on the banks of the River Danube situated in the Wachau region, Niederösterreich.

Brands Vineyard (Austr) a winery of Coonawarra in South Australia. Grape varieties: Cabernet and Shiraz. Wines sold under the Laira label.

Brand Up'52 (Hol) a well-hopped pilsener lager beer brewed by the Brand Brouwerij in Wijke.

Brandvlei Koöperatiewe Wynkelder (S.Afr) a co-operative winery (established 1955) based in Dornrivier, Worcester, Western Cape. 1400ha. (Add): Private Bag X3001, Worcester 6850. Grape varieties: Chardonnay, Chenin blanc, Colombard, Hanepoot jerepiko, Merlot, Ruby cabernet, Sauvignon blanc. Labels: Bacchanté, BC. Websites: http://www.brandvlei.co.za/http://www.bcwines.co.za

Brandy (Eng) distillation of wine made from grape must. *See also* Aguardente, Aguardiente, Armagnac, Bagaceira, Cognac, Grappa, Pisco. (Cro) = konjak/rakija, (Den) = cognac/brandy/frugtbrændevin, (Fr) = marc, (Ire) = branda, (Lat) = acquavite, (Rus) = kanyak.

Brandy Alexander (Cktl) ⅓ measure brandy, ⅓ measure (brown) crème de cacao, ⅓ measure cream. Shake over ice, strain into a cocktail glass and grate nutmeg on top. Named after Alexander the Great.

Brandy Alexander Milk Punch (Cktl) 25mls (⅛ gill) Cognac, 15mls (⅛ gill) crème de cacao, 125mls (1 gill) milk. Shake well over ice, strain into a highball glass. Top with grated nutmeg and serve with straws.

Brandy and Ginger Ale (Cktl) place 1 measure brandy in a tumbler containing 2 ice cubes. Top with ginger ale and stir.

Brandy and Soda (Cktl) place 1 measure brandy in a tumbler with 2 ice cubes and top with soda water.

Brandy Antinori (It) a well-known brandy from Antinori.

Brandy Balloon (Eng) the name given to the 'nosing glass', has a large bowl and narrow lip. Used for nosing wines during production. Is favoured by the British as a brandy glass. see Brandy Inhaler and Brandy Snifter.

Brandy Blazer (Cktl) 2 measures Cognac, 1 lump sugar, orange and lemon zest. Mix altogether in a pan, ignite, stir then extinguish. Strain into an old-fashioned glass. May add 10mls (½fl.oz) Kahlúa.

Brandy Cask Pub & brewery (Eng) a brewery (established 1995). (Add): 25 Bridge Street, Pershore, Worcestershire WR10 1AJ. Brews: Brandy Snapper 4% alc by vol., John baker Original 4.8% alc by vol., Whistling Joe 3.6% alc by vol.

Brandy Cassis Cocktail (Cktl) 1 measure brandy, ½ measure lemon juice, 1 dash crème de cassis. Shake over ice, strain into a cocktail glass. Add twist of lemon peel.

Brandy Champerelle Cocktail (Cktl) ½ measure Cognac, ½ measure Curaçao, 2 dashes Angostura. Stir over ice in a balloon glass.

Brandy Cobbler [1] (Cktl) 125mls (1 gill) brandy, 30mls (¼ gill) brown Curaçao. Shake over broken ice, strain into highball with ice. Decorate with dash lemon peel juice, 2 slices lemon, spoon and straws.

Brandy Cobbler [2] (Cktl) 1 measure brandy, 4 dashes orange Curaçao, sugar to taste. Fill 125mls (5fl.oz) wine goblet with crushed ice, add brandy, sugar and Curaçao. Stir, decorate with fruit, add sprig of mint and serve with straws.

Brandy Cocktail [1] (Cktl) 60mls (½ gill) Cognac, 3 dashes Curaçao, dash Angostura. Stir over ice, strain into a cocktail glass.

Brandy Cocktail [2] (Cktl) 40mls (⅓ gill) Cognac, 1 dash Pernod, 4 dashes brown Curaçao, 10 drops Angostura. Stir over ice. Strain into cocktail glass, serve with a cherry and dash of lemon peel juice.

Brandy Cocktail [3] (Cktl) 30mls (¼ gill) Cognac, 30mls (¼ gill) dry vermouth. Stir over ice, strain into a cocktail glass, decorate with cherry and a dash of lemon peel juice.

Brandy Cocktail [4] (Cktl) 40mls (⅓ gill) brandy, 2 dashes sugar syrup, 2 dashes Angostura. Stir over ice, strain into a cocktail glass and add twist of lemon peel.

Brandy Cocktail [5] (Cktl) ⅓ measure Cognac, ¼ measure Italian vermouth, ¼ measure Grand Marnier, 2 dashes Angostura. Shake over ice, strain into a cocktail glass. Squeeze of orange peel juice on top.

Brandy Collins (Cktl) *see* Collins, substitute brandy for spirit.

Brandy Crusta (Cktl) 40mls (⅓ gill) brandy, 20mls (⅙ gill) lemon juice, dash orange bitters, dash Angostura, ½ teaspoon powdered sugar, teaspoon plain syrup, teaspoon maraschino. Shake over ice, strain. Moisten inside of wine glass with lemon juice and sprinkle with sugar. Add mixture and serve with fruit slices and lemon peel.

Brandy Daisy (Cktl) 60mls (½ gill) brandy, 60mls (½ gill) lemon juice, 60mls (½ gill) lime juice, 30mls (¼ gill) grenadine. Shake over ice, strain into a highball and fill up with soda water. Serve with slices of fruit on top and a spoon.

Brandy de Bayo (Ch.Isles) cherry brandy, home-made by soaking cherries and raspberries in brandy with cinnamon, cloves and sugar.

Brandy de Gengivre (Ch.Isles) ginger cordial.

Brandy de Jerez (Sp) Denominación Específica. *abbr:* D.E. Method of production is controlled but the origin of the grapes is not. Grape varieties are mainly Airén with some Cayetana, Jaén and Palomino. Made by both pot and patent still methods. Ageing and blending is done in Criadera and Solera. Three styles are produced – Solera brandy de Jerez (min .of 6 months in Solera with min. of 3g./litre of congenerics), Reserva brandy de Jerez (min. of 1 year in Solera with min. of 2.5g./litre of congenerics), Gran Reserva brandy de Jerez (min. of 3 years in Solera with min. of 3g./litre of congenerics). Strength is from 34%–45% alc by vol.

Brandy del Bourgogne (It) a brandy produced by Gambarotta.

Brandy Egg Flip [1] (Cktl) 1 egg, 1 measure brandy and sugar syrup to taste. Shake and strain into a cocktail glass and add grated nutmeg.

Brandy Egg Flip [2] (Cktl) 1 measure brandy, 1 teaspoon sugar, 3 measures hot water. Place ingredients into a tumbler, stir, float a toasted biscuit on top and add grated nutmeg.

Brandy Egg Nogg (Cktl) 60mls (½ gill) brandy, 40mls (1/3 gill) rum, 1 teaspoon sugar, 1 egg, 90mls (¾ gill) milk. Shake over ice, strain into a highball. Top with grated nutmeg.

Brandy Fix (Cktl) 35mls (1½ fl.ozs) brandy, 100mls (4fl.ozs) lemon juice, 10mls (½ fl.oz) cherry brandy, 4 dashes gomme syrup. Pour into a goblet filled with crushed ice, stir slightly. Add orange and lemon slices and a cherry. Serve with straws.

Brandy Fizz (Cktl) 60mls (½ gill) brandy, 4 dashes brown Curaçao, dash grenadine, 90mls (¾ gill) lemon juice, white of egg. Shake over ice, strain into a highball and top with soda.

Brandy Flip (Cktl) *see* Brandy Egg Flip.

Brandy Float (Cktl) a measure of Cognac floating on top of a glass of water. Is achieved by placing a whisky glass of water over a pony glass of brandy. The pony glass is gently removed leaving the brandy floating on top of the water.

Brandy Gump (Cktl) ½ measure brandy, ½ measure lemon juice, 2 dashes grenadine, shake over ice and strain into a cocktail glass.

Brandy Highball (Cktl) as for Gin Highball but using brandy in place of the gin.

Brandyhum (Cktl) equal quantities of Van der Hum and brandy.

Brandy Inhaler (USA) the name often used for a balloon glass (nosing glass).

Brandy Mac Cocktail (Cktl) ½ measure brandy, ½ measure ginger wine. Shake over ice. strain into an ice-filled highball and top with soda.

Brandy Milk Punch (Cktl) 35mls (1½ fl.ozs) brandy, 50mls (2fl.ozs) milk, barspoon sugar. Shake over ice, strain into wine goblet and top with nutmeg.

Brandy Punch [1] (Cktl) 90mls (¾ gill) brandy, juice ½ lemon, sugar syrup to taste. Shake well over ice, strain into a wine goblet and top with iced soda water.

Brandy Punch [2] (Cktl) 1 measure brandy, 4 dashes curaçao. Stir with ice in a highball, top with ginger ale, add mint and fruit.

Brandy Punch [1] (Punch) Juice of 12 lemons, 4 oranges, 125mls (1gill) gomme syrup, 150mls (6fl.ozs) grenadine, 1100mls (2pints) soda water, 150mls (6fl.ozs) Cointreau, 2 bottles brandy, 425mls (¾ pint) strong cold tea. Stir well together, decorate with fruits in season.

Brandy Punch [2] (Punch) ½ bottle Cognac, 2 measures white rum, 3 measures Cointreau, 1 measure maraschino, juice 10 lemons, 300 g. (¾ lb.) sugar, 500mls (1pint) iced soda water. Stir the sugar in the lemon juice. Pour in remaining ingredients except soda. Leave to chill, add soda, decorate with fruit in season.

Brandy Rickey (Cktl) place the juice of ½ a lime and 3 ice cubes into a highball glass. Add 1½ measures brandy and top with soda and serve with twist of lime peel.

Brandy Rum (W.Ind) the name given to the Haitian rum because it is lighter and less pungent than most rums. Also applied to Barbados rum.

Brandy Sangaree (Cktl) equal parts of brandy and water with barspoon of sugar. Fill glass with crushed ice, stir in ingredients and top with grated nutmeg.

Brandy Scaffa (Cktl) equal quantities of brandy and maraschino in a cocktail glass. Stir, add 2 dashes Angostura on top and serve.

Brandy Shamparelle (Cktl) ¼ measure anisette, ¼ measure red Cointreau, ¼ measure Yellow

Chartreuse, ¼ measure brandy. Shake over ice and strain into a cocktail glass.

Brandy Shrub (Eng) place the juice of 5 lemons and the zest of 2 lemons with 2¼ litres (4pints) brandy into a bowl. Cover and stand for 3 days. Add 1.1litres (2pints) sweet Sherry and 1 kg. (2lbs.) sugar. Stir well, strain through a jelly bag and bottle. Drink as required.

Brandy Sling (Cktl) dissolve a teaspoon of powdered sugar into the juice of ½ a lemon and a little water. Add 40mls (⅓ gill) Cognac. Place into an ice-filled old-fashioned glass and top with a twist of lemon peel.

Brandy Smash (Cktl) 35mls (1½ fl.ozs) brandy, 6 leaves mint, powdered sugar. Dissolve sugar in a little water in an old-fashioned glass. Add mint and bruise to extract flavour. Add brandy, fill with crushed ice. Stir, decorate with lemon slice and serve with straws.

Brandy Snapper (Eng) a 4% alc by vol. ale brewed by the Brandy Cask Pub & Brewery, Worcestershire.

Brandy Snaps (Eng) not a drink but a type of cake! Made with sugar syrup, butter, flour and ginger.

Brandy Snifter (USA) the name given to the nosing glass (brandy balloon).

Brandy Sour (Cktl) 35mls (1½ fl.ozs) brandy, 20mls (¾ fl.oz) lemon juice, teaspoon powdered sugar. Shake well over ice, strain into a tall glass. Top with soda, add a slice of orange and a cherry.

Brandy Squirt (Cktl) 40mls (⅓ gill) brandy, 2 barspoons powdered sugar, 4 dashes grenadine. Shake over ice, strain into a highball glass, top with soda water. Decorate with a pineapple piece and a strawberry on a cocktail stick.

Brandy Swizzle (Cktl) place the juice of a lime, 1 teaspoon powdered sugar and 50mls (2fl.ozs) soda water into a collins glass over ice. Stir with a swizzle stick, add 2 dashes Angostura, 40mls (⅓ gill) gin, top with soda and serve with swizzle stick.

Brandy Toddy [cold] (Cktl) place ½ teaspoon powdered sugar and 1 teaspoon water into an old-fashioned glass. Stir, add 40mls (⅓ gill) brandy and an ice cube. Stir, add twist of lemon peel juice on top.

Brandy Toddy [hot] (Cktl) place a sugar cube into a warmed old-fashioned glass, fill ⅔ full very hot water, add 40mls (⅓ gill) brandy. Stir, decorate with lemon slice, top with grated nutmeg.

Brandy Vermouth (Cktl) ⅘ measure brandy, ⅕ measure Italian vermouth, dash Angostura. Stir over ice, strain into a cocktail glass.

Brandy Warmer (Cktl) add 1 teaspoon of Cognac to 200mls (⅓ pint) freshly brewed tea. Float a slice of lemon on top and serve with a cinnamon stick.

Brandy Warmer (Eng) a silver pot with a handle used to heat brandy in the eighteenth century for serving as a toddy.

Braník Brewery (Czec) a small brewery (established 1899) in the north west of Prague. Noted for a dark beer called Tmavé 12°, served in a bar called '*The Cave*' which is situated in the former monastery of St. Thomas and Branicky Lezák.

Branicky Lezák (Czec) a 5.3% alc by vol. straw coloured, bottled lager brewed by Braník in Prague.

Braník Straw 10% (Czec) a 4.2% alc by vol. bottled lager brewed by Braník in Prague.

Branntwein (Ger) lit: 'burnt wine', brandy.

Branntwein aus Wein (Ger) lit: 'made from wine', when found on a label it denotes that the brandy does not contain 38% alc by vol. and may not have been oak matured.

Brännvin (Den)(Swe) aquavit, distilled from potatoes the alcohol content can vary from 35% by vol. to 50% by vol.

Branoc (Eng) a 3.8% alc by vol. ale brewed by The Branscombe Vale Brewery, Devon.

Branscombe Vale Brewery [The] (Eng) a brewey (established 1992). (Add): Great Seaside Farm, Branscombe, Seaton, Devon EX12 3DP. Brews: Bab 4.6% alc by vol., Branoc 3.8% alc by vol., BVB 4.6% alc by vol., Draymans Best 4.2% alc by vol., Hells Belles 4.8% alc by vol., Summa'That 5% alc by vol (this replaces Olde Stoker which now becomes a winter ale)., Yabba Dabba Dooo 8.7% alc by vol., Royal Assent, Yo Ho ho and 101 Ale. 'E'mail: branscombe.brew@btconnect.com

Branscourt (Fr) a Cru Champagne village in the Canton de-Ville-en-Tardenois. District: Reims.

Brant Cocktail (Cktl) ¼ measure peppermint liqueur, ¾ measure brandy, dash Angostura. Shake over ice, strain into a cocktail glass. Serve with dash lemon peel juice on top.

Brantini (Cktl) 1 measure brandy, ⅔ measure gin, dash French vermouth. Stir over ice, strain into an old-fashioned glass with an ice cube and add a twist lemon peel juice.

Braquet (Fr) a red grape variety grown in the A.C. Bellet district in Provence, south-eastern France.

Bras Armé (Fr) the brand-name of a fine old Cognac from Hennessy.

Brasenose Ale (Eng) a hot drink served on Shrove Tuesday at the Brasenose College. Recipe: 3¼ litres (6 pints) hot ale, sugar to taste with 6 roasted eating apples floated on top. Also known as Lamb's Wool.

Brasilian Night (Cktl) ¾ measure vodka, ¼ measure blue Curaçao, ½ measure Batida de Coco. Shake well over ice, strain into a cocktail glass and top with chocolate powder.

Brassage (Fr) brewing.

Brasschaat Brasserie (Bel) a brewery noted for Witkap Pater, a light-coloured, bottle-conditioned, top-fermented beer.

Brasser (Fr) to brew.

Brasserie (Fr) brewery/ale-house (can also denote a simple restaurant).

Brasserie Artisanale des Alberes (Fr) a brewery. (Add): 29 Ave des Flamants Roses, 66700 Argeles-sur-Mer. Brews beers and lager. Website: http://www.cap-dona.com

Brasserie Artisanale du Dauphiné (Fr) a brewery. (Add): 33 Rue de Champ Roman, En Face de Castorama, 38400 Saint Martin d'Hères. Brews beers and lager. Website: http://www.mandrin.biz 'E'mail: brasseur@mandrin.biz

Brasserie Artisanale du Sud (Fr) a brewery. (Add): 69 Ave Frederic Mistral, 21100 Nyons. Brews beers and lager. Website: http://www.la-grihete.com 'E'mail: contact@la-grihete.com

Brasserie Artisanale la Choulette (Fr) a brewery. (Add): 16 Rue des Écoles, 59111 Hordain. Brews beers and lager. Website: http://www.lachoulette.com

Brasserie Castelain (Fr) a brewery. (Add): 13 Rue Pasteur, 62410 Bénifontaine. Brews beers and lager. Website: http://www.chti.com

Brasserie Coreff (Fr) a brewery. (Add): 1 Place de la Madelaine, 29600 Morlaix. Brews beers and lager. Website: http://www.coreff.com 'E'mail: contact@coreff.com

Brasserie de la Chapelle (Fr) a brewery. (Add): Ferme Brasserie, La Chapelle 76780 La Chapelle Saint-Ouen. Brews beers and lager. Website: http://www.northmaen.com

Brasserie de la Divatte (Fr) a brewery. (Add): Le Norestier, 44450 La Chapelle Basse Mer. Brews beers and lager. Website: http://www.brasseriedeladivatte.com 'E'mail: brasserie-de-la-divatte@club-internet.fr

Brasserie de l'Abbaye des Rocs (Bel) a brewery. (Add): 37, Chaussée Brunehault 7387 Montignies-sur-Roc. Brews beers and lager. Website: http://www.abbaye-des-rocs.com 'E'mail: abbaye.des.rocs@skynet.be

Brasserie de Silly (Bel) a brewery. (Add): Rue Ville Basse 2, 7830, Silly. Brews beers and lager. Website: http://www.silly-beer.com 'E'mail: contact@silly-beer.com

Brasserie de Vauclair (Fr) a brewery. (Add): 52210 Giey-sur-Aujon. Brews beers and lager. Website: http://www.la-choue.com 'E'mail: contact@la-choue.com

Brasserie des Géants sprl (Bel) a brewery. (Add): Rue du Castel 19, 7801bIrchoncwelz. Brews beers and lager. Website: http://www.brasseriedesgeants.com 'E'mail: info@brasseriedesgeants.com

Brasserie Distillerie du Mont Blanc (Fr) a brewery and distillery. (Add): 15, Place de la Mairie, 74310 Les Houches. Brews beers and lager. Website: http://www.brasserie-montblanc.com 'E'mail: info@brasserie-montblanc.com

Brasserie d'Oc (Fr) a brewery. (Add): RN 113 ZI, 34140 Mèze. Brews beers and lager. Website: http://www.brasseriedoc.com 'E'mail: info@brasseriedoc.com

Brasserie d'Olt (Fr) a brewery. (Add): Sébastien Blaquière, 28 Rue Sannié, 12130 St-Géniez d'Olt. Brews beers and lager.

Brasserie Du Bocq sa (Bel) a brewery. (Add): Rue de la Brasserie 4, Pumode B-5530. Brews beers and lager. Website: http://www.bocq.be 'E'mail: brasserie@bocq.be

Brasserie du Sollier (Fr) a brewery. (Add): 18570 Le Subdray, Bouhrges. Brews beers and lager. Website: http://www.sollier.fr 'E'mail: brasserie@sollier.fr

Brasserie Dubuisson & Frères (Bel) a brewery. (Add): Chaussée de Mons, 28 Pipaix. Brews beers and lager.

Website: http://www.br-dubuisson.com 'E'mail: info@br-dubuisson.com

Brasserie Duont Sprl (Bel) a brewery. (Add): Rue Basse 5, Tourpes B-7904. Brews beers and lager. Website: http://www.brasserie-dupont.com

Brasserie Duyck (Fr) a brewery. (Add): BP 6, 59144 Jenlain. Brews beers and lager. Website: http://www.duyck.com 'E'mail: comptabilite@duyck.com

Brasserie Ellezelloise (Bel) a brewery. (Add): Guinaumont 75, 7890 Ellezelles. Brews beers and lager. Website: http://www.agriss.be

Brasserie Haacht (Bel) a brewery. (Add): Provinciesteenweg, Boortmeerbeek 3190. Brews lager. Website: http://www.primus.be

Brasserie L&L Alphand (Fr) a brewery. (Add): Place du Village, 05290 Vallouise. Brews beers and lager. Website: http://www.brasserie-alphand.com

Brasserie La Saint-Pierre (Fr) a brewery. (Add): 30 Rue Principale, 67140 Saint-Pierre. Brews beers and lager. Website: http://www.lasaintpierre.com

Brasserie Lorraine SA (W.Ind) a brewery. (Add): Quartier Union, 97232 Le Lamentin, Martinique. Brews lager. Website: http://www.brasserielelorraine.com 'E'mail: info@brasserielelorraine.com

Brasserie Meteor (Fr) a brewery. (Add): 6 Rue du General Lebocq, Hockfelden 67270. Brews beers and lager. Website: http://www.brasserie-meteor.fr

Brasserie Mor Braz (Fr) a brewery. (Add): St. Léonard Nord, 56450 Thiex. Brews lager. Website: http://www.morbraz.com 'E'mail: contact@morbraz.com

Brasserie Nationale (Lux) a brewery (established 1974) by a merger of the Bofferding and Funck-Bricher Brasseries.

Brasseries de Bourbon (Fr) a brewery group. (Add): 60 Quai Ouest, Saint-Denis Cedex 97468. Brews beers and lager. Website: http://www.ladodo.com

Brasseries du Logon (Afr) a brewery in Chad noted for Gala Export Beer.

Brasseries Kronenbourg (Fr) a famous brewery group. (Add): Boulevard de l'Europe, Obernai 67212. Brews beers and lager. Website: http://www.brasseries-kronenbourg.com

Brasseur (Fr) brewer.

Brass Monkey (Eng) a limited edition ale brewed by the St. Austell Brewery, St. Austell, Cornwall to highlight the towns links with the sea.

Brass Monkey Stout (Austr) a bottled stout brewed by the Matilda Bay Brewing Company, Fremantle, Western Australia.

Bratenhöfchen (Ger) vineyard (Anb): Mosel-Saar-Ruwer. (Ber): Bernkastel. (Gro): Badstube. (Vil): Bernkastel-Kues.

Bratislava Brewery (Czec) a brewery (established 1873) based in south-east Czec.

Brau ag Brauerei (Aus) a brewery based in Linz, also owns the Schwechat Brauerei near Vienna.

Braubach (Ger) village (Anb): Mittelrhein. (Ber): Rheinburgengau. (Gro): Marksburg. (Vins): Koppelstein, Marmorberg, Mühlberg.

Braucol (Fr) a red grape variety grown in the Gaillac region. Also known as the Fer and Fer servadou.

Braucommune Freistadt (Aus) a brewery. (Add): Promenade 7, Freistadt A-4240. Brews beers and lager. Website: http://www.freistadter-bier.at 'E'mail: info@freistadt-bier.at

Brauer (Aus)(Ger) brewer.

Brauerei (Aus)(Ger) brewery.

Brauerei Alsfeld AG (Ger) a brewery. (Add): Grünberger Strasse 68, Alsfeld D-36304. Brews lager. Website: http://www.alsfelder.de 'E'mail: info@alsfelder.de

Brauereiausschank Schlenkerla (Ger) a brewery. (Add): Dominikanerstrasse 6, Bamberg D-96049. Brews beers and lager. Website: http://www.schlenkerla.de

Brauerei Baar AG (Switz) a brewery. (Add): Postfach 142, Langgasse 41 Baar CH-6341. Brews beers and lager. Website: http://www.brauereibaar.ch 'E'mail: bestellung@brauereibaar.ch

Brauerei Brinkhoff (Eng) a brewery. (Add): 1–2, North End, Swineshead, Boston, Lincolnshire PE20 3LR. Brews beers and lager. A subsidiary of Brauerei Brinkhoff GmbH.

Brauerei Egg GmbH & C° KG (Aus) a brewery. (Add): Gerbe 500, Egg A-6863. Brews beers and lager. Website: http://www.brauerei-egg.at 'E'mail: Brauerei@brauerei-egg.at

Brauerei Eichhof (Switz) a brewery. (Add): Obergrundstrasse 110, CH-6002 Luzern. Brews beers and lager. Website: http://www.eichhof.ch 'E'mail: info@eichhof.ch

Brauerei Falken AG (Switz) a brewery. (Add): Schaffhausen, CH-8201. Brews beers and lager. Website: http://www.falken.ch

Brauerei Fässla (Ger) a brewery. (Add): Obere Königsstrasse 19-21, Baburg D-96052. Brews beers and lager. Website: http://www.faessla.de 'E'mail: info@faessla.de

Brauerei Felsenau AG (Switz) a brewery. (Add): Strandweg 34, CH-3004 Bern. Brews beers and lager. Website: http://www.felsenau.ch 'E'mail: felsenau@felsenau.ch

Brauerei Fischerstube AG (Switz) a brewery. (Add): Rheingasse 45, CH-4058 Basel. Brews beers and lager. Website: http://www.uelibier.ch

Brauerei Franz Xaver Glossner & Neumarkter Mineralbrunnen (Ger) a brewery. (Add): D-92318 Neumarkt. Brews beers and lager. Website: http://www.glossner.de 'E'mail: Brauerei-franz-xaver-glossner@glossner.de

Brauerei Göller (Ger) a brewery. (Add): Wildgarten 12, Zeil am Main D-97475. Brews beers and lager. Website: http://www.brauerei-goeller.de

Brauerei Locher AG (Switz) a brewery. (Add): Brauereiplatz, CH-9050 Appenzell. Brews beers and lager. Website: http://www.appenzellerbier.ch 'E'mail: info@appenzellerbier.ch

Brauerei Müller AG (Switz) a brewery. (Add): Dynamostrasse 8, Baden CH-5400. Brews beers and lager. Website: http://www.brauerei-muller.ch

Brauerei Rosengarten AG (Switz) a brewery. (Add): Spitalstrasse 14, CH-8840, Einsiedeln. Brews beers and lager. Website: http://www.beer.ch 'E'mail: beer@beer.ch

Brauerei Schumacher GmbH (Ger) a brewery. (Add): Oststrasse 123, Düssseldorf D-40210. Brews beers and lager. Website: http://www.schumacher-alt.de

Brauerei Schützengarten AG (Switz) a brewery. (Add): St. Jakobstrasse 37, CH-9004, St. Gallen. Brews: Edelspez 2.8% alc by vol., Edelspez Premium 5.2% alc by vol., Festbier 5.2% alc by vol., Fiesta Cerveza Lager 4.8% alc by vol., Schützengarten Lagerbier 4.8% alc by vol., Schützengold Alkoholfrei, Schwarzer Bär Dunkelbier 5% alc by vol., St. Galler Klosterbräu 5.2% alc by vol., St. Galler Landbier 5% alc by vol. Website: http://www.schuetzengarten.ch

Brauerei Ziegelhof (Switz) a brewery. (Add): Gerberstrasse 4, CH-4410 Liestal. Brews beers and lager. Website: http://www.ziegelhof.ch 'E'mail: info@ziegelhof.ch

Brauerei zum Kuchlbauer GmbH & C° KG (Ger) a brewery. (Add): Römerstrasse 5-9, Abensberg D-93326. Brews beers and lager. Website: http://www.kuchlbauer.de 'E'mail: info@kuchlbauer.de

Brauerei Zwettl Karl Schwarz GmbH (Aus) a brewery. (Add): Symauer Strasse 22-25, Postfach 80, Zwettl A-3910. Brews beers and lager. Website: http://www.zwettler.de

Brauhaase Brewery (Afr) a brewery based in Togo noted for pilsener beer.

Bräuhaus (Ger) brewery.

Bräuhaus Oettingen (Ger) a brewery based in Oettingen. Brews Original Oettinger Schwarzbier.

Brähaus Sternen AG (Switz) a brewery. (Add): Hohenzornstrasse 2, Zürcherstrasse 216, Frauenfeld CH-8500. Brews beers and lager. Website: http://www.brauhaussternen.ch 'E'mail: info@brauhaus.ch

Brauneberg (Ger) village (Anb): Mosel-Saar-Ruwer. (Ber): Bernkastel. (Gro): Kurfürstlay. (Vin): Hasenläufer, Juffer, Juffer-Sonnenhr, Kammer, Klostergarten, Mandelgraben.

Brauneberg (Ger) vineyard (Anb): Mosel-Saar-Ruwer. (Ber): Bernkastel. (Gro): Michelsberg. (Vil): Hetzerath.

Brauneberg (Ger) vineyard (Anb): Mosel-Saar-Ruwer. (Ber): Bernkastel. (Gro): Michelsberg. (Vil): Rivenich.

Brauneberg (Ger) vineyard (Anb): Mosel-Saar-Ruwer. (Ber): Bernkastel. (Gro): Sankt Michael. (Vil): Bekond.

Brauneberg (Ger) vineyard (Anb): Mosel-Saar-Ruwer. (Ber): Saar-Ruwer. (Gro): Scharzberg. (Vil): Konz.

Brauneberg (Ger) vineyard (Anb): Mosel-Saar-Ruwer. (Ber): Zell/Mosel. (Gro): Goldbäumchen. (Vil): Klotten.

Brauneberg (Ger) vineyard (Anb): Mosel-Saar-Ruwer. (Ber): Zell/Mosel. (Gro): Weinhex. (Vil): Oberfell.

Braune Kupp (Ger) vineyard (Anb): Mosel-Saar-

B

Ruwer. (Ber): Saar-Ruwer. (Gro): Scharzberg. (Vil): Wiltingen.

Braunerde (Aus) the name for the brown clay soil found mainly in the Wachau region.

Bräunersberg (Ger) vineyard (Anb): Pfalz. (Ber): Mittelhaardt-Deutsche Weinstrasse. (Gro): Schnepfenflug vom Kellertal. (Vil): Kettersheim/Zellerthal.

Braunfels (Ger) vineyard (Anb): Mosel-Saar-Ruwer. (Ber): Saar-Ruwer. (Gro): Scharzberg. (Vil): Wiltingen.

Braunsdorf (Aus) a vineyard area on the banks of the River Danube in the Kremstal region.

Braunweiler (Ger) village (Anb): Nahe. (Ber): Schloss Böckelheim. (Gro): Rosengarten. (Vins): Hellenpfad, Michaeliskapelle, Schlossberg, Welterkreuz.

Bräustübl Kaltenhausen (Aus) a brewery. (Add): Salzbuhrgerstrasse 67, A-5400 Hallein-Kaltenhausen. Brews beers and lager. Website: http://www.kaltenhausen.at 'E'mail: info@kaltenhausen.at

Brautrock (Ger) vineyard (Anb): Mosel-Saar-Ruwer. (Ber): Zell/Mosel. (Gro): Grafschaft. (Vil): Bullay.

Brave Bull (Cktl) 1 jigger tequila, 25mls (1fl.oz) coffee liqueur. Pour over ice into a tall glass, stir, add a twist of lemon.

Bravado (S.Afr) the label for a red wine (Cabernet sauvignon, Merlot and shiraz blend) produced by the Rijk's Private Cellar winery, Tulbagh, Western Cape.

Braye (Ch.Isles) a traditional draught ale 3.7% alc by vol. (1037 O.G.) brewed by the Guernsey Brewery in St. Peter Port, Guernsey (now no longer produced). see Braye, Captains, Pony Ale, Sunbeam.

Braye Brewery (Ch.Isles) a brewery (opened in 1984) in Alderney. Brews from malt extract. Produces Alderney Ale 1035 O.G.

Brazil (S.Am) has five main vine-growing regions: Campanha, Campos de Cima da Serra, Serra Gaúcha, Vale do São Francisco and Vale dos Vinhedos. Grows mainly hybrid grape varieties. Wines consumed mainly locally. Also produces spirits (Pisco, Cachaça and grain spirits) and is the largest coffee-producing country in the world. Website: http://www.winesfrombrazil.com

Brazil Cocktail (Cktl) 30mls (¼ gill) dry Sherry, 30mls (¼ gill) French vermouth, dash orange bitters, 2 dashes Pernod, 2 dashes sugar syrup. Stir over ice, strain into a cocktail glass, squeeze of lemon peel juice on top.

Brazil [Coffee] (S.Am) the world's largest producer. Regions of Bahia, Parama, Santos (Bourbon Santos, Flat Bean Santos and Red Santos) and Victoria.

Bread Wine (Rus) the historical name given to Russian vodka as it was traditionally made from grain.

Breaker (Eng) a bottled malt lager 1047 O.G. brewed by Tennents (Bass) now Coors Brewers.

Breaker (Eng) a small water cask used on a boat to carry drinking water in the eighteenth century.

Breakfast (Eng) a 5% alc by vol. beer brewed by the Barum Brewery, Devon.

Breakfast Cocktail (Cktl) ½ measure Port, ¼ measure crème de cacao, ¼ measure fresh lemon juice, 2 dashes light rum, dash egg white. Shake over ice, strain into a cocktail glass and top with nutmeg.

Breakfast Coffee (Eng) the name given to light, mild-roasted coffees.

Breakfast Cup (Eng) a china drinking vessel of 300mls (½ pint) capacity, used at breakfast for tea, coffee etc.

Breakfast Egg Nogg [1] (Cktl) 60mls (½ gill) V.S.O.P. Cognac, 30mls (¼ gill) orange Curaçao, 1 fresh egg, 125mls (1 gill) milk. Shake well over ice, strain into a tumbler and add grated nutmeg.

Breakfast Egg Nogg [2] (Cktl) 40mls (⅓ gill) apricot brandy, 15mls (⅛ gill) Curaçao, 1 egg, 125mls (1 gill) milk. Blend altogether, strain into a highball glass and top with grated nutmeg.

Breakfast Rock (S.Afr) a red wine (Shiraz) produced by Andy Mitchell Wines, Greyton, Southern Cape.

Breaking Down (Eng) a term applied to the distillation of spirits to denote the adding of pure water to the spirit to reduce it to the required strength.

Breaky Bottom Vineyard (Eng) a vineyard (established 1974). Sited at Rodmell, Lewes, Sussex. 1.75ha. Grape varieties: Müller-Thurgau and Seyval blanc.

Breathalyse (Eng) to be tested on the breathalyser.

Breathalyser (Eng) an instrument used by police forces in many countries to detect the alcohol level in motor vehicle driver's blood. This is achieved by taking a breath sample with a variety of styles of equipment.

Breathalyze (USA) see Breathalyse.

Breathalyzer (USA) see Breathalyser.

Breathing (Eng) the action of wine as it matures in the bottle. Minute amounts of air pass between the cork and bottle neck during a long period of time. Also applies when the cork is drawn and the wine is allowed to 'breathe' for a period of time before it is consumed.

Breath Test (Eng) the term for the taking of a breath sample on the Breathalyser.

Brebaje (W.Ind) the name given to an Aguardiente produced in Puerto Rico.

Breckenridge Cellars (USA) the brand-name used for a range of varietal wines produced by the Giumarra Vineyards.

Brecknock Brewery (Wal) based at Ystradgynlais, Swansea Valley. Brews Valhalla Original 3.8% alc by vol. Valhalla Premium 5% alc by vol.

Breclav Brewery (Czec) an old brewery (established 1522) based in southern Czec.

Brecon (Bel) a still and sparkling mineral water imported into the U.K. by Spadel.

Brecon Carreg (Wal) a sparkling natural spring mineral water from the Brecon Beacons National Park, Llandeilo, Carmarthenshire SA19 6TT. Mineral contents (milligrammes per litre): Sodium 5.7mg/l, Calcium 47.5mg/l, Magnesium

175

16.5mg/l, Potassium 0.4mg/l, Bicarbonates 206mg/l, Chlorides 9mg/l, Sulphates 9mg/l, Nitrates 2.2mg/l, Silicates 5.1mg/l. pH 7.8 Website: http://www.breconwater.co.uk

Brecon County Ale (Wal) a 3.7% alc by vol. ale brewed by the Breconshire Brewery, Powys.

Brecon Court (Wal) a 3ha. vineyard based at Llansoy, near Usk, Monmouthshire. Produce still and sparkling wines. Grape varieties: Cabernet sauvignon, Merlot, Kerner, Pinot gris, Reichensteiner, Schönburger, Seyval blanc.

Brecon Natural Spring Water (Wal) a bottled mountain spring water from the Brecon Beacons in Mid-Wales. Still and carbonated.

Breconshire Brewery (Wal) a brewery (established 2002). (Add): Ffrwdgrech Ind Estate, Brecon, Powys LD3 8LA. Brews: Brecon County Ale 3.7% alc by vol., Golden Valley 4.2% alc by vol., Ramblers Ruin 5% alc by vol., Red Dragon 4.7% alc by vol., Winter Beacon 5.3% alc by vol. Website: http://www.breconshirebrewery.com 'E'mail: info@breconshirebrewery.com

Breda Bier (Afr) a lager beer brewed under licence from the Bierbrouwerij de Drie Hoefijzers, Holland.

Breda Brouwerij (Hol) *see* Bierbrouwerij de Drie Hoefijzers.

Breda Royal Lager (Hol) a lager beer brewed by the Bierbrouwerij de Drie Hoefijzers.

Brède [La] (Fr) a moated estate in A.C. Graves, Bordeaux. Produces dry white wine.

Brédif (Fr) a grower with cellars at Rochecorbon in A.C. Vouvray, Touraine.

Breed (Eng) a term used to describe a wine of fine quality and is distinguished for its kind.

Breedeberg (S.Afr) a varietal wine produced by the KWV.

Breede River Valley (S.Afr) a controlled region of origin in the Cape province (noted for fortified wines).

Breeland Winery (S.Afr) a winery based in Rawsonville, Western Cape. Grape varieties: Cabernet sauvignon, Chardonnay, Chenin blanc, Sémillon.

Breërrivirvallei Wines (S.Afr) *see* De Wet Co-operative.

Breganze (It) a small town in Veneto, its name also applies to six types of wine.

Breganze Bianco (It) a D.O.C. white wine from Veneto region. Made with the Pinot bianco, Pinot grigio, Riesling italico, Tocai, Sauvignon and Vespaiolo grape varieties.

Breganze-Cabernet (It) a D.O.C. red wine from Veneto region. Made with the Cabernet franc and Cabernet sauvignon grape varieties. Is classified as Superiore if it is 12% alc by vol. minimum.

Breganze-Pinot Bianco (It) a D.O.C. white wine from the Veneto region. Made from the Pinot bianco and Pinot grigio grape varieties. Is classified as Superiore if it is 12% alc by vol. minimum.

Breganze-Pinot Nero (It) a D.O.C. red wine from the Veneto region. Made with the Pinot nero grape variety. Is classified as Superiore if is 12% alc by vol. minimum.

Breganze Rosso (It) a D.O.C. red wine from the Veneto region. Made with the Cabernet franc, Cabernet sauvignon, Freisa, Groppello, Marzomina, Merlot and Pinot nero.

Breganze-Vespaiolo (It) a D.O.C. white wine from the Veneto region. Made from the Vespaiolo grape variety. Classified as Superiore if is 12% alc by vol. minimum.

Breidecker (N.Z) a white grape variety used in blending.

Breinsberg (Ger) vineyard (Anb): Pfalz. (Ber): Mittelhaardt-Deutsche Weinstrasse. (Gro): Schnepfenflug von Zellertal. (Vil): Rüssingen.

Breisach a Rh (Ger) village (Anb): Baden. (Ber): Kaiserstuhl-Tuniberg. (Gro): Vulkanfelsen. (Vins): Augustinerberg, Eckartsberg.

Breiselberg (Ger) vineyard (Anb): Nahe. (Ber): Kreuznach. (Gro): Schlosskapelle. (Vil): Windesheim.

Breisgau (Ger) bereich (Anb): Baden. (Gros): Burg Lichteneck, Burg Zähringen, Schutterlindenberg.

Breisgauer (Ger) a natural spring mineral water from Markgräfler Mineralquelle GmbH. D-79395 Neuenburg-Steinenstadt, BW. Mineral contents (milligrammes per litre): Sodium 50mg/l, Calcium 489mg/l, Magnesium 42.7mg/l, Bicarbonates 385mg/l, Chlorides 79.7mg/l, Sulphates 1042mg/l, Nitrates <1mg/l.

Breit (Ger) a term used to describe a sound wine that has no finesse.

Breitel (Aus) a vineyard site on the banks of the River Danube situated in the Wachau region, Niederösterreich.

Breitenweg (Ger) vineyard (Anb): Nahe. (Ber): Kreuznach. (Gro): Kronenberg. (Vil): Bad Kreuznach.

Brela (Euro) a wine-producing region in Dalmatia.

Bremerton (Austr) a winery based at Langhorne Creek, South Australia. Label: Racy Rosé (rosé).

Bremm (Ger) village (Anb): Mosel-Saar-Ruwer. (Ber): Zell/Mosel. (Gro): Grafschaft. (Vins): Calmont, Frauenberg, Laurentiusberg, Schlemmertröpfchen.

Bremm (Ger) village (Anb): Mosel-Saar-Ruwer. (Ber): Zell/Mosel. (Gro): Rosenhang. (Vins): Abtei, Kloster Stuben.

Breña Alta (Sp) a still natural spring mineral water from Cortijo de Jacon, Telde, Las Palmas de Gran Canaria. Mineral contents (milligrammes per litre): Sodium 45mg/l, Calcium 6mg/l, Magnesium 4mg/l, Potassium 6mg/l, Bicarbonates 105mg/l, Chlorides 20mg/l, Fluorides <0.05mg/l.

Brendan's Birthday Beer (Eng) an ale brewed by micro-brewery Lord Raglan, Nangreave, near Bury.

Brenin Bitter (Wal) a light keg bitter 1034 O.G. brewed by the Crown Brewery, Llanelli, South Wales. Contains crystal malt.

Brenner (Ger) a fungal disease that browns the vine

leaves between the veins on the basal leaves. Treated with copper sulphate.

Brenthurst Winery (S.Afr) a winery (established 1993) based in Paarl, Western Cape. 5ha. Grape varieties: Cabérnet franc, Cabernet sauvignon, Merlot, Petit verdot.

Brent Marris (N.Z) a winery based in the Wairau Valley, Marlborough, South Island. Grape varieties include: Sauvignon blanc. Label: Clocktower.

Brentwein (Ger) lit: 'burnt wine', brandy. *See also* Brandwein.

Breque (Fr) a producer of Bordeaux Mousseux based at Pain-de-Sucre, Côte de Bourg, north-eastern Bordeaux.

Bresparolo (It) the Veneto name for the white Vespaiolo grape.

Bressande [La] (Fr) a noted vineyard in the A.C. commune of Rully, Côte Chalonnaise, Burgundy.

Bressandes [Les] (Fr) a Premier Cru vineyard in the A.C. commune of Beaune, Côte de Beaune, Burgundy. 21.8ha.

Bressan Nereo (It) a winery based in Farra d'Isonzo in the Friuli-Venezia-Guilia region. Grape varieties include: Cabernet sauvignon, Malvasia, Pinot nero, Ribolla, Schioppettino, Tocai, Verduzzo. Label: Carat, N° 3 Vintage.

Bressanone (It) a term used in the Trentino-Alto-Adige region for the Valle Isarsco wines if produced in the communes of Varna and Bressanone.

Bressanone (It) a local name in the Trentino-Alto-Adige region for the Austrian white Brixen grape.

Bresse-sur-Grosne (Fr) a commune in the Mâconnais district where Mâcon Supèrieur is produced.

Brestnik (Bul) a wine producing area within the Southern Basic region.

Breton (Fr) the Touraine (Loire) name for the Cabernet franc grape variety, also known as the Bouchet, Bouchy and the Véron.

Breton Fils (Fr) récoltants-manipulants in Champagne. (Add): 12 Rue Courte-Pilate, Congy, 51270 Montmort. Produces vintage and non-vintage wines.

Brettach (Ger) village (Anb): Württemberg. (Ber): Württembergisch Unterland. (Gro): Staufenberg. (Vin): Berg.

Bretanomyces (Bot) a group of wild yeasts that can give wines an aroma of farmyard/gamey/animal tones. *See also* Bretty.

Brettanomyces bruxelliensis (Bel) a wild yeast used for making lambic beer.

Brettanomyces lambicus (Bel) a wild yeast used for making lambic beer.

Bretterins [Les] (Fr) a Premier Cru vineyard (including La Chapelle) in Beaune, A.C. commune of Auxey-Duresses, Côte de Beaune, Burgundy. 5ha.

Bretty (Austr) a slang term for the *Brettanomyces* yeasts that give the wine an aroma of farmyard.

Bretzenheim (Ger) village (Anb): Nahe. (Ber): Kreuznach. (Gro): Kronenberg. (Vins): Felsenköpfchen, Hofgut, Pastorei, Schlossgarten, Vogelsang.

Bretzfeld (Ger) village (Anb): Württemberg. (Ber): Württembergisch Unterland. (Gro): Lindelberg. (Vin): Goldberg.

Bretz Winery (USA) a winery situated on Middle Bass Island, Ohio. Produces fine hybrid wines.

Breuil [Le] (Fr) a Cru Champagne village in the Canton de Dormans. District: Épernay.

Breuil [Le] (Fr) a vineyard in the A.C. commune of Montagny, Côte Chalonnaise, Burgundy.

Breuningsweiler (Ger) village (Anb): Württemberg. (Ber): Remstal-Stuttgart. (Gro): Kopf. (Vin): Holzenberg.

Breuningsweiler (Ger) village (Anb): Württemberg. (Ber): Remstal-Unterland. (Gro): Wartbühl. (Vin): Haselstein.

Breuwan (Eng) an old Saxon word for brewer.

Brevet Royal (Fr) a 4 year old Cognac produced by Rouyer.

Bréviaire (Fr) a bottle similar in style to the bocksbeutel.

Brew (Eng) the name given to the boiling wort by the brewer. *See also* Brewing. (Ire) = grúdaireacht.

Brew (Eng) a slang term for drink.

Brew (USA) applied to the ferment in beer or lager.

Brewer (Eng) a person who makes (brews) beer. (Fr) = brasseur, (Ger) = brauer, (Hol) = brouwer, (Ire) = grúdaire, (It) = birraio, (Port) = fabricante de cerveja, (Scan) = brugga, (Sp) = cerveciro, (Wal) = darllawydd.

Brewerkz Singapore (E.Ind) a brewery. (Add): Restaurant & Microbrewery, 30 Merchant Road, 01-05/06 Riverside Point 058282 Singapore. Brews beers and lager.

Breweriana (Eng) collectable items associated with Public houses or Breweries. Usually in the form of advertising for a brewery's products.

Brewers and Licensed Retailers Association (Eng) *abbr*: B.L.R.A. trade body that promotes beer.

Brewers' Association of Scotland (Scot) an organisation. (Add): 6 St. Colme Street, Edinburgh, Midlothian EH3 6AD.

Brewer's Bitter (Eng) a cask-conditioned ale 1037 O.G. brewed by the Ind Coope Brewery, Romford, Essex.

Brewer's Bitter (Eng) a 1042 O.G. bitter ale brewed by Wortley Brewery at Wortley, near Barnsley, South Yorkshire. *See also* Wortley Best Bitter, Old Porter.

Brewer's Choice (Eng) a dark beer with a lightly hopped flavour sold in cans and 2 litre PET bottles. Brewed by the Federation Brewery, Tyneside.

Brewer's Choice (Euro) a top-fermented bitter ale 1050 O.G. brewed by Farsons Brewery in Malta.

Brewer's Droop (Eng) a slang term for impotence due to excessive alcohol consumption.

Brewer's Gold (Eng) a type of hop used in Britain for the 'dry hopping' of cask-conditioned beers. Heavy cloying aroma and flavour.

Brewers Gold (Eng) a 4.2% alc by vol. beer brewed by the Crouch Vale Brewery, Essex.

Brewer's Gold (USA) a style of Ballantine ale 1070

O.G. brewed by the Falstaff's Narrangansett Brewery, Cranston, Rhode Island.

Brewers Gold Ale (Eng) a bottled strong ale 1078 O.G. brewed by the Truman's Brewery, London.

Brewer's Pride (Eng) a bitter ale brewed by the Marston Moor Brewery at Kirk Hammerton near York.

Brewer's Society (Eng) see The Brewer's Society.

Brewers Treat (Eng) a 4.6% alc by vol. bitter ale brewed by The derby Brewing C° Ltd., Derbyshire.

Brewer Street Rascal (Cktl) 25mls (1fl.oz) Mandarine Napoléon, 10mls (½ fl.oz) vodka, 100mls (4fl.ozs) grapefruit juice, dash egg white. Shake well over ice, strain into a large wine glass. Decorate with a wedge of grapefruit.

Brewery (Eng) a building for making beer. (Aus) = brauerei, (Bel) = brasserie, (Den) = bryggeri, (Fr) = brasserie, (Hol) = brouwerij, (Ger) = brauerei, (Ire) = grúdlann, (It) = fabbrica, (Port) = fábrica de cerveja, (Sp) = cerveceria, (Swe) = bryggeri, (Tur) = bira fabrikasi, (Wal) = bragdy/darllawyd.

Brewery Bitter (Eng) a cask-conditioned bitter 1036 O.G. brewed by the Smiles Brewery in Bristol, Avon.

Brewery Conditioned (Eng) a term used for beer which is conditioned at the brewery. e.g. keg and brewery conditioned traditional ales.

Brewery Gate Bitter (Eng) a keg bitter 4.3% alc by vol. from Morrells, Oxford. See also Friars Bitter.

Brewery On Sea (Eng) a micro-brewery at Lancing, West Sussex. Brews Spinnaker Mild 3.5% alc by vol. Big Fat Santa 4.2% alc by vol.

Brewery Tap (Eng) the name given to the pub/bar usually found built into the brewery premises.

Brewex (Eng) a brewing trade fair held ever few years.

Brewhouse (Eng) a part of the brewery where the brewing of the beer takes place.

Brewhouse (Eng) a public house in Poole, Dorset. Owned by the Poole Brewery which brews its own beers. Produces cask-conditioned High Street Mild 1035 O.G. High Street Bitter 1036 O.G. Bosun 1048 O.G. Dave's Lager 1048 O.G.

Brewhouse Ale (Eng) a top bitter ale 1055 O.G. brewed by Reepham Brewery, Norfolk.

Brewhouse Bitter (Eng) a 3.8% alc by vol. bitter beer brewed by the Dunn Ploughman Brewery, Herefordshire.

Brewing (Eng) the process of boiling the wort with hops (and invert sugar if required) in beer production under pressure in a copper to flavour and sterilise the wort. (Fr) = brassage.

Brewing (Scot) the process of fermenting (with yeast) the wort for 60 hours or more in the production of malt whisky. The brewing vessels hold around 40000 gallons each.

Brewing Kettle (USA) fermenting vessel.

Brew Kettle (Eng) a vessel used to heat the wort during the brewing process, also known as a Copper.

Brewmaster Ale (Eng) an Export lager 1042 O.G. brewed by Whitbread's.

Brew 101 (Eng) a 5% alc by vol. beer from the Vaux group at Ward's Brewery, Sheffield. Has honey as an essential ingredient. see Waggle Dance.

Brew 69 (Eng) a 5.6% alc by vol. (1055 O.G.) ale from the Wye Valley Brewery, Hereford.

Brewster (Eng) an old term for a female brewer. Now used for a brewer of either sex.

Brewster Brewing C° Ltd (Eng) a brewery (established 1998). (Add): Penn Lane, Stathern, Melton Mowbray, Leicestershire LE14 4JA. Brews: Bellydancer 5.2% alc by vol., Daffy Elixir 4.2% alc by vol., Hop a Doodle 4.2% alc by vol., Hophead 3.6% alc by vol., Marquis 3.8% alc by vol., Rutalian 4.8% alc by vol., Rutterkin 4.6% alc by vol., Wicked Women 4.8% alc by vol. Website: http://www.brewsters.co.uk 'E'mail: sara@brewsters.co.uk

Brewster Sessions (Eng) the annual licensing court which meets in February. It is the main court for issuing, transferring and renewing of classes of drinks licences.

Brew Ten (Eng) a beer brewed by Bass Worthington at their Bass North plant in Tadcaster, Yorkshire.

Brew XI (Eng) a famous Midlands cask-conditioned and keg bitter brewed by Mitchells and Butlers Brewery, Birmingham. 3.9% alc by vol.

Brey (Ger) village (Anb): Mittelrhein. (Ber): Rheinburgengau. (Gro): Gedeonseck. (Vin): Hämmchen.

Brezanky (Czec) a wine-producing town based north of Prague.

Brézé (Fr) a commune near Saumur, Anjou-Saumur in the Loire region.

Brezloff (Sp) a brand of vodka produced by Cocal in Telde, Canary Islands.

Breznice Brewery (Czec) an old brewery based in Breznice, western Czec.

Bri Vineyard [La] (S.Afr) a winery. (Add): P.O. Box 180, Franschhoek 77690. Produces Blanc de la Bri, La Bri Chardonnay.

Brian O'Lynn (Eng) the London cockney rhyming slang for gin.

Briars Vineyard (Austr) a winery (established 1989). (Add): Nepean Hwy., Mount Martha, Victoria. Grape varieties: Chardonnay, Pinot noir.

Bricco Manzoni (It) a red wine from Monforte d'Alba in the Piemonte. Made from a blend of Barbera and Nebbiolo grapes.

Bricco Marun (It) a D.O.C. Barbera d'Alba wine produced by Correggia (Matteo) in Piemonte. Wine is aged in 60% new oak barriques and is unfiltered and unfined.

Bric Corderi (It) a winery based in the Langhe, Piemonte region. Grape variety: Nebbiolo.

Bric dei Banditi (It) an unoaked D.O.C. Barbera d'Asti wine produced by Martinetti (Franco) in Piemonte.

Bricher Meisterbock (Lux) a beer brewed by the Funck Brewery in Neudorf.

Brick Brewing C° Ltd (Can) a brewery. (Add): 181 King Street South, Waterloo, Ontario N2J 1P7. Brews beers and lager. Website: http://www.brickbeer.com 'E'mail: info@brickbeer.com

Brick Dust (Eng) the description given to the flavour of fine red Graves wines.

Brick House Farm Water (USA) a natural spring mineral water from Ellicott City, Maryland.

Brick Tea (Chi) also known as Pressed Tea, a tea pressed into bricks for ease of transport. Black in colour and stamped with a description of the tea. It is now rarely made although are still produced by the Tsaiao Liu Chiu Tea Brick Factory.

Bricout et Koch (Fr) a Champagne producer. (Add): 7, Route de Cramant, 51190, Avize. 4ha. Produces vintage and non-vintage wines. Vintages: 1973, 1975, 1976, 1978, 1981, 1982, 1985, 1989, 1990, 1995, 1998, 1999. Labels include Bricout Rosé, Carte Noir, Carte Or and Charles Koch.

Bricout Rosé (Fr) a pale pink, non-vintage Champagne produced by Bricout et Koch from Chardonnay and Pinot noir grapes.

Bridal Cocktail (Cktl) ³⁄₁₀ measure Saké Gozenshu, ³⁄₁₀ measure Rosse liqueur, ³⁄₁₀ measure lemon juice, 1 barspoon maraschino. Shake over ice and strain into a cocktail glass.

Brideshead Bitter (Eng) a 4% alc by vol. bitter ale brewed by York Brewery. Toft Green, North Yorkshire.

Bride's Tears (Hol) the nickname for a Goldwasser and Silberwasser.

Bridge Bitter (Eng) a 4.2% alc by vol (1042 O.G.). cask-conditioned ale brewed by Burton Bridge Brewery, Burton-on-Trent.

Bridge House (Eng) a public house next to the Tower bridge in London that brews its own ales. Produces cask-conditioned Bermondsey Bitter 1036 O.G. Special 1048 O.G. 007 1055 O.G.

Bridge of Allan Brewery (Scot) a brewery. (Add): The Brewhouse, Queens Lane, Bridge of Allan, Stirling, Stirlingshire FK9 4NY. Brews: Bannockburn., Ben Nevis., Brig O'Allan., Glencoe Wild Oat Stout., Lomond Gold Blond Ale., Sheriffmuir., Stirling Brig. Website: http://www.bridgeofallan.co.uk 'E'mail: brewery@bridgeofallan.co.uk

Bridgeport Brewing Company (USA) a brewery based in Portland, Oregon. Brews: Black Strap Stout, Blue Heron, Ebenezer Ale, ESB, India Pale Ale, Old Knucklehead, Pintail Ale, Porter, Ropewalk. Website: http://www.bridgeportbrew.com

Bridgers Gold Ale (Eng) a mixed gas smooth beer, 3.8% alc by vol. from Gibbs Mew, Salisbury, Wiltshire.

Bridge Street (Eng) a premium bitter beer from the Green Dragon, Suffolk.

Bridgeview (USA) a 74acre (33.5ha) winery in Siskiyou Mountains, Illinois Valley, Oregon. Grape varieties: Chardonnay, Gewürztraminer, Pinot gris, Pinot noir, Merlot, Riesling.

Bridgewater Ales (Eng) a brewery based in Salford. Brews Barton Best, Delph Porter, Navigation Ale.

Bridgewater Arms (Eng) a public house in Little Gaddesden, Hertfordshire that used to brew its own beers (stopped in 1990). Produces cask-conditioned best bitter 1035 O.G. Earl's Bitter 1048 O.G. Old Santa 1066 O.G.

Briedel (Ger) village (Anb): Mosel-Saar-Ruwer. (Ber): Bernkastel. (Gro): Vom Heissen Stein. (Vins): Herzchen, Nonnengarten, Schäferlay, Schlem, Weisserberg.

Briedern (Ger) village (Anb): Mosel-Saar-Ruwer. (Ber): Zell/Mosel. (Gro): Goldbäumchen. (Vin): Rüberberger-Domherrenberg.

Briedern (Ger) village (Anb) Mosel-Saar-Ruwer. (Ber): Zell/Mosel. (Gro): Rosenhang. (Vins): Herrenberg, Kapellenberg, Römergarten, Servatiusberg.

Brierley Court (Eng) a 4.6% alc by vol. limited edition ale brewed by Samuel Allsopp. Part of the Carlsberg-Tetley Tapster's Choice range.

Briesgauer Riesling (Ger) an erroneous varietal name of the Ortlieber (Knipperlé) grape.

Brie-Sous-Archiac (Fr) a commune in the Charente-Maritime département whose grapes are classed Petite Champagne (Cognac).

Brigante dei Barbi (It) a red I.G.T. wine produced from 50% Sangiovese and 50% Merlot grapes by Fattoria dei Barbi in Tuscany.

Brigg Beer (Nor) a low-alcohol beer 2.2% alc by vol.

Brighams Creek Rhine Riesling (N.Z) a dry, fruity, single vineyard white wine from Selaks.

Bright Beer (Eng) also known as brewery-conditioned beer, usually it is chilled and filtered to remove the yeasts and solids,

Brighton Punch (Cktl) ⅓ measure Bourbon whiskey, ⅓ measure brandy, ⅓ Bénédictine, juice ½ orange and lemon. Shake over ice, strain into a collins glass ½ filled with crushed ice. Top with soda water and stir. Dress with an orange and lemon slice and serve with water.

Brighton Rock (Eng) a 4% alc by vol. ale from the Dark Star Brewery in Brighton under the Skinners label.

Brightwater (N.Z) a winery based in Nelson, South Island. Grape varieties include: Riesling, Sauvignon blanc.

Brightwater Ridge (N.Z) a natural spring mineral water (established 2000).

Brights (Can) the biggest winery in Ontario. Produces mainly French-American hybrid wines.

Brigita (Czech) a lager beer brewed by the Topvar Brewery in the Topolcany region, Slovakia.

Brigitt (Cktl) ⅓ measure dry vermouth, ⅓ measure whisky, ⅓ measure Triple Sec, dash lemon juice. Stir over ice, strain into a cocktail glass. Decorate with an olive.

Brig O'Allan (Scot) the name of a beer brewed by the Bridge of Allan Brewery, Stirlingshire.

Briki (Gre) a pot for making Greek 'Turkish' coffee. (Arab) = kanaka, (Tur) = ibrik.

Briljant (Hol) a premium beer brewed by the De Kroon Brouwerij in Oirschot, Brabant.

Brillat-Savarin (Fr) an Armagnac distillery. (Add): Distillerie Armagnaçaise SA, BP. 55, 32100 Condom.

Brillet (Fr) a Cognac producer. (Add): Les Aireaux, Graves, 16120 Châteauneuf. 40ha. in Grande

Champagne and 40ha. in Petite Champagne. Produces Très Rare Heritage and Poire au Cognac (extract of Poire Williams and Eau-de-vie de Cognac).

Brilliance (Eng) a term used to describe a star-bright or crystal clear wine.

Brilliant (Eng) a term used to describe an absolutely clear drink.

Brimful Glass (Eng) a goverment-stamped, un-lined beer glass at 10fl.oz and 20fl.ozs capacities. These glasses must be full (with maximum of 5% allowed for the 'head' on the beer).

Brimmer (Eng) a term for a glass or bowl or other vessel full to the top (the brim) with liquid.

Brimont (Fr) a Cru Champagne village in the Canton de Bourgogne. District: Reims.

Brimstage Brewing (Eng) a brewery. (Add): White Star, 102 Allport Road, Bromborough, Wirral, Merseyside CH62 6AQ. Brews a variety of beers.

Brinay (Fr) a commune in the A.C. Quincy, Central Vineyards, Loire.

Brinckhoff's N°1 (Ger) a fine lager beer brewed by the D.U.B. Brauerei in Dortmund, Westphalia.

Brindar (Port)(Sp) to drink (to the health of), a toast. To toast one's health. Brinde = toast.

Brindare (It) to drink a toast.

Brindle (Wal) a 5% alc by vol. ale brewed by the Bullmastiff Brewery, South Glamorgan.

Brindis (Sp) to drink a toast.

Brindisi (It) a D.O.C. red or rosé wines produced in Southern Puglia.

Bring Your Own (Austr) a nickname for restaurants in Melbourne which are not licensed and customers have to bring their own alcoholic drink (wine etc.) to drink with their meal. Known as B.Y.O's.

Brinkhoffs 1 (Ger) a 5% alc by vol. bottled pilsner brewed by the Dortmunder Union, Dortmund.

Briolet (Fr) a slang term used for wines of Brie which are very acidic, is also used for other acidic wines.

Briones (Sp) a Zona de Crianza 2000ha. in the Rioja Alta, Rioja, north-eastern Spain. Soil: alluvial, red clay and gravel sub-soils.

Briosa (It) a natural spring mineral water brand.

Brioso (Arg) the label for a red Bordeaux blend wine (part of the Susana Balbo range) produced by the Dominio del Plata winery in the Mendoza region.

Briotett (Fr) a firm that produces crème de cassis liqueur and other fruit liqueurs in Dijon, Côte d'Or.

Brisbane (Austr) a wine region in Queensland in Eastern Australia.

Briscoe's Brewery (Eng) a micro-brewery (established 1998). (Add): 16 Ash Grove, Otley, West Yorkshire LS21 3EL. Brews: Burnsall Classic, Chevin Chaser, Irish Stout, Puddles & Barmey. 'E'mail: briscoebrewery@virgin.net

Brissac (Fr) a commune in the A.C. Coteaux de l'Aubance, Anjou-Saumur, Loire. Produces fine rosé wines from Cabernet franc and Cabernet sauvignon. Labelled as Anjou Village Brissac.

Bristol Beer Factory (Eng) a brewery (established 2000). (Add): C/o Tobacco Factory, Rayleigh Road, Southville, Bristol, Avon BS3 1TF. Brews: English Malt Ale 3.8% alc by vol., Gold 5% alc by vol., Golden Ale 3.8% alc by vol., Number7 4.2% alc by vol. Website: http://www.bristolbeerfactory.co.uk 'E'mail: enquiries@bristolbeerfactory.co.uk

Bristol Blue (Eng) an eighteenth century type of glass made in Bristol, using Colbalt oxide from Saxony to produce blue-coloured glass decanters etc.

Bristol Bottle (Eng) a mould for making bottles of claret (Bordeaux) shape. Invented by the Bristol glassmakers.

Bristol Brewery (Eng) the name for Hall's Brewery near Bristol. Produces Jacobs Best Bitter 1038 O.G. Bristol Pride 1045 O.G.

Bristol Cream (Sp) the brand-name for a dessert Cream Sherry, produced in Jerez de la Frontera by Harvey's. Sweetened Oloroso.

Bristol Dry (Sp) a brand of dry Sherry produced by Harvey's in Jerez de la Frontera.

Bristol Fino (Sp) a brand of dry Sherry produced by Harvey's in Jerez de la Frontera.

Bristol Milk (Sp) a brand of sweet Sherry produced by Harvey's in Jerez de la Frontera.

Bristol Stout (Eng) brewed by Smiles Brewery in Bristol.

Britannia (Eng) a 4.4% alc by vol. ale brewed by the Buntingford Brewery, Hertfordshire.

British Beer and Pub Association (Eng) abbr: BBPA. an organisation (established 1904) of brewers and public house owners who set codes of practice to which its members are bound to adhere to. (Add): Market Towers, 1 Nine Elms Lane, London SW8 5NQ. Website: http://www.beerandpub.com 'E'mail: web@beerandpub.com

British Bonded (Eng) a term used to describe Cognacs which travel in cask to England and are matured in London Dock warehouses. Aged in bond and a record kept. *See also* Old Landed.

British Bottlers' Institute (Eng) abbr: B.B.I. a body for the promotion and standards of glass bottling.

British Bulldog Best Bitter (Eng) a 4.3% alc by vol. best bitter beer brewed by the Westerham Brewery, C°., Kent.

British Columbia (Can) a wine region in western Canada. Has 4 designated wine regions: Okanagan Valley, Similkameen Valley, Fraser Valley, Vancouver Island.

British Columbia Distillery C°. (Can) a subsidiary of Seagram. Produces a range of Canadian whiskies.

British Compounds (Eng) a word used to describe the rectified, redistilled and flavoured spirits.

Britisher's Wine (Eng) a nineteenth century nickname given to Port.

British Fortified Wine (Eng) a new term since December 1995 for British and Irish Sherry-style wines.

British Fruit Juice Association (Eng) an organization (established 1947). (Add): The Gables, Kings

B

Caple, Hereford, Herefordshire HR1 4UD. 'E'mail: bfja@ashurstassociates.co.uk

British Gallon (Eng) British Imperial Gallon. Equal to 1.20 American gallons. Contains 160 Imperial fluid ounces (fl.ozs).

British Institute of Innkeeping (Eng) *abbr*: BII. (Add): Wessex House, 80 Park Street, Camberley, Surrey GU15 3PT. The official body for the pub trade (established in 1981) it is now known as the BII. Website: http://www.biiab.org 'E'mail: reception@bii.org

British Natural Mineral Waters Association (Eng) *abbr*: B.N.M.W.A. Associated body of the N.M.W.B.W.A. Formed to represent the interests of packers and importers of bottled natural mineral waters. *See also* B.S.D.A.

British Navy Rum (Eng) *see* Pusser's.

British Plain Spirit (Eng) a spirit produced in the U.K. e.g. gin, vodka and whisky before maturation.

British Sherry (Eng) a Sherry-style wine made in the U.K. from grape concentrate. Cream and medium styles produced (now no longer allowed). *see* British Fortified Wine.

British Soft Drinks Association (Eng) a body formed in Bristol on the 1st May 1987. Represents all makers of still, carbonated drinks, bottled waters, fruit and vegetable drinks. Includes the N.A.S.D.M., N.M.W.B.W.A. and B.N.M.W.A.

British Soluble Coffee Manufacturers Association (Eng) (Add): 6, Catherine Street, London EC4N 5AB.

British Wine (Eng) a wine made in the U.K. from grape concentrate that is imported and reconstituted. May have flavourings added.

Britta Water Filter Systems (Eng) a water filter system™ for both home and industry. (Add): P.O. Box 276, Bicester, Oxfordshire OX26 4WZ Website: http://www.britta.co.uk 'E'mail: enquiries@britta.co.uk

Britt-Brasserie de Bretagne (Fr) a brewery. (Add): Sarl. Kérouel, F-29810 Tregunc. Brews beers and lager. 'E'mail: brasserie.britt@wanadoo.fr

Britvic Soft Drinks Ltd (Eng) a firm that produces bottled fruit juices and squashes as mixers. (Add): Britvic House, Broomfield Road, Chelmsford, Essex CM1 1TU. Merged with Corona in 1987. Work with Pepsi C°. in USA. *see* Britvic 55, Carbon, Purdeys and Shandy Bass. Websites: https://www.britvic.com/ http://www.britvic.co.uk

Britvic 55 (Eng) a sparkling fruit drink from Britvic.

Britvic Mist (Eng) the name given to a range of fruit-flavoured mineral waters. Range includes apricot, damson, raspberry.

Britz (Eng) a draught sparkling water from Natural Purewater.

Britzingen (Ger) village (Anb): Baden. (Ber): Markgräflerland. (Gro): Burg Neuenfels. (Vins): Altenberg, Rosenberg, Sonnhohle.

Britzingen [ortsteil Dattingen] (Ger) village (Anb): Baden. (Ber): Markgräflerland. (Gro): Burg Neuenfels. (Vins): Altenberg, Rosenberg, Sonnhohle.

Briuwan (Ger) an old word for brewer.

Brives-sur-Charente (Fr) a commune in the Charente-Maritime département whose grapes are classed Petite Champagne (Cognac).

Brix (USA) a scale of sugar density of grape must. Operates at 17.5°C or 20°C. Invented by A.F.W. Brix in Germany in the nineteenth century. *See also* Balling and Sykes.

Brixen (Aus) a term used to describe a white grape in the Südtirol. Known as the Bressanone in Italy.

Briza Liovei (Rum) a sparkling natural spring mineral water (established 1818) from Lipova. Mineral contents (milligrammes per litre): Sodium 159.68mg/l, Calcium 114.23mg/l, Magnesium 38.65mg/l, Potassium 4.07mg/l, Bicarbonates 756.4mg/l, Chlorides 36.92mg/l, Sulphates 40.68mg/l, Nitrates 0.408mg/l, Silicates 21.4mg/l.

Brizard [Marie] (Fr) a liqueur company that produces a wide range of liqueurs. Based in the Basque country, south-western France.

BRL Hardy (Austr) the second largest producer of Australian wine (established 1992) by the merger of Berri Renmano Ltd. and Thomas Hardy and Sons Pty. Ltd. Owns and operates Chateau Reynella, Tintara Winery (McLaren Vale), Leasingham (Clare Vale), Padthaway, Berri, Renmano in South Australia, Yarra Burn in Victoria, Houghton in Western Australia, Stanley Buronga in New South Wales, Domaine de la Baume, Languedoc, France.

Brno Brewery (Czec) a brewery (established 1872) based in Brno southern Czec.

Broach (Eng) a tool for tapping casks of wine or spirits etc. Also to tap a cask.

Broaching (Eng) opening applicable to casks of wine, beer, spirits etc. Also denotes the opening of a cask to remove the contents.

Broadfield Vineyard (Eng) a vineyard (established 1972). (Add): Broadfield Court Estate, Bodenham, Herefordshire. 4.2ha. Grape varieties: 75% Reichensteiner and 25% Riesling. Vinified at Pilton Manor. *see* Bodenham.

Broadley Vineyards (USA) a 34ha winery based in the Willamette Valley, Oregon. Grape varieties: Chardonnay, Pinot noir. Label: Marcile Lorraine, Shea.

Broad Run Vineyards (USA) a winery (10ha) based near Louisville, Kentucky.

Broadside (Eng) a 4.7% alc by vol. ale brewed by Sole Bay Brewery, Southwold, Suffolk.

Broadside Ale (Eng) a strong pale ale 4.7%–6.3% alc by vol. (1068 O.G.) brewed by Adnams Sole Bay Brewery, Southwold, Suffolk.

Broadsman Bitter (Eng) a cask-conditioned bitter 1035–1037 O.G. brewed by the Woodeforde Brewery in Norfolk.

Broadstone Best Bitter (Eng) a 3.8% alc by vol. bitter beer brewed by the Broadstone Brewing C. Ltd., Nottinghamshire.

Broadstone Brewing C° Ltd (Eng) a brewery (established 1999). (Add): Wharf Road, Retford, Nottinghamshire DN22 6EN. Brews: Broadstone

181

Best Bitter 3.8% alc by vol., Charter Ale 4.6% alc by vol., Gold 5% alc by vol., Stonebridge Mild 4% alc by vol., Warhorse 4.8% alc by vol. Website: http://www.broadstonebrewery.com 'E'mail: broadstone@btconnect.com

Broadway Cocktail (Cktl) 60mls (½ gill) dry gin, 30mls (¼ gill) Italian vermouth, 2 dashes orange bitters. Shake over ice, strain into a small wine glass. Serve with a dash of orange peel juice on top.

Broadwood Cream (Eng) a 4.2% alc by vol. seasonal nitrokeg ale brewed by the King and Barnes Brewery, Horsham, West Sussex.

Broc (Fr) a small earthenware brown jug used for wine in mediaeval times.

Brocard [Jean Marc] (Fr) a négociant based Préhy, Chablis, Burgundy. Produces a range of Chablis wines and A.C. Bourgogne wines under the soil names of Jurassique, Kimmeridgien and Portlandien. Also produces Premier Crus Montmains, Vaillons, and Vau de Vey.

Brocca (It) pitcher/jug.

Brochon (Fr) a village that was part of the A.C. Côte de Nuits Villages, but is now part of Gevrey-Chambertin. 53ha.

Brockhouse (Den) a brewery. (Add): Hogevej 6, Hillerod 3400. Brews beers and lagers. Website: http://www.broeeckhouse.dk 'E'mail: kontakt@broeckhouse.dk

Brockhurst (Eng) a natural spring mineral water from Brockhurst, Surrey.

Brock Lager (Eng) a lager 1033 O.G. brewed by the Hall and Woodhouse, Dorset.

Brod Brewery (Czec) a brewery (established 1880) based in central Czec.

Brodnanka (Czec) a mild beer brewed in Uhersky.

Brody (Eng) a strong premium cider sold in clear flint glass bottles by Taunton in Somerset. 8.4% alc by vol.

Broggingen (Ger) village (Anb): Baden. (Ber): Breisgau. (Gro): Burg Lichteneck. (Vin): Kaiserberg.

Broggini (Fr) a Champagne producer. (Add): B.P.18, Chigny-lès-Roses, 51500 Rilly-la-Montagne. Négociant-manipulant. Prestige cuvée: Cuvée Emeraude.

Brohler Classic (Ger) a natural mineral water (established 1593) from Vulkaneifel, Brohl. Mineral contents (milligrammes per litre): Sodium 370mg/l, Calcium 88mg/l, Magnesium 78mg/l, Potassium 22mg/l, Bicarbonates 1208mg/l, Chlorides 190mg/l, Sulphates 110mg/l.

Brohler Highlight (Ger) a natural spring mineral water from the Friedrichsquelle. Mineral contents (milligrammes per litre): Sodium 61mg/l, Calcium 42mg/l, Magnesium 40mg/l, Potassium 11mg/l, Bicarbonates 362mg/l, Chlorides 45mg/l, Sulphates 61mg/l.

Broiling (Eng) a term used for the roasting of coffee beans. *See also* Singeing.

Broke Fordwich (Austr) a sub-region of the Hunter Valley, New South Wales. Soil: red volcanic.

Broken Leg (Cktl) stir in a suitable mug 25mls (1fl.oz) Bourbon whiskey, 60mls (2½ fl.ozs) hot apple juice, 4 raisins, stick of cinnamon, slice of lemon.

Broken Orange Pekoe (Eng) abbr: BOP a type of broken leaf grade black tea, usually used in traditional packet teas. Also can be classed: Golden Broken Orange Pekoe and Tippy Broken Orange Pekoe.

Broken Pekoe (Eng) a type of broken leaf tea grade that is used in tea bags and in packet tea.

Broken Pekoe Souchong (Eng) a type of broken tea leaf grade, small and uneven.

Broken River Wines (Austr) a winery (established 1989). (Add): Cosgrove Road, Lemnos, Victoria. Grape varieties: Cabernet franc, Cabernet sauvignon, Chenin blanc.

Broken Spur (Cktl) ¼ measure dry gin, ¼ measure sweet vermouth, 1½ measures Port wine, dash anisette, yolk of egg. Shake over ice, strain into a wine goblet.

Broken Spur Cocktail (Cktl) 40mls (⅓ gill) Port, 20mls (⅙ gill) Italian vermouth, 2 dashes Cointreau. Stir over ice, strain into a cocktail glass.

Broken Stone (S.Afr) a range of wines (Cabernet sauvignon/Cabernet Sauvignon & Shiraz/Pinotage/Sauvignon blanc) produced by the Slaley Estate, Stellenbosch, Western Cape.

Broken Tea (Eng) a small size tea grade obtained from the sieving of tea leaf. e.g. Broken Pekoe, Fannings, Dust, Broken Orange Pekoe.

Brokenwood (Austr) a winery (20ha). (Add): McDonalds Road, Pokolbin, New South Wales 2321. Grape varieties: Cabernet sauvignon, Chardonnay, Hermitage, Sémillon and Shiraz. Also has vineyards in Hunter Valley and McLaren Vale in South Australia. Labels: Graveyard Vineyard, Rayner Vineyard, The Mistress Block Vineyard and Wade Block 2.

Brokov (Eng) a sparkling alcohol-free malt drink made with ginger, nutmeg, quillia bark, white horehound, coriander by Bulmers.

Brolio Chianti (It) the most famous of the Chianti Classico estates, also where the Governo process was created.

Brombeergeist (Ger) blackberry brandy.

Brombeerlikoer (Ger) blackberry liqueur.

Bromista (Scot) a popular brand of white rum bottled by Scottish and Newcastle Breweries.

Bromius (Lat) another name for Bacchus.

Bron (Bel) a natural spring mineral water from Bron, Chaudfontaine.

Bronco Wines (USA) a winery based near Stanislaus in the Central Valley, California. Produces varietal and table wines. Labels include: Napa Creek, Napa Ridge and Two Buck Chuck.

Brondums Kummenakvavit (Den) a caraway and cinnamon flavoured akvavit produced by DDS.

Brondums Snaps (Den) a low-strength akvavit produced by DDS.

Bronte (Eng) a 4% alc by vol. ale brewed by the Goose Eye Brewery, West Yorkshire.

Brontë (Eng) a honey, spices, herbs and orange-flavouring, brandy-based liqueur made in Yorkshire. Bottled in a squat pottery jug. 34% alc by vol.

Bronte Bitter (Eng) a 4% alc by vol. bitter beer brewed by the Goose Eye Brewery, West Yorkshire.

Bronte Winery (USA) a large winery based in Paw Paw, Michigan. Produces American and hybrid wines.

Bronx (Cktl) ½ measure dry gin, ⅙ measure dry vermouth, ⅙ measure sweet vermouth, ⅙ measure orange juice, dash egg white. Shake over ice and strain into a cocktail glass.

Bronx Golden (Cktl) as for a Bronx with the addition of an egg yolk and serve in a flip glass.

Bronx Silver (Cktl) 1 measure gin, ½ measure dry vermouth, juice ½ orange, 1 egg white. Shake over ice and strain into a cocktail glass.

Bronx Terrace (Cktl) ⅔ measure dry gin, ⅓ measure dry vermouth, dash lime juice cordial. Stir over ice, strain into a cocktail glass and decorate with cherry.

Bronze (Eng) a bronze coloured ale brewed by the Derwentrose Brewery in Consett, County Durham.

Bronze Port (Austr) a full-bodied, sweet, Port-style wine from West End Wines, New South Wales. Produced from the Hermitage grape.

Brooke Bond Oxo Ltd. (Eng) famous producers of a wide range of teas and coffees based in Croydon. Brands include P.G. Tips. (tea) and Red Mountain (coffee).

Brookfields Vineyards (N.Z) a winery. (Add): 376 Brookfield Road, Napier, Hawkes Bay, North Island. 3ha. Grape varieties: Cabernet sauvignon, Merlot, Chasselas, Gewürztraminer, Müller-Thurgau, Pinot gris and Rhine riesling.

Brooklands Express (Eng) a 4.6% alc by vol. ale brewed by the Sawbridge Worth Brewery, Hertfordshire.

Brookland Valley (Austr) a winery based in the Margaret River region of Western Australia. Grape varieties include: Cabernet sauvignon, Merlot. Label: Verse 1.

Brooklyn (Cktl) 1½ measures rye whiskey, ½ measure sweet vermouth, dash Amer Picon, dash maraschino. Stir over ice and strain into a cocktail glass.

Brooklyn Brewery (USA) a brewery (established 1987) based in New York. Produces a range of seven beers including Brooklyn Lager.

Brooklyn Bridge Beer (Eng) a 4.5% alc by vol. American oak cask-conditioned ale produced using hop varieties from across the Atlantic by Brakspear, Henley-on-Thames.

Brooklyn Kümmel (Cktl) into a 125mls (5fl.oz) wine glass place some shaved ice and a slice of lemon. Pour 25mls (1fl.oz) kümmel on top.

Brooklyn Lager (USA) a 1048 O.G. lager beer from 8% crystal malt with pale malt to give body and flavour (dry hopped). Brewed by the Matt Brewery, New York.

Brooklyn Lager (USA) a 5.1% alc by vol. bottled lager brewed by the Brooklyn Brewery, New York using Hallertau and cascade hops.

Brook's Club (Eng) an old eighteenth century tea blend.

Brookside Winery (USA) a multi-owned winery based in Cucamonga, California. Wines sold under the Assumption Abbey, Brane and Brookside labels.

Brookvale Riesling (N.Z) a brand of white wine produced by the Villa Maria Winery, South Auckland.

Brookvale Riesling Sylvaner (N.Z) a medium, fruity, white wine from the Villa Maria Winery, South Auckland.

Broomelt (Lux) a vineyard site in the village of Ehnen.

Broomstick (Eng) a 4% alc by vol. ale brewed by Mauldon's Ltd., Suffolk.

Broomstick Bitter (Eng) a bitter ale brewed by the Moorhouses Brewery (Burnley) Ltd., Lancashire.

Brother Dominic (N.Z) an alcoholic beverage containing some grapes produced in 1979 by Montana Wines (had undergone process of Oenological Amelioration).

Brotherhood Winery (USA) a winery based in Hudson Valley, New York. Produces hybrid and sparkling wines. Grape varieties include: Pinot noir.

Brothers Best Bitter (Eng) a 3.9% alc by vol. bitter ale brewed by the micro-brewery Pett Brewing Company, Hastings.

Brothers Drinks (Eng) a cider company based in Somerset that produces natural and flavoured ciders.

Brothers Vineyards [The] (N.Z) a winery. (Add): Brancott Road, RD 2, Blenheim. 10ha. Grape varieties: Chardonnay, Sauvignon blanc, Sémillon. Merlot.

Brotwasser (Ger) vineyard (Anb): Württemberg. (Ber): Remstal-Stuttgart. (Gro): Wartbühl. (Vil): Stetten i.R.

Brotwasser (Ger) lit- 'bread water', a white wine of Stetten in the anbaugebiete of Württemberg. A delicate wine that gets its name from a lady who used to dip her bread into her wine year after year.

Brotzeit (Ger) elevenses/morning coffee.

Brou [Roger-Felicien] (Fr) a sparkling wine producer based in A.C. Vouvray, Touraine, Loire. (Add): Clos de l'Epinay, 37210 Vouvray.

Brouette-Bassereau (Fr) a producer of Bordeaux Mousseux based at Pain-de-Sucre, Côtes de Bourg, north-eastern Bordeaux. Wines made by the méthode traditionelle.

Broughton Best (Scot) a 3.8% alc by vol. ale brewed by the Broughton Brewery, Lanarkshire.

Broughton Brewery (Scot) a brewery (established 1979). (Add): Broughton, Biggar, Lanarkshire ML12 6HQ. Produces: Angel Organic 5% alc by vol., keg Broughton Best Ale 3.8% alc by vol (1036 O.G.)., bottled Black Douglas 5.2% alc by vol., Border Gold 6% alc by vol., Clipper IP80 4.6% alc by vol., Exciseman's 80 4.6% alc by vol., cask-conditioned Greenmantle Ale 3.9% alc by vol (1038 O.G)., Merlins Ale 4.2% alc by vol., Old Jock 6.7% alc by vol (1070 O.G)., Border Gold 6% alc by vol., Scottish Oatmeal Stout 4.2% alc by vol., The Ghillie 4.5% alc by vol., The Reiver 3.8% alc by vol. Website: http://www.broughtonales.co.uk 'E'mail: beer@broughtonales.co.uk

Brouillards [Les] (Fr) a Premier Cru vineyard [part] in the A.C. commune of Volnay, Côte de Beaune, Burgundy 6.5ha.

Brouillet (Fr) a Cru Champagne village in the Canton de Ville-en-Tardenois. District: Reims.

Brouillis (Fr) lit: 'boiling'. It is the term used in Cognac for the '*heart*' of the distillation, separated from the headings and tailings.

Brouilly (Fr) an A.C. Cru Beaujolais-Villages, Burgundy. 1217ha. under vine.

Brouwen (Hol) brew.

Brouwer (Hol) brewer.

Brouwerij (Bel)(Hol) brewery/brew-house.

Brouwerij Bockor (Bel) a brewery. (Add): Kwabrugstraat 5, B-8510. Brews beers and lager. Website: http://www.bockor.be 'E'mail: info@bockor.be

Brouwerij Der Trappisten Van Westmalle (Bel) a trappiste brewery. (Add): Antwerpsesteenweg 596, Westmalle B-2390. Brews beers and lager. Website: http://www.trappistwestmalle.be 'E'mail: info@trappistewestmalle.be

Brouwerij Fontein (Bel) a brewery. (Add): Hoogstraat 2a, Beersel, B-1650. Brews beers and lager. Website: http://www.2.resto.de 'E'mail: armand.debelder@pandora.be

Brouwerij Het Anker (Bel) a brewery. (Add): Guido Gezellelaan, 49-2800 Mechelel. Brews beers and lager. Website: http://www.hetanker.be

Brouwerij Kerkom (Bel) a brewery. (Add): Naamsesteenweg 469, Sint-Truiden B-3800. Brews beers and lager. Website: http://www.brouwerijkerkom.be 'E'mail: info@brouwerijkerkom.be

Brouwsel (Hol) mash.

Brown [J.T.S.] (USA) a Bourbon whiskey distillery based in Frankfurt, Kentucky.

Brown Ale (Eng) a bottled sweet, mild ale, usually low in alcohol, lightly hopped and dark in colour.

Brown Betty (Cktl) brandy, spices, lemon, brown sugar and strong ale. Pour into glass asnd top with toast cubes. Drunk hot or cold.

Brown Betty (Eng) the name given to the red-brown earthenware teapot.

Brown Bommer (Eng) a 3.8% alc by vol. dark ale brewed by the Sawbridge Worth Brewery, Hertfordshire.

Brown Bracer Ale (Wal) a brown ale 1033 O.G. brewed by the Crown Brewery in South Wales.

Brown Brewery (Eng) a collection of four breweries in Blackburn, Carlisle, Masham and Workington. Produce a large range of ales.

Brown Bros (Austr) *see* Brown Brothers.

Brown Brothers (Austr) a large famous family winery in Milawa, Victoria. Vineyards at King Valley, Koombhala, Milawa, Mystic Park and Whitlands. Grape varieties: Cabernet sauvignon, Chardonnay, Gewürztraminer, Merlot, Muscat, Riesling and Sémillon. Produces varietal, dessert, botrytised and fortified wines. *see* Tarrango (a red cross between the Touriga and Sultana) and Flora (a sweet yellow-gold coloured dessert wine). Also known as Brown Bros. Website: http://www.brown-brothers.com.au 'E'mail: bbmv@brown-brothers.com.au

Brown Cocktail (Cktl) ⅓ measure dry vermouth, ⅓ measure dry gin, ⅓ measure Jamaican rum, stir over ice and strain into a cocktail glass.

Brown Cow (Cktl) 1 part Kahlúa, 3 parts full-cream milk. Stir together with ice, strain into a goblet.

Brown Cow (Eng) a vodka and real chocolate milk beverage at 4% alc by vol. produced by Anglo Drinks.

Brown Cow Brewery (Eng) a brewery. (Add): Brown Cow Road, Barlow, Selby, North Yorkshire YO8 8EH. Brews a variety of beers and lager. Website: http://www.browncowbrewery..co.uk 'E'mail: susansimpson@browncowbrewery.co.uk

Brown Curaçao (USA) an orange-flavoured liqueur, with orange-brown colour. e.g. Grand Marnier, Van der Hum, etc.

Brown Distillers [Robert] (Can) a subsidiary of Seagram that produces a range of Canadian whiskies.

Brown-Forman (USA) a Bourbon whisky distillery based in Louisville, Kentucky.

Brown Frontignac (Austr) an alternative name for the Muscat à Petits Grains Rouge.

Browning (Eng) a vine complaint, usually occurs when careless pruning aimed at increasing production takes place. The vine leaves show brown stains and eventually fall off.

Browning (Eng) a wine complaint, caused through oxidation by the enzyme **Polyesterase**. Fruit if rotten acts upon tannin with free oxygen when air is in contact with the wine. Also caused by contamination of wine with metal.

Brown Muscat (Austr) a dark skinned Muscat grape variety used for making dessert wines in Victoria.

Brown Oxford Ale (Eng) a brown ale 1032 O.G. brewed by the Morrell's Brewery, Oxford.

Brown Peter Ale (Eng) a brown ale 1034 O.G. brewed by Peter Walker's Brewery, Warrington.

Brown Sherry (Eng) Sherries made by blending Olorosos with sweetening and colouring wines. Brown Sherry was popular with the Victorians whom many have said invented it.

Brown Stout (Eng) a sweet stout 1040 O.G. brewed by the Holt's Brewery, Manchester.

Brown Velvet (Cktl) ⅛ measure Port wine, ⅜ measure sweet stout. Stir lightly together in a tall glass until blended.

Brown Willy (Eng) a 1055 O.G. ale brewed by the Min Pin home-brew public house (inn) at Tintagel, North Cornwall.

Broyage (Fr) the crushing of the grapes.

Broyes (Fr) a Cru Champagne village in the Canton de Montmort. District: Reims.

Broyhan Alt (Ger) a noted malty, top-fermented bier from the Lindener-Gilde Brauerei in Hanover. 5.25% alc by vol. it has a strong hoppy flavour. Named after a sixteenth century brewer.

Brözel [Günter] (S.Afr) a noted wine producer of the Nederburg Estate.

Bru (Bel) a sparkling natural mineral water from Bru, Chevron. Mineral contents (milligrammes per litre): Sodium 8mg/l, Calcium 21mg/l, Magnesium 20mg/l, Potassium 1.5mg/l, Bicarbonates 180mg/l, Chlorides 4mg/l, Sulphates 5mg/l, Nitrates <0.2mg/l, Silicates 19mg/l.

Brubecker (Eng) a premium canned lager from Bass.

Bruce [David] (USA) a winery in Santa Cruz, California. 10.5ha. Grape varieties: Cabernet sauvignon, Petit syrah, Pinot noir, Zinfandel.

Bruce Breweries (Eng) a chain of home-brew public houses in London which are under the 'Firkin' banner.

Bruch (Ger) a brewery based in Saarbrücken. Brews Steifel Bräu (Hell and Dunkel Weizenbiers).

Bruchsal (Ger) village (Anb): Baden. (Ber): Badische Bergstrasse/Kraichgau. (Gro): Mannaberg. (Vin): Klosterberg.

Bruchsal [stadtteil Obergrombach] (Ger) village (Anb): Baden. (Ber): Badische Bergstrasse/Kraichgau. (Gro): Mannaberg. (Vin): Burgwingert.

Bruchsal [stadtteil Untergrombach] (Ger) village (Anb): Baden. (Ber): Badische Bergstrasse. (Gro): Mannaberg. (Vins): Michaelsberg, Weinhecke.

Bruck (Aus) a vineyard site on the banks of the River Danube situated in the Wachau region, Niederösterreich.

Brückchen (Ger) vineyard (Anb): Rheinhessen. (Ber): Nierstein. (Gro): Spiegelberg. (Vil): Nierstein.

Brückstück (Ger) vineyard (Anb): Mosel-Saar-Ruwer. (Ber): Zell/Mosel. (Gro): Weinhex. (Vil): Winningen.

Brüderberg (Ger) vineyard (Anb): Mosel-Saar-Ruwer. (Ber): Obermosel. (Gro): Königsberg. (Vil): Langsur.

Bruderberg (Ger) vineyard (Anb): Mosel-Saar-Ruwer. (Ber): Saar-Ruwer. (Gro): Römerlay. (Vil): Mertesdorf (ortsteil Maximin Grünhaus).

Brudersberg (Ger) vineyard (Anb): Rheinhessen. (Ber): Nierstein. (Gro): Rehbach. (Vil): Nierstein.

Bruderschaft (Ger) vineyard (Anb): Mosel-Saar-Ruwer. (Ber): Bernkastel. (Gro): Sankt Michael. (Vil): Klüsserath.

Bruderthal (Fr) an A.C. Alsace Grand Cru at Molsheim, Bas-Rhin 19ha.

Brugerolle (Fr) a Cognac producer. (Add): Cognac Brugerolle, 17160 Matha près Cognac. Produces Napoléon Aigle rouge 10 y.o. Napoleon Aigle d'Or 25–30 y.o. Très Vieux Cognac Réserve Speciale X.O. Owns no vineyards.

Bruges Tripel (Bel) a strong sweet beer from Bruges. 9.5% alc by vol.

Brugga (Scan) an old Norse word for brewer.

Bruggeman Distillerie (Bel) a large distillery based in Ghent.

Brugnola (It) a red grape variety.

Brugnon [Phillippe] (Fr) a Champagne producer. (Add): 16 Rue Carnot, 51500 Rilly-la-Montagne. Produces vintage and non-vintage Champagnes.

Brugny-Vaudancourt (Fr) a Cru Champagne village in the Canton d'Avize. District: Épernay.

Bruichladdich (Scot). A single malt distillery on the island of Islay. A strong peaty Islay malt whisky. 10 years old. 46% alc by vol. Also a 12, 15, 21 and 26 y.o. Also ages a variety of rums: Guyana 1991 (Hermitage cask-aged), Guyana 1990 (Condrieu cask-aged), Jamaica 1992 (port cask-aged), Trinidad 1992 (Madeira cask-aged).

Bruidstranen (Hol) lit: 'bride's tears', a liqueur produced by Van Zuylekom of Amsterdam. A version of Goldwasser.

Bruin Bier (Hol) brown beer (ale).

Bruins Ruin (Eng) a 5% alc by vol. ale brewed by the Beartown Brewery, Cheshire.

Bruisyard St. Peter Vineyard (Eng) a vineyard (established 1974). (Add): Church Road, Bruisyard, Saxmundham, Suffolk. 4ha. Grape variety: Müller-Thurgau.

Bruito (Port) dry.

Brükes (Ger) vineyard (Anb): Nahe. (Ber): Kreuznach. (Gro): Kronenberg. (Vil): Bad Kreuznach.

Brûlets [Les] (Fr) a wine producing village in the commune of Fuissé in A.C. Pouilly-Fuissé, Mâcon, Burgundy.

Bruley (Fr) a Vin Gris from commune of same name in the Lorraine region.

Brûlot (Fr) lit: 'firebrand', the action of placing spirit (or liqueur) into a spoon with a sugar cube, igniting it and pouring into a cup of hot black coffee. i.e. Café Brûlot au Rhum.

Brulpadda (S.Afr) the label for a Port-style wine (Pinotage and Ruby cabernet blend) produced by the Paddagang Wines winery, Tulbagh, Western Cape.

Brum (Fr) an old word for rum.

Brummie (Eng) a bottled brown ale 1032 O.G. brewed by Davenport's Brewery, Birmingham.

Brumov Brewery (Czec) an old brewery based in eastern Czec.

Brun [Edouard] & C°. (Fr) a Champagne producer (established 1898). (Add): 14 Rue Marcel Milly, 51160 B.P. 11 Aÿ-Champagne. 7ha. Négociant-manipulant. Produces : Cuvée Spéciale, Cuvée de Réserve, Cuvée Blanc de Blancs, Rosé Brut and Vintage Champagnes.

Brun [René] (Fr) a Champagne producer. (Add): 14 Place de la Libération, BP 5, 51160 Aÿ-Champagne 8ha.

Brun [Roger] (Fr) a Champagne producer. (Add): 1 Impasse de Saint-Vincent, 51160 Aÿ. Négociant-manipulant 16ha.

Brunader (Aus) a vineyard site based on the banks of the River Kamp in the Kamptal region.

Brunate (It) a Cru vineyard (25ha) based in the DOCG Barolo, La Morra, Piemonte. Grape variety:

Nebbiolo. Owned by 8 growers it has soils composed of limestone and sand.

Bründelsberg (Ger) vineyard (Anb): Pfalz. (Ber): Südliche Weinstrasse. (Gro): Trappenberg. (Vil): Schwegenheim.

Brun de Neuville [Le] (Fr) a Champagne producer. (Add): Rte. de Chantemerle, Bethon, 51260 Anglure. Coopérative-manipulant. 145 growers own 140ha.

Brundlmayer (Aus) a winery (60ha) based in the Kamptal region. (Add): Zwettler Strasse 23, 3550 Langenlois. Grape varieties: Cabernet sauvignon, Chardonnay, Grüner veltliner, Merlot, Pinot blanc, Pinot gris, Pinot noir, Riesling, Zweigelt. Produces a range of wine styles.

Brune (Bel) lit: 'brown/dark' refers to beers (average 6.5% alc by vol) that are brown-black in colour. Brewed from dark-roasted malts with a bitter-sweet flavour.

Brune et Blonde (Fr) two slopes on the Côte Rotie in the Rhône. The slopes named after the types of soils present. i.e. **Brune**: has soil of iron oxide/ **Blonde**: has soil of limestone.

Brunel 200 IPA (Eng) a 5% alc by vol. India pale ale brewed by the Butcombe brewery to celebrate the 200th anniversary (birth) of Isambard Kingdom Brunel in 2006.

Brunello (It) a red grape variety of the Sangiovese family. Used to produce Brusco dei Barbi Colombini in Tuscany. Made by a unique and long fermentation process.

Brunello di Montalcino (It) a red grape variety grown in the Tuscany region to produce a wine of the same name. Also known as Sangiovese grosso.

Brunello di Montalcino (It) a famous D.O.C.G. red wine produced from the grape of the same name in Tuscany. Vinification and ageing must occur in commune of Montalcino. Maximum yield is 56hl/ha. Must be aged for 4 years before release, (minimum of 3 years in oak casks). If aged 5 years is classified Riserva. Minimum alcohol level of 12.5% by vol. Sold in Bordeaux bottles.

Brunet (Fr) a cuvée in the vineyard of Bressandes in A.C. Beaune, Côte de Beaune, Burgundy. Is owned by the Hospices de Beaune.

Brunette Cocktail (Cktl) ⅓ measure Bourbon whiskey, ⅓ measure Kahlúa, ⅓ measure cream. Shake over ice and strain into a cocktail glass.

Brunnfeld (Aus) a vineyard area on the banks of the River Danube in the Kremstal region.

Brun Fourca (Fr) an ancient red vine grown in Palette, Provence.

Brunissure (Eng) the browning caused by a lack of pruning and hence over-production. Brown stains appear on the leaves which then fall off the vine. Can be fatal if the vine becomes exhausted.

Brünnchen (Ger) vineyard (Anb): Mittelrhein. (Ber): Rheinburgengau. (Gro): Loreleyfelsen. (Vil): Nochern.

Brunnen (Aus)(Ger) spring (water).

Brunnen BW (Ger) a natural spring mineral water from Burgbernheim, BY.

Brunnenhäuschen (Ger) vineyard (Anb): Rheinhessen. (Ber): Wonnegau. (Gro): Bergkloster. (Vil): Westhofen.

Brunnen Perle (Ger) a natural spring mineral water from Kirkel, SL.

Brunngasse (Aus) a vineyard site based on the banks of the River Kamp in the Kamptal region.

Brunngraben (Aus) a vineyard area on the banks of the River Danube in the Kremstal region.

Brunnleiten (Aus) a vineyard area on the banks of the River Danube in the Kremstal region.

Brunnthaler (Ger) a natural spring mineral water from Burgheim, BY.

Bruno Clair (Fr) a Burgundy producer based in the Côte d'Or who has holdings in Chambertin, Clos de Bèze and Gevrey-Chamberin (21ha).

Bruno Colacicchi (It) a noted red wine-producer based in the Latium region. Noted for Torre Ercolana and Romagnano.

Bruno do Rocca (It) a red I.G.T. wine produced from 55% Cabernet sauvignon and 45% Sangiovese grapes by Tenuta Vecchie Terre di Montefili in Tuscany.

Bruno Giacosa (It) a winery based in Neive, Alba in Piemonte that buys in the grapes from local vineyards. Label: Rocche di Falletto.

Bruno Negroni (It) a producer of sparkling (metodo tradizionale) wines based in Emilia-Romagna.

Bruno Paillard (Fr) a Champagne house. (Add): Rue Jacques Maritain, 51100 Reims. Produces vintage and non-vintage wines. Owns no vineyards. Vintages: 1969, 1973, 1974, 1975, 1976, 1979, 1982, 1985, 1989, 1990, 1995, 1998, 1999, 2001. Prestige Cuvée is NPU (Non Plus Ultra).

Brunor (Bel) a brown ale brewed by the Roman Brasserie near Oudenaarde.

Brunswick Cooler (Cktl) place into a highball glass the juice of a lemon, 1 teaspoon of sugar syrup, 2 lumps of ice. Add cold ginger ale, stir and serve.

Brussannes [Les] (Fr) see Brussonnes (Les).

Brüssele (Ger) the name given to the wine of Kleinbottwar, Württemberg.

Brussels Lace (Eng) the name given to the foam pattern that is left behind on the sides of the glass after the beer has been consumed.

Brussonnes [Les] (Fr) a Premier Cru vineyard [part] in the A.C. commune of Chassagne-Montrachet, Côte de Beaune, Burgundy. 17.72ha. (red and white). Also known as Bressandes (Les).

Brunswick Brewing C°. (Eng) a micro-brewery (owned by Everards) that brews The Umpire Strikes Back 4% alc by vol.

Brut (Fr) a term used to describe the driest wines, Champagne and other sparkling wines. It is drier than 'Extra dry'. A dosage of from 0g/l to 15g/l maximum is used. See also Brut Sauvage and Brut Zero.

Brut (Sp) dry (for sparkling wines).

Brut Azur (Fr) a Champagne cuvée of de Cazanove (Charles), in Épernay. See also Stradivarius.

Brut de Brut Gran Reserva de Artesania (Sp) a soft, fruity, dry cava wine produced by Cavas Hill.

Brut de Futs Hors d'Age (Fr) a style of Cognac produced by Edgard Leyrat.

Brut di Concilio (It) a sparkling (metodo tradizionale) wine produced by Lagariavini in the Trentino-Alto-Adige region north-eastern Italy.

Brut Intégrale (Fr) a term sometimes used for a completely unsugared Champagne. Also known as Brut Non-Dosé and Brut Zéro.

Brut Natur (Sp) extra dry (sparkling wine).

Brur Nature (Fr) a term to denote a completely dry Champagne with only 3 grammes of sugar or less. Also known as Dosage Zéro and Non Dosé.

Brut Non-Dosé (Fr) see Brut Intégrale and Brut Zéro.

Bruto (Port) denotes a very dry sparkling wine.

Bruto (Sp) extra dry.

Brutocao Cellars (USA) a winery based in the Mendocino County, California. Is a member of the Coro Mendocino (Zinfandel) wine group of Mendocino wineries.

Brut Quatro Vecchio (It) a sparkling (metodo tradizionale) wine made from Chardonnay and Pinot noir grapes by Castello di Bevilacqua. Min. alc. content of 12% by vol.

Brut Sans Année (Fr) abbr: B.S.A. Label of a dry Champagne made from different years.

Brut Sauvage (Fr) a non-dosage Champagne from Piper Heidsieck.

Bruttig-Fankel (Ger) village (Anb): Mosel-Saar-Ruwer. (Ber): Zell/Mosel. (Gro): Goldbäumchen. (Vin): Götterlay.

Bruttig-Fankel (Ger) village (Anb): Mosel-Saar-Ruwer. (Ber): Zell/Mosel. (Gro): Rosenhang. (Vins): Kapellenberg, Langenberg, Martinsborn, Pfarrgarten, Rathausberg, Rosenberg.

Brutus (Eng) a 5% alc by vol. ale brewed by Feast and Firkin in Leeds.

Brut Zéro (Fr) see Brut Intégrale and Brut Non-Dosé.

Bryant Family Estate (USA) a winery based in the Napa Valley, California. Grape varieties include: Cabernet sauvignon. Label: Pritchard Hill (Cabernet sauvignon).

Bryde (S.Afr) a brand label for a range of red (Shiraz) and white (Chenin-blanc and Colombard/Sauvignon blanc) wines produced by ACJ Wines, Durbanville, Western Cape.

Brydge Bitter (Eng) a 3.8% alc by vol. bitter beer brewed by the Bank Top Brewey, Lancashire.

Bryggeri (Swe) brewery.

Brympton d'Evercy (Eng) a vineyard (established 1974). 0.33ha. (Add): Yeovil, Somerset. Soil is loam pH7. Grape varieties: 50% Müller-Thurgau and 50% Reichensteiner. Also produce Apple Brandy.

Bryan Creek Vineyard (USA) the label for a red wine (Pinot noir) from Yamill County and produced by the Adelsheim winery, Oregon.

Brysons Brewery (Eng) a micro-brewery based at Morecambe, Lancashire. Brews a standard bitter and a porter ale.

B.S.D.A. (Eng) abbr: British Soft Drinks Association.

BSE (Eng) a 3.7% alc by vol. beer brewed by the Barum Brewery, Devon.

BSN Bières (Fr) the largest bottle-maker. Has 17 breweries. 2 principal components: Kronenbourg and Société Europé de Brasseries. Tiger Scotch is a well-known brand.

B.S.T. (Eng) a 4.3% alc by vol. ale brewed by the Somerset (Electric) Brewery, Somerset.

B.T.I. (USA) abbr: The Beverage Testing Institute.

Buachaill Tabhairne (Ire) barman.

Bual (Mad) a medium sweet Madeira. See also Boal.

Bubbler (USA) the glass fermentation valve known as an airlock in the U.K.

Bubbles (Eng) CO_2 gas released when sparkling wine or beer is opened.

Bubble Tea (Tai) sweetened tea with milk and tapioca balls that is drunk using a large straw!

Bubbly (Eng) a slang term for Champagne and other sparkling wines.

Bubeneck (Ger) vineyard (Anb): Pfalz. (Ber): Mittelhaardt-Deutsche Weinstrasse. (Gro): Feuerberg. (Vil): Ellerstadt.

Bubenheim (Ger) village (Anb): Rheinhessen. (Ber): Bingen. (Gro): Kaiserpfalz. (Vins): Honigberg, Kallenberg.

Bubenheim (Ger) village (Anb): Pfalz. (Ber): Mittelhaardt-Deutsche Weinstrasse. (Gro): Schnepfenflug vom Zellertal. (Vin): Hahnenkamm.

Bubenstück (Ger) vineyard (Anb): Rheinhessen. (Ber): Bingen. (Gro): Sankt Rochuskapelle. (Vil): Bingen.

Buçaco (Port) a top quality red wine produced by the Buçaco Hotel near Coimbra in Beira Alta.

Bucaramangas (S.Am) a noted coffee-producing region in Colombia.

Buccaneer Beer (Eng) a cask-conditioned bitter 1065 O.G. brewed by the Pier Hotel, a home-brew public house in Gravesend.

Buccaneer Beer (Eng) a cask-conditioned bitter 1065 O.G. brewed by the Southeastern brewery, a home-brew public house in Strood.

Buccaneer Bitter (Eng) a seasonal cask-conditioned ale brewed by Burtonwood in Warrington. Part of their Masterclass range.

Buccaneer Punch (Punch) 500mls (1 pint) Bacardi rum, 300mls (½ pint) dry white wine, 300mls (½ pint) orange juice, 150mls (¼ pint) lemon juice, 1 vanilla pod, 1 cinnamon stick, 100gms (4ozs) sliced fresh pineapple, grated nutmeg. Mix altogether, chill down, serve with orange and lemon slices.

Buccanheer (S.Afr) the label for a range of red wines (Cabernet sauvignon and Touriga nacional) produced by the Jonkeer winery, Robertson, Western Cape.

Buccia Vineyard (USA) a winery based in Conneaut, Ohio. Produces French hybrid wines.

Bucelas (Port) a DOC wine area of Portugal. Produces white wines from the Arinto grape in the Estremadura region on the plains of the river Tejo. see Camilo Alves.

Bucellas (Port) the old spelling of Bucelas.

Buchanan (Scot) producers of Strathconon (a blended malt), part of the DCL group.

B

Buchanan Best Bitter (Eng) a 3.6% alc by vol. cask-conditioned bitter brewed by the Federation Brewery, Tyneside.

Buchanan Best Scotch (Eng) a 3.6% alc by vol. mild ale from the Federation Brewery, Tyneside.

Buchanan Blend [The] (Scot) an 8 year old blended de luxe Scotch whisky produced by Buchanan and Co. 40% alc by vol.

Buchanan Original Ale (Eng) a 1045 O.G. draught or cask-conditioned bitter brewed by the Federation Brewery, Tyneside.

Buchbrunn (Ger) village (Anb): Franken. (Ber): Maindreieck. (Gro): Hofrat. (Vil): Heisser Stein.

Buchegger (Aus) a winery based in the Kremstal region. (Add): Wienbergstrasse 9, 3494 Gedersdorf. Grape varieties: Cabernet sauvignon, Grüner veltliner, Müller-Thurgau, Riesling, Neuberger, Zweigelt. Produces a range of wine styles.

Buchental (Aus) a vineyard site on the banks of the River Danube situated in the Wachau region, Niederösterreich.

Bucherburger (Switz) a red wine.

Buchholz (Ger) village (Anb): Baden. (Ber): Breisgau. (Gro): Burg Zähringen. (Vin): Sonnhalde.

Buchhorn Quelle (Ger) a natural spring mineral water from Eberstadt-Buchhorn, BW.

Buchner Filter (Eng) a straight-sided funnel which is fitted with a perforated porcelain plate. Used for filtration of wines.

Buchu Brandy (S.Afr) a liqueur brandy flavoured with the leaves of the Buchu plant.

Buck [The] (Cktl) ½ measure Cognac, ⅔ measure white crème de menthe, ⅙ measure lemon juice. Shake over ice, strain into an ice-filled collins glass, top with ginger ale and dress with seedless grapes.

Buckaroo (Cktl) into a highball glass put 35mls (1½ fl.ozs) American Bourbon and several dashes Angostura. Add ice, Coca Cola and stir.

Buckeye Ontario Special Ale (Can) a beer brewed by the Carling Brewery in Toronto.

Buckfast Wine (Eng) a tonic wine produced by Bénédictine monks in Devon from French wine, herbs and minerals.

Buckie's Brose (Cktl) ⅓ measure Scotch whisky, ⅓ measure Kahlúa, ⅓ measure cream, 1 teaspoon clear honey. Shake well over ice, strain into a cocktail glass and top with toasted oatmeal.

Buckingham (Can) a brand of dry gin produced by Hiram Walker.

Buckingham Valley Vineyards (USA) a small winery based in Buckingham, Pennsylvania. 4ha. Produces French hybrid wines.

Buck Jones Cocktail (Cktl) ¾ measure Jamaican rum, ¼ measure cream Sherry, juice ½ lime. Place altogether in an ice-filled highball glass, stir and top with ginger ale.

Buckland Best Bitter (Eng) a 4.1% alc by vol. bitter ale from micro-brewery Winchester Arms, Buckland, Portsmouth.

Buckler (Hol) a low alcohol lager 0.5% alc by vol. from Heineken.

Buckley Brewery (Wal) the oldest Welsh brewery, formerly based at Llanelli. Produces cask-conditioned ales and other styles. *see* Crown Buckley, Brain (S.A.).

Bucks County Vineyards (USA) a winery based in New Hope, Pennsylvania. Produces Chardonnay, Riesling and French hybrid wines.

Buck's Fizz (Cktl) place some ice in a highball glass. Add 25mls (1fl.oz) of fresh orange juice then top up with iced Champagne.

Buck's Fizz (Cktl) (Non-alc) in a highball glass mix equal quantities of chilled Ashbourne mineral water and fresh orange juice.

Buck's Ridge (S.Afr) a winery (established 2005) based in Tulbagh, Western Cape. 10ha. Grape varieties: Cabernet sauvignon, Mourvèdre, Petit verdot, Shiraz, Viognier, Zinfandel. Website: http://www.bucksridge.co.za

Bucktrout and Cº. (Ch.Isles) the largest wine and spirits merchants in Guernsey. Taken over by Ann Street Brewery (now Jersey Brewery) of Jersey. Bottles own brands of spirits and sherries. *See also* Guernsey Brewery 1920 Ltd., Jersey Brewery. Part of CI Traders. Website: http://www.bucktrouts.com 'E'mail: info@bucktrouts.com

Bucovina (Rum) a natural spring mineral water (established 1993). Mineral contents (milligrammes per litre): Sodium 45mg/l, Calcium 83mg/l, Magnesium 24mg/l, Potassium 4mg/l, Bicarbonates 548mg/l, Chlorides 11mg/l, Sulphates 9mg/l.

Buda (Hun) a red table wine from Budapest.

Budaer Riesling (Ger) an erroneous varietal name for the Kleinweiss white grape variety.

Budafok (Hun) the headquarters of the Hungarian State wine cellars.

Budai Zöld (Hun) a white grape variety.

Budding (Eng) the term given to the action of yeast multiplying. *see* Binary Fision.

Buddings (Eng) a 4.5% alc by vol. dark ruby spring ale brewed by the Everards Brewery.

Budejovice (Czec) the modern name for Budweis (Austro-Hungarian Empire name). *see* Ceské Budejovice.

Budejovický Budvar Brewery (Czec) a brewery (established 1895) based in Ceské Budejovice. Brews Budejovický Budvar 10%, Budejovický Budvar 12%.

Budejovický Budvar 10% (Czec) a 4% alc by vol. light, bottled lager brewed by Budejovický Budvar Brewery, Ceské Budejovice.

Budejovický Budvar 12% (Czec) a 5% alc by vol. straw coloured, bottled lager brewed by Budejovický Budvar Brewery, Ceské Budejovice.

Budelse Brouwerij BV (Hol) a small brewery. (Add): Nieuwstraat 9, Postbus 2026, AA Budel, north Brabant. Brews unpasteurised beers of same name and lager. Website: http://www.budels.nl

Budels Alt (Hol) a dark ale 5.5% alc by vol. from Budelse Brouwerij. *See also* Capucijn, Parel.

Bud Ice (USA) a 5.2% alc by vol. bottom-fermented, bottled ice beer from Anheuser-Busch, St. Louis.

Budis (Slo) a sparkling natural mineral water (established 1573). Mineral contents (milligrammes per litre): Sodium 439mg/l, Calcium 237.8mg/l, Magnesium 53.2mg/l, Potassium 52.9mg/l, Bicarbonates 1679.3mg/l, Chlorides 24.4mg/l, Sulphates 440mg/l, Fluorides 1.86mg/l.

Bud Light (USA) *abbr: see* **Bud**weiser **Light**.

Bud Mutation (USA) a natural mutation of the plant to produce different fruit than that of the parent strain.

Budoo (Jap) grape.

Budos (Fr) a commune in the A.C. Graves district of south-western Bordeaux.

Budvar (Czec) a brewery (established 1895) in Bohemia in the town of Ceské Budejovice. Produces a light and a dark 4.7% alc by vol coloured beer Budweis.

Budweis (Czec) a light-coloured beer brewed by the Budvar Brewery in Ceské Budejovice.

Budweiser Beer (USA) a 5% alc by vol. bottled lager beer produced by Anheuser-Busch, St. Louis. Name originates from the Czech town of Ceské Budejovice. Brewed with malted barley or rice and fined over beechwood chips. Brewed under licence by Watneys in England. 1044 O.G. *See also* BE. Website: http://www.budweiser.co.uk

Budweiser Budvar UK Ltd (Eng) a major well-known brewery. (Add): Hamilton House, Mabledon Place, London WC1H 9BB. Brews Budweiser lager beer. Website: http://www.original-budweiser.cz 'E'mail: sales@budvarUK.com

Budweiser Light (USA) a 4.3% alc by vol. malt beer from Anheuser-Busch, St. Louis.

Bué (Fr) a small commune in the A.C. Sancerre district of the Central Vineyards, Loire.

Buehler Vineyards (USA) a small vineyard and winery based in the Napa valley, California. 25ha. Grape varieties: Cabernet sauvignon and Sauvignon blanc. Produces varietal wines.

Buena Vida Vineyards [La] (USA) a large winery based in Springtown, Central Texas. Produces mainly hybrid wines.

Buena Vista (USA) a winery sited at Sonoma, north of San Francisco. Founded by Haraszthy (Agostan) in 1857. 1360ha. Grape varieties: Cabernet sauvignon, Chardonnay, Gamay, Gewürztraminer, Merlot, Pinot noir, Riesling, Sauvignon blanc and Zinfandel. Produces table and dessert wines. Owned by Beam Wine Estates (Allied Domecq)

Buffalo Valley Winery (USA) a winery based in Lewisburg, Pennsylvania. Produces French hybrid wines.

Buff Bitter (Lux) a beer made according to Dr. Boerhare's formulae.

Buffelskroon Wines (S.Afr) *see* Calitzdorp Vrugte en Wynkelders.

Buffet (Hol) bar.

Buffeter (Fr) to draw off wine from a cask and replace with water. *see* Servir à Buffet.

Buffethouder (Hol) bar-keeper/barman.

Buffetjuffrouw (Hol) barmaid.

Buff's Bitter (Eng) a cask-conditioned bitter 1050 O.G. brewed by the Canterbury Brewery, Kent.

Buffy (Switz) a sparkling natural spring mineral water from Adelboden. Mineral contents (milligrammes per litre): Sodium 4.8mg/l, Calcium 510mg/l, Magnesium 31mg/l, Bicarbonates 285mg/l, Chlorides 5.5mg/l, Sulphates 1150mg/l, Fluorides 0.18mg/l, Nitrates 2mg/l.

Buffy's Bitter (Eng) a bitter ale 3.9% alc by vol. brewed by the Buffy's Brewery, Norfolk.

Buffy's Brewery (Eng) a brewery (established 1993). (Add): Rectory Road, Tivetshall St. Mary, Norwich, Norfolk NR15 2DD. Brews: Buffy's Ale 5.5% alc by vol., Buffy's Bitter 3.9% alc by vol., Buffy's Hopleaf 4.5% alc by vol., Buffy's India Ale 4.6% alc by vol., Buffy's Mild 4.2% alc by vol., Buffy's Norwich Terrier 3.6% alc by vol., Buffy's Norwegian Blue 4.9% alc by vol., Buffy's 10 X 10% alc by vol., IPA 5.1% alc by vol., Mucky Duck 4.5% alc by vol., Polly's Folly 4.3% alc by vol. and Royal Divorce ale. Website: http://www.buffys.co.uk 'E'mail: buffysbrewery@evemail.net

Bugey (Fr) a V.D.Q.S. district in Savoie which produces dry white, rosé and red wines from the Altesse, Gamay, Jacquère, Mondeuse blanche, Pinot noir and Poulsard grapes.

Buggingen (Ger) village (Anb): Baden. (Ber): Markgräflerland. (Gro): Lorettoberg. (Vins): Höllberg, Maltesergarten.

Bugisu Coffee (S.Afr) a Ugandian coffee bean which produces a fine coffee with good flavour and aroma.

Bühl (Ger) vineyard (Anb): Baden. (Ber): Kairerstuhl-Tuniberg. (Gro): Attilafelsen. (Vil): Merdingen.

Bühlertal (Ger) village (Anb): Baden. (Ber): Ortenau. (Gro): Schloss Rodeck. (Vins): Engelsfelsen, Klotzberg.

Bühl [ortsteil Neusatz] (Ger) village (Anb): Baden. (Ber): Ortenau. (Gro): Schloss Rodeck. (Vins): Burg Windeck-Kostanienhalde, Sternenberg, Wolfhag.

Build (Cktl) to pour the necessary ingredients into a glass without pre-mixing.

Buisson [Le] (Fr) the brand-name for a Vin de Table from Henry Chouteau.

Buitenverwachting (S.Afr) a winery (established 1796) based in Constantia, Western Cape. 120ha. (Add): P.O. Box 281, Constantia 7848. Grape varieties: Cabernet franc, Cabernet sauvignon, Chenin blanc, Merlot, Rhine riesling, Sauvignon blanc grapes. Labels: Cap Classique, Christine, Coastal, Husseys Vlei, Meifort. Website: http://www.buitenverwachting.com

Buitléir Fiona (Ire) wine butler/sommelier.

Buitzorg (E.Ind) a coffee-producing region in Java.

Bujariego (Sp) a local grape variety grown on island of La Palma in the Canary Islands.

Bukettreich (Ger) a rich pronounced bouquet.

Bukettriesling (Ger) a grape variety from a cross between the Red riesling x Muscat St. Laurent.

Bükkalja (Hun) a wine-producing region based in northern Hungary. Is noted for white wines.

B

Bukkettraube (S.Afr) a white grape variety. Has a Muscat aroma, is light in acidity and is used for blending (of German origin).

Bukkuram (It) the label for a sweet wine produced on the island of Pantelleria by the De Bartoli winery.

Bule (Port) tea-pot.

Bulgaria (Bul) a large wine producing country. Wine production and sales were formerly controlled by Vinprom. Produces fine wines and spirits (most are exported to Russia). Key D.G.O. regions are-Northern region [Pavlikeni, Russe, Suhindol, Svischtov], Southern region [Assenovgrad, Korten, Oriachovitza, Plovdiv, Sakar and Stambolovo], Eastern region [Khan Krum, Novi Pazar, Shumen and Varna], Sub-Balkan region, South-western region [Harsovo, Melnik and Petrich Damianitza]. Grape varieties include Bordeaux varieties plus Chardonnay, Gamza, Mavrud, Melnik, Misket, Pamid and Rkatsiteli. *see* Controliran, Declared Geographical Origin.

Bulgarsko Pivo (Bul) the name of the Bulgarian State brewery. Brews Astica.

Bulk Gallon (Eng) a wine gallon. 160 Imperial fl.ozs 128 US fl.ozs. a gallon of spirit, basis for charges of Customs and Excise.

Bulk Process (Eng) the fermentation of sparkling wines in long sealed tanks instead of by the méthode traditionelle.

Bull (Eng) a premium bitter 4% alc by vol. from Hambleton Brewery, near Thirsk, Yorkshire. *See also* Old Rabey Ale, Stallion, White Boar Bitter 3.8% alc by vol.

Bullace Grape (USA) an alternative name for the Muscadine grape.

Bullage à L'Air (Fr) wine is aerated by small controlled doses of oxygen during maturation to help 'round it out'.

Bullards Old Ale (Eng) a noted old ale 1057 O.G. brewed by Norwich (Watney's) Brewery.

Bullas (Sp) a D.O. wine producing area in Murcia, Levante. Grape varieties: Monastrell, Tempranillo, Airén, Macabeo. Produces red, white and rosé wines.

Bullay (Ger) village (Anb): Mosel-Saar-Ruwer. (Ber): Zell/Mosel. (Gro): Graftschaft. (Vins): Brautrock, Graf-Beyssel-Herrenberg, Kroneberg, Kirchweingarten, Sonneck.

Bull Best Bitter (Eng) a 3.9% alc by vol. bitter beer brewed by the Blanchfield Brewery, Essex.

Bulldog (Cktl) place a lump of ice in a highball, add juice of ⅓ lemon, 90mls (⅜ gill) dry gin, sugar syrup to taste and top up with ginger ale. Stir carefully and serve. Can substitute orange instead of lemon. Also known as Bulldog Cooler.

Bulldog Ale (Eng) a bottled pale ale 6.3% alc by vol (1068 O.G). brewed by Courage. *See also* John Martin and Martin's Pale ale.

Bulldog (Eng) a 4% alc by vol. ale brewed by Drummond's Brewery, Heeley, Sheffield.

Bulldog Brand Bottled Guinness (Eng) bottled at Gibbs Mew Brewery in Salisbury, Wiltshire. Taste

stems from the maturation process: 10 days at a constant temperature of 55°F (12.7°C).

Bulldog Cooler (Cktl) *see* Bulldog.

Bulldog Export Ale (Eng) a 5% alc by vol. ale brewed by Courage.

Bulldog Highball (Cktl) ⅓ measure gin, ⅓ measure orange juice. Shake over ice, strain into a cocktail glass, top with cold ginger ale and add straws.

Bulleit Bourbon (USA) a premium straight 'frontier whiskey' amber-coloured Bourbon whiskey 40% alc by vol. produced by Diageo's Bulleit Distillery.

Bullenheim (Ger) village (Anb): Franken. (Ber): Steigerwald. (Gro): Schlosstück. (Vin): Paradies.

Bullers (Austr) a vineyard based in north-east Victoria. Produce a wide range of table wines.

Bulles (Fr) the name for the CO_2 gas bubbles in bottles of Champagne.

Bull Frog (Cktl) 35mls (1½ fl.ozs) apricot brandy, juice of a lemon. Shake over ice, strain into a cocktail glass.

Bullfrog (Eng) a 4.8% alc by vol. ale brewed by the Wizard Brewery, Warwickshire.

Bullfrog Beer (Eng) a cask-conditioned bitter 1045 O.G. brewed at the Frog and Firkin Public house in London.

Bulligny (Fr) a commune in the Côtes de Toul, Lorraine region. Produces Vins gris.

Bullion (Eng) a 4.7% alc by vol. ale brewed by the Nottingham Brewery, Nottinghamshire.

Bullion (Eng) a 4.7% alc by vol. dark, amber-coloured bitter ale from the Old Mill Brewery, Snaith, North Yorkshire.

Bullmastiff Brewery (Eng) a brewery (established 1992). (Add): Unit 14, Bessemer Close, Cardiff, South Glamorgan CF11 8DL. Brews: Best Bitter 4% alc by vol., Brindle 5% alc by vol., Gold Brew 3.8% alc by vol., Snarlsberg Lager 4.5% alc by vol., Son of a Bitch Bitter 6.5% alc by vol., Thoroughbred 4.5% alc by vol.

Bull Pup Cooler (Cktl) 35mls (1½ fl.ozs) gin, 500mls (1pint) ginger ale, juice ½ lemon. Place altogether into an ice-filled jug. Stir, serve in highball glasses with a thin strip of lemon peel.

Bullrush Wines (N.Z) a winery based at Main Road, Waimauku, Kumau. 16ha. Grape varieties: Chardonnay, Sauvignon blanc.

Bull's Blood (Hun) a popular name for robust red wine from Eger region called Egri Bikavér. Produced from Kadarka, Kéfrankos and Médoc noir grape varieties. Name used on label. From January 2001 must be bottled in Hungary and have minimum maturation of 12 months in oak. Before release must pass tasting test by Eger Wine Society.

Bulls Eye Ale (Eng) a bottled brown ale 1035 O.G. from the Greenhall Whitley Brewery, Warrington.

Bull's Eye Cocktail (Cktl) ⅓ measure brandy, ⅔ measure dry cider. Stir together in a highball glass with ice, top with ginger ale.

Bull Shot (Cktl) 1 measure vodka, 100mls (4fl.ozs) clear beef bouillon, dash lemon juice, dash Worcestershire sauce, celery salt. Pour 'on the rocks' in an old-fashioned glass, stir and serve.

190

Bull's Milk (Cktl) 90mls (¾ gill) V.S.O.P. Cognac, sugar syrup to taste, 1 part milk. Shake well over ice, strain into a tumbler, add grated nutmeg and cinnamon on top.

Bully Hill (USA) a new winery based in the Finger Lakes region. Produces varietal wines from hybrid American grapes.

Bulmers (Eng) the largest cider makers in U.K. based at The Cider Mills, Plough Lane, Hereford on the English/Welsh border. Produce Kiri and Max, N° 7 (still bottled cider), Original (draught) and Traditional (cask) ciders, also Bulmers Black. Distributes Perrier water and Orangina. Now owned by Scottish & Newcastle. see Scottish Courage. Website: http://www.bulmers.com

Bulmers Black (Eng) a 4.1% alc by vol. drink produced from malt hops and apples by Bulmers.

Bumastus (Lat) a variety of vine.

Bumper (USA) a glass or tankard filled to the brim for a toast in the seventeenth and eighteenth centuries.

Bunce's Brewery (Eng) a brewery (established 1984) in Netheravon, Wiltshire. Brews Bunce's Best 1043 O.G. Benchmark 3.5% alc by vol. green beer 4.6% alc by vol. Old Smokey 5% alc by vol. The Famous Pigswill 4% alc by vol. Sign of Spring 4.6% alc by vol.

Bunches (Eng) the trading name used by Fuller Smith and Turner's, two large stores in Surrey and London. See also Fullers.

Bundaberg (Austr) a rum producer based in Queensland. Brands include Endeavour plus Bundaberg (a golden rum sold in a distinctive square bottle at 37% alc by vol.), Overproof at 57.7% alc by vol. Black Label at 40% alc by vol.

Bundarra Vineyard (Austr) a part of Baileys of Glenrowen.

Bundenheim (Ger). Village (Anb): Rheinhessen. (Ber): Nierstein. (Gro): Domherr. (Vin): Sites not yet chosen.

Bundes-Kellerei-Inspektor (Aus) the Federal Cellar Controller Office where the vignerons have to state what type of wine and quantity was produced.

Bundesverband der Deutschen Spirituosen Industrie (Ger) a body which is associated with over 60 of the major distilleries.

Bundesweinpramierung (Ger) a competition run by the D.L.G. (German Agricultural Society) to find the top wines. Gold, silver and bronze awards are given to the best, the award to be displayed on the bottle label.

Bung (Eng) a stopper of cork, glass, metal, rubber or wood etc. used to block a bunghole.

Bungawarra Vineyard (Austr) a 20ha. vineyard. (Add): Marshall's Crossing Road, Ballandean, Queensland. Grape varieties: Cabernet sauvignon, Chardonnay, Malbec, Muscat, Pinot noir, Sémillon, Shiraz.

Bunghole (Eng) hole through which a cask is filled with beer, wine, etc. It is closed using a shive (beer) or a bung. Also used for the removal of cask's contents. See also Keyhole.

Bunn (E.Asia) the Amharic word for coffee.

Bunnahabhain (Scot) a single Islay malt whisky distillery (established 1881). Owned by the Highland Distilleries Company. 12 year old. 40% alc by vol., a 1979 20 year old at 43% alc by vol. and a single cask 1965 at 53.9% alc by vol.

Bunny Hug (Cktl) ⅓ measure Pernod, ⅓ measure whisky, ⅓ measure gin. Shake over ice, strain into cocktail glass.

Bunratty Potcheen (Ire) a 40% alc by vol. peppery, herbal potcheen spirit from Pondicherry International.

Bunter Gin (Eng) a London distilled dry gin 40% alc by vol. produced by Hayman distillers for Club Spirits, London.

Buntingford Brewery (Eng) a brewery (established 2001). (Add): Grey Brewhouse, Therfield Road, Buntingford, Hertfordshire SG8 9NW. Brews: Britannia 4.4% alc by vol., Challenger 3.8% alc by vol., Grey Partridge 4.1% alc by vol., Pargetters Mild 3.6% alc by vol., Silence 5.2% alc by vol., Western Monarch 4.3% alc by vol. Website: http://www.buntingford-brewery.co.uk 'E'mail: steve@buntingford-brewery.co.uk

Buntsandstein (Ger) the name for the sandstone soil found in Franken (Franconia).

Burberry's (Scot) a de luxe Scotch whisky 15 years old. Produced by A. Gillies and C°., a subsidiary of Amalgamated Distilled Products.

Burcom Bitter (Eng) a 4.2% alc by vol. bitter beer brewed by Willy's Brewery, South Humberside.

Burdigala (Fr) an old Roman name for the Bordeaux region.

Burdin (Fr) a famous French hybridiser noted for developing a red grape variety from a white grape original.

Burdock (Eng) a bur-like fruit from the genus *Arctium*, family **Compositae**. A weed used in the production of Dandelion and Burdock. Has heart-shaped leaves and purple flowers surrounded by hooked bristles.

Burdon (Sp) a Sherry producer based in Puerto de Santa Maria. Is part of Caballero.

Burdur Dimitiri (Tur) a white grape variety grown in southern Turkey.

Bureau Interprofessionnel des Calvados (Fr) the Committee who regulates the making of Calvados.

Bureau Interprofessionnel des Vins de Bourgogne (Fr) abbr: BIVB. the committee that regulates Burgundy wines. See also Project Burgundy. (Add): 12, Boulevard Bretonnière, B.P. 150, 21204 Beaune Cedex, France. Website: http://www.vins-bourgogne.fr 'E mail: bivb@bivb.com

Bureau National Interprofessionnel de l'Armagnac (Fr) abbr: B.N.I.A. the Armagnac governing body.

Bureau National Interprofessionnel des Calvados et Eaux-de-Vie-de-Cidre-et-de-Poire (Fr) abbr: B.N.I.C.E. Defines areas where Calvados apples and pears may be grown.

Bureau National Interprofessionnel du Cognac (Fr) abbr: B.N.I.C the Government body that controls the production and sale of Cognac. Fixed the prices for grapes, wine and new/aged distillations before 1984.

Bureau of Alcohol, Tobacco and Firearms (USA) *see* B.A.T.F.

Burette (Eng) a glass or plastic tube which is calibrated and fitted with a stopcock. Used in the testing of musts.

Burg (Ger) the old name for a fortified town.

Burg (Ger) grosslagen (Anb): Franken. (Ber): Maindreieck. (Vils): Hammelburg, Ramsthal, Saaleck, Wirmsthal.

Burg (Ger) vineyard (Anb): Baden. (Ber): Badische Bergstrasse/Kraichgau. (Gro): Mannaberg. (Vil): Heidelberg.

Burg (Ger) village (Anb): Mosel-Saar-Ruwer. (Ber): Bernkastel. (Gro): Schwarzlay. (Vins): Falklay, Hahnenschrittchen, Thomasberg, Wendelstüch.

Bürg (Ger) village (Anb): Württemberg. (Ber): Remstal-Stuttgart. (Gro): Kopf. (Vin): Schlossberg.

Burgans (Sp) a white wine produced by Bodegas Vilariño-Cambados in Val do Salnés, Rías Baixas, D.O. Galicia.

Burgas (Bul) a delimited wine-producing area based in the the Eastern region.

Burgas Prosenik (Bul) a delimited wine-producing area based in the Eastern region.

Burgaud [Jean-Marc] (Fr) a winery based in the A.C. Beaujolais Cru Morgon, southern Burgundy. (Add): Côte de Py, Morgan. 14ha.

Burgberg (Ger) vineyard (Anb): Ahr. (Ber): Walporzheim/Arhtal. (Gro): Klosterberg. (Vil): Mayschoss.

Burgberg (Ger) vineyard (Anb): Mosel-Saar-Ruwer. (Ber): Bernkastel. (Gro): Schwarzlay. (Vil): Lösnich.

Burgberg (Ger) vineyard (Anb): Mosel-Saar-Ruwer. (Ber): Saar-Ruwer. (Gro): Römerlay. (Vil): Trier.

Burgberg (Ger) vineyard (Anb): Mosel-Saar-Ruwer. (Ber): Zell/Mosel. (Gro): Weinhex. (Vil): Alken.

Burgberg (Ger) vineyard (Anb): Nahe. (Ber): Kreuznach. (Gro): Schlosskapelle. (Vil): Dorsheim.

Burgberg (Ger) vineyard (Anb): Rheinhessen. (Ber): Bingen. (Gro): Kaiserpfalz. (Vil): Ingelheim.

Burgberg (Ger) vineyard (Anb): Württemberg. (Ber): Württembergisch Unterland. (Gro): Schalkstein. (Vil): Steinheim.

Burgberg (Ger) vineyard (Anb): Württemberg. (Ber): Württembergisch Unterland. (Gro): Schozachtal. (Vil): Abstatt.

Burgberg (Ger) vineyard (Anb): Württemberg. (Ber): Württembergisch Unterland. (Gro): Schozachtal. (Vil): Auenstein.

Burg Bischofsteiner (Ger) vineyard (Anb): Mosel-Saar-Ruwer. (Ber): Zell/Mosel. (Gro): Weinhex. (Vil): Hatzenport.

Burgbronn (Ger) village (Anb): Württemberg. (Ber): Württembergisch Unterland. (Gro): Heuchelberg. (Vin): Hahnenberg.

Burg Coreidelsteiner (Ger) vineyard (Anb): Mosel-Saar-Ruwer. (Ber): Zell/Mosel. (Gro): Goldbäumchen. (Vil): Klotten.

Burgeff (Ger) the name of a large producer of Deutscher Sekt.

Burg Ehrenberg (Ger) vineyard (Anb): Baden. (Ber): Badische Bergstrasse/Kraichgau. (Gro): Stiftsberg. (Vil): Heinsheim.

Bürgel (Ger) vineyard (Anb): Rheinhessen. (Ber): Wonnegau. (Gro): Burg Rodenstein. (Vil): Flörsheim-Dalsheim.

Burgen (Ger) village (Anb): Mosel-Saar-Ruwer. (Ber): Bernkastel. (Gro): Kurfürslay. (Vins): Hasenläufer, Kirchberg, Romerberg,

Burgen (Ger) village (Anb): Mosel-Saar-Ruwer. (Ber): Zell/Mosel. (Gro): Weinhex. (Vin): Bischofstein.

Burgengau (Ger) an Untergebiete of the Oberrhein district.

Burgenland (Aus) a wine region containing Neusiedlersee, Neusiedlersee-Hügelland, Mittel-Burgenland and Süd-Burgenland. Produces both red, white and botrytised sweet wines. Also home to the area of Rust that produces Ausbruch wines.

Bergenperle (Ger) a natural spring mineral water (established 1992). Mineral contents (milli-grammes per litre): Sodium 10mg/l, Calcium 269mg/l, Magnesium 42mg/l, Potassium 5mg/l, Bicarbonates 298mg/l, Chlorides 5mg/l, Sulphates 587mg/l.

Burgenquelle (Ger) a natural spring mineral water from Reutlingen-Rommelsbach, BW.

Burgquelle-Mineralwasser (Ger) a natural spring mineral water from Brunnen 1, Volkmarsen, HE.

Burger (Ger) the name given to the white wines from Burg, Bernkastel.

Burger (USA) a white grape variety used to make white and dessert wines in California.

Burger [Le] (Fr) the Alsace name for Vin de Table wines made from the Burger-Elbling grape variety.

Burger-Elbling (Fr) a white grape variety of Alsace

Bürgergarten (Ger) vineyard (Anb): Pfalz. (Ber): Mittelhaardt-Deutsche Weinstrasse. (Gro): Meerspinne. (Vil): Haardt.

Burgerlich (Ger) denotes Bourgeois, middle-class wines.

Bürgerspital (Ger) the Holy Ghost Hospice of the Citizens in Franconia. Vineyards still support it. Produce white wines.

Burgess Best (Eng) a cask-conditioned bitter 1048 O.G. brewed by the Railway, a home-brew public house owned by Whitbread in Burgesshill, Sussex.

Burgess Brewery (S.E.Asia) a brewery based in Singapore.

Burgess Cellars (USA) a large winery based in St. Helena, Napa Valley. Owns 9.25ha. Grape varieties: Cabernet sauvignon, Chardonnay, Chenin blanc, Johannisberg riesling, Petit syrah, Pinot noir and Zinfandel. Also buys in grapes. *see* Dutton Vineyard.

Burggarten (Aus) a vineyard site on the banks of the River Danube situated in the Wachau region, Niederösterreich.

Burggarten (Ger) vineyard (Anb): Ahr. (Ber): Walporzheim/Ahrtal. (Gro): Klosterberg. (Vil): Dernau.

B

Burggarten (Ger) vineyard (Anb): Ahr. (Ber): Walporzheim/Ahrtal. (Gro): Klosterberg. (Vil): Heimersheim.

Burggarten (Ger) vineyard (Anb): Pfalz. (Ber): Mittelhaardt-Deutsche Weinstrasse. (Gro): Grafenstück. (Vil): Bockenheim.

Burggraf (Ger) vineyard (Anb): Baden. (Ber): Badische Bergstrasse/Kraichgau. (Gro): Mannaberg. (Vil): Rauenberg.

Burggraf (Ger) vineyard (Anb): Mosel-Saar-Ruwer. (Ber): Zell/Mosel. (Gro): Grasfchaft. (Vil): Alf.

Burggräfler (Aus) a term used in the Südtirol region of Italy. Known as Burgravio in Italy. Specification given to a wine obtained in the land of the former country of Tyrol.

Burg Gutenfels (Ger) vineyard (Anb): Mittelrhein. (Ber): Rheinburgengau. (Gro): Herrenberg. (Vil): Kaub.

Burghalde (Ger) vineyard (Anb): Württemberg. (Ber): Remstal-Stuttgart. (Gro): Sonnenbühl. (Vil): Weinstadt (ortsteil Beutelsbach).

Burghalde (Ger) vineyard (Anb): Württemberg. (Ber): Remstal-Stuttgart. (Gro): Sonnenbühl. (Vil): Weinstadt (ortsteil Schnait i.R.).

Burg Hammerstein (Ger) grosslagen (Anb): Mittelrhein. (Ber): Rheinburgengau. (Vils): Bad Hönningen, Dattenberg, Hammerstein, Kasbach, Leubsdorf, Leutesdorf, Linz, Rheinbrohl, Unkel.

Burghers Post (S.Afr) the label for red wine (Shiraz) produced by the Cloof winery, Darling, Western Cape.

Burg Katz (Ger) vineyard (Anb): Mittelrhein. (Ber): Rheinburgengau. (Gro): Loreleyfelsen. (Vil): St. Goarshausen.

Burglay (Ger) vineyard (Anb): Mosel-Saar-Ruwer. (Ber): Bernkastel. (Gro): Michelsberg. (Vil): Minheim.

Burglay (Ger) vineyard (Anb): Mosel-Saar-Ruwer. (Ber): Bernkastel. (Gro): Nacktarsch. (Vil): Kröv.

Burg Layen (Ger) village (Anb): Nahe. (Ber): Kreuznach. (Gro): Schlosskapelle. (Vins): Hölle, Johannisberg, Rothenberg, Schlossberg.

Burglay-Felsen (Ger) vineyard (Anb): Mosel-Saar-Ruwer. (Ber): Zell/Mosel. (Gro): Schwarze Katz. (Vil): Zell.

Burg Lichteneck (Ger) grosslagen (Anb): Baden. (Ber): Breisgau. (Vils): Altdorf, Bleichheim, Bombach, Broggingen, Ettenheim, Hecklingen, Heimbach, Herbolzheim, Kenzingen, Köndringen, Malterdingen, Mundingen, Nordweil, Ringsheim, Tutschfelden, Wagenstadt.

Burgmauer (Ger) vineyard (Anb): Mosel-Saar-Ruwer. (Ber): Bernkastel. (Gro): Probstberg. (Vil): Schweich.

Burg Maus (Ger) vineyard (Anb): Mittelrhein. (Ber): Rheinburgengau. (Gro): Loreleyfelsen. (Vil): St. Goarshausen.

Burg Neuenfels (Ger) grosslagen (Anb): Baden. (Ber): Markgräflerland. (Vils): Auggen, Bad Bellingen, Badenweiler, Ballrechten-Dottingen, Britzingen, Britzingen (ortsteil Dattingen), Feldberg, Hügelheim, Laufen, Liel, Lipburg,

Mauchen, Müllheim, Niedereggenen, Niederweiler, Obereggenen, Schliengen, Steinenstadt, Sulzburg, Zunzingen.

Burgomer Burgundec (Euro) a red wine from the Spätburgunder grape, made in the Kosovo Pilje vineyard in south Serbia.

Burgoyne and Company (Austr) a noted old-established wine exporting firm *circa* 1870 of Australia.

Burg-Quelle (Ger) a natural spring mineral water from Plaidt RP.

Burg Ravensburger Dicker Franz (Ger) vineyard (Anb): Baden. (Ber): Badische Bergstrasse/Kraichgau. (Gro): Stiftsberg. (Vil): Sulzfeld.

Burg Ravensburger Husarenkappe (Ger) vineyard (Anb): Baden. (Ber): Badische Bergstrasse/Kraichgau. (Gro): Stiftsberg. (Vil): Sulzfeld.

Burg Ravensburger Löchle (Ger) vineyard (Anb): Baden. (Ber): Badische Bergstrasse/Kraichgau. (Gro): Stiftsberg. (Vil): Sulzfeld.

Burgravio (It) *see* Burggräfler.

Burg Rheinfels (Ger) grosslagen (Anb): Mittelrhein. (Ber): Rheinburgengau. (Vil): St. Goar-Werlau.

Burg Rodenstein (Ger) grosslagen (Anb): Rheinhessen. (Ber): Wonnegau. (Vils): Bermersheim/Worms, Flörsheim-Dalsheim, Mörstadt, Ober-Flörsheim.

Burgsponheim (Ger) village (Anb): Nahe. (Ber): Schloss Böckelheim. (Gro): Rosengarten. (Vins): Höllenpfad, Pfaffenberg, Schlossberg.

Bürgstadt (Ger) village (Anb): Franken. (Ber): Mainviereck. (Gro): Not yet assigned. (Vins): Centgrafenberg, Mainhölle.

Burgstall (Aus) a vineyard site on the banks of the River Danube situated in the Wachau region, Niederösterreich.

Burgstall (Ger) vineyard (Anb): Baden. (Ber): Bodensee. (Gro): Sonnenufer. (Vil): Hagnau.

Burgstall (Ger) vineyard (Anb): Baden. (Ber): Bodensee. (Gro): Sonnenufer. (Vil): Immenstaad.

Burgstall (Ger) vineyard (Anb): Baden. (Ber): Bodensee. (Gro): Sonnenufer. (Vil): Kippenhausen.

Burgstall (Ger) vineyard (Anb): Baden. (Ber): Bodensee. (Gro): Sonnenufer. (Vil): Markdorf.

Burgstall (Ger) vineyard (Anb): Württemberg. (Ber): Kocher-Jagst-Tauber. (Gro): Kocherberg. (Vil): Criesbach.

Burgstall (Ger) vineyard (Anb): Württemberg. (Ber): Kocher-Jagst-Tauber. (Gro): Kocherberg. (Vil): Niedernhall.

Burgu (Tur) a corkscrew. *See also* Tirbuson.

Burguet [Alain] (Fr) a négociant-éleveur based at Gevrey-Chambertin, Côte d'Or, Burgundy.

Burgundac Bijeli (Ser) the name given to the Chardonnay grape that is grown in Vojvodina and Slavonia.

Burgundac Crni (Ser) a red grape variety grown in Banat, Serbia. Also known as Pinot noir.

Burgundec (Ser) a full-bodied red wine produced in Serbia.

Burgunder (Fr) the name for the Pinot noir grape in Alsace. Also known as the Spätburgunder and Frühburgunder.

B

Burgundi (Hun) the Hungarian name for the Pinot noir.

Burgundii (Euro) a fifth century kingdom of which present day Burgundy was part.

Burgundy (Fr) the famous wine region of east-central France (100kms south of Paris). Divided into 5 areas: Chablis, Côte de Nuits, Côte de Beaune, Chalonnaise, Mâconnais and Beaujolais. *See also* Côte d'Or. Produces 60% white wine and 40% red wine. Main grape varieties: Chardonnay, Gamay au jus blanc and Pinot noir. Average wine production 190–195 million bottles. *see* Bureau Interprofessionnel des Vins de Bourgogne. Website: http://www.vins-bourgogne.fr

Burgundy (USA) the name given to the Zinfandel grape in California in the middle of the twentieth century.

Burgundy (USA) *see* California Burgundy.

Burgundy Basket (USA) wine bottle cradle.

Burgundy Bishop (Cktl) 1 measure dark rum, juice ¼ lemon, 1 teaspoon powdered sugar. Shake over ice, strain into an ice-filled highball glass. Top with red Burgundy and decorate with fruit in season.

Burgundy Cask (Fr) a wine cask of 114 litres capacity.

Burgundy Cobbler (Cktl) 1 teaspoon gomme syrup, 4 dashes orange Curaçao, red Burgundy. Fill an ice-filled highball glass ⅔ with wine. Add liqueur and syrup, stir, decorate with fresh fruit and a mint sprig.

Burgundy Cocktail (Cktl) ¾ measure red Burgundy, ¼ measure Cognac, 2 dashes maraschino. Stir over ice, strain into a cocktail glass. Add slice of lemon and a cherry.

Burgundy Cup (Punch) 1 bottle Burgundy (red), 60mls (½ gill) brandy, 60mls (½ gill) maraschino, 30mls (¼ gill) brown Curaçao, 1 bottle soda water, 3 dashes Bénédictine. Stir all well together over ice in punch-bowl. Serve in large tumbler with slices of orange and lemon and fresh fruit.

Burgundy Mixture (Fr) **Copper sulphate** and **Calcium carbonate** (washing soda) used for spraying against pests and diseases.

Burgundy Mull (Punch) 1 bottle Burgundy (red), 1 wine-glass dry Sherry, 50mls (2fl.ozs) brandy, ½ bottle Blackcurrant cordial, sugar to taste, juice 3 lemons, 1.1 ltrs. (1quart) water, ground ginger. Mix altogether, heat, strain and add sliced lemons. Serve in cups.

Burgundy Punch (Punch) 450mls (¾ pint) Burgundy (red), 450mls (¾ pint) iced water, 35mls (1½ fl.ozs) Port, juice ½ lemon, 10mls (½ fl.oz) gomme syrup, 25mls (1fl.oz) orange juice. Stir altogether, decorate with orange and lemon slices.

Burgwallbronn (Ger) a natural spring mineral water from Duisburg-Walsum, NW.

Burg Warsberg (Ger) vineyard (Anb): Mosel-Saar-Ruwer. (Ber): Obermosel. (Gro): Gipfel. (Vil): Wincheringen.

Burgweg (Ger) grosslage (Anb): Franken. (Ber):

Steigerwald. (Vils): Iphofen, Markt Einersheim, Possenheim.

Burgweg (Ger) vineyard (Anb): Mosel-Saar-Ruwer. (Ber): Bernkastel. (Gro): Schwarzlay. (Vil): Traben-Trarbach.

Burgweg (Ger) grosslagen (Anb): Nahe. (Ber): Schloss Böckelheim. (Vils): Altenbamberg, Bad Münster a. St-Ebernburg, Duchroth, Niederhausen an der Nahe, Norheim, Oberhausen an der Nahe, Schlossböckelheim, Traisen, Waldböckelheim.

Burgweg (Ger) grosslagen (Anb): Rheingau. (Ber): Johannisberg. (Vils): Assmannshausen-Aulhausen, Geisenheim, Lorch, Lorchhausen, Rüdesheim.

Burgweg (Ger) vineyard (Anb): Rheinhessen. (Ber): Nierstein. (Gro): Sankt Alban. (Vil): Bodenheim.

Burgweg (Ger) vineyard (Anb): Rheinhessen. (Ber): Wonnegau. (Gro): Liebfrauenberg. (Vil): Worms.

Burgweg (Ger) vineyard (Anb): Pfalz. (Ber): Mittelhaardt-Deutsche Weinstrasse. (Gro): Grafenstück. (Vil): Kindenheim.

Burgweg (Ger) vineyard (Anb): Pfalz. (Ber): Mittelhaardt-Deutsche Weinstrasse. (Gro): Rosenbühl. (Vil): Lambsheim.

Burgweg (Ger) vineyard (Anb): Pfalz. (Ber): Mittelhaardt-Deutsche Weinstrasse. (Gro): Rosenbühl. (Vil): Weisenheim/Sand.

Burgweg (Ger) vineyard (Anb): Pfalz. (Ber): Mittelhaardt-Deutsche Weinstrasse. (Gro): Schwarzerde. (Vil): Grosskarlbach.

Burg Wildeck (Ger) vineyard (Anb): Württemberg. (Ber): Württembergisch Unterland. (Gro): Schozachtal. (Vil): Abstatt.

Burg Windeck Kastanienhalde (Ger) vineyard (Anb): Baden. (Ber): Ortenau. (Gro): Schloss Rodeck. (Vil): Bühl (ortsteil Neusatz).

Burgwingert (Ger) vineyard (Anb): Baden. (Ber): Badische Bergstrasse/Kraichgau. (Gro): Mannaberg. (Vil): Bruchsal (stadtteil Obergrombach).

Burgwingert (Ger) vineyard (Anb): Baden. (Ber): Badische Bergstrasse/Kraichgau. (Gro): Mannaberg. (Vil): Helmsheim.

Burg Zähringen (Ger) grosslagen (Anb): Baden. (Ber): Breisgau. (Vils): Buchholz, Denzlingen, Emmendingen (ortsteil Hockburg), Freiburg i.Br. (ortsteil Lehen), Glottertal, Heuweiler, Sexau, Wildtal.

Burie (Fr) a commune in the Charente-Maritime département whose grapes are classed Borderies (Cognac).

Burignon (Switz) a white wine from the Vaud canton of Chardonnes.

Buring [Leo] (Austr) a winery. (Add): Para Road, Tanunda, Barossa Valley, South Australia. Owned by Lindeman. Grapes include Cabernet sauvignon, Chardonnay, Pinot noir, Shiraz.

Burkes Brewery (Eng) a public house brewery at the Lion in Croydon, Surrey. Produces cask-conditioned Original 1034 O.G. and Best Bitter 1042 O.G.

Burke's Irish Brigade (Eng) a bottled stout brewed by Greenhall Whitley, Warrington (for export).

Burkheim (Ger) village (Anb): Baden. (Ber):

Kaiserstuhl-Tuniberg. (Gro): Vulkanfelsen. (Vins): Feuerberg, Schlossgarten.

Burkittsville Vineyards (USA) a small winery based in Burkittsville, Maryland. Produces hybrid wines.

Bürklin-Wolf (Ger) a family estate of the Palatinate (Pfalz).

Burley Fox (Austr) a winery based in New South Wales. Grape varieties: Cabernet sauvignon, Shiraz.

Burlington Bertie (Eng) a 3.3% alc by vol. ale brewed by Hobdens Wessex Brewery, Wiltshire.

Burma (Asia) a hardy variety of the Assam tea bush.

Burmarrad (Euro) a wine-producing area on the island of Malta.

Burmester (Port) a vintage Port shipper. Vintages: 1873, 1878, 1887, 1890, 1896, 1900, 1904, 1908, 1912, 1920, 1922, 1927, 1931, 1935, 1937, 1940, 1943, 1945, 1948, 1954, 1955, 1958, 1960, 1963, 1977, 1980, 1984, 1985, 1989, 1991, 1992, 1994, 1997.

Burn (Scot) the name given to the streams in the Scottish Highlands of whose clear waters are often used to make Scotch whisky.

Burn (Eng) an energy drink sold in black cans that contains taurine, guarana, glucronalactone. Produced by CCT.

Burnay Sale (Eng) the largest auction ever held of wines. 10000 pipes of Port. (565000 dozen bottles). Held for 4 days in May 1892 at Christies.

Burnbrae (Austr) a winery based in Mudgee, New South Wales.

Burnbrae Spring (Scot) a natural spring mineral water from Lennoxtown, Glasgow.

Burnett Gin (Eng) a brand of gin sold under the White Satin label. Part of Seagram. 40% alc by vol.

Burnins [Les] (Fr) a vineyard in the A.C. commune of Montagny, Côte Chalonnaise, Burgundy.

Burns Ale (Scot) a 4.7% alc by vol. cask or bottled-conditioned ale brewed by Caledonian Brewing Cº. Ltd. in Edinburgh for Burns night.

Burns Ale (Scot) a keg special ale 1036 O.G. brewed by Drybrough's Brewery, Edinburgh. Known as Burn's Scottish Ale if canned.

Burnsall Classic (Eng) a 4% alc by vol. bitter ale brewed by Briscoe's in Otley, West Yorkshire.

Burn's Scottish Ale (Scot) see Burns Ale.

Burn Stewart Distillers Ltd (Scot) a distillery (established 1988). (Add): 8 Milton Road, College Milton North, East Kilbride, Glasgow, Lanarkshire C74 5BU. Produces a range of sprits and liqueurs. Website: http://www.burnstewartdistillers.com 'E'mail: enquiries@burnstewartdistillers.com

Burnt Ale (W.Ind) an alternative name for Dunder.

Burntisland Brewery (Scot) a brewery based in Fife. Brews: Alexander's Downfall.

Burnt Spur (N.Z) a vineyard based in the Martinborough region of the North Island.

Burnt Wine (Eng) brandy.

Burntwood Bitter (Eng) a 4% alc by vol. bitter beer brewed by the Mighty Oak Brewing Cº. Ltd., Essex.

Buronator (Ger) a dark bock bier brewed by the Rosenbrauerei at Kaufbeuren, Western Germany.

Buronga Growers (Austr) a co-operative winery based in south-eastern Australia. Grape varieties include: Chardonnay, Shiraz, Verdelho. Labels include: Ashcroft.

Burot (Fr) the local Burgundy name for the white Pinot gris. See also Beurot.

Burrington Brewery (Eng) a brewery (established 2003). (Add): Homelands Business Centre, Burrington, Umberleigh, Devon EX37 9JJ. Brews: Alchemy 4.2% alc by vol., Azza Newt 5.2% alc by vol., Golden Newt-Rition 5.2% alc by vol., Newt'N'Wriggly 4.6% alc by vol., Ruby Newt 3.6% alc by vol., Tippled Newt 3.8% alc by vol. Website: http://www.burringtonbrewery.co.uk 'E'mail: info@burringtonbrewery.co.uk

Burrough's (Eng) a company that produces a range of 'mixed doubles' drinks. See also Beefeater Dry Gin.

Burrow Hill (Eng) bottle-fermented sparkling cider made in Somerset from Stoke Red apples.

Burrweiler (Ger) village (Anb): Pfalz. (Ber): Südliche Weinstrasse. (Gro): Bischofskreuz. (Vins): Altenforst, St. Annaberg, Schäwer, Schlossgarten.

Bursins (Switz) a wine-producing area in the La Côte district on the west bank of Lake Geneva.

Burslem Brewery (Eng) a subsidiary company of Ansell's Brewery.

Bursley Bitter (Eng) a cask-conditioned bitter 1040 O.G. brewed by the Five Towns Brewery, Stoke-on-Trent.

Burt Brewery (Eng) a brewery based at Ventnor, Isle of Wight. Produces cask-conditioned LB. 1030 O.G. and a variety of other beers.

Burth Brauerei (Switz) a brewery based in Liechtenstein. Part of the Sibra Group (Cardinal) Breweries.

Burton Ale (Eng) a bottled ale 1031 O.G. brewed by Greene King Brewery, eastern England.

Burton Ale (Eng) a cask-conditioned bitter 1047.5 O.G. brewed by Ind Coope Brewery, Burton-on-Trent.

Burton Ale (Eng) the general name given to beers brewed in the town of Burton-on-Trent.

Burton Bitter (Eng) a cask-conditioned bitter 1037 O.G. brewed by the Marston's Brewery, Burton-on-Trent. Also a keg version.

Burton Brewery (Eng) the Allied Breweries major brewery based at Burton-on-Trent.

Burton Bridge Brewery (Eng) a brewery (established 1982). (Add): 24 Bridge Street, Burton-on-Trent, Staffordshire DE14 1SY. Produces: cask-conditioned Bridge Bitter 4.2% alc by vol (1042 O.G.)., Burton Festival Ale 5.5% alc by vol (1055 O.G.), Burton Porter 4.5% alc by vol. (1045 O.G.)., Golden Delicious 3.8% alc by vol., Old Expensive 1065 O.G. Stairway to Heaven 5% alc by vol., Thomas Sykes Old Ale 10% alc by vol., Tickle Brain., Top Dog Stout 5% alc by vol., XL Bitter 4% alc by vol. 'E'mail: bbb@burtonbridgebrewery@fsnet.co.uk

Burtonisation (Eng) the process of Burtonising.

Burtonising (Eng) the process of adding chemicals to the brewing liquor to obtain an identical composition to true Burton liquor. Also called Burtonisation. see Burton-on-Trent.

Burton Mild (Eng) a mild beer 1033 O.G. brewed by Everards Burton Brewery.

Burton-on-Trent (Eng) the major brewing centre in England. Established because its water has a high mineral content. Ideal for the British beers. Based in Staffordshire.

Burton Porter (Eng) see Burton Bridge Brewery.

Burton Spring (Eng) a pale ale 6.2% alc by vol. (originally brewed in 1913). Re-introduced in 1995 by Marston's, Burton-on-Trent. Part of their Head Brewers Choice range.

Burton Strong Pale Ale (Eng) a 6.2% alc by vol. bottled S.P.A. brewed by Marston, Thompson & Evershed Brewery, Burton-on-Trent.

Burton Union System (Eng) a system developed in the nineteenth century of fermentation where CO_2 created by the fermentation forces liquid and yeast out of the oak casks, through swan-neck pipes into tilted troughs (barm trays) which returns the liquid to the brew but retains the yeast. Still used by the Marstons Brewery in Burton-on-Trent. see Held in Union and Union Room.

Burton Union Bottom Taps (Eng) a cask-conditioned ale from Marston's Head Brewers' Choice.

Burtonwood Brewery (Eng) a large brewery based at Bold Lane, Burtonwood, Warrington, Cheshire. Produces many styles of beer including a cask-conditioned Mild 1032 O.G. and Top Hat 1047 O.G. Smooth Mild 3% alc by vol. Bitter Smooth 3.7% alc by vol.

Burt's Brewery (Eng) a small Isle of Wight brewery at Ventnor. Brews cask-conditioned beers. LB 1030 O.G. Dark Mild 1030 O.G. VPA 1040 O.G. Needles Bitter 1049 O.G. Also Lighthouse, Old Vectis Venum, Yachtsman.

Buruk (Tur) denotes an acidic, sour wine.

Burundi Coffee (Afr) a noted Arabica coffee produced in central Africa. Has good acidity and body.

Busch (USA) a Bavarian beer brewed by Anheuser-Busch.

Buschenberg (Aus) a vineyard site on the banks of the River Danube situated in the Wachau region, Niederösterreich.

Buschenschank (Aus) a Viennese tavern owner displaying a bunch of fir-twigs on the wall of his tavern to show that his Heurige are on sale. see Heurige and Heurigen.

Buschenschanken (Aus) are Austrian wine (heurigen) inns where a bunch of fir tree branches are hung outside to tell travellers that the in is a heurigen.

Busen (Hol) an old Dutch word for heavy drinking.

Busera (Afr) a rough beer made from millet and honey.

Bush (Eng) a 3.5% alc by vol. ale from the Furze and Firkin, Streatham High Road, London.

Bush Beer (Bel) a strong, copper-coloured ale 9.5%–10% alc by vol. brewed by the Dubuisson Brasserie near Tournai.

Bushcreek Vineyards (USA) a winery based in Peebles, Ohio. Produces French-American hybrid and native wines.

Bushel Basket (Eng) the hop-picking basket used by the bushler to take the hops from the picker's crib into the large sacks.

Bushie (S.Am) the local name for 'moonshine' in Guyana.

Bushler (Eng) a man who fills the large sacks with the hops from the hop picker's cribs with his bushel basket.

Bushman's Creek (S.Afr) the label for a range of wines produced by the Cru Wines marketing company, Western Cape.

Bushmills Malt (Ire) a single malt Irish whiskey produced by the Bushmills Distillery. 10 years old. 40% alc by vol. Also a 16 year old triple wood premium malt.

Bushmills Whiskey (Ire) a smokey-flavoured Irish whiskey. Named from Northern Ireland's oldest distillery. Part of Irish Distillers.

Bushmills White Label (Ire) a grain whiskey, also known as Red Bush, produced by Bushmills Distillery.

Bushranger Cocktail (Cktl) 40mls (⅓ gill) dark rum, 20mls (⅙ gill) Dubonnet, dash Angostura. Stir over ice and strain into a cocktail glass.

Bush System (Eng) a term that describes a spur pruning system of vine-training, no wires are usually used.

Bush Tea (Afr) a beverage made from the dried beans of the shrub family Cyclopia in southern Africa.

Bushvine (S.Afr) the label for a white wine (Chenin blanc) produced by the Hazendal winery, Stellenbosch, Western Cape.

Bush Vine (S.Afr) the label for a white wine (Sauvignon blanc) produced by the Darling Cellars winery, Swartland.

Bush Vines (S.Afr) the label for a range of red wines produced by the Cloof winery, Darling, Western Cape.

Bushys (I.O.M) the name for the Mount Murray Brewery, Isle of Man.

Bushys Bitter (I.O.M) a 3.8% alc by vol. bitter beer brewed by the Mount Murray Brewery, Isle of Man.

Business as Usual (Eng) a 4.4% alc by vol. ale brewed by The Derby Brewing C° Ltd., Derbyshire.

Busslay (Ger) vineyard (Anb): Mosel-Saar-Ruwer. (Ber): Bernkastel. (Gro): Schwarzlay. (Vil): Erden.

Bus Ticket (S.Afr) the nickname for the wine certificate on South African wine bottles. The size of a postage stamp it gave authenticity to the wines contents with a series of coloured bands. **Blue**: Wine's origin, **Red**: Vintage, **Green**: Grape variety. If coloured gold then of superior quality. Now no longer used.

Butanoic Acid (Eng) C_3H_7COOH a volatile acid found in wine.

Butcher (Austr) the name used in South Australia for a 6fl.oz (150mls) glass.

Butcombe Bitter (Eng) a 4% alc. by vol (1039 O.G.). bitter ale 4% alc by vol. brewed by Butcombe Brewery, Avon.

Butcombe Blonde (Eng) a 4.3% alc by vol. beer brewed by the Butcombe Brewery, Avon.

Butcombe Brewery (Eng) a brewery (established 1978) (Add): Cox's Green, Wrington, Bristol, Avon BS40 5PA. Produces: Brunel 200 IPA 5% alc by vol., cask-conditioned Butcombe Bitter 4% alc by vol (1039 O.G), Butcombe Blond 4.3% alc by vol., Butcombe Golden Ale 4.7% alc by vol. Website: http://wwwbutcombe.com 'E'mail: guy@butcombe.com

Butcombe Gold (Eng) an ale 4.7% alc by vol. brewed by the Butcombe Brewery, Avon.

Butenwall-Quelle (Ger) a natural spring mineral water from Bocholt, NW.

Buthelezi Wines (S.Afr) a winery (established 2002) based in Cape Town. Grape varieties include: Syrah. Labels: Tutuka, W.O.

Butiliram (Bul) to bottle.

Butler (Eng) the nineteenth century servant who looked after the wine cellar.

Butler Nephew (Port) vintage Port shippers. Vintages: 1922, 1924, 1927, 1934, 1942, 1945, 1947, 1948, 1955, 1957, 1958, 1960, 1975.

Butlers Brewery (Eng) a brewery (established 2003). (Add): 23, Grimmer Way, Woodcote, Reading, Berkshire RG8 0SN. Brews: Bob 3.6% alc by vol., Old Granary Bitter 4.2% alc by vol., Oxfordshire Bitter 3.7% alc by vol., Red Fox 4% alc by vol., Skylark 4% alc by vol., Swift 4% alc by vol. 'E'mail: butlerbrew@aol.com

Butler's Friend (Eng) a corkscrew that works on the principle of two prongs that slip down each side of the cork between it and the bottle neck and ease the cork out without damage. So called because the dishonest butler would consume the good contents of the bottle and replace it with inferior wine, then replace the undamaged cork without the owners' knowledge.

Buton (It) a producer of elixir di China (a style of bitter apéritif) and liqueurs.

Butser Bitter (Eng) a 3.4% alc by vol. seasonal ale brewed by Gale's Brewery, Horndean, Hampshire.

Butt (Eng) two hogsheads capacity.

Butt (Sp) a Sherry cask with a capacity of 108 gallons (490 litres). 132 U.S. gallons.

Butt (USA) a cask measuring 126 US gallons.

Buttafuoco (It) a sweet, red sparkling wine made from the Barbera grape (plus others) in Lombardy. Sold under the D.O.C. Oltrepo Pavese.

Buttage (Fr) a method by which the soil in the vineyard is ploughed up to the vine trunk in winter as a precaution against frost.

Butte (Hun) a measure used in Tokaji-Hegyalja (13.6 litres).

Butteaux (Fr) an A.C. Premier Cru Chablis, often reclassified as the Premier Cru Montmains.

Butte County (USA) a small wine producing county in Sacramento Valley, California.

Butte Creek Winery (USA) a small winery based in Butte County. Was closed in 1976.

Bütten (Ger) the name given to the grape pickers hod in the Rheingau.

Buttered Coffee (Eng) put hot coffee in glass, add 1 measure of brandy, sugar to taste. Stir, add pat of butter on top and a stick of cinnamon to stir.

Buttered Rum (Eng) *see* Hot Buttered Rum.

Butterfly (Cktl) ⅖ measure gin, ³⁄₁₀ measure dry vermouth, ⅕ measure blue Curaçao, ⅕ measure Poire Williams. Shake over ice, strain into a flute, decorate with a twist of lemon and orange.

Butterknowle Bitter (Eng) a 1036 O.G. hoppy bitter ale, amber in colour with a malty taste from Butterknowle Brewery in County Durham.

Butterknowle Brewery (Eng) a brewery based at Lynesack, near Bishop Auckland, County Durham. Brews Black Diamond Porter 4.8% alc by vol. Butterknowle Bitter 3.6% alc by vol. Banner 4% alc by vol. Conciliation 4.2% alc by vol. Forever Amber 4% alc by vol. High Force 6.2% alc by vol. Old Ebeneezer 8% alc by vol. Old Glory 4.5% alc by vol. Lynesack Porter 5% alc by vol. Silver Lining 4% alc by vol. West Auckland Mild 3.3% alc by vol. Festival Stout. Brewery now at Castle Eden, County Durham.

Buttermilch (Aus)(Ger) buttermilk.

Buttermilk (Eng) the liquid left after the butter has been removed, has a sour taste. (Aus) = buttermilch, (Fr) = babeurre, (Ger) = buttermilch, (Hol) = karnemelk, (Ire) = blálhach, (Port) = soro de leite, (Tur) = ayran, (Wal) = enwyn.

Buttig (Hun) *see* Butte.

Buttis (Lat) cask.

Button Hook (Cktl) ¼ measure Pernod, ¼ measure Cognac, ¼ measure (white) crème de menthe, ¼ measure apricot brandy. Shake over iceand strain into a cocktail glass.

Butts Brewery (Eng) a brewery (established 1994). (Add): Unit 6a, Northfield Farm, Wantage Road, Great Shefford, Hungerford, Berkshire RG17 7BY. Brews: Barbus Barbus 4.6% alc by vol., Black guard Porter 4.5% alc by vol., Butts Traditional 4% alc by vol., Golden Brown 5% alc by vol., Jester 3.5% alc by vol., Le Butt Biére 5% alc by vol. Website: http://www.buttsbrewery.com 'E'mail: sales@buttsbrewery.com

Butts Traditional (Eng) a 4% alc by vol. bitter beer brewed by the Butts Brewery Ltd., Berkshire.

Butty Bach (Eng) a 4.5% alc by vol. ale brewed by Wye Valley Brewery, Herefordshire. Brewed specially for the Cardiff festival.

Butyl (Eng) C_4H_9OH. a higher alcohol, part of the fusel oils.

Butylene Glycol (Eng) a glycerine-related compound found in wines in small quantities.

Butyrate Acid (Eng) *see* Cheesy.

Butyric Acid (Eng) C_3H_7COOH. an acid found in spirits and in wines in small quantities.

Buur (Den) a strong beer brewed by the Thor Brewery.

Buvable (Fr) drinkable.

Buvee (Fr) old word for drinking.

Buxentinum (It) a red wine produced in south-western Italy in Roman times.

Buxeuil (Fr) a Cru Champagne village in the Canton de l'Aube. District: Château Thierry.

Buxton (Eng) a still and sparkling natural spring mineral water from St. Ann Spring, Buxton, Derbyshire (Peak District). Mineral contents (milligrammes per litre): Sodium 24mg/l, Calcium 55mg/l, Magnesium 19mg/l, Potassium 1mg/l, Bicarbonates 248mg/l, Chlorides 37mg/l, Sulphates 13mg/l, Nitrates <0.1mg/l. pH 7.4

Buxy (Fr) a Premier Cru vineyard and town of the Côte Chalonnaise in Burgundy in the commune of Montagny.

Buyers Own Bottling (Eng) *abbr*: B.O.B. alternative wording for Buyers Own Brand where the product takes the name of the Buyer (not the producer).

Buyers Own Brand (Eng) *see* B.O.B.

Buza (Egy) an alcoholic beverage distilled from fermented grapes.

Buzau (Rum) a Wallachia wine-producing district.

Buzbag (Tur) a rich, red, dry wine made from the Boguzkere grape.

Buzet (Fr) an A.C. region in the south-west of the country produces fine, full-bodied red wines.

Buzias (Rum) a natural spring mineral water from buzias City, Transylvania.

Buzias (Rum) a wine-producing area, a part of the Banat Vineyard.

Buzón (Sp) bung.

Buzz (Eng) a term meaning '*Send the bottle round*' refers to the passing of the Port.

Buzz (Eng) the label of a 5% alc by vol. lager brewed with Mexican honey by Vaux.

Buzzards Bay (USA) a brewery. (Add): 98 Horseneck Road, Westport, MA02790. Brews beers and lager. Website: http://www.buzzardsbrew.com 'E'mail: tim.coleman@buzzardsbrew.com

Buzzer Cocktail (Cktl) ¼ measure dry gin, ¼ measure sweet vermouth, 4 dashes crème de menthe, 2 dashes Angostura. Shake over ice, strain into a cocktail glass. Add a cherry.

Buzzetto (It) an alternative name for the Trebbiano toscano grape.

B.V. (USA) *abbr*: **B**eaulieu **V**ineyards, appears on their labels.

B.V.A. (Eng) *abbr*: **B**irch **V**ale **A**le 1037 O.G. brewed by the Winkle's Brewery, North Derbyshire.

BVB (Eng) a 4.6% alc by vol. ale brewed by The Branscombe Vale Brewery, Devon.

B.V.C. (Eng) *abbr*: **B**ulgarian **V**intners **C**ompany Ltd. (Add): Bridge Wharf, 156 Caledonian Road, London N1 9RD. Major Bulgarian wine importers to the U.K.

B.V.D. Cocktail (Cktl) ⅓ measure Bacardi rum, ⅓ measure dry vermouth, ⅓ measure dry gin. Shake over ice and strain into a cocktail glass.

BWC Wines (S.Afr) a winery (established 1997) based in Stellenbosch, Western Cape. (Add): 2, Blaauwklippen Meent, Stellenbosch. Grape varieties: Cabernet sauvignon, Merlot, Pinot noir, Sauvignon blanc, Syrah. Myraid, Wholeberry. Website: http://www.bwcwines.co.za

B.Y.B. (Eng) *abbr*: **B**entley's **Y**orkshire **B**itter. 1033 O.G. Brewed by the Whitbread in Sheffield.

Bybline (Egy) a sweet white wine produced in Phoencia.

Bylines (Austr) a red wine produced from 25% Cabernet sauvignon & 75% Shiraz by The Pomegranate Wine Company, South Australia.

Bynum Winery (USA) a winery based on the west side of the Russian River, Sonoma County, California. Grape varieties: Cabernet sauvignon, Chardonnay, Fumé blanc, Gewürztraminer, Pinot noir and Zinfandel.

B.Y.O. (Austr) *abbr*: *see* **B**ring **Y**our **O**wn.

Byrd Vineyards (USA) a small winery based in Myersville, Maryland. 7ha. Grape varieties: Cabernet sauvignon, Chardonnay, Gewürztraminer and Sauvignon blanc. Produces vinifera and also hybrid wines.

Byron Vineyard (USA) a vineyard. (Add): Santa Maria Valley, Santa Barbara County, California. Grape varieties: Chardonnay, Pinot noir.

Byrrh (Fr) a bitter apéritif wine, contains quinine, Peruvian bark, oils and herbs. 17% alc by vol. Produced by Violet Frères.

Byrrh-Cassis Cocktail (Cktl) 25mls (1fl.oz) Byrrh, 3 dashes crème de cassis. Stir together in an ice-filled old-fashioned glass.

Byrrh-Citron (Cktl) 60mls (½ gill) Byrrh, 20mls (⅙ gill) sirop de citron, Soda water. Stir over ice, strain into tall glass with ice. Top with soda water.

Byrrh Cocktail [1] (Cktl) 1 measure Byrrh, 1 measure dry gin. Shake well with ice, strain into a cocktail glass.

Byrrh Cocktail [2] (Cktl) ⅓ measure Byrrh, ⅓ measure dry vermouth, ⅓ measure rye whiskey. Stir with ice, strain into cocktail glass.

Byrsa (Afr) a noted fortified wine-producing area in Tunisia.

Bytca Brewery (Czec) a brewery based in Bytca in eastern Czec.

By the Neck (Eng) a slang term for a bottle of beer with the crown cork removed (not served in a glass).

Byung (Kor) bottle.

Byzantine Coffee (Eng) another name for Turkish coffee.

Byzantis (Gre) the name of a red wine from the island of Zakinthos near Peloponnese.

C

C2 (Eng) a Carling lager low alcohol beer (2% alc by vol) introduced by Coors Brewers in 2005.

Caapmans (S.Afr) the label for a red wine (Cabernet sauvignon and Merlot blend) produced by the Durbanville Hills winery, Durbanville, Western Cape.

Cab (Isr) an old hebrew measure, equal to ½ gallon, 2.3 litres. *See also* Kab.

Cabaceo (Sp) a blend of wine.

Caballero (Sp) a Sherry and brandy producer based in Puerto de Santa Maria. Sherries include Benito, Don Guisa (a Fino) and Gran Señor Choice Old Cream. Brandies include Chevalier, Decano, Sortilegio (Solera Reservas), Gran Señor (Solera gran reserva). Also produces Ponche orange and brandy liqueur.

Caballero (Sp) a pale Amontillado Sherry produced by Gonzalez Byass in Jerez de la Frontera.

Caballero [Luis] (Sp) a noted Sherry producer based in Jerez, noted for Fino Pavon.

Caballero de la Cepa (Arg) the brand-name for red and white wines from the Bodegas Flitchman.

Cabana (W.Ind) the brand-name of a white rum.

Cabana Soft Drinks (Eng) a soft drinks manufacturer based in Preston Lancashire. Produces soft drinks and mixers (on draught) through franchise.

Cabardès (Fr) an A.C. red and rosé wine-producing district in the département of Aude, Languedoc-Roussillon, southern France. 800ha. Grape varieties: ⅔ Cot, Cabernet, Merlot, ⅓ Syrah, Grenache.

Cabaret (Ch.Isles) inn/public house.

Cabaret (Fr) a liqueur stand (decanter, glassware and tray) used for liqueur service. Also for a liqueur cabinet.

Caberat (Bra) the local spelling of the Cabernet sauvignon grape.

Caberet (Fr) tavern/public house or restaurant.

Caberet (Cktl) 40mls (⅓ gill) gin, 2 dashes Angostura, 1 dash Bénédictine, 2 dashes French vermouth. Stir over ice, strain into a cocktail glass. Top with a cherry.

Caberne (Bul) the name for the Cabernet sauvignon grape.

Cabernelle (Fr) an alternative name for the Carmenère grape variety. *See also* Bouton Blanc, Carmenelle, Carbouet, Grande Vidure, Grand Carmenet.

Cabernet (Fr) the famous, superb red wine grape from Bordeaux. Is related to the Cabernet sauvignon. *See also* Cabernet Franc.

Cabernet Boché (USA) a red wine produced by the Freemark Abbey winery in the Napa Valley, California.

Cabernet Brda (Slo) a light red wine.

Cabernet Breton (Fr) the Touraine (Loire) district name for the Cabernet franc grape. *See also* Breton.

Cabernet Cygne Blanc (Austr) a 'white' Cabernet sauvignon grape variety developed by the Dorham Mann Estate in Western Australia from a freak of nature. Also known as the Cygne Blanc.

Cabernet d'Anjou Rosé (Fr) an A.C. rosé wine produced in the Anjou-Saumur district of the Loire. Produced from the Cabernet sauvignon or Cabernet franc grapes. Is a perfumed, slightly sweet wine. Min. alc. content 10% by vol.

Cabernet del Trentino (It) a D.O.C. red wine produced in the Trentino region from Cabernet sauvignon and Cabernet franc grapes.

Cabernet de Piave Riserva (It) *see* Piave Cabernet.

Cabernet di Pramaggiore (It) a D.O.C. red wine produced in Veneto. Grape varieties: Cabernet franc 90% and Merlot 10%. If aged for 3 years and 12% alc by vol. then classed Riserva.

Cabernet Franc (Fr) a classic red grape (with a high tannin content) variety used mainly in the Graves, Saint-Émilion and Pomerol districts of Bordeaux, and also to a lesser degree in the Médoc. Produces wines that have a grassy, herbaceous (young), pencil shavings and ripe red berried fruits (strawberry/raspberry/redcurrant) aromas and flavours. Also known as the Bouchet, Bouchy, Breton, Cabernet, Cabernet gris and Véron. Produces wines with an aromatic bouquet. *See also* Cabernet Gris.

Cabernet Gris (Fr) the alternative name for the Cabernet franc red grape variety.

Cabernet Levodia (Rus) a dry red wine from the Crimea Peninsular.

Cabernet Rosé (Fr) an A.C. rosé wine from the Anjou-Saumur district of the Loire, made from the Cabernet franc grape. It replaces the Anjou Coteaux de la Loire Rosé de Cabernet.

Cabernet Rosé (USA) a rosé wine produced in California from the Cabernet sauvignon grape.

Cabernet Sauvignon (Fr) the classic black grape variety of the Médoc district of Bordeaux, gives tannin, colour and body to the wine. Most widely grown grape in the world. Produces wines with a blackcurrant, cedar, cigar box, lead pencil, tobacco, mint, dark chocolate, liquorice, truffles, olives aromas and flavours. Genetic fingerprinting at the University of California at Davis indicate it

C

was a cross between Cabernet franc and Sauvignon blanc in the seventeenth century. *see* Gros Bouchet.

Cabernet Sauvignon di Miralduolo (It) a red Vino da Tavola wine from the Cabernet sauvignon grape produced in central Italy.

Cabernet Severny (Rus) a red grape variety created in Rostov, Russia through pollination of *Galan* x *Vitus amurensis*.

Cabernet Toso (Arg) a Cabernet-based wine produced by the Toso Winery at San José.

Cabeza [En] (Sp) the name for the gobelet or head pruning method of vine training.

Cabezuela (Sp) the name given to a second sedimentation of musts.

Cabido (Port) a Dão wine produced by Real Companhía Vinícola do Norte de Portugal.

Cabinet (Ger) *see* Cabinett and Kabinett.

Cabinett (Ger) a word used to describe a special reserve wine one grade up from QmP. A natural wine with no added sugar and is estate-bottled. *See also* Kabinett.

Cabinett-Wein (USA) kabinett, a wine of a kabinett standard.

Cablegram Cooler (Cktl) into a large tumbler put 2 ice cubes, juice of ½ lemon, 90mls (¼ gill) rye whiskey, dash gomme syrup. Top up with ginger ale, stir gently and serve.

Cablegram Highball (Cktl) 40mls (⅓ gill) Bourbon whiskey, 1 teaspoon of powdered sugar, juice ½ lemon. Stir well over ice, strain into an ice-filled highball glass and top with ginger ale.

Cab Mac (Austr) a light, fresh wine made from the Cabernet sauvignon grape by macération carbonique fermentation.

Cabreiroa (Sp) a natural spring mineral water from Verin, Ourense, Galicia. Mineral contents (milligrammes per litre): Sodium 47.9mg/l, Calcium 4mg/l, Magnesium 2.1mg/l, Potassium 2.7mg/l, Bicarbonates 102.7mg/l, Chlorides 10.1mg/l, Sulphates 10.3mg/l, Fluorides 0.5mg/l, Nitrates 2.1mg/l, Silicates 18.2mg/l.

Cabreo Il Borgo (It) a Super Tuscan red wine produced by Fattoria de Nozzole in Tuscany from a blend of 30% Cabernet sauvignon and 70% Sangiovese grapes. Also produce Cabreo La Pietra Chardonnay (aged and fermented in oak).

Cabrida (Sp) the label for a red wine (Garnacha 100%) produced by the Capçanes wine co-operative, Montsant, Tarragona, Cataluña.

Cabrière Estate (S.Afr) a winery (established 1982) based in Franschhoek, Western Cape. 24ha. (Add): Clos Cabrière, Cabrière Street, P.O. Box 245, Franschhoek 7690. Grape varieties: Cabernet sauvignon, Chardonnay, Pinot noir, Sauvignon blanc. Labels: Arnim, Cuvée Belle Rose, Cuvée Reserve, Haut Cabrière, Pierre Jourdan. Website: http://www.cabriere.co.za

Cabrières (Fr) a commune in the Coteaux du Languedoc district of southern France. Produces A.C. rosé Clairette du Languedoc wine (of same name) only from Carignan and Cinsault (min. 45% max. 50%) grapes. 11% alc by vol.

Cabriolet (S.Afr) the label for a red wine (Cabernet franc, Cabernet sauvignon and Merlot blend) produced by the Blaauwklippen Agricultural Estate winery, Stellenbosch, Western Cape.

Cabrusina (It) a red grape variety grown in the Veneto region.

Cacao (Fr) *see* Crème de Cacao.

Cacao (Fr)(Hol)(It) cocoa.

Cacao Disbor (Fr) a crème de cacao and vanilla-flavoured liqueur produced by Puerto Cabello.

Cacao mit Nuss (Ger) a white chocolate and hazelnut liqueur.

Cacao Torréfié (Fr) roasted chocolate, a powder of fine roasted cocoa beans which produces a dark, slightly bitter-tasting drink.

Cacao Tree (S.Am) *Theobroma cacao* a tree species whose seeds produce cocoa and chocolate.

Cacatoes Cocktail (Cktl) 1 measure Cognac, ½ measure Mandarine Napoléon, ½ measure orange juice, 3 dashes crème de banane, 3 dashes lemon juice, dash grenadine. Shake over ice, strain into cocktail glass. Top with a cherry and orange slice.

Cacc'Emmitte di Lucera (It) a D.O.C. rosé wine from Lucera in the Apulia region.

Cacchione (It) a grape variety grown in Latium.

Cáceres (Sp) a wine-producing province of the Extremadura, south-western Spain. Includes the Vino de mesa wine of Valencia de Alcántar, the Vino Comarcal wine of Cilleros, the Vino de la Tierra wines of Cañamero, Montánchez, plus the areas of Ceclavin, Cilleros, Hervós and Jerte Miajados.

Cachaça (Bra) a white sugar cane spirit. *See also* Caxaca.

Cachaça (Port) rum, also a slang term for 'fire water'.

Cachaça de Cabeca (Bra) the name given to the heads (first spirit out of the still) in cachaça production.

Cachaça Sao Francisco (Bra) a premium sugar cane spirit (rum style) produced by Seagram in Rio de Janeiro.

Cachagua Cabernet (USA) an organic Cabernet sauvignon produced by the Durney Vineyards.

Cachantun (Chile) a natural spring mineral water (blue label: sparkling/green label: light gas/red label: still). Mineral contents (milligrammes per litre): Sodium 2.1mg/l, Calcium 7.6mg/l, Magnesium 1mg/l, Potassium 0.4mg/l, Bicarbonates 10.3mg/l, Chlorides 2.8mg/l, Sulphates 8.5mg/l, Silicates 8.5mg/l.

Cachapoal (Chile) the principal wine-producing region of the Central Valley. Soil: stony alluvial. Produces good, sound wines. Grape varieties include: Cabernet sauvignon, Carmenère, Chardonnay, Merlot, Sauvignon blanc, Syrah, Viognier.

Cachar (Ind) a tea-producing area in northern India.

Cachérisation (Fr) the process of producing Vin Cacher (kosher wine). *See also* Shomrim.

Cachet (Fr) seal or mark.

Cachet Blanc (Austr) a wine produced by the Quelitaler Estate, South Australia.

200

C

Cachiri (S.Am) a rough spirit that is produced from fermented cassava. Produced in Guyana, is similar to Cajuada.

Cacho (Port) a bunch of grapes.

Cacique (Bra) a large coffee exporter who introduced into the U.K. a French (chicory) blend of coffee. Sold in powder, granule and decaffeinated form.

Cactus (Mal) a natural spring mineral water from Johan. (Add): PTD 6386 Bukit Jintan, Mukim Tanjong Sembrong VII, Batu Pahal, Johan Mineral contents (milligrammes per litre): Calcium 16mg/l, Magnesium 4.1mg/l, Potassium 1.6mg/l, Bicarbonates 83mg/l, Chlorides <1mg/l, Sulphates 7.7mg/l, Silicates 48mg/l, Nitrates 9.5mg/l. pH 7.4

Cactus (Mal) a still natural spring mineral water from Taiping. Mineral contents (milligrammes per litre): Sodium 6mg/l, Calcium 7.5mg/l, Magnesium 1.8mg/l, Potassium 4.6mg/l, Bicarbonates 248mg/l, Chlorides <1mg/l, Sulphates <3mg/l, Silicates 53mg/l. pH 7.1

Cactus (Mex) the plant used in the making of tequila. There are 2 types: Maguey and Blue Maguey (or Mezcal Azul).

Cadarca (Rum) an alternative spelling of Kadarka (a red grape).

Cadastro (Port) vineyard register.

Cadaujac (Fr) a commune within the A.C. Graves district of south-western Bordeaux.

Cadaval (Port) a white wine from Torres Vedras.

Cadbury (Eng) the label used by Kenco-Typhoo (part of Premier Beverages) for a range of drink powders. Brands include Chocolate Break, Highlights, Drinking Chocolate, Sprinklers, Cocoa, Bournvita, Malitivita.

Cadbury's Cream Liqueur (Eng) a liqueur made from chocolate, dairy cream and French brandy by Westbay Distributors in Southampton. 17% alc by vol.

Ca'd Carussin (It) a 13ha. winery based at Regione Mariano 27, 14050 San Marzano Oliveto (AT). Specialises in Barbera d'Asti wines.

Caddies Quencher (Eng) a 3.8% alc by vol. bitter sweet ale specially brewed for Greenalls by Ridleys in Essex.

Caddies Quencher (Eng) a 4.4% alc by vol. event ale brewed by Ridleys of Essex.

Caddy (Eng) see Tea Caddy.

Ca'del Bosco (It) a well-known winery based in Franciacorta, Lombardy. 31ha. Produces sparkling (metodo tradizionale) wines.

Cà del Magro (It) the label for a DOC Bianco di Custoza from the Azienda Agricola Monte del Frá, Lombardy.

Cadenas (W.Ind) originally one of the major rum producers in the West Indies based on the island of Cuba.

Cadenasso Winery (USA) a small winery based in Fairfield, Solano, California. 38ha. Grape varieties: Cabernet sauvignon, Chenin blanc and Zinfandel. Produces varietal and dessert wines.

Cadenhead [William] (Scot) a malt whisky producer based in Aberdeen. Produces Putachieside Liqueur Whisky.

Cadenza (USA) the label of a red wine produced from Bordeaux varieties by Allegro, York County, west of Susquehanna River, Pennsylvania.

Cadet (Fr) lit: 'young', the name that prefixes many vineyards in the Saint-Émilion district of Bordeaux. e.g. Château Cadet-Piola, Château Cadet-Soutard.

Cadet-Bon [Le] (Fr) a wine from the Cadet vineyards in Saint-Émilion. Is also known as Cadet-Pinaud-Bon.

Cadet-Pinaud-Bon (Fr) see Cadet-Bon (Le).

Cadière d'Azur [La] (Fr) a commune in the A.C. Bandol, Provence.

Cadillac (Fr) an A.C. of the Côtes de Bordeaux. Produces semi-sweet, white wines from the Sauvignon blanc, Sémillon and Muscadelle grapes.

Cadiolo Winery (USA) a small winery based in Escalon, Stanislaus, California. Produces table and dessert wines.

Cádiz (Sp) a province of the D.O. Andalucía. Home to the Vino de la Tierra area of Cádiz. Grape varieties: Palomino, Moscatel de chipiona, Mantúa and Perruno. White wines are produced at a minimum of 10.5% alc by vol.

Cadiz Cocktail (Cktl) ⅓ measure Fino Sherry, ⅓ measure blackberry brandy, ⅙ measure Cointreau, ⅙ measure cream. Shake over ice and strain into an ice-filled old-fashioned glass.

Cadnam Bitter (Eng) see C.B.

Cadole (Fr) a traditional vigneron's stone-built hut, is circular with a cone-shaped roof.

Cadre Noir (Fr) an A.C. Saumur méthode traditionelle range of wines from the Compagnie Française des Grands Vins Chacé (brut, demi-sec, rosé).

Cadres (Fr) a commune in the A.C. Côtes de Blaye in north-eastern Bordeaux.

Caecuban (It) see Caecubum Wine.

Caecubum Wine (It) a red wine originating from the days of the Roman Empire. From Ager Caecubus in south Latium. See also Caecuban.

Caeres (It) a red wine produced in central-western Italy during Roman times.

Caesarea (Isr) a Palestinian wine (red) written about by the Romans.

Caesarum (Ger) the name given to a beer sold in a swing top bottle (1045 O.G.).

Cafae (Thai) coffee.

Café (Hol) (Isr) café.

Cafe (Isr) coffee.

Café (Fr) a coffee shop in the seventeenth to nineteenth centuries, was operated with food. In the present day is a coffee bar or small inexpensive restaurant that serves light meals or refreshments. Also known as a bistro. (Arab) = maqha, (Aus) = café, (Chi) = kafeguan, (Cro) = kavana, (Den) = café, (Eng) = café, (Ger) = café, (Gre) = kafeteria, (Hol) = café, (Indo) = kedai kopi, (Ire) = caife, (Isr) café, (It) = caffe, (Jap) = kissaten, (Kor) = chatjip, (Port) = café, (Rus) =

kafye, (Sp) = café, (Thai) = rankafae, (Wal) = bwyty.

Café (Fr) (Port) (Sp) coffee.

Café (Fr) lit: 'one night's wine', a term used in the Côtes du Ventoux for light-styled A.C. wines that are removed from the vat and pressed before the end of fermentation.

Cafea (Rum) coffee.

Café Alexander (Cktl) blend with a scoop of crushed ice 100mls (⅕ pint) iced black coffee, 10mls (½ fl.oz) Cognac, 10mls (½ fl.oz) crème de cacao, 25mls (1fl.oz) cream. Serve in a highball glass.

Café Allemande (Liq.Coffee) using a measure of schnapps.

Café Amaretto (Liq.Coffee) using ½ measure amaretto and ½ measure Kahlúa.

Café Américaine (Liq.Coffee) using a measure of Bourbon whiskey.

Café Anglaise (Liq.Coffee) using a measure of gin.

Café Borgia (It) equal quantities of hot black espresso coffee and hot chocolate. Pour into warmed cups, top with sweetened, whipped cream and grated orange peel.

Café Brizard (USA) a coffee-flavoured liqueur.

Café Brûlot (USA) *see* Creole Café Brûlot.

Café Brûlot Diabolique (USA) as for Creole Café Brûlot using a measure of Cointreau with the brandy.

Café-Calva (Fr) a kick start to the day, black coffee with Calvados in or added to.

Café Calypso (Liq.Coffee) using a measure of Tia Maria.

Café Caribbean (Liq.Coffee) using a measure of white rum.

Café Carioca (Cktl) 25mls (⅕ gill) iced black coffee, 20mls (⅙ gill) Jamaican rum, 20mls (⅙ gill) orange juice. Stir over ice, strain into a flute glass, top with whipped cream, grated chocolate and orange zest.

Café Chimo (USA) into a large wine goblet place 1 teaspoon of Instant coffee, ½ fill with hot fresh brewed coffee (leave spoon in the glass), add 25mls (1fl.oz) maple syrup, 10mls (½ fl.oz) Cognac. Top with crème chantilly (whipped, sweetened cream).

Cafecino (Aust) a sparkling espresso coffee drink from Bickford's. *See also* Esprit.

Café com Leite (Bra) a hot drink of ½ coffee and ½ milk drunk with plenty of sugar in the morning.

Café Crème (Fr) cappuccino coffee.

Café Créole Bourbon (Fr) a method of making coffee using a filter and bain-marie. The water is heated in the bain-marie and is then poured slowly over the grounds in a filter. The resulting coffee is heated in the bain-marie. Takes approximately 1 hour to brew.

Café Curaçao (Cktl) ½ measure Kahlúa, ½ measure Triple Sec. Stir over ice in an old-fashioned glass, serve with spiral of orange peel and straws.

Café Curaçao (Liq.Coffee) using a measure of Grand Marnier.

Café Décafeiné (Fr) decaffeinated coffee.

Café d'Écosse (Liq.Coffee) using a measure of malt whisky.

Café de Olla (Mex) coffee made with brown sugar, cinnamon and cloves. Boiled and served thick.

Café de Paris (Cktl). 40mls (⅓ gill) dry gin, 15mls (⅛ gill) Pernod, 15mls (⅛ gill) cream, 1 egg white. Shake well over ice and strain into a 125mls (5fl.ozs) goblet.

Café de Paris (Fr) a sparkling wine produced by the cuve close method from CDC in Paris.

Cafeeiro (Port) the coffee bush (tree).

Café Fertig (Switz) coffee served with a measure of schnapps.

Café Filtre (Fr) filter coffee, a method of brewing coffee using a filter (paper or other). Near boiling water 96°C (204.8°F) is poured over the grounds in the filter medium.

Café Galliano (It) rub the rim of a wine glass with a lemon wedge and dip in castor sugar. Place a measure of Galliano in the glass and ignite. When the sugar has caramelised add hot coffee until ¾ full and top with double cream.

Café Glacé (Fr) iced coffee with vanilla-flavoured milk and cream (iced).

Café Gloria (Liq.Coffee) using a measure of Cognac and a vanilla pod.

Café HAG (Hol) the ™brand-name of an instant, de-caffeinised coffee. Also a ground variety.

Café Imperial (Liq.Coffee) using a measure of Mandarine Napoléon.

Café Irlandaise (Liq.Coffee) using a measure of Irish whiskey. Is also known as Gaelic coffee and Irish coffee.

Café Italienne (Liq.Coffee) using a measure of Strega.

Café Jamaique (Liq.Coffee) using a measure of Jamaican (dark) rum.

Café Kahlúa (Liq.Coffee) using a measure of Kahlúa and cream topped with grated orange zest.

Café Kiss (Eng) a 5% alc by vol. RTD canned (20cls) cappuccino and Red Square Vodka blend produced by Halewood International.

Café Liégeois [1] (Fr) iced coffee served with whipped cream.

Café Liégeois [2] (Fr) 100mls (4fl.ozs) iced coffee blended in a blender with a scoop of coffee ice cream, serve in a tall glass and top with whipped cream.

Café Mandarine (Liq.Coffee) using a measure of Mandarine Napoléon liqueur.

Café Mexicaine (Liq.Coffee) using a measure of tequila.

Café Noir (Fr) black coffee.

Café Normandie (Liq.Coffee) using a measure of Calvados.

Café-Oh (E.Asia) hot, thick, black coffee served with sugar in glasses from Thailand. Is known as Oliang if cream is added.

Café Religieux (Liq.Coffee) using a measure of Bénédictine.

Café René (Fr) the brand-name of a 12% alc by vol. bottled wine from Prosper Mafoux (named after

C

the café in the famous BBC T.V. programme 'Allo 'Allo).

Café Royal (Eng) place into a saucepan 1 orange studded with cloves, 4 pieces of orange zest and lemon zest, 1 stick of cinnamon, 125mls (¼ pint) Cognac, 75mls (3fl.ozs) Cointreau. Heat and flame. Douse with 900mls (1½ pints) strong, black coffee, sweeten with sugar cubes to taste. Serve in a demi-tasse.

Café Royal Appetizer (Cktl) 1 measure dry gin, 1 measure Dubonnet, juice ½ lemon. Shake over ice, strain into a cocktail glass.

Café Royale (Liq.Coffee) using a measure of Cognac.

Café Royale (USA) see Coffee Royale.

Café Russe (Liq.Coffee) using a measure of vodka.

Café Sanka (USA) the brand-name of a de-caffeinised instant coffee.

Cafeteira (Port) coffee pot.

Cafeteria (USA) an old Spanish name for a coffee-shop. Now denotes a self-service restaurant.

Café Tia Sole (Sp) a brand of coffee liqueur made by Campeny in Barcelona.

Cafetière (Fr) coffee pot.

Cafetière (Fr) the brand-name of the 'plunger pot' coffee-making method. Incorporates a glass jug and plunger. The grounds are placed into the jug, near boiling water 96°C (204.8°F) poured onto the grounds and the plunger placed on top. When the coffee reaches the required strength the plunger is pushed to the base of the jug to separate the coffee from the grounds.

Café Toussaint (Haiti) a 21% alc by vol. dry coffee liqueur produced by Toussaint.

Cafèzal (Port) a coffee plantation.

Cafezinho (Bra) fill a cup ¾ full with brown sugar, top with strong black coffee, usually drunk in the afternoon and evening.

Caffe (It) café/coffee.

Caffé (It) coffee.

Caffé Caraibi (It)(Liq.Coffee) using a measure of white rum, also known as Café Caribbean.

Caffé Corretto (It) an espresso coffee drunk with a dash of grappa added.

Caffé Della Casa (It)(Liq.Coffee) using a measure of Sambuca.

Caffé Espresso (It) lit: 'pressed coffee', see Espresso Coffee.

Caffé Francese (It)(Liq.Coffee) using a measure of Cognac, also known as Café Royale.

Caffeina (It) caffeine.

Caffeine (Eng) $C_8H_{10}N_4O_2$ a constituent of coffee and tea, stimulates the nervous system and respiration. See also Red Bull. (Ire) = caiféin.

Caffé Irlandaise (It)(Liq.Coffee) using a measure of irish whiskey, also known as Gaelic coffee and Irish coffee.

Caffé Italiano (It)(Liq.Coffee) using a measure of Strega.

Caffé Jamaique (It)(Liq.Coffee) using a measure of Jamaican (dark) rum. Also known as Café Jamaique.

Caffé Russo (It)(Liq.Coffee) using a measure of vodka, also known as Café Russe.

Caffé Scozzese (It)(Liq.Coffee) using a measure of Scotch whisky.

Caffettiera (It) coffee pot.

Caffrey Brewing C°. [Thomas] (Ire) a Bass brewery plant based in Belfast. Brews Caffrey's Irish Ale.

Caffrey's Irish Ale (Ire) an Irish ale 4.9% alc by vol. from Bass in their Belfast plant (Caffrey Brewing C°), also available as a 4.2% alc by vol. version.

Cafi (Ch.Isles) coffee.

Caf'tchière (Ch.Isles) coffee pot. See also Caf'tière.

Caf'tière (Ch.Isles) coffee pot. See also Caf'tchière.

Cagazal (Sp) a white grape variety grown in Rioja. Is also known as the Calagraño, Jaén, Jaina and Navés.

Ca-Gera Agricola Vinhos Alto Douro (Port) the producers of Grandelite wine.

Cagette (Fr) a trolley used in the Bordeaux region to pull between the vines which holds the harvested grapes.

Caglarsu (Tur) a natural spring mineral water from Antalya. Mineral contents (milligrammes per litre): Calcium 19mg/l, Chlorides 8.52mg/l. pH 7.59

Cagliari (It) a vineyard centre in southern Sardinia. D.O.C.'s include: Monica di Cagliari, Monica di Sardegna, Nuragus di Cagliari, Moscato di Cagliari, Malvasia di Cagliari, Nasco di Cagliari, Girò di Cagliari. Campidano produces the best red and white wines.

Cagnassó Winery (USA) a winery based in Marlboro, Hudson Valley, New York. Produces hybrid wines.

Cagnina (It) a red grape variety grown in central-eastern Italy.

Cahors (Fr) an A.C. district in the Lot département. Produces red and white wines from grapes grown on iron-rich, limestone soils. Red from the Auxerrois [max. 70%] (also known as the Côt and Malbec) plus Merlot, Tannat, Jurançon noir. Grape must was originally baked or boiled and often fortified with local brandy! See also Black Wine of Cahors.

Cahors (Fr) a red grape variety grown in small quantities in the Bordeaux region. Is also known as the Côt and Malbec.

Cahouet (Fr) see Cahove.

Cahove (Fr) an early seventeenth century name for coffee. See also Cahouet.

Caife (Ire) coffee.

Caiféin (Ire) caffeine.

Cailin Tabhaine (Ire) barmaid.

Cailleret [Le] (Fr) a Premier Cru vineyard in the A.C. commune of Puligny-Montrachet, Côte de Beaune, Burgundy 5.4ha.

Cailleret [Les] (Fr) see Cailleret (En).

Caillerets [Les] (Fr) a Premier Cru vineyard in the A.C. commune of Meursault, Côte de Beaune, Burgundy 1.3ha.

Caillerets-Dessus (Fr) a Premier Cru vineyard in the A.C. commune of Volnay, Côte de Beaune, Burgundy. 14.7ha. Also known as Les Caillerets-Dessus.

Cailles [Les] (Fr) a Premier Cru vineyard in the A.C. commune of Nuits-Saint-Georges, Côte de Nuits, Burgundy 3.8ha.

C

Caillez Lemaire (Fr) a Champagne producer. (Add): 14-25, Rue Pierre Curie, B.P. 11, 51480 Damery. Produces vintage and non-vintage wines, also Ratafia, Fine de Champagne, Marc de Champagne.

Caillier (Fr) a sixteenth century wooden drinking cup used for wine.

Caillottes (Fr) the Loire name for the dry limestone soil of the Sancerre district in the Central Vineyards.

Cailloux (Fr) the small gravel pebbles of the Haut-Médoc which retain the heat of the sun.

Cailloux (Les) (Fr) the label of a Châteauneuf-du-Pape produced by Brunel (Lucien et André), 6 Chemin du Bois de la Ville, 84230 Châteauneuf-du-Pape, southern Rhône.

Cain [Robert] Brewery (Eng) a brewery (established 1850). (Add): Stanhope Street, Liverpool, Merseyside L8 5XJ. Brews: Cain's Dark Mild 3.2% alc by vol., Cain's Finest Bitter 4% alc by vol., Cain's Finest Lager 5% alc by vol., Cain's Formidable Ale 5% alc by vol., Cain's Golden Summer Ale, Cain's IPA 3.5% alc by vol., Cain's Lager 5% alc by vol., Cain's Mayflower, Cain's Raisin Beer 5% alc by vol., Cain's Styrian Gold, Cain's Superior Stout, Cain's Traditional Bitter, Blackout Winter Warmer, Dragon Heart, Red Fox, Springbok Ale, Sundowner Ale, 2000 Millennium Ale. Taken over by Faxe Jyske Breweries, Denmark in 1992. Website: http://www.cains.co.uk 'E'mail: info@cains.co.uk

Cain Five (USA) *see* Cain Vineyard.

Cainho Branco (Port) a white grape variety grown in the Lima (sub-region of Vinho Verde).

Caíño Tinto (Sp) a red grape variety grown in the Ribeiro region of north- western Spain. Produces deep-red, sharp tasing wines. Known as Borracal in Vinho Verde, Portugal.

Caíño Blanco (Sp) a white grape variety planted in the Rias Baixas.

Cain's Dark Mild (Eng) a dark, mild ale brewed in Stanhope Street, Liverpool by Robert Cain Brewery.

Cain's Formidable Ale (Eng) a 5.1% alc by vol. ale brewed by Robert Cain Brewery, Stanhope Street, Liverpool.

Cain Vineyard (USA) a winery (established 1982) in Spring Mountain District in Napa Valley. 34ha. planted with Bordeaux grape varieties. Produces Cain Five from 63% Cabernet sauvignon, 25% Merlot, 6% Cabernet franc, 4% Malbec, 2% Petit verdot.

Caipirinha (Cktl) 1 measure cachaça, 1 lime, sugar to taste. Cut the lime into small pieces, place into an old-fashioned glass sprinkle with sugar and crush together. Fill with ice, add the cachaça and serve with a spoon.

C.A.I.R. (Gre) a co-operative winery based on the Island of Rhodes. Is the main wine-producer there.

Cairanne (Fr) a village in the A.C. Côtes du Rhône-Villages. Produces mainly red wines (with a little rosé and white wine).

Cairnbrae Wines (N.Z) a winery. (Add): Jacksons Road, RD 3, Blenheim, Marlborough. 18ha. Grape varieties: Cabernet sauvignon, Cabernet franc, Chardonnay, Riesling, Sauvignon blanc, Sémillon.

Cairngorm Brewery C° [The] (Scot) a brewery (established 2001). (Add): Unit 12, Dalfaber Ind Estate, Aviemore, Inverness PH22 1PY. Brews: Black Gold 4.4% alc by vol., Cairngorm Gold 4.5% alc by vol., Sheephaggers Gold 4.5% alc by vol., Stag 4.1% alc by vol., Trade Winds 4.3% alc by vol., Wild Cat 5.1% alc by vol. Website: http://www.cairngormbrewery.com 'E'mail: info@cairngormbrewery.com

Cairngorm Gold (Scot) a 4.5% alc by vol. ale brewed by The Cairngorm Brewery C°. Ltd, Inverness.

Cairn O'Mhor Ltd (Scot) a carbonated drinks producer. (Add): East Inchmichael, Errol, Perth, Perthshire PH2 7SP. Produces alcoholic wine, sparkling and fruit drinks. Website: http://www.cairnomhor.co.uk 'E'mail: us@cairnomhor.co.uk

Cairns Bitter Ale (Austr) a bitter beer brewed by C.U.B. in Cairns.

Caisse à Thé (Fr) tea trolley/tea chest.

Caithness Spring (Scot) a still and sparkling natural spring mineral water. (Add): Achentoul Spring Water Company, Scaraben, Berriedale, Caithness.

Caitlin's Reserve (USA) a label for a white (Chardonnay) wine produced by the Adelsheim winery, Oregon.

Cajuada (S.Am) a spirit produced from pulverised cashew nuts in Guyana.

Cake (Eng) the name given to the residue of the grapes after the juice has been extracted in a press.

Cakebread Cellars (USA) a winery based near Oakville, Napa Valley, California. 9ha. Grape varieties: Cabernet sauvignon, Chardonnay, Sauvignon blanc and Zinfandel. Produces varietal wines.

Çakirkeyif (Tur) denotes tipsy/merry.

Calabrese (It) a red grape variety grown in Sicily. Also known as the Nero d'Avola.

Calabresi Frohlich (It) a red grape variety.

Calabria (It) a natural spring mineral water from Sicilia.

Calabria (It) the southern most region of the Italian peninsular, also a peninsular in its own right. Famous for full red wines.

Caladoc (Fr) a red variety created by crossing (Grenache x Malbec).

Calados (Sp) the underground cellars of Rioja for maturing wines.

Calafia (Mex) the label used by Luis Cetto Vineyards in Guadalupe, Baja California for a range of their wines.

Calagraño (Sp) a white grape variety grown in Rioja. Also known as the Cagazal, Jaén, Jaina, Navés and the Cayetana in the Estremadura.

Calahorra (Sp) a Zona de Crianza in the Rioja Baja, north-eastern Spain.

Calamich (It) boiled must for Marsala production.

Calanda Brewery (Switz) an independent brewery based in Chur.

C

Calaretto (It) a white grape variety used in the making of Marsala.

Calatayud (Sp) a a Denominación de Origen area in province of Zaragoza. 8,500ha. Grape varieties: Garnacha tinta, Tempranillo, Mazuelo, Monastrell, Juan Ibáñez, Cabernet sauvignon, Cariñena, Chardonnay, Garnacha blanca, Malvasía, Moscatel, Romano, Viura. Produces red, white and rosé wines.

Calaveras (USA) a small wine-producing county in the Sierra foothills, California. Covers approximately 26ha.

Calcaire de Plassac (Fr) calcerous subsoil combined with clay found in the commune of Margaux in the Haut-Médoc, Bordeaux. It is unique to the commune. On the top is gravel and gravillious.

Calcareous (Eng) chalk soil. Is found in Champagne, Cognac and Jerez de la Frontera. Contains calcium carbonate.

Calcarole (It) a winery based in Verona. (Add): Guerrieri Rizzardi (Azienda Agricola), Via Verdi, 4-37011 Bardolino, Verona. Produces: Bardolino, Soave, Valpolicella and Valdadige. Website: http://www.guerrieri-rizzardi.it 'E'mail: mail@guerrieri-rizzardi.it

Calcinaia (It) a Chianti Classico estate based in Tuscany.

Calcium Carbonate (Eng) CACO$_3$ an additive used to de-acidify wines made from under-ripe grapes.

Calcium Phytate (Eng) a fining agent, also known as Aferrin.

Calcium Sulphate (Eng) CASO$_4$. see Gypsum.

Calctufa (Eng) another name for Tufa. See also Calctuff.

Calctuff (Eng) another name for Tufa. see Calctufa.

Calcutta Cup (Eng) a mixture of ½ pint (300mls) Guinness and ½ pint (300mls) tonic water.

Caldaro (It) a dry red wine from the upper Trentino-Alto-Adige. Produced around lake of same name. Also called Lago di Caldaro.

Caldaro (It) a small lake based south-west of Bolzano in the region of Trentino-Alto-Adige. Produces a red wine of same name. See also Lago di Caldaro.

Caldas de Penacova (Port) a natural spring mineral water from Penacova.

Caldener Mineralbrunnen (Ger) a natural spring mineral water from Calden-Westuffeln, HE.

Caldera (S.Afr) the label for a red wine (Grenache, Mourvèdre and Syrah blend) produced by the Fairview winery, Suider-Paarl, Western Cape.

Calder's Cream Ale (Den) a 4.5% alc by vol. Scottish nitrokeg beer from Carlsberg-Tetley.

Caldes de Bohi (Sp) a still natural spring mineral water from the Font del Bou, Barruera, Lleida. Mineral contents (milligrammes per litre): Sodium 36.2mg/l, Calcium 6.1mg/l, Magnesium 0.5mg/l, Potassium 1.5mg/l, Bicarbonates 45.8mg/l, Chlorides 24.2mg/l, Sulphates 24.9mg/l, Fluorides 1.6mg/l, Nitrates 0.1mg/l.

Caledon (S.Afr) a natural spring mineral water from Caledon, Western Cape. (Add): Quindrink (Pty) Ltd., 19, Nourse Avenue, Epping 2, Cape Town. Mineral contents (milligrammes per litre): Sodium 17mg/l, Calcium 1.9mg/l, Magnesium 1mg/l, Potassium 5mg/l, Bicarbonates 32mg/l, Chlorides 23mg/l, Sulphates 1.7mg/l. pH 6.4 (also flavoured varieties produced).

Caledon (S.Afr) a wine-producing district in the Cape Province.

Caledonia (Cktl) 25mls (1fl.oz) Glayva, 25mls (1fl.oz) Scotch whisky, juice of a lemon, dash grenadine, dash egg white. Shake over ice, strain into cocktail glass, dress with slice of lemon and a cherry and serve with straws.

Caledonia Cocktail (Cktl) ⅓ measure Cognac, ⅓ measure crème de cacao, ⅓ measure fresh milk, 1 egg yolk. Shake well over ice, strain into an ice-filled highball glass and serve with a cinnamon stick.

Caledonian (Scot) a malt and grain whisky distillery based near Edinburgh. Distill a 1976 (23 year old) malt whisky at 59% alc by vol.

Caledonian Ale (Scot) a rich ale 1077 O.G. brewed by the Lorimer and Clark's Caledonian Brewery, Edinburgh.

Caledonian Brewing Cº. Ltd [The] (Scot) a brewery (established 1869). (Add): 42 Slateford Road, Edinburgh, Midlothian EH11 1PH. Brews: Burns Ale, Edinburgh Strong Ale, Golden Promise 4.4% alc by vol., 80/-, Deuchars IPA 3.8% alc by vol., Flying Scotsman, Lorimars IPA 5.2% alc by vol., Merman XXX, Six Nations 4.2% alc by vol., Tempus Fugit. Website: http://www.caledonian-brewery.co.uk 'E'mail: info@caledonian-brewery.co.uk

Caledonian Clear (Scot) a range of sparkling Scottish spring waters with natural fruit flavours (apple, peach, raspberry, wild blackberry, pear william, red cherry, arctic strawberry).

Caledonian Spring (Scot) a sparkling, slightly acidic natural spring mineral water from Campsie Fells, Lennoxtown, Glasgow. Mineral contents (milligrammes per litre): Sodium 6.6mg/l, Calcium 27mg/l, Magnesium 6.9mg/l, Potassium <1mg/l, Bicarbonates 103mg/l, Chlorides 6.4mg/l, Sulphates 10.6mg/l, Fluorides <0.1mg/l, Nitrates <2.5mg/l, Silicates 7.6mg/l. pH 4.6

Cal'em and Filho (Port) Vintage Port shippers. Quinta da Foz. Vintages: 1935, 1947, 1948, 1955, 1958, 1960, 1963, 1966, 1970, 1975, 1977, 1980, 1982, 1983, 1985, 1986, 1991, 1994, 1995, 1997. Website: http://www.calem.pt

Calepitrimerus vitis (Lat) the grape rust mite. see *Phyllocoptes vitis* and *Acorissis*.

Calera [La] (Chile) a noted wine-producing area in the Aconcagua province, northern Chile.

Calera Wine Cº. (USA) a winery based in San Benito County, California. 9.5ha. Grape variety: Zinfandel. Noted for Zinfandel Essence (produced from botrytised grapes).

Calgalon (Sp) a white grape variety grown in Jerez de la Frontera. Is also known as the Albillo and Castellano.

Calgary Export (Can) a noted brand of beer.

Calgrano (Sp) a white grape variety used for the white, dry wines of the Rioja.

205

C

Calice (It) cup/chalice.

Calice (Port) a wine glass, a glass for Port wines and liqueurs, also a Chalice cup.

Calice de Saint Pierre [Le] (Fr) the label of a Châteauneuf-du-Pape produced by Gradassi, Avenue Impériale, 84320 Châteauneuf-du-Pape, southern Rhône. Other label is Domaine des Saint Pères.

Calichal (Mex) a mixture of pulque and lager beer at approximately a 4 to 1 ratio.

California (USA) a wine-producing state on the west coast of America. Vineyards are grouped into 6 regions: North Coast, North Central Coast, South Central Coast, Sierra Foothills, Southern California, Central Valley. All styles of wine are produced from a wide range of grape varieties including: Cabernet sauvignon, Chardonnay, Fumé blanc, Nebbiolo, Pinot noir, Riesling, Sangiovese, Sémillon, Sirah, Zinfandel. *see* Friar Junipéro Serra.

California Aleatico (USA) a medium sweet, red table wine with the Muscat aroma. Must contain 51% of the named grape variety.

California Angelica (USA) a blend of several dessert wines of the California region. Are blended to produce a very sweet wine of 10%–15% unfermented sugar. *see* Angelica.

California Barbera (USA) a varietal, full-bodied, deep coloured red wine. Must have at least 51% of the named grape. *See also* Barberone.

California Barberone (USA) lit: 'small Barbera', is a varietal with at least 51% of the Barbera grape but less than the California Barbera. *see* California Barbera.

California Brandy (USA) produced by much the same method as Cognac. Sold at about 50% alc by vol. Is blended and matured in oak casks. Has a good nose, but is more fiery than Cognac.

California Brandy Advisory Board (USA) the governing body for USA-produced brandies.

California Burgundy (USA) a deep, rich, ruby-red, full-bodied an flavoured wine. Is sold in traditional Burgundy bottles.

California Cabernet Sauvignon (USA) a varietal, full-bodied red wine of claret type. Must have at least 51% of named grape.

California Carignane (USA) a varietal, full-bodied red wine with a full aroma. Must have at least 51% of the named grape.

California Chablis (USA) a delicate, straw-coloured wine made with the Chardonnay and Pinot blanc grapes. Other varieties are used such as the Burger, Chenin blanc, Golden chasselas, Green hungarian.

California Champagne (USA) a sparkling wine made by all methods (charmat, cuve close, traditional method). Follows French labelling practices.

California Charbono (USA) a varietal, full-bodied red wine of the Burgundy style. Must have at least 51% of the named grape.

California Chardonnay (USA) a varietal, light, dry, medium-bodied white wine. Must be made from at least 51% of the named grape.

California Château Sauterne (USA) *see* Château Sauterne.

California Chenin Blanc (USA) a varietal, light, dry, medium-bodied, white wine. Must be made from 51% of named grape.

California Chianti (USA) a dry, medium-bodied, deep red and well-flavoured wine. Softer than its Italian original. Is sold in a straw-covered flask.

California Claret (USA) a dry, rich, red, medium-bodied wine bottled in the traditional Bordeaux bottle.

California Folle Blanche (USA) a dry, straw-coloured, medium-bodied wine with Chablis characteristics. Must have at least 51% of the named grape.

California Gamay (USA) a light, red, fruity wine with a good bouquet in the Beaujolais style. Must have at least 51% of the name grape.

California Grappa (USA) is distilled from grape pomace. A fiery brandy with no colour, and no aging. Also known as California Pomace.

California Grignolino (USA) a varietal, full-flavoured, red wine. Must have at least 51% of the named grape.

California Growers (USA) a large winery based at Cutler in Tulare, California. Grape varieties: Cabernet sauvignon, Emerald riesling, French colombard and Johannisberg riesling. Its varietal wines are sold under Bounty, Le Blanc and Setrakian labels. Also produces brandies. *see* Growers Old Reserve.

California Haut Sauterne (USA) *see* Haute Sauterne.

California Hock (USA) a light, dry, pale-coloured wine made from assorted grapes but having the characteristics of Hock wine.

California Lemonade (Cktl) 40mls (⅓ gill) Bourbon whiskey, juice of a lemon, 2 teaspoons powdered sugar, 2 dashes grenadine. Shake well over ice, strain into a collins glass with crushed ice. Top with soda water and decorate with slice of orange, lemon and a cherry. Serve with straws.

California Light Muscat (USA) a varietal Muscat wine. Varies from dry to very sweet but all have a Muscat aroma. Also sometimes labelled with the exact varietal. i.e. the Moscato canelli, Moscato hamburg, etc.

California Madeira (USA) made to resemble the true Madeira but tends to taste like a sweet Sherry.

California Malaga (USA) a very deep, dark amber-coloured wine made from a blend of dessert wines.

California Marsala (USA) made to resemble the true Marsala but tends to be like a very sweet Sherry.

California Mission (USA) a native red grape variety.

California Moselle (USA) a light, dry, pale-coloured wine made from assorted grapes but having the characteristics of the wines of the Mosel-Saar-Ruwer.

California Muscat Brandy (USA) distilled from Muscat wines which give it a distinctive bouquet of the Muscat grape.

California Muscatel (USA) a rich, sweet, highly

perfumed, white wine. Made from any one of the eight Muscat varieties.

California Petite Syrah (USA) a varietal, full-bodied, red wine of the Burgundy style. Must contain at least 51% of the named grape.

California Pinot Blanc (USA) a light, dry, straw-coloured wine. Must contain at least 51% of the named grape.

California Pinot Noir (USA) a varietal, full-bodied, red wine made in the Burgundy style. Must contain at least 51% of the named grape.

California Pomace Brandy (USA) *see* California Grappa.

California Port (USA) a Port-type wine made in California but now no longer allowed to use the name Port through treaties of 1968.

California Red Pinot (USA) a varietal, full-bodied, red wine of the Burgundy style. Must contain at least 51% of the named grape.

California Rhine Riesling (USA) a light, dry, pale-coloured wine. Is made from assorted grapes but has the characteristics of a Rhine wine.

California Riesling (USA) a dry, acidic, white wine made from a variety of grapes including the Emerald riesling, Grey riesling, Johannisberg riesling.

California Rosé (USA) a light-bodied, dry wine that ranges in colour from pale pink to light red. Grapes such as Cabernet, Gamay, Grenache and Grignolino are all used in the making.

California Sauterne (USA) a light, full-bodied, dry, golden wine. Is often sold as Dry Sauterne.

California Sauvignon Blanc (USA) a varietal, sweet, white wine. Must contain at least 51% of the named grape.

California Screwdriver (Cktl) 50mls (2fl.ozs) Smirnoff vodka, 200mls fresh orange juice, stir over ice and serve in a highball glass with a slice of orange.

California Sémillon (USA) a varietal, dry, fruity, white wine. Must contain at least 51% of the named grape.

California Sherry (USA) a dessert wine which is baked in the sun in large vats to give it a slightly bitter tang and nutty flavour.

California Sparkling Burgundy (USA) a sparkling red wine made from red grapes. Semi-sweet to sweet.

California Sparkling Malvasia Bianca (USA) a carbonated version of the still table wine. Made by the Charmat method.

California Sparkling Moselle (USA) a carbonated version of the still table wine. Made by the Charmat method.

California Sparkling Muscat (USA) a carbonated version of the still table wine. Made by the Charmat method.

California Sparkling Sauterne (USA) a carbonated version of the still table wine. Made by the Charmat method.

California State Board of Viticultural Commissioners (USA) a body formed in 1880 to help combat pests, improve grape cultivation and winemaking practices and to improve the economic status of the industry.

California Sweet Sauterne (USA) *see* Sweet Sauterne.

California Tokay (USA) an amber-coloured blend of sweet wines.

California Trebbiano (USA) *see* California Ugni Blanc.

California Ugni Blanc (USA) a varietal, light, dry, medium-bodied, white wine. Must contain at least 51% of the named grape. Also known as the California Trebbiano.

California Vermouth (USA) made as in Europe (French style is light in colour and dry, Italian style is amber in colour and sweet) is sold under brand names.

California White Chianti (USA) a dry, fruity, medium-bodied, white wine made from the Trebbiano and Muscat grapes. Is sold in the traditional straw-covered flasks.

California Wine Association (USA) *abbr*: C.W.A. A group of wineries based in Delano, California. Under the control of Perelli-Minetti C°. Varietal wines and brandies produced. *see* Aristocrat Brandy and Morrow Brandy.

California Wine Institute (USA) founded in February 1934. Introduced standards and helps promote Californian wines.

California Zinfandel (USA) a varietal, red, fruity and spicy wine. Must contain at least 51% of the named grape.

Calimero Cocktail (Cktl) 1 measure Cognac, 1 measure orange juice, ½ measure Grand Marnier, ½ measure Tia Maria, 2 dashes lemon juice, ½ egg white. Shake well over ice, strain into a balloon glass and dress with a slice of orange.

Câlin Cocktail (Cktl) ⅓ measure orange juice, ⅓ measure anisette, ⅓ measure Mandarine Napoléon. Shake over ice, strain into a cocktail glass, dress with a mint leaf, cherry and a slice of lime.

Calisay (Sp) a digestive liqueur made from herbs and aromatic roots, blended with pure alcohol. 32% alc by vol.

Calisaya (Sp) a bitters flavoured with quinine and calisaya bark and with a brandy base. 33% alc by vol.

Calisay Cocktail (Cktl) ½ measure Calisaya, ½ measure sweet vermouth, 2 dashes gomme syrup, 2 dashes lime juice. Shake well over ice and strain into a cocktail glass.

Calissano (It) a noted producer of D.O.C.G. Asti. Labels include Realbrut.

Calistoga (USA) a noted wine town in the northern Napa Valley, California.

Calistoga Mineral Water (USA) a sparkling natural spring mineral water from, Calistoga, California. Mineral contents (milligrammes per litre): Sodium 183.7mg/l, Calcium 1.7mg/l, Magnesium 1.7mg/l, Potassium 14.5mg/l, Bicarbonates 36.3mg/l, Chlorides 224.9mg/l, Sulphates 83.5mg/l, Fluorides 0.9mg/l, Silicates 145mg/l. pH 7.7

C

Calistoga Mountain Spring Water (USA) a natural spring mineral water from Calistoga, California. Mineral contents (milligrammes per litre): Sodium 7.8mg/l, Calcium 6.4mg/l, Magnesium 2mg/l, Potassium 4.7mg/l, Bicarbonates 36.3mg/l, Chlorides 3.5mg/l, Sulphates 1.2mg/l, Fluorides 0.2mg/l, Nitrates 0.7mg/l, Silicates 57mg/l. pH 7.64

Calistoga Spring Water (USA) a natural spring mineral water from Calistoga, California. Mineral contents (milligrammes per litre): Sodium 10.2mg/l, Calcium 4.4mg/l, Magnesium 1.9mg/l, Potassium 5.4mg/l, Bicarbonates 47.6mg/l, Sulphates 1.5mg/l. pH 7.33

Caliterra (Chile) a winery based in the Central Valley, noted for Merlot wines.

Calitor (Fr) a red grape variety grown in the southern Rhône.

Calitris quadrivalvis (Gre) the pine tree from which the resin is used to make Retsina. Called the Aleppo pine.

Calitzdorp (S.Afr) a wine and brandy-producing region based in Klein Karoo, Eastern Cape.

Calitzdorp Vrugte en Wynkelders (S.Afr) a co-opertative winery (established 1928) based in Klein Karoo, Eastern Cape. 160ha. (Add): Box 193, Calitzdorp 6660. Grape varieties: Chardonnay, Golden jerepigo, Hanepoot, Merlot, Sauvignon blanc, Shiraz, Touriga naçional. Produces varietal wines sold under the Buffelskroon Wines label. Also produces Port-style wines.

Calivine (USA) a wine importing company that represents four Californian wineries. Range includes non-alcoholic varietal wines.

Calix (Lat) wine cup. *See also* Camella.

Calizaani Fonti Bauda (It) a sparkling natural spring mineral water from Savona. Mineral contents (milligrammes per litre): Sodium 3.4mg/l, Calcium 6.4mg/l, Magnesium 1.1mg/l, Potassium 0.68mg/l, Bicarbonates 27.5mg/l, Chlorides 3.7mg/l, Sulphates 6.1mg/l, Nitrates 2.7mg/l, Silicates 10.3mg/l. pH 7.06

Calkarasi (Tur) a white grape variety grown in the Ægean.

Callahan Ridge Winery (USA) a winery based in Roseburg, Oregon. Produces a range of varietal wines.

Callao (S.Am) the word for a brewery in Peru.

Callaway Winery (USA) vineyards and winery based in Temecula in Southern California. Grape varieties: Chardonnay, Chenin blanc, Petite syrah, Sauvignon blanc, Zinfandel. Produces varietal wines. *See also* Sweet Nancy.

Callet (Sp) a red grape variety grown on the Balearic Islands.

Calliga Ktima (Gre) a dry tannic wine produced by a Cephalonian winery from Thiniatiko and Robola grapes. Sold in hand tied hessian bags.

Calliga Nostos (Gre) a red wine produced by a Cephalonian winery from Agioigitiko and Mavrodaphne grapes.

Calligas [John] (Gre) a producer of Mavrodaphne wines and Château Calligas on the island of Cephalonia.

Calligraphy (S.Afr) the label for a red wine (Cabernet franc, Cabernet sauvignon and Merlot blend) produced by the Nitida Cellars winery, Durbanville, Western Cape.

Callitheke (Eng) a drinks producer with bottling plants at Hartlepool and Upwell. Products include Aqua Libra, Ame, Dexters, Monsoon and Jive, Norfolk Punch, Purdey's.

Call of the African Eagle (S.Afr) the label for an oak-aged white wine (Chardonnay) produced by the De Wetshof Estate winery, Robertson, Western Cape.

Call Time (Eng) denotes that drinking time on licensed premises has come to an end. *see* Drinking Up Time.

Calm & Clear (Eng) the brand-name for a range of still waters. Flavours include orchard apple, summer peach, spring raspberry, arctic strawberry.

Calmont (Ger) vineyard (Anb): Mosel-Saar-Ruwer. (Ber): Zell/Mosel. (Gro): Grafschaft. (Vil): Bremm.

Calmont (Ger) vineyard (Anb): Mosel-Saar-Ruwer. (Ber): Zell/Mosel. (Gro): Grafschaft. (Vil): Ediger-Eller.

Calmus (Ger) a liqueur wine produced near Frankfurt in the nineteenth century from Botrytis-attacked grapes.

Calm Voyage (Cktl) ⅓ measure Strega, ⅓ measure white rum, ⅓ egg white, ⅙ measure passion fruit liqueur. Blend altogether with a scoop of crushed ice in a blender and pour into a flute glass.

Calò [Michele] & Figli (It) a winery based Via Masseria Vacchia, 73058 Tuglie (LE). Produces Spano (from 90% Negroamaro and 10% Malvasia Nera grapes. 60% of wine aged one year in barriques, 40% in stainless steel).

Calona Wines (Can) a winery based in British Columbia.

Caloric Punch (Scan) a tonic liqueur with a rum base.

Caloric Punch (USA) another name for Swedish Punsch. *See also* Arrack Punsch.

Calouères (Fr) a Premier Cru vineyard in the A.C. commune of Morey-Saint-Denis, Côte de Nuits, Burgundy 1.3ha.

Calpico (Jap) an alternative name for Calpis.

Calpis (Jap) a sweet, soft drink derived from milk, which has a similar taste to barley water. Is diluted with water to drink. Also known as Calpico.

Caluso Passito (It) a D.O.C. white wine produced in Caluso, Piemonte region from the Erbaluce grape. Grapes are selected and then partially dried under natural conditions until sugar content in not less that 30%. Must be aged for a minimum of 5 years.

Caluso Passito Liquoroso (It) a fortified wine from Caluso, Piemonte. Made from the grapes, musts or wines suitable to produce Caluso passito. Must be aged for a minimum of 5 years.

C

Calva (Fr) denotes an apple brandy other than A.C. Calvados.

Calvados (Fr) an apple brandy produced in Normandy and Brittany. A.C. Calvados du Pays d'Auge is made from the double distillation of apple/pear wine in pot stills. Matured in oak casks. 40% alc by vol. There are ten other regional appellations (A.R.). Ageing: 3*/3 apples = 2 years min., Vieux/Réserve = 3 years min., V.O./Vieille Réserve/V.S.O.P. = 4 years min., Extra/Napoléon/Hors d'Age = 6 years min.

Calvados Cocktail (Cktl) ⅓ measure Calvados, ⅙ measure Cointreau, ⅓ measure orange juice, ⅙ measure orange bitters. Shake over ice and strain into a cocktail glass.

Calvados Cooler Cocktail (Cktl) 20mls (⅙ gill) Calvados, juice ½ lemon, 1 teaspoon sugar. Stir well over ice in a highball glass and top with soda water.

Calvados de-la-Vallée de l'Orne (Fr) an A.R. Calvados area. see Calvados.

Calvados de l'Avranchin (Fr) an A.R. Calvados area. see Calvados

Calvados-du-Calvados (Fr) an A.R. Calvados area. see Calvados.

Calvados du Cotentin (Fr) an A.R. Calvados area. see Calvados.

Calvados du Domfrontais (Fr) an A.R. Calvados area. see Calvados.

Calvados du Mortainais (Fr) an A.R. Calvados area. see Calvados.

Calvados du Pays d'Auge (Fr) an A.C. Calvados area. see Calvados.

Calvados du Pays de Bray (Fr) an A.R. Calvados area. see Calvados.

Calvados du Pays de la Risle (Fr) an A.R. Calvados area. see Calvados.

Calvados du Pays du Merlerault (Fr) an A.R. Calvados area. see Calvados.

Calvados du Perche (Fr) an A.R. Calvados area. see Calvados.

Calvados Gilbert (Fr) a small distillery based in Milly, Normandy that produces a range of spirits from local apples. Labels include Carte Verte.

Calvados Rickey (Cktl) 20mls (⅙ gill) Calvados, juice ¼ lemon. Stir well over ice in an old-fashioned glass, top with soda water and dress with a slice of lime.

Calvados Sour (Cktl) 20mls (⅙ gill) Calvados, ½ teaspoon sugar, 2 dashes lemon juice. Shake over ice, strain into a club goblet, dress with an orange slice and a cherry.

Calvagna (It) a natural spring mineral water from Calvagna.

Calvarino (It) a D.O.C. Soave wine produced by Pieropan from 70% Garganega and 30% Trebbiano di soave grapes. See also La Rocca, Le Colombare Recioto di Soave Classico.

Calvert Distilling C°. (USA) a part of Seagram. Major distillers of Bourbon whiskey, vodka and many other spirits.

Calvet (Fr) major French négociants. (Add): 75 Cours de Médoc, 33300, Bordeaux. Ships Cognac plus Bordeaux and Burgundy wines.

Calvet et Cie (Fr) a négociant based in Beaune, Côte de Beaune, Burgundy.

Calvi (Fr) a sub-region in the north of Corsica. Produces fine A.C. red and white wines.

Calviere (Eng) a lightly sparkling, medium dry, alcoholic pear drink produced by Showerings, Shepton Mallet, Somerset (owned by Allied-Domecq).

Calypso (Eng) a rum and banana cream liqueur produced by Goldwell and Company.

Calypso (S.Afr) the brand-name of a double-distilled cane spirit.

Calypso Cocktail (Cktl) place 20mls (⅙ gill) orange Curaçao into an ice-filled highball glass and top with ginger ale.

Calypso Coffee (Liq.Coffee) using a measure of Tia Maria.

Calypso Soft Drinks (Wal) a non-alcoholic drinks manufacturer (established 1986). (Add): Spectrum Business Park, Wrexham Ind Estate, Wrexham, Clwyd LL13 9QA. Produces mineral water, fruit and carbonated soft drinks. Website: http://www.calypso.co.uk

Calypso Spring Water (Eng) a natural, sugar free, low calorie water produced in Wrexham. Available in forest fruits, orange and mango, strawberry and apple flavours.

Calzadilla (Sp) a winery in Cuenca, Castilla-La Mancha. Likely to apply for Castilla-La Mancha private D.O. status. See also Sandoval, Manzaneque, Dehesa del Carrizal, Vallegarcía, Valdepusa, Aalto, Mauro, San Román.

Cama de Lobos (Mad) one of the Island's top vineyards, also known as Camara de Lobos.

Camara de Lobos (Mad) see Cama de Lobos.

Camaralet (Fr) a red grape variety grown in the Bergerac region of south-western France.

Camarate (Port) a red grape variety also known as the Mortàgua.

Camarate (Port) a red wine made from a blend of Cabernet sauvignon, Merlot and Periquita grapes.

Camarèse (Fr) a red grape variety grown in the southern Rhône.

Camartina (It) an I.G.T. red Sangiovese and Cabernet sauvignon wine from Agricola Querciabella SpA., Greve, Chianti.

Cambas (Gre) a dry, light-coloured brandy. 40% alc by vol.

Camberley Wines (S.Afr) a winery (established 1990) based in Uniedal, Stellenbosch, Western Cape. 7ha. Grape varieties: Cabernet franc, Cabernet sauvignon, Merlot, Pinotage, Shiraz. Labels: Charisma, Philosopher's Stone. Website: http://www.camberley.co.za

Cambiaso Vineyards (USA) a Thai-owned winery based in Sonoma County, California. Grape varieties: Barbera, Cabernet sauvignon, Petite syrah and Sauvignon blanc. Produces varietal wines.

Cambodia (E.Asia) a single stemmed variety of tea bush which is used to cross with other varieties of tea bush to improve quality.

C

Cambolosa (Sp) the name of a Riojan wine produced by Bodega San Miguel in Ausejo, Rioja.

Cambrai (Austr) a winery based in Clare-Watervale, South Australia. Produces varietal wines.

Cambria Estate (USA) a winery based in the Santa Maria Valley, Santa Barbara County, California. Grape varieties include: Pinot noir. Labels: Bench Break Vineyard, Julia's Vineyard..

Cambrian Brewery (Wal) a subsidiary brewery of Ansell's based at Dolgellau, Gwynned Brewery, South Wales. Produces cask-conditioned Dark Ale 1034 O.G.

Cambridge Ale (Eng) a bottled pale ale 1052 O.G. brewed by the Paine Brewery, Cambridgeshire.

Cambridge Bitter (Eng) a 3.8% alc by vol. draught bitter from Elgood in Wisbech, Cambridgeshire.

Cambrinus Craft Brewery (Eng) a brewery (established 1997). (Add): Home Farm, Knowsley Park, Prescot, Merseyside L34 4AQ. Brews: Deliverance 4.2% alc by vol., Endurance 4.5% alc by vol., Herald 3.8% alc by vol., Yardstick 4% alc by vol. 'E'mail: cambrinus@ukonline.co.uk

Cambus (Fr) a well-known brandy producer. Produces a range of fine brandies and wines.

Cambus (Scot) the label of a 1964 31 year old Scotch malt whisky 44% alc by vol.

Camella (Lat) wine cup. *See also* Calix.

Camel Lager (Afr) a lager beer 1044 O.G. brewed by the Blue Nile Brewery in Karthoum, Sudan.

Camellia sinensis (Lat) the botanical name for the true Tea bush.

Camelot Spring (Cktl) 1 part brandy, 2 parts Merrydown Mead, 4 parts Merrydown Apple Wine, sliced apples or whole strawberries. Marinate the fruit in the mead and brandy for one hour, add wine and ice cubes. Serve in goblets.

Camel Valley Vineyards (Eng) a vineyard (established 1989). (Add): Little Denby Farm, Nanstallon, near Bodmin, Cornwall PL30 5LG. Produce a variety of red, white and sparkling wines including Kernow Noweth (bottled as a *'Nouveau'* wine in early November). Website: http://www.camelvalley.com 'E'mail: sales@camelvalley.com

Cameradi Wines (S.Afr) a winery (established 1998) based in Wellington, Stellenbosch, Western Cape. Grape varieties: Cabernet sauvignon, Shiraz.

Camera Obscura (Sp) describes a wooden structure that has a candle inside which is used to test the clarity of wines.

Camerca (S.Afr) the label for a red wine (Cabernet sauvignon 50% and Merlot 50% blend) produced by the Slanghoek Winery, Worcester, Western Cape.

Cameronbridge (Scot) a grain whisky distillery (established 1824) based in Fife, south of Dundee. Owned by Haig. *see* Cameron Brig and Old Cameron Brig.

Cameron Brig (Scot) a famous single grain whisky produced by Haig. *see* Cameronbridge and Old Cameron Brig.

Camerons Brewery (Eng) a large brewery. (Add): Lion Brewery, Hartlepool, Cleveland TS24 7QS. Bought by Wolverhampton and Dudley from Brent Walker. Produces many fine styles of beers including cask-conditioned Lion Bitter 1036 O.G. Strongarm 1040 O.G. 4% alc by vol., Crown 1040 O.G. Hansa 1036 O.G. Cameron Bitter 3.6% alc by vol. Strongarm Special 1046 O.G. Ruby Red Bitter 4% alc by vol. Website: http://www.cameronsbrewery.com

Cameron's Brewing C° (Can) a brewery. (Add): 1165 Invicta Drive, Oakville, Ontario, L6H 4M1. Brews a variety of beers and lager. Website: http://www.camersonsbrewing.com 'E'mail: info@cameronsbrewing.com

Cameron's Kick (Cktl) ½ measure Scotch whisky, ½ measure Irish whiskey, juice ½ lemon, 2 dashes Orange bitters. Shake over ice and strain into a cocktail glass.

Camerons LA (Eng) a low alcohol bitter brewed by the Lion Brewery in Hartlepool, County Durham. Sold in 500mls bottles (at less than 1% alc by vol).

Cameroon [Coffee] (W.Afr) coffee-producing country where both robustas and arabicas grown. Are both sweet and mellow in style.

Camerte (It) a red I.G.T. wine produced by Fattoria La Monacesca in the Marche from 70% Sangiovese and 30% Merlot grapes.

Camilla (Cktl) 20mls (⅙ gill) dry gin, 60mls (½ gill) camomile tea, dash French vermouth, dash Italian vermouth. Shake over ice, strain into a cocktail glass and dress with a green olive.

Camillona (It) the name of a Sauvignon blanc wine produced by Araldici Vini Piemontesi, 14040 Castel Boglione. Part of the Poderi Alasia range.

Camilo Alves (Port) produces Bucelas (only firm to do so), is sold under the Caves Velhas label. Also sells Dão wines.

Camina (Ger) a red grape variety, a cross between the Portugieser and the Spätburgunder. Has higher sugar and acidity than either of its parents.

Camino Real (Mex) a coffee-flavoured liqueur produced by Montini.

Camissa (S.Afr) the label for a red wine (Cabernet sauvignon, Merlot and Shiraz blend) produced by the Stony Brook winery, Franschhoek, Western Cape.

Camlibel (Tur) a natural spring mineral water. Mineral contents (milligrammes per litre): Chlorides 21.3mg/l, Fluorides <0.03mg/l. pH 7.86

Camomile Tea (Eng) a herbal (tissane) tea, used as a stimulant which helps relaxation.

Camorei (It) a still natural spring mineral water from Borgo San Dalmazzo (CN), Piedmonte. Mineral contents (milligrammes per litre): Sodium 4.9mg/l, Calcium 62.1mg/l, Magnesium 6.7mg/l, Potassium 1.1mg/l, Bicarbonates 284.6mg/l, Chlorides 6.5mg/l, Sulphates 15.3mg/l, Fluorides 0.02mg/l, Nitrates 19.6mg/l, Silicates 8.3mg/l. pH 7.0

Camp (S.Afr) the label for a range of wines produced by the Backsberg Cellars winery, Suider-Paarl, Western Cape.

C

Campagna (Lat) lit: 'open, un-forested land', the word from which Champagne derives.

Campagnola (It) a wine-producer based in Valgatara, Verona. Noted for Valpolicella.

Campaign for Real Ale (Eng) *abbr*: CAMRA (see).

Campanaro (It) a red wine produced by Feudi di San Gregorio from Fiano di Avellino and Greco di tufo grapes, aged for 22 months in Alliers and Tronçais oak barriques.

Campanàrio (Mad) a noted vine-growing area on the south coast.

Campanaro (It) a white wine produced from 55% Greco di Tufo and 45% Fiano di Avellino grapes by Feudi di San Gregorio in Campania. Fermented in new barriques.

Campanas [Las] (Sp) red, rosé and white wines sold under the Castillo de Tiebas label from Vinícola Navarra, north-eastern Spain.

Campanha (Bra) a wine-producing region based on the Uraguay border.

Campania (It) a wine province that includes Naples. Lies south of Latium on the west coast. *see* Lacryma Christi del Vesuvio.

Campari (It) a famous orange bitters, bright red in colour, its base is an extract of capsicum. 24% alc by vol.

Campari Apéritif (Cktl) place a good measure of Campari in an ice-filled highball glass. Top with soda, stir and dress with a slice of orange.

Campari Shakerado (Cktl) 40mls (⅓ gill) Campari shaken vigorously over ice, strained and served in a small goblet.

Campay Cocktail (Cktl) 25mls (⅕ gill) Campari, 25mls (⅕ gill) dry gin, dash gomme syrup, juice of a grapefruit. Shake well over ice, strain into a club goblet., dress with a spiral of lemon peel and serve with straws.

Campbell and Son (Scot) the former owners of Aberlour-Glenlivet Distillery, has now been taken over by Pernod-Ricard.

Campbell's (Eng) a dark, bitter keg ale 4.1% alc by vol. from Whitbread Beer C°. at their Castle Eden Brewery.

Campbells Ales (Bel) are strong bottled Christmas and Scotch ales, brewed for the Belgiums by the Whitbread Brewery in England.

Campbell's Glory (Jap) a white grape variety.

Campbells of Rutherglen (Austr) a winery based in north-east Victoria. Noted for dessert wines plus Chardonnay, Bobbie Burns Shiraz.

Campbeltown (Scot) a class of malt whisky from Campbeltown on the Mull of Kintyre. Only 2 now produced (Springbank and Glen Scotia).

Campbeltown Loch (Scot) a standard blended Scotch whisky distilled by Springbank in Campbeltown. 40% alc by vol.

Camp Coffee (Eng) a brand name coffee and chicory essence beverage drink. Is slightly sweetened.

Campden Tablets (Eng) a proprietary brand-name for small **Potassium** or **Sodium metabisulphide** tablets used by amateur winemakers to stop the growth of bacteria, moulds and yeasts which also prevents malo-lactic fermentation.

Camp du Rouss (It) a D.O.C. Barbera d'Asti wine aged in large cask and new oak barriques by Coppo (Luigi) in Piemonte.

Campeaching Wood (Mex) also known as Logwood, produces a dye often used to improve the colour of wines and liqueurs.

Campeador (Sp) a red wine produced from the Garnacha 40% and the Tempranillo 60%. Is oak-matured for 3 years then bottle-aged for 2 years. Produced by Martinez Lacuesta.

Campelo [Joaquin Miranda & Filhos] (Port) producers of Morgarinha-Bagaceira do Minho (an aguardente).

Campeny (Sp) a spirits and liqueurs producer based in Barcelona.

Campidano (It) the top vineyard in Caglian, southern Sardinia, noted for both red and white wines.

Campi Flegrei (It) a D.O.C. area in Campania where Falerno wine is produced.

Campiglia (It) one of the five towns in Cinque Terre, Liguria.

Campilho 1 (Port) a natural spring mineral water from the Fonte Campilho 1.

Campilho 2 (Port) a natural spring mineral water from the Fonte Campilho 2.

Campillo (Sp) the brand-name for the wines produced by Bodegas Campillo in Rioja.

Campo Aldea (Sp) a red wine (100% Graciano) from the Santiago Garde of Viñedos de Aldeanueva, Rioja.

Campobello (It) a Chianti Classico producer based in Tuscany.

Campo Blanco (Sp) a red wine produced by Bodegas Campo Blanco, Rioja. Made from the Garnacha and Tempranillo grape varieties.

Campo Burgo (Sp) the name of a range of red and white wines produced by Bodegas de la Torre y Lapuerta.

Campo Cartagena (Sp) a Vino de la Tierra of Murcia, south-eastern Spain. 143ha. Grape varieties are mainly Merseguera plus Monastrell, Cencibel, Airén and Pedro ximénez.

Campo de Borja (Sp) a Denominación de Origen in Aragón, north-eastern Spain. 8049ha. Grape varieties: Garnacha tinta, Tempranillo, Mazuelo, Cabernet sauvignon, Macabeo, Moscatel. Produces red, white and rosé wines.

Campo de Tarragona (Sp) one of three sub-zones in Tarragona, south-eastern Spain. Main Grape varieties: Cariñena, Garnacha, Paralleda and Xarel-lo.

Campo Eilseo (Sp) a winery in the D.O. Toro.

Campo Fiorin (It) a single vineyard Ripasso (a Vino da Tavola) red wine produced by Masi.

Camponac (Fr) the brand-name of Eschanauer. Red and white wines sold for export.

Campo Nuevo (Sp) the brand-name label used by Cenalsa in the Navarra region, north-eastern Spain.

C

Campo Rojo (Sp) a winery based in the D.O. Cariñena. Produces red and white wines.

Campos de Cima da Serra (Bra) a wine-producing region in the Rio Grande do Sul.

Campo Viejo (Sp) the brand-name for wines from the Bodegas Campo Viejo, Rioja. Both red and white wines are produced. Owned by Allied Domecq.

Campsie Spring (Scot) a natural spring mineral water from Campsie Fells, Lennoxtown, Glasgow. Mineral contents (milligrammes per litre): Sodium 6.9mg/l, Calcium 29.1mg/l, Magnesium 5.3mg/l, Potassium 0.3mg/l, Bicarbonates 102mg/l, Chlorides 11.2mg/l, Sulphates 9.1mg/l, Fluorides 0.1mg/l, Nitrates 1.2mg/l.

Campus Gold (Bel) a 6% alc by vol. top-fermented, bottle-conditioned special beer brewed by the Biertoren Brouwerij, Kampenhout.

CAMRA (Eng) *abbr*: **CAM**paign for **R**eal **A**le a British organisation (established in 1971) to promote the production of traditional cask-conditioned and bottle conditioned beers. (Add): 230 Hatfield Road, St. Albans, Hertfordshire AL1 4LW. Website: http://www.camra.org.uk 'E'mail: camra@camra.org.uk

Camsie Spring (Eng) a recognised mineral water source.

Camtrell and Cochrane (Eng) *see* C & C.

Camus (Fr) a noted Cognac producer. (Add): Camus la Grande Marque SA. 29 Rue Marguerite de Navarre, BP 19, 16101 Cognac. 100ha. 50% in the Grande Champagne and 50% in the Borderies.

Camus (Fr) a Champagne producer. (Add): 14 Rue de Bernon, 51200 Épernay.

Camus (Scot) a grain whisky distillery based at the mouth of the river Forth, eastern Scotland.

Caña (S.Am) rum.

Caña (S.Am) sugar cane from which the molasses are obtained for the production of rum.

Caña (Sp) a glass of beer.

Caña (Sp) a tall, straight-sided glass used for drinking Sherry in Jerez de la Frontera. *See also* Copita.

Canaan (S.Afr) a red grape variety.

Can Abadía (Sp) the brand-name of a dry, light, red wine produced by Raimat in Lérida.

Canada (N.Am) a wine-producing country that has three wine growing regions: Ontario, British Columbia, Nova Scotia. Ontario (the main region) has 3 designated viticultural areas: Niagara Peninsula, Pelee Island, Lake Erie North Shore. *Vitis labrusca* vines banned in 1988. Set up VQA. Also noted for Ice Wine.

Canada (Port) a measure of 2 litres capacity used in the blending of Port.

Canada Cocktail (Cktl) 35mls (1½ fl.ozs) Canadian whisky, 2 dashes Cointreau, 2 dashes Angostura, 1 teaspoon powdered sugar. Shake over ice and strain into a cocktail glass.

Canada Cup (Can) the brand-name of a Canadian whisky produced by Schenley. 40% alc by vol.

Canada Dry (Eng) *see* Canada Dry Rawlings.

Canada Dry Rawlings (Eng) producers of Canada Dry (a popular brand of ginger ale) sold in a distinctive green bottle. Also other mineral mixers and fruit juices.

Canada House (Can) a brand of Canadian rye whisky produced by the Canadian Distillers Ltd. (a subsidiary of Seagram).

Canadaigua (USA) producers of sparkling wines based in eastern USA.

Canada's Choice [Eastern Source] (Can) a natural spring mineral water. Mineral contents (milligrammes per litre): Sodium 1.1 mg/l, Calcium 56mg/l, Potassium 0.22mg/l, Nitrates 0.56mg/l.

Canada's Choice [Western Source] (Can) a natural spring mineral water. Mineral contents (milligrammes per litre): Sodium 6mg/l, Calcium 69mg/l, Potassium 0.092mg/l, Nitrates 0.21mg/l.

Cañada Seca (Arg) a wine-producing area based in southern Argentina.

Canadian Bourassa (Can) a natural spring mineral water from Toba Inlet, British Columbia. Mineral contents (milligrammes per litre): Potassium 0.4mg/l, Bicarbonates 0.1mg/l, Chlorides 0.1mg/l, Sulphates 1.2mg/l, Nitrates 0.9mg/l, Silicates 2.3mg/l.

Canadian Cherry Cocktail (Cktl) ⅓ measure rye whisky, ⅓ measure lemon juice, ⅓ measure orange juice, ⅓ measure cherry brandy. Shake over ice and strain into an ice-filled old-fashioned glass (with the rim moistened with cherry brandy).

Canadian Club (Can) a blended Canadian whisky produced by Hiram Walker and Sons Ltd. 40% alc by vol.

Canadian Cup (Can) a straight rye whisky produced by the Canadian Schenley Distilleries. 40% alc by vol.

Canadian Distillers Ltd. (Can) a subsidiary of Seagram. Produces a fine range of Canadian whiskies.

Canadian Double Distilled (Can) a brand of Canadian whisky produced by the Canadian Distillers Ltd. 40% alc by vol.

Canadian Gibson Distilleries (Can) produces a range of Canadian whiskies.

Canadian Gold (Can) a cold filtered, unpasteurised premium export beer from Canadian National Breweries.

Canadian Ice Wine (Can) a wine made to QVA standards from ripe grapes picked in mid-winter when the grapes are frozen on the vine. The yield is from 75 to 100 litres of must per tonne of grapes. Has a potential alcohol content in excess of 15% alc by vol.

Canadian Lord Calvert (Can) a brand of Canadian whisky produced by Seagram. 40% alc by vol.

Canadian Mist Distilleries Ltd. (Can) a distillery based at Collingwood, Ontario. Produces Canadian Mist (a blended Canadian whisky). 40% alc by vol.

Canadian Mountain (Can) a natural spring mineral water from Barrie, Ontario.

Canadian Music Premium Glacier Water (Can) a natural spring mineral water from Toba Bay.

Canadian Pineapple (Cktl) 60mls (½ gill) Canadian

Club whisky, juice ½ lemon, 30mls (¼ gill) pineapple juice, 2 dashes maraschino. Shake over ice, strain into an ice-filled highball glass and dress with pineapple cubes.

Canadian Rye Whisky (Can) *see* Canadian Whisky and Rye Whisky.

Canadian Schenley Distilleries Ltd. (Can) producers of Canadian Cup, Five Thirty, OFC and Order of Merit brands of whiskies. Also produces liqueurs sold under the Henkes and Ross label.

Canadian Sunset Cocktail (Cktl) ½ measure Canadian whisky, ¼ measure Strega, ¼ measure Galliano, juice of a lemon, 2 dashes grenadine. Shake all ingredients (except the grenadine) over ice, strain into a cocktail glass containing the grenadine. Do not stir.

Canadian Whisky (Can) a whisky made mainly from rye but can be made from other cereals. Can be bottled at 2 years of age. It is usually matured in charred oak casks for 5 years. Varies in alcoholic strength.

Canadoro Wines (N.Z) a winery based in New Street, Martinborough. 1.25ha. Grape varieties: Cabernet sauvignon, Chardonnay.

Canado Saludo (Cktl) 25mls (⅓ gill) Jamaican rum, 20mls (⅙ gill) orange juice, 20mls (⅙ gill) pineapple juice, 4 dashes grenadine. Shake well over ice, strain into a club goblet with a pineapple chunk, orange slice and a cherry. Serve with straws.

Canaiolo Bianco (It) a white grape variety grown in Tuscany. Known as the Drupeggio in Umbria.

Canaiolo Nero (It) a red grape variety used in the making of Chianti in the Tuscany region. Known as the '*Grape of the Estruscans*'. Has a good sugar content.

Canakin (Eng) *see* Cannikin and Canikin.

Canakkale (Tur) a vineyard based in the Thrace and Marmara regions. Produces white table wines.

Canakkale-Balikesir (Tur) a vineyard based in the Thrace and Marmara regions. Produces red wines.

Canal Ale (Eng) a 1035 O.G. beer from the micro-brewer Ryburn of Sowerby Bridge.

Canale Estate (Arg) a winery based in Río Negro, Patagonia. Grape varieties include: Merlot.

Canaletto (It) a range of wines from Casa Girelli (Add): Viale Verona 182, 38100 Trento. Grape varieties: Chardonnay, Garganega, Merlot, Montepulciano d'Abruzzo, Pinot grigio, Primotivo. 'E'mail: info@casagirelli.it

Canali (It) a natural spring mineral water from Lecce.

Canal Street Daisy (Cktl) 1 measure Bourbon whiskey, ¼ measure lemon juice, 1 measure orange juice. Stir over ice, strain into an ice-filled highball glass, top with soda water and orange slice.

Cañamero (Sp) a Vino de la Tierra wine-producing village based in the Sierra de Guadaloupe in the province of Cáceres in Extremadura that produces flor-attacked wines. Grape varieties: Alarije, Verdejo, Garnacha, Cencibel, Malvar, Albillo, Mantúa, Chelva, Provechón. 1,200ha. Red, white and rose wines produced.

Canard-Duchêne (Fr) a Champagne producer. (Add): 1, Rue Edmond Canard, Ludes, 51500 Rilly-la-Montagne. 16ha. A Grande Marque. Produces vintage and non-vintage wines. Vintages: 1943, 1947, 1949, 1952, 1955, 1957, 1959, 1961, 1962, 1964, 1966, 1969, 1970, 1971, 1973, 1975, 1976, 1979, 1982, 1983, 1985, 1988, 1990, 1995, 1998, 1999, 2000. Prestige cuvée: Charles VII Brut. Also produces N.V. Patrimoire. Part of Veuve Clicquot.

Canarias (Sp) wine producing islands. Home to the provinces of Las Palmas de Gran Canaria and Santa Cruz de Tenerife. *see* Canary Islands, Gran Canaria, Tenerife.

Cañarroyo (Sp) a white grape variety grown in central Spain.

Canary Islands (Sp) a group of Spanish islands off the West African coast. Most of the wines are consumed locally. The wine of Palma was popular in England in the seventeenth century under the name of Palma Sack. Also produces Canary Sack. Home to D.O.'s of Lanzarote, Palma (La), Tacoronte-Acentejo, Tenerife, Ycoden-Daute-Isora.

Canary Sack (Sp) a sweet wine produced in the Canary Islands from Malvasia grapes.

Canasta Cream (Sp) an old, sweet, premium Oloroso Sherry produced by Williams and Humbert.

Canastas (Sp) the baskets used in Jerez to carry the cut grapes to the winery.

Canay (It) a natural spring mineral water from Canay, Savona.

Can Casal (Sp) the brand-name of a light, dry, white wine produced by Raimat Bodegas in Lérida.

Canchales (Sp) red and white wines produced by Bodegas Riojanas S.A. Cenicero, Rioja.

Canciller (Arg) the name given to a premium range of wines produced by Griol (the State co-operative).

Can Clamor (Sp) the brand-name of a red wine produced by the Raimat Bodega in Lérida.

Candau (Fr) a wine-producing district based in A.C. Bellet, Provence.

C & C (Eng) *abbr*: **C**amtrell **&** **C**ochrane (G.B), Warwickshire, a soft drinks producer. The third largest in the U.K. which markets under the 'Club' label.

Candes (Fr) a white wine produced in the Touraine district, Loire.

C & G (Eng) *abbr*: **C**ity **&** **G**uilds, the examining body for the 717 (originally 707-3) Alcoholic Beverages certificate (now superseded by N.V.Q's and S.V.Q's).

Candia (It) the name for Crete in the thirteenth century. Wines were known as Candiae, Candy or Malvasia Candiae.

Candiae (It) *see* Candia.

Candida (Cktl) ⅓ measure Marie Brizzard, ⅓ measure Cognac, ⅓ measure double cream. Place with some crushed ice into a mixing glass, stir until foaming and strain into a cocktail glass.

Candida mycroderma (Lat) a variety of yeast, is aerobic, grows on low alcohol wines.

C

Candido (It) a 137ha. winery in Salice Salentino D.O.C. (Add): Via Armando Diaz 46, 72025 Sandonaci. Grape varieties: Aleatico, Cabernet sauvignon, Montepulciano, Negroamaro, Primitivo, Chardonnay, Garganega, Sauvignon blanc.

Candy (It) see Candia.

Cane (Eng) the name used to describe a mature vine shoot.

Canebière Cocktail (Cktl) ⅔ measure Pernod, ⅓ measure cherry brandy. Shake over ice and strain into cocktail glass.

Caneca (Port) a tankard/mug or large glass.

Caneco (Port) an oak jug that is bound with copper.

Cane Cutter (S.Am) a brand of rum produced in Guyana.

Cane End (Eng) a vineyard based in Berkshire that produces dry wines.

Cane Garden Bay (W.Ind) a noted rum distillery based in the Virgin Islands.

Canéjean (Fr) a commune in the A.C. Graves district in south-western Bordeaux.

Canela (Sp) a cinnamon-flavoured liqueur.

Canella (It) a producer of sparkling (cuve close) wines in Veneto. Also produces Prosecco di Conegliano-Valdobbiadene.

Canellino (It) the name given to the sweet-styled Frascati Superiore.

Canepa [José] (Chile) a winery based at Valparaiso, Maipo. Noted for dry Sémillon, sweet Muscadel, Sauvignon blanc, Chardonnay, Merlot and Cabernet wines.

Canephora (Afr) Coffea canephora also known as Robusta coffee. A hardy plant, it grows in low altitudes, indigenous in north-east and central Africa, Asia and South America.

Cane Spirit (Eng) a rectified spirit made from cane sugar in various countries such as South Africa, South America and the West Indies.

Canette (Fr) a drinks can (beer and soft drinks).

Canevel Spumanti (It) a sparkling wine produced in Valdobbiadene from Chardonnay, Verdiso and Prosecco grapes.

Cangas de Narcea (Sp) a Vino de Mesa of Asturias.

Cangkir (Indo) cup.

Canica (Mad) a hybrid grape variety also known as the Cunningham that has been banned from use in Madeira production.

Canikin (Eng) see Cannikin and Canakin.

Canister Beer (Eng) another name for keg beer.

Cannabis (Ger) a 4.5% alc by vol. premium pils lager beer brewed by Heaven-Bräu.

Cannavive (It) a natural spring mineral water from Duronia, Campabasso. Mineral contents (milli-grammes per litre): Sodium 7.92mg/l, Calcium 69.2mg/l, Magnesium 13.3mg/l, Potassium 1.68mg/l, Chlorides 12.4mg/l, Sulphates 14.5mg/l, Nitrates 6.3mg/l. pH 7.46

Canned (Eng) slang for drunk/intoxicated.

Canned Cocktail (Cktl) ½ measure gin, ½ measure vodka, ⅓ measure lime juice. Shake over ice, strain into a cocktail glass and dress with a slice of lime.

Cannelle (Fr) a liqueur flavoured with cinnamon.

Cannellino (It) a term that means the same as dolce (sweet) in Latium.

Cannicci (It) special wicker frames in Tuscany used to partially dry the grapes (governo) for Chianti. Also known as Castelli.

Cannikin (Eng) a small can used as a drinking vessel in the nineteenth century. See also Canakin and Canikin.

Cannonau (It) a red grape variety used to produce both dry and sweet fortified wines in Sardinia. (Fr) = Grenache, (Sp) = Garnacha.

Cannonau di Sardegna (It) a D.O.C. ruby red wine made in Sardinia from the Cannonau grape variety plus no more than 10% of Bovale grande, Bavale sardo, Carignano, Pascale di cagliari, Monica or Vernaccia di San Gimignano grapes. Must be aged 1 year in wood. If three years then Riserva. Also produce Superiore Natural Mente Secco (dry), Amabile (medium-sweet) and Dolce (sweet).

Cannonau di Sardegna Liquoroso (It) a D.O.C. vini liquoroso. 2 types are produced (secco and dolce naturale). Additional sub-denomination Oliena or Nepente di Oliena can appear on the label if grapes used are produced from Oliena or Orgosolo Rosé Cannonau di Sardegna, produced by the fermentazione in bianco.

Cannon Ball (Eng) a 5% alc by vol. ale brewed by the Merlin Brewery, Lancashire.

Cannon Bitter (Eng) a 4.2% alc by vol. bitter beer brewed by the Shoes Brewery, Herefordshire.

Cannon Brewery (Eng) a brewery based in Tadcaster, North Yorkshire. Brews Stones Creamflow.

Cannon Royall Brewery (Eng) a brewery (established 1993). (Add): Fruiterers Arms, Uphampton, Droitwich, Worcestershire WR9 0JW. Brews: Arrowhead Bitter 3.9% alc by vol., Fruiterers Mild 3.7% alc by vol., Kings Shilling 3.8% alc by vol., Muzzle Loader 4.2% alc by vol. Website: http://www.cannonroyall.co.uk 'E'mail: info@cannonroyall.co.uk

Cannubi (It) a famous Cru vineyard area (18ha) in the DOCG Barolo region of Piemonte. Owned by many growers it has soils of calcerous marl and limestone.

Canny Lad (Eng) a 4.5% alc by vol. ale from the Durham Brewery, Bowburn, Durham.

Cano [Gaspar F. Florido] (Sp) a Sherry producer based in Jerez de la Frontera.

Canoa (Sp) a wedge-shaped funnel used to fill wine casks.

Cañocazo (Sp) the alternative name for the white grape Mollar blanco.

Canoe Ridge Vineyard (USA) a winery based in Walla Walla, Columbia Valley, Oregon. Grape varieties include Chardonnay and Merlot.

Canoe Springs (Can) a natural spring mineral water. Mineral contents (milligrammes per litre): Sodium 1.2mg/l, Calcium 82mg/l, Magnesium 31mg/l, Potassium 0.85mg/l, Bicarbonates 270mg/l, Chlorides 3.8mg/l, Sulphates 7.9mg/l, Fluorides 0.23mg/l, Nitrates 1.7mg/l. pH 7.16

C

Canon (Fr) a wine measure of one sixteenth of a litre used in the eighteenth and nineteenth centuries.

Canon-Fronsac (Fr) an A.C. red wine of Bordeaux. *see* Côtes Canon-Fronsac.

Canons Grélifuges (Fr) nineteenth century cannons designed to fire into the clouds to prevent hailstorms in the Burgundy region.

Canova (It) cellar/cave/tavern.

Can Rius (Sp) the brand-name for a dry, rosé wine produced by Raimat Bodega in Lérida.

Canstatter Wasen (Ger) an autumn beer festival held in Stuttgart in the Canstatt district which specialises in the beers of Baden and Württemburg.

Cant (Eng) the end piece of the top of a cask in which the two hold the middle stave.

Cantab Bitter (Eng) a sweet-style bitter ale brewed by the Tolly Cobbold Brewery, Ipswich, Suffolk.

Cantabria (Sp) an area based in north-central Spain that produces very little wine. Home to the province of Santander and the Vinos de Mesa of Liébana (expected to apply for Vino de la Tierra status soon) and Treceño.

Cantagalo (Bra) a natural spring mineral water from the Fonte Progresso. Mineral contents (milligrammes per litre): Sodium 3.4mg/l, Calcium 6.21mg/l, Magnesium 3.03mg/l, Potassium 1.8mg/l, Chlorides 228.78mg/l, Sulphates 1.73mg/l, Fluorides 7.54mg/l, Nitrates 0.1mg/l. pH 6.25

Cantalar (Sp) a natural spring mineral water from Cantalar, Moratalla, Murcia.

Cantalupi (It) a rosé wine (Malvasia and Negroamaro blend) produced by the Conti Zecca winery Puglia.

Cantaro (Ger) a white grape hybrid cross between Seibel 2765 and the Müller-Thurgau.

Canteiro (Mad) the name given to Madeira that has been through the estufa system but has been heated in small casks. Used mainly in blending to improve wines.

Cantena (Arg) the name for Chardonnay and Cabernet sauvignon wines from Bodegas Esmeralda in Mendoza. *See also* Alamos Ridge.

Cantenac (Fr) a commune within the district of A.C. Haut-Médoc in north-western Bordeaux.

Canterbury (N.Z) a wine-producing area in the South Island.

Canterbury Ale (Eng) a cask-conditioned ale 1038 O.G. brewed by the Wiltshire Brewery, Tisbury, Wiltshire for the Canterbury Brewery in Canterbury, Kent.

Canterbury Brewery (Eng) a brewery based in Canterbury, Kent which has its beer brewed under contract by the Wiltshire Brewery of Tisbury. Produces cask-conditioned Canterbury Ale 1038 O.G. and Buff's Bitter 1050 O.G.

Canterbury Jack (Eng) a 4.5% alc by vol. cask-conditioned summer ale brewed by Shepherd Neame, Kent.

Canterie (Fr) a still natural spring mineral water from Aurelle. Mineral contents (milligrammes per litre): Sodium 4.1mg/l, Calcium 98mg/l, Magnesium 4mg/l, Potassium 1.9mg/l, Bicarbonates 269mg/l, Chlorides 3.6mg/l, Sulphates 43mg/l, Nitrates <2mg/l.

Cantharus (Lat) tankard.

Cantillon (Bel) a museum brewery in Anderlecht, Brussels that produces lambic beers.

Cantillon Rosé de Gambrinus (Bel) a 5% alc by vol. dry gueuze beer made with cherries and raspberries.

Cantimplora (Sp) water bottle.

Cantina (It) cellar.

Cantina (Sp) cellar/winery/bar.

Cantina Agricola (It) when preceded by the producer's name on the label it guarantees that the wine is made from the producers' own grapes.

Cantina Beato Bartolomeo (It) a co-operative winery (established 1950) with 1000 growers and 800ha. Based in Breganze, Veneto. Produces: Bosco Grande Merlot, Dolce San Giorgio, Kiló, Torcolato (main label: Villa Savardo). Grape varieties: uses a large variety of local and international varieties. Website: http://www.cantinabreganze.it

Cantina Christina (It) a winery. (Add): Serra Capelli 2, Neive. 6.5ha. vineyard that produces Barbaresco, Barbera d'Alba, Dolcetto d'Alba, Moscato d'Asti.

Cantina Collavini (It) a noted wine-producers based in Grave del Fruili.

Cantina Co-operative (It) denotes a wine-growers' co-operative.

Cantina del Taburno (It) a winery based in the Avellino district in the Campania region. Label: Follus Falanghina, also produces DOC Taburno.

Cantina di Montalcino (It) a winery. (Add): Loc. di Cava, 53024 Montalcino (SI). Wine estate that produces D.O.C.G. Brunello di Montalcino. Aged in Slovenian oak for a minimum of 3 months.

Cantina di Santadi (It) a co-operative winery (established 1960) on the island of Sardinia. Has 230 growers and owns 500ha. Grape varieties include: Carignano del Sulcis, Monica, Nasco, Vermentino. Label: Grotta Rossa, Latina, Rocca Rubia, Terre Brune, Tre Torri. Website: http://www.cantinadisantadi.it

Cantina di Terlano (It) a co-operative winery (established 1893) in Terlano, Trentino-Alte-Adige region. Has 100 growers and 150ha of vineyards. Grape varieties include: Chardonnay, Pinot Bianco, Sauvignon blanc. Labels: Pinot Bianco Vorberg, Sauvignon Quartz, Terlano Classico.

Cantina di Venosa (It) a winery based in Basilicata. Label: Vignali (rosé).

Cantina La Vis (It) a co-operative winery (established 1948) in the Valle dell'Adige, Trentino-Alte-Adige region. Has 1300 growers and 1350ha of vineyards. Grape varieties include: Chardonnay, Pinot grigio, Riesling.

Cantina Mascarello (It) a noted traditional wine producer based in Barolo, Piemonte.

Cantina Produttori Colterenzio (It) a co-operative winery (established 1960) in Bolzano, Trentino-Alte-Adige region. Has 310 growers and 370ha of vineyards. Grape varieties include: Chardonnay, Pinot grigio. Label: Cornell.

C

Cantina San Marco (It) a producer of Frascati wines. (Add): Via di Frascati 34, 00040, Monteporzio Cantone, Roma.

Cantina San Marco (It) a producer of sparkling (cuve close) wines in Lazio.

Cantina Sociale (It) denotes a wine-grower's co-operative.

Cantina Sociale Cellavo (It) a wine co-operative based in Sicily. Grape varieties include: Barbera, Catarratto, Inzolio, Nerello cappuccio, Nerello mascalese, Sangiovese, Trebbiano.

Cantina Sociale di Canelli (It) a noted producer of Moscato d'Asti Spumante in Piemonte.

Cantina Sociale di Dolianova (It) a wine co-operative based at Dolianova, Sardinia.

Cantina Sociale di Gambellara (It) a co-operative in Vicenza that vinifies grapes from the D.O.C. area and bottles the wines of Colli Berici. Spicailises in dry white Gambellara wines.

Cantina Sociale di Locorotondo (It) a wine co-operative based in Bari. Produces a still and sparkling version of Locorotondo.

Cantina Sociale di Santa Maria Delle Versa (It) a producer of sparkling (metodo tradizionale) wines in Lombardy.

Cantina Sociale di Soligo (It) producers of sparkling (metodo tradizionale) Prosecco wines in Veneto.

Cantina Sociale di Trapani (It) a co-operative winery based on the island of Sicily. Labels include: Forti Terre di Sicilia (Cabernet sauvignon).

Cantina Sociale di Valdobbiadene (It) producers of Prosecco di Conegliano-Valdobbiadene in Veneto.

Cantina Sociale di Vo (It) a producer of sparkling (cuve close) wines in Veneto.

Cantina Sociale S.A. Della Versa (It) a producer of sparkling (metodo tradizionale) wines in Lombardy.

Cantina Sociale Valpolicella Negrar (It) a co-operative winery (established 1933) in the Negra, Veneto region. Has 205 growers and 450ha of vineyards. Grape varieties include: Corvina, Corvinone, Rondinella. Produces a variety of local D.O.C. wines. Label: La Casetta.

Cantina Terre del Barolo (It) a winery based in the Piemonte region. Produces: DOCG Barbera d'Alba Superiore. Grape varieties include: Barbera, Nebbiolo.

Cantina Tollo Società Co-operative (It) a large wine co-operative based at Tollo in Abruzzo. Produces: Aldiano, Cagliolo, Cerasuolo, Colle Secco, Hedò, Menir, Rocca Ventosa, Valle d'Oro. Website: http://www.cantinatollo.it

Cantina Valpantena (It) a winery based in Verona. Grape varieties include: Garganega. Label: Falasco.

Cantina Valpolicella Negrar (It) see Domini Veneti.

Cantina Vinicola (It) winery, when it precedes the producer's name on a label it guarantees that the wine is made from his own and bought in grapes.

Cantine (It) when it precedes the producer's name on a label it denotes that he is a commercial producer buying grapes from growers, possibly owning vineyards himself.

Cantine del Notaio (It) a winery (established 1995) based in Rionero in Vulture, Basilicata region. Produces: D.O.C. Aglianico del Vulture.

Cantine Michele Chiarlo (It) a winery based at Calamandrana in the DOCG Barolo, Piemonte region. Label: Cannuli. Website: http://www.chiarlo.it

Cantinera (Sp) bartender. See also Cantinero.

Cantinero (Sp) bartender. See also Cantinera.

Cantinetta (It) cellar/bar.

Cantois (Fr) a commune in the Haut-Benauge, central Bordeaux.

Canton (Fr)(Switz) an area of wine production, i.e. Vaud.

Canton d'Avize (Fr) an area in the Champagne region, Contains the Grand Cru villages: Avize, Cramant, Le Mesnil-sur-Oger, Oger and Oiry. Premier Cru villages: Cuis and Grauves and the Cru villages of Brugny-Vaudancourt, Chavot-Courcourt, Mancy, Monthelon, Morangis and Moslins.

Canton d'Aÿ (Fr) an area in the Champagne region. Contains the Grand Cru villages: Ambonnay, Aÿ-Champagne, Bouzy, Louvois and Tours-sur-Marne and the Premier Cru villages: Avenay, Bisseuil, Champillon, Cumières, Dizy, Hautvillers, Mareuil-sur-Aÿ, Mutigny, Tauxières and Tours-sur-Marne and the Cru villages: Cormoyeux and Romery.

Canton de Beine (Fr) see Beine.

Canton de Bourgogne (Fr) see Bourgogne.

Canton de Braine (Fr) see Braine.

Canton de Châtillon-sur-Marne (Fr) see Châtillon-sur-Marne.

Canton de Condé-en-Brie (Fr) see Condé-en-Brie.

Canton de Dormans (Fr) see Dormans.

Canton de Fismes (Fr) see Fismes.

Canton de l'Aube (Fr) an area in the Champagne region. Contains the Cru villages: Balnot-sur-Laignes, Buxeuil, Courteron, Gye-sur-Seine, Les Riceys, Montgueux, Neuville-sur-Seine and Polisy.

Canton de Montmort (Fr) see Montmort.

Canton d'Épernay (Fr) see Épernay.

Canton de Reims (Fr) see Reims.

Canton de Sézanne (Fr) see Sézanne.

Canton d'Esternay (Fr) see Esternay.

Canton de Suippes (Fr) see Suippes.

Canton de Vertus (Fr) see Vertus.

Canton de Verzy (Fr) see Verzy.

Canton de Ville-en-Tardenois (Fr) see Ville-en-Tardenois.

Cantaoir Fhiona (Ire) grape press.

Canuck Brewery Company (Eng) a brewery based in Rowley Regis, West Midlands. Brews: Mick the Tick's 10,000th Brew.

Canuto (Sp) a narrow pipe of mahogany or olive wood, driven into the falsete prior to the wine being racked off.

Canvermoor (Eng) a company that produces a range of soft drinks. Also is a major distributor of Bulmers Strongbow Cider, Woodpecker Cider and for Red Stripe Lager.

Can-y-Delyn (Eng) a Welsh whiskey-based liqueur produced by the Hallgarten Company in London.

Canyon (Fr) a natural spring mineral water. Mineral

216

C

contents (milligrammes per litre): Sodium 13mg/l, Calcium 63mg/l, Magnesium 23mg/l, Potassium 1.8mg/l, Bicarbonates 200mg/l, Chlorides 11mg/l, Sulphates 14mg/l, Fluorides 0.02mg/l, Nitrates 2mg/l. pH 7.4

Canzem (Ger) the English spelling of the Saar vineyard of Kanzem.

Cao (Port) a red grape variety used in the production of Port to give it colour.

Caol Ila (Scot) a single malt whisky distillery based on the Isle of Islay. Is used mainly for blending of Scotch whiskies, an Islay malt whisky. (Part of the DCL group). 11 year old at 46% alc by vol., 15 year old at 43% alc by vol., also a cask-conditioned 1980 vintage 40% alc by vol.

Cap (Eng) the name given to the solid layer of skins and pips which floats on the top of fermenting red wine. Is usually broken up and submerged in the wine for maximum colour (and tannin) extraction. *See also* Chapeau and Cappello Sommerso.

Capafons-Ossó (Sp) a producer of a D.O. Priorat (Tarragona) wine called Mas de Masos from 45 year old Garnacha plus Cariñena grapes. Based at Falset they also produce a rosé made from 100% Syrah grapes.

Capaia Wines (S.Afr) a winery based in Philadelphia, Western Cape. 58ha. Grape varieties: Cabernet franc, Cabernet sauvignon, Merlot, Petit verdot. Label: Blue Hill Grove. Website: http://www.capaia.co.za

Capa Negra (Sp) a brandy produced in Jerez. Is distilled from local wines. (Add): Sandeman Hinos. y Cia, Pizzaro 10, Jerez de la Frontera. Produces Solera Reserva Capa Negra (3 year old), Brandy Reserva Capa Vieja (18 year old).

Capanelle (It) an 8ha. wine estate in Gaiole, Tuscany. Noted for Sangiovese wines.

Capanne [Le] (It) *see* Castello di Querceto.

Capataz (Sp) the head cellarman of a Spanish cellar.

Cap Bon (Afr) a principal wine-producing area in Tunisia based around Bizerta. Produces a full-bodied, dark, red wine of same name.

Capçanes (Sp) a winery based in the D.O. Montsant, Cataluña. Grape varieties include: Cariñena, Garnacha, Tempranillo. Label: Mas Collet.

Cap Classique (S.Afr) *see* Méthode Cap Classique.

Cap Colombie (S.Am) a brand of coffee produced by Nescafé from Colombian arabica beans.

Cap Corse (Fr) a full-bodied, sweet red wine apéritif flavoured with herbs and quinine from area of same name in the northern part of Corsica.

Cape American Oak (S.Afr) the label for a red wine (Pinotage) from the Isabela range produced by the Thirtytwo [32] South Ltd winery, Stellenbosch, Western Cape.

Cape Aqua (S.Afr) a natural still and sparkling mineral water. (Add): L'Arc d'Orleans, Franschhoek, Western Cape. Mineral contents (milligrammes per litre): Sodium 11mg/l, Calcium 1.1mg/l, Magnesium 2.3mg/l, Chlorides 19mg/l, Sulphates 1.7mg/l, Nitrates 2.7mg/l. pH 5.1

Cape Bay Wines (S.Afr) a winery. (Add): P.O. Box 225, Hermanus 7200. Grape varieties: Bouquet blanc, Cabernet sauvignon, Chardonnay, Chenin blanc, Colombard, Gewürztraminer, Muscadel, Merlot, Pinotage, Ruby cabernet, Sauvignon blanc, Shiraz. Labels: Admiralty House, Mellow Red.

Cape Blend (S.Afr) the label for a red wine (Merlot, Pinotage and Shiraz blend) produced by the De Waal Wines winery, Stellenbosch, Western Cape.

Cape Blend (S.Afr) the label for a red wine (Cabernet sauvignon 40%, Cabernet franc 28% and Pinotage 22% blend) produced by the Neethlingshof Estate, Stellenbosch, Western Cape.

Cape Blend (S.Afr) the label for a red wine (Shiraz 41%, Merlot and Pinotage blend) produced by the Ouoin Rock Winery, Stellenbosch, Western Cape.

Cape Boar (S.Afr) the label for a red wine (Cabernet sauvignon, Merlot and Shiraz blend) produced by the Doolhof Estate winery, Wellington, Western Cape.

Cape Bouquet (S.Afr) a medium-sweet, white wine from KWV. Is made from the Muscadelle grape.

Cape Chamonix Wine Farm (S.Afr) a winery (established 1991) based in Franschhoek, Western Cape. 50ha. Grape varieties: Cabernet franc, Cabernet sauvignon, Chardonnay, Merlot, Pinotage, Pinot noir, Sauvignon blanc. Label: Troika. Also produces Cap Classique wines. Website: http://www.chamonix.co.za

Cape Circle (S.Afr) the export label for a range of wines produced by the Rooiberg Winery, Robertson, Western Cape.

Cape Clairault (Austr) a winery based at CMB Carbunup, West Australia. Grapes include Cabernet sauvignon, Sauvignon blanc, Sémillon.

Cape Classics (S.Afr) a winery (established 1991) based in the Somerset West, Stellenbosch, Western Cape. Grape varieties includes: Chardonnay, Chenin blanc, Merlot, Pinotage, Sauvignon blanc, Shiraz. Label: Indaba. Website: http://www.capeclassics.com

Cape Coastal Vintners (S.Afr) a private export company (established 2004) based in Paarl, Western Cape. Grape varieties: Cabernet sauvignon, Chardonnay, Chenin blanc, Merlot, Pinotage, Sauvignon blanc, Shiraz. Labels: Kleinbosch, Matuba, Vineyard Specific. Website: http://www.matuba.co.za

Cape Codder (Cktl) ⅓ measure cranberry juice, ⅙ measure vodka, ⅙ measure lemon juice. Shake over ice, strain into an ice-filled old-fashioned glass and top with soda water.

Cape Cod Jack Cocktail (Cktl) ½ measure Calvados, ½ measure bilberry juice, dash gomme syrup. Stir over ice in an old-fashioned glass and serve with the stirrer.

Cape Country (S.Afr) the name given to a range of varietal wines: Pinotage, Chardonnay, Chenin blanc, Sauvignon blanc from Breede River Valley and the Coastal Region.

Cape Cross (S.Afr) the label for a red wine (Cabernet

C

sauvignon 25%, Merlot 45% and Pinotage 30% blend) produced by the Stellekaya Winery, Stellenbosch, Western Cape.

Cape Fest (S.Afr) the label for a range of wines produced by the Oranjerivier Wine Cellars winery, Lower Orange, Northern Cape.

Cape First Wines (S.Afr) a winery (established 2003) based in Somerset West, Stellenbosch, Western Cape. Grape varieties: Cabernet sauvignon, Chardonnay, Chenin blanc, Merlot, Pinotage, Pinot noir, Sauvignon blanc, Shiraz. Labels: Makana, Mill Station, Three Anchor.

Cape Forêt (S.Afr) a dry, white, cask-matured wine made from the Chenin blanc grape by KWV.

Cape Fusion (S.Afr) a red wine (Cabernet sauvignon 33%, Merlot 33%, Pinotage 33%) produced by the Asara Estate, Stellenbosch, Western Cape.

Cape Grace Winery (Austr) a winery based in the Margaret River region of Western Australia. Grape varieties include: Cabernet sauvignon.

Cape Grace Wines (S.Afr) a winery (established 1990) based in Stellenbosch, Western Cape. Grape varieties: Cabernet franc, Chardonnay, Chenin blanc, Merlot, Pinotage, Semillon, Shiraz. Website: http://www.capegracewine.co.za

Cape Harmony (S.Afr) the label for a red wine (Cabernet sauvignon, Merlot and Pinotage blend) produced by the Lorraine Private Cellar winery, Worcester, Western Cape.

Cape Haven (S.Afr) the label for a range of wines produced by the Pulpit Rock Winery, Swartland, Western Cape.

Cape Heights (S.Afr) the label for a range of wines produced by the False Bay Vineyards winery, Wellington, Western Cape.

Cape House (S.Afr) the brand-name for a South African Sherry.

Cape Hutton (S.Afr) a winery based in Stellenbosch, Western Cape. 4ha. Grape varieties: Cabernet sauvignon, Merlot. Website: http://www.capehutton.co.za

Cape Karoo (S.Afr) *see* Karoo.

Cape Legends (S.Afr) the sales and marketing organisation of Distell, Stellenbosch, Western Cape. Labels include: Allesverloren, Alto, Flat Roof Manor, Hill & Dale, Jacobsdale, Le Bonheur, Lomond, Neethlingshof, Plaisir de Merle, Stellenzicht, Theuniskraal, Tukulu, Uitkyk.

Capell's Court (S.Afr) the label for a range of wines produced by the Linton Park Wines winery, Wellington, Western Cape.

Capel Vale Winery (Austr) a winery. (Add): P.O. Box 692, Bunbury, Western Australia. 9.5ha. Grape varieties: Cabernet sauvignon, Chardonnay, Gewürztraminer, Merlot, Rhine riesling, Sauvignon blanc and Shiraz. Wines include Baudin (a Bordeaux blend). (Add): Lot 5, Stirling Estate, Capel Northwest Road, Capel, Western Australia 6271.

Cape Maiden's (S.Afr) a label for white (Chardonnay) and red (Shiraz) wines from the Juno Wine Company, Paarl.

Cape Mentelle Vineyards (Austr) a winery. (Add): P.O. Box 110, Margaret River, Western Australia.

17ha. Grape varieties: Cabernet sauvignon, Sauvignon blanc, Chardonnay, Sémillon, Merlot, Shiraz and Zinfandel. Produces varietal and table wines. Labels include: Trianders (Cabernet and Merlot blend).

Cape Mist (S.Afr) the label for a red wine (Shiraz) produced by the Tulbagh Mountain Vineyards winery, Tulbagh, Western Cape.

Cape Muscadel (S.Afr) the label for a white wine (Muscadel) produced by the De Westshof Estate winery, Robertson, Western Cape.

Capena (It) a D.O.C. dry white or sparkling wines from Latium.

Capenheimer (S.Afr) a lightly sparkling (perlé), medium-sweet, white wine (Chenin blanc 50% Colombard 50%) produced by Distell, Stellenbosch, Western Cape.

Cape Nouveau Black (S.Afr) a dry, fruity, pétillant, white wine produced by KWV.

Capensis Reserve (S.Afr) the label for a red wine (Cabernet sauvignon 62%, Merlot 31% and Pinotage 7% blend) produced by the Marklew Family Wines winery, Stellenbosch, Western Cape.

Cape Point Vineyards (S.Afr) a winery (established 1996) based in Noordhoek, Cape Point, Western Cape. 31ha. Grape varieties: Cabernet sauvignon, Chardonnay, Pinotage, Sauvignon blanc, Sémillon, Shiraz. Labels: Isliedh, Stonehaven. Website: http://www.capepointvineyards.co.za

Capercaillie (Austr) a winery based in the Hunter Valley, New South Wales. Grape varieties include: Chardonnay, Merlot, Semillon, Shiraz. Labels: Ceilidh, Ghillie.

Caperdonich (Scot) a single highland malt whisky distillery based at Rothes. 43% alc by vol.

Caperdonich Distillery Company Limited (Scot) a subsidiary of the Glenlivet Distillers Limited.

Cape Riesling (S.Afr) the name for the Crouchon grape of France.

Caperitif (S.Afr) a deep-coloured herb-flavoured apéritif made from wine blended with spirit.

Cape Roan (S.Afr) the label for a red wine (Shiraz, Cabernet sauvignon and Merlot blend) produced by the Doolhof Estate winery, Wellington, Western Cape.

Capès (W.Ind) a natural spring mineral water from Eau de Source de Dolé, Gourbeyre, Guadeloupe. Mineral contents (milligrammes per litre): Sodium 22mg/l, Calcium 58mg/l, Magnesium 24mg/l, Potassium 5.5mg/l, Bicarbonates 140mg/l, Chlorides 53mg/l, Sulphates 59mg/l, Fluorides 0.13mg/l, Nitrates 1.3mg/l. pH 6.9

Cape Smaak (S.Afr) lit: 'cape taste'. *see* Kaapse Smaak.

Cape Smoke (S.Afr) a derivative of Kaapse Smaak used nowadays for inferior brandy.

Cape Snort (S.Afr) the label for a range of wines produced by the Sentinel Vineyards winery, Stellenbosch, Western Cape.

Cape View Classic Red (S.Afr) the label for a red wine produced by the Kaapzicht Estate winery, Stellenbosch, Western Cape.

Cape Vineyards (Pty) Ltd. (S.Afr) a winery

C

(established 1994). (Add): P.O. Box 106, Rawsonville, Worcester. Formed by the amalgamation of 4 wine cellars. Grape varieties: Cabernet sauvignon, Chardonay, Chenin blanc, Malbec, Merlot, Pinotage, Ruby cabernet, Sauvignon blanc, Shiraz. Labels: Andrew Bain, Jantara, Rawson's, Wildfire. Website: http://www.cape-vineyards.com

Cape Vintage (S.Afr) the label for a red wine (Pinotage 50% and Tinto 50%) produced by Beaumont Wines winery, Walker Bay, Western Cape.

Cape Vintage (S.Afr) the label for a CWG Auction reserve Port produced by the JP Bredell winery, Stellenbosch, Western Cape.

Cape Vintage Port (S.Afr) a vintage Port-style wine produced by the Axe Hill winery, Little Karoo.

Cape White (S.Afr) the label for a white wine (Chenin blanc 80% and Chardonnay 20% blend) produced by the Stellendrift winery, Stellenbosch, Western Cape.

Cape White (S.Afr) the label for a white wine (Chenin blanc) produced by the Drostdy Wine cellar winery, Tulbagh, Western Cape.

Cape Wine Cellars (S.Afr) a winery. (Add): P.O. Box 508, Wellington, Paarl, Western Cape. Grape varieties: Cabernet sauvignon, Chardonnay, Chenin blanc, Cinsault, Merlot, Pinotage, Sauvignon blanc.

Cape Wine Centre (Eng) an information bureau. (Add): South African Wine Trade Centre, 46 Great Marlborough Street, London W1V 1DB.

Cape Winemakers Guild (S.Afr) abbr: CWG an independent association (established 1982) to promote excellence in wine making. Holds an annual wine auction since 1985. Website: http://www.capewinemakersguild.com

Cape Wines and Distillers (S.Afr) abbr: C.W. & D. A part of S.F.W. Produces varietal wines, brandies and liqueurs.

Capezzana (It) a winery based in Carmignano, Tuscany. Label: Vin Ruspo (rosé).

Capilano Springs (Can) a natural spring mineral water from Delta, British Columbia.

Capillaire (Eng) a mixture of sugar, water and egg white heated and flavoured with almond or orange flower water. Used to sweeten hot or cold drinks and punches.

Ca Pinotte (Fr) a term used in Beaujolais to denote the maturing of a good or great Cru Beaujolais.

Capireaux (Fr) a heady wine, high in alcohol that goes to one's head.

Capitala [La] (Sp) a brand of Manzanilla Sherry produced by Marqués del Real Tesoro.

Capital Ale (Eng) a cask-conditioned light mild ale 1030 O.G. brewed by Marston's Brewery, Burton-on-Trent, Staffordshire.

Capital Ale (Wal) a keg ale 1033 O.G. brewed by S.A. Brain & C°. Ltd. in Cardiff.

Capit'ale (Fr) see Freedom & Firkin.

Capitan (Sp) an Oloroso Sherry produced by Bobadilla in Jerez de la Frontera.

Capità Vidal (Sp) a winery. (Add): Vilafranca-Igualada, Km 30, 08733 El Pla del Penedés. Cava wines include: Brut Nature Banda Reserva from Parellada, Xarel-lo, Macabeo grapes.

Capitel San Rocco Rosso (It) a ripasso wine produced by Renzo Tedeschi in Valpolicella, Verona.

Capitulare de Villis (Lat) the first recorded wine laws drawn up in the eighth century during the reign of Charlemagne.

Cap M^{ac}Lear (S.Afr) a brand label for red (Cabernet sauvignon and Shiraz blend) and white (Chardonnay and Chenin blanc blend) wines produced by African Pride Wines, Constantia, Western Cape.

Capo di Stato (It) an I.G.T. red wine produced by Azienda Agricola Conte Loredan Gasparini, Via Martignano Alto, 24/A, I-31040 Venegazzù di Volpago del Montello. Grape varieties: 70% Cabernet sauvignon, 10% Cabernet franc, 10% Malbec, 10% Merlot. Matured in French oak for 2 years.

Capogreco Winery (Austr) a winery based in the Murray Valley, Victoria. Produces varietal wines from Shiraz, Cabernet sauvignon, Riesling, Mataro grapes.

Cappan (Fr) a wine-producing district based in A.C. Bellet, Provence.

Cappello Sommerso (It) lit: 'submerged cap', vinification method where the skins are kept submerged in the must for 3–5 weeks to extract maximum colour and tannin.

Cappuccino (It) a red grape variety grown in Savuto, Calabria.

Cappuccino Coffee (It) an espresso coffee topped with hot frothy milk and grated chocolate mixed with ground cinnamon sprinkled on top. Also spelt Capuccino (English spelling). (Fr) = café crème, (Ger) = cappucino, (Sp) = capuchino.

Cappucino (Ger) cappuccino coffee.

Cappucino Cocktail (Cktl) ⅓ measure Kahlúa, ⅓ measure vodka, ⅓ measure cream, dash gomme syrup. Shake well over ice and strain into a cocktail glass.

Capraldehyde (Eng) an aldehyde found in wine which contributes to the bouquet and flavour of the wine.

Capri (It) an island off the west coast that produces red, rosé and white wines.

Capri Bianco (It) a white wine made on the island of Capri from the Greco and Fiano grapes.

Capric Acid (Eng) $C_9H_{19}COOH$. an acid that is found in wine in small quantities.

Capri Cocktail [1] (Cktl) ⅓ measure Cognac, ⅓ measure Campari, ⅓ measure sweet Martini. Stir over ice, strain into cocktail glass, add ice cube and lemon peel spiral.

Capri Cocktail [2] (Cktl) 20mls (⅙ gill) créme de banane, 20mls (⅙ gill) white créme de cacao, 20mls (⅙ gill) cream. Shake over ice and strain into an ice-filled old-fashioned glass.

Capricornia (Austr) a liqueur made from tropical fruits.

Caprilla (Cktl) ¾ measure vodka, ⅛ measure dry Port, ⅛ measure cherry brandy, 2 dashes grenadine. Stir over ice, strain into cocktail glass and top with a cherry.

Caprini (Eng) the brand-name of a perry produced by Taunton Cider Company Ltd.

Caproic Acid (Eng) $C_5H_{11}COOH$. an ester that is found in wine in small quantities.

Cap Royal Blanc (Fr) the label for an A.C. Bordeaux Blanc Sec, Bordeaux. Grape varieties: Sauvignon blanc 45%, Sémillon 55%.

Caprylic Acid (Eng) $C_7H_{15}COOH$. an acid that is found in wine in small quantities.

Cap Savanna (Fr) a 43% alc by vol. golden oak-aged rum from the Savanna distillery, La Réunion.

Capstone (Eng) a 6% alc by vol. strong ale brewed by the White Star Brewery, Hampshire.

Capsule (Eng) the lead, foil or plastic covering over the top of a bottle to seal the contents from the air.

Capsule Blanche (Bel) lit: 'white top', a light-coloured beer with a very pronounced bitterness brewed by the Abbaye of Chimay Brasserie. 8% alc by vol.

Capsule Bleu (Bel) lit: 'blue top', a deep copper-coloured, well-hopped beer 9% alc by vol. brewed by the Abbaye of Chimay Brasserie.

Capsule-Congé (Fr) the foil bottle covering on a bottle of French wine that signifies that the duties have been paid and the wine can be traded freely.

Capsule Rouge (Bel) lit; 'red top', a beer 7% alc by vol. brewed by the Abbaye of Chimay Brasserie.

Captain (Ch.Isles) a draught bitter 1045 O.G. brewed by the Guernsey Brewery, St. Peter Port, Guernsey (renamed Special in 1999) now brewed on Jersey.

Captain Collins (Cktl) 25mls (⅕ gill) Canadian whisky, juice ½ lime, dash grenadine. Shake over ice, strain into an ice-filled collins glass, top with soda, stir and serve.

Captain Cook Brewery [The] (Eng) a brewery (established 1999). (Add): The White Swan, 1 West End, Stokesley, Middlesborough, Cleveland TS9 5BL. Brews: Black Porter 4.4% alc by vol., Slipway 4.2% alc by vol., Sunset 4% alc by vol. Website: http://www.thecaptaincookbrewery.co.uk

Captain Cook Brewery (N.Z) a brewery based in Auckland. Introduced beer that was filtered, pasteurised and carbonated.

Captain Morgan (W.Ind) the popular brand-name of a dark rum from Barbados, Guyana and Jamaica. 40% alc by vol. Sold by Seagram. *See also* The Dark and Stormy.

Captain Bill Bartrams Bitter (Eng) a 4.5% alc by vol. bitter ale brewed by Bartrams Brewery, Suffolk.

Captain's Bitter (Eng) a cask-conditioned bitter 1037 O.G. brewed by the Southsea Brewery, Portsmouth, Hampshire.

Captain's Blood (Cktl) 35mls dark rum, 2 teaspoons lime cordial, dash Angostura. Shake over ice and strain into a cocktail glass.

Captain's Drift (S.Afr) the label for a white (Chardonnay) and red (Shiraz) wines produced by the Nordale Winery, Robertson, Western Cape.

Captain Smith (Eng) a cask-conditioned ale brewed by the Titanic Brewery, Burslem, Stoke-on-Trent, Staffordshire.

Captains Stout (Eng) a 4.8% alc by vol. stout brewed by Bartrams Brewery, Suffolk.

Capua (It) an area in Campania where Fallerno wine is produced.

Capucijn (Hol) a bottle-conditioned abbaye beer 6.5% alc by vol. from Budel Brouwerij. *See also* Budels Alt, Parel.

Caques (Fr) willow baskets used in the Champagne region to carry the grapes (375kgs–393kgs) (150lbs–175lbs) can be held in each.

Ca'Quila (Mex) a 5.5% alc by vol. bottled drink of Mexican tequila, organic agave cactus juice and Mexican lime.

Ca'Quila Silver (Mex) a 5.5% alc by vol. bottled drink of Mexican tequila, organic agave cactus juice and Sicilian lemon.

Capuccino (Eng) *see* Cappuccino Coffee.

Capuccino (It) a cream and brandy-based liqueur 17% alc by vol.

Capuchino (Sp) cappuccino coffee.

Capuijn (Hol) a 6.5% alc by vol. ruby-red, bottled special beer brewed by the Budelse Brouwerij, Budel.

Cara (S.Afr) the label for a red wine (Cabernet sauvignon 39%, Merlot 24% and Shiraz 37% blend) part of the Jacques de Savoy range produced by the Vrede en Lust Wine Farm winery, Paarl, Western Cape.

Carabella Winery (USA) a winery based in the Willamette Valley, Oregon. Grape variety: Pinot noir.

Carabinieri Cocktail (Cktl) ⅓ measure Galliano, ⅓ measure tequila, ⅓ measure triple sec, 3 dashes lime juice, 1 egg yolk. Shake over ice, strain into an ice-filled highball glass and top with fresh orange juice, decorate with a green and red cherry and a slice of lime.

Cara Blanc (S.Afr) a dry, fragrant, light, white wine produced by Blaauwklippen Agricultural Estate from the Colombar grape.

Caracas (S.Am) a coffee-producing region in Venezuela.

Caracol (Eng) a small grade of green coffee bean, also known as a Peaberry.

Caraf (Ire) carafe.

Carafe (Fr) lit: 'decanter', a clear glass decanter used for serving wines or water at the table. Inexpensive wines are usually served '*en carafe*'. (Ire) = caraf.

Carafe Clos-Vougeot (Fr) an urn-shaped, glass decanter with a short neck.

Caraffa (It) decanter.

Carafino Wines (S.Afr) the brand-name for everyday drinking wines produced by Gilbeys Ltd.

Carafon (Fr) a small carafe of half a litre capacity or less.

Carah (S.Afr) the label for a red blend wine produced by the Tanagra Pivate Cellar winery, McGregor, Western Cape.

C

Caraïbos (W.Ind) coconut milk.

Carajillo (Sp) lit: 'little penis', the name given to a strong black coffee with a dash of brandy, drunk in the morning in northern Spain.

Caramalt (Eng) see Carapils.

Caramany (Fr) the name of a new appellation in part of the Côtes de Roussillon-Villages, south-western France.

Caramba Cocktail (Cktl) ½ measure dry gin, dash crème de framboise, dash Cherry Heering, 2 dashes grapefruit juice, 2 dashes pineapple juice. Shake over ice, strain into a club goblet and dress with a spiral of grapefruit peel and a cherry.

Caramel (Eng) used to colour spirits, wines and beers, made from burnt sugar.

Caramelised (Eng) a term sometimes used to describe the flavour of Madeira wine which acquires this taste due to the estufa system.

Caramulo (Port) a slightly acidic natural spring mineral water from Oliveira de Frades. Mineral contents (milligrammes per litre): Sodium 20.7mg/l, Calcium 3.2mg/l, Magnesium 1.2mg/l, Potassium 1.1mg/l, Bicarbonates 14.6mg/l, Chlorides 23.8mg/l, Sulphates 11mg/l, Fluorides 0.1mg/l, Silicates 13.4mg/l. pH 5.5

Carapils (Eng) used in the production of lager, a lightly kilned malt, also called Caramalt.

Cara Sposa Cocktail (Cktl) ⅓ measure Cointreau, ⅓ measure Tia Maria, ⅓ measure cream. Shake well over ice and strain into a cocktail glass.

Carat (Ger) a natural spring mineral water from Naturpark, Teutoburger Wald. Mineral contents (milligrammes per litre): Sodium 13.2mg/l, Calcium 110mg/l, Magnesium 8mg/l, Potassium 1.5mg/l, Bicarbonates 262mg/l, Chlorides 33.2mg/l, Sulphates 74mg/l, Fluorides 0.12mg/l.

Caratello (It) a barrel of 50 litres capacity.

Carawdines (Eng) a noted blender and producer of fine teas and coffees based at Berkeley Square, Bristol, Avon.

Carbách (Ire) carboy.

Carballo Galego (Sp) a white wine produced by Bodegas Salnesur, Val do Salnés, Rías Baixas, D.O. Galicia from Albariño grapes.

Carbine (Austr) a bitter stout brewed by the Castlemaine Perkins Brewery in Queensland.

Carbon (Eng) a non-alcoholic drink containing the herb absinthe, caffeine and glucose. Part of the Britvic Carbon energy drink range.

Carbonated (Eng) a term to denote drinks charged with CO_2 gas. i.e. soft drinks, bottled beers, cheap sparkling wines, etc. see Carbonates.

Carbonated Sparklers (USA) the cheapest grade of sparkling wine, the U.S. Government requires them to be labelled as such. i.e. Carbonated Hock.

Carbonated Wine (USA) wines made by artificial carbonation, both red and white wines are made in this way as well (dry to sweet styles).

Carbonates (Eng) a term which denotes artificially gassed (carbonated) drinks.

Carbon-dioxide (Eng) abbr: CO_2 gas, a non-toxic gas given off by the action of yeast on sugar. Is also used (a): as a 'blanket' on top of wines in tank to prevent oxygen attacking the wine (is heavier than oxygen) and (b): as a carbonator to cheap sparkling wines and bottled and kegged beers. (Fr) = gaz carbonique, (Ire) = dé-ocsaid carbóin, (It) = diossido di carboni/carbónico.

Carbone (It) carbonate.

Carbonell y Cía, S.A. (Sp) a producer of fine Montilla wines based in Córdoba, Montilla-Moriles.

Carbonet (Fr) an alternative name for the Carmenère grape. See also Bouton Blanc, Carbouet, Cabernelle, Carmenelle, Grande Vidure, Grand Carmenet.

Carbonic Acid (Eng) a weak acid formed by Carbon-dioxide being soluble in water. Helps to prevent oxidation during racking. Disappears at the end of fermentation with the loss of CO_2.

Carbonic Acid Gas (Eng) CO_2/Carbon-dioxide. (ire) = searbhghás carbónach.

Carbonic Maceration (Eng) see Macération Carbonique.

Carbónico (It) carbon-dioxide.

Carbonnieux (Fr) see Château Carbonnieux.

Carbonup (Austr) a district in the Margaret River region of Western Australia.

Carbouet (Fr) an alternative name for the Carmenère grape. See also Bouton Blanc, Carbonet, Cabernelle, Carmenelle, Grande Vidure, Grand Carmenet.

Carboxylase (Eng) the name given to an enzyme secreted by wine yeasts. It removes the carbon from pyruvic acid and reduces it to acetaldehyde.

Carboy (Eng) a large glass container similar to a large Italian flask. Holds 5gallons (9litres) or more. (Ire) = carbách.

Carcavelos (Port) a DOC region in southern Portugal. Produces sweet, fortified white wines from the Galego dourado grape.

Cardamaro (It) a bitter, tonic liqueur produced from herbs and wine by Giovanni Bosca in Canelli.

Cardeal (Port) a Dão wine produced by Caves Dom Teodósio.

Cardenal (Sp) the brand-name of a Sherry poduced by Valdespino.

Cardenal Cisneros (Sp) a Solera gran reserva brandy over 10 years old produced by Romate in Jerez de la Frontera.

Cardenal Mendoza (Sp) a Solera gran reserva brandy from Jerez produced by Romate in Jerez de la Frontera. 45% alc by vol.

Cardhu (Scot) a single highland malt whisky distillery based at Knockando in Morayshire. 12 year old. 40% alc by vol. Part of John Walker and Sons (owned by the DCL group). See also Cardow.

Cardicas (Cktl) ⅓ measure white rum, ⅓ measure dry white Port, ⅓ measure Cointreau. Shake well over ice and strain into a frosted cocktail glass.

Cardiff Bay Bounty Ale (Wal) a 5.5% alc by vol. ale brewed by Welsh Brewers, Cardiff.

Cardinal (Eng) a 5.2% alc by vol. ale brewed by Tolly Cobbold, Ipswich, Suffolk using Golding hops.

Cardinal (Fr) a variation of the dark kir where the white wine is replaced by red wine. See also Communiste.

Cardinal Brewery (Switz) a brewery based in Fribourg. Part of the Sibra Group (Cardinal) Breweries. Brews Top.

Cardinal Cocktail (Cktl) 40mls (⅓ gill) dry gin, 2 dashes dry vermouth, dash Campari. Stir over ice, strain into a cocktail glass and dress with a lemon peel spiral.

Cardinale Winery (USA) a winery with vineyards in both the Napa Valley and Sonoma County, California. Grape varieties include: Cabernet sauvignon.

Cardinal Punch (Punch)(Non-alc) 1100mls cranberry juice, 500mls orange juice, juice of 2 lemons, 4 bottles chilled ginger ale, stir altogether over ice and serve.

Cardinal Richard (Fr) an A.C. Muscadet Sèvre et Maine produced by Château du Cléray from a top wine tested by a team of tasters each year from a selection of vineyards.

Cardinal Sin (Eng) a 4.8% alc by vol. ale brewed by Abbey Ales Brewery in Lansdown, Bath.

Cardinel (Eng) a 4.4% alc by vol. ale brewed by the Filo Brewing Company, East Sussex.

Cardisco (It) an alternative name for the Sangiovese grape.

Cardo (Sp) a still natural spring mineral water from the Cardo Valley. Mineral contents (milligrammes per litre): Sodium 10.8mg/l, Calcium 95mg/l, Magnesium 42.3mg/l, Bicarbonates 424mg/l.

Cardouw (S.Afr) the label for a red wine produced by the Citusdal Cellars winery, Swartland, Western Cape.

Cardow (Scot) a single highland malt whisky from the same distillery as Cardhu near Knockando, Morayshire 40% alc by vol. Part of the DCL Group.

Caref Ertach Pensans (Eng) a cask-conditioned beer 1055 O.G. brewed by the Pensans Brewery, Penzance, Cornwall.

Carelle-Dessous (Fr) a Premier Cru vineyard [part] in the A.C. commune of Volnay, Côte de Beaune, Burgundy.

Carelle-Sous-la-Chapelle (Fr) a Premier Cru vineyard in the A.C. commune of Volnay, Côte de Beaune, Burgundy.

Carema (It) a D.O.C. red wine from Piemonte in a small commune near Turin. Made from the Nebbiolo grape. Produced by leaving the grapes to macerate before pressing in a room saturated with natural CO_2. Aged 4 years (2 years in oak/chestnut casks).

Carême (Fr) Lent, the Roman Catholic fasting of 40 days from Ash Wednesday to Easter when only a little food and no alcoholic beverages are consumed.

Caresse Marine (S.Afr) the label for a range of wines produced by the Wildekrans Estate, Walker Bay, Western Cape.

Caretaker of History (Eng) a 6% alc by vol. ale brewed by the Red Rose brewery, Lancashire.

Carey Cellars (USA) a winery based in the Santa Ynez Valley, Santa Barbara, California. 19ha. Grape varieties: Cabernet sauvignon, Chardonnay, Merlot and Sauvignon blanc. Produces varietal wines.

Carey Winery (USA) a winery based in Alameda, California. Produces table and dessert wines.

Cargo (Mad) the old name for sweet Madeira wine.

Cariad (USA) lit: 'darling', a label for a red wine (Cabernet sauvignon) from the Tychson Hill Vineyard, Napa Valley (part of Colgin).

Cariad (Wal) the label used for a range of white, rosé and sparkling wines produced by the Llanerch Vineyard in the Vale of Glamorgan. (Add): Hensol, Pendoylan, Vale of Glamorgan, South Wales. CF7 8JU.

Carib (W.Ind) a beer brewed by the Caribbean Development Corporation in Trinidad & Tobago.

Cariba (Eng) a carbonated, non-alcoholic, pineapple and grapefruit drink from Schweppes.

Caribbean Cay (Eng) a dark West Indian rum, 40% alc by vol. from Kilsern Distillers Ltd., Leicester.

Caribbean Champagne (Cktl) ½ measure white rum, ½ measure crème de banane. Shake over ice, strain into a Champagne flute and top with iced Champagne and add a slice of banana.

Caribbean Coffee (Liq.Coffee) using a measure of white rum.

Caribbean Cool (Eng) a range of non-alcoholic, sparkling, fruit-flavoured drinks.

Caribbean Cup (Cup) 300mls dry cider, 100mls white rum, 250mls orange juice. Mix altogether with ice, decorate with mint sprigs and orange slices.

Caribbean Sunset (Cktl) ⅓ measure gin, ⅓ measure blue Curaçao, ⅓ measure crème de banane, ⅓ measure cream, ⅓ measure lemon juice, dash grenadine. Shake all (except grenadine) over ice, strain into a cocktail glass and add the grenadine. Do not stir.

Carib Brewery (W.Ind) a brewery based in Trinidad. Brews: Allsopps, Carib Lager, F.E.S. and Skol.

Carib Lager (W.Ind) a lager beer 5.2% alc by vol (1049 O.G) brewed by the Carib Brewery in Trinidad.

Carica (Mex) a natural spring mineral water from Tapachula.

Carignan (Fr) a red grape variety grown in southern France. Is also known as the Bois dur, Carignane, Carignan noir, Cariñena, Cariñena-Mazuelo, Catalan, Crujillón, Mataro, Mazuelo, Roussillonen and Tinto mazuela.

Carignane (USA) a red grape variety used for red wines and dessert wines. See also California Carignane, Carignan and Cariñena-Mazuelo.

Carignano (It) a red grape variety grown in Latium and Sardinia.

Carignano di Sulcis (It) a D.O.C. red wine produced on Sardinia.

Carillon de L'Angélus [Le] (Fr) the second wine of [Château L'Angélus, GCC A.C. Saint-Émilion].

Carillon [Louis] (Fr) a winery (12ha) based in Puligny-Montrachet, Côte de Beaune, Burgundy. Produces: Grand Cru Bienvenues-Bâtard-Montrachet, Premier Crus of Combettes, Perrières and Referts.

C

Carine (Cktl). ¼ measure Mandarine Napoléon, ½ measure dry gin, ¼ measure Dubonnet, 3 dashes lemon juice. Stir well over ice and strain into cocktail glass.

Cariñena (Sp) a Denominación de Origen region between Madrid and Barcelona. 21,597ha. D.O. applies to red, white and rosé wines produced in the region in province of Zaragoza. Grape varieties include Cariñena (6%), Garnacha blanca, Garnacha (55%), Parellada, Tempranillo (15%), Viura (20%).

Cariñena (Sp) a red grape variety grown in the south-eastern regions of Spain. Also known as the Cariñena-Mazuelo, Mazuelo and Carignan.

Cariñena-Mazuelo (Sp) an alternative name for the Carignan.

Carinera (Sp) a red grape variety grown in the Penedés region.

Carino (It) a producer of Moscato Spumante wines in Piemonte.

Cariño (Sp) a red grape variety grown in Ribeiro.

Carioca (Bra) a strong coffee drink usually drunk watered down with hot or cold water.

Carioca (Bra) a 5% alc by vol. pale straw, bottled lager brewed by Latino do Brasil Brewery.

Carioca (Port) a weak espresso coffee.

Carioca (W.Ind) the brand-name of a rum from a distillery of same name in Puerto Rico.

Carioca Cocktail (Cktl) 25mls (⅕ gill) Cognac, 15mls (⅛ gill) Kahlúa, 20mls (⅙ gill) cream, 1 egg yolk. Blend altogether with a scoop of crushed ice in a blender, pour into a saucer glass and sprinkle with ground cinnamon.

Carisbrooke Wines (S.Afr) a winery (established 1989) based in Stellenbosch, Western Cape. 6ha. Grape varieties: Cabernet sauvignon, Merlot, Shiraz.

Caritelli (It) very small casks used for Vin Santo.

Carleton Tower (Can) a blended Canadian whisky produced by Hiram Walker. 40% alc by vol.

Carl Everson (S.Afr) the label for a range of wines produced by the Opstal Estate winery, Worcester, Western Cape.

Carling Black Label (Can) a lager beer 4.1% alc by vol. brewed by Carling O'Keefe Brewery in Toronto. Brewed in Britain under licence by Bass Charrington.

Carling Brewery (USA) noted breweries based in Baltimore, Belleville, Phoenix and Tacoma.

Carling Extra Dry (Eng) a dry version of Carling Black Label that is sold in a matt silver can. 6.5% alc by vol. Brewed by Bass under licence.

Carling O'Keefe (Can) a large brewery based in Toronto, owns Beamish Brewery in Ireland. Famous for Carling Black Label Lager.

Carlins [Les] (Fr) a vineyard. (Com): Montagny, Côte Chalonnaise, Burgundy.

Carlomagno (Sp) a red wine produced by Bodegas Carlos Serres S.A. in Rioja. Made by macération carbonique. Matured in oak 3¼ years and then in bottle. Made from 60% Tempranillo and 40% Garnacha grapes.

Carlonet (S.Afr) a Cabernet-based red wine produced by Uiterwyk.

Carlo Rossi (USA) the brand-name used by the Gallo Winery for a range of their table wines.

Carlos 1 (Sp) a 12 year old Solera gran reserva brandy, 80% pot-distilled, produced by Domecq.

Carlos 1 Imperial (Sp) a 100% Solera gran reserva pot-distilled brandy with an average age of 17 years produced by Domecq.

Carlos 111 (Sp) a 6 year old Solera gran reserva brandy produced by Domecq.

Carlos Serres (Sp) a white wine produced by Bodegas Carlos Serres, S.A. Rioja. Vinification by macération carbonique then oak and bottle matured.

Carlow Brewing C° (Ire) a brewery. (Add): The Goods Store, Station Road, Carrickfergus, County Antrim, Northern Ireland. Brews beers and lager. Website: http://www.carlowbrewing.com 'E'mail: info@carlowbrewing.com

Carlowitz (Ser) the old name for a red wine produced in Sremski Karlovici, Vojvodina.

Carlsbad (Czec) a lithiated mineral water.

Carlsbad Becher (Czec) a herbal liqueur made with spa water from Carlsbad used for the aroma and taste.

Carlsberg (Czec)(Ger) a bitter herbal digestive liqueur.

Carlsberg (Ger) vineyard (Anb): Mosel-Saar-Ruwer. (Ber): Bernkastel. (Gro): Kurfürstlay. (Vil): Veldenz.

Carlsberg Brewery (Den) a large, famous brewery (established 1947) based in Copenhagen. Also owns Holstein Brewery in Hamburg. (U.K) branch address: Jacobsen House, 140 Bridge Street, Northampton, Northamptonshire, England NN1 1PZ. *see* Carlsberg UK. Website: http://www.carlsberg.co.uk

Carlsberg Kildevaevald (Den) a still natural spring mineral water from Jydsk Kildevald. Mineral contents (milligrammes per litre): Sodium 16mg/l, Calcium 12mg/l, Magnesium 5mg/l, Potassium 2mg/l, Bicarbonates 65mg/l, Chlorides 17mg/l, Sulphates 9mg/l, Nitrates <1mg/l. pH 7.2

Carlsberg Kurvand (Den) a natural spring mineral water from Arnakke Kilde. Mineral contents (milligrammes per litre): Sodium 30mg/l, Calcium 50mg/l, Magnesium 5mg/l, Potassium 2mg/l, Bicarbonates 147mg/l, Chlorides 40mg/l, Sulphates 35mg/l, Nitrates 0.1mg/l.

Carlsberg Lager (Den) a famous lager beer brewed by the Carlsberg Brewery. Brewed under licence in many countries. Carlsberg Pilsner 1030 O.G. Carlsberg Special Brew 1080 O.G. Carlsberg Ice 5.6% alc by vol. Alcohol for Carlsberg Lager increased from 3.4% to 3.8% alc by vol.

Carlsberg 68 (Den) *see* Elephant Lager.

Carlsberg Special Brew (Den) a strong lager beer 1080 O.G. brewed by the Carlsberg Brewery in Copenhagen.

Carlsberg-Tetley (Den) half-owned by Allied-Domecq and Carlsberg.

223

C

Carlsberg UK (Eng) a brewery. (Add): Jacobsen House, 140 Bridge Street, Northampton, Northamptonshire, England NN1 1PZ. Brews: Carlsberg Export, Carlsberg Special Brew, Holstein (Alcohol Free), Holstein Export, Holstein Pils, San Miguel, Skol Lager, Skol Soper, Tetley's Bitter. Website: http://www.carlsberg.co.uk

Carlshama (Swe) a Swedish Punsch 55.5% alc by vol. Produced by the Aktiebolaget Vin & Spritcentralem.

Carlsheim (S.Afr) a Sauvignon blanc blended, dry, white wine from the Uitkyk Estate in Stellenbosch.

Carlsminde Brewery (Den) a brewery based in Nyborg.

Carlton Brut Pêcher (Fr) a white wine and peach-flavoured drink.

Carlton LA (Eng) a low alcohol lager 0.9% alc by vol. from Courage.

Carlton United Brewery (Austr) a brewery based in Melbourne. Produces Carlton, Victoria and Fosters beers.

Carl von Linné (Swe) a still natural spring mineral water from Carl von Linné, Källa. Mineral contents (milligrammes per litre): Sodium 30mg/l, Calcium 70mg/l, Magnesium 10mg/l, Potassium 4mg/l, Bicarbonates 30mg/l, Chlorides 3mg/l.

Carmaralet (Fr) a white grape variety grown in the Jurançon region in south-western France.

Carmarthen Breweries (Wal) see Castle Brewery (The).

Carmel (Isr) a large co-operative that produces wines and fruits. see Société Coopérative Vigneronne des Grands Caves.

Carmel Hock (Isr) a medium dry, white wine produced by the Carmel co-operative.

Carmeline (Fr) a liqueur cordial of herbs (now no longer produced), originally made in Bordeaux.

Carmelita (C.Am) a natural spring mineral water from Carmelita, Guatemala.

Carmelitano (Sp) a herb-flavoured, brandy-based liqueur.

Carmelith (Isr) a semi-dry, red table wine produced by the Carmel co-operative.

Carmel Road (USA) a winery based in the Monterey County district, California. Grape variety: Pinot noir. Label: Arroyo Seco.

Carmel Valley (USA) a small A.V.A. wine-producing district in Monterey County, California. 121ha. Noted for red wines produced from Cabernet sauvignon and Merlot grapes.

Carmenelle (Fr) an alternative name for the Carmenère grape. See also Bouton Blanc, Carbonet, Carbouet, Cabernelle, Grande Vidure, Grand Carmenet.

Carmenère (Fr) a lesser red grape variety grown in Bordeaux and popular in South America. Also known as Bouton Blanc, Carbonet, Carbouet, Cabernelle, Carmenelle, Grande Vidure, Grand Carmenet.

Carmenet (Fr) an alternative name for the Cabernet franc grape.

Carmenet Vineyard (USA) a winery based in Sonoma Valley, California. Grape varieties: Cabernet sauvignon, Merlot. Label: Moon Mountain Reserve.

Carmes (Fr) a popular brand of Melisse liqueur made from balm-mint.

Carmignano (It) a 150ha. wine producing zone in Tuscany, 25 km. north-west of Florence. Home to D.O.C.G. Carmignano and Carmignano Riserva, D.O.C. Barco Reale, D.O.C. Rosato di Carmignano, D.O.C. Vin Santo.

Carmignano (It) a D.O.C.G. red wine from the communes of Carmignano and Poggio a Caiano in Tuscany. Produced from a min. of 50% Sangiovese, plus 10% to 20% Cabernet sauvignon/franc, up to 10% Canaiolo nero, up to 10% Trebbiano toscano, Canaiolo bianco and Malvasia del chianti, up to 10% other authorised grapes. Cannot be sold before June 21st of the 2nd year of vintage. If aged minimum of 3 years then classed as Riserva.

Carnegie Porter (Swe) a mild beer 3.5% alc by vol. brewed by the Pripps Brewery.

Carnelian (USA) a black, hybrid grape variety developed by the University of California.

Carneros (USA) an A.V.A. of Napa Valley, California since 1983. 3,239ha. Grape varieties include Pinot noir, Chardonnay, Merlot, Syrah.

Carneros Creek Winery (USA) a winery based in the Napa Valley, California. 4ha. Grape varieties: Cabernet sauvignon, Chardonnay, Pinot noir and Zinfandel. Produces varietal wines.

Carne's Dry Stout (Eng) a stout brewed by the Cornish Brewery Company.

Carnevale [Giorgio] (It) a Moscato d'Asti producer based in Piemonte, north-western Italy.

Carnival (Cktl) ⅓ measure Cognac, ⅓ measure Lillet, ⅓ measure apricot liqueur, dash kirsch, dash orange juice. Shake over ice and strain into a cocktail glass.

Carnival (S.Afr) a range of boxed (1, 3 and 5litres) wines produced by Country Cellars Spar convenience store. Includes a rosé (Colombard and Pinotage), Grand Cru (Chenin blanc and Colombard) plus a red, late harvest and perlé varieties.

Carnivale (Eng) a 4.5% alc by vol. ale brewed by the Berrow Brewery, Somerset.

Carnmor Spring (Scot) a natural spring mineral water from Clash, Braes of Glenlivet, Ballindalloch, Banffshire.

Carnuntum (Aus) a newly created A.C. area (in 1994) that is noted for red wines. 995ha. Soil: gravel, loam, loess and sand. Main grape varieties: white (Chardonnay, Grüner veltliner, Pinot blanc, Welschriesling), red (Blaufränkisch, Cabernet sauvignon, St. Laurent, Zweigelt. Main villages: Altenburg, Berg, Bruck, Fischamend Markt, Göttlesbrunn, Hainburg, Höflein, Mannersdorf, Schwadorf and Trautmannsdorf. See also Traisnel.

Carobbio (It) a 10ha wine estate that produces a range of Chianti wines. (Add): Via San Martino a Cecione 26, 50020 Panzano in Chianti.

224

C

Carola (Fr) a carbonated natural mineral water from Alsace. (Add): SA des Eaux Minérales de Ribeauvillé, BP 7, 68150 Ribeauvillé. Mineral contents (milligrammes per litre): Sodium 131mg/l, Calcium 80mg/l, Magnesium 23mg/l, Potassium 7mg/l, Bicarbonates 427mg/l, Chlorides 60mg/l, Sulphates 145mg/l, Nitrate 1mg/l.

Carolans (Ire) a cream liqueur made from Irish whiskey, honey, Clonmel cream and chocolate. Produced in Tipperary. 17% alc by vol. see Alcoholic Yoghurt.

Carola Rouce (Fr) a natural spring mineral water from from Source du Châteaux, Ribeauville, Alsace. Mineral contents (milligrammes per litre): Sodium 103mg/l, Calcium 160mg/l, Magnesium 52mg/l, Potassium 22mg/l, Bicarbonates 505mg/l, Chlorides 76mg/l, Sulphates 205mg/l, Fluorides 0.7mg/l.

Carolinahoeve Boutique Cellar (S.Afr) a winery (established 2004) based in Wellington, Western Cape. 4ha. Grape varieties: Chenin blanc, Cinsaut, Pinotage. Produces varietal wines. Website: http://www.carolinahoeve.com

Carolina Mountain Spring Water (USA) a natural spring mineral water (established 1972) from Carolina. Mineral contents (milligrammes per litre): Sodium 4.83mg/l, Calcium 5.84mg/l, Sulphates 9.3mg/l. pH 7.6

Caroline Mountain Water (USA) a natural spring mineral water. Mineral contents (milligrammes per litre): Sodium 3.5mg/l, Calcium 6.7mg/l, Magnesium 0.34mg/l, Potassium 1.5mg/l, Fluorides 0.06mg/l. pH 6.88

Carolinen Quelle (Ger) a still and sparkling natural spring mineral water from Teutoburger Wald. Mineral contents (milligrammes per litre): Sodium 9mg/l, Calcium 230mg/l, Magnesium 55mg/l, Potassium 4mg/l, Bicarbonates 332mg/l, Chlorides 14mg/l, Sulphates 540mg/l.

Ca'Romé (It) a winery based at Ca'Romé di Romano Marengo Via Rabajà 36, 12050 Barbaresco (CN). Produces Romano Marengo Rapet D.O.C.G. Barolo.

Caroni (W.Ind) the brand-name of a white rum from Trinidad that is matured in England. See also White Magic Light.

Carousal (Eng) lit: 'a merry drinking party' a seventeenth century word.

Carouse (Eng) a seventeenth century word denoting a drinking spree (to drink freely).

Carousel (Eng) a 4% alc by vol. ale brewed by the South Port Brewery, Merseyside.

Carousel (Ger) a wrought iron turntable used for wine tasting in the Pfalz. Has spaces for up to 12 glasses. Different wines are poured into each and drinkers revolve the table to sample each.

Carpano (It) the brand-name of a famous vermouth producer. Produces Punt e Mes.

Carpano [Antonio] (It) in 1786, the Italian purported to have invented sweet vermouth. See also Noilly (Louis).

Carpathian Mountains (Rum) wine region that occupies most of central Rumania. Wine areas are situated amongst their foothills.

Carpe Diem (S.Afr) the label for a range of wines produced by the Diemersfontein Wines winery, Wellington, Western Cape.

Carpy Ranch Chardonnay (USA) a white wine produced by the Freemark Abbey winery in the Napa Valley, California.

Carpené-Malvolti (It) a famous wine and brandy producer based in the Veneto region.

Carpené-Malvolti Brut (It) a sparkling (metodo tradizionale) wine produced in Veneto by Carpené-Malvolti from Chardonnay and Pinot grapes. 12.5% alc by vol.

Carpineto (It) a Chianti Classico producer based in the Tuscany region. (Add): Dudda, 50022 Greve in Chianti (Firenze). Produces Chianti Classico and Vino Nobile di Montepulciano. Labels include: Dogajola, Farnito. Website: http://www.carpineto.com 'E'mail: info@carpineto.com

Carrabassett (USA) a natural spring mineral water (established 1988) from the Carrabassett Fault, Maine.

Carral (Sp) wine butt.

Carras [John] (Gre) a hotelier and noted wine maker based at Sithonia, Halkidiki. Produces red and white wines under the labels of Côtes du Meliton and Château Carras.

Carrasal (Arg) a label for a red wine (Cabernet sauvignon, Malbec and Merlot blend) from the Weinert winery, Mendoza.

Carrasca (S.Am) a local name for oak.

Carrascal (Sp) a district within Andalusia, has chalky soil. Also spelt Carrascol.

Carrascao (Port) a term used to describe an astringent rough red wine.

Carrascol (Sp) the alternative spelling of Carrascal.

Carrassons (Fr) the wooden staves to which the wires are attached for the Guyot system on which the vines are tied.

Carrel [Eugène] (Fr) a winery based in the A.C. Savoie. Produces: Roussette, Marestel, Jongieux (Mondeuse and Pinot noir), Jongieux Gamay Cuvée Vieilles Vignes

Carrère (Fr) an Armagnac producer. (Add): Distilleries Carrère SA. 36, Rue des Alliés, 32500 Fleurance. Produces Panache d'Or and Panache d'Or V.S.O.P.

Carricante (It) a white grape variety grown in Sicily to make dry white wines.

Carrick (N.Z) a winery in the Central Otago region, South Island. Grape varieties: Pinot gris, Pinot noir, Sauvignon blanc. Vineyards: Bannockburn.

Carrington (Austr) a label for a sparkling wine range from Orlando Wines.

Carrington Distilleries (Can) the producers of Carrington Canadian Whisky. 40% alc by vol.

Carrizal (Sp) a natural spring mineral water from San Andrés del Rabanedo, Léon. Mineral contents (milligrammes per litre): Sodium 1mg/l, Calcium 27mg/l, Magnesium 6mg/l, Bicarbonates

104mg/l, Chlorides 3mg/l, Sulphates 2mg/l, Silicates 9.3mg/l.

Carrodilla Tinto (Arg) the brand-name of a red wine produced in central Argentina.

Carrol Cocktail (Cktl) 40mls (⅓ gill) brandy, 20mls (⅙ gill) sweet vermouth. Stir over ice, strain into a cocktail glass and top with a cherry.

Carrousser (Fr) old word denoting '*to drink freely*', used in the sixteenth century.

Carr's Best Bitter (Eng) a cask-conditioned bitter beer 1041 O.G. brewed in a home-brew public house in Southampton, Hampshire. Is owned by Whitbreads.

Carr Taylor (Eng) a vineyard and winery (planted in 1973). (Add): Yew Tree Farm, Westfield, Hastings, East Sussex TN35 4SG. 8.5ha. Produces wines, spirits, beers, mineral waters. Grape varieties: Gutenborner, Kerner, Müller-Thurgau and Reichensteiner. Website: http://www.carr-taylor.co.uk 'E'mail: sales@carr-taylor.co.uk

Carruades de Château Lafite (Fr) a red wine produced at Château Lafite from vines under 12 years old.

Carrypac (Eng) a 24 can holder which has a handle at the top, the beers are held sideways.

Cars (Fr) a commune in the A.C. Côtes de Blaye in north-eastern Bordeaux.

Carsebridge (Scot) a grain whisky distillery based south of Dundee, Perthshire.

Carseolanum (It) a red wine produced in central Italy in Roman times.

Carso (It) a D.O.C. red and white wines from the Friuli-Venezia-Giulia region.

Carstairs (USA) a blended whiskey bottled by the Calvert Distillers C°. of Baltimore, Louisville. 40% alc by vol.

Carstens (Ger) a noted producer of Deutscher Sekt by the cuve close method.

Carta Blanca (Mex) the name of a beer exported to the USA.

Carta Blanca (Sp) a Fino Sherry produced by Blàzquez in Jerez de la Frontera.

Carta Blanca (W.Ind) a light-bodied rum (white label) produced in Greater Antilles, Cuba and Puerto Rico.

Carta de Oro (Sp) a red wine produced by Bodegas Berberana S.A. Oak matured for 2 years minimum and for 1 year in bottle. Also a white wine of same name.

Carta de Plata (Sp) the brand-name for red and white wines produced by Bodegas Berberana S.A. in Rioja.

Carta Nevada (Sp) a non-vintage cava wine produced by Freixenet in the Penedés region.

Carta Oro (Sp) an Amontillado Sherry produced by Blàzquez in Jerez de la Frontera.

Carta Oro (W.Ind) a brand of golden rum (gold label) coloured with caramel and produced in the Greater Antilles, Cuba and Puerto Rico.

Cartaxo (Port) an I.P.R. red wine within the I.P.R. region of the Estremadura on the plains of the Rio Tejo.

Carte Blanche (Fr) the name given to the sweeter style of Champagne from Pomméry et Greno.

Carte Blanche (Fr) a non-vintage Champagne produced by Bonnet et Fils.

Carte Blanche (Scot) a 5% alc by vol. ale brewed by the Kelburn Brewing C°., Lanarkshire.

Carte d'Argent Extra (Fr) a Cognac with 35 years of ageing from Renault Cognac. *See also* Carte Noire Extra.

Carte de Vin (Fr) wine list.

Carte d'Or Riesling (Austr) a white wine from the Yalumba Vineyard. Is crisp, spicy and aromatic.

Cartègue (Fr) a commune in the A.C. Côtes de Blaye in north-eastern Bordeaux.

Carte Noir (Fr) a non-vintage Champagne produced by Bricout et Koch from 40% Chardonnay, 20% Pinot meunier and 40% Pinot noir grapes.

Carte Noire (Eng) a 100% arabica coffee from Jacobs Suchard.

Carte Noire Extra (Fr) a Cognac (12 years old average) produced by Renault Cognac.

Carte Or (Fr) a non-vintage Champagne produced by Bricout et Koch from 40% Chardonnay and 60% Pinot noir grapes.

Carte Orange (Fr) a non-vintage Champagne produced by Napoléon from Chardonnay 40% and Pinot noir 60%.

Carte Vert (Fr) a blanc de blancs vintage Champagne produced by Chauvet in Tours-sur-Marne.

Carte Verte (Fr) a non-vintage Champagne produced by Napoléon from Chardonnay 25% and Pinot noir 75% grapes.

Cartoixa (Sp) the alternative name used in the Tarragona region for the Xarel-lo grape.

Carton (Eng) a partitioned cardboard box which normally holds 12 standard bottles of wine or spirits. *See also* Case.

Cartron (Fr) a liqueur producer based in Burgundy. Noted for Crème de Nuits and a mandarine liqueur produced from brandy and tangerine peel.

Cartuxa Evura (Port) a Tinto Reserva D.O.C. Alentejo wine produced by Eugénio de Almeida, Adega de Cartu, Evora. Originally known as Pera Manca. Made from a blend of Aragonês and Trincadeira grapes aged in oak barriques for 18 months.

Cartwright Brewery (USA) a brewery based in Portland, Oregon. Brews: Cartwright Portland Beer 5% alc by vol.

Caruso Cocktail (Cktl) ⅓ measure dry gin, ⅓ measure dry vermouth, ⅓ measure (white) crème de menthe. Stir over ice and strain into a cocktail glass.

Carvalhelhos (Port) a natural spring mineral water (established 1850) from Boticas. Mineral contents (milligrammes per litre): Sodium 52.6mg/l, Bicarbonates 140mg/l, Fluorides 3.3mg/l, Silicates 41.9mg/l. pH 7.82

Carvalho (Port) oak.

Carvalho, Ribeiro and Ferreira (Port) a distillers (established 1898) producers of Conde de Santar (a Dão wine). Does not vinify any wine. Is the

C

largest brandy maker in Portugal. Also produces Aguardente Preparada Reserva (brandy) and red and white Serraclayres (an Alentejo wine).

Carver Wine Cellars (USA) a winery based in Rolla, Missouri. Produces hybrid wines.

Carypton (W.Ind) a green-coloured swizzle drink, drunk as an apéritif.

Casa (It) a term that if it precedes producer's name on the label means he is a commercial producer who buys grapes from growers, possibly owning vineyards himself.

Casabello Wines Ltd. (Can) a winery based in Penticton, Vancouver. Also imports grapes from Washington. Wines sold in vacuum-sealed litre carafes and bottles.

Casablanca (Afr) a wine-producing region of Morocco. Contains the A.O.G. areas of Doukkala, Sahel and Zenata. Soil is mainly sandy.

Casablanca (Chile) a 130ha wine growing area situated north-west of Santiago. Noted for Sauvignon blanc and Chardonnay wines. Home to Veramonte.

Casablanca (Cktl) 35mls white rum, 25mls coconut cream, 50mls pineapple juice, 2 dashes grenadine, 2 scoops crushed ice. Blend well together in a blender and pour into a large balloon glass.

Casa Blanca (Cktl) ⅓ measure Jamaican rum, ⅛ measure Cointreau, ⅛ measure lime juice, ⅛ measure Maraschino. Shake over ice and strain into a cocktail glass.

Casablanca Cocktail (Cktl) ⅔ measure vodka, ⅓ measure advocaat, 2 dashes Galliano, 4 dashes lemon juice, 2 dashes orange juice. Shake over ice, strain into a cocktail glass and top with a slice of orange.

Casablanca Collins (Cktl) 35mls vodka, 5mls Galliano, 25mls advocaat, 10mls lemon juice, 5mls orange juice. Shake over ice, strain into an ice-filled highball glass and top with a cherry.

Casa Burmester (Port) a new D.O. red wine produced by Burmester, Douro.

Casa Cadaval (Port) a winery based in Ribatejo. Grape varieties: Cabernet sauvignon, Merlot, Pinot noir, Trincadeira, Castelão Francês (Periquita), Fernão pires.

Casa Compostela (Port) a small private firm that produces Vinhos Verdes. Has 28ha. (Add): Requiao, 4760 V.N. Familicao. Produces Casa de Compostela. Grape varieties: Azal, Loureiro, Pederña, Trajadura.

Casa da Tapada (Port) a producer of Vinho Verde from the Loureiro grape. (Add): Soc. Agricola Lda. S-Miguel de Fiscal 4700 Amares.

Casa de Cabanelas (Port) a brand of Vinho Verde produced from Azal, Loureiro, Pederña and Trajadura grapes. (Add): Bustelõ 4560 Penafiel.

Casa de Calderón (Sp) a private bodega based in Utiel-Requena in the Levante region. Produces Blanco from Macabeo, Malvasia and Meseguera grapes. Tinto from Tempranillo, Garnacha and Monastrell grapes.

Casa de Cerca (Port) a pétillant rosé wine.

Casa de Compostela (Port) a brand of Vinho Verde produced from the Casa Compostela.

Casa de la Ermita (Sp) a red wine produced from the Monastrell grape in the Jumilla region.

Casa de Penela (Port) a Vinho Verde produced from the Loureiro and Trajadura grapes. (Add): Adaúfe, 4700 Braga.

Casa de Rendufe (Port) a Vinho Verde producer based in Resende. Grape variety: Avesso.

Casa de Saima (Port) a winery based in the DOC Bairrada.

Casa de Santa Leocàdia (Port) a Vinho Verde produced mainly from the Loureiro grape. (Add): Geraz do Lima, 4900 Viana do Castelo.

Casa de Sezim (Port) a Vinho Verde producer. (Add): Nespereira, 4800 Guimaraes. Grape varieties: Loureiro, Pederña and Trajadura.

Casa de Valdaiga (Sp) a light red wine produced by VILE in Léon.

Casa de Vila Boa (Port) a Vinho Verde producer. (Add): Vila Boa de Quires, 4630 Marcode Canaveses. Main grape variety is the Azal.

Casa de Vilacetinho (Port) a Vinho Verde producer. (Add): Alpendurada, 4575 Entre-Os-Rios. Grape varieties: Azal, Loureiro, Pederña.

Casa de Vila Nova (Port) a Vinho Verde producer. Wine made from the Avesso and Pederña grapes.

Casa de Vilaverde (Port) a Vinho Verde producer. (Add): Caíde de Rei, 4620 Lousada. Grape varieties: Azal, Loureiro, Pederña.

Casa do Landeiro (Port) a Vinho Verde producer. (Add): Carreira, 4750, Barcelas. Grape varieties: Loureiro and Trajadura.

Casa Donoso (Chile) a range of wines from Domaine Oriental in the Maule Valley. Grape varieties include Sauvignon blanc, Chardonnay, Merlot, Cabernet sauvignon. Website: http://www.casadonoso.cl

Casa dos Cunhas (Port) a Vinho Verde produced by the Quinta do Belinho, Antas, 4740 Esposende from Loureiro grapes. Also a red version from the Espadeiro and Vinhao grapes.

Casa Fondata Nel (It) lit: 'Firm established in', found on a wine label.

Casa Laora (It) a winery based in the Tuscany region. Produces DOCG Chianti.

Casa Lapostolle (Port) a noted winery based in the Colchagua Valley, Central Chile. Grape varieties include: Syrah. Label: Cuvée Alexandre.

Casa Larga (USA) a winery based near Rochester in the Finger Lakes, New York. 5ha. Grape varieties: Chardonnay, Gewürztraminer and Riesling. Produces varietal wines.

Casal Bordino (It) a range of D.O. wines from Montepulciano d'Abruzzo. Grape varieties: Trebbiano, Montepulciano, Cerasuolo. Co-operative bottled.

Casal Caeiro (Sp) a white wine produced from Albariño grapes by Bodegas Castro Martín, Val do Salnés, Rías Baixas, D.O. Galicia.

Casal de Coelheira (Port) a label for a range of red wines produced from Trincadeira, Castelão francês

C

and Cabernet grapes by Centro Agricola de Tramagal in Ribatejo.

Casa de Saima (Port) a winery based in the D.O. Bairrada. Grape variety: Baga.

Casal de Vale Pradinhos (Port) an aguardiente produced by Maria Pinto de Azevedo.

Casal do Coelheira (Port) a red wine produced by Centro Agricola de Tramagal in Ribatejo from Cabernet, Castelão francês and Trincadeira grapes.

Casal do Ermízio (Port) a Vinho Verde producer. (Add): Ronfe, 4800 Guimaraes. Grape varieties: Loureiro, Pederña and Trajadura.

Casaleiro (Port) brands of Vinhos Verdes and Dão wines produced by Caves Dom Teodósio.

Casalferro (It) a non-D.O.C. wine produced by Castello di Brolio from 100% Sangiovese grapes.

Casal Garcia (Port) a brand of Vinho Verde from Quinta Avelada. Website: http://www.aveleda.pt

Casa Girelli (It) a large wine producer and merchant based in Verona. (Add): Viale Verona 182, 38100 Trento, Italy. Produces wines from around Italy. Grape varieties include: Merlot, Nero d'Avola, Primitivo. Labels: Canaletto, Virtuoso, Winemakers Collection. 'E'mail: export@girelli.it

Casalinho (Port) the brand-name of a Vinho Verde from Caves do Casalinho.

Casal Mendes (Port) a brand-name of red and white Vinho Verde wines from Caves Aliança.

Casal Miranda (Port) a brand of Vinho Verde from Louro.

Casa Lo Alto (Sp) a D.O. Utiel-Requena. Based at Venta del Moro, Valencia. Grape varieties: Tempranillo, Garnacha, Graciano, Macabeo, Chardonnay, Sauvignon blanc, Cabernet sauvignon, Cabernet franc, Syrah.

Casa Madero (Mex) *see* Bodegas de San Lorenzo.

Casamari (It) a Cistercian monastery-produced herb liqueur.

Casa Marin (Chile) a winery based in the region of San Antonio. Label: Laurel Vineyard.

Casanis (Fr) a Corsican-made pastis which is popular in France.

Casa Ranuzzi (S.Am) a producer of Inca Pisco in Lima, Peru. (Is made exclusively for McKesson Liquor C°. of New York).

Casa Real (Chile) a 100% Cabernet sauvignon wine made from 40 year old vines, matured for 18 months in French oak. Produced by Santa Rita. *See also* Medalla Real, Medalla Reserva.

Casa Rivas (Chile) a winery based in the Maria Pinto valley district of the Maipo Valley region. Grape varieties: Cabernet franc, Cabernet sauvignon, Carmenère, Merlot, Sauvignon blanc, Syrah. Website: http://www.casarivas.cl

Casa Romero (Sp) a producer and shipper of Málaga wine from Málaga, southern Spain.

Casa Santos Lima (Port) a winery based outside Silgueiros in the Dão region. Produces red and white Dão wines.

Casas del Bosque (Chile) a winery based in the Casablanca Valley. Grape varieties: Carmenère, Pinot noir, Syrah. Website: http://www.casasdelbosque.cl

Casas del Toqui (Chile) a winery based in the Cachapoal Valley, Central Chile. Has a joint venture with Château Larose Trintaudon (Bordeaux).

Casa Silva (Chile) a vineyard based in Colchagua. Grape varieties: Chardonnay, Sauvignon gris, Viognier. Label: Quinta Generacíon.

Casa Sola (It) a Chianti Classico producer based in Tuscany.

Cassavecchia (It) a red grape variety from the Campania.

Casa Vinicola (It) when it precedes a producer's name on a label denotes that he is a commercial producer buying grapes and possibly owning vineyards as well.

Casa Vinicola Bruno Giacosa (It) a winery based in the Piemonte region. Produces: DOC Dolcetto d'Alba.

Casa Vinicola Dosio (It) a wine-producer based in La Morra, Piemonte. Noted for their Barolo wines.

Casa Vinicola Giacosa Fratelli (It) a winery. (Add): Via XX Settembre 64, 12057 Neive (CN). Produces Barbera wines that are aged in French barriques.

Cascade (Eng) a 4.5% alc by vol. ale brewed by Hanby Ales Ltd., Shropshire.

Cascade (Eng) a 4% alc by vol. ale brewed by the York Brewery Company, North Yorkshire.

Cascada (Ger) a natural spring mineral water from Bad Windsheim, BY.

Cascade (USA) a hybrid red grape variety. Is also known as the Seibel 5409.

Cascade Brewery (Austr) Tasmania's main brewery.

Cascade Clear Mountain Spring Water (Can) a natural spring mineral water.

Cascade Highball (Cktl) equal quantities of sweet vermouth and crème de cassis. Stir over ice in a highball glass.

Cascade Mountain Vineyards (USA) a small winery based in the Hudson Valley, New York. 6ha. Produces hybrid wines.

Cascades (USA) a hop variety which has a minty, sweet and oily character often used for the dry-hopping of beers.

Cascade Springs (Austr) a natural spring mineral water from Cascade. Mineral contents (milligrammes per litre): Sodium 6mg/l, Calcium 70mg/l, Magnesium 40mg/l, Potassium 0.3mg/l, Bicarbonates 300mg/l.

Cascade System (Fr) an old system now no longer used in which the wine producer sells his wines at various maximum grades. The method was open to abuse and allowed many inferior wines to be sold as top A.C. wines. Has now been replaced by the 'Rendement de Base'. *See also* 'Plafond Limité de Classement'.

Cascais (Cktl) ⅔ measure Smirnoff vodka, ³⁄₁₀ measure Campari, ³⁄₁₀ measure dry Sherry. Stir well over ice, strain into cocktail glass and top with a twist of orange peel.

Cascal (Port) a white grape variety grown in Peñafiel (a sub-region of Vinho Verde).

Cascalho (Mad) the stoney soil found on the island of Madeira.

C

Cascarilla (S.Am) a popular liqueur, spirit-based and flavoured with spices and barks. 30% alc by vol.

Cascastel (Fr) a noted wine-producing village in the Corbières area of Languedoc, southern France.

Cascastel (Fr) a commune in the A.C. Fitou, southern France.

Cascastel-de-Corbières (Fr) a commune in the Corbières area of the Languedoc region, southern France. Is allowed to use the A.C. Fitou.

Cascata (It) a slightly sparkling wine produced by Castello Wines. (Wine is from Veneto).

Casa Tamaya (Chile) a winery based in the Limarí region of northern Chile.

Cascina (It) an estate (formerly known as a farmhouse). *see* Fattoria, Tenuta.

Cascina Castlèt (It) a winery based in Piedmont. Produces Policalpo and Passum wines.

Cascina L'Arbiola (It) a winery. (Add): Regione Saline 56, 14050 San Marzano Oliveto (AT). 15ha. Grape varieties: Barbera, Brachetto, Cabernet sauvignon, Chardonnay, Cortese, Moscato, Pinot noir, Dolcetto, Sauvignon blanc.

Casco (Sp) cask.

Case (Eng) a box made of wood or cardboard used to hold 12 full bottles or 24 half bottles of wines, beers or spirits. *See also* Carton.

Casea Nobre (Mad) lit: 'noble vine', denotes the permitted vines for use in the production of Madeira wines.

Casein (Eng) a protein used in the production of white wines. Used as a clarifier and as a preventative against oxidation and madeirisation. Also lightens the colour of wine.

Caseinogen (Eng) the principal protein in milk which is converted into casein by rennin.

Caseiri (Mad) *see* Caseiro.

Caseiro (Mad) a parcel of land cultivated under the old feudal system, a Caseiri pays half of his grape crop as his rent.

Casel (Eng) the spelling of Kasel (a village in the Bereich of Saar-Ruwer, Mosel-Saar-Ruwer, western Germany) in the nineteenth century.

Casellas Winery (Austr) a winery based in Riverina, New South Wales. Produces varietal and table wines.

Casenallas [Jaime Lluch] (Sp) a wine producer based in the Penedés region. (Add): Carretera de Ignalada-Sitges, Km 25, Barcelona. Produces: Junot.

Casey's Cream Ale (Eng) a 4.5% alc by vol. nitrokeg ale brewed by Shepherd Neame, Kent. *see* Bishop's Cream, Master Brew Smooth.

Casgen (Wal) cask/barrel.

Casiene (Fr) an old-style fining agent still used in the vinification of méthode ancienne in the Palette, south-eastern France.

Casier à Bouteilles (Fr) bin or bottle rack.

Casillero del Diablo (Chile) a red wine made from 100% Cabernet sauvignon grapes in central Chile by Concha y Toro. Is oak-matured 2–3 years and then bottle-aged for 2 years.

Casina Adelaide (It) a winery based in the DOCG Barolo. Website: http://www.casinaadelaide.com

Casindra Mineralbrunnen (Ger) a still natural spring mineral water from Leissing, Saxony. Mineral contents (milligrammes per litre): Sodium 137mg/l, Calcium 68.8mg/l, Potassium 9.6mg/l, Bicarbonates 505mg/l, Chlorides 68.4mg/l, Sulphates 55.4mg/l.

Casino (Cktl) ½ measure gin, ¼ measure lemon juice, ¼ measure maraschino. Shake well over ice, strain into a cocktail glass and top with a cherry.

Casino (Hun) a brand of rum.

Cask (Eng) wooden (oak, chestnut, etc.) container for beers, wines or spirits. **Sizes:** Pin 4½ gals. (20.45 litres), Firkin 9 gals. (40.90 litres), Kilderkin 18 gals. (81.80 litres), Barrel 36 gals. (163.60 litres), Hogshead 54 gals. (245.40 litres). Now are also made of metal and in metric sizes of 25 litres capacity and multiples of.

Caskade (Eng) a 4.2% alc by vol. cask-conditioned ale brewed by Oldershaw's. Grantham, Lincolnshire.

Cask Age (Eng) the time wines and spirits are left to mature in casks of wood to obtain some of the flavour of that wood, helps to soften the wines or spirits.

Cask & Codpiece (Eng) a micro-brewery at Sandown, Isle of Wight. Brews Old Codswallop 4.2% alc by vol.

Cask Breather (Eng) *see* Asperating Valve.

Cask-Conditioned (Eng) beer that is allowed to condition in the cask in the public house cellar after delivery from the brewery. Is primed with finings, sugar and dry hops and takes 2–3 days before it is ready for drinking. *See also* Primings, Tapping and Venting. *See also* Brewery Conditioned and Keg Beer.

Casking (Eng) the placing of beer, wines or spirits into a cask. *see* Étonner.

Cask Marque [The] (Eng) an organisation (established 1977). (Add): Seed Bed Centre, Severalls Park, Colchester, Essex CO4 4HT. The 'traditional' beer badge of quality, the "Consumers' Charter" was introduced by them, recommended service temperature between 10°C and 15.5°C (50°F and 60°F). Website: http://www.cask-marque.co.uk 'E'mail: info@cask-marque.co.uk

Cask Strength (Scot) at 63.5% alc by vol. the strength of the malt whisky when place into casks (Sherry, Bourbon, Port) for maturation.

Cask Tannins (Eng) the tannins extracted from wooden casks during maturation of the wine. New wood will release stronger tannins than old (used casks) wood.

Cask 23 (USA) a red wine (Cabernet sauvignon) produced by the Stags Leap Wine Cellars, Napa Valley, California. Website: http://www.CASK23.com

Casorzo d'Asti (It) a small D.O.C. region based north-east of Barbera d'Asti in Piemonte.

Caspar-Heinrich-Quelle Heilwasser (Ger) an ancient natural spring mineral water. Mineral contents (milligrammes per litre): Sodium

24mg/l, Calcium 281mg/l, Magnesium 83mg/l, Potassium 3mg/l, Bicarbonates 1125mg/l, Chlorides 38mg/l, Sulphates 104mg/l.

Casparie Schagen (Hol) a 5% alc by vol. bottled cloudy wheat beer brewed by De Drie Ringen Amersfoort Bier Brouwerij, Amersfoort.

Casque (Eng) a brandy-based, honey liqueur.

Cas-Rougeot [Le] (Fr) a Premier Cru vineyard in the A.C. commune of Monthélie, Côte de Beaune, Burgundy 0.4ha.

Cassan (Fr) a Vin de Pays area of the Hérault département in southern France. Produces red and rosé wines.

Cassayre-Forni Winery (USA) a small winery based near Rutherford, Napa Valley, California. Grape varieties: Cabernet sauvignon, Chenin blanc and Zinfandel. Produces varietal wines.

Casse (Fr) an unhealthy haze or deposit in wines. *see* Copper Casse and Iron Casse.

Casse Bleu (Fr) iron casse. Also known as Casse Ferrique.

Casse Brune (Fr) a condition that occurs in wines made from grapes that have been attacked by pourriture gris (grey rot), is treated with tannin and bisulphate.

Casse Ferrique (Fr) iron casse, also known as Casse bleu.

Cassegrain (Austr) a winery. (Add): Hastings Valley Winery, Pacific Highway, Port Macquarie, New South Wales. Grape varieties: Cabernet sauvignon, Shiraz, Chardonnay.

Casillero del Diablo (Chile) *see* Casillero del Diablo.

Cassis (Fr) a blackcurrant liqueur made chiefly in the northern Côte d'Or (Dijon plains and Arrière Côtes), Burgundy. *See also* Crème de Cassis.

Cassis (Fr) a mainly white A.C. wine area in the Côtes de Provence on on the south-eastern coast of France. Produces a little red and rosé wine. Minimum alc by vol. of 11% for all A.C. wines.

Cassis Cocktail (Cktl) ⅔ measure Bourbon whiskey, ½ measure dry vermouth, 2 dashes crème de cassis. Shake over ice and strain into a cocktail glass.

Cassis de Dijon (Fr) a fine crème de cassis produced only on the plains of Dijon in Burgundy.

Cassis-Kirsch (Fr) an apéritif. Same as Polichinelle.

Cassovar (Czec) a dark lager beer brewed by Kosice.

Casta (Port) grape (variety).

Casta Predominante (Port) lit: 'predominant grape variety'.

Castarède (Fr) an Armagnac producer who specialises in dated Armagnacs. (Add): J. Castarède, Pont-des-Bordes, 47230 Lavardac. 20ha. situated in the Bas Armagnac. Produces Château de Maniban Cuvée Speciale.

Castas Nobres (Mad) lit: 'noble varieties', the permitted grapes used in the production of Madeira (**white**): Bual, Sercial, Terrantez and Verdelho (**red**): Bastardo and Terrantez preto.

Castaway (Eng) the name of a sparkling 'cooler' produced from white wine and tropical fruit juice.

Castay Frères (Fr) an Armagnac producer. (Add):

Château de Jaulin, Bretagne d'Armagnac, 32800 Eauze.

Casteja (Fr) an Armagnac producer. Produces V.S.O.P. Grande Réserve.

Castelain Brasserie (Fr) a brewery (established 1926) based in Bénefontaine. Brews CH'TI.

Castelão (Port) a red grape variety grown in Bairrada. *see* Castelão Francês.

Castelão Francês (Port) the full name for the red grape variety Castelão. In Arrábida, Palmela: Periquita, Oeste: Mórtagua, Ribatejo: Periquita, João de Santarém, Santarém.

Castel Chandon (Arg) the brand-name used by Bodegas Proviar for a range of their wines.

Castel Danielis (Gre) a dry red table wine produced in Patras by Achaia-Clauss.

Castel del Monte (It) a D.O.C. for red, rosé and white wines from Puglia. *See also* Locorotondo, San Severo.

Castel del Monte Bianco (It) a D.O.C. white wine from Puglia in the commune of Minervino Murge and in parts of Bari. Grape varieties: Bombino bianco, Palumbo, Pampanuto, Trebbiano giallo and Trebbiano toscano.

Castel del Monte Rosato (It) a D.O.C. rosé from Puglia in the commune of Minervino Murge and in parts of Bari. Grape varieties: Bombino nero, Montepulciano, Sangiovese and Uva di troia. If aged for 3 years minimum and alc by vol. of 12.5% then classed Riserva.

Casteldrione (It) an I.G.T. red wine produced by d'Alfonso del Sordo in San Severo, Puglia from a blend of Troia, Sangiovese and Malvasia grapes.

Castelfiora (It) a noted producer of sparkling (cuve close) wines in the Marche region.

Castelino (Port) a red grape variety grown in Torres Vedras.

Castell (Ger) village (Anb): Franken. (Ber): Steigerwald. (Gro): Herrenberg. (Vins): Bauch, Feuerbach, Hohnart, Kirchberg, Kugelspiel, Reitsteig, Schlossberg, Trautberg.

Castell (Ger) village (Anb): Franken. (Ber): Steigerwald. (Gro): Schild. (Vins): Bausch, Kirschberg.

Castellana (Sp) a white grape variety.

Castellane [Vicomte de] (Fr) a Champagne producer. (Add): 57 Rue de Verdun, 51204 Épernay. Produces vintage and non-vintage wines and liqueurs. (See Vicomte Champagne Liqueur).

Castellberg (Ger) vineyard (Anb): Baden. (Ber): Kaiserstuhl-Tuniberg. (Gro): Vulkanfelsen. (Vil): Achkarren.

Castellberg (Ger) vineyard (Anb): Baden. (Ber): Kaiserstuhl-Tuniberg. (Gro): Vulkanfelsen. (Vil): Ihringen.

Castellberg (Ger) vineyard (Anb): Baden. (Ber): Markgräflerland. (Gro): Burg Neuenfels. (Vil): Ballrechten-Dottingen.

Castellblanch (Sp) producers of cava wines based in San Sadurní de Noya, Cataluña.

Castell de Vilarnau (Sp) a brut-style cava wine produced by Gonzalez Byass.

Casteller (It) a D.O.C. light red wine from the Trentino-Alto-Adige region. Produced from the Lambrusco, Merlot and Schiava grapes.

Castellero (It) a red wine produced from Nebbiolo grapes by Araldici Vini Piemontesi, 14040 Castel Boglione. Part of the Poderi Alasia range.

Castellet [Le] (Fr) a noted wine-producing commune in A.C. Bandol, Provence, southern France.

Castelli (It) another name for the Cannicci.

Castelli (It) volcanic hills.

Castellina (It) a commune of Chianti Classico Riserva.

Castellina (It) a sparkling natural mineral water from Castellina, Molise. Mineral contents (milligrammes per litre): Sodium 2.1mg/l, Calcium 54mg/l, Magnesium 2.5mg/l, Potassium 0.3mg/l, Bicarbonates 175mg/l, Chlorides 2.8mg/l, Sulphates 2.2mg/l, Fluorides 0.15mg/l, Nitrates 1mg/l, Silicates 3.5mg/l. pH 7.44

Castelli del Grevepsa (It) a co-operative winery in the DOCG Chianti Classico, Tuscany region. Produces: Clemente VIII (Chianti Classico Riserva).

Castell'in Villa (It) a Chianti Classico producer based in Tuscany.

Castelli Romani (It) a delimited wine region in Lazio. Produces mainly white wines with some red. *see* Frascati.

Castelli Romani (It) a white grape variety grown in Lombardy. Also known as the Trebbiano toscano.

Castello (Ger) a beer brewed by the Feldschlösschen Brauerei based in Hammink, Rheinfelden.

Castello (It) castle, the Italian equivalent of a French Château.

Castello (It) a natural spring mineral water from Castello. Mineral contents (milligrammes per litre): Sodium 0.94mg/l, Calcium 62.3mg/l, Magnesium 33.9mg/l, Potassium 0.12mg/l, Bicarbonates 339.1mg/l, Chlorides 0.85mg/l, Sulphates 10.5mg/l, Nitrates 5mg/l, Silicates 2.4mg/l. pH 7.5

Castello (Port) a natural spring mineral water from Pisões-Moura.

Castello Banfi S.p.A. (It) a winery. (Add): Castello di Poggio alle Mura, Montalcino, Siena. Famous producers of Brunello di Montalcino, Summus and San Angelo (Pinot grigio) wines. Label: Poggio alle Mura. Website: http://www.castellobanfi.com

Castello della Sala (It) a white wine produced by Antinori from Grechetto and Sauvignon blanc grapes.

Castello di Bevilacqua (It) a producer of sparkling (metodo tradizionale) wines in Veneto. Labels include Brut Quarto Vecchio.

Castello di Bornato (It) a noted producer of Franciacorta wine from Barbera, Cabernet franc, Merlot and Nebbiolo grapes.

Castello di Brolio (It) a winery based at Gaiole in Chianti, Tuscany. Produces D.O.C.G. Chianti and Casalferro (a 100% Sangiovese non-D.O.C.)

Castello di Cacchiano (It) a Chianti Classico estate in Gaiole, Tuscany. Owned by Ricasoli.

Castello di Gabbiano (It) a Chianti Classico producer based in the Tuscany region.

Castello di Lucignano (It) a winery based at I–53013 Gaiole in Chianti, Tuscany. Noted for D.O.C.G. Chianti Classico Riserva and I.G.T. Il Solissimo.

Castello di Luzzano (It) *see* Azienda Agricole M. and G. Fugazza.

Castello di Momaci (It) a winery based in Salento, Puglia. Label: Kreos (rosé).

Castello di Montegufoni (It) a Chianti Putto producer based in the Tuscany region.

Castello di Nieve (It) a vineyard based in Nieve, Piemonte.

Castello di Nipozzano (It) a Chianti produced by the Frescobaldi C°.

Castello di Querceto (It) a 65ha. wine estate. (Add): Via Dudda 61, Lucolena, 50020 Greve in Chianti, Tuscany. Produces Vin Santo and a range of Chianti Classico: Castello di Querceto, Il Picchio Riserva, La Capanne. Plus La Corte, Il Quercetino, Il Querciolaia, Cignale, Le Giuncaie (all I.G.T. wines). Website: http://www.castellodiquerceto.it 'E'mail: querceto@castellodiquerceto.it

Castello di San Polo (It) a winery that produces mainly Chianti Classico wines plus Cetinaia (a 100% barrique-aged Sangiovese) and Rosso dell'erta (100% Sangiovese). (Add): Rosso 1, I 53013 Gaiole, Chianti, Tuscany.

Castello di Volpaia (It) a Chianti Classico producer based at Radda, Tuscany 42ha.

Castello Montefioralle (It) a Chianti Classico producer based in the Tuscany region.

Castello Romitorio (It) a 250ha winery. (Add): Loc. Romitorio 279, 53024 Montalcino (SI). owns 35ha vineyards (D.O). Produces D.O.C.G. Brunello di Montalcino, D.O.C. Rosso di Montalcino, I.G.T. Romito del Romitorio, red and white Vino da Tavola.

Castello Vicchiomaggio (It) a winery in the DOCG Chianti Classico, Tuscany region. Labels: La Prima, Petri. Produces a DOCG Chianti Classico Riserva.

Castelmaure (Fr) a wine-producing village in the A.C. Corbières area of the Languedoc, southern France.

Castelnau (Fr) a commune in the A.C. Médoc, north-western Bordeaux. May use the A.C. Listrac designation.

Castelnuovo Berardenga (It) a commune of Chianti Classico Riserva.

Castelo de Vide (Port) a natural spring mineral water from Fonte da Mealhada 1, Castelo de Vide. pH 7.4

Castelo Rodrigo (Port) an I.P.R. region in the central east.

Castel Pujol (S.Am) Tannat and Tannat rosé wines produced by Vinos Finos J. Carrau, Monterideo, Uruguay.

Castel San Michele (It) a dry red wine made from Cabernet and Merlot grapes by the agricultural college in the Trentino-Alto-Adige region.

Castelvecchi (It) a Chianti Classico producer based in the Tuscany region.

Castets (Fr) a rare red vine variety originating from south-western France.

Castets [Les] (Fr) a Premier Cru vineyard in the A.C. commune of Saint-Aubin, Côte de Beaune, Burgundy.

Catharina (S.Afr) the label for a red wine (Shiraz 40%, Cabernet franc, Cabernet sauvignon and Nebbiolo blend) produced by the Steenberg Vineyards winery, Constantia, Western Cape.

Castiglione Falletto (It) a commune in the Barolo district of the Piemonte region.

Castilla-La Mancha (Sp) a vast wine-producing area that covers nearly 8 million hectares based in Levante and Meseta. Contains the provinces of Albacete, Ciudad Real, Cuenca, Guadalajara, Toledo. Home to D.O. zones of Almansa, La Mancha, Méntrida, Valdepeñas. Vino de la Tierra areas of Gálvez (Toledo), Manchuela, Pozohondo Siera de Alcaraz (Albacete), Sacedón-Mondéjar (Guadalajara). Vino de Mesa areas of El Bonillo (Albacete), Malpica de Tajo (Toledo).

Castilla la Vieja (Sp) a bodega de crianza based in Rueda.

Castilla-León (Sp) a wine-producing area based in the Duero Valley. Home to D.O.'s of Bierzo, Cigales, Ribera del Duero, Rueda, Toro. Vino de la Tierra areas: Cebreros (DEp of Ávila), Fermoselle-Arribes del Duero, (Salamanca/Zamora), Tierra del Vino de Zamora Valdevimbre-Los Oteros (Valladolid/León). Vino Comarcal areas of Benavente (Zamora), La Ribera del Arlanza (Burgos), La Sierra de Salamanca Valtiendas (Segovia). Vino de Mesa areas: La Ribera del Cea (León/Valladolid). Private bodegas are also selling as Vino de Mesa wines in order to allow a vintage to appear on the label. These include Vino de Mesa de Toledo, Vino de Mesa de Castilla-León.

Castille (Fr) a Champagne producer. (Add): 14 Rue des Moissons, 51100 Reims 13ha.

Castillo de Cuzcurrita (Sp) a bodega based in Rio Tirón, Rioja, north-western Spain.

Castillo de Liria (Sp) based in Valencia, the name given to a red and white wine range from Gandia Pla, S.A.

Castillo d'Mont-Blanc (Sp) the label for a rosé wine produced by Bodegas Concavins, Cataluña.

Castillo del Morro (Cub) a winery with 50ha. in Pinar del Rio. Grape varieties include Cabernet sauvignon, Tempranillo, Chardonnay, Pinot grigio. Produce still and sparkling wines.

Castillo de Manza (Sp) the label used by Vinos de Castilla in the La Mancha region.

Castillo de Melida (Sp) the brand-name of a light, red wine produced by Julián Chivite in the Navarra region, north-western Spain.

Castillo de Molina (Chile) a winery that grows Cabernet sauvignon, Merlot, Chardonnay and Sauvignon blanc grapes.

Castillo de San Diego (Sp) a white table wine produced from the Palomino grape by Bobadillo of Jerez de la Frontera.

Castillo de Tiebas (Sp) the label under which red

and white wines of Vinícola Navarra, Las Campañas in Navarra are sold.

Castillo la Torre (Sp) a cava wine produced by Freixedas in the Penedés region.

Castillon Renault (Fr) a Cognac producer. (Add): 23 Rue du Port, 16101 Cognac. Has own distillery. Owns no vineyards, buys in wines. Produces Carte Noire Extra (average 12 years old).

Castillo Perelada (Sp) a cava producer based at Perelada, Girona. Produces both vintage and non-vintage cavas. Label: Gran Claustra.

Castillo San Lorenzo Fino Clarete (Sp) a non-vintage red wine from Rioja.

Castillo Viejo (S.Am) a 130ha. wine estate at San José, north-west of Montevideo in Uruguay. Noted for Catamayor wine from Tannat or Sauvignon blanc grapes. Other grape varieties include Cabernet franc.

Castillo Ygay (Sp) a red wine produced by Bodegas Marqués de Murrieta in Rioja.

Castle Ale (Eng) a bottled special pale ale 1047 O.G. brewed by the McMullen Brewery, Hereford.

Castle Ale (Eng) a bottled special pale ale 1041 O.G. brewed by the Morrell Brewery, Oxford, Oxfordshire.

Castles Ale (Eng) a 3.7% alc by vol. ale brewed by Northumberland Brewery, North Seaton, near Ashington. 3.8% alc by vol. bitter beer brewed by the Conway Brewery, Gwynedd.

Castle Bitter (Wal) a 4.2% alc by vol. bitter ale from Dyffryn Brewery, Denbigh. *See also* Cysur Bitter, Cwrw Derwydd, Pedwar Bawd.

Castle Brewery [The] (Wal) a brewery. (Add): Carmarthen Breweries Limited, 40A Rhosmaen Street, Landeilo, Carmarthenshire. Brews: Whoosh bitter ale.

Castle Cary Vineyard (Eng) a vineyard based at Honeywick House, Castle Cary, Somerset. 1ha. Grape varieties: Huxelrebe, Madeleine angevine, Müller-Thurgau and Seyval blanc.

Castle d'Almain (Euro) a red wine from Peljesac in Dalmatia. Is also known as Dingac.

Castle Dip Cocktail (Cktl) ½ measure (white) crème de menthe, ½ measure Calvados, 3 dashes Pernod. Shake over ice, and strain into a cocktail glass.

Castle d'Or Sherry (Eng) a 15% alc by vol. Sherry bottled by St. Austell Brewery C°., Cornwall.

Castle Eden Brewery (Eng) a brewery based in County Durham. Brews Autumn Knights, Winter Knights, Rymans Reserve, Fuggles Imperial IPA, D-day Bitter, Higsons Bitter, Nimmo's XXXX, Winter Royal, Special (a bottled ale). Butterknowle Brewery now based here.

Castle Hill Sauvignon Blanc (N.Z) a dry white wine made from the Sauvignon blanc grape, matured in wood and produced by the Te Mata Vineyard.

Castle Lager (Afr) a well-hopped bottled lager brewed by the South African Breweries (S.A.B.), Johannesburg. 5% alc by vol.

Castlemaine-Perkins (Austr) a brewery based at 185 Milton Road, Brisbane. Brews XXXX.

Castlemaine-Tooheys (Austr) a new company

C

formed by the merger of the Castlemaine Brewery of Brisbane and the Toooheys Brewery of Sydney in 1980.

Castlemaine XXXX (Austr) a keg lager beer 1035 O.G. brewed by the Castlemaine-Toooheys Brewery. Brewed under licence in Wrexham by Allied Breweries. Canned version 1041-1045 O.G. 4.8% alc by vol.

Castlenau de Suduiraut (Fr) the second wine of Château Suduiraut in the commune of Preignac, A.C. Sauternes, Bordeaux.

Castle Rock (USA) a natural spring mineral water. Mineral contents (milligrammes per litre): Calcium 10mg/l, Magnesium 5mg/l, Potassium 2mg/l, Bicarbonates 64mg/l, Chlorides 2mg/l, Nitrates 1mg/l.

Castle Rock Brewery (Eng) a micro-brewery. (Add): Queensbridge Road, The Meadows, Nottingham, Nottinghamshire NG2 1NB. Brews: Black Gold 3.5% alc by vol., Elsie Mo 4.7% alc by vol., Harvest Pale Ale 3.8% alc by vol., Hemlock Bitter 4% alc by vol., Nottingham Dark Stout 4.5% alc by vol., Nottingham Gold 3.5% alc by vol., Snowwhite 4.2% alc by vol., VIP Conception Brew, Dark Stout. Website: http://www.castlerockbrewery.co.uk 'E'mail: castle.rock@btconnect.com

Castle Springs (USA) a natural spring mineral water from New Hampshire.

Castle Springs (Wal) a natural spring mineral water from Lon Parewr, Ruthin.

Castle Steamer Beer (Eng) a cask-conditioned ale 1045 O.G. brewed by the Three Tuns, a home-brew public house in Bishop's Castle, Shropshire.

Castletown Brewery (I.O.M) a brewery based in Castletown, Isle of Man that sells beers under the Castletown label. Brews: Castletown Liqueur Barley Wine 1072 O.G. Nut Brown 1036 O.G. and Red Seal 1036 O.G.

Castle Wine and Green (S.Afr) noted producers of a range of fine South African brandies.

Castra (Sp) a method of pruning useless buds on Sherry vines to help the growth of good healthy buds.

Castres (Fr) a commune in the A.C. Graves district of south-western Bordeaux.

Castrillo del Val (Sp) a Vino de Mesa wine of the province Burgos in Castilla-León.

Castrovita (Sp) a natural spring mineral water.

Cat (Afr) an alternative spelling of Khat.

Catador (Sp) wine taster.

Catalan (Fr) a Vin de Pays area in the Pyrénées-Orientales département, south-western France. Produces red, rosé and dry white wines.

Catalan (Fr)(Sp) a red grape variety also known as the Mourvèdre in France and Carignan in Spain.

Catalogue Raisonné (It) a catalogue of vines compiled by the Marchese Leopoldo (1790–1871).

Catalonia (Sp) the English spelling of Cataluña.

Cataltepe (Tur) a natural spring mineral water. Mineral contents (milligrammes per litre): Sodium 4.97mg/l, Calcium 9.62mg/l, Magnesium 1.7mg/l, Chlorides 10.3mg/l. pH 6.94

Cataluña (Sp) a Denominación de Origen region in south-eastern Spain. Provences: Barcelona, Gerona, Lleida and Tarragona. Produces red, rosé, white and Cava wines. Produces fine brandy (Mascaró) and is also famous for cork, the best in Europe. Has D.O's of Cava plus Alella, Ampurdán Costa-Brava, Conca de Barberá, Costers del Segre, Monsant, Penedés, Priorato, Tarragona, Terra Alta. Vinos de la Tierra of Bages, Vinos Comarcales of Anoia, Bajo-Ebro Montsía, Conca de Tremp.

Catalyst (Eng) a chemical agent which induces chemical changes in other substances by its presence but remains unchanged itself. Used in some wines to solidify unwanted elements in the wine.

Catalytic Agent (Eng) see Catalyst.

Catape (Fr) an alternative name for the Muscadelle grape.

Catarratto Bianco (It) a white grape variety grown in Sicily that has an aroma of flowers and honey. Is used in the production of Marsala. see Comune, Lucido.

Catawba (USA) a large red American grape variety (*Vitis labrusca*). Used for white and rosé wines and for blending in sparkling wines.

Catbells Pale Ale (Eng) a 5.2% alc by vol. pale ale brewed by the Hesket Newmarket Brewery, Cumbria.

Catechin (Eng) see Flavenoids.

Catechol (Eng) a tannin found in fruit that causes astringency in wine.

Catedral de León (Sp) the brand label for the red, rosé and white wines of VILE.

Catemario (It) see Collavini.

Catena (Arg) a winery 79ha. The Angelica vineyard in Lunlunta, Mendoza. Grape variety: Malbec. Tikal vineyard. Grape varieties: Cabernet sauvignon, Malbec, Pinot noir, Chardonnay. Produce the Alta, Catena, Alamos Ridge, Argento and Luca Vineyard ranges of wines.

Catering Tea Grading Scheme (Eng) a body whose aim is to improve the standards of tea service in the catering sector. Applies quality standards to most of the catering tea drunk.

Cathareine (Hol) a natural spring mineral water from Utrecht. Mineral contents (milligrammes per litre): Sodium 10mg/l, Calcium 43mg/l, Magnesium 3mg/l, Potassium 0.6mg/l, Bicarbonates 165mg/l, Chlorides 9.5mg/l, Sulphates 1mg/l, Nitrates mg/l.

Catharinen-Quelle Oberselter (Ger) a natural spring mineral water (established 1998). Mineral contents (milligrammes per litre): Sodium 212mg/l, Calcium 52mg/l, Magnesium 18mg/l, Potassium 7mg/l, Bicarbonates 488mg/l, Chlorides 178mg/l, Sulphates 28mg/l.

Cathcart Ridge Estate (Austr) a winery (established 1978) in Victoria. Grape varieties: Cabernet sauvignon, Hermitage, Merlot, Shiraz, Chardonnay, Muscat, late-picked Riesling.

Cathedral Cellars (S.Afr) the name for a range of wines from the K.W.V. Coastal Region on the

Western Cape. Grape varieties: Cabernet sauvignon, Merlot, Pinotage, Sauvignon blanc, Chardonnay.

Catherdral Gold (Eng) a 4.5% alc by vol. ale brewed by The Durham Brewery Ltd., County Durham.

Catherine Blossom Cocktail (Cktl)(Non-alc) 175mls orange juice, 2 scoops water ice, ½ measure maple syrup. Blend altogether in a blender, pour into a highball glass and top with soda water.

Cathérine de Medicis (Fr) a prestige cuvée Champagne of Meric (de).

Catherine's Peak (W.Ind) a natural spring mineral water (established 1992) from Jamaica. Mineral contents (milligrammes per litre): Sodium <10mg/l, Magnesium 30mg/l, Bicarbonates 103mg/l, Chlorides 7mg/l, Sulphates 10mg/l.

Catina (S.Afr) a natural spring mineral water. Mineral contents (milligrammes per litre): Sodium 3mg/l, Calcium 7mg/l, Magnesium 5mg/l, Potassium <1mg/l, Chlorides <5mg/l, Sulphates 5mg/l, Fluorides <0.2mg/l, Silicates mg/l. 24.4 pH 6.4 Website: http://www.dominique.co.za

Catiniense (It) a red wine produced on the island of Sicily during Roman times.

Cat Nap Ale (Eng) a 3.6% alc by vol. ale brewed by the Barngates Brewery Ltd., Cumbria.

Catskill Mountains (USA) a natural spring mineral water. Mineral contents (milligrammes per litre): Sodium 39mg/l, Calcium 110mg/l, Magnesium 22mg/l, Potassium 2.2mg/l, Chlorides 110mg/l, Fluorides 0.2mg/l, Nitrates 3.1mg/l. pH 6.7

Cat's Pee (Eng) a wine tasting term for the sometimes powerful and distinct aroma given off by some Sauvignon blanc wines which resemble the odour.

Cat's Water (Eng) a slang term used for gin.

Cats Whiskers (Eng) a 4.2% alc by vol. ale brewed by the Whittington Brewery, Gloucestershire.

Cattier (Fr) récoltants-manipulants in Champagne. (Add): 6 & 11 Rue Dom Pérignon, Chigny-lès-Roses, 51500 Rilly-la-Montagne. 18ha. Produces vintage and non-vintage wines. Single cuvée: Clos du Moulin.

Catto's (Scot) a blended Scotch whisky produced by James Catto & C°. Ltd. Renfrew. 40% alc by vol. Part of the International Distillers and Vintners. Also available as a 12 year old.

Catturich-Ducco (It) a producer of sparkling (metodo tradizionale) wines based in Lombardy.

Catty (Chi) the Chinese word for 'weight' from which tea 'caddy' derives.

Catz Bitters (Hol) an aromatic bitters.

Caucinianum (It) a white wine produced in central Italy during Roman times.

Caudalies (Fr) lit: 'the finish' the term given for the final 'overall' taste of a wine.

Caudin (Ch.Isles) intoxicated/tipsy. See also Chiraï.

Caudle (Eng) the name given to an ornate hot drink cup circa 1664. Usually made of silver with a lid and two handles.

Caudle (Eng) hot spiced wine or ale to which beaten egg yolk and sugar is added, made from gruel.

Cauldron Snout (Eng) a 5.6% alc by vol. stout brewed by the Darwin Brewery, Tyne & Wear.

Cauldron Stout (Eng) a 5.6% alc by vol. draught or bottled stout from a brewpub at the High Force Hotel, Teesdale, County Durham.

Caulinum (It) a red wine produced in central-western Italy during Roman times.

Caupo (Lat) innkeeper/publican.

Caupona (Lat) alehouse.

Cauquenes (Chile) a wine-producing region in southern Chile.

Cauro (Fr) a red wine produced on the island of Corsica.

Cauro (It) an I.G.T. red wine produced by Statti at Lamezia Terme, Calabria from Gaglioppo, Magliocco and Cabernet sauvignon grapes.

Cauroy-les-Hermonville (Fr) a Cru Champagne village in the Canton de Bourgogne. District: Reims.

Cautivo (Arg) a Cabernet-based wine produced by Orfila at St. Martin, Mendoza.

Caux (Fr) a Vin de Pays area in the Hérault département in southern France. Produces red, rosé and dry white wines.

Cava (Sp) cellar.

Cava (Sp) the name for Q.W.P.S.R. wines produced by the cava method. Area of D.O. zone is 30,800ha. Only from demarcated vineyards in 5 provinces: Cataluña (provinces of Gerona, Barcelona, Tarragona, Lérida), Aragón (province of Zaragoza), Navarra, La Rioja, País Vasco (provice of Alava). Most is produced in the Cataluña region. Recommended grapes are **white**: Macabeo (Viura), Xarel-lo, Parellada, Chardonnay, Subirat. **rosé**: Garnacha, Monastrell. Aged for minimum of 9 months on lees, 30 months for gran reserva wines.

Cava (Gre) denotes a high quality red or white table wine that has been given an extra long ageing process. Minimum of 2 years for white wines, 3 years for red wines.

Cava Boutari (Gre) a four year old, oak-aged, red wine produced by Boutari from the Xinomavro grape.

Cava Cambas (Gre) a smooth, golden wine aged before bottling.

Cava Carras (Gre) a range of red, rosé and dry white wines.

Cavagrande (It) a natural spring mineral water from Cavagrande, Mount Etna. Mineral contents (milligrammes per litre): Sodium 34.4mg/l, Calcium 10.4mg/l, Magnesium 7mg/l, Potassium 7.8mg/l, Chlorides 24.8mg/l, Sulphates 29.5mg/l, Fluorides 0.43mg/l. pH 7.69

Cavalier (Eng) a 4% alc by vol. ale brewed by the Clearwater Brewery, Devon.

Cavalier (S.Afr) a red wine (Cabernet franc 25%, Cabernet sauvignon 25%, Merlot 40% and Shiraz 10%) produced by Annandale Wines, Stellenbosch, Western Cape.

Cavalier (Thai) a 38% alc by vol. imperial reserve brandy produced by the United Thai Distillery, Bangkok.

Cavalier Cocktail (Cktl) 1½ measures strawberry juice, ½ measure Cinzano Bianco, ¼ measure Grand Marnier, ¼ measure white rum. Shake well over ice, strain into a highball glass, top with ginger ale, strawberry and orange slice.

Cavalier d'Asti e de Montferrato (It) a wine-brotherhood based in the Asti district of the Piemonte region, north-western Italy.

Cavalierii (Fin) a 'sparkling fruit wine' made from whiteberries by the méthode traditionelle.

Cavallino Rosso (It) the name for a brandy produced by Schweppes Italia.

Cavalotto (It) a winery based at Castiglione Falletto (district of Barolo), Piemonte. Labels: Bricco Boschis, Vigna San Giuseppe. Website: http://www.cavallotto.com

Cavalry Bottle (Eng) a leather bottle with a long strap, shaped like a German bocksbeutel. Used by the cavalry in the eighteenth and nineteenth centuries.

Cavas Conde de Caralt (Sp) Catalonian sparkling wines produced by the cava method.

Cavas del Ampurdán (Sp) a sparkling (cava) wine producer based in Ampurdán-Costa Brava, Cataluña.

Cavas de San Juan (Mex) a winery based in the valley of Río de San Juan. Produces wines under the Hidalgo label.

Cavas do Barrocão (Port) a winery based in Bairrada. Produces fine red Dão and Bairrada Garrafeiras.

Cavas Hill (Sp) a bodega based near Moja, Penedés. Produces both Cava and table wines.

Cavas Masachs (Sp) a winery based in Vilafranca del Penedés. 55ha. Produces sparkling (cava) wines under the labels of Louis Vernier and Masachs.

Cavas Mestres (Sp) a cava producer based in San Sadurní de Noya, south-east Spain. Produces Mestres

Cavas Segura Viudas (Sp) a winery based in Cataluña. Was part of the Rumasa group. Produces cava wines.

Cavatappi (It) corkscrew.

Cavaturracciolo (It) corkscrew.

Cave (Fr) cellar (underground)/winery. See also Chais.

Cave à Liqueurs (Fr) liqueur cellar, usually a cabinet or chest which is lockable, often glass-fronted.

Caveau (Fr) a small cellar, often used for fine wines.

Caveau de Gustation (Fr) tasting cellars.

Cave Beer Stout (Eng) a 4% alc by vol. stout brewed by the Newmans Brewery, Avon.

Cave Bellevue (Fr) a vineyard. (Add): Ordonnac, 33340 Lesparre, Médoc. 210ha. (Com): Ordonnac. A.C. Médoc. Cave Coopérative Ordonnac. Grape varieties: Cabernet franc 5%, Cabernet sauvignon 45% and Merlot 50%.

Cave Canterayne (Fr) a cave coopérative. (Com): Saint-Sauveur. A.C. Haut-Médoc. (Add): Saint-Sauveur 33250, Pauillac.

Cave Coopérative (Fr) wine growers co-operative association, first introduced in 1907 in southern France.

Cave Coopérative Belle Vue (Fr) a co-operative based in the commune of Ordonnac-et-Potensac. A.C. Médoc, Bordeaux 130ha.

Cave Coopérative Condom (Fr) an Armagnac-producing co-operative. (Add): Avenue des Mousqutaires, 32100 Condom.

Cave Coopérative de Bégadan (Fr) a vineyard. (Add): Cave St.Jean, Bégadan 33340 Lesparre, Médoc. 567ha. (Com): Bégadan. A.C. Haut-Médoc. Grape varieties: Cabernet franc, Cabernet sauvignon, Merlot and Petit verdot.

Cave Coopérative de Die (Fr) a co-operative winery based in southern France. Main producer of Clairette de Die.

Cave Coopérative de Liergues (Fr) a co-operative winery (established 1929) based in Villefranche, Beaujolais, Burgundy.

Cave Coopérative de Pauillac (Fr) a co-operative winery based in Pauillac, Médoc, north-western Bordeaux.

Cave Coopérative des Côtes-de-Castillon (Fr) a co-operative based in the commune of Saint-Étienne-de-Lisse. 3ha. A.C. Saint-Émilion, Bordeaux.

Cave Coopérative des Grands Vins de Fleurie (Fr) a noted co-operative based in Fleurie, Beaujolais, Burgundy.

Cave Coopérative des Grands Vins de Juliénas (Fr) (Add): 69840 Juliénas. A large co-operative of 306 members based in Juliénas, Beaujolais, Burgundy. Sells direct to négociants.

Cave Coopérative des Grands Vins Rosés (Fr) a co-operative winery of 19 members. (Add): 21 Rue de Mazy, 21160 Marsannay-la-Côte, Burgundy.

Cave Coopérative de St. Sauveur (Fr) a co-operative winery based in Canterayne.

Cave Coopérative de Vertheuil (Fr) a co-operative winery based in Châtellenie, Vertheuil.

Cave Coopérative de Vinification de Quinsac (Fr) a co-operative vineyard in the commune of Quinsac. A.C. Premières Côtes de Bordeaux. 140ha. (Add): 33360 Quinsac. Grape varieties: Cabernet franc, Cabernet sauvignon and Merlot.

Cave Coopérative la Chablisienne (Fr) a co-operative winery based in Chablis, Burgundy. (Add): 89800 Chablis.

Cave Coopérative le Vieux Colombier (Fr) a co-operative winery based at Lafon-Prignac, Prignac-en-Médoc, north-western Bordeaux.

Cave Coopérative St-Jean (Fr) a co-operative based in the commune of Bégadan. A.C. Médoc, Bordeaux. see Cave Saint-Jean.

Cave de Bailly (Fr) a wine co-operative based in the Mâconnais, southern Burgundy. Has 68 members owning 350ha. Specialises in Crémant de Bourgogne by méthode traditional.

Cave de Cairanne (Fr) a co-operative winery based in Cairanne A.C. Côtes-du-Rhône-Villages, Vaucluse. Produces: Coteau Brûlée (rose).

Cave de Chaintré (Fr) a winery based in Chaintré, Mâcon, Burgundy. (Add): Cidex 418, 71570 Chaintré. Grape variety: Chardonnay. Produces: A.C.'s Mâcon-Villages, Saint-Véran, Pouilly-Fuissé, Pouilly-Vinzalles. 'E'mail: cavedechaintre@wanadoo.fr

C

Cave de Lugny (Fr) a wine co-operative based in the Mâconnais, southern Burgundy. Has 251 members. Labels incude: Unité.

Cave de Prissé (Fr) a wine co-operative based in the Mâconnais, southern Burgundy. Has 900ha.

Cave des Cordeliers (Fr) a Burgundy négociant based in Beaune, Côte de Beaune, Burgundy.

Cave des Producteurs de Fleurie (Fr) a co-operative winery based in the A.C. Cru Beaujolais Fleurie, southern Burgundy. Labels include: Cuvée Cardinal Bienfaiteur, Cuvée Présidente Marguerite.

Cave des Producteurs Réunis (Fr) an Armagnac producer. (Add): 32100 Nogaro.

Cave des Vignérons de Buxy (Fr) a wine co-operative based in Buxy, Côte Chalonnais, Burgundy. Has 195 members and 900ha.

Cave des Vignérons de Mancey (Fr) a co-operative winery (established 1980) based in Mancey, Mâcon, Buhrgundy. (Add): B.P. 100, Route Nationale 6, 71700 Tounus. Has 12 members. 'E'mail: bdvv@wanadoo.fr

Cave de Tain (Fr) a large co-operative winery based at Tain l'Hermitage, northern Rhône.

Cave de Turkheim (Fr) a co-operative winery based in Turkheim, Alsace. Has 230 members.

Cave de Vinification des Grands Vins de Listrac (Fr) a vineyard. (Add): Listrac, Médoc, 33480 Castelnau. 160ha. Communes: Listrac and Moulis. A.C. Médoc. Grape varieties: Cabernet sauvignon, Merlot and Petit verdot.

Cave du Bourgogne (Fr) a Burgundy négociant based in Beaune, Côte de Beaune, Burgundy.

Cave Frères (Fr) an Armagnac producer. (Add): 32520 Lannepax.

Cave Grand Listrac (Fr) a co-operative winery. (Add): Listrac 33480 Castelnau-de-Médoc. A.C. Listrac. (Com): Listrac, Médoc, north-western Bordeaux.

Cave Harnois (Fr) a patent underground spiral wine cellar designed specifically for the home-owner. (U.K) = The Spiral Cellar.

Cavekane (Tur) coffee.

Cave la Châtellenie (Fr). a co-operative winery. (Add): Vertheuil 33250 Pauillac. (Com): Vertheuil. A.C. Haut-Médoc, north-western Bordeaux.

Cave la Paroisse (Fr) a co-operative winery. (Add): St-Seurin-de-Cadourne, 33250 Pauillac. (Com): St-Seurin-de-Cadourne. A.C. Haut-Médoc, north-western Bordeaux.

Cave la Rose Pauillac (Fr) a co-operative winery. (Add): Rue Maréchal-Joffre, 33250 Pauillac. (Com): Pauillac. A.C. Pauillac, Médoc, north-western Bordeaux.

Cave les Vieux Colombiers (Fr) a co-operative winery. (Add): Prignac-en-Médoc, 33340 Lesparre. (Com): Prignac. A.C. Médoc, north-western Bordeaux.

Caveman (Eng) a 5% alc by vol. ale brewed by the Kinver Brewery, West Midlands.

Cave Marquis de Saint-Estèphe (Fr) a co-operative winery in north-western Bordeaux. (Add): Saint-Estèphe, 33250 Pauillac. A.C. Saint-Estèphe. (Com): Saint-Estèphe.

Cavendish Cape (S.Afr) the name given to a range of South African Sherries from KWV.

Cavendish Manor (Eng) a vineyard (established 1972). (Add): Nether Hall, Cavendish, Suffolk. 4.2ha. Soil: boulder clay. Grape varieties include: Müller-Thurgau. Vinification at Chilford Hall, Linton, Cambridgeshire.

Cave Pavillon de Bellevue (Fr) a co-operative based in the commune of Ordonnac 33340 Lesparre. A.C. Médoc, Bordeaux.

Caverna (Sp) cavern/cellar.

Caversham Estate (Austr) a part of the Sandalford Winery, Western Australia.

Caves Acàcio (Port) the producer of Novo Mundo (a Dão wine).

Cave Saint-Brice (Fr) a co-operative winery. (Add): Saint-Yzans-de-Médoc, 33340 Lesparre. A.C. Médoc. (Com): Saint-Yzans, north-western Bordeaux.

Cave Saint-Jean (Fr) the wine co-operative: Société Coopérative de Vinification. (Add): Bégadan, 33340 Lesparre. A.C. Médoc. (Com): Bégadan, north-western Bordeaux 500ha.

Cave Saint-Roch (Fr) a co-operative winery. (Add): Queyrac, 33340 Lesparre. A.C. Médoc. (Com): Queyrac, north-western Bordeaux.

Cave Saint-Sauveur (Fr) vineyard. (Add): 33250 Pauillac. 100ha. A.C. Haut-Médoc. (Com): Saint-Sauveur-du-Médoc. Grape varieties: Cabernet sauvignon, Malbec, Merlot and Petit verdot. Owned by Coopérative Vinicole.

Caves Aliança (Port) producers of Casa Mendes (a Vinho Verde) and Dão Aliança. Also red and white Garrafeiras in Bairrada and Aliança Seco.

Cave San Jose (Port) a winery based in the DOC Estramadura. Grape varieties include: Tempranillo. Label: Viña Canchal.

Caves Borlida (Port) producers of S. Vincente (a Dão wine).

Caves Coopératives de l'Appellation Haut-Médoc Cave la Paroisse (Fr) a co-operative winery based in the commune of St-Seurin-de-Cadourne. A.C. Haut-Médoc.

Caves da Raposeira (Port) producers of sparkling wines in Lamego. Is owned by Seagram.

Caves da Silva (Port) producer of Dalva (a Dão wine) and Isabel (a traditional method sparkling wine).

Caves de Bailly (Fr) a 35 ha vineyard at Saint Bris, Le Veneux, Yonne. Produce Meurgis (an A.C. Crémant de Bourgogne).

Caves de la Reine Pédauque (Fr) a noted Burgundy shipper based in Beaune, Côte de Beaune.

Caves de Solar de S. Domingos (Port) a winery that produces Dão wines under the Dão S. Domingos label. Also red and white Bairrada wines.

Caves-de-Teilles (Fr) a commune in the A.C. Fitou region, south-western France.

Caves do Casalinho (Port) the producer of Casalinho (a brand-name of Vinho Verde).

Caves d'Olt [Les] (Fr) a large co-operative based in Parnac, Cahors. It handles nearly half of the regions wine production.

C

Caves Dom Teodósio (Port) a winery based in the Ribatejo. Producer of Dão and Vinho Verde wines under the label of Casaleiro. Also Cardeal (a Dão wine) and wines under the Serradayres label. Some of the best wines come from their own vineyards of Quinta de Almargem.

Caves Fundaçao (Port) a producer of Dão wines under the Dão Fundaçao brand-name.

Caves Império (Port) a winery that produces Painel (a Dão wine), red and white Garrafeiras, Bairrada and Impérial (a Dão wine).

Caves Messias (Port) a large wine company with wineries based the D.O.C.'s Bairrada (Quinta do Valdoeiro), Beiras, Dão, Douro (Quinta do Cachão), Terras do Sado and Vinho Verde.

Caves Pimavera (Port) a winery that produces Dão wines under the Dão Primavera label (owns no vineyards).

Cave Spring Cellars (Can) a winery (established 1986) based at Niagara Peninsula in Ontario. Produces dry Riesling and Chardonnay wines, plus Cabernet/Merlot blends.

Caves Saint Pierre [Les] (Fr) a winery. (Add): Ave. Pierre de Luxembourg, B.P. 5, 84230 Châteauneuf-du-Pape. Labels include Tiare du Pape (La), Clefs des Prelats.

Caves Sao João (Port) a winery based in Bairrada, Beira Littoal that produces full-bodied Bairrada wines.

Caves Solar das Francesas (Port) a noted shipper of Dão wines.

Caves St-Pierre (Fr) a co-operative winery based in the A.C. Châteauneuf-du-Pape. Produces a variety of A.C. wines from the Côtes-du-Rhône, Vaucluse. Labels include: Préference (A.C. Côtes-du-Rhone-Villages Rasteau).

Cave St. Martin (Lux) a leading producer of sparkling wines based at Remich.

Cave Uni-Médoc (Fr) a wine co-operative known as the Union de Caves Coopératives. (Add): Gaillan-en-Médoc, 33340 Lesparre. A.C. Médoc. (Com): Gaillan, north-western Bordeaux.

Caves Velhas (Port) a winery owned by Camilo Alves (who still produce Bucelas under this name). Also produce Dão Caves Velhas (a brand-name used for their Dão wines).

Cave Vinicole d'Eguisheim (Fr) an Alsace co-operative. (Add): 6, Grand-Rue, 68420 Eguisheim.

Cave Vinicole de Pfaffenheim (Fr) an Alsace co-operative. (Add): 68250 Rouffach.

Cave Vinicole de Puisseguin (Fr) a co-operative winery based in the commune of Puisseguin-Saint-Émilion. A.C. Saint-Émilion, Bordeaux. 570ha.

Cave Vinicole de Turckheim (Fr) an Alsace wine co-operative. (Add): 68230 Turckheim.

Cavicchioli (It) a winery based at San Prospero near Sorbara in the Emilia Romagna region. Noted for Lambrusco (still and sparkling).

Caviros (Gre) a large, noted wine-producer of Greece.

Caviste (Sp) cellar worker.

Cavit (It) a co-operative in the Trentino-Alto-Adige region. Blends, matures and bottles wines made by other co-operatives.

Cawston Vale (Eng) a fruit juice and soft drink packer based in Sudbury, Suffolk.

Caxaca (Bra) the alternative spelling of Cachaça.

Çay (Tur) tea.

Cayd (Sp) the noted Sherry-producers, Criadores Almancenistes' own brand-name: Buidores de Vinhos de Jerez.

Çaydanlik (Tur) tea-pot.

Cayetana (Sp) a white grape variety grown in western Spain to produce medium white wines. A high yielder, it is often blended with other varieties. Known as Calagraño or Cazagal in Rioja.

Çay Fincani (Tur) teacup.

Çayhane (Tur) tea house/tea shop.

Caymus Vineyard (USA) a winery (29ha) based near Rutherford, Napa Valley, California. Grape varieties: Cabernet franc, Cabernet sauvignon, Chardonnay, Malbec, Merlot, Pinot noir, Sauvignon blanc, Sémillon, Zinfandel. Produces varietals and table wines under the Liberty School label.

Cayo Verde (USA) a lime-flavoured liqueur.

Caythorpe Brewery (Eng) a brewery based in Hoveringham. Brews: Birthday Brew.

Cayuga (USA) an AVA region within the Finger Lakes, New York State.

Cayuse (USA) a winery based in the Columbia Valley, Washington state. Produces a variety of wines.

Cazagal (Sp) an alternative name for Cayetana or Calagraño grapes.

Cazanove (Fr) the brand-name of a Cognac from Cazanove. (Add): S.A. 17500 Jonzac. Also produces a range of liqueurs.

Cazeau (W.Ind) a rum distillery based in Haiti that produces Rhum Marie Colas.

Cazes Frères (Fr) a noted producer of A.C. Muscat de Rivesaltes. VdN. (Add): 4, Rue Francisco Ferrer, BP 61-66600, Rivesaltes.

Cazetiers (Fr) a Premier Cru vineyard in the A.C. commune of Gevrey-Chambertin, Côte de Nuits, Burgundy. 9.11ha. Also known as Les Cazetiers.

C.B. (Fr) abbr: Château Bottled.

CB (Eng) abbr: Cadnam Brewery based in Cadnam, New Forest, Hampshire. Produces Cadnam Bitter 1031 O.G.

C.B.A.B. (USA) abbr: California Brandy Advisory Board.

CC (USA) the label used by J.F.J Bronco Winery, California for a range of wines.

CCC (S.Afr) the label for a red wine (Cabernet franc, Cabernet sauvignon) and white (Chardonnay, Chenin blanc, Colombard) produced by Bonnievale Callar winery, Robertson, Western Cape.

C.C.G.B. (Eng) abbr: Coca Cola Great Britain.

C.C.O.V.I. (Can) abbr: Cool Climate Oenology Viticultural Institute. A teaching research institute. Part of Brook University in Niagara. Housed in Inniskillin Hall.

C.C.S.B. (Eng) abbr: Coca Cola and Schweppes Beverages Company.

C

C.C.T. (Eng) *abbr*: Common Customs Tarrif.

CDC (Fr) a producer of Café de Paris. (Add): 30, Avenue Kléber, Paris.

C.D. Pils (Ger) a pilsener lager brewed by the Dinkelacker Brauerei in Stuttgart. 5.3% alc by vol. Is unpasteurised and has a long lagering period.

Cebada (Sp) barley.

Cebreros (Sp) awarded provisional DE in 1986. (DEp). A Vino de la Tierra Castilla-León based in Ávila. 9,000ha. Main grape varieties are Garnacha, Albillo, Viura.

Cecema Punch (Punch) 850mls white rum, 500mls orange juice, 500mls pineapple juice, 1 litre iced lemonade, 150mls lemon juice, 300mls gomme syrup. Stir altogether (except lemonade). Chill down in a refrigerator, add lemonade and 2 sliced oranges.

Ceciliana (It) a sparkling natural spring mineral water from Ceciliana. Mineral contents (milligrammes per litre): Sodium 6.6mg/l, Calcium 26.43mg/l, Magnesium 11.17mg/l, Potassium 7mg/l, Bicarbonates 122mg/l, Chlorides 21.27mg/l, Sulphates 3mg/l, Fluorides 0.05mg/l, Silicates 32.3mg/l. pH 6.34

Ceclavin (Sp) a wine-producing area based in Cáceres, south-western Spain.

Cedarcreek Estate Winery (Can) a winery based in British Columbia.

Cedar Hill Wine Company (USA) a winery based in Cleveland Heights, Ohio. Produces French-American hybrid and vinifera wines under the Château Lagniappe label.

Cedar Springs (Can) a natural spring mineral water from Oro Mountain, Horseshoe Valley. Mineral contents (milligrammes per litre): Sodium 3mg/l, Calcium 41.5mg/l, Chlorides 1.11mg/l, Sulphates 12.7mg/l, Fluorides 0.2mg/l. pH 8.1

Cedarwood (Eng) a term used to describe a certain bouquet associated with the bottle maturity of a wine which has previously been fermented or stored in wood.

Cederberg Kelders (S.Afr) a winery (established 1977) based at Cederberg, Olifants River, Western Cape. 52ha. (Add): Dwarsrivier, P.O. Cederberg 7341. Grape varieties: Bukettraube, Cabernet sauvignon, Chenin blanc, Sauvignon blanc, Shiraz. Labels: Cederberger (Merlot 50%, Pinotage 30%, Shiraz 20%), V Generation. Website: http://www.cederbergwine.com

Cederlunds Torr Caloric (Swe) a Swedish Punsch 55.5% alc by vol. Produced by Aktiebolaget Vin & Spritcentralem.

Cédratine (Fr) a citrus-flavoured liqueur produced on the island of Corsica.

Cédres [Les] (Fr) a vineyard in the A.C. Châteauneuf-du-Pape, southern Rhône. Owned by Paul Jaboulet Aîné et Fils. *See also* Grappe des Papes.

Ceiling Yield (Fr) *see* Plafond Limité de Classement.

Celebes Islands Coffee (E.Ind) an Indonesian coffee which produces strong, full-flavoured coffees.

Celebrance (Eng) a 6.5% alc by vol. pale bitter ale brewed by the Aspinall Cambrinus Craft Brewery, Knowsley, Merseyside.

Celebrated Oatmeal Stout (Eng) a bottled strong stout 1050 O.G. brewed by the Samuel Smith Brewery, Tadcaster, Yorkshire.

Celebration Ale (Eng) a sweet, heavy, strong ale 1066 O.G. brewed by the Morrell's Brewery, Oxford, Oxfordshire.

Celebration Ale (Eng) a 4.6% alc by vol. bottled ale brewed by Tolly Cobbold, Suffolk to celebrate the 175th anniversary of the R.N.L.I. 4.2% alc by vol. ale brewed by the Conway Brewery, Gwynedd.

Celebration Cream (Sp) a brand of Cream Sherry produced by Domecq in Jerez de la Frontera.

Celebration Water (Arg) a natural spring mineral water from Neuquen, Cordillera de los Andes. Mineral contents (milligrammes per litre): Sodium 11mg/l, Calcium 14mg/l, Magnesium 8mg/l, Potassium 1.5mg/l, Bicarbonates 105mg/l, Chlorides 9mg/l, Sulphates 0.2mg/l, Fluorides 0.2mg/l, Nitrates 4.5mg/l. pH 8.0

Celebration Wine (USA) the name often used for sparkling wines.

Celeste (S.Afr) the label for a white wine (Sauvignon blanc) produced by the Drostdy Wine Cellar winery, Tulbagh, Western Cape.

Celina Mineralbrunnen (Ger) a natural spring mineral water from Leissling, ST.

Celis Brewery (USA) a brewery (established 1992) based in Austin, Texas. Brews: Celis Golden, Celis Grand Cru, Celis Pale Bock, Celis Raspberry, Celis White.

Celis Golden (USA) a 4.8% alc by vol. light, bottled lager brewed using Saaz hops by the Celis Brewery, Austin, Texas. A Belgian style beer.

Celis Grand Cru (USA) an 8.75% alc by vol. top-fermented, bottled special beer brewed using a variety of spices by the Celis Brewery, Austin, Texas.

Celis Pale Bock (USA) an 4.8% alc by vol. top-fermented, copper coloured, bottled ale brewed by the Celis Brewery, Austin, Texas. A Belgian style beer.

Celis Raspberry (USA) an 4.8% alc by vol. top-fermented, fruity, bottled raspberry beer brewed by the Celis Brewery, Austin, Texas using 30% wheat, a Belgian-style beer.

Celis White (USA) an 4.8% alc by vol. top-fermented, fruity, bottled white wheat beer brewed by the Celis Brewery, Austin, Texas using coriander and Curaçao orange peel, a Belgian-style beer.

Cella (Lat) cellar.

Cellah (Afr) an A.O.G. area in the wine-producing region of Gharb, Morocco.

Cellar (Eng) an underground room for the storage of beers, wines, etc. Must have a cool, constant temperature 10°C–16°C (50°F–60.8°F) with little or no vibration. (Fr) = cellier/cave, (Ger) = keller, (Hol) = kelder, (Ire) = siléan, (It) = cantina, (Lat) = cella, (Port) = adega, (Sp) = bodega, (Tur) = mahzen, (USA) = celler, (Wal) = seler.

Cellarage (Eng) the area of a cellar.

C

Cellarage (Eng) the charges levied for storing wines etc. in a cellar.

Cellar Blend (S.Afr) the label for a red wine (Cabernet sauvignon, Pinotage, Shiraz, Tinta) produced by the Cloof winery, Darling, Western Cape.

Cellar Brewery (Eng) *see* Cirencester.

Cellarcraft (Eng) the name given to the tending of wines in a hygienic manner in order to mature them and keep them in peak condition. Includes storage, temperature and hygiene. In wine-making includes filtering, fining, blending and bottling.

Cellar Door (S.Afr) the label for a range of wines produced by the Villiera Wines winery, Stellenbosch, Western Cape.

Cellarer (Eng) in the past a monastery monk who is responsible for the wine and food in the cellar.

Cellar Estates (Eng) the brand label for a range of wines from around the new and old world wine regions (85 different wines) as part of the wine range from Bestwood Cash & Carry.

Cellaret (Eng) a small cupboard, case or cabinet for storing bottles of wine. Has compartments.

Cellar Hand (S.Afr) the label for a white wine (Chenin blanc) produced by the Flagstone Winery, Somerset West, Western Cape

Cellarman's Cask (Eng) the banner used by Hardy's & Hanson's in Kimberley, Nottinghamshire for a range of ales. *see* Crazy Cow, Crowing Cock, Frolicking Farmer, Guzzling Goose, Raging Rooster, Rocking Rudolph.

Cellar Master (Eng) a person in charge of the cellars. *See also* Oinophoros, Wine Butler. (Fr) = maître de chai, (Ger) = cellermeister, (Sp) = capataz.

Cellar Masters Choice (S.Afr) the label for a red and white wine produced by the Excelsior Estate winery, Robertson, Western Cape

Cellar Selection (S.Afr) the label for a range of wines produced by Kleine Zalze Wines, Stellenbosch, Western Cape.

Cellar Series (S.Afr) the label for a range of wines (Cellar Silver, Cellar Gold, Cellar Reserve) produced by the Franschhoek Vineyards winery, Franschoek, Western Cape (originally known as La Cotte).

Cellar Vee (Eng) a 3.7% alc by vol. ale brewed by the Summerskills Brewery, Devon.

Cellar-Vie Wines (S.Afr) a winery (established 1990) based in Edleen, Western Cape. Grape varieties: Cabernet franc, Cabernet sauvignon, Malbec, Merlot, Petit verdot. Label: Commitment.

Cellatica (It) a small town in the Garda distict of Lombardy, north-west of Brescia. Also the name of red wine.

Cellatica (It) a D.O.C. red wine from the Lombardy region. Produced from Barbera 25%–30%, Incrocio terzi 10%–15%, Marzernino 20%–30% and Schiava gentile 35%–40% grapes.

Celler (USA) cellar.

Celler de Capçanes (Sp) a co-operative winery (established 1935) based in the D.O. of Monsant, Tarragona, Catalonia. Labels: Cabrida, Lasendal.

Cellerette (Eng) a large, lead-lined bucket designed to take bottles of wine and ice. Usually on a stand and lockable. Also called a wine cooler. Popular in the eighteenth and nineteenth centuries.

Celles (Fr) a commune in the Charente-Maritime département whose grapes are classed Petite Champagne (Cognac).

Cell Gen (Jap) a natural spring mineral water. Mineral contents (milligrammes per litre): Sodium 4.7mg/l, Calcium 16.1mg/l, Magnesium 1.2mg/l, Potassium 6mg/l, Bicarbonates 19.4mg/l, Chlorides 14.2mg/l, Sulphates 16.6mg/l, Fluorides 0.22mg/l. pH 7.9

Cellier (Arg) a natural spring mineral water. Mineral contents (milligrammes per litre): Sodium 134mg/l, Calcium 25mg/l, Magnesium 15mg/l, Potassium 10mg/l, Chlorides 30mg/l, Sulphates 28mg/l, Fluorides 0.6mg/l, Nitrates 44mg/l. pH 7.6

Cellier (Fr) cellar.

Cellier-aux-Moines (Fr) a vineyard in the A.C. commune of Givry, Côte Chalonnaise, Burgundy.

Cellier de Graffan (Fr) a winery based in the A.C. Corbières, south-western France. Labels: Graffan, Les Grès de Graffan.

Cellier de Marrenon (Fr) a group of co-operatives based in the southern Rhône. Produce both red and white wines.

Cellier des Demoiselles (Fr) a co-opeartive winery based in the A.C. Corbières, Languedoc-Roussillon. (Add): S.C.V. Les Maîtres Vignerons Coopérateurs, 11220 Saint-Laurent de la Cabrerisse Tournissan. Produces: white, rosé and red wines. Label: St. Laurentaise. Website: http://www.cellier-des-demoiselles.fr

Cellier des Princes [Le] (Fr) the label of a Châteauneuf-du-Pape produced by Co-operative Vinicole Intercommunale, R.N. 7, 84350 Courthézon, southern Rhône.

Cellier le Brun (N.Z) a winery. (Add): Terrace Road, P.O. Box 33, Renwick, Marlborough. 15ha. A sparkling wine producer. Produces vintage and non-vintage wines from Chardonnay, Pinot noir, Pinot meunier grapes.

Celliers (Fr) above-ground, wine stores in monasteries.

Celorico de Basto (Port) a small district in the Vinho Verde region that produces fine white wines.

Celt (Wal) a bottled ale from the Snowdonia Brewery (a micro-brewery), Gellilydan, Gwynedd.

Celtia (Afr) the name of a local bottled beer produced in Tunisia.

Celtic (Eng) a 4.2% alc by vol. ale from The Durham Brewery, Bowburn, C°. Durham. *See also* Palatinate, Sanctuary.

Celtic (Fr) a still and carbonated natural mineral water from the Vosges mountains. (Add): Celtic-S.E.A.N., 2, Place des Thermes, 67110 Niederbronn-les-Bains. Mineral contents (milligrammes per litre): Sodium 2.5mg/l, Calcium 8.8mg/l, Magnesium 2.6mg/l, Potassium 4.4mg/l, Bicarbonates 24.4mg/l,

C

Chlorides 3.3mg/l, Sulphates 8.2mg/l, Fluride 0.03mg/l, Nitrates 3.3mg/l, Iron 0.01mg/l. pH 6.61

Celtic Ale (Wal) a 4.2% alc by vol. ale brewed by Granny's, Aberystwyth.

Celtic Black (Scot) a 3.9% alc by vol. ale brewed by the Hebridean Brewery C°., Isle of Lewis.

Celtic Bright Bitter (Wal) a keg bitter 1033 O.G. brewed by the Buckley's Brewery, Llanelli, South Wales.

Celtic Gold (Eng) a 4% alc by vol. ale brewed by the Spinning Dog Brewery, Herefordshire.

Celtic Gold Lager (Wal) a lager 1046 O.G. brewed by the Silverthorne's Brewery in Cwmbran, Gwent.

Celtic Pride (Wal) a 4.5% alc by vol. ale brewed by The Rymney Brewery Ltd., Mid-Glamorgan.

Celtic Spirit C°. (Wal) a distillery based at Grove Farm, Abergavenny, Monmouthshire, Wales. Produces a range of products including Black Mountain Liqueur, Danzy Jones plus Celtic Whisky, Dragon Spirit and Llanthony Honey Liqueur. Website: http://www.celticspirit.co.uk

Celtic Spring (Eng) a natural spring mineral water from Longtown. Mineral contents (milligrammes per litre): Sodium 6mg/l, Calcium 36mg/l, Magnesium 0.2mg/l, Potassium 0.6mg/l, Bicarbonates 91mg/l, Chlorides 10mg/l, Sulphates 13mg/l, Nitrates 3mg/l. pH 7.7

Celtic Whisky (Wal) a 4 year old and 12 year old Scotch whisky produced for the Celtic Spirit C°. based at Grove Farm, Abergavenny, Monmouthshire, Wales. Both 40% alc by vol.

Celvik Extra (Bos) a natural spring mineral water from Dolac-Tesanj, Bosnia Herzegovina. Mineral contents (milligrammes per litre): Sodium 460mg/l, Calcium 144.28mg/l, Magnesium 145.8mg/l, Potassium 23.46mg/l, Bicarbonates 1756.8mg/l, Chlorides 395.47mg/l, Nitrates 0.1mg/l, Silicates 30mg/l, Strontium 1.58mg/l. pH 6.06

CENALSA (Sp) abbr: Comercializadora Exportadora Navarra de Alimentación. **S.A.** A body owned by the government, savings banks and producers' co-operatives. Conducts viticultural research. Is based in Navarra, north-eastern Spain. Trade name: Agronavarra.

Cenanthaldehyde (Eng) an aldehyde formed by oxidation of alcohols found in wine in small traces that contributes to the bouquet.

Cencibel (Sp) a red grape variety grown in the La Mancha region to produce dry red wines of 12%–14% alc by vol. Also known as the Tempranillo, Tinto fino and the Ull de llebre.

Cendré de Novembre (Fr) a rosé wine produced in the Arbois district of the Jura, central-eastern France.

Cenicero (Sp) a noted wine-producing village in the Rioja Alta, north-western Spain.

Cenizo (Sp) the local name for the first system of oidium (a dark, fine, ash-like powder that gathers on the vine stem).

Centaure (Fr) brand Cognacs produced by Rémy Martin. Either Napoléon, X.O. or Extra.

Centaurée Quinta (Fr) a proprietary brand of apéritif.

Centaury (Fr) an aromatic wine flavoured with marjoram, hyssop, tea, coriander and citrus peels.

Centenario (Sp) a 3 year old solera brandy produced by Terry.

Centenary Ale (Eng) a bottled ale brewed by the Elgood Brewery in Wisbech, Cambridgeshire to celebrate 100 years of brewing. A strong, dark brew.

Centenary Ale (Eng) a bottled ale 1080 O.G. brewed by the Mitchells Brewery, Lancaster to celebrate 100 years of brewing.

Centenary Ale (Eng) a bottled ale 1060 O.G. brewed by the Home Brewery, Nottingham to celebrate 100 years of brewing.

Centenary Ale (Eng) a 1050 O.G. ale produced by Exmoor Ales to celebrate the centenary of Somerset Cricket club.

Centenary Ale (Wal) a 3.9% alc by vol. ale brewed by The Rhymney Brewery Ltd., Mid-Glamorgan.

Centennial (USA) a 10 year old Kentucky straight sour mash Bourbon whiskey from W.L. Weller.

Centerbe (It) another name for the herb liqueur Mentaccia. Called so because 100 herbs are used in its production.

Centgericht (Ger) see Zentgericht.

Centgrafenberg (Ger) vineyard (Anb): Franken. (Ber): Mainviereck. (Gro): Not yet assigned. (Vil): Bürgstadt.

Centiliter (USA) centilitre, 0.100 part of a litre.

Centilitre (Euro) 0.100 of a litre.

Centine Rosso di Montalcino (It) a red wine produced from Brunello grapes by Costello Villa Banfi in the Tuscany region.

Centraal Brouwerij Kantoor (CBK) (Hol) a brewery. (Add): Herengracht 282, 1016 BX Amsterdam. Brews beers and lager. Website: http://www.cbk.nl 'E'mail: info@cbk.nl

Central Coast (USA) a large Californian wine-producing area between Santa Barbara and San Francisco.

Central Otago (N.Z) a wine-producing area based near Queenstown in the South Island.

Central Valley (Chile) a major wine-producing area in central Chile. Produces over half the country's wine. Home to wineries of Caliterra, Carmen, Morandi, Valdivieso.

Central Vinícola do Sul (Bra) abbr: VINOSUL S/A. a body who have helped in the development of the local wine industry.

Centrifugal Press (Eng) it works on the principle of a spin-dryer drawing the must through the sides of the drum as it spins, leaving the pomace behind. Does not crush the pips, skins or stalks.

Centrifugation (Fr) centrifuging.

Centrifuge (Euro) a unit which removes the solid matter out of grape juice. Is used in Germany in the preparation of süssreserve.

Centrifuging (Eng) see Centrifuge. (Fr) = centrifugation.

Centro Agricola de Tramagal (Port) a family winery

C

based in the Ribatejo. Noted for red wines produced from Castelão francês, Trincadeira and Cabernet grapes. Wines are bottled under the Casal do Coelheira label.

Centro de Estudos Vitivinícolas do Dão (Port) the research body in the Dão region that has laboratories in Nelas. Works with the Federação in the region.

Centurian (USA) a black grape variety developed by the University of California.

Centurians Ghost (Eng) a 5.4% alc by vol. ale brewed by the York Brewery Company Ltd, North Yorkshire.

Centurion Best Bitter (Eng) a 4.5% alc by vol. bitter beer brewed by Hadrian and Border Brewery, Tyne & Wear. *See also* Emperor Ale, Zetland Bitter.

Centurion's Ghost Ale (Eng) a 5% alc by vol. bitter ale brewed by the York Brewery, Toft Green, North Yorkshire.

Century Ale (Eng) a tawny coloured beer 4.2% alc by vol. from Hambleton Brewery, Holme-on-Swale, near Thirsk, North Yorkshire. Brewed to commemorate the 100th edition of the Darlington Drinker (newsletter of the local CAMRA branch).

Century Plant (USA) the alternative name for the agave cactus. *See also* American Aloe, Maguey and Mezcal Cacti.

Cent Vignes [Les] (Fr) a Premier Cru vineyard in the A.C. commune of Beaune, Côte de Beaune, Burgundy 23.5ha.

Cep (Fr) vine stock.

Cepa (Port) grapevine/vine stock.

Cepa (Sp) vine stock.

Cepa Borgona (Sp) a Riojan vine root-stock brought by the French in the nineteenth century. Thought to be the Pinot noir or Gamay from Burgundy.

Cepa Chablis (Sp) a Riojan vine root-stock brought by the French in the nineteenth century. Thought to be the Chardonnay from the Burgundy region.

Cépage (Fr) a vine variety (mainly applies to **Vitis vinifera**). i.e. one of the leading '*cépages*' of the Burgundy region is the Pinot noir.

Cépage Courant (Fr) the standard grape varieties for the region under the A.C. laws. i.e. Gamay in the Beaujolais.

Cépage de France (Fr) a new style wine at Vin de Pays quality but blending wines from different Vin de Pays regions.

Cépages Améliorateurs (Fr) lit: 'grape variety improvers', grape varieties that help to upgrade the quality of the finished wine.

Cépages d'Abondanse (Fr) the name used to denote heavy cropping grape varieties.

Cépages Nobles (Fr) noble grape varieties. i.e. the Riesling in the Alsace region.

Cepa Médoc (Sp) a Rioja vine root-stock brought by the French in the nineteenth century. Thought to be the Cabernet sauvignon from Bordeaux.

Cepa Velha (Port) the brand-name used by the Vinhos de Monção in the Minho for red and dry white wines.

Cep d'Or (Fr) a 15 year old Cognac produced by Jean Fillioux.

Cephalonia (Gre) an Ionian island in western Greece. Produces mainly country wines for local consumption.

Cerasol (Sp) a red grape variety grown in the Navarra, north-eastern Spain. Produces light red wines. *see* Ojo de Gallo.

Cerassella (It) a liqueur made from cherries in Pescara.

Cerasuolo (It) lit: 'cherry coloured'.

Cerasuolo (It) a D.O.C. red wine from the Abruzzi region. Made from the Montepulciano grape.

Cerasuolo di Vittoria (It) a D.O.C. red wine from Sicily. Made from the Calabrese, Frappato, Grosso nero and Mascalese grapes. Is high in alcohol.

Cerbère (Fr) a commune in the A.C. Banyuls, south-western France.

Cerceal (Mad)(Port) a white grape variety grown in Madeira to make the fortified wine Sercial. Cerceal is the old spelling originally from the Rhine. Also grown in Bairrada and Dão in Portugal. Also known as the Cerceal do Dão.

Cercié (Fr) a commune in the Beaujolais. Has A.C. Beaujolais-Villages or Beaujolais-Cercié status.

Cercle des Chevaliers du Cep (Fr) a wine society based in Châteauroux.

Cercles [En] (Fr) the name given to wines contained in casks (barrels).

Cerdon (Fr) a vineyard in the Ain département of central-eastern France. Produces red and sparkling rosé wines.

Cerelia (It) a natural spring mineral water from Cerelia, Appenin. Mineral contents (milligrammes per litre): Sodium 5.6mg/l, Calcium 119mg/l, Magnesium 10mg/l, Potassium 0.6mg/l, Bicarbonates 416mg/l, Chlorides 5.3mg/l, Sulphates 7.8mg/l, Fluorides 0.14mg/l, Nitrates 1.5mg/l, Silicates 15.8mg/l. pH 7.4

Ceremony Brandy (USA) the brand-name of a 5 or 8 year old brandy bottled by the Guild of Wineries and Distillers at Lodi in California. 40% alc by vol.

Ceres (S.Afr) a wine-producing area in the Cape Province.

Ceres Brewery (Den) the largest, independent brewery in Denmark. Is based in Aarhus. Noted for Ceres Danish Stout 7.5% alc by vol. Red Erik lager 6.5% alc by vol. Royal Export 5.8% alc by vol. Strong Brew 7.7% alc by vol.

Ceres Plus (S.Afr) a 100% pure fruit juice blended with tea (or vegetables). Flavours include: cranberry and rooibos, litchi, mango, pure grape juice, papaya and carrot. (Add): Bon Chretien Street, Ceres, 6835 S.Afr. Website: http://www.ceres.co.za

Ceret (Sp) an old name for Sherry, derived from Xera (the Greek name for Jerez).

Ceretene (It) the Roman name for Sherry.

Ceretto (It) a winery based in Alba, Piemonte, north-western Italy. Owns the Bricco Rocche Estate. Produces Barolo Brunate DOCG. Website: http://www.ceretto.com

C

Cereza (S.Am) a white fleshed grape with a pink skin grown in Argentina. Produces white and rosé wines.

Cergal (Port) the brand-name used by a brewing company based at Belas for one of their beers.

Cerist (Wal) a natural spring mineral water from Llawr Cae, Dinas Mawddwy, Powys. Mineral contents (milligrammes per litre): Sodium 3mg/l, Calcium 3.2mg/l, Magnesium 1.5mg/l, Potassium 0.4mg/l, Bicarbonates 2.8mg/l, Chlorides 8.1mg/l, Sulphates 6.6mg/l, Nitrates 0.8mg/l. pH 6.3

Cern Horà Brewery (Czec) an old brewery based in south-western Czec.

Cernay (Fr) a wine-producing village of the Haut-Rhin at the southern extreme of Alsace. Known in German as Sennheim.

Cernay-lès-Reims (Fr) a Cru Champagne village in the Canton de Beine. District: Reims.

Cerny Kozel (Czec) lit: 'black billy goat', a strong beer brewed by the Stankov Brewery.

Cérons (Fr) a commune in the A.C. Cérons in south-eastern Bordeaux.

Cérons (Fr) a commune [part] in the A.C. Graves district of south-eastern Bordeaux.

Cérons (Fr) an A.C. district of south-eastern Bordeaux on the west bank of the river Garonne, between the communes of Graves and Sauternes. Produces sweet, white wines with a hint of Botrytis cinerea. Contains the communes of Cérons, Illats and Podensac. Minimum alc. content 12.5% by vol.

Cerrement (Fr) the label for a rosé wine (Cabernet franc, Cabernet sauvignon & Merlot blend) produced by Château Puy-Servain, A.C. Bergerac.

Cerro Añon Reserva (Sp) a red wine produced by Bodegas Olarra S.A. Made from the Tempranillo 60%, Garnacha 30%, Mazuela 5% and Graciano 5% grapes.

Cerro Chapeu-Casa Pujol (S.Am) has the Rivera Vineyard (one of the highest in Uruguay at 280 metres). Noted for barrel-fermented Chardonnay, Gran Tradición (Tannat plus Cabernet sauvignon and Cabernet franc aged in new French oak) and Amat (a top of the range Tannat aged in French and USA oak).

Cerros de San Juan [Los] (S.Am) a winery based in Colonia, Uruguay Produces Fiesta de San Juan (blend of Cabernet sauvignon, Merlot and Tannat grapes), plus Cuna de Piedra (a 100% oak aged Tannat).

Cerseuil (Fr) a Cru Champagne village in the Canton de Braine. District: Soissons.

Certificate (Fr) a vintage de luxe cuvée Champagne produced by A. Charbaut et Fils from 100% Chardonnay grapes.

Certificate of Age (USA) the Government certificate guaranteeing the age of spirits produced in the USA.

Certified (USA) the brand-name for a brandy produced by Schenley Distillers.

Certosa (It) a green herb liqueur from Florence,

yellow and red versions are also produced which are sweeter. Made by the Carthusian monks.

Certosa (It) a natural spring mineral water brand.

Certosa Fonte Camarda (It) a sparkling natural spring mineral water from the Certosa Fonte Camarda. Mineral contents (milligrammes per litre): Sodium 7.8mg/l, Calcium 6.2mg/l, Magnesium 4.12mg/l, Potassium 1.2mg/l, Chlorides 14.89mg/l, Sulphates 8.4mg/l, Fluorides 0.09mg/l, Nitrates 2.7mg/l, Silicates 8.6mg/l. pH 6.38

Cervaro (It) an oak-aged, white wine produced by Antinori from the Chardonnay and Grechetto grapes.

Cerveceria (Sp) brewery/bar.

Cerveceria Leona SA (S.Am) a brewery. (Add): Kilómetro 30 via, Bogatá-Tocanpipá, Bogatá, Columbia. Brews beers and lager. Website: http://www.leona.com.co 'E'mail: info@leona.com.co

Cerveceria Moctezuma (S.Am) see Moctezuma Brewery.

Cerveceria Modelo (S.Am) a brewery based in Mexico City, Mexico that brews Corona Extra Lager 4.6% alc by vol. Negra Modelo 5.3% alc by vol.

Cervecero (Sp) brewer/beer seller.

Cerveja (Port) beer/ale.

Cerveja de Fàbrica (Port) brewery. See also Cervejaria.

Cervejaria (Port) a public house/bar. Also the name for a brewery. See also Cerveja de Fàbrica.

Cerveteri Bianco (It) a D.O.C. white wine from the communes of Cervelen, Ladispoli, Santa Marinella and Civitavecchia in Latium. Made from Barbera, Canaiolo nero, Carignano, Cesanese commune, Montepulciano and Sangiovese grapes.

Cerveteri Rosso (It) a D.O.C. red wine from the communes of Cervelen, Ladispoli, Santa Marinella and Civitavecchia in Latium. Made from Barbera, Canaiolo nero, Carignano, Cesanese commune, Montepulciano and Sangiovese grapes.

Cerveza (Sp) beer/ale.

Cerveza Negra (Sp) dark beer.

Cervione (Fr) a wine-region based in north-eastern Corsica. Produces a full-bodied red wine of same name.

Cervisa (Lat) ale/beer.

Cervisia (Fr) a barley wine made from fermented barley malt in the Middle Ages.

Cervoise (Fr) a mediaeval, un-hopped beer.

Cervoise Lancelot (Fr) a 6% alc by vol. top-fermented, bottle-conditioned, amber coloured ale brewed by Lancelot Brasserie, St. Servant.

Cesanese (It) a red grape variety grown in the Lazio region. Also known as the Cesanese commune.

Cesanese Commune (It) see Cesanese.

Cesanese di Affile (It) a red grape variety grown in Latium (Lazio).

Cesanese di Affile (It) a D.O.C. red wine from the communes of Affile, Roiate and part of Arcinazzo in the Latium (Lazio) region. Made from Barbera, Bombino bianco, Cesanese di affile, Montepulciano, Sangiovese and Trebbiano

242

C

toscano. Produced as Secco, Amabile or Dolce. D.O.C. also applies to the sparkling wines

Cesanese di Olevano Romano (It) a D.O.C. deep-ruby red wine from the communes of Olevano Romano and parts of Genazzano in the Latium (Lazio) region. Made from Barbera, Bombino bianco, Cesanese di affile, Montepulciano, Sangiovese and Trebbiano toscano grapes. Produces Secco, Amabile and Dolce. D.O.C. also applies to sparkling and semi-sparkling wines.

Cesanese di Piglio (It) a D.O.C. red wine from Latium. Made from the Barbera, Bombino bianco, Cesanese di affile, Montepulciano, Sangiovese and Trebbiano toscano grapes. Produced as either Secco, Amabile or Dolce. D.O.C. also applies to the sparkling wines.

Cesar (Fr) a natually carbonated mineral water from the Loire Valley. (Add): Eaux Minérales de St. Alban-les-Eaux s.a., F-42370 Saint-Alban-les-Eaux (Loire). Mineral contents (milligrammes per litre): Sodium 350mg/l, Calcium 220mg/l, Magnesium 70mg/l, Potassium 46mg/l, Bicarbonates 2000mg/l, Chlorides 21mg/l, Sulphates 6mg/l, Fluoride 2.45mg/l, Nitrate 0mg/l. pH 6.5

César (Fr) a red grape variety. see Céssar.

Cesar [El] (Sp) a solera brandy produced by Sanchez Romate in Jerez de la Frontera. see Conquistador, Respetable.

Cesare (It) a brand of sweet vermouth at 18% alc by vol.

Cesari (It) a winery based in the DOC Valpolicella, Veneto region. Produces a range of Valpolicella wines. Website: http://www.cesari-spa.it

Cesarini-Sforza (It) wine-producers based in Trentino-Alto-Adige region. Produces sparkling wines from the Chardonnay and Pinot grapes.

Cesky Akciovy Pipover (Czec) the Czech. Brewery Ltd. (established 1895) now known as Budweiser Budvar. Produce an alcohol-free, a light, a (10° Balling) lager for local market and 12% Balling Svetly Lezák (Premium) for export.

Ceské Budejovice (Czec) a famous Bohemian brewing town, was known as Budweis in the Austro-Hungarian Empire.

Ceské Krumlov Brewery (Czec) an old brewery based in Ceské Krumlov in south-western Czec.

Céssar (Fr) a red grape variety grown in Burgundy in the Yonne département. Used for the production of Bourgogne rouge.

Cessenon (Fr) a Vin de Pays area in the Hérault département in southern France. Produces red and white wines.

C'est la Vie (Cktl) 25mls (⅕ gill) Calvados placed into a liqueur glass, float 25mls (⅕ gill) cream on top and decorate with finely grated dark chocolate.

C'est la Vie (Lux) a sparkling (méthode traditionelle) wine produced by the House of Gales. White and rosé styles produced.

Cetina (Cro) a still natural spring mineral water from Veliko Vrilo. Mineral contents (milligrammes per litre): Sodium 4.8mg/l, Calcium 54.8mg/l,

Magnesium 14.?mg/l, Bicarbonates 107mg/l, Chlorides 12mg/l, Sulphates 14.3mg/l.

Cetinaia (It) barrique-aged red wine produced by Castello di San Polo in Tuscany from 100% Sangiovese grapes.

Ceti Standard (Fr) a type of bottle from Bordeaux, lighter than the Bordelaise Lourde.

Cetto [L.A.] Mex) the largest winery in the Valle de Guadalupe. Grape varieties: Zinfandel, Nebbiolo, Sauvignon blanc, Petit sirah.

Ceuso (It) a winery (established 1860) based on the island of Sicily. 50ha. Grape varieties: Cabernet sauvignon, Grecanico, Merlot, Nero d'Avola. Label: Scurati.

Cevada (Port) barley.

Cevennes Blanc (S.Afr) the label for a white wine (Chardonnay, Chenin blanc and Sauvignon blanc blend) produced by the La Couronne Estate winery, Franschhoek, Western Cape.

Ceylon Breakfast (Eng) a fine flavoured tea of Broken Orange Pekoe characteristics. Made from high-grown Uva Ceylon teas.

Ceylon Breweries (Sri.L) a brewery which brews Lion Lager, Stout, Pale and Jubilee Ales.

Ceylon Tea (Sri.L) although country now known as Sri Lanka, teas are known as Ceylon teas. Best regions are Dimbula, Dikoya and Nuwara Eliya (all high regions). Are blended teas with a light, delicate, lemony flavour. Usually served with lemon.

Ceylon Tea Centre (Eng) Sri Lankan tea promoting centre. (Add): 22 Regent Street, London SW1. Does research and promotion of Ceylon teas.

Ceyras (Fr) a wine-producing commune in the A.C. Clairette du Languedoc, southern France.

Cezarken (Bel) 5% alc by vol. light-coloured, bottle-conditioned special beer brewed by Crombé Brouwerij, Zottegem.

Cezve (Tur) coffee pot.

Ch. (Fr) abbr: Château.

CH (Fr) abbr: Chanteau. Found on barrels in Cognac. see Chanteau.

Cha [1] (Chi)(Kor) tea.

Cha [2] (Chi) a fermented beverage made from palm sap.

Cha (Eng) a slang for tea. i.e. "A cup of cha". Derives from the Cantonese word 'Tcha'.

Chá (Port) tea.

Chabanneau et Cie (Fr) a Cognac producer. (Add): Chabanneau et Cie, B.P. 8 16101 Cognac.

Chabiots (Fr) a Premier Cru vineyard of the A.C. commune of Morey-Saint-Denis, Côte de Nuits, Burgundy. 2.2ha.

Chablais (Switz) a wine-producing sub-district of the Vaud canton. Produces dry, heady white wines from Chasselas.

Chablis (Fr) the most northerly district of the Burgundy region. 2,600ha. Produces mainly white wines within the A.C. from the white Chardonnay grape, also some V.D.Q.S. red wines in the southern half of the district. Communes: Beines, Béru, Chablis, Chemilly-sur-Serein,

C

Chichée, Courgis, Fontenay, Fyé, La Chapelle-Vaupelteigne, Lignorelles, Ligny-le-Châtel, Maligny, Milly, Poilly-Poinchy, Préhy, Rameau, Villy and Viviers. Has four grades: Chablis Grand Cru, Chablis Premier Cru, Chablis and Petit Chablis.

Chablis (Fr) one of the four methods of pruning permitted in the Champagne region.

Chablis (USA) see California Chablis.

Chablis Cup (Cup) 1 bottle Chablis, 50mls Sherry, rind of a lemon, 10mls gomme syrup. Mix altogether in a large jug, add ice and serve in goblets.

Chablis Grand Cru (Fr) there are seven vineyards entitled to this appellation. Must have 11% alc by vol. They are: Blanchots, Bougros, Les Clos, Les Grenouilles, Les Preuses, Valmur and Vaudésir.

Chablis Moutonne (Fr) a vineyard which is of Chablis Grand Cru standard but has no official grading.

Chablis Premier Cru (Fr) there are 29 individual vineyards that are entitled to this appellation. Must have 10.5% alc by vol. They are Beauregards, Beauroy, Beugnon, Butteaux, Chapelot, Châtain, Côte de Fontenay, Côte de Jouan, Côte de Léchet, Fourchaume, Les Forêts, Les Fourneaux, Les Lys, l'Homme Mort, Mélinots, Mont de Milieu, Montée de Tonnerre, Montmains, Pied d'Aloup, Séchet, Testuit, Troesme, Vaillon (also known as Côte de Vaillon), Vaucoupin, Vau de Vey, Vaulignot, Vaulorent, Vaupulent and Vosgros (also spelt Vosgiras).

Chablis Simple (Fr) Chablis and Petit Chablis grades.

Chaboeufs [Les] (Fr) a Premier Cru vineyard in the A.C. commune of Nuits-Saint-Georges, Côte de Nuits, Burgundy. 3ha.

Chabot-Marquis de Puységur (Fr) an Armagnac producer. (Add): Compagnie Viticole des Grandes Armagnacs, Route de Bordeaux, 40190 Villeneuve de Marsan. 60ha. situated in the Bas Armagnac. Produces Chabot Blason d'Or, X.O. and Marquis de Puységur.

Chabot Vineyard (USA) a red wine (Cabernet sauvignon) produced by the Beringer Estate winery, Napa Valley, California.

Chaboud [Jean-Francois] (Fr) a producer of A.C. Saint Péray Mousseux in the Rhône. Made from Marsanne and Roussanne grapes.

Chacé (Fr) a commune in the A.C. Saumur, Anjou-Saumur, Loire. Produces red and white wines.

Ch'a Ching of Lu Yu (Chi) see Tea Scripture.

Chacolets [Les] (Fr) a vineyard in the A.C. commune of Montagny, Côte Chalonnaise, Burgundy.

Chacolí (Sp) a white, sharp, Basque wine. 8%–9% alc by vol. from area of same name in north-eastern Spain.

Chacolí de Guetaria (Sp) a D.O. region of Guipúzcoa, País Vasco, north-west Spain. 64ha. Grape varieties: Ondarrabí Zurí, Ondarrabí Beltza. see Getariako Txakolina.

Chacolí de Vizcaya (Sp) a D.O. region of Vizcaya, País Vasco, north-west Spain. 10ha. in Bakio, 56ha. in

Balmaseda. 80% of production is white from Folle blanche and Ondarrabí Zurí grapes. Some red and rosé from Ondarrabí Beltza grapes. See also Bizkaiko Txakolina.

Chacón [Miguel Velasco S.A.] (Sp) a producer of Montilla based in Montilla-Moriles.

Chadburns (Eng) see Wicket & Willow, Mansfield Brewery.

Chaddsford (USA) a vineyard (established 1982) based in Brandywine Valley, south-west of Philadelphia, Pennsylvania. 10ha. Grape varieties: Chardonnay, Pinot gris, Barbera, Riesling, Cabernet sauvignon, Cabernet franc, Merlot. Produces Merican (blend of Bordeaux varieties).

Chadely (Arab) a Mullah who, in the ninth century was purported to have discovered coffee. Also known as Scyadly.

Chadenac (Fr) a commune in the Charente-Maritime département whose grapes are classed Petite Champagne (Cognac).

Chaffots [Les] (Fr) a Premier Cru vineyard in the A.C. commune Morey-Saint-Denis, Côte de Nuits, Burgundy 1.25ha.

Chagga Coffee (Afr) the alternative name for Kilimanjaro Coffee from Tanzania. Gets its name from the Tribe who cultivate it. See also Kibo Chagga Coffee.

Chagny (Fr) a wine-town in the Mercurey district, Côte Chalonnaise, Burgundy.

Chai (Fr) an above ground storage area for wines in both bulk and bottle.

Chai de Vieillissament (Fr) wine cellars used for ageing wines.

Chai de Vin (Fr) winery.

Chaillées (Fr) the name given to the narrow terraces in the northern Rhône.

Chaillots [Les] (Fr) a Premier Cru vineyard [part] in the A.C. commune of Aloxe-Corton, Côte de Beaune, Burgundy.

Chailloux [Les] (Fr) a vineyard. (Com): Solutré-Pouilly in the A.C. Pouilly-Fuissé, Mâcon, Burgundy.

Chainmaker Mild (Eng) a 3.6% alc by vol. mild ale brewed by Enville Ales Ltd., West Midlands.

Chain of Ponds (Austr) a vineyard based in the Adelaide Hills, South Australia. Grape varieties: Pinot grigio, Sauvignon blanc, Shiraz. Labels: Black Thursday Sauvignon Blanc and Ledge Shiraz.

Chaintré (Fr) a commune in the Mâconnais district which produces A.C. Pouilly Fuissé.

Chairman's Choice (Eng) a keg bitter 1039 O.G. brewed by the Gibbs Mew Brewery, Salisbury, Wiltshire. Also known as Anchor Keg.

Chairman's Premium Select (Eng) a 4.2% alc by vol. golden hoppy-style ale brewed by Daniel Thwaites, Blackburn, Lancashire.

Chairman's Reserve (S.Afr) the label for a red wine (Cabernet sauvignon) produced by the Grangehurst Winery, Stellenbosch, Western Cape.

Chais (Fr) a building used to store wines, usually above ground but similar to a Cave or Cellar.

Chais Baumière (Fr) the label of a wine produced by

the Domaine de la Baume vineyard in the Languedoc-Roussillon. Grape varieties: Chardonnay and Merlot.

Chaix (Fr) above ground cellars.

Chakana Estate (Arg) a winery based in Luján de Cuyo, Mendoza region. Grape varieties include: Malbec. Website: http://www.chakanawines.com.ar 'E'mail: Santiago@chakanawines.com.ar

Chalambar (Austr) the label of red wine (a blend of Hermitage and other varieties) produced by Seppelt in Victoria.

Chaleira (Port) kettle.

Chalenberg (N.Z) a medium-sweet, white wine made from the Müller-Thurgau grape by the Pacific Vineyards, McLeod Road, Henderson, North Island.

Chalet Debonné Vineyards (USA) a winery based in Madison, Ohio. 16ha. Produces French hybrid and Labrusca wines.

Chalice (Eng) a religious (Christian) drinking vessel (cup).

Chalice Bridge (Austr) a winery based in the Margaret River in Western Australia. Grape varieties include: Cabernet sauvignon.

Chalié Richards (Eng) the wine company of Halewood International. Produces a range of wines including: Ocean Boulevard, Ocean Point and Orange Street.

Chalino (N.Z) a medium-sweet, white wine made from the Chasselas and Palomino grapes combined with Muscat juice. Produced by the Te Mata Winery, Hawkes Bay.

Chalk (Eng) fine calcerous soil found in the Champagne, Cognac and Andalusia (Jerez) regions. Also to a lesser extent in many other wine regions of the world. Produces fine wines. (Fr) = calcaires. *See also* Mussel Lime and Oolitic Chalk..

Chalkers Cocktail (Cktl) ⅓ measure vodka ⅓ measure Batida de Côco, ⅓ measure cream, dash egg white. Shake over ice and strain into a cocktail glass.

Chalk Hill (USA) an A.V.A. region within the A.V.A. Russian River Valley. 1,000ha. planted. *See also* Green Valley.

Chalk Hill Brewery (Eng) a brewery based in Norwich. Brews: LRN 150 to mark the 150th anniversary of Lowestoft-Reedham-Norwich railway line. Brewed from same mash as Green Jack Brewery.

Chalkhill Vineyard (Eng) a vineyard. (Add): Bowerchalke, Wiltshire. 2.5ha. Grape varieties: Bacchus, Kerner and Müller-Thurgau.

Chalk Hill Vineyard (USA) a vineyard based in the Russian River Valley, Sonoma County, California. Produces varietal wines.

Chalkis (Gre) a dry, white wine from Negropont.

Chalklands (Eng) the label used by Chilsdown for their co-operative wines.

Chalk Tufa (Fr) *see* Tufa.

Chalky Soil (Eng) soils with a heavy base of chalk (calcerous clay). (Fr) = crayeux.

Challanger APA (Eng) a 4.2% alc by vol. ale brewed by the Copper Dragon Skipton Brewery plc., North Yorkshire.

Challenge (Eng) a 4.2% alc by vol. ale brewed by Tarka Ales Ltd., Devon.

Challenger (Eng) a 5.6% alc by vol. ale brewed by the Barum brewery, Devon.

Challenger (Eng) a 3.8% alc by vol. ale brewed by the Buntingford Brewery, Hertfordshire.

Challenger Ale (Eng) a cask ale brewed using single hop variety by Ledbury Brewery Company, Herefordshire.

Challenger Ale (Eng) a 4.7% alc by vol. ale brewed by King and Barnes, Horsham, Surrey using challenger hops.

Challenger Bitter (Eng) a cask-conditioned bitter 1039 O.G. brewed by the Ashford Brewery, Ashford, Kent.

Challenger Bitter (Eng) a 4.1% alc by vol. best bitter from the Ash Vine Brewery, Trudoxhill, near Frome, Somerset.

Challes (Fr) a brand of sulphurous mineral water.

Chalone Vineyard (USA) a winery based in Monterey County, south of San Francisco, California. 50ha. Grape varieties: Chardonnay, Pinot noir. Produces varietal wines.

Chalonnaise (Fr) a red and white wine-producing district in the central Burgundy region. Has the communes of Givry, Mercurey, Montagny and Rully.

Chalonnes (Fr) a commune in the A.C. Savennières, Anjou-Saumur, Loire.

Chalon-sur-Marne (Fr) an important centre of the Champagne trade.

Chalons-sur-Vesle (Fr) a Cru Champagne village in the Canton de Fismes. District: Reims.

Chalosse Blanche (Fr) an alternative name for the white grape variety Claverie.

Chalumeau (Fr) drinking straw.

Chalumeaux [Les] (Fr) a Premier Cru vineyard in the A.C. commune of Puligny-Montrachet, Côte de Beaune, Burgundy 7ha.

Chalybeate Water (Eng) mineral waters that are either carbonated or sulphated. Acts as a stimulant and as a tonic. e.g. Passy, Vittel, St. Nectaire and Forges.

Chalybon (Gre) a biblical sweet wine made near Damascus and drunk in ancient Greece. Also known as Helbon.

Chalybon (Gre) the brand-name given to the wines from the Lebanon vineyards.

Chamakha (Rus) a red grape variety grown in Azerbaijan to produce dessert wines.

Chamarre (Fr) *see* OVS.

Chambard (Eng) a brand of wine from J.E. Mather and Sons.

Chambave (It) the local name used in Valle d'Aosta for Moscato grape.

Chambecy [Le] (Fr) a dry vintage Champagne produced by the house of Lagache-Lecourt from Chardonnay and Pinot noir grapes.

Chambers' Rosewood (Austr) a winery based in north-eastern Victoria. Is noted for dessert wines

C

(especially Tokaji), liqueur muscats and Cabernet sauvignon.

Chambertin (Fr) a Grand Cru vineyard within the A.C. commune of Gevrey-Chambertin, Côte de Nuits, Burgundy. 13ha. and is adjacent to the famous vineyard of Clos de Bèze. Has 8 Grand Crus that can use its name in prefix.

Chambertin Clos de Bèze (Fr) see Clos de Bèze.

Chambéry (Fr) an aromatic, fortified wine flavoured with herbs and sugar from the Haut-Savoie. See also Chambéryzette.

Chambéry-Citron (Cktl) 60mls Chambéry, 20mls sirop de citron. Stir over ice, strain into an ice-filled highball glass and top with soda water.

Chambéry-Fraisette (Cktl) 60mls Chambéry, 20mls Fraisette. Stir over ice, strain into an ice-filled highball glass and top with soda water.

Chambéryzette (Fr) a red, aromatic, fortified wine from the Haut-Savoie. Is made with the juice of wild strawberries. Top brands are Dolin and Gaudin.

Chamblanc (S.Afr) a demi-sec (and doux) sparkling wine made from the Clairette blanche and Colombard grapes by the Bertram Estates.

Chambolle Musigny (Fr) an A.C. commune in the Côte de Nuits, Burgundy. Has Grand Cru vineyards: Les Bonnes Mares [part] and Les Musigny 24.4ha. and the Premier Cru vineyards: Aux Beau-Bruns, Aux Combottes, Aux Échanges, Combe d'Orveau [part], Derrièrre-la-Grange, La Combe d'Orveau, Les Amoureuses, Les Baudes, Les Borniques, Les Carrièrres, Les Chabriots, Les Charmes, Les Chatelots, Les Combottes, Les Fousselottes, Les Fuées, Les Grands Murs, Les Groseilles, Les Gruenchers, Les Haut-Doix, Les Lavrottes, Les Noirots, Les Plantes and Les Sentiers. 68.35ha.

Chambon (Fr) a natural mineral water from 45340 Chambon la Forêt, Val du Loire. Mineral contents (milligrammes per litre): Sodium 10.6mg/l, Calcium 96mg/l, Magnesium 6.1mg/l, Potassium 3.7mg/l, Bicarbonates 297.7mg/l, Chlorides 22.6mg/l, Sulphates 9.3mg/l, Fluorides 0.18mg/l, Nitrates <2mg/l, Silicates 36.2mg/l. pH 7.2

Chambourcin (Fr) a red hybrid grape grown in Nantais, Loire. Resistant to many fungal diseases.

Chambraise (USA) the American spelling of Chambéryzette.

Chambre (Fr) lit: 'room', denotes in wine language 'room temperature' for the service of red wines. Ideally at 18°C–22°C. see Chambrer.

Chambrecy (Fr) a Cru Champagne village in the Canton de Ville-en-Tardenois. District: Reims.

Chambrer (Fr) derived from the French 'chambre', the term is used for bringing red wines to room temperature from cellar temperature.

Chambre Syndicate des Courtiers (Fr) a syndicate of wine brokers in Bordeaux who are responsible for the 1855 classification of Sauternes wines in Bordeaux.

Chamelion (S.Afr) a label for white (Chardonnay & Sauvignon blanc blend) and red (Cabernet sauvignon & Shiraz blend) wines from the Jordan Vineyards, Stellenbosch.

Chamery (Fr) a Cru Champagne village in the Canton de Verzy. District: Reims.

Chamisal Vineyards (USA) the label for a red wine (Pinot noir) from Califa and produced by Domaine Alfred, Edna Valley, San Luis Obispo County, California.

Chamonix Winery (S.Afr) a winery based at Franschhoek. Grape variety: Chardonnay. Website: http://www.chamonix.co.za 'E'mail: marketing@chamonix.co.za

Champagnac (Fr) a commune in the Charente-Maritime département whose grapes are classed as Petite Champagne (Cognac).

Champagne (Fr) the top A.C. (awarded 1927) sparkling wine-producing region in the world. The method of making sparkling wine was created by the monks Dom Pérignon and Dom Oudart. Is the most northerly wine region of France. Has chalk soil. Average annual production 300 million bottles. Three major regions: Montagne de Reims (in north), Vallée de la Marne (central) and Côte des Blancs (in south). Cantons: d'Avize, d'Ay, de Beine, de Bourgogne, de Braine, de Châtillon-sur-Marne, de Condé-en-Brie, de Dormans, d'Épernay, de Fismes, de l'Aube, de Montmort, de Reims, de Sézanne, de Suippes, de Vertus, de Verzy, de Ville-en-Tardenois. see Dom Pérignon, Méthode Champenoise, Méthode Traditionelle, Oolitic Chalk, Prix du Raison and Widow Cliquot. (Arab) = shambania, (Aus) = sekt, (Chi) = xiangbingjiu, (Cro) = šampanjac, (Den) = champagne, (Ger) = sekt, (Gre) = sampania, (Hol) = champagne, (Indo) = sampanye, (Ire) = seaimpéin, (Isr) = champagnia, (It) = sciampagna/spumante, (Jap) = shan pen, (Kor) = shampein, (Pol) = szampan, (Port) = champanha, (Rus) = shampanskoye, (Sp) = champaña, (Thai) = champagne, (Tur) = şampanya, (Wal) = gwin champagne. Website: http://www.champagne.fr

Champagne à Gogo (Fr) denotes that Champagne is flowing freely. Can drink as much as one likes!

Champagne & Châteaux Ltd (Eng) a wine producer (established 1989). (Add): 11 Calico House, Plantation Wharf, London SW11 3TN. Produces a variety of wines including red, white and Champagne. 'E'mail: info@champagneandchateaux.co.uk

Champagne Apple (Cktl) 1 part Champagne 1 part dry sparkling cider. Serve in the Champagne flute. Dress with an apple slice.

Champagne Beaumont des Crayères (Fr) a Champagne producer. (Add): BP 1030, 51318 Épernay. Vintages: 1990, 1992, 1995. Produces: Grande Réserve (Pinot meunier 60%, Chardonnay 25% and Pinot noir 15%). Grand Prestige (Chardonnay 40%, Pinot noir 40% and Pinot meunier 20%).Grand Rosé (Chardonnay 25%, Pinot noir 35% and Pinot meunier 40%). Fleur de Prestige vintage (Chardonnay 50%, Pinot noir 40% and Pinot meunier 10%). Fleur de Rosé vintage (Chardonnay 50%, Pinot noir 25% and Pinot meunier 25%).

246

Nostalgie vintage (Chardonnay 70% and Pinot noir 30%). Also produces Nuit d'Or. Website: http://www.champagne-beaumont.com Email: champagne-beaumont@wanadoo.fr

Champagne Bottle Sizes (Fr) Huitième: (9.4cls), Quarter (Quart): (18.75cls), Half Bottle (Demie): (37.50cls), Imperial Pint (Médium): (60cls), Bottle: (75cls), Magnum: 2 bottles (1.6ltrs), Jereboam (Jéroboam): 4 bottles (3.2ltrs), Rehoboam (Réhoboam): 6 bottles (4.8ltrs), Methuselah (Mathusalem): 8 bottles (6.4ltrs), Salmanazar: 12 bottles (9.6ltrs), Balthazar: 16 bottles (12.8ltrs), Nebuchadnezzar (Nabuchodonosor): 20 bottles (16ltrs), Salomon: (18ltrs), Sovereign: (26.25ltrs), Primato: (27ltrs), Melchisedec: (30ltrs).

Champagne Charlie (Eng) a song sung in Victorian days by George Leybourne when Champagne was very popular.

Champagne Charlie (Fr) the name given to a de luxe vintage cuvée Champagne produced by Charles Heidsieck. Minimum of 45% Chardonnay and remainder Pinot noir grapes.

Champagne Cider (Eng)(USA) the name given to sparkling cider.

Champagne Cobbler [1] (Cktl) 120mls Champagne, 2 dashes old Cognac, 1–2 dashes lemon juice, 3–4 dashes gomme syrup. Stir gently over crushed ice, serve with dash of lemon juice, slice of lemon and straws.

Champagne Cobbler [2] (Cktl) into a mixing glass place Champagne, 2 dashes sugar syrup and fruit syrup. Stir with ice, strain into highball glass filled with crushed ice, top with a dash of lemon juice, serve with straws and fruit in season.

Champagne Cocktail (Cktl) into a Champagne saucer place a cube of sugar that has been soaked with a dash of Angostura and 2 dashes of Cognac. Add slice of orange and a cherry then top with iced Champagne.

Champagne Cooler (Cktl) fill a highball glass ½ full of ice, add ½ measure of Nassau Orange Liqueur and ½ measure Martell Cognac. Top with iced Champagne.

Champagne Cork (Fr) see Agglomerated Cork. See also Patina.

Champagne Coupe (Fr) a Champagne saucer glass.

Champagne Cup [1] (Cup) into a large jug place 25mls (⅛ gill) abricotine, 25mls (⅛ gill) Curaçao, 50mls (⅜ gill) Cognac, 1 bottle iced Champagne, 500mls (1 pint) soda water. Add ice, stir well, serve with slices of fruit in season, a sprig of mint or borage and sliced cucumber.

Champagne Cup [2] (Cup) into a large jug place 1 bottle of iced dry Champagne, 60mls Cognac, 60mls maraschino, 40mls Yellow Chartreuse, 30mls gomme syrup. Stir well over ice, serve with slices of orange, lemon, cucumber and fruits in season. Top with sprig of mint.

Champagne Cup [3] (Cup) into a large jug place 1 bottle iced dry Champagne, 100mls Cognac, 75mls Grand Marnier, 25mls maraschino, 1 teaspoon powdered sugar. Stir altogether with ice, add sliced fruits in season and sprig of mint.

Champagne de Courcy (Fr) see De Courcy.

Champagne de Saint Gall (Fr) a Gremier Cru blanc de blancs from Union Champagne. Website: http://www.de-saint-gall.com

Champagne des Princes (Fr) a de luxe Grand Cru vintage cuvée Champagne produced from 100% Chardonnay and matured 6-7 years before release by De Venoge.

Champagne Deutz, Deutz and Gelderman (Fr) see Deutz.

Champagne de Venoge (Fr) see De Venoge.

Champagne Flip [1] (Cktl) shake a yolk of egg over ice, add iced Champagne and strain into a wine glass and top with grated nutmeg.

Champagne Flip [2] (Cktl) 1 egg yolk, barspoon gomme syrup, 25mls orange juice, 3 dashes Grand Marnier. Shake well together over ice, strain into a wine goblet and top with iced Champagne.

Champagne Flute (Fr) a tall slim glass for correctly serving all sparkling wines in to retain their (sparkle) bubbles. See also Coupette.

Champagne Frappé (Fr) Champagne served very cold.

Champagne Humide [La] (Fr) lit: 'damp', the name given to the northern area of Champagne. An extremely fertile strip that goes down towards Burgundy.

Champagne Julep (Cktl) place a cube of sugar in a tumbler, add 2 mint sprigs and crush together with a barspoon muddler. Add ice, and top with iced Champagne, stir gently and serve with sliced fruits in season.

Champagne Key (USA) a stainless steel device used to hold the cork whilst the wire cage is removed from the Champagne bottle.

Champagne Method (Eng) see Méthode Champenoise.

Champagne Milan (Fr) a Champagne producer (established 1864). (Add): 6, Rue d'Avize, 51190 Oger. Produces vintage and non-vintage wines. Website: http://www.Champagne-milan.com 'E'mail: info@Champagne-milan.com

Champagne Napoléon (Cktl) 25mls Mandarine Napoléon, dash orange juice, pour into Champagne flute and top with iced Champagne.

Champagne of Teas (Ind) the finest teas, said to come from the Himalayan foothills near Darjeeling.

Champagne-Orange (Cktl) an alternative name for Buck's Fizz.

Champagne Pick-me-up (Cktl) 60mls Cognac, juice ½ orange, 4 dashes Curaçao or grenadine. Shake well over ice, strain into a highball glass, top with iced Champagne and add a dash of Pernod.

Champagne Pouilleuse [La] (Fr) lit: 'good for nothing', west Champagne where the soil is poor and chalky.

Champagne Punch (Cktl) 1 teaspoon gomme syrup, juice of ½ lemon, 20mls (⅙ gill) Curaçao. Shake over ice, strain into a wine glass, top with iced

C

dry Champagne and decorate with fruits in season (1 measure of brandy can be used).

Champagne Rare (Fr) a de luxe cuvée Champagne produced by Piper-Heidsieck from 60% Chardonnay and 40% Pinot noir grapes.

Champagne Riots (Fr) *see* Champagne Wars.

Champagne Rosé-Gris (Fr) lit: 'grey Champagne', the Middle-Ages name for still Champagne. Was of a light rosé colour.

Champagne Saucer (Eng) a saucer-shaped glass used for the serving of Champagne cocktails. This type of glass was popular in the USA at the turn of the century. *see* Champagne Coupe and Coupe à Champagne Americaine.

Champagne Société de Producteurs, Mailly-Champagne (Fr) a Champagne co-operative. (Add): 51500 Rilly la Montagne. Wines made from member's grapes. Produces vintage and non-vintage wines. Owns 70ha. Vintages: 1973, 1975, 1977, 1979, 1980, 1982, 1985, 1989, 1990, 1992, 1993, 1999, 1996, 1998, 1999, 2000. De Luxe cuvée: Cuvée des Enchansons also Mailly Rosé (a non-vintage rosé Champagne).

Champagne Soil (Fr) *see* Oolitic Chalk.

Champagne Star (Eng) a device for opening Champagne. Consists of four prongs that are inserted into the four grooves in the cork and the cork is turned slowly.

Champagne Trouillard (Fr) a family Champagne-producing firm based in Épernay. Produces vintage and non-vintage wines under Cuvée Diamant label.

Champagne Velvet (Cktl) another name for Black Velvet.

Champagne Wars (Fr) 1910–1911, laws passed in 1911 after vignerons who were making wine exclusively from grapes grown in the Provence, rose up in arms against those importing cheap grapes into the Provence. Riots broke out so that laws were introduced to fix boundaries within which grapes must be grown to be entitled to be made into Champagne.

Champagnia (Isr) Champagne/sparkling wine.

Champagnisation (Eng) the name for the méthode traditionelle sparkling wine-making method.

Champagnisation (Eng) a term used in the nineteenth century for the practice of making the cork shoot out of a Champagne bottle by firstly shaking the bottle so as to cause an 'explosive' effect.

Champagnon (Fr) a still apéritif wine from the Champagne region, fortified with Cognac. Also known as Ratafia de Champagne.

Champagny-Sous-Uxelles (Fr) a commune in the Mâconnais district whose grapes can be used for making Mâcon Supérieur.

Champale (USA) a beer 6%–8% alc by vol. brewed by the Champale Brewery in Trenton, New Jersey. Also citrus and grenadine fruit flavours.

Champale Brewery (USA) a brewery based in Norfolk, Virginia.

Champale Brewery (USA) a brewery based in Trenton, New Jersey. Noted for Champale 6%–8% alc by vol.

Champalimaud (Port) producers of a single quinta Vintage Port (Quinta do Cotto) based at Cidadelhe near Régua. Also produces red and white wines including Vinhos Verdes.

Champan (Sp) the local Cataluña name for Cava wines.

Champaña (Sp) the name for Champagne.

Champanha (Bra)(Port) Champagne/sparkling wine.

Champ-Canet [Le] (Fr) a Premier Cru vineyard in the A.C. commune of Puligny-Montrachet, Côte de Beaune, Burgundy 4.6ha.

Champ-Clou (Fr) a vineyard in the A.C. commune of Rully, Côte Chalonnaise, Burgundy.

Champ de la Rose (Fr) an A.C. Bordeaux Rosé Sec wine.

Champeaux (Fr) a Premier Cru vineyard in the A.C. commune of Gevrey-Chambertin, Côte de Nuits, Burgundy 6.76ha.

Champelle (N.Z) the brand-name used by Selaks for their sparkling (méthode traditionelle) wine.

Champenise (Fr) describes a wine that has been made sparkling using the méthode traditionelle.

Champerelle (Pousse-Café) pour into a tall liqueur glass in order equal quantities of Curaçao, Anisette, Chartreuse and Cognac.

Champflower Ale (Eng) a 4.2% alc by vol. ale brewed by the Cottage Brewing C°., Somerset.

Champigneulles (Fr) a brand of bière from Champigneulles.

Champigniser (Eng) another name for the méthode traditionelle.

Champigny (Fr) a light red A.C. wine from a small vineyard near Saumur, Anjou-Saumur, Loire.

Champillon (Fr) a Premier Cru Champagne village in the Canton d'Aÿ. District: Reims.

Champimonts (Fr) *see* Champ-Pimont.

Champinski (Eng) the name for Russian sparkling wines.

Champinski (Geo) a sparkling wine produced in the Don Valley.

Champion (Ch.Isles) a 1045 O.G. best bitter brewed by the Guernsey Brewery, St. Peter Port, Guernsey (now brewed on Jersey).

Champion Ale (Eng) a bottled pale ale 1032 O.G. brewed by the Adnams Brewery, Suffolk.

Champion Ale (Eng) a bottled pale ale 1040 O.G. brewed by the Gales Brewery, in Hampshire. Brewed for the French market.

Champion Ale (Eng) a bottled pale ale 1038 O.G. brewed by the Greenall Whitley Brewery in Warrington, Cheshire.

Champion Bitters (Fin) bitters produced by the Marli C°.

Champion Mild (Eng) a mild ale 3.5% alc by vol. from Ridleys, Essex.

Championship Ale (Wal) a 5% alc by vol. ale from Brain's Brewery, Cardiff.

Champitonnois (Fr) a Premier Cru vineyard in the A.C. commune of Gevrey-Chambertin, Côte de Nuits, Burgundy. 3.97ha. Also known as Petite Chapelle.

Champlain (Can) a natural spring mineral water

C

from the Appalachian Mountains. Mineral contents (milligrammes per litre): Sodium 4mg/l, Calcium 36mg/l, Magnesium 6mg/l, Bicarbonates 140mg/l, Chlorides 1mg/l, Sulphates 13mg/l.

Champlat-Boujacourt (Fr) a Cru Champagne village in the Canton de Châtillon-sur-Marne. District: Reims.

Champlieu (Fr) a commune in the Mâconnais whose grapes may be used in the production of Mâcon Supérieur.

Champlot (Fr) a Premier Cru vineyard in the A.C. commune of Saint Aubin, Côte de Beaune, Burgundy 8ha.

Champneys Chittern Hills (Eng) a natural mountain or carbonated water from Tom Hill, Hertfordshire (source).

Champoeg Wine Cellars (USA) a winery (established 1974) based in Willamette Valley, Oregon. Grape varieties: Chardonnay, Pinot noir, White riesling, Müller-Thurgau, Gewürztraminer, Pinot gris.

Châmpogne (Ch.Isles) Champagne.

Champonnets (Fr) a Premier Cru vineyard in the A.C. commune of Gevrey-Chambertin, Côte de Nuits, Burgundy. 3.32ha.

Champonnières [Les] (Fr) a Premier Cru vineyard in the A.C. commune of Pommard, Côte de Beaune, Burgundy 3.3ha.

Champoreau (Fr) the term used for a liqueur or spirit added to milky coffee.

Champ-Pimont (Fr) a Premier Cru vineyard in the A.C. commune of Beaune, Côte de Beaune, Burgundy. 18.07ha. Also known as Champimonts.

Champs-Cains [Les] (Fr) *see* Champs-Gains (Les).

Champs-de-Coignée [Les] (Fr) a vineyard in the A.C. commune of Montagny, Côte Chalonnaise, Burgundy.

Champs Elysées (Cktl) ⅓ measure brandy, ⅓ measure Yellow Chartreuse, ⅓ measure lemon juice, dash Angostura. Shake over ice and strain into a cocktail glass.

Champs-Fulliot [Les] (Fr) a Premier Cru vineyard in the A.C. commune of Monthélie, Côte de Beaune, Burgundy 8.74ha.

Champs-Gains [Les] (Fr) a Premier Cru vineyard [part] in the commune of Chassagne-Montrachet, Côte de Beaune, Burgundy. 4.24ha. Also spelt Champs-Cains.

Champs-Toizeau [Les] (Fr) a vineyard in the A.C. commune of Montagny, Côte Chalonnaise, Burgundy.

Champtocé (Fr) a commune in the A.C. Savennières, Anjou-Saumur, Loire.

Champvoisy (Fr) a Premier Cru Champagne village in the Canton de Dormans. District: Épernay.

Champy Père et Fils (Fr) a noted Burgundy shipper (established 1720) the oldest in Burgundy. (Add): 5, Rue du Greniera Sel, 21200 Beaune. A small company with some good vineyard holdings.

Chamusca (Port) an I.P.R. wine region within central-west Ribatejo.

Chamvermeil [A.] (Fr) a producer of Crémant de Bordeaux at Château d'Arsac.

Chancay (Fr) a commune in A.C. Vouvray, Touraine, Loire.

Chance de St. Luc [La] (Fr) an A.C. Côtes du Roussillon red wine produced by Jean-Luc Colombo, La Roche, 26600 Tain l'Hermitage from Grenache, Syrah and Mourvèdre grapes.

Chancellor (USA) a red hybrid grape variety also known as the Seibel 7053.

Chancellor Cocktail (Cktl) 25mls (⅛ gill) Scotch whisky, 15mls (⅛ gill) French vermouth, 15mls (⅛ gill) Port, 2 dashes Angostura. Shake well over ice, strain into a cocktail glass and dress with a cherry.

Chancelord and De Vitis (Fr) a Cognac producer. (Add): Sarl Queron, Macqueville, 17490 Beauvais sous Matha. 50ha. in the Fins Bois. Produces Napoléon Chancelord (a 15 y.o.), Antique De Vitis (a 20 y.o.) and Age d'Or De Vitis (a 50 y.o.).

Chandesais (Fr) a Burgundy shipper based in Fontaines, Côte Chalonnaise. Specialises in the wines of the Côte d'Or, especially of the Hospices de Beaune.

Chandits [Les] (Fr) a vineyard in the A.C. commune of Montagny, Côte Chalonnaise, Burgundy.

Chandon (USA) a sparkling (traditional method) wine from Moët et Chandon's vineyards at Yountville, Napa Valley, California.

Chandon [M.] (Arg) a sparkling wine produced by Bodegas Proviar.

Chandos (N.Z) a light, sweet white wine from the Ormond Vineyard.

Chânes (Fr) a commune in the Beaujolais district. Has A.C. Beaujolais-Villages or Beaujolais-Chânes status. Also sold as Mâconnais Blanc.

Chanflor (Fr) a natural spring mineral water. Mineral contents (milligrammes per litre): Sodium 9.7mg/l, Calcium 7mg/l, Magnesium 3.9mg/l, Potassium 1.1mg/l, Bicarbonates 50mg/l, Chlorides 5.9mg/l, Sulphates 3mg/l.

Chang (Chi) an old Chinese name for wine. *See also* Li and Chiu.

Chang'aa (Afr) a slang term used for home brew in Kenya.

Changuirongo (Mex) a traditional drink of tequila and a fizzy drink with plenty of ice.

Changuirongo [The] (Cktl) place ice into a highball glass, add a measure of silver tequila and top with equal quantities of tonic water and cola.

Chanière [La] (Fr) a Premier Cru vineyard in the A.C. commune of Pommard, Côte de Beaune, Burgundy 10ha.

Chanlin (Fr) a Premier Cru vineyard [part] in the A.C. commune of Volnay, Côte de Beaune, Burgundy.

Chanlins-Bas [Les] (Fr) a Premier Cru vineyard in the A.C. commune of Pommard, Côte de Beaune, Burgundy 7.1ha.

Channe (Switz) a tin receptacle which varies in shape in each of the cantons and which preserves in full the fresh taste of the wine.

Channel Islands Cream Liqueurs (Ch.Isles) a liqueurs manufacturer. (Add): Liqueur House,

C

Pitronneries Road, St. Peter Port, Guernsey GY1 2RQ.

Chanoine Frères (Fr) a Champagne producer (established 1730) based in Reims. Produces vintage and non-vintage wines. Vintages: 1990, 1995, 1998, 1999, 2000. Website: http://www.Champagnechanoine.com 'E'mail: chanoine-freres@wanadoo.fr

Chanoyu (E.Asia) the Buddist Tea Ceremony. Lasts 2 hours and includes lunch and green teas. *See also* Koicha and Ususha.

Chanrue [Les] (Fr) a wine-producing village in the commune of Solutré-Pouilly in Pouilly-Fuissé, Mâcon, Burgundy.

Chanson Père et Fils (Fr) a Burgundy négociant-éleveur based in Beaune, Côte de Beaune. Have existing holdings such as Beaune Clos de Fèves. Also produces A.C. Chablis including Premier Cru Montmains.

Chantadu (Fr) red and white Châteauneuf-du-Pape wines produced by SCEA du Chantadu, 7 Ave. des Bosquets, 84230 Châteauneuf-du-Pape, southern Rhône.

Chantagne (Fr) a noted wine-producing village in the Savoie region of south-eastern France.

Chant de Nuit (S.Afr) the label for a white (Ferdinand de lesseps a table grape) wine produced by the Nuy Wine Cellar winery, Worcester, Western Cape.

Chant de Nuy (S.Afr) a very dry, fruity, white wine made from the Colombard, Steen and other varieties by the Nuy Co-operative, Worcester, Western Cape.

Chante Alouette (Fr) a noted white A.C. Hermitage vineyard in the northern Côtes du Rhône.

Chanteau (Fr) the name given to a partly empty barrel in Cognac production, it is used to replenish other barrels during the ageing process. Marked CH for identification.

Chante Bled (Afr) a brand of A.O.G. red wine from the Meknès in Morocco. Made from the Carignan and Cinsault grapes. Carries the A.O.G. Guerrouane. Bottled by CVM.

Chantecler (Cktl) as for a Bronx Cocktail but with the addition of 3 dashes of grenadine.

Chantemerle (Fr) a Cru Champagne village in the Canton d'Épernay. District: Épernay.

Chantenière [La] (Fr) a vineyard in the A.C. commune of Saint-Aubin, Côte de Beaune, Burgundy 10ha.

Chante-Perdrix (Fr) a Rhône wine produced by Delas at Tournon.

Chantepleure (Fr) a tube used in the Anjou district of the Loire for removing the wine from the cask.

Chantereine (Fr) a natural spring mineral water from Chelles. Mineral contents (milligrammes per litre): Sodium 7mg/l, Calcium 119mg/l, Magnesium 25mg/l, Potassium 2mg/l, Bicarbonates 430mg/l, Chlorides 18mg/l, Sulphates 52mg/l, Fluorides 0.75mg/l. pH 7.9

Chanticleer (USA) a winery based in the Napa Valley, California. Grape varieties include: Cabernet sauvignon.

Chantilly (S.Afr) a natural spring mineral water. Mineral contents (milligrammes per litre): Sodium 9mg/l, Calcium 15.2mg/l, Magnesium 7mg/l, Chlorides <5mg/l, Sulphates <5mg/l, Fluorides 0.07mg/l, Nitrates 1.5mg/l.

Chantmerle (Fr) a natural spring mineral water from Pestrin Ardèche. Mineral contents (milligrammes per litre): Sodium 13.4mg/l, Calcium 45mg/l, Magnesium 10.5mg/l, Potassium 2.1mg/l, Bicarbonates 223.3mg/l, Chlorides 2mg/l, Sulphates 6.3mg/l, Silicates 45.7mg/l.

Chantobines [Les] (Fr) an A.C. Pouilly Fumé produced by J.Pabiot et Fils, Loges 58150 Pouilly-sur-Loire.

Chantovent (Fr) a well-known vin de table from the Minervois region.

Chantre (Ger) a weinbrand produced by Eckes at Neider-Olm.

Chantré Brandy Cream Liqueur (Ger) a brand of German cream and brandy liqueur produced by a subsidiary of Peter Eckes (Merrydown is the U.K. agent) 17% alc by vol.

Chanturgues (Fr) a red wine from Clermont-Ferrand near the Côtes d'Auvergne. Made from the Gamay grape.

Chanut Frères (Fr) a négociant based at Romanèche-Thorins, Burgundy.

Chão de Areia (Port) lit: 'sandy bed', name of a wine of the Colares region, north of Lisbon 11% alc by vol.

Chaopa Valley (Chile) a wine region situated in northern Chile.

Chão Rijo (Port) lit: 'solid bed', name for a wine from the Colares region, north of Lisbon.

Chaos Marche Rosso (It) an I.G.T. red wine produced by Fattoria Le Terrazze in the Marche from 50% Montepulciano, 25% Syrah and 25% Merlot grapes.

Chapala Cocktail (Cktl) 40mls tequila, 15mls orange juice, 15mls lemon juice, dash orange flower water, 2 barspoons grenadine, shake over ice, strain into an ice-filled highball glass and add a slice of orange.

Chapeau (Fr) lit: 'cap', applies to the skins that float on top of the fermenting must (especially in red wine production).

Chapeau et Landais (Fr) an Anjou and Crèmant de Loire producer based at Chace, Loire.

Chapeau Immergé (Fr) occurs during some red wine production, the practice of keeping the cap moist by using wooden planks to keep it submerged.

Chapeau Soumergé (Fr) the grape cap (skins, pips etc.) which is submerged into the must by wicker racks so as to extract the maximum colour and tannin. *see* Chapeau.

Chapeau Tropical Lambic (Bel) a 3% alc by vol. bottled lambic fruit beer brewed using banana by De Troch Lambic Brouwerij, Ternat-Wambeek.

Chapel Ale (Eng) a 3.8% alc by vol. cask ale brewed by Clarks Brewery of Wakefield.

Chapel Down (Eng) a winery and the label for a

C

range of red, white and traditional method sparkling wines from Tenterden Vineyards in Kent. Grape varieties: Bacchus, Müller-Thurgau, Pinot noir, Riesling and Sylvaner. Also brews Curious Brew Lager 5% alc. By vol. Website: http://www.englishwinesgroup.com

Chapel Hill Cocktail (Cktl) 35mls Bourbon whiskey, 35mls Cointreau, juice ¼ lemon. Shake over ice, strain into a cocktail glass and top with a twist of orange peel.

Chapel Hill Winery (Austr) a winery. (Add): P.O. Box 194, McLaren Vale, South Australia. Has vineyards in Coonawarra. Grape varieties: Shiraz, Cabernet sauvignon, Riesling, Chardonnay. Produces The Vicar and an unwooded Chardonnay wine.

Chapelle [La] (Fr) a Premier Cru vineyard in the A.C. commune of Auxey-Duresses, Côte de Beaune, Burgundy. 12.8ha. Is now split up to form Les Bretterins and Reugne.

Chapelle [La] (Fr) a vineyard producing red wines in the A.C. Hermitage, northern Rhône.

Chapelle [La] (Fr) a Premier Cru vineyard [part] in the A.C. commune of Auxey-Duresses, Côte de Beaune, Burgundy. 5ha. Also known as Les Bretterins.

Chapelle [La] (Fr) a Premier Cru vineyard [part] in the A.C. commune of Auxey-Duresses, Côte de Beaune, Burgundy. 7.8ha. Also known as Reugne.

Chapelle-Chambertin (Fr) a Grand Cru vineyard in the A.C. commune of Gevrey-Chambertin, Côte de Nuits, Burgundy 4.06ha.

Chapelle d'Ausone (Fr) the second wine of Château Ausone, Saint-Émilion, Bordeaux.

Chapelle-de-Guinchay [La] (Fr) a commune in the Beaujolais. Has A.C. Beaujolais-Villages, or Beaujolais La Chapelle-de-Guinchay status.

Chapelle de Lafaurie [La] (Fr) the second wine of Château Lafaurie-Peyraguey, A.C. Sauternes, Bommes, Bordeaux.

Chapelle-Vaupelteigne [La] (Fr) a commune in the A.C. Chablis, northern Burgundy.

Chapelot (Fr) a Premier Cru vineyard in the A.C. Chablis, sometimes is reclassified as the Premier Cru Monteré de Tonerre.

Chapeltown Glenlivet Natural Mineral Water (Scot) a natural spring mineral water from Schold Spring, Braes of Glenlivet, Ballindalloch, Banffshire.

Chapiteau (Fr) the name for the Cognac still.

Chapître (Fr) a vineyard in the A.C. commune of Rully, Côte Chalonnaise, Burgundy.

Chaponnières [Les] (Fr) a Premier Cru vineyard in the A.C. commune of Pommard, Côte de Beaune, Burgundy 3.3ha.

Chapoutier [Max] (Fr) a noted Rhône négociant-éleveur. (Add): 18, Ave. de la République, 26600 Tain l'Hermitage.

Chappellet Vineyard (USA) a winery based in the Napa Valley, California. 41.5ha. Grape varieties: Cabernet sauvignon, Chardonnay, Chenin blanc, Gamay, Johannisberg riesling and Merlot.

Chaptal (Fr) the name of the Minister of Agriculture

in the time of Napoléon 1st. Gave his name to the system of Chaptalisation.

Chaptalisation (Fr) the addition of sugar to grape must to secure a higher degree of alcohol. The amount that can be added is strictly controlled by law. Invented by Dr. Chaptal. *see* Chaptal. *See also* Sucrage (Le). (Eng) = sugaring, (Ger) = anreicherung, (USA) = sugaring.

Chaptaliser (Fr) the name for the sugar used for Chaptalisation.

Char (Eng) a slang for tea (drink). *See also* Cha.

Character (Eng) a term used by wine tasters to denote wine with a definite and unmistakable though not necessarily outstanding, quality.

Character Amoroso (Sp) a pale-gold Sherry based on an 1895 Oloroso Solera produced by Sandeman.

Charade (S.Afr) the label for a red wine (Shiraz 60% plus Cabernet sauvignon blend) produced by the Stellen Hills Wines winery, Stellenbosch, Western Cape.

Charal (Can) a major wine-producer based in Ontario.

Charbaut [A. et Fils] (Fr) a Champagne producer. (Add): 17, Avenue de Champagne, 35 Rue Maurice Cerveaux, 51205 Épernay. 56ha. Produces vintage and non-vintage wines. Vintages: 1971, 1973, 1976, 1979, 1982, 1985, 1987, 1988, 1990, 1995, 1998, 2000. De Luxe Cuvée: Certificate.

Charbonnier (Fr) the brand-name of a French table wine range marketed by Colman's of Norwich.

Charbono (USA) a red grape variety that produces full-bodied red wines.

Charbono (USA) *see* California Charbono.

Charcoal (Eng) used to take the excess colour out of wines, especially rosés, achieved by filtering the wine through the charcoal. *See also* Activated Charcoal.

Chard Farm (N.Z) a winery (12ha). (Add): Chard Road, RD 1, Queenstown, Otago. Grape varieties: Pinot noir, Chardonnay, Gewürztraminer, Riesling, Sauvignon blanc.

Chardon (N.Z) a fruity, lightly sparkling, white wine produced by the Penfolds Winery from Müller-Thurgau grapes.

Chardonnay (Fr) one of the world's finest white grape varieties. Is used for the production of France's great dry white wines including Chablis, Champagne and Montrachet. Also known as the Arnoison, Aubaine, Beaunois, Feinburgunder, Feiner Weisser Burgunder, Morillon and Melon blanc. Produces wines that (when young) have a lemon, green apple/pear, citrus, capsicum, sap, green tomato aroma and flavour (when old and oaked) a toast, butter, butterscotch, capsicum, hazelnut, walnut, vanilla, honey, melon, tropical fruits, melon, mixed spice, tobacco and wax aromas and flavours. Said to originate from the Pinot noir and Gouais blanc grapes.

Chardonnay (USA) *see* California Chardonnay.

Chardonnay Blanc Musqué (Fr) a lesser variety of the Chardonnay grape which has a strong 'musky' aroma.

C

Chardonnay di Capezzana (It) a Chardonnay-based Vino da Tavola from central-western Italy.

Chardonnay di Miralduolo (It) a Chardonnay-based Vino da Tavola from central-western Italy.

Chardonnayle (Eng) a 5.1% alc by vol. ale brewed by Bobs Brewing Company, West Yorkshire.

Chardonnay Rosé (Fr) a lesser variety of the Chardonnay grape that has a light red skin.

Chardonne (Switz) a wine-producing district based near Lavaux in the central Vaud canton.

Charentais (Fr) a Vin de Pays area in the Charente and Charente-Maritime départements of western France. Produces red, rosé and dry white wines.

Charentais Still (Fr) an open-fired pot still used to distil Cognac in the Charente département. Holds not more that 30 hecto-litres.

Charentay (Fr) a commune in the Beaujolais district. Has the A.C. Beaujolais-Villages or Beaujolais-Charentay status.

Charente (Fr) a département of western France, north of Bordeaux where Cognac brandy is produced. The finest grapes grown for Cognac are in this département.

Charente-Maritime (Fr) a département of western France, north of Bordeaux where Cognac brandy is produced. Has part of the Petite Champagne area within its boundaries.

Charge de Bouteiller (Fr) a cellar master in the eighteenth and nineteenth centuries.

Charged Water (USA) mineral water.

Charger Lager (Scot) a canned lager 1032 O.G. brewed by the Tennants Brewery in Glasgow.

Charisma (S.Afr) the label for a red wine (Cabernet franc 65%, Merlot and Shiraz blend) produced by the Camberley Wines winery, Stellenbosch, Western Cape.

Charité [La] (Fr) a famous old vineyard at Pouilly-sur-Loire making A.C. Pouilly Fumé.

Charlemagne [Guy] (Fr) a Champagne producer based in Mesnil-sur-Ogier. Produces vintage and non-vintage Champagnes.

Charles (Cktl) ½ measure sweet vermouth, ½ measure brandy, dash Angostura. Stir over ice and strain into a cocktail glass.

Charles and Diana (Scot) a 12 year old blended de luxe Scotch whisky from Whyte and Mackay. Sold in a royal blue bottle (stein-style) and a leather-style box which is lined with satin.

Charles Chaplin Cocktail (Cktl) 35mls (1½ fl.ozs) sloe gin, 10mls (½ fl.oz) apricot brandy, 2 teaspoons lime juice. Shake over ice and strain into a cocktail glass.

Charles Collin (Fr) a Champagne producer. (Add): 27, Rue des Pressoirs, 10360 Fontette. Produces vintage and non-vintage Champagnes. Vintages: 1995, 1996, 1999, 2000. Part of Coopérative de Fontette.

Charles Coury Vineyards (USA) see Reuter's Hill Vineyard.

Charles de Batz de Montesquiou Fezenzac (Fr) the patron Saint of the Armagnac. Also known as D'Artagnan.

Charles Dennery (Fr) a brut Champagne produced by Charbaut et Fils.

Charles et Fils (Fr) récoltants-manipulants in Champagne. (Add): 4 Rue des Pervenches, Montigny-sous-Chatillon, 51700 Dormans. Produces vintage and non-vintage wines. A member of the C.V.C.

Charles Gerard (S.Afr) a white wine produced by Fairview from a blend of Sauvignon blanc and Sémillon grapes.

Charles Koch (Fr) a vintage Champagne produced by Bricout et Koch from 60% Chardonnay and 40% Pinot noir.

Charles Krug (USA) a large winery based north of St. Helena, Napa Valley, California. 498ha. Grape varieties: Cabernet sauvignon, Chenin blanc, Gewürztraminer and Johannisberg riesling. Produces varietal and dessert wines.

Charles Lefranc (USA) the brand-name used by the Almaden Vineyards in California for a range of their fine wines.

Charles Le Roi (Lux) a sparkling (méthode traditionelle) wine produced by Bernard Massard.

Charles VII Brut (Fr) a prestige cuvée Champagne produced by Canard-Duchêne.

Charleston Cocktail (Cktl) ½ measure Mandarine Napoléon, ½ measure cherry brandy. Stir over ice in a highball glass and top up with 7-Up.

Charles Wells (Eng) see Wells Brewery.

Charley Goodleg (Cktl) 20mls Galliano, 40mls tequila. Shake over ice, strain into an ice-filled sugar frosted (orange juice) highball glass and top with orange juice.

Charley's White Label (W.Ind) a light, blended rum produced in Jamaica in 1892. Now produced by Seagram.

Charlier et Fils (Fr) a Champagne producer. (Add): 4 Rue des Pervenches, 51700 Montigny-sous-Châtillon. 14ha. Produces vintage and non-vintage wines. A member of the Club Tresors de Champagne. Labels: Cuvée Carte Blanche, Cuvée Carte Noire, Cuvée 'Special Club' Millésimée. Website: http://www.champagne-charlier.com

Charlies Angel (Eng) 4.5% alc by vol. ale brewed by the Nottingham Brewery, Nottinghamshire.

Charlotte Dumay (Fr) a parcel of cuvées owned in the Renardes (2ha), Clos du Roi (0.5ha) and Les Bressandes (1ha) of Corton, Côte de Beaune, Burgundy (owned by the Hospices de Beaune).

Charm (Eng) a term used to describe an appealing wine.

Chamarré (Fr) a brand label for a range of wines (launched 2006) produced by the OVS group (consisting of 6 co-operative wineries).

Charmat (Fr) the 'cuve close' or 'tank method', invented by Eugene Charmat in 1910 for the production of sparkling wines.

Charmat [Eugène] (Fr) the inventor of the tank method (1910) of producing sparkling wines that originated from Bordeaux.

Charme (Port) a still red wine produced by the Port shippers Niepoort.

C

Charmelottes [Les] (Fr) a vineyard in the A.C. commune of Montagny, Côte Chalonnaise, Burgundy.

Charmer Original (Eng) a gin-based fruit cup cocktail from Edward Butler Vintners. 24.5% alc by vol.

Charmes [Les] (Fr) a Premier Cru vineyard in the A.C. commune of Chambolle-Musigny, Côte de Nuits, Burgundy 6ha.

Charmes-Chambertin (Fr) a Grand Cru vineyard in the A.C. commune of Gevrey-Chambertin, Côte de Nuits, Burgundy. 32.36ha., of which 19.5ha. of them is Mazoyères-Chambertin which can be sold as Charmes-Chambertin (since the name of Mazoyères-Chambertin is not well-known).

Charmes-Dessous [Les] (Fr) a Premier Cru vineyard in the A.C. commune of Meursault, Côte de Beaune, Burgundy 12.5ha.

Charmes-Dessus [Les] (Fr) a Premier Cru vineyard in the A.C. commune of Meursault, Côte de Beaune, Burgundy 15.5ha.

Charmes-la-Côte (Fr) a commune in the Côtes de Toul, Lorraine, north-eastern France. Produces Vins gris.

Charmots [Les] (Fr) a Premier Cru vineyard in the A.C. commune of Pommard, Côte de Beaune, Burgundy 3.6ha.

Charneco (Port) the name given to a wine from a sub-district of Bucelas of the same name in the sixteenth and seventeenth centuries.

Charnières [Les] (Fr) a Premier Cru vineyard in the A.C. commune of Savigny-lès-Beaune, Côte de Beaune, Burgundy.

Charnu (Fr) denotes a full-bodied wine.

Charpente (Fr) denotes a well-made wine/a wine with structure.

Charpentier [André] (Fr) a Champagne producer. (Add): 6 Rue de Mars, B.P. 467, 51066 Reims Cedex.

Charpentier [Jacky] (Fr) a Champagne producer. (Add): 88 Rue de Reuil, Villers-sous-Châtillon, 51700 Dormans. 12 ha. based in the Vallée de la Marne with Pinot noir 80%. 'E'mail: champagnejcharpentier@wanadoo.fr

Charpignat (Fr) an A.C. vineyard on the bank of lake Bourget in the Savoie region, south-eastern France.

Charpoutier (Fr) a négociant based at Tain in the Côtes du Rhône. Produces Hermitage wines under the names of Chante Alouette (white wine) and La Sizeranne (red wine). Labels: La Croix des Grives.

Charred Barrels (USA) used in the making of American whiskey, gives the whiskey colour and quality.

Charrier (Fr) a neutral and slightly pétillant mineral water.

Charrington (Eng) a large brewery that merged with Bass in 1967 to form the Bass Charrington Company. Brews: Charrington IPA 1039 O.G. Prize Medal 1035 O.G. Barley Wine 1064 O.G. Also many fine beers.

Charta (Ger) a group (established 1984) to promote wine-drinking with food, the wines must conform to Halbtroken regulations.

Charta Estate Association (Ger) an association of producers (formed July 12th 1984) based in the Rheingau who promote their wines and bottle the best in specially marked bottles. These must conform to more stringent standards than the present Government ones.

Charter Ale (Eng) a 4.6% alc by vol. ale brewed by the Broadstone Brewing C°. Ltd., Nottinghamshire.

Charter of Muri (Ger) a charter of the abbey of Mur near Zurich for viticultural practices such as planting, pruning, hoeing, etc.

Charter Pensans (Eng) an alternative name for Coref Ertach Pensans beer 1055 O.G.

Chartogne-Taillet (Fr) a Champagne producer. (Add): 37-39 Grande Rue, 51220 Merfy. 10ha. Produces Cuvée Fiacre Taillet which contains 60% Chardonnay.

Chartreuse (Fr) a herb-flavoured, green liqueur 55% alc by vol. made by Carthusian monks. A yellow sweeter version 40% alc by vol. is also made using orange and myrtle flavours. Also produced in Spain in the Tarragona region and at Voiron (Spain).

Chartreuse (Fr) a herb-based liqueur, white in colour and very rare. Produced only between 1840–1880 and 1886–1890. Created by Brother Bruno.

Chartreuse Cooler (Cktl) 25mls Green Chartreuse, 20mls lime juice. Blend together in a blender with a scoop of crushed ice, pour into a flute glass and top with iced Champagne.

Chartreuse de Château Coutet [La] (Fr) the second wine of Château Coutet, A.C. Barsac, Bordeaux.

Chartreuse Diffusion (Fr) the name of the company which distributes the Chartreuse liqueurs.

Chartreuse Liqueur Du gème Centenaire (Fr) produced in 1980 for the 900th birthday of the Chartreuse monastery 47% alc by vol.

Chartreuse Nun (Cktl) 25mls (⅛ gill) green Chartreuse in the large liqueur glass. Top with double cream and sprinkle with finely grated dark chocolate.

Chartreuse Tonic (Cktl) 25mls (⅛ gill) green Chartreuse, juice 1 lime. Stir well over ice in an old-fashioned glass, top with tonic water and dress with a slice of lime.

Chasan (Fr) a crossed grape variety between the Chardonnay and the Palomino (Listán). Grown in the Languedoc region of southern France.

Chase Bitter (Eng) a 4.4% alc by vol. bitter ale brewed by the Blythe Brewery, Staffordshire.

Chaser (Scot) the name given to a measure of spirits (usually Scotch whisky) consumed before a glass of beer. Both are purchased together. e.g. " *bitter and whisky chaser*".

Chaser Stout (Eng) a 5.1% alc by vol. stout brewed by the Highgate Brewery, West Midlands.

Chash-ka (Rus) cup.

Chassagne-Montrachet (Fr) a vineyard area

(163.92ha) in the A.C. commune of Chassagne, Côte de Beaune, Burgundy. Has the Grand Crus: Montrachet [part], Bâtard-Montrachet [part] and Criots-Bâtard-Montrachet [part] 10.8ha. Also the Premier Crus: Bois de Chassagne, Champgain, Clos de la Boudriotte, Clos Saint-Jean, L'Abbaye de Morgeot, La Maltroie, La Romanée, Les Boudriottes, Les Brussanes, Les Caillerets, Les Champs-Cain, Les Chaumées, Les Grande Montagne, Les Grandes Ruchottes, Les Macherelles, Les Ruchottes and Les Vergers.

Chassart Distillerie (Bel) a distilling company based in Chassart. Produces grain élixer and jenevers under own name.

Chasseignes [Les] (Fr) the label for a white A.C. Sancerre produced by Domaine Raimbault.

Chasselas (Fr) a white grape variety grown in southern France. Is known as the Dorin (in Vaud), Perlan (in Geneva) and Fendant (in Valais), Switzerland and the Gutedel in Baden, south-western Germany.

Chasselas Blanc (Fr) an alternative name for the Chasselas grape.

Chasselas Cioutat (Fr) a lesser variety of the Chasselas grape.

Chasselas de Fontainbleu (Fr) the local name for the Chasselas grape in central France.

Chasselas de Montauban (Fr) the local name for the Chasselas grape.

Chasselas de Thomery (Fr) a local name for the Chasselas grape.

Chasselas Doré (USA) also known as the Golden Chasselas, a white grape variety used for white wines in California. Is also known as the Palomino in Spain and the Chasselas in France.

Chasselas Musqué (Fr) a white grape variety from the Chasselas species. Has a 'musky' spicy aroma.

Chasselas Rosé (Fr) the alternative name for the Fendant rosé grape.

Chasselas Violet (Fr) a black grape variety, a variation of the white Chasselas grape.

Chasslie (Ger) a dry white wine produced in Baden from Chasselas and Gutedel grapes. Matured on the lees until march the following year after the harvest.

Chassenay d'Arce (Fr) a Champagne producer. (Add): 10110 Ville-sur-Arce. Co-opérative-manipulant. 130 growers own 300ha.

Châtains (Fr) a Premier Cru vineyard of A.C. Chablis. Is often re-classified as the Premier Cru Vaillons.

Château (Fr) castle, manor house or lodge. In a wine country it can only be used on a label if the vineyard exists, has produced wine, and has a traditional right to use the name (for list see Château). (Ger) = schloss, (It) = castello.

Château Abel-Laurent (Fr) where the white wine of Château Margaux called Pavillon blanc is vinified and aged.

Château à Lafitte (Fr) a vineyard in the A.C. Entre-Deux-Mers, Bordeaux.

Château Alphen (S.Afr) a wine-producer based in Constantia.

Château Amarande (Fr) an A.C. Bordeaux. Grape varieties: Cabernet sauvignon 20%, Merlot 80%.

Château Ambleville (Fr) the brand-name of Cognacs produced by Raymond Ragnaud.

Château Ambois (Fr) a vineyard. (Com): Saint-Georges-Saint-Émilion. A.C. Saint-Émilion, Bordeaux 1ha.

Château Andoyse du Hayot (Fr) the second wine of Château Romer du Hayot, Fargues, A.C. Sauternes, Bordeaux.

Château André-Lamothe (Fr) an A.C. Graves. (Com): Portets 6ha (red and white).

Château Andron-Blanquet (Fr) a vineyard. (Add): Saint-Éstèphe, 33250, Médoc. Cru Bourgeois. A.C. Saint-Éstèphe. (Com): Saint-Éstèphe. 15.9ha. Grape varieties: Cabernet franc, Cabernet sauvignon, Merlot and Petit verdot. Second wine is Château St-Roch.

Château Aney (Fr) a vineyard. (Add): Margaux, 33460, Médoc. Cru Bourgeois. A.C. Haut-Médoc. (Com): Cussac-Fort-Médoc. 20ha. Grape varieties: Cabernet franc, Cabernet sauvignon and Merlot.

Château Angélus (Fr) a vineyard. (Add): 33330 Saint-Émilion. A.C. Saint-Émilion Premier [B] Grand Cru Classe. (Com): Saint-Émilion. 23ha. Grape varieties: Cabernet franc 50%, Cabernet sauvignon 5% and Merlot 45%. Second wine is Le Carillon de L'Angélus.

Château Angludet (Fr) a vineyard. (Com): Cantenac. A.C. Haut-Médoc, Bordeaux. 30ha

Château Agnel (Fr) a vineyard in the A.C. Minervois. Grape variety: Syrah.

Château Anniche (Fr) a vineyard. (Com): Haux. A.C. Premières Côtes de Bordeaux, Bordeaux. (Add): 33550 Haux. Grape varieties: Cabernet 60%, Malbec 20% and Merlot 20%.

Château Anseillant (Fr) a vineyard. (Com): Pomerol. A.C. Pomerol, Bordeaux.

Château Anthonic (Fr) a vineyard. (Com): Moulis. A.C. Moulis, Bordeaux. Cru Bourgeois Supérieur 5ha.

Château Archambeau (Fr) a vineyard. (Com): Illats. A.C. Cérons, Bordeaux 4ha

Château Archambeau (Fr) a vineyard in the A.C. Graves, Bordeaux (white).

Château Arcins (Fr) a vineyard. (Com): Arcins. A.C. Haut-Médoc. (Add): Arcins, 33460 Margaux. Cru Bourgeois. Second label is Château Tour Belleville.

Château Arnaud de Jacquemeau (Fr) a vineyard. (Add): 33330 Saint-Émilion. A.C. Saint-Émilion. (Com): Saint-Émilion. 4.75ha. Grape varieties: Cabernet franc 20%, Cabernet sauvignon 10%, Malbec 10% and Merlot 60%.

Château Arnauld (Fr) a Cru Bourgeois Supérieur vineyard. (Add): Arcins, 33480 Margaux, Médoc. A.C. Haut-Médoc. (Com): Arcins. 20ha. Grape varieties: Cabernet franc, Cabernet sauvignon, Malbec, Merlot and Petit verdot.

Château Arnauton (Fr) a vineyard. (Com): Fronsac. A.C. Côtes de Fronsac, Bordeaux 11ha.

Château Arricaud (Fr) a vineyard. (Com): Landiras. A.C. Graves, Bordeaux. 12ha (white).

C

Château Augey (Fr) a 10ha vineyard. (Com): Bommes. A.C. Sauternes, Bordeaux.

Château Ausone (Fr) a vineyard 7ha. (Add): 33330 Saint-Émilion. Premier [A] Grand Cru Classé (A). A.C. Saint-Émilion. (Com): Saint-Émilion. 7ha. Grape varieties: Cabernet franc, Cabernet sauvignon, Carmemère, Merlot and Petit verdot. Second wine is Chapelle d'Ausone.

Château Austerlitz (Fr) a vineyard. (Com): Sables-Saint-Émilion. A.C. Saint-Émilion, Bordeaux 5ha.

Château aux Roquettes (Fr) a 2ha vineyard in the A.C. Saint-Émilion, Bordeaux.

Château Badette (Fr) an 8ha vineyard in the A.C. Saint-Émilion, Bordeaux.

Château Badon (Fr) a 6ha vineyard. (Com): Saint-Émilion. A.C. Saint-Émilion, Bordeaux.

Château Bagnols (Fr) a Grand Cru. A.C. Saint-Émilion. (Com): Saint-Étienne-de-Lisse. 6.5ha. Grape varieties: Cabernet franc and Merlot.

Château Bahans (Fr) the vintage and non-vintage second red wine of Château Haut-Brion (Premier Grand Cru Classé) in the Graves.

Château Bahans-Haut-Brion (Fr) *see* Château Bahans.

Château Balac (Fr) a Cru Bourgeois. (Add): 33112, St. Laurent du Médoc. A.C. Haut-Médoc. (Com): St. Laurent. 13-14ha. Grape varieties: Cabernet franc, Cabernet sauvignon and Merlot.

Château Baleau (Fr) *see* Château Côte Baleau.

Château Balestard-la-Tonnelle (Fr) a Grand Cru Classé. A.C. Saint-Émilion. (Com): Saint-Émilion. 11.41ha. Grape varieties: Cabernet franc 20%, Cabernet sauvignon 20%, Malbec 5% and Merlot 65%.

Château Balestey (Fr) a vineyard. (Com): Cérons. A.C. Graves, Bordeaux 10ha

Château Baleyron (Fr) a vineyard. (Com): St-Seurin-de-Cadourne. A.C. Haut-Médoc, Bordeaux.

Château Baloques-Haut-Bages (Fr) a vineyard. (Com): Pauillac. A.C. Pauillac, Bordeaux. Cru Bourgeois 6ha.

Château Balouet-Roailloy (Fr) a vineyard. (Add): Langon 33210. A.C. Graves. (Com): Langon. 3.9ha. Grape varieties: Cabernet franc, Merlot, Sauvignon blanc and Sémillon. *See also* Clos Dumes.

Château Barateau (Fr) a vineyard. (Com): Saint Laurent. A.C. Médoc, Bordeaux. Cru Bourgeois.7ha.

Château Barbé (Fr) a vineyard in the A.C. Premier Côtes de Blaye, Bordeaux.

Château Barbe Blanche (Fr) a vineyard. (Com): Lussac-Saint-Émilion. A.C. Lussac-Saint-Émilion, Bordeaux 8ha.

Château Barbe Morin (Fr) a vineyard. (Com): Loupiac. A.C. Loupiac, Bordeaux 5ha.

Château Barberousse (Fr) a vineyard. (Com): Loupiac. A.C. Loupiac, Bordeaux 4ha.

Château Barbet (Fr) a vineyard. (Com): Cars. A.C. Côtes de Blaye, Bordeaux.

Château Barbey (Fr) a 2ha vineyard in the A.C. Saint-Émilion, Bordeaux.

Château Barbeyron (Fr) a 4ha vineyard in the A.C. Saint-Émilion, Bordeaux.

Château Barbier (Fr) a 6ha vineyard. (Com): Fargues. A.C. Sauternes, Bordeaux.

Château Barde-Haut (Fr) a 12ha vineyard in the A.C. Saint-Émilion, Bordeaux.

Château Bardins (Fr) a vineyard. (Com): Cadaujac. A.C. Graves, Bordeaux 2ha (red and white).

Château Bardis (Fr) a vineyard. (Add): Saint-Seurin-de-Cadourne, 33250, Pauillac. A.C. Haut-Médoc. (Com): Saint-Seurin-de-Cadourne. 8ha. Grape varieties: Cabernet sauvignon 65% and Merlot 35%.

Château Bardon-Ferrand (Fr) a vineyard. (Com): St-Aignan. A.C. Côtes de Fronsac, Bordeaux 2ha.

Château Bardoulet (Fr) a 2ha vineyard in the A.C. Saint-Émilion, Bordeaux.

Château Baret (Fr) a vineyard. (Add): Villenave d'Ornon, Graves. A.C. Graves. (Com): Graves. 40ha. Grape varieties: Cabernet sauvignon, Merlot, Sauvignon and Sémillon (red and white).

Château Barjumeau-Chauviné (Fr) a 3ha vineyard. (Com): Sauternes. A.C. Sauternes, Bordeaux.

Château Barker (Austr) a winery. (Add): Albany Highway, P.O. Box 102, West Barker, Western Australia, 6324. 17ha. Grape varieties: Cabernet sauvignon, Gewürztraminer, Malbec, Merlot, Pinot noir, Rhine riesling, Sémillon and Shiraz.

Château Barrabaque (Fr) a vineyard. (Com): Fronsac. A.C. Côtes Canon-Fronsac, Bordeaux 9ha.

Château Barrail des Graves (Fr) a vineyard. (Add): Saint-Sulpice-de-Faleyrens, 33330 Saint-Émilion. A.C. Saint-Émilion. (Com): Saint-Sulpice-de-Faleyrens.

Château Barraud (Fr) a vineyard. (Com): Montagne-Saint-Émilion. A.C. Saint-Émilion, Bordeaux 4ha.

Château Barreau (Fr) a vineyard. (Add): 33330 Saint-Émilion. Grand Cru. A.C. Saint-Émilion. (Com): Saint-Émilion. Grape varieties: Cabernet franc, Malbec, Merlot.

Château Barrette (Fr) a 5ha vineyard. (Com): Sauternes. A.C. Sauternes, Bordeaux.

Château Barreyres (Fr) a vineyard. (Com): Arcins. A.C. Haut-Médoc, (Add): Arcins, 33460 Margaux. Cru Bourgeois. 62ha. Grape varieties: Cabernet sauvingnon 50%, Merlot 50%.

Château Barrieux (Fr) a vineyard. (Com): Samonac. A.C. Côtes de Bourg, Bordeaux.

Château Barthès-Pian-Médoc (Fr) a vineyard. (Com): Le Pian. A.C. Haut-Médoc, Bordeaux.

Château Bastor-Lamontagne (Fr) a vineyard. (Com): Preignac. A.C. Sauternes, Bordeaux. 38ha. Cru Bourgeois. Grape varieties: Sauvignon blanc 20%, Sémillon 80%.

Château Batailley (Fr) a Grand Cru Classé (5th). A.C. Pauillac. (Com): Pauillac. 80ha. Grape varieties: Cabernet franc, Cabernet sauvignon and Merlot.

Château Batsalle (Fr) a 4ha vineyard. (Com): Fargues. A.C. Sauternes, Bordeaux.

Château Batsères (Fr) a vineyard. (Com): Landiras. A.C. Graves, Bordeaux. 4ha (white).

Château Baudron (Fr) a vineyard. (Com): Montagne-Saint-Émilion. A.C. Montagne-Saint-Émilion, Bordeaux.

Château Bauduc (Fr) a vineyard in the A.C. Entre-Deux-Mers, Bordeaux.

C

Château Baulac-Dodijos (Fr) a vineyard. (Com): Barsac. A.C. Barsac (or Sauternes), Bordeaux 5ha.

Château Bayard (Fr) a vineyard. (Com): Montagne-Saint-Émilion. A.C. Saint-Émilion, Bordeaux 7ha.

Château Bayard (Fr) an A.C. white wine from Vienne in the département of Isère. Southern France.

Château Bayle (Fr) the original name for Château Guiraud before the 1855 classification. 100ha. (85ha) A.C. Sauternes, (15ha) A.C. Bordeaux. Produces dry white A.C. Bordeaux under the label 'G'.

Château Beafils (Fr) an A.C. Bordeaux.

Château Béard (Fr) a 5ha vineyard in the A.C. Saint-Émilion, Bordeaux.

Château Béard le Chapelle (Fr) a vineyard. (Add): Peyrelongue, Saint Laurent des Combes. Grand Cru. A.C. Saint-Émilion. (Com): Saint Laurent des Combes. 16ha. Grape varieties: Cabernet franc, Cabernet sauvignon and Merlot.

Château Beaubois (Fr) a domaine in the A.C. Costières de Nîmes, Languedoc-Roussillon. Noted for white wines from Marsanne grapes.

Château Beauchêne (Fr) a vineyard. (Com): Beautiran. A.C. Graves, Bordeaux. 5ha (red and white).

Château Beauchêne (Fr) a vineyard. (Com): Pomerol. A.C. Pomerol, Bordeaux 2ha.

Château Beaulac (Fr) a vineyard. (Com): Illats. A.C. Cérons, Bordeaux 3ha.

Château Beaulieu (Fr) a vineyard. (Com): Pomerol. A.C. Pomerol, Bordeaux 1ha.

Château Beaulieu (Fr) a vineyard. (Com): Saint-Germain-d'Esteuil. A.C. Médoc, Bordeaux. Cru Bourgeois.

Château Beau-Mayne (Fr) an A.C. Bordeaux.

Château Beau-Mayne (Fr) a Grand Cru. A.C. Saint-Émilion. (Com): Saint-Émilion. Wine is made from the young vines of the Grand Cru Classé Couvent des Jacobins.

Château Beau-Mazeret (Fr) a part of Château Grand-Mayne, A.C. Saint-Émilion, Bordeaux.

Château Beaumont (Fr) a vineyard. (Add): 33460, Margaux, Médoc. Cru Bourgeois Supérieur. A.C. Haut-Médoc. (Com): Cussac-Fort-Médoc. 146ha. Grape varieties: Cabernet franc, Cabernet sauvignon, Merlot and Petit verdot. The 2nd wine is Château Moulin d'Arvigny.

Château Beauregard (Fr) a vineyard in the A.C. Corbières, Languedoc, south-western France (red).

Château Beauregard (Fr) a vineyard. (Com): Pomerol. A.C. Pomerol, Bordeaux. 13ha. Grape varieties: Cabernet franc, Cabernet sauvignon, Malbec and Merlot.

Château Beauregard (Fr) a vineyard. (Com): Saint-Julien. A.C. Saint-Julien, Bordeaux 4ha.

Château Beaurégard Ducasse (Fr) a vineyard based in Mazères, Gironde, A.C. Graves (red and white).

Château Beau-Rivage (Fr) a vineyard. (Com): Macau. A.C. Bordeaux Supérieur.

Château Beauséjour (Fr) a vineyard. (Add): 33330 Saint-Émilion. Premier [B] Grand Cru Classé. A.C. Saint-Émilion. (Com): Saint-Émilion. 7ha. Grape varieties: Cabernet franc, Cabernet sauvignon and Merlot. The second wine is Croix de Mazerat.

Château Beauséjour (Fr) a vineyard. (Com): Montagne-Saint-Émilion. A.C. Saint-Émilion, Bordeaux 6ha.

Château Beauséjour (Fr) a vineyard. (Com): Pomerol. A.C. Pomerol, Bordeaux 2ha.

Château Beauséjour (Fr) a vineyard. (Com): Puisseguin-Saint-Émilion. A.C. Saint-Émilion, Bordeaux 14ha.

Château Beauséjour (Fr) a vineyard. (Com): Saint-Estèphe. A.C. Saint-Estèphe, Bordeaux 23ha.

Château Beau-Séjour-Bécot (Fr) a vineyard. (Add): 33330 Saint-Émilion. Premier [B] Grand Cru Classé. (Re-promoted to Premier [B] Grand Cru Classé from 1996 vintage). A.C. Saint-Émilion. (Com): Saint-Émilion. 18.5ha. Grape varieties: Cabernet franc, Cabernet sauvignon and Merlot. Website: http://www.beausejour-becot.com

Château Beauséjour-Duffau-Lagarosse (Fr) a 6.5ha. vineyard. (Com): of Saint-Émilion. A.C. Saint-Émilion, Bordeaux. Premier [B] Grand Cru Classé. Grape varieties: Merlot, Cabernet franc, Cabernet sauvignon.

Château Beausite (Fr) a vineyard. (Com): Lussac-Saint-Émilion. A.C. Saint-Émilion, Bordeaux 4ha.

Château Beau Site (Fr) a Cru Bourgeois Supérieur. A.C. Saint-Estèphe. (Com): Saint Corbian. 22ha. Grape varieties: Cabernet sauvignon 70%, Merlot 25% and Petit verdot 5%. Also known as Château Beau Site Haut Vignoble.

Château Beau-Site (Fr) a vineyard. (Com): Bourg. A.C. Côtes de Bourg, Bordeaux.

Château Beau-Site (Fr) a vineyard. (Com): Monprinblanc. A.C. Premières Côtes de Bordeaux, Bordeaux.

Château Beau Site de la Tour (Fr) an A.C. Fronsac. Second wine of the Grand Cru. A.C. Saint-Émilion. Château Gueyrot.

Château Beau Site Haut Vignoble (Fr) see Château Beau Site.

Château Beau-Soleil (Fr) a vineyard. (Com): Pomerol. A.C. Pomerol, Bordeaux 3ha.

Château Beau-Soleil (Gre) a wine estate in Porto Carras.

Château Beau Village (Fr) a vineyard in the A.C. Médoc. (Add): 33340 Cocqueques.

Château Béchereau (Fr) a 12ha. vineyard. (Com): Bommes. A.C. Sauternes, Bordeaux.

Château Bedou (Fr) a vineyard. (Com): Cars. A.C. Côtes de Blaye, Bordeaux.

Château Bégadanet (Fr) a vineyard. (Com): Bégadan. A.C. Médoc, Bordeaux 4ha.

Château Bégot (Fr) a vineyard. (Com): Lansac. A.C. Côtes de Bourg, Bordeaux.

Château Begude (Fr) an A.O.C. Limoux.

Château Belá (Slo) a vineyard based in the Stúrovo region.

Château Bélair (Fr) a vineyard. (Add): 33330 Saint-Émilion. Premier [B] Grand Cru Classé. A.C. Saint-Émilion. (Com): Saint-Émilion. 14ha. Grape varieties: Cabernet franc 40%, Merlot 60%.

C

Château Bel Air (Fr) an A.C. Bordeaux Supérieur.

Château Bel Air (Fr) a vineyard. (Add): Domaines Henri Martin, 33250, Saint-Julien, Médoc. A.C. Haut-Médoc. (Com): Saint-Julien. 35ha. Grape varieties: Cabernet sauvignon 60% and Merlot 40%.

Château Bel-Air (Fr) a vineyard in the A.C. Côtes de Blaye.

Château Bel-Air (Fr) a vineyard. (Com): Montagne-Saint-Émilion. A.C. Saint-Émilion, Bordeaux 8ha.

Château Bel-Air (Fr) a vineyard. (Com): Portets. A.C. Graves, Bordeaux. 2ha (white).

Château Bel-Air (Fr) a vineyard. (Com): Puisseguin-Saint-Émilion. A.C. Saint-Émilion, Bordeaux 11ha.

Château Bel-Air (Fr) a vineyard. (Com): Tresses. A.C. Entre-Deux-Mers (white).

Château Bel-Air (Fr) a vineyard. (Com): Saint-Morillon. A.C. Graves, Bordeaux. 3ha (white).

Château Bel-Air (Fr) a vineyard. (Com): Vayres. A.C. Graves-de-Vayres.

Château Bel-Air (Fr) a vineyard. (Com): Loupiac. A.C. Loupiac, Bordeaux 10ha.

Château Bel-Air (Fr) a vineyard. (Com): Camblanec. A.C. Premières Côtes de Bordeaux, Bordeaux (red and white).

Château Bel-Air (Fr) a vineyard. (Com): Néac. A.C. Pomerol, Bordeaux 10ha.

Château Bel-Air (Fr) a vineyard. (Com): Sainte-Croix-du-Mont. A.C. Sainte-Croix-du-Mont, Bordeaux.

Château Bel-Air Lagrave (Fr) a vineyard. (Add): Grand-Poujeaux, Moulis-en-Médoc 33480, Castelnau-en-Médoc. A.C. Moulis-en-Médoc. (Com): Moulis. 12ha. Grape varieties: Cabernet sauvignon, Merlot and Petit verdot.

Château Bel-Air-Lussac (Fr) a vineyard. (Com): Lussac-Saint-Émilion. A.C. Saint-Émilion, Bordeaux 12ha.

Château Belair-Marignan (Fr) a vineyard. (Com): Saint-Émilion. A.C. Saint-Émilion, Bordeaux.

Château Bel-Air-Marquis-d'Aligre (Fr) a vineyard. (Com): Soussans. A.C. Haut-Médoc, Bordeaux. Cru Exceptionnel. Second label is Château Bel Air Marquis de Pomereau 17ha.

Château Bel-Air-Marquis-de-Pomereau (Fr) the second wine of Château-Bel-Air-Marquis-d'Aligre.

Château Belair-Sarthou (Fr) a vineyard in the A.C. Saint-Émilion, Bordeaux 5ha.

Château Belaussel (Fr) a vineyard in the A.C. Corbières, south-western France.

Château Bel Evêque (Fr) a winery based in the A.C. Corbières, Languedoc-Roussillon. Produces: white, rosé and red wines.

Château Belgrave (Fr) a Grand Cru Classé (5ᵗʰ). A.C. Haut-Médoc. (Com): Saint-Laurent. 76ha. Grape varieties: Cabernet sauvignon 60%, Merlot 35% and Petit verdot 5%.

Château Bel-Horizon (Fr) a 2ha vineyard in the A.C. Saint-Émilion, Bordeaux.

Château Belingard (Fr) a vineyard in the A.C. Monbazillac, Bergerac, south-western France (red and sweet white).

Château Belingard (Fr) a vineyard in the A.C. Côtes de Bergerac. (Add): 17 Rue Millet, 24100 Bergerac (red and white).

Château Belle Assise Coureau (Fr) a vineyard. (Add): Saint-Sulpice-de-Faleyrens A.C. Saint-Émilion. (Com): Saint-Sulpice-de-Faleyrens. 14.6ha. Grape varieties: Cabernet franc 10%, Cabernet sauvignon 30% and Merlot 60%.

Château Bellefontaine (Fr) a vineyard. (Com): St-Pierre-de-Mons. A.C. Graves, Bordeaux. 3ha (white).

Château Bellefont-Belcier (Fr) a vineyard. (Add): Saint Laurent des Combes, 33330 Saint-Émilion. Grand Cru Classé (Promotion 2006). A.C. Saint-Émilion. (Com): Saint Laurent des Combes. 13ha. Grape varieties: Cabernet franc 20%, Cabernet sauvignon 10% and Merlot 70%.

Château Bellegrave (Fr) a vineyard. (Com): Listrac. A.C. Haut-Médoc, Bordeaux 9ha.

Château Bellegrave (Fr) a vineyard in the A.C. Saint-Émilion, Bordeaux 11ha.

Château Bellegrave-du-Poujeau (Fr) a vineyard. (Com): Le Pian. A.C. Haut-Médoc, Bordeaux. Cru Bourgeois.

Château Bellegraves (Fr) a vineyard. (Com): Pomerol. A.C. Pomerol, Bordeaux 4ha.

Château Bellerive (Fr) a vineyard. (Com): Valeyrac. A.C. Médoc, Bordeaux. Cru Bourgeois 9ha.

Château Belleroque (Fr) a vineyard. (Com): Bourg. A.C. Côtes de Bourg, Bordeaux.

Château Belle-Rose (Fr) a vineyard. (Add): 33250, Pauillac, Médoc. Cru Bourgeois. A.C. Pauillac. (Com): Pauillac. 7ha. Grape varieties: Cabernet franc, Cabernet sauvignon, Malbec and Merlot.

Château Belles Eaux (Fr) a vineyard (90ha) in the A.C. Coteaux du Languedoc. (Add): 34720 Caux. Grape varieties: Carignan, Grenache, Mourvèdre, Syrah. Labels: Domaine Belles Eaux, Sainte Hélène. Website: http://www.chateau-belleseaux.com 'E'mail: contact@chateau-belleseaux.com

Château Belles-Plantes (Fr) a vineyard in the A.C. Saint-Émilion, Bordeaux 3ha.

Château Bellevue (Fr) a vineyard in the A.C. Bergerac, south-western France (red).

Château Bellevue (Fr) a vineyard. (Com): Blaye. A.C. Côtes de Blaye, Bordeaux.

Château Bellevue (Fr) a vineyard. (Com): Cussac-Fort-Médoc. A.C. Haut-Médoc, Bordeaux 1ha.

Château Bellevue (Fr) a vineyard. (Com): Lussac-Saint-Émilion. A.C. Lussac-Saint-Émilion, Bordeaux 11ha.

Château Belle-Vue (Fr) a vineyard. (Com): Macau. A.C. Haut-Médoc, Bordeaux. Cru Bourgeois.

Château Bellevue (Fr) a vineyard. (Com): Montagne-Saint-Émilion. A.C. Montagne-Saint-Émilion, Bordeaux 4ha.

Château Bellevue (Fr) a vineyard. (Com): Pomerol. A.C. Pomerol, Bordeaux 5ha.

Château Bellevue (Fr) a vineyard. (Com): Quinsac. A.C. Premières Côtes de Bordeaux, Bordeaux.

Château Bellevue (Fr) a vineyard. (Add): 33330 Saint-Émilion. Grand Cru (demoted 2006). A.C. Saint-Émilion. (Com): Saint-Émilion. 9ha. Grape varieties: Cabernet sauvignon 25% and Merlot 75%.

C

Château Bellevue (Fr) a vineyard. (Com): Saint-Michel-de-Fronsac. A.C. Fronsac, Bordeaux.

Château Bellevue (Fr) a vineyard. (Com): Valeyrac. A.C. Médoc, Bordeaux 9ha.

Château Bellevue la Forêt (Fr) a vineyard in the A.C. Côtes du Frontonnais, Tarn-et-Garonne, south-western France. 105ha (red and rosé).

Château Bellisle Mondotte (Fr) a vineyard. (Com): Saint-Hippolyte. A.C. Saint-Émilion, Bordeaux 4ha.

Château Belloy (Fr) a vineyard. (Com): Fronsac. A.C. Côtes Canon Fronsac, Bordeaux 5ha.

Château Belon (Fr) a vineyard. (Com): Saint-Morillon. A.C. Graves, Bordeaux. 3ha (white).

Château Bel-Orme-Tronquoy-de-Lalande (Fr) a vineyard. (Com): Saint-Seurin-de-Cadourne. A.C. Haut-Médoc, Bordeaux. Cru Bourgeois 25ha.

Château Belize (Fr) a vineyard in the A.C. Minervois, Languedoc-Roussillon. Grape varieties: Carignan Grenache, Mourvèdre and Syrah. Label: Cuvée des Oliviers.

Château Benoit (USA) a winery (established 1979) based at 6580 N.E. Mineral Springs Road, Carlton, Oregon 8ha. Grape varieties: Müller-Thurgau, Sauvignon blanc, barrel-fermented Chardonnay, Pinot noir, Riesling.

Château Bensse (Fr) a vineyard. (Com): Prignac. A.C. Médoc, Bordeaux. Cru Bourgeois.

Château Béouran (Fr) a vineyard. (Com): Saint-Émilion. A.C. Saint-Émilion, Bordeaux 1ha.

Château Bergat (Fr) a vineyard. (Add): 33330 Saint-Émilion. Grand Cru Classé. A.C. Saint-Émilion. (Com): Saint-Émilion. 3ha. Grape varieties: Cabernet franc, Cabernet sauvignon and Merlot 70%.

Château Bergeron (Fr) a vineyard. (Com): Bommes. A.C. Sauternes, Bordeaux 5ha.

Château Berloz (Fr) a vineyard in the A.C. Corbières, south-western France. Label: Adagio.

Château Berliquet (Fr) a vineyard. (Add): 33330 Saint-Émilion. Grand Cru Classé A.C. Saint-Émilion. (Com): Saint-Émilion. 8.74ha. Grape varieties: Cabernet franc, Cabernet sauvignon and Merlot 70%. Second wine is Les Ailes de Berliquet.

Château-Bernard (Fr) a commune in the Charente département whose grapes are classed Grande Champagne (Cognac).

Château Bernadotte (Fr) a 7ha. vineyard based in Pauillac. A.C. Pauillac. Owned by Château Pichon-Longueville Comtesse de Lalande. Website: http://www.pichon-lalande.com

Château Bernard-Raymond (Fr) a vineyard. (Com): Portets. A.C. Graves, Bordeaux (red and white) 5ha.

Château Bernateau (Fr) a vineyard. (Add): Saint-Étienne-de-Lisse, 33330 Saint-Émilion. Grand Cru. A.C. Saint-Émilion. (Com): Saint-Étienne-de-Lisse. Grape varieties: Cabernet franc 20%, Merlot 80%.

Château Bernisse (Fr) a vineyard. (Com): Barsac. A.C. Barsac (or Sauternes), Bordeaux 3ha.

Château Bernones (Fr) a Cru Bourgeois vineyard.

(Com): Cussac-Fort-Médoc. A.C. Haut-Médoc, Bordeaux.

Château Berthenon (Fr) a vineyard. (Com): St-Paul. A.C. Côtes de Blaye, Bordeaux.

Château Berthou (Fr) a vineyard. (Com): Comps. A.C. Côtes de Bourg, Bordeaux.

Château Bertin (Fr) a vineyard. (Com): Montagne-Saint-Émilion. A.C. Montagne-Saint-Émilion, Bordeaux.

Château Bertinat-Lartigue (Fr) a vineyard. (Com): Saint-Émilion. A.C. Saint-Émilion, Bordeaux.

Château Bertineau-Goby (Fr) a vineyard. (Com): Montagne-Saint-Émilion. A.C. Saint-Émilion, Bordeaux 9ha.

Château Bertineau St. Vincent (Fr) a vineyard. (Com): Lalande de Pomerol. A.C. Lalande de Pomerol, Bordeaux.

Château Bertinerie (Fr) an A.C. Côtes de Blaye. White: 25ha of 100% Sauvignon blanc. Red: 75% Cabernet sauvignon plus Cabernet franc, Merlot.

Château Bertranon (Fr) a vineyard. (Com): Loupiac. A.C. Loupiac, Bordeaux 2ha.

Château Bessan Ségur (Fr) a vineyard in the A.C. Médoc. Cru Bourgeois.

Château Beychevelle (Fr) (Add): Saint-Julien, Beychevelle 33250, Pauillac, Médoc. Grand Cru Classé (4th). A.C. Saint-Julien. (Com): Saint-Julien. 72ha. Grape varieties: Cabernet franc 8%, Cabernet sauvignon 60%, Merlot 28% and Petit verdot 4%.

Château Bézineau (Fr) a vineyard in the A.C. Saint-Émilion, Bordeaux 13ha.

Château Bianca (USA) a winery based in Willamette Valley, Oregon. Produces varietal wines. Noted for Pinot noir.

Château Bicasse-Lartigue (Fr) a vineyard in the A.C. Saint-Émilion, Bordeaux 3ha.

Château Bicot (Fr) a vineyard. (Com): Fronsac and St-Aignan. A.C. Côtes de Fronsac, Bordeaux 3ha.

Château Bicot Latour (Fr) a vineyard. (Com): St-Aignan. A.C. Côtes de Fronsac, Bordeaux 3ha.

Château Bidou (Fr) an A.C. Bourgeais et Blayais.

Château Bigaroux (Fr) a vineyard. (Add): Saint-Sulpice-de-Faleyrens, 33330 Saint-Émilion. Grand Cru. A.C. Saint-Émilion. (Com): Saint-Sulpice-de-Faleyrens. 6ha. Grape varieties: Cabernet 10% and Merlot 90%.

Château Billeron (Fr) a vineyard in the A.C. Saint-Émilion, Bordeaux 8ha.

Château Binet (Fr) a vineyard. (Com): Parsac. A.C. Saint-Émilion, Bordeaux 9ha.

Château Biston-Brillette (Fr) a vineyard. (Com): Moulis. A.C. Moulis, Bordeaux. (Add): Moulis 33480 Castelnau-de-Médoc. Cru Bourgeois 10ha.

Château Blaignan (Fr) a vineyard. (Com): Blaignan A.C. Médoc, Bordeaux. Used to be known as Château Tafford-de-Blaignan. 45ha. Cru Bourgeois.

Château Blissa (Fr) a vineyard in the A.C. Côtes de Bourg, Bordeaux.

Château Bodet (Fr) a vineyard. (Com): Fronsac. A.C. Côtes de Canon-Fronsac, Bordeaux 10ha.

Château Boënot (Fr) a vineyard. (Com): Pomerol. A.C. Pomerol, Bordeaux 4ha.

C

Château Boiresse (Fr) a vineyard. (Com): Ayguemortes. A.C. Graves, Bordeaux. 4ha (white).

Château Bois du Roc (Fr) a vineyard. (Com): Saint-Yzans. A.C. Médoc, Bordeaux. (Add): St-Yzans-de-Médoc, 33340 Lesparre.

Château Bois-Grouley (Fr) a vineyard in the A.C. Saint-Émilion, Bordeaux 3ha.

Château Boismartin (Fr) a vineyard. (Com): Léognan. A.C. Pessac-Léognan, Bordeaux (red).

Château Bois-Rond-Grand-Corbin (Fr) a vineyard in the A.C. Saint-Émilion, Bordeaux 4ha.

Château Boissac (Fr) a vineyard. (Com): Lussac-Saint-Émilion. A.C. Lussac-Saint-Émilion, Bordeaux.

Château Bonair (Fr) a vineyard. (Com): Mérignac. A.C. Graves.

Château Bonalgue (Fr) a vineyard based in Pomerol, eastern Bordeaux.

Château Bon la Madeleine (Fr) a vineyard. (Add): 33330 Saint-Émilion. Grand Cru. A.C. Saint-Émilion. (Com): Saint-Émilion. 4ha. Grape varieties: Cabernet sauvignon 40% and Merlot 60%.

Château Bonneau (Fr) a vineyard. (Com): Montagne-Saint-Émilion. A.C. Saint-Émilion, Bordeaux 9ha.

Château Bonneau-Livran (Fr) a vineyard. (Add): St-Seurin-de-Cadourne, 33250 Pauillac, Médoc. Cru Bourgeois. A.C. Haut-Médoc. (Com): St-Seurin-de-Cadourne. 12ha. Grape varieties: Cabernet sauvignon 50% and Merlot 50%.

Château Bonnet (Fr) the label for an A.C. Bordeaux.

Château Bonnet (Fr) a vineyard in the A.C. Entre-Deux-Mers, Bordeaux. Grape varieties: Sauvignon blanc 45%, Sémillon 45%, Muscadelle 10%.

Château Bonnet (Fr) a vineyard. (Add): Saint Pey d'Armens, 33330 Saint-Émilion. Grand Cru. A.C. Saint-Émilion. (Com): Saint Pey d'Armens. 23.1ha. Grape varieties: Cabernet franc 27%, Cabernet sauvignon 11%, Malbec 2% and Merlot 60%. Second wine is Château d'Armens. A.C. Saint-Émilion.

Château Bonnet Réserve du Château (Fr) new wine, aged in new oak casks and fined with egg white from the Grand Cru. A.C. Saint-Émilion vineyard Château Bonnet.

Château Bord-Fonrazade (Fr) a vineyard in the A.C. Saint-Émilion, Bordeaux 4ha.

Château Bord-Lartigue (Fr) a vineyard in the A.C. Saint-Émilion, Bordeaux 2ha.

Château Borie-Lalande (Fr) a vineyard. (Com): Saint-Julien. A.C. Saint-Julien, Bordeaux 18ha.

Château-Bottled (Fr) see Mise-en-bouteille-au-Château. These words on a wine bottle label guarantee the authenticity of the wine. Used mainly in Bordeaux (does not guarantee quality).

Château Bouchaine (USA) a winery based in Carneros, Napa Valley, California. Grape varieties: Cabernet sauvignon, Chardonnay and Pinot noir. Produces varietal wines.

Château Bouchoc (Fr) a vineyard. (Com): Loupiac. A.C. Loupiac, Bordeaux 2ha.

Château Bouchoc (Fr) a vineyard. (Com): Sainte-Croix-du-Mont. A.C. Sainte-Croix-du-Mont, Bordeaux 3ha.

Château Boudgand (Fr) a vineyard in the A.C. Côtes de Bergerac, south-western France. (Add): 17 Rue Millet, 24100 Bergerac (red and white).

Château Boulerne (Fr) a vineyard in the A.C. Saint-Émilion, Bordeaux 9ha.

Château Bouqueyran (Fr) a vineyard. (Com): Moulis. A.C. Médoc, Bordeaux. Cru Bourgeois 2ha.

Château Bourdieu (Fr) a vineyard. (Com): Berson. A.C. Côtes de Blaye, Bordeaux. (Add): Berson, 33390 Blaye.

Château Bourgade (Fr) is part of Château Rosemount in the A.C. Haut-Médoc, Bordeaux.

Château Bourgneuf-Vayron (Fr) a vineyard. (Com): Pomerol. A.C. Pomerol, Bordeaux 8.5ha.

Château Bournac (Fr) a vineyard. (Com): Civrac. A.C. Médoc, Bordeaux. (Add): Civrac-en-Médoc, 33340 Lesparre. Cru Bourgeois. 3ha. Second label is Château La Chandelière.

Château Bournac (Fr) a vineyard. (Com): Saint-Estèphe. A.C. Saint-Estèphe, Bordeaux 3ha.

Château Bouscassé (Fr) a vineyard based in the A.C. Madiran, south-western France.

Château Bourseau (Fr) a vineyard. (Com): Lalande de Pomerol. A.C. Lalande de Pomerol, Bordeaux.

Château Bouscassé (Fr) a vineyard in the A.C. Pacherenc-de-Vic-Bilh.

Château Bouscaut (Fr) a vineyard. (Add): 33140 Pont de la Maye, Graves, Bordeaux. Grand Cru Classé. A.C. Pessac-Léognan. (Com): Cadaujac. 36.5ha. Grape varieties: Cabernet franc, Cabernet sauvignon, Merlot, Sauvignon and Sémillon. Second label: Château Valoux.

Château Bousclas (Fr) a vineyard. (Com): Barsac. A.C. Barsac (or Sauternes), Bordeaux 3ha.

Château Bousquet (Fr) a vineyard in the A.C. Graves, Bordeaux.

Château Boutisse (Fr) a vineyard. (Add): Place du Marcardieu, Saint-Christophe-des-Bardes, 33330 Saint-Émilion. A.C. Saint-Émilion Grand Cru. (Com): Saint-Christophe-des-Bardes. 16ha. Grape varieties: Cabernet 25% and Merlot 75%.

Château Bouyot (Fr) a vineyard. (Com): Barsac. A.C. Barsac (or Sauternes), Bordeaux 6ha.

Château Boyd-Cantenac (Fr) a vineyard. (Add): Cantenac, 33460 Margaux. Grand Cru Classé (3rd). A.C. Margaux. (Com): Cantenac. 20ha. Grape varieties: Cabernet franc, Cabernet sauvignon, Merlot and Petit verdot.

Château Boyrein (Fr) a vineyard. (Com): Roaillan. A.C. Graves, Bordeaux. 42ha. Grape varieties: Cabernet franc, Cabernet sauvignon, Merlot, Sauvignon and Sémillon.

Château Bragard (Fr) a vineyard. (Com): Saint-Émilion. A.C. Saint-Émilion, Bordeaux.

Château Brame-les-Tours (Fr) a vineyard. (Com): Leyssac. A.C. Saint-Estèphe, Bordeaux. (Add): Saint-Estèphe, 33250 Pauillac 6ha.

Château Branaire-Duluc-Ducru (Fr) a vineyard. (Add): 33250 Saint-Julien de Beychevelle. Grand Cru Classé (4th). A.C. Saint-Julien. (Com): Saint-Julien. 48ha. Grape varieties: Cabernet franc 75%,

Merlot 20% and Petit verdot 5%. *See also* Les 5. Website: http://www.branaire.com

Château Branas Grand Poujeaux (Fr) a vineyard. (Add): 33480 Moulis, Médoc. A.C. Moulis. (Com): Moulis. 8ha. Grape varieties: Cabernet franc, Cabernet sauvignon, Merlot and Petit verdot.

Château Branda (Fr) an A.C. vineyard in the Lussac-Saint-Émilion, Bordeaux.

Château Brandard (Fr) an A.C. Bordeaux Supérieur vineyard. (Com): Saint-Quentin de Caplon, Sainte-Foy-La-Grande.

Château Brane-Cantenac (Fr) a vineyard. (Add): 33460 Margaux, Médoc. Grand Cru Classé (2nd). A.C. Margaux. (Com): Cantenac. 85ha. Grape varieties: Cabernet franc, Cabernet sauvignon, Merlot and Petit verdot. *see* Domaine de Fontarney. Second wine is Baron de Brane. Also owns Château Notton.

Château Brane-Mouton (Fr) the original (post 1853) name of Château Mouton-Rothschild.

Château Branne (Fr) a vineyard. (Com): Montagne-Saint-Émilion. A.C. Saint-Émilion, Bordeaux 6ha.

Château Brassens-Guitteronde (Fr) a vineyard. (Com): Barsac. A.C. Barsac (or Sauternes), Bordeaux 5ha.

Château Breuil (Fr) a vineyard. (Com): St-Martin-Caussade. A.C. Côtes de Blaye, Bordeaux.

Château Briès-Caillou (Fr) a vineyard. (Com): Saint-Germain d'Esteuil. A.C. Médoc, Bordeaux.

Château Brillette (Fr) a Cru Bourgeois vineyard. (Com): Moulis. A.C. Moulis-en-Médoc. 30ha. Grape varieties: Cabernet sauvignon, Merlot and Petit verdot. Cru Bourgeois Supérieur. Label: Comte de Perier de Larsan.

Château Brissac (Fr) a vineyard in the A.C. Anjou. Anjou-Saumur, Loire (rosé and sweet white).

Château Brisson (Fr) a vineyard in the A.C. Saint-Émilion, Bordeaux 4ha.

Château Brochon (Fr) a vineyard. (Add): Ch. Saint-Marc, Barsac, 33720 Podensac. A.C. Graves. (Com): Podensac. 27ha. Grape varieties: Cabernet sauvignon, Merlot, Muscadelle, Sauvignon and Sémillon.

Château Brondelle (Fr) a vineyard. (Add): 33210 Langon. A.C. Graves. (Com): Langon. 18ha. Grape varieties: Cabernet franc, Cabernet sauvignon, Sauvignon 30% and Sémillon 70%.

Château Brousseau (Fr) a vineyard. (Com): Saint-Hippolyte. A.C. Saint-Émilion, Bordeaux.

Château Brousteras (Fr) a vineyard in the A.C. Médoc, Bordeaux.

Château Broustet (Fr) a vineyard. (Add): 33940 Barsac. Grand Cru Classé (2nd). A.C. Barsac (or Sauternes). (Com): Barsac. 16ha. Grape varieties: Muscadelle 15%, Sauvignon 35% and Sémillon 50%.

Château Brown (Fr) an A.C. Graves. (Com): Léognan. 10ha. Grape varieties: Cabernet sauvignon 65% and Merlot 35%.

Château Brown Lamartine (Fr) an A.C. Bordeaux Supérieur. Grape varieties: Cabernet sauvignon 75%, Merlot 25%.

Château Bruhaut (Fr) a vineyard. (Com): St-Pierre-de-Mons. A.C. Graves, Bordeaux. 2ha (white).

Château Brulesécaille (Fr) a vineyard. (Com): Tauriac. A.C. Côtes de Bourg, Bordeaux. (Add): 33710 Bourg-sur-Gironde. Côtes de Bourg. (Com): Tauriac.

Château Brun (Fr) a vineyard. (Add): Saint-Christophe-des-Bardes, 33330 Saint-Émilion. A.C. Saint-Émilion. (Com): Saint-Christophe-des-Bardes. 6ha. Grape varieties: Cabernet sauvignon 10% and Merlot 90%.

Château Brun-Mazeyres (Fr) a vineyard. (Com): Pomerol. A.C. Pomerol, Bordeaux 3ha.

Château Burlis (Fr) a vineyard. (Add): Vignonet, 33330 Saint-Émilion. A.C. Saint-Émilion. (Com): Vignonet. 3.19ha. Grape varieties: Cabernet franc, Cabernet sauvignon and Merlot 76%.

Château Busquet (Fr) a vineyard. (Add): Château Sansonnet, 33330 Saint-Émilion. A.C. Lussac-Saint-Émilion. (Com): Lussac-Saint-Émilion.

Château Bzenec (Czec) a sparkling wine made in the Uzhorod region.

Château Cabannieux (Fr) a vineyard. (Add): 33460 Portets, Graves. A.C. Graves. (Com): Portets. 21ha. Grape varieties: Cabernet sauvignon 40%, Merlot 60%, Sauvignon 25% and Sémillon 75%.

Château Cabezac (Fr) a négociant and vineyard in the A.C. Minervois, Languedoc-Roussillon. Grape varieties: Carignan Grenache, Mourvèdre and Syrah. Label: Cuvée Arthur. Website: http://www.chateaucabezec.com

Château Cabrières (Fr) a vineyard. (Add): Rte. d'Orange, 84230 Châteauneuf-du-Pape, Rhône. Produces red and white wines. Labels include Cuvée des Tonneleries, Les Silex.

Château Cadet-Bon (Fr) a vineyard. (Add): 33330 Saint-Émilion. Grand Cru (demoted 2006). A.C. Saint-Émilion. (Com): Saint-Émilion 3ha.

Château Cadet-Peychez (Fr) a vineyard. (Add): B.P. 24, 33330 Saint-Émilion. Grand Cru. A.C. Saint-Émilion. (Com): Saint-Émilion.

Château Cadet-Piola (Fr) a vineyard. (Add): B.P. 24, 33330 Saint-Émilion. Grand Cru Classé. A.C. Saint-Émilion. (Com): Saint-Émilion. 7ha. Grape varieties: Cabernet franc 18%, Cabernet sauvignon 28%, Merlot 51% and Pressac 3%.

Château Cadet-Pontet (Fr) a vineyard. (Add): 33330 Saint-Émilion. A.C. Saint-Émilion. (Com): Saint-Émilion. 8ha. Grape varieties: Bouchet 25%, Cabernet sauvignon 25% and Merlot 50%. Second wine of Château Pontet.

Château Cadet Soutard (Fr) a vineyard. (Add): Saint Laurent des Combes, 33330 Saint-Émilion. Grand Cru. A.C. Saint-Émilion. (Com): Saint Laurent des Combes.

Château Cadillac (Fr) a 75ha vineyard. A.C. Bordeaux Supérieur.

Château Cages (Fr) a vineyard. (Com): Illats. A.C. Cérons, Bordeaux 5ha.

Château Cahuzac (Fr) a vineyard based in the Côtes du Frontonnais.

Château Caillou (Fr) a vineyard in the A.C. Cahors, south-western France.

C

Château Caillou (Fr) a Grand Cru Classé (2ⁿᵈ). A.C. Barsac. (or Sauternes). (Com): Barsac. 15ha. Grape varieties: Sauvignon 10% and Sémillon 90%. *See also* Cru du Clocher and Domaine Sarraute.

Château Calligas (Gre) a white wine made from the Robola grape by Calligas (John) on Cephalonia.

Château Calmeilh (Fr) a vineyard on the Île de Nord, Gironde. A.C. Bordeaux Supérieur.

Château Calon (Fr) a 20ha vineyard. (Com): Montagne-Saint-Émilion. A.C. Montagne-Saint-Émilion, Bordeaux.

Château Calon Montagne (Fr) a vineyard. (Com): Saint-Georges-Saint-Émilion. A.C. Saint-Émilion, Bordeaux 3ha.

Château Calon Saint-Georges (Fr) a vineyard. (Com): Saint-Georges-Saint-Émilion. A.C. Saint-Émilion, Bordeaux 3ha.

Château Calon-Ségur (Fr) a Grand Cru Classé (3ʳᵈ). A.C. Saint-Estèphe. (Com): Saint-Estèphe. 60ha. Grape varieties: Cabernet franc 15%, Cabernet sauvignon 65% and Merlot 20%. Second wine is Marquis de Ségur.

Château Calvé-Croizet-Bages (Fr) the alternative name for Château Croizet-Bages.

Château Camail (Fr) a vineyard in the A.C. Premières Côtes de Bordeaux, Bordeaux (red and white).

Château Camarset (Fr) a vineyard. (Com): St-Morillon. A.C. Graves, Bordeaux (red and white).

Château Cambes-Kermovan (Fr) a vineyard. (Com): Bourg. A.C. Côtes de Bourg, Bordeaux.

Château Cambon (Fr) a vineyard. (Com): Blanquefort. A.C. Haut-Médoc, Bordeaux 5ha.

Château Cambon-la-Pelouse (Fr) a vineyard. (Com): Macau. A.C. Haut-Médoc, Bordeaux. Cru Bourgeois. 40ha. Grape varieties: Cabernet franc 20%, Cabernet sauvignon 30%, Merlot 50%.

Château Camensac (Fr) a Grand Cru Classé (5ᵗʰ). A.C. Haut-Médoc. (Com): Saint Laurent. 60ha. Grape varieties: Cabernet franc, Cabernet sauvignon and Merlot.

Château Cameron et Raymond-Louis (Fr) a vineyard. (Com): Bommes. A.C. Sauternes, Bordeaux 9ha.

Château Camino-Salva (Fr) a vineyard. (Com): Cussac. A.C. Haut-Médoc, Bordeaux. Cru Bourgeois.

Château Camou (Mex) a winery based in the Baja. Grape varieties include Cabernet franc, Cabernet sauvignon, Chardonnay, Chenin blanc, Malbec, Merlot, Petit verdot, Sauvignon blanc, Sémillon.

Château Camperos (Fr) a vineyard. (Com): Barsac. A.C. Barsac (or Sauternes), Bordeaux. 12ha. Also Château Mayne-Bert and Château Montalivet.

Château Camplong (Fr) a vineyard in the A.C. Corbières, south-western France. Label: Cuvée Grand Pièce.

Château Camponac (Fr) a vineyard. (Com): Pessac. A.C. Médoc, Bordeaux.

Château Candeley (Fr) a vineyard. (Add): Toutifaut, 33790 St. Antoine du Queyret. A.C. Entre-Deux-Mers. 21ha. Also produce Bordeaux Supérieur, Bordeaux Moelleux, Bordeaux Rosé.

Château Cannon (Fr) a vineyard. (Com): Fronsac. A.C. Saint-Émilion, Bordeaux. Also the commune of Saint-Michel-de-Fronsac.

Château Canon (Fr) a vineyard. (Com): Fronsac. A.C. Côtes Canon-Fronsac, Bordeaux 5ha.

Château Canon (Fr) a vineyard. (Add): 33330 Saint-Émilion. Premier [B] Grand Cru Classé. A.C. Saint-Émilion. (Com): Saint-Émilion. 18ha. Grape varieties: Cabernet franc, Cabernet sauvignon, Malbec and Merlot.

Château Canon-Boîtard (Fr) the former name for Château Canon-la-Gaffelière in Saint-Émilion.

Château Canon-Chaigneau (Fr) a vineyard. (Com): Néac. A.C. Pomerol, Bordeaux.

Château Canon de Brem (Fr) a vineyard. (Com): Fronsac. A.C. Côtes Canon-Fronsac, Bordeaux.

Château Canon la Gaffelière (Fr) a vineyard. (Add): 33330 Saint-Émilion. Grand Cru Classé. A.C. Saint-Émilion. (Com): Saint-Émilion. 19ha. Grape varieties: Cabernet franc 35%, Cabernet sauvignon 5% and Merlot 60%. *See also* Les 5. Website: http://www.neipperg.com

Château Canon-Saint-Émilion (Fr) the name that Château Canon (the Premier [B] Grand Cru Classé Saint-Émilion) is usually sold under.

Château Cantalot (Fr) a vineyard. (Com): St-Pierre-de-Mons. A.C. Graves, Bordeaux. 7ha (white).

Château Cantau (Fr) a vineyard. (Com): Illats. A.C. Cérons, Bordeaux 4ha.

Château Cantebeau-Couhins (Fr) once part of Château Couhins. A.C. Graves (mostly white wines).

Château Cantegril (Fr) a vineyard. (Com): Barsac. A.C. Barsac (or Sauternes), Bordeaux 14ha.

Château Cantelaude (Fr) a vineyard. (Com): Macau. A.C. Haut-Médoc, Bordeaux. Cru Bourgeois.

Château Canteloup (Fr) the second wine of Château Lagorce. (Com): Blaignan.

Château Canteloup (Fr) a vineyard. (Com): Fours. A.C. Côtes de Blaye, Bordeaux.

Château Canteloup (Fr) a vineyard. (Com): Saint-Estèphe. A.C. Saint-Estèphe, Bordeaux 15ha.

Château Canteloup (Fr) a vineyard. (Com): Yuroc. A.C. Premières Côtes de Bordeaux, Bordeaux.

Château Cantelouve (Fr) a vineyard. (Com): Fronsac. A.C. Côtes de Fronsac, Bordeaux 10ha.

Château Cantelys (Fr) a vineyard in the A.C. Pessac-Léognan, Graves, Bordeaux. Grape varieties: Sauvignon blanc 50%, Sémillon 50%.

Château Cantemerle (Fr) a vineyard. (Com): Saint-Gènes-de-Blaye. A.C. Côtes de Blaye, Bordeaux.

Château Cantemerle (Fr) a Grand Cru Classé (5ᵗʰ). A.C. Haut-Médoc. (Com): Macau. 21ha. Grape varieties: Cabernet franc, Cabernet sauvignon, Merlot and Petit verdot. Second wine is Villeneuve-de-Cantemerle. *see* Châteaux Baron Villeneuve de Cantemerle, Royal Médoc.

Château Cantenac (Fr) a vineyard. (Add): 33330 Saint-Émilion. Grand Cru. A.C. Saint-Émilion. (Com): Saint-Émilion. 14ha. Grape varieties: Cabernet franc 15%, Cabernet sauvignon 10% and Merlot 75%. Second wine Château Piganeau.

C

Château Cantenac-Brown (Fr) a vineyard. (Add): Cantenac, 33460 Margaux. Grand Cru Classé (2nd). A.C. Margaux. (Com): Cantenac. 32ha. Grape varieties: Cabernet franc 6%, Cabernet sauvignon 77% and Merlot 17%.

Château Canterane (Fr) a vineyard. (Add): Saint-Étienne-de-Lisse, 33330 Saint-Émilion. Grand Cru. A.C. Saint-Émilion. (Com): Saint-Étienne-de-Lisse. 10ha. Grape varieties: Cabernet franc 20%, Cabernet sauvignon 20% and Merlot 60%.

Château Cantereau (Fr) a vineyard. (Com): Libourne. A.C. Pomerol, Bordeaux.

Château Cantin (Fr) a vineyard. (Com): Saint-Christophe-des-Bardes. A.C. Saint-Émilion, Bordeaux.

Château Canuet (Fr) a vineyard. (Add): Margaux 33460. Cru Bourgeois. A.C. Margaux. (Com): Margaux. 11ha. Grape varieties: Cabernet sauvignon 50% and Merlot 50%. Second wine is Château Dupeyron.

Château Capbern-Gasqueton (Fr) a Cru Bourgeois Exceptionnel. A.C. Saint-Estèphe. 36ha. Grape varieties: Cabernet franc 20%, Cabernet sauvignon 40% and Merlot 40%. Second wine is Grand Village Capbern.

Château Cap de Faugères (Fr) a 26ha vineyard in the A.C. Côtes de Castillon, Bordeaux.

Château Cap de Fouste (Fr) a vineyard in the A.C. Côtes du Roussillon, south-western France. Grape varieties: Carignan 30%, Grenache 66% and Syrah 4%.

Château Cap-de-Haut (Fr) a vineyard. (Com): Lamarque. A.C. Médoc, Bordeaux. Cru Bourgeois.

Château Cap de Mourlin (Fr) a vineyard. (Add): 33330 Saint-Émilion. Grand Cru Classé. A.C. Saint-Émilion. (Com): Saint-Émilion. 15.2ha. Grape varieties: Cabernet franc 25%, Cabernet sauvignon 12%, Malbec 3% and Merlot 60%.

Château Cap d'Or (Fr) a vineyard. (Com): Saint-Georges-Saint-Émilion. A.C. Saint-Émilion, Bordeaux 5ha.

Château Cap du Haut (Fr) a vineyard. (Com): Moulis. A.C. Moulis, Bordeaux 7ha.

Château Capendu (Fr) a vineyard. A.C. Corbières in Languedoc-Roussillon. Labels: Cuvée Eugénie and L'Excellence. 120ha.

Château Caperot (Fr) is part of Château Monbousquet in A.C. Saint-Émilion, Bordeaux.

Château Capet-Bégaud (Fr) a vineyard. (Com): Fronsac. A.C. Côtes de Canon-Fronsac, Bordeaux 3ha.

Château Capet-Guillier (Fr) a vineyard. (Add): Saint-Hippolyte, 33330 Saint-Émilion. Grand Cru. A.C. Saint-Émilion. (Com): Saint-Hippolyte. 15ha. Grape varieties: Cabernet franc 30%, Cabernet sauvignon 10% and Merlot 60%.

Château Capet Pailhas (Fr) a vineyard. (Com): Saint-Émilion. A.C. Saint-Émilion, Bordeaux.

Château Cap-Léon-Veyrin (Fr) a vineyard. (Add): Donissan, Listrac, Médoc, 33480 Castelnau, Médoc. Cru Bourgeois Supérieur. A.C. Listrac-Médoc. (Com): Listrac. 12ha. Grape varieties: Cabernet franc, Cabernet sauvignon, Merlot and Petit verdot.

Château Carbonnieux (Fr) a vineyard. (Add): 33850 Léognan. Grand Cru Classé. A.C. Pessac-Léognan. (Com): Léognan. 70ha. Grape varieties: Cabernet franc, Cabernet sauvignon, Malbec, Merlot, Muscadelle, Petit verdot, Sauvignon and Sémillon. Second wine is Château La Tour Léognan.

Château Carcanieux (Fr) a vineyard. (Add): Terres Hautes de Carcanieux, 33340, Queyrac (Lesparre). Cru Bourgeois. A.C. Médoc. (Com): Queyrac. 25ha. Grape varieties: Cabernet franc, Cabernet sauvignon and Merlot.

Château Cardinal Villemaurine (Fr) a vineyard. (Add): Place du Marcardieu, 33330 Saint-Émilion. Grand Cru. A.C. Saint-Émilion. (Com): Saint-Émilion. 30ha. Grape varieties: Cabernet 30% and Merlot 70%.

Château Careau-Matras (Fr) a vineyard. (Add): 33330 Saint-Émilion. Grand Cru. A.C. Saint-Émilion. (Com): Saint-Émilion. 15ha. Grape varieties: Cabernet franc 30%, Cabernet sauvignon 3% and Merlot 67%.

Château Carey-Potet (Fr) a vineyard based in the A.C. Montagny, Côte Chalonnaise, Burgundy. Label: Les Bassets.

Château Carignan (Fr) a vineyard in Carignan de Bordeaux. A.C. Premières Côtes de Bordeaux. 45ha. Grape varieties: Cabernet franc 10%, Cabernet sauvignon 25, Merlot 65%.

Château Carmes-Haut-Brion (Fr) a vineyard. (Com): Pessac. A.C. Graves, Bordeaux. 2ha (red).

Château Caronne-Sainte-Gemme (Fr) a vineyard. (Com): Saint Laurent. A.C. Haut-Médoc, Bordeaux. Cru Bourgeois Exceptionnel. Also as Château Caronne-Ste-Gemme. 36ha. Grape varieties: Cabernet sauvignon 60%, Merlot 30%, Petit verdot 10%.

Château Caronne-Ste-Gemme (Fr) see Château Caronne-Sainte-Gemme.

Château Carras (Gre) a red wine produced from a blend of Cabernet sauvignon and Limnio grapes by Domaine Porto Carras. see Domaine Carras.

Château Carruades Lafite (Fr) a vineyard (discontinued in 1967) the second growth of Château Lafite (Pauillac).

Château Carteau (Fr) a vineyard. (Add): 33330 Saint-Émilion. Grand Cru. A.C. Saint-Émilion. (Com): Saint-Émilion. 12ha. Grape varieties: Cabernet franc 30%, Cabernet sauvignon 20% and Merlot 50%.

Château Carteau-Bas-Daugay (Fr) a vineyard in the A.C. Saint-Émilion, Bordeaux 4ha.

Château Carteau-Côtes-Daugay (Fr) a vineyard. (Add): 33330 Saint-Émilion. Grand Cru. A.C. Saint-Émilion. (Com): Saint-Émilion. 12.5ha. Grape varieties: Cabernet franc 30%, Cabernet sauvignon 20% and Merlot 50%.

Château Carteau-Pin-de-Fleurs (Fr) a vineyard in the A.C. Saint-Émilion, Bordeaux 3ha.

Château Cartier (Can) a noted winery based south of Toronto.

Château Caruel (Fr) a vineyard. (Com): Bourg. A.C. Côtes de Bourg, Bordeaux.

C

Château Cassagne (Fr) a vineyard. (Com): St-Michel. A.C. Côtes Canon-Fronsac, Bordeaux 4ha.

Château Cassat (Fr) a vineyard. (Com): Puisseguin-Saint-Émilion. A.C. Puisseguin-Saint-Émilion, Bordeaux.

Château Cassevert (Fr) a part of Château Grand-Mayne, A.C. Saint-Émilion, Bordeaux.

Château Castel Viaud (Fr) a vineyard. (Com): Saint-Émilion. A.C. Saint-Émilion, Bordeaux.

Château Castéra (Fr) a vineyard. (Com): Cissac. A.C. Médoc, Bordeaux (47ha under vines). Grape varieties: Cabernet franc, Cabernet sauvignon and Merlot 40%. Cru Bourgeois.

Château Castéra (Fr) a vineyard. (Com): St-Germain-d'Esteuil. A.C. Médoc, Bordeaux 30ha.

Château Catalas (Fr) a vineyard. (Com): Pujols. A.C. Graves, Bordeaux. 6ha (white).

Château Caudiet (Fr) a vineyard. (Com): Loupiac. A.C. Loupiac, Bordeaux 10ha.

Château Cauzin (Fr) a vineyard in the A.C. Saint-Émilion, Bordeaux 4ha.

Château Cazal-Viel (Fr) an A.C. St. Chinian, a private estate that produces a range of wines.

Château Cazeau (Fr) a vineyard. (Com): Gomac. A.C. Entre-Deux-Mers, Bordeaux.

Château Cazeaux (Fr) a vineyard. (Com): St-Paul. A.C. Côtes de Blaye, Bordeaux.

Château Cazebonne (Fr) a vineyard. (Com): St-Pierre-de-Mons. A.C. Graves, Bordeaux. 7ha (white).

Château Certan-de-May (Fr) an A.C. Pomerol. Once part of the estate of Vieux Château Certan 4ha.

Château Certan-Giraud (Fr) a vineyard. (Com): Pomerol. A.C. Pomerol, Bordeaux 2ha.

Château Certan-Marzelle (Fr) a vineyard. (Com): Pomerol. A.C. Pomerol, Bordeaux 4ha.

Château Chadène (Fr) a vineyard. (Com): St-Aignan. A.C. Côtes de Fronsac, Bordeaux 6ha.

Château Chaillou (Fr) a vineyard. (Com): St-Paul. A.C. Côtes de Blaye, Bordeaux.

Château Chalon (Fr) an A.C. Château Chalon, Jura, a Vin Jaune, sold in a Clavelin bottle. Wine is attacked by Flor, aged in cask for 6 years. Produced from the Savagnin grape.

Château Chambert-Marbuzet (Fr) a vineyard. (Add): Saint-Estèphe 33250. Cru Bourgeois. A.C. Saint-Estèphe. (Com): Saint-Estèphe. 30ha. Grape varieties: Cabernet sauvignon 55% and Merlot 45%.

Château Champ de Grenet (Fr) an A.C. Bordeaux. Grape varieties: Cabernet franc, Cabernet sauvignon, Merlot. The second wine of Château la Croix de Grézard.

Château Champion (Fr) a vineyard. (Add): Saint-Christophe-des-Bardes, 33330 Saint-Émilion. Grand Cru. A.C. Saint-Émilion. (Com): Saint-Christophe-des-Bardes. Second wine of Château Vieux Grand Faurie 5ha.

Château Chante Alouette (Fr) a vineyard in the A.C. Côtes de Blaye, Bordeaux.

Château Chante-Alouette (Fr) a vineyard in the A.C. Saint-Émilion, Bordeaux 6ha.

Château Chantecaille (Fr) a vineyard in the A.C. Saint-Émilion, Bordeaux 3ha.

Château Chantegrive (Fr) an A.C. Graves. 60ha. Grape varieties: Cabernet franc, Cabernet sauvignon, Merlot, Muscadelle, Sauvignon and Sémillon 5ha.

Château Chantegrive (Fr) a vineyard. (Com): Saint-Émilion. A.C. Saint-Émilion, Bordeaux.

Château Chantelet (Fr) is part of Château Larques, A.C. Saint-Émilion, Bordeaux.

Château Chanteloisseau (Fr) a vineyard. (Add): 33210 Langon. A.C. Graves. (Com): Langon. 20ha. Grape varieties: Cabernet sauvignon and Sauvignon.

Château Chanteloup (Fr) an A.C. Bordeaux blanc sec from Haux, Gironde.

Château Chantelys (Fr) a vineyard. (Com): Prignac. A.C. Médoc, Bordeaux 4ha.

Château Chapelle Madelaine (Fr) a vineyard. (Add): 33330 Saint-Émilion. Grand Cru. A.C. Saint-Émilion. (Com): Saint-Émilion 1ha.

Château Charmail (Fr) a vineyard. (Com): Saint-Seurin-de-Cadourne. A.C. Saint-Estèphe, Bordeaux. Cru Bourgeois 22ha.

Château Charron (Fr) a vineyard. (Com): St-Martin. A.C. Côtes de Blaye, Bordeaux. 30ha. Grape varieties: Sauvignon and Sémillon.

Château Charron les Gruppes (Fr) a vineyard in the A.C. Premières Côtes de Blaye, Bordeaux. Grape varieties: Cabernet sauvignon 10%, Merlot 90%.

Château Chasselauds (Fr) a vineyard. (Com): Cartelègue. A.C. Côtes de Blaye, Bordeaux.

Château Chasse-Spleen (Fr) a Cru Bourgeois Exceptionnel. A.C. Moulis. 75ha. Grape varieties: Cabernet sauvignon, Merlot and Petit verdot. Second label is L'Hermitage de Chasse-Spleen.

Château Chatain (Fr) a vineyard. (Com): Néac. A.C. Pomerol, Bordeaux.

Château Châteaufort de Vauban (Fr) a vineyard. (Com): Cussac-Fort-Médoc. A.C. Haut-Médoc, Bordeaux 3ha.

Château Chauvin (Fr) a vineyard. (Add): 137 Rue Doumer, Libourne 33500. Grand Cru Classé. A.C. Saint-Émilion. (Com): Saint-Émilion. 13ha. Grape varieties: Cabernet franc 30%, Cabernet sauvignon 10% and Merlot 60%.

Château Chaviran (Fr) a vineyard. (Com): Martillac. A.C. Graves, Bordeaux. 4ha (red).

Château Chayne (Fr) a vineyard in the A.C. Côtes de Bergerac. (Add): 17 Rue Millet, 24100 Bergerac (red and white).

Château Chêne Liège (Fr) a vineyard. (Com): Pomerol. A.C. Pomerol, Bordeaux.

Château Chênevert (Fr) a vineyard based in the commune of Mérignac, Bordeaux 5ha.

Château Chêne Vieux (Fr) a vineyard. (Com): Puisseguin-Saint-Émilion. A.C. Puisseguin-Saint-Émilion, Bordeaux 8ha.

Château Cheval Blanc (Fr) a vineyard. (Add): 33330 Saint-Émilion. Premier [A] Grand Cru Classé (A). A.C. Saint-Émilion. (Com): Saint-Émilion. 36ha. Grape varieties: Cabernet franc, Malbec and Merlot. *See also* Cheval des Andes.

Château Cheval-Brun (Fr) a vineyard in the A.C. Saint-Émilion, Bordeaux 5ha.

C

Château Chevalier (USA) a winery near St. Helena in the Napa Valley, California. 25ha. Produces table wines from the Cabernet sauvignon, Chardonnay and Johannisberg riesling grapes.

Château Chevaliers d'Ars (Fr) a wine co-operative in the commune of Arcins. A.C. Haut-Médoc, Bordeaux 25ha.

Château Cheval Noir (Fr) a vineyard. (Com): Saint-Émilion. A.C. Saint-Émilion Grand Cru, Bordeaux. Grape varieties: Cabernet franc, Cabernet sauvignon and Merlot. 3ha. Also known as Cheval Noir. Second wine Le Fer. Owned by Mahler-Bresse. Website: http://www.mahler-bresse.com 'E'mail: contact@mahler-bresse.com

Château Chevrol Bel-Air (Fr) a vineyard. (Com): Néac. A.C. Pomerol, Bordeaux.

Château Chicane (Fr) a vineyard. (Com): Toulenne. A.C. Graves, Bordeaux. 3ha (red and white).

Château Chichoye (Fr) a vineyard. (Com): Loupiac. A.C. Loupiac, Bordeaux 2ha.

Château Ciceron (Fr) a vineyard in the A.C. Corbières, south-western France. Label: L'Orangerie du XIXème.

Château Cissac (Fr) a vineyard. (Add): 33250 Pauillac. Cru Bourgeois Exceptionnel. A.C. Haut-Médoc. (Com): Cissac. Grape varieties: Cabernet, Merlot and Petit verdot 26ha.

Château Citran (Fr) a vineyard. (Add): 33480 Avensac. Cru Bourgeois Exceptionnel. A.C. Haut-Médoc. (Com): Avensan. 90ha. Grape varieties: Cabernet sauvignon 40% and Merlot 60%. Second wine is Château Moulins de Citran.

Château Clairac (Fr) a vineyard in the A.C. Côtes de Blaye, Bordeaux.

Château Clairfont (Fr) a vineyard. (Com): Margaux. A.C. Margaux, Bordeaux 8ha.

Château Clare (Austr) a vineyard estate in Clare-Watervale, South Australia. Owned by Taylors.

Château Clarke (Fr) a vineyard. (Add): 33480 Listrac-Médoc. Cru Bourgeois. A.C. Listrac. (Com): Listrac. 53ha. Grape varieties: Cabernet franc, Cabernet sauvignon, Merlot and Petit verdot. Second wine is Granges de Clarke.

Château Clauss (Gre) a red wine produced by the Achaia Clauss Winery of Patras, made with the Mavroutis grape.

Château Clauzet (Fr) a Cru Bourgeois Supérieur vineyard. (Com): Saint-Estèphe. A.C. Saint-Estèphe, Bordeaux 3ha.

Château Clément-Pichon (Fr) a Cru Bourgeois from Parempuyre, Médoc. A.C. Haut-Médoc.

Château Clerc Milon (Fr) a vineyard. (Add): 33250 Pauillac. Grand Cru Classé (5th). A.C. Pauillac. (Com): Pauillac. 30ha. Grape varieties: 10% Cabernet franc, 70% Cabernet sauvignon and 20% Merlot.

Château Climens (Fr) a Premier Grand Cru. A.C. Barsac. (or Sauternes). (Com): Barsac. 32ha. Grape variety: Sémillon 100%. Second wine is Cypres de Climens.

Château Clinet (Fr) a vineyard. (Com): Pomerol. A.C. Pomerol, Bordeaux 6ha.

Château Clos d'Amières (Fr) a vineyard. (Com): Cartelègue. A.C. Côtes de Blaye, Bordeaux.

Château Clos de Lacapère (Fr) a vineyard. (Com): Landiras. A.C. Graves, Bordeaux. 2ha (white).

Château Clos de la Tour Réserve (Fr) an A.C. Bordeaux Supérieur. Grape varieties: Cabernet franc 9%, Cabernet sauvingnon 15%, Merlot 75%, Petit verdot 1%.

Château Clos des Jacobins (Fr) an A.C. Saint-Émilion. see Clos des Jacobins.

Château Clos Figeac (Fr) a vineyard. (Add): 33330 Saint-Émilion. Grand Cru. A.C. Saint-Émilion. (Com): Saint-Émilion. 5ha. Grape varieties: Bouchet 25%, Cabernet sauvignon 15%, Merlot 60%.

Château Clos Fourtet (Fr) a vineyard. (Add): 33330 Saint-Émilion. A.C. Saint-Émilion. (Com): Saint-Émilion. Second wine is Domaine de Martialis.

Château Clos Haut-Peyraguey (Fr) a vineyard. (Com): Bommes. A.C. Sauternes, Bordeaux. (Add): 33210 Langon.

Château Closiot (Fr) a vineyard. (Com): Barsac. A.C. Barsac (or Sauternes), Bordeaux 5ha.

Château Clos Jean (Fr) a vineyard. (Com): Loupiac. A.C. Loupiac, Bordeaux 12ha.

Château Clos l'Église (Fr) a vineyard. (Com): Pomerol. A.C. Pomerol, Bordeaux.

Château Clos René (Fr) a vineyard. (Com): Pomerol. A.C. Pomerol, Bordeaux.

Château Clotte (Fr) a vineyard. (Add): 33330 Saint-Émilion. Grand Cru. A.C. Saint-Émilion. (Com): Saint-Émilion.

Château Colbert (Fr) a vineyard. (Com): Comps. A.C. Côtes de Bourg, Bordeaux.

Château Colombey (Fr) a vineyard in the A.C. Entre-Deux-Mers (white).

Château Colombier Monpelou (Fr) a vineyard. (Add): 33250 Pauillac. Cru Grand Bourgeois. A.C. Pauillac. (Com): Pauillac. 14ha. Grape varieties: Cabernet franc, Cabernet sauvignon, Merlot and Petit verdot. Second wine is Château Grand Canyon.

Château Combebelle (Fr) an A.C. Saint Chinian in Languedoc-Roussillon.

Château Commarque (Fr) a vineyard. (Com): Sauternes. A.C. Sauternes, Bordeaux 4ha.

Château Comte des Cordes (Fr) a vineyard. (Add): 33330 Saint-Émilion. (Com): Saint-Émilion. Second wine of Château Fonrazade. Grand Cru. Saint-Émilion.

Château Conseillant (Fr) a vineyard. (Com): Labarde. A.C. Médoc, Bordeaux.

Château Conseillante (Fr) a vineyard. (Com): Pomerol. A.C. Pomerol, Bordeaux.

Château Constant-Trois-Moulins (Fr) a vineyard. (Com): Macau. A.C. Haut-Médoc, Bordeaux. Cru Bourgeois.

Château Corbin (Fr) a vineyard. (Add): 33330 Saint-Émilion. Grand Cru. A.C. Saint-Émilion. (Com): Montagne-Saint-Émilion 13ha.

Château Corbin-Michotte (Fr) a vineyard. (Add): 33330 Saint-Émilion. Grand Cru Classé. A.C. Saint-Émilion. (Com): Saint-Émilion. 7.6ha.

C

Grape varieties: Cabernet franc 30%, Cabernet sauvignon 5% and Merlot 65%.

Château Corconnac (Fr) a vineyard. (Com): Saint Laurent. A.C. Médoc, Bordeaux. Cru Bourgeois.

Château Cormeil-Figeac (Fr) a vineyard. (Add): 33330 Saint-Émilion. Grand Cru. A.C. Saint-Émilion. (Com): Saint-Émilion. 20ha. Grape varieties: Bouchet 30% and Merlot 70%. Second wine is Château Magnan-Figeac. Grand Cru Saint-Émilion.

Château Cormey Figeac (Fr) a vineyard. (Com): Saint-Émilion. A.C. Saint-Émilion 10ha.

Château Corton Grancey (Fr) a Grand Cru. A.C. Corton. Côte de Beaune, Burgundy. Owned by Louis Latour, it is allowed to sell his wines under this name as he had done so before A.C. laws were introduced.

Château Cos d'Estournel (Fr) a vineyard. (Add): Saint-Estèphe 33250 Pauillac. Grand Cru Classé (2nd). A.C. Saint-Estèphe. (Com): Saint-Estèphe. 70ha. Grape varieties: Cabernet sauvignon 60% and Merlot 40%. Second wine is Château Marbuzet.

Château Cos-Labory (Fr) a vineyard. (Add): Saint-Estèphe, 33250 Pauillac. Grand Cru Classé (5th). A.C. Saint-Estèphe. (Com): Saint-Estèphe. 27ha. Grape varieties: Cabernet franc, Cabernet sauvignon, Merlot and Petit verdot.

Château Côte de Baleau (Fr) a vineyard. (Add): 33330 Saint-Émilion. Grand Cru. A.C. Saint-Émilion. (Com): Saint-Émilion. 27ha. Grape varieties: Cabernet franc 16%, Cabernet sauvignon 16% and Merlot 66%.

Château Côte de Bonde (Fr) a vineyard. (Com): Montagne-Saint-Émilion. A.C. Saint-Émilion, Bordeaux 7ha.

Château Côte de Rol-Valentin (Fr) a vineyard in the A.C. Saint-Émilion, Bordeaux 3ha.

Château Côte-Mignon-la-Gaffelière (Fr) a vineyard in the A.C. Saint-Émilion, Bordeaux 1ha.

Château Côte Montpezat (Fr) a vineyard in the Côtes de Castillon, Bordeaux. Grape varieties: Cabernet franc 20%, Cabernet sauvingnon 10%, Merlot 70%.

Château Côtes Bernateau (Fr) a vineyard. (Add): Saint-Étienne-de-Lisse, 33330 Saint-Émilion. Grand Cru. A.C. Saint-Émilion. (Com): Saint-Étienne-de-Lisse. 18ha. Grape varieties: Bouchet 25%, Cabernet sauvignon 6%, Merlot 65% and Pressac 4%.

Château Côtes de Blaignan [Cru Hontane] (Fr) a vineyard. (Com): Blaignan. A.C. Médoc, Bordeaux 5ha.

Château Cottière (Fr) a vineyard. (Com): Teuillac. A.C. Côtes de Bourg, Bordeaux.

Château Coubet (Fr) a vineyard in the A.C. Côtes de Bourg, Bordeaux.

Château Coucheroy (Fr) the second label of Château La Louvière.

Château Coucy (Fr) a vineyard. (Com): Montagne-Saint-Émilion. A.C. Saint-Émilion, Bordeaux 11ha.

Château Coudert (Fr) a vineyard in the A.C. Saint-Émilion, Bordeaux 3ha.

Château Coudert-Pelletan (Fr) a vineyard. (Add): Saint-Christophe-des-Bardes, 33330 Saint-Émilion. Grand Cru. A.C. Saint-Émilion. (Com): Saint-Christophe-des-Bardes. 6ha. Grape varieties: Cabernet franc 15%, Cabernet sauvignon 15%, Malbec 10% and Merlot 60%.

Château Coufran (Fr) a vineyard. (Add): St-Seurin-de-Cadourne, 33250 Pauillac. Cru Grand Bourgeois. A.C. Haut-Médoc. (Com): St-Seurin-de-Cadourne. 64ha. Grape varieties: Cabernet sauvignon 15% and Merlot 85%.

Château Couhins-Lurton (Fr) a vineyard. (Add): Léognan 33850. Grand Cru Classé. A.C. Pessac-Léognan. (Com): Villenave d'Ornon. 1.75ha. Grape variety: Sauvignon blanc.

Château Coujan (Fr) a vineyard in the A.C. Saint Chinian. Grape varieties: Grenache, Mourvèdre, Syrah. Label: Cuvée Bois Joli.

Château Coullac (Fr) a vineyard. (Com): Sainte-Croix-du-Mont. A.C. Sainte-Croix-du-Mont, Bordeaux 5ha.

Château Couloumet (Fr) a vineyard. (Com): Loupiac. A.C. Loupiac, Bordeaux 5ha.

Château Couperie (Fr) a vineyard. (Com): Saint-Émilion. A.C. Saint-Émilion, Bordeaux.

Château Coupe Roses (Fr) a vineyard in the A.C. Minervois, Languedoc-Roussillon. Grape varieties: Carignan, Grenache, Mourvèdre and Syrah. Label: Les Plots.

Château Courac (Fr) a vineyard in the village of Tresques, A.C. Côtes-du-Rhône

Château Courant (Fr) a vineyard. (Com): Arcins. A.C. Médoc, Bordeaux.

Château Courant-Barrow (Fr) a vineyard. (Com): Arcins. A.C. Médoc, Bordeaux. Cru Bourgeois.

Château Court les Muts (Fr) a vineyard in the A.C. Bergerac (white and red).

Château Coustet (Fr) a vineyard. (Com): Barsac. A.C. Barsac (or Sauternes), Bordeaux 6ha.

Château Coustolle (Fr) a vineyard. (Com): Fronsac. A.C. Côtes Canon-Fronsac, Bordeaux 12ha.

Château Coutelin-Merville (Fr) a vineyard. (Com): Saint-Estèphe. A.C. Saint-Estèphe, Bordeaux 11ha.

Château Coutelor la Romarine (Fr) a vineyard in the A.C. Ste-Foy Bordeaux. Grape varieties: Cabernet franc 10%, Cabernet sauvingnon 10%, Merlot 80%.

Château Coutet (Fr) a vineyard. (Com): Barsac. A.C. Barsac (or Sauternes), Bordeaux. 70ha. Grape varieties: Muscadelle 10%, Sauvignon 20% and Sémillon 70%. A Premier Grand Cru. Separated from Château d'Yquem in 1922.

Château Coutet (Fr) a vineyard. (Add): 33330 Saint-Émilion. Grand Cru. A.C. Saint-Émilion. 11ha. Grape varieties: Bouchet 45%, Cabernet sauvignon 5%, Malbec 3%, Merlot 45% and Pressac 2%.

Château Couvent-des-Jacobins (Fr) see Couvent-des-Jacobins.

Château Crabitey (Fr) a vineyard. (Com): Portets. A.C. Graves, Bordeaux. 15ha (red and white).

Château Cravignac (Fr) a vineyard. (Add): 33330 Saint-Émilion. A.C. Saint-Émilion. (Com): Saint-Émilion. 8ha. Grape varieties: Cabernet franc 35% and Merlot 65%.

C

Château Cremade (Fr) an A.C. wine based in Le Tholonet.

Château Croix-de-Justice (Fr) a vineyard. (Com): Puisseguin-Saint-Émilion. A.C. Saint-Émilion. Bordeaux 5ha.

Château Croix-du-Merle (Fr) a vineyard in the A.C. Saint-Émilion, Bordeaux 3ha.

Château Croix-Figeac (Fr) a vineyard in the A.C. Saint-Émilion, Bordeaux 3ha.

Château Croix-Peyblanquet (Fr) a vineyard in the A.C. Saint-Émilion, Bordeaux 4ha.

Château Croix-Villemaurine (Fr) a vineyard in the A.C. Saint-Émilion, Bordeaux 1ha.

Château Croizet-Bages (Fr) a Grand Cru Classé (5th). A.C. Pauillac. (Com): Pauillac. 25ha. Grape varieties: Cabernet franc, Cabernet sauvignon and Merlot. Second wine is Enclos de Monabon.

Château Croque-Michotte (Fr) a vineyard. (Add): 33330 Saint-Émilion. Grand Cru. A.C. Saint-Émilion. (Com): Saint-Émilion. 14ha. Grape varieties: Cabernet franc 10%, Cabernet sauvignon 10% and Merlot 80%.

Château Croûte-Charlus (Fr) a vineyard. (Com): Bourg. A.C Côtes de Bourg, Bordeaux. Cru Bourgeois.

Château Croûte-Mallard (Fr) a vineyard. (Com): Bourg. A.C. Côtes de Bourg, Bordeaux.

Château Cru Cantemerle (Fr) an A.C. Bordeaux Supérieur. Grape varieties: Cabernet franc 20%, Cabernet sauvingnon, Malbec and Petit verdot 12%, Merlot 88%.

Château Cru du Gravier (Fr) a vineyard. (Com): Arsac. A.C. Haut-Médoc, Bordeaux 4ha.

Château Cruscaut (Fr) a vineyard. (Com): Saint Laurent. A.C. Médoc, Bordeaux. Cru Bourgeois.

Château Crusquet de Lagarcie (Fr) a vineyard. (Com): Cars. A.C. Côtes de Blaye, Bordeaux.

Château Crusquet Sabourin (Fr) a vineyard. (Com): Cars. A.C. Côtes de Blaye, Bordeaux.

Château Cruzeau (Fr) a vineyard. (Com): St-Médard-d'Eyrans. A.C. Graves, Bordeaux. 47ha (red and white).

Château Cup (Cup) 1 bottle red Claret, 1 bottle soda water, 1 measure Cognac, 1 measure Cointreau, 2 dashes gomme syrup. Stir over ice in a mixing glass, dress with sliced lemon and cucumber.

Château Curé-Bon-la-Madeleine (Fr) a vineyard. (Add): 33330 Saint-Émilion. Grand Cru. A.C. Saint-Émilion. (Com): Saint-Émilion. 5ha. Grape varieties: Cabernet franc 10%, Malbec 10% and Merlot 80%. Now part of Château Canon.

Château Curson (Fr) a vineyard in the A.C. Crozes-Hermitage.

Château Cusseau (Fr) a vineyard. (Com): Macau. A.C. Haut-Médoc, Bordeaux. Cru Bourgeois.

Château d'Aganac (Fr) a vineyard. (Com): Ludon. A.C. Haut-Médoc, Bordeaux. 30ha. Grape varieties: Cabernet franc, Cabernet sauvignon and Merlot.

Château d'Agassac (Fr) a vineyard. (Com): Ludon. A.C. Haut-Médoc, Bordeaux. 34.8ha. Cru Bourgeois Exceptionnel.

Château d'Aiguihle (Fr) a 36ha estate of Côtes de Castillon. Planted with 80% Merlot, 10% Cabernet franc, 10% Cabernet sauvignon. Label: Comtes de Neipperg.

Château Dalem (Fr) a vineyard in A.C. Fronsac. 15ha. Grape varieties: 85% Merlot, 10% Cabernet franc, 5% Cabernet sauvignon.

Château d'Anchon (Arg) the brand-name of a dry white wine.

Château d'Anglès (Fr) a vineyard based in the A.C. La Clape, Coteaux du Languedoc.

Château d'Angludet (Fr) a vineyard. (Add): 33460 Cantenac. Cru Bourgeois Exceptionnel. (Com): Cantenac. 75ha. Grape varieties: Cabernet franc, Cabernet sauvignon, Merlot and Petit verdot. Second label is Baury.

Château d'Anice (Fr) a vineyard. (Com): Podensac. A.C. Cérons, Bordeaux 12ha.

Château d'Anseillan (Fr) a vineyard. (Com): Pauillac. A.C. Haut-Médoc, Bordeaux. Cru Bourgeois.

Château d'Aquéria (Fr) a vineyard in A.C. Tavel, southern Rhône. (Add): 30126 Tavel. Also produces A.C. Lirac. The label of the Société Civile Agricole Producteurs à Tavel.

Château d'Arbanats (Fr) a vineyard. (Com): Arbanats. A.C. Graves, Bordeaux. 6ha (white).

Château d'Arboras (Fr) a vineyard in A.C. Saint-Saturnin, Languedoc, southern France (red).

Château d'Archambeau (Fr) a vineyard in A.C. Graves, Bordeaux. Grape varieties: Cabernet sauvignon 50%, Merlot 50%.

Château d'Arche (Fr) a Cru Bourgeois Supérieur vineyard. (Add): 33290 Ludon, Médoc. A.C. Haut-Médoc. (Com): Ludon. 9ha. Grape varieties: Cabernet franc 5%, Cabernet sauvignon 45%, Carmenere 5%, Merlot 40%, Petit verdot 5%.

Château d'Arche (Fr) a Grand Cru (2nd). A.C. Sauternes. (Com): Sauternes. Grape varieties: Sauvignon 15%, Sémillon 80% and Muscadelle 5%. Second label is Château d'Arche Lafaurie.

Château d'Arche-Lafaurie (Fr) a Grand Cru Classé (2nd). A.C. Sauternes. (Com): Sauternes. 19ha. Second label of Château d'Arche.

Château d'Arche Pugneau (Fr) a vineyard. (Com): Preignac. A.C. Sauternes, Bordeaux.

Château d'Arches (Fr) a vineyard. (Com): Ludon. A.C. Haut-Médoc, Bordeaux 4ha.

Château d'Arches (Fr) a vineyard. (Com): Sauternes. A.C. Sauternes, Bordeaux. 15ha (also Château Lamothe).

Château d'Arche-Vimeney (Fr) a vineyard. (Com): Sauternes. A.C. Sauternes, Bordeaux 5ha. Grand Cru Classé vineyard. (Com): Arcins. A.C. Haut-Médoc, Bordeaux. Cru Bourgeois.

Château d'Ardennes (Fr) an A.C. Graves, at Illats, Gironde. 60ha (red and white).

Château d'Ardolou (Fr) a vineyard in the A.C. Corbières. (Add): Ribaute, 31200 Lézignan-Corbières.

Château d'Arlay (Fr) a vineyard in the A.C. Jura. Produces the famous Vin Jaune and Vin de Paille wines from Savagnin. Also Côtes du Jura red from 100% Pinot noir and a rosé from 50%–60% Pinot

C

noir, 35%–40% Trousseau, 5% Chardonnay and Savagnin.

Château d'Armailhacq (Fr) an A.C. Pauillac. (5th) Cru Classé. 57ha. Grape varieties: 50% Cabernet sauvignon, 25% Merlot, 23% Cabernet franc, 2% Petit verdot. Sold as Château Mouton d'Armailhacq until 1956, Château Mouton-Baron Philippe until 1975, Château Mouton Baronne Philippe until 1991.

Château d'Armajan-des-Ormes (Fr) a vineyard. (Com): Preignac. A.C. Sauternes, Bordeaux 7ha.

Château d'Armens (Fr) an A.C. Saint-Émilion. Second wine of Château Bonnet. Grand Cru. Saint-Émilion.

Château d'Arnauld (Fr) a vineyard. (Com): Arcins. A.C. Médoc, Bordeaux. Cru Bourgeois.

Château d'Arpayé (Fr) an A.C. Fleurie. Cru Beaujolais-Villages, Burgundy. 15ha. (Add): 69820 Fleurie.

Château d'Arrichaud (Fr) an A.C. Graves, Landiras, Gironde (red and white).

Château d'Arsac (Fr) a vineyard. (Com): Arsac. A.C. Médoc, Bordeaux. Cru Bourgeois.

Château d'Arthus (Fr) a vineyard in the A.C. Saint-Émilion, Bordeaux 4ha.

Château Dassault (Fr) a vineyard. (Add): 33330 Saint-Émilion. Grand Cru Classé. A.C. Saint-Émilion. (Com): Saint-Émilion. 30ha. Grape varieties: Cabernet franc 35%, Cabernet sauvignon 5% and Merlot 60%. Website: http://www.chateaudassault.com 'E'mail: lbv@chateaudassault.com

Château d'Augey (Fr) a vineyard. (Com): Bommes. A.C. Sauternes, Bordeaux.

Château Dauphiné Rondillon (Fr) a vineyard. (Com): Loupiac. A.C. Loupiac, Bordeaux 15ha. produces Cuvée d'Or (botrytised sweet).

Château d'Auros (Fr) a vineyard in the A.C. Graves, Bordeaux.

Château d'Aussières (Fr) a vineyard in the A.C. Corbières, south-western France, owned by Rothshild.

Château Dauzac (Fr) a vineyard. (Add): Labarde, Margaux 33460. Grand Cru Classé (5th). A.C. Margaux. (Com): Margaux. 40ha. Grape varieties: Cabernet franc, Cabernet sauvignon, Merlot and Petit verdot. Second wine is Château Labarde.

Château d'Avallrich (Fr) a vineyard in the Côtes du Roussillon, south-western France. (Add): 33270 Floirac.

Château David (Fr) a vineyard. (Add): Vensac 33590 St. Vivien de Médoc. A.C. Médoc. (Com): Vensac. 10ha. Grape varieties: Cabernet sauvignon 75% and Merlot 25%.

Château d'Aÿ (Fr) the Château of the Grand Marque Champagne house of Ayala.

Château d'Aydie (Fr) an A.C. Madiran wine produced from old vines and aged 1 year in new oak. Also produces A.C. Pacherenc-de-Vic-Bilh.

Château de Barbe (Fr) a vineyard. (Com): Villeneuve. A.C. Côtes de Bourg, Bordeaux 61.5ha.

Château de Basque (Fr) a vineyard in the A.C. Saint-Émilion, Bordeaux 3ha.

Château de Bastard (Fr) a vineyard. (Com): Barsac. A.C. Barsac (or Sauternes), Bordeaux.

Château de Beaucastel (Fr) a vineyard in the A.C. Châteauneuf-du-Pape, southern Rhône 72ha. Produced by Perrin (Francois), Courthézon, southern Rhône. Produces Les Sens de Syrah.

Château Beauchêne (Fr) a vineyard in the A.C. Côtes-du-Rhône.

Château de Beaulieu (Fr) a winery based in the A.C. Coteaux d'Aix en Provence, south-eastern France. Produces a range of red, rosé and white wines.

Château de Beaulieu (Fr) an A.C. Bordeaux rouge. (Add): 33540 Sauveterre-de-Guyenne, Bordeaux.

Château de Beaulieu (Fr) an A.C. Cabernet d'Anjou rosé from the Anjou-Saumur, Loire.

Château de Beaulieu (Fr) an A.C. Côtes-du-Rhône produced by Caves Saint Pierre under the 'La Majeure' label.

Château de Beaulieu (Fr) a winery based in the A.C. Montagne-Saint-Émilion, Bordeaux.

Château de Beaulieu (Fr) a red wine from the Coteaux du Languedoc, south-western France.

Château de Beaulon (Fr) a noted Pineau des Charentes from the Cognac region, western France.

Château de Beaune (Fr) the name for the cellars of négociants-éleveurs Bouchard Père et Fils, Burgundy.

Château de Beauregard (Fr) an A.C. Bordeaux blanc.

Château de Bel Air (Fr) a vineyard. (Com): Lalande de Pomerol. A.C. Pomerol, Bordeaux.

Château de Belle Coste (Fr) a domaine in the A.C. Costières de Nîmes, Languedoc-Roussillon. Produces white A.C. wine from 90% Roussanne and 10% Grenache blanc grapes. Also red wine from Merlot grapes.

Château de Bellet (Fr) a vineyard in the A.C. Bellet, Provence, south-eastern France, one of only two growers. *see* Château de Crémat.

Château de Bellevue (Fr) a vineyard in the A.C. Morgon. Cru Beaujolais-Villages, Burgundy. (Add): Côte de Py, Morgon (now known as the Château des Lumières).

Château de Bellevue (Fr) a vineyard. (Com): Lussac-Saint-Émilion. A.C. Lussac-Saint-Émilion, Bordeaux.

Château de Bensée (Fr) a vineyard in the A.C. Médoc, Bordeaux.

Château de Béranger (Fr) a V.D.Q.S. vineyard of Picpoul de Pinet, Languedoc.

Château de Berne (Fr) a vineyard in the A.C. Côtes de Provence, south-eastern France. Grape varieties: Cabernet sauvignon, Grenache, Syrah. Label: Cuvée Speciale.

Château de Bertranon (Fr) a vineyard. (Com): Sainte-Croix-du-Mont. A.C. Sainte-Croix-du-Mont, Bordeaux 2ha.

Château de Berzé (Fr) a vineyard in the Mâcon, Burgundy. Produces A.C. Mâcon Supérieur.

Château de Besseuil (Fr) a vineyard in Clessé, Mâconnais. Wine is sometimes attacked by botrytis.

C

Château de Beychade (Fr) a vineyard in the A.C. Côtes de Bourg, Bordeaux.

Château de Bligny (Fr) a champagne producer (propriétaire-récoltant). (Add): 10200, Bligny. Produces vintage and non-vintage wines includinding a blanc de blancs. Grape varieties Chardonnay and Pinot noir.

Château de Blissa (Fr) a vineyard. (Com): Bayon. A.C. Côtes de Bourg, Bordeaux.

Château de Blomac (Fr) a vineyard in the A.C. Minervois. (Add): 11700 Capendu. (red, rosé and white).

Château de Bluizard (Fr) a vineyard in the A.C. Beaujolais-Villages, Burgundy.

Château de Bord (Fr) a winery based in the A.C. Côtes-du-Rhône-Villages Laudun, Vaucluse. Owned by Charles Brotte. Website: http://www.brotte.com 'E'mail: export@brotte.com

Château de Bordeneuve (Fr) an Armagnac producer based in the Bas Armagnac, Gers. Produces a range of Armagnacs.

Château de Boursault (Fr) a vineyard. (Add): 51480 près d'Épernay. A Champagne producer. 16ha. Produces vintage and non-vintage brut and brut rosé. Originally owned by the Veuve Clicquot.

Château de Bousquet (Fr) a vineyard. (Com): Bourg. A.C. Côtes de Bourg, Bordeaux.

Château de Breuil (Fr) a vineyard in the A.C. Coteaux du Layon, Anjou-Saumur, Loire.

Château de Breuilh (Fr) a vineyard. (Com): Cissac. A.C. Médoc, Bordeaux. Cru Bourgeois.

Château de Brézé (Fr) a vineyard in the A.C. Saumur, Anjou-Saumur, Loire. (Add): 19260 Brézé.

Château de Brochon (Fr) a vineyard in the A.C. Haut-Médoc, Bordeaux.

Château de Brugnac (Fr) an A.C. Bordeaux Supérieur.

Château de Budos (Fr) a vineyard. (Com): Budos. A.C. Graves, Bordeaux. 9ha (red).

Château de Bussy (Fr) a vineyard in the A.C. Beaujolais-Villages, Burgundy.

Château de By (Fr) a vineyard. (Add): Bégadan, 33340 Lesparre. Cru Bourgeois. A.C. Médoc. (Com): Bégadan. 30ha. Grape varieties: Cabernet franc 10%, Cabernet sauvignon 30%, Merlot 40% and Petit verdot 20%.

Château de Cabriac (Fr) a vineyard in the A.C. Corbières, Languedoc, south-western France.

Château de Cach (Fr) a vineyard. (Com): Saint Laurent. A.C. Médoc, Bordeaux. Cru Bourgeois.

Château de Cadillac (Fr) an A.C. Bordeaux.

Château de Caiz (Fr) a vineyard in the A.C. Cahors, south-western France. (Add): Côtes d'Olt, Parnac, Lot.

Château de Calissanne (Fr) a vineyard. (Add): 13680, Lancon de Provence. A.C. Coteaux d'Aix-en-Provence.

Château Camarsac (Fr) an A.C. Bordeaux Supérieur. Grape varieties: Cabernet franc 2%, Cabernet sauvignon 46%, Merlot 52%.

Château de Camensac (Fr) see Château Camensac.

Château de Campuget (Fr) a vineyard in the A.C. Costières de Nîmes.

Château de Candale (Fr) an A.C. Haut-Médoc. Second wine of Château d'Issan.

Château de Candale (Fr) a vineyard based in Saint-Laurent-des-Combes. Grand Cru. A.C. Saint-Émilion. (Com): Saint-Émilion. Grape varieties: Cabernet franc, Malbec, Merlot.

Château de Cantenac Prieuré (Fr) see Château Prieuré Lichine.

Château de Capitol La Clape (Fr) a vineyard in the A.C. Coteaux de Languedoc, southern France. Label: Les Rocailles (rosé).

Château de Caraguilhes (Fr) a vineyard in the A.C. Corbières, south-western France. (Add): St. Laurent de la Cabrerisse, 11220 Legrasse. Grape varieties: Carignan, Grenache, Syrah. Produces organic wines. Labels: Le Jardin de Galatée and Solus.

Château de Cardaillan (Fr) a vineyard. (Add): Toulenne 33210 Langon. A.C. Graves. (Com): Toulenne. 50ha. Grape varieties: Cabernet sauvignon 80%, Merlot 20%, Sauvignon 90% and Sémillon 10%.

Château de Carignan (Fr) a vineyard. (Com): Carignan. A.C. Premières Côtes de Bordeaux. (Add): 33360 Latresne. 110ha. Grape varieties: Cabernet franc 25%, Merlot 50% and Sauvignon 25%.

Château de Carles (Fr) a vineyard. (Com): Barsac. A.C. Barsac (or Sauternes), Bordeaux 6ha.

Château de Carles (Fr) a vineyard. (Com): Fronsac. A.C. Côtes de Fronsac, Bordeaux.

Château de Carrasset (Fr) a vineyard. (Com): Lamarque. A.C. Médoc, Bordeaux. Cru Bourgeois.

Château de Castegens (Fr) a vineyard in the A.C. Côtes de Castillon. (Add): Belves de Castillon.

Château de Castex (Fr) an Armagnac producer, produces dated Armagnacs including a 14 y.o. 46% alc by vol.

Château de Cayrou (Fr) a vineyard in the A.C. Cahors, south-western France. Grape varieties: Auxerrois, Jurançon, Merlot and Tannat.

Château de Cazeneuve (Fr) a 15ha vineyard in the A.C. Coteaux du Languedoc Pic Saint-Loup. Grape varieties: Syrah, Grenache, Carignan, Mourvèdre, Roussanne, Grenache blanc.

Château de Cérons (Fr) a vineyard. (Com): Cérons. A.C. Cérons, Bordeaux. 15ha. Grape varieties: Sauvignon blanc and Sémillon.

Château de Chaintres (Fr) a vineyard in the A.C. Saumur-Champigny, Anjou-Saumur, Loire. (Add): Dampierre-sur-Loire. (red, rosé and white).

Château de Chambert (Fr) a vineyard in the A.C. Cahors, south-western France.

Château de Chamboureau (Fr) a vineyard in the A.C. Savennières. Anjou-Saumur, Loire.

Château de Champagny (Fr) a V.D.Q.S. vineyard in the Côtes Roannaises, western France. Grape variety: Gamay. (red and rosé).

Château de Chantegrive (Fr) a vineyard. (Add): Domaine de Chantegrive, Podensac 33720. A.C. Graves. (Com): Podensac. 80ha. Grape varieties: Cabernet franc, Cabernet sauvignon, Merlot, Muscadelle, Sauvignon and Sémillon.

C

Château de Chasseloir (Fr) a vineyard in A.C. Muscadet Sèvre et Maine, Nantais, Loire. (Add): 44690 St-Fiacre-sur-Maine.

Château de Chatagnéréaz (Switz) a white wine produced in Rolle, La Côte, western Switzerland by Schenk.

Château de Chenas (Fr) a winery based in the A.C. Beaujolais Cru Moulin-à-Vent, southern Burgundy. Label: Selection de la Hante.

Château de Chenbonceau (Fr) a vineyard in the A.C. Touraine, Loire. (Add): Chenonceau, Touraine. (White and sparkling [méthode traditionelle] wines).

Château de Chorley (Fr) a winery based in the A.C. Chorey-lès-Beaune, Burgundy, also holds a number of Premier Cru plots in Beaune and Pernand-Vergelesses.

Château de Clairfont (Fr) the second wine of Château Prieuré-Lichine, Grand Cru Classé (4th) Margaux, Bordeaux.

Château de Clary (Fr) a vineyard in the A.C. Côtes du Rhône, Orange, southern France.

Château de Cognac (Fr) the Château headquarters of the Otard Cognac Company in Cognac, western France.

Château de Côme (Fr) a vineyard. (Com): Saint-Estèphe. A.C. Saint-Estèphe, Bordeaux 2ha.

Château de Cornneilla (Fr) an A.C. red wine from the Côtes du Roussillon, south-western France.

Château de Coulinats (Fr) a vineyard. (Com): Sainte-Croix-du-Mont. A.C. Sainte-Croix-du-Mont, Bordeaux 3ha.

Château de Courvoisier (Fr) the headquarters of Courvoisier Cognac in Jarnac, Charente.

Château de Coye (Fr) a vineyard. (Com): Sauternes. A.C. Sauternes, Bordeaux 1ha.

Château de Crain (Fr) a vineyard in the A.C. Entre-Deux-Mers, Bordeaux (white wine).

Château de Crémat (Fr) a vineyard in the A.C. Bellet, Provence, south-eastern France, one of only two growers. see Château de Bellet.

Château de Crouseilles (Fr) a vineyard in A.C. Madiran. Grapes include Cabernet and Tannat.

Château de Crustades (Fr) a winery based in the A.C. Corbières, Languedoc-Roussillon. Produces: white, rosé and red wines.

Château de Cruzeau (Fr) a vineyard. (Add): Château-la Louvière, Léognan 33850. A.C. Graves. (Com): Léognan. 50ha. Grape varieties: Cabernet sauvignon, Merlot and Sauvignon blanc.

Château de Cujac (Fr) a vineyard. (Com): Saint-Aubin. A.C. Médoc, Bordeaux. Cru Bourgeois.

Château de Dauzay (Fr) a vineyard in the A.C. Chinon, Anjou-Saumur, Loire.

Château de Dreiborn (Lux) a sparkling wine made by the méthode traditionelle by St. Martin.

Château de Fargues (Fr) a vineyard. (Com): Fargues. A.C. Sauternes, Bordeaux. 7ha.

Château de Fayolle (Fr) a vineyard in the A.C. Bergerac (red and white wines).

Château de Ferrand (Fr) a vineyard. (Add): Saint-Hippolyte, 33330 Saint-Émilion. Grand Cru. A.C.

Saint-Émilion. (Com): Saint-Émilion. 28ha. Grape varieties: Cabernet franc 15%, Cabernet sauvignon 15% and Merlot 70%.

Château de Fesles (Fr) a vineyard in the A.C. Bonnezeaux, Anjou-Saumur, Loire, (Add): 49380 Thouarcé, Loire. Produces A.C. Bonnezeaux, A.C. Coteaux du Layon, A.C. Chaume. Website: http://www.loire@vgas.com

Château de Fieuzal (Fr) a vineyard. (Add): Au Bourg, Léognan 22850. Grand Cru Classé. A.C. Pessac-Léognan. (Com): Léognan. 16ha. Grape varieties: Cabernet sauvignon, Merlot, Petit verdot, Sauvignon and Sémillon. Second label is L'Abeille de Fieuzal.

Château de Fleurie (Fr) a vineyard in the A.C. Fleurie Cru Beaujolais-Villages, Burgundy.

Château de Fonbel (Fr) a vineyard. (Add): 33330 Saint-Émilion. Grand Cru. A.C. Saint-Émilion. (Com): Saint-Émilion. Grape varieties: Cabernet franc, Malbec, Merlot.

Château de Fonsalette (Fr) owned by Château Rayas. Produces red and white Côtes du Rhône and a Cuvée Syrah under this label.

Château de Fonscolombe (Fr) a vineyard. (Add): 13610 Le-Puy-Sainte-Réparde, Aix-en-Provence. A.C. Coteaux d'Aix-en-Provence.

Château de Fontpinot Grande Champagne (Fr) a fine Cognac 41% alc. by vol. produced by Frapin et Cie in Cognac. Also produces 20–25 y.o. Cognacs and Tres Vielle Réserve du Château.

Château de Fouilloux (Fr) a vineyard in the Cru Beaujolais-Villages of Brouilly in Burgundy. Produced by Pasquier-Desvignes.

Château de Fourques (Fr) a vineyard in the A.C. Coteaux du Languedoc, south-western France. (Add): 34980 Saint-Gely-du-Fesc.

Château de France (Fr) a vineyard. (Add): 33850 Léognan. A.C. Graves. (Com): Léognan. 31ha. Grape varieties: Cabernet 50%, Merlot 50%, Muscadelle, Sauvignon and Sémillon.

Château de Gasq (Fr) the old name for Château Palmer Grand Cru Classé (3rd). A.C. Margaux.

Château d'Egmont (Fr) a vineyard. (Com): Ludon. A.C. Haut-Médoc, Bordeaux. Cru Bourgeois.

Château de Gorsse (Fr) a vineyard. (Com): Margaux. A.C. Margaux, Bordeaux. Cru Bourgeois.

Château de Gourgazaud (Fr) a vineyard in the A.C. Minervois la Livinière, south-eastern France. (Add): 34210 La Livinière, Minervois. (red). Grape varieties: Carignan, Grenache, Mourvèdre and Syrah.

Château de Grand Pré (Fr) a vineyard in the A.C. Fleurie Cru Beaujolais-Villages, Burgundy.

Château de Grézels (Fr) a 2ha. vineyard in Cahors.

Château de Grissac (Fr) a vineyard. (Com): Prignac-Marcamps. A.C. Côtes de Bourg, Bordeaux.

Château de Guezes (Fr) a vineyard in the A.C. Côtes de Buzet, south-western France (red).

Château de Haut-Gravat (Fr) a vineyard. (Com): Bourg. A.C. Côtes de Bourg, Bordeaux.

Château de Haut-Serre (Fr) a 125ha estate with 62ha of vines in A.C. Cahors on a limestone Causse, south of Cahors.

C

Château de Hilde (Fr) a vineyard. (Com): Bèles. A.C. Graves de Bordeaux, Bordeaux.

Château de Jasson (Fr) a vineyard in the A.C. Côtes de Provence. (Add): Ete de Collobrières, 83250 La Londe-les-Maures. Grape varieties: Cinsault, Grenache, Mourvèdre, Syrah and Tibouren. Produces rosé wines under the Cuvée Eléonore label.

Château de Jau (Fr) a vineyard in the A.C. Muscat de Rivesaltes, southern France. (Add): 66600 Cases-de-Pêne. Also produces A.C. Côtes du Roussillon.

Château de Jaulin (Fr) *see* Castay Frères.

Château de Javernand (Fr) a vineyard in the Cru Beaujolais-Villages of Chiroubles in Burgundy. (Add): 69115 Chiroubles.

Château de Junca (Fr) a vineyard. (Add): Saint-Sauveur de Médoc, 33250. A.C. Haut-Médoc. (Com): Saint-Sauveur de Médoc. 9ha. Grape varieties: Cabernet sauvignon 50%, Malbec 3% and Merlot 47%.

Château de Labarde (Fr) the name given to the second wine of Château Dauzac. Also the former name of the Château.

Château de la Barde (Fr) a vineyard. (Add): Saint Laurent des Combes, 33330 Saint-Émilion. Grand Cru. A.C. Saint Laurent des Combes. 3.65ha. Grape varieties: Cabernet franc 20%, Cabernet sauvignon 10% and Merlot 70%.

Château de Labat (Fr) a vineyard. (Com): Saint Laurent. A.C. Haut-Médoc, Bordeaux. Cru Bourgeois.

Château de Labaude (Fr) an Armagnac producer. (Add): GFA de Labaude, Sorbets 32110 Nogaro. 100ha. in Bas Armagnac.

Château de l'Abbaye (Fr) a vineyard in the A.C. Fleurie Cru Beaujolais-Villages, Burgundy.

Château de l'Abbé-Gorsse-de-Gorsse (Fr) a vineyard. (Com): Margaux. A.C. Haut-Médoc, Bordeaux. Cru Bourgeois.

Château de Labégorce (Fr) a vineyard. (Com): Margaux. A.C. Margaux, Bordeaux. Cru Bourgeois.

Château de la Bidière (Fr) a vineyard in the A.C. Muscadet Sèvre et Maine, Nantais, Loire.

Château de la Bigotière (Fr) a vineyard in the A.C. Muscadet Sèvre et Maine, Nantais, Loire.

Château de la Bizolière (Fr) a vineyard in the A.C. Savenniéres, Anjou-Saumur, Loire.

Château de la Brède (Fr) a vineyard. (Com): La Brède. A.C. Graves, Bordeaux. 6ha (white).

Château de la Bridane (Fr) a vineyard. (Com): Saint-Julien. A.C. Médoc, Bordeaux. Grape variety: Cabernet sauvignon 100%. Cru Bourgeois.

Château de Lacarelle (Fr) a large vineyard in the A.C. Beaujolais-Villages, Burgundy. (Add): 69460 St-Étienne-des-Oullières.

Château de Lacaze (Fr) an Armagnac producer. (Add): Parlebosq-en-Armagnac, 40310 Gabarret. Vineyards in Bas Armagnac. Produces ***, V.S.O.P. and Hors d'Age.

Château de la Chaize (Fr) a famous vineyard and château in the Cru Beaujolais-Villages of Brouilly in Burgundy. A.C. Brouilly. (Add): 69460 Odenas.

Château de la Chartreuse (Fr) a vineyard. (Com): Preignac. A.C. Sauternes, Bordeaux 5ha.

Château de la Commanderie (Fr) a vineyard. (Com): Lalande de Pomerol. A.C. Saint-Émilion, Bordeaux.

Château de la Cour d'Argent (Fr) a vineyard. (Add): Saint-Sulpice-de-Faleyrens, 33330 Saint-Émilion. A.C. Bordeaux Supérieur.

Château de Lacouy (Fr) an Armagnac producer. 20ha. in Bas Armagnac.

Château de la Croix (Fr) a vineyard. (Com): Lormont. A.C. Premières Côtes de Bordeaux, central Bordeaux.

Château de la Croix-Millerit (Fr) a vineyard. (Com): Bayon. A.C. Côtes de Bourg, Bordeaux.

Château de la Croix-Simard (Fr) a vineyard in the A.C. Saint-Émilion, Bordeaux 1ha.

Château de la Dauphine (Fr) a vineyard in the A.C. Côtes de Fronsac, Bordeaux.

Château de la Dimerie (Fr) a vineyard in the A.C. Muscadet Sèvre et Maine, Nantais, Loire. (Add): G.F.A. Rouge Terre de la Viticulteurs au Loroux Bottereau, Loire Atlantique.

Château de la Font-du-Loup (Fr) a vineyard. (Com): Courthézon. A.C. Châteauneuf-du-Pape, southern Rhône. Produced by Mélia. Grape varieties: Cinsault, Clairette, Grenache, Grenache blanc, Mourvèdre and Rousanne.

Château de la France (Fr) an A.C. Bordeaux Supérieur. 82ha. in Beychac et Caillou. Grape varieties: 60% Merlot, 20% Cabernet franc, 20% Cabernet sauvignon. Also a rosé and clairet produced.

Château de la Fresnaye (Fr) an A.C. Cabernet d'Anjou, Anjou-Saumur, Loire.

Château de la Galissonière (Fr) a vineyard in A.C. Muscadet Sèvre et Maine, Nantais, Loire. (Add): 6, Pallet, Loire Atlantique.

Château de la Gardine (Fr) a vineyard in the A.C. Châteauneuf-du-Pape, southern Rhône. Owned by Brunel (G. et Fils). Also produces an A.C. Côtes-du-Rhône-Villages Rasteau,

Château de la Grange (Fr) a vineyard in the A.C. Premières Côtes de Blaye, north-eastern Bordeaux.

Château de la Grange (Fr) a Cognac producer. (Add): 17400 St. Jean d'Angely. Owns 90ha. Produces Bladon d'Or (15 year old) and Maxim's de Paris Cognacs.

Château de la Grave (Fr) a vineyard. (Com): Bourg. A.C. Côtes de Bourg, Bordeaux. Cru Bourgeois.

Château de la Gravière (Fr) a vineyard. (Com): Toulenne. A.C. Graves, Bordeaux. 7ha (white).

Château de la Guimonière (Fr) a vineyard in the A.C. Quarts de Chaume, Coteaux du Layon, Anjou-Saumur, Loire (sweet white).

Château de l'Aiglerie (Fr) an A.C. Anjou, Anjou-Saumur, Loire Atlantique (white wine).

Château de la Janière (Fr) a vineyard in the A.C. Muscadet Sèvre et Maine, Nantais, Loire.

Château de la Jaubertie (Fr) a winery based in the A.C. Bergerac region. Produces a range of white, red and rosé wines.

Château de la Jousselinière (Fr) a vineyard in the A.C. Muscadet Sèvre et Maine, Nantais, Loire.

270

C

Château de la Maisdonnière (Fr) an A.C. Muscadet, Nantais, Loire.

Château de la Maltroye (Fr) an estate in A.C. Chassagne-Montrachet, Côte de Beaune, Burgundy (red and white). Vineyards includes the Clos du Château (2.5ha).

Château de Lamarque (Fr) a vineyard. (Add): 33460 Margaux. Cru Bourgeois. A.C. Haut-Médoc. (Com): Lamarque. 50ha. Grape varieties: Cabernet franc, Cabernet sauvignon, Merlot and Petit verdot.

Château de la Mecredière (Fr) a vineyard in the A.C. Muscadet Sèvre et Maine, Nantais, Loire. (Add): 44190 Clisson, Loire Atlantique.

Château de la Monge (Fr) a vineyard. (Com): Bourg. A.C. Côtes de Bourg, Bordeaux.

Château de Lamothe (Fr) the fifteenth century name for Château Margaux. Premier Grand Cru Classé Margaux.

Château de la Mouchetière (Fr) a vineyard in the A.C. Muscadet Sèvre et Maine, Nantais, Loire. (Add): La Mouchetière, Le Loroux-Bottereau, Loire Atlantique.

Château de Lamourous (Fr) a vineyard. (Com): Le Pian. A.C. Haut-Médoc, Bordeaux 4ha.

Château de Lamouroux (Fr) a vineyard. (Com): Margaux. A.C. Margaux, Bordeaux. Cru Bourgeois 7ha.

Château de la Nauve (Fr) a vineyard. (Add): Saint Laurent des Combes, 33330 Saint-Émilion. A.C. Saint-Émilion. (Com): Saint Laurent des Combes. 11ha. Grape varieties: Cabernet franc, Cabernet sauvignon and Merlot 80%.

Château de Lancyre (Fr) a vineyard in the A.C. Coteaux du Languedoc Pic Saint-Loup. produces Grande Cuvée from 75% Syrah and 15% Grenache grapes.

Château de l'Annonciation (Fr) a vineyard. (Add): 33330 Saint-Émilion. Grand Cru. A.C. Saint-Émilion. (Com): Saint-Émilion. Grape varieties: Cabernet franc, Malbec, Merlot.

Château de la Nouvelle Église (Fr) a vineyard. (Com): Pomerol. A.C. Pomerol, Bordeaux.

Château de Lastours (Fr) a vineyard in the A.C. Corbières, south-western France. Label: Cuvée Simon Descamps.

Château de la Tour Penet (Fr) a vineyard in the A.C. Mâcon-Villages.

Château de la Preuille (Fr) a vineyard in the A.C. Muscadet, Nantais, Loire.

Château de la Princesse (Fr) a vineyard. (Com): Sainte-Croix-du-Mont. A.C. Sainte-Croix-du-Mont, Bordeaux 2ha.

Château de la Ragotière (Fr) a vineyard in the A.C. Muscadet Sèvre et Maine, Nantais, Loire.

Château de la Ramière (Fr) a vineyard in the A.C. Côtes du Rhône, south-eastern Rhône.

Château de la Rigodière (Fr) a vineyard in the A.C. Beaujolais, Burgundy.

Château de la Rivière (Fr) a vineyard. (Com): St-Michel. A.C. Fronsac, Bordeaux. (Add): La Rivière, 33145 St-Michel-de-Fronsac. 56ha.

Château de la Roche (Fr) a vineyard. (Com): Les Lèves et Thoumeyrogues. A.C. Saint-Foy-Bordeaux, Bordeaux (red and white).

Château de la Roche aux Moines (Fr) a vineyard. (Com): Savennières, Anjou-Saumur, Loire. A.C. Savennières. (Add): Savennières-Coulée de Serrant, Loire.

Château de la Roque (Fr) a vineyard in Fontanès, A.C. Coteaux du Languedoc-Pic-Saint-Loup. White wines are made from Marsanne, Rolle and Viognier grapes. Red wines from Grenache, Mourvèdre and Syrah grapes 42ha.

Château de la Roulerie (Fr) a vineyard. (Com): Saint-Aubin-de-Luigne. A.C. Coteaux du Layon-Chaume, Anjou-Saumur, Loire. Grape varieties: Cabernet franc, Chenin blanc.

Château de Laroze (Fr) a vineyard. (Com): Margaux. A.C. Margaux, Bordeaux 2ha.

Château de la Salagre (Fr) a vineyard in the A.C. Monbazillac, Bergerac, south-western France (sweet white).

Château de la Saule (Fr) a Premier Cru white wine vineyard, A.C. Montagny.

Château de Lascaux (Fr) a vineyard in Vacquières, A.C. Coteaux du Languedoc-Pic-Saint-Loup. Top red cuvée is produced from 90% Syrah, 10% Grenache grapes. Top white cuvée is from Marsanne, Rolle, Roussanne and Viognier grapes, vinified in barrique. 35ha. Label: Pierres d'Argent.

Château de Lastours (Fr) a vineyard. (Com): A.C. Corbières. (Add): Centre d'Aide par la Travail, 11490 Portel des Corbières.

Château de la Tuilerie (Fr) a vineyard in the Costières de Nîmes. (Add): Route de Saint-Gilles, 30000 Nîmes. Noted for Vieille Vignes white wine from 80% Grenache, 20% Marsanne & Roussanne grapes and Cuvée Eole from mainly Syrah grapes.

Château de Laubade (Fr) a producer in Bas Armagnac on a 170ha estate.

Château de Lauga (Fr) a Cru Artisan A.C. Médoc from the commune of Cusac-Fort-Médoc, Bordeaux.

Château de l'Aulée (Fr) a vineyard. (Com): Azay le Rideau. A.C. Touraine, Loire. Grape variety: Chenin blanc.

Château de l'Aumerade (Fr) a winery based in the A.C. Côtes de Provence. Produces a variety of wines (white, rosé and red). Label: Cuvée Marie-Christine (rosé). Website: http://www.sa-fabre.com E'mail: caroline.demey@sa-fabre.com

Château de Laussac (Fr) a vineyard in the A.C. Côtes de Castillon.

Château de l'Emigré (Fr) a vineyard. (Com): Cérons. A.C. Graves, Bordeaux. (Add): Route d'Illats, 33177 Cérons. 2ha. Grape varieties: Merlot, Sauvignon 35% and Sémillon 65% (red and white).

Château de l'Engarran (Fr) a vineyard based in St-Georges d'Orques, A.C. Coteaux du Languedoc. Noted for red Cuvée Quetton St-Georges and rosé and wines

Château de l'Ermitage (Fr) a vineyard. (Com): Loupiac. A.C. Loupiac, Bordeaux 2ha.

C

Château de Lescours (Fr) a vineyard. (Add): Saint-Sulpice-de-Faleyrens, 33330 Saint-Émilion. A.C. Saint-Émilion Grand Cru. (Com): Saint-Sulpice-de-Faleyrens. 21ha. Grape varieties: Merlot 70%, Cabernet franc 15%, Cabernet sauvignon 15%.

Château de l'Espérance (Fr) a vineyard. (Com): La Brède. A.C. Graves, Bordeaux. 12ha (red and white).

Château de l'Estagnol (Fr) an A.C. Côtes du Rhône. Grape variety: Bourboulenc (blanc de blancs).

Château de l'Estonnat (Fr) a vineyard. (Com): Margaux. A.C. Margaux, Bordeaux.

Château de l'Euzière (Fr) a vineyard in the A.C. Coteaux du Languedoc Pic Saint-Loup. Produces Cuvée des Escarboucles from 85% Syrah, 10% Grenache, 5% Mourvèdre and 5% Carignan grapes.

Château de l'Horte (Fr) a vineyard in the A.C. Corbières, south-western France. (Add): 11700 Montbrun. Label: Cuvée Marquis de St. Felix.

Château de l'Hospital (Fr) a vineyard. (Com): Portets. A.C. Graves, Bordeaux. 8ha. (red and white). Owned by Domaines Lafragette. Website: http://www.lafragette.com

Château de Ligré (Fr) a vineyard in the A.C. Chinon, Touraine, Loire. (Add): Ligré, 37500 Chinon.

Château de l'Ille (Fr) a vineyard in the A.C. Corbières, Languedoc-Roussillon. Grape varieties: Grenache, Mourvèdre, Syrah.

Château de Loei (Thai) the label for a reserve red wine (Syrah) produced by CPK International. *See also* Solar. Website: http://www.chateaudeloei.com

Château de l'Oiselinière (Fr) a vineyard in the A.C. Muscadet Sèvre et Maine, Nantais, Loire. (Add): Aulanière, 44190 Clisson, Loire Atlantique.

Château de Luc (Fr) a vineyard in the A.C. Corbières, south-western France. Label: Les Murets.

Château de Lucat (Fr) an A.C. Premières Côtes de Bordeaux.

Château de Lucquos (Fr) a vineyard. (Com): Barsac. A.C. Barsac (or Sauternes), Bordeaux.

Château de Lugagnac (Fr) an A.C. Bordeaux Supérieur wine. (Add): 33790 Pellegrue.

Château de Lunes (Fr) a red wine from the Coteaux du Languedoc, southern France.

Château de Lussac (Fr) a vineyard. (Com): Lussac-Saint-Émilion. A.C. Saint-Émilion, Bordeaux 25ha.

Château de Luzies (Fr) a vineyard. (Com): Barsac. A.C. Barsac (or Sauternes), Bordeaux 3ha.

Château de Maco (Fr) a vineyard. (Com): Tauriac. A.C. Côtes de Bourg, Bordeaux.

Château de Madère (Fr) a vineyard. (Com): Podensac. A.C. Médoc, Bordeaux.

Château de Maison Neuve (Fr) a winery based in the A.C. Montagne-Saint-Émilion, Bordeaux.

Château de Malendure (Fr) a vineyard. (Com): Loupiac. A.C. Loupiac, Bordeaux 3ha.

Château de Malgarni (Fr) a vineyard. (Com): Saillans. A.C. Côtes de Fronsac, Bordeaux 3ha.

Château de Maligny (Fr) a winery based in the A.C. Chablis, Burgundy. (Add): 89800, Chablis. Produces a range of Chablis wines including Premier Crus Fourchaume and Vau de Vey.

Château de Malle (Fr) a vineyard. (Add): Fermière au Pian-Médoc, Gironde. Grand Cru Classé (2nd). A.C. Sauternes. (Com): Preignac. 20ha. Grape varieties: Muscadelle 5%, Sauvignon 25% and Sémillon 70%. Second label is Domaine de Sainte-Hélene.

Château de Malleret (Fr) a vineyard. (Com): Le Pian. A.C. Haut-Médoc, Bordeaux. 60ha. Grape varieties: Cabernet franc 9%, Cabernet sauvignon 82% and Merlot 9%. Cru Bourgeois.

Château de Maniban Cuvée Speciale (Fr) a vintage Armagnac produced by Castarède. Vintages include: 1893, 1900, 1924, 1931, 1934, 1940, 1949, 1955.

Château de Manissy (Fr) a vineyard in the A.C. Tavel, southern Rhône.

Château de Marbuzet (Fr) a vineyard. (Add): Saint-Estèphe 33250 Pauillac. Cru Bourgeois. A.C. Saint-Estèphe. 7ha. Grape varieties: Cabernet sauvignon and Merlot.

Château de Marsan (Fr) an estate in the Armagnac that was run as a model farm and experimental station.

Château de Marsillac (Fr) a vineyard in the A.C. Côtes de Bourg, north-eastern Bordeaux.

Château de Mauves (Fr) a vineyard. (Add): 25, Rue François Maurice, Podensac. A.C. Graves. (Com): Podensac. 16ha. Grape varieties: Cabernet sauvignon 65% and Merlot 35%.

Château de May (Fr) a vineyard in the A.C. Graves, Bordeaux (red).

Château de Mendoce (Fr) a vineyard. (Com): Villeneuve. A.C. Côtes de Bourg, Bordeaux. (Add): 33710 Bourg.

Château de Menota (Fr) a vineyard. (Com): Barsac. A.C. Barsac (or Sauternes), Bordeaux.

Château de Mercey (Fr) an A.C. Hautes Côtes de Beaune, Burgundy. Vineyards situated near Cheilly-lès-Maranges (red and white).

Château de Mercuès (Fr) a wine producing estate and luxury hotel in Cahors. 40ha. Grape varieties: 75% Malbec, 20% Merlot, 5% Tannat.

Château de Messey (Fr) a vineyard based in the A.C. Mercurey, Côte Chalonnaise, Burgundy. Label: Les Villerouges, also produces a Premier Cru A.C. Rully: La Fosse.

Château de Meursault (Fr) an estate of 41.5ha. in the A.C. commune of Meursault in the Côte de Beaune, Burgundy (red and white).

Château de Moncontour (Fr) a vineyard in the A.C. Vouvray, Touraine. Is famous for sparkling Vouvray.

Château Mongin (Fr) an A.C. Châteauneuf-du-Pape (red) 2ha. and A.C. Côtes-du-Rhone 18ha. produced by the students at the Lycée Viticole d'Orange, 84100 Orange, France.

Château de Mons (Fr) a vineyard. (Add): Saint-Sulpice-de-Faleyrens, 33330 Saint-Émilion. A.C. Saint-Émilion. Second wine of Château du Barry. Grand Cru. Saint-Émilion.

Château de Montdespic (Fr) a vineyard in the A.C. Côtes de Castillon, Bordeaux.

Château de Montfort (Fr) an A.C. Arbois vineyard producing red, rosé and white wines in the Jura.

272

C

Château de Montgueret (Fr) an A.C. Saumur (white).

Château de Montifaud (Fr) a Cognac producer based in the Grande Champagne district, Charente.

Château de Montmelas (Fr) a vineyard in the A.C. Beaujolais-Villages, Burgundy.

Château de Montmirail (Fr) a vineyard in the A.C. Gigondas, Côtes du Rhône-Villages. (Add): B.P. 12, 84190 Vacqueyras.

Château de Montpatey (Fr) an A.C. Bourgogne Chardonnay. Label: Cuvée Marquis d'Espies.

Château de Montrabech (Fr) a vineyard in the A.C. Corbières, south-western France.

Château de Morgan (Fr) a vineyard in the A.C. Morgon. Cru Beaujolais-Villages, Burgundy.

Château de Musset (Fr) a vineyard in the Lalande de Pomerol. A.C. Lalande, Bordeaux.

Château de Myrat (Fr) a vineyard. (Com): Barsac. A.C. Barsac (or Sauternes), Bordeaux.

Château de Nages (Fr) a vineyard in the A.C. Costières de Nîmes, southern France. Produces Réserve du Château (red: 60% Grenache, 40% Syrah, white: 50% Grenache blanc, 50% Roussanne grapes), Joseph Torrès (100% Roussanne).

Château de Nairne (Fr) a vineyard. (Com): Barsac. A.C. Barsac (or Sauternes), Bordeaux.

Château de Nardon (Fr) an A.C. Bordeaux Supérieur red wine. Grape varieties: 40% Cabernet sauvignon, 40% Merlot, 20% Cabernet franc.

Château de Naujan (Fr) an A.C. Bordeaux red wine.

Château de Neuville (Fr) a vineyard in the A.C. Saint-Émilion, Bordeaux 1ha.

Château de Nevers (Fr) a vineyard in the A.C. Brouilly. Cru Beaujolais-Villages, Burgundy.

Château de Nouchet (Fr) a vineyard. (Com): Martillac. A.C. Graves, Bordeaux.

Château de Nouguey (Fr) a vineyard. (Com): Langon. A.C. Graves, Bordeaux 2ha. (white).

Château de Nouvelles (Fr) an A.C. Rancio de Rivesaltes. (Add): 11350 Tucan.

Château de Nozet (Fr) *see* Baron de L'.

Château de Pach-Lat (Fr) a vineyard in the A.C. Corbières, south-western France.

Château de Padère (Fr) a vineyard in the A.C. Côtes de Buzet, south-western France.

Château de Paillet-Quancard (Fr) a vineyard. (Com): Langoiran. A.C. Premières Côtes de Bordeaux. (Add): 33550 Langoiran. Grape varieties: Cabernet sauvignon 35% and Merlot 65%.

Château de Panigon (Fr) an A.C. Médoc. A Cru Bourgeois based in Civrac en Médoc, Gironde.

Château de Panisseau (Fr) a vineyard in the A.C. Bergerac. (Add): Thénac, 24240 Sigoulés, Dordogne. Grape variety: Sauvignon blanc.

Château de Parnay (Fr) a vineyard in the A.C. Anjou, Anjou-Saumur, Loire Atlantique (white wine).

Château de Passavant (Fr) a vineyard in the A.C. Anjou-Villages, Anjou-Saumer, Loire.

Château de Paulignan (Fr) a vineyard in the A.C. Minervois, Languedoc-Roussillon. Grape varieties: Carignan, Grenache, Mourvèdre and Syrah.

Château de Pennautier (Fr) a vineyard within the A.C. Cabardès based in the Montagne Noire foothills, in the département of Aude, southern France, uses Bordelais and Languedoc grapes.

Château de Peyre (Fr) a 1ha vineyard. (Com): Fargues. A.C. Sauternes, Bordeaux.

Château de Peyros (Fr) a vineyard in the A.C. Madiran, Pyrénées, south-western France (red).

Château de Pez (Fr) a vineyard. (Com): Moulis. A.C. Moulis, Bordeaux 40ha.

Château de Pez (Fr) a vineyard. (Add): Pez, Saint-Estèphe, 33250 Pauillac. A.C. Saint-Estèphe. (Com): Saint-Estèphe. 23.25ha. Grape varieties: Cabernet franc 15%, Cabernet sauvignon 70% and Merlot 15%.

Château de Pibarnon (Fr) a vineyard in the A.C. Bandol, Provence.

Château de Pic (Fr) a vineyard in the A.C. Premières Côtes de Bordeaux. Grape varieties: Cabernet franc 5%, Cabernet sauvignon 35%, Merlot 60%.

Château de Pick (Fr) a vineyard. (Com): Preignac. A.C. Sauternes, Bordeaux 23ha.

Château de Pierreux (Fr) a winery based in the A.C. Beaujolais Cru Brouilly, southern Burgundy. Label: Réserve du Château.

Château d'Epiré (Fr) a vineyard. (Com): Savennières, A.C. Savennières, Anjou-Saumur, Loire. Website: http://www.chateau-epire.com

Château de Pitray (Fr) a vineyard in the A.C. Côtes-de-Castillon.

Château de Pizay (Fr) a vineyard in the A.C. Morgon. Cru Beaujolais, Burgundy.

Château de Plaisance (Fr) a vineyard. (Com): Chaume. A.C. Coteaux du Layon, Anjou-Saumur, Loire.

Château de Pomès Pébérère (Fr) the labels of 10 and 20 year old Armagnacs produced in Ténarèze.

Château de Pommard (Fr) a vineyard in the A.C. Pommard, Côte de Beaune, Burgundy 20ha.

Château de Pommarède (Fr) a vineyard. (Com): Castre. A.C. Graves, Bordeaux (red and white).

Château de Portets (Fr) a vineyard. (Com): Portets. A.C. Graves, Bordeaux. 42ha (red and white).

Château de Pressac (Fr) a vineyard. (Add): Saint-Étienne-de-Lisse, 33330 Saint-Émilion. Grand Cru. A.C. Saint-Émilion. (Com): Saint-Étienne-de-Lisse. 55ha. Grape varieties: Cabernet franc 40%, Malbec and Pressac 2% and Merlot 58%. Second wine is Château Tour de Pressac.

Château de Puisseguin (Fr) a vineyard. (Com): Puisseguin-Saint-Émilion. A.C. Saint-Émilion, Bordeaux.

Château de Puligny Montrachet (Fr) a cuvée 20ha in the Premier Cru vineyard of Les Folatières, A.C. Puligny Montrachet, Côte de Beaune, Burgundy. Vineyards include: Puligny Folatières. *See also* Clos de Château.

Château de Puy-Blanquet (Fr) a vineyard. (Com): Saint-Étienne-de-Lisse. A.C. Saint-Émilion, Bordeaux.

Château de Raousset (Fr) a vineyard in the A.C. Chiroubles Cru Beaujolais-Villages, Burgundy.

Château de Ravignan (Fr) an Armagnac producer.

(Add): Domaine de Ravignan, Perique, 40190, Villeneuve de Marsan. 18ha. in Bas Armagnac.

Château de Rayne-Vigneau (Fr) a Premier Grand Cru Classé. A.C. Sauternes. (Com): Bommes. 65ha. Grape varieties: Muscadelle 10%, Sauvignon 30% and Sémillon 60%.

Château de Respide (Fr) a vineyard. (Com): St-Pierre-de-Mons. A.C. Graves, Bordeaux (white).

Château de Ribautes (Fr) a vineyard in the A.C. Corbières, south-western France.

Château de Riquewihr (Fr) a winery in the A.C. Alsace owned by Dopff et Irion. Has a number of 'domaines' within its structure. *see* Les Murailles.

Château de Rochefort (Fr) a vineyard in the A.C. Muscadet Sèvre et Maine, Nantais, Loire. (Add): Vallet, Loire Atlantique.

Château de Rochemorin (Fr) a vineyard. (Com): Léognan. A.C. Pessac-Léognan, Bordeaux (red and white).

Château de Rol (Fr) a vineyard in the A.C. Saint-Émilion, Bordeaux 5ha.

Château de Rolland (Fr) a vineyard. (Com): Barsac. A.C. Barsac (or Sauternes), Bordeaux 14ha.

Château de Romefort (Fr) a vineyard. (Com): Cussac. A.C. Médoc, Bordeaux. Cru Bourgeois.

Château de Roquebert (Fr) a vineyard. (Com): Quinsac. A.C. Premières Côtes de Bordeaux. (Add): Quinsac, 33360 Latresne. 16.4ha. Grape varieties: Cabernet, Malbec and Merlot.

Château de Roquebrune (Fr) a vineyard. (Com): Cenac. A.C. Premières Côtes de Bordeaux. (Add): 33360 Cenac. Grape varieties: Cabernet franc 33%, Cabernet sauvignon 33% and Merlot 33%.

Château de Roques (Fr) a vineyard. (Com): Puisseguin-Saint-Émilion. A.C. Saint-Émilion, Bordeaux.

Château de Roquetaillade (Fr) a vineyard. (Com): Mazères. A.C. Graves, Bordeaux (red and white).

Château de Roquetaillade (Fr) a vineyard. (Com): Ordonnac-et-Potensac. A.C. Médoc, Bordeaux 3ha.

Château de Rouanne (Fr) a winery based in the A.C. Côtes-du-Rhône-Villages Vinsobres, Vaucluse.

Château de Rouillac (Fr) a vineyard. (Add): 33170 Gradignan. A.C. Pessac-Léognan, Graves. (Com): Canéjean. 5ha. Grape varieties: Cabernet sauvignon 85% and Merlot 15%. (red). Owned by Domaines Lafragette. Website: http://www.lafragette.com

Château de Roux (Fr) a vineyard in the A.C. Côtes-de-Provence, south-eastern France. (Add): Le Cannet-des-Maures, 83340 Le Luc. (red and rosé).

Château de Rozet (Fr) a vineyard in the A.C. Pouilly Blanc Fumé, Central Vineyards, Pouilly-sur-Loire.

Château de Ruth (Fr) a vineyard in the A.C. Côtes du Rhône. Grape varieties: Carignane, Grenache and Syrah. Produced by Gabriel Meffre.

Château de Saint-Julien d'Aille (Fr) a vineyard. (Com): Vidauban. A.C. Côtes-de-Provence. (Add): B.P. 38, 83550 Vidauban.

Château de Saint Pey (Fr) a vineyard. (Add): Saint-Pey-d'Armens, 33330 Saint-Émilion. Grand Cru. A.C. Saint-Émilion. (Com): Saint-Pey-d'Armens.

16ha. Grape varieties: Cabernet franc 30%, Cabernet sauvignon 6% and Merlot 64%.

Château de Saint-Philippe (Fr) a vineyard. (Com): Saint Philippe d'Aiguille, Côtes de Castillon, eastern Bordeaux. A.C. Bordeaux Supérieur. (Add): 33350 Saint Philippe d'Aiguille.

Château de Saint Pierre (Fr) a vineyard. (Add): Saint Pierre de Mons 33210. A.C. Graves. Grape varieties: Cabernet 60%, Merlot 40%, Sauvignon 35% and Sémillon 65%

Château de Sales (Fr) a vineyard. (Com): Pomerol. A.C. Pomerol, Bordeaux. 48ha. The second wine of Château Chantalouette.

Château de Samonac (Fr) a vineyard in the A.C. Côtes de Bourg, north-eastern Bordeaux.

Château de Sancerre (Fr) a vineyard in the A.C. Sancerre, Central Vineyards, France. Grape variety: Sauvignon blanc.

Château des Annereaux (Fr) a vineyard. (Com): Lalande de Pomerol. A.C. Lalande de Pomerol, Bordeaux.

Château de Sarenceau (Fr) a vineyard in the A.C. Saint-Émilion, Bordeaux 5ha.

Château de Sarpe (Fr) a vineyard in the A.C. Saint-Émilion, Bordeaux 6ha.

Château des Arrocs (Fr) a vineyard. (Com): Langon. A.C. Graves, Bordeaux. 3ha (white).

Château de Sassay (Fr) a vineyard in the A.C. Chinon, Touraine, Loire.

Château de Savennières (Fr) a vineyard. (Com): Savennières. A.C. Savennières, Anjou-Saumur, Loire.

Château des Bachelards (Fr) a vineyard in the A.C. Fleurie Cru Beaujolais-Villages, Burgundy.

Château des Belles Graves (Fr) a vineyard. (Com): Ordonnac et Podensac. A.C. Médoc, Bordeaux.

Château des Brousteras (Fr) a vineyard. (Com): Saint-Yzans-de-Médoc. A.C. Médoc, Bordeaux. (Add): Saint-Yzans-de-Médoc, 33340 Lesparre.

Château des Cabannes (Fr) a vineyard. (Add): Saint-Sulpice-de-Faleyrens, 33330 Saint-Émilion. A.C. Saint-Émilion 5ha.

Château des Caperans (Fr) a vineyard. (Com): Cussac-Fort-Médoc. A.C. Haut-Médoc, Bordeaux 4ha. Grape varieties: Cabernet 50% and Merlot 50%.

Château des Capitans (Fr) a vineyard in the A.C. Juliénas Cru Beaujolais-Villages, Burgundy. (Add): B.P. 73- 69822 Belleville Cedex.

Château des Carmes-Haut-Brion (Fr) a vineyard. (Com): Pessac. A.C. Médoc, Bordeaux.

Château des Chaberts (Fr) a winery (30ha) based in the Coteaux Various, Provence. Produces a range of white, rosé and red wines. Label: Cuvée de Bacchus.

Château des Chambrettes (Fr) a vineyard. (Com): Pessac. A.C. Médoc, Bordeaux.

Château des Charmes (Can) a winery (established 1978) based at Saint Davids, near Niagara-on-the-Lake, Ontario. 60acres. Mainly Chardonnay, Pinot noir and Riesling grapes grown. Produces a Late-harvest Riesling.

C

Château des Combes (Fr) a vineyard. (Com): Bégadan. A.C. Médoc, Bordeaux 4ha.

Château des Combes-Canon (Fr) a vineyard. (Com): St-Michel. A.C. Côtes de Canon-Fronsac, Bordeaux 2ha.

Château des Deduits (Fr) a vineyard in the A.C. Fleurie Cru Beaujolais-Villages, Burgundy.

Château des Desmoiselles (Fr) a vineyard in the A.C. Saint-Émilion, Bordeaux 1ha.

Château des Ducs d'Epernon (Fr) see Maison du Vin, Château des Ducs d'Epernon.

Château de Ségriès (Fr) a vineyard in the A.C. Lirac, Côtes du Rhône, southern France. Also produces A.C. Tavel rosé.

Château de Seguin (Fr) an A.C. vineyard in Entre-Deux-Mers (near Lignan-de-Bordeaux). 170ha. of which 75ha. for red Bordeaux Supérieur from 50% Cabernet sauvignon, 45% Merlot, 5% Cabernet franc.

Château de Selle (Fr) a vineyard. (Add): Taradeau, 83460 Les Arcs. A.C. Côtes-de-Provence. Grape varieties: Cabernet sauvignon, Cinsault and Grenache. (red and rosé). Owned by Domaines Ott.

Château de Sérame (Fr) a vineyard in the A.C. Corbières, south-western France.

Château des Fines Roches (Fr) an A.C. Châteauneuf-du-Pape. 50ha. Grape varieties: Cinsault 5%, Grenache 70%, Mourvèdre 5% and Syrah 10% with 10% of 8 other varieties.

Château des Fougères (Fr) a vineyard. (Com): La Brède. A.C. Graves, Bordeaux 2ha. (white).

Château des Gauliers (Fr) a vineyard in the A.C. Bonnezeaux, Coteaux du Layon, Anjou-Saumur, Loire.

Château des Gondats (Fr) the second wine of Château Marquis de Terme. A 'Palus' wine.

Château des Granges (Fr) a vineyard in the A.C. Beaujolais, Burgundy.

Château des Graves (Fr) a vineyard. (Com): Portets. A.C. Graves, Bordeaux (red and white).

Château des Graves (Fr) a vineyard in the A.C. Saint-Émilion, Bordeaux 4ha.

Château des Graves-de-Mondou (Fr) a vineyard in the A.C. Saint-Émilion, Bordeaux 4ha.

Château des Gravettes (Fr) a vineyard. (Com): St. Morillon. A.C. Graves, Bordeaux.

Château des Gravières (Fr) a vineyard. (Com): Portets. A.C. Graves, Bordeaux. 5ha (red and white).

Château des Graviers d'Ellies (Fr) a vineyard. (Add): Saint-Sulpice-de-Faleyrens, 33330 Saint-Émilion. Grand Cru. A.C. Saint-Émilion. (Com): Saint-Sulpice-de-Faleyrens. 7ha. Grape varieties: Cabernet sauvignon 25% and Merlot 75%.

Château des Guerches (Fr) a vineyard in the A.C. Muscadet Sèvre et Maine, Nantais, Loire.

Château des Guillemins (Fr) a vineyard. (Com): Langon. A.C. Graves, Bordeaux. 8ha (white).

Château des Jacobins (Fr) a vineyard. (Com): Pomerol. A.C. Pomerol, Bordeaux 1ha.

Château des Jacques (Fr) a vineyard (30ha) in the A.C. Moulin-à-Vent Cru Beaujolais-Villages,

Burgundy. (Add): 71570 Romanèche-Thorins. Owned by Louis Jadot.

Château des Jaubertes (Fr) a vineyard. (Com): St-Pierre-de-Mons. A.C. Graves, Bordeaux. 6ha (red).

Château de L'Abbaye de Saint Ferme (Fr) an A.C. Bordeaux Supérieur. Grape varieties: Cabernet franc 20%, Cabernet sauvignon 40%, Merlot 40%.

Château des Labourons (Fr) a vineyard (35ha) in the A.C. Fleurie Cru Beaujolais-Villages, Burgundy. Originally known as the Château de Bellevue.

Château des Laurets (Fr) a vineyard. (Com): Puisseguin-Saint-Émilion. A.C. Puisseguin-Saint-Émilion, Bordeaux.

Château des Lucques (Fr) a vineyard. (Com): Portets. A.C. Graves, Bordeaux. 5ha (red and white).

Château des Lumières (Fr) a winery based in the A.C. Beaujolais Cru Morgon, southern Burgundy. (Add): Côte de Py, Morgon.

Château des Mailles (Fr) a vineyard. (Com): Sainte-Croix-du-Mont. A.C. Sainte-Croix-du-Mont, Bordeaux 6ha.

Château des Matards (Fr) a vineyard in the Premières Côtes de Blaye. (Add): St. Ciers sur Gironde. 43ha. Grape varieties: Ugni blanc, Sauvignon blanc, Muscat, Colombard, Merlot, Cabernet sauvignon.

Château des Mauves (Fr) a vineyard. (Com): Podensac. A.C. Cérons, Bordeaux 7ha.

Château Desmirail (Fr) a vineyard. (Add): 33460 Margaux. Grand Cru Classé (3rd). A.C. Margaux. (Com): Cantenac. 18ha. Grape varieties: Cabernet, franc, Cabernet sauvignon, Merlot and Petit verdot. Second label is Domaine de Fontarney.

Château des Moines (Fr) a vineyard. (Com): Lalande de Pomerol. A.C. Lalande de Pomerol, Bordeaux.

Château des Moines (Fr) a vineyard. (Com): Saint-Christophe-des-Bardes. A.C. Saint-Émilion, Bordeaux.

Château de Sours (Fr) a vineyard in the A.C. Entre-Deux-Mers, central Bordeaux. 24ha. Saint-Quentin-de-Baron. White from Sémillon, Muscadelle, Merlot blanc, Ugni blanc. Red from Merlot, Cabernet sauvignon, Cabernet franc. Also produces an A.C. Bordeaux rosé from 100% Merlot. Website: http://www.chateaudesours.com 'E'mail: esme@chateaudesours.com

Château Despagne (Fr) a vineyard. (Com): St-Pierre-de-Mons. A.C. Graves, Bordeaux. 4ha (white).

Château Despagnet (Fr) a vineyard. (Com): Saint-Émilion. A.C. Saint-Émilion, Bordeaux 3ha.

Château des Palais (Fr) a vineyard in the A.C. Corbières, south-western France.

Château des Peyrères (Fr) a vineyard. (Com): Landiras. A.C. Graves, Bordeaux 4ha.

Château des Peyteaux (Fr) a vineyard in the A.C. Côtes du Frontonnais, south-western France (red).

Château des Religieuses (Fr) a vineyard in the A.C. Saint-Émilion, Bordeaux 2ha.

Château des Remparts (Fr) a vineyard. (Com): Preignac. A.C. Sauternes, Bordeaux 1ha.

Château des Respide (Fr) a vineyard in the A.C.

C

Graves, Bordeaux. Grape varieties: Cabernet sauvignon 30%, Merlot 70%.

Château des Richards (Fr) a vineyard. (Com): Mombrier. A.C. Côtes de Bourg, Bordeaux.

Château des Rochers (Fr) an A.C. Bordeaux Supérieur.

Château des Rochers (Fr) part of Château Bonneau, A.C. Saint-Émilion, Bordeaux.

Château des Roches (Fr) a vineyard. (Com): Loupiac. A.C. Cérons, Bordeaux.

Château des Rochettes (Fr) a vineyard in the A.C. Anjou, Anjou-Saumur, Loire. (Add): Concourson-sur-Layon, Loire.

Château des Rocs (Fr) a vineyard. (Com): Preignac. A.C. Sauternes, Bordeaux 1ha.

Château des Rozier (Fr) a domaine in A.C. Costières de Nîmes, Languedoc-Roussillon. Noted for red wines made from Grenache grapes.

Château des Roziers (Fr) a vineyard. (Com): Montagne-Saint-Émilion. A.C. Saint-Émilion, Bordeaux 4ha.

Château des Templiers (Fr) a vineyard. (Com): Pomerol. A.C. Pomerol, Bordeaux 3ha.

Château Destieu (Fr) a vineyard. (Com): Saint-Étienne-de-Lisse. A.C. Saint-Émilion, Bordeaux.

Château Destieux (Fr) a vineyard. (Add): Saint-Hippolyte, 33330 Saint-Émilion. Grand Cru Classé. A.C. Saint-Émilion. (Com): Saint-Hippolyte. 8.27ha. Grape varieties: Cabernet 35% and Merlot 65%.

Château Destieux-Verac (Fr) a vineyard in the A.C. Saint-Émilion, Bordeaux 11ha.

Château de St. Maigrin (Fr) a Cognac producer. (Add): Saint-Maigrin, 17520 Archiac. 50ha. in the Bons Bois.

Château des Tonnelles (Fr) a vineyard. (Com): St-Aignan. A.C. Côtes de Fronsac, Bordeaux 6ha.

Château des Tourelles (Fr) a vineyard. (Add): Blaignan 33340. Cru Bourgeois. A.C. Médoc. (Com): Blaignan. 21ha. Grape varieties: Cabernet sauvignon 50% and Merlot 50%.

Château des Tours (Fr) a vineyard in the A.C. Brouilly Cru Beaujolais-Villages, Burgundy. (Add): 69830 St-Étienne-la-Varenne.

Château des Tours (Fr) a vineyard. (Com): Montagne-Saint-Émilion. A.C. Saint-Émilion, Bordeaux 59ha.

Château des Tours (Fr) a vineyard. (Com): Sainte-Croix-du-Mont. A.C. Sainte-Croix-du-Mont, Bordeaux. Also Ste. Clé du Domaine du Château Loubens.

Château des Trois Chardons (Fr) a vineyard. (Add): Cantenac, Margaux 33460. A.C. Margaux. (Com): Cantenac. 2.5ha. Grape varieties: Cabernet sauvignon 60% and Merlot 40%.

Château des Trois Moulins (Fr). A vineyard. (Com): Macau. A.C. Haut-Médoc, Bordeaux. Cru Bourgeois.

Château des Tuileries (Fr) a vineyard. (Com): Virelade. A.C. Graves, Bordeaux. 10ha (red and white).

Château de Suduiraut (Fr) a Premier Grand Cru Classé. A.C. Sauternes. (Com): Preignac. Grape varieties: Sauvignon 5% and Sémillon 95%.

Château de Suronde (Fr) a vineyard in the A.C. Quarts de Chaume, Anjou-Saumur, Loire. Top wine is Cuvée Victor Joseph.

Château des Vaults (Fr) a vineyard based in the A.C. Savennières, Anjou-Saumur, Loire Valley. Owned by Domaine du Closel.

Château de Targé (Fr) an A.C. Saumur-Champigny. (Add): 49730 Parnay, Loire.

Château de Tariquet (Fr) an Armagnac producer. (Add): P. Grassa et Fils, Château de Tariquet, 32800 Eauze. 60ha. in Bas Armagnac. Produces: Degrés Naturel range of brandies XO 49.5% alc. by vol., XO 53.3% alc. by vol. XO Cask N°6 54.9% alc. by vol., Hors d'Age 52.8% alc. by vol. and Hors d'Age Cask N°16 53.4% alc. by vol.

Château de Taste (Fr) a vineyard. (Com): Lansac. A.C. Côtes de Bourg, Bordeaux.

Château de Tastes (Fr) a vineyard. (Com): Sainte-Croix-du-Mont. A.C. Sainte-Croix-du-Mont, Bordeaux. 6ha.

Château de Terrefort-de-Fortissan (Fr) a vineyard. (Com): Villenave-d'Ornon. A.C. Graves, Bordeaux. Cru Bourgeois.

Château de Tersac (Fr) a vineyard in the A.C. Corbières, south-western France.

Château de Teuil de Nailhac (Fr) a vineyard in the A.C. Monbazillac, Bergerac.

Château de Teysson (Fr) a vineyard. (Com): Néac. A.C. Lalande de Pomerol, Bordeaux.

Château de Thau (Fr) a vineyard. (Com): Gauriac. A.C. Côtes de Bourg, Bordeaux.

Château de Tigné (Fr) a vineyard in the A.C. Anjou-Villages, Tigné, Loire. 90ha. Produced by Gérard Depaudieu.

Château de Tiregand (Fr) a vineyard. (Com): Pécharmant. A.C. Pécharmant, Bergerac. (red). (Add): Comtesse F. de Saint-Exupéry Creysse, 24100 Bergerac.

Château de Touilla (Fr) a vineyard. (Com): Fargues. A.C. Sauternes, Bordeaux 3ha.

Château de Tracy (Fr) a vineyard in the A.C. Pouilly Fumé, Central Vineyards, Loire.

Château de Triac (Fr) an Armagnac vineyard owned by Braastad.

Château de Trinquevedel (Fr) a vineyard in the A.C. Tavel. Grape varieties: Clairette, Cinsault and Grenache. Rosé wine sold in véronique bottle.

Château de Triquedina (Fr) a vineyard in A.C. Cahors. Top cuvée is Prince Probus which is aged in new oak.

Château de Valandraud (Fr) a 2.5ha vineyard based in Pomerol, Bordeaux. A.C. Pomerol. Grape varieties: 75% Merlot, 30% Cabernet franc, 5% Malbec.

Château de Valcombe (Fr) a vineyard in the A.C. Costières de Nîmes.

Château de Valfaunès (Fr) a vineyard (established 1996) in the A.C. Pic Saint-Loup, Coteaux du Languedoc. Labels: Favorite, Un Peu de Toi.

Château de Valois (Fr) a vineyard. (Com): Pomerol. A.C. Pomerol, Bordeaux 6ha.

C

Château de Valpinson (Fr) a vineyard in the A.C. Côtes du Rhône, south-eastern France.

Château de Vanisseau (Fr) a vineyard in the A.C. Bergerac (white wines).

Château de Vaudenuits (Fr) an A.C. Vouvray, Touraine, Loire (dry white and sweet sparkling [méthode traditionelle] wines). (Add): B.P. 23, 37210 Vouvray.

Château de Vaudieu (Fr) a vineyard in Courthézon, producing A.C. red and white Châteauneuf-du-Pape wine in the southern Rhône, owned by Brechet.

Château de Varennes (Fr) a vineyard in the A.C. Savennières.

Château de Viaud (Fr) a vineyard. (Com): Lalande de Pomerol. A.C. Saint-Émilion, Bordeaux.

Château de Viens (Fr) a vineyard in the A.C. Côtes de Bourg, north-eastern Bordeaux.

Château Vieux Parc (Fr) a vineyard in the A.C. Corbières, south-western France. Label: La Sélection.

Château Villegorge (Fr) a vineyard. (Com): Avensan (and Moulis). A.C. Haut-Médoc, Bordeaux. Cru Bourgeois Exceptionnel.

Château de Villenouvette (Fr) a vineyard in the A.C. Corbières, south-western Bordeaux.

Château de Villerambert (Fr) a vineyard in the A.C. Minervois, south-western France (red).

Château de Virelade (Fr) a vineyard. (Com): Arbanats. A.C. Graves, Bordeaux. 13ha (red and white).

Château de Viviers (Fr) a winery based in the A.C. Chablis, Burgundy. Produces a range of Chablis wines including Premier Crus Vaillons and Vaucoupin.

Château de Vosne Romanée (Fr) a vineyard in the A.C. commune of Vosne Romanée, Côte de Nuits, Burgundy.

Château d'Eyguem (Fr) an A.C. Bordeaux (red).

Château Deyrem Valentin (Fr) a Cru Bourgeois vineyard. (Com): Soussans-Margaux. A.C. Haut-Médoc, Bordeaux 7ha.

Château d'Hortevie (Fr) a vineyard. (Com): Saint-Julien. A.C. Saint-Julien, Bordeaux. Cru Bourgeois.

Château Dillon (Fr) a vineyard. (Add): 33290 Blanquefort. A.C. Médoc. (Com): Blanquefort. 100ha. Grape varieties: Cabernet franc, Cabernet sauvignon and Merlot.

Château d'Issan (Fr) a Grand Cru Classé (3rd). A.C. Margaux. (Com): Cantenac. 32ha. Grape varieties: Cabernet sauvignon 75% and Merlot 25%.

Château Divon (Fr) a vineyard. (Com): Saint-Georges-Saint-Émilion. A.C. Saint-Émilion, Bordeaux 4ha.

Château Doisy-Daëne (Fr) a Grand Cru Classé (2nd). A.C. Barsac (or Sauternes). (Com): Barsac. Grape varieties: Sauvignon blanc 20%, Muscadelle 10%, Sémillon 70%.

Château Doisy-Dubroca (Fr) a Grand Cru Classé (2nd). A.C. Sauternes. Now part of Château Climens, Barsac.

Château Doisy-Védrines (Fr) a Grand Cru Classé (2nd). A.C. Barsac (or Sauternes). (Com): Barsac.

30ha. Grape varieties: Sauvignon 15% and Sémillon 85%.

Château Domaine de la Rose Maréchale (Fr) a Cru Bourgeois. A.C. Médoc. (Com): St-Seurin-de-Cadourne.

Château Domeyne (Fr) a vineyard. (Com): Saint-Estèphe. A.C. Saint-Estèphe, Bordeaux 2ha.

Château Doms et Clos du Monastère (Fr) an A.C. Graves. (Com): Portets (red and white) 15ha.

Château Donissan-Veyrin (Fr) a vineyard. (Com): Listrac. A.C. Haut-Médoc, Bordeaux 6ha.

Château Donos (Fr) a vineyard in the A.C. Corbières, south-western France. Label: Cuvée Gonezinde Premier Cru.

Château Doré (Austr) a vineyard (Add): Mandurang, Victoria. Grape varieties: Riesling, Cabernet sauvignon, Shiraz. Also produce a tawny Port-style wine.

Château Doumayne (Fr) a vineyard. (Add): Château Sansonnet, 33330 Saint-Émilion A.C. Saint-Émilion. (Com): Saint-Émilion.

Château Doumens (Fr) a vineyard. (Com): Margaux. A.C. Margaux, Bordeaux. Cru Bourgeois.

Château Drouilleau Belles Graves (Fr) a vineyard. (Com): Néac. A.C. Lalande de Pomerol, Bordeaux.

Château Duarate (S.Am) a red wine produced in San Salvador.

Château du Barrail (Fr) a vineyard. (Com): Bégadan. A.C. Médoc, Bordeaux.

Château du Barrail (Fr) a vineyard. (Com): Eynesse. A.C. Saint-Foy-Bordeaux, Bordeaux.

Château du Barry (Fr) a vineyard. (Add): Saint-Sulpice-de-Faleyrens, 33330 Saint-Émilion. Grand Cru. A.C. Saint-Émilion. (Com): Saint-Sulpice-de-Faleyrens. 16ha. Grape varieties: Cabernet franc 20%, Cabernet sauvignon 10% and Merlot 70%. The second wine is Château de Mons.

Château du Basty (Fr) a vineyard in the A.C. Beaujolais-Villages, Burgundy. Wine produced by Perroud in Lantignié.

Château du Beau Vallon (Fr) a vineyard. (Com): Saint-Christophe-des-Bardes. A.C. Saint-Émilion, Bordeaux.

Château du Biac (Fr) a vineyard. (Com): Langoiran. A.C. Premières Côtes de Bordeaux. (Add): 33550 Langoiran. 10ha. Grape varieties: Cabernet franc, Cabernet sauvignon, Merlot, Muscadelle, Sauvignon and Sémillon (red 50% and white 50%).

Château du Bloy (Fr) a vineyard in the A.C. Bergerac, south-western France. (Add): Bonneville, 24230 Velines. (red, rosé, sweet white and dry white).

Château du Bluizard (Fr) a vineyard in the A.C. Beaujolais-Villages, Burgundy.

Château du Bosquet (Fr) a vineyard in the A.C. Côtes de Bourg, Bordeaux. Cru Bourgeois.

Château du Bouchet (Fr) a vineyard in the A.C. Côtes de Buzet, south-western France.

Château du Boulay (Fr) a vineyard in the A.C. Montlouis, Touraine, Loire.

Château Dubraud (Fr) an A.C. Bordeaux (red).

Château du Breuil (Fr) a Calvados distillery and

producer based in the Calvados Pays d'Auge, Normandy.

Château du Breuil (Fr) a vineyard. (Com): Bayon. A.C. Côtes de Bourg, Bordeaux.

Château du Breuil (Fr) a vineyard. (Com): Cissac. A.C. Médoc, Bordeaux 19 ha.

Château du Breuil (Fr) a vineyard in A.C. Coteaux du Layon Beaulieu, Anjou-Saumur, Loire. 32ha. Wine is produced and bottled by M. Morgat, Beaulieu-sur-Layon. Grape varieties: Chardonnay, Chenin blanc, Gamay, Pinot blanc and Sauvignon blanc.

Château du Busca (Fr) an Armagnac producer. (Add): Château du Busca Maniban, 32310 Mansecome. 30ha. in Ténarèze. Produces: Marquis de Maniban Napoléon.

Château du Calvaire (Fr) a vineyard in the A.C. Saint-Émilion, Bordeaux 12ha.

Château du Carles (Fr) a vineyard. (Com): Saillans. A.C. Côtes de Fronsac, Bordeaux 13ha.

Château du Cartillon (Fr) a vineyard, (Com): Lamarque. A.C. Haut-Médoc, Bordeaux. 20ha. Cru Bourgeois.

Château Ducasse (Fr) a vineyard. (Com): Barsac. A.C. Barsac (or Sauternes), Bordeaux 5ha.

Château du Casse (Fr) a vineyard. (Com): Pomerol. A.C. Pomerol, Bordeaux 2ha.

Château du Castera (Fr) a vineyard. (Com): Saint-Germain-d'Esteuil. A.C. Médoc, Bordeaux. Cru Bourgeois.

Château du Cauze (Fr) a vineyard. (Add): Saint-Christophe-des-Bardes, 33330 Saint-Émilion. Grand Cru. A.C. Saint-Émilion. (Com): Saint-Christophe-des-Bardes. 23ha. Grape varieties: Cabernet franc, Cabernet sauvignon and Merlot 60%.

Château du Cayrou (Fr) a vineyard in the A.C. Cahors. (Add): 46700 Puy-l'Evêque, Lot.

Château du Cèdre (Fr) a vineyard in the A.C. Cahors.

Château du Chatelard (Fr) a winery based in the A.C. Beaujolais-Villages, (Lancié), southern Burgundy. Also produces Les Vieux Granites (A.C. Cru Beaujolais Fleurie).

Château du Chayne (Fr) a vineyard in the A.C. Côtes de Bergerac, south-western France.

Château du Ducla (Fr) an A.C. Bordeaux. 85ha. Grape varieties: Cabernet franc 6%, Cabernet sauvignon 38%, Malbec 2%, Merlot 54%.

Château du Cléray-Sauvion en Eolie (Fr) a vineyard in the A.C. Muscadet Sèvre et Maine, Nantais, Loire. (Add): Sauvion Fils, 44330 Vallet, Loire. Also a major Loire négociant. *see* Cardinal Richard.

Château du Clocher (Fr) a vineyard in the A.C. Saint-Émilion, Bordeaux 3ha.

Château du Clos Renon (Fr) a vineyard. (Com): Portets. (Graves). A.C. Bordeaux Supérieur (red).

Château Ducluzeau (Fr) a vineyard. (Com): Listrac. A.C. Listrac, Bordeaux 4ha. Grape varieties: Cabernet sauvignon 20% and Merlot 80%.

Château du Cognac (Fr) the premises of Otard, Cognac producers.

Château du Coing de St-Fiacre (Fr) a vineyard in the A.C. Muscadet Sèvre et Maine, Nantais, Loire. 40ha. (Add): 44 St-Fiacre, Loire.

Château du Comte (Fr) a vineyard in the A.C. Saint-Émilion, Bordeaux 3ha.

Château du Cotelet (Fr) a vineyard in Pallet, A.C. Muscadet Sèvre et Maine, Nantais, Loire.

Château du Cros (Fr) a vineyard. (Com): Loupiac. A.C. Loupiac, Bordeaux 21ha.

Château du Croute (Fr) an A.C. Bordeaux (red).

Château Ducru Beaucaillou (Fr) a vineyard. (Add): Saint-Julien, Beychevelle, Grand Cru Classé (2nd). A.C. Saint-Julien. (Com): Saint-Julien. 50ha. Grape varieties: Cabernet franc, Cabernet sauvignon, Merlot and Petit verdot. Second wine is Château La Croix de Beaucaillou.

Château du Domaine de Descazeaux (Fr) a vineyard. (Com): Gauriac. A.C. Côtes de Bourg, Bordeaux.

Château Dudon (Fr) a vineyard. (Com): Barsac. A.C. Barsac (or Sauternes), Bordeaux 8ha.

Château Dudon (Fr) an A.C. Bordeaux (red).

Château du Ferrand (Fr) a vineyard. (Com): Saint-Émilion. A.C. Saint-Émilion, Bordeaux. (Add): 33330 Saint-Émilion.

Château du Fronsac (Fr) a vineyard. (Com): Fronsac. A.C. Côtes de Fronsac, Bordeaux 4ha.

Château du Gaby (Fr) a vineyard. (Com): St-Michel. A.C. Côtes Canon-Fronsac, Bordeaux 25ha.

Château du Galan (Fr) a vineyard. (Com): Saint Laurent. A.C. Médoc, Bordeaux. Cru Bourgeois.

Château du Glana (Fr) a vineyard. (Com): Saint-Julien. A.C. Saint-Julien, Bordeaux. Cru Bourgeois Exceptionnel.

Château du Grand Barrail (Fr) an A.C. Premières Côtes de Blaye (based in Cars) 33ha.

Château du Grand Clapeau (Fr) a vineyard. (Com): Blanquefort. A.C. Haut-Médoc, Bordeaux. (Add): 33290 Blanquefort. 11ha. Cru Bourgeois.

Château du Grand Moine (Fr) a vineyard. (Com): Lalande de Pomerol. A.C. Lalande de Pomerol, Bordeaux.

Château du Grand Moueys (Fr) a vineyard on south-facing slopes near the Garonne. A.C. Premières Côtes de Bordeaux (60ha red/40ha white).

Château du Grand Moulas (Fr) a vineyard in the A.C. Côtes du Rhône, south-western France.

Château du Grand Pierre (Fr) a vineyard in the A.C. Premières Côtes de Blaye.

Château du Grand-Saint Julien (Fr) a vineyard. (Com): Saint-Julien. A.C. Saint-Julien, Bordeaux. Cru Bourgeois.

Château du Haire (Fr) a vineyard. (Com): Preignac. A.C. Sauternes, Bordeaux 4ha.

Château Duhart Milon (Fr) *see* Château Duhart Milon Rothschild.

Château Duhart Milon Rothschild (Fr) a vineyard. (Add): 33250 Pauillac. Grand Cru Classé (4th). A.C. Pauillac. (Com): Pauillac. 50ha. Grape varieties: Cabernet franc, Cabernet sauvignon and Merlot. Second wine is Château Moulin-Duhart. Owned by Rothshild.

Château du Haut-Gravier (Fr) a vineyard. (Com): Illats. A.C. Cérons, Bordeaux 11ha.

Château du Juge (Fr) an A.C. Bordeaux Sec. (Add): 33190 Yvon Mau.

C

Château du Juge (Fr) a vineyard. (Com): Preignac. A.C. Sauternes, Bordeaux 4ha.

Château du Junca (Fr) a vineyard. (Com): St-Sauveur. A.C. Haut-Médoc, Bordeaux. (Add): St-Sauveur, 33250 Pauillac.

Château du Magnum (Fr) a vineyard in the A.C. Graves, Bordeaux (white).

Château du Marquisat (Fr) a vineyard in the A.C. Côtes de Bourg, north-eastern Bordeaux.

Château du Mayne (Fr) a vineyard. (Com): Barsac. A.C. Barsac (or Sauternes), Bordeaux 7ha.

Château du Mayne (Fr) a vineyard. (Com): Pomerol. A.C. Pomerol, Bordeaux 2ha.

Château du Mayne (Fr) a vineyard. (Com): Preignac. A.C. Sauternes, Bordeaux 2ha.

Château du Mirail (Fr) a vineyard. (Com): Portets. A.C. Graves, Bordeaux. (Add): 33460 Portets. 23ha. Grape varieties: Cabernet, Merlot and Sémillon.

Château du Mont (Fr) a vineyard. (Com): Sainte-Croix-du-Mont. A.C. Sainte-Croix-du-Mont, Bordeaux 7ha.

Château du Mont (Fr) a vineyard. (Com): Preignac. A.C. Sauternes, Bordeaux 4ha.

Château du Monthil (Fr) a vineyard. (Com): Bégadan. A.C. Médoc, Bordeaux. (Add): Bégadan, 33340 Lesparre. 20ha. Grape varieties: Cabernet sauvignon, Malbec, Merlot and Petit verdot.

Château du Moulin (Fr) a vineyard. (Com): Montagne-Saint-Émilion. A.C. Saint-Émilion, Bordeaux 6ha.

Château du Moulin du Bourg (Fr) a vineyard. (Com): Listrac. A.C. Haut-Médoc, Bordeaux 7ha.

Château du Moulin Rouge (Fr) a vineyard. (Add): Cussac-Fort-Médoc, 44460 Margaux. Cru Bourgeois. A.C. Haut-Médoc. (Com): Cussac-Fort-Médoc. 15ha. Grape varieties: Cabernet sauvignon, Malbec, Merlot and Petit verdot.

Château du Noble (Fr) a vineyard. (Com): Loupiac. A.C. Loupiac, Bordeaux 7ha.

Château du Nozay (Fr) a vineyard in the A.C. Sancerre, Central Vineyards, France. Grape variety: Sauvignon blanc.

Château du Pape (Fr) a vineyard. (Com): Preignac. A.C. Sauternes, Bordeaux 3ha.

Château du Paradis (Fr) a vineyard. (Add): Vignonet, 33330 Saint-Émilion. Grand Cru. A.C. Saint-Émilion. (Com): Vignonet. 25ha.

Château du Pavillon (Fr) a vineyard. (Com): Roaillan. A.C. Graves, Bordeaux. 6ha (white).

Château du Pavillon (Fr) a vineyard. (Com): Sainte-Croix-du-Mont. A.C. Sainte-Croix-du-Mont, Bordeaux.

Château du Petit-Moulinet (Fr) a vineyard. (Com): Pomerol. A.C. Pomerol, Bordeaux 3ha.

Château du Petit Puch (Fr) a vineyard in the A.C. Entre-Deux-Mers based at Saint Germain du Puch, Gironde.

Château du Peyrat (Fr) a vineyard. (Com): Cérons. A.C. Cérons, Bordeaux 8ha.

Château Dupeyrat (Fr) a vineyard. (Com): St-Paul. A.C. Côte de Blaye, Bordeaux.

Château du Peyrat (Fr) a vineyard. (Com): Saint Laurent. A.C. Médoc, Bordeaux. Cru Bourgeois.

Château Dupeyron (Fr) the second wine of Château Canuet.

Château Dupian (Fr) a vineyard. (Com): Le Pian. A.C. Haut-Médoc, Bordeaux. Cru Bourgeois.

Château du Pick (Fr) a vineyard. (Com): Preignac. A.C. Sauternes, Bordeaux.

Château du Planter (Fr) an A.C. Bordeaux Rouge. (Add): 33540, Sauveterre-de-Guyenne.

Château Duplessis-Fabre (Fr) a vineyard. (Com): Moulis. A.C. Moulis, Bordeaux. (Add): 33480 Moulis. Cru Bourgeois. 17ha. Grape varieties: Cabernet franc, Cabernet sauvignon, Merlot and Petit verdot.

Château Duplessis-Hauchecorne (Fr) a vineyard. (Com): Moulis. A.C. Moulis, Bordeaux. 16ha. Cru Grand Bourgeois.

Château du Pont du Bouquey (Fr) a vineyard in the A.C. Saint-Émilion, Bordeaux 3ha.

Château du Pontet (Fr) a vineyard in the A.C. Saint-Émilion, Bordeaux 3ha.

Château du Puy (Fr) a vineyard. (Com): Parsac-Saint-Émilion. A.C. Saint-Émilion, Bordeaux 6ha.

Château du Puynormand (Fr) a vineyard. (Com): Parsac-Saint-Émilion. A.C. Saint-Émilion, Bordeaux 7ha.

Château Durand-Laplagne (Fr) a vineyard. (Com): Puisseguin-Saint-Émilion. A.C. Puisseguin-Saint-Émilion, Bordeaux.

Château du Raux (Fr) a vineyard. (Add): Cussac-Fort-Médoc. 33460 Margaux. A.C. Haut-Médoc, Bordeaux. (Com): Cussac-Fort-Médoc. 10ha. Grape varieties: Cabernet sauvignon 50% and Merlot 50%.

Château Durfort-Vivens (Fr) a vineyard. (Add): 33460 Margaux. Grand Cru Classé (2nd). A.C. Margaux. (Com): Margaux. 20ha. Grape varieties: Cabernet franc 10%, Cabernet sauvignon 82% and Merlot 8%. Second wine is Domaine de Cure-Bourse.

Château du Roc (Fr) a vineyard. (Com): Barsac. A.C. Barsac (or Sauternes), Bordeaux 2ha.

Château du Roc (Fr) a vineyard. (Com): Cérons. A.C. Cérons, Bordeaux 5ha.

Château du Roc de Boissac (Fr) a vineyard. (Com): Puisseguin-Saint-Émilion. A.C. Saint-Émilion, Bordeaux.

Château du Rocher (Fr) a vineyard. (Add): Saint-Étienne-de-Lisse, 33330 Saint-Émilion. Grand Cru. A.C. Saint-Émilion. (Com): Saint-Étienne-de-Lisse. 15ha. Grape varieties: Cabernet franc 20%, Cabernet sauvignon 30% and Merlot 50%.

Château du Roy (Fr) a vineyard in the A.C. Saint-Émilion, Bordeaux 3ha.

Château du Rozay (Fr) a vineyard in the A.C. Condrieu, northern Rhône.

Château du Seuil (Fr) a vineyard. (Com): Cérons. A.C. Cérons, Bordeaux 3ha.

Château du Seuil (Fr) a vineyard in Aix-en-Provence, south-eastern France. Red, rosé and white wines produced.

Château du Suduiraut (Fr) a Premier Grand Cru

C

Classé vineyard. (Com): Preignac. A.C. Sauternes, Bordeaux.

Château du Tailhas (Fr) a vineyard. (Com): Libourne. A.C. Pomerol, Bordeaux 9ha.

Château du Taillan (Fr) a Cru Grand Bourgeois. (Add): Le Taillon-Médoc, 33320 Eysines. A.C. Haut-Médoc. (Com): Le Taillon-Médoc. 25ha. Grape varieties: Cabernet franc, Cabernet sauvignon and Merlot.

Château du Tariquet (Fr) an estate in Bas Armagnac that produces a Folle blanche Armagnac, XO and Hors d'Age.

Château du Tasta (Fr) a vineyard. (Com): Camblancs. A.C. Premières Côtes de Bordeaux. (Add): 33360 Camblancs.

Château du Tasta (Fr) a vineyard. (Com): St-Aignan. A.C. Côtes de Fronsac, Bordeaux 12ha.

Château du Tertre (Fr) an A.C. Margaux. (Com): Arsac. 45ha. Grape varieties: Cabernet franc, Cabernet sauvignon and Merlot.

Château du Testeron (Fr) a vineyard. (Com): Moulis. A.C. Haut-Médoc, Bordeaux. Cru Bourgeois.

Château Duthil-Haut-Cressant (Fr) a vineyard. (Com): Le Pian. A.C. Haut-Médoc, Bordeaux. Cru Bourgeois.

Château du Thyl (Fr) a vineyard in the A.C. Beaujolais-Villages, Burgundy.

Château du Touran (Fr) a vineyard in the A.C. Saint-Émilion, Bordeaux 4ha.

Château du Treuil de Nailhac (Fr) a vineyard. (Com): Monbazillac. A.C. Monbazillac, Bergerac.

Château du Trignon (Fr) a vineyard in the A.C. Côtes-du-Rhône-Villages Sablet, Vaucluse. Also A.C. Côtes-du-Rhône-Villages Rasteau.

Château Dutruch-Grand-Poujeaux (Fr) a vineyard. (Add): 33480 Moulis-en-Médoc. Cru Bourgeois Exceptionnel. A.C. Moulis. (Com): Moulis. 30ha. Grape varieties: Cabernet, Merlot and Petit verdot.

Château du Val de Mercy (Fr) a winery based in the A.C. Chablis, Burgundy. Produces a range of Chablis wines including Premier Crus Beauregard and Côte de Jouan.

Château du Val-d'Or (Fr) a vineyard in the A.C. Saint-Émilion, Bordeaux 3ha.

Château du Vieux Corbeau (USA) a winery based near Louisville, Kentucky.

Château du Vieux-Moulin (Fr) a vineyard. (Com): Loupiac. A.C. Loupiac, Bordeaux 9ha.

Château du Vigneau (Fr) a vineyard. (Com): St. Nicolas de Bourgueil. A.C. St. Nicolas de Bourgueil, Touraine, Loire.

Château du Violet (Fr) a vineyard. (Com): Preignac. A.C. Sauternes, Bordeaux 7ha.

Château du Vivier (Fr) a vineyard in the A.C. Fleurie Cru Beaujolais-Villages, Burgundy.

Château d'Yquem (Fr) a Premier Grand Cru Classé vineyard. (Com): Sauternes. A.C. Sauternes. 80ha. Grape varieties: Sauvignon 20% and Sémillon 80%. Average annual production 5500cases (66000bottles). Its dry white wine is Y Grec (a wine rarely seen), now owned by the LVMH Group since 1999.

Château Edem (Fr) a vineyard in the A.C. Côtes du Ventoux, Rhône Valley.

Château Esterlin (Fr) a vineyard. (Com): Barsac. A.C. Barsac (or Sauternes), Bordeaux 3ha. Also Clos d'Espagnet.

Château Étang des Colombes (Fr) a vineyard in the A.C. Corbières, Languedoc-Roussillon, south-western France. Produces: white, rosé and red wines. Label: Bois des Dames.

Château Eyquem (Fr) a vineyard. (Com): Bayon. A.C. Côtes de Bourg, Bordeaux.

Château Fagouet-Jean-Voisin (Fr) a vineyard in the A.C. Saint-Émilion, Bordeaux 6ha.

Château Faizeau (Fr) a vineyard. (Com): Montagne-Saint-Émilion. A.C. Saint-Émilion, Bordeaux 7ha.

Château Faleyrens (Fr) a vineyard in the A.C. Saint-Émilion, Bordeaux 5ha.

Château Falfas (Fr) an organic wine-producing vineyard. (Com): Bayon. A.C. Côtes de Bourg, Bordeaux 22ha.

Château Fantin (Fr) a vineyard. (Com): Saint-Jeane-de-Blaigrac. A.C. Entre-Deux-Mers, Bordeaux.

Château Fargues (Fr) a vineyard. (Com): Fargues. A.C. Sauternes, Bordeaux 62ha.

Château Farluret (Fr) a vineyard. (Com): Barsac. A.C. Barsac (or Sauternes), Bordeaux 4ha.

Château Fatin (Fr) a vineyard in the A.C. Médoc, Bordeaux. Cru Bourgeois.

Château Faurie de Souchard (Fr) a vineyard. (Add): BP. 24, 33330 Saint-Émilion. Grand Cru (demoted 2006). A.C. Saint-Émilion. (Com): Saint-Émilion. 12ha. Grape varieties: Cabernet franc 26%, Cabernet sauvignon 9% and Merlot 65%.

Château Fayau (Fr) a vineyard in the A.C. Cadillac, Bordeaux.

Château Fayolle (Fr) a vineyard in the A.C. Bergerac, south-western France (red).

Château Fellonneau (Fr) a vineyard. (Com): Macau. A.C. Haut-Médoc, Bordeaux 1ha.

Château Fernon (Fr) a vineyard. (Com): Langon. A.C. Graves, Bordeaux. 40ha (red and white).

Château Ferran (Fr) a vineyard. (Com): Martillac. A.C. Graves, Bordeaux. 3.5ha (red and white).

Château Ferrand (Fr) a vineyard. (Com): Pomerol. A.C. Pomerol, Bordeaux 11ha.

Château Ferrandat (Fr) a vineyard in the A.C. Saint-Émilion, Bordeaux 4ha.

Château Ferrande (Fr) a vineyard. (Add): 33640 Portets, Castres, Gironde. A.C. Graves. (Com): Portets. 43ha. Grape varieties: Cabernet franc, Cabernet sauvignon, Merlot, Sauvignon and Sémillon.

Château Ferrière (Fr). Grand Cru Classé (3ʳᵈ). A.C. Margaux. (Com): Margaux 26ha.

Château Feytit-Clinet (Fr) a vineyard. (Com): Pomerol. A.C. Pomerol, Bordeaux 6ha.

Château Fieuzal (Fr) a vineyard. (Com): Léognan. A.C. Pessac-Léognan, Bordeaux. 30ha. Grand Cru Classé. (white). Second wine is Château L'Abeille de Fieuzal.

Château Figeac (Fr) a vineyard. (Add): 33330 Saint-Émilion. Premier [B] Grand Cru Classé. A.C. Saint-

Émilion. (Com): Saint-Émilion. 40ha. Grape varieties: Cabernet franc, Cabernet sauvignon and Merlot. Website: http://www.chateau-figeac.com

Château Filhot (Fr) a vineyard. (Add): 33210 Sauternes. Grand Cru Classé (2nd). A.C. Sauternes. Established 1709. (Com): Sauternes. 60ha. Grape varieties: Muscadelle 4%, Sauvignon 36% and Sémillon 60%. Originally known as Château Sauternes until 1901.

Château Fleur (Slav) the brand-name of a range of full, sweet, red and white wines.

Château Fleur Cardinale (Fr) a vineyard. (Add): Saint-Étienne-de-Lisse, 33330 Saint-Émilion. Grand Cru Classé (promoted 2006). A.C. Saint-Émilion. (Com): Saint-Étienne-de-Lisse. 12ha. Grape varieties: Cabernet franc 15%, Cabernet sauvignon 15% and Merlot 70%.

Château Fleury (Fr) a vineyard. (Com): Barsac. A.C. Barsac (or Sauternes), Bordeaux 2ha. Also Château Terre-Noble.

Château Flotis (Fr) a vineyard in the A.C. Côtes du Fronton.

Château Fombrauge (Fr) a vineyard (planted circa 1618). (Add): Saint-Christophe-des-Bardes, 33330 Saint-Émilion. Grand Cru. A.C. Saint-Émilion. (Com): Saint-Christophe-des-Bardes. 75ha. Grape varieties: Cabernet franc 20%, Cabernet sauvignon 10% and Merlot 70%.

Château Fonbadet (Fr) a vineyard. (Add): 33250 Pauillac. A.C. Pauillac. (Com): Pauillac. 18ha. Grape varieties: Cabernet franc, Cabernet sauvignon, Malbec, Merlot and Petit verdot. Second wine is Château Tour du Roc Milon.

Château Foncet Lacour (Fr) the brand-name for Barton & Guestier red and white wines.

Château Foncla (Fr) a vineyard. (Com): Castres. A.C. Graves, Bordeaux. 13ha (red and white).

Château Foncroise (Fr) a vineyard. (Com): St-Selve. A.C. Graves, Bordeaux. 7ha (red and white).

Château Fondarzac (Fr) a vineyard in Naujan et Postiac, A.C. Entre-Deux-Mers, Bordeaux.

Château Fond-de-Rol (Fr) a vineyard in the A.C. Saint-Émilion, Bordeaux 1ha.

Château Fond-Razade (Fr) a vineyard in the A.C. Saint-Émilion, Bordeaux 4ha.

Château Fongaban (Fr) part of Château Mouchet A.C. Saint-Émilion, Bordeaux.

Château Fongaban (Fr) a vineyard in the A.C. Côtes de Castillon. Part of Château Mouchet A.C. Saint-Émilion, Bordeaux.

Château Fonpetite (Fr) a vineyard. (Com): Saint-Estèphe. A.C. Saint-Estèphe, Bordeaux. Cru Bourgeois.

Château Fontaneau (Fr) an A.C. Médoc vineyard (Com): Bégadan, Médoc. Grape varieties: Cabernet franc, Cabernet sauvignon, Merlot and Petit verdot.

Château Fontpinot (Fr) see Château de Fontpinot.

Château Fonpiqueyre (Fr) the name under which Château Liversan is sometimes sold.

Château Fonplégade (Fr) a vineyard. (Add): 33330 Saint-Émilion. Grand Cru Classé. A.C. Saint-

Émilion. (Com): Saint-Émilion. 19.5ha. Grape varieties: Cabernet franc 35%, Cabernet sauvignon 5% and Merlot 60%. 'E'mail: stephany.rosa@wanadoo.fr

Château Fonrazade (Fr) a vineyard. (Add): 33330 Saint-Émilion. Grand Cru. A.C. Saint-Émilion. (Com): Saint-Émilion. 15ha. Grape varieties: Cabernet franc 10%, Cabernet sauvignon 20% and Merlot 70%. Second wine is Château Comte des Cordes. 'E'mail: chateau-fonrazade@wanadoo.fr

Château Fonréaud (Fr) a vineyard. (Add): 33480 Listrac-Médoc. Cru Bourgeois. A.C. Listrac. (Com): Listrac. 45ha. Grape varieties: Cabernet sauvignon, Merlot and Petit verdot. Second wine is Chemin Royal.

Château Fonroque (Fr) a vineyard. (Add): 33330 Saint-Émilion. Grand Cru Classé. A.C. Saint-Émilion. (Com): Saint-Émilion 18ha.

Château Fontaneau (Fr) a vineyard in the A.C. Médoc in the commune of Bégadan. Grape varieties: Cabernet franc, Cabernet sauvignon, Merlot, Petit verdot.

Château Fontanet (Fr) a vineyard. (Com): Le Taillon-Médoc. A.C. Médoc, Bordeaux. Cru Grand Bourgeois.

Château Fontareche (Fr) a vineyard in the A.C. Corbières, south-western France. Label: Sélection Vieilles Vignes.

Château Fontebride (Fr) a vineyard. (Com): Preignac. A.C. Sauternes, Bordeaux 2ha.

Château Fontenil (Fr) a vineyard (established 1986) in the A.C. Fronsac, Bordeaux 8ha.

Château Fontesteau (Fr) a vineyard. (Com): Saint-Sauveur. A.C. Haut-Médoc, Bordeaux. Cru Grand Bourgeois 12ha.

Château Fontmurée (Fr) a vineyard. (Com): Montagne-Saint-Émilion. A.C. Saint-Émilion, Bordeaux 8ha.

Château-Fort (Lux) a large spirit distilling centre in Beaufort.

Château Fort de Vauban (Fr) a vineyard. (Add): 33460 Margaux. Cru Bourgeois. A.C. Haut-Médoc. (Com): Cussac-Fort-Médoc. 6ha. Grape varieties: Cabernet 40% and Merlot 60%.

Château Fortia (Fr) an historic vineyard producing red and white wines in the A.C. Châteauneuf-du-Pape, southern Rhône. It was here that the A.C. wine laws were conceived (circa 1920 – 1935). see Baron le Roy.

Château Fougeailles (Fr) a vineyard. (Com): Néac. A.C. Lalande de Pomerol, Bordeaux.

Château Fougères (Fr) a vineyard in the A.C. Saint-Émilion, Bordeaux 9ha.

Château Fouguetrat (Fr) a vineyard in the A.C. Saint-Émilion, Bordeaux 19ha.

Château Fourcas-Dupré (Fr) a vineyard. (Add): 33480 Listrac-Médoc. Cru Bourgeois Exceptionnel. A.C. Listrac. (Com): Listrac. 40ha. Grape varieties: Cabernet franc, Cabernet sauvignon and Merlot. Second wine is Château Bellevue Laffont.

Château Fourcas-Hosten (Fr) a vineyard. (Add): 33480 Listrac-Médoc. Cru Bourgeois Exceptionnel.

C

A.C. Listrac. (Com): Listrac. 40ha. Grape varieties: Cabernet franc, Cabernet sauvignon and Merlot. 'E'mail: fourcas@club-internet.fr

Château Fourcas-Loubaney (Fr) a vineyard. (Add): Moulin de Laborde, 33480, Listrac-Médoc. A.C. Listrac. (Com): Listrac. 5ha. Grape varieties: Cabernet sauvignon 60%, Merlot 30%, Petit verdot 10%.

Château Fournas-Bernadotte (Fr) an A.C. Cru-Bourgeois. 35ha. 7ha. in Pauillac and 28ha. in Haut-Médoc.

Château Fourney (Fr) a vineyard. (Add): Saint-Pey-d'Armens, 33330 Saint-Émilion, Grand Cru. A.C. Saint-Émilion. (Com): Saint-Pey-d'Armens. 12ha. Grape varieties: Cabernet franc 30%, Cabernet sauvignon 6% and Merlot 64%.

Château Fourtet (Fr) a vineyard. (Com): Saint-Émilion. A.C. Saint-Émilion, Bordeaux.

Château Franc (Fr) an A.C. Saint-Émilion. (Com): Saint-Émilion. Second wine of Château Franc-Patarabet. Grand Cru. Saint-Émilion 4ha.

Château Franc-Beau-Mazerat (Fr) a vineyard in the A.C. Saint-Émilion, Bordeaux 3ha.

Château Franc-Bigaroux (Fr) a vineyard. (Add): Vignonet, 33330 Saint-Émilion. Grand Cru. A.C. Saint-Émilion. (Com): Vignonet.

Château Franc-Cantenac (Fr) a vineyard in the A.C. Saint-Émilion, Bordeaux 1ha.

Château Franc-Cormey (Fr) a vineyard in the A.C. Saint-Émilion, Bordeaux 2ha.

Château Franc-Cros (Fr) a vineyard in the A.C. Saint-Émilion, Bordeaux 4ha.

Château Franc Grace-Dieu (Fr) a vineyard. (Add): 33330 Saint-Émilion. Grand Cru. A.C. Saint-Émilion. (Com): Saint-Émilion. 8ha. Grape varieties: Bouchet 41%, Cabernet sauvignon 7% and Merlot 52%.

Château Franc-Laporte (Fr) a vineyard in the A.C. Saint-Émilion, Bordeaux 9ha.

Château Franc-Larmande (Fr) a vineyard in the A.C. Saint-Émilion, Bordeaux 3ha.

Château Franc-la-Rose (Fr) a vineyard in the A.C. Saint-Émilion, Bordeaux 4ha.

Château Franc Maillet (Fr) a vineyard. (Com): Pomerol. A.C. Pomerol, Bordeaux 4ha.

Château Franc Mayne (Fr) a vineyard. (Add): 33330 Saint-Émilion. Grand Cru Classé. A.C. Saint-Émilion. (Com): Saint-Émilion 6.5ha.

Château Franc-Mazerat (Fr) a vineyard in the A.C. Saint-Émilion, Bordeaux 2ha.

Château Francois (Austr) the name of a small vineyard based in New South Wales. Produces varietal wines.

Château Franc-Patarabet (Fr) a vineyard. (Add): 33330 Saint-Émilion. Grand Cru. A.C. Saint-Émilion. (Com): Saint-Émilion. 5ha. Grape varieties: Cabernet franc 27.5%, Cabernet sauvignon 27.5% and Merlot 45%. Second wine is Château Franc. A.C. Saint-Émilion.

Château Franc Peilhan (Fr) a vineyard in the A.C. Saint-Émilion, Bordeaux 3ha.

Château Franc-Petit-Figeac (Fr) a vineyard in the A.C. Saint-Émilion, Bordeaux 3ha.

Château Franc-Pineuilh (Fr) a vineyard. (Add): Saint-Christophe-des-Bardes, 33330 Saint-Émilion. A.C. Saint Émilion. (Com): Saint-Christophe-des-Bardes. 8.5ha. Grape varieties: Cabernet franc 35%, Cabernet sauvignon, Malbec and Merlot 60%.

Château Franc Pipeau (Fr) a vineyard. (Add): Saint-Hippolyte, 33330 Saint-Émilion. Grand Cru. A.C. Saint-Émilion. (Com): Saint-Hippolyte. 4.5ha. Grape varieties: Cabernet franc 15%, Cabernet sauvignon 25% and Merlot 60%.

Château Franc Pourret (Fr) a vineyard in the Côtes Saint-Émilion. A.C. Saint-Émilion, Bordeaux 11ha.

Château Franc Rosier (Fr) a vineyard. (Com): Saint Hippolyte. A.C. Saint-Émilion, Bordeaux 11ha.

Château Franquet Grand Poujeaux (Fr) a vineyard. (Add): 6 Rue des Lilas, Moulis 33250. A.C. Moulis. (Com): Moulis. 6ha. Grape varieties: Cabernet franc, Cabernet sauvignon, Malbec, Merlot and Petit verdot.

Château Froquard (Fr) a vineyard. (Com): Saint-Georges-Saint-Émilion. A.C. Saint-Émilion, Bordeaux 3ha.

Château Freydefond (Fr) a vineyard in the A.C. Côtes de Castillon, Bordeaux.

Château Fuissé (Fr) a vineyard. (Com): Fuissé. A.C. Pouilly-Fuissé, Mâconnais, Burgundy.

Château Gaby (Fr) a vineyard. (Com): Fronsac. A.C. Côtes Canon-Fronsac, Bordeaux 6ha.

Château Gachet (Fr) a vineyard. (Com): Néac. A.C. Lalande de Pomerol, Bordeaux.

Château Gachon (Fr) a vineyard. (Com): Montagne-Saint-Émilion. A.C. Saint-Émilion, Bordeaux. Grape varieties: Cabernet franc 30%, Cabernet sauvignon 30%, Merlot 40%.

Château Gaciot (Fr) a vineyard. (Com): Avensan. A.C. Haut-Médoc, Bordeaux 5ha.

Château Gadeau (Fr) a vineyard. (Com): Plassac. A.C. Côtes de Blaye, Bordeaux.

Château Gadet-Plaisance (Fr) a vineyard. (Com): Montagne-Saint-Émilion. A.C. Saint-Émilion, Bordeaux 4ha.

Château Gagnard (Fr) a vineyard. (Com): Fronsac. A.C. Côtes de Fronsac, Bordeaux 11ha.

Château Gai (Can) a winery sited near the Niagara Falls. Produces a variety of wines.

Château Gaillard (Fr) a vineyard. (Com): Sables-Saint-Émilion. A.C. Saint-Émilion, Bordeaux 4ha.

Château Gaillard (Fr) a vineyard. (Add): 33330 Saint-Émilion. Grand Cru. A.C. Saint-Émilion. (Com): Saint-Émilion. 20ha. Grape varieties: Cabernet franc 20%, Cabernet sauvignon 40% and Merlot 40%.

Château Gaillard [Le] (Fr) a Premier Cru vineyard in the A.C. commune of Monthélie, Côte de Beaune, Burgundy 0.9ha

Château Gaillard-de-Gorse (Fr) a vineyard in the A.C. Saint-Émilion, Bordeaux 3ha.

Château Gallais Bellevue (Fr) a vineyard. (Com): Potensac. A.C. Haut-Médoc, Bordeaux. Cru Bourgeois. Grape varieties: Cabernet franc, Cabernet sauvingnon, Merlot.

C

Château Gamage (Fr) a 2.5ha. A.C. Entre-Deux-Mers vineyard. (Add): Lavie-Spurrier, 33550 Saint-Pey-de-Castets.

Château Garderose (Fr) a vineyard. (Com): Sables-Saint-Émilion. A.C. Saint-Émilion, Bordeaux 5ha.

Château Garraud (Fr) a vineyard in the communes of Néac and A.C. Lalande de Pomerol. A.C. Saint-Émilion, Bordeaux. Grape varieties: Cabernet franc 30%, Cabernet sauvingnon 25%, Merlot 45%.

Château Garreau (Fr) see Garreau.

Château Gastebourse (Fr) part of Château Pontet Clauzure, A.C. Saint-Émilion, Bordeaux.

Château Gaubert (Fr) a vineyard in the A.C. Saint-Émilion, Bordeaux 16ha.

Château Gaudet-le-Franc-Grâce-Dieu (Fr) a vineyard in the A.C. Saint-Émilion, Bordeaux 8ha.

Château Gaury Balette (Fr) a vineyard producing A.C. Bordeaux wines.

Château Gaussan (Fr) a vineyard in the A.C. Corbières, south-western France. Grape varieties: Grenache and Syrah.

Château Gautoul (Fr) a 30ha vineyard based in A.C. Cahors. Grape varieties: 80% Malbec, 15% Merlot, 5% Tannat.

Châteaugay (Fr) a sub-appellation of the V.D.Q.S. region of Côtes d'Auvergne near Clermont-Ferrand in central France. Produces red wines made from the Gamay grape.

Château Gay-Moulins (Fr) a vineyard. (Com): Montagne-Saint-Émilion. A.C. Saint-Émilion, Bordeaux 7ha.

Château Gazin (Fr) a vineyard. (Com): Plassac. A.C. Côtes de Blaye, Bordeaux.

Château Gazin (Fr) a vineyard. (Com): Léognan. A.C. Pessac-Léognan, Bordeaux. 7ha (red and white).

Château Gazin (Fr) a vineyard. (Com): Pomerol. A.C. Pomerol, Bordeaux. 25ha. See also Les 5. Website: http://www.gazin.com

Château Génisson (Fr) a vineyard. (Com): St-Germain-de-Graves. A.C. Premières Côtes de Bordeaux. 20ha. (Add): St-Germain-de-Graves, 33490 Saint-Macaire. Grape varieties: Cabernet 50%, Malbec 10%, Merlot 40%.

Château Genot-Boulanger (Fr) an estate in the A.C. commune of Pommard in the Côte de Beaune, Burgundy.

Château Gensonne (Fr) a vineyard. (Com): Sainte-Croix-du-Mont. A.C. Sainte-Croix-du-Mont, Bordeaux 2ha.

Château Gessan (Fr) a vineyard. (Add): Saint-Sulpice-de-Faleyrens, 33330 Saint-Émilion. Grand Cru. A.C. Saint-Émilion. (Com): Saint-Sulpice-de-Faleyrens. 7.32ha. Grape varieties: Cabernet 82% and Merlot 18%.

Château Gigault (Fr) a 25ha vineyard. (Com): Mazion. A.C. Côtes de Blaye, Bordeaux.

Château Gilette (Fr) a vineyard. (Com): Preignac. A.C. Sauternes, Bordeaux. 14ha. Cru Bourgeois. Also Domaine des Justices and Châteaux Les Rochers, Les Ramparts and Lamothe.

Château Gironde (Fr) a vineyard. (Com): Puisseguin-Saint-Émilion. A.C. Saint-Émilion, Bordeaux 4ha.

Château Gironville (Fr) a vineyard. (Com): Macau. A.C. Médoc, Bordeaux. Cru Bourgeois.

Château Giscours (Fr) a vineyard. (Add): 33460 Margaux-Labarde. Grand Cru Classé (3rd). A.C. Margaux. (Com): Labarde. 84ha. Grape varieties: Cabernet sauvignon 75% and Merlot 25%. Second wine is Château Candelaude. Label: Le Haut-Médoc de Giscours.

Château Glana (Fr) a vineyard. (Com): Saint-Julien. A.C. Saint-Julien, Bordeaux 71ha.

Château Gleon Montanié (Fr) a winery based in the A.C. Corbières, Languedoc-Roussillon. Produces: white, rosé and red wines.

Château Gloria (Fr) a vineyard. (Add): Saint-Julien Beychevelle. A.C. Saint-Julien. (Com): Saint-Julien. 45ha. Grape varieties: Cabernet franc, Cabernet sauvignon, Merlot and Petit verdot.

Château Gobinaud (Fr) a vineyard. (Com): Listrac. A.C. Listrac, Bordeaux 8ha.

Château Godeau (Fr) a vineyard in the A.C. Saint-Émilion, Bordeaux 3ha.

Château Gombaude-Guillot (Fr) a vineyard. (Com): Pomerol. A.C. Pomerol, Bordeaux 6ha.

Château Gombeau (Fr) a vineyard. (Com): Fronsac. A.C. Côtes de Canon-Fronsac, Bordeaux 4ha.

Château Gontet-Robin (Fr) a vineyard. (Add): Château Sansonnet, 33330 Saint-Émilion. A.C. Puisseguin-Saint-Émilion. (Com): Puisseguin-Saint-Émilion.

Château Gontier (Fr) a vineyard. (Com): Plassac. A.C. Côtes de Blaye, Bordeaux.

Château Gorre (Fr) a vineyard. (Com): Martillac. A.C. Graves, Bordeaux. 3ha (red and white).

Château Goudichaud (Fr) a vineyard in the A.C. Graves de Vayres, 33760, Saint-Germain-du-Puch.

Château Goujon (Fr) a vineyard. (Com): Montagne-Saint-Émilion. A.C. Saint-Émilion, Bordeaux 3ha.

Château Gouprie (Fr) a vineyard. (Com): Pomerol. A.C. Pomerol, Bordeaux 3ha.

Château Gourgazaud (Fr) a vineyard in the A.C. Minervois la Livinière. Grape varieties: Mourvèdre and Syrah. Label La Réserve.

Château Grabitey (Fr) a vineyard based in the A.C. Graves, Bordeaux.

Château Grand Abord (Fr) a vineyard. (Add): 33460 Portets. A.C. Graves. (Com): Portets. 17ha. Grape varieties: Malbec 10%, Merlot 90%, Sauvignon and Sémillon.

Château Grand Barrail (Fr) a vineyard in the A.C. Côtes de Blaye, Bordeaux.

Château Grand Barrail Lamarzelle Figeac (Fr) a vineyard. (Add): 33330 Saint-Émilion. Grand Cru. A.C. Saint-Émilion. (Com): Saint-Émilion. 19ha. Grape varieties: Cabernet franc 20%, Cabernet sauvignon 20% and Merlot 60%.

Château Grand-Berc (Fr) a vineyard in the A.C. Saint-Émilion, Bordeaux 4ha.

Château Grand Bertin de Saint-Clair (Fr) a Cru Bourgeois vineyard. (Com): Begadan, A.C. Médoc. Grape varieties: Cabernet sauvignon, Merlot.

C

Château Grand Bigaroux (Fr) a vineyard. (Add): Saint-Sulpice-de-Faleyrens, 33330 Saint-Émilion. Grand Cru. A.C. Saint-Émilion. (Com): Saint-Sulpice-de-Faleyrens. 6ha. Grape varieties: Cabernet 10% and Merlot 90%.

Château Grand'Boise (Fr) a vineyard. (Add): B.P. 2, 12530 Trets. A.C. Côtes-de-Provence, south-eastern France. (red and blanc de blanc wines). Grape varieties: Cabernet sauvignon, Cinsault, Grenache and Syrah.

Château Grand-Caillou-Noir (Fr) a vineyard in the A.C. Saint-Émilion, Bordeaux 3ha.

Château Grand Canyon (Fr) a vineyard. (Add): 33250 Pauillac. Cru Bourgeois. A.C. Pauillac. (Com): Pauillac. 8ha. Grape varieties: Cabernet franc, Cabernet sauvignon and Merlot.

Château Grand-Carretey (Fr) a vineyard. (Com): Barsac. A.C. Barsac (or Sauternes), Bordeaux 1ha.

Château Grand Caumont (Fr) a vineyard in the A.C. Corbières, south-western France. Labels: Cuvée Spéciale and Cuvée Tradition..

Château Grand Chemin (Fr) a vineyard. (Com): Cérons. A.C. Cérons, Bordeaux 4ha.

Château Grand Chemin (Fr) a vineyard. (Com): Cérons. A.C. Graves, Bordeaux 2ha. (white).

Château Grand Clapeau Olivier (Fr) a vineyard. (Com): Blanquefort. A.C. Médoc, Bordeaux. Cru Bourgeois.

Château Grand Corbin (Fr) a vineyard. (Com): Saint-Émilion. A.C. Saint-Émilion, Bordeaux. Grand Cru Classé (promoted 2006). 13.5ha. Grape varieties: Cabernet franc 22%, Cabernet sauvingnon 1%, Merlot 72%.

Château Grand-Corbin-Despagne (Fr) a vineyard. (Add): 33330 Saint-Émilion. Grand Cru Classé (promoted 2006). A.C. Saint-Émilion. (Com): Saint-Émilion. 31ha. Grape varieties: Cabernet franc 25%, Cabernet sauvignon 5% and Merlot 70%. Second wine is Château Reine-Blanche. Website: http://www.vignobles-brunot.fr 'E'mail: vignobles-brunot@wanadoo.fr

Château Grand Corbin Giraud (Fr) a vineyard in the Graves-Saint-Émilion. A.C. Saint-Émilion, Bordeaux. Grand Cru.

Château Grand Corbin Manuel (Fr) a vineyard. (Add): 33330 Saint-Émilion. Grand Cru. A.C. Saint-Émilion. (Com): Saint-Émilion. 12ha. Grape varieties: Bouchet 30%, Cabernet sauvignon 30% and Merlot 40%.

Château Grand Duroc Milon (Fr) a vineyard. (Com): Pauillac. A.C. Pauillac, Bordeaux.

Château Grande Cassagne (Fr) a domaine in the A.C. Costières de Nîmes, Languedoc-Roussillon. Noted for white wine from 90% Grenache blanc, 10% Roussanne grapes plus red wines Les Rameaux and Grande Cassagne from mainly Syrah grapes.

Château Grandes-Murailles (Fr) a vineyard in the Côtes Saint-Émilion. A.C. Grand Cru Classé Saint-Émilion, Bordeaux 2ha.

Château Grandes-Vignes-Clinet (Fr) part of Château Gombaude-Guillot, A.C. Pomerol, Bordeaux.

Château Grand Gontey (Fr) a vineyard in the A.C. Saint-Émilion, Bordeaux 4ha.

Château Grandis (Fr) a vineyard. (Com): Saint-Seurin-de-Cadourne. A.C. Haut-Médoc, Bordeaux 5ha.

Château Grand Jacques (Fr) a vineyard in the A.C. Saint-Émilion, Bordeaux 11ha.

Château Grand-Jaugueyron (Fr) a vineyard. (Com): Cantenac. A.C. Haut-Médoc, Bordeaux 3ha.

Château Grand Jour (Fr) a vineyard. (Com): Yvrac. A.C. Premières Côtes de Bordeaux.

Château Grand-Jour (Fr) a vineyard. (Com): Prignac-Marcamps. A.C. Côtes de Bourg, Bordeaux.

Château Grand Lartigue (Fr) a vineyard. (Add): 33330 Saint-Émilion. Grand Cru. A.C. Saint-Émilion. (Com): Saint-Émilion. 7ha. Grape varieties: Cabernet 25% and Merlot 75%.

Château Grandmaison (Fr) a vineyard. (Com): Léognan. A.C. Pessac-Léognan, Bordeaux. 2ha (red).

Château Grand Mayne (Fr) a vineyard. (Add): 33330 Saint-Émilion. Grand Cru Classé. A.C. Saint-Émilion. (Com): Saint-Émilion. 21ha. Grape varieties: Cabernet franc 40%, Cabernet sauvignon 10% and Merlot 50%. Website: http://www.grand-mayne.com 'E'mail: grand-mayne@grand-mayne.com

Château Grand-Mayne-Qui-Né-Marc (Fr) a vineyard. (Com): Barsac. A.C. Barsac (or Sauternes), Bordeaux 1ha.

Château Grand Mazerolles (Fr) a vineyard in the A.C. Premières Côtes de Blaye, Bordeaux.

Château Grand-Mirande (Fr) a vineyard in the A.C. Saint-Émilion, Bordeaux 6ha.

Château Grand Moulin (Fr) a vineyard in the A.C. Corbières, south-western France. Labels: Terres Rouges and Vieilles Vignes.

Château Grand Moulin (Fr) a vineyard. (Com): Saint-Seurin-de-Cadourne. A.C. Médoc, Bordeaux. Cru Bourgeois.

Château Grand Moulinet (Fr) a vineyard. (Com): Pomerol. A.C. Pomerol, Bordeaux 2ha.

Château Grand Ormeau (Fr) a 11.5ha vineyard. (Com): Lalande de Pomerol. A.C. Lalande de Pomerol, Bordeaux.

Château Grand-Peilhan-Blanc (Fr) a vineyard in the A.C. Saint-Émilion, Bordeaux 7ha.

Château Grand Pey-de-Lescours (Fr) a vineyard in the A.C. Saint-Émilion, Bordeaux 24ha.

Château Grand-Pey-Lescours (Fr) a vineyard. (Add): Saint-Sulpice-de-Faleyrens, 33330 Saint-Émilion. Grand Cru. A.C. Saint-Émilion. (Com): Saint-Sulpice-de-Faleyrens. 24ha.

Château Grand-Pontet (Fr) a vineyard. (Add): 33330 Saint-Émilion. Grand Cru Classé. A.C. Saint-Émilion. (Com): Saint-Émilion. 14.65ha. Grape varieties: Cabernet franc 15%, Cabernet sauvignon 15% and Merlot 70%.

Château Grand-Puy-Ducasse (Fr) a Grand Cru Classé (5th). A.C. Pauillac. (Com): Pauillac. 35ha. Grape varieties: Cabernet franc and Merlot. Second wine is Château Artigues-Arnaud.

C

Château Grand Puy Lacoste (Fr) a vineyard. (Add): 33250 Pauillac. Grand Cru Classé (5th). A.C. Pauillac. (Com): Pauillac. 45ha. Grape varieties: Cabernet sauvignon and Merlot. Second wine is Château Lacoste-Borie.

Château Grand Quintin (Fr) a vineyard in the A.C. Bergerac produces red and white wines. Grape varieties: Cabernet sauvignon, Sauvignon blanc.

Château Grand Renouilh (Fr) a vineyard. (Com): St-Michel. A.C. Côtes Canon-Fronsac, Bordeaux 6ha.

Château Grand-Rivallon (Fr) a vineyard in the A.C. Saint-Émilion, Bordeaux 3ha.

Château Grand-Seuil (Fr) a vineyard. (Add): Puyricard, 13100 Aix-en-Provence. A.C. Coteaux-d'Aix-en-Provence (red and rosé wines).

Château Grand-Soussans (Fr) a vineyard. (Com): Soussans. A.C. Médoc, Bordeaux 3ha.

Château Grands Sillons (Fr) a vineyard. (Com): Pomerol. A.C. Pomerol, Bordeaux 3ha.

Château Grand Travers (USA) a winery based in Grand Traverse (City), North Michigan. 18ha. Grape varieties: Chardonnay and Riesling.

Château Grand Tuillac (Fr) a vineyard in the A.C. Côtes-de-Castillon. Grape varieties: Cabernet franc 20%, Cabernet sauvignon 5%, Merlot 75%.

Château Grange Neuve (Fr) a vineyard. (Com): Pomerol. A.C. Pomerol, Bordeaux 4ha.

Château Grangeneuve (Fr) part of Château Figeac, A.C. Saint-Émilion, Bordeaux.

Château Grangey (Fr) a vineyard in the A.C. Saint-Émilion, Bordeaux 5ha.

Château Gravas (Fr) a vineyard. (Com): Barsac. A.C. Barsac (or Sauternes), Bordeaux 8ha.

Château Graves-d'Armens (Fr) a vineyard in the A.C. Saint-Émilion, Bordeaux 3ha.

Château Graves d'Arthus (Fr) a vineyard in the A.C. Saint-Émilion, Bordeaux 5ha.

Château Graves-Richeboh (Fr) a vineyard. (Com): Moulis. A.C. Moulis, Bordeaux 2ha. Grape varieties: Savignon blanc 10%, Sémiloon 90%.

Château Gravet (Fr) a vineyard in the A.C. Saint-Émilion, Bordeaux 12ha.

Château Gravet-Renaissance (Fr) a vineyard. (Add): Saint-Sulpice-de-Faleyrens, 33330 Saint-Émilion. Grand Cru. A.C. Saint-Émilion. (Com): Saint-Sulpice-de-Faleyrens. 9ha. Grape varieties: Cabernet franc 30%, Cabernet sauvignon 2%, Malbec 3% and Merlot 60%. Second wine is Les Grandes Versannes.

Château Graveyron (Fr) a vineyard. (Com): Portets. A.C. Graves, Bordeaux. 10ha (red and white).

Château Gressier-Grand-Poujeaux (Fr) a vineyard. (Add): 33480 Moulis-Médoc. A.C. Moulis. (Com): Moulis. 19ha. Grape varieties: Cabernet franc 15%, Cabernet sauvignon 35% and Merlot 50%.

Château Greysac (Fr) a Cru Grand Bourgeois. A.C. Médoc. (Com): Bégadan. 65ha. Grape varieties: Cabernet franc, Cabernet sauvignon, Malbec, Merlot and Petit verdot. (Add): Bégadan, 33340 Lesparre.

Château Grillet (Fr) the famous A.C. Château Grillet. 1.45ha. One of the smallest A.C.'s in France.

Produces 3,000 bottles of white wine per year (aged in oak) from the Viognier grape. Sited near Condrieu, northern Rhône.

Château Grillon (Fr) a vineyard. (Com): Barsac. A.C. Barsac (or Sauternes), Bordeaux 6ha.

Château Grinou (Fr) a winery based in the A.C. Bergerac. (Add): 24240 Monestier. Also produces: Le Grand Vin de Château Grinou (Merlot). 'E'mail: chateaugrinou@aol.com

Château Gris (Fr) an estate in the A.C. Nuits-Saint-Georges. Côtes de Nuits, Burgundy.

Château Grivière (Fr) a vineyard. (Add): 33340 Lesparre. A.C. Médoc. (Com): Blaignan. 19ha. Grape varieties: Cabernet franc, Cabernet sauvignon and Merlot.

Château Gros Caillou (Fr) a vineyard. (Add): Saint-Sulpice-de-Faleyrens, 33330 Saint-Émilion, Bordeaux. A.C. Saint-Émilion Grand Cru. (Com): Saint-Sulpice-de-Faleyrens. 12ha. Website: http://www.chateaugroscaillou.com 'E'mail: vigdupuy@club-internet.fr

Château Gros Jean (Fr) a vineyard. (Com): St-Aignan. A.C. Côtes de Fronsac, Bordeaux 4ha.

Château Gros-Moulin (Fr) a vineyard. (Com): Bourg. A.C. Côtes de Bourg, Bordeaux.

Château Gruaud-Larose (Fr) a vineyard. (Add): Saint-Julien-Beychevelle. Grand Cru Classé (4th). A.C. Saint-Julien. (Com): Saint-Julien. 82ha. Grape varieties: Cabernet franc, Cabernet sauvignon, Merlot and Petit verdot. Second wine is Sarget de Gruaud-Larose. *See also* Osoyoos Larose.

Château Guadet de Franc Grâce-Dieu (Fr) a vineyard in the A.C. Saint-Émilion, Bordeaux 8ha.

Château Guadet-Plaisance (Fr) a vineyard. (Add): Montagne-Saint-Émilion. 33330 Saint-Émilion. A.C. Montagne-Saint-Émilion. (Com): Montagne-Saint-Émilion.

Château Guadet St-Julien (Fr) a vineyard. (Add): 33330 Saint-Émilion. Grand Cru (demoted 2006). A.C. Saint-Émilion. (Com): Saint-Émilion. 6ha. Grape varieties: Cabernet franc, Cabernet sauvignon and Merlot 75%.

Château Guerande (Fr) a vineyard in the A.C. Muscadet Sèvre et Maine, Nantais, Loire. (Add): 44330 Vallet.

Château Guerrit (Fr) a vineyard. (Com): Tauriac. A.C. Côtes de Bourg, Bordeaux. Also known as Domaine de Guerrit.

Château Guerry (Fr) a vineyard in the A.C. Côtes de Bourg, Bordeaux. (Add): Domaine Ribet, 33450 Saint-Loubès.

Château Gueyrosse (Fr) a vineyard. (Com): Sables-Saint-Émilion. A.C. Saint-Émilion, Bordeaux 4ha. (Add): 33500 Libourne.

Château Gueyrot (Fr) a vineyard. (Add): 33330 Saint-Émilion. Grand Cru. A.C. Saint-Émilion. (Com): Saint-Émilion. 8.33ha. Grape varieties: Cabernet franc, Cabernet sauvignon and Merlot 66%. Second wine is Château Beau Site de la Tour. A.C. Fronsac.

Château Guibot-La-Fourvieille (Fr) a vineyard. (Com): Puisseguin-Saint-Émilion. A.C. Puisseguin-

Saint-Émilion, Bordeaux. 41ha. Grape varieties: Cabernet franc 5%, Cabernet sauvignon 5%, Merlot 90%.

Château Guienne (Fr) a vineyard. (Com): Lansac. A.C. Côtes de Bourg, Bordeaux.

Château Guillaumont (Fr) a vineyard. (Com): La Brède. A.C. Graves, Bordeaux. 13ha (red and white).

Château Guillemot (Fr) a vineyard. (Com): Saint-Christophe-des-Bardes. A.C. Saint-Émilion, Bordeaux 7ha.

Château Guillonnet (Fr) a vineyard. (Com): Anglade. A.C. Côtes de Blaye, Bordeaux.

Château Guillot (Fr) a vineyard. (Com): Pomerol. A.C. Pomerol, Bordeaux 5ha.

Château Guillotin (Fr) a vineyard. (Com): Puisseguin-Saint-Émilion. A.C. Saint-Émilion, Bordeaux.

Château Guillou (Fr) a vineyard. (Com): Saint-Georges-Saint-Émilion. A.C. Saint-Émilion, Bordeaux 13ha.

Château Guimbalet (Fr) a vineyard. (Com): Preignac. A.C. Sauternes, Bordeaux 1ha.

Château Guinot (Fr) a vineyard in the A.C. Saint-Émilion, Bordeaux 4ha.

Château Guionne (Fr) a vineyard. (Com): Lansac. A.C. Côtes de Bourg, Bordeaux.

Château Guiot (Fr) a vineyard in the A.C. Costières de Nîmes (white, red and rosé).

Château Guiraud (Fr) a vineyard in the A.C. Saint Chinian.

Château Guiraud (Fr) a vineyard. (Com): St-Ciers-de-Canesse. A.C. Côtes de Bourg, Bordeaux.

Château Guiraud (Fr) a Premier Grand Cru Classé. A.C. Sauternes. (Com): Sauternes. 55ha. Grape varieties: Muscadelle, Sauvignon and Sémillon. (Also grows some Cabernet sauvignon and Merlot). Original name was Château Bayle before the 1855 classification.

Château Guirouilh (Fr) an A.C. Jurançon wine, moelleux in style from the Petit manseng grape (aged in oak for 2 years).

Château Guitard (Fr) a vineyard. (Com): Montagne-Saint-Émilion. A.C. Saint-Émilion, Bordeaux.

Château Guitignan (Fr) a vineyard in the A.C. Moulis en Médoc, Bordeaux.

Château Guitteronde (Fr) a vineyard. (Com): Barsac. A.C. Barsac (or Sauternes), Bordeaux 1ha.

Château Guitteronde-Bert (Fr) a vineyard. (Com): Barsac. A.C. Barsac (or Sauternes), Bordeaux 9ha.

Château Guitteronde-Sarraute (Fr) a vineyard. (Com): Barsac. A.C. Barsac (or Sauternes), Bordeaux 4ha.

Château Hallet (Fr) a vineyard. (Com): Barsac. A.C. Barsac (or Sauternes), Bordeaux 10ha.

Château Hanteillan (Fr) a vineyard. (Add): Cissac-Médoc, 33250 Pauillac. Cru Bourgeois. A.C. Haut-Médoc. (Com): Cissac. 87ha. Grape varieties: Cabernet franc 8%, Cabernet sauvignon 45%, Merlot 42% and Petit verdot 5%. *See also* Châteaux Larrivaux, Larrivaux-Hanteillan and Tour de Vatican.

Château Harlaftis (Gre) the name of a Vin de Pays

Cabernet sauvignon or Chardonnay wine produced by Domaine Harlaftis in Attique. Website: http://www.harlaftis.gr 'E'mail: wines@harlaftis.gr

Château Hauchat (Fr) a vineyard. (Com): St-Aignan. A.C. Côtes de Fronsac, Bordeaux 1ha.

Château Hauret (Fr) a vineyard. (Com): Illats. A.C. Cérons, Bordeaux 4ha.

Château Haut-Badette (Fr) a vineyard. (Add): 37 Rue Pline-Parmentier, 33500 Libourne. A.C. Saint-Émilion. (Com): Saint-Christophe-des-Bardes. 6ha. Grape varieties: Cabernet sauvignon 10% and Merlot 90%.

Château Haut-Bages Avéyrous (Fr) a vineyard. (Add): 33250 Pauillac. A.C. Pauillac. (Com): Pauillac. 5ha. Grape varieties: Cabernet sauvignon, Merlot and Petit verdot (the second wine of Château Lynch-Bages).

Château Haut-Bages Libéral (Fr) a vineyard. (Add): Balogues, 33250 Pauillac. Grand Cru Classé (5th). A.C. Pauillac. (Com): Pauillac. 28ha. Grape varieties: Cabernet sauvignon, Merlot and Petit verdot.

Château Haut-Bages Monpelou (Fr) a vineyard. (Add): 33250 Pauillac. Cru Bourgeois Supérieur. A.C. Pauillac. (Com): Pauillac. 15ha. Grape varieties: Cabernet sauvignon 75% and Merlot 25%.

Château Haut-Bailly (Fr) a vineyard. (Add): 33850 Léognan. Grand Cru Classé. A.C. Pessac-Léognan. (Com): Léognan. 25ha. Grape varieties: Cabernet franc 10%, Cabernet sauvignon 60% and Merlot 30%. *See also* Parde de Haut-Bailly (La).

Château Haut-Ballet (Fr) a vineyard. (Com): Néac. A.C. Lalande de Pomerol, Bordeaux. Grape varieties: Cabernet franc 10%, Cabernet sauvignon 10%, Merlot 80%.

Château Haut-Barbeyron (Fr) a vineyard in the A.C. Saint-Émilion, Bordeaux 4ha.

Château Haut-Bastienne (Fr) a vineyard. (Com): Montagne-Saint-Émilion. A.C. Saint-Émilion, Bordeaux 4ha.

Château Haut Batailley (Fr) a vineyard. (Add): 33250 Pauillac. Grand Cru Classé (5th). A.C. Pauillac. (Com): Pauillac. 20ha. Grape varieties: Cabernet franc 10%, Cabernet sauvignon 65% and Merlot 25%. Second wine is Château Tour d'Aspic.

Château Haut-Bayle (Fr) an A.C. Bordeaux rouge from a co-operative winery at 33540 Saveterre-de-Guyenne. (Les Vignerons de Guyenne à Blasinon).

Château Haut Bellevue (Fr) a vineyard. (Com): Lamarque. A.C. Haut-Médoc, Bordeaux 3ha.

Château Haut-Benitey (Fr) a vineyard in the A.C. Saint-Émilion, Bordeaux 5ha.

Château Haut-Bergeron (Fr) a vineyard. (Com): Preignac. A.C. Sauternes, Bordeaux 4ha. (adjoins Château d'Yquem).

Château Haut-Bergey (Fr) a vineyard. (Add): 33850 Léognan. A.C. Pessac-Léognan. (Com): Léognan. 13.5ha. Grape varieties: Cabernet sauvignon 70% and Merlot 30% (red).

Château Haut-Berthonneau (Fr) a vineyard in the A.C. Saint-Émilion, Bordeaux 1ha.

C

Château Haut Bertinerie (Fr) a vineyard based in Cobnezais. A.C. Premières Côtes de Blaye. 4ha (red and white).

Château Haut Beychevelle Gloria (Fr) part of Château Gloria, A.C. Haut-Médoc, Bordeaux.

Château Haut-Blagnac (Fr) an A.C. Bordeaux. Produced by Carl et Fils, Lignan à Bordeaux. Grape varieties: Merlot.

Château Haut-Blaignan (Fr) a vineyard. (Com): Blaignan. A.C. Haut-Médoc, Bordeaux. Cru Bourgeois 7ha.

Château Haut Bommes (Fr) a vineyard. (Com): Bommes. A.C. Sauternes, Bordeaux.

Château Haut Bourcier (Fr) an A.C. Côte de Blaye. Grape varieties: Merlot 93% Cabernet sauvignon 7%.

Château Haut-Brega (Fr) a vineyard in the A.C. Médoc, Bordeaux.

Château Haut Breton Larigaudière (Fr) a vineyard. (Add): Soussans 33460. A.C. Margaux. (Com): Soussans. 5ha. Grape varieties: Cabernet sauvignon 70% and Merlot 30%.

Château Haut-Brignon (Fr) a vineyard. (Com): Cenac. A.C. Premières Côtes de Bordeaux, central Bordeaux.

Château Haut-Brion (Fr) a vineyard. (Add): 33600 Pessac. Premier Grand Cru Classé. A.C. Pessac-Léognan. (Com): Pessac. 43ha. Grape varieties: Cabernet franc, Cabernet sauvignon, Merlot, Sauvignon and Sémillon. see Château Bahans Haut Brion. See also D'obrion and Daubrion. Website: http://www.haut-brion.com

Château Haut-Brisson (Fr) a vineyard. (Add): 167 Avenue Maréchal Foch, B.P. 170, 33500 Libourne. Grand Cru. A.C. Saint-Émilion. (Com): Vignonet. 23ha. Grape varieties: Bouchet 10%, Cabernet sauvignon 25% and Merlot 65%.

Château Haut-Cabat (Fr) a vineyard. (Com): Anglade. A.C. Côtes de Blaye, Bordeaux.

Château Haut-Cadet (Fr) a vineyard. (Add): 33330 Saint-Émilion. A.C. Saint-Émilion. (Com): Saint-Émilion 13ha.

Château Haut-Caillou (Fr) a vineyard. (Com): Fronsac. A.C. Côtes de Canon-Fronsac, Bordeaux 3ha.

Château Haut-Canteloup (Fr) a vineyard. (Com): Couquèques. A.C. Médoc, Bordeaux. Cru Bourgeois.

Château Haut-Carmail (Fr) a vineyard. (Com): Saint-Seurin-de-Cadourne. A.C. Haut-Médoc, Bordeaux 5ha.

Château Haut-Castanet (Fr) an A.C. Bordeaux Rouge.

Château Haut-Chaigneau (Fr) a vineyard. (Com): Néac. A.C. Lalande de Pomerol, Bordeaux.

Château Haut-Chéreau (Fr) a vineyard. (Com): Lussac-Saint-Émilion. A.C. Saint-Émilion, Bordeaux 2ha.

Château Haut-Claverie (Fr) a vineyard. (Com): Fargues. A.C. Sauternes, Bordeaux 4ha.

Château Haut-Cloquet (Fr) a vineyard. (Com): Pomerol. A.C. Pomerol, Bordeaux 1ha.

Château Haut-Corbin (Fr) a vineyard. (Com): Saint-Émilion. A.C. Saint-Émilion, Bordeaux. 3.5ha. Grand Cru Classé.

Château Haut d'Allard (Fr) a vineyard in the A.C. Côtes de Bourg, Bordeaux.

Château Haut de Baritault (Fr) a vineyard. (Com): Sainte-Croix-du-Mont. A.C. Sainte-Croix-du-Mont, Bordeaux 5ha.

Château Hauterive (Fr) a vineyard. (Com): Saint-Germain-d'Esteuil. A.C. Médoc, Bordeaux. Cru Bourgeois.

Château Hautes Combes (Fr) a vineyard in the A.C. Côtes de Bourg, Bordeaux.

Château Hautes-Graves-d'Arthus (Fr) a vineyard in the A.C. Saint-Émilion, Bordeaux 9ha.

Château Haut Fabrègues (Fr) an A.C. Faugères wine produced by Saur Père et Fils. 50ha. estate. Grape varieties: Grenache, Cinsault, Carignan, Syrah and Mourvèdre.

Château Haut-Fonrazade (Fr) a vineyard in the A.C. Saint-Émilion, Bordeaux 11ha.

Château Haut-Gardère (Fr) a vineyard in the A.C. Pessac-Léognan, Graves, Bordeaux.

Château Haut Garin (Fr) a vineyard. (Com): Prignac. A.C. Haut-Médoc, Bordeaux. Cru Bourgeois.

Château Haut Gleon (Fr) a vineyard in the A.C. Corbières, south-western France.

Château Haut-Grâce-Dieu (Fr) part of Château Peyrelongue A.C. Saint-Émilion, Bordeaux.

Château Haut-Grand-Faurie (Fr) a vineyard in the A.C. Saint-Émilion, Bordeaux 4ha.

Château Haut-Gravet (Fr) a vineyard. (Add): 33330 Saint-Émilion. Grand Cru. A.C. Saint-Émilion. (Com): Saint-Émilion. Grape varieties: Cabernet franc, Malbec, Merlot.

Château Haut Grelot (Fr) a vineyard in Saint-Ciers-sur-Gironde. A.C. Premières Côtes de Blaye.

Château Haut-Gueyrot (Fr) a vineyard in the A.C. Saint-Émilion, Bordeaux 2ha.

Château Haut-Guiraud (Fr) a vineyard in the A.C. Côtes de Bourg, Bordeaux.

Château Haut-Guitard (Fr) a vineyard. (Com): Montagne-Saint-Émilion. A.C. Saint-Émilion, Bordeaux 4ha.

Château Haut-Jean-Faure (Fr) a vineyard in the A.C. Saint-Émilion, Bordeaux 7ha.

Château Haut-Jeanguillot (Fr) a vineyard in the A.C. Saint-Émilion, Bordeaux 4ha.

Château Haut Laborde (Fr) a vineyard in the A.C. Médoc, Bordeaux. Second label of Château Peyrabon.

Château Haut-Langlade (Fr) a vineyard. (Com): Parsac-Saint-Émilion. A.C. Saint-Émilion, Bordeaux 4ha.

Château Haut-Larose (Fr) a vineyard. (Com): Lussac-Saint-Émilion. A.C. Saint-Émilion, Bordeaux 5ha.

Château Haut-Lartigue (Fr) a vineyard in the A.C. Saint-Émilion, Bordeaux 3ha.

Château Haut-Lavallade (Fr) a vineyard. (Add): Saint-Christophe-des-Bardes, 33330 Saint-Émilion. A.C. Saint-Émilion. (Com): Saint-Christophe-des-Bardes.

C

12ha. Grape varieties: Cabernet franc 20%, Cabernet sauvignon 25% and Merlot 65%.

Château Haut-Logat (Fr) a vineyard. (Add): Cissac, 33250 Pauillac. A.C. Haut-Médoc. (Com): Cissac. 14ha. Grape varieties: Cabernet sauvignon 75% and Merlot 25%.

Château Haut-Luccius (Fr) a vineyard in the A.C. Lussac-Saint-Émilion, Bordeaux.

Château Haut-Macô (Fr) a vineyard. (Com): Tauriac. A.C. Côtes de Bourg, Bordeaux. 50ha. (Add): 33710 Tauriac. Grape varieties: Cabernet 70% and Merlot 30%.

Château Haut-Madère (Fr) a vineyard. (Com): Villenave d'Ornon. A.C. Graves, Bordeaux. 2ha (red).

Château Haut Madrac (Fr) a vineyard. (Add): 33250 Pauillac. A.C. Haut-Médoc. (Com): St-Saveur-du-Médoc. 40ha. Grape varieties: Cabernet 75% and Merlot 25%.

Château Haut-Maillet (Fr) a vineyard. (Com): Pomerol. A.C. Pomerol, Bordeaux 5ha.

Château Haut-Marbuzet (Fr) a vineyard. (Add): 33250 Saint-Estèphe. Cru Bourgeois Supérieur. A.C. Saint-Estèphe. (Com): Saint-Estèphe. 30ha. Grape varieties: Cabernet franc 10%, Cabernet sauvignon 40% and Merlot 50%. Second wine is Château Tour de Marbuzet.

Château Haut-Maurac (Fr) a vineyard. (Com): St-Yzans-de-Médoc. A.C. Médoc, Bordeaux. (Add): St-Yzans-de-Médoc, 33340 Lesparre.

Château Haut-Mauvinon (Fr) a vineyard in the A.C. Saint-Émilion, Bordeaux 8ha.

Château Haut-Mayne (Fr) an A.C. Graves. (Com): Cérons. 8ha. Grape varieties: Cabernet franc 50%, Cabernet sauvignon 50%, Sauvignon 25% and Sémillon 75%.

Château Haut-Mayne (Fr) a vineyard. (Com): Fargues. A.C. Sauternes, Bordeaux 2ha.

Château Haut Mazerat (Fr) a vineyard. (Add): 33330 Saint-Émilion. Grand Cru. A.C. Saint-Émilion. (Com): Saint-Émilion. 12.5ha. Grape varieties: Cabernet franc 30%, Cabernet sauvignon 10% and Merlot 60%.

Château Haut Mazeris (Fr) a vineyard. (Com): St-Michel. A.C. Côtes Canon-Fronsac, Bordeaux 6ha.

Château Haut-Merigot (Fr) a vineyard in the A.C. Entre-Deux-Mers, central Bordeaux.

Château Haut Mouleyes (Fr) a vineyard in the A.C. Entre-Deux-Mers, central Bordeaux. Grape varieties: Cabernet sauvignon, Sauvignon blanc, Sémillon. Produces red and white wines.

Château Haut-Musset (Fr) a vineyard. (Com): Parsac-Saint-Émilion. A.C. Saint-Émilion, Bordeaux 5ha.

Château Haut-Nauve (Fr) a vineyard in the A.C. Saint-Émilion, Bordeaux 3ha.

Château Haut-Nouchet (Fr) a vineyard. (Add): 33650 Labrède. A.C. Graves Supérieures. (Com): Léognan. 11ha (red and white).

Château Haut-Padarnac (Fr) a vineyard. (Com): Pauillac. A.C. Haut-Médoc, Bordeaux. Cru Bourgeois.

Château Haut-Panet-Rineuilh (Fr) a vineyard in the A.C. Saint-Émilion, Bordeaux 2ha.

Château Haut Pauillac (Fr) a vineyard. (Com): Pauillac. A.C. Médoc, Bordeaux. Cru Bourgeois.

Château Haut Peyraguey (Fr) a Premier Cru Classé vineyard. (Com): Bommes. A.C. Sauternes, Bordeaux.

Château Haut-Peyroutas (Fr) a vineyard in the A.C. Saint-Émilion, Bordeaux 2ha.

Château Haut-Piquat (Fr) a vineyard. (Add): 35570 Lussac. (Com): Lussac-Saint-Émilion. A.C. Saint-Émilion, Bordeaux. 22ha. Grape varieties: 65% Merlot, 25% Cabernet sauvignon, 10% Cabernet franc.

Château Haut-Plaisance (Fr) a vineyard. (Com): Montagne-Saint-Émilion. A.C. Saint-Émilion, Bordeaux 7ha.

Château Haut Plantey (Fr) a vineyard. (Com): Listrac. A.C. Haut-Médoc, Bordeaux 3ha.

Château Haut-Plantey (Fr) a vineyard. (Add): Saint Laurent des Combes, 33330 Saint-Émilion. Grand Cru. A.C. Saint-Émilion. (Com): Saint-Hippolyte. 9.10ha. Grape varieties: Cabernet franc 28%, Cabernet sauvignon 2% and Merlot 70%.

Château Haut-Poitou (Fr) a vineyard. (Com): Lussac-Saint-Émilion. A.C. Saint-Émilion, Bordeaux 2ha.

Château Haut-Pontet (Fr) a vineyard in the A.C. Saint-Émilion, Bordeaux 5ha.

Château Haut-Pourret (Fr) a vineyard in the A.C. Saint-Émilion, Bordeaux 5ha.

Château Haut-Pourteau (Fr) a vineyard. (Com): Lussac-Saint-Émilion. A.C. Saint-Émilion, Bordeaux 2ha.

Château Haut-Rabion (Fr) a vineyard. (Com): Vignonet. A.C. Saint-Émilion, Bordeaux. (Add): Vignonet, 33330 Saint-Émilion. 5ha.

Château Haut-Rat (Fr) a vineyard. (Com): Illats. A.C. Cérons, Bordeaux 16ha.

Château Haut-Renaissance (Fr) a vineyard. (Add): Saint-Sulpice-de-Faleyrens, 33330 Saint-Émilion. A.C. Saint-Émilion. (Com): Saint-Sulpice-de-Faleyrens. 3ha.

Château Haut Rey (Fr) a vineyard. (Com): Fronsac. A.C. Côtes de Fronsac, Bordeaux 8ha.

Château Haut Rian (Fr) a vineyard in the A.C. Premières Côtes de Bordeaux. Grape varieties: Cabernet sauvignon 30%, Merlot 70%. Also produces a white A.C. Entre-Deux-Mers. Grape varieties: Sauvignon blanc 30%, Sémillon 70%.

Château Haut-Rocher (Fr) a vineyard. (Add): Saint-Étienne-de-Lisse, 33330 Saint-Émilion. Grand Cru. A.C. Saint-Émilion. (Com): Saint-Étienne-de-Lisse. 15ha. Grape varieties: Cabernet franc 25%, Cabernet sauvignon 15% and Merlot 60%.

Château Haut-Sarpe (Fr) a vineyard. (Add): 37 Rue Pline-Parmentier, 33500 Libourne. Grand Cru Classé A.C. Saint-Émilion. (Com): Saint-Christophe-des-Bardes. 25ha. Grape varieties: Cabernet franc 30%, Cabernet sauvignon 10% and Merlot 60%. Website: http://www.j-

C

janoueix-bordeaux.com 'E'mail: info@j-janoueix-bordeaux.cm

Château Haut-Ségottes (Fr) a vineyard. (Add): 33330 Saint-Émilion. Grand Cru. A.C. Saint-Émilion. (Com): Saint-Émilion. 8.6ha. Grape varieties: Cabernet franc 40%, Cabernet sauvignon 10% and Merlot 50%.

Château Haut-Serre (Fr) a 62ha. vineyard in the A.C. Cahors, south-western France. Grape varieties: 75% Malbec, 20% Merlot, 5% Tannat.

Château Haut-Simard (Fr) a vineyard in the A.C. Saint-Émilion, Bordeaux 20ha.

Château Haut-Sociondo (Fr) a vineyard. (Com): Cars. A.C. Côtes de Blaye, Bordeaux.

Château Haut-St-Georges (Fr) a vineyard. (Com): Saint-Georges-Saint-Émilion. A.C. Saint-Émilion, Bordeaux 2ha.

Château Haut-Tayac (Fr) a vineyard. (Com): Soussans-Margaux. A.C. Haut-Médoc, Bordeaux 6ha.

Château Haut-Touran (Fr) a vineyard in the A.C. Saint-Émilion, Bordeaux 3ha.

Château Haut-Troquard (Fr) a vineyard. (Com): Saint-Georges-Saint-Émilion. A.C. Saint-Émilion, Bordeaux 3ha.

Château Haut-Troquart (Fr) a vineyard in the A.C. Saint-Émilion, Bordeaux 4ha.

Château Haut-Tuquet (Fr) a vineyard. (Com): St-Magne-de-Castillon (Côtes de Castillon). A.C. Bordeaux Supérieur.

Château Haut-Veyrac (Fr) a vineyard in the A.C. Saint-Émilion, Bordeaux 7ha.

Château Hélène (Fr) a vineyard. (Add): Barbaira, 11800 Trèbes. A.C. Corbières (red wine). Label: Pénélope.

Château Hennebelle (Fr) a vineyard. (Add): 33460 Margaux. A.C. Haut-Médoc. (Com): Lamarque. 5.5ha. Grape varieties: Cabernet sauvignon, Merlot and Petit verdot.

Château Hontemieux (Fr) an A.C. Médoc. (Com): Blaignan. Grape varieties: Cabernet sauvignon and Merlot.

Château Hornsby (Austr) a small winery at Alice Springs, Northern Territory.

Château Hortevie (Fr) a vineyard in the A.C. Médoc, Bordeaux. Cru Bourgeois.

Château Hostein (Fr) a vineyard. (Com): Saint-Estèphe. A.C. Saint-Estèphe, Bordeaux 3ha.

Château Houbanon (Fr) a vineyard. (Com): Prignac. A.C. Médoc, Bordeaux. Cru Bourgeois.

Château Houissant (Fr) a Cru Bourgeois Exceptionnel. A.C. Saint-Estèphe. (Com): Saint-Estèphe. Also sold as Château Leyssac. 20ha

Château Hourbanon (Fr) a vineyard. (Com): Prignac. A.C. Médoc, Bordeaux 6ha.

Château Hourmalas (Fr) a vineyard. (Com): Barsac. A.C. Barsac (or Sauternes), Bordeaux. 6ha. Also Château St-Marc.

Château Hourtin-Ducasse (Fr) a vineyard. (Com): Saint-Sauveur. A.C. Haut-Médoc, Bordeaux. Cru Bourgeois.

Château Houtou (Fr) a vineyard. (Com): Tauriac. A.C. Côtes de Bourg, Bordeaux.

Château Huradin (Fr) a vineyard. (Com): Cérons. A.C. Cérons, Bordeaux. 8ha. *see* Domaine du Salut.

Château Jacqueblanc (Fr) a vineyard in the A.C. Saint-Émilion, Bordeaux 20ha.

Château Jacqueminot (Fr) a vineyard in the A.C. Saint-Émilion, Bordeaux 1ha.

Château Jacquenoir (Fr) a vineyard in the A.C. Saint-Émilion, Bordeaux 4ha.

Château Jacques-Blanc (Fr) a vineyard. (Com): Saint-Étienne-de-Lisse. A.C. Saint-Émilion, Bordeaux.

Château Jamnets (Fr) a vineyard. (Com): St-Pierre-de-Mons. A.C. Graves, Bordeaux. 2ha (red and white).

Château Jany (Fr) a vineyard. (Com): Barsac. A.C. Barsac (or Sauternes), Bordeaux 2ha.

Château Jappe-Loup (Fr) a vineyard. (Com): Saint-Étienne-de-Lisse. A.C. Saint-Émilion, Bordeaux.

Château Jaubert-Peyblanquet (Fr) a vineyard in the A.C. Saint-Émilion, Bordeaux 5ha.

Château Jaugueblanc (Fr) a vineyard in the A.C. Saint-Émilion, Bordeaux 5ha.

Château Jean-Blanc (Fr) a vineyard. (Com): Saint-Pey d'Armens. A.C. Saint-Émilion, Bordeaux 6ha.

Château Jeandeman (Fr) a vineyard. (Com): Fronsac. A.C. Côtes de Fronsac, Bordeaux.

Château Jean du Mayne (Fr) a vineyard. (Com): Graves-Saint-Émilion. A.C. Saint-Émilion, Bordeaux. Grand Cru.

Château Jean-Faure (Fr) a vineyard. (Add): 33330 Saint-Émilion. Grand Cru. A.C. Saint-Émilion. (Com): Saint-Émilion. 20ha. Grape varieties: Cabernet franc 60%, Malbec 10% and Merlot 30%.

Château Jean-Galant (Fr) a vineyard. (Com): Bommes. A.C. Sauternes, Bordeaux 2ha.

Château Jean-Gervais (Fr) a vineyard in commune of Portets. A.C. Graves, Bordeaux. 25ha (red and white). Also Clos Puyjalon.

Château Jean-Laive (Fr) a vineyard. (Com): Barsac. A.C. Barsac (or Sauternes), Bordeaux 4ha.

Château Jean-Lamat (Fr) a vineyard. (Com): Sainte-Croix-du-Mont. A.C. Sainte-Croix-du-Mont, Bordeaux 4ha.

Château Jean-Marie-Cheval-Blanc (Fr) a vineyard in the A.C. Saint-Émilion, Bordeaux 2ha.

Château Jean-Pierre Gaussen (Fr) a vineyard in the A.C. Bandol, Provence. (Add): 185, Chemin de l'Argile, Quartier de la Noblesse, 83740 La Cadière d'Azur, Var.

Château Jean Voisin (Fr) a vineyard. (Add): 33330 Saint-Émilion. Grand Cru. A.C. Saint-Émilion. (Com): Saint-Émilion. 14ha. Grape varieties: Cabernet franc 25%, Cabernet sauvignon 15% and Merlot 60%.

Château Jendeman (Fr) a vineyard. (Com): St-Aignan. A.C. Côtes de Fronsac, Bordeaux 9ha.

Château Joly (Fr) a vineyard in the A.C. Saint-Émilion, Bordeaux 2ha.

Château Jolys (Fr) a vineyard in the A.C. Jurançon, south-western France.

Château Jouanin (Fr) a vineyard in the A.C. Côtes de Castillon, Bordeaux.

Château Joutan (Fr) an Armagnac producer. (Add):

40240 Betbezer, Labastide d'Armagnac. 6.5ha. in Bas Armagnac.

Château Julia Assyrtiko (Gre) a white wine produced by Kostas Lazaridis. *See also* Amethystos Cava.

Château Juliénas (Fr) a vineyard in the A.C. Juliénas Cru Beaujolais-Villages, Burgundy.

Château Junayme (Fr) a vineyard. (Com): Fronsac. A.C. Côtes Canon-Fronsac, Bordeaux 13ha.

Château Jupille (Fr) a vineyard in the A.C. Saint-Émilion, Bordeaux 2ha.

Château Jura-Plaisance (Fr) a vineyard. (Com): Montagne-Saint-Émilion. A.C. Saint-Émilion, Bordeaux 8ha.

Château Justice (Fr) a vineyard in the A.C. Saint-Émilion Grand Cru, Bordeaux 3ha. Grape varieties: Cabernet sauvignon 15%, Merlot 85%.

Château Karolus (Fr) a vineyard in the A.C. Haut-Médoc, Bordeaux.

Château Kefraya (Leb) *see* Kefraya. (Add): B.P. 16-5768 Achrafieh 1100 2070 Beyrouth-Liban. 300ha. Website: http://www.chateaukefraya.com 'E'mail: admin@chateaukefraya.com

Château Kirwan (Fr) a vineyard. (Add): 33460 Cantenac, Margaux. Grand Cru Classé (3rd). A.C. Margaux. (Com): Cantenac. 32ha. Grape varieties: Cabernet franc, Cabernet sauvignon, Merlot and Petit verdot.

Château Ksara (Leb) a winery (established 1857) based in the Bekka Valley, Lebanon. Label: Réserve du Couvent, Sunset (rosé) 300ha.

Château Labadie (Fr) a Cru Bourgeois vineyard based in Begadan in the A.C. Médoc.

Château la Barde (Fr) a vineyard. (Com): Tauriac. A.C. Côtes de Bourg, Bordeaux.

Château Labarde (Fr) a vineyard. (Com): Labarde. A.C. Médoc, Bordeaux. Second wine of Château Dauzac.

Château la Barde (Fr) a vineyard. (Com): Saint Laurent des Combes. A.C. Saint-Émilion, Bordeaux 3ha.

Château la Barrière (Fr) a 'Vin Nouveau' produced by Château Peychaud. (Com): Teuillac (Côtes de Bourg). A.C. Bordeaux. Grape varieties: Cabernet sauvignon 20% and Merlot 80%.

Château la Barthe (Fr) a vineyard in the A.C. Saint-Émilion, Bordeaux 4ha.

Château la Bastide (Fr) a vineyard in the A.C. Corbières, south-western France.

Château la Bastide (Fr) the former name of Château Dauzac, Margaux.

Château la Bastienne (Fr) a vineyard. (Com): Montagne-Saint-Émilion, A.C. Saint-Émilion. Bordeaux 15ha.

Château Labat (Fr) a vineyrad in the A.C. Haut-Médoc, Bordeaux. Grape varieties: Cabernet sauvingnon 50%, Merlot 50%.

Château Labatut-Bouchard (Fr) a vineyard. (Add): 33490 Saint-Maxant. A.C. Premières Côtes de Bordeaux. (Com): Cadillac.

Château l'Abbaye (Fr) a vineyard. (Add): 33330 Saint-Émilion. A.C. Saint-Émilion. (Com): Saint-Émilion.

Château l'Abbaye-Skinner (Fr) a vineyard. (Com): Vertheuil. A.C. Saint-Estèphe, Bordeaux.

Château l'Abbé-Gorsse-de-Gorsse (Fr) a vineyard. (Com): Margaux. A.C. Margaux, Bordeaux. 10ha. Cru Bourgeois.

Château la Bécade (Fr) a vineyard. (Com): Listrac. A.C. Haut-Médoc, Bordeaux. Cru Bourgeois 28ha

Château la Bécasse (Fr) a vineyard. (Com): Saint-Julien. A.C. Saint-Julien, Bordeaux 4ha.

Château Labégorce (Fr) a vineyard. (Add): Margaux 33460. Cru Bourgeois. A.C. Margaux. (Com): Margaux. 29.5ha. Grape varieties: Cabernet franc 5%, Cabernet sauvignon 60% and Merlot 35%.

Château Labégorce-Zédé (Fr) a vineyard. (Add): 33460 Margaux. A.C. Margaux. Cru Bourgeois Exceptionnel. (Com): Soussans. 26ha. Grape varieties: Cabernet franc 10%, Cabernet sauvignon 50%, Merlot 35% and Petit verdot 5%. Second label is Admiral.

Château la Berrière (Fr) a vineyard. (Add): 44450 La Chapelle, Basse-Mer. A.C. Muscadet Sèvre et Maine. *See also* Muscadet Saint-Clement.

Château la Bertonnière (Fr) a vineyard. (Com): Plassac. A.C. Côtes de Blaye, Bordeaux.

Château Labesse (Fr) a vineyard. (Com): Côtes du Castillon. A.C. Bordeaux Supérieur.

Château la Blancherie (Fr) a vineyard. (Com): La Brède. A.C. Graves. 20ha. Grape varieties: Cabernet sauvignon, Merlot, Sauvignon and Sémillon.

Château la Bonnelle (Fr) a vineyard. (Add): Saint-Pey-d'Armens, 33330 Saint-Émilion. Grand Cru. A.C. Saint-Émilion. (Com): Saint-Pey-d'Armens. 6.5ha. Grape varieties: Cabernet sauvignon 35% and Merlot 65%.

Château Laborde (Fr) a vineyard. (Com): Lalande de Pomerol. A.C. Saint-Émilion, Bordeaux.

Château la Borderie (Fr) a vineyard in the A.C. Côtes de Bergerac, south-western France. (Add): Route de Marmande, Bergerac (red, rosé and white).

Château la Borie (Fr) a vineyard (established 1963) in the A.C. Côtes du Rhône, south-eastern France. Website: http://www.chateau-la-borie.com 'E'mail: eric.magnat@chateau-la-borie.com

Château Laborie (Fr) a vineyard. (Com): Sainte-Croix-du-Mont. A.C. Sainte-Croix-du-Mont, Bordeaux 6ha.

Château la Bouade (Fr) a vineyard. (Com): Barsac. A.C. Barsac (or Sauternes), Bordeaux 12ha.

Château la Bouygue (Fr) a vineyard in the A.C. Saint-Émilion, Bordeaux 3ha.

Château Labrède (Fr) a vineyard. (Com): Mombrier. A.C. Côtes de Bourg, Bordeaux.

Château la Bridane (Fr) a vineyard. (Add): Cartujac, 33112 Saint Laurent, Médoc. Cru Bourgeois. A.C. Saint-Julien. (Com): Saint-Julien. 15ha. Grape varieties: Cabernet sauvignon 55% and Merlot 45%.

Château la Brouillère (Fr) a vineyard. (Com): Bommes. A.C. Sauternes, Bordeaux 4ha.

Château la Brousse (Fr) a vineyard. (Com): Saint-Martin-Caussade. A.C. Côtes de Blaye, Bordeaux.

Château Laburthe-Brivazac (Fr) a vineyard. (Com): Pessac. A.C. Graves, Bordeaux.

Château Lacabane (Fr) a vineyard. (Com): Saint-Martin-Caussade. A.C. Côtes de Blaye, Bordeaux.

Château la Cabanne (Fr) a vineyard. (Com): Soussans. A.C. Haut-Médoc, Bordeaux. Cru Bourgeois.

Château la Cabanne (Fr) a vineyard. (Com): Pomerol. A.C. Pomerol, Bordeaux. Grape varieties: Cabernet franc 20% and Merlot 80%. 9ha.

Château la Calisse (Fr) an 8ha. vineyard in the A.C. Coteaux Varois, Côtes de Provence. Grape varieties: Rolle, Cabernet sauvignon, Grenache, Syrah.

Château la Canorgue (Fr) a organic wine-producing vineyard in the A.C. Côtes de Lubéron, Vallée du Rhône.

Château la Cardonne (Fr) a vineyard. (Com): Blaignan. A.C. Médoc, Bordeaux. Cru Grand Bourgeois. 55ha. Grape varieties: Cabernet franc 5%, Cabernet sauvignon 45%, Merlot 50%.

Château la Carte (Fr) a vineyard. (Com): Saint-Émilion. A.C. Saint-Émilion, Bordeaux. Grand Cru 4.5ha.

Château La Cassagne-Boutet (Fr) a vineyard based at Cars, A.C. Premières Côtes de Blaye .

Château la Caussade (Fr) a vineyard. (Com): Sainte-Croix-du-Mont. A.C. Sainte-Croix-du-Mont, Bordeaux 5ha.

Château la Cave (Fr) a vineyard. (Com): Blaye. A.C. Côtes de Blaye, Bordeaux.

Château la Chapelle (Fr) a vineyard in the A.C. Saint-Émilion, Bordeaux 4ha.

Château la Chapelle aux Moines (Fr) a vineyard. (Add): Saint-Christophe-des-Bardes. Grand Cru. A.C. Saint-Émilion. (Com): Saint-Émilion. Grape varieties: Cabernet franc, Malbec, Merlot.

Château la Chapelle-de-Lescours (Fr) a vineyard. (Com): Saint-Sulpice-de-Faleyrens. A.C. Saint-Émilion, Bordeaux 3ha. Grape varieties: Cabernet franc, Cabernet sauvignon, Malbec and Merlot.

Château la Chapelle-Lariveau (Fr) a vineyard. (Com): St-Michel. A.C. Côtes Canon-Fronsac, Bordeaux 5ha.

Château la Chapelle-Lescours (Fr) a vineyard in the A.C. Saint-Émilion, Bordeaux 3ha.

Château la Chapelle-St-Aubin (Fr) a vineyard. (Com): Bommes. A.C. Sauternes, Bordeaux 3ha.

Château Lachesnaye (Fr) a vineyard. (Add): Cussac-Fort-Médoc, 33460 Margaux. A.C. Haut-Médoc. (Com): Cussac-Fort-Médoc. 20ha. Grape varieties: Cabernet sauvignon 50% and Merlot 50%.

Château la Chichonne (Fr) a vineyard. (Com): Pomerol. A.C. Pomerol, Bordeaux 2ha.

Château la Clare (Fr) a Cru Bourgeois. A.C. Médoc. (Com): Bégadan. 20ha. Grape varieties: Cabernet franc, Cabernet sauvignon and Merlot.

Château la Clie de Corbin (Fr) a vineyard in the A.C. Montagne-Saint-Émilion, eastern Bordeaux.

Château la Closerie-du-Grand-Poujeaux (Fr) a vineyard. (Com): Moulis. A.C. Haut-Médoc, Bordeaux. Cru Bourgeois 7ha.

Château la Clotte (Fr) a vineyard. (Com): Barsac. A.C. Barsac (or Sauternes), Bordeaux 5ha.

Château la Clotte (Fr) a vineyard. (Com): Puisseguin-Saint-Émilion. A.C. Saint-Émilion, Bordeaux 2ha.

Château la Clotte (Fr) a vineyard. (Com): Saint-Émilion. A.C. Saint-Émilion, Bordeaux. (Add): 33330 Saint-Émilion. Grand Cru Classé 4.5ha.

Château la Clotte-Grande-Côte (Fr) a vineyard in the A.C. Saint-Émilion, Bordeaux 4ha.

Château la Clusière (Fr) a vineyard. (Add): 33330 Saint-Émilion. Grand Cru. A.C. Saint-Émilion. (Com): Saint-Émilion. 4.78ha. Grape varieties: Bouchet 20%, Cabernet sauvignon 10% and Merlot 70%.

Château la Clyde (Fr) a vineyard. (Com): Langoiran. A.C. Premières Côtes de Bordeaux. (Add): 33550 Langoiran 15.5ha.

Château Lacombe-Noaillac (Fr) a vineyard based in Jau-Dignac-et-Loirac, Bordeaux. A.C. Cru Bourgeois. Second label is Les Traverses.

Château la Commanderie (Fr) an A.C. Bordeaux Mousseux.

Château la Commanderie (Fr) a vineyard. (Com): Libourne. A.C. Pomerol, Bordeaux 5ha.

Château la Commanderie (Fr) a vineyard. (Com): Pineuilh. A.C. Saint-Foy-Bordeaux, southern Bordeaux.

Château la Commanderie (Fr) a vineyard. (Add): 33330 Saint-Émilion. Grand Cru. A.C. Saint-Émilion. (Com): Saint-Émilion. 3.6ha. Grape varieties: Cabernet franc 10%, Cabernet sauvignon 5% and Merlot 85%.

Château la Commanderie (Fr) a vineyard. (Com): Saint-Estèphe. A.C. Médoc, Bordeaux.

Château la Commanderie du Queyret (Fr) a vineyard situated in the commune of Saint-Antoine-du-Queyret. 51ha. red from 60% Merlot, 30% Cabernet sauvignon, 10% Cabernet franc. 22ha. white from 50% Sémillon, 30% Sauvignon, 20% Muscadelle.

Château la Condamine (Fr) a vineyard in the A.C. Corbières, south-western France. Label: Cuvée Tradition.

Château la Condamine-Bertrand (Fr) a vineyard in the A.C. Clairette du Languedoc, south-western France.

Château Laconfourque (Fr) a vineyard. (Com): Saint-Julien. A.C. Saint-Julien, Bordeaux 1ha.

Château la Conseillante (Fr) a vineyard. (Com): Pomerol. A.C. Pomerol, Bordeaux. 12ha. Grape varieties: Cabernet franc and Merlot.

Château Lacoste-Borie (Fr) the second wine of Château Grand Puy-Lacoste.

Château la Côte-Daugay (Fr) a vineyard in the A.C. Saint-Émilion, Bordeaux 1ha.

Château la Côte-Haut-Brion (Fr) a vineyard. (Com): Talence. A.C. Graves, Bordeaux. Cru Bourgeois.

Château la Courolle (Fr) a vineyard in the A.C. Montagne-Saint-Émilion. Grape varieties: Cabernet franc, Cabernet sauvignon, Merlot.

Château la Couronne (Fr) a vineyard. (Com): Montagne-Saint-Émilion. A.C. Saint-Émilion, Bordeaux 4ha.

C

Château la Couronne (Fr) a vineyard. (Com): Pauillac. A.C. Haut-Médoc, Bordeaux. (Part of Château Haut Batailley) 3ha.

Château la Couspaude (Fr) a vineyard. (Com): Saint-Émilion. A.C. Grand Cru Classé Saint-Émilion, Bordeaux. (Add): B.P. 40, 33330 Saint-Émilion. 4.5ha.

Château la Croix (Fr) a vineyard. (Com): Néac. A.C. Saint-Émilion, Bordeaux.

Château la Croix (Fr) a vineyard. (Com): Pomerol. A.C. Pomerol, Bordeaux 8ha.

Château la Croix (Fr) a vineyard. (Com): Fronsac. A.C. Côtes de Fronsac, Bordeaux. 11ha

Château la Croix (Fr) the second wine of Château Ducru-Beaucaillou.

Château la Croix (Fr) a vineyard. (Com): Teuillac. A.C. Côte de Bourg, Bordeaux.

Château la Croix Bellevue (Fr) a vineyard. (Com): Lalande de Pomerol. A.C. Lalande de Pomerol, Bordeaux.

Château la Croix-Chantecaille (Fr) a vineyard. (Add): 33330 Saint-Émilion. Grand Cru. A.C. Saint-Émilion. (Com): Saint-Émilion. Grape varieties: Cabernet franc, Malbec, Merlot. 6ha.

Château la Croix-de-Blanchon (Fr) a vineyard. (Com): Lussac-Saint-Émilion. A.C. Saint-Émilion, Bordeaux 5ha.

Château la Croix-de-Gay (Fr) a vineyard. (Com): Pomerol. A.C. Pomerol, Bordeaux. 12ha. Grape varieties: Cabernet franc 10%, Cabernet sauvignon 10% and Merlot 80%.

Château la Croix de Grézard (Fr) an A.C. Saint-Émilion. Second wine is Château Champ de Grenet.

Château la Croix-de-la-Bastienne (Fr) a vineyard. (Com): Montagne-Saint-Émilion. A.C. Saint-Émilion, Bordeaux 2ha.

Château la Croix de la Chenevelle (Fr) a vineyard based in Levrault-Bedrienne, 33 Lalande-de-Pomerol. A.C. Lalande-de-Pomerol.

Château la Croix du Casse (Fr) a vineyard. (Com): Pomerol. A.C. Pomerol, Bordeaux.

Château la Croix du Chabut (Fr) a vineyard in the A.C. Premières Côtes de Blaye, Bordeaux.

Château la Croix Gandineau (Fr) a vineyard. (Com): Fronsac. A.C. Côtes de Fronsac, Bordeaux 5ha.

Château la Croix-St-Georges (Fr) a vineyard. (Com): Pomerol. A.C. Pomerol, Bordeaux 4ha.

Château la Croix St. Michel (Fr) a vineyard in the A.C. Côtes de Bourg, Bordeaux.

Château la Croix-Taillefer (Fr) a vineyard. (Com): Pomerol. A.C. Pomerol, Bordeaux 2ha.

Château la Croix Toulifaut (Fr) a vineyard. (Com): Pomerol. A.C. Pomerol, Bordeaux 1ha.

Château la Croizille (Fr) a vineyard in the A.C. Saint-Émilion, Bordeaux 4ha.

Château la Cure (Fr) a vineyard. (Com): Cars. A.C. Côtes de Blaye, Bordeaux.

Château la Dame Blanche (Fr) a vineyard based in the Haut-Médoc. (Add): La Taillan-Médoc, 33320 Eysines. A.C.'s Bordeaux Blanc, Bordeaux Rouge, Haut-Médoc. (Com): La Taillan. 25ha. Grape varieties: Cabernet sauvignon, Colombard, Merlot, Sauvignon blanc.

Château la Dauphine (Fr) a vineyard. (Com): Fronsac. A.C. Canon-Fronsac, Bordeaux 6ha.

Château la Décelle (Fr) a vineyard in the A.C. Côtes-du-Rhône-Villages Valréas. (Add): 26130 Saint Paul Trois Chateaux. Label: Cuvée St-Paul. 'E'mail: ladecelle@wanadoo.fr

Château la Dominante (Fr) a vineyard in the A.C. Lalande de Pomerol. 25ha. Website: http://www.chateau-la-dominante.com

Château la Dominique (Fr) a vineyard. (Add): Route de Montagne, B.P. 160, 33500 Libourne Cedex. Grand Cru Classé. A.C. Saint-Émilion. (Com): Saint-Émilion. 21ha. Grape varieties: Cabernet franc 15%, Cabernet sauvignon 15%, Malbec 10% and Merlot 60%.

Château la Ladouys (Fr) a vineyard. (Com): Saint-Estèphe. A.C. Haut-Médoc, Bordeaux 4ha.

Château la Duchesse (Fr) a vineyard. (Com): Fronsac. A.C. Canon-Fronsac, Bordeaux.

Château la Fagnouse (Fr) a vineyard in the A.C. Saint-Émilion, Bordeaux 5ha.

Château Lafargue (Fr) a vineyard based in Léognan, Bordeaux. A.C. Pessac-Léognan.

Château la Faucherie (Fr) a vineyard. (Com): Montagne-Saint-Émilion. A.C. Saint-Émilion, Bordeaux 3ha.

Château la Faure (Fr) a vineyard. (Com): Saillans. A.C. Côtes de Fronsac, Bordeaux 13ha.

Château Lafaurie (Fr) a vineyard. (Com): Néac. A.C. Lalande de Pomerol, Bordeaux.

Château Lafaurie-Peyraguey (Fr) a Premier Grand Cru Classé vineyard. (Com): Bommes. A.C. Sauternes. 22ha. Grape varieties: Muscadelle 10%, Sauvignon 30% and Sémillon 60%.

Château Laffite (Fr) a vineyard. (Com): Yvrac. A.C. Médoc, Bordeaux.

Château Laffite-Saint-Estèphe (Fr) a vineyard. (Com): Saint-Estèphe. A.C. Haut-Médoc, Bordeaux.

Château Laffitte (Fr) a vineyard. (Com): Bégadan. A.C. Médoc, Bordeaux.

Château Laffitte-Cantegric (Fr) a vineyard. (Com): Listrac, A.C. Haut-Médoc, Bordeaux. Cru Bourgeois.

Château Laffitte-Canteloup (Fr) a vineyard. (Com): Ludon. A.C. Médoc, Bordeaux.

Château Laffitte-Carcasset (Fr) a vineyard. (Add): Saint-Estèphe 33250. A.C. Saint-Estèphe. (Com): Saint-Estèphe. 25ha. Grape varieties: Cabernet franc 10%, Cabernet sauvignon 60% and Merlot 30%. Second label is Vicomtesse.

Château Laffitte Laujac (Fr) the second label of Château Laujac.

Château Lafite (Fr) see Château Lafite Rothschild.

Château Lafite Rothschild (Fr) a vineyard. (Add): 33250 Pauillac. Premier Grand Cru Classé. A.C. Pauillac. (Com): Pauillac. 100ha. Grape varieties: Cabernet franc, Cabernet sauvignon and Merlot. Second wine is Les Carruades de Lafite Rothschild.

Château Lafitte-Bordeaux (Fr) a vineyard in the A.C. Graves, Bordeaux (red).

C

Château Lafitte-Talence (Fr) a vineyard. (Com): Talence. A.C. Graves, Bordeaux (red).

Château la Fleur (Fr) an A.C. Grand Cru vineyard in Saint-Émilion, Bordeaux 5ha.

Château La Fleur-Cadet (Fr) a vineyard in the A.C. Saint-Émilion, Bordeaux 4ha.

Château la Fleur-Cravignac (Fr) a vineyard. (Add): 33330 Saint-Émilion. Grand Cru. A.C. Saint-Émilion. (Com): Saint-Émilion.

Château Lafleur de Gay (Fr) a vineyard. (Com): Pomerol. A.C. Pomerol, Bordeaux 4ha.

Château la Fleur-des-Rouzes (Fr) a vineyard. (Com): Pomerol. A.C. Pomerol, Bordeaux 4ha.

Château Lafleur du Roy (Fr) a vineyard. (Com): Pomerol, A.C. Pomerol, Bordeaux (mainly Merlot grapes).

Château Lafleur-Gazin (Fr) a vineyard. (Com): Pomerol, A.C. Pomerol, Bordeaux 4ha.

Château la Fleur Godard (Fr) an A.C. Bordeaux Côtes de Francs. Grape varieties: Cabernet franc 10%, Cabernet sauvingnon 25%, Merlot 65%.

Château la Fleur-Milon (Fr) a Cru Grand Bourgeois. A.C. Haut-Médoc. (Com): Pauillac. 13ha.

Château la Fleur Morange (Fr) a vineyard. (Add): Saint Pey d'Armens, 33330 Saint-Émilion. Grand Cru. A.C. Saint-Émilion. (Com): Saint-Émilion. 2.25ha. Website: http://www.saint-emilion-vin-grand-cru.com.fr

Château La Fleur Perron (Fr) a 15ha vineyard in Lalande de Pomerol. A.C. Lalande de Pomerol.

Château la Fleur-Perruchon (Fr) a vineyard. (Com): Lussac-Saint-Émilion. A.C. Saint-Émilion, Bordeaux 5ha.

Château la Fleur-Pétrus (Fr) a vineyard. (Com): Pomerol. A.C. Pomerol, Bordeaux 9ha.

Château la Fleur Peyrabon (Fr) a Cru Bourgeois vineyard in the A.C. Pauillac, St. Saveur, Médoc, Bordeaux.

Château la Fleur Picon (Fr) a vineyard. (Add): 33330 Saint-Émilion. Grand Cru. A.C. Saint-Émilion. (Com): Saint-Émilion. 5.58ha. Grape varieties: Cabernet franc 35% and Merlot 65%.

Château la Fleur Pourret (Fr) a vineyard. (Add): 33330 Saint-Émilion. A.C. Saint-Émilion. (Com): Saint-Émilion. 4.7ha. Grape varieties: Cabernet franc 50%, Cabernet sauvignon 25% and Merlot 25%.

Château la Fleur-St-Georges (Fr) part of Château St-Georges A.C. Saint-Émilion, Bordeaux.

Château Lafon (Fr) a vineyard. (Com): Listrac. A.C. Listrac, Bordeaux. Cru Grand Bourgeois. 7ha. Second wine is Les Hauts Marcieux.

Château Lafon (Fr) a vineyard. (Com): Sauternes. A.C. Sauternes, Bordeaux. 6ha. Also Château le Mayne.

Château Lafon-Laroze (Fr) a vineyard. (Com): Sauternes. A.C. Sauternes, Bordeaux 3ha.

Château Lafon-Menaut (Fr) a vineyard in the A.C. Léognan-Pessac, Graves. White wine.

Château Lafon-Rochet (Fr) a vineyard. (Add): 33250 Saint-Estèphe. Grand Cru Classé (4th). A.C. Saint-Estèphe. (Com): Saint-Estèphe. 55ha. Grape varieties: Cabernet franc 8%, Cabernet sauvignon

70%, Malbec 2% and Merlot 20%. Second label is Le Numéro 2 de Lafon-Rochet.

Château Lafont (Fr) a vineyard. (Com): Cartelègue. A.C. Côtes de Blaye, Bordeaux.

Château la Fontaine (Fr) a vineyard. (Com): Fronsac. A.C. Côtes de Fronsac, Bordeaux 9ha.

Château La Forêt St. Hilaire (Fr) an A.C. Bordeaux Blanc Sec, Bordeaux. Grape varieties: Sauvignon blanc 70%, Sémillon 25%, Muscadelle 5%.

Château la Fortine (Fr) a vineyard in the A.C. Saint-Émilion, Bordeaux 12ha.

Château la France (Fr) a vineyard. (Com): Blaignan. A.C. Médoc, Bordeaux. Cru Bourgeois 6ha.

Château Lafuë (Fr) a vineyard. (Com): Sainte-Croix-du-Mont. A.C. Sainte-Croix-du-Mont, Bordeaux 10ha.

Château la Gaffelière (Fr) a vineyard. (Add): 33330 Saint-Émilion. Premier [B] Grand Cru Classé. A.C. Saint-Émilion. (Com): Saint-Émilion. 25ha. Grape varieties: Cabernet franc, Cabernet sauvignon and Merlot.

Château la Galiane (Fr) a vineyard. (Com): Soussans-Margaux. A.C. Haut-Médoc, Bordeaux 5ha. Grape varieties: 50% Merlot, 45% Cabernet sauvignon, 5% Petit verdot.

Château la Ganne (Fr) a vineyard. (Com): Pomerol. A.C. Pomerol, Bordeaux 5ha.

Château Lagarde (Fr) a vineyard. (Com): Saint-Seurin-de-Cursac. A.C. Côtes de Blaye, Bordeaux.

Château la Garde (Fr) a vineyard. (Add): 45650 La Brède. A.C. Pessac-Léognan. (Com): Léognan. 39ha. Grape varieties: Cabernet franc, Cabernet sauvignon, Merlot, Sauvignon and Sémillon.

Château la Garde (Fr) a vineyard. (Com): Martillac. A.C. Pessac-Léognan, Bordeaux. 13ha (red). Grape varieties: Cabernet sauvignon 50%, Merlot 50%.

Château la Garde Roland (Fr) a vineyard. (Com): Saint-Seurin-de-Cursac. A.C. Côtes de Blaye, Bordeaux.

Château la Garélle (Fr) a Grand Cru vineyard. (Com): Saint-Émilion. A.C. Saint-Émilion, Bordeaux 12ha.

Château la Garlière (Fr) a vineyard in the A.C. Haut-Médoc, Bordeaux. Cru Bourgeois.

Château la Gigoterie (Fr) a vineyard in the A.C. Côtes de Blaye, Bordeaux.

Château la Girouette (Fr) a vineyard. (Com): Fours. A.C. Côtes de Blaye, Bordeaux.

Château Lagniappe (USA) the label used by the Cedar Hill Wine C°. based in Cleveland Heights, Ohio for their vinifera wines.

Château la Gomerie (Fr) a vineyard in the A.C. Saint-Émilion, Bordeaux 2ha.

Château la Gorce (Fr) a vineyard. (Add): Blaignan, 33340 Lesparre. A.C. Médoc (Com): Blaignan. 42ha. Grape varieties: Cabernet 70% and Merlot 30%. Second label is Château Canteloup.

Château Lagorce (Fr) a vineyard. (Com): Moulis. A.C. Moulis, Bordeaux 3ha.

Château la Gordonne (Fr) a vineyard in the A.C. Côtes de Provence (white wine).

Château la Gorre (Fr) a vineyard. (Com): Bégadan. A.C. Médoc, Bordeaux 7ha.

C

Château la Grâce-Dieu-les-Menuts (Fr) a vineyard. (Add): 33330 Saint-Émilion. Grand Cru. A.C. Saint-Émilion. (Com): Saint-Émilion. 13ha. Grape varieties: Cabernet franc 30%, Cabernet sauvignon 10% and Merlot 60%.

Château la Grande-Clotte (Fr). A vineyard. (Com): Lussac-Saint-Émilion. A.C. Saint-Émilion, Bordeaux 5ha.

Château La Grande-Maye (Fr). 20ha. vineyard in the A.C. Côtes de Castillon, Bordeaux.

Château Lagrange (Fr) a vineyard. (Com): Blaye. A.C. Côtes de Blaye, Bordeaux.

Château Lagrange (Fr) a vineyard. (Com): Bourg. A.C. Côtes de Bourg, Bordeaux.

Château Lagrange (Fr) a vineyard. (Add): Sarl, 33250 Saint-Julien, Pauillac. Grand Cru Classé (3rd). A.C. Saint-Julien. (Com): Saint-Julien. 113ha. Grape varieties: Cabernet 70% and Merlot 30%. Second wine is Les Fiefs de Lagrange.

Château la Grange (Fr) a vineyard. (Com): Pomerol. A.C. Pomerol, Bordeaux 8ha.

Château la Grange Neuve (Fr) a vineyard in the A.C. Bergerac, south-western France (red).

Château la Graulet (Fr) a vineyard. (Com): St-Cier-de-Canesse. A.C. Côtes de Bourg, Bordeaux.

Château la Grave (Fr) a vineyard in the A.C. Minervois, Languedoc-Roussillon. Grape varieties: Carignan Grenache, Mourvèdre and Syrah. Label: Cuvée Privilège.

Château la Grave (Fr) a vineyard. (Com): Sainte-Croix-du-Mont. A.C. Sainte-Croix-du-Mont, Bordeaux 6ha.

Château la Grave Figeac (Fr) (Fr) a vineyard. (Add): 33330 Saint-Émilion. Grand Cru. A.C. Saint-Émilion. (Com): Saint-Émilion. Grape varieties: Cabernet franc, Malbec, Merlot.

Château la Graves (Fr) a vineyard. (Com): Fronsac. A.C. Côtes de Fronsac, Bordeaux 3ha.

Château la Grave Trigant de Boisset (Fr) a vineyard. (Com): Pomerol. A.C. Pomerol, Bordeaux 8ha.

Château Lagravette (Fr) a vineyard. (Com): Bommes. A.C. Sauternes, Bordeaux 2ha.

Château Lagravette-Peyredon (Fr) a vineyard. (Com): Listrac. A.C. Listrac, Bordeaux 5ha.

Château la Gravière (Fr) a vineyard. (Com): Sainte-Croix-du-Mont. A.C. Sainte-Croix-du-Mont, Bordeaux 11ha.

Château la Graville (Fr) a vineyard. (Com): Sainte-Croix-du-Mont. A.C. Sainte-Croix-du-Mont, Bordeaux 4ha.

Château la Grenière (Fr) a vineyard. (Com): Lussac-Saint-Émilion. A.C. Saint-Émilion, Bordeaux 5ha.

Château Lagrezette (Fr) a 50ha. vineyard based in Caillac, Cahors. A.C. Cahors. 70% Malbec, 27% Merlot, 3% Tannat.

Château la Grolet (Fr) see Château Graulet.

Château Lague Bourdieu (Fr) a vineyard. (Com): Fronsac. A.C. Côtes de Fronsac, Bordeaux 4ha.

Château la Gurgue (Fr) a vineyard. (Add): Rue de la Tremoille, Margaux. Cru Bourgeois. A.C. Margaux. (Com): Margaux. 12ha. Grape varieties: Cabernet 55% and Merlot 40%, Petit verdot 5%.

Château la Hargue (Fr) a vineyard. (Com): Plassac. A.C. Côtes de Blaye, Bordeaux. Also produces an A.C. Bordeaux Blanc Sec. Grape variety: Sauvignon blanc 100%.

Château la Haye (Fr) a vineyard. (Add): Saint-Estèphe, 33250 Pauillac. A.C. Saint-Estèphe. (Com): Saint-Estèphe. 10ha. Grape varieties: Cabernet sauvignon, Merlot and Petit verdot.

Château Lahouilley (Fr) a vineyard. (Com): Barsac. A.C. Barsac (or Sauternes), Bordeaux 3ha.

Château la Hourcade (Fr) a vineyard. (Com): Preignac. A.C. Sauternes, Bordeaux 4ha.

Château la Houringue (Fr) a vineyard. (Com): Macau. A.C. Haut-Médoc, Bordeaux. Cru Bourgeois.

Château la Jaubertie (Fr) a vineyard. (Com): Monbazillac. A.C. Bergerac, south-western France (red and white).

Château la Lagune (Fr) a vineyard. (Add): Ludon, Médoc 33290 Blanquefort. Grand Cru Classé (3rd). A.C. Haut-Médoc. (Com): Ludon. 55ha. Grape varieties: Cabernet franc, Cabernet sauvignon, Merlot and Petit verdot. Second label is Château Ludon-Pomies-Agassac.

Château Lalande (Fr) a vineyard. (Add): 33480 Listrac-Médoc. A.C. Listrac. (Com): Listrac. 12ha. Grape varieties: Cabernet, Merlot and Petit verdot.

Château Lalande Borie (Fr) an A.C. Saint-Julien. (Com): Saint-Julien. 18ha. Grape varieties: Cabernet franc 10%, Cabernet sauvignon 65% and Merlot 25%.

Château Lalanette Ferbos (Fr) a vineyard. (Com): Cérons. A.C. Cérons, Bordeaux 5ha.

Château Lalibarde (Fr) a vineyard. (Com): Bourg. A.C. Côtes de Bourg, Bordeaux.

Château la Louvière (Fr) a vineyard. (Add): Léognan 33850. A.C. Pessac-Léognan. (Com): Léognan. 55ha. Grape varieties: Cabernet franc, Cabernet sauvignon, Merlot, Sauvignon and Sémillon (red and white), second wine is L de la Louvière.

Château la Madeleine (Fr) a vineyard. (Add): 33330 Saint-Émilion. Grand Cru. A.C. Saint-Émilion. (Com): Saint-Émilion.

Château la Magdelaine (Fr) a vineyard. (Com): Saint-Émilion. A.C. Saint-Émilion, Bordeaux 11ha.

Château Magnan la Gaffelière (Fr) a vineyard. (Add): 33330 Saint-Émilion. Grand Cru. A.C. Saint-Émilion. (Com): Saint-Émilion. vineyard. (Add): 33330 Saint-Émilion. Grand Cru. A.C. Saint-Émilion. (Com): Saint-Émilion.

Château la Marche-Canon (Fr) a vineyard. (Com): Fronsac. A.C. Côtes Canon-Fronsac, Bordeaux 2ha.

Château la Maréchaude (Fr) a commune in the Lalande de Pomerol. A.C. Saint-Émilion, Bordeaux.

Château Lamarque (Fr) a vineyard. (Com): Lamarque. A.C. Haut-Médoc, Bordeaux. Cru Grand Bourgeois. 47ha. Second wine is Réserve du Marquis d'Evry.

Château Lamarque (Fr) a vineyard. (Com): Sainte-Croix-du-Mont. A.C. Sainte-Croix-du-Mont, Bordeaux 15ha.

Château Lamartine (Fr) a vineyard. (Com):

Cantenac. A.C. Bordeaux Supérieur, Bordeaux. Grape varieties: Cabernet sauvignon and Merlot. Vinified at Château Cantenac-Brown.

Château Lamartine (Fr) a vineyard in the A.C. Côtes-de-Castillon, south-eastern Bordeaux. Grape varieties: Cabernet sauvignon, Cabernet franc, Merlot.

Château Lamarzelle (Fr) a vineyard. (Add): 33330 Saint-Émilion. Grand Cru (demoted 2006). A.C. Saint-Émilion. (Com): Saint-Émilion. 15ha. Grape varieties: Cabernet franc 20%, Cabernet sauvignon 20% and Merlot 60%.

Château la Mausse (Fr) a vineyard. (Com): St-Michel. A.C. Côtes Canon-Fronsac, Bordeaux 7ha.

Château la Mayne (Fr) a vineyard. (Com): Sables-Saint-Émilion. A.C. Saint-Émilion, Bordeaux 3ha.

Château Lambert (Fr) a vineyard. (Com): Pauillac. A.C. Médoc, Bordeaux. Cru Bourgeois.

Château Lambert (Fr) a vineyard. (Com): St-Aignans. A.C. Côtes de Fronsac, Bordeaux 3ha.

Château la-Mission-Haut-Brion (Fr) a vineyard. (Add): 33400 Talence, Graves. Grand Cru Classé. A.C. Pessac-Léognan. (Com): Talence. 20ha. Grape varieties: Cabernet franc, Cabernet sauvignon, Merlot, Muscadelle, Sauvignon and Sémillon. Website: www.mission-haut-brion.com

Château la Mondotte (Fr) a vineyard. (Add): Saint Laurent des Combes, 33330 Saint-Émilion. Grand Cru. A.C. Saint-Émilion. (Com): Saint Laurent des Combes. 4.3ha. Grape varieties: Cabernet franc 25% and Merlot 75%. Now known as Mondotte (La).

Château la Mongie (Fr) a 35ha vineyard based in Vérac, Bordeaux. Grape varieties: Merlot, Sauvignon.

Château Lamon Winery (Austr) a winery. (Add): 140 km. Post, Calder Highway, Big Hill, Bendigo, Victoria 3550 (P.O. Box 487). 4.2ha. Grape varieties: Cabernet sauvignon, Pinot noir, Chardonnay, Rhine riesling, Sémillon, Shiraz.

Château Lamorère (Fr) a vineyard. (Com): Moulis. A.C. Médoc, Bordeaux. Cru Bourgeois.

Château Lamothe (Fr) a vineyard. (Com): St-Paul. A.C. Côtes de Blaye, Bordeaux.

Château Lamothe (Fr) a vineyard. (Com): Lansac. A.C. Côtes de Bourg, Bordeaux.

Château Lamothe (Fr) a vineyard. (Com): Cadaujac. A.C. Graves, Bordeaux. 4ha (red and white).

Château Lamothe (Fr) a vineyard. (Com): Saint-Medard-d'Eyrans. A.C. Graves, Bordeaux.

Château Lamothe (Fr) a vineyard. (Add): 33250 Pauillac. Cru Grand Bourgeois. A.C. Haut-Médoc. (Com): Cissac. 50ha. Grape varieties: Cabernet franc, Cabernet sauvignon 70%, Merlot 25% and Petit verdot.

Château Lamothe (Fr) a vineyard. (Com): Gatarnos Haut. A.C. Premières Côtes de Bordeaux, central Bordeaux

Château Lamothe (Fr) a vineyard. (Com): Sauternes. A.C. Sauternes, Bordeaux. 15ha. Also Château d'Arches.

Château Lamothe (Fr) a vineyard. (Com): Sauternes.

A.C. Sauternes, Bordeaux. 14ha. Also Domaine des Justices and the Châteaux- Gilette, les Remparts and les Rochers.

Château Lamothe (Fr) a Grand Cru Classé. A.C. Sauternes. (Com): Sauternes. Grape varieties: Sauvignon 20%, Sémillon 70% and Muscadelle 10%.

Château Lamothe Bergeron (Fr) a vineyard. (Com): Cussac-Fort-Médoc. A.C. Haut-Médoc, Bordeaux. Cru Bourgeois 10ha.

Château Lamothe-Bouscaut (Fr) a vineyard. (Com): Cadaujac. A.C. Graves, Bordeaux. Cru Bourgeois.

Château Lamothe-de-Bergeron (Fr) a vineyard. (Com): Cussac-Fort-Médoc. A.C. Haut-Médoc, Bordeaux. Cru Bourgeois.

Château la Mothe et Grand Moulin (Fr) a vineyard. (Com): Saint-Seurin-de-Cadourne. A.C. Haut-Médoc, Bordeaux. (Add): Société Civile Cru Bourgeois, Saint-Seurin-de-Cadourne, 33250 Pauillac. 30ha.

Château la Mouleyre (Fr) a vineyard. (Com): Sainte-Croix-du-Mont. A.C. Sainte-Croix-du-Mont, Bordeaux 4ha.

Château la Mouline (Fr) a vineyard. (Add): 33480 Castelnau-de-Médoc. A.C. Moulis. (Com): Moulis. 15ha. Grape varieties: Cabernet franc, Cabernet sauvignon, Merlot and Petit verdot.

Château la Mourette (Fr) a vineyard. (Com): Bommes. A.C. Sauternes, Bordeaux 3ha.

Château Lamouroux (Fr) a vineyard. (Com): Cérons. A.C. Cérons, Bordeaux 10ha.

Château Lamouroux (Fr) a vineyard. (Com): Cérons. A.C. Graves Supérieur, Bordeaux. 8ha (white).

Château Landon (Fr) a vineyard. (Com): Bégadan. A.C. Médoc, Bordeaux 25ha.

Château la Nerthe (Fr) a vineyard in the A.C. Châteauneuf-du-Pape, southern Rhône. Produced by Dugas, Rte. de Sorgues, 84230 Châteauneuf-du-Pape. Other label is Clos de Beauvenir.

Château Lanessan (Fr) a vineyard. (Add): Cussac-Fort-Médoc, 33460 Margaux. Cru Bourgeois Exceptionnel. A.C. Haut-Médoc. (Com): Cussac-Fort-Médoc. 40ha. Grape varieties: Cabernet franc, Cabernet sauvignon, Merlot and Petit verdot.

Château Lanessan (Fr) a vineyard. (Com): Pauillac. A.C. Pauillac, Bordeaux.

Château Lanette (Fr) a vineyard. (Com): Cérons. A.C. Cérons, Bordeaux 5ha.

Château la Nève (Fr) a vineyard. (Com): Loupiac. A.C. Loupiac, Bordeaux 9ha.

Château Lange (Fr) a vineyard. (Com): Gradignan. A.C. Graves, Bordeaux.

Château Lange (Fr) a vineyard. (Com): Bommes. A.C. Sauternes, Bordeaux 5ha.

Château l'Angélus (Fr) a vineyard. (Com): Pomerol. A.C. Pomerol, Bordeaux 1ha.

Château Langlade (Fr) a vineyard. (Com): Parsac-Saint-Émilion. A.C. Saint-Émilion, Bordeaux 6ha.

Château Langlois (Fr) a vineyard based in Saumur, Anjou-Saumur, Loire. Produces sparkling (méthode traditionelle) wines. Owned by the Bollinger Champagne house.

Château Langoa (Fr) *see* Château Langoa Barton.

C

Château Langoa-Barton (Fr) a vineyard. (Add): Saint-Julien, Beychevelle 33250 Pauillac. Grand Cru Classé (3rd). A.C. Saint-Julien. (Com): Saint-Julien. 25ha. Grape varieties: Cabernet franc, Cabernet sauvignon, Merlot and Petit verdot.

Château Langueloup (Fr) a vineyard. (Com): Portets. A.C. Graves, Bordeaux. 2ha (red and white).

Château Laniote (Fr) a vineyard. (Com): Saint-Émilion. A.C. Saint-Émilion, Bordeaux. 5ha. (Add): 33330 Saint-Émilion. A.C. Saint-Émilion Grand Cru Classé.

Château la Noë (Fr) a vineyard in the A.C. Muscadet Sèvre et Maine, Nantais, Loire. (Add): Clos de Ferré, Vallet, Loire Atlantique.

Château Laouilley (Fr) a vineyard. (Com): Roaillan. A.C. Graves, Bordeaux. 3ha (white).

Château la Paillette (Fr) a vineyard. (Com): Sables-Saint-Émilion. A.C. Saint-Émilion, Bordeaux 3ha.

Château la Papeterie (Fr) a vineyard. (Com): Montagne-Saint-Émilion. A.C. Saint-Émilion, Bordeaux 9ha.

Château la Patache (Fr) a vineyard. (Com): Pomerol. A.C. Pomerol, Bordeaux 2ha.

Château la Pelletrie (Fr) a vineyard. (Add): Saint-Christophe-des-Bardes, 33330 Saint-Émilion. Grand Cru. A.C. Saint-Émilion. (Com): Saint-Christophe-des-Bardes. 15ha. Grape variety: Merlot 100%.

Château Lapelou (Fr) a vineyard. (Com): Barsac. A.C. Barsac (or Sauternes), Bordeaux 6ha.

Château la Perotte (Fr) a vineyard. (Com): Eyrons. A.C. Côtes de Blaye, Bordeaux.

Château la Perrière (Fr) a vineyard. (Com): Lussac-Saint-Émilion. A.C. Saint-Émilion, Bordeaux 5ha.

Château Lapeyrère (Fr) a vineyard. (Com): Sainte-Croix-du-Mont. A.C. Sainte-Croix-du-Mont, Bordeaux 5ha.

Château la Picherie (Fr) a vineyard. (Com): Montagne-Saint-Émilion. A.C. Saint-Émilion, Bordeaux 6ha.

Château Lapinesse (Fr) a vineyard. (Com): Barsac. A.C. Barsac (or Sauternes), Bordeaux 16ha.

Château Laplagnotte-Bellevue (Fr) a vineyard. (Add): Saint-Christophe-des-Bardes, 33330 Saint-Émilion. Grand Cru. A.C. Saint-Émilion. (Com): Saint-Christophe-des-Bardes. 6ha. Grape varieties: Cabernet franc 20%, Cabernet sauvignon 10% and Merlot 70%. 'E'mail: arnauddl@aol.com

Château la Plante (Fr) a vineyard. (Com): Sables-Saint-Émilion. A.C. Saint-Émilion, Bordeaux 1ha.

Château la Pointe (Fr) an A.C. Pomerol. Commune: Pomerol. 20ha. Grape varieties: Cabernet franc 20%, Malbec 5% and Merlot 75%.

Château la Providence (Fr) a vineyard. (Com): Ludon. A.C. Médoc, Bordeaux. Cru Bourgeois.

Château la Providence (Fr) a vineyard. (Com): Pomerol. A.C. Pomerol, Bordeaux 3ha.

Château la Pujade (Fr) a vineyard in the A.C. Corbières, south-western France. Label: Cuvée Charlemagne and Cuvée Gomard.

Château la Rame (Fr) a vineyard. (Com): Sainte-Croix-du-Mont. A.C. Sainte-Croix-du-Mont, Bordeaux. 20ha. Labels: Sublime.

Château la Raye (Fr) a vineyard in the A.C. Bergerac.

Château La Raze Beauvallet (Fr) a vineyard in the A.C. Médoc, Bordeaux. Grape varieties: Cabernet franc 5%, Cabernet sauvingnon 50%, Merlot 45%.

Château Larchevêque (Fr) a vineyard. (Com): Fronsac. A.C. Côtes Canon-Fronsac, Bordeaux 5ha.

Château Larcis-Ducasse (Fr) a vineyard. (Add): Saint Laurent des Bardes, 33330 Saint-Émilion. Grand Cru Classé. A.C. Saint-Émilion. (Com): Saint Laurent des Combes. 12ha. Grape varieties: Cabernet franc 30%, Cabernet sauvignon 5%, Malbec 5% and Merlot 60%.

Château la Renaissance (Fr) a vineyard. (Com): Pomerol. A.C. Pomerol, Bordeaux 1ha.

Château Laribotte (Fr) a vineyard. (Com): Preignac. A.C. Sauternes, Bordeaux 5ha.

Château Lariveau (Fr) a vineyard. (Com): Saint-Michel. A.C. Côtes Canon-Fronsac, Bordeaux.

Château la Rivière (Fr) a vineyard. (Com): Saint-Michel. A.C. Côtes Canon-Fronsac, Bordeaux. (Add): 33145 Saint-Michel-de-Fronsac.

Château Larivière (Fr) a vineyard. (Com): Blaignan. A.C. Médoc, Bordeaux 12ha.

Château Larmande (Fr) a vineyard. (Add): 33330 Saint-Émilion. Grand Cru Classé. A.C. Saint-Émilion. (Com): Saint-Émilion. 20ha. Grape varieties: Cabernet franc 30%, Cabernet sauvignon 5% and Merlot 65%.

Château la Rocaille (Fr) a vineyard in the commune Virelade. A.C. Graves, Bordeaux. 9ha (red and white).

Château la Rocaille (Fr) a vineyard. (Com): Saint-Émilion. A.C. Saint-Émilion. 5.47ha. (Add): Gueyrosse, 33500 Libourne. Grape varieties: Bouchet, Cabernet sauvignon 50% and Merlot 50%.

Château La Roche Gaby (Fr) a vineyard in the A.C. Canon-Fronsac, Bordeaux. Grape varieties: Cabernet franc 5%, Cabernet sauvingnon 10%, Merlot 85%.

Château la Rode (Fr) an A.C. Côtes de Castillon. (Add): Celliers de Canterane A.F/ 33440 Ambares (Gironde).

Château Laroque (Fr) a vineyard. (Add): Saint-Christophe-des-Bardes. A.C. Saint-Émilion Grand Cru Classé. (Com): Saint-Christophe-des-Bardes. 44ha. Grape varieties: Cabernet franc 20%, Cabernet sauvignon 15% and Merlot 65%. Website: http://www.chateau-laroque.com

Château la Roque (Fr) a vineyard. (Com): La Roque. A.C. Premières Côtes de Bordeaux, central Bordeaux.

Château la Roque (Fr) a vineyard based near Fontanès in A.C. Coteaux du Languedoc Pic Saint-Loup. Grape variety is mainly Mourvèdre. Wines produced include: Cupa Numismae, Cuvée des Vieilles Vignes.

Château la Roque de By (Fr) a vineyard. (Com): Bégadan. A.C. Médoc, Bordeaux. Cru Bourgeois.

C

Château **Larose** (Fr) a vineyard. (Com): Baurech. A.C. Entre-Deux-Mers, Bordeaux (red and white).

Château **la Rose-Capbern** (Fr) part of Château Capbern A.C. Haut-Médoc, Bordeaux.

Château **la Rose Côtes Rol** (Fr) a vineyard. (Add): 33330 Saint-Émilion. Grand Cru. A.C. Saint-Émilion. (Com): Saint-Émilion. 8.5ha. Grape varieties: Cabernet 35% and Merlot 65%.

Château **la Rose de France** (Fr) a vineyard. (Com): Saint-Julien. A.C. Saint-Julien, Bordeaux 2ha.

Château **la Rose Garamay** (Fr) see Château Livran A.C. Médoc.

Château **la Rose-Pauillac** (Fr) a Cave Co-opérative vineyard. (Com): Pauillac. A.C. Pauillac, Bordeaux. Cru Bourgeois.

Château **Larose-Perganson** (Fr) a vineyard. (Com): St Laurent du Médoc. A.C. Haut-Médoc, Bordeaux. Cru Bourgeois. Grape varieties: Cabernet sauvingnon 60%, Merlot 40%.

Château **la Rose Pourret** (Fr) a vineyard. (Add): 33330 Saint-Émilion. Grand Cru. A.C. Saint-Émilion. (Com): Saint-Émilion. 8.26ha. Grape varieties: Cabernet 50%, Merlot 50%. Website: http://www.la-rose-pourret.com

Château **Laroseraie-du-Mont** (Fr) a vineyard. (Com): Puisseguin-Saint-Émilion. A.C. Saint-Émilion, Bordeaux 4ha.

Château **la Rose Trimoulet** (Fr) a vineyard. (Add): Puisseguin-Saint-Émilion. 33330 Saint-Émilion. Grand Cru. A.C. Saint-Émilion. (Com): Puisseguin-Saint-Émilion. 5ha. Grape varieties: Cabernet franc 20%, Cabernet sauvignon 10% and Merlot 70%.

Château **Larose-Trintaudon** (Fr) a vineyard. (Com): Saint Laurent du Médoc-Gironde. A.C. Haut-Médoc, Bordeaux. Cru Grand Bourgeois. 157ha. Grape varieties: Cabernet franc 5%, Cabernet sauvignon 65%, Merlot 30%.

Château **Laroze** (Fr) a vineyard. (Add): 33330 Saint-Émilion. Grand Cru Classé. A.C. Saint-Émilion. (Com): Saint-Émilion. 30ha. Grape varieties: Cabernet franc 45%, Cabernet sauvignon 10% and Merlot 45%.

Château **Larrieu-Terrefort** (Fr) a vineyard. (Com): Macau. A.C. Haut-Médoc, Bordeaux. Cru Bourgeois 3ha.

Château **Larrivaux** (Fr) a vineyard. (Add): Cissac, Médoc 33250 Pauillac. A.C. Haut-Médoc. (Com): Cissac. 100ha. Grape varieties: Cabernet sauvignon, Malbec, Merlot and Petit verdot. (Bought by Château Hanteillan in 1979 and added to its name). see Château Hanteillan.

Château **Larrivaux-Hanteillan** (Fr) the name used by Château Hanteillan for its second wines.

Château **Larriveau** (Fr) see Château Larrivaux.

Château **Larrivet-Haut-Brion** (Fr) an A.C. Pessac-Léognan. (Com): Léognan. 16.16ha. Grape varieties: Cabernet sauvignon 60%, Merlot 40%, Sauvignon 60% and Sémillon 40%.

Château **l'Arrosée** (Fr) a vineyard. (Add): 33330 Saint-Émilion. Grand Cru Classé. A.C. Saint-Émilion. (Com): Saint-Émilion 25ha.

Château **Lartigue de Brochon** (Fr) a vineyard. (Com): St-Seurin-de-Cadourne. A.C. Médoc, Bordeaux. Cru Bourgeois. Second wine of Château Sociando Mallet.

Château **Lartique** (Fr) a vineyard. (Com): Saint-Estèphe. A.C. Saint-Estèphe, Bordeaux 2ha.

Château **Larue** (Fr) a vineyard. (Com): Parsac-Saint-Émilion. A.C. Saint-Émilion, Bordeaux 4ha.

Château **la Salette** (Fr) a vineyard. (Com): Cérons. A.C. Cérons, Bordeaux 5ha.

Château **la Salle** (Fr) a vineyard. (Com): Martillac. A.C. Graves, Bordeaux. 3ha (red and white).

Château **la Salle** (USA) a sweet, dessert wine made from the Muscat grape by the Christian Brothers at their Mont la Salle Vineyards in California. Sold in a decanter-shaped bottle.

Château **la Sartre** (Fr) an A.C. Pessac-Léognan. Commune: Léognan. 10ha. Grape varieties: Cabernet franc, Cabernet sauvignon, Malbec and Merlot.

Château **Lascombes** (Fr) a vineyard. (Add): 33460 Margaux. Grand Cru Classé (2nd). A.C. Margaux. (Com): Margaux. 83ha. Grape varieties: Cabernet sauvignon, Malbec, Merlot and Petit verdot. Second wine is Château Ségonnes.

Château **la Sergue** (Fr) a vineyard in the A.C. Pomerol, Bordeaux.

Château **la Serre** (Fr) a vineyard. (Add): 33330 Saint-Émilion. Grand Cru Classé. A.C. Saint-Émilion. (Com): Saint-Émilion. 7ha. Grape varieties: Cabernet 20%, Merlot 80%. Second wine is Clos la Tonnelle.

Château **la Solitude** (Fr) a vineyard. (Com): Martillac. A.C. Graves, Bordeaux.

Château **Lassale** (Fr) a vineyard. (Com): St-Genès. A.C. Côtes de Blaye, Bordeaux.

Château **Lassalle** (Fr) a vineyard. (Com): Potensac. A.C. Médoc, Bordeaux. Cru Bourgeois. Second wine of Château Potensac.

Château **Lassèque** (Fr) a vineyard. (Add): Saint-Hippolyte, 33330 Saint-Émilion. Grand Cru. A.C. Saint-Émilion. (Com): Saint-Hippolyte. 23ha. Grape varieties: Cabernet franc 35%, Cabernet sauvignon 20% and Merlot 45%.

Château **Lasserre** (Fr) a vineyard. (Com): Saint-Émilion. A.C. Saint-Émilion, Bordeaux. 7ha. Grand Cru Classé.

Château **Lassime** (Fr) a vineyard in the A.C. Entre-Deux-Mers at Landerrouet sur Ségur, Bordeaux.

Château **la Taure Ste-Luce** (Fr) a vineyard. (Com): Blaye. A.C. Côtes de Blaye, Bordeaux.

Château **la Terrasse** (Fr) a vineyard on the Île Verte in the river Gironde. A.C. Bordeaux Supérieur.

Château **la Tête-du-Cerf** (Fr) a vineyard. (Com): Montagne-Saint-Émilion. A.C. Saint-Émilion, Bordeaux 6ha.

Château **la Touche** (Fr) a vineyard in the A.C. Muscadet Sèvre et Maine, Nantais, Loire. (Add): Andre Vinet, Vallet, Loire Atlantique.

Château **la Tour** (Fr) a vineyard. (Com): Barsac. A.C. Barsac (or Sauternes), Bordeaux 2ha.

Château **la Tour** (Fr) a vineyard. (Com): Léognan.

C

A.C. Pessac-Léognan, Bordeaux. 4ha (red and white).

Château Latour (Fr) a vineyard. (Com): Montagne-Saint-Émilion. A.C. Saint-Émilion, Bordeaux 5ha.

Château Latour (Fr) a vineyard. (Add): 33250 Bordeaux. Premier Grand Cru Classé. A.C. Pauillac. (Com): Pauillac. 65ha. Grape varieties: Cabernet franc 4%, Cabernet sauvignon 75%, Merlot 20% and Petit verdot 1%. The second wine is Les Forts de Latour. *See also* Enclos. Website: http://www.chateau-latour.com

Château Latour (Fr) a vineyard. (Com): St. Martin-du-Puy Gironde. A.C. Bordeaux Supérieur, Bordeaux.

Château Latour à Pomerol (Fr) a vineyard. (Com): Pomerol. A.C. Pomerol, Bordeaux.

Château la Tour Baladoz (Fr) a vineyard. (Add): Saint Laurent des Combes, 33330 Saint-Émilion. Grand Cru. Saint-Émilion. (Com): Saint Laurent des Combes. 10ha. Grape varieties: Cabernet, Merlot 65% and Petit verdot.

Château la Tour-Ballet (Fr) a vineyard. (Com): Montagne-Saint-Émilion. A.C. Saint-Émilion, Bordeaux 1ha.

Château la-Tour-Bicheau (Fr) a vineyard. (Add): Portets Gironde 33640. A.C. Graves. (Com): Portets. 20ha. Grape varieties: Cabernet, Merlot, Sauvignon and Sémillon. (red and white).

Château la Tour-Blanche (Fr) a vineyard. (Com): Parsac-Saint-Émilion. A.C. Saint-Émilion, Bordeaux 3ha.

Château la Tour Blanche (Fr) a vineyard. (Add): 33340 Saint-Christoly-de-Médoc. Cru Bourgeois. A.C. Médoc. (Com): Saint-Christoly. Grape varieties: Cabernet franc 10%, Cabernet sauvignon 40% and Merlot 50%. 26ha

Château la Tour Blanche (Fr) a Premier Grand Cru Classé vineyard. (Com): Bommes. A.C. Sauternes, Bordeaux 27ha.

Château la Tour-Cantenac (Fr) a vineyard. (Com): Cantenac. A.C. Haut-Médoc, Bordeaux. Cru Bourgeois.

Château la Tour-Carnet (Fr) a Grand Cru classé (4th). A.C. Haut-Médoc. (planted circa 1407). (Com): Saint Laurent. 31ha. Grape varieties: Cabernet franc, Cabernet sauvignon, Merlot and Petit verdot.

Château la Tour Castillon (Fr) a vineyard. (Com): Saint-Christoly-de-Médoc. A.C. Médoc, Bordeaux. Cru Bourgeois.

Château la Tour-de-Bessan (Fr) part of Château la Tour-de-Mons, A.C. Haut-Médoc, Bordeaux.

Château la Tour-de-Boyrin (Fr) a vineyard. (Com): Langon. A.C. Graves, Bordeaux. 13ha (white).

Château la Tour-de-By (Fr) a vineyard. (Add): 33340 Bégadan. Cru Grand Bourgeois. A.C. Médoc. (Com): Bégadan. 61ha. Grape varieties: Cabernet franc, Cabernet sauvignon and Merlot. Second label is Château Roque-de-By.

Château la Tour de Fabrezan (Fr) a vineyard in the A.C. Corbières, south-eastern France. (red). Grape varieties: Carignan, Grenache and Syrah.

Château la Tour-de-Grenet (Fr). A vineyard. (Com): Lussac-Saint-Émilion. A.C. Saint-Émilion, Bordeaux 30ha

Château la Tour de Leyssac (Fr) a vineyard. (Com): Saint-Estèphe. A.C. Saint-Estèphe, Bordeaux 4ha.

Château la Tour de Malescasse (Fr) a vineyard. (Com): Lamarque. A.C. Haut-Médoc, Bordeaux 5ha.

Château la Tour-de-Marbuzet (Fr) a vineyard. (Com): Saint-Estèphe. A.C. Saint-Estèphe, Bordeaux.

Château la Tour de Mons (Fr) a vineyard. (Add): Soussans, 33460 Margaux. A.C. Margaux. (Com): Soussans. 40ha. Grape varieties: Cabernet franc, Cabernet sauvignon, Merlot and Petit verdot.

Château la Tour-de-Pape (Fr) a vineyard. (Com): Mérignac. A.C. Graves, Bordeaux.

Château la Tour de Pez-l'Hétéyre (Fr) a vineyard. (Com): Saint-Estèphe. A.C. Saint-Estèphe, Bordeaux 9ha.

Château la Tour de Pressac (Fr) a vineyard. (Com): Saint-Étienne-de-Lisse. A.C. Saint-Émilion, Bordeaux.

Château la Tour-des-Combes (Fr) a vineyard. (Com): Saint Laurent des Combes. A.C. Saint-Émilion, Bordeaux.

Château la Tour-de-Ségur (Fr) a vineyard. (Com): Lussac-Saint-Émilion. A.C. Saint-Émilion, Bordeaux 12ha.

Château Latour-de-Ségur (Fr) a vineyard. (Com): Lussac-Saint-Émilion. A.C. Saint-Émilion, Bordeaux 8ha.

Château la Tour des Ternes (Fr) a vineyard. (Com): Saint-Estèphe. A.C. Saint-Estèphe, Bordeaux 12ha.

Château la Tour du Haut-Caussan (Fr) a vineyard. (Com): Blaignan. A.C. Médoc, Bordeaux 6ha.

Château la Tour du Haut Moulin (Fr) a vineyard. (Com): Cussac-Fort-Médoc. A.C. Haut-Médoc, Bordeaux. Cru Grand Bourgeois. 24ha

Château la Tour du Mirail (Fr) a vineyard. (Com): Cissac. A.C. Haut-Médoc, Bordeaux. Cru Bourgeois.

Château la Tour-du-Pin-Figeac-Grand-Bélivier (Fr) a vineyard. (Add): 33330 Saint-Émilion. Grand Cru (demoted 2006). A.C. Saint-Émilion. (Com): Saint-Émilion. 10.5ha. Grape varieties: Bouchet 25% and Merlot 75%.

Château la Tour-du-Pin-Figeac-Moueix (Fr) a vineyard. (Add): 33330 Saint-Émilion. Grand Cru (demoted 2006). A.C. Saint-Émilion. (Com): Saint-Émilion. 10.5ha. Grape varieties: Cabernet franc 30% and Merlot 70%.

Château la Tour du Roc (Fr) a vineyard. (Com): Arcins. A.C. Haut-Médoc, Bordeaux 9ha.

Château la Tour du Roch Milon (Fr) a vineyard. (Com): Pauillac. A.C. Pauillac, Bordeaux 18ha.

Château la-Tour-du-Roi (Fr) an A.C. Médoc. Second wine of Château Lagrange Grand Cru Classé (3rd) Saint-Julien.

Château la Tour-Figeac (Fr) a vineyard. (Add): 33330 Saint-Émilion. Grand Cru Classé. A.C. Saint-Émilion. (Com): Saint-Émilion. 13.6ha. Grape varieties: Cabernet franc 40% and Merlot 60%. Website: http://www.latourfigeac.com

C

Château la Tour Gayet (Fr) a vineyard. (Com): St-Androny. A.C. Côtes de Blaye, Bordeaux.

Château la Tour Gilet (Fr) a vineyard. (Com): Montagne-Saint-Émilion. A.C. Saint-Émilion, Bordeaux 6ha.

Château la Tour-Guillotin (Fr) a vineyard. (Com): Puisseguin-Saint-Émilion. A.C. Saint-Émilion, Bordeaux 6ha.

Château la Tour Haut-Brion (Fr) a vineyard. (Add): 33400 Talence. Cru Classé. A.C. Pessac-Léognan. (Com): Talence 6ha.

Château la Tour Haut-Caussan (Fr) a vineyard. (Add): 33340 Blaignan-Médoc. Cru Bourgeois. A.C. Médoc. (Com): Blaignan. 9ha. Grape varieties: Cabernet sauvignon 55% and Merlot 45%.

Château la Tour Haut Vignoble (Fr) a vineyard. (Com): Saint-Estèphe. A.C. Haut-Médoc, Bordeaux 12ha.

Château la Tour l'Aspic (Fr) a vineyard. (Com): Pauillac. A.C. Haut-Médoc, Bordeaux 4ha.

Château la Tour Léognan (Fr) a vineyard. (Com): Léognan. A.C. Pessac-Léognan, Bordeaux. 7ha. (Add): Léognan 33850. Grape varieties: Cabernet franc, Cabernet sauvignon, Malbec, Merlot, Sauvignon and Sémillon. Second label of Château Carbonnieux.

Château la Tour Lichine (Fr) part of Château Capbern, A.C. Haut-Médoc, Bordeaux.

Château la Tour Marbuzet (Fr) a vineyard. (Com): Saint-Estèphe. A.C. Médoc, Bordeaux. Cru Bourgeois.

Château la Tour Marcillanet (Fr) a vineyard. (Com): Saint Laurent. A.C. Médoc, Bordeaux. Cru Bourgeois 6ha.

Château la Tour Martillac (Fr) a vineyard. (Add): Martillac, 33650 La Brède. Grand Cru Classé. A.C. Pessac-Léognan. (Com): Léognan. 23ha. Grape varieties: Cabernet franc, Cabernet sauvignon, Malbec, Merlot, Muscadelle, Petit verdot, Sauvignon and Sémillon. Also Kressmann la Tour.

Château Latour-Musset (Fr) a vineyard. (Com): Parsac-Saint-Émilion. A.C. Saint-Émilion, Bordeaux 10ha.

Château la Tour-Paquillon (Fr) a vineyard. (Com): Montagne-Saint-Émilion. A.C. Saint-Émilion, Bordeaux 8ha.

Château la Tour Pibran (Fr) a vineyard. (Com): Pauillac. A.C. Haut-Médoc, Bordeaux. Cru Bourgeois 7ha.

Château Latour-Pomerol (Fr) a vineyard. (Com): Pomerol. A.C. Pomerol, Bordeaux 9ha.

Château Latour-Pourret (Fr) a vineyard in the A.C. Saint-Émilion, Bordeaux.

Château Latour Prignac (Fr) a vineyard. (Com): Prignac. A.C. Haut-Médoc, Bordeaux 115ha.

Château la Tour Puyblanquet (Fr) a vineyard. (Com): Saint-Étienne-de-Lisse. A.C. Saint-Émilion, Bordeaux 40ha.

Château la Tour Saint-Bonnet (Fr) a vineyard. (Com): Saint-Christoly. A.C. Médoc, Bordeaux. Cru Bourgeois.

Château la Tour Saint Joseph (Fr) a vineyard. (Add): 33250 Pauillac. Cru Bourgeois A.C. Haut-Médoc. (Com): Cissac. 10ha. Grape varieties: Cabernet sauvignon 75% and Merlot 25%.

Château la Tour-Seguy (Fr) a vineyard. (Com): St-Ciers-de-Canesse. A.C. Côtes de Bourg, Bordeaux.

Château la Tour Sieujan (Fr) a vineyard. (Com): St Laurent. A.C. Médoc, Bordeaux. Cru Bourgeois.

Château la Tour-St-Georges (Fr) a part of Château St-Georges, A.C. Saint-Émilion, Bordeaux.

Château la Tour St. Pierre (Fr) a vineyard in the Côtes-Saint-Émilion. A.C. Saint-Émilion, Bordeaux.

Château la Tourte (Fr) a vineyard. (Com): Toulenne. A.C. Graves, Bordeaux. 6ha (white).

Château la Trezette (Fr) a vineyard in the A.C. Sauternes, Bordeaux.

Château Latrezotte (Fr) a vineyard. (Com): Barsac. A.C. Barsac (or Sauternes), Bordeaux 7ha.

Château Latte de Sirey (Fr) a vineyard. (Add): Saint Laurent des Combes, 33330 Saint-Émilion. A.C. Saint-Émilion. (Com): Saint Laurent des Combes. 5ha. Grape varieties: Cabernet franc, Cabernet sauvignon and Merlot 65%.

Château la Tulière (Fr) a vineyard in the A.C. Côtes de Bourg, Bordeaux.

Château la Tuque (Fr) a vineyard. (Com): Eyresse. A.C. Saint-Foy-Bordeaux, south-eastern Bordeaux.

Château l'Aubépin (Fr) a vineyard. (Com): Bommes. A.C. Sauternes, Bordeaux. Cru Bourgeois.

Château Laujac (Fr) a vineyard. (Add): Bégadan, 33340 Lesparre-Médoc. Cru Grand Bourgeois. A.C. Médoc. (Com): Bégadan. 60ha. Grape varieties: Cabernet franc, Cabernet sauvignon, Merlot and Petit verdot. Second label is Château Laffitte Laujac.

Château Launay (Fr) a vineyard. (Com): Teuillac. A.C. Côtes de Bourg, Bordeaux.

Château Launay (Fr) a vineyard at Soussac, Gironde. A.C. Entre-Deux-Mers.

Château Laurensanne (Fr) a vineyard. (Com): St-Seurin-Bourg. A.C. Côtes de Bourg, Bordeaux.

Château Laurenzane (Fr) a vineyard. (Com): Gradignan. A.C. Graves, Bordeaux.

Château Lauretan (Fr) the brand-name for red and white wines produced by the négociant-éleveur Cordier in Bordeaux. Red: Cabernet franc, Cabernet sauvignon, Merlot. White: Sauvignon blanc and Sémillon.

Château Laurette (Fr) a vineyard. (Com): Sainte-Croix-du-Mont. A.C. Sainte-Croix-du-Mont, Bordeaux 15ha.

Château la Vaisinerie (Fr) a vineyard. (Com): Puisseguin-Saint-Émilion. A.C. Saint-Émilion, Bordeaux 8ha.

Château La Valade (Fr) a vineyard. (Com): Fronsac. A.C. Côtes de Fronsac, Bordeaux 15ha.

Château Lavalière (Fr) a vineyard. (Com): Saint-Christoly. A.C. Médoc, Bordeaux.

Château Lavallade (Fr) a vineyard. (Add): Saint-Christophe-des-Bardes, 33330 Saint-Émilion. Grand Cru. A.C. Saint-Émilion. (Com): Saint-

Christophe-des-Bardes. 13ha. Grape varieties: Cabernet 25% and Merlot 75%.

Château la Varière (Fr) a vineyard in the A.C. Anjou-Villages. Grape varieties: Cabernet franc, Cabernet sauvignon. Label: La Grande Chevalerie 100% Cabernet sauvignon..

Château Laval (Fr) a vineyard in the A.C. Costières de Nîmes.

Château Lavaud la Maréchaude (Fr) a vineyard. (Com): Lalande de Pomerol. A.C. Lalande de Pomerol, Bordeaux.

Château la Venelle (Fr) a vineyard. (Com): Fronsac. A.C. Côtes de Fronsac, Bordeaux 4ha.

Château la Verrerie (Fr) a vineyard based at Puget sur Durance, 84360 Lauris. A.C. Côtes du Luberon. Second wine is Bastide la Verrerie.

Château la Vieille Cure (Fr) a vineyard. (Com): Saillans. A.C. Fronsac, Bordeaux. (Add): 331412 Villegouge. 14ha.

Château la Vieille-France (Fr) a vineyard. (Com): Portets. A.C. Graves, Bordeaux. 16ha. Grape varieties: Cabernet and Sémillon (red and white).

Château Lavignac (Fr) a vineyard. (Com): Preignac. A.C. Sauternes, Bordeaux 3ha.

Château Laville (Fr) a vineyard. (Com): Preignac. A.C. Sauternes, Bordeaux 11ha.

Château Laville Haut Brion (Fr) a vineyard. (Add): 67, Rue Peybouquey, 33400 Talence. A.C. Pessac-Léognan. (Com): Talence. 6ha. Grape varieties: 40% Sauvignon, 60% Sémillon.

Château Lavillotte (Fr) a vineyard. (Add): 33250 Vertheuil-Médoc. A.C. Saint-Estèphe. (Com): Vertheuil. 13ha. Grape varieties: Cabernet 75%, Merlot 25%.

Château Lavinot-la-Chapelle (Fr) a vineyard. (Com): Néac. A.C. Saint-Émilion, Bordeaux.

Château la Violette (Fr) a vineyard. (Com): Pomerol. A.C. Pomerol, Bordeaux 2ha.

Château la Voulte-Gasparets (Fr) a vineyard in the A.C. Corbières, south-western France. Labels: Cuvée Romain Pauc and Cuvée Réserve.

Château le Barrail (Fr) a vineyard in the A.C. Médoc, Bordeaux. Grape varieties: Cabernet sauvingnon 55%, Merlot 45%.

Château le Basque (Fr) a vineyard. (Com): Arbanats. A.C. Graves, Bordeaux (red and white).

Château le Basque (Fr) a vineyard. (Com): Lussac-Saint-Émilion. A.C. Saint-Émilion, Bordeaux.

Château le Bécade (Fr) a vineyard. (Com): Listrac. A.C. Médoc, Bordeaux. Cru Bourgeois.

Château le Bedou (Fr) a vineyard in the A.C. Côtes de Blaye, Bordeaux.

Château le Bonnat-Jeansotte (Fr) a vineyard. (Add): Saint Selve, 33650 La Brède. A.C. Graves. (Com): Saint Selve. 27ha. Grape varieties: Cabernet 65%, Merlot 35%, Sauvignon and Sémillon.

Château le Bernat (Fr) a vineyard. (Com): Puisseguin-Saint-Émilion. A.C. Saint-Émilion, Bordeaux. 6ha. Grape varieties: Merlot 70%, Cabernet sauvignon 30%.

Château le Bernet (Fr) a vineyard in the A.C. Médoc, Bordeaux.

Château le Bon Pasteur (Fr) a vineyard. (Com): Pomerol. A.C. Pomerol, Bordeaux. 7ha. Grape varieties: Merlot, Cabernet franc.

Château le Boscq (Fr) a vineyard. (Add): Saint-Christoly, 33340 Médoc. Cru Bourgeois. A.C. Médoc. (Com): Saint-Christoly. 24ha. Grape varieties: Cabernet franc, Cabernet sauvignon and Merlot.

Château le Boscq (Fr) a vineyard. (Com): Saint-Estèphe. A.C. Saint-Estèphe, Bordeaux 13ha.

Château le Bouïs (Fr) a vineyard in the A.C. Corbières, south-western France.

Château le Bourdieu (Fr) a vineyard. (Add): Vertheuil 33250 Pauillac. A.C. Haut-Médoc. (Com): Vertheuil. 51ha. Grape varieties: Cabernet franc 20%, Cabernet sauvignon 50% and Merlot 30%.

Château le Breuilh (Fr) a vineyard. (Com): Cissac. A.C. Haut-Médoc, Bordeaux.

Château le Brouillaud (Fr) a vineyard. (Com): St-Mèdard-d'Eyrans. A.C. Graves, Bordeaux. 5ha (white).

Château le Burck (Fr) a vineyard. (Com): Mérignac. A.C. Graves, Bordeaux.

Château le Caillou (Fr) a vineyard in the A.C. Côtes de Bourg, Bordeaux.

Château le Caillou (Fr) a vineyard. (Com): Pomerol. A.C. Pomerol, Bordeaux 5ha.

Château le Carillon (Fr) a vineyard. (Com): Pomerol. A.C. Pomerol, Bordeaux 4ha.

Château le Castelot (Fr) a vineyard. (Add): Saint-Sulpice-de-Faleyrens, 33330 Saint-Émilion. Grand Cru. A.C. Saint-Émilion. (Com): Saint-Sulpice-de-Faleyrens. 8.7ha. Grape varieties: Cabernet franc 20%, Cabernet sauvignon 20% and Merlot 60%.

Château le Catillon (Ch.Isles) a vineyard (established 1985) based in Grouville, Jersey. Wine is bottled in Gloucestershire (red and white wines). Also produces ciders.

Château le Cauze (Fr) a vineyard. (Com): Saint-Christophe-des-Bardes. A.C. Saint-Émilion, Bordeaux.

Château le Chais (Fr) a vineyard. (Com): Puisseguin-Saint-Émilion. A.C. Saint-Émilion, Bordeaux.

Château le Châtelet (Fr) a vineyard. (Add): 33330 Saint-Émilion. Grand Cru. A.C. Saint-Émilion. (Com): Saint-Émilion 2.5ha.

Château le Chay (Fr) a vineyard. (Com): Puisseguin-Saint-Émilion. A.C. Saint-Émilion, Bordeaux 32.5ha.

Château le Cluzet (Fr) an A.C. Bordeaux vineyard. (Add): l'Union des Producteurs de Rauzan, 33488 Gironde.

Château le Cône Moreau (Fr) a vineyard. (Com): Blaye. A.C. Côtes de Blaye, Bordeaux.

Château le Cône Sebilleau (Fr) a vineyard. (Com): Blaye. A.C. Côtes de Blaye, Bordeaux.

Château le Cône Taillasson (Fr) a vineyard. (Com): Blaye. A.C. Côtes de Blaye, Bordeaux.

Château le Coustet (Fr) a vineyard. (Com): Barsac. A.C. Barsac (or Sauternes), Bordeaux 5ha.

Château le Couvent (Fr) a vineyard in the Côtes-

C

Saint-Émilion. A.C. Saint-Émilion, Bordeaux. Grand Cru 0.6ha.

Château le Crock (Fr) a vineyard. (Add): Marbuzet Saint-Estèphe, 33250 Pauillac. Cru Bourgeois Exceptionnel. A.C. Saint-Estèphe. (Com): Saint-Estèphe. 31ha. Grape varieties: Cabernet sauvignon 65% and Merlot 35%.

Château le Cros Vernet (Fr) an A.C. Bordeaux Supérieur.

Château le Fournas (Fr) a vineyard in the comune of Saint-Sauveur. A.C. Haut-Médoc, Bordeaux. 6ha. Owned by Château Pichon-Longueville Comtesse de Lalande.

Château le Fournas Bernadotte (Fr) a vineyard. (Com): Saint-Sauveur. A.C. Haut-Médoc, Bordeaux 20ha.

Château le Gardera (Fr) the name for a red A.C. Bordeaux Supérieur produced by the négociants-éleveurs Cordier from Cabernet sauvignon and Merlot grapes.

Château le Gay (Fr) a vineyard. (Com): Pomerol. A.C. Pomerol, Bordeaux 8ha.

Château l'Église-Clinet (Fr) a vineyard. (Com): Pomerol. A.C. Pomerol, Bordeaux.

Château l'Église Vieille (Fr) a vineyard. (Com): Lamarque. A.C. Haut-Médoc, Bordeaux 3ha. Grape varieties: Cabernet 50% and Merlot 50%.

Château le Grand-Mazerolle (Fr) a vineyard. (Com): Cars. A.C. Côtes de Blaye, Bordeaux.

Château le Grand Peyrot (Fr) a vineyard. (Com): Sainte-Croix-du-Mont. A.C. Sainte-Croix-du-Mont, Bordeaux 5ha.

Château le Gravier-Gueyrosse (Fr) a vineyard. (Com): Sables-Saint-Émilion. A.C. Saint-Émilion, Bordeaux 7.5ha.

Château le Hère (Fr) a vineyard. (Com): Bommes. A.C. Barsac (or Sauternes), Bordeaux 6ha.

Château Léhoul (Fr) a vineyard. (Add): Route d'Auros, 33210 Langon. A.C. Graves. (Com): Langon. 5ha. Grape varieties: Cabernet sauvignon, Malbec, Merlot, Muscadelle, Sauvignon and Sémillon.

Château le Huzet (Fr) a vineyard. (Com): Illats. A.C. Cérons, Bordeaux 7ha.

Château le Jurat (Fr) a vineyard. (Add): 33330 Saint-Émilion. Grand Cru. A.C. Saint-Émilion. (Com): Saint-Émilion. 7.5ha. Grape varieties: Cabernet sauvignon 35% and Merlot 65%.

Château le Landat (Fr) a vineyard. (Com): Cissac. A.C. Médoc, Bordeaux. Cru Bourgeois.

Château le Mayne (Fr) a vineyard. (Com): Preignac. A.C. Sauternes, Bordeaux 13ha.

Château le Mayne (Fr) a vineyard. (Com): Puisseguin-Saint-Émilion. A.C. Saint-Émilion, Bordeaux 3ha.

Château le Mayne (Fr) a vineyard. (Com): Sauternes. A.C. Sauternes, Bordeaux. 6ha. Also Château Lafon.

Château le Menaudat (Fr) a vineyard. (Com): St-Androny. A.C. Côtes de Blaye, Bordeaux.

Château le Meynieu (Fr) a Cru Grand Bourgeois. (Add): 33250 Verteuil-Médoc. A.C. Haut-Médoc. (Com): Verteuil. 15ha. Grape varieties: Cabernet 70% and Merlot 30%.

Château le Monastère (Fr) a vineyard in the A.C. Côtes de Bourg, Bordeaux.

Château le Moulin-Rompu (Fr) a vineyard in the A.C. Côtes de Bourg, Bordeaux.

Château le Mouret (Fr) a vineyard. (Com): Fargues. A.C. Sauternes, Bordeaux 6ha.

Château Lemoyne-Lafon-Rochet (Fr) a vineyard. (Com): Le Pian. A.C. Haut-Médoc, Bordeaux 6ha.

Château le Mugron (Fr) a vineyard. (Com): Prignac-Marcamps. A.C. Côtes de Bourg, Bordeaux.

Château l'Enclos (Fr) a vineyard. (Com): Pomerol. A.C. Pomerol, Bordeaux. 9.5ha. Grape varieties: Merlot, Cabernet sauvignon, Côt.

Château Lenoir (Fr) a vineyard. (Com): Sables-Saint-Émilion. A.C. Saint-Émilion, Bordeaux 4ha.

Château Leonay (Austr) a winery. (Add): Para Road, Tanunda, South Australia, 5253. 80ha. Grape varieties: Cabernet sauvignon, Chardonnay, Malbec, Pinot noir, Rhine riesling, Sauvignon blanc, Sémillon and Shiraz. Vineyards in the Barossa Valley, Hunter River and Watervale districts.

Château Léoville-Barton (Fr) a vineyard. (Add): Saint Julien-Beychevelle 33250. Grand Cru Classé (2nd). A.C. Saint-Julien. (Com): Saint-Julien. 48ha. Grape varieties: Cabernet gris, Cabernet sauvignon, Merlot and Petit verdot. Second wine: La Réserve de Léoville Barton. Website: http://www.leoville-barton.com

Château Léoville-Las-Cases (Fr) a vineyard. (Add): Saint Julien-Beychevelle 33250. Grand Cru Classé (2nd). A.C. Saint-Julien. (Com): Saint-Julien. 97ha. Grape varieties: Cabernet franc, Cabernet sauvignon, Merlot and Petit verdot. *see* Clos du Marquis.

Château Léoville-Poyferré (Fr) a vineyard. (Add): Saint Julien-Beychevelle 33250. Grand Cru Classé (2nd). A.C. Saint-Julien. (Com): Saint-Julien. 80ha. Grape varieties: Cabernet franc, Cabernet sauvignon and Merlot. Second label is Château Moulin-Riche.

Château le Pape (Fr) a vineyard. (Com): Léognan. A.C. Pessac-Léognan, Bordeaux. 6ha (red and white).

Château le Pavillon (Fr) a vineyard. (Com): Loupiac. A.C. Loupiac, Bordeaux 4ha.

Château le Peillan (Fr) a vineyard. (Com): Saint Laurent des Combes. A.C. Saint-Émilion, Bordeaux.

Château le Pelletan (Fr) a vineyard. (Com): Saint-Quentin-de-Caplang. A.C. Saint-Foy-Bordeaux, south-eastern Bordeaux.

Château le Pey (Fr) a Cru Bourgeois vineyard in the A.C. Médoc, Bordeaux. (Add): Propiétés Compagnet, Bégadan, 33340 Lesparre-Médoc. 'E'mail: compagnetvins@wanadoo.fr

Château le Pin (Fr) a vineyard. (Com): Sainte-Croix-du-Mont. A.C. Sainte-Croix-du-Mont, Bordeaux 3ha.

Château Lépine (Fr) a vineyard. (Com): Sables-Saint-Émilion. A.C. Saint-Émilion, Bordeaux 2ha.

C

Château le Plantier (Fr) a vineyard in Bordeaux. A.C. Bordeaux.

Château le Pont-de-Pierre (Fr) a vineyard. (Com): Lussac-Saint-Émilion. A.C. Saint-Émilion, Bordeaux 3ha.

Château le Prieuré (Fr) a vineyard. (Com): Saint-Genes-de-Blaye. A.C. Côtes de Blaye, Bordeaux.

Château le Prieuré (Fr) a vineyard. (Add): 33330 Saint-Émilion. Grand Cru Classé. A.C. Saint-Émilion. (Com): Saint-Émilion. 6ha. Grape varieties: Cabernet franc 30% and Merlot 70%.

Château le Puy (Fr) a vineyard. (Com): Parsac-Saint-Émilion. A.C. Saint-Émilion, Bordeaux.

Château le Puy-St-Georges (Fr) part of Château St-Georges, A.C. Saint-Émilion, Bordeaux.

Château le Rauly (Fr) a vineyard in the A.C. Bergerac, south-western France (red).

Château le Raux (Fr) a vineyard in the commune Cussac. A.C. Haut-Médoc, Bordeaux 4ha.

Château l'Ermitage (Fr) a Cru Bourgeois vineyard in the A.C. Listrac-Médoc, Médoc, Bordeaux. (Add): 33480 Listrac.

Château l'Ermitage (Fr) a vineyard. (Com): Preignac. A.C. Sauternes, Bordeaux 7ha.

Château le Roc (Fr) a vineyard. (Com): Bourg. A.C. Côtes de Bourg, Bordeaux.

Château le Roc (Fr) a vineyard. (Com): Saint-Estèphe. A.C. Saint-Estèphe, Bordeaux. Cru Bourgeois.

Château le Roc-de-Troquard (Fr) a vineyard. (Com): Saint-Georges-Saint-Émilion. A.C. Saint-Émilion, Bordeaux 3ha.

Château le Rose-et-Monteil (Fr) a vineyard. (Com): Preignac. A.C. Sauternes, Bordeaux 5ha.

Château le Sahue (Fr) a vineyard. (Com): Preignac. A.C. Sauternes, Bordeaux 3ha.

Château les Alberts (Fr) a vineyard. (Com): Mazion. A.C. Côtes de Blaye, Bordeaux.

Château les Arrieux (Fr) a vineyard. (Com): Preignac. A.C. Sauternes, Bordeaux 5ha.

Château les Baraillots (Fr) a vineyard. (Com): Margaux. A.C. Margaux, Bordeaux.

Château les Bardes (Fr) a vineyard. (Com): Montagne-Saint-Émilion. A.C. Saint-Émilion, Bordeaux 3ha.

Château les Bardes (Fr) a vineyard. (Com): Pomerol. A.C. Pomerol, Bordeaux 2ha.

Château les Bavolliers (Fr) a vineyard. (Com): St-Christ-de-Blaye. A.C. Côtes de Blaye, Bordeaux.

Château les Bertins (Fr) a vineyard. (Com): Valeyrac. A.C. Médoc, Bordeaux.

Château les Bouysses (Fr) the name used by Les Côtes d'Olt (Cahors) for a red wine.

Château les Brandines (Fr) a vineyard in the A.C. Bergerac, south-western France (red).

Château l'Escadre (Fr) a vineyard. (Com): Cadre. A.C. Premières Côtes de Blaye, Bordeaux.

Château l'Escaley (Fr) a vineyard. (Com): Sainte-Croix-du-Mont. A.C. Sainte-Croix-du-Mont, Bordeaux 5ha.

Château les Capitans (Fr) a vineyard in the A.C. commune of Juliénas, Cru Beaujolais-Villages, Burgundy.

Château Lescarjeau (Fr) a vineyard. (Com): Saint-Sauveur. A.C. Haut-Médoc, Bordeaux 5ha.

Château les Carmes-Haut-Brion (Fr) a vineyard. (Com): Pessac. A.C. Graves, Bordeaux.

Château les Carrières (Fr) a vineyard. (Com): Montagne-Saint-Émilion. A.C. Saint-Émilion, Bordeaux 2ha.

Château les Charmettes (Fr) a vineyard. (Com): Budos. A.C. Graves, Bordeaux. 2ha (white).

Château les Chaumes (Fr) a vineyard. (Com): Fours. A.C. Côtes de Blaye, Bordeaux. (Add): 33390 Blaye.

Château les Chaumes (Fr) a vineyard. (Com): Néac. A.C. Pomerol, Bordeaux.

Château les Combes (Fr) a vineyard. (Com): Saint-Estèphe. A.C. Saint-Estèphe, Bordeaux.

Château les Côtes-Sebizeaux (Fr) a vineyard. (Com): Blaye. A.C. Côtes de Blaye, Bordeaux.

Château les Côtes-de-Gardat (Fr) a vineyard. (Com): Montagne-Saint-Émilion. A.C. Saint-Émilion, Bordeaux 5ha.

Château Lescours (Fr) a vineyard. (Com): Saint-Sulpice-de-Faleyrens. A.C. Saint-Émilion, Bordeaux.

Château les Cruzelles (Fr) a vineyard. (Com): Lalande de Pomerol. A.C. Saint-Émilion, Bordeaux.

Château Lescure (Fr) a vineyard. (Com): Lerdelais. Produces A.C. Bordeaux Mousseux.

Château les Echevins (Fr) a vineyard. (Com): Lussac-Saint-Émilion, A.C. Lussac-Saint-Émilion, Bordeaux.

Château les Essarts (Fr) a vineyard. (Com): Lussac-Saint-Émilion. A.C. Lussac-Saint-Émilion, Bordeaux.

Château les Eyguires (Fr) a vineyard. (Com): Saint-Christophe-des-Bardes. A.C. Saint-Émilion, Bordeaux.

Château les Eyquems (Fr) a vineyard. (Com): Tauriac. A.C. Côtes de Bourg, Bordeaux.

Château les Faures (Fr) an A.C. Bordeaux (red wine).

Château les Grandes Murailles (Fr) a vineyard. (Add): 33330 Saint-Émilion. Grand Cru Classé. A.C. Saint-Émilion. (Com): Saint-Émilion. 3.5ha. Grape varieties: Cabernet franc 16%, Cabernet sauvignon 16% and Merlot 66%.

Château les Grandes Versaines (Fr) a vineyard. (Com): Néac. A.C. Lalande de Pomerol, Bordeaux.

Château les Grandes-Vignes (Fr) a vineyard. (Com): Montagne-Saint-Émilion. A.C. Saint-Émilion, Bordeaux 2ha.

Château les Grandes-Vignes (Fr) a vineyard. (Com): Pomerol. A.C. Pomerol, Bordeaux 1ha.

Château les Grands Chênes (Fr) a Cru Bourgeois Supérieur A.C. Haut-Médoc (planted circa 1880).

Château les Grands-Sillons (Fr) a vineyard. (Com): Pomerol. A.C. Pomerol, Bordeaux 2ha.

Château les Grangeaux (Fr) an A.C. Bordeaux Supérieur. Grape varieties: Cabernet franc, Cabernet sauvingnon, Merlot.

Château les Granges d'Or (Fr) a vineyard. (Com): Blaignan. A.C. Médoc. Cru Bourgeois. (Add): Blaignan, 33340 Lesparre.

Château les Graves de Germignan (Fr) a vineyard. (Com): Le Taillan. A.C. Haut-Médoc, Bordeaux 3ha.

Château les Gravières (Fr) a vineyard based in Saint Sulpice de Faleyrens. Grand Cru Saint-Émilion. A.C. Saint-Émilion.

Château les Gravilles (Fr) a vineyard. (Add): 33250 Pauillac, Médoc. A.C. Haut-Médoc. (Com): Saint Sauveur du Médoc. 4ha. Grape varieties: Cabernet sauvignon 68% and Merlot 32%.

Château les Hautes-Rouzes (Fr) a vineyard. (Com): Pomerol. A.C. Pomerol, Bordeaux 2ha.

Château les Hauts de Granges (Fr) a vineyard. (Com): Salles-de-Castillon, Côtes de Castillon, eastern Bordeaux. A.C. Bordeaux Supérieur (red).

Château les Hauts de Pontet (Fr) the second label of Château Pontet Canet, A.C. Pauillac.

Château les Hauts Marcieux (Fr) the second label of Château Lafon.

Château les Jacquets (Fr) a vineyard. (Com): Saint-Georges-Saint-Émilion. A.C. Saint-Émilion, Bordeaux 5ha.

Château les Jouans (Fr) a vineyard. (Com): Saint-Sulpice-de-Faleyrens. A.C. Saint-Émilion, Bordeaux.

Château les Justices (Fr) a vineyard. (Com): Preignac. A.C. Sauternes, Bordeaux 3ha.

Château les Laurets (Fr) a vineyard. (Com): Puisseguin-Saint-Émilion. A.C. Saint-Émilion, Bordeaux 75ha.

Château les Maules (Fr) a vineyard in the A.C. Bergerac, south-western France (red).

Château les Miaudoux (Fr) a vineyard in the A.C. Bergerac.

Château les Moines (Fr) a vineyard. (Com): Blaye. A.C. Côtes de Blaye, Bordeaux.

Château les Moulins (Fr) a vineyard in the A.C. Puisseguin-Saint-Émilion, Bordeaux.

Château les Ollieux Romanis (Fr) a vineyard in the A.O.C. Corbières, south-west France.

Château les Ormes de Pez (Fr) a vineyard. (Add): Saint-Estèphe, 33250 Pauillac. Cru Grand Bourgeois. A.C. Saint-Estèphe. (Com): Saint-Estèphe. 30ha. Grape varieties: Cabernet franc, Cabernet sauvignon, Merlot and Petit verdot.

Château les Ormes Sorbet (Fr) a vineyard. (Add): 33340 Lesparre. Cru Grand Bourgeois. A.C. Médoc. (Com): Couquéques. 20ha. Grape varieties: Cabernet franc, Cabernet sauvignon, Merlot and Petit verdot.

Château le Souley-Ste Croix (Fr) a vineyard. (Add): 33250 Vertheuil. Cru Bourgeois A.C. Haut-Médoc. (Com): Vertheuil. 20ha. Grape varieties: Cabernet sauvignon 60% and Merlot 40%.

Château les Palais (Fr) a vineyard in the A.C. Corbières, south-western France. (red).

Château Lespault (Fr) a vineyard. (Com): Martillac. A.C. Graves, Bordeaux. 4.5ha. (red and white). Second label of Château La Tour Martillac.

Château les Petits Arnauds (Fr) a vineyard. (Com): Cars. A.C. Côtes de Blaye, Bordeaux.

Château l'Espigne (Fr) a vineyard based in Villeneuve Les Corbières, Languedoc, southern France. A.C. Fitou.

Château les Plantes (Fr) a vineyard. (Com): Barsac. A.C. Barsac (or Sauternes), Bordeaux 5ha.

Château les Quatre Filles (Fr) a vineyard in the A.C. Côtes-du-Rhône-Villages Cairanne, Sainte-Cécile-les-Vignes, Vacleuse. Website: http://www.chateau-4filles.com 'E'mail: contact@chateau-4filles.com

Château les Remparts (Fr) a vineyard. (Com): Preignac. A.C. Sauternes, Bordeaux. 14ha. Also Domaine des Justices and the Châteaux: Gilette, Lamothe and les Rochers.

Château les Renardières (Fr) a vineyard. (Com): Saint-Georges-Saint-Émilion. A.C. Saint-Émilion, Bordeaux 4ha.

Château les Richards (Fr) a vineyard. (Com): Cars. A.C. Côtes de Blaye, Bordeaux.

Château les Rochers (Fr) a vineyard. (Com): Preignac. A.C. Sauternes, Bordeaux 7ha.

Château les Rochers (Fr) a vineyard. (Com): Preignac. A.C. Sauternes, Bordeaux. 14ha. Also Domaine des Justices and the Châteaux: Gilette, Lamothe and les Remparts.

Château les Roches Rouges (Fr) a vineyard in the A.C. Saint-Émilion, Bordeaux.

Château Lestage (Fr) a vineyard. (Add): 33480 Listrac-Médoc. Cru Bourgeois. A.C. Listrac-Médoc. (Com): Listrac. 56ha. Grape varieties: Cabernet sauvignon, Merlot and Petit verdot. Second label is Château Caroline.

Château Lestage (Fr) a vineyard. (Com): Parsac-Saint-Émilion. A.C. Saint-Émilion, Bordeaux 8ha.

Château Lestage (Fr) a vineyard. (Com): Saint-Seurin-de-Cadourne. A.C. Haut-Médoc, Bordeaux 1ha.

Château Lestage Darquier [Grand Poujeaux] (Fr) a vineyard. (Com): Moulis, A.C. Moulis, Bordeaux. Cru Bourgeois. (Add): Moulis, 33480 Castelnau-de-Médoc. 4ha

Château Lestage-Simon (Fr) a vineyard. (Com): St-Seurin-de-Cadourne. A.C. Haut-Médoc, Bordeaux. Cru Bourgeois. (Add): St-Seurin-de-Cadourne, 33250 Pauillac. Second label is Château Troupian. Grape varieties: Cabernet franc 17%, Cabernet sauvignon 23%, Merlot 60%.

Château l'Estagnol (Fr) a vineyard in the A.C. Côtes du Rhône, south-eastern France.

Château les Templiers (Fr) a vineyard. (Com): Lalande de Pomerol. A.C. Lalande de Pomerol, Bordeaux.

Château les Trois Moulins (Fr) a vineyard in the Côtes-Saint-Émilion. A.C. Saint-Émilion, Bordeaux. Grand Cru.

Château Lestruelle (Fr) a vineyard. (Com): Saint-Yzans. A.C. Médoc, Bordeaux. 21ha. Grape varieties: Cabernet 30% and Merlot 70%. Second label is Château Plantey.

Château les Tuileries-de-Bayard (Fr) a vineyard. (Com): Montagne-Saint-Émilion. A.C. Saint-Émilion, Bordeaux 8ha.

Château les Videaux (Fr) a vineyard in the A.C. Côtes de Blaye, Bordeaux.

C

Château les Vieux-Rocs (Fr) a vineyard. (Com): Lussac-Saint-Émilion. A.C. Saint-Émilion, Bordeaux 3ha.

Château les Vignes (Fr) a vineyard. (Com): Fronsac. A.C. Côtes Canon-Fronsac, Bordeaux 2ha.

Château le Tarey (Fr) a vineyard. (Com): Loupiac. A.C. Loupiac, Bordeaux 5ha.

Château le-Tetre-de-Perruchon (Fr) a vineyard. (Com): Lussac-Saint-Émilion. A.C. Saint-Émilion, Bordeaux 3ha.

Château le Tertre Rotebœuf (Fr) a vineyard. (Add): Saint Laurent des Combes, 33330 Saint-Émilion. Grand Cru. A.C. Saint-Émilion. (Com): Saint Laurent des Combes. 5.5ha. Grape varieties: Cabernet franc 20% and Merlot 80%.

Château le Teyssier (Fr) a vineyard. (Com): Puisseguin-Saint-Émilion. A.C. Saint-Émilion, Bordeaux.

Château le Thil [Comte Clary] (Fr) a vineyard. (Com): Léognan. A.C. Pessac-Léognan, Bordeaux. 20ha. (red and white). Grape varieties: Cabernet sauvignon, Merlot, Muscadelle, Sauvignon blanc.

Château le Thou (Fr) a vineyard in the A.C. Côteaux-du-Languedoc, Languedoc-Roussillon. Grape variety: Syrah.

Château l'Étoile-Pourret (Fr) an A.C. Saint-Émilion. Part of Château la Grâce-Dieu.

Château le Tréhon (Fr) a vineyard. (Com): Bégadan. A.C. Médoc, Bordeaux. (Add): Bégadan, 33340 Lesparre. 13ha.

Château le Truch de Reignac (Fr) a vineyard. (Add): Le Truch, 33450 Saint-Loubès, Entre-Deux-Mers. A.C. Entre-Deux-Mers. Grape varieties: Merlot, Cabernet sauvignon. Wines are aged in oak.

Château le Tuquet (Fr) a vineyard. (Com): Beautiran. A.C. Graves, Bordeaux 42ha.

Château l'Évangile (Fr) a vineyard. (Com): Pomerol. A.C. Pomerol, Bordeaux. 13.67ha. Grape varieties: Cabernet franc and Merlot. Second wine Blason de l'Evangile. Owned by Rothshild.

Château le Virou (Fr) a vineyard. (Com): St-Girons. A.C. Premières Côtes de Blaye, Bordeaux.

Château Leyssac (Fr) see Château Houissant.

Château Lezin (Fr) an A.C. Bordeaux Supérieur.

Château Lezongars (Fr) a vineyard in the A.C. Premières Côtes de Bordeaux. Website: http://www.chateau-lezongars.com 'E'mail: info@chateau-lezongars.com

Château l'Hermitage (Fr) a vineyard. (Com): Couquéques. A.C. Médoc, Bordeaux 6ha.

Château l'Hermitage (Fr) a vineyard. (Com): Martillac. A.C. Graves, Bordeaux.

Château l'Hermitage (Fr) a vineyard. (Com): Montagne-Saint-Émilion. A.C. Saint-Émilion, Bordeaux 6ha.

Château l'Hermitage-Mazerat (Fr) a vineyard in the A.C. Saint-Émilion, Bordeaux 4ha.

Château l'Hôpital (Fr) a vineyard. (Com): Saint-Estèphe. A.C. Saint-Estèphe, Bordeaux 5ha.

Château Libertas (S.Afr) the label for a red wine (Cabernet and Pinotage blend) produced by the Stellenbosch Farmers' winery, Stellenbosch, Western Cape.

Château Lidonne (Fr) a vineyard. (Com): Bourg. A.C. Côtes de Bourg, Bordeaux. (Add): 33710 Bourg-sur-Gironde.

Château Lieujan (Fr) a vineyard. (Com): St-Sauveur. A.C. Haut-Médoc, Bordeaux. Cru Bourgeois. (Add): St-Sauveur, 33250 Pauillac.

Château Ligondras (Fr) a vineyard. (Com): Arsac. A.C. Margaux, Bordeaux. (Add): Arsac, 33460 Margaux.

Château Lilian Ladouys (Fr) a Cru Bourgeois. A.C. St.Estèphe. Grape varieties: 58% Cabernet sauvignon, 37% Merlot, 5% Cabernet franc. Second label is La Devise de Lilian. Part of Château Ladouys 48ha.

Château Limbourg (Fr) a vineyard. (Com): Villenave-d'Ornon. A.C. Graves, Bordeaux (red and white) 10ha.

Château Lionel Faivre (Fr) a vineyard in the A.C. Corbières, south-western France.

Château Lionnat (Fr) a vineyard. (Com): Lussac-Saint-Émilion. A.C. Saint-Émilion, Bordeaux.

Château Lion Noble d'Or (Jap) a sweet white wine made by Suntory.

Château Liot (Fr) an A.C. Barsac (or Sauternes). (Com): Barsac. Grape varieties: 10% Sauvignon, 85% Sémillon and 5% Muscadelle. 11ha.

Château Liot-Moros (Fr) a vineyard in commune of Pujols. A.C. Graves, Bordeaux. 5ha (white).

Château Liouner (Fr) a vineyard. (Com): Listrac. A.C. Listrac, Bordeaux. Cru Bourgeois. (Add): Listrac, 33480 Castelnau-de-Médoc.

Château Listrac (Fr) a vineyard. (Com): Listrac. A.C. Haut-Médoc, Bordeaux. Cru Bourgeois.

Château Liversan (Fr) a vineyard. (Add): 33250 Pauillac. Cru Grand Bourgeois. A.C. Haut-Médoc. (Com): Saint-Sauveur-du-Médoc. 50ha. Grape varieties: Cabernet franc 50%, Cabernet sauvignon 50%, Merlot and Petit verdot.

Château Livran (Fr) a vineyard. (Com): Lesparre. A.C. Médoc, Bordeaux. Cru Bourgeois. (Add): Saint-Germain-d'Esteuil, 33340 Lesparre. 40ha.

Château Lognac (Fr) a vineyard. (Com): Castres. A.C. Graves, Bordeaux. 5ha (red).

Château Lognac (Fr) a vineyard. (Com): Portets. A.C. Graves, Bordeaux.

Château L'Oiselinière de la Ramée (Fr) a vineyard in the A.C. Muscadet Sèvre et Maine, Nantais, Loire.

Château Loquey (Fr) a vineyard. (Com): Saint-Seurin-de-Cadourne. A.C. Haut-Médoc, Bordeaux 12ha.

Château Lorane (USA) a 14ha vineyard (established 1984). Grape varieties include Chardonnay, Durif, Gewürztraminer, Sauvignon blanc, Pinot noir.

Château l'Oratoire (Fr) a vineyard. (Com): Saint-Émilion. A.C. Saint-Émilion, Bordeaux. 6ha. Grand Cru.

Château Lorillard (USA) a fictitious Château used as part of a 'Kent' cigarettes advertising campaign in 1986. The Château being from the Médoc!

Château l'Ormeau-Vieux (Fr) a vineyard. (Com): Puisseguin-Saint-Émilion. A.C. Saint-Émilion, Bordeaux 7ha.

Château los Boldos (Chile) a winery based in the Cachapoal Valley, Central Chile, owned by the Massenez family of Alsace.

Château Loubens (Fr) a vineyard. (Com): Sainte-Croix-du-Mont. A.C. Sainte-Croix-du-Mont, Bordeaux. 15ha. Grape varieties: Sauvignon blanc, Sémillon and Muscadelle. *see* Château des Tours.

Château Loudenne (Fr) a vineyard. (Add): 33340 Saint-Yzans de Médoc. Cru Grand Bourgeois. A.C. Médoc. (Com): Saint-Yzans. 55ha. Grape varieties: Cabernet franc, Cabernet sauvignon, Merlot, Sauvignon 50%, Sémillon 50%. Owned by Domaines Lafragette. Website: http://www.lafragette.com

Château Loumède (Fr) a vineyard in the A.C. Côtes de Blaye, Bordeaux.

Château Loupiac-Gaudiet (Fr) a vineyard. (Com): Loupiac. A.C. Loupiac, Bordeaux. 10ha. Grape varieties: Sauvignon and Sémillon.

Château Lousteau Vieil (Fr) a vineyard. (Com): Sainte-Croix-du-Mont. A.C. Sainte-Croix-du-Mont, Bordeaux 7ha.

Château Loyac (Fr) the second wine of Château Malescot-Saint Exupéry.

Château Lucas (Fr) a vineyard. (Com): Lussac-Saint-Émilion. A.C. Saint-Émilion, Bordeaux. 9ha. Grape varieties: Cabernet franc 50%, Merlot 50%.

Château Ludeman-Lacôte (Fr) a vineyard. (Com): Langon. A.C. Graves, Bordeaux. 7ha (white).

Château Ludon-Pomiés-Agassac (Fr) a vineyard. (Com): Ludon. A.C. Médoc, Bordeaux. Cru Bourgeois. Second label of Château La Lagune.

Château Lugagnac (Fr) a vineyard. (Com): Vertheuil. A.C. Médoc, Bordeaux.

Château Lussac (Fr) a vineyard. (Com): Lussac-Saint-Émilion. A.C. Saint-Émilion, Bordeaux.

Château Lusseau (Fr) a vineyard. (Com): Ayguemortes. A.C. Graves, Bordeaux. 4ha (red).

Château Lynch-Bages (Fr) a vineyard. (Add): 33250 Pauillac. Grand Cru Classé (5th). A.C. Pauillac. (Com): Pauillac. 75ha. Grape varieties: Cabernet franc, Cabernet sauvignon and Merlot. Second wine is Château Haut-Bages Averous.

Château Lynch-Moussas (Fr) a vineyard. (Add): 33250 Pauillac. Grand Cru Classé (5th). A.C. Pauillac. (Com): Pauillac. 35ha. Grape varieties: Cabernet sauvignon 70% and Merlot 30%.

Château Lyonnat (Fr) a vineyard. (Com): Lussac-Saint-Émilion. A.C. Lussac-Saint-Émilion, Bordeaux 49ha.

Château Lyon-Perruchon (Fr) a vineyard. (Com): Lussac-Saint-Émilion. A.C. Saint-Émilion, Bordeaux 4ha.

Château Macau (Fr) a vineyard. (Com): Tauriac. A.C. Côtes de Bourg, Bordeaux.

Château Macay (Fr) a vineyard. (Com): Samonac. A.C. Côtes de Bourg, Bordeaux.

Château Mac-Carthy Moula (Fr) a vineyard. (Com): Saint-Estèphe. A.C. Haut-Médoc, Bordeaux. Cru Grand Bourgeois 6ha.

Château Macquin St-Georges (Fr) a vineyard. (Com): Saint-Georges-Saint-Émilion. A.C. Saint-Georges-Saint-Émilion, Bordeaux.

Château Macureau (Fr) a vineyard. (Com): Montagne-Saint-Émilion. A.C. Saint-Émilion, Bordeaux 6ha.

Château Madélis (Fr) a vineyard. (Com): Portets. A.C. Graves, Bordeaux. 4ha (red and white).

Château Madère (Fr) a vineyard. (Com): Podensac. A.C. Cérons, Bordeaux 12ha.

Château Madran (Fr) a vineyard. (Com): Pessac. A.C. Pessac-Léognan, Bordeaux. 3ha (red).

Château Magdelaine (Fr) a vineyard. (Add): 33330 Saint-Émilion. Premier [B] Grand Cru Classé. A.C. Saint-Émilion. (Com): Saint-Émilion. 11.5ha. Grape varieties: Cabernet franc, Merlot.

Château Magence (Fr) a vineyard. (Com): Saint-Pierre-de-Mons. (Add): 33210 Langon. A.C. Graves, Bordeaux. 30ha (white).

Château Magence-Maragnac (Fr) an A.C. Graves Supérieures. A vin liquoreux produced at Château Magence.

Château Magnan-Figeac (Fr) a vineyard. (Add): Cormeil-Figeac, 33330 Saint-Émilion. Grand Cru. A.C. Saint-Émilion. (Com): Saint-Émilion. Second wine of Château Cormeil-Figeac. Grand Cru Saint-Émilion.

Château Magnan la Gaffelière (Fr) a vineyard. (Add): 33330 Saint-Émilion. Grand Cru. A.C. Saint-Émilion. (Com): Saint-Émilion. 8ha. Grape varieties: Cabernet franc 40%, Cabernet sauvignon 10% and Merlot 50%.

Château Magneau (Fr) a 30ha. vineyard at La Brède. A.C. Graves. Mainly white wines.

Château Magnol (Fr) a vineyard. (Com): Blanquefort. A.C. Haut-Médoc, Bordeaux. Cru Bourgeois. (Add): 33290 Blanquefort.

Château Magondeau (Fr) a vineyard. (Com): Saillans. A.C. Côtes de Fronsac, Bordeaux 9ha.

Château Maillard (Fr) a vineyard. (Com): Mazères. A.C. Graves, Bordeaux. 5ha (white).

Château Maine-Blanc (Fr) a vineyard. (Com): Lussac-Saint-Émilion. A.C. Saint-Émilion, Bordeaux.

Château Maine-Marzelle (Fr) a vineyard. (Com): Saint-Savin-de-Blaye. A.C. Côtes de Blaye, Bordeaux. (Add): 33920 Saint-Savin-de-Blaye.

Château Maison Blanche (Fr) a vineyard. (Com): Montagne-Saint-Émilion. A.C. Saint-Émilion, Bordeaux. 40ha. Special cuvée is Louis Rapin (less than 10,000 bottles produced).

Château Maisonneuve (Fr) a vineyard. (Com): Parsac-Saint-Émilion. A.C. Saint-Émilion, Bordeaux 7ha.

Château Maja (USA) the brand-name used by the Conn Creek vineyard in the Napa Valley, California for one of their Chardonnay wines.

Château Malanguin (Fr) a vineyard. (Com): Parsac-Saint-Émilion. A.C. Saint-Émilion, Bordeaux.

Château Malartic-Lagravière (Fr) a vineyard. (Add): 39 Ave. de Mont-de-Marsan, Léognan. Grand Cru Classé. A.C. Pessac-Léognan. (Com): Léognan.

22ha. Grape varieties: Cabernet franc, Cabernet sauvignon, Merlot and Sauvignon. Website: http://www.malartic-lagraviere.com

Château Malécot (Fr) a vineyard. (Com): Pauillac. A.C. Pauillac, Bordeaux 7ha.

Château Malescasse (Fr) a vineyard. (Add): 33460 Lamarque. Cru Bourgeois. A.C. Haut-Médoc. (Com): Lamarque. 40ha. Grape varieties: Cabernet franc, Cabernet sauvignon and Merlot.

Château Malescot Saint-Exupéry (Fr) a vineyard. (Add): 33460 Margaux. Grand Cru Classé (3rd). A.C. Margaux. (Com): Margaux. 45ha. Grape varieties: Cabernet franc, Cabernet sauvignon, Merlot and Petit verdot.

Château Malineau (Fr) a vineyard. (Add): 33330 Saint-Émilion. Grand Cru. A.C. Saint-Émilion. (Com): Saint-Émilion. 4.89ha. Grape varieties: Bouchet, Cabernet sauvignon and Merlot 66%.

Château Malleprat (Fr) a vineyard. (Com): Martillac. A.C. Graves, Bordeaux. 3ha (white).

Château Malleret (Fr) a vineyard. (Com): Le Pian. A.C. Haut-Médoc, Bordeaux. Cru Grand Bourgeois. 22ha. Second label is Château Lemoine-Nexon.

Château Malmaison (Fr) a vineyard. (Com): Moulis. A.C. Moulis, Bordeaux 4ha.

Château Mandelot (Fr) an A.C. Hautes Côtes de Beaune based in the village of Mavilly-Mandelot, Burgundy. Grape variety: Pinot noir.

Château Mangot (Fr) a vineyard. (Add): St. Étienne-de-Lisse, 33330 Saint-Émilion. Grand Cru. A.C. Saint-Émilion. (Com): Saint-Émilion. 'E'mail: chmangot@terre.net.fr

Château Mansenoble (Fr) a vineyard in the A.C. Corbières, south-western France. Label: Réserve.

Château Manville (Eng) a 6% alc. by vol. medium sweet perry.

Château Marais (Fr) an A.O.C. Minervois.

Château Marbuzet (Fr) a vineyard. (Com): Saint-Estèphe. A.C. Saint-Estèphe, Bordeaux. Cru Bourgeois Exceptionnel. 12ha. Second label of Château Cos-d'Estournel.

Château Marchand (Fr) a vineyard. (Com): Montagne-Saint-Émilion. A.C. Saint-Émilion, Bordeaux.

Château Marcillan-Belle-Vue (Fr) a vineyard. (Com): Saint Laurent. A.C. Médoc, Bordeaux. Cru Bourgeois.

Château Margaux (Fr) a vineyard. (Add): 33460 Margaux. Premier Grand Cru Classé. A.C. Margaux. (Com): Margaux. 99ha. Grape varieties: Cabernet franc, Cabernet sauvignon, Merlot, Petit verdot and Sauvignon. *see* Pavillion Rouge du Château Margaux.

Château Margillière (Fr) a wine estate in the A.C. Coteaux Varois. Grape varieties: 80% Rolle, 20% Ugni blanc (white wines), 80% Cinsaut, 20% Grenache (rosé wines), 50% Grenache, 20% Tibouren, 20% Cabernet sauvignon, 10% Mourvèdre (red wines).

Château Margot (Fr) a vineyard. (Com): Pomerol. A.C. Pomerol, Bordeaux 1ha.

Château Maris la Livinière (Fr) a vineyard in the A.C. Minervois la Livinière. Label Comte Cathare. Red wines. Grape varieties: Carignan Grenache, Mourvèdre and Syrah.

Château Marjosse (Fr) a 6ha Vineyard in the Entre-Deux-Mers. Sells 6ha of white wine plus 36ha of Bordeaux red under the Château Marjosse label.

Château Marque (Fr) a vineyard. (Com): Saint-Seurin-de-Cadourne. A.C. Haut-Médoc, Bordeaux 1ha.

Château Marquey (Fr) a vineyard. (Add): 33330 Saint-Émilion. Grand Cru. A.C. Saint-Émilion. (Com): Saint-Émilion.

Château Marquisat de Binet (Fr) A.C. Montagne-Saint-Émilion.

Château Marquis-d'Alesme-Becker (Fr) a vineyard. (Add): 33460 Margaux. Grand Cru Classé (3rd). A.C. Margaux. (Com): Margaux. 15ha. Grape varieties: Cabernet franc, Cabernet sauvignon, Merlot and Petit verdot.

Château Marquis-de-Terme (Fr) a vineyard. (Add): 33460 Margaux. Grand Cru Classé (4th). A.C. Margaux. (Com): Margaux. 40ha. Second label is Domaine de Goudat.

Château Marsac-Séguineau (Fr) a vineyard. (Com): Soussans. A.C. Médoc, Bordeaux. Cru Bourgeois. 7ha. Second label is Gravières de Marsac.

Château Marsau (Fr) an A.C. Bordeaux Côtes de Francs. Grape variety: Merlot 100%.

Château Martinens (Fr) a Cru Grand Bourgeois. A.C. Margaux. (Com): Cantenac. 30ha. Grape varieties: Cabernet franc, Cabernet sauvignon, Merlot and Petit verdot.

Château Martinet (Fr) a vineyard. (Com): Sables-Saint-Émilion. A.C. Saint-Émilion, Bordeaux 12ha.

Château Martinon (Fr) a vineyard in the A.C. Entre-Deux-Mers, central Bordeaux (white).

Château Masburel (Fr) a vineyard (established 1740) 23ha. (Add): Fougueyrolles 33220 Ste. Foy la Grande. Produces A.C. Bergerac and A.C. Montravel. Grape varieties: Cabernet franc, cabernet sauvignon, Malbec, Merlot, Muscadelle, Sauvignon blanc, Sémillon. Website: http://www.chateau-masburel.com 'E'mail: olivia@chateau-masburel.com

Château Mascard (Fr) a vineyard. (Com): Saint Laurent. A.C. Médoc, Bordeaux. Cru Bourgeois.

Château Massereau (Fr) a vineyard. (Com): Barsac. A.C. Barsac (or Sauternes), Bordeaux 7ha.

Château Mathalin (Fr) a vineyard. (Com): Barsac. A.C. Barsac (or Sauternes), Bordeaux 11ha.

Château Matras (Fr) a vineyard. (Add): 33330 Saint-Émilion. Grand Cru Classé. A.C. Saint-Émilion. (Com): Saint-Émilion. 8.5ha.

Château Matsa (Gre) a soft, dry white wine produced by Boutari.

Château Maucaillou (Fr) a vineyard. (Add): 33480 Castelnau de Médoc. Cru Bourgeois A.C. Moulis. (Com): Moulis. 55ha. Grape varieties: Cabernet franc, Cabernet sauvignon, Merlot and Petit verdot.

Château Maucamps (Fr) a vineyard. (Com): Macau. A.C. Médoc, Bordeaux. Cru Bourgeois 3ha.

Château Maucoil (Fr) an A.C. red Châteauneuf-du-Pape, produced by Domaine Quiot (Pierre), southern Rhône. 6ha. Uses all 13 permitted grape varieties in its wines. (Add): BP07 F-84231 Châteauneuf-du-Pape. Website: http://www.chateau-maucoil.com 'E'mail: contact@chateau-maucoil.com

Château Mauconseil (Fr) a vineyard. (Com): Plassac. A.C. Côtes de Blaye, Bordeaux.

Château Mauras (Fr) a vineyard. (Com): Bommes. A.C. Sauternes, Bordeaux 13ha.

Château Maurens (Fr) a vineyard. (Com): Saint-Étienne-de-Lisse. A.C. Saint-Émilion, Bordeaux.

Château Mausse (Fr) a vineyard in the A.C. Canon-Fronsac, Bordeaux.

Château Mauvesin (Fr) a vineyard. (Com): Moulis. A.C. Moulis, Bordeaux 60ha.

Château Mauvezin (Fr) a vineyard. (Add): 33330 Saint-Émilion. Grand Cru. A.C. Saint-Émilion. (Com): Saint-Émilion. 16.7ha. Grape varieties: Cabernet franc 50%, Cabernet sauvignon 10% and Merlot 40%.

Château Mayence (Fr) a vineyard. (Com): Mazion. A.C. Côtes de Blaye, Bordeaux.

Château Mayne (Fr) a vineyard. (Com): Pomerol. A.C. Pomerol, Bordeaux 3ha.

Château Mayne-Bert (Fr) a vineyard. (Com): Barsac. A.C. Barsac (or Sauternes), Bordeaux. 12ha. Also Châteaux Camperos and Montalivet.

Château Mayne d'Anice (Fr) a vineyard. (Com): Podensac. A.C. Cérons, Bordeaux 4ha.

Château Mayne de Bernard (Fr) a vineyard in the A.C. Côtes de Bourg, Bordeaux.

Château Mayne des Carmes (Fr) the second wine of Château Rieussec, A.C. Sauternes, Bordeaux.

Château Mayne Lalande (Fr) a vineyard. (Add): Le Mayne-de-Lalande, Listrac-Médoc. A.C. Listrac-Médoc. Cru Bourgeois.

Château Mayne-Levêque (Fr) a vineyard. (Com): Podensac. A.C. Graves, Bordeaux. 15ha (red and white).

Château Mayne Vieille (Fr) a vineyard. (Com): Galgon. A.C. Côtes de Fronsac, Bordeaux 16ha.

Château Mazarin (Fr) a vineyard. (Com): Loupiac. A.C. Loupiac, Bordeaux. 16ha. Grape varieties: Sauvignon and Sémillon.

Château Mazerat (Fr) a vineyard in the A.C. Saint-Émilion, Bordeaux.

Château Mazeris (Fr) a vineyard. (Com): Saint-Michel. A.C. Côtes Canon-Fronsac, Bordeaux. (Add): 33145 Saint-Michel-de-Fronsac. 7ha

Château Mazeris Bellevue (Fr) a vineyard. (Com): Saint-Michel. A.C. Côtes Canon-Fronsac, Bordeaux 6ha.

Château Mazerolles (Fr) a vineyard. (Com): Cars. A.C. Côtes de Blaye, Bordeaux.

Château Mazeyres (Fr) a vineyard. (Com): Pomerol. A.C. Pomerol, Bordeaux. 17ha. Grape varieties: 66% Merlot, 34% Cabernet franc.

Château Méaume (Fr) a vineyard. (Com): Maransin. A.C. Bordeaux Supérieur. 25ha. Grape varieties: Cabernet franc 15%, Cabernet sauvignon 5% and Merlot 80%.

Château Médrac (Fr) a vineyard. (Com): Moulis. A.C. Moulis, Bordeaux 1ha.

Château Megnien (Fr) a vineyard. (Com): Sainte-Croix-du-Mont. A.C. Sainte-Croix-du-Mont, Bordeaux 3ha.

Château Megyer (Hun) a range of Tokaji Aszú wines produced and bottled by Megyer at an 80ha. vineyard based at Saroszatak. Grape varieties: Chardonnay, Furmint.

Château Meillant (Fr) a V.D.Q.S. wine of the Loire. (red, rosé and white). Produced in the Cher département.

Château Melnik (Czec) a sparkling wine made in the Uzhorod region.

Château Mendoce (Fr) a vineyard. (Com): Villeneuve. A.C. Côtes de Bourg, Bordeaux.

Château Menota (Fr) a vineyard. (Com): Barsac. A.C. Barsac (or Sauternes), Bordeaux. 17ha. Also Château Menota-Labat.

Château Menota-Labat (Fr) a vineyard. (Com): Barsac. A.C. Barsac (or Sauternes), Bordeaux. 17ha. Also Château Menota.

Château Mercian (Jap) a 'Grand Cru Classé' white wine produced from the Koshu grape by Sanraku Ocean based in Yamanashi near Tokyo.

Château Mercier (Fr) a vineyard. (Com): Barsac. A.C. Barsac (or Sauternes), Bordeaux 2ha.

Château Méric (Fr) a vineyard. (Add): 33650 La Brède. A.C. Graves. (Com): La Brède. 12ha. Grape varieties: Cabernet franc, Cabernet sauvignon, Malbec, Merlot, Muscadelle, Sauvignon and Sémillon.

Château Merissac (Fr) the second wine of Château Dassault. Grand Cru Classé. A.C. Saint-Émilion.

Château Merlet (Fr) an A.C. Bordeaux wine from the Entre-Deux-Mers, central Bordeaux.

Château Merlet (Fr) a vineyard in the A.C. Graves, Bordeaux.

Château Meunier St-Louis (Fr) a vineyard in the A.C. Corbières, south-western France.

Château Meynard (Fr) a vineyard. (Com): Sables-Saint-Émilion. A.C. Saint-Émilion, Bordeaux 6ha.

Château Meyney (Fr) a Cru Bourgeois Exceptionnel. A.C. Saint-Estèphe. (Com): Saint-Estèphe. 74ha. Grape varieties: Cabernet franc, Cabernet sauvignon, Merlot and Petit verdot. See also Prieur, de Meyney.

Château Michel de Montaigne (Fr) a vineyard in the A.C. Bergerac, south-western France (red).

Château Mille-Secousses (Fr) a vineyard. (Com): Bourg. A.C. Côtes de Bourg, Bordeaux.

Château Millet (Fr) a vineyard. (Add): 33460 Portets. A.C. Graves. (Com): Portets. 58ha. Grape varieties: Cabernet 40% and Merlot 60%.

Château Milon (Fr) a vineyard. (Add): Saint-Christophe-des-Bardes, 33330 Saint-Émilion. Grand Cru. A.C. Saint-Émilion. (Com): Saint-Christophe-des-Bardes. 22.91ha. Grape varieties: Cabernet franc, Cabernet sauvignon and Merlot 75%. Second label is Clos Renon.

Château Minière (Fr) a vineyard. (Com): Restigné. A.C. Bourgueil, Touraine, Loire.

Château Minuty (Fr) an A.C. rosé wine from the Côtes de Provence, south-eastern France.

Château Mirabel (Fr) a vineyard. (Com): Pujols. A.C. Graves, Bordeaux. 3ha (white).

Château Miraval (Fr) a 28ha vineyard in the A.C. Côtes de Provence. White wine is A.C. Coteaux Varois from 100% Rolle. Produces red and rosé wines are A.C. Côtes de Provence.

Château Mirefleurs (Fr) an A.C. Bordeaux Supèrieur.

Château Moderis (Fr) a vineyard. (Com): Virelade. A.C. Graves, Bordeaux. 5ha (red and white).

Château Molhières (Fr) a vineyard in the A.C. Côtes de Duras. (Add): Blancheton Frères, Duras 47120.

Château Monbazillac (Fr) a vineyard. (Com): Monbazillac. A.C. Monbazillac, Bergerac.

Château Monbousquet (Fr) a vineyard. (Add): Place Guadet, 33500 Libourne. Grand Cru Classé. A.C. Saint-Émilion. (Com): Saint-Sulpice-de-Faleyrens. 40ha. Grape varieties: Cabernet franc 40% and Merlot 60%.

Château Monbrison (Fr) a vineyard. (Add): Arsac 33460. Cru Bourgeois. A.C. Margaux. (Com): Arsac. 13ha. Grape varieties: 15% Cabernet franc, 50% Cabernet sauvignon, 30% Merlot, 5% Petit verdot. Second label is Clos Cordat.

Château Moncets (Fr) a vineyard. (Com): Néac. A.C. Saint-Émilion, Bordeaux.

Château Monconseil (Fr) a vineyard. (Com): Plassac. A.C. Côtes de Blaye, Bordeaux.

Château Moncontour (Fr) a vineyard in the A.C. Vouvray, Touraine, Loire. Produces sparkling (méthode traditionelle) wines and pétillant Vouvray.

Château Mondou (Fr) a vineyard. (Com): Saint-Sulpice-de-Faleyrens. A.C. Saint-Émilion, Bordeaux.

Château Montfollet (Fr) a vineyard in the Premières Côtes de Blaye, Bordeaux. Grape varieties: Malbec 30%, Merlot 70%.

Château Mongravey (Fr) a vineyard. (Com): Arsac. A.C. Margaux, Bordeaux. Cru Bourgeois. (Add): Arsac, 33460 Margaux.

Château Monjou (Fr) an A.C. Barsac (or Sauternes). (Com): Barsac. 9ha. Also Château Terre Noble.

Château Monlot Capet (Fr) a vineyard. (Com): Saint-Hippolyte. A.C. Saint-Émilion, Bordeaux 8ha.

Château Monpelou (Fr) a vineyard. (Com): Pauillac. A.C. Pauillac, Bordeaux 8ha.

Château Monregard Lacroix (Fr) a vineyard. (Com): Pomerol. A.C. Pomerol, Bordeaux 5ha.

Château Montagne (Isr) a dry white table wine.

Château Montaiguillon (Fr) a vineyard. (Com): Montagne-Saint-Émilion. A.C. Montagne-Saint-Émilion, Bordeaux 23ha.

Château Montaiguillon (Fr) a vineyard. (Com): Saint-Georges-Saint-Émilion. A.C. Saint-Émilion, Bordeaux 3ha.

Château Montalivet (Fr) a vineyard. (Com): Barsac. A.C. Barsac (or Sauternes), Bordeaux. 12ha. Also Châteaux Camperos and Mayne-Bert.

Château Montauriol (Fr) a vineyard. (Com): Villaudric. A.C. Côtes du Frontonnais, south-western France. (Add): 31620 Villaudric.

Château Montauriol Rigaud (Fr) a vineyard in the A.C. Corbières, south-western France. Label: Grande Réserve.

Château Montbelair (Fr) a vineyard in the A.C. Saint-Émilion, Bordeaux 2ha.

Château Montbenault (Fr) a vineyard. (Add): 49380 Faye-d'Anjou. A.C. Anjou-Villages and A.C. Coteaux du Layon. (Com): Faye-d'Anjou. Anjou-Saumur, Loire Atlantique.

Château Montbrun (Fr) a vineyard. (Com): Cantenac. A.C. Haut-Médoc, Bordeaux 9ha.

Château Montchenot (Arg) the brand-name of red and white wines produced by Bodegas Lopez Hermanos, Mendoza.

Château Monteau (Fr) a vineyard. (Com): Preignac. A.C. Sauternes, Bordeaux 9ha.

Château Montelena (USA) a vineyard (established 1882) based in the Napa Valley. (Add): 1429 Tubbs Lane, Calistoga, Napa Valley, California 94515. Produces varietal wines from the Cabernet sauvignon and Chardonnay grapes. 40ha. Website: http://www.montelena.com

Château Montespertoli (It) a D.O.C.G. Riserva wine.

Château Montesquieu (Fr) a vineyard. (Com): Puisseguin-Saint-Émilion. A.C. Puisseguin-Saint-Émilion, Bordeaux 14ha.

Château Montfin (Fr) a vineyard in the A.C. Corbières, south-western France. Labels: Cuvée Margot and Cuvée Marcel Cabanier.

Château Montfollet (Fr) an A.C. Premières Côtes de Blaye at Cars.

Château Montfort (Fr) a noted wine brotherhood based in the Jura region of eastern France.

Château Monthil (Fr) a vineyard. (Com): Bégadan. A.C. Médoc, Bordeaux. Cru Bourgeois 15ha.

Château Montlabert (Fr) a vineyard. (Add): 33330 Saint-Émilion. Grand Cru. A.C. Saint-Émilion. (Com): Saint-Émilion. 12.5ha. Grape varieties: Cabernet franc 35%, Cabernet sauvignon 15% and Merlot 50%. Second wine is La Croix Montlabert.

Château Montlau (Fr) a vineyard. (Com): Branne. A.C. Bordeaux Supérieur. (Add): 33420 Branne. (red).

Château Mont-Redon (Fr) the label of a red or white Châteauneuf-du-Pape produced by Fabre (Didier) at Château Mont-Redon, 84230 Châteauneuf-du-Pape, southern Rhône.

Château Montremblant (Fr) a vineyard in the A.C. Saint-Émilion, Bordeaux 5ha.

Château Montrose (Fr) a vineyard. (Add): 33250 Pauillac. Grand Cru Classé (2nd). A.C. Saint-Estèphe. (Com): Saint-Estèphe. 68ha. Grape varieties: Cabernet franc 10%, Cabernet sauvignon 65%, Merlot 25%. Second label is La Dame de Montrose.

Château Monturon (Fr) a vineyard. (Add): Saint Laurent des Bardes, 33330 Saint-Émilion. A.C. Saint-Émilion. (Com): Saint Laurent des Bardes. Second wine of Château Rozier. Grand Cru Saint-Émilion.

C

Château Montus (Fr) a vineyard in the A.C. Madiran, Pyrénées, south-western France. (red). Also produces A.C. Pacherenc-de-Vic-Bilh.

Château Moreau (USA) the brand-name of the Gibson vineyard of Fresno, California for a range of their wines.

Château Morillon (Fr) a vineyard in the A.C. Saint-Émilion, Bordeaux 2ha.

Château Morillon (Fr) an A.C. Bordeaux Supérieur. Grape varieties: Cabernet franc 22%, Cabernet sauvignon 22%, Malbec 6%, Merlot 50%. Also an A.C. Bordeaux Blanc Sec. Grape varieties: Sauvignon blanc 75%, Sémillon 25%.

Château Morin (Fr) a vineyard. (Com): Saint-Estèphe. A.C. Haut-Médoc, Bordeaux. Cru Grand Bourgeois 10ha.

Château Mornag (Tun) an A.C. red wine produced by Sidi Selem in Tunisia.

Château Mouchet (Fr) a vineyard. (Com): Puisseguin-Saint-Émilion. A.C. Puisseguin-Saint-Émilion, Bordeaux 10ha. See also Château Fongaban.

Château Mouchique (Fr) a vineyard. (Com): Puisseguin-Saint-Émilion. A.C. Puisseguin-Saint-Émilion, Bordeaux 4ha.

Château Moulerens (Fr) a vineyard. (Com): Gradignan. A.C. Graves, Bordeaux.

Château Moulin à Vent (Fr) a vineyard. (Com): Cérons. A.C. Cérons, Bordeaux 4ha.

Château Moulin-à-Vent (Fr) a vineyard. (Add): 33480 Moulis-en-Médoc. Cru Grand Bourgeois. A.C. Moulis. (Com): Moulis. 30ha. Grape varieties: Cabernet sauvignon, Malbec, Merlot and Petit verdot. Second label is Moulin de St-Vincent

Château Moulin-à-Vent (Fr) a vineyard. (Com): Néac. A.C. Pomerol, Bordeaux.

Château Moulin-à-Vent (Fr) a vineyard. (Com): St-Michel. A.C. Côtes Canon-Fronsac, Bordeaux 6ha.

Château Moulin Bellegrave (Fr) a vineyard. (Add): Vignonet, 33330 Saint-Émilion. Grand Cru. A.C. Saint-Émilion. (Com): Vignonet. 15ha. Grape varieties: Cabernet franc 15%, Cabernet sauvignon 15% and Merlot 70%.

Château Moulin-Blanc (Fr) a vineyard. (Com): Néac. A.C. Pomerol, Bordeaux.

Château Moulin-Blanc (Fr) a vineyard. (Com): Montagne-Saint-Émilion. A.C. Saint-Émilion, Bordeaux.

Château Moulin de Bel Air (Fr) a vineyard. (Add): Saint-Yzans-de-Médoc. A.C. Médoc. (Com): Saint-Yzans. 20ha. Grape varieties: Cabernet franc, Cabernet sauvignon and Merlot.

Château Moulin de Buscateau (Fr) a vineyard. (Add): Ordonnac, 33340 Lesparre, Médoc. A.C. Médoc. (Com): Ordonnac. 5ha. Grape varieties: Cabernet sauvignon 50% and Merlot 50%.

Château Moulin de Cantelaube (Fr) a vineyard in the A.C. Saint-Émilion, Bordeaux 3ha.

Château Moulin de Castillon (Fr) a vineyard. (Add): Le Bourg, Saint-Christoly-de-Médoc 33340. A.C. Médoc. (Com): Saint-Christoly-de-Médoc. 13ha. Grape varieties: Cabernet sauvignon, Malbec and Merlot.

Château Moulin de Ferregrave (Fr) a vineyard. (Com): Saint-Vivien-de-Médoc. A.C. Médoc, Bordeaux. (Add): Jau Dignac et Loirac, 33590 St-Vivien-de-Médoc.

Château Moulin de Gassiot (Fr) a vineyard. (Com): Sauveterre-de-Guyonne. A.C. Bordeaux Rouge. (Add): 33540 Sauveterre-de-Guyonne.

Château Moulin de Laborde (Fr) a vineyard. (Add): 33480 Listrac, Médoc. A.C. Listrac. (Com): Listrac. 8ha. Grape varieties: Cabernet sauvignon 60%, Merlot 30% and Petit verdot 10%.

Château Moulin de la Bridane (Fr) a vineyard. (Com): Pauillac. A.C. Pauillac, Bordeaux 2.5ha.

Château Moulin de Landry (Fr) a vineyard in the A.C. Côtes de Castillon, eastern Bordeaux.

Château Moulin de la Rose (Fr) a vineyard. (Add): 33250 Saint-Julien, Beychevelle. A.C. Saint-Julien. (Com): Saint-Julien. 4ha. Grape varieties: Cabernet franc, Cabernet sauvignon and Petit verdot.

Château Moulin de Pierrefitte (Fr) a vineyard. (Add): Saint-Sulpice-de-Faleyrens, 33330 Saint-Émilion. Grand Cru. A.C. Saint-Émilion. (Com): Saint-Sulpice-de-Faleyrens. 7ha. Grape varieties: Cabernet 10% and Merlot 90%.

Château Moulin de Pillardot (Fr) an A.C. Bordeaux Supérieur. Grape varieties: Cabernet sauvignon 15%, Merlot 85%.

Château Moulin des Carruades (Fr) the second wine of Château Lafite.

Château Moulin de St-Vincent (Fr) a vineyard. (Com): Moulis. A.C. Médoc, Bordeaux. Cru Bourgeois. Second label of Château Moulin-à-Vent.

Château Moulin de Taffard (Fr) a vineyard. (Add): Saint-Christoly-de-Médoc, 33340 Lesparre. A.C. Médoc. (Com): Saint-Christoly. 8ha. Grape varieties: Cabernet sauvignon and Merlot.

Château Moulin du Cadet (Fr) a vineyard. (Com): Saint-Émilion. A.C. Saint-Émilion, Bordeaux. Grand Cru Classé 5ha.

Château Moulin-du-Jura (Fr) a vineyard. (Com): Montagne-Saint-Émilion. A.C. Montagne-Saint-Émilion, Bordeaux 3ha.

Château Moulin du Vilet (Fr) a vineyard. (Com): Saint-Christophe-des-Bardes, A.C. Saint-Émilion, Bordeaux. (Add): Saint-Christophe-des-Bardes, 33340 Saint-Émilion.

Château Moulinet (Fr) a vineyard. (Com): Pomerol. A.C. Pomerol, Bordeaux 5ha. Grape varieties: Merlot, Cabernet franc, Malbec.

Château Moulin Eyquem (Fr) a vineyard in the A.C. Côtes de Bourg, Bordeaux

Château Moulin Haut-Laroque (Fr) a vineyard. (Com): Saillans. A.C. Fronsac, Bordeaux. (Add): Saillans, 33141 Villegouge.

Château Moulin Joli (Fr) see Château Les Ormes-de-Pez, A.C. Haut-Médoc, Bordeaux.

Château Moulin la Mondière (Fr) a vineyard in the A.C. Corbières, south-western France.

Château Moulin Neuf (Fr) a vineyard. (Com): Loupiac. A.C. Loupiac, Bordeaux 10ha.

C

Château Moulin-Pey-Labrie (Fr) a vineyard. (Com): Fronsac. A.C. Fronsac, Bordeaux 4ha. Grape varieties: Cabernet franc 10%, Cabernet sauvignon 20%, Merlot 70%.

Château Moulin-Riche (Fr) a vineyard. (Com): Saint-Julien. A.C. Saint-Julien, Bordeaux. Cru Bourgeois, the second label of Château Léoville-Poyferré.

Château Moulin-Rose (Fr) a vineyard. (Com): Lamarque, A.C. Haut-Médoc, Bordeaux 3ha. Cru Bourgeois.

Château Moulin Rouge (Fr) a vineyard. (Com): Cissac-Fort-Médoc. A.C. Haut-Médoc, Bordeaux. Cru Bourgeois.

Château Moulins (Fr) a vineyard. (Com): Saillans. A.C. Côtes de Fronsac, Bordeaux 16ha.

Château Moulin Saint Georges (Fr) a vineyard. (Add): 33330 Saint-Émilion. Grand Cru. A.C. Saint-Émilion. (Com): Saint-Émilion. 11ha. Grape varieties: Cabernet franc 35% and Merlot 65%.

Château Moulins-de-Calon (Fr) a vineyard. (Com): Montagne-Saint-Émilion. A.C. Saint-Émilion, Bordeaux.

Château Moulins Haut Villars (Fr) a vineyard. (Com): Fronsac. A.C. Fronsac, Bordeaux.

Château Moulis (Fr) a vineyard. (Add): 33480 Moulis-en-Médoc. Cru Bourgeois. A.C. Moulis. (Com): Moulis. 12ha. Grape varieties: Cabernet sauvignon 50% and Merlot 50%.

Château Mounic (Fr) a vineyard. (Com): Fargues. A.C. Sauternes, Bordeaux 1ha.

Château Moura (Fr) a vineyard. (Com): Barsac. A.C. Barsac (or Sauternes), Bordeaux 1ha.

Château Mourgues du Grès (Fr) a domaine in A.C. Costières de Nîmes, Languedoc-Roussillon. Produces: Les Galets Rouge (65% Syrah, 35% Grenache), Syrah Terre d'Argence, Capitelles des Mourgues and rosé wines.

Château Mouteou (Fr) a vineyard. (Com): Portets. A.C. Graves, Bordeaux. 3ha (red and white).

Château Moutin (Fr) a vineyard. (Com): Portets. A.C. Graves, Bordeaux. 1ha (red).

Château Mouton Cadet (Fr) a famous branded Claret, originally sold as an off-vintage Château Mouton Rothschild, now sold separately. *see* Mouton Cadet.

Château Mouton-Baronne-Philippe (Fr) *see* Château Mouton d'Armailhacq.

Château Mouton-Baron-Philippe (Fr) a vineyard. (Add): 33250 Pauillac. Grand Cru Classé (5th). A.C. Pauillac. (Com): Pauillac. 67ha. Grape varieties: Cabernet franc 15%, Cabernet sauvignon 65% and Merlot 20%.

Château Mouton d'Armailhacq (Fr) renamed Château Mouton-Baronne- Philippe. Cru Classé (5th) du Baronne Philippe in 1975 in honour of his late wife the late Baronne Pauline.

Château Mouton-Rothschild (Fr) a vineyard (established 1853). (Add): 33250 Pauillac. Premier Grand Cru Classé (elevated from 2nd growth in 1973). A.C. Pauillac. (Com): Pauillac. 82ha. Grape varieties: Cabernet franc 9%,

Cabernet sauvignon 77%, Merlot 12% and Petit verdot 2%. Second wine is Le Petit Mouton de Mouton-Rothschild. Château was originally known as Brane-Mouton.

Château Mouyet (Fr) a vineyard. (Com): Budos. A.C. Graves, Bordeaux. 2ha (red).

Château Musar (Leb) a red wine produced in the Bekka Valley in the Lebanon from Cabernet sauvignon, Carignan, Cinsaut, Grenache and Mourvèdre. Also produces white wine from Obaideh and Merweh grapes. Website: http://www.chateaumusar.com.lb

Château Musseau de Haut (Fr) a vineyard. (Com): St-Aignan. A.C. Côtes de Fronsac, Bordeaux 2ha.

Château Musset (Fr) a vineyard. (Com): Lalande de Pomerol. A.C. Lalande de Pomerol, Bordeaux.

Château Musset (Fr) a vineyard. (Com): Parsac-Saint-Émilion. A.C. Saint-Émilion, Bordeaux 7ha.

Château Myosotis (Fr) a vineyard in the A.C. Saint-Émilion, Bordeaux 3ha.

Château Myrat (Fr) a Grand Cru Classé (2nd). A.C. Barsac (or Sauternes). Commune: Barsac. (now no longer in production).

Château Naguet-la-Grande (Fr) a vineyard. (Com): Parsac-Saint-Émilion. A.C. Saint-Émilion, Bordeaux 5ha.

Château Nairac (Fr) a vineyard. (Add): 33720 Podensac. Grand Cru Classé (2nd). A.C. Barsac (or Sauternes). (Com): Barsac. 13ha. Grape varieties: Sauvignon 6%, Sémillon 90% and Muscadelle 4%.

Château Nairne (Fr) a vineyard. (Com): Barsac. A.C. Barsac (or Sauternes), Bordeaux.

Château Nardique la Gravière (Fr) an A.C. Entre-Deux-Mers. Grape varieties: Sauvignon blanc, Sémillon, Muscadelle.

Château Nardon (Fr) part of Domaine Laroque, A.C. Saint-Émilion, Bordeaux.

Château Naude (Fr) a vineyard. (Com): Saint-Sulpice-des-Faleyrens. A.C. Saint-Émilion, Bordeaux.

Château Négrit (Fr) *see* Vieux Château Negrit.

Château Nénin (Fr) an A.C. Pomerol. (Com): Pomerol. 28ha. Grape varieties: Bouchet 30%, Cabernet sauvignon 20% and Merlot 50%.

Chateauneuf (Fr) a naturally carbonated mineral water from the Auvergne. (Add): Compagnie Hydrothermale des Grandes Sources, 63390 Chateauneuf-les-Bains. Mineral contents (milligrammes per litre): Sodium 651mg/l, Calcium 152mg/l, Magnesium 36mg/l, Potassium 40mg/l, Bicarbonates 1799mg/l, Chlorides 215mg/l, Sulphates 195mg/l, Fluride 3mg/l, Nitrates 0mg/l.

Château-Neuf (Fr) a vineyard. (Com): Léognan. A.C. Pessac-Léognan, Bordeaux. Cru Bourgeois.

Châteauneuf (Fr) a commune in the Charente département whose grapes are classed Petite Champagne (Cognac). Wines are made into Cognac des Bois.

Châteauneuf Auvergne (Fr) a natural spring mineral water from Châteauneuf-les-Bains. Mineral contents (milligrammes per litre): Sodium

310

C

620mg/l, Calcium 160mg/l, Magnesium 40mg/l, Potassium 40mg/l, Bicarbonates 1850mg/l, Chlorides 180mg/l, Sulphates 180mg/l, Fluorides 3mg/l, Nitrates <1mg/l.

Châteauneuf-Calcernier (Fr) the old name for Châteauneuf-du-Pape. Was changed in 1850 to present name by the Marquis de Nerthe.

Châteauneuf-du-Pape (Fr) an A.C. red and white wines produced in the southern Rhône. Reds can be rich, full-bodied and alcoholic (min 12.5% by vol), produced from one or all of the 13 (includes Grenache and Grenache blanc as one variety) permitted grape varieties (red: Cinsault, Counoise, Grenache [main variety], Mourvèdre, Muscardin, Picpoul, Syrah, Terret noir, Vaccarese) and (white: Bourboulenc, Clairette, Grenache blanc, Picardan, Roussane). Whites are full-bodied, fruity and usually age well. see Baron le Roy, King of Wines and Mistral. Website: http://www.chateauneufdupape.com

Château Nexon-Lemoyne (Fr) a vineyard. (Com): Ludon. A.C. Médoc, Bordeaux. Cru Bourgeois 16ha.

Château Nodot (Fr) a vineyard in the A.C. Côtes de Bourg, Bordeaux.

Château Nodoz (Fr) a vineyard. (Com): Tauriac. A.C. Côtes de Bourg, Bordeaux.

Château Notton (Fr) a vineyard. (Com): Arsac. A.C. Haut-Médoc, Bordeaux. Cru Bourgeois. Second label of Château Brane-Cantenac.

Château Olivier (Fr) a vineyard. (Add): 33850 Léognan. Grand Cru Classé. A.C. Pessac-Léognan. (Com): Léognan. 36ha. Grape varieties: Cabernet sauvignon 70%, Merlot 30%, Sauvignon 30%, Sémillon 65% and Muscadelle 5%.

Château Ollieux Romanis (Fr) a vineyard in the A.C. Corbières, south-western France. Label: Cuvée Classique.

Château Orisse du Casse (Fr) a vineyard. (Add): Saint-Sulpice-de-Faleyrens, 33330 Saint-Émilion. Grand Cru. A.C. Saint-Émilion. (Com): Saint-Sulpice-de-Faleyrens. Grape varieties: Cabernet franc, Malbec, Merlot.

Château Pabeau (Fr) a vineyard. (Add): 33250 Saint-Seurin-de-Médoc. A.C. Haut-Médoc. (Com): Saint-Seurin-de-Cadourne. 10ha. Grape varieties: Cabernet 50% and Merlot 50%.

Château Padouen (Fr) a vineyard. (Com): Barsac. A.C. Barsac (or Sauternes), Bordeaux 10ha.

Château Pageot (Fr) a vineyard. (Com): Sauternes. A.C. Sauternes, Bordeaux 5ha.

Château Pailhas (Fr) a vineyard. (Add): Saint-Hippolyte, 33330 Saint-Émilion. A.C. Saint-Émilion. (Com): Saint-Hippolyte. 25ha. Grape varieties: Cabernet franc 8%, Cabernet sauvignon 20%, Malbec 2% and Merlot 70%.

Château Pajzos (Hun) the name of a Tokaji Aszú bottled by Pajzos R.T. Tolesva at their 63ha vineyard.

Château Palmer (Fr) a Grand Cru Classé (3rd) A.C. Margaux. (Com): Cantenac. 41ha. Grape varieties: Cabernet 60% and Merlot 40%. Second label is

Réserve du Général (now known as Alter Ego de Palmer).

Château Paloumat (Fr) a vineyard. (Com): Fargues. A.C. Sauternes, Bordeaux 2ha.

Château Paloumey (Fr) a vineyard. (Com): Ludon. A.C. Médoc, Bordeaux. (Add): 33290 Ludon. Cru Bourgeois Supérieur.

Château Panet (Fr) a vineyard. (Com): Fronsac. A.C. Côtes Canon-Fronsac, Bordeaux 4ha.

Château Panet (Fr) a vineyard in the A.C. Saint-Émilion, Bordeaux 22ha.

Château Panchille (Fr) a vineyard in the A.C. Bordeaux. Label: Cuvée Alix.

Château Panigon (Fr) a vineyard. (Com): Civrac. A.C. Médoc, Bordeaux. Cru Bourgeois 20ha.

Château Panniseau (Fr) a vineyard in the A.C. Bergerac, south-western Bordeaux (red and white).

Château Pape-Clément (Fr) a vineyard (planted 1252). (Add): Pessac, Gironde. Grand Cru Classé. A.C. Pessac-Léognan. (Com): Pessac. 27.3ha. Grape varieties: Cabernet sauvignon 65%, Merlot 35%, Muscadelle, Sauvignon and Sémillon.

Château Papetterie (Fr) a vineyard. (Com): Néac. A.C. Saint-Émilion, Bordeaux.

Château Paradis (Fr) a vineyard. (Com): Vignonet. A.C. Saint-Émilion, Bordeaux 19ha.

Château Paradis Casseuil (Fr) a vineyard in the A.C. Entre-Deux-Mers. Owned by Rothshild.

Château Parans (Fr) a vineyard in the A.C. Saint-Émilion, Bordeaux 7ha.

Château Pardaillan (Fr) a vineyard. (Com): Cars. A.C. Côtes de Blaye, Bordeaux.

Château Pardanac (Fr) a vineyard. (Com): Pauillac. A.C. Médoc, Bordeaux. Cru Bourgeois.

Château Parempuyre (Fr) a vineyard. (Com): Parempuyre. A.C. Médoc, Bordeaux. Cru Bourgeois.

Château Paret Beauséjour (Fr) an A.C. Bordeaux Supérieur.

Château Partarrieu (Fr) a vineyard commune of Fargues. A.C. Sauternes, Bordeaux 8ha.

Château Pasquier (Fr) a vineyard. (Com): Camblancs. A.C. Premières Côtes de Bordeaux. (Add): 33360 Camblancs.

Château Patache d'Aux (Fr) a vineyard. (Add): Bégadan, 33340 Lesparre, Médoc. Cru Bourgeois Supérieur. A.C. Médoc. (Com): Bégadan. 43ha. Grape varieties: Cabernet franc, Cabernet sauvignon and Merlot. Second label is Le Boscq. Website: http://www.domaines-lapalu.com 'E'mail: export@domaines-lapalu.com

Château Patarabet (Fr) part of Château Paradis, A.C. Saint-Émilion, Bordeaux.

Château Patris (Fr) a vineyard. (Add): 33330 Saint-Émilion. Grand Cru. A.C. Saint-Émilion. 10ha. Grape varieties: Cabernet sauvignon 30% and Merlot 70%.

Château Paul Blanc (Fr) a red wine produced by Mas Carlot from Syrah grapes in the A.C. Costières de Nîmes, Languedoc-Roussillon

Château Paulet (Fr) a Cognac producer. (Add):

Route de Ségonzac, B.P. 24, 16101 Cognac. Produces: Ecusson Rouge ***, Very Rare Age Inconnu, Borderies Très Vieilles plus V.S.O.P. and Premier X.O.

Château Paveil-de-Luze (Fr) a vineyard. (Add): Soussans, 33460 Margaux. Cru Grand Bourgeois. A.C. Margaux. (Com): Soussans. 23ha. Grape varieties: Cabernet sauvignon 65% and Merlot 35%. Second label is Château Coste.

Château Pavie (Fr) a vineyard. (Add): B.P. 7F, 33330 Saint-Émilion. Premier [B] Grand Cru Classé. A.C. Saint-Émilion. (Com): Saint-Émilion. 41ha. Grape varieties: Bouchet, Cabernet sauvignon and Merlot.

Château Pavie Décesse (Fr) a vineyard. (Add): B.P. 7 F, 33330 Saint-Émilion. Grand Cru Classé. A.C. Saint-Émilion. (Com): Saint-Émilion. 9.9ha. Grape varieties: Bouchet 25%, Cabernet sauvignon 15% and Merlot 60%.

Château Pavie-Macquin (Fr) a vineyard. (Add): 33330 Saint-Émilion. Premier [B] Grand Cru Classé (promoted 2006). A.C. Saint-Émilion. (Com): Saint-Émilion. 13ha. Grape varieties: Cabernet franc 15%, Cabernet sauvignon 15% and Merlot 70%.

Château Pavillon Cadet (Fr) a vineyard. (Add): 33330 Saint-Émilion. Grand Cru. A.C. Saint-Émilion. (Com): Saint-Émilion. 3.5ha.

Château Pavillon-Figeac (Fr) a vineyard in the A.C. Saint-Émilion, Bordeaux 4ha.

Château Pavillon-Fougailles (Fr) a vineyard in the A.C. Saint-Émilion, Bordeaux 1ha.

Château Pay-de-Lalo (Fr) a vineyard. (Com): Saint-Germain-d'Esteuil. A.C. Médoc, Bordeaux 2ha.

Château Pay de Pie (Fr) a vineyard. (Com): Fronsac. A.C. Côtes de Fronsac, Bordeaux.

Château Pébayle (Fr) a vineyard. (Com): Barsac. A.C. Barsac (or Sauternes), Bordeaux 5ha.

Château Pech-Latt (Fr) a vineyard in the A.C. Corbières, south-western France. Label: Sélection Vieilles Vignes.

Château Pechon-Terre-Noble (Fr) a vineyard. (Com): Barsac. A.C. Barsac (or Sauternes), Bordeaux 3ha.

Château Pech-Redon (Fr) a vineyard (40ha) based in the A.C. La Clape, Coteaux du Languedoc. Labels: La Centeurée, L'Epervier, Les Cades.

Château Pédebayle (Fr) a vineyard. (Com): St-Pierre-de-Mons. A.C. Graves, Bordeaux (white) 8ha.

Château Pedesclaux (Fr) a vineyard. (Add): 33250 Pauillac. Grand Cru Classé (5th). A.C. Pauillac. (Com): Pauillac. 18ha. Grape varieties: Cabernet franc 10%, Cabernet sauvignon 65% and Merlot 25%.

Château Peguilhem (Fr) a vineyard. (Com): Saillans. A.C. Côtes de Fronsac, Bordeaux.

Château Peillan-St-Clair (Fr) a vineyard in the A.C. Saint-Émilion, Bordeaux 6ha.

Château Peillon-Claverie (Fr) a vineyard. (Com): Fargues. A.C. Sauternes, Bordeaux 9ha.

Château Pelletan (Fr) a vineyard. (Add): Saint-Christophe-des-Bardes, 33330 Saint-Émilion. A.C. Saint-Émilion. (Com): Saint-Christophe-des-Bardes.

Château Pelletan (Fr) a vineyard. (Com): Saint Quentin-de-Caplang. A.C. Saint-Foy-Bordeaux, south-eastern Bordeaux 5ha.

Château Penin (Fr) a vineyard in the Entre-Deux-Mers. A.C. Bordeaux Supérieur (red and white) 25ha.

Château Péran (Fr) a vineyard. (Com): Langon. A.C. Graves, Bordeaux (white) 8ha.

Château Perenne (Fr) a vineyard in the Saint Genès-de-Blaye. A.C. Côtes de Blaye, Bordeaux. 60ha.

Château Pérey (Fr) a vineyard in the A.C. Saint-Émilion, Bordeaux 8ha.

Château Perin de Naudine (Fr) a vineyard. (Add): Castres-Gironde, 33640 Portets. A.C. Graves. (Com): Castres. 4.52ha. Grape varieties: Cabernet 50% and Merlot 50%.

Château Pernaud (Fr) a vineyard. (Com): Barsac. A.C. Barsac (or Sauternes), Bordeaux 17ha.

Château Perray-Jouannet (Fr) a vineyard in the A.C. Anjou-Villages, Anjou-Saumur, Loire.

Château Perrein (Fr) a vineyard. (Com): Mazion. A.C. Côtes de Blaye, Bordeaux.

Château Perron (Fr) a vineyard. (Com): Fronsac. A.C. Côtes de Fronsac, Bordeaux 3ha.

Château Perron (Fr) a vineyard. (Com): Roaillan. A.C. Graves, Bordeaux. 14ha (white).

Château Perron (Fr) a vineyard. (Com): Lalande de Pomerol. A.C. Lalande de Pomerol, Bordeaux.

Château Perroy-Jean-Blanc (Fr) a vineyard. (Com): Bommes. A.C. Sauternes, Bordeaux 7ha.

Château Perruchon (Fr) a vineyard. (Com): Lussac-Saint-Émilion. A.C. Saint-Émilion, Bordeaux.

Château Perruchot (Fr) a vineyard with holdings in the A.C. Meursault, Burgundy.

Château Pesilla (Fr) a vineyard. (Com): Landiras. A.C. Graves, Bordeaux. 4ha (white).

Château Pessan (Fr) a vineyard. (Com): Portets. A.C. Graves, Bordeaux. 40ha. Grape varieties: Cabernet franc, Cabernet sauvignon, Merlot and Sémillon.

Château Petit Bigaroux (Fr) a vineyard. (Com): Saint-Sulpice-de-Faleyrens. A.C. Saint-Émilion, Bordeaux 3ha.

Château Petit-Bois la Garelle (Fr) a vineyard. (Com): Saint-Émilion. A.C. Saint-Émilion, Bordeaux. 4.82ha. (Add): 33330 Saint-Émilion.

Château Petit Bord (Fr) a vineyard in the A.C. Saint-Émilion, Bordeaux 1ha.

Château Petit Boyer (Fr) a vineyard in A.C. Premières Côtes de Blaye. Plantings include 20% very old Malbec vines.

Château Petit-Clos (Fr) a vineyard. (Com): Montagne-Saint-Émilion. A.C. Montagne-Saint-Émilion, Bordeaux 8ha.

Château Petit-Cormey (Fr) a vineyard in the A.C. Saint-Émilion, Bordeaux 4ha.

Château Petit Faurie (Fr) a vineyard in the A.C. Saint-Émilion, Bordeaux 1ha.

Château Petit-Faurie de Souchard (Fr) a vineyard. (Com): Saint-Émilion. A.C. Saint-Émilion, Bordeaux. 19ha. Grand Cru.

C

Château Petit-Faurie de Soutard (Fr) a vineyard. (Add): 33330 Saint-Émilion. Grand Cru (demoted 2006). A.C. Saint-Émilion. (Com): Saint-Émilion. 8.88ha. Grape varieties: Cabernet franc 30%, Cabernet sauvignon 10% and Merlot 60%.

Château Petit-Faurie-Trocard (Fr) a vineyard. (Com): Saint-Émilion. A.C. Saint-Émilion, Bordeaux 4ha.

Château Petit Figeac (Fr) a vineyard. (Add): La Fleur Pourret, 33330 Saint-Émilion Grand Cru. A.C. Saint-Émilion. (Com): Saint-Émilion. 1.5ha. Grape varieties: Cabernet sauvignon 40% and Merlot 60%.

Château Petit-Frombrauge (Fr) an A.C. Saint-Émilion Grand Cru. (Add): Saint-Christophe-des-Bardes, 33330 Saint-Émilion, Bordeaux. (Com): Saint-Christophe-des-Bardes. 2ha. 'E'mail: petitfombrauge@terre.net.fr

Château Petit-Gravet (Fr) a vineyard. (Add): 33330 Saint-Émilion. Grand Cru. A.C. Saint-Émilion. (Com): Saint-Émilion. 5ha. Grape varieties: Cabernet franc 30%, Cabernet sauvignon 20% and Merlot 50%.

Château Petit-Mangot (Fr) a vineyard in the A.C. Saint-Émilion, Bordeaux 5ha.

Château Petit Mouta (Fr) a vineyard in Mazères-Langon, Gironde. A.C. Graves.

Château Petit-Refuge (Fr) a vineyard. (Com): Lussac-Saint-Émilion. A.C. Saint-Émilion, Bordeaux 4ha.

Château Petit Val (Fr) a vineyard. (Add): 33330 Saint-Émilion. Grand Cru. A.C. Saint-Émilion. (Com): Saint-Émilion. 9.5ha. Grape varieties: Cabernet franc 30%, Cabernet sauvignon 5% and Merlot 65%.

Château Petit-Village (Fr) an A.C. Pomerol. (Com): Pomerol. 11ha. Grape varieties: Cabernet franc, Cabernet sauvignon and Merlot.

Château Petray (Fr) an A.C. Bordeaux Supérieur.

Château Pétrus (Fr) the world's most famous red wine commanding the highest prices for single bottles. A.C. Pomerol. (Com): Pomerol. 11.5ha. Grape varieties: Cabernet franc 5% and Merlot 95%.

Château Peybonhomme les Tours (Fr) an A.C. Premières Côtes de Blaye at Cars, Bordeaux.

Château Peychaud (Fr) a 26ha vineyard. (Com): Teuillac. A.C. Côtes de Bourg, Bordeaux.

Château Peychez (Fr) a vineyard. (Com): Fronsac. A.C. Côtes de Fronsac, Bordeaux 4ha.

Château Peygenestou (Fr) a vineyard in the A.C. Saint-Émilion, Bordeaux 2ha.

Château Pey La Tour (Fr) an A.C. Bordeaux Supérieur red wine.

Château Peymartin (Fr) a vineyard. (Com): Saint-Julien. A.C. Saint-Julien, Bordeaux. Cru Bourgeois. 15ha. Second wine of Château Gloria.

Château Peymouton (Fr) a vineyard in the A.C. Saint-Émilion, Bordeaux 3ha.

Château Peyrabon (Fr) a vineyard. (Add): Saint-Sauveur-du-Médoc 33250. Cru Grand Bourgeois. A.C. Haut-Médoc. (Com): Saint-Sauveur-du-Médoc. 70ha. Grape varieties: Cabernet franc 23%, Cabernet sauvignon 50% and Merlot 27%. Second label is Château Haut Laborde.

Château Peyraguey-le-Rousset (Fr) a vineyard. (Com): Preignac. A.C. Sauternes, Bordeaux. 15ha. Also Cru d'Arche-Pugnau.

Château Péyran (Fr) a vineyard. (Com): Landiras. A.C. Graves, Bordeaux. 4ha (white).

Château Peyrat (Fr) a vineyard in the A.C. Premières Côtes de Bordeaux, Bordeaux. Grape varieties: Cabernet franc 10%, Cabernet sauvignon 30%, Merlot 60%.

Château Peyreau (Fr) a vineyard. (Add): 33330 Saint-Émilion. Grand Cru. A.C. Saint-Émilion. (Com): Saint-Émilion. 13.5ha. Grape varieties: Cabernet franc 25%, Cabernet sauvignon 10% and Merlot 65%. Second wine is Clos de l'Oratoire.

Château Peyrebrune (Fr) a vineyard. (Com): Cartelègue. A.C. Côtes de Blaye, Bordeaux.

Château Peyredon (Fr) a vineyard. (Com): Moulis. A.C. Moulis, Bordeaux 3ha.

Château Peyredon-Lagravette (Fr) a vineyard. (Add): 33480 Listrac-Médoc. A.C. Listrac. (Com): Listrac. 7ha. Grape varieties: Cabernet sauvignon, Malbec, Merlot and Petit verdot.

Château Peyrelongue (Fr) a vineyard. (Add): 33330 Saint-Émilion. Grand Cru. A.C. Saint-Émilion. (Com): Saint-Émilion. 10ha. Grape varieties: Cabernet franc 15%, Cabernet sauvignon 15% and Merlot 70%.

Château Peyron (Fr) a vineyard. (Com): Fargues. A.C. Sauternes, Bordeaux 4ha.

Château Peyrou (Fr) a vineyard. (Com): Saint-Étienne-de-Lisse. A.C. Saint-Émilion, Bordeaux 5ha.

Château Peyrouquet (Fr) a vineyard in the A.C. Saint-Émilion, Bordeaux 1ha.

Château Peyroutas (Fr) a vineyard. (Com): Vignonet. A.C. Saint-Émilion, Bordeaux 8ha.

Château Peyruchet (Fr) a vineyard. (Com): Loupiac. A.C. Loupiac, Bordeaux 12ha.

Château Phélan Ségur (Fr) a Cru Bourgeois Exceptionnel. A.C. Saint-Estèphe. (Com): Saint-Estèphe. 70ha. Grape varieties: 60% Cabernet franc, 10% Cabernet sauvignon, 30% Merlot.

Château Phénix (Fr) a vineyard. (Com): Pessac. A.C. Pessac-Léognan, Bordeaux.

Château Piada (Fr) a vineyard. (Com): Barsac. A.C. Barsac (or Sauternes), Bordeaux. 11ha. Also Clos du Roy.

Château Piaut (Fr) a vineyard. (Com): Barsac. A.C. Barsac (or Sauternes), Bordeaux 9ha.

Château Pibarnon (Fr) a vineyard based in A.C. Bandol, Provence. Grape variety: Mourvèdre.

Château Pibran (Fr) a vineyard. (Com): Pauillac. A.C. Haut-Médoc, Bordeaux. Cru Bourgeois 7ha.

Château Picard (Fr) a vineyard. (Com): Saint-Estèphe. A.C. Saint-Estèphe, Bordeaux. Cru Bourgeois.

Château Pichelebre (Fr) a vineyard. (Com): Fronsac. A.C. Côtes Canon-Fronsac, Bordeaux 5ha.

Château Pichon (Fr) a vineyard. (Com): Parempuyre A.C. Haut-Médoc, Bordeaux 3ha.

Château Pichon Comtesse (Fr) a vineyard. (Com): Pauillac. A.C. Pauillac, Bordeaux.

Château Pichon-Lalande (Fr) *see* Château Pichon-Longueville Comtesse de Lalande.

Château Pichon-Longueville (Fr) a Grand Cru Classé (2nd). A.C. Pauillac. (Com): Pauillac. 30ha. Grape varieties: Cabernet sauvignon 70% and Merlot 30%. Second wine is Les Tourelles de Longueville.

Château Pichon-Longueville-Baron (Fr) *see* Château Pichon-Longueville.

Château Pichon-Longueville Comtesse de Lalande (Fr) a vineyard. (Add): 33250 Pauillac. Grand Cru Classé (2nd). A.C. Pauillac. (Com): Pauillac. 62ha. Grape varieties: Cabernet franc, Cabernet sauvignon, Merlot and Petit verdot. Own Châteaux Le Fournas and Bernadotte. *See also* Réserve de la Comtesse. Website: http://www.pichon-lalande.com 'E'mail: pichon@pichon-lalande.com

Château Picon-Gravignac (Fr) a vineyard in the A.C. Saint-Émilion, Bordeaux 4ha.

Château Picque-Caillou (Fr) a vineyard. (Com): Pessac. A.C. Pessac-Léognan, Bordeaux. 14ha. Grape varieties: Cabernet franc, Cabernet sauvignon and Merlot.

Château Picque-Caillou (Fr) a vineyard. (Add): Route de Pessac, 33700 Mérignac. A.C. Graves. (Com): Mérignac. 7ha. Grape varieties: Cabernet sauvignon 50% and Merlot 50%.

Château Pidoux (Fr) a vineyard in the A.C. Saint-Émilion, Bordeaux 2ha.

Château Pierrail (Fr) an A.C. Bordeaux Supérieur. Grape varieties: Cabernet franc 5%, Cabernet sauvignon 85%, Merlot 10%.

Château Pierre Bibian (Fr) a vineyard. (Com): Listrac. A.C. Listrac, Bordeaux. Cru Bourgois 14ha.

Château Pierre-Bise (Fr) a vineyard based in Rouannères, Coteaux-du-Layon, Anjou-Saumur, Loire Valley. Label: Clos de la Soucherie.

Château Pierrousselle (Fr) a white A.C. Entre-Deux-Mers wine made from Sauvignon blanc and Sémillon grapes. (Add): 19, Avenue de Fontenille, 33360 Carignan-de-Bordeaux. Website: http://www.ginestet.fr 'E'mail: contact@ginestet.fr

Château Piganeau (Fr) a vineyard. (Add): 33330 Saint-Émilion. A.C. Grand Cru Saint-Émilion. (Com): Saint-Émilion. Second wine of Château Cantenac. Grand Cru Saint-Émilion. Website: http://www.vignobles-brunot.fr 'E'mail: vignobles-brunot@wanadoo.fr

Château Pignon-de-Gay (Fr) a vineyard. (Com): Pomerol. A.C. Pomerol, Bordeaux 2ha.

Château Pindefleurs (Fr) a vineyard. (Add): 33330 Saint-Émilion. Grand Cru. A.C. Saint-Émilion. (Com): Saint-Émilion. 10.27ha. Grape varieties: Cabernet franc and Merlot.

Château Pinet (Fr) a vineyard. (Com): Berson. A.C. Côtes de Blaye, Bordeaux.

Château Piney (Fr) a vineyard in the A.C. Saint-Émilion, Bordeaux 6ha.

Château Pingoy (Fr) a vineyard. (Com): Portets. A.C. Graves, Bordeaux. 8ha (red and white)

Château Pinon la Roquete (Fr) a vineyard. (Com): Berson. A.C. Côtes de Blaye, Bordeaux.

Château Pion (Fr) a vineyard in the A.C. Bergerac, south-western France (red).

Château Piot (Fr) a vineyard. (Com): Barsac. A.C. Barsac (or Sauternes), Bordeaux.

Château Pipeau (Fr) a vineyard. (Add): Saint Laurent des Combes, 33330 Saint-Émilion. Grand Cru. A.C. Saint-Émilion. (Com): Saint Laurent des Combes. 25ha. Grape varieties: Cabernet franc, Cabernet sauvignon and Merlot 65%.

Château Pipeau-Menichot (Fr) a vineyard in the A.C. Saint-Émilion, Bordeaux 6ha.

Château Pique-Caillou (Fr) a vineyard. (Com): Mérignac. A.C. Graves, Bordeaux.

Château Piron (Fr) an A.C. Bordeaux wine.

Château Piron (Fr) a vineyard. (Com): Parsac-Saint-Émilion. A.C. Saint-Émilion, Bordeaux 6ha.

Château Piron (Fr) a vineyard. (Com): St-Morillon. A.C. Graves, Bordeaux. 15ha (red and white).

Château Pitray (Fr) a vineyard in the A.C. Côtes de Castillon, eastern Bordeaux. Grape varieties: Cabernet franc 30%, Merlot 70%.

Château Placette du Rey (Fr) a vineyard. (Com): Fronsac. A.C. Côtes de Fronsac, Bordeaux 4ha.

Château Plagnac (Fr) a vineyard. (Com): Bégadan. A.C. Médoc, Bordeaux. 38ha. Grape varieties: Cabernet sauvignon 70% and Merlot 30%.

Château Plain-Point (Fr) a vineyard. (Com): St-Aignan. A.C. Côtes de Fronsac, Bordeaux. 12ha. Grape varieties: Cabernet franc 10%, Cabernet sauvingnon 20%, Merlot 70%.

Château Plaisance (Fr) a vineyard. (Com): Villeneuve-de-Blaye. A.C. Côtes de Bourg, Bordeaux.

Château Plaisance (Fr) a vineyard. (Com): Montagne-Saint-Émilion. A.C. Saint-Émilion, Bordeaux 20ha.

Château Plaisance (Fr) a vineyard. (Com): Parsac-Saint-Émilion. A.C. Saint-Émilion, Bordeaux 9ha.

Château Plaisance (Fr) a vineyard. (Com): Saint-Sulpice-de-Faleyrens. A.C. Saint-Émilion, Bordeaux.

Château Plantey (Fr) the second wine of Château l'Estruelle.

Château Plantey de la Croix (Fr) a vineyard. (Com): St-Seurin-de-Cadourne. A.C. Médoc, Bordeaux. Cru Bourgeois. Second wine of Château Coufran.

Château Pleytegeat (Fr) a vineyard. (Com): Preignac. A.C. Sauternes, Bordeaux 12ha.

Château Plince (Fr) a vineyard. (Com): Pomerol. A.C. Pomerol, Bordeaux. Grape varieties: Cabernet 30% and Merlot 70%. 7ha

Château Plincette (Fr) a vineyard. (Com): Pomerol. A.C. Pomerol, Bordeaux 1ha.

Château Plo du Roy (Fr) a vineyard in the A.C. Minervois, Languedoc-Roussillon. Grape varieties: Grenache, Syrah.

Château Pointe-Bouquey (Fr) a vineyard in the A.C. Saint-Émilion, Bordeaux 4ha.

Château Pomeys (Fr) a vineyard. (Add): Moulis-en-Médoc, 33480. A.C. Moulis. (Com): Moulis. 8ha. Grape varieties: Cabernet sauvignon 65% and Merlot 35%.

C

Château Pomiés-Agassac (Fr) a vineyard. (Com): Ludon. A.C. Médoc, Bordeaux. Cru Bourgeois.

Château Pommarède (Fr) a vineyard. (Com): Castres. A.C. Graves, Bordeaux. 3ha (red).

Château Pommarède-de-Bas (Fr) a vineyard. (Com): Castres. A.C. Graves, Bordeaux. 5ha (red and white).

Château Pomys (Fr) a vineyard. (Add): Leyssac, Saint-Estèphe 33250. A.C. Saint-Estèphe. (Com): Saint-Estèphe. 15ha. Grape varieties: Cabernet franc, Cabernet sauvignon, Merlot and Petit verdot.

Château Pontac (Fr) a vineyard. (Com): Loupiac. A.C. Loupiac, Bordeaux 10ha.

Château Pontac (Fr) see Château Pontac-Monplaisir.

Château Pontac-Lynch (Fr) a vineyard. (Com): Margaux. A.C. Margaux, Bordeaux 22ha.

Château Pontac-Monplaisir (Fr) a vineyard. (Add): Villenave d'Ornon 33140. A.C. Graves. (Com): Villenave d'Ornon. 14ha. Grape varieties: Cabernet sauvignon 40%, Merlot 60%, Sauvignon and Sémillon.

Château Pont-de-Figeac (Fr) a vineyard in the A.C. Saint-Émilion, Bordeaux 25ha.

Château Pont-de-Mouquet (Fr) a vineyard in the A.C. Saint-Émilion, Bordeaux 12ha.

Château Pont-de-Pierre (Fr) a vineyard. (Com): Lussac-Saint-Émilion. A.C. Saint-Émilion, Bordeaux.

Château Potensac (Fr) a Cru Bourgeois Exceptionnel vineyard in the A.C. Médoc, Bordeaux. (Add): Ordonnac, Potensac, Bordeaux.

Château Pontet (Fr) a vineyard. (Add): 41 Cours Victor-Hugo 33340. Cru Bourgeois. A.C. Médoc. (Com): Blaignan. 11ha. Grape varieties: Cabernet 50% and Merlot 50%.

Château Pontet (Fr) an A.C. Saint-Émilion. Second wine of Château Cadet-Pontet. Grand Cru Saint-Émilion, Bordeaux 4ha.

Château Pontet Barrail (Fr) a vineyard. (Com): Bégadan, A.C. Médoc, Bordeaux. Grape varieties: Cabernet franc, Cabernet sauvignon, Merlot.

Château Pontet-Canet (Fr) a vineyard. (Add): 33250 Pauillac. Grand Cru Classé (5th). A.C. Pauillac. (Com): Pauillac. 120ha. Cabernet franc, Cabernet sauvignon and Merlot. Second wine is Château Les-Hauts-de-Pontet. See also Les 5. Website: http://www.pontet-canet.com

Château Pontet Caussan (Fr) a vineyard. (Com): Blaignan. A.C. Médoc, Bordeaux. Cru Bourgeois.

Château Pontet-Clauzure (Fr) a vineyard. (Com): Saint-Émilion. A.C. Saint-Émilion, Bordeaux. Grand Cru 8ha.

Château Pontet-Fumet (Fr) a vineyard in the A.C. saint-Émilion, Bordeaux. Grape varieties: Cabernet franc 21%, Cabernet sauvingnon 7%, Merlot 72%.

Château Pontoise-Cabarrus (Fr) a vineyard. (Com): St-Seurin-de-Cadourne. A.C. Médoc, Bordeaux. Cru Grand Bourgeois 18ha.

Château Pontrousset (Fr) a vineyard in the A.C. Premières Côtes de Blaye, Bordeaux.

Château Pontus (Fr) a vineyard. (Com): Fronsac. A.C. Fronsac, Bordeaux.

Château Potelle (USA) a winery based at Mount Veeder, Napa Valley, California, noted for barrel-fermented Chardonnay.

Château Potensac (Fr) a vineyard. (Add): Ordonnac, 33340 Lesparre, Médoc, Cru Grand Bourgeois. A.C. Médoc. (Com): Ordonnac. 160ha. Grape varieties: Cabernet franc, Cabernet sauvignon and Merlot. Second wine is Château Lassalle.

Château Pouget (Fr) a vineyard. (Add): Cantenac 33460 Margaux. Grand Cru Classé (4th). A.C. Margaux. (Com): Cantenac. 10ha. Grape varieties: Cabernet franc, Cabernet sauvignon and Merlot.

Château Poujeaux (Fr) a vineyard. (Add): Moulis, 33480 Castelnau. Cru Bourgeois Exceptionnel. A.C. Moulis. (Com): Moulis. 50ha. Grape varieties: Cabernet franc, Cabernet sauvignon, Merlot and Petit verdot. Second label is Salle de Poujeaux.

Château Poujeaux-Theil (Fr) see Château Poujeaux.

Château Poumey (Fr) a vineyard. (Com): Gradignan. A.C. Graves, Bordeaux. 4ha (red and white).

Château Poyanne (Fr) a vineyard. (Com): Gauriac. A.C. Côtes de Bourg, Bordeaux.

Château Pradeaux (Fr) a vineyard in the A.C. Bandol, Provence.

Château Pressac (Fr) a vineyard in the A.C. Saint-Émilion, Bordeaux 24ha.

Château Preuilhac (Fr) a vineyard. (Com): Lesparre. A.C. Médoc, Bordeaux. Cru Bourgeois. (Add): 33340 Lesparre. 26ha.

Château Priban (Fr) a vineyard. (Com): Macau. A.C. Médoc, Bordeaux. Cru Bourgeois.

Château Prieuré-Blaignan (Fr) a vineyard. (Com): Blaignan. A.C. Médoc, Bordeaux.

Château Prieuré de Bubas (Fr) a vineyard in the A.C. Corbières, south-western France. Label: Clos Bubas.

Château Prieuré-Lescours (Fr) a vineyard. (Add): Saint-Sulpice-de-Faleyrens, 33330 Saint-Émilion. Grand Cru. A.C. Saint-Émilion. (Com): Saint-Sulpice-de-Faleyrens.

Château Prieuré-les-Tours (Fr) a vineyard in the A.C. Graves. Grape varieties: Cabernet franc 10%, Cabernet sauvignon 30%, Merlot 60%.

Château Prieuré-Lichine (Fr) a vineyard. (Add): 33460 Margaux. Grand Cru Classé (4th). A.C. Margaux. (Com): Margaux. 60ha. Grape varieties: Cabernet franc, Cabernet sauvignon, Malbec, Merlot and Petit verdot. Second wine is Château de Clairefont. See also Cloitre du Château Prieuré Lichine.

Château Prost (Fr) a vineyard. (Com): Barsac. A.C. Barsac (or Sauternes), Bordeaux 8ha.

Château Puech-Haut (Fr) a 26ha vineyard based at A.C. Saint Drézery in the Coteaux du Languedoc. Grape varieties: Syrah 70%, Carignan 25% and Grenache 5%.

Château Pugnau (Fr) a vineyard. (Com): Preignac. A.C. Sauternes, Bordeaux 3ha.

Château Puy Beney (Fr) a vineyard. (Com): Mazion. A.C. Côtes de Blaye, Bordeaux.

C

Château Puy Beney Lafitte (Fr) a vineyard. (Com): Mazion. A.C. Côtes de Blaye, Bordeaux.

Château Puy-Blanquet (Fr) a vineyard. (Add): Saint-Étienne-de-Lisse, 33330 Saint-Émilion. A.C. Saint-Émilion. (Com): Saint-Étienne-de-Lisse. 120ha.

Château Puyblanquet-Carrille (Fr) a vineyard. (Add): Place du Marcardieu, 33330 Saint-Émilion. Grand Cru. A.C. Saint-Émilion. (Com): Saint-Christophe-des-Bardes. 18ha. Grape varieties: Cabernet 25% and Merlot 75%.

Château Puy-Bonnet (Fr) a vineyard. (Com): Parsac-Saint-Émilion. A.C. Saint-Émilion, Bordeaux 5ha.

Château Puycarpin (Fr) a vineyard in the Côtes de Castillon, eastern Bordeaux. A.C. Bordeaux Supérieur.

Château Puy Castéra (Fr) a vineyard. (Add): Cissac-Médoc, 33250 Pauillac. Cru Bourgeois. A.C. Haut-Médoc. (Com): Cissac. 28ha. Grape varieties: Cabernet franc, Cabernet sauvignon, Malbec and Merlot.

Château Puyfromage (Fr) a vineyard. (Com): Saint-Cibard, Côtes de Castillon, eastern Bordeaux. A.C. Bordeaux Supérieur. (Add): 33570 Saint-Cibard, Gironde.

Château Puygéraud (Fr) a 35ha vineyard in the Côtes de Francs. A.C. Bordeaux.

Château Puy la Rose (Fr) a Cru Bourgeois vineyard in the A.C. Pauillac, Médoc, Bordeaux.

Château Puy Normand (Fr) an A.C. Montagne-Saint-Émilion. (Com): Montagne-Saint-Émilion.

Château Puy-Razac (Fr) a vineyard. (Add): 33330 Saint-Émilion. Grand Cru. A.C. Saint-Émilion. (Com): Saint-Émilion. 6ha. Grape varieties: Cabernet franc 30%, Cabernet sauvignon 30% and Merlot 40%.

Château Puy-Servain (Fr) a winery based in the A.C. Bergerac. Grape varieties: Cabernet franc, Cabernet sauvignon, Merlot, Sauvignon blanc, Sémillon. Label: Cerrement (rosé).

Château Quattre (Fr) a vineyard based in Bagat en Quercy, Cahors. A.C. Cahors.

Château Quentin (Fr) a vineyard in the A.C. Saint-Émilion 35ha.

Château Quercy (Fr) a vineyard in the A.C. Saint-Émilion, Bordeaux 4ha.

Château Queyrats (Fr) a vineyard. (Com): St-Pierre-de-Mons. A.C. Graves, Bordeaux. 34ha. Also Château St. Pierre and Clos d'Uza.

Château Queyret-Pouillac (Fr) a vineyard in the A.C. Entre-Deux-Mers, central Bordeaux. Red: 42ha. 40% Merlot, 20% Cabernet sauvignon, 20% Cabernet franc. White: 18ha.

Château Queyron (Fr) a vineyard. (Com): Cérons. A.C. Cérons, Bordeaux.

Château Queyron (Fr) a vineyard. (Com): Cantois. A.C. Entre-Deux-Mers, central Bordeaux.

Château Queyron (Fr) a vineyard in the A.C. Saint-Émilion, Bordeaux 4ha.

Château Queyron-Pin-de-Fleurs (Fr) a vineyard in the A.C. Saint-Émilion, Bordeaux 4ha.

Château Quinault (Fr) a vineyard. (Com): Sables-Saint-Émilion. A.C. Saint-Émilion, Bordeaux. 12ha. Website: http://www.chateauquinault.com

Château Quinault l'Enclos (Fr) a vineyard. (Com): Saint-Émilion. A.C. Saint-Émilion, Bordeaux. Grand Cru.

Château "R" de Rieussec (Fr) the dry white wine of Château Rieussec, A.C. Sauternes, Bordeaux.

Château Raba (Fr) a vineyard. (Com): Talence, Graves. A.C. Pessac-Léognan, Bordeaux.

Château Rabat (Fr) a vineyard in the A.C. Saint-Émilion, Bordeaux 3ha.

Château Rabaud-Promis (Fr) a vineyard. (Com): Bommes. A.C. Sauternes, Bordeaux. 30ha. Premier Grand Cru Classé.

Château Rabion (Fr) a vineyard in the A.C. Saint-Émilion, Bordeaux 5ha.

Château Rahoul (Fr) a vineyard. (Add): 33640 Portets. A.C. Graves. (Com): Portets. 17.5ha. Grape varieties: Cabernet sauvignon 30%, Merlot 70% and Sémillon 100%. Second label is Petit Rahoul.

Château Ramage-la-Batisse (Fr) a vineyard. (Com): St-Sauveur. A.C. Haut-Médoc, Bordeaux. 60ha. Cru Bourgeois Supérieur. Grape varieties: Cabernet franc, Cabernet sauvignon, Merlot and Petit verdot. second label is Château Tourteran.

Château Rasclet (Fr) a vineyard. (Com): Vignonet. A.C. Saint-Émilion, Bordeaux.

Château Raspide (Fr) a vineyard. (Com): Barsac. A.C. Barsac (or Sauternes), Bordeaux 5ha.

Château Rasque (Fr) a winery (160ha) based in the A.C. Côtes de Provence, south-eastern France. (Add): 83460 Taradeau. Grape varieties include: Cinsault, Grenache, Rolle, Syrah. Produces white, rosé and red wines. Labels: Clos Jasmin, Cuvée Alexandra, Le Clos de Madame, Pièce Noble. Website: http://www.chateau-rasque.com

Château Rausan-Ségla (Fr) a vineyard. (Add): 33460 Margaux. Grand Cru Classé (2nd) A.C. Margaux. (Com): Margaux. 49ha. Grape varieties: Cabernet franc, Cabernet sauvignon, Merlot and Petit verdot. Since 1994 known as Château Rauzan-Ségla.

Château Rauzan-Gassies (Fr) a vineyard. (Add): 33460 Margaux. Grand Cru Classé (2nd). A.C. Margaux. (Com): Margaux. 35ha. Grape varieties: Cabernet franc, Cabernet sauvignon, Merlot and Petit verdot. Second wine is Enclos de Moncabon.

Château Rauzan-Ségla (Fr) the new name for Château Rausan-Ségla since 1994.

Château Rayas (Fr) a noted 14.5ha vineyard in the A.C. Châteauneuf-du-Pape, southern Rhône. Aged vines (50-70 years old) produce both red and white wines. Red: mainly Grenache plus Syrah, Cinsault. White: Grenache blanc, Clairette. Second label is Pignan. Also a Cuvée Syrah and Château de Fonsalette from Grenache, Clairette, Chardonnay, Marsanne (A.C. Côtes du Rhône).

Château Raymond-Lafon (Fr) a vineyard. (Com): Sauternes. A.C. Sauternes, Bordeaux 5ha. (Add): 33210 Sauternes.

Château Rayne-Vigneau (Fr) a vineyard. (Com):

Bommes. A.C. Sauternes, Bordeaux. 62ha. Premier Grand Cru Classé.

Château Réal Martin (Fr) a vineyard in the A.C. Côtes de Provence. (Add): 83143 Le Val. Produces red, rosé and white wines.

Château Rebeymond-Lalibard (Fr) a vineyard. (Com): Bourg. A.C. Côtes de Bourg, Bordeaux.

Château Rebeymont (Fr) a vineyard. (Com): Bourg. A.C. Côtes de Bourg, Bordeaux.

Château Rebouquet (Fr) a vineyard. (Com): Berson. A.C. Côtes de Bourg, Bordeaux.

Château Recougne (Fr) an A.C. Bordeaux-Supérieur. Grape varieties: Cabernet franc 10%, Cabernet sauvignnon 15%, Merlot 75%.

Château Redon (Fr) a vineyard. (Com): Cissac. A.C. Médoc, Bordeaux.

Château Redortier (Fr) a winery based in the A.C. Beaumes-de-Venise, Côtes-du-Rhône-Villages. (Add): 84190 Suzette. Produces red and Muscat VdN. Label: Cuvée Sébastien. 'E'mail: chateau-redortier@wanadoo.fr

Château Régent (Fr) a vineyard in the A.C. Saint-Émilion, Bordeaux 4ha.

Château Reindent (Fr) a vineyard. (Add): Saint Laurent des Combes, 33330 Saint-Émilion. A.C. Bordeaux Supérieur (red).

Château Reine-Blanche (Fr) the second wine of Château Grand-Corbin-Despagne. Grand Cru Classé. Saint-Émilion 5ha.

Château Remy (Austr) a winery (established 1963). (Add): On Sunraysia Highway, via Ballarat, Victoria. Produces both still and sparkling wines from Cabernet sauvignon, Pinot noir, Shiraz, Chardonnay, Sauvignon blanc, Sémillon, Noble Sémillon.

Château Renaissance (Fr) a vineyard. (Com): Saint-Sulpice-de-Faleyrens. A.C. Bordeaux. (Add): Renaissance, Saint-Sulpice-de-Faleyrens, Saint-Émilion.

Château Renard (Fr) a vineyard. (Com): St-Arche-de-Fronsac. A.C. Fronsac, Bordeaux.

Château Renouil Franquet (Fr) a vineyard. (Com): Moulis. A.C. Moulis, Bordeaux 4ha.

Château Respide (Fr) a vineyard. (Com): Langon. A.C. Graves, Bordeaux. 34ha (red and white).

Château Respide (Fr) a vineyard. (Com): St-Pierre-de-Mons. A.C. Graves, Bordeaux. 4ha (white).

Château Respide (Fr) a vineyard. (Add): 33210 Toulenne. A.C. Graves. (Com): Toulenne. 11ha. Grape varieties: Cabernet 20%, Merlot 20%, Sauvignon 30% and Sémillon 30%.

Château Rêve-d'Or (Fr) a vineyard. (Com): Pomerol. A.C. Pomerol, Bordeaux 5ha.

Château Reverdi (Fr) a vineyard. (Add): Donissan Listrac 33480. A.C. Listrac. (Com): Listrac. 8ha. Grape varieties: Cabernet sauvignon, Merlot and Petit verdot.

Château Reynard (Fr) a vineyard in the A.C. Saint-Émilion, Bordeaux 4ha.

Château Reynella (Austr) a range of red and white wines produced by the Reynella Vineyards (from Cabernet sauvignon grapes, Chardonnay, Sémillon and Shiraz) in Reynella, McClaren Vale, South Australia. Label: Basket Pressed Shiraz.

Château Reynon (Fr) a vineyard. (Com): Bequey-Cadillac. A.C. Premières Côtes de Bordeaux. (Add): 33410 Bequey-Cadillac. Grape varieties: Cabernet sauvignon 50%, Merlot 50% (red) and Sauvignon blanc (white) 37ha.

Château Reysson (Fr) a vineyard. (Com): Vertheuil. A.C. Haut-Médoc, Bordeaux. Cru Bourgeois Supérieur 46ha.

Château Ribeyrolles (Fr) an A.C. Bordeaux Supérieur. Grape varieties: Cabernet franc 20%, Cabernet sauvignnon 25%, Merlot 55%.

Château Ricadet (Fr) a vineyard. (Com): Cartelègue. A.C. Côtes de Blaye, Bordeaux.

Château Ricardelle (Fr) a vineyard based in the A.C. La Clape, Coteaux du Languedoc.

Château Richard (Fr) an organic wine-producing vineyard in the A.C Bergerac. Produces white wines from Sauvignon blanc, Sémillon and Muscadelle grapes.

Château Ricaud (Fr) a vineyard. (Com): Loupiac. A.C. Loupiac, Bordeaux 36ha.

Château Richautey le Haut (Fr) a vineyard. (Com): St-Aignan. A.C. Côtes de Fronsac, Bordeaux 2ha.

Château Richelieu (Fr) a vineyard in the A.C. Fronsac, Bordeaux. Label: La Favorite de Richelieu.

Château Richeterre (Fr) see Château la Tour-de-Mons, A.C. Haut-Médoc, Bordeaux.

Château Richodey (Fr) a vineyard. (Com): St-Aignan. A.C. Fronsac, Bordeaux 2ha.

Château Richon (Isr) a Vin Blanc d'Israel, a medium dry golden white wine produced for the USA market.

Château Richon (Isr) a Vin Rouge d'Israel. Grape variety: Alicanté, a medium-sweet red wine produced for the USA market.

Château Rider (Fr) a vineyard. (Com): Bourg. A.C. Côtes de Bourg, Bordeaux.

Château Rieussec (Fr) a Premier Grand Cru Classé. A.C. Sauternes. (Com): Fargues. 60ha. Grape varieties: Sauvignon 24%, Sémillon 75% and Muscadelle 1%. Second wine is Clos l'Abère. Owned by Rothshild. See also Château "R".

Château Rigaud (Fr) a vineyard. (Com): Puisseguin-Saint-Émilion. A.C. Saint-Émilion, Bordeaux 3ha.

Château Ripeau (Fr) a vineyard. (Add): 169 Avenue Foch, B.P. 17, 33500 Libourne. Grand Cru Classé. A.C. Saint-Émilion. (Com): Saint-Émilion. 20ha. Grape varieties: Cabernet franc 25%, Cabernet sauvignon 25% and Merlot 50%.

Château Rivallon (Fr) a vineyard in the A.C. Saint-Émilion, Bordeaux 8ha.

Château Rivereau (Fr) a vineyard. (Com): Côtes de Bourg, Bordeaux.

Château Robert (Fr) a vineyard. (Com): Pomerol. A.C. Pomerol, Bordeaux.

Château Robert Franquet (Fr) a vineyard. (Com): Moulis. A.C. Moulis, Bordeaux 4ha.

Château Robin (Fr) a vineyard. (Com): Saint-Christophe-des-Bardes. A.C. Saint-Émilion, Bordeaux 4ha.

Château Robin-des-Moines (Fr) a vineyard in the A.C. Saint-Émilion, Bordeaux 5ha.

Château Roc (Fr) a vineyard in the A.C. Saint-Émilion, Bordeaux 4ha.

Château Roc de Cambes (Fr) a 10ha. vineyard in A.C. Côtes de Bourg. Grape varieties: 55% Merlot, 20% Cabernet sauvignon, 15% Cabernet franc, 10% Malbec.

Château Roc de Cazade (Fr) an A.C. Bordeaux (white).

Château Roc-de-Puynormand (Fr) a vineyard. (Com): Parsac-Saint-Émilion. A.C. Saint-Émilion, Bordeaux 6ha.

Château Rochebelle (Fr) a vineyard. (Add): Saint Laurent des Combes, 33330 Saint-Émilion. Grand Cru. A.C. Saint-Émilion. (Com): Saint Laurent des Combes. 2.45ha. Grape varieties: Cabernet 25% and Merlot 75%.

Château Rochemorin (Fr) a vineyard. (Add): Château la Louvière, Léognan 33850. A.C. Pessac-Léognan. (Com): Léognan. 55ha. Grape varieties: Cabernet sauvignon, Merlot, Sauvignon and Sémillon.

Château Roche-Morin (Fr) a vineyard. (Com): Martillac. A.C. Graves, Bordeaux. 48ha (red and and white).

Château Rocher-Beauregard (Fr) a vineyard. (Com): Pomerol. A.C. Pomerol, Bordeaux 2ha.

Château Rocher-Bellevue-Figeac (Fr) a vineyard in the A.C. Saint-Émilion, Bordeaux 8ha.

Château Rocher-Corbin (Fr) a vineyard. (Com): Montagne-Saint-Émilion. A.C. Saint-Émilion, Bordeaux 6ha.

Château Rocher-Figeac (Fr) a vineyard. (Add): 194 Route de St-Émilion, 33500 Libourne. A.C. Saint-Émilion. (Com): Saint-Émilion. 7ha. Grape varieties: Cabernet 15% and Merlot 85%.

Château Rochet (Fr) *see* Château Lafon-Rochet (an alternative name used).

Château Rocheyron (Fr) a vineyard. (Com): Saint-Christophe-des-Bardes. A.C. Saint-Émilion, Bordeaux.

Château Roc Mignon (Fr) an A.C. Bordeaux.

Château Rocs-Marchand (Fr) a vineyard. (Com): Montagne-Saint-Émilion. A.C. Montagne-Saint-Émilion, Bordeaux 9ha.

Château Roc-St-Michel (Fr) a vineyard. (Com): Saint-Émilion. A.C. Saint-Émilion, Bordeaux 4ha.

Château Roland (Fr) a vineyard. (Com): Pauillac. A.C. Pauillac, Bordeaux 5ha.

Château Roland (Fr) a vineyard. (Com): Saint-Émilion. A.C. Saint-Émilion, Bordeaux.

Château Roland la Garde (Fr) a vineyard in the A.C. Premières Côtes de Blaye, Bordeaux. Grape varieties: Cabernet franc 20%, Merlot 80%.

Château Rol de Fombrauge (Fr) a vineyard in the A.C. Saint-Émilion, Bordeaux 4ha.

Château Rolland (Fr) a vineyard. (Com): Pauillac. A.C. Médoc, Bordeaux. Cru Bourgeois.

Château Rollan de By (Fr) a vineyard. (Com): Bégadan. A.C. Médoc, Bordeaux. Cru Bourgeois. (Add): Bégadan, 33340 Lesparre.

Château Rolland-Maillet (Fr) a vineyard. (Com): Saint-Émilion, Bordeaux. A.C. Saint-Émilion Grand Cru.

Château Romain (Alg) a red wine produced in Zaccar, northern Algeria.

Château Romanin (Fr) a vineyard. (Add): 13210 St. Rémy-de-Provence (a biodynamic vineyard). A.C. Les Baux-de-Provence.

Château Romassan (Fr) a vineyard based in the A.C. Bandol, south-eastern France. Owned by Domaine Ott. Produces red and rosé wines from the Mourvèdre grape.

Château Romefort (Fr) a vineyard. (Com): Cussac-Fort-Médoc. A.C. Haut-Médoc, Bordeaux.

Château Romer du Hayot (Fr) a vineyard. (Com): Fargues. A.C. Sauternes, Bordeaux.

Château Romer-Lafon (Fr) a vineyard. (Com): Fargues. A.C. Sauternes, Bordeaux. 15ha. Grand Cru Classé (2nd).

Château Rondillon (Fr) a vineyard. (Com): Loupiac. A.C. Loupiac, Bordeaux 12ha.

Château Roquebrune (Fr) a vineyard. (Com): Cenac. A.C. Premières Côtes de Bordeaux. (Add): 33360 Cenac. Grape varieties: Cabernet franc 33%, Cabernet sauvignon 33% and Merlot 33%.

Château Roquefort (Fr) a vineyard. (Com): Haux. A.C. Premières Côtes de Bordeaux. (Add): 33550 Haux. Grape varieties: Cabernet 60%, Malbec 20% and Merlot 20%.

Château Roquegrave (Fr) a vineyard. (Add): Villeneuve Valeyrac 33340. A.C. Médoc. (Com): Valeyrac. 36ha. Grape varieties: Cabernet 70% and Merlot 30%.

Château Roquetaillade (Fr) a vineyard. (Com): Mazères. A.C. Graves, Bordeaux. 3ha (white).

Château Roquetaillade la Grange (Fr) a vineyard. (Add): Mazères, 33210 Langon. A.C. Graves. (Com): Mazères. 36ha. Grape varieties: Cabernet franc, Cabernet sauvignon, Malbec, Merlot, Petit verdot, Sauvignon and Sémillon.

Château Rosario (Fr) a vineyard. (Com): Eyzines. A.C. Graves, Bordeaux. 1ha (white).

Château Rose de Pont (Fr) a vineyard in the A.C. Médoc, Bordeaux.

Château Rose-la-Riche (Fr) a vineyard. (Com): Macau. A.C. Médoc, Bordeaux. Cru Bourgeois.

Château Rosemont (Fr) a vineyard. (Com): Labarde. A.C. Médoc, Bordeaux.

Château Rose Ste-Croix (Fr) a vineyard. (Com): Listrac. A.C. Listrac, Bordeaux 6ha.

Château Rosevale Winery (Austr) a winery based near Tanunda, Barossa Valley, South Australia. Produces varietal wines. Also in Gomersal, Barossa Valley.

Château Rostang-Haut-Carré (Fr) a vineyard. (Com): Talence. 4ha (red and white).

Château Roubinet (Fr) a vineyard. (Com): Pujols. A.C. Graves, Bordeaux. 8ha (white).

Château Roucheyron (Fr) a vineyard in the A.C. Saint-Émilion, Bordeaux 6ha.

Château Roudier (Fr) a vineyard. (Add): Château Balestard la Tonnelle, 33330 Saint-Émilion. A.C.

C

Montagne-Saint-Émilion. (Com): Montagne-Saint-Émilion 30ha.

Château Roudier (Fr) a vineyard. (Com): Montagne-Saint-Émilion. A.C. Montagne-Saint-Émilion, Bordeaux 3ha.

Château Rouet (Fr) a vineyard. (Com): Fronsac. A.C. Côtes de Fronsac, Bordeaux 3ha.

Château Rouget (Fr) a vineyard. (Com): Pomerol. A.C. Pomerol, Bordeaux 11ha.

Château Roullet (Fr) a vineyard. (Com): Fronsac. A.C. Côtes Canon-Fronsac, Bordeaux 3ha.

Château Roumieu (Fr) a vineyard. (Com): Barsac. A.C. Barsac (or Sauternes), Bordeaux. 18ha. Grape varieties: Sauvignon blanc, Sémillon, Muscadelle.

Château Roumieu-Lacoste (Fr) a vineyard. (Com): Barsac. A.C. Barsac (or Sauternes), Bordeaux 5ha.

Château Rouques (Fr) a vineyard. (Com): Puisseguin-Saint-Émilion, Bordeaux.

Château Rousselle (Fr) a vineyard. (Com): St-Ciers-de-Canesse. A.C. Côtes de Bourg, Bordeaux.

Château Rousset (Fr) a vineyard. (Com): Samonac. A.C. Côtes de Bourg, Bordeaux 25ha.

Château Roustit (Fr) a vineyard. (Com): Sainte-Croix-du-Mont. A.C. Sainte-Croix-du-Mont, Bordeaux 9ha.

Château Routas (Fr) a 45ha vineyard in A.C. Coteaux Varois. Grape varieties: Cabernet sauvignon, Chardonnay, Grenache, Rolle, Syrah, Viognier. Produces a Vin de Pays from 100% Syrah, A.C. Coteaux Varois red, Pyramus (Rolle blend), Coquelicot (60% Chardonnay, 40% Viognier grapes), Rouvière rosé.

Châteauroux (Fr) a noted wine-producing town in the Indre département, central France.

Château Royal-Médoc (Fr) the second wine of Château Cantermerle.

Château Royal Saint-Émilion (Fr) the brand name of a Co-operative in the Saint-Émilion district of eastern Bordeaux.

Château Rozier (Fr) a vineyard. (Add): Saint Laurent des Combes, 33330 Saint-Émilion. Grand Cru. A.C. Saint-Émilion. (Com): Saint Laurent des Combes. 18ha. Grape varieties: Bouchet 20%, Cabernet sauvignon 5% and Merlot 75%. Second wine is Château Monturon.

Château Rozier-Béard (Fr) a vineyard in the A.C. Saint-Émilion, Bordeaux 6ha.

Château Ruat (Fr) a vineyard. (Com): Moulis. A.C. Moulis, Bordeaux. 6ha. Second label of Château Ruat-Petit-Poujeaux.

Château Ruat-Petit-Poujeaux (Fr) a Cru Bourgeois wine of Moulis, A.C. Moulis, Bordeaux. Second label is Château Ruat.

Château Sablons (Fr) a vineyard. (Com): Montagne-Saint-Émilion. A.C. Montagne-Saint-Émilion, Bordeaux 5ha.

Château Sahuc (Fr) a vineyard. (Com): Preignac. A.C. Sauternes, Bordeaux 2ha.

Château Sahuc-Latour (Fr) a vineyard. (Com): Preignac. A.C. Sauternes, Bordeaux 4ha.

Château Saige-Fort-Manoir (Fr) a vineyard. (Com): Pessac. A.C. Pessac-Léognan, Bordeaux. 5ha (red).

Château Saint-Agraves (Fr) a vineyard. (Add): Artigues, Landiras, 33720 Podensac. A.C. Graves. (Com): Landiras. 10ha. Grape varieties: Cabernet franc, Cabernet sauvignon and Merlot.

Château Saint-Amand (Fr) a vineyard. (Com): Preignac. A.C. Sauternes, Bordeaux 7ha.

Château Saint André (Fr) the label of a Châteauneuf-du-Pape produced by a négociant in Gigondas, southern Rhône.

Château Saint-Augustin-la-Grave (Fr) a vineyard. (Com): Martillac. A.C. Graves, Bordeaux.

Château Saint Auriol (Fr) a vineyard in the A.C. Corbières. (Add): Saint-Auriol SA, Gaujac, BP 79, 11204 Lézignan-Corbières.

Château Saint-Bonnet (Fr) a vineyard. (Com): Saint-Christoly. A.C. Médoc, Bordeaux. Cru Bourgeois. 30ha. Second label is Du Moulin.

Château Saint-Christoly (Fr) a vineyard. (Add): Le Bourg, Saint-Christoly-de-Médoc A.C. Médoc. (Com): Saint-Christoly-de-Médoc. Grape varieties: Cabernet 65% and Merlot 35%. 4ha.

Château Sainte-Colombe (Fr) a vineyard in the A.C. Côtes de Castillon, Bordeaux. Grape varieties: Cabernet franc 20%, Cabernet sauvignon 10%, Merlot 70%.

Château Saint Cosme (Fr) a vineyard in the A.C. Côtes-du-Rhône. Grape varieties: Clairette, Grenache, Syrah.

Château Saint-Cyrgues (Fr) a domaine in the A.C. Costières de Nîmes, Languedoc-Roussillon. Noted for red wines made from Syrah grapes.

Château Sainte Catherine (Fr) a vineyard. (Add): Chemin de la Chapelle Sainte Catherine, B.P. 2, 33550 Paillet. 22ha. Produce A.C. Premières Côtes de Bordeaux (red and sweet white), A.C. Bordeaux (rosé and white), Cadillac, Crémant de Bordeaux (white and rosé).

Château Sainte Roseline (Fr) a vineyard in the A.C. Côtes de Provence. (Add): 83460 Les Arcs-sur-Argens.

Château Saint-Estèphe (Fr) a vineyard. (Add): Leyssac, Saint-Estèphe 33250. A.C. Saint-Estèphe. (Com): Saint-Estèphe. 12ha. Grape varieties: Cabernet franc, Cabernet sauvignon, Merlot and Petit verdot.

Château Saint Estève d'Uchaux (Fr) a vineyard in the A.C. Côtes du Rhône, south-eastern France. (Add): Uchaux-F-84100 Orange.

Château Saint Eulalie (Fr) a vineyard in the A.C. Minervois la Livinière. Label Cuvée Cantilène.

Château Saint-Florin (Fr) a vineyard at Soussac, Gironde. A.C. Entre-Deux-Mers.

Château Saint Galier (Fr) a vineyard in Graves, Bordeaux. A.C. Graves (red and white).

Château Saint Georges [Côte Pavie] (Fr) a vineyard. (Add): 33330 Saint-Émilion. Grand Cru Classé. A.C. Saint-Émilion. (Com): Saint-Émilion. 5.48ha. Grape varieties: Bouchet 33%, Cabernet sauvignon 33% and Merlot 33%.

Château Saint Jacques (Fr) a vineyard. (Add): Annexe au Château Siran, Labarde, 33460 Margaux. A.C. Bordeaux Supérieur. (Com):

C

Labarde-Médoc. 10ha. Grape varieties: Cabernet franc, Cabernet sauvignon, Merlot and Petit verdot.

Château Saint-Jean (Fr) an A.C. Bordeaux Supérieur. (Add): Saint-Médard de Guizières, Gironde.

Château Saint Jean (USA) a (55ha) winery of Kenwood, Sonoma, California. Grape varieties: Cabernet sauvignon, Chardonnay, Gewürztraminer, Johannisberg riesling, Malbec. Produces varietal, sparkling and late-harvest wines. Label: Cinq Cépages. Part of the Beringer-Blass Group now owned by Mildara Blass. *see* Domaine Beringer Blass.

Château Saint-Julien (Fr) an A.C. Médoc. Second wine of Château Lagrange. Grand Cru Classé (3rd). A.C. Saint-Julien. 3ha.

Château Saint Martin de la Garrique (Fr) (Fr) a vineyard based in the A.C. Grès de Montpellier, Coteaux du Languedoc. Label: Bronzinelle.

Château Saint-Paul (Fr) a vineyard. (Com): St-Seurin-de-Cadourne. A.C. Haut-Médoc, Bordeaux. Cru Bourgeois. (Add): St-Seurin-de-Cadourne, 33250 Pauillac. 19ha.

Château Saint Pierre (Fr) a vineyard. (Add): 33250 Saint-Julien, Beychevelle. Grand Cru Classé (4th). A.C. Saint-Julien. (Com): Saint-Julien. 20ha. Grape varieties: Cabernet franc 5%, Cabernet sauvignon 70% and Merlot 25%.

Château Saint-Pierre-Bontemps (Fr) *see* Château Saint Pierre.

Château Saint-Pierre-Sevaistre (Fr) *see* Château Saint Pierre.

Château Saint-Roch (Fr) a red Châteauneuf-du-Pape produced by Verda (Antoine) 30150 Roquemaure, southern Rhône. Labels include Cuvée Princes d'Orange.

Château Saint-Roch (Fr) a vineyard in the A.C. Lirac, southern Rhône.

Château Saint-Saturnin (Fr) a vineyard. (Com): Bégadan. A.C. Médoc, Bordeaux. Cru Bourgeois. (Add): Bégadan, 33340 Lesparre. 8ha.

Château Saint-Seurin (Fr) an A.C. Haut-Médoc. Cru Bourgeois.

Château Saint Sorlin (Fr) a Cognac producer. (Add): Saint Sorlin de Cognac, 17150 Mirambeau. 36 ha. in the Fins Bois. Produces a range of Cognacs.

Château-Salins (Fr) a wine town in Alsace. (Ger) = Salzburg.

Château Samion (Fr) a vineyard. (Com): Saint-Georges-Saint-Émilion. A.C. Saint-Émilion, Bordeaux 9ha.

Château Sansonnet (Fr) a vineyard. (Add): 33330 Saint-Émilion. A.C. Saint-Émilion Grand Cru. (Com): Saint-Émilion. 8ha. Grape varieties: Cabernet franc 20%, Cabernet sauvignon 10% and Merlot 70%.

Château Saransot-Dupré (Fr) a vineyard. (Add): Listrac-Médoc 33480. Cru Bourgeois. A.C. Listrac. (Com): Listrac. 40ha. Grape varieties: Cabernet sauvignon 60% and Merlot 40%.

Château Sauman (Fr) a vineyard in the A.C. Côtes de Bourg, Bordeaux.

Château Saupiquet (Fr) a vineyard in the A.C. Saint-Émilion, Bordeaux 1ha.

Château Sauterne (USA) a sweet white wine made from Sauvignon blanc, Sémillon and Muscadelle grapes in California.

Château Sauternes (Fr) the original name for Château Filhot until 1901.

Château Sauvage (Fr) a vineyard in Haux-Langoiran, Bordeaux. A.C. Premières Côtes de Bordeaux. Grape varieties: 60% Merlot, 30% Cabernet sauvignon, 10% Cabernet franc.

Château Sauvenelle (Fr) a vineyard. (Add): Route de St-Émilion, 33500 Libourne. A.C. Saint-Émilion. (Com): Libourne. 70ha. Grape varieties: Cabernet franc, Cabernet sauvignon and Merlot.

Château Ségonnes (Fr) the second label of Château Lascombes. Grape varieties: 65% Cabernet sauvignon, 30% Merlot, 3% Cabernet franc, 2% Petit verdot.

Château Segonzac (Fr) a vineyard. (Com): St-Genès-de-Blaye. A.C. Premières Côtes de Blaye, Bordeaux. Grape varieties: Cabernet franc 10%, Cabernet sauvignon 20%, Malbec 10%, Merlot 60%.

Château Ségur (Fr) a vineyard. (Com): Parempuyre. A.C. Haut-Médoc, Bordeaux. Cru Grand Bourgeois 30ha.

Château Ségur d'Arsac (Fr) a vineyard. (Add): 33460 Margaux. A.C. Haut-Médoc. (Com): Arsac. 260ha. Grape varieties: Cabernet franc, Cabernet sauvignon and Merlot.

Château Ségur de Cabanac (Fr) an A.C. Saint-Estèphe. Cru Bourgeois.

Château Ségur Fillon (Fr) a vineyard. (Com): Parempuyre. A.C. Haut-Médoc, Bordeaux. Cru Grand Bourgeois.

Château Semeillan-Mazeau (Fr) a vineyard. (Add): Listrac-Médoc, 33480. Cru Bourgeois. A.C. Listrac. (Com): Listrac. 12ha. Grape varieties: Cabernet sauvignon and Merlot.

Château Sénéjac (Fr) a vineyard. (Com): Le Pian. A.C. Haut-Médoc, Bordeaux. Cru Bourgeois Supérieur. 26ha. White: 100% Sémillon. Red: 60% Cabernet sauvignon, 25% Merlot, 14% Cabernet franc, 1% Petit verdot.

Château Senilhac (Fr) a vineyard. (Add): 33250 Pauillac. A.C. Haut-Médoc. (Com): Saint-Seurin-de-Cadourne. 14ha. Grape varieties: Cabernet franc, Cabernet sauvignon and Merlot.

Château Sergant (Fr) an A.C. Lalande-de-Pomerol. Bordeaux.

Château Sestignan (Fr) a vineyard. (Add): 33590 Saint Vivien-de-Médoc. Cru Bourgeois. A.C. Médoc. (Com): Jau-Dignac-Loirac. 20ha. Grape varieties: Cabernet sauvignon, Malbec, Merlot and Petit verdot.

Château Siaurac (Fr) a vineyard. (Com): Néac. A.C. Lalande de Pomerol, Bordeaux.

Château Sigalas-Rabaud (Fr) a Premier Grand Cru Classé (2nd). A.C. Sauternes. (Com): Bommes. 14ha. Grape varieties: Sauvignon 10% and Sémillon 90%.

Château Sigognac (Fr) a vineyard. (Add): 33340 Saint-Yzans-de-Médoc. Cru Bourgeois. A.C. Médoc. (Com): Saint-Yzans. 73ha. Grape

C

varieties: Cabernet franc, Cabernet sauvignon and Merlot.

Château Simard (Fr) a vineyard in the A.C. Saint-Émilion, Bordeaux 15ha.

Château Simian (Fr) a red and white Châteauneuf-du-Pape wines produced by Serguier (Yves et Fils), 84420 Piolenc, southern Rhône.

Château Simon (Fr) a vineyard. (Com): Barsac. A.C. Barsac (or Sauternes), Bordeaux 4ha.

Château Simon-Carretey (Fr) a vineyard. (Com): Barsac. A.C. Barsac (or Sauternes), Bordeaux 4ha.

Château Simone (Fr) a noted vineyard in the A.C. Palette. (Add): 13590 Meyreuil, Aix-en-Provence. Grape varieties: Clairette, Cinsault, Grenache and Mourvèdre.

Château Siran (Fr) a vineyard. (Add): 33460 Margaux. Cru Exceptionnel. A.C. Margaux. (Com): Labarde. 33ha. Grape varieties: Cabernet franc, Cabernet sauvignon, Merlot and Petit verdot. Second wine is Château Bellegarde.

Château Sissan (Fr) a vineyard in the A.C. Premières Côtes de Bordeaux, Bordeaux. Grape varieties: Cabernet franc 5%, Cabernet sauvingnon 45%, Merlot 50%.

Château Smith-Haut-Lafitte (Fr) a Grand Cru Classé. A.C. Pessac-Léognan. (Com): Martillac. 56ha. Grape varieties: Cabernet franc, Cabernet sauvignon, Merlot and Sauvignon 100%. Second wine is Hauts de Smith Haut-Lafitte. *See also* Les 5. Website: http://www.smith-haute-lafitte.com 'E'mail: f.cathiard@smith-haute-lafitte.com

Château Sociando (Fr) a vineyard. (Com): Cars. A.C. Premières Côtes de Blaye, Bordeaux.

Château Sociando-Mallet (Fr) a vineyard. (Add): 33250 Pauillac. Cru Grand Bourgeois. A.C. Haut-Médoc. (Com): Saint-Seurin-de-Cadourne. 30ha. Grape varieties: Cabernet franc 10%, Cabernet sauvignon 60% and Merlot 30%. Second wine is Château Lartigue de Brochon.

Château Soleil (Fr) a vineyard. (Com): Puisseguin-Saint-Émilion. A.C. Puisseguin-Saint-Émilion, Bordeaux 5ha.

Château Solon (Fr) a vineyard. (Com): Preignac. A.C. Sauternes, Bordeaux 4ha.

Château Soucarde (Fr) a vineyard. (Com): St-Seurin-de-Bourg. A.C. Côtes de Bourg, Bordeaux.

Château Soudars (Fr) a vineyard. (Add): 33250 Pauillac. Cru Bourgeois. A.C. Haut-Médoc. (Com): Saint-Seurin-de-Cadourne. 14ha. Grape varieties: Cabernet sauvignon 65% and Merlot 35%. Second wine is Marquis de Cadourne.

Château Soutard (Fr) a vineyard. (Add): 33330 Saint-Émilion. Grand Cru Classé. Saint-Émilion. (Com): Saint-Émilion. 28ha. Grape varieties: Cabernet franc 40% and Merlot 60%. Second wine is Clos la Tonnelle.

Château Soutard-Cadet (Fr) a vineyard in the A.C. Saint-Émilion, Bordeaux 3ha.

Château Souverain (USA) a winery based in Alexander Valley, Sonoma County, California. Produces a variety of grape varieties. Is a part of the Beringer Group (owned by Wine World Inc, a part of Nestlé). Now owned by Mildara Blass. *see* Domaine Beringer Blass.

Château Spook (Eng) the brand-name of a special bottled cider.

Château St. Ahon (Fr) a vineyard. (Com): Blanquefort. A.C. Médoc, Bordeaux. Cru Bourgeois.

Château St. Amand (Fr) a vineyard in the A.C. Sauternes, Bordeaux.

Château St-André (Fr) a vineyard. (Com): Saint-Georges-Saint-Émilion. A.C. Saint-Émilion, Bordeaux.

Château St-Antoine (Fr) an A.C. Bordeaux (red).

Château St. Bonnet (Fr) a vineyard in the A.C. Médoc, Bordeaux.

Château St-Christophe (Fr) a vineyard in the A.C. Saint-Émilion, Bordeaux 7ha.

Château St. Didier-Parnac (Fr) a vineyard in the A.C. Cahors, south-western France.

Château Ste. Anne (Fr) a vineyard in the A.C. Bandol, Provence.

Château Ste-Anne (Fr) a vineyard. (Com): St-Christoly. A.C. Médoc, Bordeaux 4ha.

Château Ste. Chapelle (USA) a winery based near Caldwell, Idaho. 60ha. Produces varietal wines.

Château Ste. Michelle (USA) a large winery in Washington, Pacific North-West. 1,280ha. Grape varieties: Cabernet sauvignon, Merlot, Chardonnay, Gewürztraminer, Riesling and Syrah. Produces varietal wines.

Château St. Georges (Fr) a vineyard in the A.C. Côtes du Rhône, south-eastern France.

Château St-Georges (Fr) a vineyard. (Com): Saint-Georges-de-Montagne. A.C. Saint-Émilion, Bordeaux. (Add): 33570 Lussac.

Château St-Georges (Fr) a vineyard. (Com): Saint-Georges-Saint-Émilion. A.C. Saint-Émilion, Bordeaux 35ha.

Château St-Georges-Macquin (Fr) a vineyard. (Com): Saint-Georges-Saint-Émilion. A.C. Saint-Émilion, Bordeaux. 17ha. Is part of Domaine de Maisonneuve.

Château St-Germain (Fr) a vineyard. (Com): Berson. A.C. Côtes de Blaye, Bordeaux.

Château St-Germain (Fr) a vineyard. (Com): Saint-Germain-d'Esteuil. A.C. Médoc, Bordeaux 2ha.

Château St-Gérôme (Fr) a vineyard. (Com): Ayguemortes. A.C. Graves, Bordeaux. 4ha (red and white).

Château St. Haon (Fr) a vineyard. (Com): Blanquefort. A.C. Haut-Médoc, Bordeaux 13ha.

Château St-Hubert (Fr) a vineyard. (Com): Saint-Émilion. A.C. Saint-Émilion, Bordeaux. Grand Cru. (Add): 33330 Saint-Émilion.

Château St-Jacques-Calon (Fr) a vineyard. (Com): Montagne-Saint-Émilion. A.C. Montagne-Saint-Émilion, Bordeaux 6ha.

Château St. Jean (USA) *see* Château Saint Jean. Vineyards Belle Terre and Rancho Alta Vista.

Château St-Julien (Fr) a vineyard. (Com): Saint-Julien. A.C. Médoc, Bordeaux.

Château St-Lô (Fr) a vineyard in the A.C. Saint-Émilion, Bordeaux 8ha.

Château St-Louis (Fr) a vineyard. (Com): Saint-Georges-Saint-Émilion. A.C. Saint-Émilion, Bordeaux 4ha.

Château St-Marc (Fr) a vineyard. (Com): Barsac. A.C. Barsac (or Sauternes), Bordeaux. 6ha. Also Château Hourmalas.

Château St-Martial (Fr) a vineyard in the A.C. Saint-Émilion, Bordeaux 2ha.

Château St-Martin (Fr) a vineyard. (Com): Listrac. A.C. Listrac, Bordeaux 2ha.

Château St-Michel (Fr) a vineyard. (Com): Barsac. A.C. Barsac (or Sauternes), Bordeaux 1ha.

Château St-Michel (Fr) a vineyard. (Com): Montagne-Saint-Émilion. A.C. Saint-Émilion, Bordeaux 2ha.

Château St. Patrice (Fr) a vineyard in the A.C. Châteauneuf-du-Pape, southern Rhône.

Château St-Paul (Fr) a vineyard. (Com): Montagne-Saint-Émilion. A.C. Montagne-Saint-Émilion, Bordeaux 5ha.

Château St. Pey (Fr) a vineyard. (Com): Saint-Émilion. A.C. Saint-Émilion, Bordeaux. Grand Cru 9ha.

Château St. Pierre (Fr) an A.C. Côtes du Roussillon (red wine).

Château St. Pierre (Fr) a vineyard. (Com): St-Pierre-de-Mons. A.C. Graves, Bordeaux. 34ha (white). Also Château Queyrats and Clos d'Aza.

Château St. Pierre (Fr) a vineyard. (Com): Montagne-Saint-Émilion. A.C. Montagne-Saint-Émilion, Bordeaux.

Château St-Pierre-de-Pomerol (Fr) a vineyard. (Com): Pomerol. A.C. Pomerol, Bordeaux.

Château St-Roch (Fr) a vineyard in the A.C. Saint-Émilion, Bordeaux 3ha.

Château St. Roch (Fr) a vineyard. (Com): Saint-Estèphe. A.C. Médoc, Bordeaux. Cru Bourgeois.

Château St-Seurin (Fr) a vineyard in the A.C. Haut-Médoc, Bordeaux.

Château Suau (Fr) a vineyard. (Com): Barsac. A.C. Barsac (or Sauternes), Bordeaux. 7ha. Grand Cru Classé (2nd).

Château Suau (Fr) a vineyard in Capian, A.C. Premières Côtes de Bordeaux (oak matured).

Château Suduiraut (Fr) a Grand Cru Classé. A.C. Sauternes. (Com): Preignac. 72ha. Grape varieties: Sauvignon 15% and Sémillon 85%. *See also* S. de Suduiraut. Website: http://www.suduiraut.com

Château Sylvain (Fr) a vineyard. (Com): Cérons. A.C. Cérons, Bordeaux 3ha.

Château Taffard-de-Blaignan (Fr) *see* Château Blaignan.

Château Tahbilk (Austr) a winery. (Add): Tahbilk, Victoria 3607. 75ha. Grape varieties: Cabernet sauvignon, Chardonnay, Chenin blanc Marsanne, Rhine riesling, Sauvignon blanc, Sémillon and Shiraz.

Château Taillefer (Fr) a vineyard. (Com): Pomerol. A.C. Pomerol, Bordeaux 18ha.

Château Talbot (Fr) a vineyard. (Add): Saint-Julien, Beychevelle 33250. Grand Cru Classé (4th). A.C. Saint-Julien. (Com): Saint-Julien. 85ha. Grape varieties: Cabernet franc, Cabernet sauvignon, Merlot and Petit verdot. *See also* Connetable Talbot.

Château Tanesse (Fr) a vineyard based in central Bordeaux owned by the négociant-éleveurs Cordier. Produces fine wines from Cabernet sauvignon, Sauvignon blanc, Sémillon and Muscadelle grapes.

Château Tanunda (Austr) a winery in the Barossa Valley, South Australia. Produces mainly varietal wines. Noted for Shiraz Filsell (oak matured for 2 years)

Château Tariquet (Fr) an A.C. Armagnac produced near Eauze, Bas Armagnac. Grape varieties: Baco, Folle blanche, Ugni blanc.

Château Tarreyre (Fr) a vineyard in the A.C. Saint-Émilion, Bordeaux 2ha.

Château Tasta (Fr) a vineyard. (Com): Saint-Aignan. A.C. Fronsac, Bordeaux.

Château Taureau (Fr) a vineyard. (Com): Lussac-Saint-Émilion. A.C. Saint-Émilion, Bordeaux 3ha.

Château Tauzinat (Fr) a vineyard in the A.C. Saint-Émilion, Bordeaux 3ha.

Château Tauzinat L'Hermitage (Fr) a vineyard. (Add): Saint-Christophe-des-Bardes, 33330 Saint-Émilion. A.C. Saint-Émilion. (Com): Saint-Christophe-des-Bardes. 12.5ha. Grape varieties: Cabernet franc 40% and Merlot 60%.

Château Tayac (Fr) a vineyard. (Com): Bayon. A.C. Côtes de Bourg, Bordeaux.

Château Tayac (Fr) a vineyard. (Add): Tayac, Soussans 33460 Margaux. Cru Bourgeois. A.C. Margaux. (Com): Soussans. 37ha. Grape varieties: Cabernet franc, Cabernet sauvignon, Merlot and Petit verdot.

Château Teillac (Fr) a vineyard. (Com): Puisseguin-Saint-Émilion. A.C. Puisseguin-Saint-Émilion, Bordeaux 7ha.

Château Templiers (Fr) a vineyard. (Com): Lalande de Pomerol. A.C. Lalande de Pomerol, Bordeaux.

Château Terfort (Fr) a vineyard. (Com): Sainte-Croix-du-Mont. A.C. Sainte-Croix-du-Mont, Bordeaux 3ha.

Château Terrefort (Fr) a vineyard. (Com): Loupiac. A.C. Loupiac, Bordeaux 8ha.

Château Terrefort-Quancard (Fr) a vineyard. (Com): St-André de Cubzac. A.C. Bordeaux.

Château Terre-Noble (Fr) a vineyard. (Com): Barsac. A.C. Barsac (or Sauternes), Bordeaux 2ha. Also Château Fleury.

Château Terre Noble (Fr) a vineyard. (Com): Barsac. A.C. Barsac (or Sauternes), Bordeaux. 9ha. Also Château Montjou.

Château Terre Rouge (Fr) a vineyard in the A.C. Médoc, Bordeaux.

Château Terrey-Gros-Caillou (Fr) a vineyard. (Add): Saint-Julien-Beychevelle, 33250. Cru Bourgeois. A.C. Saint-Julien. (Com): Saint-Julien. 14ha. Grape varieties: Cabernet 65%, Merlot 30% and Petit verdot 5%.

Château Terrien (Fr) a vineyard. (Com): Lussac-Saint-Émilion. A.C. Saint-Émilion, Bordeaux 3ha.

Château Terrier Bergerac (Fr) a vineyard in the A.C. Bergerac, south-western France (red).

Château Tessendey (Fr) a vineyard in the A.C. Côtes de Fronsac, Bordeaux.

Château Tetre Daugay (Fr) a vineyard. (Add): 33330 Saint-Émilion. Grand Cru (demoted 2006). A.C. Saint-Émilion. (Com): Saint-Émilion. 18ha. Grape varieties: Cabernet franc 30%, Cabernet sauvignon 10% and Merlot 60%. Second wine is Château de Roquefort.

Château Tetre-de-la-Mouleyre (Fr) a vineyard. (Com): Parsac-Saint-Émilion. A.C. Saint-Émilion, Bordeaux 2ha.

Château Tetre Roteboeuf (Fr) a vineyard. (Com): Saint-Émilion. A.C. Saint-Émilion, Bordeaux. (Add): 33330 Saint-Émilion.

Château Teynac (Fr) a vineyard. (Com): Saint-Julien. A.C. Saint-Julien, Bordeaux 5ha.

Château Teynac [Clos St-Julien] (Fr) a vineyard. (Com): Saint-Julien. A.C. Saint-Julien, Bordeaux 4ha.

Château Teyssier (Fr) a Grand Cru vineyard. (Com): Puisseguin-Saint-Émilion. A.C. Pusseguin-Saint-Émilion, Bordeaux 28ha.

Château Teyssier (Fr) a vineyard. (Add): Vignonet, 33330 Saint-Émilion. Grand Cru. A.C. Saint-Émilion. (Com): Vignonet. 18ha. Grape varieties: Cabernet 35%, Merlot 60% and Petit verdot 5%.

Château Thibaut (Fr) a vineyard. (Com): Fargues. A.C. Sauternes, Bordeaux 2ha.

Château Thibéaud Maillet (Fr) a vineyard. (Com): Pomerol. A.C. Pomerol, Bordeaux 2ha.

Château Thieuley (Fr) an A.C. Entre-Deux-Mers and A.C. Bordeaux Supérieur (48ha red and white). A.C. Bordeaux Blanc Sec (Grape varieties: Savignon blanc 80%, Sémillon 20%).

Château Thivin (Fr) a vineyard (19.5ha) in the A.C. Côte de Brouilly Cru Beaujolais-Villages, Burgundy. Label: La Capelle.

Château Thomé-Brousterot (Fr) a vineyard. (Com): Illats. A.C. Cérons, Bordeaux 8ha.

Château Timberlay (Fr) a vineyard. (Com): Saint-André-de-Cubzac, Gironde. A.C. Bordeaux (red and white wines).

Château Timberlay (Fr) a Grand Cru vineyard in the A.C. Saint-Émilion.

Château Tiregand (Fr) a vineyard in the A.C. Pécharmant, Bergerac, south-western France. 30ha (red).

Château Toinet Fombrauge (Fr) a vineyard in the A.C. Saint-Émilion, Bordeaux 8ha.

Château Tonneret (Fr) a vineyard in the A.C. Saint-Émilion, Bordeaux 2ha.

Château Toudenac (Fr) an A.C. Bordeaux (white).

Château Touilla (Fr) a vineyard. (Com): Fargues. A.C. Sauternes, Bordeaux 3ha.

Château Toulifant (Fr) part of Château Taillefer, A.C. Pomerol, Bordeaux.

Château Toumalin (Fr) a vineyard in the A.C. Canon-Fronsac, Bordeaux.

Château Toumilon (Fr) a vineyard. (Add): Saint Pierre-de-Mons 33210 Langon. A.C. Graves. (Com): Saint Pierre-de-Mons. 13ha. Grape varieties: Cabernet franc 30%, Cabernet sauvignon 35%, Merlot 35%, Sauvignon 40% and Sémillon 60%.

Château Tourans (Fr) a vineyard. (Com): Saint-Étienne-de-Lisse. A.C. Saint-Émilion, Bordeaux.

Château Tour Blanche (Fr) a vineyard. (Add): Saint-Christophe-des-Bardes, 33330 Saint-Émilion. Grand Cru. A.C. Saint-Émilion. (Com): Saint-Christophe-des-Bardes. 12ha. Grape varieties: Cabernet 30% and Merlot 70%.

Château Tour Carelot (Fr) a vineyard. (Com): Avensan. A.C. Haut-Médoc, Bordeaux. Cru Bourgeois. (Add): Avensan, 33480 Castelnau-de-Médoc.

Château Tour-Coutely-Saint Louis (Fr) a vineyard. (Add): Leyssac, Saint-Estèphe 33250. A.C. Saint-Estèphe. (Com): Saint-Estèphe. 5ha. Grape varieties: Cabernet franc 10%, Cabernet sauvignon 50%, Malbec 5%, Merlot 30% and Petit verdot 5%.

Château Tour de Bardes (Fr) a vineyard. (Add): Saint Laurent des Bardes, 33330 Saint-Émilion. A.C. Saint-Émilion. (Com): Saint Laurent des Bardes. The second wine of Clos Labarde.

Château Tour de Capet (Fr) an A.C. Saint-Émilion. The second wine of Château Capet-Guillier. Grand Cru Saint-Émilion.

Château Tour de Grenet (Fr) a vineyard. (Add): Lussac-Saint-Émilion. 33330 Saint-Émilion. A.C. Lussac-Saint-Émilion. (Com): Lussac-Saint-Émilion. Website: http://www.vignobles-brunot.fr 'E'mail: vignobles-brunot@wanadoo.fr

Château Tour de Mirambeau (Fr) an A.C. Bordeaux. Grape varieties: Cabernet sauvingnon 20%, Merlot 80%.

Château Tour de Pressac (Fr) a vineyard. (Add): Saint-Étienne-de-Lisse, 33330 Saint-Émilion. A.C. Saint-Émilion. (Com): Saint-Étienne-de-Lisse. The second wine of Château de Pressac.

Château Tour des Combes (Fr) a vineyard. (Add): Saint Laurent des Combes, 33330 Saint-Émilion. Grand Cru. A.C. Saint-Émilion. (Com): Saint Laurent des Combes. 17ha. Grape varieties: Cabernet franc 15%, Cabernet sauvignon 15% and Merlot 70%.

Château Tour des Gendres (Fr) a vineyard in the Bergerac region. A.C. Bergerac. Grape varieties: Sémillon and Sauvignon blanc. Produces Cuvée des Conti.

Château Tour des Termes (Fr) a vineyard. (Add): Saint Codian, Saint-Estèphe 33250 A.C. Saint-Estèphe. (Com): Saint-Estèphe. 30ha. Grape varieties: Cabernet franc, Cabernet sauvignon, Merlot and Petit verdot.

Château Tour du Haut-Moulin (Fr) a vineyard. (Add): Cussac-Fort-Médoc 33460. Cru Bourgeois Supérieur. A.C. Haut-Médoc. (Com): Cussac-Fort-Médoc. Grape varieties: Cabernet sauvignon, Merlot and Petit verdot.

Château Tour du Mirail (Fr) a vineyard. (Add): 33250 Pauillac. Cru Bourgeois. A.C. Haut-Médoc. (Com): Cussac. Grape varieties: Malbec, Merlot and Petit verdot. Second label is De Martigny.

Château Tour du-Pas-St-Georges (Fr) a vineyard. (Add): Saint-Georges-Saint-Émilion. 33330 Saint-Émilion. A.C. Saint-Georges-Saint-Émilion. (Com): Saint-Georges-Saint-Émilion 15ha.

C

Château Tour du Roc (Fr) a vineyard. (Add): Arcins, 33460 Margaux. Cru Bourgeois. A.C. Haut-Médoc. (Com): Arcins. 14ha. Grape varieties: Cabernet sauvignon 50% and Merlot 50%.

Château Tour Fortin (Fr) a vineyard. (Com): Saint-Émilion. A.C. Saint-Émilion, Bordeaux. (Add): 33330 Saint-Émilion.

Château-Tour-Grand-Faurie (Fr) a vineyard. (Add): 33330 Saint-Émilion. A.C. Saint-Émilion. (Com): Saint-Émilion. 11ha. Grape varieties: Bouchet 20%, Cabernet sauvignon 5%, Malbec 5% and Merlot 70%.

Château Tour Grand Mayne (Fr) a vineyard in the A.C. Côtes de Castillon, eastern Bordeaux.

Château Tour Granins (Fr) a vineyard. (Com): Moulis. A.C. Moulis, Bordeaux. Cru Bourgeois. (Add): Moulis 33480, Castelnau-de-Médoc.

Château Haut-Canessen (Fr) a 17ha. vineyard in the Médoc. A.C. Médoc, Bordeaux. Cru Bourgeois.

Château Tour Musset (Fr) a vineyard. (Add): Montagne-Saint-Émilion, 33330 Saint-Émilion. A.C. Montagne-Saint-Émilion. (Com): Montagne-Saint-Émilion.

Château Tournefeuille (Fr) a vineyard. (Com): Néac. A.C. Lalande de Pomerol, Bordeaux.

Château Tour Prignac (Fr) a vineyard. (Com): Prignac. A.C. Médoc, Bordeaux. Cru Bourgeois. (Add): Prignac-en-Médoc, 33340 Lesparre. Grape varieties: Cabernet sauvignon 47%, Malbec 4%, Merlot 49%.

Château Tour Renaissance (Fr) a vineyard. (Add): Saint-Sulpice-de-Faleyrens, 33330 Saint-Émilion. Grand Cru. A.C. Saint-Émilion. (Com): Saint-Sulpice-de-Faleyrens. 35ha. Grape varieties: Cabernet franc 20%, Cabernet sauvignon 10% and Merlot 70%.

Château Tour Saint Christophe (Fr) a vineyard. (Add): Saint-Christophe-des-Bardes, 33330 Saint-Émilion. Grand Cru. A.C. Saint-Émilion. (Com): Saint-Christophe-des-Bardes. 20ha. Grape varieties: Cabernet franc, Cabernet sauvignon and Merlot 66%.

Château Tour Saint-Pierre (Fr) a vineyard. (Add): 33330 Saint-Émilion. Grand Cru. A.C. Saint-Émilion. (Com): Saint-Émilion. 10ha. Grape varieties: Cabernet franc 10%, Cabernet sauvignon 10% and Merlot 80%.

Château Tourteau-Chollet-Lafitte (Fr) a vineyard. (Com): Arbanats. A.C. Graves, Bordeaux. 13ha (red and white).

Château Tourteran (Fr) a vineyard. (Com): St-Sauveur. A.C. Médoc, Bordeaux. Cru Bourgeois. Second wine of Château Ramage-La-Batisse.

Château Toutigeac (Fr) an A.C. Bordeaux Rouge.

Château Touzinat (Fr) a vineyard in the A.C. Saint-Émilion, Bordeaux 7ha.

Château Tramont (Fr) a vineyard. (Com): Arcins. A.C. Haut-Médoc, Bordeaux.

Château Trapaud (Fr) a vineyard. (Add): Saint-Étienne-de-Lisse, 33330 Saint-Émilion. Grand Cru. A.C. Saint-Émilion. (Com): Saint-Étienne-de-Lisse. 14.5ha. Grape varieties: Bouchet 30%, Cabernet sauvignon 20% and Merlot 50%.

Château Trapeau (Fr) a vineyard in the A.C. Saint-Émilion, Bordeaux 8ha.

Château Trianon (Fr) a vineyard in the Côtes-Saint-Émilion. A.C. Saint-Émilion, Bordeaux 5ha.

Château Triguedina (Fr) a vineyard in A.C. Cahors. Standard wine is produced from 70% Malbec. Prince Probus is prestige cuvée made from older vines, aged in oak barriques.

Château Trillon (Fr) a vineyard. (Com): Sauternes. A.C. Sauternes, Bordeaux. 8ha

Château Trimoulet (Fr) a vineyard. (Add): 33330 Saint-Émilion. Grand Cru. A.C. Saint-Émilion. (Com): Saint-Émilion. 17ha. Grape varieties: Cabernet franc 35%, Cabernet sauvignon 15% and Merlot 50%.

Château Trinité-Valrosé (Fr) a vineyard on the Île de Patiras in the river Gironde. A.C. Bordeaux Supérieur.

Château Trintin (Fr) part of Château Boënot in A.C. Pomerol, Bordeaux.

Château Tristant (Fr) a vineyard. (Com): Pomerol. A.C. Pomerol, Bordeaux 1ha.

Château Trocard (Fr) an A.C. Bordeaux Supérieur. A 100% Merlot wine aged in new oak casks.

Château Trois-Moulins (Fr) a vineyard. (Com): Saint-Émilion. A.C. Saint-Émilion, Bordeaux. Grand Cru 4.5ha.

Château Tronquoy-Lalande (Fr) a Cru Grand Bourgeois. A.C. Saint-Estèphe. (Com): Saint-Estèphe. 16ha. Grape varieties: Cabernet sauvignon 48%, Merlot 48% and Petit verdot 4%.

Château Troplong-Mondot (Fr) a vineyard. (Add): 33330 Saint-Émilion. Premier [B] Grand Cru Classé (promoted 2006). A.C. Saint-Émilion. (Com): Saint-Émilion. 30ha. Grape varieties: Bouchet, Cabernet sauvignon, Malbec and Merlot 70%.

Château Trotanoy (Fr) a vineyard. (Com): Pomerol. A.C. Pomerol, Bordeaux 9ha.

Château Trottevieille (Fr) a vineyard. (Add): 33330 Saint-Émilion. Premier [B] Grand Cru Classé. A.C. Saint-Émilion. (Com): Saint-Émilion. 11ha. Grape varieties: Bouchet, Cabernet and Merlot.

Château Truquet (Fr) a vineyard in the A.C. Saint-Émilion, Bordeaux 4ha.

Château Tucau (Fr) a vineyard. (Com): Barsac. A.C. Barsac (or Sauternes), Bordeaux 3ha.

Château Tuquet (Fr) a vineyard. (Com): Beautiran. A.C. Graves, Bordeaux. 26ha (red and white).

Château Turon Lanère [Dalas] (Fr) a vineyard. (Com): Loupiac. A.C. Loupiac, Bordeaux 3ha.

Château Turon Lanère [David] (Fr) a vineyard. (Com): Loupiac. A.C. Loupiac, Bordeaux 5ha.

Château Tustoc (Fr) a vineyard. (Com): Toulenne. A.C. Graves, Bordeaux. 8ha (white).

Château Tuyttens (Fr) a vineyard in the A.C. Sauternes, Bordeaux.

Château Uferic (Fr) a vineyard. (Com): Cérons. A.C. Cérons, Bordeaux 6ha.

Château Uroulat (Fr) an A.C. Jurançon wine, moelleux in style.

Château Val-Joanis (Fr) a vineyard in the V.D.Q.S.

Côtes de Luberon, south-eastern France (red, rosé and white).

Château Valley Red (N.Z) a soft, fruity, full-flavoured red wine from Nobilo's vineyard.

Château Valmont-Mayne (Fr) a vineyard. (Com): Barsac. A.C. Barsac (or Sauternes), Bordeaux 2ha.

Château Valose (Fr) an A.C. Bordeaux Supérieur (red).

Château Valoux (Fr) a vineyard. (Com): Cadaujac. A.C. Graves, Bordeaux. Cru Bourgeois. Second wine of Château Bouscaut.

Château Valrose (Fr) a vineyard in the A.C. Saint-Estephe, Haut-Médoc, Bordeaux. Label: Cuvée Alienor.

Château Vannières (Fr)) a vineyard based in A.C. Bandol, Provence.

Château Védrines (Fr) a vineyard. (Com): Barsac. A.C. Barsac (or Sauternes), Bordeaux.

Château Verdet (Fr) a vineyard. (Com): Libourne. A.C. Pomerol, Bordeaux.

Château Verdignan (Fr) a vineyard. (Add): St-Seurin-de-Cadourne, 33250 Pauillac. Cru Grand Bourgeois. A.C. Haut-Médoc. (Com): Saint-Seurin-de-Cadourne. 50ha. Grape varieties: Cabernet franc 5%, Cabernet sauvignon 50% and Merlot 45%. Second wine is Rose Maréchale.

Château Verdus et Bardis (Fr) a vineyard. (Com): St-Seurin-de-Cadourne. A.C. Haut-Médoc, Bordeaux. Cru Bourgeois. (Add): St-Seurin-de-Cadourne, 33250 Pauillac.

Château Verger (Fr) a vineyard in the A.C. Côtes de Bourg, Bordeaux.

Château Vernous (Fr) a vineyard. (Com): Lesparre. A.C. Médoc, Bordeaux 15ha.

Château Vertheuil (Fr) a vineyard. (Com): Sainte-Croix-du-Mont. A.C. Sainte-Croix-du-Mont, Bordeaux 10ha.

Château Vésinerie (Fr) a vineyard. (Com): Puisseguin-Saint-Émilion. A.C. Saint-Émilion, Bordeaux.

Château Veyrac (Fr) a vineyard. (Com): Saint-Étienne-de-Lisse. A.C. Saint-Émilion, Bordeaux 3ha.

Château Veyres (Fr) a vineyard. (Com): Preignac. A.C. Sauternes, Bordeaux 10ha.

Château Veyrin (Fr) a vineyard. (Com): Listrac. A.C. Médoc, Bordeaux. Cru Bourgeois.

Château Veyrin-Domecq (Fr) aee Château Veyrin.

Château Victoria (Fr) a vineyard. (Com): Vertheuil. A.C. Médoc, Bordeaux. Cru Bourgeois.

Château Videau (Fr) a vineyard in the A.C. Côtes de Blaye, Bordeaux.

Château Videlot (Fr) a vineyard. (Com): Libourne. A.C. Saint-Émilion, Bordeaux.

Château Vieille-Tour-la-Rose (Fr) a vineyard in the A.C. Saint-Émilion, Bordeaux 3ha.

Châteauvieux (Switz) the name of a red wine produced in Sion, Valais, western Switzerland.

Château Vieux (Arg) the brand-name of a red wine produced by Bodegas Lopez from the Cabernet sauvignon grape.

Château Vieux Blassan (Fr) an A.C. Bordeaux Supérieur.

Château Vieux Bonneau (Fr) a vineyard. (Com): Montagne-Saint-Émilion. A.C. Saint-Émilion, Bordeaux 4ha.

Château Vieux Braneyre (Fr) a vineyard. (Add): Les Gunes, Cissac-Médoc 33250 Pauillac. A.C. Haut-Médoc. (Com): Cissac. 10ha. Grape varieties: Cabernet franc, Cabernet sauvignon, Merlot and Petit verdot.

Château Vieux Cantenac (Fr) a vineyard. (Add): Cantenac, 33330 Saint-Émilion. Grand Cru. A.C. Saint-Émilion. (Com): Saint-Émilion. 5ha. Grape varieties: Bouchet, Cabernet, Merlot.

Château Vieux-Castel-Robin (Fr) a vineyard in the A.C. Saint-Émilion, Bordeaux 4ha.

Château Vieux-Ceps (Fr) a vineyard in the A.C. Saint-Émilion, Bordeaux 6ha.

Château Vieux-Château-Certan (Fr) a vineyard. (Com): Pomerol. A.C. Pomerol, Bordeaux. 13ha. Grape varieties: Cabernet franc 25%, Cabernet sauvignon 20%, Malbec 5% and Merlot 50%.

Château Vieux-Château-Landon (Fr) a vineyard. (Com): Bégadan. Bordeaux.

Château Vieux Château-St-André (Fr) a vineyard. (Add): Montagne-Saint-Émilion, 33330 Saint-Émilion. A.C. Montagne-Saint-Émilion. (Com): Montagne-Saint-Émilion.

Château Vieux Chevrol (Fr) a vineyard. (Com): Néac. A.C. Saint-Émilion, Bordeaux.

Château Vieux Clos St-Émilion (Fr) a vineyard. (Add): 33330 Saint-Émilion. Grand Cru. A.C. Saint-Émilion. (Com): Saint-Émilion. Grape varieties: Cabernet franc 25%, Cabernet sauvignon 20%, Malbec 5% and Merlot 50%.

Château Vieux Garouilh (Fr) a vineyard in the A.C. Saint-Émilion, Bordeaux 5ha.

Château Vieux Grand Faurie (Fr) a vineyard. (Add): Saint-Christophe-des-Bardes, 33330 Saint-Émilion. Grand Cru. A.C. Saint-Émilion. 10ha. Grape varieties: Cabernet franc 15%, Cabernet sauvignon 15% and Merlot 70%. Second wine is Château Champion.

Château Vieux Grenet (Fr) a vineyard in eastern Bordeaux. A.C. Bordeaux Supèrieur. Grape varieties: Cabernet sauvignon, Cabernet franc and Merlot.

Château Vieux Guadet (Fr) a vineyard. (Add): Place du Marcardieu, 33330 Saint-Émilion. Grand Cru. A.C. Saint-Émilion.

Château Vieux-Guillou (Fr) a vineyard. (Com): Saint-Georges-Saint-Émilion. A.C. Saint-Émilion, Bordeaux 4ha.

Château Vieux-Guinot (Fr) a vineyard. (Add): Saint-Étienne-de-Lisse, 33330 Saint-Émilion. Grand Cru. A.C. Saint-Émilion. (Com): Saint-Étienne-de-Lisse. 12ha. Grape varieties: Cabernet franc 45%, Cabernet sauvignon 5% and Merlot 50%.

Château Vieux-Larmande (Fr) a vineyard (Add): 33330 Saint-Émilion, Bordeaux. A.C. Saint-Émilion Grand Cru 4ha.

Château Vieux-Logis-de-Cazelon (Fr) a vineyard. (Com): Montagne-Saint-Émilion. A.C. Saint-Émilion, Bordeaux 2ha.

C

Château Vieux-Maillet (Fr) a vineyard. (Com): Pomerol. A.C. Pomerol, Bordeaux 1ha.

Château Vieux Montaiguillon (Fr) a vineyard. (Com): Saint-Georges-Saint-Émilion. A.C. Saint-Émilion, Bordeaux 3ha.

Château Vieux-Mouchet (Fr) a vineyard. (Com): Montagne-Saint-Émilion. A.C. Saint-Émilion, Bordeaux 1ha.

Château Vieux Moulin (Fr) a vineyard in the A.C. Corbières, south-western France. Label: Vox Dei

Château Vieux Moulin (Fr) a vineyard. (Com): Fronsac. A.C. Côtes de Fronsac, Bordeaux 5ha.

Château Vieux-Moulin-du-Cadet (Fr) a vineyard in the A.C. Saint-Émilion, Bordeaux 3ha.

Château Vieux-Pourret (Fr) a vineyard. (Add): 33330 Saint-Émilion. Grand Cru. A.C. Saint-Émilion. (Com): Saint-Émilion. 4.2ha. Grape varieties: Cabernet franc 25% and Merlot 75%.

Château Vieux Robin (Fr) a vineyard. (Add): Bégadan, 33340 Lesparre. Cru Bourgeois Supérieur. A.C. Médoc. (Com): Bégadan. 13ha. Grape varieties: Cabernet sauvignon 65% and Merlot 35%. Second label is Lalande Robin. Label: Bois de Lunier.

Château Vieux-Sarpe (Fr) a vineyard. (Add): 37 Rue Pline Parmentier, 33500 Libourne. Grand Cru. A.C. Saint-Émilion. (Com): Saint-Christophe-des-Bardes. 6.5ha. Grape varieties: Cabernet franc 20%, Cabernet sauvignon 10% and Merlot 70%.

Château Vignelaure (Fr) a red and rosé wine estate near Aix-en-Provence, south-eastern France. A.C. Coteaux d'Aix en Provence. Grape varieties: Cabernet sauvignon, Grenache, Syrah. Cabernet sauvignon wines are Vins de Pays des Coteaux du Verdon.

Château Vignes (Fr) a vineyard. (Com): Fronsac. A.C. Côtes de Fronsac, Bordeaux 2ha.

Château Villars (Fr) a vineyard. (Com): Saillans. A.C. Fronsac, Bordeaux. (Add): 33141 Villegouge. 12ha.

Château Villefranche (Fr) a vineyard. (Com): Barsac. A.C. Barsac (or Sauternes), Bordeaux 6ha.

Château Villegeorge (Fr) a vineyard. (Add): 33480 Castelnau de Médoc. A.C. Haut-Médoc. (Com): Avensan. 20ha. Grape varieties: Cabernet franc, Cabernet sauvignon and Merlot.

Château Villemaurine (Fr) a vineyard. (Add): B.P. N°31 au Domaine de Louiseau, 33240 Saint André de Cubzac. Grand Cru (demoted 2006). A.C. Saint-Émilion. (Com): Saint-Émilion. 8ha. Grape varieties: Cabernet 30% and Merlot 70%.

Château Villepreux (Fr) an A.C. Bordeaux Supérieur. Grape varieties: Cabernet franc 25%, Cabernet sauvingnon 25%, Merlot 50%.

Château Villerambert-Julien (Fr) a vineyard (established 1858) based in the A.C. Minervois la Livinière, Languedoc-Roussillon. Grape varieties: Carignan Grenache, Mourvèdre and Syrah.

Château Villerouge la Crémade (Fr) a vineyard in the A.C. Corbières, south-western France. Label: Evohé.

Château Vincent (Fr) a vineyard. (Com): Cantenac. A.C. Haut-Médoc, Bordeaux 1ha.

Château Vincent (Fr) a vineyard. (Com): St-Aignan. A.C. Fronsac, Bordeaux. (Add): 33126 Fronsac, Gironde. 12ha (jointly owned).

Château Vincent la Mouleyre (Fr) a vineyard. (Com): St-Aignan. A.C. Côtes Canon-Fronsac, Bordeaux 2ha.

Château Viramon (Fr) a vineyard. (Add): Saint-Étienne-de-Lisse, 33330 Saint-Émilion. Grand Cru. A.C. Saint-Émilion. 11ha. Grape varieties: Cabernet 30% and Merlot 70%.

Château Voigny (Fr) a vineyard. (Com): Preignac. A.C. Sauternes, Bordeaux. 6ha. Cru Bourgeois. Grape varieties: Sauvignon and Sémillon.

Château Vrai Canon Bouché (Fr) a vineyard in the commune Fronsac, A.C. Côtes Canon-Fronsac, Bordeaux 5ha.

Château Vrai Canon Bourret (Fr) a vineyard. (Com): Fronsac. A.C. Côtes Canon-Fronsac, Bordeaux 2ha.

Château Vrai Canon Boyer (Fr) a vineyard. (Com): St-Michel. A.C. Côtes Canon-Fronsac, Bordeaux 7ha.

Château Vraye-Croix-de-Gay (Fr) a vineyard. (Com): Pomerol. A.C. Pomerol, Bordeaux 6ha.

Château Wente (USA) a sweet white, Sauternes-style wine produced by the Wente Bros. in Livermore, California.

Château Windsor (Isr) a semi-dry, red table wine.

Château Woltner (USA) a winery based in the Howell Mountains, Saint Helena, Napa Valley, California. Produces varietal wines.

Château Xanadu (Austr) a winery. (Add): P.O. Box 99, Margaret River, Western Australia 6285. 35ha. Grape varieties: Cabernet franc, Cabernet sauvignon, Chardonnay, Sauvignon blanc and Sémillon.

Château Yaldara (Austr) a winery in the Barossa Valley, South Australia. Produces varietal wines.

Château Yarrinya Winery (Austr) a winery. (Add): Pinnade Lane, Dixons Creek, Yarra Valley, Victoria. 18ha. Grape varieties: Cabernet sauvignon, Chardonnay, Gewürztraminer, Pinot noir, Sauvignon blanc and Shiraz.

Château Yelas (N.Z) the brand-name used by Pleasant Valley Wines of Valley Road, Henderson.

Château Yerring (Austr) a winery. (Add): Melba Highway, Yerring. Grape varieties: Chardonnay, Pinot noir, Cabernet sauvignon, Merlot.

Château Yon (Fr) a vineyard. (Com): Saint-Christophe-des-Bardes. A.C. Saint-Émilion, Bordeaux.

Château Yon-Figeac (Fr) a vineyard. (Add): 33330 Saint-Émilion. Grand Cru (demoted 2006). A.C. Saint-Émilion. (Com): Saint-Émilion. 24ha. Grape varieties: Bouchet, Cabernet sauvignon and Merlot.

Château Yveline (Fr) a vineyard. (Com): Lalande de Pomerol. A.C. Lalande de Pomerol, Bordeaux.

Château Yvonne (Fr) a 6ha vineyard in commune of Parnay, Saumur-Champigny. Noted for A.C. Saumur blanc wines from Chenin blanc grapes.

Châtelain-Desjacques (Fr) the name given to an A.C. sparkling Saumur wine from the Loire.

C

Châtelaine (Fr) a female château (vineyard) owner.

Chatelaine (S.Afr) a white wine (Gewürztraminer, Riesling and Viognier blend) produced by the Altydgedacht Estate, Durbanville, Western Cape.

Châteldon (Fr) a natural sparkling mineral water from the Puy-de-Drôme. (Add): Châteldon (Puy-de-Drôme). Mineral contents (milligrammes per litre): Sodium 240mg/l, Calcium 383mg/l, Magnesium 49mg/l, Potassium 35mg/l, Bicarbonates 2075mg/l, Chlorides 7mg/l, Sulphates 20mg/l, Fluride 2mg/l, Nitrates 0mg/l. pH 6.2

Chatelots [Les] (Fr) a Premier Cru vineyard in the A.C. commune of Chambolle-Musigny, Côte de Nuits, Burgundy 2.6ha.

Châtemp (Thai) the label for a range of wines (white, rosé and red) produced by the Siam Winery, Bangtorud, Samut Sakhon.

Châtenets [Les] (Fr) a wine-producing village in the commune of Fuissé in A.C. Pouilly-Fuissé, Mâcon, Burgundy.

Chatenois (Fr) a wine town in Alsace, known in German as Kestenholz.

Chatilton (S.Afr) the label for a white wine (Chenin blanc and Sémillon blend) produced by the Hartenberg Estate winery, Northern Cape.

Châtillon-en-Diois (Fr) an A.C. region of the Rhône. Produces red, rosé and white wines from Gamay, Pinot noir, Syrah, Aligoté and Chardonnay grapes. Minimum alc by vol. (red): 11%, (white): 10%.

Châtillon-sur-Marne (Fr) a Cru Champagne village in the Canton de Châtillon-sur-Marne. District: Reims.

Châtillon-sur-Marne (Fr) a canton in the Reims district of the Champagne region. Has the Cru villages: Baslieux, Belval-sous-Châtillon, Binson-Orquigny, Champlat-Boujacourt, Châtillon-sur-Marne, Courtagnon, Cuchery, Cuisles, Jonquery, Montigny-sous-Châtillon, La Neuville-aux-Larris, Olizy-Viuolaine, Passy-Grigny, Pourcy, Reuil, Sainte-Gemme, Vandières and Villers-sous-Châtillon.

Chatjip (Kor) café.

Chaucé Gris (USA) a white grape variety grown in Santa Cruz and in Livermore, California. Also known as the Grey riesling.

Chaucer Ale (Eng) a 3.6% alc by vol. beer brewed by the Green Dragon. See also Dragon Ale, Bridge Street Bitter.

Chaudenet Gras (Fr) a lesser name for the Aligoté grape in eastern France.

Chaudfontaine (Bel) a natural spring mineral water from Thermale, Chaudfontaine. Mineral contents (milligrammes per litre): Sodium 44mg/l, Calcium 65mg/l, Magnesium 18mg/l, Potassium 2.5mg/l, Bicarbonates 305mg/l, Chlorides 35mg/l, Sulphates 40mg/l, Fluorides 0.4mg/l, Nitrates <0.1mg/l. pH 7.0

Chaudière (Fr) an onion-shaped, pot-still used in the Cognac region for distillation.

Chauffe Coeur (Fr) a 6 year old Cognac produced by Martayrol.

Chauffe Coeur Napoléon (Fr) a 10 year old Cognac produced by Martayrol.

Chaufferettes (Fr) a frost precaution used in the Burgundy region, the use of burners in the vineyards.

Chauffe-Vin (Fr) a type of holding tank (heat exchanger) used in the Cognac region.

Chaume (Fr) a vineyard in the Coteaux du Layon, Anjou-Saumur region in the Loire. Produces fine, luscious sweet (**Botrytis cinerea**) white wines from the Chenin blanc grape.

Chaumes [Les] (Fr) a Premier Cru vineyard in the A.C. commune of Vosne-Romanée, Côte de Nuits, Burgundy 7.4ha.

Chaumuzy (Fr) a Cru Champagne village in the Canton de-Ville-en-Tardenois. District: Reims.

Chautagne (Fr) a light red wine produced from the Gamay grape in the Savoie region, south-eastern France.

Chautauqua (USA) a wine region of eastern USA. A strip that follows along the south bank of Lake Erie from Buffalo west to Ohio. The Concord is the main grape variety used.

Chauvenet (Fr) a Burgundy négociant based in Nuits-Saint-Georges. Noted for Red Cap sparkling Burgundy.

Chauvet (Fr) a Champagne house. (Add): 41 Avenue de Champagne, 51150 Tours-sur-Marne. 10ha. Produces vintage and non-vintage wines. Vintages: 1971, 1973, 1976, 1979, 1982, 1985, 1989, 1990, 1992, 1995, 1996, 1998, 1999, 2000. Cuvée: Carte Vert.

Chauvet Vineyard (USA) a small vineyard based in Sonoma Valley, Sonoma County, California. Grape variety: Zinfandel.

Chavant (S.Afr) the label for a white wine (Chardonnay) produced by the Louisvale Wines winery, Stellenbosch, Western Cape.

Chave [Gérard] (Fr) a famous wine producer based in Hermitage, Rhône. Produces fine red and white Hermitage wines.

Chàvena (Port) tea cup.

Chaves (Port) a DOC wine of Trás os Montes in the north-east.

Chavey [Louis] (Fr) a winery based in the A.C. Chablis, Burgundy. Produces a range of Chablis wines including Premier Cru Vaillons.

Chavignol (Fr) a wine-producing village in A.C. Sancerre, Central Vineyards, Loire. Includes the vineyard of Les Monts Damnés.

Chavot-Courcourt (Fr) a Cru Champagne village in the Canton d'Avize. District: Épernay.

Chawan (Jap) a tea tumbler (drinking vessel).

Chay (Rus) tea.

Chazalettes and Cº. (It) noted vermouth producers based in Turin.

Chazelles [Les] (Fr) a vineyard in the A.C. commune of Montagny, Côte Chalonnaise, Burgundy.

Chéandrie (S.Afr) the label for a red wine (Chenin blanc 66% and Sémillon 34%) produced by the Lievland Estate winery, Stellenbosch, Western Cape.

Cheater (Can) a short glass that has a line marked on the side which shows ⅙ of an ounce short. It is a dishonest glass.

Cheb Brewery (Czec) a brewery based in western Czec.

Cheddar Valley (Eng) a cider produced by Thatcher's in Somerset.

Cheddar Valley Vineyards (Eng) a vineyard. (Add): Townsend Farm, Axbridge, Somerset. Planted 1974. 1.25ha.

Cheeky Pheasant (Eng) a 4.7% alc by vol. ale brewed by the George Wright Brewing C°., Merseyside.

Cheerio Cocktail (Cktl) 10mls Italian vermouth, 10mls French vermouth, 20mls dry gin, 1 tablespoon orange juice, dash orange bitters, 2 dashes absinthe. Shake over ice and strain into a cocktail glass.

Cheers (Eng) a salutation with a drink, denotes "*Good health and thank you*" (for the drink purchased for you). (Aus) = prost, (Cro) = klicanje, (Fr) = votre santé, (Ger) = prost, (It) = salute/cin-cin, (Jap) = kanpai, (Nor) = skol, (Pol) = na zdrowie, (Rus) = nazdaroye, (Scot) = slainte mhath, (Sp) = salud, (Wal) = iechyd dda.

Cheese (Eng) milled cider apples layered between a fine mesh cloth for pressing. *see* Cheese Cloth.

Cheese Cloth (Eng) a fine mesh cloth used in cider making to contain the '*cheese*' so it can be pressed to extract the juice (hence the name '*cheese*' cloth).

Cheesy (Eng) a term used to describe the characteristic element in the bouquet of an old Champagne, is caused by the presence of butyrate acid.

Chef de Cave (Fr) the head cellarman.

Chef de Culture (Fr) the vineyard foreman.

Chef du Vignoble (Fr) the head of the vineyard, chief vigneron.

Chef-Huisknecht (Hol) butler.

Chefoo (Chi) the name given to a sweet red wine, similar in style to a light, fortified wine and to a strong, aromatic white wine.

Chehalem (USA) a 29.5ha. vineyard on the Chehalem Ridge in the Willamette Valley, Oregon. Grape varieties: Chardonnay, Pinot gris, Pinot noir. Labels: Ian's Reserve, 3 Vineyard.

Cheilly-lès-Maranges (Fr) a commune in the A.C. Santenay, Côte de Beaune-Villages, Burgundy. Has the vineyards: Maranges [part], La Boutière [part], Les Maranges [part] and Les Plantes. The red wines (from the Pinot noir grape) may be sold under the Côte de Beaune-Villages label.

Cheju (S.Kor) a natural spring mineral water from Kashi-Ri, Cheju-Do. Mineral contents (milligrammes per litre): Sodium 7.18mg/l, Calcium 5.78mg/l, Magnesium 6.95mg/l, Potassium 2.8mg/l. pH 7.5

Chekov Ice (Eng) the label for a range of fruit flavour vodka-based drinks at 5.5% alc by vol. Flavours include lime, orange, watermelon, lemon.

Chehalem Vineyard (USA) a vineyard estate based in the Willamette Valley, Oregon. Grape variety: Pinot noir. Label: Rion Reserve.

Chelmer Gold (Eng) a 5% alc by vol. bottle-conditioned beer named after the river that flows past Ridleys Hartford End Brewery, Essex.

Chelmsford 800 Ale (Eng) a beer brewed by the Crouch Vale Brewery, Essex.

Chelois (USA) a red hybrid grape variety.

Chelsea Blossom (Eng) a 3.5% alc by vol. pale golden ale brewed by Orange Brewery, London to mark the Chelsea Flower Show.

Chelsea Gin (Eng) the brand-name of a dry gin produced by International Distillers and Vintners Ltd., London.

Chelsea Reach (Cktl) in a highball glass place 2 ice cubes and add 50mls vodka, 50mls orange squash and top with medium-dry cider.

Chelsea Sidecar (Cktl) ½ measure dry gin, ½ measure Cointreau, juice ¼ lemon. Shake over ice and strain into a cocktail glass.

Chelsea Sunshine (N.Z) the name given to the sugar and water solution that is added to some grape musts to increase the alcohol content.

Cheltenham (Eng) a still aperient mineral water from mid-western England.

Chemakhinsk (Rus) a major wine-producing centre in Azerbaijan.

Chemical Additives to Wines (Eng) *see* Carbon-dioxide, Gypsum, Plâtage, Phosphotage, Salage, Shellisage, Sulphur-dioxide and Tanisage.

Chemical Beer (Eng) a miss-used term for many beers, relates to the addition of minerals to waters that are mineral-deficient. The law does not allow any '*chemicals*' to be added to beers. *See also* Burtonisation and German Purity Law.

Chemilly-sur-Serein (Fr) a commune in the A.C. Chablis, Burgundy.

Chemise (Fr) the name given to the coating or deposit that collects on the inside of red wine bottles.

Chénas (Fr) a commune of the A.C. Cru Beaujolais-Villages, Burgundy. 280ha. under vines.

Chénay (Fr) a Cru Champagne village in the Canton de Fismes. District: Reims.

Chêne (Fr) oak.

Chêne (Fr) a term used to describe the oak character that wine obtains from the wooden casks.

Chenel (S.Afr) a white grape variety, a cross between the Chenin blanc and Trebbiano (Ugni blanc).

Chenet [J.P.] (Fr) a range of wines including a Cinsault rosé and a Cabernet sauvignon from the d'Oc and Côtes de Gascogne. Bottled by Les Grands Chais de France, F-67290 Petersbach.

Chénevery [Les] (Fr) a Premier Cru vineyard [part] in the A.C. commune of Morey-Saint-Denis, Côte de Nuits, Burgundy. 3.25ha.

Chénevottes [Les] (Fr) a Premier Cru vineyard [part] in the A.C. commune of Chassagne-Montrachet, Côte de Beaune, Burgundy (red and white).

Chenin Blanc (Fr) the chief white grape of the Anjou-Saumur and Touraine regions of the Loire. Makes both dry and sweet white wines with a lemon and green apple aroma and flavour when young and an apple, apricot, nuts, marzipan, straw, almond, honeysuckle, honey, wet straw aromas and flavours when old..

Chenin Blanc (USA) *see* California Chenin Blanc.

Chenin Noir (Fr) a red grape variety, also known as the Pineau d'Aunis.

Chenite (USA) a dark, rosé wine produced from the Chenin blanc and Petit syrah grapes. Produced by Cilurzo and Piconi in Temecula, California.

Chenôve (Fr) a Burgundy vineyard (1920) which used to be of 52ha. but has now been absorbed into the suburbs of Dijon (has almost disappeared).

Chenu (Fr) lit: 'the white hair of old age', a term used to denote a fine wine of old age.

Chequera Vineyard (USA) a vineyard based in the Paso Robles, San Luis Obispo County, California. Grape variety: Roussanne. Owned by the Bonny Doon Estate.

Chequer Bitter (Eng) a keg bitter 1036.5 O.G. brewed by the Davenports Brewery, Birmingham.

Chequers (Scot) a 12 year old de luxe blended Scotch whisky produced by McEwan and C°. 40% alc by vol.

Cher (Fr) a Vin de Pays area in the Loir-et-Cher département, central-western France. Produces red, rosé and dry white wines.

Chérac (Fr) a commune in the Charente-Maritime département whose grapes are classed Borderies (Cognac).

Chereau (Fr) a large producer of Muscadet in the Nantais district of the Loire region.

Cheribon (E.Ind) a coffee-producing region in Java.

Cherinac (Sp) the alternative spelling of Jeriñac.

Chéri Sling (Cktl) 50mls Chéri-Suisse, 35mls dry gin. Shake over ice, strain into a highball glass, add a dash of lime juice and top with soda.

Chéri-Suisse (Switz) a cherry and chocolate liqueur.

Cheriton Brewhouse [The] (Eng) a brewery (established 1993). (Add): Cheriton, Alresford, Hampshire SO24 0QQ. Brews: Ambler Gambler 3.9% alc by vol., Cheriton Best Bitter 4.2% alc by vol., Diggers Gold 4.6% alc by vol., Green Light 3.3% alc by vol., Pots Ale 3.8% alc by vol., Village Elder 3.8% alc by vol. 'E'mail: bestbeer1@aol.com

Chéri Tonic (Cktl) 50mls Chéri-Suisse, 25mls lime juice. Shake over ice, strain into a highball glass and top with soda water.

Cherokee Bottled Water (USA) a natural spring mineral water from Cherokee, North Carolina.

Cherristock (It) a cherry-flavoured liqueur.

Cherry (Eng) the name given to the fruit of the coffee tree because of its cherry-like appearance.

Cherry Alexander (Cktl) ½ measure cherry brandy, ½ measure crème de cacao, ¼ measure cream. Shake over ice and strain into a cocktail glass.

Cherry 'B' (Eng) a cherry wine produced by Showerings.

Cherry B Cream (Eng) a Devon cream, brandy and cherry liqueur produced by Showerings.

Cherry Bestle (Den) a local cherry-flavoured liqueur.

Cherryblock (USA) a Cabernet sauvignon wine from Sebastiani Estates Group, Sonoma Valley, California.

Cherry Blossom (Cktl) 1 part sloe gin, 1 part fruit juice, topped up with calpis.

Cherry Blossom Cocktail (Cktl) ⅗ measure brandy, ⅖ measure cherry brandy, dash lemon juice, dash grenadine, dash Curaçao. Shake over ice and strain into a cocktail glass. The glass may be frosted with cherry brandy and castor sugar.

Cherry Blossom Liqueur (Jap) a delicate pink liqueur with a strong fragrance of Japanese cherry blossoms.

Cherrybom (Port) a cherry liqueur produced by J.M. Fonseca.

Cherry Bomb (Eng) a 6% alc by vol. strong ale brewed by Hanby Ales Ltd., Shropshire.

Cherry Bounce (USA) a cordial made by boiling the strained juice of cherries. Add lemon peel, cinnamon, cloves, allspice, mace and sugar to taste. Add 250mls of brandy to every 4litres (US) of juice. Drink hot or cold.

Cherry Brandy (Eng) liqueur or brandy with a cherry flavour.

Cherry Brandy Liqueur (Euro) produced by the maceration of fruit in spirit 22%–25% alc by vol.

Cherry Brandy Punch (Punch) 500mls boiling water, juice of 2 lemons, 200grms sugar. Bring back to boil, simmer 5 minutes, add 1 bottle deep red wine, 125mls cherry brandy. Heat slowly, add slices of orange and lemon.

Cherry Brandy Vichniovaia (Rus) a cherry-based spirit.

Cherry 'B' White (Eng) a white, cherry-flavoured wine from Showerings.

Cherry Cobbler (Cktl) place 25mls cherry brandy into an ice-filled highball glass. Top with dry white wine and dress with a slice of orange.

Cherry Cocktail (Cktl) 30mls cherry syrup, 30mls ginger syrup, 2 dashes lime syrup and 1 dash Angostura. Stir over ice, strain into a highball glass, top with soda and serve with slices of orange and a cherry.

Cherry Coke (USA) a cola drink with a cherry taste produced by the Coca Cola and Schweppes Beverage Company.

Cherry Cooler (Cktl) 35mls cherry brandy, juice of ½ lemon, ½ teaspoon castor sugar. Shake well over ice, strain into a highball glass over ice and top with soda.

Cherry Cream (Hol) a 17% alc by vol. cherry-flavoured cream liqueur from Bols.

Cherry Daiquiri (Cktl) ½ measure white rum, ¼ measure cherry brandy, ¼ measure lemon juice. Shake over ice and strain into a cocktail glass.

Cherry Fizz (Cktl) ⅓ measure cherry brandy, juice ⅛ lemon. Shake over ice, strain into an ice-filled highball glass, top with soda water and a cherry.

Cherry Flavoured Brandy (USA) a brandy-based liqueur infused with cherries

Cherry Flip (Cktl) 40mls (⅓ gill) cherry brandy, 1 egg, 1 teaspoon powdered sugar, 15mls (⅛ gill) cream. Shake well over ice, strain into a flip glass and top with grated nutmeg.

C

Cherry Heering (Den) a very popular cherry-flavoured liqueur. Produced by Peter Heering.

Cherry Hill Vineyard (Eng) a vineyard (established 1966). (Add): Nettlestead, Kent. 1ha. Soil-Greensand. Grape varieties: Müller-Thurgau 98%, Siebel 13053 1% and Seyve Villard 1%. Vinified at Lamberhurst.

Cherry Julep (It) an apéritif wine produced for the USA market.

Cherry Karise (Den) a local cherry-flavoured liqueur.

Cherry Kirsberry (Den) a Danish brand-name cherry wine.

Cherry Liqueur (USA) produced from small black wild cherries by the maceration technique.

Cherry Marnier (Fr) a Dalmatia black cherry liqueur. 23% alc by vol. Produced in Paris.

Cherry Nalivika (Rus) a cherry liqueur.

Cherry Pepsi (USA) a cherry-flavoured cola drink produced by Pepsi-Cola World Wide Beverages Company.

Cherrypicker's (Eng) *see* Alford Arms.

Cherry Ricky (Cktl) place some ice in a highball glass, add juice of a small lime, 2 measures cherry brandy. Stir and top with Perrier mineral water.

Cherry Rocher (Fr) a large liqueur producer. (Add): La Côte St. André, Vienne. Produces Cherry Rocher (a cherry liqueur), Guignolet and many fruit and herb liqueurs.

Cherry Rum (Eng) a 5.5% alc by vol. flavoured bottled drink from Spilt Drinks C°., Exeter, Devon.

Cherry Rum Cocktail (Cktl) 40mls (⅓ gill) Jamaican rum, 15mls (⅛ gill) cherry brandy, 15mls (⅛ gill) cream. Shake over ice and strain into a cocktail glass.

Cherrys (Ire) part of the Guinness-controlled Irish Ale Breweries based in Waterford, south-eastern Eire.

Cherry's Bitter (Ire) a 3.7% alc by vol. draught in a can beer from Guinness.

Cherry Sling (Cktl) 40mls cherry brandy, juice ½ lemon. Stir over ice in an old-fashioned glass, top with a twist of lemon peel juice.

Cherry Sour (Cktl) place 1 measure cherry brandy into an ice-filled highball glass. Add 1 sugar cube and the juice of a lemon. Stir, top with soda water and decorate with a slice of orange and lemon.

Cherry Sour Simple (Cktl) 25mls (⅛ gill) cherry brandy in an ice-filled highball glass, top with iced lemonade and a slice of lemon.

Cherry Stock (It) a cherry liqueur produced by Stock in Trieste. 24% alc by vol. from the juice of maraska cherries.

Cherry Triple (Cktl) ⅓ measure cherry brandy, ⅓ measure Triple Sec. Stir over ice in a highball glass, add juice of ½ lemon and top with soda water.

Cherry Whiskey (Fr) a cherry-flavoured whiskey liqueur. Also known as Chesky, Gean Whiskey, Geen Whiskey, Guyne Whiskey.

Cherry Whisky (Cktl) 65mls Scotch whisky, ½ teaspoon Angostura, 1 teaspoon grenadine. Stir over broken ice, strain into a wine glass. Decorate with a cherry and a dash of lemon peel juice.

Cherry Wine Cocktail [1] (Cktl) 20mls (¾ fl.oz) Danish cherry liqueur, 20mls (¾ fl.oz) dry gin, juice ½ lime. Shake over ice and strain into a cocktail glass.

Cherry Wine Cocktail [2] (Cktl) ½ measure Danish cherry wine, ½ measure vodka, juice ½ lime. Shake over ice, strain into a cocktail glass.

Cherry Wine Collins (Cktl) 20mls (¾ fl.oz) Danish cherry wine, 20mls (¾ fl.oz) dry gin, juice ½ lime. Mix well over ice, strain into a highball glass and top with soda.

Cherson (Ukr) a wine-producing region based in the Ukraine.

Cherusker (Ger) a natural spring mineral water from Borgholzhausen, NW.

Cherveno Vino (Bul) red wine.

Cherves (Fr) a commune in the Charente-Maritime département whose grapes are classed Borderies (Cognac).

Chesapeake (Eng) a 5.5% alc by vol. ale brewed by the Newby Wyke Brewery, Lincolnshire.

Cheshire Cheese (Eng) a 4.7% alc by vol. cask-conditioned ale brewed by Ridley for Greenall outlets.

Cheshire English Pub Beer (Eng) a bottled ale 1045 O.G. produced by the Greenhall Whitley Brewery, Warrington, Cheshire for the USA market.

Chesima (E.Asia) a plant used in the production of oolong teas which gives the tea a unique flavour (often flavoured with jasmine).

Chesky (Fr) a cherry-flavoured whiskey liqueur produced by Fremy.

Chesmeh (Iran) a natural spring mineral water.

Chess (Swe) a light-styled ale 5.6% alc by vol. brewed by the Pripps Brewery.

Cheste (Sp) a Denominación de Origen wine-producing region within the province of Valencia in southern Spain. Grape varieties: Macabeo, Merseguera, Muscat, Pedro Ximénez, Planta fina and Planta nora. Produces mainly white wines.

Chester Brown (Eng) *see* Old Chester.

Chesterfield Ale (USA) a bottom-fermented, dry-hopped ale brewed by the Yuengling Brewery, Pottsville, Pennsylvania.

Chester Gold (Eng) *see* Old Glory.

Chester Rock (Eng) a 4.5% alc by vol. cask-conditioned ale brewed by Ridley for Greenall outlets.

Chesters Brewery (Eng) a brewery of Whitbreads. Known as the Manchester Trading Company and Salford Brewery. Produces cask-conditioned Chester Best Mild 1033 O.G. and Chesters Best Bitter 1034 O.G. Sold under the name of Duttons in the north of England.

Chesters Strong Ale (Eng) a 5.2% alc by vol. ale brewed by the Barngates Brewery Ltd., Cumbria.

Chestnut Ale (Eng) a 5% alc by vol. malty cask ale brewed by the Marston Brewery. Part of the Tapster's Choice range.

Chestnut Mild (Eng) a dark, keg mild 1033 O.G.

C

brewed by the John Smith Brewery in Tadcaster, Yorkshire.

Cheurlin-Dangin (Fr) a Champagne producer. (Add): 17, Grande Rue, 10110 Celles sur Ource. Produces non-vintage Champagnes. Website: http://www.cheurlin-dangin.fr

Cheurlin et Fils (Fr) a Champagne producer. (Add): 12 Rue de la Gare, Gyé-sur-Seine, 10250 Mussy-sur-Seine. 25ha. All remuage is done by hand. Top cuvée is Prestige Brut. Also produce Originel (a blanc de blancs).

Cheval Blanc (Fr) see Château Cheval Blanc.

Cheval Blanc Ambré [Le] (Can) a 5% alc by vol. bottle-conditioned special amber beer brewed by Le Cheval Blanc Brewery in Montreal.

Cheval Blanc Brewery [Le] (Can) a brewery based in Montreal. Brews: Le Cheval Blanc Ambré, Le Cheval Blanc Rousse.

Cheval Blanc Rousse [Le] (Can) a 5% alc by vol. amber coloured, bottled special red beer brewed by Le Cheval Blanc Brewery in Montreal.

Cheval des Andes (Arg) a red wine produced as a joint venture between Château Cheval Blanc (Saint-Émilion) and Roberto de la Mota (Terrazas de los Andes) in the Mendoza region.

Chevalier (Sp) a solera reserva brandy produced by Luis Caballero.

Chevalier [Yves] (Fr) a wine producer based at Turquant, Saumur, Anjou-Saumur, Loire. Noted for Saumur Mousseux.

Chevalier d'Alsace (Fr) denotes Alsatian white wines that have been made from noble grape varieties that have been gathered after the prescribed harvest date. See also Flambeau d'Alsace.

Cheval des Andes (Arg) a label from the Terrazas de los Andes Vistalba winery, Mendoza. Grape varieties: Cabernet sauvignon 60% and Malbec 40%.

Chevalier de Stérimberg [Le] (Fr) the name of a white A.C. Hermitage produced by Jaboulet Aîné in the Côtes du Rhône.

Chevalier et Fils (Fr) a Burgundy négociant based in Charney-les-Mâcon, Mâconnais, Burgundy.

Chevalier Marin (Bel) a pilsener-style beer brewed by the Artois Brasserie in Louvain.

Chevalier-Montrachet (Fr) a Grand Cru vineyard in the A.C. commune of Puligny-Montrachet, Côte de Beaune, Burgundy 7.1ha.

Chevaliers Bretvins (Fr) a noted wine brotherhood of Nantes in the western Loire. Is the fourth oldest in France (founded 1947). Is mainly concerned with the wines of Nantais. Has branches (bailliages) world-wide. The president is always the Marquis de Goulaine.

Chevaliers de la Chantepleure (Fr) a wine brotherhood based in Vouvray, Touraine, Loire.

Chevaliers de Sancerre (Fr) a wine society based in Sancerre, Central Vineyards, Loire.

Chevaliers du Sacavin (Fr) a wine brotherhood based in Angers, Anjou-Saumur, Loire.

Chevaliers du Tastevin (Fr) the Burgundy growers and wine merchants' body to promote the sale of their wines. see Tastevinage and Confrérie des Chevaliers du Tastevin.

Chevallier [Sylvain] (Fr) a 9.5ha. wine estate in Savoie. Produces A.C. Vin de Savoie Jongieux from Jacquère, plus Pinot noir version. Has 1.5ha. in the Marestel Cru of Roussette.

Cheval Noir (Fr) a vineyard in the AC. Saint-Émilion Grand Cru. see Mahler-Bresse.

Cheverny (Fr) an A.C. wine district in the Loire Valley. Produces red, rosé and white wines. Main grape is the white Romorantin. See also Cours-Cheverny.

Cheverny le Frileuse (Fr) an A.C. Cheverny wine produced from 60% Chardonnay grapes by Clos du Tue-Boeuf.

Chevier (Fr) the local name for the Sémillon grape in Bordeaux along the river Dordogne.

Chevin Chaser (Eng) a 4.3% alc by vol. pale bitter brewed by Briscoe's in Otley, West Yorkshire.

Chevre Chardonnay (S.Afr) a Chardonnay wine produced by the Fairview Estate.

Chèvres Pirreuses [Les] (Fr) a single vineyard Champagne produced by Leclerc Briant.

Chevrets [Les] (Fr) a Premier Cru vineyard in the A.C. commune of Volnay, Côte de Beaune, Burgundy 6ha.

Chevrier (USA) a barrel fermented white wine produced from Sémillon grapes by Columbia Winery, Woodinville, Washington State.

Chevrier Blanc (USA) a white wine produced by the Vichon Winery, Napa Valley, California. Made from a blend of Sauvignon blanc and Sémillon grapes.

Chevron (Bel) a natural spring mineral water from Monastère, Chevron.

Chewy (Eng) a term used to describe full-bodied wines, similar to meaty.

Cheys (Fr) the name given to the walls that retain soil in the terraced vineyards of the Côte Rôtie in the northern Rhône. Also called Murgeys.

Chhabri (Ind) a still white wine produced on an east-facing 45.5ha. vineyard in Sahyadri Valley. Made from a blend of Chardonnay, Ugni blanc and Thompson seedless grapes.

Chhang (Ind) describes a drink made from fermented millet and served in a hollowed-out bamboo stem filled with millet seed and boiling water. This ferments and the liquid is served with a bamboo straw.

Chia Fan (Chi) a noted brand of rice wine produced in Shanghai. See also Shaoh-Sing Rice Wine.

Chiai Della Furba (It) a red Vino da Tavola wine made from one third Merlot and other grape varieties in central-western Italy.

Chianti (It) a D.O.C.G. red wine from Tuscany. Districts: Arezzo, Florence, Pisa, Pistoia and Siena districts. (Coms): Chianti Classico Riserva are Barberino, Castellina, Castelnuovo Berardenga, Gaiole, Greve, Monteriggioni, Poggibonsi, Radda, San Cascaino, Tarnavelle. Produce red wines from the Canaiolo nero, Malvasia del chianti, Sangiovese (main variety) and Trebbiano toscano grapes. May now be produced from 100%

C

Sangiovese under the latest D.O.C.G. rules. Some are made using the Governo process. If minimum total alc. content is 12% by vol. and aged 2 years originally called Vecchio. If aged 3 years then Riserva – this can now be released after 2 years. Since 1996 vintage production is limited to 52.5 hl./ha. No more than 3 kgs. grapes per vine. From 2000 up to 20% of other grape varieties can be added (including Cabernet, Merlot and Syrah). see Chianti Classico, Chianti Putto and Ruffino.

Chianti (USA) see California Chianti.

Chianti Classico (It) a D.O.C.G. area founded in 1924, 8500ha. (245000 hl). see Classico and Chianti. Has a Black Cockerel (Gallo Nero) as its symbol. Minimum alc. content 12.5% by vol. If aged 2 years in cask then originally called Vecchio. Riserva can now be released after 2 years. Minimum of 3 months in bottle (27 months ageing in total). Single vineyard is identified by Vigna on label. From 1995 vintage possible to use 100% Sangiovese or to create blend with up to 15% other red varieties (Cabernet sauvignon, Canaiolo, Colorino, Malvasia nera, Merlot and Syrah – no white grapes allowed). No longer essential to include white grape varieties. Website: http://www.chianticlassico.com

Chianti Colli Arentini (It) a D.O.C.G. Chianti area that does not belong to either Chianti Classico or Chianti Putto.

Chianti Colli Fiorentini (It) a D.O.C.G. Chianti area that does not belong to either Chianti Classico or Chianti Putto.

Chianti Colline Pisane (It) a D.O.C.G. Chianti area that does not belong to either Chianti Classico or Chianti Putto.

Chianti Colli Senesi (It) a D.O.C.G. Chianti area that does not belong to either Chianti Classico or Chianti Putto.

Chiantigiana (It) a special Chianti bottle of 175 centilitres.

Chianti Magni (It) a Chianti Classico producer based in Tuscany.

Chianti Montalbano (It) a D.O.C.G. Chianti area that does not belong to either Chianti Classico or Chianti Putto.

Chianti Putto (It) a D.O.C.G. Chianti Consorzio founded in 1927. Set up by producers similar to Chianti Classico. Has a Cherub as its logo.

Chianti Rufina (It) a D.O.C.G. Chianti area 745ha. (25,700 hl) that does not belong to either Chianti Classico or Chianti Putto. Grape varieties: Canaiolo 5%–10%, Sangiovese 75%–100% plus up to 20% other varieties.

Chianti Superiore (It) a Chianti produced in the Classico district, the wine uses neither the Classico or D.O.C.G. seals. Instead it sells under the name of the producer Marchese Vittorio Frescobaldi.

Chian Wine (Gre) a dark, red, sweet, heavy wine produced on the island of Chios. Has a long historical fame.

Chiarandà del Merlo (It) a dry white wine made from the Ansonica and Chardonnay grapes on the island of Sicily by Donnafugata.

Chiarella (It) a still and sparkling natural mineral water from Plesio, Lake Como. Mineral contents (milligrammes per litre): Sodium 0.9mg/l, Calcium 40.6mg/l, Magnesium 22.1mg/l, Potassium 0.2mg/l, Bicarbonates 217.8mg/l, Chlorides 0.9mg/l, Sulphates 8.6mg/l, Fluorides 0.04mg/l, Nitrates 7.5mg/l, Silicates 4.3mg/l. pH 7.7

Chiaretto (It) lit: 'claret', very light red wines.

Chiaretto (It) pale pink, term used when describing rosé wines.

Chiaretto del Garda (It) a deep-coloured, rosé wine of the Lombardy region produced on the southern shores of Lake Garda. Made from the Sangiovese grape.

Chiarieri (It) a winery based in Tuscany. Produces a DOCG Montepulciano d'Abruzzo under the Vinum Hannibal label.

Chiarire (It) clarify.

Chiarli (It) noted wine-producers based in Modena, Emilia-Romagna, north-eastern Italy.

Chiaro (It) clear.

Chiavennasca (It) the Lombardy name for the Nebbiolo grape.

Chiba (Mor) absinthe.

Chic (It) a de luxe beer brewed by the Birra Bellizona Brewery of Ticino.

Chica (S.Am) a spirit produced from fermented maize by the Indians in Peru. Also made from molasses.

Chicago Bomb Cocktail (Cktl) ½ measure (green) crème de menthe, ½ measure (white) crème de cacao, 1 scoop vanilla ice cream. Blend together in a blender and pour into a flute glass.

Chicago Cocktail [1] (Cktl) 60mls (½ gill) brandy, 3 dashes Curaçao, dash Angostura. Stir over ice, strain into a cocktail glass. Top with iced Champagne, add a squeeze of lemon peel juice on top. Also known as a Fancy Brandy Cocktail.

Chicago Cocktail [2] (Cktl) 40mls (⅓ gill) brandy, 2 dashes triple sec, 1 dash Angostura. Sugar the rim (with orange juice) of an old-fashioned glass. Shake ingredients over ice and strain into a glass.

Chicago Fizz (Cktl) ½ measure Port, ½ measure Jamaican rum, juice ½ lemon, 1 teaspoon powdered sugar, 1 egg white. Shake well over ice, strain into an ice-filled highball glass and top with soda water.

Chicama Vineyards (USA) a winery based on Martha's Vineyard Island, Massachusetts. Produces hybrid wines.

Chicco de Caffé (It) coffee bean.

Chicha (S.Am) a beverage fermented from quinoa seeds in Bolivia and Peru.

Chichée (Fr) a commune in the A.C. Chablis, Burgundy.

Chi Chi (Cktl) 15mls vodka, 25mls coconut cream, 100mls unsweetened pineapple juice. Blend with 2 scoops of crushed ice in a blender. Serve in a large highball glass and decorate with a pineapple slice, cherry and serve with straws.

Chicken (USA) the broad general name used to include various types of native American grapes used in wine production.

Chicken Drink (Cktl) ½ measure white rum, ¼ measure apricot brandy, ¼ measure orange juice. Shake over ice, strain into a cocktail glass and dress with a slice of orange.

Chicken Ranch (USA) the label for a red wine (Cabernet sauvignon) produced by the Trinchero winery, Rutherford, Napa Valley, California.

Chickering Hall (Eng) a vineyard. (Add): Chickeringhall, Hoxne, near Eye, Suffolk. Grape variety: Müller-Thurgau.

Chiclana (Sp) an area in the Jerez Supérieur district.

Chicory (Eng) *Cicohorium Intybus* an additive to coffee blends when roasted. Makes the coffee bitter. *see* French Coffee.

Chicory Coffee (Eng) *see* Wild Chicory Coffee.

Chiddingstone (Eng) a 4% alc by vol. ale from Larkin's Brewery, Chiddingstone.

Chiddingstone Vineyard (Eng) a vineyard based in Kent. Grapes include: Pinot, Seyval, Kerner and Gutedel.

Chifney Wines (N.Z) a winery. (Add): Huangarua Road, Martinborough. 4.5ha. Grape varieties: Chardonnay, Chenin blanc, Gewürztraminer, Cabernet franc, Cabernet sauvignon, Merlot.

Chig-Ge (E.Asia) an alcoholic drink of fermented mare's milk made in Mongolia. Is similar to Koumiss.

Chignard [Michel] (Fr) a winery based in the A.C. Beaujolais Cru Fleurie, southern Burgundy. 8.5ha.

Chignin (Fr) a white table wine from the vineyards of Chignin, Savoie, south of Chambéry. Made from the Jacquère grape.

Chignin-Bergeron (Fr) a wine-producing village based in the Savoie region of south-eastern France.

Chigny-les-Roses (Fr) a Premier Cru Champagne village in the Canton de Verzy. District: Reims.

Chihuahua (Mex) a district that contains the wine-producing area of Delicías.

Chi Kung (S.E.Asia) a natural spring mineral water from Taiwan.

Chile (S.Am) a South American wine-producing country along south-eastern coast. Produces full-bodied wines from European vine species (Phylloxera-free). Five recognised areas are Atacama, Coquimbo, Aconcagua, Central Valley, Southern Region. Single varietal wines must contain 75% of grape stated (85% if for E.U. export). All are estate wines, 100% produced and bottled from one source. Ageing of wine: Special: 2 y.o. Reserve: 4 y.o. Gran Vino: 6 y.o. Main producers: Colchagua, Concha y Toro, Errazuriz, Maipo, Santa Rita. Website: http://www.winesofchile.org

Chilford Hundred (Eng) a vineyard. (Add): Chilford Hall, Linton, Cambridgeshire. Soil: loam gravel. 7.5ha. Grape varieties: Huxelrebe, Müller-Thurgau, Ortega, Schönburger and Siegerrebe.

Chilean Palm (S.Am) *Jubaea chilensis* a giant palm the sap of which is used in the making of palm wine.

Chill Blane (Eng) a 5% alc by vol. dark winter warmer brewed by Hydes Anvil, Manchester in November and December.

Chilled and Filtered (Eng) a part of the brewing process in which the beer is cooled which causes suspended proteins to separate out and then it is filtered out.

Chilled Cherry Tea (Cup) place 75mls cherry brandy, 250mls white sparkling wine and 250mls wild cherry tea into jug over ice. Stir and serve in highball glasses with cocktail cherries.

Chill Haze (Eng) a condition which can appear in cask-conditioned ales. Caused when the beer becomes too cold and the proteins separate out. Does not alter the flavour but looks unsightly. Treated by filtering.

Chilli Beer (Eng) a malt lager which has a chilli pepper added during bottling. Produced by Batemans, Lincolnshire for the USA market.

Chillier à Cidre (Ch.Isles) cider cellar.

Chillin (Eng) a 4.5% alc by vol. pineapple and grapefruit mix from Aston Manor, Birmingham.

Chillproofing (Eng) a process of chilling wines to remove excess acid and proteins. Filtered afterwards.

Chilsdown (Eng) a vineyard. (Add): The Old Station House, Singleton, Chichester, West Sussex. 5.3ha. Soil: clay, silt loam over chalk. Grape varieties: Chardonnay, Müller-Thurgau and Reichensteiner. *See also* Chalklands and Grapple.

Chiltern Ale (Eng) a 3.7% alc by vol. ale brewed by The Chiltern Brewery, Buckinghamshire.

Chiltern Brewery [The] (Eng) a brewery (established 1980). (Add): Nash Lee Road, Terrick, Aylesbury, Buckinghamshire HP17 0TQ. Produces Beechwood Bitter 4.3% alc by vol (1043 O.G.), Bodgers Barley Wine 8.5% alc by vol., cask-conditioned Chiltern Ale 3.7% alc by vol (1036 O.G)., John Handonns Ale 4.8% alc by vol., Lord Lieutenant's Ale 6% alc by vol., Three Hundreds Old Ale 5% alc by vol. Website: http://www.chilternbrewery.co.uk 'E'mail: enquiries@chilternbrewery.co.uk

Chiltern Hills (Eng) a natural mineral water from Chiltern Farm, Toms Hill Estate, Tring, Hertfordshire. Mineral contents (milligrammes per litre): Sodium 8mg/l, Calcium 104mg/l, Magnesium 1.4mg/l, Potassium 1mg/l, Bicarbonates 293mg/l, Chlorides 15mg/l, Sulphates 12mg/l, Fluorides 0.1mg/l, Nitrates 5mg/l.

Chiltern Valley Vineyard (Eng) a vineyard based in Hambledon, Oxfordshire. Grape varieties: Bacchus, Madeleine-angevine. Noted for 'noble' Bacchus, Old Luxters.

Chimay (Bel) the name given to a range of Trappist ales brewed by the Trappist monks at the Scourmont Abbaye, Forges-les-Chimay. Both bottle-conditioned and vintage dated beers are produced. Each style is distinguished by the bottle cap colour. *see* Capsule Blanche 8% alc by vol.,

Capsule Bleu 9% alc by vol. (vintage dated) and Capsule Rouge 7% alc by vol. Also Chimay Première, Chimay Cinq Cents, Chimay Grande Réserve.

Chimay Brasserie (Bel) see Chimay. An abbaye brewery based in southern Belgium, made by the monks of Château Orval, Rochefort, Westmalle, Westvleteren. Brews beers of same name. see Chimay.

Chimay Cinq Certs (Bel) an 8% alc by vol. bottle-fermented beer brewed by Chimay Brasserie.

Chimay Glass (Bel) a specially designed glass (bell-shaped with an inturned rim on a short, stumpy stem) used to serve Chimay beers.

Chimay Grande Réserve (Bel) a 9% alc by vol. bottle-fermented beer brewed by Chimay Brasserie.

Chimay Première (Bel) a 7% alc by vol. bottle-fermented beer brewed by the Chimay Brasserie using Hallertau and Yakima hops.

Chime (Eng) the end rim of a beer cask.

Chimera Ales (Eng) see the Dowton Brewery C°., Wiltshire.

Chimney Rock (USA) a winery based in the Stags Leap District, Napa Valley, California. Grape varieties include: Cabernet sauvignon.

Chimos (Gre) juice/fruit juice.

China (Asia) the main species of tea bush, has the smallest leaves of the tea bush family.

China (E.Asia) a country which has the oldest wine making records (2,500 B.C.). Main wine producing regions are Hebei, Henan, Jiangsu, Liao River, Shanxi, Sinkiang and Yangste. Is also noted for Rice wines and Tea. see C.N.C.O.F.I.E.C.

China (Fr) a liqueur produced from wild cherries in Grenoble, eastern France.

China Bisleri (It) tonic wine.

China Black (Chi) a tea from the Anhwei province, a medium leaf that gives a good quality and delicate taste.

China-China (Fr) a tonic liqueur made from spices and other ingredients including quinine. Produced by Picard et Cazot Fils in Lyons.

China-Martini (It) a bitters-apéritif 31% alc by vol. produced by Martini and Rossi. Contains quinine.

China National Cereals, Oils and Foodstuffs Import and Export Corp (E. Asia) abbr: C.N.C.O.F.I.E.C. the Chinese State monopoly that produces wines, spirits, etc. Based in Dairen, Fukien, Hupeh, Kwangsi, Kwangtung, Peking, Shanghai, Shantung and T'ien-Chin.

China Oolong Tea (Chi) the most expensive tea in the world, has a fine flavour, body and aroma.

China Tea (Chi) see Oolong, Tea Bricks and China Black.

Chinato (It) an apéritif made from Barolo wine and quinine.

Chinchón (Sp) an aniseed-flavoured aguardiente usually drunk diluted. Is similar to ouzo and pastis.

Chinese Cocktail (Cktl) 65mls Jamaican rum, 3 dashes maraschino, 3 dashes Curaçao, 3 dashes grenadine, 1 dash Angostura. Stir over ice, strain into a cocktail glass, add a cherry and squeeze of lemon peel juice on top.

Chinese Egg Nogg (Cktl) see Itchiban.

Chinese Ginseng Beer (Chi) a 4.1% alc by vol. straw coloured, bottled lager brewed by the Chinese Beer Company using ginseng, roasted wheat, ginger, glucose, maltose.

Chinese Ginseng Port Wine (Chi) a Port-style red wine flavoured with ginseng root, produced by the Talien Brewery.

Chinese Itch Cocktail (Cktl) 25mls golden rum, 20mls passion fruit juice, dash orgeat syrup, juice of a lime. Blend with a scoop of crushed ice in a blender, pour into a saucer glass and dress with a slice of lime.

Chinese Lady (Cktl) ½ measure Yellow Chartreuse, ½ measure grapefruit juice, 1 measure lemon gin. Shake well over ice and strain into a large cocktail glass.

Chinon (Fr) an A.C. wine-producing area in the Anjou-Saumur district, Loire. Produces red, rosé and white wines. Red wines have a distinct flavour of strawberries. Minimum alc by vol. 9.5%.

Chios (Gre) an island in the Aegean Sea noted for white wines.

Chipan (Bul) a delimited wine-producing region in southern Bulgaria, main grape varieties: Aligoté, Cabernet sauvignon, Dimiat, Merlot and Pinot noir.

Chipiona (Sp) the Andalusian name for a Moscatel wine and the name of district in Jerez Supérieur.

Chippewa Pride (USA) a light beer 4.37% alc by vol. brewed by the Leinentugel Brewery at Chippewa Falls, Wisconsin.

Chiquet [Gaston] (Fr) a Champagne producer based in Dizy. (Add): 912 Ave. du Général Leclerc, 51318 Épernay. récoltants-manipulants. Produce vintage and non-vintage wines. Website: http://www.gastonchiquet.com

Chiquito (Sp) the brand-name used by Bodegas García Carrión in Jumilla for red table wine.

Chira (Fr) an alternative name for the Syrah grape in south-western France.

Chiraï (Ch.Isles) intoxicated. See also Caudin.

Chirine (Rus) a red grape variety grown in Kazakhstania for the making of dessert wines.

Chiron (Aust) a de-alcoholised wine produced from Riesling grapes (less than 0.5% alc by vol).

Chiroubles (Fr) a commune in the Cru Beaujolais-Villages, Burgundy. Has 380ha. under vine.

Chisenbury Priory (Eng) a vineyard based in Wiltshire. Main grape is Bacchus.

Chisohoou (Gre) a winery in northern Greece, noted for a Xinomavro and Merlot special cuvée blend.

Chispa Cellars (USA) a small winery based in Calveras, California. Grape varieties: Ruby cabernet and Zinfandel. Produces varietal red wines.

Chispal (Arg) a natural spring mineral water. Mineral contents (milligrammes per litre): Sodium

1.4mg/l, Calcium 10.3mg/l, Magnesium 1.4mg/l, Bicarbonates 30mg/l, Sulphates 5mg/l, Fluorides 0.1mg/l, Nitrates 10mg/l.

Chiswick Bitter (Eng) a cask-conditioned bitter 1035 O.G. brewed by the Fuller's Brewery, London.

Chitry (Fr) a small wine-producing district in the Yonne département that produces red wines.

Chiu (Chi) a term for wine. *See also* Li and Chang.

Chivalry (Chi) a natural spring mineral water. Mineral contents (milligrammes per litre): Sodium 55mg/l, Calcium 79mg/l, Magnesium 30mg/l, Potassium 5mg/l, Bicarbonates 389mg/l, Chlorides 73mg/l, Sulphates <15mg/l. pH 7.5

Chivas Regal (Scot) a de luxe blended Scotch whisky (12 year old) produced by the Chivas Brothers in Aberdeen. Part of Seagram 43% alc by vol.

Chivite [Julian] (Sp) a wine producer based in Ribero del Ebro, Navarra. Noted for Parador (10 y.o. red wine), Cirbonero (5 y.o. red wine), Gran Fuedo (4 y.o. red or rosé wine) and Castillo de Melida (a young red wine). Also produces white wines.

Chiwara (S.Afr) the label for a red wine (Cabernet sauvignon, Merlot and Pinotage blend) produced by the Ashanti winery, Paarl, Western Cape. *See also* Daschbosch Wine Cellar.

Chkoua (Mor) a goatskin water bottle.

Chlorophyl (Eng) is sometimes found in white wines it gives a distinct green tinge to the wine.

Chlorose (Eng) the yellowing of the vine leaves, leaving them unable to nourish the grape. Usually shows the vine is not suited to the soil. Fertilisers are sometimes a cure.

Chmelar (Czec) lit: 'hop grower', a beer brewed by the Zatec Brewery.

Choc Dream (Cktl) ½ measure vodka, 1 measure Royal Mint Chocolate Liqueur, ⅔ measure cream. Shake well over ice, strain into a cocktail glass. Add dash of Tia Maria and sprinkle with grated chocolate on top, serve with straws and a cherry on the rim of the glass.

Chocen Brewery (Czec) a brewery based in Chocen in northern Czec.

Chocks (Eng) the wooden wedges used to secure the beer casks on stillages.

Chocla Menthe (Hol) a peppermint and cacao-flavoured liqueur produced by De Kuyper 30% alc by vol.

Chocolate (Eng) a beverage produced from the seeds of the cacao plant. *see* Xocoatl and Drinking Chocolate. (Den) = chokolade.

Chocolate Break (Eng) a powdered chocolate drink produced by Cadbury (part of Premier Beverages).

Chocolate Cocktail [1] (Cktl) 1 teaspoon chocolate powder, yolk of an egg, 30mls red Port. Stir over broken ice and pass through a strainer into a wine glass.

Chocolate Cocktail [2] (Cktl) 30mls Port, 30mls Yellow Chartreuse, 1 egg yolk, 1 teaspoon chocolate powder. Shake over ice and strain into a cocktail glass.

Chocolate Daisy (Cktl) ½ measure Port, ½ measure brandy, ½ teaspoon powdered sugar, juice ½ lemon, 4 dashes grenadine. Shake over ice, strain into an ice-filled highball glass and add sliced fruit in season.

Chocolate Flip (Cktl) ½ measure sloe gin, ½ measure brandy, 1 egg, 1 teaspoon sugar, 2 teaspoons cream. Shake over ice, strain into a flip glass and top with grated nutmeg.

Chocolate Frog Porter (Eng) a 8% alc by vol. strong porter ale brewed by the Garton Brewery, East Yorkshire.

Chocolate Heavy (Eng) a 5.5% alc by vol. dark ale brewed by the Marble Beer Brewery, Greater Manchester.

Chocolate Liqueurs (Euro) *see* Chéri-Suisse, Chocolate Suisse, Crème de Cacao, Royal Mint Chocolate Liqueur. Also Chokalu.

Chocolate Malt (Eng) a specially malted barley produced by roasting kiln-dried malt at a lower temperature than for black malt.

Chocolate Manufacturing Association and American Cocoa Research Institute (USA) an information bureau. (Add): 7900 Westpark Drive, Suit 514, McLean V.A. 22101.

Chocolate Martini (Cktl) 60mls vodka, 15mls crème de cacao, shake over ice and strain into a martini glass.

Chocolate Punch (Cktl) 25mls Kahlúa, 1½ teaspoons chocolate powder, 1 teaspoon coffee powder, 150mls milk, sugar to taste. Heat altogether, stirring until well mixed, pour into a heat-proof glass, top with whipped cream and ground cinnamon.

Chocolate Rum (Cktl) ⅓ measure Jamaican rum, ⅙ measure (white) crème de menthe, ⅙ measure crème de cacao, 4 dashes high-strength rum, 15mls cream. Shake over ice and strain into an ice-filled old-fashioned glass.

Chocolate Soldier [1] (Cktl) ⅓ measure crème de cacao, ⅓ measure brandy, ⅓ measure dry vermouth, 2 dashes orange bitters. Shake over ice and strain into a cocktail glass.

Chocolate Soldier [2] (Cktl) ½ measure dry gin, ¼ measure Dubonnet, ¼ measure lime juice. Shake over ice and strain into a cocktail glass.

Chocolate Stout (Eng) the label of a stout brewed by Arkell's Brewery, Swindon at 4.8% alc by vol. using chocolate malt.

Chocolate Stout (Eng) the label of a stout brewed by Youngs Brewery in London.

Chocolate Suisse (Switz) a chocolate-flavoured liqueur with tiny squares of chocolate floating in it. 30% alc by vol.

Chocolate Taste (Eng) a term applied to the taste of old Champagne that is past its best (usually best avoided).

Chocshots (Eng) a series of 30mls chocolate and fruit-flavoured (banana/orange/strawberry) cream drinks laced with vodka (at 20% alc by

C

vol.) and produced by Independent Distillers (UK) Ltd.

Chodov Plan Brewery (Czec) an old established brewery based in western Czec.

Chodovar (Czec) a dark, special, strong beer 13° brewed by the Chodov Plan Brewery.

Choice Madeira (Mad) may use a brand-name or word '*Madeira*' and a description. e.g. dry, medium, etc. but not the name of the grape. Must be minimum age 3 years after estufagem.

Choice Old Cameron Brig (Scot) the only single blended grain whisky which is produced by John Haig & C°. Ltd.

Choir Porter (Wal) a porter ale produced by Snowdonia Brewery (a micro-brewery) now based at Shrewsbury.

Chojungri (S.Kor) a natural spring mineral water brand. pH 6.19

Chokalu (Mex) a chocolate-flavoured, sweet liqueur 26% alc by vol.

Choko (Jap) a small ceramic tumbler used to drink hot saké.

Chokolade (Den) hot chocolate drink.

Chollet (Fr) *see* Cognac Chollet.

Chondrus crispus (Bot) a red algae used to clarify the wort during the brewing process.

Chope (Fr) a half a litre glass used for beer.

Chope (Fr) tankard.

Chopin (Pol) a 40% alc by vol. rye vodka produced and bottled in Poland by Polmos.

Chopine (Fr) a ½ litre mug/tankard (originally a ½ litre capacity measure).

Chopiner (Fr) boozer.

Chop Nut (Cktl) 15mls each of crème de banane and coconut liqueur, 25mls each of vodka and orange juice, dash egg white. Shake well over ice and strain into a large cocktail glass.

Chopp (Bra) a brand of beer.

Chopper Ale (Eng) a 3.5% alc by vol. ale from Forester and Firkin brew-pub in Stafford.

Chorey-lès-Beaune (Fr) an A.C. wine-producing village in the northern Côte de Beaune, Burgundy. Has no Premier Cru vineyards. Wines usually sold as A.C. Côte de Beaune-Villages.

Chorherrenhalde (Ger) vineyard (Anb): Baden. (Ber): Bodensee. (Gro): Sonnenufer. (Vil): Meersburg.

Chorherren Klosterneuburg (Aus) a winery (103ha) based in Klosterneuburg, Thermenregion. (Add): Am Renninger 2, 3400 Klosterneuburg. Grape varieties: Blauer portugieser, Chardonnay, Pinot blanc, Rotgipfler, St. Laurent, Traminer, Zweigelt.

Chorherrenstift Cellar (Aus) wine cellars based at Klosterneuberg that have their own shaped sekt bottles.

Chorister (Eng) a 4.5% alc by vol. ale brewed by Abbey Ales Ltd., Avon.

Chorny Doktor (Geo) a red, sweet, dessert wine from the Crimean peninsular.

Chorus (Fr) a red wine produced by Val d'Orbieu in the Languedoc-Roussillon from Carignan and Cabernet franc.

Chotapeg (Ind) the old Raj word for a glass of whisky (or other style of spirits).

Chouacheux [Les] (Fr) a Premier Cru vineyard in the A.C. commune of Beaune, Côte de Beaune, Burgundy.5.04ha.

Chouao (S.Am) often seen on a label of crème de cacao, denotes that the cacao bean comes from the Chouao region of Venezuela.

Chouchenn (Fr) the north-western French name for hydromel.

Chouffe [La] (Bel) an 8% alc by vol. top-fermented, bottle-conditioned special beer brewed by Brasserie d'Achouffe, Achouffe-Wibrin.

Chouilly (Fr) a Grand Cru Champagne village in the Canton d'Épernay. District: Épernay. Reclassified in 1985.

Choulette [La] (Fr) a bière de garde 7.5% alc by vol. Also available as Choulette Ambrée (La) at 7.5% alc by vol. from producer of same name.

Choum (E.Asia) a digestif liqueur made from fermented rice in Vietnam, if it is matured then known as Tchoung-tchoung.

Choupal (Port) the brand-label for red and white wines from Neto Costa.

Chrichton Hall Estate (USA) a winery based in Darms Lane, Napa Valley, California.

Chrisman Mill Winery (USA) a winery based in Lexington, Kentucky.

Christianabronnen (Bel) a natural spring mineral water from Christiana, Gavere.

Christian Brothers (USA) a religious brotherhood who produce wines in the Napa Valley, California. Also produce brandies. *see* Mont la Salle Vineyard. They also own the largest collection of antique and unusual corkscrews in the world. See *also* Mount Tivy Winery. Produces varietal wines.

Christian Brothers XO Rare Reserve (USA) a fine brandy produced by the Christian Brothers. Introduced in 1972.

Christian Domange (Fr) an Armagnac producer. (Add): Domaine de la Las Lannes, Bezolles 32310 Valence-sur-Baise. Produces Hors d'Age 10 year old.

Christian Dupré (Eng) the brand-name of a brandy produced for Linfood Cash and Carry, Northamptonshire 40% alc by vol.

Christian Senez (Fr) a Champagne producer. (Add): 6 Grande Rue, 10360 Fontette. Produces vintage and non-vintage Champagnes. Vintages: 1994, 1995, 1996, 1999, 2000. A member of the Copérative de Fontette. Website: http://www.contact-champagne-senez.com 'E'mail: champagne-senez@wanadoo.fr

Christianshavner Akvavit (Den) the brand-name of an akvavit produced by Peter Heering.

Christina Wine Cellars (USA) a winery based in McGregor, Iowa. Produces mainly French hybrid wines.

Christine (S.Afr) the label for a red wine (Cabernet franc, Cabernet sauvignon and Merlot blend) produced by the Buitenverwachting winery, Constantia, Western Cape.

Christinen Brunnen (Ger) a natural spring mineral

C

water (established 1966) from Bielefeld. Mineral contents (milligrammes per litre): Sodium 371mg/l, Calcium 55mg/l, Magnesium 6mg/l, Potassium 10mg/l, Bicarbonates 543mg/l, Chlorides 304mg/l, Sulphates 124mg/l, Fluorides 3mg/l, Nitrates 0.03mg/l.

Christlesee (Ger) a natural spring mineral water from Obersdorf, BY.

Christmas Ale (Eng) a strong winter ale 7.6% alc by vol. from the Blue Anchor Brewery.

Christmas Ale (Eng) the name now used by Green King for its winter ale from 1988.

Christmas Ale (Eng) a 5.5% alc by vol. seasonal winter beer brewed by Gale's Brewery, Horndean, Hampshire.

Christmas Ale (Eng) a 6% alc by vol. ale brewed by Wye Valley Brewery, Herefordshire.

Christmas Ales (Eng) festive ales brewed for the Christmas period that are usually high in alcohol.

Christmas Beer (Eng) the name of a Carlsberg lager 6.4% alc by vol.

Christmas Cheer (Punch) 500mls water, ¼ bottle Jamaican rum, 4 bottles red wine, 12 cloves, ½ teaspoon ground cinnamon, ½ teaspoon grated nutmeg. Heat water, wine, rum and spices together with a lemon studded with the cloves and bake in a hot oven for approximately 15 minutes. Serve in cups.

Christmas Cracker (Eng) a dark-brew ale 1080 O.G. brewed by the Woods Brewery in Shropshire. Made without sugars, obtains flavour from crystal and chocolate malts.

Christmas Cracker (Eng) a 6% alc by vol. beer from Teignworthy Brewery, Newton Abbot.

Christmas Cracker (Eng) a 5.5% alc by vol. cask-conditioned ale from Mitchells, 11 Moor Lane, Lancaster.

Christmas Cracker (Eng) a 6% alc by vol. strong ale brewed by the Teignworthy Brewery, Devon.

Christmas Noggin (Eng) a winter warmer ale brewed by Hoskins and Oldfield Brewery, Leicester.

Christmas Pudding Ale (Eng) a 5.5% alc by vol. cask-conditioned beer from Whitbread. Contains coriander, cinnamon bark, nutmeg, based on a seventeenth century recipe.

Christmas Reserve (Eng) a 6.6% alc by vol (1065) Christmas brew 1065 O.G. brewed by Mauldon's Ltd., Suffolk.

Christmas Ruby (Eng) a 4.7% alc by vol. Christmas ale brewed by the Millstone Brewery, Lancashire.

Christmas Special (Eng) a 7.6% alc by vol. strong Christmas ale brewed by the Blue Anchor Brewery, Cornwall.

Christmas Special (Wal) a 5% alc by vol. Christmas ale brewed by The Rhymney Brewery Ltd., Mid-Glamorgan.

Christmas Spiced Ale (Eng) a 5.1% alc by vol. Christmas ale from Bass, Burton-on-Trent.

Christmas Yule Egg Nog (Punch) 12 eggs, 200mls dark rum, 500mls milk, 500mls cream, 1litre Scotch whisky, 1kg sugar. Beat egg yolks and sugar together, beat egg whites separately and fold into yolks and sugar. Add remaining ingredients, chill and serve with grated nutmeg.

Christophe & Fils (Fr) a winery based in the A.C. Chablis, Burgundy. Produces a range of Chablis wines including Premier Cru Fourchaume.

Christophe Patrice (Fr) a winery based in the A.C. Chablis, Burgundy. Produces a range of Chablis wines including Premier Cru Montmains.

Christopher's Fino (Eng) a fine, dry, Fino Sherry from Christopher's and C°. London.

Christophorou (Cyp) a small, independent company who deal with wine production based in Limassol, south-eastern Cyprus.

Christwein (Ger) the name for a wine made from grapes gathered on December 24th and 25th.

Chronic Alcoholism (Eng) causes the diseases: Cirrhosis, Gastritis, Nephritis and Neuritis.

Chrustalni Mineralwater (Rus) a natural spring mineral water from St. Petersburg. Mineral contents (milligrammes per litre): Sodium 1100–1350mg/l, Calcium 70–90mg/l, Magnesium 50–70mg/l, Chlorides 1900–2300mg/l.

Chrüter (Switz) a herb-flavoured eau-de-vie distilled by Morand Distillerie, Martigny, Valais 40% alc by vol.

Chryseia (Port) lit: 'old', a wine produced as a joint venture between Bruno Prats and the Symington Port Group. First vintage was 1999.

Ch'ti (Fr) a 6.4% alc by vol. fruity, bottom fermented, blonde bière de garde brewed by Castelain Brasserie, Bénifontaine.

Chudleigh Organic Vineyard (Eng) a vineyard based in Old Exeter Street, Chudleigh, Devon. Produces white wines.

Chuico (Chile) a wicker-covered demi-john of 5–10 litres capacity.

Chumai (Rus) a red, dessert wine from the Moldavia region, produced from the Cabernet grape.

Chun Mee (E.Asia) a green, unfermented tea produced in Taiwan.

Chun Yang (Chi) a natural spring mineral water. Mineral contents (milligrammes per litre): Magnesium 18.2mg/l, Silicates 21mg/l.

Chupeta (Port) a drinking straw.

Chur Brauerei (Switz) a brewery based in Freuenfeld. Produces weizenbiers.

Churchaven (S.Afr) the label for a wine produced by The Winery, Stellenbosch, Western Cape.

Church Bitter (Eng) a 3.7% alc by vol. bitter ale brewed by the Leasingham Brewery, Lastingham, near Pickering, North Yorkshire.

Church Block (Austr) the brand label of the Wirra Wirra Vineyard in South Australia.

Church End Brewery [The] (Eng) a brewery (established 1994). (Add): Ridge Lane, Nuneaton, Warwickshire CV10 0RD. Brews: Cuthberts 3.8% alc by vol., Goats Milk 3.8% alc by vol., Gravediggers 3.8% alc by vol., Pooh Beer 4.3% alc by vol., Vicars Ruin 4.4% alc by vol., What the Fox Hat 4.2% alc by vol.

Church Hill (Austr) the brand-name used by the Mildara Vineyards.

C

Churchill Cocktail (Cktl) 25mls (1fl.oz) Scotch whisky, 10mls (⅓ fl.oz) Cointreau, 10mls (⅓fl.oz) Italian vermouth, dash lemon juice. Shake over ice and strain into a cocktail glass.

Churchill Graham Lda. (Port) vintage Port shippers. Vintages: 1982, 1985, 1991, 1994, 1997, 1998. Produces Quinta da Agua Alta.

Churchills (Eng) the name given to a range of bitter and lager beers from the Cornish Brewery.

Churchills Pride (Eng) an ale brewed to commemorate VE day by Hoskins in Leicester.

Church Inn (I.O.M) a micro-brewery at Uppermill, near Saddleworth. Brews: Saddleworth More, Shaftbender.

Church Parade (Cktl) 1 measure Plymouth gin, ½ measure dry vermouth, dash orange Curaçao, ½ measure orange juice. Shake over ice and strain into a cocktail glass.

Churchwards (Eng) based in Paignton. Produce Devon Mix–a draught cider.

Churleur (Fr) a word used by the Champenois for 'a drunk'.

Churn (Eng) a large container used for transporting milk. 1–10 gallons in capacity.

Chusclan (Fr) an A.C. Côtes du Rhône-Villages noted for rosé wines.

Chwart (Wal) a quart (2pints).

Chwisgi Cymraeg (Wal) lit: 'Welsh whiskey'. see Swn y Don, Swn y Mor and Welsh Whiskey Company.

Chymos (Fin) a company that produces Lakka, Polar and Villman liqueurs.

Chyorniye Glaza (Rus) lit: 'black eyes', style of 'Port' wine that is produced near Krasnodar.

C.I.A. [The] (Cktl) ⅓ measure Armagnac, ⅓ measure Cointreau, ⅓ measure Yellow Izarra. Shake over ice and strain into an ice-filled old-fashioned glass.

Ciabot Berton (It) a winery. (Add): Fraz. S. Maria 1, 12064 La Morra (Cueno). 10ha. vineyard that produces Barolo, Barbera d'Alba Bricca San Biagio, Dolcetto d'Alba, Dolcetto d'Alba Rutuin.

Ciappazzi (It) a sparkling natural spring mineral water from Ciappazzi. Mineral contents (milligrammes per litre): Sodium 448mg/l, Calcium 118mg/l, Magnesium 107mg/l, Potassium 19mg/l, Bicarbonates 1800mg/l, Chlorides 117mg/l, Sulphates 148mg/l, Fluorides 2mg/l, Nitrates 23mg/l, Silicates 44mg/l, Oxygen 905mg/l. pH 7.12

Cía Vinícola del Sur, S.A. (Sp) a producer of Montilla based in Montilla-Moriles, south-eastern Spain.

C.I.B. (Fr) abbr: Comité Interprofessionnel de la Côte d'Or et de l'Yonne pour les Vins de Bourgogne.

C.I.B.M. (Fr) abbr: Comité Interprofessionnel de Saône-et-Loire par les Vins A.O.C. de Bourgogne et de Mâcon.

C.I.B.V. (Fr) abbr: Comité Interprofessionnel de Vins de Bordeaux. (Add): 1, Cours du XXX Juillet, 33075 Bordeaux, Cedex.

C.I.C.D.R. (Fr) abbr: Comité Interprofessionnel des Vins des Côtes du Rhône.

Cicero (Cktl) ⅓ measure Honiggoscherl, ⅓ measure dry vermouth, ⅓ measure orange juice. Shake over ice, strain into a highball glass and top with iced Champagne.

Cichorium intybus (Lat) the botanical name of the chicory plant. Used as a substitute for coffee.

Ciclopi (It) noted wine-producers based near Etna on the island of Sicily.

Cider (Eng) fermented apple juice. **Dry**: 6% alc by vol. **Medium**: 4% alc by vol. **Sweet**: 2% alc by vol. See also English Farm Cider Centre and Scrumpy. (Bel) = cidre, (Ch.Isles) = cidre, (Den) = cider, (Fr) = cidre, (Ger) = apfelwein, (Ire) = leann úll ceirtlis, (It) = ucco di mele.

Cider Cocktail [1] (Cktl) ⅓ measure sparkling cider, ⅓ measure dry gin, ⅓ measure orange juice. Stir over ice and strain into a goblet.

Cider Cocktail [2] (Cktl) 90mls (¾ gill) cider, 1 dash Angostura, 3 dashes gomme syrup. Stir over ice, strain into a goblet and top with a lemon slice.

Cider Cup [1] (Cktl) into a large jug place some ice, 125mls pale Sherry, 65mls brandy, 65mls blue Curaçao, 1.1ltrs cider, rind of a lemon, stir with some ice and serve.

Cider Cup [2] (Cup) 20mls (⅙ gill) each of Calvados, Curaçao, maraschino, brandy, 1.1ltrs (2pints) cider. Stir over ice in a large jug and decorate with orange slices.

Cider Eggnog (Cktl) 1 egg, 1 teaspoon gomme syrup, 200mls (⅓ pint) milk. Shake over ice, strain into a collins glass, top with sweet cider and grated nutmeg.

Cider Glass (Eng) a stemmed, trumpet-shaped glass that was popular in the eighteenth and nineteenth centuries.

Cider Grog (Eng) heat 175mls (⅓ pint) cider and 100mls (⅕ pint) Jamaican rum together until nearly boiling, add sugar to taste and decorate with a lemon studded with some cloves.

Cider House (Eng) a building where cider in fermented and produced.

Cidéries Mignard (Fr) a noted cider producer based in Bellot. Also produces Mignard (a sparkling white grape juice).

Cidéries Réunies (Fr) one of France's largest cider companies based in Normandy, northern France. see Cidraie (La).

Cidermaster (Eng) the name for the head cider maker in a cider house.

Cidermaster (Eng) see Blackthorn Cidermaster.

Cider with Honey (Eng) a cider produced by Sheppy's Cider C°. which contains a teaspunful of clear honey in each bottle.

Cidona (Eng) old name to denote cider or apple.

Cidraie [La] (Fr) the brand-name for a range of ciders produced by Cidéries Réunies, Le Thiel, Normandy.

Cidre (Bel)(Ch.Isles)(Fr) cider.

Cidre Bouché (Fr) sparkling cider, fermented twice (naturally).

Cidre Brut (Fr) the most popular cider in France, is dry and of 4% alc by vol.

Cidre de Glace (Can) see Iced Cider.

Cidre Doux (Fr) a sweetish cider up to 3% alc by

C

vol, fermentation is stopped early so that not all the sugar is fermented.

Cidre Fermier (Fr) lit: 'farm cider'/'farmer's cider', home-produced cider, the equivalent of English 'Scrumpy'.

Cidre Mayenne (Fr) a brand of cider produced by Cidreric Volcler at Mayenne. Full title: Bouche de Volcler. see Cidreric Volcler.

Cidreric Volcler (Eng) the brand-name of ciders produced by Cidreric Volcler at Mayenne. 2 types: Cuvée Prestige Brut and Doux. See also Cidre Mayenne.

Cidrérie du Calvados [Le] (Fr) one of the largest cider producing companies of Normandy.

Cidre Sec (Fr) dry cider.

Cie des Grands Armagnacs (Fr) an Armagnac producer. (Add): Castelnau d'Auzan, 32800 Eauze.

Ciego Montero (Cuba) a natural spring mineral water. Mineral contents (milligrammes per litre): Calcium 98mg/l, Magnesium 38.9mg/l, Bicarbonates 300.5mg/l, Chlorides 61.7mg/l, Sulphates 120.2mg/l.

Cielo (S.Am) a natural spring mineral water from Peru.

Cienega (USA) a wine-producing area of San Benito, California.

Cienna (Austr) a grape variety that is a cross between Cabernet sauvignon x Sumoll.

Cierzac (Fr) a commune in the Charente-Maritime département whose grapes are classed Petite Champagne (Cognac).

Cigales (Sp) a Denominación de Origen area within Castilla-Léon. 2,063ha. Red and rosé wines are produced. Grape varieties: 50% Tempranillo (Tinta del País), 30% Garnacha, Verdejo, Viura, Palomino, Albillo.

Cigar Box (Eng) the term used to describe the aroma of some red wines (that of a wood bouquet) e.g. Spanish Rioja.

Cigare Volant [Le] (USA) a brand-name given to a wine from a blend of Grenache, Syrah and Mourvèdre from the Bonny Doon winery.

Cigel Spring Water (Slo) a sparkling natural spring mineral water from Cigelka Village, Bardejov, Slovakia. Mineral contents (milligrammes per litre): Sodium 3.6mg/l, Calcium 42.6mg/l, Magnesium 7.7mg/l, Potassium 0.66mg/l, Bicarbonates 119mg/l, Chlorides 3.49mg/l, Sulphates 30.7mg/l, Fluorides <0.05mg/l, Nitrates 15.5mg/l, Silicates 21.6mg/l. pH 7.98

Cigelka (Slo) a sparkling natural spring mineral water from Cigelka Village, Bardejov, Slovakia. Mineral contents (milligrammes per litre): Sodium 8127.9mg/l, Calcium 172.3mg/l, Magnesium 86.1mg/l, Potassium 137mg/l, Bicarbonates 216461.1mg/l, Chlorides 3761mg/l.

Cignale (It) a red I.G.T. wine produced from 90% Cabernet sauvignon and 10% Merlot by Castello di Querceto in Tuscany.

Cignano (It) a Chianti Putto producer based in the Tuscany region.

Cilandia (S.Afr) a winery (established 2002) based in Robertson, Western Cape. 60ha. Grape varieties: Cabernet sauvignon, Chardonnay, Chenin blanc, Cinsaut, Pinotage, Roobernet, Shiraz.

Cilaos (Fr) a natural spring mineral water from the island of La Réunion. Mineral contents (milligrammes per litre): Sodium 238mg/l, Calcium 110.5mg/l, Magnesium 70.5mg/l, Potassium 5.3mg/l, Bicarbonates 1298.2mg/l, Chlorides 3mg/l, Sulphates 54.7mg/l.

Cilento (It) a D.O.C. red wine produced from Aglianico grapes in Southern Italy.

Ciliegiolo (It) a red grape variety grown in the Tuscany region.

Cilleros (Sp) a Vino Comarcal wine area in the province of Cáceres, Extremadura.

Cilliers Cellars (S.Afr) the label for a red wine (Cabernet sauvignon) produced by the Stellendrift winery, Stellenbosch, Western Cape.

Cilurzo and Piconi (USA) a winery based in Temecula, California. 16.5ha. Grape varieties: Cabernet sauvignon, Chenin blanc and Petit syrah. Produces Chenite and varietal wines.

Cima Corgo (Port) the upper area of the river Douro.

Cimbalino (Port) a local coffee drink in the Douro region.

Cime Bianche (It) a natural spring mineral water. Mineral contents (milligrammes per litre): Sodium 1.5mg/l, Calcium 12mg/l, Bicarbonates 36mg/l, Sulphates 8.7mg/l. pH 7.6

Cin (USA) a noted brand of vermouth.

Cinar (Tur) a sparkling natural spring mineral water (established 1986) from Mount Uludag. Mineral contents (milligrammes per litre): Sodium 385.8mg/l, Calcium 200.4mg/l, Magnesium 85.09mg/l, Sulphates 12mg/l, Nitrates 0.97mg/l, Silicates 45.5mg/l, Iron 3.53mg/l, Aluminium 3.53mg/l, Boration 1.3mg/l, Boron 1.3mg/l, Barium 1mg/l. pH 6.33

Cincher (Cktl) 35mls cherry brandy, 35mls dry gin, Pour over crushed ice in an old-fashioned glass.

Cinciano (It) a sparkling natural spring mineral water from Cinciano. Mineral contents (milligrammes per litre): Sodium 123.2mg/l, Calcium 283mg/l, Magnesium 45.1mg/l, Potassium 8.4mg/l, Bicarbonates 1181mg/l, Chlorides 71mg/l, Sulphates 104mg/l, Fluorides 0.2mg/l, Nitrates 2.2mg/l, Silicates 20.4mg/l, Strontium 1.24mg/l. pH 6.5

Cin-Cin (It) cheers/good health. (Fr) = santé, (Ger) = prosit, (Gre) = lekhayyim, (It) = salute, (Nor) = skol, (Scot) = slàinte mhath, (Wal) = lechyd dda.

Cinco Estrelles (Sp) a Solera gran reserva brandy produced by Emilio Lustau.

Cinderella (Cktl)(Non-alc) 40mls (⅓ gill) orange juice, 40mls (⅓ gill) lemon juice, 40mls (⅓ gill) pineapple juice. Shake over ice, strain into a cocktail glass.

Cinnamaldehyde (Eng) an aldehyde found in wine which contributes to the bouquet and flavour of the wine. Is produced by the oxidation of alcohols.

Cinq-Saou (Fr) the alternative name for the Cinsault grape.

Cinqua (N.Z) the alternative name for the black hybrid grape Seibel 5455.

Cinquantenaire (Fr) the brand-name of a blend of Armagnac brandies produced by Janneau. 40% alc by vol.

Cinque Terre (It) lit: 'five villages', a small D.O.C. region situated on the narrow coastal strip of the Italian Riviera between Savona and Spezia in the Liguria region. Produces full-flavoured white wines from the Albarola, Bianchetta boscovines and Vermentino grapes. D.O.C. Towns are Biasca, Campiglia, Monterosso, Riomaggiore and Vernazza.

Cinqueterre (It) the alternative spelling presentation of Cinque Terre.

Cinque Terre Sciacchetrà (It) a D.O.C. white wine from the Cinque Terre, Liguria. Made from partially dried grapes: Albarola, Bosco and Vermentino. Can have on the label Vino dolce naturale (naturally sweet wine) when there is 4% sugar in suspension.

Cinque-Vie (Cktl) 30mls (¼ gill) each of Kirsch de Zoug, vodka, Cointreau, grapefruit juice. Shake well over ice, strain into a cocktail glass and top with a cherry.

Cinquième Cru (Fr) lit: 'fifth growths', the 1855 Médoc classification, there are 18 Châteaux on the list. Châteaux: Batailley, Belgrave, Camensac, Cantemerle, Clerc-Milon, Cos-Labory, Croizet-Bages, Dauzac, Grand-Puy-Ducasse, Grand-Puy-Lacoste, Haut-Bages-Libéral, Le Tertre, Lynch-Bages, Lynch-Moussas, Mouton-Baron Philippe, Mouton-Baronne-Philippe, Pédesclaux and Pontet-Canet.

Cinsault (Fr) a red grape variety grown in southern France that produces wines with a pepper spice, nutmeg, clove, damson, and black cherry aroma and flavours. Also known as Espagna, Hermitage, Malaga, Oltravianello and Picardin noir. *See also* Cinsaut (not to be confused with).

Cinsaut (S.Afr) a red grape variety (the Cinsaut x Pinot noir = Hermitage), known as the Blue Imperial in Australia.

Cinsaut (USA) a white grape variety used in the making of dessert wines in California. Also known as Malaga.

Cintana (It) a red grape variety grown in Sicily to produce red and rosé wines.

Cinta Oro (Sp) a Solera Reserva brandy produced by Emilio Lustau.

Cintiana (Bra) a red grape variety.

Cintoia (It) a sparkling natural spring mineral water from Cintoia. Mineral contents (milligrammes per litre): Sodium 9.4mg/l, Calcium 105mg/l, Magnesium 6mg/l, Potassium 0.8mg/l, Bicarbonates 332mg/l, Chlorides 15.1mg/l, Sulphates 11.9mg/l, Fluorides 0.1mg/l, Nitrates 1.9mg/l, Silicates 10.1mg/l. pH 7.4

Cinzano (It) a noted large vermouth-producing company based in Turin. Also produce Piemonte wines.

Cinzano Glass Collection (It) a magnificent collection of early glass in Turin.

Cinzano Winery (Austr) a winery based in Riverina, New South Wales.

Cinzia (It) a sparkling natural spring mineral water from Cinzia, Pennabilli, Pesaro. Mineral contents (milligrammes per litre): Sodium 9.5mg/l, Calcium 92mg/l, Magnesium 8.4mg/l, Potassium 0.65mg/l, Bicarbonates 317.259mg/l, Chlorides 7.8mg/l, Sulphates 13mg/l, Fluorides 0.11mg/l, Nitrates 2mg/l, Silicates 8mg/l. pH 7.4

Cirbonero (Sp) the brand-name of a 5 year old, full-bodied, red wine produced by Julián Chivite in Navarra, north-eastern Spain.

Circuito das Águas (Bra) a natural spring mineral water from the Fonte Amparo. Mineral contents (milligrammes per litre): Sodium 7.68mg/l, Calcium 6.98mg/l, Magnesium 6.46mg/l, Potassium 2mg/l, Bicarbonates 36.46mg/l, Sulphates 2.63mg/l, Fluorides 0.08mg/l, Nitrates 2.35mg/l. pH 6.0

Circulatory Vat (Port) a method of fermentation in which stainless steel vats are used. Inside these is a central column with an Archimedian screw rotated by an electric motor which carries the manta down to the bottom of the vat continuously.

Circumpotatio (Lat) to pass drinks around, passing drinks around.

Cirencester Brewery (Eng) a brewery based in Cirencester, Gloucestershire. Also known as the Cellar Brewery. Brews: cask-conditioned Down Moore Ale 1042 O.G. and Abbey Ale 1047 O.G.

Cirfandli (Hun) a white grape variety.

Ciriaco Borelli Winery (USA) *see* Borelli Winery.

Cirial (Sp) a white grape variety grown in the La Mancha region. It produces dry wines low in acidity.

Ciró (It) a Calabrian province of southern Italy. Noted for red, rosé and white wines. Old wine district whose wines are a distant descendant of Cremissa (a wine offered to athletes at the Olympic games).

Ciró Bianco (It) a D.O.C. white wine from Calabria. Produced from the Greco bianco and Trebbiano toscano grapes grown in the commune of Ciró.

Ciró Rosato (It) a D.O.C. rosé wine from Calabria. Produced from the Gaglioppo, Greco bianco and Trebbiano toscano grapes in the communes of Ciró Marina and part of Melissa Ceucoli (all in the province of Catanzaro).

Ciró Rosso (It) a D.O.C. red wine from Calabria. Produced from the Gaglioppo, Greco bianco and Trebbiano toscano grapes. If produced in communes of Ciró and Ciró Marina then entitled to the Classico designation. If total alc by vol. is 13.5% and aged 3 years then classed Riserva.

Cirrhosis (Lat) a disease of the liver associated with an excessive and continuous alcohol consumption.

Cirrus (S.Afr) the label for a red wine produced by

C

the Drostdy Wine Cellar winery, Tulbagh, Western Cape.

Cirsion (Sp) the top wine of Bodegas Roda, Rioja. Made from Tempranillo grapes.

Cisa Asinari dei Marchesi di Gresy (It) a noted vineyard based in the Barbaresco district of Piemonte.

Cisano (It) a natural spring mineral water from Calda, Bardolino, Verona.

Ciseau (Hol) a natural spring mineral water from Heerlen. Mineral contents (milligrammes per litre): Sodium 4mg/l, Calcium 68mg/l, Magnesium 8.4mg/l, Potassium 1.7mg/l, Bicarbonates 220mg/l, Chlorides 5mg/l, Sulphates 23mg/l, Nitrates 0.5mg/l.

Cisk Lager (Euro) a lager beer 1042 O.G. brewed by the Farsons Brewery in Malta.

Cissac (Fr) a commune in the A.C. Haut-Médoc, north-western Bordeaux.

Citation Brandy (USA) the brand-name of a brandy bottled by the Guild of Wineries and Distillers at Lodi, California.

Citeal (Ire) kettle.

Citeaux Monks (Fr) the owners of Clos de Vougeot, Côte de Nuits, Burgundy until the French revolution.

Citric Acid (Eng) CH₂(COOH)C(OH)COOH)CH₂COOH an additive to wines. Prevents iron casse by complexing with iron ions. (Fr) = acide citrique.

Citroen (Hol) a lemon peel-flavoured liqueur produced by De Kuyper. 30% alc by vol.

Citroengenever (Hol) a lemon-flavoured jenever (gin).

Citronen-Eis Likör (Ger) a yellow liqueur made from the juice and oil of lemon. Eis denotes that it should be drunk over ice.

Citronvand (Den) lemonade.

Citrusdal (S.Afr) a dessert wine and brandy-producing region based north of Tulbagh.

Citrusdal Koöperatiewe Wynkelders (S.Afr) a co-operative winery (established 1957) based at Citrusdal, Swartland, Western Cape. who operate as Fairtraders. 1200ha. (Add): Box 41, Citrusdal 7340. Grape varieties: Bukettraube, Cabernet sauvignon, Chardonnay, Chenin blanc, Cinsaut, Colombard, Grenache, Hanepoot jerepiko, Merlot, Muscadel, Pinotage, Red jerepiko, Sauvignon blanc, Shiraz. Labels: Cardouw, Classique Blanc Chianti, Goue Vallei, Ivory Creek, Royal Blanc, Zaximus. Website: http://www.citrusdalcellars.co.za

Citrus Spring (Eng) a sparkling spring water and 10% fruit juice (orange or lemon) produced by Britvic.

Citrus Teacup (Cktl) 850mls (1½ pints) fresh brewed tea, rind of a grapefruit, lemon, orange and apple, 1 clove. Heat altogether, strain, sweeten with sugar syrup to taste. Serve hot or cold.

City and Guilds Alcoholic Beverages Certificate (Eng) Prefix 717. Was originally prefixed 150 (1960's) and 707-3 (1970's). The original qualification for wine waiters (sommeliers). Now replaced by N.V.Q (and S.V.Q).

City Centres Breweries (Eng) a brewery (established 1978). (Add): Unit 14, Garanor Way, Portbury, Bristol, Avon BS20 7XE. Brews a variety of beers. Website: http://www.smiles.co.uk 'E'mail: info@smiles.co.uk

City Gin (Eng) a dry gin produced in 1986 by Nicholson & C°. for the 'Morning Advertiser' (now The Licensee) to raise monies for the L.V.A. schools (part of the sales donated) a limited production.

City Lager (Afr) a lager 1042 O.G. brewed by the East Africa Breweries in Tanzania.

City Lights [1] (Cktl) ½ measure Glayva, ¼ measure orange juice, ¼ measure lemon juice. Stir over ice, strain into an ice-filled highball glass, top with soda water, slice of lemon and a cherry and serve with straws.

City Lights [2] (Cktl) 1 measure Cinzano Bianco, serve in an ice-filled highball glass and top with lemonade.

City of Cambridge Brewery [The] (Eng) a brewery. (Add): Ely Road, Chittering, Cambridge, Cambridgeshire CB5 9PH. Brews: Hobson's Choice. Website: http://www.cambridge-brewery.co.uk 'E'mail: sales@cambridge-brewery.co.uk

Ciudad Real (Sp) a wine-producing area in the La Mancha region.

C.I.V.A. (Fr) abbr: Comité Interprofessionnel des Vins d'Alsace.

C.I.V.A.S. (Fr) abbr: Conseil Interprofessionnel des Vins d'Anjou et de Saumur.

C.I.V.B. (Fr) abbr: Comité Interprofessionnel des Vins de Bordeaux.

C.I.V.C. (Fr) abbr: Comité Interprofessionnel du Vin de Champagne. Was founded in 1941 to regulate the growing of the vines and the production of Champagne. (Add): 5, Rue Henri Martin, 51-Épernay.

C.I.V.C.P. (Fr) abbr: Comité Interprofessionnel des Vins de Côtes de Provence.

C.I.V.D.N. (Fr) abbr: Comité Interprofessionnel des Vins Doux Naturels.

C.I.V.G. (Fr) abbr: Comité Interprofessionnel des Vins de Gaillac.

C.I.V.L. (Fr) abbr: Comité Interprofessionnel des Vins du Languedoc.

Civitella d'Agliano (It) an I.G.T. of Latium.

C.I.V.O.N. (Fr) abbr: Comité Interprofessionnel des Vins d'Origine du Nantais.

C.I.V.O.P.N. (Fr) abbr: Comité Interprofessionnel des Vins d'Origine du Pays Nantais.

Civrac (Fr) a commune in the Bas-Médoc, A.C. Médoc, north-western France.

C.I.V.R.B. (Fr) abbr: Comité Interprofessionnel des Vins de la Région de Bergerac.

C.I.V.T. (Fr) abbr: Comité Interprofessionnel des Vins de Touraine. (Add): 19, Square Prosper Mérimée, 3700 Tours.

Clacquesin (Fr) a distillery whose products include: Crème de Cassis, Extrait des Pins (pine needle liqueur) and Clacquesin liqueur.

341

C

Cladosporium cellerae (Lat) the name given to the black-brown mould that grows on walls etc. in wine cellars. Lives off the alcoholic vapours (esters and volatile acids). *See also* **Torula compniacensis**.

Claerkampster (Hol) a monastery-produced herb liqueur 35% alc by vol.

Claeryn (Hol) a young genever produced by the Bols C°.

Clairault Estate (Austr) a winery based in the Margaret River region of Western Australia. Grape varieties include: Cabernet sauvignon.

Clair-Daü (Fr) a large estate 41.5ha. based in the Côte de Nuits, Burgundy.

Clairdie (Fr) a Clairette de Die sparkling (méthode traditionelle) wine from the Cave Coopérative Clairette de Die, Rhône.

Clairdoc (Fr) *abbr*: A.C. **Clair**ette de Langue**doc**.

Claire Baie Bottled Water (USA) a natural spring mineral water from Oak Creek, Wisconsin.

Clairelle (Fr) a natural spring mineral water from Chanterine. Mineral contents (milligrammes per litre): Sodium 7mg/l, Calcium 119mg/l, Magnesium 28mg/l, Potassium 2mg/l, Bicarbonates 430mg/l, Chlorides 18mg/l, Sulphates 18mg/l, Fluorides 0.75mg/l. pH 7.9

Clairet (Fr) lit: 'clear/bright/light', associated with the red wines of Bordeaux. Anglocised to Claret by the English when Bordeaux wines were first popular. *See also* Claret.

Clairet de Moselle (Fr) a rosé wine produced in Metz, Lorraine, north-eastern France.

Clairet-Schillerwein (Fr) an Alsace rosé wine.

Clairette (Fr) *see* Clairette Blanche.

Clairette (It) a white grape variety grown in Sardinia.

Clairette à Grains Ronde (Fr) the alternative name for the Ugni blanc in southern France.

Clairette Blanche (Fr) a white grape variety grown in southern France to produce sparkling and still white wines usually low in alcohol and acidic. Also grown in Armagnac and other countries i.e. South Africa.

Clairette de Bellegarde (Fr) an A.C. full-bodied and flavoured white wine from the area of the Costières du Gard, 25 miles south-west of Avignon near the Rhône-Sète canal. Made from the Clairette grape. Minimum alc by vol. 11%.

Clairette de Die (Fr) an A.C. dry, sparkling (méthode traditionelle) wine produced from the Clairette and Muscat à petits grains (25% max) grapes. Has a fine Muscat flavour and bouquet. Minimum alc by vol. 10% (Muscat-based) and 9% (Clairette-based). Replaced by Crémant de Die.

Clairette de Die 'Méthode Dioise Ancestrale' (Fr) usually demi-sec with a minimum 75% muscat and about 7.5% alc by vol.

Clairette de Die Mousseux (Fr) an A.C. sparkling (méthode traditionelle, no liqueur de tirage added) wine. Made from Clairette and Muscat (minimum 75%) grapes. Minimum alc by vol. 7.5% alc by vol.

Clairette de Venice (Fr) an alternative name for the Ugni blanc.

Clairette du Gaillac (Fr) a slightly-sparkling, red-rosé wine produced in the Gaillac region, Tarn département, southern France.

Clairette du Languedoc (Fr) an A.C. dry, white, acidic wine produced near Montpellier in the Midi region of the Languedoc-Roussillon. Also a semi-sweet version (Rancio) aged 3 years minimum alc by vol. 14%, (dry) = 13%. Made from the communes of Aspiran, Cabrières, Ceyras, Paulhan and Péret. *see* Clairdoc.

Clairette Egreneuse (Isr) a white grape variety.

Clairette Ronde (Fr) *see* Clairette à Grains Ronde.

Clairin (W.Ind) the local name for the white spirit (rum) from the first distillation in Haiti.

Clairvaux Koöperatiewe Wynkelders (S.Afr) a co-operative winery based at Robertson. (Add): Box 179, Robertson 6705. Noted for dessert wines and brandies. Grape varieties include Chenin blanc, Sauvignon blanc, Rhine Riesling.

Clam (Fr) a commune in the Charente-Maritime département whose grapes are classed Petite Champagne (Cognac).

Clamato Cocktail (Cktl) 1 measure vodka, ½ measure clam juice, 2 measures tomato juice. Shake over ice and strain into an ice-filled old-fashioned glass.

Clamato Juice (USA) a clam and tomato juice drink.

Clameur de Haro (Ch.Isles) a 3.6% alc by vol. ale from the R. W Randall Vauxlaurens Brewery, St. Peter Port, Guernsey.

Clan Campbell (Scot) a 12 year old blended de luxe Scotch whisky. 43% alc by vol.

Clan Dew (Eng) the brand-name of a Scotch whisky and ginger wine drink.

Clan MacGregor (Scot) a blended Scotch whisky produced by William Grant and Sons. 40% alc by vol.

Clanrana (Scot) a herb-flavoured liqueur whisky.

Clansman Cocktail (Cktl) ½ measure white rum, ½ measure apricot brandy, 1 measure orange juice, ½ measure lemon juice, dash egg white. Shake over ice, strain into a cocktail glass, dress with slices of orange, lemon and a cherry.

Clansman (Scot) a 3.9% alc by vol. ale brewed by the Hebridean Brewery C°., Isle of Lewis.

Clanwilliam (S.Afr) a brandy and dessert wine-producing region based north of Tulbagh.

Clan-y-Delyn (Eng) a whisky, honey and sugar-based liqueur produced by Hallgarten. 40% alc by vol.

Clape [La] (Fr) an A.C. district in the Aude department, is classed as part of the Coteaux du Languedoc. Produces mainly white wines.

Clara (Fr) a natural spring mineral water. Mineral contents (milligrammes per litre): Sodium 92mg/l, Calcium 60mg/l, Magnesium 23mg/l, Potassium 20mg/l, Bicarbonates 476mg/l, Chlorides 36mg/l, Sulphates 55mg/l.

Clara (Mex) a term used to denote 'clear' when applied to lager beers.

C

Clare (Austr) an area of South Australia near the towns of Clare and Watervale. Produces full, rich reds and full-bodied white wines.

Clare (Cktl) ½ measure sloe gin, ½ measure Italian vermouth, dash Cognac. Shake over ice and strain into a cocktail glass.

Claremont Winery (Can) one of the top wineries based in British Columbia.

Clarendon and Bakers Gully (Austr) part of the Coolawin Estate in South Australia.

Clare Riesling (Austr) the erroneous varietal name for the white grape Crouchen.

Clares (Eng) Chaucer's way of spelling Clairet (from his Canterbury Tales).

Claret (Eng) the name given to the red wines of Bordeaux (especially those of the Médoc). A corruption of the French word Clairet and Clairette. *See also* Clarry. (Den) = rød Bordeaux-vin.

Claret (USA) *see* California Claret.

Claret (USA) a red wine (Cabernet sauvignon) produced by the Robert Foley winery, Napa Valley, California.

Claret Cobbler (Cktl) place some ice into a large goblet, half fill with claret wine, add barspoon of gomme syrup, 4 dashes Curaçao. Stir, decorate with fruit in season, sprig of mint and serve with straws.

Claret Cocktail (Cktl) dissolve 1 teaspoon powdered sugar in 50mls soda water, add 75mls claret. Stir over ice, strain into a highball glass with ice, decorate with fruits in season, mint and cucumber peel.

Claret Cup (Cup) juice 2 oranges, juice 2 lemons, 1 bottle claret, 150mls water, 1 syphon soda water, rind of 1 orange and lemon. Boil 100grms. sugar in the water together with the rinds. Add the juices and wine and cool. Place ice into a large jug, add mix, top with soda, fruits in season, mint and sliced cucumber.

Claret de Gascogne (Fr) a rare white grape variety also known as Blanc Dame or Claret de Gers.

Claret de Gers (Fr) an alternative name for the southern French variety Blanc Dame of Claret de Gascogne.

Clarete (Port) light red wine.

Clarete (Sp) a term used to describe a light red wine from the Rioja region.

Clarete Campanas (Sp) a fine, light red wine produced by Las Campanas in the Navarra region, north-eastern Spain.

Claret Jug (Eng) a Georgian decanter-style glass container with a handle, often has a silver neck band, lid and base.

Claret Lemonade (Cktl) dissolve 2 teaspoons sugar in the juice of a large lemon in a highball glass. Top with 50mls (2fl.ozs) claret and soda water, dress with an orange and lemon slice and a cherry. Serve with straws.

Claret Punch (Cktl) 100mls (4fl.ozs) claret, 25mls (1fl.oz) lemon juice, 2 dashes orange Curaçao, 3 dashes gomme syrup. Stir over ice, strain into an ice-filled highball glass, top with ginger ale and a slice of and lemon.

Claret Punch (Punch) 1 bottle claret, 50mls (2fl.ozs) Cognac, 50mls (2fl.ozs) orange Curaçao, 1 sliced orange, 300mls (¼ pint) soda water. Stir altogether, add ice and serve.

Claret Sangaree (Cktl) 1 measure claret, juice of a lemon, 1 teaspoon castor sugar. Fill a wine glass with crushed ice, add ingredients and stir, top with an orange slice and grated nutmeg.

Clarett (Eng) the old Georgian way of spelling Claret.

Claretto (It) claret.

Clare Valley (Austr) a wine region situated north of Adelaide, South Australia, has a warm climate with soils of 'terra rossa' red sandy soil over limestone. Sub Region: Polish Hill (slatey soils).

Clare-Watervale (Austr) a wine-producing region of South Australia. Is based 90 miles north of Adelaide. Planted mainly with Cabernet, Riesling and Shiraz.

Clariano (Sp) a D.O. blanco seco wine produced from Merseguera, Tortosí and Malvasía grapes with a minimum of 11% alc by vol. Light red and tinto wines from Monastrell, Forcayat and Granacha grapes with a minimum of 12% alc by vol. White and rosado wines are Jóvenes. Red wines are Jóvenes or Crianza in style. Licoroso and rancio wines for Reserva spend 24 months in USA oak and 1 year in bottle.

Claridge (Cktl) 20mls (⅙ gill) each of Cointreau, dry gin, apricot brandy, 40mls (⅓ gill) dry vermouth. Stir over ice and strain into a cocktail glass.

Clarificaçao (Port) the clarification (fining) of wines with egg white, bentonite, etc.

Clarificants (Eng) the name given to substances used to clear wines and make them bright. *see* Bentonite, Blood, Egg White, Gelatine and Isinglass.

Clarification (Eng) the process of clarifying wines to make them clear and bright. *See also* Collage. (Fr) = clarification, (Port) = clarificaçao.

Clarifiers (Eng) fining agents (e.g. ox blood, isinglass, egg white, gelatine or bentonite).

Clarifiers (USA) long shallow pans used in San Francisco to ferment the beer in the Anchor Steam Brewery.

Clarify (Eng) to clear wine and make it bright using fining agents such as ox blood, isinglass, egg white, gelatine or bentonite.

Clarissen-Brau (Ger) a 4.6% alc by vol. beer from Dortmunder Stifts Brauerei, Dortmund, Westphalia.

Clark and Randolph Fizz (Cktl) 125mls (1 gill) gin, 35mls (1½ fl.ozs) pineapple juice, 1 egg white. Shake well over ice, strain into an ice-filled highball glass, top with soda water and serve with straws.

Clark & C° Ltd [HB] (Eng) a brewery (established 1982). (Add): 136 Westgate, Wakefield, West Yorkshire WF2 9SW. Brews: Chapel Ale 3.8% alc by vol., Classic Blonde 3.9% alc by vol., Classic Brunette 4.2% alc by vol., Golden Hommet 5%

C

alc by vol., cask-conditioned Hammerhead 1050 O.G., Henry Boon's Wakefield Ale 1038 O.G., Mulberry Tree 5% alc by vol., No Angel 4% alc by vol., Rams Revenge 4.6% alc by vol. Website: http://www.hbclark.co.uk 'E'mail: clarksbrewery@hbclark.co.uk

Clark & Telephone Vineyard (USA) the label for a red wine (Pinot noir) produced by the Belle Glos winery, Santa Maria Valley, Santa Barbara County, California.

Clarkes Hydrometer (Eng) invented in 1725 by John Clarke. Was the first accurate hydrometer using brass weights.

Clarksburg (USA) a wine-producing district in Yolo County, California.

Claro (Port) *see* Vinho Claro.

Claro de Lias (Sp) describes a clear wine obtained from the lees of the must.

Claros (Sp) bright wine.

Claros de Turbios (Sp) a wine made from the lees which accumulate in the casks and is used for blends in some cheaper Sherries.

Claro Valley (Chile) the northerly part of the Maule Valley. Home to Calina Winery, Casanova, Domaine Oriental.

Clarry (Eng) the nickname for clairet (claret) in the seventeenth and eighteenth centuries.

Clarus Canadian Springs (Can) a natural spring mineral water from Winnipeg, Manitoba.

Clary Wine (Eng) a wine made from chopped Málaga raisins and clary blossom.

Clásico (Sp) a white wine produced by Bodegas Salnesur, Val do Salnés, Rías Baixas, D.O. Galicia from Albariño grapes.

Clásico (Sp) a term used in the Tarragona region for red or sweet white dessert wines up to 14%–15% alc by vol.

Classé (Fr) denotes a wine of quality. *see* Grand Cru Classé.

Classement (Fr) classification. i.e. Classement 1855.

Classe Royale (Hol) a 5% alc by vol. bottled pilsner brewed by De Vriendenkring Bier Brouwerij.

Classic (Cktl) ½ measure brandy, ⅙ measure maraschino, ⅙ measure lemon juice, ⅙ measure orange juice. Shake over ice, strain into a sugar-rimmed (lemon juice) wine glass and add a twist of lemon peel juice.

Classic (Eng) the term used to describe top quality wines which have finesse and style. (Fr) = classé, (It) = classico.

Classic (Eng) a 4.5% alc by vol. premium best bitter brewed by the Wye Valley Brewery, Herefordshire.

Classic (Ger) a new term introduced in 2001 for dry style wines that are considered 'classic' of a particular region. *See also* Selection.

Classic (Ger) a fine lager beer brewed by the Dortmunder Kronen Brauerei of Dortmund, Westphalia 5.1% alc by vol.

Classic (S.Afr) the label for a range of blended wines (red and white) produced by the Douglas Wine Cellar winery, Douglas, Northern Cape.

Classic (S.Afr) the label for a red wine (Cabernet

sauvignon, Malbec, Merlot and Petit verdot blend) part of the Jacques de Savoy range produced by the Vrede en Lust Wine Farm winery, Paarl, Western Cape.

Classic Blanc Chianti (S.Afr) the label for a red wine (Cinsaut and Merlot blend) produced by the Citrusdal Cellars winery, Swartland, Western Cape.

Classic Blonde (Eng) 3.9% alc by vol. ale brewed by H.B. Clark & Cº. Ltd., West Yorkshire.

Classic Brunette (Eng) a 4.2% alc by vol. ale brewed by H.B. Clark & Cº. Ltd., West Yorkshire.

Classic Crystal (Ire) a natural spring mineral water from Edward Street, Lurgan, Craigavon, County Armagh, Northern Ireland.

Classico (It) lit; 'classic', the central and best area in relation to wine. To be labelled Classico the grapes must come from the delimited area. i.e. Chianti Classico, Frascati Classico, etc.

Classics Range (Eng) a new (2006) range of bitter ales (Cutty Sark, Dr's Orders, Free Spirit, Heavenly Draft, Hidden Treasure) brewed by the Hydes Brewery, Manchester.

Classic Wine Glass (Czec) a fine glass design made of Barium crystal in Bohemia. Is similar to the Baccarat design. Supplied in U.K. by: Classic Wine Club, 4, Mardon, Westfield Park, Hatch End, Middlesex. HA5 4JQ.

Classified (S.Afr) the label used by the Bartho Eksteen Family winery, Walker Bay, Western Cape for a range of wines.

Classimo (It) a term (now seldom used) to describe bottle-fermented sparkling wine. *see* Talento, Metodo Classico, Metodo Tradizionale.

Classique (S.Afr) the label for a red wine (Cabernet franc 10%, Cabernet sauvignon 60%, Merlot 30%) produced by the Du Toitskloof Winery, Worcester, Western Cape.

Classique Red (S.Afr) the label for a red wine (Merlot, Cabernet sauvignon and Cabernet franc blend) produced by the Verdôme winery, Paarl, Western Cape.

Clastidio (It) the name given to red or dry white wines from Lombardy.

Clastidium (It) a dry, white wine made from the Pinot grigio and the Pinot nero grapes. Is oak matured.

Clastido-Ballabio (It) a producer of sparkling (metodo tradizionale) wines based in Lombardy.

Claudius-Quelle (Ger) a natural spring mineral water from Trappenkamp, SH.

Clauss [Gustav] (Gre) a Bavarian refugee who in 1861 set up business in Patras and introduced the Mavrodaphne dessert wine. The business is now called the Achaia-Clauss Wine Cº. 450ha. French and Greek varietals.

Clausthaler Premium Alcoholfrei (Ger) a bottled, low-alcohol lager beer 0.5% by vol. brewed by the Binding Brauerei, Frankfurt.

Clavelin (Fr) a squat bottle used for the Jura (vin jaunes) wines of eastern France. Holds 62cls. (620mls = 21fl.ozs).

Claverie (Fr) an Armagnac producer. (Add):

344

C

Lannemaignan, 32240 Estang. 10ha. in the Bas Armagnac.

Claverie (Fr) a white grape variety grown in southern France. Also known as Chalosse Blanche.

Claverley Ale (Eng) a cask-conditioned ale brewed by Bank's Brewery.

Clavignon, Gamay Rouge (Switz) a red wine produced from the Gamay grape by Société Vinicole de Perroy in the Vaud canton.

Clavileño (Sp) a dry white wine produced by La Daimieleña in the La Mancha region.

Clay (Eng) sedimentary soil, stiff, viscous earth. (Fr) = argile.

Clay and Chalk (Eng) a soil style found in the Champagne region. (Fr) = argilo-calcaires.

Clayette (Fr) a wicker tray used in the Champagne region to hold the grape whilst éppluchage takes place.

Claymore [The] (Scot) a blended Scotch whisky produced by A. Ferguson and C°. A subsidiary of White Horse Distillers (part of DCL). 40% alc by vol.

Clayson Report (Scot) a report on the Scottish licensing laws made in 1976 by Dr. Christopher Clayson who headed the government committee. It allowed public houses to apply for regular extensions to permitted hours and be able to open all day.

Clayton's Original (Eng) a cask-conditioned ale 1048 O.G. brewed by the Fellows, Morton and Clayton Brewery (a Whitbreads home-brew public house) in Nottingham.

Clean (Eng) a term used to describe a wine which has no unnatural aroma or maladies present.

Clean Coffee (Eng) the name given to the coffee beans when they are ready for roasting.

Cleanfield Bottled Water (Tai) a natural spring mineral water from. Mineral contents (milligrammes per litre): Calcium 1.2mg/l, Magnesium 8mg/l, Potassium 1mg/l. pH 7.5

Clearick (Scot) the name for the spirit from the second distillation in malt whisk production. Also known as New Make or Spirit.

Clearly Artic (USA) a natural spring mineral water from Anchorage, Alaska.

Clearly Canadian (Eng) clear, flavoured waters: raspberry, peach, cherry and blackberry from Callithekë (the soft drinks arm of IDV).

Clearly Canadian O+2 (Can) a natural spring mineral water brand.

Clear Mountain (USA) a natural spring mineral water brand.

Clearview Estate Winery (N.Z) a winery. (Add): Clifton Road, RD 2, Te Awanga, Hastings. 6ha. Grape varieties: Chardonnay, Sauvignon blanc, Cabernet franc, Merlot.

Clearwater Brewery (Eng) a brewery (established 1999). (Add): 2 Devon Units, Torrington, Devon EX38 7HP. Brews: 1646 4.8% alc by vol., Cavalier 4% alc by vol., Olivers Nectar 5.2% alc by vol., Torridge Best 4.4% alc by vol., Village Pride 3.7% alc by vol. Website: http://www.clearwaterbrewery.com 'E'mail: info@clearwaterbrewery.com

Cleebronn (Ger) village (Anb): Württemberg. (Ber): Württembergisch Unterland. (Gro): Heuchelberg. (Vin): Michaelberg.

Clef du Vin (Euro) a device™ that claims to be able to age a glass of wine in seconds (1 year for each second the 'key' is left in the glass of wine) and is able to age any type/style of wine.

Clefs des Prelats (Fr) the label of a Châteauneuf-du-Pape produced by Caves Saint Pierre, Avenue Pierre Luxembourg, B.P. 5, 84230 Châteauneuf-du-Pape, southern Rhône. See also Tiare du Papes (La).

Clefs d'Or [Les] (Fr) the label of a Châteauneuf-du-Pape produced by Deydier (Jean), Avenue St. Joseph, 84230 Châteauneuf-du-Pape, southern Rhône.

Cleft Grafting (Sp) a style of grafting carried out on those vines which have previously been bench or field grafted and have not taken.

Clemenceau Cocktail (Cktl) ⅔ measure gin, ⅓ measure French vermouth, ⅙ measure Cointreau, 2 dashes orange bitters. Shake over ice and strain into a cocktail glass.

Clément Distillerie (W.Ind) a noted rum distillery based on the island of Martinique.

Clemente VIII (It) a winery in the DOCG Chianti Classico Riserva produced by the Castelli del Grevepesa co-operative in the Tuscany region.

Clement V (Fr) the first Avignon Pope (1305–1313) built Châteauneuf-du-Pape and owned Château Pape Clement in the Graves (1216–1314).

Clerambault [Emile] (Fr) a Champagne producer. (Add): Neuville Buxeuil, Neuville-sur-Seine, 10250 Mussy-sur-Seine. Co-operative. Produces vintage and non-vintage wines.

Clergets (Fr) an important négociant-éleveur based in Saint Aubin, Côte de Beaune, Burgundy.

Clerico (It) a winery based in the DOCG Barolo, Piemonte. Label: Pajana.

Clerics Cure (Eng) a 5% alc by vol. ale brewed by the Three Tuns Brewery, Shropshire.

Clermont-Ferrand (Fr) a town in eastern France near the Côtes d'Auvergne where Châteaugay and Chanturgues are produced from the Gamay grape, noted for its chalk soil.

Clés des Ducs (Fr) a brand of Armagnac made by the Izarra company.

Clessé (Fr) see Viré-Clessé.

Cleveland Winery (Austr) a winery (established 1984). (Add): Off Shannons Road, Lancefield, Victoria. Grape varieties: Chardonnay, Cabernet sauvignon, Pinot noir.

Clever (Czec) a sparkling natural spring mineral water from Hanácká Kyselka Prirodni. Mineral contents (milligrammes per litre): Sodium 412.4mg/l, Calcium 185.2mg/l, Magnesium 107.1mg/l, Bicarbonates 2058mg/l, Chlorides 144.2mg/l, Sulphates 0.185mg/l, Fluorides 0.63mg/l, Iron 2.45mg/l, Iodine 0.073mg/l.

Clever Endeavour (Eng) a 4.5% alc by vol. seasonal ale brewed by Hydes at 46 Moss Lane, West Manchester, Lancashire. Avaialble March and April (part of their Craft Ale range).

C

Cleversulzbach (Ger) village (Anb): Württemberg. (Ber): Württembergisch Unterland. (Gro): Staufenberg. (Vin): Berg.

Clevner (Fr) the name given to the Pinot blanc grape in Alsace. *See also* Melon de Bougogne, Muscadet. (Aus) = Weissburgunder, (Ger) = Weisser burgunder, (It) = Pinot bianco.

Clicquot [Madame] (Fr) inventor of remuage and dégorgement. *see* Veuve Clicquot.

Clicquot Rosé (Fr) a vintage rosé Champagne produced by Veuve Clicquot Ponsardin from 52% Pinot noir, 32% Chardonnay and Bouzy Rouge.

Cliff Bier (Eng) a 5.2% alc by vol. ale brewed by the Facers Brewery, Greater Manchester.

Cliff Hanger (Cktl) 1 measure Montezuma Silver Tequila stirred over ice in a highball glass. Top with bitter lemon and a slice of lemon.

Cliffhanger (Eng) a 5.5% alc by vol. porter ale from the Dark Star Brewery in Brighton under the Skinner brand label.

Cliff Lede (USA) a winery based in the Stags Leap District, Napa Valley, California. Grape varieties include: Cabernet sauvignon.

Cliftonia (Cktl) ⅓ measure Swedish Punsch, ⅓ measure Grand Marnier, ⅓ measure dry gin, ⅓ measure orange juice. Shake over ice and strain into a cocktail glass.

Clifton Road (N.Z) a vineyard. (Add): Clifton Road, Te Awanga, P.O. Box 4118, Mayfair, Hastings. 2.5ha. Grape varieties: Chardonnay, Sauvignon blanc.

Climat (Fr) a specific individual vineyard used mainly in the Côte d'Or, Burgundy (having individual climatic conditions).

Climat (Switz) a term designating a particular wine-growing area.

Climat de Corsaire (S.Afr) the label for a white wine (Chardonnay) produced by the Signal Hill winery, Cape Town, Western Cape.

Climat de la Forge (Fr) the old name used for Clos de Tart, Côte de Nuits, Burgundy.

Climat-du-Val (Fr) a Premier Cru vineyard in the A.C. commune of Auxey-Duresses, Côte de Beaune, Burgundy. 23ha. Also known as the Clos-du-Val.

Climate (Eng) appertaining to the weather, the right climate is needed to produce grapes suitable for wine production. *see* Micro-climate.

Climax Brewing C° (USA) a brewery. (Add): 112 Valley Road, Roselle Park, New Jersey 07204 1402. Brews beers and lager. Website: http://www.home.sharednet.com 'E'mail: climaxbrewing@istpage.com

Climax KY (USA) a still natural spring mineral water (established 2002) from Rockcastle Springs.. Mineral contents (milligrammes per litre): Sodium 1.21mg/l, Calcium 12.1mg/l, Magnesium 1.39mg/l, Potassium 0.718mg/l, Chlorides 2mg/l, Sulphates 5.6mg/l, Fluorides 0.05mg/l, Nitrates 1.6mg/l. pH 7.5

Clim Cav (Fr) a wine rack made from Pozzolana (a volcanic lava) quarried near Auvergne. (Add):

Sogestel 17, Boulevard du Géneral de Gaulle, 49600 Beaupréau.

Clinch's Brewery (Eng) no longer used, now known as the Glenny Brewery.

Cline Cellars (USA) a winery based in Sonoma, California. Noted for Zinfandel wines.

Clinton (USA) a red grape variety, a member of Vitis labrusca family.

Clinton Vineyards (USA) a small winery based in Hudson Valley, New York. 6ha. Noted for Seyval blanc wines.

Clip Joint (USA) a slang term for an establishment that charges high prices for drinks, etc. (overcharges).

Clipper Beer (Eng) a cask-conditioned bitter 1040 O.G. brewed by the Pier Hotel in Gravesend, Kent, and the South-eastern in Strood, Kent.

Clipper IP80 (Scot) the name of an ale brewed by Broughton Ales Ltd., Lanarkshire.

Clisse (Fr) the name for the wicker covering wrapped around demi-johns.

C.L.O.C. (Den) lit: 'best caraway in Castel', an *abbr*: **C**umin **L**iquidum **O**ptimum **C**astelli. A caraway-flavoured liqueur 31.5% alc by vol.

Cloc Brun (Den) a brown version of C.L.O.C. 38.5% alc by vol.

Clockwork Beer C° (Scot) a brewery. (Add): 1153-1155 Cathcart Road, Athos Sky Ltd., Glasgow, Lanarkshire G42 9HB. Brews a variety of beers and lager. 'E'mail: robin.graham@btconnect.com

Clohars (Fr) a noted producer of cider produced in Brittany, north-western France.

Cloister (Eng) a 4.5% alc by vol. ale brewed by The Durham Brewery Ltd., County Durham.

Cloister Liqueur (Eng) the collective name for liqueurs originally associated with monasteries.

Cloitre du Château Prieuré Lichine [Le] (Fr) wine produced by Château Prieure Lichine, Cantenac, Margaux.

Clonal Selection (Eng) the process of 'cloning' grape varieties to produce a pure species of the named grape using DNA. *see* Clone.

Clone (Eng) lit: 'a group of organisms or cells of the same genetic constitution that are descended from a common ancestor by asexual reproduction as by cuttings, grafting, etc'. The best of a species of vine which is usually resistant to disease and tolerant to climatic conditions. An improved specimen.

Cloof Estate (S.Afr) a winery (established 1997) based in Darling, Costal Region, Western Cape. 166ha. Grape varieties: Cabernet sauvignon, Chenin blanc, Cinsaut, Merlot, Pinotage, Shiraz, Tinta. Label: Burghers Post, Bush Wines, Cellar Blend, Crucible, Dusty Road. Website: http://www.cloof.co.za

Clos (Fr) a walled vineyard especially in Burgundy.

Clos [Le] (Fr) a wine-producing village in the commune of Fuissé in the A.C. Pouilly-Fuissé, Mâcon, Burgundy.

Clos [Les] (Fr) a Grand Cru vineyard of A.C. Chablis, Burgundy.

C

Clos Abadía (Sp) a full, red wine produced by Raimat in Lérida from Cabernet 50%, Garnacha 20% and Tempranillo 30%.

Clos André (S.Afr) the label for a cape classique sparkling wine produced by the High Constantia winery, Constantia, Western Cape.

Clos Apalta (Chile) a red wine produced by Casa Lapostolle, Rapel Valley, Colchagua from Merlot, Carmenère and Cabernet sauvignon grapes.

Clos Arlots (Fr) a Premier Cru vineyard of the village Premeau in the southern end of the A.C. commune of Nuits-Saint-Georges, Côte de Nuits, Burgundy. 4ha. Also known as Clos des Arlots.

Clos Avocat (Fr) a vineyard. (Com): Cérons. A.C. Cérons, Bordeaux 4ha.

Clos Badon (Fr) a Grand Cru Classé vineyard in the A.C. Saint-Émilion, Bordeaux.

Clos Barrail-du-Milieu (Fr) a vineyard. (Com): Pomerol. A.C. Pomerol, Bordeaux 2ha.

Clos Barreau (Fr) a vineyard. (Com): Fargues. A.C. Sauternes, Bordeaux 1ha.

Clos Barreyre (Fr) a vineyard. (Com): Virelade. A.C. Graves. Bordeaux. 3ha (white).

Clos Baudoin (Fr) an A.C. Vouvray. (Add): Prince Poniatowski, Vouvray 11 & LI., Loire Valley.

Clos-Baulet (Fr) a Premier Cru vineyard in the A.C. commune of Morey-Saint-Denis, Côte de Nuits, Burgundy 0.8ha.

Clos Bayard (Fr) a vineyard. (Com): Montagne-Saint-Émilion. A.C. Saint-Émilion, Bordeaux 5ha.

Clos Beaufort-Mazerat (Fr) a vineyard. (Com): Saint-Émilion. A.C. Saint-Émilion, Bordeaux 2ha.

Clos Beauregard (Fr) part of Château Taillefer, A.C. Pomerol, Bordeaux.

Clos Beau Rivage de By (Fr) a vineyard. (Com): Bégadan. A.C. Médoc, Bordeaux 5ha.

Clos Bel-Air (Fr) part of Domaine la Pointe, A.C. Pomerol, Bordeaux.

Clos Bell Rose (Fr) a vineyard. A.C. Saint-Émilion. (Add): 33330 Saint-Émilion, Bordeaux. (Com): Saint-Émilion.

Clos Belle-Vue (Fr) a vineyard. (Com): Sainte-Croix-du-Mont. A.C. Sainte-Croix-du-Mont, Bordeaux 4ha.

Clos Bellevue-Figeac (Fr) a vineyard in the A.C. Saint-Émilion, Bordeaux 3ha.

Clos Bellevue-Peyblanquet (Fr) a vineyard in the A.C. Saint-Émilion, Bordeaux 3ha.

Clos Bernachot (Fr) part of Château du Roy, A.C. Saint-Émilion, Bordeaux.

Clos Blanc (Fr) a Premier Cru vineyard in the A.C. commune of Pommard, Côte de Beaune, Burgundy. 4.3ha. Also known as Le Clos Blanc.

Clos Blanc [de Vougeot] (Fr) a Premier Cru vineyard in the A.C. commune of Vougeot, Côte de Nuits, Burgundy 1.8ha.

Clos Bonalgue (Fr) a vineyard. (Com): Pomerol. A.C. Pomerol, Bordeaux 3ha.

Clos Bourgelet (Fr) a vineyard. (Com): Cérons. A.C. Cérons, Bordeaux 7ha.

Clos Brun (Fr) a vineyard in the A.C. Saint-Émilion, Bordeaux 3ha.

Clos-Bussière (Fr) a Premier Cru vineyard in the A.C. commune of Morey-Saint-Denis, Côte de Nuits, Burgundy 3.1ha.

Clos Cabanes (Fr) a vineyard. (Com): St-Pierre-de-Mons. A.C. St-Pierre-de-Mons, Bordeaux. 4ha (white).

Clos Cabannes (Fr) a vineyard. (Com): St-Pierre-de-Mons. A.C. Graves. Bordeaux. 1ha (white).

Clos Cabrière (S.Afr) a specialist sparkling wine producer (mèthode traditionelle) based in Franschhoek. Also produces a fine brandy using the Chardonnay grapes.

Clos Canos (Fr) a vineyard in the A.C. Corbières, Languedoc-Roussillon, south-western France. Produces: white, rosé and red wines. Labels: Les Cocobirous, Tradition.

Clos Cantenac (Fr) a vineyard in the A.C. Saint-Émilion, Bordeaux 6ha.

Clos Cantermerle (Fr) a vineyard. (Com): Cérons. A.C. Cérons, Bordeaux 3ha.

Clos Caperot (Fr) a vineyard in the A.C. Saint-Émilion, Bordeaux 3ha.

Clos Casal (Sp) a dry, white wine produced by Raimat in Lérida from Chardonnay 37%, Macabeo 30% and Parellada 33%.

Clos Castelot (Fr) a vineyard in the A.C. Saint-Émilion, Bordeaux 10ha.

Clos Chantegrive (Fr) a vineyard. (Com): Podensac. A.C. Graves, Bordeaux 15ha (red and white).

Clos Chante-l'Alouette (Fr) a vineyard in the A.C. Saint-Émilion, Bordeaux 4ha.

Clos Chaudron (Fr) a vineyard in the A.C. commune of Montagny, Côte Chalonnaise, Burgundy.

Clos Cherchy (Fr) a vineyard. (Com): Pujols. A.C. Graves. Bordeaux. 4ha (white).

Clos Cloziot (Fr) a vineyard. (Com): A.C. Barsac (or Sauternes), Bordeaux 1ha.

Clos Cormey (Fr) a vineyard in the A.C. Saint-Émilion, Bordeaux 7ha.

Clos Côtes-Roland-de-Pressac (Fr) a vineyard in the A.C. Saint-Émilion, Bordeaux 2ha.

Clos Dady (Fr) a vineyard in the A.C. Sauternes, Bordeaux.

Clos Darches (Fr) a vineyard. (Com): St-Pierre-de-Mons. A.C. Graves, Bordeaux. 4ha (white).

Clos d'Armajan (Fr) a vineyard. (Com): Budos. A.C. Graves, Bordeaux. 2ha (red).

Clos d'Armens (Fr) a vineyard in the A.C. Saint-Émilion, Bordeaux 2ha.

Clos Darrouban (Fr) a vineyard. (Com): Portets. A.C. Graves. Bordeaux. 2ha (red and white).

Clos d'Arthus (Fr) a vineyard in the A.C. Saint-Émilion, Bordeaux 5ha.

Clos Dauphin (Fr) a vineyard in the A.C. Saint-Émilion, Bordeaux 2ha.

Clos Daviaud (Fr) a vineyard. (Com): Parsac-Saint-Émilion. A.C. Saint-Émilion, Bordeaux 5ha.

Clos de Amandiers (Fr) a vineyard. (Com): Pomerol. A.C. Pomerol, Bordeaux 2ha.

Clos de Barail (Fr) a vineyard. (Com): Illats. A.C. Cérons, Bordeaux 9ha.

Clos de Beauvenir (Fr) the label of a Châteauneuf-

C

du-Pape produced by Dugas, Route de Sorgues, 84230 Châteauneuf-du-Pape, southern Rhône. Other label is Château La Nerthe.

Clos de Bèze (Fr) the finest of the Grand Crus of Gevrey-Chambertin. Of 16ha. with 12 owners. Often regarded as the finest of the red Burgundies. Also classed as Chambertin-Clos de Bèze.

Clos de Bos-Lancon (Fr) a vineyard. (Com): Illats. A.C. Cérons, Bordeaux 4ha.

Clos de Breuil (Fr) a vineyard in the A.C. Montlouis, Touraine, Loire valley.

Clos de Chaumiennes (Fr) an old walled vineyard in the wine village of Pouilly-sur-Loire. Produces fine A.C. Blanc Fumé.

Clos de Ciron (Fr) a vineyard. (Com): Loupiac. A.C. Loupiac, Bordeaux 4ha.

Clos de Cray (Fr) a Chenin blanc white wine produced in A.C. Montlouis, Touraine, Loire. Bottled at La Chappelle de Cray, Lussault.

Clos de Cuminaille (Fr) a vineyard in the A.C. Saint-Joseph, northern Rhône.

Clos du Ferré (Fr) a label for an A.C. Muscadet de Sèvre et Maine Sur-Lie from Domaine Michel David.

Clos de Gamot (Fr) a vineyard in the A.C. Cahors. (Add): Rayssac, Lot département, southern France.

Clos de Gensac (Fr) a vineyard. (Com): Pujols. A.C. Graves, Bordeaux. 4ha (white).

Clos de Haute-Combe (Fr) a winery based in the A.C. Beaujolais Cru Juliénas, southern Burgundy 15ha.

Clos de Jeanlaive (Fr) a vineyard. (Com): Barsac. A.C. Barsac (or Sauternes), Bordeaux. 5ha.

Clos de la Barre (Fr) a Premier Cru vineyard in the A.C. commune of Volnay, Côte de Beaune, Burgundy. 2ha. Also known as La Barre.

Clos de l'Abbaye (Fr) a vineyard in the A.C. Bourgueil, Touraine, Loire.

Clos de l'Abbaye-de-la-Rame (Fr) a vineyard. (Com): Mazères. A.C. Graves, Bordeaux. 6ha (white).

Clos de la Bonneterie (Fr) a vineyard. (Com): Portets. A.C. Graves, Bordeaux. 4ha (red and white).

Clos de la Cavaille-Lescours (Fr) a vineyard in the A.C. Saint-Émilion, Bordeaux 1ha.

Clos de la Chaînette (Fr) a small, noted red wine vineyard based in Auxerre.

Clos de la Chance (USA) a winery based in the Napa Valley, California. Grape varieties include: Cabernet sauvignon.

Clos de la Chapelle (Fr) a vineyard in the A.C. commune of Pouilly-Fuissé, Côte Mâconnais, Burgundy.

Clos de la Commaraine (Fr) a Premier Cru vineyard in the A.C. commune of Pommard, Côte de Beaune, Burgundy 4ha.

Clos de la Coulée de Serrant (Fr) vineyard. Also known as Coulée de Serrant. (Add): Château de la Roche aux Moines, Savenniéres, Loire. A.C. Savennières-Coulée de Serrant. A famous property

that produces fine long-lived white wines from Chenin blanc grapes.

Clos de la Cure (Fr) a vineyard. (Add): 33330 Saint-Émilion. Grand Cru. A.C. Saint-Émilion. (Com): Saint-Émilion.

Clos de la Dioterie (Fr) a vineyard in the A.C. Chinon, Anjou-Saumur, Loire.

Clos de la Féguine (Fr) a cuvée of the Premier Cru vineyard Aux Cras in the A.C. Beaune, Côte de Beaune, Burgundy.

Clos de la Gravette (Fr) a vineyard. (Com): Pomerol. A.C. Pomerol, Bordeaux.

Clos de l'Anhel (Fr) a vineyard in the A.C. Corbières, south-western France. Labels: Les Dimanches, Les Terrasselles.

Clos de la Henri (Fr) a winery. (Add): 'Le Vaud Godard', Benais, 37140 Bourgueil, Loire. A.C. Bourgueil.

Clos de la Maison Blanche (Fr) a vineyard. (Com): Budos. A.C. Graves, Bordeaux. 2ha (white).

Clos de la Mare (Ch.Isles) *see* Blayney Vineyards.

Clos de la Maréchale (Fr) a Premier Cru vineyard in the village of Premeaux in the A.C. of commune Nuits-Saint-Georges, Côte de Nuits, Burgundy 9.5ha.

Clos de la Miro (Fr) a vineyard in the A.C. Corbières, south-western France.

Clos de la Mousse (Fr) a Premier Cru vineyard in the A.C. commune of Beaune, Côte de Beaune, Burgundy 3.36ha.

Clos de Langres (Fr) a vineyard in the Côte de Nuits which forms the boundary with the Côte de Beaune. Belongs to La Reine Pedauque. Produces supple fruity wines.

Clos de la Perrière (Fr) a Premier Cru vineyard in the A.C. commune of Fixin, Côte de Nuits, Burgundy. 6.53ha. Owned by Phillip Joliet.

Clos de la Perrière (Fr) a Premier Cru vineyard in the A.C. commune of Vougeot, Côte de Nuits, Burgundy.

Clos de la Point du Jour (Fr) a vineyard in the A.C. Fleurie Cru Beaujolais-Villages, Burgundy.

Clos de la Poussie (Fr) a vineyard in the A.C. Sancerre, Central Vineyards, Loire. 30ha (red and white wines). Owned by Cordier.

Clos de la Roche (Fr) a Grand Cru vineyard in the A.C. commune of Morey-Saint-Denis, Côte de Beaune, Burgundy 15.5ha.

Clos de la Roilette (Fr) a vineyard in Fleurie, A.C. Cru Beaujolais-Villages, Burgundy.

Clos de la Sablette (Fr) a vineyard in the A.C. Muscadet Sèvre et Maine, Nantais, Loire.

Clos de la Soucherie (Fr) a label for an A.C. Coteaux-du-Layon from Château Pierre-Bise, Anjou-Saumur, Loire Valley.

Clos de la Tuilerie (Fr) a vineyard. (Com): Portets. A.C. Graves, Bordeaux. 5ha (red and white).

Clos de la Vieille Forge (Fr) a vineyard. (Com): Lalande de Pomerol. A.C. Lalande de Pomerol, Bordeaux.

Clos de l'Avocat (Fr) a vineyard. (Com): Cérons. A.C. Cérons, Bordeaux 3ha.

348

C

Clos de L'Echo (Fr) the label of an A.C. Chinon wine produced by Domaine R. Couly, Chinon, Loire. *See also* Clos de L'Olive.

Clos de l'Ecu (Fr) a Premier Cru vineyard in the A.C. commune of Beaune, Côte de Beaune, Burgundy. 5ha. Also known as A l'Ecu.

Clos de l'Église (Fr) a vineyard. (Com): Lalande de Pomerol. A.C. Lalande de Pomerol, Bordeaux.

Clos de l'Église (Fr) a vineyard. (Com): Saint-Jean-de-Blaignac. A.C. Saint-Émilion, Bordeaux 17ha.

Clos de l'Émir (Alg) a red wine produced in Mascara.

Clos de L'Olive (Fr) the label of an A.C. Chinon wine produced by Domaine R. Couly, Chinon, Loire. *See also* Clos de L'Echo.

Clos de l'Oranje (S.Afr) the label for a red wine (Shiraz) produced by the Signal Hill winery, Cape Town, Western Cape.

Clos de l'Oratoire (Fr) (Add): Château Peyreau, 33330 Saint-Émilion. Grand Cru Classé. A.C. Saint-Émilion. (Com): Saint-Émilion. 9.45ha. Grape varieties: Cabernet franc 30% and Merlot 70%.

Clos de l'Oratoire des Papes (Fr) a red or white wine in the A.C. Châteauneuf-du-Pape. (Add): Ave. St. Joseph, 84230 Châteauneuf-du-Pape, southern Rhône.

Clos de los Siete (Arg) a vineyard site (has six wineries) based in the Uco Valley, Mendoza.

Clos de Mazeray (Fr) a vineyard in the A.C. Meursault, Côte de Beaune, Burgundy (red and white).

Clos de Mesnil (Fr) the incorrect spelling. *see* Krug and Clos du Mesnil.

Clos de Miaille (Fr) a vineyard in the commune Barsac. A.C. Barsac (or Sauternes), Bordeaux 1ha.

Clos de Moines (Fr) a vineyard. (Com): Lalande de Pomerol. A.C. Lalande de Pomerol, Bordeaux.

Clos de Mons (Fr) a vineyard. (Com): La Brède. A.C. Graves, Bordeaux. 3ha (red and white).

Clos de Montibeux (Switz) a white wine produced in the canton of Valais.

Clos de Naudin (Fr) a vineyard in the A.C. Saint-Émilion, Bordeaux 2ha.

Clos de Nauton (Fr) a vineyard. (Com): Fargues. A.C. Sauternes, Bordeaux 4ha.

Clos de Nouchet (Fr) a vineyard. (Com): Castres. A.C. Graves, Bordeaux.

Clos d'Épenots (Fr) a Premier Cru vineyard in the A.C. commune of Pommard, Côte de Beaune, Burgundy 3.64ha.

Clos de Pierrefeu (Fr) a vineyard. (Com): Preignac. A.C. Sauternes, Bordeaux 4ha.

Clos de Pintray (Fr) a vineyard in A.C. Montlouis, 37270 St. Martin-le-Beau, Loire.

Clos de Places (Fr) a vineyard. (Com): Arbanats. A.C. Graves, Bordeaux. 1ha (red and white).

Clos de Princes (Fr) a vineyard. (Com): Barsac. A.C. Barsac (or Sauternes), Bordeaux 2ha.

Clos de Reynard (Fr) a French-style red wine (Carignan, Cinsault, Mourvèdre) produced in California.

Clos des Abbayes (Switz) a vineyard based near Lausanne in Lavaux. Noted for the auction of its wines every December.

Clos de Sainte-Catherine (Fr) a vineyard in the A.C. Coteaux du Layon, Anjou-Saumur, Loire.

Clos des Amandiers (Fr) a vineyard in Alsace which is one of the few that sells wine using its name (vineyard). A light muscat wine with a slight almond taste.

Clos des Argillières (Fr) a Premier Cru vineyard from the village of Premeaux in the southern part of the A.C. commune of Nuits-Saint-Georges, Côte de Nuits, Burgundy 4.2ha.

Clos des Arnaud (Fr) a vineyard. (Com): Lalande de Pomerol. A.C. Lalande de Pomerol, Bordeaux.

Clos de Sarpe (Fr) a vineyard in the A.C. Saint-Émilion, Bordeaux 3ha.

Clos des Arvelets (Fr) a Premier Cru vineyard in the A.C. commune of Pommard, Côte de Beaune, Burgundy. 8.5ha. Also known as Les Arvelets.

Clos des Avaux (Fr) a cuvée in the Premier Cru vineyard of Les Avaux in the A.C. commune of Beaune, Côte de Beaune, Burgundy. Is owned by the Hospices de Beaune.

Clos des Barillères (Fr) a vineyard. (Add): Bouchereau Frères, Beauregard, Mouzillon, Loire Atlantique. A.C. Muscadet Sèvre et Maine.

Clos des Batailles (Fr) a vineyard in the A.C. Sancerre, Central Vineyards, Loire.

Clos des Brusquières (Fr) the label of a Châteauneuf-du-Pape produced by Courtil, Ave. St. Joseph, 15 Rue Ville Vieille, 84230 Châteauneuf-du-Pape, southern Rhône.

Clos des Camuzeilles (Fr) a vineyard in the A.C. Fitou, south-western France. Label: L'Embuse.

Clos des Capucins (Fr) a fine, noted vineyard of Kayserberg-Weinbach in Alsace. Owned by Faller-Frères.

Clos des Champions [Les] (Fr) a single vineyard Champagne produced by Leclerc Briant.

Clos des Chartrons (Fr) the second wine of Château Lagrange [Grand Cru Classé (3rd) A.C. Saint-Julien].

Clos-des-Chênes (Fr) a Premier Cru vineyard in the A.C. commune of Volnay, Côte de Beaune, Burgundy.

Clos des Corbières (Fr) a vineyard. (Com): Montagne-Saint-Émilion. A.C. Montagne-Saint-Émilion, Bordeaux 2ha.

Clos des Cordeliers (Fr) a vineyard. (Com): Souzay-Champigny, A.C. Saumur-Champigny, Anjou-Saumur, Loire.

Clos des Corvées (Fr) a Premier Cru vineyard in the village of Premeaux in the southern part of the A.C. commune of Nuits-Saint-Georges, Côte de Nuits, Burgundy 5.1ha.

Clos des Ducs (Fr) a Premier Cru vineyard in the A.C. commune of Volnay, Côte de Beaune, Burgundy.

Clos de Seillas (Fr) a vineyard. (Com): Gauriac. A.C. Côtes de Bourg, Bordeaux.

Clos des Épeneaux (Fr) a cuvée in the Premier Cru Les Épenots, A.C. Pommard, Côte de Beaune, Burgundy.

C

Clos des Fiétres (Fr) a vineyard within the Grand Cru Corton, Côtes de Beaune, Burgundy. Also known as Les Fiétres.

Clos des Forêts (Fr) a Premier Cru vineyard in the village of Premeaux in the southern part of the A.C. commune of Nuits-Saint-Georges, Côte de Nuits, Burgundy.

Clos des Fougères (Fr) a vineyard. (Com): Virelade. A.C. Graves, Bordeaux. 4ha (white).

Clos-des-Fourneaux (Fr) a vineyard in the A.C. commune of Mercurey, Côte Chalonnaise, Burgundy. Can use the designation Premier Cru on the bottle label.

Clos des Goisses (Fr) a single vineyard based at Mareuil-sur-Aÿ, owned by Philiponnat. Produce a de luxe vintage cuvée Champagne of the same name from 30% Chardonnay and 70% Pinot noir grapes.

Clos des Grandes Vignes (Fr) a Premier Cru vineyard [part] of the village of Premeaux in the southern part of the A.C. commune of Nuits-Saint-Georges, Côte de Nuits, Burgundy 2.1ha.

Clos des Grandes Vignes (Fr) a vineyard. (Com): Pomerol. A.C. Pomerol, Bordeaux. 6ha. Also known as Clos des Grandes Vignes-Clinet.

Clos des Grands Sillons (Fr) a vineyard. (Com): Pomerol. A.C. Pomerol, Bordeaux 3ha.

Clos des Grands Voyens (Fr) (Add): Rue de Jamproyes, 71640 Mercurey. A vineyard in the A.C. commune of Mercurey, Côte Chalonnaise, Burgundy. Can use the designation Premier Cru on the bottle label.

Clos des Gravières (Fr) a vineyard. (Com): Portets. A.C. Graves, Bordeaux. 3ha (red and white).

Clos des Gros-Chênes (Fr) a vineyard in the A.C. Saint-Émilion, Bordeaux 5ha.

Clos des Jacobins (Fr) (Add): 33330 Saint-Émilion. Grand Cru Classé. A.C. Saint-Émilion. (Com): Saint-Émilion. Grape varieties: Cabernet franc, Cabernet sauvignon and Merlot 8ha. Owned by Cordier.

Clos des Lambrays (Fr) a Grand Cru vineyard in the A.C. commune of Morey-Saint-Denis. Côte de Nuits, Burgundy. 6ha. Promoted to Grand Cru status in 1981.

Clos des Magrines (Fr) a vineyard. (Com): Puisseguin-Saint-Émilion. A.C. Puisseguin-Saint-Émilion, Bordeaux 3ha.

Clos des Maraings (Fr) a vineyard. (Com): Preignac. A.C. Sauternes, Bordeaux 3ha.

Clos des Marquis (Fr) a Châteauneuf-du-Pape produced by Royer, 23 Ave. Saint-Joseph, 84230 Châteauneuf-du-Pape, southern Rhône.

Clos des Menuts (Fr) (Add): Place du Chapitre, 33330 Saint-Émilion. Grand Cru. A.C. Saint-Émilion. (Com): Saint-Émilion. 22.5ha. Grape varieties: Cabernet franc 10%, Cabernet sauvignon 20% and Merlot 70%.

Clos des Moines (Switz) a noted vineyard based near Lausanne in Lavaux.

Clos des Montaigus (Fr) a vineyard in the A.C. commune of Mercurey, Côte Chalonnaise,

Burgundy. May use the designation Premier Cru on the bottle label.

Clos des Mouches (Fr) a Premier Cru vineyard in the A.C. commune of Beaune, Côte de Beaune, Burgundy 25.13ha.

Clos des Moulins-à-Vents (Fr) a vineyard. (Com): Cérons. A.C. Cérons, Bordeaux 5ha.

Clos des Ormes (Fr) a Premier Cru vineyard [part] in the A.C. commune of Morey-Saint-Denis, Côte de Nuits, Burgundy 4.8ha.

Clos Despagne (Fr) a vineyard. (Com): St-Pierre-de-Mons. A.C. Graves, Bordeaux. 4ha (white).

Clos d'Espagnet (Fr) a vineyard. (Com): Sauternes. A.C. Sauternes, Bordeaux 3ha. Also Château Esterlin.

Clos des Papes (Fr) the label of a Châteauneuf-du-Pape produced by Paul Avril, 13 Rte. d'Avignon, 84230 Châteauneuf-du-Pape, southern Rhône.

Clos des Pyramides (Egy) the brand-name for red and white wines usually exported to Russia.

Clos des Réas (Fr) a Premier Cru vineyard in the A.C. commune of Vosne-Romanée, Côte de Nuits, Burgundy 2.1ha.

Clos des Religieuses (Fr) a vineyard. (Com): Puisseguin-Saint-Émilion. A.C. Puisseguin-Saint-Émilion, Bordeaux 8ha.

Clos des Roches (Fr) a vineyard. (Com): Illats. A.C. Cérons. Bordeaux 2ha.

Clos des Roches (Fr) a vineyard in A.C. Sancerre, Central Vineyards, eastern Loire.

Clos des Rois (Fr) a Premier Cru vineyard [part] in the A.C. commune of Sampigny-lès-Maranges, A.C. Santenay, Côte de Beaune, Burgundy 6ha.

Clos des Sarrazins (Fr) a vineyard in the A.C. Saint-Émilion, Bordeaux 6ha.

Clos des Templiers (Fr) a vineyard. (Com): Pomerol. A.C. Pomerol, Bordeaux 1ha.

Clos des Tonnelles (Fr) a vineyard. (Com): St-Aignan. A.C. Côtes de Fronsac, Bordeaux 4ha.

Clos de Tart (Fr) a Grand Cru vineyard in the A.C. commune of Morey-Saint-Denis, Côte de Nuits, Burgundy. 7.5ha. Is owned by Maison Mommessin. *See* Climat de la Forge.

Clos de Tavannes (Fr) a Premier Cru vineyard [part] in the A.C. commune of Santenay, Côte de Beaune, Burgundy.

Clos de Terrefort (Fr) a vineyard. (Com): Loupiac. A.C. Loupiac. Southern Bordeaux 3ha.

Clos de Toumalin (Fr) a vineyard. (Com): Fronsac. A.C. Côtes Canon-Fronsac, Bordeaux 2ha.

Clos de Triguedina (Fr) a vineyard. (Add): 46700 Puy-l'Évêque, Lot. based in A.C. Cahors, southern France.

Clos de Varambond (Fr) a vineyard. (Com): Fuissé, A.C. Pouilly-Fuissé, Côte Mâconnais, Burgundy.

Clos de Vougeot (Fr) the Grand Cru vineyard in the A.C. commune of Vougeot, Côte de Nuits, Burgundy. 50ha (has some 80 individual owners). *See also* Bisson (Colonel).

Clos Domaine-Château-la-Bastienne (Fr) a vineyard. (Com): Montagne-Saint-Émilion. A.C. Montagne-Saint-Émilion, Bordeaux 2ha.

C

Clos du Alem (Fr) a vineyard. (Com): Saillans. A.C. Côtes de Fronsac, Bordeaux 10ha.

Clos du Barrail (Fr) a vineyard. (Com): Cérons. A.C. Cérons, Bordeaux 8ha.

Clos du Bois (USA) a large winery (124.5ha) based in Sonama Coast, Sonoma County, California. (Add): 19410 Geyserville Avenue, Getserville, California 95441. Vineyards in Alexander Valley and Dry Creek Valley. Grape varieties: Cabernet franc, Cabernet sauvignon, Chardonnay, Gewürztraminer, Johannisberg riesling, Malbec, Merlot, Petit verdot, Pinot grigio, Pinot noir, Shiraz. Labels: Marlstone. Website: http://www.closdubois.com

Clos du Bourg (Fr) a vineyard in the A.C. Vouvray, Touraine, Loire.

Clos du Caderet (Fr) a range of wines produced in the Côtes du Duras, South-west France from Merlot, Cabernet franc, Sauvignon blanc, Sémillon and Muscadelle grapes. *see* Cuvée Quentin.

Clos du Cailleret (Fr) a vineyard in the A.C. Puligny-Montract, Burgundy.

Clos du Calvaire (Fr) a vineyard in the A.C. Saint-Émilion, Bordeaux 2ha.

Clos du Calvaire (Fr) the label of a Châteauneuf-du-Pape produced by Domaine du Père Pape. *See also* Domaine de Grand Coulet.

Clos du Casrel (Fr) a vineyard. (Com): Néac. A.C. Lalande de Pomerol, Bordeaux.

Clos du Castel (Fr) a vineyard. (Com): Pomerol. A.C. Pomerol, Bordeaux 2ha.

Clos du Chapitre (Fr) a Premier Cru vineyard [part] in the A.C. commune of Fixin, Côte de Nuits, Burgundy. 4.79ha. The remaining part in the A.C. commune of Gevrey-Chambertin. Is entirely rented out to Domaine Gelin & Moulin.

Clos du Chapitre (Fr) a Premier Cru vineyard [part] in the A.C. commune of Gevrey-Chambertin, Côte de Nuits, Burgundy. 0.97ha. The remaining part is in the A.C. commune of Fixin.

Clos du Chatain (Fr) a vineyard. (Com): Néac. A.C. Lalande de Pomerol, Bordeaux.

Clos du Chêne Marchand (Fr) a vineyard in the A.C. Sancerre, Central Vineyards, Loire.

Clos du Chêne Vert (Fr) a vineyard in the A.C. Chinon, Anjou-Saumur, Loire.

Clos du Ciel (USA) a Chardonnay wine produced by the Peter Michael Winery, Calistoga, Napa Valley, California.

Clos du Clocher (Fr) a vineyard. (Com): Pomerol. A.C. Pomerol, Bordeaux 5ha.

Clos du Commandeur (Fr) a vineyard. (Com): Pomerol. A.C. Pomerol, Bordeaux 1ha.

Clos du Crot de la Roue (Fr) a vineyard in the A.C. Sancerre, Central Vineyards, Loire.

Clos du Fagnard (Fr) a vineyard. (Com): Pomerol. A.C. Pomerol, Bordeaux 2ha.

Clos du Gratte Sabots (Fr) a vineyard in the A.C. Sancerre, Central Vineyards, Loire.

Clos du Gros (Fr) a vineyard in the A.C. Saint-Émilion, Bordeaux 1ha.

Clos du Jaugua (Fr) a vineyard. (Com): Illats. A.C. Cérons, Bordeaux 4ha.

Clos du Marquis (Fr) (Add): 33250 Saint-Julien, Pauillac. A.C. Haut-Médoc. (Com): Saint-Julien. The second wine of Château Léoville-Las-Cases Grand Cru Classé (2nd) Saint-Julien.

Clos du Mas (Fr) a vineyard. (Com): Listrac. A.C. Listrac, Bordeaux 5ha.

Clos du Medouc (Fr) a vineyard. (Com): Sainte-Croix-du-Mont. A.C. Sainte-Croix-du-Mont, Bordeaux 2ha.

Clos Dumes (Fr) (Add): Langon 33210. A.C. Graves. (Com): Langon. *see* Château Balouet-Roailly.

Clos du Mesnil (Fr) a phylloxera-free, single vineyard (established 1698) based in Mesnil-sur-Ogier (owned by Krug). 1.85ha. Produces a vintage Blanc de Blancs De Luxe Champagne of same name. Vintages: 1979, 1980, 1981, 1982, 1983, 1984, 1985, 1986, 1990, 1992, 1995. Often mis-spelt Clos de Mesnil.

Clos du Monastère (Fr) *see* Château Doms et Clos du Monastère.

Clos du Mont Olivet (Fr) a vineyard in the A.C. Châteauneuf-du-Pape, southern Rhône. Red and white wines are produced by Les Fils de Sabon (Joseph).

Clos du Moulin (Fr) a vineyard. (Com): Saint-Christoly. A.C. Médoc, Bordeaux 8ha.

Clos du Moulin (Fr) a vineyard. (Com): Saint-Estèphe. A.C. Saint-Estèphe, Bordeaux 5ha.

Clos du Moulin-à-Vent (Fr) a vineyard. (Com): St-Pierre-de-Mons. A.C. Graves, Bordeaux. 5ha. (white).

Clos du Palais-Cardinal (Fr) a vineyard in the A.C. Saint-Émilion, Bordeaux 5ha.

Clos du Palmiers (Fr) a vineyard. (Com): Sainte-Croix-du-Mont. A.C. Sainte-Croix-du-Mont, Bordeaux 3ha.

Clos du Pape (Fr) a vineyard. (Com): La Brède. A.C. Graves, Bordeaux. 6ha (white).

Clos du Pape (Fr) a vineyard. (Com): Fargues. A.C. Sauternes, Bordeaux 5ha.

Clos du Papillon (Fr) a vineyard in the A.C. Savennières. Anjou-Saumur, Loire.

Clos du Pas de Saint Maurice (Fr) a small vineyard near Montmartre, Paris, has 3300 vines of which 80% Sémillon, 20% Sauvignon blanc, a Vin de Pays wine.

Clos du Pellerin (Fr) part of Clos Barrail-du-Milieu, A.C. Pomerol, Bordeaux.

Clos du Roc (Fr) a vineyard in the A.C. Saint-Émilion, Bordeaux 3ha.

Clos du Roi (Fr) a Grand Cru vineyard [part] in the A.C. commune of Aloxe-Corton, Côte de Beaune, Burgundy (red and white).

Clos du Roi (Fr) a Premier Grand Cru vineyard [part] in the A.C. commune of Beaune, Côte de Beaune, Burgundy 8.44ha.

Clos-du-Roi (Fr) a vineyard in the A.C. commune of Mercurey, Côte Chalonnaise, Burgundy. May use the designation Premier Cru on the bottle label.

Clos du Roy (Fr) a vineyard. (Com): Barsac. A.C. Barsac (or Sauternes), Bordeaux. 11ha. Also Château Piada.

Clos du Roy (Fr) a vineyard. (Com): Pomerol. A.C. Pomerol, Bordeaux 3ha.

Clos du Roy (Fr) an A.C. Sancerre. (Add): 18, Rue F. Gambon, 58150, Pouilly-sur-Loire, Sancerre, Central Vineyards, Loire.

Clos du Sable (Fr) a vineyard in the A.C. Saint-Émilion, Bordeaux 2ha.

Clos du Soleil (USA) the label for a white (Chardonnay) wine produced by Domaine Serene, Willamette Valley, Oregon.

Clos du Tue-Boeuf (Fr) a 16ha. vineyard in A.C Cheverny. Produces Cheverny le Frileuse from 60% Chardonnay grapes, Touraine le Brin de Chèvre from Pineau grapes, Touraine le Buisson Pouilleux Vieilles Vignes from Sauvignon blanc grapes, Touraine la Guerrerie from Cabernet franc, Cabernet sauvignon and Côt grapes, La Caillière (a Vin de Table from Pinot noir grapes).

Clos-du-Val (Fr) a Premier Cru vineyard in the A.C. commune of Auxey-Duresses, Côte de Beaune, Burgundy. 23ha. Also known as the Climat-du-Val.

Clos du Val (USA) a French-owned winery in the Napa Valley, California. (Add): 5330 Silverado Trail, Napa California 94558. Also has vineyards in Carneros. Grape varieties: Cabernet sauvignon, Chardonnay, Zinfandel. Produces varital wines. Website: http://www.closduval.com

Clos du Verger (Fr) a Premier Cru vineyard in the A.C. commune of Pommard, Côte de Beaune, Burgundy 2.55ha.

Clos du Vieux (Fr) part of Château les Eyguires, A.C. Saint-Émilion, Bordeaux.

Clos d'Uza (Fr) a vineyard. (Com): St-Pierre-de-Mons. A.C. Graves, Bordeaux 34ha (white). Also Château Queyrats and St. Pierre.

Clos d'Yvigne (Fr) a winery. (Add): Le Bourg, 2420 Gageac et Rouillac. 16ha. planted. Red wines are sold under the A.C. Côtes de Bergerac. Labels include Rouge et Noir (75% Merlot, 25% Cabernet sauvignon), Le Petit Prince (90% Merlot, 10% Cabernet franc). White wines are sold under the A.C. Bergerac . Labels include La Princesse de Clèves (50% Sauvignon blanc, 30% Sémillon, 20% Muscadelle), Cuvée Nicolas (50% Sauvignon blanc, 30% Sémillon, 20% Muscadelle). Rosé wine is sold under Côtes de Bergerac. Labels include Bel Ami (100% Merlot). A sweet white Saussignac wine is also produced (90% Sémillon, 10% Muscadelle).

Closed Wine (Eng) a wine which has still to develop. Its bouquet is still closed in.

Close Encounters Cocktail (Cktl) 50mls orange juice, 10mls Cognac, 10mls crème de fraises, 2 dashes curaçao, dash Angostura. Blend together with a scoop of crushed ice in a blender. Pour into a large goblet, dress with an orange slice on the rim of the glass.

Clos Feurus (Fr) a jointly-owned vineyard in the A.C. Saint-Émilion, Bordeaux 4ha.

Clos Floridene (Fr) (Add): Pujols/Ciron, Gironde. A.C. Graves. 17ha (mainly red).

Clos Fonrazade (Fr) a vineyard in the A.C. Saint-Émilion, Bordeaux 4ha.

Clos Fontaine (Fr) a vineyard. (Com): Fargues. A.C. Sauternes, Bordeaux 2ha.

Clos Fontelle (Fr) a vineyard in the A.C. Saint-Émilion, Bordeaux 4ha.

Clos Fourney (Fr) a vineyard in the A.C. Saint-Émilion, Bordeaux 4ha.

Clos Fourtet (Fr) a Premier [B] Grand Cru Classé. A.C. Saint-Émilion. (Com): Saint-Émilion. 21ha. Grape varieties: Cabernet franc, Cabernet sauvignon and Merlot.

Clos Franc-Larmande (Fr) a vineyard in the A.C. Saint-Émilion, Bordeaux 3ha.

Clos Gaensbroennel (Fr) a famous vineyard on a hill near Barr in Alsace.

Clos Gauthey (Fr) a Premier Cru vineyard in the A.C. commune of Monthélie, Côte de Beaune, Burgundy 1.4ha.

Clos Gerbaud (Fr) a vineyard in the A.C. Saint-Émilion, Bordeaux 1ha.

Clos Gilet (Fr) a vineyard. (Com): Montagne-Saint-Émilion A.C. Montagne-Saint-Émilion, Bordeaux 3ha.

Clos Girautin (Fr) a vineyard. (Com): Barsac. A.C. Barsac (or Sauternes), Bordeaux 1ha.

Clos Gontey (Fr) a vineyard in the A.C. Saint-Émilion, Bordeaux 32ha.

Clos Grand-Faurie (Fr) a vineyard in the A.C. Saint-Émilion, Bordeaux 4ha.

Clos Grand-Gontey (Fr) a vineyard in the A.C. Saint-Émilion, Bordeaux 4ha.

Clos Gravet (Fr) a vineyard in the A.C. Saint-Émilion, Bordeaux 11ha.

Clos Gros-Caillou (Fr) a vineyard in the A.C. Saint-Émilion, Bordeaux 3ha.

Clos Guinot (Fr) a vineyard in the A.C. Saint-Émilion, Bordeaux 6ha.

Clos Haut-Bibey (Fr) a vineyard in the A.C. Saint-Émilion, Bordeaux 2ha.

Clos Haut-Cabanne (Fr) a vineyard in the A.C. Saint-Émilion, Bordeaux 1ha.

Clos Haut-Caillou (Fr) a vineyard. (Com): Fronsac. A.C. Côtes Canon-Fronsac, Bordeaux 3ha.

Clos Haut-Cavujon (Fr) a vineyard. (Com): Lalande de Pomerol. A.C. Lalande de Pomerol, Bordeaux.

Clos Haut-Jaugueblanc (Fr) a vineyard in the A.C. Saint-Émilion, Bordeaux 1ha.

Clos Haut-Listrac (Fr) a vineyard. (Com): Puisseguin-Saint-Émilion. A.C. Puisseguin-Saint-Émilion, Bordeaux 4ha.

Clos Haut-Mazerat (Fr) a vineyard in the A.C. Saint-Émilion, Bordeaux 8ha.

Clos Haut-Mazeyres (Fr) a vineyard. (Com): Pomerol. A.C. Pomerol, Bordeaux 9ha.

Clos Haut-Montaiguillon (Fr) a vineyard. (Com): Saint-Georges-Saint-Émilion. A.C. Saint-Émilion, Bordeaux 5ha.

Clos Haut-Peyraguey (Fr) a Premier Grand Cru. A.C. Sauternes. (Com): Bommes 25ha.

Clos Haut-Peyraguey (Fr) a vineyard. (Com): Barsac. A.C. Barsac (or Sauternes), Bordeaux.

Clos Haut-Robin (Fr) a vineyard in the A.C. Saint-Émilion, Bordeaux 4ha.

Clos Haut-Troquard (Fr) a vineyard in the A.C. Saint-Georges-Saint-Émilion. A.C. Saint-Émilion, Bordeaux 1ha.

Closing Time (Eng) the time when the sale of alcoholic beverages is not permitted between licensing hours. After 'time' has been called, (10 minutes for full on-licence and 30 minutes for restaurant license) it is permitted to consume those drinks that were purchased during permitted hours, after which the licenced premises must be vacated.

Clos Jacqueminot (Fr) a vineyard in the A.C. Saint-Émilion, Bordeaux 4ha.

Clos Jamnet (Fr) a vineyard. (Com): La Brède. A.C. Graves, Bordeaux. 4ha (white).

Clos Jauguet (Fr) a vineyard. (Com): Barsac. A.C. Barsac (or Sauternes), Bordeaux 1ha.

Clos Jaumard (Fr) a vineyard in the A.C. Saint-Émilion, Bordeaux 2ha.

Clos Jean-de-Maye (Fr) a vineyard. (Com): Portets. A.C. Graves, Bordeaux. 5ha (red and white).

Clos Jean Dubos (Fr) a vineyard. (Com): Pujols. A.C. Graves, Bordeaux. 2ha (white).

Clos Jean Guillot (Fr) a vineyard in the A.C. Saint-Émilion, Bordeaux 1ha.

Clos Jean-Voisin (Fr) a vineyard in the A.C. Saint-Émilion, Bordeaux 3ha.

Clos la Barde (Fr) a vineyard. (Add): Saint Laurent des Bardes, 33330 Saint-Émilion. Grand Cru. A.C. Saint-Émilion. (Com): Saint Laurent des Bardes. 4.5ha. Grape varieties: Cabernet 40% and Merlot 60%.

Clos l'Abeilley (Fr) the second wine of Château Rayne-Vigneau, Bommes, A.C. Sauternes, Bordeaux.

Clos la Bouade (Fr) a vineyard. (Com): Barsac. A.C. Barsac, (or Sauternes), Bordeaux 3ha.

Clos la Bourrue (Fr) part of Château Haut-Jean-Faure, A.C. Saint-Émilion, Bordeaux.

Clos la Cabanne (Fr) a vineyard. (Com): Puisseguin-Saint-Émilion. A.C. Puisseguin-Saint-Émilion, Bordeaux 4ha.

Clos La Chance (USA) a winery based in the Central Coast, Saratoga, California. Grape varieties: Chardonnay, Grenache, Syrah.

Clos la Chance Winery (USA) utilise a winery in Scotts Valley, Santa Cruz Mountains, California for their wines.

Clos Lacombe (Fr) a vineyard. (Com): Pomerol. A.C. Pomerol, Bordeaux 2ha.

Clos la Coutale (Fr) an A.C. Cahors vineyard. (Add): 46700 Puy-l'Évêque, Lot.

Clos la Croix (Fr) a vineyard in the A.C. Saint-Émilion, Bordeaux 6ha.

Clos la Croix-Figeac (Fr) a vineyard in the A.C. Saint-Émilion, Bordeaux 4ha.

Clos la Fleur-Figeac (Fr) A.C. Saint-Émilion Grand Cru, part of Château Haut-Jean-Faure, A.C. Saint-Émilion, Bordeaux.

Clos la Fleur Figeac (Fr) a vineyard. (Add): Château La Tour du Pin Figeac, 33330 Saint-Émilion. A.C. Saint-Émilion. (Com): Saint-Émilion. 3.66ha.

Grape varieties: Cabernet franc 35% and Merlot 65%.

Clos Laforest (Fr) a vineyard. (Com): Saint-Christoly. A.C. Médoc, Bordeaux 4ha.

Clos la Glaye (Fr) a vineyard in the A.C. Saint-Émilion, Bordeaux 4ha.

Clos la Madeleine (Fr) a vineyard. (Add): Château la Gaffelière, 33330 Saint-Émilion. Grand Cru Classé. A.C. Saint-Émilion. (Com): Saint-Émilion. 2ha. Grape varieties: Cabernet franc and Merlot.

Clos Lamagine (Fr) a vineyard. (Com): St-Pierre-de-Mons. A.C. Graves, Bordeaux. 6ha (white).

Clos la Marche (Fr) a vineyard. (Com): Fronsac. A.C. Côtes Canon-Fronsac, Bordeaux 2ha.

Clos la Maurasse (Fr) a vineyard. (Com): Langon. A.C. Graves, Bordeaux. 8ha. Grape varieties: Cabernet sauvignon 45%, Malbec 10%, Merlot 45%, Sauvignon 50% and Sémillon 50%.

Clos Lamothe (Fr) a vineyard. (Com): Portets. A.C. Graves, Bordeaux. 5ha (red and white).

Clos-Landry (Fr) a Premier Cru vineyard in the A.C. commune of Beaune, Côte de Beaune, Burgundy. 1.98ha. Also known as Tiélandry.

Clos Lapachère (Fr) a vineyard. (Com): Barsac. A.C. Barsac (or Sauternes) 4ha.

Clos la Perrière (Fr) generic and single vineyard Sancerre wines produced by Pierre Archambault.

Clos l'Arabey (Fr) a vineyard. (Com): Sainte-Croix-du-Mont. A.C. Sainte-Croix-du-Mont, Bordeaux 2ha.

Clos l'Arieste (Fr) a vineyard. (Com): Preignac. A.C. Sauternes, Bordeaux 3ha.

Clos la Rose (Fr) a vineyard. (Com): Pomerol. A.C. Pomerol, Bordeaux 3ha.

Clos Larrivat (Fr) a vineyard. (Com): Sainte-Croix-du-Mont. A.C. Sainte-Croix-du-Mont, Bordeaux 3ha.

Clos la Soulatte (Fr) a vineyard. (Com): Pomerol. A.C. Pomerol, Bordeaux 2ha.

Clos la Tonnelle (Fr) the second wine of Château La Serre, Grand Cru Classé Saint-Émilion.

Clos la Tonnelle (Fr) the second wine of Château Soutard, Grand Cru Classé Saint-Émilion.

Clos la-Tour-Cluchon (Fr) a vineyard. (Com): Portets. A.C. Graves, Bordeaux. 4ha (red and white).

Clos la Vallée-du-Roi (Fr) a vineyard. (Com): Montagne-Saint-Émilion. A.C. Montagne-Saint-Émilion, Bordeaux 3ha.

Clos l'Avocat (Fr) a vineyard. (Com): Cérons. A.C. Graves, Bordeaux. 3ha (white).

Clos le Couvent (Fr) a vineyard. (Com): Saint-Émilion. A.C. Saint-Émilion, Bordeaux. Grand Cru.

Clos L'Église (Fr) a 17ha. vineyard in the A.C. Côte de Castillon, Bordeaux.

Clos L'Église (Fr) a vineyard. (Com): Pomerol. A.C. Pomerol, Bordeaux 5ha.

Clos l'Église Clinet (Fr) a vineyard. (Com): Pomerol. A.C. Pomerol, Bordeaux 4ha.

Clos le Haut-Crabitan (Fr) a vineyard. (Com): Sainte-Croix-du-Mont. A.C. Sainte-Croix-du-Mont, Bordeaux 2ha.

C

Clos Léhoul (Fr) a vineyard. (Com): Langon. A.C. Graves, Bordeaux. 4ha (white).

Clos le Pas-St-Georges (Fr) a vineyard in the commune Saint-Georges-Saint-Émilion. A.C. Saint-Émilion, Bordeaux 6ha.

Clos les Arrivaux (Fr) a vineyard in the commune Sainte-Croix-du-Mont. A.C. Sainte-Croix-du-Mont, Bordeaux 3ha.

Clos les Grands-Champs (Fr) a vineyard. (Com): Pomerol. A.C. Pomerol, Bordeaux 5ha.

Clos les Hautes Bretonnières (Fr) a winery. (Add): Joseph Hallereau, Les Chaboissières, Vallet, Loire. A.C. Muscadet Sèvre et Maine, Nantais, Loire.

Clos les Moines (Fr) a vineyard. (Com): Couquéques. A.C. Médoc, Bordeaux 10ha.

Clos les Perriers (Fr) a vineyard in the A.C. Sancerre, Central Vineyards, Loire.

Clos les Santenots (Fr) see Santenots (Les).

Clos l'Étoile (Fr) a vineyard. (Com): Lalande de Pomerol. A.C. Lalande de Pomerol, Bordeaux.

Clos l'Évêque (Fr) a vineyard. (Add): Château d'Estroyes, 71640 Mercurey. A vineyard. (Com): Mercurey. A.C. Mercurey, Côte Chalonnaise, Burgundy.

Clos Liché (Fr) a vineyard. (Com): St-Pardon-de-Conques. A.C. Graves, Bordeaux. 3ha (white).

Clos Louloumet (Fr) a vineyard. (Com): Toulenne. A.C. Graves, Bordeaux. 3ha (white).

Clos Magne Figeac (Fr) a vineyard. (Add): 33450 Saint-Sulpice-et-Cameyrac. A.C. Saint-Émilion. (Com): Saint-Sulpice-et-Cameyrac. 5.5ha. A.C. Grape varieties: Cabernet franc and Merlot.

Clos Maisonneuve (Fr) a vineyard. (Com): Parsac-Saint-Émilion. A.C. Saint-Émilion, Bordeaux 2ha.

Clos Malverne (S.Afr) a winery (established 1988) based in Stellenbosch, Western Cape. 25ha. (Add): P.O. Box 1887, Devon Valley, Stellenbosch. Grape varieties: Cabernet sauvignon, Chardonnay, Merlot, Pinotage, Sauvignon blanc, Shiraz. Labels: Auret Cape Blend, Devonet, Shepherd's Creek Classic. Websites: http://www.closmalverne.co.za/http://wwwcapeblend.co.za

Clos Mandillot (Fr) a vineyard. (Com): Saint-Christoly. A.C. Saint-Émilion, Bordeaux.

Clos Marcilly (Fr) a vineyard in the A.C. commune of Mercurey, Côte Chalonnaise, Burgundy. May use the designation Premier Cru on the bottle label.

Clos Mariout (Egy) a vineyard that produces fine, full-flavoured white wines.

Clos Matamir (Egy) a vineyard that produces fine, full-flavoured red wines.

Clos Maurice (Fr) a vineyard. (Com): Saint-Sulpice-de-Faleyrens. A.C. Saint-Émilion, Bordeaux 1ha.

Clos Mayne-Lamouroux (Fr) a vineyard. (Com): Barsac. A.C. Barsac (or Sauternes), Bordeaux 2ha.

Clos Mazeyres (Fr) a vineyard. (Com): Pomerol. A.C. Pomerol, Bordeaux 6ha.

Clos Mercier (Fr) a vineyard. (Com): Barsac. A.C. Barsac (or Sauternes), Bordeaux 3ha.

Clos Micot (Fr) a Premier Cru vineyard in the A.C. commune of Pommard, Côte de Beaune, Burgundy 3.9ha.

Clos Mireille (Fr) a Blanc de Blancs wine produced by Domaine Ott in the A.C. Côtes de Provence, south-eastern France. Grape varieties: Sauvignon, Sémillon and Ugni blanc.

Clos Monplaisir (Fr) a vineyard in the A.C. Saint-Émilion, Bordeaux 2ha.

Clos Montesquieu (Fr) a vineyard. (Com): Montagne-Saint-Émilion. A.C. Montagne-Saint-Émilion, Bordeaux 3ha.

Clos Morteil (Fr) a vineyard. (Com): Bégadan. A.C. Médoc, Bordeaux 4ha.

Clos Napolon (Fr) a Premier Cru vineyard in the A.C. commune of Fixin, Côte de Nuits, Burgundy. 1.75ha. Also known as Aux Cheusots.

Clos Nardian (Fr) a 1.52ha. vineyard based in Saint-Émilion, Bordeaux. A.C Saint-Émilion. Grape variety: 100% Merlot. Also has vineyards in the A.C. Entre-deux-mers.

Clos Nardin (Fr) a vineyard. (Com): St-Michel. A.C. Côtes Canon-Fronsac, Bordeaux. 1ha.

Clos Nouchet (Fr) a vineyard in the commune in the Castres. A.C. Graves, Bordeaux. 3ha (red).

Clos Pailhas (Fr) a vineyard in the A.C. Saint-Émilion, Bordeaux 3ha.

Clos Pasquette (Fr) a vineyard in the A.C. Saint-Émilion, Bordeaux 3ha.

Clos Patarabet (Fr) a vineyard in the A.C. Saint-Émilion, Bordeaux 1ha.

Clos Patarabet-la-Gaffelière (Fr) a vineyard in the A.C. Saint-Émilion, Bordeaux 2ha.

Clos Patris (Fr) a vineyard in the A.C. Saint-Émilion, Bordeaux 1ha.

Clos Pegase Winery (USA) a vineyard based in St. Helena, Napa. Vineyards at Los Carneros, Lake County and Napa Valley. Grape varieties: Cabernet sauvignon, Chardonnay, Fumé blanc, Merlot, Petite sirah, Sauvignon blanc, Sémillon. Label: Mitsuko's Vineyard.

Clos Petit Corbin (Fr) a vineyard. (Add): 33330 Saint-Émilion. A vineyard. (Com): Saint-Émilion. A.C. Saint-Émilion, Bordeaux.

Clos Petite Bellane (Fr) a vineyard in the A.C. Valréas, Côtes-du-Rhône-Villages. (Add): 84602 Valréas. Produces Les Echalas. Website: http://www.clos-petite-bellane.com 'E'mail: info@clos-petite-bellane.com

Clos Petit-Figeac (Fr) a vineyard in the A.C. Saint-Émilion, Bordeaux 3ha.

Clos Petit Mauvinon (Fr) a vineyard. (Add): Saint-Sulpice-de-Faleyrens, 33330 Saint-Émilion. A.C. Saint-Émilion. (Com): Saint-Sulpice-de-Faleyrens. 4ha. Grape varieties: Cabernet sauvignon 35% and Merlot 65%.

Clos Peyret (Fr) a vineyard. (Com): Preignac. A.C. Sauternes, Bordeaux 1ha.

Clos Pezat (Fr) a vineyard in the A.C. Saint-Émilion, Bordeaux 1ha.

Clos Piganeau (Fr) a vineyard in the A.C. Saint-Émilion, Bordeaux 1ha.

Clos Plaisance (Fr) a vineyard. (Com): Parsac-Saint-Émilion. A.C. Saint-Émilion, Bordeaux 9ha.

Clos Pleville (Fr) a vineyard. (Com): Pomerol. A.C. Saint-Émilion, Bordeaux 1ha.

Clos Plince (Fr) a vineyard in the Sables-Saint-Émilion. A.C. Saint-Émilion, Bordeaux 1ha.

Clos Pourret (Fr) part of Clos Petit-Figeac, A.C. Saint-Émilion, Bordeaux.

Clos Pressac (Fr) a vineyard. (Com): Saint-Étienne-de-Lisse. A.C. Saint-Émilion, Bordeaux 7ha.

Clos Prieur (Fr) a Premier Cru vineyard [part] in the A.C. commune of Gevrey-Chambertin, Côte de Nuits, Burgundy 1.98ha.

Clos Puyjalon (Fr) a vineyard. (Com): Portets. A.C. Graves, Bordeaux. 25ha (red and white). Also Château Jean-Gervais.

Clos René (Fr) a vineyard. (Com): Pomerol. A.C. Pomerol, Bordeaux 10ha.

Clos Rol de Fombrauge (Fr) a vineyard. (Com): Saint-Christophe-des-Bardes. A.C. Saint-Émilion, Bordeaux 4ha.

Clos Roque d'Aspes (Fr) a vineyard in the A.C. Faugères, Languedoc-Roussillon. Grape varieties: Grenache, Mourvèdre, Syrah.

Clos Roucheyron (Fr) a vineyard in the A.C. Saint-Émilion, Bordeaux 1ha.

Clos Rousseau (Fr) a Premier Cru vineyard in the A.C. commune of Santenay, Côte de Beaune, Burgundy.

Clos Saint André (Fr) the label of a Châteauneuf-du-Pape produced by Deville et Fils, 4 et 6 Ave. du Général de Gaulle, 84230 Châteauneuf-du-Pape, southern Rhône.

Clos Saint-Denis (Fr) a Grand Cru vineyard of the commune of Morey-Saint-Denis, Burgundy 6.5ha.

Clos Sainte Magdeleine (Fr) a vineyard in the A.C. Cassis, Provence, south-eastern France.

Clos Saint-Jacques (Fr) a Premier Cru vineyard in the A.C. commune of Gevrey-Chambertin, Côte de Nuits, Burgundy. 6.92ha. Also sold as Village Saint-Jacques.

Clos Saint-Jean (Fr) a Premier Cru [part] in the A.C. commune of Chassagne-Montrachet, Côte de Beaune, Burgundy 14.36ha.

Clos Saint Jean (Fr) the label of red Châteauneuf-du-Pape wine produced by Maurel et Fils, 8 Chemin de la Calade, 84230 Châteauneuf-du-Pape, southern Rhône.

Clos Saint Julien (Fr) a vineyard. (Add): 33330 Saint-Émilion. Grand Cru. A.C. Saint-Émilion. (Com): Saint-Émilion. 20ha. Grape varieties: Cabernet franc, Cabernet sauvignon and Merlot.

Clos Saint-Marc [Les] (Fr) a Premier Cru vineyard in the village of Prémeaux in the southern part of the A.C. commune of Nuits-Saint-Georges, Côte de Nuits, Burgundy 0.9ha.

Clos Saint Martin (Fr) a vineyard. (Add): Château Côte-Baleau, 33330 Saint-Émilion. Grand Cru Classé. A.C. Saint-Émilion. (Com): Saint-Émilion. 3.5ha. Grape varieties: Cabernet franc, Cabernet sauvignon and Merlot.

Clos Saint Michel (Fr) the label of a Châteauneuf-du-Pape produced by Mousset (Guy), La Prieuré, Saint-Joseph, 84700 Sorgues, southern Rhône.

Clos Saint-Paul (Fr) a vineyard in the A.C. commune of Givry, Côte Chalonnaise, Burgundy.

Clos Saint-Pierre (Fr) a vineyard in the A.C. commune of Givry, Côte Chalonnaise, Burgundy.

Clos Salmon (Fr) a vineyard in the A.C. commune of Givry, Côte Chalonnaise, Burgundy.

Clos Sentouary (Fr) a vineyard. (Com): St-Pierre-de-Mons. A.C. Graves, Bordeaux. 2ha (white).

Clos Sicard (Fr) a vineyard in the A.C. Saint-Émilion, Bordeaux 4ha.

Clos Simard (Fr) a vineyard. (Com): Saint-Émilion. A.C. Saint-Émilion, Bordeaux 4ha.

Clos Sorbés [Les] (Fr) a Premier Cru vineyard in the A.C. commune of Morey-Saint-Denis, Côte de Nuits, Burgundy 3.3ha.

Clos St-André (Fr) a vineyard. (Com): Pomerol. A.C. Pomerol, Bordeaux 2ha.

Clos St-Anne (Fr) part of Château Taillefer, A.C. Pomerol, Bordeaux.

Clos St-Émilion (Fr) a vineyard in the A.C. Saint-Émilion, Bordeaux 7ha.

Clos St-Hilaire (Fr) a vineyard. (Com): Portets. A.C. Graves, Bordeaux. 6ha (red and white).

Clos St. Jacques (Fr) a vineyard. (Add): Sté. Civile du Domaine de la Folie, 71150 Chagny. A vineyard in the A.C. commune of Rully, Côte Chalonnaise, Burgundy.

Clos St-Jean (Fr) a vineyard. (Com): Pujols. A.C. Graves, Bordeaux. 8ha (white).

Clos St-Martin (Fr) a vineyard. (Com): Saint-Émilion. A.C. Saint-Émilion, Bordeaux. 6ha. Grand Cru Classé.

Clos St-Robert (Fr) a vineyard. (Com): Barsac. A.C. Barsac (or Sauternes), Bordeaux 1ha.

Clos St-Robert (Fr) a vineyard. (Com): Pujols. A.C. Graves, Bordeaux. 30ha (red and white).

Clos St-Valéry (Fr) a vineyard in the A.C. Saint-Émilion, Bordeaux 3ha.

Clos Tasta (Fr) a vineyard. (Com): St-Aignan. A.C. Côtes de Fronsac, Bordeaux.

Clos Teynac-Rival (Fr) a vineyard. (Com): Lussac-Saint-Émilion. A.C. Saint-Émilion, Bordeaux 3ha.

Clos Toulifaut (Fr) part of Château Boënot, A.C. Pomerol, Bordeaux.

Clos Triguedina (Fr) a vineyard in the A.C. Cahors in south-western France.

Clos Trimoulet (Fr) a vineyard. (Add): 33330 Saint-Émilion. Grand Cru. A.C. Saint-Émilion. (Com): Saint-Émilion. 8ha. Grape varieties: Cabernet franc 10%, Cabernet sauvignon 10% and Merlot 80%.

Clos Valentin (Fr) a vineyard in the A.C. Saint-Émilion, Bordeaux 4ha.

Clos Verdet-Monbousquet (Fr) a vineyard. (Com): Saint-Émilion. A.C. Saint-Émilion, Bordeaux 5ha.

Clos Vert Bois (Fr) a vineyard in the A.C. Saint-Émilion, Bordeaux 4ha.

Clos Viaut (Fr) a vineyard. (Com): St-Pardon-de-Conques. A.C. Graves, Bordeaux. 2ha (white).

Clos Viaut (Fr) a vineyard. (Com): St-Pierre-de-Mons. A.C. Graves, Bordeaux. 9ha (white).

Clos Vieux Capot (Fr) a vineyard. (Com): Fronsac. A.C. Côtes Canon-Fronsac, Bordeaux 2ha.

Clos Vieux-Maillet (Fr) a vineyard. (Com): Pomerol. A.C. Pomerol, Bordeaux 2ha.

Clos Vieux-Pontet (Fr) a vineyard in the A.C. Saint-Émilion, Bordeaux 1ha.

Clos-Voyen (Fr) a Premier Cru vineyard in the A.C. commune of Mercurey, Côte Chalonnaise, Burgundy. Is also known as Les Voyens.

Clotted Cream (Eng) see Devonshire Cream.

Clou [Le] (Fr) a vineyard in the A.C. commune of Montagny, Côte Chalonnaise, Burgundy.

Cloud Burst Cocktail (Cktl) 25mls (1fl.oz) dry gin, 20mls (¾ fl.oz) crème de noyau, juice ½ lime, juice ½ lemon, dash egg white. Shake over ice, strain into an ice-filled highball glass. Top with soda water, lemon slice and 5mls (¼ fl.oz) parfait amour.

Cloud Buster Cocktail (Cktl) place 25mls (⅕ gill) vodka into a flute glass with 2 small ice cubes, top with iced Champagne and spiral of lemon.

Clouded Yellow Ale (Eng) a 4.8% alc by vol. ale brewed by the St. Austell Brewery C°. Ltd., Cornwall.

Cloudiness (Eng) is caused by either a drastic change in temperature, from unwanted continuation of fermentation, from excess protein or bacterial action. Treated by fining.

Cloud Mist (Chi) the name given to the tea grown in the Lu Shan Botanic Garden in the Szechwan Province. Is served to visiting Western VIP's. Was originally reserved for the Emperor's use only.

Cloud Nine (Eng) a 4.2% alc by vol. cask-conditioned ale brewed by the Six Bells Brewery, Bishop's Castle, Shropshire.

Cloud Seeding (Eng) the action of spraying clouds with silver iodide to create rainfall away from the vineyards which might turn into hail storms over the vineyards. Either practiced with aircraft or rockets in those areas of greatest risk. (Burgundy in France and Penedés in Spain are examples).

Clouds Vineyards (S.Afr) a winery (established 2002) based in Stellenbosch, Western Cape. 2.5ha. Grape variety: Savignon blanc. Website: http://www.cloudsguesthouse.com

Cloud Valley Wines (Austr) a vineyard (established 1983). (Add): Red Hill, Shoreham Road, Red Hill South, Victoria. Grape varieties: Cabernet sauvignon and Chardonnay.

Cloudy (Eng) see Cloudiness.

Cloudy Bay (N.Z) a winery. (Add): Jacksons Road, Blenheim. 50ha. Grape varieties: Chardonnay, Sauvignon, Sémillon, Merlot, Cabernet sauvignon, Cabernet franc. Noted for their Sauvignon blanc varietal wine, late-harvest Riesling, Pelorus (méthode traditionelle).

Cloudy Sky (Cktl) place 2 ice cubes into a highball glass, add juice of ½ lime, 90mls (¾ gill) sloe gin. Stir and top with ginger ale.

Clouet [André] (Fr) a Champagne producer. (Add): 8 Rue Gambetta, Bouzy, 51150 Tours-sur-Marne. Produces Prestige cuvee: Un Jour de 1911, also a Brut rosé and vintage cuvée.

Clouseaux [Les] (Fr) a vineyard in the A.C. commune of Montagny, Côte Chalonnaise, Burgundy.

Cloux (Fr). A vineyard in the A.C. commune of Rully, Côte Chalonnaise, Burgundy.

Clovaillon (Fr) a Premier Cru vineyard in the A.C. commune of Puligny-Montrachet, Côte de Beaune, Burgundy 5.5ha.

Clove Cocktail (Cktl) ⅓ measure Italian vermouth, ⅙ measure sloe gin, ⅙ measure muscatel wine. Stir over ice and strain into a cocktail glass.

Clovelly Wines (S.Afr) a winery (established 2000) based in the Stellenbosch, Western Cape. 3ha. Grape varieties include: Cabernet sauvignon, Chardonnay, Chenin blanc, Cinsaut, Merlot. Label: Triangle. Website: http://www.clovellywines.com

Clover Club [1] (Cktl) 40mls (⅓ gill) gin, 20mls (⅙ gill) French vermouth, 1 teaspoon raspberry syrup, juice of lime, egg white. Shake over ice and strain into a small goblet.

Clover Club [2] (Cktl) 2 measures gin, 1 measure grenadine, 1 measure lemon juice, 1 egg white. Shake well over ice, and strain into a cocktail glass.

Clover Club Royal (Cktl) 65mls (½ gill) dry gin, 30mls (¼ gill) grenadine, 30mls (¼ gill) lemon juice, 1 egg yolk. Shake well over ice and strain into a cocktail glass.

Cloverdale (USA) a wine-producing district in the Russian River Valley, California.

Cloverfield Private Cellar (S.Afr) a winery (established 1920) based in Robertson, Western Cape. 120ha. Grape varieties: Chardonnay, Chenin blanc, Sauvignon blanc, Shiraz. Label: Four Clover, Winemaker's Selection.

Clover Hill (Austr) the name used for a sparkling wine produced by Taltarni from the Pipers' River region, Tasmania. 100% Chardonnay.

Clover Leaf Cocktail (Cktl) as for Clover Club but with 2 sprigs of mint shaken with the cocktail. Decorate with a sprig of mint.

Cloying (Eng) a term given to a sweet wine the sweetness of which tends to be overpowering to the other properties of the wine.

Club (Eng) licensed premises that differ from full On-licenses. There are two classes: [a] the club that operates the same as a public house with a full On-licence and the same licensing hours but the clientele must be members. e.g. The Royal British Legion Club, Workingmen's Club. [b] the club that has a Club licence and is owned by the members, opening to suit the club's activities. e.g. Golf Club, Rugby Club. All visitors to clubs must have been signed in by a paid-up member and must be accompanied by the member whilst on the club premises.

Club (Indo) a still natural spring mineral water from Desa Lemahbang, Pandaan, Sukorejo, Indonesia. Mineral contents (milligrammes per litre): Sodium 8.7mg/l, Calcium 20.4mg/l, Magnesium 13.3mg/l, Potassium 3.4mg/l, Bicarbonates 152.6mg/l, Chlorides 4.8mg/l, Sulphates 5.1mg/l, Fluorides 0.23mg/l, Nitrates 0.05mg/l. pH 7.2

Club Amontillado (Sp) a brand of Amontillado Sherry produced by Harvey in Jerez de la Frontera. Now known as Club Classic.

C

Club Bitter (Eng) a 3.9% alc by vol. bitter beer brewed by The Concertina Brewery, South Yorkshire. % alc by vol.

Club Bottle (Fr) the name given to the bottles used for the sparkling Blanc Foussy wine of Vouvray, Touraine, Loire.

Club Classic (Sp) the new name for Club Amontillado Sherry from Harveys in Jerez de la Frontera.

Club Cocktail [1] (Cktl) 60mls (½ gill) Scotch whisky, 3 dashes grenadine, 2 dashes Angostura. Stir over ice, strain into a cocktail glass, add a cherry and squeeze of lemon peel juice on top.

Club Cocktail [2] (Cktl) 40mls (⅓ gill) dry gin, 20mls (⅙ gill) sweet vermouth. Stir over ice, strain into a cocktail glass, add a cherry and olive.

Club Cooler (Cktl) 40mls (⅓ gill) Italian vermouth, 20mls (⅙ gill) grenadine, dash lemon juice, 250mls (½ pint) soda water. Stir over ice in a highball glass and serve with a squeeze of lemon peel juice.

Club des Amis du Vin de Bordeaux (Fr) a wine society based in Bordeaux.

Club de Viticulteurs Champenois (Fr) founded in 1971 by a group of récoltants-manipulants to improve the quality of non-vintage wines by limiting the amount of vintage wines its members may produce. abbr: C.V.C.

Club Goblet (Eng) a short footed tulip glass 200mls (6⅔ fl.ozs) used for cocktails and fruit juices.

Club Lager Beer (Afr) a lager beer brewed by the Accra Brewery in Ghana.

Club Licence (Eng) see Club.

Clubman (S.Afr) the brand-name of a mint-flavoured punch (a wine apéritif).

Clubman [The] (Cktl) 25mls Irish Mist, 100mls orange juice, dash egg white. Shake over ice, strain into an ice-filled highball glass and trickle blue Curaçao down the inside of the glass.

Club 19 (Can) the brand-name of a Canadian whisky imported by Kilsern Distillers, Leicester.

Club Room (Eng) a private room within licenced premises where clubs and societies can meet and drink in private.

Club Rose (Cktl) ½ measure Calvados, 1 measure rye whisky, ½ measure lime cordial, dash grenadine, dash egg white. Shake well over ice and strain into a cocktail glass.

Club Select (S.Afr) the label for a white wine (Sémillon) produced by the Nitida Cellars winery, Durbanville, Western Cape.

Club Soda (USA) the name for a Soda syphon.

Club Tawny Port (Port) a fine old Tawny Port from Graham's Port shipping company.

Club Tresor de Champagne (Fr) a group of Champagne Récoltant-Manipulants (established 1971) who produce a special vintage cuvee which if it passes a 'jury' tasting is awarded the Cuvée 'Special Club'. (Add): 44, Avenue Jean Jaurès, 51200 Épernay. Members: Paul Bara, Yves Beautrait, Roland Champion, Charlier et Fils, Marc Chauvet, Forget-Chemin, Fresnet-Juillet, Pierre Gimonnet et Fils, Gosset Brabant, Goutorbe, Grongnet, Bernard Hatté et Fils, Marc Hérrart, Hervieux Dumez, Janisson Baradon et Fils, Juillet-Lallement, Lamiable, Larmandier Père et Fils, J.Lassalle, Launois Père et Fils, A.Margaine, José Michel et Fils, Nomine Renard, Vazart Coquart, Voirin-Desmoulins. 'E'mail: contact@clubtresorsdechampagne.com

Club Weisse (Ger) a sparkling wheat beer 5.2% alc by vol. brewed by the Spätenbräu Brauerei in Munich.

Cluster (USA) a hop variety which has a mild bitterness and bland flavour.

Clyde Distillers Ltd. (Scot) a distillery based in Glasgow. Produces King's Royal blended Scotch whisky 43% alc by vol.

Clynelish (Scot) a single malt whisky distillery at Bora, Sutherland. A new distillery under the same name has recently been built nearby by the DCL. Group. 43% alc by vol.

C.M. (Fr) abbr: Co-operative-Manipulant. C.I.V.C. registered members initials on a Champagne label. Name belongs to a co-operative of top producers.

C.N.C.O.F.I.E.C. (Chi) abbr: China National Cereals, Oils, Foodstuffs ImPorts and Export Corp.

Cnoc (Scot) a 12 year old malt whisky. 40% alc by vol.

CO₂ (Eng) the chemical symbol for **Carbon-dioxide**. 1 Carbon atom and 2 Oxygen atoms, a by-product of fermentation.

Coach House Brewing C° (Eng) a brewery (established 1991). (Add): Wharf Street, Howley, Warrington, Cheshire WA1 2DQ. Brews: Autumn Ale 5% alc by vol., Dick Turpin 4.2% alc by vol., Gunpowder Strong Mild 3.8% alc by vol., Honey Pot 3.8% alc by vol., Innkeepers Special Reserve 4.5% alc by vol., Ostlers Summer Ale 4% alc by vol., Post Horn Premium Ale 5% alc by vol. Website: http://www.coach-house-brewing.co.uk 'E'mail: djbcoachhouse@hotmail.com

Coaching Inn (Eng) an old picking-up or setting-down point for horse drawn coach passengers. Usually offers food, drink and accommodation.

Coachman (Cktl) ½ measure Cognac and ½ measure Port.

Coa-Dor (USA) a cloth bag into which coffee grounds are placed and then are put into near-boiling water to brew the coffee.

Coahuila (Mex) a region that contains the wine-producing districts of Parras and Saltillo.

Coalesce (S.Afr) the label for a Bordeaux-style red wine (Cabernet franc, Cabernet sauvignon, Malbec, Merlot and Petit verdot blend) produced by the Gerhard Britz winery, Walker Bay, Western Cape.

Coal Porter (Eng) a 4.5% alc by vol. porter brewed by Bartrams Brewery, Suffolk.

Coalporter Beer (Eng) a cask-conditioned ale 1048 O.G. brewed by a public house in Bristol.

Coalville Vineyard (Austr) a winery (established 1975). (Add): Moe South Road, Moe South, Victoria. Grape variety: Cabernet sauvignon.

C

Coarse (Eng) a term used in wine tasting for wines with a rough texture.

Coast (S.Afr) the label for a range of wines marketed by the PicardiRebel drinks chain, Western Cape.

Coastal (S.Afr) the label for a range of white wines (Chenin blanc and Sauvignon blanc) produced by the Buitenverwachting winery, Constantia, Western Cape.

Coastal Belt (S.Afr) a major wine-producing area in the south west.

Coaster (Cktl) place several dashes of Angostura bitters into a spirit glass, swirl and discard. Add 1 measure of gin and serve with soda water.

Coaster (Eng) a stand usually of silver, cork, cardboard or wood used to stand bottles, glasses or decanters on to prevent drips of wine or beer staining the tables. (Fr) = dessous.

Coastliner (Eng) an ale brewed by Skinner's Brewery, Truro, Cornwall.

Coast 2 Coast (Eng) a 5% alc by vol. ale brewed by the Derwentrose Brewery in Consett, County Durham.

Coatepec (Mex) a noted coffee-producing region in southern Mexico.

Coatepec Coffee (Mex) a coffee from Vera Cruz. Is a rich, full-flavoured coffee that can be drunk on its own.

Coates and Cº. (Eng) the distillers of Plymouth gin at the Blackfriars Distillery in Plymouth, Devon.

Coates Gaymers (Eng) a major cider-making firm based in Somerset.

Coates Somerset L.A. (Eng) a low alcohol cider from Showering. 0.9% alc by vol.

Coating (Eng) a deposit that is sometimes found on the inside of red wine bottles. (Fr) = chemise.

Cobalt Oxide (Eng) a mineral from Saxony used in glass making to produces a blue glass called Bristol Blue. Used for decanters and wine glasses in the seventeenth and eighteenth centuries.

Cobanpinar (Tur) a still natural spring mineral water. Mineral contents (milligrammes per litre): Sodium 21.4mg/l, Calcium 12.4mg/l, Magnesium 5.34mg/l, Potassium 3.8mg/l, Chlorides 33mg/l, Sulphates 31mg/l, Fluorides 0.2mg/l, Nitrates 1mg/l.

Cobaw Ridge (Austr) a winery (established 1985). (Add): Perc Boyers Lane, East Pastonia via Kyneton, Victoria. Grape varieties: Chardonnay, Cabernet sauvignon, Shiraz.

Cobblers (USA) a drink for warm weather, made from wine or spirits, fresh fruits and ice shavings. Served in a highball glass. (Den) = vindrink med frugtstykker.

Cobbler's Hill (S.Afr) a red wine (Cabernet franc, Cabernet sauvignon and Merlot blend) produced by the Jordan Vineyards, Stellenbosch.

Cobb Mountain (USA) a still natural spring water (established circa 1850) from Calso Spring. Mineral contents (milligrammes per litre): Sodium 5mg/l, Calcium 8.9mg/l, Magnesium 2.4mg/l, Potassium 3.4mg/l, Bicarbonates 29mg/l, Chlorides 2mg/l, Sulphates 2mg/l, Fluorides 0.11mg/l, Nitrates 5mg/l. pH 7.3

Cobbold's IPA (Eng) a 4.2% alc by vol. light golden best bitter brewed by Tolly Cobbold in Suffolk.

Cobbold's 250 Special (Eng) a light golden in colour, 6% alc by vol. premium bottled beer from Tolly Cobbold in Suffolk. Brewed to mark the 250th year anniversary of Ipswich brewery in 1996.

Cobnut Ale (Eng) an ale brewed by Samuel Allsopp in Burton (part of the Tapster's Choice range).

Cobnut Brown Ale (Eng) a bottled brown ale brewed by Tolly Cobbold, Suffolk.

Cobos (Sp) a producer of Montilla wines in Montilla-Moriles.

Cobra (Ind) the name of a 5% alc by vol. bottled lager beer sold in 650mls bottles. Brewed by Mysore Brewery, Bangalore.

Cobra (Cktl) 1 measure Southern, Comfort, ½ measure Parfait Amour, ½ measure Jack Daniels. Shake over ice, serve in an ice-filled goblet and decorate with a cherry on a stick.

Cobra Beer (Eng) a beer 5% alc by vol. brewed by Cobra Beer Ltd. London.

Cobra Beer Ltd (Eng) a brewery (established 1989). (Add): Alexander House, 14–16 Peterborough Road, Fulham, London SW6 3BN. Produces under licence: Cobra Beer 5% alc by vol. King Cobra 8% alc by vol and Bilimoria Wine. *See also* Mysore Brewery. Website: http://www.cobrabeer.com 'E'mail: cobrabeer@cobrabeer.com

Coca (Fr) cola.

Coca (S.Am) a Peruvian shrub whose leaves are used for infusion in alcohol, wine or as a tisane, has strong stimulative (narcotic) powers.

Cocabelos (Sp) a wine-producing area in Galicia. Produces red and white wines.

Coca Cola (USA) a ™ Cola created in America, now produced under licence world-wide. Non-alcoholic and carbonated it was invented by Dr. John Pemberton in 1886. Formed the C.C.S.B. with the Schweppes Cº. in 1986. (U.K). Charter Place, Vine Street, Uxbridge, Middlesex UB8 1EZ. *See also* Hajime. Websites: http://www.cokecce.co.uk/http://www.coca-cola.co.uk

Coca Cola and Schweppes Beverages Company (Eng) *abbr*: C.C.S.B. Formed by a merger of Coca Cola and Schweppes. Is the largest soft drinks company in the U.K.

Cocal (Sp) liqueur producers based in Telde, Canary Islands.

Cocoa Bean (Eng) the cocoa seed from which chocolate and cocoa powder is manufactured. (Ire) = crann coco.

Cocao Shells (Eng) used to make a substitute cocoa drink, the powder was infused (similar to coffee).

Cocchi (It) a noted producer of Moscato d'Asti based in Piemonte, north-western Italy.

Coccocciola (It) a white grape variety grown in Abruzzi. Also spelt Cococciola.

Cochem (Ger) village (Anb): Mosel-Saar-Ruwer. (Ber): Zell/Mosel. (Gro): Goldbäumchen. (Vins): Bischofstuhl, Herrenberg, Hochlay, Klostergarten, Pinnerkreuzberg, Schlossberg, Sonnenberg.

C

Cochem (Ger) village (Anb): Mosel-Saar-Ruwer. (Ber): Zell/Mosel. (Gro): Rosenhang. (Vins): Arzlay, Nikolausberg, Rosenberg.

Cochero (Hol) a banana and cream-based liqueur 14.9% alc by vol.

Cochineal (S.Am) a grub (or beetle) that attacks the vine, feeding on its sap. This weakens the plant and eventually kills it. Oil emulsions prevent it.

Cochiry (S.Am) a beer made from sweet potatoes in Guyana.

Cochylis (Lat) the eggs of a night-flying moth whose caterpillars eat the blossoms and later the bunches of grapes. Treated by lead arsenate and other insecticides. *see* Eudemis, Pyralis.

Cock-a-Doodle (Cktl)(Non-Alc) shake 3 parts grape juice, 3 parts lemon juice, 1 part lime cordial, 1 part gomme syrup, and a dash of grenadine over ice, strain into a highball glass and decorate with lime slice and black grape halves.

Cock-Ale (Eng) a mixture of spirits fed to fighting cocks in the eighteenth century. This would also be consumed by the winning punters with a number of tail feathers in the drink showing the number of ingredients in the drink. Tale is often suggested as being the origination of Cocktail.

Cock & Bull (N.Z) a brewery. (Add): P.O.Box 82-008, Highland Park, Auckland New Zealand. Brews beers and lager. Website: http://www.cockandbull.co.nz 'E'mail: info@cockandbull.co.nz

Cock & Hoop (Eng) a 4.3% alc by vol. ale brewed by the Nottingham Brewery, Nottinghamshire.

Cockburn (Port) Vintage Port shippers. Vintages: 1870, 1872, 1873, 1875, 1878, 1881, 1884, 1887, 1890, 1894, 1896, 1900, 1904, 1908, 1912, 1927, 1935, 1947, 1950, 1955, 1960, 1963, 1967, 1970, 1975, 1977, 1982, 1983, 1985, 1991, 1994, 1997, 2000, 2003. Single Quinta is the Quinta da Eira Velha: (1978). Owned by Allied-Domecq.

Cockburn Smithies (Port) vintage Port shippers. *see* Cockburn.

Cocked Ale (Eng) the Yorkshire dialect that denotes a fresh, foaming beer.

Cockerel (Eng) the name of a nitrokeg beer brewed by Courage.

Cocker Hoop (Eng) a 4.8% alc by vol. cask-conditioned bitter from Jennings Brothers, Castle Brewery, Cockermouth. Named after the river Cocker.

Cock-eyed (Eng) a slang term for a nineteenth century term for drunk, intoxicated.

Cockle Pippin Ale (Eng) an ale brewed using apple juices from Samuel Allsopp Brewery in Burton (part of their Tapster's Choice range).

Cockleroaster (Eng) brewed at Christmas by Furgusons of Plymouth. *See also* Dartmoor Best, Dartmoor Millennium.

Cock O'The North Liqueur C° (Scot) a distillery (established 1998). (Add): Aboyne Castle, Aboyne, Aberdeenshire AB34 5JP. Produces malt, Scotch whiskies and liqueurs. Website: http://www.cockothenorth.com 'E'mail: sales@cockothenorth.co.uk

Cock Robin Bitter (Eng) a keg bitter brewed by the Robinson Brewery in Stockport.

Cockspur Five Star (W.Ind) a 2 year old golden rum produced by West India Rum Refinery, Barbados.

Cockspur Old Gold (W.Ind) a 5 year old rum produced by West India Rum Refinery, Barbados.

Cockspur V.S.O.R. (W.Ind) a 10 year old rum produced by West India Rum Refinery, Barbados.

Cocktail (Eng) a combination of mixed drinks. Can be alcoholic or non-alcoholic. *see* Betsy Flannigan, Cock-Ale, Glamour Cocktails and Pousse Cafés. (Aus) = cocktail, (Chi) = jiweijiu, (Cro) = koktel, (Den) = cocktail, (Fr) = apéritif, (Ger) = cocktail, (Gre) = kokteil, (Hol) = cocktail, (Indo) = cocktail, (Ire) = manglam, (Isr) = cocktail, (It) = cocktail, (Jap) = kakuteru, (Kor) = kakteil, (Port) = coquetel, (Rus) = kaktyeel, (Sp) = coctel, (Thai) = kruangdeum, (Wal) = anogydd.

Cocktail Age (USA) 1920–1935.

Cocktail Carine (Cktl) ½ measure gin, ¼ measure Mandarine Napoléon, ¼ measure Dubonnet, dash lemon juice. Shake over ice and strain into a cocktail glass.

Cocktail Cherry (Eng) two kinds, **red**: in maraschino or **green**: in Curaçao or crème de menthe. Used as a cocktail decoration.

Cocktail Hour (USA) the name given to the apéritif hour (pre-dinner) when cocktails are normally consumed.

Cocktail Mixes (USA) prepared cocktail mixes (fruit juices etc.) that only need the addition of the spirit to complete them.

Cocktail Party (Eng) a pre-meal party where apéritifs (cocktails) are served with canapés (hors d'œuvre) to stimulate the appetite.

Cocktail Shaker (Eng) an implement for mixing cocktails with ice to cool them quickly. Has a lid and strainer built in. Usually made of silver, E.P.N.S. or stainless steel.

Cocktail Sherry (USA) the name given to a dry, Sherry-type drink made from a variety of grapes.

Cocktail Stick (Eng) a small pointed stick of wood or plastic used either for impaling fruit (cherries, pineapple) or onions, olives, etc. which are placed in a drink (cocktail) or used for canapés.

Coco (Ch.Isles)(Wal) cocoa.

Cócó (Ire) cocoa.

Cocoa (Eng) a commercially produced powdered drink made from the cocoa bean. It is mixed with hot milk or water and sweetened to taste. *See also* Chocolate. (Aus) = kakao, (Ch.Isles) = coco, (Cro) = kakao, (Fr) = cacao, (Ger) = kakao, (Ire) = coco, (Pol) = kakao, (Sp) = cacao, (Wal) = coco.

Coco Braziliana (W.Ind) a coconut-flavoured liqueur.

Cococciola (It) a local white grape variety from the Abruzzo region which has an aroma and flavour of apricots and apples. Also spelt Coccocciola.

Coco Fresh (It) a coconut-flavoured liqueur from Francoli.

Cocogif (W.Ind) a coconut-flavoured liqueur.

CoCoGif (Fr) a coconut liqueur produced by Giffard, 49240 Avrille, Angers.

Coco Loco Cocktail (Cktl) 2 measures coconut water, ½ measure white rum, ½ measure apricot brandy, ½ measure coconut milk. Blend with a scoop of crushed ice in a blender. Pour into a coconut shell, dress with powdered cinnamon and serve with straws.

Coconut Breeze (Cktl) 35mls (1½ fl.ozs) dark rum, 20mls (¾ fl.oz) pineapple juice, 20mls (¾ fl.oz) coconut milk, dash maraschino, dash orgeat syrup. Shake over ice and strain into a cocktail glass.

Coconut Cocktail (Cktl) ½ measure coconut milk, ¼ measure white rum, ⅛ measure triple sec, ⅛ measure gomme syrup. Stir over ice.

Coconut Daiquiri (Cktl) 50mls (2fl.ozs) lime juice, 25mls (1fl.oz) coconut liqueur, 10mls (½ fl.oz) white rum, dash egg white. Shake over ice and strain into a cocktail glass.

Coconut Liqueur (W.Ind) a white rum flavoured with essences from macerated coconuts.

Coconut Milk (Eng) the juice obtained by pressing the coconut kernel flesh. (Fr) = lait de coco, (W.Ind) = caraïbos.

Coconut Shell Cocktail (Cktl) a shell shaped as a cup, top quarter removed, flesh scooped out, blend with 40mls (⅓ gill) tequila, juice ¼ lemon, 25mls (⅕ gill) coconut cream, 2 dashes Maraschino and a scoop of crushed ice. Serve in the shell with straws and spoon.

Coconut Tequila Cocktail (Cktl) 40mls (⅓ gill) tequila, juice ¼ lemon, 2 dashes Maraschino, 20mls (⅙ gill) coconut cream, scoop crushed ice. Blend altogether in blender, serve in a flute glass.

Coconut Tumble Cocktail (Cktl) 35mls (1½ fl.ozs) white rum, 25mls (1fl.oz) coconut cream, 20mls (¾ fl.oz) Cointreau, dash grenadine. Stir well over ice. Pour into a coconut shell. Dress with cherries and serve with straws.

Coco Oco Cocktail (Cktl) (Non-alc) ½ measure coconut cream, juice of ¼ lemon, ¼ teaspoon Angostura, 4 dashes maraschino, 75mls (3fl.ozs) milk. Blend with a scoop of crushed ice in a blender. Strain into a goblet. Dress with a cherry.

CocoRibe (USA) a coconut milk and white Virginian rum liqueur from Cincinnati, Ohio. 23% alc by vol.

Cocoron (Hol) a coconut-flavoured liqueur produced by De Kuyper.

Cocteaux [Michel] (Fr) a Champagne producer. (Add): Grande Rue, 51260 Montgenost. 8.5ha. (6.5ha. Chardonnay, 2.5ha. Pinot noir).

Coctel (Sp) cocktail.

Cocui (S.Am) see Cocuy.

Cocur (Ukr) a white grape variety grown in the Ukraine.

Cocuy (S.Am) a brandy distilled from fermented sisal roots in Venezuela. See also Cocui.

Coda di Volpe Bianco (It) lit: 'wolf's tail', a white grape variety (so named because the bunches of grapes curl up at the tip – just like the tail of a wolf) grown in the Campania region. Gives perfumed, strong, vinous, straw-coloured dry wines.

Cod Bottle (Eng) a mineral bottle with a marble in the neck to retain the pressure, often coloured to stop being used by rival companies.

Coddington (Eng) a vineyard based in Herefordshire. Grape varieties: Bacchus, Kerner, Ortega.

Code du Vin (Fr) in Burgundy forbids more than the addition of 9 kilogrammes of sugar per 3 hectolitres of must and 200 kilogrammes per hectare.

Códega (Port) a white grape variety. Known as the Alva (Portalegre), Roupeiro (Douro), Siria (Beiras).

Code of Hammurabi (Arab) the first wine laws of Babylonia in 2,000 B.C.

CODERUM (W.Ind) abbr: Comité de Défense et d'Organisation du Marché du Rhum.

Codex Laureshamensis (Ger) a list of vineyards donated to the abbey of Lorsch by St. Nazarius in 764 A.D. (consisted of vineyards of most of the present day regions along the Rhine).

Codlings (Eng) old English cider-making apples. Made very fine cider.

Codo (Port) a white grape variety grown in Beiras.

Codorníu [Anna de] (Sp) a producer (established 1872) of sparkling Cava wines by the metodo tradicional in south-eastern Spain. Website: http://www.codorniu.com

Codswallop (Eng) the name for the mallet that was used to hammer the marble into the Cod mineral bottles.

Coebergh (Hol) a distillery that produces Jenevers and liqueurs. Part of Heineken.

Coefficient of Valorization (Port) part of the method of scoring marks during a tasting of Vinhos Verdes by multiplying the points scored during the tasting according to the type of wine.

Coères [Les] (Fr) a vineyard in the A.C. commune of Montagny, Côte Chalonnaise, Burgundy.

Coeur de Lion (Cyp) a red table wine produced by Keo in Limassol.

Coeur de Rouge (S.Afr) a red wine (blend of Cabernet 80% and Merlot 20%) from the Audacia Estate in Stellenbosch, Western Cape.

Coeur du Lion (Fr) an A.C. Calvados du Pays d'Auge distilled in a wood-fired pot-still. Aged in Sherry and Port casks. Produced by Drouin. see Pomme Prisonnière (La).

Co-Ferment (Eng) part of the complex proteins (enzymes) which together with the apoferment form the holoferment.

Coffea (Lat) a coffee tree species for the genus Rubicaea of which there are 60–100 species.

Coffea abeokutae (Lat) a variety of the coffee tree grown mainly in Africa. see Coffea.

Coffea arabica (Lat) a species of the coffee tree. Grows mainly in hilly regions 600–2000 metres and produces the finest coffes. See also Bourbon Coffee and Coffea.

Coffea arabusta (Lat) a hybrid coffee bean from Arabica and Robusta cross.

Coffea canephora (Lat) a species of the coffee tree. Also known as the Robusta. see Coffea.

C

Coffea congensis (Lat) a variety of the coffee tree grown mainly in West Africa. *see* Coffea.

Coffea devevrei (Lat) a variety of the coffee tree grown mainly in West Africa. *see* Coffea.

Coffea eugenioides (Lat) a variety of coffee tree grown mainly in West Africa. *see* Coffea.

Coffea excelsa (Lat) a variety of the coffee tree whose bean produces a dark roast. Grown mainly in West Africa. *see* Coffea.

Coffea liberica (Lat) a variety of the coffee tree. Grown mainly in West Africa. *see* Coffea.

Coffea robusta (Lat) a variety of **Coffea canephora**. Produces a dark, bitter coffee. Is more resistant to disease than Arabica and grows at altitudes of sea level to 600 metres. *see* Coffea.

Coffea stenophylla (Lat) a variety of the coffee tree grown mainly in West Africa. *see* Coffea.

Coffee (Eng) a beverage produced from the roasted and ground bean (kernel) of the Coffea tree. Strength of the roast and blending will influence the strength of brew. There are three main types-Brazil, Milds and Robustas. *See also* Acorn Coffee and Pure Coffees. (Arab) = qahwa, (Aus) = kaffee, (Chi) = kafei, (Cro) = kava, (Den) = kaffe, (Fr) = café, (Ger) = kaffee, (Gre) = kafes, (Hol) = koffie, (Indo) = kopi, (Ire) = caife, (Isr) = cafe, (It) = caffe, (Jap) = koohii, (Kor) = keopi, (Port) = café, (Rus) = kofye, (Sp) = café, (Thai) = cafae, (Wal) = coffi.

Coffee Amaretto (Liq.Coffee) using ½ measure amaretto and ½ measure Tia Maria. Top with whipped cream.

Coffee and Brandy Liqueur (USA) a liqueur made from a blend of Colombian coffee and brandy. 35% alc by vol.

Coffee Bags (Eng) fresh ground coffee in mesh bags, usually medium ground to prevent grinds escaping. Produces mainly medium brews.

Coffee Bean (Eng) the kernel of the coffee cherry. (Cro) = zrno kave, (It) = chicco di caffé.

Coffee Berry Disease (Eng) a strain of **Colletotrichum coffeanum** a major coffee disease that lives in the bark tissue of the coffee tree. Is dispersed by rain splash.

Coffee Bestle (Den) a coffee-flavoured liqueur.

Coffee Borgia (Liq.Coffee) *see* Café Borgia.

Coffee Break (USA) the time allocated around mid-morning (11a.m.) when coffee (and biscuits) are consumed. *see* Elevenses and Tea Break.

Coffee Brewing Methods (Eng) boiling/filtering/infusion/percolating and steaming. *see* Al Fresco, Automatic Drip, Espresso, Filter, Neapolitain Pot, Percolator, Turkish and Vacuum.

Coffee Bush Diseases (Lat) *see* **Colletotrichum coffeanum, Hemileia vastatrix and Stephanoderes hamjei.**

Coffee Cherry (Eng) the name given to the fruit of the Coffea tree. Has an outer skin, parchment, silverskin and 2 beans (seeds).

Coffee Cobbler (Cktl) 25mls (⅕ gill) Cognac, 2 dashes sugar syrup, fresh brewed coffee. Stir over ice, strain into an ice-filled highball glass. Top with a dash of Port wine and serve with straws.

Coffee Cocktail [1] (Cktl) ⅔ measure Port wine, ⅓ measure brandy, 2 dashes orange Curaçao, yolk of egg. Shake over ice and strain into a cocktail glass.

Coffee Cocktail [2] (Cktl) 20mls (⅙ gill) Cognac, 40mls (⅓ gill) Port, 1 egg yolk, 1 teaspoon gomme syrup. Shake over ice, strain into a small wine goblet and top with grated nutmeg. Also known as Law's Cocktail.

Coffee Compliment (Eng) powderd milk substitute produced by Cadbury (part of Premier Beverages).

Coffee Diablo (Fr) heat together 2 cloves, 25mls (1fl.oz) Cognac, 10mls (½fl.oz) Cointreau, piece of orange and lemon zest over a low flame until nearly boiling. Ignite and pour over hot black coffee in a heat-proof glass or cup.

Coffee-Flavoured Brandy (USA) a brandy-based liqueur infused with coffee beans.

Coffee Flip (Cktl) 1 egg, 1 teaspoon sugar, 25mls (⅕ gill) brandy, 25mls (⅕ gill) Port, 2 teaspoons cream. Shake over ice, strain into a flip glass. Top with grated nutmeg.

Coffee Grasshopper (Cktl) ⅓ measure coffee liqueur, ⅓ measure crème de menthe (white), ⅓ measure cream. Shake over ice and strain into an ice-filled old-fashioned glass.

Coffee Grinder (Eng) *see* Coffee Mill.

Coffee Grinds (Eng) *see* Grinds or Coffee Grounds.

Coffee Grounds (Eng) the roasted beans after they have been ground (cut up) for brewing. *See also* Grinds.

Coffee Leaf Rust (Eng) **Hemileia vastatrix** an obligate parasite to coffee that forms orange pustules on the underside of leaves. The postules contain spores. Heavy infection can kill the plant.

Coffee Liqueurs (Eng) a spirit-based, coffee-flavoured liqueurs. Range in alc. content from 17%–35% by vol. Best known are Bahia, Coffee Bestle, Illy, Kahlúa, Kamok, Pasha and Tia Maria.

Coffee Machines (Eng) manual or automatic units which aid the brewing of coffee from the roasted, ground bean. *see* Coffee Brewing Methods.

Coffee Mill (Eng) a machine (hand or mechanical) used to grind the roasted coffee beans prior to brewing the coffee as a beverage. The size of the grind depending on the method of brewing used (filter, perculator, Turkish, vacuum, etc.). (Fr) = moulin de café.

Coffee Morning (Eng) an event organised to raise monies for charity where coffee is served for a nominal fee.

Coffee Nog (Eng) for two persons. 2 measures Cognac, 2 teaspoons cocoa powder, 2 teaspoons sugar, 1 measure crème de cacao, 2 egg yolks, 1 measure whipped cream. Pour 200mls strong black coffee into a saucepan, add ingredients (except cream) heat slowly. Stir, pour into heat-proof glasses, top with cream and grated nutmeg.

Coffee Royale (USA) 125mls strong hot black coffee, 35mls brandy, sugar cube. Heat a 250 ml. goblet, place coffee into glass. Put bowl of a teaspoon over coffee, place sugar cube into bowl. Pour brandy over sugar and then ignite sugar and brandy in bowl of spoon. Stir into coffee and serve.

Coffee Sour (Cktl) 40mls (⅓ gill) Tia Maria, 20mls (⅙ gill) lemon juice, 1 teaspoon powdered sugar, ½ egg white. Shake well over ice, strain into a sour glass.

Coffee Sport (USA) a coffee liqueur which is similar in style to Crème de Café.

Coffeestone (S.Afr) the label for a red wine (Cabernet sauvignon) produced by the Graham Beck Wines winery, Franschhoek, Western Cape.

Coffee Substitutes (Eng) ingredients that are roasted and ground and used as a substitute for coffee or as an additive to coffee to bulk out and flavour. Main ones are acorn, carrot, cereals, chick pea, chicory, dandelion root, date, fig, lupin and soya.

Coffee Syrup Nog (Eng) hot milk mixed with coffee essence and golden syrup to taste.

Coffee Tree (Eng) a name for the **Coffea** from the family **Rubicaea**. 60–100 species.

Coffee Year (Eng) commences each year from 1st October to 30th September.

Coffeina (It) caffeine.

Coffey (Eng) the seventeenth century word used for coffee.

Coffey [Aeneas] (Ire) an Irish excise officer who in 1831 invented and registered the patent for the 'Coffey Still', a continuous still. See also Stein (Robert).

Coffey Still (Ire) a continuous still invented by Aeneas Coffey. See also Coffey [Aeneas], Stein [Robert].

Coffi (Wal) coffee.

Cofield Wines (Austr) a winery (established 1990) based at Distillery Road, Wahgunyah, Victoria. Produces a range of red, white, fortified and méthode traditionelle wines. Grape varieties: Chardonnay, Pinot noir.

Cófra Tae (Ire) tea chest.

Cognac (Fr) a commune in the Charente département whose grapes are classed Borderies (Cognac).

Cognac (Fr) a commune in the Charente département whose grapes are classed Grande Champagne (Cognac).

Cognac (Fr) a spirit distilled from wine in the Charente region of western France. Region was defined in 1909, has its own A.C. and rated the best brandy in the world. Crus of Grande Champagne, Petite Champagne, Borderies, Fins Bois, Bons Bois and Bois Ordinaires. See also Fine Champagne and Vignobles a Double Fin. Website: http://www.Cognac.fr

Cognac Authentique (Fr) the name given to Cognac brandy that is less than four years old.

Cognac Chollet (Fr) a Cognac producer. (Add): Le Planty, Boutiers-Saint-Trijan, 16100 Cognac. 18ha. in Fins Bois. Produces a wide range of fine Cognacs.

Cognac Coupling (Cktl) 1 measure old Cognac, ½ measure tawny Port, ¼ measure Pernod, 4 dashes

lemon juice. Shake over ice, strain into an ice-filled old-fashioned glass. Serve with straws.

Cognac des Bois (Fr) the name for the lesser Cognac areas of Borderies, Fins Bois, Bons Bois and Bois Ordinaires.

Cognac Grades and Ageing (Fr) is classified according to age (of the youngest brandy in the blend). The blend must be at least two years old before it can be exported. Grades are: *** and V.S. (min. of 2 years in wood), V.S.O.P. (4 years in wood) XO (6 years in wood). Generally they are much older. Age is guaranteed only for first 6 years. Others include Old Liqueur which may have been matured in wood for 20, 30 or 40 plus years. (Also known as Extra Vieille, Napoléon, etc). see Compte System

Cognac Mint Frappé Cocktail (Cktl) ½ measure Cognac, ½ measure crème de menthe. Stir well over ice, strain into an ice-filled highball glass. Add crushed mint leaves and serve with straws.

Cognac Orange Cocktail (Cktl) 1 measure orange juice, ½ measure Cognac. Stir over ice in a highball glass. Dress with a slice of orange and serve with straws.

Cognathèque [La] (Fr) a famous specialist brandy shop based in the town of Cognac, Charente. (Add): 10, Place Jean Monnet, 16100 Cognac. Has a large range of Cognacs, Pineau des Charentes and regional liqueurs for sale. Website: http://www.cognatheque.com 'E'mail: info@cognatheque.com

Cognoscenti (It) connoisseur.

Cohobate (Eng) to redistil a number of times returning the distilate to the still with the residue.

Coigns (Scot) a term used for chocks to hold casks in place.

Coing (Fr) quince brandy, a stone fruit brandy.

Cointreau (Fr) a clear triple sec orange liqueur. Produced by Les Distilleries Cointreau, 49 St-Barthelemy d'Anjou, Angers. Also distilled in Vilafranca del Penedés, Spain. Made from dried bitter orange peel and sweet orange peel. 40% alc by vol.

Cointreau Rocks (Cktl) in a small tumbler pour 75mls (3fl.ozs) Cointreau over ice cubes. Add 3 dashes of Angostura, stir, decorate with slice of lemon.

Coka (Gre) cola.

Coka Cola (Indo) cola.

Cokanski Merlot (Ser) a red wine produced in the north-east near the Hungarian border.

Coke (Eng) abbr: of Coca Cola.

Coke High (Cktl) in a small glass put 1 measure rye whisky, add ice and a slice of orange. Top up with Coca Cola.

Col (Fr) term used during the fining process where the wine is clarified prior to bottling. Wine remains 'sur col' for several weeks or months.

Cola (Afr) a seed which contains caffeine. Is used as a colouring agent and flavouring agent (bitter) in beverages.

Cola (USA) a non-alcoholic red-brown carbonated

drink made from a secret blend of essences and other flavours. Top brands Coca Cola and Pepsi Cola. (Arab) = cola, (Chi) = kele, (Den) = cola, (Fr) = coca, (Ger) = cola, (Gre) = coka, (Hol) = cola, (Indo) = coka cola, (Ire) = cola, (Isr) = cola, (Jap) = koora, (Kor) = cola, (Rus) = kola, (Thai) = cola.

Cola de Mono (Chile) a mixture of milk, coffee, vanilla and aguardiente (flavoured with anis) served at Christmas, drunk hot or cold.

Cola de Pescado (Sp) isinglass.

Cola Lips (Eng) a 5% alc by vol. Cola drink produced by the Lanchester Group, C°. Durham.

Colares (Port) a DOC area of Portugal. Produces red and white wines, sited in 'the ocean' of the river Tejo in the region of Estremadura. See also Ramisco Vine.

Colas [Marie] (W.Ind) a rum distillery based at Port au Prince, Haiti. Produces Rhum Citadelle.

Colatje (Hol) a term used if a kleintje beer is served in a colatje glass.

Colatje Glass (Hol) a small (baby) beer glass.

Colchagua Valley (Chile) a province (9518ha) and wine-producing area in the Central Zone. Grape varietie include: Cabernet sauvignon, Carmenère, Chardonnay, Merlot, Sauvignon blanc, Syrah, Viognier.

Colchester Fino (Sp) the brand-name of a dry Sherry marketed by Lay & Wheeler. Produced by Vinícola Hidalgo in Sanlúcar de Barrameda.

Colcord Winery (USA) a winery based in Paris, Kentucky. 14ha. Produces French-American hybrids and Vinifera wines.

Cold Bottling (Eng) a term used to describe wines, beers, etc. that do not go through pasteurisation after bottling. The wines, beers, etc. are usually passed through a membrane filter or treated with SO_2 to ensure sterility (all equipment must be hygienically clean and sterile).

Cold Cactus Cocktail (Cktl) ⅔ measure tequila, ⅔ measure vodka, ⅛ measure blue curaçao, juice ½ lemon, dash egg white. Shake over ice, strain into a highball glass and top with soda.

Cold Comfort (Eng) a 3.9% alc by vol. ale brewed by the Facers Brewery, Greater Manchester.

Cold Compound Gin (Eng) a cheaply produced gin by adding chemically-made juniper flavoured essence to the alcohol.

Cold Deck Cocktail (Cktl) 1 measure brandy, ½ measure (white) crème de menthe, ½ measure sweet vermouth. Stir over ice and strain into a cocktail glass.

Cold Duck (Cktl) equal quantities of red Burgundy and iced Champagne.

Cold Duck (Ger) the American name for Kalte Ente sparkling red wine.

Cold Duck (USA) a mixture of sweet pink sparkling wines from the mid-west.

Cold Duck 5th Avenue (S.Afr) a sparkling rosé wine made from Steen, Clairette blanche and Pinotage grapes by the SFW (medium-sweet).

Cold Duck St. Louis (S.Afr) a rosé sparkling wine

made from Grenache, Cinsault and Clairette blanche grapes by Gilbeys Ltd. (sweet).

Col de Venti (It) a natural spring mineral water from Muccia (Macerata).

Cold Ginger Tea (Cktl) 250mls (½ pint) cold tea, 250mls (½ pint) dry ginger ale, 25mls (1fl.oz) stem ginger syrup, 1 measure whisky, 6 cloves. Infuse tea with cloves, cool. Add remaining ingredients, cool and decorate with sliced stem ginger.

Coldie (Austr) a slang term used for a cold can/bottle of beer.

Colding (Ger) a brand of rum produced by Hansen in Flensburg.

Cold Mix System (USA) a method of making gin as an alternative to the Head System.

Cold Ridge (Austr) a natural spring mineral water from. Mineral contents (milligrammes per litre): Sodium 17mg/l, Calcium 2mg/l, Magnesium 3mg/l, Potassium 2mg/l, Bicarbonates 19mg/l, Chlorides mg/l.

Cold Soaking (USA) the practice of storing the freshly harvested grapes, after de-stalking in a blanket of CO_2 at 10°C–15°C for 4–6 days before fermentation. The process aids extraction of colour without tannins.

Cold Spring Brewing (USA) a brewery based in Cold Spring, Minnesota. Is noted for Colonie, Fox De Luxe, Gameinde and Kegelbräu.

Cold Sterile Filtration (Eng) the process of filtering wine through fine sheet membrane filters to remove yeast cells. Does not affect the finished wine.

Cold Stream Hills (Austr) a winery (established 1985) based at Lot 6 Maddens Lane, Gruyere, Coldstream, Victoria. Grape varieties: Chardonnay, Cabernet sauvignon, Merlot, Pinot noir. Website: http://www.coldstreamhills.com.au

Cold Turkey (USA) a slang term used for giving up an addiction all at once instead of being weaned off the habit. i.e. An alcoholic.

Col du Cygne (Fr) the name given to the pipe that the Cognac vapours pass through before reaching the cooling coil (condenser).

Coldwater Creek (USA) a brand label of the Fetzer Winery, California.

Coleburn (Scot) a single malt whisky distillery (established 1896) on Rothes Road, outside Elgin. Owned by DCL. company. 43% alc by vol.

Coleraine (Ire) a light blend of grain whiskey from Colereine in north-eastern Eire.

Coleraine Cabernet Merlot (N.Z) a wine from Te Mata, Hawkes Bay. Deep coloured, soft and elegant. see Elston Castle Hill.

Coleraine Wines (S.Afr) a winery (established 1998) based in Suider-Paarl, Western Cape. 30ha. Grape varieties: Cabernet sauvignon, Cinsaut, Merlot, Ruby cabernet, Shiraz. Labels: Culraithin, Fire Engine Red. Website: http://www.coleraine.co.za

Cole Ranch Vineyard (USA) a vineyard based in Mendocino County in California. 16.5ha. Grape variety: Johannisberg riesling.

C

Coles (Sp) a Vino de Mesa wine from the province of Ourense in Galicia.

Colfax (USA) a natural spring mineral water from Colfax, Iowa. Mineral contents (milligrammes per litre): Sodium 380mg/l, Calcium 180mg/l, Magnesium 91mg/l, Potassium 8.8mg/l, Bicarbonates 293mg/l, Chlorides 29mg/l, Sulphates 1900mg/l, Fluorides 2.5mg/l, Silicates 7.4mg/l. pH 7.4

Colforte (It) an I.G.T. Merlot de Venezia wine (part of the Gamma range) produced by Bolla. Aged 4 months in French oak.

Colgin (USA) a winery based in the Napa Valley, California. Grape varieties include: Cabernet sauvignon. Labels: Cariad (Tychson Hill Vineyard), Herb Lamb Vineyard.

Colheita [1] (Port) vintage.

Colheita [2] (Port) a tawny Port from a single vintage with a minimum of seven years aging. Date of bottling is on the label.

Coligny (Fr) a Cru Champagne village in the Canton de Vertus. District: Châlons.

Colin-Deléger (Fr) a winery based in Chassagne-Montrachet, Côte de Beaune, Burgundy. Label: Chassagne en Remilly.

Colio Estate Wines (Can) a winery based in Harrow, Ontario. Grape varieties: Goldburger, Limberger, Riesling, Traminer.

Coliseo Corregedor (Sp) the brand-name of a Sherry produced by the Valdespino C°.

Collage (Fr) clearing wine of its sediment.

Collar (Eng) an area between the measure line of a glass and the beer surface.

Collar (Fr) to clarify a wine in cask.

Collar (USA) the name given to the foamy top to a glass of beer.

Collard Brothers (N.Z) a vineyard and winery. (Add): 303 Lincoln Road, Henderson, North Island. 14ha. Grape varieties: Cabernet franc, Cabernet sauvignon, Chardonnay, Gewürztraminer, Merlot, Müller-Thurgau, Rhine riesling, Sauvignon blanc and Sémillon.

Collard-Chardelle (Fr) a Champagne producer. Vintages: 1995, 1996. Website: http://www.collard-chardelle.fr

Collar Label (Eng) the label found on the neck of a bottle of beer, spirits or wine. (Fr) = collerette.

Collavini (It) a noted winery based at Corno di Rosazzo in the Friuli-Venezia Giulia region. Buys in grapes as it owns no vineyards. Also known as Catemario. Produces cuve close sparkling wines.

Collection Erté (Fr) an exclusive Cognac produced by Corvoisier (only 1000 bottles produced).

College Ale (Eng) a dark winter warmer cask-conditioned ale 1073 O.G. (7.4% alc by vol.) brewed by the Morrell Brewery of Oxford.

College Ale (Eng) a term formerly used to describe strong beers brewed in the colleges of the older universities.

College Bottles (Eng) the name for early wine bottles with the seal of the college embossed on them. Eighteenth and early nineteenth century.

College Fino (Eng) a fine, Fino Sherry from the Dolamore stable in London.

College Winery (Austr) a winery. (Add): P.O. Box 588, Wagga Wagga, New South Wales 2650. 13ha. Grape varieties: Cabernet franc, Cabernet sauvignon, Chardonnay, Merlot, Pinot gris, Rhine riesling and Traminer.

Collemattoni (It) a small wine estate of 6ha. Produces D.O.C.G. Brunello di Montalcino, D.O.C. Rosso di Montalcino, Grappa di Brunello.

Colle-Musquette (Fr) an alternative name for the Muscadelle grape.

Collerette (Fr) describes the label seen on some wine bottle necks, known as the Collar label in England. *See also* Cravate.

Collery (Fr) a Champagne producer. (Add): 4 Rue Anatole, 51160 Aÿ. 9ha. Produces vintage and non-vintage wines. Vintages: 1945, 1947, 1959, 1964, 1966, 1969, 1970, 1971, 1973, 1974, 1976, 1979, 1980, 1981, 1982, 1985, 1989, 1990, 1995, 1996, 1998, 1999, 2001.

Colletotrichum coffeanum (Lat) the Coffee Berry Disease, a fungus that attacks the berry (cherry) of the coffee tree especially the Coffea Arabica variety.

Collezione Italiana (It) winery based in Tuscany. Produces a DOCG Montepulciano d'Abruzzo.

Coleys Black Dog (Eng) a 5.2% alc by vol. ale brewed by the Tring Brewery C°. Ltd., Hertfordshire.

Colli (It) lit: 'hill wine'.

Colli (It) an old term, that when applied to Marsala, denotes 2 years of ageing and 18% alc by vol.

Colli Albani (It) a D.O.C. white wine from Latium. Made from Bonvino, Cacchione, Giallo, Malvasia del lazio, Malvasia rossa, Trebbiano toscano and Verde grapes. Vinification has to take place in the area of production. Graded Superiore if total alc by vol. is 12.5%. D.O.C. also applies to the naturally sparkling wines.

Colli Berici (It) a D.O.C. red wine from Veneto. 3 red wines are named after principal grape variety used. Colli Berici Cabernet, Colli Berici Merlot and Colli Berici Tocai Rosso.

Colli Berici (It) a D.O.C. white wines of Veneto. 4 white wines are named after principal grape variety used. Colli Berici Garganega, Colli Berici Pinot Bianco, Colli Berici Sauvignon and Colli Berici Tocai Bianco.

Colli Bolognesi dei Castelli Medioevali (It) *see* Colli Bolognesi di Monte San Pietro.

Colli Bolognesi di Monte San Pietro (It) a D.O.C. red wines from Emilia-Romagna. Grape varieties: Barbera, Merlot, Cabernet. Red wines are named after the principal grape variety used. If the Barbera has total alc. content of 12.5% and aged 3 years (1 year in wood) then graded Riserva.

Colli Bolognesi di Monte San Pietro (It) a D.O.C. white wine from Emilia-Romagna. 6 wines are produced – Pignoletto, Bianco, Pinot bianco, Riesling italico, Sauvignon, Chardonnay. The Bianco is made from Albana and Trebbiano

C

romagnola grapes. Pignoletto is also available as a semi-sparkling version.

Colli Cimini (It) an I.G.T. of Latium.

Colli del Transimeno Bianco (It) a D.O.C. white wine from Umbria. Made from the Grechetto, Malvasia del chianti, Trebbiano toscano 60%, Verdicchio and Verdello grapes. Produced by the Order of Malta monks at the Castello Magione, Perugia.

Colli del Trasimeno Rosso (It) a D.O.C. red wine from Umbria. Made from Cigliegiolo, Gamay, Malvasia del chianti, Sangiovese 60%–80% and Trebbiano toscano grapes. Produced by the Order of Malta monks at the Castello Magione, Perugia.

Colli di Bolzano (It) a D.O.C. red wine from Trentino-Alto-Adige. Made from Lagrein, Pinot nero and Schiave grapes.

Colli di Catone (It) a winery based at Monteporzio Catone in the Latium region. Noted for Frascati wines.

Colli di Congeliano (It) a dry white wine from the Treviso provence of Venetia. Made from the Prosecco grape.

Colli di Faenza (It) a D.O.C. wine area of Emilia-Romagna.

Colli di Imola (It) a D.O.C. wine area of Emilia-Romagna.

Colli di Lapio (It) a vineyard in the DOCG Fiano di Avellino, Campania. Grape variety: Fiano di Avellino.

Colli di Luna (It) a D.O.C. for Vermentino in Liguria.

Colli di Parma (It) a D.O.C. wine area of Emilia-Romagna.

Colli di Rimini (It) a D.O.C. wine area of Emilia-Romagna.

Colli di Scandiano E di Canossa (It) a D.O.C. wine area of Emilia-Romagna.

Colli di Tuscolo (It) a winery based in Latium. Noted for Frascati Classico wines.

Colli Euganei (It) a district within the provence of Padova in Veneto. Has 17 communes producing red and white wines. The vineyards are in the Euganean hills.

Colli Euganei Bianco (It) a D.O.C. white wine from Veneto. Made from the Garganega, Pinella, Pinot bianco, Riesling italico, Sauvignon, Seprina and Tocai grapes. If total alc. content is 12% by vol. and aged for minimum of 6 months then graded Superiore. D.O.C. also applies to sparkling wines produced to specifications.

Colli Euganei Moscato (It) a D.O.C. white wine from Veneto. Made from the Moscato bianco grape. D.O.C. also applies to sparkling wines produced according to specifications.

Colli Euganei Rosso (It) a D.O.C. red wine from Veneto. Made from Barbera, Cabernet franc, Cabernet sauvignon, Merlot and Raboso veronese grapes. If total alc. content is 12% by vol. and aged minimum 12 months then graded Superiore. D.O.C. applies to sparkling wines produced according to specifications.

Colligny Père et Fils (Fr) a Champagne producer

based in Épernay. Wine made by Lanson International, Épernay.

Colli Lanuvini (It) a D.O.C. white wine from Latium. Made from Bellone, Bonvino, Malvasia bianca di candia, Puntinata and Trebbiano grapes. Produced in communes of Genzano and part of Lanuvio in the Alban hills.

Colli Morenici Mantovani del Garda (It) a D.O.C. red, rosé and white wines from Lombardy. Red and rosé made from 30%–60% Rossanella, 20%–50% Rondinella and 10%–30% Negrara trentina. White made from 20%–25% Garganega, 20%–25% Trebbiano giallo and 10%–40% Trebbiano nostrano. If rosé total alc. content equals 11.5% by vol. then graded Chiaretto.

Collina della Vedova (It) a D.O.C. red barrique-aged Barbera wine produced by Alfiero Boffa, San Marzano Oliveto, Piemonte.

Colline di Caldaro (It) a red wine produced near Lake Caldaro from the Pinot noir and Schiave grapes.

Colline Novaresi (It) a D.O.C. area in Piemonte.

Collines de la Moure (Fr) a Vin de Pays area in the Hérault département in southern France. Produces red, rosé and dry white wines.

Collines Rhodaniennes (Fr) a Vin de Pays area based in the northern Rhône valley in the départements of Ardèche, Drôme, Isère and the Loire. Produces red, rosé and dry white wines.

Colline Teatine (It) an I.G.T. of Abruzzo.

Collins (USA) *see* John Collins and Tom Collins. Can also be made from other spirits. ie. Whisky Collins.

Collins Glass (USA) a tall, narrow, plain straight-sided glass (12fl.ozs).

Collins Lemon Gin (USA) a lemon-flavoured gin produced by Seagram.

Collio (It) a small D.O.C. area west of Goriza in Friuli-Venezia Giulia that produces white and some sparkling wines. *see* Collio Goriziano, Flysch.

Collio Cabernet Franc (It) *see* Collio Goriziano.

Collio Goriziano (It) a D.O.C. red and white wines from Friuli-Venezia Giulia, 7 white wines named after the principal grape variety used. Collio Goriziano-Malvasia, Pinot Bianco, Pinot Grigio, Riesling Italico, Sauvignon, Tocai and Traminer. 3 red wines: Collio Goriziano Cabernet Franc, Merlot and Pinot Nero.

Collio Malvasia (It) *see* Collio Goriziano.

Collio Merlot (It) *see* Collio Goriziano.

Collio Pinot Bianco (It) *see* Collio Goriziano.

Collio Pinot Grigio (It) *see* Collio Goriziano.

Collio Pinot Nero (It) *see* Collio Goriziano.

Colli Orientali del Friuli (It) a D.O.C. red and white wines from Friuli-Venezia Giulia. 8 white wines named after the principal grape. Colli Orientali del Friuli: Picolit, Pinot Bianco, Pinot Grigio, Ribolla, Riesling Renano, Sauvignon, Tocai and Verduzzo. 4 red wines. Colli Orientali del Friuli- Cabernet, Merlot, Pinot Nero and Refosco. If reds are aged a minimum of 2 years then can be classed Riserva. If white Picolit aged for 2 years minimum can also be classed Riserva.

C

Collio Riesling Italico (It) *see* Collio Goriziano.

Collio Sauvignon (It) *see* Collio Goriziano.

Collio Tocai (It) *see* Collio Goriziano.

Collio Traminer (It) *see* Collio Goriziano.

Collioure (Fr) an A.C. red wine from Banyuls, Roussillon in the Midi. Produced from the Carignan and Grenache grapes.

Colli Piacentini Malvasia (It) a D.O.C. white wine from the Emilia Romagna region. Made from the Malvasia grape. D.O.C. also applies to a Frizzante or Spumante version.

Collison's (S.Afr) a leading brand of double-distilled cane spirit.

Colli Tortonesi (It) a D.O.C. district of Piemonte. Produces red, white and sparkling wines.

Colli Tortonesi Barbera (It) a D.O.C. red wine from Piemonte. Made from Barbera plus up to 15% of Bonarda, Dolcetto and Freisa grapes. If alc. content is 12.5% by vol. and aged 2 years (1 year in oak-chestnut) then graded Superiore.

Colli Tortonesi Cortese (It) a D.O.C. white wine from Piemonte. Made from Cortese grapes. Has a slight bitter taste of almonds.

Colli Trevigiani (It) a Vino da Indicazione area. Equivalent to the French Vin de Pays. Now includes Malbec and Wildbacher.

Colloids (Eng) gelatinous substances that are used as finings. e.g. bentonite, egg white, gelatine, isinglass and oxblood.

Colmar (Fr) a wine town of Alsace. Also the scene of an annual wine fair.

Cölner Hofbräu (Ger) a famous tavern in Cologne noted for its beers and hospitality. Originated in the sixteenth century.

Colne Spring Ale (Eng) a strong bottled ale 1082 O.G. brewed by Benskins Brewery, Watford.

Colobel (USA) a red hybrid grape variety also known as Seibel 8357.

Colodra (Sp) wine measure.

Cologne Spirit (Eng) *see* Silent Spirit.

Coloma Wine Cellars (USA) a small winery based near Lodi, San Joaquin, California. Produces varietal and dessert wines.

Colomb (Fr) the name for the Colombar grape used in the Armagnac region.

Colomba (Fr) a 5% alc by vol. unpasteurised bottled white beer produced in Corsica by the Pietra Brewery.

Colombaio di Cencio (It) a 17ha. wine estate based in Gaiole. Grape varieties include: Sangiovese, Cabernet and Merlot. Produces: Super-Tuscan Il Futuro.

Colomba Platino (It) a white wine produced by Corvo in Sicily. *See also* Prima Goccia.

Colombar (Fr) a white grape variety that is sensitive to Oidium. Needs much sulphur spraying which results in a harsh wine. It can produce highly alcoholic wines. Used mainly in Cognac where it is known as the Pied-Tendre. Also known as the Bon blanc in Dauphiné. *See also* Blanquette.

Colombard (Fr) another spelling of Colombar.

Colombare Recioto di Soave Classico [Le] (It) first produced in 1870 by Pieropan. Now D.O.C.G. *See also* Calvarino, Rocca (La).

Colombe Cathare (Fr) the name for an A.C. Blanquette de Limoux produced by Jean Demolombe.

Colombia (S.Am) a small wine-producing country with 1,000ha. under vines. Produces mainly sweet dessert wines. Also produces Aguardiente, rum, brandy and rectified spirits. *See also* Colombia Coffee.

Colombia Coffee (S.Am) a rich, low-acid coffee with a wine flavour, one of the best coffees from the high Andes. Used mainly for blending. Main regional varieties are Armenias, Bogotas, Bucaramangas, Excelso, Hibanos, Manizales and Medellins.

Colombier (Fr) an alternative spelling of the white Colombar grape.

Colombier (Fr) a commune within the A.C. Monbazillac in the Bergerac region. (sweet white).

Colombo [Jean Luc] (Fr) a winery based in Cornas, La Roche, Tain l'Hermitage. Wines include Terres Brûlées, Les Ruchets, La Louvée, Les Collines Rhodanniennes.

Colombo (It) a natural spring mineral water from Sorgente, Rocche di Valletti.

Colombo Special (Cktl) 1 measure gin, ½ measure crème de menthe, ½ measure lemon juice, dash egg white. Shake well over ice and strain into a cocktail glass.

Colomé (Arg) a winery (120ha) based in the Calchaqui Valley, Salta, northern Mendoza. Is one of the world's highest vineyards. Grape varieties: Cabernet sauvignon, Malbec, Petit verdot, Syrah, Tannat, Tempranillo, Tourigo nacional. Website: http://www.bodegacolome.com 'E'mail: info@bodegacolome.com

Colonnara (It) a co-operative winery (established 1959) in the Marches region. Has 190 growers and 260ha of vineyards. Grape varieties include: Verdicchio. Labels: Cuprese, Romitello delle Mandriole, Tufico, Vigna San Marco.

Colona Winery (N.Am) the largest winery in British Columbia. Is owned by the Nabisco Company.

Colonel Pepper's Lemon Ale (Eng) an ale made using ground black pepper and lemon peel. Made exclusively with Target hops by Whitbread.

Colonel's Choice [The] (Eng) an 8.5% alc by vol. bottled beer from the Morrell Brewery in Oxford. Brewed to honour the brewery president's 80th birthday.

Colong (E.Asia) a semi-green, light, delicate tea with a fruity scented aroma, should be drunk without milk or sugar.

Colonial Cocktail (Cktl) ¾ measure dry gin, ¼ measure grapefruit juice, 4 dashes maraschino. Shake over ice, strain into a cocktail glass and top with an olive.

Colonial Sugar Refining Company (Austr) the largest rum distillery in Australia, based in Pyrmont, Sydney. Rums are produced from Queensland molasses.

C

Colonie (USA) a light, malty beer brewed by the Cold Spring Brewery in Cold Spring, Minnesota.

Colonna (It) *see* Montecompatri-Colonna.

Colonnara (It) a sparkling (metodo tradizionale) Verdicchio from the Marche region.

Colonnara Marche Srl. (It) a winery (established 1959) with 300ha. vineyards and 180 associates. (Add): Via Mandriole 2, 60034 Cupramontana (AN). Produces Verdicchio under Cuprese label, Tornamagno, plus 3 Spumantes- Brut Metodo Classico Millesimato, Charmat (from Verdicchio grapes) and Charmat Dolce (from Verdicchio and moscato grapes).

Colony Village Winery (USA) a winery based in Iowa. Produces mainly French hybrid wines.

Color (Sp) colour wine. *See also* Paxerete.

Colorado Cocktail (Cktl) ½ measure kirsch, ½ measure cherry brandy, ¼ measure cream. Shake well over ice and strain into a cocktail glass.

Colorado Crystal (USA) a natural spring mineral water (established 1986) from Colorado. Mineral contents (milligrammes per litre): Sodium 1mg/l, Chlorides 1.2mg/l, Sulphates 2mg/l. pH 7.0

Colorado Mountain Vineyards (USA) a winery based in Colorado. 8ha. Grape varieties: Chardonnay, Gewürztraminer and Riesling. Also buys in grapes from California.

Colorants (Fr) the colours in red wines from tannins, anthocyanins, anthocyanols, etc.

Colorino (It) a red grape variety used in Chianti to give colour to the wine.

Coloroll Glassware (Eng) one of the largest producers of drinking glasses. Formerly Dema Glass.

Color Wine (Sp) *see* Arrope, Paxerete, Sancocho, Color, Vino do Color.

Colour Deposit (Eng) a wine malady, an almost black deposit, often adhering to the side of the bottle during natural maturation. Can be reduced by an extra addition of SO^2.

Colour's Best (Eng) an ale brewed by the Mildmay Brewery, Holbeton, near Plymouth.

Col Sandago (It) an estate winery based in Veneto. Produces red, white and sparkling Prosecco wines.

Col Solare (USA) a Cabernet sauvignon, Merlot and Syrah wine produced by Antinori and Château Ste. Michelle in Columbia Valley, Washington State. First vintage was in 1995.

Coltassala (It) a red Vino da Tavola wine from Castello di Volpaia in Chianti (Classico) estate at Radda, Tuscany. Made from 100% Sangiovese grapes.

Colt 45 (USA) a malt beer 1047.O.G. brewed by the Colt Breweries of America. Brewed under licence by Courage's Brewery U.K.

Columba Cream (Scot) a 17% alc by vol. Scotch whisky liqueur flavoured with honey and cream.

Columbard (Fr) an alternative spelling of the white grape variety Colombar.

Columbia Crest Winery (USA) a winery based in Columbia Valley, Washington. Produces Cote de Columbia range of wines. Grape varieties include Chardonnay, Grenache, Lemberger and Merlot.

Columbia Winery (USA) a winery based in Woodinville, Washington State. Grape varieties: Cabernet, Chardonnay, Gewürztraminer, Merlot, Pinot noir, Riesling, Sémillon and Syrah. Labels include Chevrier, Milestone and Red River.

Columbia Valley (USA) the largest wine area in Washington State, has a dry, stony, desert-like terrain which requires irrigation to support vines. Two sub-appellations in this area are Walla Walla, Yakima Valley.

Columbus (Aus) a well-hopped beer 5.4% alc by vol. brewed by the Steigel Brauerei in Salzburg.

Columbus (Hol) a 9% alc by vol. bottle-conditioned, unpasteurised, unfiltered special beer brewed by 't IJ Brouwerij, Amsterdam.

Columbus Cocktail (Cktl) 1½ measures dry vermouth, ½ measure Angostura bitters. Shake over ice and strain into an ice-filled goblet.

Columella (S.Afr) the label for a red wine (Shiraz and Mourvèdre blend) produced by the Sadie Family winery, Swartland, Western Cape.

Column Stacking (Eng) a method of stacking beer crates, one on top of the other. Used for certain wooden and plastic crates. *See also* Bond Stacking.

Colungo (Sp) a local style of anis found in southern Spain near Sorontondo.

Comarca de Falset (Sp) one of the three sub-zones in Tarragona. The soil is of granite, limestone and loam. Main Grape varieties: Cariñena, Garnacha and Tempranillo.

Combeau/Normandin-Girard/de Laage (Fr) a Cognac producer. (Add): 28, Rue des Ponts, 16140 Aigre. Produces Cognac Pascal Combeau, Cognac Normandin, Cognac Girard and Cognac de Laage.

Combe-aux-Moines (Fr) a Premier Cru vineyard in the A.C. commune of Gevrey-Chambertin, Côte de Nuits, Burgundy. 4.78ha. Also sold as La Combe-aux-Moines.

Combe House (Eng) a vineyard (established 1979) based at Broad Oak, Heathfield, East Sussex. 0.8ha. Grape varieties: ⅔ Müller-Thurgau and ⅓ Seyval blanc.

Comber Distilleries (Ire) an old distillery based in Belfast, Northern Ireland that closed in 1953.

Combes (Fr). In Burgundy (the Côte d'Or) name for the minor valleys that deeply indent the Côte.

Combes [Les] (Fr) a vineyard in the A.C. commune of Montagny, Côte Chalonnaise, Burgundy.

Combes [Les] (Fr) a Premier Cru vineyard in the A.C. commune of Saint-Aubin, Côte de Beaune, Burgundy.

Combes Bitter (Eng) a cask-conditioned ale 1041 O.G. brewed by Watney's Brewery.

Combes-Dessus [Les] (Fr) a Premier Cru vineyard in the A.C. commune of Pommard, Côte de Beaune, Burgundy 2.8ha.

Combettes [Les] (Fr) a Premier Cru vineyard in the A.C. commune of Puligny-Montrachet, Côte de Beaune, Burgundy 6.7ha.

Combibloc (Eng) a patented carton packaging for beverages.

C

Combibo (Lat) to drink to the full. Also a fellow drinker.

Combinado (Sp) the alternative name for Mitad y Mitad.

Combination (Cktl) ½ measure dry gin, ¼ measure French vermouth, ¼ measure Amer Picon, ½ measure lemon juice, ½ measure orange Curaçao. Shake over ice, strain into a cocktail glass and sprinkle with grated nutmeg.

Combination (S.Afr) the label for a white wine (Chenin blanc and Sauvignon blanc blend) produced by the Kaapzicht Estate winery, Stellenbosch, Western Cape.

Combined Harvest (Eng) a 4.4% alc by vol. unique beer brewed by the Bateman's Brewery from a mixture of barley, oats, rye and wheat.

Comblanchien (Fr) a commune which is part of the Côte de Nuits-Villages. It is not allowed to use name as its own A.C.

Comblizy (Fr) a Cru Champagne village in the Canton de Dormans. District: Épernay.

Combo Cocktail (Cktl) 40mls (⅓ gill) French vermouth, 4 dashes brandy, 2 dashes Curaçao, dash Angostura, 1 teaspoon powdered sugar. Shake over ice and strain into an ice-filled old-fashioned glass.

Combottes (Fr) a Premier Cru vineyard in the commune A.C. Gevrey-Chambertin, Côte de Nuits, Burgundy. 4.9ha. Also sold as Aux Combottes.

Combottes [Les] (Fr) a Premier Cru vineyard in the A.C. commune of Chambolle-Musigny, Côte de Nuits, Burgundy 0.65ha.

Comburg Minerale (Ger) a natural spring mineral water from Brunnen VII, Schwäbisch Hall, BW.

Combustible Matter (Eng) the compounds of must. Starch, Protein, Pectin, Cellulose, Acids, Tannin, Colouring, Vitamins, Enzymes and other unknown substances.

Come Back Marion (Cktl) ⅗ measure dry gin, ³⁄₁₀ measure grapefruit juice, ¹⁄₁₀ measure orgeat syrup, dash fraises du bois. Shake over ice and strain into a cocktail glass.

Comédie [La] (Fr) the name of Hennessy Cognacs' Paradise cellar. Once used as a theatre, hence the name. Has the largest collection of old Cognacs.

Comercializadora Exportadora Navarra de Alimentación S.A. (Sp) *abbr*: CENALSA an organisation to promote the produce and wines of the Navarra region. Is owned by the provincial government and companies. Trade name is Agronavarra.

Comercial Pirineos (Sp) a major wine-producer based in Rioja.

Comet [The] (Cktl) 1 measure brandy, ⅓ measure Van der Hum, ⅔ measure grapefruit juice. Shake over ice, strain into a cocktail glass and add a drop of lemon peel juice.

Comfortably Numb (Eng) a 5% alc by vol. ale brewed by Triple FFF Brewery, Four Marks, near Alton, Hampshire.

Comfort American (Cktl) 25mls (1fl.oz) Southern Comfort, 10mls (½ fl.oz) lime cordial, 10mls {½ fl.oz) Campari, dash egg white. Shake well over ice, strain into an ice-filled highball glass and top with American ginger ale.

Comfort Coffee (Liq.Coffee) using a measure of Southern Comfort.

Comfort Colada (Cktl) 50mls pineapple juice, 35mls Southern Comfort, 25mls coconut cream. Shake over crushed ice. Serve in a cocktail glass, decorate with pineapple.

Comfort Collins (Cktl) 1 measure Southern Comfort, juice ¼ lemon. Serve over ice in a tall glass, top with lemonade and decorate with a lemon wedge.

Comforter (Cktl) 1 measure dry gin, 1 measure Dry Martini. Shake over ice, strain into a cocktail glass, add a dash of dry Sherry and zest of lemon.

Comissão de Viticultura da Região dos Vinhos Verdes (Port) *abbr*: C.V.R.V.V. The headquarters in Oporto of the Vinhos Verdes Commission. It analyses samples, researches into yeasts and bulk production of yeast which is distributed to co-operatives.

Comissão de Viticultura Região de Colares (Port) a body that has now been absorbed by the Junta Nacional do Vinho.

Comissão Interprofessional da Região Demarcada do Douro (Port) *abbr*: C.I.R.D.D. New organisation in the Douro. Look after Port wine appellation and the other denominations of the Douro region. Head office is at Peso da Régua.

Comissão Vitivinicola da Região do Dão (Port) formed in 1948. The official quality control station for the whole of the Dão region. All wines have to be submitted for testing.

Comitato Nazionale Per la Tutela Delle Denominazione d'Origine (It) a national committee. Consists of 28 members plus a chairman. Chosen by the Ministry of Agriculture in collaboration with the Ministry of Industry and Commerce.

Comité Consultatif Viti-Vinicole (E.C.) a consultative committee for wine growing and wine making.

Comité d'Action Viticole, nous Arretêrons les Importations (Fr) a body of southern wine producers whose aim is to stop the importation of Italian wines. Based at Sète was first formed in the early 1970's.

Comité d'Aménagement des Hautes-Côtes (Fr) a group formed to promote the wines of the Hautes-Côtes by organising wine tastings and tourist routes etc.

Comité de Défense et d'Organisation du Maché du Rhum (W.Ind) *abbr*: CODERUM. A body formed in 1960 in Martinique to arrange contracts and prices between producers and imPorters. *See also* FENARUM.

Comité d'Experts (Fr) an old governing body of Alsace for control and production of Alsace wines.

Comité Interprofessionnel de la Côte d'Or et de l'Yonne Pour les Vins de Bourgogne (Fr) *abbr*:

C

C.I.B. Body for the promotion and control of Chablis and Burgundy wines. (Add): Rue Henri-Dunant, 21200 Beaune.

Comité Interprofessionnel de Saône-et-Loire Pour les Vins A.O.C. de Bourgogne et de Mâcon (Fr) *abbr*: C.I.B.M. A body for the promotion of the wines of Mâcon and Burgundy.

Comité Interprofessionnel des Vins d'Alsace (Fr) *abbr*: C.I.V.A. 1962 Protective committee of merchants and growers to control and promote Alsace wines. (Add): 8 Place de Lattre-de-Tassigny, 68003 Colmar Cedex.

Comité Interprofessionnel des Vins d'Anjou (Fr) *abbr*: C.I.V.A. Body for the promotion of Loire wines.

Comité Interprofessionnel des Vins de Bourgogne et Mâcon (Fr) a body for the promotion of Mâconnais and Burgundy wines. *abbr*: C.I.B.M. (Add): Maison du Tourisme, Ave. du Maréchal-de-Latte-de-Tassigny, 71000, Mâcon.

Comité Interprofessionnel des Vins de Gaillac (Fr) a body set up to promote and control the wines of Gaillac. *abbr*: C.I.V.G. (Add): 8 Rue du Père Gibrat, 81600 Gaillac.

Comité Interprofessionnel des Vins de la Région de Bergerac (Fr) a body formed for the promotion and control of Bergerac wines. *abbr*: C.I.V.R.B. (Add): 2 Place du Docteur-Cayla, 24100, Bergerac.

Comité Interprofessionnel des Vins des Côtes de Provence (Fr) a body for the promotion of the wines of Provence. *abbr*: C.I.V.C.P. (Add): 3 Ave. Jean-Jaurès, 83460 Les-Arcs-sur-Argens.

Comité Interprofessionnel des Vins des Côtes du Rhône (Fr) a body for the promotion of the wines of the Rhône. *abbr*: C.I.C.D.R. (Add): Maison du Tourisme et du Vin, 41 Cours Jean-Jaurès, 84000 Avignon, southern Rhône.

Comité Interprofessionnel des Vins de Touraine (Fr) a body for the promotion and control of the wines of Touraine, Loire. *abbr*: C.I.V.T. (Add): 19 Square Prosper Mérimée, 37000 Tours.

Comité Interprofessionnel des Vins d'Origine du Nantais (Fr) a body for the promotion of the wines of western Loire. *abbr*: C.I.V.O.N. (Add): 17 Rue des Etats, 44000 Nantes. Branch for Muscadet is based at Maison des Vins, Bellevue, 44690 La Haie Fouassière.

Comité Interprofessionnel des Vins Doux Naturels (Fr) a body for the promotion of VdN wines of southern France. *abbr*: C.I.V.D.N. (Add): 19 Ave. de Grande-Bretagne, 66000 Perpignan.

Comité Interprofessionnel du Vin de Bordeaux (Fr) a body for the promotion of Bordeaux wines. *abbr*: C.I.V.B.

Comité Interprofessionnel du Vin de Champagne (Fr) a body formed on April 12th 1941 to regulate the growing of the vines and the production of Champagne. *abbr*: C.I.V.C. (Add): 5, Rue Henri Martin, 51-Épernay.

Comité National de Pineau (Fr) a body for the promotion of pineau des charentes based in Cognac. (Add): 45 Ave. Victor Hugo, 16100 Cognac.

Comité Régional d'Action Viticole (Fr) *abbr*: CRAV a body of growers and wine makers formed to protect French wine production from modernisation and cheap imports from other countries.

Comité Professionnel du Bourgogne (Fr) a body based in Burgundy for the promotion of Burgundian wines.

Comité Vin (Fr) wine committee.

Command (Cyp) the brand-name used by the Loël Company for a range of Cyprus sherries.

Commander (Cktl) ⅓ measure Cognac, ⅓ measure Port, ⅓ measure lemon juice, shake over ice, strain into an ice-filled highball glass and top with sparkling mineral water.

Commandaria (Cyp) a rich, sweet, dessert wine made in south east of the island. Made from dried out Xynisteri grapes and then flavoured with cloves and resin and with scented woods which are suspended in the wine in a bag. Becomes tawny as it ages in solera, matured 12 years or more, not fortified. Q.W.P.S.R. in 1993.

Commandaria St. John (Cyp) the full title for Commandaria that gets its name from the Crusades when it was given to any of the injured knights whilst they were recuperating in Cyprus.

Commanderie de Champagne (Fr) a wine brotherhood based in the Champagne region.

Commanderie de Champagne de l'Ordre des Coteaux (Fr) a wine brotherhood based in the Champagne region.

Commanderie de la Bargemone (Fr) a vineyard. (Com): St. Cannat. A.C. Coteaux d'Aix en Provence, south-eastern France.

Commanderie de l'Île de France des Anysetiers du Roy (Fr) a noted wine brotherhood based in Paris.

Commanderie de Sauternes-Barsac (Fr) a wine brotherhood of the Sauternes and Barsac.

Commanderie des Chevaliers de Tursan (Fr) a wine brotherhood based in south-western France. Promotes the wines of the region.

Commanderie des Grands Vins d'Amboise (Fr) a wine brotherhood based in Touraine, Loire.

Commanderie des Nobles Vins du Jura et Gruyère de Comté (Fr) a noted wine society for the promotion of Jura wines.

Commanderie des Vins et Spiriteux de France (Fr) a society based in Paris for French wines and spirits.

Commanderie de Tavel (Fr) the wine brotherhood of Tavel in the southern Rhône.

Commanderie du Bontemps de Médoc et des Graves (Fr) a wine brotherhood of the Médoc and Graves.

Commanderie du Bontemps de Sainte-Croix-du-Mont (Fr) a wine brotherhood of the Sainte-Croix-du-Mont, Bordeaux.

Commanderie du Bontemps de Sauternes et de Barsac (Fr) a wine brotherhood for the wines of Sauternes and Barsac based in Bordeaux.

C

Commanderie du Taste-Saumur (Fr) a wine brotherhood for the wines of Saumur based in the Loire region.

Commando (S.Afr) the brand-name for a brandy produced by Castle Wine and Green.

Comme [La] (Fr) a Premier Cru vineyard in the A.C. commune of Santenay, Côte de Beaune, Burgundy.

Commende Majeure de Roussillon pour Garder le Devoir et le Droit de la Vigne et du Vin (Fr) a wine society for the promotion and improvement of the wines of the Roussillon.

Commerce (Fr) a term applied to a blend of kirsch with an eau-de-vie or neutral alcohol.

Commercial Wines (Eng) a wine trade term for wines that can be bought and sold in large quantities at a reasonable profit.

Commerciante (It) dealer/trader.

Comm. G.B. Burlotto (It) a winery (established 1850). (Add): Via Vittorio Emanuele, 12060 Verduno (CN) 11ha. vineyard. Produce white Langhe Dives (Sauvignon blanc grape) and red wines Barolo Cannubi, Barbera Monngliero, Barbera Neirane, Dolcetto d'Alba Neirane, Barbera d'Alba Boscato, Langhe Mores, Langhe Nebbiolo, Verduno Pelaverga.

Comminutes (Eng) an alternative name for fruit drinks where the fruit is pulverised or 'comminuted'.

Commitment (S.Afr) the label for a red wine (Cabernet sauvignon 54% plus Cabernet franc, Malbec, Merlot and Petit verdot) produced by Cellar-Vie Wines winery, Edleen, Western Cape.

Commodity Wine (Eng) a general term for basic wines, those other than A.C./D.O.C./Qmp/etc.

Commodore (Cktl) ⅔ measure rye whiskey, ⅓ measure lime juice, 2 dashes orange bitters, sugar to taste. Shake over ice, strain into a cocktail glass. Add sugar to taste.

Commodore (Fr) the name of the Grande Cuvée Champagne produced by the De Castellane Champagne house.

Commodore Cocktail (Cktl) 25mls (1fl.oz) Bourbon whiskey, 10mls (½ fl.oz) lemon juice, 2 dashes Angostura, dash gomme syrup. Shake over ice and strain into a cocktail glass.

Common (Eng) a term used to describe a wine as sound but lacking any finesse.

Common Clean (W.Ind) the name given to light-bodied styles of rum produced in a continuous still.

Common Customs Tariff (Eng) abbr: C.C.T. Associated with wine exports to E.C. countries. Payable per hectolitre. Some countries are exempt.

Common Dry (Mad) an old-style name used for Sercial (now no longer used).

Common Man's Glass (Eng) the term given to the continental glass of the seventeenth and eighteenth century that was mass produced.

Common Rich (Mad) an old-style name used for Malmsey. Now no longer used.

Commonwealth Winery (USA) a winery based in Plymouth, Massachusetts that produces hybrid and vinifera wines.

Commun (Fr) denotes a wine with no character.

Commune (Fr) a township or the administrative council or parish in France.

Communiste (Fr) a variation of the drink kir in Burgundy (red wine replaces the white) also, known as a Cardinal.

Community Pub (Eng) the name given to a public house that is the only pub serving a rural area, housing estate, etc. and is considered as a part of that community.

Como (Gre) the name given to a red, fortified wine from the island of Syra.

Comondor (Aus) a red wine produced mainly from Cabernet sauvignon by Hans Nittnaus, Gols.

Compagnie de la Vallée de la Loire (Fr) the largest producer of Muscadet wines in the Nantais region of the Loire.

Compagnie des Mousquetaires d'Armagnac (Fr) a wine brotherhood based in the Armagnac region.

Compagnie des Produits de Gascogne (Fr) an Armagnac producer based in Ténarèze and Bas Armagnac. Noted for the De Montal brand of Armagnac brandy.

Compagnie des Trois Épis [La] (Fr) a brewery based in Paris. Brews L'Épi Blanc, L'Épi Noir, L'Épi Rouge beers.

Compagnie d'Honneur des Sorciers et Birettes (Fr) a wine society based in Anjou, Loire.

Compagnie du Sarto (Fr) a wine brotherhood based in the Savoie region of south-eastern France.

Compagnons de Bordeaux (Fr) a wine brotherhood based in Bordeaux.

Compagnons du Beaujolais (Fr) a wine brotherhood for the wines of Beaujolais, Burgundy.

Compagnons du Loupiac (Fr) a wine society based in Loupiac, Bordeaux.

Compagnons du Pintou (Fr) a wine society based in Auvergne.

Compagnons Hauts-Normands du Gouste-Vin (Fr) a wine society based in Paris.

Companhia Cacique de Café Soluvel (Bra) the largest producer of instant coffee in Brazil.

Companhia dos Vinhos Messias (Port) producers of Messias Seco.

Companhia União Fabril Potuense (Port) abbr: C.U.F.P. Company formed by a merger of Oporto Breweries. Brews Crystal (a pilsener-style lager beer).

Compañía Española Promotora de la Exportación, S.A. (Sp) a major wine-producer based in the Rioja region.

Compañía Mata (Sp) a noted producer and exporter of Málaga wines.

Compañía Ron Bacardi (W.Ind) originally one of the main producers of rum on the island of Cuba before the revolution.

Compañía Vinícola del Norte de España (Sp) abbr: C.V.N.E. (Add): Costa del Vino 21-Haro, La Rioja. 480ha. Grape varieties: Garnacha 10%, Graciano 5%, Mazuelo 10%, Tempranillo 60% and Viura 15%. Produces 65% red wine, 33% white wine.

C

••

Compartimenti (It) provinces.

Competidor (Sp) a solera reserva brandy produced by Terry (de).

Complantation (Fr) lit: 'vine by vine', the process of vine management in a vineyard. Grapes are harvested separately according to the vine's age, vines removed and replanted when past best and vineyards completely replanted after land rested for a minimum of 2 years (no new vines planted for the last 8 years prior to 'grubbing' up).

Compléter (Switz) late picked.

Completer (Switz) a rare white grape variety from Grison and Herrschaft. Produces a rich, sweet wine.

Complex (Eng) a term often used to describe wines that have many smells and tastes. Is usually applied to fine wines.

Complexa (Mad) a *Vitis vinifera* cross black grape variety used in the production of Madeira. A new variety of Tinta negra mole.

Complexity (Eng) a term used to describe the different nuances of bouquet and taste in a wine.

Comportes (Fr) wooden containers used for transporting the grapes from the vineyard to the winery. Hold 40–50 kilogrammes of grapes. Are round with dowling handles.

Compotatio (Lat) a drinking party.

Compotation (Eng) a seventeenth century term for drinking together in company.

Compotor (Lat) fellow drinker. *See also* Combibo.

Compound Beverages (USA) these are made by combining either a fermented beverage or a spirit with flavouring substances.

Compound Gin (USA) a mixture of neutral spirits and extract or oil of juniper and other botanicals.

Compounding (Eng) a method of extracting flavours from ingredients to make spirits.

Comprad (Mac) a natural spring mineral water (established 1994) from Macedonia. Mineral contents (milligrammes per litre): Calcium 82mg/l, Magnesium 91.2mg/l, Sulphates 98.8mg/l, Fluorides 0.3mg/l, Nitrates 6.83mg/l.

Comps (Fr) a commune in the A.C. Côtes de Bourg in north-eastern Bordeaux.

Compte O (Fr) a term used for distilled Armagnac on May 1st of the following year after Compte 00 and for Cognac on April 1st of the following year after Compte 00.

Compte OO (Fr). a term used for newly distilled Armagnac in September and October till April 30th of the following year and for Cognac till March 31st of the following year.

Comté de Signargues (Fr) a village in the A.C. Côtes du Rhône-Villages (awarded 2004). Produces mainly red wines (with a little rosé and white wine).

Compte System (Fr) a system devised for the ageing of A.C. brandies (Armagnac and Cognac). Works on a series of numbers from 00 to 6. After 00 (see Compte 00) the brandy is raised one number per year spent in wood. e.g. a 'Compte 4' will have spent 4 years in cask. *See also* Acquit Jaune d'Or.

Comptoir (Fr) bar/counter.

Comptoir des Vins du Maroc (Afr) *abbr*: CVM. A Belgo-Moroccan company which has sole marketing rights for Moroccan wines sold under names of Chantebled, Ourika and Tarik.

Comte André de Montpezat (Fr) the brand name used by Les Côtes d'Olt for a red wine.

Comte d'Argelas (Fr) the label of a Châteauneuf-du-Pape (Add): La Vinothèque, 9 Rue de la République, 84230 Châteauneuf-du-Pape, southern Rhône.

Comte de Champagne (Fr) the label used by Taittinger for their De Luxe vintage cuvée Champagne made from 100% Chardonnay and for a vintage rosé made from 100% Pinot noir.

Comte de Guyon (Fr) the label of an Armagnac produced by Château Lassalle in Maupas, Gers, near Estang, Grand Bas Armagnac.

Comte de Lauvia (Fr) an Armagnac producer. Produces a range of Armagnacs including vintage brandies.

Comte de Lauze (Fr) the label of a Châteauneuf-du-Pape produced by Carré, 7 Ave. des Bosquets, 84230 Châteauneuf-du-Pape, southern Rhône.

Comte de Vogüé (Fr) a vineyard. (Com): Le Musigny, Côte de Nuits, Burgundy. *see* Domaine Comte de Vogüé.

Comte de Wormeldange (Lux) a producer of sparkling (méthode traditionelle) and pétillant wines.

Comtesse de Roseval (Fr) the brand name of a Crémant de Bourgogne produced by Labour, Gontard, Nuits-Saint-Georges, Côte de Nuits, Burgundy.

Comte Tolosan (Fr) a Vin de Pays area in the Haute-Garonne near Toulouse. Produces red, rosé and dry white wines.

Comune (It) describes a grape grown in Sicily that is related to the white grape Catarratto.

Coñac (Sp) a brandy which is dark, sweet and high in alcohol.

Coñac Corriente (Sp) rough, local brandy.

Cona Coffee (Eng) a brand-name unit for making coffee by the vacuum process.

Conari (S.Afr) the label for a non-vintage red wine (Cabernet sauvignon) produced by the Mons Ruber Estate winery, Little Karoo.

Conca (It) a red wine produced near the Bay of Sorrento in the Campania region. Made from the Aglianico, Canaiolo, Malvasia and Sangiovese grapes.

Conca de Barberá (Sp) a Denominación de Origen wine-producing region in Cataluña. 6,500ha. Red, rosé and white wines produced. Most of production is white. Grape varieties: 30% Macabeo, 35% Parellada, 20% Trepat (Garnacha trepat), 10% Ull de llebre (Tempranillo), Garnacha, Cabernet sauvignon, Merlot.

Conca del Huelva (Sp) a Denominación de Origen wine-producing region in south-western Spain on the Portuguese border.

Conca de Tremp (Sp) a Vino Comarcal wine from the province Lleida in Cataluña.

Conca d'Ora (Cktl) ⅝ measure dry gin, ⅛ measure cherry brandy, ⅛ measure maraschino, ⅛ measure triple sec, orange peel. Shake over ice and strain into a cocktail glass.

Concannon (USA) a winery based in the Livermore Valley, Alameda, California. 75ha. Grape varieties: Cabernet sauvignon, Petit sirah, Sauvignon blanc, Zinfandel.

Concentrated Wine (Hol) an old Dutch description of brandy which was shipped to Holland. Originally made to save freight charges. *see* 'Soul of the Wine'.

Concentrato (It) a concentrated grape must that is used for correcting wines.

Concept (S.Afr) the label for a Grand Vin white (Chardonnay and Chenin blanc blend) and Grand Vin red (blend) produced by the Saxenberg winery, Stellenbosch, Western Cape.

Concept Wines (S.Afr) a range of wines under the labels: French Kiss, Joseph's Hat, Nicole's Hat and Sunset Hat. Produced by the Ashanti winery, Paarl, Western Cape.

Concertina Brewery [The] (Eng) a brewery. (Add): 9a, Dolcliffe Road, Mexborough, South Yorkshire S64 9AZ. Brews: Ariel Four Square 5.3% alc by vol., Bengal Tiger 4.5% alc by vol., Best Bitter 4% alc by vol., Club Bitter 3.9% alc by vol., New Imperial 4.6% alc by vol., Old Dark Attic 4% alc by vol.

Concha [La] (Sp) a dry Amontillado Sherry produced by Gonzalez Byass in Jerez de la Frontera, Cadiz.

Concha y Toro [Viña] (Chile) the largest wine firm with over 1040ha. in the Maipo Valley (has several Bodegas). Noted brands it produces are Cassillero del Diablo, Marqués de Casa, Terrunyo, Trio Merlot and St. Emiliana. Also has holdings in the Cachapoal Valley (Peumo Vineyard).

Conching (S.Am) the process of developing the flavour in the chocolate (cocao) bean after fermentation.

Conchita Cocktail (Cktl) 25mls (1fl.oz) tequila, 25mls (1fl.oz) grapefruit juice, 2 dashes lemon juice. Shake over ice and strain into a cocktail glass with 2 ice cubes.

Concierto (It) a herb liqueur made by the Maiori Nuns of Amalfi Riviera.

Conciliation (Eng) a 4.2% alc by vol. (1042 O.G.) full-flavoured premium ale from Butterknowle Brewery, Lynesack, near Bishop Auckland, County Durham. *See also* High Force.

Conçillon et Fils (Fr) a major liqueur producer based in the Loire region.

Concise (Switz) a wine-producing area in the northern Vaud canton. Produces red and white wines.

Conclave Cocktail (Cktl) (Non-alc) ¾ measure orange juice, ¼ measure raspberry syrup, ½ measure milk. Shake over crushed ice, strain into an ice-filled highball glass, dress with a slice of orange and serve with straws.

Concoction (Eng) a mixture of drinks etc. that does not conform to a set recipe.

Concongello Vineyards (Austr) *see* 'Bests Great Western'.

Concord (USA) a blue-black grape variety of North America, very sweet and can withstand severe winters. Used for blending and religious wines. American native vine stock.

Concord Cocktail (Cktl) ¼ measure Calvados, ¼ measure Grand Marnier, ½ measure orange juice. Stir with ice, strain into a club goblet, top with iced Champagne and decorate with a cube of pineapple.

Concorde (Eng) a slightly sparkling British wine produced by Allied-Domecq.

Concours Agricole (Fr) a wine classification competition.

Concurso Nacional de Vinhos Engarrafados (Port) a nationwide competition organised by the Junta in which the producers own wines take part and are awarded prizes by a qualified jury.

Condado (Sp) county.

Condado de Huelva (Sp) a Denominación de Origen of the Huelva province in Andalucía, south-western Spain. D.O. applies to white wines produced in the region. 8,000ha. Grape varieties: Garrido fino, Listán, Mantúa, Palomino and Zalema. Some Moscatel but not for D.O. wines. Three styles of wine are produced: Condado Pálido (lightly fortified to 15.5% alc by vol.), Condado Viejo (fortified from 17%–23% alc by vol.) and Condado Joven Afrutado (white wine made from Zalema grape, 11%–14% alc by vol.). Pálido and Viejo are aged in Solera.

Condado de Niebla (Sp) lit: 'country of mist', an old name for the D.O. Huelva province in south-western Spain.

Condado de Rosal (Sp) a wine producing area on the river Miño in western Spain. Produces mainly red wines from the Caiño, Espadeiro and Tintarrón grapes.

Condado do Tea (Sp) one of four sub-regions of Rías Baixas in Galicia. *See also* O Rosal, Sotomayor, Val do Salnés.

Condal (Sp) the brand-name for the wines of Bodegas Rioja Santiago.

Condé (S.Afr) the label for a range of red wines (Cabernet sauvignon/Syrah) produced by the Stark-Condé Wines winery, Stellenbosch, Western Cape.

Conde S.A. [Rafael Cruz] (Sp) a producer of Montilla based in Córdoba.

Conde de Caralt (Sp) a bodega based in San Sadurní de Noya. Produces Cava and table wines.

Conde de Haro (Sp) a white cava wine produced by Bodegas Muga in the Rioja region.

Conde de la Salceda (Sp) the label of wines from Viña Salceda S.A., Rioja. The Tinto is oak matured for 2-3 years and also 3 years in bottle. Also produce a Gran Reserva.

Conde de Los Andes (Sp) a red Gran Reserva Rioja wine produced by Federico Paternina at Ollauri.

Conde de Osborne (Sp) a 20 year old solera gran reserva brandy produced by Osborne.

C

Conde de Santar (Port) an estate-produced wine from the Dão region.

Conde de Siruela (Sp) a winery based in the D.O. Ribera del Duero.

Conde Duque (Sp) an 8 year old solera gran reserva brandy produced by Gonzalez Byass.

Conde-en-Brie (Fr) a canton in the district of Château Thierry in the Champagne region. Has the Cru villages: Aisne, Barzy-sur-Marne, Baule-en-Brie, Passy-sur-Marne and Trelou-sur-Marne.

Condé Estate (S.Afr) a winery based in the Stellenbosch region, Western Cape. Grape varieties include: Cabernet sauvignon.

Condemine [La] (Fr) a vineyard in the A.C. commune of Montagny, Côte Chalonnaise, Burgundy

Condensed Milk (Eng) milk which is evaporated in a vacuum to reduce the water content up to 50%. Usually sold canned, sweetened or unsweetened.

Condenser (Eng) the part of the distilling process that turns the vapour (alcohol) back into liquid.

Conders Bend Wines and Estates (N.Z) a winery. (Add): Raparua Road, Blenheim. Produces still and méthode traditionelle white wines from Chardonnay, Riesling, Sauvignon blanc grapes.

Condesa de Leganza (Sp) a winery based in the La Mancha, central Spain. Grape varieties: Cabernet sauvignon, Tempranillo. Label: Finca Los trenzones.

Condessa (Wal) a liqueur manuyfacturer (established 1969). (Add): Bryn Maethlu, Llanfaethlu, Anglesey, Gwynedd LL65 4NW. Produces a range of liqueurs including Welsh Cream Liqueur 16% alc by vol. Website: http://www.condessa.com 'E'mail: sales@condessa.co.uk

Condessa Welsh Cream Liqueur (Wal) a 16% alc by vol. cream liqueur made using whisky, chocolate, vanilla and banana. Produced in Anglesey.

Condestable (Sp) a solera gran reserva brandy produced by Gil Galan in Jerez de la Frontera.

Conde Valdemar (Sp) *see* Bodegas Martinez Bujanda

Condition (Eng) a part of the beer-making process in which the newly made beer is 'primed' and conditioned. CO_2 gas is dissolved into beer during this process to give it 'condition'.

Condom (Fr) the commercial centre of the Armagnac brandy region, Gers département.

Condomois (Fr) a Vin de Pays area in the Gers département. Produces red, rosé and dry white wines.

Condrieu (Fr) a famous A.C. region in the Rhône. Only white wines are produced from the Viognier grape on terraced vineyards. Wines are full-bodied, often with a touch of pétillance and sweetness in a good vintage. *See also* Château Grillet.

Conestoga Vineyards (USA) a winery based in Birchrunville, Pennsylvannia. Produces Labrusca and French hybrid wines.

Confluence (S.Afr) the label for a white wine (Chenin blanc and Colombard blend) produced by the Douglas Wine Cellar winery, Douglas, Northern Cape.

Confraria dos Enofilos da Bairrada (Port) a Bairrada fraternity who help to promote and enhance the quality of the wines.

Confraternità della Cheer (It) a wine brotherhood.

Confraternità d'la Tripa (It) a wine brotherhood.

Confrérie (Fr) brotherhood. A wine organisation in France for the promotion and enjoyment of the wines of a specific district or region.

Confrérie de Bacchus et d'Icare (Fr) a wine society based in Lyon.

Confrérie de Chevaliers du Cep (Fr) a wine society based in Verdigny.

Confrérie de Guillon (Switz) a wine brotherhood.

Confrérie des Alambics Charentais (Fr) a wine society for the promotion of Cognac brandy based in the Cognac region.

Confrérie des Baillis de Pouilly-sur-Loire (Fr) a wine brotherhood based in Pouilly-sur-Loire, Central Vineyards, Loire.

Confrérie des Chevaliers de la Canette (Fr) a wine brotherhood based in Deux Sèvres.

Confrérie des Chevaliers de la Chantepleure (Fr) a wine brotherhood based in Vouvray, Touraine, Loire.

Confrérie des Chevaliers de la Syrah et Roussette (Fr) a wine brotherhood of the Rhône.

Confrérie des Chevaliers des Cuers de Baril (Fr) a wine brotherhood based in Loches. Mâconnais, Burgundy.

Confrérie des Chevaliers du Sacavin (Fr) a wine brotherhood based in Angers, Anjou-Saumur, Loire.

Confrérie des Chevaliers du Tastevin (Fr) the oldest wine brotherhood based at the Clos de Vougeot in Burgundy. *See also* Tastevinage.

Confrérie des Chevaliers Rabelaisiens de Belgique (Bel) a wine brotherhood.

Confrérie des Compagnons de la Capucine (Fr) a wine society based at Toul.

Confrérie des Comtes de Nice et de Provence (Fr) a wine society based in Provence.

Confrérie des Domaines [La] (Fr) a co-operative winery based in the A.C. Chablis, Burgundy. Produces a range of Chablis wines including Premier Crus Fourchaume, Mont de Milieu and Vaillons.

Confrérie des Échansons de Vidauban (Fr) a wine brotherhood based in the Provence region, south-eastern France.

Confrérie des Grandgousiers (Fr) a brotherhood of Touraine. Meetings held in Amboise in the Loire Valley.

Confrérie des Hospitaliers de Pomerol (Fr) a wine society for the promotion of Pomerol wines based in Bordeaux.

Confrérie des Trois Ceps (Fr) a wine society based in the Yonne.

Confrérie des Vignerons de la Canette (Fr) a wine society based in Bouille-Loretz.

Confrérie des Vignerons de St-Vincent-de-Mâcon (Fr) a wine brotherhood of the Mâcon, Burgundy.

Confrérie des Vignolants de Neuchâtel (Switz) a

C

wine brotherhood of Neuchâtel, western Switzerland.

Confrérie des Vin Gousiers d'Anjou (Fr) a wine society based in Anjou, Loire.

Confrérie du Gosier-sec de Clochemerle (Fr) a fraternity founded in Beaujolais in 1961.

Confrérie du Vin de Cahors (Fr) a wine society based in Cahors.

Confrérie Saint-Étienne (Fr) a wine society based in Alsace.

Confrérie Saint Vincent des Vignerons de Mâcon (Fr) a wine brotherhood based in the Mâconnais, Burgundy.

Confrérie Saint Vincent des Vignerons de Tannay (Fr) a wine brotherhood based in the Nièvre département, central France.

Confrérie Saint-Vincent et Disciples de la Chante Fluté de Mercurey (Fr) a fraternity founded in Mercurey, Côte Chalonnaise, Burgundy in 1972. Has a yearly tasting by 5 experts to select the best wines, Has Chante-fluté on the bottle label.

Confrérie Saint-Vincent et Disciples de la Confréries Vigneronnes (Fr) wine brotherhoods.

Confrérie Vineuse des Piliers Chablisiens (Fr) a wine fraternity founded in 1952 which meets 4 times a year for the promotion of Chablis wines.

Confrérie Vineuse des Tire-Douzil (Fr) a wine brotherhood based in the Vienne département, Loire.

Congé (Fr) documents which indicate that internal taxes have been paid. Usually accompany wines and spirits. Different types used for different styles of wines and spirits. See also Capsule-Congé.

Congenerics (Eng) see Congeners.

Congeners (Eng) the composition of wines and spirits etc. Made up of alcohols, esters, acids, fusil oils etc. that give bouquet and flavour.

Conghurst Vineyard (Fr) a vineyard based in Conghurst Oast, Hawkhurst, Kent. 0.5ha. Grape varieties: Chasselas and Regner.

Congius (Lat) a measure in Roman times approximately equal to an Imperial gallon.

Congo (Chi) see Congou.

Congou (Chi) a course-leaf grade of 'black tea'. Also spelt Congo.

Congregazione (It) co-operative.

Congy (Fr) a Cru Champagne village in the Canton de Montmort. District: Épernay.

Conhaque (Bra) a liqueur.

Coniano (It) a sparkling natural spring mineral water. Mineral contents (milligrammes per litre): Sodium 668mg/l, Calcium 176mg/l, Magnesium 64mg/l, Potassium 21mg/l, Bicarbonates 1836.6mg/l, Chlorides 348.1mg/l, Sulphates 179mg/l, Nitrates 0.6mg/l, Silicates 18.2mg/l, Strontium 4.8mg/l. pH 6.7

Conical Fermentation Vessel (Eng) a tall cylinder with a tapered lower end, the fermenting brew is kept agitated by air injection.

Coniston Bluebird (Eng) a 4.5% alc by vol. ale brewed by Refresh UK plc., Oxfordshire.

Coniston Brewing Company (Eng) a brewery (established 1995). (Add): Coppermines Road, Coniston, Cumbria LA21 8HL. Brews: Blacksmith Ale 5% alc by vol., Bluebird Bitter 3.6% alc by vol (a bottle-conditioned bitter made with Challenger hops)., Bluebird Exp 4.2% alc by vol., Old Man Ale 4.2% alc by vol. Website: http://www.conistonbrewery.com 'E'mail: sales@conistonbrewery.com

Conn Creek (USA) a winery based near Rutherford, Napa Valley, California. Grape varieties: Cabernet sauvignon, Chardonnay and Zinfandel. Produces varietal wines.

Connecticut (USA) the home to many small wineries producing mainly French hybrid wines.

Connemara (Ire) a pure double pot-stilled, peated, single malt Irish whiskey from the Cooley Distillery in Dundalk.

Connétable Talbot (Fr) the second wine of Château Talbot [Grand Cru Classé (4th). A.C. Saint-Julien].

Connétablie de Guyenne (Fr) a wine brotherhood for the wines of the Guyenne in south-eastern Bordeaux. Members are devoted to the promotion of sweet white wines.

Connoisseur (Fr) one who appreciates and knows of the fine things of life. (It) = cognoscenti.

Cono (Sp) the name used in Màlaga and Valencia for Tino.

Conos (Sp) the name given to large wooden, truncated, conical-shaped vats. See also Tino.

Cono Sur (Chile) a single vineyard estate in Casablanca Valley, south of San Fernando where mainly Pinot noir is grown by Concha y Toro. Label: Ocio. Also has holdings in the Cachapoal Valley (Vision label). Also produces: Viognier. Website: http://www.conosur.com

Conqueror Ale (Eng) a cask-conditioned ale 1066 O.G. brewed by the Axe Vale Brewery, Devon.

Conquest (Austr) a wine made from a blend of Sémillon, Colombard and Chenin blanc produced by Norman's in South Australia.

Conquest (Eng) a 3.8% alc by vol. ale brewed by the Blindmans Brewery, Somerset.

Conquistador (Sp) a solera brandy produced by Sanchez Romate. See also Abolengo, Cesar (El), Tres Espadas.

Conradie Family Vineyards (S.Afr) a winery (established 2004) based in Worcester, Western Cape. 91ha. Grape varieties: Cabernet franc, Cabernet sauvignon, Chardonnay, Chenin blanc, Colombard, Crouchen, Merlot, Muscadel, Pinotage, Red muscadel. Website: http://www.conradie-vineyards.co.za

Conradsminde Glassworks (Den) a glassworks which produced many of the early drinking vessels in the eighteenth and nineteenth centuries.

Conroi (Cktl) ¾ measure rye whiskey, ⅛ measure apricot brandy, ⅛ measure crème de banane, ¾ measure orange juice. Shake over ice and strain into a cocktail glass.

Conrotto Winery (USA) a winery based in Santa Clara, California. Produces ordinary table wines.

Conroy's Angel (Eng) a 4.8% alc by vol. beer brewed by a micro-brewery in County Durham.

C

Consecha (Sp) *see* Consecho.

Consecha Special (Arg) a brand of sparkling wine produced by the Bodegas Norton.

Consecho (Sp) crop or vintage.

Conseil des Échansons de France (Fr) a wine society based in Paris.

Conseil Interprofessionnel des Vins d'Anjou et Saumur (Fr) a body for the promotion of the wines of Anjou-Saumur, Loire. *abbr*: C.I.V.A.S. (Add): 21 Boulevard Foch, 49000 Angers.

Conseil Interprofessionnel des Vins de Fitou, Corbières et Minervois (Fr) a body for the promotion of wines of the Midi. (Add): R.N.113, 11200 Lézignan-Corbières.

Conseil Interprofessionnel des Vins du Languedoc (Fr) *abbr*: CIVL a body for the promotion of the wines of the Languedoc, southern France.

Conseil Interprofessionnel du Vin de Bordeaux (Fr) *abbr*: C.I.V.B a body for the promotion of Bordeaux wines. (Add): 3 Cours du 30 Juillet, 33075 Bordeaux.

Consejo Regulador de la Denominación de Origen (Sp) the organisation for the defence, control and promotion of a Denominación de Origen.

Consejo Regulador de la Denominación de Origen Califcada (Sp) the organisation for the defence, control and promotion of Rioja wines. (Add): C/ Estambrera, 52. 26006 Logroño, Spain. Website: http://www.riojawine.com 'E'mail: info@riojawine.com

Consenso (USA) a varietal Sangiovese produced in the Napa Valley, California.

Consentinum (It) a red wine produced in southern Italy during Roman times.

Conservation des Vins (Fr) the process and culture of the correct cellering and storage of wines until they reach maturity and perfection.

Conservato (It) a wine to which concentrated or boiled wine has been added.

Consilience Winery (USA) a winery based in the Santa Rita Hills, Santa Barbara County, California. Grape variety: Pinot noir. Label: Ashley's Vineyard.

Consistorial (Sp) a solera brandy produced by Emilio Hidalgo. *See also* Gobernador.

Consort (Afr) a brand of double-distilled cane spirit.

Consorzio (It) a local growers' association with legal standing.

Consorzio Per la Difesa dei Vini Tipici Barolo e Barbaresco (It) a local consorzio. Seal is seen on some bottles of wine as **Barbara**: ancient tower and **Barolo**: golden lion in blue field.

Consorzio Vino Chianti Classico (It) formed on 14th June 1924, it as a black cockerel as logo (the ancient crest of Lega del Chianti).

Consorzio Viticoltori Associati del Vulture (It) a co-operative (established 1978) based in the village of Barile, Basilicata. Has 700 members. Produces D.O.C. Aglianico del Vulture.

Conspirare (S.Afr) a winery (established 2002) based in Stellenbosch, Western Cape. 24ha. Grape varieties: Cabernet franc, Cabernet sauvignon, Merlot.

Constantia (S.Afr) a coastal wine region. *see* Groot Constantia.

Constantia (S.Afr) an old name for a rich, sweet, liqueur-type wine from Groot Constantia vineyards, produced from the Muscat grape. Grapes are left to dry on the vine before harvesting to produce and wine of 15% alc. b vol. and mature in French oak for two years. Sold in 50cls hand-blown bottles to resemble the original bottle first created in the seventeenth century.

Constantia de Tulbagh (S.Afr) the old name for the Montpellier du Sud winery. *See also* Montpellier de Tulbagh.

Constantia Glen (S.Afr) a winery (established 2000) based in Constantia, Western Cape. 29ha. Grape varieties: Cabernet franc, Cabernet sauvignon, Malbec, Merlot, Petit verdot, Sauvignon blanc. Website: http://www.constantiaglen.com

Constantia Rood (S.Afr) the label for a red wine (Cabernet sauvignon, Merlot and Pinotage blend) produced by the Groot Constantia Estate winery, Constantia, Western Cape.

Constantia Uitsig (S.Afr) a winery (established 1988) based in Constantia, Western Cape. 32ha. (Add): P.O. Box 402, Constantia 7848. Grape varieties include Cabernet sauvignon, Cabernet sauvignon, Chardonnay, Merlot, Sauvignon blanc, Sémillon. Labels: Contantia Red, Constantia White. Website: http://www.uitsig.co.za

Constantinovka (Rus) a wine-producing centre in the River Don area. Produces mainly white wines.

Constanza (Rum) a wine-producing region based in the Dobruja region.

Consulat de la Vinée de Bergerac (Fr) a wine society based in the Bergerac region.

Consulat de Septimanie (Fr) a wine brotherhood of the Languedoc.

Consume (Eng) to swallow or drink, to devour, to take in by mouth into the body.

Consumo (Port) denotes ordinary table wine/vin ordinaire.

Contact Process (Eng) the addition of finely ground tartrate crystals to cooled wine. This is stirred for 16 hours and the tartrates can then be removed. Reduces the wines's acidity.

Contadino (It) vineyard worker.

Contado do Tea (Sp) one of four sub-regions in D.O. Rías Baixas. Grape varieties are 90% Albariño plus 7% Treixadura, plus 3% Loureiro, Torrontés and local red varieties.

Container Beer (Eng) the brewery name for keg or bright beer.

Contea di Scalfani (It) a zone located in the province of Palermo, Sicily. Granted D.O.C. in August 1996.

Contemporary (Austr) a blend based on Chardonnay produced by Ryecroft in South Australia.

Conterno Fantino (It) a winery based in the DOCG Barolo, Piemonte. Label: Sori Ginestra.

Conterno [Giacomo] (It) a winery based in Monforte d'Alba, Piemonte.

Contessa Rosa Nature (It) a sparkling (metodo tradizionale) wine produced by Fontanafredda in

C

Piemonte. Made from Chardonnay and Pinot grapes. Minimum alc by vol. 11.5%.

Conte Vaselli (It) producers of Orvieto in the Umbria region.

Conteville Winery (Austr) a winery based in the Swan Valley. Grape varieties: Cabernet, Hermitage and Riesling.

Conthey (Switz) a wine-producing village based near Sion in the Valais département. Noted for Fendant wines.

Contichinno (Austr) a coffee, cream and rum liqueur produced by the Continental Distillers.

Conticream (Austr) a chocolate, cream and Scotch whisky liqueur produced by the Continental Distillers.

Contière [La] (Fr) a Premier Cru vineyard in the commune of Ladoix-Serrigny, A.C. Aloxe-Corton, Côte de Beaune, Burgundy.

Conti Forest Hill (Austr) a vineyard. (Add): 18 Km, West Mount Barker Muir Highway, Forest Hill, P.O. Box 49, Western Australia 6324. 22ha. Grape varieties: Cabernet sauvignon and Rhine riesling.

Contigu au (Fr) lit: 'adjoining the', seen on a bottle label.

Conti Guerrieri Rizzardi (It) a winery with 100ha. vineyards. (Add): Azienda Agricola Piazza Guerrieri 1, 37011 Bardolino, Verona. Produces Tacchetto.

Conti Loredan-Gasparini (It) a sparkling (metodo tradizionale) wine producer based in Veneto.

Continental Blend Coffee (Eng) a dark, full roast which produces a strong, dark, rich coffee. Ideal for after dinner drinking.

Continental Cocktail (Cktl) ⅓ measure dark rum, ⅓ measure crème de menthe (white), juice ¼ lemon, ½ teaspoon gomme syrup. Shake over ice, strain into a cocktail glass and top with a twist of lemon peel juice.

Continental Distillers (Austr) a large distilling company noted for cream liqueurs. *see* Contichinno and Conticream.

Continental Flavoured Rum (W.Ind) a rum produced only in Jamaica. Is aromatic and has a 'pineapple' flavour. Germans often use it for their Rum Verschnitt.

Continental Lager (Eng) a lager beer 1034 O.G. brewed by Davenports Brewery, Birmingham.

Continentality (Eng) the difference between winter and summer temperatures.

Continental's Charter Oak (USA) the brand-name of a Bourbon whiskey 40% alc by vol.

Continental Sour (Cktl) as for Brandy Sour but with a dash of claret on top.

Continental Vineyards (USA) a vineyard based in San Luis Obispo County, California. Grape variety: Zinfandel.

Continental Winery (N.Z) a winery. (Add): Okaika, Northland. 4.3ha. Grape varieties: Baco 22, Breidecker, Grey riesling, Niagara and Reichensteiner.

Contino (Sp) the name given to a single-vineyard, Alavesa red wine produced by the Compañia Vinícola del Norte de España in the Rioja Alta.

Continuato (It) continuous still.

Continuous Fermentation (Eng) a beer brewing process where the wort is passed continuously through a concentration of yeast.

Continuous Method (Eng) describes the sparkling wine method where wine is passed through a series of 5 tanks, all of which are under different pressures. Still wine, yeast and sugar enters the first tank, sparkling wine emerges from the fifth tank. Total time: 3–4 weeks. Also known as the Russian Method.

Continuous Screw Press (Fr) a rather harsh type of press that is only used for vin de table and wines for distilling.

Continuous Still (Eng) *see* Coffey Still, Patent Still and Stein (Robert).

Conti Royal (USA) the brand-name of a brandy produced by the East-Side Winery Co-operative in Lodi, California.

Conti Royale (USA) the brand-name used by the East-Side Winery Co-operative in Lodi, California for their fine wines.

Conti Sanminiatelli (It) a Chianti Classico producer based in Greve in Tuscany.

Conti Serristori (It) a Chianti Classico producer based in Percussina in Firenze, Tuscany.

Conti Zecca (It) a winery based in the Salento region of Puglia. Grape varieties include: Malvasia, Negroamaro. Label: Cantalupi (rosé).

Contra Costa (USA) a northern district of California. Produces fine white table wines, red and dessert wines 395ha.

Contrado del Santo (It) an I.G.T. red wine produced by d'Alfonso del Sordo in San Severo, Puglia from 80% Troia and 20% Montepulciano grapes.

Contraetiqueta (Sp) in Rioja the name given to the back label on a wine bottle that specifies the type of wine.

Contratto (It) wine producers at Canelli, Piemonte. Also produce brandies and sparkling (metodo tradizionale) wines including Sabauda Riserva and Bacco d'Oro.

Contraviesa-Alpujarra (Sp) a Vino de la Tierra of Granada in Andalucía. Grape varieties: Garancha tinta, Jaén blanco, Mantúa, Pedro ximénez, Tempranillo, Vigiriega (Vijiriego), Perruno. Red, rosé (both 12% alc by vol.) and white (11% alc by vol.) wines are produced. Some are Rancio in style.

Contrex (Fr) a still natural mineral water (established 1760) from Contrexville in the Vosges mountains, Alsace. (Add): 18, Rue de Courcelles, 75382 Paris cedex 08. Mineral contents (milligrammes per litre): Sodium 7mg/l, Calcium 451mg/l, Magnesium 66mg/l, Potassium 3mg/l, Bicarbonates 386mg/l, Chlorides 6mg/l, Sulphates 1058mg/l, Fluoride 0.32mg/l, Nitrates 1mg/l.

Controliran (Bul) above D.G.O. Equivalent to A.C. in France. Wine has to be approved by a tasting panel. May add Reserve if aged in oak (white: 3 years/red: 4 years).

C

Controllata e Garantita (It) lit: 'controlled and guaranteed' *see* D.O.C.G.

Conumdrum (USA) a white wine from a blend of Sauvignon blanc, Sémillon, Chardonnay, Muscat canelli. Produced by Caymus Vineyard, Napa Valley, California.

Convalmore-Glenlivet (Scot) a single malt whisky distillery based near Dufftown, Banffshire. Part of the DCL. Group. Produces an 18 year old malt 45% alc by vol.

Convenience Cask (Eng) the name for plastic bag containers in cardboard boxes, used for dispensing wine in large quantities. Helps to keep the air out. *See also* Bag-in-the-Box.

Con Vento (It) a white wine produced by Tenuta del Terriccio from Sauvignon blanc grapes.

Convento de Alpendurada (Port) a producer of Vinho Verde wine based at Alpendurada 4575 Entre-Os-Rios.

Conviction (Eng) a 3.8% alc by vol. ale brewed by the Edale Brewery C°., Cumbria.

Convivio (It) a winery based in Tuscany. Produces a DOCG Montepulciano d'Abruzzo.

Conway Brewery (Wal) a brewery (established 2003). (Add): Bryn Dinas, Woodlands, Gyffin, Conway, Gwynedd LL32 8LT. Brews: Castle Bitter 3.8% alc by vol., Celebration Ale 4.2% alc by vol., Honey Fayre 4.5% alc by vol. Website: http://www.conwaybrewery.co.uk 'E'mail: enquiries@conwaybrewery.co.uk

Cooch Behar Cocktail (Cktl) shake together a small tomato juice with 25mls pepper vodka over ice and strain into an ice-filled old-fashioned glass.

Cooil (I.O.M.) a 4.2% alc by vol. pilsner-style lager brewed by Okell's at their Kewaigue Brewery, near Douglas.

Cooil Honda (I.O.M) a 4.7% alc by vol. bottled Manx lager brewed by Okell's at their Kewaigue Brewery, near Douglas to celebrate the 50th anniversary of the Honda bike company.

Cook Brewery (Eng) now no longer brewing but is a distributor for Ridley's Brewery. (Add): Halstead, Essex.

Cooked (Eng) a term used in tasting to describe a sweet, heavy smell.

Cooking Bitter (Eng) a 3.6% alc by vol. bitter ale brewed by the Davis'es Brewing C°. Ltd., Rutland.

Cooks New Zealand (N.Z) a winery. (Add): Paddy's Road, Te Kauwhata, North Island. 400ha. at Te Kauwhata and Fernhill. Grape varieties: Cabernet sauvignon, Chardonnay, Chauche gris, Chenin blanc, Merlot, Müller-Thurgau, Pinot noir, Sauvignon blanc, Sémillon, Sylvaner.

Cool (Eng) a brand of light-style, low-alcohol cider produced by the Taunton Cider C°. Has no artificial colouring or flavouring.

Coolabah (Austr) the brand-name of a range of cask and flagon wines produced by the Orlando Winery, South Australia.

Coolart Valley Vineyard (Austr) a winery (established 1981). (Add): Thomas Road, Red Hill, Off Red Hill Road, Victoria. Grape varieties: Cabernet sauvignon, Merlot, Chardonnay, Riesling.

Coolawin (Austr) a winery. (Add): Grants Gully Road, Clarendon, South Australia 5157. 50ha. at Clarendon and Bakers Gully in Adelaide Hills and at Woods Point. Grape varieties: Cabernet sauvignon, Rhine riesling and Shiraz.

Cool Banana (Cktl) 25mls crème de banane, 15mls triple sec, 10mls grenadine, 25mls double cream, dash egg white. Shake over ice and strain into a cocktail glass.

Cool Blonde [The] (Ger) the Berliners' name for their Champagne-like beer called Berliner Weisse.

Cool Blue (Ger) a still and sparkling natural spring mineral water (established 1908) from the Haaner Felsenquelle. Mineral contents (milligrammes per litre): Sodium 3.2mg/l, Calcium 17.6mg/l, Magnesium 25.2mg/l, Potassium 181mg/l, Bicarbonates 37mg/l, Chlorides 100mg/l.

Cool Blue (N.Z) a natural spring mineral water from Putaruru.

Cool Breeze (Cktl) 25mls Cognac, 75mls cream, 10mls Grand Marnier, 2 dashes maraschino cherry juice. Shake over ice and strain into a cocktail glass.

Cool Caribbean Cocktail (Cktl) 10mls (½ fl.oz) crème de banana, 25mls (1fl.oz) coconut liqueur. Stir over ice in a highball glass, top with orangeade, dress with a slice of orange and 2 cherries.

Cool Cask (Eng) a new 'real ale' served at 10°C (50°F) brewed at ScotCo's Tyneside subsidiary. Aimed at cask beer drinkers who enjoy a cooler drink. Full name is Theakston's Cool Cask.

Cool Climate Oenology and Viticultural Institute (Can) *see* C.C.O.V.I.

Cool Cup (Cup) 400mls (¾ pint) sweet Sherry, 500mls (1pint) dry cider, juice and zest of a small lemon, 25mls (⅛ gill) sugar syrup, pinch grated nutmeg. Stir altogether, chill down, add mint and sliced cucumber, top with a syphon of iced soda water and serve.

Cooler (USA) a mixed drink of spirit, ginger ale or soda, syrup and dressed with crushed ice and fruit in season.

Cooler Club (E.Ind) a slightly sparkling, pineapple and passion fruit flavoured drink produced by Mather in conjunction with a Bangkok firm in Thailand.

Coolex (Ken) a natural spring mineral water from Kenya.

Cooley Distillery (Ire) a distillery (established 1987) based in Riverstown, Co. Louth, Dundalk. Began whiskey distilling in 1989 and started to bottle and sell in 1993. All whiskies are double distilled. **Single malt**: Connemara, Tyrconnell (The) **Grain blends**: Erin's Isle, Inishowen, Kilbeggan, Locke's, Millars.

Coolgardie Safe (Austr) a cupboard or box with wetted hessian sacking draped over it used for keeping drinks (and food) cool by evaporation.

C

Cool Luc (USA) a natural spring mineral water from North Winconsin.

Cool Ridge (Austr) a natural spring mineral water. Mineral contents (milligrammes per litre): Sodium 17mg/l, Calcium 2mg/l, Magnesium 3mg/l, Potassium 2mg/l, Bicarbonates 19mg/l, Chlorides 30mg/l.

Coolserve (Eng) a refrigeration unit that chills bottles of white wines. Holds up to 14 litres. Marketed by Gilbeys.

Coolship (USA) in brewing a container for cooling the wort after it passes through the hop strainer.

Cool Spring (Can) a light, low-alcohol beer 3.9% alc by vol. brewed by the Labatt Brewery.

Cool Springs (USA) a natural spring mineral water from Parkersburg, West Virginia.

Cool Valley (Ind) a natural spring mineral water from Chennai. Mineral contents (milligrammes per litre): Sodium 17mg/l, Calcium 4mg/l, Magnesium 17mg/l, Potassium 2.9mg/l, Bicarbonates 28mg/l, Chlorides 17mg/l, Sulphates 4mg/l, Nitrates 0.03mg/l, Silicates 5mg/l, Iron 28mg/l. pH 6.3

Coomassie (Cktl) 40mls (⅓ gill) dry Sherry, 20mls (⅙ gill) Cognac, 1 barspoon icing sugar, 1 egg yolk, 2 dashes Angostura. Shake well over ice, strain into a highball glass, top with grated nutmeg and cinnamon.

Coonawarra (Austr) a famous wine district (8 miles x 1 mile) in South Australia. 350km. south-east of Adelaide, 400km. west of Melbourne which was first planted with vines in the 1980's. Contains the Terra Rossa (sandstone under-pinned with limestone). Wineries include Balnaves, Hollick, Katnook, Lindemans, Mildara, Majella, Penfolds, Penley, Petaluma, Rymill, Wynns. Mainly red grape varieties (Cabernet sauvignon, Shiraz), whites include Chardonnay and Riesling.

Coonawarra Cabernet Sauvignon (Austr) a full-flavoured red wine with a strong bouquet from the Rosemount Estate vineyards in New South Wales.

Coonawarra Shiraz (Austr) a full, peppery aromatic red wine with a touch of sweetness from the Rosemount Estate vineyards in New South Wales.

Cooper (Eng) cask or barrel maker.

Cooper (Eng) a mixture of equal parts stout and porter.

Cooper (Eng) a merchant who is employed in the testing and bottling of wine.

Cooperage [1] (Eng) the building where casks (barrels) are made. See also Coopery.

Cooperage [2] (Eng) the craft of the cooper.

Cooperage [3] (Eng) the fee charged by a cooper for his work.

Cooper Ale (Eng) a 4.8% alc by vol. ale brewed by the Hook Norton Brewery C°. Ltd., Oxfordshire.

Cooperativa (Sp) a co-operative winery.

Cooperativa Agricoltura Cinque Terre (It) a co-operative winery based in the Cinque Terre, Liguria region. Has 300 growers. Grape varieties include: Albarola, Bosco, Vermentino. Labels: Costa da Posa, Costa de Campu, Costa de Sera, Manarola.

Cooperativa de Manjavacas (Sp) a large co-operative bodega winery based in La Mancha. Uses the label Zagarrón for its wines.

Cooperativa de Ribero del Duero (Sp) a large co-operative winery based in Peñafiel. Is noted for Protos (a 5 year old, cask-aged red wine).

Cooperativa de Vila Nova Tazem (Port) a large co-operative winery belonging to SOGRAPE.

Cooperativa Interlocal de Alesanco (Sp) a modern winery based in Logroño, Rioja. Operates on a continuous vinification method (Torre Vinaria).

Cooperativa Jesus Nazareno (Sp) a co-operative winery based in Barco. Produces Gran Vino Godello (a white varietal wine) and Valdouro (a red wine from Garnacha and Vencia grapes).

Cooperativa la Purisima (Sp) a large co-operative winery in the Yecla region. Produces red, rosé and white wines.

Cooperativa la Seca (Sp) the only co-operative winery based in the La Rueda region. Produces Palido and Dorada (flor-affected wines) and Cuatro Rayas and Veliterra (white wines).

Cooperativa San Raphael (Arg) a large co-operative which deals mainly in concentrated grape must and ordinary bulk wines.

Cooperativa Santa Rita (Sp) a co-operative winery based in Fuenterobles, Utiel-Requena, Levante.

Cooperativa San Valero (Sp) a co-operative winery based near Zaragoza in Cariñena. Produces mainly table wines.

Cooperativa Vinícola de Cenicero, B. 'Santa Daria' (Sp) a co-operative winery (Add): Ctra de Logroño, s/n, Cenicero (la Rioja). 800ha. Grape varieties: Garnacha, Graciano, Malvasia, Mazuelo, Tempranillo and Viura. Produces Santa Daria and Valdemontan.

Cooperativa Vinícola de Labastida (Sp) see Labastida.

Cooperativa Vinícola del Penedés (Sp) abbr: COVIDES has wineries at San Cugat and San Sadurní in Cataluña, south-eastern Spain.

Cooperativa Vinícola del Ribeiro (Sp) a winery based in Rivadavia. Produces low-alcohol white wines.

Cooperativa Vinicola Produttori Verdicchio Monte Schiavo (It) abbr: C.V.P.V. a co-operative winery based at Moie di Maiolati in the Marche region.

Cooperativa Vitivinicola Nueva California Ltda (Arg) a winery based in the Mendoza region, eastern Argentina. Website: http://www.patagoniawines.com 'E'mail: californ@rcc.com.ar

Co-operative (Eng) a winery or cellar belonging jointly to a number of small producers. (Fr) = coopérative, (It) = cooperativa, (Sp) = cooperativa.

Coopérative (Fr) co-operative.

Coopérative d'Armagnac 'Gerland' (Fr) an Armagnac co-operative. (Add): Route de Bordeaux, 49190 Villeneuve-de-Marsan.

Coopérative de Fontette (Fr) a Champagne co-operative winery (established 1952). (Add): 10360 Fontette. Has 95 members.

Coopérative de L'Union des Proprietaires de Vins Fins (Fr) a wine co-operative of the commune of Gevrey-Chambertin in the Côte de Nuits, Burgundy.

Coopérative de Montagne (Fr) a co-operative vineyard and winery in the commune of Montagne-Saint-Émilion. A.C. Saint-Émilion, Bordeaux 145ha.

Coopérative des Vins Fins (Fr) a wine co-operative of the commune Morey-Saint-Denis in the Côte de Nuits, Burgundy.

Coopérative Intercommunale de Vinification (Fr) a co-operative winery. (Add): Prignas en Médoc, 33340. A.C. Médoc. (Com): Lesparre. 290ha. Grape varieties: Cabernet franc, Cabernet sauvignon and Merlot.

Coopérative-Manipulant (Fr) abbr: C.M. on a Champagne bottle label denotes a co-operative producer's wine.

Coopérative Régionale de Vins de Champagne (Fr) abbr: C.R.V.A. A Champagne co-operative consisting of 680 vignerons. Sells under the trade-name of Jacquart.

Coopératives de Pressurage (Fr) a Champagne co-operative that presses the grapes only.

Coopératives de Pressurage et Vinification (Fr) a Champagne co-operative that presses the grapes and makes the initial still wine.

Coopératives de Pressurage, Vinification et Champanisation (Fr) a Champagne co-operative that presses the grapes, produces the still wines and Champagne and sells it.

Copérative Vinicole de Cuis (Fr) a co-operative Champagne producer (established 1947). (Add): 11, Rue de Champagne, 51530 Cuis. Has 95 membersProduces vintage and non-vintage Champagnes. Label: De Blémond.

Co-operative Wine Farmers' Association (S.Afr) abbr: K.W.V. Formed in 1918 at the time of the two Gladstone Acts.

Cooper Mountain Vineyards (USA) a 35ha. vineyard based in Willamette Valley, Oregon. Grape varieties: Pinot noir, Chardonnay, Pinot gris.

Coopers (Eng) a 3.5% alc by vol. ale brewed by the Wickwar Brewing Cº. Ltd., Gloucestershire.

Coopers Ale (Scot) a 3.2% alc by vol. beer from Maclay.

Coopers Bell (Eng) a seasonal ale brewed by Frederic Robinson Ltd., Unicorn Brewery, Stockport, Cheshire (available in September).

Coopers Best Extra Stout (Austr) a 6.8% alc by vol. deep-black, top-fermented, bottle-conditioned Stout brewed by Coopers Brewery Ltd., Leabrook, Adelaide.

Coopers Brewery Ltd. (Austr) a brewery (established 1862). (Add): P.O. Box 46, Regency Park, 5942, Leabrook, Adelaide. Produces bottle-conditioned beers fermented in wooden casks. Best Extra Stout 6.8% alc by vol. Thomas Cooper's Finest Export 4.9% alc by vol. and Sparkling Ale 5.8% alc by vol. Website: http://www.coopers.com.au 'E'mail: coopers@coopers.com.au

Cooper's Finest Export [Thomas] (Austr) a 4.9% alc by vol. gold-straw coloured, top-fermented, bottled ale brewed by Coopers Brewery Ltd., Leabrook, Adelaide.

Coopers Creek Vineyard (N.Z) a winery. (Add): 601 State Highway 16, Huapai, Kumeu. 18ha. Grape varieties: Cabernet sauvignon, Chardonnay, Gewürztraminer, Merlot, Pinot noir, Chenin blanc, Riesling, Sauvignon blanc, Sémillon. Noted for late-harvest Riesling and méthode traditionelle.

Coopers Fruit (Cktl) ⅓ measure Mandarine Napoléon, ⅓ measure vodka, ⅓ measure crème de banane. Shake well over ice, strain into a cocktail glass, dress with a slice of banana, lemon and a cherry.

Coopers Sparking Ale (Austr) a 5.8% alc by vol. top-fermented, bottle-conditioned ale brewed by Coopers Brewery Ltd., Leabrook, Adelaide.

Cooperstown Cocktail [1] (Cktl) a Martini Cocktail, shaken with 2 sprigs of fresh mint.

Cooperstown Cocktail [2] (Cktl) as for [1] with addition of half a teaspoon of orange bitters.

Cooperstown Brewing Cº (USA) a brewery (established 1995). (Add): River St. P.O. Box 276, Milford NY13807. Brews a variety of beers. Website: http://www.cooperstownbrewing.com

Coopery (Eng) the alternative word for Cooperage.

Co-op Fairbourne Springs (Wal) a natural spring mineral water from Churchstoke, Montgomeryshire, Powys. Mineral contents (milligrammes per litre): Sodium 31.2mg/l, Calcium 55mg/l, Magnesium 4.4mg/l, Potassium 8.2mg/l, Chlorides 19.1mg/l, Sulphates 45.7mg/l, Fluorides <0.1mg/l. pH 7.85

Coorg (Ind) a coffee-producing region in central India.

Coors Brewers (Eng) the new name for Bass Brewers from 2001.

Coors Brewery [Adolf] (USA) a brewery based at Golden, Colorado. Brews: Coors Extra Gold. Also Irish Red Ale under licence from Letts Brewery in Southern Ireland.

Coors Extra Gold (USA) a light coloured, bottled, premium pilsener lager 5% alc by vol. brewed by Adolf Coors Brewery, Golden, Colorado.

Cooymans (Hol) a noted liqueur producer. (Add): P.O. Box 416, 5201 AK Den Bosch. Produces many fine liqueurs.

Copa (Lat) barmaid.

Copa (Sp) wine glass.

Copa de Oro (Cktl) 25mls (1fl.oz) tequila, 25mls (1fl.oz). Grand Marnier, 1 egg, 1 teaspoon castor sugar. Shake well together, strain into a wine glass, top with round orange slice and straws.

Copeaux [Les] (Fr) a term used to describe wood shavings, chips and granules used during/after vinification.

Copella (Eng) an apple juice drink from Taunton Cider Cº. Ltd., Somerset produced at the Boxford Farm, Suffolk.

C

Copenheering (Cktl) ⅓ measure Peter Heering Cherry brandy, ⅔ measure vodka, dash lime and lemon juice. Stir over ice and strain into a cocktail glass.

Copère (Bel) a top-fermented beer brewed by the Dinant Brasserie.

Copertino (It) a D.O.C. red wine from Southern Puglia. Produced from the Negroamaro grape.

Copetin (Bra) a vermouth served in Brazil as a gesture of hospitality usually in the 'vermouth hour' between 5–6 p.m. especially in Buenos Aires.

Cope-Williams [Romsey Vineyards] (Austr) a winery (established 1977). (Add): Glenfern Road, Romsey, Victoria. Grape varieties: Cabernet franc, Cabernet sauvignon, Merlot, Pinot noir, Chardonnay, Riesling.

Cophe (Rus) coffee. *See also* Kofé.

Copinet [Jacques] (Fr) a Champagne producer. (Add): 11 Rue de l'Ormeau, 51260 Mongenost. 6ha. (5.7ha. Chardonnay, 0.3ha. Pinot noir).

Copita (Sp) a rosebud-shaped Sherry glass, also a name for a glass of Sherry. *See also* Caña.

Copo (Port) cup/tumbler/drinking glass.

Copo de Agua (Port) water glass/glass of water.

Copo de Vinho (Port) wine glass/glass of wine.

Coppa da Sciampagna (It) a saucer (Champagne) glass.

Coppa Para Vino (Sp) wine glass.

Copper (Eng) *see* Kettle.

Copper (Fr) a 7.6% alc by vol. amber coloured, bottom-fermented, bottled beer brewed by Schutzenberger Brasserie, Schiltigheim.

Copper Ale (Eng) a seasonal ale brewed by the Hook Norton Brewery, Banbury, Oxon.

Copper Beech (Sp) the name of a rich, sweet, brown Sherry from Harveys.

Copper Casse (Eng) a wine malady, produces an orange brown deposit which dissolves when the wine is oxygenated. Wine has a high copper content and is treated with blue finings.

Copper Dragon Skipton Brewery (Eng) a brewery (established 2002). (Add): Snaygill Ind Estate, Skipton, North Yorkshire BD23 2AR. Brews: Best Bitter 3.8% alc by vol., Black Gold 3.7% alc by vol., Challanger APA 4.2% alc by vol., Golden Pippen 3.7% alc by vol., Stout 1816 4.1% alc by vol. Website: http://www.copperdragon.uk.com 'E'mail: post@copperdragon.uk.com

Copperhead (Eng) a draught cider from Gaymer, Bristol.

Copperino (Cktl) ⅓ measure Kahlúa, ⅓ measure cream, ⅓ measure Galliano. Shake over ice, strain into a cocktail glass and add grated nutmeg on top.

Copper Sulphate (Eng) CUSO₄ used to remove hydrogen sulphide smells in wine. Legal limit 1mg per litre. Caution is required as it also promotes oxidation.

Copper Syrup (Eng) a concentrated malt extract used in the copper to extend the brew length or to alter the gravity.

Copperwinkle (Eng) a 4% alc by vol. cask/bottle

conditioned ale brewed by the Swale Brewery, Sittingbourne.

Coppo [Luigi] (It) a noted producer of D.O.C. Barbera d'Asti in Piemonte. Wines include L'Avoccata, Camp du Rouss, Pomorosso.

Coppoolse Finlayson Winery (S.Afr) a large winery (established 1991) based in Stellenbosch, Western Cape. Grape varieties: Cabernet franc, Chardonnay, Cinsaut, Merlot, Pinotage, Sauvignon blanc, Shiraz, Steen. Labels: Kaya, Nandi, Shaka, Songloed. Website: http://www.cfwines.co.za

Copus Cup (Punch) place 1 litre bitter ale, 500mls Cognac, 150mls crème de noyau, 200gms sugar, juice ½ lemon into a saucepan and heat gently. Serve warm with a slice of toast coated with grated nutmeg and cloves floated on top.

Coq (Fr) a 3–4 year old Cognac produced by Jean Fillioux.

Coq [Le] (Eng) a bottled, super-strength Imperial Extra Double Stout brewed by Harveys of Lewes, East Sussex. Takes over a year to brew and is named after a Belgian brewer who exported stout from England to Russia in the early 19th century.

Coquelicot (Fr) a white wine produced in the A.C. Coteaux Varois by Château Routas from 60% Chardonnay and 40% Viognier grapes.

Coques Courtes (Fr) the 2 short shoots on the main branches of the Taille-Genre Bordelaise vine training system.

Coquetel (Port) cocktail.

Coquimbo (Chile) northern vineyards in Chile.

Coquinero (Sp) a brand of dry, nutty Sherry produced by Osborne.

Coquito Cocktail (Cktl) blend 10mls (½ fl.oz) Cherry Heering, 25mls (1fl.oz) white rum, 10mls (½ fl.oz) coconut cream and 75mls (3fl.ozs) fresh cream with a scoop of crushed ice in a blender, pour into a highball glass and serve with straws.

Cora (It) a vermouth made in Turin.

Corail Bulles (Fr) a natural spring mineral water from Ste. Cécile. Mineral contents (milligrammes per litre): Sodium 23mg/l, Calcium 44mg/l, Magnesium 24mg/l, Potassium 2mg/l, Bicarbonates 287mg/l, Chlorides 5mg/l, Sulphates 3mg/l, Nitrates 1mg/l. pH 7.6

Coral (Mad) the name for a local brand of beer brewed on the island.

Coralba (It) a sparkling natural spring mineral water from Coralba. Mineral contents (milligrammes per litre): Sodium 0.4mg/l, Calcium 54mg/l, Magnesium 21mg/l, Potassium 0.3mg/l, Bicarbonates 255mg/l, Chlorides 0.8mg/l, Sulphates 8.6mg/l, Nitrates 2mg/l, Silicates 3.4mg/l, Oxygen 4.7mg/l. pH 8.0

Coral Reef (Cktl) 1 part Warnick's Advocaat, 2 parts pineapple juice, 1 part lime juice. Stir together over ice in a highball glass and dress with a cherry.

Cora-Quelle (Ger) a natural spring mineral water from Cora-Brunnen, Erkrath, NW.

Cora Villa Costa (It) a producer of sparkling (cuve close) wines in the Piemonte region. Noted for Moscato d'Asti.

C

Corbans (N.Z) a winery. (Add): 426-448 Great North Road, Henderson. Vineyards at Te Kauwhata, Tolga Bay, Gisborne, Hawkes Bay and Marlborough. Grape varieties: Chardonnay, Chenin blanc, Cabernet sauvignon, Merlot, Pinot noir. Noted for botrytised Riesling wines. Labels include Cooks, Longridge, Stoneleigh.

Corbeaux [Les] (Fr) a Premier Cru vineyard in the A.C. commune of Gevrey-Chambertin, Côte de Nuits, Burgundy 3.12ha.

Corbes (Fr) a red grape variety grown in the Bergerac region.

Corbet (Fr) a négociant based in Morey-Saint-Denis, Côte de Nuits, Burgundy.

Corbières (Fr) an A.C. wine area of the Languedoc-Roussillon situated on the foothills of the Pyrénées with Carcassonne in the north-west. Produces mainly red wines at 11% alc by vol. minimum.

Corbières du Roussillon (Fr) an A.C. red wine from the Corbières area in the Roussillon region of south-eastern France.

Corby Distillery (Can) a producer of Canadian whisky.

Corby's Reserve (USA) the brand-name for a blended whiskey.

Corc (Wal) cork.

Corcho (Sp) cork/stopper.

Corconte (Sp) a natural spring mineral water.

Corcova Crianza (Sp) a 100% Tempranillo wine produced by Bodegas Megía e Hijos [J.A.] in Valdepeñas.

Corcyn (Wal) to cork (a bottle).

Cor de Amora (Eng) a style of perry and raspberry drink 5.4% alc by vol. from Showerings. Brand-name is Zazou. See also Douardo.

Cordeliers (Fr) a noted producer of A.C. Bordeaux Mousseux based in Saint-Émilion, eastern Bordeaux.

Cordial (Eng) a stimulating drink. (Den) = hjertestyrkning/likor, (It) = cordiale.

Cordial (Eng) a filtered, non-alcoholic, fruit squash.

Cordial (Scot) the nickname for whisky.

Cordial Campari (It) a light-yellow dessert liqueur obtained from the distillation of raspberries and brandy. 37.5% alc by vol.

Cordial Daisy (Cktl) ¾ measure Cherry brandy, ¼ measure Triple Sec, juice ¼ lemon. Stir well over shaved ice in a highball glass and top with soda water.

Cordiale (It) cordial.

Cordial Glass (USA) a thistle-shaped glass of 100mls (4fl.oz) capacity.

Cordial Médoc (Fr) a blend of Curaçao, crème de cacao and Cognac 44% alc by vol.

Cordial Reby (Fr) a liqueur with Cognac base. Brown in colour.

Cordials (USA) the American name for liqueurs.

Cordier (Fr) a famous négociant and grower in Bordeaux. Owns the following vineyards: Châteaux Gruaud Larose, Meyney, Plagnac, Tanesse and Talbot, Clos de la Poussie, Clos des Jacobins and Labottière.

Cordillera (Chile) a red wine produced by Torres in Curicó from Cariñena, Syrah and Merlot grapes. Aged in French oak for 9 months.

Córdoba (S.Am) a noted wine-producing area in central Argentina.

Córdoba (Sp) a province of Andalucía, a wine area of southern Spain in which D.O. Montilla-Moriles is the most famous district. Produces highly alcoholic, Sherry-type wines which are unfortified. Also home to the Vino Comarcal area of Villaviciosa.

Cordoba Winery (S.Afr) a winery (established 1982) based in Helderberg, Stellenbosch, Western Cape. 31ha. Grape varieties: Cabernet franc, Cabernet sauvignon, Chardonnay, Merlot, Shiraz. Labels: Crescendo, Mount Claire Mountain Red. Website: http://www.cordobawines.co.za

Cordon (Fr) a method of growing vines invented by Dr. Guyot using a permanent stump with horizontal and vertical shoots growing from it.

Cordon Argent (Fr) the name given to fine old Cognacs.

Cordon Bleu (Fr) a non-vintage group of Champagnes produced by De Venoge. Brut *Sélect*: Chardonnay 25%, Pinot noir 50%, Pinot meunier 25% matured for 3 years before release. Brut *Millésiemé*: Chardonnay 15%, Pinot noir 70%, Pinot meunier 15%. matured for 5–6 years before release. *Demi-Sec*: 25% Chardonnay, 50% Pinot noir, Pinot meunier 25% matured for 3 years before release.

Cordon Bleu (Fr) a noted fine old liqueur Cognac from Martell.

Cordon d'Alsace (Fr) a blended Alsatian wine that was produced for USA market. Mainly of Sylvaner blend (now no longer produced).

Cordon de Royat (Fr) a method of vine training in which a main branch is trained ⅔ metre high with 2–3 buds on each shoot.

Cordon Jaune (Fr) see Grand Marnier.

Cordon Negro (Sp) a vintage sparkling wine produced by the Frexinet Cº. Distinguished by its black matt bottle, produced by the cava method.

Cordon Rosé (Fr) a fine vintage rosé Champagne produced by G.H. Mumm from ⅓ Chardonnay and ⅔ Pinot noir grapes. Vintages: 1976, 1979, 1982, 1985, 1988, 1989, 1990, 1995.

Cordon Rouge (Fr) a popular non-vintage, brut Champagne produced by G.H. Mumm.

Cordon Rubis (Fr) a light-style Cognac produced by Martell in Cognac that has an average cask-age of 20 years.

Cordon Vert (Fr) a non-vintage, demi-sec Champagne produced by G.H. Mumm.

Coref Ertach Pensans (Eng) a fine ale 1055 O.G. brewed by Pensans Brewery, Cornwall for the Penzance Heritage fortnight. Also Charter Pensans.

Coreff Ambrée (Fr) a 6.5% alc by vol. unpasteurised, amber coloured, top-fermented, bottle-conditioned ale brewed by Des 2 Rivières Brasserie, Morlaix.

Coreff Brune (Fr) a 6.5% alc by vol. unpasteurised,

top-fermented, bottle-conditioned, brown ale brewed by Des 2 Rivières Brasserie, Morlaix.

Corent (Fr) a rosé wine from the Côtes d'Auvergne in eastern France made from the Gamay grape.

Corenwijn (Hol) lit: 'corn wine', a clean grain spirit (similar to schnapps) made from barley, maize and rye. 40% alc by vol. Also spelt Korenwijn.

Corenwijn (Hol) the brand-name used by the Bols Company for a Moutwijn distilled without juniper.

Corenwyn (Hol) a triple-distilled, wood-aged, all-grain corenwijn.

Corfu (Gre) an island in the western Ionian islands of Greece. Produces mainly Vin de Pays-style wines.

Corgi (Fr) a species of barley malt from the Triumph varieties that gives good sugar yields.

Corgo (Port) the name given to the Port district of the Douro river. Is divided into 2 regions: Baixo (lower) and Cima (upper).

Corgolin (Fr) a commune in the Côte de Nuits-Villages which uses that A.C. and is not allowed to use its own name as a separate A.C.

Cori Bianco (It) a D.O.C. white wine from Latium, produced from Bellone, Malvasia di candia, Trebbiano giallo and Trebbiano toscano grapes. From the commune of Cori and part of Cisterna.

Corinth (Chile) a seedless table grape which is used to produce dessert wines.

Corinto Nero (It) a red grape variety grown on the Lipari Islands, Sicily.

Corio (Austr) the brand-name for a whiskey produced by the United Distillers.

Coriole Winery (Austr) a winery based in McLaren Vale, Southern Vales, South Australia. Produces varietal wines.

Cori Rosso (It) a D.O.C. red wine from Latium. Made from Cesanese, Montepulciano and Nero buono di cori grapes. From the commune of Cori and part of Cisterna.

Corison Winery (USA) the label of a wine produced by Phelps, Napa Valley, California. (Add): 987 St. Helena Highway, California 94574. Website: http://www.Corison.com

Cork (Eng) usually made from the bark of the Portuguese or Spanish cork oak (*Quercus suber*). Is used to seal the necks of wine bottles allowing minute quantities of oxygen into the wine over a prolonged period of time. *See also* Agglomerated Cork. (Fr) = bouchon. Website: http://www.corkmasters.com

Cork (Ire) a town in southern ireland famous for its glass.

Corkage (Eng) a charge levied by restaurants to customers for bringing in their own wines to be opened and consumed in the restaurant.

Cork Borer (Eng) a brass instrument used for boring holes in cork, metal or plastic bungs (or stoppers) to enable any size of spile or airlock to be fitted to a cask.

Cork Distillery C°. (Ire) originally formed in 1867 by the amalgamation of the Daly, Green, North

Mail, Old Middleton and Watercourse Distilleries. Is now part of the Irish Distillers Group Ltd.

Cork Dry Gin (Ire) a dry gin produced by the Irish Distillers Group at the Cork Distillery C°.

Corked (Eng) a slang term for drunk/intoxicated.

Corked Wine (Eng) a rare occurrence, caused by a diseased cork which is immediately detectable by an unpleasant smell in the cork and a fungus-like taste in the wine. *See also* Cork Taint, Wet Cork. (Fr) = bouchonné.

Corker (Eng) an instrument used by amateur wine makers to fit around cylindrical corks in home-made wines that need maturation and therefore need laying down.

Corkette (Eng) a patented device that is used to remove corks from bottles of wine. Consists of a hollow needle which is pushed through the cork into the bottle and then air is pumped into the bottle with the aid of the handle to build up pressure in the bottle to force out the cork.

Cork Flogger (Eng) the name given to a flat piece of hard wood used to ram a softened cork flush home in the neck of the bottle. *See also* Boot.

Corkiness (Eng) a wine malady. Smell of damp, autumnal woodlands, usually from a bad cork. Caused by the mould **Aspergillius**.

Cork Oak (Euro) **Quercus suber** a species of oak tree. *see* Cork.

Cork Pin (Eng) a decorative pin and chain used to hold the extracted cork around the neck of the wine bottle or decanter for inspection.

Cork Press (Euro) an implement for compressing the corks before they are placed in the bottle (neck). Used in the late eighteenth and early nineteenth centuries.

Corkscrew (Eng) implement for extracting the cork from a bottle of wine. There are many designs since its invention in the seventeenth century. (Arab) = mibram, (Aus) = korkenzieher, (Chi) = pingsaizuan, (Den) = proptrækker, (Fr) = tire-bouchon, (Ger) = korkzieher/korkenzieher, (Gre) = tirbousson, (Hol) = kurketrekker, (Indo) = pencabut gabus botol, (Isr) = mehaletz, (It) = cavatappi/cavaturacciolo, (Jap) = koruku nuki, (Kor) = taraesongkot, (Port) = saca-rolhas, (Rus) = shtopor, (Sp) = tira buzon/saca corcho, (Thai) = teeperdjookkuad, (Tur) = tirbuson, (Wal) = allwedd castrel.

Cork Taint (Eng) a condition caused by chlorine-based products used in and around wineries known as 2,4,6 Tri-chloro-anisole (*abbr:* TCA). Professional wine tasters can detect its presence at a ratio of 3:1,000000,000000! *See also* Corked Wine.

Cork Weevil (Eng) an insect that attacks the cork wood, sometimes found in wine-bottle corks.

Corky (Eng) a term to describe a wine that has been contaminated by a faulty cork.

Corky's (Eng) a brand name for flavoured vodka shots 20% alc by vol. produced by Global brands. Website: http://www.corkysays.com 'E'mail: corkys@globalbrands.co.uk

C

Cormicy (Fr) a Cru Champagne village in the Canton de Bourgogne. District: Reims.

Cormondrèche (Switz) a noted vineyard in the Neuchâtel district of western Switzerland.

Cormoyeux (Fr) a Cru Champagne village in the Canton d'Aÿ. District: Reims.

Cornalin (Switz) a red grape variety grown in Valais.

Cornas (Fr) an A.C. red wine region of central-western Rhône, on the river Isère. Wines made from the Syrah grape, minimum alc by vol. 10.5%.

Corn Base (Jap) a Bourbon-style whiskey produced by Nikka. *see* Rye Base.

Corn Beer (Eng) a 6.5% alc by vol. seasonal cask and bottle-conditioned ale from King and Barnes, Horsham, West Sussex.

Corn Circle Organic Ale (Eng) a 4.7% alc by vol. ale brewed by Wychwood Brewery at Eagle Maltings, Witney, Oxfordshire.

Cornell Cocktail (Cktl) 1 measure dry gin, 4 dashes maraschino, 2 dashes lemon juice, 1 egg white. Shake well over ice and strain into a cocktail glass.

Cornerea [La] (Fr) a white wine producer in southern Piemonte, wines produced from the Arneis grape.

Cornerstone (S.Afr) the label for a red wine (Cabernet sauvignon 40%, Merlot 20% and Shiraz 40% blend) produced by the Reyneke Wines winery, Stellenbosch, Western Cape.

Cornevent (Fr) a vineyard in the A.C. commune of Montagny, Côte Chalonnaise, Burgundy.

Corney and Barrow (Eng) a noted, old-established firm of wine merchants. (Add): 12, Helmet Row, London, EC1V 3QJ. Produce fine '*house wines*'.

Corn Grits (USA) cracked corn used for making beer.

Cornifesto (Port) a grape grown before phylloxera in the Douro, found now in small quantities only.

Cornish Best Bitter (Eng) a cask-conditioned and keg bitter 1042 O.G. brewed by the Cornish Brewery C°. in Redruth, Cornwall. Was originally known as the Devenish Brewery.

Cornish Blonde (Eng) a 5% alc by vol. ale brewed by the Skinner's Brewery C°. Ltd., Cornwall.

Cornish Brewery Company (Eng) *see* Devenish Brewery.

Cornish Coaster (Eng) a 3.6% alc by vol. ale brewed by Sharp's Brewery in Cornwall.

Cornish Corgi (Eng) a 4.5% alc by vol. ale brewed by The Dog House Brewery, Cornwall.

Cornish Cream Ale (Eng) a 3.6% alc by vol. ale brewed by the St. Austell Brewery C°. Ltd., Cornwall.

Cornish Cyder Farm (Eng) a cyder house and distillery based near Truro that distills a cider brandy.

Cornish Knocker (Eng) a 4.5% alc by vol. dark golden, flowery, fruity ale brewed by Skinner's Brewing Co. in Truro.

Cornish Mead C° (Eng) a drinks manufacturer (established 1959). (Add): The Mead House, Newlyn, Penzance, Cornwall TR18 5QF. Produces mead, wines and fruit wines. Website: http://www.cornishmead.co.uk

Cornish Original (Eng) a beer brewed by the Cornish Brewery C°.

Cornish Rebellion (Eng) a 4.8% alc by vol. traditional cask-conditioned bitter brewed by the Redruth Brewery, Cornwall.

Cornish [Scrumpy Callestock] Cider Farm [The] (Eng) a cider farm (established 1982). (Add): based Penhallow, Truro, Cornwall TR4 9LW. Produces cider, wines and spirits. Website: http://www.thecornishciderfarm.co.uk 'E'mail: info@thecornishciderfarm.co.uk

Cornish Steamer (Eng) a 4% alc by vol. ale brewed by the Ring 'O' Bells Brewery, Cornwall.

Cornish Storm (Eng) a lager beer (launched 2005) brewed by the Skinners Brewery, Truro.

Cornish Wreckers Scrumpy (Eng) a cask cider produced by Countryman in Devon.

Corn Liquor (USA) the old western America name for corn whiskey.

Cornouaille (Fr) a region in Brittany awarded A.O.C. for cider in 1996. *See also* Auge.

Corn Rose (Eng) a 3.6% alc by vol. cask-conditioned ale brewed by the Steampacket Brewery, Knottingley, Yorkshire.

Cornwell Cocktail (Cktl) 40mls (⅓ gill) dry gin, 20mls (⅙ gill) Seville orange bitters. Shake well over ice, strain into a cocktail glass, add the peel of an olive and squeeze of lemon peel juice on top.

Corn Whiskey (USA) a fiery whiskey made from a mash containing 80% maize or more with little or no ageing.

Coromandel Valley (Austr) a wine-producing district based in South Australia.

Coro Mendocino (USA) the label for a red wine (Zinfandel blend) individually produced by each of a group of 11 wineries (Brutocao Cellars, Dunnewood Cellars, Eaglepoint Ranch Winery, Fetzer Vineyards & Golden Vineyards, Graziano Family Wines, McDowell Valley Vineyards, McNab Ridge Winery, Mendocino Wine Company, Oracle Oaks Winery, Pacific Star Winery, Parducci Wine Cellars) based in the Mendocino County. The wine has a common label with the name of the winery and the Zinfandel must be 40% to 70% of the wine with up to 10% of the remaining single or blend of (Barbera, Carignane, Charbono, Dolcetto, Petite sirah, Primotivo, Sangiovese and Syrah) and a maximum of 16% alc by vol.

Corona (It) a sparkling natural spring mineral water from Corona. Mineral contents (milligrammes per litre): Sodium 31.8mg/l, Calcium 12.1mg/l, Magnesium 13.6mg/l, Potassium 0.9mg/l, Bicarbonates 125mg/l, Chlorides 33.7mg/l, Sulphates 7mg/l, Nitrates 1.8mg/l, Silicates 10mg/l. pH 6.7

Coronado Brewing (USA) a brewery. (Add): 170 Orange Avenue, California CA 92118. Brews a variety of beers. Website: http://www.coronadobrewingcompany.com

C

Corona Extra (S.Am) a 4.6% alc by vol. bottled lager beer brewed by the Modelo Brewery (Cerveceria Modelo), Mexico City, Mexico.

Coronas (Sp) a red wine made from 25% Monastrell and 75% Ull de llebre grapes by Torres in Penedés, aged in American oak for 1 year.

Corona Soft Drinks (Eng) a famous soft drinks company that has merged with Beecham Soft Drinks C°. and then joined with Britvic. Now known as Britvic Corona.

Coronata (It) a white wine from Genoa in north-western Italy. Made from the Vermentino grape.

Coronation (Bel) a pale, strong ale brewed by the Wielemans Brasserie in Brussels.

Coronation Cocktail [1] (Cktl) 60mls (½ gill) brandy, 3 dashes Curaçao, 2 dashes Peach bitters, 2 dashes peppermint. Stir over ice, strain into a cocktail glass with a squeeze of lemon peel on top.

Coronation Cocktail [2] (Cktl) 25mls (1fl.oz) each of dry vermouth, Dubonnet, dry gin. Stir over ice and strain into a cocktail glass.

Coronation Cocktail [3] (Cktl) 30mls (¼ gill) Sherry, 30mls (¼ gill) French vermouth, 1 teaspoon Maraschino, 1 teaspoon Angostura. Shake over ice and strain into a cocktail glass.

Coronation Crystal (Cktl) 1 bottle dry white wine, 3 glasses Marsala, 1 bottle soda water, sliced lemon. Mix all together, leave for 2 hours, sweeten to taste and serve iced.

Coronator Doppelbock (Ger) a strong lager 7.5% alc by vol. from Arcobräu Brauerei in Bavaria.

Coronet (Ger) a natural spring mineral water from Bochum, NW.

Coronet VSQ (USA) a premium label brandy produced by the Schenley Distillers in California.

Coron Père et Fils (Fr) a négociant-éleveur based in Beaune. Owns 4ha. in the A.C. Beaune.

Corowa (Austr) a wine-producing area based in New South Wales which produces mainly sweet, fortified wines.

Corps (Fr) body (i.e. richness in alcohol and other substances).

Corpse-Reviver [1] (Cktl) 10mls (½fl.oz) Calvados, 25mls (1fl.oz) marc brandy, 10mls (½fl.oz) sweet vermouth. Stir over ice, strain into a cocktail glass and add a twist of lemon peel.

Corpse Reviver [2] (Cktl) ¼ measure gin, ¼ measure Triple Sec, ¼ measure lemon juice, ¼ measure Swedish Punsch, dash Pernod. Shake over ice and strain into a cocktail glass.

Corpse Reviver [3] (Cktl) ⅓ measure Cognac, ⅓ measure Fernet Branca, ⅓ measure Peppermint Schnapps. Shake over ice and strain into a cocktail glass.

Corpse Reviver [4] (Cktl) ¼ measure dry gin, ¼ measure Cointreau, ¼ measure China Martini, ¼ measure lemon juice, dash Pernod. Shake over ice and strain into a cocktail glass.

Corpse Reviver [5] (Cktl) ½ measure Cognac, ½ measure Calvados, ¼ measure sweet vermouth. Shake over ice and strain into a cocktail glass.

Corpse Reviver [6] (Cktl) ⅓ measure Cognac, ⅓ measure orange juice, ⅓ measure lemon juice, dash grenadine. Shake over ice, strain into a flute glass, top with iced Champagne and a slice of orange.

Corpse Reviver (USA) a pick-me-up cocktail.

Corquete (Sp) a knife with a curved tip used in the harvesting of the grape.

Corrales Winery (USA) a winery based in Corrales, New Mexico. Produces mainly table wines.

Corralillo (Chile) a winery based in San Antonio. Grape varieties includes: Cabernet sauvignon, Malbec, Merlot. Label: Matetic Vineyards.

Corral Tinto Rioja (Sp) a red wine produced by Bodegas Corral S.A. Alta, Rioja. Is oak and bottle-matured.

Correas (Arg) a winery based at Tupungato, Maipú, Mendoza. Grape varieties: Torrontés, Syrah, Malbec, Sangiovese, Cabernet sauvignon.

Correct (Eng) a term used to describe a wine with all the right characteristics for its type and origin. Not necessarily a fine wine.

Correction (Eng) the addition of sugar, acid, tannin or the removal of excess acid or tannin in wines. Also the blending of wines. Practised to maintain uniformity and improve the wine. Strict laws to this practice vary from country to country.

Corredor (Sp) wine broker.

Correggia [Matteo] (It) a D.O.C. Barbera d'Alba producer in Piemonte. Wines include Bricco Marun.

Corretto (It) a coffee and grappa drink.

Corrida (Sp) the brand-name for a range of Spanish wines distributed in the U.K. by Stowells of Chelsea, London. Produced by José Lopez Bertran, Tarragona. Are sold in Spain under the Vinate label.

Corroborar (Sp) to fortify/to strengthen.

Corsé (Switz) (Fr) full-bodied and high in alcohol.

Corsendonk Agnus (Bel) a bottle conditioned pale ale 8% alc by vol. brewed by the Brouwerij du Bocq, Purnode for Corsendonk.

Corsendonk Pater (Bel) a bottle conditioned dark beer brewed by the Brouwerij du Bocq, Purnode for Corsendonk.

Corsica (Fr) an island producing red and rosé wines usually strong and aromatic. A.C: Vin de Corse. Has six sub-regions: Calvi, Coteaux d'Ajaccio, Figari, Patrimonio, Porte Vecchio and Sartène. Local grapes include Niellucio, Sciacarerllo.

Corsican Bounty Cocktail (Cktl) ½ measure Mandarine Napoléon, 1 measure Malibu, 1 measure lemon juice, dash orgeat, dash egg white. Shake well over ice, strain into a cocktail glass, top with a slice of lemon and a green cocktail cherry.

Cortaccio (It) the label of a 100% Cabernet sauvignon wine from Villa Cafaggio in Tuscany.

Cortado (Sp) a Sherry-style between an Amontillado and an Oloroso, classified as Un, Dos, Tres, Cuarto.

Cortaillod (Switz) a red wine of the Neuchâtel

C

region from the Pinot noir grape. Also a pink wine called Cortaillod Oeil de Perdrix.

Cortaillod Oeil de Perdrix (Switz) *see* Cortaillod.

Corte (Fr) a wine district of central Corsica that produces full-flavoured wines.

Corte (Port) the name given to the process of treading grapes, denotes the first treading which crushes the grapes to release the best juice.

Corte [La] (It) a red I.G.T. wine produced from 100% Sangiovese grapes by Castello di Querceto in Tuscany.

Corte Majoli (It) a winery based in the Veneto region. Produces: DOC Valpolicella, DOC Amarone della Valpolicella.

Cortes (Sp) a still natural spring mineral water. Mineral contents (milligrammes per litre): Sodium 6.4mg/l, Calcium 81.9mg/l, Magnesium 7.2mg/l, Potassium 0.7mg/l, Bicarbonates 268.4mg/l, Chlorides 8.7mg/l, Sulphates 17.6mg/l, Fluorides <1mg/l, Nitrates 7mg/l.

Cortes de Cima Vineyards (Port) winery. Website: http://www.cortesdecima.pt 'E'mail: cortesdecima@ip.pt

Cortese (It) a white grape variety grown in Piemonte and Liguria.

Cortese [Giuseppe] (It) a small wine producer based in Barbaresco, Piemonte (has vineyards on Rabaya Hill).

Cortese di Galvi (It) a D.O.C.G. white wine from Piemonte produced from the Cortese grape. A D.O.C. applies to the sparkling wine produced by the natural process from musts or wines according to the regulations.

Cortese Spumante (It) a D.O.C. sparkling wine from Piemonte. *see* Colli Tortonesi Cortese.

Corton (Fr) a Grand Cru vineyard in the A.C. commune of Aloxe-Corton, Côte de Beaune, Burgundy. Many climats within the vineyard use the name. i.e. Corton-Bressandes, Corton-Charlemagne. Also known as Le Corton. Part lies in the A.C. commune of Pernand-Vergelesses (red and white).

Corton-Bressandes (Fr) a Grand Cru climat in the vineyard of Corton, A.C. Aloxe-Corton, Côte de Beaune, Burgundy. Also known as Les Bressandes.

Corton Charlemagne (Fr) a Grand Cru climat [part] in the vineyard of Corton, A.C. Aloxe-Corton, Côte de Beaune, Burgundy. Part is also in the A.C. commune of Pernand-Vergelesses. Is also known as Le Charlemagne. (red and white) 25ha.

Corton-Chaumes (Fr) a Grand Cru climat [part] in the vineyard of Corton, A.C. Aloxe-Corton, Côte de Beaune, Burgundy. Is also known as Les Chaumes (red and white).

Corton Clos du Roi (Fr) a Grand Cru climat in the vineyard of Corton, A.C. Aloxe-Corton, Côte de Beaune, Burgundy (red and white).

Corton-Combes (Fr) a Grand Cru climat [part] in the vineyard of Corton, A.C. Aloxe-Corton, Côte de Beaune, Burgundy. Is also known as Les Combes. (red and white).

Corton En Pauland (Fr) *see* Corton-Pauland.

Corton-Fiètres (Fr) a Grand Cru climat in the vineyard of Corton, A.C. Aloxe-Corton, Côte de Beaune, Burgundy. Is also known as Les Fiètres.

Corton-Grèves (Fr) a Grand Cru climat in the vineyard of Corton, A.C. Aloxe-Corton, Côte de Beaune, Burgundy. Is also known as Les Grèves. (red and white).

Corton-Languettes (Fr) a Grand Cru climat [part] in the vineyard of Corton, A.C. Aloxe-Corton, Côte de Beaune, Burgundy. Also known as Les Languettes (red and white).

Corton La Vigne-au-Saint (Fr) a Grand Cru climat in the vineyard of Corton, A.C. Aloxe-Corton, Côte de Beaune, Burgundy (red and white).

Corton-Maréchaudes (Fr) a Grand Cru climat [part] in the vineyard of Corton, A.C. Aloxe-Corton, Côte de Beaune, Burgundy. Is also known as Les Maréchaudes (red and white).

Corton-Meix (Fr) a Grand Cru climat [part] in the vineyard of Corton, A.C. Aloxe-Corton, Côte de Beaune, Burgundy. Is also known as Les Meix (red and white).

Corton-Meix-Lallemant (Fr) a Grand Cru climat [part] in the vineyard of Corton, A.C. Aloxe-Corton, Côte de Beaune, Burgundy. Is also known as Les Meix-Lallemant (red and white).

Corton-Pauland (Fr) a Grand Cru climat [part] in the vineyard of Corton, A.C. Aloxe-Corton, Côte de Beaune, Burgundy. Is also known as Corton-En-Pauland or En Pauland (red and white).

Corton-Perrières (Fr) a Grand Cru climat in the vineyard of Corton, A.C. Aloxe-Corton, Côte de Beaune, Burgundy. Also known as Les Perrières (red and white).

Corton-Pougets (Fr) a Grand Cru climat [part] in the vineyard of Corton, A.C. Aloxe-Corton, Côte de Beaune, Burgundy. 9.82ha. Also known as Les Pougets (red and white).

Corton-Renardes (Fr) a Grand Cru climat in the vineyard of Corton, A.C. Aloxe-Corton, Côte de Beaune, Burgundy. Also known as Les Renardes (red and white).

Coruba (W.Ind) a brand of dark rum produced in Jamaica by the Rum Company (Jamaica) Ltd.

Coruche (Port) an I.P.R. wine of the I.P.R. region Ribatejo.

Corucho (Port) a new red wine produced by Quinta do Noval, D.O. Douro.

Çorum (Tur) a wine-producing area in northern Turkey. Produces mainly white wines.

Corvedale Brewery (Eng) a brewery (established 1999). (Add): The Sun Inn, Corfton, Craven Arms, Shropshire SY7 9DF. Brews: Dark & Delicious 4.6% alc by vol., Normans Pride 4.3% alc by vol., Secret Hope 4.5% alc by vol. Website: http://www.thesuninn.netfirms.com/corvedale.htm

Corvée [La] (Fr) a vineyard in the A.C. commune of Montagny, Côte Chalonnaise, Burgundy.

Corvées-Paget [Les] (Fr) a Premier Cru vineyard in the village of Prémeaux in the southern part of the A.C. commune of Nuits-Saint-Georges, Côte de Nuits, Burgundy 1.6ha.

385

C

Corvina (It) a red grape variety grown in the Veneto region. Also known as Cruina. Makes light red wines.

Corvina Veronese (It) a red wine grape used in the making of Bardolino wine.

Corvinone (It) a clone of Corvina, has thick skinned, open bunches but has less vigour than Corvina.

Corvo (It) a large producer of red and white wines based near Palermo in Sicily. *White*: Prima Goccia, Colomba Platino. *Red*: Vino Fiore, Duca Enrico.

COS (It) a winery based on the island of Sicily. Label: Cerasuolo di Vittoria.

COS (Pol) *abbr*: "*ut vinum habeat Colorem, Odorem et Saporem*" an old term used to describe the tokay wines of Hungary suitable for buying, is the abbreviation of Latin expression, which means that wine should have colour, scent and taste.

Cosbys (Eng) a 3.7% alc by vol. ale brewed by the Bells Brewery, Leicestershire.

Cosecha (Sp) harvest/vintage.

Cosecha Propia (Sp) own harvest/grapes.

Cosechero (Sp) denotes a small vineyard owner.

Cosentino (USA) a winery based in the Napa Valley, California. Grape varieties include: Cabernet sauvignon. Label: M Coz Meritage.

Cos-Labory (Fr) *see* Château Cos-Labory.

Cosmos Cocktail (Cktl) ⅔ measure fresh cream, ⅓ measure coconut cream, 2 measures tropical fruit drink, 6 fresh strawberries, blend altogether in a blender with a scoop of crushed ice, strain into a goblet and top with a strawberry.

Cossack (Eng) a vodka produced by Booth's C°. 40% alc by vol.

Cossack Cooler (Cktl) in a highball glass filled with ice, add 1 measure Cossack vodka, fill with equal amounts of ginger ale and medium dry cider. Garnish with a slice of lemon and rub the glass rim with a mint leaf.

Cossart Gordon (Mad) a Madeira company that produces under the '*Good Company*' label, as well as Cossarts.

Cosson [Gilles] (Fr) a Cognac producer. (Add): SARL La Grange Neuve, Guimps, 16300 Barbezieux. 50ha. Grande Champagne 35%, Petite Champagne 65%. Produces Très Vieille Réserve Fine Champagne 25 year old, Blason Fine Champagne 10 year old.

Costa Blanca (Sp) the name used by García Poveda in Alicante for a range of wines.

Costa Rica Coffee (W.Ind) a mild coffee with a strong nutty flavour. The beans are blue-green in colour. Gives a fine brew with low acidity, good body and flavour.

Costasera (It) a south-facing district within the Valpolicella region that is noted for its grapes used for amarone wines.

Coste [Pierre] (Fr) a négociant-éleveur based in Langon, Bordeaux.

Costers del Segre (Sp) a D.O. region inland near the town Lérida in Cataluña. 3,800ha. Split into 4 sub-zones: Artesa, Les Garrigues, Raïmat, Valls de Riu Corb. Grape varieties: Cabernet sauvignon,

Cariñena, Chardonnay, Garnacha blanca, Garnacha tinta, Macabeo, Mazuelo, Merlot, Monastrell, Parellada, Ull de llebre (Tempranillo or Gotim Bru), Trepat, Xarello. An experimental vineyard area so no irrigation allowed. Red, white and rosé wines produced.

Costières de Nîmes (Fr) an A.C. area in north-east Languedoc. Produces mainly red and rosé wines, plus some white. Before 1985 known as Costières du Gard. Grape varieties: Grenache, Mourvèdre, Syrah, Cabernet sauvignon, Merlot, Grenache blanc, Marsanne, Roussanne, Rolle, Ugni blanc, Bourboulenc, Maccabéo, Clairette.

Costières du Gard (Fr) a V.D.Q.S. red wine region of Languedoc. Since 1988 known as A.C. Costières de Nîmes.

Costières Mas Carlot (Fr) an A.C. red wine produced from Grenache and Syrah grapes in the A.C. Costières de Nîmes, Languedoc-Roussillon by Mas Carlot.

Costmary (Euro) *Chrysanthemum balsamuta* an old herb used for flavouring ale in the Middle-Ages of the family Compositae. Leaves only were used.

Costrel (Eng) a leather or earthenware flask which held water, wine or beer and was carried on a waist-belt in the Middle-Ages.

Costyn Vineyard (Wal) a vineyard (established 1978) based at Cosheston, Pembroke Dock, Dyfed. 0.35ha. Grape varieties: Madeleine angevine, Müller-Thurgau, Reichensteiner, Wrotham Pinot, plus others.

Côt (Fr) an alternative name for the Malbec/Auxerrois name in the Loire and Cahors. *see* Côt Noir.

Côte (Fr) slope/side of hill.

Côte [La] (Switz) a wine-producing district in the canton of Vaud, south-western Switzerland.

Coteau Brûlée (Fr) the label for a rosé wine produced by the Cave de Cairanne winery, Côtes-du-Rhône, Vaucluse.

Coteau de Migraine (Fr) a vineyard which produces red wine in Auxerre in the Yonne département, northern Burgundy 18.5ha.

Coteaux (Fr) hillside.

Coteaux Cathares (Fr) a Vin de Pays area in the Aude département in central-southern France. Produces red and rosé wines.

Coteaux Cévenois (Fr) a Vin de Pays area of the Gard département in south-western France. Produces red, rosé and dry white wines.

Coteaux Champenois (Fr) a new name for the still wine produced in the Champagne region. Was known as Vin Nature de Champagne but now E.C. regulations prevent the use of the old name.

Coteaux d'Aix-en-Provence (Fr) an A.C. region in southern France. Produced red, rosé and white wines from the Carignan, Cinsault, Clairette, Counoise, Mourvèdre, Muscat and Ugni blanc grapes. Received A.C. status in 1984.

Coteaux d'Ajaccio (Fr) an A.C. red, rosé and white wines of the Ajaccio region of Corsica.

Coteaux d'Ancenis (Fr) a Loire vineyard area around

C

the town of Ancenis which produces red and rosé wines from the Gamay grape. V.D.Q.S. status. The same vineyard produces Muscadet Coteaux de la Loire.

Coteaux de Baronnies (Fr) a Vin de Pays area in the Drôme département in south-eastern France.

Coteaux de Carthage (Afr) the brand-name for red and rosé wines made by the UCCVT in Tunisia.

Coteaux de Cèze (Fr) a Vin de Pays area within the Gard département in south-western France. Produces red, rosé and dry white wines.

Coteaux de Die (Fr) an A.C. area in the same production zone as sparkling Clairette de Die. Produces still white wines from Clairette grapes.

Coteaux de Fenouillèdes (Fr) a Vin de Pays area within the Pyrénées-Orièntales département in south-western France.

Coteaux de Fontcaude (Fr) a Vin de Pays area within the Hérault département in southern France. Produces red, rosé and dry white wines.

Coteaux de Glanes (Fr) a Vin de Pays area within the Lot département in southern France.

Coteaux de Gresivaudan (Fr) a Vin de Pays area in the Isère département, central-eastern France.

Coteaux de Kefraya [Les] (Leb) a 250ha. vineyard in the Bekaa Valley. Grape varieties: Cabernet sauvignon, Cinsault, Syrah, Grenache, Mourvèdre. *See also* Coteaux du Kefraya.

Coteaux de Ksara (Leb) a brand of white wine produced in Lebanon.

Coteaux de la Cabrerisse (Fr) a Vin de Pays area within the Aude département in central-southern France. Produces red and rosé wines.

Coteaux de la Cité de Carcassonne (Fr) a Vin de Pays area within the Aude département in central-southern France.

Coteaux de la Loire (Fr) a separate A.C. within the region of Anjou-Saumur, Loire (for rosé).

Coteaux de la Loire-Rosé de Cabernet (Fr) an A.C. rosé wine made from the Cabernet franc grape in the Coteaux de la Loire.

Coteaux de la Méjanelle (Fr) a V.D.Q.S. wine-producing district in the Hérault département. Produces white wines.

Coteaux de l'Ardèche (Fr) a Vin de Pays area within the Ardèche département in south-east France.

Coteaux de l'Aubance (Fr) an A.C. white wines. Separate A.C. in the district of Anjou-Saumur of the Loire. Produces sweet white wines from the Chenin blanc grape.

Coteaux de l'Aubance-Rosé de Cabernet (Fr) an A.C. rosé from the Anjou-Saumur region of the Loire. Made from the Cabernet franc grape.

Coteaux de Lézignanais (Fr) a Vin de Pays area within the Aude département in central-southern France. Produces red and rosé wines.

Coteaux de Libron (Fr) a Vin de Pays area within the Hérault département in southern France. Produces red, rosé and dry white wines.

Coteaux de Mascara (Alg) an A.O.G. wine-producing area in the Oran département. Produces red, rosé and white wines.

Coteaux de Miramont (Fr) a Vin de Pays area within the Aude département in central-southern France. Produces red and rosé wines.

Coteaux de Murviel (Fr) a Vin de Pays area within the Hérault département in southern France. Produces red and rosé wines.

Coteaux de Narbonne (Fr) a Vin de Pays area within the Aude département in central-southern France. Produces red and rosé wines.

Coteaux d'Enserune (Fr) a Vin de Pays area within the Hérault département in southern France. Produces mainly red wines.

Coteaux de Patras (Gre) a medium-dry white wine made from the grape Rhoditis, produced in Peloponnese.

Coteaux de Peyriac (Fr) a Vin de Pays area within the Aude département in central-southern France. Produces red and rosé wines.

Coteaux de Pierrevert (Fr) an A.C. rosé wine from near the River Durance, north of Manosque in the Rhône.

Coteaux de Quercy (Fr) a Vin de Pays area within the Lot département in south-western France. Produces red and rosé wines.

Coteaux de Saint-Christol (Fr) an A.C. red wine-producing district in Languedoc-Roussillon region, southern France.

Coteaux de Saumur (Fr) an A.C. within the Anjou-Saumur district of the Loire.

Coteaux de Saumur-Rosé de Cabernet (Fr) an A.C. rosé of the Saumur region of Anjou-Saumur in the Loire. Made from the Cabernet franc (now sold as A.C. Cabernet rosé).

Coteaux-des-Baux-en-Provence (Fr) an A.C. wine-producing region in south-eastern France. Produces red, rosé and a litle white wine. Received A.C. in 1985.

Coteaux des Fenouillèdes (Fr) a Vin de Pays area in the Pyrénées-Orièntales département in south-western France.

Coteaux de Termenès (Fr) a Vin de Pays area within the Aude département in the Languedoc-Roussillon region, southern France.

Coteaux de Tlemcen (Alg) an A.O.G. wine-producing area in the Oran département. Produces red, rosé and white wines.

Coteaux de Touraine (Fr) a wine region of the central Loire. Wines produced are Bourgueil, St. Nicolas de Bourgueil, Vouvray and Montlouis.

Coteaux de Touraine (Fr) an A.C. red, rosé and white wines designation which is now no longer used.

Coteaux de Touraine Mousseux (Fr) an A.C. sparkling wine of the Touraine region of the Loire (now no longer used as A.C. designation).

Coteaux de Vérargues (Fr) an A.C. wine-producing in the Coteaux du Languedoc, southern France. Produces red and rosé wines.

Coteaux Diois (Fr) granted A.C. in 1994 for still wines in the Rhône.

Coteaux du Cap Corse (Fr) an A.C. red, rosé dry and semi-sweet white wines from Corsica. Also VdN. (from Muscat and Vermentino grapes).

C

Coteaux du Cher et de l'Arnon (Fr) a Vin de Pays area in the Cher and Indre départements of western France. Produces red, rosé and white wines.

Coteaux du Giennois (Fr) a 154ha. A.C. wine area of the Loire between Orléans and Pouilly-sur-Loire. Produces red and white wines from Gamay, Pinot noir and Sauvignon blanc.

Coteaux du Kefraya (Leb) the former name for Château Kefraya in the Lebanon. *See also* Coteaux de Kefraya.

Coteaux du Khanguet (Afr) a noted wine-producing area in Tunisia.

Coteaux du Languedoc (Fr) an A.C. of the Languedoc in the Midi, southern France. Grape varieties: Bourboulenc, Carignan and Cinsault (maximum 50%), Clairette, Grenache (rouge and blanc), Marsanne, Mourvèdre, Picpoul, Roussanne, Rolle and Syrah. Received A.C. in 1985. Has 7 sub-region A.C.'s: Gres de Montpellier, La Clape, Pézenas, Pic St. Loup, Terrasses de Béziers, Terrasses du Larzac, Terres de Sommières. Has 168 communes including: Cabrières, La Clape, Méjanelle, Montpeyroux, Picpoul de Pinet, Pic Saint-Loup, Quatourze, Saint-Christol, Saint-Drézery, Véragues, Saint-Georges-d'Orques, Saint-Saturnin.

Coteaux du Layon (Fr) a separate A.C. within the region of Anjou-Saumur of the Loire. Produces fine, sweet (**Botrytis cinerea**) wines from the Chenin blanc. *see* Coteaux du Layon-Chaume and Quarts de Chaume.

Coteaux du Layon-Chaume (Fr) an A.C. sweet white wine of the Anjou-Saumur region. *see* Coteaux du Layon. Minimum alc by vol. 13%.

Coteaux du Layon-Rosé de Cabernet (Fr) an A.C. rosé wine made from the Cabernet franc grape in the Anjou-Saumur region of the Loire. Now sold as A.C. Cabernet rosé.

Coteaux du Littoral Audois (Fr) a Vin de Pays area within the Aude département in central-southern France. Produces red and rosé wines.

Coteaux du Loir (Fr) an A.C. wines of Touraine, Loire. Dry or medium white from Chenin blanc. Red and rosé from Gamay, Cabernet franc, Côt.

Coteaux du Loiret (Fr) an old A.C. red, rosé and white wines of the Loire.

Coteaux du Lubéron (Fr) *see* Côtes du Lubéron.

Coteaux du Lyonnaise (Fr) an A.C. red, rosé and white wines produced near Lyon in the Rhône region.

Coteaux du Pont-du-Gard (Fr) a Vin de Pays area within the Gard département in south-western France. Produces red, rosé and dry white wines.

Coteaux du Salagou (Fr) a Vin de Pays area within the Hérault département in southern France. Produces red and rosé wines

Coteaux du Salavès (Fr) a Vin de Pays area within the Gard département in south-western France. Produces red, rosé and dry white wines.

Coteaux du Tessalah (Alg) a wine-producing area in the Oran département. Produces red, rosé and white wines.

Coteaux du Tricastin (Fr) a A.C. red wine district on the left bank of the Rhône. 12 communes produce light red wines. Grape varieties: Carignan, Cinsault, Grenache, Mourvèdre and Picpoul.

Coteaux du Vendômois (Fr) a V.D.Q.S. red, rosé and white wines produced north of Blois in the Loire.

Coteaux du Vidourle (Fr) a Vin de Pays area within the Gard département in south-western France. Produces red, rosé and dry white wines.

Coteaux du Zaccar (Alg) a wine-producing area in the Alger département. Produces red, rosé and white wines.

Coteaux et Terrasses de Montauban (Fr) a Vin de Pays area in the Tarn-et-Garonne département, south-western France. Produces red and rosé wines.

Coteaux Flaviens (Fr) a Vin de Pays area within the Gard département of south-western France. Produces red, rosé and dry white wines.

Coteaux Mascara (Alg) a principal wine-producing area in the Oran département.

Coteaux Varois (Fr) an A.C. area within the Var département in Provence, south-eastern France. Produces red, rosé and dry white wines. 1,800ha. Awarded A.C. in 1993. Grape varieties include: Rolle, Viognier, Cabernet sauvignon, Carignan, Cinsaut, Grenache, Mourvèdre, Syrah, Tibouren.

Côte Blonde (Fr) the name for half of the Côte Rôtie district in the northern Rhône. So named because of the light coloured soil, composed of silico-calcerous. *see* Côte Brune.

Côte Brune (Fr) the name for half of the Côte Rôtie district of the northern Rhône. So named because of the brown coloured soil, a brownish clay. *see* Côte Blonde.

Côte Catalane (Fr) a Vin de Pays area within the Pyrénées-Orièntales département in south-western France.

Côte Chalonnaise (Fr) a region (900ha) in the southern half of Burgundy. Has 3 A.C. **red districts**: Givry, Mercurey, and Rully. 1 A.C. **white district**: Montagny. The red wines made from the Pinot noir, the white from the Chardonnay and Pinot blanc.

Côte d'Azur de la Côte d'Or (Fr) *see* Domaine de Bévy.

Côte de Beaune (Fr) the southern half of the Côte d'Or in Burgundy. Noted for Grand Cru white wines made with the Chardonnay grape. All white Grand Crus (except Musigny) are found here. Home to Corton and Premier Cru red wines made from the Pinot noir. *See also* Côte de Nuits, Hospices de Beaune.

Côte de Beaune-Villages (Fr) an A.C. red wines produced from the Pinot noir grape from communes within the Côte de Beaune in the southern half of the Côte d'Or, Burgundy. Minimum alc by vol. of 10.5%.

Côte de Brouilly (Fr) an A.C. Cru Beaujolais-Villages, Burgundy. Has 310ha. under vines.

Côte de Columbia (USA) a range of wines produced by Columbia Crest Winery, Columbia Valley,

C

Washington. Grapes include Grenache and Lemburger.

Côte de Dijon (Fr) an area based north of the A.C. Fixin, Côte de Nuits, Burgundy. Was once a top growth region. Now planted mainly with the Gamay grape.

Côte de Fontenay (Fr) an A.C. Premier Grand Cru Chablis. Often is re-classified as the Premier Cru Fourchaume.

Côte de la Mouleyre (Fr) a vineyard in the A.C. Saint-Émilion. (Add): Saint-Christophe-des-Bardes, 33330 Saint-Émilion. (Com): Saint-Christophe-des-Bardes.

Côte de Léchet (Fr) a Premier Cru vineyard in the A.C. Chablis, Burgundy.

Côte de Nuits (Fr) the northern half of the Côte d'Or in Burgundy. Noted for Grand Cru red wines made with the Pinot noir grape. All red Grand Crus (except Corton) are found here. *See also* Côte de Beaune.

Côte de Nuits-Villages (Fr) previously known as Vins Fins de la Côte de Nuits. Consists of the communes: Brochon, Fixin, Prissey, Corgolin and Comblanchien. The latter three cannot use their commune names as a separate A.C. Grape variety: Pinot noir. Minimum alc by vol. 10.5% red and 11% white.

Côte de Parnasse (Gre) the name for red and white wines from Hatikoi.

Côte des Bar (Fr) a region (7000ha) within the A.C. Champagne containing the villages of Bar sur Aube, Bar sur Seine, Bayel and Les Riceys.

Côte des Blancs (Fr) a vineyard area of the Champagne region. Produces white grapes (Chardonnay) for Champagne production.

Côte des Colombes (USA) a vineyard based in Banks, Oregon. 4ha. Produces Vitis vinifera wines.

Côte des Prés-Girots (Fr) a Premier Cru vineyard in the A.C. Chablis. Often reclassified as Premier Cru Les Fourneaux.

Côte d'Or (Fr) lit: 'golden hills', a top wine area of Burgundy. Consists of the Côte de Nuits in the northern half and the Côte de Beaune in the south.

Côte Droit (Cktl) ³⁄₁₀ measure Mandarine Napoléon, ³⁄₁₀ measure orange juice, ¹⁄₁₀ measure Calvados, ³⁄₁₀ measure Dubonnet. Shake well together over ice, strain into a highball glass with ice, top with a cherry and slice of orange.

Côte Hyot (Fr) a red wine produced in the Savoie region in south-eastern France.

Coterie (Fr) set or group. i.e. group of vine growers.

Coterie des Closiers de Montlouis (Fr) a wine society based in the Touraine district of the Loire.

Côte Roannaise (Fr) a V.D.Q.S. red and rosé wines produced in the Loire département, central France. Produced from the Gamay grape. Minimum alc by vol. 9%.

Côte Rôtie (Fr) a district in the northern Rhône. Made up of the Côte Blonde and Côte Brune. Villages: Ampuis, Tupin and Semons (vineyards are terraced). Grape varieties: Syrah for red and Viognier for white.

Côte Rôtie (Fr) a Premier Cru vineyard in the A.C. commune of Morey-Saint-Denis, Côte de Nuits, Burgundy 0.4ha.

Côte Rouvre [La] (Fr) a large vineyard in Avallon, Yonne département. Produces red and white wines.

Côtes (Fr) hills/vineyard slopes.

Côtes Canon-Fronsac (Fr) an A.C. district in central-eastern Bordeaux on the right bank of the river Gironde. Grape varieties: Cabernet franc, Cabernet sauvignon, Malbec and Merlot. Minimum alc by vol. 11%.

Côtes Catalanes (Fr) a Vin de Pays area in the Pyrénées-Orièntales département. Includes the canton of Rivesaltes.

Côtes d'Agly (Fr) an A.C. Vin doux Naturel from the Roussillon region on the Pyrénées border.

Côtes d'Auvergne (Fr) a V.D.Q.S. district near Clermont-Ferrand in central France. Produces red, rosé and white wines. 5 sub-regions: Boudes, Chateaugay, Corent, Chanturge and Madargues. Grape varieties: Chardonnay, Gamay à jus blanc and Pinot noir.

Côtes de Bergerac Moelleux (Fr) an A.C. sweet white wine from the Bergerac region of western France (12%–15% alc by vol).

Côtes de Blaye (Fr) an A.C. district in north-eastern Bordeaux. Also known as the Blaye. (Coms): Anglade, Berson, Blaye, Blaye-Plassac, Cadres, Cars, Cartelègue, Eyrons, Fours, Mazion, Plassac, St-Androny, St-Christ-de-Blaye, St-Genès, St-Genès-de-Blaye, St-Girons, St-Martin-Caussaude, St-Paul and St-Seurin-Cursac. Red wines of minimum alc by vol. 10.5%, also white wines. *See also* Premières Côtes de Blaye.

Côtes de Bordeaux (Fr) a new (2006) A.C. consisting of the Côtes de Blaye, Côtes de Bourg, Côtes de Castillon, Côtes de Francs and Premières Côtes de Bordeaux. *See also* Côtes de Bordeaux Saint-Macaire.

Côtes de Bordeaux Saint-Macaire (Fr) an A.C. white wine district in the southern region of Bordeaux. Sweet white wines. Minimum alc by vol. 11.5%.

Côtes de Bourg (Fr) an A.C. district in the north-eastern Bordeaux. Also known as the Bourg. (Coms): Bayon, Bourg, Comps, Gauriac, Lansac, Samonac, Prignac-Marcamps, Monbrier, St-Ciers-de-Canesse, St-Seurin-Bourg, Pugnac, Tauriac and Teuillac. Red wines of minimum alc by vol. 10.5%, also white wines. *See also* Bourgeais.

Côtes de Brian (Fr) a Vin de Pays area within the Hérault département in southern France.

Côtes de Bruhlois (Fr) a Vin de Pays area within the Lot-et-Garonne département in south-western France.

Côtes de Buzet (Fr) an A.C. area based south-east of Bordeaux. Produces mainly red with some white wines. Minimum alc by vol. 10%. *see* Cuvée Napoléon.

Côtes de Castillon (Fr) an A.C. red wine region in the south-eastern part of Bordeaux (since 1989). Wines often sold under the A.C. Bordeaux Supérieur designation. 2,945ha.

C

Côtes de Céressou (Fr) a Vin de Pays area within the Hérault département in southern France. Produces red, rosé and dry white wines.

Côtes de Duras (Fr) an A.C. red and white wine-producing region based east of Bergerac. Grape varieties: Cabernet, Malbec, Mauzac, Muscadelle, Sauvignon blanc and Sémillon. Minimum alc by vol. 10.5%.

Côtes de Francs (Fr) an A.C. red wine area in Bordeaux with 3 communes: Francs, Saint-Cibard, Tayac. *see* Bordeaux Côtes de Franc.

Côtes de Fronsac (Fr) a small A.C. district in eastern Bordeaux. Red wines only.

Côtes de Gascogne (Fr) a Vin de Pays area within the Gers département in central-southern France.

Côtes de Gien (Fr) a V.D.Q.S. area between Orléans and Pouilly-sur-Loire in the Loire. Produces red and white wines.

Côtes de la Malepère (Fr) a V.D.Q.S. red and rosé wines from the region of Carcassonne in the Aude département.

Côtes de Lastours (Fr) a Vin de Pays area in the Aude département in central-southern France.

Côtes de Meliton (Gre) an A.O.Q.S. red, white and rosé wines, main estate is Château Carras.

Côtes de Millau (Fr) a Vin de Pays area of southern France.

Côtes de Montestruc (Fr) a Vin de Pays area within the Gers département in central-southern France.

Côtes de Montravel (Fr) an A.C. white (medium-sweet) wine-producing district of the Bergerac region. Minimum alc by vol. 12%.

Côtes de Pérignan (Fr) a Vin de Pays area within the Aude département in central-southern France.

Côtes de Prouille (Fr) a Vin de Pays area in the Aude département in central-southern France.

Côtes de Provence (Fr) an A.C. of Provence. Fine wines in which some 12 vineyards can use the designation Grand Cru. Red, rosé and white wines produced (received A.C. in 1977).

Côtes de Rol (Fr) a vineyard. (Com): Saint-Émilion. A.C. Saint-Émilion, Bordeaux 4ha.

Côtes de Saint-Mont (Fr) a V.D.Q.S. area within the Gers département in central-southern France. Produces red, rosé and white wines.

Côtes de Saussignac (Fr) an A.C. commune in the Côtes de Bergerac, south-western France. Produces sweet wines.

Côtes de Thau (Fr) a Vin de Pays area within the Hérault département in southern France. Produces red, rosé and dry white wines.

Côtes de Thongue (Fr) a Vin de Pays area within the Hérault département in southern France. Produces red, rosé and white wines.

Côtes de Toul (Fr) a 90ha. area producing a light A.C. rosé wine (Vins Gris) from gamay, Pinot noir, Pinot meunier, Auxerrois and Aubin, plus white and red wines.

Côtes de Toul (Fr) a V.D.Q.S. wine produced in Lorraine near Nancy. Light red, rosé and white wines produced. Sited within the communes of Blénod-les-Toul, Bruley, Bulligny, Charmes-la-Côte, Dongermain, Écouvres, Lucey and Mont-le-Vignoble.

Côtes d'Olt [Les] (Fr) the only large co-operative based in A.C. Cahors, south-western France. 512 members. Grape varieties: Malbec, Merlot, Tannat. Sells under the brand-names of Côtes d'Olt, Comte André de Montpezat and Château les Bouysses.

Côtes du Brulhois (Fr) a V.D.Q.S. since 1984, red and rosé wines produced from Bordeaux and indigenous grapes.

Côtes du Cabardès et de l'Orbiel (Fr) a V.D.Q.S. red and rosé wine-producing area in the Languedoc. Lies in the Aude département part of the Coteaux du Languedoc, south-western France.

Côtes du Condomois (Fr) a Vin de Pays area within the Lot-et-Garonne département in central-southern France.

Côtes du Couchois (Fr) a district (240ha) within the Burgundy region. Produces wines under the A.C. Bourgogne-Côtes-du-Couchois (Coms): Couches, Dracy-lès-Couches, Saint Jean de Trézy, Saint Maurice les Couches, Saint Pierre de Varennes and Saint Sernin du Plain. Grape variety: Pinot noir.

Côtes du Forez (Fr) a V.D.Q.S. district in central Rhône, southern France. Grape variety: Gamay rouge à jus blanc.

Côtes du Fronton (Fr) a small A.C. red wine-producing district in south-western France. Grape variety mainly Negrette with Cabernets, Gamay and Syrah. Min. alc by vol. 10.5%.

Côtes du Frontonnaise (Fr) *see* Côtes du Fronton.

Côtes du Haut-Roussillon (Fr) a Vin Doux Naturel from the Roussillon region of southern France.

Côtes du Jura (Fr). A.C. wine region at the foot of the Jura mountains in eastern France. Noted for *Vin de paille* (straw wine) and *Vin jaune* (yellow wine) from the commune of Arbois. Red, rosé and white wines produced.

Côtes du Jura Mousseux (Fr) sparkling wines produced by méthode traditionelle (or méthode gaillaçoise) in the Savoie region in south-eastern France. Made from Chardonnay and Pinot blanc grapes.

Côtes du Lubéron (Fr) an A.C. region of the Rhône. Produces red, rosé and dry white wines.

Côtes du Marmandais (Fr) an A.C. district near Marmande in the Lot-et-Garonne département in south-western France. Produces red wines from the Abouriou grape, plus a little white and rosé wine. Minimum alc by vol. 10%.

Côtes du Meliton (Gre) an A.O.Q.S. wine-producing area in Macedonia. Produces red, rosé and white wines. *see* Carras. Also spelt Côtes de Meliton.

Côtes du Rhône (Fr) a large wine region in southern France. Noted for heady red wines. Produces all styles of wines. Covers the départements of Ardèche, Drôme, Gard, Vaucluse, Rhône and the Loire. Minimum alc by vol. of 11%. *see* Château Grillet, Châteauneuf-du-Pape, Condrieu, Cornas, Côte Rôtie, Crozes-Hermitage, Gigondas,

C

Hermitage, Lirac, Saint-Joseph, Saint-Péray and Tavel. Website: http://www.vins-rhone.com

Côtes du Rhône-Villages (Fr) an A.C. designation of the central Rhône region. Communes can use their own name or Côtes du-Rhône-Villages A.C. 19 Villages: Cairanne, Chusclan, Comté de Signargues, Laudun, Massif d'Uchaux, Plan de Dieu, Puymeras, Rasteau, Rochegude, Roaix, Rousset-les-Vignes, Sablet, Séguret, St. Gervais, St. Maurice-sur-Eygues, St. Pantaléon-les-Vignes, Valréas, Vinsobres and Visan. Website: http://www.vins-rhone.com

Côtes du Roussillon (Fr) an A.C. wine-producing region in south-eastern France. Produces red, rosé white and VdN wines. Grape varieties: Carignan, Cinsault, Grenache, Lledoner pelut, Macabeo and Mourvèdre.

Côtes du Roussillon-Villages (Fr) an A.C. red wines from the better parts of the Roussillon region in south-eastern France. Minimum alc by vol. 12%.

Côtes du Tarn (Fr) a Vin de Pays area within the Lot-et-Garonne département in central-southern France.

Côtes du Ventoux (Fr) an A.C. district of the eastern Rhône. Produces red, rosé and white wines. Also A.C. Mazan (a VdL).

Côtes du Vidourle (Fr) a Vin de Pays area within the Gard département in the Languedoc-Roussillon region.

Côtes du Vivarais (Fr) a V.D.Q.S. district in the south of the Massif Centrale. Produces light red, rosé and white wines.

Côtes et Pied de Côtes (Fr) lit: 'hillsides at the foot of the slopes', a zone of production in the Saint-Émilion, Bordeaux.

Côtes Frontonnais (Fr) see Côtes du Fronton.

Côtes Roannaises (Fr) a V.D.Q.S. red and rosé wine-producing area in the Loire. Grape variety: Gamay St. Romain à jus blanc. Also known as Vin de Renaison.

Côtes Rocheuses (Fr) a cave co-opérative based in Saint-Émilion, Bordeaux. Part of Royal Saint-Émilion. 775ha. in total.

Côtes Saint-Émilion (Fr) a district within the A.C. Saint-Émilion, Bordeaux.

Côte St. André (Fr) a white wine from Vienne in Dauphiny in the Isère département, south-eastern France.

Cotesti (Rum) Focsani red and white table wines.

Cotignac (Fr) a quince-flavoured liqueur 14.8% alc by vol.

Cotilia (It) a natural spring mineral water brand.

Cotleigh Brewery (Eng) a brewery (established 1979). (Add): Ford Road, Wivellscombe, Taunton, Somerset TA4 2RE. Brews: Barn Owl Bitter 4.5% alc by vol., Golden Eagle 4.2% alc by vol., Old Buzzard 4.8% alc by vol (1048 O.G). , Tawny Bitter 3.8% alc by vol (1040 O.G)., also Hawkshead 5.5% alc by vol., Nutcracker 1036 O.G., WB Bitter 1037 O.G., Red Nose Reindeer, Harrier Spa 3.6% alc by vol., Snowy Ale (a winter ale), Magpie. Website: http://www.cotleighbrewery.co.uk 'E'mail: sales@cotleighbrewery.co.uk

Cotnari (Rum) a noted wine region producing sweet botrytised wines from Feteasca Alba, Francusa, Grasa, Tamaîoasa grapes.

Cotnari (Rum) a strong natural wine based on the Grasa grape which is subject to **Botrytis cinerea**. Produced in the Cotnari region.

Côt Noir (Fr) an alternative name for the Malbec (or Auxerrois) grape in Cahors.

Coto de Imaz (Sp) a red wine produced by Bodegas El Coto, S.A. Rioja. Made from the Tempranillo grape (oak-matured), a vintage style is also produced.

Côto de Mamoelas (Port) a D.O.C. bottle-fermented Vinho Verde (Alvarhino) wine produced by the Provam co-operative.

Cotswold Brewing Company (Eng) a brewery based in Cirencester, Gloucester. Brews: Monkey's Fist a very strong British beer sold in Champagne-style bottle with a cork and wire).

Cotswold Cottage Cider (Eng) a dry or medium-sweet cider produced by the Frampton Village Cider C°.

Cotswold Spring (Eng) a still (blue cap) and sparkling (green cap) natural spring mineral water (established 1994). (Add): Dodington Ash, Chipping Sodbury, BS37 6RX. Mineral contents (milligrammes per litre): Sodium 9mg/l, Calcium 133mg/l, Magnesium 4mg/l, Potassium 1.5mg/l, Bicarbonates 261mg/l, Chlorides 22mg/l, Sulphates 59mg/l, Nitrates 11.2mg/l. pH 7.8

Cotswold Way (Eng) a 4.2% alc by vol. ale brewed by the Wickwar Brewing C°. Ltd., Gloucestershire.

Cottabus (Gre) see Kottabos.

Cottage Brand (Eng) a herb farm based near Canterbury, Kent. Produces a wide range of herb teas.

Cottage Brewing Company (Eng) a brewery (established 1994). (Add): The Old Cheese Dairy, Hornblottom Road, Lovington, Castle Carey, Somerset BA7 7PS. Brews: Champflower Ale 4.2% alc by vol., Golden Arrow 4.5% alc by vol., G.W.R. 5.4% alc by vol., Wheeltappers Ale 4% alc by vol., S & D Bitter 4.4% alc by vol. Normans Conquest 7% alc by vol. (a barley wine), Old Freckled Ken 4.5% alc by vol., S & D 4.4% alc by vol., Southern Bitter 3.7% alc by vol.

Cottage Vineyards (USA) a winery based in Marlboro, Hudson Valley, New York. Produces American and hybrid wines.

Cottanera (It) a winery based on the island of Sicily. Label: L'Ardenza Mondeuse. Website: http://www.cottanera.it

Cotte [La] (S.Afr) the prestige label of the Franschhoek Co-operative.

Cotto [Vino] (It) lit: 'cooked wine', i.e. concentrated, a speciality of a few regions.

Cottonwood Canyon (USA) a winery based in the Santa Maria Valley, Santa Barbara County, California. Grape variety: Pinot noir. Label: Sharon's Vineyard.

Cottonwood Valley (Austr) a natural spring mineral

391

C

water. Mineral contents (milligrammes per litre): Sodium 24mg/l, Calcium 12mg/l, Magnesium 15mg/l, Potassium 5mg/l, Bicarbonates 158mg/l, Chlorides 27mg/l.

Cottorella (It) a sparkling natural spring mineral water from Cottorella. Mineral contents (milligrammes per litre): Sodium 3.92mg/l, Calcium 96mg/l, Magnesium 2.1mg/l, Potassium 0.35mg/l, Bicarbonates 305mg/l, Chlorides 9mg/l, Sulphates 6mg/l, Nitrates 0.4mg/l, Silicates 4mg/l. pH 7.4

Cotturi and Sons (USA) a winery based in Sonoma County, California. Grape varieties: Cabernet sauvignon, Chardonnay, Gewürztraminer, Johannisberg riesling, Pinot noir, Sémillon and Zinfandel. Produces varietal wines.

Couche (Ch.Isles) the name given to the pulp (cheese) residue left from the apples after the juice has been extracted in cider production.

Couche Père et Fils (Fr) a Champagne producer. (Add): 29, Grande Rue, 10110 Buxeuil. Produces vintage and non-vintage Champagnes. Vintages: 1995, 1996, 1997, 1998, 1999, 2000. 'E'mail: champagne.coucher@wanadoo.fr

Couches (Fr) a commune of A.C. Bourgogne Côtes du Couchois.

Couchey (Fr) a commune which joins Marsannay-la-Côte and has its wines under the same A.C.

Couderc (Fr) a famous French hybridiser, a grape named after him is grown in Brazil.

Couderc (Sp) a rootstock used in Tarragona, a cross between *Vitis riparia* and *Vitis berlandieri*.

Coudert Père et Fils (Fr) a winery based in the A.C. Cru Beaujolais Fleurie, southern Burgundy. Label: Clos de la Roilette.

Cougar's Cooler (Cktl) ½ measure vodka, ½ measure Oolgaard blueberry liqueur, 1 measure lemon juice. Shake well over ice, strain into a 350 ml. (12fl.oz) highball glass filled with ice, garnish with a cherry and slices of citrus fruits.

Couillebaud [Rémy] (Fr) a Cognac producer. (Add): Nle 141 Malvielle, Moulidars, 16290 Hiersac. 22ha. in the Fins Bois. Produces ***, V.S.O.P. and Napoléon.

Coulage (Fr) leakage, loss of liquid from a cask.

Coulange-la-Vineuse (Fr) a vineyard producing red wine in Auxerre in the Yonne département in north-central France.

Coulant (Fr) lit: 'flowing', term used to describe an easy drinking wine.

Coulée de Serrant (Fr) a noted vineyard at Savennières (first planted in 1130 by Cistercian monks) which has its own A.C. Produces a light, rich white wine from Chenin blanc grapes on volcanic soil. Alo knwn as Clos de la Coulée de Serrant. see Roche-aux-Moines (La).

Couleuse (Fr) a term used in the Champagne region for a sparkling wine that has lost its gas.

Coulommes-la-Montagne (Fr) a Cru Champagne village in the Canton de Ville-en-Tardenois. District: Reims.

Coulonges (Fr) a commune in the Charente-

Maritime département whose grapes are classed Petite Champagne (Cognac).

Coulure (Fr) a vine malady caused by rain and mineral deficiency in the soil that can have a disastrous effect at the crucial stage of blossoming. The blossoms fall off and berries become stunted. There is no real cure but careful fertilising will help.

Couly Dutheil (Fr) a noted producer of Chinon wines in the Anjou-Saumur, Loire. (Add): 12 Rue Diderot BP. 234, 37502 Chinon.

Counoise (Fr) a red grape variety of the Rhône, used for its vinosity, freshness and bouquet.

Counseil Interprofessionnel des Vins de Bordeaux (Fr) abbr: C.I.V.B. The controlling body for Bordeaux wines. (Add): 1 Cours du XXX Juliet, 33075 Bordeaux, Cedex.

Count Agusta (S.Afr) a winery based in Franschhoek. Grape variety: Chardonnay.

Count Currey Cocktail (Cktl) 40mls (⅓ gill) gin, 1 teaspoon powdered sugar. Shake over ice, strain into a Champagne flute and top with iced Champagne.

Counterpoint (USA) the second label of a wine produced by the Laurel Glen Vineyard, Hopland, Sonoma, California.

Count Rossi (Cktl) place 2 ice cubes in a small tumbler. Top with 40mls (⅓ gill) dry Martini and 40mls (⅓ gill) sweet Martini vermouths. Squeeze lemon rind over, stir and serve with a slice of orange.

Country Best Bitter (Eng) a 4.3% alc by vol. bitter beer brewed by McMullen & Sons Ltd., Hertfordshire.

Country Bitter (Eng) a cask-conditioned bitter 1036 O.G. brewed by the Queen Victoria home-brew public house in London.

Country Bitter (Eng) a cask-conditioned bitter 1041 O.G. brewed by McMullen's Brewery of Hertford, Hertfordshire.

Country Bitter (Eng) a keg bitter beer 1036 O.G. brewed by Usher's Brewery in Wiltshire.

Country Brew (Eng) a bottled pale ale 1050 O.G. brewed by Ridley's Brewery in Essex.

Country Bumpkin (Eng) a 6% alc by vol. ale brewed by the Country Life Brewery, Devon.

Country Cider (Eng) a low-strength cider produced by Merrydown C°. in Sussex.

Country Club Cooler (Cktl) place 2 dashes of grenadine into a collins glass with 50mls (2fl.ozs) soda water. Stir, add 2 ice cubes, 50mls (2fl.ozs) dry vermouth, top with ginger ale and a spiral of orange zest.

Country Creek (USA) a natural spring mineral water from Midland, Michigan.

Country Dale (Eng) liquid U.H.T. milk sold in individual cartons by Cadbury (part of Premier Beverages).

Country Girl (Gre) the name given to a range of medium-dry, red, rosé and white wines produced by Tsantali.

Country Life Brewery (Eng) a brewery (established

C

1998). (Add): The Big Ship, Abbotsham, Bideford, Devon EX39 5AP. Brews: Country Bumpkin 6% alc by vol., Golden Pig 4.7% alc by vol., H.B. 10% alc by vol., Laceys Real lager 5.2% alc by vol., Old Appledore 3.7% alc by vol., Wallop 4.4% alc by vol. Website: http://www.countrylifebrewery.co.uk 'E'mail: simon@countrylifebrewery.co.uk

Countryman Cider (Eng) a cider producer (established 1858). (Add): Felldownhead, Milton Abbot, Tavistock, Devon PL19 0QR. Company which produces fine ciders. Is helped by the St. Austell Brewery who have shares in the company. Specialises in still ciders (Cornish Wreckers, Devon Gold, Ploughmans and Scrumpy).

Country Manor (Eng) a still perry produced by the Goldwell C°.

Country Satin (Eng) a liqueur of Devon cream, malt whisky and British wine produced by the Goldwell C°.

Country Wine (Bul) describes wines produced from a blend of two grape varieties (stated on the label).

Count Thibaut lV (Fr) purported to have brought the Chardonnay grape back to Champagne from the Crusades in the Middle-East.

County Ale (Eng) a cask-conditioned champion ale 1050 O.G. brewed by Ruddles Brewery. Has won the Brewex Supreme Championship on two occasions.

County Creek Winery (USA) a vineyard and winery based in Telford, Pennsylvania. Produces American and hybrid Vinifera wines.

County Hamley (Austr) a winery. (Add): Bookmark Ave, & 28th Street Renmark, South Australia 5341. 2ha. Grape varieties: Cabernet sauvignon, Chardonnay, Merlot, Pinot noir, Ruby and Sauvignon blanc.

Coupage (Fr) the vatting or blending of wines to produce a good, standard wine. *See also* Assemblage.

Coup d'Après (Fr) a term for a large glass of wine consumed after the soup course at a meal in the nineteenth century.

Coup d'Avant (Fr) a pre-meal drink (apéritif) drunk just before the meal which began in the nineteenth century.

Coup de l'Étrier (Fr) stirrup cup, an eighteenth and nineteenth century drink of wine given to a rider before his journey home. *See also* Trou Normand.

Coup de Milieu (Fr) a drink of spirits served in the middle of a meal. i.e. Calvados (in Normandy) and Marc (in Champagne). *See also* Trou Normande.

Coup de Vin (Fr) the amount of wine that can be drunk in a single swallow (gulp).

Coupé (Fr) a blended wine.

Coupe (Fr) a Champagne saucer.

Coupe à Champagne Américaine (Fr) a Champagne saucer glass.

Coupe à Thée (Ch.Isles) teacup.

Coupe en Vitesse (Fr) lit: 'a quick one' (drink).

Coupé Souche (Fr) the name given to the large, long handled secateurs used to cut the shoots and fruit branches of the vine.

Coupette (Fr) a small Champagne flute.

Couprie (Fr) a Cognac producer. (Add): Ets. Couprie, La Roumade 16300 Ambleville/Barbezieux. 22ha. in Grande Champagne. Produces X.O. Très Vieille Réserve 20 year old and Très Vieux Cognac d'Age 42 year old.

Courage Brewery (Eng) a large company that has 3 breweries at Bristol, Reading and Tadcaster (John Smiths). Produces many famous beers including cask-conditioned Directors 1046 O.G. Simonds Keg Bitter 1036 O.G. Harp Lager 1032 O.G. Hofmeister 1036 O.G. Kronenbourg 1064 O.G. Colt 45 1047 O.G. Bulldog 1068 O.G. and Russian Stout 1100 O.G. Also brews Festivale. Bought by Elders IXL in 1986. Taken over by Scottish & Newcastle. Now known as Scottish Courage. Bristol brewery closed down in May 1999.

Courage Russian Imperial Stout (Eng) a strong, medium bitter beer with a long history. Has a long bottle maturation of 2 years bottle-conditioned 1100 O.G. Brewed by Courage's. *See also* Russian Stout.

Courant (Chile) a two year old wine.

Courant (Fr) a term used in Alsace to denote other than noble grapes.

Courantin (S.Am) a fruit rum produced in Guyana with a taste and aroma of spices and fruit.

Courbe de Fermentation (Fr) the record of temperature and density of a vat of must/wine during fermentation.

Courbu (Fr) a red grape variety grown in the Tursan region, south-western France, also grown in the Jurançon

Courbut Blanc (Sp) a white grape variety also known as the Ondarrabi zuria.

Courcelles-Sapicourt (Fr) a Cru Champagne village in the Canton de Ville-en-Tardenois. District: Reims.

Courgis (Fr) a commune in the A.C. Chablis, Burgundy.

Courjeonnet (Fr) a Cru Champagne village in the Canton de Montmort. District: Épernay.

Courmas (Fr) a Cru Champagne village in the Canton de Ville-en-Tardenois. District: Reims.

Courmayeur Fonte Youla (It) a sparkling natural spring mineral water from the Fonte Youla, Courmayeur. Mineral contents (milligrammes per litre): Sodium 1mg/l, Calcium 533mg/l, Magnesium 66mg/l, Potassium 2mg/l, Bicarbonates 176mg/l, Chlorides <1mg/l, Sulphates 1420mg/l, Fluorides <1mg/l, Nitrates <2mg/l. pH 7.4

Cour Pavillon [La] (Fr) the brand-name used by Gilbeys for their red and white Bordeaux wines.

Cours-Cheverny (Fr) an A.C. dry white wine from the Touraine district in the Loire. Produced by the Romaratin production method.

Courson (Fr) a term used to describe short spur pruning.

Court (Fr) denotes a short, unbalanced wine.

C

Courtagnon (Fr) a Cru Champagne village in the Canton de Châtillon-sur-Marne. District: Reims.

Courtakis (Gre) a wine merchant who is noted for his dark red Nemean wine.

Courte à Cot (Fr) a style of pruning used in the Sauternes district in south-western Bordeaux. The vines are severly pruned.

Couteron (Fr) a Cru Champagne village in the Canton de l'Aube. District: Château Thierry.

Courthiézy (Fr) a Cru Champagne village in the Canton de Dormans. District: Épernay.

Courtier (Fr) a wine broker, one who visits vignerons and keeps them in touch with the market. A liaison between the vignerons and négociants.

Courtiers de Campagne (Fr) country winebrokers who send wines of interest to the wine merchants (négociants). Receives a percentage of the price of the purchase from their client.

Courtillier Musqué (Fr) another name for the Huxelrebe grape. Also known as the Muscat courtillier.

Court Lane Vineyard (Eng) a vineyard (established 1979) based at Ropley, Hampshire. 0.08ha. Grape varieties: Huxelrebe, Madeleine angevine, Müller-Thurgau and Reichensteiner.

Court Noué (Fr) a virus that turns vine leaves yellow so that they become mis-shapen, shoots grow laterally and become short and stunted. Is transmitted in the soil by parasites. (Eng) = fan-leaf.

Court Royal (Eng) a variety of cider apple.

Court Royal (Eng) a bottled cider made from a single variety of apple called Court Royal. Produced by Dunkertons Cider Mill, Pembridge, Herefordshire.

Courvoisier (Fr) a Cognac producer. (Add): B.P. 59, 16200 Jarnac. Largest seller of Cognac. Top is Extra Vieille 50–60 year old.

Cous (Lat) the name of an Aegean island noted for its wines in Roman times.

Cousin Jack's (Eng) a beer brewed by St. Austell, Cornwall from a mix of malted barley, rye and First Gold hops.

Cousinerie de Bourgogne (Fr) a wine fraternity founded in 1960 in Savigny-lès-Beaune in the Côte d'Or, Burgundy. Has members world-wide. Meets four times per year.

Cousiño Macul (Chile) a wine estate based near Santiago. Grape varieties: Cabernet sauvignon, Chardonnay and Sémillon. Wines are sold under Don Luis and Don Matias labels.

Coutier [R.H] (Fr) a Champagne producer. (Add): 7, Rue Henri III, 51150 Ambonnay. Produces both vintage and non-vintage Champagnes and a Graqnd Cru Brut Rosé.

Couvent des Jacobins (Fr) vineyard. (Add): 33330 Saint-Émilion. Grand Cru Classé. A.C. Saint-Émilion. (Com): Saint-Émilion. 9ha. Grape varieties: Cabernet franc, Cabernet sauvignon and Merlot.

Couversets (Fr) a Châteauneuf-du-Pape produced by Quiot at Ave. Baron le Roy, 84230 Châteauneuf-du-Pape, southern Rhône. Other labels include Arnevals (Les), Domaine du Vieux Lazaret.

Cova da Beira-Port (Port) an I.P.R. region in the central-east. *see* Beira Interior.

Covadonga Cocktail (Cktl) 35mls (1½ fl.ozs) Campari, 25mls (1fl.oz) Italian vermouth, 10mls (½ fl.oz) grenadine, 25mls (1fl.oz) orange juice, dash Angostura. Shake over ice, strain into a club goblet and dress with an orange slice.

Covanegra (Sp) the brand-name used by the Bodegas García Carrión in the Jumilla region for a range of their red, rosé and white wines.

Covell Estate Wines (N.Z) a winery. (Add): Troutbeck Road, Galatea, Murupara, Bay of Plenty. 6ha. Grape varieties: Pinot noir, Chardonnay, Merlot, Riesling, Cabernet sauvignon.

Cover Crops (USA) plants (other than vines) planted in and around organic and bio-dynamic vineyards to improve soils and encourage beneficial insects.

Covered Wagon (Cktl) 35mls (1½ fl.ozs) tequila, 25mls (1fl.oz) French vermouth, juice ½ lime, dash grenadine. Shake over ice and strain into a cocktail glass.

COVIDES (Sp) *abbr*: **Co**operativa **Vi**nícola **del** Penedés. Produce Duc de Folie.

Covino Special (Cktl) ½ measure Cognac, ½ measure Noilly Prat. Stir over ice, strain into a cocktail glass and top with a twist of lemon peel juice.

Cow (Eng) a cream-based liqueur of low alcoholic strength.

Cowboy Cocktail (Cktl) 40mls (⅓ gill) Scotch whisky, 20mls (⅙ gill) cream. Shake over ice and strain into a cocktail glass.

Cowlin Wines (S.Afr) a winery (established 2001) based in Simondium, Paarl, Western Cape. 17ha. Grape varieties: Cabernet sauvignon, Chardonnay, Merlot, Mourvèdre, Sauvignon blanc, Shiraz, Viognier. Labels: Jack's Jug, Noble Hill, Poodle's Passion. Website: http://www.cowlinwines.co.za

Cowper (Wal) cooper/cask maker.

Cowra Vineyard (Austr) a winery with 242ha. on the bank of the Lachlan river. Grape varieties: Chardonnay, Verdelho.

Cowslip Tea (Eng) a herbal tea which is a good aid to sleep. *see* Tissanes.

Cow's Nipple (Chi) *see* Niunai.

Coxley Vineyard (Eng) a vineyard. (Add): Coxley, Near Wells, Somerset. Grape variety: Seyval blanc.

Cox's Katy (Eng) a 3.5% alc by vol. medium cider produced by Thatcher's based in Sandford, north Somerset. A single variety cider apple cider. *See also* Spartan, Tremlett's Bitter.

Cox's Ruin (Cktl) 1 part Pimms No.1, 3 parts lemonade, dash Cointreau Mix over ice in a highball glass. Dress with a slice of cucumber and orange.

Cox's Yard (Eng) a micro-brewery based in Stratford upon Avon. Owned by Charles Wells of Bedford. Brews Jester Ale.

Coxwains Special Bitter (Eng) a 4.9% alc by vol. special bitter ale brewed by Willy's Brewery, South Humberside.

C

Coyame (Mex) a natural spring mineral water from Catemaco.

Coy Private Reserve (USA) a beer 1039 O.G. brewed by the Coy Brewing Company.

CPK International (Thai) a winery and distillery. (Add): 165 Moo 10, Tambol Rongjik, Amphoe Phurua, Loei Province. Produces: Château de Loei and Victory brandy.

Crabbers' Nip (Eng) a barley wine 1066 O.G. brewed by the Devenish Brewery (now ceased being produced).

Crabbie (Scot) a de-luxe blended Scotch whisky distilled and blended by John Crabbie and C°. in Edinburgh. 8 year old. 43% alc by vol.

Crabbie's Green Ginger Wine (Scot) the only ginger wine matured in oak casks from Crabbie and C°. Edinburgh.

Crab Farm Winery (N.Z) a winery. (Add): 511 Main Road, North Bayview, Napier. 12.5ha. Grape varieties: Pinot noir, Cabernet sauvignon, Chardonnay, Merlot, Gewürztraminer, Sauvignon blanc.

Crabutet Noir (Fr) an alternative name for the Merlot grape.

Crachoir (Fr) spittoon.

Cracked Corn (USA) a cereal used in the making of some beers. *See also* Corn Grits.

Cracked Ice (USA) broken ice from a block or from large cubes.

Cracker Ale (Eng) a 3.9% alc by vol. ale brewed by the Barnsgates Brewery Ltd., Cumbria.

Crackling (Eng) an ale brewed by Beowulf Brewery, Yardley, Birmingham.

Crackling (S.Afr) a semi-sweet, pétillant wine from the SFW Centurin Harvest Wines.

Crackling Rosé (USA) a slang term for the pétillant rosés of Portugal.

Crackling Wines (USA) a North American name for sparkling wines made by CO_2 injection to give a slight sparkle.

Crack Shot (Eng) a 5.5% alc by vol. bottled beer produced for Sir Thomas Ingleby of Ripley Castle. Devised from a seventeenth century recipe by the Daleside Brewery, Harrogate, North Yorkshire.

Cracovia (Pol) a 42% alc by vol. vodka distilled in Cracow.

Cradle (Eng) a wicker, straw or metal basket used for bringing red wines from the cellar for decanting. Allows the handler to keep the bottle horizontal whilst the cork is being removed. *see* Burgundy Basket and Wine Cradle.

Crafter (Eng) a low alcohol bitter beer from McMullens of Hertford. 1% alc by vol. Brewed using traditional copper-lined oak vats, East Anglian malt, Kentish hops.

Craftsman Ale (Eng) a premium cask ale 4.2% alc by vol. (1042 O.G.) brewed by Thwaites, Blackburn, Lancashire.

Cragganmore (Scot) a single malt whisky distillery based on the river Spey. A highland malt whisky. 45% alc by vol. Also a 12 year old at 40% alc by vol.

Cragganmore Spring (Scot) a natural spring mineral water from Fanellan, Kiltarlity, Beauly, Inverness.

Craggy Range Winery (N.Z) a winery (90ha) based in Martinborough North Island. (Add): P.O.Box 8749, Havelock North. Has vineyards in Te Muna. Grape varieties: Pinot noir, Sauvignon blanc. Label: Te Muna Road. *See also* Family of Twelve. Website: http://www.craggyrange.co.nz

Craibillon (Fr) a small (0.65 ha) vineyard in the village of Brochon, now part of the A.C. Gevrey-Chambertin in the Côte de Nuits, Burgundy.

Craic (Ire) a 5.5% alc by vol. drink produced from Irish spirit, elderflower, spring water and natural extracts.

Craido en Cava (Sp) lit: 'born in the cellar', applied to Spanish sparkling wines, a poet's description of wine made by the masters of the craft.

Craie (Fr) chalk (soil).

Craig [Elijah] (USA) a Baptist preacher, reputedly the first man to have made Bourbon whiskey in Scott County, Kentucky in 1789.

Craig Avon Vineyard (Austr) a winery (established 1986). (Add): Craig Avon Lane, Merricks North, Victoria. Grape varieties: Cabernet sauvignon, Pinot noir, Chardonnay.

Craigellachie-Glenlivet (Scot) a single malt whisky distillery in Speyside. Produces a 16 year old whisky. Owned by Peter Mackie. 40% alc by vol.

Craiglee Vineyard (Austr) a winery. (Add): Tullamarine Fwy., Victoria. Grape varieties: Cabernet sauvignon, Pinot noir, Shiraz, Chardonnay.

Craigmore (Austr) a winery based in Mudgee, New South Wales. Produces varietal and Port-style wines.

Craipillot (Fr) a Premier Cru vineyard in the A.C. commune of Gevrey-Chambertin, Côte de Nuits, Burgundy. 2.75ha.

Cramant (Fr) a Grand Cru Champagne village in the Canton d'Avize. District: Épernay. Renowned for Blanc de Blancs.

Cramant Bonnaire (Fr) a vintage Champagne produced by Bonnaire. Vintages: 1934, 1947, 1949, 1952, 1955, 1959, 1961, 1964, 1966, 1969, 1971, 1973, 1975, 1976, 1979, 1982, 1985, 1989, 1990, 1995, 1998, 1999, 2001.

Crambambull (Cktl) ale, rum, sugar and whisked egg served hot or cold.

Cranberry Charge (Eng) a 5.3% alc by vol. flavoured alcoholic beverage from Whitbread Beer C°. under the Shott's Alcoholic Seltzer label.

Cranberry Ice (Eng) a 5.5% alc by vol. mixed vodka drink from Halewood International. *See also* Red Square, Reloaded Red Square.

Crane (S.Afr) the label for a range of red (Merlot) and white (Colombard) wines produced by the Goedverwacht Estate winery, Robertson, Western Cape.

Crane Brewery [The] (Eng) *see* Twickenham Fine Ales Ltd.

Crane Sundancer (Eng) a 3.7% alc by vol. ale brewed by Twickenham Fine Ales Ltd., Middlesex.

C

Cranmore Vineyard (Eng) a vineyard (established 1967) near Yarmouth in the Isle of Wight. 3ha. Soil: clay. Grape varieties: Gutenborner 15%, Müller-Thurgau 75% and Weisser burgunder 10%.

Crann Cócó (Ire) cocoa bean.

Crapula (Lat) intoxicated/drunken.

Crapulant (Eng) drunken/suffering from intemperance.

Crapulentus (Lat) drunk/intoxicated.

Crapuloso (Port) drunken/intoxicated.

Crapulous (Eng) denotes a person in an intoxicated state.

Cras [Les] (Fr) a Premier Cru vineyard [part] in the A.C. commune of Chambolle-Musigny, Côte de Nuits, Burgundy. 4.5ha. Also known as Les Gras.

Cras [Les] (Fr) a Premier Cru vineyard in the A.C. commune of Meursault, Côte de Beaune, Burgundy 4.8ha.

Cras [Les] (Fr) a Premier Cru vineyard [part] in the A.C. commune of Vougeot, Côte de Nuits, Burgundy. 4.2ha. Also known as Les Gras.

Crasse de Fer (Fr) a soft ferruginous sandstone found in Saint-Émilion, Bordeaux.

Crate (Eng) a container of wood or plastic holding 12 or 24 pint or half pint (250mls/500mls) bottles of beer respectively. Usually applies to beers but cider, minerals and wine can also be carried.

Crater (Sp) a red wine produced from Listán negra and Negramoll grapes by Bodegas Buten, Tenerife.

Crato Branco (Port) a white grape variety grown in the Algarve.

Crato Preto (Port) a red grape variety grown in the Algarve.

Cratur [The] (Scot) lit: 'the creature', the gaelic nickname for Scotch whisky.

CRAV (Fr) abbr: Comité Régional d'Action Viticole.

Cravate (Fr) see Courette.

Crawford (Scot) a noted Scotch whisky distillers based in Leith. Now part of DCL.

Crawford River (Austr) a winery (established 1975). (Add): Condah, Victoria. Grape varieties: Cabernet sauvignon, Merlot, Riesling, Sauvignon blanc, Sémillon.

Crawford's Five Star Scotch Whisky (Scot) a de-luxe blended Scotch whisky produced by Archibald and Aikman Crawford in Leith.

Crayère [Le] (Fr) a co-operative winery in Bethon in the southern Marne département. see Saint Simon.

Crayères (Fr) the chalk caves built by the Romans in Champagne.

Crayères [Les] (Fr) a single vineyard Champagne produced by Leclerc Briant.

Crayeux (Fr) chalky (soil).

Crazies (Eng) a white table wine from Joyous Garde Vineyard, Wargrove, Berkshire.

Crazy (Eng) an egg-based drink produced by Townend of Hull, Yorkshire.

Crazy (Ind) a lager beer 1064 O.G. brewed by the Vinedale Brewery in Hyderabad.

Crazy Cow (Eng) a 4.1% alc by vol. seasonal cask-conditioned porter stout brewed by Hardys and Hansons, Kimberley, Nottingham. Part of the Cellarman's Cask range. see Frolicking Farmer, Grasshopper, Guzzling Goose, Red Rooster, Rocking Rudolph.

Crazy Horse (Cktl) ½ measure crème de banane, ½ measure fraises des bois, 1 measure Scotch whisky. Shake over ice, strain into a Champagne flute, top with iced Champagne, decorate with slices of lime, orange and wild strawberries. Finish with a mint sprig.

Creaca (Rum) a grape variety also known as Banater riesling, Kreaca, Kriacza and Zakkelweiss.

Cream [1] (Eng) the fat of milk found floating on the top of fresh milk. see Clotted Cream, Devon Cream, Double Cream, Single Cream, Whipping Cream. (Arab) = laban, (Aus) = sahne, (Chi) = naiyou, (Cro) = vrhnje/krema, (Den) = fløde/creme, (Fr) = crème, (Den) = fløde/creme, (Ger) = rham/sahne, (Gre) = krema galaktos, (Hol) = room, (Indo) = krim, (Ire) = uachtar, (Isr) = katzefet, (It) = panna/fiore di latte, (Jap) = kuriimu, (Kor) = krim, (Port) = crème/nata, (Rus) = kryem/sleefkee, (Sp) = crema, (Thai) = cream, (Wal) = hufen.

Cream (Eng) the name given to the precipitation from a brew of tea when it cools. Contains caffeine, Theaflavins and Thearubigins.

Cream (Eng) a 4.7% alc by vol. bitter beer brewed by Roosters Brewing C°. Ltd., North Yorkshire.

Cream (Eng) a term given to Sherry that is heavily sweetened.

Cream Ale (USA) a blend of ale and lager beer. Main producers are the Genesee Brewery, Rochester, New York.

Cream Beer (USA) see Creamy Beer.

Creamer (Eng) a machine that removes (separates) the cream from the milk in a dairy.

Creamer (Eng) a small plastic individual portion pot of liquid U.H.T. cream used for coffee.

Creamer (USA) powdered milk substitute used for coffee.

Cream Fizz (Cktl) 90mls (¾ gill) gin, juice of lemon, 15mls (⅛ gill) cream, teaspoon sugar syrup. Shake well over ice, strain into a highball glass and top with soda water.

Creaming (Eng) the term used to describe a wine that has a slight mousse (sparkle).

Cream Label Stout (Eng) a bottled stout 1038 O.G. brewed by Watneys.

Cream Liqueurs (Eng) a combination of cream, spirit and flavourings. e.g. Bailey's Irish Cream, Devonshire Cream Liqueur, Merlyn.

Cream of the Barley (Scot) see Stewart's Cream of the Barley.

Cream of the Century (Sp) a deep-gold Sherry produced by Wisdom and Warter in Jerez de la Frontera.

Cream Puff (Cktl) 40mls (⅓ gill) dark rum, 20mls (⅙ gill) cream, 2 dashes gomme syrup. Shake over ice, strain into an ice-filled highball glass and top with soda water.

C

Cream Sherry (Eng) a very sweet Sherry, an Oloroso sweetened with Paxerete.

Cream Soda (USA) a vanilla-flavoured, non-alcoholic carbonated drink.

Cream Stout (Eng) a name often used for English stout. Now can no longer be used because of Trade Descriptions Act, as it contains no cream. *See also* Milk Stout.

Cream Stout (Wal) a bottled sweet stout 1040 O.G. brewed by the Felinfoel Brewery in South Wales. *see* Cream Stout.

Creamy Beer (USA) a carbonated beer, either bottled, canned or on draught.

Creamy Orange Cocktail (Cktl) 20mls Cognac, 25mls sweet Sherry, 30mls cream. Shake over ice and strain into a cocktail glass.

Creamy Screwdriver (Cktl) 40mls (⅓ gill) vodka, 125mls (1 gill) orange juice, 1 egg yolk, 2 dashes gomme syrup. Blend altogether with a scoop of crushed ice and pour into a collins glass.

Creata (Rum) a white grape variety grown in the Banat Vineyard (Tomnatec and Teremia Mare) for the production of white wines. Is also known as Riesling de Banat.

Crébillon (Fr) an alternative spelling of Craibillon.

Crécelle (Fr) lit: 'rattle', the new method of mechanical riddling of Champagne bottles which is replacing remuage by hand. (Eng) = gyropalette, (Sp) = girasol.

Crédo [Le] (Fr) a Vin de Pays red wine from 50% Cabernet sauvignon, 50% Merlot. Produced in the Côtes de Roussillon area.

Creedy Bitter (Eng) *see* Creedy Valley.

Creedy Valley (Eng) a brewery (established 1984) based in Crediton, Devon. Produces cask-conditioned Creedy Bitter 1036 O.G. and Tun Bitter 1041 O.G.

Creekside Vineyards (USA) a winery and distillery. (Add): 1894, Six Mile Road, Murphys, California. Produces apple brandy, grappa.

Creemore Springs Brewery (Can) a brewery. (Add): 139 Mill Street, Creemore, Ontario L0M 1G0. Brews a variety of beers. Website: http://www.creemoresprings.com 'E'mail: thefolks@creemoresprings.com

Creep Show (Eng) a special beer brewed by Crouch Vale Brewery for Hallowe'en.

Crema [1] (Sp) cream.

Crema [2] (Sp) a term used to describe a sweet Málaga wine.

Crema de Mandarine (Sp) a mandarine liqueur produced by the Cocal Cº. in Telde, Canary Islands.

Crémant (Fr) a term once denoting a creamy foam on top of wine in association with light sparkling wines which have less carbonation than Champagne. Originally associated with Cramant village in Champagne. From 1994 this term will be reserved solely for Crémant A.C. wines from elsewhere in France with a minimum of 3.5 atmospheres. 160 kg. grapes for 100 litres of must.

Crémant (Fr) a wine-producing district in Bellet, Provence, south-eastern France.

Crémant d'Alsace (Fr) an A.C. sparkling wine made by the méthode traditionelle. Grape varieties: Riesling, Pinot blanc, Pinot gris, Pinot auxerrois, Chardonnay and Pinot noir. Aged for a minimum of 9 months before dégorgement. Minimum alc by vol. 10% (8.5% must be natural). Introduced in 1976.

Crémant de Bordeaux (Fr) an A.C. Bordeaux méthode traditionelle wine. Minimum of 9 months on lees. Grape varieties: Sauvignon blanc, Sémillon, Muscadelle, Cabernet franc, Cabernet sauvignon, Carmenère, Malbec, Merlot, Petit verdot.

Crémant de Bourgogne (Fr) a light sparkling dry wine from Burgundy made by the méthode traditionelle. Can be red, rosé or white with the white A.C. only being made from the Chardonnay grape.

Crémant de Cramant (Fr) a unique sparkling™ (méthode traditionelle) wine produced by G.H. Mumm Champagne house in Champagne. Is a Blanc de Blancs with a lighter sparkle. Mumm use an agraffe to hold the cork in place as opposed to the usual wire cage.

Crémant de Die (Fr) an A.C. méthode traditionelle wine since March 1993. Yield- 50 hl./ha. Grape variety: Clairette. Replaced A.C. Clairette de Die.

Crémant de Limoux (Fr) an A.C. méthode traditionelle wine from the hinterland of the Languedoc. Grape varieties: Mauzac plus min. 30% Chardonnay and Chenin blanc but not more than 20% of either.

Crémant de Loire (Fr) a new title for A.C. sparkling wines of the Saumur and Touraine districts of the Loire. Grape varieties: Chardonnay, Chenin blanc, Sauvignon blanc, Cabernet franc, Pinot noir. Minimum alc by vol. 10% (8.5% must be natural).

Crémant de Luxembourg (Lux) an A.C. méthode traditionelle wine since 1991. Grape varieties: Elbling, Pinot blanc, Pinot noir, Riesling.

Crémant des Moines (Fr) a non-vintage Champagne produced by Besserat de Bellefon from 20% Chardonnay and 80% Pinot noir grapes.

Crémant F. Kobus (Fr) *see* St. Odile.

Crema Vinera [La] (USA) a winery based in the Sonoma County, California. Grape varieties: Cabernet sauvignon, Chardonnay and Pinot noir. Produces varietal wines.

Crème (Fr) cream.

Crème (Port) cream. *See also* Nata.

Crème au Calvados (Fr) a 17% alc by vol. Calvados and dairy cream liqueur.

Crème Brûlée (Fr) a liqueur with the flavour of the dessert crème brûlée sold in an art deco bottle.

Crème d'Almond (USA) another name for Crème de Noyau.

Crème d'Amandes (Fr) a sweet almond-flavoured liqueur.

Crème d'Ananas (Fr) a pineapple liqueur made by maceration 30% alc by vol.

Crème de Banane (Fr) a banana-flavoured liqueur made by infusion and maceration 30% alc by vol.

Crème de Cacao (Fr) a cocoa-flavoured liqueur made from cacao beans. 25%–30% alc by vol. *see* Chouao.

Crème de Café (Cktl) ⅓ measure coffee brandy, ⅓ measure cream, ⅙ measure dark rum, ⅙ measure anisette. Shake well over ice and strain into an ice-filled old-fashioned glass.

Crème de Café (Fr) a liqueur made from spirit extracts of coffee, coloured brown and sweetened. 26%–31% alc by vol.

Crème de Cassis (Fr) a blackcurrant liqueur produced in Burgundy. Made from both infusion and maceration methods (18%–25% alc by vol). Fine crème de cassis has a vintage date because it will lose its fine flavour.

Crème de Ciel (Hol) an orange liqueur similar to Curaçao, light blue in colour.

Crème de Fraises (Fr) a strawberry liqueur made from both cultivated and wild strawberries by both infusion and maceration.

Crème de Fraises des Bois (Fr) a liqueur made from wild strawberries.

Crème de Framboises (Fr) a liqueur made from raspberries by both infusion and maceration methods.

Crème de Gin (Cktl) ¾ measure dry gin, ¼ measure (white) crème de menthe, juice ¼ lemon, 2 teaspoons orange juice, 1 egg white. Shake well over ice, strain into a cocktail glass.

Crème de Grand Marnier (Fr) a cream and Grand Marnier liqueur from the Grand Marnier company.

Crème de Guignolet (Fr) a cherry liqueur made in Dijon (guignol = punch).

Crème de Kobai (Jap) a liqueur produced from Japanese plums.

Crème de la Crème (Fr) lit: 'cream of the cream', term given to the finest wines etc.

Crème de la Crème (Cktl) 1 teaspoon sugar, 1 measure brandy, 1½ measures Cointreau, 2 dashes double cream, 1 dash orange bitters. Shake, pour over crushed ice into a cocktail glass, top with soda water and a slice of orange.

Crème de Mandarine (USA) a liqueur produced from tangerine peel. Is produced by the infusion method 30% alc by vol.

Crème de Menthe (Fr) a peppermint-flavoured liqueur, is colourless when it leaves the still, sold without colour or green 30% alc by vol.

Crème de Mokka (Fr) a light brown coffee-flavoured liqueur.

Crème de Myrtilles (Fr) a liqueur made from wild bilberries from the mountains of France.

Crème de Noisette (Fr) a hazelnut-flavoured liqueur made by the infusion method 30% alc by vol.

Crème de Noix (Fr) a walnut-flavoured liqueur from Périgord. Produced by the infusion method 30% alc by vol.

Crème de Noyau (Fr) a peach kernel-flavoured liqueur 30% alc by vol.

Crème de Noyaux (USA) *see* Crème de Noyau.

Crème de Noyeau (Fr) an almond-flavoured liqueur, pink or white in colour.

Crème de Nuits (Fr) a double crème de cassis liqueur produced by Cartron in Nuits-Saint-Georges, Burgundy 17% alc by vol.

Crème de Pecco (Hol) a tea-flavoured liqueur, medium-sweet and colourless.

Crème de Poire (Fr) a pear-flavoured liqueur.

Crème de Prunelle (Fr) a plum-flavoured liqueur, is plum-green in colour, made by infusion and maceration 40% alc by vol.

Crème de Rhum (Cktl) ½ measure white rum, ⅓ measure crème de banane, ⅓ measure orange squash. Shake over ice, strain into a cocktail glass, add a cherry and slice of lemon.

Crème de Roses (Fr) a liqueur made from the oil of rose petals, vanilla and citrus oils. Pink in colour.

Crème des Barbades (Fr) an eau-de-vie, flavoured with spices (cloves, cinnamon and mace) and citrus peel.

Crème de Tête (Fr) a label term used in Sainte-Croix-du-Mont until banned in 1973. Denoted the use of **Botrytis cinerea**-attacked grapes in the wine.

Crème de Tête (S.Afr) the label for a noble late harvest wine (Muscat d'Alexandrie) produced by the Signal Hill winery, Cape Town, Western Cape.

Crème de Thé (W.Ind) an old Martinique liqueur made in the nineteenth century from cane syrup sweetened with cane sugar and flavoured with tea.

Crème de Vanille (USA) a vanilla-flavoured liqueur made by the infusion method from Mexican vanilla beans. 30% alc by vol.

Crème de Violette (USA) a violet-flavoured liqueur obtained from the oil of violets and vanilla by the infusion method and blending 30% alc by vol.

Crémerie (Fr) dairy.

Crémeux (Fr) creamy.

Crème Yvette (USA) a liqueur made from Parma violets (violet in colour 32% alc by vol).

Crémier (Fr) dairyman.

Cremière (Fr) dairywoman (milkmaid).

Cremocha (USA) a sweet, coffee-flavoured liqueur produced by the Barengo Winery in San Joaquin, California.

Creole Café Brûlot (USA) 500mls (1pint) strong hot coffee, 125mls (¼ pint) brandy, 1 whole orange peel in spiral, cinnamon stick, vanilla pod, 12 cloves, 4 sugar cubes. Place all in bowl (except coffee), heat, ignite and baste with a ladle letting flaming liquor cascade into bowl. Add hot coffee, infuse 3 minutes, strain and serve.

Creole Cocktail (Cktl) 1 measure Jamaican rum, 4 dashes lemon juice, 1 dash Tabasco sauce, salt and pepper. Shake well over ice, strain into an ice-filled old-fashioned glass, top with iced beef bouillon and stir.

Creole Cooler (Cktl) 200gms crushed pineapple, 500ml milk, 50ml orange juice, 25ml lime juice. Combine pineapple and juices in jug, add sugar to taste, add milk, mix well, chill and serve.

C

Creole Lady (Cktl) ½ measure Bourbon whiskey, ½ measure Boal Madeira, 4 dashes grenadine. Stir over ice, strain into a cocktail glass, decorate with red and green cherries.

Crépitant (Fr) a term used to describe the slight fizz (pétillance) in some wines from Crépy in Savoie.

Crépy (Fr) an A.C. white wine from Savoie in south-eastern France. The wine is often slightly pétillant due to the fact it is raised on the lees. Made from the Chasselas grape. 9.5% alc by vol. Is sold in tall green bottles. *see* Crépitant.

Crequi (Sp) a Solera gran reserva brandy produced by Barbadillo.

Crescenz (Ger) growth. *See also* Kresenz.

Cressier (Switz) a noted vineyard based in the Neuchâtel district of western Switzerland.

Cresta Bella (USA) the brand-name used by the Gibson Vineyards in California for their wines.

Cresta Blanca (USA) a part of the Guild Co-operative, Livermore Winery the north coast of California.

Cresta Doré (N.Z) the brand-name of a dry white wine produced by the McWilliams Winery in Hawkes Bay.

Crested Ten (Ire) a blend of malt and grain whiskies produced by Jameson.

Crest Lager (Eng) a lager brewed by Charles Wells, Bedford, sold mainly by supermarkets in cans and PET bottles.

Creta (Gre) a dry white wine produced on the island of Crete.

Cretan Malvasia (Port) another name for the Malmsey grape.

Creta Olympias (Gre) a winery based at Peza, Heraklion, Crete. Produces Peza V.Q.P.R.D. (red and white) plus Creta Nobile (red), Cretan Country (red and white).

Crete (Gre) a large island which produces local red, rosé and white wines. Grape varieties: Kotsifali, Liatiko, Mandilari, Vilana. Main areas: Archanes, Dafnes, Peza, Sitia.

Crets [Les] (Fr) a vineyard in the A.C. commune of Montagny, Côte Chalonnaise, Burgundy.

Creu (Fr) the seventeenth century spelling of Cru from the verb Croître (to grow).

Creusots [Les] (Fr) an old name for the Premier Cru vineyard Clos Napoléon in the A.C. commune of Fixin, Côte de Nuits, Burgundy.

Creux (Fr) denotes a thin wine that lacks body.

Creux de la Net (Fr) a Premier Cru vineyard [part] in the A.C. commune of Pernand-Vergelesses, Côte de Beaune, Burgundy 5ha.

Creysse (Fr) a commune within the A.C. district of Pécharmant in northern Bergerac (red wine).

Crezenz (Ger) lit: 'the growth of'.

Criadera (Sp) the nursery, contains the younger Sherries waiting to go into the Solera system.

Criado (Sp) matured.

Criado y Embotellado Por (Sp) grown and bottled by.

Crianza (Sp) lit: 'ageing', red wine is 2 y.o. (oak aged 6 months). White and rosé are a minimum of 1 y.o.

Crianza (Sp) young brandy nurseries.

Crianza Bajo Velo (Sp) lit: 'ageing under film', applied to Vino de Crianza wines, a method of ageing wines in sealed casks or vats away from the air.

Crianza en Botella (Sp) denotes the ageing in bottle of wine. Is applied to Vino de Crianza wines.

Crianza en Madera (Sp) denotes the ageing in cask, applied to Vino de Crianza wines.

Crianza en Roble (Sp) denotes ageing in oak, applied to Vino de Crianza wines.

Crianza Grabazán Limousin (Sp) a wine produced in Rías Baixas, D.O. Galicia by Agro de Bazán in Val do Salnés.

Crib (Eng) a large sheet of cloth used in hop picking to collect the hops. *see* Bushler.

Cribari and Sons (USA) a label owned by the Guild Wineries and Distilleries in California.

Crichton Hill Estate (USA) a winery. (Add): 1150, Darms Lane, Napa, California. Produces varietal wines including Chardonnay.

Cricketer's (Eng) the name of a special reserve gin from Seagram. 40% alc by vol. Sold with different cricketing scenes on the labels (recipe includes fresh limes).

Cricket Pitch (S.Afr) the label for a red wine (Cabernet sauvignon 40% and Merlot 60% blend) produced by the Welbedacht Wines winery, Wellington, Western Cape.

Crickley Windward (Eng) a vineyard based at Little Wircombe, Gloucestershire. Small producer of English Table wine. Grape variety: Seyval blanc.

Criesbach (Ger) village (Anb): Württemberg. (Ber): Kocher-Jagst-Tauber. (Gro): Kocherberg. (Vins): Burgstall, Hoher Berg, Sommerberg.

Criffel Ale (Scot) a 4.6% alc by vol. ale brewed by Sulwath Brewers Ltd., Kirkcudbrightshire.

Crilles [Les] (Fr) a vineyard in the A.C. Sancerre, Central Vineyards, Loire.

Crillon Cocktail (Cktl) 25mls (⅕ gill) Noilly Prat, 15mls (⅛ gill) Campari, 15mls (⅛ gill) eau-de-vie-de-poire. Shake over ice, strain into an ice-filled old-fashioned glass, dress with an orange and lemon spiral.

Crimea (Geo) *see* Crimean Peninsular.

Crimean Peninsular (Geo) an important wine region which produces most styles of wines.

Crimmins Ranch (USA) a small vineyard based near Healdsburg, California. Grape variety: Sauvignon blanc.

Crimson Cocktail (Cktl) 40mls (⅓ gill) gin, 15mls (⅛ gill) lemon juice, 4 dashes grenadine, shake over ice, strain into a cocktail glass and float a little Port wine on top.

Crio-Extraxtion (Eng) the process of freezing partially botrytised grapes to freeze any remaining water in the grape juice to increase the sugar content of the must.

Criolla Chica (Arg) a native white grape variety that corresponds roughly to the Californian Mission. Found mainly in La Rioja. Also known as Negra Corriente.

C

Criolla Grande (Arg) a pink skinned grape variety, widely found in Mendoza. Also known as Criolla Sanjuanina.

Criolla Sanjuanina (Arg) *see* Criolla Grande.

Crios de Susana Balbo (Arg) the label for a range of wines (white, rosé and red) produced by the Dominio del Plata winery in the Mendoza region.

Criots-Bâtard-Montrachet (Fr) a Grand Cru vineyard in the A.C. commune of Chassagne-Montrachet, Côte de Beaune, Burgundy 1.4ha.

Cripple Cock (Eng) the brand-name of a cider produced by the Saffron Cider C°. in Radwater, Essex.

Crippledick (Eng) an 11.7% alc by vol. special bottled beer brewed by the St.Austell Brewery, Cornwall.

Crisp (Eng) a term to describe a white wine that has a pronounced acidity without being sharp. e.g. Mosel wines.

Crisp Dry (S.Afr) the label for a dry white wine (Chenin blanc) from the Meander range of wines produced by the Groot Eiland Winery, Worcester, Western Cape.

Crispen (Eng) the name of a 4% alc by vol. cider produced by Bulmer (increased from 3% alc by vol.)

Cristal (C.Am) a natural spring mineral water from Heredia, Costa Rica. Mineral contents (milligrammes per litre): Sodium 5.8mg/l, Calcium 14.8mg/l, Magnesium 7.9mg/l, Potassium 2.8mg/l, Sulphates 8mg/l, Fluorides 0.1mg/l. pH 7.7

Cristal (Chile) a white grape variety.

Cristal (Port) a pilsener-style lager beer brewed by the C.U.F.P.

Cristal (Peru) a 5% alc by vol. straw coloured, bottled premium lager beer brewed by Backus Y. Johnson Brewery, Lima.

Cristal (Sp) the label used by Castellblanch for their 'brut' and 'extra' sparkling wines.

Cristal Agua Purificada (Mex) a natural spring mineral water. Mineral contents (milligrammes per litre): Chlorides 18mg/l, Sulphates 8mg/l. pH 6.5

Cristal Aiken (Hol) the brand-name of a well-hopped pilsener lager beer 5% alc by vol. brewed in Limburg.

Cristal Brut (Fr) a vintage de luxe cuvée Champagne produced by Louis Roederer from 45% Chardonnay and 55% Pinot noir grapes.

Cristal Bulles (Fr) a natural spring mineral water from Orléans. Mineral contents (milligrammes per litre): Sodium 11.2mg/l, Calcium 71mg/l, Magnesium 5.5mg/l, Potassium 3.2mg/l, Bicarbonates 250mg/l, Chlorides 20mg/l, Sulphates 5mg/l, Nitrates 1mg/l. pH 7.5

Cristal da Estancia (Bra) a natural spring mineral water from Estancia. Mineral contents (milligrammes per litre): Sodium 3.4mg/l, Calcium 10mg/l, Magnesium 5.65mg/l, Potassium 1mg/l, Bicarbonates 352mg/l, Chlorides 6.57mg/l, Nitrates 20mg/l. pH 6.9

Cristal Floquet (Fr) an orange-flavoured colourless Curaçao made by the firm of Floquet.

Cristalina (Bra) a natural spring mineral water. Mineral contents (milligrammes per litre): Sodium 22mg/l, Calcium 5.78mg/l, Magnesium 2.68mg/l, Potassium 3.9mg/l, Bicarbonates 68.12mg/l, Chlorides 9.84mg/l, Sulphates 2.5mg/l, Fluorides 0.27mg/l, Nitrates 6.8mg/l. pH 6.18

Cristaline (Fr) the brand™ name for a group of natural mineral waters sourced around France.

Cristaline [1] (Fr) a still natural spring mineral water from Aurele, Jandun. Mineral contents (milligrammes per litre): Sodium 3.5mg/l, Calcium 106mg/l, Magnesium 3.8mg/l, Potassium 1.8mg/l, Bicarbonates 272mg/l, Chlorides 3.8mg/l, Sulphates 58.9mg/l, Nitrates <2mg/l. pH 7.2

Cristaline [2] (Fr) a still natural spring mineral water from Bondoire, Loches. Mineral contents (milligrammes per litre): Sodium 17.7mg/l, Calcium 86mg/l, Magnesium 3mg/l, Potassium 1.7mg/l, Bicarbonates 256mg/l, Chlorides 23mg/l, Sulphates 6mg/l, Nitrates 16mg/l.

Cristaline [3] (Fr) a still natural spring mineral water from Elénore. Mineral contents (milligrammes per litre): Sodium 21mg/l, Calcium 56mg/l, Magnesium 9.7mg/l, Potassium 1.3mg/l, Bicarbonates 188mg/l, Chlorides 41mg/l, Sulphates 21mg/l, Nitrates <1mg/l. pH 7.8

Cristaline [4] (Fr) a still natural spring mineral water from Lucheux. Mineral contents (milligrammes per litre): Sodium 7.2mg/l, Calcium 96mg/l, Magnesium 2.2mg/l, Potassium 0.7mg/l, Bicarbonates 284mg/l, Chlorides 15mg/l, Sulphates 5mg/l. pH 7.0

Cristaline [5] (Fr) a still natural spring mineral water from Rieudière, St. Michel de Montjoie. Mineral contents (milligrammes per litre): Sodium 8.1mg/l, Calcium 3.2mg/l, Magnesium 1.7mg/l, Potassium 0.8mg/l, Bicarbonates 15.2mg/l, Chlorides 17.4mg/l, Sulphates 2.5mg/l.

Cristaline [6] (Fr) a still natural spring mineral water (established 1989) from Roc. Mineral contents (milligrammes per litre): Sodium 4.4mg/l, Calcium 70mg/l, Magnesium 2.1mg/l, Potassium 1.6mg/l, Bicarbonates 200mg/l, Chlorides 8mg/l, Sulphates 15.3mg/l, Nitrates <2mg/l. pH 7.7

Cristaline [7] (Fr) a still natural spring mineral water from Sainte-Cécile. Mineral contents (milligrammes per litre): Sodium 23mg/l, Calcium 44mg/l, Magnesium 24mg/l, Potassium 2mg/l, Bicarbonates 287mg/l, Chlorides 5mg/l, Sulphates 3mg/l, Nitrates 1mg/l. pH 7.6

Cristaline [8] (Fr) a still natural spring mineral water from St-Cyr. Mineral contents (milligrammes per litre): Sodium 11.2mg/l, Calcium 71mg/l, Magnesium 5.5mg/l, Potassium 3.2mg/l, Bicarbonates 250mg/l, Chlorides 20mg/l, Sulphates <5mg/l, Nitrates 1mg/l. pH 7.45

C

Cristaline [9] (Fr) a still natural spring mineral water from St. Jean-Baptiste, Busigny. Mineral contents (milligrammes per litre): Sodium 8mg/l, Calcium 80mg/l, Magnesium 8mg/l, Potassium 2mg/l, Bicarbonates 263mg/l, Chlorides 12mg/l, Sulphates 13mg/l, Nitrates 0.6mg/l.

Cristaline [10] (Fr) a still natural spring mineral water from St. Médard. Mineral contents (milligrammes per litre): Sodium 44mg/l, Calcium 43mg/l, Magnesium 11mg/l, Potassium 2.3mg/l, Bicarbonates 180mg/l, Chlorides 76mg/l, Sulphates 6mg/l, Nitrates 1mg/l. pH 7.5

Cristaline [11] (Fr) a still natural spring mineral water from Ste-Sophie. Mineral contents (milligrammes per litre): Calcium 63mg/l, Magnesium 26mg/l, Bicarbonates 493mg/l, Chlorides 33mg/l, Sulphates 60mg/l, Nitrates <2mg/l.

Cristaline [12] (Fr) a still natural spring mineral water from Vitale, Montpeyroux. Mineral contents (milligrammes per litre): Sodium 11.9mg/l, Calcium 90.3mg/l, Magnesium 14.7mg/l, Potassium 1mg/l, Bicarbonates 302mg/l, Chlorides 21mg/l, Sulphates 23mg/l, Nitrates 10mg/l.

Cristaline [13] (Fr) a still natural spring mineral water from Vosgia. Mineral contents (milligrammes per litre): Sodium 3mg/l, Calcium 6.4mg/l, Magnesium 1.2mg/l, Potassium 0.5mg/l, Bicarbonates 20mg/l, Chlorides 3mg/l, Sulphates 5mg/l, Nitrates 4mg/l. pH 6.5

Cristaline [14] (Fr) a still natural spring mineral water from Doye, Nantua. (Add): Source de la Doye, 01130 Nantua. Mineral contents (milligrammes per litre): Sodium 8mg/l, Calcium 64.2mg/l, Magnesium 3.3mg/l, Potassium 2mg/l, Bicarbonates 195mg/l, Chlorides 18mg/l, Sulphates 10mg/l, Nitrates 4mg/l, Silicates 2mg/l. pH 7.8

Cristaline – Eau de Source Pétillante (Fr) the sparkling version of the still natural spring mineral waters.

Cristaline des Grands Bois (Fr) a still natural spring mineral water. Mineral contents (milligrammes per litre): Sodium 11mg/l, Calcium 124mg/l, Magnesium 25mg/l, Potassium 3.5mg/l, Bicarbonates 420mg/l, Chlorides 16mg/l, Sulphates 60mg/l. pH 7.6

Cristalline (Can) a natural spring mineral water. Mineral contents (milligrammes per litre): Sodium 11mg/l, Calcium 35mg/l, Magnesium 22mg/l, Potassium 4mg/l, Bicarbonates 46mg/l, Chlorides 71mg/l, Sulphates 8mg/l.

Cristallo (Switz) a still and sparkling natural spring mineral water from Cristalloquelle, Lostorf SO. (red label: sparkling/green label: low gas/blue label: still). Mineral contents (milligrammes per litre): Sodium 19.9mg/l, Calcium 115mg/l, Magnesium 40mg/l, Potassium 1.8mg/l, Bicarbonates 306mg/l, Chlorides 11.5mg/l, Sulphates 211mg/l, Fluorides 1.4mg/l, Nitrates 1.8mg/l.

Cristal Monopole Bel) a natural spring mineral water from Cristal, Aarschot.

Cristal Pinot Brut (It) a sparkling (metodo tradizionale) wine produced by Maggi in Lombardy.

Cristalp Saxon (Switz) a still natural spring mineral water from Saxon. Mineral contents (milligrammes per litre): Sodium 19.9mg/l, Calcium 115mg/l, Magnesium 40mg/l, Potassium 1.8mg/l, Bicarbonates 306mg/l, Chlorides 11.5mg/l, Sulphates 211mg/l, Fluorides 1.4mg/l, Nitrates 1.8mg/l.

Cristal Springs (Can) a still natural spring mineral water from Oak Ridges, Moraine, Ontario. pH 7

Cristo [El] (Sp) a nineteenth-century name given to a 3,500 gallon cask. Now known as El Maestro.

Cristom Vineyards (USA) vineyards based in Willamette Valley, Oregon. Contains the Louise Vineyard. Grape varieties: Chardonnay, Pinot noir, Pinot gris. Labels: Marjorie Vineyard, Mt. Jefferson Cuvée.

Critéuil-la-Magdeleine (Fr) a commune in the Charente département whose grapes are classed Grande Champagne (Cognac).

Critone (It) an I.G.T. white wine produced by Librandi in Calabria from 90% Chardonnay and 10% Sauvignon blanc grapes.

Crljenak Kastteljanski (Cro) a local black grape variety which is the ancestor of the Zinfandel.

Crni (Slo) black, also name of red wine grape variety. *see* Crno.

Crno (Slo) a red grape variety. *see* Crni.

Croak & Stagger (Eng) a 5.6% alc by vol. ale brewed by the Frog Island Brewery, Northamptonshire.

Croaker Beer (Eng) a cask-conditioned ale 1050 O.G. brewed by the Frog and Frigate public house in Sheffield, Yorkshire.

Croatia (Cro) a northern wine region on the Dalmatian coast reaching around the Adriatic sea to the Italian border. Key regions: Adriatic Islands, Istria, Kontinentalna Hrvatska. Grape varieties: Grk, Plavac Mali, Cabernet sauvignon, Merlot, Pinot noir, Posip, Marastina, Kékfrankos, Laski rizling, Rafosk, Zweigelt.

Croatina (It) a red grape variety grown in the Piemonte region.

Crobhaing Fhionchaor (Ire) bunch of grapes.

Crochet (Fr) vine training method similar to gobelet, used for young vines where the fruiting canes are pruned short.

Crock Bottle (Eng) a stone bottle used since Roman times to keep wine cool in warm climates.

Crocked (Eng) a slang term for drunk/intoxicated.

Crodo Lisiel (It) a still natural spring mineral water from the Crodo Springs, Lisiel, Formazzo. Mineral contents (milligrammes per litre): Sodium 5.5mg/l, Calcium 60.3mg/l, Magnesium 7.3mg/l, Potassium 3.2mg/l, Bicarbonates 103.2mg/l, Chlorides 1.8mg/l, Sulphates 102.5mg/l, Nitrates 3.9mg/l, Silicates 8.6mg/l. pH 7.64

Croeschen Riesling (S.Afr) a locally produced white grape variety that produces light wines.

Croffta Vineyard (Wal) a noted vineyard (established 1975). (Add): Groes-Faen, Pontyclun, Mid-Glamorgan. 1.25ha. Grape varieties: Madeleine-angevine, Müller-Thurgau and Seyval blanc.

Croft (Port) vintage Port shippers. Vintages: 1870, 1872, 1875, 1878, 1881, 1884, 1885, 1887, 1890, 1894, 1896, 1897, 1900, 1904, 1908, 1912, 1917, 1920, 1922, 1924, 1927, 1935, 1942, 1945, 1950, 1955, 1960, 1963, 1966, 1970, 1975, 1977, 1980, 1982, 1985, 1991, 1994, 1997, 2000, 2003. Owned by Gilbey's. Also produce a range of wines and sherries as well as Ports. Single quinta is the Quinta da Roeda.

Croft (Sp) a Sherry, brandy and wine producer. (Add): Rancho Croft Ctra, Circunvalcion 636,3, Apartado 414, Jerez de la Frontera. Owns 290ha. of vineyards and wineries. Sherry brand-names include Palo Cortado and Delicado. Brandy Croft: Solera Reserva brandy, Solera Privada: Solera gran reserva brandy. Owned by Gilbey's.

Crofters (Eng) a 4% alc by vol. bitter beer brewed by the Filo Brewing Company, East Sussex.

Croft Particular (Sp) a brand-name of a pale Amontillado Sherry produced by Croft.

Crofty (Eng) a 3.6% alc by vol. cask ale brewed by the Redruth Brewery in Cornwall.

Croisière (Fr) the name of a range of fruit flavoured sparkling wines from Jenks Brokerage. Flavours include peach, cherry, Curaçao.

Croître (Fr) see Creu.

Croix de Mazerat (Fr) a vineyard in Saint-Émilion. A.C. Saint-Émilion. (Com): Saint-Émilion. The second wine of Château Beauséjour. Grand Cru Classé Saint-Émilion.

Croix de Salles (Fr) the name for a range of Armagnacs including a ***, V.S.O.P. and 12 y.o. blend produced by H. Dartigalongue et Fils at Nogaro in the Bas Armagnac.

Croix des Bouquets (W.Ind) a distillery based in Haiti. Produces Rhum Champion.

Croix de Touraine (Fr) a V.D.Q.S. wine no longer produced under this label.

Croix de Touraine Mousseux (Fr) a V.D.Q.S. sparkling wine now no longer produced.

Croix Maron [Chevalier de la] (Fr) is reputed to have invented the Bonne Chauffe (second distillation) for brandy in the sixteenth century in Cognac.

Croix Montlabert [La] (Fr) the second wine of Château Montlabert. Grand Cru Saint-Émilion.

Croix-Noires [Les] (Fr) a Premier Cru vineyard in the A.C. commune of Pommard, Côte de Beaune, Burgundy 1.2ha.

Croizet [Pierre] (Fr) a Cognac producer. (Add): Lantin, 16200 Jarnac. 30ha. in the Fins Bois. Produces a range of Cognacs.

Croizet Eymard (Fr) a Cognac producer. (Add): B.P. 3, 16720 Saint Merne-lès-Carrières, 16200 Jarnac. 150ha. in the Grande Champagne. Produces Age Inconnu and Réserve Royale.

Crombé Brouwerij (Bel) a brewery (established 1798) based in Zottegem. Brews: Cezarken, Egmont, Oud Zottegems Bier, Zottegemse Grand Cru.

Cromwell Bitter (Eng) a cask-conditioned bitter 1037 O.G. brewed by Marston Brewery near York.

Cromwell's Hat (Eng) a 6% alc by vol. strong ale brewed by the Springhead Brewery, Nottinghamshire.

Crone's Cider (Eng) a cider producer (established 1984). (Add): Fairview, Fersfield Road, Kenninghall, Norwich, Norfolk NR16 2DP. Produces a range of ciders, fruit and vegetable juices. Website: http://www.crones.co.uk 'E'mail: info@crones.co.uk

Crop Circle (Eng) a 4.2% alc by vol. bottled best bitter brewed by the Hop Back Brewery, Downtown, Salisbury.

Cropton Brewery (Eng) a brewery (established 1984). (Add): Woolcroft, Crompton, Pickering, North Yorkshire YO18 8HH. Brews: Backwoods, Endeavour Ale 3.6% alc by vol., Honey Gold 4.2% alc by vol., Honey Farm Bitter, King Billy 3.6% alc by vol., Monkmans Slaughter 6% alc by vol., Rudolph's Revenge 4.6% alc by vol., Scoresby Stout 4.2% alc by vol., (bottle conditioned) Two Pints Ale 4% alc by vol., Uncle Sam's 4.4% alc by vol., Yorkshire Moors 4.6% alc by vol. Website: http://www.cromptonbrewery.co.uk 'E'mail: info@cromptonbrewery.co.uk

Croser (Austr) a sparkling wine produced by Petaluma in South Australia.

Cross (Eng) a new variety of vine obtained by cross-pollination of 2 varieties of the same species i.e. Vitis vinifera. e.g. Riesling x Sylvaner = Müller-Thurgau.

Crossbow (Cktl). ⅓ measure Cointreau, ⅓ measure gin, ⅓ measure crème de cacao. Shake over ice and strain into a cocktail glass.

Cross Buttock Ale (Eng) a 4.5% alc by vol. autumn ale brewed by the Jennings Brothers Castle Brewery, Cockermouth, Cumbria.

Crosspoint (USA) a winery based in Monterey County, California. Grape variety: Pinot noir.

Crossroads Wine Company (N.Z) a winery. (Add): Korokipo Road, SH 50 Fernhill, Napier. 5ha. Main grape is the Riesling.

Crotta di Vegneron (It) a co-operative winery (established 1980) in the Valle d'Aosta, Piemonte region. Has 120 growers and 30ha of vineyards. Grape varieties include: Dolcetto, Freisa, Gamay, Pinot gris. Labels: Chambave, Crotta di Vegneron, Muscat, Nus.

Crouchen (Austr) a white grape variety. Also known as the Clare riesling.

Crouch Vale Brewery (Eng) a brewery (established 1981). (Add): 12 Redhills Road, South Woodham Ferrers, Chelmsford, Essex CM3 5UP. Brews: Black Water Mild 3.7% alc by vol., Brewers Gold 4.1% alc by vol., Chelmsford 800 Ale, Crouch Best Bitter 4.1% alc by vol., Essex Boys 3.5% alc by vol., SAS 1048 O.G. Woodham Bitter 1035.5 O.G. Santa's Revenge, 39 Steps 3.9% alc by vol. and

Willie Warmer. Website: http://www.crouch-vale.co.uk 'E'mail: info@crouch-vale.co.uk

Croupe (Fr) a ridge where vines grow. i.e. Margaux.

Crouzet Henriette (Fr) the label of a Châteauneuf-du-Pape produced by Crouzet at 4 Bis, Chemin du Bois de la Ville, 84230 Châteauneuf-du-Pape, southern Rhône.

Crow [Dr. James] (USA) built the first distillery in Frankfurt Kentucky in 1835. Now a modern distillery making Old Crow Bourbon.

Crowing Cock (Eng) a 4.2% alc by vol. cask-conditioned bitter brewed by Hardys and Hansons, Kimberley Brewery, Nottingham. Part of the Cellarman's Cask range.

Crow Light (USA) the brand-name of a light, blended whiskey. 40% alc by vol.

Crown (USA) the name for the cap (chapeau) during the fermentation process.

Crown Ale (Eng) an ale brewed for the Queen's Silver Jubilee by the Cameron's Brewery in Hartlepool, County Durham. 1040 O.G.

Crown Ale (Eng) a special ale at 5.5% alc by vol. brewed by the Potton Brewing Company for the Golden Jubilee of Queen Elizabeth 2nd in 2002.

Crown Ale (Eng) a pale ale (bottled) 1039 O.G. brewed by Greene King Brewery, East Anglia.

Crown Beer (E.Asia) a lager beer brewed by the Oriental Brewery in Seoul, South Korea.

Crown Bitter (Eng) a bitter beer brewed by Bass Charrington at their Cape Hill Brewery.

Crown Brewery (Eng) a brewery. (Add): 56 Langsett Road, Sheffield, South Yorkshire S6 2UB. Brews a variety of beers and lager. Website: http://www.crownbrewery.com 'E'mail: reception@hillsboroughhotel.com

Crown Brewery (Wal) merged with Buckley's in 1989. *see* Crown Buckley.

Crown Buckley (Wal) a brewery based in South Wales that used to brew for the Miner's clubs. Based in Pontyclun, Mid-Glamorgan and supplies the clubs in the area. Formed in 1989 by a merger of Crown Brewery, Pontyclun and Buckley's, Llanelli. Brews Brenin 1034 O.G. Brown Bracer 1033 O.G. Great Western 1041 O.G. Black Prince, Merlin, St. Davids Ale, Sunbeam. Merged with S.A. Brain in 1997. Now known as S.A. Brain & C°. Ltd.

Crown Cork (USA) a patented metal bottle cap now used for most bottled carbonated beverages.

Crown Dry (Kor) a lager beer 5.1% alc by vol. from the Chosun Brewery.

Crown Graft (Eng) a style of grafting where the scion is inserted at the crown of the stock.

Crowning (USA) a term used to describe the using of the Crown corks to cap pressure beers in bottle.

Crowning Glory (Eng) a 6.8% alc by vol. strong ale brewed by the Leyden brewery, Lancashire.

Crown Jewel (Eng) the brand-name of a 50% alc by vol. triple distilled de luxe London dry gin from Beefeater in London.

Crown of Crowns (Ger) a famous brand name liebfraumilch from the firm of Langenbach.

Crown Point Bitter (Eng) a cask-conditioned bitter 1038 O.G. brewed by the Crown Point Inn, Seal Chart, Kent.

Crown Point Inn (Eng) a home-brew public house in Seal Chart, Kent. Brews Crown Point Bitter.

Crown Royal (Can) a de luxe 10 year old blended Canadian whisky 40% alc by vol. Produced by Seagram.

Crown Russe Vodka (USA) a vodka produced by Calvert Distilling C°. (part of Seagram) 30% alc by vol.

Crown Viking (Eng) a brand-name used by Dema Glass for a popular style of their glassware.

Crow's Nest (Eng) a 4.8% alc by vol. cask ale produced by the Flagship Brewery, Chatham Dockyard, Dartford.

Crows Nest (S.Afr) a winery (established 2003) based in Paarl, Western Cape. 11ha. Grape varieties: Cabernet sauvignon, Chardonnay, Merlot, Sauvignon blanc, Syrah. Labels: La Karnel, Marcel de Reuck, Torres Claude.

Crow Valley Bitter (Wal) a 4.2% alc by vol. bitter beer brewed by the Cwmbran Brewery, Gwent.

Crow Valley Stout (Wal) a 4.2% alc by vol. stout brewed by the Cwmbran Brewery, Gwent.

Croydon Vineyard Residential Estate (S.Afr) a winery (established 2005) based in Tokai, Stellenbosch, Western Cape. 7ha. Grape varieties: Cabernet franc, Cabernet sauvignon, Merlot, Pinotage, Shiraz. Website: http://www.croydon-estate.co.za

Crozes-Hermitage (Fr) an A.C. within the district of Hermitage in the central Rhône. Has 11 communes in 350ha. situated in the northern end of Hermitage (red and white wines) minimum alc by vol. 11%.

Cru (Fr) growth, the soil on which the vine is grown. *see* Premier Cru, Grand Cru, Creu and Crus. (It) = ronco.

Cru Abraham (Fr) a vineyard. (Com): Sainte-Croix-du-Mont. A.C. Sainte-Croix-du-Mont, Bordeaux 4ha.

Cru Arrançon-Boutoc (Fr) a vineyard. (Com): Preignac. A.C. Sauternes, Bordeaux 3ha.

Cru Artisan (Fr) a term used in the Haut-Médoc and Médoc for rank below Cru Bourgeois. Denoted properties of 1ha–5ha. Wines are submitted for tasting after a minimum period of 15 months. Property is totally responsible for the viticulture, vinification, ageing, bottling and marketing. Since 1994 denotes property of 8ha–10ha.

Cru au Verre (Fr) *see* Cruover.

Cru Baboye (Fr) a vineyard. (Com): Fargues. A.C. Sauternes, Bordeaux 2ha.

Cru Barberousse (Fr) *see* Château Barberousse.

Cru Baret-les-Arrivaux (Fr) a vineyard. (Com): Sainte-Croix-du-Mont. A.C. Sainte-Croix-du-Mont, Bordeaux 3ha.

Cru Barjumeau (Fr) a vineyard. (Com): Sauternes. A.C. Sauternes, Bordeaux 3ha.

Cru Barraillot (Fr) a vineyard. (Com): Margaux. A.C. Margaux, Bordeaux 3ha.

Cru Barrette (Fr) a vineyard. (Com): Fargues. A.C. Sauternes, Bordeaux 1ha.

Cru Barrouet (Fr) a vineyard. (Com): Pujols. A.C. Graves, Bordeaux. 3ha (white).

Cru Bas-Peyraguey (Fr) a vineyard. (Com): Preignac. A.C. Sauternes, Bordeaux 2ha.

Cru Batsalle (Fr) a vineyard. (Com): Fargues. A.C. Sauternes, Bordeaux 1ha.

Cru Baylieu (Fr) a vineyard. (Com): Fargues. A.C. Sauternes, Bordeaux 7ha.

Cru Bel-Air (Fr) a vineyard. (Com): Illats. A.C. Cérons, Bordeaux 3ha.

Cru Bel-Air (Fr) a vineyard. (Com): Preignac. A.C. Sauternes, Bordeaux 2ha.

Cru Bel-Air Mareil (Fr) a vineyard. (Com): Ordonnac-et-Potensac. A.C. Médoc, Bordeaux. 3ha.

Cru Bellevue-Mondotte (Fr) a vineyard in the A.C. Saint-Émilion, Bordeaux 2ha.

Cru Bergeron (Fr) a vineyard. (Com): Preignac. A.C. Sauternes, Bordeaux 4ha.

Cru Berlière (Fr) a vineyard. (Com): Parsac-Saint-Émilion. A.C. Saint-Émilion, Bordeaux 4ha.

Cru Bernisse (Fr) a vineyard. (Com): Barsac. A.C. Barsac (or Sauternes), Bordeaux 1ha.

Cru Bibian Darriet (Fr) a vineyard. (Com): Listrac. A.C. Haut-Médoc, Bordeaux 2ha.

Cru Bichons (Fr) a vineyard. (Com): La Brède. A.C. Graves, Bordeaux. 5ha (red and white).

Cru Bignon (Fr) a vineyard. (Com): Bommes. A.C. Sauternes, Bordeaux 1ha.

Cru Bilbey (Fr) a vineyard in the A.C. Saint-Émilion, Bordeaux 6ha.

Cru Biquet (Fr) a vineyard in the A.C. Saint-Émilion, Bordeaux 4ha.

Cru Bordesouilles (Fr) a vineyard. (Com): Preignac. A.C. Sauternes, Bordeaux 3ha.

Cru Boritz (Fr) a vineyard. (Com): St-Pierre-de-Mons. A.C. Graves, Bordeaux 4ha. (white).

Cru Bourgeois (Fr) the classification of 58 Médoc wines below the 5th growths of the 1855 classification. Wines are of good quality and carry A.C. Haut-Médoc (or A.C. communes) and A.C. Médoc. Since 1978 must not be less than 7ha. in size, wine to be made on the property and submitted for official tasting before being awarded the designation. In January 2001 the first official classification of Cru Bourgeois of the Médoc was introduced and finalised in 2003. It created three categories: Cru Bourgeois, Cru Bourgeois Supérieur, Cru Bourgeois Exceptionnel. Will be revised every 10 years. Each Château will have to apply for status.

Cru Bourgeois Exceptionnel (Fr) the new (2003) grading for top Cru Bourgeois wines grown within the A.C.'s of the Haut-Médoc, Bordeaux. Will be revised every ten years. *see* Cru Bourgeois, Cru Bourgeois Supérieur.

Cru Bourgeois Supérieur (Fr) a new classification (2003) for A.C.'s of the Haut-Médoc Bordeaux. Aged in wood. Superior to a Cru Bourgeois. Will be revised every ten years. *see* Cru Bourgeois, Cru Bourgeois Exceptionnel.

Cru Bousclas (Fr) a vineyard. (Com): Barsac. A.C. Barsac (or Sauternes), Bordeaux 4ha.

Cru Boutoc (Fr) a vineyard. (Com): Preignac. A.C. Sauternes, Bordeaux 5ha.

Cru Boutoc (Fr) a vineyard. (Com): Sauternes. A.C. Sauternes, Bordeaux 2ha.

Cru Boutreou (Fr) a vineyard. (Com): Preignac. A.C. Sauternes, Bordeaux 1ha.

Cru Bouyon (Fr) a vineyard. (Com): Pujols. A.C. Graves, Bordeaux. 2ha (white).

Cru Brouillaou (Fr) a vineyard. (Com): Podensac. A.C. Cérons, Bordeaux 11ha.

Cru Calens (Fr) a vineyard. (Com): Beautiran. A.C. Graves, Bordeaux. 6ha (white).

Cru Camegaye (Fr) a vineyard. (Com): Landiras. A.C. Graves, Bordeaux. 2ha (white).

Cru Camelong (Fr) a vineyard. (Com): Bommes. A.C. Sauternes, Bordeaux 1ha.

Cru Canteloup (Fr) a vineyard. (Com): Blaignan. A.C. Médoc, Bordeaux 2ha.

Cru Capital Monte Fontana (It) a sweet Recioto wine produced by Renzo Tedeschi in Valpolicella, Veneto.

Cru Caplane (Fr) a vineyard. (Com): Bommes. A.C. Sauternes, Bordeaux 2ha.

Cru Caplane (Fr) a vineyard. (Com): Sauternes. A.C. Sauternes, Bordeaux 5ha.

Cru Carbonnieu (Fr) a vineyard. (Com): Bommes. A.C. Sauternes, Bordeaux 6ha.

Cru Cardeneau (Fr) a vineyard. (Com): Saillans. A.C. Côtes de Fronsac, Bordeaux 10ha.

Cru Castagnet (Fr) a vineyard. (Com): Virelade. A.C. Graves, Bordeaux. 3ha (white).

Cru Chanyeloisseau (Fr) a vineyard. (Com): Langon. A.C. Graves, Bordeaux 5ha (white).

Cru Chauvin (Fr) a vineyard. (Com): Sauternes. A.C. Sauternes, Bordeaux 2ha.

Cru Chêne-Vert (Fr) a vineyard. (Com): Parsac-Saint-Émilion. A.C. Parsac-Saint-Émilion, Bordeaux 7ha.

Cru Chercy (Fr) a vineyard. (Com): Pujols. A.C. Graves, Bordeaux. 2ha (white).

Cruchinet (Fr) an alternative name for the Chenin blanc grape.

Crucial Brew (W.Ind) a strong version of Red Stripe Lager 1038 O.G. from Jamaica. Brewed by Charles Wells in England under licence. *see* Red Stripe Crucial Brew.

Crucible (S.Afr) the label for a red wine (Shiraz) produced by the Cloof winery, Darling, Western Cape.

Cru Classé (Fr) classified growths. In Bordeaux the ratings that the vineyards were given. Médoc 1855 (*See also* Château Mouton Rothschild), Graves 1953 and 1959, Saint-Émilion 1955 (revised at regular 10 year intervals), Sauternes 1855.

Cru Claverie (Fr) a vineyard. (Com): Sauternes. A.C. Sauternes, Bordeaux 2ha.

Cru Cleyrac (Fr) a vineyard. (Com): Cérons. A.C. Cérons, Bordeaux 5ha.

Cru Cluziot (Fr) a vineyard. (Com): Barsac. A.C. Barsac (or Sauternes), Bordeaux 1ha.

C

Crucoli (It) a wine-producing commune in the Calabria district. Is noted for red, rosé and white Ciró wines.

Cru Commarque (Fr) a vineyard. (Com): Bommes. A.C. Sauternes, Bordeaux 1ha.

Cru Commarque (Fr) a vineyard. (Com): Sauternes. A.C. Sauternes, Bordeaux 6ha.

Cru Commet-Magey (Fr) a vineyard. (Com): Preignac. A.C. Sauternes, Bordeaux 4ha.

Cru Commet-Magey-Briatte (Fr) a vineyard. (Com): Preignac. A.C. Sauternes, Bordeaux 4ha.

Cru Côtes-du-Fayan (Fr) a vineyard. (Com): Puisseguin-Saint-Émilion. A.C. Puisseguin-Saint-Émilion, Bordeaux 8ha.

Cru Côtes-Pressac (Fr) a vineyard in the A.C. Saint-Émilion, Bordeaux 2ha.

Cru Côtes-Roland (Fr) a vineyard in the A.C. Saint-Émilion, Bordeaux 2ha.

Cru Côtes-Veyrac (Fr) a vineyard in the A.C. Saint-Émilion, Bordeaux 2ha.

Cru Coussères (Fr) a vineyard. (Com): Fargues. A.C. Sauternes, Bordeaux 1ha.

Cru Coustet (Fr) a vineyard. (Com): Barsac. A.C. Barsac (or Sauternes), Bordeaux 1ha.

Cru d'Arche-Pugnau (Fr) a vineyard. (Com): Preignac. A.C. Sauternes. (Add): 33210 Langon, Bordeaux 15ha. Also Château Peyraguey-la-Rousset.

Cru d'Arrançon (Fr) a vineyard. (Com): Preignac. A.C. Sauternes, Bordeaux 5ha.

Cru de Barboye (Fr) a vineyard. (Com): Bommes. A.C. Sauternes, Bordeaux 2ha.

Cru de Bérot (Fr) a vineyard. (Com): Arbanats. A.C. Graves, Bordeaux. 2ha (white).

Cru de Bizeaudon (Fr) a vineyard. (Com): Ludon. A.C. Médoc, Bordeaux. Cru Bourgeois.

Cru de Borderie (Fr) a vineyard. (Com): Portets. A.C. Graves, Bordeaux. 5ha (red and white).

Cru de Bouley (Fr) a vineyard. (Com): Illats. A.C. Cérons, Bordeaux 4ha.

Cru de Boutec (Fr) a vineyard. (Com): Illats. A.C. Cérons, Bordeaux 5ha.

Cru de Braze (Fr) a vineyard. (Com): Illats. A.C. Cérons, Bordeaux 7ha.

Cru de Cabiro (Fr) a vineyard. (Com): Illats. A.C. Cérons, Bordeaux 3ha.

Cru de Cadenne (Fr) a vineyard. (Com): Pujols. A.C. Graves, Bordeaux. 5ha (white).

Cru de Cap-de-Hé (Fr) a vineyard. (Com): Pujols. A.C. Graves, Bordeaux 2ha (white).

Cru de Gaillardet (Fr) a vineyard. (Com): Sainte-Croix-du-Mont. A.C. Sainte-Croix-du-Mont, Bordeaux 1ha.

Cru de Gonthier (Fr) a vineyard. (Com): Portets. A.C. Graves, Bordeaux. 3ha (red and white).

Cru de Guerisson (Fr) a vineyard. (Com): Sainte-Croix-du-Mont. A.C. Sainte-Croix-du-Mont, Bordeaux 3ha.

Cru de Haut-Blanc (Fr) a vineyard. (Com): Pujols. A.C. Graves, Bordeaux. 1ha (white).

Cru de Haute-Mayne (Fr) a vineyard. (Com): Cérons. A.C. Cérons, Bordeaux 3ha.

Cru de la Cave (Fr) a vineyard. (Com): Preignac. A.C. Sauternes, Bordeaux 2ha.

Cru de la Chatolle (Fr) a vineyard. (Com): St. Laurent. A.C. Médoc, Bordeaux. Cru Bourgeois.

Cru de la Colonie (Fr) the second wine of Château Malescot-Saint-Exupéry. Grand Cru Classé (3rd). A.C. Margaux, Bordeaux.

Cru de la Côte Doré (Fr) a vineyard. (Com): Sainte-Croix-du-Mont. A.C. Sainte-Croix-du-Mont, Bordeaux 2ha.

Cru de la Girouette (Fr) a vineyard. (Com): Fours. A.C. Côtes de Blaye, Bordeaux.

Cru de Lamoigon (Fr) a vineyard. (Com): Pujols. A.C. Graves, Bordeaux. 3ha (white).

Cru de la Nouvelle-Église (Fr) a vineyard. (Com): Pomerol. A.C. Pomerol, Bordeaux 2ha.

Cru de la Poste (Fr) a vineyard. (Com): Virelade. A.C. Graves, Bordeaux. 4ha (white).

Cru de la Sablière (Fr) a vineyard. (Com): Loupiac. A.C. Loupiac, Bordeaux 4ha.

Cru de la Vigne du Diable (Switz) a vineyard based in Cortaillod, Neuchâtel (white).

Cru de l'Église (Fr) a vineyard. (Com): Virelade. A.C. Graves, Bordeaux. 2ha (white).

Cru de l'Hermitage (Fr). A vineyard. (Com): Budos. A.C. Graves, Bordeaux. 8ha (red).

Cru de Lionne (Fr) a vineyard. (Com): Illats. A.C. Cérons, Bordeaux 7ha.

Cru de Lubat (Fr) a vineyard. (Com): St-Pierre-de-Mons. A.C. Graves, Bordeaux. 8ha (white).

Cru de Mahon (Fr) a vineyard. (Com): Preignac. A.C. Sauternes, Bordeaux 2ha.

Cru de Menjon (Fr) a vineyard. (Com): Illats. A.C. Cérons, Bordeaux 3ha.

Cru de Montagne (Fr) a vineyard. (Com): Sainte-Croix-du-Mont. A.C. Sainte-Croix-du-Mont, Bordeaux 5ha.

Cru de Montalivet (Fr) a vineyard. (Com): Barsac. A.C. Barsac (or Sauternes), Bordeaux.

Cru de Perret (Fr) a vineyard. (Com): Bommes. A.C. Sauternes, Bordeaux 2ha.

Cru de Peyre (Fr) a vineyard. (Com): Fargues. A.C. Sauternes, Bordeaux 1ha.

Cru de Pistoulet-Peyraguey (Fr) a vineyard. (Com): Bommes. A.C. Sauternes, Bordeaux 2ha.

Cru de Portails (Fr) a vineyard. (Com): Landiras. A.C. Graves, Bordeaux. 2ha (white).

Cru de Rouquette (Fr) a vineyard. (Com): Loupiac. A.C. Loupiac, Bordeaux 8ha.

Cru des Deux Moulins (Fr) a vineyard. (Com): Illats. A.C. Cérons, Bordeaux 4ha.

Cru des Deux-Moulins (Fr) a vineyard. (Com): St-Christoly. A.C. Médoc, Bordeaux 13ha.

Cru des Graves (Fr) a vineyard. (Com): Portets. A.C. Graves, Bordeaux. 4ha (red and white).

Cru des Graves (Fr) a vineyard in the A.C. Saint-Émilion, Bordeaux 2ha.

Cru des Guizats (Fr) a vineyard. (Com): Pujols. A.C. Graves, Bordeaux. 2ha (white).

Cru des Moulins-à-Vent (Fr) a vineyard. (Com): Cérons. A.C. Cérons, Bordeaux. 12ha. Has 2 owners: 3ha. and 9ha.

Cru des Parrajots (Fr) a vineyard. (Com): Illats. A.C. Graves, Bordeaux 3ha.

Cru des Plantes (Fr) a vineyard. (Com): Landiras. A.C. Graves, Bordeaux. 14ha (white).

Cru des Ptolemées (Egy) a brand of white wine produced by Gianaclis Vineyards at Abú-Hummus.

Cru des Terrefort (Fr) a vineyard. (Com): Loupiac. A.C. Loupiac, Bordeaux 4ha.

Cru des Terrefort Pierre Noire (Fr) a vineyard. (Com): Loupiac. A.C. Loupiac, Bordeaux 3ha.

Cru des Terres Rouges (Fr) a vineyard. (Com): Barsac. A.C. Barsac (or Sauternes), Bordeaux 2ha.

Cru des Tonnelles (Fr) a vineyard. (Com): St-Aignan. A.C. Côtes de Fronsac, Bordeaux 3ha.

Cru de Troupian (Fr) a vineyard. (Com): Saint-Estèphe. A.C. Saint-Estèphe, Bordeaux 2ha.

Cru de Vieux-Château Landon (Fr) a vineyard. (Com): Bégadan. A.C. Médoc, Bordeaux 20ha.

Cru Druenn (Fr) a vineyard. (Com): Barsac. A.C. Barsac (or Sauternes), Bordeaux 2ha.

Cru du Braneyre (Fr) the second wine of Château d'Arche, A.C. Sauternes, Bordeaux.

Cru du Caladis (Fr) a vineyard. (Com): Portets. A.C. Graves, Bordeaux. 7ha (red and white).

Cru du Canet (Fr) a vineyard. (Com): Sainte-Croix-du-Mont. A.C. Sainte-Croix-du-Mont, Bordeaux 3ha.

Cru du Carrefour (Fr) a vineyard. (Com): Sauternes. A.C. Sauternes, Bordeaux 1ha.

Cru Ducas (Fr) a vineyard. (Com): Illats. A.C. Cérons, Bordeaux 2ha.

Cru Ducasse (Fr) a vineyard. (Com): Fargues. A.C. Sauternes, Bordeaux 2ha.

Cru du Chalet (Fr) a vineyard. (Com): Barsac. A.C. Barsac (or Sauternes), Bordeaux. 2ha.

Cru du Chalet (Fr) a vineyard. (Com): Preignac. A.C. Sauternes, Bordeaux 1ha.

Cru du Clocher (Fr) a red wine produced by Château Caillou. Grand Cru Classé (2nd). A.C. Barsac, Bordeaux.

Cru du Couet (Fr) a vineyard. (Com): St-Pierre-de-Mons. A.C. Graves, Bordeaux. 2ha (white).

Cru du Grand Chênes (Fr) a vineyard. (Com): Cérons. A.C. Cérons, Bordeaux 3ha.

Cru du Haire (Fr) a vineyard. (Com): Preignac. A.C. Sauternes, Bordeaux 6ha.

Cru du Haut-Claron (Fr) a vineyard. (Com): St-Morillon. A.C. Graves, Bordeaux. 3ha (white).

Cru du Hère (Fr) a vineyard. (Com): Preignac. A.C. Sauternes, Bordeaux 2ha.

Cru du Moulin-à-Vent (Fr) a vineyard. (Com): Illats. A.C. Cérons, Bordeaux 2ha.

Cru du Moulin-à-Vent (Fr) a vineyard. (Com): Landiras. A.C. Graves, Bordeaux 3ha. (white).

Cru du Moulin de Laborde (Fr) a vineyard. (Com): Listrac. A.C. Listrac, Bordeaux 7ha.

Cru du Moulin Neuf (Fr) a vineyard. (Com): Preignac. A.C. Sauternes, Bordeaux 1ha.

Cru du Moulins-à-Vent (Fr) a vineyard. (Com): Cérons. A.C. Graves, Bordeaux 3ha. (white).

Cru du Moulin Vieux (Fr) a vineyard. (Com): Loupiac. A.C. Loupiac, Bordeaux 5ha.

Cru du Noulin (Fr) a vineyard. (Com): Cérons. A.C. Cérons, Bordeaux 3ha.

Cru du Pageot (Fr) a vineyard. (Com): Bommes. A.C. Sauternes, Bordeaux 4ha.

Cru du Perliques (Fr) a vineyard. (Com): Illats. A.C. Cérons, Bordeaux 3ha.

Cru du Pin (Fr) a vineyard. (Com): Sainte-Croix-du-Mont. A.C. Sainte-Croix-du-Mont, Bordeaux 2ha.

Cru du Placey (Fr) a vineyard. (Com): Barsac. A.C. Barsac (or Sauternes), Bordeaux 1ha.

Cru du Roc (Fr) a vineyard. (Com): Couquéques. A.C. Médoc, Bordeaux 2ha.

Cru du Terrefort (Fr) a vineyard. (Com): Sainte-Croix-du-Mont. A.C. Sainte-Croix-du-Mont, Bordeaux 2ha.

Cru du Violet (Fr) a vineyard. (Com): Preignac. A.C. Sauternes, Bordeaux 1ha.

Cru du Violet-et-Lamothe (Fr) a vineyard. (Com): Preignac. A.C. Sauternes, Bordeaux 5ha.

Cru Duzan (Fr) a vineyard. (Com): Barsac. A.C. Barsac (or Sauternes), Bordeaux 1ha.

Crue (Fr) the old word for a flask or bottle.

Cruet (Fr) a mediaeval name for a flask used for the wine or water for the Eucharist.

Cruet (Fr) an A.C. vineyard based on the right bank of the river Isère in the Savoie region, south-eastern France.

Cru Exceptionnel (Fr) a grading used in the Graves for certain wines not quite of Grand Cru standard. See also Cru Bourgeois Exceptionnel.

Cru Eyquem (Fr) a vineyard. (Com): La Brède. A.C. Graves, Bordeaux. 5ha (white).

Cru Ferrandat (Fr) a vineyard in the A.C. Saint-Émilion, Bordeaux 1ha.

Cru Fillau (Fr) a vineyard. (Com): Fargues. A.C. Sauternes, Bordeaux 4ha.

Cru Fort Médoc (Fr) a vineyard. (Com): Cussac-Fort-Médoc. A.C. Haut-Médoc, Bordeaux. 50ha. Grape varieties: Cabernet 50% and Merlot 50%.

Cru Franc-Mazerat (Fr) a vineyard in the A.C. Saint-Émilion, Bordeaux 2ha.

Cru Franc-Roxier (Fr) a vineyard in the A.C. Saint-Émilion, Bordeaux 3ha.

Cru Galad (Fr) a vineyard. (Com): Cérons. A.C. Graves, Bordeaux. 1ha (white).

Cru Gavach (Fr) a vineyard. (Com): Fargues. A.C. Sauternes, Bordeaux 3ha.

Cru Gavailles (Fr) a vineyard. (Com): Preignac. A.C. Sauternes, Bordeaux 2ha.

Crugny (Fr) a Cru Champagne village in the Canton de Fismes. District: Reims.

Cru Grand Bourgeois (Fr) a 1978 classification for certain properties which includes the rules of Cru Bourgeois plus the requirement to age young wine in oak casks. Nine properties were classified: Châteaux Greysac, La Cardonne, La Tour de By, Laujac, Les Ormes Sorbet, Loudenne, Patache d'Aux, Potensac and Sigognac. See also Cru Grand Bourgeois Exceptionnel. see Cru Bourgeois Supérieur.

Cru Grand Bourgeois Exceptionnel (Fr) a 1978 classification. As for Cru Grand Bourgeois but

C

Châteaux must be sited in communes that contain Grand Cru Classé (1855) vineyards in the Haut-Médoc. *see* Cru Bourgeois Exceptionnel.

Cru Grand-Carretey (Fr) a vineyard. (Com): Barsac. A.C. Barsac (or Sauternes), Bordeaux 6ha.

Cru Grand Champ (Fr) a vineyard. (Com): Pomerol. A.C. Pomerol, Bordeaux.

Cru Grand-Jauga (Fr) a vineyard. (Com): Barsac. A.C. Barsac (or Sauternes), Bordeaux 2ha.

Cru Grand-Mazeyres (Fr) a vineyard. (Com): Pomerol. A.C. Pomerol, Bordeaux 2ha.

Cru Grotte-d'Arcis (Fr) a vineyard in the A.C. Saint-Émilion, Bordeaux 3ha.

Cru Guillem-du-Rey (Fr) a vineyard. (Com): Preignac. A.C. Sauternes, Bordeaux 7ha.

Cru Gutteronde (Fr) a vineyard in the commune in Barsac. A.C. Barsac (or Sauternes), Bordeaux 1ha.

Cru Haut-Buhan (Fr) a vineyard. (Com): Illats. A.C. Cérons, Bordeaux 7ha.

Cru Hautes Plantes (Fr) a vineyard. (Com): Landiras. A.C. Graves, Bordeaux. 3ha (white).

Cru Haut-Grand-Faurie (Fr) a vineyard in the A.C. Saint-Émilion, Bordeaux 1ha.

Cru Haut-Gravette (Fr) a vineyard. (Com): St-Morillon. A.C. Graves, Bordeaux 3ha. (white).

Cru Haut-Groupey (Fr) a vineyard. (Com): Pomerol. A.C. Pomerol, Bordeaux 2ha.

Cru Haut-Lagueritte (Fr) a vineyard. (Com): Bommes. A.C. Sauternes, Bordeaux 2ha.

Cru Haut la Hountasse (Fr) a vineyard. (Com): Illats. A.C. Cérons, Bordeaux 8ha.

Cru Haut-Larrivat (Fr) a vineyard. (Com): Sainte-Croix-du-Mont. A.C. Sainte-Croix-du-Mont, Bordeaux 3ha.

Cru Haut-Mayne (Fr) a vineyard. (Com): Cérons. A.C. Cérons, Bordeaux 2ha.

Cru Haut-Medouc (Fr) a vineyard. (Com): Sainte-Croix-du-Mont. A.C. Sainte-Croix-du-Mont, Bordeaux 3ha.

Cru Haut-Piquan (Fr) a vineyard. (Com): Sauternes. A.C. Sauternes, Bordeaux 1ha.

Cru Haut-Reys (Fr) a vineyard. (Com): La Brède. A.C. Graves, Bordeaux. 3ha (red and white).

Cru Hontane (Fr) *see* Château Côtes de Blaignan, A.C. Médoc, Bordeaux.

Cru Hourmalas (Fr) a vineyard. (Com): Barsac. A.C. Barsac (or Sauternes), Bordeaux 2ha.

Crúim (Ire) milk.

Cruina (It) an alternative name for Corvina in Veneto.

Cru Janot-Bayle (Fr) a vineyard. (Com): Budos. A.C. Graves, Bordeaux. 8ha (red).

Cru Jauguet (Fr) a vineyard. (Com): Barsac. A.C. Barsac (or Sauternes), Bordeaux 5ha.

Cru Jeanguillot (Fr) a vineyard in the A.C. Saint-Émilion, Bordeaux 2ha.

Cru Jeannonier (Fr) a vineyard. (Com): Bommes. A.C. Sauternes, Bordeaux 3ha.

Crujidera (Sp) a red grape variety grown in southern Spain.

Crujillón (Sp) a black grape variety related to the Carignan and Mazuelo.

Cru Jubilé (Fr) a vineyard in the A.C. Saint-Émilion, Bordeaux 2ha.

Cru Junka (Fr) a vineyard. (Com): Preignac. A.C. Sauternes, Bordeaux 3ha.

Cru la Bernisse (Fr) a vineyard. (Com): Barsac. A.C. Barsac (or Sauternes), Bordeaux 3ha.

Cru la Bouchette (Fr) a vineyard. (Com): Bommes. A.C. Sauternes, Bordeaux 1ha.

Cru la Bouchette (Fr) a vineyard. (Com): Preignac. A.C. Sauternes, Bordeaux 2ha.

Cru Labrousse (Fr) a vineyard. (Com): Barsac. A.C. Barsac (or Sauternes), Bordeaux 2ha.

Cru la Cabane (Fr) a vineyard. (Com): Pujols. A.C. Graves, Bordeaux. 4ha (white).

Cru la Capère (Fr) a vineyard. (Com): Landiras. A.C. Graves, Bordeaux. 4ha (white).

Cru la Chapelle (Fr) a vineyard. (Com): Parsac-Saint-Émilion. A.C. Parsac-Saint-Émilion, Bordeaux 7ha.

Cru la Côte (Fr) a vineyard. (Com): Fargues. A.C. Sauternes, Bordeaux 5ha.

Cru la Croix-Blanche (Fr) a vineyard. (Com): Montagne-Saint-Émilion. A.C. Saint-Émilion, Bordeaux 2ha.

Cru Lafon (Fr) a vineyard. (Com): St-Pierre-de-Mons. A.C. Graves, Bordeaux. 2ha (white).

Cru Lagardan (Fr) a vineyard. (Com): Pomerol. A.C. Pomerol, Bordeaux.

Cru la Garelle (Fr) a vineyard in the A.C. Saint-Émilion, Bordeaux 1ha.

Cru la Girouette (Fr) a vineyard. (Com): Cantelègue. A.C. Côtes de Blaye, Bordeaux.

Cru l'Agnet (Fr) a vineyard. (Com): Bommes. A.C. Sauternes, Bordeaux 2ha.

Cru Lagrange (Fr) a vineyard. (Com): Pomerol. A.C. Pomerol, Bordeaux.

Cru la Grave (Fr) a vineyard. (Com): Sainte-Croix-du-Mont. A.C. Sainte-Croix-du-Mont, Bordeaux 2ha.

Cru la Gravière (Fr) a vineyard. (Com): Preignac. A.C. Sauternes, Bordeaux 2ha.

Cru Lahonade-Peyraguey (Fr) a vineyard. (Com): Bommes. A.C. Sauternes, Bordeaux 2ha.

Cru la Hounade (Fr) a vineyard. (Com): Pujols. A.C. Graves, Bordeaux. 2ha (white).

Cru Lalot (Fr) a vineyard. (Com): Preignac. A.C. Sauternes, Bordeaux 6ha.

Cru la Mainionce (Fr) a vineyard. (Com): Pujols. A.C. Graves, Bordeaux. 3ha (white).

Cru la Médicine (Fr) a vineyard. (Com): St-Pierre-de-Mons. A.C. Graves, Bordeaux. 2ha (white).

Cru Lamothe (Fr) a vineyard. (Com): Sauternes. A.C. Sauternes, Bordeaux 6ha.

Cru la Mouleyre (Fr) a vineyard. (Com): Sainte-Croix-du-Mont. A.C. Sainte-Croix-du-Mont, Bordeaux 3ha.

Cru Landarey (Fr) part of Château Hennebelle, A.C. Haut-Médoc, Bordeaux.

Cru Lanère (Fr) a vineyard. (Com): Sauternes. A.C. Sauternes, Bordeaux 1ha.

Cru Langa (Fr) a vineyard. (Com): Cussac. A.C. Haut-Médoc, Bordeaux 3ha.

Cru Lanusquet (Fr) a vineyard. (Com): Fargues. A.C. Sauternes, Bordeaux 2ha.

Cru **Lapinesse** (Fr) a vineyard. (Com): Barsac. A.C. Barsac (or Sauternes), Bordeaux 7ha.

Cru **la Pinesse** (Fr) a vineyard. (Com): Barsac. A.C. Barsac (or Sauternes), Bordeaux 2ha.

Cru **la Rame** (Fr) a vineyard. (Com): Sainte-Croix-du-Mont. A.C. Sainte-Croix-du-Mont, Bordeaux 6ha.

Cru **Lardite** (Fr) a vineyard. (Com): Arbanats. A.C. Graves, Bordeaux. 4ha (white).

Cru **Larode** (Fr) a vineyard. (Com): Sauternes. A.C. Sauternes, Bordeaux 1ha.

Cru **la Rose** (Fr) a vineyard. (Com): Puisseguin-Saint-Émilion. A.C. Puisseguin-Saint-Émilion, Bordeaux 5ha.

Cru **Larragay** (Fr) a vineyard. (Com): Listrac. A.C. Haut-Médoc, Bordeaux 2ha.

Cru **Larroucat** (Fr) a vineyard. (Com): Pujols. A.C. Graves, Bordeaux. 2ha (white).

Cru **Larrouquey** (Fr) a vineyard. (Com): Cérons. A.C. Cérons, Bordeaux 7ha.

Cru **la Terce** (Fr) a vineyard. (Com): Budos. A.C. Graves, Bordeaux. 2ha (red).

Cru **la Tour-Fonrazade** (Fr) part of Château Haut-Fonazade, A.C. Saint-Émilion, Bordeaux.

Cru **la Tuilerie** (Fr) a vineyard. (Com): Landiras. A.C. Graves, Bordeaux. 2ha (white).

Cru **l'Aubépin** (Fr) a vineyard. (Com): Bommes. A.C. Sauternes, Bordeaux 10ha.

Cru **l'Aubépine** (Fr) a vineyard. (Com): Bommes. A.C. Sauternes, Bordeaux 3ha.

Cru **l'Aubépins** (Fr) a vineyard. (Com): Sauternes. A.C. Sauternes, Bordeaux 3ha.

Cru **le Bécasse du Ferrey** (Fr) part of Château Ferrey Gros Caillou, A.C. Haut-Médoc, Bordeaux.

Cru **le Bourut** (Fr) a vineyard. (Com): Pujols. A.C. Graves, Bordeaux. 2ha (white).

Cru **le Franc-Rival** (Fr) a vineyard. (Com): Lussac-Saint-Émilion. A.C. Saint-Émilion, Bordeaux 2ha.

Cru **le Haut Bommes** (Fr) a vineyard. (Com): Bommes. A.C. Sauternes, Bordeaux 0.5ha.

Cru **le Monteil** (Fr) a vineyard. (Com): Arsac. A.C. Médoc, Bordeaux. Cru Bourgeois Supérieur.

Cru **le Pageot** (Fr) a vineyard. (Com): Bommes. A.C. Sauternes, Bordeaux 2ha.

Cru **le Roc** (Fr) a vineyard. (Com): Preignac. A.C. Sauternes, Bordeaux 1ha.

Cru **le Rousseau** (Fr) a vineyard. (Com): Bommes. A.C. Sauternes, Bordeaux 2ha.

Cru **les Arroucats** (Fr) a vineyard. (Com): Sainte-Croix-du-Mont. A.C. Sainte-Croix-du-Mont, Bordeaux 2ha.

Cru **les Cailloux** (Fr) a vineyard. (Com): Bommes. A.C. Sauternes, Bordeaux 2ha.

Cru **Lescourt** (Fr) a vineyard. (Com): Listrac. A.C. Haut-Médoc, Bordeaux 2ha.

Cru **les Graves** (Fr) a vineyard. (Com): Toulenne. A.C. Graves, Bordeaux 4ha.

Cru **les Graves** (Fr) a vineyard. (Com): Barsac. A.C. Barsac (or Sauternes), Bordeaux 1ha.

Cru **les Guizats** (Fr) a vineyard. (Com): Pujols. A.C. Graves, Bordeaux. 2ha (white).

Cru **les Mengets** (Fr) a vineyard. (Com): Pujols. A.C. Graves, Bordeaux. 2ha (white).

Cru **les Pinsas** (Fr) a vineyard. (Com): Pujols. A.C. Graves, Bordeaux. 2ha (white).

Cru **les Quints** (Fr) a vineyard. (Com): Barsac. A.C. Barsac (or Sauternes), Bordeaux 1ha.

Cru **les Rochers** (Fr) a vineyard. (Com): Preignac. A.C. Sauternes, Bordeaux 2ha.

Cru **les Rocs** (Fr) a vineyard. (Com): Pujols. A.C. Graves, Bordeaux. 2ha (white).

Cru **Lestage** (Fr) a vineyard. (Com): Landiras. A.C. Graves, Bordeaux. 4ha (white).

Cru **les Tourelles** (Fr) a vineyard. (Com): Blaignan. A.C. Médoc, Bordeaux 15ha.

Cru **les Tuileries** (Fr) a vineyard. (Com): Fargues. A.C. Sauternes, Bordeaux 1ha.

Cru **le Tarey** (Fr) a vineyard. (Com): Sainte-Croix-du-Mont. A.C. Sainte-Croix-du-Mont, Bordeaux 5ha.

Cru **le Tinan** (Fr) a vineyard. (Com): Illats. A.C. Cérons, Bordeaux 3ha.

Cru **Lioy** (Fr) a vineyard. (Com): Budos. A.C. Graves, Bordeaux. 3ha (red).

Cru **Madéro**t (Fr) a vineyard. (Com): Podensac. A.C. Cérons, Bordeaux. 11ha (has 2 owners).

Cru **Magnaud** (Fr) a vineyard. (Com): La Brède. A.C. Graves, Bordeaux. 5ha (red and white).

Cru **Mahon** (Fr) a vineyard. (Com): Bommes. A.C. Sauternes, Bordeaux 1ha.

Cru **Mahon** (Fr) a vineyard. (Com): Preignac. A.C. Sauternes, Bordeaux 2ha.

Cru **Majans** (Fr) a vineyard. (Com): Cérons. A.C. Cérons, Bordeaux 3ha.

Cru **Marc** (Fr) a vineyard. (Com): Illats. A.C. Cérons, Bordeaux 5ha.

Cru **Marges Dusseau** (Fr) a vineyard. (Com): Loupiac. A.C. Loupiac, Bordeaux 4ha.

Cru **Massiot** (Fr) a vineyard. (Com): Martillac. A.C. Graves, Bordeaux. 2ha (white).

Cru **Mauras** (Fr) a vineyard. (Com): Bommes. A.C. Sauternes, Bordeaux 3ha.

Cru **Mauvin** (Fr) a vineyard. (Com): Preignac. A.C. Sauternes, Bordeaux 6ha.

Cru **Mayne d'Eyquem** (Fr) a vineyard. (Com): La Brède. A.C. Graves, Bordeaux. 5ha (red and white).

Cru **Maynine** (Fr) a vineyard. (Com): Illats. A.C. Cérons, Bordeaux 3ha.

Cru **Medouc** (Fr) a vineyard. (Com): Sainte-Croix-du-Mont. A.C. Sainte-Croix-du-Mont, Bordeaux 4ha.

Cru **Medouc la Grave** (Fr) a vineyard. (Com): Sainte-Croix-du-Mont. A.C. Sainte-Croix-du-Mont, Bordeaux 2ha.

Cru **Menate** (Fr) a vineyard. (Com): Barsac. A.C. Barsac (or Sauternes), Bordeaux 1ha.

Cru **Mercier** (Fr) a vineyard. (Com): Barsac. A.C. Barsac (or Sauternes), Bordeaux 1ha.

Cru **Miaille** (Fr) a vineyard. (Com): Barsac. A.C. Barsac (or Sauternes), Bordeaux 1ha.

Cru **Miselle** (Fr) a vineyard. (Com): Preignac. A.C. Sauternes, Bordeaux 3ha.

Cru **Monteil** (Fr) a vineyard. (Com): Bommes. A.C. Sauternes, Bordeaux 3ha.

Cru **Monteils** (Fr) a vineyard. (Com): Preignac. A.C. Sauternes, Bordeaux 1ha.

Cru **Montjoie** (Fr) a vineyard. (Com): Preignac. A.C. Sauternes, Bordeaux 2ha.

Cru **Morange** (Fr) a vineyard. (Com): Virelade. A.C. Graves, Bordeaux. 2ha (red and white).

Cru **Mothes** (Fr) a vineyard. (Com): Fargues. A.C. Sauternes, Bordeaux 8ha.

Cru **Moulie de la Glorie** (Fr) a vineyard. (Com): Illats. A.C. Cérons, Bordeaux 2ha.

Cru **Moulin-à-Vent** (Fr) a vineyard. (Com): Illats. A.C. Cérons, Bordeaux 16ha.

Cru **Mourens** (Fr) a vineyard in the A.C. Saint-Émilion, Bordeaux 2ha.

Cru **Mouret** (Fr) a vineyard. (Com): Fargues. A.C. Sauternes, Bordeaux 3ha.

Cru **Mussotte** (Fr) a vineyard. (Com): Fargues. A.C. Sauternes, Bordeaux 1ha.

Cru **Napoléon** (Fr) a vineyard in the A.C. Saint-Émilion, Bordeaux 2ha.

Cru **Nodoy** (Fr) a vineyard. (Com): Virelade. A.C. Graves, Bordeaux. 5ha (red and white).

Cruover (Fr) a unit invented by Jacques Fourès in 1979. Is a dispenser where fine wines are decanted into the multi-units and kept fresh using nitrogen even though some of the wines have been dispensed. Enables fine wines to be sold 'by the glass' without deteriorating. Has 15 separate units. (Fr) = Cru au Verre, (USA) = Cruvinet.

Cru **Passérieux** (Fr) a vineyard. (Com): Barsac. A.C. Barsac (or Sauternes), Bordeaux 3ha.

Cru **Patarabet** (Fr) a vineyard in the A.C. Saint-Émilion, Bordeaux 1ha.

Cru **Patiras** (Fr) a vineyard. (Com): Toulenne. A.C. Graves, Bordeaux. 2ha (white).

Cru **Paysan** (Fr) an old Cru grading rank below Cru Artisan (now no longer used).

Cru **Peillot** (Fr) a vineyard. (Com): Sainte-Croix-du-Mont. A.C. Sainte-Croix-du-Mont, Bordeaux 2ha.

Cru **Perran** (Fr) a vineyard. (Com): Landiras. A.C. Graves, Bordeaux. 3ha (white).

Cru **Petit-Gontey** (Fr) a vineyard in the A.C. Saint-Émilion, Bordeaux 2ha.

Cru **Petit-Grillon** (Fr) a vineyard. (Com): Barsac. A.C. Barsac (or Sauternes), Bordeaux 2ha.

Cru **Peyraguey** (Fr) a vineyard. (Com): Preignac. A.C. Sauternes, Bordeaux 8ha.

Cru **Peyroutene** (Fr) a vineyard. (Com): Cérons. A.C. Cérons, Bordeaux 4ha.

Cru **Pezeau** (Fr) a vineyard. (Com): Beautiran. A.C. Graves, Bordeaux. 3ha (red).

Cru **Pian** (Fr) a vineyard. (Com): Barsac. A.C. Barsac (or Sauternes), Bordeaux 2ha.

Cru **Pilote** (Fr) a vineyard. (Com): Fargues. A.C. Sauternes, Bordeaux 3ha.

Cru **Pinaud** (Fr) a vineyard. (Com): Cérons. A.C. Cérons, Bordeaux 4ha.

Cru **Pinaud** (Fr) a vineyard. (Com): Cérons. A.C. Graves, Bordeaux. 2ha (white).

Cru **Piney** (Fr) a vineyard in the A.C. Saint-Émilion, Bordeaux 1ha.

Cru **Piquey** (Fr) a vineyard. (Com): Bommes. A.C. Sauternes, Bordeaux 1ha.

Cru **Plaisance** (Fr) a vineyard in the A.C. Saint-Émilion, Bordeaux 6ha.

Cru **Planton** (Fr) a vineyard. (Com): Barsac. A.C. Barsac (or Sauternes), Bordeaux 1ha.

Cru **Plateau-Jappeloup** (Fr) a vineyard in the A.C. Saint-Émilion, Bordeaux 3ha.

Cru **Pontet-Chappez** (Fr) a vineyard. (Com): Arsac. A.C. Haut-Médoc, Bordeaux 4ha.

Cru **Pouteau** (Fr) a vineyard. (Com): Fargues. A.C. Sauternes, Bordeaux 2ha.

Cru **Pouton** (Fr) a vineyard. (Com): Preignac. A.C. Sauternes, Bordeaux 2ha.

Cru **Puydomine** (Fr) a vineyard. (Com): Bommes. A.C. Sauternes, Bordeaux 2ha.

Cru **Richard Barbe** (Fr) a vineyard in the commune Bommes. A.C. Sauternes, Bordeaux 2ha.

Cru **Ripaille** (Fr) a vineyard. (Com): Preignac. A.C. Sauternes, Bordeaux 1ha.

Cru **Rol-de-Frombrauge** (Fr) a vineyard in the A.C. Saint-Émilion, Bordeaux 4ha.

Cru **Roudet** (Fr) a vineyard. (Com): Pujols. A.C. Graves, Bordeaux. 5ha (white).

Crus (Fr). Growths. When applied to vineyards denotes the production of the vineyard. The wines produced are usually classified into Crus. e.g. Grand Cru, Premier Cru, Grand Cru Classé etc. *see* Croître.

Cru **Sabade-Terrefort** (Fr) a vineyard. (Com): Sauternes. A.C. Sauternes, Bordeaux 2ha.

Crusader (Eng) a 4.4% alc by vol. ale brewed by the Milestone Brewery C°., Nottinghamshire.

Crusader Premium Bitter (Eng) a 4.9% alc by vol. summer bitter ale brewed by the Pilgrim Brewery, Reigate, Surrey.

Cru **Sadout** (Fr) a vineyard. (Com): Virelade. A.C. Graves, Bordeaux. 6ha (red and white).

Cru **Sarraguey** (Fr) a vineyard. (Com): Virelade. A.C. Graves, Bordeaux. 5ha (red and white).

Crus Artisans (Fr) *see* Cru Artisan.

Crus Bourgeois (Fr) *see* Cru Bourgeois.

Crus Bourgeois Supérieures (Fr) an old Médoc grading now no longer used.

Crus Classés (Fr) *see* Cru Classé.

Cruse (Eng) the name for a water jug in the Middle Ages.

Cruse et Fils Frères (Fr) négociants-éleveurs based in Bordeaux and in Nuits-Saint-Georges, Burgundy.

Crus Exceptionnels (Fr) *see* Cru Exceptionnel.

Crush Bar (Fr) the nickname given to a theatre bar used for serving drinks during the interval at a performance.

Crushed Glass (N.Z) a material (mainly from wine bottles) being used as an experimental mulch to reflect sunlight to the grapes.

Crusher (Eng) a machine that bursts or crushes the grapes to allow the juice to run freely. Replaces the practice of treading the grapes.

Crushing (Eng) the method of extracting the juice from fruit as opposed to pressing which squeezes out the juice. The crushing only breaks the skins and allows the free run juice to be removed. *see* Pressing.

Crushing Station (USA) a press-house.

C

Crus Non Côtes (Fr) a term used in the Champagne region to describe the lower-priced growths from vineyards in the Marne.

Cru Soula (Fr) a vineyard. (Com): Fargues. A.C. Sauternes, Bordeaux 4ha.

Crus Paysans (Fr) see Cru Paysan.

Crust (Eng) in fermentation the name given to the cap of skins etc. on top of the fementing must.

Crust (Port) the sediment in a bottle of Vintage or Crusted Port.

Crusta (Cktl) a mixed drink with the glass rim rubbed with either orange or lemon peel and dipped in powdered sugar.

Crusta Glass (USA) similar to a small wine glass used for serving Crustas.

Crustas (Cktl) 60mls (½ gill) spirit, juice ½ lemon or orange, 2 dashes maraschino, 2 dashes Angostura. Shake over ice, strain into a crusta glass which has been rubbed with lemon or orange peel and dipped on sugar.

Crusted Port (Port) a blended Port wine bottled after two years, has almost the same qualities as a Vintage Port and needs laying down to mature when it will 'throw' a crust (sediment). Is a blend of different years' wines.

Cru St-Louis (Fr) a vineyard. (Com): Couquéques. A.C. Médoc, Bordeaux 3ha.

Cru St-Michel (Fr) a vineyard. (Com): Barsac. A.C. Barsac (or Sauternes), Bordeaux 1ha.

Cru St-Roch (Fr) a vineyard. (Com): Illats. A.C. Cérons, Bordeaux 2ha.

Cru St-Romain (Fr) a vineyard. (Com): Loupiac. A.C. Loupiac, Bordeaux 4ha.

Cru St-Sardeau (Fr) a vineyard. (Com): Fargues. A.C. Sauternes, Bordeaux 2ha.

Crust Test (Eng) see Wet Smell.

Cru Terrefort (Fr) a vineyard. (Com): Bommes. A.C. Sauternes, Bordeaux 4ha.

Cru Terrefort (Fr) a vineyard. (Com): Pujols. A.C. Graves, Bordeaux. 3ha (white).

Cru Thibaut (Fr) a vineyard. (Com): Fargues. A.C. Sauternes, Bordeaux 7ha.

Crutin (It) see Infernotti.

Cru Toumilon (Fr) a vineyard. (Com): St-Pierre-de-Mons. A.C. Graves, Bordeaux. 2ha (white).

Cru Tucan (Fr) a vineyard. (Com): Barsac. A.C. Barsac (or Sauternes), Bordeaux 2ha.

Cru Tucou (Fr) a vineyard. (Com): Preignac. A.C. Sauternes, Bordeaux 1ha.

Cruvajo (It) a single varietal grappa produced from the pomace of a grape of same name by Fratelli Brunello, Vincenza.

Cru Verdon (Fr) a vineyard. (Com): Valeyrac. A.C. Medoc, Bordeaux 3ha.

Cru Videau (Fr) a vineyard. (Com): Pujols. A.C. Graves, Bordeaux. 6ha (white).

Cru Vigne-Vieille (Fr) a vineyard. (Com): Barsac. A.C. Barsac (or Sauternes), Bordeaux 3ha.

Cruvinet (USA) see Cruover.

Cru Vineyards (Eng) the best vineyards, vineyards that have above average, soils, climate, etc. (Aus) = rieden.

Cru Voltaire (Fr) a vineyard. (Com): Cérons. A.C. Cérons, Bordeaux 4ha.

Cru Wines (S.Afr) a production and marketing company (established 2004) based in Paarl, Western Cape. Labels: Alpen Hill, Bushman's Creek, Dolphin Bay, Due South, Klippendale, Kosie Möller Wines, Rickety Bridge, Rising River, Something Else, Withof.

Cruzan (W.Ind) the brand-name used on all rum labels produced by the government-run distillery (Virgin Islands Rum Industries Ltd.) in the Virgin Islands.

Cruzan Rum (W.Ind) see Cruzan.

Cruzcampo (Sp) the label of a 5% alc by vol. pilsner lager brewed in Seville.

Cruzeta (Port) a system of growing vines, the first ergonomic system, the grapes grow at the ideal height for gathering. see Barra, Spur.

Cruziero (Port) a natural spring mineral water from Luso. Mineral contents (milligrammes per litre): Sodium 10.2mg/l, Calcium 19.6mg/l, Magnesium 12.4mg/l, Potassium 5.8mg/l, Bicarbonates 126mg/l, Chlorides 16.5mg/l, Sulphates 1.6mg/l, Fluorides 0.2mg/l, Silicates 13.6mg/l. pH 6.9

C.R.V.C. (Fr) abbr: Coopérative Régionale de Vins de Champagne.

Cryoextraction (Eng) during vinification the chilling of the grape to the point where watery unripe fruit is frozen and passes through the press uncrushed. The emerging juice is concentrated and richer in all the grape constituents (including sugar).

Cryomaceration (Eng) during fermentation describes the process of skin contact with the must that is temperature controlled.

Cryptococcus (Lat) a slime yeast that can attack and spoil wine, caused through poor hygiene.

Cryptogamic (Eng) non-flowering plant i.e. Fungi. (Fr) = cryptogamique.

Cryptogamic Diseases (Eng) the fungal diseases associated with the vine (oïidium, mildew, black rot, grey rot, etc.). (Fr) = maladies cryptogamiques.

Cryptogamique (Fr) cryptogamic.

Crystal (Bra) a natural spring mineral water from the Fonte Ycuara. Mineral contents (milligrammes per litre): Sodium 22.36mg/l, Calcium 6.22mg/l, Magnesium 9.06mg/l, Potassium 1.83mg/l, Bicarbonates 122.12mg/l, Sulphates 1.2mg/l, Fluorides 0.52mg/l. pH 7.22

Crystal (E.Afr) a natural spring mineral water from Djibouti. Mineral contents (milligrammes per litre): Sodium 15mg/l, Calcium 0.3mg/l, Magnesium 3.2mg/l, Potassium 3.4mg/l, Bicarbonates 0.3mg/l, Chlorides 25.2mg/l, Sulphates 12.7mg/l.

Crystal (Eng) see Lead Crystal.

Crystal (Eng) a natural spring mineral water from the Saint George's Well, Silk Hill, Swan Lane, Long Hanborough, Oxfordshire.

Crystal (Fr) a still natural spring mineral water. Mineral contents (milligrammes per litre): Sodium 17mg/l, Calcium 18mg/l, Magnesium

C

14mg/l, Potassium 1mg/l, Chlorides 21.6mg/l, Sulphates 10mg/l, Nitrates 2.5mg/l. pH 7.6

Crystal (Mau) a natural spring mineral water from Mauritius. Mineral contents (milligrammes per litre): Sodium 17mg/l, Calcium 18mg/l, Magnesium 14mg/l, Potassium 1mg/l, Chlorides 21.6mg/l, Sulphates 10mg/l, Nitrates 2.5mg/l. pH 7.0

Crystal (USA) the name used in America for the Budvar beer of Czec.

Crystal [Le] (Fr) the brand-name used by Berger for their clear anis.

Crystal Ale (Eng) an export IPA 1038 O.G. brewed by Matthew Brown Brewery in Blackburn, Lancashire.

Crystal Ale (Eng) a keg and bottled ale 1030 O.G. brewed by Eldridge Pope Brewery in Dorset.

Crystal Beach (Can) a wine region.

Crystal Beer (Can) a dry (bitter) beer brewed by the Labatt Brewery.

Crystal Bitter (Eng) easy drinking bitter from Eldridge Pope. *See also* Eldridge Pope Best Bitter 3.8% alc by vol.

Crystal Canadian (Can) a sparkling natural spring mineral water (established 1819). Mineral contents (milligrammes per litre): Sodium 12mg/l, Calcium 16mg/l, Magnesium 9mg/l, Potassium 1mg/l, Bicarbonates 65mg/l, Chlorides 29mg/l, Sulphates 9mg/l.

Crystal Clear Oke (USA) a pure, clear style of okolehao.

Crystal Dry (Fr) a Cognac producer. (Add): Castel Sablons, Saint Maigrin, 17520 Archiac. 80ha. in the Fins Bois.

Crystal Falls (Wal) a natural spring mineral water from Blaen Twyni Farm, Glyntawe, Penycae, Powys. Mineral contents (milligrammes per litre): Sodium 5.2mg/l, Calcium 10.5mg/l, Magnesium 0.9mg/l, Potassium 0.3mg/l, Bicarbonates 1mg/l, Chlorides 12mg/l, Fluorides 0.03mg/l, Nitrates 0.1mg/l. pH 6.3

Crystal Geyser Natural Alpine (USA) a natural spring mineral water from the Crystal Geyser Roxane Source. Mineral contents (milligrammes per litre): Calcium 40mg/l, Magnesium 8mg/l, Bicarbonates 110mg/l, Chlorides 2mg/l, Nitrates <0.5mg/l.

Crystal Geyser Natural Spring (USA) a natural spring mineral water from Olancha. Mineral contents (milligrammes per litre): Sodium 13mg/l, Calcium 27.4mg/l, Magnesium 6mg/l, Potassium 2mg/l, Chlorides 6.5mg/l, Sulphates 36.7mg/l, Nitrates 0.6mg/l. pH 7.9

Crystal Geyser Water (USA) a natural spring mineral water (established 1977) from Calistoga. Mineral contents (milligrammes per litre): Sodium 130mg/l, Calcium 12mg/l, Magnesium 3.1mg/l, Potassium 8.7mg/l, Chlorides 260mg/l, Sulphates 2.6mg/l.

Crystal Gin (Can) a brand of dry gin produced by Hiram Walker.

Crystal Ice (Eng) a 5% alc by vol. ale brewed by the Highgate Brewery, West Midlands.

Crystallisation (Eng) the precipitation of tartaric acid. *see* Crystals.

Crystal Malt (Eng) a barley malt for brewing. Is placed in a pre-heated kiln at a high temperature to produce a glossy finish. It enhances the body of the finished beer and gives it a 'reddish' colour..

Crystal Organic Water (Austr) a still natural spring mineral water from Mount Grove Mountain. Mineral contents (milligrammes per litre): Sodium 3.3mg/l, Calcium 35mg/l, Magnesium 3.2mg/l, Potassium 0.43mg/l, Chlorides 3.7mg/l, Sulphates 3.3mg/l.

Crystals (Eng) found in white and red wines, caused by the precipitation of tartaric acid and others due to long storage at cold temperatures. Disappears if wine is brought to room temperature for a short while. Harmless.

Crystal Slipper (Cktl) ¾ measure dry gin, ¼ measure crème Yvette, 2 dashes orange bitters. Stir over ice and strain into a cocktail glass.

Crystal Spring (Austr) a still natural spring mineral water from Mount Lofty, Adelaide, South Australia. Mineral contents (milligrammes per litre): Sodium 24mg/l, Calcium 2mg/l, Magnesium 4mg/l, Potassium 2mg/l, Bicarbonates 8mg/l, Chlorides 45mg/l, Sulphates 4mg/l.

Crystal Spring (USA) a brand of rum produced by Felton and Son in New England.

Crystal Spring Mineral Water (Wal) a natural mineral water bottled by the Carmarthen Water C°. in south-western Wales.

Crystal Springs (USA) a natural spring mineral water.

Crystal Tropical (Bra) a still, acidic natural spring mineral water. Mineral contents (milligrammes per litre): Sodium 7.2mg/l, Calcium 0.62mg/l, Magnesium 0.94mg/l, Potassium 6.2mg/l, Bicarbonates 8.1mg/l, Chlorides 11.71mg/l, Sulphates 1.95mg/l, Fluorides 0.59mg/l, Nitrates 2.75mg/l. pH 5.38

Crystal Water (Sri.L) a natural spring mineral water.

Crystal Wheat Beer (Eng) a 5% alc by vol. wheat beer brewed by the Three Rivers Brewing C°. Ltd., Cheshire.

Csàszarkörte (Hun) a fruit brandy made from pears.

Csopaki Furmint (Hun) a full-bodied dry white wine similar to Tokaji.

C.S.R. (Austr) *abbr*: Colonial Sugar Refining C°.

C.T.C. (E.Asia) *abbr*: Crushing, Tearing and Curling, the name for a machine which cuts the tea leaf up after it has been withered (dried).

CT de Waal (S.Afr) the label for a red wine (Pinotage) produced by the De Waal Wines winery, Stellenbosch, Western Cape.

C.T.G.S. (Eng) *abbr*: Catering Tea Grading Scheme.

Ctrl (Eng) a new RTD lemon-flavoured vodka 3% alc by vol. produced by Anglo Drinks Ltd. Also produces a blue coloured version.

C2 (Eng) a low alcohol (2% alc by vol) lager beer brewed by Carling.

Cu (Chi) vinegar.

Cuach (Scot) *see* Quaich.
Cuadrilla Forestera (Sp) the name given to a group of grape pickers.
Cuarenta-y-Tres (Sp) a yellow herb liqueur made from 43 different herbs in Cartagena. 31.5% alc by vol. Also known as Licor 43.
Cuartillo (Sp) a specific amount of wine, measured by volume 1/32 arroba.
Cuatrao Rayas (Sp) s superior wine, made from over 60% Verdejo grapes by Cooperativa La Seca in La Rueda.
Cuatro Año (Sp) denotes 4 years in cask before bottling.
Cuatro Palmas (Sp) a mark on a Sherry butt shaped like a palm, it denotes an old Fino Sherry.
Cuatro Rayas (Sp) lit: 'four stokes', the marks on a Sherry butt used to denote the destiny of wine. Here it is destined to be distilled.
Cuauhtémoc Brewery (S.Am) a brewery based in Monterrey, Mexico which also has a third share in the Yucateca Brewery. Brews Bohemia, Tecate.
C.U.B. (Austr) *abbr*: Foster/**C**arlton & **U**nited **B**rewery, a large brewing company with breweries based in Ballarat, Brisbane, Cairns, Darwin, Geelong and Melbourne.
Cuba (W.Ind) a white rum-producing island in the Caribbean.
Cuba (Chile)(Port) cask/barrel/vat. (Fr) = cuvée.
Cuba (Port)(Sp) stainless steel or concrete vats used in the production of Port (and still) wines.
Cubaexport (W.Ind) a light rum distillery based on the island of Cuba.
Cuba Libre (Cktl) place 35mls (1½ fl.ozs) white rum, 1 bottle cola in a small highball glass, add ice, stir lightly and top with a squeeze of a ¼ fresh lime.
Cuba Libre Supreme (Cktl) in an ice-filled collins glass place 1 measure of Southern Comfort, juice of ½ lime and spent lime shell, stir and top with Coca Cola.
Cuban Cocktail (Cktl) ½ measure brandy, ¼ measure apricot brandy, ¼ measure lime juice. Shake over ice and strain into a cocktail glass.
Cuban Coffee (W.Ind) a smooth, mellow and somewhat spicey coffee with a smokey taste and aroma from Cuba.
Cuban Ron (W.Ind) the nickname for white rum from the island of Cuba.
Cuban Special (Cktl) 25mls (⅕ gill) white rum, 60mls (½ gill) pineapple juice, juice ½ lime, 2 dashes Cointreau. Shake over ice, strain into a cocktail glass, top with a pineapple cube and cherry.
Cubas de Calor (Mad) describes concrete tanks between 20,000 litres and 50,000 litres in capacity with a stainless steel coil in the centre. Used for Estufagem.
Cubero (Sp) cooper/cask maker.
Cubitainer (Fr) a small plastic container for transporting bulk wines from 5 litres to 33 litres in capacity.
Cucamonga (USA) a Californian wine region which contains the districts of Los Angeles, San Bernardino and Riverside. Produces table and dessert wines.
Cucamonga Winery (USA) a large winery based in Cucamonga, California. Grape varieties: Cabernet sauvignon, Johannisberg riesling, Petit syrah and Zinfandel. Produces varietal wines.
Cucharadita (Sp) teaspoon.
Cuchery (Fr) a Cru Champagne village in the Canton de Châtillon-sur-Marne. District: Reims.
Cuchulain Shiraz (Austr) a rich red wine produced by the Setanta Vineyard, Adelaide Hills, South Australia.
Cuckmere (Eng) a vineyard (established 1973) based at the English Wine Centre, Drusillas Corner, Alfriston, Eastern Sussex. 0.33ha. Grape varieties: Huxelrebe, Müller-Thurgau, Seyval blanc plus others.
Cuckmere Haven Best Bitter (Eng) a bitter brewed by a micro-brewery in Cuckmere Haven, Eastbourne.
Cuckoo (Eng) a 4.3% alc by vol. ale brewed by Mauldon's Ltd., Suffolk.
Cucugnan (Fr) a Vin de Pays area within the Aude département in central-southern France. Produces red and rosé wines.
Cudzik [Daniel F] (USA) the inventor (1975) of the '*stay-on*' ring-pull tab on drinks cans.
Cuenca (Sp) a wine-producing area in the La Mancha region.
Cuero (Sp) a pigskin used to hold wine.
Cueros (Sp) *see* Cuero.
Cuers (Fr) a wine-producing village in the Côtes de Provence, south-eastern France. Produces rosé wines.
Cuervo [José] (Mex) a noted producer of tequila sold under the same name. Owned by the Diageo group.
Cues (Ger) an old English spelling of Kues, Mosel-Saar-Ruwer.
Cuesta (Sp) a brand of Sherry shipped by Saccone and Speed. Produced in Puerto de Santa Maria. Brands include Troubador (part of Caballero).
Cuevo (Mex) the brand-name for a tequila. 38% alc by vol.
Cuff and Buttons (USA) the name given to Southern Comfort liqueur whiskey in the 1870's (meant 'white tie and tails').
Cufic Vines (Eng) a vineyard (established 1973) based at Tuttors Hill, Cheddar, Somerset. 0.20ha. Grape varieties: Gewürztraminer, Huxelrebe, Madeleine angevine, Müller-Thurgau 90%, Reichensteiner, Seyval blanc and others.
Cugat (Sp) a noted white wine-producing area based in Cataluña.
Cuil Hill (Scot) a 3.6% alc by vol. ale brewed by Sulwath Brewers Ltd., Kirkcudbrightshire.
Cuiller à Thé (Fr) teaspoon.
Cuirim (Ire) barrel/bottle.
Cuis (Fr) a Premier Cru Champagne village in the Canton d'Avize. District: Épernay.
Cuisles (Fr) a Cru Champagne village in the Canton de Châtillon-sur-Marne. District: Reims.

C

Cuit (Fr) a wine that has been heated or cooked. i.e. Marsala.

Cuka (Indo) vinegar.

Culaton (It) a word used in the Piemonte region for the lees in the bottom of a bottle of wine.

Culbertson (USA) a winery based in San Diego, California. Produces varietal wines.

Culemborg Wines (S.Afr) varietal wines produced by Union Wines in Wellington, Western Cape.

Cul en l'Air (Fr) lit: 'bottom up', how Champagne used to be sold (before remuage), the sediment was found in the neck of the bottle resting on the cork.

Culha (Bra) see Yerba Maté.

Cullens Willybrup (Austr) a vineyard based in the Margaret River region. (Add): P.O. Box 17, Cowaramup, Western Australia. 20ha. Grape varieties: Cabernet franc, Cabernet sauvignon, Chardonnay, Merlot, Pinot noir, Rhine riesling, Sauvignon blanc and Sémillon. Label: Diana Madeline.

Culleus (Lat) a leather pouch used for carrying beverages (wine, water, etc).

Culligan (Fr) a natural spring mineral water. Mineral contents (milligrammes per litre): Sodium 34mg/l, Calcium 48mg/l, Magnesium 11mg/l, Potassium 1mg/l, Bicarbonates 183mg/l, Chlorides 50mg/l, Sulphates 16mg/l. pH 7.8

Culligans (Ch.Isles) a 4% alc by vol. light-coloured, nitrogenated Irish ale from the Guernsey Brewery, St. Peter Port, Guernsey.

Cully (Switz) a noted vineyard based in Lavaux.

Culm (Scot) the dried sprouts of the malted barley which are removed before being milled into grist.

Cul-Net (Fr) a term used in the Champagne region, denotes 'to drink in one gulp'.

Culraithin (S.Afr) the label for red wines produced by the Coleraine Wines winery, Suider-Paarl, Western Cape.

Cul Sec (Fr) denotes extremely dry.

Cultivar (Eng) a variety of plant that was produced from natural species and is maintained by cultivation.

Cultivars (S.Afr) vine varieties. see Cultivar.

Cultivation d'Grappes (Fr) viniculture.

Cultive á l'Ancienne (Fr) a term which denotes that traditional viticultural methods are used.

Cultured Yeasts (Eng) yeast strains that have been cloned and produced to be added to grape musts (that have been freed from any natural yeasts present of the skins) to produce a typical wine of the region.

Culture Large (Eng) denotes a method of training the vines high and planted wide apart.

Culullus (Lat) a goblet. See also Poterium.

Cumberland Ale (Eng) a bitter ale 1040 O.G. brewed by Jennings in Cumbria. See also Cumbrian Ale, Jennings Bitter.

Cumbrero (Sp) a red Rioja from the Bodegas Montecillo.

Cumbrian Ale (Eng) a mild strength bottled ale from Jennings in Cumbria.

Cumbrian Natural Mineral Water (Eng) a natural spring mineral water from Armathwaite, Cumbria.

Cumières (Fr) a Premier Cru Champagne village in the Canton d'Aÿ. District: Reims.

Cumin Liquidum Optimum Castelli (Den) see C.L.O.C.

Cumulus (S.Afr) the label for a white wine (Chenin blanc) produced by the Drostdy Wine Cellar winery, Tulbagh, Western Cape.

Cunachos (Sp) the name used in the Rioja region for 22 kilogramme wicker baskets used for grape harvesting.

Cune (Sp) a red Rioja table wine produced by C.V.N.E. in the Alta region. Produced from the Garnacha 20%, Mazuelo 5%, Tempranillo 60% and Viura 15%. Website: http://www.cvne.com

Cuneo Cellars (USA) a vineyard based in the Eola Hills, Oregon. Grape varieties: Cabernet sauvignon, Pinot noir, Merlot, Nebbiolo.

Cunningham (Mad) a red grape variety, also known as the Canica.

Cunning Stunts (Eng) a strong bottled ale 9.5% alc by vol. from Ballards Brewery, Sussex. see Gone Fishing, Wassail Ale.

Cup (Eng) an alternative name for the chalice used to hold the wine for the Eucharist.

Cup (Eng) a bar measure which equals 250mls (8fl.ozs)

Cup (Eng) a china drinking vessel with a handle for holding hot liquids such as tea, coffee, cocoa. Capacities of 100mls (⅙ pint), 200mls (⅓ pint) and 300mls (½ pint). (Arab) = funjan, (Aus) = tasse, (Chi) = beizi, (Den) = kop/kopje, (Fr) = tasse, (Ger) = tasse, (Gre) = ambix/flitzani, (Indo) = cangkir, (Ire) = cupán, (Isr) = sefel, (It) = tazza, (Jap) = koppu, (Kor) = kup, (Port) = copo, (Rus) = chash-ka, (Sp) = taza, (Thai) = tuay.

Cup (USA) a long refreshing drink used as an apéritif, made of either Champagne, cider, wine or fortified wines. see Champagne Cup, Dancer's Cup, Peace Cup, Cider Cup. (Den) = kold punch.

Cup (USA) a measure of 8 U.S.fl.ozs.

Cupada (Sp) vatting or blending. (Fr) = coupage.

Cupaje (Sp) see Cupada.

Cupán (Ire) cup.

Cupán caife (Ire) coffee cup.

Cupán Tae (Ire) tea cup.

Cup Bearer (Eng) a servant who fills the wine cups and serves them in a royal household. (Fr) = échanson.

Cup Crillon Cocktail (Cktl) 25mls (1fl.oz) white rum, 5mls (¼ fl.oz) each of crème de cassis and Grand Marnier, dash lemon juice. Shake over ice. Strain into a highball glass, top with ginger ale, cherry and spiral of lemon peel.

Cuperly (Fr) a Champagne producer. (Add): 2 Rue Ancienne Église, 51380 Verzy. Récoltants-manipulants. Produces vintage and non-vintage wines.

Cuper's Gardens (Eng) eighteenth century tea gardens.

C

Cupertino (USA) a small wine-producing area in Santa Clara County, California.

Cupid's Best Bitter (Eng) a bitter ale brewed by Matthew Brown, Scottish Courage for Valentine's day.

Cupid's Bow (Cktl) ¼ measure gin, ¼ measure Aurum, ¼ measure Forbidden Fruit liqueur, ¼ measure passion fruit juice. Shake over ice and strain into a cocktail glass.

Cup of Cha (Eng) a slang term for a cup of tea.

Cuprea (Eng) a vineyard based in Devon. Grape variety: Kerner.

Cups (USA) *see* Cup.

Curaçao (W.Ind) a liqueur made from bitter oranges from the island of Curaçao. Now made in many styles and colours (blue, brown, green, purple and red) mainly in France and Holland. 40% alc by vol.

Curaçao Cocktail (Cktl) ¾ measure Scotch whisky, ½ measure lemon juice, ¼ measure white Curaçao. Shake over ice, strain into a cocktail glass.

Curaçao Triple Sec (Hol) a clear orange liqueur, drier and stronger than Curaçao. Produced by many companies including Bols.

Curate's Choice (Eng) a 4.8% alc by vol. bitter brewed by Exe Valley Brewery, Silverton, Devon.

Curate's Downfall (Eng) a 4.3% alc by vol. beer brewed by the Lastingham Brewery, Lastingham, near Pickering, North Yorkshire.

Cure d'Attalens (Switz) a white wine produced in Lavaux.

Curicó Valley (Chile) a wine-producing region in southern Chile, home to Echeverría winery.

Curieux et Courtois des Chevaliers de Saint-Bacchus (Fr) a noted wine brotherhood based in Paris.

Curing (Eng) *see* Kilning.

Curing (Eng) the word used to denote the preparation of the coffee beans, one of two methods are used. Wet or Dry method.

Curious Brew Brut (Eng) a light 5% alc by vol. bottled lager beer brewed by Chapel Down Wines and refermented using East Anglian malt, Cascade and Saaz hops and French sparkling wine yeasts.

Curler Blend (Scot) a brand of Scotch whisky once produced by Arthur Bell and Sons.

Currant Abbey (S.Afr) the label for a red wine (Ruby cabernet) produced by the Oude Wellinton Estate winery, Wellington, Western Cape.

Curtis Distillery (Eng) a distillery. (Add): London EC1P 1BJ. Distillers of Curtis gin 43% alc by vol. Part of Stewart and Son.

Curtis Distillery (Scot) a distillery based in Dundee. Distillers of Curtis blended Scotch whisky 40% alc by vol. Part of Stewart and Son.

Curtis Gin (Eng) a London Dry gin 43% alc by vol. produced by the Curtis Distillery, London. Part of Stewart and Son.

Cusanushaus (Ger) *see* Cusanusstift.

Cusanusstift (Ger) a charitable foundation established at Kues (the town opposite Bernkastel) on the river Mosel. Depends on the produce of the Bernkasteler vineyard.

Cusenier (Fr) a famous French liqueur company producing most types of popular liqueurs.

Cushman (Cktl) ¼ measure dry vermouth, ¾ measure dry gin. Shake over ice and strain into an ice-filled goblet.

Cushy Butterfield (Eng) a 4.4% alc by vol. brown ale brewed by Foundry and Firkin brew-pub.

Cusquena (Peru) a bottled 5% alc by vol. lager beer from a brewery of same name.

Cussac (Fr) a small commune in the Haut-Médoc. Wines may be sold under the A.C. Saint-Julien (adjoining commune)' or A.C. Haut-Médoc, Bordeaux. *see* Cussac-Fort-Médoc.

Cussac-Fort-Médoc (Fr) the full title for the commune of Cussac, Médoc, Bordeaux.

Customs (Eng) a charge made on alcohol and other goods imported into any country. (Fr) = douane.

Cut (Eng) the adulteration of a better quality wine with an inferior one (or water) to increase its bulk.

Cuthberts (Eng) a 3.8% alc by vol. ale brewed by The Church End Brewery, Warwickshire.

Cuthberts Cross (Eng) a 4.7% alc by vol. ale brewed by The Durham brewery Ltd., County Durham.

Cut Kümmel (Cktl) into a small wine glass place some shaved ice and slice of lemon, pour 25mls (⅙ gill) kümmel on top then a dash of Scotch whisky.

Cutolo Rionero (It) a sparkling natural spring mineral water. Mineral contents (milligrammes per litre): Sodium 72.4mg/l, Calcium 50mg/l, Magnesium 13.1mg/l, Potassium 29mg/l, Bicarbonates 298mg/l, Chlorides 34mg/l, Sulphates 54mg/l, Fluorides 0.88mg/l, Nitrates 26.4mg/l, Silicates 78mg/l. pH 6.05

Cutting (Port) a term used in the Douro region to describe the treading of the grapes for Port wine. i.e. 40 men to 'cut' a 20 pipe lagar.

Cutting Wine (USA) poor quality wines used to lower the quality of better wines to make both saleable at a lower price.

Cutty Sark (Eng) a classic bitter ale (part of the Classics Range) brewed by the Hydes Brewery, Manchester.

Cutty Sark (Scot) a blended Scotch whisky produced in Glasgow by Berry Brothers and Rudd. 43% alc by vol. Also an 18 year old version.

Cutty Twelve (Scot) a de luxe version of Cutty Sark Scotch whisky produced in Glasgow by Berry Brothers and Rudd. 43% alc by vol.

Cuva (Sp) a large cask used in the Rioja region that contains 25,000 litres (5,500 gallons).

Cuvage (Fr) an alternative word for the Cuvaison.

Cuvaison (Fr) the period of the first violent fermentation during which the must remains in contact with the grape skins to obtain colour and tannin. An aerobic fermentation, it applies only to red wines. Also known as Cuvage.

Cuvaison Inc. (USA) a large winery based near Calistoga, Napa Valley, California. 166ha. Grape varieties: Cabernet sauvignon, Chardonnay and Merlot. Produces varietal wines.

C

Cuvaison Winery (USA) a 160ha. winery at Carneros, Napa Valley, California. Grape varieties include: Chardonnay, Merlot.

Cuve (Fr) a vat/tun/cask produced from a variety of materials (wood, glass-fibre, glass, stainless steel, etc.).

Cuveau (Fr) a small vat.

Cuve Close (Fr) a method of making sparkling wines by having the second fermentation in pressurised tanks. The wine is then filtered under pressure and bottled. (Eng) = cuve nature/tank method, (Fr) = charmat, (It) = metodo charmat, (Sp) = gran vas.

Cuvedor Riserva (It) a brandy produced by Fabbri.

Cuvée (Fr) lit: 'vatful', a specific blend of wines from more than one vat of a similar style, usually the best. Premier Cuvée means the best of a commune. Tête de Cuvée means the best batch of a vintage. (Port) = cuba.

Cuvée Alexandra (Fr) a rosé wine produced by Château Rasque, A.C. Côtes de Provence.

Cuvée Alexandre (Chile) a red wine produced by Casa Lapostolle, Rapel Valley from Merlot grapes. *See also* Clos Apalta.

Cuvée Amazone (Fr) a de luxe cuvée Champagne produced by Palmer & C°. from 50% Chardonnay and 50% Pinot noir grapes. New name is Lady Palmer.

Cuvée Ameena (S.Afr) the label for a red wine (Syrah) produced by the Vin d'Orrance winery, Little Karoo, Western Cape.

Cuvée Anaïs (S.Afr) the label for a white wine (Chardonnay) produced by the Vin d'Orrance winery, Little Karoo, Western Cape.

Cuvée Antwerpen '93' (Bel) *see* Cuvée De Koninck.

Cuvée Anniversaire (Fr) an Armagnac produced by Samalens from brandies of the Bas Armagnac up to 100 years old.

Cuvée Baccarat (Fr) a de luxe prestige cuvée Champagne produced by Henriot.

Cuvée Bévy (Fr) the name applied to wines made at Bévy in the Hautes Côtes de Nuits, Burgundy.

Cuvée Brut (S.Afr) the label for a white wine (Chenin blanc and Colombard blend) produced by the Klein Parys Vineyards winery, Suider-Paarl, Western Cape.

Cuvée Burr (S.Afr) a red wine (Cabernet sauvignon) produced by thr Mount Rozier winery, Stellenbosch.

Cuvée Cape (S.Afr) the label for a red wine (Pinotage 80% and Chenin blanc 20% blend) produced by the Môreson winery, Franschhoek, Western Cape.

Cuvée Centenaire (Fr) the bottom grade of wine from Salins du Midi.

Cuvée Charles Joseph (Fr) the label for an A.C. Côtes-du-Rhone-Villages Vinsobres (red) from Domaine du Moulin, Vinsobres, Vaucluse.

Cuvée Cinquantenaire (Fr) a prestige Champagne cuvée produced by Perrier (Joseph).

Cuvée Clos Syrah Léone (Fr) a red wine produced from 95% Syrah and 5% Mourvèdre grapes by Domaine Peyre-Rose. A.C. Coteaux du Languedoc.

Cuvée Col du Débat (Fr) the label for an A.C. Côtes-du-Rhone-Villages Cairanne (red) from Domaine les Hautes Cances, Cairanne, Vaucluse.

Cuvée Commodore (Fr) a vintage de luxe cuvée Champagne produced by De Castellane from 25% Chardonnay and 75% Pinot noir grapes.

Cuvée de Bacchus (Fr) a label for a rosé wine (Cinsault and Grenache) produced by Château des Chaberts, Coteaux Various, Provence.

Cuvée de Boisdauphin (Fr) the label of a Châteauneuf-du-Pape produced by Jacumin (Pierre), Rte. de Sorgues, 84230 Châteauneuf-du-Pape, southern Rhône.

Cuvée de Centenaire (Fr) a vintage de luxe cuvée Champagne produced by George Goulet from 60% Chardonnay and 40% Pinot noir grapes.

Cuvée de Ciney Blond (Bel) a 7% alc by vol. yellow-gold, top-fermented, bottled beer brewed by Union Brouwerij, Jumet.

Cuvée de Haute Pierre (Fr) the label of a Châteauneuf-du-Pape produced by négociant Delas in Tournon-sur-Rhône.

Cuvée de Koninck (Bel) an 8% alc by vol. bottled beer brewed by De Koninck Brouwerij, Antwerp. Originally brewed as Cuvée Antwerpen '93'.

Cuvée de la Reine (Fr) a de luxe cuvée Champagne produced by Marie Stuart from a blend of vintages.

Cuvée de la Reine Jeanne (Fr) the label of a red and white Châteauneuf-du-Pape produced by négociant Ogier et Fils, Ave. Louis-Boudin, 84800, L'Isle-sur-la-Sorgue.

Cuvée de l'Ermitage (Bel) a strong, amber-coloured ale 8° brewed by the Union Brasserie in Heinaut.

Cuvée de Prestige (Fr) a vintage de luxe cuvée Champagne produced by De Courcy.

Cuvée des Celtes (Fr) an A.C. Muscadet Sèvre et Maine. (Add): La Chapelle-Heulin, Loire Atlantique. Sur Lie.

Cuvée des Echansons (Fr) a de luxe cuvée Champagne produced by Champagne Société de Producteurs, Mailly-Champagne from a blend of vintages. 25% Chardonnay and 75% Pinot noir grapes.

Cuvée des Escarboucles (Fr) an A.C. Coteaux du Languedoc Pic-Saint-Loup red wine produced by Château de l'Euzière from 85% Syrah, 10% Grenache and 5% Mourvèdre grapes.

Cuvée des Roys (Fr) a vintage de luxe cuvée Champagne produced by Duval Leroy from 80% Chardonnay and 20% Pinot noir grapes.

Cuvée des Seigneurs de Ribeaupierre (Fr) a Gewurztraminer-based wine produced by Trimbach in Ribeauvillé, Alsace.

Cuvée des Sommeliers (Fr) the label of a Châteauneuf-du-Pape produced by Mestre (Jacques), Rte. de Bédarrides, 84230 Châteauneuf-du-Pape, southern Rhône.

Cuvée des Templiers (Fr) a rich red wine produced by Domaine le Clos des Cazeaux, Vacqueyras, Côtes-du-Rhône-Villages.

Cuvée d'Estevenas (Fr) the label for an A.C. Côtes-du-Rhone-Villages Cairanne (red) from Domaine Rabasse Charavin, Cairanne, Vaucluse.

Cuvée des Tonneleries (Fr) the label used by Château Cabrières for one of their Châteauneuf-du-Pape wines.

Cuvée d'Exception (Fr) a de luxe vintage cuvée Champagne produced by Lang-Biemont.

Cuvée Diamant (Fr) the label of a vintage and non-vintage Champagne from Chanmpagne Trouillard.

Cuvée Douceur (Fr) an off-dry (20 grammes dosage) non-vintage Champagne from the house of E. Barnaut aged for 4-5 years before release.

Cuvée Ducale (Fr) a style of Champagne produced by Ducale in Damery.

Cuvée du Conclave des Cardinaux (Fr) the label of a Châteauneuf-du-Pape used by Barnaud (Paul), 2 Rte. d'Avignon, 84230 Châteauneuf-du-Pape, southern Rhône.

Cuvée du Majoral (Fr) the label of a Châteauneuf-du-Pape produced by Brun (Avril Juliette), 8 Ave. Pasteur, 84230 Châteauneuf-du-Pape, southern Rhône. *See also* Juliette Avril.

Cuvée du Millenaire (Fr) a Champagne produced by Drappier from 55% Pinot noir, 40% Chardonnay, 5% Pinot meunier. 80% Grand Cru.

Cuvée du Vatican (Fr) the label of a Châteauneuf-du-Pape produced by Diffonty, Rte. de Courthézon, B.P. 33, 10, Route de Courthézon, F-84230 Châteauneuf-du-Pape, southern Rhône. 'E'mail: cuvee_du_vatican@mnet.fr

Cuvée Duvault-Blocher (Fr) a wine produced from the second picking of Domaine de la Romanée-Conti in the 1930's in honour of the domaine's founder. *See also* Vosne-Romanée Premier Cru.

Cuvée Edmond [La] (Fr) a non-vintage Champagne from the house of E. Barnaut. Produced from a blend of quality years of 40% Chardonnay, 40% Pinot noir and 20% Pinot meunier.

Cuvée El Campanario (Sp) a red wine produced by Abadía Retuerta in Ribera del Duero from 100% Tempranillo grapes. Has 4 weeks maceration and 1 year in new Limousin 300litre barrels.

Cuvée Elisabeth Salmon Rosé (Fr) a vintage cuvée Champagne produced by Billecart-Salmon.

Cuvée El Palomar (Sp) a red wine produced by Abadía Retuerta in Ribera del Duero from 50% Tempranillo and 50% Cabernet grapes. Spends 9 months in French and USA oak.

Cuvée Elysée Millésimé (Fr) a vintage de luxe cuvée Champagne produced by Oudinat-Jeanmaire in Épernay from 100% Chardonnay grapes.

Cuvée Emeraude (Fr) a prestige cuvée Champagne produced by Broggini in Rilly-la-Montagne.

Cuvée Emile Peynaud (Fr) a rich red wine produced in honour of the late Professeur Emile Peynaud by the Mas de Daumas Gassac vineyard.

Cuvée Eugène Mercier (Fr) a non-vintage dry Champagne from the house of Mercier.

Cuvée Eugénie (Fr) a red wine aged in oak for 16 months produced by Château Capendu, A.C. Corbières from 70% Syrah and 30% Carignan grapes.

Cuvée Flamme (Fr) sparkling red, rosé and white wines produced by the méthode traditionelle from Chenin blanc or Cabernet franc grapes. Produced by Gratien & Meyer, Saumur, Loire and matured for 4 years in bottle.

Cuvée Forrets Diverses (USA) the label for a white (Chardonnay) wine produced by the Hammacher winery, Willamette Valley, Oregon.

Cuvée Frederic Ejile (Fr) a Riesling wine produced by Trimbach in Ribeauvillé, Alsace.

Cuvée Gastronomique (Fr) a middle grade of wine from Salins du Midi.

Cuvée Grand Couronnement Brut (Fr) a vintage de luxe cuvée Champagne produced by De Telmont from 100% Chardonnay grapes.

Cuvée Grand Siècle (Fr) a de luxe cuvée Champagne produced by Laurent-Perrier from a blend of vintages of 55% Chardonnay and 45% Pinot noir grapes.

Cuvée Irene (Fr) an A.C. Muscadet Sèvre et Maine wine produced in Nantais, Loire.

Cuvée Jamais Content (Fr) an A.C. Coteaux du Languedoc Pic-Saint-Loup red wine produced by Domaine de Mortiès from 60% Syrah, 20% Mourvèdre, 10% Grenache and 10% Carignan grapes.

Cuvée Jean d'Alibert (Fr) an A.C. red wine from Minervois, southern France.

Cuvée 'L' (USA) a red wine (Cabernet sauvignon) produced by the Lewis winery, Napa Valley, California.

Cuvée Léa Felsch (Fr) the label for an A.C. Côtes-du-Rhône-Villages Cairanne (red) from Domaine Catherine le Gœuil, Cairanne, Vaucluse.

Cuvée Les Cistes (Fr) a red wine produced from 85% Syrah and 15% Grenache in A.C. Coteaux du Languedoc by Domaine Peyre-Rose.

Cuvée Liesse d'Harbonville (Fr) a vintage cuvée produced by Ployez-Jacquemart from 100% Pinot noir grapes.

Cuvée Lila (Ger) the brand-name sparkling dry sekt from the Riesling grape made by Deinhard and C°.

Cuvée Longue Garde (Fr) an A.C. Bandol red wine produced by Domaine Lafran-Veyrolles. from 100% Mourvèdre grapes.

Cuvée Lynette (S.Afr) the label for a red wine (Pinot noir) produced by the Weening & Barge Winery, Stellenbosch, Western Cape.

Cuvée Madelaine (Fr) an A.C. Muscadet Sèvre et Maine. Produced by the Compagnie de la Vallée de la Loire.

Cuvée Marguerite Brut Millésime (Fr) a vintage produced from Chardonnay 75% and Pinot noir 25% by the house of Vollereaux.

Cuvée Marie-Christine (Fr) the label of a rosé wine produced by Château de l'Aumerade, A.C. Côtes-de-Provence.

Cuvée Marquise de la Tourette (Fr) a Rhône wine A.C. Hermitage (white and red) produced by Delas at Tournon.

Cuvée Melchoir de Joanis (Fr) the label of a Châteauneuf-du-Pape produced by Granget (Bernard), at Dom. de Husson, 84350 Courthézon, southern Rhône.

Cuvée Mélodie (Fr) the label of a Châteauneuf-du-Pape produced by Mme. Vve. Camille Serre, Dom. de Saint Préfert, 84230 Châteauneuf-du-Pape, southern Rhône. Other label: Tenue de Soirée (vineyard now changed owners).

Cuvée Mosaïque (Fr) a vintage rosé vin de garde Champagne produced by Jacquart.

Cuvée Mythique [La] (Fr) a red wine produced by Val d'Orbieu in the Languedoc-Roussillon from Mourvèdre, Syrah, Grenache, Carignan, Cabernet sauvignon.

Cuvée Napa (USA) the label of a vintage or blanc de blancs/blanc de noirs sparkling (méthode traditionelle) wine produced from the French firm Mumm in California. Grape varieties: Chardonnay, Pinot noir, Pinot gris, Pinot meunier. Owned by Seagram. Sold in the USA as Cuvée Prestige.

Cuvée Napoléon (Fr) a red wine from Buzet, aged in new oak barrels for 6–9 months.

Cuvée Nicolas François Billecart (Fr) a prestige cuvée Champagne produced by Billecart-Salmon.

Cuvée Nominée (Fr) a vintage Champagne produced by Jacquart from 60% Chardonnay, 40% Pinot noir.

Cuvée One (Austr) a sparkling (méthode traditionelle) wine from Yalumba Winery, Eden Valley Road, Angaston, South Australia. Grape varieties: Chardonnay, Pinot noir.

Cuvée Oriu (Fr) a red wine from Domaine de Torraccia, Corsica. Grapes: Nielluccio 80%, Sciacarello 20%.

Cuvée Orpale (Fr) a blanc de blancs Champagne from Union Champagne.

Cuvée Perfection (Fr) a non-vintage Champagne produced by Jacquesson et Fils.

Cuvée Philippine (Fr) the label for a rosé wine produced by the Domaine de la Sauveuse, A.C. Côtes-de-Provence.

Cuvée Prestige (Fr) a non-vintage de luxe cuvée Champagne produced by A. Desmoulins from 50% Chardonnay and 50% Pinot noir grapes.

Cuvée Princes d'Orange (Fr) the label of a Châteauneuf-du-Pape produced by Château Saint-Roch, 30150 Rocquemaure, southern Rhône.

Cuvée Privée (Fr) private selection/non-vintage wine sold by the proprietor.

Cuve 4ème Centenaire (Fr) a prestige cuvée Champagne of Gosset.

Cuvée Quentin (Fr) a sweet white wine produced from Sémillon, Sauvignon blanc and Mauzac grapes by Clos du Cadaret, Côtes du Duras, South-west France.

Cuvée Quetton St-Georges (Fr) a red A.C. Coteaux du Languedoc wine produced by Château de l'Engarran.

Cuvée Quint (S.Afr) the label for a red wine (Shiraz) produced by the Weening & Barge Winery, Stellenbosch, Western Cape.

Cuvée Régence (Fr) the top grade of wine from Salins du Midi.

Cuvée Renaissance (Fr) a classification of Château Grillet in northern Rhône.

Cuvée Renommée (Fr) brut and rosé Champagnes from Pinot noir and Chardonnay grapes.

Cuvée R.G. (Fr) *abbr*: René Greffart, a blanc de blancs cuvée Champagne produced by Marie Stuart.

Cuvée Rive Gauche (Fr) a wood-aged red A.C. Gaillac wine from the co-operative Labastide-de-Levis.

Cuvée Rubis (Fr) a non-vintage rosé Champagne produced by Palmer and Company.

Cuvée S (Fr) a vintage de luxe cuvée Champagne produced by Salon from 100% Chardonnay grapes.

Cuvée Saint Agnès (Fr) an A.C. Coteaux du Languedoc Pic-Saint-Loup red wine produced by Ermitage Pic Saint-Loup from 70% Syrah, 20% Grenache and 10% Mourvèdre grapes.

Cuvée Sauvage (USA) a Chardonnay wine fermented on its own wild yeast in small oak barrels from the Franciscan Vineyard.

Cuvée Sébastion (Fr) a full (cuvee prestige) red wine produced by Château Redortier, A.C. Côtes-du-Rhône-Villages.

Cuvée Signée Chatellier (Fr) a de luxe cuvée vintage Champagne produced by De St. Marceaux & C°. from 87% Chardonnay and 13% Pinot noir grapes.

Cuvée Sir Winston Churchill (Fr) a de luxe cuvée vintage Champagne created in 1975 and produced by Pol Roger in a black (magnum) bottle to commemorate Sir Winston Churchill. Vintages: 1975, 1979, 1985, 1986, 1990, 1995.

Cuvée 'Spécial Club' (Fr) *see* Club Tresor de Champagne.

Cuvée St. Amands (Bel) a dark, strong ale brewed in Bavikhove, western Flanders.

Cuvée St-Christophe (Fr) the label for an A.C. Beaumes-de-Venise (red) from Domaine de Cassan, Beaumes-de-Venise, Vaucluse.

Cuvée St-Martin (Fr) the label for an A.C. Beaumes-de-Venise (red) from Domaine de la Ferme St-Martin, Beaumes-de-Venise, Vaucluse.

Cuvée St-Paul (Fr) the label for an A.C. Côtes-du-Rhône-Villages Valréas (red) from Château la Décelle, Valréas, Vaucluse.

Cuvée St. Vincent (Fr) a blanc de blancs Champagne produced by Legras.

Cuvée Terry Lynn (S.Afr) the label for a rosé wine (Shiraz) produced by the Weening & Barge Winery, Stellenbosch, Western Cape.

Cuvée Third [III] (Fr) a de luxe blanc de blancs cuvée Champagne produced by Lang-Biemont from a blend of vintages.

Cuvée Tradition Brut Vendange (Fr) a vintage Champagne made from Chardonnay 70%, Pinot noir 15%, Pinot meunier 15% and produced by the house of Vollereaux.

Cuvée Trésor (Fr) a wood-aged brut méthode traditionelle wine from Bouvet-Ladubay, Saumur, Loire. Also a demi-sec version.

Cuvée Victoire (Fr) a de luxe cuvée Champagne produced by Martel.

Cuvée Victor Joseph (Fr) a top cuvée produced by

Château de Suronde in the A.C. Quarts de Chaume, Anjou-Saumur, Loire.

Cuvée Vieille Vignes (Fr) the label for an A.C. Côtes-du-Rhône-Villages Cairanne (red) from Domaine les Hautes Cances, Cairanne, Vaucluse.

Cuvée Vulcano (Aus) a red wine from 75% Blaufränkisch and 25% Cabernet grapes. Produced by Hans Igler in Deutschkreutz, Central Burgenland.

Cuvée William Deutz (Fr) a vintage cuvée Champagne produced by Deutz from 30% Chardonnay, 60% Pinot noir and 10% Pinot meunier grapes.

Cuve Nature (Eng) the English name for Cuve Close.

Cuveno Vino (Slo) selected wine. see Vrhunsko Vino.

Cuverie (Fr) fermentation cellar/winery.

Cuvette (Eng) a small shallow drinking vessel (cup) used in the seventeenth century.

Cuvier (Fr) fermentation rooms, a mis-spelling of Cuverie.

Cuviller (Fr) an alternative name for the Cinsault grape.

Cuvillo (Sp) a Sherry bodega based at Puerto de Santa Maria. Noted for a wide range of Sherries.

Cuya (Arg) a wine-producing region of central Argentina. Has the sub-regions of: La Rioja, San Juan and Mendoza (north/central/south).

Cuytes (Sp) an alternative name for Vino de Color.

Cuzco (S.Am) the name for an ancient Inca village in Peru where old vineyards are situated.

Cuzcurrita (Sp) a noted wine-producing village based in the Rioja Alta, north-eastern Spain.

CVBG (Fr) noted négociants whose brands include Dourthe Frères. Have over 20 exclusive Châteaux.

C.V.C. (Fr) abbr: Club de Viticulteurs Champenois. An organisation devoted to maintaining quality standards amongst Champagne growers.

Cvicek (Slo) abbr: Slovenia light red/dark rosé wine that is low in alcohol. Produced in Posavje.

C.V.M. (Afr) abbr: Comptoir des Vins du Maroc (Morocco).

C.V.N.E. (Sp) abbr: Compañia Vinícola del Norte de España. Wine producer in the Alta region of Rioja.

CVP-2001 (S.Afr) a red wine (Shiraz) produced by the Annandale Wines, Stellenbosch, Western Cape.

C.V.P.V. Maiolati (It) abbr: see Cooperativa Vinicola Produttori Verdicchio Monte Schiavo.

C.V.R.V.V. (Port) abbr: Comissao de Viticultura da Região dos Vinhos Verdes. Viticultural Commission for the region of Vinhos Verdes.

C.W.A. (USA) abbr: California Wine Association.

C.W. & D. (S.Afr) abbr: Cape Wines and Distillers. Part of SFW.

CWG (S.Afr) abbr: Cape Winemakers Guild.

CWG Black South Easter (S.Afr) the label for a red wine (Cabernet sauvignon 50% Merlot 50%) produced by the Flagstone Winery, Somerset West, Western Cape.

Cwmbran Brewery (Wal) a brewery (established 1999). (Add): Gorse Cottage, Graig Road, Upper Cwmbran, Cwmbran, Gwent NP44 5AS. Brews: Blackcurrant Stout 4% alc by vol., Crow Valley

Bitter 4.2% alc by vol., Crow Valley Stout 4.2% alc by vol., Double Hop 4% alc by vol., Drayman's Bitter 3.5% alc by vol., Drayman's Choice 3.8% alc by vol., Drayman's Gold 3.8% alc by vol., Easter Bunny 4.5% alc by vol., 4 Seasons 4.8% alc by vol., Full Malty 4.8% alc by vol., Golden Wheat 4.5% alc by vol., Pink Panther 4.5% alc by vol., Santa's Tipple 5% alc by vol., VC 3.8% alc by vol. Website: http://www.cwmbranbrewery.co.uk 'E'mail: Cwmbran@btinternet.com

Cwm Dale (Wal) a carbonated mineral water with a natural lemon flavour from South Wales.

Cwm Deri Vineyard (Wal) a vineyard based in Martletwy, Pembrokeshire. Grape varieties include: Gewürztraminer, Madeleine angevine, Seyval blanc. Produces wines, fruit liqueurs and meads. Labels include Derwen, Dewi Sant, Landsker, Sir Benfro.

Cwpan (Wal) cup (tea).

Cwrw (Wal) ale/beer.

Cwrw Derwydd (Wal) a 3.9% alc by vol. ale from Bragdy Dyffryn Brewery, Denbigh. See also Cysur Bitter, Castle Bitter, Pedwar Bawd.

Cwrw Haf (Wal) a 4.2% alc by vol. ale brewed by the Hurns Brewing C°., West Glamorgan.

Cwrw Tudno (Wal) a 5% alc by vol. ale from the Plassey Brewery, Eyton, near Wrexham.

Cyathus (Lat) wine ladle.

Cyclades Islands (Gre) southern islands of Greece that produce highly alcoholic white wines. Isles of Paros and Thira are main wine producers.

Cyclops (Eng) a 5.3% alc by vol. ale brewed by the Milton Brewery Cambridge Ltd., Cambridgeshire.

Cyder (Eng) the old way of spelling cider (from Hebrew Schekar). See also Sicera.

Cyder Fizz (Cktl) 20mls (⅙ gill) Calvados placed into an ice-filled highball glass, top with ½ sparkling sweet cider and ½ dry Champagne.

Cyder Royal (Eng) a medium-dry, extra strength cider produced by the Whiteways C°. Exeter, Devon.

Cyder Soup (Punch) place into a punch bowl 500mls Calvados, 1litre dry sparkling cider, juice of 3 oranges, 1 syphon soda water. Add ice cubes, stir and decorate with slices of apple and orange.

Cyder with Rose (Cktl) 1 measure Calvados, ¼ measure grenadine. Stir together in an ice-filled highball glass, top with dry sparkling cider, serve with an apple slice and straws.

Cydrax (Eng) a non-alcoholic, apple-based, sparkling drink from the Whiteways C°. Exeter, Devon.

Cydweithredol (Wal) co-operative.

Cyfuniad Sych (Wal) a dry white wine produced by Gwinllan Pant Teg, Llanishen, Cardiff.

Cygne Blanc (Austr) an alternative name for the Cabernet Cygne Blanc.

Cygnet Cellars (USA) a small winery based in San Benito County, California. Grape varieties: Carignane and Zinfandel. Produces varietal wines.

Cymbium (Lat) cup. See also Pocullum.

Cynar (It) a quinine-flavoured apéritif made from artichokes 18% alc by vol.

C

Cynful (Ch.Isles) a 3.5% alc by vol. mild ale brewed by R.W. Randalls Brewery, Guernsey.

Cynhaeaf Gwin (Wal) vintage (wine).

Cynthiana (USA) see Norton.

Cyprès de Climens (Fr) the second wine of Château Climens, A.C. Barsac, Bordeaux.

Cyprus (Cyp) a large wine producing island in the eastern Mediterranean. Noted for highly alcoholic wines and Commandaria. Regions: Paphos and Troodos produce most of the countries finest wines. Limassol is main wine centre.

Cyprus Sherry (Cyp) Sherry-type wines which include fino, medium and cream styles. Producers are Etko, Haggipavlo, Keo, Loël and Sodap.

Cyprus Trade Centre (Eng) a promotional office for the wines of Cyprus. (Add): 213, Regent Street, London W1R 8DA. Wine information.

Cyriakusberg (Ger) vineyard (Anb): Franken. (Ber): Maindreieck. (Gro): Hofrat. (Vil): Sulzfeld.

Cyser (Eng) an apple juice and honey-based mead that is similar in taste to Sherry. Dry and sweet styles produced.

Cystine (Eng) an amino acid found in wines that is formed by yeasts.

Cysur Bitter (Wal) a 3.6% bitter ale from Bragdy Dyffryn Brewery in Denbigh. See also Castle Bitter, Cwrw Derwydd, Pedwar Bawd.

Cytrnówka (Pol) a lemon-flavoured vodka produced by Polmos 40% alc by vol.

Czamillonberg (Aus) a large vineyard area situated in the south-eastern corner of Austria on the Slovenian border. Produces quality white wines.

Czarine (Cktl) ½ measure vodka, ¼ measure apricot brandy, ¼ measure dry vermouth, dash Angostura. Stir over ice and strain into a cocktail glass.

Czaroff (Eng) a proprietary brand of vodka. 40% alc by vol.

Czar Simeon (Bul) the label of a 100% Cabernet sauvignon wine produced by Domaine Boyar from vineyards in Vinenka, west of Suhindol. Spends 3 years in oak.

Czechmate Saaz (Eng) a 4.2% alc by vol. ale flavoured with saaz hops and brewed by Enville Ales Ltd., West Midlands.

Czechoslovakia (Czec) former country of the Eastern Bloc, noted mainly for pilsner beer (and other styles). Has three main wine-producing regions of Bohemia (west), Moravia (central) and Slovakia (east) wines produced from Vitis vinifera stock are mainly consumed in the country.

Czerniawianka (Pol) a natural spring mineral water from Czerniawa. Mineral contents (milligrammes per litre): Sodium 23mg/l, Calcium 65mg/l, Magnesium 50mg/l, Potassium 2.8mg/l, Bicarbonates 976mg/l, Fluorides 1.2mg/l.

Czopowe (Pol) a 'tap tax' imposed on the sale of beer, mead and spirits in the sixteenth century.

D.A. (Austr) *abbr*: Dinner Ale.

D.A.B. (Ger) *abbr*: Dortmunder Actien Brauerei, a brewery (established 1868) based in Dortmund Westphalia, Germany. (The largest brewery in Germany).

D.A.B. (Ger) *abbr*: Dortmunder Actien Beer, a light beer brewed at the Dortmunder Actien Brauerei in Dortmund Westphalia, Germany.

D.A.B. Altbier (Ger) a famous altbier brewed by D.A.B. is milder than the Düsseldorf variety.

D.A.B. Diät Pils (Ger) a 4.9% alc by vol. bottled diet pilsner brewed by D.A.B.

D.A.B. Export (Ger) a fine Dortmunder bottled export beer 5.1% alc by vol. brewed by D.A.B.

D.A.B. Original (Ger) a 5% alc by vol. bottom-fermented beer brewed by D.A.B.

D.A.B. Pilsener (Ger) a 4.8% alc by vol. bottled pilsener brewed by D.A.B.

D.A.B. Strong (Ger) a 4.9% alc by vol. bottled pilsener brewed by D.A.B.

Dabinet (Eng) a variety of cider apple.

Dabug (Ger) vineyard (Anb): Franken. (Ber): Maindreieck. (Gro): Not yet assigned. (Vil): Randersacker.

Dabuki (Isr) a local red grape variety.

DAC (Aus) *abbr*: Districtus Austriae Controllatus.

Da Capo (Fr) a special cuvée red wine produced by Domaine de Pegau, Châteauneuf-du-Pape, southern Rhône using all 13 permitted grape varieties.

Dachgewann (Ger) vineyard (Anb): Rheinhessen. (Ber): Nierstein. (Gro): Gutes Domtal. (Vil): Zornheim.

D'Achouffe (Bel) a brewery (established 1982) based in Achouffe-Wibrin. Brews: La Vieille Salme.

Dachsberg (Ger) vineyard (Anb): Rheingau. (Ber): Johannisberg. (Gro): Erntebringer. (Vil): Winkel.

Dachsberg (Ger) vineyard (Anb): Rheingau. (Ber): Johannisberg. (Gro): Steinmacher. (Vil): Schierstein.

Dachsberg (Ger) vineyard (Anb): Württemberg. (Ber): Württembergisch Unterland. (Gro): Heuchelberg. (Vil): Brackenheim.

Dachsberg (Ger) vineyard (Anb): Württemberg. (Ber): Württembergisch Unterland. (Gro): Heuchelberg. (Vil): Haberschlacht.

Dachsbuckel (Ger) vineyard (Anb): Baden. (Ber): Badische Bergstrasse/Kraichgau. (Gro): Mannaberg. (Vil): Heidelberg.

Dachsteiger (Ger) vineyard (Anb): Württemberg. (Ber): Württembergisch Unterland. (Gro): Lindelberg. (Vil): Harsberg (ortsteil Neuholz)

Dachsteiger (Ger) vineyard (Anb): Württemberg. (Ber): Württembergisch Unterland. (Gro): Lindelberg. (Vil): Michelbach a. W.

Dachsteiger (Ger) vineyard (Anb): Württemberg. (Ber): Württembergisch Unterland. (Gro): Lindelberg. (Vil): Untersteinbach.

Dackenheim (Ger) village (Anb): Pfalz. (Ber): Mittelhaardt-Deutsche Weinstrasse. (Gro): Kobnert. (Vins): Kapellgarten, Liebesbrunnen, Mandelröth.

Daffodil Beer (Eng) a bottled beer brewed by Tollemache & Cobbold Brewery Ltd., Cliff Brewery, Ipswich, Suffolk for the Marie Cure Cancer Centre.

Daffy's Elixir (Eng) the nickname for gin in the eighteenth century.

Daflora (Bra) a natural spring mineral water. Mineral contents (milligrammes per litre): Sodium 13.92mg/l, Calcium 29.16mg/l, Magnesium 20.46mg/l, Potassium 3.84mg/l, Bicarbonates 13.92mg/l, Chlorides 1.96mg/l, Sulphates 0.17mg/l, Fluorides 0.38mg/l, Nitrates 1.48mg/l. pH 6.2

Dafnes (Gre) a wine producing area on Crete that produces A.O.C. dessert wine and dry A.O.Q.S. red wine from the red Liatiko grape.

Da Fonseca (Port) the main producer (founded in Azeitao in 1834) of wine in Setúbal and Dão.

Dafty Elixer (Eng) a 4.2% alc by vol. ale brewed by the Brewster Brewing C°. Ltd., Leicestershire.

Dagen Lager (Eng) a continental-style lager brewed by the Burtonwood Brewery, Warrington, Cheshire.

Daggio (It) a natural spring mineral water from Daggio, Introbio, Como (CO), Lombardy. Mineral contents (milligrammes per litre): Sodium 1.5mg/l, Calcium 7.9mg/l, Magnesium 2mg/l, Potassium 0.7mg/l, Bicarbonates 40.9mg/l, Chlorides 0.9mg/l, Sulphates 4.6mg/l, Nitrates 1.4mg/l, Silicates 6.5mg/l. pH 7.7

Daghestan (Arm) a fine wine-producing area in Armenia.

Daglig Snaps (Den) the brand-name of an akvavit.

D'Agostini (USA) a winery based in the Shenandoah Valley, Amador, California. 52ha. Grape variety: Zinfandel.

Dags (Eng) leather bottles in the shape of old pistols, used as an imitation pistol to ward off highwaymen, especially at night. Carried spirits or ale and could also be used as a club.

Daguin (Fr) an Armagnac producer. (Add): Rue Guynemer, 32000 Auch.

Dahdi (Ind) a style of fermented milk.

Daheuiller [Claude] (Fr) a noted sparkling wine producer based at Varrains, Saumur, Anjou-Saumur, Loire.

Dahls Brewery (Nor) a brewery based in Trondheim. Brews Tuborg under licence.

Dahra (Alg) a noted wine-producing area based in the Oran département.

Daiga Brewery [The] (Lith) a brewery. (Add): Pramones St 37, Alytus LT-4580 Lithuania. Brews a variety of beers and lagers.

Dailuaine (Scot) a single malt whisky distillery at Carron Burn. Owned by Dailuaine-Talisker Ltd. A 16 year old highland malt whisky. 40% alc by vol.

Daily Mail (Cktl) ⅓ measure rye whiskey, ⅓ measure Amer Picon, ⅓ measure orange squash, 3 dashes orange bitters. Shake over ice and strain into cocktail glass.

Daimiel (Sp) an important wine centre of La Mancha region of central Spain.

Daimieleña [La] (Sp) a noted wine co-operative based in La Mancha. Produces Clavileño (a dry white wine).

Daiquiri [1] (Cktl) 35mls (1½ fl.ozs) Bacardi White Label, juice of ½ lime, ½ teaspoon sugar. Combine sugar with lime juice, put in shaker with ice and rum, shake well and strain into a cocktail glass.

Daiquiri [2] (Cktl) 50mls (2fl.ozs) Bacardi White Label, 15mls (½ fl.oz) lime juice, 1 teaspoon grapefruit juice, 1 teaspoon sugar, 1 teaspoon maraschino. Combine sugar with lime and grapefruit juice, add ice, maraschino and rum, shake well, strain into a cocktail glass.

Daiquiri [3] (Cktl) 50mls (2fl.ozs) Bacardi White Label, 2 dashes Curaçao, juice ½ lime, 1 teaspoon sugar, 1 teaspoon grapefruit juice. Combine sugar and juices, add other ingredients, shake over ice and strain into a cocktail glass.

Daiquiri [4] (Cktl) ¾ measure white rum, ¾ measure lemon juice, 3 dashes gomme syrup, shake well over ice and strain into a cocktail glass.

Daiquiri (W.Ind) a demerara white (non-matured) rum.

Daiquiri Banane (Cktl) ¾ measure lemon juice, ⅛ measure white rum, ⅛ measure gomme syrup, ½ ripe banana, blend all together and serve over ice in a highball glass.

Daiquiri Blossom (Cktl). ½ measure white rum, ½ measure fresh orange juice, dash maraschino, shake over ice and strain into a cocktail glass.

Daiquiri Liberal (Cktl) ⅔ measure white rum, ⅓ measure sweet vermouth, dash Amer Picon, stir over ice and strain into a cocktail glass.

Daiquiri Mambi (Cktl) 35mls (1½ fl.ozs) Bacardi White Label, juice ½ lime, 1 teaspoon sugar, place all in a jug with plenty of ice, stir until cold and serve in a 125mls (5fl.oz) goblet.

Dairen (Chi) a branch of the China National Cereals, Oils and Foodstuffs Import and Export Corporation. Uses Hung Mei brand. Produces a cider.

Dairy (Eng) a place where cows are milked, where milk is stored, or where milk products are produced.

Daisies (Cktl) an American drink from spirit, raspberry syrup, lemon juice, soda and fruit. Serve over crushed ice in highball glasses.

Daisy Fizz (Cktl) 1 measure brandy, ½ measure orange juice, juice ½ lime and lemon. Shake over ice, strain into a highball glass and top with soda water.

Daisy Spring (Mal) a still natural spring mineral water from Bukit Jerakah. Mineral contents (milligrammes per litre): Sodium 2.8mg/l, Calcium 4.73mg/l, Magnesium 0.38mg/l, Potassium 4.85mg/l, Bicarbonates 97.5mg/l, Chlorides 7.1mg/l, Sulphates 1mg/l. pH 6.2

Dajeeling Tea (Ind) the mis-spelling of Darjeeling Tea.

Daktari (Hol) a banana and white rum liqueur, made for Matthew Clark by De Kuyper. Also known as Banana Daktari.

Dalberg (Ger) village (Anb): Nahe. (Ber): Kreuznach. (Gro): Pfarrgarten. (Vins): Schlossberg, Sonnenberg, Ritterhölle.

Dale Monopole (Bel) a natural spring mineral water from Verlinden, Lubeek.

Dalesice Brewery (Czec) a brewery based in southern Czec.

Daleside Blonde (Eng) a 3.9% alc by vol. ale brewed by the Daleside Brewwery, North Yorkshire.

Daleside Brewery (Eng) a brewery (established 1985). (Add): Camwal road, Starbeck, Harrogate, North Yorkshire HG1 4PT. Brews: Crack Shot, Daleside Blonde 3.9% alc by vol., FCP Ale, Greengrass Old Rogue Ale 4.5% alc by vol., Monkey Wrench 5.4% alc by vol., Morocco Ale 5.5% alc by vol., Old Legover 4.1% alc by vol., Old Lubrication 4.1% alc by vol., Pride of England 4% alc by vol., Ripon Jewel Ale 5.9% alc by vol., Shrimpers 4.1% alc by vol., St. Georges Ale 4.1% alc by vol. 'E'mail: enquiries@dalesidebrewery.plus.com

D'Alfonso del Sordo (It) a winery based in Puglia. Produces IGT Guado San Leo (made from the Uva di troia grape). Website: http://www.dalfonsodelsordo.it

Dalheim (Ger) village (Anb): Rheinhessen. (Ber): Nierstein. (Gro): Gutes Domtal. (Vins): Altdörr, Kranzberg, Steinberg.

Dali (Chi) a natural spring mineral water from Dali. Mineral contents (milligrammes per litre): Calcium 74mg/l, Magnesium 39.7mg/l, Potassium 9.9mg/l, Silicates 31.5mg/l. pH 7.6

Dalila (Cezc) a medium-dark lager beer brewed at the Samson Brewery in Ceské Budejovice.

Dalintober (Scot) a single highland malt whisky that was bottled in 1905.

Dalla Cia Wine Company (S.Afr) a winery (established 2004) based in Stellenbosch, Western Cape. Grape varieties: Cabernet sauvignon, Chardonnay, Merlot, Viognier. Label: Giogio. Website: http://www.dallacia.com

Dallas Dhu (Scot) a single malt whisky distillery on the outskirts of Forres in Morayshire. A highland malt whisky, part of the DCL group 43% alc by vol.

Dalla Valle Maya (USA) a winery based in the Napa

D

Valley, California. Grape varieties include: Cabernet sauvignon.

Dalmaciajavino (Euro) a co-operative based at Split that produces a wide range of wines.

Dalmatia (Euro) a wine region which produces red wines from the Cabernet, Gamay, Merlot and Pinot noir grapes. Also noted for Opolo, a rosé from the Plavac grape.

Dalmatia Maraschino (Euro) a cherry-flavoured liqueur.

Dalmatian Islands (Euro) see Dalmatia.

Dalmatian Oak (Sp) an oak used for wine vats in the Rioja region.

Dalmau (Sp) see Bodegas Marqués de Murietta.

Dalmore (Scot) a single malt whisky distillery at Alness, Ross-shire, a highland malt whisky. Owned by Whyte and Mackay Ltd. Produces 8, 12 and 20 year old varieties. 40% alc by vol.

Dalsheim (Ger) village (Anb): Rheinhessen. (Ber): Wonnegau. (Gro): Burg Rodenstein. see Flörsheim-Dalsheim.

Da Luca (It) a winery in the DOCG Barbera d'Asti, Piemonte region. Label: Alto.

Dalva (Port) a grande reserve sparkling (traditional method) wine produced by Caves da Silva. Also the name for their Dao wines.

Dalwhinnie (Scot) a single malt whisky distillery from town of same name. Produce a 12 year old highland malt whisky 43% alc by vol. Part of the DCL group.

Dalwhinnie Vineyard (Austr) a winery (established 1976). (Add): Taltarni Road, Moonambel, Victoria. Grape varieties: Chardonnay, Cabernet sauvignon, Shiraz.

Dalwood Vineyard (Austr) a vineyard based in New South Wales. Part of the Penfolds Vineyards.

Daly Distillery [B] (Ire) a whiskey distillery based in Tullamore. Produces Knappogue Castle 51.

Damacana (Tur) a demi-john.

Damalatmak (Tur) a word to denote 'to pour slowly'.

Damas (Iran) a red grape variety.

Damaschino (It) a white grape variety grown in Sicily.

Damascus (Arab) a hilly wine-producing region of northern Syria.

Damas do Campo (Cktl) ⅓ measure Bacardi White Label, ⅓ measure Campari, ⅓ measure anis, 2 dashes grenadine. Stir over ice, strain, add a slice of orange and a cherry.

Damash (Iran) a natural spring mineral water from the Damash Spring. Mineral contents (milligrammes per litre): Sodium 6mg/l, Calcium 28.8mg/l, Magnesium 3.84mg/l, Potassium 1mg/l, Chlorides 6mg/l, Sulphates 10mg/l, Fluorides 0.1mg/l, Nitrates 1.5mg/l. pH 7.3

Damassine (Fr) an A.C. fruit spirit made from small red damassine plums. Produced by Caves de Soyhières in the Jura.

Damavand (Iran) a sparkling natural spring mineral water (established 1977) from Ala-Damavand. Mineral contents (milligrammes per litre): Sodium 4.58mg/l, Calcium 56.41mg/l,

Magnesium 15.36mg/l, Potassium 0.62mg/l, Bicarbonates 212mg/l, Chlorides 5.99mg/l, Sulphates 10.65mg/l, Fluorides 0.14mg/l, Nitrates 7.57mg/l. pH 7.32

Damblat (Fr) an Armagnac producer. (Add): Rue République, Castelnau d'Auzan, 32800 Eauze. 40% alc by vol.

Dame-Jeanne (Fr) a wide-waisted covered glass wicker jar which holds 2.5ltrs–45.5ltrs used for storing Madeira (a demi-john).

Dame Noir (Fr) the local name in Cahors for the Jurançon grape.

Damenwein (Aus) a zuckerhütl wine (medium-sweet).

Damery (Fr) a Cru Champagne village in the Canton d'Épernay. District: Reims.

Dames de la Charité (Fr) a cuvée in the A.C. commune of Pommard, Côte de Beaune, Burgundy (owned by the Hospices de Beaune).

Dames Hautes (Fr) an exclusive estate of Geisweiler in the A.C. commune of Nuits-Saint-Georges, Côte de Nuits, Burgundy.

Dames Hospitalières (Fr) a cuvée in the A.C. commune of Pommard, Côte de Beaune, Burgundy (owned by the Hospices de Beaune).

Dampt [Daniel] (Fr) a winery based in the A.C. Chablis, Burgundy. Produces a range of Chablis wines including Premier Crus: Côte de Léchet and Les Lys.

Da Mhile (Scot) the gaelic for 2000. A whisky made from English and Scottish barley, the first to distill an organic Scotch whisky. Made at Springbank Distillery, Campbeltown, Argyll by a West Wales farmer from Llandysul.

Damianitza (Bul) a winery based in the Struma Valley. Grape varieties include: Cabernet sauvignon, Merlot, Rubin. Label: Redark, Uniqato.

Damien Distillery (W.Ind) a distillery on the isle of Haiti that produces Barbancourt.

Damijan Podversic (It) a winery based in Gorizia in the Friuli-Venezia-Guilia region. Labels: Kaplija.

Damilano (It) a family winery based in the Piedmonte region of north-western Italy. Produces a variety of wines including a Barolo from the Cannubi vineyard.

Damitmak (Tur) to distill.

Damm-Bier (Sp) the label of a lager brewed by Estrella-Damm in Barcelona.

Dämmerschoppen (Ger) denotes an evening drink/cocktail.

Dammheim (Ger) village (Anb): Pfalz. (Ber): Südliche Weinstrasse. (Gro): Bischofskreuz. (Vin): Höhe.

Damn Brewery (Sp) a brewery based in Barcelona. Brews Damn lager 5.4% alc by vol.

Damn-the-Weather (Cktl) ⅓ measure dry gin, ⅓ measure sweet vermouth, ⅙ measure orange juice, 4 dashes Cointreau. Shake over ice and strain into a cocktail glass.

Damoisel V.S.O.P. (Fr) a 15 year old Cognac produced by Rouyer 40% alc by vol.

Damon Pils (Bel) a 4% alc by vol. bottled pilsner lager.

422

Damoy [Julien] (Fr) a Rhône négociant based at 1 Rue des Oliviers, 94320 Thiais.

Dampierre (Fr) a commune of Coteaux de Saumur, produces mainly white wines with some red.

Dampierre [Comte Audoin de] (Fr) a Champagne producer. (Add): 5 Grande Rue, 51140 Chenay par Reims. Marque Auxiliare. Produces vintage and non-vintage wines.

Dampierre [Comte de] (Fr) a Cognac producer. (Add): Château de Plassac, 17240 Plassac. 30ha. in the Bons Bois.

Damscheid (Ger) village (Anb): Mittelrhein. (Ber): Rheinburgengau. (Gro): Schloss Schönburg. (Vins): Frankenhell, Goldemund, Sonnenstock.

Damselfly (Eng) the label of a 5% alc by vol. lager brewed with elderflower by Young and C°. of London.

Damson Beer (Eng) a beer brewed by the Lakeland Brewing Company.

Damson Beer (Eng) a bottle-conditioned beer brewed by the Strawberry Bank Brewery, Masons Arms.

Damson Cream (Eng) an egg-based drink produced by Townend of Hull.

Dancer (Eng) a 4.2% alc by vol. ale brewed by Northern Brewing, Cheshire.

Dancer's Cup (Cktl) place ice into a large jug, add a measure of orgeat, and a wine glass of brandy. Fill jug with cider and soda water, stir well and decorate with lemon slices.

Dandelion (Eng) *Taraxcum officinale*. Family: *Compositae* a weed used to produce Dandelion and Burdock. Leaves only used.

Dandelion and Burdock (Eng) a non-alcoholic carbonated drink produced by A.G. Barr.

Dandelion Coffee (Eng) a coffee made from the dried and roasted roots of young dandelions that are ground and infused for 10 minutes in boiling water. Use same amount as for normal coffee.

Dandy (Cktl) ½ measure Dubonnet, ½ measure rye whiskey, dash Angostura, 3 dashes Cointreau. Stir over ice, strain into a cocktail glass, add a piece of orange and lemon peel.

Danebury Vineyard (Eng) a vineyard based in Hampshire, noted for dry Auxerrois wines.

Danfold's (S.Afr) the export label for wine produced by the Klein Constantia Estate winery, Constantia, Western Cape.

D'Angelo (It) a winery (established 1930) based at Rionero in Vulture in the Basilicata region. Produces: D.O.C. Aglianico del Vulture.

D'Angelo Estate Wines (Can) a winery based at Amhertsburg, Lake Erie north shore, Ontario. Grape varieties include Pinot noir, Chardonnay.

Danglade [L. et Fils] (Fr) a Bordeaux négociant, well known for Saint-Émilion and Pomerol wines.

Danie de Wet (S.Afr) noted wine producer based in Robertson. Grape variety: Chardonnay. Labels: Bateleur, Giyani, Limestone Hill, Reserve Call of the African Eagle.

Danielis (Gre) a red wine produced by Achaia Clauss.

Daniel Leclerc et Fils (Fr) a Champagne producer (7.5ha). (Add): Maison Rouge, 10110 Polisot. Produces vintage and non-vintage Champagnes. Vintages: 1995, 1996, 1999, 2000, 2001. 'E'mail: Champagne_daniel_leclerc@hotmail.fcom

Danielli (Cktl) ⅗ measure vodka, ³⁄₁₀ measure dry vermouth, ¹⁄₁₀ measure Campari, Stir over ice and strain into a cocktail glass.

Daniel's Hammer (Eng) a 5% alc by vol. golden ale brewed by Daniel Thwaites at the Star Brewery, Blackburn, Lancashire.

Daniel Thwaites (Eng) *see* Thwaites Brewery.

Danir de Wet (S.Afr) the label for a range of wines produced by the De Wetshof Estate winery, Robertson, Western Cape.

D'anis (Den) a liqueur produced by Danish Distilleries from extracts of anise and natural spices.

Danish Distilleries (Den) *abbr*: D.D.S. De Danske Spritfabrikker. Main producer of akvavit. Based at Aalborg.

Danish Dynamite (Eng) a 5% alc by vol. ale brewed by Stonehenge Ales (Bunces Brewery) Ltd., Wiltshire.

Danish Gin Fizz (Cktl) ¾ measure dry gin, ¼ measure Cherry Heering, 3 dashes kirsch, juice ½ lime, barspoon gomme syrup. Shake well over ice, strain into an ice-filled highball glass and top with soda water.

Danish Light (Eng) a 0.9% alc by vol. beer from the Federation Brewery, Newcastle.

Danish Light Lager (Den) a low alcohol lager 0.6% alc by vol. brewed in Copenhagen.

Danish Mary (Cktl) 75mls (3fl.ozs) tomato juice, 25mls (1fl.oz) akvavit, 2 dashes Worcestershire sauce, 2 dashes lemon juice, dash celery salt. Shake over ice and strain into an ice-filled highball glass.

Danish Whiskey (Den) a whiskey distilled in a patent still.

Dank Cellar (Eng) a description of a cellar that is unfit for wine storage (denotes that it is damp, cold and musty).

Dannon (USA) a natural spring mineral water from Diamond Springs, Graysville. PA.

Danny Brown Ale (Eng) a brown ale 1034 O.G. brewed by Daniel Thwaites.

Danny's Special Cocktail (Cktl) 25mls (⅕ gill) Jack Daniels Bourbon, 15mls (⅛ gill) triple sec, 2 dashes orange Curaçao, juice ½ lemon. Stir over ice, strain into a 125mls (5fl.oz) goblet.

Dánosi Leánkya (Rum) an alternative name for Feteasca Alba and Grasa. Known as Királyleánkya in Hungary.

Dansk LA (Den) a low alcohol lager 0.9% alc by vol. brewed by Carlsberg-Tuborg at their Wiibroes Brewery, Elsinore.

Danskvand (Den) soda water/mineral water.

Danzern Grillenparz Dantzig (Fr) a herb liqueur with gold leaf. Is similar to Goldwasser 45% alc by vol.

Danziger Goldwasser (Den) a herb-flavoured liqueur, clear, with fine cut gold leaf added, flavoured with aniseed and caraway. Also made in West Berlin. *See also* Bruidstranen.

Danzig Silverwasser (Den) has not been produced since the Second World War. Similar to Danziger goldwasser but contains silver flakes.

Danzka Vodka (Den) a 40% alc by vol. 100% grain neutral spirit distilled by Danish Distilleries.

Danzy Jones (Wal) a 40% alc by vol. old style mellow whisky liqueur produced by the Celtic Spirit C°. based at Grove Farm, Abergavenny, Monmouthshire. *See also* Black Mountain Liqueur, Celtic Whisky.

Dão (Port) a DOC wine-producing district in northern Portugal. Produces predominantly red wines. Main Grape varieties: red wines: Touriga nacional, Tinta roriz and Encruzado, white wines: Bical (Borrado das moscas), Cerceal do Dão, Malvasia fina and Rabo de Ovelha.

Dão Adegas Cooperativas (Port) the name used by the União das Adegas Cooperativas do Dão for their Dão wines.

Dão Aliança (Port) a Dão wine produced by Caves Aliança.

Dão Caves Velhas (Port) the brand-name used by Caves Velhas for their Dão wines.

Dão Ferreira Malaquias (Port) a Dão wine produced by Ferreira Malaquias.

Dão Fundação (Port) are Dão wines produced by Caves Fundação.

Dão Primavera (Port) are Dão wines produced by the Caves Primavera.

Dão S. Domingos (Port) are Dão wines produced by Caves de Solar de S. Domingos.

Daose (Ch.Isles) a drinking bout. Also spelt Dosaïe.

Dão Serra (Port) a Dão wine produced by J. Serra and Sons.

Daphnes (Gre) the name given to red and rosé wines produced on the isle of Crete made from the Liatiko grape.

Dapple Sparkler (Cktl) 2 parts Dubonnet, 1 part cider, 1 part lemonade. Stir on ice in a highball glass and decorate with a slice of apple.

Darb Cocktail (Cktl) ⅓ measure dry gin, ⅓ measure apricot brandy, ⅓ measure French vermouth, juice ¼ lemon. Shake over ice and strain into a cocktail glass.

Dar Bel Amri (Afr) a noted red wine-producing area near Rabat in Morocco. *See also* Dar Bel Hamri.

Dar Bel Hamri (Afr) the alternative spelling of Dar Bel Amri.

D'Arbis (Fr) a commune in the Haut-Benauge, central Bordeaux.

Daredevil (Eng) a winter ale 7.1% alc by vol. from Everards.

D'Arenberg (Austr) a winery. (Add): Osbourne Road, MᶜLaren Vale, South Australia 5171. 78ha. Grape varieties: Cabernet sauvignon, Chardonnay, Grenache, Palomino, Riesling and Shiraz. Produces: The Hermit Crab (Marsanne, Viognier), The Laughing Magpie (Shiraz, Viognier), The Money Spider (Roussanne).

Daresbury's Quintessential Dry Gin (Eng) the label of a 45% alc by vol. gin.

Darioush (USA) a winery based in the Napa Valley, California. Grape varieties include: Cabernet sauvignon, Merlot. Label: The Signature.

Dario Raccaro (It) a winery based in Cormons in the Friuli-Venezia-Guilia region.

Darjeeling (Ind) a famous tea plantation of northern India, produces high quality teas with a '*Muscatel*' aroma and flavour. Broken orange pekoe grade. *See also* Dajeeling Tea.

Darjeeling Oolong Phoobsering (Ind) one of the world's most expensive teas with a maximum of only 50kgs produced annually.

Darjon Vineyards (N.Z) a winery. (Add): North Eyre Road, Swannanoa, North Canterbury. 2ha.

Dark (Wal) the name given to the mild beers of South Wales.

Dark Aishoerer (Eng) a 4.7% alc by vol. ale brewed by the White Star Brewery, Hampshire.

Dark & Delicious (Eng) a 4.6% alc by vol. dark ale brewed by the Covedale Brewery, Shropshire.

Dark Beer (Eng) a general term for mild ales and other deep-coloured beers. (Bel) = brune, (Den) = mørkt øl, (Ger) = dunkel.

Dark Corner (Austr) a winery based in South-Eastern Australia. Grape varieties include: Durif, Shiraz.

Dark Delight (Eng) a 6% alc by vol. strong dark ale brewed by the Downton Brewery Ltd., Wiltshire.

Dark de Triomphe (Fr) a stout produced by micro-brewery Paris Real Ale Brewery's Frog and Rost Bif in Saint Denis, Paris. *see* Inseine Bitter.

Dark Fields (Eng) the label for a red wine (Dunkelfelder 50% Pinot noir, 50%) produced by the Hidden Spring Vineyards.

Dark Forest (Eng) a 5% alc by vol. dark ale brewed by Rockingham Ales, Cambridgeshire.

Dark Golden (Sp) *abbr*: D.G. an old classification of Sherry (raya).

Dark Horse (S.Afr) the label for a red wine (Shiraz) produced by the Flagstone Winery, Somerset West, Western Cape.

Dark Horse Porter (Eng) a 5% alc by vol. porter ale produced from an original nineteenth century recipe by Ushers of Trowbridge. *See also* 1824 Particular.

Dark Island (Scot) a 4.6% alc by vol. dark ale brewed by the Atlas Brewery, Argyll.

Dark Island Ale (Scot) a 4.6% alc by vol. dark ruby-red ale brewed by the Orkney Brewery in the village of Quoyloo using Goldings and Omega hops.

Dark Lager (Scan) a deep-coloured lager beer using roasted barley malt. (Den) = lagerøl.

Dark Lord (Eng) a 5% alc by vol. dark ale brewed by George Bateman & Son Ltd., Lincolnshire.

Dark Mild (Eng) a dark mild ale brewed by the Blackawton Brewery, Rowden, near Dartmouth.

Dark Mild (Eng) a 3% alc by vol. dark mild ale brewed by George Bateman & Son Ltd., Lincolnshire.

Dark Mild (Eng) a 4% alc by vol. dark mild ale brewed by the Hogs Back Brewery, Surrey.

Dark Mild (Eng) a 4% alc by vol. dark mild ale brewed by the White Brewing C°., East Sussex.

Dark Moor (Scot) a 4.5% alc by vol. ale brewed by the Kelburn Brewing C°., Lanarkshire.

Darkness (Eng) a 4.2% alc by vol. dark ale brewed by the Acorn Brewery, South Yorkshire.

Dark Roast (Eng) a 5% alc by vol. dark ale brewed by the Old Luxters Brewery, Oxfordshire.

Dark Ruby Mild (Eng) a bottle-conditioned mild ale brewed by the Sarah Hughes Brewery, Beacon Hotel, Sedgley, near Dudley, West Midlands (1095 O.G) 6% alc by vol.

Dark Secret (Eng) a 4.3% alc by vol. ale brewed by The Durham Brewery Ltd., County Durham.

Dark Star (Eng) a 5.8% alc by vol. ale brewed by the Barum Brewery, Devon.

Dark Star Ale (Eng) a bottled sediment ale 1050 O.G. brewed by Pitfield's Brewery, London.

Dark Star Brewing C° (Eng) a brewery (established 1995). (Add): Moonhill Farm, Antsy, Haywards Heath, West Sussex. Uses two labels: Skinners, Dark Star. Skinners label: Ale Trail Mild 3.5% alc by vol. Brighton Rock 4% alc by vol. Penguin Stout 4.2% alc by vol. Cliffhanger Porter 5.5% alc by vol. Pavillion Beast 6% alc by vol. Dark Star label: Black Hole 6% alc by vol. Espresso Stout 4.2% alc by vol., Dark Star 5% alc by vol., Hophead, Original, Solstice 4% alc by vol. Website: http://www.darkstarbrewing.co.uk 'E'mail: info@darkstarbrewing.co.uk

Dark Stranger (Eng) a 4.4% alc by vol. dark ale brewed by the Teme Valley Brewery, Wiltshire.

Darktribe Brewery (Eng) a brewery based at Gunness, near Scunthorpe, North Lincolnshire. Brews: Terrier beer 4.2% alc by vol. Full Astern 3.8% alc by vol.

Dark Wheat Mild (Eng) a 3.6% alc by vol. dark mild ale brewed by the TigerTops Brewery, West Yorkshire.

Darley Brewery (Eng) a brewery now owned by Vaux of Sunderland. Noted for cask-conditioned Thorne Best Bitter 1038 O.G. Based at Thorne in south Yorkshire.

Darling Cellars (S.Afr) a winery based in Darling, Swartland, Coastal region. Grape varieties: Bukettraube, Cabernet sauvignon, Chenin blanc, Cinsaut, Grenache, Pinotage, Sauvignon blanc, Shiraz. Labels: Black Granite, Bush Vine, DC Range, Flamingo Bay, For My Friends, Old Block, Onyx, Quercus Gold, Six Tonner, Terra Hutton, Zantsi Natural Sweet.

Darling Estate (Austr) a winery (established 1990) based at Whitfield-Myrtleford Road, Chestnut, Victoria. Grape varieties: Chenin blanc, Pinot noir.

Darlington Wines (Eng) specialist bag-in-box wines (established 1981). (Add): Crown House, North Circular Road, London NW10 7PN. Designed for Pubs, Hotels, etc. Wines dispensed from patented equipment installed in the premises. 'E'mail: sales@darlingtonwines.com

Darllaw (Wal) to brew (beer).

Darllawdy (Wal) brewery.

Darllawydd (Wal) brewer.

Dar Natury (Pol) a natural spring mineral water.

Daroca (Sp) a Vino Comarcal of Zaragoza in Aragón.

Produces red wines that are high in alcohol. 13%–16% alc by vol.

Darona [Pierre] (Fr) a noted producer of A.C. Saint-Péray Mousseux in the Côtes du Rhône.

Dart (Swe) a dark, malty beer 5.6% alc by vol. brewed by the Pripps Brewery.

D'Artagnan (Fr) the Patron Saint of Armagnac, also known as Charles de Batz de Montesquiou Fezenzac.

Dartigalongue et Fils (Fr) an Armagnac producer. (Add): 32110 Nogaro. Produces a range of Armagnac brandies.

Dartmoor (Eng) the brand-name of a keg bitter 1037 O.G. and a lager 1036 O.G. brewed by Thompson's Brewery of Ashburton in Devon.

Dartmoor Best Bitter (Eng) a bitter ale brewed by Furgusons of Plymouth. See also Cockleroaster, Dartmoor Strong, Dartmoor Millenium.

Dartmoor Best Bitter (Eng) a 3.9% alc by vol. bitter ale brewed by the St. Austell Brewery C°. Ltd., Cornwall.

Dartmoor IPA (Eng) a 4% alc by vol. India pale ale brewed by the Princetown Breweries Ltd., Devon.

Dartmoor Millenium (Eng) a beer brewed by Furgusons of Plymouth to celebrate their 1000th brew. See also Cockleroaster, Dartmoor Best Bitter, Dartmoor Strong.

Dartmoor Spring (Eng) a still and sparkling natural spring mineral water bottled at source (Lower Hurston Farm) near Chagford, Devon.

Dartmoor Strong (Eng) a strong ale brewed by Furgusons of Plymouth. See also Cockleroaster, Dartmoor Best Bitter, Dartmoor Millenium.

Daru Spirit (Sri.L) see Madhvi.

Darwin Brewery (Eng) a brewery. (Add) 63 Back Tatham Street, Sunderland, Tyne & Wear SR1 2QE. Brews: Blew Cap Pilsner 4.8% alc by vol., Cauldron Snout 5.6% alc by vol., Durham Light Ale 4% alc by vol., Evolution Ale 8.3% alc by vol., Extinction Ale 8.3% alc by vol., Feethams Farewell 3.7% alc by vol., Flag Porter 5% alc by vol., Forest XB 4.2% alc by vol., Ghost Ale 4.1% alc by vol., Imperial Stout 7% alc by vol., Killer Bee 6% alc by vol., Penshaws Pint 4.1% alc by vol., Poominator 4.8% alc by vol., Profs Pint 4.1% alc by vol., Richmond Ale 4.2% alc by vol., Saints Sinner 4% alc by vol., Smugglers Mild 4% alc by vol., Stokoe's Trophy 3.8% alc by vol., Sunderland Best 3.9% alc by vol. Website: http://www.darwinbrewery.com 'E'mail: info@darwinbrewery.com

Darwin Stubby (Austr) a 2.25 litre bottle of Northern Territory Draught produced in Darwin by C.U.B. and Swan (also colloquial name for a 37cls bottle).

Dasani (USA) a natural spring mineral water.

Daschbosch Wine Cellar (S.Afr) a winery (established 1956) based in Rawsonville, Worcester, Western Cape. 890ha. Grape varieties: Cabernet franc, Cabernet sauvignon, Chardonnay, Hanepoot, Merlot, Pinotage, Ruby cabernet, Sauvignon blanc. Labels: Louwshoek-Voorsorg, Nectar de Provision, Welgevonde. Website: http://www.daschbosch.co.za

D

Dash (Wal) a nickname given to the Worthington Dark Mild (1034 O.G) in Swansea, South Wales.

Dash (USA) a measure for a cocktail (approx. ⅙ teaspoon).

Dasher (USA) a special type of stopper which is used for making cocktails that only allows small amounts out of the bottle.

Dashers Beer (Eng) a cask-conditioned beer 1040 O.G. brewed by the Fox and Hounds public house in Stottesdon, Shropshire.

Dasher Stopper (USA) *see* Dasher.

Dash of Bitters (Cktl) adding a '*dash*' of bitters (Angostura, Amer Picon, etc.) to a cocktail.

Dashwood (N.Z) the label used by Vavasour Wines Ltd., Redwood Pass, Awatere Valley, Marlborough for their wine range.

Dassie's (S.Afr) the label for a range of wines produced by the Botha Wine Cellar winery, Worcester, Western Cape.

Dated Ports (Port) denotes Ports of an indicated age, bottled in Oporto and sold as 10, 20, 30, 40 or over 40 years only. The 10 year old Ports may not necessarily contain 10 year old Port but as long as they pass an Instituto do Vinho do Porto blind tasting and conform to the character of a 10 year old then may be labelled as such.

Dated Solera System (Mad) used since the Phylloxera outbreak where the oldest wine (date) in the system is used on the label.

Date of Harvest (Port) refers to Port that has been in wood for at least 7 years, then bottled. Must bear vintage date, year of bottling and indication that it has been aged in cask.

Dattenberg (Ger) village (Anb): Mittelrhein. (Ber): Rheinburgengau. (Gro): Burg Hammerstein. (Vin): Gertrudenberg.

Dattier (Austr) a white grape variety also known as Waltham Cross.

Dattingen (Ger) a village in the anbaugebiet of Baden. *see* Britzingen.

Daubhaus (Ger) vineyard (Anb): Ahr. (Ber): Walporzheim/Arhtal. (Gro): Klosterberg. (Vin): Ahrweiler (red wine).

Daubhaus (Ger) grosslage (Anb): Rheingau. (Ber): Johannisberg. (Vils): Flörsheim, Hochheim, Kostheim, Wicker.

Daubhaus (Ger) vineyard (Anb): Rheinhessen. (Ber): Bingen. (Gro): Abtey. (Vil): Appenheim.

Daubhaus (Ger) vineyard (Anb): Rheinhessen. (Ber): Nierstein. (Gro): Güldenmorgen. (Vil): Oppenheim.

Daubrion (Fr) an ancient spelling of Château Haut-Brion, Graves, Bordeaux. *See also* D'obrion.

Dauner (Ger) a natural spring mineral water from the Dauner Quelle 1, Daun, RP. Mineral contents (milligrammes per litre): Sodium 818mg/l, Calcium 142mg/l, Magnesium 192mg/l, Potassium 33mg/l, Bicarbonates 3478mg/l, Chlorides 66mg/l.

Dauner Urquelle (Ger) a natural spring mineral water from the Dauner Quelle III, Daun, RP.

Dauphin de Château Guiraud [Le] (Fr) the second wine of Château Guiraud, A.C. Sauternes, Bordeaux.

Dausenau (Ger) village (Anb): Mittelrhein. (Ber): Rheinburgengau. (Gro): Lahntal. (Vin): Hasenberg.

Dautenheim (Ger) village (Anb): Rheinhessen. (Ber): Wonnegau. (Gro): Sybillenstein. (Vin): Himmelacker.

Dautenpflänzer (Ger) vineyard (Anb): Nahe. (Ber): Kreuznach. (Gro): Schlosskapelle. (Vil): Münster-Sarmsheim.

Dauvissat [Jean & Sébastien] (Fr) a winery based in the A.C. Chablis, Burgundy. Produces a range of Chablis wines including Premier Cru Montmains.

Davalos (Arg) a 2365metres high winery in Molinos, Salta. Produces a Malbec-Cabernet sauvignon based wine from 100 year old vines from a 9ha. Colomé vineyard.

Davenports (Eng) *see* Higate Brewery Ltd.

Davenports Brewery (Eng) a famous brewery based in Birmingham noted for its '*Beer at home*' service. Closed in January 1989 by the parent group Greenall Whitley. Produced many noted beers including Brummie Brown 1032 O.G. Chequer Bitter 1036.5 O.G. Continental Lager 1033.9 O.G. Drum Bitter 1036.5 O.G. Top Brew De Luxe 1074 O.G. and Jager Lager 1032 O.G.

Davenport Vineyards (Eng) a vineyard and winery (established 1991). (Add): Limney Farm, Castle Hill, Rotherfield, East Sussex TN6 3RR. Grape varieties: Auxerrois, Pinot noir. Produces a wide range of wines (red, rosé, white and sparkling). Website: http://www.davenportvineyards.co.uk 'E'mail: will@davenportvineyards.co.uk

Dave's Lager (Eng) a lager 1048 O.G. brewed by the Brewhouse Brewery in Dorset.

David Arthur Estate (USA) a winery based in the Napa Valley, California. Grape varieties include: Cabernet sauvignon. Label: Elevation 1147.

David et Foillard (Fr) a négociant based at Saint Georges de Reneins in the Burgundy region.

David-Quelle (Ger) a natural spring mineral water from Bad Peterstal, BW.

David's Old Crofter's Bitter (Eng) a bitter beer brewed by the home-brew public house 'First in Last out' in Hastings, Sussex.

Daview Vineyards (S.Afr) a winery (established 1994) based in Nooder-Paarl, Western Cape. 24ha. Grape varieties: Cabernet sauvignon, Merlot, Shiraz. Label: Par Excellence. Website: http://www.frostwine.com

Davina (Mac) a still natural spring mineral water from Davina, Macedonia. Mineral contents (milligrammes per litre): Sodium 18.98mg/l, Calcium 102.6mg/l, Magnesium 112.7mg/l, Potassium 2.14mg/l, Bicarbonates 201.3mg/l, Chlorides 255mg/l, Sulphates 7.06mg/l, Fluorides 0.4mg/l, Nitrates 0.45mg/l. pH 7.5

Davis'es Brewing Company (Eng) *see* Grainstore Brewery [The].

Davisons (Eng) the trading name used for over 85 specialist wine Off-licenses that belong to J.T. Davies and Sons.

Davewn Springs (Can) a natural spring mineral water

(established 1994) from Middlebro, Manitoba. Mineral contents (milligrammes per litre): Sodium 6.1mg/l, Calcium 12.5mg/l, Magnesium 4.63mg/l, Potassium 0.69mg/l, Bicarbonates <40mg/l, Chlorides 13mg/l, Sulphates <9mg/l, Fluorides 0.1mg/l, Nitrates 4.63mg/l.

Dawes Soft Drinks (Eng) a family-run soft drinks manufacturer based in Paignton, Devon.

Dax (Fr) a natural spring mineral water from Elvina. Mineral contents (milligrammes per litre): Sodium 126mg/l, Calcium 125mg/l, Magnesium 30.1mg/l, Potassium 19.4mg/l, Bicarbonates 164.7mg/l, Chlorides 155mg/l, Sulphates 365mg/l, Fluorides 1.4mg/l, Nitrates 0.8mg/l. pH 7.25

Day by Day (Cktl) ⅓ measure Mandarine Napoléon, ⅓ measure Scotch whisky, ⅓ measure sweet vermouth. Shake well over ice and strain into a cocktail glass.

Daydream Cocktail (Cktl) 40mls (⅓ gill) brandy, 1 teaspoon maraschino, 1 teaspoon brown Curaçao, 1 teaspoon Angostura. Stir over ice, strain into a cocktail glass, serve with dash of Champagne, a cherry and a dash of lemon peel juice.

Daylight Robbery (Eng) an ale brewed by Everards of Leicester.

Dazed and Confused (Eng) a 4.6% alc by vol. ale brewed by Triple FFF Brewery, Four Marks, near Alton, Hampshire.

Dazzler (Eng) a 4.5% alc by vol. ale brewed by the Ossett Brewing C°. Ltd., West Yorkshire.

DB Bitter (N.Z) a 4% alc by vol. canned brown lager brewed by DB Breweries, Auckland.

DB Breweries (N.Z) a large brewery based in Auckland. (Add): 1 Bairds Road, Atahuhu, Auckland. Brews: DB Bitter, DB Draught, DB Export Dry, DB Export Gold, Mako. Website: http://www.db.co.nz

DB Draught (N.Z) a 4% alc by vol. light, malty canned lager brewed by DB Breweries, Auckland.

DB Export Dry (N.Z) a 5% alc by vol. premium bottled/canned lager brewed by DB Breweries, Auckland.

DB Export Gold (N.Z) a 4% alc by vol. light, malty, canned lager brewed by DB Breweries, Auckland.

DB Natural (N.Z) an ale brewed by DB South Island Breweries. See also DB Export Dry.

DB South Island Breweries (N.Z) a brewery based in the South Island. Brews: DB Export Dry, DB Natural.

D.C.L. (Eng) abbr: Distillers Company Limited. Large company owning many of the Scotch whisky distilleries.

D.D. (Eng) abbr: Double Diamond. Famous for Ind Coope Pale ale.

D-Day Ale (Eng) a 4.8% alc by vol. ale brewed by Young's Wandsworth plant to commemorate D-Day.

D-Day Anniversary Ale (Eng) a 6.3% alc by vol. ale from Courage (5,000 bottles made to commemorate the 50 year anniversary)

D-Day Bitter (Eng) a bitter ale brewed to commemorate the invasion of Europe in 1944.

Made using a 50 y.o. recipe by the Castle Eden Brewery, C°. Durham. see Higson's Bitter, Fuggles Imperial IPA, Ryman's Reserve.

DDS (Den) abbr: see Danish Distilleries.

DE (Sp) abbr: see Denominación Específica.

Dea (Pol) a still and sparkling natural spring mineral water from Polczyn Zdroj (red Label: sparling/green Label: still). Mineral contents (milligrammes per litre): Sodium 6mg/l, Calcium 65.73mg/l, Magnesium 9.72mg/l, Potassium 1.5mg/l, Bicarbonates 226mg/l, Chlorides 12mg/l, Sulphates 25mg/l, Fluorides 0.3mg/l. pH 7.9 Website: http://www.deawater.com

De-Acidification (Eng) the removal of excess acid in wine by the addition of calcium carbonate or other calcium compounds to neutralise the acids.

Dead Arm Disease (Eng) an English vine disease. see Eutypiose.

Dead Frogge (S.Afr) the label for a white wine (Chardonnay) produced by the Jonkeer winery, Robertson, Western Cape.

Dead Stock (Eng) a term used to describe wine maturing in a restaurant's cellar the value of which adds nothing to the 'cash flow'. Also applies to over-stocking of bottles of spirits, liqueurs, beers, etc. that will not be used for a long time.

Dead Wash (W.Ind) the name given to the distilling mash in the production to rum that is made up of Limings and Dunder.

Deakin's Red Admiral (Eng) a beer brewed by the Mansfield Brewery. see Deakin's Red Squirrel, Deakin's Royal Stag, Deakin's Wild Boar, Deakin's Yule Brew.

Deakin's Red Squirrel (Eng) a 4.4% alc by vol. ale from the Mansfield Brewery.

Deakin's Royal Stag (Eng) a 4.5% alc by vol. coppery coloured autumn brew from Mansfield Brewery using a blend of new season hops and dark malt (600 barrels brewed over a 6 week period).

Deakin's Wild Boar (Eng) a 6% alc by vol. seasonal ale from the Mansfield Brewery.

Deakin's Yule Brew (Eng) a 6% alc by vol. winter warmer cask-conditioned bitter from Mansfield Brewery. Named after a turn of the century brewer Sydney Deakin.

Dealul-Mare (Rum) a wine region producing good red and white wines from the Cabernet sauvignon, Pinot noir and Welschriesling grapes.

De-amination (Eng) the break down of protein into amino acids and the removal of the nitrogen-containing group of atoms. Poisonous amyl alcohol is produced during this process.

Dean's Gate (Cktl) ½ measure Drambuie, ½ measure white rum, ¼ measure lime juice cordial. Stir over ice, strain into a cocktail glass and add a twist of orange.

Deanston Mill (Scot) a single malt whisky distillery based at Deanston in Perthshire. Matured and bottled by Longman Distillers, Glasgow. A 17 year old highland malt whisky. 40% alc by vol. Part of the Invergordon Distillers.

Death in the Afternoon (Eng) the great author Ernest Hemmingway's special: "Pour one jigger of absinthe into a Champagne glass, add iced Champagne until it attains the proper opalescent milkiness. Drink three to five of these slowly".

D'Eau (Pak) a bottled tap water (established 2002). Mineral contents (milligrammes per litre): Sodium 42mg/l, Calcium 40mg/l, Magnesium 14mg/l, Potassium 5mg/l, Chlorides 48mg/l, Sulphates 73mg/l. pH 7.51

Deauville Cocktail [1] (Cktl) 60mls (½ gill) dry gin, 2 dashes lime juice, 2 dashes plain syrup. Shake over ice, strain into a cocktail glass and serve with a dash of lemon peel juice.

Deauville Cocktail [2] (Cktl) 30mls (¼ gill) each of Cointreau, brandy, Calvados, lemon juice. Shake well over ice and strain into a cocktail glass.

Deaver Ranch (USA) a vineyard based in the Shenandoah Valley, Amador County, California. 41.5ha. Grape variety: mainly Zinfandel.

De Azevado [Maria Pinto] (Port) a producer of Casal de Vale Pradinhos (an aguardente).

De Bahèzre de Lanlay (Fr) a cuvée in the Premier Cru vineyard of Les Charmes-Dessus in the A.C. commune of Meursault-Charmes, Côte de Beaune, Burgundy. Is owned by the Hospices de Beaune 0.5ha.

De Bakker Brewery (USA) a brewery based in Marin County, California. Noted for De Bakker Pale Ale 5.2% alc by vol. and Dry Porter 5.2% alc by vol.

De Bartoli (It) a winery based at Samperi, near Marsala in Sicily. Labels include: Bukkuram.

De Beauceyrac [Philippe] (Fr) a Cognac producer. (Add): La Bergerie, N137, 17150 Mirambeau. 160ha. mainly in the Fins Bois. Produces a range of Cognacs.

De Bersac [Guy] (Fr) a Cognac producer. (Add): Domaine du Chillot, Saint-Preuil, 16130 Segonzac. Produces Grande Fine Champagne 10 year old and Très Vieille Fine Cognac 25 years old.

De Bertelli (It) a producer of D.O.C. Barbera d'Asti wines in Piemonte. Labels include: Montetusa and Giarone.

De Bêthe d'Jus Fruit (Ch.Isles) a drink made with pomegranates. Non-alcoholic.

De Beukelaer (Bel) producers of Élixir d'Anvers in Antwerp. Owns the rights to Élixir de Spa liqueur from Spa town in Walloon Hills.

De Bie (Bel) a brewery (established 1992) based at Watou. Brews: Zatte Bie.

Debina (Gre) a white grape variety grown in Epirus. Produces Zitsa (a naturally sparkling dry, medium or sweet white wine).

De Blémond (Fr) the label for the Champagne Coopérative Vinicole de Cuis.

De Block (Bel) a brewery (established 1887). (Add): Nieuwbaan 92, Merchtem, B-1785. Brews: a range of beers and lager including Satan Gold, Satan Red. Website: http://www.satanbeer.com

De Bortoli Winery (Austr) a winery. (Add): De Bortoli Road, Bilbul, New South Wales. 60ha. Grape varieties: Colombard, Grenache, Muscat gordo blanco, Muscat hamburg, Sémillon and Shiraz. Produce Sacred Hill series of wines plus Black Noble and Noble One (both dessert wines) and Vat 4 (Petit verdot). Website: http://www.debortoli.com.au

Déboucher (Fr) uncork/open.

Débouchier (Ch.Isles) to uncork/remove a cork.

Débourbage (Fr) a term used in the making of white wines to denote the delaying of the fermentation for 24 hours after pressing. This allows time for the juice to clear so that it can be drawn off leaving the coarse sediment behind. (Ger) = entschleimen, (Sp) = desfangado.

Débourrement (Fr) the term used to describe the buds of the vine which form after the leaves, allows growth before the flowering parts develop.

Debrö (Hun) a wine region in Eger that produces Debröi Hàrslevelü.

Debröi Hàrslevelü (Hun) a medium sweet white wine with a good bouquet produced in the Eger district from the Hàrslevelü grape.

Deb's Delight (Cup) 1 bottle Lutomer riesling, 40mls (⅓ gill) maraschino, 20mls (⅙ gill) Cointreau, 20mls (¼ gill) gomme syrup. Stir altogether over ice, top with soda water, sliced orange, pineapple cubes and a mint sprig.

Debutante (S.Afr) the label for a red wine (Cabernet sauvignon and Merlot blend) produced by the Jacaranda Estate winery, Wellington, Western Cape.

Debuttage (Fr) the removal of soil away from the roots of the vine to form a basin to absorb the spring rainfall.

Decaff (Eng) a slang term for decaffeinated coffee.

Decaffeinated [Coffee] (Eng) see Decaffeinised Coffee. Some of the caffeine may be extracted using **Dichloroethylene** or **Trichloroethylene**. Chlorinated solutions and used before being roasted (green coffee). See also Secoffex Water Process. (Sri.L) = luaka.

Decaffeinised Coffee (Eng) coffee which has had the caffeine removed. Brands H.A.G. (Hol), Maxima (Ger) and Sanka (USA). See also Decaffeinated Coffee.

Decano (Sp) a solera brandy produced by Luis Caballero.

Decant (Eng) the removal of wine from the bottle leaving the sediment behind. Port and old red wines especially need decanting. Also allows the wine to 'breathe' before drinking. White wine may need decanting if tartrates are present. Wines are decanted into a decanter or other suitable clean receptacle.

Decantae (Wal) a still and sparkling mineral water from source near Mount Snowdon, North Wales. (Add): Trofarth Industries, Trofarth, Conway, North Wales. Mineral contents (milligrammes per litre): Sodium 7.7mg/l, Calcium 10.6mg/l, Magnesium 4.8mg/l, Potassium 0.6mg/l, Bicarbonates 46mg/l, Chlorides 11mg/l, Sulphates 17.5mg/l, Nitrates 1mg/l, Fluoride <0.1mg/l. pH 6.8

Decantare (It) decanting.

D

Decantation (Fr) decanting.

De Canteneur (Fr) a Champagne producer. (Add): Château de Canteneur, 79, Avenue de Champagne, 51200 Épernay.

Decanter (Eng) a glass container usually of lead crystal for decanting wines into. Also can be used for spirits and fortified wines. Differs from a carafe in that it has a stopper. (Hol) = karaf.

Décanter (Fr) to decant.

Decanter Label (Eng) bottle tickets. Early ones made of parchment, bone, wood, ivory etc. Are used to indicate the contents of the decanter. Also used in the eighteenth century to indicate the contents of dark-coloured wine bottles that were used as decanters. When glass decanters became the vogue then labels were made of precious metals, porcelain, enamel and silk. *see* Nig.

Decanter Magazine (Eng) a popular monthly magazine (first published in 1975) for both the public and trade. Deals with wines and spirits, also specialises in vintage and auction reports. Has many M.W's contributing articles. (Add): Priory House, 8 Battersea Park Road, London SW8 4BG. Website: www.decanter.com 'E'mail: editorial@decantermagazine.com

Decanter Wagon (Eng) a small, wheeled unit with 2–3 fixed coasters. Used for passing wine decanters around the dining table. Eighteenth and nineteenth centuries.

Décànteur (Ch.Isles) decanter.

Decantevin [The] (Eng) a patented mechanical decanting machine from Yeo Ratcliffe & Dawe, Sheepcote Farm, Wooburn Common, Bucks.

Decanting (Eng) *see* Decant. (Fr) = decantiran, (It) = decantare.

Decanting Cradle (Eng) a mechanical cradle for decanting wines. Is also known as a Port tilter.

De Carabantes [Francisco] (Chile) a missionary who was supposedly one of the first to introduce vines to Chile in the sixteenth century.

De Carli (It) a Chianti Classico producer based in Tuscany.

De Castaigne and C° [Philippe] (Fr) a Cognac producer. (Add): Domaine de Lafont, 16200 Jarnac. 40ha. in the Fins Bois. Produces a range of Cognacs including V.S., V.S.O.P., 25 year old Réserve Ancienne, 40 year old Extra Vieux, 1893 & 1850 Grande Fine Champagnes.

De Casta Rosado (Sp) a rosé wine produced by Torres in Penedés, Catalunya. Made originally from 40% Cariñena and 60% Garnacha grapes but now (2004) from 65% Garnacha and 35% Mazuelo grapes.

De Castellane (Fr) a Champagne producer (established 1895). (Add): 57 Rue de Verdun, 51200 Épernay. Produces vintage and non-vintage wines. Vintages: 1971, 1973, 1975, 1976, 1979, 1980, 1981, 1986, 1988, 1989, 1990, 1995, 1998, 2000, 2001. Top cuvee: Cuvée Commodore. Website: http://www.castellane.com 'E'mail: visites@castellane.com

De Cazanove [Charles] (Fr) a Champagne producer. (Add): 1, Rue des Cotelles, B.P. 118, 51204 Épernay. Produces vintage and non-vintage wines. Vintages: 1981, 1985, 1989, 1990, 1995, 1998, 2000, 2001. Prestige cuvee: Stradivarius, Cuvée: Brut Azur.

Deceitful Cocktail (Cktl) ½ measure gin, ¼ measure apricot brandy, ⅛ measure green Curaçao, ⅛ measure lemon juice. Shake over ice, strain into a cocktail glass and top with a cherry.

Dechantsberg (Ger) vineyard (Anb): Mosel-Saar-Ruwer. (Ber): Zell/Mosel. (Gro): Goldbäumchen. (Vil): Treis-Karden.

De Chassey [Guy] (Fr) a Champagne producer. (Add): 1 Place de la Demi Lune, 5100 Louvois, Marne. Produces vintage and non-vintage wines.

De Chaunac (USA) a hybrid red grape variety used to make dark red wines.

Deci (Switz) a standard ⅒ litre glass used for wine in Switzerland.

Decín Brewery (Czec) a brewery based in north-western Czec.

Deckrot (Ger) a red grape variety, a cross between Rülander and Teinturier grapes. Makes an excellent colour blending wine.

De Clairveaux (Fr) a Champagne produced by Marne & Champagne, 51200 Épernay.

Déclaration de Récolte (Fr) the declaration of the vintage in Burgundy.

Declared Geographical Origin (Bul) *abbr*: D.G.O. Wines must have the geographical origin and grape variety stated on label. May add Reserve if aged in oak (**white**: 2 years, **red**: 3 years). Special Reserve: as Reserve but from best cuvées, some are aged in new oak. *See also* Controliran, Country Wine. (Fr) = vin de pays.

Déclassement (Fr) the down-grading of wines that do not reach the required standards of an A.C.

De Clieu (W.Ind) a young French naval officer who transported the first coffee seedling to the Caribbean (Island of Martinique) from France in 1723.

Decocta (Lat) a cold drink.

Decoction (Eng) the extraction of water soluble substances from botanicals by boiling.

Decoction (Eng) the name for the essence or liquor that results from decoction.

Decoction (Euro) a method of mashing used for lager beers (in the U.K. the infusion method is used), usually done in 3 steps with staged temperature rises.

De Compagnie (S.Afr) a winery (established 2002) based in Wellington, Western Cape. 16ha. Grape varieties: Cabernet franc, Cabernet sauvignon, Merlot. Label: Privaatkeur. Website: http://www.decompagnie.co.za

De Couleur Oeil de Pedrix (Fr) lit: 'partridge's eye colour', a grade of rosé wine.

De Courcy Père et Fils (Fr) a Champagne producer. (Add): 1 Place André Tritant, 51150 Bouzy. Produces vintage and non-vintage wines and Coteaux Champenois N.V. Vintages: 1971, 1973, 1976, 1979, 1982, 1985, 1989, 1990, 1995, 1998, 1999, 2001. *See also* Mary Rose.

D

Décuvage [1] (Fr) the drawing off of the fermenting must from the skins after the first violent fermentation. Also known as Décuvaison.

Décuvage [2] (Fr) the racking of the fermenting (red) wine from the pomace so that the pomace can be pressed and used for Piquette.

Décuvaison (Fr) *see* Décuvage.

De Dolle Brouwers (Bel) lit: 'the mad brewers', a brewery (established 1980). (Add): Roeselaretraat 12b, B-8600, Esen-Diksmuiden. Brews: Boskeun 7% alc by vol. Dulle Teve 10% alc by vol. Oeral 6% alc by vol. Bitter, Oerbier 7.5% alc by vol. dark beer. 'E'mail: de.dolle@proximedia.be

De Dool Brouwerij (Bel) a brewery (established 1994) based in Helchteren. Brews: Ter Dolen.

De Doorns Co-operative (S.Afr) a co-operative winery (established 1968) based in Worcester, Western Cape. (Add): De Doorns Wine Cellars, Box 129, De Doorns 6857. Grape varieties: Cabernet sauvignon, Chardonnay, Chenin blanc, Colombard, Hanepoot, Red muscadel, Produces varietal wines. Label: Roodehof Dry Red.

Dédoublage (Fr) the removal of the double shoots/buds in spring. *See also* Ébourgonnage, Ébrossage, Échtonnage, Évasivage.

De Drie Horne Bier Brouwerij (Hol) *see* De 3 Horne Bier Brouwerij

De 3 Horne Bier Brouwerij (Hol) a brewery (established 1991) based at Kaatsheuvel. Brews: Antonius Abt, Bockaar Triple Bock, Drakenbloed, Horn's Bock, 't Lempke, Trippelaer, Wolluk Bier.

De Draak (Hol) a 5% alc by vol. bottle-conditioned special beer brewed by De Schelde Brouwerij, 's-Gravenpolder. Contains coriander. Brewed to mark 600th anniversary of Hotel de Draak in Bergen op Zoom.

De Drie Kruizen Brouwerij (Hol) a brewery (established 1991) based in Westmaas. Brews: Karthuizer Dubbel.

De Drie Ringen Amersfoort Bier Brouwerij (Hol) a brewery (established 1989) based in Amersfoort. Brews: Bokbier, Casparie Schagen, Meibok, Panelenbier, Veens Nat.

Deep (Eng) a term used to describe a wine that is either deep in colour, bouquet or flavour. i.e. Has layers of flavour underlying each other (a fine wine).

Deeping Ales (Eng) a micro-brewery at Market Deeping, near Stamford, Kent. Brews: Deeping Red Hill, Deeping Snow, Gunpowder, St. George's.

Deeping Red Hill (Eng) a 4.1% alc by vol. beer brewed by Deeping Ales micro-brewery.

Deeping Snow (Eng) a 5% alc by vol. beer brewed by Deeping Ales micro-brewery.

Deep Riverrock (Ire) a natural spring mineral water from Tullynacross, Northern Ireland. Mineral contents (milligrammes per litre): Sodium 24.7mg/l, Calcium 40mg/l, Magnesium 30.5mg/l, Potassium 2mg/l, Bicarbonates 254mg/l, Chlorides 24.3mg/l, Sulphates 32.5mg/l, Nitrates 2.8mg/l.

Deep Rock (USA) a natural spring mineral water (established 1896) from Denver, Colorado. Mineral contents (milligrammes per litre): Calcium mg/l, Magnesium mg/l, Fluorides mg/l.

Deep Rock Crystal Drop (USA) a natural spring mineral water.

Deep Rock Fontenelle (USA) a natural spring mineral water.

Deep Sea Cocktail (Cktl) 30mls (¼ gill) Old Tom gin, 30mls (¼ gill) French vermouth, dash orange bitters, dash absinthe. Shake well over ice, strain into a cocktail glass, add an olive and squeeze of lemon peel juice.

Deep Shaft Stout (Eng) the label of a stout produced by the Freeminer Brewery.

Deep Slade Dark (Wal) a 4% alc by vol. dark ale brewed by the Hurns Brewing C°. West Glamorgan.

Deep Spring (Austr) a natural spring mineral water from Sydney. Mineral contents (milligrammes per litre): Sodium 25mg/l, Calcium 2mg/l, Magnesium 4mg/l, Potassium 5mg/l, Bicarbonates 5mg/l, Chlorides 50mg/l.

Deep Spring (N.Z) a natural spring mineral water from Taupo. Mineral contents (milligrammes per litre): Sodium 7.8mg/l, Calcium 2.7mg/l, Potassium 3.8mg/l. pH 6.5

Deep Valley Cocktail (Cktl) 25mls (1fl.oz) blue Curaçao, 25mls (1fl.oz) dry gin, 35mls (1½ fl.ozs) pineapple juice, 2 dashes lemon juice. Stir over ice in a collins glass, top with soda water, lemon peel spiral and cherry.

Deerfield Ranch Winery (USA) a winery based in the Russian River Valley, Sonoma County, California. Also has vineyards in the Bennett Valley. Grape variety: Pinot noir. Labels: Cohn Vineyard, Jemrose Vineyard.

Deerfield Wine Cellars (USA) a winery based in Edenton, North Carolina. Produces Scuppernong wines.

Deer Park (USA) a natural spring mineral water from Deer Park, Maryland. Mineral contents (milligrammes per litre): Sodium 1.1mg/l, Calcium 26.6mg/l, Magnesium 2.6mg/l, Potassium 0.4mg/l, Bicarbonates 88.8mg/l, Chlorides 0.7mg/l, Sulphates 1.8mg/l. pH 8.05

Deer Park (USA) an slightly acidic natural spring mineral water from Pennsylvania. pH 5.5

Deeside Spring Water (Scot) a natural spring mineral water from Pannanich Wells, Ballater.

Defence of the Realm Act (Eng) *see* D.O.R.A.

De Fère [Charles] (Fr) a producer of sparkling wines, uses grapes from just outside the regions of Champagne and the Loire.

Defiance (Eng) a 4.1% alc by vol. ale brewed by Everards to commemorate St. George's Day in 1998.

Deerfield Ranch (USA) a winery based in the North Coast region, California. Grape varieties include: Cabernet sauvingnon. Label: DRX Meritage.

Deetlefs Estate (S.Afr) a winery (established 1822) based in Rawsonville, Western Cape. 100ha. Grape varieties: Chardonnay, Chenin blanc, Merlot,

430

D

Muscat d'alexandrie, Pinotage, Sauvignon blanc, Sémillon, Shiraz, Weisser riesling. Label: Stonecross. Website: http://www.deetlefs.com

De Friese Brouwerij (Hol) a brewery (established 1985) based at Sneek. Brews: Us Heit Twels Pilsner, Us Heit Twels Bokbier.

Defrutum (Lat) the name given to a new wine (or must) that has been boiled down.

De Gans Bier Brouwerij (Hol) a brewery (established 1998) based in Goes. Brews: Ganze Bier, Ganze Bokbier, Kerstbier, Maneblussertje, Zomer Bokbier, Zot Manneke.

Degerloch (Ger) village (Anb): Württemberg. (Ber): Remstal-Stuttgart. (Gro): Weinsteige. see Stuttgart.

Dégorgement (Fr) the release of the sediment from Champagne bottles either by hand and a keen eye or by firstly freezing the neck in dry ice and then releasing the plug of frozen wine with the sediment embodied in the ice. Invented by the Widow Clicquot in the nineteenth century. (Sp) = Degorjat.

Dégorgement à la Volée (Fr) denotes hand extraction of the sediment. see Dégorgement.

Dégorgement Automatique (Fr) the extraction by machine of the sediment in Champagne after it has been frozen. see Dégorgement.

Dégorgement Tardive (Fr) abbr: D.T. late disgorging, used by Jacquesson on their Champagne labels to indicate when the wine was disgorged from the sediment.

Dégorgeur (Fr) a skilled worker who releases the crown cork or unclips the first cork of a Champagne bottle to remove the deposit or frozen plug. see Dégorgement.

Degorjat (Sp) disgorging. The removal of the sediment from a bottle of cava wine. See also Degüelle. (Fr) = dégorgement.

De Gouberville [Gilles] (Fr) a nobleman who, in 1553 made the first Calvados.

De Goudon Boom Brouwerij (Bel) an abbaye brewery (established 1889) based in Bruges. Brews: Brugs Tarwebier, Brugse Tripel, Steenbrugge Dubbel, Steenbrugge Tripel.

De Graal (Bel) a brewery. (Add): Wim Saeyens, Brouwerij De Graal, Warande 15, Brakel B-9660. Brews a variety of beers and lager. Website: http://www.degraal.be 'E'mail: info@degraal.be

Degré Alcoolique (Fr) a term to express the degrees of alcohol as a percentage of volume (alc by vol.). The percentage by volume must be included on a bottle label for sale in the E.C.

Degree Days (USA) the University of California at Davis devised this climate zone (5 zones) system. Based on heat summation (a measure of degree days during the vine's annual period of growth) from April 1st to October 31st. Each days temperature is averaged, 10°C is subtracted and the total averaged over a number of years.

De Grendel (S.Afr) a winery (established 1720) based in Durbanville, Western Cape. 104ha. Grape varieties: Cabernet franc, Cabernet sauvignon, Chardonnay, Chenin blanc, Grenache, Malbec, Merlot, Mourvèdre, Petit verdot, Pinotage, Sauvignon blanc, Shiraz, Viognier. Website: http://www.degrendel.co.za

Degrés Naturels (Fr) a range a high strength Armagnacs (XO 49.5% alc by vol., XO 53.3% alc by vol. XO Cask N°6 54.9% alc by vol., Hors d'Age 52.8% alc by vol. and Hors d'Age Cask N°16 53.4% alc by vol.) produced by Château de Tarquet.

De Groene Heuwel (S.Afr) the export label for a range of wines produced by the Linton Park Wines winery, Wellington, Western Cape.

Degüelle (Sp) disgorging of the cava wine before the licor de expedeción is added, the sparkling wine is then bottled and corked. See also Removido, Desgüelle.

Degustacao (Bra) easy drinking wine.

Degustación (Sp) enjoyment of wine etc.

Degustar (Port) to taste wine (a liquid).

Dégustation (Fr) wine tasting.

De Halve Maan Brouwerij (Hol) a brewery (established 1991) based in Hulst. Brews: Jopen.

De Helderberg Koöperatiewe Wijnmakerij Beperkt (S.Afr) see Helderberg Co-operative.

Dehesa del Carrizal (Sp) a winery based in Ciudad Real, Castilla-La Mancha. Likely to apply for Castilla-La Mancha private D.O. status. See also Calzadilla, Sandoval, Manzaneque, Valdepusa', Vallegarcía, Aalto, Mauro, San Román.

Dehlinger Vineyard (USA) a winery based in the Russian River Valley, Sonoma, California. 6ha. Grape varieties: Cabernet sauvignon, Chardonnay and Zinfandel. Produces varietal wines.

Dehours (Fr) a Champagne producer. (Add): 1-2 Rue de la Chapelle, 51700 Cerseuil. 40ha.

Deidesheim (Ger) village (Anb): Pfalz. (Ber): Mittelhaardt-Deutsche Weinstrasse. (Gro): Hofstück. (Vin): Nonnenstück.

Deidesheim (Ger) village (Anb): Pfalz. (Ber): Mittelhaardt-Deutsche Weinstrasse. (Gro): Mariengarten. (Vins): Grainhübel, Herrgottsacker, Hohenmorgen, Kalkofen, Kieslberg, Langenmorgen, Leinhöhle, Mäushöhle, Paradiesgarten.

Deidesheim (Ger) village (Anb): Pfalz. (Ber): Mittelhaardt-Deutsche Weinstrasse. (Gro): Schnepfenflug an der Weinstrasse. (Vin): Letten.

Deinhard (Ger) a famous wine merchants based in Koblenz that produce Green Label, Hanns Christof and Docktor wines.

Deinhock (Ger) a medium-dry red tafelwein from Deinhard of Koblenz.

Deinmoselle (Ger) a light white QbA. wine from Deinhard of Koblenz.

Deipnosophistae (Egy) a major written work on food and wine in ancient Egypt written in the third century by Athenaeus.

De Jersey (Fr) a producer of A.C. Saumur in Anjou-Saumur, Loire.

De-Juicing (USA) the removal of the free-run juice before the grapes are pressed. (Fr) = égouttage.

De Keersmaecker Lambic Brasserie (Bel) a brewery based at Koddegem, northern Belgium. Brews: Mort Subite range of beers.

D

Dekeleia (Gre) the name given to the red and white wines produced near Marathon.

Dekker's Valley (S.Afr) the label for a range of wines: white (Chenin blanc) and red (Pinotage) produced by the Mellast winery, Paarl, Western Cape.

De Kluis Brasserie (Bel) a brewery based in Hoegaarden, noted for white beers: Hoegaards Wit, Peeterman and Bénédict (an abbaye-style beer) plus Hougaerdes Das, Julius, De Verboden Vrucht. Also known as Hoegaards Brasserie.

De Koninck (Bel) an unpasteurised all-malt ale 5.2% alc by vol. which is made by top-fermentation. Similar in style to German altbier. Served on draught.

De Koninck Brasserie (Bel) a brewery (established 1833). (Add): Mechelsesteenweg 291, Antwerp B-2018. Noted for top-fermented beers. see De Koninck. Website: http://www.dekoninck.be 'E'mail: info@dekoninck.com

De Koninck-Proost (Bel) a small lambic brewery based in Dworp. Noted for cherry beer.

De Krans (S.Afr) a winery (established 2004) based in Stellenbosch, Western Cape. Grape varieties: Cabernet sauvignon, Chardonnay, Chenin blanc, Gewürztraminer, Hanepoot, Merlot, Pinotage, Ruby cabernet, Tempranillo, Tinta barocca, Touriga, White jerepigo, White muscadel. Labels: Golden Harvest, Heritage Collection, Relishing Red, Red Stone Reserve. Website: http://www.dekrans.co.za

De Kroon Bier Brouwerij (Hol) the 'Crown' Brewery (established 1627) of Oirschot, North Brabant. Brews: Briljant, Oirschots Witbier.

De Kuyper (Hol) a large distillery producing genever and a wide range of liqueurs in Schiedam. Website: http://www.dekuyper.com

De la Boe [Dr. Franciscus] (Hol) is purported to have invented gin in Leiden in the sixteenth century.

De la Calle [Manuel] (Sp) a noted Sherry producer based in Jerez de la Frontera.

Delacote [Henry] (Fr) a Cognac producer based at Saint-Hilaire. Produces a variety of Cognacs.

De La Cuesta [José] (Sp) a fine Sherry producer based in Jerez de la Frontera. Noted for Troubadour (a pale dry, Fino Sherry).

Delaforce (Port) vintage Port shippers. Vintages: 1870, 1873, 1875, 1878, 1881, 1884, 1887, 1890, 1894, 1896, 1900, 1904, 1908, 1912, 1917, 1919, 1920, 1927, 1935, 1945, 1947, 1950, 1955, 1958, 1960, 1963, 1966, 1970, 1975, 1977, 1980, 1982, 1985, 1992, 1994, 1997, 2000, 2003. see Quinta da Corte.

De Lagrange [Gaston] (Fr) a Cognac producer. (Add): Rue de la Pierre Levée, Château Bernard, 16100 Cognac. 60ha. in Fins Bois 75% and Bois Ordinaires 25%. Formed in 1949 by union of Antier and Pomerol Cognac houses. Owned by Martini.

De Lahaye (Fr) a Champagne producer based in Épernay. Produces vintage and non-vintage wines including Jacqueline (a non-vintage brut rosé).

Delaire Vineyards (S.Afr) a winery (established 1982) based in Stellenbosch, Western Cape. 19ha. (Add): Box 3058, Stellenbosch 7602. Grape varieties: Cabernet franc, Cabernet sauvignon, Chardonnay, Merlot, Sauvignon blanc. Label: Botmaskop. Website: http://www.delairewinery.co.za

Delamain (Fr) Cognac producers. (Add): Delamain & C°. B.P. 16, 16200, Jarnac. Produces Vesper Grande Champagne, Pale and Dry Grande Champagne (average age is 25 years), Réserve de la Famille, Très Venerable. Owns no vineyards. All Cognacs bought in are from the Grande Champagne.

Delamotte [Père et Fils] (Fr) a Champagne producer. (Add): 5 Rue de la Brèche, 51190 Mesnil-sur-Oger. 5ha. Produces vintage and non-vintage wines.

Delano (USA) a vine-growing town in Kern, San Joaquin Valley, California.

Dela Premium (Asia) a natural spring mineral water from Matatirtha, Nepal. Mineral contents (milligrammes per litre): Calcium 44mg/l, Magnesium 8mg/l, Bicarbonates 145mg/l, Chlorides 6mg/l. pH 7.6

Delaroy (Fr) a Champagne producer. (Add): 14 Rue de Bernon, 51200 Épernay.

De La Rue (Ch.Isles) a cream liqueur based on chocolate and Guernsey cream from the Channel Island Cream Liqueur.

Delas Frères (Fr) a wine négociant-éleveurs based in the Rhône at Tournon. (Add): 2A L'Olivet, 07300 Tournon-sur-Rhône.

Delatite (Austr) a winery (established 1982) based at Stoney's Road, Mansfield, Off Buller Road, Victoria. Grape varieties: Cabernet franc, Cabernet sauvignon, Malbec, Merlot, Pinot noir, Shiraz, Chardonnay, Gewürztraminer, Riesling, Sauvignon blanc.

De la Torre y Lapuerta (Sp) a principal wine-producer based in Rioja, north-eastern Spain.

Delaware (USA) a native white grape variety (*Vitis labrusca*), has a pale yellow juice and soft skin. Considered the best north American species, used for dry, semi-dry and sparkling wines. Gives juice with high sugar content.

Délayer (Fr) diluting.

Delbeck (Fr) a Champagne producer based at 8 Rue Piper, Reims. Was a Grande Marque.

Del Carrascal (Sp) a Palo Cortado Sherry from Valdespino.

Del Duque (Sp) an Amontillado Sherry produced by Gonzalez Byass in Jerez de la Frontera, Cadiz. Aged for 30 years. Part of their Rare Old Solera range.

De l'Eau d'Cannelle (Ch.Isles) cinnamon water. 2 parts brandy, 1 part water, sugar to taste and cinnamon. Heat together and serve hot or cold.

De Leeuw Brouwerij (Hol) a brewery (established 1886) based in Valkenburg, Limburg. Noted for unpasteurised beers Super Leeuw and Donker. Also Leeuw Dortmunder, Bockbier, Pilsener, Valkenburgs Witbier, Winter Wit, Jubileeuw, Meibock, Oud Bruin, Venloosch Alt.

Delegats Winery (N.Z) a winery. (Add): Hepburn Road, Henderson. Grape varieties: Cabernet sauvignon, Merlot, Chardonnay, Gewürztraminer, Sauvignon blanc and Sémillon. Labels include Oyster Bay.

Delestage (Fr) the draining of the juice from the grape cap and pumping it back over during vinification.

De Leuwen Jagt (S.Afr) the label for a range of red wines produced by the Seidelberg Estate, Paarl, Western Cape.

Delfonte (Bra) a sparkling natural spring mineral water (established 2004) from Val do Paraiba. Mineral contents (milligrammes per litre): Sodium 9mg/l, Calcium 11.93mg/l, Magnesium 2.55mg/l, Potassium 2.63mg/l, Bicarbonates 77.81mg/l, Chlorides 0.53mg/l, Sulphates 2.1mg/l, Fluorides 0.13mg/l, Nitrates 0.1mg/l, Silicates 11.51mg/l. pH 7.95

Delgado (Sp) the term used to describe a thin Sherry.

Delgado Zuleta (Sp) a noted Sherry and brandy producer. (Add): Carmen 32, Sanlúcar de Barrameda. Labels include: La Goya (Sherry), Monteagudo (solera brandy) Goyesco (solera reserva brandy).

Delheim Wines (S.Afr) a winery (148ha) based in Stellenbosch (and in Simonsberg), Western Cape. (Add): P.O. Box 10, Koelenhof 7605. 120ha. Grape varieties: Cabernet sauvignon, Chardonnay, Chenin blanc, Gewürztraminer, Merlot, Pinotage, Pinot blanc, Riesling, Sauvignon blanc, Shiraz. Produces a Chardonnay Sur-Lie. Labels include: Edelspatz, Heeren Wijn, Spatzendreck, Vera Cruz. Website: http://www.delheim.com

Delicado (Sp) the label for a Fino Sherry produced by Crofts.

Délicat (Fr) delicate, an elegant, well-balanced wine that is not harsh or coarse, usually low in alcohol.

Delicate (Eng) a wine taster's term for a light, rather thin, full wine that is not great but fine and elegant.

Délicatesse (Fr) delicacy. *see* Délicat.

Delicatessen (USA) a hybrid red grape variety developed in Texas.

Delicator (Ger) a doppelbock beer produced by the Hofbräuhaus Brauerei of Munich.

Delicato Vineyards (USA) a large winery based near Manteca, San Joaquin, California. Produces varietal and dessert wines.

Delicato Winery (Euro) a large noted winery based in Malta.

Delice de Melon (Fr) a melon-based liqueur producd by Lou Catalou in Provence.

Delicías (Mex) a noted wine-producing area in the Chihuahua district.

Deliciosa (Sp) a Manzanilla Sherry from Valdespino.

De-Lite-Ful (S.Afr) the label for a range of wines produced by the WestCorp International, Olifants River, Western Cape.

Delikat (Ger) a delicate wine.

DeLille (USA) a winery based in the Columbia Valley, Washington State. Grape varieties include: Syrah. Label: Doyenne.

Delimited Areas (Eng) certain areas whose regional name is given to the wine or spirit produced within the geographical limits of the region.

De Lindeboom Bier Brouwerij (Hol) a brewery (established 1869) based in Neer. Brews: Gouverneur, Lente Bock.

Delirium Tremens (Eng) *see* D.T.'s.

Delirium Tremens (Bel) a 9% alc by vol. bottled special beer which is fermented three times and brewed by Huyghe, Melle.

Delisle (W.Ind) a noted rum distillery based on the island of Guadeloupe.

Deliverance (Eng) a 4.2% alc by vol. pale bitter brewed by the Aspinall Cambrinus Craft Brewery, Knowsley, Merseyside.

Dell'Alpe (It) a natural spring mineral water from Lissa Spring, Mount Pasubio.

Della Valle [Pietro] (It) the man who introduced coffee into Italy in the seventeenth century.

Dellchen (Ger) vineyard (Anb): Nahe. (Ber): Schloss Böckelheim. (Gro): Burgweg. (Vil): Norheim.

Dellchen (Ger) vineyard (Anb): Nahe. (Ber): Schloss Böckelheim. (Gro): Rosengarten. (Vil): Mandel.

Dellhofen (Ger) village (Anb): Mittelrhein. (Ber): Rheinburgengau. (Gro): Schloss Schönburg. (Vins): Römerkrug, St. Wernerberg.

Dellrust Wines (S.Afr) a winery (established 1998) based in Helderberg, Stellenbosch, Western Cape. 97ha. Grape varieties: Cinsaut, Jerepigo, Merlot, Pinotage, Sauvignon blanc, Shiraz, Tinta barocca. Labels: Steen & Groen, Three Vines. Website: http://www.dellrust.co.za

Dell'Ugo (It) a Chianti Putto producer based in Tuscany.

Del Mar Ranch (USA) a brand of dry white wine produced by the Monterey Vineyard in Monterey County, California.

Delmonico [1] (Cktl) ⅖ measure dry gin, ⅕ measure dry vermouth, ⅕ measure sweet vermouth, ⅕ measure brandy. Stir over ice, strain into a delmonico glass and add a twist of lemon peel.

Delmonico [2] (Cktl) ⅗ measure dry gin, ⅖ measure dry vermouth, dash orange bitters. Stir over ice, strain into a delmonico glass and add a twist of lemon peel.

Delmonico (USA) a type of cocktail glass. 100mls–125mls (4fl.ozs–5fl.ozs) capacity that is short and stubby (a small version of a highball glass), also known as a '*juice*' glass.

Del Monte (Eng) a firm that produces a range of canned and Tetra-pack fruit juices.

Deloach Vineyards (USA) a winery based in the Russian River Valley, Sonoma, California. 51ha. Grape varieties: Chardonnay, Gewürztraminer, Cabernet sauvignon, Pinot noir and Zinfandel. Produces varietal wines. Owned by Boisset.

Délor [A. et Cie] (Fr) a wine négociant of Bordeaux, holds some of the largest stocks of classic wine growths in Bordeaux.

Delorme [André] (Fr) a Burgundy négociant based at Rully, Côte Chalonnaise, Burgundy. Produces fine wines and Crémant de Bourgogne.

D

Delorme-Meulien (Fr) *see* Delorme (André).

Delord (Fr) an Armagnac producer. (Add): Delord Frères, Lannepax 32190 Vic-Fezensac. 20ha. in Bas Armagnac. Produces Delord vintage 1942 and Delord 20 Ans d'Age.

Delot [Maurice] (Fr) a Champagne producer. (Add): 1 Place de l'Église, Celles-sur-Ource, 10110 Bar-sur-Seine 10ha.

Del Pedro (Austr) the brand-name of a Sherry produced by Reynella.

Delphinette (Switz) a green-coloured, multi-herb liqueur.

Delph Porter (Eng) a porter ale brewed by Bridgewater Ales in Salford.

Delph Strong Ale (Eng) a beer 1054 O.G. brewed by Bathams at their Delph Brewery in Brierly Hill, Staffs.

Del Produttore all'Origine (It) estate bottled.

Delta (Egy) a natural spring mineral water. Mineral contents (milligrammes per litre): Sodium 36mg/l, Calcium 25.5mg/l, Magnesium 14.5mg/l, Potassium 3.5mg/l, Bicarbonates 205mg/l, Chlorides 12mg/l, Sulphates 12mg/l, Fluorides 0.2mg/l, Silicates 22mg/l.

Delta (Ger) a natural spring mineral water from the Delta-Quelle, Steinheim-Vinsebeck, NW.

Delta Domaines (Fr) a group based in southern France, made up of ten Master Growers. A marketing company and office of oenology from L'Aude, L'Hérault, Roussillon and Corbiéres regions.

De Luxe (Can) a blended Canadian whisky produced by Jas Barclay and C°. Part of Hiram Walker.

De Luxe (Fr) first class.

De Luxe Scotch Whisky (Scot) a blended Scotch whisky with a high proportion of malt whiskies in the blend.

De Luze [A. et Fils] (Fr) négociants and growers in Bordeaux.

Dema Glass (Eng) one of the largest British producers of drinking glasses. (Add): Pottery Lane, Chesterfield, Derbyshire S41 9BH. Now known as Coloroll Glassware.

De Malliac [J.] (Fr) an Armagnac producer. (Add): Ste. Fermière du Château de Malliac, Montreal du Gers 32250. 5ha. in Ténarèze.

Demand Valve (Eng) *see* Aspirating Valve or Cask Breather.

De Marcilly Frères [P.] (Fr) a Burgundy négociant based in Beaune, Côte de Beaune.

De Martinez (Mex) a brand-name for a tequila.

De Martino (Chile) a winery based in the Maule Valley. Grape varieties include: Malbec, Pinot noir, Zinfandel.

Demay Wine Cellars (USA) a winery based in Hammondsport, Finger Lakes, New York. Produces native and hybrid wines.

Demels (Aus) a famous coffee house in Vienna.

Demerara Distillers (S.Am) a subsidiary of the Guyana Distilleries, Guyana.

Demerara Rum (S.Am) the name given to the dark, pungent rum from British Guyana.

De Meric (Fr) a Champagne producer. (Add): 17 Rue Gambetta, 51160 Aÿ. 15ha. Prestige cuvée: Cathérine de Medicis.

Demestica (Gre) a light, dry, red or white wine made in Patras. Produced by Achaia-Clauss.

De Meye Vineyard (S.Afr) a winery (established 1998) based in Muldersvlei, Stellenbosch. Grape varieties: Cabernet sauvignon, Chardonnay, Merlot, Pinotage, Shiraz. Labels: Blend, River, Trutina. Website: http://www.demete.co.za

Demi (Fr) half (i.e. demi-tasse = half cup, demi-sec = half dry), when applied to beer is for a 30 centilitre glass of beer.

Demi-Barrique (Fr) half a Bordeaux barrique 112litres.

Demie (Fr) a small bottle of (37.5 centilitres) capacity used in the Champagne region. *see* Champagne Bottle Sizes. Also known as a Half Bottle.

Demi John (Fr) a wide-waisted, covered glass jar for storing wines. Holds from 2.25litres to 45litres (½ a gallon to 10 gallons) depending on area.

Demi-Mesure (Fr) half measure.

Demi-Muids (Fr) oak vats used for storing vermouth. 585litres (130gallons). In Champagne = 2000litres.

Demineralized Water (Eng) used to reduce spirits to correct strength.

Demi-Queue (Fr) a half queue, a Burgundy cask of 228 litres.

Demir Kapija (Ser) a noted wine-producing district based in Macedonia.

De Misa (Sp) a brandy and Sherry producer based in Jerez.

Demi-Sec (Fr) half dry, fairly sweet (dosage 35g/l to 50g/l maximum). *See also* Dosage.

Demi-Tasse (Fr) lit: 'half cup', a small china cup used for serving coffee after a dinner meal. Capacity 100mls (⅛ pint), derived from the small cups used in the Middle-east for Turkish-style coffee.

Demockaat (Hol) a coffee and advocaat-flavoured liqueur produced by Bols.

Demoiselle (Fr) a term used for a measure of spirits in western France.

Demoiselle (Fr) a Champagne producer. (Add): 42 Ave. de Champagne, 51200 Épernay. Négociant-manipulant. 43ha. Produces vintage and non-vintage wines.

Demoiselles [Les] (Fr) a vineyard in the Sancerre-Chavignol, Central vineyards district in the Loire.

Demolombe [Jean] (Fr) a producer of A.C. Blanquette de Limoux under the Colombe Cathare label.

Demon Beer (Switz) a 12% alc by vol. pale ale.

Demon brew (Eng) a 4.4% alc by vol. ale from the Wye Valley Brewery, Hereford. Part of Dorothy Goodbody's Seasonal Ale range.

De Montal (Fr) a brand of Armagnac produced by Compagnie des Produits de Gascogne, Auch, Gers. Produces V.S.O.P. and Armagnac de Montal. 40% alc by vol.

Dempsey Brewery (Ire) a brewery (established

1983) based in Dublin. Noted for cask-conditioned Dempsey's Real Ale 1037 O.G. and Dublin Pride 1040 O.G.

Dempsey Cocktail (Cktl) 60mls (½ gill) gin, 40mls (⅓ gill) Calvados, 1 teaspoon grenadine, 2 dashes absinthe. Shake over ice and strain into a cocktail glass.

De Muller (Sp) a noted wine-producer based in Scala Dei, Tarragona who uses the label name of Solimar for his red and white wines.

Denaka Danish Vodka (USA) a vodka launched by Whitbread in North America, sold in a triangular-shaped bottle. 40% alc by vol.

Denaturant (Eng) a chemical (or colouring) added to alcohol to ensure it is unfit to drink so avoiding the excise duty that would otherwise be payable.

De Nauroy (Fr) a Champagne producer. (Add): Chute des Eaux, 51140 Prouilly. Négociant-manipulant. 5.5ha. Produces vintage and non-vintage wines.

Denbies Wine Estate (Eng) a 114ha vineyard and winery (established 1986) in Mole Valley, Surrey. (Add): London Road, Dorking, Surrey RH5 6AA. 20 grape varieties including Auxerrois, Chardonnay, Dornfelder, Huxelrebe, Müller-Thurgau, Optima, Pinot blanc, Pinot gris, Pinot meunier, Pinot noir, Reichensteiner, Riesling. Website: http://www.denbieswineestate.com

Denée (Fr) a commune in the A.C. Coteaux de l'Aubance, Anjou-Saumur, Loire.

De Neuville (Fr) a wine-producer based at St-Hilaire-St-Florent, Anjou-Saumur, Loire. Noted for Saumur Mousseux.

De Nève Brasserie (Bel) a brewery based in Schepdaal, central Belgium. Taken over by the Belle-Vue Brewery. Produces filtered beers.

Denice (Fr) a commune in the Beaujolais. Has A.C. Beaujolais-Villages or A.C. Beaujolais-Denice status.

Denino Umpqua River Estate (USA) a winery based in Roseburg, Oregon. Grape varieties include: Chenin blanc.

Denisa (Cktl) 35mls (1½ fl.ozs) lemon vodka, 20mls (¾ fl.oz) Galliano, 20mls (½ fl.oz) fresh cream, scoop lemon ice cream. Blend all together and serve in a large goblet.

Denizli (Tur) a noted wine-producing vineyard in the Aegean. Produces white wines.

Denman Winery (Austr) a winery based in the Hunter Valley, New South Wales. Grape varieties: Sémillon, Shriaz.

Denneboom (S.Afr) a winery (established 35ha) based in Windmeul, Paarl, Western Cape. Grape varieties: Cabernet sauvignon, Pinotage, Shiraz.

Denoix (Fr) a liqueur producer based in Brive in the Perigord-Quercy region. Produces: Liqueur de Jus de Noix Vertes, Fenouillette and Roc Amadour.

Denominaçao de Origem Controlada (Port) *abbr*: D.O.C. a grade replacing R.D. identified by the Selo de Origem. Areas granted this appellation are Algarve, Bairrada, Bucelas, Carcavelos, Colares, Dão, Douro, Setúbal, Vinho Verde.

Denominación de Origen (Sp) *abbr*: D.O. run on similar lines to France's Appellation Contrôlée laws governing wine production.

Denominación de Origen Calificada (Sp) *abbr*: DOCa. The highest classification of wine, first granted this was Rioja in 1991.

Denominación de Origen Provisional (Sp) *abbr*: DOp. describes those wines that are seeking promotion. A substantial number of bodegas are required to provide wine of the right quality, until then the wine is still Vino de la Tierra.

Denominación Específica (Sp) *abbr*: DE/DEp. a classification which can be awarded to a Vino de la Tierra on its way up towards a D.O. Legally wines are still classified as Vino de la Tierra. De = Brandy de Jerez, DEp = Cebreros (Ávila, Castilla-León).

Denominazione di Origine Controllata (It) *abbr*: D.O.C. the Italian equivalent of France's Appellation Contrôlée. Laws include specific grapes, traditional methods, limited yields, proper ageing, adequate records, tasting panels etc. Formed in 1963.

Denominazione d'Origine Controllata e Garantita (It) *abbr*: D.O.C.G. the top award given to certain wines only within the D.O.C. zones. Must be of a very high standard and pass stringent tests. Bottles sealed with government seal. *see* Albana di Romagna, Asti, Barbaresco, Barolo, Brunello di Montalcino, Carmignano, Chianti, Chianti Classico, Gattinara, Recioto di Soave, Sagrantino di Montefalco, Taurasi, Torgiano Rosso Riserva, Vernaccia di San Gimignano, Vino Nobile di Montepulciano.

Denominazione di Origine Semplice (It) *abbr*: D.O.S. an old wine control standard which was below D.O.C. (now no longer used).

Densimeter (Eng) also referred to as a mustimeter or saccharometer, used to test the grape must density. A hollow, cylindrical float that has a ball beneath it and above it a graduated rod.

Densimètre (Fr) densimeter.

Density (Eng) the specific gravity of a liquid when compounded with an equal amount of distilled water.

Dent Brewery (Eng) a brewery (established 1990). (Add): Cowgill, Dent, Cumbria LA10 5PQ. Brews: Aviator Ale 4% alc by vol., Dent Bitter 3.7% alc by vol., Kamikaze 5% alc by vol., Ramsbottom 4.5% alc by vol., T'Owd Tup 6% alc by vol. Website: http://www.dentbrewery.co.uk 'E'mail: paul@dentbrewery.co.uk

Denzlingen (Ger) village (Anb): Baden. (Ber): Breisgau. (Gro): Burg Zähringen. (Vins): Eichberg, Sonnhalde.

Deoch (Ire) a small amount of poteen offered to a possible business dealer to encourage him to quote a fair price.

Deoch-an-Dorius (Scot) an expression used for a drink offered to a departing guest.

Dé-ocsaid Carbóin (Ire) Carbon-dioxide/CO_2.

De Oegstgeester Wijnkooperij (Hol) a noted, old established firm of wine merchants. (Add): De Kempenoerstraat 77 Oegstgeest, Netherland 2341 GJ.

D

Deograzia (It) a natural spring mineral water from Deograzia.

Deo Optimo Maximo (Fr) see D.O.M.

DEp (Sp) see Denominación Específica.

Départ de la Végétation [Le] (Fr) the first sign that the growers have of the condition of the vines after the winter and spring frosts. see Austried.

Département (Fr) department, an administrative subdivision, equivalent of an English county.

Department of Scientific and Industrial Research (N.Z) abbr: D.S.I.R. conducts tests and analysis on wines.

Dépose (Fr) trade mark (from déposer = to testify), to guarantee.

Deposit (Eng) the sediment which many red and some white wines throw whilst in bottle. In white wine it is usually tartrate crystals which are harmless but in red wines it is the tannin and colouring matter which tastes bitter and unpleasant. Wines are decanted to remove the sediment.

Deposito (Port) a large vat or tank for blending and storing wines.

Depositos (Sp) the name for large, resin-lined, cement fermentation vats placed underground to assist cold fermentation. Approximately 1,000 hectolitres capacity, used mainly in the Cataluña region.

Dépôt (Fr) sediment. see Tartrate Crystals and Tannins.

Dépouillé (Fr) a term used to describe a wine of some age that has no body or colour left.

Depourissage (Fr) the term used for the gathering of the botrytised grapes off the bunches on the vines over a period of weeks.

De Primer Año (Sp) are Rioja wines sold in the year of production.

Depth (Eng) the term to describe the depth of flavour a wine has and to its depth of interest.

Depth Bomb Cocktail (Cktl) 30mls (¼ gill) brandy, 30mls (¼ gill) Calvados, 1 teaspoon grenadine, 2 teaspoons lemon juice. Shake well over ice and strain into a cocktail glass.

Derby Brewing C° [The] (Eng) a brewery (established 2004). (Add): Masons Place Business Park, Nottingham Road, Derby, Derbyshire DE21 6AQ. Brews: Brewers Treat 4.6% alc by vol., Business as Usual 4.4% alc by vol., Old Intentional 5% alc by vol., That's Life 4.5% alc by vol., Tickety Boo 4.3% alc by vol., Triple Hop 4.1% alc by vol. Website: http://www.derbybrewing.co.uk 'E'mail: sales@derbybrewing.co.uk

Derby Cocktail [1] (Cktl) 60mls (½ gill) brandy, 2 dashes Curaçao, 2 dashes maraschino, 2 dashes Angostura. Stir over ice, strain into a cocktail glass, top with iced Champagne, cherry and squeeze of lemon peel juice.

Derby Cocktail [2] (Cktl) 50mls (2fl.ozs) gin, 2 dashes peach juice, 2 sprigs mint. Shake over ice and strain into a cocktail glass.

Derby Daiquiri (Cktl) 40mls (⅓ gill) white rum, 25mls (⅕ gill) orange juice, juice ¼ lime, 1 teaspoon sugar. Blend with a scoop of crushed ice and pour into a Champagne flute.

Derby Day (Sp) a brand of Fino Sherry produced by Romate in Jerez de la Frontera.

Derby Fizz (Cktl) 1 measure Scotch whisky, 1 egg, 1 teaspoon powdered sugar, 4 dashes Cointreau, juice ½ lemon. Shake over ice, strain into an ice-filled highball glass and top with soda water.

Derby Winner (Cktl) ⅓ measure vodka, ⅓ measure eau-de-vie-de-poire, ⅓ measure triple sec, dash lime juice. Shake over ice, strain into a cocktail glass, dress with a slice of lime and a cherry.

Derde Heuvel Rood (S.Afr) the label for a light red wine produced by the Uitvlucht Co-operative Winery, Little Karoo, Western Cape.

De Redcliffe (N.Z) a winery. (Add): Rd 1, Lyons Road, Pokeno. 19ha. Grape varieties: Chardonnay, Sauvignon blanc, Sémillon, Pinot noir.

De Ridder Stadsbrouwerij (Hol) a brewery (established 1857) based in Maastricht, South Limburg. Brews: Ridder Maltezer 6.5% alc by vol. Ridder Pilsner Bier 5% alc by vol. Vos 5% alc by vol. Wieckse Wit 5% alc by vol.

De Rigueur (S.Afr) the label for a red wine (Cabernet sauvignon, Merlot and Shiraz blend) produced by the JP Bredell winery, Stellenbosch, Western Cape.

Dermatophora necatrix (Lat) a fungus (family: Pourridié) that attacks the vine roots. see Armillaria Root-rot.

Dermond [Paul-Louis] (Fr) a sparkling wine-producer based in Saumur, Anjou-Saumur, Loire.

Dernau (Ger) village (Anb): Ahr. (Ber): Walporzheim/Ahrtal. (Gro): Klosterberg. (Vins): Burggarten, Goldkaul, Hardtberg, Pfarrwingert, Schieferlay.

Deroldego (It) a red grape variety grown in the Trentino-Alto Adige.

Dérouillat (Fr) a Champagne producer. (Add): 23, Rue des Chapelles, 51530 Monthelon. Propriétaire-Récoltant. Produces vintage and non-vintage wines also produces Ratafia and Marc de Champagne. Labels: Cuvée Arthémia, Cuvée Fanette, Cuvée Réservéee l'Espirit. Website: http://www.champagne-derouillat.fr.st 'E'mail: champagne.derouillat@wanadoo.fr

Derrière-la-Grange (Fr) a Premier Cru vineyard in the A.C. commune of Chambolle-Musigny, Côte de Nuits, Burgundy 0.73ha.

Derrière Saint-Jean (Fr) a Premier Cru vineyard in the A.C. commune of Pommard, Côte de Beaune, Burgundy 1.2ha.

Dertig (Hol) thirsty (dorst = thirst).

Dertingen (Ger) village (Anb): Baden. (Ber): Badische Frankenland. (Gro): Tauberklinge Mandelberg. (Vin): Sonnenberg.

De Rust Wines (S.Afr) the label for a range of wines made by the Mooiuitsig Wynkelders.

Dervin [Michel] (Fr) a Champagne producer.(Add): 7 Rue du Pressoir, 51480 Cuchery. Négociant-manipulant 5ha.

Derwen (Wal) oak.

Derwent Deep (Eng) a beer brewed by the Derwentrose Brewery in Consett, County Durham.

D

Derwentrose Brewery (Eng) a micro-brewery based at the Grey Horse in Consett, County Durham. Brews: Coast2Coast, Steel Town Bitter, Red Dust, Derwent Deep, Gold, Bronze, Swordmaker.

De Sacy [Louis] (Fr) a Champagne producer. (Add): 6 Rue de Verzenay, BP 2, 51380 Verzy. Négociant-manipulant. 30ha. Prestige cuvée: Grand Soir.

De Saint Gall (Fr) a Champagne producer. Produces vintage and non-vintage wines. Vintages: 1990, 1995, 1998.Website: http://www.de-saint-gall.com

Desavinho (Port) a vine malady, also known as Coulure.

Descampe (Bel) a large distillery in Gembloux.

Descamps Brasserie (Fr) a brewery based at Monceau St. Waast in the Nord département. Produces top-fermented beers.

De Schaapskooi Trappiste Brouwerij (Hol) a brewery (established 1884) based in Berkel-Enschot. Brews: La Trappe, La Trappe Dubbel, La Trappe Quadrupel.

Des Chais des Grands Armagnacs [Castagnon] (Fr) an Armagnac producer. (Add): Route de Toulouse, 32110 Nogaro.

De Schelde Brouwerij (Hol) a brewery (established 1993) based in 's-Gravenpolder. Brews: De Draak, De Zeezuiper, Lamme Goedzak, Merck Toch Hoe Sterck.

Desclieux (Fr) a Frenchman who introduced the coffee plant to the West Indies (Martinique) in the eighteenth century. The alternative spelling of De Clieu.

Descombes-Callot (Fr) a vineyard (established 1927) based in Morgon, Beaujolais. (Add): 69910 Coghard. Produces Grape variety: Gamay. A.C. Cru Beaujolais Morgon.

Descorchar (Sp) to uncork a bottle.

Des 2 Rivières (Fr) a brewery based in Morlaix. Brews: Coreff Ambrée, Coreff Brune.

Deserpia (Sp) a method of ensuring that the heavy rains of October and November are conserved by making a ridge around the vines to ensure the vines get water. Mainly applicable to the Sherry region. See also La Serpia.

Desert Gold (Eng) an 8.2% alc by vol. extra strong cider from Bulmers. Gold tinted in colour.

Desert Healer (Cktl) ⅓ measure gin, ½ measure cherry brandy, juice of an orange. Shake over ice, strain into an ice-filled highball glass and top ginger beer.

Desertnoe Vino (Rus) dessert wine.

Desertno Vino (Slo) dessert wine.

Desert Storm (Eng) a 4% alc by vol. ale brewed by the Storm Brewing C°. Ltd., Cheshire.

Desfangado (Sp) clarification. (Fr) = débourbage, (Ger) = entschleimen.

Desfontsoyes Fontette (Fr) a Champagne producer. (Add): Coopérative Fontette, Champagne Charles Colin, 10360 Fontette.

Desgalhar (Port) to prune.

Desgüelle (Sp) the disgorging of cava wines. (Fr) = dégorgement. see correct spelling Degüelle.

Désherbage (Fr) the controlled process of weeding around and between the vines.

Desiderio (It) a red I.G.T. wine produced from 100% Merlot by Avignonesi in Tuscany.

Desiderius (S.Afr) the label for a methode cap classique wine (Chardonnay 60% and Pinot noir 40% blend) part of the Pongrácz range from Distell, Western Cape.

De Silly Brasserie (Bel) a brewery (established 1854) based in Silly. Brews Double Enghien Blonde.

Desiree (Cktl) 1 measure gin, ½ measure crème de noyau, ¼ measure lemon juice, 3 dashes Maraschino. Shake over ice and strain into a cocktail glass.

De Sleutel (Hol) a hoppy beer 6% alc by vol. brewed by the Heineken Brouwerij.

Desliar (Sp) racking.

Desloch (Ger) village (Anb): Nahe. (Ber): Schloss Böckelheim. (Gro): Paradiesgarten. (Vins): Hengstberg, Vor der Hölle.

Desmazières [Laurent] (Fr) a Champagne producer. (Add): 9 Rue Dom Pérignon, B.P. 15, 51500 Chigny-lès-Roses.

De Smedt Brouwerij (Bel) a brewery (established 1790) based in Operwijk. Brews: Napoléon, Dikkenek (top-fermented bottled beer under licence from Brouwerij Dikkenek NV in Hasselt).

Desmoiselle (Fr) a Champagne produced by Vranken at 42 Ave. de Champagne, Épernay.

Desmond and Duff (Scot) a blended Scotch whisky distillers based in Edinburgh. Produce a blend and a 12 year old de luxe blend mainly for the U.S.A. market.

Desmoulins [A.] (Fr) a Champagne producer. (Add): 44 Ave. Foch, 51201 Épernay. Produces non-vintage wines. Label: Cuvée Prestige.

Desnoes and Geddes Ltd. (W.Ind) a large brewery (established 1918) based in Kingston, Jamaica. Brews: Dragon Stout and Red Stripe lager.

De Sonnenberg (S.Afr) the label for a range of wines marketed by the Premium Cape Wines company, Stellenbosch, Western Cape.

De Soto [José] (Sp) a famous Sherry and brandy producer based in Jerez de la Frontera. Produces fine Sherries of all styles. Labels include: Fino Soto, Soto and Ponch, Soto. Solera brandy: Brandy Soto, Solera Reserva brandy: Palatino, Solera gran reserva brandy: Señorial.

De Sousa et Fils (Fr) a Champagne producer n the Côte des Blancs. (Add): 12, Place Léon-Bourgeois 51190 Avize. 6.5ha. Vintages: 1997, 1998.

Desperados (Fr) a lager 5.9% alc by vol. enhanced with a shot of tequila and citrus extract. Produced by Brasserie Fischer in Schiltigheim.

Desperate Dan (Cktl) 25mls (⅛ gill) Campari and 125mls (1gill) pineapple juice. Stir over ice in a highball glass and dress with a slice of orange.

Des Seigneurs (Fr) a 3-year-old Armagnac produced by Paluel-Marmont.

Dessertvin (Den) dessert wine.

Dessert Wines (Eng) usually applied to fortified sweet wines such as Port, Sherry, Madeira etc. as opposed to table wines. Can also be applied to such sweet wines as Sauternes and Trockenbeerenauslese

D

which are unfortified. (Den) = dessertvin. (Rus) = desertnoe vino, (Slo) = desertno vino.

Dessilani (It) one of the top producers of Gattinara D.O.C.G. wines in the Piemonte region.

Dessous (Fr) coaster.

Dessous de Bouteille (Fr) a bottle coaster.

Dessous de Verre (Fr) a drinking glass coaster.

Destalking (Eng) the removal of the grapes from the stalks to prevent an accumulation of tannin in the must. (Fr) = égrappage, (Ger) = gerbelt.

De Stel (Hol) a Dutch governor who planted the Constantia vineyard and gave his name to Stellenbosch in South Africa.

Destileria Huasteca (Mex) a rum distillery that produces Potosi (a range of rums including Oro, Anejo and Blanco).

Destille (Ger) a Berlin expression for a hard-drinking bar that specialises in spirits.

Destino (S.Afr) the label for a red wine (Cabernet sauvignon and Merlot blend) produced by the Gusto Wines winery, Stellenbosch, Western Cape.

Destiny (S.Afr) the label for a red wine (Shiraz) produced by the Mont Destin winery, Paarl, Western Cape.

De St. Mardeaux & Cº. (Fr) a Champagne producer. (Add): 2-4 Ave. du Général Giraud, 51100 Reims. Produces vintage and non-vintage wines. Top vintage cuvée: La Cuvée Signée Chatellier.

Destreilles (Fr) a Cognac producer. (Add): Vignobles des Treilles, Le Taire, 16360 Baignes. 60ha. 25% in Petite Champagne, 50% in Fins Bois, 25% in Bon Bois. Produces *** Destreilles (3–4 old), Napoléon Destreilles (10–15 years old) and Vieux Réserve du Vignerons (30 plus years old).

Destroyer (Eng) a 4% alc by vol. ale brewed by the Flagship Brewery, Chatham Dockyard, Dartford. £10.00 per cask being donated to a fund to save World War II HMS Cavalier from scrapheap.

Desvignes Aîné (Fr) a négociant based in La Chapelle Pontanevaux, Burgundy.

Desvinador (Sp) de-juicer (used to crush the grapes).

De Telmont (Fr) a Champagne producer. (Add): 1 Ave. de Champagne, B.P. 17, Damery, 51316 Éperney. 25ha. Produces vintage and non-vintage wines. Top vintage De Luxe cuvée: Cuvée Grand Couronnement.

Détendu Wines (S.Afr) a winery (established 1995) based in Paarl, Western Cape. 33ha. Grape varieties: Cabernet sauvignon, Chardonnay, Merlot, Pinotage, Shiraz. Produces varietal wines.

De Terrazas [Bartoloméo] (Chile) a missionary who was supposedly one of the first to introduce vines into Chile in the sixteenth century.

De Terry (Sp) see Terry.

Déthune [Paul] (Fr) a Champagne producer based in Ambonnay. Produces vintage and non-vintage Champagnes. Label: Princesse des Thunes.

De Toren Private Cellar (S.Afr) a winery (20ha) based at Vlottenburg, Stellenbosch, Western Cape. Grape varieties: Cabernet franc, Cabernet sauvignon, Malbec, Merlot, Petit verdot. Labels: Fusion V, and letters of the Greek alphabet (Alpha 2001/Gamma 2002, Delta 2003). Website: http://www.de-toren.com

De Torens (Bel) lit: 'the towers', old name for Geens Distillery.

De Trafford (S.Afr) a winery (established 1992) based in Helderberg, Stellenbosch, Western Cape. 5ha. Grape varieties: Cabernet franc, Cabernet sauvignon, Chenin blanc, Merlot, Pinotage, Shiraz. Labels: Blueprint, Elevation 393, Straw Wine. Website: http://www.detrafford.co.za

De Troch Brasserie (Bel) a brewery based in Wambeek, north Belgium.

Dettelbach (Ger) village (Anb): Franken. (Ber): Maindreieck. (Gro): Honigberg. (Vils): Berg-Rondell, Sonnenleite.

Dettling (Switz) a liqueur producer based in Brunnen. Noted for a kirsch produced from black cherries 40% alc by vol.

Detzem (Ger) village (Anb): Mosel-Saar-Ruwer. (Ber): Bernkastel. (Gro): Sankt Michael. (Vins): Maximiner Klosterlay, Würzgarten.

Deuce (Eng) a sugar-free, non-alcoholic fruit juice, blends include: apple base with cranberry and raspberry/orange base with orange and guava produced by the Schweppes company.

Deuchars I.P.A. (Scot) a 3.8% alc by vol. I.P.A. from The Caledonian Brewery Cº. Ltd., Edinburgh. See also 80/-, Golden Promise.

De Urdiñola [Francisco] (Mex) a Spanish captain who planted the first vineyard at Parras de la Fuente.

Deus (Bel) a bottled 'vintage' beer (in a magnum Champagne-style bottle) from Flander.

Deuslay (Ger) vineyard (Anb): Mosel-Saar-Ruwer. (Ber): Zell/Mosel. (Gro): Rosenhang. (Vil): Mesenich.

Deutelsberg (Ger) grosslage (Anb): Rheingau. (Ber): Johannisberg. (Vils): Erbach, Hattenheim, Estate.

Deutsche Landwirtschafts-Gesellschaft (Ger) abbr: D.L.G. (established 1885) grants awards to wines, a Federal organisation, recognised by the E.C. Given only to quality wines.

Deutscher Devil (Cktl) ⅓ measure schnapps, ⅓ measure brandy, ⅓ measure orange juice, dash gomme syrup. Shake over ice, strain into a cocktail glass and top with an orange slice.

Deutscher Rum (Ger) a rum distilled from German-grown sugar beet molasses and sugar beet juice.

Deutscher Sekt (Ger) a sparkling wine made from at least 80% of German wine.

Deutscher Tafelwein (Ger) table wine (not to be confused with the E.C Aus Ländern der E.W.G.). Produced from the regions of Rhein, Mosel, Main, Neckar and Oberrhein. see Untergebiete Zones.

Deutsches Erzeugnis (Ger) on a label denotes 'Product of Germany'.

Deutsches Weinlesefest (Ger) a Pfalz wine festival held in Neustadt in October.

Deutsches Weinsiegel (Ger) a quality seal that appears on the neck label of those wines that have obtained a certain standard in test.

Deutsches Weintor (Ger) German wine gate, the start of the Deutsche Weinstrasse. On the border of Alsace at Schweiger, Pfalz.

D

Deutsche Weinstrasse (Ger) German wine route, wine walk from Bockenheim to Scheweigen. 80 kilometres long.

Deutschherrenberg (Ger) vineyard (Anb): Mosel-Saar-Ruwer. (Ber): Bernkastel. (Gro): Münzlay. (Vil): Zeltingen-Rachtig.

Deutschherrenberg (Ger) vineyard (Anb): Mosel-Saar-Ruwer. (Ber): Saar-Ruwer. (Gro): Römerlay. (Vil): Trier.

Deutschherrenköpfchen (Ger) vineyard (Anb): Mosel-Saar-Ruwer. (Ber): Saar-Ruwer. (Gro): Römerlay. (Vil): Trier.

Deutsch-Kreutz (Aus) a wine-producing area in the Mattersburg district.

Deutz & Geldermann (Fr) a Champagne producer. (Add): 16 Rue Jeanson, 51160, Aÿ. A Grande Marque. 42ha. Produces vintage and non-vintage wines. Vintages: 1919, 1920, 1921, 1924, 1925, 1926, 1928, 1929, 1931, 1934, 1936, 1938, 1945, 1947, 1948, 1949, 1953, 1955, 1959, 1961, 1962, 1964, 1966, 1969, 1970, 1973, 1976, 1976, 1979, 1981, 1982, 1985, 1988, 1989, 1990, 1995, 1996, 1998, 2000. De Luxe vintage cuvee: Cuvée William Deutz (Chardonnay 35%, Pinot meunier 10%, Pinot noir 55%). Website: http://www.contact-champagne-senez.com 'E'mail: champagne.senez@wanadoo.fr

Deuxièmes Crus (Fr) the second growths in Bordeaux. Châteaux: Brane-Cantenac, Cos-d'Estournel, Ducru-Beaucaillou, Durfort-Vivens, Gruard-Larose, Lascombes, Léoville-Barton, Léoville-Lascases, Léoville-Poyferré, Montrose, Pichon-Longueville Baron de Pichon, Pichon-Longueville Comtesse de Lalande, Rauzan-Gassies, Rausan-Ségla. see Cru.

Deuxièmes Crus de Sauternes (Fr) the second growths in Sauternes and Barsac (Bordeaux). There are 13 château in this classification: Château Broustet, Château Caillou, Château d'Arche, Château de Malle, Château de Myrat, Château Doisy-Daëne, Château Doisy-Dubroca, Château Doisy-Védrines, Château Filhot, Château Lamothe, Château Nairac, Château Suau.

Deuxièmes Premiers Crus (Fr) a Bordeaux classification. see Deuxièmes Crus.

Deuxième Taille (Fr) the third pressing of the Champagne grapes (now no longer used).

Deux Verres Reserve (USA) the label for a red wine (Pinot noir) produced by the Torii Mor winery, Willamette Valley, Oregon.

Deva (Sp) a 50% alc by vol. lime green/yellow coloured absinthe.

De Vaca [Alvar Nuñez Cabeza] (Sp) the man who discovered Florida and introduced Sherry to the USA.

De Vaete Bockbier (Hol) an 8% alc by vol. ruby-red, top-fermented, bottle-conditioned bock beer brewed by De Vaete Brouwerij, Lewedorp.

De Vaete Brouwerij (Hol) a brewery (established 1993) based at Lewedorp. Brews: De Vaete Bockbier, Bruin's Ale.

Devanha Brewery (Scot) a brewery (established

1982) based in north-eastern Scotland. Brews: cask-conditioned Pale Eighty 1042 O.G. XB 1036 O.G. and XXX 1042 O.G.

Dévastateur [Le] (Fr) lit: 'the devastator', the nickname for the Phylloxera vastatrix vine louse by 19th Century French scientists.

Devaux [Vve.A.] (Fr) a Champagne producer. (Add): Domaine de Villeneuve, 10110 Bar-sur-Seine. 12 cooperatives (800 growers owning 1,400ha. in 54 different growths). Vintages include 1985, 1988, 1990, 1995, 1998, 2000. Labels include: Rosé Intense (100% Pinot noir).

Deveaux (Fr) a liqueur made from brandy, cream, hazelnuts, herbs and cocoa 17% alc by vol.

Devenish Brewery (Eng) breweries in Weymouth, Dorset and Redruth in Cornwall. Produce many fine beers including cask-conditioned John Devenish 1032 O.G. Cornish 1042 O.G. Wessex 1042 O.G. Newton's Ale 1032 O.G. Saxon 1033 O.G. Falmouth Bitter 1038 O.G. and John Groves 1034 O.G. Also Grünhalle Lager 1036 O.G. and Great British Henry.

De Venoge (Fr) a Champagne producer (establisheded 1837). (Add): 46 Ave. de Champagne, 51204 Épernay Cedex. 18ha. Produces vintage and non-vintage wines. Produces: Champagne des Princes (a vintage cuvée) and Cordon Bleu (a non-vintage Champagne Brut Millésimé, Brut Sélect, Demi-Sec), Blanc de Blancs Brut, Blanc de Noirs (Pinot noir 80%, Pinot meunier 20%) and Brut Rosé (Chardonnay 20%, Pinot noir 60%, Pinot meunier 20%). Vintages: 1971, 1973, 1975, 1979 1980, 1983, 1985, 1988, 1989, 1990, 1995, 1996, 1998, 2001. Also specialises in B.O.B. Champagnes. Website: http://www.Champagnedevenoge.com

De Verboden Vrucht (Bel) an 8.8% alc by vol. top-fermented, bottle-conditioned special beer brewed with coriander by De Kluis Hoegaarden.

Devereux (S.Afr) the label for a white wine (Chenin blanc) produced by the Glen Carlou winery, Paarl, Western Cape.

Deveron Valley Scottish Spring (Scot) a natural spring mineral water from the Deveron Valley.

Deversorium (Lat) inn/public house.

De Vilanova [Arnaud] (Fr) a fourteenth century professor in the University of Montpellier who is believed to have rediscovered the art of distillation.

De Vilanova [Arnàu] (Sp) a Catalan chemist born 1820 who invented herb tinctures (similar to liqueurs).

De Villamont [Henry] (Fr) a Burgundy négociant based at Savigny-lès-Beaune, Côte de Beaune. Part of the Schenk group of Switzerland.

De Villiers Wines (S.Afr) a winery based in Paarl, Western Cape. Grape varieties: Cabernet sauvignon, Chardonnay, Chenin blanc, Pinotage, Riesling, Sauvignon blanc, Shiraz. Website: http://www.devwines.co.za

Devil's Cauldron (Eng) a vineyard (established 1977) based at Ransley Farm, High Halden, Kent. 1.5ha. Grape variety: Gutedel.

Devil's Cocktail [1] (Cktl) ½ measure dry vermouth, ½ measure Port, 2 dashes lemon juice. Shake with ice and strain into a cocktail glass.

Devil's Cocktail [2] (Cktl) 30mls (¼ gill) Cognac, 30mls (¼ gill) crème de menthe (green). Shake over ice, strain into a cocktail glass, add pinch of cayenne pepper on top.

Devil's Disciple (Cktl) place some ice into an old-fashioned glass. Add 25mls (1fl.oz) crème de menthe, 25mls (1fl.oz) Dubonnet, 50mls (2fl.ozs) tonic water, stir and finish with a slice of orange.

Devils Elbow (Eng) a 3.6% alc by vol. ale brewed by the Hexhamshire Brewery, Northumberland.

Devil's Gulch Vineyard (USA) the label for a red wine (Pinot noir) produced by the Dutton Goldfield winery, Marin County, California.

Devil's Kiss (Eng) a 7% alc by vol. amber coloured keg and bottled bitter beer brewed by Carlsberg at Alloa.

Devil's Kiss (Eng) a 5.2% alc by vol. ale from Allsopp Brewery.

Devil's Lair (Austr) a winery in the Coastal Region of Margaret River, Western Australia. Grape varieties include: Cabernet sauvignon, Chardonnay.

Devil's Tail (Cktl) 1 measure dark rum, ½ measure vodka, ⅛ measure grenadine, ⅛ measure apricot brandy, juice ¼ lime. Blend altogether with a scoop of crushed ice. Pour into a flute glass, top with iced Champagne and a twist of lime peel.

Devils Water (Eng) a 4.2% alc by vol. ale brewed by the Hexhamshire Brewery, Northumberland.

Devin (Bul) an alkaline, still natural spring mineral water from West Rhodopa Mountain, Spring B5, Devin. Mineral contents (milligrammes per litre): Sodium 65.5mg/l, Calcium 1.6mg/l, Potassium 1.59mg/l, Bicarbonates 85.4mg/l, Chlorides 3.5mg/l, Sulphates 20.6mg/l, Fluorides 4mg/l, Silicates 45.6mg/l. pH 9.4

De Vin Seu (Ch.Isles) elderflower Champagne.

Devise de Lilian [La] (Fr) the second label of Château Lilian Ladouys.

De Vit Brasserie [René] (Bel) a brewery based in Lembeek, central Belgium.

Devizes Bitter (Eng) a cask-conditioned bitter 1030 O.G. brewed by the Wadworth's Brewery in Wiltshire.

Devlin Wine Cellars (USA) a small winery based in Santa Cruz, California. Grape varieties: Cabernet sauvignon, Chardonnay, Pinot blanc and Zinfandel. Produces varietal wines.

De Vogüé (Fr) a famous noted wine producer based in Musigny, Côtes de Nuits, Burgundy.

Devoir Parisien des Compagnons du Beaujolais (Fr) formed by exiled Beaujolais compatriots in Paris. Promotes the region and its wines.

Devon (Rus) a natural spring mineral water. Mineral contents (milligrammes per litre): Calcium 14–30mg/l, Bicarbonates 200–350mg/l.

Devon Best (Eng) a keg bitter 1036 O.G. brewed by the Blackawton Brewery in Devon.

Devon Cream Ale (Eng) a 3.6% alc by vol. ale brewed by the St. Austell Brewery Cº. Ltd., Cornwall.

Devon Crest (S.Afr) the label for a red wine (Cabernet sauvignon 69% and Merlot 31% blend) produced by the Meinert Wines winery, Stellenbosch, Western Cape.

Devon Dawn (Eng) a 4.5% alc by vol. beer brewed for the new millennium by Exe Valley Brewery, Silverton, Devon.

Devon Dew (Eng) the original name for Minton Spring water.

Devonet (S.Afr) the label for red wine (Merlot and Pinotage blend) produced by the Clos Malverne winery, Stellenbosch, Western Cape.

Devon Glory (Eng) a 4.7% alc by vol. ale brewed by the Exe Valley Brewery, Silverton, Devon.

Devon Gold (Eng) a 4.1% alc by vol. beer brewed by Blackawton Brewery in Devon.

Devon Gold Cider (Eng) a medium-dry or medium-sweet cider produced by Countryman in Devon.

Devon Hills (Eng) a natural spring mineral water from Chulmleigh, Devon. Mineral contents (milligrammes per litre): Sodium 17mg/l, Calcium 26mg/l, Magnesium 14mg/l, Potassium 1.6mg/l, Bicarbonates 120mg/l, Chlorides 24mg/l, Sulphates 10.2mg/l, Nitrates 0.2mg/l.

Devon Hill Winery (S.Afr) a winery (established 1996) based in Stellenbosch, Western Cape. 46ha. Grape varieties: Cabernet sauvignon, Merlot, Pinotage, Sauvignon blanc, Shiraz. Labels: Blue Bird, Four Stars. Website: http://www.devonhill.co.za

Devonia Cocktail (Cktl) 100mls sparkling cider, 50mls gin, 2 dashes orange bitters. Stir lightly over ice and strain into a highball glass.

Devon Mix (Eng) the name of a draught cider produced by Churchwards in Paignton, Devon.

Devon Rocks (S.Afr) a winery (established 1988) based in Stellenbosch, Western Cape. 3.5ha. Grape varieties: Pinotage, Shiraz. Website: http://www.devonrocks.co.za

Devonshire Cream (Eng) clotted cream, full cream milk (from Guernsey or Jersey cattle) that has been heated gently so that the cream thickens. It is then skimmed off the top of the milk.

Devonshire Cyder (Eng) a cider produced by the Whiteways Cº. Has no additives, artificial colouring or flavourings.

Devonshire Royal Cream (Eng) a brandy and whisky-based cream liqueur produced in Plymouth, Devon 17% alc by vol.

Devon Special (Eng) a cask-conditioned bitter 1043 O.G. brewed by the Mill Brewery in Newton Abbot.

Devon Summer (Eng) a 3.9% alc by vol. seasonal ale from the Exe Valley Brewery, Silverton, Devon (June–August).

Devon Valley Estate (S.Afr) the vineyards of Bertrams Wines in the Stellenbosch region.

Devout Stout (Eng) the name for a stout brewed by the Alcazar Brewery, Nottinghamshire.

De Vriendenkring Bier Brouwerij (Hol) a brewery that brews Classe Royal (part of Breda).

D

Dew (Austr) a natural spring mineral water from North Queensland. Mineral contents (milligrammes per litre): Sodium 2mg/l, Calcium 14mg/l, Magnesium 0.4mg/l, Potassium 1.8mg/l, Bicarbonates 9mg/l, Chlorides 3mg/l, Sulphates <5mg/l.

DeWaal Wines (S.Afr) a winery (established 1682) based in Stellenbosch, Western Cape. 120ha. (Add): Box 15, Vlottenburg, 7604. Grape varieties: Cabernet sauvignon, Chardonnay, Chenin blanc, Merlot, Pinotage, Sauvignon blanc, Shiraz. Labels: Cape Blend, Hill, CT de Waal, Standard Uiterwyk, Top of the Hill, Uiterwyk Young Vines. Website: http://www.dewaal.co.za

Dewar [John] (Scot) a Perth man who is supposed to have introduced the blending of whisky by adding all the remnants of his casks together. *see* Dewar's.

Dewar's (Scot) a blended malt, produced by John Dewar and Sons Ltd., Perth. 40% alc by vol. Part of DCL.

Dewar's Ancestor de Luxe Scotch Whisky (Scot) a de luxe blended Scotch whisky produced by Dewar's of Perth. Is known as Dewar's Ne Plus Ultra in Canada.

Dewar's Ne Plus Ultra (Can) *see* Dewar's Ancestor De Luxe Scotch Whisky.

Dewar's White Label (Scot) a famous blended Scotch whisky from Dewar's of Perth.

Dew Drops (Ind) a natural spring mineral water from Muradnagar. Mineral contents (milligrammes per litre): Sodium 24mg/l, Calcium 58mg/l, Magnesium 44mg/l, Potassium 22mg/l, Bicarbonates 466mg/l, Chlorides 10mg/l, Sulphates 9.6mg/l, Nitrates 0.6mg/l. pH 7.1

De Wet Co-operative (S.Afr) a co-operative winery (established 1946) based in the Breede River Valley, Robertson, Western Cape. 60 members (1000ha). (Add): Box 16, De Wet 6853. Grape varieties: Chardonnay, Chenin blanc, Gewürztraminer, Hanepoot, Pontac, Red muscadel, Riesling, Sauvignon blanc. Produces Petillant Fronté and varietal wines sold under the Breërivievallei Wines label. Website: http://www.worcesterwinelands.co.za

De Wetsberg (S.Afr) the label for a range of wines produced by the Excelsior Estate winery, Robertson, Western Cape.

De Wetshof Estate (S.Afr) a winery (established 1949) based in Robertson, Western Cape. 180ha. (Add): Dewetshof Box 31, Robertson 6705. Produces a Chardonnay Sur-Lie and varietal wines. Grape varieties: Chardonnay, Gewürztraminer, Muscat de Frontignan, Pinot noir, Riesling, Sauvignon blanc grapes. Labels: Bateleur, Blanc de Wet, Bon Vallon, Call of the African Eagle, Cape Muscadel, Danir de Wet, Edeloes, Limestone Hill, Naissance, Nature in Concert. Website: http://www.dewetshof.co.za 'E'mail: info@dewestshof.co.za

Dewi Sant (Wal) a dry blended white wine produced by the Cwm Deri Vineyard, Martletwy, Pembrokeshire.

Dewmiel (Scot) a herb and whisky-based liqueur. 40% alc by vol.

Dew of Ben Nevis (Scot) a 40 year old single malt whisky 40% alc by vol. produced by the Ben Nevis distillery, Fort William.

Dexheim (Ger) village (Anb): Rheinhessen. (Ber): Nierstein. (Gro): Gutes Domtal. (Vin): Doktor.

Dexters (Eng) a low-calorie hypotomic after-sport drink containing nutra-sweet from Callitheke.

Dextrin (Eng) fermentable sugar in malted barley for beer and whisky production.

Dextrocheck (Eng) a tablet used for testing the residual sugar in still wine before dosage occurs. Applied mainly in home-made wine production.

Dextrose (Eng) $C_6H_{12}O_6$ (fruit sugar) also known as grape sugar. *see* Glucose.

De Yuma (Sp) the name given to the must obtained from the first light pressing of the grapes.

Deza Collection (S.Afr) the export label for a range of wines from Oaklands Wine Exporters, Western Cape.

Dézaley (Switz) a top quality A.O.C. dry white wine made from the Chasselas grape in the Canton of Vaud.

Dezberg (Ger) vineyard (Anb): Württemberg. (Ber): Württembergisch Unterland. (Gro): Salzberg. (Vil): Eberstadt.

Dezberg (Ger) vineyard (Anb): Württemberg. (Ber): Württembergisch Unterland. (Gro): Salzberg. (Vil): Gellmersbach.

Dezize-les-Maranges (Fr) a village within the commune of Santenay, Côte de Beaune, Burgundy.

De Zoete Inval Estate (S.Afr) a winery (established 1976) based in Suider-Paarl, Western Cape. 20ha. (Add): P.O. Box Suider Paarl 7625. Grape varieties: Cabernet sauvignon, Chardonnay, Merlot, Pinotage, Sauvignon blanc, Shiraz. Labels: Eskdale, Yvette. Website: http://www.dezoeteinval.co.za

DFJ Vinhos (Port) the name given to a range of 36 plus wines from Quinta Fonte Bela near Cartaxo in the Ribatejo which used to vinify grapes from over 1,500ha. of vineyards (now has just 65ha. and is converted into a bottling centre). Grape varieties: Alvarinho, Chardonnay, Fernão pires, Cabernet, Trincadeira, Tinta roriz, Touriga nacional. Wine labels include Senda do Vale, Manta Preta, Vale de Rosas, Grand d'Arte.

D-Fructose (Eng) a monosaccharide found in grape must.

D.G. (Sp) *abbr*: Dark Golden (colour grade for Raya Sherries).

DGB (S.Afr) a winery (established 1942) based in Wellington, Western Cape. Produces fortified and table wines. Website: http://www.dgb.co.za

D.G.I. (Fr) *abbr*: Direction Générale des Impôts.

Dgin (Ch.Isles) gin.

Dgin dé Prunelles (Ch.Isles) sloe gin.

D.G.O. (Bul) *abbr*: Declared Geographical Origin.

Dharmapuri (Ind) a wine-producing area.

D. Henriet-Bazin (Fr) a Champagne producer. (Add): Villers-Marmery, Marne. Vintages: 1994, 1995, 1998, 2000.

Dhoros (Cyp) a village on the south-eastern side of the island that produces grapes for Commandaria.

Diabetiker Wein (Ger) a very dry white wine, low in residual sugar, suitable for diabetics.

Diablo Cocktail (Cktl) ⅗ measure white apéritif Port, ⅖ measure Italian vermouth, 3 dashes lemon juice. Shake over ice and strain into a cocktail glass.

Diablo Vista (USA) a winery based in Solano, California. Grape varieties: Cabernet sauvignon, Chardonnay and Zinfandel. Produces varietal wines.

Diabolo Cocktail [1] (Cktl) 30mls (¼ gill) brandy, 30mls (¼ gill) French vermouth, 3 dashes orange Curaçao, 2 dashes Angostura. Stir over ice, strain into a cocktail glass, top with squeeze lemon juice and add cherry and an olive. Also known as Youngman.

Diabolo Cocktail [2] (Cktl) as for Diabolo Cocktail but omit the orange Curaçao and use brown Curaçao instead.

Diabolo Cocktail [3] (Cktl) ⅔ measure white rum, ⅙ measure French vermouth, ⅙ measure Cointreau, 2 dashes Angostura. Shake over ice, strain into a cocktail glass with a little crushed ice and a squeeze of orange peel juice on top.

Diacetyl (Eng) a glycerin-related compound found in wine in small quantities.

Diactyl (Eng) is produced by ***Lactobacilli***, gives the wine a bitter taste.

Diagalves (Port) the predominant white grape variety of Alentejo.

Diago Great Britain (Eng) a large brewery (established 1795). (Add): Park Royal Brewery, London NW10 7RR. Brews a wide range of beers and lager including Guinness. Website: http://www.diago.com 'E'mail: udv@uk.cmp-int.com

Diam (Fr) a new ™ 'cork' stopper patented by the Sabaté company to combat 2,4,6-trichloro-anisole and reduction.

Diamant (Bos) a natural spring mineral water from Tesanj, Bosnia and Herzegovina. Mineral contents (milligrammes per litre): Sodium 15mg/l, Calcium 64.92mg/l, Magnesium 47.62mg/l, Potassium 0.78mg/l, Bicarbonates 429.44mg/l, Chlorides 2.13mg/l, Sulphates 34mg/l, Fluorides 0.7mg/l, Nitrates 0.88mg/l, Silicates 19mg/l, Oxygen 7.54mg/l. pH 6.8

Diamant (Ger) a natural spring mineral water from the Diamant-Quelle, Schwollen, RP. Mineral contents (milligrammes per litre): Sodium 16mg/l, Calcium 49.8mg/l, Magnesium 24.8mg/l, Potassium 1.7mg/l, Chlorides 13.6mg/l, Sulphates 29mg/l, Nitrates 0.1mg/l.

Diamant Bleu (Fr) a de luxe vintage cuvée Champagne produced by Heidsieck Monopole from an equal blend of black and white grapes. Launched in 1967 with the 1961 vintage.

Diamante (It) a natural spring mineral water from Sassari, Sardinia.

Diamante (Sp) a red wine from the Bodegas Franco-Españolas. Made from the Garnacha 25%, Mazuelo 15% and Tempranillo 60%. Matured in oak for 1½ years and in bottle ½–1 year.

Diammonium Phosphate (Bio) a yeast nutrient added to grape musts to encourage fermentation.

Diamond (Austr) a still natural spring mineral water from Tasmania. Mineral contents (milligrammes per litre): Sodium 3.3mg/l, Calcium 35mg/l, Magnesium 3.2mg/l, Potassium 0.43mg/l, Chlorides 3.7mg/l, Sulphates 3.3mg/l.

Diamond (S.Am) a rum distillery based in Guyana.

Diamond (USA) a white hybrid grape variety.

Diamond Bitter (Eng) a keg bitter 1033 O.G. brewed by the Ind Coope Brewery in Burton-on-Trent.

Diamond Beer Brewing C° (Fin) a brewery. (Add): Sirrkuja 4E, 00940 Helsinki. Brews a variety of beers and lager.

Diamond Black (Eng) a 5% alc by vol. bottled cider and blackcurrant drink produced by Matthew Clark Taunton Cider Company, Somerset.

Diamond Blush (Eng) a 6% alc by vol. pink cider from Matthew Clark Taunton Cider Company. *See also* Diamond Orange (5% alc by vol.), Diamond White, Diamond Zest.

Diamond Cocktail (Cktl) 20mls (⅙ gill) each of dry gin, brown Curaçao, rum. Shake over ice, strain into a cocktail glass and serve with a dash lemon peel juice.

Diamond Creek (USA) a winery (established 1972) based near Calistoga, Napa Valley, California. 8.25ha. Grape variety: Cabernet sauvignon. Wines sold under Gravelly Meadow, Red Rock Terrace and Volcanic Hill labels. Website: http://www.diamondcreekvineyards.com

Diamond Dipper (Punch) 300mls (½ pint) dry Cinzano, 300mls (½ pint) vodka. Stir in a punch bowl, add 3 bottles Perrier water, dress with lemon and lime slices.

Diamond Export (Scot) a bottled ale 1042 O.G. brewed by the Alloa Brewery. If on draught then called Alloa Export.

Diamond Fizz (Cktl) 40mls (⅓ gill) gin, juice ½ lemon, teaspoon powdered sugar. Shake over ice, strain into an ice-filled highball glass and top with iced Champagne.

Diamond Heavy (Scot) a keg ale 1036 O.G. brewed by the Alloa Brewery.

Diamond Ice Cider (Eng) a 6.9% alc by vol. cider from Matthew Clark Taunton Cider Company.

Diamond Liquors (S.Am) a noted rum Distillery based in Guyana.

Diamond Mountain District (USA) a wine-producing district based in the Napa Valley, California.

Diamond Mountain Ranch (U.S.A) a red wine produced by Sterling Vineyards, Napa Valley, California from 62% Cabernet sauvignon, 20% Merlot, 9% Cabernet franc, 9% Petit verdot.

Diamond Red (Eng) a 5.4% alc by vol. bottled alcoholic drink containing caffeine and taurine from Matthew Clark.

Diamond Valley Vineyards (Austr) a winery (established 1969) based at 2130 Kinglake Road,

D

St. Andrews. Grape varieties: Chardonnay, Riesling, Cabernet sauvignon, Pinot noir.

Diamond White (Eng) a strong, 8.4% alc by vol. bottled white cider produced by Matthew Clark Taunton Cider Company, Somerset.

Diamond Zest (Eng) a 5% alc by vol. citrus lemon fruit drink from Matthew Clark Taunton Cider Company, Somerset.

Diana (Ger) a red grape variety cross (Silvaner x Muller-Thurgau) grown in eastern Germany.

Diana (USA) a native red grape variety (*Vitis labrusca*) used for making varietal wines.

Diana Cocktail [1] (Cktl) fill a cocktail glass with crushed ice, place 25mls (⅕ gill) white crème de menthe into the glass, then float liqueur Cognac on top.

Diana Cocktail [2] (Cktl) as for [1] but substitute schnapps for the crème de menthe.

Diana Madeline (Austr) a red (Cabernet sauvignon and Merlot blend) wine produced by the Cullen Estate, Western Australia.

Diana Quelle (Ger) a natural spring mineral water from Rosbach vor der Höhe, HE.

Diane de Poitiers (Fr) a non A.C. sparkling (méthode traditionelle) wine produced at a Haut-Poitou Co-operative from 100% white Chardonnay grapes, also a brut rosé version.

Dias d'Avila (Bra) an acidic natural spring mineral water from Dias d'Avila, Bahia. Mineral contents (milligrammes per litre): Sodium 6.9mg/l, Calcium 0.5mg/l, Magnesium 0.59mg/l, Potassium 0.21mg/l, Bicarbonates 9.61mg/l, Chlorides 6.69mg/l, Sulphates 2mg/l. pH 4.9

Diastase (Eng) the enzyme complex which causes the starch in malted barley to be converted into invert sugar (hydrolises the starch).

Diastasis (Eng) *see* Diastase.

Diatomaceous Earth (Eng) made up of minute animals which is used in fining wines, also known as Bentonite. *See also* Kieselguhr, Montmorillonite and Tierra de Vino.

Diät Pils (Ger) a high-alcohol, low carbohydrate beer 6% alc by vol. Brewed in west Germany. e.g. Holsten from Hamburg.

Di Castacciaro [Tommaso] (It) the Calmaldolese monk who is reputed to have turned water into wine in the thirteenth century.

Dickel [George] Cascade Distillery (USA) a distillery based near Tullahoma, Coffee County, Tennessee. Produces Tennessee whiskey (a sour mash whiskey filtered through charcoal).

Dickens (Eng) a 4% alc by vol. ale brewed by the Mauldon's Brewery, Suffolk.

Dickens Own (Eng) a cask-conditioned bitter 1042 O.G. brewed by the Tooley Street Brewery in Central London. *See also* Dickens Own Special.

Dickens Own Special (Eng) a cask-conditioned bitter 1050 O.G. brewed by the Tooley Street Brewery in Central London. *See also* Dickens Own.

Dickkopp (Ger) vineyard (Anb): Pfalz. (Ber): Mittelhaardt-Deutsche Weinstrasse. (Gro): Feuerberg. (Vil): Ellerstadt.

Dick Turpin (Eng) a 4.2% alc by vol. ale brewed by the Coach House Brewing C°. Ltd., Cheshire.

Didier (W.Ind) a natural spring mineral water from Font de France on the French island of Martinique. Mineral contents (milligrammes per litre): Calcium 137mg/l, Magnesium 113mg/l, Potassium 14mg/l, Bicarbonates 1280mg/l, Sulphates 6mg/l.

Didier Lefèvre (Fr) a propriètaire-viticulteur Champagne producer. (Add): 13, Quai de la Villa, B.P. 1055, 51319 Épernay. Produces non-vintage Champagnes including Brut Tradition, Brut Blanc de Blancs Grand Cru, Brut Rosé and Demi-Sec. Website: http://www.Champagne-lefevre.com 'E' Mail: Champagne.d.lefèvre@Hexanet.fr

Didiers [Les] (Fr) a Premier Cru vineyard of the village Prémeaux in the southern end of the A.C. commune of Nuits-Saint-Georges, Côte de Nuits, Burgundy 2.8ha.

Die (Fr) *see* Clairette de Die.

Diebels Alt (Ger) a 4.8% alc by vol. altbier from Diebels Brauerei, Issum near Düsseldorf. Well-made and full-flavoured.

Diebels Brauerei (Ger) a famous altbier brewery (established 1878) based at Issum, near Düsseldorf. Brews: Diebels Alt, Diebels Light.

Diebels Light (Ger) a 2.7% alc by vol. light altbier brewed by Diebels Brauerei, Issum, near Düsseldorf.

Die Bergkelder (S.Afr) a famous wine cellars based in Stellenbosch, Western Cape. Stocks most of the top South African wines. (Add): P.O. Box 5001, Stellenbosch 7600. *see* Fleur du Cap.

Dieblesberg (Ger) vineyard (Anb): Württemberg. (Ber): Württembergisch Unterland. (Gro): Salzberg. (Vil): Affaltrach.

Dieblesberg (Ger) vineyard (Anb): Württemberg. (Ber): Württembergisch Unterland. (Gro): Salzberg. (Vil): Löwenstein (ortsteil Hösslinsülz).

Dieblesberg (Ger) vineyard (Anb): Württemberg. (Ber): Württembergisch Unterland. (Gro): Salzberg. (Vil): Willsbach.

Dieblich (Ger) village (Anb): Mosel-Saar-Ruwer. (Ber): Zell/Mosel. (Gro): Weinhex. (Vin): Heilgraben.

Dieboldshausen (Fr) the German name for the Alsace wine town of Le Bonhomme.

Diebolt-Vallois (Fr) a Champagne producer in the Côte des Blancs. (Add): 84, Rue Neuve, 51530 Cramant. Vintages: 1996, 1997. Produces: Blanc des Blancs and Brut Prestige.

Die Breedekloof (S.Afr) the export label for a range of wines produced by the Viljoendrift wines winery, Robertson, Western Cape.

Diedersdorfer Schlossquell Mineralbrunnen (Ger) a natural spring mineral water from Diedersdorf bei Zossen, BB.

Diedesfeld (Ger) village (Anb): Pfalz. (Ber): Mittelhaardt-Deutsche Weinstrasse. (Gro): Pfaffengrund. (Vin): Berg.

Diedesfeld (Ger) village (Anb): Pfalz. (Ber): Mittelhaardt-Deutsche Weinstrasse. (Gro): Rebstöckel. (Vins): Johanniskirchel, Ölgässel, Paradies.

D

Diedesheim (Ger) village (Anb): Baden. (Ber): Badische Bergstrasse/Kraichgau. (Gro): Stiftsberg. (Vin): Herzogsberg.

Die Drostdyse Koöperatiewe Wynkelder (S.Afr) *see* Drostdyse Koöperatiewe Wynkelder.

Diefenbach (Ger) village (Anb): Württemberg. (Ber): Württembergisch Unterland. (Gro): Stromberg. (Vin): König.

Dieffert (Lux) a vineyard site in the village of Stadtbredimus.

Diekirch Brasserie (Lux) the largest brewery based in Diekirch.

Dielheim (Ger) village (Anb): Baden. (Ber): Badische Bergstrasse/Kraichgau. (Gro): Mannaberg. (Vins): Rosenberg, Teufelskopf.

Diem (Aus) a winery based in the Weinviertel. (Add): 2223 Hohenruppersdorf 118. Grape varieties: Grüner veltliner, Muller-Thurgau, Pinot blanc, Zweigelt.

Diemeltaler Quelle (Ger) a natural spring mineral water from Warburg-Germete, NW. Mineral contents (milligrammes per litre): Sodium 12mg/l, Calcium 125mg/l, Magnesium 35mg/l, Potassium 2mg/l, Bicarbonates 357mg/l, Chlorides 24mg/l, Sulphates 154mg/l.

Diemersdal (S.Afr) the label for a range of red and white wines from African Terroir winery, Paarl, Western Cape.

Diemersdal Vineyard (S.Afr) a winery (established 1698) based in Durbanville, Western Cape. 172ha. (Add): P.O. Durbanville 7550. Grape varieties: Cabernet franc, Cabernet sauvignon, Chardonnay, Merlot, Pinotage, Sauvignon blanc, Shiraz. Labels: Elixir, Matys, Private Collection. Produces varietal wines bottled by KWV.

Diemersfontein Wines (S.Afr) a winery (established 2001) based in Wellington, Cape Town, Western Cape. 180ha. Grape varieties: Cabernet franc, Cabernet sauvignon, Mourvèdre, Petit verdot, Pinotage, Shiraz, Viognier. Labels: Carpe Diem, Heaven's Eye, Maiden's Prayer, Summer Lease. Website: http://www.diemersfontein.co.za

Dienheim (Ger) village (Anb): Rheinhessen. (Ber): Nierstein. (Gro): Güldenmorgen. (Vins): Falkenberg, Herrenberg, Höhlchen, Kreuz-Siliusbrunnen, Tafelstein.

Dienheim (Ger) village (Anb): Rheinhessen. (Ber): Nierstein. (Gro): Krötenbrunnen. (Vins): Herrengarten, Paterhof, Schloss.

Dierbach (Ger) village (Anb): Pfalz. (Ber): Südliche Weinstrasse. (Gro): Guttenberg. (Vin): Kirchhöh.

Diersburg (Ger) village (Anb): Baden. (Ber): Ortenau. (Gro): Fürsteneck. (Vins): Kinzigtäler, Schlossberg.

Die Sparsamen (Ger) a natural spring mineral water from Diemeltaler Quelle, Warburg.

Die Stonsdorferei (Ger) a distillery owned by Koerner. Produces Enzian.

Diestro (Sp) a Jerez brandy producer. Produces Ponche.

Diesus (It) a bitter apéritif made by Barbero.

Dietale (Austr) a dry, diet beer brewed by C.U.B. in Victoria.

Diet (Eng) a term seen on many branded drinks, usually denotes that the product is a low calorie version.

Diet Coke (USA) a low-calorie version of the famous Coca Cola.

Dietenbronner Quelle (Ger) a natural spring mineral water from Lazarus-Quelle, Schwendi-Dietenbronn, BW.

Dietenbronner Quelle Gourmet (Ger) a natural spring mineral water. Mineral contents (milligrammes per litre): Sodium 6.15mg/l, Calcium 50.1mg/l, Magnesium 29.2mg/l, Potassium 1.03mg/l, Bicarbonates 305mg/l, Chlorides 1.73mg/l, Sulphates 8.9mg/l.

Diet Fresca (Eng) *see* Fresca.

Diethylene Glycol (Eng) a sweet syrupy liquid used as an anti-freeze in motor vehicles, has a high S.G. an illegal additive in wines (used to sweeten them) is poisonous. Associated with scandal in Austria in 1985.

Diethylpyrocarbonate (Eng) a wine preservative. *see* Baycovin.

Dietlingen (Ger) village (Anb): Baden. (Ber): Badische Bergstrasse/Kraichgau. (Gro): Hohenberg. (Vins): Keulebuckel, Klepberg.

Diet Pepper (USA) a low-calorie version of the Dr. Pepper drink.

Diet Pepsi (USA) a low-calorie version of the famous Pepsi Cola.

Diet Pils (Ger) *see* Diät Pils.

Die Tweede Droom (S.Afr) the label for a range of white wines (Chardonnay and Chenin blanc) produced by the Groot Parys winery, Paarl, Western Cape.

Dietzenbach (Ger) village (Anb): Hessische Bergstrasse. (Ber): Umstadt. (Gro): Not yet assigned. (Vin): Wingertsberg.

Dieu Donné (S.Afr) a natural still and sparkling mineral water from the Constantia Valley, Western cape. Mineral contents (milligrammes per litre): Sodium 42mg/l, Calcium 34mg/l, Magnesium 0.05mg/l, Potassium 7mg/l, Chlorides 78mg/l, Sulphates 22mg/l, pH 7.1

Dieu Donné De Lucque Vineyards (S.Afr) a winery (established 1984) based in Franschhoek, Western Cape. 40ha. (Add): P.O. Box 94, Franschhoek 7690. Produces varietal wines. Grape varieties: Cabernet sauvignon, Chardonnay, Chenin blanc, Merlot, Pinotage, Sauvignon blanc, Shiraz. Label: Maingard Brut Methode Cap Classique. Website: http://www.diendonnevineyards.com

Diez Hermanos (Port) a noted vintage Port shipping company.

Diez Hermanos (Sp) a noted Sherry producer based in Jerez de la Frontera. Brand of Sherry from Diez Merito. Range: Favorito Palma, Figaro, Imperial Fino, La Torera, Oloroso, Realengo and Victoria Regina.

Diez Merito (Sp) produces a range of Sherries under the labels of Don Zolio, Diez Hermanos. Also Mayorazgo Solera brandy, Marqués de Merito Solera Reserva brandy, Gran Duque d'Alba Solera gran reserva brandy.

D

Digby [Sir Kenelm] (Eng) a gentleman who is said to have invented the glass bottle in the year 1600.

Digestif (Eng) an aid to digestion, applied to herb liqueurs.

Digestive (Eng) see Digestif.

Diggers Gold (Eng) a 4.6% alc by vol. ale brewed by The Cheriton Brewhouse, Hampshire.

Dignac et Loirac (Fr) a commune in the Bas Médoc, north-western Bordeaux.

Dijamant (Bos) a natural spring mineral water from Ilidzanski Dijamant, Bosnia and Herzegovina. Mineral contents (milligrammes per litre): Sodium 118mg/l, Calcium 358mg/l, Magnesium 107mg/l, Potassium 7.8mg/l, Bicarbonates 1330mg/l, Chlorides 129mg/l, Sulphates 307mg/l, Fluorides 0.39mg/l, Strontium 1.1mg/l.

Diki-Diki (Cktl) 30mls (¼ gill) Calvados, 15mls (⅛ gill) Caloric Punsch, 15mls (⅛ gill) grapefruit juice. Shake over ice and strain into a cocktail glass.

Dikke Mathilde (Bel) a 6% alc by vol. amber-coloured, top-fermented, bottled ale brewed by the Strubbe Brasserie, Ichtegem.

Dikkenek (Bel) a 5.1% alc by vol. bottled special ale brewed by De Smedt Brouwerij, Opwijk.

Dikoya (Sri.L) a tea-producing region in the High region.

Diktiner (Ger) a rich herb liqueur similar to Bénédictine, green, red and yellow versions are produced.

Dilijan (Arm) a sparkling natural spring mineral water (established 1999) from Dilijan, Armenia. Mineral contents (milligrammes per litre): Sodium 36.55mg/l, Calcium 4.2mg/l, Magnesium 1.6mg/l. pH 6.7

Dillatini (Cktl) as for a Dry Martini but adding a dilly bean instead of an olive.

Diluer (Fr) to dilute/water down.

Dilute (Eng) to make weaker in strength (flavour or alcohol) by the addition of water or other weaker substance.

Dilution (Eng) the act of diluting (the thinning or weakening of a solution).

Di Mauro [Paolo] (It) a noted wine producer based in Latium who specialises in red wines.

Dimbach (Ger) vineyard (Anb): Württemberg. (Ber): Württembergisch Unterland. (Gro): Lindelberg. (Vin): Schlossberg.

Dimbula (Sri.L) a tea-producing region in the High region.

Dimiat (Bul) a white grape variety which produces dry fruity wines with a green tinge, grown mainly in the south and east. Also spelt Dimyat.

Di Montezemolo [Paolo Codero] (It) a noted wine producer based in the La Morra district of Barolo, Piemonte.

Dimple Haig (Scot) a 12 year old de luxe Scotch whisky produced by John Haig and C°. at Markinch. See also Pinch-bottle.

Dimples (Cktl) ½ measure Dimple Haig Scotch whisky, ½ measure apple juice, dash green

Chartreuse. Shake over ice, strain into an ice-filled highball glass, top with a dash of soda and sprig of mint.

Dimrit (Tur) a white grape variety grown in central Anatolia.

Dimyat (Bul) see Dimiat.

Dinah Cocktail (Cktl) 25mls Bourbon whiskey, juice ¼ lemon, 2 dashes gomme syrup. Shake well over ice, strain into a cocktail glass and top with a mint leaf.

Dinant Brasserie (Bel) a brewery based in Dinant. Produces the top-fermented beer Copère.

Dinastía Vivanco Museum (Sp) a wine museum based at the Vivanco winery, in Briones, Rioja. Website: http://www.dinastiavivanco.es 'E'mail: infomuseo@dinastiavivanco.es

Dindarella (It) a red grape variety used in the production of Toar Valpolicella.

Dingac (Cro) a strong red wine made from the Plavac grape in Croatia. Full bodied and high in alcohol.

Ding-a-ling (Scot) a slang request for a tot of Bell's Scotch whisky.

Dinka (Hun) a widely planted white grape variety. Also known as Kevedinka, Kövidinka, Ruzica.

Dinkarebe (Aus) an old red grape variety that is little used now-a-days.

Dinkel Acker (Ger) a bier produced by the Dinkelacker Brauerei in Stuttgart.

Dinkelacker Brauerei (Ger) a noted brewery of Stuttgart in south-west Germany. Noted for Sanwald brand and C.D. beers.

Dinner Ale (Austr) abbr: D.A. a pale, hoppy lager brewed by the Tooth's Brewery in New South Wales.

Dinner Ale (Austr) a low-gravity ale 4.75% alc by vol. produced by the Cooper Brewery in Adelaide. Is wood-fermented and bottle-conditioned.

Dinner Ale (Eng) a rare low-gravity bottled beer made by a second mash of malt.

Di Notte (It) a range of two white wines: Soave Superiore D.O.C. and Pinot Grigio delle Venezia I.G.T. and two red wines: Valpolicella D.O.C. and Merlot delle Venezia I.G.T. Produced by Pasqua in Verona.

Dinstlgut Loiben (Aus) a winery (400ha) based in the Wachau. (Add): Unterloiben 51, 3601 Dürnstein. Grape varieties: Blauer portugieser, Chardonnay, Grüner veltliner, Müller-Thurgau, Riesling, Zweigelt. Produces a range of dry and sweet (botrytised) wines.

Diod (Wal) a drink.

Diod Fain (Wal) a small beer.

Diod Feddwol (Wal) alcoholic drink, liquor.

Diod Gadarn (Wal) strong drink.

Diodi (Wal) to give a drink.

Diod Lemon (Wal) lemonade.

Diodlestr (Wal) tankard (beer).

Diognières [Les] (Fr) a vineyard in the A.C. Hermitage, northern Rhône.

Dionysia (Gre) ancient Greek festivals to the God Dionysos.

Dionysius (Gre) an alternative spelling of Dionysos.

D

Dionysos (Gre) an ancient Greek God of wine. *See also* Bacchus.

Dionysos Cocktail (Cktl) 25mls (⅕ gill) Metaxa brandy, 1 teaspoon honey. Shake well over ice, strain into a large liqueur glass and float 20mls (⅛ gill) cream on top.

Dionysus (Gre) an alternative spelling of Dionysos.

Diosig (Rum) a noted white wine-producing vineyard.

Diossido di Carbonio (It) carbon-dioxide.

Dioxymalic Acid (Eng) a wine acid formed due to the oxidation of tartaric acid.

Dioxytartaric Acid (Eng) a wine acid formed due to the oxidation of tartaric acid.

Di Palma (It) a partly organic 10ha. vineyard based in Rionero in Vulture, Basilicata region. Produces: D.O.C. Il Nibbio Grigio Aglianico del Vulture.

Diploma Beer (N.Z) a beer brewed by the Dominion Brewery.

Diplomat (Czec) a dark, hoppy, full, strong lager 18°. Brewed by Gambrinus in Pilsen.

Diplomat Cocktail (Cktl) 15mls (⅛ gill) each of pineapple syrup, Italian vermouth, French vermouth. Stir over ice, strain into a cocktail glass, serve with dash of lemon peel juice and a cherry.

Diplomate Cocktail (Cktl) 40mls (⅓ gill) French vermouth, 40mls (⅓ gill) Italian vermouth, 2 dashes maraschino. Stir over ice, strain into a cocktail glass, add a cherry and squeeze of lemon peel on top.

Dipoda (It) a sparkling natural spring mineral water. Mineral contents (milligrammes per litre): Sodium 33.04mg/l, Calcium 40.96mg/l, Magnesium 20.7mg/l, Potassium 3mg/l, Bicarbonates 224.48mg/l, Chlorides 37.88mg/l, Sulphates 23.7mg/l, Fluorides 0.46mg/l, Silicates 21.262mg/l. pH 7.3

Dipping Rod (Eng) an alternative name for a Dipstick.

Dipso (Eng) a slang expression to describe a person who is suffering from dipsomania.

Dipsomania (Eng) an uncontrollable craving for alcohol.

Dipsomaniac (Eng) a victim of dipsomania.

Dipstick (Eng) a thin calibrated rod dipped into a cask of ale through the spile hole to measure the contents. Also known as a Dipping rod.

Direct Distillation (USA) a method of producing flavoured spirits such as gin by putting the botanicals above the still so that the alcoholic vapours percolate through the botanicals extracting their flavour.

Direction Générale des Impôts (Fr) *abbr*: D.G.I. a group which maintains the control and marketing of wines.

Director's Bitter (Eng) a strong bitter 1046 O.G. brewed by Courage in Bristol.

Director's Blend (Eng) a brand of tea produced by Melroses (part of Kenco-Typhoo).

Director's Choice (USA) a dry red wine produced by the Golden Rain Tree Winery in Wadesville, Indiana.

Director's Live Ale (Eng) a 4.8% alc by vol. cask-conditioned ale brewed by Courage (sold in 50cls bottles).

Director's Winter Warmer (Eng) a 5.5% alc by vol. winter warmer from Scottish Courage. Available November and December at their Bristol Brewery.

Diren (Tur) a wine producer based at Tokat. Produces: Dorntal (dry white), Vadi (medium white), Karmen (dry red), Lokal (dry rosé).

Dirkzwager (Hol) a distillery noted for genever.

Dirler-Cadé (Fr) a winery (established 1871) based in Bergholz, Alsace. 20ha. Grape varieties include: Muscat, Riesling. Produces Grand Cru wines.

Dirmstein (Ger) village (Anb): Pfalz. (Ber): Mittelhaardt-Deutsche Weinstrasse. (Gro): Schwarzerde. (Vins): Herrgottsacker, Jesuitenhofgarten, Mandelpfad.

Dirty (Eng) a term applied to a wine that has an unpleasant off-smell or off-taste, usually due to poor vinification or bad bottling.

Dirty Dick's (Eng) a 4.1% alc by vol. ale brewed by Young's. Part of the Carlsberg-Tetley Tapster's Choice range.

Dirty Habit (Cktl) 1 measure Southern Comfort, 1 measure amaretto stirred over ice in an old-fashioned glass.

Dirty Socks (Eng) a wine tasting term used to describe a wine with a cheesy (and often sour) white wine.

Dirwest (Wal) abstinence (from alcohol).

Disa (S.Afr) the label for a range of wines produced by the Porterville Cellars winery, Swartland, Western Cape.

Disappointed Lady (Cktl) ½ measure crème de noyau, ½ measure Tia Maria, ½ measure brandy, ½ measure orange juice, dash egg white. Shake over ice, strain into a cocktail glass, add a dash of grenadine and a little grated nutmeg on top.

Disbor (Fr) a liqueur producing company based in Bordeaux. (Add): 17 Cours de Luze, Bordeaux. Produces a large range of liqueurs and eau-de-vie.

Disc [The] (Eng) the wine-taster's name for the meniscus.

Disciples Brew (Eng) a bitter ale brewed by Original Brewing Company in Hertfordshire.

Disco Dancer (Cktl) 2 parts Johnnie Walker Red Label, 2 parts peach brandy, 6 parts orange juice, dash Grenadine, dash egg white. Shake over ice, strain into a highball filled with ice and dress with a slice of orange.

Discovery (Eng) an 8.2% alc by vol. slightly carbonated cider from Symonds, Hereford. A cider *'nouveau'* (from the first press of the season).

Discovery (Eng) a light-coloured cask-conditioned ale 3.9% alc by vol. brewed by the Fullers Brewery, London (also a bottled version at 4.2% alc by vol).

Discovery (S.Afr) the label for a red (Pinotage 70% and Shiraz 30% blend) and white (Chenin blanc and Colombard blend) wines produced by the Spier winery, Stellenbosch, Western Cape.

Discovery Golden Ale (Eng) a 4.5% alc by vol. light

coloured golden ale brewed by Charles Wells, Bedford.

Disgorgement (Eng) *see* Dégorgement.

Disibodenberg (Ger) vineyard (Anb): Nahe. (Ber): Schloss Böckelheim. (Gro): Paradiesgarten. (Vil): Odernheim.

Dislaren (Ind) a natural spring mineral water (established 2001).

Disos (Gre) the name given to red and white wines produced from grapes grown in Greece by a Cheshire based company. Red: Moschofilero, Pavlos, Savatiano. White: Agiorgitiko, Mandilaria.

Dispore Kamma Boutique Winery (S.Afr) a winery (established 2002) based in Caledon, Western Cape. Grape varieties: Cabernet sauvignon, Merlot, Shiraz. Grapes also brought in.

Distell (S.Afr) formerly Distillers and SWF. (Add): P.O. Box 184, Stellenbosch 7599, West Cape. Vinified from the two corporate-owned wineries of Bergkelder and Adams Tas. Brands include: Autumn Harvest Crackling, Capenheimer, Cellar Cask, Château Libertas, Drostdy-Hof, 5th Avenue Cold Duck, Flat Roof Manor, Fleur du Cap, Graça, Grand Mousseux, Grûnberger, Hill & Dale, Kellerprinz, Kupferberger Auslese, Libertas, Monis, Oom Tas, Obikwa, Oracle, Overmeer, Sedgwick's, Ship Sherry, Table Mountain, Tassenberg, Taverna, Two Ocveans, Virginia, Zonnenbloem. Website: http://www.distell.co.za

Distill (USA) *see* Distillation.

Distillata (USA) a natural spring mineral water.

Distillate (Eng) the product of distillation.

Distillateur (Fr) distiller.

Distillation (Eng) the application of heat which extracts alcohol from fermented liquids. *See also* Jeber.

Distillation (Fr) distillation.

Distillato di Vennacia (It) is similar to Marc de Bourgogne.

Distilled Beverages (Eng)(USA) the name given to spirits which results in pure distillation of fermented beverages.

Distilled Gin (USA) a gin which has been flavoured by passing the vapours through the 'gin head' to extract the flavours. *see* Direct Distillation.

Distilled Water (Eng) water that has been boiled and the steam condensed into pure water. (Sp) = agua destilada.

Distiller (Fr) to distill.

Distilleria (It) distillery.

Distilleria Nardini (It) based in Vicenza, distills a range of grappas.

Distilleria Poli (It) a boutique distillery that specialises in a range of single varietal grappas.

Distillerie (Fr) distillery.

Distillerie Ambulante (Fr) a mobile distillery that looks similar to a steam tractor engine.

Distillerie Camel (It) producer of Fogolar (brandy and grappa).

Distillerie Carrère (Fr) an Armagnac producer. (Add): 36 Rue des Alliés, 32500 Fleurance.

Distillerie Chantal (Fr) a single distillery Bons Bois

Cognac produced by Cognac Louis Royer, B.P. 12, 16200 Jarnac.

Distillerie d'Aumagne (Fr) a single distillery Fins Bois Cognac produceed by Cognac Louis Royer, B.P. 12, 16200 Jarnac.

Distillerie de la Côte Basque (Fr) a distillery based in the Pyrénées. Produces Izarra.

Distillerie de la Métairie (Fr) a Cognac producer. (Add): Mazière Guimps, 16300 Barbezieux. 14ha. in the Petite Champagne.

Distillerie de l'Ecole (Fr) a single distillery Petite Champagne Cognac produced by Cognac Louis Royer, B.P. 12, 16200 Jarnac.

Distillerie des Moisans (Fr) Cognac producers. (Add): Les Moisans-Sireuil, 16440 Roullet Saint-Estèphe. 20ha. in the Grande Champagne and 40ha. in the Fins Bois. Produces a wide range of Cognacs.

Distillerie des Rhums Agricoles (W.Ind) *see* D.R.A.

Distillerie des Saules (Fr) a single distillery Borderies Cognac produced by Cognac Louis Royer, B.P. 12, 16200 Jarnac.

Distillerie du Peyrat (Fr) a Cognac distillery based in Houlette, Charente. (Add): Le Peyrat, 16200 Houlette. Produces fine Cognacs and Pineau des Charentes. 'E'mail: peyrat@wanadoo.fr

Distillerie Janot (Fr) a liqueur distillery. (Add): 13782 Aubagne-en-Provence. *see* La Sainte Baume.

Distillerie les Magnolias (Fr) a single distillery Grande Champagne Cognac produced by Cognac Louis Royer, B.P. 12, 16200 Jarnac.

Distillerie Montmorency Ltee (Can) a producer of a range of Canadian whiskies (a subsidiary of Seagram).

Distillerie Riunite (It) a liqueur producer based in Milan, noted for Galliano.

Distillerie Rougé Sumagne (Fr) a Cognac producer. (Add): 17770 Brizambourg. 56ha. in the Fins Bois. Produces wide range of Cognacs including V.S.O.P, Napoléon and X.O.

Distilleries Associées Belges (Bel) a distillery. (Add): Jumet, near Charleroi. Produces: Liqueur aux Fraises and Sève de Sapin.

Distillerie Stock (It) a large brandy producer. (Add): Distillerie Stock Sp.A. Trieste. Produces a V.S.O.P. oak-aged brandy.

Distillers Agency Limited (Scot) the export branch of D.C.L. based near Edinburgh. Has the licence for Rosebank and King George IV.

Distillers Company Limited (Scot) *abbr*: D.C.L. major whisky distillers. Owns many famous brand-names including: White Horse, VAT 69, Johnnie Walker, Haig. Taken over by Guinness in 1986.

Distillers Corporation (S.Afr) producers of Oude Meester liqueur brandy. *see* Oude Meester Group.

Distiller's Safe (Scot) *see* Whisky Safe.

Distinction (Port) the brand-name of a reserve Port produced by Croft.

Distinction Ale (Eng) a 5.1% alc by vol. ale produced by Bass.

Distinctive (Eng) a term to describe a wine that has a positive character.

D

Distinctive Drinks company [The] (Eng) a brewery and drinks manufacturer. (Add): The old Dairy, Broadfield Road, Sheffield, South Yorkshire S8 0XO. Produces lager beer and cocktail drinks. Website: http://www.distinctivedrinks.com 'E'mail: nicky@distinctivedrinks.com

Distingué (Fr) a term used to denotes a fine wine that has finesse and quality.

Distinguished (Eng) a term used by the wine experts to describe the most distinguished wines. Used only for the finest wines of superb quality.

Districtus Austriae Controllatus (Aus) abbr: DAC a new control system developed in the Weinviertel region and applied to unoaked, dry Grüner veltliner wines. Each wine has to undergo a rigid blind tasting to ensure it reaches the required standards of the DAC.

Ditchingham Ale (Eng) a cask-conditioned ale from Marston's Head Brewer's Choice.

Ditchling Vineyard (Eng) a vineyard (established 1979). (Add): Claycroft, Beacon Road, Ditchling, Sussex. 3ha. Grape varieties: Müller-Thurgau, Ortega and Reichensteiner.

Dittelsheim-Hessloch (Ger) village (Anb): Rheinhessen. (Ber): Wonnegau. (Gro): Pilgerpfad. (Vins): Edle Weingärten, Geiersberg, Kloppberg, Leckerberg, Liebfrauenberg, Mönchhube, Mondschien, Pfaffenmütze.

Dividend (USA) the part of the cocktail after it has been poured out that is left in the shaker or jug.

Divine (Eng) a 9.6% alc by vol. bottle-conditioned winter ale brewed by Ballard's Brewery, Nyewood Petersfield, Hampshire.

Divine (Eng) a range of bottled, crushed-fruit juices (apricot, banana, blackcurrant and mango) produced by the Divine Drinks Company.

Divining Rod (Eng) a rod, usually a forked hazel twig which is used to find water underground. Is said to dip when held over any water. Also known as a Dowsing Rod.

Dixie (Cktl) 1 measure dry gin, ½ measure dry vermouth, juice ¼ orange, ¼ measure absinthe. Shake over ice and strain into a cocktail glass.

Dixie Brewery (USA) a brewery based in New Orleans that produces a beer of the same name.

Dixie Julep (Cktl) 40mls (⅓ gill) Bourbon whiskey, 1 teaspoon powdered sugar. Place into an ice-filled collins glass and stir until frosted on the outside, dress with mint sprigs and serve with straws.

Dixie Whiskey (Cktl) 25mls (⅙ gill) Bourbon whiskey, 2 dashes crème de menthe (white), 2 dashes Curaçao (white), 1 dash Angostura, dash gomme syrup, shake over ice and strain into cocktail glass.

Dixon (Port) vintage Port shippers. Vintages: 1884, 1887, 1890.

Dizy (Fr) a Premier Cru Champagne village in the Canton d'Aÿ. District: Reims.

Dizzy Blonde (Eng) a 4.5% alc by vol. ale brewed by the Glentworth Brewery, South Yorkshire.

Djakoro (Cro) a northern wine-producing town in Croatia.

Djaousse (Rus) a white grape variety grown in Tadzhikistania. Used to produce dessert wines.

Djemsheed [Shah] (M.East) the old Persian (Iran) version of who first discovered wine.

Djeudyjelÿa (Ser) a noted wine-producing area in Macedonia.

Djimma (Afr) an important coffee-producing region of Ethiopia.

Djougue (Ch.Isles) pitcher/jug. See also Ecueul.

D'la Bièthe Gengivre (Ch.Isles) ginger beer.

D'Lemonade (Ch.Isles) fresh lemonade.

D.L.G. (Ger) abbr: Deutsche Landwirtschaft Gesellschaft, the German agricultural society.

Dlugopolanka (Pol) a natural spring mineral water from Dlugopole, Zdroj. Mineral contents (milligrammes per litre): Sodium 13.5mg/l, Calcium 93.6mg/l, Magnesium 36.3mg/l, Potassium 6.5mg/l.

D'Montana (Mal) a still natural spring mineral water from Lenggeng. Mineral contents (milligrammes per litre): Sodium 4mg/l, Calcium 29mg/l, Magnesium 1mg/l, Potassium 2mg/l, Bicarbonates 46mg/l, Chlorides 10mg/l, Sulphates 1mg/l, Fluorides <1mg/l. pH 7.4

DNA (Austr) a 5% alc by vol. spring water spritzer from Herres, a naturally fermented wine base with lime and thyme flavouring.

D'N'B Stinger (Eng) pre-mixed bottled alcoholic drink containing dandelion and burdock. Produced by the Federation Brewery, Lancaster Road, Dunston Indust. Estate, Newcastle, Tyne and Wear.

Dniepropetrovsk (Ukr) a wine-producing centre on the river Dnieper in the Ukraine.

D'n Schele Os (Hol) a 7.5% alc by vol. unfiltered, unpasteurised, bottle-conditioned triple beer brewed by Maasland Brouwerij, Oss.

D.O. (Sp) abbr: Denominación de Origen.

Dobbelen Bruinen (Bel) a double-brown ale brewed by the Roman Brasserie in Mater near Oudenaarde.

Dobber (Eng) a 6.5% alc by vol. winter warmer brewed by Marble Brewery, Manchester.

Doble Pasto (Sp) a red wine, high in alcohol, fermented on two lots of lees. The wine is usually sold for blending with thin, weak wines. Produced in central and southern Spain, especially in Alicante and Utiel-Requena. Often exported to eastern Europe.

Döbling (Aus) a noted vineyard area in the Wien region (has rich chalk soil).

Dobo [Captain Istvan] (Hun) circa 1552 leader of the Magyar defenders of Eger. Bull's Blood was named after the red wine his troops were seen drinking.

Dobra Voda (Czec) a still natural spring mineral water from Hrady. Mineral contents (milligrammes per litre): Sodium 9mg/l, Calcium 6.6mg/l, Magnesium 10mg/l, Potassium 10.6mg/l, Bicarbonates 109.9mg/l, Chlorides 2.8mg/l, Sulphates 4.8mg/l, Fluorides 0.7mg/l, Nitrates 0.1mg/l.

D

Dobrawa (Pol) a natural spring mineral water. Mineral contents (milligrammes per litre): Sodium 1.25mg/l, Calcium 55.2mg/l, Magnesium 29.6mg/l, Potassium 0.85mg/l, Bicarbonates 286.8mg/l, Chlorides 5.32mg/l, Sulphates 20mg/l, Fluorides 0.1mg/l.

Dobricic (Cro) a local red grape variety.

D'Obrion (Fr) the ancient spelling of Château Haut-Brion in the Graves, Bordeaux. *See also* Daubrion.

Dobruska Brewery (Czec) a brewery based in northern Czec.

Dob's Best Bitter (Eng) a 4.1% alc by vol. bitter ale brewed by the Exe Valley Brewery, Silverton, Devon.

D.O.C. (It) *abbr:* **D**enominazione di **O**rigine **C**ontrollata. Also as DOC.

D.O.C. (Port) *abbr:* **D**enominacao de **O**rigem **C**ontrolada. Also as DOC.

D.O.Ca (Sp) *abbr:* **D**enominación de **O**rigen **Ca**lificada. Also as DOCa.

Doçar (Port) a red grape variety grown in Monçao (a sub-region of the Vinhos Verdes).

Doce (Port) sweet.

D.O.C.G. (It) *abbr:* **D**enominazione di **O**rigine **C**ontrollata e **G**arantita. Also as DOCG.

Dock Glass (Eng) a glass used for drinking Port in the nineteenth century.

Dock Street Bohemian Pilsner (USA) a 5.3% alc by vol. bottled pilsner brewed by the Dock Street Brewing C°. in Bala Cynwyd, Philadelphia.

Dock Street Brewing C°. (USA) a brewery (established 1986) based in Bala Cynwyd, Philadelphia. Brews: Dock Street Bohemian Pilsner, Dock Street Illuminator.

Dock Street Illuminator (USA) a 7.5% alc by vol. bottom-fermented, bottled double bock beer brewed by the Dock Street Brewing C°. in Bala Cynwyd, Philadelphia.

Docktor (Ger) *see* Doctor and Bernkasteler Docktor.

Docteur Peste (Fr) a vineyard based in the commune of the A.C. Corton in the Côte de Beaune, Burgundy (owned by the Hospices de Beaune 1ha). Corton Bressandes, 0.5ha. Clos du Roi, 0.4ha. Fiètre, 0.1ha. Les Grèves, 1ha. Les Chaumes and 1ha. Voirosses.

Doctor (Ger) vineyard (Anb): Mosel-Saar-Ruwer. (Ber): Bernkastel. (Gro): Badstube. (Vil): Bernkastel-Kues.

Doctor Gullys Winter Ale (Eng) a 5.2% alc by vol. winter ale brewed by the Malvern Hills Brewery, Worcestershire.

Doctor Pepper (USA) *see* Dr. Pepper.

Doctor's Cocktail (Cktl) 20mls (⅛ gill) each of lemon juice, orange juice, Swedish Punsch. Shake over ice and strain into a cocktail glass.

Doctor's Orders Best Bitter (Eng) a 5% alc by vol. bitter ale brewed by the Fenland Brewery, Chatterais, Cambridgeshire.

Dodecanese Islands (Gre) a group of islands of which Rhodes is the chief wine producer in south-eastern Greece near the Turkish coast.

Dodoma (Afr) a region in Tanzania that produces full-bodied red wines, especially noted are those from the Holy Ghost Fathers.

Doeppel Kümmel (Ger) high strength kümmel.

Doerflinger Wine Cellars (USA) a winery based in Bloomsburg, Central Pennsylvania.

Dog (Eng) a slang name used locally in Newcastle for Newcastle Brown Ale.

Doga (It) a cask stave.

Dog and Parrot (Eng) a public house in Newcastle-on-Tyne which brews its own beer (owned by Whitbread). Produces a cask-conditioned Scotswood Ale 1036 O.G. and Wallop 1046 O.G.

Dogbolter (Eng) a 5.6% alc by vol. ale brewed by Felon & Firkin, Great George Street, Leeds, West Yorkshire.

Dogbolter Ale (Austr) originally a heavily hopped pale ale matured in local oak casks. 5.2% alc by vol. Brewed by the Matilda Bay Brewing C°. Ltd., Freemantle. Style now changed to a Special Dark Lager.

Dog Bolter Ale (Eng) a cask-conditioned ale 1060 O.G. brewed by the Ferret and Firkin home-brew public house in London.

Dogh (Afg) a refreshing mint and yoghurt drink.

Dog House Brewery [The] (Eng) a brewery (established 2001). (Add): Scorrier, Redruth, Cornwall TR16 5BN. Brews: Bitter 4% alc by vol., Bow Wow 5% alc by vol., Cornish Corgi 4.5% alc by vol., Dozy Dawg 4.4% alc by vol., Retriever 3.9% alc by vol., Snoozy Suzy 4.3% alc by vol. 'E'mail: starhawk@dsl.pipex.com

Dog's Bollocks (Eng) a 6.5% alc by vol. bottled ale from Wychwood Brewery, Eagle Maltings, Witney, Oxfordshire.

Dog's Nose (Eng) a glass of beer with a dash of gin in it, an old naval drink.

Dog Water (USA) a natural spring mineral water.

Do Hospital [El] (Port) a commune in the Dão region.

Dojon (Fr) an almond and Cognac flavoured liqueur produced by Serres in Toulouse.

Doktor (Ger) vineyard (Anb): Rheinhessen. (Ber): Nierstein. (Gro): Gutes Domtal. (Vil): Dexheim.

Doktor (Ger) vineyard (Anb): Pfalz. (Ber): Südliche Weinstrasse. (Gro): Trappenberg. (Vil): Venningen.

Doktorberg (Ger) vineyard (Anb): Mosel-Saar-Ruwer. (Ber): Saar-Ruwer. (Gro): Romerlay. (Vil): Waldrach.

Doktorgarten (Ger) vineyard (Anb): Baden. (Ber): Kaiserstuhl-Tuniberg. (Gro): Vulkanfelsen. (Vil): Ihringen (ortsteil Blankenhornsberg).

Dökülgen (Tur) a red grape variety grown in southern Turkey.

Dolamore Ltd (Eng) a college wine merchant that has branches in Oxford (1) and Cambridge (2). Also a shop in Craven Road, London W2.

Dolce (It) very sweet.

Dolceacqua (It) lit: 'sweet water', a red wine from Ligurian region, made from the Dolcetto, Rossese and Vermentino grapes. Also gives its name to wines. *see* Rossese di Dolceacqua.

Dolce Amaro (It) a wine apéritif with a bitter-sweet

almond taste 10.5% alc by vol. made from old family recipes of D'Elia family in Naples.

Dolce Grande Giorgio (It) a sweet white wine fermented in acacia wood casks by the Cantina Beato Bartolomeo co-operative, Breganze, Veneto.

Dolce Naturale (It) naturally sweet wine.

Dolcetto (It) a red grape variety.

Dolcetto (It) a D.O.C. red wine from the Piemonte region. Named after the grape variety.

Dolcetto d'Acqui (It) a D.O.C. red wine from Piemonte. Made in the commune of Acqui Terme from the Dolcetto grape. If 12.5% alc by vol. and aged for at least 1 year then classed Superiore.

Dolcetto d'Alba (It) a D.O.C. red wine from Piemonte. Made in the communes of Alba and Barolo and 23 others in province of Cuneo from the Dolcetto grape. If 12.5% alc by vol. and aged for 1 year then classed Superiore.

Dolcetto d'Asti (It) a D.O.C. red wine from Piemonte in the commune of Asti. Made from the Dolcetto grape. If 12.5% alc by vol. and aged 1 year then classed Superiore.

Dolcetto delle Langhe Monregalesi (It) a D.O.C. red wine from Piemonte. Made from the Dolcetto grape. If 12.5% alc by vol. and aged for 1 year then classed Superiore.

Dolcetto di Diano d'Alba (It) a D.O.C. red wine from Piemonte. Made from the Dolcetto grape. If 12.5% alc by vol. and aged for minimum 1 year then classed Superiore.

Dolcetto di Dogliani (It) a D.O.C. red wine from Piemonte. Made from the Dolcetto grape. If 12.5% alc by vol. and aged for 1 year or more then classed Superiore.

Dolcetto di Ovado (It) a D.O.C. red wine from Piemonte. Made from the Dolcetto grape. If 12.5% alc by vol. and aged for minimum 1 year then classed Superiore.

Dôle (Switz) a red wine made from the Pinot noir and Gamay grape varieties. Light and soft it is produced in the Valais region.

Dolfi (Fr) a famous eau-de-vie liqueur producer.

Dolgesheim (Ger) village (Anb): Rheinhessen. (Ber): Nierstein. (Gro): Krötenbrunnen. (Vins): Kreuzberg, Schützenhütte.

Dolia (Lat) the name given to ancient fermenting jars.

Dolias (Gre) an ancient greek container lined with pitch to store and carry wines.

Dolin (Fr) a company in the Haut-Savoie, that produces dry, aromatic apéritif wines. e.g. Chambéry and Chambéryzette.

D'Oliveiras (Mad) a Funchal-based Madeira shipper.

Dolle [Peter] (Aus) a winery based in the Kamptal region. (Add): Herrengasse 2, 3491 Strass. Grape varieties: Cabernet sauvignon, Grüner veltliner, Pinot blanc, Pinot noir, Riesling, Zweigelt. Label: Cuvée Année.

Dolomiti (It) a still natural spring mineral water from Valli del Pasubio. Mineral contents (milligrammes per litre): Sodium 1.3mg/l, Calcium 23.8mg/l, Magnesium 8.7mg/l, Potassium 0.7mg/l, Bicarbonates 94.6mg/l, Chlorides 1.1mg/l, Sulphates 22mg/l, Nitrates 3.4mg/l, Silicates 7.3mg/l. pH 8.18

Dolores Cocktail (Cktl) ⅓ measure Spanish brandy, ⅓ measure cherry brandy, ⅓ measure crème de cacao, shake over ice, strain into a cocktail glass and top with a cherry.

Dolphi (Fr) a fruit liqueur producer based in Strasbourg, Alsace.

Dolphin Bay (S.Afr) the label for a range of wines produced by the Cru Wines marketing company, Western Cape.

Dolphin Bitter (Eng) a cask-conditioned bitter 1038 O.G. brewed by the Poole Brewery in Dorset.

Dolphin Brewery (Eng) a brewery (established 2000). (Add): 48 St. Michaels Street, Shrewsbury, Shropshire SY1 2EZ. Brews a variety of beers and stout. Website: http://www.thedolphinbrewery.co.uk 'E'mail: brewers@thedolphinbrewery.co.uk

Doluca (Tur) a large private winery that produces a variety of wines from local and French grape varieties. Website: http://www.doluca.com

D.O.M. (Fr).abbr: **D**eo **O**ptimo **M**aximo, on the Bénédictine liqueur label means 'To God, most good, most great'.

Domain Durban (Fr) a noted producer of A.C. Muscat de'Beaumes de Venise in the Côtes du Rhône-Villages, south-eastern France.

Domaine (Fr) a privately owned vineyard, estate, field.

Domaine (S.Afr) the label for a red wine (Cabernet sauvignon and Carignan blend) produced by the Goede Hope Estate winery, Stellenbosch, Western Cape.

Domaine A (Austr) a winery based in Heathcote, Victoria. Label: Lady A (Fume blanc).

Domaine Abelanet (Fr) a vineyard in the A.C. Fitou, south-western France.

Domaine A.F. Gros (Fr) a vineyard in the Grand Cru A.C. Richbourg. (Add): A.F. Gros, Pommard, Côte d'Or. Website: http://www.af-gros.com

Domaine Alain Gautheron (Fr) a winery based in the A.C. Chablis, Burgundy. Produces a range of Chablis wines including Premier Cru Les Fourneaux.

Domaine Alary (Fr) a vineyard in the Côtes-du-Rhône-Villages Cairanne, Cairanne, south-eastern France. Grape varieties: Counoise, Grenache and Syrah. Labels: La Font d'Estévenas, La Jean de Verde.

Domaine Alfred (USA) a winery based in the Edna Valley, San Luis Obispo County, California. Grape variety: Pinot noir. Label: Chamisal Vineyards.

Domaine Allée-de-Lescours (Fr) a vineyard in the A.C. Saint-Émilion, Bordeaux 4ha.

Domaine Amouroux (Fr) a négociant producing Châteauneuf-du-Pape. (Add): Ave. St. Joseph, 84230 Châteauneuf-du-Pape, southern Rhône. Other label is Sang des Pierres (Le).

Domaine André Brunel (Fr) a producer of Châteauneuf-du-Pape based at 6 Chemin du Bois, Laville, 84230 Châteauneuf-du-Pape, southern Rhône.

D

Domaine Andron (Fr) a vineyard. (Com): St-Selve. A.C. Graves, Bordeaux. 3ha (white).

Domaine Aonghusa (Fr) a vineyard in the A.C. Corbières, south-western France. Label: Laval.

Domaine Arretxea (Fr) a vineyard in the A.C. Irouléguy, south-western France.

Domaine Arzac (Fr) a vineyard. (Com): St-Selve. A.C. Graves, Bordeaux. 2ha (white).

Domaine Aucoeur (Fr) a winery based in the A.C. Beaujolais Cru Morgon, southern Burgundy. Label: Cuvée Prestige.

Domaine Auther (Fr) a noted A.C. vineyard based in Alsace. (Add): 4, Route du Vin, 67650 Blienshwiller. Grape variety: Riesling.

Domaine Bacchus (Fr) a 'minature' Champagne museum open 1st April–30th October. (Add); 4, Rue Bacchus, 51480 l'Echelle Reuil. Website: http://www.Domaine-Bacchus.com 'E'mail: info@domaine-bacchus.com

Domaine Bachelier (Fr) a winery based in the A.C. Chablis, Burgundy. Produces a range of Chablis wines including Premier Cru Les Fourneaux.

Domaine Baillat (Fr) a vineyard in the A.C. Corbières, south-western France. Label: Cuvée Emilien Baillat.

Domaine Balland-Chapuis (Fr) a vineyard in the A.C. Sancerre, Central Vineyards. (Add): 18300 Bué-en-Sancerre, Cher, France. Grape variety: Sauvignon blanc, Pinot noir. 'E'mail: info@balland-chapuis.com

Domaine Balloquet (Fr) a winery based in the A.C. Beaujolais Cru Brouilly, southern Burgundy (owned by Louis Jadot).

Domaine Barat (Fr) a winery based in the A.C. Chablis, Burgundy. Produces a range of Chablis wines including Premier Crus Côte de Lêchet and Vaillons.

Domaine Baratin (Fr) a winery based in the A.C. Beaujolais Cru Brouilly, southern Burgundy.

Domaine Basse Ville (Fr) an A.C. Muscadet Sèvre et Maine from La Chapelle-Heulin, Nantais, Loire 22ha.

Domaine Bastide Blanche (Fr) an A.C. wine from the Côtes-de-Provence, south-eastern France.

Domaine Beaumont (Fr) a winery based in the A.C. Lirac, southern Rhône. (Add): Chemin de la Filature, 30126 Lirac. Also produces A.C. Tavel rosé.

Domaine Belegarde (Fr) a vineyard in the AC. Jurançon south-western France.

Domaine Bellevue (Fr) a vineyard. (Com): Toulenne. A.C. Graves, Bordeaux. 1ha (white).

Domaine Belles Eaux (Fr) a label for a series of wines (Pays de Caux) produced by Château Belles Eaux, Coteaux du Languedoc.

Domaine Beringer Blass (USA) a new 'super' estate which includes the properties of Beringer Vineyards, Château St.Jean, Château Souverain, Meridian and Mildara Blass.

Domaine Bernard Defaix (Fr) a winery based in the A.C. Chablis, Burgundy. Produces a range of Chablis wines including Premier Crus Côte de Lêchet and Les Vaillons.

Domaine Bernard Robert (Fr) a Champagne producer. (Add): Rue de l'Orme, 10200 Voigny. Produces non-vintage Champagnes. Label: Le Creizot.

Domaine Berrod (Fr) a winery based in the A.C. Beaujolais Cru Moulin-à-Vent, southern Burgundy.

Domaine Berthet-Rayne (Fr) producer of Châteauneuf-du-Pape based at Rte. de Roquemaure, 84350 Courthézon, southern Rhône.

Domaine Berthoumieu (Fr) a winery based in the A.C. Madiran, south-western France. Also produces A.C. Pacherenc-de-Vic-Bilh.

Domaine Besson (Fr) a winery based in the A.C. Chablis, Burgundy. Produces a range of Chablis wines including Premier Crus Montmains and Vaillons.

Domaine Billaud-Simon (Fr) a winery based in the A.C. Chablis, Burgundy. Produces a range of Chablis wines including Premiers Cru Montée de Tonnerre and Vaillons. Website: http://www.billaud-simon.com

Domaine Boingnères (Fr) Armagnac producers. (Add): M. et Mme. Léon Lafitte, Le Freche, 40190 Villeneuve de Marsan 19ha.

Domaine Bois de Boursan (Fr) the label of red and white Châteauneuf-du-Pape wines produced by Versino, Quartier Saint Pierre, 84230 Châteauneuf-du-Pape, southern Rhône.

Domaine Bonnardot [Jean Roger] (Fr) a vineyard (19ha) based in Villiers La Fay, Côtes de Nuits, Burgundy. (Add): Rue de l'Ancienne Cure, 21700 Villiers La Faye. Grape variety: Pinot noir.

Domaine Bonneau de Martray (Fr) a producer of A.C. Corton and Corton-Charlemagne in the Côte de Beaune, Burgundy.

Domaine Bonneteau-Guesselin (Fr) an A.C. Muscadet Sèvre et Maine from La Haye-Fouassière, Nantais, Loire 20ha.

Domaine Borie de Maurel (Fr) a vineyard in the A.C. Minervois and A.C. Minervois la Livinière, Languedoc-Roussillon. Produces Espirit d'Automne, Rêve de Carignan and La Féline. Grape varieties: Carignan, Grenache and Syrah.

Domaine Bosquets des Papes (Fr) the label of red or white Châteauneuf-du-Pape wines produced by Boiron (Maurice), Rte. d'Orange, 84230 Châteauneuf-du-Pape, southern Rhône.

Domaine Bottled (Fr) lit: 'bottled in the vineyard's cellars', the Burgundy equivalent of the Bordeaux Château bottled.

Domaine Bouvachon-Nominé (Fr) an A.C. red Châteauneuf-du-Pape produced in Orange, southern Rhône.

Domaine Boyar (Bul) a company that represents 4 Bulgarian wineries: Suhindol, Preslav, Burgas, Stara Zagora in U.K. Range includes Premium Oak, Premium Cuvée, Premium Reserve, Solitaire.

Domaine Brahms Wineries (S.Afr) a winery (established 1998) based in Windmeul, Paarl, Western Cape. 15ha. Grape varieties: Cabernet sauvignon, Chenin blanc, Merlot, Pinotage, Ruby cabernet, Shiraz. Labels: Judex Provisional Judgement, Quartet.

Domaine Brana (Fr) a vineyard in the A.C. Irouléguy, south-western France.

Domaine Bru-Baché (Fr) a vineyard in the A.C. Jurançon. Label: Cuvée des Casterasses.

Domaine Bruno Cormerais (Fr) a noted producer of A.C. Muscadet Sèvre et Maine. (Add): La Chambaudière, 44190 Saint-Lumine-de-Clisson, Pays-Nantais, Loire. 14ha. Produces: Cuvée des Chefs (Haute Expression Granit) 1995, Granite de Clisson. *See also* Domaine de la Chambaudière.

Domaine Brusset (Fr) a winery based in Cairanne A.C. Côtes-du-Rhône-Villages. Grape varieties include: Grenache, Syrah. Labels: Coteaux des Travers, Vendange Chabrille. Website: http://www.domainebrusset.fr

Domaine Caillol (Fr) a vineyard in the A.C. Cassis. Côtes-de-Provence, south-eastern France.

Domaine Caillou Rouley (Fr) a vineyard. (Com): Podensac. A.C. Cérons, Bordeaux. 8ha.

Domaine Calot (Fr) a winery based in the A.C. Beaujolais Cru Morgon, southern Burgundy. Label: Tête de Cuvée.

Domaine Calvel (Fr) a vineyard in the A.C. Corbières, south-western France.

Domaine Capion (Fr) a vineyard based in the Vin de Pays de l'Heurault. (Add): 34150 Capion. Grape varieties include: Chardonnay. Label: Le Sorbier.

Domaine Capmartin (Fr) a vineyard in the A.C. Pacherenc-de-Vic-Bilh, south-western France.

Domaine Carmantran (Fr) a vineyard in the A.C. Côtes du Fronton.

Domaine Carneros (Fr) a vineyard owed by Taittinger that produces sparkling wines.

Domaine Carneros (USA) a winery based in Carneros, northern California. Grape variety: Pinot noir. Label: Avante Garde, The Famous Gate.

Domaine Carras Grande Reserve (Gre) a red wine produced by Domaine Porto Carras from Cabernet sauvignon, Cabernet franc and Limnio grapes.

Domaine Carras Limnio (Gre) a red wine produced by Domaine Porto Carras from Limnio and Cabernet sauvignon grapes.

Domaine Carré-Courbin (Fr) a winery based in the A.C. Beaune, Côte de Beaune, Burgundy.

Domaine Carros (Fr) a vineyard. (Com): St-Selve. A.C. Graves, Bordeaux. 2ha (white).

Domaine Castelnaud (Fr) a vineyard. (Com): St-Pierre-de-Mons. A.C. Graves, Bordeaux. 2ha (white).

Domaine Castera (Fr) a vineyard in the A.C. Jurançon, south-western France. Grape variety: Petit manseng. Label: Cuvée Privilège.

Domaine Catherine le Gœuil (Fr) a winery based in the A.C. Côtes-du-Rhône-Villages Cairanne Vaucluse. Labels: Cuvée Léa Felsch, Cuvée Marie Rouvière.

Domaine Cauhapé (Fr) a vineyard in the A.C. Jurançon, south-western France. Label: Chante des Vignes, Symphonie de Novembre, Ballet d'Octobre.

Domaine Cazal (Fr) a vineyard in the A.C. Minervois, Languedoc-Roussillon. Grape varieties: Carignan, Grenache, Mourvèdre and Syrah. Label: Cuvée le Pas de Zarat.

Domaine Cazal-Viet (Fr) a Vin de Pays winery based in the Pays d'Oc. Grape varieties include: Viognier.

Domaine Chagnoleau (Fr) a vineyard (14ha) and Cognac distillery based in Le Gua, Charente. (Add): 52, Rue Croix de Châlons, 17600 Le Gua. Grape varieties: Cabernet, Colombard, Merlot, Ugni blanc. Produces a range of Cognacs, Pineau des Charentes and Vin de Pays Charentais.

Domaine Chamfort (Fr) a winery based in the A.C. Côtes-du-Rhône-Villages Sablet, Vaucluse.

Domaine Chandon (USA) a winery at One California Drive, Yountville, Napa Valley, (also in Carneros) California, belonging to Möet et Chandon of France. Produces sparkling wines from Chardonnay, Pinot blanc, Pinot meunier and Pinot noir grapes by the méthode traditionelle. Range includes Blanc de noirs, Domaine Chandon Étoile (a blend of 1984 and 1986). Also produces: Ramel Road Reserve.

Domaine Chandon (Austr) a vineyard (established 1985) based at Green Point, Maroondah Highway, Coldstream, Yarra valley. Produces a range of still and sparkling wines from Chardonnay and Pinot noir grapes. Labels include: Z*D. Website: http://www.greenpointwines.com

Domaine Chante-Alouette-Cormeil (Fr) a winery. (Add): Château Gueyrosse, Libourne 33500. Grand Cru. A.C. Saint-Émilion. Commune: Saint-Émilion. 18ha. Grape varieties: Cabernet franc 20%, Cabernet sauvignon 20% and Merlot 60%.

Domaine Chante Cigale (Fr) a vineyard producing red and white A.C. Châteauneuf-du-Pape in the southern Rhône. Owned by Sabon (Favier), Ave. Louis Pasteur, 84230 Châteauneuf-du-Pape, southern Rhône.

Domaine Chante Perdrix (Fr) a Châteauneuf-du-Pape produced by Nicolet Frères, 84230 Châteauneuf-du-Pape, southern Rhône.

Domaine Chapoton (Fr) a winery based in the A.C. Côtes-du-Rhône-Villages Rochegude, Vaucluse.

Domaine Charbay (USA) a winery based in the Napa Valley, California. Grape varieties: Cabernet franc, Cabernet sauvignon. Also produces brandy.

Domaine Charpentier (Fr) an A.C. Muscadet Sèvre et Maine from Le Louroux-Bottereau, Nantais, Loire 17ha.

Domaine Château Lichten (Switz) a Loèche Ville vineyard that produces Valais-style wines.

Domaine Chaume-Arnaud (Fr) a winery based in the A.C. Côtes-du-Rhône-Villages Vinsobres, Vaucluse. Label: La Cadène.

Domaine Chevalier Métrat (Fr) a winery based in the A.C. Beaujolais Cru Morgon, southern Burgundy.

Domaine Chevrot (Fr) a vineyard in the A.C. Marenges, Bordeaux. (Add): 71150 Cheilly-les-Maranges. Website: http://www.chevrot.fr

Domaine Chiron (Fr) an A.C. Muscadet Sèvre et Maine from Mouzillon, Nantais, Loire 16ha.

Domaine Christian Moreau Père et Fils (Fr) a

winery based in the A.C. Chablis, Burgundy. Produces a range of Chablis wines including Premier Cru Vaillon.

Domaine Christian Perrin (Fr) a vineyard (10ha) based in Ladoix Serrigny, Burgundy. (Add): 14, Avenue de Corton, 21550 Ladoix Serrigny. Grape variety: Pinot noir. Produces a range of Burgundies including A.C. Ladoix 'Les Briquottes', Premier Crus Ladoix, 'Les Gréchone et Foutrières', Les Joyeuses' and A.C. Premier Cru Aloxe-Corton 'Les Boutières'. 'E'mail: domaineperrinchristian@club-internet.fr

Domaine Clair-Daü (Fr) a large estate in the Côte d'Or of which 27ha. is in the commune of Marsannay. Produces the famous Rosé de Marsannay.

Domaine Clavel (Fr) a winery based in the A.C. Côtes-du-Rhône-Villages St-Gervais, Vaucluse. (Add): 38200 St-Gervais. Label: Signature. Website: http://www.domaineclavel.com 'E'mail: clavel@domaineclavel.com

Domaine Colombier (Fr) a winery based in the A.C. Crozes-Hermitage, Northern Rhône. Label: Cuvée Gaby.

Domaine Comte Georges de Vogüé (Fr) a famous wine-producer based in the commune of Chambolle-Musigny who owns part of the vineyards of Musigny (7.2ha.) and others 12.ha. in total (2.7ha. Bonnes-Mares/0.56ha. Chambolle-Musigny 'Les Amoureuses'/0.34ha. Chambolle-Musigny 'Les Baudes and Les Fuées'/1.8ha. Chambole-Musigny).

Domaine Condorcet (Fr) the label of a Châteauneuf-du-Pape produced by Bouche-Audibert in Châteauneuf-du-Pape, southern Rhône.

Domaine Constant (Fr) a vineyard in the A.C. Bergerac.

Domaine Cosse (Fr) a vineyard. (Com): Fargues. A.C. Sauternes, Bordeaux 6ha.

Domaine Coteau (USA) a winery based in the Yamhill County, Oregon. Grape variety: Pinot noir.

Domaine Croix-de-Grézard (Fr) a vineyard. (Com): Lussac-Saint-Émilion. A.C. Saint-Émilion, Bordeaux 2ha.

Domaine Cullilleon (Fr) a vineyard in the A.C. Saint-Joseph, northern Rhône. Grape variety: Syrah. Label: Les Pierres Sêches.

Domaine d'Ahera (Cyp) the name given to a light, red wine produced by the Keo Cº. in Limassol.

Domaine Damanieu (Fr) a vineyard. (Com): Sainte-Croix-du-Mont. A.C. Sainte-Croix-du-Mont, Bordeaux 3ha.

Domaine Dampt (Fr) a vineyard in the A.C. Chablis, Burgundy. (Add): 89700 Collan.

Domaine Danielle Laurent Soléna (USA) a winery based in the Willamette Valley, Oregon. Grape variety: Pinot noir.

Domaine Daniel Magnien (Fr) a vineyard based in Saint-Sernin-du-Plain, Côtes de Chouchois. Produces A.C. Bourgogne-Côtes-du-Couchois. Grape variety: Pinot noir.

Domaine d'Arriailh (Fr) a vineyard. (Com): Montagne-Saint-Émilion. A.C. Saint-Émilion, Bordeaux 4ha.

Domaine d'Artois (Fr) a vineyard in the A.C. Amboise Touraine-Mesland, Loire. A red wine produced from the Gamay grape. (Add): 7 Quai des Violettes, Amboise, Touraine.

Domaine de Augiers (Fr) a vineyard. (Com): Comps. A.C. Côtes de Bourg, Bordeaux.

Domaine d'Aupilhac (Fr) 23ha. vineyard in Montpeyroux. A.C. Terrasses du Lazerac, Coteaux du Languedoc-Montpeyroux. Grape varieties: Mourvèdre, Syrah, Carignan, Grenache. Also produces Vin de Pays du Mont Baudile from 100% aged Carignan.

Domaine de Baban (Fr) an A.C. Châteauneuf-du-Pape produced by Riché (Claude), 27 Ave. Général de Gaulle, 84230 Châteauneuf-du-Pape, southern Rhône. Other label is Domaine Riché.

Domaine de Bablut (Fr) a vineyard in Brissac in the A.C. Anjou, Anjou-Saumur, Loire.

Domaine de Bachellary (Fr) a Vin de Pays d'Oc produced near Béziers, Montpellier from 50% Merlot, 50% Syrah. Oak aged for 4 months.

Domaine de Badon-Patarbet (Fr) a vineyard in the A.C. Saint-Émilion, Bordeaux 2ha.

Domaine de Bardoulet (Fr) a vineyard in the A.C. Saint-Émilion, Bordeaux 3ha.

Domaine de Barraud (Fr) a vineyard. (Com): Montagne-Saint-Émilion. A.C. Saint-Émilion, Bordeaux 4ha.

Domaine de Bayard (Fr) a vineyard. (Com): Montagne-Saint-Émilion. A.C. Saint-Émilion, Bordeaux 8ha.

Domaine de Beauregard (Fr) an A.C. Muscadet Sèvre et Maine from Mouzillon, Loire 19ha.

Domaine de Beaurenard (Fr) a 31ha vineyard estate in the A.C. Châteauneuf-du-Pape, southern Rhône. Produces red and white wines. Red wine 'Boisrenard' is from 70–90 year old vines. Also produces an A.C. Côtes-du-Rhône-Villages Rasteau (Les Argiles Bleues).

Domaine de Bel-Air (Fr) a vineyard. (Com): Samonsac. A.C. Côtes de Bourg, Bordeaux.

Domaine de Bel Air (Fr) an A.C. Muscadet des Côtes de Grand-Lieu from Saint-Aignan-de-Grand-Lieu, Loire 6ha.

Domaine de Bel Air (Fr) 13ha. winery in Cravant. Produces A.C. Chinon- La Fosse aux Loups, Le Bois d'Arcon (from 60 year old vines).

Domaine de Belair (Fr) an A.C. Bordeaux Rouge.

Domaine de Bellevue (Fr) a vineyard. (Com): St-Selve. A.C. Graves, Bordeaux. 4ha (white).

Domaine de Bellevue (Fr) a vineyard in the A.C. Touraine. Grape variety: Sauvignon blanc.

Domaine de Bellivière (Fr) a vineyard (8ha) that produces A.C. Jasnières and Coteaux du Loire wines. Wines include Cuvée du Rouge Gorge (Pineau d'Aunis), Coteaux du Loire Cuvée de l'Effraie, Jasnières Les Rosiers, Jasnières Elixir de Tuf.

Domaine de Ben Naceaur (Afr) a brand of red wine produced in Morocco by the Société Socovin, Casablanca.

Domaine de Bequin (Fr) a vineyard. (Com): Portets. A.C. Graves, Bordeaux. 8ha (red and white).

Domaine de Berlière (Fr) a vineyard. (Com): Parsac-Saint-Émilion. A.C. Saint-Émilion, Bordeaux 3ha.

Domaine de Bévy (Fr) a large vineyard in the Hautes-Côtes de Nuits. Owned by Maison Geisweiler. 76.5ha. It produces fine light wines. The slopes of Bévy have a fine micro-climate and it is often known as the Côte d'Azur de la Côte d'Or.

Domaine de Biéville (Fr) a vineyard in the A.C. Chablis, Burgundy.

Domaine de Biot (Fr) a vineyard. (Com): Arbanats. A.C. Graves, Bordeaux. 4ha (red and white).

Domaine de Bois Dauphin (Fr) the label of a Châteauneuf-du-Pape produced by Jean Marchand, 21 Rte. d'Orange, 84230 Châteauneuf-du-Pape, southern Rhône.

Domaine de Bois d'Yver (Fr) a winery based in the A.C. Chablis, Burgundy. Produces a range of Chablis wines including Premier Crus Beauregard and Montmain.

Domaine de Bonne (Fr) a vineyard. (Com): Gauriac. A.C. Côtes de Bourg, Bordeaux.

Domaine de Bonneau (Fr) a vineyard. (Com): Montagne-Saint-Émilion. A.C. Saint-Émilion, Bordeaux 4ha.

Domaine de Bosquet (Fr) a light white wine produced in the Salins du Midi from Cabernet sauvignon grapes.

Domaine de Bouche (Fr) a vineyard. (Com): Samonac. A.C. Côtes de Bourg, Bordeaux.

Domaine de Bourdac (Fr) a vineyard. (Com): Illats. A.C. Cérons, Bordeaux 7ha.

Domaine de Bourg-Neuf (Fr) a vineyard. (Com): Pomerol. A.C. Pomerol, Bordeaux 1ha.

Domaine de Breton (Fr) a vineyard. (Com): Saint Martial. A.C. Côtes de Bordeaux Saint Macaire.

Domaine de Brochon (Fr) a vineyard. (Com): Arbanats. A.C. Graves, Bordeaux. 5ha (red and white).

Domaine de Brondelle (Fr) a vineyard. (Com): Langon. A.C. Graves, Bordeaux. 2ha (white).

Domaine de Brouillaud (Fr) a vineyard. (Com): St-Médard-d'Eyrans. A.C. Graves, Bordeaux. 7ha (white).

Domaine de Bujan (Fr) a vineyard. (Com): Gauriac. A.C. Côtes de Bourg, Bordeaux.

Domaine de By (Fr) a vineyard. (Com): Bégadan. A.C. Médoc, Bordeaux 31ha.

Domaine de Cabasse (Fr) a vineyard in the A.C. Côtes-du-Rhône-Villages Ségurat. Grape varieties: 55% Grenache, 45% Syrah. Label: Cuvée Cassa Bassa.

Domaine de Cabrières (Fr) a name now replaced by Château Cabrières.

Domaine de Cantereau (Fr) a vineyard. (Com): Pomerol. A.C. Pomerol, Bordeaux 1ha.

Domaine de Caplane (Fr) a vineyard. (Com): Sauternes. A.C. Sauternes, Bordeaux 5ha.

Domaine de Cassagnoles (Fr) a red A.C. Gaillac wine produced by the co-operative Rabastens.

Domaine de Cassah (Fr) a vineyard. (Com): Pusseguin-Saint-Émilion. A.C. Saint-Émilion, Bordeaux 6ha.

Domaine de Cassan (Fr) a winery based in the A.C. Beames-de-Venise, Côtes-du-Rhône, Vaucluse. Label: Cuvée St-Christophe (red).

Domaine de Cassanel (Fr) an Armagnac producer. *see* Pallas S.A. (San Gil).

Domaine de Casseuil (Fr) a vineyard. (Com): Langon. A.C. Graves, Bordeaux. 4ha (white).

Domaine de Castel Oualou (Fr) a vineyard in the A.C. Lirac, southern Rhône. (Add): 30150 Roquemaure, Gard.

Domaine de Castera (Fr) a vineyard in the A.C. Jurançon, south-western France. Label: Cuvée Privilège.

Domaine de Chantegrolle (Fr) an A.C. Muscadet Sèvre et Maine. (Add): J. Poiron et Fils, 44690, Chateau-Thébaud, France.

Domaine de Chante-Perdix (Fr) a vineyard estate in the A.C. Châteauneuf-du-Pape, southern Rhône.

Domaine de Chevalier (Fr) a vineyard. (Add): 33850 Léognan. Grand Cru Classé. A.C. Pessac-Léognan. Commune: Pessac-Léognan. 18ha. Grape varieties: Cabernet franc 5%, Cabernet sauvignon 65% and Merlot 30%.

Domaine de Chevilly (Fr) a vineyard based in the A.C. Quincy, Central Vineyards, Loire Valley.

Domaine de Christoly (Fr) a vineyard. (Com): Prignac-Marcamps. A.C. Côtes de Bourg, Bordeaux.

Domaine de Ciron (Fr) a vineyard. (Com): Pujols. A.C. Graves, Bordeaux. 5ha (white).

Domaine de Clare (Fr) a vineyard. (Com): Landiras. A.C. Graves, Bordeaux. 3ha (white).

Domaine de Clastron (Fr) a vineyard in the A.C. Côtes-de-Provence. 28ha. (Add): 83920 La Motte. Grape varieties: Cabernet sauvignon, Cinsault, Grenache and Syrah.

Domaine de Closel (Fr) a vineyard in the A.C. Savennières, Anjou-Saumur, Loire. *See also* Château des Vaults.

Domaine de Colonat (Fr) a winery based in the A.C. Beaujolais Cru Morgon, southern Burgundy. Label: Les Charmes Cuvée Roche-Briday

Domaine de Corrigot (Fr) a non-vintage brut white Champagne made from Pinot noir and Pinot meunier by the house of Vollereaux.

Domaine de Coste Chaude (Fr) a winery based in the A.C. Côtes-du-Rhône-Villages Visan, Vaucluse. Labels: L'Argentière, La Rocaille.

Domaine de Couitte (Fr) a vineyard. (Com): Preignac. A.C. Sauternes, Bordeaux 3ha.

Domaine de Coullander (Fr) a vineyard. (Com): Sainte-Croix-du-Mont. A.C. Sainte-Croix-du-Mont, Bordeaux 1ha.

Domaine de Courbon (Fr) a vineyard. (Com): Toulenne. A.C. Graves, Bordeaux. 4ha (white).

Domaine de Courniaud (Fr) a vineyard. (Com): Montagne-Saint-Émilion. A.C. Saint-Émilion, Bordeaux 5ha.

Domaine de Courniaud-Lussac (Fr) a vineyard. (Com): Lussac-Saint-Émilion. A.C. Saint-Émilion, Bordeaux 3ha.

Domaine de Courteillac (Fr) a red A.C. Bordeaux

Supérieur, Bordeaux. Grape varieties: Cabernet franc 10%, Cabernet sauvingnon 20%, Merlot 70%.

Domaine de Coussergues (Fr) an estate in the Languedoc-Roussillon noted for a red wine from Grenache, Merlot and Syrah grapes.

Domaine de Coyeux (Fr) a winery based in the A.C. Beaumes-de-Venise, Côtes-du-Rhône, Vaucluse.

Domaine de Cristia (Fr) an A.C. red and white Châteauneuf-du-Pape wines produced in Courthézon, southern Rhône. (Add): 33, Faubourg St. Georges, 84350 Courthézon. Website: http://www.cristia.com 'E'mail: domainecristia@hotmail.com

Domaine de Curebourse (Fr) the second wine of Château Dufort-Vivens, [Grand Cru Classé (2nd) A.C. Margaux].

Domaine de Darrouban (Fr) a vineyard. (Com): Portets. A.C. Graves, Bordeaux. 5ha (red and white).

Domaine de Duerre (Fr) a winery based in the A.C. Côtes-du-Rhône-Villages St-Maurice, Vaucluse.

Domaine de Durban (Fr) (Add): 84190 Beaumes-de-Venise, Vaucluse. A vineyard in the A.C. Beaumes-de-Venise, Côtes du Rhône-Villages, south-eastern France.

Domaine de Durce (Fr) a vineyard. (Com): Portets. A.C. Graves, Bordeaux. 3ha. (red and white). Also Domaine de Papoula.

Domaine de Farguerol (Fr) an A.C. Châteauneuf-du-Pape produced by Revoltier (Joseph et Fils), Ave. Louis Pasteur, B.P. 19, 84230 Châteauneuf-du-Pape, southern Rhône.

Domaine de Faye (Fr) a vineyard. (Com): Portets. A.C. Graves, Bordeaux. 3ha (red and white).

Domaine de Fief Guerin (Fr) a vineyard in the A.C. Muscadet Sèvre et Maine, Nantais, Loire.

Domaine de Fonbonne (Fr) a vineyard. (Com): Teuillac. A.C. Côtes de Bourg, Bordeaux.

Domaine de Fonbonne-Agassac (Fr) a vineyard. (Com): Ludon. A.C. Médoc, Bordeaux. Cru Bourgeois.

Domaine de Fontarney (Fr) the second wine of Château Brane-Cantenac [Grand Cru Classé (2nd). Margaux].

Domaine de Fontavin (Fr) an A.C. red Châteauneuf-du-Pape wine produced by Chouvet (Michel) at Rte. de Pécoulette, 84350 Courthézon, southern Rhône.

Domaine de Fontmurée (Fr) a vineyard. (Com): Montagne-Saint-Émilion. A.C. Saint-Émilion, Bordeaux 10ha.

Domaine Fontsainte (Fr) a vineyard in the A.C. Corbières, south-western France. Label: Cuvée du Centurion.

Domaine de Fouquet (Fr) a vineyard. (Com): Saint-Émilion. A.C. Saint-Émilion, Bordeaux 6ha.

Domaine de Fourn (Fr) an A.C. Blanquette de Limoux, Languedoc, south-western France.

Domaine de Freigate (Fr) a vineyard in the A.C. Bandol, Provence, south-eastern France.

Domaine de Fussiacus (Fr) a winery based in the A.C. Pouilly-Fuissé, Côte Maçônnaise, Burgundy.

Domaine de Fussignac (Fr) an A.C. Bordeaux Supérieur, Bordeaux Blanc and Bordeaux Mousseux.

Domaine de Gaillat (Fr) a vineyard. (Com): Langon. A.C. Médoc, Bordeaux.

Domaine de Gamage (Fr) a vineyard. (Com): Saint-Pey-de-Castets. A.C. Bordeaux Supérieur. (Add): Saint-Pey-de-Castets, 33350 Castillon la Bataille.

Domaine de Gardennes (Fr) a vineyard. (Com): Illats. A.C. Cérons, Bordeaux 3ha.

Domaine de Godons (Fr). (Add): Rte. de Sancerre, 18300 Sury-en-Vaux. A vineyard in the A.C. Sancerre, Central Vineyards, Loire.

Domaine de Grand Moine (Fr) a vineyard. (Com): Lalande de Pomerol. A.C. Lalande de Pomerol, Bordeaux.

Domaine de Grand Mouton (Fr) a winery based in the A.C. Muscadet de Sèvre et Maine, Loire-Atlantique. Label: Grand Mouton.

Domaine de Grange Grillard (Fr) an A.C. Arbois vineyard in Jura producing red, rosé and white wines.

Domaine de Grangeneuve (Fr) a vineyard in the A.C. Coteaux du Tricastin. Grape varieties: Cinsault, Grenache and Syrah.

Domaine de Graulet (Fr) a vineyard. (Com): Plassac. A.C. Côtes de Blaye, Bordeaux.

Domaine de Gravette (Fr) a vineyard. (Com): St-Morillon. A.C. Graves, Bordeaux. 15ha (white).

Domaine de Grimon (Fr) a vineyard. (Com): Saint-Georges-Saint-Émilion. A.C. Saint-Émilion, Bordeaux 5ha.

Domaine de Guérin (Fr) a vineyard. (Com): Castres. A.C. Graves, Bordeaux. 4ha (red).

Domaine de Guerrit (Fr) a vineyard. (Com): Tauriac. A.C. Côtes de Bourg, Bordeaux.

Domaine de Guirauton (Fr) a vineyard. (Com): St-Morillon. A.C. Graves, Bordeaux. 6ha (red and white).

Domaine de Haut-Barbey (Fr) a vineyard in the A.C. Saint-Émilion, Bordeaux. 2ha.

Domaine de Haut-Blanc (Fr) a vineyard. (Com): Pujols. A.C. Graves, Bordeaux (white).

Domaine de Haut-Courneau (Fr) a vineyard. (Com): Portets. A.C. Graves, Bordeaux. 10ha (red and white).

Domaine de Haut-Marchand (Fr) a vineyard. (Com): Montagne-Saint-Émilion. A.C. Saint-Émilion, Bordeaux 4ha.

Domaine de Haut-Pignin (Fr) a vineyard. (Com): Pomerol. A.C. Pomerol, Bordeaux 2ha.

Domaine de Haut-Tropchaud (Fr) a vineyard. (Com): Pomerol. A.C. Pomerol, Bordeaux 1ha.

Domaine de Herbauges (Fr) a winery based in the A.C. Muscadet Côtes Grand-Lieu, Loire-Atlantique. 40ha. Label: Fief de Guérin.

Domaine de Hourbanon (Fr) a Cru Bourgeois. A.C. Médoc. 15ha. Grape varieties: Cabernet franc, Cabernet sauvignon and Merlot.

Domaine de Husson (Fr) the label of a Châteauneuf-du-Pape produced by Granget in Courthézon, southern Rhône.

Domaine de Jarras (Fr) an A.C. rosé wine produced by Listel in the Midi, southern France.

Domaine de Jaussans (Fr) a vineyard. (Com): Illats. A.C. Cérons, Bordeaux 8ha.

Domaine de Jean-Marie (Fr) a vineyard in the A.C. Saint-Émilion, Bordeaux 2ha.

Domaine de la Bastide Neuve (Fr) a vineyard in the A.C. Côtes de Provence. Produces red and rosé wines. Noted for Cuvée d'Antan and Cuvée des Anges.

Domaine de la Baume (Fr) the home vineyard of Chais Baumière in the Languedoc-Roussillon. Noted for Merlot.

Domaine de l'Abbaye-Skinner (Fr) a vineyard. (Com): Vertheuil. A.C. Médoc, Bordeaux. Cru Bourgeois.

Domaine de la Bégude (Fr) a vineyard in the A.C. Bandol, Provence.

Domaine de Labeillon (Fr) a vineyard. (Com): St-Pierre-de-Mons. A.C. Graves, Bordeaux. 2ha (white).

Domaine de la Bergerie (Fr) a vineyard based in Champ-sur-Layon, A.C. Coteaux-du-Layon, Anjou-Saumur, Loire.

Domaine de la Biscarelle (Fr) the label of A.C. Châteauneuf-du-Pape produced by Bouyer (Gérard), Quartier du Grès, 84100 Orange, southern Rhône.

Domaine de la Blancherie (Fr) a vineyard. (Com): La Brède. A.C. Graves, Bordeaux. 10ha (white).

Domaine de la Bodinière (Fr) an A.C. Muscadet Sèvre et Maine, domaine bottled. (Add): La Bodinière, Vallet, Loire Atlantique.

Domaine de la Boissoneuse (Fr) a vineyard in the A.C. Chablis, Burgundy.

Domaine de Labouade-Rambaud (Fr) a vineyard. (Com): Barsac. A.C. Barsac (or Sauternes), Bordeaux 1ha.

Domaine de la Bretonnière (Fr) a vineyard in the A.C. Muscadet Sèvre et Maine, Nantais, Loire. Domaine bottled.

Domaine de la Brune (Fr) a winery based in the A.C. Beaumes-de-Venise, Côtes-du-Rhône, Vaucluse.

Domaine de Lacapère (Fr) a vineyard. (Com): Landiras A.C. Graves, Bordeaux. 2ha (white).

Domaine de la Cassemichère (Fr) a vineyard in the A.C. Muscadet Sèvre et Maine, Nantais, Loire. Domaine bottled.

Domaine de la Cateau (Fr) a vineyard in the A.C. Saint-Émilion, Bordeaux 3ha.

Domaine de la Chambaudière (Fr) an A.C. Muscadet Sèvre et Maine produced by Domaine Bruno Cormerais, Saint-Lumine de Clisson, Nantais, Loire. See also Domaine Bruno Cormerais.

Domaine de la Chapelle (Fr) a vineyard based in Couches, Côtes de Chouchois. (Add): Eguilly, 71490 Couches. Produces A.C. Bourgogne-Côtes-du-Couchois. Grape varieties: Aligoté, Chardonnay, Gamay, Pinot noir. Label: Chante Fluté.

Domaine de la Chapelle (Fr) a vineyard. (Com): Preignac. A.C. Sauternes, Bordeaux 3ha.

Domaine de la Chapelle (Fr) a vineyard in the A.C. Saint-Émilion, Bordeaux 3ha.

Domaine de la Chapelle des Bois (Fr) a winery based in the A.C. Beaujolais Cru Fleurie, southern Burgundy.

Domaine de la Chaponne (Fr) a winery based in the A.C. Beaujolais Cru Morgon, southern Burgundy.

Domaine de la Charbonnière (Fr) the label of a red A.C. Châteauneuf-du-Pape produced by Maret, Rte. de Courthézon, 84230 A.C. Châteauneuf-du-Pape, southern Rhône.

Domaine de la Charmoise (Fr) a 50ha vineyard at Soings on the edge of Sologne. A.C. Touraine. (Add): La Charmoise, 41230 Soings. Grape varieties: Sauvignon blanc, Gamay.

Domaine de la Charpenterie (Fr) an A.C. Muscadet Sèvre et Maine produced at Le Landreau, Nantais, Loire.

Domaine de la Chartreuse (Fr) a vineyard in the A.C. Côtes du Rhône, southern France.

Domaine de la Chartreuse (Fr) a label used by Aujoux at Saint Georges de Renins, Rhône for an A.C. Châteauneuf-du-Pape.

Domaine de la Chauvillière (Fr) a noted Pineau des Charentes producer in Cognac.

Domaine de la Chevalerie (Fr) a vineyard in the A.C. Bourgueil, Touraine, Loire. (Add): Restign, 37140.

Domaine de la Citadelle (Fr) a vineyard. (Com): Illats. A.C. Cérons, Bordeaux 4ha.

Domaine de la Citadelle (Fr) a Vin de Pays de Vaucluse from Minèrbes in the Lubéron, southern Rhône. 45ha. of Cabernet sauvignon, Merlot, Chardonnay grapes.

Domaine de la Clastre (Fr) the label of an A.C. Châteauneuf-du-Pape produced by Domaine Bernard (Michel). See also Domaine de la Serrière, Domaine Ferrand.

Domaine de la Clotte (Fr) a vineyard. (Com): Montagne-Saint-Émilion. A.C. Saint-Émilion, Bordeaux 5ha.

Domaine de Lacoste (Fr) a vineyard. (Com): Sainte-Croix-du-Mont. A.C. Sainte-Croix-du-Mont, Bordeaux 2ha.

Domaine de la Conciergerie (Fr) a winery based in the A.C. Chablis, Burgundy. Produces a range of Chablis wines including Premier Cru Montmains.

Domaine de la Coste (Fr) a red and rosé wine vineyard based at Saint Christol in A.C. Coteaux du Languedoc.

Domaine de la Côte de l'Ange (Fr) an A.C. Châteauneuf-du-Pape produced by Mestre at Quartier La Font du Pape, 84230 Châteauneuf-du-Pape, southern Rhône.

Domaine de la Cour (Fr) a vineyard in the A.C. Muscadet Sèvre et Maine. Domaine bottled. (Add): 44 Chapelle-Heulin, Loire Atlantique.

Domaine de la Courrège (Fr) a vineyard. (Com): Illats. A.C. Graves, Bordeaux. Grape varieties: Cabernet sauvignon, Merlot (red and white).

Domaine de la Courtade (Fr) a vineyard at La Courtade, Porquerolles. A.C. Côtes de Provence.

Red: 17ha. of Mourvèdre, Grenache, Syrah. White: 13ha. of Rolle, Sémillon.

Domaine de la Coustarelle (Fr) a vineyard. (Add): 46220 Frayssac. A vineyard in the A.C. Cahors, south-western France.

Domaine de la Croix (Fr) a vineyard. (Com): Langon. A.C. Graves, Bordeaux 4ha. (white).

Domaine de la Croix (Fr) a vineyard. (Com): Ordonnac. A.C. Médoc, Bordeaux 16ha.

Domaine de la Croix-Mazerat (Fr) a vineyard in the A.C. Saint-Émilion, Bordeaux 2ha.

Domaine de la d'Argis (Fr) an A.C. Arbois vineyard producing red, rosé and white wines in the Jura.

Domaine de la Dimerie (Fr) a vineyard in the A.C. Muscadet Sèvre et Maine, Nantais, Loire.

Domaine de la Faubretière (Fr) a vineyard in the A.C. Muscadet Sèvre et Maine, Nantais, Loire.

Domaine de la Ferme St-Martin (Fr) a winery based in the A.C. Beaumes-de-Venise, Côtes-du-Rhône, Vaucluse. Labels: Cuvée St-Martin (red), Les Terres Jaunes.

Domaine de la Fèvrie (Fr) a vineyard in the A.C. Muscadet Sèvre et Maine, Nantais, Loire.

Domaine de la Foliette (Fr) an A.C. Muscadet Sèvre et Maine from La Haye-Fouassière, Nantais, Loire 22ha.

Domaine de Lafon (Fr) a vineyard. (Com): Prignac. A.C. Médoc, Bordeaux 3ha.

Domaine de la Font-du-Loup (Fr) a vineyard in the A.C. Châteauneuf-du-Pape, southern Rhône 12.5ha.

Domaine de la Font du Roi (Fr) the label of an A.C. Châteauneuf-du-Pape wines produced by Mousset (Jacques) at Les Fines Roches, 84230 Châteauneuf-du-Pape, southern Rhône.

Domaine de la Forêt (Fr) a vineyard. (Com): Preignac. A.C. Sauternes, Bordeaux 21ha.

Domaine de la Fruitière (Fr) a vineyard in the A.C. Muscadet Sèvre et Maine, Nantais, Loire.

Domaine de la Gaffelière (Fr) a vineyard in the A.C. Saint-Émilion, Bordeaux 2ha.

Domaine de la Ganolière (Fr) an A.C. Muscadet Sèvre et Maine from Gorges, Nantais, Loire 9ha.

Domaine de Lagardenne (Fr) an Armagnac producer based in the Bas-Armagnac, Gers. Produces vintage and non-vintage Armagnacs.

Domaine de la Garrelière (Fr) a 20ha winery in A.C. Chinon Grape varieties include Cabernet franc, Gamay, Sauvignon blanc.

Domaine de la Gautronnière (Fr) an A.C. Muscadet Sèvre et Maine from La Chapelle-Heulin, Nantais, Loire.

Domaine de la Genetière (Fr) a vineyard in the A.C. Tavel, southern Rhône. Label: Cuvée Raphaël.

Domaine de la Girafe (Fr) a vineyard. (Com): Portets. A.C. Graves, Bordeaux. 7ha (red and white).

Domaine de la Gleyre (Fr) a vineyard. (Com): Pujols. A.C. Graves, Bordeaux. 2ha (white).

Domaine de la Goulbaudière (Fr) an A.C. Muscadet Sèvre et Maine from Vallet, Nantais, Loire 15ha.

Domaine de la Grand'Cour (Fr) a winery based in the A.C. Beaujolais Cru Fleurie, southern Burgundy. Label: Cuvée l'Exception.

Domaine de la Grande Bellane (Fr) an organic red wine-producing vineyard in the A.C. Valréas, Côtes-du-Rhône.

Domaine de la Grande Olivette (Fr) a Vin de Pays de Mont Bouquet, an oak aged red wine produced from Cabernet sauvignon, Syrah, Cinsault, Merlot, Grenache.

Domaine de la Grange (Fr) an A.C. Muscadet Sèvre et Maine from Mouzillon, Nantais, Loire. Produced by Hardy (Dominique) 19ha.

Domaine de la Grange (Fr) an A.C. Muscadet Sèvre et Maine from Mouzillon, Nantais, Loire. Produced by Luneau-Papin (Pierre) 19ha.

Domaine de Lagraulet (Fr) an Armagnac produced by the Domaine de Lasgraves.

Domaine de la Grave (Fr) a vineyard. (Com): St-Selve. A.C. Graves, Bordeaux. 3ha (white).

Domaine de la Grenaudière (Fr) an A.C. Muscadet Sèvre et Maine from Maisdon-sur-Sèvre, Nantais, Loire 26ha.

Domaine de la Guillaudière (Fr) an A.C. Muscadet Sèvre et Maine from Corcoué-sur-Logne, Nantais, Loire 5ha.

Domaine de la Haute Carizière (Fr) an A.C. Muscadet Sèvre et Maine from La Haye-Fouassière, Nantais, Loire 9ha.

Domaine de la Haute-Faucherie (Fr) a vineyard. (Com): Montagne-Saint-Émilion. A.C. Saint-Émilion, Bordeaux 3ha.

Domaine de la Haute Févrie (Fr) an A.C. Muscadet Sèvre et Maine from Maisdon-sur-Sèvre, Nantais, Loire 15ha.

Domaine de la Hautière (Fr) a vineyard in the A.C. Muscadet Sèvre et Maine, Nantais, Loire.

Domaine de la Houssais (Fr) an A.C. Muscadet Sèvre et Maine from Le Landreau, Nantais, Loire 10ha.

Domaine de la Janesse (Fr) an A.C. red or white Châteauneuf-du-Pape produced by Sabon (Aîmé) at Chemin du Moulin, 84350 Courthézon, southern Rhône.

Domaine de la Jaufrette (Fr) an A.C. Châteauneuf-du-Pape produced by Chastan (A. et Fils) at Chemin de la Gironde, 84100 Orange, southern Rhône.

Domaine de Lajorty (Fr) an A.C. Graves. (Com): Langon. *see* Château Balouet-Roailloy.

Domaine de la Lagune (Fr) a vineyard. (Com): Bégadan. A.C. Médoc, Bordeaux 5ha.

Domaine de la Landelle (Fr) an A.C. Muscadet Sèvre et Maine from Le Loroux-Bottereau, Nantais, Loire 12ha.

Domaine de la Levraudière (Fr) an A.C. Muscadet Sèvre et Maine from La Chapelle-Heulin, Nantais, Loire.

Domaine de Lalibarde (Fr) a vineyard. (Com): Bourg. A.C. Côtes de Bourg, Bordeaux.

Domaine de la Lande (Fr) a vineyard in the A.C. Bourgueil. 9ha. Grape variety: Cabernet franc.

Domaine de la Loge (Fr) a vineyard in the A.C.

Muscadet Sèvre et Maine. (Add): 44330 Vallet, Loire Atlantique.

Domaine de Lamaçonne (Fr) a vineyard. (Com): Montagne-Saint-Émilion. A.C. Saint-Émilion, Bordeaux 3ha.

Domaine de la Madone (Fr) a winery based in the A.C. Beaujolais Cru Fleurie, southern Burgundy. (Add): La Madone, 69820 Fleurie. 'E'mail: domainedelamadone@wanadoo.fr

Domaine de la Maladière (Fr) the brand label used by William Fèvre in Chablis, Burgundy.

Domaine de la Martinière (Fr) an A.C. Muscadet Sèvre et Maine from La Chapelle-Heulin, Nantais, Loire 28ha.

Domaine de la Marelle (Fr) an A.C Gigondas based in the Côtes-du-Rhône, south-eastern France.

Domaine de la Mavette (Fr) a vineyard in the A.C. Gigondas. (Add): 84190 Gigondas. Grape varieties: Grenache, Syrah.

Domaine de Lambert (Fr) a red Languedoc estate wine (102ha.) owned by GFA Lambert. Leased to Baron Philippe de Rothschild SA. Grape varieties: Cabernet sauvignon, Cabernet franc, Merlot, Grenache, Syrah.

Domaine de la Mandelière (Fr) a winery based in the A.C. Chablis, Burgundy. Produces a range of Chablis wines including Premier Crus: Les Fourchaume, Fourneaux, Mont de Milieu, Montmains, Montée de Tonnerre. Owned by Jean Durup (see Durup [Jean]).

Domaine de l'Amandine (Fr) a winery based in the A.C. Côtes-du-Rhône-Villages Séguret, Vaucluse.

Domaine de l'Ameillaud (Fr) a winery based in the A.C. Côtes-du-Rhône-Villages Cairanne, Vaucluse.

Domaine de la Mercy-Dieu (Fr) a vineyard in the A.C. Sancerre, Central Vineyards, France. Grape variety: Sauvignon blanc.

Domaine de la Meulière (Fr) a winery based in the A.C. Chablis, Burgundy. Produces a range of Chablis wines including Premier Crus Les Fourneaux and Monts de Milieu. 'E'mail: Chablis.meuliere@wanadoo.fr

Domaine de la Militière (Fr) a vineyard based at 14, Rue de la Militière, 37270 Montlouis, Loire. A.C. Montlouis.

Domaine de la Millière (Fr) an A.C. Châteauneuf-du-Pape produced by Arnaud (Michel) at Quartier Cabrières-Le Grès, 84100 Orange, southern Rhône.

Domaine de la Minière (Fr) an A.C. Muscadet Sèvre et Maine from Monnières, Nantais, Loire.

Domaine de la Mordorée (Fr) an A.C. red Châteauneuf-du-Pape produced by Delorme at Chemin des Oliviers, 30126 Tavel, southern Rhône. Also produces A.C. Tavel rosé.

Domaine de Lamothe (Fr) fine distillers of Armagnac based in Canon-Bordeaux. Noted for Gauvin 40% alc by vol.

Domaine de la Motte (Fr) a winery based in the A.C. Chablis, Burgundy. Produces a range of Chablis wines including Premier Crus Beauroy and Vau-Ligneau.

Domaine de la Motte (Fr) a vineyard in the A.C. Coteaux du Layon, Anjou-Saumur, Loire.

Domaine de la Motte (Fr) a winery based in the A.C. Beaujolais Cru Brouilly, southern Burgundy.

Domaine de la Mouchetière (Fr) a vineyard in the A.C. Muscadet Sèvre et Maine. (Add): 44430 Loroux-Bottereau, Vallet, Loire Atlantique.

Domaine de la Mouleyre (Fr) a vineyard in the A.C. Saint-Émilion, Bordeaux 5ha.

Domaine de la Muraille (Fr) an A.C. Muscadet Sèvre et Maine from Le Landreau, Nantais, Loire 10ha.

Domaine de l'Angebert (Fr) a vineyard in the A.C. Muscadet Sèvre et Maine, Nantais, Loire.

Domaine de la Noé-Bachelon (Fr) an A.C. Muscadet Sèvre et Maine from Loroux-Bottereau, Nantais, Loire.

Domaine de la Noirie (Fr) a vineyard. (Com): Morgon. A.C. Morgon Cru Beaujolis-Villages, Burgundy.

Domaine de la Paulière (Fr) a winery based in the A.C. Chablis, Burgundy. Produces a range of Chablis wines including Premier Crus Montée de Tonnerre and Montmains.

Domaine de la Perrière (Fr) a vineyard. (Add): La Perrière, 37500 Cravant-les-Coteaux. A vineyard in the A.C. Chinon, Anjou-Saumur, Loire.

Domaine de la Perrière (Fr) a vineyard in the A.C. Sancerre, Central Vineyards (Add): 18300 Verdigny, France. Grape variety: Sauvignon blanc. 'E'mail: info@domainelaperriere.com a vineyard in the A.C. Sancerre, Central Vineyards, France. Grape variety: Sauvignon blanc.

Domaine de la Petite Bastide (Fr) an A.C. Châteauneuf-du-Pape produced by Diffonty at 84230 Châteauneuf-du-Pape, southern Rhône. *See also* Domaine des Terres Blanches.

Domaine de la Pinède (Fr) an A.C. red or white Châteauneuf-du-Pape from Coulon (George) at Rte. de Sorgues, 84230 Châteauneuf-du-Pape, southern Rhône.

Domaine de la Pinte (Fr) an estate in A.C. Arbois, Jura that produces still wines and Vin de Paille.

Domaine de Laplaigne (Fr) a vineyard. (Com): Puisseguin-Saint-Émilion. A.C. Saint-Émilion, Bordeaux 7ha.

Domaine de la Presidente (Fr) a winery based in the A.C. Côtes-du-Rhône-Villages Cairanne, Vaucluse. Labels: Collection Gallifay, Grands Classiques. Also produces a red Vin de Pays de la Principauté d'Orange wine from 70% Grenache, 30% Carignan.

Domaine de la Prévosse (Fr) a winery based in the A.C. Côtes-du-Rhône-Villages Valréas, Vaucluse.

Domaine de la Prose (Fr) a vineyard (28ha) based in St-Georges d'Orques, in the A.C. Grès de Montpellier, Coteaux du Languedoc. Labels: Les Cadières, Les Embruns.

Domaine de la Proutière (Fr) an A.C. Muscadet Sèvre et Maine from Gorges, Nantais, Loire 20ha.

Domaine de la Quilla (Fr) an A.C. Muscadet Sèvre et Maine from La Haye-Fouassière, Nantais, Loire 28ha.

Domaine de Laraude (Fr) a vineyard in the commune Sauternes. A.C. Sauternes, Bordeaux 2ha.

Domaine de l'Ardennerie (Fr) a vineyard in the A.C. Muscadet Sèvre et Maine. (Add): 44450 La Chapelle, Basse-Mer, Loire.

Domaine de la Rectorie (Fr) a vineyard in the A.C. Collioure and Banyuls. Based at Banyuls-sur-mer it produces red, rosé and fortified wines from Carignan 40% and Grenache 60%.

Domaine de la Renjardière (Fr) a vineyard in the A.C. Côtes du Rhône, southern France.

Domaine de l'Arieste (Fr) a vineyard. (Com): Preignac. A.C. Sauternes, Bordeaux 8ha.

Domaine de la Rinière (Fr) an A.C. Muscadet Sèvre et Maine from Le Landreau, Nantais, Loire 13ha.

Domaine de l'Arjolle (Fr) a vineyard within the Vin de Pays des Côtes de Thongue, Languedoc. Grape varieties: Cabernet sauvignon, Merlot and Syrah.

Domaine de Larnavey (Fr) a vineyard. (Com): St-Selve. A.C. Graves, Bordeaux. 2ha (red).

Domaine de la Roche-Marot (Fr) a vineyard in the A.C. Bergerac, south-western France.

Domaine de la Rocherie (Fr) an A.C. Muscadet Sèvre et Maine from Le Landreau, Nantais, Loire 10ha.

Domaine de la Rose (Fr) a vineyard in the A.C. Saint-Émilion, Bordeaux 2ha.

Domaine de la Rossignole (Fr) a vineyard in the A.C. Sancerre, Central Vineyards, France. Grape variety: Sauvignon blanc.

Domaine de la Roudette (Fr) a vineyard. (Com): Sauternes. A.C. Sauternes, Bordeaux 2ha.

Domaine de la Rouillère (Fr) a vineyard in the A.C. Côtes-de-Provence, south-eastern France. (Add): St-Tropel, Gassin-Var.

Domaine de la Salle (Fr) a vineyard. (Add): Château Sansonnet, 33330 Saint-Émilion. A.C. Saint-Émilion. Commune: Saint-Émilion.

Domaine de la Saulzaie (Fr) an A.C. Muscadet Sèvre et Maine from La Chapelle-Basse-Mer, Nantais, Loire 16ha.

Domaine de la Sauvesuse (Fr) a winery based in the A.C. Côtes-de-Provence, south-eastern France. Label: Cuvée Philippine.

Domaine de la Sensive (Fr) an A.C. Muscadet Sèvre et Maine from Haute-Goulaine, Nantais, Loire. 9ha.

Domaine de la Serrière (Fr) an A.C. Châteauneuf-du-Pape from Bernard (Michel). *See also* Domaine de la Clastre, Domaine Ferrand.

Domaine de Lasgraves (Fr) an Armagnac producer. (Add): 10 Impasse, Andrée Cherier 40000 Mont de Marsan. 8ha. in Bas Armagnac. Produces Domaine de Lagraulet and Domaine de Martiques.

Domaine de la Sionnière (Fr) a winery based in the A.C. Beaujolais Cru Moulin-à-Vent, southern Burgundy.

Domaine de la Solitude (Fr) an A.C. Châteauneuf-du-Pape from Lançon (Pierre) at La Rte. de Bédarrides, 84230 Châteauneuf-du-Pape, southern Rhône. 33.5ha (red and white).

Domaine de la Solitude (Fr) Commune: Léognan.

23ha. (Add): 33650 Martillac. A.C. Pessac-Léognan. Grape varieties: Cabernet franc, Cabernet sauvignon, Merlot, Sauvignon 50% and Sémillon 50%.

Domaine de la Soucherie (Fr) a vineyard in the A.C. Coteaux du Layon, Anjou-Saumur, Loire.

Domaine de Lassalle (Fr) a vineyard. (Com): La Brède. A.C. Graves, Bordeaux. 6ha (red and white).

Domaine de la Suffrène (Fr) a vineyard in the A.C. Bandol, Provence 45ha.

Domaine de la Tour Bajole (Fr) a vineyard based in Saint-Maurice-les Couches, Côtes de Chouchois. Produces A.C. Bourgogne-Côtes-du-Couchois. Grape variety: Pinot noir.

Domaine de la Tour de Bon (r) a vineyard in the A.C. Bandol, Provence.

Domaine de la Tourmaline (Fr) an A.C. Muscadet Sèvre et Maine from Saint-Fiacre, Nantais, Loire 25ha.

Domaine de la Tour Vert (Fr) a vineyard (17ha) and Cognac distillery (established 1969) based in Jarnac, Charente. (Add): 8, Rue de l'Eglise, Foussignac, 16200 Jarnac. Produces a range of Cognacs and Pineau des Charentes.

Domaine de la Trappe (Alg) a red wine produced in the south-eastern region of Algeria.

Domaine de la Treille (Fr) an A.C. Fleurie. Cru Beaujolais-Villages, Burgundy.

Domaine de la Tuilière (Fr) a vineyard in the A.C. Côtes-de-Provence. (Add): Pourcieux, 83470 Maximin (red and rosé).

Domaine de Latuque Bel Air (Fr) a vineyard in the A.C. Côtes de Castillon, Bordeaux.

Domaine de l'Aurière (Fr) a vineyard in the A.C. Muscadet Sèvre et Maine. (Add): Vallet, Loire Atlantique.

Domaine de la Vialle (Fr) a vineyard in the A.C. Côtes du Rhône, southern France. Produces A.C. Châteauneuf-du-Pape.

Domaine de la Vieille Chausée (Fr) an A.C. Muscadet Sèvre et Maine from Château-Thébaud, Nantais, Loire 22ha.

Domaine de la Vieille-Cloche (Fr) a vineyard in the A.C. Saint-Émilion, Bordeaux 4ha.

Domaine de la Vieille-École (Fr) a vineyard. (Com): Pomerol. A.C. Pomerol, Bordeaux 1ha.

Domaine de la Vieille Julienne (Fr) an A.C. red Châteauneuf-du-Pape from Daumen (Maxime) at Le Grès, 84100 Orange, southern Rhône.

Domaine de la Villaudière (Fr) a vineyard in the A.C. Sancerre, Central Vineyards, France. Grape variety: Sauvignon blanc.

Domaine de la Voulte (Fr) a vineyard in the A.C. Corbières, Languedoc, south-western France.

Domaine de la Vougeraie (Fr) a vineyard holding created in 1999 by Jean-Claude Boisset to market his vineyard wines in Burgundy.

Domaine de l'Echasserie (Fr) an A.C. Muscadet Sèvre et Maine from Vallet, Nantais, Loire 9ha.

Domaine de l'Ecu (Fr) an organic sur-lie wine-producing vineyard in Le Landreau, A.C. Muscadet Sèvre et Maine, Nantais, Loire.

Domaine de l'Églantière (Fr) a winery based in the A.C. Chablis, Burgundy. (Add): Maligny 89800, Chablis. Produces a range of Chablis wines including Premier Crus l'Homme Mort and Montmains.

Domaine de l'Église (Fr) a vineyard. (Com): Pomerol. A.C. Pomerol, Bordeaux. The oldest estate in Pomerol 7ha.

Domaine de l'Épinay (Fr) a vineyard in the A.C. Vouvray, Touraine, Loire. Produces sparkling (méthode traditionelle) wines.

Domaine de l'Escaley (Fr) a 2ha vineyard in the commune of Sainte-Croix-du-Mont. A.C. Croix-du-Mont, Bordeaux.

Domaine de l'Hôpital (Fr) a vineyard. (Com): Castres. A.C. Graves, Bordeaux. 3ha (red).

Domaine de l'Hortus (Fr) a 32ha. vineyard in A.C. Coteaux du Languedoc-Pic Saint-Loup. Produces red wines (Grande Cuvée and La Bergerie) from Syrah, Mourvèdre and Grenache grapes. Also produces Bergerie de l'Hortus (rosé), Grande Cuvée Blanc (Vin de Pays du Val de Montferrand) from Viognier and Chardonnay grapes fermented in barrel.

Domaine de l'Hospitalet (Fr) a vineyard based in the A.C. Coteaux du Languedoc. Noted for white Château de l'Hospitalet produced from Bourboulenc, Roussanne and Rolle grapes.

Domaine de l'Hyvernière (Fr) a vineyard in the A.C. Muscadet Sèvre et Maine, Nantais, Loire.

Domaine de l'If (Fr) a vineyard. (Com): Sainte-Croix-du-Mont. A.C. Sainte-Croix-du-Mont, Bordeaux 3ha.

Domaine de l'Ile Margaux (Fr) a vineyard in the Ile de la Tour de Mons, Gironde. A.C. Bordeaux Supérieur 16ha.

Domaine de l'Olivette (Fr) a winery based in the A.C. Côtes-du-Rhône-Villages Chusclan, Vaucluse. Label: Excellence.

Domaine de l'Origan (Fr) the label of an A.C. Châteauneuf-du-Pape produced by Bravay.

Domaine de l'Orme (Fr) a winery based in the A.C. Chablis, Burgundy. Produces a range of Chablis wines including Premier Cru Beauroy.

Domaine de Louisot (Fr) a vineyard. (Com): Virelade. A.C. Graves, Bordeaux. 4ha (white).

Domaine de Louqsor (Fr) a vineyard. (Com): Sainte-Croix-du-Mont. A.C. Sainte-Croix-du-Mont, Bordeaux 1ha.

Domaine Delubac (Fr) a winery based in the A.C. Côtes-du-Rhône-Villages Cairanne, Vaucluse. Label: L'Authentique Delubac, Les Brunneau.

Domaine de Magnol (Fr) a vineyard. (Com): Blanquefort. A.C. Haut-Médoc, Bordeaux 9ha.

Domaine de Maisonneuve (Fr) a vineyard. (Com): Saint-Georges-Saint-Émilion. A.C. Saint-Émilion, Bordeaux 17ha.

Domaine de Marchandise (Fr) a vineyard in the A.C. Côtes-de-Provence. (Add): 83520 Roquebrune-sur-Argens (red and rosé).

Domaine de Marcoux (Fr) an A.C. Châteauneuf-du-Pape from Armenier at 3, Chemin du Clos, 84230 Châteauneuf-du-Pape, southern Rhône.

Domaine de Maron (Fr) a vineyard. (Com): Landiras. A.C. Graves, Bordeaux. 2ha (red).

Domaine de Marquisat (Fr) a vineyard. (Com): Lansac. A.C. Côtes de Bourg, Bordeaux.

Domaine de Martialis (Fr) the second wine of Château Clos Fourtet, A.C. Saint-Émilion.

Domaine de Martinoles (Fr) a winery based in St. Hilaire, southern France. Produces a sparkling (méthode traditionelle) wine.

Domaine de Martiques (Fr) an Armagnac produced by Domaine de Lasgraves.

Domaine de Mathalin (Fr) a vineyard. (Com): Barsac. A.C. Barsac (or Sauternes), Bordeaux 1ha.

Domaine de Matourne (Fr) a vineyard in the A.C. Côtes-de-Provence. (Add): 83780 Flayosc.

Domaine de Mayrac (Fr) a vineyard in the Vin de Pays de Haut Vallée de l'Aude. Grape varieties: Cabernet franc, Cabernet sauvignon and Merlot.

Domaine de Menaut Larrouquey (Fr) a vineyard. (Com): Cérons. A.C. Cérons, Bordeaux 12ha.

Domaine de Meriguet (Fr) a vineyard in the A.C. Cahors, south-western France.

Domaine de Metivier (Fr) a vineyard. (Com): Ayguemortes. A.C. Graves, Bordeaux. 3ha (white).

Domaine de Mongenan (Fr) a vineyard. (Com): Portets. A.C. Graves, Bordeaux. 5ha (red and white).

Domaine de Montagnette (Fr) a vineyard in the A.C. Côtes-du-Rhône.

Domaine de Monteils (Fr) a vineyard. (Com): Preignac. A.C. Sauternes, Bordeaux 7ha.

Domaine de Montifaud (Fr) a Cognac producer. (Add): Jarnac, Champagne 17520 Archaic. 50ha. in the Petite Champagne.

Domaine de Montmeix (Fr) a winery in the A.C. Meursault, Côte de Beaune, Burgundy.

Domaine Demontmerot Père et Fils (Fr) a vineyard based in Dracy-les-Couches, Côtes de Chouchois. Produces A.C. Bourgogne-Côtes-du-Couchois. Grape variety: Pinot noir.

Domaine de Montpertuis (Fr) an A.C. Châteauneuf-du-Pape from Jeune (Paul) at 7, Ave. Saint-Joseph, 84230 Châteauneuf-du-Pape, southern Rhône. Red and white.

Domaine de Montremblant (Fr) a vineyard in the A.C. Saint-Émilion, Bordeaux 5ha.

Domaine de Mortiers Gobin (Fr) a vineyard in the A.C. Muscadet Sèvre et Maine, Nantais, Loire. (Add): Robert Brosseau La Haye Fouassière.

Domaine de Mortiès (Fr) a vineyard in the A.C. Coteaux du Languedoc Pic-Saint-Loup. Produces Cuvée Jamais Content from Syrah, Mourvèdre, Grenache and Carignan grapes.

Domaine de Mouchac (Fr) a single vineyard in the Bas Armagnac. The grapes grown are produced into Armagnac by Janneau.

Domaine de Mounic (Fr) a vineyard. (Com): Fargues. A.C. Sauternes, Bordeaux 1ha.

Domaine de Mourchon (Fr) a vineyard in the A.C. Séguret, Côtes-du-Rhône-Villages. (Add): 84110 Séguret. Produces: Grande Réserve, Tradition. Website: http://www.domainedemourchon.com

Domaine de Musset (Fr) a vineyard. (Com): Lalande-de-Pomerol. A.C. Lalande-de-Pomerol, Bordeaux.

Domaine de Nalys (Fr) an A.C. Châteauneuf-du-Pape based at Rte. de Courthézon, southern Rhône. 52ha. (red and white wines). Other label La Crau. *see* Dufays (Doctor).

Domaine de Nerleux (Fr) an A.C. Saumur-Champigny based at 49 St. Cyr-en-Bourg.

Domaine de Noriou-Lalibarde (Fr) a vineyard. (Com): Bourg. Côtes de Bourg, Bordeaux.

Domaine de Palestor (Fr) an A.C. red Châteauneuf-du-Pape produced in Orange, southern Rhône.

Domaine de Pallus Beauséjour (Fr) a vineyard in the A.C. Chinon, Touraine, Loire. (Add): 37500 Cravant-les-Coteaux, Loire.

Domaine de Pampelune (Fr) a vineyard in commune of Sainte-Croix-du-Mont. A.C. Sainte-Croix-du-Mont, Bordeaux 3ha.

Domaine de Panisse (Fr) a vineyard estate in the A.C. Châteauneuf-du-Pape, southern Rhône.

Domaine de Paousset (Fr) an A.C. Chiroubles. Cru Beaujolais-Villages, Burgundy.

Domaine de Papoula (Fr) a vineyard. (Com): Portets. A.C. Graves, Bordeaux. 3ha. (red and white). Also Domaine de Durce.

Domaine de Parenteau (Fr) a vineyard. (Com): Sainte-Croix-du-Mont. A.C. Sainte-Coix-du-Mont, Bordeaux 4ha.

Domaine de Pasquette (Fr) a vineyard in the A.C. Saint-Émilion, Bordeaux 5ha.

Domaine de Patache (Fr) a vineyard. (Com): Bégadan. A.C. Médoc, Bordeaux 36ha.

Domaine de Pellehaut (Fr) a Vin de Pays des Côtes de Gascogne vineyard in south-eastern France. Produces red and rosé wines.

Domaine de Pérey (Fr) a vineyard in the A.C. Saint-Émilion, Bordeaux 2ha.

Domaine de Petror (Fr) a vineyard in commune of Gauriac. A.C. Côtes de Bourg, Bordeaux.

Domaine de Piaugier (Fr) a winery based in the A.C. Côtes-du-Rhône-Villages Sablet, Vaucluse. Label: Les Briguières.

Domaine de Plantat (Fr) a vineyard. (Com): St-Morillon. A.C. Graves, Bordeaux. 9ha (red and white).

Domaine de Plantes (Fr) a vineyard. (Com): Landiras. A.C. Graves, Bordeaux. 4ha. (white).

Domaine de Pont-le-Voy (Fr) a winery based in the A.C. Côtes-du-Rhône-Villages Laudun, Vaucluse. Label: Les Lauzes

Domaine de Prouzet (Fr) a vineyard. (Com): Illats. A.C. Cérons, Bordeaux 7ha.

Domaine de Rambaud (Fr) a vineyard. (Com): Lussac-Saint-Émilion. A.C. Saint-Émilion, Bordeaux 3ha.

Domaine de Rasignani (Fr) a vineyard in the A.C. Vin de Corse, Corsica. Label: Cuvée Terra Nostra (Niellucciu).

Domaine de René (Fr) a vineyard. (Com): Pomerol. A.C. Pomerol, Bordeaux 3ha.

Domaine de Rey (Fr) a vineyard in the A.C. Saint-Émilion, Bordeaux 4ha.

Domaine de Ribereau (Fr) a vineyard. (Com): Pugnac. A.C. Côtes de Bourg, Bordeaux.

Domaine de Rieux (Fr) a vineyard in the Vin de Pays des Côtes de Gascogne. (Add): St-Amand-Eauze, 32800 (Gers), France.

Domaine de Rimauresq (Fr) a vineyard. (Com): Pignans. A.C. Côtes-de-Provence, south-eastern France. (Add): 83790, Pignans. (red, rosé and white). Grape varieties include: Cinsault, Tibouren. Label: Rimauresco (rosé).

Domaine de Rivière (Fr) a vineyard in the A.C. Saint-Émilion, Bordeaux 5ha.

Domaine de Robert (Fr) a vineyard. (Com): Pomerol. A.C. Pomerol, Bordeaux 4ha.

Domaine de Roby (Fr) a vineyard. (Com): Loupiac. A.C. Loupiac, Bordeaux 5ha.

Domaine de Rol (Fr) a vineyard in the A.C. Saint-Émilion, Bordeaux 3ha.

Domaine de Roudier (Fr) a vineyard. (Com): Montagne-Saint-Émilion. A.C. Saint-Émilion, Bordeaux 7ha.

Domaine de Saint Baillon (Fr) a vineyard in the A.C. Côtes-de-Provence, south-eastern France. (Add): Flassans 83340 Le Luc.

Domaine de Saint Préfert (Fr) an A.C. Châteauneuf-du-Pape produced by Mme. Vve. Camille Serre, 84230 Châteauneuf-du-Pape, southern Rhône. Other labels: Cuvée Mélodie, Tenue de Soirée (now changed ownership).

Domaine de Saint Siffrein (Fr) an A.C. red Châteauneuf-du-Pape produced by Chastan (Claude), 84100 Orange, southern Rhône.

Domaine des Alysses (Fr) a 12ha vineyard in A.C. Coteaux Varois. Grape varieties: Chardonnay (Vin de Pays), plus Carignan, Grenache, Syrah and Cabernet sauvignon.

Domaine des Anguilleys (Fr) a vineyard. (Com): Bégadan. A.C. Médoc, Bordeaux. 8ha. Part of Château Vieux Robin.

Domaine des Arcades (Fr) a vineyard. (Com): Morgon. A.C. Morgon. Cru Beaujolais-Villages, Burgundy.

Domaine des Aspras (Fr) a vineyard in the A.C. Côtes-de-Provence, south-eastern France.

Domaine de Saumarez (Fr) a vineyard (established 2002) based in St-Georges d'Orques, in the A.C. Grès de Montpellier, Coteaux du Languedoc. 10ha. Labels: Cuvée S.

Domaine des Bateliers (Fr). A vineyard in the A.C. Cahors, south-western France. (Add): Courbenac, 46700 Puy l'Evêque.

Domaine des Baumard (Fr) a vineyard in the A.C. Savennières, Anjou-Saumur, Loire. Website: http://www.baumard.fr

Domaine des Beaumard (Fr) a Crèmant de Loire producer based at Rochefort-sur-Loire.

Domaine des Boulières (Fr) a vineyard in the A.C. Corbières, south-western France..

Domaine des Brissons de Laage (Fr) a Cognac producer. (Add): Reaux, 175000 Jarnac. 72ha. in the Petite Champagne. Produces and sells its own Cognacs.

Domaine des Buissonnes Fr) a vineyard in the A.C. Sancerre, Central Vineyards, France. Grape variety: Sauvignon blanc.

Domaine des Burdelines (Fr) a winery based in the A.C. Beaujolais Cru Moulin-à-Vent, southern Burgundy.

Domaine des Cambes (Fr) *see* Roc des Cambes.

Domaine des Carabiniers (Fr) a winery based in the A.C. Tavel, southern Rhône.

Domaine d'Escausses (Fr) a vineyard in the A.C. Gaillac, south-western France. Label: La Vigne Mythique.

Domaine des Causses et Saint-Eynes (Fr) a vineyard. (Com): St-Laurent-des-Arbes and Saint Victor-la-Coste. A.C. Lirac, Gard, southern France.

Domaine des Chanssaud (Fr) an A.C. red or white Châteauneuf-du-Pape produced by Jaume (Patrick), 84100 Orange, southern Rhône.

Domaine des Chant'Alluettes (Fr) an A.C. Pouilly Fumé. (Add): Pouilly-sur-Loire, 58150, France.

Domaine des Charbotières (Fr) a sweet white wine produced in the A.C. Coteaux de l'Aubance. Bottled at St-Jean des Mauvrets, 49320 Brissac. Clos des Huttières is a noted vineyard.

Domaine des Chausselières (Fr) an A.C. Muscadet Sèvre et Maine from Le Pallet, Nantais, Loire 18ha.

Domaine des Chenevières (Fr) a winery based in the A.C. Chablis, Burgundy. Produces a range of Chablis wines including Premier Cru Fourchaume.

Domaine de Chezelles (Fr) a vineyard in the A.C. Touraine, Loire Valley. Grape variety: Sauvignon blanc.

Domaine des Cigalons (Fr) an A.C. Châteauneuf-du-Pape from Raymond (Emile) at Quartier les Sinards, 84350 Courthézon, southern Rhône.

Domaine des Clones (Fr) a vineyard. (Com): Pomerol. A.C. Pomerol, Bordeaux 2ha.

Domaine des Comtes de Lupfen (Fr) a noted wine-producer based at Kientzheim, Kaysersberg, Haut-Rhin, Alsace.

Domaine des Comtes (Fr) a vineyard in the A.C. Meursault Premier Cru vineyard Les Charmes. Wines produced under biodymanic conditions.

Domaine des Coteaux des Travers (Fr) a winery based in the A.C. Côtes-du-Rhône-Villages Rasteau, Vaucluse. Label: Cuvée Prestige.

Domaine des Cotelins (Fr) a vineyard in A.C. Sancerre, Central Vineyards, Loire.

Domaine des Cottereaux (Fr) a vineyard in the A.C. Sancerre, Central Vineyards, Loire.

Domaine des Crais (Fr) a vineyard (10ha) based in Leynes, Beaujolais, southern Burgundy. (Add): 71570 Leynes. Grape varieties: Chardonnay, Gamay. Produces: A.C. Beaujolais-Leynes and A.C. Saint-Véran. 'E'mail: domainedescrais@wanadoo.fr

Domaine des Dépendances Cru Jaugueblanc (Fr) a vineyard in the A.C. Saint-Émilion, Bordeaux 3ha.

Domaine des 2 Anes (Fr) a vineyard in the A.C. Corbières, south-western France. Label: L'Enclos, Les Cabrioles, Fontanilles..

Domaine des Dorices (Fr) a vineyard in the A.C. Muscadet Sèvre et Maine, Nantais, Loire.

Domaine de Sème (Fr) a vineyard in the A.C. Saint-Émilion, Bordeaux 4ha.

Domaine des Escaravailles (Fr) a winery based in the A.C. Côtes-du-Rhône-Villages Rasteau, Vaucluse. Labels: La Ponce (Rasteau), Le Ventabren (Cairanne).

Domaine des Escardos (Fr) a vineyard in the A.C. Saint-Émilion, Bordeaux 7ha.

Domaine des Espiers (Fr) a winery based in the A.C. Côtes-du-Rhône-Villages Sablet, Vaucluse.

Domaine des Févries (Fr) an A.C. Muscadet Sèvre et Maine from Maisdon-sur-Sèvre, Nantais, Loire 12ha.

Domaine des Fontaines (Fr) a vineyard A.C. Moulin-à-Vent. Cru Beaujolais, southern Burgundy.

Domaine des Fontenettes (Fr) a vineyard based in Saint-Sernin-du-Plain, Côtes de Chouchois: Produces A.C. Bourgogne-Côtes-du-Couchois. Grape variety: Pinot noir.

Domaine des Forges (Fr) a vineyard based at St. Aubin-de-Luigne, A.C. Coteaux-du-Layon, Anjou-Saumur, Loire. Also produces A.C. Anjou wines.

Domaine des Frusseaux (Fr) an A.C. Muscadet Sèvre et Maine from Château-Thébaud, Nantais, Loire 9ha.

Domaine des Gaillardins (Fr) a vineyard. (Com): St-Selve. A.C. Graves, Bordeaux. 4ha (white).

Domaine des Gautronnières (Fr) a vineyard in the A.C. Muscadet Sèvre et Maine, Nantais, Loire.

Domaine des Genèves (Fr) a winery based in the A.C. Chablis, Burgundy. Produces a range of Chablis wines including Premier Crus Mont de Milieu and Vacoupin.

Domaine Gérard Charvet (Fr) a winery based in the A.C. Beaujolais Cru Moulin-à-Vent, southern Burgundy. Label: La Réserve d'Amelie.

Domaine des Grandes Perrières (Fr) a vineyard in the A.C. Sancerre, Central Vineyards, France. Grape variety: Sauvignon blanc.

Domaine des Grands Bois Chagneau (Fr) a vineyard. (Com): Néac. A.C. Lalande de Pomerol, Bordeaux.

Domaine des Grands-Champs (Fr) a vineyard. (Com): Montagne-Saint-Émilion. A.C. Saint-Émilion, Bordeaux 4ha.

Domaine des Grands Fers (Fr) a winery based in the A.C. Beaujolais Cru Fleurie, southern Burgundy.

Domaine des Grands-Pairs (Fr) a vineyard. (Com): Lussac-Saint-Émilion. A.C. Saint-Émilion, Bordeaux 2ha.

Domaine des Grands Primeaux (Fr) an A.C. Muscadet Sèvre et Maine from Le Pallet, Nantais, Loire 12ha.

Domaine des Grand'Terres (Fr) an A.C. Muscadet Sèvre et Maine from La Chapelle-Heulin, Nantais, Loire 21ha.

Domaine des Gravières (Fr) a vineyard. (Com): Portets. A.C. Graves, Bordeaux. 2ha (red).

Domaine des Greniers (Fr) an A.C. Muscadet Sèvre et Maine from Saint-Fiacre, Nantais, Loire 8ha.

Domaine des Hautes-Pémions (Fr) a vineyard in the A.C. Muscadet Sèvre et Maine, Nantais, Loire.

Domaine des Hautes Perrières (Fr) a vineyard in the A.C. Muscadet Sèvre et Maine, Nantais, Loire.

Domaine des Herbages (Fr) an A.C. Muscadet des Côtes de Grand-Lieu. (Add): Bouaye, 44830 Nantais, Loire 32ha.

Domaine des Hoscottières (Fr) a vineyard in the A.C. Muscadet Sèvre et Maine, Nantais, Loire.

Domaine des Justices (Fr) a vineyard. (Com): Preignac. A.C. Sauternes, Bordeaux. 14ha. Also Châteaux Gilette, Lamothe, Remparts and Les Rochers.

Domaine des Lambertins (Fr) a vineyard. (Com): Vacqueyras. A.C. Côtes du Rhône Villages, Rhône.

Domaine des Lanquières (Fr) a winery based in the A.C. Corbières, Languedoc-Roussillon. Produces: white, rosé and red wines.

Domaine des Lauzières (Fr) an A.C. Coteaux-des-Baux-en-Provence. (red and rosé). (Add): 13890 Mouries.

Domaine des Lucques (Fr) a vineyard. (Com): Portets. A.C. Graves, Bordeaux. 7ha (red and white).

Domaine des Malandes (Fr) a winery based in the A.C. Chablis, Burgundy. Produces a range of Chablis wines including Premier Crus Fourchaume and Vau de Vey.

Domaine des Marronniers (Fr) a winery based in the A.C. Chablis, Burgundy. Produces a range of Chablis wines including Premier Crus Côte de Jouan and Montmains.

Domaine des Mortiers-Gobin (Fr) an A.C. Muscadet Sèvre et Maine from La Haye-Fouassière, Nantais, Loire.

Domaine des Mouilles (Fr) a vineyard. (Com): Juliénas. A.C. Juliénas Cru Beaujolais-Villages, Burgundy.

Domaine des Moulins-à-Vent (Fr) a vineyard. (Com): Illats. A.C. Cérons, Bordeaux 9ha.

Domaine des Murettes (Fr) a vineyard in the A.C. Minervois la Livinière, Languedoc-Roussillon. Grape varieties: Carignan, Grenache, Mourvèdre and Syrah. Label: Cuvée des Cimes.

Domaine des Nizas (Fr) a vineyard in the A.C. Coteaux du Languedoc. Owned by Clos du Val (USA).

Domaine des Noës (Fr) an A.C. Muscadet Sèvre et Maine from Le Pallet, Nantais, Loire.

Domaine des Noyers (Fr) a vineyard. (Com): Sainte-Croix-du-Mont. A.C. Sainte-Croix-du-Mont, Bordeaux 7ha.

Domaine des Ollieux (Fr) a vineyard in the A.C. Corbières, Languedoc, south-western France.

Domaine Despagnet (Fr) a vineyard in the A.C. Saint-Émilion, Bordeaux 3ha.

Domaine des Pèlerins (Fr) an A.C. Muscadet Sèvre et Maine from Vallet, Nantais, Loire.

Domaine des Pères de l'Église (Fr) a vineyard in the A.C. Châteauneuf-du-Pape. (Add): SCEA Paulette Gradassi et Fils, 2, Avenue Impériale, Châteauneuf-du-Pape 84230 France. Uses all 13 permitted grape varieties.

Domaine des Perrières (Fr) an A.C. Muscadet Sèvre et Maine from Mouzillon, Nantais, Loire 13ha.

Domaine Desperrier Père et Fils (Fr) a winery based in the A.C. Beaujolais Cru Moulin-à-Vent, southern Burgundy. Label: Cuvée des Greneriers.

Domaine des Pierres Noires (Fr) a vineyard in the A.C. Muscadet Sèvre et Maine, Nantais, Loire.

Domaine des Places (Fr) a vineyard. (Com): Arbanats. A.C. Graves, Bordeaux. 3ha (red and white).

Domaine des Plagnes (Fr) an A.C. Châteauneuf-du-Pape from Maffret at La Font du Pape, 84230 Châteauneuf-du-Pape, Rhône.

Domaine des Pontifes (Fr) a vineyard in the A.C. Châteauneuf-du-Pape, southern Rhône.

Domaine des Quatre Routes (Fr) an A.C. Muscadet Sèvre et Maine from Maisdon-sur-Sèvre, Nantais, Loire 16ha.

Domaine des Quarres (Fr) a vineyard in the A.C. Coteaux de Layon Faye. (Add): Vignoble Bidet, 49750 Rablay-sur-Layon.

Domaine des Rebourgères (Fr) an A.C. Muscadet Sèvre et Maine from Maisdon-sur-Sèvre, Nantais, Loire 13ha.

Domaine des Relagnes (Fr) an A.C. Châteauneuf-du-Pape from Boiron at Rte. de Bédarrides, B.P. 44, 84230 Châteauneuf-du-Pape, southern Rhône. Red and white.

Domaine des Rochelles (Fr) a red wine produced at Saint-Jean-des-Mauvrets, 49320 Brissac-Quinc, from Cabernet franc and Cabernet sauvignon grapes. A.C. Anjou-Villages.

Domaine des Rochers (Fr) a vineyard. (Com): Côtes de Castillon. A.C. Bordeaux Supérieur, Bordeaux.

Domaine des Rochers (Fr) an A.C. Muscadet Sèvre et Maine from Mouzillon, Vallet, Nantais, Loire.

Domaine des Roches Neuves (Fr) an A.C. Saumur-Champigny, Loire. Vines situated on Terres Chaudes (clay and limestone).

Domaine des Rochettes (Fr) a vineyard in the A.C. Anjou, Anjou-Saumur, Loire. Grape variety: Cabernet franc.

Domaine des Rocs (Fr) a vineyard. (Com): Lussac-Saint-Émilion. A.C. Saint-Émilion, Bordeaux 8ha.

Domaine des Rozets (Fr) an A.C. Châteauneuf-du-Pape produced by Vergniaud (Dominique), Orange, southern Rhône.

Domaine des Saints Pères (Fr) an A.C. Châteauneuf-du-Pape from Gradassi, Ave. Impériale, 84230 Châteauneuf-du-Pape, southern Rhône. Other label is Calice de Saint Pierre (Le).

Domaine des Sarrots (Fr) a vineyard. (Com): St-Pierre-de-Mons. A.C. Graves, Bordeaux. 2ha (white).

Domaine des Schistes (Fr) a vineyard based in the A.C. Côtes du Roussillon, Languedoc-Roussillon, southern France.

Domaine des Sénéchaux (Fr) an A.C. Châteauneuf-du-Pape from Raynaud, 1 Rue de la Nouvelle-Poste, B.P. 27, 84230 Châteauneuf-du-Pape, southern Rhône.

Domaine des Souchons (Fr) a vineyard (13.5ha) in the A.C. Morgon Cru-Villages, Beaujolais, Burgundy. Grape variety: Gamay.

Domaine d'Esteau (Fr) a part of Château Fontesteau in the A.C. Haut-Médoc, Bordeaux.

Domaine des Templières (Fr) a vineyard. (Com): Lalande-de-Pomerol. A.C. Lalande de Pomerol, Bordeaux.

Domaine des Temps Perdus (Fr) a winery based in the A.C. Chablis, northern Burgundy.

Domaine des Terres Blanches (Fr) a vineyard. (Add): 13210 Saint-Rémy-de-Provence. A.C. Coteaux-des-Baux-en-Provence (white).

Domaine de St-Georges (Fr) a winery based in the A.C. Côtes-du-Rhône-Villages Chusclan, Vaucluse.

Domaine des Tourelles (Leb) a vineyard (4ha) based in the Bekka Valley. Grape varieties include: Cabernet sauvignon, Merwah, Obeideh, Syrah. Label: Marquis des Beys.

Domaine des Trois Chènes (Fr) a vineyard in A.C. Muscadet Sèvre et Maine, Nantais, Loire.

Domaine des Trois Monts (Fr) a vineyard based in Nyon, Côtes de Chouchois. Produces A.C. Bourgogne-Côtes-du-Couchois. Grape variety: Pinot noir.

Domaine des Trois Noyers (Fr) a vineyard in the A.C. Sancerre, Central Vineyards, Loire. (Add): Verdigny-en-Sancerre.

Domaine des Trois Versants (Fr) an A.C. Muscadet Sèvre et Maine from Maisdon-sur-Sèvre, Nantais, Loire 11ha.

Domaine de Surget (Fr) a vineyard. (Com): Néac. A.C. Lalande de Pomerol, Bordeaux.

Domaine des Valery (Fr) a winery based in the A.C. Chablis, Burgundy. Produces a range of Chablis wines including Premier Cru Vau de Vey.

Domaine des Vergnes (Fr) a vineyard. (Com): Portets. A.C. Graves, Bordeaux. 3ha (red and white).

Domaine des Vieilles Pierres (Fr) a vineyard in the A.C. Pouilly Fuissé. (Add): 71960 Vergisson. Produces: Les Crays (vieilles vignes).

Domaine des Vignes du Tremblay (Fr) a winery (10ha) based in Romanèche-Thorins, Beaujolais, southern Burgundy. Produces: A.C. Moulin-á-Vent and A.C. Beaujolais.

Domaine des Villots (Fr) a vineyard in the A.C. Sancerre, Central Vineyards, Loire.

Domaine de Terrebrune (Fr) an A.C. Bandol wine produced near Ollioules from Mourvèdre, Cinsault and Grenache grapes.

Domaine de Terre Ferme (Fr) the label of an A.C. Châteauneuf-du-Pape produced by négociant-producteur Domaine Bérard Père et Fils at 84370 Bédarrides, Châteauneuf-du-Pape, southern Rhône.

Domaine de Terrefort (Fr) an A.C. Bordeaux Supérieur.

Domaine de Terrefort (Fr) a vineyard. (Com): Sauternes. A.C. Sauternes, Bordeaux 3ha.

Domaine de Terre Mégère (Fr) a Vin de Pays d'Oc vineyard based at Cournonsec. Grape varieties: Cabernet sauvignon, Grenache, Viognier.

Domaine de Teycheney (Fr) a vineyard. (Com): Virelade. A.C. Graves, Bordeaux. 2ha (white).

Domaine de Teychon (Fr) a vineyard. (Com): Arbanats. A.C. Graves, Bordeaux. 4ha (white).

Domaine de Thalabert (Fr) an A.C. Crozes-Hermitage, Rhône. Produced by Jaboulet Aîné et Fils.

Domaine de Thibar (Afr) a vineyard at Thibarine in Tunisia. Produces wines under Thibar label. Also a 40% alc by vol. herb and date liqueur digestive.

Domaine Ticier (Fr) a winery based in the A.C. Chablis, Burgundy. (Add): Courgis F-89800. Produces a range of Chablis wines including Premier Cru Montmains. 'E'mail: taupe2@wanadoo.fr

Domaine de Torraccia (Fr) a vineyard (established 1960) and based near Porto Vecchio on the island of Corsica. Grape varieties include: Nielluccio and Sciarello. Label: Cuvée Oriu.

Domaine de Toumalin (Fr) a vineyard. (Com): Fronsac. A.C. Côtes de Canon-Fronsac, Bordeaux 2ha.

Domaine de Tourtouil (Fr) a vineyard in the A.C. Tavel, Rhône.

Domaine de Trapeau (Fr) a vineyard in the A.C. Saint-Émilion, Bordeaux 3ha.

Domaine de Treilhes (Fr) a vineyard in the Languedoc. Produces A.C. Blanquette de Limoux.

Domaine de Trepesson (Fr) a 2ha vineyard in the commune of St-Michel. A.C. Côtes de Canon-Fronsac, Bordeaux.

Domaine de Trévallon (Fr) originally A.C. Coteaux-des-Baux-en-Provence. Now Vin de Pays des Bouches du Rhône due to percentage of Cabernet sauvignon in the wine. 50%–60% Cabernet sauvignon plus Syrah. (Add): 13150 Saint-Étienne-du-Grès.

Domaine de Trians (Fr) a 20ha. vineyard in A.C. Coteaux Varois. Grape varieties: Grenache, Syrah, Cabernet sauvignon, Ugni blanc, Sémillon, Rolle, Viognier. Produces 60% red, 20% white and 20% rosé wines.

Domaine de Valmont (Switz) a red wine produced by Schenk in Salvagnin, Vaud from the Gamay and Pinot noir grapes.

Domaine de Valori (Fr) a vineyard in the A.C. Châteauneuf-du-Pape, southern Rhône. (Add): 13890 Mouries (red and white).

Domaine de Vauroux (Fr) a winery based in the A.C. Chablis, Burgundy. Produces a range of Chablis wines including Premier Crus Montée de Tonnerre and Montmains.

Domaine de Verquière (Fr) a winery based in the A.C. Côtes-du-Rhône-Villages Sablet, Vaucluse.

Domaine de Viaud (Fr) a vineyard. (Com): Lalande de Pomerol. A.C. Lalande de Pomerol, Bordeaux.

Domaine de Viaud (Fr) a vineyard. (Com): Pugnac. A.C. Côtes de Bourg, Bordeaux.

Domaine de Villeneuve (Fr) an A.C. Châteauneuf-du-Pape produced by Arnoux et Fils in Orange, Châteauneuf-du-Pape, Rhône.

Domaine de Vincent (Fr) a vineyard. (Com): St-Aignan. A.C. Côtes de Fronsac, Bordeaux 4ha.

Domaine d'Ognoas (Fr) an Armagnac producer. Produces a range of Armagnacs including vintage brandies.

Domaine d'Ormesson (Fr) a vineyard that produces

D

a Merlot and Cabernet sauvignon blended wine called L'Enclos in Lézignan. A.C. Languedoc-Roussillon.

Domaine Drouhin (USA) a winery in Willamette Valley, Oregon (part of Drouhin in Burgundy, France), noted for its Chardonnay and Pinot noir varietal wines. Label: Arthur, Laurène.

Domaine Drouhin-Laroze (Fr) a noted winery based in Chambertin, Côtes de Nuits, Burgundy. Produces Grand Cru and Premier Cru wines. 'E'mail: drouhin-laroze@wanadoo.fr

Domaine du Barque (Fr) a vineyard. (Com): St-Selve. A.C. Graves, Bordeaux. 6ha (red).

Domaine du Basque (Fr) a vineyard. (Com): Pujols. A.C. Graves, Bordeaux. 3ha (white).

Domaine du Beauregard (Fr) a vineyard based in Saint-Sernin-du-Plain, Côtes de Chouchois. Produces A.C. Bourgogne-Côtes-du-Couchois. Grape variety: Pinot noir.

Domaine du Beau-Site (Fr) a vineyard. (Com): Portets. A.C. Graves, Bordeaux. 3.5ha (red and white).

Domaine du Bois Bruley (Fr) an A.C. Muscadet Sèvre et Maine from Saint-Fiacre, Nantais, Loire 17ha.

Domaine du Bois-Joly (Fr) an A.C. Muscadet Sèvre et Maine from Pallet, Nantais, Loire 18ha.

Domaine du Bois Pothier (Fr) a winery (12ha) based in Ternand, Beaujolais, southern Burgundy. (Add): Le Berthier, 69620 Ternand. Grape varieties: Chardonnay, Gamay. Produces: a range of A.C. Beaujolais wines. Labels include: Brut Berchoux and La Torche.

Domaine du Bonat (Fr) a vineyard. (Com): St-Selve. A.C. Graves, Bordeaux. 5ha (white).

Domaine du Born (Fr) a vineyard. (Com): Sainte-Croix-du-Mont. A.C. Sainte-Croix-du-Mont, Bordeaux.

Domaine du Bosc (Fr) a vineyard in the Hérault département. Produces Vin de Pays (red and white) from Cabernet sauvignon, Cinsault, Merlot, Sauvignon blanc and Syrah grapes.

Domaine du Boscq (Fr) a vineyard. (Com): St-Morillon. A.C. Graves, Bordeaux. 2ha (white).

Domaine Dubost (Fr) a winery based in the A.C. Beaujolais Cru Brouilly, southern Burgundy. Labels: Cuvée de Vieilles Vignes, Prieuré du Tracot (A.C.'s Brouilly and Morgon).

Domaine du Bougan (Fr) a vineyard. (Com): Sainte-Croix-du-Mont. A.C. Sainte-Croix-du-Mont, Bordeaux 3ha.

Domaine du Bourg (Fr) a vineyard. (Com): Néac. A.C. Lalande de Pomerol, Bordeaux.

Domaine du Bourg (Fr) a vineyard in the A.C. Saint-Émilion, Bordeaux 2ha.

Domaine du Bousquillon (Fr) a vineyard in the A.C. Coteaux du Tricastin.

Domaine du Breuil de Segonzac (Fr) an exclusive 15 year old vieille réserve Grande Fine Champagne Cognac. Grapes grown in one parcel of Chez Collet vineyard, Segonzac.

Domaine du Brindin (Fr) an A.C. Muscadet Sèvre et Maine from Saint-Léger-les-Vignes, Nantais, Loire 8ha.

Domaine du Bugat (Fr) a vineyard. (Com): Sainte-Croix-du-Mont. A.C. Sainte-Croix-du-Mont, Bordeaux 3ha.

Domaine du Caillou (Fr) a vineyard. (Com): Cérons. A.C. Cérons, Bordeaux 5ha.

Domaine du Caillou (Fr) an A.C. red and white Châteauneuf-du-Pape produced by Pouizin (Claude) at Courthézon, southern Rhône.

Domaine du Cardneau (Fr) a vineyard. (Com): Saillans. A.C. Côtes de Fronsac, Bordeaux 6ha.

Domaine du Castel (Isr) a vineyard based in Israel. Website: http://www.castel.co.il 'E'mail: castel@castel.co.il

Domaine du Cayron (Fr) a winery based in the A.C. Gigondas, Côtes-du-Rhône, southern France.

Domaine du Chai (Fr) a vineyard. (Com): Fours. A.C. Côtes de Blaye, Bordeaux.

Domaine du Chalt Pouilly (Fr) a vineyard (established 1983) based in the Mâconnais, southern Burgundy. (Add): Les Gerbeaux, 71960 Solutré-Pouilly. 8ha. Produces: A.C. Pouilly-Fuissé and A.C. Saint-Véran. Website: http://www.domaineduchaletpouilly.com 'E'mail: contact@domaineduchaletpouilly.com

Domaine du Champ-Chapron (Fr) an A.C. Muscadet des Coteaux de la Loire, Nantais, Loire.

Domaine du Chardonnay (Fr) a winery based in the A.C. Chablis, Burgundy. Produces a range of Chablis wines including Premier Crus Montée de Tonnerre and Montmains.

Domaine du Chasseloir (Fr) a vineyard in the A.C. Muscadet Sèvre et Maine, Nantais, Loire.

Domaine du Chatain (Fr) a vineyard. (Com): Montagne-Saint-Émilion. A.C. Saint-Émilion, Bordeaux 3ha.

Domaine du Chatain (Fr) a vineyard. (Com): Néac. A.C. Lalande de Pomerol, Bordeaux.

Domaine du Château Miraudet (Fr) a vineyard based in Dracy-les-Couches, Côtes de Chouchois. Produces A.C. Bourgogne-Côtes-du-Couchois. Grape variety: Pinot noir.

Domaine du Chay (Fr) a vineyard. (Com): Loupiac. A.C. Loupiac, Bordeaux 12ha.

Domaine Duclaux (Fr) an A.C. red Châteauneuf-du-Pape produced by Quiot at Ave. Baron le Roy, 84230 Châteauneuf-du-Pape, southern Rhône.

Domaine du Cléray (Fr) a vineyard in the A.C. Muscadet Sèvre et Maine, Nantais, Loire.

Domaine du Clos du Roi (Fr) an A.C. red Châteauneuf-du-Pape produced at Le Prieuré Saint-Joseph, 84700 Sorgues, southern Rhône.

Domaine du Closel (Fr) a vineyard in the A.C. Savennières. (Add): 49170 Savennières. Labels: Clos du Papillon, Les Caillarières. Website: http://www.savennieres-closel.com

Domaine du Clos Fratin (Fr) a vineyard in the A.C. Vosne-Romanée, Burgundy. Owned by Albert Bichot.

Domaine du Colombier (Fr) a vineyard in the A.C. Sancerre, Central Vineyards, France. Grape variety: Sauvignon blanc. Label: Clos des Bouffants.

Domaine du Couprat (Fr) a vineyard. (Com): Saillans. A.C. Côtes de Fronsac, Bordeaux 5ha.

Domaine du Courreau (Fr) a vineyard. (Com): St-Médard-d'Eyrans. A.C. Graves, Bordeaux. 3ha (red and white).

Domaine du Courreau (Fr) a vineyard. (Com): St-Morillon. A.C. Graves, Bordeaux. 3ha (white).

Domaine du Coy (Fr) a vineyard. (Com): Sauternes. A.C. Sauternes, Bordeaux 3ha.

Domaine du Crampilh (Fr) a vineyard in the A.C. Madiran south-western France (red).

Domaine du Crêt Gonin (Fr) a winery based in the A.C. Beaujolais Cru Morgon, southern Burgundy.

Domaine du Demi-Boeuf (Fr) an A.C. Muscadet des Côtes de Grand-Lieu from La Limouzinière, Nantais, Loire 16ha.

Domaine du Devoy (Fr) an A.C. Lirac. (Add): St-Laurent-des-Arbes, 30126 Tavel, Gard.

Domaine du Druc (Fr) a vineyard. (Com): Landiras. A.C. Graves, Bordeaux. 2ha (white).

Domaine du Faucaudat (Fr) a Cognac producer. (Add): Gilbert Ricard, 16130 Juillac le Coq. 12ha. in Grande Champagne.

Domaine du Freyron (Fr) a vineyard. (Com): Cérons. A.C. Cérons, Bordeaux 3ha.

Domaine du Gaël (Fr) a vineyard. (Com): Sainte-Croix-du-Mont. A.C. Sainte-Croix-du-Mont, Bordeaux 2ha.

Domaine du Galet des Papes (Fr) an A.C. Châteauneuf-du-Pape produced by Mayard, Rte. de Bédarrides, 84230 Châteauneuf-du-Pape, southern Rhône.

Domaine du Gourdins (Fr) a vineyard. (Com): Sables-Saint-Émilion. A.C. Saint-Émilion, Bordeaux 1ha.

Domaine du Grand-Abord (Fr) a vineyard. (Com): Portets. A.C. Graves, Bordeaux. 5ha (white).

Domaine du Grand Beaupré (Fr) a vineyard (established 1974) based in Narbonne, southern France. (Add): 11100 Narbonne. 54ha. Grape varieties: Cabernet sauvignon, Chardonnay, Merlot. Sauvignon blanc, Viognier.

Domaine du Grand-Bigaroux (Fr) a vineyard in the A.C. Saint-Émilion, Bordeaux 2ha.

Domaine du Grand Clos (Fr) a vineyard in the A.C. Bourgueil, Touraine, Loire.

Domaine du Grand Coulet (Fr) an A.C. red Châteauneuf-du-Pape produced by Domaine du Père Pape. See also Clos du Calvaire.

Domaine du Grand Crès (Fr) a vineyard in the A.C. Corbières, Languedoc-Roussillon, south-western France. Label: Cuvée Majeure.

Domaine du Grand-Faurie (Fr) a commune in the A.C. Saint-Émilion, Bordeaux 4ha.

Domaine du Grand Ferré (Fr) an A.C. Muscadet Sèvre et Maine from Vallet, Nantais, Loire 8ha.

Domaine du Grand-Gontey (Fr) a vineyard in the A.C. Saint-Émilion, Bordeaux 4ha.

Domaine du Grand Mouton (Fr) an A.C. Muscadet Sèvre et Maine from Saint-Fiacre, Nantais, Loire 23ha.

Domaine du Grand Ormeau (Fr) a vineyard. (Com): Néac. A.C. Lalande de Pomerol, Bordeaux.

Domaine du Grand Tinel (Fr) an A.C. red and white Châteauneuf-du-Pape produced by Jeune (Elie) at B.P. 58, 84230 Châteauneuf-du-Pape, southern Rhône.

Domaine du Grand Veneur (Fr) an A.C. red and white Châteauneuf-du-Pape produced by Jaume (Alain) at Rte. de Châteauneuf-du-Pape, 84100 Orange, southern Rhône.

Domaine du Granit (Fr) a winery based in the A.C. Beaujolais Cru Moulin-à-Vent, southern Burgundy.

Domaine du Gros' Noré Fr) a vineyard in the A.C. Bandol, Provence.

Domaine du Guette-Soleil (Fr) a winery based in the A.C. Chablis, Burgundy. Produces a range of Chablis wines including Premier Cru Vosgros.

Domaine du Haut-Badon (Fr) a vineyard in the A.C. Saint-Émilion, Bordeaux 3ha.

Domaine du Haut Bourg (Fr) an A.C. Muscadet des Côtes de Grand-Lieu, Nantais, Loire.

Domaine du Haut-Cloquet (Fr) a vineyard. (Com): Pomerol. A.C. Pomerol, Bordeaux 1ha.

Domaine du Haut des Terres Blanches (Fr) an A.C. Châteauneuf-du-Pape produced by Diffonty at Châteauneuf-du-Pape, southern Rhône. See also Domaine de la Petite Bastide.

Domaine du Haut Planty (Fr) an A.C. Muscadet Sèvre et Maine from Le Landreau, Nantais, Loire 17ha.

Domaine Dujac (Fr) owners and producers of many great wines. Sited at Morey-Saint-Denis. Wines such as Clos de la Roche, Clos Saint-Denis.

Domaine du Jau (Fr) a vineyard. (Com): St-Morillon. A.C. Graves, Bordeaux. 3ha (white).

Domaine du Joncier (Fr) a vineyard based in the A.C. Lirac, southern Rhône.

Domaine du Labrande (Fr) a vineyard. (Com): Saillans. A.C. Côtes de Fronsac, Bordeaux 5ha.

Domaine du Landreau-Village (Fr) an A.C. Muscadet Sèvre et Maine from from Vallet, Nantais, Loire 13ha.

Domaine du Léonard (Fr) a vineyard. (Com): Puisseguin-Saint-Émilion. A.C. Saint-Émilion, Bordeaux 9ha.

Domaine du Lucrabey (Fr) a vineyard. (Com): Cussac. A.C. Haut-Médoc, Bordeaux 5ha.

Domaine du Mas Blanc (Fr) an A.C. Banyuls, south-western France. Vin-Doux-Naturel. (Add): 66650 Banyuls-sur-Mer.

Domaine du May (Fr) a vineyard. (Com): Portets. A.C. Graves, Bordeaux. 5ha (red and white).

Domaine du Mayne (Fr) a vineyard. (Com): Langon. A.C. Graves, Bordeaux. 3ha (white).

Domaine du Merle (Fr) a vineyard based in the Mâconnais, Burgundy. (Add): Sens, 71240 Sennecey-le-Grand. Grape varieties: Chardonnay, Gamay, Pinot noir. Produces: A.C. Bourgogne (white and red) and A.C. Passe-Tout-Grains.

Domaine du Montteillet (Fr) a vineyard in the A.C. Saint-Joseph, Northern Rhône. (Add): 42410 Chavanay. 'E'mail: stephane.montez@worldonline.fr

Domaine du Mouchez (Fr) a vineyard. (Com):

Fronsac. A.C. Côtes de Canon-Fronsac, Bordeaux 7ha.

Domaine du Moulin (Fr) a winery based in the A.C. Côtes-du-Rhône-Villages Vinsobres, Vaucluse. Label: Cuvée Charles Joseph.

Domaine du Nozay (Fr) a vineyard in the A.C. Sancerre, Central Vineyards, France. Grape variety: Sauvignon blanc.

Domaine du Parc (Fr) an A.C. Muscadet des Côtes de Grand-Lieu, Nantais, Loire 13ha.

Domaine du Pasquet (Fr) a vineyard. (Com): Loupiac. A.C. Loupiac, Bordeaux.

Domaine du Pavillion (Fr) a vineyard in the A.C. Pommard, Burgundy (owned by Albert Bichot).

Domaine du Pavillion de Chauannes (Fr) an A.C. Côte de Brouilly. (Add): 69430 Quincié-en-Beaujolais.

Domaine du Pégau (Fr) an A.C. red and white Châteauneuf-du-Pape produced by Féraud at Ave. Impériale, 84230 Châteauneuf-du-Pape, southern Rhône.

Domaine du Père Caboche (Fr) an A.C. Châteauneuf-du-Pape produced by Boisson at Rte. de Courthézon, 84230 Châteauneuf-du-Pape, southern Rhône (red and white).

Domaine du Père Pape (Fr) an A.C. red and white Châteauneuf-du-Pape produced by Mayard at 24 Ave. le Roy, 84230 Châteauneuf-du-Pape, southern Rhône.

Domaine Duperneau (Fr) a vineyard. (Com): Bommes. A.C. Sauternes, Bordeaux 3ha.

Domaine du Petit Clos (Fr) a vineyard in the A.C. Saint-Émilion, Bordeaux 4ha.

Domaine du Petit-Gontey (Fr) a vineyard in the A.C. Saint-Émilion, Bordeaux 3ha.

Domaine du Petit-Gueyrot (Fr) a vineyard in the A.C. Saint-Émilion, Bordeaux 2ha.

Domaine du Petit Metris (Fr) an A.C. Coteaux du Layon. Quarts de Chaume. Anjou-Saumur, Loire.

Domaine du Pibarnon (Fr) a 45ha estate based in A.C. Bandol south-eastern France. Produces red wines from Mourvèdre plus 5% Grenache grapes, rosé from 50% Cinsault plus Mourvèdre grapes, white wine from Clairette, Bourboulenc, Marsanne, Roussanne, Viognier and Petit Manseng grapes.

Domaine du Plantey (Fr) a vineyard. (Com): Castres. A.C. Graves, Bordeaux. 3ha (red and white).

Domaine du Poujol (Fr) a vineyard based in the A.C. Grès de Montpellier, Coteaux du Languedoc. Label: Podio Alto.

Domaine du Pourra (Fr) a winery based in the A.C. Côtes-du-Rhône-Villages Séguret, Vaucluse. Label: Cuvée Mont-Bayon.

Domaine du Prieuré d'Amilhac (Fr) a Vin de Pays des Côtes de Thongue produced from 15 year old vines.

Domaine du Puits Fleuri (Fr) a vineyard based in Saint-Maurice-les Couches, Côtes de Chouchois. Produces A.C. Bourgogne-Côtes-du-Couchois. Grape variety: Pinot noir.

Domaine du Puynormond (Fr) a vineyard. (Com):

Parsac-Saint-Émilion. A.C. Saint-Émilion, Bordeaux 5ha.

Domaine du Reys (Fr) a vineyard. (Com): La Brède. A.C. Graves, Bordeaux. 3ha. Grape varieties: Cabernet 35%, Merlot 65%, Sauvignon 35% and Sémillon 65% (red and white).

Domaine Durieu (Fr) an A.C. red and white Châteauneuf-du-Pape produced at 10 Ave. Baron le Roy, 84230 Châteauneuf-du-Pape, southern Rhône. 21ha. Produces: Réserve Lucil Avril.

Domaine du Rochoy (Fr) a vineyard in the A.C. Sancerre, Central Vineyards, France. Grape variety: Sauvignon blanc.

Domaine du Roudier (Fr) a vineyard. (Add): Montagne-Saint-Émilion, 33330 Saint-Émilion. A.C. Montagne-Saint-Émilion. Commune: Montagne-Saint-Émilion.

Domaine du Roux (Fr) a vineyard in the A.C. Saint-Émilion, Bordeaux 2ha.

Domaine du Salut (Fr) the name for the wine of Château Huradin. A.C. Cérons, Bordeaux.

Domaine du Sancy (Fr) an A.C. Muscadet Sèvre et Maine from Maisdon-sur-Sèvre, Nantais, Loire 15ha.

Domaine du Sapeur (Fr) a vineyard. (Com): Portets. A.C. Graves, Bordeaux. 4ha (red and white).

Domaine du Single (Fr) a vineyard in the A.C. Cahors, south-western France.

Domaine du Sorbief (Fr) an A.C. Arbois-Pupillin vineyard in Jura that produces red, rosé and white wines.

Domaine du Touron (Fr) a winery based in the A.C. Montbazillac, Bergerac. Grape varieties: Sauvignon blanc, Sémillon.

Domaine du Trillol (Fr) a vineyard in the A.C. Corbières, south-western France.

Domaine du Val Fleury (Fr) an A.C. Muscadet Sèvre et Maine from Le Loroux-Bottereau, Nantais, Loire.

Domaine du Ventois (Fr) an A.C. Muscadet Sèvre et Maine from Saint-Fiacre, Nantais, Loire.

Domaine du Vieux Chai (Fr) an A.C. Muscadet Sèvre et Maine from La Haye-Fouassière, Nantais, Loire.

Domaine du Vieux Cyprès (Fr) an A.C. Châteauneuf-du-Pape produced by Dorvin at 84100 Orange, southern Rhône.

Domaine du Vieux Foudre (Fr) a vineyard (6ha) based in Nyon, Côtes de Chouchois. (Add): 5, Route de Nyon, 71510 St. Sincernin du Plain. Produces A.C. Bourgogne-Côtes-du-Couchois. Grape varieties: Aligoté, Pinot noir. 'E'mail: vieuxfoudre@wanadoo.fr

Domaine du Vieux Lazaret (Fr) an A.C. Châteauneuf-du-Pape from Quiot at Ave. Baron le Roy, 84230 Châteauneuf-du-Pape, southern Rhône. Red and white.

Domaine du Vieux-Moulin-de-Calon (Fr) a vineyard. (Com): Montagne-Saint-Émilion. A.C. Saint-Émilion, Bordeaux 1ha.

Domaine du Vieux Relais (Fr) a domaine in the A.C. Costières de Nîmes, Languedoc-Roussillon. Noted for red wines: Tradition from 50% Grenache and

50% Syrah grapes and Sélection from 80% Mourvèdre and 20% Grenache grapes.

Domaine du Vieux Télégraphe (Fr) a noted A.C. Châteauneuf-du-Pape from Brunier et Fils at BP 5, 84370 Bédarrides, southern Rhône. 52ha (red and white). Labels include: Le Pigeoulet, Vieux Mas des Papes Télégramme. Owns the Domaines: La Roquète and Les Pallières. 'E'mail: vignobles@brunier.fr

Domaine du Vignots (Fr) a vineyard. (Com): Sainte-Croix-du-Mont. A.C. Sainte-Croix-du-Mont, Bordeaux 2ha.

Domaine du Viking (Fr) a vineyard in A.C. Vouvray, Touraine, Loire. Produces Cuvée Aurélie. Bottled at the domaine by Gauthier-l'Homme, Melotin, 37380 Reugny.

Domaine du Vissoux (Fr) a winery (30ha) based in Saint-Léger in the A.C. Beaujolais, southern Burgundy. Produces: A.C. Fleurie and A.C. Moulin-á-Vent. Labels include: Poncié (Fleurie), Rochègres (Moulin-à-Vent).

Domaine Emmanuel Darnaud (Fr) a vineyard in the A.C. Crozes-Hermitage, northern Rhône. Grape variety: Syrah. Label: Les Trois Chênes.

Domaine Étienne (Fr) a vineyard. (Com): St-Morillon. A.C. Graves, Bordeaux. 2ha (white).

Domaine Evharis (Gre) a winery based at Nemea on mainland Greece that produces sparkling wines by the traditional method. Grape varieties: Moscofilero and Roditis. Label: Boheme.

Domaine Fabrice Mousset (Fr) an A.C. red and white Châteauneuf-du-Pape produced by Mousset at 84230 Châteauneuf-du-Pape, southern Rhône 4ha.

Domaine Familiale (Fr) a Calvados distillery based in the A.C. Calvados Pays d'Auge, Normandy. Produces vintage Calvados.

Domaine Faurmarie (Fr) a vineyard (established 1986) based in the A.C. Grès de Montpellier, Coteaux du Languedoc. Labels: L'Ecrit Vin, Les Mathilles.

Domaine Ferrand (Fr) an A.C. red Châteauneuf-du-Pape produced by Bravay at Chemin de Saint-Jean, 84100 Orange, southern Rhône.

Domaine Fèvre (Fr) a winery based in the A.C. Chablis, Burgundy. Produces a range of Chablis wines including Premier Crus Fourchaume and Fourchaume-Vaulorent. 'E'mail: fevregilles@wanadoo.fr

Domaine Fiou (Fr) a vineyard in the A.C. Sancerre, Central Vineyards, France. Grape variety: Sauvignon blanc.

Domaine Filliatreau (Fr) an A.C. Saumur-Champigny based at Chaintres, Dampierre-sur-Loire. Includes vieilles vignes Saumur-Champigny and Château Fouquet.

Domaine Florimond (Fr) a vineyard. (Com): Berson. A.C. Côtes de Blaye, Bordeaux. (Add): 33390 Berson, Blaye.

Domaine Font-Caude (Fr) a red wine producing vineyard in A.C. Coteaux du Languedoc-Montpeyroux in the Hérault département,

southern France. Noted for Les Boissières (Grenache) and Esprit de Font-Caude (Syrah).

Domaine Font de Michele (Fr) an A.C. red and white Châteauneuf-du-Pape from Jean et Michel Gonnet at 14 Impasse des Vignerons, 84370 Bédarrides, southern Rhône. 30ha. Other label is Source aux Nymphes (La). Website: http://www.terre.net.fr/egonnet 'E' Mail: egonnet@terre.net.fr

Domaine Franc-Baudron (Fr) a vineyard. (Com): Montagne-Saint-Émilion. A.C. Saint-Émilion, Bordeaux 6ha.

Domaine François Laget (Fr) an A.C. red Châteauneuf-du-Pape produced by Laget-Royer at 19 Ave. Saint-Joseph, 84230 Châteauneuf-du-Pape, southern Rhône. 16ha. Other label is Domaine Pontificale.

Domaine François Monnot (Fr) a vineyard based in Saint-Sernin-du-Plain, Côtes de Chouchois. Produces A.C. Bourgogne-Côtes-du-Couchois. Grape variety: Pinot noir.

Domaine Frapin Grande Fine Champagne (Fr) a fine Cognac produced by Frapin et Cie.

Domaine Fussiacus (Fr) a vineyard in the A.C. Pouilly-Fuissé, Mâconnaise.

Domaine Gadant et François (Fr) a vineyard based in Saint-Maurice-les Couches, Côtes de Chouchois. Produces A.C. Bourgogne-Côtes-du-Couchois. Grape variety: Pinot noir. Label: Le Clos Voyen.

Domaine Garcin Layouni (Fr) a winery based in the A.C. Tavel, southern Rhône. (Add): Chemin des Cravailleux, 30126 Tavel. Owns Domaine de la Genestière.

Domaine Geisweiler (Fr). *see* Geisweiler et Fils.

Domaine Gérard Charvin (Fr) an A.C. Châteauneuf-du-Pape produced by Charvin at Chemin Maucoil, 84100 Orange, southern Rhône.

Domaine Gerovassiliou (Gre) a winery based in Avaton.

Domaine Gibaut (Fr) an A.C. Touraine vineyard on the Cher, Loire. Grape variety: Sauvignon blanc.

Domaine Gilles Desvignes (Fr)) a vineyard based in Couches, Côtes de Chouchois. Produces A.C. Bourgogne-Côtes-du-Couchois. Grape variety: Pinot noir. Label: Les Courtaillards.

Domaine Gilles Gaudet (Fr) a 13ha vineyard (established 1890) based in Saint-Sernin-du-Plain, Côtes de Chouchois. (Add): 3, Rue de la Fontaine, 71510 Saint-Sernin-du-Plain. Produces A.C. Bourgogne-Côtes-du-Couchois. Grape varieties: Chardonnay, Pinot noir.

Domaine de Granoupiac (Fr) a vineyard (established 1982) based in the A.C. Terrasses du Larzac, Coteaux du Languedoc. Label: Les Cresses.

Domaine Gresser [André et Rémy] (Fr) an Alsace wine producer. (Add): 2, Rue de l'Ecole, Andlau 67140 Barr.

Domaine Hatzimichalis (Gre) a winery at Farma Atlantis, Agriotiko. (Add): 13th klm National Road, 145 64 N Kifissia. Range of varietal wines include Chardonnay, Cabernet sauvignon, Merlot.

Domaine Haut-Caillate (Fr) a 2ha. vineyard in the commune of Saint-Georges-Saint-Émilion. A.C. Saint-Émilion, Bordeaux.

Domaine Haut-Callens (Fr) a vineyard. (Com): Beautiran. A.C. Graves, Bordeaux. 3ha (red).

Domaine Haut-Corbière (Fr) a vineyard. (Com): Sables-Saint-Émilion. A.C. Saint-Émilion, Bordeaux 2ha.

Domaine Haute-Rouchonne (Fr) a vineyard in the A.C. Saint-Émilion, Bordeaux 4ha.

Domaine Haut-Guillennay (Fr) a vineyard. (Com): Sables-Saint-Émilion. A.C. Saint-Émilion, Bordeaux. 2ha.

Domaine Haut-Patarabet (Fr) a part of Clos Chante-l'Alouette, A.C. Saint-Émilion, Bordeaux.

Domaine Haut-Trimoulet (Fr) a vineyard in the A.C. Saint-Émilion, Bordeaux 5ha.

Domaine Haut-Vachon (Fr) a vineyard in the A.C. Saint-Émilion, Bordeaux 4ha.

Domaine Helios (Gre) a winery based at Nemea on mainland Greece. Label: Nemea Grande Reserve.

Domaine Henri-Gouges (Fr) a noted winery based in Nuits-St-Georges, Côtes de Nuits, Burgundy. Produces a range of fine Burgundies including: Premier Cru: Clos des Porrets.

Domaine Henri Rebourseau (Fr) a winery (established 1919) based in the Grand Cru A.C. Gevrey Chambertin, Burgundy. (Add): 10, Place du Monument, 21220 Gevrey Chambertin. Website: http://www.rebourseau.com

Domaine Hervé Azo (Fr) a winery based in the A.C. Chablis, Burgundy. Produces a range of Chablis wines including Premier Cru Vau de Vey.

Domaine Huet (Fr) a vineyard in the A.C. Vouvray, Loire. Produces an organic Vouvray sec under its Le Mont label.

Domaine Jacob Frerebeau (Fr) a winery (14ha) based in Changey-Echeuronne, Côte de Beaune, Burgundy. (Add): 50 Grande Rue, 21420 Changey-Echeuronne. Grape varieties: Aligoté, Chardonnay, Pinot noir. Produces a range of Burgundy wines including A.C. Grand Cru Corton-Vergennes and A.C. Premier Cru Savigny Lavières.

Domaine Jacques Sallé (Fr) a vineyard in the A.C. Quincy, Central Vineyards, Loire Valley. Label: Silice de Quincy.

Domaine Jaune (Fr) a winery based in the A.C. Côtes-du-Rhône-Villages Vinsobres, Vaucluse.

Domaine Jean Bousquet SH (Arg) a winery based in the Mendoza region, eastern Argentina. Website: http://www.jeanbousquet.com 'E'mail: jeanbousquet1@slatinos.com.ar

Domaine Jean-Claude Bessin (Fr) a winery based in the A.C. Chablis, Burgundy. Produces a range of Chablis wines including Premier Cru Fourchaume.

Domaine Jean-Claude Martin (Fr) a winery based in the A.C. Chablis, Burgundy. Produces a range of Chablis wines including Premier Cru Beauregards.

Domaine Jean Collet et Fils (Fr) a winery based in the A.C. Chablis, Burgundy. Produces a range of Chablis wines including Premier Crus Montée de Tonnerre and Montmains.

Domaine Jean-Goulley & Fils (Fr) a winery based in the A.C. Chablis, Burgundy. Produces a range of Chablis wines including Premier Crus Fourchaume and Montmains.

Domaine Jean-Jacques Girard (Fr) a winery in the A.C. Savigny-lès-Beaune, Côte de Beaune, Burgundy.

Domaine Jean-Marc et Jocelyne Seguin (Fr) a vineyard based in Saint-Sernin-du-Plain, Côtes de Chouchois. Produces A.C. Bourgogne-Côtes-du-Couchois. Grape variety: Pinot noir.

Domaine Jean-Robert (Fr) a vineyard. (Com): Preignac. A.C. Sauternes, Bordeaux 1ha.

Domaine Jobard-Morey (Fr) a winery in the A.C. Meursault, Côte de Beaune, Burgundy.

Domaine Joblet (Fr) a winery based in the A.C. Givry, Côte Chalonnaise, Burgundy. Label: Clos de la Servoisine.

Domaine Juliette Avril (Fr) an A.C. red Châteauneuf-du-Pape. (Add): 8 Rte. d'Avignon, 84230 Châteauneuf-du-Pape, southern Rhône. 22ha. See *also* Cuvée du Majoral.

Domaine Klipfel (Fr) a vineyard in Alsace. 34ha. (Add): 67140 Barr.

Domaine la Barnouine (Fr) a vineyard in the A.C. Châteauneuf-du-Pape. (Add): Cave Éric Robbe, Quartier des Sinards, 84350 Courthézon, southern Rhône.

Domaine la Bastide Saint Dominique (Fr) an A.C. Châteauneuf-du-Pape produced by Bonnet at 84350 Courthézon, southern Rhône.

Domaine la Beillonne (Fr) a vineyard in the A.C. Saint-Émilion, Bordeaux 2ha.

Domaine la Borie (Fr) a vineyard. (Com): Saillans. A.C. Côtes de Fronsac, Bordeaux 6ha.

Domaine la Bouvaude (Fr) a winery based in the A.C. Côtes-du-Rhône-Villages Rousset-les-Vignes, Vaucluse.

Domaine Lacour [Fabrice] (Fr) a vineyard (9ha) based in Couches, Côtes de Chouchois. (Add): 71490 Couches. Produces A.C. Bourgogne-Côtes-du-Couchois. Grape variety: Pinot noir.

Domaine la Crau des Papes (Fr) an A.C. red Châteauneuf-du-Pape produced by Puget at Clos du Mont de Vies, Châteauneuf-du-Pape, southern Rhône 24ha.

Domaine la Croix Palanne (Fr) an Armagnac producer based in the Bas Armagnac, Gers. Produces vintage and other Armagnacs.

Domaine la Croix St-Laurent (Fr) a vineyard in the A.C. Sancerre, Central Vineyards, France. Grape variety: Sauvignon blanc.

Domaine Lacroix-Vanel (Fr) a vineyard based in the A.C. Pézanas, Coteaux du Languedoc. Label: Clos Mélanie.

Domaine Lafond (Fr) a winery based in the A.C. Tavel, southern Rhône. (Add): Route des Vignobles, 30126 Tavel. Label: Roc-Epine.

Domaine Lafran-Veyrolles (Fr) a 10ha. winery at La Caudière-d'Azur, Var in Provence. Produces A.C. Bandol wines. Cuvée Longue Garde is made using 100% Mourvèdre grapes.

D

Domaine La Garancière (Fr) a winery based in the A.C. Côtes-du-Rhône-Villages Séguret. (Add): Clos du Joncuas 84190 Gigondas. Website: http://www.vigneron-independant.com/membres/clos-du-joncuas

Domaine la Grange des Pères (Fr) a 10ha Vin de Pays vineyard (based near Mas de Daumas Gassac). Grape varieties include Marsanne for white wines, Syrah, Mourvèdre and Cabernet sauvignon for red wines.

Domaine La Grange Tiphaine (Fr) vineyard based in the A.C. Montlouis, Touraine, Loire Valley.

Domaine la Grave (Fr) an A.C. Graves. (Add): 33460 Portets. Commune: Portets. 7ha. Grape varieties: Cabernet sauvignon 50%, Merlot 50% and Sémillon 100%.

Domaine Lagrave de Bertin (Fr) an A.C. Bordeaux Supérieur.

Domaine la Jouchère (Fr) a Premier Cru vineyard in the A.C. Chablis, Burgundy.

Domaine Lamarche (Fr) a winery based in the Grand Cru A.C. Vosne-Romanée, Burgundy. (Add): 9, Rue des Communes, 21700 Vosne-Romanée. Holds and produces a range of Grand Cru wines (Vougeot and Vosne-Romanée). Website: http://www.domaine-lamarche.com 'E'mail: domainelamarche@wanadoo.fr

Domaine la Mereuille (Fr) an A.C. Châteauneuf-du-Pape produced by Bouyer (Michel) at Quartier Le Grès, 84100 Orange, southern Rhône 5ha.

Domaine la Moussière (Fr) a vineyard in A.C. Sancerre, Central Vineyards, Loire.

Domaine la Payrère (Fr) a vineyard. (Com): St-Selve. A.C. Graves, Bordeaux. 5ha (red and white).

Domaine la Place (Fr) a vineyard in the A.C. Madiran, south-western France.

Domaine la Pointe (Fr) a vineyard. (Com): Pomerol. A.C. Pomerol, Bordeaux 4ha.

Domaine la Raze (Fr) a vineyard in the A.C. Bergerac, south-western France. (red).

Domaine La Rocalie (Fr) a winery based in the A.C. Tavel, southern Rhône.

Domaine Laroche (Fr) a noted winery based in the A.C. Chablis, Burgundy. (Add): 89800 Chablis. Produces a range of Chablis wines including Grand Cru: Les Clos and Premier Crus Fourchaume (Vieilles Vignes) and Vaillons (Vieilles Vignes). Websites: http://www.michellaroche.com/http://www.larochewines.com 'E' mail: info@michellaroche.com

Domaine la Roquette (Fr) a vineyard (29ha) based in the A.C. red and white Châteauneuf-du-Pape produced by Brunier at 2 Ave. Louis Pasteur, 84230 Châteauneuf-du-Pape, southern Rhône. Grape varieties: Bourboulenc, Clairette, Grenache, Grenache blanc, Mourvèdre, Roussane, Syrah. Owned by Domaine du Vieux Télégraphe. 'E'mail: http://www.vignobles@brunier.fr

Domaine Larreyda (Fr) a vineyard in the A.C. Jurançon, south-western France which is noted for its sweet white wines.

Domaine Larrouquey (Fr) a vineyard. (Com): Cérons. A.C. Cérons, Bordeaux 5ha.

Domaine la Solitude (Fr) a vineyard. (Com): Martillac. A.C. Graves, Bordeaux. 6ha (red and white).

Domaine la Soumade (Fr) a vineyard in the A.C. Rasteau, Côtes-du-Rhône-Villages.

Domaine la Suffrène (Fr) a vineyard based in the A.C. Bandol, Provence, south-eastern France. Grape varieties include: Mourvèdre.

Domaine la Tourmone (Fr) a vineyard in the A.C. Vacqueyras. Produces Maître de Chais and Trésor du Poête. Grape varieties – Grenache, Mourvèdre and Syrah.

Domaine Laurier (USA) a winery based in the Russian River Valley, Sonoma, California. Grape varieties: Cabernet sauvignon, Chardonnay, Johannisberg riesling, Pinot noir and Sauvignon blanc. Produces varietal wines.

Domaine la Voltonnerie (Fr) a vineyard in the A.C. Sancerre, Central Vineyards, France. Grape variety: Sauvignon blanc.

Domaine le Breton (Fr) a vineyard. (Com): Massugas. A.C. Saint-Foy-Bordeaux, Bordeaux.

Domaine le Clos de Caveau (Fr) a vineyard in the A.C. Vacqueyras, Côtes-du-Rhône-Villages.

Domaine le Clos des Cazaux (Fr) a vineyard in the A.C. Vacqueyras, Côtes-du-Rhône-Villages. Label: Cuvée des Templiers.

Domaine le Cossu (Fr) a vineyard. (Com): Podensac. A.C. Cérons, Bordeaux 5ha.

Domaine le Devois (Fr) a vineyard based in the A.C. Coteaux du Languedoc. Grape variety: Syrah.

Domaine le Fief Joyeux (Fr) an A.C. Muscadet Sèvre et Maine. Produced by Donatien Bahuaud.

Domaine Leflaive (Fr) a winery (whose vineyards are biodynamic) based in Puligny, Côte de Beaune, Burgundy. Grand Crus: Bâtard, Bienvenues, Chevaler, Montrachet. Premier Crus: Clavoillon, Purcelles.

Domaine le Galatin (Fr) a vineyard in the A.C. Bandol. Produces: white, rosé and red wines. Grape varieties: Cinsault, Grenache and Mourvèdre.

Domaine le Malaven (Fr) a winery based in the A.C. Tavel, southern Rhône. (Add): Route de la Commanderie, 30126 Tavel.

Domaine le Père Caler (Fr) an A.C. Châteauneuf-du-Pape produced by Avril (Maurice) at Rte. de Sorgues, 84230 Châteauneuf-du-Pape, southern Rhône.

Domaine le Puy du Maupas (Fr) a winery based in the A.C. Côtes-du-Rhône-Villages Vinsobres, Vaucluse.

Domaine le Roc des Anges (Fr) a vineyard in the A.C. Côtes de Roussillon-Villages. Produces a biodynamic wine under the Rouge Segna de Cor label.

Domaine Lerys (Fr) a vineyard in the A.C. Corbières, south-western France.

Domaine le Sang des Cailloux (Fr) a winery based in the A.C. Vacqueyras, Côtes-du-Rhône, southern France. Label: Cuvée Lopy.

Domaine les Beaux Regards (Fr) a vineyard in the A.C. Sancerre, Central Vineyards, France. Grape variety: Sauvignon blanc.

D

Domaine les Bernard (Fr) a vineyard. (Com): Saillans. A.C. Côtes de Fronsac, Bordeaux 4ha.

Domaine les Cailloux du Paradis (Fr) a 6ha vineyard in Touraine. All wines produced are sold as Vin de Table or Vin de Pays de Loire et Cher. Wines include Plume d'Ange (Sauvignon blanc), Alkimya (botrytised Menu Pineau), red wines from Cabernet franc, Cabernet sauvignon, Gamay de Chaudenay, Côt, Plantet.

Domaine les Cluchets (Fr) a vineyard. (Com): Langon. A.C. Graves, Bordeaux. 4ha (white).

Domaine les Côtes de la Roche (Fr) a winery (20ha) based in the A.C. Beaujolais Crus of Chénas, Juliénas, Moulin-á-Vent, Saint-Amour, southern Burgundy.

Domaine les Gallimardes (Fr) an A.C. Châteauneuf-du-Pape produced by Giraud at Ave. Impériale, 84230 Châteauneuf-du-Pape, Rhône 18ha.

Domaine les Genêts (Fr) a vineyard. (Com): Montagne-Saint-Émilion. A.C. Saint-Émilion, Bordeaux 3ha.

Domaine les Goubert (Fr) a winery based in the A.C. Côtes-du-Rhône-Villages Sablet, Vaucluse.

Domaine les Grandes Vignes (Fr) an A.C. Bonnezeaux wine bottled at Thouarcé by Vaillant.

Domaine les Hautes Cances (Fr) a winery based in the A.C. Côtes-du-Rhône-Villages Cairanne, Vaucluse. (Add): SCEA Achàry-Astart, 84290 Cairanne. Labels: Cuvée Col du Débat, Cuvée Vieilles Vignes. Website: http://www.hautescances.com

Domaine les Jays (Fr). A.C. Bordeaux Supérieur.

Domaine les Marcottes (Fr) a vineyard. (Com): Sainte-Croix-du-Mont. A.C. Sainte-Croix-du-Mont, Bordeaux 4ha.

Domaine les Mascaronnes (Fr) an A.C. Châteauneuf-du-Pape produced by Palazzi (Jacky) at Quartier les Mascaronnes, 84230 Châteauneuf-du-Pape, southern Rhône.

Domaine le Soulida (Fr) an A.C. Châteauneuf-du-Pape produced by Brunel (Max) at Les Marines, 84230 Châteauneuf-du-Pape, southern Rhône.

Domaine le Souverain (Fr) a winery based in the A.C. Côtes-du-Rhône-Villages Séguret, Vaucluse.

Domaine les Pallières (Fr) a vineyard in the A.C. Gigondas. Côtes du Rhône-Villages, south-eastern France. 25ha. Grape varieties: Cinsault 15%, Grenache 65%, Mourvèdre 10% and Syrah 10%. Label: Au/petit Bonheur—Les Pallières (rosé). Owned by Domaine du Vieux Télégraphe.

Domaine les Roches des Garants (Fr) a winery based in the A.C. Beaujolais Cru Fleurie, southern Burgundy. Label: Les Moriers.

Domaine Lestang (Fr) a vineyard. (Com): St-Selve. A.C. Graves, Bordeaux. 5ha (red and white).

Domaine le Vieux Moulin (Fr) a winery based in the A.C. Tavel, southern Rhône.

Domaine Lignon Minervois (Fr) a vineyard in the A.C. Minervois, Languedoc-Roussillon. Grape varieties: Carignan, Grenache, Mourvèdre and Syrah. Label: Les Vignes d'Antan.

Domaine Long-Depaquit (Fr) a vineyard in the A.C. Chablis, Burgundy (domaine bottled). Owned by Albert Bichot. Produces a range of Chablis wines including Premier Crus Forêt and Les Vaucopins.

Domaine Lou Fréjau (Fr) an A.C. red and white Châteauneuf-du-Pape produced by Chastan (Serge) at Chemin de la Gironde, 84100 Orange, southern Rhône.

Domaine Louis-Fabry (Fr) a vineyard in the A.C. Corbières, south-western France. Label: Le Pountil.

Domaine Louis Moreau (Fr) a winery based in the A.C. Chablis, Burgundy. Produces a range of Chablis wines including Premier Crus Vaillons and Valignot.

Domaine Lucien Barrot et Fils (Fr) an A.C. Châteauneuf-du-Pape produced by Barrot. (Add): Chemin du Clos, 84230 Châteauneuf-du-Pape, southern Rhône 19ha.

Domaine Maby (Fr) a vineyard in A.C. Tavel, southern Rhône. 44ha. Wine sold under the name of Forcadière (La).

Domaine Magnien (Fr) a vineyard (9.25ha) based in Saint-Sernin-du-Plain, Burgundy. (Add): Cromey-le-Haut, 71510 Saint-Sernin-du-Plain. Produces: A.C. Santenay Premier Cru Clos Rousseau, A.C. Bourgogne Côtes du Couchois, A.C. Maranges Côte-de-Beaune. Label: Clos des Condemines.

Domaine Maillard (Fr) a vineyard based in the A.C. Savigny-lès-Beaune, Côte de Beaune, Burgundy.

Domaine Maréchal-Caillot (Fr) a winery based in Bligny-lès-Beaune, Côte de Beaune, Burgundy.

Domaine Marey-Monse (Fr) a négociant-éleveur based in the Côte d'Or, Burgundy.

Domaine Marguerite de Bourgogne (Fr) a vineyard based in Couches, Côtes de Chouchois. Produces A.C. Bourgogne-Côtes-du-Couchois. Grape variety: Pinot noir.

Domaine Martin (Fr) a vineyard. (Com): Roaillan. A.C. Graves, Bordeaux. 2ha (white).

Domaine Martin (Fr) a winery based in the A.C. Côtes-du-Rhône-Villages Rasteau, Vaucluse. Label: Les Sommets de Rasteau.

Domaine Matassa (Fr) a vineyard (established 2001) in the Vin de Pays des Côtes Catalanes, Roussillon, south-western France. Grape varieties: Grenache gris, Maccabeu.

Domaine Mathieu (Fr) an A.C. red and white Châteauneuf-du-Pape produced by Mathieu at Rte. de Courthézon, B.P. 32, 84230 Châteauneuf-du-Pape, southern Rhône.

Domaine Mercouri (Gre) a winery based in Letrina.

Domaine Métrat et Fils (Fr) a winery based in the A.C. Beaujolais Cru Fleurie, southern Burgundy. Label: La Roilette

Domaine Michel Bernard (Fr) an A.C. Châteauneuf-du-Pape wine producer at La Serrière, Rte. de Sérignan, 84100 Orange, southern Rhône. Labels include Domaine de la Clastre, Domaine de la Serrière, Domaine Ferrand, Château Beauchêne.

Domaine Michel David (Fr) a winery (established 1937) based at Le Landreau, A.C. Muscadet Sèvre et Maine, Loire Atlantique. 30ha. Label: Clos de Ferré.

D

Domaine Michel et Marc Rossignol (Fr) a winery (established 1961) based in Volnay, Côte de Beaune, Burgundy. (Add): Rue de l'Abreuvoir, 21190 Volnay. Grape varieties: Chardonnay, Pinot noir. Produces a range of Burgundy wines including: A.C. Côte de Beaune 'Clos de Pierres Blanches, A.C. Premier Cru Monthelie 'Les Champs Fulliots', A.C. Premier Cru Pommard 'Les Chanlins' and A.C. Volnay. 9ha. Website: http://www.m-rossignol.fr 'E'mail: marcrossignol2@wanadoo.fr

Domaine Michel Juillot (Fr) a winery (30ha) in the A.C. Mercurey, Côte Chalonnaise, Burgundy. Labels: Les Champs, Premier Cru Clos des Barraults.

Domaine Millet (Fr) a winery based in the A.C. Chablis, Burgundy. Produces a range of Chablis wines including Premier Cru Vaucoupin.

Domaine Millet (Fr) an A.C. Châteauneuf-du-Pape produced by Millet at Ave. Impériale, 84230 Châteauneuf-du-Pape, southern Rhône 8ha.

Domaine Montahuc (Fr) an A.C. St. Jean de Minervois wine.

Domaine Montjoie (Fr) a vineyard in the A.C. Corbières, Languedoc, south-western France.

Domaine Montmija (Fr) a vineyard in the A.C. Corbières, south-western France.

Domaine Moss Wood (Austr) a vineyard at Willyabrup, West Australia. Produces a Sémillon from Margaret River plus Cabernet sauvignon, Pinot noir and Chardonnay wines.

Domaine Moulin-Tacussel (Fr) an A.C. red Châteauneuf-du-Pape produced by Moulin at 10 Ave. des Bosquets, 84230 Châteauneuf-du-Pape, southern Rhône.

Domaine Mucyn (Fr) a vineyard in the A.C. Crozes-Hermitage, Northern Rhône. Grape variety: Syrah.

Domaine Müller (Aus) a winery (43ha) based in Gross St. Florian, West-Oststeiermark. (Add): Gussendorf 5, 8522 Gross St. Florian. Grape varieties: Blauer wildbacher, Cabernet sauvignon, Chardonnay, Pinot blanc, Pinot gris, Sauvignon blanc, Welschriesling, Zweigelt. Produces a range of dry and sweet wines (including Schilcherwein).

Domaine Mumm (USA) the name given to the Californian branch of G.H. Mumm (Californian Champagne). Produced from 40% Chardonnay and 60% Pinot noir grapes.

Domaine Normand (Fr) a vineyard. (Com): Saillans. A.C. Côtes de Fronsac, Bordeaux 13ha.

Domaine Norte Dame des Pallières (Fr) a winery based in the A.C. Côtes-du-Rhône-Villages Rasteau, Vaucluse.

Domaine Ogereau (Fr) a vineyard based at St. Lambert du Lattay, A.C. Coteaux-du-Layon, Anjou-Saumur, Loire.

Domaine Oriental (Chile) a winery (140ha) based in Maule Valley, Talca. Noted for Cabernet sauvignon wines. Labels include: Casa Donoso.

Domaine Ott (Fr) a vineyard based in Provence, southern France. Label: Clos Mireille.

Domaine Pagnotta (Fr) a vineyard based in the A.C. Rully, Côte Chalonnaise, Burgundy. Label: La Crée

(Premier Cru), also an A.C. Premier Cru Mercurey Voyens.

Domaine Palga Raffault (Fr) a vineyard in the A.C. Chinon, Anjou-Saumur, Loire. (Add): Roguinet, 37420 Savigny-en-Veron, Loire.

Domaine Palivós (Gre) a winery based at Nemea on mainland Greece. Label: Terre Leone.

Domaine Pasquet (Fr) a vineyard. (Com): Escoussans. A.C. Entre-Deux-Mers, Bordeaux.

Domaine Patarabet-la-Gaffelière (Fr) a vineyard in the A.C. Saint-Émilion, Bordeaux 2ha.

Domaine Patrice Magni (Fr) a vineyard based in the A.C. Châteauneuf-du-Pape.

Domaine Paul Autard (Fr) an A.C. red and white A.C. Châteauneuf-du-Pape produced by Autard at Rte. de Châteauneuf-du-Pape, 84350 Courthézon, southern Rhône 12ha.

Doamine Paul Bruno (Chile) the label for Cabernet sauvignon, Cabernet franc or Merlot wines produced by Viña Aquitania, Maipo, Santiago.

Domaine Pélaniquié (Fr) a winery based in the A.C. Tavel, southern Rhône. (Add): 7, Rue du Vernet, 30290 St. Victor La Coste. Also produces an A.C. Côtes-du-Rhône-Villages Laudun.

Domaine Perges (Fr) an A.C. Châteauneuf-du-Pape produced by Nicolet at 8 Ave. Saint-Joseph, 84230 Châteauneuf-du-Pape, southern Rhône.

Domaine Perin de Naudine (Fr) an A.C. Graves. (Add): 33640 Portets, Castres-Gironde. (Com): Castres. 4.52ha. Grape varieties: Cabernet 50% and Merlot 50%. (red). *see* Château Perin de Naudine.

Domaine Petit-Basque (Fr) a vineyard in the A.C. Saint-Émilion, Bordeaux 2ha.

Domaine Petit-Camusat (Fr) a Champagne producer. (Add): 14, Rue de l'Église, 10300 Noe les Mallets. Produces non-vintage Champagnes.

Domaine Peyre-Rose (Fr) a 24ha. vineyard in Saint-Pargoire, A.C. Grès de Montpellier, Coteaux du Languedoc. Produces Cuvée (Clos) des Cistes, Cuvée (Clos) Syrah Léone.

Domaine Philippe et Valérie Jeannot (Fr) a vineyard based in Saint-Sernin-du-Plain, Côtes de Chouchois. Produces A.C. Bourgogne-Côtes-du-Couchois. Grape variety: Pinot noir.

Domaine Piccinini (Fr) a vineyard in the A.C. Minervois la Livinière. Label is Cuvée Line et Laetitia. Grape varieties: Carignan, Grenache, Mourvèdre and Syrah.

Domaine Pierre Bouthenet (Fr)) a vineyard based in Couches, Côtes de Chouchois. Produces A.C. Bourgogne-Côtes-du-Couchois. Grape variety: Pinot noir. Label: La Creuse.

Domaine Pierre Giraud (Fr) an A.C. Châteauneuf-du-Pape produced by Giraud at Ave. Impériale, 84230 Châteauneuf-du-Pape, southern Rhône. Other label is Domaine les Gallimardes.

Domaine Pierre Usseglio (Fr) an A.C. red and white Châteauneuf-du-Pape produced by Usseglio at Rte. d'Orange, Châteauneuf-du-Pape, southern Rhône 10ha.

Domaine Pillebourse (Fr) a vineyard. (Com): Saillans. A.C. Côtes de Fronsac, Bordeaux 3ha.

D

Domaine Pinson (Fr) a winery based in the A.C. Chablis, Burgundy. Produces a range of Chablis wines including Premier Cru Mont-de-Milieu and Vaugiraut.

Domaine Pontificial (Fr) the label of an A.C. Châteauneuf-du-Pape produced by Domaine Francois Laget in southern Rhône.

Domaine Porto Carras (Gre) a 450ha. winery based at Halkidiki, northern Greece. Grape varieties: Cabernet franc, Cabernet sauvignon, Cinsault, Grenache, Limnio, Merlot, Petite syrah, Rhoditis, Sauvignon blanc and Ugni blanc. *See also* Château Carras, Carras (John).

Domaine Rabasse Charavin (Fr) a winery based in the A.C. Côtes-du-Rhône-Villages Cairanne, Vaucluse. Label: Cuvée d'Estevenas.

Domaine Rabiéga (Fr) a vineyard in A.C. Côtes de Provence. Produces red and rosé wines. Noted for Cuvée Clos d'Ière I and III. Website: http://www.rabiega.com

Domaine Rabion-Pailhas (Fr) a vineyard in the A.C. Saint-Émilion, Bordeaux 4ha.

Domaine Raimbault (Fr) a vineyard in the A.C. Sancerre. Produces white wines under the Les Chasseignes label.

Domaine Raoul Gautherin (Fr) a winery based in the A.C. Chablis, northern Burgundy.

Domaine Raymond Usseglio (Fr) an A.C. Châteauneuf-du-Pape produced by Usseglio at Rte. de Courthézon, B.P. 29, Châteauneuf-du-Pape, southern Rhône.

Domaine Régis Champier (Fr) a winery based in the A.C. Beaujolais Cru Brouilly, southern Burgundy.

Domaine Reverdy-Ducroux (Fr) a vineyard in the A.C. Sancerre, Central Vineyards. (Add): Verdigny-en-Sancerre, Cher, France. Grape variety: Sauvignon blanc. Labels: Beau Roy, La Renardière, Les Chaumes, Les Perriers.

Domaine Ribet (Fr) *see* Château Guerry.

Domaine Richaud (Fr) a winery based in the A.C. Côtes-du-Rhône-Villages Cairanne, Vaucluse.

Domaine Riché (Fr) an A.C. red and white Châteauneuf-du-Pape produced by Riché at 27 Ave. Général-de-Gaulle, 84230 Châteauneuf-du-Pape, southern Rhône.

Domaine Richeaume (Fr) a vineyard in the A.C. Côtes de Provence, south-eastern France.

Domaine Rimbert (Fr) a vineyard based in St-Chinian. Noted for red Mas au Schist wine.

Domaine Roc de Cailloux (Fr) a winery in the A.C. Buzet, south-western France.

Domaine Roche-Audran (Fr) a winery based in the A.C. Côtes-du-Rhône-Villages Visan, Vaucluse. Label: Père Mayeux.

Domaine Roger Perrin (Fr) an A.C. red and white Châteauneuf-du-Pape produced by Perrin at Rte. de Châteauneuf-du-Pape, La Berthaude, 84100 Orange, southern Rhône 11ha.

Domaine Roger Sabon (Fr) an A.C. red and white Châteauneuf-du-Pape produced by Sabon (Roger et Fils) at Ave. Impériale, 84230 Châteauneuf-du-Pape, southern Rhône. 15ha. Website: http://www.rogersabon.com02.com 'E'mail: roger.sabon@wanadoofr

Domaine Roland (Fr) a vineyard. (Com): Langon. A.C. Graves, Bordeaux. 3ha (white).

Domaine Rose-Dieu (Fr) an A.C. Côtes-du-Rhône vineyard from the Plan de Dieu, Vaucluse.

Domaine Rossignol-Février (Fr) a winery (9.65ha) based in Volnay, Côte de Beaune, Burgundy. (Add): 21190 Volnay. Grape varieties: Chardonnay, Pinot noir. Produces A.C. Pommard 'Les Petits Noizons', A.C. Volnay, A.C. Premier Cru Volnay-Robardelle,

Domaine Roy Frères (Fr) a winery (11.5ha) based in Auxey-Duresses, Côte de Beaune, Burgundy. (Add): 21190 Auxey-Duresses. Produces: A.C. Premier Crus Auxey-Duresses 'Les Duresses' and 'Le Val'. Also produces Marc de Bourgogne. Website: http://www.domaine.roy.free.fr

Domaine Saint-Andeol (Fr) a vineyard in the A.C Cairanne, Côtes-du-Rhône-Villages.

Domaine Saint-Andrieu (Fr) a 25ha. vineyard in Montpeyroux, A.C. Coteaux du Languedoc-Montpeyroux. Produces Les Roches Blanches, Les Marnes Bleues (80% Mourvèdre), L'Yeuse Noir (70% Mourvèdre).

Domaine Saint Benoit (Fr) an A.C. red and white Châteauneuf-du-Pape produced by Cellier at Quartier les Gallimardes, 84230 Châteauneuf-du-Pape, southern Rhône 26ha.

Domaine Sainte-Marie des Crozes (Fr) a winery based in the A.C. Corbières, Languedoc-Roussillon. Produces: white, rosé and red wines.

Domaine Saint Gayan (Fr) a vineyard in the A.C. Gigondas, Côtes-du-Rhône-Villages. (Add): 84190 Gigondas. Produces A.C. Rasteau. Website: http://www.saintgayan.com

Domaine Saint-Jean (Fr) a vineyard in the A.C. Côtes-de-Provence, south-eastern France. (Add): Vignobles Maille, 83570 Carcès.

Domaine Saint Joseph (Fr) a vineyard in the A.C. Corbières, Languedoc, south-western France.

Domaine Saint-Maurice (Fr) a vineyard in the A.C. Corbières, Languedoc, south-western France.

Domaine Saint-Prix (Fr) a winery based in the A.C. Chablis, Burgundy. Produces a range of Chablis wines including Premier Crus Beauroy and Montmains.

Domaine Sarda-Mallet (Fr) a 5ha. vineyard in south-western France. Wines qualify for both A.C. Rivesaltes and A.C. Côtes du Roussillon. Grape varieties: Grenache blanc, Maccabeu, Malvoisie, Mourvèdre, Syrah, Grenache.

Domaine Saupiquet (Fr) a vineyard in the A.C. Saint-Émilion, Bordeaux 2ha.

Domaine Saurrute (Fr) the dry white wine from Château Caillou [Grand Cru Classé (2nd). Barsac].

Domaines de Villemajou (Fr) vineyards in the A.C. Corbières, Languedoc, south-western France.

Domaines du Château de Riquewihr (Fr) only allocated to Dopff et Irion wines of Château Riquewihr in Alsace of the vineyards Les Sorueres, Amandiers, Maguisards and Murailles.

D

Domaine Séguinot-Bordet (Fr) a winery based in the A.C. Chablis, Burgundy. (Add): Maligny F-89800. Produces a range of Chablis wines including Premier Crus Fourchaume and Vaillons.

Domaine Seigneur de Renouard (Fr) a winery based in the A.C. Côtes-du-Rhône-Villages Séguret, Vaucluse.

Domaine Sénéchaux (Fr) an A.C. red and white Châteauneuf-du-Pape, southern Rhône. Produces both red and white wines.

Domaine Serene (USA) a vineyard based in the Willamette Valley, Oregon. (Add): 6555 Hilltop Lane, Oregon 97114. Grape varieties: Chardonnay, Pinot gris, Pinot noir. Labels: Etoile, Evenstad Reserve, Grace Vineyard. Website: http://www.domaineserene.com

Domaine Servin (Fr) a winery based in the A.C. Chablis, Burgundy. Produces a range of Chablis wines including Premier Crus Montée de Tonnerre and Vaillons.

Domaines Faiveley (Fr) a winery based in the A.C. Gevrey-Chambertin, Côtes de Nuits, Burgundy.

Domaines Font-Sainte (Fr) vineyards in the A.C. Corbières, Languedoc, south-western France.

Domaine Sigalas (Gre) a winery based on the island of Santorini.

Domaine Siouvette (Fr) a winery based in the A.C. Côtes de Provence, south-eastern France. (Add): Canton de Saint-Tropez, 83310 La Mole. Produces white, rosé and red wines. 'E'mail: sylvaine.sauron@wanadoo.fr

Domaine Skouras (Gre) a winery based at Nemea on mainland Greece. Label: Megas Oenos.

Domaines Lafragette (Fr) family-owned vineyards based in the Bordeaux region. Château de l'Hospital (A.C. graves), Château de Rouillac (A.C. Pessac-Léognan) and Château Loudenne (A.C. Médoc). Website: http://www.lafragette.com

Domaines Michel Bernard (Fr) owned by Boisset. Noted for wide range of southern Rhône wines.

Domaines Ott (Fr) a family-owned winery based in the Côtes de Provence. Produces Château de Selle, Château Romassan and Clos Mireille. Sold in special shaped bottles.

Domaines Paul Mas (Fr) a winery based in the Pays d'Oc, southern France. Grape varieties include: Chardonnay, Merlot, Syrah, Viognier. Labels: Hidden Hill, La Forge Estate.

Domaines Piron (Fr) a winery based in the A.C. Beaujolais Cru Morgon, southern Burgundy. 'E'mail: dominiquepiron@domaines-piron.fr

Domaines Robert Guiraud (Fr) a Bordeaux négociant. (Add): B.P. 31, 33240 St. André-de-Cubzac, Gironde. Distributes Château Moulin de Bel-Air exclusively.

Domaines Rolet (Fr) a 53 ha estate in A.C. Arbois, Jura. Produces still wines and Vin de Paille.

Domaines Schlumberger (Fr) wineries based in the A.C. Alsace. Label: Cuvée Anne.

Domaine Sigaux (Fr) a vineyard (established 1760) 30ha. in the A.C. Brouilly, Cru Beaujolais-Villages.

Domaine St André de Figuière (Fr) a vineyard in A.

C. Côtes de Provence. Produces red, rosé and white wines, including a Grande Cuvée Vieilles Vignes from 100 year old Carignan grapes.

Domaines Tatiarra (Austr) a winery based in Heathcote, Victoria.

Domaine St. Demetrios (USA) a winery based near St. Helena, Napa Valley, California. Grape varieties: Cabernet sauvignon, Chardonnay, Chenin blanc, Gamay, Johannisberg riesling and Sauvignon blanc. Produces varietal wines.

Domaine St-Amant (Fr) a winery based in the A.C. Beaumes-de-Venise, Côtes-du-Rhône, Vaucluse. Label: Grangeneuve.

Domaine Ste. Anne (Fr) a winery based in the A.C. Côtes-du-Rhône-Villages St.-Gervais, Vaucluse.

Domaine Ste. Michelle (USA) the sparkling wine division of Château Ste. Michelle, Washington.

Domaine St. Eulalie (Fr) a vineyard in the A.C. Minervois, south-western France.

Domaine St. Gayan (Fr) a vineyard in the A.C. Gigondas, Côtes du Rhône-Villages, south-eastern France.

Domaine St-Jean-de-Béard (Fr) a vineyard in the A.C. Saint-Émilion, Bordeaux 4ha.

Domaine St. Roman d'Esclans (Fr) a vineyard in the A.C. Côtes-de-Provence, south-eastern France.

Domaine Suteau (Fr) a vineyard in the A.C. Muscadet Sèvre et Maine, Nantais, Loire.

Domaine Tarbia (Fr) an Armagnac producer based in the Bas Armagnac, Gers. Produces vintage and other Armagnacs.

Domaine Tauzinat (Fr) a vineyard in the A.C. Saint-Émilion, Bordeaux 3ha.

Domaine Tchit (Fr) a vineyard. (Com): Fargues. A.C. Sauternes, Bordeaux 1ha.

Domaine Tempier (Fr) a vineyard in the A.C. Bandol, Provence, south-eastern France (red and rosé wines).

Domaine Terre Megère (Fr) a vineyard based in the A.C. Grès de Montpellier, Coteaux du Languedoc. Label: Les Dolomies.

Domaine Testut (Fr) a winery based in the A.C. Chablis, Burgundy. (Add): 89800 Chablis. Produces a range of Chablis wines including Premier Cru Montée de Tonnerre.

Domaine Thomas (Fr) a vineyard based in the A.C. Saint-Véran.

Domaine Tixier (Fr) a winery based in the A.C. Chablis, Burgundy. Produces a range of Chablis wines including Premier Cru Montmains (vieilles vignes).

Domaine Tolot Beaut (Fr) a winery based in the A.C. Chorley-lès-Beaune, Côte de Beaune, Burgundy.

Domaine Tour Saint Michel (Fr) an A.C. Châteauneuf-du-Pape produced by Fabre (Henri) at Quartier de Condorcet, 84230 Châteauneuf-du-Pape, southern Rhône.

Domaine Tremblay-Bouchard (Fr) a vineyard based in the A.C. Chablis.

Domaine Trintignant (Fr) an A.C. red and white Châteauneuf-du-Pape produced by Trintignant in Châteauneuf-du-Pape, southern Rhône 8ha.

D

Domaine Vacheron (Fr) a 34ha vineyard at 1 Rue de Puits Poulton, 18300 Sancerre, Loire. A.C. Sancerre.

Domaine Vachon (Fr) a vineyard in the A.C. Saint-Émilion, Bordeaux 3ha.

Domaine Vessigaud (Fr) a vineyard based in the Mâconnais, southern Burgundy. (Add): Hameau 'Pouilly', 71960 Solutré. Grape variety: Chardonnay. Produces: A.C.'s Mâcon-Fuissé, Mâcon-Solutre, Pouilly-Fuissé. Website: http://www.DomaineVessigaud.com

Domaine Villesseche (Fr) a red wine from the A.C. Côtes-du-Rhône.

Domaine Vincent Giradin (Fr) négociant-éleveur based in the A.C. Meursault, Côte de Beaune, Burgundy. Has many holdings in the Côte d'Or including Grand Cru and Premier Cru vineyards. (Add): Les Champs Lins, BP 48, 21190 Meursault. Website: http://www.vincentgiradin.com 'E'mail: vincent.giradin@vincentgiradin.com

Domaine Viret (Fr) a winery based in the A.C. Côtes-du-Rhône-Villages St. Maurice, Vaucluse. Labels: Emergence, Maréotis.

Domaine Vistalba (Arg) a winery at Luján de Cuyo, Mendoza. Grape varieties: Malbec, Cabernet sauvignon, Sémillon, Sauvignon blanc, Merlot, Malbec.

Domaine Viticoles (Fr) a large co-operative winery based in Salins du Midi, south-western France 1,700ha.

Domaine Viticole Schlumberger (Fr) an Alsace wine producer. (Add): 100 Rue Theodore Deck, 68500 Guebwiller.

Domaine Wardy (Leb) a vineyard (established 1999) based near the Bekka Valley. Grape varieties include: Muscat, Viognier. Produces varietal wines.

Domaine Weinbach (Fr) a Grand Cru vineyard in A.C. Alsace. Owned by Théo Faller. Grape varieties: Gewurztraminer, Riesling, Tokay pinot gris. Labels: Clos des Capucins 'Cuvée Sainte-Catherine' Tokay Pinot Gris, 'Cuvée Théo' Gewurztraminer.

Domaine William Fèvre (Fr) a winery based in the A.C. Chablis, Burgundy. Produces a range of Chablis wines including Premier Cru Fourchaume. Label: Vignoble de Vaulorent.

Domaine Yves Cuilleron Bassenon (Fr) a vineyard based in the A.C. Côte-Rôtie, Northern Rhône.

Domaine Zind-Humbrecht (Fr) a vineyard in the A.C. Alsace. 26.5ha. (Add): Wintzenheim, 68000 Colmar.

Domäne (Ger) usually a state-owned or state-managed vineyard or property.

Domäne Baron Geymüller (Aus) a winery based in the Kremstal region. (Add): Dinstlgut Loiben, Hollenburg 57, 3506 Krems. Grape varieties: Chardonnay, Grüner veltliner, Müller-Thurgau, Riesling, Neuberger, Zweigelt. Produces a range of wine styles.

Domänerat (Ger) State-managed vineyards.

Domange [Christian] (Fr) an Armagnac producer. (Add): Domaine de Las Lannes, Bezolles, 32310 Valence-sur-Baise. Produces Hors d'Age 10 year old.

Domazlice Brewery (Czec) an old brewery (established 1341) based in western Czec.

Domberg (Ger) vineyard (Anb): Nahe. (Ber): Kreuznach. (Gro): Schlosskapelle. (Vil): Waldlaubersheim.

Domberg (Ger) vineyard (Anb): Nahe. (Ber): Schloss Böckelheim. (Gro): Paradiesgarten. (Vil): Sobernheim.

Dombeya Vineyards (S.Afr) a winery (established 2002) based in Die Boord, Stellenbosch, Western Cape. 15ha. Grape varieties: Cabernet sauvignon, Chardonnay, Merlot, Sauvignon blanc. Website: http://www.dombeya.co.za

Domblick (Ger) grosslage (Anb): Rheinhessen. (Ber): Wonnegau. (Vils): Hohen-Sülzen, Mölsheim, Monsheim, Offstein, Wachenheim.

D.O.M. Cocktail (Cktl) 40mls (⅓ gill) gin, 20mls (⅙ gill) orange juice, 15mls (⅛ gill) Bénédictine. Shake over ice and strain into a goblet.

Domdechaney (Ger) vineyard (Anb): Rheingau. (Ber): Johannisberg. (Gro): Daubhaus. (Vil): Hochheim.

Domdechaney (Ger) lit: 'deanery', a vineyard within the village of Hochheim, 10.3ha. (100%) of which is proposed to be classifed as Erstes Gewächs.

Dôme [Le] (Fr) a 1.72ha. vineyard in Saint-Émilion, Bordeaux. A.C. Saint-Émilion. Grape varieties: 60%–65% Cabernet franc, 35%–40% Merlot.

Domecq (Sp) a brandy producer. (Add): Pedro Domecq SA, San Ildefonso No 3, Jerez 30. Wines from Estremadura, Huelva and La Mancha. Produces: Fundador (3 y.o.), Hispano, San Quintin, Tres Cepas (2 y.o.) (Solera brandies), Carlos III (6 y.o. Solera Reserva brandy), Marqués de Domecq, Carlos I (12 y.o.), Carlos I Imperial (Solera gran reserva brandy). Also produce a range of Sherries.

Domecq (Sp) a great Sherry family (own 2,600ha of vineyards in Jerez de la Frontera). Noted Sherry-brands include: Bolivar, Celebration, Double Century, Imperial 1914, La Ina, MDV, Napoleon, Nelson, Rio Viejo and Sibarita. Also a noted brandy producer.

Domecq Domain (Sp) the brand-name for red and white wines produced by the Bodegas Domecq, S.A. Rioja.

Domecq Double Century (Sp) the brand-name for a light dry Sherry produced by Domecq in Jerez.

Domein Doornkraal (S.Afr) a winery (established 1890) based in De Rust, Little Karoo. 35ha. Grape varieties: Cabernet sauvignon, Chenin blanc, Jerepigo, Merlot, Sémillon, Tinta, Touriga nacional, White jerepigo. Labels: Kannaland, Kaptein, Kuierwyn, Luitenant, Majoor, Pinta, Tickled Pink. Website: http://www.doornkraal.co.za

Dômek (Tur) to pour a drink.

Domesday Ale (Eng) 1143 O.G./15.86% alc. by vol ale brewed by Cornish Brewery to commemorate the 900th anniversary of the Domesday book.

Domesday English Wine (Eng) produced by St. George's English Wines, Waldron Vineyards, near

475

Heathfield. Produced to commemorate the 900th anniversary of the Domesday Book.

Domestic Spumante (USA) an American-type of sparkling wine, Carbon-dioxide is added artificially.

Domgarten (Ger) vineyard (Anb): Mosel-Saar-Ruwer. (Ber): Zell/Mosel. (Gro): Weinhex. (Vil): Winningen.

Dom Grossard (Fr) a style of Champagne produced by Jeeper in Damery.

Dom Henriques (Mad) the label used by Tarquinio Lomelino for their range of Madeiras.

Domherr (Ger) vineyard (Anb): Mosel-Saar-Ruwer. (Ber): Bernkastel. (Gro): Michelsberg. (Vil): Piesport.

Domherr (Ger) grosslage (Anb): Rheinhessen. (Ber): Nierstein. (Vils): Budenheim, Essenheim, Gabsheim, Klein-Winternheim, Mainz-Drais, Mainz-Finthen, Ober-Olm, Saulheim, Schornsheim, Stadecken-Elsheim, Udenheim.

Domherrenberg (Ger) vineyard (Anb): Mosel-Saar-Ruwer. (Ber): Saar-Ruwer. (Gro): Römerlay. (Vil): Trier.

Domherrenberg (Ger) vineyard (Anb): Mosel-Saar-Ruwer. (Ber): Zell/Mosel. (Gro): Schwarze Katz. (Vil): Zell.

Domherren-Quelle (Ger) a natural spring mineral water from Rhens, RP.

Domina (Ger) a red grape variety, a cross between the Portugieser and the Spätburgunder. Produces sound wines.

Dominance (Eng) a 5.5% alc by vol. pale bitter brewed by the Aspinall Cambrinus Craft Brewery, Knowsley, Merseyside.

Domingas Ranch (USA) the former name used for the Beatty Ranch Vineyard in the Napa Valley, Sonoma, California.

Dominica (W.Ind) a coffee-producing island that produces strong-flavoured and full-bodied coffees.

Dominicus Fino (Eng) a fine, dry, Fino Sherry from the Peter Dominic wine shops.

Dominikanerberg (Ger) vineyard (Anb): Mosel-Saar-Ruwer. (Ber): Saar-Ruwer. (Gro): Römerlay. (Vil): Kasel.

Dominikanerberg (Ger) vineyard (Anb): Mosel-Saar-Ruwer. (Ber): Saar-Ruwer. (Gro): Römerlay. (Vil): Morscheid.

Dominio de Fontana (Sp) a winery based in the La Mancha region. Grape varieties include: Tempranillo.

Dominio del Plata S.A (Arg) a winery based in the Mendoza region, eastern Argentina. Grape varieties: Bonarda, Cabernet sauvignon, Chardonnay, Malbec, Sauvignon blanc, Syrah, Tempranillo, Torrentés. Labels: Anubis, Ben Marco, Crios de Susana Balbo, Susana Balbo. Website: http://www.dominiodelplata.com.ar 'E'mail: info@dominiodelplata.com.ar

Dominio de Pingus (Sp) a famous new winery based in Monasterio, Ribera del Duero, Castille. (Add): S.L.R.E: 7602 VA Quintanilla de Onesimo

(Valladolid). Pruduces D.O. Pingus 14% alc by vol. and Flor de Pingus (the second wine) from Tempranillo, Tinto fino grapes. Wines are hand picked, destalked and single grape selected. Hand crushed and wood-fermented.

Dominio de Valdepusa (Sp) a winery in the province of Toledo, Castilla-La Mancha. Likely to be the first private D.O. in Spain. *See also* Calzadilla, Sandoval, Manzaneque, Dehesa del Carrizal, Vallegarcía, Aalto, Mauro, San Román.

Dominion (N.Z) a company in Aukland who invented continuous fermentation. It is the second largest brewing group in the country.

Dominion Ale (Can) a bottom-fermented beer brewed in Newfoundland by the Dominion Brewery.

Dominion Wine Company (S.Afr) a winery (established 2002) based in Stellenbosch, Western Cape. Grape varieties: Cabernet sauvignon, Chardonnay, Chenin blanc, Jerepigo, Merlot, Pinotage, Sauvignon blanc, Sémillon, Shiraz, Tinta, Touriga nacional. Labels: African Gold, Harvest Moon, Imvelo, Kaapslig (Daglig/Naglig), Keteka, Kleinbok, Red cabernet, Rolling Hills, Sugar Bush Ridge, Welgedacht. Website: http://www.dominionwineco.co.za

Dominique (S.Afr) the label for a red wine (Cabernet franc 15%, Cabernet sauvignon 55% and Merlot 30% blend) produced by the Louisvale Wines winery, Stellenbosch, Western Cape.

Domini Veneti (It) a winery (established 1933) based in the Negrar district of Veneto region. Produces a variety of local wines. 500ha. Website: http://www.cantinanegrar.it

Dominode [La] (Fr) a Premier Cru vineyard in the A.C. commune of Savigny-lès-Beaune, Côte de Beaune, Burgundy.

Dominus (USA) a California wine (Cabernet sauvignon) produced jointly by Moueix (Christian) and 2 sisters: Lail (Robin) & Smith (Marcia) in Yountville. The first wine was produced in 1983.

Dom Kölsch (Ger) a 4.8% alc, by vol. bottled straw beer brewed by the Dom Brauerei, Cologne.

Domlay (Ger) vineyard (Anb): Ahr. (Ber): Walporzheim/Ahrtal. (Gro): Klosterberg. (Vil): Walporzheim.

Dommelsch Bier Brouwerij (Hol) a brewery (established 1744) based in Dommelen. Brews: a Pils, Oud Bruin, Bokbier, Dominator, alcohol-free malt beer.

Dommelsch Dominator (Hol) a 6% alc by vol. malty bock beer brewed by the Dommelsch Bier Brouwerij, Dommelen

Dommelsch Malt (Hol) a 0.1% alc by vol. alcohol-free beer brewed by the Dommelsch Bier Brouwerij, Dommelen

Dommelsch Oud Bruin (Hol) a 2% alc by vol. old brown special beer brewed by the Dommelsch Bier Brouwerij, Dommelen.

Dommelsch Pilsener (Hol) a 5% alc by vol. pilsener

brewed by the Dommelsch Bier Brouwerij, Dommelen.

Domoshni (Rus) home-made (wine).

Dom Oudart (Fr) 1654–1742 Frère Jean Oudart, the person who is reputed to have discovered the secrets of Champagne and introduced the liqueur de tirage and cork stoppers (which replaced the original oil-soaked hemp stoppers) to Champagne production.

Dom Pérignon (Fr) 1668–1715 Pierre Pérignon, a blind Bénédictine monk who as cellar master of the cellars at Hautvillers Abbey, invented the process of second fermentation in the bottle which put the bubbles in Champagne. *See also* Dom Oudart and Pérignon [Pierre].

Dom Pérignon (Fr) a de luxe vintage cuvée Champagne from Moët et Chandon. Sold in a distinctive old-style Champagne bottle and only produced in exceptional vintages.

Dom Pers (Fr) a slang expression for Dom Pérignon. *See also* Dom Pom.

Dom Pom (Eng) a slang expression for Dom Pérignon. *See also* Dom Pers.

Domprobst (Ger) vineyard (Anb): Mosel-Saar-Ruwer. (Ber): Bernkastel. (Gro): Münzlay. (Vil): Graach.

Dom Ruinart (Fr) a Champagne producer (established 1729). Range includes a 100% Grand Cru Blanc de Blancs, Rosé and R. de Ruinart from 48% Chardonnay, 52% Pinot noir. Vintages: 1986, 1988, 1990, 1995. Website: http://www.ruinart.com

Domski (Rus) a white wine produced in the Crimea.

Dom Yago Rosado (Sp) a naturally sparkling, medium-dry, rosé wine produced by Dom Yago using the cuve close method. Is sold under the Gran-Vas label.

Doña Ana (Sp) a solera brandy produced by Garvey in Jerez de la Frontera. *See also* Tauro, Valderrama.

Doña Antonia Personel Reserve (Port) a fine old Tawny Port from Ferreira shippers.

Donabaum (Aus) a winery based in the Wachau. (Add): Zornberg 4, 3620 Spitz. Grape varieties: Grüner veltliner, Muskateller, Riesling. Produces a range of dry and sweet (botrytised) wines.

Doña Blanca (Port) *see* Doña Branco.

Doña Branco (Port)(Sp) a white grape variety grown in the Dão and Galicia regions. Also known as Doña Blanca, Moza Fresca.

Don Agustin (Sp) a solera brandy produced by Agustin Blazquez in Jerez de la Frontera. *see* Felipe II, Tres Medallas.

Dona Juana (Sp) a brand of Sherry produced by Sanchez Romate.

Don Anselmo (It) a D.O.C. Aglianico del Vulture produced by Paternoster in Basilicata. Oak aged (50% in barrique, 50% in wooden vats).

Donata (It) a sparkling natural spring mineral water from Donata, Pisa, Tuscany. Mineral contents (milligrammes per litre): Sodium 97.8mg/l, Calcium 198.8mg/l, Magnesium 71.9mg/l, Potassium 3.2mg/l, Bicarbonates 110.2mg/l, Chlorides 70.9mg/l, Sulphates 7.2mg/l, Nitrates 0.6mg/l, Silicates 27mg/l. pH 6.4

Donat Mg (Slo) a natural spring mineral water from Rogaska Slatina. Mineral contents (milligrammes per litre): Sodium 1570mg/l, Calcium 362mg/l, Magnesium 1040mg/l, Potassium 17mg/l, Chlorides 74.4mg/l, Sulphates 2092mg/l, Fluorides 0.17mg/l, Nitrates 0.1mg/l, Strontium 9.8mg/l.

Donatus (S.Afr) the label for a range of white wines (Chenin blanc, Sémillon, Sauvignon blanc) produced by the Dornier Wines winery, Stellenbosch, Western Cape.

Donau (Ger) an untergebiete of the Bayern district.

Donauland (Aus) lit: 'Danube land', a wine-producing region situated on the river Danube, north-west of Vienna. 2815ha. Soil: gravel, loam and loess. Main grape varieties: white (Grüner veltliner, Pinot blanc, Riesling, Royer veltliner) red (Blauburger, Blauer portugieser, Zweigelt). Main villages: Fels, Grossriedenthal, Hohenwarth, Kirchberg, Klosterneuburg, Königsbrunn, Sieghartskirchen, St. Ardrä and Trasdorf. *see* Klosterneuburg.

Donauleiten (Aus) a vineyard site on the banks of the River Danube situated in the Wachau region, Niederösterreich.

Donau Perle (Bul) lit: 'pearl of the Danube', a full white wine made in the Danube basin from the Fetiaska grape.

Donaupoint (Aus) a vineyard site on the banks of the River Danube situated in the Wachau region, Niederösterreich.

Don Carlo (It) a sparkling natural spring mineral water from Don Carlo, Salerno. Mineral contents (milligrammes per litre): Sodium 15.2mg/l, Calcium 189mg/l, Magnesium 25.5mg/l, Potassium 3.7mg/l, Bicarbonates 683mg/l, Chlorides 23.5mg/l, Sulphates 14.4mg/l, Nitrates 3.1mg/l, Silicates 8.4mg/l. pH 6.68

Don Cayetano (Chile) a vineyard based in the Rapel Valley. Grape varieties: Sauvignon blanc.

Don Cortez (Eng) the brand name for Grants of St. James Spanish wines. Made famous in the 1960's for their advertising slogan '*Ten bobs the bottle*'.

Don Darias (Sp) a brand label for a variety of white and red Spanish wines.

Donetskaya Vodka (Ukr) a vodka produced in Donetsk.

Don Felipe (Sp) a noted Sherry producer of Jerez de la Frontera.

Don Feliz (Sp) a solera gran reserva brandy produced by José Estevez in Jerez de la Frontera.

Don Fino (Sp) a dry, Fino Sherry produced by Sandeman.

Don García (Sp) the brand-name used by Bodegas García Carrión in Jumilla for a range of red, rosé and white wines.

Dongermain (Fr) a commune in the Côtes de Toul. Lorraine. Produces Vins gris.

Dongine (Fr) the local name used in Bugey for the Mondeuse grape.

Don Gonzalo (Sp) a dry Oloroso Sherry from Valdespino.

Don Guisa (Sp) a brand of Fino Sherry produced by Caballero.

D

Don Jacobo (Sp) the brand-name for wines produced by Bodegas Corral S.A., Alta region, Rioja.

Donjon (Fr) a brandy and almond-flavoured liqueur produced by Benoit Serres in Toulouse.

Don José (Sp) a soft Oloroso Sherry produced by Romate.

Donker (Hol) a sweet, full-bodied, 'old brown' beer brewed by the De Leeuw Brouwerij in Valkenburg, Limburg.

Donkey Box (Eng) part of a public house, a snug that seats less than 12 people.

Don Luis (Chile) a light, red, Cabernet-based wine produced by Cousiño Macul.

Don Luis (Sp) a wine produced by the Bodegas Bardón in Ribera Baja from 60% Tempranillo and other grapes.

Don Luis (Sp) a classic old Amontillado Sherry produced by Burdon (J.W).

Don Matias (Chile) a tannic, dark, Cabernet-based red wine produced by Cousiño Macul.

Don Miguel (Chile) a brand of white wine produced by Torres from Gewürztraminer and Riesling grapes.

Donna Antonia (Port) a vintage character Port produced by Ferreira shippers.

Donnafugata (It) a famous wine estate based in Sicily. Produces: Ben Ryé (dessert wine), Chiarandà (dry white wine), Contessa Entellina Milleunanotte. Grape varieties: Ansonica, Chardonnay, Moscato. Website: http://www.donnafugata.it

Donna Madda (It) a red wine produced by Fattoria San Francesco in Calabria, aged for 6–8 months in barrique.

Donna Maria Vineyards (USA) a winery based near Windsor, Sonoma, California. 63ha. Grape varieties: Gewürztraminer, Pinot noir and Zinfandel. Produces varietal wines.

Don Narciso (Sp) an 8 year old brandy produced by Mascaró in Vilafranca, Penedés.

Donnaz (It) a D.O.C. red wine from the Val d'Aosta region. Made from the Nebbiolo plus 15% of Freisa, Neyret and Vien de nus. From the communes: Bard, Donnaz, Perloz and Pont St. Martin. Must be aged for 3 years (2 in oak or chestnut).

Don Nazario Ortiz Garza (Mex) a brandy and wine producer based at Soltillo, Coahuila. Also has vineyards in Aguascalientes.

Donnici (It) a D.O.C. red or rosé wine from Calabria. Made from the Gaglioppa 50%, Greco nero, Malvasia bianca, Montonico bianco and Pecorella grapes.

Donnington Brewery (Eng) a brewery (established 1865). (Add): Stow-in-the-Wold, Cheltenham, Gloucestershire GL54 1EP. Produces: cask-conditioned XXX Dark Mild and bottled Double Dunn 1042 O.G./4.1% alc by vol. 2 draught bitters: BB (Best Bitter), SBA (Special Bitter Ale).

Donnybrook (Ire) a drunken, rowdy brawl, so named after the nineteenth century Donnybrook fair, an annual event until 1855. Based near Dublin.

Donovan (Austr) a winery (established 1981) at Pomonal Road, Victoria. Noted for its varietals Riesling and Shiraz.

Don Pablo Cocktail (Cktl) 20mls (⅙ gill) golden rum, juice ¼ lime, 40mls (⅓ gill) tomato juice, dash Tabasco sauce, celery salt and pepper. Stir well over ice, strain into an ice-filled collins glass and dress with a stick of celery.

Don Pavral (Port) the label of a late-bottled vintage Port.

Don Pepe (Sp) a natural spring mineral water from Aldeatejada, Salamanca. Mineral contents (milligrammes per litre): Sodium 12.4mg/l, Calcium 50mg/l, Magnesium 12.8mg/l, Potassium 0.79mg/l, Bicarbonates 150mg/l, Chlorides 46mg/l, Sulphates 5mg/l.

Don Q (W.Ind) the brand-name of a Puerto Rican rum distilled by Serralles at Ponce.

Don Ramon (Sp) a full-bodied red wine made with the Garnacha grape by Vincente Suso y Perez in Cariñena, north-eastern Spain.

Don Ramos (Sp) a brand of Fino Sherry produced by Bodegas Don Ramos, Jerez de la Frontera.

Don River Valley (Rus) a wine region that produces red, white and sparkling wines. see Donski.

Don Sebastiani (USA) a winery based in Sonoma County, California. Labels include: Fusée, Pepperwood grove and Smoking Loon.

Donski (Rus) a sparkling wine exported to USA, produced near Rostov in the Don River Valley region.

Don Suero (Sp) a fruity, red, oak-aged wine produced by VILE in León.

Don Thomas (Sp) the brand-name of a Sherry produced by Valdespino.

Don't Panic (Eng) a 4.2% alc by vol. ale brewed by the Spectrum Brewery, Norfolk.

Donzelinho (Port) a white grape variety used in the making of Port.

Donzelinho Tinto (Port) a red grape variety used in the making of Port.

Don Zoilo (Sp) the world's most expensive range of Sherries produced by Diez-Merito, Diego-Fernandez Herrera, 16, Jerez de la Frontera. Also produce brandies (Gran Duque d'Alba is a brand).

Dooars (Ind) a tea plantation area in northern India.

Dooley's (Eng) a toffee cream liqueur from United Brands.

Doolhof Estate (S.Afr) a winery (established 1996) based in Wellingston, Western Cape. 35ha. Grape varieties: Cabernet sauvignon, Chardonnay, Merlot, Pinotage, Sauvignon blanc, Shiraz. Labels: Cape Boar, Cape Roan, Maiden's Prayer, Renaissance, Signatures. Website: http://www.doolhof.com

Doom Bar Bitter (Eng) a bitter ale 4% alc by vol. brewed by Sharp's Brewery in Cornwall.

Doorley's XO (W.Ind) a rum produced in Barbados. Has an Oloroso finish.

Doornkaat (Ger) a brand of kornbranntwein from Norden in north-west Germany. Also called Frisian country wine.

D

Doornkraal (S.Afr) a vineyard based in Klein Karoo. Produces varietal and dessert wines.

Doosberg (Ger) vineyard (Anb): Rheingau. (Ber): Johannisberg. (Gro): Gottesthal. (Vil): Östrich.

Doosberg (Ger) a vineyard within the village of Östrich, 137.9ha. (27.8%) of which is proposed to be classified as Erstes Gewächs.

Dop-Brandy (S.Afr) a brandy made by distilling the residue grape pulp from the wine process. (Fr) = marc, (It) = grappa.

Dopff-au-Moulin (Fr) producers of sparkling Alsace wines based at Riquewihr, Alsace. 77ha.

Dopff et Irion (Fr) noted viticulturalists of Alsace. (Add): Château de Riquewihr, 68340 Riquewihr. 37ha.

Doppelbock (Ger) lit: 'double bock', an extra-strong bock bier 7.5% alc by vol. from Scherdel Brauerei. see Eisbock, Salvator, Weisse Dunkel, Weisse Hell, Weizen.

Doppelbock Dunkel (Ger) a dark double bock bier from the Andechs Brauerei in Erling-Andechs, Bavaria. Has a rich malty aroma and flavour.

Doppelbock Hell (Ger) a double bock bier from the Andechs Brauerei in Erling-Andechs, Bavaria. A rich malty brew.

Doppelbogen (Ger) the 'double guyot' method of vine training. See also Einzelbogen.

Doppelkaramelbier (Ger) a malty bier enriched with sugar.

Doppelkorn (Ger) a spirit derived from mashed corn, sometimes flavoured with herbs 38% alc by vol.

Doppelmagnum (Ger) lit: 'double magnum' a jeroboam.

Doppelohm (Ger) a cask of the Rhine and Mosel holding 300 litres (66 gallons).

Doppelstück (Ger) a large oak fermenting cask.

Doppelweizen (Ger) a spirit derived from mashed wheat.

Doppo Cedro (It) a lemon-flavoured liqueur.

Doquet-Jeanmarie (Fr) a Champagne producer. Récoltants-manipulants (Add): Route de Voipreux, 51130 Vertus. Produces vintage and non-vintage wines.

Dor [A.E.] (Fr) a Cognac producer. (Add): 14 Bis Rue J. Moreau, 16200 Jarnac. 22ha. vineyards in Petite Champagne. Produces Hors d'Age (35–60 y.o.) and Trés Vieille Grande Champagne (30–60 y.o. the oldest), Roi de Rome, Louis Philippe, Prince Albert, Prince Impériale, Excellence.

D.O.R.A. (Eng) abbr: Defence Of the Realm Act a law which restricted pub opening hours during wartime.

Dorada (Sp) a flor-attacked, vino de licor, rancio style, tawny-gold wine produced in D.O. Rueda. 15% alc by vol. the wine is aged for four years (two of which must be in oak).

Doradillo (Austr) a white grape variety grown in Riverland in South Australia. One of the varieties used to make brandy.

Doran Lager (Can) a lager beer brewed by the Doran Brewery.

Dorchester Bitter (Eng) a cask-conditioned ale 1033 O.G. brewed by Eldridge Pope Brewery in Dorchester, Dorset.

Dordogne [River] (Fr) a river running along the west coast of France in Bordeaux. Joins the river Garonne to form the river Gironde.

Doreen's Delight (Punch)(Non-alc) 1 bottle Eisberg (alcohol-free) wine, 500mls (1 pint) Cydrax (alcohol-free) cider, 250mls (½ pint) lemonade, 175mls (⅓ pint) dry ginger, 2 teaspoons rum essence. Stir with ice, dress with sliced apples and lemons.

D'Orfin (Fr) a sparkling wine producer based in Aigre. All styles of wine are produced.

Dorfprozelten (Ger) village (Anb): Franken. (Ber): Mainviereck. (Gro): Not yet assigned. (Vin): Predigtstuhl.

Dorham Mann Estate (Austr) a winery based in Western Australia. See also Cabernet Cygne Blanc.

Doria (It) a wine producer based in Oltrepo Pavese in the Lombardy region. Produces sparkling wines by the Tank method.

Dorin (Switz) the local name for the white Chasselas grape in the Vaud region. see Dorin Epesses, Fendant, Dorin Lutry, Perlan, Dorin Vaud.

Dorin (Switz) the generic name for all white wines from the canton of Vaud.

Dorin Epesses (Switz) the local name for the white Chasselas grape in the Vaud region. See also Dorin, Dorin Lutry, Dorin Vaud, Fendant, Perlan.

Dorin Lutry (Switz) the local name for the white Chasselas grape in the Vaud region. See also Dorin Epesses, Dorin Vaud, Fendant, Perlan.

Dorin Vaud (Switz) the local name for the white Chasselas grape in the Vaud region. See also Dorin, Dorin Epesses, Dorin Lutry, Fendant, Perlan.

Dörlers Kiwi-Fruit Winery (N.Z) a winery based at Tawa Road, Kumeu, Ph 412-9723. Produces a medium-dry Kiwi-fruit wine 10.2% alc by vol.

Dormalt (Eng) a method of malting using a continuous conveyor.

Dormans (Fr) a Champagne Canton. District of Épernay. Contains the Cru villages: Boursault, Champvoisy, Comblizy, Dormans (Chavenay, Try, Vassy and Vassieux), Festigny, Le Breuil, Le Mesnil-le-Hutier, Leuvrigny, Mareuil-le-Port, Nesle-le-Repons, Oeuilly, Port à Binson, Soilly, Troissy-Bouquigny, Verneuil and Vincelles.

Dormans (Fr) a Cru Champagne village in the Canton of Dormans. District: Épernay.

Dormershire (S.Afr) a winery (established 1996) based in Belleville, Stellenbosch, Western Cape. 7ha. Grape varieties: Cabernet sauvignon, Sauvignon blanc, Shiraz. Produces varietal wines.

Dorna (Rum) a natural spring mineral water from Karpates. Mineral contents (milligrammes per litre): Sodium 22mg/l, Calcium 360mg/l, Magnesium 11.8mg/l, Potassium 2.8mg/l, Bicarbonates 3500mg/l, Chlorides 10.2mg/l.

Dorn-Dürkheim (Ger) village (Anb): Rheinhessen. (Ber): Nierstein. (Gro): Rheinblick. (Vins): Hasensprung, Römerberg.

D

Dornfelder (Ger) a grape with a red coloured flesh created in 1956 as a result of crossing Helfensteiner x Heroldrebe.

Dorner (Aus) a vineyard site based on the banks of the River Kamp in the Kamptal region.

Dornier Wines (S.Afr) a winery (established 2002) based in Stellenbosch, Western Cape. 67ha. Grape varieties: Cabernet franc, Cabernet sauvignon, Chenin blanc, Merlot, Sauvignon blanc, Sémillon, Shiraz. Label: Donatus. Website: http://www.dornierwines.co.za

Dornot (Fr) a white wine produced in Lorraine.

Dornpfad (Ger) vineyard (Anb): Rheinhessen. (Ber): Nierstein. (Gro): Domherr. (Vil): Gabsheim.

Dorntal (Tur) a dry white wine produced by Diren, Tokat.

Doron (Isr) a dry white table wine.

Dorothy Goodbody's Seasonal Ales (Eng) the name given to a range of seasonal ales from the Wye Valley Brewery, Herefordshire. Includes Springtime Bitter (April, May), Golden Summertime Ale (July, August), Glowing Autumn Delight Ale (September-November), Wintertime Ale (January-February), Wholesome Stout (March), Father Christmas Ale (December). *see* the Wye Valley Brewery.

Dörrenbach (Ger) village (Anb): Pfalz. (Ber): Sudliche Weinstrasse. (Gro): Guttenberg. (Vin): Wonneberg.

Dörscheid (Ger) village (Anb): Mittelrhein. (Ber): Rheinburgengau. (Gro): Herrenberg. (Vins): Kupferflöz, Wolfsnack.

Dorset Brewing Company (Eng) a brewery (established 1996). (Add): Weymouth Brewers Quay, Hope Square, Weymouth, Dorset DT4 8TR. Brews: Durdle Door 5% alc by vol., Jurrestic 4.7% alc by vol., Silent Knight 5.9% alc by vol., Summer Knight 3.8% alc by vol., Weymouth Best Bitter 4% alc by vol., Weymouth Harbour Master 3.6% alc by vol., Weymouth JD 1742 4.2% alc by vol., Weymouth Steam Bear 4.5% alc by vol. 'E'mail: giles@quaybrewery.com

Dorset Original IPA (Eng) a cask-conditioned bitter 1041 O.G. brewed by the Eldridge Pope Brewery in Dorchester, Dorset.

Dorset Best (Eng) a 4.1% alc by vol. cask-conditioned bitter brewed by Badger Brewery, Dorset. Now known as Badger Best Bitter.

Dorset Gold (Eng) a 4.5% alc by vol. ale brewed by JC & RH Palmer Ltd., Dorset.

Dorset Spring (Eng) a natural spring mineral water from Coombe Farm, Old Coombe, Lower Brimley, Stoke Abbot, Beaminster, Dorset.

Dorsheim (Ger) village (Anb): Nahe. (Ber): Kreuznach. (Gro): Schlosskapelle. (Vins): Burgberg, Goldloch, Honigberg, Jungbrunnen, Klosterpfad, Laurenziweg, Nixenberg, Pittermännchen, Trollberg.

Dorst (Hol) thirst (dertig = thirsty).

Dort (Bel) a style of malty beer with a density of more than 5°, is less hopped than a Dortmunder and produced without the use of maize.

Dort (Hol) a malty beer 6.5% alc by vol. brewed by the Gulpen Brouwerij in Gulpen, Limburg.

Dortmund Actien Bier (Ger) *abbr:* D.A.B. a beer made in the Dortmund Actien Brauerei in Dortmund, Westphalia. A light beer with a fine hop flavour.

Dortmunder (Ger) a golden beer between a Pilsener and Münchener in flavour 5.2% alc by vol. Brewed in Dortmund.

Dortmunder Actien Brauerei (Ger) also known as D.A.B. A brewery based Dortmund, Westphalia. The biggest in Germany, it produces other styles of German beers and is noted for altbier and export.

Dortmunder Export (Ger) a famous beer from the breweries of Dortmund in West Germany. *see* D.A.B. Export, Hansa Export, Ritter Export, Stifts Export, Thier Export, Dortmunder Kronen Export and D.U.B. Export.

Dortmunder Hansa (Ger) a brewery of Dortmund in Westphalia. Part of the D.A.B. Produces fine Export and a light Pilsener beers.

Dortmunder Kronen (Ger) the oldest brewery in Dortmund, Westphalia. Noted for fine beers. *see* Pilskrone, Classic and Dortmunder Kronen Export.

Dortmunder Kronen Export (Ger) a very fine Dortmunder export beer brewed by the Dortmunder Kronen Brauerei in Dortmund, Westphalia 5% alc by vol.

Dortmunder Ritter (Ger) a brewery (established 1889) based in Dortmund, Westphalia. Owned by the D.U.B. Schultheiss. *see* Ritter Export, Ritter First.

Dortmunder Stifts (Ger) a small brewery (established 1867) based in Dortmund, Westphalia. Owned by Watney Mann of G.B. Produces sweetish beers of good quality. *see* Stifts Export, Stifts Pils.

Dortmunder Thier (Ger) a small brewery in Dortmund, Westphalia. Produces full-bodied malty beers. *see* Thier Export.

Dortmunder Union (Ger) a medium strength bier brewed by the D.U.B.

Dortmunder Union Brauerei (Ger) *abbr:* D.U.B. a large brewery in Rheinische Street, Dortmund, Westphalia. Produces a fine range of beers. *see* D.U.B. Export, Siegel Pils and Brinckhoffs N°1.

Dörzbach (Ger) village (Anb): Württemberg. (Ber): Kocher-Jagst-Tauber. (Gro): Kocherberg. (Vin): Altenberg.

D.O.S. (It) *abbr:* **D**enominazione di **O**rigine **S**emplice, a plain denomination no longer used since the D.O.C. laws.

Dosage (Fr) after Champagne has been disgorged (dégorgement) it is quite dry so a dosage, which consists of a varying amount of syrup (fortified grape must) is often added. The amount of dosage will decide on the class of Champagne. Brut Nature/Non Dosé/Dosage Zero: 3grms, Extra Brut: 6grms, Brut: 15grms, Extra Sec: 12grms–20grms, Sec: 17grms–35 grms, Demi-Sec: 33grms–50grms, Doux: 50grms plus.

Dosage Zero (Fr) a term to denote a completely dry Champagne with only 3grms of sugar or less. Also known as Brut Nature and Non Dosé.

Dosaïe (Ch.Isles) a drinking bout. *See also* Daose.

Dos Cortados (Sp) a brand of dry Oloroso Sherry from Williams and Humbert, Jerez de la Frontera.

Dos Equis (S.Am) lit: 'two crosses', a Vienna-style amber lager. 4.8% alc by vol. brewed by Moctezuma Brewery, Monterrey, Mexico.

Dos Equis Special Lager (S.Am) lit; 'two crosses', a 4.8% alc by vol. straw coloured lager brewed by the Moctezuma Brewery, Monterrey, Mexico.

Dosio (It) a producer of sparkling (metodo tradizionale) wines in Piemonte.

Dos Lustros (Sp) a método tradicional sparkling wine produced in San Sadurní de Noya by Castellblanch S.A. From 40% Parellada, 20% Xarel-lo, 40% Macabeo. Spends 24 months on lees.

Dos Rayas (Sp) lit: 'two strokes'. when applied to a Sherry butt denotes wines destined to become Olorosos. *see* Raya.

Dossenheim (Ger) village (Anb): Baden. (Ber): Badische Bergstasse/Kraichgau. (Gro): Rittersberg. (Vin): Ölberg.

Dos Viñedos (Sp) *see* Bodegas Palacios Remondo.

Dotzheim (Ger) village (Anb): Rheingau. (Ber): Johannisberg. (Gro): Steinmächer. (Vin): Judenkirch.

Douardo (Eng) a style of perry and tropical fruit flavoured drink 5.4% alc by vol. from Showerings. Brand-name is Zazou. *See also* Cor de Amora.

Double (Eng) a double measure of spirits = 2 tots. (Den) = dobbelt mål spiritus.

Double Ale (Eng) a term for a stronger brewed beer than an ordinary beer.

Double Aum (Ger) a wine cask of 300 litres. *see* Doppelohm.

Double Brown Ale (Eng) a brown ale 1037 O.G. brewed by the Bateman's Brewery in Lincolnshire.

Double Brown Beer (Eng) a keg bitter ale 1041 O.G. brewed by the John Smith Brewery.

Double Cabernet (S.Afr) the label for a red (Cabernet sauvignon, Ruby cabernet and Sauvignon blanc blend) wine produced by the Nordale Winery, Robertson, Western Cape.

Double Century (Sp) a famous range of Sherries produced by Domecq in Jerez de la Frontera.

Double Century Ale (Scot) a bottled ale 1054 O.G. brewed by the William Younger Brewery in Edinburgh to celebrate their bi-centenary of brewing in 1949.

Double Chance Bitter (Eng) a cask-conditioned ale 1039 O.G. brewed by the Malton's Brewery in north Yorkshire.

Double Chocolate Stout (Eng) a bottled or draught stout brewed by Youngs using hops, yeast, chocolate and chocolate malt.

Double D (Eng) the nickname for Double Diamond.

Double Dagger Ale (Eng) a pale ale 1050 O.G. brewed by the Oak Brewery in Cheshire.

Double Diamond (Eng) *abbr*: D.D. a famous old pale ale 1043 O.G. brewed by Ind Coope in Burton-on-Trent. Originates from an old cask-conditioned Burton ale recipe. *See also* Double D.

Double Donn Bitter (Eng) a bottled special bitter 1042 O.G. brewed by the Donnington Brewery in the Cotswolds.

Double Dragon (Wal) a cask-conditioned bitter 1042 O.G. brewed by the Felinfoel Brewery in Llanelli (the first beer to be canned).

Double Eagle (Eng) a 4.8% alc by vol. cask winter ale brewed under licence by Tring Brewery in Hertfordshire for The Vintage Hallmark Ale Company in Norwich.

Double Enghien (Bel) a dry, full-bodied saison ale 7.5% alc by vol. brewed by the Dupont Brasserie in Tourpes. *See also* Saison de Silly, Silly Scotch.

Double Enghien Blonde (Bel) a 7.5% alc by vol. straw, top-fermented, bottle-conditioned special beer brewed by De Silly Brouwerij, Silly.

Double Header (Eng) a 5.3% alc by vol. ale brewed by the RCH Brewery, Avon.

Double Helix (Eng) a 5.3% alc by vol. ale from Tomlinson's Brewery, Pontefract (a micro-brewery).

Double Hop (Eng) a premium ale 5% alc by vol. brewed by the Robinson's Unicorn Brewery, Stockport, Cheshire.

Double Hop (Wal) a 4% alc by vol. bitter beer brewed by the Cwmbran Brewery, Gwent.

Double L. Vineyard (USA) the label for a red wine (Pinot noir) produced by the Morgan winery, Santa Lucia Highlands, Monterey County, California.

Double Magnum (Fr) a four-bottle capacity bottle of red wine from the Bordeaux region. *See also* Jereboam.

Double Maxim Ale (Eng) a brown ale 1044 O.G. (4.2% alc by vol.–4.7% alc by vol.) brewed by Vaux Brewery in Sunderland. Also a nitro-keg version.

Double Millennium (Eng) a 5.5% alc by vol. hoppy beer brewed by the Cotleigh Brewery, Wiveliscombe, Somerset.

Double Pony (Ch.Isles) a strong ale brewed and bottled by the Guernsey Brewery Cº. Ltd., St. Peter Port, Guernsey (now no longer produced).

Double Q [QQ] (Scot) a blended 12 year old Scotch whisky distributed by the Montrose Whisky Company.

Double Royal Ale (Eng) a 4.2% alc by vol. limited edition bottled ale from Brain's Brewery in Cardiff. Brewed to commemorate the centenary celebrations for the Royal Monmouthshire Royal Engineers.

Double Springs (USA) a Bourbon whiskey distillery based in Louisville, Kentucky.

Double Standard Sour (Cktl) ½ measure gin, ½ measure Bourbon whiskey, juice ½ lemon, 2 dashes grenadine, 2 dashes gomme syrup. Shake over ice, strain into a sour glass, top with a cherry and a slice of lemon.

Double Star Ale (Eng) a pale ale 1040 O.G. brewed by the Charles Wells Brewery in Bedford.

Double Stout (Eng) a 4.8% alc by vol. smooth seasonal stout brewed by Hook Norton Brewery, Banbury, Oxon.

D

Double Strong Ale (Wal) a bottled strong ale 1075 O.G. brewed by the Felinfoel Brewery in Llanelli, South Wales. Sold as Hercules in the USA.

Double Swan (Eng) a 4.5% alc by vol. ale brewed by Elgood & Sons Ltd., Cambridgeshire.

Doublet (Fr) a species of barley malt of the Triumph variety that gives good sugar yields.

Double Top Ale (Eng) a brown ale 1033 O.G. brewed by the Higson's Brewery in Liverpool, Lancashire.

Double Whisky (Scot) a mark found on a hydrostatical bubble used to measure alcoholic strengths.

Double Zero Seven [007] (Cktl) 40mls (⅓ gill) Bacardi White Label, juice of ¼ lemon and ½ lime, 20mls (⅙ gill) sweet vermouth, dash gomme syrup. Shake over ice, strain into a cocktail glass, dress with a slice of orange and mint sprig.

Double Zero Seven [007] (Eng) a cask-conditioned bitter 1055 O.G. brewed by the Bridge House home-brew public house in London.

Doubling (USA) the name given to the process of re-distilling after the first distillation in whiskey production.

Douce Noire (Fr) a red grape variety found in the Savoie region. Also known as Charbono.

Doucillon (Fr) a white grape variety grown in the Bandol district of Provence.

Doudet Naudin (Fr) a Burgundy négociant based at Savigny-lès-Beaune, Burgundy.

Dou Dou Fizz (Cktl)(Non-alc) 1 measure coconut cream, 1 measure lemon juice, 1 egg white, ½ measure gomme syrup. Blend with a scoop of ice in a blender, pour into a goblet, top with soda and a slice of lemon.

Douelle (S.Afr) the label for a red wine (Cabernet franc, Cabernet sauvignon and Merlot blend) produced by the Welgemeend Estate winery, Suider-Paarl, Western Cape.

Dough (Iran) a refreshing, flavoured yoghurt drink.

Douglas (Scot) see Gordon Highland Scotch Ale.

Douglas Green (S.Afr) wine merchants and winery of Paarl, Western Cape. Sell many wines under own label, plus many top South African and European wines. (Add): Box 3337, Cape Town. Grape varieties: Cabernet sauvignon, Chardonnay, Cinsaut, Colombard, Merlot, Pinotage, sauvignon blanc, Shiraz. Labels: Cape Ruby, Faces of Africa, St. Agustine (a wood-aged red wine). Owned by DGB. Website: http://www.douglasgreen.co.za

Douglas Koöperatiewe Wynmakery (S.Afr) vineyards based at Douglas. (Add): Box 47, Douglas 8730. Produces varietal wines.

Douglas Laing Whiskies (Scot) malt whiskies producers. (Add): Douglas House, 18 Lynedoch Crescent, Glasgow G3 6EQ. Labels: Old Malt Cask, Platinum, Premier Barrel and Provenance. Website: http://www.douglaslaing.com

Douglas Scotch (Fr) the name given to Gordon's Scotch whisky (Belgium) when it crosses the border into France.

Douglas Wine Cellar (S.Afr) a winery (established 1968) based in Douglas, Northern Cape. 360ha.

Grape varieties: Cabernet sauvignon, Chardonnay, Chenin blanc, Colombard, Jerepigo, Johannisberger red, Johannisberger white, Shiraz. Labels: Classic Red, Classic White, Confluence, Grand Cru, Provin. Website: http://wwwgwk.co.za

Douil (Fr) large tubs used in the Médoc which are filled with grapes to take them from the vineyards to the winery by cart.

Doukkala (Afr) an A.O.G. wine-producing area in the region of Casablanca, Morocco.

Doura Branca (Port) a white grape variety grown in the Dão region. Is derived from the Riesling. Produces light, fruity, young wine.

Douradinha (Port) a white grape variety grown in Peñafiel (a sub-region of Vinho Verde).

Dourado (Port) a white grape variety grown in the Entre Minho e Douro, used in the making of Vinhos Verdes.

Dourdon-Viellard (Fr) a Champagne producer. (Add): 7, Rue du Château, 51480 Reuil. Produces non-vintage Champagnes.

Douro (Port) a D.O.C. region producing Port and still wines. Home to Barca Velha. Soil: schist and crystalline rock. Grape varieties include Tinta Barroca, Tinta Roriz, Tinta Nacional, Touriga Nacional, Cabernet sauvignon, Sauvignon blanc.

Douro Bake (Port) a hot taste that is associated with some Port wines produced in very hot summers.

Douro Cask (Port) see Douro Pipe.

Douro e Tras os Montes (Port) demarcated regions of Portugal. see Tras os Montes.

Douro Pipe (Port) holds 550 litres (450ltrs of wine and 100ltrs of brandy). See also Pipe.

Douro [River] (Port) a river on whose banks are grown the grapes that go to make Port wine. Northern Portugal. see Duero.

Dourthe Frères (Fr) the principal brand of CVBG in Bordeaux. Produces A.C. Bordeaux (Grape varieties: Cabernet sauvignon & Merlot) and Bordeaux Blanc Sec (Grape varieties: Sauvignon blanc, Sémillon).

Dousico (Gre) an alternative spelling of Douzico.

Douwe Egberts (Hol) famous coffee producers based at Royal Factories, Utrecht, Holland. Is noted for Moccona (an instant coffee brand).

Doux (Fr) sweet (in wines the sugar content is 45g/l or more).

Douzanelle (Fr) an alternative name for the Muscadelle grape in south-western France.

Douzico (Tur) a clear aniseed-flavoured spirit, similar to Ouzo. See also Dousico.

Dover Vineyards (USA) a winery based in Westlake, Ohio. Produces mainly Concord wines.

Dow (Hun) the grape pulp (paste) from the grape of Tokaji Aszú, the dow goes into the puttonyos.

Dow (Port) vintage Port shippers. Vintages: 1870, 1872, 1873, 1875, 1878, 1881, 1884, 1887, 1890, 1892, 1896, 1899, 1904, 1908, 1912, 1917, 1919, 1920, 1924, 1927, 1931, 1934, 1935, 1945, 1947, 1950, 1955, 1960, 1963, 1966, 1970, 1972, 1975, 1977, 1980, 1983, 1985, 1991, 1994, 1995, 1997, 2000, 2003.

Owned by Symington Family Estates. *see* Quinta do Bomfim.

Dow Brewery (Can) *see* Dow's Ale.

Down Cocktail (Cktl) ⅔ measure dry gin, ⅓ measure sweet vermouth, dash orange bitters. Shake over ice, strain into a cocktail glass and top with an olive.

Downsouth Estate (Austr) a winery based in the Frankland River region of Western Australia. Grape varieties include: Cabernet franc, Cabernet sauvignon.

Downers Vineyard (Eng) a vineyard based at Fulking, Henfield, Sussex. 2.2ha. Grape variety: Müller-Thurgau.

Downham Bitter (Eng) *see* Downham Brewery.

Downham Brewery (Eng) a home-brewery at the Castle hotel, Downham Market, Norfolk. Brews: Downham Bitter 1036 O.G. and Old 1048 O.G. Uses malt extract.

Down Moore Ale (Eng) a cask-conditioned premium ale 1042 O.G. brewed by the Cirencester Brewery in Gloucestershire.

Downpour (Eng) a 4.6% alc by vol. summer ale brewed by Brakspear's Brewery (also known as the Henley Brewery), Henley-on-Thames, Oxon. Available July and August.

Down Royal (Ire) a public house brewery in Lisburn, County Antrim, Northern Ireland. Produces a cask-conditioned Export 1043 O.G.

Down St. Mary Vineyard (Eng) a vineyard. (Add): Down St. Mary, near Crediton, Devon. Produces white wines.

Down to Earth (S.Afr) the label for a white (Sauvignon blanc, Sémillon and Chenin blanc blend) and red blend wines produced by the Villiera Wines winery, Stellenbosch, Western Cape.

Dowton Brewery C° (Eng) a brewery (established 2003). (Add): Unit 11, Dowton Ind Estate, Dowton, Salisbury, Wiltshire SP5 3HU. Brews: Chimera Gold 4.3% alc by vol., Chimera IPA 6.8% alc by vol., Chimera Red 4.6% alc by vol., Chimera Wheat Porter 4.4% alc by vol., Dark Delight 6% alc by vol., Raspberry Wheat 4.5% alc by vol.

Downy Mildew (Eng) *Peronosporaceae*.

Dow Porter (Can) a creamy-style porter brewed by Carling in Toronto.

Dow's Ale (Can) an export ale brewed by the Dow's brewery. Exported to the USA.

Dowsing Rod (Eng) *see* Divining Rod.

Doyen d'Age (Fr) a 20–30 year old Armagnac produced by Lafontan.

Dozy Dawg (Eng) a 4.4% alc by vol. ale brewed by The Dog House Brewery, Cornwall.

D.P.A. (Eng) *abbr:* Derby Pale Ale a keg mild 1033 O.G. brewed by the Mitchells and Butlers Brewery.

D-Pils (Ger) a 4.9% alc by vol. bottled diet pilsner brewed by Wicküler Brauerei, Wuppertal.

D.R.A. (W.Ind) *abbr:* Distillerie des Rhums Agricoles in Martinique. Produces La Favorite (a popular brand of rum).

Draaihoogte Vineyard (S.Afr) a vineyard based in Paarl. Grapes are sold to wineries.

Drab (Hol) the sediment or lees. *See also* Droesem.

Drachenblut (Ger) lit: 'dragon's blood', a red wine made from the Spätburgunder grape in Siebengebirge, Mittelrhein.

Drachenbrunnen (Ger) vineyard (Anb): Nahe. (Ber): Schloss Böckelheim. (Gro): Burgweg. (Vil): Waldböckelheim.

Drachenfels (Ger) vineyard (Anb): Mittelrhein. (Ber): Siebengebirge. (Gro): Petersberg. (Vil): Königswinter.

Drachenfels (Ger) vineyard (Anb): Mittelrhein. (Ber): Siebengebirge. (Gro): Petersberg. (Vil): Rhöndorf.

Drachenstein (Ger) vineyard (Anb): Rheingau. (Ber): Johannisberg. (Gro): Burgweg. (Vil): Rüdesheim.

Drachm (Eng) 3mls (⅛ fl.oz) also known as a Fluid Dram.

Drachselsrieder Schlossbraeu (Ger) a brewery. (Add): Hofmark 1, Drachselried D-94256. Brews a variety of beers and lagers. Website: http://www.schlossbraeu.de 'E'mail: info@schlossbraeu.de

Dracs (Eng) the middle ages name for a mixed drink of coarse spirit and other ingredients in the taverns (usually amongst sailors).

Dracy-les-Couches (Fr) a commune of A.C. Bourgogne Côtes du Couchois.

Draff (Scot) the residue from the wort in whisky production, used as cattle food. (Eng) = draft.

Draft (Eng) the name for the spent barley after brewing in the brewery. (Scot) = draff.

Draft Beer (Eng) denotes beer drawn from a barrel or keg by tap or suction.

Draft Brewed (USA) on a beer bottle label denotes the contents have been brewed by traditional cask beer methods.

Dragasani (Rum) a region south of the Carpathian Mountains, noted for Muskat-Ottonel.

Dragon (W.Ind) a strong, medium-sweet stout 1070 O.G. brewed by the Desnoes and Geddes Brewery in Jamaica.

Dragon Ale (Eng) a 5.5% alc by vol. ale brewed by the Green Dragon in East Anglia. Also brews Bridge Street Bitter, Chaucer Ale.

Dragon Black Beer (Eng) a beer brewed by Wells Brewery in Bedford.

Dragon Cider Company (Wal) a cider-producing factory based at Hirwaun, West Glamorgan. Produces: Thatcher's Ruin.

Dragonfly (Austr) a red (Cabernet sauvignon and Merlot blend) wine produced by the Willow Ridge Estate, Western Australia.

Dragonhead Stout (Scot) a 4% alc by vol. stout brewed by The Orkney brewery, Orkney.

Dragon Heart (Eng) a 5% alc by vol. ale brewed in March by the Cain Brewery Stanhope Street, Liverpool.

Dragon in the Clouds (Cktl) ⅓ measure Mandarine Napoléon, ⅙ measure lime juice, ³⁄₁₀ measure fresh orange juice, ³⁄₁₀ measure gin. Shake well over ice and strain into a Champagne flute.

Dragon Lady Cocktail (Cktl) 1 measure orange juice, ¾ measure white rum, dash curaçao, dash grenadine. Stir well over ice, strain into an ice-filled highball glass, dress with a cherry and a slice of orange.

Dragon Punch (Cktl) 60mls (½ gill) brandy, 60mls (½ gill) dry Sherry, 300mls (½ pint) stout, 300mls (½ pint) lager, 1 bottle dry Champagne (iced). Mix well together over ice and decorate with slices of lemon.

Dragon's Blood (Eng) a barley wine brewed by the Flowers Brewery.

Dragons Blood (Eng) a 5.2 ale brewed by the Kemptown Brewery C°. Ltd., East Sussex.

Dragon's Blood (Ger) the name given to the wine from the vineyards around Königswinter called Drachenfels where, according to legend, Siegfried slew the dragon then bathed in its blood.

Dragon's Breath (Wal) a 6% alc by vol. strong ale brewed by the Plassey Brewery, Eyton, Clwyd.

Dragon Seal (Chi) a medium dry white wine 12% alc by vol. from French and Chinese grape varieties. Produced by a union of Pernod-Ricard and Beijing Friendship Winery.

Dragon's Eye (Chi) a white grape variety grown in the Tianjin and Hebei regions. *see* Loong Yan.

Dragon's Fury (Wal) a cask-conditioned ale brewed by Bragdy Clwyd Brewery, Denbigh, North Wales.

Dragon Slayer (Eng) a 4.5% alc by vol. dark beer brewed by Banks and Taylor, Shefford, Bedfordshire to celebrate St. George's day.

Dragons Smoke Stout (Eng) a stout brewed by Beowulf Brewery, Yardley, Birmingham.

Dragon Spirit (Wal) a 30% alc by vol. flavoured spirit produced by the Celtic Spirit C°. based at Grove Farm, Abergavenny, Monmouthshire using Welsh elderberry and rowan.

Dragon's Tale (Eng) a 4.5% alc by vol. ale brewed by the Marston Brewery, Staffordshire.

Dragon's Teeth (Eng) a beer brewed by Archers Brewery in Swindon, Wiltshire for Wetherspoons.

Dragon Stout (W.Ind) a 7.5% alc by vol. dark, top-fermented, bottled stout brewed in Kingston, Jamaica by Desnoes and Geddes Ltd.

Dragon's Well (Chi) a green tea from the Hangchow area, has a thick curled leaf which is still curled by hand.

Dragon Tree (S.Afr) the label for a white wine (Cabernet sauvignon, Merlot, Pinotage, Shiraz blend) produced by the Flagstone Winery, Somerset West, Western Cape.

Drahtrahmenerziehung (Ger) a method of vine training using wire frames.

Drainers (Eng) stainless steel vats with sieves to allow the juice to drain out before pressing.

Drakenbloed (Hol) a 9% alc by vol. bottle-conditioned special tripel beer brewed by De Drei Horne Bier Brouwerij, Kaatsheuvel for De Bockaar.

Drakensig Wines (S.Afr) a winery (established 1999) based in Simondium, Paarl, Western Cape. 13ha. Grape varieties: Cabernet sauvignon, Merlot, Pinotage, Sauvignon blanc, Shiraz. Label: Marais Viljoen.

Drakenstein (S.Afr) a still and sparkling natural spring mineral water from Franschhoek, Western Cape. Mineral contents (milligrammes per litre): Sodium 5.9mg/l, Calcium 0.5mg/l, Magnesium 0.3mg/l, Potassium 0.7mg/l, Chlorides 8mg/l, Sulphates 0.6mg/l, Fluorides <0.1mg/l, Nitrates <0.1mg/l. pH 6.4

Drakenstein Co-operative (S.Afr) a co-operative winery (established 1906) based in Paarl. (Add): Box 19, Simondium, 7670. Produces varietal wines.

Drake Port (Eng) the brand-name of Port bottled by Avery's of Bristol. Old Tawny style.

Drakes Cocktail (Cktl) ⅔ measure Plymouth gin, 10mls (½ fl.oz) crème de framboise, dash egg white, 2 dashes lemon juice. Shake over ice, strain into a cocktail glass and dress with a slice of lemon.

Dram (Scot) a slang term for a measure of spirits (usually whisky). i.e. "*a wee dram*" (a small measure).

Dramblat (Fr) an Armagnac producer. (Add): Maison Damblat, Castelnau d'Auzan 32240. 15ha. Produces Millesimes.

Drambuie (Scot) the oldest whisky liqueur (established 1906). (Add): Hillwood House, Corstorphine, Edinburgh, Midlothian EH12 6UX. Made from whisky, heather, honey and herbs. 40% alc by vol. Website: http://www.drambuie.com

Drambuie Eggnog (Cktl) 3 egg yolks creamed together with a teaspoon of sugar until smooth. Stir in 40mls (⅓ gill) Sherry, 90mls (⅔ gill) Drambuie, 175mls (⅓ pint) vanilla ice cream, 500mls (1 pint) milk. Mix well, add whipped egg whites and grated nutmeg.

Drambuie Swizzle (Cktl) 25mls (⅛ gill) Drambuie, juice ½ lime, 1 teaspoon sugar. Stir over crushed ice in a highball glass, top with soda water and mint sprig.

Drank (Eng) has consumed liquid (past tense of drink).

Drank (Hol) beverage/drink (also spirits).

Dranken (Hol) drinks.

Drankkwast (Hol) lemon squash.

Drankwinkel (S.Afr) wine shop/store.

Drankzuchtig (Hol) dipsomaniac.

Drapeau (Fr) pipes used for cooling (or heating) the fermenting must.

Drappier [André] (Fr) a Champagne producer. (Add): Grande Rue, Urville, 10200 Bar-sur-Aube. 35ha. Produces vintage and non-vintage wines. Vintages: 1973, 1976, 1979, 1981, 1982, 1983, 1985, 1988, 1989, 1990, 1995, 1998, 2000. Labels: Grande Sendrée (De Luxe Cuvée) and Valdes Desmoiselles (a vintage rosé).

Draught (Eng) the term used to denote a portion of liquid to be drunk. May be used as a slang term i.e. "*Draught of ale*".

Draught (Scot) *see* Draught "a wee draught", a small measure of whisky.

Draught Beer (Eng) either cask-conditioned or brewery conditioned beers. Beers that are drawn from a cask or keg. (Den) = fadøl.

Draught Excluder (Eng) a high gravity winter ale 1070. O.G. brewed by the Chudley Brewery in London.

Draught Mild (Eng) a 3.2% alc by vol. draught mild in a can from Thwaites (Daniel), Blackburn.

Draw Off (Eng) denotes the removal of liquid from a cask. Usually off the lees. i.e. racking, decanting, syphoning.

Drawwell Bitter (Eng) a 3.9% alc by vol. bitter beer brewed by Hanby Ales of Wem, Shropshire.

Dray (Eng) originally a horse-drawn cart but now a motorised vehicle used for transporting and delivering ales.

Drayman (Eng) the name for the driver and his assistants who delivered casks of ale to public houses on a dray.

Drayman's (S.Afr) a brewery. (Add): P.O. Box 1648, Silverton, Pretoria 0127. Brews a variety of beers and lager. Website: http://www.draymans.com 'E'mail: info@draymans.co.za

Draymans Best (Eng) a 4.2% alc by vol. best bitter brewed by The Branscombe Vale Brewery Ltd., Devon.

Drayman's Bitter (Wal) a 3.5% alc by vol. bitter ale brewed by the Cwmbran Brewery, Gwent.

Drayman's Choice (Eng) a low-gravity bitter beer brewed by the Mansfield Brewery, Nottinghamshire.

Drayman's Choice (Wal) a 3.8% alc by vol. ale brewed by the Cwmbran Brewery, Gwent.

Drayman's Gold (Wal) a 3.8% alc by vol. ale brewed by the Cwmbran Brewery, Gwent.

Draytons (Austr) an estate winery in the Hunter Valley, New South Wales. Grape varieties: Chardonnay, Hermitage and Sémillon.

Dr. Cameron's (Eng) a British wine and whisky drink produced by the Wham Company.

Dr. Cook Cocktail (Cktl) ⅓ measure dry gin, juice ¼ lemon, dash maraschino, 1 egg white. Shake over ice and strain into a 125mls (5fl.oz) goblet.

Dreadnought (Eng) a 1080 O.G. light coloured ale from Clarks of Wakefield, Yorkshire.

Dreadnought (Eng) a 4.5% alc by vol. ale brewed by the Nottingham Brewery, Nottinghamshire.

Dreamcatcher (Eng) a 4.7% alc by vol. ale brewed by the Bells brewery, Leicestershire.

Dreamcatcher (Eng) a cask ale brewed by the Wychwood Brewery, Eagle Maltings, Witney, Oxfordshire (part of their Character Ale range).

Dream Cocktail (Cktl) 1 measure brandy, ½ measure Cointreau, 2 dashes anisette. Shake over ice and strain into a cocktail glass.

Dreamview Hill (S.Afr) a winery (established 2004) based in Somerset West, Western Cape. 4ha. Grape varieties: Cabernet franc, Cabernet sauvignon, Merlot. Label: Redstone. Website: http://www.capelands.com

Drèche (Fr) *see* Draft.

Dreck (Austr) a little known red wine grape from the Bakersfield region.

Dreckly (Eng) a 4.8% alc by vol. ale brewed by the Ring 'O' Bells Brewery, Cornwall.

Dregs (Eng) lees, particles remaining in the bottom of a drink. i.e. coffee grounds, tea leaves, tannin, tartrate crystals etc.

Dreher [Anton] (It) name appears only on a brewing group jointly controlled by Whitbread and Heineken.

Dreher Brauerei (Aus) a brewery founded by Anton Dreher. Produced the first modern lager beer. Breweries in Vienna (Schwechat), Czec. (Michelob, Bohemia), Hungary (Budapest) and Italy (Trieste).

Dreher Neto [Carlos] (Bra) a leading wine producer in the country.

Dreibogen-Quelle (Ger) a natural spring mineral water from Eichendorf-Adldorf, BY.

Dreikönigs Bier (Switz) lit: 'three king beer', a beer brewed by the Hürlimann Brauerei in Zürich. A Starkbier 6.5%. alc by vol.

Dreikönigsquelle (Ger) a natural spring mineral water from Bad Hönningen, Rheinbrohl, RP. Mineral contents (milligrammes per litre): Sodium 13mg/l, Calcium 67mg/l, Magnesium 21mg/l, Potassium 1.8mg/l, Bicarbonates 726mg/l, Chlorides 22mg/l, Sulphates 44mg/l, Fluorides 0.27mg/l.

Dreikönigswein (Ger) the name given to wines made from grapes picked on the sixth day of January (twelfth night).

Dreimanner (Czec) a white grape variety.

Dreimännerwein (Ger) lit: 'three man wine', the name given to wine produced in the Saar-Ruwer from the Elbling grape. In good years the wine is austere but in poor years it takes 2 men to hold the third down to make him drink it (hence the name).

Dreis (Ger) village (Anb): Mosel-Saar-Ruwer. (Ber): Bernkastel. (Gro): Schwarzlay. (Vin): Johannisberg.

Dreiser Sprudel (Ger) a natural spring mineral water from Dreiser Weiher, Dreis-Brück, Vulkaneifel, RP. Mineral contents (milligrammes per litre): Sodium 302mg/l, Calcium 183mg/l, Magnesium 241mg/l, Potassium 38.3mg/l, Bicarbonates 2553mg/l, Chlorides 17mg/l, Sulphates 18mg/l, Fluorides 0.34mg/l, Nitrates 0.3mg/l.

Drench (Eng) a branded bottled drinking water from Britvic.

Dressing (Eng) a term used to denote the labelling and foiling of wine and beer bottles.

Dressler Brauerei (Ger) a subsidiary brewery of the Holstein Brauerei Hamburg, situated in Bremen. Noted for lager beers.

Dr. Hexters Healer (Eng) a 5% alc by vol. ale brewed by the West Berkshire Brewery C°. Ltd., Berkshire.

Dr. Hogg Muscat (N.Z) a white dessert wine grape.

Dried Milk (Eng) skimmed milk (of its cream) that is evaporated by the use of heated cylinders, freeze-drying, etc.

Drie Fonteiner Brasserie (Bel) a brewery based in Beersel, central Belgium.

Drie Hoefijzers Brasserie (Bel) lit: 'three horseshoes', a brewery based in Breda. Brews: Dutch Skol Lager.

Driesprong (S.Afr) wine estate.

Drifter (Eng) tropical or strawberry flavoured wine coolers from the Global Beer Company in Old Hasland Road, Chesterfield.

Drigo (Ch.Isles) drink/grog.

Drik (Den) beverage/drink.

Drikke en Rus (Den) to become drunk, intoxicated.

Drink (Eng) to swallow liquid, absorb, to take intoxicating liquor.

Drink a Person Under the Table (Eng) a term used to denote that one person can consume more alcoholic drink than another.

Drinkbaar (Hol) potable.

Drinkebroer (Hol) drinker/tippler.

Drinken (Hol) to drink.

Drinkers Paradise Ltd (Eng) a distillers (established 1997). (Add): 129 Castlehaven Road, Kentish Town, London NW1 8SJ. Produces a wide range of spirits. 'E'mail: cannabisvodka@yahoo.co.uk

Drinkgelag (Hol) a drinking bout.

Drink Gold (Bos) a natural spring mineral water from Mihalj Spring, Praca, Bosnia and Herzegovina. Mineral contents (milligrammes per litre): Sodium 147.2mg/l, Calcium 276.55mg/l, Fluorides 0.42mg/l, Iron 3.2mg/l, Manganese 1.13mg/l. pH 7.0

Drinking Chocolate (Eng) a drink made with milk/water and chocolate, usually a commercially produced preparation in powder form.

Drinking N°1 (Rus) a still, alkaline natural spring mineral water (established 2002). Mineral contents (milligrammes per litre): Sodium >60mg/l, Calcium 40-60mg/l, Magnesium 10-15mg/l, Potassium >1mg/l, Bicarbonates 115-150mg/l, Chlorides 20-30mg/l, Sulphates 115-150mg/l, Fluorides >1.2mg/l, Iodone >60mg/l, Oxygen <9mg/l. pH 8.5

Drinking in Stereo (Eng) a slang term for a person with a drink in each hand.

Drinking Straw (Eng) a thin tube of metal, straw, paper, wood, glass, plastic, etc. used for drinking liquids from a vessel. They are especially used for many cocktails that have ice or fruit in them.

Drinking Table (Eng) a kidney-shaped table produced in Georgian times for drinking and serving wines, spirits, etc.

Drinking up Time (Eng) the time permitted by law for the consumption on licensed premised of those drinks purchased during permitted hours. 10 minutes in England and Wales, 15 minutes in Scotland and Isle of Man, 30 minutes in Northern Ireland. In restaurants it is 30 minutes.

Drinking Vouchers (Eng) a slang term used in the north of England for sterling paper money (£5, £10, £20 and £50). Usually are referred to by the note's colour. i.e. a £5 note would be described as a "*blue drinking voucher*".

Drinking Water (Eng) potable water. (Pol) = woda do picia, (Sp) = agua potable.

Drink Mixer (Eng) *see* Blender.

Drinks Can (Eng) a general name for the container (with a ring pull opening system) to hold both alcoholic and non-alcoholic drinks. (Fr) = canette.

Drink Shrink (Eng) a slang term for a drunk who want to psycho-analyse all those around him/her!

Drink With the Flies (Austr) a term to denote a person drinking on their own (a lone drinker).

Drioli (It) a liqueur producer based in Venice. Noted for Maraschino.

Drip-Feed Irrigation (Eng) the practice of watering vineyards in the New World with fine tubes that supply a small but constant supply of water. Banned in the E.C.

Drip Mat (Eng) another name for a Beer Mat.

Dripolator (USA) a method of coffee making in which very hot water is percolated through coffee grounds.

Drip Tray (Eng) a plastic or metal tray fitted under draught beer taps to catch the ullages (overflow).

Drivers (Eng) non-alcoholic, 150mls bottles of simulated drinks i.e. gin and tonic, whisky and ginger, rum and coke. distributed by Britvic Canada Dry.

Driving Force (Eng) a 1027 O.G. cask-conditioned real ale. Distributed by the north-east co-operative Legendary Yorkshire Heroes.

Dr. Konstantin Frank (USA) a winery (established 1962) based in the Finger Lakes region of the New York State.

Dr. Loosen [Ernst] (Ger) a wine estate in the middle Mosel. Produces all styles of wines including The Naked Grape. Website: http://www.drloosen.com

Dr. Ludo (Slo) a still and sparkling natural mineral water. Website: http://www.drludo.com

Dr. Milton's (Eng) an old eighteenth century tea blend.

Droë Rooi (S.Afr) dry red.

Droesem (Hol) lees/sediment. *See also* Drab.

Droë Wit (S.Afr) dry white.

Droë Wit (S.Afr) a dry, white, fruity wine made from Colombard and Steen grapes by the Opstal estate.

Droin [Jean-Paul et Benoit] (Fr) a winery based in the A.C. Chablis, Burgundy. Produces a range of Chablis wines including Premier Cru Montée de Tonnerre.

Droit de Banvin (Fr) the start of the harvest.

Dr. Okells IPA (I.O.M) a 4.5% alc by vol. India pale ale brewed by Okell & Sons Ltd., Isle of Man.

Dromana Estate (Austr) a winery (established 1982) based at Harrison's Road, Dromana, Victoria. Grape varieties: Cabernet sauvignon, Merlot, Pinot noir, Chardonnay, Sauvignon blanc.

Drôme (Fr) département of the Côtes du Rhône.

Dromersheim (Ger) village (Anb): Rheinhessen. (Ber): Bingen. (Gro): Sankt Rochuskapelle. (Vins): Honigberg, Kapellenberg, Klosterweg, Mainzerweg, Bergkelder.

Dronck (Eng) a seventeenth century spelling of drunk, intoxicated.

D

Dronkaard (Hol) drunkard.

Dronken (Hol) drunken/tipsy.

Dronkenschap (Hol) drunkenness.

Droog (S.Afr) dry.

Drop Inn (S.Afr) *see* Drop in Wines.

Drop in Wines (S.Afr) a large stores group that sells wines under the Drop Inn, Springlands and Vintner's Choice labels.

Drosophila melanogaster (Lat) vinegar fly.

Drosselborn (Ger) vineyard (Anb): Rheinhessen. (Ber): Bingen. (Gro): Abtey. (Vil): Appenheim.

Drostdy (S.Afr) the name for a range of South African Sherries from the Drostdy-Koöperatiewe Wynkelder.

Drostdy-Hof Wines (S.Afr) *see* Drostdy Koöperatiewe Wynkelder (Die).

Drostdy Koöperatiewe Wynkelder [Die] (S.Afr) a co-operative winery (established 1804) based in Tulbagh (the oldest South African co-op). (Add): Die Drostdy Koöperatiewe Wynkelders, Box 85, Tulbagh 6820. Grape varieties: Cabernet sauvignon, Carignan, Chardonnay, Chenin blanc, Cinsaut, Merlot, Palomino, Pinotage, Pinot noir, Sauvignon blanc, Sémillon, Shiraz, Ugni blanc, Viognier. Labels: Adelpracht, Celeste, Cirrus, Cumulus, Drostdy-Hof Wines, Stein Select, Witzenberg Wines. Website: http://www.drostdywines.co.za

Drostdy Pale Dry (S.Afr) a pale, dry Fino South African Sherry produced by the Die Drostdy Koöperatiewe.

Drouhin [Christian] (Fr) a producer of A.C. Calvados du Pays d'Auge. *see* Pomme Prisonière (La), Coeur du Lion. Also produces Pommeau.

Drouhin [Joseph et Cie] (Fr) a négociant-éleveur (established 1880) based in Beaune, Burgundy. 63ha. Also produces A.C. Chablis and Chablis Premier Crus Montmains and Vaillons. Website: http://www.drouhin.com

Drovers (Eng) a 4.1% alc by vol. bitter brewed by the Wood Brewery, Winstantow, Shropshire.

Drovers Bitter (Wal) a bitter ale brewed by Flannery's in Aberystwyth.

Drown One's Sorrows [To] (Eng) a term used to denote a person drinking alcohol to forget their troubles.

Dr. Pepper (USA) a famous soft drink Company. *see* Doctor Pepper.

Dr's Orders (Eng) a classic bitter ale (part of the Classics Range) brewed by the Hydes Brewery, Manchester.

DR Stephens (USA) a winery based in the Napa Valley, California. Grape varieties include: Cabernet sauvignon. Label: Moose Valley Vineyard.

Dr. Thirsty's Beetlejuice (Eng) now known as Z.

Druid's Ale (Wal) a cask-conditioned strong ale brewed by the Silverthorne Brewery in South Wales.

Druids Ale (Eng) a 3.9% alc by vol. ale brewed by Leatherbritches Brewery, Fenny Bentley, near Ashbourne.

Druid's Delight (Cktl) 125mls (1 gill) mead, 25mls (⅛ gill) French vermouth. Stir over ice, strain into a highball glass, dress with a mint leaf and a lemon slice.

Druid's Fluid (Eng) a 5% alc by vol. ale brewed by the Wizard Brewery, Warwickshire.

Druids Special (Eng) *see* Ancient Druids.

Druif (Hol) grape.

Druivennat (Hol) grape juice. *See also* Druivesap.

Druivenpers (Hol) wine-press.

Druivesap (Hol) grape juice. *See also* Druivennat.

Drum (Eng) a 5.8% alc by vol. perry from Taunton Cider Company Ltd.

Drum Bitter (Eng) a keg bitter 1036.5 O.G. brewed by the Davenport's Brewery in Birmingham.

Drum Bitter (Eng) a keg bitter 1034 O.G. brewed by the Tetley Brewery in Leeds.

Drumgray Highland Cream (Scot) *see* Mrs Walker's Drumgray Highland Cream.

Drumguish (Scot) the label of a 40% alc by vol. highland Speyside malt whisky.

Drum Malting (Eng) a malting system developed in the 1950's using revolving drums to germinate and heat the barley. *see* Saladin Box.

Drummonds (USA) a 4.5% alc by vol. premium lager from Evansville, Indiana. *See also* Eagle (The).

Drummond's Brewery (Eng) a micro-brewery based at London Road, Heeley, Sheffield. Brews: Pale Ale 3.5% alc by vol. Bulldog 4% alc by vol. Drummond's Dregs 4.5% alc by vol. Drummond Bitter 4.5% alc by vol. Mild and a winter warmer.

Drummond's Dregs (Eng) a 4.5% alc by vol. premium ale brewed by Drummond's Brewery, Heeley, Sheffield.

Druniguisk (Scot) a single malt whisky distilled at The Speyside Distillery Cº.

Drunk (Eng) a slang term to describe a person who is under the influence of alcohol. (Ger) = betrunken, (Port) = ébrio.

Drunken Duck (Eng) a 3.9% alc by vol. ale brewed by the George Wright Brewing Cº., Merseyside.

Drunkometer (USA) the equivalent of the U.K. Breathalyser in America.

Drupe (Lat) the botanical name for the coffee-tree cherry (fruit).

Drupeggio (It) a white grape variety grown in Umbria. Name for Canaiolo Bianco in Orvieto.

Druskininku (Lith) a natural spring mineral water from Druskininkai. Mineral contents (milligrammes per litre): Sodium 236mg/l, Calcium 100mg/l, Magnesium 28.5mg/l, Potassium 10-230mg/l, Chlorides 470mg/l, Sulphates 18mg/l.

Druskininku Hermis (Lith) a natural spring mineral water from Druskininkai. Mineral contents (milligrammes per litre): Sodium 410mg/l, Calcium 80mg/l, Magnesium 27mg/l, Potassium 8mg/l, Bicarbonates 340mg/l, Chlorides 660mg/l, Sulphates 33mg/l.

Druskininku Rasa (Lith) a natural spring mineral water from Druskininkai. Mineral contents (milligrammes per litre): Sodium 449-539mg/l, Calcium 179-218mg/l, Magnesium 55-73mg/l, Potassium 6.5mg/l, Bicarbonates 170-205mg/l, Chlorides 1153-1385mg/l, Sulphates 32-43mg/l.

Druskininhu Rita (Lith) a natural spring mineral water from Druskininkai. Mineral contents (milligrammes per litre): Sodium 690-1200mg/l, Calcium 150-320mg/l, Magnesium 50-120mg/l, Bicarbonates 300-360mg/l, Chlorides 1200-2500mg/l, Sulphates 10-60mg/l.

Dr. Willkomm Liebfraumilch (Ger) a noted Liebfraumilch QbA. white wine from the Pfalz. Bottled in Bernkastel-Kues, Mosel-Saar-Ruwer.

DRX Meritage (USA) a label for a red wine (Cabernet sauvignon) from the Deerfield Ranch winery, North Coast, California.

Dry (Eng) when applied to wines it denotes one which has been fermented out. A wine that has no unfermented sugar remaining in the wine. (Den) = tør, (Fr) = sec.

Dry (S.Afr) a classification of wine. Has 4 grammes per litre of sugar or less.

Dry Americano Cocktail (Cktl) 25mls (⅕ gill) Noilly Prat, 25mls (⅕ gill) Campari. Stir over ice, strain into a cocktail glass and add ice and a slice of orange.

Dry Blackthorn Cider (Eng) the brand-name of a noted dry cider 5% alc by vol. from Taunton, Somerset.

Drybrough (Scot) a brewery in Edinburgh owned by Watneys. Produces: cask-conditioned Pentland 1036 O.G. Eighty 1042 O.G. Scotch 1034 O.G. Burn's Special 1036 O.G. Original 1042 O.G. and Scottish Pride Lager 1032 O.G.

Dry Buccaneer (Cktl) 1 measure white rum, 1 measure dry Dubonnet, 1 measure dry ginger. Fill a highball with ice, add all the ingredients, stir and decorate with a slice of orange.

Dry Cane (W.Ind) the brand-name of a white rum matured by Courage Breweries 40% alc by vol.

Dry Cherry Vodka (Pol) a semi-sweet cherry-flavoured vodka produced by Polmos 40% alc by vol.

Dry Cider Premium Press (Eng) the label of a cider produced by Thatchers, Somerset.

Dry Co-operative Cellar (Euro) denotes a collecting station for the grower's grapes which are sorted (and often pressed), then distributed for vinification at other cellars. Is popular in Germany.

Dry Creek (USA) a winery (established 1972) based in Healdsburg, Sonoma, California. 21ha. (Add): 3770 Lambert Bridge Roade, Healdsburg, CA 95448. Grape varieties: Cabernet sauvignon, Chardonnay, Chenin blanc, Petit syrah and Zinfandel. Produces varietal wines. Website: http://www.drycreekvineyard.com 'E'mail: dcv@drycreekvineyard.com

Dry Creek Valley (USA) a wine-producing region in Sonoma County, California. Noted for Fumé blanc.

Dry Don (Sp) a brand of Amontillado Sherry produced by Sandeman.

Dry Farming (USA) no artificial irrigation, only natural rainfall.

Dry Fly (Eng) a brand of Amontillado Sherry shipped by Findlater's of London.

Dry Gin (Eng) produced in England and America it is light in flavour and body but has a good dry, aromatic aroma and taste.

Dry Hopping (Eng) the addition of a handful of dry hops to a finished brew when in cask to give the beer a hop aroma. *See also* Primmings.

Drying Up (Eng) a term applied to wines that have lost their freshness and fruit through age in the bottle.

Dry Lustau (Sp) the brand-name for a range of dry Sherries produced by Lustau in Jerez.

Dry Martini (Cktl) 60mls (2½ fl.ozs) dry gin, 2 dashes dry vermouth. Stir over ice, serve straight or '*on the rocks*', adding a twist of lemon or an olive. *see* Martini. (Den) = tør martini.

Dry Martini (It) the brand-name of a dry vermouth from Martini and Rossi.

Dry Martini Cocktail (Eng) a ready-mixed drink produced by Gordon's in London.

Dry Melody (Cktl) ⅘ measure vodka, ⅒ measure Fraises des Bois, ⅒ measure Mandarine liqueur. Shake over ice and strain into a cocktail glass.

Dry Method (Eng) a method of removing the coffee beans from the fruit by drying the fruit in the sun then removing the beans with a hulling machine. *See also* Wet Method.

Dry Millenary (Cktl) ⅗ measure Gilbey's gin, ⅕ measure Cinzano Americano, ⅕ measure Rosé Cinzano, dash Cinzano dry. Stir over ice and strain into a cocktail glass.

Dry Monopole (Fr) the brand-name for Heidsieck and C°. non-vintage Champagne.

Drynke (Eng) an old English spelling of drink in the sixteenth century.

Dry Presidente (Cktl) 35mls (1½ fl.ozs) each of Bacardi white label, dry vermouth. Stir with ice, strain into a cocktail glass, twist a slice of orange over glass and dress with an olive.

Dry River Wines (N.Z) a vineyard. (Add): Puruatanga Road, P.O. Box 72, Martinborough. 4ha. Grape varieties: Gewürztraminer, Pinot gris, Riesling. Noted for Botrytised Riesling.

Dry Sack (Sp) a registered trade mark of Sherry shippers Williams and Humbert. A medium Sherry.

Dry Sauterne (USA) *see* California Sauterne.

Dry Seco (Sp) a light delicate Fino Sherry from Sandeman. *See also* Don Fino, Soleo.

Drystone Cider (Eng) a cider produced by the Symonds Cider C°. in Hereford. Also known as Symonds Drystone Cider.

Dry Stout (Eng) a 4.2% alc by vol. stout brewed by O'Hanlon's Brewery C°. Ltd., Devon

Dry Tang (Port) the label for a white Port produced by Cockburns.

Dry Vermouth (Fr) colour varies from clear to light gold. Now also made in Italy.

Dry Wine (Eng) a term to denote a wine that has no residual sugar with a fresh acidity. (Fr) = vin sec/vin brut, (Ger) = trockenwein, (Ire) = fion neamh-mhilis.

Dry Wit Sherry (USA) the brand-name used by the Llords and Elwood Winery in California for a range of their sherries.

D.S.I.R. (N.Z) *abbr: see* **D**epartment of **S**cientific and **I**ndustrial **R**esearch.

D.T. (Fr) *abbr:* **D**égorgement **T**ardive.

dt (Eng) a non-alcoholic stimulating drink containing taurine, caffeine, ginseng and vitamins from Virgin. Available in 3 versions **blue**: mixed fruits, **green**: lemon, **purple**: sea breeze. Also alcoholic version containing vodka. *see* nt.

D.T.'s (Eng) *abbr:* **D**ilemous **T**reminous, the shakes from over indulgence in alcohol.

Duakademon (Eng) the name for a beer brewed by the Ballard's Brewery, Hampshire.

Duas Quintas (Port) a red wine produced from 2 quintas: Quinta da Erramoira and Quinta dos Bons Ares by Ramos Pinto in the Douro.

D.U.B. (Ger) *abbr:* **D**ortmunder **U**nion **B**rauerei.

Dubac (Fr) a brandy produced by Landy Frères.

Du Baril (Switz) a red wine produced in Salvagnin from the Gamay and Pinot noir grapes.

Du Barry (Cktl) ⅗ measure gin, ⅖ measure dry vermouth, 2 dashes Angostura. Shake over ice, strain into a cocktail glass and dress with a slice of orange.

Dubbel (Bel) a dark-brown beer 7% alc by vol. brewed by the Westmalle Brasserie.

Dubbele Graan (Hol) a term used for a genever distilled with juniper. *See also* Gebeide and Dubbel Gebeide.

Dubbel Gebeide (Hol) *see* Gebeide and Dubbele Graan.

D.U.B. Export (Ger) an export beer brewed by the D.U.B. in Westphalia.

Dublin Brewing Company (Ire) a brewery. (Add): 141-146 North King Street, Smithfield, Dublin 7. Brews: Beckett's Gold, Maeve's Crystal Wheat. Website: http://www.dublinbrewing.com 'E'mail: info@dublinbrewing.com

Dublin Distillers (Ire) formerly William Jameson and C°. Now closed down.

Dublin Pride Ale (Ire) a bottled export ale 1040 O.G. brewed by the Dempsey Brewery in Dublin. Brewed for the USA market.

Du Bocq Brasserie Centrale (Bel) a brewery based in Purnode and Marbaix. Noted for their Saison beer, Winston (pale styled beer), Gauloise [La] (Ambrée, Blonde and Brune), St. Benoit Brune, Rubens Rood and Triple Moine.

Duboeuf [Georges] (Fr) a Beaujolais négociant based at Romanèche-Thorins, Beaujolais, Burgundy.

Duboka (Yug) a natural spring mineral water from Serbia and Montenegro.

Du Bon (Cktl) 40mls (⅓ gill) Dubonnet, 20mls (⅙ gill) dry gin, juice of ½ lemon. Stir over ice in a highball glass, top with lemonade and a lemon slice.

Dubonnet (Fr) a bitter vermouth made from the Carignan, Grenache and Malvoisie muscat grapes and flavoured with quinine and bitter bark. Also produce a red and blonde version 17% alc by vol.

Dubonnet Blonde (Fr) a white version of the famous Dubonnet vermouth.

Dubonnet Cassis (Cktl) ⅔ measure red Dubonnet, ⅓ measure crème de cassis. Stir over ice in a highball glass and top with Perrier water.

Dubonnet-Citron (Cktl) 60mls (½ gill) Dubonnet, 20mls (⅙ gill) sirop de citron, soda water and ice. Stir over ice and strain into a highball glass over ice.

Dubonnet Cocktail [1] (Cktl) 10mls (½ fl.oz) dry gin, 25mls (1fl.oz) Dubonnet. Stir over ice, strain into a cocktail glass and add a squeeze lemon peel juice on top.

Dubonnet Cocktail [2] (Cktl) 40mls (⅓ gill) Dubonnet, 20mls (⅙ gill) dry Sherry, 3 dashes orange bitters. Shake well over ice and strain into a cocktail glass.

Dubonnet Fizz (Cktl) 1 measure Dubonnet, ½ measure cherry brandy, 25mls (1fl.oz) lemon juice, 25mls (1fl.oz) orange juice, 1 egg white. Shake well together over ice, strain into a highball glass with ice, top with soda water, serve with straws and muddler.

Dubonnet Mint Julep (Cktl) crush some mint leaves with ice in a highball glass. Add 25mls crème de menthe, top with Dubonnet Blonde and serve with straws.

Dubonnet Royal (Cktl) ⅓ measure dry gin, ⅔ measure Dubonnet, 2 dashes Angostura, 2 dashes orange bitters, 1 dash pastis. Stir together over ice except pastis, strain into a cocktail glass, add pastis and dress with a cherry.

Dubor and C°. (Fr) brandy producers.

Dubravka (Ser) a red wine produced in eastern Serbia.

Dubroca [Louis] (Fr) a Bordeaux négociant-éleveur. (Add): Domaine de Ribet, St. Loubes 33450. Has properties in the Médoc.

Dubuisson Brouwerij (Bel) a brewery (established 1769) based near Tournai, Pipaix. Noted for Bush Beer.

Dubuque Star (USA) a beer 4.8% alc by vol. brewed by the Pickett Brewery in Dubuque, Iowa.

Duc [Le] (Fr) a popular brand of Normandy cider from the Duché de Longueville Ciderie.

Duca d'Asti (It) a producer of sparkling (metodo tradizionale) wines based in Calamandrana Asti, Piemonte. The labels include Granduca Brut.

Duca di Castelmonte (It) a winery based on the island of Sicily. Label: Fiorile (rosé).

Duca di Salaparuta (It) a winery based on the island of Sicily, owned by Corvo. Label: Duca Enrico.

Duca Enrico (It) a red wine produced by Corvo in Sicily. *See also* Vino Fiore.

Ducale (It) a still natural spring mineral water from Monte Zuccone. Mineral contents (milligrammes per litre): Sodium 3mg/l, Calcium 12.5mg/l, Magnesium 1.3mg/l, Potassium 0.4mg/l, Bicarbonates 39.7mg/l, Chlorides 3.8mg/l, Sulphates 6.9mg/l, Nitrates 1.9mg/l, Silicates 5.4mg/l. pH 8.3

Duca Sanfelice (It) a red wine produced by Librandi in Calabria.

Ducastaing (Fr) an Armagnac producer. (Add): 32190 Vic-Fezensac. Ténarèze. Produces Bernard V11 X.O. 10 year old, Duc d'Aquitaine 10 year old and B.B. Martine V.S.O.P. 5 year old.

Duc d'Aquitaine (Fr) a 10 year old Armagnac produced by Ducastaing.

Duc de Berry Rouge (S.Afr) a blended red wine made with the Cinsault 40% and Shiraz 60% grapes by the Eikendal vineyards in Stellenbosch.

Duc de Folie (Sp) a cava wine produced by COVIDES from 40% Parallada, 30% Xarel-lo, 30% Macabeo. Spends 24 months on lees.

Duc de Lavigny (Fr) a Champagne producer. (Add): 23 Rue Roger Catillon, 02400 Château Thierry. Under the control of Pannier.

Duc d'Enghien (Fr) a vin mousseux produced by Reinevald (De), Rue Banlin, 33310 Lormont.

Duc de Niçoise (Cyp) a sparkling dry wine produced by the Keo C°.

Du Chadé (Ch.Isles) a hot cider drink from Jersey, made from equal quantities of milk and cider 300mls (½ pint) plus 2 eggs, heated but not boiled.

Duché de Longueville Cidery (Fr) a fine cider-producing company based near Dieppe on the river Scie in Normandy, northern France. Produces Le Duc brand ciders and Duche de Longueville: a single estate cider made from Gros Oeillet apples.

Duchess (USA) a native white grape variety suitable for late picking because of its thick skin.

Duchess Cocktail (Cktl) ⅓ measure pastis, ⅓ measure dry vermouth, ⅓ measure sweet vermouth. Stir over ice and strain into a cocktail glass.

Duchesse (Bel) a natural spring mineral water from Duchesse, Spontin.

Duchesse (Bra) a white grape variety also known as the Riesling de Caldas.

Duchesse Anne (Fr) a 6.5% alc by vol. deep-gold coloured, triple-fermented, bottle-conditioned special beer brewed by Bernard Lancelot Brasserie, St. Servant-sur-Oust.

Duchesse de Bourgogne (Bel) a 6.2% alc by vol. top-fermented Old Brown Flanders beer brewed by Verhaeghe Vichte.

Duchroth (Ger) village (Anb): Nahe. (Ber): Schloss Böckelheim. (Gro): Burgweg. (Vins): Felsenberg, Feuerberg, Kaiserberg, Königsfels, Rothenberg, Vogelschlag.

Duchy Bitter (Eng) a bottled ale 3.7% alc by vol (1037 O.G). brewed by the St. Austell Brewery C°. Ltd., Cornwall.

Duchy Original (Eng) a drink blended from English fruit and herbs from the Duchy of Cornwall estate. N°1 (red, lightly sparkling) and N°3 (white) versions.

Duck & Dive (Eng) a 3.7% alc by vol. ale brewed by the Mallard Brewery, Nottinghamshire.

Duck Decanter (Eng) a style of decanter that is shaped like a sitting duck. Has an oval body and wide neck at a 45° angle from the body, also has a looped handle.

Duckhorn Vineyards (USA) a small winery based near St. Helena, Napa Valley, California. Grape varieties: Cabernet sauvignon, Merlot and Sauvignon blanc. Produces varietal wines. Label: Patzimaro Vineyard.

Duckling (Eng) a 4.2% alc by vol. ale brewed by the Mallard Brewery, Nottinghamshire.

Duckling Bitter (Eng) a cask-conditioned bitter brewed by the Mallard Brewery, Carlton, Nottingham. See also Waddlers Mild.

Duck Muck (Austr) a red wine from the Wild Duck Creek Estate winery, Heathcote, Victoria.

Duck n Dive (Eng) a 4.6% alc by vol. ale brewed by the Six Bells Brewery, Shropshire.

Duck Pond Cellars (USA) a vineyard (established 1986) based in Willamette Valley. Grape varieties: Pinot noir, Chardonnay, Merlot.

Ducks Folly (Eng) a 5.2% alc by vol. ale brewed by the Goddards Brewery, Isle of Wight.

Duck Walk Vineyards (USA) a winery based in the North Fork of Long Island, New York State. Grape variety: Pinot noir.

Ducs d'Esmé, Prinal, Guy Labarde (Fr) a Cognac producer. (Add): Ste Brugerolle S.A. 17160 Matha.

Duckstein (Ger) a 4.9% alc by vol. lager/ale brewed by Holstein, copper gold in colour, it is brewed like an ale, stored and dispensed like a lager.

Dudognon [Raymond] (Fr) a Cognac producer. (Add): Lignières-Sonneville, 16130 Segonzac. 29ha. in Grande Champagne. Produces a range of Cognacs including Réserve des Ancestres.

Duenn (Ger) denotes ordinary thin wine.

Duero (Port) the river Douro (Portuguese spelling).

Dufays [Doctor] (Fr) a pioneer of macération carbonique method of fermentation who died in 1978. Was the owner of Domaine de Nalys in Châteauneuf-du-Pape, southern Rhône.

Duff Gordon (Sp) noted shippers of Sherry and brandy. Owned by Osborne and based at Puerto de Santa Maria. Labels include Duff Gordon, El Cid, Fino Feria and Santa Maria.

Dufftown–Glenlivet (Scot) a single malt whisky distillery near Dufftown in Banffshire (owned by Arthur Bell and Sons). A highland malt whisky. 15 year old, 43% alc by vol.

Dufouleur Pères et Fils (Fr) a Burgundy négociant based at Nuits-Saint-Georges, Côte de Nuits, Burgundy.

Duft (Ger) fragrant.

Duftig (Ger) fine bouquet/fragrance.

Du Gin de Prunelles (Ch.Isles) sloe gin.

Du Gin d'Orange (Ch.Isles) orange cordial.

Duhat (E.Ind) known as the Java plum. Used for making fruit wines in the Phillipines.

Duilleog Tae (Ire) tea leaf.

Duivelsbier (Bel) lit: 'devil's beer', a dark gueuze-type beer brewed by the Vander Linden Brouwerij in Halle, central Belgium.

Dujardin Fine (Ger) a weinbrand that has been matured for 8 years, distilled at Urdingen on the lower Rhine.

D

Dujardin Imperial (Ger) a weinbrand distilled at Urdingen on the lower Rhine.

Dujardin Scale (Fr) a hydrometer, approximately half reading of the Balling scale. i.e. 1.039 O.G. equals 10° Balling and 4.5° Dujardin.

Dukang (Chi) a natural spring mineral water. Mineral contents (milligrammes per litre): Silicates 50mg/l.

Duke (Bel) a natural spring mineral water from Duke, Francorchamps. Mineral contents (milligrammes per litre): Sodium 5mg/l, Calcium 10mg/l, Magnesium 6mg/l, Potassium 0.5mg/l, Bicarbonates 30mg/l, Chlorides 7mg/l, Sulphates 33mg/l.

Duke (Eng) the domestic servants nickname for gin.

Duke Cocktail [1] (Cktl) ½ measure Drambuie, ¼ measure orange juice, ¼ measure lemon juice. Shake well together, strain into a wine glass and add a dash of Champagne.

Duke Cocktail [2] (Cktl) 1 egg, 20mls (⅙ gill) Cointreau, 15mls (⅛ gill) lemon juice, 4 dashes orange juice, 2 dashes maraschino. Shake over ice, strain into a flute glass and top with chilled Champagne.

Duke of Cambridge Verdelho (Mad) a medium to dry Madeira produced by the Blandy Brothers.

Duke of Clarence (Mad) a brand of Malmsey produced by Blandy in Funchal.

Duke of Cumberland Bual (Mad) a medium to sweet Madeira produced by the Blandy Brothers.

Duke of Northumberland (Eng) a 5% alc by vol. ale from Northumberland Brewery in Ashington (a micro-brewery).

Duke of Sussex Sercial (Mad) a medium dry Madeira produced by the Blandy Brothers.

Duke of Wellington (Sp) a top class range of Sherries and a solera reserva brandy produced by Bodegas Internacionales.

Dulce (It) sweet.

Dulce (Sp) sweet.

Dulce Apagado (Sp) grape must arrested from fermentation by the addition of alcohol. see Mistelle.

Dulce de Alimbar (Sp) a solution of wine and invert sugar used for sweetening pale sherries.

Dulce Negro (Sp) a sweet style of Málaga.

Dulce Pasa (Sp) a sweetening wine used in the making of Sherry. Is made from the Palomino grape.

Dulle Teve (Bel) lit: 'crazy bitch'. a 10% alc by vol. top-fermented, bottle-conditioned special beer brewed by De Dolle Brouwers, Esen-Diksmuide. Dry-hopped, unpasteurised and unfiltered.

Dullgärten (Ger) vineyard (Anb): Mosel-Saar-Ruwer. (Ber): Obermosel. (Gro): Königsberg. (Vil): Igel.

Dumangin [Jean] (Fr) a Champagne producer. (Add): 23 Rue Sainte Agathe, 51500 Chigny-lès-Roses.

Dumb (Eng) a term used to describe a wine that is under-developed.

Dumbarton Distillery (Scot) a grain whisky distillery based north-west of Glasgow.

Dumbuck (Scot) a heavily peated malt whisky that was produced by the Littlemill Distillery (now no longer available).

Dumfries Octocentenary Ale (Scot) an ale brewed by the Scottish Brewers to commemorate the 800th birthday celebrations of the town of Dumfries.

Dummy Daisy (Cktl)(Non-alc) 1 measure raspberry syrup, ½ measure lime juice, 1 teaspoon sugar. Shake over crushed ice and pour into a cocktail glass.

DuMOL (USA) a winery based in the Green Valley, Sonoma County, California. Grape varieties include: Chardonnay, Pinot noir.

Dumont [Daniel] (Fr) a Champagne producer. (Add): 11 Rue Gambetta, 51500 Rilly-la-Montagne.

Du Moulin (Fr) a bière brewed by the Ricour Brasserie.

Dunaris Heilwasser (Ger) a natural spring mineral water from Daun, RP. Mineral contents (milligrammes per litre): Sodium 771.4mg/l, Calcium 95.86mg/l, Magnesium 126.6mg/l, Potassium 31.2mg/l, Bicarbonates 2687mg/l, Chlorides 58.48mg/l, Sulphates 43.85mg/l, Fluorides 0.34mg/l, Lithium 1mg/l, Ammonium 2.6mg/l, Silicates 74.96mg/l.

Dunbar (Jap) a brand of whiskey produced by Kiran Seagram.

Dunbar Sweet Stout (Scot) a sweet stout brewed and bottled by the Belhaven Brewery C°. Ltd. in Dunbar.

Duncan Brewery (USA) a small brewery based in Auburndale, Florida.

Duncarrig (Ire) a natural spring mineral water brand.

Dundee Hills (USA) a wine sub-region of the State of Oregon.

Dunder (W.Ind) the skimmings from the sugar boilers which is added to the molasses in the fermentation vats for rum. Also known as Burnt Ale.

Dunderhead (Eng) an old English nickname for an alcoholic who gets drunk on rum.

Dune (Sp) the new name for Luncheon Dry Sherry produced by Harvey in Jerez, a very pale dry Fino Sherry.

Dunedin Brewery (USA) a brewery. (Add): 937 Douglas Avenue, Dunedin, Florida 34698-4945. Brews a variety of beers and lager. Website: http://www.dunedinbrewery.com

Dunglass (Scot) a lightly peated malt whisky that was produced by the Littlemill distillery (now no longer available).

Dunhill Century Blend (Scot) a blended whisky sold only by the cask from I.D.V.

Dunhill Old Master Finest Scotch Whisky (Scot) a de luxe Scotch whisky produced for Alfred Dunhill of London by the International Distillers and Vintners.

Dunhill '71 (Cktl) ⅓ measure brandy, ⅓ measure crème de banane, ⅓ measure Royal Orange Liqueur. Shake over ice, strain into a cocktail glass and float cream on top.

Dunhill '74 (Cktl) ½ measure dry gin, 1/10 measure peach brandy, 2/10 measure apricot brandy, 1/10 measure orange squash, 1/10 measure lemon barley water, 1 egg white. Shake over ice, strain into cocktail glass, add ½ slice of orange and lemon.

Dunkel (Ger) lit: 'dark', refers to the colour of beers, usually Münchener beers, most being quite high in alcohol.

Dunkeld Atholl Brose (Scot) a 35% alc by vol. sweet, herb-flavoured Scotch whisky liqueur.

Dunkelfelder (Ger) an alternative name for the French red-fleshed grape variety Teinturier. (Sp) = Tintorera.

Dunkel Spezial (Ger) a dark, mature, Münchner-style beer 5.6% alc by vol. brewed by the Riegele Brauerei in Augsburg.

Dunkel Weisse (Ger) dark wheat beer 5.1% alc by vol. from Arcobräu Brauerei in Bavaria.

Dunkerton's Cider C° (Eng) cider producers (established 1981). (Add): Luntley, Pembridge, Leominster, Herefordshire HR6 9ED. Produces farmhouse medium-dry or medium-sweet cider (5% alc by vol.), Traditional Dry Cider 7% alc by vol. and Perry. Also produces organic ciders. Website: http://www.dunkertons.co.uk

Dunkerton's Traditional Dry Cider (Eng) a 7% alc by vol. organic dry cider from Dunkerton's, Hereford.

Dunkery Vineyard (Eng) a winery based in Somerset. Noted for Riesling and Ehrenfelser.

Dunmow Priory (Eng) a vineyard based in Essex. Produces Flitch Reserve.

Dunnewood Cellars (USA) vineyards and winery in Ukiah, Mendocino County. Noted for Sauvignon blanc, Chardonnay and oak aged Cabernet sauvignon, Merlot, Zinfandel. Also produce the Coastal series of wine. Is a member of the Coro Mendocino (Zinfandel) wine group of Mendocino wineries.

Dunn Forest Vineyard (USA) the label for a red wine (Pinot noir) produced by the Airlie winery, Willamette Valley, Oregon.

Dunn Plowman Brewery (Eng) a brewery. (Add): Arrow Court Ind Estate, Lower Hergest, Kington, Herefordshire HR5 3ER. Brews: Brewhouse Bitter 3.8% alc by vol., Early Riser 4% alc by vol., Kingdom Bitter 4.5% alc by vol., Thomas Bewick Bitter 3.7% alc by vol.

Dunn Vineyards (USA) a winery based at Howell Mountain, Napa Valley, California. Noted for Cabernet sauvignon.

Dunny Cocktail (Cktl) ½ measure Drambuie, ½ measure Islay malt whisky, 2 dashes lime juice. Shake over ice, strain into a cocktail glass and dress with a slice of lime.

Dunphy's (Ire) a blend of light pot still whiskey and Midleton grain. Matured in charred American oak casks.

Dun's Surprise (Cktl) ½ measure Cointreau, ½ measure (green) Crème de Menthe. Shake over ice, strain into a Sherry Elgin glass and float double cream on top.

Dun Tumas (Euro) a white grape variety grown on the island of Malta.

Dupeyron [J.] (Fr) an Armagnac producer. (Add): Ryst-Dupeyron, B.P. 58, 32100 Condom, Ténarèze.

Du Plessis (S.Afr) the label for a range of red wines produced by the Havana Hills winery, Phildelphia, Western Cape.

Duplin Wine Cellars (USA) a winery based at Rose Hill, North Carolina. Produces French-American hybrid wines.

Dupont Brasserie (Bel) a brewery based in Tourpes. Noted for top-fermented Saison Dupont and Abbaye de la Moinette (an Abbaye-style beer).

Dupratt Vineyard (USA) a vineyard based on the west side of the Anderson Valley, California. 3ha. Grape variety: Zinfandel.

Du Preez Estate (S.Afr) a winery (established 1995) based in Rawsonville, Western Cape. 300ha. Grape varieties: Cabernet sauvignon, Chardonnay, Chenin blanc, Merlot, Petit verdot, Ruby cabernet, Sauvignon blanc, Shiraz. Labels: Dry Creek, Hendrik Lodewyk, Polla's Red, Red Stone, Rockfield.

Dupuy (Fr) a Cognac producer. (Add): 32 Rue de Boston, P.O. Box 62, 16102, Cognac.

Duque Braganca (Port) a 20 year old tawny Port from A.A. Ferreira Port shippers.

Duque d'Alba (Sp) the name given to a range of brandies from Diez Merito.

Duque de Sevilla (Sp) a full-bodied, cask-aged, red wine from the Vincente Suso y Perez vineyards in Carinena, north-eastern Spain.

Duquesne (USA) a brewing company based in Cleveland, Ohio.

Duquesne (W.Ind) a distillery producing a white rum called Genippa on Martinique. Also Grand Case and Val d'Or (both dark rums).

Dur (Fr) hard.

Durango Cocktail (Cktl) ½ measure tequila, ½ measure grapefruit juice, 2 dashes orgeat. Shake over ice, strain into an ice-filled highball glass, top with Perrier water and mint sprig.

Duras (Fr) a region of south-eastern Bordeaux.

Duras (Fr) a red grape variety grown in Gaillac that produces deep coloured wines.

Durbach (Ger) village (Anb): Baden. (Ber): Ortenau. (Gro): Fürsteneck. (Vins): Berghaupten, Bermersbach, Bottenau, Diersburg, Durbach, Erlach, Gengenbach, Hofweier, Lautenbach, Nesselried, Niederschopfheim, Nussbach, Offenburg (ortsteil Zell-Weierbach), Offenburg (ortsteil Fessenbach), Oberkirch, Oberkirch (ortsteil Haslach), Ödsbach, Ohlsbach, Ortenberg, Rammersweier, Reichenbach, Ringelbach, Stadelhofen, Tiergarten, Ulm, Zunsweier.

Durbanville (S.Afr) a district north-east of Cape Town. Has two wine estates: Meerendal and Diemersdal.

Durbanville Hills Winery (S.Afr) a winery (established 1998) based at Rhinofields, Durbanville, Western Cape. 770ha. Grape varieties: Cabernet sauvignon, Chardonnay, Merlot, Pinotage, Sauvignon blanc,

D

Shiraz. Labels: Biesjes Craal, Caapmans, Luipaardsberg, Premium Range, Rhinofields. Website: http://www.durbanvillehills.co.za

Durchgegoren (Ger) lit: 'fully fermented', the term is now no longer allowed on a wine label.

Durchriesling (Aus) coulure.

Durdle Door (Eng) a 5% alc by vol. ale brewed by the Dorset Brewing Company, Dorset.

Durella (It) a white grape variety grown in Veneto.

Durello Spumante Brut (It) a sparkling (metodo tradizionale) wine produced by A.G. Santi in Veneto.

Durendal Wines (S.Afr) the brand-name of wines from the Spier Estate in Stellenbosch.

Duresse (Fr) a Premier Cru vineyard in the A.C. commune of Monthélie, Côte de Beaune, Burgundy 10.3ha.

Duresses [Les] (Fr) a Premier Cru vineyard in the A.C. commune of Auxey-Duresses, Côte de Beaune, Burgundy 10.6ha.

Durette (Fr) a commune in the Beaujolais. Has A.C. Beaujolais-Villages or Beaujolais-Derette status.

Durham Ale (Eng) a cask-conditioned bitter 1036 O.G. brewed by the Whitbread Brewery at Castle Eden.

Durham Brewery C° Ltd [The] (Eng) a brewery (established 1994). (Add): Unit 5a, Bowburn North Ind Estate, Bowburn, Durham, County Durham DH6 5PF. Brews: Bedes Gold 4.2% alc by vol., Benedictus 8.4% alc by vol., Bishops Gold 4.5% alc by vol., Black Abbot 5.3% alc by vol., Black Velvet 4% alc by vol., Bonny Lass 3.9% alc by vol., Canny Lad 4.3% alc by vol., Cathedral Gold 4.5% alc by vol., Celtic 4.2% alc by vol., Cloister 4.5% alc by vol., Cuthberts Cross 4.7% alc by vol., Dark Secret 4.3% alc by vol., Durham County 4.4% alc by vol., Evensong 5% alc by vol., Frost Bite 3.6% alc by vol., Green Goddess 3.8% alc by vol., Invincible 4.5% alc by vol., Magnificat 6.5% alc by vol., Magnus 3.8% alc by vol., Nine Alters 5.2% alc by vol., Priors Gold 4.5% alc by vol., Sanctuary 6% alc by vol., Scimitar 4.1% alc by vol., Sunstroke 3.6% alc by vol., Temptation 10% alc by vol., White Amarillo 4.1% alc by vol., White Angel 4.1% alc by vol., White Bishop 4.8% alc by vol., White Bullet 4.4% alc by vol., White Crystal 4.3% alc by vol., White Friar 4.5% alc by vol., White Gem 3.9% alc by vol., White Gold 4% alc by vol., White Herald 3.9% alc by vol., White Magic 7% alc by vol., White Saphire 4.5% alc by vol., White Velvet 4.2% alc by vol. Website: http://www.durham-brewery.co.uk 'E'mail: gibbs@durham-brewery.co.uk

Durham County (Eng) a 4.4% alc by vol. ale brewed by The Durham Brewery C°. Ltd., County Durham.

Durham Light Ale (Eng) a 4% alc by vol. ale brewed by the Darwin Brewery, Tyne & Wear.

Durif (Austr) a red grape variety, thought also to be the same as Petit syrah, high in tannin and resistant to downy mildew. Spelt Duriff in parts of USA.

Duriff (USA) a red grape variety of California. *see* Durif.

Dürkheimer Wurstmarkt (Ger) a Pfalz wine festival held at Bad Dürkheim in September.

Durney Vineyard (USA) an organic winery based in the Carmel Valley. (Add): Heller Estate, Carmel Valley, Monterey, California. 29ha. Grape varieties: Cabernet sauvignon, Chardonnay, Chenin blanc, Gamay beaujolais, Johannisberg riesling, Rosé of Cabernet. Produces varietal wines. *see* Cachagua Cabernet.

Durnstein (Aus) a village of the Wachau, known for white wines of the same name.

Duro (Sp) a term used to describe a hard Sherry.

Duroc (Fr) a brandy négociant.

Dürrenberg (Ger) vineyard (Anb): Baden. (Ber): Markgräflerland. (Gro): Lorettoberg. (Vil): Schallstadt-Wolfenweile.

Dürrenzimmern (Ger) village (Anb): Württemberg. (Ber): Württembergisch Unterland. (Gro): Heuchelberg. (Vin): Mönchsberg.

Dürrn (Ger) village (Anb): Baden. (Ber): Badische Bergstrasse/Kraichgau. (Gro): Hohenberg. (Vin): Eichelberg.

Durst (Ger) thirst.

Dürsten (Ger) to be thirsty.

Durstig (Ger) thirsty.

Durstina-Brunnen (Ger) a natural spring mineral water from Dorsten, NW.

Durup [Jean] (Fr) a major négociant-éleveur based at Domaine de l'Eglantière Maligny, Chablis. Labels: La Paulière and Les Valery. Also has cuvées in many of the Côte d'Or vineyards.

Dusi Ranch (USA) a vineyard based near Templeton, San Luis Obispo, California. 16.5ha. Grape variety: Zinfandel.

Dusi Vineyard (USA) on a label denotes the source of Mastantuono Winery Zinfandel as from the Dusi Ranch in San Luis Obispo, California.

Düssel Alt (Ger) a full-flavoured altbier from Düsseldorf, west Germany.

Dust (Eng) a type of broken tea leaf grade used in the making of tea bags, part usually broken off during manufacture, gives a good thick liquor.

Dust (USA) a term often used in California for the soil.

Dusty (Eng) a term used to describe a wine that has a cellar-like smell with a high tannin content.

Dusty Miller (Austr) an alternative name used for the Pinot meunier grape.

Dusty Road (S.Afr) the label for a range of wines produced by the Cloof winery, Darling, Western Cape.

Dutch Coffee (Liq.Coffee) using a measure of genever gin.

Dutch County Wine Cellars (USA) a winery based in Lenhartsville, Pennnsylvania.

Dutch Courage (Eng) the name given to gin by the soldiers of James 1st as it gave them 'courage' to go into battle!

Dutch Courage Cocktail (Cktl) 1 measure dry gin, dash orange bitters, shake over ice, strain into a large liqueur glass and float a ½ measure of double cream on top.

D

Dutchess (USA) a white, hybrid grape variety developed at Dutchess County in New York State.

Dutch Gin (Hol) Hollands, Genever or Shiedam gin, are full-flavoured, full-bodied and possess a clean malty aroma and taste.

Dutch-Norman Bottle (Fr) a bottle-shape which is used for Calvados (70cls capacity).

Dutch Trade Winds Cocktail (Cktl) ⅓ measure dry gin, ⅙ measure Curaçao, ⅙ measure lemon juice, 2 dashes Gomme syrup. Shake over ice and strain into a cocktail glass.

Dutch Whiskey (Hol) a whiskey made by the patent still method.

Duties (Eng) taxes on goods.

Du Toitskloof Koöperatiewe Wynkelder (S.Afr) a co-operative winery (established 1962) based in Worcester, Western Cape. 17 members. (Add): Box 55, Rawsonville 6854. Grape varieties: Cabernet franc, Cabernet sauvignon, Chardonnay, Merlot, Sauvignon blanc, Sémillon, Shiraz. Labels: Classique, Rouge. Website: http://www.dutoitskloof.com

Duttenberg (Ger) village (Anb): Württemberg. (Ber): Württembergisch Unterland. (Gro): Staufenberg. (Vin): Schön.

Dutton Goldfield (USA) a winery based in the Marin County, northern California. Also has vineyards in the Russian River Valley, Sonoma County. Grape variety: Pinot noir. Labels: Devil's Gulch Vineyard, Dutton Ranch (Sanghietti Vineyard).

Duttons (Eng) a cask-conditioned bitter 1034 O.G. brewed by the Chester Brewery in the north of England.

Dutton Vineyard (USA) a vineyard based in the lower Russian River Valley. 21ha. Grape variety: Chardonnay (used for the Burgess Cellars Chardonnay).

Duttweiler (Ger) village (Anb): Pfalz. (Ber): Mittelhaardt-Deutsche Weinstrasse. (Gro): Pfaffengrund. (Vins): Kalkberg, Kreuzberg, Mandelberg.

Duty (Eng) taxes levied by Customs and Excise.

Duty Free (Eng) denotes goods bought on an outward journey which are free of duties.

Duty Free Shop (Eng) a shop sited on board a ship etc. or at an airport or port. Sells alcoholic drinks etc. free of duties (taxes).

Duval (Eng) a vermouth made by the British wine method and flavoured with herbs and quinine.

Duval (It) a subsidiary of Martini & Rossi that produces Pastis under the Duval label.

Duval-Leroy (Fr) a Champagne producer. (Add): B.P. 37, 51130 Vertus. 140ha. Produces vintage and non-vintage wines. Vintages: 1973, 1975, 1976, 1978, 1981, 1982, 1985, 1988, 1990, 1995, 1996, 2000. De Luxe cuvée is Cuvée des Roys also label: Fleur de Champagne.

Duvel (Bel) straw, top-fermented, bottle-conditioned, strong beer 8.5% alc by vol. brewed by the Moorgat Brasserie, Breendonk-Puurs.

Duvel Brasserie (Bel) home (founded 1871) to the Moorgat Brasserie in Breendonk-Puurs. Is noted for top-fermented beers: Duvel 8.5% alc by vol. and Maredsous brewed for the Maredsous monastery. Also produces Vedett. Website: http://www.duvel.com

Du Veron [D.] (Fr) a Cognac producer. (Add): Mesnac, 16370, Cherves Richemont, Cognac. 20ha. in Fins Bois.

Du Vin Brulaï (Ch.Isles) mulled wine.

Du Vin Pimentaï (Ch.Isles) spiced wine.

Duxoup Winery (USA) a small winery in Sonoma County that produces 2000 cases of wine per year. Grapes varieties: Carignan, Charbono, Sangiovese, Syrah.

Duyck Brasserie (Fr) a brewery based near Valenciennes that brews top-fermented beers. Jenlain Bière de Luxe 20° (deep bronze-coloured beer which is filtered but not pasteurised).

Dvine (Rus) a white grape variety grown in Armenia, used mainly in the production of brandy.

D'Vine (S.Afr) the export label for a range of wines produced by the Swartland Wine Cellar winery, Swartland, Western Cape.

Dvur Kràlové Nad Labem (Czec) a brewery based in northern Czec.

Dwain Glyndur (Wal) a 4.2% alc by vol. ale brewed by the Hurns Brewing C°., West Glamorgan.

Dwarsrivier Kelders (S.Afr) the other name for the Cederberg Kelders.

Dŵr (Wal) water.

Dŵr Bywiol (Wal) water of life.

Dwyka Hills (S.Afr) the label for a red wine (Shiraz) produced by the New Cape Wines winery, Paarl, Western Cape.

Dylans (Wal) an ale brewed by Dylan Thomas' Boathouse, Langharne, West Wales.

Dylan's Smooth (Wal) a cask-conditioned ale brewed by S.A. Brain.

Dynamite Cocktail (Cktl) ½ measure Cognac, ½ measure Grand Marnier, 1 measure orange juice, shake over ice, strain into a flute glass, top with iced Champagne and dress with an orange slice on the rim of glass and add a cherry.

Dynamite Stout (Eng) a 4.5% alc by vol. stout from Firecracker & Firkin, Crawley, London.

Dynamo (Eng) a very strong white bottled cider 7.5% alc by vol.

Dynasty (Chi) a medium-dry, white wine from the Kian Diam Cong Lu wine farm in Tianju. Made from the Dimlat, Muscat de Hamburg, Homique and Dragon's eye grapes. A joint venture between the Chinese government and Rémy Martin.

E (Eng) *abbr*: Worthington 'E', a keg bitter 1041 O.G. brewed by the Bass Breweries.

E.A. (Ger) *abbr*: Erzeuger-Abfüllung/estate bottled.

Eagle (Cktl) 8 parts gin, 1 part parfait amour, 2 parts lemon juice, dash egg white. Shake well with ice and strain into a wine goblet.

Eagle [The] (USA) a 5.2% alc by vol. premium lager from Evansville, Indiana. *See also* Drummondo.

Eagle Bitter (Eng) a cask-conditioned bitter ale 1035 O.G. brewed by the Charles Wells Brewery in Bedford.

Eagle Brewery (Wal) a wholesale company who took over the Powys Brewery to brew Samuel Powell Traditional bitter 1040 O.G. in central Wales. *see* Powell.

Eagle L.A. (Eng) a low alcohol bitter beer 0.9% alc by vol. brewed by Charles Wells Brewery in Bedford.

Eaglepoint Ranch Winery (USA) a winery based in the Mendocino County, California. Is a member of the Coro Mendocino (Zinfandel) wine group of Mendocino wineries.

Eagle Point Vineyard (USA) a small vineyard based at Talmage, Mendocino County, California. Grape variety: Zinfandel.

Eagle Rare (USA) the brand-name of a 10 year old Kentucky Bourbon whiskey distilled by Sazerac at the Old Prentice Distillery, Lawrenceburg, Kentucky. 50.5% alc by vol.

Eagle's Cliff (S.Afr) the label for a range of red and white wines produced by the New Cape Wines winery, Paarl, Western Cape. Also an Eagle's Cliff Reserve range produced.

Eagle's Dream (Cktl) ¾ measure dry gin, ¼ measure Crème Yvette, ¼ measure lemon juice, 1 egg white, 2 dashes gomme syrup. Shake over ice and strain into a goblet and top with a cherry.

Eagle Stout (Afr) a bitter stout 1068 O.G. brewed by the Golden Guinea Breweries in Nigeria.

Eaglet Cocktail (Cktl) 1 measure Mandarine Napoléon in a flute glass and top with iced, dry Champagne.

Eagle Vale (Austr) a winery based in the Margaret River region of Western Australia. Grape varieties include: Cabernet sauvignon, Merlot.

Eagle Vlei (S.Afr) a winery (established 1997) based in the Stellenbosch, Western Cape. 11ha. Grape varieties: Cabernet sauvignon, Merlot, Pinotage. Website: http://www.eaglevlei.co.za

Ealu (Eng) a mediaeval word for ale, beer. *See also* Alu, Alofat.

E and K Wine Company (USA) a winery based in Sandusky, Ohio. Produces vinifera and French-American hybrid wines.

Earl Grey (Eng) a blend of China and Darjeeling teas, has a large leaf and is delicately scented with oil of bergamot (very fragrant). Jacksons still make the original blend given to Earl Grey by a Chinese Mandarin.

Earl's Bitter (Eng) a cask-conditioned bitter ale 1048 O.G. brewed by the Bridgewater Arms, Herts.

Earl's Bitter (Eng) a bitter ale brewed by the Wortley Arms (a micro-brewery), near Barnsley, South Yorkshire.

Earl Soham Brewery (Eng) a brewery (established 1986). (Add): Earl Soham, Woodbridge, Suffolk IP13 7RT. Brews: Albert Ale 4.4% alc by vol., Empress of India 4.7% alc by vol., Gannet Mild 3.3% alc by vol., Jolabrugg 5.2% alc by vol., Pale Ale 4% alc by vol., Sir Rogers Porter 4.2% alc by vol., Victoria Bitter 3.6% alc by vol. Website: http://www.earlsohambrewery.co.uk 'E'mail: thebrewer@earlsohambrewery.co.uk

Early Bird Spring Hop Ale (Eng) a 4.3% alc by vol. light coloured, hoppy, fragrant seasonal ale brewed by Shepherd Neame, Faversham, Kent (available March to June).

Early Burgundy (USA) a black grape variety grown in California, now slowly being phased out.

Early Doors (Eng) a term used for early opening time in the north of England especially in Lancashire.

Early-Landed Cognac (Eng) refers to Cognac brandies that have been sold to British wine merchants who then age and bottle them after 15–20 years in cask.

Early Riser (Eng) a 4% alc by vol. ale brewed by the Dunn Plowman Brewery, Herefordshire.

Early Times (USA) the brand-name of a Bourbon whiskey.

Earth (S.Afr) the label for a red wine (Pinotage, Shiraz and Cabernet sauvignon blend) from the Elements range of wines produced by the Hartswater Wine Cellar winery, Hartswater, Northern Cape.

Earthquake (Cktl) 25mls (⅛ gill) tequila, 2 dashes Campari, 4 dashes grenadine, scoop crushed ice. Blend altogether, strain into a flute glass, decorate with fresh strawberries and orange segments.

EartH2O (USA) a natural spring mineral water from Opal Springs, Culver, Oregon. Mineral contents (milligrammes per litre): Fluorides 0.11mg/l, Nitrates 0.15mg/l. pH 7.9

Earthquake Cocktail (Cktl) ⅓ measure Pernod, ⅓ measure dry gin, ⅓ measure whisky. Shake over ice and strain into a cocktail glass.

Earthy (Eng) a term applied to wines which have a special flavour due to the kind of soil on which the grapes grow. It can apply to fine wines such as red Graves.

Easley Winery (USA) a winery based in Indianapolis, Indiana. Produces French hybrid wines.

East (Afr) a wine-producing region based in Morocco, contains the A.O.G. areas of Angad and Berkane. Has alluvial soil.

East African Breweries (Afr) one of the largest breweries in Kenya. (Add): P.O. Box 30161, Nairobi, Kenya. Brews a variety of beers and lagers including Tusker Lager. It also has shares in the Tanzania Breweries. Website: http://www.eabrew.com 'E'mail: kbl@kenyabreweries.co.ke

East and West Cocktail (Cktl) ½ measure medium Sherry, ½ measure vodka. Shake over ice and strain into a cocktail glass and decorate with an olive.

East Anglian English Wine Fair (Eng) a wine festival held each year in August at Ipswich, Suffolk.

East Anglian Wine Growers' Association (Eng) a body that conducts research and education to help improve English wine standards.

Eastcote Ale (Eng) a cask-conditioned bitter ale 1041 O.G. brewed by the Banks and Taylor Brewery, Bedfordshire.

Easter Ale (Eng) a cask-conditioned ale brewed by Bank's Brewery.

Easter Ale (Wal) a seasonal ale brewed by S.A. Brain & C°. Ltd. in Cardiff.

Easter Ale (Wal) a 4.3% alc by vol. ale brewed by The Rymney Brewery Ltd., Mid-Glamorgan.

Easter Bunny (Wal) a 4.5% alc by vol. ale brewed by the Cwmbran Brewery, Gwent.

Eastern Brewing (USA) a brewery based in Hammonton.

Eastern Promise (Punch)(Non-alc) 250mls cold jasmine tea, 150mls bitter lemon, 40mls pineapple juice, 15mls orange squash. Stir over crushed ice in a large jug, dress with slices orange and pineapple.

Eastern Region (Bul) the second most important area producing mainly white wines. Key D.G.O. areas are Khan Krum, Novi Pazar, Shumen, Varna.

Eastern Vineyards (N.Z) a vineyard that used to produce grapes in the Waitakere Ranges (now has closed down).

Easter Special (Eng) a 7.6% alc by vol. strong ale brewed by the Blue Anchor Brewery, Cornwall.

East India (Mad) the quality name sometimes seen on the label of a Madeira bottle, this is a 'lot' name.

East India Cocktail [1] (Cktl) 60mls (½ gill) brandy, 2 dashes Curaçao, 2 dashes maraschino, 2 dashes Angostura. Stir over ice and strain into a cocktail glass, add a cherry and squeeze of lemon peel juice. Pineapple juice can be added instead of maraschino.

East India Cocktail [2] (Cktl) ½ measure dry vermouth, ½ measure dry Sherry, 1 dash orange bitters. Shake over ice and strain into a cocktail glass.

East India Sherry (Eng) a Brown Sherry that was shipped from home to the Far East and back. Journey allowed the Sherry to mature during the long voyage.

East Kent Goldings (Eng) a 4.2% alc by vol. ale brewed by the Pitfield Brewery (London), London.

East Kent Goldings (Eng) an English hop variety which has a full aroma and flavour.

East Lancs (Eng) a pale ale 1036 O.G. brewed by the Thwaites Brewery in Blackburn.

Easton (USA) a small winery based near Shenandoah Valley, Sierra Foothills, California. Grape varieties: Cabernet sauvignon.

East-Side Winery (USA) a grower's co-operative based near Lodi, California. Grape varieties: Emerald riesling, Sémillon and Zinfandel. Produces table and dessert wines under the Angelica Antigua, Conti Royale, Gold Bell and Royal Host labels.

East Street Cream (Eng) a 5% alc by vol. strong bitter brewed by RCH Brewery, West Hewish, near Weston-Super-Mare, Somerset.

Eastwood & Sanders Ltd [Fine Ales] (Eng) a brewery. (Add): Units 3–5, Heathfield Ind Estate, Heathfield Street, Elland, West Yorkshire HX5 9AE. Brews: 1872 Porter (Gold Medal) 6.5% alc by vol., Bargee 3.8% alc by vol., Best Bitter 4% alc by vol., Beyond the Pale 4% alc by vol., First Light 3.5% alc by vol., Nettle Thresher 4.4% alc by vol. 'E'mail: admin@eastwood-sanders.fsnet.co.uk

Easy as Pie (Cktl) equal quantities of Luardo Passione Ambra and apple schnapps served chilled in a shot glass.

Easy Rider (Eng) a 4.3% alc by vol. ale brewed by the Kelham Island Brewery, South Yorkshire.

Eatanswill Old (Eng) a 4% alc by vol. old ale brewed by Mauldon's Ltd., Suffolk.

Eau (Fr) water.

Eau (Fr) a still mineral water from St. Leger.

Eau Claire (Mal) a natural spring mineral water from Titi Akar, Kedah, Malaysia. Mineral contents (milligrammes per litre): Sodium 4.3mg/l, Calcium 41mg/l, Magnesium 4.4mg/l, Potassium 9.9mg/l, Bicarbonates 153mg/l, Chlorides 1mg/l, Sulphates 745mg/l, Fluorides 0.2mg/l. pH 6.9

Eau d'Arque Busade (Fr) the alternative spelling of Eau d'Arquebuse.

Eau d'Arquebuse (Fr) a medicinal liqueur once produced in Lyons. *See also* Eau d'Arque Busade.

Eau de Chamonix (S.Afr) a natural spring mineral water. Mineral contents (milligrammes per litre): Sodium 11.8mg/l, Calcium 2.2mg/l, Magnesium 1.2mg/l, Potassium 0.95mg/l, Chlorides 15.4mg/l, Sulphates 0.3mg/l, Fluorides <0.1mg/l, Nitrates 0.62mg/l.

Eau de Gruau (Fr) oatmeal water, a nutritional beverage similar in style to barley water.

Eau de la Barbade (Fr) a Bordeaux-produced herb liqueur similar in style to Chartreuse.

Eau de Ma Tante (Hol) lit: ' water of my aunt', an orange-based Dutch liqueur.

Eau de Mélisse (Fr) a melissa (lemon balm) cordial, a spirit distilled from melissa.

Eau de Mélisse des Carmes Boyer (Fr) an élixer of

alcohol, angelica, melissa, cloves, lemon, spices and cress. Sold in medicine bottles by Renouard Larivière, Paris, it is drunk diluted with water or on a sugar cube, it relieves nervous tension, fatigue and travel sickness.

Eau de Montagne (Fr) a natural spring mineral water from the Pyrénées-Atlantiques. Mineral contents (milligrammes per litre): Sodium 1.7mg/l, Calcium 91.5mg/l, Magnesium 35.1mg/l, Potassium 0.35mg/l, Bicarbonates 425.78mg/l, Chlorides 3.3mg/l, Sulphates 20.1mg/l, Fluorides 0.14mg/l, Nitrates 4.93mg/l, Silicates 6mg/l. pH 7.45

Eau de Noix Serres (Fr) a liqueur made from the extract of walnuts (harvested in June), produced by Serres in Toulouse.

Eau de Seltz (Fr) soda water.

Eau de Source (Fr) a still mineral water from Dax. (Add): Groupe Thermes Adour, Bd des Sports, BP 363, 40108 Dax cedex. Mineral contents (milligrammes per litre): Nitrates 0mg/l.

Eau de Source des Montagnes d'Auvergne (Fr) a still mineral water from the Auvergne. (Add): 9-11, Rue Georges Enesco, 94008 Creteil cedex. Mineral contents (milligrammes per litre): Sodium 2.7mg/l, Calcium 4.1mg/l, Magnesium 1.7mg/l, Potassium 0.9mg/l, Bicarbonates 25.8mg/l, Chlorides 0.9mg/l, Sulphates 1.1mg/l, Nitrates 0mg/l. pH 7.3

Eau de Source de Montagne des Alpes (Fr) a still mineral water from Roche des Écrins. (Add): 9-11, Rue Georges Enesco, 94008 Creteil Cedex. Mineral contents (milligrammes per litre): Sodium 1.4mg/l, Calcium 63mg/l, Magnesium 10.2mg/l, Potassium 0.4mg/l, Bicarbonates 173.2mg/l, Chlorides <1mg/l, Sulphates 51.3mg/l, Nitrates 2mg/l. pH 7.6

Eau de Source de Montagne-Pyrénées (Fr) a natural spring mineral water. Mineral contents (milligrammes per litre): Sodium 35mg/l, Calcium 49mg/l, Magnesium 12mg/l, Potassium 1mg/l, Bicarbonates 186mg/l, Chlorides 54mg/l, Sulphates 17mg/l, Nitrates 5mg/l. pH 7.8

Eau de Source de Montagne-Source Centrale (Fr) a natural spring mineral water from Issy-les-Moulineaux. Mineral contents (milligrammes per litre): Sodium 31mg/l, Calcium 48mg/l, Magnesium 11mg/l, Potassium 1mg/l, Bicarbonates 183mg/l, Chlorides 44mg/l, Sulphates 16mg/l, Nitrates 3mg/l. pH 7.3

Eau de Source de Mont Blanc (Fr) a slightly acidic, sparkling natural spring mineral water. Mineral contents (milligrammes per litre): Sodium 1.6mg/l, Calcium 27.6mg/l, Magnesium 2.6mg/l, Potassium 1.9mg/l, Bicarbonates 64.2mg/l, Chlorides <1mg/l, Sulphates 32.5mg/l, Nitrates <2mg/l. pH 5.3

Eau de Source [des Oliviers] (Fr) a natural spring mineral water. Mineral contents (milligrammes per litre): Sodium 14mg/l, Calcium 157mg/l, Magnesium 21mg/l, Potassium 1.6mg/l, Bicarbonates 367mg/l, Chlorides 47mg/l, Sulphates 135mg/l, Nitrates 3.6mg/l. pH 7.6

Eau de Source [Idre!] (Fr) a natural spring mineral water. Mineral contents (milligrammes per litre): Sodium 18mg/l, Calcium 118mg/l, Magnesium 30mg/l, Potassium 7mg/l, Bicarbonates 403mg/l, Chlorides 39mg/l, Sulphates 85mg/l, Fluorides 1mg/l, Nitrates 1mg/l. pH 7.1

Eau de Source Leader Price (Fr) a natural spring mineral water from Nouvelle Calédonie. Mineral contents (milligrammes per litre): Sodium 5.2mg/l, Calcium 0.05mg/l, Magnesium 14.7mg/l, Potassium 0.1mg/l, Nitrates 0.38mg/l. pH 7.8

Eau de Table (Fr) table water.

Eau-de-Vie (Fr) lit: 'water of life', name given for spirits. Distillates.

Eau-de-Vie-Blanche (Fr) denotes white spirits, non cask matured. i.e. kirsch. See also Blanche d'Armagnac.

Eau-de-Vie-d'Alisier (Fr) a fruit brandy made from rowanberries.

Eau-de-Vie-d'Andaye (Fr) a type of marc brandy made in the Basque area near Hendaye, southern France.

Eau-de-Vie-de-Baie-d'Alisier (Fr) a rowanberry eau-de-vie.

Eau-de-Vie-de-Baie-de-Houx (Fr) an eau-de-vie made from the holly berry.

Eau-de-Vie-de-Baie-de-Sureau (Fr) an elderberry-based eau-de-vie.

Eau-de-Vie-de-Charente (Fr) Cognac brandy.

Eau-de-Vie-de-Cidre (Fr) Calvados. Distillate of cider.

Eau-de-Vie-de-Coing (Fr) a fruit brandy made from quinces.

Eau-de-Vie-de-Danzig (Fr) the French version of the German Danziger Goldwasser.

Eau-de-Vie-de-Fraise (Fr) a strawberry brandy, a distillate from strawberries 44.5% alc by vol.

Eau-de-Vie-de-Framboise (Fr) a raspberry-flavoured liqueur.

Eau-de-Vie-de-Genévrier (Fr) a juniper-based eau-de-vie (similar to gin).

Eau-de-Vie-de-Gentiane (Fr) an eau-de-vie made from gentian root.

Eau-de-Vie-d'Eglantine (Fr) an eau-de-vie flavoured with the dog rose.

Eau-de-Vie-de-Grain (Fr) a term applied to spirits distilled from grain. i.e. whisky.

Eau-de-Vie-de-Groseille (Fr) a fruit brandy made from white or red currants.

Eau-de-Vie-de-Houx (Fr) a fruit brandy made from hollyberries.

Eau-de-Vie-de-Kirsch (Fr) a fruit brandy made from fermented cherry juice and kernels 40% alc by vol.

Eau-de-Vie-de-Lie (Switz) a liqueur made from the lees of wine casks.

Eau-de-Vie-de-Marc (Fr) a brandy produced from the pomace of wine. It is produced in most wine regions.

Eau-de-Vie-de-Marc-de-Champagne (Fr) a brandy made from the wine produced by the pressing of the pomace in Champagne.

E

Eau-de-Vie-de-Mirabelle (Fr) a fruit brandy made from mirabelle plums 44.5% alc by vol.

Eau-de-Vie-de-Mûre (Fr) a fruit brandy made from blackberries.

Eau-de-Vie-de-Mûre Sauvage (Fr) a fruit brandy made from wild blackberries.

Eau-de-Vie-de-Myrtille (Fr) a fruit brandy made from bilberries.

Eau-de-Vie-de-Nèfle (Fr) a medlar-based eau-de-vie.

Eau-de-Vie-de-Pêche (Fr) a fruit brandy made from peaches.

Eau-de-Vie-de-Poire (Fr) a liqueur distilled from fermented pear juice, William or Bartlett varieties used.

Eau-de-Vie-de-Prune (Fr) a fruit brandy distilled from plum juice 40% alc by vol.

Eau-de-Vie-de-Prunelle (Fr) a fruit brandy made from sloes.

Eau-de-Vie-de-Quetsch (Fr) a fruit brandy made from Switzen plums 44.5% alc by vol.

Eau-de-Vie-de-Reineclaude (Fr) a fruit brandy made from greengages.

Eau-de-Vie-de-Sapin (Fr) an eau-de-vie made from pine needles.

Eau-de-Vie-de-Sorbier (Fr) a fruit brandy made from sorb apples.

Eau-de-Vie-de-Sureau (Fr) a fruit brandy made from elderberries.

Eau-de-Vie-de-Vin (Fr) the name given to any spirit distilled from wine.

Eau-de-Vie-de-Vin-de-Champagne (Fr) a fine de Marne, brandy made from the last pressing of grapes (rebêche) in Champagne.

Eau d'Orge (Fr) barley water.

Eau Douce (Fr) fresh water.

Eau du Robinet (Fr) tap water.

Eau Frappé (Fr) iced water.

Eau Froid (Fr) cold water.

Eau Gazeuse (Fr) soda water/sparkling water.

Eau Glacée (Fr) iced water.

Eau Miellée (Fr) a drink made from honey, spirits and water.

Eau Minérale (Fr) mineral water.

Eau Minérale des Pyrénéees (Fr) a natural spring mineral water from Font Picant, Pyrénées. Mineral contents (milligrammes per litre): Sodium 59.5mg/l, Calcium 90.5mg/l, Magnesium 33.5mg/l, Potassium 4.7mg/l, Bicarbonates 551mg/l, Chlorides 11.6mg/l, Sulphates 39.8mg/l.

Eau Minérale Naturelle (Fr) the A.C. of mineral waters. Given by the government to waters with therapeutic qualities. e.g. Evian, Vichy, Volvic.

Eau Nuptile (Fr) a popular eighteenth century eau-de-vie.

Eau Plate (Fr) tap water.

Eau Potable (Fr) drinking water.

Eau Rougie (Fr) half red wine and half water mixed.

Eau Royale (Pac) a natural spring mineral water from Paopao, French Polynesia.

Eaux de Source (Fr) a government grading of mineral waters that are not quite as high in theraputic qualities as eau minérale naturelle.

Eaux-de-Vie (Fr) an Alsace name for alcools blancs or eau-de-vie.

Eaux Mineralés de Carbonnieux (Fr) a label term used by the Bénédictine owners of Château Carbonnieux in the Graves district of Bordeaux so as to sell their wines in Moslem Turkey in the eighteenth century.

Eauze (Fr) an important town in the Gers département where Armagnac is produced.

E.B. (Eng) *abbr:* **E**state **B**ottled (on a French wine label).

Ebbrezza (It) drunkenness/intoxication.

Ebbro (It) drunk.

E.B. Specjal (Pol) triple filtered bottled pils.

Eben (Aus) a vineyard area on the banks of the River Danube in the Kremstal region.

Ebenezer Ale (USA) an ale brewed by the Bridgeport Brewing Company, Portland, Oregon.

Ebeneezer's Surprise (Eng) a bottled beer brewed by Ruddles Brewery, Leicester. Part of their Ruddles Character Ale range.

Ebenrain (Ger) vineyard (Anb): Baden. (Ber): Badische Frankenland. (Gro): Tauberklinge. (Vil): Lindelbach.

Eberbach (Ger) village (Anb): Baden. (Ber): Badische Bergstrasse/Kraichgau. (Gro): Stiftsberg. (Vin): Schollerbuckel.

Ebereschen-Branntwein (Ger) a brandy made from rowanberries, red in colour.

Eberfürst (Ger) vineyard (Anb): Württemberg. (Ber): Württembergisch Unterland. (Gro): Salzberg. (Vil): Eberstadt.

Eberle Winery (USA) a winery based in the Paso Robles, San Luis Obispo County, California. (Add): 5.5kms east of Route 101 off Highway 46 East Paso Robles, CA 93447. Grape varieties: Cabernet sauvignon, Chardonnay, Merlot, Syrah, Viognier. Website: http://www.eberlewinery.com

Ebersberg (Ger) vineyard (Anb): Rheinhessen. (Ber): Nierstein. (Gro): Sankt Alban. (Vil): Bodenheim.

Ebersberg (Ger) vineyard (Anb): Rheinhessen. (Ber): Nierstein. (Gro): Spiegelberg. (Vil): Nierstein.

Eberstadt (Ger) village (Anb): Württemberg. (Ber): Württembergisch Unterland. (Gro): Salzberg. (Vins): Dezberg, Eberfürst, Sommerhalde.

Eberstädter (Ger) a natural spring mineral water from Steinberg-Quelle, Eberstädt-Buchhorn, BW.

Ebibo (Lat) to drink up/to drain your glass.

Ebony (Eng) a bottled dark ale 1067 O.G. brewed by the Greenhall Whitley Brewery. *see* Old Chester.

Ebony (S.Afr) the label for a blended red wine produced by the Asara Estate winery, Stellenbosch, Western Cape.

Ebony (W.Ind) a dark lager beer 9% alc by vol. brewed by the Bank's Brewery in Barbados. *See also* Stallion Stout.

Ébourgonnage (Fr) a term used to describe the removal of the shoots/buds in spring. *See also* Dédoublage, Ébrossage, Échtonnage, Évasivage.

Ebrietas (Lat) drunkenness.

Ebringen (Ger) village (Anb): Baden. (Ber): Markgräflerland. (Gro): Lorettoberg. (Vin): Sommerberg.

E

Ébrio (Port) drunk/intoxicated.

Ebriolus (Lat) tipsy.

Ebriositas (Lat) alcoholic/addiction to drink.

Ebriosus (Lat) drunkard.

Ebritzstein (Aus) a vineyard area on the banks of the River Danube in the Kremstal region.

Ebrius (Lat) intoxicated/drunk. *See also* Potus, Vinolentus.

Ebro [River] (Sp) a river of northern Spain in the Rioja region.

Ébrossage (Fr) a term used to describe the removal of the shoots/buds in spring. *See also* Dédoublage, Ébourgonnage, Échtonnage, Évasivage.

E.B. Specjal (Pol) triple filtered bottled pils.

Ebulam (Eng) a strong ale flavoured with juniper and elderberries produced in the Middle-Ages.

Ebulam (Scot) a 6.5% alc by vol. ale brewed by Heather Ale Ltd., Lanarkshire.

Ebulliscope (Eng) an instrument used to measure the quantity of alcohol present in a liquid by noting the boiling point of the liquid. Alcohol boils at a lower temperature 78°C (172.4°F) than water 100°C (212°F). Is measured using a set quantity at a set atmospheric pressure.

Ébullition (Fr) lit: 'boiling', term often used for the first violent fermentation when it has the appearance of boiling.

Ebulum (Eng) *see* Ebulam.

Eccelsa (It) a natural spring mineral water from San Marino, Riparotta.

Eccleshall Brewing C° [The] (Eng) a brewery (established 1995). (Add): The George Inn, Castle Street, Eccleshall, Stafford, Staffordshire ST21 6DF. Brews: Monkey Magic 3.4% alc by vol., Original, Premium 4.4% alc by vol., Slaters Bitter 3.6% alc by vol., Supreme, Top Totty 4% alc by vol. Website: http://www.thegeorgeinn.freeserve.co.uk 'E' mail: information@thegeorgeinn.freeserve.co.uk

Échanson (Fr) lit: 'cup bearer', a person who pours the wine for a dignitary.

Échansonnerie des Papes (Fr) the wine brotherhood of Châteauneuf-du-Pape, southern Rhône.

Echar (Sp) to pour.

Ech Chaafi (Afr) a natural spring mineral water from Nouakchott, Mauritania. Mineral contents (milligrammes per litre): Sodium 34.8mg/l, Calcium 16.3mg/l, Magnesium 5.1mg/l, Potassium 3.1mg/l, Bicarbonates 106mg/l. pH 7.8

Échebrune (Fr) a commune in the Charente-Maritime département whose grapes are classed Petite Champagne (Cognac).

Échelle des Crus (Fr) the Champagne region's classification of grapes (vineyard areas). Grand Cru = 100%, Premier Cru = 90%–99% and Cru = 80%–89% (percentage of price fixed for grapes each year by C.I.V.C.).

Echézeaux (Fr) a top Grand Cru vineyard in the A.C. commune Vosne-Romanée, Côte de Nuits, Burgundy 30ha.

Echmiadzin (Arm) a wine-producing centre in Armenia.

Echt (Aus)(Ger) genuine or right, often seen on a beverage label. *See also* Echte.

Echt (Pol)(Est) a style of kümmel crystallize (sugar has been added and has crystallised).

Echte (Hol) genuine, often seen on a genever label.

Echter-Rum (Ger) a high-proof imported rum.

Échtonnage (Fr) a term used to describe the removal of the shoots/buds in spring. *See also* Dédoublage, Ébourgonnage, Ébrossage, Évasivage.

Echt Stonsdorfer (Ger) a woodberry fruit juice and herb liqueur (43 herbs in total).

Echunga Hock (Austr) the first wine made in the colonies of Australia to H.M. Queen Victoria via Lord Stanley the then Secretary of State for the Colonies. The wine was first sent in 1845.

Eck (Ger) vineyard (Anb): Ahr. (Ber): Walporzheim/Ahetal. (Gro): Klosterberg. (Vil): Altenahr.

Eckartsberg (Ger) vineyard (Anb): Baden. (Ber): Kaiserstuhl-Tuniberg. (Gro): Vulkanfelsen. (Vil): Breisach.a.Rh.

Eckberg (Ger) vineyard (Anb): Baden. (Ber): Kaiserstuhl-Tuniberg. (Gro): Vulkanfelsen. (Vil): Bötzingen.

Eckberg (Ger) vineyard (Anb): Baden. (Ber): Ortenau. (Gro): Schloss Rodeck. (Vil): Baden-Baden.

Eckelsheim (Ger) village (Anb): Rheinhessen. (Ber): Bingen. (Gro): Rheingrafenstein. (Vins): Eselstreiber, Kirchberg, Sonnenkopfchen.

Eckes (Ger) distillers based at Neider-Olm. Producers of Chantre (a Weinbrand), Edelkirsch, Klosterberg and Sechsamtertropfen.

Eckte (Ger) *see* Echt.

Eckweg (Ger) vineyard (Anb): Hessische Bergstrasse. (Ber): Starkenburg. (Gro): Schlossberg. (Vil): Heppenheim (including Erbach and Hambach).

Eclaircissage (Fr) the thinning of actual bunches of grapes around véraison in August.

Eclipse (Cktl) ⅔ measure sloe gin, ⅓ measure dry gin, 2 dashes lemon juice. Shake over ice and strain into a cocktail glass that has an olive and 2 teaspoons of grenadine in (do not stir).

Eclipse (Eng) a 4.2% alc by vol. ale brewed by the Blindmans Brewery Ltd., Somerset.

Eclipse (W.Ind) a 2 year old rum produced by Mount Gay in Barbados.

Écloseaux (Fr) a vineyard in the A.C. commune of Rully, Côte Chalonnaise, Burgundy.

Eco de Los Andes (Arg) a natural spring mineral water. Mineral contents (milligrammes per litre): Sodium 10.4mg/l, Calcium 30mg/l, Magnesium 3mg/l, Potassium 3.9mg/l, Bicarbonates 79.3mg/l, Chlorides 5.3mg/l, Sulphates 44.2mg/l, Nitrates <3mg/l.

École du Vin (Fr) wine school/wine academy.

Economiser (Eng) *see* Autovac.

Écossais (Fr) denotes Scotch (either Scotch Whisky or Scotsman).

Écoulage (Fr) racking of wines.

Écouvres (Fr) a commune in the Côtes de Toul, Lorraine. Produces Vins gris.

Eco Warrier (Eng) a 4.5% alc by vol. organic lager

E

brewed by the Pitfield Brewery, Shoreditch, London.

Eco Water Predela (Bul) a still natural spring mineral water from the National Park, Pirin. Mineral contents (milligrammes per litre): Sodium 6.2mg/l, Calcium 8.8mg/l, Magnesium 3.2mg/l, Potassium 0.25mg/l, Bicarbonates 48.8mg/l, Chlorides 2.6mg/l, Sulphates 4.5mg/l, Fluorides 0.2mg/l. pH 7.7

Ecoyen Tinto (Sp) a brand of red wine that is aged for 2 years in cask and 1 year in bottle. Produced by Señorio de Sarría in Navarra.

Ecu [À l'] (Fr) a Premier Cru vineyard in the A.C. commune of Beaune, Côte de Beaune, Burgundy. 5ha.

Ecuador (S.Am) a coffee-producing country that grows Arabica and Robusta coffees. Produces acidic coffees for blending.

Écueil (Fr) a Cru Champagne village in the Canton de Ville-en-Tardenois. District: Reims.

Écueul (Ch.Isles) jug/pitcher. *See also* Djougue.

Ecusson Rouge Three Star (Fr) a Cognac produced by Château Paulet.

Edale Brewery C° (Eng) a brewery (established 2003). (Add): Ruskin Villa, Hope Road, Edale, Derbyshire S33 7ZE. Brews: Appeal 4.5% alc by vol., Conviction 3.8% alc by vol., Kinder Croft 4% alc by vol., Kinder Downfall 5% alc by vol., Kinder Right to Roam 3.9% alc by vol., Kinder Trespass 4% alc by vol., Loxley Gold 4.5% alc by vol., Mitigation 4.2% alc by vol., Ringing Roger 6% alc by vol., Samuel Berrys IPA 5.1% alc by vol., Stannington Stout 5% alc by vol., Stouter 5% alc by vol., Volenti 5.2% alc by vol. Website: http://www.edalebrewery.co.uk

Edaphology (Eng) the study of the relationship between the plants and the soil.

Eddig (Den) vinegar.

Eddystone (Eng) a 4.8% alc by vol. cask-conditioned bitter brewed by Sutton (South Hams Brewery), Plymouth, Devon.

Edea (It) a natural spring mineral water.

Edel (Ger) noble.

Edel (Sp) the label of a lager brewed by Estrella-Damm in Barcelona.

Edelauslese (Ger) an old designation for 'noble select wine' (now no longer used).

Edelbeerenauslese (Ger) an old designation for wine made from extraordinary individual grapes which have not dried out thus preventing classification as a trockenbeerenauslese (now no longer used).

Edelberg (Ger) vineyard (Anb): Baden. (Ber): Badische Frankenland. (Gro): Tauberklinge. (Vil): Tauberbischofsheim.

Edelberg (Ger) vineyard (Anb): Mosel-Saar-Ruwer. (Ber): Bernkastel. (Gro): Schwarzlay. (Vil): Enkirch.

Edelberg (Ger) vineyard (Anb): Nahe. (Ber): Schloss Böckelheim. (Gro): Paradiesgarten. (Vil): Lauschied.

Edelberg (Ger) vineyard (Anb): Nahe. (Ber): Schloss Böckelheim. (Gro): Paradiesgarten. (Vil): Meddersheim.

Edel Bier (Ger) *see* Feuerfest Edel Bier.

Edelbräu L.A. (Eng) a low-alcohol lager 1% alc by vol. brewed by Lees. Sold in bottle.

Edelbräu Lager (Eng) a lager beer 1052 O.G. from Lees Brewery, Manchester.

Edelfäule (Ger) *Botrytis cinerea*/noble rot, also known as Eingeschrumpften. *see* Trockenbeerenauslese.

Edelfrau (Ger) vineyard (Anb): Franken. (Ber): Maindreieck. (Gro): Not yet assigned. (Vil): Homburg.

Edelfraulein (Aus) a sweet estate-bottled white wine from Wachau district. Made from the Muscat ottonel grape.

Edelgewächs (Ger) an old term for 'noble growths', best vintages.

Edelkeur (S.Afr) *Botrytis cinerea*, noble rot.

Edelkeur (S.Afr) a sweet, white, dessert wine made from botrytis-attacked grapes produced by the Nederburg Estate in Paarl.

Edelkirsch (Ger) a liqueur produced by Ekes distillery from mascara cherries.

Edel Laat oes Superior (S.Afr) a rich, dessert wine made from Steen grapes which have been botrytis-attacked. Produced by the M°Gregor Co-operative.

Edelmann (Ger) vineyard (Anb): Rheingau. (Ber): Johannisberg. (Gro): Erntebringer. (Vil): Mittelheim.

Edelmann (Ger) vineyard (Anb): Rheingau. (Ber): Johannisberg. (Gro): Honigberg. (Vil): Mittelheim.

Edelmann (Ger) vineyard (Anb): Rheinhessen. (Ber): Nierstein. (Gro): Sankt Alban. (Vil): Mainz.

Edeloes (S.Afr) late-harvest.

Edeloes (S.Afr) a sweet, white, dessert wine produced from Riesling botrytis-attacked grapes by the De Wetshof Estate in Robertson.

Edelreife (Ger) over-ripe, associated with edelfäule.

Edelrood (S.Afr) a red wine made with the (Cabernet sauvignon 60% and Merlot 40%) Nederburg Estate, Westeren Cape.

Edelspatz (S.Afr) the label for a late harvest white wine (Riesling) produced by the Delheim winery, Stellenbosch, Western Cape.

Edelspez (Switz) a 2.8% alc by vol. bier brewed by Brauerei Schützengarten AG, St. Gallen. Also a Edelspez premium 5.2% alc by vol.

Edelsuesse (Ger) great, natural, noble sweetness.

Edeltropfen (S.Afr) a medium-sweet, white wine made from a blend of Riesling and Steen grapes by the Nederburg Estate in Paarl.

Edelwein (Ger) an old designation for 'noble wine' (now no longer used).

Edelwein Gold (USA) a sweet white wine produced by the Freemark Abbey winery in the Napa Valley, California.

Edelweiss (It) a pale gold liqueur, herb-flavoured and sweetened with crystallised sugar on a twig standing in the bottle. Is similar in style to Fior d'Alpi.

Edelweiss (USA) a beer 4.8% alc by vol. brewed by the Pickett Brewery in Dubuque, Iowa.

Edelzwicker (Fr) noble blend, in Alsace denotes a blend of noble grape varieties to make a wine.

500

E

Eden (Isr) a natural spring mineral water. Mineral contents (milligrammes per litre): Sodium 32mg/l, Calcium 26mg/l, Magnesium 18mg/l, Potassium 3.5mg/l, Bicarbonates 198mg/l, Chlorides 24mg/l, Sulphates 6mg/l, Nitrates 15mg/l. pH 7.8

Edena (Fr) a natural spring mineral water from the French island of La Réunion. Mineral contents (milligrammes per litre): Sodium 7.5mg/l, Calcium 10mg/l, Magnesium 6.8mg/l, Potassium 1.3mg/l, Bicarbonates 84.2mg/l, Chlorides 6.3mg/l, Sulphates 3mg/l, Fluorides 0.08mg/l, Nitrates 3.4mg/l.

Eden Bitter (Eng) a 3.6% alc by vol. bitter brewed by Whitbread at Castle Eden, County Durham.

Eden Crest (S.Afr) a part of the Christo Wiese Portfolio. Grape varieties: Cabernet sauvignon, Chardonnay, Chenin blanc, Merlot, Pinotage. Label: Cape Blend.

Eden Dorénaz (Switz) a natural spring mineral water from Dorénaz. Mineral contents (milligrammes per litre): Sodium 4mg/l, Calcium 34.5mg/l, Magnesium 3.1mg/l, Potassium 0.7mg/l, Chlorides <0.1mg/l, Sulphates 32.8mg/l.

Eden Falls (Eng) a natural spring water from Armathwaite, Cumbria.

Edenhof (S.Afr) the label for a range of red wines (Cabernet sauvignon/Cabernet sauvignon-Merlot/Shiraz) produced by the Schalkenbosch Wines winery, Tulbagh, Western Cape.

Edenkoben (Ger) village (Anb): Pfalz. (Ber): Südliche Weinstrasse. (Gro): Schloss Ludwigshöhe. (Vins): Bergel, Blücherhöhe, Heidegarten, Heilig Kreuz, Kastaniengarten, Kirchberg, Klostergarten, Mühlberg, Schwarzer Letten.

Eden Pure Ale (Eng) a 4.4% alc by vol. ale brewed by the Sharps Brewery, Cornwall as a joint venture with the Eden Project.

Eden Pure Fruit Juices (Ger) the brand-name used for a range of unfermented water and sugar-free fruit juices, serve diluted or straight. Imported into U.K. by Leisure Drinks, Derby.

Eden Valley Road (Austr) a winery in South Australia in the Hill-Smith Estate. (Add): Angastron, South Australia 5353.

Eden Valley Shiraz (Austr) a white wine from the Château Leonay vineyard in South Australia.

Eder (Aus) a winery based in the Kamptal region. (Add): Mühlplatz 1, 3484 Grafenwörth. Grape varieties: Grüner veltliner, Muskat ottenel, Neuburger, Pinot blanc, Riesling, Zweigelt. Produces a range of wine styles.

Ederra Rioja (Sp) the brand wines of the Bodegas Bilbainas, S.A. Alta region, Rioja.

Édes (Hun) sweet.

Edesheim (Ger) village (Anb): Pfalz. (Ber): Südliche Weinstrasse. (Gro): Ordensgut. (Vins): Forst, Mandelhang, Rosengarten, Schloss.

Edes Szamorodni (Hun) a sweet style of szamorodni wines that can be matched to a Tokaji aszú.

Edgar's Golden Ale (Eng) a 4.3% alc by vol. ale brewed by the Vale Brewery, Haddenham, Buckinghamshire.

Edge (N.Z) a natural spring mineral water from Canterbury Plains, South Island. Mineral contents (milligrammes per litre): Sodium 6.9mg/l, Calcium 12mg/l, Magnesium 1.9mg/l, Potassium 0.7mg/l, Chlorides 3.9mg/l, Sulphates 3.6mg/l, Nitrates 0.26mg/l, Silicates 18mg/l. pH 7.9

Edgefield Winery (USA) a winery based in Oregon. Grape varieties: Riesling, Pinot gris, Pinot noir, Chardonnay, Cabernet, Merlot, Zinfandel. Produces still, sparkling and Port-style wines.

Edge of Darkness (Scot) a 7% alc by vol. strong ale brewed by the Far North Brewery, Caithness.

Ediger-Eller (Ger) village (Anb): Mosel-Saar-Ruwer. (Ber): Zell/Mosel. (Gro): Grafschaft. (Vins): Bienenlay, Calmont, Elzogberg, Engelströpfchen, Feuerberg, Höll, Osterlämmchen, Pfaffenberg, Pfirsichgarten, Schützenlay.

Edi Kante (It) a winery based in Duino Aurisina in the Friuli-Venezia-Guilia region.

Edi Keber (It) a winery based in Cormons in the Friuli-Venezia-Guilia region.

Edina (Slo) a still and sparkling natural spring mineral water from Rogaska Slatina. Mineral contents (milligrammes per litre): Sodium 69.4mg/l, Calcium 80mg/l, Magnesium 83mg/l, Bicarbonates 707mg/l, Chlorides 6mg/l, Sulphates 110.3mg/l.

Edinburgh Strong Ale (Scot) a 6.4% alc by vol. bottled ale from the Caledonian Brewing C°. Ltd. in Edinburgh.

Edingen (Ger) village (Anb): Mosel-Saar-Ruwer. (Ber): Obermosel. (Gro): Königsberg. (Vins): Not yet chosen.

Edins X.O. (USA) a natural spring mineral water. Mineral contents (milligrammes per litre): Sodium 7.9mg/l, Calcium 49mg/l, Magnesium 6.1mg/l, Potassium 20mg/l, Sulphates 15mg/l, Oxygen 150mg/l. pH 8.0

Edirne-Kirklareli (Tur) a vineyard based in the Thrace and Marmara region. Produces white wines.

Edle Weingärten (Ger) vineyard (Anb): Rheinhessen. (Ber): Wonnegau. (Gro): Pilgerpfad. (Vil): Dittelsheim-Hessloch.

Edmeades Vineyard (USA) a winery based in the Anderson Valley, Mendocino County, California. 14.5ha. Grape varieties: Cabernet sauvignon, Chardonnay, French colombard, Gewürztraminer, White riesling and Zinfandel. Produces varietal wines and Ice wine.

Edna Valley (USA) an A.V.A. vine-growing district in San Luis Obispo, California. Planted with Chardonnay plus Syrah, Marsanne, Roussanne, Viognier grapes. Home to Corbett Canyon, Edna Valley Vineyards, Seven Peaks.

Edna Valley Vineyards (Fr) a winery in San Luis Obispo, California. (Add): 2585 Biddle Ranch Road, San Luis Obispo, Ca 93401. Grape varieties: Chardonnay and Pinot noir. Produces varietal wines. Website: http://www.ednavalley.com

Edouard Brun (Fr) a Champagne producer. (established 1898). (Add): 14, Rue Marcel

Mailly, B.P. 11, 51160 Aÿ. 7ha. Produces vintage and non-vintage wines.

Edouard Robinson (Eng) a honey-flavoured drink produced by the Cornish Mead C°.

Edouard VII (Fr) a 150th anniversary Grande Champagne Cognac produced by Mouni (Denis). Recreated the Cognac Edouard VII drank using detailed blending notes from the 1890's. Only 750 bottles produced.

Edradour Distillery C° Ltd (Scot) a single malt whisky distillery based at Pitlochry, Perthshire. Produces a 10 year old highland malt whisky. Produced by S. Campbell & Sons Ltd. (Part of Pernod-Ricard). *See also* Signatory Vintage Scotch Whisky C° Ltd.

Edrington Group [The] (Scot) distillers (established 1887). (Add): West Kinfauns, Perth, Perthshire PH2 7XZ // 2500 Great Western Road, Glasgow Lanarkshire G15 6RW. Produces whiskes, rum, gin and other spirits. Website: http://www.edringtongroup.com 'E'mail: group@edrington.co.uk

Ed's Baby (Cktl) ⅒ measure banana liqueur, 5/10 measure white rum, 2/10 measure Curaçao, 2/10 measure cherry brandy, juice of a lime. Shake over ice and strain into a cocktail glass.

Ed's Reserve (S.Afr) the label for a dry white wine produced by the Thelma Mountain Vineyards winery, Stellenbosch, Western Cape.

Educación (Sp) the blending and maturing of new wines.

Edward Lloyd's Coffee House (Eng) a coffee house based in London in the eighteenth century in Lombard Street. Was visited by ship owners and marine insurance brokers. Led to the formation of the headquarters of Lloyd's of London.

Edwards & Chaffey Winery (Austr) a winery (established 1850) situated 7 km. north of McLaren Vale in South Australia. Grape varieties include Cabernet, Pinot noir, Shiraz, Chardonnay. Wines sold under the Edwards & Chaffey Section 353 label.

Edwin Taylor's Extra Stout (Eng) a 4.5% alc by vol. stout brewed by the B & T Brewery Ltd., Bedfordshire.

Eesterivier Valleise Koöperatiewe Wynkelder (S.Afr) a co-operative winery based in Stellenbosch. (Add): Box 2, Vlottenburg 7604. Produces varietal wines, also makes Hanseret Wines.

Efe (Tur) a natural spring mineral water. Mineral contents (milligrammes per litre): Sodium 100.119mg/l, Calcium 100.2mg/l, Magnesium 55.91mg/l, Bicarbonates 488mg/l, Sulphates 32.388mg/l, Nitrates 1.164mg/l, Silicates 13.9mg/l.

Efes (Tur) a 5% alc by vol. straw coloured, bottled pilsener brewed by Efes Brewery, Istanbul.

Efes Brewery (Tur) breweries based in Izmir and Istanbul which are noted for pilsener and dark beers.

Effervescence (Eng) the bubbling effect which occurs when a gas (CO_2) is released from a liquid. To give off bubbles. *See also* Bead and Mousse. (Fr) = effervescent.

Effervescent (Fr) effervescence.

Efringen-Kirchen (Ger) village (Anb): Baden. (Ber): Markgräflerland. (Gro): Vogtei Rötteln. (Vins): Kirchberg, Oelberg, Sonnhohle, Steingässle.

E.G. (Eng) *abbr*: named after the **E**ynesbury **G**rant. the name for a draught ale 1047 O.G. brewed by Paines and C°. in St. Neots, Cambridgeshire.

Égalisage (Fr) the blending of wines from different vats in Bordeaux and Burgundy.

Eger (Hun) a town 137 kms north-east of Budapest. Is the centre of the vineyards that produces the reknowned Egri Bikavér wine. *see* Bull's Blood. Grape varieties: Kardarka, Kékfrankos, Leànyka and Médoc noir.

Egeria (It) a slightly acidic sparkling natural spring mineral water from Egeria. Mineral contents (milligrammes per litre): Sodium 48mg/l, Calcium 94.9mg/l, Magnesium 23.6mg/l, Potassium 58mg/l, Bicarbonates 494.1mg/l, Chlorides 31.9mg/l, Sulphates 27mg/l, Fluorides 1.6mg/l, Nitrates 33mg/l, Silicates 85.6mg/l, Strontium 1.5mg/l, Oxygen 7.2mg/l. pH 5.73

Eggenberg (Aus) a Weinviertel winery that produces light red and white wines.

Eggenberg Brewery (Czec) a brewery (established 1895) based in Ceský Krumlov, privatised in 1991. Brews: straw lager 12% alc by vol. and 10% alc by vol., a dark beer 10% alc by vol. and a diet beer.

Eggenberger Schlossbrauerie (Aus) a small brewery based at Vorchdorf, between Salzburg and Linz. *see* Urbock 23°.

Eggenberger Urbock 23° (Aus) a 9.9% alc by vol. gold coloured, bottled bock beer brewed by Eggenberg Brewery, Vorchdorf. Also known as Urbock 23.

Eggenberg 10% (Czec) a 3% alc by vol. pale, straw coloured, bottled lager brewed by Eggenberg Brewery, Ceský Krumlov.

Egger (Eng) a pilsener lager from H. Augustin, an Austrian drink importer based in Kensington.

Egger Brauerei (Switz) a brewery based in Worb.

Eggert (Ger) a liqueur producer. (Add): 3116 Bevensen, Luneburger Heide.

Egg Flip (Cktl) an alternative name for Eggnog.

Egg Harbor (USA) a wine region near Atlantic City in the district of New Jersey.

Egg Lemonade (Cktl)(Non-alc) juice of a lemon, 2 teaspoons powdered sugar, 1 egg. Shake over ice and strain into an ice-filled highball glass, top with soda water and serve with straws.

Eggnog (Cktl) 80mls (⅔ gill) brandy, 1 dash rum, 90mls (¾ gill) milk, 1 egg, 1 teaspoon sugar. Shake over ice and strain into a tumbler and add a dash of nutmeg on top. Can use gin, rum or whisky in place of brandy. (Den) = æggepunch, (Hol) = advocaat.

Egg Nogg (USA) an alternative spelling of Eggnog.

Egg Noggin (Eng) an old name for an Eggnog.

Eggnog Glass (USA) a straight-sided glass of 225mls (8fl.oz) capacity.

E

Egg Sour (Cktl) 1 measure brandy, 1 measure orange juice, 1 egg, 1 measure lemon juice, teaspoon Gomme syrup. Shake over ice and strain into a goblet.

Egg Sour (Cktl)(Non-alc) juice ½ lemon, 1 egg, sugar syrup to taste. Shake well over ice and strain into a wine glass and add a splash of soda.

Egg White (Eng) used as a fining agent, a little wine is whisked with the whites and this is added to the wine, which, as it sinks to the bottom takes impurities with it.

Egill Skallagrimsson (Ice) a brewery based at Reykjavik that brews Polar beer.

Egils Bergvatten (Ice) a natural spring mineral water from Reykjavik. Mineral contents (milligrammes per litre): Sodium 10.2mg/l.

Eglantine Vineyard (Eng) a vineyard (established 1980) based at Eglantine House, Ash Lane, Costock, near Loughborough, Leicestershire. 1.5ha. Grape varieties: Madeleine angevine 65%, Müller-Thurgau and Seyval blanc.

Egli [Augusto] (Sp) a wine producer based in Valencia. Produces red and white wines.

Egly-Ouriet (Fr) a Champagne producer based in Ambonnay. Produces vintage and non-vintage Champagnes.

Egmont (Bel) a 6.8% alc by vol. bottled triple beer brewed by the Crombé Brouwerij, Zottegem.

Égouttage (Fr) the removal of the free-run juice before the grapes are pressed. (USA) = de-juicing.

Égrappage (Fr) the process of removing the stalks from the grapes before fermentation, used especially for white wines. *See also* Éraflage.

Égrappé (Fr) a mixture of grapes (red) with some of the stalks left in to increase the tannin content of must.

Égrappoir (Fr) a machine used to de-stalk grapes before pressing, also name for a person in pre-machine days who performed the same task.

Egri Bikavér (Hun) a renowned, robust red wine of the Eger district, known as Bull's blood. Made from a combination of Kardarka, Kékfrankos and Médoc noir grapes. *see* Bull's Blood and Dobo (Captain Istvan).

Egri Kadarka (Hun) a red grape and wine from the vineyards of Eger.

Egri Leányka (Hun) a light, soft white wine from the local grape variety of same name.

Egri Leànyka (Hun) a white grape variety also known as the Luglianca bianca in Italy.

Egringen (Ger) village (Anb): Baden. (Ber): Markgräflerland. (Gro): Vogtei Rötteln. (Vin): Sonnhohle.

Eguisheim (Fr) a wine commune of the Haut-Rhin in Alsace.

Egyptian Vineyards and Distillers Company (Egy) a state-run co-operative that has vineyards near Alexandria. Noted for Omar Khayyam (a red wine) and range of brandies.

Ehllers Estate (USA) a small winery based near Napa Valley, California. Grape varieties: Cabernet sauvignon.

Ehn [Ludwig] (Aus) a winery based in the Kamptal region. (Add): Bahnstrasse 3, 3550 Langenlois. Grape varieties: Chardonnay, Grüner veltliner, Pinot blanc, Pinot noir, Riesling. Produces a range of wine styles.

Ehnen (Lux) a wine village on the river Moselle. Vineyards: Kelterberg, Broomelt, Wousselt.

Ehrenberg (Ger) vineyard (Anb): Mosel-Saar-Ruwer. (Ber): Saar-Ruwer. (Gro): Römerlay. (Vil): Waldrach.

Ehrenfels (Aus) a vineyard area on the banks of the River Danube in the Kremstal region.

Ehrenfelser (Ger) a white, late-ripening grape variety, a cross between the Riesling and Sylvaner. Produces fruity wines.

Ehrenhausen (Aus) a wine-producing area in Südsteiermarken.

Ehrenstetten (Ger) village (Anb): Baden. (Ber): Markgräflerland. (Gro): Lorettoberg. (Vins): Oelberg, Rosenberg.

Ehrentrudis Spätburgunder Weissherbst (Ger) must be, according to a Baden-Württemberg decree of the 4 July 1973 for Badener rosé wines of quality or Pradikat made from Blauer Spätburgunder, grown in the Bereich of Kaiserstühl-Tuniberg.

Ehrle Brothers Winery (USA) a winery based in Iowa that produces mainly French hybrid wines.

Eh-up! It's Christmas (Eng) a 4.7% alc by vol. festive winter warmer ale brewed by the Barnsley Brewery Company of Elsecar, South Yorkshire.

Ehrwein (Ger) very fine wine.

Eibelstadt (Ger) village (Anb): Franken. (Ber): Maindreieck. (Gro): Not yet assigned. (Vins): Kapellenberg, Mönchsleite.

Eibensbach (Ger) village (Anb): Württemberg. (Ber): Württembergisch Unterland. (Gro): Heuchelberg. (Vin): Michaelsberg.

Eich (Ger) village (Anb): Rheinhessen. (Ber): Nierstein. (Gro): Krötenbrunnen. (Vin): Goldberg.

Eichbaum Brauerei (Ger) a brewery based in Mannheim. Brews: Dunkels Weizen and Hefe Wiezen.

Eichbaum Dunkels Weizen (Ger) a 5% alc by vol. dark bottle-conditioned wheat beer brewed by Eichbaum Brauerei in Mannheim.

Eichbaum Hefe Weizen (Ger) a 5% alc by vol. cloudy bottle-conditioned wheat beer brewed by Eichbaum Brauerei in Mannheim.

Eichberg (Aus) a vineyard site on the banks of the River Danube situated in the Wachau region, Niederösterrich.

Eichberg (Aus) a vineyard site based on the banks of the River Kamp situated in the Kamptal region.

Eichberg (Fr) an A.C. Alsace Grand Cru vineyard at Eguisheim, Haut-Rhin 57.6ha.

Eichberg (Ger) vineyard (Anb): Baden. (Ber): Breisgau. (Gro): Burg Zähringen. (Vil): Denzlingen.

Eichberg (Ger) vineyard (Anb): Baden. (Ber): Breisgau. (Gro): Burg Zähringen. (Vil): Glottertal.

Eichberg (Ger) vineyard (Anb): Baden. (Ber): Breisgau. (Gro): Burg Zähringen. (Vil): Heuweiler.

E

Eichberg (Ger) vineyard (Anb): Baden. (Ber): Kaiserstuhl-Tuniberg. (Gro): Vulkanfelsen. (Vil): Oberrotweil.

Eichbühel (Aus) a vineyard area on the banks of the River Danube in the Kremstal region.

Eiche (Ger) oak (tree).

Eichelberg (Aus) a vineyard site based on the banks of the River Kamp situated in the Kamptal region.

Eichelberg (Ger) lit: 'acorn hill', name used for seven vineyards in Germany.

Eichelberg (Ger) vineyard (Anb): Baden. (Ber): Badische Bergstrasse/Kraichgau. (Gro): Hohenberg. (Vil): Dürrn.

Eichelberg (Ger) village (Anb): Baden. (Ber): Badische Bergstrasse/Kraichgau. (Gro): Stiftsberg. (Vin): Kapellenberg.

Eichelberg (Ger) village (Anb): Württemberg. (Ber): Württembergisch Unterland. (Gro): Salzberg. (Vin): Hundsberg.

Eichelberg (Ger) vineyard (Anb): Baden. (Ber): Badische Bergstrasse/Kraichgau. (Gro): Stiftsberg. (Vil): Sinsheim (stadtteil Hilsbach).

Eichelberg (Ger) vineyard (Anb): Rheinhessen. (Ber): Bingen. (Gro): Rheingrafenstein. (Vil): Fürfeld.

Eichelberg (Ger) vineyard (Anb): Rheinhessen. (Ber): Bingen. (Gro): Rheingrafenstein. (Vil): Neu-Bamberg.

Eichelberg (Ger) vineyard (Anb): Württemberg. (Ber): Württembergisch Unterland. (Gro): Stromberg. (Vil): Lienzingen.

Eichensteiner Mineralwasser (Ger) a natural spring mineral water from Naila, BY.

Eichenzeller Natur-Brunnen (Ger) a natural spring mineral water from Eichenzell-Lütter, HE. Mineral contents (milligrammes per litre): Sodium 7.4mg/l, Calcium 69mg/l, Magnesium 22mg/l, Potassium 2.6mg/l, Bicarbonates 219mg/l, Chlorides 6.3mg/l, Sulphates 92mg/l, Fluorides 0.44mg/l.

Eichert (Ger) vineyard (Anb): Baden. (Ber): Kaiserstuhl-Tuniberg. (Gro): Vulkanfelsen. (Vil): Jechtingen.

Eichhof Brauerei (Switz) a brewery based in Lucerne.

Eichstetten (Ger) village (Anb): Baden. (Ber): Kaiserstuhl-Tuniberg. (Gro): Vulkanfelsen. (Vins): Herrenbuck, Lerchenberg.

Eichtersheim (Ger) village (Anb): Baden. (Ber): Badische Bergstrasse/Kraichgau. (Gro): Stiftsberg. (Vin): Sonnenberg.

Eichwäldele (Ger) vineyard (Anb): Baden. (Ber): Ortenau. (Gro): Schloss Rodeck. (Vil): Obersasbach.

Eico-Quelle (Ger) a still and sparkling natural spring mineral water from Eico-Quelle, Wallhausen. (blue label: sparkling/red label: low gas/green label: still). Mineral contents (milligrammes per litre): Sodium 25.8mg/l, Calcium 128mg/l, Magnesium 90mg/l, Potassium 29mg/l, Bicarbonates 474mg/l, Chlorides 15.8mg/l, Sulphates 396mg/l, Fluorides 1.93mg/l, Nitrates 1.9mg/l.

Eiderdown (Cktl) 1 part dry gin, 4 parts apple wine.

Stir together with ice, strain into a goblet and garnish with a twist of lemon peel.

Eierlikoer (Ger) egg flip, the best known type in which the alcohol is only brandy is called Eiweinbrand.

Eifel-Quelle (Ger) a natural spring mineral water from Krayerquelle, Brohl. Mineral contents (milligrammes per litre): Sodium 59mg/l, Calcium 103mg/l, Magnesium 65.2mg/l, Potassium 12.5mg/l, Bicarbonates 717mg/l, Chlorides 19.3mg/l, Sulphates 62mg/l, Fluorides 0.4mg/l, Nitrates 1mg/l, Silicates 23mg/l.

Eiffel Tower [The] (Fr) a brand name for a French wine for the American market. The name designed to appeal to the Americans in place of the complicated French label names!

Eigenbaugewächs (Aus) from the maker's own vineyards.

Eigenbauwein (Aus) estate-produced, describes a producer who sells his own wines.

Eigene Abfüllung (Ger) bottled by the producer.

Eigengewächs (Ger) growth.

Eight Bells (Cktl) ½ measure dark rum, ¼ measure dry vermouth, ¼ measure Van der Hum, ¼ measure orange and lemon squash. Shake over ice and strain into a cocktail glass and top with grated nutmeg.

Eight Bore Special (Eng) a premium bitter 4% alc by vol. brewed by the Raisdale Sparging and Brewing Company.

Eighteen Fifty Nine [1859] Porter (Eng) a 4.8% alc by vol. cask-conditioned or bottled porter brewed by Harvey Brewery in Lewes using Fuggles and Goldings hops.

Eighteen Fifty One [1851] (Eng) a 10.2% alc by vol. limited edition ale brewed by the St. Austell Brewery, St. Austell, Cornwall to mark the birth of the brewery.

Eighteen Forty Five [1845] Celebration (Eng) a 6.3% alc by vol. bottle-conditioned strong ale brewed by Fullers at the Griffin Brewery, Chiswick, London. Also a cask version.

Eighteen Forty Nine [1849] (Eng) a 4.5% alc by vol. limited edition bottled beer brewed by Holt in Manchester. 17,000 bottles produced to mark company's 150th anniversary.

Eighteen Forty Three [1843] (Eng) a lager 1042 O.G. brewed by the Arkell Brewery in Swindon, Wiltshire. Name comes from the year the brewery was founded.

Eighteen Seventytwo [1872] Porter (Eng) a 6.5% alc by vol. gold medal porter brewed by Eastwood & Sanders Ltd (Fine Ales, West Yorkshire).

Eighteenth Amendment (USA) a law passed in June 1919 to introduce Prohibition.

Eighteen Twelve [1812] Vodka (Eng) a vodka produced by Nicholson and Cº. Ltd., London. (A subsidiary of Stewart and Son).

Eighteen Twenty [1820] Gin Liqueur (Eng) a sweetened gin 40% alc by vol. with citrus flavours produced by the Hayman Distillery.

Eighteen Twenty Four [1824] Particular (Eng) a

E

strong winter ale 6% alc by vol. Brewed with barley by Ushers of Trowbridge. *See also* Dark Horse Porter.

Eighty Shilling [80/-] Ale (Scot) an ale brewed by the Drybrough Brewery in Edinburgh.

Eighty Shilling [80/-] Ale (Scot) a cask-conditioned ale brewed by the Tomintoul Brewery.

Eighty Shilling [80/-] Export (Scot) a beer brewed by the Belhaven Brewery in Dunbar, East Lothian. *see* Eighty shilling [80/-] Ale.

Eighty Shilling [80/-] Export Ale (Scot) a premium bottled ale 4.1% alc by vol. from the Caledonian Brewing Company Ltd., Edinburgh. Sometimes called Export. *See also* Deuchars, Golden Promise.

Eighty Shilling Export Ale (Scot) a premium bottled ale 4% alc by vol. brewed by Maclay & Cº. Ltd., Thistle Brewery, Alloa.

Eightythree [83] (Can) a blended Canadian whisky produced by Seagram to commemorate Joseph Seagram's acquisition of his distillery in 1983.

Eikehof Vineyard (S.Afr) a vineyard based in Franschhoek, Stellenbosch, Western Cape. 43ha. Grape varieties include: Cabernet sauvignon, Chardonnay, Merlot, Sauvignon blanc, Shiraz. Website: http://www.zeplins.com

Eikendal Vineyards (S.Afr) a winery (established 1981) based in Stellenbosch, Western Cape. 65ha. Grape varieties: Cabernet franc, Cabernet sauvignon, Chardonnay, Chenin blanc, Merlot, Pinotage, Sauvignon blanc, Shiraz. Labels: Classique, Rouge. Website: http://www.eikendal.com

Elefantøl (Den) a beer with a high alohol content, also known as Exportøl and Luksusøl.

Eilfingerberg (Ger) lit: 'eleven finger hill', name derived from the time during Lent when the abbot allowed the testing of the wine with the fingers only. A monk was purported to have said *"One needs eleven fingers!" see* Eilfingerberg Klosterstück.

Eilfingerberg Klosterstück (Ger) vineyard (Anb): Württemberg. (Ber): Württembergisch Unterland. (Gro): Stromberg. (Vil): Maulbronn.

Eimeldingen (Ger) village (Anb): Baden. (Ber): Markgräflerland. (Gro): Vogtei Rötteln. (Vin): Sonnhohle.

Eimer (Aus) bucket of wine.

Eimsheim (Ger) village (Anb): Rheinhessen. (Ber): Nierstein. (Gro): Krötenbrunnen. (Vins): Hexelberg, Römerschanze, Sonnenhang.

Einbeck (Ger) a city where the beer 'bock' was first brewed, a corruption of 'beck' by the people of Munich.

Einbecker Brauhaus AG (Ger) a brewery. (Add): Papenstrasse 4–7, Einbeck D-37574. Produces bock beer, Einbecker Mai-Ur-Bock and lagers. Also known as the Einbecker Brauerei. Website: http://www.einbecker.com 'E'mail: info@einbecker.com

Einbecker Mai-Ur-Bock (Ger) a 6.5% alc by vol. bock beer produced by the Einbecker Brauhaus in lower Saxony.

Einfachbieres (Ger) weak German beers with an alcoholic strength of between 4.5% and 5.5% by vol.

Eingeschrumpften (Ger) an alternative name for Edelfäule.

Einhorn Lager (Eng) a keg lager 1035 O.G. brewed by the Robinson Brewery in Stockport.

Einöd (Aus) a vineyard area based in the Kitzeck district of Süd-Steirmark that has some of the world's steepest growning vines (80°).

Einselthum (Ger) village (Anb): Pfalz. (Ber): Mittelhaardt-Deutsche Weinstrasse. (Gro): Schnepfenflug vom Zellertal. (Vins): Klosterstück, Kreuzberg.

Einspänner (Aus) the name for a Viennese coffee served in a tall glass, topped with whipped cream.

Einzelbogen (Ger) the single guyot vine-training system. *See also* Doppelbogen.

Einzellage (Ger) site, one individual vineyard, divided up between different owners but must use the vineyard name.

Eis (Ger) iced.

Eisacktaler (It) a German term which means D.O.C. of Valle Isarco in Trentino-Alto-Adige (white wine).

Eisack Valley (It) a principal wine-producing district in the Süd-Tirol (known in Italian as the Valle d'Isarco).

Eisberg (Fr) an alcohol-free 0.05% alc by vol. medium dry white wine, low in calories and slightly sparkling.

Eisberg (Ger) an alcohol-free 0.05% alc by vol. medium white wine, low in calories and slightly sparkling. Also a peach flavoured version.

Eisbock (Ger) a style of doppelbock, the beer is frozen to remove some of the water to produce a strong beer 13.2% alc by vol. Produces a rich flavour. *see* Kulminator.

Eisele Vineyard (USA) a vineyard based near Calistoga, Napa Valley, California. 8.5ha. Grape variety: Cabernet sauvignon.

Eisele Vineyard [Volker] (USA) a small vineyard based in Chile's Valley, Napa Valley, California. Grape variety: Zinfandel. Wine sold under Page Mill label. Part of the Araujo Estate.

Eisenberg (Aus) a wine district within the region of south Burgenland. Produces mainly white wines with some reds.

Eisenquelle Kastelruth (It) a natural spring mineral water from the Eisenquelle Kastelruth, Bozen. Mineral contents (milligrammes per litre): Sodium 1.5mg/l, Calcium 108mg/l, Magnesium 44.3mg/l, Potassium 1.26mg/l, Bicarbonates 83mg/l, Sulphates 385mg/l, Fluorides 0.4mg/l, Silicates 4.3mg/l.

Eisenstadt (Aus) a wine-producing district in Burgenland near the Leitha Mountains. Produces mainly white wines.

Eisental (Ger) village (Anb): Baden. (Ber): Ortenau. (Gro): Schloss Rodeck. (Vins): Betschgräbler, Sommerhalde.

Eisenwasser Innichen (It) a natural spring mineral water from Eisenwasser Innichen. Mineral

505

E

contents (milligrammes per litre): Sodium 11.1mg/l, Calcium 516mg/l, Magnesium 92mg/l, Potassium 2.7mg/l, Bicarbonates 260mg/l, Chlorides 3mg/l, Sulphates 1430mg/l, Fluorides 0.5mg/l, Silicates 9.5mg/l, Strontium 4.5mg/l.

Eiserne Hand (Ger) vineyard (Anb): Rheinhessen. (Ber): Nierstein. (Gro): Krötenbrunnen. (Vil): Guntersblum.

Eisfeld (Aus) a vineyard area on the banks of the River Danube in the Kremstal region.

Eisingen (Ger) village (Anb): Baden. (Ber): Badische Bergstrasse/Kraichgau. (Gro): Hohenberg. (Vins): Klepberg, Steig.

Eiskorn (Ger) a flavoured kornbranntwein.

Eis-Liköre (Ger) when found on a liqueur bottle label, denotes that the contents are best drunk iced 'on the rocks'.

Eiswasser (Aus)(Ger) iced water.

Eiswein (Aus) must be made exclusively from frozen grapes (minimum -7°C [20°F] both during harvest and pressing). Minimum must weight 25° KMW. Wine must be bottled in Austria and cannot be sold before 1st May of year following the harvest. The use of additional Pradikats such as Spätlese, Auslese etc. is forbidden. see Prädikatsweine. See also Schneewein.

Eiswein (Ger) ripe grapes which have been frozen whilst on the vine. The water freezes but the juice does not, rarely occurs, but when it does produces luscious sweet wines. Gathered at between -6°C and -8°C [18°F–22°F] and crushed whilst still frozen. Used to have Pradikat gradings added, i.e. Auslese Eiswein, but now must be sold as a single Pradikat. Since 1982 a minimum of 110° Oeschle.

Eiswürfel (Ger) ice.

Eiszeitquell (Ger) a still and sparkling natural spring mineral water from D-72768 Reutlingen-Rommelsbach, BW. (blue label: sparkling/red label: low gas/green label: still). Mineral contents (milligrammes per litre): Sodium 6.9mg/l, Calcium 135mg/l, Magnesium 35mg/l, Potassium 3.8mg/l, Bicarbonates 354mg/l, Chlorides 3.2mg/l, Sulphates 200mg/l, Fluorides 0.6mg/l, Nitrates 0.3mg/l, Silicates 29.2mg/l, Iron 1.4mg/l, Strontium 1.15mg/l. pH 7.04 Website: http://www.eiszeitquelle.de 'E'mail: sammelaktion@eiszeitquell.de

Eitcheld Process (Fr) a method of fermentation.

Eitelsbach (Ger) a wine village on the River Ruwer.

Eitelsbacher Karthäuserhofberer (Ger) a wine that is noted for having the smallest label in Germany.

Ejarque Rebollar (Sp) a private bodega based in Utiel-Requena area in the Levante.

Éjetonnement (Fr) see Évasivage.

Ekenroth (Ger) village (Anb): Nahe. (Ber): Kreuznach. (Gro): Schlosskapelle. (Vins): Felsenberg, Hölle.

Ekko (Cktl) a 10mls (½ fl.oz) each of Mandarine Napoléon and vodka, juice of ½ lemon, 1 dash grenadine. Shake well over ice and strain into a cocktail glass, add a cherry and a twist lemon peel.

Eksi (Tur) sour/very acidic. See also Kekre.

Ekstreme (Eng) a 6% alc by vol lager from Courage, sold in a blue bottle.

E.K.U. Brauerei (Ger) abbr: Erste Kulmbacher Actienbrauerei, a brewery in Kulmbach. Makes one of the world's strongest beers EKU 28. See also Kulminator.

E.K.U. 28 (Ger) an 11% alc by vol. strong amber-coloured bock beer brewed by E.K.U. Brauerei in Kulmbach.

Elaberet Estate (Afr) a winery based in northern Ethiopia.

Elaboracíon (Sp) the initial blending of brandy.

Elaborado (Sp) see Montilla-Moriles.

Eladorado y Aejado Por (Sp) made and aged by.

Elandsberg (S.Afr) the export label for a range of wines produced by the Viljoendrift wines winery, Robertson, Western Cape.

Elan Vineyard (Austr) a winery (established 1985) based at 17 Turner's Road, Bittern, Victoria. Grape varieties: Cabernet sauvignon, Merlot, Shiraz.

Elba (It) an island between Tuscany on the mainland and Corsica. Produces both red and white wines. Sometimes the wines taste of a tang of the sea.

Elba (S.Afr) the label for a red wine (Malbec, Mourvèdre, Sangiovese and Viognier blend) produced by the Backsberg Cellars winery, Suider-Paarl, Western Cape.

Elba Bianco (It) a D.O.C. white from the island of Elba. Made from the Trebbiano toscano grapes. D.O.C. also applies to the naturally sparkling wines made according to regulations.

Elba Rosso (It) a D.O.C. red wine from the island of Elba. Made from the Canaiolo, Sangiovese and Trebbiano toscano bianco grapes.

Elbling (Ger) a white grape variety which is used in some of the wine-producing regions, gives a high yield. Also known as the Knipperlé. See also Albling, Alben, Grober, Grobriesling, Kleinberger, Kleinelbling and Kleinpereich.

El Botellon (Sp) lit: 'the big bottle', a slang term used by under-age Spanish drinkers for the large plastic cola bottles that are filled with alcoholic drinks to disguise them.

Elbrus (Rus) a still and sparkling natural spring mineral water from Nalchik. Mineral contents (milligrammes per litre): Calcium 78mg/l, Magnesium 11.7mg/l, Bicarbonates 219mg/l, Chlorides 19mg/l, Sulphates 39mg/l.

El Calvador (Fr) the name of a Spanish galleon of the Armada which was shipwrecked on the Normandy coast from which Calvados takes its name.

El Cañar (Sp) a still natural spring mineral water from Spring Cañar 2, Jaraba, Zaragoza. Mineral contents (milligrammes per litre): Sodium mg/l, Calcium mg/l, Magnesium mg/l, Potassium mg/l, Bicarbonates mg/l, Chlorides mg/l, Sulphates mg/l, Fluorides mg/l, Nitrates mg/l.

El Cántaro (Arg) a still and sparkling natural spring mineral water (established 1993) from Buenos Aires. Mineral contents (milligrammes per litre): Sodium 50mg/l.

506

E

El Carrizal (Sp) a natural spring mineral water.

El Castano (Ven) a natural spring mineral water from Maracay. Mineral contents (milligrammes per litre): Magnesium 1.8mg/l, Bicarbonates 28mg/l, Chlorides 4.2mg/l, Sulphates 1mg/l, Fluorides 0.06mg/l. pH 7.6

El Cep (Sp) the name of a 200ha cava winery in Sant Sadurni d'Anoia. Labels include: Marqués de Gelida.

El Cerro (Cktl) 20mls (¾ fl.oz) Galliano, 25mls (1 fl.oz) light rum, 25mls (1 fl.oz) dark rum, 20mls (¾ fl.oz) Curaçao, 50mls (2 fl.ozs) pineapple juice, dash grenadine. Shake over ice and strain into an ice-filled highball glass, decorate with a pineapple ring, fresh strawberry and straws.

El Cesar (Sp) a 5-year-old brandy produced by Romate.

El Cíd (Sp) a brand of Amontillado Sherry produced by Duff Gordon.

Elciego (Sp) a noted wine-producing village based in the Alavesa district of Rioja, north-eastern Spain.

El Coto (Sp) the name for red and white wines produced by the Bodegas El Coto, S.A. Rioja.

El Cuadrado (Sp) the name given to a Fino Sherry from Vinícola Hidalgo in Sanlúcar de Barrameda, Jerez.

El Degirmeni (Tur) coffee grinder.

Elderberry (Eng) a wild fruit that produces fruit wines which are similar to heavy red wines (juice was sometimes used to improve the body of grape wines though now no longer practiced). The flowers are used to produce home-made wines (produces a Gewürztraminer-style wine).

Elderberry Fruit Beer (Eng) a 4.7% alc by vol. cask or bottled wheat beer brewed by the St. Peter's Brewery, St. Peter's Hall, South Elmham St. Peter, near Bungay, Suffolk.

Elderflower (Eng) a popular flower (of the elderberry tree) used in the making of dry home-made wines. Produces a wine similar in bouquet to that of the Gewürztraminer.

Elderflower Tea (Eng) a fragrant herbal tea that aids cold cures.

Elderton (Austr) a winery based at Tanunda Road, Nurioopta, South Australia. Grape varieties: Cabernet sauvignon, Hermitage, Pinot noir.

El Diablo Cocktail (Cktl) 1½ measures tequila, ¾ measure crème de cassis, juice of ½ lime. Stir over ice in a highball glass together with the spent lime shell, top with ginger ale and serve with straws.

El Dorado (S.Am) golden, white or dark demerara rums produced by Demerara Distillers, 44 Kingston, Georgetown. Also a 15 year old Special Reserve.

Eldorado (Cyp) the name given to a rich white and an oak-aged, old tawny liqueur wine 17.5% alc by vol.

Eldorado (USA) a natural spring mineral water from Eldorado, Colorado.

Eldorado (USA) a sub A.V.A. vine growing county within the Sierra Foothills in California.

Eldorado Cocktail (Cktl) 40mls (⅓ gill) tequila, 25mls (⅕ gill) lemon juice, teaspoon honey. Shake well over ice and strain into a collins glass with ice and add a slice of orange.

Eldorado Wines (S.Afr) a winery (established 1999) based in the Windmeul, Paarl, Western Cape. 1ha. Grape varieties: Cabernet sauvignon, Merlot, Syrah. Label: Aquila. Website: http://www.eldorado.co.za

Eldridge Pope Brewery (Eng) a brewery (established 1833). (Add): Weymouth Avenue, Dorchester, Dorset DT1 1QT. Produces many fine beers including Thomas Hardy Ale 1125 O.G. Britain's strongest beer. Also produced are cask-conditioned Royal Oak 1048 O.G. Dorset Original IPA 1041 O.G. Pope's 1880 1041 O.G. Green top 1042 O.G. Crystal Bitter 1034 O.G. Faust Pilsener 1035 O.G. Sold under the Huntsman Ales name. Also owns 12 retail wine outlets in the Dorset area and J.B. Reynier in London. Website: http://www.eldridge-pop.co.uk 'E'mail: webenquiries@eldridge-pope.co.uk

Eleanor of Aquitaine (Fr) a French Queen who in 1152A.D. married Henry 2nd of England. Brought the vineyards of Bordeaux and Gascony under English control and introduced French wines in quantity into England.

Electra (Eng) a 4.5% alc by vol. ale brewed by the Milton Brewery Cambridge Ltd., Cambridgeshire.

Electra (USA) the name of a California Orange Muscat wine produced by Quady, Madera. *See also* Elysium, Starboard.

Electric Light Ale (Eng) a 3.7% alc by vol. beer from the Hull Brewery, North Humberside.

Electric Pump (Eng) a beer dispenser. Two types: **Free flow pumps** which switch on by a pressure switch that senses when the tap is opened and the **Displacement-type pump** which has a calibrated measuring container where the beer is displaced when a button is pressed (latter is sealed by Customs and Excise).

Electric White (Eng) an 8.4% alc by vol. strong white cider from Lanchester of Durham.

Electropura (Mex) a natural spring mineral water from Tlálplan.

Élegance (Fr) a term to describe a wine of good vintage having delicacy and lightness, but does not promise longevity.

Elegancia (Scot) a single malt highland malt whisky 40% alc by vol. produced by The Macallan distilleries. Aged in Oloroso and Fino Sherry casks there are dated (1991) and 12 y.o. versions currently produced.

Elegant (Eng) a term used by a wine taster to describe a wine of breeding but not with such high praise as to be distinguished.

Elegante Dry Fino (Sp) a brand of Fino Sherry produced by Gonzalez Byass in Jerez.

Element (Austr) the label for a red (Cabernet sauvignon) wine produced by the Sandalford Estate, Western Australia.

Elemental (S.Afr) the label for a red wine (Shiraz and Viognier blend) produced by the Boschheim winery, Stellenbosch, Western Cape.

Elements (S.Afr) the label for a range of wines (Earth/Fire/Rain) produced by the Hartswater Wine Cellar winery, Hartswater, Northern Cape.

Elena Fucci (It) a winery based in Barile, Basilicata region. Produces: D.O.C. Aglianico del Vulture.

Elephantenwein (Ger) a wine made from grapes that are so hard that an elephant would be required to crush them, made in the villages of Tübingen and Reutlingen.

Elephant Kinjia (Afr) a coffee brand from the Blackburn Estate, northern Tanzania.

Elephant Lager (Den) an export lager 7.2% alc by vol. 1062 O.G. brewed by the Carlsberg Brewery in Copenhagen. Imported into England as Carlsberg 68.

Elephants (Eng) a grade of coffee bean, those that are too large or have grown together in the coffee cherry.

Elephant Trail (S.Afr) the label for a red wine (Pinotage and Shiraz blend) from the Isabela range produced by the Thirtytwo [32] South Ltd winery, Stellenbosch, Western Cape.

Elephant Trip (S.Afr) the export label for Daschbosch Wine Cellar Worcester, Western Cape.

Eleus (Lat) a word used for Bacchus. *See also* Bassareus, Bromius, Dionysos, Dionysus, Eleleus, Euhan, Euan, Euhius, Euius, Lacchus, Lyaeus and Thyoneus.

Élevage (Fr) a term for the time between completion of fermentation and bottling when the wine is 'looked after', an important time in viniculture (Aus) = ausbau.

Elevation 1147 (USA) a red wine (Cabernet sauvignon) produced by the David Arthur winery, Napa Valley, California.

Elevation 393 (S.Afr) the label for a quality red wine (Cabernet franc, Cabernet sauvignon, Merlot and Shiraz) produced by the De Trafford Wines winery, Stellenbosch, Western Cape.

Élevé (Fr) a label term which denotes 'grown'.

Eleven (Eng) a light, medium-sweet Sherry designed as a mixer from Harveys of Bristol.

Elevenses (Eng) an informal slang term for morning coffee, usually served at 11a.m. but can be any time around that hour.

Éleveur (Fr) grower. *see* Négociant-Éleveur.

Elfenlay (Ger) vineyard (Anb): Mittelrhein. (Ber): Rheinburgengau. (Gro): Gedeonseck. (Vil): Boppard.

El Gaitero (Sp) a noted brand of cider produced in Chacolí, north-eastern Spain.

El Hierro (Sp) *see* Hierro (El).

Elgee Park (Austr) a winery (established 1972) based at Junction Road, Merricks, North Victoria. Grape varieties: Chardonnay, Cabernet sauvignon, Cabernet franc, Merlot.

Elgin (S.Afr) the label for a white wine (Chardonnay) produced by the Neil Ellis Wines, Stellenbosch, Western Cape.

Elgin Glass (Eng) a small slim-waisted glass used for fortified wines and liqueurs.

Elgin Vintners (S.Afr) a winery (established 2003)

based in the Elgin, Western Cape. 42ha. Grape varieties: Cabernet sauvignon, Pinot noir, Sauvignon blanc.

El Goléa (Alg) a natural spring mineral water from El Maniaa. Mineral contents (milligrammes per litre): Sodium 25mg/l, Calcium 26mg/l, Magnesium 10mg/l, Potassium 5mg/l, Bicarbonates 118mg/l, Chlorides 21mg/l, Sulphates 43mg/l.

Elgood & Sons (Eng) a brewery (established 1795). (Add): North Brink Brewery, Wisbech, Cambridgeshire PE13 1LN. Brews: Barleymead 4.6% alc by vol., Bitter End (The), Black Dog 3.6% alc by vol., Cambridge Bitter 3.8% alc by vol., Centenary Ale, Double Swan 4.5% alc by vol., Fenman Bitter 1033 O.G., Fenman Pale Ale 3.6% alc by vol., Golden Newt 4.1% alc by vol., Greyhound Strong Bitter 4.2% alc by vol., Highway, Mad Dog 4.4% alc by vol., Mellow Mild, North Brink porter 5% alc by vol., Old Black Shuck 4.5% alc by vol., Old Smoothy Bitter Fenman 3.8% alc by vol., Old Smoothie Mild 3.6% alc by vol., Old Wagg 4% alc by vol., Pageant Ale 4.3% alc by vol., Reinbeer, Russet Ale 1032 O.G., Thin Ice 4.7% alc by vol., Wenceslas Winter Warmer 7.5% alc by vol. Website: http://www.elgoods-brewery.co.uk 'E'mail: info@elgoods-brewery.co.uk

Elham Park (Eng) a vineyard. (Add): North Elham, Dereham, Norfolk. 3ha. Soil: gravel loam. Grape varieties: Müller-Thurgau 60%, Madeleine angevine plus a variety of others. Produces Elham Parker Müller-Thurgau.

Elham Parker Müller-Thurgau (Eng) *see* Elham House.

Elham Valley Vineyards (Eng) a vineyard (established 1981) based at Breach, Barham, Kent. 0.75ha. Grape varieties: Chasselas, Kerner, Madeleine angevine, Müller-Thurgau and Seyval blanc. Produces Pendant (a blended wine).

Elias Wineries (Isr) *see* Eliaz Wineries (alternative spelling).

Eliaz Wineries (Isr) a group of wineries, the best based in Binyamina.

Elijah Craig (USA) an 18 year old single barrel Bourbon whiskey, also a 12 year old version.

Elims Spring Water (Afr) a natural spring mineral water from Kenya.

Eliqua (Sp) a natural spring mineral water from Font d'Elca, Salem, Valencia. Mineral contents (milligrammes per litre): Sodium 5.6mg/l, Calcium 63.8mg/l, Chlorides 14mg/l.

Elisa (Cktl) ⅛ measure sweet vermouth, ½ measure light rum, ⅛ measure apricot brandy, ⅛ measure Amaro. Stir over ice and strain into a Champagne flute, top with iced Asti Spumanti, add the zest of an orange and a cherry.

Elisabethanberg (Ger) vineyard (Anb): Baden. (Ber): Bodensee. (Gro): Sonnenufer. (Vil): Hilzingen.

Elisabethenberg (Ger) vineyard (Anb): Baden. (Ber): Bodensee. (Gro): Sonnenufer. (Vil): Singen.

Elisabethenquelle Heilwasser (Ger) a sparkling natural spring mineral water. Mineral contents

E

(milligrammes per litre): Sodium 519mg/l, Calcium 469mg/l, Magnesium 97mg/l, Potassium 29mg/l, Bicarbonates 730mg/l, Chlorides 719mg/l, Sulphates 1106mg/l, Fluorides 1mg/l, Nitrates 0.4mg/l.

Eliseevskaya (Rus) a natural spring mineral water from Stavropol Territory, Northern Causasus. Mineral contents (milligrammes per litre): Sodium 1100–1400mg/l, Potassium 1100–1400mg/l, Bicarbonates 1400–2200mg/l, Chlorides 250–700mg/l, Sulphates 600–1100mg/l.

Elisenberg (Ger) vineyard (Anb): Mosel-Saar-Ruwer. (Ber): Bernkastel. (Gro): Kurfürstlay. (Vil): Mülheim.

Elisenberg (Ger) vineyard (Anb): Mosel-Saar-Ruwer. (Ber): Bernkastel. (Gro): Kurfürstlay. (Vil): Veldenz.

Elitness (Ger) a natural spring mineral water from Baruth Quelle, Baruth/Mark, BB.

Élixer (Fr) the old term used to describe liqueurs.

Élixer d'Amorique (Fr) a herb liqueur produced near Lannion in north-western France.

Élixer d'Anvers (Bel) a yellow-green, bitter-sweet liqueur made from herbs by De Beuckelaer 34.5% alc by vol.

Élixer de Garrus (Fr) a brand of elixir produced by Picard et Cazot Fils, Lyons. Made from spirits, vanilla, saffron, maidenhead fern and orange flower water.

Élixer de la Chartreuse (Fr) a brand of elixir produced by Picard et Cazot Fils, Lyons.

Élixer de la Marshal d'Estrées (Fr) a digestif considered to be the original recipe for Chartreuse (green), produced in the eighteenth century. *see* Élixer de Santé.

Elixer dell'Eremita (It) a herb-flavoured liqueur made by the Camaldoli order.

Élixer de Monbazillac (Fr) a nickname for the sweet wine of Bergerac.

Elixer de Mondorf (Lux) a liqueur which originates from the nineteenth century.

Élixer de Santé (Fr) lit: 'elixir of health', (1764) forerunner of Green Chartreuse. *see* Élixer de la Marshal d'Estrées.

Élixer des Braves (Fr) a brand of elixir produced by Picard et Cazot Fils, Lyons.

Élixer de Spa (Bel) a pale green-yellow herb liqueur produced by the Capuchin monks in the town of Spa.

Élixer de Table (Fr) an old name for liqueurs used as digestifs.

Elixer di China (It) a sweet colourless liqueur made from aniseed.

Élixer du Mont Ventoux (Fr) a herb liqueur produced in Avignon.

Elixer Longae Vitae (Ger)(Hol) an alternative name for Pommeranzen bitters.

Élixers (Fr) liqueurs made from the finest distillates.

Élixer Végétal (Fr) an 80% alc by vol. version of the Élixer de Santé, sold in a small bottle it is used as a medicinal liqueur.

Élixer Vital (Fr) a brand of elixir produced by Picard et Cazot Fils, Lyons, southern France.

Elixir (Eng) the English spelling of Elixer.

Elixir (S.Afr) a noble late harvest sauvignon blanc wine produced by the African Terroir winery, Paarl, Western Cape.

Elizabethan (Eng) a pale, dry, Fino Sherry from Avery's of Bristol.

Elizabethan Barley Wine (Eng) a strong pale ale 1090 O.G. brewed by the Harvey's Brewery in Lewes, Sussex (occasionally sold in draught form).

Elizabethan Mead (Eng) the brand-name of a mead produced by Lamb and Watt of Liverpool.

El Jardinero Cocktail (Cktl) ¾ measure white rum, ½ measure Sambuca, ¼ measure lime juice. Shake well over ice and strain into a scooped out marrow shell and serve with straws.

Elk (Hol) oak.

Elk Cove Vineyards (USA) a small winery based in Gaston, Willamette Valley, Oregon. 8ha. Grape varieties: Chardonnay, Pinot gris, Pinot noir, Riesling, Cabernet sauvignon, Gewürztraminer. Label: Mount Richmond.

Elkersberg (Ger) vineyard (Anb): Nahe. (Ber): Schloss Böckelheim. (Gro): Paradiesgarten. (Vil): Alsenz.

Elkhorn Peak (USA) a winery based in the Napa Valley, California. Grape variety: Pinot noir. Label: Fagan Creek Vineyard.

Elkhorn Ridge Vineyards (USA) a winery based in the Willamette Valley, Oregon. Grape variety: Pinot noir. Website: http://www.elkhornridgevineyards.com

Elk's Own (Cktl) 1 measure Bourbon whiskey, ½ measure port, juice ¼ lemon, 1 egg white, dash gomme syrup. Shake over ice and strain into a cocktail glass and decorate with piece of pineapple.

Ella Drinks C° (Scot) a fruit and vegetable drinks manufacturer (established 1999). (Add): Alloa Business Centre, Alloa, Clackmannanshire FK10 3SA. Website: http://www.bouvrage.com 'E'mail: anne.thompson@sol.co.uk

Ellagic Acid (Eng) is obtained from the wooden casks, absorbed by the wines that are matured in them, a simple tannin that causes astringency in the wine.

Ellenz-Poltersdorf (Ger) village (Anb): Mosel-Saar-Ruwer. (Ber): Zell/Mosel. (Gro): Goldbäumchen. (Vins): Alterberg, Kurfürst, Ruberberger Domherrenberg.

Ellenz-Poltersdorf (Ger) village (Anb): Mosel-Saar-Ruwer. (Ber): Zell/Mosel. (Gro): Rosenhang. (Vins): Silberberg, Woogberg.

Ellergrub (Ger) vineyard (Anb): Mosel-Saar-Ruwer. (Ber): Bernkastel. (Gro): Schwarzlay. (Vil): Enkirch.

Ellerstadt (Ger) village (Anb): Pfalz. (Ber): Mittelhaardt-Deutsche Weinstrasse. (Gro): Feuerberg. (Vins): Bubeneck, Dickkopp, Sonnenberg.

Ellerstadt (Ger) village (Anb): Pfalz. (Ber): Mittelhaardt-Deutsche Weinstrasse. (Gro): Hofstück. (Vin): Kirchenstück.

E

Ellevin [Jean-Pierre] (Fr) a winery based in the A.C. Chablis, Burgundy. Produces a range of Chablis wines including Premier Cru Vaucoupin.

Ellhofen (Ger) village (Anb): Württemberg. (Ber): Württembergisch Unterland. (Gro): Salzberg. (Vins): Altenberg, Althälde, Rauzenberg.

Elliot Winery (Austr) a winery based in Hunter Valley, New South Wales. Their vineyard is called Oakville.

Ellis [Neil] (S.Afr) a winery based at Devon Valley Road, Stellenbosch, Western Cape. Produces varietal wines including Cabernet franc, Cabernet sauvignon, Merlot, Pinot noir, Chardonnay, Sauvignon blanc.

Ellisse Cocktail (Cktl) 1 measure Cognac, dash Angostura, dash Strega. Stir over ice and strain into an ice-filled highball glass, top with ginger ale and lemon peel spiral.

Ellis Vineyard (USA) the label used by the Mark West Vineyards, Russian River Valley, California.

Ellmendingen (Ger) village (Anb): Baden. (Ber): Badische Bergstrasse/Kraichgau. (Gro): Hohenberg. (Vin): Keulebuckel.

Ellner [Charles] (Fr) a Champagne producer based at 1 & 6 Rue Côte Legris, 51207 Épernay Cedex. 52ha. Produces vintage wines. Vintages: 1986, 1987, 1988, 1989, 1990, 1993, 1995, 1996, 1998, 2000. Vintage cuvées: Séduction, Charles Ellner.

El Maestro (Sp) the name given to a large cask known in the nineteenth century as El Cristo.

Elmer Mineralwasser (Switz) a still and sparkling natural spring mineral water from Elm, Glarus. (blue label: sparkling/white label: still). Mineral contents (milligrammes per litre): Sodium 3mg/l, Calcium 114mg/l, Magnesium 7mg/l, Bicarbonates 240mg/l, Chlorides <1mg/l, Sulphates 120mg/l, Fluorides <0.1mg/l, Nitrates <1mg/l.

Elmer T. Lee (USA) a single barrel Bourbon whiskey from Leestown in Frankfort. 90° US proof (45% alc by vol.).

El Metraya (Cktl) 25mls (1 fl.oz) Tia Maria, 10mls (½ fl.oz) dark rum, 75mls (3 fl.ozs) cane syrup. Shake well over ice and pour into a goblet.

El Mezcal (Mex) the brand-name of a tequila.

Elmham Park Vineyard (Eng) a vineyard (established 1971) based in Norfolk. 3ha. Grape varieties: Madeleine angevine 20% and Müller-Thurgau 80%.

Elmhurst Spring (Eng) a natural spring mineral water from Elmhurst Spring (Borehole 1), Litchfield, Staffordshire.

El Montecillo (Sp) see Bodegas El Montecillo.

Elongated Wine (Eng) a term used to describe a wine that has been increased by the addition of water to reduce the alcoholic strength for purposes of Excise duty.

Eloro (It) the name for D.O.C. red and white wines produced in Sicily near Noto and Ragusa.

El Paso Winery (USA) a winery based in Ulster Park, Hudson Valley, New York.

El Pepino Cocktail (Cktl) 25mls (1 fl.oz) golden rum, 10mls (½ fl.oz) triple sec, 35mls (1½ fl.ozs) each of pineapple juice and orange juice, 1 dash grenadine. Stir well over ice and strain into a scooped-out marrow shell and serve with straws.

Elpersheim (Ger) village (Anb): Württemberg. (Ber): Kocher-Jagst-Tauber. (Gro): Tauberberg. (Vins): Mönchsberg, Probstberg.

El Pinalito (Sp) a still natural spring mineral water. Mineral contents (milligrammes per litre): Sodium 300.7mg/l, Calcium 24.6mg/l, Magnesium 5.2mg/l, Potassium 16.4mg/l, Bicarbonates 892.2mg/l, Chlorides 4.3mg/l, Sulphates 8mg/l, Fluorides 2.1mg/l, Nitrates 0.5mg/l.

El Portell, MP (Sp) a still natural spring mineral water from El Portell, Monserrat, Valencia. Mineral contents (milligrammes per litre): Sodium 23.6mg/l, Calcium 95.4mg/l, Magnesium 12.2mg/l, Bicarbonates 257.4mg/l, Chlorides 38.4mg/l, Sulphates 49.1mg/l.

El Porvenir de los Andes (Arg) a winery based in the Salta region, northern Argentina. Website: http://www.bodegaselporvenir.com 'E'mail: info@bodegaselporvenir.com

El Presidente (Cktl) 40mls (⅓ gill) rum, 15mls (⅛ gill) pineapple juice, 15mls (⅛ gill) grenadine and juice of a lime. Shake over ice and strain into a cocktail glass.

El Presidente Cocktail (Cktl) ⅗ measure rum, ⅕ measure Curaçao, ⅕ measure dry vermouth, dash grenadine. Shake over ice and strain into a cocktail glass and decorate with a twist orange peel.

Elqui (Chile) a principal wine region in the north, producing fine wines.

El Rocío (Sp) a 15% alc by vol. Manzanilla Sherry produced by Gonzalez Byass in Jerez de la Frontera, Cadiz.

Elroy's Pawt (S.Afr) a sweet, fortified red wine (Cabernet sauvignon and Merlot blend) produced by Alto Ego Wines, Tulbagh, Western Cape.

Els (Ger) a bitters made by the Hennekens Distillery at Beck.

El Salvador (C.Am) a coffee-producing country that produces mainly Arabica beans.

Elsäss (Ger) the name for the Alsace region in the nineteenth century. See also Ilsace.

Elsässer Wein (Ger) the name for the wines of Alsace to distinguish them from the Rhine wines.

Elsäss-Lothringen (Ger) the German name for Alsace-Lorraine.

Elsbethen-Quelle (Ger) a natural spring mineral water from Pfeffenhausen, BY.

El Scrumpy (Eng) the name given to an oak matured cider produced by Inch's Cider of Winkleigh, Devon.

Elsenz (Ger) village (Anb): Baden. (Ber): Badische Bergstrasse/Kraichgau. (Gro): Stiftsberg. (Vin): Spiegelberg.

Elsie Mo (Eng) a 4.7% alc by vol. ale brewed by the Castle Rock Brewery, Nottinghamshire.

E

Elsinore (Austr) a winery based in Granite Belt, Queensland.

Elskebitter (Hol) a bitter beer.

Elster (Ger) vineyard (Anb): Pfalz. (Ber): Mittelhaardt-Deutsche Weinstrasse. (Gro): Mariengarten. (Vil): Forst.

Elston (N.Z) the label for a Chardonnay wine produced by Te Mata in Hawkes Bay. *see* Castle Hill, Coleraine.

Elterberg (Lux) a vineyard site in the village of Wormeldange.

Eltham Vineyards (Austr) a winery. (Add): Shaw's Road, Arthur's Creek, Yarra Valley. Grape varieties: Cabernet sauvignon, Pinot noir, Chardonnay.

Eltina Sprudel (Ger) a natural spring mineral water from Eberstadt-Buchhorn, BW.

Eltville (Ger) village (Anb): Rheingau. (Ber): Johannisberg. (Gro): Heiligenstock. (Vin): Sandgrub.

Eltville (Ger) village (Anb): Rheingau. (Ber): Johannisberg. (Gro): Steinmächer. (Vins): Langenstück, Rheinberg, Sandgrub, Sonnenberg, Taubenberg.

El Viejito (Mex) a producer of tequila of same name 47% alc by vol.

Elvina (Fr) a natural mineral water from Dax.

Elvio Cogno (It) a winery. (Add): Loc. Ravera 2, 12060 Novello (CN). 7ha. planted. Produces D.O.C.G. Barolo plus Barbera d'Alba, Dolcetto d'Alba, Langhe Rosso and white Vino da Tavola.

Elvira (USA) a white grape variety produced from *Vitis riparia* and *Vitis labrusca* cross that is slowly being replaced.

Elvot (Eng) an old English cider-making apple.

Elysium (USA) a black muscat sweet dessert wine from Quady. *See also* Electra, Starboard.

Elzévia (Fr) a de luxe vintage Champagne (100% Chardonnay) produced by Esterlin, Épernay. Vintages: 1999.

Elzogberg (Ger) vineyard (Anb): Mosel-Saar-Ruwer. (Ber): Zell/Mosel. (Gro): Grafschaft. (Vil): Ediger-Eller.

El Zorzal Cocktail (Cktl) ½ measure anisette, ½ measure white rum, 1 measure orange juice, dash grenadine. Shake well over ice and strain into an ice-filled old-fashioned glass, dress with a pineapple slice, orange slice and cherry.

Embassy Royal (Cktl) ½ measure Bourbon whiskey, ¼ measure Drambuie, ¼ measure sweet vermouth, 2 dashes orange squash. Shake over ice and strain into a cocktail glass.

Embolicaire (Sp) a black grape variety grown in central Spain.

Embotellado (Sp) bottled.

Embres-et-Castelmaure (Fr) a noted wine-producing village based in the A.C. Corbières district of Languedoc, south-western France.

Embriaguaz (Port) intoxication/drunken.

Emerald Cocktail (Cktl) 40mls (⅓ gill) gin, 15mls (⅛ gill) green crème de menthe, dash Angostura, dash lemon juice, ½ egg white. Shake over ice and strain into a cocktail glass and top with a green cherry.

Emerald Dry (USA) *see* Emerald Riesling.

Emerald Forest (Austr) a still natural spring mineral water from Kulnurra, NSW. Mineral contents (milligrammes per litre): Sodium 9.9mg/l, Calcium 0.16mg/l, Magnesium 1.33mg/l, Potassium 0.22mg/l, Bicarbonates 2mg/l, Chlorides 4.26mg/l. Website: http://www.geocities.com/emeraldforest.au

Emerald Isle Cocktail (Cktl) ⅓ measure dry gin, 4 dashes green crème de menthe, 3 dashes Angostura. Stir over ice and strain into a cocktail glass.

Emerald Riesling (USA) a white grape variety developed by the University of California at Davis and grown in the Paul Masson Vineyards. High yielding it produces dry white wines, a cross between Muscadelle x Riesling, also referred to as Emerald Dry.

Emerald Sparkler (Cktl) 1 part Midori liqueur, 3 parts Champagne. Pour Midori and Champagne in a saucer glass and decorate with a green cherry.

Emerald Swizzle (Cktl) into an ice-filled highball glass place 1 measure Midori, 2 measures dry Cinzano. Stir, top with lemonade and serve with straws.

Emer Chardonnay (Austr) a dry white wine produced by the Setanta Vineyard, Adelaide Hills, South Australia.

Emeringes (Fr) a commune in the Beaujolais. Has the A.C. Beaujolais-Villages of Beaujolais-Emeringes status.

Emerlingtal (Aus) a vineyard area on the banks of the River Danube in the Kremstal region.

Emerson Cocktail (Cktl) ¾ measure gin, ¼ measure sweet vermouth, juice ½ lemon, 4 dashes maraschino. Shake over ice and strain into a cocktail glass.

Emeryville (USA) a vine-growing city in Almeda County, California.

Émet (Ch.Isles) cider press.

Emilia (Cktl) ½ measure Bacardi rum, ¼ measure apricot brandy, ¼ measure Grand Marnier, dash orange bitters. Stir over ice and strain into a cocktail glass.

Emilia Romagna (It) a wine region around Bologna, south of River Po. Wines include: D.O.C. & Vino da Tavola Lambrusco, D.O.C. Sangiovese di Romagna, D.O.C. Trebbiano di Romagna and D.O.C.G. Albana di Romagna.

Emilie May (Austr) the label for a red (Cabernet sauvignon) wine produced by the Woodlands Estate, Western Australia.

Emilio Lustau (Sp) *see* Lustau.

Eminencia (Sp) a 6-year-old brandy produced by Palomino y Vergara S.A. Colon 1-25, Jerez de la Frontera, Cadiz.

Emir (Tur) a red grape variety grown in Middle Anatolia.

Emita d'Espiells (Sp) an estate-bottled white wine produced by Juvé y Camps in San Sadurní de Noya, Cataluña, north-eastern Spain.

Emma Green (Cktl) ³⁄₁₀ measure dry gin, ¹⁄₁₀ measure Amaretto di Saronno, ¹⁄₁₀ measure blue Curaçao, ¹⁄₁₀

E

orange juice, ⁹/₁₀ measure sparkling wine, dash egg white. Shake well over ice and strain, add sparkling wine and a slice of lime.

Emmendingen [ortsteil Hochberg] (Ger) village (Anb): Baden. (Ber): Briesgau. (Gro): Burg Zähringen, (Vin): Halde.

Emmerdale Ale (Eng) a 4.2% alc by vol. bitter ale brewed by the Black Sheep brewery, Yorkshire.

Emmets (Ire) a brand of cream liqueur produced by Emmet & Company 17% alc by vol.

E-Motif (Fr) a Bordeaux company of wine-makers formed to produce gaudy labels for bottled French wines for the American Market (e.g. Fusion Red/Exciting White).

Emperatriz Eugenia (Sp) a solera reserva brandy produced by Emilio Lustau in Jerez de la Frontera.

Empéreur (Fr) a brand of Grande Champagne Cognac produced by Lafont de Saint-Preuil.

Emperor (Austr) a red grape variety that is sometimes used in small quantities in USA for brandy production.

Emperor Ale (Eng) an ale brewed by the Hadrian Brewery at Tyneside. *See also* Centurion Best Bitter.

Emperor's Brandy [The] (Eng) a name given to Corvoisier Cognac after casks of it were found on his ship in 1815 when he was fleeing to America.

Empilage (Fr) the rest period for Champagne, gives the wine a chance to settle down after the disturbance of dégorgement which cannot be skimped if quality is the aim.

Empire Cocktail (Cktl) ¼ measure gin, ¼ measure Calvados, ¼ measure apricot brandy. Shake well over ice and strain into a cocktail glass.

Empire Glory (Cktl) ½ measure rye whiskey, ¼ measure lemon juice, ¼ measure ginger wine, 3 dashes grenadine. Shake well over ice and strain into a cocktail glass.

Emporadà-Costa Brava (Sp) a a Denominación de Origen based in south-eastern Spain on the French border.

Empress of India (Eng) a 4.7% alc by vol. ale brewed by the Earl Soham Brewery, Suffolk.

Empress of India (Eng) a 6% alc by vol. strong ale brewed by the Fernanders Brewery, West Yorkshire.

Empress Springs (Can) a still and slightly alkaline natural spring mineral water (established 2002) from Saanich Penninsula. Mineral contents (milligrammes per litre): Sodium 71.9mg/l, Calcium 70.8mg/l, Chlorides 26.9mg/l, Sulphates 7.74mg/l, Fluorides 0.31mg/l, Nitrates 0.004mg/l, Silicates mg/l. pH 8.32

Emrich Bier (Ger) a brewery based in Kusel. Brews: Jäger Pils, Export and Dunkel beers.

Emsland Quelle (Ger) a natural spring mineral water (established 1983) from Haselünne, NI. Mineral contents (milligrammes per litre): Sodium 418mg/l, Calcium 30mg/l, Magnesium 9.1mg/l, Potassium 10.4mg/l, Bicarbonates 247mg/l, Chlorides 578mg/l, Sulphates 21mg/l.

EMS Mineral Water (Chi) a natural spring mineral water from Emei Shan. Mineral contents (milligrammes per litre): Calcium 64.7mg/l, Silicates 14.21mg/l. pH 7.9

Emstaler Brunnen (Ger) a natural spring mineral water from Bad Camberg-Oberselters, HE. Mineral contents (milligrammes per litre): Sodium 194mg/l, Calcium 68.9mg/l, Magnesium 19.7mg/l, Potassium 8.2mg/l, Chlorides 188mg/l, Fluorides 0.37mg/l.

Emu (Austr) a brand-name used by the Swan Brewery for their Emu Export Lager and Emu Bitter (a lager beer).

Emu (Austr) a bulk shipper in South Australia.

Emu Bitter (Austr) *see* Emu.

Emu Export Lager (Austr) *see* Emu.

Emu Winery (Austr) a winery based in Reynella in Southern Vales, South Australia.

Emva Cream (Cyp) a famous brand of Cyprus sweet Sherry 15% alc by vol. produced by the Etko C°. (A subsidiary of Haggipavlu in Limassol). Grape varieties: Mavro, Xiniseri.

Ename Dubbel (Bel) a 6.5% alc by vol. bottle-conditioned double abbaye beer from Saint-Salvator Ename Abbaye, brewed by the Roman Brouwerij, Oudenaarde-Mater.

Ename Tripel (Bel) a 9% alc by vol. bottle-conditioned triple abbaye beer from Saint-Salvator Ename Abbaye, brewed by the Roman Brouwerij, Oudenaarde-Mater.

Enantio (It) the new name for the black grape variety Lambrusco a Foglia Frastagliata.

Enate Rosado (Sp) a rosé wine produced in the Somontano region from 100% Cabernet sauvignon grapes.

En Cailleret (Fr) a Premier Cru vineyard [part] in the A.C. commune of Chassagne-Montrachet, Côte de Beaune, Burgundy. 5.49ha. Also known as Les Cailleret.

En Caradeux (Fr) a Premier Cru vineyard [part] in the A.C. commune of Pernand-Vergelesses, Côte de Beaune, Burgundy 20ha.

Encépagement (Fr) vine varieties planted in a particular vineyard.

Enchada (Mad) a tool which is a cross between a hoe and a pick for tending the vineyard soil.

En Champans (Fr) a Premier Cru vineyard in the A.C. commune of Volnay, Côte de Beaune, Burgundy. 11.3ha. Also known as Les Champans.

Enclos (Fr) the name for the vines that surround the château and its winery in Bordeaux.

Enclos [l'] (Fr) an A.C. red wine produced by Domaine d'Ormesson from Merlot and Cabernet sauvignon grapes in the Languedoc-Roussillon.

Encostas de Aire (Port) a DOC wine within the I.P.R. region of Estremadura.

Encostas da Nava (Port) an I.P.R. region south of River Douro.

Encruzado (Port) a white grape variety grown in the Dão and Vinho Verde regions.

Endeavour (Austr) the brand-name of a rum produced by Bundaberg in Queensland.

Endeavour Ale (Eng) a 3.6% alc by vol. ale brewed by the Cropton Brewery, North Yorkshire.

E

En de l'El [L'] (Fr) a white grape variety grown in the Gaillac region of south-western France.

Endersbach (Ger) village (Anb): Württemberg. (Ber): Remstal-Stuttgart. (Gro): Wartbühl. (Vins): Happenhalde, Wetzstein.

Endersbach (Ger) village (Anb): Württemberg. (Ber): Remstal-Stuttgart. see Weinstadt.

Endikos Diateremenon (Gre) lit: 'mature quality wine', found on the bottle label. See also Endikos Diatirimenon.

Endikos Diatirimenon (Gre) the alternative spelling of Endikos Diateremenon.

Endingen (Ger) village (Anb): Baden. (Ber): Kaiserstuhl-Tuniberg. (Gro): Vulkanfelsen. (Vins): Engelsberg, Steingrube, Tannacker.

Endocarp (Eng) the botanical name for the parchment in a coffee cherry.

Endurance (Eng) a 4.5% alc by vol. ale brewed by the Cambrius Craft Brewery, Merseyside.

Energiser (Eng) a compound added to slow or reluctant fermentations to reactivate the yeast.

En Ergots (Fr) see Ergots.

Energy 69 (Eng) a branded non-sparkling, non-alcoholic drink (below 0.5% alc by vol) which gives drinkers a high energy burst, used as a cocktail mixer or straight drink.

Enfant-Jésus (Fr) a part of the Premier Cru vineyards of Les Grèves, in the Côte de Beaune (owned by Bouchard Père).

Enfants de Gayant (Fr) a brewery (established 1920) based in Douai. Brews: La Bière du Démon, Bière du Désert.

Enfer d'Arvier (It) a red wine from the Val d'Aosta. Made from the Dolcetto, Neyret, Petit-rouge and Viendenus grapes. Must age for minimum 1 year in wooden casks holding no more than 3 hl.

Enforcado (Port) a method of lacing vines through the branches of trees.

Engadi (Cyp) an ancient vineyard based in southern Cyprus that was written about in the Bible (Solomon's Song of Songs, Chapter 1, verse 14).

Engageat Blanc (Fr) an alternative name for the Folle blanche grape.

Engarrafado na Origem (Port) estate bottled.

Engelberg (Fr) an A.C. Alsace Grand Cru vineyard at Dahlenheim, Bas-Rhin 11ha.

Engelbert-Brunnen (Ger) a natural spring mineral water from Bocum, NW.

Engelbert Neu (Ger) a natural spring mineral water from Bochum, NW.

Engelbräu (Ger) a 5% alc by vol. Bavarian wheat beer from the Engelbräu Brauerei.

Engelbrecht-Els Proprietor's Blend (S.Afr) the label for a red wine (Cabernet sauvignon 60%, Shiraz 20% plus Malbec, Merlot and Petit verdot blend) produced by the Ernie Els Wines winery, Stellenbosch, Western Cape.

Engelgrube (Ger) vineyard (Anb): Mosel-Saar-Ruwer. (Ber): Bernkastel. (Gro): Michelsberg. (Vil): Neumagen-Dhron.

Engelmannsberg (Ger) vineyard (Anb): Rheingau.

(Ber): Johannisberg. (Gro): Deutelsberg. (Vil): Hattenheim.

Engelmannsberg (Ger) a vineyard within the village of Hattenheim, 14.1ha (74.5%) of which is proposed to be classified as Erstes Gewächs.

Engelsberg (Ger) vineyard (Anb): Baden. (Ber): Kaiserstuhl-Tuniberg. (Gro): Vulkanfelsen. (Vil): Endingen.

Engelsberg (Ger) village (Anb): Franken. (Ber): Mainviereck. (Gro): Not yet assigned. (Vin): Klostergarten.

Engelsberg (Ger) vineyard (Anb): Rheinhessen. (Ber): Nierstein. (Gro): Spiegelberg. (Vil): Nackenheim.

Engelsberg (Ger) vineyard (Anb): Rheinhessen. (Ber): Wonnegau. (Gro): Domblick. (Vil): Offstein.

Engelsberg (Ger) vineyard (Anb): Pfalz. (Ber): Südliche Weinstrasse. (Gro): Herrlich. (Vil): Herxheim bei Landau.

Engelsfelsen (Ger) vineyard (Anb): Baden. (Ber): Ortenau. (Gro): Schloss Rodeck. (Vil): Bühlertal.

Engelstadt (Ger) village (Anb): Rheinhessen. (Ber): Bingen. (Gro): Kaiserpfalz. (Vins): Adelpfad, Römerberg.

Engelstein (Ger) vineyard (Anb): Mittelrhein. (Ber): Rheinburgengau. (Gro): Gedeonseck. (Vil): Boppard.

Engelstein (Ger) vineyard (Anb): Mittelrhein. (Ber): Rheinburgengau. (Gro): Gedeonseck. (Vil): Spay.

Engelströpfchen (Ger) vineyard (Anb): Mosel-Saar-Ruwer. (Ber): Zell/Mosel. (Gro): Grafschaft. (Vil): Ediger-Eller.

Engeltjpipi (S.Afr) the label for a sweet botrytised white wine (Sémillon, Chenin blanc and Riesling blend) produced by the Twee Jongegezellen Estate winery, Tulbagh, Western Cape.

En Genêt (Fr) a Premier Cru vineyard in the A.C. commune of Beaune, Côte de Beaune, Burgundy 4.32ha.

Enggass (Ger) vineyard (Anb): Mosel-Saar-Ruwer. (Ber): Bernkastel. (Gro): Sankt Michael. (Vil): Thörnich.

Engineers Arms Brewery C° (Eng) a brewery (established 2001). (Add): Engineers Arms, 66 High Street, Henlow, Bedfordshire SG16 6AA. Brews: Bing 4.8% alc by vol.

England (Eng) a country which produces wines, mainly white in style, fairly acidic and light in body. Main grape varieties include Chardonnay (south), Huxlrebe, Madeleine-angevine, Müller-Thurgau, Pinot noir (south), Reichensteiner, Schönburger. Relies heavily on the weather which in most years is insufficient to produce wines of quality (although climate change is producing improvements). In certain years sweet wines are made. See also E.V.A., British Wines.

Englands Glory (Eng) a 4.3% alc by vol. ale brewed by the Highgate Brewery Ltd., West Midlands.

English Ale (Eng) a bottled beer 1042 O.G. brewed by Whitbreads Brewery, is low in carbohydrates and so suitable for diabetics.

E

English Bishop (Punch) bake an orange with 12 cloves, cut into quarters. Place in bowl and top with a bottle of heated Port. Add sugar, return to heat, cover for ½ hour, add 125mls (1 gill) rum, ground ginger and cinnamon to taste.

English Bolo (Cktl) 125mls (1 gill) manzanilla, juice ½ lemon, ¼ teaspoon sugar, ¼ teaspoon ground cinnamon. Mix sugar, cinnamon and lemon juice together in an old-fashioned glass, add ice and Sherry, stir and serve.

English Breakfast Tea (Eng) a blend of Ceylon (Sri Lanka) and Indian small leaf teas that gives a full-bodied tea.

English Coffee (Liq.Coffee) using a measure of dry gin.

English Factory House (Port) *see* Feitoria Inglesa.

English Farm Cider Centre (Eng) a cider farm based in Lewes, East Sussex. Has a collection of 200 bottled/draught ciders available for tasting.

English Highball (Cktl) ⅓ measure brandy, ⅓ measure Italian vermouth, ⅓ measure gin. Shake over ice and strain into an ice-filled highball glass, top with soda water and a twist of lemon peel juice.

English London Dry (USA) a style of dry gin.

English Malt Ale (Eng) a 3.8% alc by vol. ale brewed by the Bristol Beer Factory, Avon.

English Market (USA) a dry gin, the brand-name of the Old Mr. Boston Distillers of Boston, Massachusetts.

English Mead (Eng) a mead commissioned by the National Maritime Museum to mark the 400th anniversary of the Spanish Armada's arrival in Britain. Produced by Lurgashall Winery in West Sussex from naturally fermented honey and yeast, fortified with brandy (aged 1 year).

English Mountain (USA) a natural spring mineral water (established 1830) from Chestnut Hill, Dandridge, Tennessee. Mineral contents (milligrammes per litre): Calcium 22mg/l, Magnesium 4.3mg/l. pH 7.7

English Mountain (Eng) a natural spring mineral water from Armathwaite, Cumbria.

English Rose (Cktl) ½ measure dry gin, ¼ measure apricot brandy, ¼ measure French vermouth, 4 dashes grenadine, 2 dashes lemon juice. Shake over ice, strain into a sugar-rimmed cocktail glass and top with a cherry.

English Rose Cream Liqueur (Eng) a liqueur made with crush ½ rose petals, cream and alcohol.

English Vineyards Association Limited (Eng) from 1st April 1996 known as the United Kingdom Vineyards Association.

English Vineyards Certification Trade Mark (Eng) the A.C. equivalent for the wines of England.

English Wine (Eng) a wine made from freshly gathered grapes grown in England and vinified without any preservative. *see* British Wine.

English Wine Producers (Eng) a winery (established 1993). (Add): P.O. Box 5729, Market Harborough, Leicestershire LE16 8WX. Produces a variety of red, white and sparkling wines. Website: http://www.englishwineproducers.com 'E'mail: info@englishwineproducers.com

English Wines Group plc (Eng) wine and beer producers (established 2002). (Add): Tenterden Vineyard, Small Hythe, Tenterden, Kent TN30 7NG. Produces a range of wines, beers, fruit and vegetable juices. Website: http://www.englishwinesgroup.com 'E'mail: sales@englishwinesgroup.com

Engweg (Ger) vineyard (Anb): Württemberg. (Ber): Kocher-Jagst-Tauber. (Gro): Kocherberg. (Vil): Niedernhall.

Engweg (Ger) vineyard (Anb): Württemberg. (Ber): Kocher-Jagst-Tauber. (Gro): Kocherberg. (Vil): Weissbach.

Enigma (Eng) a new (2005) seasonal beer brewed by Frederic Robinson Brewery at 4.7% alc by vol.

Eniséli (Geo) a white grape variety grown in the Georgia region, mainly used in the production of brandy.

Enivrer (Fr) intoxicate.

Enkirch (Ger) village (Anb): Mosel-Saar-Ruwer. (Ber): Bernkastel. (Gro): Schwarzlay. (Vins): Batterieberg, Edelberg, Ellergrub, Herrenberg, Monteneubel, Steffensberg, Weinkammer, Zeppwingert.

En la Chaîne-Carteau (Fr) a Premier Cru vineyard [part] in the A.C. commune of Nuits-Saint-Georges, Côte de Nuits, Burgundy 2.6ha.

En l'Orme (Fr) a Premier Cru vineyard in the A.C. commune of Beaune, Côte de Beaune, Burgundy 2.02ha.

En l'Ormeau (Fr) a Premier Cru vineyard in the A.C. commune of Volnay, Côte de Beaune, Burgundy. 4.3ha. Also known as L'Ormeau.

Enmore (S.Am) a rum distillery based in Guyana.

Enocarboj (It) a noted wine co-operative based in Sciassa, Sicily.

Enoch's Hammer (Eng) a cask-conditioned bitter 1080 O.G. from Sair, a home-brew public house in Linthwaite, Huddersfield.

Enologia (Sp) the study of wine.

Enologica Valtellinese (It) a wine producer in the Valtellina region noted for their Valtellina, Grumello and Inferno wines.

Enologix (USA) a computerized programme ™ analyses the constituents of wines to assess the wine's quality. Created by Leo McCloskey the programme is able to assess the quality of the wine for keeping (maturing) by analising its anthocyanins. The database has the analysis of over 10,000 wines.

Enology (Eng) an alternative spelling of oenology (the study of wine).

Enoteca (It) a wine library where wines are shown, tasted and sold.

Enoteca Permanente (It) a wine library in the Grinzano Castle near Alba. Wines of the region are on show and for tasting.

Enotecnio (It) oenological consultant.

Enotria La Lastra (It) a winery based in the DOCG Vernaccia di San Gimignano in the Tuscany region.

En Pauland (Fr) a Premier Cru vineyard [part] in the A.C. commune of Aloxe-Corton, Côte de Beaune, Burgundy.

E

En Remilly (Fr) a Premier Cru vineyard in the A.C. commune of Saint-Aubin, Côte de Beaune, Burgundy 2ha.

Enrichment (Eng) the sugaring of the grape must. (Fr) = chaptalisation, (Ger) = anreichern.

En Saussilles (Fr) a Premier Cru vineyard in the A.C. commune of Pommard. Côte de Beaune, Burgundy. 3.8ha. Is also known as Les Saussilles.

Ensch (Ger) village (Anb): Mosel-Saar-Ruwer. (Ber): Bernkastel. (Gro): Sankt Michael. (Vins): Mühlenberg, St. Martin, Sonnenlay.

Enselberg (Ger) vineyard (Anb): Baden. (Ber): Kaiserstuhl-Tuniberg. (Gro): Vulkanfelsen. (Vil): Bischoffingen.

Enselberg (Ger) vineyard (Anb): Baden. (Ber): Kaiserstuhl-Tuniberg. (Gro): Vulkenfelsen. (Vil): Jechtingen.

Ensheim (Ger) village (Anb): Rheinhessen. (Ber): Bingen. (Gro): Adelberg. (Vin): Kachelberg.

Ensign (Eng) a 'take home' bitter from Wells Brewery, Bedford.

Ensign (Eng) a 4.2% alc by vol. cask-conditioned ale from the Flagship Brewery, Chatham Dockyard, Dartford.

Ensingen (Ger) village (Anb): Württemberg. (Ber): Württembergisch Unterland. (Gro): Stromberg. (Vin): Schanzreiter.

Ensinger Mineralwasser (Ger) a sparkling natural spring mineral water. (red label: sparkling/blue label: light gas). Mineral contents (milligrammes per litre): Sodium 28.8mg/l, Calcium 528mg/l, Magnesium 124mg/l, Potassium 6.9mg/l, Bicarbonates 403mg/l, Chlorides 28.9mg/l, Sulphates 1463mg/l, Nitrates 2.1mg/l.

Ensinger Schiller Heilwasser (Ger) a natural spring mineral water. Mineral contents (milligrammes per litre): Sodium 19.7mg/l, Calcium 425mg/l, Magnesium 160mg/l, Potassium 6.6mg/l, Chlorides 35mg/l, Sulphates 1330mg/l, Fluorides 0.44mg/l.

Ensinger Schiller Quelle (Ger) a natural spring mineral water from Ensingen. Mineral contents (milligrammes per litre): Sodium 33.7mg/l, Calcium 585mg/l, Magnesium 102mg/l, Potassium 7.42mg/l, Bicarbonates 362mg/l, Chlorides 28.1mg/l, Sulphates 1560mg/l, Fluorides 0.47mg/l.

Ensinger Urquelle (Ger) a still and sparkling natural spring mineral water (established 1999) from Ensingen. (red label: sparkling/blue label: light gas/green label: still). Mineral contents (milligrammes per litre): Sodium 7.1mg/l, Calcium 81.9mg/l, Magnesium 40mg/l, Chlorides 7.2mg/l, Sulphates 36mg/l.

Ente [Benoit] (Fr) a winery (3ha) based in Puligny, Côte de Beaune, Burgundy. Produces Premier Crus: Champs Gain, Folatières.

Entee (Austr) a natural spring mineral water from The Gardens, Darwin, Northern Territory. Mineral contents (milligrammes per litre): Sodium 5mg/l, Calcium 7mg/l, Magnesium 10mg/l, Potassium 1mg/l, Bicarbonates 35mg/l, Chlorides 5mg/l. pH 7.5

Enterprise Wines (Austr) a winery based in the Clare Valley, South Australia. Grape varieties: Cabernet sauvignon, Fumé blanc and Rhine riesling. Produces varietal wines.

Enthopio (S.Afr) the label for a red wine (Pinotage plus Cabernet franc, Merlot and Shiraz blend) produced by the Vriesenhof Vineyards winery, Stellenbosch, Western Cape.

Entire (Eng) a form of porter ale called Entire Butts. Brewed to incorporate three separate beers in one butt or cask: a pale ale, a brown ale and a stock ale. In the early eighteenth century sold as Three Thirds or Three Threads.

Entire Bitter (Eng) a cask-conditioned bitter 1043 O.G. brewed by the Holt, Plant and Deakin Brewery.

Entire Butts (Eng) see Entire.

Entire Stout (Eng) a 4.5% alc by vol. stout brewed by the Hop Back Brewery, Salisbury, Wiltshire.

Entonneurs Rabelaisiens (Fr) a wine society based in Chinon, Loire.

Entonnoir à Porto (Fr) wine funnel, a device used for decanting Port. The end of the funnel is rested against the side of the decanter so that the wine does not gather air as it is decanted.

Entournerier (Fr) an alternative name for the Syrah grape.

Entre Blanc et Rouge (Fr) a grade of rosé wine made from a blend of red and white wine.

Entre-Deux-Mers (Fr) lit: 'between two seas' a large wine area within the Bordeaux region that lies between the rivers Garonne and Dordogne Produces A.C. white wines and A.C. Bordeaux reds.

Entre-Deux-Mers Haut Benauge (Fr) a white wine A.C. see Haut Benauge.

Entre Fino (Sp) a term used to describe a Fino Sherry that is lacking in distinction.

Entre Minho e Douro (Port) a demarcated region of Portugal, Vinho Verde is the main wine produced.

Entre Ríos (Arg) a wine-producing area west of Sante Fé.

Entschleimen (Ger) the process of letting the freshly pressed must stand to let the solids settle to the bottom. (Fr) = débourbage, (Sp) = desfangado.

Entschleimung (Aus) the Austrian spelling of Entschleimen.

Envase (Sp) bottling.

Enveloppe (Fr) a straw case that was used to protect bottles, cardboard has now mainly replaced the straw (is banned in USA).

Enverado (Sp) term used in D.O. Ribeiro to describe under ripe wines. Must be between 8% – 9% alc by vol.

En Verseuil (Fr) a Premier Cru vineyard in the A.C. commune of Volnay, Côte de Beaune, Burgundy 18ha.

Enville Ale (Eng) a type of India pale ale brewed from honey, spring water, yeast and malt by the Enville Ales Brewery (1046 O.G) 4.8% alc by vol.

Enville Ales Brewery (Eng) a brewery (established 1992). (Add): Cox Green, Hollies Lane, Enville,

E

Stourbridge, West Midlands DY7 5LG. Brews: Anniversary Ale 4.5% alc by vol., Chainmaker Mild 3.6% alc by vol., Czechmate Saaz 4.2% alc by vol., Enville Ale–O.G 4.5% alc by vol., Enville Gargoyle 4.5% alc by vol., Enville White 4.2% alc by vol., Enville womanizer 5.6% alc by vol., Ginger Beer 4.6% alc by vol., Gothic Ale 5.2% alc by vol., Maidens Ruin 6% alc by vol., Nailmaker Mild 4% alc by vol., Old Porter 4.5% alc by vol., Phoenix Indian Pale Ale 4.8% alc by vol. Website: http://www.envilleales.com 'E'mail: info@envilleales.com

Envites (Lat) a sub-genus of the Vitis species of *Ampelidacae* of which grapes for wine production are members.

Envy (Austr) a 150mls non-vintage bottled wine produced by BRL Hardy. Part of the Seven Deadly Sins range. *See also* Flirt, Greed.

Envy (Ch.Isles) a 4.8% alc by vol. bitter ale brewed by the Randalls Brewery, St. Peter Port, Guernsey.

Enwyn (Wal) buttermilk.

Enxebre (Sp) a white wine produced by Bodegas Salnesur, Val do Salnés, Rías Baixas, D.O. Galicia from Albariño grapes.

Enz [River] (Ger) a tributary of the river Neckar in Württemberg. Soil: shell limestone.

Enzian (Ger) a term used to signify gentian-flavoured liqueurs (enzian means gentian), also used in Austria and Bavaria.

Enzian Calisay (Sp) a sweet, pale gold liqueur based on gentian and other herbs.

Enz Vineyards (USA) a winery based in San Benito, California. 12.5ha. Grape varieties: Chasselas, Pinot St. Georges and Zinfandel. Produces varietal wines and Limestone (a flavoured apéritif wine).

Enzymes (Eng) a group of substances found in animals and plants which decompose carbon compounds.

Eocene (It) clay schist soils.

Eola Hills Wine Cellars (USA) a winery based in Oregon. Grape varieties: Cabernet sauvignon, Chardonnay, Gamay, Gewürztraminer, Pinot gris, Pinot noir, Riesling, Sauvignon blanc.

EOS Estate Winery (USA) a winery. (Add): Paso Robles, California 93447. Grape varieties include: Chardonnay, Petite syrah. Produces EOS Tears of Dew (a late harvest Moscato). Website: http://www.eosvintage.com

E.P. (Eng) a limited edition ale brewed by the St. Austell Brewery, St. Austell, Cornwall to mark the Eden Project. Full name is E.P. Hothouse Ale.

Epee (Cktl) ¾ measure Cognac, ¼ measure sweet vermouth. Stir well with ice and strain into a cocktail glass.

Épenots (Fr) a Premier Cru vineyard of the A.C. commune of Pommard, Côte de Beaune, Burgundy. 8.06ha. Also spelt Epenottes (les).

Épenottes [Les] (Fr) *see* Épenots.

Épernay (Fr) an important Champagne centre, the headquarters of many of the Grandes Marques. Canton d'Épernay has the Grand Cru village of Chouilly [white], Premier Cru villages: Chouilly [red] and Pierry, and Cru villages of Damery,

Épernay, Fleur-la-Rivière, Mardeuil, Moussy, Saint-Martin-d'Ablois, Vaucienne, Venteuil and Vinay.

Épernay (Fr) a Cru Champagne town in the Canton d'Épernay. District: Épernay.

Épesses (Switz) a dry white wine producing village in the Vaud canton.

E.P. Hothouse Ale (Eng) *see* E.P.

Épi Blanc [L'] (Fr) a 5.6% alc by vol. pale, light straw coloured, top-fermented, bottled special beer brewed by La Compagnie des Trois Épis, Paris (contains oats). *See also* Épi Noir [L'], Épi Rouge [L'].

Epicatechin (Eng) *see* Flavenoids.

Epicentre (S.Afr) the label for a red (Cabernet sauvignon 70% plus others) wine produced by the Nick and Forti's Wines winery, Western Cape.

Epieds (Fr) a region in the A.C. Saumur, Anjou-Saumur, Loire. Produces red and white wines.

Epinette Blanche (Fr) an alternative name for the Chardonnay grape.

Epinettes (Fr) the scissor-like cutters used to cut off the bunches of grapes in Champagne.

Épineuil (Fr) a village in the Yonne, noted for Vin gris.

Épi Noir [L'] (Fr) a 5.6% alc by vol. orange-straw coloured, top-fermented, bottled special beer brewed by La Compagnie des Trois Épis, Paris (includes buckwheat). *See also* Épi Blanc [L'], Épi Rouge [L'].

Épinottes [Les] (Fr) a Premier Cru vineyard of A.C. Chablis. Often is reclassified as the Premier Cru Mélinots.

Épi Rouge [L'] (Fr) a 5.6% alc by vol. medium-brown, top-fermented, bottled special beer brewed by La Compagnie des Trois Épis, Paris. *See also* Épi Blanc [L'], Épi Noir [L'].

Epirus (Gre) a red and white wine-producing region in north-western Greece. Grape varieties: Debina, Zitsa (white) and Cabernet sauvignon (red).

Epirus (Gre) a white grape variety grown in Attica.

Episcopal (Cktl) ½ measure yellow Izarra, ½ measure green Izarra. Pour over crushed ice and serve in a goblet with straws.

Epitrapezio Krasi (Gre) table wine.

Épluchage (Fr) the picking out of rotten and broken black grapes from the picked bunches especially in the Champagne region.

Epoch V (Eng) a crisp dry white wine from Tenterden Vineyards, Kent.

Epondage (Fr) the pruning of dead twigs and suckers off the vine, usually done in November.

Epotare (Lat) drink-up/booze-up.

Eppalock Ridge (Austr) a winery based on Metcalfe Pool Road, Lake Eppalock, Victoria. Grape varieties: Cabernet sauvignon, Pinot noir, Shiraz, Chardonnay, Sémillon.

Eppelsheim (Ger) village (Anb): Rheinhessen. (Ber): Wonnegau. (Gro): Bergkloster. (Vin): Felsen.

Eppingen (Ger) village (Anb): Baden. (Ber): Badische Bergstrasse/Kraichgau. (Gro): Stiftsberg. (Vin): Lerchenberg.

Eptinger (Switz) a still and sparkling natural spring mineral water from Quelle Birch, Eptingen. (red label: sparkling/green label: light gas/blue label: still). Mineral contents (milligrammes per litre): Sodium 4.2mg/l, Calcium 510mg/l, Magnesium 117mg/l, Bicarbonates 278mg/l, Chlorides 3mg/l, Fluorides 1.8mg/l, Nitrates <0.1mg/l.

Equil (Indo) a natural spring mineral water from West Java. Mineral contents (milligrammes per litre): Sodium 9mg/l, Calcium 9.5mg/l, Magnesium 8.2mg/l, Potassium 1.2mg/l, Bicarbonates 68.6mg/l, Chlorides 0.9mg/l, Sulphates 2.4mg/l, Nitrates <0.2mg/l. pH 7.2

Équilibré (Fr) harmonious, a well-balanced wine.

Equinox (Eng) a cask-conditioned autumn ale brewed by Everards Brewery, Leicester.

Equipe 5 (It) a group formed by five independent producers. Noted for a wide range of sparkling (metodo tradizionale) wines.

Equi Valley (Chile) a wine district in northern Chile.

Éraflage (Fr) the separating of the grapes from the stalks. See also Égrappage.

Eral (Sp) a red wine produced by Bodegas José Palacios, Alta region in Rioja. Made from Garnacha 60% and Tempranillo 40%. Reservas and Gran Reservas are oak matured and then bottle matured.

Erath Vineyards (USA) a vineyard based in Willamette Valley, Oregon. Grape varieties: Pinot Gris, Pinot noir. Labels: Estate Selection, Prince Hill.

Éraville (Fr) a commune in the Charente département whose grapes are classed Grande Champagne (Cognac).

Erbach (Ger) village (Anb): Rheingau. (Ber): Johannisberg. (Gro): Deutelsberg. (Vins): Hohenrain, Honigberg, Marcobrunn, Michelmark, Schlossberg, Siegelsberg, Steinmorgen.

Erbacher Vineyards (USA) a winery based in Roxburg, Connecticut. Produces mainly French hybrid grapes.

Erbaluce (It) a white wine grape variety.

Erbaluce di Caluso (It) a D.O.C. white wine from Piemonte. Made from the Erbaluce grape grown in the commune of Caluso and others.

Erbalus di Caluso (USA) a white grape variety grown in California to make dessert wines.

Erbarola (It) the Ligurian name for the white Albarola grape.

Erben (Ger) estate of/heirs of.

Erbes-Büdesheim (Ger) village (Anb): Rheinhessen. (Ber): Bingen. (Gro): Adelberg. (Vins): Geisterberg, Vogelsang.

Erdbeergeist (Ger)(Switz) strawberry brandy, a soft fruit brandy.

Erdeck (Tur) a wine-producing area in north-western Turkey. Produces red and white wines.

Erdelega (Eng) a vineyard based in Ardleigh, Essex.

Erden (Ger) village (Anb): Mosel-Saar-Ruwer. (Ber): Bernkastel. (Gro): Schwarzlay. (Vins): Busslay, Herrenberg, Prälat, Treppchen.

Erdevik (Ser) a wine-producing area in Fruška Gora, Vojvodina.

Erdig (Ger) earthy.

Erdinger Pikantus Weizenbock (Ger) a 7.3% alc by vol. dark bottle-conditioned wheat bock beer brewed by the Erdinger Weiss Brauerei.

Erdinger Weissbier (Ger) a 5.3% alc by vol. straw bottle-conditioned wheat beer said to have a citric tang. Brewed by the Erdinger Weiss Brauerei.

Erdinger Weissbier Dunkel (Ger) a 5.6% alc by vol. dark bottle-conditioned wheat beer brewed by the Erdinger Weiss Brauerei.

Erdinger Weissbier Kristallklar (Ger) a 5.3% alc by vol. filtered wheat beer brewed by the Erdinger Weiss Brauerei.

Erdinger Weiss Brauerei (Ger) a brewery in Erding that produces a range of beers including: Weissbier, Hefe Weissbräu, Kristal Weizen, Kristallklar, Pikantus Weizenbock.

Erdmannhausen (Ger) village (Anb): Württemberg. (Ber): Württembergisch Unterland. (Gro): Schalkstein. (Vin): Neckarhälde.

Erdöbénye (Hun) a wine-producing village based in the southern foot-hills.

Erdschüssl (Aus) a vineyard area on the banks of the River Danube in the Kremstal region.

Erdut (Cro) a wine-producing town based in northern Croatia.

Erévan (Arm) a white grape variety grown in Armenia that is used mainly in brandy production.

Ergersheim (Ger) village (Anb): Franken. (Ber): Steigerwald. (Gro): Schlosstück. (Vin): Altenberg.

Ergonomic System (Eng) vine growing (bio-technological).

Ergots (Fr) a Premier Cru vineyard in the A.C. commune of Gevrey-Chambertin, Côte de Nuits, Burgundy. 1.17ha. Also known as En Ergots.

Eric's Brewery (Wal) a brewery based in Pontypridd, Mid Glamorgan. Brews: Renown Ale 4% alc by vol. Restoration 4.3% alc by vol. Recked 'Em 5.2 % alc by vol. Rejoice 6% alc by vol.

Eric's Half Century Ale (Wal) a beer brewed by McMullen of Hertfordshire to commemorate 50 years of service of Eric Mansfield (10,000 bottles only).

Eridge Vale (Eng) a strong dry cider sold by the wholesalers Landmark.

Erie Brewery (USA) a brewery based in Erie.

Erikli (Tur) a natural spring mineral water. Mineral contents (milligrammes per litre): Chlorides 10.65mg/l, Fluorides 0.088mg/l. pH 7.13

Erikois (Fin) a term denoting 'special' (in relation to beer).

Erinose (Eng) a tiny mite that forms blisters on flower clusters, leaves and grapes. Many vines are now resistant to it.

Erin's Isle (Ire) a double distilled Irish whiskey produced by Cooley in Dundalk.

Eriophyes vitis (Lat) the name given to the grape bud mite. See also Acariosis.

Eriosoma lanigera (Lat) see Apple Blight.

Eristoff Red (Austr) a 20% alc by vol. liqueur.

Eritire (Afr) one of three main wine-producing regions in Ethiopia. See also Abadir-Dukem and Guder.

Erkenbrecht (Ger) vineyard (Anb): Pfalz. (Ber): Mittelhaardt-Deutsche Weinstrasse. (Gro): Rebstöckel. (Vil): Neustadt an der Weinstrasse.

Erlabrunn (Ger) village (Anb): Franken. (Ber): Maindreieck. (Gro): Ravensburg. (Vin): Weinsteig.

Erlach (Ger) village (Anb): Baden. (Ber): Ortenau. (Gro): Fürsteneck. (Vin): Renchtäler.

Erlach (Switz) a red wine produced from the Bienne vineyards in Berne.

Erlau (Hun) a wine district that produces red and white wines.

Erlenbach (Ger) village (Anb): Württemberg. (Ber): Württembergisch Unterland. (Gro): Staufenberg. (Vin): Kazberg.

Erlenbach (Switz) a principal vineyard based in Zurich.

Erlenbach a. Main (Ger) village (Anb): Franken. (Ber): Mainviereck. (Gro): Not yet assigned. (Vin): Hochberg.

Erlenbach bei Marktheidenfeld (Ger) village (Anb): Franken. (Ber): Maindreieck. (Gro): Not yet assigned. (Vin): Krähenschnabel.

Erlen Brauerei (Switz) an independent brewery based in Glarus.

Erligheim (Ger) village (Anb): Württemberg. (Ber): Württembergisch Unterland. (Gro): Stromberg. (Vin): Lerchenberg.

Ermida (Port) a red wine produced by Real Companhía Vinícola do Notre de Portugal.

Ermine Ale (Eng) a 4.2% alc by vol. ale brewed by Oldershaw Brewery in Lincolnshire.

Ermita d'Espiells (Sp) a wine produced by Juvé y Camps in San Sadurní de Noya, Barcelona.

Ermitage (Fr) a light rosé wine produced in the eighteenth century. A blend of Auvernat red wine and light wines from the eastern Loire and Orléans (now no longer produced).

Ermitage (Fr) the French spelling of Hermitage in the Côtes de Rhône, southern France.

Ermitage (Switz) the name for the white French grape variety Marsanne.

Ermitage (Switz) a speciality of the Valais canton, a dry generous wine.

Ermitage [L'] (USA) a sparkling prestige cuvée produced by the Roederer Estate in Anderson Valley, California.

Ermitage du Pic Saint-Loup (Fr) a vineyard in A.C. Coteaux du Languedoc Pic-Saint-Loup. Produces: Cuvée Saint Agnès from 70% Syrah, 20% Grenache and 10% Mourvèdre grapes.

Ernie Els Wines (S.Afr) a winery (established 1999) based in the Stellenbosch, Western Cape. 72ha. Grape varieties: Cabernet sauvignon, Malbec, Merlot, Mourvèdre, Petit verdot, Pinotage, Shiraz. Labels: Labels: Engelbrecht-Els Proprietor's Blend, Ernie Els, Frontier, Guardian Peak. Website: http://www.ernieelswines.com

Ernsbach (Ger) village (Anb): Württemberg. (Ber): Kocher-Jagst-Tauber. (Gro): Kocherberg. (Vin): Flatterberg.

Ernst (Ger) village (Anb): Mosel-Saar-Ruwer. (Ber): Zell/Mosel. (Gro): Goldbäumchen. (Vins): Feuerberg, Kirchlay.

Ernst & CO Wines (S.Afr) a winery (established 2004) based in the Stellenbosch, Western Cape. 12ha. Grape varieties: Cabernet sauvignon, Chardonnay, Chenin blanc, Merlot, Sauvignon blanc. Labels: Imbazo, Timbili. Website: http://www.ernstco.co.za

Ernst & Julio Gallo (USA) see Gallo.

Erntebringer (Ger) grosslage (Anb): Rheingau. (Ber): Johannisberg. (Vils): Geisenheim, Johannisberg, Estate, Mittelheim, Winkel.

Erolzthaler (Switz) the name of a brandy-producing company based in Ormalingen. Produces apple-based brandies.

Eros Cocktail (Cktl) ⅓ measure Cointreau, ⅓ measure Calvados, ⅓ measure sweet vermouth, dash grenadine, dash lemon juice. Shake well over ice and strain into a cocktail glass.

Erpolzheim (Ger) village (Anb): Pfalz. (Ber): Mittelhaardt-Deutsche Weinstrasse. (Gro): Kobnert. (Vin): Kirschgarten.

Erpolzheim (Ger) village (Anb): Pfalz. (Ber): Mittelhaardt-Deutsche Weinstrasse. (Gro): Rosenbühl. (Vins): Goldberg, Keiselberg.

Errazuriz-Panquehue (Chile) a winery with vineyards in Aconcagua, Casablanca Valley and Mataquito Valley. Varietal wines sold under the Errazuriz Estate label. See also Viña Errazuriz. Labels include: La Cumbre, The Blend, Wild Ferment.

Ersatz Genever (Hol) a rare type of gin.

Ersingen (Ger) village (Anb): Baden. (Ber): Badische Bergstrasse/Kraichgau. (Gro): Hohenberg. (Vin): Klepberg.

Erste Kulmbacher Actienbrauerei (Ger) a brewery based in Kulmbach, west Germany. Brews Kulminator, one of the strongest beers in the world. see E.K.U.

Erste Lage (Aus) a term introduced in 1992 to denotes the 'First Site'.

Erster Nebel (Aus) the label for a red wine (Blaufränkisch and Nebbiolo blend) produced by the Triebaumer [Paul] winery, Rust, Burgenland.

Erstes Gewächs (Ger) first approved in 1997, denotes first growth wines based on calorific assessments made by the Geisenheim Institute. Must be 100% Riesling, dry, hand-picked from classified vineyards with a max. yield of 50 hl./ha. and with a potential alc by vol. of 12% min. Wines are tasted. Includes 18 villages and 49 vineyards. See also Vereinigung der Charta Weingüter.

Erusbacher Bräu (Switz) a brewery. (Add): Brauerei Sorg & Schädeli, Büttikerstrasse3, Villmergen CH-5612. Brews a variety of beers and lager. Website: http://www.erusbacher.ch 'E'mail: bier@erusbacher.ch

Erven Lucas Bols (Hol) a Dutch distiller of the sixteenth century who invented kümmel. see Bols.

Erzeugerabfüllung (Aus) produced and bottled by the producer.

Erzeuger Abfüllung (Ger) from the producer's own estate, produced and bottled by the producer. May

E

blend 25% of another vineyard and 15% of another grape or vintage with his own.

Erzgrupe (Ger) vineyard (Anb): Nahe. (Ber): Schloss Böckelheim. (Gro): Burgweg. (Vil): Bad Münster a. St.-Ebernburg.

Erzingen (Ger) village (Anb): Baden. (Ber): Bodensee. *see* Klettgau.

Es (Indo) ice.

Esa (Swe) yeast.

E.S.B. (Eng) *abbr*: Extra Special Bitter a 4.7% alc by vol. bitter beer brewed by the Berrow Brewery, Somerset.

E.S.B. (Eng) *abbr*: Extra Special Bitter 1055.75 O.G. Brewed by the Fullers Brewery in London. Export version 1060 O.G.

E.S.B. (Eng) *abbr*: Extra Special Bitter 1044.8 O.G. Brewed by the Mitchells Brewery of Lancaster.

ESB (USA) a beer brewed by the Bridgeport Brewing Company, Portland, Oregon.

Escalas (Sp) scales of the solera system.

Escalon (USA) the central region of the Central Valley in California. Produces dessert and table wines.

Escande (Fr) a Cognac producer. (Add): Domaine de Courpe, 17150 Mirambeau, près Cognac. 22ha. in Fins Bois. Produces Hors d'Age X.O. 25 years old.

Escanyavella (Sp) an alternative name for the Merseguera grape.

Escape (S.Afr) the label for a range of wines produced by the Kanu Wines winery, Stellenbosch, Western Cape.

Escarchardo (Port) an aniseed-flavoured liqueur containing sugar crystals in the bottle.

Escarpment (N.Z) a winery based in the Te Muna district of Martinborough, North Island. Grape varieties: Chardonnay, Pinot blanc, Pinot gris, Pinot noir. Label: Kupe.

Escava (Port) a depression made around the base of the vine in the Douro region. Fertiliser is put in and then covered over.

Escharchado (Port) *see* Escarchardo (an alternative spelling).

Eschbach (Ger) village (Anb): Baden. (Ber): Markgräflerland. (Gro): Lorettoberg. (Vin): Maltesergarten.

Eschbach (Ger) village (Anb): Pfalz. (Ber): Südliche Weinstrasse. (Gro): Herrlich. (Vin): Hasen.

Eschelbach (Ger) village (Anb): Baden. (Ber): Badische Bergstrasse/Kraichgau. (Gro): Stiftsberg. (Vin): Sonnenberg.

Eschelbach (Ger) village (Anb): Württemberg. (Ber): Württembergisch Unterland. (Gro): Lindelberg. (Vin): Schwobajörgle.

Eschenau (Ger) village (Anb): Württemberg. (Ber): Württembergisch Unterland. (Gro): Salzberg. (Vin): Paradies.

Eschenauer (Fr) a noted Bordeaux négociant-éleveur and owner of Châteaux Smith Haut-Lafitte and Rausan-Ségla (based in Martillac, Gironde).

Eschen Vineyard (USA) a vineyard based in Shenandoah Valley, Amador, California. 8.5ha. Grape variety: Zinfandel.

Escherndorf (Ger) village (Anb): Franken. (Ber):

Maindreieck. (Gro): Kirchberg. (Vins): Berg, Fürstenberg, Lump.

Escondido (USA) a wine district in San Diego, southern California which produces sparkling, table and dessert wines.

Escorial (Ger) a yellow or green herb liqueur similar to Chartreuse.

Escoussans (Fr) a commune in the Haut-Benauge, Bordeaux.

Escritório Comercial de Portugal (Bra) an information bureau on Portuguese wines. (Add): Avenida Paulista, 2001-6°. Andar-Salus 1604/7-Caixa Postal 22045-(CEP-01311), S. Paulo.

Escrivains (Fr) a vine pest in mediaeval times.

Escubac (Sp) a brandy-based cordial which contains sugar, liquorice, cinnamon, raisins and sugar. Also known as Ratafia.

Escudo Rosé (Port) a still, dry, pale rosé wine.

Escusseaux [Les] (Fr) a Premier Cru vineyard in the A.C. commune of Auxey-Duresses, Côte de Beaune, Burgundy 6.43ha.

Eselsberg (Ger) vineyard (Anb): Franken. (Ber): Maindreieck. (Gro): Kirchberg. (Vil): Stammheim.

Eselsberg (Ger) vineyard (Anb): Württemberg. (Ber): Württembergisch Unterland. (Gro): Kirchenweinberg. (Vil): Flein.

Eselsbuckel (Ger) vineyard (Anb): Pfalz. (Ber): Südliche Weinstrasse. (Gro): Guttenberg. (Vil): Nierderotterbach.

Eselshaut (Ger) vineyard (Anb): Pfalz. (Ber): Mittelhaardt-Deutsche Weinstrasse. (Gro): Meerspinne. (Vil): Mussbach.

Eselspfad (Ger) vineyard (Anb): Rheinhessen. (Ber): Bingen. (Gro): Abtey. (Vil): Appenheim.

Eselstreiber (Ger) vineyard (Anb): Rheinhessen. (Ber): Bingen. (Gro): Rheingrafenstein. (Vil): Eckelsheim.

Esgana Cão (Port) lit: 'dog strangler', a white grape variety grown in Bucelas, Douro and Vinho Verde. Also known as Esganoso, Sercial.

Esganose (Port) a white grape variety grown in the Vinho Verde region, also spelt Esganoso.

Esganoso (Port) a white grape variety grown in Peñafiel (a sub-region of the Vinho Verde), is also spelt Esganose. An alternative name for the Esgana Cão.

Eshald Well Brewery (Eng) a brewery (established 1828) as Henry Bentley & Cº. in Woodlesford, near Leeds. Noted for B.Y.B. (Bentley Yorkshire Bitter) and Timothy.

Eshkol Kosher Winery (S.Afr) a winery (established 2003) based in the Wellington, Western Cape. 15ha. Grape varieties: Cabernet sauvignon, Chardonnay, Chenin blanc, Cinsaut, Merlot, Pinotage, Ruby cabernet, Shiraz. Labels: Cellar Masters Choice, Eshkol, Kiddush, King Solomon. Website: http://www.eshkol.co.za

Eskdale (S.Afr) the label for a range of red wines produced by the De Zoete Inval Estate winery, Suider-Paarl, Western Cape.

Eskdale Winegrowers (N.Z) a winery. (Add): Main

Road, Eskdale, P.O. Box 77, Bayview, Napier. 4ha. Grape varieties: Cabernet sauvignon, Chardonnay, Gewürztraminer.

Esker (Can) a natural spring mineral water from Northern Quebec. Mineral contents (milligrammes per litre): Sodium 2.25mg/l, Calcium 20.9mg/l, Magnesium 3.3mg/l, Potassium 0.75mg/l, Bicarbonates 76.4mg/l, Sulphates 6.8mg/l, Nitrates 0.13mg/l.

Eskie (Austr) a nickname given to a portable Thermos flask™ used to keep beer cool.

Eskisehir-Nevsehir (Tur) a vineyard based in Middle Anatolia. Produces white wines.

Esk Valley (N.Z) a winery at 735 Main Road, Bay View, Hawkes Bay, North Island. 5.5ha. planted for the Glenvale Winery. Grape varieties include Cabernet, Malbec, Merlot and Chardonnay. The wines for Glenvale are sold under Esk Valley label. Other labels include The Terraces (45% Malbec, 35% Merlot, 20% Cabernet franc grapes) and Black Label.

Esmagamento (Port) the crushing of the grapes.

Esmeralda (Arg) a wine producer based at Córdoba, noted for St. Felician (a Cabernet-based wine).

Esola Vineyard (USA) a vineyard based in the Shenandoah Valley, Amador, California. 8.5ha. Grape variety: Zinfandel.

Espada (Sp) a method of vine training used in the Sherry region. *see* Spade.

Espadeiro (Sp) a black grape variety grown in Rías Baixas, Galicia.

Espadeiro de Basto (Port) a black grape variety grown in the Basto (a sub-region of Vinho Verde). Produces deep coloured red wines.

Espagna (Fr) an alternative name for the Cinsault grape.

Espalier (Fr) a method of vine training using a firm base with vertical shoots rising upwards from 2 horizontal arms.

Espar (Fr) a red grape variety also known as the Mourvèdre.

Esparato Grass (Sp) the grass used to make mats to lay out the Sherry grapes to dry in the sun in the Almijar in Andalusia.

Esparato Mats (Sp) *see* Esparato Grass.

Esparte (Austr) an old name for the Mourvèdre grape.

Esper (Ger) vineyard (Anb): Pfalz. (Ber): Mittelhaardt-Deutsche Weinstrasse. (Gro): Schnepfenflug vom Kellertal. (Vil): Kerzenheim.

Espinardo (Sp) a Vino de Mesa wine from Murcia, south-eastern Spain.

Espirito (Port) a brand of brandy from Fonseca.

Espirituoso (Port) a term used to denote a beverage that is high in alcohol (beer, wine, etc).

Espirraque (Sp) the name used to denote the third pressing that occurs in the small Jerez vineyards. *See also* Prensa.

Esplendido (Sp) a solera brandy with a minimum age of 3 years. Produced by Garvey S.A.

Esporão (Sp) a 370ha winery in Alentejo. Estate is in Reguengos de Monsaraz. White wines from Roupeiro, red wines from Periquita. Grape varieties: Aragonez, Arinto, Basterdo, Cabernet sauvignon, Periquita, Roupeiro, Touriga nacional and Trincadeira. Website: http://www.esporao.com

Espreso (Sp) espresso coffee.

Espresso (USA) an Italian coffee liqueur made in Ancona. *see* Illy Coffee Liqueur 30% alc by vol.

Espresso Coffee (It) a coffee drink made by forcing steam under pressure through the coffee grounds then topping with frothy hot milk. *See also* Cappuccino Coffee (often wrongly spelt Expresso). (Fr) = expresso, (Ger) = espresso, (Sp) = espreso.

Espresso Coffee Liqueur (It) a coffee flavoured liqueur made with espresso brewed coffee.

Espresso-Dek (Eng) the name given to a coffee made from a blend of 100% arabica beans from Twinings. Part of the Lavazza range of coffees.

Espresso Stout (Eng) a stout at 4.2% alc by vol. brewed by the Dark Star Brewing C°.

Esprit (Fr) the name given to a Cognac that is above 84% alc by vol.

Esprit (Aust) a sparkling natural fruit drink produced by Beckford's. *See also* Cafécino.

Esprit Cocktail (Cktl) 25mls (⅙ gill) Armagnac brandy, 20mls (⅙ gill) crème de noyau, 2 dashes (white) crème de cacao, stir over ice and strain into an ice-filled old-fashioned glass.

Esprit d'Amour (W.Ind) the local name for 'moonshine' on the island of St. Lucia.

Esprit de Font-Caude (Fr) a red wine produced from Syrah grapes by Domaine Font-Caude in Montpeyroux.

Esprit de France (Fr) an Armagnac producer. Is noted for Palvel Marmont and Des Seigneurs (a 3 year old).

Espumante (Port) sparkling.

Espumantes Naturais (Port) the traditional method (for sparkling wine production).

Espumoso (Sp) sparkling.

Esquerre-Bounoure (Fr) an Armagnac producer. (Add): Place des Maures, 32000 Auch. Based in the Haut Armagnac.

Esquitxagos (Sp) a white grape variety grown in Tarragona.

Essais (Fr) cups used in the middle-ages for tasting the royal wine to check if free from poisoning. Used by the royal taster.

Es Savi (Afr) a natural spring mineral water from Nouakchott, Mauritania. Mineral contents (milligrammes per litre): Sodium 20.8mg/l, Calcium 13.9mg/l, Magnesium 3.8mg/l, Potassium 6.2mg/l, Bicarbonates 66mg/l, Chlorides 14.5mg/l, Sulphates 6.2mg/l. pH 7.4

Esselborn (Ger) village (Anb): Rheinhessen. (Ber): Wonnegau. (Gro): Bergkloster. (Vin): Goldberg.

Essence (Eng) describes brewed coffee that has most of the moisture removed by evaporation. Often sold slightly sweetened. *see* Camp.

Essence of Lockjaw (USA) a slang term used in the eastern states for applejack brandy.

Essencia (Eng) *see* Eszencia.

Essenheim (Ger) village (Anb): Rheinhessen. (Ber): Nierstein. (Gro): Domherr. (Vins): Römerberg, Teufelspfad.

Essentuky N°17 (Rus) a natural spring mineral water. Mineral contents (milligrammes per litre): Sodium 3687.4mg/l, Calcium 139.2mg/l, Magnesium 70.8mg/l, Potassium 11.2mg/l, Bicarbonates 6246.4mg/l, Chlorides 2532mg/l, , Sulphates 2.8mg/l, Strontium 2mg/l, Iodine 1.3mg/l, Silicates 23mg/l, Boron 44.2mg/l, Barium 4mg/l, Hydrobromide 6mg/l.

Essentuky-2 Novaya (Rus) a natural spring mineral water brand.

Essentuky-4 (Rus) a natural spring mineral water brand.

Essenz (Hun) essence. *see* Tokaji Essenz.

Essex Ale (Eng) a bottled light ale 1030 O.G. brewed by the Ridley Brewery in Essex.

Essex Boys (Eng) a 3.5% alc by vol. ale brewed by the Crouch Vale Brewery, Essex.

Essex Porter (Eng) a winter warmer from Crouch Vale, Chelmsford, Essex.

Essig (Aus)(Ger) vinegar.

Essigstich (Ger) denotes a wine with a flavour of vinegar.

Essingen (Ger) village (Anb): Pfalz. (Ber): Südliche Weinstrasse. (Gro): Trappenberg. (Vins): Osterberg, Rossberg, Sonnenberg.

Esslingen (Ger) village (Anb): Württemberg. (Ber): Remstal-Stuttgart. (Gro): Weinsteige. (Vins): Ailenberg, Kirchberg, Lerchenberg, Schenkenberg.

Estaçao de Viticultura Amandio Galhano (Port) *abbr*: E.V.A.G. a research station for the whole of the Vinho Verde region.

Estaçao Vitivinícola da Bairrada (Port) formed in 1897, a government run experimental station.

Estaçao Vitivinícola de Beira Litoral (Port) the research station based in Anadia, Bairrada that advises wine growers and helps to improve techniques.

Estación de Viticultura y Enología (Sp) a body that administers the Consejo Regulador quality control of Spanish wines.

Estación de Viticultura y Enología de Navarra (Sp) *abbr*: EVENSA checks wines before D.O. seal is awarded. Also a research station (viticultural research and research into rootstock). Owns 5 vineyards.

Estagel (Fr) a red wine from the A.C. Côtes du Roussillon-Villages in south-eastern France.

Estàgio (Mad) the name given to the rest period that Madeira wine goes through after it leaves the Estufa.

Estàgio (Port) lit: 'wine in the making', vinification.

Estalagem (Port) a small hotel or country inn.

Estaminet (Fr) a small bar or café usually of a shabby nature that was popular in the nineteenth century.

Estancia Vineyard [La] (USA) a small vineyard based in Salinas Valley, Monterey, California (also has vineyards at Keyes Canyon Ranches, Paso Robles, Sao Luis Obispo). Grape varieties include: Cabernet sauvignon, Chardonnay and Pinot noir. Labels: Pinnacles Ranches, Stonewall Vineyard.

Estanciero (Arg) a red wine from the Mendoza region.

Estanza (Ger) pure 100% juice drinks with added vitamins. Flavours include apple, orange, pink grapefruit, summer fruit, ten fruit, vegetable blend.

Estate (Ger) village (Anb): Mosel-Saar-Ruwer. (Ber): Saar-Ruwer. (Gro): Scharzberg. (Vins): Scharzhofberger, Schlagengraben, Schlossberg.

Estate (Ger) village (Anb): Rheingau. (Ber): Johannisberg. (Gro): Deutelsberg. (Vin): Steinberg.

Estate (Ger) village (Anb): Rheingau. (Ber): Johannisberg. (Gro): Erntebringer. (Vins): Schloss Johannisberg, Schwartzenstein, Vogelsang.

Estate (Ger) village (Anb): Rheingau. (Ber): Johannisberg. (Gro): Honigberg. (Vin): Schloss Vollrads.

Estate Bottled (Eng) wine bottled by the vineyard owner, producer. *see* (Fr) = mise-en-bouteille-au-château/mise-en-bouteille-au-domaine, (Ger) = erzeuger abfüllung, (It) = nel'origine/imbottigliato alla'origine/messo in bottiglia.

Estate Cuvée (USA) the label for a red wine (Pinot noir) produced by the Sokol Blosser winery, Dundee Hills, Oregon.

Estates (W.Ind) a term applied to Jamaican and British West Indies sugar plantations where the best materials for distilling rum are obtained.

Estate Selection (USA) the label for a red wine (Pinot noir) produced by the Erath winery, Willamette Valley, Oregon.

Estate Vineyard (USA) a winery based in the Willamette Valley, Oregon. Grape variety: Pinot noir.

Estate Wine (S.Afr) the label for a red wine (Cabernet sauvignon, Merlot and Pinotage blend) produced by the Remhoogte Estate winery, Stellenbosch, Western Cape.

Estatuto de la Viña del Vino y de Los Alcoholes (Sp) 1970 regulations that apply to the whole of Spain. All wine produced must conform to these.

Esterhazy (Aus) a family-owned vineyard in Ausbruch and Burgenland. Produces white wines of fine quality.

Esterification (Eng) production of wine esters, helps soften old wines by reducing the acidity during the process of esterification.

Esterlin (Fr) a Champagne producer. (Add): 2 Rue du Château Mancy, 51530 Épernay. Coopérative-manipulant. 125 growers own 120ha. Produce vintage and non-vintage wines. Label: Cuvée de Prestige Elzévia (100% Chardonnay).

Esternay (Fr) a canton based in the Champagne district of Épernay has the Cru villages of Bethon and Chantemerle.

Esters (Eng) a combination of acids and alcohol which gives wines its bouquet.

Est! Est!! Est!!! (It) a D.O.C. white wine from the Latium region. Made from Trebbiano toscano 65%, Malvasia bianco toscana and Rossetto grapes. Vinification can take place within the production area and commune of Viterbo. Also known as Moscatelo. *see* Montefiascone and Bishop Fugger.

Esteva (Port) a red wine from the Douro produced by Ferreira (Port house), cold fermented.

Estève [Jacques] (Fr) a Cognac producer. 45ha.

Estevez [José] (Sp) a producer of solera brandies. Labels include: Sautu, Ruiz, Guadal, El Tutor, Don Feliz, Tartesio.

Estonian Viru Valge (Rus) a brand of vodka 40% alc by vol.

Estoril (Cktl) 25mls (⅕ gill) Bacardi White Label rum, 2 dashes orgeat syrup, 2 dashes lemon juice, dash amaretto. Shake well over ice and strain into a highball glass, top with soda water, dress with a slice of lemon and serve with straws.

Estoril (Port) a district in Carcavelhos, allowed to use that designation.

Estrada Winery (USA) a small winery based in the Mesilla Valley, New Mexico. Produces table wines.

Estrangey (Fr) an alternative name for the Malbec grape.

Estrangle-Chien (Fr) lit: 'dog strangler', an obscure name for the Mourvèdre grape in southern France.

Estrella [River] (USA) a large winery based in Shandon, San Luis Obispo, California. 291ha. Grape varieties: Cabernet sauvignon, Chardonnay, Johannisberg riesling, Muscat blanc and Syrah. Produces varietal wines.

Estrella-Damm (Sp) a brewery based in Barcelona. Brews Voll-Damm, Bock-Damm, Damm-Bier, Edel, Xibeca.

Estremadura (Port) a wine-producing region based north-west of Lisbon with over 50,000ha. of vineyards. Has the DOC wines: Alcobaça, Alenquer, Arruda, Bucelas, Carcavelos, Colares, Obidos, Encostas d'Aire, Lourinha and Torres Vedras. Produces red and full-bodied white wines.

Estufa (Mad) lit: 'stove', the name for a room where Madeira wine is held at a high temperature 45C when it is made to give it the special 'cooked' flavour.

Estufado (Mad) lit; 'to stew', the process of heating Madeira wine in an Estufa.

Estufa do Sol (Mad) houses where the Madeira is stored and heated by the sun only.

Estufagem (Mad) invented by a monk, it is a method of heating the wine of Madeira (see Estufa) to compensate for the loss of travelling that the wine obtained passing over the Equator many times giving the original wine its 'cooked' flavour.

Estuary (S.Afr) the label for a white wine (Sauvignon blanc) produced by the Mountain River Wines winery, Paarl, Western Cape.

ESX Best (Eng) a 4.3% alc by vol. bitter ale from Ridleys, Essex, also available in bottle.

Eszencia (Hun) a rare wine produced in exceptional years from the free-run juice of pure aszú affected grapes (100kgs of botrytised grapes required to produce 1litre of wine). *See also* Tokaji Aszú Eszencia. (Eng) = essencia.

Etalon (Ukr) a brewery (established 2002) based near the town of Kiev, brews mainly weissbier (wheat beer) 5% alc by vol..

Étampé (Fr) lit: 'stamped'/'branded', is associated with the marking of corks as a guarantee of the bottles contents.

Etaulier (Fr) an alternative name for the Malbec grape.

Etchart (Arg) the name given to a producer of varietal wines in Cafayate, Salta, north-west Argentina. Grape varieties: Cabernet sauvignon, Chardonnay, Torrontes.

Etchmiadzine (Arm) a white grape variety grown in Armenia.

Eternal Water (N.Z) a still natural spring mineral water from Whakatane, Bay of Plenty. Mineral contents (milligrammes per litre): Calcium 23mg/l, Magnesium 10mg/l, Bicarbonates 34mg/l, Silicates 85mg/l. pH 7.0

Et Fille (USA) a winery based in the Oregon State. Grape varieties include: Pinot noir. Labels: Palmer Creek Vineyard, Seven Springs.

Ethanal (Eng) CH_3CHO an aldehyde produced from oxidation of ethanol (molecular weight of 44 and S.G. of 0.78).

Ethanoic Acid (Eng) CH_3COOH a volatile acid found in wine.

Ethanol (Eng) C_2H_5OH the main alcohol produced by the yeast Sacchromyces ellipsoideus, converting grape sugar into Ethyl alcohol and CO_2 [molecular weight of 46 and a freezing point -133°C (-207.4°F) and boiling point 78.3°C (172.94°F). S.G. = 0.79044 at 20°C (68°F)]. *See also* Ethynol. *See also* Bioethanol.

Ethel Duffy Cocktail (Cktl) ⅓ measure Cointreau, ⅓ measure brandy, ⅓ measure white crème de menthe. Shake over ice and strain into a cocktail glass.

Ethelene (Eng) the hormone that makes fruit ripen.

Ethereal Oils (Eng) important for coffee aroma, are released during the roasting process.

Etherel (Eng) a term only applied to a superb wine with an excellent bouquet and character.

Etherium (Eng) a Victorian registered trade-mark, lead-free vitrious enamel glazed earthenware used for holding drinking water.

Ethers (Eng) the minute etheral qualities which form the bouquet of a wine or spirit together with the esters.

Ethiopian Coffee (Afr) the home of Arabica coffee, produces robust, tangy and winey coffee. The coffee is often roasted with cloves or cinnamon and stirred with a Tena-adam branch to add flavour. Drink with rock salt. e.g. Longberry Harar resembles Mocha and Ethiopian Mocha. (3 regions: Djimma, Kaffa and Sidamo). *See also* Abyssinian Coffee.

Ethiopian Mocha (Afr) a style of coffee that resembles Mocha.

Ethyl acetate (Eng) $CH_3COOC_2H_5$ an ester of ethyl alcohol and acetaldehyde. Has a smell similar to nail varnish. In strong concentrations is unpleasant and indicates that the wine is turning to vinegar. Apple, pear, peach and strawberry aromas.

Ethyl alcohol (Eng) C_2H_5OH see Ethanol, alcohol produced by the fermentation of yeast on sugar.

Ethylene glycol (Eng) caused the 1985 Austrian Wine Scandal. See also Diethylene Glycol.

Ethyl ethanoate (Eng) caused by acetic fermentation, gives a sweet vinegary aroma to the wine.

Ethyl mercaptan (Eng) occasionally found in wines, it is detected by a sewage related odour.

Ethyl pyrocarbonate (Eng) the result of a combination of ethyl alcohol and CO_2 during bottle fermentation and storage of sparkling wines. The more pyrocarbonate is formed the longer the bead (bubbles) will rise.

Etichetta (It) label.

Etichetta Nera (It) lit: 'black label', a brandy produced from equal quantities of pot and continuous stills by Vecchia Romagna (aged for 3–5 years).

Etienne Le Riche (S.Afr) a winery and wine cellar. (Add): P.O. Box 6295, Stellenbosch. Grape varieties: Cabernet sauvignon, Merlot.

Etiqueta (Sp) label.

Etiquetta Blanca (Sp) a 4 year old white wine produced by Marqués de Murrieta S.A. in the Rioja Alta.

Etiquetta Blanca (Arg) a white wine produced by Bodegas Suter.

Etiquetta Marron (Arg) a red wine produced by Bodegas Suter.

Etiquette (Fr) bottle label.

Etko (Cyp) a subsidiary wine producing company of Haggipavlu, based in Limassol, south-eastern Cyprus.

Etna (It) a red and white wines produced in the vineyards around Mount Etna in Sicily.

Etna Bianco (It) a D.O.C. white wine from Sicily. Made from the Carricante, Catarratto bianco, Minella bianca and Trebbiano grapes. Produced in 20 communes in the province of Catania. If has a minimum of 11.5% alc by vol. and produced from 80% Carricante grapes in the Milo commune then classed Superiore.

Etna Rosato (It) a D.O.C. rosé wine from Sicily. Made from Nerello mantellato and Nerello mascalese grapes. Produced in 20 communes in the province of Catania.

Etna Rosso (It) a D.O.C. red wine from Sicily. Made from Nerello mantellato and Nerello mascalese grapes. Produced in 20 communes in the province of Catania.

Étoffé (Fr) describes a well conserved wine with fine qualities.

Étoges (Fr) a Cru Champagne villages in the Canton de Montmort. District: Épernay.

Étoile (Fr) a vineyard district in the Jura. Noted for A.C. Vin Jaune and Vin de Paille wines. Grape varieties: Chardonnay and Savagnin.

Etoile (USA) a label for a white (Chardonnay) wine produced by Domaine Serene, Willamette Valley, Oregon.

Étoile Mousseux [L'] (Fr) a sparkling (Charmat method) A.C. wine produced in Étoile, Savoie.

Eton Blazer (Cktl) ⅘ measure dry gin, ⅕ measure kirsch, juice of ½ lemon, 4 dashes gomme syrup. Shake well over ice, strain into an ice-filled highball glass and top with soda water.

Étonner (Fr) casking, the pouring of liquids into a cask.

Étournelles (Fr) a Premier Cru vineyard in the A.C. commune of Gevrey-Chambertin, Côte de Nuits, Burgundy 2ha.

Étraire de l'Adui (Fr) a red grape variety formerly grown in Savoie and the southern Rhône. Also spelt Étraire de la Dui.

Étraire de la Dui (Fr) an alternative spelling of Étraire de l'Adui.

Étranger (Fr) an alternative name for the Malbec grape.

Et Rates (Eng) evapotranspiration rates that measure the vine's water uptake.

Étrechy (Fr) a Premier Cru Champagne village in the Canton de Vertus. District: Châlons. Red grapes (Premier Cru) and white grapes (Cru).

Etrigny (Fr) a commune in the Mâconnais region where Mâcon Supérieur may be produced.

Etschtaler (It) a German name used in the Südtirol region. see Valdadige Bianco or Valdadige Rosso.

Ettal Abbaye Brauerei (Ger) a brewery based in Ettal. Brews: Ettaler Curator.

Ettaler Curator Dunkler Doppelbock (Ger) a 7% alc by vol. dark double bock beer brewed by the Ettal Abbaye Brauerei, Ettal.

Ettalier (Ger) a herb liqueur made at Kloster Ettal, made in a green (dry) or yellow (sweet) style.

Ettaro (It) 1 hectare (2.471 acres).

Ettenheim (Ger) village (Anb): Baden. (Ber): Breisgau. (Gro): Burg Lichteneck. (Vin): Kaiserberg.

Ettenheim [ortsteil Wallburg] (Ger) village (Anb): Baden. (Ber): Breisgau. (Gro): Schutterlindenberg. (Vin): Kirchberg.

Etter (Switz) a noted eau-de-vie producer based in Zoug.

Ettolitro (It) 1 hectolitre or 100 litres.

Etude (USA) a small winery based in Carneros, California. Grape varieties: Cabernet sauvignon, Pinot noir.

Euan (Lat) a word used for Bacchus. See also Dionysos, Dionysus, Bassareus, Bromius, Eleleus, Euhan, Euhius, Euius, Lacchus, Lyaeus and Thyoneus.

Eubea (It) a winery based in the Basilicata region. Produces: D.O.C. Aglianico del Vulture.

Euboea (Gre) an island of central Greece. Produces red and white wines mainly for home consumption.

Eucario Gonzalez (Mex) a producer of tequila of same name.

Eucharist (Lat) a Christian religious ceremony (the last supper) during which wine is offered together with bread.

E

Euchariusberg (Ger) vineyard (Anb): Mosel-Saar-Ruwer. (Ber): Saar-Ruwer. (Gro): Scharzberg. (Vil): Konz.

Euchariusberg (Ger) vineyard (Anb): Mosel-Saar-Ruwer. (Ber): Saar-Ruwer. (Gro): Scharzberg. (Vil): Mennig.

Eudemis (Fr) the grape-berry moth, similar to the Cochylis. *see* Pyralis.

Eugenio Bustos (Arg) a wine-producing area in central Argentina.

Euhan (Lat) a word used for Bacchus. *See also* Dionysos, Dionysus, Bassareus, Bromius, Eleleus, Euan, Euhius, Lacchus, Lyaeus and Thyoneus.

Euhius (Lat) a word used for Bacchus. *See also* Dionysos, Dionysus, Bassareus, Bromius, Eleleus, Euhan, Euan, Euius, Lacchus, Lyaeus and Thyoneus.

Euius (Lat) a word used for Bacchus. *See also* Dionysos, Dionysus, Bassareus, Bromius, Eleleus, Euhan, Euan, Euhius, Lacchus, Lyaeus and Thyoneus.

Eulengrund (Ger) vineyard (Anb): Franken. (Ber): Steigerwald. (Gro): Kapellenberg. (Vil): Schmachtenberg.

Euler Landpils (Ger) a brand of lager beer.

Eumelan (USA) a red grape variety grown in the eastern states.

Eumryosu (Kor) beverage/drink.

Eurageot (Fr) the Bordeaux name for the Folle blanche grape.

Euregio (Hol) a natural spring mineral water from Pompput 4, Heerlen. Mineral contents (milligrammes per litre): Sodium 4mg/l, Calcium 68mg/l, Magnesium 8.4mg/l, Potassium 1.7mg/l, Bicarbonates 220mg/l, Chlorides <0.4mg/l, Sulphates 23mg/l.

Eureka (It) a still natural spring mineral water from Fonte della Madonnina. Mineral contents (milligrammes per litre): Sodium 33.5mg/l, Calcium 66.5mg/l, Magnesium 30.1mg/l, Potassium 3mg/l, Bicarbonates 311mg/l, Chlorides 59.6mg/l, Nitrates 24.3mg/l, Silicates mg/l. pH 7.3

Euroblend (Euro) table wine (vin de table and tafelwein) produced from a blend of E.C. wines. Usually blended and bottled in Germany.

Europadorf (Aus) *see* Alberndorf.

European Cellars (Eng) an Allied-Domecq and Whitbread-owned company. Labels include: Black Tower, Calvet, Don Cortez, Langenbach and Piemontello.

Euro Perl (Ger) a natural spring mineral water brand.

Euroquell (Ger) a natural spring mineral water from Schwollen RP. Mineral contents (milligrammes per litre): Sodium 8.4mg/l, Calcium 40.8mg/l, Magnesium 20.9mg/l, Potassium 0.8mg/l, Bicarbonates 157.4mg/l, Chlorides 14.9mg/l, Sulphates 28.2mg/l.

Eussenheim (Ger) village (Anb): Franken. (Ber): Maindreieck. (Gro): Rosstal. (Vin): First.

Eusson Poiré (Fr) a 2% alc by vol. perry that is slightly pink in colour.

Eutypa (Lat). *see* Eutypiose.

Eutypiose (Lat) a new fungal vine disease, known as the dead arm or dying arm in Australia. Discovered in France in 1977 in the Cognac region, 1988 in Burgundy. Also referred to as Eutypa. Attacks the vine where it has been pruned. Pervades the whole plant and there is no treatment at present.

Eva (Eng) an apple juice from Evia (Agencies), sold in 200mls slim packs and cartons.

Eva (Cktl) ¼ measure crème de violettes, ⅛ measure Caperatif, ⅛ measure orange juice, ⅛ measure lemon juice, ⅛ measure grenadine, dash Pernod. Shake over ice and strain into a cocktail glass.

Eva (Sp) a Solera gran reserva brandy produced by Barbadillo. *See also* Extra.

E.V.A. (Eng) *abbr*: English Vineyards Association, offers a seal of quality to English wines.

E.V.A.G. (Port) *abbr*: Estacao de Viticultura Amandio Galhano.

Evans (Cktl) 50mls (2 fl.ozs) rye whiskey, dash Curaçao, dash apricot brandy. Stir over ice and strain into a cocktail glass.

Evans and Tate (Austr) a winery. (Add): Swan St. West Swan, Western Australia 6055. 24ha. Grape varieties: Cabernet sauvignon, Chardonnay, Merlot, Sauvignon blanc, Sémillon, Shiraz, Traminer. Label: Redbrook.

Evan Williams (USA) an 8 year old Kentucky Bourbon whiskey produced by Old Evan Williams Distillery, Bardstown, Kentucky. Also produces a vintage single barrel version.

Evaporated Milk (Eng) a tinned (canned) milk, unsweetened, from which some of the water has been removed (evaporated).

Evaporation (Eng) occurs during maturation of a wine in cask, the ullage must be filled frequently to help reduce evaporation of wine (or spirits) and alcohol. Also prevents spoilage.

Évasivage (Fr) the de-suckering of the vine and general tidying up (usually done in May). Also known as Dédoublage, Ébourgonnage, Ébrossage, Échtonnage, Éjotonnement.

Evel (Port) a red wine produced by Real Companhía Vinícola do Norte de Portugal near Vila Real, Tras-os-Montes.

Evelita (Port) a wine produced in Lafoes.

Evenos (Fr) a commune of which part is in the A.C. Bandol, south-eastern France.

EVENSA (Sp) *abbr*: Estación de Viticultura y Enología de Navarra.

Evensen Winery (USA) a small winery based in the Napa Valley, California. 8.5ha. Grape variety: Gewürztraminer.

Evensong (Eng) a 5% alc by vol. a brewed by The Durham Brewery Ltd., County Durham.

Evenstead Reserve (USA) the label for a red wine (Pinot noir) produced by Domaine Serene, Willamette Valley, Oregon.

Évent (Fr) describes a wine that is over-oxidised (either in cask or bottle). *see* Gout d'Éventé.

Eventide Cellar (S.Afr) a winery based in the Wellington region. Grape varieties include: Cabernet sauvignon.

E

Everards Brewery (Eng) a brewery (established 1849). (Add): Everard Way, Castle Acres, Narborough, Leicester, Leicestershire LE19 5BY. Produces: Buddings 4.5% alc by vol., Old Original 1050 O.G. Red Crown 1034.5 O.G. Defiance 4.1% alc by vol. Nutcracker, Old Bill Winter Warmer, Daylight Robbery, 2XM, Lazy. Daze. *see* Old Burton Brewery and The Brunswick Brewing C°. Website: http://www.everards.co.uk 'E'mail: mail@everards.co.uk

Everards Beacon Bitter (Eng) a cask-conditioned bitter from Everards Brewery, Leicester.

Everest (Afr) a natural spring mineral water from Kenya.

Evergreen Cocktail (Cktl) 25mls (1 fl.oz) tequila, 10mls (½ fl.oz) green crème de menthe, 5mls (¼ fl.oz) Galliano, 75mls (3 fl.ozs) pineapple juice. Stir over ice, strain into a goblet and dress with a sprig of mint.

Everybody's Irish (Cktl) 25mls (⅛ gill) Irish whiskey, 1 barspoon green Chartreuse, 1 barspoon green crème de menthe. Stir over ice, strain into a cocktail glass and dress with an olive.

Evian (Fr) a still natural spring mineral water (established 1878) from Cachet Spring, Evian-lès-Bains (at the foot of Mont Blanc). Mineral contents (milligrammes per litre): Sodium 5mg/l, Calcium 78mg/l, Magnesium 24mg/l, Potassium 1mg/l, Bicarbonates 357mg/l, Chlorides 4.5mg/l, Sulphates 10mg/l, Nitrates 3.8mg/l, Silicates 13.5mg/l. pH 7.2 Website: http://www.evian.com

Évier (Fr) a fourteenth century large jug or pitcher.

Evita (Pol) a natural spring mineral water from Biskupiec. Mineral contents (milligrammes per litre): Sodium 5mg/l, Calcium 95.5mg/l, Magnesium 14.2mg/l, Potassium 1.9mg/l, Bicarbonates 336mg/l, Chlorides 8.5mg/l, Sulphates 30mg/l, Fluorides 0.3mg/l.

Evolution (Eng) a 4% alc by vol. cask ale from Darwin Brewery, Crook, County Durham.

Evora (Port) an I.P.R. wine within the I.P.R. Alentejo.

Ewer (Eng) a decanter with a handle (jug shaped). (Fr) = aiguiere.

Ewig Leben (Ger) grosslage (Anb): Franken. (Ber): Maindreieck. (Vil): Randersacker. (Vins). Marsberg, Pfülben, Sonnenstuhl, Teufelskeller.

Ex-Bier (Switz) an alcohol-free lager brewed by the Feldschlösschen Brauerei.

Ex-Cellars (Eng) means that duty and V.A.T. do not become payable until wine etc has been cleared from bond.

Excellence (Bel) a 7% alc by vol. cider from Cidre Stassen S.A. (part of Bulmer).

Excellence (Fr) an 1889 distilled Cognac produced by A.E. Dor in Jarnac 35% alc by vol.

Excellence (Jap) a brand of whiskey produced by Suntory.

Excellent (Austr) the brand-name of a locally produced brandy.

Excelsior (Eng) a 5.2% alc by vol. ale brewed by the Ossett Brewing C°. Ltd., West Yorkshire.

Excelsior (Fr) a winery based in Le Landreau, Muscadet Sèvre et Maine, Loire Atlantique. Produces Le Clos de Noelles an A.C. Muscadet Sèvre et Maine 30ha.

Excelsior (S.Am) a grade of coffee that produces a rich, strong, smooth brew. Grown in Colombia.

Excelsior Estate (S.Afr) a wine estate (established 1859) based in Ashton, Rombertson, Western Cape. 170ha. (Add): P.O. Aston, 6715, Robertson. Grape varieties: Cabernet sauvignon, Chardonnay, Merlot, Shiraz, Viognier. Labels: Paddock, Purebred, De Westsberg, Stonehurst. Owned by the De Wet Brothers. Website: http://www.excelsior.co.za

Excelsious Wines (S.Afr) a winery (established 1997) based in the Vrendal, Oliphants River, Western Cape. 112ha. Grape varieties: Cabernet sauvignon, Chardonnay, Merlot, Shiraz.

Excise (Eng) a tax on liquor produced in the country of production. *see* Duty, Customs and Excise.

Exciseman's 80 (Scot) a 4.6% alc by vol. 80/- ale brewed by Broughton Ales Ltd., Lanarkshire.

Excise Officer's Dram (Eng) produced by Cromdale (a subsidiary of Macallan) from a blend of malt whiskies. Sold in a 250mls hip flask-style bottle 40% alc by vol.

Exclusiv (Ger) the name given to describe a premium beer of the Astra brand produced by the Bavaria-St-Pauli Brauerei in Hamburg.

Exclusive [L'] (Fr) special numbered limited edition cuvée of Champagne produced for the year 2000 by Ruinart. Produced from a blend of six Grand Cru vintage Chardonnays. The magnums are sold in a silver plate holder.

Excoriose (Lat) a fungal disease that attacks the branches of the vine which is treated by using copper suphate.

Exeter Old Bitter (Eng) a 4.8% alc by vol. bitter brewed by the Exe Valley Brewery, Silverton, Devon.

Exe Valley Bitter (Eng) a 3.7% alc by vol. bitter from Exe Valley Brewery, Silverton, Devon.

Exe Valley Brewery (Eng) a brewery (established 1984). (Add): Silverton, Exeter, Devon EX5 4HF. Brews: Autumn Glory 4.5% alc by vol., Barons Dark 4.1% alc by vol., Barons Hopsit 4.1% alc by vol., Curate's Choice 4.8% alc by vol., Devon Dawn 4.5% alc by vol., Devon Glory 4.7% alc by vol., Devon Summer 3.9% alc by vol., Dob's Best Bitter 4.1% alc by vol., Exe Valley Bitter 3.7% alc by vol., Exeter Old Bitter 4.8% alc by vol., Mr. Shepherds Crook 4.7% alc by vol., Spring Beer 4.3% alc by vol., Winter Glow 6% alc by vol. Website: http://www.siba-southwest.co.uk/breweries/exvalley/index.ttm 'E'mail: exevalley@supanet.com

Exhibition (Eng) a bottled brown ale 1042 O.G. Brewed by the Harvey Brewery in Sussex.

Exhibition (Eng) a cask-conditioned/keg bitter 1042 O.G. Brewed in Newcastle.

Exhibition (Eng) a cask-conditioned ale 1051 O.G. brewed by the Smiles Brewery in Bristol.

Exhibition (Wal) a cask-conditioned ale 1054 O.G. brewed by the Silverthorne Brewery, South Wales.

Exhibition (Wal) a light mild 1034 O.G. brewed by the Border Brewery in North Wales.

Exhibition Cider (Eng) an 8.2% alc by vol. strong dry cider from Taunton Cider Company in Somerset.

Exigence d'Yon Mau (Fr) an A.C. Bordeaux Supérieur, Bordeaux. Grape varieties: Cabernet sauvignon 50%, Merlot 50%.

Exit (Eng) a bitter lemon drink claimed to clear alcohol from the system twice as fast as normal.

Exmoor (Eng) the name given to a range of beers produced at the Golden Hill Brewery, Wiveliscombe, Somerset.

Exmoor Ale (Eng) a cask-conditioned bitter 3.8% alc by vol (1039 O.G.) brewed by the Exmoor Ales Golden Hill Brewery in Somerset.

Exmoor Ales Ltd (Eng) a brewery (established 1980). (Add): Golden Hill Brewery, Wiveliscombe, Taunton, Somerset TA4 2NY. Brews: Exmoor Ale 3.8% alc by vol., Exmoor Beast 6.6% alc by vol., Exmoor dark (1042 O.G.), Exmoor Exmas 5% alc by vol., Exmoor Fox 4.2% alc by vol., Exmoor Gold 4.5% alc by vol., Exmoor Hart 4.8% alc by vol., Exmoor Hound Dog 4% alc by vol., Exmoor Stag 5.2% alc by vol., Exmoor Wildcat 4.4% alc by vol. Also Exmoor 1000. Website: http://www.exmoorales.co.uk 'E'mail: info@exmoorales.co.uk

Exmoor Beast (Eng) a dark winter warmer ale 6.6% alc by vol. from Exmoor Ales Golden Hill Brewery, Wiveliscombe, Somerset.

Exmoor Dark (Eng) a 1042 O.G. bitter-sweet ale brewed by the Exmoor Ales Golden Hill Brewery, Wiveliscombe, Somerset.

Exmoor Exmas (Eng) a strong ruby beer brewed from 100% whole malt mash 1058 O.G. (6% alc by vol.) brewed for Christmas 1993 by the Exmoor Ales Golden Hill Brewery, Wiveliscombe, Somerset. Modern version at 5% alc by vol.

Exmoor Fox (Eng) a 4.2% alc by vol. ale brewed by the Exmoor Ales Golden Hill Brewery, Wiveliscombe, Somerset.

Exmoor Gold (Eng) a light gold in colour, strong smooth bitter beer. Brewed at the Exmoor Ales Golden Hill Brewery in Wiveliscombe, Somerset. Draught at 4.5% alc by vol. bottled at 5% alc by vol. Originally known as Exmoor 1000.

Exmoor Hart (Eng) an ale 4.8% alc by vol. brewed by the Exmoor Ales Golden Hill Brewery, Wiveliscombe, Somerset.

Exmoor Hound Dog (Eng) an ale 4% alc by vol. brewed by the Exmoor Ales Golden Hill Brewery, Wiveliscombe, Somerset.

Exmoor Stag (Eng) an ale 5.2% alc by vol. brewed by the Exmoor Ales Golden Hill Brewery, Wiveliscombe, Somerset.

Exmoor 1000 (Eng) produced at the Exmoor Ales Golden Hill Brewery, Wiveliscombe, Somerset as it was the 1000th brew since opening in 1979, now known as Exmoor Gold.

Exmoor Wildcat (Eng) a 4.4% alc by vol. brown ale brewed by the Exmoor Ales Golden Hill Brewery, Wiveliscombe, Somerset.

Expédier en Fût (Fr) a term used to describe a wine being despatched into the wood (cask).

Explorer (Eng) a bottled and draught beer at 4.3% alc by vol brewed by the Adnams Brewery.

Explorer Vodka (Den) a vodka brand-name used by Aktiebolaget Vin and Spritcentralem.

Exportacien (Sp) to export.

Exportador (Sp) an exporter.

Export Akvavit (Den) a Madeira-flavoured akvavit.

Export Ale (Scot) a Scottish export ale 4% alc by vol. from Maclay's in Alloa. *see* Scotch Ale.

Export Beer (Eng) the term used for premium beers that may or may not be exported. Usually bottled beers. *see* Export Beer (Scot)

Export Beer (Ger) nothing to do with the export trade, it refers to the strength of the beer 12.5% alc by vol–14% alc by vol.

Export Beer (Scot) the name for either bottled or cask-conditioned ales which may be exported. *see* Eighty Shilling Export [80/-].

Export Cassis (Fr) another name for the apéritif Vermouth-Cassis.

Export Gold (Eng) a barley wine 1070 O.G. brewed by Watney Mann, London.

Exportøl (Den) export ale, an alternative name for Elefantøl.

Expresiones (Arg) the label for a range of red wines (Cabernet sauvignon and Malbec/Cabernet sauvignon and Shiraz blends) produced by the Finca Flichman winery in the Mendoza region.

Expresivo (Arg) the label for a red wine (part of the BenMarco range) produced by the Dominio del Plata winery in the Mendoza region.

Express Cocktail (Cktl) 25mls (1fl.oz) Scotch whisky, 25mls (1fl.oz) sweet vermouth, dash orange bitters. Stir over ice and strain into a cocktail glass.

Expressed Juice (Eng) the must after pressing the juice.

Expresso (Fr) espresso coffee.

Expresso Coffee (USA) the American way of spelling of Espresso coffee.

Exquitxagos (Sp) an alternative name for the Merseguera grape.

eXSB (Eng) a 5.5% alc by vol. bitter ale brewed by the Bazens Brewery, Greater Manchester.

Exshaw (Fr) a Cognac producer. (Add): Exshaw S.A., 127 Boulevard Denfert-Rochereau 16100 Cognac. Produces Cognac Exshaw N° 1. and Cognac Exshaw Age d'Or. Is part of Otard.

Extaler (Ger) a natural spring mineral water from Exertal, Rinteln. Mineral contents (milligrammes per litre): Sodium 10.3mg/l, Calcium 350mg/l, Magnesium 56.7mg/l, Potassium 1.6mg/l, Bicarbonates 265mg/l, Chlorides 14.9mg/l, Sulphates 864mg/l, Fluorides 0.1mg/l, Nitrates 7mg/l.

Extinction Ale (Eng) an 8.3% alc by vol. ale brewed by Darwin Brewery, Crook, County Durham. Made using a lost yeast and recipe originally used by Scarborough and Whitby Brewery.

Extra (Fr) on an Armagnac label denotes a minimum of 5 years of age.

E

Extra (Fr) a Cognac term found on a brandy label, denotes that the brandy has been at least 75 years in cask.

Extra (Scot) the name given to a keg lager 1044 O.G. brewed by Tennent's Brewery.

Extra (Sp) a solera gran reserva brandy produced by Barbadillo. *See also* Eva.

Extra Ale (Scot) a strong ale 1085 O.G. brewed by Borve House in the Isle of Lewis.

Extra Belle Réserve (Fr) a Cognac produced by Monnet.

Extra Bitter (Eng) the former name of the Dutchy keg bitter 1044 O.G. brewed by the St. Austell Brewery in Cornwall.

Extra Choice Old Tawny (Port) a fine old Tawny Port from Cockburn, Martinez and Mackenzie.

Extract (Eng) in wine the sugar-free extract matter left after the wine has been fined, is also called Total Extract.

Extracteur à Bouchon (Fr) cork extractor.

Extra Droog (S.Afr) extra dry.

Extra Dry (S.Afr) a wine classification, must contain 2.5 grammes per litre of sugar or less. *See also* Extra-Sec and Extra Droog.

Extra Dry Gin (USA) denotes a gin that has drier-tasting flavourings (botanicals) than dry gin.

Extra Gammal (Swe) a Swedish Punsch 55.5% alc by vol. Produced by Aktiebolaget Vin and Spritcentralem.

Extra Gold (USA) a 5% alc by vol. premium lager from Coors, Colorado.

Extrait de Malt (Fr) malt extract.

Extrait des Pins (Fr) a pine needle-flavoured liqueur produced by Clacquesin. Also known as Sapindor or Liqueur des Pins.

Extra Light (S.Afr) the label for a white wine (Crouchen and Hanepoot blend) produced by the Simonsvlei International winery, Suider-Paarl, Western Cape.

Extra Light Beer (Eng) a cask-conditioned/keg bitter 1031 O.G. brewed by Bass Breweries for the north of England.

Extra Light Beer (USA) a very low alcohol beer (see Light Beer), has a strong hop flavour.

Extra Light Bitter (Eng) a low alcohol bitter 0.9% alc by vol. brewed by Youngs of London.

Extralite (Eng) a low carbohydrate ale 1030 O.G. brewed by the Wadworth Brewery in Wiltshire.

Extra Nº 9 (Fr) a 1914 distilled Cognac produced by A.E. Dor. Stored in demi-johns after 50 years of ageing.

Extra Old (W.Ind) the label of a rum (blend of 5–10 years old) from Mount Gay, Barbados.

Extra Pale Ale (Eng) a 4.2% alc by vol. pale ale brewed by the Nottingham Brewery, Nottinghamshire.

Extra Parés Balt (Sp) a cava wine from the Cavas Parés Balt, Pachs de Penedés.

Extra Reserve Madeira (Mad) blended, youngest wine, must be a minimum of 15 years old after

Estufagem. If grape variety stated must contain 85% of named variety.

Extra Sec (Fr) denotes less dry than brut.

Extra-Sec (S.Afr) a wine classification, must contain 2.5 grammes of sugar per litre or less. Also Extra dry.

Extra Special Bitter (Eng) a bottled bitter 1038 O.G. brewed by the Simpkiss Brewery, Brierley Hill in Staffordshire.

Extra Special Bitter (Eng) *see* E.S.B.

Extra Viejo (Arg) extra old.

Extremadura (Sp) a region of central Spain on the Portuguese border. Covers the provinces of Cáceres and Badajoz. Makes up part of the Meseta Central. Home to the Vino de la Tierra wines of Cañamero, Montánchez (Cáceres), Matanegra, Ribera Alta de Guadiana, Ribera Baja de Guadiana, Tierra de Barros (Badajoz). Vino Comarcal areas of Azuaga, La Serena (Budajoz), Cilleros (Cáceres). Vino de Mesa wine of Valencia de Alcántar (Cáceres).

Extrísimo (Sp) a sweet white wine from Masía Bach in the Penedés, Catalan.

Eyachtal-Quelle (Ger) a natural spring mineral water from Horb-Mühringen, BW.

Eyelids of Buddha (Chi) an old Chinese name for tea (leaves are shaped like eyelids).

Eye of a Newt (Eng) a special ale brewed by the Ash Vine Brewery for Hallowe'en.

Eye-Opener (Cktl) 20mls (⅛ gill) each of liqueur brandy, crème de menthe and absinthe, 1 whole egg. Shake well over ice, strain into a cocktail glass and top with a pinch of cayenne pepper.

Eye Opener Cocktail (Cktl) 1 measure white rum, 1 egg yolk, 1 barspoon each of Pernod, Cointreau and crème de cacao (white), teaspoon gomme syrup. Shake over ice and strain into a flip glass.

Eye Openers (USA) an early slang term for cider and beer, also for an alcoholic drink taken early in the morning.

Eye Water (Eng) the nickname for gin from the London printers.

Eylenbosch Brasserie (Bel) a brewery based in Schepdaal in northern Belgium, noted for dry lambic-style beers.

Eynesbury Giant (Eng) a strong bitter brewed by the Paines Brewery in St. Neots, Cambridgeshire. Named after a local giant caller James Toller who was 8 foot 6 inches tall.

Eyrie Vineyards (USA) a winery (established 1966) in Willamette Valley, Oregon in the Pacific North-West. 20.5ha. Grape varieties: Chardonnay, Muscat Ottonel, Pinot gris, Pinot meunier and Pinot noir. Produces varietal wines.

Eyrons (Fr) a commune in the A.C. Côtes de Blaye in north-eastern Bordeaux.

Eyzines (Fr) a commune in the A.C. Graves district of south-western Bordeaux.

Ezerja (Hun) an alternative spelling of the Ezerjó grape.

Ezerjó (Hun) the principal white grape of the Mór region. Produces dry golden wines. e.g. Móri ezerjó.

FAB (Eng) *abbr*: **F**lavoured **A**lcoholic **B**everage, describes a wide variety of drinks usually sold in bottled form. *see* Bacardi Breezer, Smirnoff Mule, VK, Metz, Hooch, WKD.

Fabbrica [di Birra] (It) brewery.

Faber (Ger) a white grape variety, a cross between Weissburgunder and Müller-Thurgau, is early ripening and gives a fruity muscat-type bouquet, also known as the Faberrebe.

Faber (Ger) a noted producer of sekt made by the cuve close method.

Faberrebe (Ger) *see* Faber.

Fabia (It) a sparkling natural spring mineral water from Fabia. Mineral contents (milligrammes per litre): Sodium 13.98mg/l, Calcium 133.9mg/l, Magnesium 5.4mg/l, Potassium 1.21mg/l, Bicarbonates 381.3mg/l, Chlorides 25.58mg/l, Sulphates 28.44mg/l, Nitrates 18mg/l, Silicates 8.98mg/l, Strontium 0.91mg/l. pH 7.42

Fabrini (It) a producer of sparkling (metodo tradizionale) wines Verdicchio, Vernaccia di Serrapetrona and sparkling red wine in the Marche region.

Fabrizia (It) a still and sparkling natural spring mineral water from Passo Abate-Serricella (green label: sparkling/blue label: still). Mineral contents (milligrammes per litre): Sodium 9.7mg/l, Calcium 4mg/l, Magnesium 1.58mg/l, Potassium 0.65mg/l, Bicarbonates 23.79mg/l, Chlorides 11.01mg/l, Sulphates 8.2mg/l, Nitrates 5.97mg/l, Silicates 4.67mg/l. pH 6.4

Fabrizio Bianchi (It) a red I.G.T. wine produced from 100% Sangiovese grapes by Castello di Monsanto in Tuscany.

Fabuloso (Sp) a 3-year-old brandy produced by Palomino y Vergara S.A.

Facama Vineyard (S.Am) a vineyard based in Inca, Peru. Produces everyday table wines.

Facers Brewery (Eng) a brewery (established 2003). (Add): Unit 6, Knoll Street Ind Park, Knoll street, Salford, Greater Manchester M7 2BL. Brews: 50 Degrees of Bitterness 4% alc by vol., Anthem 3.9% alc by vol., Cliff Bier 5.2% alc by vol., Cold Comfort 3.9% alc by vol., Head Strong 4.9% alc by vol., Jas Summer Ale 3.9% alc by vol.'E'mail: dave@facers.co.uk

Faces of Africa (S.Afr) the label for a range of wines (Colombard & Chardonnay), (Cinsaut & Pinotage) produced by the Douglas Green winery.

Fachbach (Ger) village (Anb): Mittelrhein. (Ber): Rheinburgengau. (Gro): Lahntal. (Vin): Sites not yet chosen.

Fächern (Ger) vineyard (Anb): Mosel-Saar-Ruwer. (Ber): Zell/Mosel. (Gro): Weinhex. (Vil): Niederfell.

Facon [La] (Fr) a traditional French lager 1046 O.G. brewed by Groupe Saint Arnould Brasseries at Lille, Boulogne and Saint Ormer.

Façon de Venise (Fr) lit: 'in the fashion of Venice', name for wine glasses made in France, Holland, England, etc (around 1500–1700 A.D).

Faconnières [Les] (Fr) a Premier Cru vineyard in the A.C. commune of Morey-Saint-Denis, Côte de Nuits, Burgundy 1.7ha.

Factory House [The] (Port) based in Oporto, the building was built in 1870's for the Port Factors: the British who were shipping Port to the U.K. Now used for meetings of the Port shippers (traditionally male only). *see* Feitoria Inglesa. Members are Cockburn Smithes & Cia Lda., Croft & Cia Lda., Delaforce Sons & Cia Vinhos S.A.R.L., Graham W. & J. & C°., Guimaraens (Vinhos) S.A.R.L., (Fonseca's Port), Martinez Gassiot & Cia Lda., Robertson Brothers & Cia Lda., Sandeman & Cia Lda., Silva & Cosens Ltd. (Dows Port), Taylors, Fladgate & Yeatman, Vinhos S.A.R.L. and Warres & Cia Lda.

Fad (Den) in association with beer and lager denotes draught.

Fad (Ger) insipid.

Fadøl (Den) draught beer.

Fagins (Eng) a 4.1% alc by vol. ale brewed by the Itchen Valley Brewery, Hampshire.

Fagotière [La] (Fr) the label of a Châteauneuf-du-Pape produced by Chastan (Pierry) at Domaine Palestor, 84100 Orange, southern Rhône.

Fahnbach (Aus) a vineyard site based on the banks of the River Kamp situated in the Kamptal region.

Fahnberg (Aus) a vineyard site based on the banks of the River Kamp situated in the Kamptal region.

Fahr (Ger) village (Anb): Franken. (Ber): Maindreieck. (Gro): Kirchberg. (Vins): Assorted parts of vineyards.

Fahrberg (Ger) vineyard (Anb): Mosel-Saar-Ruwer. (Ber): Zell/Mosel. (Gro): Weinhex. (Vil): Kattenes.

Fahrberg (Ger) vineyard (Anb): Mosel-Saar-Ruwer. (Ber): Zell/Mosel. (Gro): Weinhex. (Vil): Kobern-Gondorf.

Fahrberg (Ger) vineyard (Anb): Mosel-Saar-Ruwer. (Ber): Zell/Mosel. (Gro): Weinhex. (Vil): Moselsürsch.

Faible (Fr) thin wine, in Cognac refers to a weak brandy added to new Cognac to help 'reduce' it down.

F

Failsworth Brewery (Eng) a brewery (established 1982) in Manchester, Lancs. Produces cask-conditioned Failsworth Original 1037 O.G. and Failsworth Strong 1044 O.G.

Fair and Warmer (Cktl) ⅓ measure dark rum, ⅓ measure Italian vermouth, ⅙ measure Curaçao. Stir over ice and strain into a cocktail glass.

Fairbank Cocktail (Cktl) 30mls (¼ gill) dry gin, 30mls (¼ gill) French vermouth, 2 dashes Noyau Rose, 2 dashes orange bitters. Stir over ice, strain into a cocktail glass and add a squeeze of lemon peel juice on top.

Fairbank's Cocktail (Cktl) 25mls (1fl.oz) rye whiskey, 5mls (¼ fl.oz) apricot brandy, dash Angostura. Stir over ice and strain into an old-fashioned glass.

Faire Champoreau (Fr) a slang term to denote a Cognac added to a café au lait (coffee with milk).

Fairfield Vineyards (Austr) a vineyard. (Add): Murray Valley Highway, Rutherglen, Victoria. Grape varieties: Trebbiano, Cabernet sauvignon, Durif, Shiraz.

Fairhall Dry Red (N.Z) a red wine produced by Montana Wines, the country's most popular red wine, made from a blend of Cabernet sauvignon and Pinotage grapes. Has a dry aroma and full, fruity sweetness.

Fairhead (S.Afr) the label for a red wine (Chenin blanc 40% Viognier 60% blend) produced by the Joostenberg Wines winery, Paarl, Western Cape.

Fairlie's Light Highland Liqueur (Scot) a 24% alc by vol. liqueur produced by Glenturret.

Fairlight (Ger) a 2.9% alc by vol. light pilsner beer brewed by Krombacher Brauerei, Kreuztal-Krombach.

Fairtrade Agreement (World) an organisation that ensures that growers receive a fair price for their crops including wine-producing grapes, coffee, tea, etc.

Fairvalley Farmworkers Association (S.Afr) a winery (established 1997) based in Paarl, Western Cape. 18ha. Grape varieties: Chenin blanc, Pinotage, Sauvignon blanc.

Fairview (S.Afr) a large wine estate and winery (established 1693) based in the Suider-Paarl, Coastal Region 300ha (also has vineyards in Swartland). (Add): Box 583, Suider-Paarl 7625. Grape varieties: Barbera, Cabernet sauvignon, Carignan, Chardonay, Chenin blanc, Gamay, Grenache, Malbec, Mourvèdre, Nebbiolo, Pinotage, Primotivo, Sangiovese, Sémillon, Shiraz, Viognier, Zinfandel. Labels: Agostinelli, Akkerbos, Beacon Block, Bored Doe, Caldera, Charles Gerard, Chevre Chardonnay, Cyril Back Goat d'Afrique, Goat Door, Goats do Roam in Villages, Goats du Roam, Cyril Back, Jakkalsfontein, La Beryl, Oom Pagal, Pegleg, Primo, Red Seal, Weisser Riesling. Also marketed as The Goats do Roam Wine Company. Website: http://www.fairview.co.za

Fairy Belle (Cktl) ¾ measure dry gin, ¼ measure apricot brandy, 1 barspoon grenadine, 1 egg white. Shake over ice and strain into a cocktail glass.

Faisca (Port) the brand-name of a carbonated rosé wine produced by J.M. da Fonseca.

Faithful Hound (S.Afr) the label for a red wine (Cabernet sauvignon 53% and Merlot 34% plus Cabernet franc, Malbec and Shiraz blend) produced by the Mulderbosch Vineyards winery, Stellenbosch, Western Cape.

Faito (It) a sparkling natural spring mineral water from Faito. Mineral contents (milligrammes per litre): Sodium 12mg/l, Calcium 73mg/l, Magnesium 18mg/l, Potassium 9mg/l, Bicarbonates 311.1mg/l, Chlorides 16.6mg/l, Sulphates 12.6mg/l, Fluorides 0.2mg/l, Nitrates 1.6mg/l, Silicates 20.1mg/l. pH 7.5

Faiveley [J.] (Fr) a négociant-éleveur (established 1825) based at Nuits-Saint-Georges, Côte de Nuits, Burgundy. Has vineyards in the Côte d'Or, Givry (Champ-Lalot) and Mercurey. Website: http://www.bourgognes-faiveley.com

Fajouet Jean Voisin (Fr) the second wine of Château Voisin. Grand Cru Saint-Émilion. See also Voisin (Jean).

Fal (Scot) the Scots gaelic for the spade that is used to cut peat from the peat bogs. (Ire) = slane.

Fala (S.E. Asia) a natural spring mineral water from Taiwan.

Falanda (Sp) the name given to an Oloroso Sherry produced by Harveys of Bristol.

Falandy-Liandry (Fr) a Cognac producer. (Add): 6 Rue Barbezieux, 16100 Cognac.

Falanghina Greco (It) a white grape variety with high acidity used in the production of white Falerno made in Campi Flegrei, Mondragone, Capua or Sessa Aurunca in Campania.

Falaso (It) the label for a white wine from the Cantina Valpantena, Verona.

Falchini [Roberto] (It) a noted sparkling (metodo tradizionale) wine producer based in Tuscany.

Falcoaria (Port) a red wine produced by Quinta do Casal Branco from a blend of Trincadeira preta and Castelão francês grapes.

Falcon (Pak) a natural spring mineral water (established 1999) from Lahore. Mineral contents (milligrammes per litre): Sodium 28mg/l, Calcium 50mg/l, Magnesium 46mg/l, Potassium 2.4mg/l, Bicarbonates 152mg/l, Chlorides 6mg/l, Sulphates 20mg/l, Fluorides 0.8mg/l, Nitrates 0.6mg/l. pH 7.8

Falcon (It) a beer brewed by the Falcon Brewery in Sicily.

Falcon Ales (Eng) the brand-name for a range of beers brewed by the Isle of Man Breweries (formerly the Falcon Brewery).

Falcon Brewery (Eng) now known as the Isle of Man Breweries, Isle of Man.

Falcon Lager (Eng) a canned lager 1032 O.G. brewed by Allied Breweries solely for Victoria wine shops.

Falerio dei Colli Ascolani (It) a D.O.C. white wine from the Marches. Made from 80% Trebbiano toscano with Malvasia toscano, Passerina, Pecorino, Pinot bianco and Verdicchio grapes.

F

Falerno (It) a modern product of the ancient Falernum (red version: Aglianico grapes/white version: Falanghina grapes).

Falerno Del Massico Bianco Vigna Caracci (It) a white wine produced from 100% Falanghina grapes by Villa Matilde in Campania.

Falernum (It) a favourite wine of ancient Rome. Produced between Rome and Naples. Was a heavy yellow wine. *See also* Falerno.

Falernum (W.Ind) a flavouring syrup for drinks (3% alc by vol) made of syrup, ginger, spices and limes. Clear, it is used on the Isle of Barbados in the British West Indies.

Falesco (It) a winery based in the Umbria region. Label: Vitiano.

Falkenberg (Ger) vineyard (Anb): Mosel-Saar-Ruwer. (Ber): Bernkastel. (Gro): Michelsberg. (Vil): Piesport.

Falkenberg (Ger) vineyard (Anb): Nahe. (Ber): Schloss Böckelheim. (Gro): Paradiesgarten. (Vil): Alsenz.

Falkenberg (Ger) vineyard (Anb): Rheinhessen. (Ber): Nierstein. (Gro): Güldenmorgen. (Vil): Dienheim.

Falkenbergquelle (Ger) a natural spring mineral water from Löhne. Mineral contents (milligrammes per litre): Sodium 25mg/l, Calcium 218mg/l, Magnesium 59mg/l, Potassium 2.6mg/l, Bicarbonates 297mg/l, Chlorides 43mg/l, Sulphates 525mg/l.

Falken Brauerei (Switz) a brewery based in Schaffhausen. Part of the Interbera group.

Falken Brewery (Swe) a brewery based in Falkenberg in south-western Sweden, the second largest brewery in the country.

Falkenstein (Aus) a wine district in the region of Niederösterreich. Produces mainly white wines. *See also* Weinviertel.

Falkensteiner Hofberg (Ger) vineyard (Anb): Mosel-Saar-Ruwer. (Ber): Saar-Ruwer. (Gro): Scharzberg. (Vil): Konz.

Falklay (Ger) vineyard (Anb): Mosel-Saar-Ruwer. (Ber): Bernkastel. (Gro): Schwarzlay. (Vil): Burg.

Falklay (Ger) vineyard (Anb): Mosel-Saar-Ruwer. (Ber): Bernkastel. (Gro): Vom Heissen Stein. (Vil): Reil.

Fall Bright (Eng) the term given to a wine or beer that becomes clear on its own, usually after a long period in cask, does not need any finings.

Fall Creek Vineyards (USA) a 27ha Hill County estate winery based in Tow, south-western Texas. Noted for Cabernet sauvignon, Chardonnay, Sauvignon blanc wines.

Fallen Angel (Cktl) ¾ measure gin, 2 dashes crème de menthe, juice of ¼ lemon or lime juice, dash Angostura. Shake over ice and strain into a cocktail glass.

Fallen Company [The] (Eng) a distillery that produces a range of crafted vodkas under the Fallen label including: The Hero (French and American grain distillates,), The Innocent (French grain spirits, sugar cane and Scottish malted barley) and The Outlaw (French wheat, Mexican blue agave, Caribbean sugar and peated islay malt). Website: http://www.thefallencompany.com

Faller [Robert et Fils] (Fr) a noted wine producer and shipper based in Ribeauvillé, Alsace.

Faller Frères (Fr) a noted Alsatian wine shipper based in Kayserberg.

Falletto di Serralunga (It) a Cru vineyard (7ha) in the DOCG Barolo near Serralunga, Piemonte. Grape variety: Nebbiolo. Owned by the Azienda Agricola Falletto di Bruno Giacosa.

Falling Down Water (Eng) a slang term used in northern England for beer (or other alcoholic drinks).

Falling Stone (Eng) a 4.2% alc by vol. ale brewed by the World Top Brewery, East Yorkshire.

Falloises [Les] (Fr) a Premier Cru vintage blanc de blancs Champagne produced from vieilles vignes by the house of François Vallois.

Falloux [Denis] (Fr) a wine producer based at Le Puy-Notre-Dame in the Saumur district of Anjou-Saumur, Loire. Noted for Saumur Mousseux.

Falls City Brewery (USA) a brewery based in Louisville.

Falmouth Bitter (Eng) a keg bitter 1038 O.G. brewed by the Cornish Brewery Company in Dorset.

Falooda (Ind) a rose syrup-flavoured milk drink often served with ice cream and other sweet ingredients.

Flase Bay Vineyards (S.Afr) a winery (established 2002) based in Wellington, Western Cape. 40ha. Grape varieties: Cabernet franc, Cabernet sauvignon, Chardonnay, Grenache, Merlot, Mourvèdre, Petit verdot, Shiraz. Labels: Cape Heights, Hoop Huis, Paarl Heights, Peacock Ridge, Post Stones, Vals Baai, Waterkloof. Owned by Boutinot U.K.

False Pedro (Sp) a white grape variety also known as Cañocazo.

Falsete (Sp) the tight-bunged hole near the bottom of the cask at the front, a canuto is driven into this prior to racking.

Falstaff Mild (Eng) a cask-conditioned (and keg) light mild 1032 O.G. brewed by the Tetley Brewery. Also known as Best or Scotch depending on the region, *see* Best Mild and Scotch Mild.

Falstaff Pale (Eng) a 4% alc by vol. ale brewed by by the Ossett Brewing C°. Ltd., West Yorkshire.

Famiglia Quattrochi Winery (Arg) a winery based in the Mendoza region, eastern Argentina. Website: http://www.bodegaquattrochi.com.ar

Familia Cassone (Arg) a winery based in the Mendoza region, eastern Argentina. Website: http://www.familiacassone.com.ar 'E'mail: bodegacassone@familiacassone.com.ar

Familia Zuccardi (Arg) a winery (established 1956) based in the Mendoza region, eastern Argentina. Grape varieties include: Cabernet sauvignon, Caladoc, Malbec, Marselan, Syrah, Tempranillo, Viognier. Labels: Santa Julia, Zuccardi Q, Zuccardi Zeta. Website: http://www.familiazuccardi.com 'E'mail: info@familiazuccardi.com

F

Family Ale (Eng) an old name for bottled pale bitter beers.

Family Ale (Eng) a 2.2% alc by vol. cask-conditioned light bitter dinner ale brewed by Harveys Brewery, Lewes, East Sussex. Bottled version is 2% alc by vol.

Family Home Estate (USA) a vineyard based in the Napa Valley. Home to the Origin Napa winery.

Family of Twelve (N.Z) a group of 12 vineyards who have joined forces to market their wines. The wineries are: Ata Rangi, Craggy Range, Felton Road, Fromm, Kumeu River, Lawson's Dry Hills, Nautilus, Neudorf, Pallister Estate, Pegasus Bay, The Milton Vineyard, and Villa Maria. Website: http://www.familyoftwelve.co.nz

Family Reserve (S.Afr) the label for a range of wines produced by the Jonkeer winery, Robertson, Western Cape.

Family Reserve (S.Afr) the label for a range of varietal wines (Cabernet sauvignon, Sauvignon blanc and Shiraz) produced by Kleine Zalze Wines, Stellenbosch, Western Cape.

Family Reserve Heatherleigh (S.Afr) the label for a sweet white wine (Muscat d'Alexandrie 50%, Chenin blanc 40% and Sauvignon blanc 10% blend) produced by the Waterford Estate winery, Stellenbosch, Western Cape.

Famous Crazy (USA) a natural spring mineral water from Mineral Wells, Texas. Mineral contents (milligrammes per litre): Sodium 909mg/l, Calcium 38mg/l, Magnesium 22mg/l, Potassium 5mg/l, Bicarbonates 360mg/l, Chlorides 178mg/l, Sulphates 1540mg/l, Fluorides <0.02mg/l, Nitrates 0.19mg/l. pH 8.1

Famous Grouse Experience (Scot) a blended Scotch whisky (established 1775) produced by Matthew Gloag and Sons. (Add): Glenturret, Crieff, Perthshire PH7 4HA. (Part of Highland Distilleries Company). 40% alc by vol. Also a 1987 Vintage Malt at 40% alc by vol (now replaced by a 10 year old malt). and Islay Cask Finish at 40% alc by vol. Website: http://www.famousgrouseexperience.com 'E'mail: enquiries@famousgrouse.com

Famous Natural Deep Well (USA) a natural spring mineral water from Mineral Wells, Texas. Mineral contents (milligrammes per litre): Sodium 284mg/l, Calcium 38mg/l, Magnesium 15mg/l, Potassium 2mg/l, Bicarbonates 488mg/l, Chlorides 145mg/l, Sulphates 168mg/l, Fluorides 0.18mg/l, Nitrates 0.14mg/l. pH 8.2

Famous Pigswill [The] (Eng) a 4% alc by vol. beer brewed by Bunce's Brewery, Netheravon, near Salisbury. See also Benchmark, Old Smokey.

Famous Premium (USA) a natural spring mineral water from Mineral Wells, Texas. Mineral contents (milligrammes per litre): Sodium 3mg/l, Magnesium <1mg/l, Potassium <1mg/l, Bicarbonates 6mg/l, Chlorides 2mg/l, Sulphates 1mg/l, Fluorides <0.02mg/l, Nitrates <0.01mg/l. pH 6.3

Famous Taddy Porter (Eng) a bottled porter 1050 O.G. brewed by the Sam Smith Brewery in Tadcaster, Yorkshire.

Fancy Brandy Cocktail (Cktl) another name for a Chicago Cocktail.

Fancy Free Cocktail (Cktl) 35mls (1½ fl.ozs) rye whiskey, dash orange bitters, 2 dashes maraschino, dash Angostura. Shake over ice and strain into cocktail glass rimmed with powdered sugar.

Fancy Gin Cocktail (Cktl) ⅓ measure gin, dash Angostura, 2 dashes Cointreau, 2 dashes gomme syrup. Shake over ice, strain into a cocktail glass and top with a twist of lemon peel juice.

Fancy Gin Smash (Cktl) as for Gin Smash but the glass is filled with shaved ice and decorated with fruits and a sprig of mint. Serve with straws and a spoon.

Fancy Whiskey Cocktail (Cktl) ⅓ measure Bourbon whiskey, 1 dash Angostura, 2 dashes Cointreau, 2 dashes gomme syrup. Shake over ice, strain into a cocktail glass and top with a twist of lemon peel juice.

Fanega (Sp) a measurement used in Málaga (1 acre equals 1.5 Fanegas).

Fanez de Minaya (Sp) the label of a solera and solera gran reserva brandy produced by Barbadillo in Jerez de la Frontera.

Fangos (Austr) a principal liqueur producer who produces many styles of liqueurs.

Fanleaf Virus (Eng) a disease (virus) of the vine. see Court Noué.

Fannings (Eng) a type of broken tea leaf grade, small leaf between B.P and Dust in size that is usually used in teabags. Name derived from the way the 'fannings' that were on the floor were 'fanned' into piles.

Fanta (USA) a non-alcoholic, still or sparkling, orange or icy lemon drink produced by the Coca Cola C°.

Fantaisie (Fr) if found on a label denotes synthetic products have been used.

Fantaisie (Fr) a term applied to kirsch made from neutral alcohol, natural kirsch and other ingredients.

Fantasia Cocktail (Cktl) 25mls (⅕ gill) green Chartreuse, 20mls (⅙ gill) vodka, 15mls (⅛ gill) grapefruit juice, 4 dashes cherry brandy. Stir over ice and strain into a frosted cocktail glass, dress with an orange slice and a cherry.

Fantasia Ramazzotti (It) a banana-flavoured liqueur.

Fantasio Cocktail (Cktl) 40mls (⅓ gill) brandy, 15mls (⅛ gill) maraschino, 15mls (⅛ gill) white crème de menthe, 15mls (⅛ gill) dry vermouth. Stir over ice and strain into a cocktail glass.

Fantesca Estate (USA) a winery based in the Spring Mountain District, Napa Valley, California. Grape varieties include: Cabernet sauvignon.

F.A.Q. (Austr) abbr; Fair Average Quality.

Fara (It) a D.O.C. red wine from Piemonte. Produced in the commune of Novara from 40% Bonarda, 30%–50% Nebbiolo and 10%–30% Vespolina grape varieties. Must be aged for 3 years (at least 2 years in oak/chestnut casks).

Fare la Birra (It) brew.

Fares (Fr) a vineyard based in Vienne, Isère département. Produces red wines.

Fare Thee Well Cocktail (Cktl) ⅓ measure dry gin, ⅙ measure dry vermouth, dash sweet vermouth, dash Cointreau. Shake over ice and strain into a cocktail glass.

Farewell (Eng) an alternative term sometimes used in place of aftertaste.

Farfelu Vineyard (USA) a small vineyard based in Flint Hill, Virginia. 5ha. Produces French hybrid and vinifera wines.

Fargo Ale (Eng) a bottled strong ale 1046 O.G. (5% alc by vol.) brewed by Charles Wells at the Eagle Brewery, Havelock Street, Bedford.

Fargo Velvet (Eng) fully matured, smooth, 5% alc by vol. ale from the Charles Wells Brewery, Havelock Street, Bedford.

Fargues (Fr) a commune in the Sauternes district of Bordeaux, wines are sold under the A.C. Sauternes.

Farmakas (Cyp) a natural spring mineral water. Mineral contents (milligrammes per litre): Sodium 39mg/l, Calcium 28mg/l, Magnesium 9mg/l, Potassium 0.1mg/l, Bicarbonates 140mg/l, Chlorides 21mg/l, Sulphates 46mg/l, Nitrates <1mg/l. pH 7.6

Farmer Boys (Eng) a 3.6% alc by vol. ale brewed by the Blencowe Brewing C°., Rutland.

Farmer Mineral (Switz) a natural spring mineral water brand.

Farmer's Ale (Eng) a bottled bitter 1036 O.G. brewed by the McMullen Brewery in Hertford.

Farmer's Ale (Eng) a cask-conditioned bitter 1038 O.G. brewed by the Oakhill Brewery, Bath, Wiltshire.

Farmer's Glory (Eng) a cask-conditioned 1046 O.G. or bottled 4.5% alc by vol. ale brewed by the Wadworth Brewery in Devizes, Wiltshire.

Farmer's Joy (Eng) a 4.5% alc by vol. ale brewed by the Verulam Brewery, Hertfordshire.

Farmer's Joy (Cktl)(Non-alc) 75mls (3 fl.ozs) tomato juice, 1 egg yolk, dash lemon juice, celery salt, milled pepper, Worcestershire sauce. Shake well over ice, strain into an old-fashioned glass and serve with a stick of celery.

Farmhouse Ale (Eng) a 3.5% alc by vol. ale brewed by the Oakleaf Brewing C°. Ltd., Hampshire.

Farmhouse Bitter (Wal) a bitter ale 1039 O.G. brewed by the Plassey Brewery, Eyton, near Wrexham in Clwyd.

Farm Stout (Eng) a sweet stout 1035 O.G. brewed by the Greene King Brewery in East Anglia.

Farm Winery Bill (USA) a law passed in 1968 in Pennsylvania that prevents wineries producing in excess of 100000 U.S. gallons of wine per year.

Far Niente Winery (USA) a winery (established 1885). (Add): Oakville, Napa Valley, California. Grape varieties: Chardonnay, Cabernet sauvignon.

Farne Island (Eng) a 4% alc by vol. ale brewed by the Hadrian & Border Brewery, Tyne & Wear.

Far North Brewery (Scot) a brewery (established 1998). (Add): Melvich, Thurso, Caithness KW14 7YJ. Brews: Edge of Darkness 7% alc by vol., Fast

reactor 4.8% alc by vol., Real Mackay 3.8% alc by vol., Splitstone Pale Ale 4.2% alc by vol. Website: http://www.smoothhound.co.uk/hotels/melvich 'E'mail: farnorthbrewery@aol.com

Faro (Bel) a lambic beer (sweetened version).

Faro (Fr) a low-alcohol, sour beer which is often sweetened.

Faro (It) a D.O.C. red and rosé wines made by Palarion from the Nerello, Nocera and Cintana grapes in Sicily.

Faros (Euro) a smooth dry red wine from Hvar Island.

Farris (Nor) a natural spring mineral water from Kong Olavskilde, Larvik. Mineral contents (milligrammes per litre): Sodium 400mg/l, Calcium 26mg/l, Magnesium 30mg/l, Potassium 15mg/l, Bicarbonates 300mg/l, Chlorides 590mg/l, Sulphates 15mg/l, Silicates 14mg/l. pH 7.0

Farse (Iran) a wine-producing province in northern Iran.

Farsons Brewery (Euro) a brewery (established 1927). Full name is Simonds Farsons Cisk on the island of Malta. Brews top-fermented and pasteurised beers. see Blue Label, Brewer's Choice, Farsons Strong and Hop Leaf.

Farsons Strong (Euro) a 6.7% alc by vol. top-fermented, bottled ale brewed by Simonds Farsons Cisk, Mriehel, Malta.

Fartó (Sp) a white grape variety grown in Alicante.

Fass (Ger) cask.

Fässer (Aust) the name given to a large fermenting and maturing vessel for wine.

Fässerlay (Ger) vineyard (Anb): Mittelrhein. (Ber): Rheinburgengau. (Gro): Gedeonseck. (Vil): Boppard.

Fassle (Ger) a small cask of 5 litres in capacity, similar to a Spanish porrón, requires a steady hand to drink from.

Fass N° (Ger) cask number.

Fast Reactor (Scot) a 4.8% alc by vol. ale brewed by the Far North Brewery, Caithness.

Fat (Eng) a term usually applied to dry white wines that lack acidity but have plenty of fruit.

Fat Apple (Eng) a 5% alc by vol. cider produced by Bass at Burton-on-Trent.

Fatal Distraction (Eng) a 4.5% alc by vol. draught bitter ale brewed by the Hardys and Handons Brewery, Nottinghamshire.

Fat Bastard (S.Afr) the export label for a red (Shiraz) and white (Chardonnay and Sauvignon blanc blend) wines produced in Robertson, Western Cape.

Fat Bastard (Fr)(USA) a brand name for a French Chardonnay wine produced by Gabriel Meffre group for the American market. The name designed to appeal to the Americans in place of the complicated French label names!

Fatboys (Eng) a 6% alc by vol. dark cider from the Gaymer Group, made using dark sugar. See also Kells Edge, Ice Dragon.

Fat Cat (Eng) a 4.2% alc by vol. golden bitter. Part of the Carlsberg-Tetley Tapster's Choice range.

Fat God's Mild (Eng) a beer brewed by the Queens Head Brewery, Evesham, Worcestershire.

Father Christmas (Eng) a 5% alc by vol. ale brewed by the Itchen Valley Brewery, Hampshire.

Father Christmas Ale (Eng) a (1078 O.G) 8% alc by vol. Christmas ale from the Wye Valley Brewery, Hereford (available in December). Part of the Dorothy Goodbody's Seasonal Ales.

Father of California Viticulture (USA) see Count Agoston Haraszthy.

Fathers Pride (Eng) a 4.5% alc by vol. ale brewed by the Highwood Brewery Ltd., north-east Lincolnshire.

Fatima (Slo) a natural spring mineral water. Mineral contents (milligrammes per litre): Sodium 4.3mg/l, Calcium 65.8mg/l, Magnesium 11.3mg/l, Potassium 1.6mg/l, Bicarbonates 228.8mg/l, Chlorides 2.5mg/l, Sulphates 24.6mg/l, Nitrates 2mg/l. pH 7.3

Fatra (Slo) a sparkling natural spring mineral water (established 1928). Mineral contents (milligrammes per litre): Sodium 823mg/l, Calcium 42.16mg/l, Magnesium 47.3mg/l, Potassium 19.6mg/l, Bicarbonates 2461mg/l, Chlorides 34.2mg/l, Sulphates 134mg/l, Fluorides 0.55mg/l, Silicates 14.3mg/l, Ammonium 30mg/l.

Fatsu (Tur) a natural spring mineral water. Mineral contents (milligrammes per litre): Sodium 2.9mg/l, Calcium 14mg/l, Potassium 1.1mg/l, Chlorides 3mg/l, Fluorides 0.12mg/l. pH 6.2

Fattigmands Snaps (Den) a noted brand of akvavit.

Fattoria (It) farm/vineyard/estate. see Cascina, Maso.

Fattoria Colle Alodole (It) a winery in the DOCG Sagrantino di Montefalco, Umbria region. Label: Fattoria di Milziade Antano.

Fattoria dei Pagliaresi (It) a Chianti Classico producer based in Siena, Tuscany.

Fattoria delle Lodoline (It) a Chianti Classico producer based in Vagliagli, Tuscany.

Fattoria dell'Ugo (It) a Chianti Putto producer based in Tuscany.

Fattoria de Nozzole (It) a wine estate owned by Folonari, based at Nozzole in Tuscany. Montemasso is a single high altitude estate vineyard. Produce Cabreo Il Borgo (a super Tuscan wine from a blend of 70% Sangiovese, 30% Cabernet sauvignon), Cabreo La Pietra Chardonnay, plus D.O.C.G. Chianti Classico Riserva Ducale Oro.

Fattoria di Petroio (It) a winery. (Add): Via Mocenni 7, 53033 Quercegrossa (SI). Has 13ha. of vines (12ha. are D.O.C.G.). Noted for Chianti Classico Riserva.

Fattoria La Monacesca (It) a winery based in the Marche. Produces I.G.T. Mirum (100% Verdicchio) and Camerte (70% Sangiovese grosso, 30% Merlot).

Fattoria La Ripa (It) a winery. (Add): Casella Postale n-1, 50020 San Donato in Poggia (FI). Produces Chianti Classico, Vin Santo, Grappa. Noted for Super Tuscan Santa Brigida.

Fattoria le Pici (It) a Chianti Classico producer based in San Gusine, Tuscany.

Fattoria Le Terrazze (It) a winery based in the Marche. Produces I.G.T. Chaos Marche Rosso.

Fattoria Mancini (It) a winery that produces a DOC Colli Pesaresi. Grape varieties include: Sangiovese.

Fattoria Montellori (It) a Chianti Putto producer based in Tuscany.

Fattoria Nico (It) see Illuminati.

Fattoria Ormanni (It) a 60ha. wine estate based in Chianti Classico, Poggibonsi, Tuscany. Produces I.G.T. Julius, D.O.C.G. Chianti Classico and Chianti Classico Riserva.

Fattoria Paradiso (It) a winery based at Bertinoro in the Emilia-Romagna region 30ha.

Fattoria Pasolini dall'Onda (It) a winery. (Add): 50021 Barberino Val d'Elsa (FI). Wineries in Tuscany and Emilia-Romagna. Produce San Zanobi, Chardonnay and Chardonnay-Pinot Grigio I.G.T. wines from Tuscany, Vin Santo di Toscana. Also D.O.C.G. Chianti Riserva, Chianti Classico Riserva and D.O.C. Sangiovese di Romagna Superiore.

Fattoria San Francesco (It) a winery based in Cirò, Calabria. 70ha. (60ha. of Gaglioppo, 10ha. Greco grapes). Produce Donna Madda, Ronco dei Quattroventi.

Fattoria Saulina (It) a Chianti Putto producer based in Tuscany.

Fattoria Villa S. Andrea (It) a winery. (Add): Via di Fabbrica 63–50020 Montefiridolfi S. Casciano V.P. (FI). 50ha. Noted for Chianti Classico D.O.C.G.

Faucha (Aus) a vineyard area on the banks of the River Danube in the Kremstal region.

Fauconberg Wine Stores (Eng) the trading name for one of J.T. Davies retail wine and spirit outlets in Chiswick, London.

Faugères (Fr) an A.C. commune in the Coteaux du Languedoc, Midi. Produces red and white wines. Grape varieties: Grenache, Carignan, Cinsaut, Mourvèdre, Syrah. Minimum 11% alc by vol.

Fäul (Ger) mouldy/foul.

Faure [Michel] (Fr) a V.S.O.P. Armagnac produced in the Bas Armagnac by Michel Faure 40% alc by vol.

Fausta (It) a natural spring mineral water from Fausta.

Faust Brauerei (Ger) a famous brewery based in Bavaria noted for pilsener lagers. see Faust Lager.

Faustianum (It) a red wine produced in central-western Italy during Roman times.

Faustine (Fr) a natural spring mineral water from Saint-Alban-les-Eaux.

Faustino (Sp) a brand-name for the Bodegas Faustino Martinez S.A., Oyón, Rioja. Many grades are produced.

Faustino I (Sp) a tinto gran reserva produced by Bodegas Faustino Martinez S.A. 12.5% alc by vol. Produced from Graciano 15%, Mazuelo 15% and Tempranillo 70% grapes.

Faustino IV (Sp) a red reserva wine produced by Bodegas Faustino Martinez S.A.

Faustino V (Sp) the brand-label for red and white wines produced by the Bodegas Faustino Martinez, Rioja. (Red): 20% Garnacha, 80% Tempranillo. (White): Viura 100%. Also a rosé version.

Faustino Rivero Ulecia, S.A. (Sp) a winery. (Add): Ctra Garray, Km 73, Arnedo La Rioja. 30ha. Grape varieties: Garnacha 50%, Tempranillo 30% and Viura 20%. Wines: Red 70%, Rosé 20% and White 10%. Website: http://www.faustinorivero.com

Faust Lager (Eng) a pilsener lager 1035 O.G. brewed by the Eldridge Pope Brewery in Dorchester, Dorset. Also an Export version 1042 O.G. and a Diät Pils 1035 O.G. All brewed under licence from the Faust Brauerei in Bavaria.

Fauvelots (Fr) a grade of rosé to red wine.

Fauvet (Fr) an alternative name for the Pinot gris grape.

Faventinum (It) a white wine produced in north-eastern Italy during Roman times.

Faverolles (Fr) a Cru Champagne village in the Canton de Ville-en-Tardenois. District: Reims.

Favorita (It) a red grape variety grown in Alba and Piemonte. Is also used to lighten Barbera wines.

Favorita [La] (Fr)(W.Ind) a popular brand of rum produced on the island of Martinique by D.R.A.

Favorito (Port) a fine old tawny Port from Smith Woodhouse Port shippers.

Favorito (Sp) a brand of Oloroso Cream Sherry from the Diez Hermanos range produced by Diez Merito.

Favourite Cocktail [1] (Cktl) ⅓ measure gin, ⅓ measure apricot brandy, ⅓ measure dry vermouth, 2 dashes lemon juice. Shake over ice and strain into a cocktail glass.

Favourite Cocktail [2] (Cktl) ½ measure gin, ½ measure Cognac, 3 dashes grenadine, 2 dashes lemon juice. Shake well over ice, strain into a cocktail glass and dress with a slice of lemon.

Faxe Fad (Den) a bottled lager 4.5% alc by vol. brewed by the Faxe Jyske Breweries in Denmark. *see* Fad.

Faxe Jyske Breweries (Den) own Higsons Brewery. Produce an unpasteurised beer called Faxe Fad, bottled lager 4.5% alc by vol. Other beers include Scandia, Odin, Supermalt. *see* Fad. Took over Cain (Robert) Brewery in 1992.

Fayal (Port) a vineyard in the Azores that produced wines under label of same name (now no longer in operation).

Faye d'Anjou (Fr) an A.C. commune in the Coteaux du Layon, Anjou-Saumur, Loire.

Fayre Ladye (Cktl) 1 measure dry gin, ⅙ measure crème de violette, ⅓ measure Grand Marnier, ⅙ measure pink crème de noyau, ⅓ measure lemon juice, dash egg white. Shake over ice and strain into a cocktail glass.

Fay Vineyard (USA) a vineyard based near Yountville, Napa Valley, California. 50ha. Grape variety: Cabernet sauvignon.

Fazendas (Bra) the coffee farms.

Fazi-Battaglia (It) a noted producer of Verdicchio dei Castelli di Jesi D.O.C. from the Marche region and Vino Nobile di Montepulciano D.O.C.G. The main winery is based at Castelplanio. 650ha. Labels include: Le Moie.

F.B. (Eng) *abbr*: **F**rench **B**ottled.

FC (Eng) a bottled ale brewed by the Marstons Brewery.

F.D. (Sp) *abbr*: **F**laverscenia **D**orada.

Feast Ale (Eng) a 4.3% alc by vol. ale brewed by the Feast & Firkin, Woodhouse Lane, Leeds.

Feast & Firkin (Eng) a micro-brewery at Woodhouse Lane in Leeds. Brews: Brutus 5% alc by vol. Feast Ale 4.3% alc by vol. Gladiator's Courage 3.5% alc by vol. Phalanx 4.3% alc by vol.

Feather Cocktail (Cktl) ¾ measure sweet vermouth, ¼ measure dry vermouth, ½ measure Pernod. Shake over ice and strain into a cocktail glass.

Feather Light (Eng) a 4.1% alc by vol. light ale brewed by the Mallard Brewery, Nottinghamshire.

Fécamp (Fr) home of the Bénédictine monastery where the drink of the same name is made. *see* Bénédictine.

FeCoVitA Coop. Ltda (Arg) a co-operative winery based in the Mendoza region, eastern Argentina. Website: http://www.fecovita.com 'E'mail: export@fecovita.com

Federaçao dos Vinicultores do Dão (Port) a body founded in 1942 to improve the standards of quality and labelling of Dão wines.

Federal Institute for Viticulture (Ger) sited at Siebeldingen in the Pfalz.

Federation Brewery (Eng) a specialist Club Brewery (established 1919) and also known as the Northern Clubs' Federation Brewery. Brewery sited in Lancaster Road, Dunston Indust. Estate, Gateshead, Tyne and Wear. Produces only processed beers. Noted for Ace (standard draught lager) 1032 O.G., Ace of Clubs: Brown Ale, bottled Export Ale, Export IPA 4.4% alc by vol., LCL (premium bottled Pils) 1036 O.G. Medallion Lager 1036 O.G. and a bottled sweet Federation Stout 1043 O.G. D'N'B Stinger. Website: http://www.federation-brewery.co.uk 'E'mail: enquiries@federation-brewery.co.uk

Fédération Nationale de Producteurs de Rhum (Fr) *abbr*: FENARUM the French equivalent of CODERUM in Martinique, West Indies.

Federation of Licensed Victuallers Associations (Eng) an organisation (established 1992). (Add): 126 Bradford Road, Brighouse, West Yorkshire HD6 4AU. Website: http://www.fiva.co.uk 'E'mail: admin@fiva.fsbusiness.co.uk

Federation of Sherry and Spirit Producers (Sp) *abbr*: F.E.V.Y.B.A. a body for industrial and home market affairs.

Federation of the Retail Licensed Trade (NI) (Ire) an organization (established 1890). (Add): 91 University Street, Belfast, County Antrim, Northern Ireland BT7 1HP. Website: http://www.ulsterpubs.com 'E'mail: enquiries@ulsterpubs.com

Federica della Fonte S.Giacomo (It) a slightly alkaline natural spring mineral water. Mineral contents (milligrammes per litre): Sodium 85mg/l, Magnesium 3.89mg/l, Potassium 1.7mg/l, Bicarbonates 124.4mg/l, Chlorides 73.7mg/l, Sulphates 18.8mg/l, Fluorides 0.425mg/l, Nitrates 3.99mg/l, Silicates 15mg/l. pH 8.3

Federico Paternina (Sp) wine bottler (Add): Avd. Santo Domingo, N°11, Haro (La Rioja). Has no vineyards, buys in wines: 72% red, 11% rosé and 17% white. Labels include Banda Dorada (white), Banda Azul (red), Conde de los Andes (red), Rinsol (white) and Viña Vial (red).

Federico Prima (It) an I.G.T. barrique-aged red wine produced by Gualdo del Re in Suvereto, Maremma, Tuscany from Merlot, Cabernet and Sangiovese grapes.

Federspiel (Aus) a term used in Wachau to describe the category of fresh medium-bodied wines. 11%–12% alc by vol. (must not exceed 12.5% alc by vol.) minimum sugar level of 17° KMW. Equivalent to German Kabinett. *See also* Steinfeder, Smaragd.

Federweissen Festival (Ger) *see* Fest des Federweissen.

Federweisser (Aus) fermenting must.

Federweisser (Ger) a milky-white, still-fermenting, strong, young wine drunk in Germany by the local residents.

Fée [La] (Fr) a 70% alc by vol. grassy green coloured absinthe, launched in July 2000.

Feeny's (Eng) an Irish cream liqueur 17% alc by vol. produced by Kilsern Distillers in Leicester. Also available in banana flavour.

Feethams Farewell (Eng) a 3.7% alc by vol. ale brewed by the Darwin Brewery, Tyne & Wear.

Fefiñanes (Sp) a white wine prodced by Bodegas Palacio de Fefiñanes, Val do Salnés, Rías Baixas, D.O. Galicia.

Fefiñanes Palacio (Sp) an oak-aged, white wine produced by Marqués de Figueroa in Zona del Albariño, Galicia, north-western Spain.

Fehér (Hun) white.

Féherbór (Hun) white wine.

Fehérburgundi (Hun) a white grape variety grown in south-western Hungary. Known as the Pinot blanc in France.

Feher Szagos (USA) a white grape variety used in the making of dessert wines in California.

Feilbingert (Ger) village (Anb): Nahe. (Ber): Schloss Böckelheim. (Gro): Paradiesgarten. (Vins): Bocksberg, Feuerberg, Höchstes Kreuz, Kahlenberg, Königsgarten.

Feiler-Artinger (Aus) a winery (19ha) based in Rust, Neusiedlersee-Hügelland, Burgenland. (Add): Hauptstrasse 3, 7071 Rust. Grape varieties: Blaufränkisch, Cabernet sauvignon, Chardonnay, Merlot, Pinot blanc, Traminer, Welschriesling, Zweigelt. Label: Solitaire.

Fein (Ger) fine.

Feinburgunder (Aus) an Austrian name for the Chardonnay. *See also* Morillon.

Feine (Ger) fine, a pre 1971 designation on wine labels.

Feiner Weisser Burgunder (Ger) the local name for the Chardonnay grape.

Feinste (Ger) finest.

Feints (Scot) the '*lasts*' from a pot still used for whisky and grain spirits. The '*firsts*' are called 'Foreshots' and between the two is called '*the Heart*'.

Feis (Ch.Isles) a tot or dram of drink. *See also* Lache.

Feist (Port) vintage Port shippers. Vintage: 1922, 1980, 1982, 1983, 1985, 1987, 1991, 1994, 1997.

Feiteiras Vineyards (S.Afr) a winery (established 2003) based in Bot River, Walker Bay, Western Cape. 4.5ha. Grape varieties: Cabernet sauvignon, Merlot, Mourvèdre, Petit verdot, Shiraz, Verdelho. Website: http://www.feiteiraswines.co.za

Feitoria Inglesa (Port) a club building based in Oporto. Originally was a factory system. British had extra-territorial rights. Members are partners in British Port firms (Oporto-based). *see* Factory House (The).

Felanitx (Sp) a major wine-producing area on Majorca, Balearic Isles.

Feldbach (Aus) a wine-producing area in southern Austria.

Feldberg (Ger) village (Anb): Baden. (Ber): Markgräflerland. (Gro): Burg Neuenfels. (Vin): Paradies.

Feldebro (Hun) a wine-producing village in Debröi that produces sweet white Hárslevelü wine.

Feldschlösschen Malz Light (Ger) a 0% alc by vol. diet beer brewed by the Feldschlösschen Spezialbier Brauerei in Hammink, Rheinfelden.

Feldschlösschen Spezialbier Brauerei (Switz) a large brewery. (Add): Brauereistrasse 2, Hamminkeln, Rheinfelden, D-46499. Brews a variety of beers and lagers and is noted for Castello, Fledschlössschen Malz Light. Website: http://www.feldschloessen-brauerei.de 'E'mail: info@feldschloessen-brauerei.de

Feliciano (Sp) a deep straw-coloured Cream Sherry produced by Wisdom and Warter in Jerez de la Frontera.

Felicitation Cocktail (Cktl)(Non-alc) ⅓ measure tomato juice, ⅓ measure orange juice, ⅓ measure blackcurrant juice, 1 egg yolk. Blend together with a scoop of crushed ice in a blender and serve in a flute glass with an orange slice on rim.

Felicité (S.Afr) the label for a rosé wine (Pinot noir) produced by the Newton Johnson Wines winery, Walker Bay, Western Cape.

Felicity (S.Afr) the label for a red wine (Cabernet sauvignon, Merlot and Cabernet franc blend) produced by the Tanagra Pivate Cellar winery, McGregor, Western Cape.

Féline [La] (Fr) A red wine produced by Domaine Borie de Maurel. Grape variety: Carignan.

Felinfoel Brewery C° [The] (Wal) a famous Welsh brewery (established 1878). (Add): Farmers Row, Felinfoel, Llanelli, Carmarthenshire, dyfed SA14 8LB. Noted for cask-conditioned/keg Double Dragon 1041 O.G. (the first beer to be canned), Cream Stout 1040 O.G. Nut Brown 1032 O.G. John Brown 1032 O.G. and St. David's Porter 1036 O.G. Website: http://www.felinfoel-brewery.com 'E'mail: enquiries@felinfoel-brewery.com

Felipe 11 (Sp) a noted brandy produced by Agustín Blázquez.

Felix García Gómez (Sp) a producer and exporter of Málaga wines.

Fell (Ger) village (Anb): Mosel-Saar-Ruwer. (Ber): Bernkastel. (Gro): Probstberg. (Vin): Maximiner Burgberg.

Fellbach (Ger) village (Anb): Württemberg. (Ber): Remstal-Stuttgart. (Gro): Weinsteige. (Vins): Gips, Goldberg, Herzogenberg, Hinterer, Berg, Lämmler, Mönchberg, Wetzstein.

Fellbacher Herbst (Ger) a Württemberg wine festival held at Fellbach in October.

Fellerich (Ger) village (Anb): Mosel-Saar-Ruwer. (Ber): Obermosel. (Gro): Gipfel. (Vin): Schleidberg.

Fellini Cocktail (Cktl) 50mls (2fl.ozs) Eisberg alcohol-free wine, 50mls (2fl.ozs) peach liqueur. Stir over crushed ice and strain into a Paris goblet.

Fellini Cocktail (Cktl)(Non-alc) 50mls (2fl.ozs) Eisberg alcohol-free wine, 50mls (2fl.ozs) peach juice. Stir over crushed ice and strain into a Paris goblet.

Fellow's Bitter (Eng) a cask-conditioned bitter 1040 O.G. brewed by the Whitbread home-brew public house Fellows, Morton and Clayton in Nottingham (made with malt extract).

Fellows, Morton and Clayton (Eng) a home-brew public house owned by Whitbread, based in Nottingham. Produces a cask-conditioned Clayton's Original 1048 O.G. and Fellow's Bitter 1040 O.G.

Fellrunner (Eng) a 4.3% alc by vol. traditional ale brewed by Jennings Brothersat the Castle Brewery, Cockermouth, Cumbria.

Fellrunners (Eng) a standard draught bitter from the Robinson Unicorn Brewery, Stockport, Cheshire.

Fells Manzanilla (Sp) the label for a Manzanilla Sherry produced by Rafael O'Neale of Jerez de la Frontera.

Felluga [Marco] (It) a north-east Italian producer based near the border. Produces a wide range of wines including Tocai, Pinot grigio, Pinot nero, Cabernet.

Felon & Firkin Brewery (Eng) a brewery based in Great George Street, Leeds, West Yorkshire. Brews: Bobby Ale 5% alc by vol. Felon Bitter 4.3% alc by vol. Fuzz Ale 3.5% alc by vol. Dogbolter 5.6% alc by vol.

Felon Bitter (Eng) a 4.3% alc by vol. bitter from the Felon & Firkin Brewery, Leeds. *see* Bobby Ale.

Fels (Ger) vineyard (Anb): Mosel-Saar-Ruwer. (Ber): Saar-Ruwer. (Gro): Scharzberg. (Vil): Könen.

Fels (Ger) vineyard (Anb): Nahe. (Ber): Kreuznach. (Gro): Schlosskapelle. (Vil): Windesheim.

Fels (Ger) vineyard (Anb): Nahe. (Ber): Schloss Böckelheim. (Gro): Rosengarten. (Vil): St. Katharinen.

Fels (Ger) vineyard (Anb): Rheinhessen. (Ber): Bingen. (Gro): Rheingrafenstein. (Vil): Frei-Laubersheim.

Fels (Lux) a vineyard site in the village of Grevenmacher.

Felsberg (Lux) a vineyard site in the village of Wintrange.

Felsen (Ger) vineyard (Anb): Rheinhessen. (Ber): Wonnegau. (Gro): Bergkloster. (Vil): Eppelsheim.

Felsenau Brauerei (Switz) a small brewery based in Bern.

Felsenberg (Ger) vineyard (Anb): Nahe. (Ber): Kreuznach. (Gro): Schlosskapelle. (Vil): Eckenroth.

Felsenberg (Ger) vineyard (Anb): Nahe. (Ber): Schloss Böckelheim. (Gro): Burgweg. (Vil): Duchroth.

Felsenberg (Ger) vineyard (Anb): Nahe. (Ber): Schloss Böckelheim. (Gro): Burgweg. (Vil): Oberhausen an der Nahe.

Felsenberg (Ger) vineyard (Anb): Nahe. (Ber): Schloss Böckelheim. (Gro): Burgweg. (Vil): Schlossböckelheim.

Felseneck (Ger) vineyard (Anb): Nahe. (Ber): Kreuznach. (Gro): Pfarrgarten. (Vil): Gutenberg.

Felseneck (Ger) vineyard (Anb): Nahe. (Ber): Kreuznach. (Gro): Pfarrgarten. (Vil): Wallhausen.

Felseneck (Ger) vineyard (Anb): Nahe. (Ber): Schloss Böckelheim. (Gro): Burgweg. (Vil): Bad Münster a. St-Ebernburg.

Felsen Export (Ger) a fine beer produced by the Felsenkeller Brauerei of Beerfelden in Hesse.

Felsengarten (Ger) vineyard (Anb): Baden. (Ber): Bodensee. (Gro): Sonnenufer. (Vil): Überlingen.

Felsengarten (Ger) vineyard (Anb): Württemberg. (Ber): Württembergisch Unterland. (Gro): Schalkstein. (Vil): Besigheim.

Felsengarten (Ger) vineyard (Anb): Württemberg. (Ber): Württembergisch Unterland. (Gro): Schalkstein. (Vil): Hessigheim.

Felsenkeller Brauerei (Ger) a small brewery of Beerfelden in Hesse. Produces fine beers, including Herforder Pils, pilseners and bocks.

Felsenkopf (Ger) vineyard (Anb): Mosel-Saar-Ruwer. (Ber): Bernkastel. (Gro): Michelsberg. (Vil): Trittenheim.

Felsenköpfchen (Ger) vineyard (Anb): Nahe. (Ber): Kreuznach. (Gro): Kronenberg. (Vil): Bretzenheim.

Felsenquelle-Fonte Randa (Ger) a sparkling natural spring mineral water from Felsen Quelle, in Malsfeld. Mineral contents (milligrammes per litre): Sodium 37mg/l, Calcium 137.5mg/l, Magnesium 41mg/l, Potassium 7.9mg/l, Bicarbonates 539mg/l, Chlorides 36mg/l, Sulphates 88mg/l.

Felsensteiner (Ger) a natural spring mineral water. Mineral contents (milligrammes per litre): Sodium 258mg/l, Calcium 1.5mg/l, Magnesium 0.5mg/l, Potassium 4.7mg/l, Bicarbonates 397mg/l, Chlorides 116mg/l.

Felsensteyer (Ger) vineyard (Anb): Nahe. (Ber): Schloss Böckelheim. (Gro): Burgweg. (Vil): Niederhausen an der Nahe.

Felsentreppche (Ger) vineyard (Anb): Mosel-Saar-Ruwer. (Ber): Bernkastel. (Gro): Schwarzlay. (Vil): Wittlich.

Fels Krone Alt (Ger) a 4.8% alc by vol. alt beer brewed by the Lindener Gilde Brauerei, Unna.

Fels Krone Kölsch (Ger) a 4.9% alc by vol. kölsch straw beer brewed by the Lindener Gilde Brauerei, Unna.

Fels Krone Pilsner (Ger) a 4.8% alc by vol. straw pilsener brewed by the Lindener Gilde Brauerei, Unna.

Felslay (Ger) vineyard (Anb): Mosel-Saar-Ruwer. (Ber): Saar-Ruwer. (Gro): Römerlay. (Vil): Mertesdorf.

Felstar (Eng) the brand-name for wine from the vineyards (established 1966) based at Crick's Green, Felstead, Essex. (4.35ha). Grape varieties: Chardonnay, Madeleine angevine, Müller-Thurgau, Pinot noir and Seyval blanc.

Felstar Brewery (Eng) a brewery (established 2001). (Add): Felstead Vineyard, Crix Green, Felstead, Dunmow, Essex CM6 3ST. Brews a variety of beers and lager. Website: http://www.eastanglianbrewers.com 'E'mail: felstarbrewery@sepernet.com

Felton and Son (USA) a distillery of New England rum including Crystal Spring and Pilgrim brands.

Felton-Empire (USA) vineyards based at Santa Cruz, California. Has vineyards at Beauregard, Hallcrest and Vine Hill. Grape varieties: Gewürztraminer, White riesling. Produces table and dessert (botrytis) wines.

Felton Road (N.Z) a winery. *See also* Family of Twelve.

Femage (Fr) the renting out of a domaine or vineyard in Burgundy.

Femmes et Vins de Bourgogne (Fr) a co-operative winery based in the A.C. Montagny, Côte Chalonnaise, Burgundy. Label: Premier Crus: Les Coères and Les Crets. Website: http://www.fevb.net

FENARUM (Fr) *abbr*: **Fé**dération **N**ationale de Producteurs de **Rhum**.

FENAVI (Port) *abbr*: National Federation of Independent Growers, a small group whose aim is to be in complete control of their own grapes. Produce and bottle their own wines from fruit grown in their own vineyards.

Fen Chiu (Chi) a grain spirit produced from wheat and millet in Sing Hua village, Shansi province.

Fendant (Switz) a white wine grape known as the Chasselas in France and the Gutedel in Germany. *See also* Bon Blanc, Dorin, Perlan.

Fendant de Sion (Switz) a local name for the Chasselas grape in the Valais region. *See also* Fendant du Valais and Fendant Vert.

Fendant du Valais (Switz) a local name for the Chasselas grape in the Valais region. *See also* Fendant de Sion and Fendant Vert.

Fendant Vert (Switz) a local name for the Chasselas grape in the Valais region. *See also* Fendant de Sion and Fendant du Valais.

Fendant Wine (Switz) a white wine, best known in the Valais region, made from the Fendant (Chasselas) grape.

Feni Fenix (Bra) a natural spring mineral water from the Fonte do Amanhecer. Mineral contents (milligrammes per litre): Sodium 5.8mg/l, Calcium 4.74mg/l, Magnesium 1.25mg/l, Potassium 2.6mg/l, Bicarbonates 36.52mg/l, Chlorides 0.3mg/l, Sulphates 0.44mg/l,

Fluorides 0.047mg/l, Nitrates 2.27mg/l, Silicates 16.77mg/l. pH 6.53

Fenland Brewery (Eng) a brewery (established 2003). (Add): Unit 2, Fielview, Cowbridge Hall Road, Little Downham, Ely, Cambridgeshire CB6 2UQ. Brews: Babylon Banks 4.1% alc by vol., Doctors Orders Best Bitter 5% alc by vol., Fenland Brewery Bitter, Osier Cutter 4.2% alc by vol., Rabbit Poacher 3.8% alc by vol., Sparkling Wit 4.5% alc by vol., St. Andrews 3.9% alc by vol., Winter Warmer 5.2% alc by vol. Website: http://www.elybeer.co.uk 'E'mail: enquiries@elybeer.co.uk

Fenland Fizzer (Cktl) 25mls (1fl.oz) Tia Maria, 25mls (1fl.oz) vodka. Stir over ice, strain into a highball glass with ice, top up with cola and add a slice of lemon.

Fenman Bitter (Eng) a keg bitter 1033 O.G. brewed by the Elgood Brewery in Wisbech, Cambridgeshire.

Fenman Pale Ale (Eng) a 3.6% alc by vol. pale ale brewed by Elgood & Sons Ltd., Cambridgeshire.

Fennel Water (Eng) *see* Fenouillette (a fennel-flavoured liqueur).

Fenn Valley Vineyards (USA) a winery based in Fennsville, Michigan. Noted for Riesling wines.

Fenouillette (Fr) a fennel-based liqueur produced by Denoix of Brive.

Fensai (Chi) a natural spring mineral water. Mineral contents (milligrammes per litre): Sodium 12.8mg/l, Calcium 40.9mg/l, Potassium 1.2mg/l, Silicates 27mg/l.

Fentimans Beggars Brew (Eng) a 1.2% alc by vol. botanically brewed beer from Gaymers. *See also* Fentimans Ginger Brew.

Fentimans Ginger Brew (Eng) a 1.2% alc by vol. botanically brewed beer from Gaymers. *See also* Fentimans Beggars Brew.

Fenton Acres (USA) a winery based in the Russian River Valley, Sonoma County, California. Grape variety: Chardonnay.

Fer (Fr) a red grape variety grown in Bergerac, in Gaillac where it is called Braucol, in Madiran where it is called Pinenc. Also known as Fer Servadou.

Fer [Le] (Fr) the second label wine produced by Château Cheval Noir. A.C. Saint Émilion Grand Cru.

Ferat [Pascale] (Fr) a Champagne producer. (Add): 14 Rue de Bernon, 51200 Épernay. Produces mainly Chardonnay wines.

Ferdinand Schumacher Brauerei (Ger) a brewery of Düsseldorf, western Germany in the Oststrasse. Produces fine altbier. *see* Schumacker Altbier.

Fèrebrianges (Fr) a Cru Champagne village in the Canton de Montmort. District: Épernay.

Fergies Choice (Eng) a 3.8%–4.5% alc by vol. ale from the Strangeway's Brewery, Manchester.

Fergie's Fizz (Cktl) ½ measure Cointreau, ½ measure cherry brandy. Shake over ice, strain into a flute glass and top with Champagne.

Fergusson's Winery (Austr) a winery. (Add): Wills Road, Yarra Glen, Victoria, 3775, Australia. 6ha. Grape varieties: Cabernet franc, Cabernet

F

sauvignon, Chardonnay, Marsanne, Pinot noir, Rhine riesling, Shiraz.

Fergusons (Eng) a 5% alc by vol. nitrokeg ale brewed by Morland Brewery, Abingdon, Oxford.

Feria (Sp) a spectacular celebration of Jerez to start the harvest of the grapes.

Fermage [En] (Fr) the term used when a négociant dictates to a château wine producer how they require the wine to be produced (grapes grown, cépage, viniculture, etc.)

Fermé (Fr) a firm, full wine which possesses a hardness when mature that it should have lost. *See also* Fermenté.

Ferme-Brasserie de Gaillon (Fr) a brewery. (Add): F-77540 Courpalay. Brews a variety of beers and lager.

Ferme-Brasserie Schoune (Can) a brewery. (Add): 2075 Ste-Catherine, Saint-Polycarpe, Quebec L0P1X0. Brews a variety of beers. Website: http://www.schoune.com 'E'mail: brasserie@schoune.com

Ferment (Eng) from the Latin (fervere = to boil) denotes the process of yeasts on sugars to produce alcohol and CO_2.

Fermentare (It) to ferment.

Fermentation (Eng)(Fr) the action of a ferment. (Ger) = gärung.

Fermentation Alcoolique (Fr) alcoholic fermentation – the process of yeasts turning the grape sugars into alcohol and carbon-dioxide.

Fermentation Lock (Eng) also known as an airlock. A valve used in the fermentation of home-made wines (and with barrel-fermented wines) which allows CO_2 gas to escape but prevents the entry of any contamination (air or bacterial). Uses a water seal as the airlock.

Fermentation Malolactique (Fr) malo-lactic fermentation, the action of lactic bacteria on the harsh malic acid to convert it to the softer lactic acid.

Fermentazione (It) the fermentation process.

Fermentazione in Bianco (It) removing the skins from the must for white wines.

Fermentazione Naturale (It) natural fermentation, either in tank or metodo tradizionale, but the former most likely.

Fermenté (Fr) a firm full wine which possesses a hardness when mature that it should have lost. *See also* Fermé.

Fermented Beverages (USA) the name given to beverages made from grain or fruits with alcoholic strengths that range from 7%–14% alc by vol.

Fermented Milk (Eng) a method of preserving milk which alters the flavour and appearance. *See also* Dahdi, Huslanka, Lad Anzebadi, Mazyn and Taetta.

Fermenting (Eng) the action of fermentation.

Fermentor (USA) a vessel in which the fermentation takes place in the production of whiskey.

Fermentum (Lat) yeast/to ferment.

Fermoselle-Arribes del Duero (Sp) a Vino de la Tierra Castilla-León situated between Salamanca and Zamora. 5,000ha. of vines. Red, rosé and white wines are produced from Garnacha tinta, Malvasía and Rufete grapes plus Juan García, Bobal, Tinta de toro, Tinto de Madrid secondary grape varieties.

Fermoy Estate (Austr) a winery based in the Margaret River region of Western Australia. Grape varieties include: Cabernet sauvignon.

Fernandes Brewery (Eng) a brewery (established 1996). (Add): The Old Malt House, 5 Avison Yard, Kirkgate, Wakefield, West Yorkshire WF1 1UA. Brews: Empress of India 6% alc by vol., Harvest Gold 3.9% alc by vol., Malt Shovel Mild 3.8% alc by vol., Moodies Mild 6% alc by vol., Triple O 3.9% alc by vol., Wakefield Pride 4.5% alc by vol. Also brews Old Bridge Bitter, Star Stout, Great Northern. Website: http://www.fernandes-brewery.gowyld.com

Fernandez Distillery (W.Ind) rum distilleries based on the islands of Puerto Rico and Trinidad.

Fernandez Vat 19 (W.Ind) a golden rum produced by the Fernandez Distillery on the island of Puerto Rico.

Fernando A. de Terry (Sp) a Sherry and brandy producer (Add): Santísima Trinidad, 2 y 4 11500, Puerto de Santa Maria. Sherry labels include St. Michael's Fino.

Fernando de Castilla (Sp) a solera gran reserva brandy produced by Castilla.

Fernand Pernot (Fr) a négociant-éleveur based in the Côte d'Or, Burgundy.

Fernão Pires (Port) a white grape variety grown in Estremadura, Ribatejo and in Bairrada where it is called Maria Gomes. Also used in Californian dessert wines.

Fernbrook (Can) a natural spring mineral water (established 1984) from Shelburne, Ontario.

Fernet (It) a herbal bitters digestif made by Martini & Rossi in Turin 45% alc by vol.

Fernet Branca (Fr) a producer in St-Louis, Haut-Rhin, Alsace of a liqueur of same name (Fleurs des Alpes and Branca Menthe).

Fernet Branca (It) a bitters, has a medicinal flavour and aroma. Produced in Turin 40% alc by vol.

Fernet Branca Cocktail (Cktl) ½ measure Fernet Branca, ½ measure sweet vermouth, 1 measure brandy. Shake over ice and strain into a cocktail glass.

Fernet Branca Menta (It) a mint-flavoured bitters from the Fratelli Branca Distilleries S.p.A.

Fernet Cocktail (Cktl) 30mls (¼ gill) Fernet Branca, 30mls (¼ gill) Cognac, 1 dash Angostura, 2 dashes gomme syrup. Stir over ice, strain into a cocktail glass and top with a squeeze of lemon peel juice.

Fernet Gambarotti (It) a herb-flavoured liqueur produced by the Gambarotta di Inga & C. S.p.A., Serravalle Scrivia.

Fernet Menthe (Cktl) ⅔ measure Fernet Branca, ⅓ measure (green) crème de menthe. Stir together over ice and strain into a cocktail glass (a pick-me-up).

F

Fernets (Cktl) the name given to cocktails which have Fernet Branca in the recipe.

Ferngrove Vineyards Estate (Austr) a winery based in the Frankland River region of Western Australia. Grape varieties include: Cabernet sauvignon, Merlot. Label: Majestic.

Fernhill (N.Z) part of the Cooks Winery.

Fernhill Spring Water (Wal) a spring water from Llechyrd, Ceredigon.

Ferral (Mad) a white grape variety used in the making of Madeira.

Ferrana (Alg) a white grape variety.

Ferrand [Pierre] (Fr) a Cognac producer. (Add): La Nerolle, 16130 Ségonzac. 27ha. in the Grande Champagne. Produces Réserve Ancestrale, Sélection des Anges.

Ferrara Winery (USA) a small winery based in Escondido, San Diego, California. Produces varietal and dessert wines.

Ferrarelle (It) a sparkling natural spring mineral water from the Ferrarelle Spring, Caserta, Ricarta, Campania. Mineral contents (milligrammes per litre): Sodium 49mg/l, Calcium 362mg/l, Magnesium 18mg/l, Potassium 43mg/l, Bicarbonates 1372mg/l, Chlorides 21mg/l, Sulphates 6mg/l, Fluorides 0.8mg/l, Nitrates 5mg/l, Silicates 81mg/l. pH 6.1

Ferrari (It) producers of sparkling (metodo tradizionale) wines from the Trentino area of the Venetian region in north-eastern Italy, all are estate-bottled. Also produce still wines.

Ferrari-Carano (USA) a winery based in the Alexander Valley, Sonoma County, California. Grape varieties: Cabernet sauvignon.

Ferrari Cocktail (Cktl) ⅔ measure French vermouth, ⅓ measure amaretto. Stir over ice in a highball glass and dress with a lemon slice.

Ferratum (Eng) a mediaeval wine produced in southern England, was classed as a tonic wine because of its iron content.

Ferraud [Piere] (Fr) a négociant-éleveur. (Add): 31 Rue Maréchale Foch, 69823 Belleville. Deals in Beaujolais and Mâconnais wines.

Ferraz Lda. (Mad) a noted producer of Madeira wines.

Ferreira [A.A.] (Port) vintage Port shippers. Vintages: 1894, 1896, 1897, 1900, 1904, 1908, 1912, 1917, 1920, 1924, 1927, 1935, 1937.

Ferreira [A.A. Sucrs] (Port) vintage Port shippers. Vintages: 1945, 1955, 1960, 1963, 1966, 1970, 1975, 1977, 1980, 1982, 1983, 1985, 1987, 1991, 1994, 1997, 2000, 2003.

Ferreira [Raul & Filho] Lda. (Port) own Quinta do Barao, the only remaining vineyard in Carcalvelos.

Ferreira dos Santos (Port) a producer of Dão wines based in Povolide and Viseu.

Ferreira Malaquias (Port) a producer of Dão wines under the Dão Ferreira Malaquias label.

Ferren (Sp) a red grape variety grown in the Galicia region.

Ferrer (Sp) a wine-producer based in Mallorca, produces mainly red wines.

Ferrerinha (Port) the brand-name of a light red wine produced by Ferreira.

Ferrero Vineyard (USA) a small winery based in Shenandoah Valley, Amador, California. 8.5ha. Grape variety: Zinfandel.

Ferret Ale (Eng) a cask-conditioned bitter 1045 O.G. brewed by the Ferret and Firkin home-brew public house in London.

Ferret and Firkin (Eng) a home-brew public house in London. Produces Dogbolter 1060 O.G. Ferret Ale 1045 O.G. and a Stout 1036 O.G.

Ferret y Mateu (Sp) a noted cava and still wine producer based in the Penedés. Produces Viña Laranda Blanco.

Ferric Casse (Eng) a problem caused by a high iron content in the wine resulting in cloudiness and a deposit forming, cured by adding blue finings (forbidden in some countries).

Ferro China (It) an aromatic bitters similar to Fernet Branca produced in Milan 21% alc by vol.

Ferro-China Bisteri (It) see Ferro-China.

Ferrol (Sp) see Ferrón.

Ferrón (Sp) a black grape variety grown in Galicia and Ribeiro. Also called Ferrol.

Ferrugineuse Incomparable (Fr) a natural spring mineral water from Asperjoc.

Ferruginous Clay (Sp) iron-rich clay soil found in the Rioja region of north-western Spain.

Ferry (S.Afr) the label for a range of wines: white (Chenin blanc 20% and Colombard 80%) and red (Pinotage 60% and Ruby cabernet 40%) produced by the Merwespont Winery, Robertson, Western Cape.

Ferrymans Gold (Eng) a 4.4% alc by vol. ale brewed by the Loddon Brewery, Berkshire.

Fer Servadou (Fr) a white grape variety grown in the Côtes du Marmandais. see Fer. Also known as the Braucol and Pinenc.

Fertilia (Bel) a natural spring mineral water from Roosdaal. Mineral contents (milligrammes per litre): Sodium 10.1mg/l, Calcium 101mg/l, Magnesium 13mg/l, Potassium 3.9mg/l, Bicarbonates 230mg/l, Chlorides 51mg/l, Sulphates 68.8mg/l, Silicates 28mg/l.

Fervere (Lat) to boil, the word from which ferment derives.

F.E.S. (Eng) abbr: see Foreign Extra Stout.

Fesq (Austr) a principal distillers and liqueur producer.

Fessenbach (Ger) village (Anb): Baden. see Offenburg.

Fess Parkey Winery (USA) a winery based in the Santa Barbara County, California. Grape variety: Pinot noir.

Festa de la Verena (Sp) a 'vintage festival' which occurs in Sitges, Barcelona.

Festbier (Ger) a 5.6% alc by vol. winter beer brewed by the Engelbräu Brauerei.

Festbier (Switz) a 5.2% alc by vol. bier brewed by Brauerei Schützengarten AG, St. Gallen.

Fest des Federweissen (Ger) the Federweissen festival, a wine festival held in Landau in the Pfalz in the Autumn.

539

F

Festigny (Fr) a Cru Champagne village in the Canton de Dormans. District: Épernay.

Festival Ale (Eng) a cask-conditioned bitter 1055 O.G. brewed by the Burton Bridge Brewery in Burton-on-Trent.

Festival Ale (Eng) a 1042 O.G. light golden bitter with a hoppy aroma from Clarks of Wakefield, Yorkshire.

Festival Ale (Eng) a keg bitter 1039 O.G. brewed by the Greenall Whitley Brewery in Warrington, Cheshire. Also sold in bottle 1042 O.G.

Festival Ale (Eng) a pale ale 1050 O.G. brewed by the King and Barnes Brewery in Sussex.

Festival Ale (Eng) a cask-conditioned ale 1052 O.G. brewed by the Woodeforde Brewery in Norfolk.

Festivale (Eng) a special beer brewed by the Courage Brewery for the 1986 Great Western Beer Festival.

Festivale (Eng) a special ale brewed by the Iceni Brewery, Ickburgh, near Thetford for the Norwich and Norfolk festival.

Festival Mild (Eng) a 4.8% alc by vol. dark, full-bodied mild ale brewed by Gales Brewery, Horndean, Hampshire.

Festival Stout (Eng) a beer brewed by the Butterknowle Brewery, Lynesack, near Bishop Auckland, County Durham.

Festival Wines (S.Afr) the label used by Gilbeys Ltd. for their varietal wines.

Festive (Eng) a 5% alc by vol. seasonal ale produced by King & Barnes, Horsham, West Sussex. Also a bottle-conditioned version.

Festive (Eng) a 5% alc by vol. bottled premium style lager brewed by J.W. Lees, Manchester.

Festive Ale (Eng) a 9.9% alc by vol. ale brewed by Ballard's, Rogate, near Petersfield.

Festive Wines (USA) the general name given to sparkling wines.

Fest Rund um die Naheweinstrasse (Ger) a festival held in each of the greater communities of the Nahewein route during the end of August.

Festrus (Cktl) ⅓ measure Grand Marnier, ⅓ measure Smirnoff vodka, ⅓ measure bitter Cinzano. Stir over ice, strain into a cocktail glass, add a twist of orange peel and a cherry.

Feteasca (Rum) a white grape variety which produces full-bodied wines. Also grown in (Bul) = Fetiaska, (Ger) = Mädchentraube, (Hun) = Mädchentraube, (Mol) = Mädchentraube, (Ukr) = Mädchentraube.

Feteasca Alba (Rum) a white grape variety grown in central and eastern Rumania. Also known as Leànyka.

Feteasca de Tîrnave (Rum) a white wine from the Tîrnave region.

Feteasca Neagra (Rum) a red grape variety grown in Husi near the Russian border in eastern Rumania.

Feteasca Regala (Rum) a white grape variety produced by crossing Grasa x Feteasca Alba. Also known as Kir Lyle Nyka in Hungary.

Fête de la Fleur (Fr) a festival held in June of each year in Bordeaux to celebrate the appearance of the flowers on the vines.

Fête de la Veraison (Fr) a mediaeval-style festival to celebrate the colouring of the grapes in Châteauneuf-du-Pape, held over the first full weekend each August.

Fête des Vignerons (Switz) see Vevey Festival.

Fête du Biou (Fr) held on the first Sunday of September annually, the great vintage celebration of Arbois.

Fetiaska (Bul) a white grape variety which produces medium-dry white wines. (Hun) = Leànyka, (Mol) = Fetiaska/Fetjaska, (Rum) = Feteasca.

Fetiaska (Mol) a dry white wine from Moldavia.

Fetjaska (Mol) see Fetiaska (another spelling of).

Feto com Màquina (Port) a large, strong caffè latte.

Fett (Ger) lit: 'fat', a full, big wine.

Fettercairn (Scot) a single malt whisky distillery based on the east coast of Scotland. A highland malt whisky 43% alc by vol.

Fettgarten (Ger) vineyard (Anb): Mosel-Saar-Ruwer. (Ber): Zell/Mosel. (Gro): Schwarze Katz. (Vil): Zell-Merl.

Fettlers Fancy (Eng) a 4% alc by vol. ale brewed by the Goldcar Brewery, West Yorkshire.

Fetzer Vineyards (USA) a winery based at Redwood Valley, Mendocino, California. 83ha. Also has vineyards in the Santa Maria Valley, Santa Barbara County. Grape varieties: Cabernet sauvignon, Carignane, Chardonnay, Chenin blanc, Gewürztraminer, Johannisberg riesling, Petit syrah, Sauvignon blanc and Zinfandel. Varietal and table wines sold under the Bel Arbes, Coldwater Creek and Valley Oaks labels. see Sundial. Is a member of the Coro Mendocino (Zinfandel) wine group of Mendocino wineries. Website: http://www.fetzer.com

Feudi di San Gregorio (It) a winery (established 1986) based in Campania. 200ha. Grape varieties: Aglianico, Falanghina, Fiano di Avellino, Greco di tufo, Piedirosso, Sangiovese. Produces: Taurasi, Serpico (a pre-phylloxera wine), Privilegio Fiano di Avellino, Campanaro wines.

Feudo Principi di Butera-Zonin (It) a winery based on the island of Sicily. Label: Deliella.

Feuer (Ger) vineyard (Anb): Pfalz. (Ber): Mittelhaardt-Deutsche Weinstrasse. (Gro): Rebstöckel. (Vil): Hambach.

Feuerbach (Ger) village (Anb): Baden. (Ber): Markgräflerland. (Gro): Vogtei Rötteln. (Vin): Steingässle.

Feuerbach (Ger) vineyard (Anb): Franken. (Ber): Steigerwald. (Gro): Herrenberg. (Vil): Castell.

Feuerbach (Ger) village (Anb): Württemberg. (Ber): Remstal Stuttgart. (Gro): Weinsteige. see Stuttgart.

Feuerberg (Ger) vineyard (Anb): Baden. (Ber): Kaiserstuhl-Tuniberg. (Gro): Vulkanfelsen. (Vil): Burkheim.

Feuerberg (Ger) vineyard (Anb): Mosel-Saar-Ruwer. (Ber): Zell/Mosel. (Gro): Goldbäumchen. (Vil): Ernst.

Feuerberg (Ger) vineyard (Anb): Mosel-Saar-Ruwer. (Ber): Zell/Mosel. (Gro): Grafschaft. (Vil): Ediger-Eller.

Feuerberg (Ger) vineyard (Anb): Nahe. (Ber): Schloss Böckelheim. (Gro): Burgweg. (Vil): Bad Münster a. St-Ebernburg.

Feuerberg (Ger) vineyard (Anb): Nahe. (Ber): Schloss Böckelheim. (Gro): Burgweg. (Vil): Duchroth.

Feuerberg (Ger) vineyard (Anb): Nahe. (Ber): Schloss Böckelheim. (Gro): Paradiesgarten. (Vil): Feilbingert.

Feuerberg (Ger) vineyard (Anb): Rheinhessen. (Ber): Wonnegau. (Gro): Bergkloster. (Vil): Flomborn.

Feuerberg (Ger) grosslage (Anb): Pfalz. (Ber): Mittelhaardt-Deutsche Weinstrasse. (Vils): Bad Dürkheim, Bobenheim am Berg, Ellerstadt, Gönnheim, Kallstadt, Weisenheim am Berg.

Feuerfest Brauerei (Ger) a brewery based in Treuchtlingen, Bavaria. Noted for strong beers e.g. Edel Bier. Also known as Schäffbräu.

Feuerfest Edel Bier (Ger) a strong long-lagered beer 11% alc by vol. which is sold in numbered and sealed bottles and is brewed by the Feuerfest Brauerei in Treuchtlingen, Bavaria.

Feuerheerd (Port) vintage Port shippers. Vintages: 1870, 1872, 1873, 1875, 1878, 1881, 1884, 1887, 1890, 1894, 1896, 1900, 1904, 1908, 1912, 1917, 1920, 1924, 1927, 1942, 1943, 1944, 1945, 1951, 1955, 1957, 1960, 1963, 1966, 1970, 1974, 1977, 1980, 1985, 1987, 1991, 1994, 1997, 2003.

Feuerlay (Ger) vineyard (Anb): Mittelrhein. (Ber): Rheinburgengau. (Gro): Gedeonseck. (Vil): Boppard.

Feuermännchen (Ger) vineyard (Anb): Pfalz. (Ber): Mittelhaardt-Deutsche Weinstrasse. (Gro): Höllenpfad. (Vil): Neuleiningen.

Feuerstein (Ger) vineyard (Anb): Franken. (Ber): Maindreieck. (Gro): Not yet assigned. (Vil): Röttingen.

Feuersteinrossel (Ger) vineyard (Anb): Nahe. (Ber): Schloss Böckelheim. (Gro): Paradiesgarten. (Vil): Oberndorf.

Feuerwant (Ger) lit: 'fire wall', a local name for the wine of Beutelsbach in Württemberg, west Germany.

Feuillaison (Fr) when the leaves begin to appear on the vines.

Feuillatte [Nicolas] (Fr) a Champagne producer, (Add): B.P. 210, Chouilly, 51206 Épernay. 1800ha. owned by 5000 co-operative members, founded in 1972. Produces vintage: 1988, 1990, 1996, 1998 and non-vintage wines including a Rosé de Saignée. Special cuvees: Cuvée Speciale, Palmes d'Or, Palmes d'Or Rosé from Chardonnay 20%, 40% Pinot noir grapes (Bouzy), 20% Pinot meunier grapes (Riceys). Website: http://www.feuillatte.com 'E'mail: service-visites@feuillatte.com

Feuilles de Thé (Fr) tea leaves.

Feuille de Tilleul (Hun) an alternative name for the Hárslevelü.

Feuilles Mortes (Fr) the local name for the yellow-green Burgundy bottles.

Feuillette (Fr) a capacity measure of a barrel of Chablis between 112litres–140litres (175bottles average). Various sizes, Burgundy 114litres, Chablis 132litres.

Feuillette Bourgogne (Fr) a Burgundy cask holding 114litres.

Feuillette Chablais (Fr) a Chablis cask hold 132litres.

Feurig (Ger) lit: 'fiery', denotes a red wine with a high alcohol content.

Fevanti (Fr) a continental cider mousseux sold in a black and gold bottle.

Fever (Eng) a 5.5% alc by vol. cranberry carbonate with vodka, peach and lime juice. Produced by Round Imports.

Fever Thermometer (USA) the nickname for the signs that acetobacteria are present in a wine and it is turning to vinegar. *See also* Pulse.

Fèves [Les] (Fr) a Premier Cru vineyard in the A.C. commune of Beaune, Côte de Beaune, Burgundy 4.4ha.

Fèvre [William] (Fr) a winery based in the A.C. Chablis, Burgundy. Produces a range of Chablis wines including Premier Cru Vaillons.

F.E.V.Y.B.A. (Sp) *abbr: see* Federation of Sherry and Spirit Producers.

Fez (Afr) a wine-producing region in Morocco.

F.F. (Den) *abbr:* Fine Festival, a beer 7.75% alc by vol. brewed by the Tuborg Brewery. Also known as Royal Denmark.

F.F. Ferraz Lda. (Mad) a company that ships Madeira wines to the U.K.

Ffynnon Gran (Wal) a natural spring mineral water from Dolgran, Pencader, Carmarthenshire.

Ffynnon Las (Wal) a vineyard based at Lampeter Road, Aberaeron, Dyfed. Produce white wines.

FGL Lager (Eng) a 4.2% alc by vol. lager beer brewed by the Highgate Brewery Ltd., West Midlands.

FGL Wine Estates (Austr) owned by Fosters Breweries a company that owns and markets many of Australia's finest wineries including Lindemanns, Penfolds, Rosemount and Wolf Blass.

FGR Riesling (Austr) *abbr:* Forty Grammes Residual, a white Riesling wine produced by the Wellington winery, Tasmania.

F.I. (USA) *abbr:* Fratt Industries, the brand-name of a brandy bottled by a company of same name.

Fiano (It) an aromatic white grape variety grown in the Puglia region, has a delicate aroma of toasted hazelnuts and flavour of ripe pears, peaches and apricots.

Fiano di Avellino (It) a white grape variety grown in Campagnia. Also a DOCG white wine of same name.

Fiaschetteria (It) a shop that sells wines.

Fiaschi (It) straw-encased flasks.

Fiasco (It) a wicker-wrapped bottle used for Italian wines. 2litres in size, usually smaller versions are called Mezzofiasco (they hold 1litre). Generic Chianti is sold in this style of bottle.

Fiasque (Fr) wine flask.

Fibber McGee (Cktl) 35mls (1½ fl.ozs) dry gin, 10mls (½ fl.oz) sweet vermouth, 10mls (½ fl.oz) grapefruit juice, 2 dashes Angostura. Stir with ice,

F

strain into a cocktail glass and add a twist of lemon peel.

Fichage (Fr) the tying up of the vine canes to secure them.

Fiche de Dégustation (Fr) wine tasting notes.

Fichots [Les] (Fr) a Premier Cru vineyard in the A.C. commune of Pernand-Vergelesses, Côte de Beaune, Burgundy 11ha.

Fiçi (Tur) cask/barrel.

Ficklin Vineyard (USA) a winery of San Joaquin in California. Produces dessert wines and Tinta Port-style wine.

Fiddlers Elbow (Eng) a 4.5% alc by vol. ale brewed by Refresh UK plc., Oxfordshire.

Fiddler's Elbow (Eng) a 4% alc by vol. ale brewed from malted barley and wheat by Wychwood Brewery, Eagle Maltings, Witney, Oxfordshire.

Fiddlestix Vineyard (USA) the label for a red wine (Pinot noir) produced by the Ortman winery, Santa Rita Hills, Santa Barbara County, California.

Fiddletown (USA) a sub A.V.A. in the Sierra Foothills, Sacramento Valley, California.

Fidesser (Aus) a winery based in Platt, Weinviertel. (Add): 2051 Platt 6. Grape varieties: Frühroter veltliner, Grüner veltliner, Muskateller, Roter veltliner, Sauvignon blanc.

Fié (Fr) an ancient white grape variety grown in the Loire (also known as the Fiét).

Fief de Guérin (Fr) a label for an A.C. Muscadet Côtes de Grandlieu from Domaine de Herbauges.

Fiée de Lois (Fr) a natural spring mineral water from Prahecq. Mineral contents (milligrammes per litre): Sodium 17mg/l, Calcium 89mg/l, Magnesium 31mg/l, Potassium 2mg/l, Bicarbonates 360mg/l, Chlorides 28mg/l, Sulphates 47mg/l, Fluorides 1mg/l, Nitrates 0.05mg/l. pH 7.2

Fiefs de Lagrange [Les] (Fr) an A.C. Saint Julien. Second wine of Château Lagrange.

Fiefs Vendéens (Fr) a Vin de Pays area in the Vendée département in western France.

Fiege Brauerei [Moritz] (Ger) a brewery (established 1878) based in Bochum. Brews: Bläck Mäx.

Fieille dé Thée (Ch.Isles) tea leaf.

Field Grafting (Eng) the grafting of European vine-stock onto the roots of American vine-stock in the vineyard as opposed to the method of bench-grafting.

Fierce Bull (Punch) heat gently until very hot one bottle red Castle d'Almain and sugar to taste, add 125mls (1gill) brandy and grated nutmeg, remove from heat and stir in a beaten egg.

Fierté Wines (S.Afr) a former winery (95ha) based in Rawsonville, Worcester, Western Cape. Grape varieties: Chardonnay, Chenin blanc, Colombard, Merlot, Ruby cabernet, Riesling, Sauvignon blanc, Sémillon, Shiraz. A supplier to Goudini Wines.

Fiesta (Sp) the label used by Bodegas García Carrión in the Jumilla region for their Sangría.

Fiesta Cerveza Lager (Switz) a 4.8% alc by vol. lager beer brewed by Brauerei Schützengarten AG, St. Gallen.

Fiesta Cocktail [1] (Cktl) 25mls (⅕ gill) white rum, 15mls (⅛ gill) lemon juice, 3 dashes Cointreau, dash grenadine, dash gomme syrup. Stir well over crushed ice, strain into a flute glass, top with soda water and dress with a lemon peel spiral.

Fiesta Cocktail [2] (Cktl) ½ measure white rum, ¼ measure dry vermouth, ¼ measure Calvados. Shake well over ice and strain into a cocktail glass.

Fiesta de la Vendimia (Sp) a vintage fête for Sherry, the celebration for the start of the harvest. Lasts 4 days. see Saint Ginés de la Jara.

Fiesta Punch (Punch) 1 bottle sweet white wine, 1 bottle soda water, 1 can unsweetened pineapple juice, 75mls (3 fl.ozs) lemon juice, sugar to taste. Dissolve sugar in fruit juices, add wine, chill. Add mix to bowl containing ice, add soda and float sliced fruit on top.

Fiét (Fr) see Fié.

Fiétres [Les] (Fr) a vineyard within the Grand Cru A.C. Corton, Côte de Beaune, Burgundy. Also known as Clos des Fiétres.

Fifteen Eighty Three [1583] (Sp) an oak-aged D.O. Galicia white wine produced by Bodegas Palacio de Fefiñanes in Val do Salnés, Rías Baixas.

Fifth (USA) a bottle size 25.36 U.S. fl.ozs (⅘ quart).

Fifth Avenue (USA) a type of tall, thin cocktail glass.

Fifth Avenue Cocktail (Pousse Café) pour in order ½ measure crème de cacao, ½ measure apricot brandy, ⅙ measure cream.

Fifth Growths (Fr) the Bordeaux Haut-Médoc Grand Crus. see Cinquième Crus.

Fifth Sense (Eng) a bottled ale brewed by the Holts Brewery, Manchester.

Fifty Eight [58] (Can) a blended Canadian whisky produced by Hiram Walker.

Fifty Degrees of Bitterness (Eng) a 4% alc by vol. bitter ale brewed by the Facers Brewery, Greater Manchester.

Fifty-Fifty (Cktl) 1 measure dry gin, 1 measure French vermouth. Stir together with ice and strain into a cocktail glass.

Fifty One to One a [51-1a] (Sp) a nutty brown bone-dry Amontillado Sherry produced by Domecq, Macharnudo, Jerez.

Fifty to One [50-1] (Eng) a winter ale brewed by the Mildmay Brewery, Holbeton, near Plymouth.

Figarella (Fr) large wine-producers of Corsica. 192ha. A.C. Corse-Calvi. Grape varieties: Carignan, Cinsault, Nielluccio and Sciacarello. (Red, rosé and white wines).

Figari (Fr) an A.C. sub-region of Corsica.

Figaro (Sp) a brand of medium-dry Sherry from the Diez Hermanos range produced by Diez Merito.

Figgy's Brew (Eng) a 4.5% alc by vol. ale brewed by Skinner's Brewery, Truro, Cornwall.

Fighting Cocks Brewery (Eng) a small brewery based at Grantham, Lincolnshire.

Figi (S.Pac) a natural spring mineral water from Viti Levu, Figi. Mineral contents (milligrammes per litre): Calcium 17mg/l, Magnesium 13mg/l, Bicarbonates 140mg/l, Silicates 83mg/l. pH 7.5

Figs (Eng) a blended coffee additive, they are roasted, makes the coffee stronger, more bitter with an underlying sweetness. *see* Viennese Coffee.

Figula (Hun) a winery based in Balatonfüred. Grape varieties include: Cabernet sauvignon. Label: New Generation.

Figurehead Cape Blend (S.Afr) the label for a red wine (Cabernet franc, Cabernet sauvignon, Malbec Merlot and Pinotage blend) produced by the Raka winery, Walker Bay, Western Cape.

Filament (Eng) a 4.3% alc by vol. ale brewed by the Filament and Firkin, Tyneside.

Filament & Firkin (Eng) a micro-brewery pub based in Tyneside. Brews: Bayonet, Filament, Floodlight.

Filby [The] (Cktl) ⅔ measure dry gin, ⅓ measure dry vermouth, ⅓ measure Amaretto di Saronno, ⅓ measure Campari. Stir with ice and add a twist of orange.

Filette [1] (It) a sparkling natural spring mineral water from Filette, Guarcino. Mineral contents (milligrammes per litre): Sodium 2.9mg/l, Calcium 66.13mg/l, Magnesium 2.43mg/l, Potassium 0.4mg/l, Bicarbonates 204.3mg/l, Chlorides 9.23mg/l, Sulphates 3.62mg/l, Oxygen 9.28mg/l, Nitrates 0.61mg/l, Silicates 2.4mg/l. pH 7.6

Filette [2] (It) a sparkling natural spring mineral water from Filette, Guarcino. Mineral contents (milligrammes per litre): Sodium 3.3mg/l, Calcium 77.4mg/l, Magnesium 1.3mg/l. pH 7.6

Filfar (Cyp) a bitter orange liqueur usually bottled in stone jugs.

Filipetti (It) a producer of sparkling (cuve close) wines in the Piemonte region.

Filipoquelle Haigerloch (Ger) a natural spring mineral water. Mineral contents (milligrammes per litre): Sodium 48.3mg/l, Calcium 604mg/l, Magnesium 51.3mg/l, Bicarbonates 362mg/l, Chlorides 51.3mg/l, Sulphates 1406mg/l.

Filippi Winery (USA) a winery based in Cucamonga, California. 133ha. Produces a wide range of varietal, sparkling and dessert wines.

Fillette (Fr) a slang term for a half-bottle of wine. *see* Anjou Fillette.

Fillette d'Anjou (Fr) aee Anjou Fillette.

Fillette de Touraine (Fr) aee Anjou Fillette.

Filliers (Bel) jenever and liqueur producers. (Add): Bachte-Maria-Leerne, near Saint-Martens-Latem.

Fillioux [Jean] (Fr) a Cognac producer. (Add): La Pouyade, Juillac-le-Coq, 16130 Segonzac.16ha. in Grande Champagne. Produces Cep d'Or: 15 y.o., Coq d'Or: 3–4 y.o., Réserve Familiale: over 45 y.o. also noted for receiving the Cep d'Or award for quality (the only Cognac ever to do so).

Fillossero (It) phylloxera vastatrix.

Film Yeast (Eng) the alternative name for flor.

Filo Brewing Company (Eng) a brewery. (Add): 14-15 Hight Street, Old Town, Hastings, East Sussex TN34 3EY. Brews: Cardinel 4.4% alc by vol., Crofters 4% alc by vol., Ginger Tom 4.2% alc by vol., Gold Premium 4.8% alc by vol. Website: http://www.thefilo.co.uk 'E'mail: mike@thefilo.co.uk

Fils (Fr) sons.

Filsen (Ger) village (Anb): Mittelrhein. (Ber): Rheinburgengau. (Gro): Marksburg. (Vin): Pfarrgarten.

Filsinger Vineyards (USA) a winery based in Temecula, California. 25ha. Grape varieties: Chardonnay, Petit syrah, Sauvignon blanc, White riesling, Zinfandel. Produces varietal wines.

Filter (Eng) a paper or metal unit used to restrain the solid matter from the liquid (coffee, wine, beer, etc.) after infusion, brewing, fermenting, etc. *See also* Membrane Filter.

Filter Coffee (Eng) a method of making coffee where the grounds are placed in a filter and boiling water is poured or sprayed (automatic) over them to percolate through to produce coffee on the other side of filter.

Filtering (Eng) to remove the unwanted particles in wine or beer to leave it bright. *See also* Hippocrate's Sleeve.

Filter Tubes (Eng) fine, medium or coarse fibre tubes fitted with a plastic cap at one end to stop the wine from by-passing the filter medium. Is used to give a final 'polish' to the wine.

Filtrage (Fr) percolation.

Filtrato Dolce (It) lit: 'sweet filtrate', grape must filtered and chilled in southern Italy then shipped to northern Italy for making vermouth and Vino da Tavola wines. Made from the Moscato grape on the island of Pantelleria.

Filtre (Fr) filter. *see* Café Filtre.

Filtrer (Fr) percolate.

Filtrier-Geschmack (Ger) lit: 'filter taste', describes a wine with an asbestos taste.

Filzen (Ger) village (Anb): Mosel-Saar-Ruwer. (Ber): Saar-Ruwer. (Gro): Scharzberg. (Vins): Altenberg, Herrenberg, Liebfrauenberg, Pulchen, Steinberger, Unterberg, Urbelt.

Fin (Fr) fine/delicate.

Fina (Port) a white grape variety of the Malvasia strain, used in the making of white Port.

Final Gravity (Eng) normally about (1008–1015 S.G) the higher the amount then the sweeter the beer, the term applies to the end of fermentation.

Final Whistle (Eng) a 3.9% alc by vol. bottle-conditioned ale from the York Brewery, Toft Green, North Yorkshire. Brewed to celebrate the 1998 World Cup.

Finca (Sp) (S.Am) estate.

Finca Alma (Arg) a winery based in the Mendoza region, eastern Argentina. Website: http://www.fincaalma.com.ar 'E'mail: info@fincaalma.com.ar

Finca de Valpiedra (Sp) *see* Bodegas Martinez Bujanda.

Finca el Retiro (Arg) a winery based in Mendoza. Noted for Sangiovese, Bonarda, Malbec and Tempranillo wines.

Finca Flichman SA (Arg) a winery (established 1910) based in Tupungato, Mendoza (owned by SOGRAPE) Grape varieties: Cabernet sauvignon, Chardonnay, Malbec, Shiraz.

Labels: Expresiones, Paisaje de Tupungato. Website: http://www.flichman.com.ar 'E'mail: international@flichman.com.ar

Finca La Celia S.A (Arg) a winery based in the Mendoza region, eastern Argentina. Website: http://www.fincalacelia.com.ar 'E'mail: info@fincalacelia.com.ar

Finca la Linda (Arg) a winery based in Luján de Cuyo, Mendoza. Grape varieties: Chardonnay, Sémillon, Malbec, Syrah.

Finca Las Moras (Arg) a winery based in the Tullum Valley, San Juan district, Cuyo region, eastern Argentina. Grape varieties: Bonarda, Cabernet sauvignon, Chardonnay, Malbec, Sauvignon blanc, Shiraz. Website: http://www.fincalasmoras.com

Finca los Trenzones (Sp) the name for a vineyard rosé wine (Tempranillo) from the Contessa de Leganza winery, La Mancha.

Finca Norte (Arg) a winery based in the Villa Atuel, Mendoza. Grape variety: Syrah.

Fincas (S.Am) the name given to the coffee farms in the Spanish speaking, Latin-American countries, also known as Haciendas.

Finca Sophenia (Arg) a winery (established 1997) based in Tupungato, Mendoza. Grape varieties include: Cabernet sauvignon, Malbec, Merlot. Labels: Altosur, Sophenia Synthesis. Website: http://www.sophenia.com.ar 'E'mail: consultas@sophenia.com.ar

Finca y Bodega Carlos Pulenta (Arg) a winery based in the Mendoza region, eastern Argentina. Website: http://www.carlospulentawines.com 'E'mail: iouet@cpwines.com

Fin de Bouche (Fr) lit: 'finale', a term associated with wine tasting, final taste (after-taste).

Findlater, Mackie Todd and Cº. Ltd. (Scot) a company which produces Marlodge (a blended malt whisky) and Findlater's range of Sherries.

Findlater's (Eng) noted London wine merchants. Ship Dry Fly Amontillado, Tia Lola, River Fly, May Fly and Lake Fly Sherries (part of Findlater, Mackie Todd and Cº Ltd).

Findlays (Scot) a natural spring mineral water from Pitcox, East Lothian. Mineral contents (milligrammes per litre): Sodium 12.1mg/l, Calcium 55mg/l, Magnesium 20mg/l, Potassium 0.9mg/l, Bicarbonates 151mg/l, Chlorides 21mg/l, Sulphates 0.6mg/l. pH 7.2

Findling (Ger) a white grape variety, a mutation of the Müller-Thurgau.

Findling (Ger) vineyard (Anb): Rheinhessen. (Ber): Nierstein. (Gro): Spiegelberg. (Vil): Nierstein.

Fine (Eng) to add finings to a cask of beer or wine. see Fining.

Fine (Fr) denotes a brandy of no great distinction.

Finéagar (Ire) vinegar.

Fine à l'Eau (Bel) a brandy and mineral water.

Fine and Dandy (Cktl) ¾ measure dry gin, ¼ measure Cointreau, juice ¼ lemon, dash Angostura. Shake over ice, strain into a cocktail glass and top with a cherry.

Fine Bourgogne (Fr) a fine mark brandy made from the lees and sediment of Burgundy wines, matured in oak casks.

Fine Champagne (Fr) the finest Cognac brandy, a blend of Grande and Petite Champagne Cognacs. Minimum of 50% Grande Champagne.

Fine de Bordeaux (Fr) an eau-de-vie distilled from Bordeaux wine.

Fine de la Maison (Fr) denotes 'house brandy' or 'bar brandy'.

Fine de Marne (Fr) an eau-de-vie-de-vin-de-Champagne, marc brandy produced in Champagne from last (rebêche) pressings.

Fine Festival (Den) the local name for Royal Denmark (a lager beer 7.75% alc by vol.) brewed by the Tuborg Brewery in Copenhagen.

Fine Fettle (Eng) a cask-conditioned ale brewed by Bank's Brewery.

Fine Fettle (Eng) a 4.8% alc by vol. ale brewed by the Ossett Brewing Cº. Ltd., West Yorkshire.

Finegr (Wal) vinegar.

Fine Lachamp (Fr) a prune and nut liqueur produced by the Germain Cº. in southern France.

Fine Leaf Fannings (Eng) a grade of black tea from the smallest leaf size, produces the most strength and colour.

Fine Ligne (Fr) a natural spring mineral water from Belles Roches. Mineral contents (milligrammes per litre): Sodium 38mg/l, Calcium 15mg/l, Magnesium 8mg/l, Potassium 2mg/l, Bicarbonates 162mg/l, Chlorides 7.2mg/l, Sulphates 10.6mg/l, Nitrates <0.5mg/l.

Fine Maison (Fr) the brandy of the 'house' or 'restaurant'.

Fine Marivaux (Sp) a 3 year old brandy produced by Mascaró.

Finé Natural Artesian Water (Jap) a still natural mineral water (established 1998) from Shuzenji. Mineral contents (milligrammes per litre): Sodium 8.7mg/l, Calcium 9.7mg/l, Magnesium 4.7mg/l, Potassium 1.7mg/l, Bicarbonates 52.8mg/l, Chlorides 5.3mg/l, Sulphates 5.7mg/l, Silicates 76.2mg/l. pH 7.6 Website: http://www.drinkfine.com

Finenc (Fr) a red grape variety grown in Madiran.

Fine Old Malmsey (Mad) a Madeira wine produced by Rutherford and Miles.

Fine Pyrénées (Fr) an angelica-based liqueur produced by Serres in Toulouse.

Fines Roches [Les] (Fr) part of the Châteauneuf-du-Pape vineyard area in the southern Rhône.

Fine Soft Day (Eng) a 4% alc by vol. ale brewed by the Iceni Brewery, Norfolk.

Finesse (Eng) a wine taster's term for a wine which has breed or class, a wine which is more than ordinary in quality, an elegant wine.

Finesse (Sp) a pale Cream Sherry produced by Harvey in Jerez de la Frontera.

Finest Madeira (Mad) may use a brand-name or word 'Madeira' and a description e.g. dry, medium, but not the name of the grape. Must be of minimum age of 3 years after Estufagem.

Finest Tippy Golden Flowery Orange Pekoe (Eng)

abbr: FTGFOP a fine grade of Broken Orange Pekoe black tea.

Fine Wine (Eng) a top quality wine, one with breeding and all the right characteristics.

Finger Lakes (USA) a wine district of the New York region that takes its name from the shape of its lakes (67 wineries) 10400ha. on sandy soils. Main regions are: Cayuga, Keuka and Seneca. Main grape varieties grown: Cabernet franc, Cabernet sauvignon, Chardonnay, Gewurztraminer, Merlot, Pinot noir and Riesling together with local *Vitis labrusca.* Also known as the Five Finger Lakes.

Fingers (USA) a term for a measure of spirits. i.e. 3 fingers is the span of 3 fingers up the glass which will be the measure.

Finggan (Egy) an Egyptian coffee cup.

Finian's Irish Red Ale (Ire) a 4.6% alc by vol. ale brewed at County Meath, near Dublin using Alfa Super Styrian hops, East Kent Goldings and Cascade hops.

Fining (Eng) the clarifying of a wine or beer in a cask or tank, [egg white, isinglass, nylon powder, ox blood, gelatine and some clays (bentonite) are used for the purpose]. *see* Colloids and Kieselguhr. *See also* Tierra de Lebrija.

Finish (Eng) the after-taste a wine leaves in the mouth, describes the length of the taste after the wine has been swallowed (or spat out into a spittoon).

Finish (Eng) a term used to describe the appearance of wine or beer. *See also* Polish.

Finishing Yeast (Eng) *Saccharomyces oviformis* used in sparkling (traditional method) wine production.

Finisimo Currito (Sp) a Fino Sherry produced at Bodegas Internacionales S.A., Jerez.

Finiuin (Ire) vine.

Finiúnach (Ire) vineous.

Finkel (Nor) a type of gin spirit.

Finkenbach Quelle (Ger) a natural spring mineral water. Mineral contents (milligrammes per litre): Sodium 0.9mg/l, Calcium 11.5mg/l, Magnesium 3mg/l, Potassium 2.8mg/l, Bicarbonates 51mg/l, Chlorides 1.3mg/l, Sulphates 2mg/l, Fluorides 0.1mg/l.

Fink Winery (USA) a winery based in Dundee, Michigan. Produces hybrid wines.

Finlaggen Ale (Scot) a 3.7% alc by vol. ale brewed by Islay Ales, Argyll.

Finlandia (Fin) a clean, neutral vodka 47% alc by vol (distilled from barley) from Finnish National Distillers at the Rajamaki distillery, sold in a frosted, 'rippled' bottle. Two flavoured versions: cranberry and lime both at 40% alc by vol (originally 37.5% alc by vol.)

Finnegans (Eng) a nitro-keg beer 3.8% alc by vol. from Ridley Brewery, Chelmsford, Essex. Originally brewed at 4.5% alc by vol.

Finnesko & Firkin (Eng) the new name for the Reindeer home-brew pub, Dereham Road, Norwich.

Finnish National Distillers (Fin) based at the Rajamaki distillery. Produces Finlandia vodka.

Finnor (Cktl) 25mls (1fl.oz) Cointreau, 25mls (1fl.oz) rye whiskey, juice of half lemon, orange tonic, dash grenadine. Blend the whiskey, Cointreau and lemon juice into an ice-filled highball glass, stir in orange tonic and add grenadine, garnish with a slice of orange and cherry.

Finn Spring (Fin) a still natural spring mineral water (established 1995) from Syrinharju. Mineral contents (milligrammes per litre): Sodium 20mg/l, Calcium <3.9mg/l, Magnesium 1.1mg/l, Bicarbonates 26mg/l, Chlorides 2mg/l, Sulphates 3mg/l, Nitrates <0.6mg/l. pH 6.5

Finn Valley (Eng) a vineyard (established 1972). (Add): Cherrybank Estates, Otley, Ipswich, Suffolk. 4.2ha. Soil: heavy boulder clay. Grape variety: Müller-Thurgau.

Fino (Sp) the driest Sherry, pale in colour, light and dry, attacked by flor 17% alc by vol. *see* Flor, Manzanilla, *Saccharomyces beticus.*

Fino Apitivi (Sp) an extra-dry Fino Sherry produced by the Sandeman Company.

Fino Bandera (Sp) a dry Fino Sherry from Bodegas M. Gilluque.

Fino Camborio (Sp) a Fino Sherry produced by De Terry, Jerez de la Frontera.

Fino Campero (Sp) the Spanish name given to a Fino Sherry known as Fino Soto in Great Britain.

Fino Chiquilla (Sp) the brand-name of a Fino Sherry produced by Marqués de Misa.

Fino Cristal (Sp) a brand of Fino Sherry produced by Sanchez Romate.

Fino Feria (Sp) a pale Fino Sherry produced by Duff Gordon in Puerto de Santa Maria.

Fino Imperial (Sp) the label of a dry Fino Sherry produced by Diez-Merito in Jerez.

Fino Mac (Cktl) 25mls (1fl.oz). ginger wine, 50mls (2fl.ozs) dry Sherry. Stir over ice and strain into a cocktail glass.

Fino Marismeño (Sp) a brand of Fino Sherry produced by Romate in Jerez de la Frontera.

Fino Martini (Cktl) ½ measure dry gin, ¼ measure Fino Sherry. Stir over ice, strain into a cocktail glass and add a twist of lemon peel juice on top.

Fino Olivar (Sp) a Fino Sherry produced by Wisdom & Warter.

Fino Pavon (Sp) a brand of Fino Sherry produced by Luis Caballero, Jerez de la Frontera.

Fino Quinta (Sp) a fine old Fino Sherry from Osborne and Cº.

Fino San Patricio (Sp) a brand of Fino Sherry produced by Garvey's in Jerez de la Frontera.

Fino Soto (Eng) the name used in Great Britain for a light Fino Sherry from Sandeman known as Fino Campero in Spain.

Fino Soto (Fr) a fine Fino Sherry produced by José de Soto, Jerez de la Frontera.

Fino Valley (N.Z) a winery based in Henderson, North Island. 3ha. Noted for Alphonse Lavalee (a sweet red, high-alcohol wine).

Fins Becs (Fr) denotes a person with a finely tuned nose (smell).

F

Fins Bois (Fr) the fourth Cru of Cognac which covers 35.5% of region.

Finsbury Distillery (Eng) the home of Stone's Original Green Ginger Wine in north London.

Finsprit (Den) the brand-name of an akvavit produced by D.D.S.

Fiole du Pape [La] (Fr) the label of a Châteauneuf-du-Pape produced by négociant Brotte in Châteauneuf-du-Pape, southern Rhône. *See also* Père Anselme, Flascoulet (Le).

Fion (Ire) wine.

Fionchaor (Ire) grape.

Fioncheannai (Ire) vintner.

Fion Dearg (Ire) red wine.

Fion den Scoth (Ire) vintage wine.

Fion Éadrom (Ire) light wine.

Fion Geal (Ire) white wine.

Fionghloine (Ire) wine glass.

Fionghort (Ire) vineyard.

Fion Milis (Ire) sweet wine.

Fionnar (Scot) a natural spring mineral water from Achmony Farm, Drumnadrochit, Inverness.

Fion Neamh-Mhilis (Ire) dry wine.

Fioralcól (Ire) pure alcohol.

Fiorano (It) a red wine produced by Boncampagni Ludovisi in Latium.

Fior d'Alpe (It) a very sweet, spicy liqueur, made from such herbs as mint, thyme, marjoram, hyssop, juniper etc. Has a sprig of herb inside bottle on which the sugar crystallises 46% alc by vol. Also called Fior d'Alpi.

Fior d'Alpi (It) *see* Fior d'Alpe 40% alc by vol.

Fior di Mandorla (Cktl) ⁵⁄₁₀ measure white rum, ³⁄₁₀ measure sweet vermouth, ¹⁄₁₀ measure apricot brandy, ¹⁄₁₀ measure amaretto. Shake over ice and strain into a cocktail glass.

Fiore (It) a high quality grape must.

Fioruisce (Ire) fresh water/spring water.

Fior Uisce (Ire) a still and sparkling natural spring mineral water (established 2003) from Tourmakeady, County Mayo (green label: sparkling/blue label: still). Mineral contents (milligrammes per litre): Sodium 107.2mg/l, Calcium 95.7mg/l, Magnesium 9.64mg/l, Potassium 22mg/l, Bicarbonates 196mg/l, Chlorides 56mg/l, Sulphates 314mg/l, Fluorides 0.167mg/l, Silicates 16.1mg/l, Strontium 2.7mg/l. pH 7.8

Fioupe Cocktail (Cktl) 30mls (¼ gill) Cognac, 30mls (¼ gill) Italian vermouth, 1 teaspoon Bénédictine. Stir over ice, strain into a cocktail glass, add a cherry and a squeeze of lemon peel juice on top.

Fire (S.Afr) the label for a sweet rosé wine (Chenin blanc and Pinotage blend) from the Elements range of wines produced by the Hartswater Wine Cellar winery, Hartswater, Northern Cape.

Fire Bellied Toad (Eng) a 5% alc by vol. cask ale brewed by the Frog Island Brewery, The Maltings, Westbridge, St. James Road, Northampton.

Fire Box (Eng) a 6% alc by vol. premium bottle-conditioned bitter brewed by RCH Brewery, West Hewish, Somerset.

Fire Brigade (Eng) a 3.8% alc by vol. ale from the Mordue Brewery, North Shields, Tyne & Wear.

Firecracker (Eng) a 5.8% alc by vol. bottled ale brewed by the Harvey Brewery, Lewes, Sussex.

Firecracker (Eng) the name for a beer brewed by micro-brewery Firecracker & Firkin, Brighton Road, Crawley.

Fire Cracker (Punch) 1 bottle red wine, 550mls (1pint) water, 200g. (½ lb) sugar, 2 lemons, 4 sticks cinnamon, 4 cloves. Boil the water with sugar, lemon juice, cloves and cinnamon for 5 minutes, add wine, heat slowly to boiling point and serve.

Firecracker & Firkin (Eng) a micro-brewery in Brighton Road, Crawley. Brews: Firecracker 4.3% alc by vol. Dynamite Stout 4.5% alc by vol. Gunpowder 5% alc by vol. Rocket 3.5% alc by vol.

Fired Earth (S.Afr) the label for a LVB Port-style wine (Shiraz 48% plus Touriga, Pinotage and Tinta blend) produced by the Villiera Wines winery, Stellenbosch, Western Cape.

Fire Devil Cocktail (Cktl) 30mls (¼ gill) sloe gin, 30mls (¼ gill) French vermouth, 30mls (¼ gill) Italian vermouth, 2 dashes Angostura. Stir over ice, strain into a cocktail glass and serve with a dash of lemon peel juice.

Fire Engine Red (S.Afr) the label for red wine (Cinsaut, Merlot and Ruby cabernet blend) produced by the Coleraine Wines winery, Suider-Paarl, Western Cape.

Fireman's Sour (Cktl) 35mls (1½ fl.ozs) golden rum, 10mls (½ fl.oz) grenadine, 25mls (1fl.oz) lime juice, 2 dashes gomme syrup. Shake over ice, strain into a large cocktail glass, top with a splash of soda water and decorate with a slice of orange and a cherry.

Firenze (It) the Italian spelling of Florence.

Fireside Port (Austr) a Port-style wine produced by Miranda Wines in New South Wales.

Firestead (USA) a winery based in the Willamette Valley, Oregon. Grape variety: Pinot noir.

Firestone Vineyard (USA) a large winery on the Solvang Plateau in the Santa Ynez Valley, Santa Barbara, California. 125ha. Grape varieties: Cabernet sauvignon, Chardonnay, Gewürztraminer, Johannisberg riesling, Merlot and Pinot noir. Produces varietal and table wines.

Firewater (USA) the old American Indian name for whiskey (as it gave a burning sensation as they swallowed it).

Firefly (Eng) a 3.7% alc by vol. ale brewed by the O'Hanlon's Brewery Cº. Ltd., Devon.

Firgas (Sp) a natural spring mineral water from Firgas, Gran Canaria. Mineral contents (milligrammes per litre): Sodium 62.9mg/l, Calcium 79.7mg/l, Magnesium 41.4mg/l, Potassium 10.1mg/l, Bicarbonates 513.8mg/l, Chlorides 44.7mg/l, Sulphates 28.2mg/l, Silicates 113.1mg/l.

Fire Gully (Austr) a winery based in the Margaret River in Western Australia. Grape varieties include: Cabernet sauvignon.

F

Firkin (Eng) a nine gallon (40.5litres) beer cask.

Firkin (Eng) the name given to a chain of public houses that brew their own beers in London under the Bruce name.

Firkin 98 (Eng) a 4.5% alc by vol. cask-conditioned lager brewed by the Foundry & Firkin in Sheffield to celebrate the 1998 World Cup.

Firkin Special Brew (Eng) *see* F.S.B.

Firm (Eng) a term used to describe wines that have a good constitution, held up with a certain amount of acidity and tannin.

Firme (Sp) a word used to describe a stable Sherry.

Firn (Ger) a tired, woody, madeirised wine.

Firnriesling (USA) a white grape variety, a cross between White Riesling and Muscat St. Laurent.

First (Chi) a natural spring mineral water. Mineral contents (milligrammes per litre): Sodium 22.3mg/l, Calcium 53.8mg/l, Magnesium 19mg/l, Potassium 2mg/l, Bicarbonates 217.5mg/l, Chlorides 15.1mg/l, Sulphates 47.5mg/l, Fluorides 0.33mg/l. pH 7.9

First (Ger) vineyard (Anb): Baden. (Ber): Badische Frankenland. (Gro): Tauberklinge. (Vil): Reicholzheim.

First (Ger) vineyard (Anb): Franken. (Ber): Maindreieck. (Gro): Rosstal. (Vil): Eussenheim.

First (S.E.Asia) a still natural spring mineral water from the Philippines. Mineral contents (milligrammes per litre): Sodium 40mg/l, Calcium 48mg/l, Magnesium 14mg/l, Bicarbonates 259mg/l, Chlorides 15mg/l, Sulphates 17mg/l. pH 7.0

First Aid Cocktail (Eng) a slang term for a '*double brandy*'.

FirstCape Vineyards (S.Afr) a winery (established 2002) based in the Paarl, Western Cape. Grape varieties: Cabernet sauvignon, Chardonnay, Chenin blanc, Colombard, Merlot, Pinotage, Sémillon, Shiraz. Website: http://www.firstcape.com

First Cask (Scot) an unblended cask of a 16 year old Glen Mhor highland malt whisky bottled on 31st September 1978 46% alc by vol.

First Chop (Chi) the name given to finest quality tea which is gathered in April and May.

First Class (USA) the label for a red wine (Pinot noir) produced by the Benton Lane winery, Oregon.

First Edition (Eng) an 8.4% alc by vol. cider from Taunton Cider, Norton Fitzwarren, Somerset.

First Gold (Eng) a new variety of dwarf hop, *See also* Herald, Pioneer.

First Gold (Eng) a 3.8% alc by vol. special ale named after the new dwarf hop variety it is brewed with. From the Butterknowle Brewery, Lynesack, County Durham.

First Growths [1] (Fr) the top five château classified in the Bordeaux Haut-Médoc, *see* Premier Grand Cru Classé.

First Growths [2] (Fr) the top clasification of Sauternes and Barsac in Bordeaux, *see* Premier Cru Classé Sauternes.

Firstland Vineyards (N.Z) a winery based in Gimblett Road, Hawkes Bay. Grape varieties: Cabernet sauvignon, Chardonnay, Sauvignon blanc, Shiraz.

First Light (Eng) a 3.5% alc by vol. light ale brewed by Eastwood & Sanders Ltd. (Fine Ales), West Yorkshire.

First Light (Eng) a 4.3% alc by vol. seasonal ale brewed by the Hook Norton Brewery, Banbury, Oxon.

First Light (Scot) a 4.3% alc by vol. ale brewed by the Fyfe Brewing C°., Fife.

First Marriage (Scot) the term used during whisky production for the marrying of the malt whiskies. *See also* Marriage.

First Night (Cktl) ¼ measure Tia Maria, ¼ measure Van der Hum, ¼ measure brandy, 1 barspoon cream. Shake over ice and strain into a cocktail glass.

First Season Vine (Fr) a name given to the vines like the Pinots that ripen early, are young maturing and degenerate quickly.

First Sighting (S.Afr) the label for a range of varietal wines from Agulhas Wines, Bredasdorp, Southern Cape.

Fiscanensis (Fr) an élixer made by the monks of Fècamp, the original name of Bénédictine.

Fisch (Ger) village (Anb): Mosel-Saar-Ruwer. (Ber): Obermosel. (Gro): Gipfel. (Vins): Sites not yet chosen.

Fischer (Ger) vineyard (Anb): Franken. (Ber): Maidreieck. (Gro): Not yet assigned. (Vil): Frickenhausen am Main.

Fischer Brasserie (Fr) a brewery (established 1821) based in Schiltigheim. Brews: Desperados, Fischer Tradition, Kingston.

Fischer [Christian] (Aus) a winery based in Sooss, Thermenregion. (Add): Hauptstrasse 33, 2500 Sooss. Grape varieties: Cabernet sauvignon, Pinot noir, Riesling, Traminer, Zweigelt.

Fischerpfad (Ger) vineyard (Anb): Rheinhessen. (Ber): Nierstein. (Gro): Rheinblick. (Vil): Alsheim.

Fischer [Richard] (Aus) a winery based in Leobersdorf, Thermenregion. (Add): Enzensfelder Strasse 16, 2544 Leobersdorf. Grape varieties: Cabernet sauvignon, Pinot noir, Scheurebe, Zweigelt. Produces a range of dry and sweet wines.

Fischingen (Ger) village (Anb): Baden. (Ber): Markgräflerland. (Gro): Vogtei Rötteln. (Vin): Sonnhohle.

Fisherman Ale (Eng) a seasonal old brown ale 1042 O.G. 4.5% alc by vol. brewed by the Adnams Sole Bay Brewery in Suffolk.

Fisherman's (S.Afr) the label for a sweet white wine (Hanepoot) produced by the Wamakersvallei Winery, Wellington, Western Cape.

Fisherman's Whopper (Eng) a 4.3% alc by vol. malty event ale brewed by Ridley Brewery, Hartford End, Chelmsford, Essex. Available in July.

Fisherrow Brewery (Scot) a brewery. (Add): Unit 11–12, Duddington Park, Edinburgh, Midlothian EH15 3NX. Brews a variety of beers and lager.

F

Website: http://www.fisherrow.co.uk 'E'mail: sales@fisherrow.co.uk

Fisher Vineyards (USA) a winery based near Santa Rosa, Sonoma County, California. 8ha. Grape varieties: Cabernet sauvignon, Chardonnay, Sauvignon blanc. Produces varietal wines. Label: Wedding Vineyard.

Fish Glue (USA) a slang term for isinglass.

Fish Hoek (S.Afr) the label for a range of wines produced by the Flagstone Winery, Somerset West, Western Cape

Fish House Punch (Punch) 2¼ litres (4pts) Jamaican rum, 1100mls (2pts) Cognac, 2¼ litres (4pts) water, 300grms (¾ lb) loaf sugar, juice 2 lemons, 1 wine-glass peach brandy. Heat all together and serve.

Fish T'Ale (Eng) a cask-conditioned ale 1036 O.G. brewed by the home-brew public house the Flounder and Firkin based in London.

Fismes (Fr) a canton in the Champagne region. Has the Cru villages: Châlons-sur-Vesle, Chenay, Crugny, Hermonville, Hourges, Pévy, Prouilly, Trigny, Unchair and Vandeuil.

Fita Azul (Port) a brand-name for a sparkling wine.

Fitger (USA) the brand-name used by Schell in New Ulm, Minnesota for their range of light beers.

Fitou (Fr) a commune within the A.C. Fitou region, Languedoc, south-western France. Produces red wines.

Fitou (Fr) an A.C. wine region near Corbières, Languedoc-Roussillon. Produces red and white wines (Coms): Cascastel, Caves-de-Treilles, Fitou, Lapalme, Leucate, Paziols, Treilles, Tuchan and Villeneuve-les-Corbières. Minimum alc. 12% by vol.

Fitusberg (Ger) vineyard (Anb): Rheingau. (Ber): Johannisberg. (Gro): Steinmacher. (Vil): Oberwalluf.

Fiuggi (It) a sparkling natural spring mineral water from Fiuggi. Mineral contents (milligrammes per litre): Sodium 6.4mg/l, Calcium 15.9mg/l, Magnesium 6.3mg/l, Potassium 4.4mg/l, Bicarbonates 81.7mg/l, Chlorides 13.9mg/l, Sulphates 6mg/l, Nitrates 7mg/l, Silicates 12.8mg/l. pH 6.8

Fiuza-Bright (Port) a vineyard in Ribatejano. Grape varieties include: Cabernet sauvignon, Merlot, Chardonnay and Sauvignon blanc. Produces: red, white and rosé wines.

Five Alive Lite (Eng) a mixed citrus drink containing an artificial sweetener (no added sugar) produced by Refreshment Spectrum.

Five Bridge Bitter (Eng) a 3.8% alc by vol. bitter beer brewed by the Mordue Brewery Ltd., Tyne & Wear.

Five Crowns (Port) a brand of tawny Port produced by Graham Port shippers, Oporto.

Five Finger Lakes (USA) *see* Finger Lakes.

Five Flags (Bel) a 5% alc by vol. bottled premium lager.

Five Hundred [500] (Eng) a special ale 1090–1100 O.G. brewed by the Watney Coombe Reid Brewery to celebrate 500 years of brewing in 1987.

Five Hundred [500] Year Celebration Ale (Eng) a 1104 O.G. ale brewed by Watney Coombe Reid. Sold in 250mls (½ pint) bottles.

Five Kings (Eng) the kings of Cyprus, Denmark, England, France and Scotland who, in 1363, were invited to a banquet by the mayor of London (Sir Henry Picard) to discuss and help improve the English wine trade.

Five-O-One [501] (Sp) a brand of Fino Sherry produced by De Terry in Puerto de Santa Maria.

Five Rings (Eng). 4.1% alc by vol. golden event ale brewed by Ridleys Hartford End Brewery, Chelmsford, Essex (available in September).

Five Rivers (USA) a winery based in the Santa Barbara County, California. Grape variety: Pinot noir.

Five Senses (S.Afr) the export label for a range of wines produced by the Overhex Private Cellar winery, Worcester, Western Cape.

Five Soldiers (S.Afr) the label for a white wine (Chardonnay) produced by the Rustenberg Wines winery, Stellenbosch, Western Cape.

Five Star (Switz) a de luxe beer brewed by the Hürlimann Brauerei in Zurich.

Five Star Bitter (Eng) a keg bitter 1043 O.G. brewed by the Home Brewery in Nottingham.

Five Star Rhum (W.Ind) a straight unblended 7 year old vintage spirit from Haiti.

Five Thirty (Can) a Canadian whisky produced by the Canadian Schenley Distilleries Ltd. 40% alc by vol.

Five Towns Brewery (Eng) a brewery (established 1983) based at Hanley in Staffordshire. Noted for cask-conditioned Bursley Bitter 1040 O.G. and Bennet's Strong Ale 1057 O.G.

Five X (Eng) a cask-conditioned ale 1044 O.G. brewed by the Shepherd Neame Brewery in Kent.

Five X (Eng) an 1105 O.G. ale brewed by Greene King. Oak matured for 5 years.

F.I.V.S. (Fr) *abbr:* The International Federation of Wine and Spirit Merchants.

Fix (Gre) a well-known brand of lager beer.

Fixed Acids (Eng) the principal fixed acids (non-volatile) to be found in wine are: tartaric, malic, succinic and lactic.

Fixer (Cktl) ¼ measure brandy, ¼ measure prunelle, ¼ measure crème de noyau, ⅛ measure cream. Shake over ice and strain into a cocktail glass.

Fixes (Cktl) spirit, lemon, sugar, water and fruit, served in a highball glass with shaved ice.

Fixin (Fr) a commune in the north of the Côte de Nuits, sited around the hamlet of Fixey. Has its own A.C. and also part of the A.C. Côte de Nuits. Has 6 Premier Crus: Aux Cheusots, Clos de la Perrière, Clos du Chapitre, Les Arvelets, Les Hervelets and Les Meix-Bas. 22.14ha. Has a good micro-climate and 131ha vineyards. Also sells part of the wine under the A.C. Côte de Beaune-Villages.

Fizz (Cktl) 5 parts iced sparkling wine to 1 part grenadine served in a flute (or tall) glass.

Fizz (Eng) a slang term for sparkling wine.

Fizzes (Cktl) spirit, lemon, sugar and soda water

served in a tall glass with ice cubes, usually consumed in the mornings.

Fizz Glass (USA) a tumbler-shaped glass 175mls–250mls (6fl.ozs–8fl.ozs) capacity.

Fjord Cocktail (Cktl) 25mls (⅛ gill) Cognac, 15mls (⅛ gill) each of akvavit, orange juice, lime juice, 4 dashes grenadine. Shake well over ice and strain into an ice-filled old-fashioned glass.

Flabby (Eng) a term to describe a wine that lacks balanced acidity.

Flaccianello della Pieve (It) a Cru vineyard (10ha) in the DOCG Chianti Classico, near Panzano, Tuscany. Grape varity: Sangiovese. Owned by the Fondtodi winery, the wine does not hold the DOCG classification (because it is produced from 100% Sangiovese).

Flach (Ger) lit: 'flat', describes a wine that possesses no outstanding characteristics.

Fläche (Ger) vineyard (Anb): Nahe. (Ber): Kreuznach. (Gro): Kronenberg. (Vil): Bad Kreuznach. (n.b. is not an Einzellagen).

Flacon (Fr) bottle/flask/flagon.

Flacon d'Exception (Fr) the name for a magnum of old vintage Champagne disgorged to order produced by Pommery et Gréno.

Fladderack (Hol) a citrus-flavoured brandewijn.

Flag Ale (Austr) a dark ale brewed by the Toohey's Brewery in New South Wales.

Flagey-Échezeaux (Fr) a noted wine town within the Côte de Nuits, Burgundy. see Échezeaux and Grand-Échezeaux.

Flagon (Eng) a quarter bottle of 39fl.ozs used for beers and cider.

Flag Porter (Eng) a 5% alc by vol Victorian porter ale brewed by Darwin Brewery, Crook, County Durham using yeast from a bottled beer from an 1825 shipwreck.

Flagship (S.Afr) the label for a Bordeaux-style red wine (Cabernet sauvignon, Malbec, Merlot and Petit verdot blend) produced by the Ernie Els Wines winery, Stellenbosch, Western Cape.

Flagship (S.Afr) the label for a red wine (50% Cabernet sauvignon and 50% Merlot blend) produced by the Havana Hills winery, Philadelphia, Western Cape.

Flagship (S.Afr) the label for a red wine (Syrah) produced by the Spice Route Wine Company, Swartland, Western Cape.

Flagship Brewery (Eng) a brewery based at Chatham Dockyard, Dartford. Brews: Capstan, Crow's Nest, Destroyer, Ensign, Futtock, Gang Plank, Spring Pride, Nelson's Blood, Friggin in the Riggin. Now known as the Nelson Brewing Company.

Flag Speciale (Afr) a beer 12.5° Plato brewed in Benin.

Flagstone Vineyard (S.Afr) a winery (established 1998) based at Two Roads, Somerset West, Western Cape. 130ha. Grape varieties: Cabernet sauvignon, Chardonnay, Chenin blanc, Merlot, Morio Muscat, Pinotage, Pinot noir, Sauvignon blanc, Shiraz. Labels: BK5, Cellar Hand, CWG Black South Easter, Dark Horse, Fish Hoek, Free

Run, Heywood House, Longitude, Mary le Bow, Noon Gun, Semaphore, The Backchat Blend, The Berrio, The Glass Carriage, The Last Word, The Music Room, The Poetry Collection, The Wallflower, Two Roads, Writer's Block. Website: http://www.flagstonewinery.co.za

Flambeau d'Alsace (Fr) a white wine of Alsace from noble grapes, gathered after certain prescribed date. Also Chevalier d'Alsace.

Flambé Cocktail (Cktl) 1 measure dry vermouth, 1 measure lemon juice. Stir over ice and strain into a saucer glass with crushed ice. Place a small slice of lemon on top and coat with a teaspoon of flaming Galliano.

Flamboyant Cocktail (Cktl) 1 measure golden rum, 1 measure crème de cacao, juice ¼ orange, 1½ measures pineapple juice, dash grenadine, 2 dashes lime juice. Shake over ice, strain into an ice-filled highball glass. Top with a slice of lime and a pineapple cube and serve with straws.

Flame Muscat (USA) a relation of the Muscat true grape. See also Red Hanepoot.

Flamenco (S.Afr) the label for a sparkling wine (Muscadel and Merlot) produced by the Rooiberg Winery, Robertson, Western Cape.

Flames Over New Jersey Punch (Punch) heat a bottle of applejack brandy with 200gms (½ lb) sugar, add 1 barspoon Angostura and ignite. Finally add 550mls (1pint) barley water, stir and serve in toddy mugs.

Flame Seedless (Austr)(USA) a red table grape variety.

Flame Tokay (USA) a white grape variety used for making dessert wines in California.

Flaming Cocktail (Cktl) another name for a traditionally-served Sambuca.

Flaming Ferrari (Cktl) a '*potent*' concoction consisting of 75mls (3fl.ozs) white rum, 75mls (3fl.ozs) dark rum, 25mls (1fl.oz) Grand Marnier, 25mls (1fl.oz) green Chartreuse. Blend rums and Grand Marnier together in a large cockail glass, ignite and drink through a straw whilst adding the green Chartreuse.

Flaming Glögg (Punch) stir well together 1 bottle akvavit, 1 bottle claret, 300mls (½ pint) orange juice, ginger root, 6 cloves, stick of cinnamon and the rind of an orange and lemon. Into a scooped-out ½ orange shell (the rim having been dipped in sugar) put some akvavit and set alight. Float on top of the wine and spice mixture for 2 minutes then overturn the orange shell and serve.

Flamingo (Cktl) 25mls (1fl.oz). Bourbon whiskey, 20mls (¾ fl.oz) crème de banane, 50mls (2fl.ozs) orange juice, 20mls (¾ fl.oz) lemon juice, 2 dashes grenadine, dash egg white. Shake over ice, strain into old-fashioned glass and decorate with a slice of orange and a cherry.

Flamingo Bay (S.Afr) the label for a range of wines produced by the Darling Cellars winery, Swartland.

Flamingo Cocktail [1] (Cktl) ¼ measure gin, ¼ measure apricot brandy, juice ½ lime, 4 dashes

F

grenadine. Shake well over ice and strain into a cocktail glass.

Flamingo Cocktail [2] (Cktl) 20mls (¾ fl.oz) vodka, 20mls (¾ fl.oz) Campari, shake over ice, strain into a flute glass, top with iced Champagne and dress with a slice of orange.

Flaminia (It) a natural spring mineral water from Flaminia.

Flanagan [Betsy] (USA) an Irish lady who is purported to have invented the cocktail. *see* Cocktail.

Flanders Crock Ale (Bel) a bottle-conditioned ale 7.2% alc by vol. from the Sterkens Brauerei.

Flannery's (Wal) a micro-brewery based in Aberystwyth (took over Bragdy Dyffryn). Brews: Granny's Flan 3.8% alc by vol. Celtic Ale 4.2% alc by vol. Oatmeal Stout 4.2% alc by vol. Dr. Johnsons draught, Drovers Bitter, Four Thumbs, Rheidol Reserve.

Flannigans (Ire) the label of a cream and Irish whiskey liqueur 15% alc by vol.

Flap (Cktl) 1 measure of brandy topped with soda water.

Flasca (Lat) flask/bottle.

Flasce (Eng) the mediaeval word for flask/bottle.

Flasche (Aus)(Ger) bottle.

Flaschen Bordeaux (Ger) a Bordeaux bottle.

Flaschengärung (Ger) bottle fermented (sparkling wines). *See also* Traditionelle Flaschengärung.

Flaschenkrank (Ger) bottle-sickness.

Flaschenschild (Ger) label.

Flascoulet [Le] (Fr) the label of a Châteauneuf-du-Pape produced by the négociant Brotte in Châteauneuf-du-Pape, southern Rhône. Bottle shaped in the old style with a slightly twisted appearance. *See also* Père Anselme, Fiole du Pape (La).

Flash Cocktail (Cktl) 60mls (½ gill) gin, 1 teaspoon absinthe, 1 teaspoon Angostura. Shake over ice, strain into a cocktail glass, serve with a cherry and a dash of lemon peel juice.

Flash Cooler (Eng) a refrigerated unit connected to the drink supply line near to the dispense tap. Serves the drink in the line at a pre determined temperature. Usually applied to beer, lager and cider.

Flash of Lightning (Eng) an old slang term for gin.

Flash Pasteurisation (Eng) a reliable method of passing wine through a heat exchanger where it is rapidly heated to 95°C (203°F) for 1–2 seconds and then rapidly cooled.

Flask (Eng) a style of jug or bottle. (Fr) = gourde, (Ger) = flasche, (Hol) = fles, (Lat) = flasca.

Flask (Eng) a vacuum container for keeping drinks either hot or cold. *see* Thermos.

Flaske (Den) bottle.

Flaske (Fr) a fourteenth century word for flask, bottle. *See also* Flasket, Flasque, Flasquet and Flaxe.

Flasket (Fr) a small flask or bottle, name often given to a hip flask. *See also* Flaske, Flasque, Flasquet and Flaxe.

Flasque (Fr) an old mediaeval word for flask or bottle. *See also* Flaske, Flasket, Flasquet and Flaxe.

Flasquet (Fr) an old mediaeval word for a flask or bottle. *See also* Flaske, Flasket, Flasque and Flaxe.

Flat (Eng) a term applied to sparkling wines that have lost their mousse, also applied to wines that have a lack of acidity on the finish (lifeless).

Flatbac (Eng) a 4.2% alc by vol. ale brewed by Bazens Brewery, Greater Manchester.

Flat Bean Santos (Bra) a variety of Santos pure coffee.

Flat Beer (Eng) a description of a beer that has lost its carbonation (draught or bottled).

Flat Cap (Eng) a 4% alc by vol. ale brewed by the Bank Top Brewery Ltd., Lancashire.

Flatterberg (Ger) vineyard (Anb): Württemberg. (Ber): Kocher-Jagst-Tauber. (Gro): Kocherberg. (Vil): Ernsbach.

Flatterberg (Ger) vineyard (Anb): Württemberg. (Ber): Kocher-Jagst-Tauber. (Gro): Kocherberg. (Vil): Forchtenberg.

Flavanol (Eng) a group of pigments which give the yellow colour to white wines.

Flavenoids (USA) the name given to phenolic substances (flavouring compounds) found in wines by Dr. Len McCloskey Ph.D. who owns the Felton-Empire Winery in Santa Cruz, mid-California. Five found on the skins of grapes are: Catechin, Epicatechin, Quercetin, Reservatrol, Rutin. *see* Oenin.

Flaverscenia dorada (Sp) *abbr:* F.D. a new type of disease transmitted by a mosquito-like insect in north-eastern Spain. Prevents fruit production, turns foliage yellow (to date has no known cure).

Flavia (It) a sparkling natural spring mineral water from Flavia. Mineral contents (milligrammes per litre): Sodium 0.64mg/l, Calcium 59.6mg/l, Magnesium 26.5mg/l, Potassium 0.24mg/l, Bicarbonates 271.5mg/l, Chlorides 0.61mg/l, Sulphates 28.6mg/l, Fluorides 0.1mg/l, Nitrates 1.1mg/l, Silicates 3.5mg/l. pH 7.45

Flavones (Eng) the alternative name for anthoxanthins.

Flavor (USA) the American spelling of Flavour.

Flavored Brandy (USA) a brandy-based liqueur which has an infusion of named fruit as flavouring.

Flavored Gin (USA) a sweet gin usually flavoured with either citrus or botanicals. i.e. orange, lemon, lime or mint.

Flavored Rums (USA) spirits which have a mixture of flavourings added after fermentation and before distillation to give the finished spirit such flavours as Sherry, Madeira, almond etc.

Flavored Vodka (USA) a sweetened and flavoured vodka, usually flavoured with citrus fruits, mint or grape juice.

Flavored Wines (USA) *see* Pop Wines.

Flavour (Eng) the taste experienced in the mouth from drink, food, etc. can be pleasant or unpleasant. *see* Finish and After-taste.

Flaxe (Fr) a mediaeval word for flask. *See also* Flaske, Flasket, Flasque and Flasquet.

Fleece and Firkin (Eng) a home-brew public house

F

based in Bristol (owned by Halls). Noted for cask-conditioned Coal Porter 1048 O.G. Best Bristol 1045 O.G. Bootlace 1038 O.G. and Dogbolter 1060 O.G.

Fleece 500 (Eng) a 4.3% alc by vol. ale, the 500th guest ale of the Golden Fleece public house in Tiverton.

Fleein (Scot) an old word meaning drunk.

Flehingen (Ger) village (Anb): Baden. (Ber): Badische Bergstrasse/Kraichgau. (Gro): Stiftsberg. (Vin): Lerchenberg.

Flein (Ger) village (Anb): Württemberg. (Ber): Württembergisch Unterland. (Gro): Kirchenweinberg. (Vins): Altenberg, Eselsberg, Sonnenberg.

Fleischmann (USA) a Bourbon whiskey distillery based on the Indiana border in Kentucky.

Fleischmann Preferred (USA) the brand-name of a blended whiskey 40% alc by vol.

Fleischtraube (Ger) lit: 'fleshy or pulpy', the name for the red grape variety Trollinger.

Flemlingen (Ger) village (Anb): Pfalz. (Ber): Südliche Weinstrasse. (Gro): Bischofskreuz. (Vins): Herrenbuckel, Vogelsprung, Zechpeter.

Flerchinger Vineyards (USA) vineyards based in Hood River County, Oregon. Grape varieties: Chardonnay, Cabernet sauvignon, Riesling, Grenache, Merlot.

Fles (Hol) bottle.

Fleshy (Eng) a term used to describe wines with plenty of fruit and body.

Flessebakje (Hol) coaster.

Fletcherism (USA) the practice of drinking in small sips to aid the digestion (this together with chewing food thoroughly), invented by Horace Fletcher (1840–1919) an American nutritionalist.

Flétri (Switz) a term for withered **Botrytis cinerea** attacked grapes used to make sweet wines.

Fleur (Eng) an alternative name for **Mycodermae**.

Fleur (USA) a winery based in Carneros, northern California. Grape variety: Pinot noir.

Fleuraison (Fr) the flowering of the vine (May-June in northern hemisphere). (Eng) = floraison. Vintage usually takes place 100 days after flowering.

Fleur de Bière (Fr) a 40% alc by vol. eau-de-vie made using beer by Bertrand, Uberach, Alsace.

Fleur de Cap Wines (S.Afr) the brand-name for the Die Bergkelder Estate, Stellenbosch, Western Cape varietal wines, Coastal region. Grape varieties: Cabernet sauvignon, Chardonnay, Chenin blanc, Merlot, Pinotage, Riesling, Sauvignon blanc, Sémillon, Shiraz, Viognier. Owned by Distell. Website: http://www.fleurducap.co.za

Fleur de Champagne (Fr) a vintage Champagne produced by Duval-Leroy, 69 Ave. de Bammental, 51130 Vertus.

Fleur du Lys (Fr) the name of an A.C. Blanquette de Limoux produced by Producteurs de Blanquette de Limoux.

Fleurie (Fr) an A.C. Cru Beaujolais-Villages, Burgundy. Has 850ha under vines.

Fleuron [Le] (USA) the brand-name label used by the Joseph Phelps Vineyards for a range of varietal and table wines.

Fleurs de Vin (Fr) **Mycodermae vini** a fungus which develops on low-alcoholic wines, appears as a whitish film on ullaged wines.

Fleury-la-Rivière (Fr) a Cru Champagne village in the Canton d'Épernay. District: Épernay.

Flexerne Fruit Farm (Eng) a vineyard (established 1965). (Add): Fletching Common, Newick, Sussex. 1.2ha Soil: sand. Grape variety: Müller-Thurgau. Vinification by Merrydown Wine C°.

Fleys (Fr) a commune in the A.C. Chablis, Burgundy.

Fliers (Eng) the name given to the dead yeasts (lees) on unracked wine that lift from the bees occasionally, especially if an un-disgorged bottle of Champagne is opened. see Beeswine.

Flietre (Fr) the name for the Syrah grape in the Drôme, Rhône.

Flight of the Fish Eagle (S.Afr) a 38% alc by vol., 3 y.o. cask matured 100% pot-stilled brandy produced by Distill in Stellenbosch, Western Cape.

Fliniaux [Roland] (Fr) a Champagne producer. (Add): 1 Rue Léon-Bourgeois, 51160 Aÿ. 4ha. Produces vintage and non-vintage wines. Vintages: 1973, 1976, 1985, 1989, 1990, 1995, 1996, 1997, 1998, 1999.

Flint Glasses (Eng) an old nickname for cut-glass.

Flinty (Eng) a term describing a dry, clean white wine which has a special bouquet, and a particular finish on the palate. e.g. Pouilly Fumé.

Flip Pot (USA) the American name for the neapolitain pot (coffee-making method). See also Machinetta.

Flips (Cktl) spirit, sugar, egg yolk and nutmeg, shaken over ice, strained and served in a small glass.

Flirt (Austr) 150mls bottled sparkling Chardonnay wine produced by BRL Hardy. Part of the Seven Deadly Sins range. See also Envy, Greed.

Flitch Reserve (Eng) a dry table wine produced by Dunmow Priory in Essex.

Flitz (It) a natural spring mineral water from Flitz, Villnöss, Bozen. Mineral contents (milligrammes per litre): Sodium 1.4mg/l, Calcium 96mg/l, Magnesium 44mg/l, Potassium 0.13mg/l, Sulphates 1470mg/l, Fluorides 2.4mg/l, Iron 219.4mg/l, Manganese 10.65mg/l, Zinc 1.575mg/l, Aluminium 14.35mg/l, Hydrobromide 16mg/l.

Flitzani (Gre) cup.

Flives (Fr) a grade of rosé wine produced in the seventeenth century in northern France.

Floated Liqueurs (USA) the name for pousse-cafés.

Floater (USA) a long drink consisting of soda covered with a measure of liqueur or brandy poured in carefully over a spoon.

Floaters (Eng) the term used for odd 'bits' seen suspended in the wine, results from fruit pulp, filtering medium, casks or corks.

Floaters (Eng) a slang term used for the tea leaves that float on top of the brewed tea. Usually caused through poor brewing (water not boiling, insufficient infusion) or poor quality tea (the stem of the tea leaf).

Floats (Eng) used on wines in tanks to stop air contaminating the wine.

Floc (Fr) a fortified, unfermented grape juice apéritif wine from the Gers département in southern France 16%–18% alc by vol.

Flocculate (Eng) see Flocculent.

Flocculation (Eng) see Flocculent.

Flocculent (Eng) a term used to describe the deposit after fermentation that is easily disturbed. Also referred to as Flocculate and Flocculation.

Floc de Gascogne (Fr) see Floc.

Fløde (Den) cream.

Flogger (Eng) a wooden implement for corking bottles. see Boot and Flogger.

Flöhpeter (Ger) a term used for very sour (acidic) wines, are so sour that any fleas that bit the drinker would die due to the acid in the blood. Flöh = flea.

Flomborn (Ger) village (Anb): Rheinhessen. (Ber): Wonnegau. (Gro): Bergkloster. (Vins): Feuerberg, Goldberg.

Flonheim (Ger) village (Anb): Rheinhessen. (Ber): Bingen. (Gro): Adelberg. (Vins): Bingerberg, Klostergarten, La Roche, Pfaffenberg, Rotenpfad.

Flood Irrigation (Eng) the practice in the 'New World' of flooding vineyards in dry areas with water to saturate the ground (simulating heavy rainfall). Now superceded by drip-feed irrigation. Banned in the E.C.

Floodlight (Eng) a 3.5% alc by vol. ale brewed by the Filament and Firkin, Tyneside.

Floor Malting (Eng) the traditional method of germinating the barley (malting) on wooden floors where the barley is turned with wooden spades and forks to dispel excess heat. See also Saladin Box.

Floozy (Fr) see Freedom & Firkin.

Flor (Sp) lit: 'flower', a yeast growth on some Sherries which gives a white film and produces Fino Sherry. The yeast is *Saccharomyces ellipsoideus beticus* which feeds at alcohol levels of 15.2%–15.4% by vol. on air, glycerine, alcohol and fusel oils. Killed at 16.3%–16.4% alc by vol. See also Voile. (Eng) = flowers of wine.

Flora (USA) a white grape variety produced as a cross of Gewürztraminer x Sémillon.

Flora (Austr) the label of a rich, golden-coloured wine produced from late-picked flora grapes (cross between Gewürztraminer and Sémillon) by Brown Brothers Winery.

Flora Blanche [La] (Eng) the brand-name used by J.R. Parkington's to describe a sweet (and medium-sweet) white wine from the A.C. Premières Côtes de Bordeaux.

Flora di Alpi (It) see Fior d'Alpi – a mis-spelling of.

Flora di Monteuliveto (It) a herb liqueur produced in the monastery in Monteuliveto.

Floradora Cooler (Cktl) into a highball glass place the juice of a lime, 1 teaspoon powdered sugar, 15mls (⅛ gill) grenadine, 50mls (2fl.ozs) soda water. Stir, fill with ice and add 40mls (⅓ gill) dry gin and top with ginger ale.

Floraison (Eng) see Fleuraison.

Floralies (Fr) a natural spring mineral water. Mineral contents (milligrammes per litre): Sodium 22mg/l, Calcium 36mg/l, Magnesium 22mg/l, Potassium 1.5mg/l, Bicarbonates 263mg/l, Chlorides 4mg/l, Sulphates 4mg/l, Nitrates <1mg/l. pH 7.7

Flora Spring Wine C°. (USA) a winery based at 1978, West Zinfandel Lane, St. Helena, Napa Valley, California. 91ha. Grape varieties include Johannisberg riesling, Chardonnay, Sauvignon blanc, Pinot noir. Produces Triology: a blend of Cabernet sauvignon, Cabernet franc and Merlot, plus single vineyard wines Wild Boar Cabernet sauvignon, Rutherford Hillside Reserve Cabernet sauvignon.

Flor de Pingus (Sp) the second wine of the Dominio de Pingus in Ribera del Duero. See also Pingus.

Flor do Douro (Port) a red grape variety used in the making of Port to give fruit and body.

Floreal (S.Afr) the label for a range of white (Chenin blanc, Crouchen and Muscat blend) and red (Malbec and Merlot blend) wines produced by the Onderkloof winery, Stellenbosch, Western Cape.

Floreal (Sp) the name given to a range of red, white and rosado wines from Gandia Pla S.A. in Valencia.

Floreffe Blond (Bel) a 6.5% alc by vol. light amber, top-fermented, bottle-conditioned abbaye-style special beer from Lefèbvre in Quenast. See also Floreffe Double, Floreffe la Meilleure, Floreffe Triple.

Floreffe Dubbel (Bel) a 7% alc by vol. top-fermented, bottle-conditioned abbaye-style double beer from Lefèbvre in Quenast. See also Floreffe Blond, Floreffe la Meilleure, Floreffe Triple.

Floreffe la Meilleure (Bel) an 8% alc by vol. brown-red, top-fermented, bottle-conditioned abbaye-style special beer spiced with rich aromatics from Lefèbvre in Quenast. See also Floreffe Blond, Floreffe Double, Floreffe Triple.

Floreffe Triple (Bel) a 7.5% alc by vol. pale, top-fermented, bottle-conditioned abbaye-style triple beer from Lefèbvre in Quenast. See also Floreffe Blond, Floreffe Double, Floreffe la Meilleure.

Florens-Louis Brut (Fr) the label of a prestige cuvée Champagne produced by Piper-Heidsieck.

Flores Hermanos (Sp) a producer and exporter of Málaga wines.

Florida (Cktl) 25mls (1fl.oz). Galliano, 35mls (1½ fl.ozs) dry gin, 10mls (½ fl.oz) Campari, 100mls (4fl.ozs) grapefruit juice. Shake well over ice, strain into an ice-filled highball glass and top with soda and a slice of orange.

Florida (USA) a wine-producing state in south-eastern America. Produces mainly Muscadine wines.

F

Florida Cocktail [1] (Cktl) 1 part dry gin, 1 part pineapple juice, 1 part sweet vermouth. Shake well over ice and strain into a cocktail glass.

Florida Cocktail [2] (Cktl)(Non-alc) juice of ½ lemon, juice of ½ orange, 3 dashes Angostura, 2 dashes gomme syrup. Shake well over ice and strain into a cocktail glass.

Florida Cocktail [3] (Cktl)(Non-alc) 50mls (2fl.ozs) gomme syrup, 90mls (3½ fl.ozs) grapefruit juice, 35mls (1½ fl.ozs) orange juice, 2 dashes lemon juice, pinch salt. Shake together with ice, strain into a highball glass filled with crushed ice, top with soda water and decorate with sprig of mint.

Florida Cocktail [4] (Cktl) ¼ measure dry gin, ⅛ measure kirsch, ¼ measure Cointreau, ½ measure orange juice, 4 dashes lemon juice. Shake over ice and strain into a cocktail glass.

Florida Daiquiri (Cktl) 25mls (⅛ gill) white rum, juice of a lime, dash maraschino. Blend altogether with a scoop of crushed ice in a blender, pour into a flute glass and top with a cherry.

Florida Gold (Eng) the brand-name of an orange juice produced by Chevron. No additives or colourings (juice is flash frozen).

Florimont (Fr) a 15ha A.C. Alsace Grand Cru vineyard at Ingersheim, Haut-Rhin.

Florio (It) a noted brandy and wine producer.

Florisgaarden Wit (Bel) a beer with fruits. 3% alc by vol. Produced using peaches and raspberries.

Florita (Austr) a vineyard in Watervale, South Australia. Owned by the Leo Buring C°.

Flörsheim (Ger) village (Anb): Rheingau. (Ber): Johannisberg. (Gro): Daubhaus. (Vin): Herrnberg.

Flörsheim-Dalsheim (Ger) village (Anb): Rheinhessen. (Ber): Wonnegau. (Gro): Burg Rodenstein. (Vins): Bürgel, Frauenberg, Goldberg, Hubacker, Sauloch, Steig.

Flor Sherry (Sp) a Sherry-style, dry wine made from the Palomino grape that has been attacked by flor yeasts.

Flossmoor Brewery (USA) a brewery. (Add): 1035 Sterling Avenue, Flossmoor, Illinois 60422. Brews a variety of beers and lager. Website: http://www.flossmoorstation.com

Flounder and Firkin (Eng) a home-brew public house in London. Produces: cask-conditioned Dogbolter 1060 O.G. Fish T'Ale 1036 O.G. Whale Ale 1045 O.G. Apiarist's Delight 4.6% alc by vol.

Flowerdale Winery (Austr) a winery (established 1976). (Add): Whittlesea-Yea Road, Flowerdale, Yarra Valley. Grape varieties: Chenin blanc, Chardonnay, Traminer, Pinot noir.

Flower-Honey (Eng) a tasting term often used to describe the sweet taste of old Vouvray or other sweet honeyed wines.

Flowering (Sp) the term used to describe the growth of flor yeasts on Sherry.

Flower Liqueurs (Jap) liqueurs made from tea and rose petal, blue gentian, cherry blossom etc.

Flowers (Eng) the name used by Whitbreads for some of their southern beers and their West Midlands trading company. Noted for cask-conditioned Flowers IPA 1036 O.G., Flowers Original 4.4% alc by vol.

Flowers of Wine (Eng) the alternative name for Flor.

Flowers Vineyard (USA) a winery based in the Sonama County, California. (Add): 28500 Seaview Road, Cazadero, California 95421. Grape varieties include: Pinot noir. Label: Andreen-Gale Cuvée. Website: http://www.flowerswinery.com 'E'mail: info@flowerswinery.com

Flowery (Eng) the term used to describe the bouquet of certain wines, likened to the scent of flowers. Fine Mosels have this particular quality as also do some Riesling wines.

Flowery Orange Pekoe (Eng) abbr: FOP a grade of unbroken tea leaf, the youngest leaf with tips.

Flownes Neck (Eng) a cider produced on Luscombe Farm, Buckfastleigh, south Devon.

Fl.oz (Eng) abbr: Fluid Ounce one twentieth of an Imperial pint. 20fl.ozs = 1pint/568mls (approx).

Fl.oz (USA) abbr: Fluid Ounce one sixteenth of a U.S. pint. 16 fl.ozs = 1 U.S. pint = 473mls.

Fluchtig (Ger) light/empty.

Fluffy Duck (Cktl) 25mls (1fl.oz). dry gin, 25mls (1fl.oz). advocaat, 10mls (½ fl.oz) Cointreau, 20mls (¾ fl.oz) orange juice. Build into an ice-filled highball glass, stir in soda water, add straws and a stirrer.

Fluid Dram (Eng) a 3mls (⅛ fl.oz). See also Drachm.

Fluidised Bed Roaster (Eng) used in coffee production in the roasting process, lifts the coffee beans into a jet of hot air which roasts them between 3–10 minutes.

Fluoridation (Eng) the addition of fluoride to the drinking water supply to help prevent tooth decay.

Flurbereinigung (Ger) involves the pulling together of small vineyards and to reconstruct them into larger units. The costs of this operation are shared between the state and the owners and are funded by a 'per litre tax' called the stabilisierungsfonds. Used to increase the root-stock after phylloxera.

Flushes (Eng) a tip of 2 tea bush leaves and open bud (the portion of the bush which is used in tea making).

Flussbach (Ger) village (Anb): Mosel-Saar-Ruwer. (Ber): Bernkastel. (Gro): Schwarzlay. (Vin): Reichelberg.

Flute (Fr) a tall Champagne glass. See also Flûte d'Alsace.

Fluteau (Fr) a Champagne producer based in Gyé-sur-Seine. Produces vintage and non-vintage Champagnes. Website: http://www.fleuryjs.free.fr/ Champagne-fluteau

Flûte d'Alsace (Fr) the bottle used for Alsatian wines. Is the same shape and colour as the Mosel wine bottle but is approximately two centimetres taller. See also Flute.

Flyer (Eng) a term for a particle floating in wine.

Flying Dog Brewery (USA) a brewery. (Add): 2401 Blake Street, Denver, Colorado 80205. Brews a variety of beers and lager. Website: http://www.flyingdogales.com

Flying Dutchman (Cktl) 1 measure dry gin, dash Cointreau. Shake well over ice and strain into an ice-filled old-fashioned glass.

Flying Grasshopper (Cktl) ⅓ measure vodka, ⅓ measure (green) crème de menthe, 1/3 measure (white) crème de cacao. Stir over ice and strain into a cocktail glass.

Flying High (Cktl) 35mls (1½ fl.ozs) Booth's High & Dry gin, 25mls (1fl.oz). orange juice, 25mls (1fl.oz). cherry brandy, 4 dashes lemon juice, dash Angostura, 1 egg white. Shake over ice and strain into a wine glass.

Flying Horse (Ind) a premium lager beer 1052 O.G. brewed by the United Breweries in Bangalore.

Flying Scotsman (Cktl) ½ measure Scotch whisky, ½ measure Italian vermouth, dash Angostura, 2 dashes gomme syrup. Stir over ice and strain into a cocktail glass.

Flying Scotsman (Scot) a 5.1% alc by vol. ale brewed by Caledonian Brewery based in Edinburgh.

Flying Tiger (Cktl) 35mls (1½ fl.ozs) Bacardi Gold Label rum, 10mls (½ fl.oz) gin, 1 teaspoon grenadine, 2 dashes Angostura. Shake well with ice and strain into a cocktail glass.

Flying Winemaker (Eng) a term used to describe consultants or winemakers who travel from one region to another to make or advise on viticulture and vinification.

Flynn & Williams (Austr) a winery (established 1981) based at Flynn's Lane, Kyneton, Victoria. Grape variety: 100% Cabernet sauvignon.

Flynn Vineyards (USA) vineyards (established 1982) based in Willamette Valley, Oregon. Noted for sparkling wines. Grape varieties: Pinot noir, Chardonnay, Pinot gris.

Flysch (It) a mixture of crumbly marl and sandstone found in the foothills of the Collio Mountains.

FMC (S.Afr) the label for a white wine (Chenin blanc) produced by the Ken Forrester Wines winery, Stellenbosch, Western Cape.

Foam (Eng) the name given to the formation of bubbles which collect briefly at the top of a glass of sparkling wine. Also known as the Mousse.

Foam (USA) *see* Foam Collar.

Foam Collar (USA) a name given to the frothy head on a glass of beer.

Foaming Cocktail (USA) any cocktail that has had egg white added so that when shaken over ice produces a '*head*' of foam.

Foaming Head (Eng) the 'froth' on the top of a glass of beer.

Fob (Eng) the excessive froth seen when serving keg beer or lager beer. Occurs from over carbonation or if there is an air leak in the connections especially in cask-conditioned ales.

F.O.B. (Eng) *abbr*: **F**reight **O**n **B**oard.

Foch (USA) a red grape variety hybrid developed in Alsace, France.

Fockink (Ger) the producers of a noted brand of kümmel liqueur.

Focsani (Rum) a wine region noted for white wines from the Riesling grape, and also dessert wines from the Murfatler Hills. Includes the areas of Cotesti, Nicoresti and Odobesti.

Foehn (Ger) *see* Föhn.

Fog Cutter Cocktail (Cktl) ⅓ measure dark rum, ⅓ measure lemon juice, ⅙ measure dry gin, ⅙ measure brandy, juice of ½ an orange, 2 barspoons orgeat syrup. Shake over ice, strain into an ice-filled highball glass and top with a dash of sweet Sherry.

Fog Cutters (USA) an early American slang term for cider and beer.

Fog Horn Cocktail (Cktl) 25mls (⅓ gill) dry gin, juice ½ lime. Shake well over ice, strain into an ice-filled highball glass, top with ginger ale and a slice of lime.

Fogolar (It) a brandy produced by Distillerie Camel.

Fogoneu (Sp) a red grape variety grown on the Balearic Islands, also called Callet.

Föhn (Aus)(Ger) a warm southerly wind that blows across Lake Constance in Baden.

Fohrenberg (Ger) vineyard (Anb): Baden. (Ber): Bodensee. (Gro): Sonnenufer. (Vil): Meersburg.

Fohrenberg (Ger) vineyard (Anb): Baden. (Ber): Bodensee. (Gro): Sonnenufer. (Vil): Stetten.

Fohrenberg (Ger) vineyard (Anb): Baden. (Ber): Kaiserstuhl-Tuniberg. (Gro): Vulkanfelsen. (Vil): Ihringen.

Foil (USA) the metal or tinfoil capsules on Champagne and sparkling wine bottles.

Foire aux Vins (Fr) lit: 'wine fair/sale', an event, usually held in September–November when last year's vintages are sold off (at bargain prices) to make ready for new stock. French supermarchés often hold foire aux vins in non-wine-producing regions.

Foire aux Vins d'Orange (Fr) the Orange wine fair held on the Saturday closest to the middle of January in Orange, southern France. Shows off and judges the new wines of the region.

Fol (It) a noted producer of sparkling (cuve close) wines in Veneto.

Folatières [Les] (Fr) a Premier Cru vineyard in the A.C. commune of Puligny-Montrachet, Côte de Beaune, Burgundy 3.4ha.

Folded Edge (Eng) a name given to the base of drinking glasses made in the seventeenth century which is turned under at the base.

Foley Winery (USA) a winery based in the Santa Rita Hills, Santa Barbara County, California. Grape variety: Pinot noir. Label: Rancho Santa Rosa.

Folgasão (Port) a white grape variety used in the production of Port. Also known as the Terrantez.

Folha de Figo (Bra) lit: 'fig leaf', a red grape variety.

Folk Hero (Ser) a sparkling mineral water bottled in Serbia.

Folle Blanche (Fr) a white grape variety which gives a pale acid wine that is low in alcohol. It is grown in France under many names. Picpoul in Cognac and Armagnac and Gros plant in the Loire. Also Avillo, Engageat blanc, Euragest and Picapoll blanc.

Folle Blanche (USA) *see* California Folle Blanche.

F

Folle Noire (Fr) a red grape variety grown in Bellet, Provence. Is also known as the Fuella nera.

Folly Ale (Eng) a 5% alc by vol. ale brewed by The Wharfedale Brewery, North Yorkshire.

Folly Gold (Eng) a 5% alc by vol. golden ale brewed by The Wharfedale Brewery, North Yorkshire.

Fómhar an Fhiona (Ire) vintage.

Fómharai Fionchar (Ire) grape picker.

Fond (Ger) a stabilization fund formed by weinwirtschaftsgesetz to increase wine quality, help guarantee the grower a realistic price, increase wine publicity and to store wine.

Fonda (Sp) inn/tavern.

Fond de Culotte (Cktl) 35mls (1½ fl.ozs) Suze, 10mls (½ fl.oz) crème de cassis. Add to ice in a Paris goblet and top with a little water if required.

Fondé (Fr) founded.

Fondillón (Sp) a D.O. red wine produced from 100% Monastrell grapes with 16% alc by vol. Unique to Alicante.

Fonsana Somosierra (Sp) a still mineral water from La Cabrera.

Fonseca (Port) vintage Port shippers. Vintages: 1870, 1873, 1878, 1881, 1884, 1887, 1890, 1896, 1900, 1904, 1908, 1912, 1920, 1922, 1924, 1927, 1934, 1945, 1948, 1955, 1960, 1963, 1966, 1970, 1975, 1977, 1980, 1983, 1985, 1992, 1994, 1995, 1997, 1998, 2000, 2003. *See also* Guimaraens.

Fonseca, [J.M.Da] (Port) a family firm based in Estremadura. Produces a wide range of wines.

Fon7es (Port) a natural spring mineral water from Covilha. Mineral contents (milligrammes per litre): Sodium 2.5mg/l, Calcium 5.3mg/l, Magnesium 0.9mg/l, Potassium 0.5mg/l, Bicarbonates 38mg/l, Chlorides 1.9mg/l, Sulphates 4.4mg/l, Fluorides 0.2mg/l. pH 6.1

Font (It) (Sp) fountain.

Font Agudes (Sp) a still natural spring mineral water from Arbúcies. Mineral contents (milligrammes per litre): Sodium 44.7mg/l, Calcium 52.9mg/l, Magnesium 15.1mg/l, Potassium 2.6mg/l, Bicarbonates 264.5mg/l, Chlorides 21.2mg/l, Sulphates 45.3mg/l, Fluorides 1.3mg/l, Nitrates 1.6mg/l.

Fontainbleu (Fr) an alternative name for the Golden chasselas grape.

Fontainbleu Special (Cktl) ⅗ measure Cognac, ⅗ measure anisette, ⅕ measure French vermouth. Shake over ice and strain into a cocktail glass.

Fontaine (Fr) fountain.

Fontaine de la Reine (Fr) a natural spring mineral water from Castelnau de Brassac, Tarn. Mineral contents (milligrammes per litre): Sodium 2.8mg/l, Calcium 3.2mg/l, Magnesium 0.4mg/l, Potassium 0.35mg/l, Bicarbonates 7.5mg/l, Chlorides 3mg/l, Sulphates 1mg/l, Nitrates 5.5mg/l. pH 6.1

Fontaine de la Reine Naturelle (Fr) a natural spring mineral water. Mineral contents (milligrammes per litre): Sodium 0.139mg/l, Calcium 0.325mg/l, Magnesium 0.016mg/l, Potassium 0.012mg/l, Bicarbonates 0.02mg/l, Chlorides 0.082mg/l, Sulphates 0.098mg/l, Fluorides 6.1mg/l, Silicates 0.01mg/l.

Fontaine Jolival (Fr) a natural spring mineral water from Vœuillet et Giget 16. Mineral contents (milligrammes per litre): Sodium 16.6mg/l, Calcium 46mg/l, Magnesium 33mg/l, Potassium 3.9mg/l, Bicarbonates 253mg/l, Chlorides 18mg/l, Sulphates 59mg/l, Fluorides 1mg/l, Nitrates <0.01mg/l. pH 7.6

Fontalba (It) a sparkling natural spring mineral water from Fontalba. Mineral contents (milligrammes per litre): Sodium 12.5mg/l, Calcium 25.8mg/l, Magnesium 6.9mg/l, Potassium 1.4mg/l, Bicarbonates 84.6mg/l, Chlorides 16.6mg/l, Sulphates 29.7mg/l, Nitrates 1.2mg/l, Silicates 13.8mg/l. pH 6.96

Fontana (Bel) a natural spring mineral water from Pearl, Maarkedal.

Fontana (Med) a natural spring mineral water from Malta. Mineral contents (milligrammes per litre): Sodium 15mg/l, Calcium 35mg/l, Chlorides 65mg/l, Fluorides 0.8mg/l, Nitrates 5mg/l.

Fontana Candida (It) a noted Frascati Classico producer.

Fontanaccio (It) a sparkling natural spring mineral water from Reiti, Lazio. Mineral contents (milligrammes per litre): Sodium 4.7mg/l, Calcium 102.2mg/l, Magnesium 2.7mg/l, Potassium 0.6mg/l, Bicarbonates 311mg/l, Chlorides 12mg/l, Sulphates 6.2mg/l, Fluorides 0.1mg/l, Nitrates 0.7mg/l, Silicates 5.5mg/l, Oxygen 9.5mg/l. pH 7.4

Fontana di Dio (Aus) a natural spring mineral water.

Fontanafredda (It) a famous winery in Alba, Piemonte in north-western Italy. (Add): Via Alba, 15–12050 Serralunga d'Alba, Italy. Produces a wide range of fine quality still and sparkling wines. *see* Serralunga d'Alba. Website: http://www.fontanafredda.it 'E'mail: info@fontanafredda.it

Fontanaro (Ger) a white grape variety cross between the Rieslaner and the Müller-Thurgau.

Fontanel (Fr) a natural spring mineral water. (Add): Eau de Source Poiraudière, La Roche sur Yon Vendée. Mineral contents (milligrammes per litre): Sodium 39.6mg/l, Calcium 36.3mg/l, Magnesium 10.9mg/l, Potassium 2.2mg/l, Sulphates 41.2mg/l, Fluorides 0.34mg/l, Silicates 39mg/l. pH 7.4

Fontanella (N.Z) a sparkling (méthode traditionelle) wine made from the Pinot meunier grape. Made by the Mission Vineyards near Napier in the Hawkes Bay region.

Fontainis Karl Eugen Quelle (Ger) a sparkling natural spring mineral water from Fontanis Mineralquellen, Sachsenheim-Spielberg. Mineral contents (milligrammes per litre): Sodium 45mg/l, Calcium 568mg/l, Magnesium 92.9mg/l, Potassium 8.7mg/l, Bicarbonates 326mg/l, Chlorides 40.7mg/l, Sulphates 1530mg/l, Fluorides 0.2mg/l, Nitrates 0.3mg/l, Silicates 18.8mg/l, Strontium 10.9mg/l.

F

Fontanis Natürliches Mineralwasser (Ger) a sparkling natural spring mineral water from Fontanis Mineralquellen, Sachsenheim-Spielberg. (white label: spakling/blue label: light gas). Mineral contents (milligrammes per litre): Sodium 38mg/l, Calcium 600mg/l, Magnesium 89mg/l, Potassium 8.4mg/l, Bicarbonates 340mg/l, Chlorides 38mg/l, Sulphates 1530mg/l, Fluorides 0.15mg/l.

Fontdalt (Sp) a natural spring mineral water. Mineral contents (milligrammes per litre): Sodium 4.6mg/l, Calcium 50.1mg/l, Magnesium 14.6mg/l, Potassium 0.5mg/l, Bicarbonates 164.9mg/l, Chlorides 11.6mg/l, Sulphates 41.1mg/l, Fluorides 0.1mg/l, Nitrates 1.6mg/l.

Font del Pi (Sp) a still natural spring mineral water. Mineral contents (milligrammes per litre): Sodium 28.1mg/l, Calcium 77.7mg/l, Magnesium 70.5mg/l, Potassium 1.4mg/l, Bicarbonates 300.7mg/l, Chlorides 22.7mg/l, Sulphates 233.3mg/l, Fluorides 0.9mg/l, Nitrates 11.7mg/l.

Font del Regàs (Sp) a still, slightly alkaline natural spring mineral water from Arbúcies (Girona). Mineral contents (milligrammes per litre): Sodium 13.5mg/l, Calcium 32.9mg/l, Magnesium 4.1mg/l, Potassium 1.6mg/l, Bicarbonates 129.2mg/l, Chlorides 7.2mg/l, Sulphates 10.2mg/l, Fluorides 0.5mg/l, Nitrates 1mg/l, Silicates 17.9mg/l. pH 8.8

Font del Subira (Sp) a natural spring mineral water from Osor, Girona.

Font d'Or (Sp) a natural spring mineral water from Saint Hilari Sacalm, Massif of Montseny (Girona). Mineral contents (milligrammes per litre): Sodium 8.3mg/l, Calcium 24mg/l, Magnesium 3.9mg/l, Potassium 1.6mg/l, Bicarbonates 62.2mg/l, Chlorides 4.6mg/l, Sulphates 14.8mg/l, Fluorides 0.2mg/l, Nitrates 20.9mg/l, Silicates 14.2mg/l. pH 8.2

Fonte (Bra)(Isr)(It)(Sp) fountain.

Fonte dei Medici (It) a natural spring mineral water from Vescina.

Fonte del Faro (It) a natural spring mineral water. Mineral contents (milligrammes per litre): Sodium 63.1mg/l, Calcium 1134.8mg/l, Magnesium 9.3mg/l, Potassium 4.6mg/l, Bicarbonates 312.7mg/l, Chlorides 162.2mg/l, Sulphates 40.1mg/l, Nitrates 3.2mg/l, Silicates 8.8mg/l.

Fonte della Buvera (It) a natural spring mineral water from Fonte della Buvera. Mineral contents (milligrammes per litre): Sodium 0.9mg/l, Calcium 13mg/l, Magnesium 0.8mg/l, Potassium 0.3mg/l, Bicarbonates 36.6mg/l, Chlorides 0.9mg/l, Sulphates 6.9mg/l, Nitrates 1.6mg/l, Silicates 8mg/l. pH 7.7

Fonte della Madonnina della Calabria (It) a natural spring mineral water from Fonte della Madonnina.

Fonte della Virtù (It) a natural spring mineral water brand.

Fonte delle Alpi (It) a sparkling natural spring mineral water. Mineral contents (milligrammes per litre): Sodium 1.2mg/l, Magnesium 0.3mg/l, Potassium 0.5mg/l, Chlorides 0.2mg/l, Sulphates 2.4mg/l. pH 6.8

Fonte delle Rocce (It) a natural spring mineral water brand.

Fonte del Lupo (It) a sparkling natural spring mineral water from Fonte del Lupo. Mineral contents (milligrammes per litre): Sodium 4mg/l, Calcium 3.2mg/l, Magnesium 1.4mg/l, Potassium 0.35mg/l, Bicarbonates 8.9mg/l, Chlorides 4.3mg/l, Sulphates 2.5mg/l, Nitrates 8.5mg/l, Silicates 4mg/l. pH 7.0

Fonte del Parco (It) a sparkling natural spring mineral water from Fonte del Parco. Mineral contents (milligrammes per litre): Sodium 5.5mg/l, Calcium 75mg/l, Magnesium 7.5mg/l, Potassium 1.1mg/l, Bicarbonates 258.2mg/l, Chlorides 3.2mg/l, Sulphates 17.6mg/l, Nitrates 1.4mg/l, Silicates 2.8mg/l, Oxygen 7.7mg/l. pH 7.72

Fonte di Alice (It) a sparkling natural spring mineral water from Fonte di Alice. Mineral contents (milligrammes per litre): Sodium 96.1mg/l, Calcium 57.2mg/l, Magnesium 23.1mg/l, Potassium 3mg/l, Bicarbonates 363mg/l, Chlorides 70.6mg/l, Sulphates 50.5mg/l, Fluorides 0.1mg/l, Strontium 2.2mg/l, Silicates 22.2mg/l. pH 7.8

Fonte Diana (It) a natural spring mineral water from Diana.

Fonte di Palme (It) a sparkling natural spring mineral water from Fonte di Palme. Mineral contents (milligrammes per litre): Sodium 22.8mg/l, Calcium 104.21mg/l, Magnesium 23.04mg/l, Potassium 1.41mg/l, Bicarbonates 305mg/l, Chlorides 36.21mg/l, Sulphates 51.5mg/l, Fluorides 0.43mg/l, Nitrates 40.5mg/l, Silicates 17.55mg/l, Oxygen 10.28mg/l. pH 7.21

Fonte di Tito (It) a natural spring mineral water from Firenze.

Fonte Abrau (It) a natural spring mineral water from Fonte Abrau. Mineral contents (milligrammes per litre): Sodium 0.8mg/l, Calcium 26mg/l, Magnesium 12.5mg/l, Potassium 0.2mg/l, Bicarbonates 140mg/l, Silicates 25.4mg/l. pH 8.1

Fonte Allegra (It) a sparkling natural spring mineral water from Salo, Brescia. Mineral contents (milligrammes per litre): Sodium 27.1mg/l, Calcium 65.5mg/l, Magnesium 23.3mg/l, Potassium 1.9mg/l, Bicarbonates 363.1mg/l, Chlorides 11.3mg/l, Sulphates 7.8mg/l, Nitrates 0.5mg/l, Silicates 16mg/l. pH 7.62

Fonte Alpinaia (It) a still and sparkling natural spring mineral water. Mineral contents (milligrammes per litre): Sodium 3.6mg/l, Calcium 24.7mg/l, Magnesium 4.4mg/l, Potassium 1mg/l, Bicarbonates 86mg/l, Chlorides 1.2mg/l, Sulphates 17.1mg/l, Fluorides 0.07mg/l, Nitrates 2.1mg/l, Silicates 6.6mg/l. pH 8.2

Fonte Alta (It) a natural spring mineral water from Romani I.

F

Fonte Angelica (It) a natural spring mineral water from Angelica.

Fonte Annia (It) a natural spring mineral water from Paradiso di Pocenia, Udine, Friuli. Mineral contents (milligrammes per litre): Calcium 53mg/l, Magnesium 23.7mg/l, Bicarbonates 183mg/l, Sulphates 75mg/l, Nitrates 4mg/l. pH 7.87

Fonte Antica dei Bagni di Barbarano (It) a natural spring mineral water from Fonte Antica.

Fonte Argentiera (It) a slightly acidic, sparkling natural spring mineral water from Frigurin. Mineral contents (milligrammes per litre): Sodium 2.85mg/l, Calcium 0.8mg/l, Magnesium 0.85mg/l, Potassium 0.25mg/l, Bicarbonates 5.3mg/l, Chlorides 3.1mg/l, Sulphates 0.8mg/l, Nitrates 3.2mg/l, Silicates 1.6mg/l, Oxygen 8.566mg/l. pH 5.9

Fonte Aura (It) a sparkling natural spring mineral water from Fonte Aura. Mineral contents (milligrammes per litre): Sodium 8.03mg/l, Calcium 132.4mg/l, Magnesium 6.1mg/l, Potassium 1.08mg/l, Bicarbonates 368.2mg/l, Chlorides 15.73mg/l, Sulphates 40.2mg/l, Nitrates 16.9mg/l, Silicates 8.73mg/l, Strontium 1.43mg/l, Oxygen 1.6mg/l. pH 7.36

Fontecabras (Sp) a still natural spring mineral water from Jaraba, Zaragona. Mineral contents (milligrammes per litre): Calcium 93mg/l, Magnesium 38.9mg/l, Bicarbonates 300.7mg/l, Chlorides 56.7mg/l, Sulphates 130.3mg/l.

Fonte Caiçara (Bra) a natural spring mineral water (established 2001) from Bela Vista de Goiás. Mineral contents (milligrammes per litre): Calcium 0.8mg/l, Magnesium 0.24mg/l, Potassium 0.09mg/l, Chlorides 0.081mg/l, Fluorides 0.017mg/l, Nitrates 0.04mg/l.

Fonte Caudana (It) a sparkling natural spring mineral water from Fonte Caudana. Mineral contents (milligrammes per litre): Sodium 2.64mg/l, Calcium 7.59mg/l, Magnesium 3.32mg/l, Potassium 0.73mg/l, Chlorides 1.43mg/l, Sulphates 4.22mg/l, Nitrates 3.49mg/l. pH 7.61

Fonte Celta (Sp) a natural spring mineral water (established 1903) from Céltigos, Galicia. Mineral contents (milligrammes per litre): Sodium 89.5mg/l, Calcium 26.5mg/l, Magnesium 1.8mg/l, Potassium 4.3mg/l, Bicarbonates 288.3mg/l, Chlorides 27.2mg/l, Sulphates 9.3mg/l, Fluorides 1mg/l, Silicates 33mg/l. Also spelt Fontecelta.

Fontecelta Gaseada (Sp) a sparkling natural spring mineral water from Céltigos, Galicia. Mineral contents (milligrammes per litre): Sodium 79.4mg/l, Calcium 19.6mg/l, Magnesium 1.7mg/l, Potassium 3.2mg/l, Bicarbonates 225mg/l, Chlorides 27.2mg/l, Sulphates 11.2mg/l, Fluorides 0.9mg/l, Nitrates <0.02mg/l.

Fonte Cerreto (It) a natural spring mineral water from Fonte Cerreto.

Fontechiara (It) a sparkling natural spring mineral water from Medesano, Parma. Mineral contents (milligrammes per litre): Sodium 76.5mg/l, Calcium 48.7mg/l, Magnesium 31.8mg/l, Potassium 3mg/l, Bicarbonates 353.8mg/l, Chlorides 9.6mg/l, Sulphates 111.5mg/l, Nitrates 6.1mg/l, Oxygen 2.99mg/l. pH 7.5

Fonte Corte Paradiso (It) a natural spring mineral water from Fonte Paradiso. Mineral contents (milligrammes per litre): Sodium 3.18mg/l, Calcium 71.6mg/l, Magnesium 27mg/l, Potassium 0.74mg/l, Bicarbonates 266mg/l, Sulphates 54.7mg/l. pH 7.65

Fontedoro (It) a slightly acidic, sparkling natural spring mineral water from Nunzio III, Oppido Mamertino, Reggio Calabria. Mineral contents (milligrammes per litre): Sodium 6mg/l, Calcium 4.8mg/l, Magnesium 1.4mg/l, Potassium 0.8mg/l, Bicarbonates 16.5mg/l, Chlorides 10mg/l, Sulphates 4.2mg/l, Fluorides 0.2mg/l, Nitrates 2mg/l, Silicates 5mg/l. pH 5.6

Fonte Elisa (It) a natural spring mineral water. Mineral contents (milligrammes per litre): Sodium 10mg/l, Calcium 99.8mg/l, Magnesium 2.8mg/l, Potassium 1.6mg/l, Bicarbonates 308mg/l, Chlorides 18mg/l, Sulphates 17.5mg/l, Nitrates 6.3mg/l, Silicates 9.9mg/l. pH 7.35

Fonte Gabinia (It) a sparkling natural spring mineral water from Gabinia. Mineral contents (milligrammes per litre): Sodium 11.2mg/l, Calcium 23.5mg/l, Magnesium 11.11mg/l, Potassium 10.5mg/l, Bicarbonates 119.1mg/l, Chlorides 17.31mg/l, Sulphates 4.49mg/l, Fluorides 0.11mg/l, Nitrates 22.82mg/l, Silicates 18.1mg/l, Oxygen 6.67mg/l. pH 6.9

Fontegal (Port) a white grape variety grown in Beiras.

Fonte Garbarino (It) a sparkling natural spring mineral water from Lurisia. Mineral contents (milligrammes per litre): Sodium 10.5mg/l, Calcium 22mg/l, Magnesium 0.7mg/l, Potassium 1.4mg/l, Bicarbonates 70mg/l, Oxygen 7.7mg/l. pH 7.1

Fonte Gaudianello (It) a slightly acidic, sparkling natural spring mineral water from Potenza. Mineral contents (milligrammes per litre): Sodium 130mg/l, Calcium 140mg/l, Magnesium 51mg/l, Potassium 47.2mg/l, Bicarbonates 877mg/l, Chlorides 36.8mg/l, Sulphates 117mg/l, Nitrates 2.4mg/l, Silicates 100mg/l, Strontium 1.8mg/l. pH 5.75

Fonte Geu (It) a natural spring mineral water from Udine.

Fonte Gioiosa (It) a natural spring mineral water from Quarona Sesia. Mineral contents (milligrammes per litre): Sodium 4.5mg/l, Calcium 4.91mg/l, Magnesium 0.87mg/l, Potassium 0.41mg/l, Bicarbonates 14.33mg/l, Chlorides 1.73mg/l, Sulphates 6.24mg/l, Nitrates 6.54mg/l, Silicates 15.4mg/l. pH 6.11

Fonte Giulia (It) a slightly acidic natural spring mineral water from Aanguillara Sabazia, Rome, Lazio. Mineral contents (milligrammes per litre):

F

Sodium 57.7mg/l, Calcium 92.5mg/l, Magnesium 23.6mg/l, Potassium 77.5mg/l, Bicarbonates 537.3mg/l, Chlorides 37.3mg/l, Sulphates 49mg/l, Fluorides 1.4mg/l, Nitrates 2.6mg/l, Silicates 73.8mg/l, Strontium 1.4mg/l. pH 5.73

Fonte Grande (Sp) a natural spring mineral water from La Coruña. Mineral contents (milligrammes per litre): Sodium 5.8mg/l, Calcium 0.9mg/l, Magnesium 1mg/l, Potassium 0.2mg/l, Bicarbonates 9.1mg/l, Chlorides 9.2mg/l, Silicates 9.1mg/l. pH 6.4 Also spelt Fontegrande.

Fonte Guizza (It) a sparkling natural spring mineral water from Scorze, Venezia. Mineral contents (milligrammes per litre): Sodium 7.1mg/l, Calcium 46mg/l, Magnesium 31mg/l, Potassium 1.1mg/l, Bicarbonates 296mg/l, Chlorides 2.8mg/l, Sulphates 4.6mg/l, Silicates 17mg/l. pH 7.67

Fonteide (Sp) a still natural spring mineral water from Galería el Mundo, La Orotava, Santa Cruz de Tenerife. Mineral contents (milligrammes per litre): Sodium 19.1mg/l, Calcium 7mg/l, Magnesium 3.7mg/l, Potassium 8.6mg/l, Bicarbonates 58mg/l, Chlorides 16.7mg/l, Sulphates 3.2mg/l, Fluorides 0.2mg/l, Nitrates 12.2mg/l.

Fonte Ijui (Bra) a natural spring mineral water (established 1926) from Ijui. Mineral contents (milligrammes per litre): Sodium 9.39mg/l, Calcium 5.31mg/l, Magnesium 6.2mg/l, Potassium 0.7mg/l, Bicarbonates 254.35mg/l, Chlorides 2.43mg/l, Sulphates 5.72mg/l, Fluorides 1.16mg/l, Nitrates 5.77mg/l. pH 8.0

Fonte Ilaria (It) a natural spring mineral water from Lucca.

Fonte Itala (It) a slightly acid, sparkling natural spring mineral water from Fonte Itala. Mineral contents (milligrammes per litre): Sodium 71.5mg/l, Calcium 58.3mg/l, Magnesium 14.9mg/l, Potassium 28.8mg/l, Bicarbonates 390mg/l, Chlorides 17.8mg/l, Sulphates 40.2mg/l, Fluorides 1.1mg/l, Nitrates 18.7mg/l, Silicates 85.7mg/l. pH 5.85

Fontel (Fr) a natural mineral water from the Vendée. (Add): 25, bd de l'Industrie, 85000 La-Roche-sur-Yon. Mineral contents (milligrammes per litre): Sodium 38mg/l–39.6mg/l, Calcium 36.3mg/l–38mg/l, Magnesium 9.6mg/l–10.9mg/l, Potassium 2.2mg/l–2.5mg/l, Bicarbonates 0mg/l–150mg/l, Silicates 39mg/l. pH 6.9

Fonte Laura (It) a sparkling natural spring mineral water (established 1995) from Fontelaura, Plesio, Como. Mineral contents (milligrammes per litre): Sodium 1.7mg/l, Calcium 46.4mg/l, Magnesium 22.4mg/l, Potassium 0.7mg/l, Bicarbonates 237.9mg/l, Chlorides 1.4mg/l, Sulphates 10.1mg/l, Nitrates 5.9mg/l, Silicates 5.5mg/l. pH 7.8

Fonte Lidia (It) a slightly alkaline, sparkling natural spring mineral water from Sant Andrea, Fonte Lidia. Mineral contents (milligrammes per litre):

Sodium 202mg/l, Calcium 4.6mg/l, Magnesium 2.8mg/l, Potassium 1.8mg/l, Bicarbonates 455mg/l, Chlorides 9.5mg/l, Sulphates 65mg/l, Silicates 42.5mg/l, Oxygen 3.57mg/l. pH 9.3

Fonte Lieta (It) a sparkling natural spring mineral water from Lieta. Mineral contents (milligrammes per litre): Sodium 10.9mg/l, Calcium 39.5mg/l, Magnesium 3.8mg/l, Potassium 0.2mg/l, Bicarbonates 132mg/l, Chlorides 3mg/l, Sulphates 24.5mg/l, Silicates 3mg/l, Oxygen 4.5mg/l. pH 7.7

Fonte Lonera (It) a natural spring mineral water from Lonera. Mineral contents (milligrammes per litre): Sodium 0.3mg/l, Calcium 26.4mg/l, Magnesium 12.9mg/l, Potassium 0.15mg/l, Bicarbonates 137mg/l, Chlorides 0.7mg/l, Sulphates 3.4mg/l. pH 7.6

Fonte Maddalena (It) a natural spring mineral water from Ardea, Rome.

Fonte Margherita (It) a sparkling natural spring mineral water from Margherita. Mineral contents (milligrammes per litre): Sodium 308mg/l, Calcium 225mg/l, Magnesium 131mg/l, Potassium 32mg/l, Bicarbonates 1409mg/l, Chlorides 115mg/l, Sulphates 485mg/l. pH 6.27

Fonte Meo (It) a sparkling natural spring mineral water from Gavignano, Rome. Mineral contents (milligrammes per litre): Sodium 11.92mg/l, Calcium 23.5mg/l, Magnesium 7.71mg/l, Potassium 10.42mg/l, Bicarbonates 119mg/l, Chlorides 11.8mg/l, Sulphates 5mg/l, Fluorides 0.1mg/l, Nitrates 13.12mg/l, Silicates 17.5mg/l, Oxygen 9.25mg/l. pH 7.08

Fontemilla (Sp) a still natural spring mineral water from Sierra de Guadalajara. Mineral contents (milligrammes per litre): Sodium 4.1mg/l, Calcium 80.2mg/l, Magnesium 23.1mg/l, Potassium 0.9mg/l, Bicarbonates 315.4mg/l, Chlorides 12.3mg/l, Sulphates 26.7mg/l, Fluorides 0.2mg/l, Nitrates 10.8mg/l.

Fontemura (It) a sparkling natural spring mineral water from Fontemura. Mineral contents (milligrammes per litre): Sodium 14.8mg/l, Calcium 69.7mg/l, Magnesium 24.4mg/l, Potassium 2.4mg/l, Bicarbonates 292.8mg/l, Chlorides 10.2mg/l, Sulphates 54.6mg/l, Nitrates 0.9mg/l, Silicates 15.2mg/l. pH 7.5

Fontenac (Sp) a 12 year old brandy produced by Torres in the Penedés region, Cataluña.

Fonte Napoleone (It) a slightly alkaline, sparkling natural spring mineral water from Fonte Napoleone. Mineral contents (milligrammes per litre): Sodium 15.5mg/l, Calcium 3.7mg/l, Magnesium 2.1mg/l, Potassium 0.8mg/l, Bicarbonates 12.4mg/l, Chlorides 25mg/l, Sulphates 5.2mg/l, Silicates 12.2mg/l. pH 5.6

Fontenay (Fr) a commune in the A.C. Chablis, Burgundy.

Fonteneige (Fr) a still natural spring mineral water from Source de Moulettes. Mineral contents (milligrammes per litre): Sodium 1.4mg/l, Calcium 63mg/l, Magnesium 10.2mg/l,

Potassium 0.4mg/l, Bicarbonates 173.2mg/l, Chlorides 1mg/l, Sulphates 51.3mg/l, Nitrates 2mg/l. pH 7.6

Fontenoce (It) a still and sparkling natural spring mineral water (established 1995) from Parenti, Cosenza. (red label: sparkling/blue label: still). Mineral contents (milligrammes per litre): Sodium 5.8mg/l, Calcium 16.01mg/l, Magnesium 4.85mg/l, Potassium 3.4mg/l, Bicarbonates 64.5mg/l, Chlorides 9.93mg/l, Sulphates 11.4mg/l, Fluorides 0.11mg/l, Nitrates 2.2mg/l, Silicates 17.4mg/l. pH 7.69

Fontenova (It) a sparkling natural spring mineral water from Fontenova. Mineral contents (milligrammes per litre): Sodium 5.18mg/l, Calcium 8.52mg/l, Magnesium 31.32mg/l, Potassium 0.41mg/l, Bicarbonates 180.2mg/l, Chlorides 3.2mg/l, Sulphates 12.2mg/l, Nitrates 2.04mg/l, Silicates 28.5mg/l, Oxygen 9.2mg/l. pH 7.5

Fontenova (Sp) a natural spring mineral water (established 1904). Mineral contents (milligrammes per litre): Sodium 723.2mg/l, Calcium 14.8mg/l, Potassium 46.7mg/l, Bicarbonates 2030mg/l, Chlorides 29.6mg/l, Fluorides 12.6mg/l, Lithium 2.9mg/l, Silicates 61.8mg/l.

Fonteny [Le] (Fr) a Premier Cru vineyard in the A.C. commune of Gevrey-Chambertin, Côte de Nuits, Burgundy 3.8ha.

Fontepatri (It) a sparkling natural spring mineral water from Lastra a Signa, Firenze. Mineral contents (milligrammes per litre): Sodium 81mg/l, Calcium 74.8mg/l, Magnesium 27.2mg/l, Potassium 1.6mg/l, Bicarbonates 421mg/l, Chlorides 47mg/l, Sulphates 54mg/l, Fluorides 0.5mg/l, Nitrates 0.8mg/l, Silicates 12.2mg/l, Oxygen 6.4mg/l. pH 7.4

Fonte Perna della Certosa (It) a sparkling natural spring mineral water from Certosa. Mineral contents (milligrammes per litre): Sodium 7.36mg/l, Calcium 3.8mg/l, Magnesium 1.82mg/l, Potassium 1.12mg/l, Chlorides 14.19mg/l, Sulphates 5.1mg/l, Fluorides 0.09mg/l, Nitrates 1.7mg/l, Silicates 15.52mg/l. pH 5.9

Fonte Pocenia (It) a natural spring mineral water from Udine.

Fonte Preistorica (It) a sparkling natural spring mineral water from Montefortino (AP). Mineral contents (milligrammes per litre): Sodium 11.28mg/l, Calcium 91.95mg/l, Magnesium 28.02mg/l, Potassium 2.39mg/l, Bicarbonates 390.5mg/l, Sulphates 31.08mg/l. pH 7.45

Fonte Primavera (It) a still natural spring mineral water from Popoli, Pescara. Mineral contents (milligrammes per litre): Sodium 4.87mg/l, Calcium 82.76mg/l, Magnesium 17.98mg/l, Potassium 1.38mg/l, Bicarbonates 340.91mg/l, Chlorides 14.4mg/l, Sulphates 25.17mg/l, Fluorides 0.15mg/l, Nitrates 3.24mg/l, Silicates 4.28mg/l. pH 7.3

Fonter (Sp) a still natural spring mineral water from Girona. Mineral contents (milligrammes per litre): Sodium 11.4mg/l, Calcium 27mg/l, Magnesium 0.9mg/l, Potassium 5.4mg/l, Bicarbonates 100.5mg/l, Chlorides 12.7mg/l, Sulphates 17.2mg/l, Fluorides 0.1mg/l, Nitrates 9.5mg/l.

Fonte Randa (Aus) a sparkling natural spring mineral water from Urquelle in Kobersdorf, Burgenland. Mineral contents (milligrammes per litre): Sodium 16.8mg/l, Calcium 83.7mg/l, Magnesium 12.7mg/l, Potassium 2.57mg/l, Bicarbonates 338mg/l, Chlorides 5.5mg/l, Sulphates 14mg/l.

Fonte Reale di Valdieri (It) a natural spring mineral water from Valdieri, Cuneo.

Fonte Regina (It) a sparkling natural spring mineral water from Regina. Mineral contents (milligrammes per litre): Sodium 288mg/l, Calcium 160mg/l, Magnesium 109mg/l, Potassium 10mg/l, Bicarbonates 1726mg/l, Chlorides 6.3mg/l, Sulphates 94mg/l, Strontium 1.4mg/l.

Fonte Rey (It) a sparkling natural spring mineral water from Aosta. Mineral contents (milligrammes per litre): Sodium 1.7mg/l, Calcium 72.2mg/l, Magnesium 9.6mg/l, Potassium 2.4mg/l, Bicarbonates 96.4mg/l, Sulphates 137mg/l. pH 7.8

Fonternel (S.Afr) a spicy, white, medium-sweet wine made from a blend of Muscat d'Alexandrie, Muscadelle and Steen grapes by the Nederburg Estate in Paarl.

Fontès (Fr) a wine-producing commune in the A.C. Clairette du Languedoc, south-western France.

Fontesana (It) a natural spring mineral water from Fontesana. Mineral contents (milligrammes per litre): Sodium 38.5mg/l, Calcium 125mg/l, Magnesium 25.5mg/l, Sulphates 76mg/l. pH 7.35

Fonte San Moderanno (It) a sparkling natural spring mineral water from San Moderanno. Mineral contents (milligrammes per litre): Sodium 37.94mg/l, Calcium 55.2mg/l, Magnesium 30.72mg/l, Potassium 2.45mg/l, Bicarbonates 317.2mg/l, Chlorides 10.64mg/l, Sulphates 63.25mg/l, Fluorides 0.1mg/l, Nitrates 0.26mg/l, Silicates 9.5mg/l, Oxygen 9.2mg/l. pH 7.03

Fonte Santa Barbara (It) a sparkling natural spring mineral water from Santa Barbara di Lurisia, Cuneo. Mineral contents (milligrammes per litre): Sodium 2.7mg/l, Potassium 1mg/l, Bicarbonates 15.2mg/l, Silicates 5.2mg/l. pH 6.9

Fonte Santa Chiara (It) a sparkling natural spring mineral water from Santa Chiara. Mineral contents (milligrammes per litre): Sodium 22mg/l, Calcium 91mg/l, Magnesium 13mg/l, Potassium 1.7mg/l, Bicarbonates 228mg/l, Sulphates 86mg/l, Fluorides 0.21mg/l, Nitrates 1.1mg/l, Silicates 6.1mg/l. pH 7.53

Fonte Santafiora (It) a sparkling natural spring mineral water from Arezzo, Tuscany. Mineral contents (milligrammes per litre): Sodium 108mg/l, Calcium 76.4mg/l, Magnesium 30mg/l, Potassium 3.2mg/l, Bicarbonates 390.4mg/l, Chlorides 121.1mg/l, Sulphates 53.2mg/l, Nitrates 13mg/l, Silicates 20.5mg/l. pH 7.6

Fonte Santagata (It) a sparkling natural spring mineral water from Caserta, Campania. Mineral contents (milligrammes per litre): Sodium 47mg/l, Calcium 270mg/l, Magnesium 18mg/l, Potassium 36mg/l, Bicarbonates 1049mg/l, Chlorides 19mg/l, Sulphates 4mg/l, Fluorides 1mg/l, Nitrates 7mg/l, Silicates 63mg/l. pH 6.0

Fonte Santa Lucia (Bra) a slightly acidic, sparkling natural spring mineral water. Mineral contents (milligrammes per litre): Sodium 4.8mg/l, Calcium 1.68mg/l, Magnesium 1.77mg/l, Potassium 1.42mg/l, Bicarbonates 12.4mg/l, Chlorides 6.81mg/l, Nitrates 4.5mg/l. pH 5.1

Fonte Santa Ursula (Bra) a natural spring mineral water. Mineral contents (milligrammes per litre): Sodium 5.76mg/l, Calcium 6.93mg/l, Magnesium 1.28mg/l, Potassium 4.27mg/l, Bicarbonates 38.4mg/l, Chlorides 1.02mg/l, Sulphates 0.1mg/l, Fluorides 0.05mg/l, Nitrates 9.4mg/l.

Fontessa Elm (Switz) a sparkling natural spring mineral water from Elm. (red label: sparkling/blue label: light gas). Mineral contents (milligrammes per litre): Sodium 3mg/l, Calcium 114mg/l, Magnesium 7mg/l, Bicarbonates 280.6mg/l, Chlorides <1mg/l, Sulphates 120mg/l, Fluorides <0.1mg/l, Nitrates <0.1mg/l.

Fonte Tavina (It) a sparkling natural spring mineral water from Fonte Tavina. Mineral contents (milligrammes per litre): Sodium 10.6mg/l, Calcium 83.2mg/l, Magnesium 25.8mg/l, Potassium 1.8mg/l, Bicarbonates 363mg/l, Chlorides 9.1mg/l, Sulphates 26.5mg/l, Nitrates 9.5mg/l, Silicates 14.2mg/l. pH 7.64

Fonte Tullia (It) a still natural spring mineral water from Tullia. Mineral contents (milligrammes per litre): Sodium 3.4mg/l, Calcium 68mg/l, Magnesium 8.4mg/l, Potassium 1.2mg/l, Bicarbonates 216mg/l, Chlorides 5.5mg/l, Sulphates 26mg/l, Fluorides 0.74mg/l, Silicates 8.5mg/l. pH 7.66

Fonte Umbria (It) a still natural spring mineral water from Umbria. Mineral contents (milligrammes per litre): Sodium 28.2mg/l, Calcium 5.4mg/l, Magnesium 1.3mg/l, Potassium 6.6mg/l, Bicarbonates 90.3mg/l, Chlorides 19.7mg/l, Sulphates 90.3mg/l, Fluorides 0.6mg/l, Nitrates 8.7mg/l.

Fonte Valle Realle (Isr) a natural spring mineral water. Mineral contents (milligrammes per litre): Sodium 3.21mg/l, Calcium 86.18mg/l, Magnesium 15.33mg/l, Potassium 0.9mg/l, Bicarbonates 320.1mg/l, Chlorides 3.91mg/l, Sulphates 16.14mg/l. pH 7.3

Fonte Vijrgin (It) a natural spring mineral water from Salo, Brescia.

Fonte Visciolo (It) a sparkling natural spring mineral water from Visciolo. Mineral contents (milligrammes per litre): Sodium 67.8mg/l, Calcium 56mg/l, Magnesium 12.11mg/l, Potassium 17.8mg/l, Bicarbonates 302mg/l, Chlorides 26.2mg/l, Sulphates 67.6mg/l, Fluorides 0.93mg/l, Nitrates 23.7mg/l, Silicates 63.34mg/l. pH 6.8

Fonteviva (It) a sparkling natural spring water from Volpara 2, Massa, Tuscany. Mineral contents (milligrammes per litre): Sodium 3.9mg/l, Calcium 8.8mg/l, Magnesium 2.67mg/l, Potassium 0.2mg/l, Bicarbonates 30.5mg/l, Chlorides 9.1mg/l, Sulphates 3.3mg/l, Fluorides 0.04mg/l, Nitrates 0.87mg/l, Silicates 5.75mg/l, Oxygen 9.31mg/l. pH 6.9

Fonte Vivia (It) a slightly acidic natural spring mineral water from Vivia. pH 5.5

Fontfort (Fr) a natural spring mineral water (established 1894). Mineral contents (milligrammes per litre): Sodium 1110mg/l, Calcium 106mg/l, Magnesium 93mg/l, Potassium 120mg/l, Bicarbonates 3800mg/l, Chlorides 115mg/l, Sulphates 1.7mg/l, Nitrates <1mg/l.

Fonti di Crodo (It) a sparkling natural spring mineral water from Crodo Springs, Fomazzo, Piemonte. Mineral contents (milligrammes per litre): Sodium 2mg/l, Calcium 526mg/l, Magnesium 48.5mg/l, Potassium 5.9mg/l, Bicarbonates 73mg/l, Chlorides <0.5mg/l, Sulphates 1420mg/l, Fluorides 0.3mg/l, Nitrates <1mg/l, Silicates 7.61mg/l, Strontium 9.7mg/l. pH 7.6

Fonte Feja (It) a natural spring mineral water from Fonti Feja.

Fonti Levissima (It) a still or sparkling mineral water bottled at source in Cepina Sondrio.

Fonti San Bernardo (It) a still mineral water from the springs of Garessio, there is also a sparkling style bottled.

Font Jaraba (Sp) a still natural spring mineral water from Jaraba, Zaragoza. Mineral contents (milligrammes per litre): Sodium 42.5mg/l, Calcium 100.3mg/l, Magnesium 40.9mg/l, Potassium 2.5mg/l, Bicarbonates 301.3mg/l, Chlorides 65.7mg/l, Sulphates 158.4mg/l, Fluorides 0.3mg/l, Nitrates 12.4mg/l. Also spelt Fontjaraba.

Font Lys (Sp) a natural spring mineral water from Manuel, Valencia.

Fontoira (Sp) a still natural spring mineral water from Fontoria, Sanxenxo, Galicia. Mineral contents (milligrammes per litre): Sodium 9.3mg/l, Calcium 40.6mg/l, Magnesium 7.4mg/l, Bicarbonates 152.4mg/l, Chlorides 12.6mg/l, Sulphates 6.3mg/l.

Fontoise (Fr) a natural spring mineral water from Source de la Poiraudière. Mineral contents (milligrammes per litre): Sodium 39.6mg/l, Calcium 36.3mg/l, Magnesium 10.9mg/l, Potassium 2.2mg/l, Sulphates 41.2mg/l, Fluorides 0.34mg/l, Silicates 39mg/l. pH 7.4

F

Fontovova (Sp) a naturally sparkling mineral water from the Verin Valley.

Font Picant (Sp) a sparkling natural spring mineral water from Amer, Girona. Mineral contents (milligrammes per litre): Sodium 62.7mg/l, Calcium 114.6mg/l, Magnesium 47.7mg/l, Potassium 5.3mg/l, Bicarbonates 673mg/l, Chlorides 10.5mg/l, Sulphates 49.1mg/l, Fluorides 0.5mg/l, Nitrates mg/l. Also spelt Fontpicant

Font Salem (Sp) a natural spring mineral water from Font d'Elca, Salem, Valencia.

Font Selva (Sp) a natural spring mineral water from Sant Hilari Sacalm, Massif of Montseny, Girona. Mineral contents (milligrammes per litre): Sodium 49.7mg/l, Calcium 33.9mg/l, Magnesium 5mg/l, Potassium 7.1mg/l, Bicarbonates 215.8mg/l, Chlorides 12.4mg/l, Sulphates 10.6mg/l, Silicates 22.5mg/l.

Fontselva (Sp) a still natural spring mineral water from Valencia. Mineral contents (milligrammes per litre): Sodium 41.1mg/l, Calcium 35.3mg/l, Magnesium 5.4mg/l, Potassium 0.8mg/l, Bicarbonates 206.2mg/l, Chlorides 10.6mg/l, Sulphates 9.6mg/l, Fluorides 0.3mg/l, Nitrates 0.1mg/l.

Font Sol (Sp) a still and sparkling natural spring mineral water from Aguas de Sierra Sanchis-Partida el Moreal, La Font de la Figuera, Valencia. Mineral contents (milligrammes per litre): Sodium 80.1mg/l, Calcium 118mg/l, Magnesium 51mg/l, Potassium 2.9mg/l, Bicarbonates 239mg/l, Chlorides 134.5mg/l, Sulphates 239mg/l, Fluorides 0.6mg/l, Nitrates 9.1mg/l, Silicates 12.8mg/l.

Font Sorda-Son Coco (Sp) a natural spring mineral water from Alaró, Balearic Isles. Mineral contents (milligrammes per litre): Sodium 27.9mg/l, Calcium 83.3mg/l, Magnesium 26.2mg/l, Potassium 1.5mg/l, Bicarbonates 342mg/l, Chlorides 63.8mg/l, Sulphates 13.2mg/l, Fluorides 0.3mg/l, Nitrates 2.1mg/l.

Font Vella (Sp) a still natural spring mineral water from Sant Hilari, Sacalm, Girona. Mineral contents (milligrammes per litre): Sodium 13.1mg/l, Calcium 40.9mg/l, Magnesium 7.8mg/l, Bicarbonates 153mg/l, Chlorides 10.9mg/l, Sulphates 13.8mg/l. pH 7.62

Fonty's Pool (Austr) a winery based in the Pemberton region of Western Australia. Grape varieties include: Cabernet sauvignon.

Fonxesta (Sp) a still natural spring mineral water from Lancara, Lugo, Galicia. Mineral contents (milligrammes per litre): Sodium 9.5mg/l, Calcium 8.1mg/l, Magnesium 1.6mg/l, Potassium 1.1mg/l, Bicarbonates 38.2mg/l, Chlorides 7.8mg/l, Sulphates 2.5mg/l, Fluorides 0.1mg/l, Nitrates 4.6mg/l, Silicates 22mg/l.

Food & Drink Federation (Eng) an organisation (established 1986). (Add): 6 Catherine Street, London WC2B 5JJ. Website: http://www.fdf.org.uk 'E'mail: generalenquiries@fdf.org.uk

Food Lion Drinking Water (USA) a natural spring mineral water from Abington.

Footed Glass (USA) the name given to a glass that has a wide base and stem.

Footlights Ale (Scot) a special ale brewed to commemorate the Edinburgh Festival in 1997. Part of Tapster's Choice range from Carlsberg-Tetley.

Foot of Africa (S.Afr) the label for a range of varietal wines produced by Kleine Zalze Wines, Stellenbosch, Western Cape.

Footprint (S.Afr) a label for a range of varietal wines produced by African Pride Wines, Constantia, Western Cape.

F.O.P. (Eng) *abbr*: Flowery Orange Pekoe a black tea grade.

Foppiano Vineyards (USA) a winery in the Russian River Valley, Sonoma County, California. 83ha. Grape varieties: Cabernet sauvignon, Chardonnay, Chenin blanc, French colombard, Petit syrah, Pinot noir and Zinfandel. Produces varietal wines.

Foral (Port) the label of a red wine produced by Caves Aliança.

Forastera (It) a white grape variety and white wine from the island of Ischia in southern Italy.

Forastera (Sp) a white grape variety grown in the Canary Islands.

Forastero (S.Am) a grade of coffee bean which is classed as a common grade and is fermented longer with its pulp from the pod to give average flavour. *See also* Criollo.

Forbidden Fruit (USA) a liqueur made from a type of grapefruit called a shaddock (pomelo), made with brandy and honey 32% alc by vol sold in a round (spherical) bottle.

Forcadière [La] (Fr) the name of an A.C. Tavel rosé wine produced by Domaine Maby.

Forcayat (Sp) a red grape variety grown in the Valencia region.

Force 8 (Eng) a 5% alc by vol. seasonal beer brewed by Gale's Brewery, Horndean, Hampshire.

Force 135 (Ch.Isles) a light ale 3.6% alc by vol. brewed by the Jersey Brewery and lauched on 9th May 2005 to celebrate the 60th Anniversary of the liberation of the Channel Islands after the Second World War (named after the British Army task force that liberated the islands).

Forceful (Eng) a term used to describe a wine that is assertive and has tannin and acidity.

Forchtenberg (Ger) village (Anb): Württemberg. (Ber): Kocher-Jagst-Tauber. (Gro): Kocherberg. (Vin): Flatterberg.

Fordítás (Hun) *see* Tokaji Fordítás.

Foreign Extra Stout (E.Asia) a Guinness stout brewed under contract by the Amarit Brewery in Thailand.

Foreign Extra Stout (W.Ind) *abbr*: F.E.S. a Guinness-type brew (1073 O.G) higher than regular Guinness, with a sharp acidity due to the introduction of some older Guinness into the brew to create lactic acid by fermentation, is then pasteurised.

Forellenwein (Ger) a brand of white table wine produced by Deinhard in Koblenz.

Foreshots (Scot) the first part of the distillation which is returned because it contains impurities. Only the 'heart' is kept, the end of the distillation is called the 'feints'.

Forest Brown (Eng) a famous brown ale 1032 O.G. brewed by the Whitbread Brewery.

Forest Crimmins Ranch (USA) see Crimmins Ranch.

Forester (Eng) the brand-name of a cider from Linfood Cash & Carry, Northamptonshire.

Forester (Eng) a 4.1% alc by vol. ale brewed by the Acorn Brewery, South Yorkshire.

Forester's Delight (Cktl) 35mls (1½ fl.ozs) Cointreau, 35mls (1½ fl.ozs) Bourbon whiskey, 2 dashes lemon juice, 2 dashes blue Curaçao. Shake over ice, strain into a sugar-rimmed flute glass and top with a cherry.

Forest Gold (Eng) an ale brewed by the micro-brewery Red Shoot, Linwood, Hampshire.

Forest Hill (Austr) a winery based in the Great Southern region of Western Australia.

Forest Lager (Eng) a lager beer 1038 O.G. brewed in the New Forest Brewery, Cadnam, Hampshire.

Forestville (USA) a wine-producing town in the Russian River Valley, California.

Forest XB (Eng) a 4.2% alc by vol. bitter ale brewed by the Darwin Brewery, Tyne & Wear.

Foret (Fr) see Gimlet.

Foretaste (Eng) the experience, albeit limited, that a person has of a wine before it is taken in the mouth, is created by the senses of sight, smell and knowledge of the wine.

Forêts (Fr) an A.C. Premier Cru Chablis. Often reclassified as the Premier Cru Montmains.

Forever Amber (Eng) a 4% alc by vol. ale brewed by the Butterknowle Brewery, Lynesack, Durham.

Forge Bitter (Eng) a 4.2% alc by vol. seasonal beer produced using an oak fermented by Hydes Anvil, Manchester. Also brew Victory Ale.

Forgeron [Michel] (Fr) a Cognac producer. (Add): Chez Richon, 16130 Segonzac. Owns 11ha. in the Grande Champagne.

Forgeron Winery (USA) a winery based in Elmira, Willamette Valley, Oregon. Produces vinifera wines.

Forges (Fr) a chalybeate mineral water.

Forget-Brimont (Fr) a Champagne producer (négociant-manipulant and récoltant-manipulant). (Add): 51500 Craon de Ludes. Labels include Carte Blanche Brut.

Forget-Chemin (Fr) a Champagne producer (12ha). (Add): 15, Rue Victor Hugo, B.P. 8, 51500 Ludes-le-Coquet. Récoltant-Manipulant. Produces vintage and non-vintage wines. Vintages: 1995, 1999. A member of the Club Tresors de Champagne. Labels: Cuvée 'Special Club' Millésimée.

Foris Vineyard (USA) a winery. (Add): Rogue Valley, Oregon. Grape varieties: Chardonnay, Gewürztraminer, Merlot, Pinot gris, Pinot noir.

Formaldehyde (Eng) an aldehyde found in wine that contributes to the bouquet and flavour of the wine.

Forman Winery (USA) a winery based near Saint Helena, Napa Valley, California. 21ha. Grape varieties: Merlot and Sauvignon blanc. Produces varietal wines.

Formianum (It) a red wine produced in central western Italy during Roman times.

Formic Acid (Eng) H.COOH an acid found in wines in minute traces.

Formidable (Sp) the label of a solera reserva brandy produced by Gil Galan.

Formosa Dourada (Port) a white grape variety grown in Alentejo.

Formosa Oolong (E.Asia) a tea that has a large leaf and a unique peach fragrance, produced in Taiwan.

Formosa Peak (S.Afr) the label for a red wine (Cabernet sauvignon & Shiraz blend) produced by the Fairview winery, Suider-Paarl, Western Cape.

Formula 1 (Cktl) 25mls (⅛ gill) Bell's Scotch whisky, 15mls (⅛ gill) Galliano, 40mls (⅓ gill) orange juice, 2 dashes lime juice. Shake well over ice, strain into an ice-filled highball glass, top with soda water and an orange slice and serve with straws.

Formula 2 (Cktl) ⅓ measure sweet Martini, ⅓ measure dry Martini, juice of ½ grapefruit, dash tonic water. Mix in a highball glass, decorate with slices of orange, lemon, grapefruit and cherry.

For My Friends (S.Afr) the label for a red wine (Shiraz) produced by the Darling Cellars winery, Swartland.

Forneret (Fr) cuvées in the vineyards of Les Marconnets [0.8 ha] and Les Peuillets [1 ha] of A.C. Savigny-lès-Beaune, Burgundy (owned by the Hospices de Beaune).

Fornterutoli (It) a Chianti Classico producer based in Tuscany.

Föroya Bjór (Den) a brewery. (Add): FO-700 Klakksvik, Faeroe Isles. Brews a variety of beers and lagers. Website: http://www.foroya-bjor.com 'E'mail: fb@foroya-bjor.fo

For Planter's Punch (USA) a label statement on dark rum bottles to denote a suitable drink that particular rum can be used for.

Forrester (Port) a Port shipper. see Offley Forrester Boa Vista.

Forrester & Firkin (Eng) a micro-brewery pub at Stafford. Brews: Chopper Ale 3.5% alc by vol.

Forrester Estate (N.Z) a winery. (Add): Blicks Road, Renwick, Marlborough. 16ha. Grape varieties: Chardonnay, Riesling, Sauvignon blanc, Sémillon, Cabernet franc, Cabernet sauvignon, Merlot.

Forsellina (It) a red grape variety grown in the Veneto region.

Forshaw (Eng) owners of Burtonwood Regional Brewery. see Burtonwood.

Forst (Ger) vineyard (Anb): Nahe. (Ber): Kreuznach. (Gro): Kronenberg. (Vil): Bad Kreuznach.

Forst (Ger) village (Anb): Pfalz. (Ber): Mittelhaardt-Deutsche Weinstrasse. (Gro): Mariengarten. (Vins): Elster, Freundstück, Jesuitengarten, Kirchenstück, Musenhang, Pechstein, Ungeheuer.

Forst (Ger) village (Anb): Pfalz. (Ber): Mittelhaardt-Deutsche Weinstrasse. (Gro): Schnepfenflug an der Weinstrasse. (Vins): Bischofsgarten, Stift, Süsskopf.

Forst (Ger) vineyard (Anb): Pfalz. (Ber): Südliche Weinstrasse. (Gro): Ordensgut. (Vil): Edesheim.

Forstberg (Ger) vineyard (Anb): Ahr. (Ber): Walporzheim/Ahrtal. (Gro): Klosterberg. (Vil): Ahrweiler.

Forstberg (Ger) vineyard (Anb): Mittelrhein. (Ber): Rheinburgengau. (Gro): Burg Hammerstein. (Vil): Leutesdorf.

Forstberg (Ger) vineyard (Anb): Württemberg. (Ber): Württembergisch Unterland. (Gro): Wunnenstein. (Vil): Gronau.

Forstberg (Ger) vineyard (Anb): Württemberg. (Ber): Württembergisch Unterland. (Gro): Wunnenstein. (Vil): Oberstenfeld.

Försterlay (Ger) vineyard (Anb): Mosel-Saar-Ruwer. (Ber): Bernkastel. (Gro): Schwarzlay. (Vil): Lösnich.

Forstgrube (Ger) vineyard (Anb): Württemberg. (Ber): Württembergisch Unterland. (Gro): Stromberg. (Vil): Illingen.

Forstgrube (Ger) vineyard (Anb): Württemberg. (Ber): Württembergisch Unterland. (Gro): Stromberg. (Vil): Rosswag.

Förstina St. Maria-Brunnen (Ger) a natural spring mineral water. Mineral contents (milligrammes per litre): Sodium 37mg/l, Calcium 565mg/l, Magnesium 62mg/l, Potassium 14.5mg/l, Bicarbonates 1068mg/l, Chlorides 39mg/l, Sulphates 795mg/l, Fluorides 1.9mg/l.

Forstreiter (Aus) a winery based in the Kremstal region. (Add): Hollenburg 13, 3506 Krems-Hollenburg. Grape varieties: Grüner veltliner, Riesling, Neuberger, Pinot gris, Zweigelt. Label: Grüner Veltliner Exklusiv. Produces a range of wine styles.

Forstweg (Ger) vineyard (Anb): Pfalz. (Ber): Südliche Weinstrasse. (Gro): Bischofskreuz. (Vil): Walsheim.

Fort (Fr) strong.

Forta (Ger) a white grape variety, a cross between Madeleine angevine and Silvaner, gives high sugar.

Fortana (It) a red grape variety grown in Emilia-Romagna, known as Uva d'Oro in Romagna.

Fortant de France (Fr) a winery. (Add): 278 Ave. du Maréchal Juin, 34200 Sète. Name given to a range of Vin de Pays d'Oc varietal wines from Cabernet sauvignon, Grenache, Merlot, Syrah, Chardonnay, Sauvignon blanc.

Fortediga (It) a winery based in the Tuscany region. Grape varieties include: Cabernet sauvignon, Merlot, Sangiovese. Label: Maremma.

Forte's Fizz (Cktl) 25mls (1fl.oz) vodka, 25mls (1fl.oz) cassis. Place in a highball with ice, top with iced Champagne, stir and decorate with a slice of lemon.

Fort Garry Ltd. (Can) a subsidiary of Seagram. Produces a fine range of Canadian whiskies.

Forth Brewery Cº (Scot) a brewery. (Add): Eglington, Kelliebank, Alloa, Clackmannanshire FK10 1NU. Brews a variety of beers and lager. Website: http://www.forthbrewery.co.uk 'E'mail: duncankellock@forthbury.freeserve.co.uk

Forth Flyer (Cktl) 25mls (1fl.oz). Glayva, 10mls (½fl.oz) blue Curaçao, 10mls (½ fl.oz) Galliano, 100mls (4fl.ozs) ginger ale. Stir over ice in a slim jim glass, dress with a lemon and orange slice and serve with straws.

Fourth Growths (Eng) the Bordeaux Haut-Médoc Grand Crus. *see* Quatrième Crus.

Fortification (Eng) the addition of brandy to wine. *see* Fortified.

Fortified (Eng) a wine that has had its alcohol level raised by the addition of brandy. The spirit may be added before, during or after natural fermentation and is added to raise the alcohol level above that which yeast can work 18% by vol.

Fortified (S.Afr) denotes wines which have had their alcohol content increased to 16% alc by vol. with spirits.

Fortified British Wine (Eng) the name by which British 'Sherry-style' wines will be known by from 1996.

Fortifying (Eng) the adding of brandy to wine. *see* Fortified.

Fort Ile (W.Ind) a rum distillery based in Guadeloupe.

Fortino Winery (USA) a winery based in southern Santa Clara, California. Grape varieties: Barbera, Cabernet sauvignon, Charbono, Carignane, Petit syrah and Ruby cabernet. Produces fine varietal wines.

Fortin Plaisance (Fr) a vineyard in the A.C. Saint-Émilion, Bordeaux 5ha.

Fortis (Ger) a natural spring mineral water. Mineral contents (milligrammes per litre): Sodium 7.8mg/l, Calcium 138mg/l, Magnesium 26.7mg/l, Potassium 8.1mg/l, Bicarbonates 329mg/l, Chlorides 0.27mg/l, Sulphates 59.4mg/l.

Fortius (Sp) the label for a rosé (Merlot and Tempranillo blend) wine from Bodegas Valcarlos, Navarra. Also a rosé Fortius Selección (Cabernet sauvignon).

Fort Laudedale (Cktl) ⅓ measure dark rum, ⅓ measure sweet vermouth, juice ¼ lemon and lime. Shake well over ice, strain into an ice-filled old-fashioned glass and top with a slice of orange.

Fortress (Eng) a cask ale produced by Mitchells in Lancaster.

Fort Schuyler (USA) a top and bottom-fermented beer brewed by the West End Brewing Cº. in Utica, New York.

Forts de Latour [Les] (Fr) the second wine of Château Latour in the commune of Pauillac, Haut-Médoc, Bordeaux.

Fortuna Quelle (Ger) a sparkling natural spring mineral water from Eichenzell. Mineral contents (milligrammes per litre): Sodium 30mg/l, Calcium 380mg/l, Magnesium 48mg/l,

Potassium 11.7mg/l, Bicarbonates 787mg/l, Chlorides 41mg/l, Sulphates 502mg/l, Fluorides 1.1mg/l.

Forty Eight (Cktl) ⅕ measure apricot brandy, ⅕ measure orange Curaçao, ⅕ measure dry vermouth, ⅖ measure dry gin, dash lemon juice. Shake over ice and strain into a cocktail glass.

Forty-Five South [45] (N.Z) the brand-name of a whiskey produced by Wilson's Distillery in Dunedin.

Forty Four [44] Special (Eng) a 4.5% alc by vol. beer brewed by the Blackawton Brewery in Devon.

Forty Niner (Eng) a bitter 4.9% alc by vol. 1049 O.G. brewed by the Ringwood Brewery in Hampshire.

Forty Seven (Den) an amber-coloured beer brewed by Carlsberg C47 that commemorates when Carlsberg was founded in 1947 (5.5% alc by vol).

Fortytwo [42] (Eng) a 4.2% alc by vol. ale brewed by the Spectrum Brewery, Norfolk.

Fortytwo [42] Below (N.Z) a vodka produced by Bacardi

Forum Humuli (Ger) a famous hop market in Hamburg.

Forward (Eng) a term used to describe a wine with a well-marked aroma and taste and qualities earlier than expected.

Forzato (It) a term used to describe a wine produced from over-ripe grapes.

Fossanova (It) a Cistercian liqueur made from herbs.

Fosse [La] (Fr) a vineyard in the A.C. commune of Rully, Côte Chalonnaise, Burgundy.

Fosse aux Loups [La] (Fr) a Cru A.C. Chinon produced by Domaine de Bel Air in Cravant, Touraine. *See also* Le Bois d'Arcon.

Fossi (It) a Chianti Classico producer based in Tuscany.

Foster Burgess Winery (USA) a winery based in Freeport, Florida. Produces Muscadine wines.

Foster/Carlton & United Breweries Ltd. (Austr) *abbr*: C.U.B. Brewery based in Carlton, Melbourne. *See also* FGL Wine Estates. Owns: Berlinger Blass, Coldstream Hills, Devil's Lair, Eaglehawk, Jamiesons Run, Lindemans, Mildara, Penfolds, Rosemount Estate, Saltram, Seaview, Seppelt, Tollana, Wolf Blass, Wynns, Yellowglen.

Foster's (Austr) a famous gold-straw, bottled/canned lager 5% alc by vol. brewed by the Foster/Carlton & United Breweries Ltd., (C.U.B.), Carlton, Melbourne.

Foster's Draught (Eng) a lager beer 1035 O.G. brewed by under licence by Watney's Mortlake Brewery in London.

Foster's Ice Beer (Austr) a 5% alc by vol. gold-straw ice pilsner beer brewed by the Foster/Carlton & United Breweries Ltd., (C.U.B.), Carlton, Melbourne.

Foudre (Fr) huge casks (200hl to 300hl) for storing wine.

Fouesnant (Fr) a noted growth of cider from Brittany, north-western France.

Fougères (Fr) an A.C. red wine-producing region of the Languedoc-Roussillon, south-western France.

Foulage (Fr) the breaking of the crust during vinification, nowadays done mechanically. Also known as Pigeage.

Foulage au Pied (Fr) the crushing of the grapes by foot.

Foulage Méchanique (Fr) the mechanical pressing of the grapes.

Foulage Méchanique à Cylindres (Fr) cylinder presses, also known as Égrappoir à Tambour.

Foulage Méchanique Centrifuge (Fr) centrifugal presses, also known as Égrappoir Centrifuge.

Foule [En] (Fr) a term used to denote the practice of planting vines haphazardly.

Foulograppe (Fr) the alternative name for an Égrappoir.

Fouloir (Fr) a long revolving tube that extracts the juice out of the grapes, used in the Sauternes district of Bordeaux.

Foul-Pipe (Ire) in a whiskey distillery the pipe that returns the condensate from the Lyne arm to the still.

Foundation-BK5 (S.Afr) the label for a red wine (Pinot noir) produced by the Flagstone Winery, Somerset West, Western Cape.

Founder's Ale (Eng) a cask-conditioned ale 1045 O.G. (4.5% alc by vol.) brewed by the Usher Brewery of Trowbridge in Wiltshire.

Founders Brewery (N.Z) a brewery. (Add): Founders Historic Park, P.O. Box 1489, 87 Athawhai Drive, Nelson. Brews a variety of beers and lager. Website: http://www.biobrew.co.nz 'E'mail: info@biobrew.co.uk

Founder's Rock (Austr) the label for a Cabernet sauvignon produced by the Katnook Vineyard winery, Coonawarra, South Australia.

Foundry & Firkin (Eng) a micro-brewery based in Sheffield. Brewed Firkin 98 (a cask-conditioned lager) to celebrate the 1998 World Cup.

Fountain (Eng) a controlled and '*tapped*' natural source of spring water. (It) = fonte, (Fr) = fontaine, (Sp) = font/fonte.

Fountain (USA) a natural spring mineral water from Keyser, West Virginia.

Fountaingrove (USA) a former winery of a religious sect before prohibition. Today is a brand of Martini & Prati.

Fountainhead (USA) a natural spring mineral water. Mineral contents (milligrammes per litre): Calcium 9mg/l, Magnesium 3mg/l, Fluorides 0.41mg/l. pH 7.5

Fouquerand (Fr) a vineyard in the A.C. commune of Savigny-lès-Beaune, Burgundy (owned by the Hospices de Beaune).

Fouquet [André] (Fr) a viticulteur-récoltant based in Vouvray, Touraine, Loire. (Add): 47 Rue Gambetta, 37210. Produces fine A.C. Vouvray wines.

Four Ale Bar (Eng) a public bar from the days when ale was sold at 4 old pennies a quart (hence the name).

Four Bells Navy Rum (Eng) a dark rum produced by Charles Lamb of London 40% alc by vol.

Fourchaume (Fr) an A.C. Premier Cru Chablis. Often

has the Premier Cru vineyards of Vaupulent, Côte de Fontenay, Valorent and l'Homme-Mort reclassified to this vineyard name.

Four Clover (S.Afr) the label for white wine (Chardonnay, Chenin blanc and Sauvignon blanc blend) produced by the Cloverfield Private Cellar winery, Robertson, Western Cape.

Four Cousins (S.Afr) the label for a range of 1ltr bottled wines produced by the Van Loveren Private Cellar winery, Robertson, Western Cape.

Fourderaine (Fr) a sloe-flavoured, home-made liqueur produced by soaking sloes (which have been pricked many times) in marc. *See also* Sloe Gin.

Four K Bitter [4K] (Eng) *see* Four Keys.

Four Keys (Eng) a home-brew public house in Sussex that produces 4K Bitter 1036 O.G. and Stallion 1045 O.G.

Four K Mild [4K] (Eng) a 3.8% alc by vol. mild ale brewed by the Keltek Brewing C°. Ltd., Cornwall.

Fourneaux [Les] (Fr) a Premier Cru A.C. Chablis. Often has the Premier Crus of Morein and Côte des Prés-Girots reclassified as its vintage.

Fournier (Sp) a still natural spring mineral water from La Garriga, Barcelona. Mineral contents (milligrammes per litre): Sodium 21.3mg/l, Calcium 85mg/l, Magnesium 26.3mg/l, Potassium 1.5mg/l, Bicarbonates 321.2mg/l, Chlorides 16.5mg/l, Sulphates 53.3mg/l, Fluorides 0.2mg/l, Nitrates 0.1mg/l.

Fournier [Charles] (USA) ran the Gold Seal Vineyards at Hammondsport in New York State. Was chief wine-maker of Veuve-Clicquot until 1934.

Fournières [Les] (Fr) a Premier Cru vineyard in the A.C. commune of Aloxe-Corton, Côte de Beaune, Burgundy.

Fournier Père et Fils (Fr) a winery. (Add): B.P. 7, Chaudoux, 18300 Verdigny-en-Sancerre. Produces A.C. Sancerre wines.

Four Pack (USA) a slang term for a pack of cans or bottles of beer containing 4 cans. *See also* 'Six Pack'.

Fourrey & Fils (Fr) a winery based in the A.C. Chablis, Burgundy. Produces a range of Chablis wines including Premier Crs Mont de Milieu and Vaillons.

Four Rivers Brewery (Eng) a brewery based in Newcastle-on-Tyne. Brews: Moondance Bitter 3.8% alc by vol. Rowan 4.2% alc by vol. premium ale, Halfside 4.8% alc by vol. winter warmer.

Four Roses (USA) a brand-name of a blended Bourbon whiskey produced by the Four Roses Distilling C°. in Baltimore, Lawrenceburg 40% alc by vol.

Four Row Barley (Eng) the poorest of the barleys for the brewing of beer, refers to the number of rows of grain per ear. *See also* Two Row and Six Row.

Four Seasons (Austr) the brand-name of a whiskey produced by United Distillers.

Four [4] Seasons (Wal) a 4.8% alc by vol. special ale brewed by the Cwmbran Brewery, Gwent.

Four Sheets to the Wind (Eng) an old naval slang description used to describe someone under the influence of alcohol who is *'all over the place'* as sails are on a ship in a strong wind.

Four Sisters (S.Afr) the label for a methode cape classique sparkling wine produced by the Ruitersvlei Wines winery, Suider-Paarl, Western Cape.

Foursome (Eng) the local name given to large cans of beer from the Bank's Brewery in Wolverhampton.

Four Stars (S.Afr) the label for a red wine (Pinotage 40%, Merlot 30% plus Cabernet sauvignon and Shiraz) produced by the Devon Hill Winery, Stellenbosch, Western Cape.

Fourteen-Eighteen [14–18] h (Gre) a light rosé wine produced by Yannis Paraskevopolous at the Gaia Winery, Nemea from Aghiorgitiko grapes. Spends 14–18 hours on the skins.

Fourth Degree (Cktl) a Martinez cocktail with a dash of absinthe and a cherry (less 30mls gin and 15mls French vermouth).

Fourth Growths (Fr) the Bordeaux Haut-Médoc Grand Crus.

Fourth of July (Cktl) ⅕ measure Kahlúa, ⅕ measure Bourbon whiskey, ⅕ measure Galliano, ⅕ measure orange juice, ⅕ measure cream. Place the whiskey and Galliano into a warm cocktail glass, flame, shake in some ground cinnamon, whilst still flaming, strain, mix in remaining ingredients and add a cherry.

Four Thumbs (Wal) a strong pale ale from the Dyffryn Brewery, north Wales. *see* Pedwar Bawd.

Fourtyfour [44] Special (Eng) a 4.5% alc by vol. ale brewed by the Blackawton Brewery, Cornwall.

Fortynine [49] er (Eng) a 4.9% alc by vol. ale brewed by the Ringwood Brewery Ltd., Hampshire.

Four X (Eng) an Old ale 1040 O.G. brewed by the Burt Brewery in the Isle of Wight (bottled as a 4X Brown).

Four X (Wal) a cask-conditioned mild 1036 O.G. brewed by the Crown Brewery in Pontyclun, Mid Glamorgan.

Four X (Wal) a cask-conditioned mild 1030 O.G. brewed by the Border Brewery, Wrexham.

Four X (Eng) *see* XXXX.

Four X Porter (Eng) a 4.7% alc by vol. porter brewed by the Ringwood Brewery Ltd., Hampshire.

Four XXXX (Eng) a cask-conditioned bitter 1045 O.G. brewed by the Mansfield Brewery in the East Midlands.

Fourteen Eightytwo [1482] (S.Afr) the label for a red wine (Cabernet sauvignon, Merlot and Shiraz blend) produced by the Mont Destin winery, Paarl, Western Cape.

Fousselottes [Les] (Fr) a Premier Cru vineyard in the A.C. commune of Chambolle-Musigny, Côte de Nuits, Burgundy 4ha.

Fousslach (Lux) a vineyard site in the village of Bech-Kleinmacher.

Fowler's Wee Heavy Ale (Scot) a strong bottled ale 1070 O.G. brewed by the Belhaven Brewery of Dunbar for Tennent-Caledonian.

F

Fox Ale (Eng) a 4.6% alc by vol. ale brewed by Banks's Brewery.

Fox and Firkin (Eng) a home-brew public house in London. Produces: cask-conditioned Bruce's Bitter 1045 O.G. Dogbolter 1060 O.G. and Vixen 1036 O.G.

Fox and Hounds (Eng) a home-brew public house near Royston in Hertfordshire. Noted for Hogshead Bitter 1043 O.G. Nog 1040 O.G. and Nathaniel's Special 1034 O.G.

Fox and Hounds (Eng) a home-brew public house in Stottesdon, Shropshire. Produces cask-conditioned Dasher's Draught 1040 O.G.

Fox and Newt (Eng) a home-brew public house owned by Whitbread in Leeds. Noted for cask-conditioned Old Willow 1046 O.G. and Burley 1036 O.G.

Foxen (Austr) a winery in the Santa Ynez Valley, Santa Barbara County, California. Vineyard is Rothbury. Noted for Pinot noir and Viognier grapes that are fermented and aged in barrel. Also has vineyards in the Santa Maria Valley. Label: Bien Nacido Vineyard.

Foxes Island Wines (N.Z) a winery. (Add): Rapaura Road, RD 3, Blenheim. 4.5ha. Grape variety: Chardonnay.

Foxfield Brewery (Eng) a brewery (established 1996). (Add): Prince of Wales, Broughton-on-Furness, Cumbria LA20 6BX. Brews a variety of beers and lagers. Website: http://www.princeofwalesfoxfield.co.uk 'E'mail: drink@princeofwalesfoxfield.co.uk

Fox Grape (USA) the name given to the American native grape variety *Vitis riparia* in the nineteenth century when domesticated, hence the term 'foxy wines'.

Foxiness (USA) a term used to describe the very pronounced grapey flavour to be found in wines produced from American native grape varieties in the eastern states (especially from the *Vitis riparia*).

Fox River Cocktail (Cktl) 1 measure Bourbon whiskey, ¼ measure crème de cacao, 4 dashes Angostura. Stir over ice and strain into a cocktail glass.

Fox's Nob (Eng) a 4.4% alc by vol. session beer (bottled % alc by vol) brewed by Highgate and Walsall Brewery. Has now been renamed Highgate Bitter.

Foxwhelp (Eng) an excellent variety of cider apple, very sweet with little acidity.

Foxy (USA) a taste description of wines made from *Vitis riparia* grapes. see Fox Grape and Foxiness.

Fraai Uitzicht 1798 (S.Afr) a winery (established 1798) based in Robertson, Western Cape. 10ha. Grape varieties: Cabernet sauvignon, Merlot, Shiraz. Website: http://www.fraaiuitzicht.com

Fracia (It) a D.O.C. red wine from Valtellina in Lombardy. Produced from Nebbiolo grapes.

Fractional Blending (Eng) a term used for the solera system where a proportion of each years wine is taken from casks in a tier system so that a portion

is drawn off each year and replaced by wine from the following year.

Fragny (Fr) a wine-producing village of the Roussette de Savoie, south-eastern France.

Fragrant (Eng) a term used to describe a very pronounced and pleasing aroma in a wine.

Frais (Fr) lit: 'fresh or cool', when applied to wine is seen on the label as 'servir très frais'. Means 'serve well chilled'.

Fraise (Fr) a strawberry spirit liqueur 43% alc by vol.

Fraise d'Anjou (Fr) a strawberry brandy produced in western France.

Fraise de Bois (Fr) a liqueur flavoured with wild strawberries.

Fraise de Bois Dolfi (Hol) a Dutch strawberry liqueur produced from wild strawberries.

Fraise Royale (Cktl) 2 fresh strawberries, dash fraise liqueur, iced Champagne. Blend strawberries with liqueur, pour into a flute and top with iced Champagne.

Fraises Fizz (Cktl) ⅜ measure gin, ⅜ measure crème de fraises, juice ¼ lemon, 2 dashes gomme syrup. Shake over ice, strain into an ice-filled highball glass, top with soda water, slice of strawberry and squeeze of lemon peel juice.

Fraisette Cornu (Fr) a non-alcoholic strawberry syrup.

Framboise (Fr) a raspberry spirit liqueur 43% alc by vol.

Framboise (Bel) a lambic beer which has raspberries added to start a new fermentation 6% alc by vol.

Framboise de Bordeaux (Fr) a raspberry liqueur produced by Marie Brizzard. Made by maceration and distillation 20% alc by vol.

Frambozen (Bel) the name given to lambic fruit beers usually made from cherries or raspberries.

Frambozenbrandewijn (Hol) a raspberry-flavoured brandy.

Frambrosia (USA) a raspberry dessert wine produced by the Oak Knoll Winery, Hillsboro, Willamette Valley, Oregon.

Framersheim (Ger) village (Anb): Rheinhessen. (Ber): Nierstein. (Gro): Petersberg. (Vins): Hornberg, Kreuzweg, Zechberg.

Framework of Hospitality [The] (Eng) an old English slang saying that advocated three sips of a drink instead of one gulp especially for spirits (brandy and rum) when offered at a host's house.

Framingham Wine Company (N.Z) a 13ha winery. (Add): Conders Bend Road, Marlborough, Box 37, Renwick. Grape varieties: Rhine riesling, Sauvignon blanc, Chardonnay, Cabernet sauvignon, Cabernet franc, Merlot, Malbec, Shiraz.

Frampton Village (Eng) a dry (and medium-sweet) cider produced by the Frampton Village Cider Company, Hereford.

Frampton Village Cider Company (Eng) a cider producers based on the banks of the Gloucester and Sharpness Canal in Frampton Village, Herefordshire. Produces Cotswold Cottage and Frampton Village Ciders.

Franc (Fr) clean tasting.

F

Francavilla (It) a white grape variety grown in the Puglia region.

Franc de Goût (Fr) a term for the refreshing, clean taste of a wine.

France (Fr) the country that produces the top wines of the World, has many regions which lead with their style and are imitated by most other countries. *see* Alsace, Armagnac, Bordeaux, Burgundy, Champagne, Cognac, Jura, Loire, Midi, Rhône, Roussillon. *See also* Appellation Contrôlée, V.D.Q.S., Vin de Pays and Vin de Table.

Francerre (Eng) a range of sparkling non-alcoholic fruit juices with no artificial additives from Copak Drinks (apple, apple and blackcurrant, red and white grape juices).

Franche-Comté (Fr) a Vin de Pays area in the Jura département in eastern France. Produces red, rosé and dry white wines.

Franchette (Arg) a full red table wine produced by the Andean Vineyards in Mendoza.

Franchetti (It) a winery based on the island of Sicily. Label: Passopisciaro.

Francia (It) a famous Cru vineyard (14ha) in the DOCG Barolo owned by the Giacomo Conterno winery. Soil: calcerous marl, iron and sand. Grape variety: Nebbiolo. Wines: Barolo Casina Francia, Barolo Monfortino Riserva.

Franciacorta (It) a D.O.C. red wine of good flavour produced in the Garda district of Lombardy.

Franciacorta (It) a D.O.C.G. sparkling wine, aged for minimum of 25 months (18 on lees). Vintage spends 37 months in bottle, 30 months on lees. Brut, extra brut, rosé, demi-sec.

Franciacorta Pinot (It) a D.O.C. white wine made in the Garda district of Lombardy from the Pinot bianco grape. D.O.C.G. applies to bottle-fermented sparkling wine made from Chardonnay, Pinot bianco, Pinot nero grapes. Bottle aged for a min. 37 months for vintage, 25 months for N.V.

Franciacorta Rosso (It) a D.O.C. red wine from the Garda district of Lombardy. Made from 20%–30% Barbera, 40%–50% Cabernet franc, 10%–15% Merlot and 15%–20% Nebbiolo grapes.

Franciscan Vineyard (USA) a large winery based near Oakville Estate, Rutherford, Napa Valley, California. 250ha. Grape varieties: Cabernet sauvignon, Chardonnay and White riesling. Produces varietal wines.

Francis Tannahill (USA) a small winery based in Oregon State. Grape varieties: Chardonnay, Gewürztraminer, Pinot noir, Syrah. Label: The Hermit.

Franco-British Basin of Chalk (Eng) caused by a drying up of the sea 69 million years ago over northern France and southern England in places over 1000 feet deep. Kent, Sussex and the Champagne district lies on it.

Franco-Españolas S.A. (Sp) *see* Bodegas Franco-Españolas S.A.

Franco-Fiorina (It) a winery based in Alba, Piemonte, produces wines from bought-in grapes.

François de Salins (Fr) a cuvée in the Grand Cru vineyard of A.C. Corton-Charlemagne, Côte de Beaune, Burgundy. Is owned by the Hospices de Beaune.

François Vallois (Fr) a Premier Cru Champagne producer. (Add): 10, Avenue des Comtes de Champagne, 51130 Bergères-les-Vertus, Marne. Produces: Blanc des Blancs, Brut Tradition (Chardonnay 90%/Pinot noir 10%), Demi-Sec, Les Falloises 'Vieilles Vignes Blanc des Blancs', Brut Rosé, Rosé de Saignée (Pinot noir 100%) and Ratafia Rosé. Vintages: 1998, 2000, 2002. Website: http://www.Champagne-vallois-francois.com 'E' Mail: Champagne.vallois.francois@wanadoo.fr

Francoli (It) a liqueur producer based in Gattinara.

Franconia (Ger) a wine region. Most easterly of all regions, lies on the river Main. *see* Anbaugebiete, Franken and Fränkisch.

Franconia (It) the local name used in Friuli for Blaufränkisch.

Francorvm (Fr) the old Latin name for Fronsac and name for A.C. Fronsac wines from the Société du Château de la Rivière, 33145 Saint Michel de Fronsac.

Franco Toros (It) a winery based in Cormons in the Friuli-Venezia-Guilia region. Grape varieties include: Tocai, Pinot bianco

Frangelico (It) a liqueur made with berries, herbs and hazelnuts 23% alc by vol. produced by InSpirit Brands. *See also* Toussaint Coffee Liqueur, Opal Nera Black Sambuca, Teichenné Schnapps.

Frank [Dr. Konstantin] (USA) the founder of the New York State Vinifera Winery.

Franken (Ger) was the most easterly of the anbaugebiet (of the old Western Germany). *see* Franconia.

Franken (Ger) anbaugebiet (Bers): Bayer, Bodensee, Maindreieck, Mainviereck, Steigerwald. Produces 98% white and 2% red wines. Main grape varieties are Müller-Thurgau 47% and Silvaner 28%.

Frankenberg (Ger) vineyard (Anb): Baden. (Ber): Badische Frankenland. (Gro): Tauberklinge. (Vil): Lauda.

Frankenberg (Ger) vineyard (Anb): Baden. (Ber): Badische Frankenland. (Gro): Tauberklinge. (Vil): Marbach.

Frankenberg (Ger) village (Anb): Franken. (Ber): Steigerwald. (Gro): Schlosstück. (Vin): Herrschaftsberg.

Frankenbrunnen Hochstein-Quelle (Ger) a still and sparkling natural spring mineral water (established 1924) from Neustadt, Aisch. Mineral contents (milligrammes per litre): Sodium 61.2mg/l, Calcium 256.5mg/l, Magnesium 61.2mg/l, Potassium 5.2mg/l, Bicarbonates 356mg/l, Chlorides 82mg/l, Sulphates 600mg/l, Fluorides 0.12mg/l, Nitrates 0.23mg/l.

Frankenbrunnen Silvana-Quelle (Ger) a sparkling natural spring mineral water (established 1989) from Fichtelgebirge. Mineral contents (milligrammes per litre): Sodium 9mg/l, Calcium

F

73mg/l, Magnesium 11mg/l, Potassium 2mg/l, Bicarbonates 256mg/l, Chlorides 9mg/l, Sulphates 19mg/l.

Frankenbrunnen Theresien-Quelle (Ger) a sparkling natural spring mineral water (established 1786) from Fräkische, sale, Rhönvorstadt. Mineral contents (milligrammes per litre): Sodium 507mg/l, Calcium 110mg/l, Magnesium 40mg/l, Potassium 30mg/l, Bicarbonates 582mg/l, Chlorides 630mg/l, Sulphates 205mg/l.

Frankenheim Alt (Ger) a 4.8% alc by vol. altbier brewed by Frankenheimer Brauerei in Düsseldorf, west Germany. Has a red-brown colour and full hop flavour.

Frankenhell (Ger) vineyard (Anb): Mittelrhein. (Ber): Rheinburgengau. (Gro): Schloss Schönburg. (Vil): Damscheid.

Frankenjack (Cktl) ⁹⁄₁₀ measure dry gin, ³⁄₁₀ measure dry vermouth, ¹⁄₁₀ measure apricot brandy, ¹⁄₁₀ measure Cointreau. Stir over ice, strain into a cocktail glass and top with a cherry.

Frankenland (Ger) an alternative name for Franken (Franconia).

Frankenmarkter Mineralwasser (Aus) a sparkling natural spring mineral water (red label: sparkling/blue label: light gas). Mineral contents (milligrammes per litre): Sodium 4.5mg/l, Calcium 37.13mg/l, Magnesium 15.64mg/l, Bicarbonates 195.5mg/l, Chlorides 0.85mg/l, Sulphates 9.9mg/l, Nitrates 0.6mg/l, Silicates 38mg/l. pH 7.0

Frankenmuth Brewery (USA) a brewery (established 1987) based in Frankenmuth Michigan. Brews: Frankenmuth Pilsener.

Frankenmuth Pilsener (USA) a 5.18% alc by vol. bottled pilsner brewed by the Frankenmuth Brewery, Frankenmuth, Michigan.

Frankenriesling (Ger) the erroneous varietal name for the white grape Green silvaner.

Frankenstein (Fr) an A.C. Alsace Grand Cru vineyard in Dambach-la-Ville, Bas-Rhin 53ha.

Frankenstein (Ger) vineyard (Anb): Rheinhessen. (Ber): Wonnegau. (Gro): Sybillenstein. (Vil): Freimersheim.

Frankental (Fr) a black grape variety also known as the Black Hamburg.

Frankentha (Ger) vineyard (Anb): Rheingau. (Ber): Johannisberg. (Gro): Steil. (Vil): Assmannshausen.

Frankenthal (Fr) a black grape variety also known as the Trollinger.

Frankenthaler (Ger) an erroneous varietal name for the red grape Trollinger.

Franken Traube (Ger) another name for the Silvaner grape.

Frankenwein (Ger) the wine of Franken (Franconia) also called Steinwein. From Stein Vineyards.

Franken Wine Festivals (Ger) see Fränkisches Weinfest-Volkach, Fränkisches Weinfest Sulzfeld, Winzerfest-Klingenberg, Winzerfest-Würzburg.

Franken Wine Route (Ger) known as the Bocksbeutelstrasse.

Frankenwinheim (Ger) village (Anb): Franken. (Ber): Maindreieck. (Gro): Not yet assigned. (Vin): Rosenberg.

Frank Family Vineyards (USA) a winery based in Rutherford, Napa Valley. Grape varieties: Cabernet sauvignon, Chardonnay, Sangiovese, Zinfandel. Label: Winton Hill 40ha.

Frankfort (USA) a town based in north Kentucky, the home to many famous Bourbon whiskey distilleries.

Frankfort Distilling C°. (USA) a distillery based in Athertonville, Kentucky. Produces Antique (a Kentucky Bourbon whiskey 40% alc. by vol). Part of Seagram.

Frankfurt Diat Pils (Ger) a lager beer brewed by the Henninger-Brauerei in Frankfurt for the Courage Brewery in London.

Frankfurt/Main (Ger) village (Anb): Rheingau. (Ber): Johannisberg. (Gro): Not yet assigned. (Vin): Lohberger Hang.

Frank Hill Cocktail (Cktl) ½ measure brandy, ½ measure cherry brandy. Shake over ice, strain into a cocktail glass, top with a cherry and a twist of lemon peel juice.

Frankinja Crna (Slo) a local name for the Gamay noir à jus blanc.

Frankinja Modra (Slo) a local name for the Gamay noir à jus blanc.

Fränkisch (Aus)(Ger) lit: 'Franconian' the name medieval name used for noble grape varieties in the region.

Fränkischer Landwein (Ger) one of seventeen Deutsche Landwein zones.

Fränkisches Weinfest-Sulzfeld (Ger) a Franken wine festival held at Sulzfeld in August.

Fränkisches Weinfest-Volkach (Ger) a Franken wine festival held at Volkach in the middle of August.

Frankland (Austr) a wine region in the province of Western Australia that has a moderate climate and a variety of soil types including gravely granitic loams. Also known as Frankland River.

Frankland Estate (Austr) a winery based in Frankland, Western Australia. Label: Isolation Ridge.

Frankland River (Austr) see Frankland.

Frankland River Estate (Austr) a vineyard (94ha) based in the Frankland River, Western Australia. Grape varieties include: Cabernet sauvignon. Label: Olmo's Reward. Is owned by Houghton Vineyards, Western Australia.

Franklin County (USA) a wine-producing region of Arkansas.

Franklin Heritage (USA) a natural spring mineral water from Franklin, Tennessee.

Franklin's Brewery (Eng) a brewery (established 1980) based in Harrogate, North Yorkshire that brews Blotto a seasonal ale.

Frankovka (Slo) a red wine produced in Vojvodina from the grape of the same name. Also known as Blaufränkisch.

Frankweiler (Ger) village (Anb): Pfalz. (Ber): Südliche Weinstrasse. (Gro): Königsgarten. (Vins): Biengarten, Kalkgrube.

F

Frans (S.Afr) see Fransdruif.

Franschhoek Koöpatief (S.Afr) a co-operative winery (established 1945) based in Franschhoek, Western Cape. (Add): Box 52, Franschhoek 7690. Grape varieties: Cabernet sauvignon, Chardonnay, Chenin blanc, Crouchen, Hanepoot, Merlot, Petit verdot, Pinotage, Sauvignon blanc, Sémillon, Shiraz. Labels: Anvil, Cellar Reserve, Cellar Gold, Cellar Silver, La Cotte. Website: http://www.franschhoek-vineyards.co.za

Franschhoek Valley (S.Afr) a wine-producing area situated east of the Stellenbosch, Western Cape. see Vignerons de Franschhoek.

Fransdruif (S.Afr) the name for the Palomino grape used in the making of South African Sherry. Also called Frans. see White French.

Fransola (Sp) a new name (in 1990) for Gran Viña Sol Green Label from Torres. Named after its single vineyard of origin. 25ha. Grape variety: Sauvignon blanc.

Franta's Rules (Czec) a Falstaffian code of taverns, named after a tap-room in Pilsen.

Franzenheim (Ger) village (Anb): Mosel-Saar-Ruwer. (Ber): Saar-Ruwer. (Gro): Römerlay. (Vin): Johannisberg.

Franzensberger (Ger) vineyard (Anb): Baden. (Ber): Ortenau. (Gro): Fürsteneck. (Vil): Offenburg (ortsteil Fessenbach).

Franzensberger (Ger) vineyard (Anb): Baden. (Ber): Ortenau. (Gro): Fürsteneck. (Vil): Ortenberg.

Franzia Brandy (USA) the brand-name for a brandy produced by the Franzia Brothers Winery, Ripon, San Joaquin Valley, California 40% alc by vol.

Franzia Brothers Winery (USA) a family winery in Ripon, San Joaquin Valley, California. Produces varietal and sparkling wines, also brandies. Owned by Coca Cola C°.

Franziskaner (Ger) vineyard (Anb): Baden. (Ber): Kaiserstuhl-Tuniberg. (Gro): Attilafelsen. (Vil): Oberimsingen.

Franziskaner Hefe Weissbier (Ger) a 5% alc by vol. bottle-conditioned wheat beer brewed by the Spätenbräu Brauerei in Munich.

Franziskaner Hefe Weissbier Dunkel (Ger) a 5% alc by vol. dark bottle-conditioned wheat beer brewed by the Spätenbräu Brauerei in Munich.

Franziskaner Kristallklar (Ger) a 5% alc by vol. filtered weizenbier brewed by the Spätenbräu Brauerei in Munich.

Franziskus (Ger) a pale bock bier 6.7% alc by vol. brewed by the Spätenbräu Brauerei in Munich.

Franz Joseph Jubelbier (Ger) a 5.5% alc by vol. dark beer brewed by the Franz Joseph Sailer Brauerei, Marktoberdorf.

Franz Joseph Sailer Brauerei (Ger) a brewery based at Marktoberdorf. Brews: Franz Joseph Jubelbier.

Französicher Landwein (Ger) the equivalent to the French Vin de Pays wines.

Fraoch (Scot) an old heather-flavoured ale 'beer'.

Fraoch (Scot) a 5% alc by vol. heather ale brewed by Heather Ale Ltd., Lanarkshire.

Fraoch Heather Ale (Scot) a 5% alc by vol. heather-flavoured ale brewed by Maclay & C°. at the Thistle Brewery in Alloa. See also Heather Ale.

Frapin (Fr) a famous Cognac producer based in Segonzac 137ha. in the Grande Champagne. Produces Château de Fontpinot Grande Champagne and Domaine Frapin Grande Fine Champagne.

Frappato (It) a red grape variety used in Sicily.

Frappato di Vittoria (It) a sweet, dessert, red wine produced near Ragusa in Sicily from the Frappato grape.

Frappé (Fr) iced or very cold, a term used for serving sparkling wines or for liqueurs that are served with crushed ice.

Frappé (Eng) a 4.5% alc by vol. fruit flavoured drinks suspended in crushed ice from Spilt Drink Company. 3 flavours: lemon, orange, tropical fruit.

Frappuccino (USA) the name™ for an iced cappuccino coffee produced by the Starbucks Coffee Company.

Frasassi (It) a sparkling natural spring mineral water from Piagge del Prete. Mineral contents (milligrammes per litre): Sodium 19.2mg/l, Calcium 93mg/l, Magnesium 3.8mg/l, Potassium 1.8mg/l, Bicarbonates 281mg/l, Chlorides 19.9mg/l, Sulphates 25.5mg/l, Strontium 2.6mg/l, Silicates 9.1mg/l. pH 7.5

Frascalli (Bra) a natural spring mineral water (established 1999).

Frascati (It) a D.O.C. white wine from Latium. Made from the Bellone, Bonvino, Greco, Malvasia bianca di candia, Malvasia del lazio and Trebbiano toscano grapes. Produced in the commune of Frascati and others. Secco, Amabile and Dolce styles produced. For the latter, 2 varieties of **Botrytis cinerea (muffa nobile)** attacked grapes are used. If alc. content is 12% by vol. minimum then classed Superiore. The D.O.C. also applies to sparkling wines. see Classico. Also known as Vini dei Castelli Romani.

Frasco (Sp) a small bottle/flask.

Fraser Blue (Austr) a natural spring mineral water from Queensland. Mineral contents (milligrammes per litre): Sodium 19.2mg/l, Calcium 8.3mg/l, Magnesium 2.3mg/l, Potassium 0.7mg/l, Bicarbonates 43.5mg/l, Sulphates 5mg/l.

Fraser Valley (Can) a designated wine region in British Columbia.

Frasinetti and Sons (USA) a winery based in Sacramento, California. Produces table and dessert wines.

Frasqueira (Port) a bottle case/crate.

Fratelli (It) brothers.

Fratelli Barale (It) a long-standing Barolo producing winery in the Piemonte region.

Fratelli Branca (USA) a version of the Italian bitters (Fernet Branca) produced for the American market.

Fratelli Brunello (It) a family run distillery in Vicenza. Specialise in single varietal grappas including Crujavo which is made from the pomace of a rare local variety of same name, plus Moscato Fior d'Arancio (orange blossom muscat).

F

Fratelli Cora [G. and L.] (It) a sparkling (metodo tradizionale) wine producer based in the Piemonte region. Labels include: Royal Ambassador Brut.

Fratelli d'Angelo (It) see d'Angelo.

Fratelli Oddero (It) noted vineyard owners and producers of Barolo based at La Morra, Barolo, Piemonte.

Fratelli Pasqua (It) sparkling wine producers based in Verona.

Fratelli Pedrotti (It) producers of sparkling (metodo tradizionale) wines in the Trentino-Alto Adige region.

Fratelli Pisoni (It) producers of sparkling (metodo tradizionale) wines in the Trentino-Alto Adige region.

Fratelli Vita (Bra) a natural spring mineral water. Mineral contents (milligrammes per litre): Sodium 5.76mg/l, Calcium 8.93mg/l, Magnesium 1.28mg/l, Potassium 4.27mg/l, Bicarbonates 38.4mg/l, Chlorides 1.02mg/l, Sulphates 0.1mg/l, Fluorides 0.05mg/l, Nitrates 9.4mg/l. pH 6.02

Fratt Industries Ltd. (USA) a distillery based in Delano, California. Producers of F1 Brandy.

Frauenbach (Aus) a vineyard area on the banks of the River Danube in the Kremstal region.

Frauenberg (Ger) vineyard (Anb): Baden. (Ber): Markgräflerland. (Gro): Burg Neuenfels. (Vil): Mauchen.

Frauenberg (Ger) vineyard (Anb): Mosel-Saar-Ruwer. (Ber): Zell/Mosel. (Gro): Grafschaft. (Vil): Bremm.

Frauenberg (Ger) vineyard (Anb): Mosel-Saar-Ruwer. (Ber): Zell/Mosel. (Gro): Grafschaft. (Vil): Neef.

Frauenberg (Ger) vineyard (Anb): Rheinhessen. (Ber): Wonnegau. (Gro): Burg Rodenstein. (Vil): Flörsheim-Dalsheim.

Frauenfeld Brauerei (Switz) a noted brewery based in Frauenfeld, eastern Switzerland.

Frauengärten (Aus) a vineyard site on the banks of the River Danube situated in the Wachau region, Niederösterreich.

Frauengarten (Ger) vineyard (Anb): Rheinhessen. (Ber): Nierstein. (Gro): Krötenbrunnen. (Vil): Wintersheim.

Frauengrund (Aus) a vineyard area on the banks of the River Danube in the Kremstal region.

Frauenholzener Mineralbrunnen (Ger) a natural spring mineral water. Mineral contents (milligrammes per litre): Sodium 7.5mg/l, Calcium 89mg/l, Magnesium 21.8mg/l, Potassium 3mg/l, Bicarbonates 373mg/l, Fluorides 0.62mg/l.

Frauenländchen (Ger) vineyard (Anb): Pfalz. (Ber): Mittelhaardt-Deutsche Weinstrasse. (Gro): Höllenpfad. (Vil): Kleinkarlbach.

Frauenpoint (Aus) a vineyard site on the banks of the River Danube situated in the Wachau region, Niederösterreich.

Frauenstein (Ger) village (Anb): Rheingau. (Ber): Johannisberg. (Gro): Steinmacher. (Vins): Herrenberg, Homberg, Marschall.

Frauenweingärten (Aus) a vineyard site on the banks of the River Danube situated in the Wachau region, Niederösterreich.

Frauenzimmer (Ger) vineyard (Anb): Württemberg. (Ber): Württembergisch Unterland. (Gro): Salzberg. (Vil): Lehrensteinsfeld.

Frauenzimmern (Ger) village (Anb): Württemberg. (Ber): Württembergisch Unterland. (Gro): Heuchelberg. (Vins): Kaiserberg, Michaelsberg.

Fräulein Frankfurt (Cktl) 1 measure gin, ⅓ measure cherry brandy, ⅓ measure crème de noyau, ⅓ measure lemon juice. Shake well over ice and strain into a cocktail glass.

Fray Junipero (USA) a wine pioneer, a Dominican missionary who planted around the missions of California the vines he had brought from Spain.

Freal (Aus) a vineyard site on the banks of the River Danube situated in the Wachau region, Niederösterreich.

Frecciarossa (It) wines made by a single family (the Odero family). Produce red, rosé and slightly sweet white wines around a village near Casteggio in Lombardy.

Frechau (Aus) a vineyard area on the banks of the River Danube in the Kremstal region.

Freckenfeld (Ger) village (Anb): Pfalz. (Ber): Südliche Weinstrasse. (Gro): Guttenberg. (Vin): Gräfenberg.

Freddie Fudpucker Cocktail (Cktl) 25mls (⅕ gill) tequila gold, 125mls (1gill) orange juice. Pour over ice in a highball glass, add 1 teaspoon of Galliano on top and a cherry.

Frederick Johnson Winery (USA) a winery based in Westfield, Chautauqua, New York. Produce wines mainly from the Concord grape.

Frederic Robinson's Brewery (Eng) see Robinson [Frederic].

Frederic Robinson's Old Tom Strong Ale (Eng) an 8.5% alc by vol. classic winter warmer cask-conditioned or bottled ale brewed by Frederic Robinson at the Unicorn Brewery, Stockport.

Frederics (Eng) a 5% alc by vol. premium bottled beer, light golden in colour, from an all malt grist recipe it is dry hopped. Produced by independent Stockport brewer Frederic Robinson at the Unicorn Brewery.

Frederik (Est) a brewery. (Add): As Viru Olu, 45301 Haljala, Lääne-Virumaa, Estonia. Brews a variety of beers and lager. Website: http://www.frederik.ee 'E'mail: frederik@frederik.ee

Fredine le Roux Wines (S.Afr) a winery (established 2004) based in Caledon, Walker Bay, Western Cape. Grape varieties: Cabernet sauvignon, Chenin blanc, Grenache.

Fredonia (USA) a black grape variety, the juice used for blending with Concord must.

Fredrikstad Brewery (Nor) a brewery based in Fredrikstad, south-eastern Norway.

Freebooter (Eng) a 4% alc by vol. ale brewed by the Jolly Boat Brewery (Bideford) Ltd., Devon.

Freedom (Fr) see Freedom & Firkin.

Freedom & Firkin (Fr) a micro-brewery based in

Paris. Brews: cask Dogbolter 5.6% alc by vol. Also Floozy, Capit'ale and Freedom (all at 4.3% alc by vol).

Freedom Brewing C°. (Eng) a micro-brewery (established 1995). (Add): 11 Galena Road, Hammersmith, London W6 0LT. Brews Freedom Lager 5.4% alc by vol. Freedom Pilsner 5% alc by vol. Fresh Natural Beer, a US-style Red Ale, Pale Ale, Wheat Beer, Freedom Organic 4.8% alc by vol. Freedom Organic Pilsner 5% alc by vol. Website: http://www.freedombrewery.com 'E'mail: info@freedombrewery.com

Freedom Hill Wines (S.Afr) a winery (established 1997) based in Uniedal, Paarl, Western Cape. 19ha. Grape varieties: Cabernet sauvignon, Merlot, Pinotage, Shiraz. Labels: Liberty, Shibul. Website: http://www.freedomhill.co.za

Free Flow (Eng) a pressurised keg which is connected to a small on/off tap. beer flows when the tap is opened. Used to serve keg or top pressure beer.

Free House (Eng) a public house which is not connected (tied) to a brewery and which can offer beers etc. from different breweries and outlets. see Tied House.

Freemark Abbey Winery (USA) a winery based near Saint Helena, Rutherford, Napa Valley, California. Produces: Cabernet Boché, Sycamore Vineyards Cabernet Sauvignon, Carpy Ranch Chardonnay and Edelwein Gold. Grape varieties: Chardonnay, Johannisberg riesling, Cabernet sauvignon, Merlot and Petit syrah. Label: Sycamore Vineyard.

Freeminer Brewery (Eng) a brewery (established 1992). (Add): Whimsey Road, Steam Mills, Cinderford, Gloucestershire GL14 3JA. Brews: Freeminer Bitter 4% alc by vol., Deep Shaft Stout, Gold Standard, Shakemantle, Speculation 4.8% alc by vol., Strip and At It 4% alc by vol., Trafalgar IPA 6% alc by vol., Waterloo 4.5% alc by vol. Website: http://www.freeminer.com 'E'mail: info@freeminer.com

Free Run (S.Afr) the label for a white wine (Sauvignon blanc) produced by the Flagstone Winery, Somerset West, Western Cape.

Free Run Wine (Fr) the juice from partially crushed and destalked grapes which is fermented out. Produces the best wine.

Free Silver Cocktail (Cktl) ⅓ measure dry gin, ⅓ measure dark rum, ⅓ measure lemon juice, dash gomme syrup, 2 teaspoons milk. Shake over ice, strain into an ice-filled highball glass and top with soda water.

Free SO₂ (Eng) unbound **Sulphur-dioxide** active in wine as a bacteriacide.

Free Spirit (Eng) a 4.8% alc by vol. classic bitter ale (part of the Classics Range) brewed by the Hydes Brewery, Manchester.

Freeze Dried Coffee (Eng) an instant coffee made from fresh brewed coffee and dried freezing in a vacuum (lyophilisation).

Freezomint (Fr) a mint digestive liqueur 27% alc by vol. Produced by the Cusenier C°.

Freiburg (Ger) village (Anb): Baden. (Ber): Markgräflerland. (Gro): Lorettoberg. (Vins): Jesuitenschloss, Steinler.

Freiburger Weintage (Ger) a Baden wine festival held at Freiburg in June annually.

Freiburg i. Br. (Ger) village (Anb): Baden. (Ber): Breisgau. (Gro): Burg Zähringen. (Vin): Schlossberg.

Freiburg i. Br. (Ger) village (Anb): Baden. see Freiburg.

Freie Weingärtner Wachau (Aus) lit: 'free wine-growers of Wachau', a co-operative winery (600ha) based in Dürnstein, Wachau. (Add): 3601 Dürnstein. Has 778 members. Grape varieties: Chardonnay, Grüner veltliner, Müller-Thurgau, Neuburger, Pinot blanc, Riesling, Sauvignon blanc, Zweigelt. Produces a range of dry and sweet (botrytised) wines.

Freihand (Ger) a term used for those wines that are sold from the cellars directly to the purchasers through brokers.

Freiherr (Ger) baron.

Freiherr von Brentano (Ger) a family estate in Winkel, Rheingau.

Frei-Laubersheim (Ger) village (Anb): Rheinhessen. (Ber): Bingen. (Gro): Rheingrafenstein. (Vins): Fels, Kirchberg, Reichskeller, Rheingrafenberg.

Freimersheim (Ger) village (Anb): Rheinhessen. (Ber): Wonnegau. (Gro): Sybillenstein. (Vin): Frankenstein.

Freimersheim (Ger) village (Anb): Pfalz. (Ber): Südliche Weinstrasse. (Gro): Trappenberg. (Vin): Bildberg.

Freinsheim (Ger) village (Anb): Pfalz. (Ber): Mittelhaardt-Deutsche Weinstrasse. (Gro): Rosenbühl. (Vin): Goldberg.

Freisa (It) a red wine grape variety grown in the Piemonte. Produces a sparkling red wine called Freisa. Two clones: Freisa Grossa, Freisa Piccola.

Freisa (It) a sparkling red wine made from the Freisa grape in the Piemonte.

Freisa d'Asti (It) a D.O.C. red wine from Piemonte. Made from the Freisa grape. If alc. 11.5% by vol. and aged for minimum 10–11 months then classed Superiore. D.O.C. also applies to the naturally sparkling wines produced in the specific region. Spumante or Frizzante.

Freisa di Chieri (It) a D.O.C. red wine from Piemonte. Made from the Freisa grape throughout the commune of Chieri and others. Either dry or semi-sweet- Freisa Secco or Amabile. If aged for 10–11 months and alc. content 11.5% by vol. then classed Superiore.

Freisa di Chieri (It) a D.O.C. which can be applied to sparkling and semi-sparkling wines obtained by re-fermenting the natural sugar left in the sweet wine kept by filtration or refrigeration.

Freisa Grossa (It) a large red berried grape variety, a clone of the Freisa.

Freisamer (Ger) a white grape variety, a cross between the Silvaner and the Ruländer. Gives full neutral wines.

Freisa Piccola (It) small red berried grape variety, a clone of the Freisa.

Freisheim (Ger) village (Anb): Pfalz. (Ber): Mittelhaardt-Deutsche Weinstrasse. (Gro): Kobnert. (Vins): Musikantenbuckel, Oschelskopf, Schwarzes Kreuz.

Freising Court Brauerei (Ger) a brewery that is noted for Huber Weisses wheat beer.

Freitas Martins Caldeira Lda. (Mad) a noted shipper of Madeira wines to the United Kingdom.

Freixedas [José] (Sp) a producer of sparkling (cuve close) wines including Castillo la Torre.

Freixenet (Sp) a major sparkling wine producer. Wines made by the cava method in Catalonia, San Sadurni de Noya, Barcelona. Noted for Cordon Negro, Brut Nature, Brut Rosé and Carta Nevada Extra.

Fremantle Bitter Ale (Austr) a 4.9% alc by vol. top-fermented, bottled ale brewed by the Mathilda Bay Brewery (C.U.B.), Stirling Highway in Fremantle, Western Australia.

Fremersberger Feigenwäldchen (Ger) vineyard (Anb): Baden. (Ber): Ortenau. (Gro): Schloss Rodeck. (Vil): Sinzheim.

Fremières [Les] (Fr) a Premier Cru vineyard in the A.C. commune of Morey-Saint-Denis, Côte de Nuits, Burgundy 2.4ha.

Fremiers [Les] (Fr) a Premier Cru vineyard in the A.C. commune of Volnay, Côte de Beaune, Burgundy 4.9ha.

Fremiets (Fr) a Premier Cru vineyard in the A.C. commune of Volnay, Côte de Beaune, Burgundy. 6.5ha. Also known as Les Fremiets.

Fremlins Bitter (Eng) a 3.5% alc by vol. traditional draught ale brewed by Ridley at the Hartford End Brewery, Essex.

Fremlins Brewery (Eng) is Whitbread's Kent Brewery in Faversham. Noted for keg AK 1032 O.G. and Trophy Bitter 1035 O.G.

French (Eng) when applied to drinks usually denotes a dry, white vermouth such as Noilly Prat, Dubonnet, etc.

French Apéritifs (Fr) appetisers, long drinks usually served with cold water. see Dubonnet-Citron, Picon Grenadine, Polichinelle, Curaçao.

French Coffee (Eng) a coffee blend that usually has roasted chicory added which gives it a bitter taste.

French Colombard (USA) a white grape variety grown in California to produce dry white wines.

French Connection [1] (Cktl) 35mls (1½ fl.ozs) amaretto, 35mls (1½ fl.ozs) brandy. Build into an ice-filled old-fashioned glass.

French Connection [2] (Cktl) build 25mls (1fl.oz) Glayva into an ice-filled slim jim glass and stir in Perrier water.

French Egg Nogg (Fr) see Lait de Poule.

French Emperor (Cktl) ⅔ measure Mandarine Napoléon, ⅓ measure green crème de menthe, dash egg white. Stir, add ice and top up with soda water.

French Farm (N.Z) a winery. (Add): French Farm Valley Road, RD 2, Akaroa, Canterbury. Grape varieties: Pinot noir, Chardonnay.

French Fruit (Cktl) 5mls (¼ fl.oz) each of Mandarine Napoléon, Southern Comfort, orange juice. Fill a highball glass with ice, add ingredients and stir.

French Grape (S.Afr) the local name for the Palomino vine.

French Green Dragon Cocktail (Cktl) ½ measure Cognac, ½ measure green Chartreuse. Shake well over ice and strain into a cocktail glass.

French Kiss (S.Afr) a sweet white wine (Chenin blanc) produced under the Concept Wines label by the Ashanti winery, Paarl, Western Cape.

French Oak (Fr) the oak used in the making of wine and spirit casks usually from the forests of Limousin, Monlezun, Nevers and Tronçais. Imparts a vanillin flavour to the wine or spirit.

French Pousse Café (Pousse Café) in a liqueur glass pour in order: ¼ measure green Chartreuse, ¼ measure maraschino, ¼ measure cherry brandy, ¼ measure kümmel (do not stir).

French Rabbit (Fr) a new range (2005) of vin de pays wines sold in recyclable Tetra-Pak™ by J.P. Boisset in Burgundy.

French Roots (Fr) a Vin de Table range of French wines bottled in the Bordeaux region. (Add): 19, Avenue de Fontenille 33360 Carignan-de-Bordeaux. Website: http://www.frenchroots-wine.com

French Rose (Cktl) ⅗ measure dry gin, ⅕ measure cherry brandy, ⅕ measure dry vermouth. Stir over ice and strain into a cocktail glass.

French Seventyfive (75) [1] (Cktl) 1 jigger brandy, juice 1 lemon, 1 teaspoon sugar. Shake over ice, strain into a highball glass and top with iced Champagne.

French Seventyfive (75) [2] (Cktl) 50mls (2fl.ozs) dry gin, juice of ½ lemon, 1 teaspoon sugar. Shake well with ice, strain into a highball glass and top with iced Champagne.

French Sherbert (Cktl) place into a flute glass 3 dashes Cognac, 3 dashes kirsch, dash Angostura. Stir, add a scoop of water ice and top with iced Champagne.

French Sherbert (USA) the nickname for Champagne.

French Smeller's (Fr) the nickname for government agents who smelt out coffee smugglers in the seventeenth century travelling to Germany.

French Vermouth (Fr) is drier than Italian vermouth (white and dry), the base wine is stored in thick oak casks, then allowed to spend some time outside to allow exposure to sea air. Has a spicey aroma. see Gin and French.

Frénette (Fr) a low-alcohol fermented beverage made from ash leaves, sugar and roasted chicory. A second fermentation takes place in the bottle to give a sparkle similar to lemonade. See also Ash Drink.

Frères du Cênes (Fr) a Cognac producer. (Add): Distillerie Merlet, St. Sauvant, 17610 Chaniers. 40ha. Situated in the Borderies 50% and Fins Bois 50%.

F

Frés (Eng) a 4% alc by vol. blond cider produced by Matthew Clark Taunton.

Fresca (Eng) a low-calorie diet grapefruit-flavoured drink from the Coca Cola C°.

Frescca (Bra) a sparkling natural spring mineral water from Fonte São Francisco, Cotia. Mineral contents (milligrammes per litre): Sodium 8.98mg/l, Calcium 10.31mg/l, Magnesium 1.61mg/l, Potassium 2.77mg/l, Bicarbonates 63.22mg/l, Chlorides 1.78mg/l, Sulphates 0.7mg/l, Fluorides 0.18mg/l, Nitrates 0.2mg/l. pH 6.68 Website: http://www.cotiafoods.com.br

Frescobaldi [Marchese Vittorio] (It) wine producers based in Florence, Tuscany. Noted for Chianti Ruffina. 540ha. Also produces sparkling (metodo tradizionale) wines.

Fresh (Eng) the term that describes a young wine which has not lost its charm.

Fresh Brew (Eng) the brand-name for a tea produced by Kenco-Typhoo.

Freshers Special (Eng) a 5.5% alc by vol. special ale brewed by Bazens Brewery, Greater Manchester.

Fresh Water (Eng) a description of potable water that has derived from a spring, tap or well. (Ire) = fioruisce.

Freshwells Spring (Eng) a natural spring mineral water (established 1999).

Fresk (Arg) a natural spring mineral water. Mineral contents (milligrammes per litre): Sodium 70mg/l, Calcium 60mg/l, Magnesium 5mg/l, Potassium 7mg/l, Chlorides 15mg/l, Sulphates 13mg/l, Fluorides 0.7mg/l. pH 7.2

Freslier [André] (Fr) a noted producer of pétillant wines based in the A.C. Vouvray area, Touraine, Loire.

Fresnet-Juillet (Fr) a Champagne producer. (Add): 10, Rue de Beaumont, 51380 Verzy. 8ha. Produces vintage and non-vintage wines. Vintages: 1995, 1996, 1997, 1999. A member of the Club Tresors de Champagne. Labels: Cuvée 'Special Club' Millésimée Premier Cru.

Fresno (USA) the Fresno-San Joaquin Valley, California, the southern part of the Great Valley. Produces most of Californias' dessert wines with some table and sparkling wines.

Fresno State (USA) abbr: California State University based at Fresno where practical training in viticulture and oenology occurs.

Fret (Eng) to undergo a secondary fermentation after the wine has been fermented and racked. A small ring of bubbles appears and the wine slowly ferments, caused through sugar still remaining or a malo-lactic fermentation.

Frettenheim (Ger) village (Anb): Rheinhessen. (Ber): Wonnegau. (Gro): Pilgerpfad. (Vin): Heil.

Freudenlese (S.Afr) a special late harvest wine produced by Hazendal.

Freudenstein (Ger) village (Anb): Württemberg. (Ber): Württembergisch Unterland. (Gro): Stromberg. (Vin): Reichshalde.

Freudental (Ger) vineyard (Anb): Baden. (Ber):

Ortenau. (Gro): Fürsteneck. (Vil): Ortenberg.

Freudental (Ger) village (Anb): Württemberg. (Ber): Württembergisch Unterland. (Gro): Stromberg. (Vin): Kirchberg.

Freu Hé (Bel) a natural spring mineral water. Mineral contents (milligrammes per litre): Sodium 14mg/l, Calcium 17mg/l, Magnesium 3.5mg/l, Potassium 1mg/l, Bicarbonates 80mg/l, Chlorides 5mg/l, Sulphates 18mg/l, Nitrates <0.2mg/l, Silicates 18mg/l.

Freundstück (Ger) vineyard (Anb): Pfalz. (Ber): Mittelhaardt-Deutsche Weinstrasse. (Gro): Mariengarten. (Vil): Forst.

Freycinet Estate (Austr) a vineyard. (Add): Lot 1, Gnaraway Road, Margaret River, Western Australia. 8ha. Grape varieties: Cabernet franc, Cabernet sauvignon, Chardonnay, Chenin blanc, Merlot, Sauvignon blanc and Sémillon. Also holdings in Tasmania.

Freydenlund (Nor) a brand of beer. 1042 O.G.

Freyersbacher (Ger) a natural mineral water from the Black Forest. (Add): Brunnen-Union St. Christophorus GmbH. Betreib: Freyersbacher Mineralquellen 77737 Bad Peterstal/Schwarzwald. Mineral contents (grammes per litre): Sodium 0.331g/l, Calcium 0.326g/l, Magnesium 0.0724g/l, Potassium 0.0244g/l, Bicarbonates 1.635g/l, Chlorides 0.0295g/l, Sulphates 0.475g/l.

Freyersbacher Alexanderquele (Ger) a natural spring mineral water (established 1838) from Peterstal. Mineral contents (milligrammes per litre): Sodium 153mg/l, Calcium 144mg/l, Magnesium 31mg/l, Potassium 24mg/l, Bicarbonates 747mg/l, Chlorides 19mg/l, Sulphates 190mg/l, Fluorides 2.4mg/l.

Freyersbacher Scharzwälder (Ger) a natural spring mineral water (established 1838) from Peterstal. Mineral contents (milligrammes per litre): Sodium 331mg/l, Calcium 326mg/l, Magnesium 72.4mg/l, Potassium 24.4mg/l, Bicarbonates 1635mg/l, Chlorides 29.5mg/l, Sulphates 475mg/l, Fluorides 2.4mg/l.

Freyung (Aus) lit: 'without water', the name given to 1968 eiswein (one of the first produced for a long while).

Frey Vineyards (USA) a vineyard based in Redwood Valley, Mendocino, California (30 acres of their own vineyards). Grape varieties: Cabernet sauvignon, Carignan, Pinot noir, Syrah, Zinfandel, Gewürztraminer, Sauvignon blanc.

Friand (Fr) applies to a young wine that is fresh, fruity and has a good flavour.

Friar John Cor (Scot) a monk who in 1494 produced the first acquavitae.

Friar's Ale (Eng) a keg bitter 1036 O.G. brewed by the Morrell Brewery in Oxford.

Friars Bitter (Eng) a 3.3% alc by vol. bitter ale from the Morrell Brewery in Oxford. See also Brewery Gate Bitter.

Friarwood Ltd (Eng) a distillers (established 1967). (Add): 26 New Kings Road, Fulham, London SW6 4ST. Produces a variety of spirits and alcoholic drinks. Website: http://www.friarwood.com 'E'mail: sales@friarwood.com

Friary Meux Brewery (Eng) a brewery based in Goldaming, Surrey. Part of the Ind Coope Breweries. Noted for Treble Gold 1052 O.G.

Frick [Pierre et Fils] (Fr) an Alsace wine producer. (Add): 5 Rue de Baer, 68250 Pfaffenheim.

Frickenhausen (Ger) village (Anb): Württemberg. (Ber): Remstal-Stuttgart. (Gro): Hohenneuffen. (Vin): Schlossteige.

Frickenhausen am Main (Ger) village (Anb): Franken. (Ber): Maindreieck. (Gro): Not yet assigned. (Vins): Fischer, Kapellenberg, Markgraf, Babenberg.

Frida (It) a natural spring mineral water from Cimbro di Vergiate, Lombardy. Mineral contents (milligrammes per litre): Sodium 4.6mg/l, Calcium 47.14mg/l, Magnesium 10.98mg/l, Potassium 1.85mg/l, Bicarbonates 160.43mg/l, Chlorides 5.7mg/l, Sulphates 20.64mg/l, Fluorides 0.04mg/l, Nitrates 17.55mg/l, Silicates 10mg/l. pH 7.8

Friday 13th (Eng) a 4.2% alc by vol. ale brewed by the Hogs Back Brewery Ltd., Surrey.

Friedberger (Aus) a winery based in Bisamberg, Weinviertel. (Add): Hauptstrasse 17, 2102 Bisamberg. Grape varieties: Grüner veltliner, Pinot blnc, Riesling.

Friedelsheim (Ger) village (Anb): Pfalz. (Ber): Mittelhaardt-Deutsche Weinstrasse. (Gro): Hofstück. (Vins): Gerümpel, Rosengarten.

Friedelsheim (Ger) village (Anb): Pfalz. (Ber): Mittelhaardt-Deutsche Weinstrasse. (Gro): Schnepfenflug an der Weinstrasse. (Vins): Bischofsgarten, Kreuz, Schlossgarten.

Friedman-Tnuva (Isr) a noted winery that produces red, rosé and white wines.

Friedrich Christian Heilwasser (Ger) a sparkling natural spring mineral water. Mineral contents (milligrammes per litre): Sodium 621mg/l, Calcium 233mg/l, Magnesium 81.9mg/l, Potassium 18.3mg/l, Bicarbonates 1488mg/l, Chlorides 728mg/l, Sulphates 21mg/l, Fluorides 0.47mg/l, Silicates 31.4mg/l.

Friedrich Laibach (S.Afr) the label for a red wine (Cabernet sauvignon 64%, Cabernet franc, Merlot and Petit verdot blend) produced by the Laibach Vineyards winery, Stellenbosch, Western Cape.

Friedrich Wilheim Gymnasium (Ger) a charitable estate in the Rheingau. 46ha. (Gro): Burgweg. (Vins): Rothenberg and Kläuserweg.

Friendship Cocktail (Cktl) ⅓ measure gin, ⅓ measure orange Curaçao, ⅓ measure lemon juice. Shake over ice, pour into a cocktail glass, dress with a slice of orange and lemon.

Friesa (It) a grape variety grown in Piemonte that produces dry wines. See also Freisa.

Friesengeist (Ger) a (herb) mint liqueur from the Frisian part of Germany 45% alc by vol. Produced by Johann Eschen.

Friesenheim (Ger) village (Anb): Baden. (Ber):

Breisgau. (Gro): Schotterlindenberg. (Vin): Kronenbühl.

Friesenheim (Ger) village (Anb): Rheinhessen. (Ber): Nierstein. (Gro): Gutes Domtal. (Vins): Altdörr, Bergpfad, Knopf.

Friesenrock (Aus) a vineyard site based on the banks of the River Kamp situated in the Kamptal region.

Frigola (Sp) a thyme-flavoured liqueur from the Balearic Islands.

Frij (Austr) a heavy vinyl bag with a drawstring top used to keep drinks cool.

Frincusa (Rum) a white grape variety.

Frio (Mex) chilled. See also Helado.

Frionnes [Les] (Fr) a Premier Cru vineyard in the A.C. commune of Saint-Aubin, Côte de Beaune, Burgundy.

Frisch (Ger) fresh/sprightly.

Frische (Ger) freshness.

Frische Brise (Ger) a natural spring mineral water from Billetal Quelle, Reinbek.

Frisco Sour (Cktl) 10mls (½ fl.oz) Bénédictine, 35mls (1½ fl.ozs) Bourbon whiskey, 10mls (½ fl.oz) lime juice, 10mls (½ fl.oz) lemon juice. Shake over ice, strain into a large cocktail glass and decorate with slices of lemon and lime.

Frisia (It) a sparkling natural spring mineral water from Piuro, Lombardy. Mineral contents (milligrammes per litre): Sodium 2.57mg/l, Calcium 16.9mg/l, Magnesium 2.59mg/l, Potassium 2.72mg/l, Bicarbonates 48mg/l, Chlorides 1.8mg/l, Sulphates 15.9mg/l, Nitrates 4.75mg/l, Silicates 9.43mg/l. pH 7.3

Frisian Coffee (Liq.Coffee) from Germany, made with friesengeist (which is set alight). Serve black.

Frisian Country Wine (Ger) see Doornkaat.

Frisians (Ger) early seventh century merchants who navigated the river Rhine and took the German wines to western ports in U.K., Iberia and France.

Frisk (Nor) a natural spring mineral water from Trio bryggeri Skien, Telemark.

Frisk Lager (Eng) a low-carbohydrate lager 1033 O.G. brewed by the Vaux Brewery in Sunderland.

Frithsden (Eng) a vineyard. (Add): Berkhampsted, Hertfordshire. 1ha. Soil: heavy loam with flint and chalky subsoil. Grape varieties: Müller-Thurgau, Pinot meunier, Pinot noir, Ruländer and Weissburgunder (vinification at Gamlingay Vineyards).

Fritsch [Karl] (Aus) a winery based in Kirchberg am Wagram, Donauland. (Add): Oberstockstall 24, 3470 Kirchberg am Wagram. Grape varieties: Grüner veltliner, Pinot noir, Riesling, Welschriesling. Produces a range of wines including eiswein.

Fritz Kupelwieser (It) an old established winery based in Salurn, Süd-Tirol (Trentino-Alto Adige).

Friularo (It) a black grape variety grown in the Veneto region. Also name of red table wine made from same grape.

Friuli-Venezia Giulia (It) one of the smallest regions that borders Austria to the north and has the Adriatic sea to the south.

F

Frize (Port) a sparkling natural spring mineral water (established 1994) from Frize, Vila Flor. Mineral contents (milligrammes per litre): Sodium 741mg/l, Calcium 116mg/l, Magnesium 35.2mg/l, Bicarbonates 2393mg/l, Chlorides 145mg/l, Silicates 26.7mg/l. pH 6.4

Frizzante (It) slightly sparkling. See also Frizzantino. (Fr) = pétillant, (Ger) = spritzig.

Frizzantino (It) refers to a wine with a barely noticable prickle. See also Frizzante.

Frobishers Juices (Wal) a soft drinks manufacturer (established 1999). (Add): Sun House, Llantrisant Business Park, Llantrisant, Pontyclun, Mid Glamorgan CF72 8LF. Produces a variety of fruit and vegetable juices. 'E'mail: sales@frobishers.com

Froccs (Hun) a light white wine mixed with soda water as a thirst quencher.

Froehn (Fr) an A.C. Alsace Grand Cru vineyard in Zellenberg, Haut-Rhin. 13ha.

Frog (Scot) the name used in the Orkneys to describe the top layer of peat which is used in malt whisky production. See also Moss, Yarpie

Frog and Firkin (Eng) a home-brew public house in London. Noted for cask-conditioned Bullfrog 1045 O.G. Dogbolter 1060 O.G. and Tavistock 1036 O.G.

Frog and Frigate (Eng) a home-brew public house in Southampton. Noted for Croaker 1050 O.G. and Frog's Original 1040 O.G.

Frog and Parrot (Eng) a home-brew public house owned by Whitbread in Sheffield. Noted for cask-conditioned Old Croak 1035 O.G. Reckless Bitter 1046 O.G. Roger's Special 1065 O.G. all using malt extract. Also Hope & Glory 4.2% alc by vol.

Frog Hill (S.Afr) a range of red (Cabernet, Merlot and Shiraz blend) and white (Chenin blanc) wines from the Anura Vineyards, Paarl, Western Cape.

Frog Island Brewery (Eng) a brewery (established 1994). (Add): The Maltings, Westbridge, St. James Road, Northampton, Northamptonshire NN5 5HS. Brews: Best Bitter (Cask) 3.8% alc by vol., Croak and Stagger (bottle-conditioned) 5.6% alc by vol (1056 O.G)., Draught 5.8% alc by vol., Fire Belly Toad 5% alc by vol., Natterjack 4.8% alc by vol., Seasonal Ales, Shoemaker 4.2% alc by vol. Website: http://www.frogislandbrewery.co.uk 'E'mail: beer@frogislandbrewery.co.uk

Frog's Leap (USA) a small organic winery based near Rutherford, Napa Valley, California. (Add): 8815 Conn Creek Road, Rutherford CA 94573. Grape varieties: Cabernet sauvignon. Website: http://www.frogsleap.com

Froher Weingarten (Ger) vineyard (Anb): Mittelrhein. (Ber): Bacharach. (Gro): Schloss Reichenstein. (Vil): Niederheimbach.

Fröhlich (Ger) vineyard (Anb): Rheinhessen. (Ber): Wonnegau. (Gro): Sybillenstein. (Vil): Bechenheim.

Fröhliche Weinberg [Der] (Ger) a play by Carl Zuckemeyer. 'The Merry Vineyard'.

Frohnwingert (Ger) vineyard (Anb): Pfalz. (Ber): Südliche Weinstrasse. (Gro): Kloster Liebfrauenberg. (Vil): Oberhausen.

Frohnwingert (Ger) vineyard (Anb): Mittelrhein. (Ber): Rheinburgengau. (Gro): Burg Rheinfels. (Vil): St. Goar-Werlau.

Froichots [Les] (Fr) a Premier Cru vineyard in the A.C. commune of Morey-Saint-Denis, Côte de Nuits, Burgundy.

Frolicking Farmer (Eng) a 4.2% alc by vol. seasonal beer brewed by Hardy's and Hanson's at their Kimberley Brewery, Nottinghamshire (available July to September). Part of the Cellarman's cask range.

Fröllern (Aus) a vineyard area on the banks of the River Danube in the Kremstal region.

Fromenteau (Fr) a white table grape sometimes used to produce wine. Produces flat, sweet wines.

Fromont [Jean-Claude] (Fr) a winery based in the A.C. Chablis, Burgundy. Produces a range of Chablis wines including Premier Crus Beauroy and Montmains.

Fromentot (Fr) an alternative name for the Pinot gris grape.

Fromm Winery (N.Z) a winery. (Add): Corner Godfrey & Middle Renwick Roads, Blenheim. 4.5ha. Grape varieties: Pinot noir, Merlot, Malbec, Cabernet franc, Cabernet sauvignon, Sangiovese, Syrah, Chardonnay. See also Family of Twelve.

Frondator (Lat) vine-pruner.

Fron Goch (Wal) a brand of Welsh whiskey in a glass cabinet (old).

Fronhof (Ger) vineyard (Anb): Pfalz. (Ber): Mittelhaardt-Deutsche Weinstrasse. (Gro): Schenkenböhl. (Vil): Bad Dürkheim.

Fronsac (Fr) an A.C. red wine commune in eastern Bordeaux.

Fronsadais (Fr) wines of the Fronsac commune in Bordeaux. Are heavy meaty wines.

Frontenac Vineyard (USA) a winery based in Paw Paw, Michigan. Produces a variety of alcoholic beverages including wines.

Frontier (S.Afr) the label for a red wine (Cabernet sauvignon, Merlot and Shiraz blend) produced by the Ernie Els Wines winery, Stellenbosch, Western Cape.

Frontignac (Fr) an A.C. vin doux naturel produced from the Frontignan grape in the Languedoc-Roussillon region of the Pyrénées in southern France.

Frontignan (Fr) see Muscat de Frontignan.

Frontignan (Fr) a type of bottle used in Bordeaux, especially Pauillac and Sauternes.

Fronton (Fr) a wine-producing area in the Haut-Garonne, south-western France. Produces A.C. red, rosé and white wines. see Côtes du Fronton.

Front Street Brewery [The] (Eng) a small brewery (established 2005) based in Binham, Norfolk. Brews: Binham Cheer, Callum's Ale and Unity.

Frost (Eng) a weather condition that is feared by the wine producers especially when the vines start to bud. Is combatted by such methods as aspersion-spraying vines with water or heating the vineyards with fire or smudge pots. In Germany can help produce Eiswein.

Frostbite Cocktail (Cktl) ⅓ measure tequila, ⅓ measure (white) crème de cacao, ⅓ measure cream. Shake over ice, strain into a cocktail glass and top with grated nutmeg.

Frost Bite (Eng) a 3.6% alc by vol. ale brewed by The Durham Brewery, County Durham.

Frostbiter (Eng) a cask-conditioned ale 1055 O.G. brewed by the home-brew Ancient Druids public house in Cambridge.

Frosted Coffee Hawaii (USA) a 550mls (1pint) cold strong black coffee, 300mls (½ pint) pineapple juice, 1 block vanilla ice cream. Blend altogether in a blender until smooth and foamy and serve with straws.

Frosted Glass (Cktl) a glass in which the rim has been dipped in egg white, lemon juice or other and then in sugar to give a frosted appearance. Also can apply to a glass which has been chilled in a refrigerator to chill cocktails down without the aid of ice.

Frostgeschmack (Ger) lit: 'frosty flavour', a wine that has been made from frost-affected grapes.

Frost Vineyards (S.Afr) the old name for the Daview Vineyards.

Frosty Amour (Cktl) ⅓ measure Smirnoff vodka, ⅓ measure Southern Comfort, ⅓ measure apricot brandy, dash parfait amour, dash crème de banane. Shake over ice, strain into a highball glass, fill with 7-Up and serve with straws.

Frosty Dawn (Cktl) ⅓ measure white rum, ⅙ measure maraschino, ⅙ measure falernum syrup, ⅓ measure orange juice. Shake over ice and strain into a cocktail glass.

Frosty Jacks (Eng) the label of a white cider from Aston Manor, Birmingham. Two versions: Extra Strong 8.4% alc by vol. Extra Strength 7.5% alc by vol.

Frosty Lime Cocktail (Cktl)(Non-alc) ¾ measure grapefruit juice, ¾ measure mint syrup, scoop of lime sorbet. Blend altogether in a blender. Pour into a saucer glass, dress with a lemon slice and mint leaf and serve with straws.

Froth (Eng) also known as the '*head*', the foamy bubbles seen on the top of a glass of beer.

Froth Blower (Cktl) 25mls (⅕ gill) dry gin, 4 dashes grenadine, 1 egg white. Shake well over ice and strain into a cocktail glass.

Frothing (Eng) an upsurge of bubbles and debris at the start of fermentation. Causes tiny particles to be lifted up by CO_2 gas bubbles and to froth over.

Froth Law (Eng) a slang term for that part of the Weights and Measures Act that requires a pint of beer to consist of a minimum of 95% liquid and maximum of 5% foaming head (froth).

Froupe Cocktail (Cktl) ½ measure brandy, ½ measure Italian vermouth, 4 dashes Bénédictine. Stir well over ice and strain into a cocktail glass.

Frozen Apple Cocktail (Cktl) ⅚ measure Calvados, ⅙ measure lime juice, 2 dashes gomme syrup, ½ egg white. Blend together with a scoop of crushed ice and serve in a flute glass.

Frozen Berkeley (Cktl) ¾ measure white rum, ¼ measure brandy, 2 barspoons passion fruit juice, juice ¼ lemon. Blend with a scoop of crushed ice in a blender and pour into a flute glass.

Frozen Daiquiri (Cktl) 35mls (1½ fl.ozs) white rum, juice ½ lime, dash maraschino, dash gomme syrup. Blend on high speed in a blender with a scoop of crushed ice, pour into a highball glass and serve with straws.

Frozen Matador (Cktl) ⅗ measure tequila, ⅗ measure pineapple juice, juice ¼ lime. Blend altogether with a scoop of crushed ice. Pour into an old-fashioned glass and dress with a pineapple cube.

Frozen Mint Daiquiri [1] (Cktl) ⅕ measure white rum, juice ¼ lime, 6 mint leaves, 1 barspoon gomme syrup. Blend together with a scoop of crushed ice and pour into an old-fashioned glass.

Frozen Mint Daiquiri [2] (Cktl) 25mls (1fl.oz) white rum, 10mls (½ fl.oz) white crème de menthe, 10mls (½ fl.oz) lime juice. Blend together with a scoop of crushed ice in a blender, pour into a saucer glass and dress with mint leaves.

Frozen Pineapple Daiquiri [1] (Cktl) ⅕ measure Bacardi White Label rum, juice ¼ lemon, 2 dashes gomme syrup, 4 pineapple cubes. Blend altogether in a blender with a scoop of crushed ice and pour into a flute glass.

Frozen Pineapple Daiquiri [2] (Cktl) 25mls (1fl.oz) white rum, 10mls (½ fl.oz) lime juice, 3 dashes Cointreau, 2 pineapple slices. Blend altogether in a blender with a scoop of crushed ice, pour into a saucer glass, dress with a pineapple cube and a cherry.

Frozen Scotch Cocktail (Cktl) 25mls (⅕ gill) Scotch whisky, 25mls (⅕ gill) lemon juice, dash Angostura, dash Cointreau, 4 dashes gomme syrup, 3 pineapple cubes. Blend altogether with a scoop of crushed ice in a blender, pour into an old-fashioned glass and dress with a pineapple cube.

Frozen Southern Comfort (Cktl) 25mls (⅕ gill) Southern Comfort, juice ½ lime, ½ teaspoon sugar. Blend together with a scoop of crushed ice in a blender, pour into a saucer glass and serve with straws.

Frozen Spirits Cocktail (Cktl) ¾ measure brandy, ¼ measure white rum, 1 egg yolk, teaspoon gomme syrup, 2 dashes lemon juice. Blend altogether with a scoop of crushed ice in a blender and pour into a flute glass.

Frozen Steppes (Cktl) 25mls (1fl.oz) vodka, 10mls (½ fl.oz) crème de cacao, scoop vanilla ice cream. Blend well together and serve in a small goblet with straws.

Frozen Strawberry Cocktail (Cktl) 20mls (⅙ gill) crème de fraises, 20mls (⅙ gill) tequila, dash lemon juice, 4 strawberries. Blend altogether in a blender with a scoop of crushed ice, pour into a saucer glass, dress with a strawberry and lemon slice.

Fruchsftlikors (Ger) a spirit that is flavoured with a single fruit extract.

Fruchtaromalikors (Ger) on a label denotes that there are no additives used.

Fruchtig (Ger) fruity.

Fruchtschaumwein (Ger) a sparkling lemonade flavoured with fruit juice.

Fructexport (Rum) the old government exporting agency.

Fructose (Eng) $C_6H_{12}O_6$ fruit sugar, is easily fermentable by yeast into alcohol and CO_2.

Frugtjuice (Den) fruit juice.

Frühburgunder (Ger) a red grape variety (an early-ripening Pinot strain) used in the Ahr and the Rheinhessen regions.

Frühjahrsbierfest (Ger) a springtime beer festival held in Munich. Begins on Saint Joseph's day.

Früh Kölsch (Ger) a 4.8%–5.5% alc by vol. kölsch beer brewed by Cölner Hofbräu Brauerei, Früh, Cologne. (Cologne Court Brewery).

Frühlingsplätzchen (Ger) vineyard (Anb): Nahe. (Ber): Schloss Böckelheim. (Gro): Paradiesgarten. (Vil): Monzingen.

Frühmess (Ger) vineyard (Anb): Pfalz. (Ber): Südliche Weinstrasse. (Gro): Kloster Liebfrauenberg. (Vil): Glieszellen-Gleishorbach.

Frühmesse (Ger) vineyard (Anb): Rheinhessen. (Ber): Nierstein. (Gro): Rheinblick. (Vil): Alsheim.

Frühmessler (Ger) vineyard (Anb): Baden. (Ber): Ortenau. (Gro): Schloss Rodeck. (Vil): Sinzheim.

Frühroter Veltliner (Aus) a white grape variety, also known as the Malvasier.

Fruit Ale (Eng) a 3.5% alc by vol. beer from the Fruit & Firkin in Bracknell.

Fruit & Firkin (Eng) a micro-brew pub in Bracknell. Brews: Passion Ale 4.3% alc by vol., Fruit Ale 3.5% alc by vol and Frutti Tutti Ale 5% alc by vol.

Fruit Beers (Eng) see Lambic Beers.

Fruit Brandies (Euro) spirits distilled from fermented fruit juices and fruit kernels 40%–44.5% alc by vol.

Fruit Cups (Cktl) non-alcoholic fruit drinks based on fruit juices, diluted squashes or cordials. Usually served chilled in a large bowl and put in tumblers, dressed with sliced fruit.

Fruité (Fr) fruity.

Fruiterers Mild (Eng) a 3.7% alc by vol. ale brewed by the Cannon Royall Brewery Ltd., Worcestershire.

Fruit Flavour Concentrates (USA) permitted fruit extracts added to wines to give fruit flavours.

Fruit Juice (Eng) the liquid content of fresh fruits, extracted by pressing the fruits. (Den) = frugtjuice.

Fruit Lemonade (Cktl)(Non-alc) 60mls (½ gill) lemon juice and 60mls (½ gill) orange juice, grenadine to taste. Mix well together, top with non-alcoholic cider and garnish with mint and serve chilled.

Fruitopia (USA) the name given to a range of still fruit drinks produced by C.C.S.B. Flavours include citrus, blackcurrant, apple & tangerine, passion fruit & lemon, mango & banana, vanilla.

Fruit Punch (Cktl)(Non-alc) 50mls (2fl.ozs) orange juice, 35mls (1½ fl.ozs) lemon juice, 35mls (1½ fl.ozs) pineapple juice, 2 dashes grenadine. Stir over ice, strain into a goblet with ice and dress with fruit in season.

Fruits of The Forest (Eng) a 4.5% alc by vol. ale brewed by Rockingham Ales, Cambridgeshire.

Fruit Spirits (Eng) alcohols made from fruit-based wines. i.e. strawberry, cherry, raspberry etc.

Fruit Squashes (Eng) a sweetened liquid fruit concentrate, usually diluted before drinking.

Fruit Tea (Eng) a hot (or cold) beverage produced from fruit acids and fruit flavourings, can also be flavoured with herbs. see Tisanes. (Ire) = toradh tae.

Fruit Wines (Eng) wines produced from any fruit other than grapes. Usually sugar and yeast have to be added before fermentation.

Fruity (Eng) a term for a wine which has a definite flavour and aroma of fresh fruit. Most fine young wines are 'fruity'.

Fruity (S.Afr) the label for a red (Cinsaut) and white (Chenin blanc) wines from the Meander range of wines produced by the Groot Eiland Winery, Worcester, Western Cape.

Frusinate (It) an I.G.T. of Latium.

Fruska Gora (Ser) a key wine district in Vojvodina, Serbia, south of the River Danube. Has many noted wineries based within its boundaries. Grape varieties: Gewürztraminer, Sauvignon blanc, Sémillon.

Fruskogoraki Biser (Ser) a light demi-sec sparkling white wine from Serbia.

Frutti Tutti Ale (Eng) a 5% alc by vol. ale from the Fruit & Firkin in Bracknell.

Frydenlunds Brewery (Nor) a famous Norwegian brewery based in Oslo. Produces bock biers and Tuborg lager under licence.

Fryer's Cove Vineyards (S.Afr) a winery (established 1999) based in Stellenbosch, Western Cape. 6ha. Grape varieties: Cabernet sauvignon, Merlot, Pinot noir, Sauvignon blanc. Label: Richard Fryer.

Fryns (Bel) a company that produces a wide range of fruit liqueurs and Jenever.

FSB (Eng) abbr: Firkin Special Brew 1058 O.G. beer brewed by the Bosham Brewery in West Sussex.

FTGFOP (Eng) abbr: Finest Tippy Golden Flowery Orange Pekoe a fine grade of Broken Orange Pekoe black tea.

Fuchs (Ger) vineyard (Anb): Mosel-Saar-Ruwer. (Ber): Saar-Ruwer. (Gro): Scharzberg. (Vil): Saarburg.

Fuchsberg (Ger) vineyard (Anb): Rheingau. (Ber): Johannisberg. (Gro): Burgweg. (Vil): Geisenheim.

Fuchsberg (Ger) a vineyard within the village of Geisenheim, 44.4ha (12.6%) of which is proposed to be classified as Erstes Gewächs.

Fuchsen (Ger) vineyard (Anb): Nahe. (Ber): Kreuznach. (Gro): Schlosskapelle. (Vil): Laubenheim.

Fuchshöhle (Ger) vineyard (Anb): Mosel-Saar-Ruwer. (Ber): Zell/Mosel. (Gro): Weinhex. (Vil): Kobern-Gondorf.

F

Fuchsloch (Aus) a vineyard site based on the banks of the River Kamp situated in the Kamptal region.

Fuchsloch (Ger) vineyard (Anb): Mosel-Saar-Ruwer. (Ber): Obermosel. (Gro): Gipfel. (Vil): Wincheringen.

Fuchsloch (Ger) vineyard (Anb): Rheinhessen. (Ber): Nierstein. (Gro): Petersberg. (Vil): Gau-Odernheim.

Fuchsloch (Ger) vineyard (Anb): Pfalz. (Ber): Mittelhaardt-Deutsche Weinstrasse. (Gro): Hofstück. (Vil): Hochdorf-Assenheim.

Fuchsloch (Ger) vineyard (Anb): Pfalz. (Ber): Mittelhaardt-Deutsche Weinstrasse. (Gro): Hofstück. (Vil): Rödersheim-Gronau.

Fuchsmantel (Ger) vineyard (Anb): Pfalz. (Ber): Mittelhaardt-Deutsche Weinstrasse. (Gro): Schenkrenböhl. (Vil): Bad Dürkheim.

Fuchsmantel (Ger) vineyard (Anb): Pfalz. (Ber): Mittelhaardt-Deutsche Weinstrasse. (Gro): Schenkenböhl. (Vil): Wachenheim.

Füder (Ger) a cask for storing wine 1000litres (250gallons).

Füder N° (Ger) cask number.

Fudger Cream Ale (Eng) a 4.5% alc by vol. cask-conditioned ale brewed by Lees (J.W.), Manchester using Welsh fudge from Anglesey.

Fuddling Cup (Austr) a winery based in Western Australia. Grape varieties include: Cabernet sauvignon. 'E'mail: info@fuddlingcup.com

Fuées [Les] (Fr) a Premier Cru vineyard in the A.C. commune of Chambolle-Musigny, Côte de Nuits, Burgundy 6.2ha.

Fuella (Fr) an alternative name for the Folle blanche grape grown in the Bellet district of Provence, south-eastern France.

Fuella Nera (Fr) a red grape variety grown in the Bellet district of Provence, south-eastern France. Also known as the Folle noire.

Fuelle (Ger) denotes a rich, fine wine.

Fuencaliente (Sp) a light red wine produced on the Canary Islands. Has 12%–15% alc by vol.

Fuenmayor (Sp) a noted wine-producing village of the Rioja region in north-eastern Spain.

Fuensanta (Sp) a still and sparkling natural spring mineral water from Fuensanta de Buyeres, Nava, Astuhrias. Mineral contents (milligrammes per litre): Sodium 9.9mg/l, Calcium 63.3mg/l, Magnesium 8.3mg/l, Potassium 2.5mg/l, Bicarbonates 198.3mg/l, Chlorides 8.3mg/l, Sulphates 38.4mg/l.

Fuente (Sp) spring (water) see Agua de Fuente.

Fuente Alhamilla (Sp) a still natural spring mineral water. Mineral contents (milligrammes per litre): Sodium 70mg/l, Calcium 12mg/l, Magnesium 7mg/l, Potassium 4.3mg/l, Chlorides 50mg/l, Sulphates 49mg/l, Fluorides 0.3mg/l, Nitrates 0.2mg/l.

Fuente Alta (Sp) a natural spring mineral water from Vila flor, Tenerife.

Fuentecilla (Sp) a still natural spring mineral water from Paraje Fuente del Fraile, Tarazona de la Mancha, albacete. Mineral contents (milligrammes per litre): Sodium 27mg/l, Calcium 80mg/l, Magnesium 24mg/l, Potassium 1mg/l, Bicarbonates 312mg/l, Chlorides 34mg/l, Sulphates 33mg/l, Fluorides 0.5mg/l, Nitrates 27mg/l.

Fuente del Marquesado (Sp) a still natural spring mineral water from Huerta del Marquesado, Cuenca. Mineral contents (milligrammes per litre): Sodium 0.8mg/l, Calcium 70.5mg/l, Magnesium 18.5mg/l, Potassium 0.5mg/l, Bicarbonates 267.7mg/l, Chlorides 1.9mg/l, Sulphates 27.4mg/l, Fluorides 0.1mg/l, Nitrates 2mg/l.

Fuente del Val (Sp) a still natural spring mineral water from Fonteval 2, Mondariz, Pontevedra. Mineral contents (milligrammes per litre): Sodium 28mg/l, Calcium 22.8mg/l, Magnesium 6.3mg/l, Potassium 3.8mg/l, Bicarbonates 127.1mg/l, Chlorides 18.9mg/l, Sulphates 3.5mg/l, Fluorides 0.3mg/l, Nitrates 22.3mg/l.

Fuentedueñas (Sp) a natural spring mineral water from Fuentedueñas, Mula, Murcia.

Fuente en Segures (Sp) a still natural spring mineral water from Benasal, Castellón. Mineral contents (milligrammes per litre): Sodium 2.7mg/l, Calcium 92.2mg/l, Magnesium 4.4mg/l, Potassium 1.2mg/l, Bicarbonates 267.2mg/l, Chlorides 5.1mg/l, Sulphates 29.2mg/l, Fluorides 0.1mg/l, Nitrates 3.2mg/l.

Fuente Fria (Sp) a natural spring mineral water brand.

Fuente Liviana (Sp) a still natural spring mineral water from Huerta del Marquesado, Cuenca. Mineral contents (milligrammes per litre): Sodium 0.8mg/l, Calcium 64.9mg/l, Magnesium 17mg/l, Potassium 0.5mg/l, Bicarbonates 252.6mg/l, Chlorides 1.8mg/l, Sulphates 19.5mg/l, Nitrates 0.9mg/l, Silicates 3.4mg/l. pH 7.42

Fuente Madre (Sp) a natural spring mineral water from Los Chorchalejos, Los Navalmorales, Toledo.

Fuente Piña (Sp) a natural spring mineral water from Finca Casa Gallur – El Angosto, Caudete, Albacete.

Fuente Primavera (Sp) a still natural spring mineral water from S. Antonio de Requena, Valencia. Mineral contents (milligrammes per litre): Sodium 20.7mg/l, Calcium 86.6mg/l, Magnesium 23.3mg/l, Potassium 1.3mg/l, Bicarbonates 295.3mg/l, Chlorides 39.7mg/l, Sulphates 43mg/l, Fluorides 0.1mg/l, Nitrates 16.5mg/l, Silicates 6.9mg/l.

Fuenteror (Sp) a still natural spring mineral water (established 1916) from Hoya de la Palma, Tenor, Las Palmas, Gran Canaria. Mineral contents (milligrammes per litre): Sodium 28mg/l, Calcium 12mg/l, Magnesium 9mg/l, Potassium 5mg/l, Bicarbonates 95mg/l, Chlorides 26mg/l, Sulphates 11mg/l, Nitrates 19mg/l.

Fuente Sante (Sp) a natural spring mineral water from Asturia. Mineral contents (milligrammes per litre): Sodium 15.9mg/l, Calcium 71.3mg/l,

F

Magnesium 10.9mg/l, Potassium 4.4mg/l, Bicarbonates 222.2mg/l, Chlorides 9.3mg/l, Sulphates 56.5mg/l, Silicates 3.3mg/l. pH 7.0

Fuentevera (Sp) a natural spring mineral water from Finca Hinojosa de Abajo-Calera y Chozas, Toledo.

Fuente Vidrio (Sp) a natural spring mineral water from Caravaca, Murcia.

Fuenzalida Eyzaguirre (Chile) a noted wine exporter based in Santiago.

Fuerteventura (Sp) one of three islands that make up Las Palmas de Gran Canaria, Canarias. *See also* Gran Canaria, Lanzarote.

Fufluns (It) the Etruscans' God of wine.

Fugari (Fr) a white wine from Sartene in Corsica.

Fugger [Bishop] (Ger) Bishop John Fugger of Ausburg, Swabia who in 1110AD on a visit to Rome he sent his servant ahead to test the wines of the inns on route and chalk Est! (good) or Non Est! (is not good) on the wall. At Montefiascone the wine was so good he chalked Est!Est!!Est!!! The Bishop arrived there in early 1111 and stayed for the rest of his life, never reaching Rome. *see* Est!Est!!Est!!!

Fuggle Ale (Eng) the label of an ale brewed by micro-brewery Fuggle & Firkin, Oxford.

Fuggle & Firkin (Eng) a micro-brewery based in Oxford. Brews Fuggle Ale, Hop Head.

Fuggle-Dee-Dum (Eng) a 4.8% alc by vol. ale brewed by the Goddards Brewery, Isle of Wight.

Fuggles (Eng) a popular traditional variety of hop which gives good bitterness to beers.

Fuggles Chocolate Mild (Eng) a beer made at the Whitbread Cheltenham site (contains the essence of cocoa as well as chocolate barley).

Fuggles Imperial Ale (Eng) produced by Whitbread at the Castle Eden Brewery in County Durham. 5.5% alc by vol. Based on an I.P.A. of the 19th century using 100% Worcestershire fuggles hops. *See also* Ryman's Reserve, D-Day Bitter, Higson's Bitter.

Fugi (Jap) a natural spring mineral water (established 1929) from Shimobe, Yamanashi Prefecture.

Fuglsang Brewery (Den) a brewery based in Haderslev that is noted for draught, unpasteurised beers.

Fugsland Soda Water (Den) a natural spring mineral water from Haderslev. Mineral contents (milligrammes per litre): Sodium 500mg/l.

Fuhrgassl-Huber (Aus) a winery based in the Wien region. (Add): 1190 Neustif am Walde 68. Grape varieties: Grüner veltliner, Müller-Thurgau, Pinot gris, Welschriesling, Zweigelt. Produces a range of wine styles. Noted for its Heurige wines.

Fuissé (Fr) a commune in the A.C. Pouilly-Fuissé district of the Mâconnais in the Burgundy region. Top vineyards: Château Fuissé, Clos de la Chapelle, Clos de Varabond, Le Clos, Les Brûlets, Les Châtenets, Les Perrières, Les Vignes-Blanches, Menetrières and Versarmières.

Fukien Loh Chiu (Chi) a noted brand of rice wine produced in Shantung province from yellow rice. *See also* Shaoh-Sing Rice Wine.

Fulda [Bishop of] (Ger) a German Bishop who is purported to have let his grapes rot on the vine because he was so lazy. He then gave the rotten grapes to the peasants who made wine with them. The elixir that was produced was the forerunner of Sauternes and Trockenbeerenauslese.

Fuldataler (Ger) a natural spring mineral water from Malsfeld. Mineral contents (milligrammes per litre): Sodium 139mg/l, Calcium 362mg/l, Magnesium 108mg/l, Potassium 17.8mg/l, Bicarbonates 1418mg/l, Chlorides 70mg/l, Sulphates 400mg/l.

Full (Austr) a slang term for a drunken person.

Full (Eng) a term used for a wine that is big in taste and not light or watery.

Full Astern (Eng) a 3.8% alc by vol. light summer ale brewed by the Darktribe Brewery, Scunthorpe.

Full-Bodied (Eng) a term applied to wines with a rich bouquet that are high in fruit and alcohol.

Full Circle (Eng) a 4.5% alc by vol. ale brewed by the West Berkshire Brewery Cº., Berkshire.

Full Circle (S.Afr) the label for a red wine (Shiraz, Mourvèdre and Viognier blend) produced by the Saronsberg Cellar winery, Tulbagh, Western Cape.

Fülle (Ger) plenty of richness in great wines.

Fuller L.A. (Eng) a low alcohol bitter 1% alc by vol. from the Fullers Brewery, London.

Fullers (Eng) the trading name for a 56-strong group of Off-Licenses used by Fuller Smith and Turner PLC.

Fullers Brewery (Eng) a brewery based at the Griffith Brewery, Chiswick in London. Noted for cask-conditioned Chiswick Bitter 1035.7 O.G. Discovery, London Pride 1041.5 O.G. and Golden Pride 1090 O.G. Mr. Harry, Summer Ale, India Pale Ale, Old Winter Ale, Organic Honey Dew, Vintage Ale 8.5% alc by vol., 1845 Celebration, Ted & Bens Organic Beer, Hock (a cask-conditioned Mild).

Füllig (Ger) full-bodied.

Full Malty (Scot) a seasonal barley, wheat and oat cask ale brewed by the Maclay Brewery based in Alloa.

Full Malty (Wal) a 4.8% alc by vol. malt ale brewed by the Cwmbran Brewery, Gwent.

Full Mash (Eng) a 1038 O.G. bitter produced by the Trough Brewery in Bradford.

Full Monty (Eng) a cask-conditioned ale brewed by Bank's Brewery to celebrate the 50th anniversary of VE day.

Full Monty (Eng) a 5% alc by vol. ale brewed by the Glentworth Brewery, South Yorkshire.

Full Monty Mild (Eng) a 3.7% alc by vol. mild brewed by Foundry & Firkin, Sheffield.

Full Roast (Eng) a dark roasted coffee that has a slightly bitter taste (popular in Italy).

Füllwein (Ger) topping up with wine, wine used to top up casks after racking or through evaporation.

Full Wine (Eng) denotes a wine of good body.

Fulschette (Lux) a vineyard site in the village of Wellenstein.

Fumarium (It) an ancient hot room used for wines

579

F

that were exposed to smoke in order to improve them.

Fumé (Fr) smoked, refers to the 'bloom' on the grape which gives it a smokey appearance. i.e. Fumé Blanc.

Fumé Blanc (USA) the alternative name for the Sauvignon blanc.

Fumet (Fr) a definite bouquet.

Fumeux (Fr) a spirity or heady wine.

Fumé Vert (N.Z) a wine from the Babich Vineyard in Auckland. Has a herb flavour and aroma with a smokey touch.

Fumigation (Eng) the burning of a sulphur wick in a wine barrel to destroy bacteria. (Fr) = méchage.

Fumin (It) a red grape variety grown in Valle d'Aosta.

Fumosity (Eng) a term used to describe the heady vapours that are given off by some wines when they are poured out.

Fun and Games (Cktl) ½ measure gin, ¼ measure blackcurrant cordial, ¼ measure lemon juice, dash Angostura. Shake over ice, strain into a cocktail glass and serve with a small segment of lemon.

Funapple (Cktl)(Non-alc) place 2 dashes Angostura and 2 dashes rum essence into a large ice-filled highball glass. Top with non-alcoholic cider or sparkling apple juice and dress with an apple slice.

Funchal (Mad) the principal wine town where Madeira wine is aged and stored.

Funck-Bricher Brasserie (Lux) *see* Brasserie Nationale. Brews: Bricher Meisterbock.

Fundador (Sp) a 3 year old solera brandy produced by Domecq 40% alc by vol.

Fundanum (It) a red wine produced in central-western Italy in Roman times.

Fund d'Böta (It) the wine left in the bottle. Not drunk the same day.

Fundillón (Sp) a red wine produced from 100% Monastrell grapes. Is wood aged for 15 years. Produced only in good years.

Fun Drinks (UK) Ltd (Eng) distillers (established 1997). (Add): Unit 5, Staden Lane business Park, Staden Lane, Ashbourne Road, Buxton, Derbyshire SK17 9RZ. Produces a variety of spirits and liqueurs.

Fungicide (Eng) a maufactured fungus destroyer.

Fungus (Eng) a mushroom or allied plant, spongy or morbid growth.

Funjan (Arab) cup.

Funkenberg (Ger) vineyard (Anb): Mosel-Saar-Ruwer. (Ber): Zell/Mosel. (Gro): Goldbäumchen. (Vil): Münden.

Funky Llama (Arg) a vineyard based in the Mendoza region

Fun Pub (Eng) a term used in the 1980's to describe a public house with bright lights, loud music and catering for young customers.

Funtana Abbarghente (It) a natural spring mineral water from Funtana Abbarghente.

Funtasy (Ger) a bottled beer and cola mixed drink from the Steffens Brauerei, St. Severinsberg.

Funte Fria (It) a sparkling natural spring mineral

water from Funte Fria. Mineral contents (milligrammes per litre): Sodium 90mg/l, Calcium 22.2mg/l, Magnesium 8.6mg/l, Potassium 2.16mg/l, Bicarbonates 91.5mg/l, Chlorides 128.48mg/l, Sulphates 15.1mg/l, Fluorides 0.28mg/l, Nitrates 14.56mg/l, Silicates 40mg/l. pH 7.43

Furapane (It) a natural spring mineral water brand.

Furdyna [Michel] (Fr) a Champagne producer. (Add): 13, Rue Trot, 10110 Celles-sur-Ource. Vintages: 1995, 1996, 1997, 1998, 1999. Grape variety: Pinot noir 100% Produces: Blanc de Noirs.

Fürfeld (Ger) village (Anb): Rheinhessen. (Ber): Bingen. (Gro): Rheingrafenstein. (Vins): Eichelberg, Kapellenberg, Steige.

Furfural (Eng) an aldehyde obtained from oak casks. Part of the congeners, cask matured spirits.

Furgusons (Eng) a brewery based in Plymouth. Brews: Dartmoor Best Bitter, Dartmoor Strong, Cockleroaster, Dartmoor Millenium (a medium-strength pale ale brewed at Christmas).

Furthner Steig (Aus) a vineyard area on the banks of the River Danube in the Kremstal region.

Furlotti (Arg) a fine winery based in Mendoza.

Furmint (Hun) the famous white grape used mainly in the making of Tokaji. There are other Hungarian wines made with the Furmint grape and it usually appears on the label following the name of the district. Produces wines with an aroma and flavour of apples and acid (young) nuts and honey (old). (Aus) = Gelber furmint/Gelber moseler/Mosler/Zapfeter/Zapfner, (Rom) = Grasa, (Slov) = Sipon.

Furmint (N.Z) a spicey, fruity white wine made by the Te Mata Vineyards.

Furore (Cktl) ³⁄₁₀ measure brandy, ³⁄₁₀ measure Lillet, ⅓ measure Aurum, ¹⁄₁₀ measure orange juice. Shake over ice and strain into a cocktail glass.

Fürst Bismark (Ger) a kornbranntwein made from rye and wheat only by Fürstlich von Bismark'sche, Brennerei GmBh, Friedrichsruh.

Fürst Bismark Quelle (Ger) a natural spring mineral water (established 1871) from Sachsenwald. Mineral contents (milligrammes per litre): Sodium 10mg/l, Calcium 60mg/l, Magnesium 3.9mg/l, Bicarbonates 183mg/l, Chlorides 14.3mg/l, Sulphates 16mg/l.

Fürstenberg (Ger) vineyard (Anb): Franken. (Ber): Maindreieck. (Gro): Kirchberg. (Vil): Escherndorf.

Fürstenberg (Ger) vineyard (Anb): Mittelrhein. (Ber): Bacharach. (Gro): Schloss Stahleck. (Vil): Oberdiebach.

Furstenberg Wines (S.Afr) a winery (established 2004) based in Stellenbosch, Western Cape. Grape varieties: Cabernet sauvignon, Chardonnay. Website: http://www.furstenberg.com

Fürstenbrunn (Ger) a natural spring mineral water from Fürstenbrunn-Quelle, Lehnin, Brandenbuhrg. Mineral contents (milligrammes per litre): Sodium 6.5mg/l, Calcium 34.2mg/l, Bicarbonates 116mg/l.

Fürsteneck (Ger) grosslage (Anb): Baden. (Vils): Berghaupten, Bermersbach, Bottenau, Diersburg, Durbach, Erlach, Gengenbach, Hofweier, Lautenbach, Nesselried, Niederschopfheim, Offenburg, (ortsteil Zell-Weierbach), Offenbach (ortsteil Fessenbach), Oberkirch, Oberkirch (ortsteil Haslach), Ödsbach, Ohlsbach, Ortenberg, Rammersweier, Reichenbach, Ringelbach, Stadelhofen, Tiergarten, Ulm, Zunsweier.

Fürstenlager (Ger) vineyard (Anb): Hessische Bergstrasse. (Gro): Starkenburg. (Vil): Bensheim-Auerbach.

Furstentum (Fr) an A.C. Alsace Grand Cru vineyard at Kientzheim & Sigolsheim, Haut-Rhin 27.65ha.

Fürstenthaler Quelle (Ger) a natural spring mineral water from Berlin.

Fürstlich Fürstenbergische Brauerei (Ger) a noted brewery (established 1283). (Add): International Division, Postplatz 1-4, Donaueschingen, Baden D-78166. Produces Fürstenberg 5% alc by vol., Fürstenberg Premium Pilsner 4.8% alc by vol. Website: http://www.fuerstenberg.de 'E'mail: int.division@fuerstenberg.de

Fürst van Louny (Czec) a 4.5% alc by vol. dark, bottled lager brewed by the Louny Brewery, Louny.

Fürst Von Metternich (Ger) the name of a dry (Riesling) sparkling white wine.

Fürst Wallerstein Brauhaus (Ger) a brewery. (Add): Berg 78, Wallerstein D-86757. Brews a variety of beers and lagers. Website: http://www.fuerst-wallerstein.de

Fursty Ferret (Eng) a golden brown cask-conditioned ale brewed by the Gribble Inn, Oving, Chichester.

Fürwirth [Fritz] (Aus) a winery based in Klöch, Süd-Oststeiermark. (Add): Deutsch-Haseldorf 46, 8493 Klöch. Grape varieties: Chardonnay, Gewürztraminer, Pinot blanc, Zweigelt.

Furze (Eng) a 4.3% alc by vol. ale from the Furze and Firkin, Streatham High Road, London.

Furze and Firkin (Eng) a micro-brew pub in Streatham High Road, London. *see* Bush, Furze, Rambler.

Fuschsgeschmack (Aus) a term for a wine with a 'foxy' taste produced from hybrid grapes.

Fusée (USA) a label for the Don Sebastiani winery, Sonoma Country, California.

Fusel Oils (Eng) higher alcohols. Alcohol (not Ethyl) found in spirits and in minute traces in some wines (Propyl, Butyl, Amyl, Hexyl and Heptyl) can be toxic in high amounts.

Fusiko Epitrapexio Nero (Gre) a natural spring mineral water. Mineral contents (milligrammes per litre): Sodium 1.49mg/l, Calcium 97.45mg/l, Magnesium 0.71mg/l, Potassium 0.39mg/l, Bicarbonates 283.66mg/l, Chlorides 5.94mg/l, Sulphates 1.96mg/l. pH 7.59

Fusilier (Wal) a 4.5% alc by vol. ale brewed by Plassey Brewery at Eyton, bottled by the Hanby Brewery.

Fusion V (S.Afr) a flagship red wine (Cabernet franc, Cabernet sauvignon, Malbec, Merlot and Petit verdot) aged in 50% new French oak from the De Toren Private Cellar winery, Stellenbosch.

Fussell's Bitter (Wal) a cask-conditioned bitter 1038 O.G. brewed by the Bass Brewery in Cardiff.

Fuste (Ch.Isles) keg. *See also* P'tit barri.

Fusto (It) a wooden barrel.

Fusty (Eng) denotes musty/damp/mouldy smelling.

Fût (Fr) a hogshead cask holding 225 litres, also known as a Pièce.

Fûts Roux (Fr) casks that are between 5 and 10 years old (neither new or old). Used for Cognac maturation.

Futtock (Eng) a 5.2% alc by vol. cask ale from the Flagship Brewery, Chatham Dockyard, Dartford.

Futura (It) a sparkling natural spring mineral water from Dipodi. Mineral contents (milligrammes per litre): Sodium 24.5mg/l, Calcium 42.5mg/l, Magnesium 15.6mg/l, Potassium 2.25mg/l, Bicarbonates 207.4mg/l, Chlorides 25.4mg/l, Sulphates 21.5mg/l, Fluorides 0.12mg/l, Silicates 25.3mg/l, Strontium 1.41mg/l. pH 7.72

Futurity Cocktail (Cktl) ½ measure sweet vermouth, ½ measure sloe gin, 2 dashes Angostura, stir over ice and strain into a cocktail glass.

Fuzz Ale (Eng) 3.5% alc by vol. ale brewed by Felon & Firkin, Great George Street, Leeds, West Yorkshire.

Fuzzy Navel (Cktl) place 1 measure of Peach County schnapps into an ice-filled highball glass, top with 2 measures orange juice and a slice of orange.

FX Matt's Premium (USA) the label of a 4.5% alc by vol. lager.

Fyfe Brewing Cº (Scot) a brewery (established 1995). (Add): 469 High Street, Kirkcaldy, Fife KY1 2SN. Brews: Auld Alliance 4% alc by vol., First Light 4.3% alc by vol., Fyfe Fyre 4.8% alc by vol., Lion Slayer 4.2% alc by vol., Rope of Sand 3.7% alc by vol., Weiss Squad 4.5% alc by vol. 'E'mail: fyfebrew@blueyonder.co.uk

Fyfe Fyre (Scot) a 4.8% alc by vol. ale brewed by the Fyfe Brewing Cº., Fyfe.

Fyfield Hall Vineyard (Eng) a vineyard (established 1976) based in Essex. 2.25ha. Grape variety: Müller-Thurgau.

Fylde Ale (Eng) a beer brewed by the Hart Brewery (a micro-brewery) at Little Eccleston, near Preston, Lancashire.

Fynew Ales Ltd (Scot) a brewery (established 2001). (Add): Loch Fyne, Cairndow, Argyll PA26 8BJ. Brews: Highlander 4.8% alc by vol., Maverick 4.2% alc by vol., Pipers Gold 3.8% alc by vol. Website: http://www.fyneales.com 'E'mail: jonny@fyneales.com

Fyresdal (Nor) a slightly acidic, still natural spring mineral water from Fyresdal, Kildevann, Telemark. Mineral contents (milligrammes per litre): Sodium 1.6mg/l, Calcium 3mg/l, Magnesium 0.4mg/l, Potassium 0.5mg/l, Bicarbonates 13mg/l, Chlorides 1.6mg/l, Sulphates 3.5mg/l, Fluorides 0.2mg/l. pH 5.9

G

G (Fr) an A.C. Bordeaux white wine produced by Château Guiraud.

G (Sp) *abbr:* **G**olden, the colour grade for Oloroso and Palo Cortado Sherries.

Gaamez (Sp) an alternative name for the Gamay noir à jus blanc.

Gabarnac (Fr) a commune in the Premières Côtes de Bordeaux, central Bordeaux.

Gables Collins (Cktl) ⅔ measure vodka, ⅓ measure crème de noyau, juice ¼ lemon, 15mls (⅛ gill) pineapple juice, shake over ice, strain into an ice-filled collins glass, top with soda, a slice of lemon and a pineapple chunk.

Gablinger (USA the brand-name used by Rheingold for their 'light' beers.

Gabriela (Sp) the alternative name for Mantúo de Pila.

Gabriel Boudier (Fr) a distillery and liqueur producer based in Dijon, Burgundy.

Gabro (It) an I.G.T. red Cabernet-based wine produced by Villa Monte Rico, Suvereto, Maremma, Tuscany.

Gabsheim (Ger) village (Anb): Rheinhessen. (Ber): Nierstein. (Gro): Domherr. (Vins): Dornpfad, Kirchberg, Rosengarten.

Gadd's (Eng) the brand-name for ales and beers brewed by the Ramsgate Brewery, Kent.

Gaeiras (Port) a full-bodied, dry, red wine produced in Obidos, Estremadura.

Gaelic Coffee (Liq.Coffee) *see* Irish Coffee.

Gaelic Cow (Cktl) place 35mls (1½ fl.ozs) Glayva into a highball containing hot milk and top with a teaspoon of honey if required.

Gaensefurther Schloss Quelle (Ger) a natural spring mineral water (established 1876). Mineral contents (milligrammes per litre): Sodium 48mg/l, Calcium 235mg/l, Magnesium 81mg/l, Potassium 6mg/l, Bicarbonates 323mg/l, Chlorides 306mg/l, Sulphates 329mg/l.

Gafé (S.Asia) the word for coffee in Thailand.

Gaffel Brauerei (Ger) a brewery (established 1302) based in Cologne. Brews: Gaffel Kölsch 4.8% alc by vol.

Gagarin Blue (Eng) a red grape variety of Russian origin named by Barrington Brock in 1965.

Gager (Aus) a winery based in Deutschkreutz, Mittel-Burgenland. (Add): Karrnergasse 8, 7301 Deutschkreutz. Produces a range of wines. Label: Cuvée Quatro.

Gaggia [Archille] (It) the inventor of the espresso coffee machine in 1946.

Gagliole (It) a 5ha wine estate in Castellina, noted for a Sangiovese wine.

Gaglioppo (It) a red grape variety in Calabria, known locally as Aglianico, Arvino, Lacrima nera, Magliocco, Mantonico nero.

Gaia (It) a sparkling natural spring mineral water from Ancona. Mineral contents (milligrammes per litre): Sodium 22mg/l, Calcium 88.9mg/l, Magnesium 3.3mg/l, Potassium 1.8mg/l, Bicarbonates 274.5mg/l, Chlorides 19.8mg/l, Sulphates 29.2mg/l, Nitrates 6.2mg/l, Silicates 8.9mg/l. pH 7.3

Gaia Estate (Gre) a winery based in the Peloponnese. Produces: A.O.C. Nemea, A.O.C. Santorini, Notios red and white wines.

Gaia Entrepot (Port) the district in Vila Nova de Gaia where the wine lodges are situated.

Gaia Pipe (Port) storage casks in Vila Nova de Gaia for Port (550litres in capacity).

Gaillac (Fr) a red grape variety grown in Gaillac, south-western France.

Gaillac (Fr) an A.C. region near Bordeaux that produces red, rosé, sparkling, pétillant and white wines. Grape varieties: Gaillac, Negrette, Ouras and Syrah (red). L'En de l'El, Mauzac, Muscadelle, Ondenc, Sauvignon and Sémillon (white). If wine has 10.5% alc by vol. then Gaillac. If 12% alc by vol. then Premières Côtes de Gaillac.

Gaillac Mousseux (Fr) an A.C. sparkling (méthode gaillaçoise) wine produced in Gaillac, western France.

Gaillaçoise (Fr) a sparkling wine method where no sugar or liqueur de tirage is added, fermentation is stopped by filtration.

Gaillac Perlé (Fr) a slightly sparkling white wine produced in the Gaillac region of western France.

Gaillard (N.Z) a white hybrid grape variety.

Gain d'Espace (Fr) an ice-bucket stand, a holder that attaches itself to the table to avoid a free-standing ice-bucket stand at the table, used for Champagne, white wine etc.

Gaiole (It) a commune of Chianti Classico Riserva.

Gairé (Fr) a nineteenth century Cognac producer.

Gaisberg (Aus) a vineyard area on the banks of the River Danube in the Kremstal region.

Gaisberg (Aus) a vineyard site based on the banks of the River Kamp situated in the Kamptal region.

Gaisböhl (Ger) vineyard (Anb): Pfalz. (Ber): Mittelhaardt-Deutsche Weinstrasse. (Gro): Hofstück. (Vil): Ruppertsberg.

Gaisburg (Ger) village (Anb): Württemberg. (Ber): Remstal-Stuttgart. *see* Stuttgart.

G

Gaispfad (Ger) vineyard (Anb): Mosel-Saar-Ruwer. (Ber): Bernkastel. (Gro): Schwarzlay. (Vil): Traben-Trarbach.

Gaja (It) a producer based in Barbaresco, Piemonte. see Azienda Agricola di Angelo Gaja.

Gajum (It) a natural spring mineral water from Gajum. Mineral contents (milligrammes per litre): Sodium 1mg/l, Calcium 59.7mg/l, Magnesium 9.2mg/l, Potassium 0.4mg/l, Bicarbonates 205mg/l, Chlorides 1.2mg/l, Sulphates 12mg/l, Nitrates 9.5mg/l, Silicates 4.5mg/l. pH 7.8

Gala (Gre) milk.

Gala Caffé (It) a coffee liqueur produced by the Stock C°., Trieste 26% alc by vol.

Gala Coffee & Tea Ltd (Eng) a coffee and tea manufacturer (established 1986). (Add): Mill House, riverside Ind Estate, Dartford, Kent DA1 5BS. Produces a wide range of coffees and teas. Website: http://www.gala-coffee-tea.co.uk 'E'mail: gala@gala-coffee-tea.co.uk

Galactic (Eng) relating to milk.

Galactometer (Eng) an instrument similar to a hydrometer used for measuring the relative density of milk, used to determine fat content.

Galactozyme (Fr) see Galazyme.

Gala Export Beer (Afr) a light beer brewed by the Brasseries du Logone, Chad.

Galamus (Fr) a tawny-coloured, sweet dessert wine from the Roussillon region, southern France.

Galantskloof (S.Afr) the label for a red wine (Shiraz) produced by the Keissenkraal Vineyards winery, Walker Bay, Western Cape.

Galão (Port) a large, weak caffé latte.

Galati (Rum) a white wine-producing area.

Galaxy (Gre) a natural spring mineral water from Kreta. Mineral contents (milligrammes per litre): Sodium 12.6mg/l, Calcium 46.5mg/l, Magnesium 10.2mg/l, Potassium 0.4mg/l, Bicarbonates 177mg/l, Chlorides 21.3mg/l, Sulphates 11mg/l, Nitrates 3.1mg/l. pH 7.6

Galaxy (USA) a brand of whiskey produced by Seagram.

Galazyme (Fr) lightly fermented milk, frothy in appearance. Is also known as Galactozyme.

Galbena (Rum) a white grape variety grown near Foscani in eastern Romania.

Galea (Sp) a still natural spring mineral water from Meres-Siero, Asturias. Mineral contents (milligrammes per litre): Sodium 9mg/l, Calcium 56.1mg/l, Magnesium 15.1mg/l, Potassium 5.8mg/l, Bicarbonates 224.5mg/l, Chlorides 14.8mg/l, Sulphates 19.4mg/l, Fluorides 0.3mg/l, Nitrates 1mg/l.

Galego Dourado (Port) a white grape variety used in the production of Carcavelos. Produces wines high in alcohol.

Galerie (Fr) coaster.

Galerie de Vin (Fr) wine coaster.

Galeries (Fr) part of the chalk caves in Champagne used for the storage of maturing wines. see Oolitic Chalk.

Gales [George] Brewery (Eng) a brewery (established 1847). (Add): The Hampshire Brewery, Horndean, Hampshire PO8 0DA. Noted for Prize Old Ale 1095 O.G. Treble Seven 1034 O.G. Southdown Bitter 1040 O.G. Nourishing Stout 1034 O.G. Champion Ale 1040 O.G. Tudor Ale 1051 O.G. Anniversary Ale 4% alc by vol. Best Bitter 3.8% alc by vol. Butser Bitter 3.4% alc by vol. Christmas Ale 5.5% alc by vol., Festival Mild, Force 8 5% alc by vol. Hampshire Glory 4.3% alc by vol. Harvest Ale 4.5% alc by vol. Horndean Special Bitter 4.8% alc by vol. GB 4% alc by vol. Millennium Ale, Old Nick 7.2% alc by vol., Trafalgar Ale 4.2% alc by vol. Trafalgar 2000 and Winter Brew. Website: http://www.gales.co.uk 'E'mail: thebrewery@gales.co.uk

Galestrino (It) a local Tuscany name for the small silica pebbles found in the schistous clay soil in the Chianti district. Is also known as Galestro.

Galestro (It) see Galestrino.

Galestro (It) a white Vino da Tavola made from the Malvasia, Sauvignon blanc and Trebbiano grapes in Tuscany.

Galets Rouges [Les] (Fr) a red A.C. Costières de Nîmes wine produced from 65% Syrah, 35% Grenache grapes by Château Mourgues du Grès in the Languedoc-Roussillon

Galets Roulés (Fr) large boulder-style stones found in Châteauneuf-du-Pape and the southern Rhône.

Galgenberg (Aus) a vineyard site based on the banks of the River Kamp situated in the Kamptal region.

Galgenberg (Ger) vineyard (Anb): Nahe. (Ber): Kreuznach. (Gro): Kronenberg. (Vil): Bad Kreuznach (ortsteil Bosenheim).

Galgenberg (Ger) vineyard (Anb): Rheinhessen. (Ber): Bingen. (Gro): Rheingrafenstein. (Vil): Hackenheim.

Galgenberg (Ger) vineyard (Anb): Rheinhessen. (Ber): Bingen. (Gro): Sankt Rochuskapelle. (Vil): Badenheim.

Galgenberg (Ger) vineyard (Anb): Pfalz. (Ber): Südliche Weinstrasse. (Gro): Guttenberg. (Vil): Kandel.

Galgenwein (Ger) lit: 'gallows wine', refers to a strong, harsh, fiery wine, which, it is said, "Can choke a drinker and so the gallows rope is not needed!"

Galgon (Fr) a commune in the A.C. Côtes de Fronsac, Bordeaux.

Galibert (Fr) a famous French hybridiser.

Galicia (Sp) a district in north-western Spain. Produces Vinhos Verdes similar to those in Portugal. Has the Denominaciónes de Origen (23876ha): Rías Baixas, Ribeira Sacra, Ribeiro, Valdeorras, Val de Monterrei. Vino de la Tierra of Valle del Miño-Ourense. Vino Comarcal areas: Betanzos, Ribeira do Ulla (A Coruña and Pontevedra), O Bolo (Ourense), Península de Marrazo (Pontevedra).

Galil (Isr) a dry white wine produced in the Galilee region.

Galilee (Isr) a wine-producing region. Noted for red and white wines.

Galion Brewery (E.Ind) a brewery based in Medan, Sumatra. Brews: Galion (a pilsener-style beer).

G

Galius (Fr) an A.C. Grand Cru Saint-Émilion, Bordeaux produced by the Union des Producteurs de St.Émilion. Grape varieties: Cabernet franc 30%, Cabernet sauvignon 10%, Merlot 60%.

Gall (Ger) a chemist who pioneered the addition of sugar (non-grape) to grape must.

Gallagher and Burton (USA) the brand-name for a blended Bourbon whiskey bottled by Gallagher and Burton Cº. Baltimore 40% alc by vol.

Gallagher's Choice (Austr) a red (Cabernet sauvignon) wine produced by the Woody Nook Estate, Western Australia.

Galland (Aus) a liqueur producer based in Vienna. Produces a fine range of liqueurs.

Galleano Winery (USA) a winery based in Cucamonga, California. Grape variety: Zinfandel.

Galleon Wine (Eng) a large Off-Licence chain owned by the Bass group.

Galleron (USA) a winery based in the Napa Valley, California. Grape varieties include: Cabernet sauvingnon. Label: Morisoli Vineyard.

Galliano (It) a spicy, herb-flavoured liqueur from Livorno. Also known as Liquore Galliano. 35% alc by vol. Produced by the Distillerie Riunite, Solano.

Galliano's Golden Cup (Punch) 1litre hot tea, 1¼ litres orange juice, 200mls Galliano, cinnamon stick, sugar syrup. Heat all together, strain, garnish with mint leaves and orange slices and serve hot.

Gallic Acid (Eng) an acid obtained during storage in wooden casks.

Gallic Coffee (Liq.Coffee) see Gaelic Coffee (alternative spelling of in USA).

Gallice (Lat) see Spiritus. Vini de Gallice.

Gallimard Père et Fils (Fr) a Champagne producer. (Add): 18-20, Rue Gaston Cheq, Le Magny, BP 23, 10340 Les Riceys. Produces vintage and non-vintage Champagnes.

Gallization (Ger) term for chaptalisation. Named after the German chemist Gall, adding sugar to grape must to raise the alcohol level. see Anreicherung (Ger), Chaptalisation (Fr).

Gallo (It) a sparkling natural spring mineral water from Gallo. Mineral contents (milligrammes per litre): Sodium 32mg/l, Calcium 95.09mg/l, Magnesium 32.6mg/l, Potassium 3.6mg/l, Bicarbonates 457.64mg/l, Chlorides 29.2mg/l, Sulphates 26.9mg/l, Fluorides 0.41mg/l, Nitrates 1.43mg/l, Silicates 17.5mg/l, Oxygen 4.84mg/l. pH 7.13

Gallo d'Oro (It) a wine-producer based in Piemonte. Is noted for Verbeso (white wine) and Barbaresco.

Gallo [Ernst & Julio] (USA) a large winery (established 1933) in San Joaquin Valley, California. Produces nearly 40% of total Californian wine output. Produce table, sparkling and dessert wines from a large variety of grapes. Labels include: Laguna Valley, Sycamore Canyon. Has contracts with wineries in Sonoma and Napa Valley. See also Livingstone Cream.

Gallo Family (USA) a winery based in the Sonoma County, California. Grape variety: Pinot noir. Label: Sonoma Reserve.

Gallon (Eng) an Imperial measure. Equals 8pints or 4quarts, 1.2 USgallons, 4.54litres. 277.42 cubic inches. (Wal) = galwyn.

Gallon (USA) a US Gallon. Equals 0.83Imperial gallons.3.79litres. 231 Cubic inches.

Gallonage (Eng) the total amount in gallons.

Gallo Nero (It) lit: 'black cockerel', the seal of the Consorzio for Chianti Classico wines.

Gallo of Sonoma (USA) a winery based in the Dry Creek Valley, Sonoma County, California. Label: Frei Vineyard.

Gallop Hill (S.Afr) a winery based in Paarl, Western Cape. 20ha. Grape varieties: Cabernet sauvignon, Sauvignon blanc, Shiraz. Label: The First Chukka. Website: http://www.gallophill.co.za

Gallo's Thunderbird (USA) a popular flavoured and fortified 'Pop' wine at about 10% alc by vol.

Galloway (Scot) a natural spring mineral water from Dumfries. Mineral contents (milligrammes per litre): Sodium 10mg/l, Calcium 42mg/l, Potassium 1.2mg/l, Chlorides 22mg/l. pH 7.6

Galloway Gold (Scot) a 5% alc by vol. golden ale brewed by the Sulwath Brewers Ltd., Kirkcudbrightshire.

Gallweys (Ire) a liqueur based on whiskey, honey, herbs and coffee 31% alc by vol.

Galon (Fr) the mediaeval word for gallon. See also Jalon.

Galpin Peak (S.Afr) the label for a red wine (Pinot noir) produced by the Bouchard Finlayson winery, Walker Bay, Western Cape. Also a Tête de Cuvée Galpin Peak.

Galvanina (It) an ancient (100BC) sparkling natural spring mineral water from La Galvanina. Mineral contents (milligrammes per litre): Sodium 36mg/l, Calcium 135mg/l, Magnesium 23mg/l, Potassium 2.3mg/l, Bicarbonates 445mg/l, Chlorides 27mg/l, Sulphates 68mg/l, Fluorides 0.4mg/l, Nitrates 9mg/l. pH 7.06

Gálvez (Sp) a Vino de la Tierra of La Mancha in the province of Toledo. Produces red wines from Garnacha tinta and Cencibel.

Galvez Fizz (Cktl) 35mls (1½ fl.ozs) dry gin, 35mls (1½ fl.ozs) cream, 1 egg white, 3 dashes grenadine, dash orange flower water, juice of a lemon, barspoon sugar. Shake well over ice, strain into a highball glass and top with lemonade.

Galway (Ire) a natural spring mineral water from Galway. Mineral contents (milligrammes per litre): Sodium 15mg/l, Calcium 104mg/l, Magnesium 11mg/l, Potassium 1.1mg/l, Bicarbonates 334mg/l, Chlorides 32mg/l, Sulphates 22mg/l. pH 7.2

Galway Grey (Cktl) ⅓ measure vodka, ⅓ measure Cointreau, ⅓ measure crème de cacao, ⅓ measure lime juice. Stir, float cream on top and add a twist of orange.

Galwyn (Wal) gallon 8pints (4.54litres).

Gamage (Fr) a label for an A.C. Entre-deux-Mers white wine (100% Sauvignon blanc).

Gamaret (Switz) a red grape variety produced as a result of crossing Gamay x Reichensteiner.

G

Gamashara (Rus) a red grape variety popular in Azerbaijan (between Armenia and Caspian Sea).

Gamay (Fr) a red grape variety grown mainly in the Beaujolais, Rhône and the Loire that produces wines with an aroma and flavour of cherry, raspberry, apricots ripe bananas. *see* Gamay Noir à Jus Blanc. (Aus) = blaufränkisch, (Hun) = kékfrankos.

Gamay (USA) *see* California Gamay and Napa Gamay.

Gamay à Feuille Ronde (Fr) an alternative name for the Melon de bourgogne.

Gamay à Jus Coloré (Fr) lit: 'Gamay with coloured juice', a red grape variety grown in southern Burgundy. Known also as the Gamay Teinturier. Also spelt Gamay au Jus Coloré.

Gamay au Jus Blanc (Fr) *see* Gamay Noir à Jus Blanc.

Gamay au Jus Coloré (Fr) *see* Gamay à Jus Coloré.

Gamay Beaujolais (USA) a red grape variety grown in California, a clone of the Pinot noir.

Gamay Blanc à Feuilles Rondes (Fr) an alternative name for the Muscadet grape.

Gamay Crni (Cro) a red grape variety grown in Istria, Croatia.

Gamay de Liverdun (Fr) a red grape variety grown in the Côtes de Toul, Lorraine.

Gamay de Toul (Fr) a red grape variety grown in the Côtes de Toul, Lorraine.

Gamay Fréau (Fr) a red skinned grape with red flesh grown in the Loire.

Gamay Noir à Jus Blanc (Fr) lit: 'Gamay with white juice', a red grape variety grown in the Beaujolais, Loire and Rhône. *see* Gamay. Also known as Blaufränkisch, Borgogna crna, Bourgignon noir, Frankinja crna, Frankinja modra, Gaamez, Gamay au jus blanc, Gamay rond, Gamé, Kékfrankos, Limberger, Napa gamay and Petit gamai.

Gamay Rond (Fr) an alternative name for the Gamay noir à jus blanc.

Gamay Rosé (USA) a rosé wine produced in California from the Gamay Beaujolais grape.

Gamay St. Romain à Jus Blanc (Fr) a red grape variety grown in the Côtes Roannaises, Loire.

Gamay Teinturier (Fr) *see* Gamay à Jus Coloré.

Gamba (Port) the brand-name of a Vinho Verde from Borges & Irmao, sold in flasks.

Gambach (Ger) village (Anb): Franken. (Ber): Maindreieck. (Gro): Rosstal. (Vin): Kalbenstein.

Gambarotta (Fr) producers of Brandy del Bourgogne.

Gambarotta di Inga (It) liqueur producers based in Serravalle, Scrivia. Produce Fernet Gambarotta (a herb liqueur 43% alc. by vol).

Gambellara (It) a small town half-way between Verona and Vicenza, also the name of a white wine.

Gambellara (It) a A D.O.C. white wine from Veneto. Made from the Garganega and Trebbiano nostrano grapes. If total alc. content is 11.5% by vol. then classed Superiore.

Gambia Distillers Ltd. (Afr) distillers of a range of spirits based in Kanifing, Gambia.

Gambrinus (Bel) a legendary Flemish king who is supposed to have invented beer.

Gambrinus (Czec) a brewery (established 1870) in Pilsen. Known as Erste Pilsner Actienbrauerei (First Plzen Brewery Ltd). Amalgamated with two others, privatised it is now part of Pilsner Urquell, the largest brewing group. Brews Pilsener Lager called Svetovar and Gambrinus 4.9% alc by vol. Also Diplomat, a strong, dark Lager beer with a good hop flavour. *see* Pilsner Urquell, Plzenský Prazdroj.

Gambrinus Brauerei Weiden (Ger) a brewery. (Add): Keplerstrasse 15-23, Weiden D-92637. Brews a variety of beers and lagers. Website: http://www.gambrinus-weiden.de

Gambrinus C° [The] (USA) a brewery. (Add): 14800 San Pedro, Third Floor, san Antonio TXT8232. Brews beers and lager. Website: http://www.gambrinus.com

Gambrinus Dark 10% (Czec) a 3.8% alc by vol. bottled, dark lager brewed by Gambrinus, Plzenský Prazdroj, Plzen.

Gambrinus Straw 10% (Czec) a 4.1% alc by vol. bottled, pale straw lager brewed by Gambrinus, Plzenský Prazdroj, Plzen.

Gambrinus Straw 12% (Czec) a 5% alc by vol. bottled, pale straw lager brewed by Gambrinus, Plzenský Prazdroj, Plzen.

Gamé (Bul) an alternative name for the Blaufränkisch grape.

Gamebird (Port) a brand of both tawny and ruby Ports from Robertson.

Gamekeeper's Autumn Ale (Eng) a 4.7% alc by vol. winter warmer ale from Carlsberg-Tetley (part of the Tapster's Choice range).

Gamel (Nor) a brand of aquavit.

Game Set and Match (Eng) a 3.8% alc by vol. ale brewed by the Bank Top Brewery Ltd., Lancashire.

Gamet (Fr) the name used for the Gamay grape in the seventeenth and eighteenth centuries.

Gamla (Isr) the name given to a range of Israeli wines produced in the Golan Heights Winery, Galilee. Range includes: Cabernet sauvignon, Chardonnay, Sangiovese and Sauvignon blanc.

Gamla Slottskällans Bryggeri AB (Swe) a brewery. (Add): Märstagatan 10-12, 753 23 Uppsala. Brews beers and lagers. Website: http://www.slottskallan.se

Gamle Carlsberg (Den) also known as 'Old Carlsberg', a Münchener-style lager beer.

Gamlingay (Eng) a vineyard. (Add): Near Sandy, Bedfordshire. 4.5ha. Soil: green sand. Grape varieties: Faber, Müller-Thurgau, Reichensteiner, Rieslaner, Scheurebe.

Gammel Dansk (Den) a style of alcoholic bitters distilled from a variety of berries, herbs and spices (including gentian) 38% alc by vol.

Gammelholm Snaps (Den) the brand-name of an akvavit.

Gammel Porter (Den) a medium-sweet imperial stout 6.1% alc by vol. brewed by Carlsberg.

Gampal (Port) a white grape variety grown in Torres Vedras.

Gamza (Bul) a red grape variety which produces a full rich red Beaujolais-style of wine. (Hun) = Kadarka.

G

Gamza (Bul) a red wine produced near northern Sofia from the grape of same name.

Gancia (It) major wine producers near Asti in the Piemonte region. Noted for D.O.C.G. Asti and vermouths.

Gancia [Carlo] (It) the creator of Asti Spumante in the nineteenth century.

Gandesa Terralta (Sp) a Denominación de Origen region near Priorato, Catalonia. Produces red wines from the Cariñena, Garnacha and Macabeo grapes.

G and G (Jap) a brand of whiskey produced by the Nikka Distilleries.

Gandia PLA S.A. (Sp) a wine producer based at Valencia. Produces wines under the Castillo de Liria and Floreal labels.

Gangadine Cocktail (Cktl) ⅓ measure gin, ⅓ measure white crème de menthe, ⅓ measure Oxygénée Cusenier, 2 dashes framboise syrup. Shake over ice and strain into a cocktail glass.

Gang Plank (Eng). 5.8% alc by vol. cask ale produced by the Flagship Brewery, Chatham Dockyard, Dartford.

Gangster Cocktail (Cktl) 30mls (¼ gill) brown Curaçao, 30mls (¼ gill) brandy. Shake over ice, strain into a cocktail glass, serve with a cherry and a dash of lemon peel juice.

Gannaru (Euro) a red grape variety grown on the island of Malta.

Gannet Mild (Eng) a 3.3% alc by vol. mild ale brewed by the Earl Soham Brewery, Suffolk.

Gäns (Ger) vineyard (Anb): Mosel-Saar-Ruwer. (Ber): Zell/Mosel. (Gro): Weinhex. (Vil): Kobern-Gondorf.

Gänsberg (Ger) vineyard (Anb): Baden. (Ber): Ortenau. (Gro): Schloss Rodeck. (Vil): Neuweier.

Ganshalt (Aus) a vineyard area on the banks of the River Danube in the Kremstal region.

Gantry [1] (Eng) the area behind a bar where spirits are displayed.

Gantry [2] (Eng) the framework to hold a cask of ale.

Ganze Bier (Hol) a 5.5% alc by vol. bottle-conditioned ale brewed by De Gans Bier Brouwerij, Goes.

Ganze Bokbier (Hol) a 7.5% alc by vol. bottle-conditioned bock beer brewed by De Gans Bier Brouwerij, Goes.

Gaolers Ale (Eng) the name for an ale brewed by the Alcazar Brewery, Nottinghamshire.

Garabana (Iran) a large flagon used during early Persian times.

Garafoes (Port) wine containers for bulk selling, usually they are returnable.

Garage Wines (Fr) the name given to a range of wines produced in small quantities that sell for very high prices, found mainly in the Bordeaux region.

Garagiste (Fr) the nickname given to small Bordeaux producers whose total production could fit in their garage!

Garance (Fr) a type of plant (also known as the madder wort) from which can be brewed a style of beer.

Garaway's Coffee House (Eng) founded in 1615, purported to have been the first coffee house to serve tea.

Garbi (Sp) *see* Llebeig.

Garboon (Eng) the name given to the spittoon used by professional coffee tasters to deposit the coffee they are assessing.

Garcés Silva (Chile) a winery based in the Lydia district of San Antonio. Label: Amayana. Website: http://www.vgs.cl

Garceta (Sp) a finely woven sack that is used to slow down wine that is being transferred into a cask.

Garchères [Les] (Fr) a vineyard in the A.C. commune of Montagny, Côte Chalonnaise, Burgundy.

Garci (Tun) an acidic, natural spring mineral water (established 1968). Mineral contents (milligrammes per litre): Sodium 435mg/l, Calcium 192mg/l, Magnesium 54mg/l, Potassium 16mg/l, Bicarbonates 1229mg/l, Chlorides 426mg/l, Sulphates 65mg/l. pH 5.5

Garcia Caribbean Cream (Hol) a Jamaican rum and cream liqueur from Cooymans 14.9% alc by vol.

García Poveda (Sp) a large bodega based in Alicante, produces wines under the Costa Blanc label.

Garçon de Comptoir (Fr) barman.

Garco Wine Company (USA) a winery based in St. Louis, Missouri.

Garcy (Fr) a commune in the Central Vineyards region of the Loire, produces A.C. Pouilly Fumé.

Gard (Fr) a département of the Languedoc-Roussillon, including the Plaine du Vistre and the Plaine du Vidourle. Noted for Costières and Clairette de Bellegarde. *See also* Costières-du-Gard.

Garda (It) the name given to wines that are grown near Lake Garda in northern Italy. Moniga-del-Garda and Chiaretto-del-Garda.

Garda Bresciano (It) a D.O.C. red, rosé, rosé spumante, and dry white wines. Red wine produced from blend of Groppello, Sangiovese, Marzemino and Barbera grapes. White from Rhine riesling and Italian riesling grapes. Separate D.O.C. for Groppello.

Garden Creek Ranch (USA) a vineyard based in Alexander Valley, Sonoma County, California. 17ha. Grape varieties: Cabernet sauvignon and Gewürztraminer. Produces varietal wines.

Garden Gully (Austr) a winery (established 1985) based at Western Highway, Great Western, Victoria. Grape varieties: Chardonnay, Gewürztraminer, Riesling, Shiraz. Produces still and sparkling (traditional method) wines.

Garden Party (Cktl) 10mls (½ fl.oz) Vaapukka liqueur, Champagne. Pour liqueur into Champagne flute and top with iced Champagne.

Gardet and Cº. (Fr) a Champagne producer. (Add): 13 Rue Georges Legros, Chigny lès Roses, 51500 Rilly La Montagne. Produces vintage and non-vintage wines. Vintages: 1973, 1975, 1976, 1979, 1982, 1983, 1988, 1989, 1990, 1993, 1995, 1996, 1998, 1999.

G

Gareisa (It) a natual sparkling mineral water. (Add): Fonti di San Maurizio s.a.s. Roccaforte, Mondovi (Cuneo). Mineral contents (milligrammes per litre): Sodium 9.5mg/l, Calcium 27mg/l, Magnesium 2.1mg/l, Potassium 2.5mg/l, Bicarbonates 100mg/l, Chlorides 1mg/l, Sulphates 19mg/l, Silicate 19mg/l. pH 7.5

Garenne (Fr) a Premier Cru vineyard in the A.C. commune of Puligny-Montrachet, Côte de Beaune, Burgundy 0.4ha.

Garfoli (It) a noted Verdicchio dei Castelli di Jesi producer based at Loreto.

Garganega (It) a white grape variety grown around Lake Garda in northern Italy, the Garganega di Gambellara is a sub-variety.

Garganega di Gambellara (It) a sub-variety of Garganega. Produces a dry white wine of same name from the province of Vicenza in the Venetia (Verona).

Gargle (Eng) lit: 'to rinse out the mouth with liquid', a slang term for a drink in the north of England.

Gargoyle Cocktail (Cktl) ⅓ measure dry gin, ⅓ measure Cointreau, ⅓ measure Cognac. Stir well over ice and strain into a cocktail glass.

Garibaldi Dolce (It) *see* G.D.

Gärkammer (Ger) vineyard (Anb): Ahr. (Ber): Walporzheim/Ahrtal. (Gro): Klosterberg. (Vil): Walporzheim.

Garlic (Eng) if present on the bouquet of a wine then denotes the presence of sorbic acid.

Garnacha (Sp) a black grape variety used in Rioja, Navarre, Madrid, La Mancha, Somontano, Tarragona, Campo de Borja, Penedés. It ripens late and is resistant to Oïidium. Also produces white grapes depending on method of cultivation. (See Garnacha blanca). Also known as the Alicante, Garnacha tinta, Garnach tinto, Grenache, Granaccia, Llandoner, Roussillón tinto, Tinta aragonés and Uva di spagna.

Garnacha Blanca (Sp) a white grape variety grown in Cataluña and Rioja, also known as Grenache blanc.

Garnacha de Alicante (Sp) a red grape variety grown in the Galicia region.

Garnacha Negra (Sp) a red grape variety grown in the Penedés region.

Garnacha Paluda (Sp) a red grape variety grown in Alella, near Barcelona, south-eastern Spain. A variant of the Garnacha tinta. Also spelt Garnacha peluda. The grapes are darker and thicker skinned than Garnacha tinta. Also known as Lladoner pelut.

Garnacha Peluda (Sp) an alternative spelling of the Garnacha paluda.

Garnacha Tinta (Sp) a red grape variety grown in the Rioja region. *see* Garnacha.

Garnacha Tintorera (Sp) a red grape variety grown in the southern regions of Spain. An alternative name for Alicante bouschet.

Garnacho Tinto (Sp) an alternative name for Garnacha.

Garnatxa (Sp) a sweet, orange-red coloured wine made in Ampurdán Costa Brava by the same method as vin de paille from 100% Garnacha grapes. Full name is Garnatxa d'Empordà. Also produced in Tarragona. Achieves 15% alc by vol. Stored for 5–10 years in a combination of tank, oak and bottle.

Garnet (It) a desirable colour in the red wines of northern Italy.

Garnet Point (N.Am) a winery based in South Eastern Australia. Grape varieties: Cabernet sauvignon and Shiraz.

Garnet Point (USA) a winery based in California. Grape varieties: Cabernet sauvignon, Merlot, Zinfandel, Chardonnay, Chenin blanc.

Garnheath (Scot) a grain spirit once produced by Inver House Distillers at Airdrie, West Lothian.

Garnheath (Scot) a 1972 dated, 27 year old malt whisky from Compass Box 59% alc by vol.

Garnier (Fr) a famous liqueur firm owned by Bénédictine. Produces a range of fruit liqueurs including abricotine.

Garoa (Sp) a red Riojan wine from the Bodegas Velazquez.

Garofoli (It) a winery based at Loreto in the Marches. (Add): Casa Vinicola Gioacchino Garofoli Spa, Via Arno, 9-60025, Loreto. Owns 60ha. of vineyards. Noted for Verdicchio dei Castelli di Jesi Classico Superiore wines. Label: Podium. Website: http://www.garofolivini.it 'E'mail: mail@garofolivini.it

Garolla (Fr) an alternative name for the Égrappoir.

Garollières [Les] (Fr) *see* Jarolières (Les).

Garonne (S.Afr) a dessert wine made from the Rhine riesling and Steen grapes by the Villiera Estate in Paarl.

Garonne [River] (Fr) a river that runs to the west coast of France in Bordeaux. Joins with the river Dordogne to form the river Gironde.

Garoto (Port) a small black coffee (Portuguese espresso) served with milk, can also denote a small cappuccino coffee.

Garrafa (Sp) carafe/bottle.

Garrafão (Port) a large bottle.

Garrafa Termos (Port) Thermos flask™.

Garrafeira (Port) if found on a wine label denotes best wine of that year. Top quality. Sometimes a little wine of another year is blended in to add body. **Red**: aged 2 years before bottling plus 1 year in bottle. **White**: aged 6 months before bottling plus 6 months in bottle.

Garreau (Fr) an Armagnac producer. (Add): Charles Garreau et ses Enfants, SARL, Château Garreau, 40240 Labastide d'Armagnac. 21ha. in Bas Armagnac.

Garrido Fino (Sp) a white grape variety grown in south-western Spain (Huelva).

Garrigos (Sp) wine-producers and bottlers based in Valencia.

Garrigues (Fr) the name given to moorland in the Languedoc-Roussillon region of south-western France.

G

Garró (Sp) red grape variety from the Catalonia region.

Garrut (Sp) a rare red grape variety grown in Cataluña that produces aromatic wines, high in tannin.

Gärtchen (Ger) vineyard (Anb): Mosel-Saar-Ruwer. (Ber): Bernkastel. (Gro): Michelsberg. (Vil): Piesport.

Gartenlay (Ger) vineyard (Anb): Mittelrhein. (Ber): Rheinburgengau. (Gro): Burg Hammerstein. (Vil): Leutesdorf.

Gartl (Aus) a vineyard area on the banks of the River Danube in the Kremstal region.

Gärtling (Aus) a vineyard area on the banks of the River Danube in the Kremstal region.

Garton Brewery (Eng) a brewery (established 2001). (Add): Station House, Station Road, Garton on the Wolds, Driffield, East Yorkshire YO25 3EX. Brews: Chocolate Frog Porter 8% alc by vol., Goodnight Vienna IPA % alc by vol., Liquid Lobotomy Stout 8% alc by vol., Old Buffer Dark Mild 4.5% alc by vol., Stunned Mullet Bitter 5% alc by vol., Woldsman Bitter 4.5% alc by vol. 'E'mail: gartonbrewery@aol.com

Gärung (Ger) fermentation.

Garvey (Sp) a noted Sherry and brandy producer based in Jerez de la Frontera. Was owned by Rumasa. Sherry range includes: Tio Guillermo, La Lidia, San Patricio and Ochavico.

Gary Farrell Winery (USA) a winery (established 2000) based in the Russian River Valley, Sonoma County, California. Grape varieties include: Cabernet sauvignon, Chardonnay, Merlot, Pinot noir, Zinfandel.

Garza Cellars [La] (USA) a 4ha.vineyard based in Roseburg, Oregon. Grape varieties: Cabernet sauvignon, Chardonnay, Merlot.

G.A.S. (Rum) *abbr*: **G**aspodaniile **A**gricole de **S**tat, a state agricultural enterprise.

Gas Blanketing (Eng) a treatment of wine in which air in an ullaged vat is replaced with CO_2 or nitrogen, prevents attack by acetobacter and oxidation.

Gas Chromatography (Eng) a process which measures the chemical content of substances by turning them into gases (by heating), used to measure the blood alcohol level in drunken drivers.

Gascosa (Port) mineral water/fizzy drink/pop.

Gaseosa (Sp) mineral water.

Gaseoso (Sp) the name given to a sparkling wine produced by an injection of CO_2 gas.

Gasificado (Sp) CO_2 injected sparkling wines.

Gas Light [The] (Cktl) 35mls Scotch whisky, 10mls Italian vermouth, dash orange Curaçao. Shake well over ice and strain into an ice-filled goblet. Add 5mls Drambuie and garnish with a twist of orange.

Gaspo (Fr) a buttermilk drink which is popular in Auvergne.

Gaspodaniile Agricole de Stat. (Rum) *see* G.A.S.

Gässel (Ger) vineyard (Anb): Pfalz. (Ber): Mittelhaardt-Deutsche Weinstrasse. (Gro): Pfaffengrund. (Vil): Geinsheim.

Gassificato (It) artificially gas injected with CO_2.

Gassosa (It) the general term for sparkling drinks.

Gasteiner (Aus) a still and sparkling natural spring mineral water (established 1929) from Bad Gastein. (green label: sparkling/blue label: light gas/pink label: still). Mineral contents (milligrammes per litre): Sodium 15mg/l, Calcium 24.05mg/l, Magnesium 2.19mg/l, Potassium 2.3mg/l, Bicarbonates 66.51mg/l, Chlorides 7.23mg/l, Sulphates 34mg/l, Fluorides 0.58mg/l, Nitrates 5.6mg/l, Silicates 13.4mg/l, Barium <2mg/l. Website: http://www.gasteiner.at

Gastenklinge (Ger) vineyard (Anb): Württemberg. (Ber): Remstal-Stuttgart. (Gro): Wartbühl. (Vil): Strümpfelbach.

Gasthaus (Ger) guesthouse/Inn.

Gaston Burtin (Fr) a Champagne producer based in Épernay F-51200.

Gaston Chiquet (Fr) a Champagne producer (established 1746). (Add): 912, Avenue du Général Leclerc, B.P. 1019, 51530 Dizy. 22ha. Propriétaire-Récoltant. Produces vintage and non-vintage wines. Vintages: 1995, 1996, 1997, 1999. A member of the Club Tresors de Champagne. Labels: Cuvée 'Special Club' Millésimée. 'E'mail: info@gastonchiquet.com

Gastritis (Eng) a disease of the stomach caused through chronic alcoholism.

Gastropub (Eng) a slang term for a public house with an up-maket dining area and which concentrates on its food than its beers.

Gatao (Port) the brand-name of a Vinho Verde produced by Soc. Vinhos Borges & Irmao, Porto-Portugal.

Gate (Eng) the name for the home-brew public house The Lee, Buckinghamshire. Produces Carr's Best Bitter 1041 O.G.

Gate (Eng) a home-brew public house owned by Whitbread in Southampton noted for cask-conditioned Three Bar 1035 O.G. and Five Bar 1050 O.G.

Gatehouse Wines (N.Z) a winery. (Add): Jowers Road, West Melton, RD 6, Christchurch. 4ha. Grape varieties: Chardonnay, Gewürztraminer, Riesling, Pinot noir, Cabernet sauvignon, Merlot, Malbec.

Gatinois (Fr) a Champagne producer. (Add): 7 Rue Marcel Mailly, 51056 Aÿ-Champagne. Produces a blanc de noirs and Grand Cru brut réserve.

Gato Cocktail (Cktl) 25mls (⅙ gill) gin, 4 dashes gomme syrup, 6 strawberries. Blend together with a scoop of crushed ice in a blender, strain into a saucer glass and dress with a strawberry.

Gattinara (It) a commune in the provence of Vercelli, Piemonte.

Gattinara (It) a D.O.C.G. red wine from Piemonte. Made from the Nebbiolo grape plus Vespolina (0%–4%) and Bonarda (0%–10%). Has to age 3 years of which 2 years is in oak/chestnut casks. Is a dry wine with slight bitter taste.

G

Gatz Altbier (Ger) a 4.8% alc by vol. altbier brewed by the Gayzweiler Brauerei, Düsseldorf.

Gatzweiler Brauerei (Ger) a brewery in Düsseldorf. Owned by Zum Schlüssel. Produces Gatz Altbier 4.8% alc by vol.

Gatzweiler Alt (Ger) a fine altbier brewed by the Gatzweiler Brauerei in Düsseldorf. Is a bitter, light, slightly acid brew.

Gau-Algesheim (Ger) village (Anb): Rheinhessen. (Ber): Bingen. (Gro): Abtey. (Vins): Goldberg, Johannisberg, Rothenberg, St. Laurenzikapelle, Steinert.

Gau-Bickelheim (Ger) village (Anb): Rheinhessen. (Ber): Bingen. (Gro): Kurfürstenstück. (Vins): Bockshaut, Kapelle, Sankopf.

Gau-Bischofsheim (Ger) village (Anb): Rheinhessen. (Ber): Nierstein. (Gro): Sankt Alban. (Vins): Glockenberg, Herrnberg, Pfaffenweg.

Gaucho (Cktl) ½ measure Dutch gin, ½ measure Hespiridina, dash Angostura. Shake over ice, strain into an ice-filled old-fashioned glass and decorate with a slice of orange.

Gaudenziana (It) a sparkling natural spring mineral water from Gaudenziana. Mineral contents (milligrammes per litre): Sodium 1.7mg/l, Calcium 25.4mg/l, Magnesium 1.9mg/l, Potassium 1.7mg/l, Bicarbonates 73.7mg/l, Chlorides 0.5mg/l, Sulphates 12.7mg/l, Nitrates 3.2mg/l, Silicates 8.1mg/l. pH 7.88

Gaudenzio (It) a producer of Moscato d'Asti Spumante in the Piemonte region.

Gaudi (Ind) the name given to a drink produced from the crystallised residue left from Sidhu by Ancient Indians.

Gaudianello (It) a sparkling natural spring mineral water from Gaudianello. Mineral contents (milligrammes per litre): Sodium 129mg/l, Calcium 152mg/l, Magnesium 52mg/l, Potassium 48mg/l, Bicarbonates 940mg/l, Chlorides 38mg/l, Sulphates 122mg/l, Nitrates 3mg/l, Silicates 100mg/l. pH 5.79

Gaudichots [Les] (Fr) a Premier Cru vineyard in the A.C. commune of Vosne-Romanée, Côte de Nuits, Burgundy 5.8ha.

Gaudin (Fr) a company based in the Haut-Savoie, eastern France that produces dry, aromatic apéritif wines i.e. Chambéry and Chambéryzette.

Gaudium (Sp) a red wine produced by Marqués de Cáceres from a blend of old vine Tempranillo, Grenache and Graciano grapes.

Gauersheim (Ger) village (Anb): Pfalz. (Ber): Mittelhaardt-Deutsche Weinstrasse. (Gro): Schnepfenflug vom Zellertal. (Vin): Goldloch.

Gaugrehweiler (Ger) village (Anb): Nahe. (Ber): Schloss Böckelheim. (Gro): Paradiesgarten. (Vin): Graukatz.

Gauguin Cocktail (Cktl) ⅙ measure white rum, ⅙ measure passion fruit syrup, ⅙ measure lemon juice, ⅙ measure lime juice. Blend altogether with a scoop of crushed ice, pour into an old-fashioned glass and top with a cherry.

Gau-Heppenheim (Ger) village (Anb): Rheinhessen. (Ber): Nierstein. (Gro): Petersberg. (Vins): Pfarrgarten, Schlossberg.

Gauitsch (Aus) a vineyard area based in the Kitzeck district of Süd-Steirmark.

Gauloise (Fr) a very old apéritif drink, made in three styles: dry, medium and sweet.

Gauloise Ambrée [La] (Bel) a 6.5% alc by vol. amber coloured, top-fermented, bottle-conditioned, special beer brewed by Du Bocq Brasserie Centrale in Purnode.

Gauloise Blonde [La] (Bel) a 7% alc by vol. top-fermented, bottled, straw coloured beer brewed by Du Bocq Brasserie Centrale in Purnode.

Gauloise Brune [La] (Bel) a 9% alc by vol. top-fermented, bottled, strong brown-coloured beer brewed by Du Bocq Brasserie Centrale in Purnode.

Gau-Odernheim (Ger) village (Anb): Rheinhessen. (Ber): Nierstein. (Gro): Petersberg. (Vins): Fuchsloch, Herrgottspfad, Ölberg, Vogelsang.

Gauranum (It) a red wine produced in central Italy during Roman times.

Gauriac (Fr) a commune in the A.C. Côtes de Bourg in north-eastern Bordeaux.

Gautheron [Alain] (Fr) a winery based in the A.C. Chablis, Burgundy. Produces a range of Chablis wines including Premier Cru Vaucoupin.

Gauthier (Fr) a Champagne producer. (Add): 12 Boulevard Lundy, B.P. 163, 51016 Reims.

Gautier (Fr) a Cognac producer. (Add): 28 Rue des Ponts, 16140 Aigre. Produces X.O. Gold.

Gautier [Laurent] (Fr) a négociant-éleveur based at Savigny-lès-Beaune, Côte de Beaune, Burgundy.

Gautscher (Aus) a vineyard site based on the banks of the River Kamp situated in the Kamptal region.

Gauvin (Fr) a vineyard based in the A.C. Volnay-Santenots. Is owned by the Hospices de Beaune (based in the Santenots vineyard).

Gauvin (Fr) the brand-name of an Armagnac produced by Domaine de Lamothe.

Gau-Weinheim (Ger) village (Anb): Rheinhessen. (Ber): Bingen. (Gro): Kurfürstenstück. (Vins): Geyersberg, Kaisergarten, Wissberg.

Gavernia (It) a natural spring mineral water from Terme Gavernia 3, Casazza (BG). Mineral contents (milligrammes per litre): Sodium 11.5mg/l, Calcium 112mg/l, Magnesium 30.1mg/l, Potassium 0.92mg/l, Bicarbonates 332.5mg/l, Sulphates 140.6mg/l, Fluorides 0.73mg/l, Silicates 10.8mg/l, Strontium 14.7mg/l. pH 7.95

Gavi (It) *see* Cortese di Gavi.

Gavilan (Mex) a noted distillery based in Jalisco. Produces Tequila Especial 40% alc by vol.

Gavine (S.Afr) a leading brand of double-distilled cane spirit.

Gavnø Gods Kilde (Den) a natural spring mineral water from Gavnø Gods Kilde.

Gavotte (S.Afr) a red wine blend of Cabernet and Shiraz grapes which is produced by the Villiera Estate, Paarl. Also a white (blanc de noirs) version produced.

Gavriche (Eng) a chocolate cream liqueur sold in a

chocolate brown bottle. Produced by Vine Products, contains chocolate, cream and cherry kirsch.

Gay Lussac (Fr) the inventor of a hydrometer named after him that measures the volume of alcohol on a scale of 0° water–100° pure alcohol.

Gaymer Group (Eng) formed on 5th May 1992 due to a take in of Showerings, Vine Products and Whiteways. (Add): Whitchurch Lane, Bristol. Brands include Copperhead, Olde English. Now part of Matthew Clark Taunton. Produces: Addlestone's 5% alc by vol., Gaymers Finest Spiced Cyder, Olde English Cyder, Orchard Reserve 6.8% alc by vol., Original Cider 4.55% alc by vol.

Gaymers Finest Spiced Cyder (Eng) a cider produced by the Gaymer Group from a blend of ginger, cinnamon, orange juice and cider (sold in 1 litre bottles).

Gaymers Olde English Cyder (Eng) a brand of cider produced by the Gaymer Group.

Gaza (Isr) a Palestine wine written about in Roman times.

Gaz Carbonique (Fr) the French for **Carbon-dioxide**, CO_2.

Gazéifié (Fr) a term for artificially carbonated sparkling wines.

Gazela (Port) the brand-name of a vinho verde wine.

Gazeux (Fr) aerated.

Gaziantep (Tur) a vineyard noted for red and white wines based in eastern Turkey.

Gazino (Tur) beer house/pub (usually with entertainment).

Gazoz (Tur) denotes a sparkling soft drink (non-alcoholic) i.e. pop, ginger beer, lemonade.

GB (Eng) a 4% alc by vol. cask-conditioned ale brewed by Gales Brewery, Horndean, Hampshire.

GB (Eng) a 4.4% alc by vol. lager from the **G**et **B**rewing subsidiary of Whitbread.

G.B. (Eng) abbr: The initials of the **G**reengate **B**rewery in Manchester. see G.B. Mild.

GB Bronwater (Bel) a natural spring mineral water from Saint Léger. Mineral contents (milligrammes per litre): Sodium 92mg/l, Calcium 60mg/l, Magnesium 23mg/l, Potassium 20mg/l, Bicarbonates 476mg/l, Chlorides 36mg/l, Sulphates 55mg/l.

G.B. Mild (Eng) a mild beer 1032 O.G. formerly brewed by the Greengate Brewery in Manchester. Now brewed by Lees (J.W.) in Manchester.

GBOP (Eng) abbr: **G**olden **B**roken **O**range **P**ekoe a grade of Broken Orange Pekoe black tea.

G.D. (It) abbr: **G**aribaldi **D**olce, the old-style name given to Marsala, denotes 2 years ageing and 18% alc by vol.

G.D.C. (Eng) abbr: **G**eneva **D**ouble **C**urtain.

Gean Whisky (Scot) a black cherry whisky, is also spelt Geen Whisky. See also Cherry Whisky.

Geary Brewing C°. [D.L.] (USA) a micro-brewery (established 1983), sold first beer in 1986. Based at Portland, Maine, Philadelphia.

Geary's American Ale (USA) a 4.8% alc by vol. gold

coloured, top-fermented, bottled ale brewed by the Geary Brewing Company in Portland, Maine, Philadelphia.

Geary's London Style Porter (USA) a 4.2% alc by vol. dark, top-fermented, bottled porter brewed by the Geary Brewing Company in Portland, Maine, Philadelphia. Produced using English malts plus Cascade, Goldings and Willamette hops.

Geary's Pale Ale (USA) a 4.5% alc by vol. copper coloured, top-fermented, bottled ale brewed by the Geary Brewing Company in Portland, Maine, Philadelphia.

Geb de Koninck Brasserie (Bel) a brewery based in Dwarp, central Belgium.

Geb de Vit Brasserie (Bel) a brewery based in Asse, north Belgium.

Gebeide (Hol) a term used for a jenever distilled from juniper. See also Dubbele Graan and Dubbel Gebeide.

Gebiet (Ger) a vine-growing region. e.g. Rheinhessen. see Anbaugebiete.

Gebietsweinmarkt der Ahr (Ger) a wine festival held at Ahrweiler each May.

Gebietswinzergenossenschaft (Ger) regional co-operative. See also Bezirkswinzergenossenschaft.

Gebirgsbitter (Ger) a brandy with additional aromatic and bitter ingredients. Brown or green in colour.

Gebling (Aus) a vineyard area on the banks of the River Danube in the Kremstal region.

Gebweiler (Fr) the German name for the Alsace town of Guebwiller.

Gecht [A.] de Luxe Brandy (USA) the brand-name of a brandy bottled by Liquors C°. of America 40% alc by vol.

Gecko Ridge (S.Afr) a winery based in Stellenbosch, Western Cape (owned by Pernod-Ricard) Grape varieties: Cabernet sauvignon, Chardonnay. Produces varietal wines.

Geddelsbach (Ger) village (Anb): Württemberg. (Ber): Württembergisch Unterland. (Gro): Lindelberg. (Vin): Schneckenhof.

Gedeonseck (Ger) grosslage (Anb): Mittelrhein. (Ber): Rheinburgengau. (Vils): Boppard, Brez, Rhens, Spay.

Gedera (Isr) the viticultural centre of Israel which produces most types of wines.

Geelong (Austr) a wine-producing area in Victoria.

Geens (Bel) a distillery based in Aarschot. Produces a large range of liqueurs and a genever, also owns French vineyards and produces French table wines.

Geen Whisky (Scot) see Gean Whisky.

Gefällig (Ger) a pleasing, harmonious wine.

Geffard [Henri] (Fr) a Cognac producer. (Add): Verriers, 16130 Segonzac. 25ha. in the Grande Champagne. Produces a wide range of fine Cognacs.

Gefüllt (Ger) full, rich wine.

Geheelonthouder (Hol) teetotaler.

Gehot Bosch Winery (S.Afr) a winery (established 2005) based in Bot River, Walker Bay, Western Cape. Grape variety: Cabernet sauvignon.

G

Gehrig's Winery (Austr) a winery. (Add): Murray Valley Highway, Barnawatha, Victoria. Grape varieties: Cabernet sauvignon, Pinot noir, Shiraz, Chardonnay, Chenin blanc, Riesling.

Gehrn (Ger) vineyard (Anb): Rheingau. (Ber): Johannisberg. (Gro): Steinmacher. (Vil): Rauenthal.

Gehrn (Ger) a vineyard within the village of Rauenthal, 17.1ha. (79.5%) of which is proposed to be classified as Erstes Gewächs.

Gehvé (Iran) coffee.

Geiersberg (Ger) vineyard (Anb): Rheinhessen. (Ber): Bingen. (Gro): Adelberg. (Vil): Armsheim.

Geiersberg (Ger) vineyard (Anb): Rheinhessen. (Ber): Wonnegau. (Gro): Pilgerpfad. (Vil): Dittelsheim-Hessloch.

Geiershöll (Ger) vineyard (Anb): Rheinhessen. (Ber): Nierstein. (Gro): Domherr. (Vil): Klein-Winternheim.

Geinsheim (Ger) village (Anb): Pfalz. (Ber): Mittelhaardt-Deutsche Weinstrasse. (Gro): Pfaffengrund. (Vin): Gässel.

Geisberg (Ger) vineyard (Anb): Mosel-Saar-Ruwer. (Ber): Bernkastel. (Gro): Michelsberg. (Vil): Rivenich.

Geisberg (Ger) vineyard (Anb): Mosel-Saar-Ruwer. (Ber): Saar-Ruwer. (Gro): Scharzberg. (Vil): Ockfen.

Geisberg (Ger) vineyard (Anb): Mosel-Saar-Ruwer. (Ber): Saar-Ruwer. (Gro): Scharzberg. (Vil): Schoden.

Geisberg (Ger) vineyard (Anb): Mosel-Saar-Ruwer. (Ber): Zell/Mosel. (Gro): Schwarze Katz. (Vil): Zell.

Geisberg (Ger) vineyard (Anb): Nahe. (Ber): Schloss Böckelheim. (Gro): Rosengarten. (Vil): Bockenau.

Geisburger (Fr) a lesser white grape variety grown in Alsace.

Geisenheim (Ger) village (Anb): Rheingau. (Ber): Johannisberg. (Gro): Burgweg. (Vins): Fuchsberg, Mäuerchen, Mönchspfad, Rothenberg.

Geisenheim (Ger) village (Anb): Rheingau. (Ber): Johannisberg. (Gro): Erntebringer. (Vins): Kilzberg, Klaus, Klauserweg, Schlossgarten.

Geisenheim Institute (Ger) a noted institute for vine breeding and grafting. see Omega Graft.

Geisha (Cktl) equal quantities of plum wine, cranberry juice and Champagne.

Geissberg (Ger) vineyard (Anb): Rheinhessen. (Ber): Bingen. (Gro): Kaiserpfalz. (Vil): Heidesheim.

Geissenkopf (Ger) vineyard (Anb): Nahe. (Ber): Schloss Böckelheim. (Gro): Paradiesgarten. (Vil): Niedermoschel.

Geissenkopf (Ger) vineyard (Anb): Nahe. (Ber): Schloss Böckelheim. (Gro): Paradiesgarten. (Vil): Obermoschel.

Geisskopf (Ger) vineyard (Anb): Pfalz. (Ber): Mittelhaardt-Deutsche Weinstrasse. (Gro): Schwarzerde. (Vil): Kirchheim.

Geist (Ger) the term to describe types of fruit liqueurs, distilled from unfermented berries, apricots, peaches plus the addition of alcohol. See also Wasser.

Geisterberg (Ger) vineyard (Anb): Rheinhessen. (Ber): Bingen. (Gro): Adelberg. (Vil): Erbes-Bürdesheim.

Geisweiler et Fils (Fr) noted Burgundy shippers based at Nuits-Saint-Georges. Owns 70% of the vineyards in the Hautes Côtes de Nuits. see Domaine Geisweiler.

Gekkeikan (Jap) a liqueur made from a special kind of plum which gives a luscious flavour.

Gekkeikan (Jap) a small brewery near Kyoto that produces Namazake and Horin Jyunmai Dai Ginjyo Sakés.

Gélas et Fils [Ets] (Fr) an Armagnac producer based in Ténarèze. (Add): Ave. Bergès, 32190 Vic-Fezensac.

Gelatine (Eng) used as a finings for wines, a little wine is mixed with the dissolved gelatine and then poured in the wine. As it sinks impurities in the wine are taken to the bottom.

Gelber Furmint (Aus) an alternative name for the Furmint grape.

Gelber Moseler (Aus)(Ger) another name for the Furmint grape used in Germany and Austria.

Gelber Ortlieber (Aus) another name for the Knipperlé grape.

Gelber Traminer (Aus) an alternative name for the rosé-coloured Traminer grape. Also regional (Styria) name for the Gewürztraminer.

Gelendshik (Rus) a wine region of the Crimean Peninsular.

Gelin [Pierre] (Fr) a négociant-éleveur based in the Côte d'Or. (Add): 62 Rte. des Grands Crus, 21220 Gevrey-Chambertin, Burgundy.

Gellewza (Euro) a red grape variety grown on the island of Malta. Also known as the Mammolo.

Gellmersbach (Ger) village (Anb): Württemberg. (Ber): Württembergisch Unterland. (Gro): Salzberg. (Vin): Dezberg.

Gelo (Port) ice.

Geltsfreund (Aus) a vineyard site based on the banks of the River Kamp situated in the Kamptal region.

Gelynis Vineyard (Wal) 0.65 ha vineyard at Treffogan, Cardiff. Produces Taff Trail sparkling white wine.

Gem (Eng) a 4.1% alc by vol. ale brewed by Bath Ales, Webbs Heath, Kingswood, Avon.

Gemarkung (Ger) wine town or village. See also Weinbauort and Gemeinde.

Gemberbier (Hol) ginger beer.

Gem City Vineland Compagny (USA) a winery based in Nauvoo, Illinois. Produces Labrusca wines.

Gemeaux Cherbaudes [Les] (Fr) a Premier Cru vineyard in the A.C. commune of Gevrey-Chambertin, Côte de Nuits, Burgundy.

Gemeinde (Ger) another name for a wine producing village. See also Weinbauort and Gemarkung.

Gemeinde (USA) a mild beer brewed by the Cold Spring Brewery based in Cold Spring, Minnesota.

Gemello Winery (USA) a winery based in Santa Clara, California. Grape varieties: Barbera, Petit syrah and Zinfandel. Produces varietal wines.

Geminianum (It) a red wine produced in south-western Italy during Roman times.

Gemischter Satz (Aus) denotes a wine made from a variety of grape species grown on a single vineyard.

Gemma (It) a natural spring mineral water from Endine.

Gemma d'Abeto (It) a pine needle-flavoured liqueur produced by the Servite friars near Florence.

Gemmingen (Ger) village (Anb): Baden. (Ber): Badische Bergstrasse/Kraichgau. (Gro): Stiftsberg. (Vin): Vogelsang.

Gemmrigheim (Ger) village (Anb): Württemberg. (Ber): Württembergisch Unterland. (Gro): Schalkstein. (Vins): Neckarberg, Wurmberg.

Gemstone (USA) a winery based in Yountville in the Napa Valley, California. Grape varieties include: Cabernet sauvingnon.

Gemtree (Austr) a winery based in the McLaren Vale, South Australia. Grape variety: Shiraz. Label: Bloodstone.

Genalpy (Fr) a herb-flavoured liqueur produced in Paris.

Genders Winery (Austr) a winery based in McLaren Vale, South Australia.

Génépi des Alpes (Switz) an orange-flavoured liqueur.

Générac (Fr) an area of vinification for A.C. wines of the Costières du Gard, Languedoc, south-western France.

Generala (It) an oak aged D.O.C. Barbera d'Asti Superiore produced by Bersano in Piemonte.

General Alvear (Arg) a wine-producing area in southern Argentina.

General Bilimoria (Eng) the brand label of a range of Languedoc wines designed for the Indian restaurant market (ideal wth hot, spicy foods), named after the father of Karan Bilimoria the label's creator. see Cobra Beer Ltd.

General Brewing (Can) a brewery based in Vancouver.

General Brewing Anchor Steam Beer (USA) a brewery based in San Francisco.

General Foods (Eng) a large company based at Ruscote Avenue, Banbury, Oxon. OX16 7QU. Produces a wide range of ground and instant coffees including Master Blend, Maxwell House and Mellow Bird's.

General Harrison's Egg Nogg (Cktl) 1 egg, sugar syrup to taste, juice of a lemon, fresh milk. Shake well over ice, strain into a highball glass and top with grated nutmeg.

General Kalashnikov's Vodka (Rus) the new name for Kalashnikov vodka.

Général Muteau (Fr) a cuvée in the vineyard of Volnay le Village, A.C. Volnay, Côte de Beaune, Burgundy (owned by the Hospices de Beaune) 0.8ha.

General Sutter Kirsch (Switz) the brand-name used by the Nebiker Distillery based in Sissach.

Generation (Eng) a 4% alc by vol. pale ale brewed by Hook Norton Brewery, Banbury, Oxon.

General Toussaint L'Ouverture (W.Ind) a 25.5% alc by vol. coffee liqueur from Haiti.

General Wine Company [The] (Gre) formed by Yiannis and Milhalis Boutaris. Has two wineries: Kyr-Yianni (28ha) for red wines (Xinomavro, Merlot, Syrah) and Vergoritis for white wines (Rhoditis, Chardonnay, Gewurztraminer, Sauvignon blanc).

General Wolfe 1759 Maple Ale (Eng) a 4.5% alc by vol. ale brewed by the Westerham Brewery Cº. Ltd., Kent.

Génération (Fr) a prestige non-vintage Champagne aged for 5 years in the cellars from the house of Lecomte Père et Fils.

Généreux (Fr) a generous wine, one with plenty of alcohol, a fortified sweet wine.

Generic (Eng) a wine name which is not related to the wine's origin. e.g. vin rosé, sparkling wine. This term is also used to denote a district wine such as Saint-Émilion, Médoc etc. (Fr) = générique.

Generic Bottling (Eng) a term that refers to the bottling of wines from a specific area. i.e. Sauternes, Saint-Émilion, Graves, Médoc, etc.

Generic Wine (Eng) wine sold under a commune name of an appellation. e.g. Saint-Émilion, Sauternes, Graves etc.

Générique (Fr) describes a regional A.O.C. wine that has no communal appellation or cru. (Eng) = generic.

Generosa (It) a natura. spring mineral water from Generosa. Mineral contents (milligrammes per litre): Sodium 57mg/l, Magnesium 40.8mg/l, Potassium 24mg/l, Bicarbonates 550.9mg/l, Nitrates 42mg/l, Silicates 12mg/l. pH 6.5

Generosos (Port) strong, sweet, fortified wines such as Port, Madeira, Moscatel, Setúbal.

Generous (Eng) denotes a wine that is mouth-filling, rich and warm in vitality and alcohol.

Genesee (USA) a brewery in Rochester, New York. Produces American Cream Ale 4.7% alc by vol. and Twelve Horse 5% alc by vol.

Genesis (Isr) a natural spring mineral water from Edi Gedi Spring, Jordan Mountains.

Genesis Green (Eng) a vineyard based at Wickhambrook in Suffolk.

Genesis Vineyard (S.Afr) a vineyard based in Stellenbosch. Grape variety: Chardonnay.

Genet [Michel] (Fr) a Champagne producer. (Add): 22 Rue des Partelaines, 51530 Chouilly. Produces vintage and non-vintage wines.

Geneva (Hol) the Dutch name for juniper and for gin. see Jenever.

Geneva (Switz) the local name for the Chasselas grape which produces light and slightly sparkling wines.

Geneva (Switz) the smallest canton. Produces mainly light, dry and slightly pétillant wines. Red wines are produced from the Gamay grape.

Geneva Double Curtain (Eng) abbr: G.D.C. a method of vine cultivation, high wire trellis system (vines are trained to height of 5 feet, allows optimum photosynthesis).

G

Genever (Hol) juniper, also the old name for gin. *see* Geneva and Jenever.

Genever Coffee (Liq.Coffee) melt a knob of butter in a pan and add 10grms castor sugar, dissolve, then add 12 juniper berries, flame with 25mls Hollands gin and douse with 200mls hot black coffee, pour into mug and top with whipped cream.

Genevières [Les] (Fr) a Premier Cru vineyard in the A.C. commune of Morey-Saint-Denis, Côte de Nuits, Burgundy 0.9ha.

Genevrette (Fr) a wine made from junipers berries, drunk for medicinal purposes.

Genevrières-Dessous [Les] (Fr) a Premier Cru vineyard in the A.C. commune of Meursault, Côte de Beaune, Burgundy.

Genevrières-Dessus [Les] (Fr) a Premier Cru vineyard in the A.C. commune of Meursault, Côte de Beaune, Burgundy 7.7ha.

Gengenbach (Ger) village (Anb): Baden. (Ber): Ortenau. (Gro): Fürsteneck. (Vins): Kinzigtäler, Nollenköpfle.

Genheim (Ger) village (Anb): Nahe. (Ber): Kreuznach. (Gro): Schlosskapelle. (Vin): Rossel.

Genièvre (Fr) juniper, also the old name for gin.

Genippa (W.Ind) the brand-name of a white rum sold by Duquesne in Martinique.

Genmai Cha (Asia) a leaf tea style which has toasted rice kernels added that produces a light, fragrant tea.

Genoa Cocktail (Cktl) 25mls (⅛ gill) grappa, 15mls (⅛ gill) Sambuca, 15mls (⅛ gill) dry vermouth. Shake over ice and strain into an ice-filled balloon glass.

Genopy des Alpes (Fr) a digestive liqueur produced in Grenoble, eastern France.

Gensac-la-Pallue (Fr) a commune in the Charente département whose grapes are classed Grande Champagne (Cognac).

Gensingen (Ger) village (Anb): Rheinhessen. (Ber): Bingen. (Gro): Sankt Rochuskapelle. (Vin): Goldberg.

Genté (Fr) a commune in the Grande Champagne district of Cognac, Charente.

Gentian (Eng) *Gentiana lutea* an ingredient in many herb liqueurs and apéritifs, bitter in flavour, it possesses digestive properties.

Gentiane (Fr)(Switz) a bitter liqueur digestif made from gentian and spirits. *see* Liqueur de Gentiane Sauvage, Suze.

Gentil (Fr) a lesser white grape variety of the Pinot family grown in Alsace.

Gentil (Fr) no real legal definition, the old Alsace name for noble, used for wines made with the Traminer and Gewurztraminer. Gentil Aromatique is the term now used for spicey wines.

Gentil Aromatique (Fr) an old name for the grape variety Gewurztraminer in Alsace.

Gentile-Groppellone (It) a variety of the red grape Groppello.

Gentilhomme [Le] (Eng) a 1 year old brandy imported by Kilsern Distillers of Leicester 36% alc by vol.

Gentilini (Gre) a 4ha. winery based in Cephalonia, white wine is made from Robola with Tsaoussi and Sauvignon blanc.

Gentilshommes de Fronsac (Fr) a wine brotherhood for the promotion of the wines of Fronsac, eastern Bordeaux.

Gentle (Eng) a term used to describe a wine as being unassertive and mild, pleasant to drink.

Gentle Ben Cocktail (Cktl) ⅓ measure vodka, ⅓ measure dry gin, ⅓ measure tequila. Shake over ice, strain into an ice-filled highball glass, top with fresh orange juice, a slice of orange and a cherry.

Gentleman Jack (USA) the label of a double filtered Bourbon whiskey 40% alc by vol.

Gentleman Jack (Eng) a 5% alc by vol. bottled strong ale brewed by Shepherd Neame.

Gentling (Eng) a term to describe the maturing of wines in casks, especially the hard tannic red wines of Spain.

Genuense (It) a white wine produced in north-western Italy during Roman times.

Genuina Lindoya (Bra) a natural spring mineral water from Serra da Mantiqueira. Mineral contents (milligrammes per litre): Sodium 8.2mg/l, Calcium 5.09mg/l, Magnesium 2.24mg/l, Potassium 2.5mg/l, Bicarbonates 43.95mg/l, Chlorides 1.54mg/l, Sulphates 0.54mg/l, Fluorides 0.25mg/l, Nitrates 4.21mg/l. pH 6.24

Geoffroy [Alain] (Fr) a winery based in the A.C. Chablis, Burgundy. Produces a range of Chablis wines including Premier Crus Fourchaume and Vau-Ligneau.

Geoffroy [René] (Fr) a Champagne producer. (Add): 150 Rue de Bois-de-Jots, Cumières, 51480 Daméry. 13ha. Vintages: 1988, 1990, 1991, 1995, 1996, 1997, 1998, 1999, 2001.

Geographe (Austr) a sub-region of Western Australia situated north of Margaret River.

Geographic Indications (Austr) abbr: G.I., a classification of areas (62 in total) according to climate and terroir.

Geokchai (Rus) a major wine-producing centre in Azerbaijan.

Geordie Pride (Eng) a 4.2% alc by vol. beer from Mordue Brewery, North Shields, Tyne & Wear.

George and Chestnut Teal (Austr) the brand-name of an Australian Sherry.

George Bateman & Son Ltd (Eng) *see* Bateman [George] & Son Ltd.

George Dickel Cascade Distillery (USA) a distillery based near Tullahoma, Coffee County, Tennessee. Produces Tennessee whiskey (a sour mash whiskey filtered through charcoal).

George Dickel Tennessee Sour Mash (USA) a sour mash whiskey produced by the Dickel (George) Cascade Distillery in Coffee County, Tennessee. Is filtered through activated charcoal, made from sugar maple wood. Two versions: Ivory label 7–10 year old, Ebony label: 6–7 year old.

George [EARL] (Fr) a winery based in the A.C.

Chablis, Burgundy. Produces a range of Chablis wines including Premier Cru Beauregards. 'E'mail: fevregilles@wanadoo.fr

George IV (Scot) a blended Scotch whisky produced by the DCL group 43% alc by vol.

George Gale & C° Ltd (Eng) *see* Gales [George] Brewery.

George Roullet (Fr) a Cognac producer based in the Grande Champagne, District: Charente.

George's (Wal) a large West Wales wholesaler who deals with Ansells Brewery. Has its own keg bitter George's Best 1037 O.G. which is brewed in Burton-on-Trent.

George's Best (Eng) a 4.4% alc by vol. best bitter ale brewed by Mauldon's Ltd., Suffolk.

Georges de Latour (USA) a private reserve Cabernet sauvignon wine produced by the Beaulieu Vineyards.

George's Home Brewed Ale (Eng) a bottled pale ale 1042 O.G. brewed by Courage, named after the Bristol Brewery that makes it.

Georges de Latour Private Reserve (USA) a red wine (Cabernet sauvignon) produced by the Beaulieu Vineyard, Napa Valley, California.

George Wright Brewing C° (Eng) a brewery (established 2003). (Add): 11 Diamond Business Park, Sandwash Close, Rainford, St. Helens, Merseyside WA11 8LU. Brews: Cheeky Pheasant 4.7% alc by vol., Drunken Duck 3.9% alc by vol., IPA 4.5% alc by vol., Kings Shillin' 4.5% alc by vol., Mizzen Mast 4.4% alc by vol., Winter Sun 4.2% alc by vol. Website: http://www.georgewrightbrewing.co.uk 'E.mail: george.dove@georgewrightbrewing.co.uk

Georgia (USA) a wine-producing state in south-eastern America. Produces mainly Concord and Muscadine wines.

Georgia (Geo) the main wine country between the Black and Caspian seas. Produces most styles of wines especially sparkling.

Georgia Mint Julep (Cktl) ⅓ measure brandy, ⅔ measure peach brandy, 1 teaspoon sugar, 2 sprigs mint. Crush mint and sugar together with a drop of water in a highball glass. Add ice and spirits, stir and dress with mint leaves and serve with straws.

Georgia Mountain Water (USA) a natural spring mineral water.

Georgian Rczaziteli (Rus) a white grape variety. *See also* Rcakziteli.

Georgie Porgie (Eng) a 3.7% alc by vol. session ale brewed by the Nursery Brewery, Keynsham, near Bristol.

Georg Scheu (Ger) a hybridiser who produced the Huxelrebe 1927 and the Scheurebe 1916.

Georg-Viktor-Quelle Heilwasser (Ger) a natural spring mineral water. Mineral contents (milligrammes per litre): Sodium 41.7mg/l, Calcium 202mg/l, Magnesium 103mg/l, Potassium 4.2mg/l, Chlorides 7.9mg/l, Sulphates 55.9mg/l, Fluorides 0.3mg/l, Iron 1.078mg/l.

Geppling (Aus) a vineyard site based on the banks of the River Kamp situated in the Kamptal region.

Geraci (It) a sparkling natural spring mineral water from Fonti di Pizzo Argentaria, Parco Naturale delle Madonie. Mineral contents (milligrammes per litre): Sodium 5.5mg/l, Calcium 6.6mg/l, Magnesium 2.53mg/l, Potassium 1mg/l, Bicarbonates 5.88mg/l, Chlorides 10.7mg/l, Sulphates 19.2mg/l, Nitrates 1.08mg/l, Silicates 10.9mg/l. pH 6.3

Geradstetten (Ger) village (Anb): Württemberg. (Ber): Württembergisch Unterland. (Gro): Wartbühl. (Vins): Litchenberg, Sonnenberg.

Geranium Odour (Eng) a wine malady, caused by the attack of **Lacto-bacillus** on sorbic acid. Occurs due to a lack of hygiene and has a smell of **Pelargonium**.

Gérant (Fr) an agent in Bordeaux who is responsible for the sale of wine from a Château.

Gérard Bertrand (Fr) a winery based in the A.C. Corbières, Languedoc-Roussillon. Grape varieties include: Mourvédre, Syrah. Label: Terroir.

Gerard 157 (N.Z) a white hybrid grape variety.

Gerasia (It) a natural spring mineral water from Ali, Messina, Sicily. Mineral contents (milligrammes per litre): Sodium 18.2mg/l, Calcium 34.4mg/l, Magnesium 7.3mg/l, Potassium 2.35mg/l, Bicarbonates 91.5mg/l, Chlorides 19.5mg/l, Sulphates 39.5mg/l, Nitrates 1mg/l, Silicates 20.4mg/l. pH 7.42

Gerbaude [La] (Fr) the traditional meal supplied by the vigneron to his vineyard and winery workers at the end of the harvest. Also spelt Gerbebaude.

Gerbebaude (Fr) an alternative spelling of Gerbaude.

Gerebelt (Ger) destalking of grapes.

Gerber Foods Soft Drinks Ltd (Eng) a soft drinks manufacturer (established 1983). (Add): 78 Wembdon Road, Bridgwater, Somerset TA6 7QR. Produces fruit and vegetable juices. Website: http://www.gerberfoods.com 'E'mail: info@gerberfoods.com

Gerente (Sp) the name given to a bodega manager.

Gerfroy (Fr) a natural spring mineral water. Mineral contents (milligrammes per litre): Sodium 127.6mg/l, Calcium 83.1mg/l, Magnesium 8.8mg/l, Potassium 0.7mg/l, Bicarbonates 398mg/l, Chlorides 50.5mg/l, Sulphates 111.6mg/l. pH 7.8

Gerhard Britz (S.Afr) a formery winery based in Hermanus, Walker Bay, Western Cape. Grape varieties: Cabernet franc, Cabernet sauvignon, Malbec, Merlot, Petit verdot, Sémillon. Label: Coalesce.

Gerhardt [Jakob] (Ger) a wine grower and merchant based in Nierstein. Market wines of Staatliche Weinbaudomäne Rheinhessia (state-owned vineyard of Rheinhessia) plus many northern German, French and other countries.

Gerichtstal (Aus) a vineyard site based on the banks of the River Kamp situated in the Kamptal region.

Gering (Ger) rather poor wine.

Gerk (Euro) the alternative spelling of Grk.

Gerlachsheim (Ger) village (Anb): Baden. (Ber): Badische Frankenland. (Gro): Tauberklinge. (Vin): Herrenberg.

G

Gerlingen (Ger) village (Anb): Württemberg. (Ber): Remstal-Stuttgart. (Gro): Weinsteige. (Vin): Bopser.

Germain (Fr) a liqueur producer based in St. Florent-sur-Auzonnet, southern France. Famous for Auzonnet, Fine Lachamp, Gorges du Tarn, Ravanello and Verveine du Rouvergue liqueurs.

Germain [Francois] (Fr) a Burgundy négociant-éleveur based in Beaune, Côte de Beaune, Burgundy.

Germain [H. et Fils] (Fr) a Champagne producer. (Add): 38 Rue de Reims, 51500 Rilly-La-Montagne. 80ha. Produces vintage and non-vintage wines. Vintages: 1971, 1973, 1975, 1976, 1979, 1981, 1982, 1983, 1986, 1988, 1990, 1995, 1996, 1998, 1999, 2000. De Luxe vintage cuvée: Grande Cuvée Venus Brut. Prestige Cuvée: Présidente.

Germain [Jean] (Fr) a négociant-éleveur based in Meursault, Côte d'Or, Burgundy. (Add): 9 Rue de la Barre, 21190 Meursault.

Germain Robin (USA) a distillery (established 1982). A grappa and brandy producer based in Mendocino County. Some brandies are aged in Limousin oak. 1,200 bottles of Anno Domini 2,000. Also an Anno Domini 2001. Both distilled from Pinot noir grapes. Also produce a 100% Colombard single barrel and grappa from Muscat and Zinfandel plus a 100% Viognier.

German Band Cocktail (Cktl) 40mls (⅓ gill) schnapps (Steinhäger), 20mls (⅙ gill) blackberry liqueur, dash bitters. Stir over ice and strain into a chilled cocktail glass.

German Coffee (Liq.Coffee) using a measure of kirsch.

German Gin (Ger) a light-flavoured gin with a hint of sweetness.

Germania (Ger) a low alcohol lager 0.9% alc by vol. from the Schwithein Bravarie.

German Purity Law (Ger) a 1516 law to control the production of beer. The Reinheitsgebot.

German Whiskey (Ger) a medium-flavoured whiskey made from a variety of grains (continuous stilled).

German Wine Gate (Ger) see Deutsches Weintor.

German Wine Law (Ger) law passed in 1971, gave strict controls on the production and labelling of German wines, partly reviewed in 1994.

German Wine Route (Ger) see Deutsche Weinstrasse.

Germany (Ger) the most northerly European wine-producing country. Produces mainly white wines which are, in the main, sweet in style. Some red wine is produced but this tends to be austere and is consumed locally. A sparkling wine called **sekt** is also produced. In 2001 two new wine terms were introduced to describe German dry wines. **Classic**: will cover dry style wines that are considered 'classic' of a particular region. **Selection**: will be used for dry style, top class wines from select sites. The front wine label must be simplified and should include one of the new terms plus the grape variety, vintage, region/site

plus the producer. see Amtliche Prüfungsnummer and Anbaugebiete for regions.

Germeta Quelle (Ger) a natural spring mineral water (established circa 1679) from Germete, NRW. Mineral contents (milligrammes per litre): Sodium 15mg/l, Calcium 210mg/l, Magnesium 43mg/l, Potassium 6mg/l, Bicarbonates 400mg/l, Chlorides 8mg/l, Sulphates 420mg/l.

Germeta Urquell (Ger) a natural spring mineral water. Mineral contents (milligrammes per litre): Sodium 14.2mg/l, Calcium 502mg/l, Magnesium 78.4mg/l, Potassium 3.3mg/l, Chlorides mg/l.

Germignac (Fr) a commune in the Charente-Maritime département whose grapes are classed Petite Champagne (Cognac).

Germigny (Fr) a Cru Champagne village in the Canton de Ville-en-Tardenois. District: Reims.

Germination (Eng) a term for barley after it has germinated (sprouts shoots to convert the starch into fermentable sugars) see Green Malt.

Gerolsheim (Ger) village (Anb): Pfalz. (Ber): Mittelhaardt-Deutsche Weinstrasse. (Gro): Schwarzerde. (Vins): Klosterweg, Lerchenspiel.

Gerolsteiner (Ger) a still (stille) and sparkling (sprudel) natural spring mineral water from Gerolstein. Mineral contents (milligrammes per litre): Sodium 119mg/l, Calcium 347mg/l, Magnesium 108mg/l, Potassium 10.8mg/l, Bicarbonates 1817mg/l, Chlorides 39.7mg/l, Sulphates 36.3mg/l, Fluorides 0.21mg/l, Nitrates 5.1mg/l, Silicates 40.2mg/l, Strontium 2.9mg/l. pH 7.0

Gerona (Sp) an area in the northern province which produces a variety of wine styles.

Geronimo (Cktl) 25mls (1fl.oz) each of white rum, orange juice, pineapple juice, 10mls (½ fl.oz) lime juice, dash Angostura, dash grenadine, shake well over ice, strain into an ice-filled collins glass and dress with a slice of pineapple and orange.

Geropiga (Port) a natural Port or special liquid made to sweeten other Portuguese wines. Also spelt Jeropiga.

Gerovassiliou (Gre) a 30ha. winery based at Epanomi, Thessaloniki. Grape varieties: Sauvignon blanc, Chardonnay, Viognier, Malagusia, Assyrtiko, Merlot, Syrah, Grenache.

Gers (Fr) a département in south-western France. Most of the wine is used in the production of Armagnac or in blending.

Gerst (Hol) barley.

Gerstel Lager (Hol) a low-alcohol lager 0.8% alc by vol. brewed by the Henninger Brauerei and imported into Britain by Courage.

Gesundbrunnen (Afr) a still natural spring mineral water from Namibia. Mineral contents (milligrammes per litre): Calcium 154mg/l, Magnesium 71mg/l, Chlorides 7.8mg/l, Sulphates 7.8mg/l, Fluorides 0.3mg/l, Nitrates 11.4mg/l, Hydrogene-Phosphate 2.9mg/l. pH 7.3

Gertrudenberg (Ger) vineyard (Anb): Mittelrhein. (Ber): Rheinburgengau. (Gro): Burg Hammerstein. (Vil): Dattenberg.

G

Gerümpel (Ger) vineyard (Anb): Pfalz. (Ber): Mittelhaardt-Deutsche Weinstrasse. (Gro): Hofstück. (Vil): Freidelsheim.

Gerümpel (Ger) vineyard (Anb): Pfalz. (Ber): Mittelhaardt-Deutsche Weinstrasse. (Gro): Mariengarten. (Vil): Wachenheim.

Geschmack (Ger) a term meaning taste. e.g. Nachgeschmach: aftertaste.

Gesellmann (Aus) a winery (17ha) based in Deutschkreutz, Mittel-Burgenland. (Add): Langegasse 65, 7301 Deutschkreutz. Grape varieties: Blaufränkisch, Cabernet sauvignon, Chardonnay, Merlot, Pinot noir, St. Laurent, Zweigelt. Labels: Bela Rex, Creitzer, Hochacker, Opus Eximium, Steinriegel.

Gesellschaft mit beschränkter Haftung (Ger) see GmbH.

Gesertifiseer (S.Afr) certified, found on the 'bottle stamp' of South African wines to certify that the contents are genuine. see Wine and Spirit Board.

Gesetz über Massnahmen auf dem Gebiete der Weinwirtschaft (Ger) formed the Fond law and regulations that govern German viticulture. Rules about setting up new plantations. abbr: Weinwirtschaftsgesetz.

Gestühl (Ger) vineyard (Anb): Baden. (Ber): Kaiserstuhl-Tuniberg. (Gro): Vulkanfelsen. (Vil): Jechtingen.

Gestühl (Ger) village (Anb): Baden. (Ber): Kaiserstuhl-Tuniberg. (Gro): Vulkanfelsen. (Vin): Leiselheim.

Getariako Txakolina (Sp) a 64ha. D.O. (established May 1990) vineyard area in the province of Guipúzcoa (Gipuzkoa) in the zone of País Vasco. Grape varieties used to produce Txakoli are Ondarribí Zuri (89%), Ondarribí Beltza (11%). 89% of wine produced is white. A small amount of red and a little rosé are also produced. All Txakoli wines are Jóvenes in style. Also known as Chacolí de Getaria.

Getashan (Arm) a dessert wine produced in Armenia.

Getaufer (Ger) watered wine.

Getränk (Aus)(Ger) beverage/drink.

Getränke (Ger) drinks.

Geur (Hol) aroma.

Gevrey-Chambertin (Fr) a top A.C. commune in the Côte de Nuits, Burgundy. Has 8 Grand Crus: [Chambertin, Chambertin-Clos de Bèze, Chapelle-Chambertin, Charmes-Chambertin, Griotte-Chambertin, Latricières-Chambertin, Mazoyères-Chambertin and Mazys (Mazis)-Chambertin] 96.37ha. plus 23 Premier Cru vineyards: [Au Closeau, Aux Combottes, Bel-Air, Champeaux, Champitennois (or Petite Chapelle), Champonnet, Cherbaudes, Clos du Chapitre, Clos-Prieur, Clos Saint-Jacques, Combe-au-Moine, Craipillot, En Ergot, Étournelles, Issarts (or Plantigone), La Perrière, Lavaut, Le Fonteny, Les Cazetiers, Les Corbeaux, Les Goulots, Poissenot and Varoilles] 83.61ha.

Gewächs (Ger) vineyard of.

Geweerloop (Hol) barrel/vat.

Gewoon (Hol) lit: 'normal', a term used to denote a 25mls glass.

Gewürz (Ger) means spicy, applied to a variety of the Traminer grape called the Gewürztraminer.

Gewürzgärtchen (Ger) vineyard (Anb): Rheinhessen. (Ber): Bingen. (Gro): Sankt Rochuskapelle. (Vil): Horrweiler.

Gewürzgarten (Ger) vineyard (Anb): Rheinhessen. (Ber): Bingen. (Gro): Rheingrafenstein. (Vil): Hackenheim.

Gewurztraminer (Fr) the French (Alsace) spelling of Gewürztraminer, also used in many ‚New World' countries.

Gewürztraminer (Ger) lit: 'spicy traminer', a white grape variety that produces wines with an aroma and taste of spice (ginger and cinnamon), lychees, tropical fruits, herbs, roses. Can also be attacked by noble rot to produce luscious sweet wines. First produced in the Trentino-Alto Adige and now used in the Rhine, Alsace, Austria and New World. Spelt Gewurztraminer in France. see Gelber Traminer, Gentil Aromatique, Traminer, Weisser Traminer.

Geyer Brewery (USA) a brewery based in Frankenmuth, Michigan. Is noted for krausened beers that are fermented in open iron tanks.

Geyerhof (Aus) a winery based in the Kremstal region. (Add): Oberfucha 3, 3511 Furth. Grape varieties: Grüner veltliner, Riesling, Malvasier, Neuberger, Zweigelt. Produces a range of wine styles.

Geyersberg (Ger) vineyard (Anb): Rheinhessen. (Ber): Bingen. (Gro): Abtey. (Vil): Sankt Johann.

Geyersberg (Ger) vineyard (Anb): Rheinhessen. (Ber): Bingen. (Gro): Kurfürstenstück. (Vil): Gau-Weinheim.

Geyersberg (Ger) vineyard (Anb): Rheinhessen. (Ber): Wonnengau. (Gro): Gotteshilfe. (Vil): Bechtheim.

Geyser Peak Winery (USA) a large winery based in Sonoma County, California. 166ha. (Add): 22281 Chianti Road, Geyserville, California 95441. Produces a range of wine styles from a large variety of grapes. Owns Kuimelis Vineyard, also owns vineyards in the Russian River Valley. Label: Block Collection. Website: http://www.geyserpeakwinery.com

Geyserville (USA) a noted wine town in the Alexander Valley, Sonoma County, California.

Geyserville (USA) the label for a red wine (Carignane 18%, Petite syrah 8%, Zinfandel 74% blend) produced by the Ridge Vineyard winery, Cupertino, California.

Gezuckert (Ger) sugared. i.e. verbessert, or improved.

G.F.B. (Eng) a 3.5% alc by vol. ale brewed by the Hop Back Brewery.

Ghadeer (Jor) a natural spring mineral water from Petra, Sharah Mountains. Mineral contents (milligrammes per litre): Sodium 34.5mg/l, Calcium 54mg/l, Magnesium 24mg/l, Potassium 0.7mg/l, Bicarbonates 220mg/l, Chlorides 50mg/l, Sulphates 22mg/l. pH 7.3

596

G

Gharb (Afr) a wine-producing region in Morocco. Contains the A.O.G. areas of Chellah, Gharb, Zaer and Zemmour. Soil: sandy.

Gharb (Afr) an A.O.G. area within the region of Gharb in Morocco.

Ghemme (It) a D.O.C.G. red wine from Piemonte. Made from the Bonarado novarese 15%, Nebbiolo 60%–80% and Vespolina 10%–30%. Has to age 4 years (3 years in oak/chestnut cask).

Gherardi (Austr) a winery based in the Margaret River region of Western Australia.

Ghezala (Afr) a noted co-operative based in Tunisia. One of 14 that belongs to the UCCVT.

Ghiaccio (It) ice.

Ghioroc (Rum) a wine-producing area, part of the Banat Vineyard.

Ghirgentina (Euro) a white grape variety grown on the island of Malta. Known as the Inzolia in Sicily.

Ghost Ale (Eng) a 4.1% alc by vol. ale brewed by the Darwin Brewery, Tyne & Wear.

Ghost Buster (Eng) a 5.1% alc, by vol. ale which has the appearance of bright green slime. Brewed by the Fox and Newt in Leeds, West Yorkshire.

Ghost Gum (S.Afr) the label for a red wine (Cabernet franc, Cabernet sauvignon, Merlot and Petit verdot blend) produced by the Stony Brook winery, Franschhoek, Western Cape.

Ghost on the Rim (Eng) a 4.5% alc by vol. ale brewed by the Anglo Dutch Brewery, West Yorkshire.

Ghost Tree (S.Afr) the label for a rosé wine (Cabernet and Chenin blanc blend) produced by the Sylvan Vale Vineyards winery, Stellenbosch, Western Cape.

Ghurdjurni (Rus) a white table wine produced in the region of Georgia.

G.I. (Austr) *abbr:* **G**eographical Indications.

Gi (Eng) *abbr:* **gi**ll.

Giacomo Conterno (It) a winery based in Serralunga in the Piemonte region. Produces: Barolo Cascina Francia and Barolo Monfortino Riserva.

Giaconda (Austr) a winery (established 1982) based 9kms from Beechworth, Victoria. Grape varieties: Cabernet sauvignon, Pinot noir, Chardonnay.

Giada (It) a natural spring mineral water from Giada.

Gianaclis Vineyard (Egy) a noted winery based at Abú-Hummus, north-west of the Nile Delta. Produces mainly white wines with a little red. *see* Cru des Ptolemées and Reine Cléopatre (both white wines).

Giant Filtered Drinking water (USA) a bottled spring mineral water from Washington.

Giant Springs (USA) a natural spring mineral water from Giant Springs Heritage State Park, Great Falls, Montana. Mineral contents (milligrammes per litre): Calcium 88mg/l, Magnesium 31mg/l, Bicarbonates 246mg/l, Sulphates 148mg/l, Fluorides 0.6mg/l, Nitrates 0.5mg/l. pH 7.6

Giara (It) a sparkling natural spring mineral water from Giara. Mineral contents (milligrammes per litre): Sodium 54mg/l, Calcium 11.22mg/l, Magnesium 8.99mg/l, Potassium 2.6mg/l, Bicarbonates 56.1mg/l, Chlorides 73.14mg/l, Sulphates 14.39mg/l, Fluorides 0.2mg/l, Nitrates 25.2mg/l, Silicates 28.5mg/l. pH 6.87

Giardinella (It) a still and sparkling natural spring mineral water from Sorgente 'Giardinella'. (pink label: sparkling/blue label: still). Mineral contents (milligrammes per litre): Sodium 9.3mg/l, Calcium 74.2mg/l, Magnesium 19.2mg/l, Potassium 0.7mg/l, Bicarbonates 292.8mg/l, Chlorides 23.4mg/l, Nitrates 0.1mg/l. pH 7.1

Giardini (Eng) a herbal fruit drink produced by Bulmers and sold in a blue glass bottle. Blend of pear and lemon juices, burnet, heartease, gentian, feverfew and elder.

Giarone (It) a barrique-aged D.O.C. Barbera d'Asti wine produced by De Bertelli in Piemonte.

Giascosa Bruno (It) a large winery based in Piemonte. Noted for Barbaresco, Barbera d'Alba, Barolo and Nebbiolo d'Alba wines.

Gibberellic Acid (Eng) a sugar-based natural acid which is added to barley that has been steeped in water to encourage embryo development in the malting process.

Gibbons (USA) the brand-name used by the Lion Brewery in Wilkes-Barre, Pennsylvania for a range of their beers.

Gibbs Mew (Eng) a brewery based in Salisbury, Wiltshire. Also owns Seymour Soft Drinks in Sherbourne, Dorset. Noted for cask-conditioned Wiltshire Bitter 1036 O.G. Salisbury Best 1042 O.G. Bishop's Tipple 1066 O.G. Chairman's Choice 1039 O.G. Moonraker Brown 1032 O.G. and Sarum Special 1048 O.G.

Gibbston Valley Wines (N.Z) a winery. (Add): Main Queenstown-Cromwell Highway, SH 6, Gibbston, RD 1, Queenstown. 3.5ha. Grape varieties: Pinot noir, Riesling, Sauvignon blanc, Gewürztraminer, Pinot gris, Chardonnay, Sauvignon blanc, Müller-Thurgau.

Gibier (Fr) lit: 'game', a term used to denote older red wines that have a pronounced aroma, '*ripe or well hung*'.

Gibó (It) the name used by Giovanni Bosca for a range of vermouths, Marsalas and sparkling wines.

Giboudot Blanc (Fr) a lesser name for the Aligoté grape in southern France.

Gibralta Springs (Can) a natural spring mineral water from Gibralta Springs. Mineral contents (milligrammes per litre): Sodium 3mg/l, Calcium 80mg/l, Magnesium 25mg/l, Potassium 2mg/l, Bicarbonates 290mg/l, Chlorides 5mg/l, Sulphates 6mg/l, Nitrates 1.4mg/l. pH 7.2

Gibson (Cktl) ⅔ measure dry gin, ⅓ measure dry vermouth. Stir together with ice and strain into a cocktail glass. Add a pearl onion. Another version has a piece of garlic in place of the onion!

Gibson Vineyards (USA) a winery based in Fresno, California. Produces generic table and dessert wines which are sold under the Château Moreau, Cresta Bella and Gibson Vineyards labels.

Giddy Ass (Eng) a barley wine from the Steampacket Brewery in West Yorkshire.

Giebelhöll (Ger) vineyard (Anb): Mittelrhein. (Ber): Rheinburgengau. (Gro): Lahntal. (Vil): Weinähr.

Giesen Wine Estate (N.Z) a winery. (Add): Burnham School Road, N°5 RD, P.O. Box 11066 Christchurch. 35ha. Grape varieties: Riesling, Chardonnay, Müller-Thurgau, Sauvignon blanc, Cabernet franc, Cabernet sauvignon, Pinot noir, Merlot. Website: http://www.giesen.co.nz

Giesler (Fr) a Champagne producer. Produces vintage and non-vintage wines. Vintages: 1900, 1904, 1906, 1911, 1914, 1921, 1926, 1928, 1934, 1937, 1941, 1943, 1945, 1947, 1949, 1952, 1953, 1955, 1959, 1961, 1962, 1964, 1966, 1969, 1970, 1971, 1973, 1975, 1978, 1982, 1985, 1990, 1991, 1995, 1996, 1997, 1998, 1999, 2000, 2001.

Giessen (Aus)(Ger) to pour.

Gieten (Hol) to pour.

Giffard (Fr) a distillery (established 1855) based in Anjou-Saumur, Loire. Produces a wide range of liqueurs. Noted for Menthe Pastille at 24% alc by vol.

Giggle Water (USA) a slang term used for Champagne or other sparkling wines, especially in the 1920's–1930's.

Gigondas (Fr) an A.C. red and rosé wine district of the southern Rhône 1,250ha. Reds are full-bodied. Grape varieties include Grenache, Syrah, Mourvèdre, Cinsault.

Gilbert Holl Distillery & Craft Brewery (Fr) a brewery and distillery. (Add): 8 Avenue Jacques Preiss, F-68340 Riquewhr. Produces sprits, beers and lager. Website: http://www.gilbertholl.com 'E'mail: info@gilbertholl.com

Gilberts (Port) a vintage Port producer, controlled by Burmester. Vintages: 1963, 1984, 1985, 1991, 1994, 1997, 2003.

Gilbey [S.A.] (Fr) a Bordeaux négociant-éleveurs and owners of Château Loudenne.

Gilbey [W.A.] (Eng) a large wines and spirits merchants. (Add): Gilbey House, Fourth Avenue, Harlow Essex. CM20 1DX. (Part of IDV).

Gilbey Canada Ltd. (Can) a large distillery which produces a range of Canadian whiskies etc. Pallister Distillers is a subsidiary company.

Gilbey Distillers and Vintners (S.Afr) *see* Gilbeys Ltd.

Gilbeys Distillers & Vintners (Pty) Ltd. (S.Afr) a large wine merchant based in Stellenbosch. (Add): Box 137, Stellenbosch 7599. Wines sold under a large variety of labels such as Alphen, Bertrams, Klein Zalze, Montagne, Stellenvale etc. A subsidiary of W. & A. Gilbey, London.

Gilbey Vintners (Eng) a distillery based in Harlow, Essex. Produces a range of spirits including gin and Smirnoff vodka (under licence from the USA). *See also* Gilbey (W.A).

Gilde Brauerei (Ger) a brewery based in Hanover. Brews: Ratskeller (a lager sold in a flip-top bottle), Diät Pils 6.2% alc by vol. Pils 5.5% alc by vol. Deluxe Bier 5.1% alc by vol. Bölkstoff 4.9% alc by vol.

Gilde de Saint-Vincent de Belgique (Bel) a wine brotherhood.

Gilde Diät Pils (Ger) a 6.2% alc by vol. lager brewed by the Gilde Brauerei.

Gildenbier (Bel) a Münchener-style dark beer brewed at the Diest Brasserie. Is matured for 9 months.

Gilden Kölsch (Ger) a 4.8% alc by vol. kölsch beer brewed by the Gilden Kölsch Brauerei, Cologne.

Gilde Taffel (Nor) the brand-name of an akvavit produced by the A/S Vinmonopolet.

Giles Vineyard (USA) a small independent vineyard based in Sonoma County, California. 2.5ha. Grape varieties include: Chardonnay.

Gil Galan (Sp) a brandy producer based in Jerez de la Fontera. Solera Reserva brandies include Condestable, Formidable, Legislador, Romancero.

Gilga Wines (S.Afr) a winery (established 1998) based in Vlottenburg, Stellenbosch, Western Cape. Grape variety: Syrah. Website: http://www.gilga.com

Gilka Kümmel (Ger) a caraway and cumin-flavoured liqueur made in Berlin 40% alc by vol.

Gill (Eng) *abbr*: Gi. 5fl.ozs ¼ imperial pint (125mls).

Gill (Eng) a slang term for "*Let's go for a gill*", a term used in the north for "*Let's go for a drink*". Used to mean '*½ pint of beer*'.

Gillan Estate Wines (N.Z) a winery. (Add): Rapaura Road, P.O. Box 482, Blenheim. 15ha. Grape varieties: Sauvignon blanc, Chardonnay, Merlot. Produce still and traditional method wines.

Gille (Fr) a mediaeval word for vat, tub.

Gillenza (Euro) a black grape variety grown on the island of Malta. Is known as the Mammolo in Italy.

Gillespies (Sp) a 4% alc by vol. draught or canned draught malt stout from Scottish & Newcastle in Edinburgh. Revival of the Dumbartonshire Brewery which operated from 1810–1952.

Gillet [Jean-Pierre] (Fr) a producer of sparkling Vouvray based at Parcay-Meslay, Touraine, Loire.

Gillies and C°. (Scot) a company based in Glasgow. Produces Royal Culross (a blended malt whisky).

Gill Measure (Eng) graded to allow the measuring of such fractions as ½ gill, ⅓ gill, ¼ gill, ⅕ gill and ⅙ gill (now no longer used as only metric measures are now legal).

Gilmour [Duncan] (Eng) an old brewery based in Sheffield. Brews: Balaclava (a strong ale), a Milk and Oatmeal Stout.

Gilon (Isr) a sweet, dark, dessert wine which is similar in style to Málaga.

Gilroy (USA) a vine-growing district in southern Santa Clara, California.

Gilroy Cocktail (Cktl) ½ measure gin, ½ measure cherry brandy, juice ¼ lemon, dash orange bitters, 4 dashes dry vermouth. Shake well over ice and strain into a cocktail glass.

Gilt Edge (Austr) the brand-name of a whiskey produced by Gilbeys.

Gimblett Gravels (N.Z) a new appellation based on soil types. 800ha. of vines in Hawkes Bay, North Island consisting of 34 wineries and growers. A minimum of 95% of the grapes must be from Gimblett Gravels.

Gimbsheim (Ger) village (Anb): Rheinhessen. (Ber): Nierstein. (Gro): Krötenbrunnen. (Vins): Liebfrauenthal, Sonnenweg.

Gimeux (Fr) a commune based in the Charente-Maritime département whose grapes are classed Grande Champagne (Cognac).

Gimileo (Sp) a wine-producing village in the Rioja Alta, north-eastern Spain.

Gimlet (Cktl) ⅔ measure dry gin, ⅓ measure lime juice cordial, shake over ice, strain into an ice-filled highball glass and add a good splash of soda.

Gimlet (Eng) a sharp, pointed metal implement used to penetrate casks and often used to remove corks from bottles. (Fr) = foret.

Gimmeldingen (Ger) village (Anb): Pfalz. (Ber): Mittelhaardt-Deutsche Weinstrasse. (Gro): Meerspinne. (Vins): Biengarten, Kapellenberg, Mandelgarten, Schlössel.

Gimonnet [Pierre et Fils] (Fr) a Champagne producer (established 1750). (Add): 1 Rue de la République, 51200 Épernay. Récoltants-manipulants. 25ha. Produce vintage and non-vintage wines. Vintages: 1995, 1996, 1997, 1998, 1999, 2000. A member of the Club Tresors de Champagne. Labels include: Brut Fleuron and Brut Gastronome (both 100% Chardonnay), Brut Oenophile (100% Chardonnay but no dosage), Cuvée Spécial Millésimé (100% Chardonnay). Website: http://www.champagne-gimonnet.com

Gin (Eng) the rectified neutral spirit distilled from any grain, potato or beet and flavoured with Juniper. *see* London Dry, Plymouth Dry and Old Tom. (Fr) = genièvre, (Ger) = wacholder-schnaps, (Hol) = jenever, (It) = ginepro, (Port) = genebra, (Sp) = ginebra, (Wal) = jin.

Gin Acts (Eng) first passed in 1736, was designed to help reduce the amount of gin shops and to make the spirit too expensive for the working classes to drink. It put a tax on gin and introduced the need for a licence to sell spirits.

Gin Alexander (Cktl) also known as Princess Mary. *see* Alexander.

Gin Aloha (Cktl) ½ measure dry gin, ½ measure Cointreau, 15mls (⅛ gill) pineapple juice, dash orange bitters. Shake well over ice and strain into a cocktail glass.

Gin and Bitters (Cktl) *see* Pink Gin.

Gin and French (Cktl) ½ measure of dry gin and ½ measure of French (dry white) vermouth. Stir over ice and strain into a cocktail glass.

Gin and It (Cktl) ½ measure dry gin and ½ measure Italian (sweet red) vermouth,tir over ice, strain into a cocktail glass and top with a cocktail cherry. Also known as a Gin and Italian. (Den) = gin og sød.

Gin and Italian (Cktl) *see* Gin and It.

Gin and Sin (Cktl) 25mls (⅕ gill) dry gin, 25mls (⅕ gill) lemon juice, 15mls (⅛ gill) orange juice, dash grenadine. Shake over ice and strain into a cocktail glass.

Gin and Tansy (Eng) is produced by macerating a bunch of tansy in a bottle of gin for 3–4 weeks. Served 'on the rocks'.

Gin and Tonic (Cktl) 1 measure of dry gin placed into an ice-filled highball glass. Top with soda water and a slice of lemon.

Gin & Vodka Association of Great Britain (Eng) an organisation (established 1950). (Add): Cross Keys House, Queen Street, Salisbury, Wiltshire SP1 1EY. Website: http://www.ginvodka.org.uk 'E'mail: gva@ginvodka.org.uk

Gin Aurum (Cktl) ³⁄₁₀ measure aurum, ⁴⁄₁₀ measure gin, ³⁄₁₀ measure lemon juice, dash grenadine. Shake over ice and strain into a cocktail glass.

Ginger Brandy (Eng) place 50grms of peeled ginger root into 1litre of brandy, store for 6-8 weeks, strain and use.

Gin Buck (Cktl) 25mls (⅕ gill) dry gin, juice ½ lemon. Place into an ice-filled highball glass, stir and top with ginger ale.

Gin Cobbler (Cktl) gin, barspoon sugar, 4 dashes orange Curaçao, fill a medium sized wine glass with ice, add a measure of gin, sugar and Curaçao. Stir, decorate with fruit, add a sprig of mint and serve with straws.

Gin Cocktail [1] (Cktl) 40mls (⅓ gill) gin, 2 dashes brown Curaçao, 1 dash Angostura bitters. Stir over ice, strain into a cocktail glass and decorate with a cherry and a dash of lemon peel juice.

Gin Cocktail [2] (Cktl) 2 measures gin, 3 dashes orange bitters, shake over ice, strain into a cocktail glass and add a twist of orange peel.

Gin Cooler (Cktl) place ½ teaspoon powdered sugar and 50mls (2fl.ozs) soda water into a collins glass. Stir, add ice and 40mls (⅓ gill) dry gin. Top with soda water and decorate with a spiral of orange peel and lemon peel.

Gin Crusta (Cktl) 40mls (⅓ gill) dry gin, 1 teaspoon maraschino, 1 dash Angostura, 1 dash orange bitters, 1 teaspoon syrup. Shake over ice, strain. Moisten inside of wine glass with lemon juice and with ½ teaspoon of sugar, serve with spiral of lemon peel and slices of fresh fruit.

Gin Daisy (Cktl) 60mls (½ gill) dry gin, 15mls (⅛ gill) lemon juice, 15mls (⅛ gill) grenadine. Shake over ice, strain into a highball glass and fill with soda water and serve with slices of fresh fruit.

Gin de Prunelles (Ch.Isles) sloe gin. *See also* Du Gin de Prunelles.

Ginder (Bel) a beer (abbaye-style) brewed by the Artois Brasserie in Louvain.

Ginebra (Sp) gin.

Ginepro (It) gin (juniper).

Ginepy (It) a green or white liqueur with an anise flavour.

Ginestet (Fr) noted Bordeaux négociants.

Gin Fix (Cktl) 60mls (2½ fl.ozs) gin, 25mls (1fl.oz) lemon juice, teaspoon gomme syrup. Build into a wine goblet filled with crushed ice. Stir lightly, add a slice of lemon and serve with straws.

Gin Fizz (Cktl) 35mls (1½ fl.ozs) dry gin, 1 teaspoon sugar. Stir together with ice until sugar has dissolved and top up with soda water in a highball glass.

Ginger Ale (Eng) carbonated water, ginger extract and sugar. Is non-alcoholic. e.g. American Dry, Canada Dry, Dry Ginger, etc. (Den) = sodavand med ingefærsmag.

Ginger Ale Cup (Cktl) 1 litre ginger ale, 1 tablespoon sugar, 60mls (½ gill) brandy, 30mls (¼ gill) lime juice, 30mls (¼ gill) maraschino, 2–3 dashes Bénédictine. Stir over ice, strain and serve in a highball glass with lemon/orange slices and sprigs of mint.

Ginger Beer (Eng) ginger, sugar, water and yeast (fermented), cream of tartar, tartaric acid or lemon essence may be included (alcohol content is below 2% by vol.).

Ginger Beer (Eng) a 4.6% alc by vol. ale brewed by Enville Ales Ltd., West Midlands.

Ginger Brandy (Eng) a ginger-flavoured brandy. Has a deep, tawny colour.

Ginger Fizz (Cktl)(Non-alc) 300mls (½ pint) cold tea, juice of an orange and ½ a lemon, sugar to taste, ginger ale. Stir all together over ice and decorate with a slice of orange.

Ginger Flavoured Brandy (USA) a brandy based liqueur infused with ginger root.

Ginger Highball (Cktl) 40mls (⅓ gill) Bourbon whiskey stirred over ice in a highball glass, top with ginger ale and a piece of ginger root.

Ginger Liqueur (Hol) made from ginger roots steeped in spirit.

Ginger Marble (Eng) a 4.5% alc by vol. ale brewed by Marble Beer, Greater Manchester.

Ginger Mist Cocktail (Cktl) 2 measures Irish Mist in an ice-filled highball glass, top with ginger ale and a squeeze of lemon peel juice.

Ginger Rum Tea (Cktl) pour 25mls (⅕ gill) dark rum into a cup of black tea and top with a piece of preserved ginger. Can be served hot or cold.

Ginger Snap (Eng) a dark wheat beer containing root ginger brewed by Salopian Brewery in Shrewsbury, Shropshire.

Ginger Square (Cktl) 25mls (1fl.oz) ginger brandy, 25mls (1fl.oz) ginger ale. Stir both together and build into an ice-filled highball glass.

Ginger Tea (Eng) *see* Cold Ginger Tea.

Ginger Tom (Eng) a 4.2% alc by vol. ale brewed by the Filo Brewing Company, East Sussex.

Ginger Tom (Eng) a ginger beer 5% alc by vol. (1050 O.G.) from Midsummer Leisure.

Ginger Wine (Eng) a grape wine base with ginger and spices, herbs and fruits added. *see* Crabbie's and Stones.

Gin Gin (Cktl) equal measures of Booth's gin, Crabbie's Green Ginger Wine and orange squash. Shake over ice and strain into a large cocktail glass.

Ginginha (Port) fruit wines.

Gin Head (Eng) a unit at the point where freshly distilled vapours have to pass through. Is packed with juniper and botanicals, the flavour of which is extracted by the vapour as it passes through.

Gin Highball (Cktl) 20mls (⅙ gill) gin, 20mls (⅙ gill) soda water. Place a lump of ice into a highball, add gin and soda and serve with slice of lemon.

Gini (Bel) a lemon and tonic drink produced by Boire Citron Français in 20cls cans.

Ginjinha (Port) cherry brandy.

Gin Julep (Cktl) as for Mint Julep but substituting gin for brandy.

Gin Lane (Eng) the name of Hogarth's famous eighteenth century painting depicting the deprivation of gin drinking of the age.

Gin Long Drink (Fin) a gin and grapefruit drink.

Gin Milk Punch (Cktl) 50mls (2fl.ozs) dry gin, 200mls (⅓ pint) milk, 1 teaspoon powdered sugar. Shake over ice, strain into a collins glass and top with grated nutmeg.

Gin og Sød (Den) Gin an It (cocktail).

Gin Palace (Eng) an eighteenth and early nineteenth century name given to the more respectable public houses of the time.

Gin Punch (Punch) 300mls (½ pint) gin, 150mls (¼ pint) maraschino, juice of 3 lemons. Blend together, chill down. Serve in chilled highball glasses with ice, top with soda water and dress with a lemon peel spiral.

Gin Ricky [1] (Cktl) 1 measure dry gin, juice of 1 lime. Build into an ice-filled old-fashioned glass, add spent lime shell and stir in soda water.

Gin Ricky [2] (Cktl) 50mls (2fl.ozs) dry gin, juice ½ lemon. Place ice into a small tumbler, stir in ingredients, add rind of lemon and top with soda water.

Gin Sangaree (Cktl) dissolve ½ teaspoon of powdered sugar in 1 teaspoon of water in a highball glass. Add ice and 50mls (2fl.ozs) gin. Top with soda water, float 15mls (⅛ gill) Port on top and dress with grated nutmeg.

Ginseng Beer (Chi) a 4.8% alc by vol. beer produced by the Zhao Qing Brewery in the Guangdong province. Brewed using spring water from the Dinghu mountains. Contains malt, rice, hops and ginseng.

Ginseng Ju (E.Asia) a liqueur produced by Jinro of Seoul, South Korea. Has a large piece of ginseng root in each bottle.

Ginseng Piu Chiew (E.Asia) a type of choum, infused with a root native to North Vietnam. Various types: Ruou Cuc (chrysanthemum), Ruou Tam (slightly sparkling) and Ruou Tiêt dê (alcohol and goat's blood).

Ginseng Ruou Cuc (E.Asia) *see* Ginseng Piu Chiew.

Ginseng Ruou Tam (E.Asia) *see* Ginseng Piu Chiew.

Ginseng Ruou Tiêt Dê (E.Asia) *see* Ginseng Piu Chiew.

Ginseng Tea (E.Asia) a tissane produced from the ginseng root, is drunk for its aphrodisiac properties.

Gin Sling (Cktl) add to a large tumbler containing a large piece of ice, juice ¾ lemon, ½ tablespoon powdered sugar, 1 measure gin. Top with water, float a dash of Angostura on top and decorate with a slice of lemon.

G

Gin Sling [Hot] (Cktl) dissolve a sugar cube in 150mls (¼ pint) hot water in an old-fashioned glass. Add 1 measure dry gin, stir, top with grated nutmeg and a lemon slice.

Gin Smash (Cktl) dissolve a little sugar in 1 measure of water, 1 measure gin, 3 sprigs of mint and ice. Shake well together, strain into a wine glass, dress with fruit in season and serve with a spoon.

Gin Sour (Cktl) 50mls (2fl.ozs) gin, juice ½ lemon, ½ teaspoon sugar, dash egg white. Shake well with ice and strain into a cocktail glass.

Gin Squirt (Cktl) 1 measure dry gin, 1 teaspoon grenadine, 1 teaspoon gomme syrup. Stir over ice, strain into an ice-filled highball glass. Top with soda water and dress with a pineapple cube and a fresh strawberry.

Ginstbronnen (Bel) a natural spring mineral water from Ginst, Scheldwindeke.

Ginstbergbronnen (Bel) a natural spring mineral water from Ginstberg, Scheldewindeke.

Gin Swizzle (Cktl) 25mls (1fl.oz) gin, 10mls (½ fl.oz) lime juice, 2 dashes gomme syrup, 2 dashes Angostura. Build into a 300mls (12fl.oz) glass filled with crushed ice, fill glass with soda water and serve with a small swizzle stick.

Gin Thing (Cktl) 1 measure dry gin, juice ½ lime. Pour into an ice-filled highball glass, stir and top with ginger ale.

Gin Toddy (Cktl) place ½ teaspoon sugar and 2 teaspoons water into a highball glass. Stir, add 50mls (2fl.ozs) dry gin and ice cubes. Stir and add a twist of lemon peel juice.

Gin Toddy [Hot] (Cktl) place a sugar cube into an old-fashioned glass, fill ⅔ boiling water. Add 50mls (2fl.ozs) dry gin, slice of lemon and top with grated nutmeg.

Gin Tropical (Cktl) ¾ measure gin, ½ measure passion fruit juice, juice ¼ orange and lemon. Shake over ice, strain into an ice-filled highball glass, top with soda water, stir, add a dash of blue Curaçao, dress with a cherry and serve with straws.

Gioia di Colle Rosso (It) a D.O.C. red wine produced from Primitivo grapes in Southern Italy.

Giol (Arg) a large state-owned co-operative in the province of Maipu. Deals with bulk wines and has a premium range under the Canciller label.

Giogio (S.Afr) the label for a red wine (Cabernet sauvignon 70% and Merlot 30%) produced by the Dalla Cia Wine Company, Stellenbosch, Western Cape.

Gioiosa della Valsesia (It) a sparkling natural spring mineral water from Gioiosa della Valsesia. Mineral contents (milligrammes per litre): Sodium 4.22mg/l, Calcium 5.88mg/l, Magnesium 0.93mg/l, Potassium 0.43mg/l, Bicarbonates 15.68mg/l, Chlorides 2mg/l, Sulphates 6.1mg/l, Nitrates 7.5mg/l, Silicates 15.43mg/l. pH 6.03

Giovanni (Austr) a red (Cabernet sauvignon) wine produced by the Sinclair Estate, Western Australia.

Gipfel (Ger) grosslage (Anb): Mosel-Saar-Ruwer. (Ber): Obermosel. (Vils): Bitzengen, Fellerich, Fisch, Helfant-Esingen, Kirf, Köllig, Kreuzweiler, Meurich, Nittel, Oberbillig, Onsdorf, Palzem, Portz, Rehlingen, Soest, Tawern, Tammels, Wasserliesch, Wehr, Wellen, Wincheringen.

Gips (Ger) vineyard (Anb): Württemberg. (Ber): Remstal-Stuttgart. (Gro): Weinsteige. (Vil): Fellbach.

Gips (Ger) vineyard (Anb): Württemberg. (Ber): Remstal-Stuttgart. (Gro): Weinsteige. (Vil): Stuttgart (ortsteil Untertürkheim).

Gipsy [1] (Cktl) ⅓ measure Bénédictine, ⅔ measure vodka, dash Angostura. Shake over ice and strain into a cocktail glass.

Gipsy [2] (Cktl) ¼ measure Mandarine Napoléon, ¾ measure Cognac, ¾ measure dry gin, ¾ measure cherry brandy. Shake together with ice in a highball glass, top with tonic water and garnish with a slice of orange and a cherry.

Gipsy's Brew (Punch) 550mls (1pint) gin, 1.1ltrs. (1quart) ale, 2 x 15cms (6ins) roots of horseradish. Mix gin and ale, grate in horseradish, stand for 3 days, strain and bottle. Considered to be good for arthritis.

Gir (It) a red grape variety grown in Sardinia.

Giradet Wine Cellars (USA) winery (established 1971). 7.5ha. based in Roseburg, Oregon. Grape varieties: Pinot noir, Cabernet sauvignon, Chardonnay, Riesling, White zinfandel, Baco noir, Seyval blanc.

Girardin Brasserie (Bel) a brewery based in St-Ulricks-Kapelle in northern Belgium. Noted for its fruity lambic beers.

Girasols (Sp) lit: 'sunflower' metal racks which are mechanical and replace the old pupîtres which were operated by hand (remuage). Used for all cava wines in Spain. *see* Crecelles, Giro-Palettes and Gyropalettes. Holds 540 bottles.

Giraud [Paul] (Fr) a Cognac producer. (Add): Bouteville, 16120 Châteauneuf. 28ha. in the Grande Champagne. Produces a wide range of Cognacs.

Giraudeau [Yves] (Fr) a small producer of Muscadet based at Pont-James, St. Colomban, Nantes, Loire.

Girault-Artois (Fr) a crèmant de Loire producer based at Amboise, Loire.

Girelli (It) a producer of sparkling (metodo tradizionale) wines based in Veneto.

Girgentina (Euro) a white grape variety grown on the island of Malta. Also known as the Insolia.

Girl's Wines (Eng) usually applied to the sweet white wines such as Sauternes and Barsac. *see* Lady's Wine.

Girò (It) a red grape variety grown in Sardinia, produces sweet, soft, velvety still and dessert wines.

Girò di Cagliari (It) a D.O.C. red wine from Sardinia. Made from the Girò grape from the province of Cagliari. Vinification and ageing must occur in the region. 4 types produced: Dolce naturale, Secco, Liquoroso dolce naturale and Liquoroso secco. The last two are fortified and if aged for 2 years (1 year in wood) then classed Riserva. Grapes can dry on vines or on frames.

G

Girò di Sardegna (It) a red dessert wine of Sardinia.

Gironde [River] (Fr) a river in western France in the Bordeaux region. Is made up of the rivers Dordogne and Garonne and runs to the Bay of Biscay. Has the Médoc along its west bank.

Girone (It) a name used in Sardinia for the Bovale grande red grape.

Giro-Palettes (Fr) the name for the crecelles (automatic remueur). See also Girasols, Giro-Pallets and Gyropalettes.

Giro-Pallets (Eng) the name for the automatic remueurs. See also Crecelles, Giro-Palettes and Gyropalettes.

Girrawheen (Austr) a winery based in the Granite Belt, Queensland.

Girvan Distillery (Scot) a grain whisky distillery based in south-west Scotland.

Gisborne (N.Z) an area on the east coast of the North Island noted for quality Müller-Thurgau wines.

Gisselbrecht [Louis] (Fr) a noted Alsace wine producer based in Dambach-la-Ville 5ha.

Gist (Hol) yeast.

Gisten (Hol) ferment.

Gisting (Hol) fermentation.

Gitana [La] (Sp) a brand of Manzanilla Sherry produced by Vinícola Hidalgo in Sanlúcar de Barrameda.

Giulia (It) a slightly acidic, sparkling natural spring mineral water from Rome. Mineral contents (milligrammes per litre): Sodium 53mg/l, Calcium 90mg/l, Magnesium 21.3mg/l, Potassium 74mg/l, Bicarbonates 510mg/l, Chlorides 44mg/l, Sulphates 47mg/l, Fluorides 1.4mg/l, Nitrates 4.6mg/l, Silicates 102mg/l, Strontium 2.4mg/l. pH 5.75

Giumarra Vineyards (USA) a winery based near Bakersfield, Kern County, California. 1,660ha. Grape varieties: Cabernet sauvignon, Chardonnay and Zinfandel. Produces varietal wines.

Giunone (It) a natural spring mineral water from Sorgente, Brentella.

Giustina-Leitac (It) see Leitacher.

Giustro di Notri (It) an I.G.T. Cabernet and Merlot blend red wine produced by Villa Monte Rico, Suvereto, Maremma, Tuscany.

G.I.V. (It) abbr: Gruppo Italiano Vini.

Give Us A Try (Eng) a 4.1% alc by vol. dark event ale brewed by Ridleys Hartford End Brewery, Chelmsford, Essex. Available in March.

G.I.VI.S.O. (Fr) abbr: Groupement d'Intéret Économique des Vignerons du Sud-Ouest.

Givreur [Le] (Bel) a commercial™ automatic 'glass froster', frosts drinking glasses so enhancing presentation.

Givry (Fr) a district within the Côte Chalonnaise in southern Burgundy. Produces A.C. red wines from the Pinot noir grape and some white wines.

Givry-les-Loisy (Fr) a Cru Champagne village in the Canton de Vertus. District: Reims.

G.L. (Fr) abbr: Gay Lussac.

G.L.A.A.S. (Eng) abbr: Greater London Alcohol Advisory Service, a body who with Alcohol Concern ran a campaign of 'Think before you drink' to promote moderate drinking in the early 1980's.

Glacé (Fr) chilled.

Glace [à la] (Fr) a method of dégorgement using dry ice to freeze the neck of the bottle. See also Volée (A La).

Glaceau Smart Water (USA) a natural spring mineral water.

Glaceau Vitamin Water (USA) a vapourised, distilled water enriched with vitamins and minerals.

Glacé Noir (Can) the label for a red wine (Pinot noir) produced by the Warm Lake Estate, Niagara Escarpment.

Glacial Moraine (Eng) a soil containing medium and large boulders which were deposited during the Ice Age.

Glaciar (Arg) a vapourised, distilled water fortified with vitamins and minerals. Mineral contents (milligrammes per litre): Sodium 10mg/l, Calcium 20.7mg/l, Bicarbonates 18.1mg/l, Chlorides 36.3mg/l.

Glaciar (Port) a natural spring mineral water from Manteigas. Mineral contents (milligrammes per litre): Sodium 1.9mg/l, Calcium 0.9mg/l, Bicarbonates 5.8mg/l, Chlorides 1.5mg/l, Silicates 8 mg/l. pH 6.0

Glacier Brewhouse (USA) a brewery. (Add): 737 W 5th Avenue, Suite 110, Anchorage, Alaska 99501. Brews a variety of beers and lager. Website: http://www.glacierbrewhouse.com 'E'mail: info@glacierbrewhouse.com

Glacier Mint (Cktl) 1 dash P.L.J., 25mls (1fl.oz) vodka, 10mls (½ fl.oz) green crème de menthe. Stir with ice, strain into a sugar-rimmed glass and decorate with a sprig of mint.

Glacier Water (Austr) a still and sparkling natural spring mineral water from the Highlands of Victoria. Mineral contents (milligrammes per litre): Sodium 8mg/l, Calcium 4mg/l, Magnesium 3.5mg/l, Potassium 1mg/l, Bicarbonates 28mg/l, Chlorides 8.5mg/l. Website: http://www.glacier.com.au

Glaçon(s) (Fr) ice.

Glad Eye (Cktl) 40mls (⅓ gill) Pernod, 30mls (¼ gill) Peppermint Get. Shake well over ice and strain into a cocktail glass.

Gladiator (Eng) a 3.8% alc by vol. ale brewed by the Hadrian & Border Brewery, Tyne & Wear.

Gladiador (Sp) a solera reserva brandy produced by Real Tesoro.

Gladiator's Courage (Eng) a 3.5% alc by vol. ale brewed by Feast & Firkin, Leeds.

Gladstone Bitter (Eng) a 4.3% alc by vol. cask and 5% alc by vol. bottled bitter from McMullens in Hertfordshire.

Gladstone Vineyard and Winery (N.Z) a winery. (Add): Gladstone Road, P.O. Box 2, Gladstone, Wairapa. 3ha. Grape varieties include: Sauvignon blanc.

Glaetzer Wines (Austr) a winery based in the Barossa Valley, South Australia. Grape varieties include:

Cabernet sauvignon, Shiraz. Labels: Amon Ra, Godolphin.

Glamis 90 (Scot) 25 year old Scotch whiskies blended to commemorate the H.M. Queen Mother's 90th birthday. Sold in a crystal decanter.

Glamour Cocktails (Eng) the name given to colourful cocktails designed for female and young drinkers that are usually decorated with toys and trimmings as part of the garnish.

Glan Usk (Wal) a dry gin produced by the Brecon Brewery Company in south Powys.

Glasgow Flip (Cktl) *see* Lover's Dream.

Glashäger (Ger) a sparkling natural spring mineral water from Quellental bei Glashägen, Bad Doberahn. Mineral contents (milligrammes per litre): Sodium 10mg/l, Calcium 94mg/l, Magnesium 8mg/l, Potassium 1mg/l, Bicarbonates 240mg/l, Chlorides 27mg/l, Sulphates 77mg/l.

Glass (Ire) a term used for a half pint of beer.

Glass (Eng) a clear vessel used for holding cold beverages for drinking, the clearness of the glass allows the full appreciation of the drink's colours and its shape will help in the appreciation of the bouquet. *see* Crystal Glass and Glass Excise Acts. (Fr) = verre, (Ire) = gloire, (It) = coppa, (Port) = copo, (Sp) = coppa.

Glass Balloon (USA) the American name for the vacuum method of coffee brewing.

Glass Cloth (Eng) a soft cloth made of linen used for the drying and polishing drinking glasses.

Glass Cork (Eng) *see* Vino-Lok.

Glass Excise Acts (Eng) 1745 a tax levied on glass according to the weight of materials used in manufacture. Glass became light and elegant. *see* Rococo.

Glassing (Eng) a slang term used for the offensive criminal action of pushing a beer glass into the face of an opponent in a public house brawl.

Glass of Beer (Eng) a request for a half pint of draught ale (mild or bitter). (Ire) = gloine leann.

Glass of Wine (Eng) a request for a 125mls measure of wine. (Fr) = verre du vin, (Ire) gloine fhióne.

Glass Ring (Eng) found on the neck of early flasks or decanters so that the cork could be secured with string.

Glastonbury Ales (Eng) a brewery (established 2001). (Add): Unit 10, Wessex Park, Somerton Business Park, Somerton, Somerset TA11 6SB. Brews: Golden Chalice 4.8% alc by vol., Hedgemonkey 4.6% alc by vol., Lady of the Lake 4.2% alc by vol., Mysterytor 3.8% alc by vol. Website: http://www.glastonburyales.com 'E'mail: glastonburyales@ukonline.com

Glastwr (Wal) milk and water.

Glatt (Ger) smooth.

Glatzen (Ger) vineyard (Anb): Franken. (Ber): Maindreieck. (Gro): Kirchberg. (Vil): Neuses.

Glatzer (Aus) a winery based in Göttlesbrunn, Carnuntum. (Add): 2464 Göttlesbrunn 76. Grape varieties: Blaufränkisch, Cabernet sauvignon, Chardonnay, Zweigelt. Label: Gotisprun.

Glayva (Scot) a famous whisky-based liqueur flavoured with herbs and spices 35% alc by vol.

Glayva Belgravia Special (Cktl) 1 measure Glayva, 1 measure dry vermouth. Stir with ice in a highball glass, top up with cola and finish with a slice of lemon.

Glayva Celebration (Cktl) 25mls (1fl.oz) Glayva, 25mls (1fl.oz) passion fruit juice. Stir together with ice, strain into a flute glass and top with iced Champagne.

Glayva Champagne Cocktail (Cktl) soak a cube of sugar with Angostura in a highball glass. Add 10mls (½ fl.oz) Glayva and top with iced dry Champagne.

Glayva Champagne Punch (Punch) 100mls (⅙ pint) each of Glayva, Cognac, maraschino, 200gms (½ lb.) sugar, 1litre (2pints) Perrier water, 1litre (2 pints) Champagne. Mix together in a punch bowl over ice and add fruits in season.

Glayva Ciderific (Cktl) bring 1litre (2pints) cider to the boil, remove from the heat and add 50mls (⅖ gill) Glayva. Pour into mugs, add a knob of butter, lemon slice, cinnamon stick and clove to each mug.

Glayva Cider Punch (Punch) 75mls (3fl.ozs) Glayva, 1litre (2pints) chilled sweet cider, 200mls (⅓ pint) soda water, 75mls (3fl.ozs) dry Sherry, 25mls (1fl.oz) lemon juice. Mix together in a punch bowl over ice. Flavour with nutmeg and sugar and decorate with apple slices and borage.

Glayva Collins (Cktl) 25mls (1fl.oz) Glayva, 100mls (4fl.ozs) soda water, 50mls (2fl.ozs) lemon juice, 10mls (½ fl.oz) gomme syrup. Place ingredients into an ice-filled 250mls (10fl.oz) highball glass. Stir, top with soda water, lemon slice and serve with straws.

Glayva Gleam (Cktl) 25mls (⅕ gill) Glayva, 15mls (⅛ gill) orange Curaçao, ½ egg white, dash lemon juice. Shake well over ice and strain into a cocktail glass.

Glayva Highball (Cktl) pour 25mls (1fl.oz) Glayva into an ice-filled highball glass. Stir in 100mls (4fl.ozs) dry ginger ale and top with a twist of lemon.

Glayva Horses Neck (Cktl) place 25mls (1fl.oz) Glayva in a 250mls (10fl.oz) slim jim glass with a lemon peel spiral on inside, top with ginger ale and a dash of Angostura.

Glayva Hot Toddy (Cktl) place 1 teaspoon of brown sugar and 1 measure of Glayva into a 300mls (½ pint) mug. Top with boiling water, stir, add a lemon slice and a teaspoonful of honey.

Glayva Iceberg (Cktl) in a 250mls (10fl.oz) slim jim glass place some ice and 35mls (1½ fl.ozs) Glayva. Stir in chilled milk and top with grated nutmeg.

Glayva Mai Tai (Cktl) 25mls (1fl.oz) golden rum, 25mls (1fl.oz) white rum, 10mls (½ fl.oz) Glayva, 5mls (¼ fl.oz) lime juice, dash grenadine. Build into a large, ice-filled old-fashioned glass. Decorate with a cherry and mint and serve with straws.

Glayva Old Fashioned (Cktl) place a sugar cube in

G

an old-fashioned glass. Soak with Angostura, add enough water to dissolve the sugar. Fill with ice, add 25mls (⅙ gill) Glayva, dress with an orange slice and a cherry.

Glayva Passion (Cktl) ⅓ measure Glayva, ⅓ measure Scotch whisky, ⅓ measure passion fruit juice. Shake over ice and strain into a large cocktail glass.

Glayva Sour (Cktl) 35mls (1½ fl.ozs) Glayva, 50mls (2fl.ozs) lemon juice, 10mls (½ fl.oz) sugar, dash egg white. Shake over ice and strain into an ice-filled large goblet.

Glayva Sunset (Cktl) 25mls (1fl.oz) Glayva, 25mls (1fl.oz) amaretto, 100mls (4fl.ozs) orange juice. Shake together over ice, strain into a 250mls (10fl.oz) slim jim glass. Add a dash grenadine and an orange slice and serve with straws.

Glayva Tammy (Cktl) ½ measure Glayva, ½ measure Glenlivet malt whisky. Stir with ice in an old-fashioned glass and dress with a twist of lemon peel juice.

Glayva Tropical Punch (Punch) 2 bottles Glayva, 700mls (1¼ pints) passion fruit juice, 700mls (1¼ pints) orange juice, 150mls (¼ pint) lemon squash. Mix together and chill for 2 hours, pour into a punch bowl with ice, add 1 litre (2pints) Perrier water and fruit in season.

Glazebrook Vineyard (N.Z) a winery based in Hawkes Bay, North Island Grapre varieties: Cabernet sauvignon, Merlot. Label: Ngatarawa Wines.

Gleichenberger Johannisbrunnen (Aus) a sparkling natural spring mineral water (established 1678) from Johannisbrunnen-Hof, Straden, Steiermark. (blue label: sparkling/yellow label: low gas). Mineral contents (milligrammes per litre): Sodium 1020mg/l, Calcium 187mg/l, Magnesium 107.7mg/l, Potassium 44mg/l, Bicarbonates 3420mg/l, Chlorides 279mg/l, Fluorides 1.4mg/l, Iron 6.32mg/l.

Gleisseln (Aus) a vineyard site based on the banks of the River Kamp situated in the Kamptal region.

Gleisweiler (Ger) village (Anb): Pfalz. (Ber): Südliche Weinstrasse. (Gro): Bischofskreuz. (Vin): Hölle.

Gleiszellen-Gleishorbach (Ger) village (Anb): Pfalz. (Ber): Südliche Weinstrasse. (Gro): Kloster Liebfrauenberg. (Vins): Frühmess, Kirchberg.

Glen Albyn (Scot) a single malt whisky distillery on the banks of the Caledonian canel basin. Owned by MacKinleys and Birnie Ltd. Produce a 15 year old whisky at 45% alc by vol. A highland malt.

Glenallachie (Scot) a single highland malt whisky distillery based north-west of Dufftown. Produce a 12 years old. 43% alc by vol. Part of Charles MacKinlay & Cº.

Glenallan Spring (Scot) a natural spring mineral water from Blackford, Perthshire.

Glenalwyn (Austr) a winery based in the Swan Valley, Western Australia.

Glenburgie-Glenlivet (Scot) a single highland malt whisky distillery. Owned by J. and C. Stodart Ltd. Produce a 16 year old whisky at 45% alc by vol (part of Hiram Walker).

Glenburn (N.Z) a small winery in the Kumeu area of Riverhead.

Glen Burn (Scot) a single highland malt whisky distillery based at Leith. Produces a 10 year old whisky 40% alc by vol.

Glenburn Spring (Scot) a natural spring mineral water from Lennoxtown, Glasgow.

Glencadam (Scot) a single highland malt whisky distillery based near to the river Esk, half a mile out of Brechen. Owned by Hiram Walker Group. Produces a 14 year old whisky 45% alc by vol.

Glencairn Spring (Scot) a natural spring mineral water from Campsie Fells, Lennoxtown, Glasgow. Mineral contents (milligrammes per litre): Sodium 6mg/l, Calcium 26mg/l, Magnesium 6mg/l, Potassium <1mg/l, Bicarbonates 81mg/l, Chlorides 7mg/l, Sulphates 10mg/l, Fluorides 0.1mg/l, Nitrates 3mg/l.

Glen Calder Fine Old Scotch Whisky (Scot) a de luxe Scotch whisky which is blended by Gordon and MacPhail of Elgin 40% alc by vol.

Glen Carlou Vineyard (S.Afr) a winery (established 1984) based in Klapmuts, Paarl, Western Cape. 70ha. Grape varieties: Cabernet franc, Cabernet sauvignon, Chardonnay, Merlot, Pinot noir, Sauvignon blanc, Shiraz, Touriga, Viognier, Zinfandel. Labels: Grand Classique, Tortoise Hill. Website: http://www.glencarlou.co.za

Glencoe (Scot) a vatted malt whisky. Produced by R.N. MacDonald & Cº. at the Ben Nevis Distillery. 8 year old 56% alc by vol.

Glencoe Wild Oat Stout (Scot) the name for a stout brewed from wild oats by the Bridge of Allan Brewery, Ltd., Stirlingshire.

Glendale Spring (Afr) a natural spring mineral water from Glendale, Zimbabwe. Mineral contents (milligrammes per litre): Sodium 16mg/l, Calcium 65.7mg/l, Magnesium 29.5mg/l, Potassium 4.2mg/l, Bicarbonates 354mg/l, Chlorides 11.6mg/l, Sulphates 17.6mg/l, Fluorides 0.1mg/l, Nitrates 0.6mg/l. pH 7.5

Glendale Spring (Scot) a natural spring mineral water from Blackford, Tayside, Perthshire. Mineral contents (milligrammes per litre): Sodium 26.5mg/l, Calcium 32.1mg/l, Magnesium 7.3mg/l, Potassium 0.9mg/l, Bicarbonates 152mg/l, Chlorides 26mg/l, Sulphates 11mg/l, Fluorides 0.1mg/l, Nitrates 1.7mg/l. pH 7.4

Glen Darbach (Scot) a 12 year old malt (Speyside) whisky 40% alc. b vol. Produced by Burn Stewart Distillers for Marks and Spensers.

Glen Deveron (Scot) a single highland malt whisky distillery owned by William Lawson. Produce a 5, 10 and 15 year old at 43% alc by vol.

Glendeveron (Scot) another name for the malt whisky MacDuff.

Glen Distilleries of Cork (Ire) a distilling company based in Cork, Eire that closed in 1925.

Glendronach (Scot) a single highland malt whisky distillery based in the valley of Forgue, 9 miles from Huntley in Aberdeenshire. Owned by William Teacher and Sons Ltd. 8, 12 and 18 year

G

old produced. Also a 15 year old, 100% of which is matured in Sherry casks.

Glen Drummond (Scot) a vatted malt whisky. Blended Speyside malts. Produced by Melrose-Drover of Leith.

Glendullan (Scot) a single highland malt whisky distillery based at Dufftown. Part of M^{ac}Donald Greenlees,

Gleneagles (Scot) a natural spring mineral water from The Maltings, Blackford, Tayside, Perthshire.

Gleneagles Maltings (Scot) a natural spring mineral water (established 1979). (Add): The Maltings, Moray Street, Blackford, Auchterarder, Perthshire PH4 1QF. Owned by Highland Spring. Website: http://www.highland-spring.com 'E'mail: enquiries@highland-spring.com

Glenelg (W.Ind) a natural spring mineral water from Glenelg, Granada. Mineral contents (milligrammes per litre): Calcium 35mg/l, Magnesium 41mg/l.

Glen Elgin (Austr) an estate belonging to Tulloch Vineyards based near Polkobin, New South Wales.

Glen Elgin (Scot) a single highland malt whisky distillery near Longmorn, Elgin in Morayshire. Owned by White Horse Distilleries. Produce an 8 year and 12 year old malt whisky 43% alc. by. vol (part of the DCL group).

Glen Ellen (USA) a noted wine town in the Sonoma Valley, California.

Glen Ellen Winery (USA) a small winery based in the Sonoma Valley, California. 13.5ha. Grape varieties: Cabernet sauvignon, Chardonnay.

Glenesk (Scot) a single highland malt whisky distillery from the Hillside Distillery, near Montrose, Angus. Produce a 12 year old whisky. Also 1982 40% alc by vol. cask-conditioned whisky. Licence held by William Sanderson & Son.

Glenfarclas (Scot) a single highland malt whisky distillery based near Marypark, Ballindalloch in Banffshire. Owned by J. and G. Grant. Produces an 8, 10, 12, 15, 21, 25 and 30 year old, 105° Proof (cask strength) plus Glenhaven 17 year old. Also known as Glenfarclas-Glenlivet.

Glenfarclas-Glenlivet (Scot) *see* Glenfarclas.

Glenfiddich (Scot) a natural spring mineral water from Dufftown, Banffshire.

Glenfiddich (Scot) a a world reknown single highland malt whisky distillery (established 1886) based at Dufftown in Banffshire. Owned by the Grant family. Produce an 8, 12, 15, 18 and 50 year old whisky. 40% alc by vol. Also a 12 y.o. Caoran Rerserve 45% alc by vol., 18 y.o. Ancient Reserve and Malt Whisky Liqueur at 40% alc by vol. Website: http://www.glenfiddich.com

Glenfinnan (Scot) a 12 year old blended malt whisky.

Glen Flagler (Scot) a single malt whisky distillery once produced by Moffat. Now owned by Inver House Distillers, based at Airdrie. A lowland malt whisky.

Glenforres (Scot) a vatted malt whisky blended from the output of the Edradour Distillery. Owned by the Glenforres Glenlivet Distillery C°. Distributed by William Whiteley and C°. 43% alc by vol.

Glen Foyle (Scot) a single malt whisky distillery, a highland malt whisky.

Glenfyne (Scot) a single malt whisky distillery based near Loch Fyne. A highland malt whisky.

Glen Garioch (Scot) a single highland malt whisky distillery based in Meldrum. Owned by Morrison Bowmore Distillers in Aberdeenshire. Produce a 21 year old, 43% alc by vol. Also a 1972 vintage.

Glengarr (Scot) a natural spring mineral water from Westown Farm, Sorn, Ayrshire.

Glengarry Winery (Austr) a winery based in Tasmania.

Glenglassaugh (Scot) a single highland malt whisky distillery based in north-eastern Scotland near the river Deveron (now closed).

Glengoyne (Scot) a single highland malt whisky distillery based near Dumgoyne, Stirlingshire. Owned by the Lang Brothers. Produce an 8 and 10 year old at 40% alc by vol. Also a 17 year old at 43% alc by vol., a 25 year old Vintage Reserve and a Vintage 1971 at 48.5% alc by vol. (only 2100 bottles produced). Website: http://www.glengoyne.com

Glen Grant (Scot) a single highland malt whisky distillery near the village of Rothes in Morayshire. Owned by The Glenlivet Distillers, a part of the Seagram empire. Produce an 8 year old at 56% alc by vol. 10 year old, 15 year old at 40% and 56% alc by vol. 21 year old at 40% alc by vol. and a 25 year old at 40% alc by vol. Known as Glen Grant-Glenlivet.

Glen Grant-Glenlivet (Scot) *see* Glen Grant.

Glenhurst (S.Afr) the label for a range of wines produced by the Ouoin Rock Winery, Stellenbosch, Western Cape.

Glenkeith-Glenlivet (Scot) a single highland malt whisky distillery in Keith. Owned by the Chivas Brothers. Produce a 10 and 12 year old malt, 45% alc by vol. Also a 1983 vintage at 43% alc by vol. (Part of Seagram).

Glen Kella (I.O.M) a single malt white whiskey, re-distilled from Kella Distillers. 40% alc by vol. Originally known as Kella White.

Glenkinchie (Scot) a single malt whisky distillery in the Glen of Kinchie. Owned by John Haig and C°. Produce a 10 year old 40% and 43% alc by vol. and a 13 year old whisky 45% alc by vol. A lowland malt (part of DCL group).

Glenleven (Scot) a blended malt whisky. 12 year old, 6 different malts. Produced by John Haig and C°. Ltd.

Glenlivet (Scot) the most famous glen in Scotland on the Speyside. Produces the finest highland malt whiskies.

Glenlivet [The] (Scot) *see* The Glenlivet.

Glenlivet and Glen Grant Distillers Limited (Scot) an amalgamation of Glen Grant and George and J.G. Smith. Later on then became known as the Glenlivet Distillers Limited.

Glenlivet Distillers Limited (Scot) originally known as Glenlivet and Glen Grant Distillers Limited (owned by Seagram).

Glenlivet Spring Water [The] (Scot) the label of a sparkling spring water.

Glenlochy (Scot) a single malt whisky distillery, a rare highland malt.

Glenlossie-Glenlivet (Scot) a single highland malt whisky distillery based 4 miles outside Elgin in Morayshire (owned by the D.C.L. Group). Produce a 21 year old whisky at 45% alc by vol.

Glenloth Winery (Austr) a vineyard based in Reynella, Southern Vales, New South Wales. Grape varieties: Cabernet sauvignon, Shiraz.

Glenmark Wines (N.Z) a winery. (Add): Weka Plains, Mackenzies Road, N°3 RD, Amberley, Waipara. 8ha. Grape varieties: Chardonnay, Riesling, Cabernet sauvignon.

Glen Mhor (Scot) a single highland malt whisky distillery based in Inverness. Produce an 8 year old whisky (part of the DCL group) 40% alc by vol.

Glen Mist (Scot) a whisky-based liqueur flavoured with herbs, spices and honey. Matured in whisky casks. 2 styles: Red seal 40% alc by vol. and dry in taste and Gold seal 23% alc by vol. and sweet in taste.

Glen Mister (Cktl) 1 measure Glen Mist, 1 measure Roses lime juice. Shake together over ice, strain into a highball glass and add tonic or bitter lemon to taste.

Glenmorangie (Scot) a single highland malt whisky distillery (established 1853) based in Coy, Tain, Ross-shire. (Add): Macdonald House, 18 Westerton Road, Broxburn, West Lothian EH52 5AQ. Owned by MᵃᶜDonald and Muir. Produce a 10 and 18 year old whisky at 43% alc by vol. plus a single barrel 1972 vintage. Madeira, Sherry and Port wood casks used. A 15 year old is aged in white American oak casks. Website: http://www.glenmorangie.com 'E'mail: pmiles@glenmorangieplc.co.uk

Glen Moray (Scot) a single highland malt whisky distillery based near Elgin in Morayshire. Owned by MᵃᶜDonald and Muir. Produce a 10, 12 and 17 year old whisky at 43% alc by vol. plus a 1966 vintage and a 1959 vintage (500 bottles only).

Glenmore (USA) a Bourbon whiskey distillery based in Louisville and on the Indiana border in Kentucky. Produce a Bourbon whiskey of same name 40% alc by vol.

Glen Moriston Estates (Scot) whisky distillers based in Glenmoriston, Invermoriston, Loch Ness. *see* Old Farm.

Glenny Brewery (Eng) a brewery (established 1983) based in Witney, Oxfordshire. Produce a cask-conditioned Witney Bitter 1037 O.G. and Wychwood Best Bitter 1044 O.G. *see* Clinch's Brewery.

Glen Oran (Scot) the old name used for Glen Ord malt whisky distillery.

Glenora Wine Cellars (USA) a winery (established 1974) based in Dundee in the AVA Seneca, Finger Lakes region of New York State.

Glen Ord (Scot) a single highland malt whisky distillery (formerly known Glen Oran). Produced by Dewar's. 12 year old, 43% alc by vol.

Glen Orrin (Scot) a natural spring mineral water

from the highlands of Scotland. Mineral contents (milligrammes per litre): Sodium 9mg/l, Calcium 61mg/l, Magnesium 5mg/l, Potassium 2.5mg/l, Bicarbonates 246mg/l, Chlorides 15mg/l, Sulphates 8mg/l, Nitrates 9mg/l. pH 7.0

Glenpatrick (Ire) a natural spring mineral water from Tipperarary. Mineral contents (milligrammes per litre): Sodium 13mg/l, Calcium 123mg/l, Magnesium 19mg/l, Potassium 1mg/l, Bicarbonates 363mg/l, Chlorides 18mg/l, Sulphates 16mg/l, Nitrates 10mg/l.

Glen Rosa (S.Afr) the label for a red wine (Merlot, Cabernet franc and Cabernet sauvignon blend) produced by the Schalkenbosch Wines winery, Tulbagh, Western Cape.

Glen Rossie (Scot) a blended Scotch whisky produced by Laing 37.5% alc by vol.

Glen Rothes (Scot) a single highland malt whisky distillery (established 1879) based near Rothes in Morayshire. Owned by the Highland Distillers Ltd. Produce an 8 year old whisky, 43% alc by vol. Also 1972, 1974, 1979, 1992 vintages. Known as the Glen Rothes-Glenlivet. Website: http://www.theglenrothes.com

Glen Rothes-Glenlivet (Scot) *see* Glen Rothes.

Glenrowan (Austr) a wine-producing area in north-eastern Victoria. Noted for heavy full red wines.

Glen Scotia (Scot) a single Campbeltown malt whisky distillery based at Campbeltown, Mull of Kintyre. Produce a 5 and 8 year old whisky. 43% alc by vol. Produced by Amalgamated Distilled Products.

Glenside (Scot) a blended Scotch whisky produced by Laing 37.5% alc by vol.

Glen Spey (Scot) a single malt whisky distillery based north of Inverness. Produces an 8 year old highland malt whisky at 43% alc by vol. Part of International Distillers and Vintners.

Glen Talloch (Scot) an 8 year old single highland malt whisky distilled in Scotland and bottled in Holland from Carmichael and Sons, Aidrie 43% alc by vol.

Glentauchers (Scot) a single highland malt whisky distillery based north of Dufftown.

Glenturret (Scot) a single highland malt whisky distillery. Produce 8, 12 and 15 year old malt whiskies 43% alc by vol.

Glenturret Fairlie's (Scot) a 24% alc by vol. malt whisky liqueur from Glenturret.

Glenturret Original Malt Liqueur (Scot) a 35% alc by vol. malt whisky liqueur from Glenturret.

Glentworth Brewery (Eng) a brewery (established 1996). (Add): Glentworth House, Crossfield Lane, Skellow, Doncaster, South Yorkshire DN6 8PL. Brews: Dizzy Blonde 4.5% alc by vol., Full Monty 5% alc by vol., Light Year 3.9% alc by vol. 'E'mail: glentworth.brewery@btopenworld.com

Glenugie (Scot) a single highland malt whisky distillery based near Peterhead. Produces a 14 year old at 45% alc by vol. whisky and a 1966 vintage.

Glenury-Royal (Scot) a single highland malt whisky distillery based south of Aberdeen.

G

Glenvale Winery (N.Z) a winery. (Add): Main Road, Bay View, Hawkes Bay. 75 ha of which 20 are at Bay View and 50 at Esk Valley.

Glenview Wines (S.Afr) a winery (established 1998) based in Paarl, Western Cape. Grape varieties: Chenin blanc, Merlot. Produces varietal wines. Website: http://www.glenview.co.za

Glen Wood (S.Afr) a winery (established 2000) based in Franschhoek, Western Cape. 21.5ha. Grape varieties: Chardonnay, Merlot, Pinotage, Sauvignon blanc, Shiraz. Label: Vignerons Reserve. Website: http://www.glenwood.co.za

Glenwood Inglewood (USA) a natural spring mineral water from California.

Gleukos (Gre) sweet wine.

Gleumes (Ger) a 4.9% alc by vol. altbier brewed by Arthur Gleumes Brauerei, Krefeld.

Glewinski (Eng) a range of vodka cocktails at 37.5% alc by vol. Flavours include: raspberry, strawberry, chocolate and vanilla.

Glimmerschiefer (Ger) slate soil mainly found in Franken.

Gloag [Matthew] & Son Ltd. (Scot) a distillery based in Perth. Noted whisky producer. Products also include a traditional distilled London gin 40% alc by vol.

Gloag's Gin (Scot) a 40% alc by vol. London gin distilled by Gloag (Matthew) & Son, Perth.

Globe (Wal) a home-brew public house based in Fishguard, Dyfed. Noted for cask-conditioned Black Fox 1038 O.G. (using malt extract).

Glöck (Ger) vineyard (Anb): Rheinhessen. (Ber): Nierstein. (Gro): Auflangen. (Vil): Nierstein.

Glockenberg (Ger) vineyard (Anb): Rheinhessen. (Ber): Nierstein. (Gro): Sankt Alban. (Vil): Gau-Bischofsheim.

Glockenzehnt (Ger) vineyard (Anb): Pfalz. (Ber): Mittelhaardt-Deutsche Weinstrasse. (Gro): Meerspinne. (Vil): Mussbach.

Glögg (Punch) 1 bottle red wine, 1 bottle medium Sherry, 75gms (3ozs) powdered sugar, ½ bottle brandy, 8 dashes Angostura. Heat, pour into mugs containing raisins and unsalted almonds.

Gloine (Ire) glass (drinking).

Gloine Fhióne (Ire) glass of wine.

Gloine Seirise (Ire) copita/Sherry glass.

Gloire de Montpellier (Fr) USA root stock used for grafting in the Rhône.

Gloom Chaser [1] (Cktl) ¼ measure grenadine, ¼ measure Grand Marnier, ¼ measure white Curaçao, ¼ measure lemon juice. Shake over ice and strain into a cocktail glass.

Gloom Chaser [2] (Cktl) 25mls (1fl.oz) dry vermouth, 35mls (1½ fl.ozs) gin, ½ teaspoon grenadine, 2 dashes Pernod. Shake over ice and strain into a cocktail glass.

Gloom Lifter [1] (Cktl) ⅔ measure Scotch whisky, ⅓ measure brandy, juice ½ lemon, 2 dashes gomme syrup, 4 dashes raspberry syrup, ½ egg white. Shake over ice, and strain into an ice-filled highball glass.

Gloom Lifter [2] (Cktl) 25mls (⅓ gill) Irish whiskey, juice of ½ lemon, 2 dashes gomme syrup, 1 egg white. Shake over ice and strain into a cocktail glass.

Gloom Raiser (Cktl) 20mls (⅙ gill) dry gin, 20mls (⅙ gill) Noilly Prat, 2 dashes grenadine, 2 dashes absinthe. Stir over ice, strain into a cocktail glass and add a squeeze lemon peel juice on top.

Gloria (Ger) a white grape variety, a cross between the Sylvaner and the Müller-Thurgau. An early ripener which gives good sugar but has a neutral flavour.

Gloria Ferrer (USA) a winery based in the Carneros, California. Grape variety: Pinot noir. Label: José S. Ferrer.

Gloria Mundi (Mad) a popular bone-dry Sercial Madeira produced by Leacocks and Cº. for the USA market.

Glorioso (Sp) a red wine produced by Bodegas Palacio in the Rioja Alavasa, north-eastern Spain.

Glorious Goldings (Eng) a single varietal hop bitter ale 4% alc by vol. from Whitbread.

Glorious Twelfth (Scot) a de luxe blended Scotch whisky of 12 years old minimum. Produced by John Buckmaster and Sons 43% alc by vol.

Glottertal (Ger) village (Anb): Baden. (Ber): Breisgau. (Gro): Burg Zähringen. (Vins): Eichberg, Roter Burg.

Glover's Vineyard (N.Z) vineyard. (Add): Gardner Valley Road, RD 1, Upper Moutere, Nelson. 2ha. Grape varieties: Cabernet sauvignon, Pinot noir, Sauvignon blanc.

Glowing Autumn Ale (Eng) a 4.5% alc by vol. (1044 O.G.) ale from the Wye Valley Brewery, Hereford. Available from September–November (part of Dorothy Goodbody's Seasonal Ales).

Glucometer (Eng) a scaled hydrometer for measuring the sugar content in liquids. i.e. in grape must. (Fr) = glucomètre.

Glucomètre (Fr) glucometer.

Gluconic Acid (Eng) a wine acid formed from Eudemised grapes.

Gluconobacter (Bio) *Gluconobacter oxydans* a bacteria found on grape skins and wine musts that feeds off glucose to form acetic acid.

Gluco-Oenometer (Port) an instrument used in Port production to test the sugar levels in the musts. *See also* Glucometer.

Glucose (Eng) $C_6H_{12}O_6$ simple grape sugar that combines with fructose to form sucrose. Enzymes secreted by the wine yeasts convert it into alcohol and CO_2.

Glühwein (Ger) a mulled wine, spiced and sweetened, uses lemon zest, ginger, cinnamon, cloves, sugar and a little water. Heat together and infuse 5 minutes, strain and serve as hot as possible.

Glun (Fr) a commune of the A.C. Saint-Joseph in the northern Rhône.

Glutamic Acid (Eng) an amino acid found in wine, formed by the yeasts.

Gluten & Wheat Free (Eng) a 4.2% alc by vol. special diet ale brewed by Hambleton Ales, North Yorkshire.

G

Glutinous Rice Chiew (Chi) a style of rice wine.

Glycerine (Eng) an oil residue used as a non-fermentable sweetener, is found naturally in wines and spirits as a by-product of plant oils. (Fr) = glycérine. *See also* Glycerol.

Glycérine (Fr) glycerine.

Glycerol (Eng) $C_2H_5(OH)_3$ (molecular weight 92) a by-product of fermentation which develops in early stages. S.G. 1.2613 at 20°C. (Fr) = glycérol. *See also* Glycerine.

Glycérol (Fr) glycerol.

Glycine (Eng) an amino acid found in wine formed by the yeasts.

Glycolysis (Eng) the decomposition of glucose or glycogen into simpler compounds.

Glycuronic Acid (Eng) a wine acid formed from eudemised grapes.

Glyndwr (Wal) a natural spring mineral water from Llandre. Mineral contents (milligrammes per litre): Sodium 13.6mg/l, Calcium 10.1mg/l, Magnesium 3.4mg/l, Potassium 0.4mg/l, Bicarbonates 10.1mg/l, Chlorides 25mg/l, Sulphates 24.7mg/l, Fluorides 0.01mg/l.

Glyndwr Vineyard (Wal) a 1.5ha vineyard at Glyndwr House, Llanblethian, Cowbridge. Produces red, white and sparkling wines.

G.M.A. (Fr) *abbr:* Grandes Maisons d'Alsace.

G.m.b.H. (Ger) *abbr:* Gesellschaft mit beschränkter Haftung, denotes a limited liability company. (Eng) = Ltd.

GMS (Austr) *abbr:* Grenache, Mataro and Shiraz, the particular grapes in a blend.

GM 6494 (Asia) small red berried hybrid grape variety with red flesh grown in Mongolia. Produces fruity, light ruby-coloured red wines.

Gnangara Vineyards (Austr) part of the Evans and Tate Winery, Western Australia.

Gnu Bru (Eng). 4.5% alc by vol. beer brewed by the Finnesko and Firkin Brewery in Norwich (formerly known as the Reindeer Brewery). *See also* Red Nose.

Goacher [P&D J] Brewery (Eng) a brewery (established 1983). (Add): The Brewery, Unit 8, Tovil Green Business Park, Maidstone, Kent ME15 6TA.. Noted for cask-conditioned Maidstone Light 1036 O.G. Maidstone Ale 1040 O.G. and Goacher's-1066 1066 O.G.

Goat d'Afrique (S.Afr) a red wine made from organically grown Shiraz from the Fairview Estate.

Goat Door (S.Afr) a Chardonnay wine produced by the Fairview Estate.

Goats do Roam (S.Afr) a red wine from Charles Rack of Fairview the name of which was created as a 'joke' against the wine makers of the Côtes-du-Rhône in southern France!

Goats do Roam in Villages (S.Afr) a white a red variety (of blended grapes) wine from the Fairview Estate.

Goats Milk (Eng) a 3.8% alc by vol. ale brewed by The Church End Brewery Ltd., Warwickshire.

Goaty (Eng) a term used to describe some wines made from the Traminer grape that has a rich animal-like flavour.

Goeie Tye (S.Afr) the export label for a range of wines produced by the Rooiberg Winery, Robertson, Western Cape.

Gobelet (Fr) a method of cultivating vines on a vertical trunk, with branches rising and spreading to form the shape of a goblet, hence the name. Bush formation. (Sp) = en cabeza/en vaso.

Gobelet (Fr) goblet, a wide-rimmed drinking vessel. *See also* Paris Goblet and Tastevin.

Gobelet [Dom] (Fr) the cellar master of Clos de Vougeot at the time of the French Revolution.

Gobelsberger Haide (Aus) a vineyard site based on the banks of the River Kamp situated in the Kamptal region.

Gobernador (Sp) a solera brandy from Emilio Hidalgo. *See also* Consistorial.

Gobillard [Paul] (Fr) a Champagne producer. (Add): Château de Pierry, 423 Rue de Bacchus, Pierry 51200 Épernay. Négociant-manipulant. 5 ha of vineyards. Vintages include: 1983, 1988.

Goblet (Eng) a drinking vessel either of metal or glass with a large bowl and stem. (Fr) = gobelet.

Gochsheim (Ger) village (Anb): Baden. *see* Kraichtal.

Goccia (It) a carbonated natural mineral water from the Friuli. (Add): S. Andrea S.p.A. Piacenza Stablimento Goccia di Carnia, Forni Avoltri, Udine, Fruili. Mineral contents (milligrammes per litre): Sodium 1.1mg/l, Calcium 20.5mg/l, Magnesium 4.6mg/l, Potassium 0.2mg/l, Bicarbonates 78mg/l, Chlorides 0.2mg/l, Sulphates 3.1mg/l, Nitrates 1.6mg/l. pH 8.25

Goccia Azzurra (It) a natural spring mineral water from Diana, S. Gregorio d'Ippona, Vibo Valenzia.

Goccia Blu (It) a still natural spring mineral water. Mineral contents (milligrammes per litre): Sodium 19.2mg/l, Calcium 93mg/l, Magnesium 3.8mg/l, Potassium 1.8mg/l, Bicarbonates 281mg/l, Chlorides 19.9mg/l, Sulphates 25.5mg/l, Strontium 2.6mg/l, Silicates 9.1mg/l. pH 7.0

Goccia Diamante (It) a natural spring mineral water from Piave.

Goccia di Carnia (It) a natural spring mineral water from Fonte di Fleons. Mineral contents (milligrammes per litre): Sodium 1.2mg/l, Calcium 17.6mg/l, Magnesium 4mg/l, Potassium 0.2mg/l, Bicarbonates 79mg/l, Chlorides 0.3mg/l, Sulphates 2.8mg/l, Nitrates 1.6mg/l. pH 8.34

Göcklingen (Ger) village (Anb): Pfalz. (Ber): Südliche Weinstrasse. (Gro): Herrlich. (Vin): Kaiserberg.

Göcklingen (Ger) village (Anb): Pfalz. (Ber): Südliche Weinstrasse. (Gro): Kloster Liebfrauenberg. (Vin): Herrenpfad.

Göcseji Barna (Hun) the brand-name of a beer brewed by the Nagykanizsa Brewery.

Godailler (Fr) a term used in the Champagne region to denote the visit to a café (pub).

Goddards (Eng) a 4% alc by vol. bitter ale brewed by the Goddards Brewery, Isle of Wight.

Goddards Brewery (Eng) a brewery (established

G

1992). (Add): Barnsley Farm, Bullen Road, Ryde, Isle of Wight PO33 1QF. Brews: Ale of Wight 4% alc by vol., Ducks Folly 5.2% alc by vol., Fuggle-Dee-Dum 4.8% alc by vol., Goddards 4% alc by vol., Inspiration 5.2% alc by vol., Iron Horse 4.8% alc by vol., Jubilation 4% alc by vol., Special Bitter, Winter Warmer 5.2% alc by vol. Website: http://www.goddards-brewery.co.uk 'E'mail: office@goddards-brewery.co.uk

Godehard (Ger) a natural spring mineral water. Mineral contents (milligrammes per litre): Sodium 320mg/l, Calcium 100mg/l, Magnesium 27mg/l, Bicarbonates 150mg/l, Chlorides 550mg/l.

Godello (Sp) a white grape variety grown in Galicia. Produces fragrant, fresh wines high in acidity.

Godendorf (Ger) village (Anb): Mosel-Saar-Ruwer. (Ber): Obermosel. (Gro): Königsberg. (Vin): Sites not yet chosen.

Godet (Fr) a Cognac producer. (Add): Godet Frères, 1 Rue du Duc, La Rochelle 17003. Produces V.S.O.P. Fine Champagne Gastronome 7–9 year old Cognac.

Godfather (Cktl) 20mls (¾ fl.oz) amaretto, 35mls (1½ fl.ozs) Scotch whisky. Build into an ice-filled old-fashioned glass.

Godfathers (Eng) a 3.8% alc by vol. cask-conditioned ale brewed by the Itchen Valley Brewery in Alresford.

Godfrey's Lemon Schnapps (Sp) a 20% alc by vol. lemon schnapps made in Barcelona. Also available in peach, apple and cranberry flavours.

Godmother (Cktl) 1 part amaretto, 1 part vodka, build into an ice-filled old-fashioned glass.

Godolphin (Austr) the label for a red wine (Shiraz-Cabernet sauvignon) produced by the Glaetzer winery, Barossa Valley, south Australia.

Godo Shusei (Jap) a whiskey producer.

Godoy Cruz (Arg) a wine-producing area in the Mendoza region.

Godramstein (Ger) village (Anb): Pfalz. (Ber): Südliche Weinstrasse. (Gro): Königsgarten. (Vins): Klostergarten, Münzberg.

Godrich and Petman (Eng) a retail Off-Licence owned by Eldridge Pope.

God's Garden (Ger) the German nickname for the Rheinhessen because of its fertility and wealth.

Godsun Chudley (Eng) two breweries that merged in 1984. Based in London. Produces: cask-conditioned Godson's Black Horse 1048 O.G. Stock Ale 1085 O.G. Chudley's Local Line 1038 O.G. Wilmot's Hop Cone 1042 O.G. Lord's Strong 1048 O.G. and Draught Excluder 1070 O.G.

Gods Wallop Christmas Ale (Eng) a 4.3% alc by vol. Christmas ale brewed by the Westerham Brewery C°. Ltd., Kent using Bramling Cross, First Gold and Cascade hops and spices (cinnamon, cloves and ginger).

Goede Hoop Estate (S.Afr) a winery and estate (established 1928) based in Kuils River, Stellenbosch, Western Cape. (Add): P.O. Kuils River, 7580. 80ha. Grape varieties: Cabernet sauvignon, Carignan, Merlot, Pinotage, Sauvignon blanc, Shiraz. Labels: Domaine, Private Collection. Website: http://www.goedehoop.co.za

Goedgeloof Vineyards (S.Afr) a part of the Spier Estate.

Goedevertrouw Estate (S.Afr) a winery (established 1990) based in Bot River, Walker Bay, Western Cape. 8ha. Grape varieties: Cabernet sauvignon, Chardonnay, Pinotage, Pinot noir, Sauvignon blanc. Label: Pardoemps.

Goedverwacht Wine Estate (S.Afr) a winery (established 1994) based in Roberstson, Western Cape. 110ha. (Add): P.O. Box 128, Bonnievale 6730, Robertson. Grape varieties: Chardonnay, Colombard, Sauvignon blanc. Labels: Acre of Stone, Crane, Great Expectations, Maxim, The Good Earth, Triangle. Website: http://www.goedeverwacht.co.za

Goerg [Paul] (Fr) a Champagne producer. (Add): 4 Place du Mont Chenil, 51130 Vertus. Coopérative-manipulant. 112 growers owning 125ha.

Goetheberg (Ger) vineyard (Anb): Mittelrhein. (Ber): Rheinburgengau. (Gro): Lahntal. (Vil): Obernhof.

Goff's Brewery (Eng) a brewery (established 1994). (Add): 9 Isbourne Way, Winchcombe, Cheltenham, Gloucestershire GL54 5NS. Brews: Black Knight, Jouster 4% alc by vol., White Knight beers. Website: http://www.goffs.biz 'E'mail: brewery@goffs.biz

Go Get Oxygenated (S.Afr) a natural spring mineral water. Mineral contents (milligrammes per litre): Sodium 6mg/l, Calcium 43mg/l, Magnesium 34mg/l, Potassium 4mg/l, Chlorides 11mg/l, Sulphates 16mg/l, Fluorides 0.08mg/l, Nitrates 2.8mg/l. pH 7.2

Goglet (Ind) a large, long-necked, porous, earthenware bottle used for cooling drinking water. Also spelt Gurglet and Guglet.

Gôiya (S.Afr) the label for a range of wines produced by the WestCorp International, Olifants River, Western Cape.

Golan Heights Winery (Isr) a winery based on the Golan Heights, north-eastern Israel. Grape varieties: Cabernet sauvignon, Sangiovese, Sauvignon blanc. Labels include: Gamla.

Golcuv Jeníkov Brewery (Czec) a noted brewery based in central Czec.

Gold (Eng) a 5% alc by vol. ale brewed by the Barum Brewery, Devon.

Gold (Eng) a 5% alc by vol. golden ale brewed by the Bristol Beer Factory, Avon.

Gold (Eng) a 5% alc by vol. golden ale brewed by the Broadstone Brewing C°. Ltd., Nottinghamshire.

Gold (Eng) a gold coloured ale brewed by the Derwentrose Brewery in Consett, County Durham.

Gold Acquette (Eng) see Acquette d'Or.

Gold Ale (Eng) a 5% alc by vol. golden ale brewed by the Old Luxters Brewery, Oxfordshire.

Goldaqua (Hun) an alkaline still and sparkling natural spring mineral water. Mineral contents (milligrammes per litre): Sodium 79mg/l, Calcium 228mg/l, Magnesium 58mg/l, Potassium 4.4mg/l, Bicarbonates 24mg/l,

Chlorides 5mg/l, Sulphates 29mg/l, Fluorides 0.1mg/l, Silicates 63mg/l. pH 9.2

Goldatzel (Ger) vineyard (Anb): Rheingau. (Ber): Johannisberg. (Gro): Erntebringer. (Vil): Johannisberg.

Goldbächel (Ger) vineyard (Anb): Pfalz. (Ber): Mittelhaardt-Deutsche Weinstrasse. (Gro): Mariengarten. (Vil): Wachenheim.

Goldbäumchen (Ger) grosslage (Anb): Mosel-Saar-Ruwer. (Ber): Zell/Mosel. (Vils): Briedern, Bruttig-Fankel, Cochem, Ellenz-Poltersdorf, Ernst, Klottern, Moselkern, Münden, Pommern, Senheim, Treis-Karden.

Gold Beach (Eng) a 3.8% alc by vol. summer beer brewed by the Hart Brewery at Little Eccleston, near Preston.

Goldbeerenauslese (Ger) an old term for a wine between beerenauslese and trockenbeerenauslese, the wine being not quite up to trocken-beerenauslese quality (now no longer used).

Gold Bell (USA) a brand-label used by the East-Side Winery, California for their generic wines.

Goldberg (Aus) vineyard areas (2) on the banks of the River Danube in the Kremstal region.

Goldberg (Aus) the label for a red wine (Blaufränkisch) produced by the Heinrich [Johann] winery, Mittel-Burgenland.

Goldberg (Ger) lit: 'golden hill', the name used for a vineyard usually in a south facing position. There are 32 vineyards in Germany with this name.

Goldberg (Ger) vineyard (Anb): Baden. (Ber): Badische Bergstrasse/Kraichgau. (Gro): Mannaberg. (Vil): Mingolsheim und Langenbrücken.

Goldberg (Ger) vineyard (Anb): Baden. (Ber): Badische Bergstrasse/Kraichgau. (Gro): Stiftsberg. (Vil): Sinsheim (stadtteil Weiler).

Goldberg (Ger) vineyard (Anb): Mosel-Saar-Ruwer. (Ber): Saar-Ruwer. (Gro): Scharzberg. (Vil): Wawern.

Goldberg (Ger) vineyard (Anb): Mosel-Saar-Ruwer. (Ber): Zell/Mosel. (Gro): Goldbäumchen. (Vil): Pommern.

Goldberg (Ger) vineyard (Anb): Rheingau. (Ber): Johannisberg. (Gro): Erntebringer. (Vil): Mittelheim.

Goldberg (Ger) vineyard (Anb): Rheinhessen. (Ber): Bingen. (Gro): Abtey. (Vil): Gau-Algesheim.

Goldberg (Ger) vineyard (Anb): Rheinhessen. (Ber): Bingen. (Gro): Kaiserpfalz. (Vil): Jugenheim.

Goldberg (Ger) vineyard (Anb): Rheinhessen. (Ber): Bingen. (Gro): Kurfürstenstück. (Vil): Vendersheim.

Goldberg (Ger) vineyard (Anb): Rheinhessen. (Ber): Bingen. (Gro): Sankt Rochuskapelle. (Vil): Gensingen.

Goldberg (Ger) vineyard (Anb): Rheinhessen. (Ber): Bingen. (Gro): Sankt Rochuskapelle. (Vil): Horrweiler.

Goldberg (Ger) vineyard (Anb): Rheinhessen. (Ber): Nierstein. (Gro): Domherr. (Vil): Udenheim.

Goldberg (Ger) vineyard (Anb): Rheinhessen. (Ber): Nierstein. (Gro): Gutes Domtal. (Vil): Nieder-Olm.

Goldberg (Ger) vineyard (Anb): Rheinhessen. (Ber): Nierstein. (Gro): Gutes Domtal. (Vil): Undenheim.

Goldberg (Ger) vineyard (Anb): Rheinhessen. (Ber): Nierstein. (Gro): Krötenbrunnen. (Vil): Alsheim.

Goldberg (Ger) vineyard (Anb): Rheinhessen. (Ber): Nierstein. (Gro): Krötenbrunnen. (Vil): Eich.

Goldberg (Ger) vineyard (Anb): Rheinhessen. (Ber): Nierstein. (Gro): Krötenbrunnen. (Vil): Mettenheim.

Goldberg (Ger) vineyard (Anb): Rheinhessen. (Ber): Wonnegau. (Gro): Bergkloster. (Vil): Esselborn.

Goldberg (Ger) vineyard (Anb): Rheinhessen. (Ber): Wonnegau. (Gro): Bergkloster. (Vil): Flomborn.

Goldberg (Ger) vineyard (Anb): Rheinhessen. (Ber): Wonnegau. (Gro): Burg Rodenstein. (Vil): Flörsheim-Dalsheim.

Goldberg (Ger) vineyard (Anb): Rheinhessen. (Ber): Wonnegau. (Gro): Gotteshilfe. (Vil): Osthofen.

Goldberg (Ger) vineyard (Anb): Rheinhessen. (Ber): Wonnegau. (Gro): Liebfrauenmorgen. (Vil): Worms.

Goldberg (Ger) vineyard (Anb): Rheinhessen. (Ber): Wonnegau. (Gro): Pilgerpfad. (Vil): Monzernheim.

Goldberg (Ger) vineyard (Anb): Pfalz. (Ber): Mittelhaardt-Deutsche Weinstrasse. (Gro): Höllenpfad. (Vil): Grünstadt.

Goldberg (Ger) vineyard (Anb): Pfalz. (Ber): Mittelhaardt-Deutsche Weinstrasse. (Gro): Rosenbühl. (Vil): Erpolzheim.

Goldberg (Ger) vineyard (Anb): Pfalz. (Ber): Mittelhaardt-Deutsche Weinstrasse. (Gro): Rosenbühl. (Vil): Freinsheim.

Goldberg (Ger) vineyard (Anb): Pfalz. (Ber): Mittelhaardt-Deutsche Weinstrasse. (Gro): Rosenbühl. (Vil): Weisenheim/Sand.

Goldberg (Ger) vineyard (Anb): Pfalz. (Ber): Mittelhaardt-Deutsche Weinstrasse. (Gro): Schwarzerde. (Vil): Bisserheim.

Goldberg (Ger) vineyard (Anb): Württemberg. (Ber): Remstal-Stuttgart. (Gro): Weinsteige. (Vil): Fellbach.

Goldberg (Ger) vineyard (Anb): Württemberg. (Ber): Württembergisch Unterland. (Gro): Lindelberg. (Vil): Bretzfeld.

Goldberg (Ger) vineyard (Anb): Württemberg. (Ber): Württembergisch Unterland. (Gro): Lindelberg. (Vil): Pfedelbach.

Goldberg (Ger) vineyard (Anb): Württemberg. (Ber): Württembergisch Unterland. (Gro): Lindelberg. (Vil): Verrenberg.

Goldberg (Ger) vineyard (Anb): Württemberg. (Ber): Württembergisch Unterland. (Gro): Lindelberg. (Vil): Windischenbach.

Goldberger (Aus) a white grape variety (a cross between the Welschriesling x Orangentraube) is susceptable to botrytis cinerea.

Gold Bier (Eng) a premium bottled lager from Bass.

Gold Bitter (Wal) a keg bitter 1043 O.G. brewed by the Buckley Brewery in South Wales.

G

Gold Blend (Eng) the ™brand-name of a instant coffee produced by Nestlé, a decaffeinated version is also available.

Goldblume (Ger) vineyard (Anb): Mosel-Saar-Ruwer. (Ber): Zell/Mosel. (Gro): Weinhex. (Vil): Löf.

Goldbräu (Aus) a beer 5% alc by vol. brewed by the Steigl Brauerei in Salzburg.

Gold Brew (Wal) a 3.8% alc by vol. ale brewed by S.A. Brain & C°. Ltd., South Glamorgan.

Goldbühel (Aus) a vineyard area on the banks of the River Danube in the Kremstal region.

Goldburger (Aus) a white grape variety produced by crossing Welschriesling x Orangetraube.

Gold Cadillac (Cktl) 20mls (¾ fl.oz) Galliano, 20mls (¾ fl.oz) crème de cacao (white), 50mls (2fl.ozs) cream. Shake well over ice and strain into a cocktail glass.

Gold Cap (Eng) a fine, old, tawny Port from Balls Brothers of London.

Goldcar Brewery (Eng) a brewery (established 2001). (Add): Swallow Lane, Goldcar, Huddersfield, West Yorkshire HD7 4NB. Brews: Bitter, Dark mild 3.4% alc by vol., Fettlers Fancy 4% alc by vol., Pennine Gold 3.9% alc by vol., Weavers Delight 4.8% alc by vol., Winkle on the Porter 4.7% alc by vol. 'E'mail: goldcarbrewery@btconnect.com

Gold Coconut Cocktail [1] (Cktl) ½ measure maraschino, ½ measure Cognac, 1 measure orange juice, dash egg white. Shake well over ice, strain into a cocktail glass and top with a cherry.

Gold Coconut Cocktail [2] (Cktl) ½ measure maraschino, ½ measure Malibu, 1 measure orange juice, dash egg white. Shake well over ice, strain into a cocktail glass and top with a dash of Grenadine (do not stir).

Gold Crest (Can) a blended Canadian whisky produced by Hiram Walker.

Gold Crest Food & beverages Ltd (Eng) tea and coffee manufacturer (established 1995). (Add): P.O. Box 35, Liverpool, Merseyside L18 8EP. 'E'mail: goldcrestexports@aol.com

Gold Cross (Eng) a pilsner lager 1030–1034 O.G. produced by Importers (Alliance) Limited, Alma Road, Reigate, Surrey.

Gold Digger (Eng) a 4% alc by vol. ale brewed by the Bank Top Brewery Ltd., Lancashire.

Gold Dragon (Wal) a vintage medium-dry cider 7.5% alc by vol. produced by Symonds of Hereford, Cardiff. Sold in 1litre PET™ bottles. See also Black Dragon, Red Dragon, Silver Dragon.

Gold Eagle Bitter (Eng) a keg bitter 1034 O.G. brewed by the Charles Wells Brewery in Bedford.

Goldeck (Aus) a brand of sparkling wine produced by Schlumberger in Vöslau.

Goldemund (Ger) vineyard (Anb): Mittelrhein. (Ber): Rheinburgengau. (Gro): Schloss Schönburg. (Vil): Damscheid.

Goldemund (Ger) vineyard (Anb): Mittelrhein. (Ber): Rheinburgengau. (Gro): Schloss Schönburg. (Vil): Oberwessel.

Golden (Eng) a 5.4% alc by vol. golden ale brewed by the Greenwich Meantime Brewing C°. Ltd., London.

Golden (Sp) see 'G', a colour grade for Oloroso and Palo Cortado Sherry.

Golden Age (Scot) a de luxe blended Scotch whisky produced by Haig 43% alc by vol.

Golden Age of Steam (Eng) a 4.2% alc by vol. ale brewed by the Somerset (Electric) brewery, Somerset.

Golden Ale (Eng) a cask-conditioned ale 1050 O.G. brewed by the Archers Brewery in Swindon, Wiltshire.

Golden Ale (Eng) a 3.8% alc by vol. golden ale brewed by the Bristol Beer Factory, Avon.

Golden Ale (Eng) a keg pale ale 1039 O.G. brewed by the Holden Brewery in the Black Country.

Golden Ale (Eng) a light ale 1030 O.G. brewed by the Ridley Brewery in Essex.

Golden Ale (Eng) a 4.7% alc by vol. ale brewed by St. Peters Brewery, South Elmham, Suffolk.

Golden Arrow (Eng) a 4.5% alc by vol. ale from the Cottage Brewing Company, West Lydford, near Yeovil, Somerset.

Golden Bahaï (Cktl) into a highball glass place 2 measures dry gin, 2 measures Cinzano, juice ½ lemon, dash gomme syrup. Stir in an egg yolk, top with pineapple juice and dress with fresh fruit in season.

Golden Barret (Scot) the brand-name of a 5 year old blended Scotch whisky 43% alc by vol.

Golden Beneagles (Scot) a blended Scotch whisky from Peter Thomson (Perth) Ltd 43% alc by vol.

Golden Best Mild (Eng) a light mild ale 1033 O.G. brewed by the Timothy Taylor Brewery in Keighley, Yorkshire.

Golden Bough (Eng) a 4.5% alc by vol. pale hoppy cask bitter ale brewed by Burtonwood in Warrington. Available March to May. Part of their Masterclass range.

Golden Broken Orange Pekoe (Eng) abbr: GBOP a grade of Broken Orange Pekoe black tea.

Golden Brown (Eng) a 5% alc by vol. ale brewed by the Butts Brewery Ltd., Berkshire.

Golden Bull (Eng) a 4.2% alc by vol. ale brewed by the Blanchfield Brewery, Essex.

Golden Cadillac (Cktl) see Gold Cadillac.

Golden Cadillac (Cktl) 25mls (1fl.oz) (white) crème de cacao, 25mls (1fl.oz) cream, 25mls (1fl.oz Galliano. Shake over ice and strain into a saucer-type glass.

Golden Cap (Eng) a blended whisky produced by the Palmer Brewery in Bridport, Dorset from a 50–50 blend of North British and Glen Grant.

Golden Chalice (Eng) a 4.8% alc by vol. ale brewed by Glastonbury Ales, Somerset.

Golden Champion Ale (Eng) a 4.6% alc by vol. cask summer ale brewed by Badger Brewery, Dorset. Also a bottled version 5% alc by vol.

Golden Chasselas (USA) see Chasselas Doré.

Golden Circle (Austr) a natural spring mineral water.

Golden Cock (Chi) a natural spring mineral water. Mineral contents (milligrammes per litre): Sodium 13.2mg/l, Silicates 15mg/l. pH 7.2

Golden Cock Gin (Nor) s smooth locally produced gin.

Golden Dawn Cocktail (Cktl) ¼ measure Calvados, ¼ measure apricot brandy, ¼ measure gin, ¼ measure orange juice, dash grenadine. Shake altogether (except the grenadine), strain into a cocktail glass and add grenadine.

Golden Daze (Cktl) ¾ measure gin, ¼ measure peach brandy, juice ½ orange. Shake over ice and strain into a cocktail glass.

Golden Delicious (Eng) a 3.8% alc by vol. ale brewed by the Blythe Brewery, Staffordshire.

Golden Delicious (Gre) the name given to a sweet white liqueur wine produced by Tsantali. A red version is known as Red Delicious.

Golden Delirious (Eng) a 4.5% alc by vol. ale brewed by the Hobdens Wessex Brewery, Wiltshire.

Golden Dream (Cktl) ¼ measure Cointreau, ¼ measure Galliano, ¼ measure orange juice, ¼ measure cream. Shake over ice and strain into a cocktail glass.

Golden Eagle (Cup) 1 bottle Tiger Milk, 20mls (⅙ gill) Curaçao, 20mls (⅙ gill) Cognac, 3 dashes maraschino, juice of 1 lemon and 2 oranges. Chill well, pour into an ice-filled jug, top with a 400mls (¾ pint) of soda water and serve.

Golden Eagle (Eng) a 4.2% alc by vol. ale brewed by the Cotleigh Brewery, Somerset.

Golden Eagle (Ind) a lager beer 1050 O.G. brewed by the Mohan Meakin Brewery in Simla Hills, Solan.

Golden Eagle (Ind) a natural spring mineral water from Solan. Mineral contents (milligrammes per litre): Sodium 1.3mg/l, Calcium 22mg/l, Magnesium 37mg/l, Potassium 2mg/l, Bicarbonates 196mg/l, Chlorides 2mg/l, Sulphates 34mg/l, Fluorides 0.15mg/l, Silicates 16mg/l.

Goldene Luft (Ger) vineyard (Anb): Rheingau. (Ber): Johannisberg. (Gro): Daubhaus. (Vil): Wicker.

Goldene Luft (Ger) vineyard (Anb): Rheinhessen. (Ber): Nierstein. (Gro): Rehbach. (Vil): Nierstein.

Goldener Oktober (Ger) a Rhine wine produced by St. Ursula (brand).

Goldenes Horn (Ger) vineyard (Anb): Rheinhessen. (Ber): Bingen. (Gro): Rheingrafenstein. (Vil): Siefersheim.

Goldeneye Vineyards (USA) the label used by Duckhorn Vineyards based near St. Helena, Napa Valley, California for their Pinot noir wine produced from Obester Winery in Mendocino's Anderson Valley. Label: Migration.

Golden Fizz (Cktl) 1 egg yolk, 90mls (¾ gill) gin, 1 teaspoon sugar syrup, juice of lemon. Shake well over ice, strain into a highball and top with soda water.

Golden Fling Cocktail (Cktl) ⅓ measure Galliano, ⅓ measure golden rum, ⅓ measure pineapple juice. Shake well over ice, strain into a highball glass, top with bitter lemon and dress with fruit in season.

Golden Frappé (Cktl) 125mls (1 gill) Port wine, juice 2 oranges, juice ¼ lemon, 1 teaspoon sugar. Stir juices and sugar together in a collins glass, add crushed ice and port.

Golden Gate Cocktail (Cktl) 25mls (⅕ gill) white rum, 4 dashes dry Sherry. Stir over ice, strain into cocktail glass and dress with a lemon peel spiral.

Golden Gin (USA) a gin that has been aged in wood and has a golden hue colour.

Golden Gleam (Cktl) ⅓ measure Grand Marnier, ⅓ measure brandy, ⅙ measure lemon juice, ⅙ measure orange juice. Shake over ice and strain into a cocktail glass.

Golden Glory Ale (Eng) a 4.5% alc by vol. summer ale brewed by Badger at the Hall and Woodhouse Brewery, Dorset.

Golden Glory Cocktail (Cktl) ⅓ measure dry Martini, ⅓ measure Scotch whisky, ⅓ measure medium Sherry. Stir over ice, strain into a cocktail glass and top with a squeeze of orange peel juice.

Golden Goose (Eng) a 4.5% alc by vol. ale brewed by the Goose Eye Brewery Ltd., West Yorkshire.

Golden Guinea (Fr) a sparkling wine from the Saumur in the Anjou-Saumur district of the Loire. Made by the cuve close method using the Chenin blanc and Muscatel dosage. Brut or Demi-sec.

Golden Guinea Breweries (Afr) a brewery based in Nigeria. Produces: Eagle Stout and Eagle Lager.

Golden Harvest (S.Afr) the label for a white wine (Gewürztraminer 50% and Hanepoot 50%) produced by the De Krans winery, Calitzdorp, Little Karoo.

Golden Heart (Hol) a 30% alc by vol. sweet, herb-flavoured liqueur with pieces of gold flake added. Produced by De Kuyper (a type of goldwasser).

Golden Hill Brewery (Eng) a brewery (established 1980) based in Wiveliscombe, Somerset. Noted for cask-conditioned Exmoor Ale 1039 O.G. Now known as Exmoor Ales.

Golden Honey (Eng) a 4.5% alc by vol. ale brewed by Hanby Ales Ltd., Shropshire.

Golden Hornet (Eng) a 5% alc by vol. ale brewed by HB Clark & C°. Ltd., West Yorkshire.

Golden IPA (Eng) a bottled pale ale 1040 O.G. brewed by the Burt Brewery in Ventnor on the Isle of Wight.

Golden Jackal (Eng) a 3.7% alc by vol. golden ale brewed by the Wolf Brewery Ltd., Norfolk.

Golden Lady Cocktail (Cktl) ⅓ measure brandy, ⅓ measure orange gin, ⅙ measure lemon juice, ⅙ measure grapefruit juice. Shake over ice and strain into a cocktail glass.

Golden Lager (Iraq) a lager beer brewed by the government-owned brewery based in Baghdad. 11.5° Balling.

Golden Lance (Eng) a 3.8% alc by vol. ale brewed by the Keltek Brewing C°. Ltd., Cornwall.

Golden Lemonade (Cktl)(Non-alc) juice 1 lemon, 2 teaspoons of powdered sugar, 1 egg yolk. Shake over ice, strain into an ice-filled highball glass, top with Perrier water and slices of orange, lemon and a cherry.

G

Golden Lion (Eng) a 4.5% alc by vol. ale brewed by Bobs Brewing Company Ltd., West Yorkshire.

Golden Medallion (Cktl) ⅓ measure old Cognac, ⅓ measure Galliano, ⅓ measure orange juice, dash egg white. Shake over ice, strain into a cocktail glass and add zest of orange.

Golden Mild (Eng) a draught mild beer from the McMullen in Hertford.

Goldmuskateller (Ger) the name for the Moscato giallo grape variety in the Südtirol (Trentino-Alto Adige).

Golden Mustang (S.Afr) a medium-sweet wine produced by the SFW from the Muscat d'Alexandrie and White cinsault grapes.

Golden Newt (Eng) a 4.6% alc by vol. pale coloured ale brewed with malted barley, wheat, rye and oats by Elgood & Sons North Brink Brewery in Wisbech, Cambridgeshire.

Golden Newt-Rition (Eng) a 5.2% alc by vol. ale brewed by the Burrington Brewery, Devon.

Golden Nut Mild (Eng) a 3.4% alc by vol. mild ale brewed by the Three Tuns Brewery, Shropshire.

Golden Oke (USA) a golden type of Okolehao.

Golden Oldie (Eng) the nickname given to Nimmo's XXXX.

Golden Original (Eng) a draught lager 4% alc by vol. from Lees, Middleton Junction.

Golden Pale (Eng) an organic pale ale 4% alc by vol. from the Caledonian Brewing Company.

Golden Pig (Eng) a 4.7% alc by vol. golden ale brewed by the Country Life Brewery, Devon.

Golden Pippin (Eng) a 3.7% alc by vol. ale brewed by the Copper Dragon Skipton Brewery Ltd., North Yorkshire.

Golden Pippins (Eng) an old English cider-making apple.

Golden Pride Ale (Eng) a bottled pale ale 9.2% alc by vol (1090 O.G) brewed by the Fullers Brewery in London.

Golden Promise (Scot) a top Scottish barley considered perfect for brewing that gives medium sugar yields. Includes varieties: Halcyon, Kaskade, Kym, Magie, Pipkin and Tweed.

Golden Promise (Scot) the oldest organic cask beer 1050 O.G. (4.4% alc by vol.). Produced by the Caledonian Brewing C°. Ltd., Edinburgh. *See also* Deuchars 80/-.

Golden Rain Tree Winery (USA) a winery based in Wadesville, Indiana. Produces hybrid blends. Noted for Director's Choice (a dry red wine).

Golden Rum (W.Ind) a style of rum from Cuba, Puerto Rico and the Virgin Islands. Is aged for 3 years and coloured with caramel (light-bodied) 40% alc by vol.

Golden Salamander (Eng) a 4.5% alc by vol. ale brewed by the Salamander Brewing Company Ltd., West Yorkshire.

Golden Screw (Cktl) 25mls (⅛ gill) dry gin, 50mls (⅖ gill) orange juice, dash Angostura. Stir altogether in an ice-filled old-fashioned glass and dress with an orange slice.

Golden Slipper (Cktl) ⅓ measure advocaat, ⅓ measure gin, ⅓ measure orange juice, dash gomme syrup, dash egg white. Shake well over ice and strain into a cocktail glass.

Golden Slipper (Pousse Café) place in a liqueur glass in order: 1 egg yolk, 20mls (⅙ gill) yellow Chartreuse, 20mls (⅙ gill) goldwasser.

Golden Slipper Cocktail (Cktl) ⅔ measure apricot brandy, ⅓ measure yellow Chartreuse. Stir over ice, strain into a cocktail glass and float an unbroken egg yolk on top.

Golden Spring (Eng) a 4% alc by vol. ale brewed by the Blindmans Brewery Ltd., Somerset.

Golden Star (Chi) the brand-name used by T'ien-chin.

Golden Summer Ale (Eng) a 4% alc by vol. ale brewed by Robert Cain in Liverpool.

Golden Summertime Ale (Eng) an 4.3% alc by vol. (1042 O.G.) ale from Wye Valley Brewery, Hereford. Available June–August (part of Dorothy Goodbody's Seasonal Ales).

Golden Tang (Cktl) ¼ measure Strega, ½ measure vodka, ⅛ measure crème de banane, ⅛ measure orange squash. Shake over ice, strain into a cocktail glass and add a cherry.

Golden Tea (Cktl) heat gently 75mls (3 fl.ozs) strong tea with 25mls (1fl.oz) arak and 75mls (3fl.ozs) cream. Stir continuously, add 2 egg yolks that have been beaten with 3 teaspoons of sugar. Stir, pour into a heat-proof glass and serve with a cinnamon stick.

Golden Tequila (Mex) a wood-aged silver tequila that has taken on a golden hue, known as Tequila Anejo.

Golden Thread (Eng) a 5% alc by vol. ale brewed by the Salopian Brewing C°. Ltd., Shropshire.

Golden Tip (Eng) a grade (quality) of tea from the Assam tea bush (dark leaves) which is produced in its second flush.

Golden Triangle (S.Afr) the label for a range of wines produced by the Stellenzicht Vineyards winery, Stellenbosch, Western Cape.

Golden Tulip (S.Afr) a still natural spring mineral water. Mineral contents (milligrammes per litre): Sodium 5mg/l, Calcium <0.5mg/l, Magnesium <0.5mg/l, Potassium <1mg/l, Chlorides 9mg/l, Sulphates <5mg/l, Fluorides <0.05mg/l.

Golden Valley (Ind) a natural spring mineral water from Trivandrum. Mineral contents (milligrammes per litre): Sodium 8mg/l, Calcium 8mg/l, Magnesium 4mg/l, Potassium 4mg/l, Bicarbonates 50mg/l, Chlorides 10mg/l, Sulphates 4mg/l, Fluorides 0.2mg/l, Silicates 2mg/l. pH 7.0

Golden Valley (S.Afr) the brand label of the Jonkheer Farmer's Winery.

Golden Valley (Wal) a 4.2% alc by vol. ale brewed by the Breconshire Brewery, Powys.

Golden Velvet (Can) a straight rye Canadian whisky produced by Gilbey Canada Ltd.

Golden Vineyards (USA) a winery based in the Mendocino County, California (owned by Fetzer Vineyards). Is a member of the Coro Mendocino (Zinfandel) wine group of Mendocino wineries.

G

Golden Vintage (S.Afr) the label for a semi-sweet white wine (Chenin blanc) produced by the Klein Parys Vineyards winery, Suider-Paarl, Western Cape.

Golden Weissbier (Ger) a 5.3% alc by vol. wheat beer brewed by Altöttingen.

Golden West Beer (Can) a beer brewed by the Carling O'Keefe Brewery.

Golden Wheat (Wal) a 4.5% alc by vol. wheat beer brewed by the Cwmbran Brewery, Gwent.

Goldfassl (Aus) the brand-name used by Ottakringer Harmer Brauerei in Vienna for their beers.

Goldfield (Eng) a 4.2% alc by vol. ale brewed by Hambleton Ales, North Yorkshire.

Goldfüsschen (Ger) vineyard (Anb): Mittelrhein. (Ber): Siebengebirge. (Gro): Petersberg. (Vil): Niederdollendorf.

Goldgrübchen (Ger) vineyard (Anb): Mosel-Saar-Ruwer. (Ber): Zell/Mosel. (Gro): Rosenhang. (Vil): Mesenich.

Goldgrube (Ger) vineyard (Anb): Mosel-Saar-Ruwer. (Ber): Bernkastel. (Gro): Schwarzlay. (Vil): Traben-Trarbach (ortsteil Wolf).

Goldgrube (Ger) vineyard (Anb): Nahe. (Ber): Schloss Böckelheim. (Gro): Rosengarten. (Vil): Rüdesheim.

Goldgrube (Ger) vineyard (Anb): Nahe. (Ber): Schloss Böckelheim. (Gro): Paradiesgarten. (Vil): Staudernheim.

Goldgrube (Ger) vineyard (Anb): Rheinhessen. (Ber): Nierstein. (Gro): Gutes Domtal. (Vil): Köngernheim.

Goldgrube (Ger) vineyard (Anb): Pfalz. (Ber): Mittelhaardt-Deutsche Weinstrasse. (Gro): Grafenstück. (Vil): Bockenheim.

Gold Harp Light Special (S.E.Asia) an all-malt brew launched in 1975. Brewed by an associate company of Guinness (brewed in Malaya).

Goldie (Eng) a barley wine 1085 O.G. brewed by the Eldridge Pope Brewery in Dorset.

Goldie Cocktail (Cktl) ⅓ measure white rum, ⅓ measure orange juice, ¼ measure Cointreau, ¼ measure Cherry Heering. Shake over ice, strain into a highball glass, top with orangeade and dress with a spiral of orange peel.

Goldihops (Scot) a 3.8% alc by vol. golden ale brewed by the Kelburn Brewing C°., Lanarkshire.

Golding Ale (Eng) a barley wine 1075 O.G. brewed by the King and Barnes Brewery in Sussex. Named after the Goldings hop used in its making.

Goldings (Eng) a traditional hop variety which gives good bitterness to beers.

Goldings Harvest Ale (Eng) a 5% alc by vol. ale produced by Shepherd Neame in Faversham, Kent. Produced to celebrate the local hop festival season in October.

Goldings Summer Hop Ale (Eng) a 4.7% alc by vol. bitter ale brewed by Shepherd Neame, Faversham, Kent using Kentish and Goldings hops.

Golding Years (Eng) a 5.9% alc by vol. single hopped beer brewed by RCH Brewery, at West Hewish, near Weston-Super-Mare, Somerset.

Goldkaul (Ger) vineyard (Anb): Ahr. (Ber): Walporzheim/Ahrtal. (Gro): Klosterberg. (Vil): Dernau.

Gold Keg (Can) a malty lager brewed by the Labatt Brewery, Ontario.

Goldkenn (Switz) the name given to a 100% Swiss chocolate and cream liqueur sold in a golden ingot-shaped bottle 18% alc by vol.

Goldkupp (Ger) vineyard (Anb): Mosel-Saar-Ruwer. (Ber): Bernkastel. (Gro): Sankt Michael. (Vil): Mehring.

Goldkupp (Ger) vineyard (Anb): Mosel-Saar-Ruwer. (Ber): Bernkastel. (Gro): Sankt Michael. (Vil): Longen.

Goldkupp (Ger) vineyard (Anb): Mosel-Saar-Ruwer. (Ber): Bernkastel. (Gro): Sankt Michael. (Vil): Lörsch.

Gold Label (Can) a blended Canadian whisky produced by Jas Barclay and C° (a subsidiary of Hiram Walker).

Gold Label (Ch.Isles) a brand of blended Scotch whisky bottled by Bucktrout & C°. Ltd., St. Peter Port, Guernsey 43% alc by vol.

Gold Label (Eng) a barley wine 1098 O.G. brewed by the Whitbread Brewery in Sheffield, Yorkshire.

Gold Label (Eng) a lager beer 1045 O.G. from Grünhalle.

Gold Label (Hol) a lager beer brewed by Amstel Brouwerij.

Gold Label Lager (Eng) a keg lager 1036 O.G. brewed by the Whitbread Brewery in Sheffield, Yorkshire.

Gold Label Rum (W.Ind) a deeper coloured rum than the silver label variety. Has a slightly sweet taste with a strong 'rum' flavour.

Goldlack (Ger) a spätlese wine from the Herrgottströpfchen range of wines from Jakob Gerhardt, Nierstein.

Gold Lager (Den) a lager 1045 O.G. brewed by Tuborg in Copenhagen.

Goldlay (Ger) vineyard (Anb): Mosel-Saar-Ruwer. (Ber): Bernkastel. (Gro): Vom Heissen Stein. (Vil): Pünderich.

Goldlay (Ger) vineyard (Anb): Mosel-Saar-Ruwer. (Ber): Bernkastel. (Gro): Vom Heissen Stein. (Vil): Reil.

Goldlay (Ger) vineyard (Anb): Mosel-Saar-Ruwer. (Ber): Zell/Mosel. (Gro): Weinhex. (Vil): Niederfell.

Goldlay (Ger) vineyard (Anb): Mosel-Saar-Ruwer. (Ber): Zell/Mosel. (Gro): Weinhex. (Vil): Oberfell.

Gold Lion (Cktl) ⅔ measure Nassau Orange Liqueur, ⅙ measure orange juice, ⅙ measure lemon juice. Shake well with ice, strain into a cocktail glass, decorate with a slice of orange and lemon.

Goldloch (Ger) vineyard (Anb): Nahe. (Ber): Kreuznach. (Gro): Schlosskapelle. (Vil): Dorsheim.

Goldloch (Ger) vineyard (Anb): Pfalz. (Ber): Mittelhaardt-Deutsche Weinstrasse. (Gro): Schnepfenflug vom Kellertal. (Vil): Gauersheim.

G

Gold Medal (S.Am) a brand of demerara rum produced by Banks DIH Ltd. in Guyana. Is aged for 2½ years in cask.

Gold Peak (USA) the label used by the Lamont Winery, California for their range of low-priced wines.

Goldpfad (Ger) vineyard (Anb): Rheinhessen. (Ber): Wonnegau. (Gro): Liebfrauenmorgen. (Vil): Worms.

Gold Premium (Eng) a 4.8% alc by vol. ale brewed by the Filo Brewing Company, East Sussex.

Gold Premium Smooth (Eng) a 4.7% alc by vol. nitro-keg lager brewed by Daniel Thwaites, Lancashire.

Goldriesling (Ger) a white grape variety, a cross between the White riesling and the Muscat precoce de Courtiller. Also known as the Riesling doré and the Knipperlé.

Gold Seal (USA) a large New York state winery owned by Seagrams. Is sited on the west shore of Lake Keuka (formerly known as the Urbana Wine C°).

Gold Seal Vineyards (USA) a leading vineyard of the Fingers Lakes region in the New York district.

Goldschläger (Switz) a 40% alc by vol. cinnamon schnapps with 24 carat gold leaf flakes.

Gold Standard (Eng) a 5% alc by vol. ale brewed from First Gold hops by the Freeminer Brewery.

Gold Star (Isr) an ale-type beer brewed by a Canadian backed brewery 12° Balling.

Gold Star Ale (Eng) a light ale 1034 O.G. brewed by the Shipstone Brewery in Nottingham.

Gold Star Soft Drinks Ltd (Eng) a carbonated soft drinks manufacturer. (Add): 4 Abbotts Close, Easatway, Lee Mill Ind Estate, Ivybridge, Devon PL21 9GA. Produces carbonated soft drinks and mineral waters. Website: http://www.goldstardrinks.co.uk 'E'mail: enquiries@goldstardrinks.co.uk

Gold Strike (Hol) produced by Bols, a schnapps-style liqueur containing cinnamon and 24 carat gold flakes (part of Allied-Domecq).

Goldstückchen (Ger) vineyard (Anb): Rheinhessen. (Ber): Bingen. (Gro): Adelberg. (Vil): Armsheim.

Goldthorn Brewery (Eng) a brewery. (Add): Imex Unit 60, Sunbeam Street, Wolverhampton, West Midlands WV2 4NU. Brews a variety of beers and lager. Website: http://www.goldthornbrewery.co.uk 'E'mail: paul@goldthornbrewery.co.uk

Gold Time Cocktail (Cktl) ⅓ measure golden rum, ⅓ measure egg yolk, ⅓ measure pineapple juice, dash lemon juice. Shake well over ice, strain into a cocktail glass, top with a cherry, lemon slice and serve with straws.

Goldtröpfchen (Ger) vineyard (Anb): Mosel-Saar-Ruwer. (Ber): Bernkastel. (Gro): Michelsberg. (Vil): Piesport.

Gold Vodka (Pol) a cask-matured vodka, may be matured for up to 10 years.

Goldwasser (Den) see Danziger Goldwasser.

Goldwasser (Pol) a vodka that dates from 16th century, flavoured with gypsy rose, valerian root, sandalwood and rosewood infused in aniseed-flavoured vodka which has 23 carat gold leaf added after the second distillation.

Goldwater Estate (N.Z) a winery. (Add): 18 Causeway Road, Putiki Bay, Waiheke Island. 5ha. Grape varieties: Cabernet franc, Cabernet sauvignon, Chardonnay, Merlot, Sauvignon blanc. Labels include: New Dog.

Goldwell (Eng) a Kent-based firm that produces Beachcomber Cream Liqueur, Calypso, Country Manor English Perry and Country Satin.

Golf (Cktl) 25mls (1fl.oz) gin, 10mls (½ fl.oz) dry vermouth, dash Angostura. Stir over ice, strain into a cocktail glass and serve with an olive.

Golfan (Fr) a wine-producing district in Bellet, Provence.

Goliath (Eng) a cask ale brewed by the Wychwood Brewery, Eagle Maltings, Witney, Oxfordshire. Part of their Character Ale range.

Gollebour (Lux) a vineyard site in the village of Machtum.

Gollenberg (Ger) vineyard (Anb): Pfalz. (Ber): Südliche Weinstrasse. (Gro): Trappenberg. (Vil): Bellheim.

Gollenberg (Ger) vineyard (Anb): Pfalz. (Ber): Südliche Weinstrasse. (Gro): Trappenberg. (Vil): Knittelsheim.

Gollop (Eng) a nineteenth century term for eating or drinking quickly.

Golubok (Sp) the brand-name of a vodka produced by Palomino y Vergara S.A. in Jerez.

Gomera [La] (Sp) one of the islands of Santa Cruz de Tenerife, Canarias. Also a Vino de la Tierra wine area of Tenerife.

Gomes [Luís] (Vinhos) Lda. (Mad) a noted firm of Madeira shippers.

Gomes [Marcelo] & Cia Lda. (Mad) a noted shipper of Madeira to the U.K.

Gomez [Felix Garcia] (Sp) a producer and exporter of Málaga wines.

Gomme Exir (Fr) a barley sugar-flavoured sirop.

Gomme Syrup (Fr) a non-alcoholic syrup used for sweetening cocktails.

Gönc (Hun) small tokaji casks. see Gonczi, Gyöncz and Gönz.

Gonczi (Hun) small casks into which the juice for Tokaji is run for ageing. see Gönc, Gyöncz and Gönz.

Gondeville (Fr) a commune in the Charente-Maritime département whose grapes are classed Grande Champagne (Cognac).

Gonet [Francois] (Fr) a Champagne producer. (Add): Rue du Stade, 51190 Mesnil-sur-Oger. Récoltants-manipulants. Produces vintage and non-vintage wines.

Gonet [Michel] (Fr) a Champagne producer. (Add): Ave. Jean Jaurès, 51190 Avize. Récoltants-manipulants. Produces vintage and non-vintage wines. Vintages: 1990, 1995, 1998, 1999.

Gonet [Philippe] (Fr) a Champagne producer. (Add): 1 et 3, Rue de la Brèche d'Oger, 51190 Le Mesnil su Oger. Propriétaire-Récoltant. Produces

G

vintage and non-vintage wines. Vintages: 1995, 1998. Labels: Roy Soleil Grand Cru, Spécial Club Blanc de Blancs Grand Cru. Website: http://www.champagne-philippe-gonet.com 'E;mail: info@champagne-philippe-gonet.com

Gönnheim (Ger) village (Anb): Pfalz. (Ber): Mittelhaardt-Deutsche Weinstrasse. (Gro): Feuerberg. (Vin): Martinshöhe.

Gönnheim (Ger) village (Anb): Pfalz. (Ber): Mittelhaardt-Deutsche Weinstrasse. (Gro): Hofstück. (Vins): Klostergarten, Mandelgarten, Sonnenberg.

Gontchi (Rus) a red dessert wine grape grown in Tadzhikistania.

Gontenbad (Switz) a sparkling natural spring mineral water from Gontenbad. Mineral contents (milligrammes per litre): Sodium 2.7mg/l, Calcium 100mg/l, Magnesium 18mg/l, Bicarbonates 1160mg/l, Chlorides 4mg/l, Fluorides <0.1mg/l, Nitrates 2mg/l.

Gönz (Hun) see Gönc, Gonczi and Gyöncz.

Gonzales (USA) a town in Salina Valley, Monterey, California. Is home to one small winery.

Gonzales [Miguel] (USA) a winery based in New Mexico. Produces table wines.

Gonzalez [Eucario] (Mex) a producer of tequila of same name.

Gonzalez Byass (Sp) a brandy and Sherry producer. (Add): Manuel M. Gonzalez 12, Jerez de la Frontera, Cadiz. Source of base wine is in La Mancha and Jerez de la Frontera. **brandies**: Soberano 2 year old, Insuperable a 5 year old, Conde Duque 8 year old and Lepanto 15 year old plus. **sherries**: Alfonso, Apostoles, Del Duque, El Rocío, La Concha, Matusalem, Nectar Cream, Noe, San Domingo and Tio Pepe. Also own Wisdom and Warter in Jerez de la Frontera. Also produce Beronia Rioja, Castell de Vilarnau cava wine. See also Gonzalez y Dubosc. Website: http://www.gonzalezbyass.com

Gonzalez Byass (Sp) vintage Port shippers. Vintages: 1896, 1900, 1904, 1908, 1912, 1917, 1920, 1945, 1955, 1960, 1963, 1967, 1970, 1975, 1977, 1980, 1985, 1991, 1994, 1997, 2003. Also produces fine brandies and sherries.

Gonzalez y Dubosc (Sp) a wine-producer based in Catalonia. Produce cava sparkling wines in caves of Segura Viudas. Sold in U.K. under the Jean Perico label. A marque owned by Gonzalez Byass.

Good Company (Mad) the brand-name for Madeira wines produced by Cossart Gordon.

Good Earth (Sing) a bottled pure drinking water (Sodium 1mg/l). (Add): Royal Queen Pte. Ltd., 138 Cecil Street, 09-01A Cecil Court, Singapore 069538.

Good Elf (Eng) a 4.9% alc by vol. seasonal cask ale brewed by Daniel Thwaite, Lancashire.

Good King Senseless (Eng) a 5.2% alc by vol. ale brewed by the Vale Brewery C°., Buckinghamshire.

Goodnight Cocktail (Cktl) ⅓ measure gin, ⅓ measure vodka, ⅓ measure rye whiskey, dash crème de noyau. Stir over ice and strain into a cocktail glass.

Goodnight Kiss (Cktl) consists of a Cherry 'B' topped up with cider.

Goodnight Vienna IPA (Eng) a 8% alc by vol. India pale ale brewed by the Garton Brewery, East Yorkshire.

Good Old Boy (Eng) a 4% alc by vol. ale brewed by the West Berkshire Brewing C°. Ltd., Berkshire.

Goodridge Castle (Eng) a 4.4% alc by vol. ale brewed by the Springhead Brewery, Nottinghamshire.

Goods (Eng) a term used to describe the contents of the mash tun. see Grist and Liquor.

Goorjuani (Geo) a dry white wine from the Rion Valley district of the Georgia region.

Goose Ale (Eng) a cask-conditioned beer 1036 O.G. brewed by the Goose and Firkin home-brew public house in London.

Goose and Firkin (Eng) a home-brew public house in London. Produces: Borough 1045 O.G. Dogbolter 1060 O.G. and Goose Ale 1036 O.G. All brewed with malt extract.

Goose Eye Brewery (Eng) a brewery (established 1991). (Add): Ingrow Bridge, South Street, Keithley, West Yorkshire BD21 5AX. Brews: Barm Pot 3.8% alc by vol., Bronte 4% alc by vol., Bronte Bitter 4% alc by vol., Golden Goose 4.5% alc by vol., No Eye Deer 4% alc by vol., Over & Stout 5.2% alc by vol., Pommies Revenge 5.2% alc by vol (1060 O.G.)., Special (or Wharfdale) Ale 4.5% alc by vol (1045 O.G.), Wonkey Donkey 4.3% alc by vol. Website: http://www.goose-eye-brewery.co.uk 'E'mail: enquiries@goose-eye-brewery.co.uk

Göppinger (Ger) a natural spring mineral water. Mineral contents (milligrammes per litre): Sodium 438mg/l, Calcium 313mg/l, Magnesium 65mg/l, Potassium 32mg/l, Chlorides 70.1mg/l.

Göppinger St. Christophorus Heilwasser (Ger) a natural spring mineral water. Mineral contents (milligrammes per litre): Sodium 331mg/l, Calcium 323mg/l, Magnesium 59mg/l, Potassium 26mg/l, Chlorides 46.4mg/l, Sulphates 71.1mg/l, Fluorides 0.57mg/l.

Gordo (Austr) a white grape variety that produces delicate, aromatic wines. Also known as Gordo blanco.

Gordo (Sp) a term used to describe a fat Sherry (depends on strength). See also Gordura.

Gordo Blanco (Sp) an alternative name for the Muscat of Alexandria. See also Gordo.

Gordon Bennett (Eng) a 4.1% alc by vol. ale brewed by the Belvoir Brewery, Leicestershire.

Gordon [Duff] (Sp) noted shippers of Sherry, owned by Osborne and based at Puerto de Santa Maria. Produces: El Cid, Fino Feria and Santa Maria.

Gordon Finest Gold (Scot) a 10% alc by vol. bottled ale brewed by McEwan Fountain Brewery, Edinburgh.

Gordon Highland Scotch Ale (Scot) a 8.6% alc by vol. bottled ale brewed by McEwan Fountain Brewery, Edinburgh, sold on the French market as Douglas.

Gordon's (Eng) a range of gins and vodkas produced by Gordon & C°. Ltd. Distillery. Part of DCL. C°.

Ltd. Range includes Gordon's 37.5% alc by vol., Gordon's Export Strength London Dry 43% alc by vol.

Gordons Ale (Scot) a strong bottled ale 9.5% alc by vol. brewed by the Scottish and Newcastle Brewery for Belgium.

Gordon's Cup (Cktl) in a large glass filled with ice add ½ glass of Gordon's gin, ½ glass port. Top with tonic water or lemonade, garnish with a slice of cucumber, slice of lemon and crushed mint leaves.

Gordon's Scotch Ale (Scot) a 7% alc by vol. ale brewed by McEwans. Available in Belgium.

Gordura (Sp) describes '*fatness*' in an Oloroso Sherry. Has rich vinosity. *See also* Gordo.

Gore-Browne (Eng) a pioneer of modern English wine-making. Started the Beaulieu Abbey Vineyard.

Gorgée (Fr) sup.

Gorges (Fr) a noted village in the Sèvre et Maine, Loire Atlantique. Produces fine Muscadet Sèvre et Maine wines.

Gorges de l'Hérault (Fr) a vin de pays area in the Hérault département in southern France.

Gorges du Tarn (Fr) a herb liqueur produced by Germain Distillery in southern France.

Gorges et Côte de Millau (Fr) a V.D.Q.S. region producing red, rosé and dry white wines from the bank of the River Tarn.

Gorilka (Ukr) a vodka flavoured with lime flower honey.

Gornac (Fr) a commune in the Haut Benauge, central Bordeaux.

Gornie Radgona (Slo) a white wine produced in the Slovenia region.

Gorno Bania 1 (Bul) an alkaline natural spring mineral water (established 1958) from Gorna Bania. Mineral contents (milligrammes per litre): Sodium 33.5mg/l, Calcium 4mg/l, Potassium 0.5mg/l, Bicarbonates 67mg/l, Chlorides 5mg/l, Sulphates 18.8mg/l, Fluorides 0.11mg/l, Silicates 42.6mg/l, Barium 1mg/l, Boration 1mg/l. pH 9.7

Gorny Doubnyak (Rus) a bitter liqueur made from ginger, galangal, angelica, clove, acorns and oak shavings.

Goron (Switz) a red Valais wine that has not passed the stringent tests to enable it to be called Dôle.

Goronsoe (S.Kor) a natural spring mineral water brand. pH 6.7

Gorska (E.Euro) a still and sparkling natural spring mineral water (established 2004) from Durmitor Heights, Trnskot Konopiste, Macedonia. Mineral contents (milligrammes per litre): Sodium 4.5mg/l, Calcium 26.5mg/l, Magnesium 3.5mg/l, Potassium 3.7mg/l, Bicarbonates 112.8mg/l, Chlorides 1.5mg/l, Sulphates 1.9mg/l, Fluorides 0.9mg/l. pH 6.0

Gorzaika (Pol) low-alcoholic vodkas produced in the eleventh and twelfth centuries as medicines.

Gospel Green Sussex Cyder (Eng) a vintage sparkling cider produced in Sussex 8% alc by vol.

Gospodaniile Agricole de Stat (Rum) *abbr*: G.A.S the State Agricultural Enterprise.

Gössenheim (Ger) village (Anb): Franken. (Ber): Maindreieck. (Gro): Rosstal. (Vin): Arnberg.

Gösser (Aus) a 5% alc by vol. straw coloured, bottled lager beer brewed by Steierbräu AG, Graz.

Gösser Brauerei (Aus) a brewery based at Leoben, the headquarters are opposite to the Renaissance Bénédictine Abbey, is noted for Steirisch Pils and Stiftsbräu beers.

Gosset (Fr) a Champagne producer. A Grande Marque (established 1584). (Add): 69 Rue Jules Blondeau, BP7, 51160 Aÿ. Produce vintage and non-vintage wines. Vintages: 1914, 1919, 1921, 1923, 1926, 1928, 1929, 1934, 1939, 1947, 1952, 1953, 1955, 1959, 1961, 1964, 1966, 1969, 1970, 1971, 1973, 1975, 1976, 1979, 1981, 1982, 1983, 1985, 1988, 1989, 1990, 1995, 1996, 1997, 1998, 1999, 2000. Hand remuage only. De Luxe vintage cuvée: Grande Millésime, Gosset Brabant Rosé, Gosset Celebris Rosé. Prestige cuvée: Cuvée 4ème Centenaire. Website: http://www.champagne-gosset.com 'E'mail: info@champagne-gosset.com

Gosset-Brabant (Fr) a Champagne producer (established 1930). (Add): 23, Boulevard de Lattre de Tassigny, 51160 Aÿ. 9.5ha.13ha. Produces vintage and non- vintage wines. Vintages: 1995, 1996, 1997, 1999. A member of the Club Tresors de Champagne. Labels: Cuvée Gabriel 'Special Club' Millésimée (Chardonnay 30%, Pinot noir 70%). 'E'mail: gusset-brabant@wanadoo.fr

Gota (Sp) virgin wine, the alternative name for Vino de Yema.

Gothe (Bra) a white grape variety.

Gothic Ale (Eng) a 5.2% alc by vol. ale brewed by Enville Ales Ltd., West Midlands.

Gotim Bru (Sp) lit: 'brown bunch', the local name for the Ull de llebre or Tempranillo grape in Costers del Segre, Cataluña.

Gotisprun (Aus) the label for a red wine (Blaufränkisch, Cabernet sauvignon and Zweigelt blend) produced by the Glatzer winery, Göttlesbrunn, Carnuntum.

Gottenheim (Ger) village (Anb): Baden. (Ber): Kaiserstuhl-Tuniberg. (Gro): Attilafelsen. (Vin): Kirchberg.

Götterlay (Ger) vineyard (Anb): Mosel-Saar-Ruwer. (Ber): Zell/Mosel. (Gro): Goldbäumchen. (Vil): Bruttig-Fankel.

Gottesacker (Ger) vineyard (Anb): Baden. (Ber): Markgräflerland. (Gro): Burg Neuenfels. (Vil): Hügelheim.

Gottesacker (Ger) vineyard (Anb): Pfalz. (Ber): Südliche Weinstrasse. (Gro): Trappenberg. (Vil): Altdorf.

Gottesfuss (Ger) vineyard (Anb): Mosel-Saar-Ruwer. (Ber): Saar-Ruwer. (Gro): Scharzberg. (Vil): Wiltingen.

Gottesgarten (Ger) vineyard (Anb): Rheinhessen. (Ber): Nierstein. (Gro): Gutes Domtal. (Vil): Selzen.

G

Gotteshilfe (Ger) grosslage (Anb): Rheinhessen. (Ber): Wonnegau. (Vils): Bechtheim, Osthofen.

Gottesthal (Ger) grosslage (Anb): Rheingau. (Ber): Johannisberg. (Vils): Estate, Östrich.

Gotto d'Oro (It) a modern winery based in Latium. Is noted for Marino (a dry white wine).

Gottschelle (Aus) a vineyard area on the banks of the River Danube in the Kremstal region.

Gott's Vineyard (USA) a vineyard which sells its grapes (Zinfandel) to the Monteviña Winery in the Shenandoah Valley, California.

Göttweig (Aus) a wine-producing abbey based near Krems.

Götzenberg (Ger) vineyard (Anb): Württemberg. (Ber): Remstal-Stuttgart. (Gro): Weinsteige. (Vil): Stuttgart (ortsteil Uhlbach).

Götzenberg (Ger) vineyard (Anb): Württemberg. (Ber): Württembergisch Unterland. (Gro): Wunnenstein. (Vil): Kleinbottwar.

Götzenborn (Ger) vineyard (Anb): Rheinhessen. (Ber): Bingen. (Gro): Abtey. (Vil): Wolfsheim.

Götzenfels (Ger) vineyard (Anb): Nahe. (Ber): Schloss Böckelburg. (Gro): Burgweg. (Vil): Bad Münster a. St-Ebernburg.

Götzenfels (Ger) vineyard (Anb): Nahe. (Ber): Schloss Böckelheim. (Gro): Burgweg. (Vil): Norheim.

Götzhalde (Ger) vineyard (Anb): Baden. (Ber): Badische Bergstrasse/Kraichgau. (Gro): Stiftsberg. (Vil): Neckarzimmern.

Gouais (Fr) a white grape popular in the seventeenth and eighteenth centuries used in the production of verjuice.

Goudallier (Ch.Isles) to drink alcoholic beverages. *See also* Goudélair.

Goudélair (Ch.Isles) to drink alcoholic beverages. *See also* Goudallier.

Goudenband Special Provisie (Bel) a bottle conditioned brown ale 6.5% alc by vol. brewed by Liefmans Brasserie in Oudenaarde. Matured for 8–12 months and bottled before the fermentation is completed.

Goudenboom (Bel) a brewery. (Add): Langestraat 45, Brugge B-8000. Produces a variety of beers and lagers. Website: http://www.bruggetripel.be

Gouden Carolus (Bel) a 7.5% alc by vol. top-fermented, strong, dark bottled ale brewed by the Het Anker Brasserie in Mechelen.

Goudge (Arg) a wine-producing area in the south of Argentina.

Goudini Co-operative (S.Afr) a co-operative winery and vineyards (established 1948) based in Goudini, Western Cape. 1040ha. (Add): Box 132, Rawsonville 6845, Worcester. Grape varieties: Cabernet sauvignon, Chardonnay, Chenin blanc, Cinsaut, Clairet blanche, Colombard, Hanepoot, Merlot, Pinotage, Ruby cabernet, Shiraz. Produces: Umfiki and a range of varietal wines. Website: http://www.goudiniwines.co.za

Goudoulin (Fr) a brand of Armagnac produced by Veuve J. Goudoulin in the Bas Armagnac.

Goudron (It) tar, applies to the bouquet and taste in Barolo wines.

Goue Vallei (S.Afr) a winery based in Citrusdal. Grape varieties include: Bukettraube, Cabernet sauvignon, Chenin blanc, Chardonnay, Sauvignon blanc, Merlot, Pinotage. Label: Impala.

Gough Brothers (Eng) a large chain of retail off-licences owned by the Seagram Distillers PLC.

Gouglou (Fr) a free 'night' club organised by the vineyard owner for their harvest staff during the period of the harvest in Bordeaux.

Gouguenheim Winery (Arg) a winery based in the Mendoza region, eastern Argentina. Website: http://www.gouguenheimwinery.com.ar

Goujan (Fr) an alternative name for the Pinot meunier grape.

Goulburn Valley (Austr) an area of Victoria around the town of Nagambia. Produces quality red and white table wines. Grapes include Marsanne.

Gould Campbell (Port) vintage Port shippers. Vintages: 1870, 1872, 1873, 1875, 1878, 1881, 1884, 1885, 1887, 1890, 1892, 1896, 1900, 1904, 1908, 1912, 1917, 1920, 1922, 1924, 1927, 1934, 1942, 1945, 1947, 1955, 1960, 1963, 1966, 1970, 1975, 1977, 1980, 1983, 1985, 1991, 1994, 1995, 1997, 2000, 2003. Owned by Symingtons.

Goulet [George] (Fr) a Champagne producer. (Add): 2-4 Ave. du Général Giraud, 51100 Reims. 15ha. Produces vintage and non-vintage wines. Vintages: 1921, 1926, 1928, 1934, 1937, 1941, 1943, 1945, 1947, 1949, 1952, 1953, 1955, 1959, 1961, 1962, 1964, 1966, 1969, 1970, 1971, 1973, 1975, 1976, 1979, 1981, 1985, 1988, 1990, 1995, 1996, 1997, 1998, 1999, 2001. De Luxe vintage cuvée: Cuvée de Centenaire.

Gouleyance (Fr) denotes a quaffing wine, an easy drinking wine.

Goulistane (Rus) a white grape variety grown in Turkmenistania. Used in the production of fortified wines.

Goulot (Fr) the name given to the bottle neck.

Goulots [Les] (Fr) a Premier Cru vineyard in the A.C. commune of Gevrey-Chambertin, Côte de Nuits, Burgundy.

Goumenissa (Gre) a dry, light-bodied, red wine produced by Boutari from the Negoska and Xinomavro grapes. Has some wood-ageing.

Goundrey Estate (Austr) a winery based in the Great Southern Region, Western Australia. Grape varieties include: Cabernet sauvignon, Merlot. Label: Homestead.

Gourd (Afr) a bottle or flask made from the dried shell of the bottle gourd.

Gourdjaani (Geo) a white wine produced in Takhetia region in Georgia.

Gourdoux (Fr) an alternative name for the Malbec grape.

Goureau (Fr) a cuvée in the Poruzots vineyard, A.C. Meursault, Côte de Beaune, Burgundy. Is owned by the Hospices de Beaune.

Gouresses [Les] (Fr) a vineyard in the A.C. commune of Montagny, Côte Chalonnaise, Burgundy.

Gourmand (Fr) a person who is devoted to food and drink (eats and drinks to excess). *See also* Gourmet.

Gourmel [L.] (Fr) a Cognac producer. (Add): B.P. 194, 16100 Cognac. 75ha. in Grande Champagne and 13ha. in Fins Bois. Produces L'Age des Fleurs 12 year old, L'Age des Épices 15 year old, L'Ages des Fruits (young and fruity) and Quintessence 21 year old.

Gourmet (Fr) a person who enjoys good food and drink, one who has a cultured palate. *See also* Gourmand.

Gourmet (Fr) a winebroker. *See also* Courtier.

Gouron [René] (Fr) a noted producer of Touraine rosé pétillant wine based in Chinon, Loire.

Gourry de Chadeville (Fr) a Cognac producer. (Add): SARL Gourry de Chadeville, 16130 Segonzac. 16ha. in the Grande Champagne. Produces Très Vieux 18–20 year old.

Gourzouf (Rus) a pink dessert wine from the southern Crimea.

Gout (Eng) a disease of the eighteenth and nineteenth centuries which was attributed to alcohol.

Goût (Fr) taste.

Goût Américan (Fr) fairly sweet, sparkling wines which are sweeter than French dosage.

Goût Anglais (Fr) dry taste.

Goût de Bois (Fr) woody taste.

Goût de Bouchon (Fr) corky tasting wine.

Goût de Capsule (Fr) taste and smell of the lead capsule.

Goût de Chêne (Fr) oaky taste.

Goût de Cuivre (Fr) taste of copper, applicable to brandy (Cognac) after distillation but passes after a year or so in oak.

Goût de Ferment (Fr) denotes that the wine is not ready to drink as it is still in the process of fermentation.

Goût de Fox (Fr) *see* Goût de Renard.

Goût de Grêle (Fr) lit: 'taste of hail', applied to wines that have been made from grapes damaged by hailstones before the harvest, applies especially to Burgundy wines. The hail bruises the skins and mildew forms which gives a curious objectionable flavour.

Goût de Lie (Fr) a yeasty taste that often renders a wine flat and unpleasant, signifies prolonged contact with lees.

Goût de Lumière (Fr) a term used to describe the maderising effect of a light-struck wine.

Goût de Moisi (Fr) musty taste.

Goût de Paille (Fr) straw taste.

Goût de Pierre à Fusil (Fr) a flinty taste to be found in Chablis.

Goût de Piqué (Fr) wine going towards vinegar.

Goût de Rafle (Fr) a term used to describe a wine that tastes of stems or vine stalks.

Goût de Rancio (Fr) bottle-stink.

Goût de Renard (Fr) lit: 'foxiness', the taste obtained from the **Vitis labrusca** grape in America. Also known as Goût de Fox.

Goût de Silex (Fr) earthy taste often found in white Burgundy wines.

Goût de Souris (Fr) mousy taste.

Goût de Taille (Fr) uncouth taste, made from the final pressing of the grapes.

Goût de Terroir (Fr) earthy taste.

Goût d'Éventé (Fr) flat taste, a taste wine obtains from old casks or badly cleaned casks. *see* Éventé.

Goute (Ch.Isles) a small sip of a drink.

Goût Française (Fr) sweet taste.

Goutorbe [Henri] (Fr) a Champagne producer. (Add): 9, Bis Rue Jeanson, F-51160, Aÿ. Récoltants-manipulants. 15ha. Produces vintage and non-vintage wines. Vintages: 1971, 1973, 1974, 1975, 1976, 1979, 1980, 1982, 1985, 1988, 1990, 1995, 1996, 1997, 1998, 1999, 2000. De Luxe vintage cuvée is Special Club. Also produces Cuvées: Traditionelle, Prestige and Rosé. Website: http://www.champagne-henri-goutorbe.com 'E'mail: info@champagne-henri-goutorbe.com

Goût Parisien (Fr) a description of the style of wine preferred by the inhabitants of Paris. Wines which are usually high in alcohol.

Goutte d'Or (Fr) a fine quality Meursault wine produced in the late eighteenth century.

Goutte d'Or (S.Afr) the label for a botrytised white wine (Sémillon 80%, Sauvignon blanc 20%) produced by the Beaumont Wines winery, Walker Bay, Western Cape.

Goutte d'Or [La] (Fr) a vineyard in the A.C. commune of Meursault, Côte de Beaune, Burgundy 5.3ha.

Gouveio (Port) a white grape variety used in the making of white Port.

Gouveiro (Mad) an alternative name for the Verdelho grape.

Gouverneur (Hol) a 5% alc by vol. pilsner brewed by De Lindeboom Bier Brouwerij, Neer.

Gouverneurs (S.Afr) the label for a range of red and white wines (including reserves) produced by the Groot Contantia Estate winery, Constantia, Western Cape.

Government Stamped (Eng) the crown and a number issued by H.M. Customs and Excise when they have tested glasses and carafes used for beers, ciders and for spirit measures.

Governo all'Uso Toscano (It) a Tuscan oenological procedure, bunches of grapes are dried indoors, then crushed, heated and added to the fermenting must in November, December and January after the harvest. 3% of total grapes (Canaiolo, Colorino and Sangiovese).

Governo Method (It) *see* Governo all'Uso Toscano.

Governor (Eng) an ale brewed by the Hull Brewery, North Humberside.

Gower Spring (Wal) a natural spring mineral water from Staffal Haegr Farm, Llanrhidian, Swansea.

Goya [La] (Sp) a Manzanilla Pasada Sherry produced by Delgado Zuleta.

Goyesco (Sp) a solera reserva brandy produced by Delgado Zuleta.

Graach (Ger) village (Anb): Mosel-Saar-Ruwer. (Ber): Bernkastel. (Gro): Münzlay. (Vins): Abtsberg, Dompprobst, Himmelreich, Josephshöfer.

G

Graan (Hol) denotes a Jenever made from grain only.

Graben (Ger) vineyard (Anb): Mosel-Saar-Ruwer. (Ber): Bernkastel. (Gro): Badstube. (Vil): Bernkastel-Kues.

Graben (Slo) a vineyard in Posavje that has over 20 different grape varieties that make over 50 wines.

Grabner-Schierer (Aus) a winery based in Sooss, Thermenregion. (Add): Hauptstrasse 55, 2500 Sooss. Grape varieties: Blauer portugieser, Grüner veltliner, Pinot blanc, Riesling, Rotgipfler, Zweigelt.

Graca (S.Afr) a dry white wine made from the Cape riesling and Sémillon grapes produced by the SFW. Is slightly pétillant.

Gra-Car (It) a liqueur which is similar in style to Chartreuse. Produced by the monks at Grand Chartreuse, Grenoble.

Grace Cup (Eng) a cup of wine passed around the table at the end of a meal in the eighteenth century.

Grace Family Vineyards (USA) vineyards based in Saint Helena, Napa Valley, California. Noted for high quality red wine produced solely from Cabernet sauvignon using bio-dynamic principles (approximately 200 cases per year produced).

Graceful (Eng) a term that describes a wine as being stylish and elegant in character.

Graceful Cocktail (Cktl) 1 measure (green) crème de menthe, stir over ice, strain into a cocktail glass, top with cream and sprinkle with grated chocolate.

Graceland Vineyard (S.Afr) a winery (established 1997) based in Stellenbosch, Western Cape. 10ha. Grape varieties: Cabernet sauvignon, Merlot, Shiraz. Label: Three Graces (also varietal wines). Website: http://www.gracelandvineyards.com

Gracerry Vineyards (Austr) *see* Stanton and Killeen.

Grace Vineyard (USA) the label for a red wine (Pinot noir) produced by Domaine Serene, Willamette Valley, Oregon.

Gracia Winery (Chile) a winery (established 1993) based in the Bío-Bío Valley, southern Chile, also has vineyards in the Cachapoal Valley. Grape varieties: Chardonnay, Pinot noir. Website: http://www.graciawinery.cl

Gracia Hermanos S.A. (Sp) a winery based in Montilla. Produces fine Montilla-Moriles wines.

Graciana (Sp) an alternative spelling of Graciano.

Graciano (Sp) a red grape variety grown in Navarre and Rioja. Late budder, low yielder and also prone to mildew. (Fr) = Morrastel, (Sp) = Tinta miúda, (USA) = Xeres.

Graciosa (Port) a DOC wine area and island in the Azores.

Gradazione Alcolica Complessiva (It) a term meaning 'total alcohol content'.

Gradi (It) grade. *see* Gradi Alcool.

Gradi Alcool (It) percentage of alcohol by volume in a beverage (100% as pure alcohol).

Gradi Alcoolico (It) lit: 'alcoholic grade' *see* Gradi Alcool.

Gradignan (Fr) a commune in the A.C. Graves region in south-western Bordeaux.

Graduate (Eng) a cask beer 5% alc by vol. brewed by the Morrell Brewery, Oxford. Bottle-conditioned version is 5.2% alc by vol.

Graeff Light (Ger) a clear drink made from grape juice, wine and water 0.05% alc by vol.

Graf (Ger) Count (title).

Graf Arco (Ger) a Bavarian lager sold by Gibbs Mew in Great Britain. Known as Bollbier Hell in bottle form.

Graf-Bernhard-Quelle (Ger) a natural spring mineral water.

Graf Beyssel-Herrenberg (Ger) vineyard (Anb): Mosel-Saar-Ruwer. (Ber): Zell/Mosel. (Gro): Grafschaft. (Vil): Bullay.

Graf Eberhard Kuenberg (It) a winery based in Schloss Sallegg, Kaltern, Trentino-Alto Adige. 25ha.

Grafenberg (Ger) vineyard (Anb): Mosel-Saar-Ruwer. (Ber): Bernkastel. (Gro): Michelsberg. (Vil): Neumagen-Dhron.

Grafenberg (Ger) vineyard (Anb): Nahe. (Ber): Schloss Böckelheim. (Gro): Rosengarten. (Vil): Sponheim.

Gräfenberg (Ger) vineyard (Anb): Rheingau. (Ber): Johannisberg. (Gro): Geiligenstock. (Vil): Kiedrich.

Gräfenberg (Ger) vineyard (Anb): Pfalz. (Ber): Südliche Weinstrasse. (Gro): Guttenberg. (Vil): Freckenfeld.

Gräfenberg (Ger) vineyard (Anb): Württemberg. (Ber): Remstal-Stuttgart. (Gro): Kopf. (Vil): Schorndorf.

Gräfenberg (Ger) vineyard (Anb): Württemberg. (Ber): Württembergisch Unterland. (Gro): Heuchelberg. (Vil): Kleingartach.

Gräfenberg (Ger) vineyard (Anb): Württemberg. (Ber): Württembergisch Unterland. (Gro): Heuchelberg. (Vil): Leingarten.

Gräfenberg (Ger) vineyard (Anb): Württemberg. (Ber): Württembergisch Unterland. (Gro): Heuchelberg. (Vil): Neipperg.

Gräfenberg (Ger) vineyard (Anb): Württemberg. (Ber): Württembergisch Unterland. (Gro): Heuchelberg. (Vil): Niederhofen.

Gräfenberg (Ger) vineyard (Anb): Württemberg. (Ber): Württembergisch Unterland. (Gro): Heuchelberg. (Vil): Nordheim.

Gräfenberg (Ger) vineyard (Anb): Württemberg. (Ber): Württembergisch Unterland. (Gro): Heuchelberg. (Vil): Nordheim.

Gräfenberg (Ger) vineyard (Anb): Württemberg. (Ber): Württembergisch Unterland. (Gro): Heuchelberg. (Vil): Schwaigern.

Gräfenberg (Ger) a vineyard within the village of Kiedrich, 10.6ha. (91.5%) of which is proposed to be classified as Erstes Gewächs.

Grafensprung (Ger) vineyard (Anb): Baden. (Ber): Ortenau. (Gro): Schloss Rodeck. (Vil): Obersrot.

Grafenstück (Ger) grosslage (Anb): Pfalz. (Ber): Mittelhaardt-Deutsche Weinstrasse. (Vils): Bockenheim, Kindenheim, Obrigheim.

Gräfin Mariannen-Quelle (Ger) a natural spring

mineral water. Mineral contents (milligrammes per litre): Sodium 9mg/l, Calcium 45mg/l, Magnesium 40mg/l, Potassium 6mg/l, Bicarbonates 293mg/l, Chlorides 5mg/l, Sulphates 55mg/l.

Graf Rudolf Quelle (Ger) a natural spring mineral water from Wagenfeld. Mineral contents (milligrammes per litre): Sodium 22.1mg/l, Calcium 107mg/l, Magnesium 11mg/l, Potassium 2.5mg/l, Bicarbonates 456mg/l, Chlorides 15.3mg/l, Sulphates 1.1mg/l.

Grafschaft (Ger) grosslage (Anb): Mosel-Saar-Ruwer. (Ber): Zell/Mosel. (Vils): Alf, Beuren, Bremm, Bullay, Ediger-Eller, Neef, Nehren, St.Aldegund, Zell-Merl.

Grafschafter Sonnenberg (Ger) vineyard (Anb): Mosel-Saar-Ruwer. (Ber): Bernkastel. (Gro): Kurfürstlay. (Vil): Veldenz.

Grafting (Eng) a method used to attach young vine stems (scions) onto disease-resistant root stocks to help combat Phylloxera. *see* Bench Grafting, Cleft Grafting, Crown Graft, Field Grafting, Greffe, Greffe Anglaise and Omega Grafting.

Gragnano (It) a dark, rich, red, fruity wine from the Campania region.

Graham [W & J] (Port) vintage Port shippers. Vintages: 1870, 1872, 1873, 1875, 1878, 1880, 1881, 1884, 1885, 1887, 1890, 1892, 1894, 1886, 1887, 1900, 1901, 1904, 1908, 1912, 1917, 1920, 1924, 1927, 1935, 1942, 1945, 1948, 1955, 1958, 1960, 1963, 1966, 1970, 1975, 1977, 1980, 1982, 1983, 1985, 1991, 1994, 1995, 1997, 2000, 2003. Produces a range of Port styles. Owned by Symingtons. *See also* The Tawny. Website: http://www.grahams-port.com

Graham Beck Wines (S.Afr) a winery (established 1983) based in Franschhoek (198ha) and Robertson (156ha), Western Cape. (Add): Madeba Farm, P.O. Box 724, Robertson. Grape varieties: Cabernet franc, Cabernet sauvignon, Chardonnay, Merlot, Muscadel, Pinotage, Pinot noir, Sauvignon blanc, Shiraz, Viognier. Labels: Anthony's Yard, Barrel Select, Coffeestone, Lonehill, Peasant's Run, Pinno, Railroad Red, Rhona, The Andrew, The Cornerstone, The Joshua, The Old Road, The William.

Graham Cocktail (Cktl) ¼ measure sweet vermouth, ¼ measure dry vermouth. Stir well over ice and strain into a cocktail glass.

Graham Reserve [Avondale] (S.Afr) a red blend wine produced by the Avondale winery, Paarl, Western Cape.

Graham's Emperor (Port) a fine, old, Tawny Port from Graham Port Shippers.

Grain (Ger) vineyard (Anb): Pfalz. (Ber): Mittelhaardt-Deutsche Weinstrasse. (Gro): Rebstöckel. (Vil): Neustadt an der Weinstrasse.

Grain Alcohol (Eng) ethanol, containing approximately 10% of water, made from a distillation of fermented grains.

Grain Alcohol (USA) the name used for gin, vodka, etc.

Grain de Café (Fr) coffee bean.

Grain d'Orge (Fr) a 8% alc by vol. golden straw coloured, top-fermented, bottled ale brewed by the Jeanne d'Arc Brasserie, Ronchin.

Grainer (Ger) the local name for red wine from the town of Kleinheppach in Württemberg.

Grainhübel (Ger) vineyard (Anb): Pfalz. (Ber): Mittelhaardt-Deutsche Weinstrasse. (Gro): Mariengarten. (Vil): Deidesheim.

Grain Neutral Spirits (USA) pure spirits, the name for any of the distillates which are distilled to over 190° U.S. Proof (95% alc by vol.) e.g. gin and vodka.

Gráinnin Eorna (Ire) barleycorn/grain of barley.

Grains Nobles (Fr) *see* Sélection de Grains Nobles.

Grain Spirits (USA) neutral spirits distilled from a fermented mash of grain and stored in oak containers.

Grain Storm (Eng) a 4.2% alc by vol. ale brewed by the Millstone Brewery, Lancashire.

Grain Store Brewery [The] (Eng) a brewery (established 1994). (Add): Davis'es Brewing Company, Station Approach, Oakham, Rutland LE15 6RE. Brews: Cooking Bitter 3.6% alc by vol., 1050 5% alc by vol., Rutland Beast 5.3% alc by vol., Rutland Panther 3.4% alc by vol., Steamin Billy 4.3% alc by vol., Triple B 4.2% alc by vol., V.P. which commemorates the 1000th guest ale served at the Queens Head, Sutton Bassett and Ten Fifty. Website: http://www.rutnet.co 'E'mail: grainstorebry@aol.com

Grain Whisky (Scot) a whisky made from grains (mainly wheat) other than barley (not malted). Used for blending with malt whiskies to produce blended Scotch whisky. *See also* Old Cameron Brig.

Graisse (Fr) a flat, oily, faded wine, a diseased wine caused by rod-shaped bacteria. Often occurs in Champagne in the wine from the last pressing, the wines lose some of their sugar and increase in acidity. (Sp) = hilo.

Graisse Blanc (Fr) an alternative name used for the Plant de graisse white grape grown in Armagnac.

Graisse des Vins (Fr) occurs in white wines as a result of harsh pressing the grapes, wine is left cloudy. Necessary to add tannin to clear the sediment. Also known as ropiness.

Graisse Roussanne (Fr) an alternative name for the Ugni blanc grape.

Grampian's Nessie (Scot) a cask-conditioned ale from the Tomintoul Brewery.

Gramp Winery (Austr) a winery owned by Orlando, Reckitt and Colman in the Barossa Valley.

Grana (Sp) a solera reserva brandy produced by Bodegas 501. *See also* Tercios, 501 Etiqueta Negra.

Granaccia (It) an alternative name for the Garnacha (Grenache) grape.

Granacha (It) an alternative name for the Garnacha (Grenache) grape.

Granada [1] (Cktl) 25mls (1fl.oz) each of Mandarine Napoléon, Campari, dry gin, 50mls (2fl.ozs) lemon juice. Shake well over ice and strain into a cocktail glass.

Granada [2] (Cktl) 25mls (1fl.oz) each of Mandarine Napoléon, Campari, dry gin, 50mls (2fl.ozs) lime juice cordial. Shake well with ice, strain into a highball glass, add ice, top with lemonade, lemon slice and serve with straws.

Granada (Sp) a province of D.O. Andalucía. Home to the Vino de la Tierra area of Contraviesa-Alpujarra.

Granado (W.Ind) the brand-name of a distilled white rum from a distillery of same name in Puerto Rico.

Gran Alanís (Sp) a white wine produced from Treixadura and Torrontés grapes by Bodega AlanIs, Ribeiro.

Gran Albina (Sp) a Rioja wine produced by Bodegas Riojanas. Aged in 100% new oak from Tempranillo, Garnacha and Mazuelo grapes grown in Cincero.

Granary Bitter (Eng) a cask-conditioned bitter ale 1038 O.G. brewed by the Reepham Brewery in Norfolk.

Granàt (Czec) lit: 'garnet', a beer brewed by the Hora Brewery based in South Morana, Cerna.

Granato (It) a term used to describe the colour of red wines. Deep ruby with golden tinges around the edges.

Granbazán Amba (Sp) a wine produced in Rías Baixas, D.O. Galicia by Agro de Bazán in Val do Salnés.

Granbazán Verde (Sp) a wine produced in Rías Baixas, D.O. Galicia by Agro de Bazán in Val do Salnés.

Gran Canaria (Sp) one of three islands that make up the Las Palmas de Gran Canaria, Canarias. See also Lanzarote, Fuerteventura.

Gran Canaria-El Monte (Sp) a Vino de la Tierra area of Gran Canaria, Canary Islands.

Gran Canciller (Sp) a 10 year old brandy produced by Palomino y Vergara S.A., Calon 1–25, Jerez de la Frontera, Cadiz.

Gran Capitán (Sp) a solera gran reserva brandy produced by Bobadilla.

Gran Caus Rosado (Sp) a rosé wine from the Penedés region of Catalonia, produced from 100% Merlot grapes.

Gran Claustro (Sp) a top of the range vintage sparkling wine produced from Chardonnay and Macabeo grapes of the Castillo Perlada C°.

Gran Coronas (Sp) a fine red reserva wine from Torres, Penedés, produced from Cabernet sauvignon 85% and Ull de llebre (Tempranillo) 15%.

Gran Coronas Black Label (Sp) a fine oak aged red wine from Torres, Penedés, produced from Cabernet sauvignon 70%, Cabernet franc 10% and Ull de llebre 20%. Now known as Mas la Plana.

Gran Crémant Semi Seco (Sp) a slightly sweet-tasting, sparkling white wine that has a dry finish. Produced by the Marqués de Monistrol.

Grand Armagnac Janneau (Fr) an Armagnac producer. (Add): Janneau Fils SA, 50 Ave. d'Acquitaine, 32100 Condom. Produces Janneau Tradition 4–5 years old.

Grand Arôme (W.Ind) the name given to those rums that are produced from molasses, fermented with dunder, coloured with caramel and slow fermented for 8–12 days. Known as Plummer or Wedderburn on the island of Jamaica.

Grand'Arte (Port) a dry white Vinho Regional Estremadura wine produced by DFJ Vinhos in the Ribatejo. White is from Alvarinho and Chardonnay grapes, red is from Touriga francesca grapes.

Grand Bois [Le] (Fr) a wine-producing district in A.C. Bellet, Provence.

Grand Carmenet (Fr) an alternative name for the Carmenère grape. See also Bouton Blanc, Carbonet, Carbouet, Cabernelle, Carmenelle, Grande Vidure.

Grand Casse (W.Ind) a 'Silver Label' rum that has been aged for three years (derived from Rhum Duquesne production) in Martinique.

Grand Chasseur Estate [Le] (S.Afr) a vineyard based in Robertson. (Add): P.O. Box 439, Robertson 6705. Produces varietal wines.

Grand Chemarin [Le] (Fr) a vineyard in the commune of Bué, A.C. Sancerre, Central Vineyards, Loire.

Grand Cidre Bouché (Fr) stoppered cider.

Grand Classique (S.Afr) the label for a red wine (Merlot blend) from Glen Calou winery, Paarl, Western Cape.

Grand Clos (Fr) an A.C. Bourgueil red wine vineyard in the Loire.

Grand Conseil de Bordeaux (Fr) a wine society based in Bordeaux.

Grand Constance (S.Afr) the label for a sweet red and white (Muscat de Frontignan) wine produced by the Groot Constantia Estate, Western Cape.

Grand Cordon (Fr) a prestige Champagne of G.H.Mumm. Replaced the Cuvée René Lalou. 50% Chardonnay from Avize and Cramant, 50% Pinot noir from Ambonnay, Aÿ, Verzenay. See also Mumm de Mumm.

Grand Cour (Fr) a vineyard in A.C. Fleurie Cru Beaujolais-Villages, Burgundy.

Grand Cru (Bel) a white beer brewed from wheat and oats from the De Kluis Brasserie 7.5% alc by vol.

Grand Cru (Eng) a 5% alc by vol. cold-filtered continental-style premium lager brewed by Young's.

Grand Cru (Fr) lit: 'great growth', in Alsace denotes a specific vineyard site. Once it has been designated any producer wishing to use the 'Grand Cru' on his/her label may do so if the grapes come only from that vineyard with a minimum specified natural sugar content and they are restricted to 65 hl/ha. maximum yield. Produced from noble grapes (Gewurztraminer, Muscat, Pinot gris, Pinot noir and Riesling) and be tested in bottle by a tasting panel. Also known as Grand Vin. (Ger) = gross gewäch.

Grand Cru (Fr) the top rating for 17 Champagne villages. 100%. see Échelle des Crus.

Grand Cru (Fr) the top grading of Burgundy wines, the Tête de Cuvée.

G

Grand Cru (S.Afr) great growth, producers own rating.

Grand Cru (S.Afr) the label for a late harvest sweet white wine (Steen) produced by the Douglas Wine Cellar winery, Douglas, Northern Cape.

Grand Cru Bourgeois (Fr) applies to Claret. Further classification in 1978. 41 châteaux in total. Vineyard must be not less than 7ha. in size, wine must be made at the property and submitted for taste testing. *See also* Cru Bourgeois, Grand Cru Bourgeois Exceptionnel (ow no longer used).

Grand Cru Bourgeois Exceptionnel (Fr) applies to Claret. Further classification in 1978. 18 châteaux in total. Vineyard must be not less than 7ha. in size, wine must be made and bottled at the property, oak aged and submitted for taste testing. *See also* Cru Bourgeois, Grand Cru Bourgeois (now no longer used).

Grand Cru Classé (Fr) top classification of vineyards in Bordeaux. Barsac 1855, Graves 1953 and 1959, Médoc 1855, Saint-Émilion 1955 (reviewed every 10 years) and Sauternes 1855.

Grand Cru Vineyards (USA) a winery in the Alexander Valley, Sonoma County, California. Grape varieties: Cabernet sauvignon, Chenin blanc, Gewürztraminer and Sauvignon blanc. Produces varietal wines.

Grand Cumberland (Austr) a sweet liqueur made with Passion fruit, golden in colour.

Grand Deluge [Le] (S.Afr) *see* Roodezandt Koöperatiewe Wynmakery.

Grand Detour (USA) the label for a red wine (Pinot noir) produced by the Landmark winery, Sonoma County, California.

Grand d'Oc (Fr) new regional designation in the Vin de Pays d'Oc, South France in 2001. A selection of red and white wines will be taste tested. To qualify the wines must be aged for a minimum of 12 months and bottled in the region.

Grand Domaine Jean-Voisin (Fr) a vineyard in the commune of Saint-Émilion. A.C. Saint-Émilion, Bordeaux 2ha.

Grand Duque de Alba (Sp) winery. (Add): Bodegas Zolio Ruiz-Mateos S.A. C/Porvera 48, Jerez de la Frontera. Source of base wine is Jerez. Produces Gran Duque de Alba 25–30 year old.

Grande Année (Fr) a prestige cuvée Champagne of Bollinger produced from 65% Pinot noir, 35% Chardonnay.

Grande Cassagne (Fr) a Syrah-based wine produced in the A.C. Costières de Nîmes, Languedoc-Roussillon by Château Grande Cassagne.

Grande Champagne (Fr) the classical area of Cognac. The ultimate in quality of brandy together with Fine Champagne. Covers 14.4% of the Cognac region. (Coms): Ableville, Angeac-Champagne, Bonneuil, Bourg-Charente, Bouteville, Château-Bernard, Cognac, Critéuil-la-Magdeleine, Eraville, Gensac-la-Pallue, Genté, Gimeux, Gondeville, Juillac-le-Coq, Lignières-Sonneville, Mainxe, Malaville, Merpins, Salles-d'Angles, Saint-Brice, Saint-Fort-sur-le-Né, Saint-Même, Saint-Preuil, Ségonzac, Touzac, Verrières and Viville.

Grande Cuvée Venus Brut (Fr) a de luxe cuvée vintage Champagne produced by Germain et Fils from 50% Chardonnay and 50% Pinot noir grapes.

Grande Dame [La] (Fr) a de luxe vintage cuvée Champagne produced by Veuve Clicquot Ponsardin from 33% Chardonnay and 66% Pinot noir grapes.

Grande Dame Rosé [La] (Fr) the top cuvée of Veuve Clicquot. Produced using 38% Chardonnay from Grand Crus of Avize, Oger, Le Mesnil-sur-Oger, 62% Pinot noir from Grand Crus of Vezernay, Verzy, Ambonnay, Bouzy, Aÿ, plus 13.3% of Pinot noir red wine from Clos Colin.

Grande Fine Ancestrale (Fr) a 4–5 year old Cognac produced by Menard.

Grande Liqueur (Fr) a green (or yellow) herb liqueur, the green is dry and yellow is sweet.

Grandelite (Port) a wine produced by Ca-Gera Agricola Vinhos Alto Douro.

Grande Marque Impériale (Fr) a vintage cuvée Champagne produced by Abele.

Grande Millésime (Fr) a de luxe vintage cuvée Champagne produced by Gosset from 66% Chardonnay and 33% Pinot noir grapes.

Grand Empereur (Fr) a well-known brand of brandy.

Grand Enclos du Château de Cérons (Fr) a vineyard in the commune of Cérons. A.C. Cérons, Bordeaux. 11ha.

Grande Pièce [La] (Fr) a vineyard in the A.C. commune of Montagny, Côte Chalonnaise, Burgundy.

Grande Pompée [La] (Fr) a vineyard in the A.C. Saint-Joseph, Rhône, southern France.

Grande Réserve (Fr) an old designation in Alsace for *'late picked'*, same grade as spätlese in Germany. *See also* Réserve Spéciale.

Grande Réserve (Lux) the top grading of wines.

Grandes Pagos de Castilla (Sp) lit: 'great estates of Castile', a new group of wineries formed in 2000 by producers who grow grapes or use methods that do not allow their wines to have D.O. status. Are working to develop individual *'private D.O.'* status.

Grandes Appellations (Fr) a famous, well-known and consistent A.C. wines. e.g. Médoc, Graves, Sauternes.

Grande Sendrée (Fr) a de luxe cuvée Champagne produced by Drappier (André).

Grandes-Lolières [Les] (Fr) a Premier Cru vineyard in the A.C. commune of Ladoix-Serrigny, A.C. Aloxe-Corton, Côte de Beaune, Burgundy.

Grandes Maisons d'Alsace (Fr) *abbr*: G.M.A. formed by association of eight top quality wine-producing houses of Alsace to promote their wines.

Grandes Marques (Fr) lit: 'great brand' or 'famous name'. The top Champagne houses. Houses are Ayala, Billecart-Salmon, Bollinger, Canard-Duchêne, Deutz, Heidsieck-Henriot, Heidsieck Monopole, Krug, Lanson, Laurent-Perrier, Mercier, Moët et Chandon, Mumm (G.H.), Perrier

(Joseph et Fils), Perrier-Jouët, Piper Heidsieck, Pol Roger, Pomméry et Greno, Prieur (Ch. & A.), Roederer (Louis), Ruinart Père et Fils, Salon, Taittinger and Veuve Clicquot-Ponsardin. *See also* Petites Marques.

Grandes-Ruchottes (Fr) a Premier Cru vineyard [part] in the A.C. commune of Chassagne-Montrachet, Côte de Beaune, Burgundy. 0.64ha. Also known as Les Grandes-Ruchottes.

Grandes Terra Alta (Sp) s Terra Alta.

Grandes Versannes [Les] (Fr) the second wine of Château Gravet-Renaissance, Grand Cru A.C. Saint-Émilion.

Grande Vidure (S.Am) an alternative name for the red grape variety Carmenère in Chile. *See also* Bouton Blanc, Carbonet, Carbouet, Cabernelle, Carmenelle, Grand Carmenet.

Grandes Vignes de Roy [Les] (Fr) a vineyard in the A.C. Rasteau, Côtes-du-Rhône-Villages.

Grand Firepeak Cuvée (USA) the label for a red wine (Pinot noir) produced by the Baileyana winery, San Luis Obispo County, California.

Grand-Formats (Fr) the collective name for large bottle sizes (magnums and above).

Grandin (Fr) producers of a range of vintage and non-vintage A.C. Crémant de Loire wines including demi-sec, brut, brut rosé.

Grandjo (Port) a wine produced in Lafoes by Real Companhía Vinícola do Norte de Portugal.

Grandma (Eng) an old ale and mild ale mixed, half and half.

Grandma (Eng) a sweet stout and old ale mix in the Midlands.

Grand Macnish (Scot) the label of a blended Scotch whisky 40% alc by vol.

Grand Marnier (Fr) a famous Curaçao with a Cognac base. Two versions produced, Cordon Rouge: Fine Champagne Cognac, red brown in colour and Cordon Jaune: lower quality brandy, lower in alcohol and pale yellow. Also a Crème de Grand Marnier.

Grand Marnier-Lapostolle (Fr) a famous liqueur producer. Produces Grand Marnier.

Grandma's Chocolate Secret (Eng) a chocolate-flavoured liqueur from Berentzen Distillers, Hailsham, Sussex.

Grandma's Vanilla Secret (Eng) a vanilla-flavoured liqueur from Berentzen Distillers, Hailsham, Sussex.

Grand Mousseux (Fr) a term used when a Champagne has the highest pressure in bottle producing a lot of sparkle on pouring.

Grand Mousseux (S.Afr) sweet (vin doux) sparkling wines produced since 1929.

Grand Mousseux Wines (S.Afr) a brand of sparkling wines produced by the SFW.

Grand Mouton (Fr) the label for an A.C. Muscadet de Sèvre et Maine Sur-Lie from Domaine de Grand Mouton.

Grand Musigny (Fr) an old division of the Grand Cru vineyard of Musigny. The other division was Petit Musigny.

Grand Noir (Fr) a red fleshed grape variety used in the making of dessert wines in California and Australia. Produced from Aramon and Petit bouschet. Also known as Grand noir de la Calmette. (Sp) = Gran negro.

Grand Noir de la Calmette (Fr) *see* Grand Noir.

Grand Nord Cocktail (Cktl). ½ measure green Chartreuse, ½ measure vodka. Stir over ice in an old-fashioned glass.

Grand Old Parr (Scot) *see* Old Parr.

Grand Pacific Vineyards (USA) a winery based in Marin, near San Francisco, California. Grape varieties: Chardonnay, Merlot and Sauvignon blanc. Produces varietal wines.

Grand Passion Cocktail (Cktl) ⅔ measure dry gin, ⅓ measure passion fruit juice, 2 dashes Angostura. Shake over ice and strain into a cocktail glass.

Grand Pavillon [Le] (S.Afr) a sparkling blanc de blancs wine from a blend of Chardonnay with Cape riesling or Cruchen and Sémillon grapes. Produced by Boschendal.

Grand Pompe [Le] (Fr) an A.C. Saint-Joseph red wine from Jaboulet Aîné in the Côtes du Rhône.

Grand Premier Cru (Lux) classification of wines. *See also* Marque Nationale.

Grand Prix Cocktail (Cktl) 25mls (1fl.oz) vodka, 20mls (¾ fl.oz) dry vermouth, 5mls (¼ fl.oz) Curaçao, dash lemon juice, dash grenadine. Shake well over ice, strain into a goblet and serve with straws.

Grand Provence (S.Afr) a winery (22ha) based in Franschhoek, Western Cape (originally known as Agusta). Grape varieties: Cabernet sauvignon, Chardonnay, Chenin blanc, Hanepoot, Merlot, Sauvignon blanc, Shiraz. Label: Angels Tears (Pink/Red/White).

Grand Quetsch Cocktail (Cktl) 25mls (⅛ gill) Grand Marnier, 15mls (⅛ gill) quetsch, 15mls (⅛ gill) orange juice. Stir together over ice, strain into a flute glass filled with crushed ice and top with a squeeze of orange peel juice.

Grand Réserve (Fr) a wine with over 11% alc by vol.

Grand Reserve (S.Afr) the label for a red wine (Cabernet sauvignon 98% and Merlot 2%) produced by the Delheim winery, Stellenbosch, Western Cape.

Grand River Winery (USA) a winery based in Madison, Ohio. 8ha. Is planted with Vitis vinifera and hybrid vines.

Grand Rouge (S.Afr) the label for a red wine (Cabernet sauvignon and Merlot blend) produced by the Bovlei Winery, Wellington, Western Cape.

Grand Rouge (S.Afr) the label for a red wine (Merlot based blend) produced by the Franschhoek Vineyards winery, Franschhoek, Western Cape.

Grand Rouge de Constance (S.Afr) the label for a red wine (Cabernet franc, Pontac and Tinta blend) produced by the Signal Hill winery, Cape Town, Western Cape.

Grand Roussillon (Fr) a region in southern France, famous for sweet and fortified wines. e.g. Banyuls, Rivesaltes, Maury, Côtes du Roussillon.

G

Grand Royal Fizz (Cktl) 50mls (2fl.ozs) dry gin, juice ½ lemon, juice ½ orange, 3 dashes gomme syrup, 2 dashes maraschino, 10mls (½ fl.oz) cream. Shake over ice, strain into an ice-filled highball glass, top with soda water and stir.

Grand-Saint-Bernard (Switz) an alpine plant liqueur. 2 versions: *Jaune* = 41% alc by vol. *Verte* = 45% alc by vol. Produced by Morand Distillerie, Martigny, Valais.

Grands Bois (Fr) a still natural spring mineral water from Fismes. Mineral contents (milligrammes per litre): Sodium 11mg/l, Calcium 124mg/l, Magnesium 25mg/l, Potassium 3.5mg/l, Bicarbonates 420mg/l, Chlorides 16mg/l, Sulphates 60mg/l.

Grands-Champs [Les] (Fr) a Premier Cru vineyard in the A.C. commune of Auxey-Duresses, Côte de Beaune, Burgundy 4.86ha.

Grands Crus (Fr) a classification of Bordeaux wines. *see* Classification of Bordeaux.

Grands Crus Classés (Fr) *see* Classification of Bordeaux.

Grands-Échezeaux (Fr) a Grand Cru vineyard in the A.C. commune Vosne-Romanée, Côte de Nuits, Burgundy 9.2ha.

Grand Siècle Alexandra (Fr) a prestige cuvée of Champagne house Laurent-Perrier.

Grand Slam (Cktl) ¼ measure sweet vermouth, ¼ measure dry vermouth, ½ measure Swedish Punsch. Stir over ice and strain into a cocktail glass.

Grand Slam Cocktail (Cktl) ¼ measure Irish whiskey, ¼ measure Glayva, ¼ measure dry gin, ¼ measure Cointreau, ½ measure orange juice, dash grenadine. Shake well over ice, pour into a large goblet, dress with an orange slice, blue cherry and serve with straws.

Grand Soir (Fr) a prestige cuvée Champagne from de Sacy (Louis).

Grandson (Switz) a red and white wine-producing area in northern Vaud.

Grand Springs (USA) a natural spring mineral water from Mount Carmel Range, Virginia.

Granduca Brut (It) a sparkling (metodo tradizionale) wine produced by Duca d'Asti, Piemonte.

Granducato (It) a Chianti Classico producer based in Siena, Tuscany.

Grand Union Brewery (Eng) a brewery (established 2002). (Add): 10 Abenglen, Betam Road, Hayes, Middlesex UB3 1SS. Brews: Grand Union Bitter 3.7% alc by vol., Grand Union Gold 4.2% alc by vol., Grand Union Special 4.5% alc by vol., Honey Porter 4.9% alc by vol., Kolsch Style 4.8% alc by vol., Stout 4.8% alc by vol. Website: http://www.gubrewery.co.uk 'E'mail: info@gubrewery.co.uk

Gran Duque de Alba (Sp) an amber-coloured, solera gran reserva brandy produced by Don Zolio in Jerez de la Frontera (part of Diez-Merito).

Grand Val (USA) the second wine of Clos du Val, Napa Valley, California.

Grand Vin (Fr) an Alsace grading which can only be used on wines coming from superior grape varieties and containing 11% alc by vol. Also referred to as Grand Cru.

Granel (Sp) the name given to a white wine produced in bulk by Bodega Cooperativa de Ribeiro.

Gran Enologica (Sp) a fine red wine produced by Rioja Santiago S.A., Rioja.

Granfiesta (Austr) a brand of Australian Sherry produced by Quelltaler in Clare Watervale, South Australia.

Gran Fuedo (Sp) the brand-name of a 4 year old red wine produced by Bodegas Julián Chivite in Navarra, also the name of a rosé (rosado) wine made from 100% Garnacha grapes.

Gran Garvey (Sp) a solera gran reserva brandy produced by Garvey. *See also* Lacre Oro, Rango.

Grange (Austr) the new name for Grange Hermitage from 1991 vintage.

Grange Hermitage (Austr) a noted red wine from the Penfold Cº. vineyards in South Australia. Created by Max Schubert who used USA oak barrel ageing on ripe Shiraz grapes from the Barossa Valley. From 1991 vintage will be named Grange.

Grangehurst Winery (S.Afr) a winery (14ha) based in Stellenbosch, Western Cape. (Add): P.O. Box 206, Stellenbosch 7599. Grape varieties: Cabernet sauvignon, Merlot, Pinotage. Labels: Chairman's Reserve, CWG Auction Reserve, Nikela. Website: http://www.grangehurst.co.za

Grängesbergs Brewery (Swe) a brewery based in Grängesberg, central Sweden. Produces fine lager beers.

Granila al Caffé (It) an iced coffee with 'frozen' egg white, it is eaten with rum.

Granite (Fr) soil composition suitable for grape cultivation, consists of granitic sand. i.e. Northern Rhône, Pays Nantais and Beaujolais.

Granite Brewery [The] (Can) a brewery. (Add): 245 Eglinton Ave.E., Toronto, Ontario M4P 3B7. Brews a variety of beers and lager. Website: http://www.granitebrewery.ca 'E'mail: ron@granitebrewery.ca

Granite de Clisson (Fr) an A.C. Muscadet Sèvre et Maine from Domaine Bruno Cormerais (aged up to 5 years in oak).

Granite Belt (Austr) a wine region in Queensland.

Granja (Port) an I.P.R. wine produced within Alentejo.

Granja Nuestra Señora de Remelluri [La] (Sp) a 40ha. vineyard. (Add): Labastida, Alavesa, Rioja. Produces Remelluri (a red estate wine from 10% Mazuela, 80% Tempranillo and 10% Viura).

Granja Remelluri [La] (Sp) *see* Granja Nuestra Señora de Remelluri (La).

Granja União (Bra) a label used by Indústria Comércio e Navegação, Sociedade Vinícola Rio Grandense, Ltda. for red and white wines.

Granjo (Port) a naturally sweet white wine.

Gran Manzeda (Eng) a fine Manzanilla Sherry from Balls Brothers of London.

G

Granmonte Asoke Valley Estate Farm Vineyards (Thai) a winery based at Khao Yai. Grape varieties: Chenin blanc, Shiraz. Produces varietal wines.

Gran Negro (Sp) a red grape variety grown in Galicia. Also known as Grão Negro. (Fr) = Grand noir.

Granny's Flan (Wal) a 3.8% alc by vol. ale brewed by Granny's, Aberystwyth.

Grano (Sp) the berry of the grape, a single grape.

Grano d'Oro (Sp) a liqueur produced from dates.

Gran Orden de Caballeros del Vino (Sp) a wine fellowship created by Vino de España in 1985. Created to honour people in the wine trade who have given outstanding personal service to the furtherance of Spanish wines.

Gran Provence (S.Afr) a sparkling, medium-sweet, white wine made from Clairette blanche and Steen grapes by Union Wines.

Gran Reserva (Sp) a term used in Jerez for D.O. brandy that guarantees that the youngest spirit in the blend is 3 years old. Aged using the Solera system.

Gran Reserva (Sp) produced only in exceptional vintages. Red wines matured 2 years in cask, 3 years in bottle (or vice versa), white and rosé wines matured 4 years with a minimum of 6 months in bottle. see Crianza, Reserva, Vino Joven.

Gran Sangre de Toro (Sp) a fine oak aged red wine from Torres, Penedés. Produced from Cariñena 25% and Garnacha 70%, Syrah 5%.

Grans Brewery (Nor) a brewery based in Sandefjord in south-eastern Norway.

Gran Señor (Sp) a solera gran reserva brandy produced by Caballero (Luís).

Gran Señor Choice Old Cream (Sp) a brand of Cream Sherry produced by Caballero (Luis).

Grans-Fassian (Ger) a winery based in Trittenheim, Mosel-Saar-Ruwer. Grape variety: Riesling. Produces a variety of wine styles.

Grans Muralles (Sp) a fine red wine from the Torres stable. 32ha. Grape varieties: Garnacha, Garró, Monastrell, Samsó.

Gran Solera (Sp) a rich old Oloroso Sherry from Harvey that is completely dry in taste.

Gran Spumante (It) a dry sparkling wine from the Pinot grape made by the metodo tradizionale.

Grant Burge (Austr) a winery based in the Barossa Valley. (Add): Sturt Highway, via Tanunda, South Australia. Grape varieties: Cabernet sauvignon, Chardonnay, Shiraz. Label: Holy Trinity.

Grantham Stout (Eng) a 4.3% alc by vol. stout brewed by the Oldershaw Brewery, Lincolnshire.

Gran Torres (Sp) a brandy and orange liqueur produced by the Torres Cº. in Penedés.

Grant [William and Sons] (Scot) a famous Scotch whisky distillery based in Banffshire. Produces Highland and Lowland malt whiskies. see Glenfiddich, Grant's Royal, Standfast, Balvenie (The).

Grant's (Scot) a 12 year old de luxe Scotch whisky. Is a re-designed and re-named version of Grant's Royal from Grant (William and Sons) 43% alc by vol.

Grantschen (Ger) village (Anb): Württemberg. (Ber): Württembergisch Unterland. (Gro): Salzberg. (Vin): Wildenberg.

Grant's Morello Cherry Brandy (Eng) a Kent-made liqueur 25% alc by vol.

Grants of St. James (Eng) a London based wine merchants famous for their 'Don Cortez' Spanish wines. See also Soir (Le).

Grant's Royal (Scot) see Grant's.

Grant's Standfast (Scot) a blended Scotch whisky from Grant (William and Sons), Banffshire.

Granules (Eng) a style of instant coffee produced by freeze drying, the resulting powder is shaped into granules to imitate ground coffee.

Gran Val (USA) the label used by the Clos du Val Wine Cº. for their range of varietal wines.

Granvás (Sp) the cuve close sparkling wine method (the second fermentation carried out in a sealed container and not in the bottle), the cork carries an oval on the base.

Gran-Vas (Sp) see Dom Yago Rosado.

Gran Viña Sol (Sp) a fine white wine from Torres, Penedés. Produced from Chardonnay 85% and Parellada 15%.

Gran Viña Sol Green Label (Sp) a fine white wine from Torres, Penedés. Produced from Parellada 70% and Sauvignon blanc 30%. Re-named Fransola.

Gran Vino (Chile) a wine older than six years before bottling.

Gran Vino Godello (Sp) a very dry, white varietal wine produced by the Cooperativa Jesus Nazareno 13.5% alc by vol.

Gran Vino Para Banquetes (Chile) a label term 'great wine for banquets'.

Gran Vino Tinto (Chile) a red wine produced by Undurraga.

Grão Negro (Sp) an alternative name for Gran Negro.

Grão Vasco (Port) the brand-name for red and white Dão wines blended and matured by SOGRAPE at Viseu.

Grapa (Sp) the name given to a metal hook that retains the temporary corks during sparkling (cava) wine manufacture. (Fr) = agrafe.

Grape(s) (Eng) the fruit of the *Vitis vinifera* that produces the raw material for wine making. A wide variety of species is grown around the world. see Vitis. (Arab) = inab, (Aus) = trauben, (Chi) = putao, (Cro) = grožde/grožnja, (Den) = vindrue, (Fr) = graine de raisin/raisin, (Ger) = trauben, (Gre) = rhax, (Gre) = stafili, (Hol) = druif, (Indo) = anggur, (Ire) = fionchaor, (Isr) = anav, (It) = uva/uvas/chicco d'uva, (Jap) = budoo, (Kor) = podo, (Lat) = uva/baca/acinum, (Pol) = winogrono, (Port) = uva/uvas, (Rus) = veenagrat, (Sp) = uva/uvas, (Thai) = arngoon, (Tur) = üzüm, (Wal) = grawnwin.

Grape [The] (Eng) a slang term for wine. See also Juice of the Grape.

Grape Brandy (Eng) any other brandy produced from the distillation of wine other than Cognac or Armagnac. *see* Aguardiente, Bagaceira, Grappa and Marc.

Grape Bud Mite (Eng) *Eriophyes vitis*. *see* Acariosis.

Grape Certificate Program (USA) formed by the University of California in 1952 to certify authentic grape varieties.

Grape Cocktail (Cktl)(Non-alc) 30mls (¼ gill) grape juice, 30mls (¼ gill) plain syrup, 2 slices fresh fruit, dash Angostura. Stir over ice, strain into a highball glass and fill with soda water.

Grape Crusher (Eng) the general term for a unit which presses the whole grape to extract the juice. *see* Grape Mill. (Ire) = cantaoir fhiona.

Grapefruit Champagne (Cktl)(Non-alc) 40mls (⅓ gill) grapefruit juice, 3 dashes lemon juice, dash Gomme syrup. Shake well over ice, strain into a flute glass and top with iced lemonade.

Grapefruit Cocktail (Cktl) ½ measure grapefruit juice, ½ measure gin, dash gomme syrup. Shake over ice and strain into a cocktail glass.

Grapefruit Nog (Cktl) 75mls (3 fl.ozs) grapefruit juice, 35mls (1½ fl.ozs) brandy, 25mls (1fl.oz) lemon juice, 1 egg, 2 teaspoons honey. Blend altogether with a scoop of crushed ice and pour into an ice-filled highball glass.

Grape Leafhoppers (USA) insects that attack the cell structure of the leaf, causes defoliation and turns grapes to raisins through too much sunshine.

Grape Mash (USA) grape juice, skins and pips used for red wines so that at the start of fermentation, the tannin and colour are extracted.

Grape-Mill (USA) another name for the grape crusher.

Grape of the Estruscans (It) *see* Canaiolo Nero.

Grape Pie (USA) the grape pulp after juice extraction.

Grape Press (Eng) *see* Grape Crusher.

Grape Rust Mite (Eng) *Calepitrimerus vitis, Phyllocoptes vitis*. *See also* **Acariosis**.

Grape Seed Tannins (Eng) bitter tannins that are extracted when the must is left on the skins and seeds for a long time (20 days or more).

Grape Spirit (Eng) brandy.

Grape Sugar (Eng) glucose $C_6H_{12}O_6$ and Dextrose are grape sugars. (Ire) = siúcra fionchaor.

Grape Vodka Froth (Cktl) ⅗ measure vodka, ⅕ measure grape juice, ⅕ measure lemon juice, 1 egg white. Shake well over ice and strain into a 125mls (5fl.ozs) goblet.

Grapey (Eng) the term used to describe the flavour and bouquet given off by certain grape varieties. If the flavour is too pronounced the wines usually lack subtlety.

Grappa (It) the Italian equivalent of French marc. After grape juice has been removed, residue is fermented and distilled to produce a harsh brandy. Also made from distilled wine. Can be both Pot or Patent stilled, flavoured with a sprig of rue as an infusion.

Grappa (S.Am) a spirit flavoured with aniseed, distilled from cane sugar 45% alc by vol. Produced in Colombia and Ecuador.

Grappa (USA) *see* California Grappa.

Grappa Blanche (W.Ind) the name given to a rum produced in Martinique that has no cask ageing.

Grappa Bochino (It) an oak-aged grappa produced in Friuli, pale-gold in colour.

Grappa d'Or (Switz) golden grape.

Grappa Julia (Eng) the brand-name of a grappa produced by Stock Distilleries in Trieste, Piemonte 40% alc by vol.

Grappa Strega (Cktl) ½ measure grappa, ½ measure Strega, 3 dashes lemon juice, 3 dashes orange juice. Shake well over ice and strain into a cocktail glass.

Grappe (Fr) a bunch of grapes.

Grappe des Papes [La] (Fr) the label of a Châteauneuf-du-Pape produced by Jaboulet in Tain-l'Hermitage, Drôme. Other label is Cédres (Les).

Grappes d'Or (Fr) a three star Cognac produced by Dupuy.

Grapple (Eng) the name used by Chilsdown for a ½ apple and ½ Chilsdown wine.

Grappling Hook (Cktl) equal quantities of red wine, Port wine and brandy shaken over ice and strained into a cocktail glass.

Grappolo (It) a bunch of grapes.

Grapput (Fr) an alternative name for the red grape variety Bouchalès.

Grapy (Eng) the term applied to the aroma and flavour of a wine which is reminiscent of the grapes used.

Gras (Fr) ropey, a condition (malady) of the wine. Is also used to describe a rich, round, robust wine. *see* Rope.

Gras [Les] (Fr) *see* Cras (Les).

Grasa (Rum) the local name for the Furmint grape.

Grasa di Cotnari (Rum) the equivalent of the Hungarian Furmint. Produced from the Grasa grape.

Grasevina (Cro) a fine medium white wine from Croatia. Made from the Grasevina (Welschriesling) grape. *See also* Grassevina.

Grasgeschmack (Aus) denotes a taste of green plants, usually derived from unripe grapes or those that have been overpressed.

Graspa (It) the Venetian spelling of grappa.

Grassl [Hans] (Aus) a winery based in Göttlesbrunn, Carnumtum. (Add): Am Graben 4 & 6, 2464 Göttlesbrunn. Grape varieties: Blaufränkisch, Chardonnay, Pinot blanc, Zweigelt.

Grassevina (Cro) a local name for the Welschriesling. *See also* Grassica and Grasevina.

Grasshopper [1] (Cktl) 20mls (¾ fl.oz) green crème de menthe, 20mls (¾ fl.oz) white crème de cacao, 20mls (¾ fl.oz) light cream. Shake well with ice and strain into a cocktail glass.

Grasshopper [2] (Cktl) in a liqueur glass pour in ½ measure crème de menthe then ½ measure crème de cacao, do not stir.

Grasshopper (Eng) a 3.6% alc by vol. seasonal cask-conditioned ale brewed by Hardy's and Hanson's, Kimberley, Nottingham. Part of the Cellarman's cask range.

Grasshopper Kentish Bitter (Eng) a 4.8% alc by vol. bitter beer brewed by the Westerham Brewery C°. Ltd., Kent.

Grassica (Cro) a local name for the white grape variety Welschriesling. *See also* Grassevina.

Grassnitzberg (Aus) a Cru vineyard area situated on the Slovakian border.

Grassy (Eng) a term used mainly for wines made from the Gewürztraminer, Sauvignon blanc and Scheurebe grapes which have a grassy type of fruitiness.

Gratacul (It) the name of a grappa flavoured with the dog rose.

Gratallops Project (Sp) a scheme to grub up native vines and replant with French varieties in the regions of Catalunya and Tarragona.

Graticci (It) straw mats used for drying the grapes for Passito wines.

Gratien [Alfred] (Fr) a Champagne producer. (Add): 30 Rue Maurice Cervaux, 51210 Épernay. Produces vintage and non-vintage wines. Vintages: 1904, 1906, 1926, 1928, 1929, 1933, 1934, 1937, 1938, 1942, 1943, 1945, 1947, 1949, 1952, 1953, 1955, 1959, 1961, 1962, 1964, 1966, 1969, 1970, 1971, 1973, 1976, 1979, 1982, 1983, 1985, 1988, 1989, 1990, 1995, 1996, 1998, 1999, 2000. Labels: Cuvée Brut Classique, Cuvée Paradis Brut, Cuvée Paradis Brut Rosé, Millésime. Website: http://www.alfredgratien.com 'E'mail: contact@alfredgratien.com

Gratien et Meyer (Fr) négociants in Anjou-Saumur. Produce fine sparkling wines by the méthode traditionelle. (Add): Route de Montsoreau, B.P. 22-49401 Saumur-Cedex. Cuvée Paradis includes specially selected wines from 1995 vintage. *See also* Royal Framboise.

Gratiesti (Rus) a dessert wine produced from the Rcakzitelli grape in the Moldavia region.

Gratitude [La] (S.Afr) a dry white wine from the Steen and Clairette blanche grapes. Produced by SFW at their Libertas winery.

Gratte-Cul (Fr) a flavoured spirit made from the dog rose.

Grattamacco (It) a wine estate in Bolgheri, Tuscany. Noted for barrique-aged Grattamacco Rosso produced from Merlot, Sangiovese and Cabernet grapes.

Grauburgunder (Ger) *see* Grauerburgunder.

Grau Clevner (Fr) a local name for the Pinot blanc grape.

Grauer Burgunder (Aus) an alternative name for the Pinot Gris grape.

Grauerburgunder (Aus)(Ger) a local name for the Pinot Gris grape.

Grauer Riesling (Ger) an erroneous varietal name for the red Ruländer.

Graukatz (Ger) vineyard (Anb): Nahe. (Ber): Schloss Böckelheim. (Gro): Paradiesgarten. (Vil): Gaugrehweiler.

Graukatz (Ger) vineyard (Anb): Nahe. (Ber): Schloss Böckelheim. (Gro): Paradiesgarten. (Vil): Kalkofen.

Graukatz (Ger) vineyard (Anb): Nahe. (Ber): Schloss Böckelheim. (Gro): Paradiesgarten. (Vil): Münsterappel.

Graukatz (Ger) vineyard (Anb): Nahe. (Ber): Schloss Böckelheim. (Gro): Paradiesgarten. (Vil): Niederhausen an der Nahe.

Graukatz (Ger) vineyard (Anb): Nahe. (Ber): Schloss Böckelheim. (Gro): Paradiesgarten. (Vil): Oberhausen an der Nahe.

Graukatz (Ger) vineyard (Anb): Nahe. (Ber): Schloss Böckelheim. (Gro): Paradiesgarten. (Vil): Winterborn.

Graukatz (Ger) vineyard (Anb): Rheinhessen. (Ber): Bingen. (Gro): Rheingrafenstein. (Vil): Tiefenthal.

Graumönch (Ger) lit: 'grey monk', the German name for the Pinot gris. Also known as the Grey Friar in Hungary.

Grauvernatsch (It) the Germanic name for a red wine from the Südtirol region. Known as Schiava grigia in Italy.

Grauves (Fr) a Premier Cru Champagne village in the Canton d'Avize. District: Épernay (red and white grapes).

Grave del Friuli (It) a D.O.C. red wines from Friuli-Venezia Giulia. The name is followed by the grape variety. Grave del Friuli Cabernet, Grave del Friuli Merlot and Grave del Friuli Reposco. Also name for white wines: Grave del Friuli Pinot bianco, Grave del Friuli Pinot grigio, Grave del Friuli Tocai and Grave del Friuli Verduzzo. Vinification can take place in the Udine and Pordenone provences and several communes.

Gravedigger Ale (Eng) a mild ale brewed by Church End Brewery in Warwickshire..

Gravedigger Beer (Eng) a cask-conditioned bitter 1050 O.G. brewed by the home-brew public houses Pier Hotel in Gravesend and the Southeastern in Strood.

Gravediggers (Eng) a 3.8% alc by vol. ale brewed by The Church End Brewery Ltd., Warwickshire.

Gravel (Fr) *see* Graves (a wide area of Bordeaux, has soil of a gravelly nature).

Gravel (USA) a term used for the tartrate crystals which appear in wines that have been chilled and precipitated out.

Gravel Hill (S.Afr) the label for a red wine (Shiraz) produced by the Hartenberg Estate winery, Northern Cape.

Gravello (It) a red wine produced by Librandi in Calabria from 60% Gaglioppo and 40% Cabernet sauvignon grapes.

Gravelly Meadow (USA) the brand-name used by the Diamond Creek Winery for one of their styles of wines from the vineyard of that name. Grapes include: Cabernet sauvignon.

Graves (Fr) a commune in the Charente département whose grapes are classed Petite Champagne (Cognac).

Graves (Fr) a large wine district in Bordeaux on the S.W. bank of the river Garonne around and to the south of Bordeaux town. Named after its gravel soil. Produces fine red and white wines. (Coms):

G

Arbanats, Aîguemortes, Beautiran, Budos, Castres, Cadaujac, Canéjean, Cérons, Eyzines, Gradignan, La Brède, Landiras, Langon, Léognan (own A.C. with Pessac), Martillac, Mazères, Mérignac, Pessac (own A.C. with Léognan), Podensac, Portets, Pujols, Ropaillan, St-Mèdard d'Eyrans, St-Morillon, St-Pardons-de-Conques, St-Pierre-de-Mons, St-Selve, Toulenne, Villenave-d'Ornon and Virelade.

Graves Bonne Terre (Fr) the brand-name for a dry white wine from Sichels.

Graves de Saint-Émilion (Fr) a small Saint-Émilion district, name derives from the soil (gravel).

Graves de Vayres (Fr) a district south of the Côtes de Fronsac in the Bordeaux region. Produces red and white wines.

Graves et Sables Anciens (Fr) lit: 'gravel with sand', a production zone in Saint-Émilion, south-eastern Bordeaux.

Graves Saint-Émilion (Fr) see Graves de Saint-Émilion.

Graves Supérieures (Fr) denotes a white wine from the A.C. Graves that has attained 12% alc by vol. by natural fermentation.

Gravier (Fr) gravelly soil.

Gravières [Les] (Fr) a Premier Cru vineyard [part] in the A.C. commune of Santenay, Côte de Beaune, Burgundy.

Gravillons (Fr) a coarse gravel soil in the commune of Margaux in Bordeaux, is grittier than the sandy topsoil (found underneath).

Gravina (It) the brand-name of a well-known grappa.

Gravina (It) a D.O.C. white wine produced from Greco and Malvasia grapes in Puglia (near the Basilicata region). Wine is lemon fresh and high in acidity. Town of Gravina is coolest in Puglia. Leading producer is Botromagno.

Graviscanum (It) a red wine produced in central-western Italy during Roman times.

Gravitas (Fr) a wine with weight, body.

Gravity (Eng) a measure of the beer's density. see Original Gravity.

Gravity (Eng) the name given to method of dispensing beer direct from the cask behind the bar.

Grawnwin (Wal) grapes.

Gray Dutchess (USA) see Grey Riesling.

Graylyn (Austr) a winery based in the Margaret River, Western Australia.

Gray Mont Estate Winery (Can) vineyards are based at Lake Okanagan, British Columbia. Grape varieties: Gewürztraminer, Pinot gris.

Gray Riesling (USA) the alternative name for the Chauche gris. See also Trousseau, Grey Riesling.

Gräzer (Aus) a white grape variety which is little used nowadays. Is also known as the Banater riesling.

Grazia (It) a natural spring mineral water from Grazia.

Graziano Family Wines (USA) a winery based in the Mendocino County, California. Is a member of the Coro Mendocino (Zinfandel) wine group of Mendocino wineries.

Graziola (It) a Moscato d'Asti Spumante producer based in the Piemonte region.

Great (Eng) a term used to describe a wine which has no flaws and has real distinction.

Great Bear (USA) a natural spring mineral water (established 1888) from Onondaga County, New York. Mineral contents (milligrammes per litre): Sodium 1.7mg/l, Calcium 1.3mg/l, Magnesium 1mg/l, Potassium 0.7mg/l, Bicarbonates 5.5mg/l, Chlorides 1.4mg/l, Sulphates 5.3mg/l. pH 6.57

Great Belly (Eng) a variety of cider apple.

Great British Beer Festival (Eng) an annual celebration run by the CAMRA organisation which has up to 250 different beers for tasting.

Great British Heavy (Eng) a strong bitter beer brewed by the Cornish Brewery C°. in Devon.

Great Bustard (Eng) a standard draught bitter from Gibbs Mew, Salisbury, Wiltshire.

Great Bustard (Eng) a 4.8% alc by vol. ale brewed by Stonehenge Ales (Bunces Brewery) Ltd., Wiltshire.

Great Canadian (Can) the name of a naturally fermented cider produced by Great Canadian Cider Exporters Ltd., Vancouver, British Columbia.

Great Cask (Ger) sited in the castle at Heidelberg in Baden (holds 220,000litres).

Great Central Valley (USA) a wine area of California. Produces mainly sweet dessert wines.

Great Cockup Porter (Eng) a 3% alc by vol. porter brewed by the Hesket Newmarket Brewery, Cumbria.

Great Dane (Eng) a 4.6% alc by vol. ale brewed by Stonehenge Ales (Bunces Brewery) Ltd., Wiltshire.

Great Dane [The] (Den) a lager brewed by the Faxe Brewery. Imported to the U.K. in 500mls cans by Danish Bacon Company.

Great Eastern (Eng) a 4.3% alc by vol. ale brewed by Woodforde's Ltd., Norfolk.

Great Expectations (S.Afr) the label for a white wine (Chardonnay) produced by the Goedverwacht Estate winery, Robertson, Western Cape

Greater London Alcohol Advisory Service (Eng) see G.L.A.A.S.

Greater Perth (Austr) a wine sub-region of Western Australia which has a hot, dry climate and produces mainly sweet and fortified wines.

Greatest Reform Act (USA) the name given to the Prohibition of the USA in 1919–1933. See also Noble Experiment.

Great Growth (Fr) a term used to describe the top classified wines from Bordeaux and Burgundy. (Fr) = grand cru, (Ger) = gross gewäch.

Great Guns Cocktail [1] (Cktl) 20mls (⅙ gill) Dubonnet, 15mls (⅛ gill) dry vermouth, 15mls (⅛ gill) pale Sherry, 2 dashes Angostura. Stir over ice, strain into a cocktail glass, serve with a cherry and a dash of lemon peel juice on top.

Great Guns Cocktail [2] (Cktl).(2) as for [1] using orange bitters and orange peel juice instead of Angostura and lemon peel juice.

Great Lakes Brewing C° [The] (USA) a brewery. (Add): 2516 Market Avenue, Cleveland, Ohio

44113. Brews beers and lager. Website: http://www.greatlakesbrewing.com 'E'mail: info@greatlakesbrewing.com

Great Northern (Eng) a 4.1% alc by vol. beer brewed by the Fernandes Brewery, Kirkgate, Wakefield, West Yorkshire.

Great Northern Bitter (Eng) a keg/canned bitter 1036 O.G. brewed by the Watney Mann, Truman breweries.

Great Plain (Hun) the largest wine-producing area that stretches from the Rumanian border to the river Danube.

Great River Winery (USA) a winery based in the Hudson Valley, New York. Noted for French hybrid and Marlboro sparkling wines.

Great Southern (Austr) a wine area in the south of Western Australia which has the coastal sub-regions of Albany and Denmark. See also Margaret River, Swan Valley.

Great Stour Brewery (Eng) a brewery based in Canterbury. Produced a 3-pack of bottled beers featuring the political leaders (early 90's). Contained: John's Judicious Juice, Tony's Trustworthy Tipple, Paddy's Proportional Pint.

Great Thirst [The] (USA) the years of Prohibition 1919–1933 were often called this mainly due to the lack of beer.

Great Tsar (Ger) a triple distilled 100% grain vodka from Asmussen 37.5% alc by vol.

Great Wall Chinese Vodka (Chi) the brand-name of the first vodka produced in China (1976). Made from mineral water and golden wheat 40% alc by vol.

Great Wall White Wine (Chi) a white wine produced from the Loong Yan (Dragon's Eye) grape by the Great Wall Wineries in Hebei.

Great Wall Wineries (Chi) a large winery based in Hebei. Produces dry fragrant white wines from the Loong Yan grape. See also Dragon's Eye.

Great Western (Austr) an area in Victoria noted for a wide range of fine sparkling wines under the Great Western and Seppelts labels. Also Avoca which is noted for still light wines.

Great Western (USA) the brand-name used by the Pleasant Valley Wine Cº. for their California Champagne range.

Great Western Beer Festival (Eng) the name for a commercial beer festival held annually in Bristol for beers and lagers.

Great Western Bitter (Wal) a keg bitter 1041 O.G. brewed by the Crown Brewery in South Wales.

Great Western Real Ale (Eng) abbr: G.W.R. a 5.4% alc by vol. ale from the Cottage Brewing Company, West Lydford, near Yeovil, Somerset.

Great Western Winery (Austr) winery in Seppelts. (Add): Western Highway, Great Western, Victoria.

Grecanico Dorato (It) a white grape variety grown in Sicily.

Grechetto Bianco (It) a white grape variety grown in Umbria. Also known as Greghetto, Greco, Greco Spoletino, Greco Bianco di Perugia.

Grechetto di Todi (It) a white Vino da Tavola from the Grechetto grape produced in Todi, Umbria.

Grecian Urn (Gre) the name given to a dry red and a dry white table wine from Tsantali.

Greco (It) an aromatic white grape variety with floral aromas and citrus flavours, grown mainly in central Italy. Known as the Grechetto in Tuscany.

Greco Bianco (It) a white grape variety grown in Calabria.

Greco Bianco di Perugia (It) an alternative name for the Grechetto Bianco.

Greco di Bianco (It) a sweet white wine made from semi-dried grapes in Calabria.

Greco di Gerace (It) a white grape variety used in the making of fine dessert wines of the same name in Calabria.

Greco di Gerace (It) a golden amber dessert wine from Calabria. It has an orange blossom nose, is high in sugar and alcohol 16%–17% by vol.

Greco di Tufo (It) a dry white wine produced in the Campania region from Greco grape.

Greco di Tufo (It) a D.O.C. white wine from Campania. Made from the Coda di Volpe bianco and Greco di tufo grapes. Vinification can take place throughout the province of Avellino. D.O.C. also applies to the sparkling wines obtained according to the regulations.

Greco Giallo (It) the Latium region name for the white Trebbiano giallo grape variety.

Greco Hermanos (Arg) wine-producers based in Mendoza. Produces Oro del Rhin (a dry white wine).

Greco Nero (It) a red grape variety grown in Calabria.

Greco Spoletino (It) an alternative name for the Grechetto Bianco.

Greece (Gre) a very old wine producing country in north eastern Mediterranean. Noted for dessert wines and resin-flavoured 'Retsina'. See also Demestica. 4 major areas: (1) Macedonia and Thrace (including O.P.A.P. wine regions of Amindeo, Goumenissa, Naoussa, Côtes de Meliton). (2) Central Greece-Attica, Epirus, Thessaly (including Ankialos, Metsovo, Rapsani, Zitsa). (3) Peloponnese (including Patras, Mantineia, Nemea). (4) Islands. see A.O.Q.S. A.O.C. T.A. Reserva: Q.W.P.S.R. + 2 years ageing (white), 3 years (red). Grande Reserve: Q.W.P.S.R. + 3 years ageing (white), 4 years (red). Cava: high quality table wine + 2 years ageing (white), 3 years (red).

Greed (Austr) a 150mls bottled Shiraz wine produced by BRL Hardy. Sold under the banner of Seven Deadly Sins. See also Envy, Flirt.

Greek Islands [The] (Gre) see Crete, Muscat de Samos, Santorini.

Greek Wine Information Bureau (Eng) information centre. (Add): The Old Vicarage, Newstead Abbey Park, Nottingham. NG15 8GE.

Green (Eng) the term applied to wines that are young and tart. i.e. Vinhos Verdes.

Greenalls Grand (Eng) a 4.1% alc by vol. cask-conditioned ale brewed by Ridley for Greenall outlets.

Greenall [G & J] (Eng) a distillers (established 1761). (Add): P.O. Box 3, Causeway Distillery, Loushers Lane, Warrington, Cheshire WA4 6RY. Produces tequila and vodka. Is owned by the De Vere Group plc.Website: http://www.gjgreenall.com 'E'mail: info@gigreenall.com

Greenall Whitley (Eng) a large brewery based in Warrington. Also owns the Wem Brewery in Shropshire and the Shipstone Brewery in Nottingham. Noted for bottled Bulls Eye Brown 1035 O.G. Champion Ale 1038 O.G. Grünhalle Lager 1035 O.G. Keg Festival 1039 O.G. Old Chester 1067 O.G. Old Glory 1074 O.G. Red Rose Stout 1074 O.G. and D.B. Pils 1038 O.G.

Green and Red Vineyard (USA) a winery based in the Napa Valley, California. 3ha. Grape variety: Zinfandel.

Greenback Cocktail (Cktl) ⅔ measure gin, ⅙ measure (green) crème de menthe, ⅙ measure lemon juice. Shake over ice and strain into an ice-filled old-fashioned glass.

Green Bean (Eng) the name given to the unroasted coffee beans.

Green Beer (Eng) unmatured raw materials used in the brewing process which have been converted to a liquid produce '*green beer*' which is then matured for a further period.

Green Beer (Eng) a 4.6% alc by vol. green-coloured seasonal beer brewed by Bunce's Brewery, Netheravon, Wiltshire. Available March, April, May.

Greenbriar (Cktl) ⅓ measure dry vermouth, ⅔ measure dry Sherry, dash peach bitters, stir over ice, strain into a cocktail glass and add a sprig of mint.

Green Bottle Ltd. (Eng) a brewery that brews Alesman Bitter 3.7% alc by vol. at the Worth Brewery, Keighley, Yorkshire.

Green Buck Cocktail (Cktl) 25mls (⅕ gill) Metaxa brandy, juice ½ lemon, shake over ice, strain into an ice-filled highball glass, top with ginger ale and float a teaspoonful of ouzo on top.

Green Bullet (Eng) a limited edition cask ale from Castle Eden Brewery. Made from Chariot barley and the New Zealand Green Bullet hop which gives a gentle nutty flavour 5.2% alc by vol.

Green Chartreuse (Fr)(Sp) a potent herb-flavoured liqueur originally made to treat cholera victims in 1832.

Green Coffee (Eng) coffee beans before they are dried and roasted.

Green Death (USA) a beer brewed by the Rainier Brewery in Seattle, Washington. Has a green label, hence the name 7.25% alc by vol.

Green Devil Cocktail (Cktl) 40mls (⅓ gill) dry gin, 15mls (⅛ gill) green crème de menthe, juice of ¼ orange, shake over ice, strain into an ice-filled highball glass and top with mint leaves.

Green Dragon (Eng) a small brewery based in East Anglia. Brews: Chaucer Ale, Dragon Ale, Bridge Street Bitter.

Green Dragon (Cktl) ½ measure dry gin, ¼ measure green crème de menthe, ⅛ measure kümmel, ⅛ measure lemon juice, shake over ice and strain into a cocktail glass.

Green Dragon Cocktail (Cktl) 40mls (⅓ gill) Pernod, 40mls (⅓ gill) milk, 20mls (⅙ gill) gomme syrup, shake over ice and strain into an ice-filled highball glass.

Greene King (Eng) a brewing company (established 1779) that has breweries in Bury St. Edmunds, Biggleswade and Furneux Pelham. (Add): Abbot House, Westgate Brewery, Bury St. Edmunds, Suffolk IP33 1QT. Noted for cask-conditioned Abbot Ale 1048 O.G. Farm Stout 1035 O.G. Harvest Brown 1031 O.G. King Keg 1038 O.G. St. Edmund 1060 O.G. Strong Suffolk 1056 O.G./6% alc by vol. and Yeoman 1038 O.G. Ruddles County 4.3% alc by vol. Mad Judge. *See also* Old 5X and The Beer to Dine For. Website: http://www.greeneking.co.uk

Green Fairy (Eng) the nickname for absinthe, *see* La Fée.

Green Fairy (Ger) a Hapsburg absinthe, lime and lemon or cranberry bottled drink 5.4% alc by vol.

Greenfield (USA) a wine town in the Salinas Valley, Monterey, California.

Green Fizz [1] (Cktl) 50mls (2fl.ozs) gin, juice ½ lemon, 4 dashes green crème de menthe, 4 dashes gomme syrup, 1 egg white. Shake over ice, strain into an ice-filled highball glass and top with soda.

Green Fizz [2] (Cktl) 1 part lime juice, 2 parts white wine. Stir together in an ice-filled highball glass and top with sparkling Ashbourne water.

Green Ginger Wine (Eng) produced by the Finsbury Distillery. Brand-name is Stone's. Made from dried grapes, fortified and powdered pure root ginger is added. Matured for 9 months in oak vats.

Green Ginger Wine (Scot) produced by Crabbie's since 1801.

Green Goddess (Eng) a 3.8% alc by vol. ale brewed by The Durham Brewery, County Durham.

Green Goddess (Eng) an egg-based drink produced by Townend of Hull.

Green Goddess (Fr) a nickname given to Pernod because of its colour.

Green Gold (Eng) a 4.3% alc by vol. ale brewed by the Oakleaf Brewing C°. Ltd., Hampshire.

Green Goose (Eng) a bitter brewed by the Woodbury Brewery at Great Whitley, Worcestershire.

Green Grape (S.Afr) a white grape variety also known as the Groendruif.

Greengrass Old Rogue Ale (Eng) a 4.5% alc by vol. ale brewed by the Daleside Brewery Ltd., North Yorkshire.

Green Gunpowder (Eng) a tea from China and Formosa, the leaf has the appearance of gunpowder (curled leaf). *see* Pin Head. Called Pearl Tea in China. Low in caffeine.

Greenhall Ltd. (Eng) distillers based in Warrington, Lancashire. Produces: 1761 and Bombay London Dry Gins and Vladivar Vodka.

Green Harvesting (Euro) the process in poor (wet), years of removing the some of the grapes from the vine to increase the chances of the remaining grapes ripening.

Green Highlander (Scot) a 5 year old blended Scotch whisky.

Greenhop Ale (Eng) a 4.2% alc by vol. ale brewed by the Skinner's Brewery C°. Ltd., Cornwall.

Green Hope (Cktl) ½ measure vodka, ⅛ measure crème de banane, ¼ measure Bols green Curaçao, ⅛ measure grape juice, dash lemon juice. Shake over ice, strain into a cocktail glass and add a cherry.

Green Hornet (Cktl) 50mls (2fl.ozs) vodka, juice of a lime. Shake over ice, strain into an ice-filled highball glass, top with soda water and a slice of lime.

Green Hungarian (USA) a white grape variety grown in California to make dessert and white table wines.

Green Island (Afr) a brand of cane spirit from Mauritius.

Green Jack Brewery (Eng) a brewery based at Oulton Broad. Brews LRN 150 to mark the 150th anniversary of Lowestoft-Reedham-Norwich railway line. Brewed from same mash as Chalk Hill Brewery.

Green Label (Austr) a strong bitter 4.56% alc by vol. brewed by the Cascade Brewery in Tasmania.

Green Label (Eng) a bottled XXXXXX ale 1040 O.G. brewed by the Wadworth Brewery in Wiltshire.

Green Label (Eng) a keg/tank mild 1034 O.G. originally brewed by Scottish Courage in Halifax, Yorkshire (bottled/canned version 1038 O.G.).

Green Label (Ger) a well-known brand of Bereich Bernkastel QmP. produced by Deinhard in Koblenz.

Green Lager (Den) a bottled green lager distributed by the Premium Beer and Wine Company.

Green Lady (Cktl) ½ measure dry gin, ⅓ measure green Chartreuse, ⅓ measure yellow Chartreuse. Shake over ice, strain into a cocktail glass and top with a slice of lime.

Green Light (Eng) a 3.3% alc by vol. light ale brewed by The Cheriton Brewhouse, Hampshire.

Green Malt (Eng) the name for germinated barley before it is transferred to the kiln for drying.

Green Mamba (Eng) a 5.3% alc by vol. drink from Aston Manor, Birmingham. Combination of Snake Bite and exotic fruits.

Green Man (Eng) a 4% alc by vol. ale brewed by the Bartrams Brewery, Suffolk.

Greenmantle Ale (Scot) a 3.9% alc by vol (1038 O.G) cask-conditioned ale brewed by the Broughton Brewery. See also Old Jock, Scottish Oatmeal Stout.

Greenmeadows (N.Z) vineyards based in the Hawke's Bay region, owned by Marist Fathers who produce red and white wines and liqueurs.

Green Mist (Cktl) ¼ measure Italian vermouth, ¼ measure French vermouth, ¼ measure Galliano, ¼ measure green Chartreuse. Stir over ice and strain into a cocktail glass.

Green Muse (USA) the name given for absinthe 'The water of the star wormwood'.

Greenness (Eng) a term applied to those wines that are young and not ready for drinking.

Green Opal (Cktl) ½ measure Pernod, ½ measure dry gin, ½ measure anisette. Shake over ice and strain into a cocktail glass.

Green Point (Austr) a winery owned by Moët et Chandon (Domaine Chandon) at Green Point, Coldstream, Yarra Valley, Victoria. Noted for sparkling wines made by traditional methods from Chardonnay and Pinot noir grapes.

Green Room (Cktl) ⅔ measure dry vermouth, ⅓ measure brandy, 2 dashes orange Curaçao, stir over ice and strain into a cocktail glass.

Green's (Port) vintage Port shippers.

Green Seal (W.Ind) a brand of dark rum produced by Wray and Nephew on the island of Jamaica.

Green Silvaner (Ger) a white grape variety also known as Franken-riesling, Monterey riesling and Sonoma riesling.

Greensleeves (Eng) a green liqueur made from brandy and flavoured with peppermint.

Green Snake [The] (Rus) a nickname given to alcohol in Russia.

Green's Vineyard (Eng) a vineyard. (Add): Ongar Farms Ltd., Green's Moreton, Essex. 1.75ha. Grape varieties: Huxelrebe, Kerner, Müller-Thurgau, Scheurebe, Schönburger and Wurzer.

Greenstone (S.Afr) the label for a white wine (un-oaked Chenin blanc) produced by the Napier Winery, Wellington, Western Cape.

Green Swizzle (Cktl) as for Gin Swizzle but with 2 barspoons of green crème de menthe (other spirits may be used instead of gin).

Green Sylvaner (Ger) see Green Silvaner.

Green Tea (Eng) the designation for unfermented tea from China, Japan and Taiwan. Leaves are stemmed and dried straight after harvest and heat-treated to prevent fermentation. After drying the leaves are rolled and broken into their various sizes. Drink without milk.

Green Tea (Jap) a cold, non-alcoholic green tea beverage. see Hajime, Namcha, O-i Ocha and Wakamusha.

Green Tea Liqueur (Jap) a liqueur made from matcha powdered tea essence and gyokuro rolled tea, also called O-Cha.

Green Tea Powder (Jap) the original instant tea! made from tea extracts, also known as soluble tea.

Green Time (S.E.Asia) a natural spring mineral water from Taiwan.

Green Top Ale (Eng) a bottled export ale 1042 O.G. brewed by the Eldridge Pope Brewery in Dorchester, Dorset.

Green Tye Brewery (Eng) a brewery (established 1999). (Add): Green Tye, Much Hadham, Hertfordshire SG10 6JP. Brews a variety of beers including stout. Website: http://www.gtbrewery.co.uk 'E'mail: info@gtbrewery.co.uk

Green Valley (USA) one of two A.V.A. areas within the Russian River Valley. 1,000acres (454.5ha) planted. Home to Iron Horse, Marimar Torres Estate. See also Chalk Hill.

Green Valley Cyder (Eng) based in Clyst Valley near Exeter, Devon. Produce still, vintage cider.

Green Valley Vineyards (USA) a winery based in Hermann, Missouri. Produces mainly hybrid wines.

Green Vodka (Pol) made by steeping zubrowka grass in Polish vodka, has a delicate aromatic bouquet. The bottle often contains a stem of the grass.

Green Whiskey (USA) the name given to the spirit after it has been distilled and before it is matured. Is colourless.

Greenwich Meantime Brewing C° (Eng) a brewery (established 2000). (Add): 2 Penhall Road, Greenwich, London SE7 8RX. Brews: Golden 5.4% alc by vol., IPA 6.9% alc by vol., Rosley Beer 5% alc by vol., Veanor 5% alc by vol., Wheat Beer 5% alc by vol. Website: http://www.meantimebrewing.com 'E'mail: Alistair@meantimebrewing.com

Green Wine (Eng) young wines. i.e. Portuguese Vinhos Verdes.

Green Wine (S.Afr) the label for a red wine (Pinotage) produced by the Southern Cape Vineyards winery, Barrydale, Little Karoo

Greenwood's (Eng) the West Crown Brewery in Newark, Nottingham. Brews: Greenwood's N° 8 and N° 10 beers.

Greffage (Fr) the grafting of European vine stock onto American root stock. *see* Phylloxera vastatrix.

Greffe (Fr) graft.

Greffe Anglaise (Fr) lit: 'English graft', a whip and tongue graft. *see* Graft.

Greghetto (It) an alternative name for the Grechetto Bianco.

Grégoire [Henri-Lucius] (Fr) a producer of Crémant de Bourgogne based at Davaye, Burgundy.

Greguniedda (It) a sweet dessert wine produced in Oristano, Sardinia.

Greifenberg (Ger) vineyard (Anb): Rheinhessen. (Ber): Bingen. (Gro): Adelberg. (Vil): Sulzheim.

Greifenlau Brauerei (Ger) a brewery based in Bamburg that produces rauchbiers.

Greiner (Ger) vineyard (Anb): Württemberg. (Ber): Remstal-Stuttgart. (Gro): Kopf. (Vil): Kleinheppach.

Greiveldange (Lux) a wine village on the river Moselle. Vineyard sites: Huette, Herrenberg.

Greiveldange (Lux) one of six co-operatives belonging to Vinsmoselle.

Greke Wyne (Eng) the sixteenth century spelling of Greek Wine (the fortified and sweet wines of Greece).

Grêle (Fr) lit: 'hail', the enemy of the wine grower, late summer hail storms when the grapes are very ripe can devastate a vineyard in a matter of seconds! *see* Go *see* Goût de Grêle.

Gremi (Geo) a white grape variety grown in Georgia, is used in the production of brandy.

Gremillet [J.M.] (Fr) a Champagne producer (established 1978) based in Balnot sur Laignes. 18ha. Produces vintage and non-vintage wines.

Gremio dos Exportadores (Port) the Portuguese official body which controls quality and production of wines for export.

Grenache (Fr) a good quality red grape grown in the southern Rhône and other regions of southern France plus the Rioja in Spain. Produces wines with aromas and flavours of pepper, spice, raspberry, blackberry, plum, damson, bitter chocolate, jam and linseed oil. (See Garnacha, Garnacho). Also grown in Italy (Granaccia/ Guarnaccia, Tocai Rosso), North Africa and California. Also known as the Alicante, Alicante Grenache, Aragón, Cannonau, Garnacha, Garnache, Granaccia, Grenache nera, Grenache noir, Roussillon tinto, Tinto aragonés, Tocai rosso and Uva di spagno.

Grenache Blanc (Fr) a white grape variety grown in southern France. (Sp) = Garnacha blanca.

Grenache de Logroño (Sp) an alternative name for Tempranillo.

Grenache Nera (Sp) an alternative name for the Grenache grape.

Grenache Noir (Fr) an alternative name for the Grenache grape.

Grenache Rosé (USA) a rosé wine produced in California from the Grenache grape.

Grenadier (Eng) a brand of dry gin produced by Findlater, Mackie Todd and C°. Ltd. for Whitmore & Bayley. 40% alc by vol.

Grenadier [1] (Cktl) 25mls (1fl.oz) Cognac, 25mls (1fl.oz) ginger wine, teaspoon powdered sugar. Shake well with ice and strain into a cocktail glass.

Grenadier [2] (Cktl)(Non-alc) 20mls (⅛ gill) grenadine, juice ½ orange. Shake over ice, strain into an ice-filled highball glass, top with tonic water and an orange slice.

Grenadière [La] (Fr) an A.C. Coteaux du Languedoc Pic-Saint-Loup wine produced by Mas Brugière from 60% Syrah, 20% Mourvèdre and 20% Grenache grapes.

Grenadine (Fr) a non-alcoholic red syrup made from pomegranates.

Grenadine Cocktail (Cktl) 3 parts grenadine, 6 parts gin, 1 part lemon juice, 3 dashes orange bitters. Shake well with ice and strain into a cocktail glass.

Grenadine Rickey (Cktl)(Non-alc) 35mls (1½ fl.ozs) grenadine, juice ½ lime. Stir over ice in a highball glass, top with soda water and a slice of lime.

Grenadine Shake Cocktail (Cktl)(Non-alc) 1 measure pineapple juice, 1 measure grenadine, ½ measure lemon juice, 1 egg white. Blend with a scoop of crushed ice in a blender. Pour into a club goblet, top with lemonade, dress with a cherry and sprig of mint.

Grendals (Eng) a 5.8% alc by vol. winter warmer brewed by Beowulf, Yardley, Birmingham.

Grenenmacher (Lux) one of six co-operatives, is a part of Vinsmoselle.

Grenon (Fr) a Cognac producer. (Add): Dom-Pierre-sur-Charente, 17610 Chaniers. 32ha. in the Petite Champagne and Borderies.

G

Grenouilles (Fr) an A.C. Grand Cru Chablis, Burgundy.

Gren Vino Sanson (Sp) a dark, sweet Málaga Lágrima made with the Lágrima (tear) must by Hijos de Antonio Barceló. Sold under the Barcarles label.

Grenzach (Ger) village (Anb): Baden. (Ber): Markgräflerland. (Gro): Vogtei Rötteln. (Vin): Hornfelsen.

Grenzquell (Ger) a dry malt beer from the Bavaria-St. Pauli in Hamburg. Is marketed in the USA by Olympia.

Grès de Montpellier (Fr) a new (2003) sub-region A.C. within the A.C. Coteaux du Languedoc based on its climate and soil (includes La Méjanelle, Picpoul de Pinet, St-Christol, St-Drézéry, St-Georges d'Orques and Vérangues)..

Grésigny (Fr) vineyard based in the A.C. commune of Rully, Côte Chalonnaise, Burgundy.

Gressier Grand Poujeaux (Fr) a vineyard in the commune of Moulis. A.C. Haut-Médoc, Bordeaux. Cru Bourgeois.

Greth (Ger) vineyard (Anb): Mosel-Saar-Ruwer. (Ber): Zell/Mosel. (Gro): Rosenhang. (Vil): Treis-Karden.

Greuth (Ger) village (Anb): Franken. (Ber): Steigerwald. (Gro): Schild. (Vin): Bastel.

Greve (It) a commune of Chianti Classico Riserva.

Grevenmacher (Lux) a wine village on the river Moselle in the north. Vineyard sites: Fels, Groerd, Rosenberg. Soil: marl and mussel-lime (chalk).

Grèves [Les] (Fr) a Premier Cru vineyard (including La Vigne de l'Enfant Jesus) in the A.C. commune of Beaune, Côte de Beaune, Burgundy 31.68ha.

Grewenich (Ger) village (Anb): Mosel-Saar-Ruwer. (Ber): Obermosel. (Gro): Königsberg. (Vin): Sites not yet chosen.

Grey Champagne (Fr) the old name for still Champagne that had a light rosé colour.

Grey Friar (Fr) an alternative name for the Pinot gris.

Grey Goose Vodka (Fr) a 40% alc by vol. multiple grain (wheat, rye, barley, corn) vodka. Owned by Bacardi.

Greyhound (Eng) a 5.2% alc by vol. strong cask bitter from Elgood & Sons Brewery, Wisbech, Cambridgeshire.

Greyhound (Eng) a home-brew public house of the Clifton Inns C°. Noted for cask-conditioned Streatham Strong 1047 O.G. and Greyhound Special 1037 O.G.

Greyhound Special (Eng) see Greyhound.

Grey Mould (USA) a botrytis attack on red grapes. see Pourriture gris.

Grey Partridge (Eng) a 4.1% alc by vol. ale brewed by the Buntingford Brewery, Hertfordshire.

Grey Pinot (USA) an American name for the Pinot gris.

Grey Riesling (USA) a white grape variety grown in California to make average white wines. See also Chauche Gris, Gray Riesling and Grey Dutchess.

Grey Rot (Bot) Pourriture gris the rot (botrytis found on red grape varieties) which is found in damp conditions and lowers the quality of the grape must, the cure is good climatic conditions. (Fr) = gris, (USA) = grey mould.

Greystone (USA) the label name used by the Perelli-Minetti Winery.

Grgich Hills (USA) a large winery based near Rutherford, Napa Valley, California. 58ha. Grape varieties: Chardonnay, Johannisberg riesling, Zinfandel. Produces varietal wines.

Gribble Ale (Eng) a cask-conditioned ale brewed by Gribble Inn, Oving, Chichester.

Gribble Inn (Eng) a micro-brewery based at Oving, Chichester. Brews: cask ales including Fursty Ferret, Gribble Ale, Reg's Tipple.

Gribena (Sp) the name of a Riojan wine produced by Propiedad Grial, S.L. Avda. Estacion, 28 26360 Fuenmayor, Rioja.

Griechische (Aus) lit: 'Greek', a white grape variety which is now no longer planted.

Gries (Fr) a lesser white grape variety grown in Alsace.

Griesbacher First Class Mineralwasser (Ger) a sparkling natural spring mineral water from Bad Griesbach, Schwarzwald. (blue label: sparkling/green label: light gas). Mineral contents (milligrammes per litre): Sodium 198mg/l, Calcium 305mg/l, Magnesium 72.5mg/l, Bicarbonates 1617mg/l, Chlorides 14.4mg/l, Sulphates 165mg/l, Nitrates 0.02mg/l.

Grieskirchen AG (Aus) a brewery. (Add): Stadtplatz 14, Postfach 109, 4710 Grieskirchen. Brews a variety of beers and lagers. Website: http://www.grieskirchner.at 'E'mail: office@grieskirchner.at

Griffi (It) a red I.G.T. wine made from the Cabernet sauvignon 50% and Prugnolo gentile 50% in central-western Italy by Avignonesi.

Griffin Vineyards (USA) see Hop Kiln Winery. 21ha.

Grifforin (Fr) an alternative name for the Malbec grape.

Grigia (It) a variety of the Schiave gentile red grape.

Grigio-Verde (Cktl) ½ measure grappa, ½ measure crème de menthe, stir together over ice and strain into a cocktail glass.

Grignan (Fr) a herb liqueur made by Trappist monks, similar to Chartreuse 45% alc by vol.

Grignolino (It) a red wine grape variety of excellent quality grown in the Piemonte region. Produces a wine of unmistakable bouquet.

Grignolino (It) a red wine from the Piemonte region named after the red grape variety of same name.

Grignolino (USA) see California Grignolino.

Grignolino d'Asti (It) a D.O.C. red wine from Piemonte. Made from the Grignolino grape. Produced throughout the 35 communes in the province of Asti.

Grignolino del Monferrato Casalese (It) a D.O.C. red wine from Piemonte. Made from the Grignolino grape, grown within the 35 communes in Monteferrato Casalese.

Grignolino Rosé (USA) a rosé wine produced from the Grignolino grape in California.

Grill (Aus) a winery based in Fels am Wagram,

634

G

Donauland. (Add): Untere Marktstrasse 19, 3481 Fels am Wagram. Grape varieties: Chardonnay, Grüner veltliner, Riesling, Zweigelt.

Grillage (Fr) in Beaujolais the pumping over and submerging of the cap to keep it wet.

Grillo (It) a white grape variety grown in Sicily, used in the making of Marsala.

Grimbergen Blond (Bel) a 7% alc by vol. top-fermented, bottled abbaye-style beer brewed by the Union Brasserie, Jumet.

Grimbergen Optimo Bruno (Bel) a 10% alc by vol. top-fermented, bottled dark abbaye-style beer brewed by the Union Brasserie, Jumet.

Grimbergen Triple (Bel) a 9% alc by vol. top-fermented, bottled abbaye-style beer brewed by the Union Brasserie, Jumet.

Grimbergen Brasserie (Bel) *see* Grimbergen.

Grimberian (Eng) a 3.7% alc by vol. bitter ale brewed by Tomlinson in Pontefract.

Grimsby (Can) a wine district between Niagara and Crystal Beach.

Grinds (Eng) the name given to ground coffee after the beans have been roasted and cut (ground) up, size can vary from coarse to very fine.

Gringet (Fr) a grape variety used in the production of Mousseux de Savoie-Ayze. Also known as Savagnin.

Grinzing (Aus) a famous white wine produced outside Vienna from a region of same name.

Griotte-Chambertin (Fr) a Grand Cru vineyard in the A.C. commune of Gevrey-Chambertin, Côte de Nuits, Burgundy 5.6ha.

Griottes [Les] (Fr) a vineyard in A.C. Pouilly Fumé, Central Vineyards, Loire. (Add): 18 Rue F. Gambon, 58150 Pouilly-sur-Loire.

Griottine (Switz) a 37% alc by vol. cherry and griottes liqueur from Morand Distillerie, Martigny, Valais.

Grip (Eng) a term that is applied to a wine that has a good finish and if red has tannin and acidity.

Gripe Water (Eng) a liquid used for 'winding' babies, contains 4.5% alc by vol. caraway-flavoured, it relieves colic.

Gris (Fr) grey rot.

Gris Cordelier (Fr) an alternative name for the Pinot gris.

Gris de Boulaouane (Afr) a 'grey wine' produced in Morocco and bottled by CVM.

Gris de Gris (Fr) an A.C. rosé wine from Provence produced by Listel.

Gris de Guerrouane (Afr) a brand of pale, dry rosé wine from Morocco. Grape varieties: Carignan and Cinsault, a 'grey wine'. Carries the A.O.G. Guerrouane, bottled by CVM.

Gris-Meunier (Fr) a red grape variety grown in the Touraine district of the Loire. Related to the Pinot meunier.

Grist (Eng) milled malted barley used for brewing and whisky making.

Grist Case (Eng) a hopper that holds the ground malt (grist).

Grist Hopper (Scot) another name for the grist case.

Grist Mill (Eng) a unit for grinding grain (especially barley) into grist.

Grizzly's (Ch.Isles) a specially hopped beer that was brewed by the Guernsey Brewery, St. Peter Port, Guernsey (for a local hotel – The Collinette).

Grk (Euro) a strong white wine which is very dry, not unlike a natural Sherry, made from a grape of same name on the island of Korcula. Also spelt Gerk.

Grobe (Aus) lit: 'rough one' the name given to grapes that produced average, everyday drinking wines.

Grober (Ger) an alternative name for the Elbling grape.

Grobriesling (Ger) an alternative name for the Elbling grape.

Grodziska (Pol) a sparkling natural spring mineral water from Grodziska Wlkp. Mineral contents (milligrammes per litre): Sodium 5mg/l, Calcium 70.5mg/l, Magnesium 8.75mg/l, Bicarbonates 231.8mg/l, Chlorides 12mg/l, Sulphates 20mg/l.

Groendruif (S.Afr) an alternative name for the Green grape.

Groenkloof (S.Afr) the label for a white wine (Sauvignon blanc) produced by the Neil Ellis Wines, Stellenbosch, Western Cape.

Groenkloof Drankhandelaars Dry Red (S.Afr) a blended red wine made from 25% Cinsault, 50% Pinotage and 25% Tinta barocca produced by the Mamreweg Co-operative.

Groenkloof Drankhandelaars Wines (S.Afr) a brand label name used by the Mamreweg Wynkelders Koöperatief.

Groerd (Lux) a vineyard site in the village of Grevenmacher.

Grog (Austr) a slang term for any alcoholic beverage.

Grog (Cktl) 1 measure dark rum, 2 cloves, lump of sugar, lemon juice, stick of cinnamon. Place all in an old-fashioned glass, top with boiling water and stir.

Grog (Eng) a British navy term for rum, derived from grogram (cloak) which was worn by its officer Edward Vernon (1684–1757).

Grog (Fr) toddy.

Grog Blossom (Austr) a slang name for the red nose of a heavy drinker.

Groggy (Eng) unsteady, comes from the old naval word meaning under the influence of alcohol (grog).

Grogier (Ch.Isles) tipple. *See also* Bevounnair.

Grognard [Le] (Liq.Coffee) put a teaspoon of castor sugar in a Paris goblet. Add 20mls (⅙ gill) Mandarine Napoléon and flambé. Add hot coffee, top with fresh cream and garnish with tangerine peel.

Groisl (Aus) a vineyard site based on the banks of the River Kamp situated in the Kamptal region.

Grokje (Hol) toddy.

Grolla (Aus) a wooden drinking vessel, consists of a hollowed out log which is filled with assorted beverages that are drunk through holes in the side of the vessel with the aid of straws. Can be served hot or cold. Used by one or more persons together (aids friendship). (It) = grolle.

Grolle (It) a round, decorated wooden vessel used for serving and drinking hot Alpine punch. (Aus) = grolla.

Grolleau (Fr) a red grape variety used in the making of rosé wines in the Anjou district of the Loire. Also spelt Groslot.

Grolsch Bier Brouwerij Nederland BV (Hol) a brewery (established 1615). (Add): Brouwerijstraat 1, Postbus 55, 7500AB, Enschede-Groenlo, Gelderland. Noted for pot-stoppered Grolsch Premium Pilsener Lager plus Amber, Special Malt, Oud Bruin, Herfst Bok, Lente Bok, Winter Vorst, Zomergoud. Website: http://www.grolsch.nl

Grolsch Oud Bruin (Hol) a 2.5% alc by vol. bottled old brown beer brewed by the Grolsch Bier Brouwerij, Enschede-Groenlo.

Grolsch Premium Pilsener (Hol) a 5% alc by vol. unpasteurised bottled beer sold in a pot-stoppered bottle, a pilsener beer brewed by the Grolsch Bier Brouwerij, Enschede-Groenlo.

Grolsch Special Malt (Hol) a 0.1% alc by vol. bottled alcohol-free beer brewed by the Grolsch Bier Brouwerij, Enschede-Groenlo.

Grolsheim (Ger) village (Anb): Rheinhessen. (Ber): Bingen. (Gro): Sankt Rochuskapelle. (Vin): Ölberg.

Grom (Ser) a red wine produced in southern Serbia.

Grombalia (Afr) a co-operative winery owned by the UCCVT.

Grombalia (Afr) a major wine-producing district in Tunisia.

Gronau (Ger) village (Anb): Württemberg. (Ber): Württembergisch Unterland. (Gro): Wunnenstein. (Vin): Forstberg.

Grön Curaçao (Nor) a green-coloured Curaçao.

Grongnet (Fr) a Champagne producer (established 1885). (Add): 41, Grande Rue, 51270 Etoges. Récoltant-Manipulant. Produces vintage and non-vintage wines. Vintages: 1995, 1996, 1997, 1999. A member of the Club Tresors de Champagne. Labels: Champagne CARPE DIEM, Cuvée 'Special Club' Millésimée. 'E'mail: champagnegrongnet@wanadoo.fr

Gron Tuborg (Den) lit: 'Green Tuborg' a pilsener-style lager 3.7% alc by vol. brewed by Carlsberg.

Groot (Hol) lit: 'large', a term used to describe a 30cls glass.

Groot Constantia Estate (S.Afr) a winery and vineyards (established 1685) based in Constantia, Langoed, Western Cape. 90ha. (Add): Groot Constantia State Estate, Private Bag, Constantia 7848. (owned by the South African Government). Grape varieties: Cabernet sauvignon, Chardonnay, Malbec, Merlot, Muscat de Frontignan, Pinotage, Sauvignon blanc, Shiraz, Touriga. Labels: Cap Classique, Constantia Rood, Grand Constance, Gouverneurs, Reserve. Website: http://www.grootconstantia.co.za

Groot Constantia State Estate (S.Afr) *see* Groot Constantia Estate.

Groot Eiland Koöperatiewe Wynkelder (S.Afr) a co-operative winery (established 1962) based in Goudini, Worcester, Western Cape. 1000ha. Grape varieties: Cabernet sauvignon, Chardonnay, Chenin blanc, Cinsaut, Colombard, Merlot, Pinotage, Shiraz. Labels: Crisp Dry, Fruity (red and white), Honigtrauber, Meander. Website: http://www.grooteiland.co.za

Groote Post Vineyard (S.Afr) a winery (established 1999) based in Darling, Western Cape. 117ha. Grape varieties: Cabernet sauvignon, Chardonnay, Chenin blanc, Merlot, Pinot noir, Sauvignon blanc, Shiraz. Label: Old Man's Blend. Website: http://www.grootepost.com

Groot Parys (S.Afr) a winery (established 1699) based in Paarl, Western Cape. 64ha. Grape varieties: Chardonnay, Chenin blanc, Colombard, Hanepoot, Ruby cabernet, Sémillon. Label: Die Tweede Droom. Website: http://www.grootparys.co.za

Groot Toren (S.Afr) a dry, white wine made from a blend of Colombard, Steen and Weisser riesling grapes by the McGregor Co-operative. Is matured in wood.

Groppello (It) a red wine grape variety also known as the Rossignola. Used in the making of Valpolicella in Veneto.

Groppellone (It) *see* Groppello.

Gros Auxerrois (Fr) an alternative name for the Muscadet (Melon de Bourgogne) grape.

Gros Bouchet (Fr) a name used in the Saint-Émilion district of Bordeaux for the Cabernet sauvignon grape.

Gros Cabernet (Fr) the local name in Bordeaux for the Cabernet franc.

Groseille (Fr) redcurrant syrup.

Groseilles [Les] (Fr) a Premier Cru vineyard in the A.C. commune of Chambolle-Musigny, Côte de Nuits, Burgundy 1.5ha.

Gros Galets (Fr) a term given to pudding stones in Châteauneuf-du-Pape, southern Rhône.

Groslot (Fr) a red grape variety grown in the Anjou district of the Loire used in the making Rosé d'Anjou. Also spelt Grolleau.

Gros Manseng (Fr) a white grape variety grown in Béarn and Jurançon.

Gros Manzenc (USA) a red grape variety grown in California.

Gros Noir (Fr) an alternative name for the Malbec grape.

Gros Noiren (Fr) the local name for the Pinot noir in the Arbois, Jura.

Gros-Pin (Fr) a wine-producing district in Bellet, Provence.

Gros Plant (Fr) a white acidic grape variety grown in Nantais district of the Loire. Produces an acidic V.D.Q.S. wine of same name, has a flavour of unripe apples and pears. Also known as the Folle blanche in Cognac and elsewhere in France.

Gros Plant Doré d'Aÿ (Fr) a variety of the Pinot noir grape grown in the Champagne region.

Gros Plant du Nantais (Fr) a V.D.Q.S. dry, white, acidic wine made from the Gros plant grape in the Nantais district of the Loire. *see* Gros Plant du Pays Nantais.

Gros Plant du Pays Nantais (Fr) now known as Gros Plant du Nantais.

Gros Producteurs (Fr) vine varieties which produce large quantities, but not fine quality wines.

Gros Rhin (Fr) the local Alsace name for the Silvaner grape.

Gross [Alois] (Aus) a winery (15ha) based in Ehrenhausen, Süd-Steiermark. (Add): Ratch an der Weinstrasse 10, 8461 Ehrenhausen. Grape varieties: Chardonnay, Gewürztraminer, Muskateller, Pinot blanc, Pinot gris, Sauvignon blanc, Traminer, Zweigelt. Produces a range of dry and sweet wines.

Gross (Ger) lit: 'great', denotes a wine that is of fine quality.

Grossa (It) a red grape variety grown in the Trentino-Alto Adige region for making Lago di Caldaro.

Grossachsen (Ger) village (Anb): Baden. (Ber): Badische Bergstrasse/Kraichgau. (Gro): Rittersberg. (Vin): Sandrocken.

Grossbottwar (Ger) village (Anb): Württemberg. (Ber): Württembergisch Unterland. (Gro): Wunnenstein. (Vins): Harzberg, Lichtenberg.

Grosse Montagne (W.Ind) a very popular brand of rum produced on the island of Guadeloupe by Simonnet.

Grosser Hengelberg (Ger) vineyard (Anb): Mosel-Saar-Ruwer. (Ber): Bernkastel. (Gro): Michelsberg. (Vil): Neumagen-Dhron.

Grosser Herrgott (Ger) vineyard (Anb): Mosel-Saar-Ruwer. (Ber): Bernkastel. (Gro): Kurfürstlay. (Vil): Wintrich.

Grosser Stollen (It) a natural spring mineral water from Grosser Stollen, S. Vigilio. Mineral contents (milligrammes per litre): Sodium 4.09mg/l, Calcium 8.61mg/l, Magnesium 1.87mg/l, Potassium 1.23mg/l, Bicarbonates 31mg/l, Sulphates 9mg/l, Fluorides 1.2mg/l.

Grosser Wein (Aus) the label for a white (Chardonnay) wine produced by the Schaflerhof winery, Traiskirchen, Thermenregion.

Grosses Stangl (Aus) a vineyard site based on the banks of the River Kamp situated in the Kamptal region.

Grosses Terres (Fr) the very best soil of the Sancerre in the Central Vineyards, Loire, almost brown in colour with some yellow brown (clay).

Grosset (Austr) a winery based in the Clare Valley, South Australia. Grape varieties include: Chardonnay, Pinot noir, Riesling, Sémillon. Label: Polish Hill.

Gross Gebirg (Aus) a vineyard area on the banks of the River Danube in the Kremstal region.

Gross Gewäch (Ger) great growth. (Fr) = grand cru.

Grossheppach (Ger) village (Anb): Württemberg. (Ber): Remstal-Stuttgart. (Gro): Kopf. (Vin): Wanne.

Grossheppach (Ger) village (Anb): Württemberg. (Ber): Remstal-Stuttgart. (Gro): Wartbühl. (Vins): Steingrüble, Zügernberg.

Grossheubach (Ger) village (Anb): Franken. (Ber):

Mainviereck. (Gro): Not yet assigned. (Vin): Bischofsberg.

Gross Highland Winery (USA) a winery based in Absecon, New Jersey. Is noted for its sparkling (Charmat method) wines.

Gross-Höflein (Aus) a wine-producing area in the Eisenstadt district.

Grossier (Fr) a big but hard, coarse wine.

Grossingersheim (Ger) village (Anb): Württemberg. (Ber): Württembergisch Unterland. (Gro): Schalkstein. (Vin): Schlossberg

Gros Sirops (Fr) molasses.

Grosskarlbach (Ger) village (Anb): Pfalz. (Ber): Mittelhaardt-Deutsche Weinstrasse. (Gro): Schwarzerde. (Vins): Burgweg, Osterberg.

Grosslage (Ger) an area formed by a number of vineyards. May be a village or not. A number of grosslagen make up a bereich.

Grosslagenfrei (Ger) no grosslagen, not yet assigned to a grosslage (associated with a weinbauort).

Grosslangheim (Ger) village (Anb): Franken. (Ber): Steigerwald. (Gro): Schlossberg. (Vin): Kiliansberg.

Grosslay (Ger) vineyard (Anb): Mosel-Saar-Ruwer. (Ber): Zell/Mosel. (Gro): Goldbäumchen. (Vil): Müden.

Gross Lees (Fr) the sediment in the wine before bottling.

Grossman [The] (USA) an all purpose lead crystal glass which has a fill-line at 100mls (4fl.ozs)

Grossmulde (Ger) vineyard (Anb): Württemberg. (Ber): Remstal-Stuttgart. (Gro): Kopf. (Vil): Beinstein.

Grossniedesheim (Ger) village (Anb): Pfalz. (Ber): Mittelhaardt-Deutsche Weinstrasse. (Gro): Schwarzerde. (Vin): Schafberg.

Grosso Nero (It) a red grape variety grown in Sicily.

Grossostheim (Ger) village (Anb): Franken. (Ber): Mainviereck. (Gro): Heiligenthal. (Vins): Reischklingeberg, Harstell.

Grossriedental (Aus) a wine district within the Donauland region noted for its eisweins.

Grossrinderfeld (Ger) village (Anb): Baden. (Ber): Badische Frankenland. (Gro): Tauberklinge. (Vin): Beilberg.

Gross-Umstadt (Ger) village (Anb): Hessische Bergstrasse. (Ber): Umstadt. (Gro): no Grosslagen. (Vins): Steingerück, Herrnberg.

Gross-Und Kleinfischlingen (Ger) village (Anb): Pfalz. (Ber): Südliche Weinstrasse. (Gro): Trappenberg. (Vin): Kirchberg.

Grossvernatsch (It) a Germanic name for the red wine grape known as the Schiava grossa in the Südtirol. Also known as the Trollinger.

Grosswallstadt (Ger) village (Anb): Franken. (Ber): Mainviereck. (Gro): Not yet assigned. (Vin): Lützeltalerberg.

Gross-Winternheim (Ger) village (Anb): Rheinhessen. (Ber): Bingen. (Gro): Kaiserpfalz. (Vins): Bockstein, Heilighäuschen, Klosterbruder, Schlossberg.

Gros Verdot (Fr) a red grape variety grown in

G

Bordeaux, also found in Argentina and Chile, South America.

Gros Vidure (Fr) the alternative name for the Cabernet franc.

Groth (USA) a winery based in the Oakville, Napa Valley, California. Grape varieties: Cabernet sauvignon.

Grottaferrata (It) a wine town based south of Frascati in the Latium region noted for white wines.

Grötzingen (Ger) village (Anb): Baden. (Ber): Badische Bergstrasse/Kraichgau. (Gro): Hohenberg. (Vins): Lichtenberg, Turmberg.

Grounds (Eng) the alternative name for the (coffee) grinds.

Groupement des Grandes Liqueurs de France (Fr) an inner court of the Syndicat National des Fabricants de Liqueurs which consists of 13 of France's biggest liqueur producers producing internationally-known brands of liqueurs.

Groupement d'Intéret Économique des Vignerons du Sud-Oeust (Fr) abbr: G.I.VI.S.O. a group of co-operatives from the A.C. districts of south-western France (Buzet, Cahors, Gaillac, Jurançon and Madiran).

Groupement Interprofessionnel des Vins de l'Ile de Corse (Fr) the wine council for the control of Corsican wines. (Add): 6, Rue Gabriel-P,ri 20000 Bastia, Corsica.

Groupe Saint Arnould (Fr) a family-based brewery at Lille, Boulogne and Saint Omer. Brews: La Facon, Bière Saint Omer.

Grouts (USA) the name for the tea leaves after brewing.

Grove Mill Wine Company (N.Z) a winery. (Add): Waihopai Valley Road, P.O. Box 67, Renwick, Marlborough. 25ha. Grape varieties: Chardonnay, Riesling, Sauvignon blanc and Pinotage wines.

Grover Gulcg Winery (USA) a winery based in Soquel, Santa Cruz, California. Produces varietal wines.

Grover Vineyards (Ind) vineyards based in the Nandu Hills, Bangalore. 120acres (54.5ha) of which 90acres (41ha) are Pergola trained. Produces: Grovers Red (Cabernet sauvignon/Shiraz), Grovers White (Clairette), Grovers Rosé.

Groves Oatmeal Stout (Eng) a stout brewed by the Quay Brewery, Hope Square, Weymouth.

Grower's Old Reserve (USA) the brand-name of a brandy produced by the California Grower's Winery in Cutler, California.

Growlin' Gator (USA) a 4.5% alc by vol. lager made in Florida. Brewed and bottled in Alligator Alley using Saaz and domestic hops, barley, yeast and Florida Spring water.

Growth (Fr) can mean a vineyard normally classed as a Great Growth, produces the best wines.

Grozet (Scot) a 5% alc by vol. ale brewed by Heather Ale Ltd., Lanarkshire.

Grub (Aus) a vineyard site based on the banks of the River Kamp situated in the Kamptal region.

Gruber (Ger) an alternative name for the Sylvaner grape.

Grúdaire (Ire) brewer.

Grúdaireacht (Ire) brew (ale).

Grudge Bitter (Eng) a 4.6% alc by vol. bitter from Lowestoft, Suffolk. Brewed as a protest against the Euro threat to guest ales.

Grúdlann (Ire) brewery.

Gruel (Eng) a drink of thin porridge made by boiling oatmeal in water or milk.

Gruenchers [Les] (Fr) a Premier Cru vineyard [part] in the A.C. commune of Chambolle-Musigny, Côte de Nuits, Burgundy 3ha.

Gruenchers [Les] (Fr) a Premier Cru vineyard [part] in the A.C. commune of Morey-Saint-Denis, Côte de Nuits, Burgundy 0.6ha.

Gruener Veltliner (Aus) the main white grape variety grown in Burgenland, produces fresh, spicey, fruity wines with a high acidity. Wines are often used as sturm for the heurigen inns. Is also spelt Grüner veltliner. Also known as the Grüner muskateller. (Czec) = Veltlin zelene, (Ger) = Veltlinske zelené, (Hun) = Veltlini/Zöldveltelini, (Slo) = Veltlin zelene/Veltliske zelen (Yug) = Veltliske zelené.

Gruet et Fils (Fr) a Champagne producer. (Add): Rue de Chemin Neuf, Bethon, 51260 Anglure. A Coopérative-manipulant (60 growers owning 95ha.).

Gruet Winery (USA) a winery (established 1984) based in Alberquerque, New Mexico. Grape varieties: Pinot noir, Chardonnay. Produces still and sparkling wines.

Gruit (Eng) a mixture of aromatic herbs used for flavouring beer.

Grume (Fr) the name used in Burgundy for the grape berry (single grape).

Grumello (It) a sub-district of Lombardy, in the foothills of the Alps, in the Valtellina Valley. Produces red wines of the same name from the Nebbiolo grape.

Grumier [Maurice] (Fr) a Champagne producer. (Add): Rte. d'Arty, 51480 Venteuil.

Grumpling Old Ale (Eng) a 4.6% alc by vol. ale brewed by the Vale Brewery C°., Buckinghamshire.

Grumpy Cow (Eng) a cask bitter brewed by Morrells Brewery, Oxford.

Grün (Ger) young/green/immature.

Grunbach (Ger) village (Anb): Württemberg. (Ber): Remstal-Stuttgart. (Gro): Kopf. (Vin): Berghalde.

Grunbach (Ger) village (Anb): Württemberg. (Ber): Remstal-Stuttgart. (Gro): Wartbühl. (Vin): Klingle.

Grünberger Stein (S.Afr) a white wine sold in the familiar German stein bottle from Die Bergkelder Ltd, Stellenbosch.

Grünberger Wines (S.Afr) wines made by the Die Bergkelder in Stellenbosch (varietal wines).

Gründelbach (Ger) village (Anb): Württemberg. (Ber): Württembergisch Unterland. (Gro): Stromberg. (Vins): Steinbachhof, Wachtkopf.

Gründel's (Ger) an alcohol-free pilsner beer from Carlsberg.

Gründen (Aus) a vineyard site on the banks of the River Danube situated in the Wachau region, Niederösterreich.

G

Grundersbacher Schlosskellerei Thun (Switz) noted producers of sparkling wines.

Grundheim Wines (S.Afr) a winery (established 1995) based in Little Karoo. 25ha. Grape varieties: Chenin blanc, Jerepigo, Muscat, Muscadel, Ruby cabernet, Tinta.

Grundkataster (Aus) the land register.

Grünerberg Quelle (Ger) a natural spring mineral water (established 1977) from Brandenburg. Mineral contents (milligrammes per litre): Sodium 36mg/l, Calcium 125mg/l, Magnesium 13.9mg/l, Potassium 2.7mg/l, Bicarbonates 371mg/l, Chlorides 31mg/l, Sulphates <1mg/l, Silicates 32mg/l.

Grüner Burgunder (Aus) an alternative name for the Neuburger grape.

Grüner Hainer (Aus) a little used red grape variety.

Grüner Husar (Aus) a medium-dry, white wine produced from the Grüner veltliner by Sepp Hold in St. Georgen.

Grüner Muskateller (Aus) an old name for the Gruener veltliner.

Grunern (Ger) village (Anb): Baden. (Ber): Markgräflerland. (Gro): Lorettoberg. (Vins): Altenberg, Schlossberg.

Grüner Veltliner (Aus) *see* Gruener Veltliner.

Grünhalle Lager (Ch.Isles) a lager beer brewed by Randall's Brewery (now the Jersey Brewery) in Jersey. Now brewed under licence by Greenall Whitley Brewery in Warrington and Devenish Brewery. Bottled/keg and Export Gold.

Grünhaus (Ger) a Ruwer estate in the Mosel-Saar-Ruwer, wines are known as Maximin Grünhauser because the vineyard was once the property of St. Maximin Abbey in Trier.

Grünling (Ger) an alternative name for the Sylvaner grape.

Grunnengold (Ger) the brand-name of an E.C. blended table wine 9.3% alc by vol.

Grünsilvaner (Rum) a white wine.

Grünstadt (Ger) village (Anb): Pfalz. (Ber): Mittelhaardt-Deutsche Weinstrasse. (Gro): Höllenpfad. (Vins): Bergel, Goldberg, Honigsack, Hütt, Klostergarten, Röth, St. Stephan, Schloss.

Grupo de Exportadores (Sp) a group that was based in Jerez de la Frontera (now disbanded), has been replaced by the Asociacíon de Criadores Exportadores de Vino de Jerez.

Grupo de Exportadores de Vinos de Navarra (Sp) a promotional body. (Add): Yanguas Miranda 27, Pamplona, a body for the promotion of Navarra wines.

Grupo dos Sete (Port) a body for the promotion of Portuguese wines. SOGRAPE, Quinta da Avelada, Caves Alianca, Caves Messias, José Maria da Fonseca.

Grupo Mahou San Miguel (Sp) a brewery. (Add): Paseo Imperial 32, Madrid 28005. Brews beers and lager. Website: http://www.mahou-sanmiguel.com

Gruppo Italiano Vini (It) *abbr*: G.I.V. helps promote Italian wine drinking.

Gruta (Sp) cavern.

Gruzinskoe Vino (Geo) a wine produced in the Georgia region.

Gryphon (Eng) a 5% alc by vol. ale brewed by the Wentworth Brewery, South Yorkshire.

Gsellgericht (Aus) a vineyard site based on the banks of the River Kamp situated in the Kamptal region.

Gsellmann & Gsellmann (Aus) a wine estate based in the Neusiedlesee, Burgenland. (Add): Obere Hauptstrasse 28/38, 7122 Gols. Produces both red wines and white wines.

Guadal (Sp) a Solera brandy produced by Esteve (José). *See also* Sautu.

Guadaloupe Valley Winery (USA) a winery based in New Braunfels, south-west Texas.

Guadalquivir [River] (Sp) mouth of which Sanlúcar de Barrameda is situated. Here Manzanilla Sherries are matured.

Guadalupe (Mex) a wine-producing region in Baja California. Has the wineries of Luis Cetto Vineyards and Productos Vinicola.

Guadalupe (Sp) an Amontillado Sherry produced by La Riva in Jerez de la Frontera.

Guadelete [River] (Sp) a river in the Andalusia (Sherry) region.

Guadeloupe (Cktl) 1 measure Mardi Gras, dash lime cordial. Shake over ice, strain into an ice-filled highball glass and top with soda water.

Guadeloupe Rum (W.Ind) a dark, full-bodied dry rum with a burnt flavour.

Guadiana [River] (Sp) (Port) a river that runs through both Spain and Portugal.

Guado al Tasso (It) an I.G.T. barrique-aged red wine produced from Cabernet, Merlot and Syrah grapes by Belvedere in Bolgheri, Tuscany.

Gual (Sp) a local grape grown on the island of La Palma in the Canary Islands.

Gualdo del Re (It) a 20ha. wine estate based in Suvereto, Tuscany. Produces a Sangiovese wine of same name plus Federico Prima.

Guarapita (S.Am) the local name given to rum mixed with fruit juice in Venezuela.

Guarapo (W.Ind) a fermented sugar-cane drink similar to beer.

Guardian Peak (S.Afr) a winery (established 1998) based in Stellenbosch, Western Cape. Grape varieties: Cabernet sauvignon, Grenache, Merlot, Mourvèdre, Shiraz, Syrah. Owned by Ernie Els Wines. Label: Frontier. Website: http://www.guardianpeak.com

Guards (Cktl) ⅓ measure sweet vermouth, ⅔ measure dry gin, 3 dashes orange Curaçao, stir over ice and strain into a cocktail glass.

Guarnaccia (It) a red grape variety grown in Campania and the island of Ischia.

Guarnaccia Bianca (It) a white grape variety grown in Pollino, Calabria.

Guaruzo (Chile) a beer produced from fermented rice.

Guasti (USA) the label used by Perelli-Minetti winery for a range of their wines.

Guatemala Coffee (C.Am) a fairly smooth, mellow coffee which has a tangy after-taste, has good acidity and bouquet.

Guder (Afr) one of three wine-producing regions in Ethiopia. *See also* Eritire and Abadir-Dukem.

Guebwiller (Fr) a town in the Haut-Rhin region of Alsace. (Ger) = Gebweiler.

Guenoc Winery (USA) vineyards and winery based in Middletown, California. Grape varieties: Cabernet sauvignon, Chardonnay. Labels include Langtry.

Guépie (Fr) an alternative name for the Muscadelle grape.

Guera [La] (It) a D.O.C. Barbera d'Asti wine barrique-aged by Il Mongetto in Piedmont.

Guerbé [Jean] (Fr) a Cognac producer. (Add): Maison Guerbé et Cie, Hameau de L'Echalotte, Juillac le Coq, 16130 Segonzac. 34ha. in Grande Champagne. Produces Logis 5 year old.

Guérets [Les] (Fr) a Premier Cru vineyard in the A.C. Aloxe-Corton, Côte de Beaune, Burgundy.

Guernsey Brewery 1920 Ltd. (Ch.Isles) a brewery (established 1920) based in St. Peter Port, Guernsey. Was noted for Pony Ale 1037.7 O.G. Milk Stout 1042 O.G. Stein Lager 1048 O.G. LBA Mild 1037.7 O.G. Captain 1045 O.G. Champion 1045 O.G. Sunbeam 1042–1048 O.G. Braye 1035–1039 O.G. Taken over by Ann Street Brewery (now Jersey Brewery). *See also* Grizzly's. (Now ceased brewing all brewing conducted at the Jersey Brewery).

Guernsey Cream Liqueur (Ch.Isles) a cream-based, brandy and amaretto flavoured liqueur produced in Guernsey 17% alc by vol.

Guerrieri-Rizzardi (It) a large Veneto wine producer. Produces most wine styles of the region. (Add): 37011 Bardolino, Verona. has 3 vineyards: Poiega, Tacchetto and Costeggiola lie in the heart of the Classico areas of Valpolicella, Bardolino and Soave.

Guerrouane (Afr) an A.O.G. wine-producing area in Meknès Fez, Morocco

Guest Ales (Eng) describes a range of 'visiting' beers that a public house may introduce for sale, not permanently on their list.

Gueule de Bois (Fr) lit; 'wooden throat', a term used for a hangover.

Gueutrange (Fr) a name given to red and white wines from Lorraine.

Gueux (Fr) a Cru Champagne village in the Canton de Ville-en-Tardenois. District: Reims.

Gueze (Bel) a blend of 2 lambic beers which re-ferment to produce a good CO_2 bead. Is a fruity beer 5.5% alc by vol.

Gueze Lambic (Bel) a local Brussels beer often sweetened by adding a lump of sugar and dash of grenadine.

Gugge (Aus) a vineyard site based on the banks of the River Kamp situated in the Kamptal region.

Guggenheim (Cktl) 1 measure dry vermouth, dash orange bitters, 2 dashes Fernet Branca, shake over ice and strain into a cocktail glass.

Guglet (Ind) *see* Goglet.

Guglielmo Winery (USA) a winery based in Santa Clara, California. 34ha. Grape varieties: Barbera, Burgundy, Petite sirah, Ruby cabernet, Zinfandel. Also has vineyards in Morgan Hill. Produces varietal wines.

Güglingen (Ger) village (Anb): Württemberg. (Ber): Württembergisch Unterland. (Gro): Heuchelberg. (Vins): Kaiserberg, Michaelsberg.

Guido Berlucchi (It) a producer of sparkling (metodo tradizionale) wines based in Lombardy. Labels include: Cuvée Imperiale, Max Rosé and Pas Dosé.

Guigal (Fr) the famous Côte Rôtie wine producer (45ha) in the northern Rhône. Has 3 Cru properties: Turque (le), Mouline (la), Landonne (la) and has holdings in the A.C. Hermitage. Also owns Vidal Fleury.

Guignolet (Fr) a cherry brandy produced in Angers from the Guigne (a small black cherry) an eau-de-vie.

Guignolet d'Anger (Fr) a cherry-flavoured liqueur from the Anjou-Saumur district of the Loire.

Guignolet d'Anjou (Fr) a cherry-flavoured liqueur made in the Loire 16% alc by vol.

Guignolet de Bourguignon (Fr) a cherry brandy produced in Dijon in Burgundy.

Guigone de Salins (Fr) a cuvée in the A.C. Beaune, Côte de Beaune, Burgundy. Is owned by the Hospices de Beaune.

Guilbaud Frères (Fr) a noted producer of Muscadet wines. (Add): Mouzillon 44300 Vallet, Loire Atlantique.

Guild Ale (Eng) a bottled beer brewed by Thwaites Brewery, Blackburn, Lancashire to mark 1992 Preston Guild Celebrations. Happens every 20 years.

Guild Blue Ribbon Brandy (USA) the brand-name of a brandy bottled by the Guild of Wineries and Distillers in Lodi, California.

Guildhive (Fr) a slang term used for kill-devil in the early twentieth century.

Guildhive (W.Ind) the name given to a sugar cane distillery.

Guild of Cellarmasters (Eng) a professional organisation. (Add): 107, Carterhatch Lane, Enfield, Middlesex.

Guild of Master Victuallers [The] (Eng) a professional organisation (established 1990). (Add): 19 Warren Drive, Elm Park, Hornchurch, Essex RM12 4QZ.

Guild of Professional Toastmasters (Eng) a professional organisation. (Add): 12, Little Bornes, Alleyn Park, Dulwich, London SE21 8SE.

Guild of Sommeliers (Eng) a professional organisation. (Add): Standish, Rockshaw Road, Merstham, Surrey.

Guild of Wineries and Distilleries (USA) a San Joaquin co-operative producing brandy, table, dessert and sparkling wines in California. Also owns the Cresta Blanca in Mendocino, California. Uses the Cribari and Sons, Roma, Tavola and Winemaster labels.

Guilford Farm Vineyard (USA) a winery based in Stanley, Virginia. Produces French hybrid and vinifera wines.

Gui Lin (Chi) a natural spring mineral water from Guilin. Mineral contents (milligrammes per litre): Sodium 0.9mg/l, Calcium 19.2mg/l, Magnesium 4.5mg/l, Bicarbonates 68.3mg/l, Chlorides 3.1mg/l, Sulphates 13.5mg/l, Silicates 3.2mg/l. pH 7.0

Guillan (Fr) an alternative name for the Muscadelle grape.

Guillan Musqué (Fr) an alternative name for the Muscadelle grape.

Guillan Rouge (Fr) an alternative name for the Malbec grape.

Guillotine [La] (Bel) a 9.3% alc by vol. triple fermented, bottled beer brewed by Huyghe in Melle.

Guilty (Ch.Isles) a 5.2% alc by vol. stout brewed by Randalls Brewery, St. Peter Port, Guernsey. Originally known as Randalls Stout.

Guimaraens (Port) vintage Port shippers. Vintages: 1952, 1957, 1958, 1961, 1962, 1964, 1965, 1967, 1968, 1987, 1991, 1992, 1995, 1998. Not a single Quinta Port. The second wine of the Fonseca Port shippers.

Guimps (Fr) a commune in the Charente département whose grapes are classed Petite Champagne (Cognac).

Guindado (S.Am) a fermented cherry liqueur produced in Uruguay.

Guinea Fowl (S.Afr) the label for a red wine (Shiraz, Cabernet sauvignon and Merlot blend) produced by the Saxenberg winery, Stellenbosch, Western Cape.

Guinea Gold (Eng) a 4.5% alc by vol. light, gold cask ale brewed by Hardy's and Hanson's at their Kimberley Brewery, Nottingham in June, July and August. Part of their Cellarman's Cask range. Based on bottled Guinea Gold.

Guinea Gold (Eng) a bottled light ale 1032 O.G. brewed by the Hardy's and Hanson's Brewery in Nottingham.

Guinevere's Champion (Cktl) 2 parts Merrydown mead, 2 parts vodka, splash Curaçao. Pour into a frosted highball glass, add ice and slice of orange.

Guingette (Ch.Isles) a small Inn.

Guinness [Arthur] Brewery (Ire) breweries in Dublin and in Park Royal, London. Brews a naturally conditioned stout. 14 other breweries around the world. Also produces Harp Lager and controls Irish Ale Breweries. Took over DCL in 1986. See also Surger Unit. Website: http://www.guinness.com

Guinness Cooler (Cktl) in a large tumbler containing a piece of ice add ⅙ measure Dubonnet, ⅓ liqueur glass each of Curaçao and crème de cacao. Fill glass with baby Guinness and decorate with a spiral of lemon peel.

Guinness Draught (Ire) a 4.1% alc by vol. canned draught-style stout brewed by Guinness in Dublin.

Guinness Foreign Extra Stout (Ire) a 7.5% alc by vol. stout brewed from unmalted roasted barley in Dublin by Guinness.

Guinness Special Edition (Ire) a 5% alc by vol. bottled stout brewed by Guinness in Dublin.

Guinness Special Export Stout (Ire) an 8% alc by vol. strong bottled stout brewed by Guinness in Dublin.

Guinness Stout (Ire) a 5% alc by vol. bottled stout brewed for the Continent using roasted malt by Guinness in Dublin.

Guinness Tan (Eng) a Guinness and draught bitter ale (half and half).

Guissare (Rus) a red grape variety used for dessert wine production in Tadzhikistania.

Guita [La] (Sp) the brand-name of a Manzanilla Sherry produced by Sanchez de Alba.

Guitar (Sp) a pale Cream Sherry produced by Domecq in Jerez.

Güitig (Ecu) a natural spring mineral water from Las Fuentes de Tasalia. Mineral contents (milligrammes per litre): Sodium 147mg/l, Calcium 46mg/l, Magnesium 148mg/l, Potassium 8mg/l, Bicarbonates 1120mg/l, Sulphates 23mg/l.

Guitton-Figerou and C° (Fr) a nineteenth century Cognac producer.

Guizza (It) a natural spring mineral water from Guizza.

Gulden Anker (Hol) a jenever produced by Allied Breweries.

Gulden Draak (Bel) a 10.5% alc by vol. top-fermented, bottle-conditioned, dark barley wine brewed by Van Steenberge in Ertvelde.

Güldenkern (Ger) vineyard (Anb): Württemberg. (Ber): Württembergisch Unterland. (Gro): Schalkstein. (Vil): Rietenau.

Güldenmorgen (Ger) grosslage (Anb): Rheinhessen. (Ber): Nierstein. (Vils): Dienheim, Oppenheim.

Güldenmorgen (Ger) vineyard (Anb): Rheinhessen. (Ber): Nierstein. (Gro): Gutes Domtal. (Vil): Zornheim.

Guldental (Ger) village (Anb): Nahe. (Ber): Kreuznach. (Gro): Schlosskapelle. (Vins): Apostelberg, Hipperich, Hölle, Honigberg, Rosenteich, St. Martin, Sonnenberg, Teufelsküche.

Guldenzoll (Ger) vineyard (Anb): Hessische Bergstrasse. (Ber): Starkenburg. (Gro): Schlossberg. (Vil): Heppenheim including Erbach and Heimbach.

Gulder Lager (Afr) a lager beer 1047 O.G. brewed by the Kumasi Brewery in Ghana.

Gulder Lager (Afr) a lager beer 1047 O.G. brewed by the Nigerian Breweries Ltd. in Nigeria.

Guld Export (Den) also known as Carlsberg Gold Export. A pilsener-style beer 4% alc by vol.

Gulfa (Arab) a natural spring mineral water from the United Arab Emirates. Mineral contents (milligrammes per litre): Sodium 14mg/l, Calcium 4.8mg/l, Magnesium 6.7mg/l, Potassium 1.1mg/l, Bicarbonates 21mg/l, Chlorides 52mg/l, Sulphates 13mg/l, Fluorides 0.5mg/l, Nitrates 1.7mg/l. pH 7.7 Website: http://www.gulfa.net

Gulfi (It) a winery based on the island of Sicily. Label: Nero Bufaleffj.

G

Gulp (Eng) to swallow quickly/drink fast.

Gulp! (Eng) a 3.5% alc by vol. ale brewed by the Milk Street Brewery, Somerset.

Gulpener Bier Brouwerij BV (Hol) a brewery (established 1825). (Add): Rijksweg 16, 62701 AE Gulpen. Produces: Dort 6.5% alc by vol. and X-pert 5% alc by vol. Korenwolf 5% alc by vol. Pilsner %5 alc by vol. All are unpasteurised beers. Website: http://www.gulpener.nl 'E'mail: info@gulpener.nl

Gulpener Korenwolf (Hol) a 5% alc by vol. bottled, unfiltered, unpasteurised wheat beer brewed by Gulpener Bier Brouwerij, Gulpen, south Limburg. Brewed using spices and elderberry blossom. *see* Coors Brewers Ltd.

Gulpener Pilsner (Hol) a 5% alc by vol. bottled pilsner brewed by the Gulpener Bier Brouwerij, Gulpen, south Limburg.

Gulpers (Eng) a slang term used in the Royal Navy to obtain one large mouthful of a shipmate's rum issue.

Gul Rose Liqueur (Tur) the brand-name of a rose-flavoured liqueur.

Güls (Ger) village (Anb): Mosel-Saar-Ruwer. (Ber): Zell/Mosel. (Gro): Weinhex. (Vins): Bienengarten, Im Röttgen, Königsfels, Marienberg.

Gumbsheim (Ger) village (Anb): Rheinhessen. (Ber): Bingen. (Gro): Kurfürstenstück. (Vin): Schlosshölle.

Gümmel (Cktl) 1 measure High and Dry gin, 1 measure kümmel. Shake over ice and strain into a cocktail glass.

Gumpoldskirchen (Aus) a wine-producing district within the region of Niederösterreich. Produces both red and white wines.

Gumpoldskirchner (Aus) a fruity white wine of the Baden district.

Gumpoldskirchner Königssekt (Aus) a brand of sekt produced by Inführ.

Gum Syrup (Eng) a plain syrup used for sweetening cocktails.

Gumza (Bul) the alternative spelling of Gamza.

Gundelsheim (Ger) village (Anb): Württemberg. (Ber): Württembergisch Unterland. (Gro): Staufenberg. (Vin): Himmelreich.

Gundersheim (Ger) village (Anb): Rheinhessen. (Ber): Wonnegau. (Gro): Bergkloster. (Vins): Höllenbrand, Konigstuhl.

Gundheim (Ger) village (Anb): Rheinhessen. (Ber): Wonnegau. (Gro): Bergkloster. (Vins): Hungerbiene, Mandelbrunnen, Sonnenberg.

Gundlach-Bundschu Vineyard C°. (USA) a winery based in the Rhinefarm Vineyard, Sonoma Valley, California. 46ha. Grape varieties: Cabernet sauvignon, Gewürztraminer, Johannisberg riesling, Kleinberger riesling, Merlot, Pinot noir and Zinfandel. Produces varietal wines.

Gun-Flint (Fr) a taste of the wines of the Loire, especially of the wines from the Central Vineyards. (Pouilly Fumé and Sancerre).

Gunn Estate (N.Z) a winery. (Add): 85 Ohiti Road, RD 9, Hastings. 15ha. Grape varieties: Cabernet sauvignon, Merlot, Chardonnay, Sauvignon blanc.

Gun Park Dark (Eng) a 3.4% alc by vol. dark ale brewed by the Wentworth Brewery, South Yorkshire.

Gunpowder (Chi) a grade of tea/young teas. *see* Green Gunpowder.

Gunpowder (Eng) a beer brewed by Deeping Ales micro-brewery, Kent.

Gunpowder (Eng) a 5% alc by vol. ale from Firecracker & Firkin, Crawley, London.

Gunpowder Mild (Eng) a mild ale brewed by the Coach House of Warrington.

Gunpowder Strong Mild (Eng) a 3.8% alc by vol. mild ale brewed by the Coach House Brewing C°. Ltd., Cheshire.

Guntersblum (Ger) village (Anb): Rheinhessen. (Ber): Nierstein. (Gro): Krötenbrunnen. (Vins): Eiserne Hand, Sankt Julianenbrunnen, Sonnenberg, Sonnenhang, Steinberg.

Guntersblum (Ger) village (Anb): Rheinhessen. (Ber): Nierstein. (Gro): Vogelsgärten. (Vins): Authental, Bornpfad, Himmelthal, Kreuzkapelle, Steig-Terrassen.

Günterslay (Ger) vineyard (Anb): Mosel-Saar-Ruwer. (Ber): Bernkastel. (Gro): Michelsberg. (Vil): Minheim.

Günterslay (Ger) vineyard (Anb): Mosel-Saar-Ruwer. (Ber): Bernkastel. (Gro): Michelsberg. (Vil): Piesport.

Güntersleben (Ger) village (Anb): Franken. (Ber): Maindreieck. (Gro): Ravensburg. (Vin): Sommerstuhl.

Guntrum [Louis] (Ger) a family wine-producer based in Nierstein, Rheinhessen.

Guozhi (Chi) juice/fruit juice.

Gurdzhaani (Geo) a white wine from the Georgia region.

Gurglet (Ind) *see* Goglet.

Gurgling Jug (Eng) a solid silver fish-shaped jug donated by Plymouth Gin. Is used as a perpetual trophy for the field gunners competition at the Royal Tournement.

Gurpegui (Sp) *see* Bodegas Gurpegui.

Gurten Brauerei (Switz) a brewery based in Bern, part of the Feldschlösschen group.

Gusano Worm (Mex) the alternative name used for the agave worm. *See also* Maguey Worm.

Gush (Eng) a term meaning 'to fob'.

Güssinger (Aus) a natural spring mineral water from Vitaquelle, Gerersdorf, Sulz. Mineral contents (milligrammes per litre): Sodium 292.2mg/l, Calcium 114.6mg/l, Magnesium 24.55mg/l, Potassium 15.79mg/l, Bicarbonates 1049.5mg/l, Chlorides 126.6mg/l, Sulphates 5.85mg/l, Fluorides 1.2mg/l, Silicates 40.6mg/l, Boron 8.86mg/l.

Gustation (Eng) the art (skill) of tasting, faculty of taste.

Gustatory (Eng) denotes the enjoyment of wine.

Gustillo (Sp) a vineyard. (Add): Avda Cenicero No.50, Fuenmayor (La Rioja). 50ha. Grape varieties: Garnacha 10%, Tempranillo 80% and Viura 10%. Produces 100% red wine.

G

Gusto (It) flavour.

Gusto Wines (S.Afr) a winery (established 2001) based in Stellenbosch, Western Cape. Grape varieties: Cabernet sauvignon, Merlot, Sauvignon blanc. Label: Destino.

Güstrover Schlossquell (Ger) a sparkling natural spring mineral water from Mecklenburg. Mineral contents (milligrammes per litre): Sodium 16.1mg/l, Calcium 98.1mg/l, Magnesium 12.2mg/l, Potassium 2.1mg/l, Bicarbonates 322mg/l, Chlorides 20.1mg/l, Sulphates 40.2mg/l, Fluorides 0.3mg/l, Nitrates <0.5mg/l.

Gut (Ger) good.

Gut Alsenhof (Ger) vineyard (Anb): Baden. (Ber): Ortenau. (Gro): Schloss Rodeck. (Vil): Lauf.

Gutedel (Ger) a white grape variety grown in the Baden Anbaugebiete. Known as the Chasselas in France and the Fendant in Switzerland. Also called the Gutedelrebe and Markgräfler.

Gutedelrebe (Ger) a white grape variety grown mainly in the Baden Anbaugebiete.

Gutenberg (Ger) village (Anb): Nahe. (Ber): Kreuznach. (Gro): Pfarrgarten. (Vins): Felseneck, Römerberg, St. Ruppertsberg, Schlossberg, Schloss Gutenberg, Sonnenlauf.

Gutenberg (Ger) vineyard (Anb): Rheingau. (Ber): Johannisberg. (Gro): Honigberg. (Vil): Winkel.

Gutenborner (Ger) a white grape variety, a cross between the Müller-Thurgau x Chasselas Napoleon.

Gutenhölle (Ger) vineyard (Anb): Nahe. (Ber): Schloss Böckelheim. (Gro): Rosengarten. (Vil): Hüffelsheim.

Gutental (Ger) vineyard (Anb): Nahe. (Ber): Kreuznach. (Gro): Kronenberg. (Vil): Bad Kreuznach.

Gutes Domtal (Ger) grosslage (Anb): Rheinhessen. (Ber): Nierstein. (Vils): Dalheim, Dexheim, Friesenheim, Hahnheim, Köngernheim, Lörzweiler, Mommenheim, Nackenheim, Nieder-Olm, Nierstein, Selzen, Sörgenloch, Undenheim, Weinolsheim, Zornheim.

Gutleuthaus (Ger) vineyard (Anb): Rheinhessen. (Ber): Nierstein. (Gro): Güldenmorgen. (Vil): Oppenheim.

Gutsabfüllung (Ger) bottled by the producer (estate bottled), replaced erzeugerabfüllung since 17th December 1992.

Gutswein (Ger) village wine.

Gutsy (Eng) a term applied to wines that are full in body, fruit and alcohol.

Guttenberg (Ger) grosslage (Anb): Pfalz. (Ber): Südliche Weinstrasse. (Vils): Bad Bergzabern, Dierbach, Dörrenbach, Freckenfeld, Kandel, Kapsweyher, Minfeld, Niederotterbach, Oberotterbach, Schweigen-Rechtenbach, Schweighofen, Steinfeld, Vollmersweiler.

Gutturnio dei Colli Piacentini (It) a D.O.C. red wine from the Emilia-Romagna. Made from the Barbera and Bonarda grapes in the defined area in the province of Piacenza.

Gutturnium (It) a large cup, the Gutturnio is named after this cup.

Guyana Distilleries (S.Am) a distillery based at Uitvlugt, Guyana. Demerara Distillers is its subsidiary company. Is noted for the rum brands Blue Seal, High and Dry, High Wine Bonded and Ordinary El Dorado.

Guyana Liquor Corporation (S.Am) a company (established 1976) as a holding company for Demerara Distillers, Diamond Liquors and Guyana Distilleries in Guyana.

Guy De Forez (Fr) a Champagne producer. (Add): Route de Tonnerre, 10340 Les Riceys. Produces vintage and non-vintage Champagnes. Vintages: 1995, 1996, 1997, 1999, 2000. Labels include: Rosé des Riceys.

Guy Fawkes (Eng) a 4.8% alc by vol. bitter ale brewed by Mitchells at 11 Moor Lane, Lancaster for November.

Guyne (Fr) see Cherry Whisky.

Guyon [Comte de] (Fr) an Armagnac producer. (Add): Guyon de Pampetonne, Château de Lassalle, Maupas en Armagnac. Produces Comte de Guyon Hors d'Age 10 and 15 year old Armagnac.

Guyot [Dr.] (Fr) the inventor of the method of growing vines to best advantage to produce the best crops. see Guyot Simple, Guyot Double and Bogen.

Guyot à Queue (Fr) a vine training method.

Guyot Double (Fr) a method of vine pruning and growing, consists of 2 branches with up to 6 buds on each. (Ger) = doppelbogen.

Guyot Double Médocaine (Fr) the style of vine pruning (Guyot double) used in the Médoc, Bordeaux.

Guyot Poussard (Fr) the style of vine pruning used in Saint-Émilion, Bordeaux.

Guyot Simple (Fr) a method of vine pruning and growing, consists of 1 branch with 3–4 buds and a reserve bud for the following year. (Ger) = einzelbogen.

Guy Testaud (Fr) a Cognac producer. (Add): Plaisance, NW Lamerac, 16300 Barbezieux-St-Hilaire. 20ha. 20% Grande Champagne and 80% Petite Champagne. Produces V.S.O.P. 7 year old, Napoléon X.O. 12 year old, Hors d'Age 20 year old.

Guzbag (Tur) the state monopoly approved name for rosé wines produced in Trakya.

Güzel Koku (Tur) bouquet/aroma (of a wine).

Güzelpinar (Tur) a natural spring mineral water from Beylýk Forest. Mineral contents (milligrammes per litre): Calcium 10mg/l, Magnesium 2.4mg/l, Chlorides 31mg/l, Sulphates 34.35mg/l, Fluorides 0.05mg/l, Nitrates 2mg/l. pH 7.3

Guzzle (Eng) to consume (drink or food) excessively and quickly.

Guzzler (Eng) a fast drinker.

Guzzler (Eng) a 3.6% alc by vol. ale brewed by the York brewery Company Ltd., North Yorkshire.

Guzzling Goose (Eng) a 4.4% alc by vol. chestnut-coloured seasonal cask ale from Hardy's and Hanson's Kimberley Brewery, Nottingham.

Brewed in October and November (part of the Cellarman's Cask range).

Gwalic (Fr) a natural spring mineral water from St. Alix. Mineral contents (milligrammes per litre): Sodium 33.3mg/l, Calcium 8mg/l, Magnesium 10.2mg/l, Potassium 4mg/l, Bicarbonates 84.2mg/l, Chlorides 37mg/l, Sulphates 20mg/l, Silicates 0.5mg/l.

Gwangechunsoo (Kor) mineral water.

Gwatkins Cider (Eng) a dry cider produced at Morehampton Farm, Herefordshire.

Gweinydd Gwin (Wal) wine waiter/sommelier.

Gwendolyn (S.Afr) the label for a red wine (Shiraz 60% and Merlot 40% blend) produced by the Saxenberg winery, Stellenbosch, Western Cape.

Gwent Ales (Wal) now known as the Silverstone Brewery.

Gwin (Wal) wine.

Gwin Champagne (Wal) Champagne/sparkling wine.

Gwinllan (Wal) vineyard.

Gwinllan Ffynnon Las (Wal) a small vineyard based at Heol Llyswen, Lampeter Road, Aberaeron. Grape varieties: Madeleine angevine, Reichensteiner, Schönburger, Seyval blanc. Produces red and white wines under the Ffynnon Las label.

Gwinllan Pant Teg (Wal) a vineyard. (Add): 69 Station Road, Llanishen, Cardiff. Produces Gwin Pefriog, Cyfuniad Sych.

Gwin o Cymru (Wal) Welsh wine.

Gwin Pefriog (Wal) quality sparkling white wine produced by Gwinllan Pant Teg, Llanishen, Cardiff from Kerner and Kerling grapes.

Gwinwryf (Wal) grape press.

Gwinwydden (Wal) grape vine.

Gwirod (Wal) liquor.

G.W.R. (Eng) *abbr*: **G**reat **W**estern **R**eal ale.

Gwydr Gwin (Wal) wineglass.

Gwyn (Wal) white.

Gwyn Gwin (Wal) white wine.

Gye-sur-Seine (Fr) a Cru Champagne village in the Canton de l'Aube. District: Château Thierry.

Gyle (Eng) a term to describe a batch of beer from one brewing. *see* Gyle Label.

Gyle Label (Eng) the label (usually coloured) attached to each keg or cask to identify the batch number of the brew and to allow publicans to recognise which beers to use first. Also known as the Gyle Ticket.

Gyle Ticket (Eng) an alternative name for the Gyle Label.

Gymkhana (Ind) a lager beer 1045 O.G. brewed by the Mohan Meakin Brewery in Simla Hills, Solan.

Gyokuro Rikyu (Jap) a low-alcohol liqueur based on green tea and brandy.

Gyöncz (Hun) a cask used in the Hegyalja region which produces Tokaji. Holds approx. 35 gallons. *See also* Gönc.

Gyöngyös Estate (Hun) producer of still and sparkling red and white table wines produced in the region of same name. Grapes include Chardonnay, Sauvignon blanc.

Gypsies Kiss (Liq.Coffee) made with a measure of Galliano.

Gypsum (Eng) *Calcium sulphate* CASO₄ added to the grape must (especially to increase acidity).

Gypsy (S.Afr) the label for a red wine (Grenache, Pinotage and Shiraz blend) produced by the Ken Forrester Wines winery, Stellenbosch, Western Cape.

Gypsy Cocktail [1] (Cktl) ⅛ measure Bénédictine, ⅔ measure vodka, dash Angostura. Stir with ice and strain into a cocktail glass.

Gypsy Cocktail [2] (Cktl) ½ measure sweet vermouth, ½ measure gin. Stir over ice and strain into a cocktail glass.

Gypsy's Kiss (Cktl) 1 measure Irish Mist, ½ measure vodka, 2 measures orange juice, 2 dashes lemon juice, dash gomme syrup, dash egg white. Shake well over ice. Strain into a cocktail glass, top with a slice of orange and lemon.

Gyropalettes (Fr) the alternative name for Crecelles (auto remuage).

Gyrovagues (Eng) the mediaeval name for monks who used their guises to travel begging food and drink. They were heavy drinkers.

Gyuu (Jap) milk. Also spelt Nyuu.

H

Ha. (Fr) *abbr:* Hectare.

Haacht Brouwerij (Bel) a brewery (established 1898) based at Boortmeerbeek. Brews: Tongerlo and Tongerlo Dubbel, both Norbertine Abbaye beers, the Abbaye of Tongerlo was founded in 1133.

Haagen (Ger) village (Anb): Württemberg. (Ber): Kocher-Jagst-Tauber. (Gro): Tauberberg. (Vin): Schafsteige.

Haagen Lager (Eng) a keg lager beer 1032 O.G. brewed by the Greenall Whitley Brewery in Warrington, Cheshire.

Haake-Beck Brauerei (Ger) an associate company of the Beck's Brauerei in Bremen. Produces: Kreusenbier (a sediment beer) and Seefartbier.

Haaner Felsenquelle (Ger) a still and sparkling natural spring mineral water (established BC3000). (blue label: sparkling/green label: still). Mineral contents (milligrammes per litre): Sodium 23.4mg/l, Calcium 76.4mg/l, Magnesium 17.5mg/l, Potassium 3.4mg/l, Bicarbonates 186mg/l, Chlorides 44.2mg/l, Sulphates 101mg/l. Website: http://www.haanerfelsenquelle.de

Haaner Felsenquelle Natürliches Heilwasser (Ger) a sparkling natural spring mineral water (established BC3000). Mineral contents (milligrammes per litre): Sodium 22.3mg/l, Calcium 72.8mg/l, Magnesium 16.62mg/l, Potassium·3.32mg/l, Bicarbonates 164.8mg/l, Chlorides 55mg/l, Sulphates 86.4mg/l, Fluorides 0.13mg/l, Silicates 17.5mg/l. Website: http://www.haanerfelsenquelle.de

Haarberg-Katzensteg (Ger) vineyard (Anb): Rheinhessen. (Ber): Bingen. (Gro): Rheingrafenstein. (Vil): Wöllstein.

Haardt (Ger) the continuation of the French Vosges Mountains that shelter the Palatinate area of western Germany.

Haardt (Ger) village (Anb): Pfalz. (Ber): Mittelhaardt-Deutsche Weinstrasse. (Gro): Meerspinne. (Vins): Bürgergarten, Herrenletten, Herzog, Mandelring.

Haberschlacht (Ger) village (Anb): Württemberg. (Ber): Württembergisch Unterland. (Gro): Heuchelberg. (Vin): Dachsberg.

Habillage (Fr) the term used to describe the capsuling of Champagne bottles.

Habsburg-Husar (Aus) a white wine produced from the Grüner veltliner grape by Sepp Höld based at St. Georgen.

Habzö (Hun) sparkling.

Hacienda Monasterio (Sp) a 68ha vineyard (established 1992) in the D.O. Ribera del Duero.

Haciendas (S.Am) the alternative name for the Fincas.

Hacienda Vineyard (USA) a winery based in Sonoma County, California. Grape varieties: Cabernet sauvignon, Chardonnay, Gewürztraminer, Pinot noir and Zinfandel. Also owns vineyards in the Russian River Valley.

Hackenheim (Ger) village (Anb): Rheinhessen. (Ber): Bingen. (Gro): Rheingrafenstein. (Vins): Galgenberg, Gewürzgarten, Kirchberg, Klostergarten, Sonnenberg.

Hacker Marzen (Ger) a specially brewed dark bier from the Hacker-Pschorr Brauerei.

Hacker-Pschorr Brauerei (Ger) a famous brewery based in Munich that is noted for Hacker Marzen.

Hackler-Poitín (Ire) *abbr:* H.P. 40% alc by vol. Irish spirit drink from the Cooley Distillery, County Louth.

Hadda (Arab) a natural spring mineral water from Saudi Arabia. Mineral contents (milligrammes per litre): Sodium 90mg/l, Calcium 24mg/l, Magnesium 1.2mg/l, Potassium 1.7mg/l, Bicarbonates 207mg/l, Chlorides 33mg/l, Sulphates 27.2mg/l. pH 7.15

Häder (Ger) vineyard (Anb): Württemberg. (Ber): Remstal-Stuttgart. (Gro): Wartbühl. (Vil): Rommelshausen.

Häder (Ger) vineyard (Anb): Württemberg. (Ber): Remstal-Stuttgart. (Gro): Wartbühl. (Vil): Stetten i R.

Haderburg (It) a sparkling (metodo tradizionale) wine producer based in Piemonte.

Hadders Headbanger (Eng) a 5% alc by vol. ale brewed by the Vale Brewery C°., Buckinghamshire.

Hadratstall (Aus) a vineyard area on the banks of the River Danube in the Kremstal region.

Hadrian (Eng) a still and sparkling natural spring mineral water. (Add): Hadrian Spring Water Company, Riversdale Road, Southwick, Northumbria. SR5 3JG. Mineral contents (milligrammes per litre): Sodium 22mg/l, Calcium 107mg/l, Magnesium 47mg/l, Potassium 2.2mg/l, Chlorides 47mg/l, Sulphates 157mg/l, Nitrates 29mg/l, Fluorides <0.2mg/l. pH 7.2

Hadrian Brewery (Eng) a brewery (established 1987) based in Tyneside (ceased in 1997). Brewed: Centurion Best Bitter, Emperor Ale, Zetland Bitter. Premises now home to Four Rivers.

Hadrian & Border Brewery (Eng) a brewery

(established 2000). (Add): Unit 11, Hawick crescent Ind Estate, Newcastle-upon-Tyne, Tyne 7 Wear NE6 1AS. Brews: Centurian 4.5% alc by vol., Farne Island 4% alc by vol., Gladiator 3.8% alc by vol., Legion 4.2% alc by vol., Reiver IPA 4.4% alc by vol., Secret Kingdon 4.3% alc by vol. 'E'mail: border@rompart.freeserve.co.uk

Haewai Meadery & Wind Gardens (N.Z) a brewery. (Add): 236 Houghton Bay Road, Houghton Bay, Wellington. Brews a variety of beers and lager. Website: http://www.windgardens.co.nz

Hafle Vineyards (USA) large vineyards and wineries based in Columbus and Springfield. Produces French-American hybrid wines.

Häfnerhaslach (Ger) village (Anb): Württemberg. (Ber): Württembergisch Unterland. (Gro): Stromberg. (Vin): Heiligenberg.

HAG (Ger) a famous brand of de-caffeinised coffee from Hag of AG Bremen.

Hagebuttenlikoer (Ger) a liqueur made from rosehips, yellow in colour.

Hagel en Donder (Hol) lit- 'hail and thunder', a Frisian sweet brandewijn that is flavoured with anis.

Hagelsberg (S.Afr) the label for a red wine (Merlot) produced by the Middelvlei Estate winery, Stellenbosch, Western Cape.

Hagen (Aus) a winery based in the Kremstal region. (Add): Seilerweg 45, 3500 Krems-Rehberg. Grape varieties: Grüner veltliner, Müller-Thurgau, Riesling, Neuberger. Produces a range of wine styles.

Hägenich (Ger) vineyard (Anb): Baden. (Ber): Badische Bergstrasse/Kraichgau. (Gro): Mannaberg. (Vil): Wiesloch.

Haggipavlu (Cyp) a large winery based in Limassol, south-eastern Cyprus that trades under the Etko label. Produces wines and spirits including Angias brandy.

Haggis Ale (Eng) a 4.2% alc by vol. whisky-flavoured bitter ale (for Burns night) from Burt's Brewery, Isle of Wight.

Hagnau (Ger) village (Anb): Baden. (Ber): Bodensee. (Gro): Sonnenufer. (Vin): Burgstall.

Hahn (Ger) vineyard (Anb): Mittelrhein. (Ber): Bacharach. (Gro): Schloss Stahlech. (Vil): Bacharach.

Hahn (Ger) vineyard (Anb): Nahe. (Ber): Schloss Böckelheim. (Gro): Paradiesgarten. (Vil): Rehborn.

Hähnchen (Ger) vineyard (Anb): Rheinhessen. (Ber): Bingen. (Gro): Adelberg. (Vil): Bornheim.

Hahnen (Ger) vineyard (Anb): Pfalz. (Ber): Mittelhaardt-Deutsche Weinstrasse. (Gro): Rosenbühl. (Vil): Weisenheim/Sand.

Hahnenberg (Ger) vineyard (Anb): Württemberg. (Ber): Württembergisch Unterland. (Gro): Heuchelberg. (Vil): Burgbronn.

Hahnenkamm (Ger) vineyard (Anb): Pfalz. (Ber): Mittelhaardt-Deutsche Weinstrasse. (Gro): Schnepfenflug vom Zellertal. (Vil): Bubenheim.

Hahnenschrittchen (Ger) vineyard (Anb): Mosel-Saar-Ruwer. (Ber): Bernkastel. (Gro): Schwarzlay. (Vil): Burg.

Hahn Estates (USA) a winery based in the Central Coast, Monterey, California. (Add): P.O. Drawer C-37700 Foothill Road, Soldad CA 93960. Grape varieties: Cabernet sauvignon, Chardonnay, Syrah. Website: http://www.HahnEstates.com

Hahnheim (Ger) village (Anb): Rheinhessen. (Ber): Nierstein. (Gro): Gutes Domtal. (Vins): Knopf, Moosberg.

Hahnhölle (Ger) vineyard (Anb): Nahe. (Ber): Schloss Böckelheim. (Gro): Paradiesgarten. (Vil): Niedermoschel.

Hahn Premium (Austr) the name of an additive-free, 5% alc by vol. bottled premium lager beer produced from 100% malted barley brewed by Lion Nathan, Sydney. Is matured for 4 weeks.

Haid (Aus) vineyard sites (2) based on the banks of the River Kamp situated in the Kamptal region.

Haider (Aus) wine producer (10 ha). (Add): Seegasse 16, 7142 Illmitz. Grape varieties: Blaufränkirsch, Bouvier, Cabernet sauvignon, Neuburger, Sauvignon blanc, Scheurebe, Welschriesling, Zweigelt. Produces a variety of white, sweet white and red wines.

Haie Fouassière [La] (Fr) a village in the central Muscadet Sèvre et Maine district in Nantais, Loire. Produces some of the finest wines. Home of the Muscadet Maison du Vin.

Haig [John] (Scot) John Haig and C°. Ltd., Markinch. Major Scotch whisky blenders. *see* Dimple Haig, Glenleven, Golden Age and Old Cameron Brig. Part of DCL.

Haight Wineries (USA) a small winery based in Liotchfield, north-western Connecticut. 8ha. Grape varieties: Chardonnay, Foch, Riesling.

Hainault (Austr) a vineyard based at Walnut Road, Bickley 6076, West Australia. Grape varieties: Cabernet sauvignon, Chardonnay, Gewürztraminer, Merlot, Pinot noir.

Hainburg (Aus) a wine-producing area based on the right-bank of the river Danube. Produces mainly white wines.

Hainfeld (Ger) village (Anb): Pfalz. (Ber): Südliche Weinstrasse. (Gro): Ordensgut. (Vins): Kapelle, Kirchenstück, Letten.

Hainhölzer (Ger) the brand-name used by August Schmidt for a range of kornbranntwein.

Hair of the Dog (Eng) a slang term for a drink of the same that caused the hangover of person requesting it. i.e. if they had been drinking brandy all night then they would have a brandy as 'the hair of the dog'.

Hair of the Dog (Eng) a 4.5% alc by vol. ale from Ryburn Brewery, Sowerby Bridge, near Halifax, West Yorkshire.

Hair of the Dog Cocktail (Cktl) 25mls (1fl.oz) Scotch whisky, 35mls (1½ fl.ozs) cream, 10mls (½ fl.oz) honey. Shake together with ice and strain into a cocktail glass.

Hair of the Hog (Eng) a 3.5% alc by vol. ale brewed by the Hogs Back Brewery Ltd., Surrey.

H

Hair Raid (Eng) a 4.2% alc by vol. seasonal ale brewed by Hydes at 46 Moss Lane, West Manchester, Lancashire. Available May and June. Part of their Craft Ale range.

Hair Raiser (Cktl) 25mls (1fl.oz) vodka, 25mls (1fl.oz) Dubonnet, fill a highball glass with ice, stir in ingredients, top up with tonic to taste and serve with slice of lemon.

Haiti Coffee (W.Ind) often a harsh, earthy coffee with a strong aroma and good acidity. Is a good blender with the softer coffee of South America.

Haiti Rum (W.Ind) a medium dark rum, not as pungent as the Jamaican rums, sometimes called brandy rums. Pot stilled 40% alc by vol.

Hajime (Jap) a branded, bottled non-alcoholic green tea produced by the Coca Cola company.

Hajos (Hun) a noted wine-producing town in Mecsek, southern Hungary. Its Cabernet sauvignon wines are of sound quality.

Hakovo (Bul) a wine-producing region in southern Bulgaria, main grape varieties are Dimiat, Mavrud, Merlot and Tamianka.

Hakushu Distillery (Jap) one of the largest distilleries in the world owned by Suntory.

Hakutsuru (Jap) a famous brand of saké.

Halav (Isr) milk.

Halb Extra Liqueur (Ger) a less bitter version of the liqueur Halb Schimmegespann.

Halbfuder (Ger) a Mosel cask holding 500litres (110gallons).

Halbrot (Switz) a rosé wine made from black and white grapes.

Halb Schimmegespann (Ger) a liqueur which gets its name from a half bitter and half sweet taste. Herb-flavoured. See also Halb Extra Liqueur.

Halbstück (Ger) a round barrel that holds 600litres, used in the Palatinate region.

Halbtrocken (Aus) lit: 'half-dry', wines can have up to a maximum of 12g/l of residual sugar.

Halbtrocken (Ger) lit: 'half dry', medium dry.

Halb und Drittel Bau (Aus) lit: 'half and one third cultivation', a tenant of a leased vineyard would give the landlord third or half of his crop instead of payment for rent.

Halb und Halb (Ger) a liqueur, a blend of Curaçao and orange bitters.

Halcyon (Eng) a species of barley malt of the Golden promise variety that gives medium sugar yields.

Halcyon Days (Eng) a cask-conditioned ale brewed by Bank's Brewery.

Halcyon Daze (Austr) a winery (established 1982) at Uplands Road, Chirnside Park, Yarra Valley. Grape varieties: Cabernet sauvignon, Chardonnay, Merlot, Riesling.

Halde (Ger) the local name for the wine of Schait in Württemberg, made from the Sylvaner grape.

Halde (Ger) vineyard (Anb): Baden. (Ber): Breisgau. (Gro): Burg Zähringen. (Vil): Emmendingen (ortsteil Hochburg).

Halde (Ger) vineyard (Anb): Pfalz. (Ber): Mittelhaardt-Deutsche Weinstrasse. (Gro): Rosenbühl. (Vil): Weisenheim/Sand.

Halde (Ger) vineyard (Anb): Württemberg. (Ber): Remstal-Stuttgart. (Gro): Weinsteige. (Vil): Stuttgart (ortsteil Cannstatt).

Halde (Ger) vineyard (Anb): Württemberg. (Ber): Württembergisch Unterland. (Gro): Stromberg. (Vil): Illingen.

Halde (Ger) vineyard (Anb): Württemberg. (Ber): Württembergisch Unterland. (Gro): Stromberg. (Vil): Mühlhausen.

Halde (Ger) vineyard (Anb): Württemberg. (Ber): Württembergisch Unterland. (Gro): Stromberg. (Vil): Rosswag.

Haldengut Brauerei (Switz) a brewery based in Winterthur that is noted for its Albanibräu.

Hale and Hearty Brewery (Eng) a brewery based in Surrey. Brews: Rocking Robin, Upper Ale, Wicket Bitter.

Hale Cellars (USA) a winery based in Los Alamos Valley, Santa Barbara, California. 142ha. Produces varietal wines.

Haleeb (Arab) milk.

Halenberg (Ger) vineyard (Anb): Nahe. (Ber): Schloss Böckelheim. (Gro): Paradiesgarten. (Vil): Monzingen.

Halewood International Ltd (Eng) distillers (established 1978). (Add): The Sovereign Distillery, Wilson Road, Huyton, Liverpool, Merseyside L36 6AD. Produces a variety of sprits, liqueurs and cider. Also owns Chalié Richards. Website: http://www.halewood-int.com 'E'mail: admin@halewood-int.co.uk

Half (Ire)(Scot) a request for a measure of malt whisky and grain (blended) whisky.

Half and Half (Cktl) 50mls (2fl.ozs) sweet vermouth, 50mls (2fl.ozs) dry vermouth. Pour into an old-fashioned glass with ice and a twist of lemon.

Half-and-Half (Eng) an equal quantity of two beers in a pint (usually mild and bitter ales).

Half and Half (Ger) a liqueur, a blend of Curaçao and orange bitters.

Half-Bocoy (Sp) see Media Bocoy.

Half-Bota (Sp) see Media Bota.

Half-Bottle (Eng) contains half the amount of a standard bottle. (U.K) = 12fl.ozs (350mls), (USA) = 15.5fl.ozs

Half Bottle (Eng) the alternative name for the Champagne Demie bottle.

Half Gassed (USA) a slang term for intoxicated.

Half-Jack (S.Afr) a flat, pocket-sized bottle of alcoholic beverage. See also Hip Flask.

Half-om-Half (Hol) a liqueur, a blend of Curaçao and orange bitters. Produced by De Kuyper 30% alc by vol.

Halfpenny Green Vineyards (Eng) vineyards based in the West Midlands. Grape variety: Huxelrebe.

Half-Pint (USA) a cocktail measure of 250mls or 8fl.oz cup (0.25 quart).

Halfside (Eng) a 4.8% alc by vol. winter warmer ale from Four Rivers Brewery, Newcastle-on-Tyne.

Halfsoet Hanepoot (S.Afr) an amber-coloured, dessert wine made from the Muscadelle grape by the Klawer Co-operative.

H

Halfsoet Wyn (S.Afr) semi-sweet wine.

Halifax Harlot (Cktl) 1 measure Mandarine Napoléon, ¼ measure Galliano, dash orange juice. Shake well over ice, strain into a flute glass and top with iced Champagne.

Halkidas (Gre) a red wine produced on the island of Euboea.

Halkidiki Peninsula (Gre) a wine-producing island in Macedonia, grows the Limnio grape.

Hall and Woodhouse Brewery (Eng) a brewery (established 1777). (Add): The Brewery, Blanford St. Mary, Blandford Forum, Dorset DT11 9LS. It specialises in canned beers and soft drinks using the Panda name. Noted for cask-conditioned Hector's Bitter 1034 O.G. Badger Best 1041 O.G. Tanglefoot 1048 O.G. Malthouse Keg 1033 O.G. Newe Timer, Brock Lager 1033 O.G. and bottled Stingo 1066 O.G. Also canned Skona Lager 1032 O.G. Website: http://www.badgerales.com 'E'mail: beermarketing@hall-woodhouse.co.uk

Hallau (Switz) a village in the Schaffhausen canton, eastern Switz.

Hallburg (Ger) village (Anb): Franken. (Ber): Maindreieck. (Gro): Not yet assigned. (Vin): Schlossberg.

Hallcrest Vineyard (USA) *see* Felton-Empire.

Hall Cross (Eng) *see* Stocks Brewery.

Hallebühl (Aus) the label for a red wine (Zweigelt, Blaufränkisch and Cabernet sauvignon blend) produced by the Umathum winery, Burgenland.

Hallelujah Brandy (Rus) an orange-flavoured, brandy-based liqueur.

Hallerbräu Lager (Eng) an unpasteurised, filtered lager beer 1042 O.G. brewed by the Phillips Brewery, Buckinghamshire.

Haller's County Fair (USA) the brand-name of a Bourbon whiskey.

Hallertauer (Eng) a 4% alc by vol. beer brewed by the York Brewery Company Ltd., North Yorkshire.

Hallertaus (Ger) a species of hops grown in Bavaria. Has a spicy, full flavour and aroma, often used for dry-hopping beers.

Hallgarten (Eng) a famous wine and liqueur producer based in north London, noted for Royal Mint Chocolate series of liqueurs.

Hallgarten (Ger) village (Anb): Rheingau. (Ber): Johannisberg. (Gro): Mehrhölzchen. (Vins): Hendelberg, Jungfer, Schönhell, Würzgarten.

Hallmint Cocktail (Cktl) ½ measure Cognac, ½ measure Royal Mint Chocolate liqueur, 2 dashes Cointreau. Stir with ice and strain into a cocktail glass.

Hall's Brewery (Eng) a brewery originally based in Oxford which ceased brewing in 1952. Now owned by Allied Breweries who use its name for their West Country public houses. Produce in Burton-on-Trent a cask-conditioned Harvest Bitter 1037 O.G. and Barleycorn 1033 O.G. for sale in the public houses.

Hall's Bristol Brewery (Eng) part of the Allied Breweries' Hall's set up. Brews: cask-conditioned Jacob's Pride 1038 O.G. and Bristol Pride 1045 O.G.

Hall's Plympton Brewery (Eng) part of the Allied Breweries' Hall's set up. Brews: cask-conditioned Plympton Best 1039 O.G. and Plympton Pride 1039 O.G.

Halmei (Rum) a wine-producing region in the district of Siebenbürgen.

Haloze (Euro) a large winery in the city of Ptuj on the banks of the river Danube. Noted for a demi-sec Sauvignon blanc, Traminer and Laski rizling.

Halstead (USA) a natural spring mineral water from Speedwell, TN.

Haltingen (Ger) village (Anb): Baden. (Ber): Markgräflerland. (Gro): Vogtei Rötteln. (Vin): Steige.

Haltnau (Ger) vineyard (Anb): Baden. (Ber): Bodensee. (Gro): Sonnenufer. (Vil): Meersburg.

Halve Maan [The] (Bel) a brewery. (Add): Walglein 26, Brugge 8000. Brews a range of beers and lagers. Website: http://www.halvemaan.be 'E'mail: info@halvemaan.be

Hama (Lat) a water-bucket.

Hamacher Vineyard (USA) a vineyard based in Oregon.

Hamar Brewery (Nor) a brewery based in Hamar, eastern Norway.

Hamarteff (Isr) a large winery based in southern Israel.

Hambach (Ger) village (Anb): Pfalz. (Ber): Mittelhaardt-Deutsche Weinstrasse. (Gro): Pfaffengrund. (Vin): Römerbrunnen.

Hambach (Ger) village (Anb): Pfalz. (Ber): Mittelhaardt-Deutsche Weinstrasse. (Gro): Rebstöckel. (Vins): Feuer, Kaiserstuhl, Kirchberg, Schlossberg.

Hambledon (Eng) a wine from the Mill Down Vineyards, Hambledon, Portsmouth, Hampshire. 3.25ha. Grape varieties: Auxerrois, Chardonnay, Pinot noir and Seyval blanc.

Hambleton Best Bitter (Eng) a 3.6% alc by vol. bitter beer brewed by Hambleton Brewery, Holme-on-Swale, near Thirsk, North Yorkshire.

Hambleton Bitter (Eng) a 4% alc by vol. bitter beer brewed by the Itchen Valley Brewery, Hampshire.

Hambleton Ales (Eng) a brewery (established 1991). (Add): Holme-on-Swale, Thirsk, North Yorkshire YO7 4JE. Brews: Bull, Gluten & Wheat Free 4.2% alc by vol., Goldfield 4.2% alc by vol., Hambleton Bitter 3.6% alc by vol., Nightmare 5% alc by vol., Stallion 4.2% alc by vol., Stud 4.3% alc by vol. Also brews White Boar and Old Raby Ale. Website: http://www.hambletonales.co.uk 'E'mail: sales@hambletonales.co.uk

Hambusch (Ger) vineyard (Anb): Mittelrhein. (Ber): Bacharach. (Gro): Schloss Stahleck. (Vil): Bacharach/Steeg.

Hameau de Blagny (Fr) a Premier Cru vineyard in the A.C. commune of Puligny-Montrachet, Côte de Beaune, Burgundy 4ha.

Hamedan (Iran) a wine-producing region in the north of the country.

Hamelin Bay (Austr) a winery based in the Margaret River, Western Australia. Grape varieties include:

Cabernet sauvignon, Merlot, Shiraz. Label: Rampant Red.

Hamilton Russell Vineyards (S.Afr) a winery (established 1975) based in Hemel-en-Aarde, Walker Bay, Overberg. 52ha. (Add): Oude Hemel en Aarde, P.O. Box 158, Hermanus 7200. Grape varieties: Chardonnay, Pinot noir. Produces varietal wines. Is the most southerly of South Africa's vineyards

Hamilton's (Austr) a family winery at Barossa and Adelaide, South Australia.

Hamilton [Richard] Winery (Austr) a winery based in Clare-Watervale, Southern Vales, South Australia.

Hamlet [The] (Cktl) ½ measure Aalborg akvavit, ½ measure Peter Heering. Stir over ice and strain into a cocktail glass.

Hamlet Glasses (Eng) a brand-name for a range of glasses produced by the Dema Glass Company.

Hamlet Hill Vineyard (USA) a vineyard based in Pomfret, Connecticut. Produces mainly French hybrid grapes.

Hamm (Ger) village (Anb): Mosel-Saar-Ruwer. (Ber): Saar-Ruwer. (Gro): Scharzberg. (Vin): Altenberg.

Hamm (Ger) vineyard (Anb): Mosel-Saar-Ruwer. (Ber): Zell/Mosel. (Gro): Weinhex. (Vil): Koblenz (ortsteil Moselweiss).

Hamm (Ger) vineyard (Anb): Mosel-Saar-Ruwer. (Ber): Zell/Mosel. (Gro): Weinhex. (Vil): Winningen.

Hamm (Ger) vineyard (Anb): Nahe. (Ber): Schloss Öckelheim. (Gro): Burgweg. (Vil): Waldböckelheim.

Hämmchen (Ger) vineyard (Anb): Mittelrhein. (Ber): Rheinburgengau. (Gro): Gedeonseck. (Vil): Brey.

Hammel (Switz) a vine grower and merchant based at Rolle, La Côte.

Hammelburg (Ger) village (Anb): Franken. (Ber): Maindreieck. (Gro): Burg. (Vins): Heroldsberg, Trautlestal.

Hammelhoden (Ger) an erroneous varietal name for the red grape variety Trollinger (hammel = castrated ram/hoden = testicles).

Hammerhead Ale (Eng) a strong ale 1050 O.G. brewed by the Clark Brewery in Wakefield, Yorkshire.

Hammerstein (Ger) village (Anb): Mittelrhein. (Ber): Rheinburgengau. (Gro): Burg Hammerstein. (Vins): Hölle, In den Layfelsen, Schlossberg.

Hammerstein (Ger) vineyard (Anb): Mosel-Saar-Ruwer. (Ber): Saar-Ruwer. (Gro): Römerlay. (Vil): Trier.

Hammerton's Porter (Eng) a highly-hopped porter 1038 O.G. brewed by the Watney Combe Reid Brewery in London.

Hammet [Emile] et Fils (Fr) a Champagne producer. (Add): 16 Rue Nicolas Philiponnat, 51160 Aÿ. 4ha. Négociant-manipulant.

Hammond (W.Ind) the local name for 'moonshine rum' on St. Kitts.

Hammondsport Wine Company (USA) a winery based in the Finger Lakes district, New York. Noted for bottle-fermented, sparkling wines.

Hammurabi (M.East) the King of Babylon. *see* Laws of Hammurabi.

Hampden Distillery (W.Ind) a rum distillery based in north-western Jamaica, produces rum which is usually used for blending.

Hampshire Brewery (Eng) a brewery (established 1992). (Add): 6-8 Romsey Ind Estate, Greatbridge Road, Romsey, Hampshire SO51 0HR. Brews: Bees Knees 4.5% alc by vol., Bohemian Rhapsody 5% alc by vol., Good King Censlas 5% alc by vol., Ironside 4.2% alc by vol., King Alfred Strong Best Bitter 3.8% alc by vol., Laughing Leprechaun Stout 4.5% alc by vol., Lionheart 4.5% alc by vol., Merlins Magic 5% alc by vol., Pendragon 4.8% alc by vol., Penny Black Porter 4.5% alc by vol., Ploughmans Punch 4.5% alc by vol., Porky & Best 4.5% alc by vol., Pride of Romsey 5% alc by vol., Seduction 4.5% alc by vol., Strong Best Bitter 3.8% alc by vol., 1066 6% alc by vol. Website: http://www.hampshirebrewery.com 'E'mail: online@hampshirebrewery.com

Hampshire Glory (Eng) a 4.3% alc by vol. seasonal ale brewed by Gale's Brewery, Horndean, Hampshire.

Hampshire Rose (Eng) a 4.2% alc by vol. ale brewed by the Itchen Valley Brewery, Hampshire.

Hana (Arab) bar.

Hanácká Kyselka (Czec) a sparkling natural spring mineral water from Horni Mostinice. Mineral contents (milligrammes per litre): Sodium 277.8mg/l, Calcium 270mg/l, Magnesium 71.4mg/l, Potassium 16.67mg/l, Bicarbonates 1645mg/l, Chlorides 185.4mg/l, Sulphates 0.25mg/l, Fluorides 1.91mg/l, Iron 3.87mg/l, Silicates mg/l.

Hanácká Kyselka Prirodni (Czec) a natural spring mineral water from Brodek. Mineral contents (milligrammes per litre): Sodium 412.4mg/l, Calcium 185.2mg/l, Magnesium 107.1mg/l, Bicarbonates 2058mg/l, Chlorides 144.2mg/l, Sulphates 0.185mg/l, Fluorides 0.63mg/l, Iron 2.45mg/l.

Hanby Ales (Eng) a brewery (established 1988). (Add): New Brewery, Aston Park, Soulton Road, Wem, Shropshire SY4 5SD. Brews: All Seasons 4.2% alc by vol., Blackmagic Mild 4% alc by vol., Cascade 4.5% alc by vol., Cherry Bomb 6% alc by vol., Drawwell Bitter 3.9% alc by vol., Golden Honey 4.5% alc by vol., Hanby's Premium 4.6% alc by vol., Joy Bringer 6% alc by vol., Nutcracker 6% alc by vol., Old Wemian 4.9% alc by vol., Rainbow Chaser 4.3% alc by vol., Scorpio Porter 4.5% alc by vol., Shropshire Stout 4.4% alc by vol., Taveners Ale 5.3% alc by vol., Wem Special 4.4% alc by vol. Also brews Peter Piper and Pickled Pam. Website: http://www.hanbyales.co.uk 'E'mail: jack@hanbyales.co.uk

Hancock Brewery (Den) a brewery based in Viborg, north Jutland.

Hancock's Brewery (Wal) a Cardiff brewery now

H

owned by Bass Worthington which operates as Welsh Brewers.

Hancock's HB (Wal) a bitter ale 1037 O.G. brewed by the Welsh Brewers.

Hancock Sour (Cktl) 35mls (1½ fl.ozs) Bourbon whiskey, 4 dashes gomme syrup, 2 dashes Jamaican rum, juice of a small lime. Stir well over ice, strain into a highball glass, top with soda water and decorate with fruit in season.

Hancock's PA (Wal) a light mild ale 1033 O.G. brewed by the Welsh Brewers.

Hancock's Reserve (USA) a 88.9° US proof single barrel Bourbon whiskey produced by Ancient Age, Leestown, Frankfort.

Hand [Peter] Brewery (USA) a noted brewery based in Chicago. Brews Van Meritt beers.

Handicap Cocktail (Cktl) 30mls (¼ gill) Grand Marnier, 1 wine-glass fruchtschaumwein. Stir well over ice, strain into a large wine glass and add a slice of lemon.

Handicask (Eng) a patented lightweight cask made of plastic.

Handle (Eng) a customer's request for a glass mug with a handle.

Handley Winery (USA) a winery based in the Anderson Valley, Mendocino County, California. Grape variety: Pinot noir.

Handpull (Eng) see Handpump.

Handpump (Eng) also known as the Handpull or the Beer Engine. Used for the dispensing of beer in the bar.

Handthal (Ger) village (Anb): Franken. (Ber): Steigerwald. (Gro): Not yet assigned. (Vin): Stollberg.

Hanepoot (S.Afr) a white grape variety which has a high sugar content and good body. Used for making dessert wines in Klein Karoo. Is also known as the Hanepoot Jerepigo, Jerepigo and Muscat of Alexandria.

Hanepoot Jerepigo (S.Afr) an alternative name for the Hanapoot. See also Jerepigo.

Hangen-Weisheim (Ger) village (Anb): Rheinhessen. (Ber): Wonnegau. (Gro): Bergkloster. (Vin): Sommerwende.

Hanging Rock Winery (Austr) a winery (established 1987) based in Victoria. Grape varieties: Chardonnay, Gewürztraminer, Sauvignon blanc, Shiraz (produces still and sparkling wines).

Hangover (Eng) an indisposition due to a heavy drinking bout. (Hol) = malessere.

Hang Time (USA) the period after the grapes have fully ripened when the bunches of grapes are left on the vine to lose some of the water and so concentrate the sugars. Also known as Physiological Ripening.

Hangtown (USA) the brand-name used for a range of red and white wines produced by the Boeger Winery in Eldorado, California.

Hankavan-Lithia (Arm) a sparkling natural spring mineral water. Mineral contents (milligrammes per litre): Sodium 1370mg/l, Calcium 265mg/l, Magnesium 126mg/l, Potassium 100mg/l, Bicarbonates 2950mg/l, Chlorides 1765mg/l, Sulphates 214mg/l, Nitrates 0.1mg/l, Silicates 167mg/l, Lithium 5.45mg/l, Hydrobromide 1.5mg/l, Iodine 2mg/l.

Hankavan-2 (Arm) a sparkling natural spring mineral water. Mineral contents (milligrammes per litre): Sodium 19.2mg/l, Calcium 252mg/l, Magnesium 16.7mg/l, Potassium 2.7mg/l, Bicarbonates 1117mg/l, Chlorides 3mg/l, Sulphates 11.2mg/l, Fluorides 0.48mg/l, Nitrates 3.8mg/l, Silicates 45mg/l.

Hankin Wines (Austr) a winery (established 1976) at Johnson's Lane, Northwood, Victoria. Grape varieties: Cabernet sauvignon, Chardonnay, Merlot, Sauvignon blanc, Sémillon, Shiraz.

Hanky Bannister (Scot) the producers of a blended Scotch whisky of the same name based in Leith, Edinburgh, Midlothian.

Hanky-Panky (Cktl) ½ measure gin, ½ measure Italian vermouth, 2 dashes Fernet Branca. Stir over ice, strain into a cocktail glass and a squeeze of lemon peel juice on top.

Hannan's (Austr) the brand-name used by the Swan Brewery for lager and stout brewed at their Kalgoorlie plant.

Hannan's Lager (Austr) see Hannan's.

Hannan's Stout (Austr) see Hannan's.

Hannen Alt (Ger) an altbier brewed by Hannener Brauerei, Mönchengladbach. Soft, dark and delicate 4.8% alc by vol.

Hannener Brauerei (Ger) a brewery (established 1725) based in Mönchengladbach since. Brews: Hannen Alt.

Hannesen (Ger) noted producers of Perlwein.

Hanneton (Eng) a beetle that attacks the roots of the vine and slows down its growth, cured with the treatment of sulphur around the roots, similar to the vespere beetle.

Hannetot Grand Maison (Fr) a vineyard in the commune of Léognan. A.C. Pessac-Léognan, Bordeaux. 5ha (red).

Hanns Christof (Ger) the brand-name of a Liebfraumilch from the shippers Deinhard and C°. Koblenz.

Hann's Creek Estate (Austr) a winery (established 1987) based at Kentucky Road, Merricks North, Victoria. Grape varieties: Cabernet sauvignon, Chardonnay, Pinot noir, Riesling, Shiraz.

Hanns Kornell Champagne Cellars (USA) see Kornell Champagne Cellars.

Hansa Bier (Ger) a brewery based in Bad Sassendorf. Brew: Hansa Pils.

Hansa Brauerei (Ger) a brewery based in Dortmund, Westphalia.

Hansa Brewery (Afr) a brewery based in Namibia, noted for pilsener lager beer.

Hansa Brewery (Nor) a brewery based in Bergen, western Norway. Brews Heineken under licence.

Hansa Export (Ger) a Dortmunder export beer brewed by the Dortmunder Hansa Brauerei in Dortmund, Westphalia.

Hansa Lager (Eng) a lager beer 1036 O.G. brewed

under licence by the Cameron's Brewery in Hartlepool, County Durham.

Hansa Pils (Ger) a pilsener lager beer brewed by the Dortmunder Hansa Brauerei in Dortmund, Westphalia.

Hansa Pils (Ger) a 4.8% alc by vol. pilsner brewed by Hansa Bier, Bad Sassendorf.

Hansa Pilsener (Afr) a lager beer brewed by the Hansa Brewery in Namibia.

Hansa Pilsener (S.Afr) a lager beer brewed by the South African Breweries.

Hansa Urbock (Afr) a dark bock beer 1080 O.G. brewed by the Hansa Brewery in Namibia.

Hansenberg (Ger) vineyard (Anb): Rheingau. (Ber): Johannisberg. (Gro): Erntebringer. (Vil): Johannisberg.

Hansen Caribbean Rum C°. (W.Ind) a rum producer based on Ariba. Produces White Cap 38% alc by vol.

Hansen GmbH & C°. (Ger) a large rum producer based in Flensburg. Produces rums under the labels: Balle, Colding, Hansen, Nissen, Old Schmidt and Président.

Hanseret Wines (S.Afr) the brand-name for table wines produced by the Eesterivier Valleise Co-operative in Stellenbosch.

Hansjakob [Heinrich] (Ger) a priest who in 1881 founded the Baden wine co-operative.

Hansje in de Kelder (Hol) lit: 'Hans in the cellar' (or Jack in the box), an old Dutch liqueur served as a discreet method used to announce a pregnancy in the family. The mother-to-be would blush when her turn came to sip the wine.

Hanson Brewery (Eng) part of the Wolverhampton Brewery. Closed their Dudley Brewery and switched to Bank's Brewery, Wolverhampton where Hanson's Mild will be produced. Produces cask-conditioned beers.

Hanssen's Brasserie (Bel) a brewery based in Dworp, central Belgium.

Hanusovice Brewery (Czec) a brewery based in northern Czec.

Hanweiler (Ger) village (Anb): Württemberg. (Ber): Remstal-Stuttgart. (Gro): Kopf. (Vin): Berg.

Hanweiler (Ger) village (Anb): Württemberg. (Ber): Remstal-Stuttgart. (Gro): Wartbühl. (Vin): Maien.

Hanwood Winery (Austr) a part of the McWilliams Vineyards in Riverina, New South Wales. 87ha. Grape varieties: Cabernet sauvignon, Chardonnay, Malbec, Pinot noir, Rhine riesling and Shiraz.

Hanzell Winery (USA) a winery based in Sonoma County, California. Grape varieties: Chardonnay and Pinot noir. Produces varietal wines.

Haomen (Chi) a natural spring mineral water. Mineral contents (milligrammes per litre): Potassium 1.9mg/l, Bicarbonates 255mg/l, Silicates 22.5mg/l.

Hapkin (Bel) an 8.5% alc by vol. top-fermented, bottle-conditioned special Duvel beer brewed by the Louwaege Brewery, Kortemark.

Happenhalde (Ger) vineyard (Anb): Württemberg. (Ber): Remstal-Stuttgart. (Gro): Wartbühl. (Vil): Endersbach.

Happs Winery (Austr) vineyard. (Add): P.O. Dunsborough, Western Australia 6281. Grape varieties: Cabernet sauvignon, Chardonnay, Merlot, Shiraz and Verdelho. Winery at Commonage Road, Yallingup, Margaret River, Western Australia.

Happy 'B' Farm Winery (USA) a winery based in Forsyth, Georgia. Produces wines mainly from the Concord and Muscadine grapes.

Happy Birthday (Cktl) 5mls (¼ fl.oz) Bacardi rum, 20mls (¾ fl.oz) Bols Johannisbeerlikoer, 2 dashes peach juice, 2 dashes pineapple juice. Build into a highball glass, top with Champagne, add a slice of lemon and cherry.

Happy Day (Scot) a term for a pint of beer made up using 400mls (⅔ pint) of light ale with a nip-sized bottle of strong ale (a wee heavy).

Happy Horse (Cktl) 25mls (1fl.oz) White Horse Scotch whisky, 50mls (2fl.ozs) grapefruit juice, dash grenadine, dash egg white. Shake with ice, strain into a small goblet and add a slice of orange.

Happy Hour (Eng) a term used for the early part of the evening during licensed hours when drinks are offered at a reduced price to attract customers and hopefully keep them when the hour ends and normal prices return.

Happy Major (Eng) a 4% alc by vol. cask-conditioned ale brewed by the Steampacket Brewery, Knottingley, Yorkshire.

Happy Medium (Cktl) ⅛ measure Lillet, ⅛ measure orange squash, ¼ measure Pimm's N°1, ¼ measure gin, ¼ measure Cointreau. Shake over ice and strain into a cocktail glass.

Happy Valley (Austr) an estate based in Hunter Valley, New South Wales. Owned by Drayton.

Happy Youth (Cktl) 10mls (½ fl.oz) cherry brandy, 35mls (1½ fl.oz) fresh orange juice, 1 lump sugar, Champagne. Place sugar in a Champagne flute with the orange juice and cherry brandy, stir and top up with iced Champagne.

Hapsburg (Bulg) a range of absinthes: 72.5% alc by vol. or a Super Deluxe Extra at 85% alc by vol.

HAP3AH (Rus) a natural spring mineral water. Mineral contents (milligrammes per litre): Sodium 359mg/l, Calcium 300mg/l, Magnesium 80mg/l, Potassium 200mg/l, Bicarbonates 1000mg/l, Sulphates 300mg/l.

Harald Jensen Taffel Akvavit (Den) the brand-name of a famous akvavit 45% alc by vol.

Haras de Pique (Chile) a winery based in the Maipo Valley. Grape varieties include: Cabernet sauvignon, Carmenère. Label: Albis.

Haraszthy [Count Agoston] (USA) an early (1849) pioneer of *Vitis vinifera* vineyards in California, considered by many as the father of Californian viticulture.

Haraszthy and Sons (USA) a winery based in Sonoma Valley, California. Grape varieties: Johannisberg riesling, Pinot noir and Zinfandel. Produces varietal wines.

Harboes Brewery (Den) a brewery based in Fakse.

Harbor Winery (USA) a winery based in Sacramento, California. Grape varieties: Chardonnay and Zinfandel. Produces varietal wines.

Harbourne Vineyard (Eng) a vineyard (established 1980) based at Harbourne Lane, High Halden, Ashford, Kent. 1.2ha. Grape varieties: Madeleine angevine, Müller-Thurgau, Reichensteiner and Seyval blanc.

Harcourt Valley (Austr) a winery. (Add): Calder Highway, Harcourt, Victoria 3453. 6ha. Grape varieties: Cabernet sauvignon, Chardonnay, Pinot noir, Rhine riesling, Shiraz.

Hard (Eng) a term used by wine tasters for a wine without much charm. Many wines which are 'hard' when young develop suppleness in time. The hardness is due to the tannin in the wine.

Hard Bean (Eng) denotes the best type of coffee bean (top quality), has good body and acidity.

Hard Cider (USA) a term for rough, alcoholic cider.

Hardenstein Brunnen (Ger) a natural spring mineral water. Mineral contents (milligrammes per litre): Sodium 359mg/l, Calcium 5.9mg/l, Magnesium 5.8mg/l, Potassium 0.9mg/l, Chlorides 311mg/l, Fluorides 2.5mg/l.

Hardie (Scot) a higland malt and Scotch whisky distiller. Part of DCL. Noted for The Antiquary.

Hardington Brewery (Eng) a brewery based in the Brewers Arms, South Petherton, Somerset. Noted for cask-conditioned Somerset Special 1043 O.G. and keg Landsdorf Lager 1034 O.G.

Hard Liquor (USA) a slang term for spirits (especially whiskey, rum, brandy and gin).

Hardt (Ger) vineyard (Anb): Württemberg. (Ber): Kocher-Jagst-Tauber. (Gro): Tauberberg. (Vil): Weikersheim.

Hard Tackle (Eng) a 4% alc by vol. limited edition ale brewed by the Pharoah and Firkin micro-brew pub in Fulham, London. Brewed to mark the rugby Five Nations Championship in 1998.

Hardtberg (Ger) vineyard (Anb): Ahr. (Ber): Walporzheim/Ahrtal. (Gro): Klosterberg. (Vil): Dernau.

Hardtberg (Ger) vineyard (Anb): Ahr. (Ber): Walporzheim/Ahrtal. (Gro): Klosterberg. (Vil): Rech.

Hard Water (Eng) denotes water that has a high dissolved mineral content and is very alkaline. Tea and coffee takes much longer to brew in hard waters. See also Soft Water.

Hardy [A.] (Fr) a Cognac producer. (Add): B.P. 27, 147 Rue Basse de Croun, 16100 Cognac. Noted for: Noces de Perle, Noces de Diamant, Noces d'Or–a 50 year old Cognac and *** Red Corner.

Hardy Country Bitter (Eng) a 4.2% bitter beer (cask or bottle-conditioned) from Eldridge Pope. Also called Thomas Hardy Country Bitter.

Hardy's Ale (Eng) see Thomas Hardy's Ale.

Hardy's and Hanson's (Eng) a brewery (established 1832). (Add): The Brewery, Kimberley, Nottingham, Nottinghamshire NG16 2NS. Noted for Blackamoor Stout 1044 O.G. Guinea Gold 1032 O.G. Special Brown 1036 O.G. Starbright IPA 1039 O.G. Rocking Rudolph, Raging Rooster, Peddlar's Pride, Guinea Gold, Guzzling Goose, Fatal Distraction 4.5% alc by vol., Frolicking Farmer, Millram Ale, Old Kim, Original Gravity, Peak Perfection, Spring Hop, Summer Swallow, Vintage 1832, Ye Old Trip Ale 4.3% alc by vol. Website: http://www.hardysandhansons.plc.uk 'E'mail: info@hardysandhansons.plc.uk

Hardy's Coronet Tawny (Austr) a well-matured old tawny Port-style wine.

Hardy's Winery (Austr) a winery. (Add): Reynella Road, Reynella, South Australia. Also McLaren Vale Winery, Main Road, McLaren Vale. Has vineyards in the Barossa Valley, Clare-Watervale, Riverland and Southern Vales. Produces a wide range of wines and port-style wines from Cabernet sauvignon, Chardonnay, Fumé blanc, Shiraz. See also Arras and Banrock Station Sparkling Shiraz 14.5% alc by vol.

Hargesheim (Ger) village (Anb): Nahe. (Ber): Kreuznach. (Gro): Kronnenberg. (Vins): Mollenbrunnen, Straussberg.

Harghita (Rum) a sparkling natural spring mineral water from Kraiten in Harghita, Transylvania. Mineral contents (milligrammes per litre): Sodium 68.3mg/l, Calcium 113.4mg/l, Magnesium 69.4mg/l, Potassium 11.1mg/l, Bicarbonates 854mg/l, Chlorides 2mg/l, Sulphates <1mg/l, Fluorides 0.2mg/l.

Hargrave Vineyard (USA) a winery based at North Fork, Long Island. Grape varieties: Chardonnay and Pinot noir. Produces varietal wines.

Hari-Kiri Cooler (Cktl) into a large tumbler place 60mls (½ gill) whisky and the juice of ½ a lemon with a little sugar syrup. Add ½ soda water and ½ Vichy water, stir, decorate with seasonal fruits and serve with a spoon.

Harkamp (Aus) a winery based in Süd-Steiermark. (Add): Flamberg 46, 8505 St. Nikolai. Grape varieties include: Pinot gris, Riesling, Zweigelt.

Harlan Estate (USA) a winery based in Oakville, Napa Valley, California that produces a cult red wine from Cabernet sauvignon, Merlot and Cabernet franc grapes.

Harlem Cocktail (Cktl) ⅔ measure dry gin, ⅓ measure pineapple juice, 2 dashes maraschino. Shake well over ice, strain into a cocktail glass and decorate with pineapple chunks.

Harling (Eng) a vineyard at East Harling in Norfolk.

Harmanlamak (Tur) tea blending/to blend teas.

Harman's Road Estate (Austr) a winery based in the Margaret River region of Western Australia. Grape varieties include: Cabernet sauvignon.

Harmatviz (Hun) a natural spring mineral water from Budapest. Mineral contents (milligrammes per litre): Sodium 120mg/l, Calcium 163mg/l, Magnesium 60mg/l, Potassium 13.2mg/l, Bicarbonates 560mg/l, Chlorides 130mg/l, Sulphates 281mg/l, Fluorides 2.8mg/l, Silicates 32.3mg/l. pH 5.0

Harmonisch (Ger) denotes a harmonious, well-balanced wine.

Harmony (S.Afr) a blended red wine produced by the AfricanTerroir winery, Paarl, Western Cape.

Haro (Sp) a town in the centre of the Rioja Alta.

Harper Distillery (USA) a Bourbon whiskey distillery based in Louisville, Kentucky.

Harp Extra (Ire) a 1041 O.G. lager brewed by the Guinness Brewery in Dublin.

Harp Irish Lager (Ire) a 4.3% alc by vol. lager brewed by the Guinness Brewery in Dublin and under license in U.K. by Hydes Brewery.

Harp Lager (Ire) a 4.3% alc by vol lager brewed by the Guinness Brewery in Dublin. Brewed under licence by Scottish and Newcastle Brewery and the Courage Brewery.

Harpoon (Cktl) 1 measure Scotch whisky, ½ measure Mandarine Napoléon, juice of 2 tangerines, 1 teaspoon castor sugar. Stir with ice, strain into a highball glass and top with soda, add a twist of tangerine peel and ice.

Harpoon Brewery [The] (USA) a brewery. (Add): 306 Northern Avenue, Boston MA02210. Brews beers and lager. Website: http://www.harpoonbrewery.com 'E'mail: jcox@harpoonbrewery.com

Harp Premier (Eng) the British name for Harp Export which is sold overseas.

Harras de Pirque (Chile) produces wines under the Pirque Estate label. Grapes include Cabernet/Merlot, Chardonnay and Sauvignon blanc grown in the Maipo Valley.

Harre (Bel) a natural spring mineral water from Harre, Werbomont-Ferrières.

Harriague (S.Am) a red grape variety grown in Uruguay, known as theTannat in France.

Harrier S.P.A. (Eng) a 3.6% alc by vol. cask-conditioned special pale ale brewed by the Cotleigh Brewery in Wiveliscombe, Somerset.

Harrilds Kildevand (Den) an acidic natural spring mineral water from Harrild Kilde, Brande. Mineral contents (milligrammes per litre): Sodium 11mg/l, Calcium 3.5mg/l, Magnesium 3mg/l, Potassium 1.3mg/l, Bicarbonates <10mg/l, Chlorides 20mg/l, Sulphates 13mg/l, Fluorides <0.1mg/l, Nitrates 5.8mg/l, Silicates 7.9mg/l. pH 5.0

Harringtons Brewery Nelson (N.Z) a brewery. (Add): 53 Beach Road, Richmond. Brews a variety of beers and lager. Website: http://www.harringtonsbrewery.co.nz 'E'mail: craig@harringtonsbrewery.co.nz

Harrison Cocktail (Cktl) 40mls (⅓ gill) gin, 20mls (⅙ gill) lemon or lime juice, ½ teaspoon powdered sugar, 1 teaspoon Angostura. Shake over ice and strain into a cocktail glass.

Harris Teeter (USA) a natural spring mineral water from North Carolina.

Harrity (Cktl) 25mls (1fl.oz) Canadian whisky, dash gin, dash Angostura. Stir over ice and strain into a cocktail glass.

Harrod's Guides (Eng) information guides that used to be published through the Decanter Magazine on subjects such as brandy, Champagne, liqueurs, Sherry, whisky, etc.

Harrogate (Eng) a still sulphurous mineral water from northern England.

Harry Halfyard (Eng) a 4.5% alc by vol. smooth bronze-coloured ale from Shepherd Neame in Kent.

Harry Jacks Ale (Eng) a 4.1% alc by vol. ale brewed by the Three Rivers Brewing C°. Ltd., Cheshire.

Harry Lauder Cocktail (Cktl) ½ measure Scotch whisky, ½ measure sweet vermouth, 2 dashes gomme syrup. Stir over ice and strain into a cocktail glass.

Harry Mahlo Signature Series Cabernet Shiraz (Austr) a wine from the Yalumba vineyard in South Australia. Named after the master cooper at Yalumba.

Harry's Cocktail (Cktl) ⅔ measure gin, ⅓ measure Italian vermouth, dash Pernod. Shake well over ice, strain into a cocktail glass, decorate with mint sprigs and a stuffed olive.

Harry Vederchi (Eng) a 4.8% alc by vol. seasonal ale brewed by Hydes at 46 Moss Lane, West Manchester, Lancashire available January and February, is a part of their Craft Ale range.

Harsberg [ortsteil Neuholz] (Ger) village (Anb): Württemberg. (Ber): Württembergisch Unterland. (Gro): Lindelberg. (Vins): Dachsteiger, Spielbühl.

Harsh (Eng) this is the term used for extreme hardness in a wine when it is very astringent, some wines will lose this quality in time.

Hárslevelü (Hun) a species of grape used to a small degree in Tokaji with the Muskotly and the main grape the Furmint. Also known as Feuille de Tilleulé. (Czec) = Lipovina, (Ger) = Lindenblättrige.

Harsovo (Bul) a D.G.O. area of south-western region, having Controliran status for Melnik.

Harstell (Ger) vineyard (Anb): Franken. (Ber): Mainviereck. (Gro): Heiligenthal. (Vil): Grossostheim.

Hart (Ger) hard/acid/even vinegary.

Hartberg (Aus) a vineyard site on the banks of the River Danube situated in the Wachau region, Niederösterreich.

Hart Brewery (Eng) a micro-brewery at Little Eccleston, near Preston, Lancashire. Brews: Fylde Ale, Gold Beach, Maysons Premier, Retriever Legend, Road to Rome, Squirrel's Hoard, Steaming Jack.

Hartcliffe Bitter (Eng) brewed by the Ross Brewing C°. in Bristol. Also brews: Ross's Pale Ale, Uncle Igor.

Hartenberg Estate (S.Afr) a winery (established 1978) based in Stellenbosch, Western Cape. (Add): Box 69, Koelenhof 7605. Grape varieties: Cabernet sauvignon, Chardonnay, Chenin blanc, Colombard, Gewürztraminer, Jerepigo, Merlot, Pinotage, Ruby cabernet, Sauvignon blanc, Shiraz, Zinfandel. Labels: Chatillon, CWG Auction Reserve Gravel Hill, The McKenzie, The Stork. Website: http://www.hartenbergestate.com

Hartford Winery (USA) a winery based in the Sonoma Coast, Sonoma County, California. Grape variety: Pinot noir.

Hartington Bitter (Eng) a 4% alc by vol. session bitter from Whim Ales in Hartington, Derbyshire.

Hartington IPA (Eng) a 4.5% alc by vol. India pale ale brewed by Whim Ales Ltd., Hartington, Derbyshire.

Hartley Brandy (USA) the brand-name of a brandy produced by the United Vintners, Lodi, California.

Hartley's Brewery (Eng) a brewery based in Ulverston, Cumbria. Produces XB Bitter 1040 O.G.

Hartmann [André et Fils] (Fr) an Alsace wine producer. (Add): 11 Rue Roger-Frémaux, 68420 Voegtlinshoffen.

Hartridge (Austr) a winery based in the south-west coastal plain, Western Australia.

Hartridge Island Brewery (Eng) a brewery based in Newport, Isle of Wight. Brews: Nipper 1038 O.G., Newport Best Bitter 1045 O.G., Wight Winter Warmer.

Hartridges Soft Drink (Eng) soft drinks producer (established 1988). (Add): Head Office, West Street, Hambledon, Waterlooville, Hampshire PO7 4SN. Produces a seletion of exotic fruits and fruit blends including: cranberry, cranberry and apple, passion fruit and orange, pineapple and coconut. Website: http://www.hartridges.co.uk 'E' mail: hartridges@msn.com

Hartsman Lager (Eng) a lager beer 1035 O.G. brewed by the McMullen's Brewery in Hertford, Hertfordshire.

Hartswater Wine Cellar (S.Afr) a winery based in Hartswater, Northern Cape. Grape varieties: Cabernet sauvignon, Chenin blanc, Colombard, Pinotage, Red jerepigo, Ruby cabernet, Shiraz. Labels: Elements (Earth & Fire), Hinterland, Thunder.

Hart Vineyards (USA) a winery based in Temecula, California. Grape varieties: Cabernet sauvignon, Chardonnay, Sauvignon blanc and Zinfandel. Produces varietal wines.

Hartwall Brewery (Fin) breweries based in Lappeenranta, south-eastern Finland, Turku, south-western Finland and Vaasa, western Finland.

Hartwell Vineyards (USA) a winery based in the Stags Leap District, Napa Valley, California. (Add): 5795 Siverado Trail, Napa. CA 94558. Grape varieties: Cabernet sauvignon. Website: http://www.hartwellvineyards.com

Harty Brewery (Ire) a brewery based in Blessington, Co. Kildare. Produces Harty's Lager 1039 O.G.

Hartz Mineral Water (Austr) a still and sparkling natural spring mineral water from the Huon Region. Website: http://www.hartz.com.au

Harvard Cocktail [1] (Cktl) 30mls (¼ gill) brandy, 30mls (¼ gill) Italian vermouth, dash gum syrup, 2 dashes Angostura. Stir well over ice, strain into a cocktail glass and add a squeeze of lemon peel on top.

Harvard Cocktail [2] (Cktl) ⅔ measure dry gin, ⅓ measure French vermouth, dash Pernod, 2 dashes grenadine. Shake well over ice and strain into a cocktail glass.

Harvard Cooler (Cktl) 1 measure applejack brandy, barspoon gomme syrup, juice of lemon or lime. Shake well together over ice, strain into a highball glass and top up with soda water.

Harvest (Eng) the gathering of the grapes. (Fr) = vendange, (Ger) = ernte, (Hol) = oogst, (Ire) = fómhar fionchaor, (It) = raccolto, (Lat) = messis, (Port) = colheita, (Sp) = vendimiar, (Wal) = cynhaeaf.

Harvest Ale (Eng) a bottled brown ale 1031 O.G. brewed by the Greene King Brewery, Bedfordshire.

Harvest Ale (Eng) a 4% alc by vol. seasonal ale produced by King and Barnes in Horsham, West Sussex. Top-fermented, bottle-conditioned version is 4.5% alc by vol.

Harvest Ale (Eng) a bottled, 1996 vintage, limited edition, pale ale 11.5% alc by vol. Brewed by the Lees Brewery, Middleton, Manchester using Man's Otter malted barley and East Kent Goldings hops.

Harvest Ale (Eng) a 5% alc by vol. seasonal ale brewed by Shepherd Neame, Kent.

Harvest Ale (Eng) a 4.5% alc by vol. seasonal ale brewed by Gale's Brewery, Horndean, Hampshire.

Harvest Banns (Fr) a famous ceremony held during the official declaration of the harvest. *See also* Ban de Vendage.

Harvest Bitter (Eng) a cask-conditioned bitter ale 1037 O.G. brewed by the Hall's Brewery in Burton-on-Trent.

Harvest Bitter (Eng) a 4.3% alc by vol. bitter ale produced using honey by the Highwood micro-brewery in Barnetby, Lincolnshire.

Harvest Festival (Eng) a 4.5% alc by vol. seasonal ale brewed by Green Bottle Ltd., Worth Brewery, Keighley, Yorkshire.

Harvest Gold (Eng) a 3.9% alc by vol. ale brewed by the Fernanders Brewery, West Yorkshire.

Harvest Golden Ale (Wal) a special limited edition ale from Bass in Cardiff using Northdown and Challenger Hops. 4.7% alc by vol.

Harvest Moon Brewery (USA) a brewery. (Add): 75th Street South, Belt MT59412. Brews a range of beers and lager. Website: http://www.harvestmoonbrew.com 'E'mail: john@harvestmoonbrew.com

Harvest Pale (Eng) a 3.8% alc by vol. ale brewed by the Castle Rock brewery, Nottinghamshire.

Harvest Scrumpy (Eng) a 5.5% alc by vol. cloudy cider produced by Bulmers of Hereford. Part of their Heritage range.

Harvest Wine Company (N.Z) a winery. (Add): Bell Road, P.O. Box 911, Gisborne. Producers of cider plus Chardonnay and Riesling wines.

Harvest Wine Group (Eng) consists of 11 vineyards, produce over half the English wines (mainly dry white wines).

Harvey (Scot) part of DCL, holds the licence for the Aultmore Distillery near Keith, a highland malt whisky.

Harvey [John] (Sp) a noted Sherry producer. (Add): Arcos 53, Apartado 494, Jerez de la Frontera.

Owns the De Terry and Palomino y Vergara bodegas. Sherry brands include Bristol Cream, Club Classic, Finesse, Dune (was Luncheon Dry), Isis, Merienda and Tico. Part of Allied-Domecq. *see* Harveys of Bristol (U.K. agents).

Harvey & Son [Lewes] Brewery (Eng) a brewery (established 1790). (Add): The Bridge Wharf Brewery, 6, Cliff High Street, Lewes, East Sussex. BN7 2AH. Brews for Beards of Lewes. Noted for Blue Label 1038 O.G. Elizabethan 1090 O.G. Exhibition Brown 1042 O.G. and Sussex Stout 1030 O.G. Family Ale 2.2% alc by vol. (bottled version 2% alc by vol.) Old Ale 3.6% alc by vol. Tom Paine 5.5% alc by vol. Also Jubilee Ale, 1859 Porter. Website: http://www.harveys.org.uk 'E'mail: info@harveys.org.uk

Harvey Cowpuncher (Cktl) 1½ measures Galliano and fresh milk. Pour Galliano into an ice-filled highball glass and top up with iced milk.

Harveys Bristol Cream (Sp) a famous cream Sherry shipped by Harveys of Bristol, sold in a Bristol blue glass bottle.

Harveys Bristol Milk (Sp) a very sweet Sherry shipped by Harveys of Bristol.

Harveys Brunel Blend (Sp) a fine, old, Oloroso Sherry produced by Harveys to celebrate the Great Western Railway's 150th anniversary in 1985.

Harveys Isis (Sp) the new name for John Harvey Sherry from Harvey in Jerez de la Frontera.

Harveys of Bristol (Eng) a noted wine importers and bottlers based in Bristol. (Add): 12 Denmark Street, Bristol BS1 5DQ. Produce Sherries, Ports and Madeiras. The U.K. agents for Harveys in Jerez de la Frontera. Part of Allied-Domecq.

Harveys Ouse Booze (Eng) a beer brewed by Harvey and Son, Lewes, East Sussex to commemorate the flooding of the river in winter 2000/2001.

Harveys Tom Paine (Eng) a 5.5% alc by vol. amber-coloured bottled ale brewed by Harvey and Son, Lewes, East Sussex.

Harvey's Vintage Port (Port) vintage Port shippers. Vintages: 1958, 1962.

Harvey Wallbanger (Cktl) 50mls (2fl.ozs) vodka, 100mls (4fl.ozs) orange juice. Shake over ice, strain into an ice-filled highball glass, float 2 teaspoons of Galliano on top and serve with straws.

Harviestoun Brewery (Scot) a brewery (established 1984). (Add): Alva Ind Estate, Alva, Clackmannanshire FK12 5DQ. Brews: Bitter & Twisted 3.8% alc by vol., Indian Summer IPA 4.1% alc by vol., Liberation Ale., Old Engine Oil 4.4% alc by vol., Ptarmigan 4.5% alc by vol., Schiehallion 4.8% alc by vol., Turnpike 4.1% alc by vol. Owned by The Caledonian Brewing Company. 'E'mail: harviestoun@tak21.com

Harwood Distilleries Ltd. (Can) a distillery based in Vancouver. Produces Harwood Canadian whisky 45% alc by vol.

Harwood's Porter Ale (Ire) a 5.2% alc by vol. cask-conditioned porter from Guinness.

Harxheim (Ger) village (Anb): Rheinhessen. (Ber): Nierstein. (Gro): Sankt Alban. (Vins): Börnchen, Lieth, Schlossberg.

Harzberg (Ger) vineyard (Anb): Württemberg. (Ber): Württembergisch Unterland. (Gro): Wunnenstein. (Vil): Grossbottwar.

Harzberg (Ger) vineyard (Anb): Württemberg. (Ber): Württembergisch Unterland. (Gro): Wunnenstein. (Vil): Hof und Lembach.

Harzberg (Ger) vineyard (Anb): Württemberg. (Ber): Württembergisch Unterland. (Gro): Wunnenstein. (Vil): Oberstenfeld.

Harzberg (Ger) vineyard (Anb): Württemberg. (Ber): Württembergisch Unterland. (Gro): Wunnenstein. (Vil): Winzerhausen.

Harzer Bergbrunnen (Ger) a natural spring mineral water from Langelsheim. Mineral contents (milligrammes per litre): Sodium 43.8mg/l, Calcium 15.8mg/l, Magnesium 5.1mg/l, Potassium 1.2mg/l, Bicarbonates 65.3mg/l, Chlorides 49.5mg/l, Sulphates 28.8mg/l.

Harzer Grauhof (Ger) a natural spring mineral water (established 1877) from grauhof/Harz. Mineral contents (milligrammes per litre): Sodium 16mg/l, Calcium 116mg/l, Magnesium 10mg/l, Bicarbonates 305mg/l, Chlorides 32mg/l, Sulphates 64mg/l.

Harz-Quell Brunnen (Ger) a natural spring mineral water from Bad Suderode. Mineral contents (milligrammes per litre): Sodium 10.9mg/l, Calcium 88.2mg/l, Magnesium 16.3mg/l, Potassium 1.3mg/l, Bicarbonates 223.9mg/l, Chlorides 21.6mg/l, Sulphates 87.8mg/l, Fluorides 0.13mg/l.

Hasandede (Tur) a red grape variety.

Hascombe Vineyard (Eng) a vineyard. (Add): Goldalming, Surrey. 2.5ha. Soil: green sand on bargate. Grape varieties: Müller-Thurgau 60% and Seyval blanc 40%.

Hasekamp (Hol) a major distiller of jenever.

Haselgrove (Austr) a winery. (Add): P.O. Box 231, Foggo Road, McLaren Vale 5171, South Australia. Grape varieties include Cabernet sauvignon, Merlot, Shiraz, Chardonnay.

Haselstaude (Ger) vineyard (Anb): Baden. (Ber): Breisgau. (Gro): Schutterlindenberg. (Vil): Kippenheim.

Haselstaude (Ger) vineyard (Anb): Baden. (Ber): Breisgau. (Gro): Schutterlindenberg. (Vil): Mahlberg.

Haselstaude (Ger) vineyard (Anb): Baden. (Ber): Breisgau. (Gro): Schutterlindenberg. (Vil): Sulz.

Haselstein (Ger) vineyard (Anb): Württemberg. (Ber): Remstal-Stuttgart. (Gro): Wartbühl. (Vil): Breuningsweiler.

Haselstein (Ger) vineyard (Anb): Württemberg. (Ber): Remstal-Stuttgart. (Gro): Wartbühl. (Vil): Winnenden.

Hasen (Ger) vineyard (Anb): Pfalz. (Ber): Südliche Weinstrasse. (Gro): Herrlick. (Vil): Eschbach.

Hasenberg (Ger) vineyard (Anb): Baden. (Ber): Kaiserstuhl-Tuniberg. (Gro): Vulkanfelsen. (Vil): Königschaffhausen.

Hasenberg (Ger) vineyard (Anb): Mittelrhein. (Ber): Rheinburgengau. (Gro): Lahntal. (Vil): Bad Ems.

Hasenberg (Ger) vineyard (Anb): Mittelrhein. (Ber): Rheinburgengau. (Gro): Lahntal. (Vil): Dausenau.

Hasenbiss (Ger) vineyard (Anb): Rheinhessen. (Ber): Wonnegau. (Gro): Gotteshilfe. (Vil): Osthofen.

Hasen-Bräu Brauerei (Ger) a brewery based in Augsburg. Brews: Weisser Hase.

Hasenlauf (Ger) vineyard (Anb): Rheinhessen. (Ber): Wonnegau. (Gro): Bergkloster. (Vil): Bermersheim.

Hasenläufer (Ger) vineyard (Anb): Mosel-Saar-Ruwer. (Ber): Bernkastel. (Gro): Kurfürstlay. (Vil): Brauneberg.

Hasenläufer (Ger) vineyard (Anb): Mosel-Saar-Ruwer. (Ber): Bernkastel. (Gro): Kurfürstlay. (Vil): Burgen.

Hasensprung (Ger) vineyard (Anb): Baden. (Ber): Badische Bergstrasse/Kraichgau. (Gro): Hohenberg. (Vil): Walzbachtal (ortsteil Jöhlingen).

Hasensprung (Ger) vineyard (Anb): Rheingau. (Ber): Johannisberg. (Gro): Honigberg. (Vil): Winkel.

Hasensprung (Ger) vineyard (Anb): Nahe. (Ber): Kreuznach. (Gro): Pfarrgarten. (Vil): Wallhausen.

Hasensprung (Ger) vineyard (Anb): Rheinhessen. (Ber): Bingen. (Gro): Kaiserpfalz. (Vil): Jugenheim.

Hasensprung (Ger) vineyard (Anb): Rheinhessen. (Ber): Nierstein. (Gro): Rheinblick. (Vil): Dorn-Dürkheim.

Hasensprung (Ger) vineyard (Anb): Rheinhessen. (Ber): Wonnegau. (Gro): Pilgerpfad. (Vil): Bechtheim.

Hasensprung (Ger) a vineyard within the village of Winkel, 103.8ha. (19.2%) of which is proposed to be classified as Erstes Gewächs.

Hasenzeile (Ger) vineyard (Anb): Pfalz. (Ber): Mittelhaardt-Deutsche Weinstrasse. (Gro): Rosenbühl. (Vil): Weisenheim/Sand.

Haskovo (Bul) a delimited wine-producing area in the Southern Basic region. Noted for Merlot wines.

Haslach (Ger) village (Anb): Baden. *see* Oberkirch.

Hassel (Aus) a vineyard site based on the banks of the River Kamp situated in the Kamptal region.

Hassel (Ger) vineyard (Anb): Rheingau. (Ber): Johannisberg. (Gro): Deutelsberg. (Vil): Hattenheim.

Hasseltse Koffie (Bel) a variation of Irish coffee.

Hassendean (N.Z) a medium-dry, white wine produced by the Ormond Vineyard, North Island.

Hasseröder (Ger) a premier pils brewed by Hasseröder Brauerei, Wernigerode.

Hassia (Ger) a natural spring mineral water (established 1875) from Bad Viebell. Website: http://www.hassia.com

Hassmannsberg (Ger) vineyard (Anb): Pfalz. (Ber): Mittelhaardt-Deutsche Weinstrasse. (Gro): Grafenstück. (Vil): Bockenheim.

Hassmersheim (Ger) village (Anb): Baden. (Ber): Badische Bergstrasse/Kraichgau. (Gro): Stiftsberg. (Vin): Kirchweinberg.

Hastings (N.Z) a wine area on the east coast of the North Island.

Hastings Glasses (Eng) the brand-name for a range of glasses produced by the Dema glass company.

Hasty Cocktail (Cktl) ½ measure dry gin, ¼ measure dry vermouth, ⅙ measure Pernod, 4 dashes grenadine. Stir over ice and strain into a cocktail glass.

Hatay (Tur) a vineyard based in southern Turkey that produces good quality red wines.

Hatcher Winery (USA) a winery based in the Willamette Valley, Oregon. Grape variety: Pinot noir.

Hatschbourg (Fr) a 47.36ha vineyard in A.C. Alsace Grand Cru, Hattstatt and Voegtlinshoffen, Haut-Rhin.

Hatswell (Eng) a vineyard in Washfield, Tiverton, Devon.

Hat Trick (Wal) a summer ale brewed by Brain & C°. Ltd., 49 St. Mary Street, Cardiff Centre.

Hattenheim (Ger) village (Anb): Rheingau. (Ber): Johannisberg. (Gro): Deutelsberg. (Vins): Engelmannsberg, Hassel, Heiligenberg, Mannberg, Nussbrunnen, Pfaffenberg, Schützenhaus, Wisselbrunnen.

Hatter's Mild (Eng) a 3.3% alc by vol. cask-conditioned mild brewed by Robinson Ltd., Unicorn Brewery, Stockport, Manchester.

Hatvey (Cub) a 4.8% alc by vol. straw coloured, cloudy, bottled lager beer brewed by the Mayabe Brewery, Holguin.

Hatzenport (Ger) village (Anb): Mosel-Saar-Ruwer. (Ber): Zell/Mosel. (Gro): Weinhex. (Vins): Burg Bischofsteiner, Kirchberg, Stolzenberg.

Hatzimichalis (Gre) a winery at Farma Atalantis Agrotiki, 13th klm National Road, 1456 N. Kifissia. Produces red and white wines from Cabernet sauvignon, Chardonnay, Merlot.

Haubenberg (Ger) vineyard (Anb): Rheinhessen. (Ber): Nierstein. (Gro): Domherr. (Vil): Saulheim.

Hauer (Aus) a part-time vine grower owning around a hectare of vineyard or less who sells his grapes to larger producers or a co-operative winery.

Hauerinnung (Aus) a wine co-operative based at Traismauer.

Hauerzeche (Aus) wine growers' guild.

Haugsdorf (Aus) a district in the Weinviertel that produces light-styled wines.

Hauptlese (Ger) the name given to the general harvest that takes place between the vorslese and the spätlese.

Hausbergen (Aus) a vineyard area on the banks of the River Danube in the Kremstal region.

Hausbrauerei Feierling (Ger) a brewery. (Add): Gerberau 46, Freiburg D-79098. Brews beers and lagers. Website: http://www.altgiessen.de 'E'mail: info@feierling.de

Hausen/Z (Ger) village (Anb): Württemberg. (Ber): Württembergisch Unterland. (Gro): Heuchelberg. (Vins): Jupiterberg, Staig, Vogelsang.

Hausgiebel (Ger) vineyard (Anb): Nahe. (Ber): Kreuznach. (Gro): Schlosskapelle. (Vil): Windesheim.

Haus Österreich Trocken Sekt (Aus) a dry, sparkling wine made by the cuve close method by the Kremser Winzergenossenschaft at Krems.

H

Haustrunk (Ger) a family drink, made from grapes with a very low sugar content. Cannot be made into wine or sold.

Haut (Fr) lit: 'high', a term meaning a superior quality wine or growth at a high altitude.

Hautains [En] (Fr) a method of vine training used in south-western France. Vines are grown up on wooden or metal stakes, supported by a cross-piece 2 metres from the ground.

Haut-Armagnac (Fr) a sub-region of Armagnac in the Gers département.

Haut-Bages-Avéros (Fr) see Château Haut-Bages-Avéros.

Haut-Bailly (Fr) see Château Haut-Bailly.

Haut Batailley (Fr) see Château Haut Batailley.

Haut-Beaujolais (Fr) the northern half of the Beaujolais region from the river Nizerand to the Mâconnais. Has granite soil and the Cru Beaujolais-Villages within its boundaries.

Haut-Benauge (Fr) a wine-producing district in the A.C. Entre-Deux-Mers. (Coms): Cantois, D'Arbis, Escoussans, Gornac, Ladaux, Mourens, Soulignac, St. Pierre-de-Bat, Targon.

Haut-Bommes (Fr) the second wine of Clos Haut-Peyraguey, Bommes, A.C. Sauternes, Bordeaux.

Haut Cabrière (S.Afr) the label for a range of wines produced by the Cabrière Estate winery, Franschhoek, Western Cape.

Haut-Comtat (Fr) an A.C. for 6 villages in a hilly area known as Les Baronnies in the Côtes du Rhône. Produces red and rosé wines.

Haut-Dahra (Alg) a wine-producing area in the Alger département (mostly red wines).

Haut de Sèvre [Le] (Fr) a vineyard in the A.C. Muscadet Sèvre et Maine. (Add): 44190 Clisson, Loire Atlantique.

Haute Normande (Fr) the name for a bottle which is similar in style to the Bordeaux bottle, used for Roussillon wines and Calvados.

Haute Provence Vineyards (S.Afr) a winery. (Add): P.O. Box 211, Franschhoeck 7690. Grape varieties include Cabernet sauvignon, Chardonnay, Chenin blanc, Sauvignon blanc, Sémillon.

Hauterive en Pays d'Aude (Fr) a Vin de Pays area of the Aude département in southern France.

Hautes Bretonnières [Les] (Fr) a vineyard in the A.C. Muscadet Sèvre et Maine, Nantais, Loire.

Hautes Côtes (Fr). Part of the Côte d'Or on the upper part of the Côte. Comprises of the Hautes Côtes de Nuits and the Hautes Côtes de Beaune. Comprises 28 communes.

Hautes Côtes de Beaune (Fr) on the south-western part of the Côte d'Or. Produces some fine wines under the A.C. Bourgogne Haut-Côtes de Beaune.

Hautes Côtes de Nuits (Fr) on the north-western part of the Côte d'Or. Produces fine wines under the A.C. Bourgogne Haut-Côtes de Nuits. see Geisweiler.

Haut Espoir (S.Afr) a winery (established 1999) based in Franchhoek, Western Cape. 12ha. Grape varieties: Chardonnay, Sauvignon blanc, Sémillon, Shiraz, Syrah rosé. Produces varietal wines. Website: http://www.hautespoir.com

Hautes Tiges (Fr) in Calvados denotes the standard system of pruning resulting in a classic spaced orchard (opposite = Basses Tiges).

Haute Vallée de l'Aude (Fr) a Vin de Pays area of the Aude département in southern France. Produces red, rosé and dry white wines which have now been granted A.C. Limoux.

Haute Vallée de l'Orb (Fr) a Vin de Pays area of the Hérault département in southern France.

Haut-Lieu [Le] (Fr) a famous vineyard in A.C. Vouvray. (Add): Huet Viticulteur, Le Haut-Lieu, Vouvray, Touraine, Loire.

Haut-Médoc (Fr) the finest area within the Bordeaux region (3347ha). Produces the finest red wines. A.C. communes: Listrac, Margaux, Moulis, Pauillac, Saint-Estèphe, Saint-Julien and the Haut-Médoc itself (7% Cru Classé).

Haut Montravel (Fr) an A.C. commune in the Côtes de Bergerac, produces medium-sweet white wines.

Haut Mornag (Afr) the brand-name for red and rosé wines from the UCCVT in Tunisia.

Haut Pays (Fr) situated in south-western France. see Languedoc.

Haut Poitou (Fr) a V.D.Q.S. area near Anjou, Anjou-Saumur, Loire. Produces mainly white wines from the Chardonnay and Sauvignon blanc grapes. Also produces a little red and rosé wine.

Haut Provence Vineyard (S.Afr) a vineyard based in Franschhoek. (Add): P.O. Franschhoek 7690. Produces varietal wines.

Haut-Pruliers [Les] (Fr) a Premier Cru vineyard in the A.C. commune of Nuits-Saint-Georges, Côte de Nuits, Burgundy 4.5ha.

Haut-Rhin (Fr) lit: 'high Rhine', a region of southern Alsace. see Bas Rhin.

Hautrive en Pays de l'Aude (Fr) a Vin de Pays area in the Aude département, southern France. Produces red, rosé and dry white wines.

Haut Roche (Fr) a vineyard based in the Petite Champagne district of Cognac, Charente-Maritime.

Haut Sauterne (USA) a Californian sweet white wine made from the Sauvignon blanc, Sémillon and Muscadelle grapes.

Hauts de Badens (Fr) a Vin de Pays area in Badens, Aude département, southern France. Produces red and rosé wines.

Hauts de Smith [Les] (Fr) the second wine of Château Smith-Haut-Lafite.

Hauts-Doix [Les] (Fr) a Premier Cru vineyard in the A.C. commune of Chambolle-Musigny, Côte de Nuits, Burgundy 1.75ha.

Hauts-Jarrons [Les] (Fr) a Premier Cru vineyard in the A.C. commune of Savigny-lès-Beaune, Côte de Beaune, Burgundy.

Hauts-Marconnets [Les] (Fr) a Premier Cru vineyard in the A.C. commune of Savigny-lès-Beaune, Côte de Beaune, Burgundy.

Hautvillers (Fr) the abbey in Champagne where Dom Pérignon is supposed to have developed the second fermentation in bottle when he was cellar master there in 1670's. A Bénédictine Abbey.

Hautvillers (Fr) a Premier Cru Champagne village in the Canton d'Aÿ. District: Reims.

Havana (Cktl) ½ measure apricot brandy, ¼ measure gin, ¼ measure Swedish Punsch, dash lemon juice. Shake over ice and strain into a cocktail glass.

Havana Beach (Cktl) 1 measure white rum, 1 measure pineapple juice, 2 dashes gomme syrup. Shake over ice and strain into a sugar-rimmed cocktail glass.

Havana Club (W.Ind) the label of a 3 year old Cuban white rum 40% alc by vol. Also Havana Club Anejo Reserva, Havana Club 7 year old.

Havana Cocktail (Cktl) *see* Havana Special.

Havana Hills (S.Afr) a winery (established 1999) based in Milnerton, Philadelphia, Western Cape. Grape varieties: Cabernet sauvignon, Chardonnay, Merlot, Sauvignon blanc, Shiraz. Labels: Du Plessis, Flagship, Havana Hills, Khanya, Lime Road.

Havana Special (Cktl) 35mls (1½ fl.ozs) Bacardi White Label. 25mls (1fl.oz) pineapple juice, ½ teaspoon sugar. Shake well together over ice and strain into a highball glass filled with ice.

Havelock (Cktl). 60mls (½ gill) brandy, 125mls (1gill) ginger ale in a goblet with a lump of ice.

Havlíckuv Brod (Czec) a brewery based in central Czec.

Havstryger Aalborg (Den) the brand-name of an akvavit produced by DDS.

Hawaiian Beach (USA) a drink of half grapefruit juice and half pineapple juice.

Hawaiian Brandy (Cktl) 40mls (⅓ gill) Calvados, 20mls (⅙ gill) pineapple juice, dash Maraschino, dash lemon juice, ½ teaspoon sugar. Shake well over ice and strain into a cocktail glass.

Hawaiian Cocktail (Cktl) ½ measure gin, ½ measure orange juice, dash orange Curaçao. Shake over ice and strain into a cocktail glass.

Hawaiian Coffee (Cktl) blend with a scoop of crushed ice in a blender 25mls (⅕ gill) white rum, 50mls (⅖ gill) pineapple juice and 125mls (1gill) cold black coffee. Pour into a highball glass and serve with straws.

Hawaiian Coffee (USA) fresh brewed coffee to which is added ⅓ part hot coconut milk topped with whipped cream and dressed with toasted dessicated coconut on top.

Hawaiian Spring Natural Water (USA) a natural spring mineral water (established 1981) from Mouna Loa, Hawaii. Mineral contents (milligrammes per litre): Sodium 6mg/l, Calcium 7.2mg/l, Magnesium 3.3mg/l, Potassium 2.2mg/l, Bicarbonates 44mg/l, Sulphates 4mg/l. pH 7.7

Hawaii Cocktail (Cktl) 1 measure dry gin, ¾ measure pineapple juice, ¼ measure grenadine, dash egg white. Shake well over ice and strain into a cocktail glass.

Hawaii Coffee (USA) a coffee with a mild, smooth butter taste and a good aroma, not usually blended. The best is Kona coffee.

Hawaii Water (USA) a natural spring mineral water from Oahu, Hawaii.

Hawequas (S.Afr) the label for a red wine (Cabernet sauvignon, Merlot and Shiraz blend) produced by the Mont du Toit Kelder winery, Wellington, Western Cape.

Hawk Crest (USA) the label used by the Stag's Leap Wine Cellars, Napa Valley, California for a range of their varietal wines.

Hawker (Eng) a noted producer of sloe gin based in Plymouth, Devon.

Hawkes Bay (N.Z) a wine-producing area on the east coast of the North Island. 2,339ha. Districts: Matua Valey, Trinity Hill. Grape varieties: Cabernet sauvignon, Merlot, Cabernet franc, Malbec, Shiraz.

Hawkesbridge Wines and Estates (N.Z) a winery. (Add): Hawkesbury Road, P.O. Box 9, Renwick, Marlborough. 16ha. Grape varieties: Chardonnay, Müller-Thurgau, Sauvignon blanc.

Hawkshead (Eng) a 5.5% alc by vol. ale brewed using English and German hops by Cotleigh Brewery, Wiveliscombe to commemorate the 18th birthday of the brewery. Also a limited bottled edition.

Hawkshead Brewery (Eng) a brewery (established 2002). (Add): Town End, Hawkshead, Ambleside, Cumbria LA22 0JU. Brews: Hawkshead Best Bitter 4.2% alc by vol., Hawkshead Bitter 3.7% alc by vol., Hawkshead Gold 4.4% alc by vol., Hawkshead Premium 4.8% alc by vol., Hawkshead Red 4.6% alc by vol., Overstone Pale Ale 4.1% alc by vol. Website: http://www.hawksheadbrewery.co.uk 'E'mail: info@hawksheadbrewery.co.uk

Hawthorn Brewery (Eng) a brewery (established 1987) based at Stourbridge, Worcestershire.

Hawthorne Strainer (Eng) a wire-rimmed strainer for cocktails that fits over the mouth of mixing jugs.

Häxli (Switz) the term for a small bottle of beer.

Hayat (Tur) a still natural spring mineral water from the Taurus Mountains. Mineral contents (milligrammes per litre): Sodium 2.3mg/l, Calcium 51mg/l, Magnesium 9mg/l, Potassium 0.4mg/l, Bicarbonates 179mg/l, Chlorides 2.9mg/l, Sulphates 8.2mg/l, Nitrates 3.4mg/l, Silicates 4.3mg/l. pH 8.0

Haymaker (Eng) a 5% alc by vol. summer cask (summer) and bottled (all year) pale ale brewed by the Hook Norton Brewery, Banbury in Oxfordshire using Goldings hops.

Hayman Distillers (Eng) a distillery. (Add): Eastways Park, Witham, Essex CM8 3YE. Produces a range of spirits, liqueurs and spirit-based drinks including: 1820 Gin Liqueur 40% alc by vol, Sir Walt's Liqueur 40% alc by vol. Website: http://wwww.hayman-distillers.co.uk 'E'mail: sales@hayman.co.uk

Haynes Vineyard (USA) a small vineyard based in the Wild Horse Valley, Napa Valley, California. Grape variety: Chardonnay.

Haytime Summer Ale (Eng) a limited edition summer ale brewed by McMullen of Hertford.

H

Haywood Winery (USA) vineyards based Los Chamizal in the Sonoma County, California. Grape varieties: Cabernet sauvignon, Chardonnay, Riesling, Zinfandel. Produces varietal wines.

Haze (Eng). *see* Chill Haze.

Hazelburn Distillery (Scot) an old Campbeltown malt whisky distillery now no longer in production.

Hazeley Down (Eng) a still or sparkling mineral water from Hazeley Road, Twyford, Winchester, Hampshire.

Hazelmere (Austr) a winery based in Clare-Watervale, Southern Vales, South Australia.

Hazendal Estate (S.Afr) a winery (established 1699) based in Stellenbosch, Western Cape. 68ha. (Add): Hazendal Langoed, Kuils River 7580. Grape varieties: Cabernet sauvignon, Chardonnay, Chenin blanc, Merlot, Pinotage, Sauvignon blanc, Shiraz. Labels: Bushvine, Freudensee, Klein Hazen, Konynwijn, Marvol, The Last Straw. Website: http://www.hazendal.co.za

Hazendal Langoed (S.Afr) *see* Hazendal Estate.

Hazes (Eng) in a wine can be caused by metal contamination, suspended starch, micro-organisms, pectin particles, hydro-colloids or protein/cellulose tissue particles. Are cleared by various treatment methods.

Hazy Dayz (Wal) a vodka-based lemonade and orangeade RTD drink from the Hurns Beer Company, South Wales 5% alc by vol.

H.B. (Eng) a 10% alc by vol. strong ale brewed by the Country Life Brewery, Devon.

H.B. (Ger) *abbr*: Hofbräuhaus Brauerei a state-owned former brewery of Bavaria which developed German bock beer, also made popular the weizenbier in southern Germany.

H.B. (Nor) *abbr*: *see* Homebum.

H.B. (Wal) *abbr*: Hancock's Bitter a 1037 O.G. bitter brewed by Welsh Brewers in Cardiff.

H. Blin & Cº (Fr) a Champagne producer. (Add): B.P. 35, 51700 Vincelles. Produces vintage and non-vintage wines. 'E'mail: contact@champagne-blin.com

Hb Oktoberfest (Ger) a 5.7% alc by vol. lager produced by Hofbrau in München from the Tetnang hop.

HD2O (USA) a natural spring mineral water from Blue Ridge, Georgia.

HdV (USA) *abbr*: Hyde de Villaine.

H.E. (Eng) *abbr*; Hartford End a cask-conditioned bitter 1045 O.G. brewed by the Ridley Brewery in Essex.

Head (Eng) the frothy, foamy top to a glass of beer. (USA) = collar.

Headache Makers (Austr) a slang term for red wines that are high in alcohol.

Head and Cold Mixing System (USA) a method used to flavour gin with botanicals.

Headbanger (Eng) a cask-conditioned ale 1065 O.G./6.3% alc by vol. brewed by Archers Brewery in Swindon, Wiltshire.

Headcorn Vineyards (Eng) vineyards based in Kent.

Produces: Wealden White (a medium dry white wine produced from Reichensteiner, Seyval blanc, Müller-Thurgau grapes).

Headcracker (Eng) a bottled full-bodied strong pale ale 7% alc by vol. from Woodforde's Norfolk Ales.

Header Tank (Eng) the storage tank for the liquor (water) in a brewery.

Headford Ridge (Eng) a cider producer based in the West County that produces Headford Ridge Bin 5.

Headford Ridge Bin 5 (Eng) a bottled cider produced by Headford Ridge, West Country using Brown Snout, Ball's Bittersweet and Yarlington Mill apples.

Headings (Fr) the beginning of distillation of Cognac, they are removed by the distiller and only the '*heart*' is retained (he latter part is called '*tailings*').

Head Injection Tap (Eng) *abbr*: H.I.T a ™ device for producing the perfect '*head*' on a pint of Foster's beer patented by Scottish and Newcastle Breweries.

Headless Horseman (Cktl) 50mls (2fl.ozs) vodka, 3 dashes Angostura. Pour into an ice-filled collins glass, top with ginger ale, stir and add a slice of orange.

Headless Peg (Eng) a 4.5% alc by vol. bitter ale brewed by the Bowland Beer Company, Lancashire.

Headmaster (Eng) a 5.2% alc by vol. ale brewed by the Mordue Brewery Ltd., Tyne & Wear.

Head Method (USA) a method of gin production, the alcoholic vapours pass through the still head which contains the botanicals.

Head of the Bourbon Family (USA) the name given to the Bourbon whiskey '*Old Grandad*'.

Head Over Heels (Austr) a winery based in Western Australia. Grape varieties include: Cabernet sauvignon, Merlot.

Heads (Fr) *see* Headings.

Headstrong (Eng) a 5.2% alc by vol (1048 O.G) bitter ale brewed by the Blackawton Brewery, Cornwall.

Head Strong (Eng) a 4.9% alc by vol. ale brewed by the Facers Brewery, Greater Manchester.

Head Tank (Eng) *see* Header Tank.

Heady (Eng) a term for a wine that is high in alcohol.

Healdsburg (USA) a town based between the Dry Creek and Alexander Valleys in the Russian River Valley, Sonoma County, California. Has many of the regions wineries there.

Health (Chi) a natural spring mineral water. Mineral contents (milligrammes per litre): Sodium 15mg/l, Calcium 15mg/l, Magnesium 2.5mg/l, Potassium 3mg/l, Bicarbonates 80mg/l, Chlorides 9mg/l, Sulphates 5mg/l. pH 8.0

Heart Breaker (Eng) a 4.1% alc by vol. seasonal ale brewed with a high percentage of crystal malt and English Challenger hops by the Charles Wells Brewery in Bedford, Bedfordshire, available February.

Hearth Warmer (Eng) a 6% alc by vol. strong ale

brewed by the Teme Valley Brewery, Worcestershire.

Heart of Oak (Eng) a 4.5% alc by vol. ale brewed by the Oakleaf Brewing C°. Ltd., Hampshire.

Heart's Desire (Cktl) ⅓ measure Bacardi, ⅓ measure Swedish Punsch, ⅓ measure grapefruit juice, 2 dashes Grand Marnier. Shake over ice and strain into a cocktail glass.

Heart Starter (Cktl) 1 measure gin in a highball glass of iced water, add 1 teaspoon Andrews liver salts and drink quickly.

Heart Starter (Eng) slang term for the first alcoholic drink of the day.

Hearty (Eng) a term that describes a red wine as being warm, high in alcohol and robust.

Heathcote (Austr) a wine region of Victoria, has a sandstone sub-soil and moderate climate.

Heathcote Estate (Austr) a winery based in Heathcote, central Victoria. Grape varieties include: Shiraz.

Heathcote Winery (Austr) a winery. (Add): 183–185 High Street, Heathcote, Victoria. Grape varieties: Chardonnay, Chenin blanc, Pinot noir, Shiraz.

Heather Ale (Scot) a traditional Scottish drink, originally known as fraoch, it was made using heather and drunk from cattle horns.

Heather Ale Ltd (Scot) a brewery (established 2003). (Add): Cragmill Brewery, Sandford Road, Strathaven, Lanarkshire ML10 6PB. Brews: Alba 7.5% alc by vol., Ebulam 6.5% alc by vol., Fraoch 5% alc by vol., Grozet 5% alc by vol., Reiver 3.8% alc by vol. Website: http://www.heatherale.co.uk 'E'mail: info@heatherale.co.uk

Heather Cream Scotch Whisky Liqueur (Scot) a malt whisky and cream liqueur produced by R. Carmichael & Sons Ltd (part of the Inver House Distillers Ltd), Airdrie, Lanarkshire 17% alc by vol.

Heather Mist Cocktail (Cktl) 50mls (2fl.ozs) lemon mix, 25mls (1fl.oz) Scotch whisky, 5mls (¼ fl.oz) Cointreau, dash grenadine. Shake over ice, strain into a cocktail glass and add a twist of lemon.

Heather Spring (Scot) a natural spring mineral water from Lennoxtown, Glasgow.

Heat Summation (USA) the alternative name for Degree Days.

Heat Treatment (Eng) a treatment to wines to de-nature proteins 15 minutes at 75°C (167°F), can alter the flavour of the wines so it should be used with caution.

Heaven-Bräu (Ger) a brewery that brews Cannabis a 4.5% alc by vol. pilsner.

Heaven, Hell and Purgatory (Eng) the name given to the taverns outside of Westminister Hall in mediaeval times.

Heavenly Chaos (S.Afr) the label for a red wine (Merlot, Cabernet sauvignon, Cabernet franc and Shiraz blend) produced by the Tanagra Pivate Cellar winery, M°Gregor, Western Cape.

Heavenly Cream (Sp) a rich old Oloroso Sherry from Burden, Puerto de Santa Maria.

Heavenly Draft (Eng) a classic bitter ale (part of the Classics Range) brewed by the Hydes Brewery, Manchester.

Heaven on Earth (S.Afr) the label for a Vin de Paille wine (Muscat d'Alexandrie) produced by the Stellar Winery, Olifants River, Western Cape.

Heaven Sent (Eng) a 4.5% alc by vol. ale brewed by the Salopian Brewing C°. Ltd., Shropshire.

Heaven's Eye (S.Afr) the label for a red wine (Cabernet franc, cabernet sauvignon, Petit verdot and Shiraz blend) produced by the Diemersfontein Wines winery, Wellington, Western Cape.

Heavitree Brewery (Eng) a brewery (established 1790). (Add): Trood Lane, Matford, Exeter, Devon EX2 8YP. Brews a variety of beers.

Heavy (Eng) a term applied to a full-bodied wine without much distinction, the heaviness is usually due to an excess of alcohol.

Heavy Beer (Scot) a term used for a medium gravity beer 1034–1039 O.G. which is light in colour.

Heavy Bodied Rums (USA) the name given to rums from Barbados, British Guyana, Jamaica, Martinique, New England and Trinidad.

Heavy Dark Rum (W.Ind) a full-bodied Puerto Rican rum which is dark and pungent.

Heavyweight Brewing C° (USA) a brewery. (Add): 1701 Valley Road, Ocean Township New Jersey 7712. Brews beers and lager. Website: http://www.heavyweightbrewing.com

Heba (Ser) a natural spring mineral water from Bujanovac, Serbia & Montenegro.

Hebei (Chi) a noted wine-producing region.

Hebridean Brewing C° (Scot) a brewery (established 2002). (Add): Stornoway, Isle of Lewis HS1 2RA. Brews: Berserker Export Pale Ale 7.5% alc by vol., Celtic Black 3.9% alc by vol., Clansman 3.9% alc by vol., Islander 4.8% alc by vol., Seeforth Ale 4.2% alc by vol. Website: http://www.hebridean-brewery.co.uk 'E'mail: sales@hebridean-brewery.co.uk

Hebridean Liqueurs (Scot) a liqueur producer. (Add): 44 Campbell Street, Helensburgh, Dunbartonshire G84 8XZ. Produces a variety of liqueurs. Website: http://www.hebridean-liqueurs.co.uk 'E'mail: roylewis@hebridean-liqueurs.co.uk

Hé Bron (Hol) a natural spring mineral water from Hoensbroek. Mineral contents (milligrammes per litre): Sodium 8mg/l, Calcium 97mg/l, Magnesium 17mg/l, Potassium 4.2mg/l, Bicarbonates 390mg/l, Chlorides 5mg/l, Sulphates 12mg/l, Nitrates 0.5mg/l.

Hebsack (Ger) village (Anb): Württemberg. (Ber): Remstal-Stuttgart. (Gro): Wartbühl. (Vin): Litchenberg.

Hecho (Sp) lit: 'made' a complete wine ready for bottling and shipping.

Hechtl Plus Sauerstoff (Ger) a sparkling natural spring mineral water (established 1998) from Ingolstadt. Mineral contents (milligrammes per litre): Sodium 4.82mg/l, Calcium 86mg/l, Magnesium 34.8mg/l, Potassium 1.52mg/l, Bicarbonates 430.2mg/l, Chlorides 0.8mg/l, Sulphates 21.7mg/l, Fluorides 0.13mg/l, Nitrates

H

0.15mg/l, Oxygen 20mg/l. pH 7.4 Website: http://www.hechti-plus-sauerstoff.de

Heckenklescher (Aus) lit: 'hedge crasher' the old nickname for the wine made from the Blauer wildbacher grape variety in that it was easy to drink and made its drinkers unsteady on their feet when they went into the fresh air to relieve themselves!

Hecker Pass Winery (USA) a winery based near Gilroy, Santa Clara, California. 6ha. Grape varieties: Carignan, Ruby cabernet and Zinfandel. Produces table and dessert wines.

Hecklingen (Ger) village (Anb): Baden. (Ber): Breisgau. (Gro): Burg Lichteneck. (Vin): Schlossberg.

Hectare (Fr) 2.471acres (10,000square metres).

Hecto (Euro) *abbr:* **Hecto**litre.

Hectolitre (Fr)) *abbr:* Hl. equals 100litres (22gallons).

Hectolitres of Pure Alcohol (Euro) *abbr:* H.L.P.A an expression used for measuring a given quantity of alcohol in a given quantity of spirit. *See also* L.P.A.

Hector's Bitter (Eng) a cask-conditioned bitter 1034 O.G. brewed by Hall and Woodhouse Brewery in Dorset.

Hector Stagnari (S.Am) a 10ha vineyard close to Montevideo and 25ha around Salto. Grape varieties include Gewürztraminer, Merlot, Syrah, Tannat.

Hedekilden (Den) a natural spring mineral water from Jydsk Kildevæld.

Hedelfingen (Ger) village (Anb): Württemberg. (Ber): Remstal-Stuttgart. (Gro): Weinsteige. (Vin): *see* Stuttgart.

Hedgehog (Eng) a cask-conditioned ale brewed by Poole Brewery, Poole.

Hedgemonkey (Eng) a 4.6% alc by vol. ale brewed by Glastonbury Ales, Somerset.

Hedges and Butler (Eng) major importers and distributors of fine wines and spirits in the U.K. (Add): Three Mill Lane, Bromley-by-Bow, London E3 3DU. *see* Hirondelle.

Hedges Cellars (USA) a 2.7ha Syrah-based vineyard on Red Mountain, Columbia Valley.

Hedging (Sp) a method of planting vines in the Sherry region, vines are planted 1 metre apart and 2 metres between rows so that the tractors can pass along. Vines are trained on wires.

Hedonic Scale (USA) a scoring system developed by the BTI in New York for scoring on a wine tasting: 0–1 [dislike extremely], 2–3 [dislike strongly], 4–5 [dislike slightly], 6–7 [neutral], 8–9 [like slightly], 10–11 [like strongly], 12–13 [like extremely].

Hedonism (Scot) a 10 year old, limited edition, grain whisky produced from a blend of two different distilleries (Cambus in Clackmannanshire and Caledonian in Edinburgh) by Compass Box, Edinburgh. 43% alc by vol.

Hedonist (Eng) a 3.8% alc by vol. ale brewed by the Wylam Brewery Ltd., Tyne & Wear.

Hedvin (Den) fortified wine.

Heeley [James and Sons] (Eng) a nineteenth century corkscrew producer based in Birmingham who patented many fine examples.

Heel Stone (Eng) a 4.3% alc by vol. ale brewed by Stonehenge Ales (Bunces Brewery) Ltd., Wiltshire.

Heeltap (Eng) derived from the lift or wedge of leather used to increase the height of shoe heel in the eighteenth century. Used for the draining of wine or spirits at the bottom of the glass. A heeltap glass has no foot. '*no heeltaps*' means that glasses have to be drained before putting down.

Heeltap (Eng) a nineteenth century term for the dregs left in the bottom of a glass after drinking, usually has sediment in.

Heeltap Glass (Eng) *see* Heeltap.

Heemskerk Vineyard (Austr) a winery. (Add): Pipers Brook, Tasmania 7254. Office: P.O. Box 1408, Launcestron, Tasmania 7250. 25 ha, Grape varieties: Cabernet sauvignon, Chardonnay, Pinot noir and Rhine riesling.

Heerbach (Ger) a still and sparkling natural spring mineral water (established 1986). Mineral contents (milligrammes per litre): Sodium 8mg/l, Calcium 36mg/l, Magnesium 7mg/l, Potassium 2mg/l, Bicarbonates 142mg/l, Chlorides 7mg/l, Sulphates 9mg/l.

Heerenrood (S.Afr) a red wine blend of Shiraz and Cabernet grapes produced by the Groot Constantia Estate.

Heerenwijn (S.Afr) a light, dry, white wine made from a blend of Colombard and Steen grapes by Delheim Wines.

Heering [Peter] (Den) the producer of Cherry Heering and akvavit (under the Christianshavner label) also Cloc and San Michele liqueurs.

Heering's Cherry Brandy (Den) originally known as Cherry Heering. Cherry brandy 24.5% alc by vol. *see* Heering (Peter).

Heerkretz (Ger) vineyard (Anb): Rheinhessen. (Ber): Bingen. (Gro): Rheingrafenstein. (Vil): Neu-Bamberg.

Heerkretz (Ger) vineyard (Anb): Rheinhessen. (Ber): Bingen. (Gro): Rheingrafenstein. (Vil): Siefersheim.

Hefe (Ger) yeast.

Hefebrand (Ger) the distillation of wine residue.

Hefebranntwein (Ger) a brandy which has been distilled from the residue left after wine production.

Hefefrei (Ger) lit: 'yeast free', a filtered weizen beer (wheat) that is free of yeast.

Hefegeschmack (Ger) yeasty tasting, not a fashionable term.

Hefetrub (Ger) lees.

Hefe-Weissbier (Ger) an unfiltered wheat beer 5.6% alc by vol. from the Paulaner Brauerei, Münich.

Hefe Weisse (Ger) a cloudy Löwen weisse wheat beer, drunk with the yeast in suspension from Löwenbräu. *See also* Krystal, Löwen Weisse.

Hefeweizen (Ger) a weizenbeer (wheat) with a sediment 5% alc by vol. Produced by the Riegele Brauerei in Augsburg.

Hefeweizen (Ger) a weizenbeer (wheat) 5.1% alc by vol. from Schöfferhofer Brauerei. *See also* Weizen.

Hegewisch Wines (S.Afr) a winery (established 2002) based in the Robertson, Western Cape. 60ha. Grape varieties: Cabernet sauvignon, Chardonnay, Merlot, Pinotage, Shiraz.

Heggies Vineyard (Austr) a 209ha vineyard site in Adelaide Hills. Owned by the Hill-Smith family. Grape varieties: Cabernet franc, Cabernet sauvignon, Chardonnay, Merlot, Rhine riesling.

Hegykozsegi Tanac (Hun) wine council, responsible for determining and guaranteeing quality. Includes representatives from local authorities, growers, traders, bottlers).

Heida ((Switz) the local name for the Traminer grape. *See also* Heiden.

Heide (Ger) vineyard (Anb): Pfalz. (Ber): Südliche Weinstrasse. (Gro): Ordensgut. (Vil): Weyher.

Heidegarten (Ger) vineyard (Anb): Pfalz. (Ber): Südliche Weinstrasse. (Gro): Schloss Ludwigshöhe. (Vil): Edenkoben.

Heidelbeergeist (Ger) a liqueur made from bilberries, either by distilling the fermented juice or by mixing the berries with alcohol.

Heidelberg (Ger) village (Anb): Baden. (Ber): Badische Bergstrasse/Kraichgau. (Gro): Mannaberg. (Vins): Burg, Dachsbuckel, Herrenberg.

Heidelberg (Ger) village (Anb): Baden. (Ber): Badische Bergstrasse/Kraichgau. (Gro): Rittersberg. (Vins): Heiligenberg, Sonnenseite ob der Bruck.

Heidelberg Lager (Afr) a dark, sweet lager beer brewed by the Intercontinental Breweries.

Heidelsheim (Ger) village (Anb): Baden. (Ber): Badische Bergstrasse/Kraichgau. (Gro): Mannaberg. (Vin): Altenberg.

Heiden ((Switz) the local name for the Traminer grape. *See also* Heida.

Heidesheim (Ger) village (Anb): Rheinhessen. (Ber): Bingen. (Gro): Kaiserpfalz. (Vins): Geissberg, Höllenberg, Steinacker.

Heid Heezy (Cktl) ⅓ measure M^{ac}Kinlays Original, ⅓ measure orange juice, ⅓ measure sparkling wine. Build together in an ice-filled old-fashioned glass and dress with a slice of orange.

Heidiland (Switz) a still and sparkling natural spring mineral water from Mels. Mineral contents (milligrammes per litre): Sodium 4mg/l, Calcium 83mg/l, Magnesium 34mg/l, Bicarbonates 126mg/l, Sulphates 249mg/l, Fluorides 1mg/l, Nitrates <1mg/l. Website: http://www.heidilandwater.ch

Heidsieck (Fr) three separate Champagne houses. *see* Heidsieck (Charles), Heidsieck Monopole, Piper Heidsieck.

Heidsieck [Charles] (Fr) a Champagne producer. (Add): 12 Allée du Vignoble, RN 15, Murigny 51061 Reims. A Grande Marque. 100ha. (80ha. with Piper-Heidsieck). Produces vintage and non-vintage wines. Vintages: 1900, 1904, 1906, 1911, 1914, 1917, 1921, 1923, 1926, 1928, 1929, 1933, 1934, 1937, 1943, 1945, 1947, 1949, 1952, 1953, 1955, 1959, 1961, 1962, 1964, 1966, 1969, 1971, 1973, 1975, 1976, 1979, 1981, 1983, 1985, 1988, 1989, 1990, 1992, 1993, 1994, 1995, 1996, 1998, 1999, 2000. Also produces a '*dated*' non-vintage Champagne: *dates*: 1993, 1995 1996, 1998, 1999, 2000.

Heidsieck Monopole (Fr) a Champagne producer. (Add): 5, Place Général Gouraud, 51100 Reims. A Grande Marque. 327ha. (some with Mumm). Produces vintage and non-vintage wines. Vintages: 1900, 1904, 1906, 1911, 1913, 1920, 1921, 1923, 1926, 1928, 1929, 1933, 1934, 1937, 1941, 1943, 1945, 1947, 1949, 1952, 1953, 1955, 1958, 1959, 1961, 1962, 1964, 1966, 1969, 1971, 1973, 1975, 1976, 1979, 1982, 1985, 1988, 1990, 1995, 1996, 1998, 1999, 2000, 2001. De Luxe vintage cuvee: Diamant Bleu. *See also* Blanc des Millénaires.

Heil (Ger) vineyard (Anb): Rheinhessen. (Ber): Bingen. (Gro): Kurfürstenstück. (Vil): Wallertheim.

Heil (Ger) vineyard (Anb): Rheinhessen. (Ber): Wonnegau. (Gro): Pilgerpfad. (Vil): Frettenheim.

Heilbronn (Ger) village (Anb): Württemberg. (Ber): Württembergisch Unterland. (Gro): Kirchenweinberg. (Vins): Altenberg, Sonnenberg.

Heilbronn (Ger) village (Anb): Württemberg. (Ber): Württembergisch Unterland. (Gro): Staufenberg. (Vins): Stahbühl, Stiftsberg, Wartberg.

Heilbronner Herbst (Ger) a Württemberg wine festival held at Heilbronn in September.

Heilbronn [ortsteil Klingenberg] (Ger) village (Anb): Württemberg. (Ber): Württembergisch Unterland. (Gro): Heuchelberg. (Vins): Schlossberg, Sonntagsberg.

Heileman Brewery (USA) breweries based in La Crosse, Wisconsin and St. Paul. Noted for Mickey's, Old Style and Special Export (a krausened beer).

Heilgarten (Ger) vineyard (Anb): Mittelrhein. (Ber): Bacharach. (Gro): Schloss Stahleck. (Vil): Manubach.

Heilgraben (Ger) vineyard (Anb): Mosel-Saar-Ruwer. (Ber): Zell/Mosel. (Gro): Weinhex. (Vil): Dieblich.

Heiligenbaum (Ger) vineyard (Anb): Rheinhessen. (Ber): Nierstein. (Gro): Auflagen. (Vil): Nierstein.

Heiligenberg (Ger) vineyard (Anb): Baden. (Ber): Badische Bergstrasse/Kraichgau. (Gro): Rittersberg. (Vil): Heidelberg.

Heiligenberg (Ger) vineyard (Anb): Baden. (Ber): Badische Frankenland. (Gro): Tauberklinge. (Vil): Krautheim.

Heiligenberg (Ger) vineyard (Anb): Baden. (Ber): Badische Frankenland. (Gro): Tauberklinge. (Vil): Krautheim (ortsteil Klepsau).

Heiligenberg (Ger) vineyard (Anb): Nahe. (Ber): Schloss Böckelheim. (Gro): Paradiesgarten. (Vil): Weiler bei Monzingen.

Heiligenberg (Ger) vineyard (Anb): Rheingau. (Ber): Johannisberg. (Gro): Deutelsberg. (Vil): Hattenheim.

Heiligenberg (Ger) vineyard (Anb): Pfalz. (Ber): Südliche Weinstrasse. (Gro): Mandelhöhe. (Vil): Maikammer.

H

Heiligenberg (Ger) vineyard (Anb): Württemberg. (Ber): Württembergisch Unterland. (Gro): Stromberg. (Vil): Häfnerhaslach.

Heiligenberg (Ger) vineyard (Anb): Württemberg. (Ber): Württembergisch Unterland. (Gro): Stromberg. (Vil): Schützingen.

Heiligenborn (Ger) vineyard (Anb): Pfalz. (Ber): Mittelhaardt-Deutsche Weinstrasse. (Gro): Schnepfenflug vom Zellertal. (Vil): Albisheim.

Heiligenhaus (Ger) vineyard (Anb): Rheinhessen. (Ber): Nierstein. (Gro): Domherr. (Vil): Saulheim.

Heiligenhäuschen (Ger) vineyard (Anb): Mosel-Saar-Ruwer. (Ber): Saar-Ruwer. (Gro): Römerlay. (Vil): Morscheid.

Heiligenhäuschen (Ger) vineyard (Anb): Mosel-Saar-Ruwer. (Ber): Saar-Ruwer. (Gro): Römerlay. (Vil): Riveris.

Heiligenhäuschen (Ger) vineyard (Anb): Mosel-Saar-Ruwer. (Ber): Saar-Ruwer. (Gro): Römerlay. (Vil): Waldrach.

Heiligenhäuschen (Ger) vineyard (Anb): Rheinhessen. (Ber): Bingen. (Gro): Kaiserpfalz. (Vil): Jugenheim.

Heiligenkirche (Ger) vineyard (Anb): Pfalz. (Ber): Mittelhaardt-Deutsche Weinstrasse. (Gro): Grafenstück. (Vil): Bockenheim.

Heiligenkreuz (Aus) *see* Stift Heiligenkreuz.

Heiligenpfad (Ger) vineyard (Anb): Rheinhessen. (Ber): Bingen. (Gro): Adelberg. (Vil): Wendelsheim.

Heiligenstein (Aus) a vineyard site based on the banks of the River Kamp situated in the Kamptal region.

Heiligenstein (Ger) vineyard (Anb): Baden. (Ber): Badische Bergstrasse/Kraichgau. (Gro): Mannaberg. (Vil): Mühlhausen.

Heiligenstein (Ger) vineyard (Anb): Baden. (Ber): Ortenau. (Gro): Schloss Rodeck. (Vil): Neuweier.

Heiligenstock (Ger) grosslage (Anb): Rheingau. (Ber): Johannisberg. (Vils): Eltville, Kiedrich.

Heiligenthal (Ger) grosslage (Anb): Franken. (Ber): Mainviereck. (Vils): Grossostheim, Wenigumstadt.

Heiligenzell (Ger) village (Anb): Baden. (Ber): Breisgau. (Gro): Schutterlindenberg. (Vin): Kronenbühl.

Heiliger Blutberg (Ger) vineyard (Anb): Rheinhessen. (Ber): Wonnegau. (Gro): Sybillenstein. (Vil): Weinheim.

Heiliger Dreikönigswein (Ger) the name given to wine made from grapes picked on the same day that the Three Wise Men visited the infant Jesus.

Heilighäuschen (Ger) vineyard (Anb): Rheinhessen. (Ber): Bingen. (Gro): Kaiserpfalz. (Vil): Gross-Winternheim

Heilighäuschen (Ger) vineyard (Anb): Pfalz. (Ber): Mittelhaardt-Deutsche Weinstrasse. (Gro): Schnepfenflug vom Zellertal. (Vil): Stetten.

Heiligkreuz (Ger) vineyard (Anb): Rheinhessen. (Ber): Wonnegau. (Gro): Pilgerpfad. (Vil): Bechtheim.

Heilig Kreuz (Ger) vineyard (Anb): Pfalz. (Ber): Südliche Weinstrasse. (Gro): Schloss Ludwigshöhe. (Vil): Edenkoben.

Heilig Kreuz (Ger) vineyard (Anb): Württemberg. (Ber): Kocher-Jagst-Tauber. (Gro): Kocherberg. (Vil): Belsenberg.

Heilquelle St. Leonhard (It) a natural spring mineral water from Passeier, Bozen. Mineral contents (milligrammes per litre): Sodium 31mg/l, Calcium 81mg/l, Magnesium 7.8mg/l, Potassium 3.2mg/l, Bicarbonates 295mg/l, Chlorides 11mg/l, Sulphates 37mg/l, Fluorides 1.3mg/l, Iron 7.65mg/l, Silicates 5mg/l.

Heilwasser (Ger) a mineral water with medicinal properties (high in minerals).

Heim (Fr) an Alsace producer. (Add): 68111 Westhaltau. Combined growers vineyards total 92ha.

Heimbach (Ger) village (Anb): Baden. (Ber): Breisgau. (Gro): Burg Lichteneck. (Vin): Bieninberg.

Heimberg (Ger) vineyard (Anb): Nahe. (Ber): Schloss Böckelheim. (Gro): Burgweg. (Vil): Schlossböckelheim.

Heimersheim (Ger) village (Anb): Ahr. (Ber): Walporzheim/Ahrtal. (Gro): Klosterberg. (Vins): Burgarten, Kapellenberg, Landskrone.

Heimersheim (Ger) village (Anb): Rheinhessen. (Ber): Wonnegau. (Gro): Sybillenstein. (Vin): Sonnenberg.

Heineken (Hol) a famous Dutch (Amsterdam) lager brewed under licence in over 20 countries. Brewed in the U.K. by Whitbread Brewery. 1033 O.G. Also an imported bottled Export 1048 O.G.

Heineken Netherlands Brouwerijen BV (Hol) famous breweries based at Zoeterwoude and s'Hertogenbosch. (Eng Add): Melbury House, 51, Wimbledon Hill Road, London SW19 7QW. Lager beers brewed under licence in most countries. *see* Heineken, Amstel. Website: http://www.heineken.com

Heineken Oud Bruin (Hol) a 2.5% alc by vol. bottled old brown beer brewed by Heineken Netherlands Brouwerij, Zoeterwoude.

Heineken Pilsner (Hol) a 5% alc by vol. bottled pilsner brewed by Heineken Netherlands Brouwerij, Zoeterwoude.

Heineman (USA) a winery based in Put-in-Bay, Ohio. Produces wines made from American vines.

Heinrich [Gernot] (Aus) a winery (12 ha) based in Gols, Neusiedlersee (Add): Baumgarten 60, 7122 Gols. Grape varieties: Blaufränkisch, Cabernet sauvignon, Chardonnay, Merlot, Neuburger, Pinot blanc, Pinot gris, St. Laurent, Syrah, Zweigelt. Produces a range of white, sweet white and red wines.

Heinrich [Johann] (Aus) a winery based in Deutschkreutz, Mittel-Burgenland. (Add): Karrnergasse 59, 7301 Deutschkreutz. Grape varieties: Blaufränkisch, Cabernet sauvignon, Pinot noir. Label: Goldberg.

Heinrichhaus (USA) a winery based in St. James, Missouri. Produces wines from American vines.

Heinr. Reissdorfer Brauerei (Ger) a brewery (established 1894) based in Cologne. Brews: Reissdorf Kölsch.

Heinsheim (Ger) village (Anb): Baden. (Ber): Badische Bergstrasse/Kraichgau. (Gro): Stiftsberg. (Vin): Burg Ehrenberg.

Heisser Stein (Ger) vineyard (Anb): Franken. (Ber): Maindreieck. (Gro): Hofrat. (Vil): Buchbrunn.

Heisterberg (Ger) vineyard (Anb): Mittelrhein. (Ber): Siebengebirge. (Gro): Petersberg. (Vil): Niederdollendorf.

Heitersbrünnchen (Ger) vineyard (Anb): Rheinhessen. (Ber): Neirstein. (Gro): Sankt Alban. (Vil): Bodenheim.

Heitersheim (Ger) village (Anb): Baden. (Ber): Markgräflerland. (Gro): Lorettoberg. (Vins): Maltesergarten, Sonnhohle.

Heitz Vineyards (USA) fine vineyards sited in St. Helena, Napa Valley, California. Also known as Martha May's Vineyard. 17ha. Grape varieties: Cabernet sauvignon and Chardonnay. Produces varietal, sparkling and dessert wines.

Heizenleithen (Aus) a vineyard site on the banks of the River Danube situated in the Wachau region, Niederösterreich.

Helado (Mex) chilled. *See also* Frio.

Helbon (Gre) a sweet white wine drunk in ancient Greece, was produced near Damascus, also known as Chalybon.

Held (Ger) vineyard (Anb): Mosel-Saar-Ruwer. (Ber): Bernkastel. (Gro): Probstberg. (Vil): Kenn.

Held (Ger) vineyard (Anb): Mosel-Saar-Ruwer. (Ber): Bernkastel. (Gro): Sankt Michael. (Vil): Köwerich.

Held (Ger) vineyard (Anb): Mosel-Saar-Ruwer. (Ber): Bernkastel. (Gro): Sankt Michael. (Vil): Pölich.

Held (Ger) vineyard (Anb): Mosel-Saar-Ruwer. (Ber): Obermosel. (Gro): Königsberg. (Vil): Mesenich.

Held (Ger) vineyard (Anb): Pfalz. (Ber): Mittelhaardt-Deutsche Weinstrasse. (Gro): Schwarzerde. (Vil): Bisserheim.

Heldenbräu Lager (Eng) a 1032 O.G. lager brewed by Whitbread for the north west of England.

Heldenspruit (S.Afr) a natural spring mineral water. Mineral contents (milligrammes per litre): Sodium 38mg/l, Calcium 7.35mg/l, Magnesium 5.02mg/l, Potassium 1.53mg/l, Bicarbonates 40mg/l, Chlorides 59mg/l, Sulphates 5mg/l, Fluorides 0.1mg/l, Nitrates 2.4mg/l.

Helderberg Co-operative (S.Afr) co-operative vineyards based in Stellenbosch. (Add): De Helderberg Koöperatiewe Wijnmakerij Beperkt, P.O. Firgrove 7110. Produces varietal wines.

Helderkruin Wine Cellar (S.Afr) a winery (established 1997) based in the Stellenbosch, Western Cape. 100ha. Grape varieties: Cabernet sauvignon, Chardonnay, Chenin blanc, Merlot, Petit verdot, Pinotage, Sauvignon blanc, Shiraz. Labels: Ben du Toit, Yellow Cellar.

Held in Union (Eng) a Victorian term to describe the Burton Union System where all the pieces of equipment used in the system were 'held in union'. The large fermenting rooms were called 'union rooms'.

Helenenkloster (Ger) vineyard (Anb): Mosel-Saar-Ruwer. (Ber): Bernkastel. (Gro): Kurfürstlay. (Vil): Mülheim.

Helenen Quelle (Ger) a sparkling natural spring mineral water. Mineral contents (milligrammes per litre): Sodium 280mg/l, Calcium 130mg/l, Magnesium 50mg/l, Bicarbonates 270mg/l, Chlorides 50mg/l, Sulphates 780mg/l.

Helenen Quelle Heilwasser (Ger) a natural spring mineral water. Mineral contents (milligrammes per litre): Sodium 724mg/l, Calcium 312mg/l, Magnesium 244mg/l, Potassium 15.1mg/l, Chlorides 608mg/l, Sulphates 22mg/l, Fluorides 0.22mg/l, Iron 6.21mg/l.

Helfant-Esingen (Ger) village (Anb): Mosel-Saar-Ruwer. (Ber): Ober-Mosel. (Gro): Gipfel. (Vin): Kapellenberg.

Helfensteiner (Ger) a red grape variety produced by crossing Frühburgunder x Trollinger. Ripens early and has a neutral flavour but is susceptible to coulure. Parent of Dornfelder.

Heligan Honey (Eng) a 4% alc by vol. ale brewed by the Skinner's Brewery C°. Ltd., Cornwall.

Helions Vineyard (Eng) a vineyard (established 1979). (Add): Helions, Bumpstead, Haver Hill, Suffolk. 0.5ha. Grape varieties: Müller-Thurgau, Reichensteiner.

Hell (Cktl) 25mls (1fl.oz) brandy, 25mls (1fl.oz) crème de menthe. Shake over ice, strain into a cocktail glass and top with cayenne pepper.

Hell (Ger) pale, a word sometimes used when ordering a pale Münchner bier.

Hella Mineralbrunnen (Ger) a natural spring mineral water from Trappenkamp. Mineral contents (milligrammes per litre): Sodium 8.2mg/l, Calcium 51.2mg/l, Magnesium 3.6mg/l, Bicarbonates 145.4mg/l.

Hellanbach (Eng) a lager brewed by the Original Brewing Company, Hertfordshire.

Hellenic Brewery (Gre) a noted brewery based in Athens.

Hellenpfad (Ger) vineyard (Anb): Nahe. (Ber): Schloss Böckelheim. (Gro): Rosengarten. (Vil): Braunweiler.

Heller Beer (Eng) a cask-conditioned bitter 1060 O.G. brewed by the home-brew public house Royal Inn at Horsebridge.

Heller Brauerei (Ger) a brewery (established 1678) based in Bamberg. Brews: Aecht Schenkerla Rauchbier.

Heller Estate (USA) a label for organic wines for the Durney Vineyards, Carmel Valley, California. Website: http://www.hellerestate.com

Helles Bier (Ger) *see* Urbräu

Hellfire (Eng) a cask-conditioned ale 1063 O.G. brewed by the Victoria Brewery, Ware, Hertfordshire.

Hell For Leather (Eng) a 5.2% alc by vol. beer brewed by the Ash Vine Brewery, Trudoxhill, Somerset. Part of their Ultimate Pub Nightmare series.

Hellgate Special (Eng) a cask-conditioned beer formerly brewed at the Unicorn (home-brew pub) in Shropshire.

Helligenborn (Ger) vineyard (Anb): Mosel-Saar-

Ruwer. (Ber): Saar-Ruwer. (Gro): Scharzberg. (Vil): Serrig.

Hello (Ind) a natural spring mineral water. Mineral contents (milligrammes per litre): Sodium 38mg/l, Calcium 18mg/l, Magnesium 12mg/l, Potassium 1.8mg/l, Bicarbonates 50mg/l, Chlorides 25mg/l, Sulphates 16mg/l, Fluorides 0.5mg/l. pH 7.6

Hells Belles (Eng) a 4.8% alc by vol. ale brewed by The Branscombe Vale Brewery, Devon.

Hellwegquelle (Ger) a natural spring mineral water. Mineral contents (milligrammes per litre): Sodium 71mg/l, Calcium 200mg/l, Magnesium 28mg/l, Potassium 7mg/l, Bicarbonates 488mg/l, Chlorides 77mg/l, Sulphates 266mg/l.

Helmholz Vineyard (USA) a vineyard based in Alexander Valley, California. Grape variety: Cabernet sauvignon. Grapes are vinified at the Veedercrest Winery.

Helmsheim (Ger) village (Anb): Baden. (Ber): Badische Bergstrasse/Kraichgau. (Gro): Mannaberg. (Vin): Burgwingert.

Helopeltis theivora (Lat) the tea mosquito, a serious pest on the African continent and other tea producing countries.

Helshoogte (S.Afr) lit: 'the heights of hell' a mountain and wine district within the Stellenbosch region.

Helshoogte Vineyards (S.Afr) a winery (established 2000) based in Stellenbosch, Western Cape. 7ha. Grape varieties: Cabernet franc, Cabernet sauvignon, Merlot. Label: Isa. Website: http://www.helshoogte.co.za

Helston Brewery (Eng) *see* Blue Anchor.

Helvellyn Gold (Eng) a 4% alc by vol. ale brewed by the Hesketh Market Brewery, Cumbria.

Helvita Sangría [U.K.] (Eng) a subsidiary of the Swiss company Helvita Corporation set up in June 1985. Markets Wins Sangría.

Hemel-en-Aarde Valley Wines (S.Afr) the brand-name for the Hamilton Russell Vineyards.

Hemeling Lager (Eng) a light lager 1030.7 O.G. brewed by Bass.

Hemelzicht (S.Afr) a winery (established 1998) based in Onrusrivier, Walker Bay, Western Cape. 16ha. Grape varieties: Cabernet sauvignon, Chardonnay, Malbec, Sauvignon blanc, Shiraz.

Hemileia vastatrix (Lat) leaf rust, a fungus that attacks the leaves of the coffee bush (especially the arabica variety). *See also* Coffee Leaf Rust.

Hemingway (Cktl) 25mls (⅙ gill) Pernod placed into a flute glass, top with iced Champagne.

Hemisphere (Eng) latitudes (north) 35°N to 50°N and (south) 23°S to 40°S. The main latitude bands that are ideal for the growing of grapes suitable for wine making.

Hemisphere (S.Afr) the label for a range of wines produced by the Lost Horizons Premium Wines winery, Suider-Paarl, Western Cape.

Hemling Lite (Eng) *see* Hemeling Lager.

Hemlock Bitter (Eng) a 4% alc by vol. bitter ale brewed by the Castle Rock Brewery, Nottinghamshire.

Hempje Licht Op (Hol) lit: 'lift up your petticoat', a liqueur produced by Van Zuylekom of Amsterdam.

Hemsbach (Ger) village (Anb): Baden. (Ber): Badische Bergstrasse/Kraichgau. (Gro): Rittersberg. (Vin): Herrnwingert.

Hemus (Bul) a medium sweet white wine from Karlovo.

Henan (Chi) a noted wine-producing region.

Henchard Bitter (Eng) a cask-conditioned bitter ale 1045 O.G. brewed by the Bourne Valley Brewery in Hampshire.

Hendelberg (Ger) vineyard (Anb): Rheingau. (Ber): Johannisberg. (Gro): Mehrholzchen. (Vil): Hallgarten.

Hendred Vineyard (Eng) a vineyard (established 1973) based at East Hendred, Wantage, Oxon, Oxfordshire. 1.4ha. Grape variety: Reichensteiner.

Hendrick's (Scot) a distillery, produces a variety of sprits including gin, vodka and whiskies. Owned by William Grant & Sons.

Hendrik Lodewyk (S.Afr) the label for a red wine (Petit verdot) produced by the Du Preez Estate winery, Worcester, Western Cape.

Hengelo Brouwerij (Hol) a brewery based in eastern Holland, noted for Hengelo Pilsner.

Hengelo Pilsener (Hol) the name used by the Artois Brasserie of Belgium for their beer brewed in the Hengelo Brouwerij, eastern Holland.

Hengelweine (Aus) the name given to wines that were sold by the growers that produced them. Derived from the branches that were hung outside their houses to show that they had wines to sell.

Hengl-Hasselbrunner (Aus) a winery based in the Wien region. (Add): Ingasegasse 10, 1190 Wien-Döbling. Grape varieties: Grüner veltliner, Müller-Thurgau, Pinot gris, Riesling, St. Laurent, Welschriesling, Zweigelt. Produces a range of wine styles.

Hengst (Fr) a 75.78ha A.C. Alsace Grand Cru vineyard in Wintzenheim, Haut-Rhin. Grape varieties include: Tokay Pinot Gris.

Hengstberg (Ger) vineyard (Anb): Nahe. (Ber): Schloss Böckelheim. (Gro): Paradiesgarten. (Vil): Desloch.

Hen Harrier (Eng) a 4% alc by vol. ale brewed by the Bowland Beer Company Ltd., Lancashire.

Henkell (Ger) a noted producer of sekt by the cuve close method.

Henkell Trocken (Ger) a brand of sparkling wine produced in 3 styles: standard with platinum foil, brut with gold foil and rosé with silver foil tops.

Henkenberg (Ger) vineyard (Anb): Baden. (Ber): Kaiserstuhl-Tuniberg. (Gro): Vulkanfelsen. (Vil): Oberrotweil.

Henkes (Can) a brand-name used by the Canadian Schenley Distilleries Ltd. for a range of liqueurs.

Henkes (Hol) a distiller of Jenever.

Henke Winery (Austr) a winery (established 1969). (Add): Henke's Lane, Victoria. Grape varieties: Cabernet, Shiraz.

H

Henley Brewery (Eng) see Brakspear's.

Hennekens (Ger) a distillery based at Beck. Produces Els (a bitters).

Hennessy (Fr) a Cognac producer. (Add): Societé Jas Hennessy and C°., 1 Rue de la Richonne, 16101 Cognac. Produces Paradis: rarest eaux-de-vie aged slowly in oak, X.O: over 100 eaux-de-vie, Privilège V.S.O.P: over 60 Cognacs matured in barrel, V.S: a blend of over 40 full-bodied eaux-de-vie. see Hennessy (Richard).

Hennessy [Maurice] (Fr) an Irishman who introduced the Star rating system for quality in Cognac brandies in 1865.

Hennessy [Richard] (Fr) an Irishman who, at the age of 26, settled in the Charente region, left the army and became an eau-de-vie dealer. Settled in Cognac and exported to Ireland and Great Britain. Founder of the Hennessy firm.

Henniez (Switz) a still and sparkling natural spring mineral water from Henniez. (Add): Henniez SA, CH-1525, Henniez. (red label: sparkling/green label: low gas/blue label: still). Mineral contents (milligrammes per litre): Sodium 7mg/l, Calcium 106mg/l, Magnesium 19mg/l, Potassium 1mg/l, Bicarbonates 392mg/l, Chlorides 8mg/l, Sulphates 13mg/l, Nitrates 16mg/l, Fluoride 0.1mg/l.

Henniger Brauerei (Ger) a well-known Frankfurt brewery noted for Kaiser Pilsener, Highlander and long lagered Export beer.

Henniger Export (Ger) see Henniger.

Henniger Hellas SA (Gre) three breweries which produce Aegean lager 5% alc by vol. Based in Atalanti, Thessaloniki and Iraklion on Crete.

Henniger Pils (Ger) a pilsener lager 1044 O.G. brewed by Henniger Brauerei in Frankfurt. Imported into Britain by Courage.

Henri Bourgeois (Fr) a wine producer based in the A.C. Sancerre, Central Vineyards, Loire Valley. Grape varieties: Pinot noir, Sauvignon blanc. Label: Les Jeannettes.

Henri Goutorbe (Fr) a Champagne producer. (Add): 9 Bis, Rue Jeanson, F-51160 Aÿ. 20ha. Produces vintage and non-vintage wines. 20ha. Produces: Brut Cuvée Tradition (Chardonnay 25%, Pinot noir 70%, Pinot meunier 5%), Le Spécial Club Millésimé Grand Cru (Chardonnay 25%, Pinot noir 75%) Vintages: 1997, 1998,1999. A member of the Club Tresors de Champagne. Website: http://www.Champagne-henri-goutorbe.com

Henri Marchant (USA) the brand-name used by the Gold Seal Winery in the Finger Lakes for their range of American-grape wines.

Henriot (Fr) a Champagne producer based in Reims. Owned by Charles Heidsieck. (Add): 3 Place des Droits de l'Homme, 51100 Reims. A Grande Marque. Produces vintage and non-vintage wines. Vintages: 1973, 1975, 1976, 1979, 1982, 1983, 1985, 1988, 1989, 1990. Blanc de blancs cuvee: St. Vincent. Prestige cuvees: Cuvée Baccarat, Réserve Baron Philippe de Rothschild, Cuvée des Enchanteleurs. 'E'mail: contact@Champagne-henriot.com

Henriot 'Réserve Baron Philippe de Rothschild' (Fr) a vintage Champagne produced by Henriot. Vintages: 1903, 1905, 1911, 1921, 1928, 1929, 1934, 1937, 1939, 1941, 1943, 1945, 1947, 1949, 1952, 1953, 1955, 1959, 1961, 1964, 1966, 1969, 1971, 1973, 1975, 1976, 1979, 1982, 1983, 1985, 1988, 1989, 1990, 1995, 1996, 1998, 1999, 2000.

Henriot Royal Wedding Cuvée (Fr) a non-vintage brut Champagne produced by Henriot of Reims for the Royal wedding in 1986.

Henriques and Henriques (Mad) a Funchal-based Madeira shipper.

Henry II (Eng) a King of England who, in 1152, married Queen Eleanor of Aquitaine and inherited the vineyards of Bordeaux and Gascony.

Henry Boon Ale (Eng) a bitter ale 1038.5. O.G. brewed by the Clark's Wakefield Brewery (named after the brewery founder).

Henry Brasserie (Fr) a brewery based in Bazincourt sur Saulx. Brews: La Saulx.

Henry Estate Winery (USA) a winery based near Umpaqua Valley, Oregon. Grape varieties: Cabernet sauvignon, Chardonnay, Gewürztraminer, Müller-Thurgau, Pinot gris, Pinot noir, Riesling. Label: Barrel Select.

Henry McKenna (USA) a brand of Bourbon whisky produced by Seagram.

Henry of Pelham (Can) a winery based in Niagara Peninsula, Ontario. Grape variety: Baco noir, Chardonnay, dry Riesling.

Henry on Thames (Eng) a 4.5% alc by vol. seasonal summer ale brewed by Brakspear, Henley-on-Thames, Oxon.

Henry's Hampton (Eng) a 4.4% alc by vol. seasonal ale brewed by Hydes at 46 Moss Lane, West Manchester, Lancashire. Available July and August. Part of their Craft Ale range.

Henry's I.P.A (Eng) a 3.8% alc by vol. dark ale brewed by Wadworth & C°., Northgate, Wiltshire.

Henry Weinhard's Private Reserve (USA) a premium lager brewed by the Blitz-Weinhard Brewery in Portland, Oregon.

Henry Williamson (Eng) a 4.8% alc by vol. ale brewed by Tarka Ales Ltd., Devon.

Henschke (Austr) a winery based in Keyneton, South Australia. Grape varieties: Cabernet sauvignon, Shiraz, Sémillon.

Hen's Dream (Cktl)(Non-alc) 1 egg, juice of ½ lemon, juice of ½ orange, 2 dashes grenadine. Shake over ice, strain into a cocktail glass and decorate with a twist of lemon zest.

Henshall Disk (Eng) a patented corkscrew circa 1795 invented by the Rev. Samuel Henshall. It had a disk at the top of the screw to prevent the tip of the screw passing through the base of the cork.

Hen's Tooth (Eng) a 6.5% alc by vol. bottle conditioned ale brewed by Morland Brewery, Abingdon, Oxfordshire.

Hépar (Fr) a still natural spring mineral water. Mineral contents (milligrammes per litre): Sodium 14mg/l, Calcium 555mg/l, Magnesium

110mg/l, Bicarbonates 403mg/l, Sulphates 1479mg/l, Nitrates 3.9mg/l. pH 7.0

Heppenheim [including Erbach and Hambach] (Ger) village (Anb): Hessische Bergstrasse. (Ber): Starkenberg. (Gro): Schlossberg. (Vins): Eckweg, Guldenzoll, Maiberg, Stemmler, Steinkopf, Zentgereich.

Heppenstein (Ger) vineyard (Anb): Mosel-Saar-Ruwer. (Ber): Saar-Ruwer. (Gro): Scharzberg. (Vil): Ockfen.

Heppingen (Ger) village (Anb): Ahr. (Ber): Walporzheim/Ahrtal. (Gro): Klosterberg. (Vin): Berg.

Heppinger (Ger) a sparkling natural spring mineral water from Bad Neuenahr. Mineral contents (milligrammes per litre): Sodium 856mg/l, Calcium 115.9mg/l, Magnesium 164.8mg/l, Potassium 52.7mg/l, Bicarbonates 2891mg/l, Chlorides 244.7mg/l, Sulphates 188mg/l, Nitrates 1.13mg/l.

Heppinger Extra (Ger) a sparkling natural spring mineral water. Mineral contents (milligrammes per litre): Sodium 651mg/l, Calcium 137mg/l, Magnesium 196mg/l, Potassium 35.8mg/l, Bicarbonates 2687mg/l, Chlorides 185mg/l, Sulphates 122mg/l, Fluorides 0.58mg/l, Lithium 1.1mg/l, Silicates mg/l, Antimony 1.1mg/l, Boron 6.9mg/l.

Hepplethwaite Cocktail (Cktl) 25mls (⅛ gill) white rum, 20mls (⅙ gill) crème de fraises, dash lemon juice. Shake over ice, strain into a cocktail glass and top with a strawberry slice.

Heptyl (Eng) a higher alcohol. Part of the Fusil oils.

Hepworth & C° Brewers Ltd (Eng) a brewery (established 2001). (Add): Chipman House, The Railway Yard, Nightingale Road, Horsham, West Sussex RH12 2NW. Brews beers whose labels are featured under the Beer Station brand including: Blond Organic Lager 5.1% alc by vol., Iron House 4.8% alc by vol., Pullman 4.2% alc by vol., Sussex Light Ale 3.5% alc by vol. Website: http://www.thebeerstation.co.uk 'E'mail: mail@thebeerstation.co.uk

Herald (Eng) a 3.8% alc by vol. ale brewed by the the Cambrinus Craft Brewery, Merseyside.

Herald (Eng) a new variety of dwarf hop. See also First Gold, Pioneer.

Herald Ale (Ire) see Herald Brewery.

Herald Bitter (Eng) a 4.2% alc by vol. bitter beer brewed by the Port Mahon Brewery, South Yorkshire.

Herald Brewery (Ire) a small free trade brewery (established 1983) based in Northern Ireland. Noted for Herald Ale 1036 O.G. which is sold under blanket pressure.

Herard [Paul] (Fr) a Champagne producer. (Add): Neuville-sur-Seine, 10250, Mussy-sur-Seine. Récoltants-manipulants. Produces vintage and non-vintage wines. Vintages: 1971, 1975, 1976, 1979, 1982, 1983, 1985, 1988, 1990, 1995, 1998, 2001.

Heras [Las] (Arg) a wine producing area in the Mendoza region.

Heraud [Ets] (Fr) a Cognac producer. (Add): Saint-André-de-Lidon, 17260 Gemonzac. Has 15ha. in the Bons Bois. Produces a wide range of Cognacs.

Héraud [L'] (Fr) a Cognac producer. (Add): Domaine de Lasdoux, Angeac-Charente, 16120 Châteauneuf-sur-Charente. 62ha. in the Petite Champagne. Produces a wide range of Cognacs by natural production methods (a single vineyard).

Hérault (Fr) a département of the Languedoc-Roussillon, in the low plain of Hérault and Orb (Vin de Pays de l'Hérault). Much wine produced used for the making of vermouth.

Herb (Ger) bitter, found on a beer label or on Mosel wines but here more akin to 'dry'.

Herbal (Eng) a term used to describe wines that have been matured in a cask.

Herbal Dew (Eng) a mixed herbal and fruit drink range, several versions available

Herbal Tea (Eng) teas made from leaves other than tea leaves, also known as Tissanes. (Ire) = leabhar tae.

Herbe aux Vers (Fr) lit: 'worm herb'. see Mugwort.

Herbemont (Mad) a hybrid grape variety which is now banned from use in Madeira production, also planted widely in Brazil.

Herberg (Hol) public house/inn/tavern.

Herbergier (Hol) innkeeper.

Herbert Beaufort (Fr) a Champagne producer (established 1820). (Add): 28 & 32 Rue de Tours, B.P. 7, 51150 Bouzy. 16.6ha. Produces vintage and non-vintage wines also Bouzy Blanc and Bouzy Rouge. 'E'mail: BEAUFORT-HERBERT@wanadoo.fr

Herb Lamb Vineyard (USA) a red wine (Cabernet sauvignon) produced by the Colgin winery, Napa Valley, California.

Herb Liqueurs (Eng) one or more varieties of herbs steeped in spirit, there are many combinations. see Élixers.

Herb Maté (S.Am) the mis-spelling of Yerba Maté.

Herbolzheim (Ger) village (Anb): Baden. (Ber): Badische Bergstrasse/Kraichgau. (Gro): Stiftsberg. (Vin): Berg.

Herbolzheim (Ger) village (Anb): Baden. (Ber): Breisgau. (Gro): Burg Lichteneck. (Vin): Kaiserberg.

Herbsaint (Fr) an aniseed-flavoured spirit.

Hercegovina (Euro) a large wine-producing region.

Herculane (Rum) a sparkling natural spring mineral water. Mineral contents (milligrammes per litre): Sodium 1.1mg/l, Calcium 53mg/l, Magnesium 3.1mg/l, Potassium 0.3mg/l, Bicarbonates 153mg/l, Chlorides 5.4mg/l, Sulphates 17.4mg/l, Fluorides 0.03mg/l, Nitrates 3.7mg/l, Silicates 4.1mg/l, Iron 1.03mg/l, Oxygen 6.8mg/l. pH 7.95

Hercules (Wal) an American export name for a bottled double strong ale 1075 O.G. brewed by the Felinfoel Brewery, Llanelli.

Hercules Cocktail (Cktl) ½ measure Cognac, ½ measure amaretto, 1 measure orange juice, 3 dashes grenadine. Stir well over ice in a highball glass, dress with orange and lemon peel spirals.

H

Herdade (Port) farm.

Herdade do Esporao (Port) a large winery based near Reguengos de Monsarez, Alentejo. 350ha. Grape varieties: Cabernet sauvignon, Diagalves, Mantuedo, Perrum, Roupeiro, Arinto, Trincadeira, Aragonez.

Herdade do Monte da Ribeira (Port) a winery (1000ha) based in Vidigueira, Alentejo. Label: Quatro Caminhos.

Herdade do Mouchão (Port) a winery (25ha) based in Alentejo. Grape varieties: Alicante bouschet, Aragonez, Moreto, Touriga nacional, Trincadeira, Syrah. Produces its wines by traditional methods (including foot-tredding the grapes).

Heredad Montsarra (Sp) a bodega based in the Penedés region that produces varietal white wines.

Heredos de Enrique Bilbao-Bodegas Ramón Bilbao (Sp) one of the main wine-producers based in Rioja. see Bodegas Ramón Bilbao.

Hereford Bitter (Eng) see Herefordshire Ales.

Hereford Cows (USA) a cream liqueur.

Hereford Pale Ale (Eng) a 4% alc by vol. pale ale brewed by the Wye Valley Brewery Ltd., 69 St. Owen Street, Hereford, Herefordshire.

Herefordshire Ale (Eng) a new brewery (established 1985) based in Hereford. Noted for cask-conditioned Hereford Bitter 1038 O.G.

Herefordshire Country Perry (Eng) a 4.5% alc by vol. perry produced by Westons, Much Marcle in Herefordshire.

Herefordshire Olde Bull (Eng) a 3.9% alc by vol. ale brewed by the Spinning Dog Brewery, Herefordshire.

Hereford Traditional (Eng) a full-bodied cider produced by Bulmers of Hereford from bitter sweet apples (part of their Heritage range).

Herencia Remondo (Sp) a white wine made from mainly Viura grapes. Produced by the Bodegas José Palacios. Also available as red or rosé from 60% Garnacha, 10% Mazuelo, 5% Graciano grapes.

Hereti (Geo) a white wine produced by Tsinandali winery in the Republic of Georgia from the Rkatsitely grape grown in Kakheti region.

Here Tonight (Cktl) ½ measure Parfait Amour, ½ measure blue Curaçao, 1 measure cream. Shake well over ice and strain into a cocktail glass.

Hereward Brewery (Eng) a brewery based in Market Deeping, Lincolnshire. Founded in 1983. Brews a Bitter 1038 O.G. and Hereward Warrior 1055 O.G.

Hereward Warrior (Eng) a cask-conditioned ale 1055 O.G. brewed by the Hereward Brewery, Market Deeping, Lincolnshire.

Here XVIII (S.Afr) a sparkling, dry white wine made from the Steen and Sémillon grapes by Die Bergkelder.

Herforder Brauerei (Ger) a well-known brewery from Herford, Westphalia. Noted for well-matured pilsener lagers.

Herforder Pils (Ger) a long-matured pilsener lager 4.9% alc by vol. brewed by the Herforder Brauerei in Westphalia.

Herforder Pils (Ger) a 4.8% alc by vol. pilsner brewed by the Felsenkeller Brauerei, Herford.

Herfst Bok (Hol) a 6.5% alc by vol. warming, ruby red, seasonal beer brewed by Grolsch at Enschede-Groenlo, Gelderland. Available in Autumn.

Hergenfeld (Ger) village (Anb): Nahe. (Ber): Kreuznach. (Gro): Pfarrgarten. (Vins): Herrschaftsgarten, Mönchberg, Sonnenberg.

Hergersweiler (Ger) village (Anb): Pfalz. (Ber): Südliche Weinstrasse. (Gro): Kloster Liebfrauenberg. (Vin): Narrenberg.

Hering (Fr) an Alsace wine producer. (Add): 6 Rue de Docteur-Sultzer 67140 Barr.

Heriot (Fr) a species of barley malt from the Triumph variety that gives a good sugar yield.

Heriot Brewery (Scot) a cask-conditioned 80/- ale brewed by Tennent's Brewery, named after their Edinburgh brewery.

Heritage (Can) a brand of Canadian whisky produced by the Canadian Distillers Ltd (part of Seagram).

Heritage (Eng) the brand-name of a coffee produced by Lyons Tetley, a blend of arabica beans from Columbia, Central America and East Africa that are medium-roasted to produce a smooth coffee.

Heritage (Eng) a range of three ciders produced by Bulmers of Hereford. see Harvest Scrumpy, Number Seven, Hereford Traditional.

Heritage (Fr) a range of wines produced by Baron Philippe de Rothschild SA. Labels include: Baron Nathaniel (Pauillac), Baron Henri (Médoc), Baron Carl (Saint-Émilion), Baronne Thérèse (Entre-Deux-Mers), Baronne Charlotte (Graves Blanc), Baronne Mathilde (Sauternes).

Heritage Ale (Eng) a 4.8% alc by vol. Burton pale ale from the Bass Museum micro-brewery, Burton-on-Trent.

Heritage Ale (Wal) a malt extract ale 1038 O.G. brewed by the home-brew public house in Cardiff owned by Whitbread.

Heritage Ales (Eng) took over the Tisbury Brewery, Tisbury, Wiltshire in February 2001. New beers introduced include 5% alc by vol. Heritage.

Heritage Bitter (Eng) a cask-conditioned bitter ale 1036 O.G. brewed by the Phillips Brewery in Buckinghamshire.

Heritage Brewery (Eng) a brewery based at Burton-on-Trent. Brews include: Linda and Stephen Wedding Ale.

Heritage Farm Vineyard (Austr) a winery (established 1974). (Add): Murray Valley Highway, Cobram, Victoria. Produces a range of sweet and fortified wines.

Heritage Gaston Briand la Paradis (Fr) a 90 year old Cognac produced by Ragnaud Sabourin.

Heritage Mme. Paul Ragnaud (Fr) a vintage 1903 Cognac produced by Ragnaud Sabourin.

Heritage Vineyard (Austr) a winery based in the Barossa Valley, South Australia.

Heritage Vineyards (USA) a winery based in West Milton, Ohio. Produces wines from American and French-American hybrid vines.

H

Heritier-Guyot (Fr) a Burgundy négociant based at Dijon. Produces Crème de Cassis and fine wines.

Herman Joseph's (USA) a premium beer with a strong hop flavour brewed by the Coors Brewery in Golden, Colorado.

Hermannhof Winery (USA) a winery based in Hermann, Missouri.

Hermann J. Weimer (USA) a winery based in the Finger Lakes, New York State. Grape variety: Pinot noir.

Hermannshöhle (Ger) vineyard (Anb): Nahe. (Ber): Schloss Böckelheim. (Gro): Burgweg. (Vil): Niederhausen an der Nahe.

Hermanos Solera (Sp) a dry Málaga produced by Scholtz.

Hermaphrodite Screw (Eng) a patent method corkscrew which has a central raising screw which is female to the inner shank and male to the outer barrel. Invented by Edward Thomason in 1802.

Hermes (Cyp) a fine dry, red wine produced by Loël in Limassol.

Herm Harrier (Cktl) 2 measures orange juice, 1 measure sloe gin, ½ measure Grand Marnier. Shake over ice and strain into a flute glass.

Hermitage (Austr) the alternative name for the Syrah grape.

Hermitage (Fr) an A.C. district in the northern Rhône that is noted for its terraced vineyards, uses the Syrah grape variety for red wines, Roussanne and Marsanne for the whites. *See also* Crozes Hermitage and Ermitage.

Hermitage (Fr) a Cognac producer based in the Grande Champagne district, Charente.

Hermitagé (Fr) a term used until the end of the nineteenth century for those red wines that had received the addition of red Hermitage wines to give added colour and body.

Hermitage (S.Afr) an alternative name for the Cinsault grape. *See also* Cinsaut which can have the same name.

Hermitage [l'] (Fr) vineyards (120ha) in the commune of Tain in the northern Rhône in the Hermitage region.

Hermitage Brewery (Eng) a small brewery attached to the Sussex Brewery public house in West Sussex. Noted for cask-conditioned Best Bitter 1048 O.G. Bitter 1040 O.G. Lumley Old Ale 1050 O.G. Mild 1034 O.G. and Triple X 1044 O.G.

Hermit Crab Marsanne Viognier [The] (Austr) a Rhône-style white wine from the D'Arenberg winery.

Hermonville (Fr) a Cru Champagne village in the Canton de Fismes. District: Reims.

Hermosillo (Mex) a wine-producing area in the Sonora district.

Hernsberg (Ger) vineyard (Anb): Hessische Bergstrasse. (Ber): Starkenburg. (Gro): Wolfsmagen. (Vil): Bensheim.

Hero (Euro) the brand-name of a non-alcoholic sparkling fruit drink range: orange, lemon, bitter lemon, cassis, strawberry, cherry. Combines 10% juice with sparkling water.

Heroes (Eng) a premium bitter ale brewed by Beowulf Brewery, Yardley, Birmingham.

Heroldrebe (Ger) a red grape variety, a cross between Portugieser x Limberger. Produces light neutral wines, low sugar content, late-ripener (the parent of the Dornfelder).

Heroldsberg (Ger) vineyard (Anb): Franken. (Ber): Maindreieck. (Gro): Burg. (Vil): Hammelburg.

Herlod Wines (S.Afr) a winery (established 1999) based in Herold, Outeniqua, Little Karoo. 6ha. Grape varieties: Pinot noir, Shiraz.

Heron (S.Afr) the label for a white wine (Chenin blanc and Viognier blend) and red wine (Shiraz and Petit verdot blend) produced by the Riverstone Vineyards winery, Worcester, Western Cape.

Heron and Brearley (I.O.M) brewers on the island. Breweries in Douglas and Castletown (The Okell Brewery).

Heron Hill Vineyards (USA) a winery based in the Finger Lakes, New York. 12ha. Grape varieties: Chardonnay and Riesling. Produces varietal wines.

Heron Ridge (S.Afr) a winery (established 1997) based in Helderberg, Stellenbosch, Western Cape. 4ha. Grape varieties: Cabernet sauvignon, Shiraz. Produces varietal wines.

Heron's Flight (N.Z) a winery. (Add): Sharp Road, RD 2, Matakana, Warkworth. 4.5ha. Grape varieties: Cabernet sauvignon, Chardonnay, Merlot, Merlot blush.

Herradura (Mex) a producer of a tequila of the same name.

Herrather Jungbrunnen (Ger) a natural spring mineral water. Mineral contents (milligrammes per litre): Sodium 8.1mg/l, Calcium 57.2mg/l, Magnesium 17.2mg/l, Potassium 7.5mg/l, Bicarbonates 281mg/l, Chlorides 5.4mg/l, Sulphates 9.8mg/l, Fluorides 0.3mg/l, Nitrates <1mg/l.

Herrenberg (Ger) lit: 'the lord's (or master's) hill', a popular vineyard name in Germany (37 individual sites are so named).

Herrenberg (Ger) grosslage (Anb): Franken. (Ber): Steigerwald. (Vil): Castell.

Herrenberg (Ger) grosslage (Anb): Mittelrhein. (Ber): Rheinburgengau. (Vils): Dörscheid, Kaub.

Herrenberg (Ger) vineyard (Anb): Ahr. (Ber): Warporzheim/Ahrtal. (Gro): Klosterberg. (Vil): Rech.

Herrenberg (Ger) vineyard (Anb): Baden. (Ber): Badische Bergstrasse/Kraichgau. (Gro): Mannaberg. (Vil): Heidelberg.

Herrenberg (Ger) vineyard (Anb): Baden. (Ber): Badische Bergstrasse/Kraichgau. (Gro): Mannaberg. (Vil): Leimen.

Herrenberg (Ger) vineyard (Anb): Baden. (Ber): Badische Frankenland. (Gro): Tauberklinge. (Vil): Gerlachsheim.

Herrenberg (Ger) vineyard (Anb): Baden. (Ber): Badische Frankenland. (Gro): Tauberklinge. (Vil): Oberschüpf.

Herrenberg (Ger) vineyard (Anb): Baden. (Ber): Breisgau. (Gro): Burg Lichteneck. (Vil): Nordweil.

Herrenberg (Ger) vineyard (Anb): Franken. (Ber): Steigerwald. (Gro): Not yet assigned. (Vil): Oberschwarzach.

Herrenberg (Ger) vineyard (Anb): Mosel-Saar-Ruwer. (Ber): Bernkastel. (Gro): Kurfürstlay. (Vil): Kesten.

Herrenberg (Ger) vineyard (Anb): Mosel-Saar-Ruwer. (Ber): Bernkastel. (Gro): Nacktarsch. (Vil): Kröv.

Herrenberg (Ger) vineyard (Anb): Mosel-Saar-Ruwer. (Ber): Bernkastel. (Gro): Probstberg. (Vil): Schweich.

Herrenberg (Ger) vineyard (Anb): Mosel-Saar-Ruwer. (Ber): Bernkastel. (Gro): Schwarzlay. (Vil): Enkirch.

Herrenberg (Ger) vineyard (Anb): Mosel-Saar-Ruwer. (Ber): Bernkastel. (Gro): Schwarzlay. (Vil): Erden.

Herrenberg (Ger) vineyard (Anb): Mosel-Saar-Ruwer. (Ber): Saar-Ruwer. (Gro): Römerlay. (Vil): Kasel.

Herrenberg (Ger) vineyard (Anb): Mosel-Saar-Ruwer. (Ber): Saar-Ruwer. (Gro): Römerlay. (Vil): Mertesdorf (ortsteil Maximin Grünhaus).

Herrenberg (Ger) vineyard (Anb): Mosel-Saar-Ruwer. (Ber): Saar-Ruwer. (Gro): Römerlay. (Vil): Trier.

Herrenberg (Ger) vineyard (Anb): Mosel-Saar-Ruwer. (Ber): Saar-Ruwer. (Gro): Scharzberg. (Vil): Filzen.

Herrenberg (Ger) vineyard (Anb): Mosel-Saar-Ruwer. (Ber): Saar-Ruwer. (Gro): Scharzberg. (Vil): Mennig.

Herrenberg (Ger) vineyard (Anb): Mosel-Saar-Ruwer. (Ber): Saar-Ruwer. (Gro): Scharzberg. (Vil): Ockfen.

Herrenberg (Ger) vineyard (Anb): Mosel-Saar-Ruwer. (Ber): Saar-Ruwer. (Gro): Scharzberg. (Vil): Schoden.

Herrenberg (Ger) vineyard (Anb): Mosel-Saar-Ruwer. (Ber): Saar-Ruwer. (Gro): Scharzberg. (Vil): Serrig.

Herrenberg (Ger) vineyard (Anb): Mosel-Saar-Ruwer. (Ber): Zell/Mosel. (Gro): Goldbäumchen. (Vil): Cochem.

Herrenberg (Ger) vineyard (Anb): Mosel-Saar-Ruwer. (Ber): Zell/Mosel. (Gro): Grafschaft. (Vil): Alf.

Herrenberg (Ger) vineyard (Anb): Mosel-Saar-Ruwer. (Ber): Zell/Mosel. (Gro): Rosenhang. (Vil): Briedern.

Herrenberg (Ger) vineyard (Anb): Mosel-Saar-Ruwer. (Ber): Zell/Mosel. (Gro): Rosenhang. (Vil): Valwig.

Herrenberg (Ger) vineyard (Anb): Nahe. (Ber): Schloss Böckelheim. (Gro): Paradiesgarten. (Vil): Boos.

Herrenberg (Ger) vineyard (Anb): Nahe. (Ber): Schloss Böckelheim. (Gro): Paradiesgarten. (Vil): Rehborn.

Herrenberg (Ger) vineyard (Anb): Nahe. (Ber): Schloss Böckelheim. (Gro): Paradiesgarten. (Vil): Staudernheim.

Herrenberg (Ger) vineyard (Anb): Rheingau. (Ber): Johannisberg. (Gro): Steinmacher. (Vil): Frauenstein.

Herrenberg (Ger) vineyard (Anb): Rheinhessen. (Ber): Nierstein. (Gro): Güldenmorgen. (Vil): Dienheim.

Herrenberg (Ger) vineyard (Anb): Rheinhessen. (Ber): Nierstein. (Gro): Güldenmorgen. (Vil): Oppenheim.

Herrenberg (Ger) vineyard (Anb): Rheinhessen. (Ber): Wonnegau. (Gro): Burg Rodenstein. (Vil): Ober-Flörsheim.

Herrenberg (Ger) vineyard (Anb): Pfalz. (Ber): Mittelhaardt-Deutsche Weinstrasse. (Gro): Höllenpfad. (Vil): Kleinkarlbach.

Herrenberg (Ger) vineyard (Anb): Pfalz. (Ber): Mittelhaardt-Deutsche Weinstrasse. (Gro): Honigsöckel. (Vil): Ungstein.

Herrenberg (Ger) vineyard (Anb): Pfalz. (Ber): Südliche Weinstrasse. (Gro): Bischofskreuz. (Vil): Nussdorf.

Herrenberg (Ger) vineyard (Anb): Pfalz. (Ber): Südliche Weinstrasse. (Gro): Guttenberg. (Vil): Minfeld.

Herrenberg (Lux) a vineyard site in the village of Greiveldange.

Herrenberg (Lux) a vineyard site in the village of Nertert.

Herrenberger (Ger) vineyard (Anb): Mosel-Saar-Ruwer. (Ber): Saar-Ruwer. (Gro): Scharzberg. (Vil): Ayl.

Herrenberger (Ger) vineyard (Anb): Mosel-Saar-Ruwer. (Ber): Saar-Ruwer. (Gro): Scharzberg. (Vil): Wawern.

Herrenbuck (Ger) vineyard (Anb): Baden. (Ber): Kaiserstuhl-Tuniberg. (Gro): Vulkanfelsen. (Vil): Eichstetten.

Herrenbuckel (Ger) vineyard (Anb): Pfalz. (Ber): Südliche Weinstrasse. (Gro): Bischofskreuz. (Vil): Flemlingen.

Herrengarten (Ger) vineyard (Anb): Rheinhessen. (Ber): Nierstein. (Gro): Krötenbrunnen. (Vil): Dienheim.

Herrengarten (Ger) vineyard (Anb): Rheinhessen. (Ber): Nierstein. (Gro): Krötenbrunnen. (Vil): Oppenheim.

Herrenhäuser Brauerei (Ger) a brewery of Hanover in western Germany. Noted for mature pilsener lagers and Kosher pilsner at 4.9% alc by vol. Brewed from barley left untouched during Passover.

Herrenhäuser Pilsener (Ger) a pilsener lager brewed by the Herrenhäuser Brauerei in Hanover. A long lagered beer 5.2% alc by vol.

Herrenletten (Ger) vineyard (Anb): Pfalz. (Ber): Mittelhaardt-Deutsche Weinstrasse. (Gro): Meerspinne. (Vil): Haardt.

Herrenmorgen (Ger) vineyard (Anb): Pfalz. (Ber): Mittelhaardt-Deutsche Weinstrasse. (Gro): Feuerberg. (Vil): Bad Dürkheim.

Herrenpfad (Ger) vineyard (Anb): Pfalz. (Ber): Südliche Weinstrasse. (Gro): Kloster Liebfrauenberg. (Vil): Göcklingen.

H

Herrenpfad (Ger) vineyard (Anb): Pfalz. (Ber): Südliche Weinstrasse. (Gro): Kloster Liebfrauenberg. (Vil): Heuchelheim-Klingen.

Herrenrood (S.Afr) a red wine produced by Groot Constantia.

Herrenstubengesellschaft (Fr) the Guild of Burgesses in Alsace, the original name of the Confrérie Saint-Étienne.

Herrenstück (Ger) vineyard (Anb): Baden. (Ber): Kaiserstuhl-Tuniberg. (Gro): Vulkanfelsen. (Vil): Bickensohl.

Herrentisch (Ger) vineyard (Anb): Baden. (Ber): Breisgau. (Gro): Schutterlindenberg. (Vil): Lahr.

Herrentrost (Aus) a vineyard area on the banks of the River Danube in the Kremstal region.

Herrenwingert (Ger) vineyard (Anb): Pfalz. (Ber): Südliche Weinstrasse. (Gro): Guttenberg. (Vil): Steinfeld.

Herrenzehntel (Ger) vineyard (Anb): Nahe. (Ber): Schloss Böckelheim. (Gro): Paradiesgarten. (Vil): Weiler bei Monzingen.

Herrgards (Swe) a whisky, Sherry and caraway-flavoured aquavit. Is matured in Sherry casks.

Herrgottsacker (Ger) vineyard (Anb): Pfalz. (Ber): Mittelhaardt-Deutsche Weinstrasse. (Gro): Höllenpfad. (Vil): Kleinkarlbach.

Herrgottsacker (Ger) vineyard (Anb): Pfalz. (Ber): Mittelhaardt-Deutsche Weinstrasse. (Gro): Mariengarten. (Vil): Diedesheim.

Herrgottsacker (Ger) vineyard (Anb): Pfalz. (Ber): Mittelhaardt-Deutsche Weinstrasse. (Gro): Schwarzerde. (Vil): Dirmstein.

Herrgottshaus (Ger) vineyard (Anb): Rheinhessen. (Ber): Nierstein. (Gro): Domherr. (Vil): Klein-Winternhaus.

Herrgottspfad (Ger) vineyard (Anb): Rheinhessen. (Ber): Nierstein. (Gro): Petersberg. (Vil): Gau-Odernheim.

Herrgottsrock (Ger) vineyard (Anb): Mosel-Saar-Ruwer. (Ber): Saar-Ruwer. (Gro): Scharzberg. (Vil): Pellingen.

Herrgottströpfchen (Ger) lit: 'drops of heaven', the name of a range of wines produced by Jakob Gerhardt. see Blaulack, Goldlack, Lilalack and Weisslack.

Herri Mina (Fr) a 2ha vineyard in the Pyrénées foothills A.C. Irouléguy.

Herrijunga Cider (Swe) a brewery. (Add): Östergåtdsgatan 11, 524 32 Herrijunga. Brews a variety of beers and lagers. Website: http://www.herrijungacider.se 'E'mail: knotor@herrijungacider.se

Herrlesberg (Ger) vineyard (Anb): Württemberg. (Ber): Württembergisch Unterland. (Gro): Kirchenweinberg. (Vil): Neckarwestheim.

Herrliberg (Switz) one of the principal vineyards in Zürich.

Herrlich (Ger) grosslage (Anb): Pfalz. (Ber): Südliche Weinstrasse. (Vils): Eschbach, Göcklingen, Herxheim bei Landau, Herxheimweyher, Ilbesheim, Impflingen, Insheim, Leinsweiler, Mörzheim, Rohrbach, Wollmesheim.

Herrmannsberg (Ger) vineyard (Anb): Nahe. (Ber):

Schloss Böckelheim. (Gro): Burgweg. (Vil): Niederhausen an der Nahe.

Herrnberg (Ger) vineyard (Anb): Hessische Bergstrasse. (Ber): Umstadt. (Gro): Not yet assigned. (Vil): Gross-Umstadt.

Herrnberg (Ger) vineyard (Anb): Rheingau. (Ber): Johannisberg. (Gro): Daubhaus. (Vil): Flörsheim.

Herrnberg (Ger) vineyard (Anb): Rheingau. (Ber): Johannisberg. (Gro): Daubhaus. (Vil): Hochheim.

Herrnberg (Ger) vineyard (Anb): Rheinhessen. (Ber): Nierstein. (Gro): Sankt Alban. (Vil): Gau-Bischofsheim.

Herrnwingert (Ger) vineyard (Anb): Baden. (Ber): Badische Bergstrasse/Kraichgau. (Gro): Rittersberg. (Vil): Hemsbach.

Herrnwingert (Ger) vineyard (Anb): Baden. (Ber): Badische Bergstrasse/Kraichgau. (Gro): Rittersberg. (Vil): Sulzbach.

Herrnwingert (Ger) vineyard (Anb): Hessische Bergstrasse. (Ber): Starkenburg. (Gro): Rott. (Vil): Bensheim-Schönberg.

Herrschaft (Switz) a small wine-producing district bordering Austria and Liechtenstein, grows Blauburgunder and Completer vines.

Herrschaftsberg (Ger) vineyard (Anb): Franken. (Ber): Steigerwald. (Gro): Schlosstück. (Vil): Frankenberg.

Herrschaftsberg (Ger) vineyard (Anb): Franken. (Ber): Steigerwald. (Gro): Schlosstück. (Vil): Ippesheim.

Herrschaftsgarten (Ger) vineyard (Anb): Nahe. (Ber): Kreuznach. (Gro): Pfarrgarten. (Vil): Hergenfeld.

Hersbrucker Hallertau (Eng) a single varietal ale brewed by Wadworth & Cº. Ltd., Northgate Brewery in Devizes, Wiltshire (between 9th and 20th August).

Herstell (Aus) a vineyard site on the banks of the River Danube situated in the Wachau region, Niederösterreich.

Herte Kamp Jenever (Bel) the brand-name for a jenever produced by Bruggeman.

Herten (Ger). Village. (Anb): Baden. (Ber): Markgräflerland. (Gro): Vogtei Rötteln. (Vin): Steinacker.

Hertford Club 100 (Eng) a bitter ale brewed by McMullen Brewery, Hertford to celebrate the centenary of the Hertford Club.

Hertingen (Ger) village (Anb): Baden. (Ber): Markgräflerland. (Gro): Vogtei Rötteln. (Vin): Sonnhohle.

Hertmannsweiler (Ger) village (Anb): Württemberg. (Ber): Remstal-Stuttgart. (Gro): Wartbühl. (Vin): Himmelreich.

Hertog Jan (Hol) a range of top-fermenting beers brewed at the Arcen Bier Brouwerij, Arcen, Limburg. Brews Pilsener, Bockbier, Dubbel, Tripel, Grand Prestige, Meibock, Primator.

Hertog Jan Bockbier (Hol) a 6.5% alc by vol. bottled ruby-red bock beer brewed by Arcen Bier Brouwerij, Arcen, Limburg.

Hertog Jan Dubbel (Hol) a 7% alc by vol. bottle-

H

conditioned double beer brewed by Arcen Bier Brouwerij, Arcen, Limburg.

Hertog Jan Gran Prestige (Hol) a 10% alc by vol. bottle-conditioned barley wine brewed by Arcen Bier Brouwerij, Arcen, Limburg.

Hertog Jan Meibock (Hol) a 7% alc by vol. bottled straw spring beer brewed by Arcen Bier Brouwerij, Arcen, Limburg.

Hertog Jan Oud Bruin (Hol) a 2% alc by vol. bottled dark old brown beer brewed by Arcen Bier Brouwerij, Arcen, Limburg.

Hertog Jan Pilsener (Bel) a 5% alc by vol. bottom-fermented pilsener brewed by the Artois Brasserie, Louvain.

Hertog Jan Primator (Hol) a 6% alc by vol. bottled de-luxe pilsner brewed by Arcen Bier Brouwerij, Arcen, Limburg.

Hertog Jan Tripel (Hol) a 8.5% alc by vol. bottle-conditioned triple beer brewed by Arcen Bier Brouwerij, Arcen, Limburg.

Herukka (Fin) a blackcurrant liqueur.

Hervelets [Les] (Fr) a Premier Cru vineyard in the A.C. commune of Fixin, Côte de Nuits, Burgundy 3.83ha.

Hervieux-Dumez (Fr) a Champagne producer. (Add): 6, Rue de Châtillon, 51500 Sacy. 9ha. Produces vintage and non-vintage wines. Vintages: 1995, 1996, 1997, 1999. A member of the Club Tresors de Champagne. Labels: Cuvée 'Special Club' Millésimée (Chardonnay 50%, Pinot meunier 20%, Pinot noir 30%). 'E'mail: hervieuxdumez@aol.com

Hervós (Sp) a wine-growing area in Càceres, south-western Spain.

Herxheim/Berg (Ger) village (Anb): Pfalz. (Ber): Mittelhaardt-Deutsche Weinstrasse. (Gro): Kobnert. (Vins): Himmelreich, Honigsack, Kirchenstück.

Herxheim ber Landau (Ger) village (Anb): Pfalz. (Ber): Südliche Weinstrasse. (Gro): Herrlich. (Vin): Engelsberg.

Herxheimweyher (Ger) village (Anb): Pfalz. (Ber): Südliche Weinstrasse. (Gro): Herrlich. (Vin): Am Gaisberg.

Herzchen (Ger) vineyard (Anb): Mosel-Saar-Ruwer. (Ber): Bernkastel. (Gro): Vom Heissen Stein. (Vil): Briedel.

Herzegovina (Euro) a small region which produces good white wines including Mostarska Zilavka.

Herzfeld (Ger) vineyard (Anb): Pfalz. (Ber): Mittelhaardt-Deutsche Weinstrasse. (Gro): Kobnert. (Vil): Leistadt.

Herzhaft (Ger) hearty.

Herzlay (Ger) vineyard (Anb): Mosel-Saar-Ruwer. (Ber): Bernkastel. (Gro): Schwarzlay. (Vil): Bausendorf.

Herzog (Ger) vineyard (Anb): Pfalz. (Ber): Mittelhaardt-Deutsche Weinstrasse. (Gro): Meerspinne. (Vil): Haardt.

Herzogenberg (Ger) vineyard (Anb): Württemberg. (Ber): Remstal-Stuttgart. (Gro): Weinsteige. (Vil): Fellbach.

Herzogenberg (Ger) vineyard (Anb): Württemberg. (Ber): Remstal-Stuttgart. (Gro): Weinsteige. (Vil): Stuttgart (orsteil Cannstatt).

Herzogenberg (Ger) vineyard (Anb): Württemberg. (Ber): Remstal-Stuttgart. (Gro): Weinsteige. (Vil): Stuttgart (ortsteil Untertürkheim).

Herzogsberg (Ger) vineyard (Anb): Baden. (Ber): Badische Bergstrasse/Kraichgau. (Gro): Stiftsberg. (Vil): Binau.

Herzogsberg (Ger) vineyard (Anb): Baden. (Ber): Badische Bergstrasse. (Gro): Stiftsberg. (Vil): Diedesheim.

Herzog Wigbert Quelle (Ger) a natural spring mineral water. Mineral contents (milligrammes per litre): Sodium 115mg/l, Calcium 124mg/l, Magnesium 27.1mg/l, Potassium 17.4mg/l, Bicarbonates 598mg/l, Chlorides 122mg/l, Sulphates 43mg/l.

Hesket Newmarket Brewery (Eng) a brewery (established 1988). (Add): Old Crown barn, Hesket Newmarket, Wigton, Cumbria CA7 8JG. Brews: Autumn Ale 4.7% alc by vol., Blencathra Bitter 3.4% alc by vol., Catbells Pale Ale 5.2% alc by vol., Great Cockup Porter 3% alc by vol., Helvellyn Gold 4% alc by vol., Old Carrock Strong Ale 6.5% alc by vol., Scaffeld Bond (Spring) 4% alc by vol., Skiddaw Special Bitter 3.5% alc by vol. Website: http://www.hesketbrewery.co.uk 'E'mail: info@hesketbrewery.co.uk

Hesperidina (Sp) a low-alcohol drink made from orange and lemon skins.

Hessen Quelle (Ger) a natural spring mineral water. Mineral contents (milligrammes per litre): Sodium 320mg/l, Calcium 242mg/l, Magnesium 42.4mg/l, Potassium 33.5mg/l, Bicarbonates 1296mg/l, Chlorides 294mg/l, Sulphates 49mg/l. Website: http://www.hassia.com

Hessens Brauerei (Ger) a brewery based in Wächterbach. Brews: Wächterbacher Doppel Bock.

Hessern (Ger) vineyard (Anb): Mittelrhein. (Ber): Rheinburgengau. (Gro): Loreleyfelsen. (Vil): St. Goarshausen.

Hess Estate (USA) a winery based in the Napa Valley, California. Grape varieties: Cabernet sauvignon.

Hesse Wine (Ger) the name given to the wine of the Rheinhessen.

Hessheim (Ger) village (Anb): Pfalz. (Ber): Mittelhaardt-Deutsche Weinstrasse. (Gro): Schwarzerde. (Vin): Lange Els.

Hessian Fly (Eng) *Mayetiola destructor* a small Dipterous fly whose larvae damage corns (barley, rye, wheat) family: *Donyidae*.

Hessigheim (Ger) village (Anb): Württemberg. (Ber): Württembergisch Unterland. (Gro): Schalkstein. (Vins): Felsengarten, Käsberg, Katzenöhrle.

Hessische Bergstrasse (Ger) anbaugebiet (Bers): Umstadt, Starkenburg. 400ha. Main grape is Riesling.

Hessische Bergstrasse Information Service (Ger) a wine information service. (Add): Weinbauverband

Hessische Bergstrasse, V. Königsberger Strasse 4. 6148 Heppenheim/Bergstrasse.

Hessische Bergstrasse Wine Festivals (Ger) Bergsträsser Weinmarkt. Bergsträsser Winzerfest.

Hessische Forschung-Sanstalt für Wein-Obst-und Gartenbau (Ger) a research wine school in Geisenheim, Rheingau.

Hessweg (Ger) vineyard (Anb): Nahe. (Ber): Schloss Böckelheim. (Gro): Paradiesgarten. (Vil): Odernheim.

Het Anker Brasserie (Bel) a brewery (established 1471) based in Mechelen. Brews: Golden Carolus.

Het Elfde Gebod (Hol) a 7% alc by vol. bottled special beer brewed by Arcen Bier Brouwerij, Arcen.

Het Ijs (Hol) ice.

Het Kapittel Abt (Bel) a 10% alc by vol. straw-coloured abbaye beer brewed by Van Eecke Brasserie, Watou.

Het Kapittel Prior (Bel) a 9% alc by vol. bottle-conditioned, brown abbaye beer brewed by Van Eecke Brasserie, Watou.

Het Pint (Scot) a traditional New Year drink that consists of ale, whisky, eggs, nutmeg and sugar.

Hetzerath (Ger) village (Anb): Mosel-Saar-Ruwer. (Ber): Bernkastel. (Gro): Michelsberg. (Vin): Brauneberg.

Heublein Inc. (USA) a liqueur producer based in Connecticut. Owner's of the Smirnoff trade name.

Heublein's (USA) a wine company who through Christies of London, organise wine auctions in the USA. see Heublin Inc.

Heuchelberg (Ger) grosslage (Anb): Württemberg. (Ber): Württembergisch Unterland. (Vils): Brackenheim, Brackenheim (ortsteil Botenheim), Burgbronn, Cleebronn, Dürrenzimmern, Eibensbach, Frauenzimmern, Güglingen, Haberschlacht, Hausen/Z, Heilbronn, (ortsteil Klingenberg), Kleingartach, Leingarten, Hassenbachhausen, Meimsheim, Neipperg, Niederhofen, Nordhausen, Nordheim, Pfaffenhofen, Schwaigern, Stetton a. H., Stockheim, Weiler/Z, Zaberfeld.

Heuchelheim/Frankenthal (Ger) village (Anb): Pfalz. (Ber): Mittelhaardt-Deutsche Weinstrasse. (Gro): Schwarzerde. (Vin): Steinkopf.

Heuchelheim-Klingen (Ger) village (Anb): Pfalz. (Ber): Südliche Weinstrasse. (Gro): Kloster Liebfrauenberg. (Vin): Herrenpfad.

Heunisch (Aus) an ancient red grape variety rarely grown now.

Heurige (Aus) a light white wine, young wine, new wine.

Heurigen (Aus) an inn or tavern where the Heurige (young wines) are consumed (created around 1784 by Emporer Joseph II who officialised the practice) owner can only sell his own wines, also known as Heurizes. See also Alter, Buschenschank and Sturm.

Heurizes (Aus) see Heurigen.

Heuweiler (Ger) village (Anb): Baden. (Ber): Breisgau. (Gro): Burg Zähringen. (Vin): Eichberg.

Hewish IPA (Eng) a 3.6% alc by vol. India pale ale brewed by the RCH Brewery, Avon.

Hewitson (Austr) a winery based at 4 Mann Street, Hyde Park, South Australia. Owns vineyards in the Barossa Valley and McLaren Vale. Grape varieties include Shiraz, Mourvèdre, Riesling. Labels: Ned and Henry's, Old Garden, The Mad Hatter

Hewitts (Ire) a blend of malt and grain whiskies from Midleton, Cork.

Hewitt Vineyard (USA) a winery based in Rutherford, Napa Valley, California. Grape varieties include: Cabernet sauvignon.

Hex (Fr) see Pernod Hex.

Hexelberg (Ger) vineyard (Anb): Rheinhessen. (Ber): Nierstein. (Gro): Krötenbrunnen. (Vil): Eimsheim.

Hexenbock (Switz) a ruby-coloured beer brewed by the Hurlimann Brauerei.

Hexhamshire Brewery (Eng) a brewery (established 1992). (Add): Leafields, Hexham, Northumberland NE46 1SX. Brews: Devils Elbow 3.6% alc by vol., Devils Water 4.2% alc by vol., Old Humbug 5.5% alc by vol., Shire Bitter 3.8% alc by vol., Whaps Weasel 4.8% alc by vol. 'E'mail: ghb@hexhamshire.co.uk

Hexose (Eng) the name given to sugars that contain 6 carbon [C$_6$] atoms (e.g. fructose and glucose).

Hex Valley (S.Afr) a natural spring mineral water from Hex Valley, Cape. Mineral contents (milligrammes per litre): Sodium 1.8mg/l, Calcium <0.5mg/l, Magnesium <0.5mg/l, Potassium <1mg/l, Chlorides <5mg/l, Sulphates <5mg/l, Fluorides <0.05mg/l, Nitrates <0.3mg/l. pH 5.7

Hex Vom Dasenstein (Ger) vineyard (Anb): Baden. (Ber): Ortenau. (Gro): Schloss Rodeck. (Vil): Kappelrodeck.

Hexyl (Eng) a higher alcohol, part of the fusil oils.

Hey Diddle Diddle (Eng) a 4.7% alc by vol. light hopped ale brewed by the Nursery Brewery, Keynsham, near Bristol.

Heylzu Herrnsheim (Ger) a famous estate based in Nierstein. 30ha. Grape variety: Riesling 55%.

Heytesbury (Austr) a red (Cabernet sauvignon) wine produced by the Vasse Felix Estate winery, Western Australia.

Heyvaert Brasserie (Bel) a brewery based in Asse, northern Belgium.

Heywood House (S.Afr) the label for a barrel-fermented white wine (Sauvignon blanc) produced by the Flagstone Winery, Somerset West, Western Cape.

Heywoods (Wal) a dry cider produced in Tregarth, north Wales.

Hhd (Eng) abbr: Hogshead.

Hi (Jap) a soft textured whiskey produced by Nikka for young adults.

Hi-Ball Glass (USA) an alternative spelling for the Highball Glass.

Hibernian Special (Cktl) ⅓ measure dry gin, ⅓ measure green Curaçao, ⅓ measure Cointreau, dash lemon juice, shake over ice and strain into a cocktail glass.

Hibiki (Jap) a whiskey produced by Suntory using 30 different malts from a single distillery. See also Yamazaki.

H

Hi-Brau (Ch.Isles) *see* Stein Lager.
Hickinbotham Family Vineyard (Austr) a vineyard. (Add): Straughton Vale Road, Anakie, Victoria 3221. 15ha. Grape varieties: Cabernet franc, Cabernet sauvignon, Chardonnay, Dolcetto, Riesling, Pinot noir, Shiraz.
Hicks Special (Eng) a strong draught cask-conditioned bitter 1050 O.G. brewed by the St. Austell Brewery in St. Austell, Cornwall.
Hicks Strong (Eng) a 5% alc by vol. strong ale brewed by the St. Austell Brewery in St. Austell, Cornwall.
Hidalgo (Mex) a wine-producing area in northern Mexico.
Hidalgo [Emilio] (Sp) a brandy producer. Solera brandies: Consistorial, Gobernador, Magistral Etiqueta Rioja, Solera Reserva brandy: Magistral Etiqueta Negra, Solera gran reserva brandy: Privilegio.
Hidden Agenda (S.Afr) the label for a range of wines produced by the Hidden Valley winery, Stellenbosch, Western Cape.
Hidden Brewery [The] (Eng) a brewery (established 2003). (Add): Wylye Road, Dinton, Salisbury, Wiltshire SP3 5EU. Brews: Hidden Depths 4.6% alc by vol., Hidden Fantasy 4.6% alc by vol., Hidden Pint 3.8% alc by vol., Hidden Quests 4.2% alc by vol., Hidden Spring 4.5% alc by vol., Old Scrum 4.1% alc by vol. Website: http://www.thehiddenbrewery.co.uk 'E'mail: sales@thehiddenbrewery.co.uk
Hidden Spring (USA) a natural spring mineral water from Vermont.
Hidden Spring Vineyards (Eng) a vineyard. (Add): Cross Road, Horam, East Sussex. Produces Sussex Sunset (a rosé wine), Dark Fields (50% Pinot noir and 50% Dunkelfelder).
Hidden Treasure (Eng) a classic bitter ale (part of the Classics Range) brewed by the Hydes Brewery, Manchester.
Hidden Valley (S.Afr) a winery (established 1995) based in Die Boord, Stellenbosch, Western Cape. 30ha. Grape varieties: Cabernet sauvignon, Chenin blanc, Merlot, Pinotage, Sauvignon blanc, Shiraz, Viognier. Labels: CWG Auction Reserve, Hidden Agenda. Website: http://www.hiddenvalleywines.com
Hidden Valley (S.Afr) the label for range of wines produced by the Luddite Wines winery, Walker Bay, Western Cape.
Hielo (Sp) ice.
Hierochloe Odorata (Pol) the name given to the grass used in Zubrowka vodka, also known as Zubrowka grass or Bison grass.
Hierro [El] (Sp) one of the islands of Santa Cruz de Tenerife, Canarias. A D.O. wine zone of Tenerife. *See also* Gomera (La), Palma (La).
Hiervandaan (S.Afr) the label for a red wine (Carignan, Grenache noir, Mourvèdre, Shiraz and Viognier blend) produced by the Solms-Delta winery, Franschhoek, Western Cape.
High (Eng) a term used to denote a state of altered consciousness induced by alcohol (or drugs).
High and Dry (Eng) a London Dry gin produced by

the Booth's Distilling Company (part of The Distillers C°. Ltd).
High and Dry (S.Am) a brand of demerara rum produced in Guyana by the Guyana Distilleries.
Highball (Cktl) spirit, ginger ale or soda served in a tall glass with ice.
Highball Glass (Eng) a straight-sided glass used for holding highballs. Of 150mls, 200mls, 250mls or 300mls (6fl.ozs, 8fl.ozs, 10fl.ozs or 12fl.ozs) capacity. *See also* Hi-Ball.
High Constantia (S.Afr) a winery (established 1683) based in Groot Constantia. (Add): Puck's Glen, Groot Constantia Road, Constantia, Western Cape. 7ha. Grape varieties: Cabernet franc, Cabernet sauvignon, Chardonnay, Pinot noir. Labels: Clos André, Sebastiaan.
High Commissioner (Scot) a brand of Scotch whisky 37.5% alc by vol. from Glen Catrine.
High Culture System (Aus) a system of vine training invented by Professor Lenz Moser. Vines are planted 1.2 metres apart in rows 3 metres apart and trailed on wires 1.2 metres above the ground. Hochkultur. *see* Lenz-Moser (Dr).
High Diver (Cktl) 1 measure Montezuma Silver Tequila in a highball on ice, top with lemonade and a slice of lemon.
High Dyke (Eng) a 3.9% alc by vol. ale brewed by the Oldershaw Brewery, Lincolnshire.
High Energy Mix (Eng) a 5.5% alc by vol. vodka energy drink. Produced by Imperial Drinks, Hertfordshire.
Higher Alcohols (Eng) also known as Fusil Oils, are more toxic alcohols than Ethyl alcohol. They include: Amyl, Propyl, Isobutyl.
Highfield Estate (N.Z) a 13ha. winery based at Brookby Road, Blenheim, Marlborough. Grape varieties: Chardonnay, Sauvignon blanc, Cabernet sauvignon, Merlot. Still and traditional method sparkling wines.
High 5ive (S.Afr) the label for a red wine (Cabernet franc, Cabernet sauvignon, Merlot, Petit verdot and Shiraz blend) produced by the Virgin Earth winery, Little Karoo, Western Cape.
High Force (Eng) a smooth strong pale ale 6.2% alc by vol./1060 O.G. from the Butterknowle Brewery, Lynesack, near Bishop Auckland, County Durham.
High Gables (S.Afr) the export label for wine produced by the Klein Constantia Estate winery, Constantia, Western Cape.
Highgate & Walsall Brewing Company (Eng) a brewery (established 1898) formerly part of Bass, Mitchells and Butlers. (Bought out Walsall's Highgate Brewery). Now privately owned as the Highgate Brewery Ltd. Brewed: Highgate Dark Mild 3.2% alc by vol. Highgate Bitter 3.7% alc by vol. Highgate Old Ale 5.3% alc by vol. Saddlers Celebrated Best Bitter 4% alc by vol. Fox's Nob 3.5% alc by vol. keg Balti Beer plus a 4.6% alc by vol. Lager. *see* Higate Brewery Ltd.
Highgate Brewery Ltd (Eng) a brewery. (Add): Sandymount Road, Walsall, West Midlands WS1

3AP. Brews: B.Fuggled 6% alc by vol., Beezone Honey Beer 3.8% alc by vol., Chaser Stout 5.1% alc by vol., Crystal Ice 5% alc by vol., Davenports Original bitter 4% alc by vol., Davenports Premium Bitter 4.5% alc by vol., Englands Glory 4.3% alc by vol., FGL Lager 4.2% alc by vol., Fox's Nob 4.4% alc by vol., Fox's Nob (bottle) 4% alc by vol., Highgate Dark Mild 3.2% alc by vol., Highgate Lager 3.8% alc by vol., Highgate Mild 3.2% alc by vol., Highgate Special Bitter 3.8% alc by vol., Highgate Whisky Beer 4.6% alc by vol., IPA 4.4% alc by vol., Old Ale Winter Warmer 5.35% alc by vol., Red Dragon 4% alc by vol., Saddlers Premium Bitter 4.3% alc by vol. Website: http://www.highgatebrewery.com 'E'mail: info@highgatebrewery.com

Highgate Bitter (Eng) a 3.7% alc by vol. bitter brewed by Highgate & Walsall Brewing Company. Originally called Fox's Nob.

Highgate Dark (Eng) a dark mild 3.2% alc by vol. from the Highgate & Walsall Brewing Company. Now known as Highgate Dark Mild.

Highgate Dark Mild (Eng) the new name for Highgate Dark.

Highgate Mild (Eng) a mild beer 1036 O.G. brewed by the Highgate & Walsall Brewing Company. Renamed Highgate Dark Mild.

Highgate Old Ale (Eng) a 5.1% alc by vol. winter warmer ale brewed by the Highgate & Walsall Brewing Company (draught and bottled).

High Gravity Brewing (USA) a method of brewing to a high strength and then diluting to required strength, used for the making of light beers.

High Hat Cocktail (Cktl) ¾ measure Scotch whisky, ¼ measure cherry brandy, ½ measure lemon juice. Shake over ice, strain into a cocktail glass and dress with a cherry.

High House Farm Brewery (Eng) a brewery (established 2003). (Add): Matfen, Newcastle-upon-Tyne, Tyne & Wear NE20 0RG. Brews: Auld Hemp 3.8% alc by vol., Nel's Best 4.2% alc by vol. Website: http://www.highhousefarmbrewery.co.uk 'E'mail: info@highhousefarmbrewery.co.uk

High Juice (Eng) a range of orange and lemon squashes from Countrywide Catering Distributors using the Country Range label. Sold in 5 litre packs they contain 35% natural fruit juice.

Highland (Afr) a natural spring mineral water (established 1997) from Uganda. Mineral contents (milligrammes per litre): Sodium 19.5mg/l, Calcium 14mg/l, Magnesium 10.8mg/l, Potassium 3.4mg/l, Chlorides 20mg/l, Nitrates 5mg/l. pH 7.1

Highland Coffee (Liq.Coffee) using a measure of Drambuie.

Highland Command (Scot) a brand of blended Scotch whisky sold through the Victoria Wines Off Licenses 37.2% alc by vol.

Highland Cooler (Cktl) into a collins glass place ½ teaspoon of powdered sugar and a little water. Stir, add ice and 40mls (⅓ gill) Scotch whisky, top with ginger ale and decorate with a spiral of orange peel over the rim of the glass.

Highland Cream (Scot) a limited edition, 18 year old, blended Scotch whisky (at least 45% malt whisky) produced by Teacher's.

Highland Daisy (Cktl) ⅔ measure Scotch whisky, 1 measure gomme syrup, juice ½ lime, lemon and an orange. Serve over crushed ice in a goblet, decorate with strips of lime, lemon and orange zest.

Highland Distilleries C°. (Scot) a company that through other subsidiaries owns Scottish Cream blends, Red Hackle and Langs. Brands include Bunnahabhain, Highland Park, Tamdhu, and The Famous Grouse.

Highlander (Ger) a 5.3% alc by vol. rauchbier (smoked beer) brewed by the Henninger Brauerei, Frankfurt am Main using whisky malt.

Highlander (Scot) a 4.8% alc by vol. ale brewed by Fyne Ales Ltd., Argyll.

Highlander Whisky Beer (Eng) a 4.6% alc by vol. beer brewed by the Highgate Brewery Ltd., West Midlands.

Highland Fling [1] (Cktl) ⅔ measure Scotch whisky, ⅓ measure sweet vermouth, 2 dashes orange bitters. Stir over ice, strain into a cocktail glass and top with an olive.

Highland Fling [2] (Cktl) 1 measure Scotch whisky, 1 measure strong assam tea (cold), ½ measure lemon juice, dash gomme syrup. Stir over ice, strain into a highball glass, top with ginger ale and serve with straws.

Highland Gathering [The] (Scot) a special reserve Scotch whisky from Lombard Scotch Whisky Ltd. in Glasgow. Produce an 8, 12 and 21 year old.

Highland Harvest (Scot) an organic Scotch whisky 40% alc by vol. (a blend of 3 organic malts and an organic grain whiskey) produced by the Organic Spirits Company, Haddington.

Highland Malts (Scot) a single malt whiskies produced north of a line drawn from Greenock to Dundee (light and full-flavoured whiskies).

Highland Manor Winery (USA) a winery based in Jamestown, Tennessee. Wines produced from American vines.

Highland Milk Punch (Cktl) 40mls (⅛ gill) Scotch whisky, 125mls (1gill) milk, dash gomme syrup. Shake well over ice, strain into a large goblet, top with grated nutmeg.

Highland Park (Scot) a single highland malt whisky distillery situated outside Kirkwall in the Isle of Orkney. Owned by James Grant and C°. Produces 12 year old malt at 40% alc by vol., 14 year old 46% alc by vol., 18 year old at 43% alc by vol. and 25 year old at 53.5% alc by vol. A 1967 vintage and 1968 vintage at 43% alc by vol. Part of Highland Distilleries C°.

Highland Poacher (Scot) a blended Scotch whisky for Chalié Richards 40% alc by vol.

Highland Pride (Scot) the label of a blended Scotch whisky.

Highland Prince (Eng) a blended Scotch whisky produced by Edward Butler in London 37.2% alc by vol.

Highland Queen (Scot) a blended Scotch whisky produced by MᵃᶜDonald and Muir. Has a high proportion of Glenmorangie and Glen Moray in the blend 40% alc by vol.

Highland Queen Grand Reserve (Scot) a 15 year old de luxe Scotch whisky produced by MᵃᶜDonald and Muir 40% alc by vol.

Highland Queen Supreme (Scot) a 21 year old rare de luxe Scotch whisky produced by MᵃᶜDonald and Muir 40% alc by vol.

Highland Spring (Scot) a still and carbonated natual water bottled in the Ochil Hills, Perthshire. (Add): Highland Spring, Blackford, Perthshire. Mineral contents (milligrammes per litre): Sodium 4.5mg/l, Calcium 32mg/l, Magnesium 8mg/l, Potassium 0.5mg/l, Bicarbonates 133mg/l, Chlorides 5mg/l, Sulphates 7mg/l, Nitrates <2mg/l. pH 7.8 Website: http://www.highland-spring.com

High Level Brown Ale (Eng) a deep-coloured strong brown ale, sold in cans and bottles. Brewed by the Federation Brewery, Tyneside.

High Life Lager (Eng) a lager beer 1032 O.G. brewed by the Ind Coope Brewery in Romford, Essex.

Highlights (Eng) a brand-name™ of a powdered chocolate drink produced by Cadburys (part of Kenco-Typhoo).

Highly Prestigious Ale (Eng) *abbr*: HPA an ale 4.5% alc by vol. brewed by the Hydes Brewery, Manchester, Lancs.

High Mountain Supreme (W.Ind) one of the three grades of coffee produced on Jamaica, a pure coffee of fine body, acidity and aroma. *See also* Blue Mountain and Red Mountain.

High Peak Porter (Eng) a porter produced by the Whim Brewery in Derbyshire.

High Point Brewing Cº Inc (USA) a brewery. (Add): 22 Park Place, Butler, New Jersey 07405. Brews beers and lager. Website: http://www.ramsteinerbeer.com 'E'mail: comments@ramsteinerbeer.com

High Proof (USA) spirits which have alcohol content near absolute alcohol. e.g. gin, vodka, brandy used for fortification of wines.

High Quality Mineral Water (Chi) a natural spring mineral water. Mineral contents (milligrammes per litre): Sodium 65mg/l, Potassium 14.5mg/l, Bicarbonates 260mg/l, Silicates 37.3mg/l. pH 7.4

High Road (Eng) a 7.3% alc by vol. strong ale brewed by the Beckstones Brewery, Cumbria.

High Roast (Eng) a dark roasted coffee in which the bitter aspects of the coffee are accentuated. Much of the original flavour is lost.

High Street Mild (Eng) a cask-conditioned mild ale 1035 O.G. brewed by the Brewhouse Brewery in Dorset.

High Summer Bitter (Eng) a 4.6% alc by vol. bitter from the McMullen Brewery, Hertfordshire.

High Tea (Eng) an early evening substantial meal (usually cooked) at which tea is served as the beverage instead of alcohol.

High-Toned (Eng) describes a wine as having a bouquet with a volatile character.

High Tor (USA) a vineyard based in the Hudson River Valley. Produces red and rosé wines from hybrid grapes and white wine from the Delaware grape.

Highway (Eng) a low-alcohol ale 1% alc by vol. brewed by the Elgood Brewery, Wisbech, Cambridgeshire, the alcohol is removed by reverse osmosis.

Highwaymans (Eng) a vineyard estate near Risby, Bury St. Edmunds in Suffolk. 10ha. Owned by Macrae Farms. Grape varieties: Müller-Thurgau, Pinot noir and others. *see* Abbey Knight.

High Weald Winery (Eng) the first winery in the U.K. founded by Cº. Lindlar to provide a marketing and wine-making consultancy service. (Add): Little Telpits Farm, Grafty Green, Kent.

High Wine (S.Am) a brand of demerara rum produced in Guyana by the Guyana Distilleries.

High Wines (Eng) the useful spirits obtained in distillation after the heads and tails have been removed.

Highwood Brewery (Eng) a brewery (established 1995). (Add): Melton Highway, Barnetby, North East Lincolnshire DN38 6AA. Brews: Tom Wood's Best Bitter 3.5% alc by vol, Bomber County 3.5% alc by vol., Fathers Pride 4.5% alc by vol., Jolly Ploughman 5% alc by vol., Old Timber 4.5% alc by vol., Harvest Bitter 4.3% alc by vol (made with honey)., Jolly Ploughman 5% alc by vol., Shepherd's Delight 4.3% alc by vol. Website: http://www.tom-wood.com 'E'mail: tomwood@tom-wood.com

Hignin (Fr) an alternative name for the Syrah grape. *See also* Hignin noir.

Hignin Noir (Fr) an alternative name for the Syrah grape. *See also* Hignin.

Higsons Bitter (Eng) a bitter beer brewed by the Castle Eden Brewery in County Durham.

Higsons Brewery (Eng) a brewery based in Liverpool, Lancashire. Noted for Stingo 1078 O.G. bottled beer and Prost Lager 1031 O.G. Is owned by Faxe Jyske Breweries, Denmark.

Hijos (Sp) lit: 'sons of'.

Hijos de A. Barceló (Sp) a producer and exporter of Málaga, Ribera del Duero (Viña Mayor).

Hijos de Alberta Gutiérrez (Sp) a noted winery based in Serrada, Valladolid, north-western Spain.

Hijos de Antonio Barceló (Sp) a winery based in the D.O.Ca. Rioja. Label: Glorioso. Website: http://www.habarcelo.es 'E'mail: harbarcelo@ harbarcelo.es

Hijos de José Suárez Villalba (Sp) a producer and exporter of Málaga.

Hilchenfest (Ger) a Rheingau wine festival held at Lorch in June.

Hildebrand Brauerei (Ger) a brewery based in Pfungstadt. Brews: Pfungstädter Edel Pils.

Hildenbrand Wine & Olive Estate (S.Afr) a winery (established 1998) based in Wellington, Western Cape. 18ha. Grape varieties: Cabernet sauvignon, Chardonnay, Chenin blanc, Sémillon, Shiraz. Label: Stellenbosch. Website: http://www.wine-estate-hildenbrand.co.za

Hildegardisberg (Ger) vineyard (Anb): Rheinhessen.

H

(Ber): Bingen. (Gro): Adelberg. (Vil): Bermersheim v.d.H.

Hildegardisbrünnchen (Ger) vineyard (Anb): Nahe. (Ber): Kreuznach. (Gro): Schlosskapelle. (Vil): Bingen-Bingerbrück.

Hilden Ale (Ire) *see* Hilden Brewery.

Hilden Brewery (Ire) a brewery (established 1981) based in Lisburn, near Belfast. Noted for cask-conditioned Hilden Ale 1040 O.G. (also sold in bottle as a naturally conditioned ale).

Hildon (Eng) a still and sparkling natural spring mineral water from the Hildon Estate, Hampshire. Mineral contents (milligrammes per litre): Sodium 7.7mg/l, Calcium 97mg/l, Magnesium 1.7mg/l, Bicarbonates 136mg/l, Chlorides 16mg/l, Sulphates 4mg/l, Fluorides <0.02mg/l, Nitrates 26.5mg/l.

Hiliostos (Eng) a 5% alc by vol. special pale ale from Tigertops Brewery, Sheffield.

Hill & Dale (S.Afr) a winery based in Stellenbosch, Western Cape. Grape varieties: Cabernet sauvignon, Chardonnay, Merlot, Pinotage, Sauvignon blanc, Shiraz. Website: http://www.hillanddale.co.za

Hill Billy Highball (Cktl) 50mls (2fl.ozs) corn whiskey served over ice in a highball glass. Top with sparkling mineral water and a twist of lemon peel juice.

Hill Country Appellation (USA) one of six A.V.A. wine regions based in Texas. Has 15000 square miles of vineyards.

Hillcrest Estate (S.Afr) a winery (established 2002) based in Durbanville, Western Cape. 25ha. Grape varieties: Cabernet sauvignon, Chardonnay, Merlot, Sauvignon blanc. Produces varietal wines.

Hillcrest Vineyard (USA) a winery based in Roseburg, Oregon in the Pacific North-West. 12ha. Noted for Riesling and bottle-fermented Cabernet sauvignon..

Hillcrest Spring Water (USA) a natural spring mineral water from Hillcrest Spring Water Inc., Big Horn range, Wyoming. Mineral contents (milligrammes per litre): Calcium 47.2mg/l, Magnesium 16.4mg/l, Potassium 2.7mg/l, Fluorides 0.17mg/l.

Hillebrand Estate Winery (Can) a winery based in Niagara. Grape varieties: Chardonnay, Riesling.

Hillesheim (Ger) village (Anb): Rheinhessen. (Ber): Nierstein. (Gro): Krötenbrunnen. (Vins): Altenberg, Sonnheil.

Hillfoot Vineyard (Eng) a vineyard based at Beenham, near Reading, Berkshire. 3.25ha. Grape varieties: Müller-Thurgau and Seyval blanc.

Hillgrove Vineyard (Eng) vineyard (established 1977). (Add): Swanmore, Hampshire. 3.5ha. Grape varieties: Madeleine angevine, Müller-Thurgau, Pinot meunier, Seyval blanc, Triomphe d'Alsace and Zweigeitrebe.

Hillinger (Aus) vineyard based in the Neusiedlersee (Add): Untere Hauptstrasse 35, 7093 Jois.

Hill of Gold Winery (Austr) a winery. (Add): Henry Lawson Drive, Mudgee, New South Wales 2850. 12ha. Grape varieties: Chardonnay and Pinot noir.

Hill of Grace (USA) a famous vineyard owned by Henschke and based in the Eden Valley. *See also* Mount Edelstone.

Hill's Absinthe (Czec) a 70% alc by vol. bright green coloured absinthe.

Hillside (Scot) a single highland malt whisky distillery based on the east coast of Scotland 40% alc by vol.

Hillside Select (USA) a red wine (Cabernet sauvignon) produced by the Shafer winery, Napa Valley, California.

Hill-Smith Estate (Austr) a winery. (Add): P.O. Box 10, Angaston, South Australia. 8ha. Grape varieties: Cabernet sauvignon, Chardonnay, Malbec, Riesling, Sauvignon blanc, Sémillon, Shiraz and Viognier. Vineyards: Koomanda, Old Triangle, Old Winery and The Home.

Hill, Thompson and Cº. (Scot) a Scotch whisky distillers. Part of the Glenlivet Distillers. Brand-names include Longman, Queen Anne and Something Special.

Hill Winery (USA) a winery based in the Napa Valley, California. 250ha. Grape varieties: Cabernet sauvignon, Chardonnay. Produces varietal wines.

Hi-Lo (Austr) a diabetic beer brewed by the Toohey's Brewery under the Miller's label.

Hilo (Sp) a flat, oily, faded wine, a diseased wine. (Fr) = graisse.

Hilsbach (Ger) *see* Sinsheim.

Hilton Brewery (Eng) the name of breweries in 2 home-brew public houses in Kent: The Pier Hotel, Gravesend and the Southeastern in Strood. Noted for cask-conditioned Buccaneer 1065 O.G Clipper 1040 O.G. Gravedigger 1050 O.G. Lifebuoy 1075 O.G. and Pirate Porter 1036 O.G.

Hilton Glasses (Eng) a brand-name for a style of glasses produced by the Dema Glass Company.

Hilzingen (Ger) village (Anb): Baden. (Ber): Bodensee. (Gro): Sonnenufer. (Vin): Elisabethenberg.

Himalaia (Bra) a slightly acidic natural spring mineral water from Fonte da Capela. Mineral contents (milligrammes per litre): Sodium 0.2mg/l, Calcium 0.3mg/l, Magnesium 0.31mg/l, Potassium 2.02mg/l, Bicarbonates 5.42mg/l, Chlorides 0.153mg/l, Sulphates 0.04mg/l, Fluorides 0.024mg/l, Nitrates 0.39mg/l. pH 5.4

Himalayan [1] (Ind) a natural spring mineral water. Mineral contents (milligrammes per litre): Sodium 20mg/l, Calcium 62mg/l, Magnesium 15mg/l, Potassium 4mg/l, Bicarbonates 263mg/l, Chlorides 8mg/l, Fluorides 0.2mg/l, Nitrates 4mg/l. pH 7.3

Himalayan [2] (Ind) a natural spring mineral water. Mineral contents (milligrammes per litre): Sodium 8.6mg/l, Calcium 49mg/l, Magnesium 35mg/l, Potassium 1.1mg/l, Bicarbonates 246mg/l, Chlorides 8mg/l, Fluorides 0.9mg/l, Nitrates <0.01mg/l. pH 7.7

Himalayan [3] (Ind) a natural spring mineral water. Mineral contents (milligrammes per litre): Sodium mg/l, Calcium 15mg/l, Magnesium

19mg/l, Potassium 2mg/l, Bicarbonates 210mg/l, Chlorides 22mg/l, Fluorides 0.2mg/l, Nitrates 4mg/l. pH 7.6

Himalayan Dew (Nep) a natural spring mineral water (established 2004) from Matatirtha, Nepal.

Himalayan Natural Spring (Nep) a still natural spring mineral water from Mount Langtang, Himalaya, Nepal. Mineral contents (milligrammes per litre): Sodium 0.9mg/l, Calcium 1.4mg/l, Magnesium 0.47mg/l, Potassium 0.7mg/l, Bicarbonates 4.3mg/l, Chlorides 3.34mg/l, Sulphates 0.2mg/l, Nitrates 1.11mg/l. pH 6.8

Himbeer (USA) a raspberry-flavoured liqueur 30% alc by vol.

Himbeergeist (Ger) an eau-de-vie made from raspberries 32% alc by vol.

Himmelacker (Ger) vineyard (Anb): Rheinhessen. (Ber): Wonnegau. (Gro): Sybillenstein. (Vil): Dantenheim.

Himmelberg (Ger) vineyard (Anb): Baden. (Ber): Badische Bergstrasse/Kraichgau. (Gro): Stiftsberg. (Vil): Michelfeld.

Himmelchen (Ger) vineyard (Anb): Ahr. (Ber): Walporzheim/Ahrtal. (Gro): Klosterberg. (Vil): Walporzheim.

Himmelgarten (Ger) vineyard (Anb): Nahe. (Ber): Kreuznach. (Gro): Kronenberg. (Vil): Bad Kreuznach (ortsteil Ippesheim).

Himmelreich (Aus) a vineyard area on the banks of the River Danube in the Kremstal region.

Himmelreich (Aus) a vineyard site on the banks of the River Danube situated in the Wachau region, Niederösterreich.

Himmelreich (Ger) vineyard (Anb): Baden. (Ber): Badische Bergstrasse/Kraichgau. (Gro): Mannaberg. (Vin): Ubstadt-Weiher (ortsteil Stettfeld).

Himmelreich (Ger) vineyard (Anb): Baden. (Ber): Badische Bergstrasse/Kraichgau. (Gro): Mannaberg. (Vil): Zeutern.

Himmelreich (Ger) vineyard (Anb): Mosel-Saar-Ruwer. (Ber): Bernkastel. (Gro): Münzlay. (Vil): Graach.

Himmelreich (Ger) vineyard (Anb): Mosel-Saar-Ruwer. (Ber): Bernkastel. (Gro): Münzlay. (Vil): Zeltingen-Rachtig.

Himmelreich (Ger) vineyard (Anb): Mosel-Saar-Ruwer. (Ber): Zell/Mosel. (Gro): Grafschaft. (Vil): St. Aldegund.

Himmelreich (Ger) vineyard (Anb): Pfalz. (Ber): Mittelhaardt-Deutsche Weinstrasse. (Gro): Kobnert. (Vil): Herxheim/Berg.

Himmelreich (Ger) vineyard (Anb): Württemberg. (Ber): Remstal-Stuttgart. (Gro): Wartbühl. (Vil): Baach.

Himmelreich (Ger) vineyard (Anb): Württemberg. (Ber): Remstal-Stuttgart. (Gro): Wartbühl. (Vil): Hertmannsweiler.

Himmelreich (Ger) vineyard (Anb): Württemberg. (Ber): Württembergisch Unterland. (Gro): Lindelberg. (Vil): Langenbeutlingen.

Himmelreich (Ger) vineyard (Anb): Württemberg.

(Ber): Württembergisch Unterland. (Gro): Lindelberg. (Vil): Siebeneich.

Himmelreich (Ger) vineyard (Anb): Württemberg. (Ber): Württembergisch Unterland. (Gro): Staufenberg. (Vil): Gundelsheim.

Himmelsberger (Ger) a natural spring mineral water. Mineral contents (milligrammes per litre): Sodium 15.7mg/l, Calcium 40.5mg/l, Magnesium 8.4mg/l, Potassium 2.4mg/l, Bicarbonates 195mg/l, Chlorides 3.3mg/l, Sulphates 2mg/l.

Himmelsberger Classic Quelle (Ger) a natural spring mineral water. Mineral contents (milligrammes per litre): Sodium 37.2mg/l, Calcium 48.6mg/l, Magnesium 8.3mg/l, Bicarbonates 257mg/l, Chlorides 15.3mg/l.

Himmelstadt (Ger) village (Anb): Franken. (Ber): Maindreieck. (Gro): Rosstal. (Vin): Kelter.

Himmelsteige (Aus) the brand-name of a white wine produced in the Wachau region from Grüner veltliner grapes.

Himmelthal (Ger) vineyard (Anb): Rheinhessen. (Ber): Nierstein. (Gro): Vogelsgärten. (Vil): Guntersblum.

Hinckley Springs (USA) a natural spring mineral water brand.

Hine (Fr) a Cognac producer. (Add): Cognac Hine S.A, 16 Quai de l'Orangerie, 16200 Jarnac. Produces Antique 25 year old, Old Vintage 30–35 year old, Triomphe 40 year old, Rare and Delicate V.S.O.P., Signature and a family vintage Cognac.

Hine Antique (Fr) a famous brand of Cognac (average 20–25 years old) produced by Hine.

Hi Nikka (Jap) a brand of whiskey produced by the Nikka Distilleries.

Hinkelstein (Ger) vineyard (Anb): Nahe. (Ber): Kreuznach. (Gro): Kronenberg. (Vil): Bad Kreuznach.

Hinkley and Schmidt (USA) a natural spring mineral water from Palomar Mountain, Southern Carolina. Mineral contents (milligrammes per litre): Sodium 12mg/l, Calcium 16mg/l, Magnesium 6mg/l, Potassium 4.2mg/l, Bicarbonates 80mg/l, Chlorides 9mg/l, Sulphates 10mg/l. pH 7.6

Hinman Vineyards (USA) a winery (established 1979) based in Oregon. Grape varieties: Chardonnay, Pinot gris, Gewürztraminer, Pinot noir, late-harvest Riesling.

Hintenaus (Aus) a vineyard site based on the banks of the River Kamp situated in the Kamptal region.

Hinter der Burg (Aus) a vineyard site on the banks of the River Danube situated in the Wachau region, Niederösterreich.

Hintere Klinge (Aus) vineyard (Anb): Württemberg. (Ber): Remstal-Stuttgart. (Gro): Sonnenbühl. (Vil): Weinstadt (ortsteil Endersbach).

Hintere Pointen (Aus) a vineyard area on the banks of the River Danube in the Kremstal region.

Hinterer Berg (Ger) vineyard (Anb): Württemberg. (Ber): Remstal-Stuttgart. (Gro): Weinsteige. (Vil): Fellbach.

Hinterkirch (Ger) vineyard (Anb): Rheingau. (Ber):

H

Johannisberg. (Gro): Steil. (Vil): Assmannshausen-Aulhausen.

Hinterkirschen (Aus) a vineyard site on the banks of the River Danube situated in the Wachau region, Niederösterreich.

Hinterland (S.Afr) the label for a range of wines produced by the Hartswater Wine Cellar winery, Northern Cape.

Hinterseiber (Aus) a vineyard site on the banks of the River Danube situated in the Wachau region, Niederösterreich.

Hinters Kirchel (Aus) a vineyard area on the banks of the River Danube in the Kremstal region.

Hinzerling Vineyards (USA) a winery based in Prosser, Washington. 9ha. Grape varieties: Cabernet sauvignon, Chardonnay, Gewürztraminer and Riesling. Produces varietal wines.

Hip Flask (Eng) a small, flat bottle of glass or metal used to carry spirits in the pocket. Approximately 175mls–300mls (6fl.ozs–10fl.ozs) capacity. see Flasket.

Hipperich (Ger) vineyard (Anb): Nahe. (Ber): Kreuznach. (Gro): Schlosskapelle. (Vil): Guldental.

Hipping (Ger) vineyard (Anb): Rheinhessen. (Ber): Nierstein. (Gro): Rehbach. (Vil): Nierstein.

Hippocras (Eng) the name of a mead produced in Cornwall.

Hippocras (Gre) an ancient (fifth century B.C) Greek wine made by Hippocrates, was flavoured with cinnamon and honey often mentioned in poetry. see Hippocrates' Sleeve.

Hippocrates' Sleeve (Gre) the name given to the woollen filter through which the wine Hippocras was passed to clear it of its debris.

Hiram Walker (Can) a large Company that owns many brewing, distilling and wine-making outlets including Ardbeg, Glencadam, Miltonduff-Glenlivet. Now part of Allied-Domecq Spirits and Wine.

Hirondelle (Cyp) a brand-name for wines produced by the Etko C°.

Hirondelle (Eng) the brand-name of Hedges and Butler's Liebfraumilch QbA.

Hirsch (Aus) a winery (16ha) based in the Kamptal region. (Add): 3493 Kammern 25. Grape varieties: Cabernet sauvignon, Grüner veltliner, Pinot blanc, Pinot noir, Riesling, Zweigelt.

Hirschau (Ger) village (Anb): Württemberg. see Kressbronn am Bodensee Tübingen.

Hirschberg (Ger) vineyard (Anb): Baden. (Ber): Badische Frankenland. (Gro): Tauberklinge. (Vil): Werbach.

Hirschgarten (Ger) a famous 7000 seater beer garden in Münich that serves Augustiner beers.

Hirschlay (Ger) vineyard (Anb): Mosel-Saar-Ruwer. (Ber): Bernkastel. (Gro): Probstberg. (Vil): Longuich.

Hirschquelle Vital (Ger) a natural spring mineral water from D-75385 Bad Teinach-Zavelstein, Schwarzwald. Mineral contents (milligrammes per litre): Sodium 261mg/l, Calcium 216mg/l, Magnesium 29.2mg/l, Potassium 11.6mg/l, Bicarbonates 1343mg/l, Chlorides 41.5mg/l, Sulphates 85mg/l, Nitrates 1.7mg/l, Fluorides 1.04mg/l.

Hirtengarten (Ger) vineyard (Anb): Mosel-Saar-Ruwer. (Ber): Obermosel. (Gro): Gipfel. (Vil): Oberbillig.

Hirtenhain (Ger) vineyard (Anb): Nahe. (Ber): Kreuznach. (Gro): Kronnenberg. (Vil): Bad Kreuznach (ortsteil Bosenheim).

Hirtzberger (Aus) a winery (12ha) based in the Wachau. (Add): Kremsere Strasse 8, 3620 Spitz an der Donau. Grape varieties: Grüner veltliner, Pinot blanc, Pinot gris, Riesling. Produces a range of dry and sweet (botrytised) wines.

Hiru 3 Racimos (Sp) a special red wine made from vines pruned to yield only 3 bunches of grapes each produced by Bodegas Luis Cañas, Rioja.

Hirzenach (Ger) village (Anb): Mittelrhein. (Ber): Rheinburgengau. (Gro): Not yet assigned. (Vin): Probsteiberg.

His Eminence's Choice (Port) an old tawny Port, a brand-name of the Delaforce Company.

His Master's Choice (S.Afr) the label for a white wine (Viognier) and Red wine (Shiraz) produced by the Ridgeback Wines winery, Paarl, Western Cape.

Hispano (Sp) a solera brandy produced by Domecq. See also San Quintin.

Hissar-Krasnovo (Bul) an alkaline natural spring mineral water (established BC2000) from Hissaria. Mineral contents (milligrammes per litre): Sodium 88.8mg/l, Calcium 2.7mg/l, Potassium 0.6mg/l, Bicarbonates 97.6mg/l, Chlorides 10.7mg/l, Sulphates 67.1mg/l, Fluorides 5.6mg/l, Silicates 57.7mg/l. pH 9.1 Website: http://www.bulgarianwater.com

Histidine (Eng) an amino acid found in wine that is formed by the yeast.

Hi Summer (Eng) a 3.2% alc by vol. seasonal light ale brewed by Green Bottle Ltd., Worth Brewery, Keighley, Yorkshire.

H.I.T. (Eng) abbr: see Head Injection Tap™

Hite (S.Kor) a 4.5% alc by vol lager-style beer brewed by the Hite Brewery.

Hitohada (Jap) body temperature, the temperature that saké should be drunk.

Hits the Spot (Eng) a 4% alc by vol. light seasonal golden ale brewed by Hydes Brewery, 46 Moss Lane, West Manchester, Lancashire.

Hitzendorf (Aus) a wine-producing area in Weststeiermark.

Hitzlay (Ger) vineyard (Anb): Mosel-Saar-Ruwer. (Ber): Saar-Ruwer. (Gro): Römerlay. (Vil): Kasel.

Hizo Koshu (Jap) producer of Chozo Saké.

HJT (Austr) abbr: Harry J. Tinson, a wine-maker at Keenan Road, Glenrowan, Victoria whose initials are seen on some labels. Grape varieties: Cabernet sauvignon, Chardonnay, Pinot noir, Riesling.

Hlinskov Cechàch Brewery (Czec) a brewery based in central Czec.

Hlohovec Brewery (Czec) an old brewery based in south-eastern Czec.

H

H.L.P.A. (Eng) *abbr:* Hectolitres of Pure Alcohol.

H.M.R. (USA) *abbr:* Hoffman Mountain Ranch. A small winery based near Paso Robles, San Luis Obispo, California. 50ha. Grape varieties: Cabernet sauvignon, Chardonnay and Zinfandel.

H.O.B. (Eng) *abbr:* Hoskins and Oldfield Bitter a cask-conditioned Bitter 1041 O.G. brewed by the Hoskins and Oldfield Brewery in Leicester.

Hobec (Hol) a strong lager beer 1048 O.G. sold in embossed green glass bottles of 440mls.

Hobdens Wessex Brewery (Eng) a brewery (established 2001). (Add): Farm Cottage, Norton Ferris, Warminster, Wiltshire BA12 7HT. Brews: Best Bitter 4% alc by vol., Big Finnish 9% alc by vol., Burlington Bertie 3.3% alc by vol., Golden Delirious 4.5% alc by vol. 'E'mail: wessexbrewery@tinyworld.co.uk

Hobgoblin (Eng) the name of a beer brewed by Refresh UK plc., Oxfordshire.

Hobgoblin (Eng) a 5.5% alc by vol. bottled real ale from Wychwood Brewery, Witney, Oxfordshire. A malty, fruity chocolate beer. *see* Wychwood Bitter.

Hob Nobs Original (Eng) a single varietal hop ale from Whitbread. Produced using the same ingredients as Hob Nob™ Biscuits: wheat, rolled oats, sugar and raising agent (yeast).

Ho Bryan (Eng) Samuel Pepys' written name for Château Haut Brion (circa 1663).

Hobson's Brewery C° (Eng) a brewery (established 1993). (Add): Cloebury Mortimer, Kidderminster, Worcestershire DY14 8RD. Brews: Hobsons Best Bitter 3.8% alc by vol., Hobsons Manor Ale 4.2% alc by vol., Hobsons Mild 3.2% alc by vol., Old Henry 5.2% alc by vol., Town Crier 4.5% alc by vol. Website: http://www.hobsons-brewery.co.uk

Hobson's Choice (Eng) a 4.1% alc by vol. light golden ale brewed by The City of Cambridge Brewery.

Hoch (Ger) vineyard (Anb): Rheinhessen. (Ber): Nierstein. (Gro): Sankt Alban. (Vil): Bodenheim.

Hochäck (Aus) a vineyard area on the banks of the River Danube in the Kremstal region.

Hochbenn (Ger) vineyard (Anb): Pfalz. (Ber): Mittelhaardt-Deutsche Weinstrasse. (Gro): Hochmess. (Vil): Bad Dürkheim.

Hochberg (Ger) vineyard (Anb): Baden. (Ber): Kaiserstuhl-Tuniberg. (Gro): Vulkanfelsen. (Vil): Jechtingen.

Hochberg (Ger) vineyard (Anb): Franken. (Ber): Mainviereck. (Gro): Not yet assigned. (Vil): Erlenbach a. Main.

Hochberg (Ger) vineyard (Anb): Franken. (Ber): Mainviereck. (Gro): Not yet assigned. (Vil): Klingenberg.

Hochberg (Ger) vineyard (Anb): Rheinhessen. (Ber): Wonnegau. (Gro): Liebfrauenmorgen. (Vil): Worms.

Hochburg (Ger) *see* Emmendingen.

Hochdorf-Assenheim (Ger) village (Anb): Pfalz. (Ber): Mittelhaardt-Deutsche Weinstrasse. (Gro): Hofstück. (Vin): Fuchsloch.

Hochdorf Brauerei (Switz) a small independent brewery based in Hochdorf.

Hochfeinste (Ger) an old term used on wine bottle label to denote '*very finest*' (now illegal).

Hochgericht (Ger) vineyard (Anb): Pfalz. (Ber): Mittelhaardt-Deutsche Weinstrasse. (Gro): Grafenstück. (Vil): Obrigheim.

Hochgericht (Ger) vineyard (Anb): Pfalz. (Ber): Südliche Weinstrasse. (Gro): Trappenberg. (Vil): Altdorf.

Hochgewächs (Ger) superb/superior vineyard or growth.

Hochgrassnitzberg (Aus) a Cru vineyard area situated on the Slovakian border in the Styria region.

Hochheim (Ger) a village in the eastern end of the Rheingau whose wines gave the name 'Hock' to the Rhine wines. The shortened version of 'Hockamore' was the Victorian name for the wines of the district (Queen Victoria's favourite wine). *See also* Hock.

Hochheim (Ger) village (Anb): Rheingau. (Ber): Johannisberg. (Gro): Daubhaus. (Vins): Berg, Domdechaney, Herrnberg, Hofmeister, Hölle, Kirchenstück, Stein, Königin, Viktoriaberg, Reichestal, Sommerheil, Steilweg.

Hochheimer Weinfest (Ger) a Rheingau wine festival held at Hochheim in July.

Hochkultur (Ger) a viticultural system. *see* High Culture and Lenz Moser.

Hochlay (Ger) vineyard (Anb): Mosel-Saar-Ruwer. (Ber): Zell/Mosel. (Gro): Goldbäumchen. (Vil): Cochem.

Hochmess (Ger) grosslage (Anb): Pfalz. (Ber): Mittelhaardt-Deutsche Weinstrasse. (Vils): Bad Dürkheim, Ungstein.

Hochrain (Aus) a vineyard area on the banks of the River Danube in the Kremstal region.

Hochrain (Aus) vineyard areas (2) on the banks of the River Danube situated in the Wachau region, Niederösterreich.

Hochriegel (Aus) a brand of dry sparkling wine produced by Kattus.

Hochsatze (Aus) a vineyard area on the banks of the River Danube in the Kremstal region.

Hochstadt (Ger) village (Anb): Pfalz. (Ber): Südliche Weinstrasse. (Gro): Trappenberg. (Vin): Rotenberg.

Hochstätten (Ger) village (Anb): Nahe. (Ber): Schloss Böckelheim. (Gro): Paradiesgarten. (Vin): Liebesbrunnen.

Höchstes Kreuz (Ger) vineyard (Anb): Nahe. (Ber): Schloss Böckelheim. (Gro): Paradiesgarten. (Vil): Feilbingert.

Hochstrasse (Aus) a vineyard site based on the banks of the River Kamp situated in the Kamptal region.

Hochstrasser (Aus) a vineyard site on the banks of the River Danube situated in the Wachau region, Niederösterreich.

Hochwart (Ger) vineyard (Anb): Baden. (Ber): Bodensee. (Gro): Sonnenufer. (Vil): Reichenau.

Hock (Eng) the former name for a malty dark cask-conditioned mild ale brewed by the Fullers Brewery in London 3.2% alc by vol.

H

Hock (Ger) the mis-spelling of Hochheim. *see* Hoch.

Hockamore (Eng) the seventeenth and eighteenth century spelling of the word Hochheim from which Hock derives. *see* Hochheim.

Hock Cup [1] (Cktl) into a large jug place some ice, 1 measure of Curaçao, 2 measures brandy, 1 bottle Hock (Rhine wine), 1 bottle soda water. Stir well and decorate with fruit in season, mint or borage and cucumber peel.

Hock Cup [2] (Cktl) 1 bottle hock (Rhine wine), 30mls (¼ gill) maraschino, 60mls (½ gill) brandy, 30mls (¼ gill) kümmel, 40mls (⅓ gill) Yellow Chartreuse, 550mls (1 pint) soda water. Stir in a bowl with plenty of ice, strain, serve in large tumblers with lemon, orange and fresh fruit slices on top.

Hockenmühle (Ger) vineyard (Anb): Rheinhessen. (Ber): Bingen. (Gro): Sankt Rochuskapelle. (Vil): Ockenheim.

Hockfeine (Ger) extra fine (now no longer used).

Hockfeinste (Ger) lit: 'best of all', old term for Mosel wines (now no longer used).

Hockhams (Eng) a light apple wine 8.3% alc by vol. from Symonds of Herefordshire.

Hock Sparkler (Cktl) 3 bottles hock (Rhine wine), 1 bottle sekt, 100mls (4fl.ozs) brandy, 1 melon or other fresh fruit. Cube the melon or slice the fruit, place in a large bowl with some sugar and the wine. Leave 1 hour, add sekt and the rest of the ingredients. serve with ice and fruit.

Hockweiler (Ger) village (Anb): Mosel-Saar-Ruwer. (Ber): Saar-Ruwer. (Gro): Römerlay. (Vin): Sites not yet chosen.

Hocus Pocus (Austr) a red (Cabernet sauvignon) wine produced by the Petalon Estate, Western Australia.

Hodge's Weardale Brewhouse (Eng) a micro-brewery. (Add): Crook, County Durham. Brews: Hodge's Cask Ale 4.1% alc by vol. Taken over by Brewlab, beers now brewed under the Darwin Brewery label.

Hoegaarden Brasserie (Bel) a brewery based in Hoegaarden. Noted for Hoegaarden Wit (wheat beer) and Grand Cru. Also known as the De Kluis Brasserie, Hoegaarden.

Hoegaarden Forbidden Fruit (Bel) a strong ale 9% alc by vol. from the De Kluis Brasserie, Hoegaarden.

Hoegaarden Grand Cru (Bel) a strong blonde beer 8.5% alc by vol. from the De Kluis Brasserie, Hoegaarden.

Hoegaarden Speciale (Bel) a 5.6% alc by vol. top-fermented, bottle-conditioned wheat beer brewed by De Kluis Brasserie, Hoegaarden.

Hoegaarden Wit (Bel) a white beer brewed by the De Kluis Brasserie, Hoegaarden. Brewed from wheat and oats and tastes of Curaçao and coriander 5% alc by vol.

Hoeilaart (Bel) a town in Belgium that produces wines from grapes grown under glass, sold and consumed locally.

Hoë Krans Wynmakery (S.Afr) *see* Krans Estate (Die).

Hoe Langer Hoe Liever (Hol) lit: 'the longer the better', a liqueur produced by Van Zuylekom of Amsterdam.

Hoeppslei (Ger) vineyard (Anb): Mosel-Saar-Ruwer. (Ber): Saar-Ruwer. (Gro): Scharzberg. (Vil): Serrig.

Hofberg (Ger) vineyard (Anb): Württemberg. (Ber): Kocher-Jagst-Tauber. (Gro): Kocherberg. (Vil): Möckmühl.

Hofberg (Ger) vineyard (Anb): Württemberg. (Ber): Kocher-Jagst-Tauber. (Gro): Kocherberg. (Vil): Siglingen.

Hofberg (Ger) vineyard (Anb): Württemberg. (Ber): Kocher-Jagst-Tauber. (Gro): Kocherberg. (Vil): Widdern.

Hofberger (Ger) vineyard (Anb): Mosel-Saar-Ruwer. (Ber): Bernkastel. (Gro): Michelsberg. (Vil): Neumagen-Dhron.

Hofbräu Münchnen (Ger) a brewery based in Munich. Brews: Urbräu plus two draught lagers: Hofbräu Premium Bier 5% alc by vol. Hofbräu Export 4.3% alc by vol. Bottled beers: Hofbräu München Dunkelgold 5.5% alc by vol. Hofbräu Pils 4.9% alc by vol. Hofbräu Original 4.9% alc by vol. Hofbräu Weissbier, Münchner Kindl Weissbier.

Hof Brauerei (Switz) a small brewery based in Wil.

Hofbräuhaus (Ger) a brewer of weizen (wheat) beers. *see* H.B. Also can contain a beer celler within the brewery complex.

Hofbräuhaus Brauerei (Ger) a brewery (established 1589) based in Munich. Originally known as the Court Brauerei by Elector William of Bavaria.

Hofen (Ger) village (Anb): Württemberg. (Ber): Remstal-Stuttgart. (Gro): Weinsteige. *see* Stuttgart.

Hofen (Ger) village (Anb): Württemberg. (Ber): Württembergisch Unterland. (Gro): Stromberg. (Vin): Lerchenberg.

Hoffman House Cocktail (Cktl) ⅔ measure dry gin, ⅓ measure dry vermouth, 2 dashes orange bitters. Stir over ice, strain into a cocktail glass and top with an olive.

Hoffmann (Aus) a winery based in Traismauer, Traisental. (Add): Özelt-Hof, Oberndorfer Strasse 41, 3133 Traismauer. Grape varieties include: Grüner veltliner.

Hoffmann Mountain Ranch (USA) *see* H.M.R.

Hoffmans (Austr) a winery. (Add): Para Road, North Para, (P.O. Box. 37), Tanunda, South Australia. 40ha. Grape varieties: Cabernet sauvignon, Frontignan, Rhine riesling and Shiraz.

Hofgarten (Ger) vineyard (Anb): Nahe. (Ber): Kreuznach. (Gro): Kronenberg. (Vil): Bad Kreuznach.

Hofgut (Ger) vineyard (Anb): Nahe. (Ber): Kreuznach. (Gro): Kronenberg. (Vil): Bretzenheim.

Hofkellerei (Ger) wine cellar of a Royal Court.

Hof Lager (Den) a lager beer 1042 O.G. from Carlsberg brewed in Great Britain.

Hofmeister (Ger) vineyard (Anb): Rheingau. (Ber): Johannisberg. (Gro): Daubhaus. (Vil): Hochheim.

Hofmeister Lager (Eng) a keg lager beer 1036 O.G. brewed by Courage. Also a canned version 1032 O.G.

Hofrat (Ger) grosslage (Anb): Franken. (Bers): Maindreieck, Buchbrunn. (Vils): Kitzingen, Mainstockheim, Marktbreit, Repperndorf, Segnitz, Sulzfeld.

Hofstätter [J.] (It) a fine winery based in Rathausplatz, Südtirol.

Hofsteige (Ger) vineyard (Anb): Württemberg. (Ber): Remstal-Stuttgart. (Gro): Hohenneuffen. (Vil): Metzingen.

Hofstetten Brauerei (Aus) a small brewery based in St. Martin.

Hofstraaty Winery (S.Afr) a winery (established 2002) based in Malmesbury, Swartland, Western Cape. Grape varieties: Barbera, Cabernet sauvignon, Merlot, Shiraz. Produces varietal wines.

Hofstadt (Aus) a vineyard site based on the banks of the River Kamp situated in the Kamptal region.

Hofstatt (Aus) vineyard sites (3) based on the banks of the River Kamp situated in the Kamptal region.

Hofstück (Ger) vineyard (Anb): Franken. (Ber): Maindreieck. (Gro): Hofrat. (Vil): Mainstockheim.

Hofstück (Ger) grosslage (Anb): Pfalz. (Ber): Mittelhaardt-Deutsche Weinstrasse. (Vils): Deidesheim, Ellerstadt, Friedelsheim, Gönnheim, Hochdorf-Assenheim, Meckenheim, Niederkirchen, Rödersheim-Gronau, Ruppertsberg.

Hof und Lembach (Ger) village (Anb): Württemberg. (Ber): Württembergisch Unterland. (Gro): Wunnenstein. (Vins): Harzberg, Lichtenberg.

Hofweier (Ger) village (Anb): Baden. (Ber): Ortenau. (Gro): Fürsteneck. (Vin): Kinzigtäler.

Hoggleys (Eng) a brewery (established 2003). (Add): 30 Mill Lane, Kislingbury, Northampton, Northamptonshire NN7 4BD. Brews: Kislingbury Bitter 4% alc by vol., Mill Lane Mild 4% alc by vol., Northamptonshire Bitter 4% alc by vol., Solstice Stout 5% alc by vol. Website: http://www.hoggleysbrewery.co.uk 'E'mail: hoggleys@hotmail.com

Hog Goblin (Eng) a 4.6% alc by vol. ale brewed by the Slaughter House Brewery Ltd., Warwickshire.

Högl [Josef] (Aus) a winery (4.5ha) based in the Wachau. (Add): Viessling 31, 3620 Spitz an der Donau. Grape varieties: Chardonnay, Grüner veltliner, Muskateller, Riesling. Produces a range of dry and sweet (botrytised) wines.

Hog Rider (Eng) a 4% alc by vol. ale brewed by the Slaughter House Brewery Ltd., Warwickshire.

Hog's Back Brewery (Eng) a brewery (established 1992). (Add): Manor Farm, The St, Tongham, Farnham, Surrey GU10 1DE. Brews: Advent Ale 4.4% alc by vol., APB 3.5% alc by vol., Autumn Seer 4.8% alc by vol., Dark Mild 4% alc by vol., Friday 13th 4.2% alc by vol., Hair of the Hog 3.5% alc by vol., Hop Garden Gold 4.6% alc by vol., OTT 6% alc by vol., Rip Snorter 5% alc by vol., Santa's Wobble 7.5% alc by vol., Spring Call 4% alc by vol., Summer This 4.2% alc by vol., Traditional English Ale 4.2% alc by vol., Xhibition Stout 4.5% alc by vol. also Tongham English Ale (T.E.A.) 4.2% alc by vol. Website: http://www.hogsback.co.uk 'E'mail: info@hogsback.co.uk

Hogsback Montaine (S.Afr) a natural spring mineral water (established 1998) from Hogsback, Eastern Cape. Mineral contents (milligrammes per litre): Sodium 7mg/l, Calcium 6.3mg/l, Magnesium 1.7mg/l, Potassium <1mg/l, Chlorides <5mg/l, Sulphates <5mg/l, Fluorides 0.43mg/l, Nitrates <0.3mg/l. pH 6.6

Hogshead (Eng) *abbr*: Hhd a cask 247litres (54gallons).

Hogshead (Fr) cask Bordeaux 220litres (48gallons).

Hogshead (Port) cask 267litres (57gallons).

Hogshead (Sp) cask 256 litres (56gallons).

Hogshead (W.Ind) cask 256litres (56gallons).

Hogue Cellars [The] (USA) a winery (established 1982) based in the Washington State. Grape varieties: Cabernet sauvignon, Chardonnay, Chenin blanc, Gewürztraminer, Merlot, Riesling, Sauvignon blanc, Sémillon.

Hohberg (Ger) vineyard (Anb): Baden. (Ber): Badische Bergstrasse/Kraichgau. (Gro): Stiftsberg. (Vil): Neckarmühlbach.

Hohberg (Ger) vineyard (Anb): Rheinhessen. (Ber): Nierstein. (Gro): Gutes Domtal. (Vil): Weinolsheim.

Hohberg (Ger) vineyard (Anb): Rheinhessen. (Ber): Nierstein. (Gro): Sankt Alban. (Vil): Lörzweiler.

Höhe (Ger) vineyard (Anb): Pfalz. (Ber): Südliche Weinstrasse. (Gro): Bischofskreuz. (Vil): Dammheim.

Hoheburg (Ger) vineyard (Anb): Pfalz. (Ber): Mittelhaardt-Deutsche Weinstrasse. (Gro): Hofstück. (Vil): Ruppertsberg.

Hohe Eiche (Ger) vineyard (Anb): Württemberg. (Ber): Württembergisch Unterland. (Gro): Kirchenweinberg. (Vil): Talheim.

Höhefeld (Ger) village (Anb): Baden. (Ber): Badische Frankenland. (Gro): Tauberklinge. (Vin): Kemelrain.

Hohenäcker (Aus) a vineyard area on the banks of the River Danube in the Kremstal region.

Hohenberg (Ger) grosslage (Anb): Baden. (Ber): Badische Bergstrasse/Kraichgau. (Vils): Berghausen, Bilfingen, Dietlingen, Dürrn, Eisingen, Ellmendingen, Ersingen, Grötzingen, Hohenwettersbach, Karlsruhe-Durlach, Söllingen, Walzbachtal (ortsteil Jöhlingen), Weingarten, Wäschbach.

Hohenberg (Ger) vineyard (Anb): Württemberg. (Ber): Württembergisch Unterland. (Gro): Heuchelberg. (Vil): Pfaffenhofen.

Hohenberg (Ger) vineyard (Anb): Württemberg. (Ber): Württembergisch Unterland. (Gro): Heuchelberg. (Vil): Weiler/Z.

Hohenberg (Ger) vineyard (Anb): Württemberg. (Ber): Württembergisch Unterland. (Gro): Heuchelberg. (Vil): Zaberfeld.

Hohenbühl (Ger) vineyard (Anb): Franken. (Ber): Steigerwald. (Gro): Schlosstück. (Vil): Seinsheim.

Hoheneck (Aus) a vineyard site based on the banks of the River Kamp situated in the Kamptal region.

Hoheneck (Ger) village (Anb): Württemberg. (Ber): Württembergisch Unterland. (Gro): Schalkstein. *see* Ludwigsburg.

Hoheneck (Ger) village (Anb): Württemberg. (Ber):

Württembergisch Unterland. (Gro): Wunnenstein. *see* Ludwigsburg.

Hohenhaslach (Ger) village (Anb): Württemberg. (Ber): Württembergisch Unterland. (Gro): Stromberg. (Vins): Kirchberg, Klosterberg.

Hohenmorgen (Ger) vineyard (Anb): Pfalz. (Ber): Mittelhaardt-Deutsche Weinstrasse. (Gro): Mariengarten. (Vil): Deidesheim.

Hohenneuffen (Ger) grosslage (Anb): Württemberg. (Ber): Remstal-Stuttgart. (Vils): Beuren, Frickenhausen, Kappishäusern, Kohlberg, Linsenhofen, Metzingen, Neuffen, Weilheim.

Hohenrain (Ger) vineyard (Anb): Rheingau. (Ber): Johannisberg. (Gro): Deutelsberg. (Vil): Erbach.

Hohenrain (Ger) vineyard (Anb): Pfalz. (Ber): Südliche Weinstrasse. (Gro): Bischofskreuz. (Vil): Knöringen.

Hohenrain (Ger) a vineyard within the village of Erbach, 17.1ha. (33.9%) of which is proposed to be classified as Erstes Gewächs.

Hohensachsen (Ger) village (Anb): Baden. (Ber): Badische Bergstrasse/Kraichgau. (Gro): Rittersberg. (Vin): Stephansberg.

Hohenstein (Ger) village (Anb): Württemberg. (Ber): Württembergisch Unterland. (Gro): Stromberg. (Vin): Kirchberg.

Hohen-Sülzen (Ger) village (Anb): Rheinhessen. (Ber): Wonnegau. (Gro): Domblick. (Vins): Kirchenstück, Sonnenberg.

Hohenwettersbach (Ger) village (Anb): Baden. (Ber): Badische Bergstrasse/Kraichgau. (Gro): Hohenberg. (Vin): Rosengarten.

Hoher Berg (Ger) vineyard (Anb): Württemberg. (Ber): Kocher-Jagst-Tauber. (Gro): Kocherberg. (Vil): Criesbach.

Hoher Berg (Ger) vineyard (Anb): Württemberg. (Ber): Kocher-Jagst-Tauber. (Gro): Kocherberg. (Vil): Künzelsau.

Hoher Berg (Ger) vineyard (Anb): Württemberg. (Ber): Kocher-Jagst-Tauber. (Gro): Kocherberg. (Vil): Ingelfingen.

Hoher Berg (Ger) vineyard (Anb): Württemberg. (Ber): Kocher-Jagst-Tauber. (Gro): Kocherberg. (Vil): Niedernhall.

Höhere Bundeslehranstalt und Bundesamt für Wein und Obstbau (Aus) the Austrian school of viticulture based in Klosterneuburg. Conducts research on vines and wines and developed grapes such as the Zweigelt. *See also* Klosterneuburg Mostwaage.

Höhereck (Aus) a vineyard site on the banks of the River Danube situated in the Wachau region, Niederösterreich.

Hoher Herrgott (Ger) vineyard (Anb): Baden. (Ber): Badische Frankenland. (Gro): Tauberklinge. (Vil): Külsheim.

Hoher Rain (Aus) a vineyard area on the banks of the River Danube in the Kremstal region.

Höhlchen (Ger) vineyard (Anb): Rheinhessen. (Ber): Nierstein. (Gro): Güldenmorgen. (Vil): Dienheim.

Hohlenstein (Aus) a vineyard site based on the banks of the River Kamp situated in the Kamptal region.

Höhlgraben (Aus) vineyard areas (2) on the banks of the River Danube in the Kremstal region.

Hohnart (Ger) vineyard (Anb): Franken. (Ber): Steigerwald. (Gro): Herrenberg. (Vil): Castell.

Ho Ho (Eng) a 5% alc by vol. cranberry juice RTD drink produced by Bass for Christmas (part of the Hooper's Hooch range).

Hokkaido (Jap) a single malt whiskey produced by Nikka.

Hokkaido Cocktail (Cktl) a 35mls (1½ fl.ozs) dry gin, 25mls (1fl.oz) saké, 10mls (½ fl.oz) Cointreau. Shake well over ice and strain into a cocktail glass.

Hokusetsu (Jap) a small brewery that produces Ongakushu and Junmai Dai-Ginjo Sakés.

Holanda (Sp) a raw grape spirit 65% alc by vol. *See also* Holanda Columna.

Holanda Columna (Sp) a spirit made in the patent (continuous) still at 65%–70% alc by vol. used in brandy production.

HOLBA a.s. (Czec) a brewery (established 1874). (Add): Pivovarská 261, Hanusovice 788 33. Brews beers and lagers. Website: http://www.holba.cz 'E'mail: obchodni@holba.cz

Holdenried Vineyards (USA) a vineyard based in Kelseyville, Lake County, California. 146ha. Grape variety: Cabernet sauvignon.

Holden's Brewery (Eng) a brewery (established 1920). (Add): George Street, Woodsetton, Dudley, West Midlands DY1 4LN. Noted for cask-conditioned Black Country Bitter 1039 O.G. Keg Golden 1039 O.G. and bottled Master Ale 1080 O.G. Holden's Mild. Was known as the Hopden Brewery. Website: http://www.holdensbrewery.co.uk 'E'mail: holdens.brewery@virgin.net

Hole Hearted (Eng) a 4.7% alc by vol. ale brewed by the Oakleaf Brewing C°. Ltd., Hampshire.

Hole-in-One (Cktl) 50mls (2fl.ozs) Scotch whisky, 25mls (1fl.oz) dry vermouth, juice ¼ lemon, 2 dashes orange bitters. Shake over ice and strain into a cocktail glass.

Holes Bay (Eng) a 4.5% alc by vol. cask-conditioned ale brewed by Poole Brewery, Poole.

Holešovice Brewery (Czec) a brewery in Prague that is noted for pale lagers.

Holiday Lager Beer (Can) a lager beer brewed by the Carling O'Keefe Brewery, Toronto.

Höll (Ger) vineyard (Anb): Franken. (Ber): Maindreieck. (Gro): Kirchberg. (Vil): Obereisenheim.

Höll (Ger) vineyard (Anb): Mosel-Saar-Ruwer. (Ber): Zell/Mosel. (Gro): Grafschaft. (Vil): Ediger-Eller.

Höll (Ger) vineyard (Anb): Nahe. (Ber): Kreuznach. (Gro): Pfarrgarten. (Vil): Spabrücken.

Höll (Ger) vineyard (Anb): Nahe. (Ber): Schloss Böckelheim. (Gro): Burgweg. (Vil): Bad Münster a. St. Ebernburg.

Hollabrunn (Aus) a noted wine-producing area in the Weinviertel. Produces light-styled wines.

Holland (Hol) has a small wine-producing area (12

vineyards) around the city of Maastrict. *see* Apostelhoeve and Thiessen.

Hollander Liqueur Cocktail (Cktl) ½ measure Hollands gin, ½ measure grape juice, ½ measure apricot brandy. Shake over ice and strain into cocktail glass.

Hollands (Eng) an early name for gin.

Hollands (Sp) the first distillation of Spanish brandy, it is distilled at a temperature below 65°C and distilled at a higher temperature for the second time.

Hollands Gin (Hol) a clean, malty gin used mainly in the making of cocktails.

Höllberg (Ger) vineyard (Anb): Baden. (Ber): Markgräflerland. (Gro): Burg Neuenfels. (Vil): Hügelheim.

Höllberg (Ger) vineyard (Anb): Baden. (Ber): Markgräflerland. (Gro): Lorettoberg. (Vil): Buggingen.

Höllberg (Ger) vineyard (Anb): Hessische Bergstrasse. (Ber): Starkenburg. (Gro): Rott. (Vil): Bensheim-Auerbach.

Höllberg (Ger) vineyard (Anb): Rheinhessen. (Ber): Bingen. (Gro): Rheingrafenstein. (Vil): Siefersheim.

Hölle (Ger) vineyard (Anb): Mittelrhein. (Ber): Rheinburgengau. (Gro): Burg Hammerstein. (Vil): Hammerstein.

Hölle (Ger) vineyard (Anb): Mosel-Saar-Ruwer. (Ber): Saar-Ruwer. (Gro): Scharzberg. (Vil): Wiltingen.

Hölle (Ger) vineyard (Anb): Mosel-Saar-Ruwer. (Ber): Zell/Mosel. (Gro): Grafschaft. (Vil): Alf.

Hölle (Ger) vineyard (Anb): Nahe. (Ber): Kreuznach. (Gro): Schlosskapelle. (Vil): Burg Layen.

Hölle (Ger) vineyard (Anb): Nahe. (Ber): Kreuznach. (Gro): Schlosskapelle. (Vil): Eckenroth.

Hölle (Ger) vineyard (Anb): Nahe. (Ber): Kreuznach. (Gro): Schlosskapelle. (Vil): Guldental.

Hölle (Ger) vineyard (Anb): Nahe. (Ber): Kreuznach. (Gro): Schlosskapelle. (Vil): Rümmelsheim.

Hölle (Ger) vineyard (Anb): Nahe. (Ber): Kreuznach. (Gro): Schlosskapelle. (Vil): Windesheim.

Hölle (Ger) vineyard (Anb): Nahe. (Ber): Schloss Böckelheim. (Gro): Paradiesgarten. (Vil): Alsenz.

Hölle (Ger) vineyard (Anb): Rheingau. (Ber): Johannisberg. (Gro): Daubhaus. (Vil): Hochheim.

Hölle (Ger) vineyard (Anb): Rheingau. (Ber): Johannisberg. (Gro): Erntebringer. (Vil): Johannisberg.

Hölle (Ger) vineyard (Anb): Rheingau. (Ber): Johannisberg. (Gro): Steinmacher. (Vil): Schierstein.

Hölle (Ger) vineyard (Anb): Rheinhessen. (Ber): Bingen. (Gro): Abtey. (Vil): Sprendlingen.

Hölle (Ger) vineyard (Anb): Rheinhessen. (Ber): Bingen. (Gro): Rheingrafenstein. (Vil): Wöllstein.

Hölle (Ger) vineyard (Anb): Rheinhessen. (Ber): Bingen. (Gro): Rheingrafenstein. (Vil): Wonsheim.

Hölle (Ger) vineyard (Anb): Rheinhessen. (Ber): Bingen. (Gro): Sankt Rochuskapelle. (Vil): Pfaffen-Schwabenheim.

Hölle (Ger) vineyard (Anb): Rheinhessen. (Ber): Nierstein. (Gro): Domherr. (Vil): Saulheim.

Hölle (Ger) vineyard (Anb): Rheinhessen. (Ber): Nierstein. (Gro): Spiegelberg. (Vil): Nierstein.

Hölle (Ger) vineyard (Anb): Rheinhessen. (Ber): Wonnegau. (Gro): Sybillenstein. (Vil): Weinheim.

Hölle (Ger) vineyard (Anb): Pfalz. (Ber): Südliche Weinstrasse. (Gro): Bischofskreuz. (Vil): Gleisweiler.

Hölle (Ger) a vineyard within the village of Hochheim, 48.9ha. (60.1%) of which is proposed to be classified as Erstes Gewächs.

Hölle (Ger) a vineyard within the village of Johannisberg, 20.9ha. (29.7%) of which is proposed to be classified as Erstes Gewächs.

Hollejo (Sp) grapeskin.

Höllenberg (Ger) lit: 'hellish hill'.

Höllenberg (Ger) vineyard (Anb): Nahe. (Ber): Schloss Böckelheim. (Gro): Paradiesgarten. (Vil): Nussbaum.

Höllenberg (Ger) a vineyard within the village of Assmannshausen, 43.4ha. (46.1%) of which is proposed to be classified as Erstes Gewächs.

Höllenberg (Ger) vineyard (Anb): Rheingau. (Ber): Johannisberg. (Gro): Steil. (Vil): Assmannshausen-Aulhausen.

Höllenberg (Ger) vineyard (Anb): Rheinhessen. (Ber): Bingen. (Gro): Kaiserpfalz. (Vil): Heidesheim.

Höllenbrand (Ger) vineyard (Anb): Nahe. (Ber): Kreuznach. (Gro): Kronenberg. (Vil): Bad Kreuznach (ortsteil Bosenheim).

Höllenbrand (Ger) vineyard (Anb): Rheinhessen. (Ber): Wonnegau. (Gro): Bergkloster. (Vil): Gundersheim.

Hollenburgern (Aus) a vineyard area on the banks of the River Danube in the Kremstal region.

Höllenpfad (Ger) vineyard (Anb): Nahe. (Ber): Kreuznach. (Gro): Pfarrgarten. (Vil): Wallhausen.

Höllenpfad (Ger) vineyard (Anb): Nahe. (Ber): Schloss Böckelheim. (Gro): Rosengarten. (Vil): Burgsponheim.

Höllenpfad (Ger) vineyard (Anb): Nahe. (Ber): Schloss Böckelheim. (Gro): Rosengarten. (Vil): Roxheim.

Höllenpfad (Ger) grosslage (Anb): Pfalz. (Ber): Mittelhaardt-Deutsche Weinstrasse. (Vils): Battenberg, Grünstadt, Kleinkarlbach, Mertesheim, Neuleiningen.

Höllenweg (Ger) vineyard (Anb): Rheinhessen. (Ber): Bingen. (Gro): Kaiserpfalz. (Vil): Ingelheim.

Hollerin (Aus) a vineyard site on the banks of the River Danube situated in the Wachau region, Niederösterreich.

Höllhagen (Ger) vineyard (Anb): Baden. (Ber): Markgräflerland. (Gro): Lorettoberg. (Vil): Kirchhofen.

Hollick Wines (Austr) a winery based at Main Road, Coonawarra, South Australia. Grape varieties include: Cabernet sauvignon, Merlot.

Höllisch Feuer (Ger) vineyard (Anb): Württemberg. (Ber): Württembergisch Unterland. (Gro): Stromberg. (Vil): Vaihingen.

Hollister (USA) a noted wine-producing town based in San Benito County, California.

Hollow (Eng) a term applied to wines which lack flavour after showing promise on the nose.

Holly Bush Vineyard (Eng) a vineyard (established 1982) based at Brockenhurst, Hampshire. 0.5ha. Grape variety: Seyval villard.

Holly Spirit (Fr) *see* Houx.

Hollywood Cocktail (Cktl) 30mls (¼ gill) dry gin, 15mls (⅛ gill) French vermouth, 15mls (⅛ gill) Italian vermouth, 2 dashes brown Curaçao. Stir over ice, strain into a cocktail glass, serve with a cherry and a dash of lemon peel juice.

Holoferment (Eng) denotes the whole fermentation.

Holsten Brauerei (Ger) a brewery. (Add): Holstenstrasse 224, Hamburg D-22765. Produces Holstein Diät Pils lager beer. Now part of the Carlsberg Brewery (2004). Website: http://www.holstein.de 'E'mail: info@holstein.de

Holsten (Ger) northern Germany's biggest selling beer, brewed in Hamburg. Noted for Moravia Pils 4.9% alc by vol. Pure 6 5.6% alc by vol. and Diät Pils 1045 O.G. Also Holsten Export lager 1045 O.G. (4.9% alc by vol.) brewed under licence by Watneys.

Holsten Diät Pils (Ger) a famous pilsener lager beer 6% alc by vol. brewed by the Holsten Brauerei in Hamburg.

Holsten Premium Pilsner (Ger) a 4.8% alc by vol. bottled pilsner brewed by Holsten Brauerei, Hamburg.

Holsten UK Ltd (Eng) a brewery (established 1952) under licence from the Holsten Brauerei, Hamburg. (Add): Reeve House, Parsonage Square, Station Road, Dorking, Surrey RH4 1UP. Brews Holsten beers. Website: http://www.holsten.co.uk

Holstein Cocktail (Cktl) ½ measure Cognac, ½ measure blackberry brandy, dash Amer Picon. Shake over ice and strain into a cocktail glass.

Holt [Joseph] Brewery (Eng) a brewery based in Manchester. (Add): Derby Brewery, Empire Street, Cheetham, Manchester. Noted for Fifth Sense, Holtenbrau 1033 O.G., Humdinger 1849 3.5% alc by vol., Maple Moon, Regal Lager 1039 O.G. 1849 (4.5% alc by vol.) and Sixex 1064 O.G., Thunder Holt and Touchwood.

Holtenbrau Lager (Eng) a light lager beer 1033 O.G. brewed by the Holt Brewery in Manchester.

Holtland (Ger) a low alcohol lager brewed using traditional methods. Packaged in Holland, sold in recycled cans 0.4% alc by vol.

Holt, Plant and Deakin (Eng) a pub group (established 1984) an Ansells Black Country C°. running public houses in the region. Noted for cask-conditioned Holts Mild 1036.5 O.G. (brewed by Tetley-Walker Brewery in Warrington) and Entire 1043 O.G. (brewed in Oldbury).

Holt Vineyard [The] (Eng) a vineyard based at Woolton Hill, Newbury, Berkshire. 0.5ha. Grape varieties: Madeleine angevine and Müller-Thurgau. Produces wines under the Woodhay label.

Holunderbeerlikoer (Ger) a liqueur made from ripe elderberries.

Holy Grail (Eng) a beer brewed by the Black Sheep Brewery, Masham.

Holy Joe (Eng) a 4.9% alc by vol. ale brewed by the Yates Brewery, Isle of Wight.

Holy Moley (Eng) a 4.7% alc by vol. ale brewed by the Moles Brewery, Wiltshire.

Holy Water (Eng) water that has been blessed by a priest for use in symbolic rituals of purification.

Holy Water (N.Z) a natural spring mineral water.

Holzäcker (Aus) a vineyard area on the banks of the River Danube in the Kremstal region.

Holzapfel Feld (Aus) a vineyard site on the banks of the River Danube situated in the Wachau region, Niederösterreich.

Holzapfel [Karl] (Aus) a winery based in the Wachau. (Add): 3610 Joching. Grape varieties: Grüner veltliner, Müller-Thurgau, Pinot blanc, Riesling, Zweigelt. Produces a range of dry and sweet (botrytised) wines and fruit-based schnapps.

Holzeg (Aus) a vineyard site based on the banks of the River Kamp situated in the Kamptal region.

Holzen (Ger) village (Anb): Baden. (Ber): Markgräflerland. (Gro): Vogtei Rötteln. (Vin): Steingässle.

Holzenberg (Ger) vineyard (Anb): Württemberg. (Ber): Remstal-Stuttgart. (Gro): Kopf. (Vil): Breuningsweiler.

Holzenberg (Ger) vineyard (Anb): Württemberg. (Ber): Remstal-Stuttgart. (Gro): Kopf. (Vil): Winnenden.

Holzgasse (Aus) a vineyard area on the banks of the River Danube in the Kremstal region.

Holzgeschmack (Ger) woody taste.

Homberg (Ger) vineyard (Anb): Rheingau. (Ber): Johannisberg. (Gro): Steinmacher. (Vil): Frauenstein.

Homberg (Ger) vineyard (Anb): Rheinhessen. (Ber): Nierstein. (Gro): Petersberg. (Vil): Albig.

Homberg (Ger) vineyard (Anb): Rheinhessen. (Ber): Nierstein. (Gro): Petersberg. (Vil): Bechtolsheim.

Homburg (Ger) village (Anb): Franken. (Ber): Maindreieck. (Gro): Not yet assigned. (Vins): Edelfrau, Kallmuth.

Home Brew (Eng) a term used for any beer, wine, etc. that is produced in a person's own home for consumption there, it can not by law be offered for sale without a licence.

Home Brewed Ale (Eng) a bottled brown ale 1036 O.G. brewed by the Home Brewery in Nottingham.

Home Brewed Ale (Eng) an ale brewed from a kit (or raw ingredients) at a person's home. *see* Home Brew.

Home Brewery (Eng) a brewery based in Nottingham. Noted for cask-conditioned Five Star 1043 O.G. (also Mild 1036 O.G. and Bitter 1038 O.G. Bottled Centenary 1060 O.G. Little John 1070 O.G. Luncheon Ale 1034 O.G. and Robin Hood 1045 O.G. Bottled Home-brewed Brown Ale 1036 O.G.

Home Brew House (Eng) a term used for a Public house that brews its own ales.
Home Brew Public House (Eng) *see* Home Brew House.
Homeburn (Nor) a spirit produced from sugar and yeast, also known as H.B.
Homenaje (Sp) a rosé wine produced by the Bodegas Marco Real, Navarra from 100% Garnacha grapes.
Homer (Isr) an old Hebrew (bible) name for fresh young unmixed wine.
Homestead (Austr) a Cabernet sauvignon and Merlot blend wine from the Goundrey Estate, Western Australia.
Homestead Cocktail (Cktl) ⅔ measure gin, ⅓ measure sweet vermouth. Stir over ice, strain into a cocktail glass and top with a slice of orange.
Hometz (Isr) vinegar.
Home Vineyard [The] (Austr) a vineyard based in the Barossa valley, owned by the Hill-Smith Estate 4ha.
Hominy (USA) prepared cereal for brewing beer.
Homique (Chi) a white grape variety grown in the Tianjin region.
Hommel Bier (Bel) a hoppy beer from west Flanders 7.5% alc by vol.
Hommelsberg (Lux) a vineyard site in the village of Wintrange.
Homme-Mort [L.] (Fr) a Premier Cru vineyard of A.C. Chablis, often is reclassified as the Premier Cru Fourchaume.
Homogenise (Eng) in relation to milk: to break up the fat globules in milk or cream so that they are evenly distributed through the whole and stay in that state throughout, produced under high pressure (3,000 lbs. per sq.in.) also spelt Homogenize.
Homogenize (USA) the American spelling of Homogenise.
Home Ranch (USA) a winery based in the Napa Valley, California. Grape varieties: Cabernet sauvignon.
Homs (Arab) a hilly wine-growing area in northern Syria.
Homtini (S.Afr) a red wine (Shiraz with a small percentage of Viognier) produced by Anthony de Jager Wines, Paarl, Western Cape.
Hondarrabi Beltza (Sp) a light, berried grape variety grown in the Basque.
Hondarrabi Zuri (Sp) a local dark berried grape variety grown in Chacolí.
Honegar (Eng) an old fourteenth century medicinal drink made from vinegar and honey, also known as Oxymel or Pharmacopeia.
Honeos (Gre) a natural spring mineral water from Thetis. Mineral contents (milligrammes per litre): Sodium 19.2mg/l, Calcium 42.9mg/l, Magnesium 31.4mg/l, Potassium 0.8mg/l, Bicarbonates 258.4mg/l, Chlorides 22.5mg/l, Sulphates 14.4mg/l, Nitrates 9.9mg/l. pH 7.7
Honest (Eng) a term used to describe a wine as ordinary, decent and well-made.
Honey (Arab) a natural spring mineral water from Saudi Arabia. Mineral contents (milligrammes per litre): Sodium 38mg/l, Calcium 8mg/l, Magnesium 3.8mg/l, Potassium 0.8mg/l, Bicarbonates 86mg/l, Chlorides 15mg/l, Sulphates 17mg/l, Fluorides 0.6mg/l, Nitrates 0.6mg/l. pH 7.5
Honey Ale (Eng) a 5% alc by vol. organic ale brewed by the Pitfield Brewery, London with a dash of ginseng.
Honey and Orange Cream Coffee (Eng) 1 orange (peel and juice), 450mls (¾ pint) hot coffee, 25mls (1fl.oz) clear honey, 25mls (1fl.oz) double cream. Add the juice to the hot coffee, sweeten with honey, chill, pour into glasses, swirl with cream and decorate with peel.
Honey Brandy (Eng) the name given to the spirit obtained from distilled mead.
Honey Dew (Eng) old name for Organic Honey Dew brewed by Fuller's.
Honeyed (Eng) a term used to describe a wine as having some bottle age, fragrance and taste similar to the fine wines of Sauternes.
Honey Farm Bitter (Eng) a 4.2% alc by vol. bottle conditioned bitter ale from Cropton Brewery, Pickering, North Yorkshire.
Honey Fayre (Wal) a 4.5% alc by vol. ale brewed by the Conway Brewery Ltd., Gwynedd.
Honey Gold (Eng) a 4.2% alc by vol. ale brewed by the Cropton Brewery, North Yorkshire.
Honeymoon (Cktl) ⅓ measure applejack brandy, ⅓ measure Bénédictine, ⅓ measure lemon juice, 3 dashes orange Curaçao. Shake over ice and strain into cocktail glass.
Honeymoon Cocktail [1] (Cktl)(Non-alc) 25mls (⅕ gill) apple juice, 25mls (⅕ gill) orange juice, juice ¼ lime, 2 teaspoons clear honey. Shake well over crushed ice, strain into a flute glass, dress with a cherry and spiral of orange peel.
Honeymoon Cocktail [2] (Cktl)(Non-alc) as for [1] but substituting maple syrup for the clear honey.
Honeymoon Cocktail [3] (Cktl)(Non-alc) blend half a banana, 50mls orange juice, 175mls yoghurt, 15mls liquid honey, 2 barspoons soft brown sugar, pour into a highball glass and decorate with banana slice.
Honey Porter (Eng) a 4.9% alc by vol. porter brewed by the Grand Union Brewery, Middlesex.
Honey Pot (Eng) a 3.8% alc by vol. ale brewed by the Coach House Brewing C°. Ltd., Cheshire.
Honeysuckle Cocktail (Cktl) 25mls (⅕ gill) golden rum, juice of a lime, 1 teaspoon clear honey. Shake well over ice and strain into a cocktail glass.
Honeysweet Coffee (Cktl) dissolve a teaspoon of clear honey in 200mls (⅓ pint) of hot, freshly brewed coffee. Chill down, when cool add a dash of Angostura bitters and a pinch of grated nutmeg. Shake over ice, strain into a highball glass and top with whipped cream.
Honey Water (Mex) a name for the aguamiel (the sap of the agave cactus).
Honeywood Winery (USA) a winery (established

H

1934) based at Salem, Oregon. Grape varieties: Pinot noir, Riesling, Chardonnay, Muscat.

Hong (Chi) a natural spring mineral water from Xianyang.

Honig (Ger) honey.

Honigartig (Ger) honey-like aroma and taste.

Honigberg (Ger) lit: 'honey hill/honey slope'.

Honigberg (Ger) grosslage (Anb): Franken. (Ber): Maindreieck. (Vil): Dettelbach.

Honigberg (Ger) grosslage (Anb): Rheingau. (Ber): Johannisberg. (Vils): Mittelheim, Estate, Winkel.

Honigberg (Ger) vineyard (Anb): Mosel-Saar-Ruwer. (Ber): Bernkastel. (Gro): Kurfürstlay. (Vil): Maring-Noviand.

Honigberg (Ger) vineyard (Anb): Nahe. (Ber): Kreuznach. (Gro): Kronenberg. (Vil): Bad Kreuznach (ortsteil Winzenheim).

Honigberg (Ger) vineyard (Anb): Nahe. (Ber): Kreuznach. (Gro): Schlosskapelle. (Vil): Dorsheim.

Honigberg (Ger) vineyard (Anb): Nahe. (Ber): Kreuznach. (Gro): Schlosskapelle. (Vil): Guldental.

Honigberg (Ger) vineyard (Anb): Rheingau. (Ber): Johannisberg. (Gro): Deutelsberg. (Vil): Erbach.

Honigberg (Ger) vineyard (Anb): Rheinhessen. (Ber): Bingen. (Gro): Abtey. (Vil): Nieder-Hilbersheim.

Honigberg (Ger) vineyard (Anb): Rheinhessen. (Ber): Bingen. (Gro): Abtey. (Vil): Sprendlingen.

Honigberg (Ger) vineyard (Anb): Rheinhessen. (Ber): Bingen. (Gro): Adelberg. (Vil): Sulzheim.

Honigberg (Ger) vineyard (Anb): Rheinhessen. (Ber): Bingen. (Gro): Kaiserpfalz. (Vil): Bubenheim.

Honigberg (Ger) vineyard (Anb): Rheinhessen. (Ber): Nierstein. (Gro): Krotenbrunnen. (Vil): Ludwigshöhe.

Honigberg (Ger) vineyard (Anb): Rheinhessen. (Ber): Bingen. (Gro): Sankt Rochuskapelle. (Vil): Biebelsheim.

Honigberg (Ger) vineyard (Anb): Rheinhessen. (Ber): Bingen. (Gro): Sankt Rochuskapelle. (Vil): Dromersheim.

Honiggoscherl (Aus) the local name for a lesser white grape variety.

Honiglerrebe (Aus) an ancient white grape variety which is little used nowadays.

Honiglikoer (Ger) honey-based liqueur.

Honigsack (Ger) vineyard (Anb): Pfalz. (Ber): Mittelhaardt-Deutsche Weinstrasse. (Gro): Höllenpfad. (Vil): Grünstadt.

Honigsack (Ger) vineyard (Anb): Pfalz. (Ber): Mittelhaardt-Deutsche Weinstrasse. (Gro): Kobnert. (Vil): Herxheim/Berg.

Honigsäckel (Ger) grosslage (Anb): Pfalz. (Ber): Mittelhaardt-Deutsche Weinstrasse. (Vil): Ungstein.

Honigtrauber (S.Afr) the label for a white wine (Chenin blanc and Colombard blend) produced by the Groot Eiland Winery, Worcester, Western Cape.

Honolulea (Cktl) ½ measure Irish whiskey, ¼ measure orange Curaçao, ¼ measure lemon juice, dash gomme syrup. Shake over ice, strain, decorate with a slice of orange and cherry.

Honolulu Cocktail [1] (Cktl) 2 measures gin, 1 measure orange juice, 1 measure pineapple juice, dash orange blossom, dash sugar. Shake over crushed ice and strain into a cocktail glass.

Honolulu Cocktail [2] (Cktl) ⅓ measure Bénédictine, ⅓ measure dry gin, ⅓ measure maraschino. Stir over ice and strain into a cocktail glass.

Honorable (Sp) a 20 year old brandy from Torres, distilled from Ugni blanc grapes and aged in Limousin oak.

Hooch (Eng) a slang word for drink.

Hooch (USA) a slang word for gin.

Hooch (Eng) *see* Hoopers Hooch.

Hooch Light (Eng) a 4.7% alc by vol. low calorie version of Hooch produced by Bass.

Hood River Vineyards (USA) a winery (established 1984) based in Yamhill County, Oregon. 5ha. Grape varieties: Pinot noir, Chardonnay, Riesling, Pinot gris, Müller-Thurgau.

Hoogland (S.Afr) the label for a red wine (Shiraz) produced by the Pella Wines winery, Stellenbosch, Western Cape.

Hoogstraten Porter (Bel) an amber coloured bottle conditioned ale (not porter) from Sterkens Brauerei 6.5% alc by vol.

Hooijberg (Hol) a bock-style beer 6% alc by vol. brewed by the Heineken Brouwerij.

Hook Ale (Eng) a bottled mild ale 1032 O.G. brewed by the Hook Norton Brewery, Banbury, Oxfordshire.

Hooker (Eng) a 4.5% alc by vol. ale brewed by George Bateman & Son Ltd., Lincolnshire.

Hooker (USA) a slang for a draught of alcoholic drink, especially spirits.

Hook Norton Brewery (Eng) a brewery (established 1849). (Add): Brewery Lane, Hook Norton, Banbury, Oxfordshire OX15 5NY. Brews: Cooper Ale 4.8% alc by vol., Double Stout 4.8% alc by vol., First Light 4.3% alc by vol., Haymaker 5% alc by vol., Hooky Bitter 3.6% alc by vol., Hooky Dark 3.2% alc by vol., cask-conditioned Old Hooky 4.6% alc by vol (1049 O.G)., Steaming On 4.4% alc by vol., 303 AD 4% alc by vol., Twelve Days 5.5% alc by vol. Plus bottled Hook Ale 1032 O.G. Jack Pot 1036 O.G. Jubilee 1049 O.G. VI 4% alc by vol. Website: http://www.hooky.co.uk 'E'mail: info@hook-norton-brewery.co.uk

Hookway Vineyard (Eng) a vineyard based in Hookway, Surrey 1.2ha.

Hooky Bitter (Eng) a 3.6% alc by vol. bitter ale brewed by the Hook Norton Brewery, Oxfordshire.

Hooky Dark (Eng) a 3.2% alc by vol. dark mild ale brewed by the Hook Norton Brewery, Oxfordshire.

Hoo La La (Eng) a 5% alc by vol. limited RTD summer World Cup bottled fruit drink from a blend of lemon, lime, orange and peach. From Hooper's Hooch.

Hooligan (Eng) a 4.3% alc by vol. ale brewed by the Roosters Brewing C°. Ltd., North Yorkshire.

Hoop (Pol) a natural spring mineral water from

bielsk Podlaski. Mineral contents (milligrammes per litre): Sodium 10.9mg/l, Calcium 90.1mg/l, Magnesium 18.9mg/l, Potassium 1.3mg/l, Bicarbonates 390mg/l, Chlorides 6.2mg/l, Sulphates 1.5mg/l, Fluorides 0.2mg/l.

Hoopenburg Wines (S.Afr) a winery (established 1992) based in the Stellenbosch, Western Cape. 34ha. Grape varieties: Cabernet sauvignon, Chardonnay, Merlot, Pinotage, Pinot noir, Sauvignon blanc, Shiraz. Labels: Preview, South Barrel Camber. Website: http://www.hoopenburg.com

Hooper (Eng) an alternative name for a cooper (cask maker), derived from the metal hoops that hold the staves together.

Hooper's Hooch (Eng) the brand-name for an RTD alcoholic fruit drink produced by Bass. Range includes lemonade (made with real lemon juice) 4.7% alc by vol., apple 5% alc by vol. orange, blackcurrant, grapefruit 5.1% alc by vol. *See also* Ho Ho, Hoo La La, Hooch Light, Reef, Smooch.

Hooper's Hoola (Eng) a 5% pineapple and grapefruit juice drink from Bass.

Hoop Huis (S.Afr) the label for a range of wines produced by the False Bay Vineyards winery, Wellington, Western Cape.

Hoopla (Cktl) ¼ measure brandy, ¼ measure Lillet, ¼ measure Cointreau, ¼ measure lemon juice. Shake over ice and strain into a cocktail glass.

Hooray Henley (Eng) a 4.6% alc by vol. cask-conditioned ale brewed by Brakspear, Henley-on-Thames, Oxon. Part of the Brewers Selection range.

Hooray Henry (Eng) a 4.6% alc by vol. cask-conditioned ale brewed by Brakspear, Henley-on-Thames, Oxon.

Hootch (USA) a slang term for illicitly distilled spirits, also for alcoholic drink. Word derived from the Tlingit Hootchinoo Indian tribe that distilled a type of liquor. *See also* Hooch.

Hoots Mon (Cktl) ½ measure Scotch whisky, ¼ measure sweet vermouth, ¼ measure Lillet. Stir over ice and strain into a cocktail glass.

Hoots Mon Cocktail (Cktl) ⅗ measure Scotch whisky, ¼ measure sweet vermouth, ¼ measure Bénédictine. Stir over ice, strain into an ice-filled cocktail glass and top with a twist of lemon peel juice.

Hop (Eng) ***Humulus lupulus*** flowering vine, plant used in beer making to give bitterness and help preserve the beer. The female plant only is used (fertilized for ales/sterile for lagers). *see* Bramlin Cross, East Kent Goldings, First Gold, Fuggles, Goldings, Hallertaus, Northdown, Saaz Target, Tettnang, and Whitbread Goldings are some examples. (Fr) = houblon, (Ger) = hopfo, (Den) = hop, (It) = luppolo, (Port) = lúpulo, (Sp) = lúpulo.

Hop a Doodle Do (Eng) a 4.2% alc by vol. ale brewed by the Brewster Brewing C°. Ltd., Leicestershire.

Hop & Glory (Eng) a label of a 5% alc by vol. pale straw-coloured beer brewed by Ash Vine Brewery, Trudoxhill, near Frome, Somerset.

Hop Back (Eng) in brewing, equipment that separates the spent hops from the wort (hop strainer). (USA) = hop jack.

Hop Back Best (Eng) a 4% alc by vol. bitter beer brewed by the Hop Back brewery plc., Wiltshire.

Hop Back Brewery plc (Eng) a brewery (established 1987). (Add): Unit 22-24, Batten Road Ind Estate, Downton, Salisbury, Wiltshire SP5 3HU. Brews: Crop Circle 4.2% alc by vol., Entire Stout 4.5% alc by vol., GFB 3.5% alc by vol., Hop Back Best 4% alc by vol., Hopleaf Bitter, Summer Lightning 5% alc by vol., Thunder Storm. Website: http://www.hopback.co.uk 'E'mail: info@hopback.co.uk

Hop Bine (Eng) a hop grower's name for the hop plant.

Hop Character (Eng) the aroma and flavour given to a beer from certain types of hops.

Hop Cone (Eng) a term for the hop flower head.

Hop Demon (Eng) a 4.2% alc by vol. triple-hopped seasonal ale brewed by Brakspear.

Hop Devil (Eng) a 3.9% alc by vol. ale brewed by Rockingham Ales, Cambridgeshire.

Hope & Glory (Eng) a 4.2% alc by vol. cask-conditioned ale, brewed by the Frog & Parrot brew-pub in Sheffield to celebrate the 1998 World Cup.

Hope Marguerite (S.Afr) the label for a white wine (Chenin blanc barrel reserve) produced by the Beaumont Wines winery, Walker Bay, Western Cape.

Höpertsbour (Lux) a vineyard site in the village of Remich.

Hop Extract (Eng) the flavouring obtained from hops including oils sold in pellet form, added to the wort during brewing, replaces the dried hops.

Hopfenbitter (Ger) a brandy made slightly bitter by the addition of hop cones.

Hopfengrund (Aus) a vineyard area on the banks of the River Danube in the Kremstal region.

Hopfenperle (Aus) a dark, full-bodied beer 13°, brewed by the Schwechat Brauerei.

Hopfenperle (Switz) a lager beer brewed by the Feldschlösschen Group Brauerei. Also brewed under licence in the U.K. by the North Country Breweries, Hull, Yorkshire.

Hop Field (Eng) *see* Hop Garden and Hop Yard.

Höpfigheim (Ger) village (Anb): Württemberg. (Ber): Württembergisch Unterland. (Gro): Schalkstein. (Vin): Königsberg.

Hopfo (Ger) hop.

Hopf Weisse Export (Ger) a wheat beer 5% alc by vol. from Hopf Brauerei in the Bavarian Alps.

Hop Garden (Eng) the name given to the hop field in Kent.

Hop Garden Gold (Eng) a 4.6% alc by vol. ale brewed by the Hogs Back brewery Ltd., Surrey.

Hophead (Eng) a 3.6% alc by vol. ale brewed by the Brewster Brewing C°. Ltd., Leicestershire.

Hophead (Eng) the name of a beer brewed by the Dark Star Brewing C°. Ltd., West Sussex.

Hop Head (Eng) the label of a beer brewed by the Fuggle & Firkin, Oxford.

Hôpital Saint-Jean (Fr) a museum based at Angers in the Loire, has a display of bottles and glasses and a twelfth century cellar which is now a wine museum.

Hop Jack (USA) an American name for the hop back.

Hop Kiln (Eng) also known as the oast house, used for drying the hop cones.

Hop Kiln Winery (USA) a winery based at the Griffin Vineyards, Russian River Valley, Sonoma County, California. Grape varieties: French colombard, Gewürztraminer, Petite syrah and Zinfandel.

Hopkins and Company (Scot) a highland malt and Scotch whisky distillery. Part of DCL. Brands include Oban and Old Mull.

Hopland (USA) a wine town in Ukiah, Mendocino County, California. Has two large wineries based there.

Hopleaf (Eng) a 3.5% alc by vol. bitter from the Hopback Brewery, Salisbury, Wilts.

Hopleaf (Eng) a 4.5% alc by vol. ale brewed by the Buffy's Brewery, Norfolk.

Hop Leaf Ale (Euro) a pale ale 1040 O.G. brewed by the Farsons Brewery on the island of Malta.

Hop'n'Gator (USA) a beer flavoured with lime, launched in 1970 by the Pittsburgh Brewery.

Hop off the Press (Ch.Isles) a special 4.5% alc by vol. limited edition bitter ale brewed by R.W. Randalls Brewery, St. Peter Port, Guernsey to commemorate the opening of the local newspaper's (Guernsey Press & Star) new building on 13th October 2005.

Hop Oil (Eng) the chemical extract from the female hop flower.

Hop Nouvelle (Eng) a 4.1% alc by vol. seasonal ale brewed by the Terne Valley Brewery, Knightwick, Worcestershire. Available mid October–November. Made using Fuggles, Challenger, Mathon Goldings, Bird Goldings, Northdown hops. Each hop makes a different Hop Nouvelle Ale. *See also* This, That, T'Other, Wat Wassail.

Hoppe (Hol) a distillery based in Schiedam (part of Heineken) that produces jenever and a range of liqueurs.

Hopped-Wort (Eng) the name given to the wort after the hops have been strained through the hop back.

Hop Pellets (Eng) compacted from natural hops, used in brewing with the same results as natural hops, makes transportation easier.

Hopper (Eng) a low alcohol beer 0.9% alc by vol. from Gibbs Mew Brewery, Salisbury, Wiltshire.

Hoppers Ale (Eng) a 4.4% alc by vol. ale brewed by the Rother Valley Brewing C°. Ltd., East Sussex.

Hoppers Bitter (Eng) a 4.2% alc by vol. cask bitter from Burtonwood in Warrington. brewed during July 1st to August 30th.

Hop Pillow (Eng) a sleep-inducing pillow stuffed with fresh hops, the oil contained in the flowers has narcotic effects!

Hoppin Mad (Eng) a 4.2% alc by vol. bitter ale brewed by the Wylam Brewery Ltd., Tyne & Wear.

Hopping (Eng) the adding of hops to the wort.

Hopping Mad (Eng) an ale brewed by Woods Brewery, Winstanlow, Shropshire.

Hoppit Classic Bitter (Eng) a 3.5% alc by vol. bitter ale brewed by the Loddon Brewery, Berkshire.

Hop Pocket (Eng) an elongated sack containing fresh hops 166lbs (75kgs).

Hoppy Easter (Eng) a 4.3% alc by vol. light coloured bitter brewed by Ridleys Hartford End Brewery, Chelmsford, Essex (available in April).

HopScotch (Eng) a 4.1% alc by vol. cask ale brewed by Summerskill Brewery, Plymouth.

HopScotch (Scot) a seasonal cask ale brewed by the Maclay Brewery of Alloa in October.

Hop Strainer (Eng) *see* Hop Back and Hop Jack.

Hop Toad (Cktl) ½ measure Bacardi White Label, ½ measure apricot brandy, juice ½ lime. Stir over ice and strain into a cocktail glass.

Hop Up (USA) a slang term for a heavy drinking bout or party (especially of beer drinking).

Höpürdetmek (Tur) to slurp/to drink noisily and heavily.

Hopwood Estate (Austr) part of the Tisdall Winery based in Victoria. Grapes come from the Rosbercon Vineyard.

Hop Yard (Eng) the south-west Midlands name for a hop field.

Horam Manor (Eng) a vineyard (established 1963). (Add): Horam, Heathfield, East Sussex. Planted 1963–1966. 1.2ha. Soil: clay, sandy loam over sandstone. Grape varieties: Huxelrebe 8%, Müller-Thurgau 90% and 2% others.

Horchata (Sp) orgeat/iced drink.

Horchata de Chufas (Sp) a sweet, milky 'tiger nut' drink.

Hordeum vulgar (Lat) barley.

Hörecker (Ger) vineyard (Anb): Mosel-Saar-Ruwer. (Ber): Saar-Ruwer. (Gro): Scharzberg. (Vil): Kanzem.

Horgazuela (Sp) the alternative name used for the Palomino grape grown in Puerto de Santa Maria, Jerez.

Horice Brewery (Czec) a brewery based in northern Czec.

Horin Jyunmai Dai Ginjyo (Jap) a saké produced by the Gekkeikan Brewery, near Kyoto.

Horizontal Cylindrical Press (Eng) a type of grape press that consists of a cylinder with a plate at each end which are linked by chains. As the drum rotates the chains are shortened, drawing the plates together so crushing the grapes. The must passes through slits in the sides of the drum while the chains keep the pulp loose.

Horizontal Tasting (Eng) a tasting of wines of different origins but of the same age.

Horizon Winery (USA) a small winery based near Santa Rosa, Sonoma County, California. Grape variety: Zinfandel.

Horkheim (Ger) village (Anb): Württemberg. (Ber): Württembergisch Unterland. (Gro): Staufenberg. (Vin): Stiftsberg.

Horlicks (Eng) a famous™ brand-name of a malted milk drink, sold in powder form, it is diluted

H

with hot milk, also available in a chocolate-flavoured form.

Horn (Ger) vineyard (Anb): Rheinhessen. (Ber): Bingen. (Gro): Kaiserpfalz. (Vil): Ingelheim.

Horn (Ger) vineyard (Anb): Rheinhessen. (Ber): Wonnegau. (Gro): Domblick. (Vil): Wachenheim.

Horn (Ger) vineyard (Anb): Pfalz. (Ber): Mittelhaardt-Deutsche Weinstrasse. (Gro): Saumagen. (Vil): Kallstadt.

Hornberg (Ger) vineyard (Anb): Rheinhessen. (Ber): Nierstein. (Gro): Petersberg. (Vil): Framersheim.

Hörnchen (Ger) vineyard (Anb): Nahe. (Ber): Kreuznach. (Gro): Pfarrgarten. (Vil): Wallhausen.

Hörnchen (Ger) vineyard (Anb): Nahe. (Ber): Kreuznach. (Gro): Schlosskapelle. (Vil): Laubenheim.

Hörnchen (Ger) vineyard (Anb): Nahe. (Ber): Kreuznach. (Gro): Schlosskapelle. (Vil): Waldlaubersheim.

Horndale Winery (Austr) a winery based near Reynella, Southern Vales, South Australia. Produces varietal, table and dessert wines.

Horndean Special Bitter (Eng) *see* H.S.B.

Hornfelsen (Ger) vineyard (Anb): Baden. (Ber): Markgräflerland. (Gro): Vogtei Rötteln. (Vil): Greuzach.

Hornimans and Cº. Ltd. (Eng) noted producers of a wide range of fine teas. (Add): 325, Oldfield Lane, Greenford, Middlesex.

Hörnle (Ger) vineyard (Anb): Württemberg. (Ber): Remstal-Stuttgart. (Gro): Kopf. (Vil): Korb.

Hörnle (Ger) vineyard (Anb): Württemberg. (Ber): Remstal-Stuttgart. (Gro): Kopf. (Vil): Waiblingen.

Horn's Bock (Hol) a 7% alc by vol. bottle-conditioned, dark-amber bock bier brewed by De Drie Horne Bier Brouwerij, Kaatsheuvel.

Horny Bull (Cktl) in a shot glass place 1 measure of vodka, layer a measure of tequila on top with 2-3 drops of Angostura bitters finally top with a measure of white rum.

Horny Toad (Ch.Isles) an ale brewed by the Tipsy Toad Town House, St. Helier in Jersey.

Horrenberg (Ger) village (Anb): Baden. (Ber): Badische Bergstrasse/Kraichgau. (Gro): Mannaberg. (Vin): Osterberg.

Horrheim (Ger) village (Anb): Württemberg. (Ber): Württembergisch Unterland. (Gro): Stromberg. (Vin): Klosterberg.

Horrweiler (Ger) village (Anb): Rheinhessen. (Ber): Bingen. (Gro): Sankt Rochuskapelle. (Vins): Gewürzgärtchen, Goldberg.

Hors Classé (Fr) unclassified.

Hors d'Age (Fr) lit: 'beyond recorded age', applied to Cognac brandies.

Hors d'Age (Fr) on an Armagnac label indicates a minimum age of 5 years.

Horsebridge Best (Eng) a cask-conditioned bitter 1045 O.G. brewed by the Royal Inn Brewery (a home-brew public house) in Horsebridge.

Horse Mountain Wines (S.Afr) a winery (established 1997) based in Windmeul, Paarl, Western Cape. 45ha. Grape varieties: Cabernet franc, Cabernet sauvignon, Merlot, Pinotage, Sémillon, Shiraz. Labels: Michele, Quagga Ridge. Website: http://www.horsemountains.com

Horsepower (Eng) a one-off beer brewed by Hambleton Brewery, Holme-on-Swale, north Yorkshire using phoenix hops, brewed to mark the move to new premises.

Horse's Collar (Cktl) spiral of orange peel moistened in rum, dusted with brown sugar. Place in a mug, add 6 cloves (prepared in the same way). Place mug on stove, when hot flame. Allow to burn until the edges of peel brown. Add 2 measures rum, top with boiling water and float butter on top.

Horse's Neck (Cktl) 60mls (½ gill) of spirit, spiral of lemon placed in a highball glass, add ice and top with ginger ale.

Horsham Ale (Eng) a 4.5% alc by vol. ale brewed with brown malt by King and Barnes of Sussex.

Horsham Best Bitter (Eng) a 3.8% alc by vol. bitter ale brewed by King W J & Cº., West Sussex.

Horsham Old Ale (Eng) a 4.6% alc by vol. ale brewed by the Weltons Brewery, West Sussex.

Horsing (Eng) *see* Stillage.

Hörstein (Ger) village (Anb): Franken. (Ber): Mainviereck. (Gro): Reuschberg. (Vin): Abtsberg.

Horta de Nazaré (Port) a light red wine produced from a blend of 50% Trincadeira preta and 50% Castelão francês grapes by Quinta de Santo André in Ribatejo.

Horton Estate (Eng) a vineyard based in Dorset.

Horton Vineyards (USA) vineyards based in Virginia in A.V.A. of Monticello. Grape varieties include: Viognier, Syrah, Touriga nacional.

Hosbag (Tur) a state monopoly-approved name for red and white wines produced in Trakya.

Hoskins and Oldfield Brewery (Eng) a brewery (established 1984) based in Leicester. Noted for HOB Bitter 1041 O.G. *see* Hoskins Brewery.

Hoskins Brewery (Eng) a brewery based in Leicester. Noted for cask-conditioned Penn's Ale 1045 O.G. and Old Nigel 1060 O.G. Hoskins Bitter, Tom's Gold. Originally known as the Hoskins and Oldfield Brewery. Taken over by Archers of Swindon in 2001.

Hospice du Rhone (USA) a wine festival (of Rhône-style American wines) held in late May each year in the Paso Robles region of California. Website: http://www.hospicedurhone.org

Hospices de Beaujeu (Fr) the name given to the red wines from the Beaujolais hills sold to benefit the Beaujeu hospital.

Hospices de Belleville (Fr) a hospice based in Belleville (south of Mâcon) in Beaujolais founded in the thirteenth century by the Duke of Orléans that has vineyards (donated by benefactors) whose wines are sold in aid of the hospital. Vineyard includes 6ha in the Cru Fleurie under Cuvée Clothilde Galliardon.

Hospices de Beaune (Fr) built in 1443 by Nicholas Rolin as a charitable hospital for the poor. Based in the town of Beaune, Côte de Beaune, Burgundy

690

H

(owns over 60ha of fine vineyards consisting of 39 appellations) in the Côte de Beaune. Produces over 39 different wines which are auctioned (in barrels) on the third Sunday in November in Beaune (can only be bid for by Burgundian négocants). The proceeds used for the running of the hospital. Also known as the Hôtel-Dieu. *see* Paulée de Meursault.

Hospices de Nuits (Fr) similar to the Hospices de Beaune but situated in the Côte de Nuits in Nuits-Saint-Georges, Burgundy, has many plots of fine vineyards in the Côte de Nuits. Auction takes place on Palm Sunday.

Hospitalet de Llobregat (Sp) a Vino de Mesa wine from the province of Barcelona in Cataluña.

Hospitaliers de Pomerol (Fr) a brotherhood of the wine producers of Pomerol in Bordeaux.

Hösslinsülz (Ger) village (Anb): Württemberg. (Ber): Württembergisch Unterland. (Gro): Salzberg. *see* Löwenstein.

Host (Eng) a term used to describe licensees and their spouses, usually used by the trade press. *see* Mine-Hosts.

Hostan (Czec) a brewery based in in Znojmo. Brews: Hostan 10%, Hostan 11%, Hostan 12%, Hostan Granát.

Hostan 11% (Czec) a 4.4% alc by vol. bottled lager brewed by the Hostan Brewery in Znojmo.

Hostan 10% (Czec) a 4% alc by vol. straw coloured, bottled lager brewed by the Hostan Brewery in Znojmo.

Hostan 12% (Czec) a 5% alc by vol. gold coloured, bottled lager brewed by the Hostan Brewery in Znojmo.

Hostan Granát (Czec) a 3.8% alc by vol. dark bottled lager brewed by the Hostan Brewery in Znojmo.

Hostelry (Eng) a nickname for a public house, old name for public house with accommodation.

Hot (Eng) a term used to describe a 'baked' wine, a wine made in a hot climate that has a cooked taste.

Hot Applejack Sling (Cktl) fill a tumbler ½ full with barley water and sugar syrup. Add 90mls (¾ gill) applejack brandy or Calvados, squeeze of lemon peel on top, stir and top with grated nutmeg.

Hot Apple Toddy (Cktl) strain juice of a baked apple, add a little sugar syrup and hot water, 90mls (¾ gill) Calvados, top with boiling water and grated nutmeg.

Hot Bottling (Eng) denotes a wine that is bottled immediately after pasteurisation whilst it is still hot. Is decreasing in popularity as it affects the freshness and delicacy of the wine.

Hot Brandy Flip [1] (Cktl) beat a whole egg with 1 teaspoon of sugar and 25mls (⅕ gill) brandy. Pour into a mug, top with hot milk, stir and dust with grated nutmeg.

Hot Brandy Flip [2] (Cktl) place 125mls (1gill) black coffee, 25mls (⅕ gill) Cognac, 40mls (⅓ gill) Port into a saucepan and heat. Pour over an egg yolk beaten with a teaspoon of sugar (stirring well), serve in a heat-proof glass topped with

grated nutmeg.

Hot Break (USA) the brewers name for substances in the wort, that when boiled, coagulate into insoluble materials.

Hot Brick Toddy (Cktl) pour 25mls (⅕ gill) Scotch whisky with sugar to taste into a mug. Add a pat of butter, cinnamon stick and top up with boiling water, stir and serve hot.

Hot Bullshot (Cktl) 25mls (⅕ gill) Vodka, juice of _ lemon, dash Tabasco, 1 teaspoon Worcestershire sauce. Add to a cup of hot consommé, stir and serve.

Hot Bush (Cktl) an ideal nightcap. 1 measure Scotch whisky mixed with sugar to taste, cloves and boiling water. Place in a mug, stir and drink hot.

Hot Buttered Rum (Cktl) 1 measure dark rum, lump sugar, 10grms (½ oz) butter, cloves. Place in old-fashioned glass and top with boiling water.

Hot Buttered Wine (Cktl) heat 75mls (3fl.ozs) Muscatel wine with 75mls (3fl.ozs) water. Pour into a mug, add 10 gms. (½ oz.) butter and teaspoon of maple syrup. Stir and top with grated nutmeg.

Hot Egg Nogg (Cktl) 1 egg, 1 measure brandy, 1 measure rum, 1 teaspoon sugar. Place in a highball glass, top with hot milk, stir and grate nutmeg on top.

Hotel (Austr) public house.

Hotel (Eng) a licensed or unlicensed establishment with a full meal service plus accommodation.

Hôtel-Dieu (Fr) *see* Hospices de Beaune.

Hotel Plaza (Cktl) ⅓ measure dry gin, ⅓ measure French vermouth, ⅓ measure Italian vermouth. Stir over ice, strain into a cocktail glass and decorate with a crushed slice of pineapple.

Hot Irishman (Ire) an 22% alc by vol. drink of ready mixed coffee and Irish whiskey.

Hot Jamaican Cow (Cktl) pour 200mls (⅓ pint) heated milk into a warmed mug, add 25mls (⅕ gill) coffee liqueur, stir and serve.

Hot Jamaica Punch (Cktl) into a highball pour 1 measure Jamaican rum, ½ tablespoon sugar, dash Angostura, ¾ measure lemon juice, 3 cloves, slice of lemon. Top up with boiling water, stir and serve.

Hot Liquor (Eng) during the brewing process the hot liquor (water) is sparged onto the grist in the mash tun.

Hot Maceration (Eng) grapes are heated to 80°C (176°F) for ½ hour, this dissolves the colour from skins but not the tannin, they are then cooled and pressed. As it can lose colour later, they are often blended with traditional red wines.

Hot Orange Tea (Cktl) heat 300mls (½ pint) of Mandarin orange tea with 40mls (⅓ gill) Jamaican rum, 200mls (⅓ pint) orange juice. Stir, pour into heat-proof glasses and serve with orange slices.

Hot Pants (Cktl) ¾ measure tequila, ¼ measure peppermint schnapps, ⅛ measure grapefruit juice, 2 dashes gomme syrup. Shake over ice and strain into a salt-rimmed, ice-filled old-fashioned glass.

Hot Press Wine (USA) a method of heating grapes,

H

the grape must and cap to speed up the extraction of colour without tannin, has a slightly 'cooked' flavour.

Hot Rum Cow (Cktl) blend together 25mls (⅕ gill) light rum, dash Angostura, dash vanilla essence, teaspoon powdered sugar, 300mls (½ pint) hot milk. Pour into a mug and top with grated nutmeg.

Hot Rum Grog (Cktl) in a goblet place a little boiling water and dissolve 2 barspoons of demerara sugar. Add 10mls (½fl.oz) lemon juice, 2 cloves, 35mls (1½fl.ozs) dark rum, grated nutmeg and stir. Top up with boiling water and serve with a cinnamon stick.

Hot Scotch Toddy (Cktl) 50mls (2fl.ozs) Scotch whisky, 10mls (½ fl.oz) lemon juice, dash Angostura, teaspoon honey, teaspoon of powdered sugar, 75mls (3fl.ozs) boiling water. Mix ingredients in a silver tankard, pour into a 175mls (6fl.oz) stemmed glass, add a slice of lemon and serve with a napkin.

Hot Spiced Rum (Cktl) 125mls (1gill) Old Jamaican rum, 3 lumps sugar, boiling water. Stir together. Top with 10 gms (½ oz) butter and a teaspoon of mixed spices, stir well and serve.

Hot Springs (Cktl) 50mls (2fl.ozs) dry white wine, 10mls (½ fl.oz) pineapple juice, 2 dashes maraschino, dash orange bitters. Shake over ice and strain into a cocktail glass.

Hotte (Fr) a wooden hod-like receptacle for the carrying of picked grapes in Bordeaux, truncated cone shape.

Hottiches (Fr) a type of Hotte used in Alsace.

Hot Toddy (Cktl) 1 measure of desired spirit, 1 teaspoon powdered sugar. Fill a medium-sized goblet with boiling water together with spirit and sugar. Stir, add a slice of lemon and dust with grated nutmeg.

Hotx Hotxa Edan (Fr) lit: 'chill before serving', found on a rosé Basque wine label (usually from Irouléguy).

Houblon (Fr) hop.

Houdini Ale (Eng) a 4.4% alc by vol. ale brewed to commemorate the link between Houdini and Carlsberg-Tetley in 1911. Part of the Tapster's Choice range.

Hougaerdse Das (Bel) a 5% alc by vol. dark straw, top-fermented, bottle-conditioned beer brewed by De Kluis Brasserie, Hoegaarden.

Houghton's Verdell (Austr) a dry white wine made from the Verdelho grape by Houghtons.

Houghton Vineyard (Austr) a winery. (Add): Dale Road, Middle Swan, Western Australia 6056. 264ha. in Swan Valley, Frankland River and Moondah Brook. Has vineyards in Frankland and Margaret River. Grape varieties: Cabernet sauvignon, Chardonnay, Chenin blanc, Malbec, Merlot, Rhine riesling, Shiraz and Verdelho. Labels: Gladstones, HRB and Jack Mann. Owns the Frankland River Estate.

Houla Houla (Cktl) ⅔ measure dry gin, ⅓ measure orange juice, 3 dashes orange Curaçao. Shake over ice and strain into a cocktail glass.

Hourges (Fr) a Cru Champagne village in the Canton de Fismes. District: Reims.

Hourglass (USA) a winery based in the Napa Valley, California. Grape varieties include: Cabernet sauvignon.

Houringue [La] (Fr) a vineyard in the commune of Margaux, A.C. Haut-Médoc, Bordeaux. Part of Château Giscours 18ha.

Hour of the Wolf (Rus) the nickname for opening time in Russia.

House of Commons N°1 (Scot) a 12 year old blended Scotch whisky produced by Buchanan & C°. for the House of Commons 43% alc by vol.

House of Horrors (Eng) a nineteenth century gimmick Public house in London owned by Whitbread.

House of Lords (Scot) an 8 year old blended Scotch whisky produced by Glenforres Glenlivet Distillery C°. William Whitelay and C°, Pitlochry. 40% alc by vol (now owned by Pernod Ricard).

House of Stuart (Scot) a brand of Scotch whisky 40% alc by vol. Produced by the House of Stuart Bonding C°. Ltd., Alexandria, Dunbartonshire.

House Wine (Eng) the wine of the establishment, often is of of a basic quality and is served by the glass or carafe.

Houston Brewing C° (Scot) a brewery (established 1997). (Add): South Street, Houston, Johnstone, Renfrewshire PA6 7EN. Brews: Barochan 4.1% alc by vol., Killellan 3.7% alc by vol., St. Peter's Well 4.2% alc by vol., Texas 4.5% alc by vol. Website: http://www.houston-brewing.co.uk 'E'mail: ale@houston-brewing.co.uk

Houx (Fr) an alcool-blanc white alcohol made from the holly-berry in the Alsace region, also known as Holly Spirit.

Howard Park (Austr) a winery based at Margaret River and Great Southern, Western Australia. Also has vineyards in Great Southern region. Grape varieties: Chardonnay, Cabernet franc, Cabernet sauvignon, Merlot, Pinot noir, Riesling, Semillon and Shiraz wines. Labels: Leston Vineyard, MadFish, Scotsdale Vineyard. Website: http://www.howardparkwines.com.au

Howcroft (Austr) a winery based on the Limestone Coast.

Howell Mountain (USA) an A.V.A. of Napa Valley since 1983. 283ha. Grape varieties include Cabernet sauvignon, Chardonnay, Zinfandel. Wineries include Beringer, Duckhorn.

Howf (Scot) the name for a public house in the sixteenth century.

Howling Wolf (Ger) a 40% alc by vol. blend of German schnapps and aged brandy flavoured with oranges from Asmussen.

How's Your Father (Eng) a 4.6% alc by vol. summer ale with a tangy lemon flavour brewed by Vaux Breweries.

Hoxton Heavy Bitter (Eng) a cask-conditioned bitter 4.8% alc by vol. brewed by the Pitfield Brewery in Shoreditch, London.

Hoyo del Mazo (Sp) one of three zone in D.O. Palma.

H

See also Fuencaliente, Vinos de Tea. Produces sweet Malvasia and a good red from Negramoll and Alumenco grapes.

H.P. (Ire) *see* Hackler Poitín.

HPA (Eng) *abbr: see* **H**ighly **P**restigious **A**le.

H.P.A. (Eng) a beer brewed by the Wye Valley Brewery in Herefordshire.

Hpnotiq (Fr) a blue coloured, 17% alc by vol. liqueur (vodka, Cognac and tropical fruits) created in 2001.

H.P.W. (Cktl) *abbr:* **H**arry **P**ayne **W**hitney 30mls (¼ gill) dry gin, 40mls (⅓ gill) Italian vermouth, slice of orange. Shake well over ice and strain into a cocktail glass.

Hrad (Czec) the name for a white wine from Bzenee.

Hradec Kràlové Brewery (Czec) a brewery based in northern Czec.

H.S.B. (Eng) *abbr:* Horndean **S**pecial **B**itter 4.8% alc by vol (1051 O.G.) brewed by Gales Brewery in Horndean, Hampshire. *see* Pentagel.

HSB (Eng) 4.8% alc by vol. bitter ale produced by Shepherd Neame, Faversham, Kent.

HSD (Eng) a 5% alc by vol. ale brewed by the St. Austell Brewery C°. Ltd., Cornwall.

Hsiang Hsueh (Chi) a noted brand of rice wine from Shanghai. *see* Shaoh-Sing Rice Wine.

H2Go (N.Z) a natural spring mineral water. Mineral contents (milligrammes per litre): Sodium mg/l, a natural spring mineral water from Aramoho. Mineral contents (milligrammes per litre): Sodium 8.4mg/l, Calcium 18mg/l, Magnesium 4mg/l.

H2O Alps (Aus) a natural spring mineral water. Mineral contents (milligrammes per litre): Sodium 3.5mg/l, Calcium 207mg/l, Magnesium 41.96mg/l, Potassium 2mg/l, Fluorides 0.79mg/l.

H2ola (S.Am) a natural spring mineral water from Ecuador. Mineral contents (milligrammes per litre): Sodium 44mg/l, Calcium 36.87mg/l, Magnesium 4.87mg/l, Potassium 1mg/l, Chlorides 14mg/l, Sulphates 12.36mg/l.

H2Only (USA) a natural spring mineral water (established 1997) from Jefferson County, Tennessee.

H2 Zero (Eng) a natural spring mineral water.

Hua Dong (Chi) a wine Company based at Quingdao that is owned by the People's Republic of China. Produces: Tsingtao Riesling and Chardonnay wines.

Hualong (Chi) a natural spring mineral water from Hualong. Mineral contents (milligrammes per litre): Sodium 18.2mg/l, Calcium 118.2mg/l, Magnesium 24.3mg/l, Potassium 1.2mg/l, Bicarbonates 262.4mg/l, Silicates 12.8mg/l. pH 7.7

Huapai Soil (N.Z) loam soil.

Huarpe Wines (Arg) a winery based in the Mendoza region, eastern Argentina. Website: http://www.huarpewines.com 'E'mail: mht@huarpewines.com

Huasco (Chile) a principal wine region that produces all types of wines.

Hua Tiao (Chi) a noted brand of rice wine from Shanghai. *see* Shaoh-Sing Rice Wine.

Huatusco (Mex) a coffee producing region.

Hubacker (Ger) vineyard (Anb): Rheinhessen. (Ber): Wonnegau. (Gro): Burg Rodenstein. (Vil): Flörsheim-Dalsheim.

Hubberg (Ger) vineyard (Anb): Baden. (Ber): Badische Bergstrasse/Kraichgau. (Gro): Rittersberg. (Vil): Weinheim.

Huber Brewery (USA) a brewery based in Monroe, Wisconsin. Is noted for Augsburger, Huber Rheinlander, Old Chicago and Regal Bräu.

Huber Rheinlander (USA) a beer 4.5% alc by vol. brewed by the Huber Brewery.

Hubert de Claminger (Fr) a Champagne producer. (Add): Rémy Galichet, 51150 Bouzy.

Hubert [Michel] (Fr) a Calvados producer based in the A.C. Calvados Pays d'Auge. (Add): 61230 La Fresnaie-Fayel, Normandy.

Hubertsborn (Ger) vineyard (Anb): Mosel-Saar-Ruwer. (Ber): Zell/Mosel. (Gro): Weinhex. (Vil): Koblenz (ortsteil Lay).

Hubertus (Hun) a bitter herb-flavoured liqueur.

Hubertusberg (Ger) vineyard (Anb): Mosel-Saar-Ruwer. (Ber): Obermosel. (Gro): Gipfel. (Vil): Nittel.

Hubertusberg (Ger) vineyard (Anb): Mosel-Saar-Ruwer. (Ber): Obermosel. (Gro): Gipfel. (Vil): Onsdorf.

Hubertusberg (Ger) vineyard (Anb): Mosel-Saar-Ruwer. (Ber): Saar-Ruwer. (Gro): Römerlay. (Vil): Waldrach.

Hubertusberg (Ger) vineyard (Anb): Mosel-Saar-Ruwer. (Ber): Saar-Ruwer. (Gro): Scharzberg. (Vil): Irsch.

Hubertusbräu (Aus) a noted beer brewed by the Hubertus Brauerei.

Hubertus Brauerei (Aus) a small independent brewery based at Laa, near the Czec border. Brews: Hubertusbräu.

Hubertuslay (Ger) vineyard (Anb): Mosel-Saar-Ruwer. (Ber): Bernkastel. (Gro): Schwarzlay. (Vil): Bausendorf.

Hubertuslay (Ger) vineyard (Anb): Mosel-Saar-Ruwer. (Ber): Bernkastel. (Gro): Schwarzlay. (Vil): Kinheim.

Hubertus Sprudel (Ger) a natural spring mineral water from Hubertusquelle, Bad Hönningen. Mineral contents (milligrammes per litre): Sodium 740mg/l, Calcium 80mg/l, Magnesium 100mg/l, Potassium 40mg/l, Bicarbonates 1850mg/l, Chlorides 370mg/l, Sulphates 170mg/l, Fluorides 0.8mg/l.

Huber Weisses (Ger) a 5.3% alc by vol. bottle-conditioned wheat beer brewed by Freising Court Hofbräuhaus.

Hübsch (Ger) a nice delicate wine.

Huckle My Buff (Eng) a hot drink made of brandy, beer and egg that is favoured in Sussex.

Hudepohl Brewery (USA) a brewery based in Cincinnati, Ohio. Noted for Burger, Hofbräu and Tap.

Hudor (Gre) water.

H

Hudson (Arg) a winery near Buenos Airès. Owns vineyards in San Rafael, Mendoza. *see* Bianchi.

Hudson and Cooper (Eng) a brand-name used by Vine Products Ltd. for British Sherry.

Hudson Bay Cocktail (Cktl) 20mls (⅙ gill) dry gin, 15mls (⅛ gill) each of cherry brandy, Jamaican rum, orange juice, juice ¼ lime. Shake over ice and strain into a cocktail glass.

Hudson River Valley (USA) a wine region of eastern America. 15 miles out of Newburgh, New York. Concord, Delaware and Catawba grape varieties are grown. Produces red, rosé and sweet white wines.

Hudson's Bay (S.Am) the brand-name of a demerara rum from Guyana. Is bottled in the U.K.

Hudson's Bay Cº. (Can) a distillery based in Winnipeg. Produces a range of Canadian whiskies (a subsidiary of Seagram).

Hudson Valley Wine Company (USA) a major winery based in the Hudson River Valley.

Huelva (Sp) a wine province of Andalucía, south-western Spain on the border with Portugal. Home to the D.O. zone of Condado de Huelva.

Huesgen [Adolf] GmbH (Ger) a noted wine company based at D-5580, Traben-Trarbach, Mosel-Saar-Ruwer. Produces wines of all qualities.

Huet [Gaston] (Fr) a noted producer of sparkling A.C.Vouvray in Touraine, Loire.

Huet [S.A.] (Fr) a viticulteur based in Le Haut-Lieu, Vouvray, Loire. Produces A.C.Vouvray wines.

Huette (Lux) a vineyard site in the village of Greiveldange.

Hufen (Wal) cream.

Hüffelsheim (Ger) village (Anb): Nahe. (Ber): Schloss Böckelheim. (Gro): Rosengarten. (Vins): Gutenhölle, Monchberg, Steyer.

Huffkin (Eng) a 4.4% alc by vol. ale brewed by the Ringwood Brewery Ltd., Hampshire.

Hugel (Fr) a famous wine négociant-éleveur of Alsace. (Hugel Père et Fils). Based at 68340 Riquewihr 26ha (one of the region's top producers). Website: http://www.hugel.com

Hügelheim (Ger) village (Anb): Baden. (Ber): Markgräflerland. (Gro): Burg Neuenfels. (Vins): Gottesacker, Höllberg, Schlossgarten.

Hugel Père et Fils (Fr) *see* Hugel.

Hugget (Scot) a term for a hogshead.

Hugsweier (Ger) village (Anb): Baden. (Ber): Breisgau. (Gro): Schutterlindenberg. (Vin): Kronenbühl.

Huguenac (S.Afr) a brand of brandy produced by the Huguenot Wine Farmers.

Huguenot Wine Farmers (S.Afr) a wine and brandy producing Co-operative.

Hugues and Louis Bétault (Fr) a cuvée in the Les Grèves vineyard, A.C. Beaune, Côte de Beaune, Burgundy (owned by the Hospices de Beaune).

Hugues de Beauvignac (Fr) a white Picpoul de Pinet wine produced at the cooperative at Pomérols.

Hühnerberg (Ger) vineyard (Anb): Mosel-Saar-Ruwer. (Ber): Bernkastel. (Gro): Schwarzlay. (Vil): Traben-Trarbach.

Huia Vineyards (N.Z) a winery (established 1996) based in Marlborough, South Island that produces sparkling and still wines. Grape varieties: Chardonnay, Gewurztraminer, Pinot gris, Pinot meunier, Pinot noir, Riesling.

Huile de Vénus (Fr) a popular eau-de-vie in the eighteenth century that is now no longer produced.

Huisbaas (Hol) landlord.

Huiswyn (S.Afr) a dry, white wine made from a blend of Kerner and Steen grapes. Is produced by the Lievland Estate.

Huitième (Fr) the smallest bottle size of (9.4 centilitres) capacity used in the Champagne region. *see* Champagne Bottle Sizes.

Hula-Hula (Cktl) 40mls (⅓ gill) dry gin, 20mls (⅛ gill) orange juice, dash gomme syrup. Shake over ice and strain into a cocktail glass.

Hull [Charles] (Eng) a noted corkscrew maker of the nineteenth century. Made many new inventions for extracting corks which are now highly collectable.

Hullabaloo Best (Eng) a 4.2% alc by vol. best bitter brewed by the Loddon Brewery, Berkshire.

Hull Brewery (Eng) a brewery based at Kingston-upon-Hull (renamed the North Country Breweries in 1972).

Hull Brewery (USA) a brewery based in New Haven.

Hull Brewery Company (Eng) a brewery based in North Humberside. Brews: Amber Ale, Electric Light Ale 3.7% alc by vol. Governor, Old Millenium 4.1% alc by vol.

Hulstkamp (Hol) a producer of old jenever.

Hultgren and Stamperton (USA) a winery based in the Russian River Valley, Sonoma County, California. Grape varieties: Cabernet sauvignon, Chardonnay. Produces varietal wines.

Humagne (Switz) the name for a rare red or white grape variety grown in Valais and Vaud.

Humagne (Switz) a red or white wine produced from the grape of the same name in Valais and Vaud. Has the full tang of its native vineyard.

Humblot (Fr) a vineyard in the A.C. Meursault, Côte de Beaune, Burgundy (owned by the Hospices de Beaune).

Humboldt (Sp) a sweet, Port-style dessert wine produced by the Viña Norte wine co-operative and named after the eighteenth century German botanist Alexander von Humboldt.

Humbro (S.Afr) the label for a red (Red jerepigo) and white (hanepoot) wines produced by the Simonsvlei International winery, Suider-Paarl, Western Cape.

Humbug Reach (Austr) a winery based in Tasmania.

Humdinger 1849 (Eng) a 3.5% alc by vol. ale (flavoured with honey), brewed by Holts Brewery, Manchester.

Humidity (Eng) a cellar condition of air moisture that assists cork-stoppered wines during the aging process. A humidity level of between 70% and 90% is recommended but with some air-flow to prevent mould developing. *see* Hygrometer.

Hummelberg (Ger) vineyard (Anb): Baden. (Ber):

Badische Bergstrasse/Kraichgau. (Gro): Mannaberg. (Vil): Östringen.

Hummelberg (Ger) vineyard (Anb): Baden. (Ber): Breisgau. (Gro): Burg Lichteneck. (Vil): Keuzingen.

Hummelberg (Ger) vineyard (Anb): Baden. (Ber): Breisgau. (Gro): Burg Lichteneck. (Vil): Wagenstadt.

Humper (Ger) a glass from Bavaria, which is shaped like a concave barrel without a stem.

Humpolec Brewery (Czec) an old brewery based in central Czec.

Humpty Dumpty Brewery (Eng) a brewery. (Add): Church Road, Reedham, Norwich, Norfolk NR13 3TZ. Brews a variety of beers and bottled beers. Website: http://www.humptydumptybrewery.co.uk 'E'mail: mick@humptydumptybrewery.co.uk

Hund (Aus) a vineyard site based on the banks of the River Kamp situated in the Kamptal region.

Hundert (Ger) vineyard (Anb): Mittelrhein. (Ber): Rheinburgengau. (Gro): Schloss Schonburg. (Vil): Langscheid.

Hundertgulden (Ger) vineyard (Anb): Rheinhessen. (Ber): Bingen. (Gro): Abtey. (Vil): Appenheim.

Hundred Acre Estate (USA) a winery based in the Napa Valley, California.

Hundred Pipers (Scot) a blended Scotch whisky produced by the Chivas Brothers 40% alc by vol.

Hundsberg (Ger) vineyard (Anb): Württemberg. (Ber): Württembergisch Unterland. (Gro): Salzberg. (Vil): Eichelberg.

Hundsberg (Ger) vineyard (Anb): Württemberg. (Ber): Württembergisch Unterland. (Gro): Salzberg. (Vil): Weiler.

Hundskopf (Ger) vineyard (Anb): Rheinhessen. (Ber): Nierstein. (Gro): Petersberg. (Vil): Albig.

Hungària (Hun) a non-vintage sparkling wine, demi-sec, extra-dry and rosé styles are produced.

Hungària (Hun) a strong pale lager-style beer brewed by the Köbànya Brewery.

Hungarovin (Hun) a state-owned wine trust based near Budapest. Its main function is to cellar and bottle the wines from co-operatives and farms.

Hungary (Hun) a large east European wine-producing country that produces most styles of wines. Famous for Tokaji and Bull's Blood. Regions: Northern Hungary [Bükkalja, Eger, Màtraalja and Tokaji-Hegyalja], Northern Transdanubia [Aszar-Neszmely, Badacsony, Balatonfüred-Csopak, Balatonmellek, Mór, Somló and Sopron], Southern Transdanubia [Mecsekalja, Szekszàrd and Villàny-Siklós] and The Great Plain [Alföld].

Hungerberg (Ger) vineyard (Anb): Württemberg. (Ber): Remstal-Stuttgart. (Gro): Kopf. (Vil): Winterbach.

Hungerbiene (Ger) vineyard (Anb): Rheinhessen. (Ber): Wonnegau. (Gro): Bergkloster. (Vil): Gundheim.

Hungerford Hill (Austr) a Hunter Valley Estate and Coonawarra Winery. Grape varieties: Cabernet sauvignon, Chardonnay.

Hung Mei (Chi) the brand-name used by Dairen.

Hung Mei Chinese Port Wine (Chi). A tonic and digestive wine produced by Dairen.

Hungriger Wolf (Ger) vineyard (Anb): Nahe. (Ber):

Kreuznach. (Gro): Kronenberg. (Vil): Bad Kreuznach.

Hunky-dory (Eng) a seasonal ale brewed by Hydes Brewery, Moss Side, Manchester.

Hunnenstein (Ger) vineyard (Anb): Mosel-Saar-Ruwer. (Ber): Zell/Mosel. (Gro): Weinhex. (Vil): Alken.

Hunolsteiner (Ger) vineyard (Anb): Nahe. (Ber): Schloss Böckelheim. (Gro): Paradiesgarten. (Vil): Merxheim.

Hünsrück (Ger) lit: 'dog's-back' a mountain range in the Nahe district. The river Nahe rises in the Hünsrück. It separates the river Nahe from the river Mosel.

Hünsrück Quelle (Ger) a natural spring mineral water from the Nahe.

Hunt [Roope] (Port) a vintage Port shipper whose brand-name is Tuke Holdsworth.

Hunter Ale (Austr) a light, fruity beer 3.41% alc by vol. brewed by the Castlemaine Toohey Brewery in New South Wales.

Hunter Brewery (Austr) a brewery based in Newcastle (owned by Toohey's of Sydney).

Hunter Cocktail (Cktl) ⅓ measure cherry brandy, ⅔ measure rye whiskey. Stir over ice and strain into a cocktail glass.

Hunter Estate Winery (Austr) a winery. (Add): Hermitage Road, Pokolbin, New South Wales 2321. 91.1ha. Grape varieties: Cabernet sauvignon, Chardonnay, Pinot noir, Rhine riesling, Sémillon, Shiraz and Traminer.

Hunter Riesling (Austr) an erroneous varietal name for the Sémillon.

Hunter River (Austr) a top wine region in New South Wales. Not affected by **Phylloxera**. Produces fortified and table wines.

Hunter River White Burgundy (Austr) a full-bodied white wine produced by the Lindemans Winery in Hunter River, New South Wales.

Hunters (N.Z.) a small 18ha winery based in Rapaura Road, Blenheim, Marlborough, South Island. Grape varieties: Cabernet sauvignon, Pinot noir, Chardonnay, Riesling, Sauvignon blanc. Produces still and traditional method sparkling wines.

Hunters Farms (USA) a small vineyard based in the Sonoma Valley, California. 16.5ha. Grape variety: Chardonnay. Grapes are vinified at Château St. Jean.

Hunters Moon (Eng) a 3.9% alc by vol. ale brewed by the Bowland Beer Company Ltd., Lancashire.

Hunter Valley (Austr) a famous wine region situated north of Sydney, has deep volcanic sub-soils and warm, humid climate. Sub-regions: Broke Fordwich. Estates include Brokenwood, Drayton's, Lake's Folly, Rothbury and Tyrrells.

Hunter Valley Hermitage (Austr) a full-bodied red wine from the Wyndham Estate in New South Wales.

Hunter Valley Riesling (Austr) an erroneous name for the Sémillon grape.

Hunter Vodka (Pol) also known as Mysliwska 43%

alc by vol. a vodka flavoured with herbs, rectified juniper distillates. Produced by Polmos.

Hunting Family (S.Afr) a range of wines (Chardonnay/Cabernet sauvignon & Merlot/ Merlot/Pinotage/Shiraz) produced by the Slaley Estate, Stellenbosch.

Hunting Lodge (Eng) the brand-name of a British Sherry from Linfood Cash and Carry, Northamptonshire.

Hunting Port (Port) a tawny Port produced by Harveys of Bristol.

Huntington Estate (Austr) a winery. (Add): Cassilis Road, Mudgee, New South Wales 2850. 42ha. Grape varieties: Cabernet sauvignon, Chardonnay, Merlot, Pinot noir, Sémillon and Shiraz.

Huntleigh Vineyards (Austr) a vineyard (established 1975). (Add): Tunne Cliffes Lane, Heathcote, Victoria. Grape varieties: Cabernet sauvignon, Shiraz, Gewürztraminer.

Hunts (Eng) the brand-name used on of a range of soft drinks by Beecham Products of Brentford, Middlesex.

Huntsman (Cktl) ¾ measure vodka, ¼ measure Jamaican rum, juice ½ lime, dash gomme syrup. Shake over ice and strain into a cocktail glass.

Huntsman Ales (Eng) see Eldridge Pope.

Huntsman Ales (Eng) a design used by Tetleys Brewery in the north of England.

Hunyadi Janos (Hun) a natural spring mineral water (established 1863) from Hunyadi Janos. Mineral contents (milligrammes per litre): Sodium 4680mg/l, Calcium 483mg/l, Magnesium 2930mg/l, Potassium 40mg/l, Bicarbonates 940mg/l, Chlorides 611mg/l, Sulphates 22170mg/l, Fluorides 1.4mg/l, Silicates 12.9mg/l. pH 7.5

Hunza Water (Pak) a natural spring mineral water (established 2003) from the Hunza Valley.

Hupeh (Chi) a branch of Dairen.

Hupperath (Ger) village (Anb): Mosel-Saar-Ruwer. (Ber): Bernkastel. (Gro): Schwarzlay. (Vin): Klosterweg.

Hurbanovo Brewery (Czec) a brewery (established 1967) based in south-eastern Czec.

Hurdle Creek Vineyard (Austr) a part of the Brown Brothers in Victoria.

Hurley's Ale (Eng) a 4.8% alc by vol. beer from Whitbread at the Castle Eden Brewery in County Durham.

Hürlimann Brauerei (Switz) a brewery based in Zürich that brews the world's strongest naturally fermented beer (Samichlaus 14% alc by vol). see Hürlimann Sternbrau and Five Star.

Hürlimann Sternbräu (Eng) a strong lager brewed by the Shepherd Neame Brewery, Kent, Brain's Brewery, Wales, Jersey Brewery, Jersey, Channel Islands under licence from Hürlimann in Switzerland.

Hurns Brewing Company (Wal) a brewery and large independent beer, cider and wine wholesaler. (Add): Unit 3, Century Park, Swansea, West Glamorgan SA6 8RP. Brews: Cwrw Haf 4.2% alc by vol., Dwain Glyndur 4.2% alc by vol., Merlin Stout

4.2% alc by vol. Also produces Taffy Apple and Hazy Dayz–a vodka based fruit drink range (flavours include lemonade and orangeade). Website: http://www.hurns.co.uk 'E'mail: info@hurns.co.uk

Hurricane Glass (Eng) an alternative name for a pina colada glass.

Hurricane Harvest English Wine (Eng) produced to commemorate the hurricane of October 16th 1987 by St. George's Vineyard, Waldron, East Sussex. Launched on October 16th 1988.

Hurricane Punch (Cktl) 35mls (1½ fl.ozs) dark rum, 35mls (1½ fl.ozs) lemon juice, 50mls (2fl.ozs) passion fruit juice, 5mls (¼ fl.oz) gomme syrup. Shake over ice, strain into an ice-filled highball glass, add a splash of soda water, decorate with a slice of lemon and serve with straws.

Husch Vineyards (USA) a small winery based in the Anderson Valley, Mendocino County, California. 14.5ha. Grape varieties: Cabernet sauvignon, Chardonnay, Gewürztraminer and Pinot noir. Produces varietal wines.

Husets Vin (Den) open wine.

Husi (Rum) a wine-producing area based near the Russian border. Produces white wines of the same name.

Huslanka (Rus) a style of fermented milk from southern Russia.

Husseys Vlei (S.Afr) the label for a range of wines produced by the Buitenverwachting winery, Constantia, Western Cape.

Hustler (Eng) the name for the Hustler Lager C° Brewery based in Southend-on-Sea. Brew Hustler 147.

Hustler 147 (Eng) a 1045–1050 O.G. top grade lager produced by the Hustler Lager C°.

Husumer (Ger) a natural spring mineral water from Husum. Mineral contents (milligrammes per litre): Sodium 15.5mg/l, Calcium 78mg/l, Magnesium 3.3mg/l, Potassium 1.1mg/l, Bicarbonates 220mg/l, Chlorides 27.5mg/l, Sulphates 22mg/l, Silicates 26mg/l.

Hutcheson (Port) producers of a vintage Port. Vintages: 1960, 1970, 1974, 1977, 1978, 1980, 1982, 1983, 1985, 1987, 1991, 1994, 1997, 2003. Controlled by Barros.

Huthlee Estate Vineyard (N.Z) a winery. (Add): 84 Montana Road, RD 5, Hastings. 5.56ha. Grape varieties: Cabernet franc, Cabernet sauvignon, Merlot. Specialise in red wines.

Hütt (Ger) vineyard (Anb): Pfalz. (Ber): Mittelhaardt-Deutsche Weinstrasse. (Gro): Höllenpfad. (Vil): Grünstadt.

Hüttberg (Ger) vineyard (Anb): Rheinhessen. (Ber): Nierstein. (Gro): Sankt Alban. (Vil): Mainz.

Hüttbühel (Aus) a vineyard site based on the banks of the River Kamp situated in the Kamptal region.

Hütte (Ger) vineyard (Anb): Mosel-Saar-Ruwer. (Ber): Saar-Ruwer. (Gro): Scharzberg. (Vil): Oberemmel.

Hüttenberg (Ger) vineyard (Anb): Nahe. (Ber): Schloss Böckelheim. (Gro): Rosengarten. (Vil): Roxheim.

H

Hüttenheim (Ger) village (Anb): Franken. (Ber): Steigerwald. (Gro): Schlosstück. (Vin): Tannenberg.

Hüttenviertel (Aus) a dry, white wine from the Grüner veltliner grape. Is produced by the Augustine monks at Klosterneuburg, Vienna. Is often recommended as a diabetic wine.

Hutter [Franz] (Aus) a winery based in Feldbach, Süd-Oststeiermark. (Add): Reiting 2, 8330 Feldbach. Grape varieties: Chardonnay, Pinot blanc, Traminer, Sauvignon blanc, Zweigelt.

Hutter [Friedrich] (Aus) a winery based in the Wachau. (Add): St. Pöltener Strasse 385, 3512 Mautern. Grape varieties: Grüner veltliner, Pinot gris, Riesling, Zweigelt. Produces a range of dry and sweet (botrytised) wines.

Hütte-Terrassen (Ger) vineyard (Anb): Rheinhessen. (Ber): Bingen. (Gro): Adelberg. (Vil): Bornheim.

Huttingen (Ger) village (Anb): Baden. (Ber): Markgräflerland. (Gro): Vogtei Rötteln. (Vin): Kirchberg.

Hutton's Jamaica Rum (W.Ind.) the brand-name of a white rum produced in Jamaica.

Hutweg (Aus) a vineyard site based on the banks of the River Kamp situated in the Kamptal region.

Huxelrebe (Ger) a white grape variety, a hybrid cross between the Weisser gutedel and the Courtillier musqué. First produced in 1927 by George Schen at the Landesanstadt für Rebenzüchtung in Alzey.

Huyghe (Bel) a family brewery (established 1906) based in Melle. Brews: Delirium Tremens, La Guillotine.

Huzzar (Ire) a brand of vodka produced by the Irish Distillers Group.

Hvantchkara (Geo) a red grape variety grown in Georgia to produce fine dessert wines.

Hvar (Euro) a wine-producing island off the Dalmatian coast.

Hvidtol (Den) a tax-free beer, medium density, low in alcohol 1.3% alc by vol. brewed by the United Breweries. Also called a dark white ale (Morkt brew).

Hvidvin (Den) white wine.

Hybrid (Eng) a cross vine. e.g. a cross between European and American vines. (Fr) = hybride.

Hybride (Fr) hybrid.

Hyde de Villaine (USA) abbr: HdV, the premium wine label produced by the Hyde Vineyards, Napa Valley, California.

Hydes Anvil (Eng) see Hydes Brewery.

Hydes Black (Eng) 3.5% alc by vol. smooth nitrokeg black beer from Hydes Brewery, West Manchester, Lancashire.

Hydes Brewery (Eng) a brewery (established 1863). (Add): 46 Moss Lane West, Manchester, Greater Manchester M15 5PH. Noted for cask-conditioned Anvil Strong 1080 O.G. and Amboss Lager 1036 O.G. Also Anvil Bitter, Light, Mild, Smooth, Berry Good Ale, Hydes Black 3.5% alc by vol. Insulation 5% alc by vol., Jekyll's Gold 4.3% alc by vol. Rampant Ram 4.3% alc by vol. Ruby Ratchet's Porter 5.3% alc by vol, Mad Ferret 4.3% alc by vol. Maris Gold 4% alc by vol. Berry Good Ale 5.3% alc by vol., Chill Blane 5% alc by vol., The Craft Ale range includes Hair Raid, Harry Vederchi, Henry's Hampton, Harp Irish Lager 4.3% alc by vol., Hits the Spot, Rocket Fuel. Also brews HPA 4.5% alc by vol., Hunky-dory, Kalt Pilsner, Tickety-boo, Clever Endeavor, Made in Manchester range (Perfection 4.8% alc by vol), Usual, Your Bard (also Classics Range: Cutty Sark, Dr's Orders, Free Spirit 4.8% alc by vol., Heavenly Draft, Hidden Treasure). Also brews under licence: Boddington's cask beers, Whitbread Trophy and Harp Lager. Website: http://www.hydesbrewery.com 'E'mail: mail@hydesbrewery.com

Hydes XXXX (Eng) a 6.8% alc by vol. dark winter warmer from Hydes Anvil Brewery, 46 Moss Lane, West Manchester, Lancashire.

Hyde Vineyard (USA) a winery based in the Carneros district of the Napa Valley, California. Grape varieties include: Cabernet sauvignon, Chardonnay, Merlot, Syrah. Label: HdV, Proprietry Red.

Hydraulic Press (Eng) a grape press, consists of a slatted wooden vat with a plate on top. Grapes are placed in the vat and the plate is forced upon them. The must is collected beneath the slats.

Hydr8 (Wal) a natural spring mineral water from the Brecon Beacons. Mineral contents (milligrammes per litre): Sodium 8mg/l, Calcium 31mg/l, Magnesium 6mg/l, Potassium 7mg/l, Chlorides 16mg/l, Sulphates 5mg/l, Nitrates 3mg/l, Silicates 8mg/l.

Hydria (Gre) a large water jug used in ancient Greece (and Rome).

Hydro-Colloids (Eng) colloidal particles in wine which are surrounded by a film of absorbed water. If they all have the same electrical charge in a wine, they remain suspended and cause hazing.

Hydrogen Sulphide (Eng) H_2S the 'rotten egg' odour that wine sometimes obtains after fermentation, often found on opening the bottle.

Hydrolysis (Eng) a reaction caused by an enzyme, involves a chemical compound and water, resulting in other compounds. i.e. the conversion of sucrose to glucose and fructose caused by the enzyme invertase.

Hydrolyzable Tannins (Eng) obtained from wooden casks.

Hydromel (Eng) the old English word for mead. See also Chouchenn.

Hydromella (Eng) a mead produced in Anglo-Saxon times.

Hydrometer (Eng) an instrument to measure the density of alcohol or sugar in wine, beer, spirit or must. see Balling, Brix, Clarkes, Dujardin Scale, Gay Lussac, O.I.M.L., Oechsle, Sykes.

Hydrometer Act (Eng) 1818 adopted Bartholomew Sykes' hydrometer as the unit for measuring the alcoholic content of all alcoholic beverages.

Hydrostatical Bubbles (Eng) glass bubbles engraved with different numbers to measure the strength of spirits. Used as a rough measure to see if spirits have been tampered with during transit.

H

Hydroxydase (Fr) a sparkling natural spring mineral water from Marie Christine, Nord le Breuil sur Couze. Mineral contents (milligrammes per litre): Sodium 1945mg/l, Calcium 213.2mg/l, Magnesium 243mg/l, Potassium 192.2mg/l, Bicarbonates 6722.2mg/l, Chlorides 367mg/l, Sulphates 10.8mg/l, Fluorides 0.2mg/l, Boron 3mg/l. pH 6.8

Hydroxymethylfurfural (Lat) is found in small traces in Madeira and Sherry-style wines.

Hygeia (Eng) a 4.6% alc by vol. ale brewed by the Ventnor Brewery Ltd., Isle of Wight.

Hygrometer (Eng) an instrument used to measure the humidity levels in a wine cellar.

Hymettus (Gre) a honey-scented, delicate, dry white wine and red wine.

Hypocras (Fr) a spiced wine of cloves, cinnamon, aniseed, saffron, pepper, ginger and sugar. Dates back to Louis XIV.

Hyson (Chi) a grade of China tea.

I

I am 1 (S.Afr) a red wine (Cabernet franc, Cabernet sauvignon, Merlot and Shiraz) produced by the Amani Vineyards, Stellenbosch, Western Cape.

Ian Macleod Distillers Ltd (Scot) a distillery (established 1936). (Add): Russell House, Dunnet Way, Broxburn, West Lothian EH52 5BU. Produces whiskies (malt and grain) and other spirits. Website: http://www.ianmacleod.com 'E'mail: info@ianmacleod.com

Iaoue (Ch.Isles) water. *See also* Iaue.

Iaoue d'Orge (Ch.Isles) barley water.

I.A.S. (Rum) *abbr*: Interprinderile Agricole de Stat, the State Agricultural Enterprise. *See also* G.A.S. (The old-style name for I.A.S.).

Iata Valley (Chile) a wine district based in southern Chile.

Iaue (Ch.Isles) water, *See also* Iaoue.

Iberia (Euro) a peninsular that contains the wine-producing countries of Spain and Portugal.

Iberia Cream (Sp) a blend of fine Pedro ximénez and Oloroso Sherries produced by Romate.

Ibera (Bra) an alkaline natural spring mineral water. Mineral contents (milligrammes per litre): Sodium 96.43mg/l, Calcium 0.42mg/l, Magnesium 0.01mg/l, Potassium 0.28mg/l, Bicarbonates 96.07mg/l, Chlorides 2.96mg/l, Sulphates 43.43mg/l, Fluorides 0.55mg/l, Nitrates 0.16mg/l. pH 10.03

Ibis (S.Afr) the label for a red wine (Cinsaut, Ruby cabernet and Merlot blend) produced by the Schalkenbosch Wines winery, Tulbagh, Western Cape.

Ibiza (Sp) a wine-producing island that produces highly alcoholic wines mainly from co-operative vineyards.

Ibrik (Tur) a small brass or tin lined copper pots for making Turkish coffee. (Arab) = kanaka, (Gre) = briki.

Iby [Anton] (Aus) a winery (10ha) based in Horitschon, Mittel-Burgenland. (Add): Kirchengasse 4a, 7312 Horitschon. Grape varieties: Blaufränkisch, Cabernet sauvignon, Merlot, Pinot noir, Zweigelt. Produces a variety of wines.

Ica (S.Am) a wine-producing area in Peru. The noted Facama vineyard is in the region.

I Can't Remember (Eng) a 6.8% alc by vol. strong ale brewed by Stumpy's Brewery, Hampshire.

Icarus (Eng) a 4.5% alc by vol. ale brewed by the Blindmans Brewery, Somerset.

I.C.C.A. (USA) *abbr*: The International Correspondence of Corkscrew Addicts the guild of corkscrew collectors formed by the Christian Brothers of California.

Ice (Eng) frozen water at 0°C (32°F) or lower, used to cool drinks down quickly by adding to or surrounding with the ice. (Arab) = thalej, (Chi) = bing, (Cro) = led, (Den) = is, (Fr) = glaçon/glaçons, (Ger) = eiswürfel, (Gre) = pagos, (Hol) = het ijs, (Indo) = es, (Ire) = leac, (Isr) = kerah, (It) = ghiaccio, (Jap) = koori, (Kor) = uleum, (Port) = gelo, (Rus) = lyot, (Sp) = hielo, (Thai) = namkaeng.

Ice Age (Can) a natural spring mineral water from Alpine Creek, Toba Inlet, British Columbia.

Ice Beer (Can) fully fermented beer chilled to -4°C (24.8°F) during brewing. At this point crystals form and concentrate the various flavours within it. The Labatt Brewery granted patent rights for the ice beer by US patent office.

Iceberg (N.Am) a vodka produced in Newfoundland.

Iceberg (Cktl) in a highball glass place some ice cubes, 50mls vodka, add a dash of Pernod and stir.

Iceberg Cocktail (Cktl) 25mls (⅕ gill) Galliano, 20mls (⅙ gill) triple sec, scoop orange water ice. Blend altogether in a blender and serve in a Champagne flute with straws.

Ice Blue (Ice) a still natural spring mineral water from Thorlakshofn. Mineral contents (milligrammes per litre): Sodium 11.6mg/l, Calcium 5.5mg/l, Magnesium 2.5mg/l, Potassium 0.7mg/l, Chlorides 13.9mg/l, Sulphates 3.9mg/l, Nitrates <0.12mg/l. pH 7.9

Ice-Bock (Ger) a strong beer with an O.G. of 25.

Icebreaker Cocktail (Cktl) 1½ measures tequila, ½ measure grapefruit juice, 10mls Cointreau, dash grenadine, scoop of crushed ice. Blend altogether in a blender and serve with crushed ice in a Champagne flute.

Ice Bucket (Eng) a container which is usually insulated and is used for holding ice in the bar.

Ice Cap (Cktl) 25mls (1fl.oz) brandy, 20mls (¾ fl.oz) crème de cacao, 1 teaspoon of cream. Shake over ice and strain into 125mls (5fl.oz) wine glass.

Içecek (Tur) beverage/drink.

Ice Cold (Austr) a term for a glass of lager.

Ice Cream Flip (Cktl) 25mls Cointreau, 25mls maraschino, 1 egg, 1 scoop vanilla ice cream. Blend altogether in a blender and serve in a large goblet.

Ice Cream Soda (USA) soda water, milk, flavourings and ice cream served together in a tall glass.

I

Iced Bishop (Punch) 1 bottle Champagne, 125mls tea (lime blossom), 125mls gomme syrup, slice of orange and lemon. Mix altogether, chill down, add 125mls brandy and serve over crushed ice in old-fashioned glasses.

Iced Cider (Can) a cider produced from apples crushed at -25°C which produces a sweet cider at approximately 12% alc by vol.

Iced Coffee (Eng) fresh brewed coffee, cooled, sweetened with sugar syrup, served over ice and top with whipped cream.

Iced Coffee Fillip (Cktl) 200mls strong black coffee, 15mls Tia Maria. Stir over ice and strain into a highball glass.

Iced Dragon (Eng) a strong white cider from the Gaymer Group. *See also* Fatboys, Kells Edge.

Iced Mint Tea (Eng) steep 12 mint sprigs in 2 cups of boiling water for 30minutes. Strain, cool and combine with 1litre cold water in a large jug. Add sugar to taste and serve in tall glasses with ice and garnish with a spiral of lemon peel and mint sprigs.

Iced Tea (Eng) freshly brewed tea, cooled, sweetened with sugar syrup, served over ice with a slice of lemon. Proprietary iced teas are also flavoured with fruits.

Iced Water (Eng) water chilled down in a refrigerator but containing no ice cubes. (Aus) = eiswasser, (Fr) = eau glacée/eau frappé, (Ger) = eiswasser, (Ire) = uisce oighrithe, (Sp) = agua helada.

Ice Gold (Eng) a lager beer from Brent Walkers' Hartlepool Brewery 3% alc by vol.

Iceland Artic (Ice) a natural spring mineral water (established 2000). Mineral contents (milligrammes per litre): Sodium 11.6mg/l, Calcium 5.5mg/l, Magnesium 2.5mg/l, Potassium 0.7mg/l, Chlorides 13.9mg/l, Sulphates 3.9mg/l, Nitrates <0.12mg/l. pH 7.9

Iceland Spring (Ice) a natural spring mineral water (established 1990) from Heidmonk. Mineral contents (milligrammes per litre): Sodium 11.5mg/l, Calcium 4.5mg/l, Magnesium 0.92mg/l, Potassium 0.5mg/l, Chlorides 10.9mg/l, Sulphates 5mg/l, Fluorides 0.2mg/l, Nitrates <0.1mg/l.

Ice Mist (Swe) a slightly alkaline natural spring mineral water from Aqua Terrena, Morarp. Mineral contents (milligrammes per litre): Sodium <9.8mg/l, Calcium <3.3mg/l, Magnesium <0.95mg/l, Potassium <0.8mg/l, Fluorides <0.06mg/l. pH 8.7

Ice Mountain (USA) a natural spring mineral water (established 1859) from Mount Zircon, Maine. Mineral contents (milligrammes per litre): Sodium 1.1mg/l, Calcium 1.3mg/l, Magnesium 1.3mg/l, Potassium 0.8mg/l, Bicarbonates 46.1mg/l, Chlorides 1.1mg/l, Sulphates 4.7mg/l. pH 6.98

Ice Machine (Eng) a machine (refrigerated) which automatically produces ice cubes (in various shapes depending on the make of the machine) suitable for drinks.

Iceni Brewery (Eng) a brewery (established 1995). (Add): 3, Foulden Road, Ickburgh, Thetford, Norfolk IP26 5HB. Brews: Festivale (for the Norwich and Norfolk festival)., Fine Soft Day 4% alc by vol., Man of Norfolk 4.2% alc by vol., Raspberry Wheat Beer at 5% alc by vol. Website: http://www.icenibrewery.co.uk 'E'mail: icenibrewe@aol.com

Ice Pick (Eng) an implement (either hammer-shaped or rod-shapped) used to chip pieces of ice from large blocks for drinks, especially cocktails.

Ice River Springs (USA) a natural spring mineral water from Feversham, Lake Ontario.

Ice Saints (Fr) sometimes referred to by growers (Servatius, Boniface and Sophid) whose days occur in mid-May, the time when late frosts can seriously damage the vine. *see* Saints.

Ice Scoop (Eng) an implement for picking up and transferring crushed and shaved ice from container to glass.

Ice Shaver (Eng) a special implement for taking off slivers of ice from a large block so that they can be used to cool down drinks quickly.

Ice Tongs (Eng) an implement for handling ice from the ice bucket to the glass or cocktail shaker etc.

Ice Valley (Eng) a natural spring mineral water from Shepley, Huddersfield.

Icewater (Can) a natural spring mineral water from Alberta.

Ice Water (USA) drinking water cooled by refrigeration (or by the addition of ice cubes).

Ice Wine (Can) a wine made to VQA standards from ripe grapes picked in mid-winter when the grapes are frozen on the vine. The yield is from 75–100litres of must per tonne of grapes. Has a potential alcohol content in excess of 15% alc by vol.

Ice Wine (Ger) *see* Eiswein.

Ichbien (Cktl) ¾ measure Cognac, ¼ measure Grand Marnier, yolk of egg, 3 measures milk. Shake well over ice, strain into a 125mls goblet and grate nutmeg on top.

Ichiban Shirori (Jap) lit: 'first pressings' a brewing process where the ingredients are only pressed once during extraction of the malt sugars. Process was created by and is only used by the Kirin Brewery.

Içilen Sey (Tur) beverage/drink.

Içki (Tur) drink.

Içkili (Tur) a licensed restaurant, also denotes 'a drink'.

Içme (Tur) mineral water/spring drinking water.

Icod (Sp) a white wine 11%–13% alc by vol. produced on the Canary Islands.

Icon (Eng) a 4.2% alc by vol. ale brewed by the Salopian Brewing C°. Ltd., Shropshire.

I.C.S. (Eng) *abbr*: **I**n **C**an **S**ystem.

Ida (Czec) a natural spring mineral water (established 1932) from Nachod. Mineral contents (milligrammes per litre): Sodium 69.32mg/l, Calcium 73.67mg/l, Magnesium 21.87mg/l, Potassium 8.78mg/l, Bicarbonates 395.1mg/l, Chlorides 9.56mg/l, Fluorides 0.197mg/l, Nitrates 2.99mg/l, Silicates 30.02mg/l.

I

Idaho (USA) a lesser wine-producing region in the Pacific North-West.

Idaho Ice (USA) a natural spring mineral water from Elk River, Idaho.

Ideal (Cktl) 25mls (1fl.oz) gin, 10mls (½ fl.oz) grapefruit juice, 10mls (½ fl.oz) dry vermouth, 1 teaspoon powdered sugar, 2 dashes Angostura. Shake over ice, strain into a cocktail glass and add a cherry.

Ideas of March (Eng) a 4.7% alc by vol. ale brewed from Progress hops by the Rudgate Brewery, York.

Idig (Ger) vineyard (Anb): Pfalz. (Ber): Mittelhaardt-Deutsche Weinstrasse. (Gro): Meerspinne. (Vil): Königsbach.

Idiom (S.Afr) a winery (established 2003) based on the Hottentots Holland Mountains, Sir Lowry's Pass, Western Cape. 32ha. Grape varieties: Cabernet franc, Cabernet sauvignon, Merlot, Mourvèdre, Sangiovese, Shiraz, Viognier, Zinfandel. Label: Bordeaux Blend. Website: http://www.idiom.co.za

Idrea (It) a natural spring mineral water from Pradidali Bassa.

Idrel (Fr) a natural spring mineral water from Fiée des Lois. Mineral contents (milligrammes per litre): Sodium 17mg/l, Calcium 89mg/l, Magnesium 31mg/l, Potassium 2mg/l, Bicarbonates 360mg/l, Chlorides 28mg/l, Sulphates 47mg/l, Fluorides 1mg/l, Nitrates <0.05mg/l. pH 7.2

Idris Ginger Beer (Eng) a non-alcoholic ginger beer sold in 180mls glass bottles from Britvic.

I.D.V. (Eng) abbr: International Distillers and Vintners C°.

Idyll Blush (Austr) a rosé wine made from the Shiraz grape from the Idyll Vineyard, Moorabool, Victoria.

Idyll Vineyard (Austr) a vineyard (established 1966). (Add): Ballan Road, Moorabool, Victoria, 3221. Grape varieties: Cabernet sauvignon, Chardonnay, Gewürztraminer and Shiraz. Labels include Idyll Blush, Bone Idyll.

Iechyd Dda (Wal) cheers!/good health.

Ifri [1] (Alg) a still natural spring mineral water. Mineral contents (milligrammes per litre): Sodium 15.8mg/l, Calcium 65.5mg/l, Magnesium 18.5mg/l, Potassium 2.1mg/l, Bicarbonates 263mg/l, Chlorides 19mg/l, Sulphates 35mg/l, Nitrates <2mg/l, Silicates 8.7mg/l. pH 7.2

Ifri [2] (Alg) a slightly acidic sparkling natural spring mineral water. Mineral contents (milligrammes per litre): Sodium 15.8mg/l, Calcium 65.5mg/l, Magnesium 15.8mg/l, Potassium 2.1mg/l, Bicarbonates 221mg/l, Chlorides 19mg/l, Sulphates 35mg/l, Nitrates <2mg/l, Silicates 8.7mg/l. pH 5.38

Igea (It) a natural spring mineral water from Igea.

Igel (Ger) village (Anb): Mosel-Saar-Ruwer. (Ber): Obermosel. (Gro): Königsberg. (Vin): Dullgäten.

Ightham Vineyard (Eng) a vineyard (established 1972). (Add): Ivy Hatch, Kent. 1.25 ha. Grape variety: Müller-Thurgau.

Igler (Aus) a winery (10ha) based in Deutschkreutz, Mittel-Burgenland. (Add): Langegasse 49, 7301 Deutschkreutz. Grape varieties: Blaufränkisch, Cabernet sauvignon, Pinot noir, St. Laurent. Label: Vulcano.

Igloos (Port) the name given to the large concrete domes that are used to store wines for short periods. see Baloes.

I Grilli di Villa (It) the name for a blended red wine produced by Terre di Ginestra in San Cipirello.

I.G.T. (It) abbr: Indicazione Geografica Tipici.

Iguazu (Arg) lit: 'great waters', the name of a 5.2% alc by vol. malt brew lager.

Ihringen (Ger) village (Anb): Baden. (Ber): Kaiserstuhl-Tuniberg. (Gro): Vulkanfelsen. (Vins): Castellberg, Fohrenberg, Kreuzhalde, Schlossberg, Steinfelsen, Winklerberg.

Ihringen [ortsteil Blankenhornsberg] (Ger) village (Anb): Baden. (Ber): Kaiserstuhl-Tuniberg. (Gro): Vulkanfelsen. (Vin): Doktorgarten.

Iianhuashan (Chi) a natural spring mineral water. Mineral contents (milligrammes per litre): Silicates 29.3mg/l.

III aC (Sp) a limited edition (2001 vintage) D.O.Ca. Rioja from Bodegas Beronia.

Ijalba (Sp) an organic winery in Rioja that produces a 100% Maturana or 100% Graciano wine.

IJ-Bockbier (Hol) a 6.5% alc by vol. bottle-conditioned, seasonal, dark-brown bock beer brewed by 't IJ Brouwerij, Amsterdam.

Ijs (Hol) ice.

Ika Cocktail (Cktl) 40mls (⅓ gill) gin, 20mls (⅙ gill) grenadine. Stir over ice, strain into a cocktail glass and serve with a dash of lemon peel juice on top.

IKB (Eng) a 4.5% alc by vol. bitter ale brewed by the Wickwar Brewing C°. Ltd., Gloucestershire.

Ikhalezi (S.Afr) the label for a white wine (Chenin blanc) produced by the Springfontein winery, Walker Bay, Western Cape.

Ikon Vodka (Rus) a 40% alc by vol. vodka that is quadruple distilled.

Iksir (Tur) elixir/liqueur.

Ilbesheim (Ger) village (Anb): Pfalz. (Ber): Südliche Weinstrasse. (Gro): Herrlich. (Vin): Rittersberg.

Île Bouchard (Fr) an island in the river Gironde, Bordeaux, produces both red and white wines.

Ileburger Sachsenquelle (Ger) a natural spring mineral water. Mineral contents (milligrammes per litre): Sodium 12mg/l, Calcium 71mg/l, Magnesium 11mg/l, Potassium 2mg/l, Bicarbonates 259mg/l, Chlorides 14mg/l, Sulphates 14mg/l.

Ileburger Schlossbrunnen (Ger) a natural spring mineral water. Mineral contents (milligrammes per litre): Sodium 9.7mg/l, Calcium 70.4mg/l, Magnesium 9.5mg/l, Potassium 2.6mg/l, Chlorides 13.9mg/l, Fluorides 0.48mg/l.

Île de Beauté (Fr) a Vin de Pays area on Corsica, produces red, rosé and white wines.

Île-de-France (Fr) caused by an earthquake 20 million years ago. Raised the level of the chalk ground approx 300feet (95metres). The Franco-

British basin of chalk was split and tertiary deposits settled on the surface 11 million years ago. The Champagne region is situated on this.

Île de Ré (Fr) part of the Bois Ordinaires in the Cognac district of the Charente-Maritime département, western France.

Île-des-Vergelesses (Fr) an area of 97ha in the commune of Pernand in the Côte d'Or, Burgundy. Produces white wines of finesse and distinction. Has a Premier Cru vineyard in the A.C. Pernand-Vergelesses.

Île-des-Vergelesses (Fr) a Premier Cru vineyard in the A.C. commune of Pernand-Vergelesses, Côte de Beaune, Burgundy 9.2ha.

Île des Vignes (Eng) the old Norman name for the Isle of Ely in Cambridgeshire.

Île d'Oléron (Fr) part of the Bois Ordinaires in the Cognac district of the Charente-Maritime département, western France.

Île du Nord (Fr) an island in the river Gironde, Bordeaux, produces mainly red wines.

Île Fumadelle (Fr) an island in the river Gironde, Bordeaux, produces red wines under commune of Soussans, A.C. Haut-Médoc, Bordeaux.

Île Margaux (Fr) an island in the river Gironde, Bordeaux, produces mainly red wines.

Île Nouvelle (Fr) an island in the river Gironde, Bordeaux, produces red and white wines. Also known as the Île Sanspain.

Île Patiras (Fr) an island in the river Gironde, Bordeaux, produces red and white wines.

Île Sanspain (Fr) *see* Île Nouvelle.

Îles de la Gironde (Fr) the collective name for the group of islands off the Haut-Médoc in the river Gironde, Bordeaux. *see* Îles Bouchard, du Nord, Fumadelle, Margaux, Nouvelle (Sanspain), Patiras and Île Verte, produces red and white wines.

Île Verte (Fr) an island in the river Gironde, Bordeaux, produces red and white wines.

Il Falcone (It) a red D.O.C. Castel del Monte wine produced from 70% Nero di troia and 30% Montepulciano grapes by Rivera in Andria, Puglia.

Ilidzanski Dijamant (Euro) a natural spring mineral water from Bosnia and Herzegovina. Mineral contents (milligrammes per litre): Sodium 118mg/l, Calcium 358mg/l, Magnesium 107mg/l, Potassium 7.8mg/l, Bicarbonates 1330mg/l, Chlorides 129mg/l, Sulphates 307mg/l, Fluorides 0.39mg/l, Strontium 1.1mg/l.

Ilina (Euro) a still natural spring mineral water from Ilina s.Velmej, Macedonia. Mineral contents (milligrammes per litre): Sodium 5.8mg/l, Calcium 187.2mg/l, Magnesium 36.8mg/l, Potassium 9mg/l, Bicarbonates 701.5mg/l, Chlorides 3.3mg/l, Sulphates 13.1mg/l, Fluorides 0.1mg/l, Nitrates 0.3mg/l. pH 7.03

Ill [River] (Fr) the river that runs through the Alsace region, a tributary of the river Rhine. *see* Ilsace.

Illats (Fr) a commune within the district of A.C. Cérons in south-western Bordeaux, produces sweet white wines.

Illicium anisatum (Lat) the botanical name for badiane, a form of anise from China used in the making of pastis.

Illingen (Ger) village (Anb): Württemberg. (Ber): Württembergisch Unterland. (Gro): Stromberg. (Vins): Forstgrube, Halde, Lichtenberg, Schanzreiter.

Illinois (USA) a large wine-producing state, has many wineries producing most styles of wines from French hybrid and *Vitis vinifera* vines.

Illmitz (Aus) a wine-producing area in the Eisenstadt district.

Il Poggiolo di E. Roberto Cosimi (It) a winery. (Add): Loc. Il Poggiolo 259, 53024 Montalcino (SI). Winery that produces D.O.C.G. Beato Brunello di Montalcino. Made from Sangiovese grosso grapes and is aged for 2 years in new 500 litre Allier oak casks.

Illuminati (It) a 50 ha winery based at Controguerra in Abruzzo. Controls Fattoria Nico, noted for Montepulciano d'Abruzzo.

Illustre Cour des Seigneurs de la Corbière (Fr) a wine society based in the Midi.

Illva (It) a famous Amaretto di Saronno producer.

Illy Coffee (It) a popular brand of Italian coffee.

Illy Coffee Liqueur (It) a coffee liqueur produced in Ancona from the famous Illy coffee 30% alc by vol.

Il Mongetto (IT) a winery based in Piedmont. Produces La Guera (D.O.C. Barbera d'Asti barrique-aged wine).

Il Nibbio Grigio (It) lit: 'grey kite' a D.O.C. Aglianico del Vulture wine produced by Di Palme in Basilicata.

Ilok (Cro) a major wine town in northern Croatia.

Il Palagione sas di Monica Rota & c (It) a winery based in the DOCG Vernaccia di San Gimignano in the Tuscany region. Label: IGT Antajr (20% Cabernet sauvignon, 20% Merlot, 60% Sangiovese), Hydra. Website: http://www.ilpalagione.com 'E'mail: info@ilpalagione.com

Il Querciolaia (It) a red I.G.T. wine produced from 65% Sangiovese and 35% Cabernet sauvignon grapes by Castello di Querceto in Tuscany.

Ilsace (Fr) the original name from which Alsace derives, from the river Ill (a tributary of the Rhine). *See also* Elsass.

Ilsfeld (Ger) village (Anb): Württemberg. (Ber): Württembergisch Unterland. (Gro): Schozachtal. (Vin): Rappen.

Ilsfeld (Ger) village (Anb): Württemberg. (Ber): Württembergisch Unterland. (Gro): Wunnenstein. (Vin): Lichtenberg.

Ilsfeld [ortsteil Schozach] (Ger) village (Anb): Württemberg. (Ber): Württembergisch Unterland. (Gro): Kirchenweinberg. (Vins): Mühlberg, Roter Berg, Schelmenklinge.

Il Solissimo (It) an I.G.T. red wine produced by Castello di Lucignano, Gaiole in Chianti, Tuscany.

Imbazo (S.Afr) the label for a range of wines produced by the Ernst & CO Wines winery, Stellenbosch, Western Cape.

Im Berg (Aus) a vineyard site on the banks of the River Danube in the Kremstal region.

Imbibe (Eng) to drink.

Imbik (Tur) pot still.

Imbottare (It) put in barrels.

Imbottigliare (It) to bottle/bottled up.

Imbottigliato (It) bottled.

Imbottigliato all'Origine (It) bottled in the region of origin. Estate bottled.

Imbottigliato Nello Stabilemento Della Ditta (It) bottled on the premises of the firm.

Imbuteliat (Rum) bottled.

Imbuvable (Fr) undrinkable.

Indalo (S.Afr) a label for a red wine (Cabernet sauvignon) from the Swartland winery based in the Stellenbosch, Western Cape.

Imesch (Switz) a red wine produced in Sion, Valais canton. Produced from the Pinot noir grape.

Im Felseneck (Ger) vineyard (Anb): Nahe. (Ber): Schloss Böckelheim. (Gro): Rosengarten. (Vil): Bockenau.

Im Füchschen (Ger) a brewery at 28, Ratingerstrasse, Düsseldorf, noted for altbier. see Im Füchschen Altbier.

Im Füchschen Altbier (Ger) a fine hoppy altbier brewed by the Im Füchschen Brauerei in Düsseldorf.

Im Grossen Feld (Aus) a vineyard site on the banks of the River Danube in the Kremstal region.

Im Heubusch (Ger) vineyard (Anb): Pfalz. (Ber): Mittelhaardt-Deutsche Weinstrasse. (Gro): Schnepfenflug vom Kellertal. (Vil): Morschheim.

Imiglykos (Gre) a range of red and white, medium-sweet table wines produced by Tsantali.

Im Innern Thalland (Aus) a vineyard site on the banks of the River Danube in the Kremstal region.

Immature Spirits Act (Eng) states that no spirits may be sold in Great Britain under 3 years old.

Immengarten (Ger) vineyard (Anb): Pfalz. (Ber): Südliche Weinstrasse. (Gro): Mandelhöhle. (Vil): Maikammer.

Immenhof Heidequelle (Ger) a still natural spring mineral water (established 1995) from Immenhof Heidequelle, Hützel. Mineral contents (milligrammes per litre): Sodium 4.9mg/l, Calcium 14.5mg/l, Magnesium 1.61mg/l, Potassium 0.64mg/l, Chlorides 8mg/l, Sulphates 1.51mg/l, Nitrates <0.01mg/l. pH 6.9

Immenstaad (Ger) village (Anb): Baden. (Ber): Bodensee. (Gro): Sonnenufer. (Vin): Burgstall.

Immesheim (Ger) village (Anb): Pfalz. (Ber): Mittelhaardt-Deutsche Weinstrasse. (Gro): Schnepfenflug vom Kellertal. (Vin): Sonnenstück.

Immiscible (Eng) unmixable, denotes two or more liquids that are incapable of being mixed to a homogeneous substance. i.e. oil and water.

Immortal Memory (Scot) the label of a blended Scotch whisky 40% alc by vol.

Imnauer Apollo (Ger) a sparkling natural spring mineral water. (red label: sparkling/blue label: low gas). Mineral contents (milligrammes per litre): Sodium 29mg/l, Calcium 519mg/l, Magnesium 44.9mg/l, Potassium 4.1mg/l, Bicarbonates 481.7mg/l, Chlorides 35.5mg/l, Sulphates 1065mg/l, Fluorides 0.53mg/l, Nitrates 0.03mg/l.

Imnauer Fürstenquellen (Ger) a still and sparkling natural spring mineral water. (red label: sparkling/green label: low gas/blue label: still). Mineral contents (milligrammes per litre): Sodium 22.1mg/l, Calcium 410mg/l, Magnesium 55.6mg/l, Potassium 7.4mg/l, Bicarbonates 625mg/l, Chlorides 44.2mg/l, Sulphates 710mg/l, Fluorides 0.5mg/l, Nitrates 0.6mg/l.

Imnauer Fürstenquellen Eugenie-Quelle (Ger) a sparkling natural spring mineral water. Mineral contents (milligrammes per litre): Sodium 27mg/l, Calcium 378mg/l, Magnesium 56mg/l, Potassium 6.4mg/l, Bicarbonates 940mg/l, Chlorides 53.5mg/l, Fluorides 0.51mg/l, Nitrates 1.8mg/l, Strontium 1.2mg/l, Silicates 14.02mg/l.

Imnauer Fürstenquellen Heilfüllung (Ger) a sparkling natural spring mineral water. Mineral contents (milligrammes per litre): Sodium 40mg/l, Calcium 369mg/l, Magnesium 57mg/l, Potassium 18mg/l, Bicarbonates 976mg/l, Chlorides 76.2mg/l, Sulphates 347mg/l, Fluorides 0.48mg/l, Nitrates 8.2mg/l, Silicates 17mg/l.

Im Neuberg (Ger) vineyard (Anb): Nahe. (Ber): Schloss Böckelheim. (Gro): Rosengarten. (Vil): Bockenau.

Impala (S.Afr) the label for a range of wines produced at Goue Vallei in Citrusdal.

Im Paschingerin (Aus) vineyard sites (2) on the banks of the River Danube in the Kremstal region.

Imperator (Hol) an all-malt, lightly hopped, unpasteurised beer 6.3% alc by vol. Brewed by the Brand Brouwerij in Wijlre, Limburg.

Imperial (Can) a blended Canadian whiskey produced by Hiram Walker.

Imperial (Chi) a grade of medium aged tea.

Imperial (Cktl) ⅓ measure Mandarine Napoléon, ⅓ measure dry gin, ⅙ measure amaretto, ⅙ measure Sambuca, 1 dash lemon juice. Shake well over ice and strain into a cocktail glass.

Imperial (Eng) see Impériale (8 bottle capacity).

Imperial (Iran) a white grape variety from the Tauris region.

Imperial (Jap) a brand of whiskey produced by the Suntory C°.

Impérial (Port) a red wine produced by the Caves Império.

Impérial (Port) the brand-name for a 20 year old tawny Port from Seagram, a partner to Royal (a 10 year old tawny port).

Imperial (Scot) a single highland malt whisky distillery operated by the Dailuaine-Talisker distilleries Ltd. Part of the DCL Group. Produces an 18 year old malt 43% alc by vol. and a 1979 vintage.

Imperial (Sp) a brand of fine old matured red wine from the Rioja of Reserva and Gran Reserva classification. Produced by C.V.N.E.

703

Imperial (Sp) a sparkling natural spring mineral water. Mineral contents (milligrammes per litre): Sodium 1138mg/l, Potassium 52.7mg/l, Bicarbonates 2196mg/l, Chlorides 602mg/l, Sulphates 53.7mg/l, Fluorides 7.8mg/l.

Imperial Bitter (Eng) a keg bitter 1042 O.G. brewed by the Tetley Brewery for north-eastern England.

Imperial Blend (Eng) a brand of fine teas produced by Ridgways C°.

Imperial Bounty (Austr) the brand-name for red and white dessert wines.

Imperial Cocktail (Cktl) 1 part dry vermouth, 1 part gin, 2 dashes maraschino, 1 dash Angostura. Stir over ice, strain into a cocktail glass and decorate with a cherry.

Imperial Drinks (Eng) a company based at Bishops Stortford in Hertfordshire. Markets: Hi Energy Mix, Raw Spirit Mix, Baux Bier.

Impériale (Fr) a large bottle that holds between 6–9 bottles. Claret is sometimes matured in them 1½ gallons (6½ litres).

Imperial Fino (Sp) a brand of Fino Sherry from the Diez Hermanos produced by Diez Merito.

Imperial Fizz (Cktl) ¾ measure Scotch whisky, ¼ measure Bacardi White Label, juice ½ lemon. Shake over ice, strain into an ice-filled highball glass and top with a dash of soda water.

Imperial Nineteen Fourteen [1914] (Sp) an old Oloroso Sherry produced by Domecq.

Imperial Old Ale (Eng) a dark barley wine 1096 O.G. brewed by the Banks Brewery in Wolverhampton, Staffordshire.

Imperial Pale (Scot) a bottled pale ale 1030 O.G. brewed by the Maclays Brewery in Alloa, Clackmannanshire.

Imperial Pint (Eng) a 4% alc by vol. ale brewed by the Anglo Dutch Brewery, West Yorkshire.

Imperial Pint (Fr) a Champagne bottle (20fl.ozs) capacity which is now no longer produced.

Imperial Pop (Eng) a drink made from ginger, lemon juice, sugar and cream of tartar, fermented with yeast.

Imperial Russian Stout (Rus) a strong beer 1096–1108 O.G. First brewed in 1781 for the Czar in St. Petersberg. Brewed for the U.K. by Courage Brewery. *See also* Russian Stout.

Imperial Scotch Whisky [The] (Ch.Isles) the brand-name for a Scotch whisky imported and bottled by Le Riches (now C.I. Traders) Stores of Jersey and Guernsey 43% alc by vol.

Imperial Stout (Eng) a high gravity stout exported in the nineteenth century to Russia. Also produced in Denmark and Finland. Brewed by Courage.

Imperial Stout (Eng) a 7% alc by vol. stout brewed by the Darwin Brewery, Tyne & Wear.

Imperial Stout (Eng) a stout 7% alc by vol. from the Smith (Samuel) Brewery in Tadcaster, Yorkshire.

Imperial Tawny (Port) a full-bodied Tawny Port from Sandeman shippers (20 year old).

Imperial Vinícola Limitada (Port) a noted shipper of Dão wines.

Imperio Grand Reserva (Sp) a 5 year old brandy produced by Terry.

Impesa (Mad) first pressing.

Impflingen (Ger) village (Anb): Pfalz. (Ber): Südliche Weinstrasse. (Gro): Herrlich. (Vin): Abtsberg.

Imp. Gal. (Eng) *abbr*: **Imp**erial **Gal**lon. Also Imp. Gall.

Imp. Gall. (Eng) *abbr*: **Imp**erial **Gall**on. Also Imp. Gal.

Impigno (It) a white grape variety grown in Puglia.

Impotable (Fr) undrinkable.

Impregnation Method (Eng) a method of making sparkling wines by putting the wine into a pressurised tank then injecting CO_2 gas into it. It is then bottled under pressure. When opened, gives off large bubbles and goes '*flat*' quickly.

Improvement of Musts (Eng) *see* Chaptalisation.

Im Renner (Aus) a vineyard site based on the banks of the River Kamp situated in the Kamptal region.

Im Röttgen (Ger) vineyard (Anb): Mosel-Saar-Ruwer. (Ber): Zell/Mosel. (Gro): Weinhex. (Vil): Güls.

Im Röttgen (Ger) vineyard (Anb): Mosel-Saar-Ruwer. (Ber): Zell/Mosel. (Gro): Weinhex. (Vil): Winningen.

Im Saherken (Aus) a vineyard site on the banks of the River Danube in the Kremstal region.

Imsdal (Nor) a sparkling natural spring mineral water from Kilden i Imsdalen. Mineral contents (milligrammes per litre): Sodium 0.9mg/l, Calcium 9.9mg/l, Magnesium 0.4mg/l, Potassium 0.5mg/l, Bicarbonates 31.2mg/l, Chlorides 0.6mg/l, Sulphates 2.9mg/l, Silicates 7mg/l. pH 7.5

Im Sonnenschein (Ger). Vineyard. (Anb): Pfalz. (Ber): Südliche Weinstrasse. (Gro): Königsgarten. (Vil): Siebeldingen.

Im Stein (Ger) vineyard (Anb): Franken. (Ber): Maindreieck. (Gro): Rosstal. (Vil): Karlstadt.

Im Talheim (Aus) a vineyard site on the banks of the River Danube in the Kremstal region.

Imvelo (S.Afr) the label for a range of varietal wines (Sauvignon blanc/Cabernet sauvignon) marketed by the Premium Cape Wines company, Stellenbosch, Western Cape.

Ina [La] (Sp) a pale dry Fino Sherry produced and bottled by Domecq (Pedro) S.A.

Inab (Arab) grape.

I.N.A.O. (Fr) *abbr*: **I**nstitut **N**ational des **A**ppellations d'**O**rigine des Vins et Eaux-de-Vie.

Inanda (S.Afr) the label for a red wine (Cabernet franc, Cabernet sauvignon and Merlot blend) produced by the Yonder Hill winery, Stellenbosch, Western Cape (part of WestCorp International).

Inaqva (Euro) a still natural spring mineral water from the Osogovo Mountains, Macedonia. Mineral contents (milligrammes per litre): Sodium 3.41mg/l, Calcium 3.9mg/l, Magnesium 0.47mg/l, Potassium 1.4mg/l, Bicarbonates 31.12mg/l, Chlorides 5mg/l, Sulphates 8.02mg/l, Fluorides 0.1mg/l. pH 7.1

InBev (Bel) a large brewing company formed with the amalgamation of Interbrew and AmBev.

(Add): Brouwerijplein 1, B-3000 Leuven. Brews a large range of beers and lager. Website: http://www.inbev.com

In Bond (Eng) *see* Bond.

In Bond Shop (W.Ind) duty free shop.

Inca Cocktail [1] (Cktl) ⅙ measure Plymouth gin, ⅙ measure French vermouth, ⅙ measure dry Sherry, 2 dashes orange bitters, 2 dashes orgeat syrup. Stir well over ice, strain into a cocktail glass, add a piece of pineapple and squeeze of orange peel on top.

Inca Cocktail [2] (Cktl) 15mls (⅛ gill) each of dry Sherry, French vermouth, gin, 1 teaspoon plain syrup, 1 teaspoon orange bitters. Stir over ice, strain into a cocktail glass, serve with a dash of orange peel juice and a cherry.

Inca Cocktail [3] (Cktl) ¼ measure dry Sherry, ¼ measure dry gin, ¼ measure French vermouth, ¼ measure Italian vermouth, dash orgeat, dash Campari. Shake over ice and strain into a cocktail glass.

In Can System (Eng) *abbr:* I.C.S. a plastic device fitted into the bottom of a canned beer/lager that on opening the can, is triggered to produce a creamy head on the top of the drink.

Inca Pisco (Peru) a well-known brand of pisco sold in black bottles moulded in the shape of an Indian head. Produced by Casa Ranuzzi.

INCAVI (Sp) *abbr:* **IN**stituto **CA**tal n de **VI**no, also spelt Institut Catala de la Vinya i del Vi.

Inchgower (Scot) a single highland malt whisky distillery near Buckie in Banffshire (owned by Arthur Bell and Sons Ltd). Produces a 12 year old malt 40% alc by vol.

Inch's Cider (Eng) a cider producer based at Winkleigh, Devon. Produces: Stonehouse (a strong dry cider), El Scrumpy (an oak matured cider) and White Lightning (taken over by Bulmer in 1996).

Incider Cocktail (Cktl) Pour 25mls (⅕ gill) Bourbon whiskey into an ice-filled old-fashioned glass, top with dry sparkling cider and a slice of apple.

Inciuccarsi (It) to become intoxicated (drunk).

Incognito (Cktl) ³⁄₁₀ measure Cognac brandy, ⁶⁄₁₀ measure Lillet, ¹⁄₁₀ measure apricot brandy, dash Angostura. Stir over ice and strain into a cocktail glass.

Income Tax (Cktl) ⅕ measure sweet vermouth, ⅕ measure dry vermouth, ⅕ measure dry gin, juice ¼ lemon, dash of Angostura. Shake over ice and strain into a cocktail glass.

Incorruptible Champagne Cocktail (Cktl) (Non-alc) 10mls (½ fl.oz) orange juice, 25mls (1 fl.oz) grapefruit juice. Shake over ice, strain into a Champagne flute and top with chilled lemonade.

Incrocio (It) crossing

Incrocio Terzi N.1. (It) a red grape variety grown in Lombardy, a cross between the Barbera and Cabernet franc.

Incrocio Manzoni 2.15 (It) a grape variety produced by crossing Prosecco x Cabernet sauvignon.

Incrocio Manzoni 6.0.13 (It) a white grape variety, a cross between Riesling x Pinot blanc.

Incrustation (Eng) a term used to describe the forming of a '*crust*' sediment in red wines. i.e. port, claret, etc.

Indaba (S.Afr) the label for a varietal red and white wine range produced by Cape Classics, Stellenbosch, Western Cape.

Indaia (Bra) a natural spring mineral water from Indaia, Bahia. Mineral contents (milligrammes per litre): Sodium 1.2mg/l, Calcium 17.09mg/l, Magnesium 9.29mg/l, Potassium 1.4mg/l, Bicarbonates 101.4mg/l, Chlorides 5.74mg/l, Fluorides 0.14mg/l, Nitrates 2.4mg/l. pH 7.6

Indalo (S.Afr) the label for a range of wines produced by the Swartland Wine Cellar winery, Swartland, Western Cape.

Ind Coope Brewery (Eng) a part of Allied Breweries. Originally two breweries based at Burton and Romford in Essex. Merged in 1961 with Ansells and Tetley Walker. Produce many fine cask conditioned, keg and bottled beers. *see* Double Diamond, Skol.

In Den Felsen (Ger) vineyard (Anb): Nahe. (Ber): Schloss Böckelheim. (Gro): Burgweg. (Vil): Schlossböckelheim.

In Den Layfelsen (Ger) vineyard (Anb): Mittelrhein. (Ber): Rheinburgengau. (Gro): Burg Hammerstein. (Vil): Hammerstein.

In Den Siebzehn Morgen (Ger) vineyard (Anb): Nahe. (Ber): Kreuznach. (Gro): Kronenberg. (Vil): Bad Kreuznach (ortsteil Winzenheim).

Independence (Scot) a 3.8% alc by vol. ale brewed by the Inveralmond Brewery Ltd., Perthshire.

Independence Day Punch (Punch) blend together in a large punch-bowl 800grms (2lbs) powdered sugar, 500mls (1pint) lemon juice, add 3 bottles claret, 1 bottle Cognac, 1 bottle Champagne, stir, add 6 sliced lemons, ice cubes and serve.

Independencia (Sp) a 10 year old solera gran reserva brandy produced by Osborne.

Independent Distillers (UK) Ltd (Eng) a distilling company. (Add): Oxon, SN7 8WX. Produces a variety of sprits, Chocshots, Jaii, Tatto, Vodka Mudshake, Vodka Twistee Shots and Woodstock Bourbon Cola. Website: http://www.independentdistillers.co.uk 'E'mail: enquiries@independentdistillers.co.uk

Independent Family Brewers of Britain (Eng) an organisation (established 1993). (Add): Albury House, The St. Albury, Guildford, Surrey GU5 9AE. Website: http://www.familybrewers.co.uk 'E'mail: rflynn@gemgroup.com

In der Eben (Aus) a vineyard site based on the banks of the River Kamp situated in the Kamptal region.

In der Gais (Aus) a vineyard site on the banks of the River Danube in the Kremstal region.

India (Ind) a large tea, coffee, wine and spirit producing country in central southern Asia. Wines produced for over 2,000 years in the regions: Dharmapuri, Kodaikanal, Madras and Penukanda. Vines of ***Vitis vinifera*** grafted on American root stock. *see* Omar Khayyam.

India Export Pale Ale (Eng) a 5.5% alc by vol. pale ale from Marston's, Burton-on-Trent. One of four beers in the '*Head Brewers Choice*' range.

Indiana (USA) a wine-producing state, produces mainly French hybrid wines.

Indiana Bones (Eng) a winter warmer ale from Summerskill Brewery, Plymouth.

Indian Breakfast (Ind) a blend of tea from the Assam province that has a distinct malty flavour.

Indian Cocktail (Cktl) 15mls (⅛ gill) each of whisky, Italian vermouth, gin, ½ teaspoon each of brown Curaçao, orange bitters and Cointreau, stir over ice and strain into a cocktail glass and serve with a dash of lemon peel juice.

Indian Coffee (Ind) mainly from the southern regions: Mysore, Tamil Nadu, Kerala Niligri, Coorg and Malabar. Produces a full-bodied taste and acidity.

Indianhead (Eng) an ale brewed by Redruth Brewery in Cornwall.

Indian Hills (USA) a natural spring mineral water from Murphy, North Carolina.

Indian Market (Mad) an old-style name for Madeira wine (sweet). Now no longer used.

Indian Quinine Water (Eng) the original name for tonic water.

Indian Summer Cocktail (Cktl) 1 measure white rum, 1 measure dry gin, 1½ measures coconut milk, 1 measure Malibu, 1 measure cream, scoop crushed ice, blend altogether in a blender. Pour into a highball glass, dress with a cherry, coconut slice and serve with straws.

Indian Summer IPA (Scot) a 4.1% alc by vol. India pale ale brewed by the Harviestoun Brewery, Clackmannanshire.

Indian Summer Pale Ale (Eng) a 4.2% alc by vol. ale brewed by the Swale Brewery, Sittingbourne.

Indian Teas (Ind) main production regions: Assam, Dooars, Cacher, Darjeeling, Kerala, Niligiri and Mysore.

Indian Tonic Water (Eng) see Indian Quinine Water.

India Pale Ale (Eng) the name originally applied to strong pale ales brewed to mature on the long sea voyage to India in the late eighteenth and early nineteenth centuries. Shipwrecked casks were retrieved and drunk, creating a home demand for more. Term now applies to draught bitters of ordinary quality and also for bottled beers of same strength.

Indicacao de Proveniência Regulamentada (Port) abbr: I.P.R. Denotes quality wines from 32 named regions. Identified by the Selo de Origem. Is equivalent to V.D.Q.S. in France.

Indication of Age (Port) applied to Tawny Ports that have been aged for 10, 20, 30 or over 40 years. Label must carry indication of age, year of bottling and state that it has been aged in cask.

Indicazione Geografica Tipici (It) abbr: I.G.T. Introduced in 1992 but was rejected as not registered with E.C. Name altered and accepted for 1996. Of Vina da Tavola category but with indication of area. see Vino da Indicazione.

Indigo Extra (Eng) bottled drink that is a mixture of peach, taurine, the Chinese herb schizandra, caffeine and glucose.

Indio Oscura (Mex) a Viennese-style lager beer.

Individual Berry Selected (USA) the American equivalent to the German trockenbeerenauslese with a sugar range of 32°–45° Balling.

Individual Bunch Selected (USA) the American equivalent to the German auslese or beerenauslese with a sugar range of 26°–32° Balling.

Individual Paddock (Austr) the brand-name of the Rothburg Estate vineyards in the Hunter Valley.

I.N.D.O. (Sp) abbr: Instituto Nacional de Denominaciones de Origen.

Indo (Viet) a natural spring mineral water.

Indonesian Coffee (E.Ind) the best is from Java, the Celebes Islands and Sumatra, with Bali and Timor producing good arabica coffee. They have a mellow flavour with a strong aroma.

Indonesian Teas (E.Ind) teas used mainly for blending.

Indre-et-Loire (Fr) a Vin de Pays area in Touraine in the Jardine de la France (Garden of France). Produces red, rosé and dry white wines.

Indústria Comércio e Navegção, Sociedade Vinícola Rio Grandense, Ltda. (Bra) the largest wine producer in Brazil. Produces both red and white wines under the Granja União label.

Industria Licorera de Bolivar (S.Am) a state-owned distillery based at Cartagena, Columbia. Produces Ron Popular, Três Esquinas, Gins and Aguardiente.

Industrias de la Fermentacíon (Mex) a large winery based in Saltillo, Coahuila.

Inebriate (Eng) to make drunk/intoxicate.

Inebriated Person (Eng) drunken person, usually defines a habitually drunken person.

Inebriety (Eng) drunkeness.

Inesquelle (Ger) a natural spring mineral water from Löhne. Mineral contents (milligrammes per litre): Sodium 25mg/l, Calcium 469mg/l, Magnesium 62mg/l, Potassium 2.9mg/l, Bicarbonates 254mg/l, Chlorides 121mg/l, Sulphates 1070mg/l.

Infanta Isabela (Port) a 10 year old dated Tawny Port from Rozés.

Infants Vintage Seco (Port) a wine produced by Caves Sao João.

I.N.F.E. (Sp) abbr: Instituto Nacional de Fomento de la Exportación.

Infectious Degeneration (Eng) a virus-like disease that attacks the vines. see Court Noué and Fanleaf.

Infernet (Fr) a red wine produced by Château Routas in the A.C. Coteaux Varois.

Inferno (It) a sub district of the Lombardy region in the foothills of the Alps in the Valtellina Valley. Produces red wines of the same name from the Nebbiolo grape.

Infernotti (It) secret cellars in the Piemonte region, also known as Crutin.

Infiascato (It) put in flasks.

Infiascato alla Fattoria (It) bottled in flasks at the winery.

Infinitus Vineyards (Arg) vineyards based in the Rio Negro, Patagonia. Grape varieties: Cabernet sauvignon, Chardonnay, Sémillon, Merlot.

Infinity (N.Z) a natural spring mineral water from Waiwera Resort.

I

Inführ (Aus) one of the countries leading sparkling wine producers. Produces: Gumpoldskirchner Königssekt, Ritter von Dürnstein trocken sekt.

Infuse (Eng) the action of steeping a solid in a liquid to extract the colour and flavour. i.e. coffee, tea, liqueurs.

Infused Wines (Austr) commercial wines that have had fruit concentrates added to enhance the natural flavours of the wines. *see* Nautico.

Infuser (Eng) a technical description of a tea maker. i.e. tea pot. *see* Tea Maker.

Infuser (Fr) to infuse. *See also* Tissane.

Infuseur à Thé (Fr) tea ball. *See also* Boule à Thé.

Infusion (Eng) the action of extracting the flavour and colour from a solid into a liquid. i.e. tea, liqueurs etc. Also during brewing applies to the extraction of the fermentable materials from the grist. *see* Decoction.

Infusionar (Sp) lit: 'to brew a cup of tea'.

Infusions (Eng) an alternative name for Tisanes.

Ing (Aus) *abbr*: **Ing**enieur.

Ingannacane (It) an alternative name for the Sangiovese grape.

Ingelfingen (Ger) village (Anb): Württemberg. (Ber): Kocher-Jagst-Tauber. (Gro): Kocherberg. (Vin): Hoher Berg.

Ingelheim (Ger) village (Anb): Rheinhessen. (Ber): Bingen. (Gro): Kaiserpfalz. (Vins): Burgweg, Höllenweg, Horn, Kirchenstück, Lottenstück, Pares, Rabenkopf, Rheinhöhe, Rotes Kreuz, Schlossberg, Schloss Westerhaus, Sonnenberg, Sonnenhang, Steinacker, Täuscherspfad.

Ingenieur (Aus) *abbr*: Ing, a wine qualification awarded to graduates from viticultural colleges. *see* Ing.

Inghams Winery (Austr) a winery based in the Barossa Valley, South Australia. Grape varieties: Cabernet sauvignon, Riesling, Shiraz. Labels: O'Leary Walker, Para River.

Ingieten (Hol) to infuse.

Ingieting (Hol) infusion.

Inglenook (USA) a vineyard in the Napa Valley, California. Grape varieties: Cabernet sauvignon, Charbono, Chardonnay, Chenin blanc, French colombard, Gewürztraminer, Johannisberg riesling, Sauvignon blanc, Pinot noir and Zinfandel. Produces quality still, sparkling and dessert wines.

Inglewood Vineyard (S.Afr) a vineyard based in the Coastal Region. Grape varieties include: Cabernet sauvignon, Chardonnay, Zinfandel.

Ingrandes (Fr) a commune in the A.C. Savennières, Anjou-Saumur, Loire.

Ingwerlikoer (Ger) a ginger liqueur.

Ingwe Vineyard (S.Afr) a winery (established 1998) based in the Somerset West, Western Cape. Grape varieties: Cabernet sauvignon, Chardonnay, Malbec, Merlot, Petit verdot, Sauvignon blanc, Shiraz. Labels: Amelho, Ingwe (48% Cabernet sauvignon and 52% Merlot).

Inhal.O (Can) a bottled, treated (purified) water brand.

Inishowen (Ire) a double distilled whiskey produced by Cooley in Dundalk.

Initiale Extra (Fr) a blend of V.O. Grande Champagne and Borderies eaux-de-vie from Corvoisier.

Initial Series (S.Afr) the label for a range of wines produced by the Jean Daneel Wines winery, Napier, Southern Cape.

Injection Method (Eng) the process of pumping of CO_2 gas into wine to make it sparkle.

Injerto (Sp) vine graft.

Inkará (S.Afr) the label for a range of red wines (Cabernet sauvignon and Shiraz) produced by the Bon Courage Estate winery, Robertson, Western Cape.

Inkawu (S.Afr) the export label for a range of wines produced by the Laibach Vineyards winery, Stellenbosch, Western Cape.

Inkeepers Special Reserve (Eng) a 4.5% alc by vol. ale brewed by the Coach House Brewing C°. Ltd., Cheshire.

Inkelhöll (Ger) vineyard (Anb): Nahe. (Ber): Schloss Böckelheim. (Gro): Paradiesgarten. (Vil): Lettweiler.

Ink Street (Cktl) ⅓ measure rye whiskey, ⅓ measure orange juice, ⅓ measure lemon juice. Shake over ice and strain into a cocktail glass.

Inky (Eng) a term used to describe the deep red wines of Bordeaux, northern Rhône, Rioja etc. especially when they are young.

Inky Cocktail (Cktl) 40mls (⅓ gill) Port wine, 20mls (⅙ gill) brandy, 20mls (⅙ gill) blackcurrant cordial, dash lemon juice. Shake over ice, strain into an ice-filled highball glass and top with soda water.

Inländerrum (Aus) the name given in the 1930's to Kunstrum, contained between 1%–2% rum only (less than rumverschnitt).

Inländischem Schaumwein (Ger) a wine produced in Germany from any red, rosé or white wine from any part of the world.

Inman Family (USA) a winery based in the Russian River Valley, Sonoma County, California. Grape variety: Pinot noir. Label: Olivet Grange Vineyard.

Inn (Eng) a licensed hostelry that caters for travellers by giving them refreshment and accommodation. (Port) = albergue.

Innausen (Aus) a vineyard site on the banks of the River Danube in the Kremstal region.

In Schiefern (Aus) a vineyard site on the banks of the River Danube in the Kremstal region.

In Schrötten (Aus) a vineyard site on the banks of the River Danube in the Kremstal region.

Innere Leiste (Ger) vineyard (Anb): Franken. (Ber): Maindreieck. (Gro): Not yet assigned. (Vil): Würzburg.

Innis & Gunn Brewing C° (Scot) a brewery (established 2003). (Add): P.O. Box 17246, Edinburgh, Midlothian EH11 1YR. Brews a variety of beers. *see* Oak-Aged Ale 6.6% alc by vol. Website: http://www.innisandgunn.com 'E'mail: dougal.sharpe@innisandgunn.com

Innisfail Vineyards and Winery (Austr) a winery

(established 1981). (Add): Cross Street, Batesford, Off Midland Highway, Victoria. Grape varieties: Cabernet sauvignon, Chardonnay, Riesling.

Inniskillin (Can) a small winery based at Niagara, Ontario. Produces both hybrid and Vitis vinifera wines. Grape varieties: Pinot gris, Riesling, Sauvignon blanc. Specialises in Ice Wines.

Inn Sign (Eng) a signboard positioned outside a public house or Inn showing its name (often drawn/painted from the days when most people could not read) with the name of the brewery which owns it (or Free House).

Innswood (W.Ind) a rum distillery based on the island of Jamaica. Produces dark rums.

Inocente (Sp) a brand of Fino Sherry produced by Valdespino at Jerez.

Inopiio (Gre) winery.

Inositol (Eng) a vitamin found in most wines.

Insalus (Sp) a sparkling natural spring mineral water. Mineral contents (milligrammes per litre): Sodium 11.2mg/l, Calcium 161.9mg/l, Magnesium 20.9mg/l, Potassium 1.3mg/l, Bicarbonates 152.5mg/l, Chlorides 15.4mg/l, Sulphates 367.4mg/l, Fluorides 0.1mg/l, Nitrates 4.8mg/l.

Inseine Bitter (Fr) a beer brewed by Paris Real Ale Brewery's Frog & Rost Bif (a micro-brewery) in Saint Denis, Paris. *see* Dark de Triomphe.

Insel Heylesern Wert (Ger) vineyard (Anb): Mittelrhein. (Ber): Bacharach. (Gro): Schloss Stahleck. (Vil): Bacharach.

Insensible Ferment (Eng) the name given to the slight fermentation that takes place after the first fermentation, also known as the malo-lactic fermentation.

Insheim (Ger) village (Anb): Pfalz. (Ber): Südliche Weinstrasse. (Gro): Herrlich. (Vin): Schäfergarten.

Insignia (USA) the name of a wine produced by Phelps, Napa Valley, California.

Insilteoir Tae (Ire) tea infuser.

Insosso (Port) a term which denotes a tasteless, insipid wine.

Inspecteurs de la Repression des Fraudes (Fr) inspectors for the A.C. to *see* that the rules are conformed to. They issue Acquits Verts.

Inspector's Ale (Eng) a 4.2% alc by vol. ale from the Station Hotel micro-brewery, Easingwold.

Inspiration (Cktl) ¼ measure Calvados, ¼ measure gin, ¼ measure Grand Marnier, ¼ measure dry vermouth, stir over ice, strain into a cocktail glass and add a cherry.

Inspiration (Eng) a 5.2% alc by vol. ale brewed by the Goddards Brewery, Isle of Wight.

Inspire (S.Afr) a winery based in the Western Cape. Grape varieties include: Cabernet sauvignon.

Inspissated Wine (Eng) a flavouring or colouring wine that can be either unfermented grape juice or boiled down must.

Instant Coffee (Eng) fresh brewed coffee which is either freeze dried, roller dried or vacuum dried. *see* Washington (G.), Kato (Sartori) and Lyophilization. Also known as soluble coffee.

Institue Nazionale per la Tutela del Brandy Italiano (It) the body that has set standards for the wine used as the distillate, the distillation process and the amount of ageing required for brandy in Italy.

Institut Algérien de la Vigne et du Vin (Alg) *see* I.V.V.

Institut Catalán de la Vinya i el Vi (Sp) *see* INCAVI.

Institute of Brewing & Distilling [The] (Eng) an organisation (established 1886). (Add): 33 Clarges Street, London, W1Y 8EE. Website: http://www.ibd.org.uk 'E'mail: enquiries@ibd.org.uk

Institute of Masters of Wine Limited (Eng) the controlling body for the Masters of Wine. (Add): Black Swan House, Kennet Wharf Lane, London EC4V, 3BE.

Institut Für Schnittreben (Aus) an institute of vine cuttings based in Vöslau.

Institut National des Appellations d'Origine des Vins et Eaux-de-Vie (Fr) the authority who set and monitor the French wine and spirit laws and classifications. I.N.A.O. *See also* Appellation Contrôlée.

Instituto Catal n de Vino (Sp) *abbr*: INCAVI a body responsible to INDO and the Departement of Agriculture in Cataluña. Experiment in drip irrigation, soils and vine training with wires.

Instituto Commercio Estero (It) Institute of Foreign Commerce a body that gives a seal to all Italian wines exported to the USA and Canada which indicates that the wine has met the Italian regulations.

Instituto do Vinho da Madeira (Mad) *abbr*: I.V.M. *see* Madeira Wine Institute.

Instituto do Vinho do Porto (Port) *abbr*: I.V.P an institute (established 1933) that follows Port production and tests quality under government directions.

Instituto Nacional de Denominaciónes de Origin (Sp) *abbr*: I.N.D.O. Legislative body for the control of vine cultivation and wine production attached to the Ministry of Agriculture. *see* Consejo Regulador de la Denominación de Origin.

Instituto Nacional de Fomento de la Exportación (Sp) *abbr*: I.N.F.E. (Add): Paseo de la Castellana, 14, Madrid 28046. A body for the promotion of Spanish wines.

Instituto Nacional de Vitivinicultura (Arg) *abbr*: I.N.V. A body (established 1959) to control all commercial practices and production methods, analyses wine and grape samples.

Instituto Regionale della Vita e del Vino (It) a Sicilian organisation designed to assist the vine growers with every aspect of wine production from vine to bottle. Also for the promotion of Sicilian wines.

Instituto Talento Metodo Classico (It) the new *'talento'* mark will apply only to prestige wines that will be recognised on a level with Champagne and Cava. Instituto includes producers of Alto Adige, Friuli Classico, Oltrepó Pavese, Trento D.O.C.

Instituto Valenciano de Viticultura y Enología (Sp) *abbr*: I.V.V.E. an institute (established 1910).

Supervised vineyards after Phylloxera, tests new products and analyses samples for export certification.

Instow Gold (Eng) a 3.8% alc by vol. golden ale brewed by Tarka Ales Ltd., Devon.

Insulation (Eng) a 5% alc by vol. dark bitter ale brewed by the Hydes Brewery, Manchester.

Insuperable (Sp). A 5 year old solera reserva brandy produced by Gonzalez Byass.

Intercellular Fermentation (Fr) a style of fermentation where the whole grape is fermented without oxygen where fermentation takes place within the grape, is also known as macération semi-carbonique.

Intercontinental Breweries (S.Afr) a brewery (established 1973) noted for lager beers (1040–1050 O.G.) Heidelberg Lager and Sportsman Lager.

Intaba (Arg) the label for a range of wines from Durbanville in Western Cape. Range includes Chardonnay, Cabernet sauvignon, Merlot, Pinotage.

Integra-Thermoplastic Elastomer (Austr) *abbr:* T.P.E. a patented brand of plastic cork produced near Adelaide. Has a slightly ridged exterior to prevent turning in the bottle.

Interbrew UK Ltd (Eng) a brewery and major distributor of beer brands (established 1990). (Add): Porter Tun House, 500 Capability Green, Luton, Bedfordshire LU1 3LS. Brands include Bass Ale, Boddingtons, Brahma, Castlemaine XXXX, Hoegaarden, Murphy's Irish Stout, Staropramen, Stella Artois, Tennents Lager (part of Interbrew SA owned by InBev). Website: http://www.interbrew.co.uk

Intercontinental Brands (ICB) Ltd (Eng) a drinks manufacturer and distributor (established 1990). (Add): 4 Sceptre House, Hornbeam Square, Hornbeam Business Park, Harrogate, North Yojrkshire HG2 8PB. Produces cider and lager. Website: http://www.icbrands.co.uk 'E'mail: sales@icbrands.co.uk

Interleven (Scot) the name of a 1979 vintage lowland malt whisky 40% alc by vol.

International Beer Convention (Ger) a Munich-based group who hold competitions and research projects with a view of upgrading beer-drinking, the members call themselves 'The Notables'.

International Brewers Guild (Eng) an organisation. (Add): 8 Ely Place, Holborn, London EC1N 6SD.

International Coffee Agreement (Eng) inaugurated in 1962 at the United Nations in New York. Was reviewed and updated by the International Coffee Organisation at their headquarters in London. Agreement included the limitation of production, supply, importation and exportation of coffee and to promote the consumption of coffee of both producing and non-producing members (now no longer in existence). *see* Freetrade.

International Coffee Organisation (Eng) an organisation (established 1968), (Add): 22 Berner's Street, London W1T 3DD. Formed to organise and administor the International Coffee Agreement and to promote and research coffee production and drinking. Website: http://www.ico.org 'E'mail: info@ico.org

International Correspondance of Corkscrew Addicts (USA) *see* I.C.C.A.

International Distillers and Vintners Ltd. (Eng) distillers. (Add): 1 York Gate, Regents Park, London. NW1. Produces Chelsea Gin and many brands of Scotch whisky including Justerini and Brooks, Dunhill, Catto's and Gilbey.

International Standards Organisation (Euro) *see* I.S.O. and I.S.O. Glass.

International Tea Committee Ltd (Eng) an organisation (established 1933). (Add): Sir John Lyon House, 5 High Timber Street, London EC4V 3NH. Website: http://www.inttea.com 'E'mail: info@inttea.com

International Wine and Food Society [The] (Eng) a society founded by André Simon that meets regularly for the appreciation of good food and wine. (Add): 9 Fitzmaurice Place, Berkeley Square, London W1X 6JD. Website: http://www.iwfs.org 'E'mail: sec@iwfs.org

Interprinderile Agricole de Stat (Rum) *see* I.A.S.

Intoxicate (Eng) causes a person to be in a state of euphoria to stupor from alcoholic drink with loss of control of motion and inhibitions. *see* Inebriate.

Intoxicated (Eng) a person who is drunk/inebriated.

Intra (Chi) a herbal tonic produced to a Chinese formula with 23 herbs and botanicals. Ingredients include aloe vera, bee pollen, ginseng.

I.N.V. (Arg) *abbr:* Instituto Nacional de Vitivinicultura.

Invalid Port (S.Afr) a soft, ruby red Port-style wine with a fine grapey flavour.

Invechiata (It) refers to aged grappa.

Invecchiato (It) aged.

Inveralmond Brewery (Scot) a brewery (established 1987). (Add): 1 Inveralmond Way, Perth, Perthshire PH1 3UQ. Brews: Independence 3.8% alc by vol., Lia Sale 4.7% alc by vol., Ossian's Ale 4.1% alc by vol., Thrappledouser 4.3% alc by vol. Website: http://www.inveralmond-brewery.co.uk 'E'mail: info@inveralmond-brewery.co.uk

Inverarity [The] (Scot) a 10 year old single speyside malt whisky from Aultmore, Inverarity Vaults Ltd 40% alc by vol.

Inverarity Islay (Scot) a 10 year old Islay vatted malt whisky from Inverarity Vaults Ltd 40% alc by vol.

Inverarity Vaults Ltd. (Scot) produces Ancestral, Inverarity (The) and Inverarity Islay whiskies.

Invergordon (Scot) a grain whisky distillery based north of Inverness.

Inver House (Scot) a major brand-name of a blended Scotch whisky. Produced by Inver House Distilleries, Airdrie. *see* William Davidson and C° 43% alc by vol.

Inver House Distillers (Scot) a distillery (established 1964). (Add): Moffat Distillery, Towers Road, Airdrie, Lanarkshire ML6 8PL. Produces a variety of whiskies and other spirits. Website: http://www.inverhouse.com 'E'mail: enquiries@inverhouse.com

I

Inverey Malt Whisky (Scot) a vatted malt whisky 40% alc by vol. produced by Burn Stewart Distillers for Marks and Spensers.

Inverleven (Scot) a malt whisky distillery based on the mouth of the river Clyde near Glasgow. 40% alc by vol. A lowland malt whisky (part of Hiram Walker).

Invertase (Eng) an enzyme in yeast that converts (inverts) the unfermentable sugars sucrose and sacchrose into fermentable (invert) sugar.

Invert Sugar (Eng) sugar which has been treated with acids to make it fermentable by yeast. *See also* Invertase.

Investment (Eng) the process of laying down vintage Port and fine red wines bought young to mature in quality and value for later sale or drinking. Can also apply to fine white wines and Champagne.

Invicta Bitter (Eng) a cask conditioned bitter 1044 O.G. brewed by the Shepherd Neame Brewery. Now known as Kent's Best Invicta Ale.

Invincible (Eng) a 4.5% alc by vol. ale brewed by The Durham Brewery Ltd., County Duhrham.

In Vino Veritas (Lat) lit: 'in wine there is truth'. Denotes that people who are drunk usually speak the truth!

Inycon (It) an IGT vineyard estate based in Sicily. Grape varieties: Aglianinco, Cabernet sauvignon, Chardonnay, Merlot, Nero d'avola.

Inzolia (It) a white grape variety grown in Sicily for the making of Marsala and also in Tuscany.

Inzolia Bianca (USA) a white grape variety grown in California to make dessert wines.

Io (Thai) a natural spring mineral water.

Iodine (Eng) used in wine making to detect the presence of starch in hazy wines.

Io Furmint (Hun) a white grape variety used exclusively in the making of Tokaji aszú.

Ioli (Gre) a still and sparkling natural spring mineral water from Mount Iti, Lamia. Mineral contents (milligrammes per litre): Sodium 8.2mg/l, Calcium 54.1mg/l, Magnesium 31.5mg/l, Potassium 0.8mg/l, Bicarbonates 267.5mg/l, Chlorides 13.5mg/l, Sulphates 15mg/l, Nitrates 6.2mg/l. pH 7.3

Iona (S.Afr) the label for range of wines produced by the Luddite Wines winery, Walker Bay, Western Cape.

Iona Estate (S.Afr) a winery (35ha) based in Grabouw, Elgin, Western Cape. Grape varieties: Cabernet sauvignon, Chenin blanc, Merlot, Mourvèdre, Petit verdot, Sauvignon blanc, Shiraz, Viognier. Website: http://www.iona.co.za

Iona (USA) genus: *Vitis labrusca* a lesser red grape (native) variety used in the making of varietals.

Ion Exchange (Eng) treatment of wines used for tartrate stabilisation by removing potassium and calcium ions and replacing with sodium (now banned by the E.C).

Ionian Islands (Gre) the islands of western Greece-Corfu, Zante, Levakas, Cephalonia. Produce mainly country style wines.

Ion Mineral Water (Jap) an alkaline natural spring mineral water. Mineral contents (milligrammes per litre): Sodium 16mg/l, Calcium 12mg/l, Magnesium 5.2mg/l, Potassium 0.6mg/l. pH 9.0

Iowa (USA) a wine-producing state that produces wines mainly from French hybrid varieties.

I.P. (It) *abbr*: Italia Particolare.

I.P.A. (Eng) *abbr*: India Pale Ale.

I.P.A. (Eng) a 4.2% alc by vol. dry hoppy ale produced by Gales Brewery, Hampshire.

I.P.A. Bitter (Eng) a 3.5% alc by vol. bitter ale from Ridleys, Essex.

I Pavé de l'Ours (Bel) a honeyed ale from the Binchoise Brasserie in Wallonia 9% alc by vol.

IPA Twist (Eng) a 3.6% alc by vol. India pale ale brewed by the Blanchfield Brewery, Essex.

I.P.1. (Ger) *abbr*: a table grape used in German crossings. Is a cross between the Chasselas and Muscat of Hamburg.

Iphofen (Ger) village (Anb): Franken. (Ber): Steigerwald. (Gro): Burgweg. (Vins): Julius-Eckter-Berg, Kalb, Kronsberg.

I Piani (It) a dry, cherry-red wine named after the area in the Nurra region of Sardinia.

Ipiros (Gre) a region that produces red and white pétillant wines.

Ipocras (Eng) the author Geoffrey Chaucer's way of spelling Hypocras in his book: The Canterbury Tales.

I Portali (It) an I.G.T. white wine produced by Basilium in Basilicata from 100% Greco grapes.

Ippesheim (Ger) village (Anb): Franken. (Ber): Steigerwald. (Gro): Schlontück. (Vin): Herrschaftsberg.

I.P.R. (Port) *abbr*: Indicacao de Proveniência Regulamentada (similar to V.D.Q.S. in France).

Ipswich Special Bitter (Eng) a bitter ale brewed by the Tolly Cobbold Brewery in Ipswich.

Ipswich Town Pride 1992 (Eng) a bottled beer brewed by Tolly Cobbold named after the brewery in Ipswich. 1048 O.G. (4.6% alc by vol.) A premium beer from 100% malt and using Goldings hops (limited edition with only 400 firkins made).

Iraleska (Euro) a natural spring mineral water from Belarus.

Iran (M.East) one of the earliest places where viticulture occurred. Then known as Persia. Vineyards in the northern provinces of East Azerbaijan, Farse, Hamedan, Khorasan, Lorestan, Teheran, West Azerbaijan and Zanjan. A wide variety of medium-sweet and dessert wines are produced for the home market mainly from the Thompson seedless grape.

Irancy (Fr) a village near Chablis in northern Burgundy. Produces red and rosé wines from the César grape. *See also* Bourgogne Irancy.

Iran Intravend (Iran) a natural spring mineral water (established 2002) from Gahar. Mineral contents (milligrammes per litre): Sodium 7mg/l, Calcium 55mg/l, Magnesium 24mg/l, Bicarbonates 280mg/l, Chlorides 6.5mg/l, Sulphates 2.5mg/l, Nitrates 2mg/l, Silicates 6.5mg/l. pH 7.3

I

Ireland (Ire) an island that is famous for its stouts (home of Guinness) and whiskies. A small amount of wine is produced near Cork. *see* Mayville.

Iris Cocktail (Cktl) ⅔ measure gin, ⅓ measure lemon juice, 1 teaspoon powdered sugar. Shake well over ice, strain into a cocktail glass and decorate with a mint sprig.

Irish Ale Breweries (Ire) a Guinness-controlled group of which Allied Breweries own a third. Runs 3 breweries in Ireland: Cherrys, Macardles and Smithwicks.

Irish Breakfast (Ind) a blend of teas from the Assam province. Produces a strong, thick, rich tea.

Irish Cheer Cocktail (Cktl) 25mls (1fl.oz) Irish whiskey, 5mls (¼ fl.oz) sweet vermouth. Stir over ice and strain into a cocktail glass.

Irish Coffee (USA) 35mls (1½ fl.ozs) Irish whiskey, 125mls (5 fl.ozs) strong hot black coffee, 1 teaspoon sugar, 1 spoonful whipped cream. Into a warmed glass place the sugar and coffee, stir, add whiskey and top with the cream.

Irish Cow (Ire) a liqueur made from Irish whiskey, double cream and chocolate by Baileys in Dublin.

Irish Distillers Group Ltd. (Ire) controls the Irish whiskey industry by an amalgamation of John Power and Son, John Jameson and Son and the Cork Distillery C°.

Irish Handshake (Cktl) 2 parts Irish whiskey, 1 part green Curaçao, 1 part fresh cream. Shake well over ice and strain into a cocktail glass.

Iris Hill (USA) a winery based in the Oregon State. Grape variety: Pinot noir.

Irish Mist (Ire) a whiskey-based liqueur flavoured with herbs and honey 35% alc by vol. Produced in Tulach Mhor.

Irish Moss (Eng) a mixture of 2 marine algae used to clarify beer during brewing.

Irish Moss (USA) a liqueur similar to Rock and Rye, but flavoured with Irish moss. Is produced by Leroux.

Irish Nigger (Pousse Café) into a liqueur glass pour in order – ½ measure crème de cacao, ½ measure (green) crème de menthe.

Irish Punch (Cktl) ½ lemon studded with 12 cloves, 1 measure Irish whiskey, 1 teaspoon sugar, hot water. Heat altogether, strain into a wine glass.

Irish Red Ale (Ire) *see* Killian.

Irish Rickey (Cktl) 50mls (2 fl.ozs) Irish whiskey, juice ½ lime. Pour into an ice-filled highball glass, top with soda water and a slice of lime.

Irish Russet Ale (Fr) a highly carbonated ale produced in France.

Irish Shillelagh (Cktl) ⅓ measure Irish whiskey, ⅙ measure sloe gin, ⅙ measure dark rum, juice ½ lemon, dash gomme syrup. Shake over ice, strain into an old-fashioned glass and decorate with fruits in season.

Irish Stout (Eng) a 4.5% alc by vol. stout brewed by Briscoe's in Otley, West Yorkshire.

Irish Velvet (Ire) a liqueur based on Irish whiskey, strong black coffee and sugar.

Irish Velvet (Ire) a package to make Irish Coffee.

Contains freeze-dried coffee, Irish whiskey, sugar and sweeteners. Produced by Irish Distillers. Need to add water and cream.

Irish Whiskey (Ire) a whiskey produced from malted barley, cereals, water and yeast. Triple pot-stilled, blended and matured in used Sherry butts. The oldest pot-stilled whiskey. *see* Bushmills Whiskey, Jameson, Midleton Distillery, Tullamore Dew.

Irish Whiskey Cocktail (Cktl) a ⅘ measure Irish whiskey, ¹⁄₁₀ measure Pernod, ¹⁄₁₀ measure Cointreau, 2 dashes maraschino, dash Angostura. Stir well over ice, strain into a cocktail glass and decorate with an olive.

Irish Whiskey Sour (Cktl) 50mls (2 fl.ozs) Irish whiskey, juice of small lemon, teaspoon sugar, white of egg. Shake juice, sugar and egg white well over ice, pour into a highball glass, add the whiskey and a little soda.

Irisquelle (Ger) a natural spring mineral water from Löhne. Mineral contents (milligrammes per litre): Sodium 25mg/l, Calcium 343mg/l, Magnesium 91mg/l, Potassium 2.7mg/l, Bicarbonates 228mg/l, Chlorides 58mg/l, Sulphates 975mg/l.

Irmos Unidos (Port) an aguardente brandy produced by the Caves Sao João.

Irn-Bru (Eng) a famous non-alcoholic (0.01% alc by vol.) soft drink first produced in 1901 in the north of England by Barr (A.G.). Website: http://www.irn-bru.co.uk

Iron Casse (Eng) a wine malady, a fine greyish-white deposit looking like yeast. Caused by a high iron content in the wine, citric acid or blue fining will rectify. Also known as Casse Bleu and Casse Ferrique.

Iron City (USA) a beer brewed by the Pittsburgh Brewery, Pittsburgh, Pennsylvania.

Ironbridge Stout (Eng) a 5% alc by vol. stout brewed by the Salopian Brewing Company, 67 Mytton Oak Road, Shrewsbury, Shropshire.

Ironhorse (Can) a malt liquor brewed by the Pacific Western Brewing company in Vancouver using spring water 5.7% alc by vol.

Iron Horse (Eng) a 4.8% alc by vol. ale brewed by the Goddards Brewery, Isle of Wight.

Iron Horse Ranch and Vineyard (USA) a 46 ha. winery based in the Russian River Valley, Sonoma County, California. Grape varieties: Cabernet sauvignon, Chardonnay, Pinot noir, Sauvignon blanc and Zinfandel. Produces sparkling wines from Pinot noir and Chardonnay. Labels include Vrais Amis, Wedding Cuvée. Laurent-Perrier has an interest.

Iron House (Eng) a 4.8% alc by vol. ale brewed by Hepworth & C°. Brewers Ltd., West Sussex.

Iron Knob Riesling (Austr) a fruity, dry Riesling wine produced by the Longview Vineyard, Adelaide Hills, South Australia.

Iron Lady (Cktl) 1 measure vodka, ½ measure Sambuca, 1 measure orange juice. Frost the top of a highball glass with castor sugar, add spirals of lemon and orange peel and ice, add ingredients, stir and top up with Irn-bru or Lucozade.

Ironman (Eng) a 4.8% alc by vol. ale brewed by Ridgeway Brewing, Berkshire.

I

Iron Oak (Eng) cold filtered oak-matured draught cider 5.2% alc by vol. from Inch's, Devon.

Ironside (Eng) a 4.2% alc by vol. ale brewed by the Hampshire Brewery, Hampshire.

Ironstone Vineyards (Austr) a winery based in West Australia. Grape varieties: Cabernet sauvignon, Shiraz, Chardonnay, Sémillon.

Ironstone Vineyards (USA) the label used by Kautz Vineyards, Murphys, California for their Cabernet franc, Chardonnay and Merlot. Based in Calaveras County, Sierra Foothills. Website: http://www.ironstonevineyards.com 'E'mail: wine@hwcg.co.uk

Iron Town (Eng) a 3.8% alc by vol. ale brewed by the Beckstones Brewery, Cumbria.

Irouléguy (Fr) an A.C. white, rose and red wines of the Basses Pyrénées region. *see* Béarn. The production is controlled by one co-operative. Minimum alc by vol. 10%, maximum 14%.

Irpinska (Ukr) a natural spring mineral water from Irpen. Mineral contents (milligrammes per litre): Sodium 21.8mg/l, Calcium 47.1mg/l, Magnesium 12.8mg/l, Bicarbonates 244mg/l, Sulphates 2.9mg/l.

Irrache (Sp) a major wine-producer of north-eastern Navarra.

Irrbling (Aus) a vineyard site based on the banks of the River Kamp situated in the Kamptal region.

Irrigazione a Zampillo (It) a method of irrigation of vineyards where the soil between the vines is sprayed with water from above.

Irroy (Eng) the brand-name of a Champagne that was popular in Victorian times. Based at Reims. A Grande Marque. Second label of the Taittinger Champagne house.

Irsai Olivér (Hun) *see* Irsay Oliver.

Irsay Oliver (Slo) a cross of the Muscat grape in Slovakia (Muscat x Frankovka). Known as Irsai Olivér in Hungary.

Irsch (Ger) village (Anb): Mosel-Saar-Ruwer. (Ber): Saar-Ruwer. (Gro): Scharzberg. (Vins): Hubertusberg, Sonnenberg, Vogelsang.

Irsee Abbaye Brauerei (Ger) a brewery based at Irsee im Allgäu. Brews: Irseer Klosterbräu Lager.

Irseer Klosterbräu (Ger) a 5.6% alc by vol. unfiltered dark lager brewed by the Irsee Abbaye Brauerei, Irsee im Allgäu.

Irshavskoje (Ukr) a white table wine produced near Cherson in the Ukraine.

Irvine's White (Austr) a white grape variety used in the making of sparkling wines. A distant cousin of the Folle blanche.

Irving Cocktail (Cktl) ½ measure dry gin, ¼ measure Calisaya, ¼ measure dry vermouth. Shake over ice, strain into a cocktail glass and top with a slice of orange.

Is (Den) ice.

Isa (S.Afr) the label for a red wine (Merlot 60% plus Cabernet franc and Cabernet sauvignon blend) produced by the Helshoogte Vineyards winery, Stellenbosch, Western Cape.

Isabeau (S.Afr) a white wine (Chardonnay 40%, Sémillon 60%) produced by the Allée Bleu winery, Franschhoek, Western Cape.

Isabel (Port) a rosé wine produced by the Caves da Silva.

Isabel Estate (N.Z) a winery based in Marlborough, South Island. Grape variety: Pinot noir.

Isabelita (Eng) a fine, dry, Fino Sherry from Harvey's of Bristol.

Isabella (Mad) a hybrid grape variety which was used in the production of Madeira wines but has now been banned.

Isabella (S.Afr) the label for a white wine (Chardonnay) produced by the Muratie Estate winery, Stellenbosch, Western Cape.

Isabella (USA) a black grape variety grown in the north. Also spelt Isabelle.

Isabelle [1] (Fr) a still natural spring mineral water from Brittany. (Add): SEMA 29520 Saint-Goazec. Mineral contents (milligrammes per litre): Calcium 1.6mg/l, Magnesium 2.2mg/l, Potassium 0.6mg/l, Bicarbonates 6.1mg/l, Sulphates 4mg/l, Fluorides 0.05mg/l, Nitrates 6mg/l, Silicates 4.8mg/l.

Isabelle [2] (Fr) a natural spring mineral water from Brittany. (Add): SEMA 29520 Saint-Goazec. Mineral contents (milligrammes per litre): Sodium 12.9mg/l, Calcium 2mg/l, Magnesium 2mg/l, Potassium 0.4mg/l, Bicarbonates 246mg/l, Chlorides 21mg/l, Sulphates 5mg/l, Nitrates 4mg/l, Silicates 5mg/l.

Isabelle [3] (Fr) a natural spring mineral water from Brittany. (Add): SEMA 29520 Saint-Goazec. Mineral contents (milligrammes per litre): Sodium 12.5mg/l, Calcium 1.5mg/l, Magnesium 2.2mg/l, Potassium 0.5mg/l, Bicarbonates 3.5mg/l, Chlorides 20mg/l, Sulphates 3mg/l, Nitrates 5mg/l. pH 5.4

Isabelle (USA) an alternative spelling of Isabella.

Isabelle Morgan (USA) the name for a red wine (Pinot noir) produced by the Au Bon Climat winery, California.

Isabellita (Cktl) 35mls (1½ fl.ozs) Amontillado Sherry, 10mls (½ fl.oz) peach brandy, 10mls (½ fl.oz) vodka. Stir with ice, strain onto ice in a highball, top up with lemonade, decorate with zest of large lemon and orange.

Isbre (Nor) a still natural spring mineral water from Hardanger Fjord. Mineral contents (milligrammes per litre): Sodium 1mg/l, Calcium 2.6mg/l, Magnesium 0.24mg/l, Sulphates 1.2mg/l, Nitrates 0.21mg/l. pH 6.7

I.S.C. (USA) *abbr*: Italian Swiss Colony.

Ischia (It) a southern island in Campania region. Known as the 'Green Island' because of its numerous pinewoods. It is the longest island in the Bay of Naples. D.O.C. is applicable to red and white wines. *see* Forastera and Biancolella.

Ischia Bianco (It) a D.O.C. white wine from Campania. Made from the Biancolella and Forastera grapes.

Ischia Bianco Superiore (It) a D.O.C. white wine from Campania. Made from the Biancolella,

Lombardy, Molise, Piemonte, Sardinia, Sicily, Trentino-Alto Adige, The Marches, Tuscany, Umbria, Valle d'Aosta and Veneto.

Itata (Chile) a wine region of southern Chile. Produces sound table wines.

Itchen Valley Brewery (Eng) a brewery (established 1997). (Add): Shelf House, New Farm Road, Alresford, Hampshire SO24 9QE. Brews: Fagins 4.1% alc by vol., Father Christmas 5% alc by vol., Godfathers, 3.8% alc by vol (cask conditioned)., Hambleden Bitter 4% alc by vol., Hampshire Rose 4.2% alc by vol., Pure Gold 4.8% alc by vol., Tea Clipper 4.2% alc by vol., Treacle Stout 4.4% alc by vol., Wat Tyler 5% alc by vol., Wykehams Glory 4.3% alc by vol. Website: http://www.itchenvalley.co.uk 'E'mail: info@itchenvalley.com

Itchiban (Cktl) a Chinese egg nogg, 1 fresh egg, 1 teaspoon crème de cacao, 1 teaspoon Bénédictine, 60mls (½ gill) brandy, shake well over ice, strain into a highball glass, top with full-cream milk and grated nutmeg.

I Ti (Chi) see I-Ty.

It's Not Bitter (Eng) a 4.9% alc by vol. ale brewed by the Oakleaf Brewing C°. Ltd., Hampshire.

Ituri (Afr) a coffee-producing region in Zaire.

I-Ty (Chi) a Chinese gentleman who discovered wine, he is reputed to have discovered it in China 2200 B.C. Also spelt I Ti.

Itza Paramount (Cktl) ½ measure dry gin, ¼ measure Drambuie, ¼ measure Cointreau. Stir over ice, strain into a cocktail glass and top with a cherry.

Iuvarella (It) the Pollino, Calabria name for the white Malvasia bianca grape variety.

Ivanhoe (Eng) a 5.2% alc by vol. ale brewed by Ridgeway Brewing, Berkshire.

Ivernel (Fr) a Champagne producer. (Add): 4 Rue Jules Lobet, 51160 Aÿ. 2 ha. Produces vintage and non-vintage wines. Vintages: 1971, 1973, 1976, 1979, 1982, 1985, 1988, 1990, 1995, 1998, 1999, 2001.

Ivérouogn (Ch.Isles) drunkard (alcoholic), also spelt Ivraon.

Ivérouognise (Ch.Isles) drunkeness (alcoholism).

Iverskaia (Rus) a slightly alkaline, sparkling natural spring mineral water (established 2002). Mineral contents (milligrammes per litre): Sodium >50mg/l, Calcium 30-50mg/l, Magnesium 9->15mg/l, Potassium >5mg/l, Bicarbonates 90-125mg/l, Chlorides 15-25mg/l, Sulphates 90-125mg/l, Fluorides >1.2mg/l, Oxygen <9mg/l. pH 8.5

Ives Noir (USA) a black grape variety used in the northern states, also known as Bordo.

I.V.M. (Mad) abbr...
Ivory Creek (S.A...) produced b... Swartland, W...
I.V.P. (Port) abbr:
Ivraon (Ch.Isles...
Ivre (Fr) drunk...
Ivresse (Fr) int...
Ivrogne (Fr) s...
Ivrognerie (Fr...
I.V.V. (Alg) ab... Vin. see V.A...
I.V.V.E. (Sp) ... Enología.
Ivy du Toit ... (Chardon... Sémillon... Private C...
I.W. Harpe... whiskey...
Izaak Walto... Roberts...
Izarra (Fr)... Armag... sugar...
Iziun (Ru...
Izmir (Tu... produ...
Izsàki (... Hung... Kada...
Izvir (S... Slov... litr... Ma... Bic... Sul... 0.1...
Izvor... M... Sc... 4... 1...
Izvo...

Forastera and San lunardo grapes. Has a higher alcoholic content than Ischia Bianco.

Ischia Rosso (It) a D.O.C. red wine from Campania. Made from the Barbera, Garnaccia and Piedirosso grapes.

Isenhower (USA) a winery based in the Walla Walla, Columbia Valley, Washington State. (Add): 3471 Pranger Road, Walla Walla, Washington 99 362. Grape varieties include: Syrah. Label: River Beauty. Website: http://www.isenhowercellars.com 'E'mail: info@isenhowercellars.com

Isimljanskoje Ygristoje (Rus) a dry sparkling wine produced in the Krasnodar region.

Isinglass (Eng) fish gelatine often made from the swim bladder of the sturgeon, used as a fining agent for wines and beers.

Is It Yourself (Eng) a 4.2% alc by vol. ale brewed by the Sawbridge Worth Brewery, Hertfordshire.

Iskendiriye (Bul) an alternative name for the Muscat of Alexandria grape.

Iskra (Bul) the brand-name of a méthode traditionelle sparkling wine. Red, rosé and white varieties are produced.

Iskriashto Vino (Bul) sparkling wine.

Islamic Wine (Eng) an old nineteenth century nickname for coffee.

Island Cask (Eng) a blend of Jamaican rum, British wine and blackcurrant from Mather in Leeds 18% alc by vol.

Island Cream Grog (Punch) 75mls (3fl.ozs) Jamaican rum, 200mls (7fl.ozs) boiling water. Mix together in a mug, sweeten to taste, top with whipped cream and grated nutmeg.

Islander (Scot) a 4.8% alc by vol. ale brewed by the Hebridean Brewery C°., Isle of Lewis.

Islander (Scot) a blended Scotch whisky produced by Bells.

Island Fruits (Eng) a range of non-alcoholic, carbonated fruit drinks produced by Schweppes.

Island Malts (Scot) the name given to malt whiskies produced in the Scottish Islands. Those from Islay, Scapa, Orkney (Highland Park), Jura and Skye (Talisker).

Island Vines (Cyp) a range of red and white wines produced by SODAP.

Islay (Scot) an island in the Hebrides which produces classic malt whiskies which have a pronounced peat reek. see Ardbeg, Bowmore, Bruichladdich, Bunnahabhain, Caol Ila, Lagavulin, Laphroaig and Port Ellen.

Islay Ales (Scot) a brewery (established 2004). (Add): The Brewery, Islay House Square, Bridgend, Isle of Islay, Argyll PA44 7NZ. Brews: Black Rock Ale 4.2% alc by vol., Finlaggen Ale 3.7% alc by vol. Website: http://www.islayales.com 'E'mail: info@islayales.com

Islay Cask Finish (Scot) a Famous Grouse blended Scotch whisky matured in old Islay malt whisky casks 40% alc by vol.

Islay Mist (Scot) a vatted malt produced by Long John International. First produced by D. Johnson

and C°. Has a high proportion of Laphroaig. An 8 year old 40% alc by vol.

Islay Water (Scot) a natural spring mineral water from Maol Dubh, Laggan Estate, Isle of Islay.

Isle of Arran (Scot) a single malt whisky from a distillery at Lochranza, Isle of Aran 40% alc by vol.

Isle of Arran Distillers (Scot) a distillery (established 1995). (Add): Enterprise House, Springkerse Business Park, Stirling, Stirlingshire FK7 7UF. Produces a range of whiskies. Website: http://www.arranwhisky.com 'E'mail: info@arranwhisky.com

Isle of Ely Vineyard (Eng) a vineyard (established 1972). (Add): Wilburton, Ely, Cambridgeshire. Soil- Sandy clay loam. 1.1 ha. Grape varieties: Chardonnay, Müller-Thurgau and Wrotham pinot. Produces: St. Etheldreda white.

Isle of Jura (Scot) an island in the Hebrides from which the famous malt whisky of same name is produced. Classed as a highland malt but with characteristics of Islay malt.

Isle of Jura (Scot) a single highland malt whisky distillery on the Isle of Jura. Owned by Charles Mackinlay and C°. Produces: 8 year old, 10 year old and a 26 year old. 43% alc by vol. also Isle of Jura Season 1882, Superstition 40% alc by vol. and 1984 (a 19 y.o. malt to commemorate the birth of George Orwell). Website: http://www.isleofjura.com

Isle of Man Breweries (I.O.M) formed as a result of a merger between Castletown Brewery and Okells in 1988. Took over Drinks Distributors (I.O.M) Ltd. in 1994. see Falcon Brewery.

Isle of Pines (Cktl) 50mls (2fl.ozs) Bacardi White Label, 10mls (½ fl.oz) grapefruit juice, ½ teaspoonful sugar. Combine juice with sugar, add rum, shake well with ice and strain into a cocktail glass.

Isle of Skye (Scot) an 8 year old Scotch whisky 40% alc by vol. produced by Macleod's in Edinburgh. Website: http://www.ianmacleod.com

Isle of Skye Brewing C° [Leann An Eilein] Ltd (Scot) a brewery (established 1995). (Add): The Pier, Ulg, Portree, Isle of Skye IV51 9XP. Brews a range of beers. Website: http://www.skyebrewery.co.uk 'E'mail: info@skyebrewery.co.uk

Isle of Skye Natural Mineral Water (Scot) a natural spring mineral water from Flodigarry Boreholes 1 & 2, Flodigarry Staffin.

Isliedh (S.Afr) the label for a white wine (Sauvignon blanc) produced by the Cape Point Vineyards winery, Cape Point, Western Cape.

I.S.O. (Euro) abbr: International Standards Organisation. see I.S.O. Glass and I.S.O. Tank Container.

Iso-Amyl Alcohol (Eng) a higher alcohol (part of the fusil oils).

Isobutyl Alcohol (Eng) C_4H_9OH a higher alcohol (part of the fusil oils).

I Sodi di S Niccolo (It) a red Vino da Tavola wine produced from 85% Sangioveto and 15%

Malvasia nera grapes by Castellare di Castellina in Tuscany.

I.S.O. Glass (Eng) a wine glass designed by the I.S.O. which best suits wine drinking. (Is deep-bowled and tulip-shaped to allow all the characteristics of the wine to be best shown).

Isolabella (It) a liqueur of the same style as Fior d'Alpi.

Isoleucine (Eng) an amino acid found in wines, formed by the yeasts.

Isonzo (It) a D.O.C. red (2) and white (8) wines from Friuli-Venezia region. Name is followed by grape. Reds: Cabernet sauvignon and Merlot. Whites: Friulano, Istriana, Pinot bianco, Pinot grigio, Renano, Sauvignon, Tocai and Traminer aromatico. Vinification can occur in Gorizia and Cervignano.

Isosceles (USA) a red wine produced from Cabernet sauvignon, Cabernet franc and Merlot grapes by Justin Vineyards and Winery, 11680 Chimney Rock Road, Paso Robles, California.

I.S.O. Tank Container (Eng) a 20000litre container for the transportation of wine, usually of stainless steel. Can be a single container or of multiple compartments.

Ispanyol Sarabi (Tur) lit: 'Spanish Sherry'.

Isparta (Tur) a wine-producing region in south-western Turkey. Produces red and white wines.

Isparta-Icel-Burdur (Tur) a noted vineyard based in the Isparta region. Produces medium-dry white wines.

Ispirato (Tur) alcohol/spirit.

Israel (Isr) an ancient wine-producing country in the Middle-East. Wine-making recorded 3000 years B.C. Most styles of wines are produced, mainly in co-operatives. Regions are Gallilee, Jerusalem Environs, Negev, Sydoo-Gezer and Zikhron-Yaacov.

Israel Gin (Isr) a light-style, medium-sweet gin (patent-stilled).

Israeli Distillers (Isr) a leading spirit and wine-producing company.

Israeli Wine Institute (Isr) formed in 1957 and based at Rehovat. Experiments with vines, conducts quality tests on wines and research into viticulture and viniculture.

Is Rock (Ice) a natural spring mineral water.

Issarts (Fr) a Premier Cru vineyard of the A.C. commune Gevrey-Chambertin in the Côte de Nuits, Burgundy. 1.82 ha. Is also known as Plantigone.

Istein (Ger) village (Anb): Baden. (Ber): Markgräflerland. (Gro): Vogtei Rötteln. (Vin): Kirchberg.

Istituzione del Comitato Nazionale Per la Tutela delle Denominazioni di Origine (It) the national institute for the protection of the denomination of origin. Body of 28 members and a President. Promotes and checks guaranteed and controlled wines.

Istra Bitters (Cro) an orange bitters which is similar

in style to Campa
and soda water.

Istria (Cro) a wine
wines from the
noir and Refosco

Istrita (Rum) a wi
of Dealul-Mare V

Itaipu (Bra) a natu
Branco Acre. M
litre): Sodium
Magnesium 5
Bicarbonates 1
Fluorides 0.0
41mg/l. pH 6

Italia (Aust) a w
used in wine

Italian Bottle Gr
bottles and
indicate the
Celsius.

Italian Coffe
containing S

Italian Gin (It
patent-still

Italian Institut
wine info
House, 20

Italian Job (
Lincolnshi
of the Jolly

Italianski Ri
white Wel

Italiansky Ri
Welschrie

Italian Som
40mls (
of crush

Italian Sw
winery
County
(United
winery
sauvig
Zinfan
under

Italian Sv
for a
Lodi,

Italian V
is sw
colou

Italia Pa
lowe

Italijan
kno

Italvini
the

Italy (
wo
Ab
Ca
Ve

J

J (USA) a Chardonnay and Pinot noir sparkling wine produced by the Jordan Vineyard and Winery in Sonoma County, California (first released in 1990).

Jaargang (Hol) vintage. *See also* Wijnoogst.

Jablonec (Czec) a brewery based in northern Czec, produces full-bodied, lager beers.

Jaboulet Aîné et Fils (Fr) a noted family wine-merchant of the Rhône based at Tain. Also producers of A.C. Hermitage. *see* Chapelle (La).

Jaboulet-Vercherre (Fr) a Burgundy négociant-éleveur based at 5 Rue Colbert, 21200 Beaune.

Jabulani (S.Afr) the label for a range of wines (Cabernet sauvignon & Merlot/Shiraz/Chardonnay) produced by the South African Premium Wines winery, Sandton, Western Cape.

Jacaranda Estate (S.Afr) a winery (established 1993) based on in Wellington, Western Cape. 2.8ha. Grape varieties: Cabernet sauvignon, Chenin blanc, Jerepigo, Merlot. Label: Debutante.

Jacivera (Sp) an alternative name for the Tempranillo grape.

Jac-Jan Vineyard (USA) a winery based in Ohio. Produces wines from French hybrid wines.

Jack (Eng) a style of leather-covered bottles used for beers and cider in the sixteenth century.

Jack and Jill (Slo) a whiskey produced in Slovenia from imported Scotch malts and local grains.

Jack Daniel (USA) a sour mash whiskey. The oldest registered distillery in the USA based in Lynchburg, Tennessee 45% alc by vol.

Jack Frost (Eng) a winter ale brewed by the Pitfield Brewery, Shoreditch, London.

Jackie O's Rose (Cktl) 40mls (⅓ gill) Bacardi, juice ½ lime, dash Triple Sec. Shake over ice and strain into a cocktail glass.

Jack-in-the-Box (Cktl) ½ measure pineapple juice, ½ measure applejack brandy, dash Angostura. Shake over ice and strain into a cocktail glass.

Jack London Vineyard (USA) *see* London Vineyard.

Jack O Legs (Eng) a 4.2% alc by vol. ale brewed by the Tring Brewery C°. Ltd., Hertfordshire.

Jack Pot Bitter (Eng) a bottled best bitter 1036 O.G. brewed by the Hook Norton Brewery, Oxfordshire.

Jack Rabbit (USA) a label name for a range of wines produced in California including Chardonnay/Merlot/White Zinfandel.

Jack Rabbit Cocktail (Cktl) 40mls (⅓ gill) Calvados, 30mls (¼ gill) each of maple syrup, orange juice, lemon juice. Shake over ice and strain into a cocktail glass.

Jack Ranch (USA) the label for a red wine (Pinot noir) from the Edna Valley, produced by the York Mountain Winery, San Luis Obispo County, California.

Jack Rose [1] (Cktl) juice of ½ large lime, 1 teaspoon grenadine, 35mls (1½ fl.ozs) applejack or Calvados. Shake over ice and strain into a cocktail glass.

Jack Rose [2] (Cktl) 40mls (⅓ gill) Calvados, 30mls (¼ gill) lemon juice, 6 dashes grenadine. Shake over ice, strain into a cocktail glass and serve with a dash lemon peel juice.

Jack's Ale (Eng) a 3.8% alc by vol. bitter ale brewed by the Windsor Castle Brewery, West Midlands.

Jack's Jug (S.Afr) the label for red wine (Cabernet sauvignon, Merlot and Shiraz blend) produced by the Cowlin Wines winery, Paarl, Western Cape.

Jackson Estate (N.Z) a 38ha winery based at Jacksons Road, Blenheim, Marlborough. Grape varieties: Chardonnay, Riesling, Sauvignon blanc, Pinot noir. *See also* Runnymede Island.

Jackson Park Vineyard (USA) a winery based in the Bennett Valley, Sonoma County, California. Part of Artisans & Estates.

Jacksons of Piccadilly (Eng) a noted tea producer of a wide range of teas. (Add): 1 West Smithfield, London.

Jacksonville Winery (USA) a winery based in south-western Oregon. Produces wines from the Valley View Vineyard.

Jack's River (S.Afr) the label for an un-wooded white wine (Chardonnay) produced by the Beaumont Wines winery, Walker Bay, Western Cape.

Jack's Special (Cktl)(Non-alc) 200mls (7fl.ozs) pineapple juice, 1 dash lemon juice, 12 strawberries. Blend well together with 1 scoop of crushed ice in a blender, pour into a large goblet and dress with a sliced strawberry.

Jack Zeller (Cktl) ½ measure Dubonnet, ½ measure Old Tom gin. Stir over ice and strain into a cocktail glass.

Jacobain (Fr) an alternative name for the Malbec grape.

Jacob Brewery (USA) a brewery based in New Bedford.

Jacobert (Fr) a noted eau-de-vie producer based in Colmar, Alsace.

Jacobi 1880 (Ger) a weinbrand produced in Stuttgart, western Germany.

Jacob Lee Winery (USA) a small winery based in Bordentown, New Jersey. Produces wines from American vines.

J

Jacobs Best Bitter (Eng) a bitter beer 1038 O.G. brewed by the Jacobs Brewery in Nailsea, near Bristol, Avon.

Jacobs Brewery (Eng) a brewery (established 1980) at Nailsea near Bristol, Avon that was taken over by the Halls Brewery in 1984. Produces Jacobs Best Bitter.

Jacob's Creek (Austr) a famous brand-name used by Orlando Winery for a range of their wines. Grape varieties include: Cabernet sauvignon, Chardonnay, Shiraz (owned by Pernod Ricard).

Jacobsdal Estate (S.Afr) a winery (100ha) based in Kuilsriver, Stellenbosch, Western Cape. (Add): Kuils River 7580. Grape varieties: Cabernet sauvignon, Chenin blanc, Pinotage, Sauvignon blanc. Produces varietal wines. Website: http://www.jacobsdal.co.za

Jacobsdal Wynkelder (S.Afr) see Bloemendal Estate.

Jacobs Royale (Eng) the brand-name of a coffee produced from a blend of Colombian beans by Jacobs Suchard.

Jacobs Suchard (Eng) a coffee producing company based at Jacobs Suchard House, Blenheim Road, Epsom, Surrey KT19 9AP. Brands include Carte Noire, Swing, Night and Day, Maestro Lorenzo, Jacobs Royale.

Jacobs Well Spring Water (Eng) a natural spring water from Bristol, sold in Bristol blue glass bottles.

Jacobus Petrus (S.Afr) the label for a red wine (Shiraz) produced by the Blyde Wines winery, Paarl, Western Cape.

Jacquart (Fr) a Champagne co-operative. (Add): 5 Rue Gosset, B.P. 467, 51066 Reims. 900 growers own 1,000ha. Wines made from members' grapes. Produces vintage and non-vintage wines. Vintages: 1970, 1973, 1975, 1976, 1978, 1979, 1980, 1981, 1982, 1983, 1985, 1986, 1987, 1988, 1989, 1990, 1992, 1995, 1996, 1998, 1999, 2000, 2001. Labels include Cuvée Nominée (brut and rosé), La Nominée du Millénaire, Onctueuse Cuvée (a rosé), Cuvée Mosaïque (a blanc de blancs and rosé). abbr: C.R.V.C.

Jacquart [André] (Fr) a Champagne producer. (Add): 5 Ave. de la République, Mesnil-sur-Oger, 51190 Avize. 18ha. Récoltant-manipulant. Produces vintage and non-vintage wines. Vintages: 1973, 1975, 1976, 1979, 1982, 1983, 1985, 1989, 1990, 1995, 1996, 1997, 1998, 1999, 2000.

Jacqueline (Fr) a rosé, non-vintage Champagne produced by De Lahaye in Épernay.

Jacquère (Fr) a white grape variety grown in the Savoie region, produces wines with a smoky, fruity scented aroma and acidic flavour.

Jacquère Chardonnay (Fr) a white grape variety grown in the Savoie region.

Jacques Bonet Brandy (USA) the brand-name of a brandy produced by the United Vintners, Lodi, California.

Jacques de Savoy (S.Afr) the label for a range of wines produced by the Vrede en Lust Wine Farm winery, Paarl, Western Cape.

Jacques Gaillard (Bra) a white grape variety.

Jacquesson et Fils (Fr) a Champagne producer. (Add): 68 Rue du Colonel Fabien, 51530 Dizy. 33ha. Produces vintage and non-vintage wines. Vintages: 1970, 1971, 1973, 1975, 1976, 1979, 1982, 1983, 1985, 1988, 1989, 1990, 1995, 1996, 1997, 1998, 1999, 2000. De Luxe vintage cuvée: Signature, non-vintage cuvée: Cuvée Perfection, Cuvée 730.

Jacquesson [Paul] (Fr) a winery in the A.C. Rully, Côte Chalonnaise, Burgundy 11ha.

Jacquet (Mad) an alternative spelling of Jacquez.

Jacquez (Mad) a white grape variety used in the making of Madeira (now banned from use), also used as grafting stock in USA. Is also spelt Jacquet.

Jaculillo (It) a red grape variety grown in Gragnano, Campania. Produces light red wines of the same name.

Jade (Eng) a 4.6% alc by vol. organic ale brewed by the Castlemain Brewery.

Jade Cocktail (Cktl) 25mls Jamaican rum, 2 dashes green crème de menthe, 2 dashes Cointreau, juice ¼ lime, 2 dashes gomme syrup. Shake over ice, strain into a cocktail glass, dress with a slice of lime.

Jade Mountain (USA) a winery based in Cloverdale, Sonoma County, California. 13ha. Grape varieties: Cabernet sauvignon and Johannisberg riesling. Produces varietal wines.

Jadot [Louis] (Fr) a noted Burgundy négociant-éleveur (established 1859). (Add): 5 Rue Samuel Legay, 21200 Beaune. Owns approximately 22ha of vineyards in the Côte d'Or, Burgundy all of which are of Grand Cru status. Labels include: Château des Jacques (A.C. Beaujolais Cru Moulin-à-Vent), Domaine Balloquet (A.C. Beaujolais Cru Brouilly), Les Charmes (A.C. Beaujolais Cru Morgon), Les Michelons (A.C. Beaujolais Cru Moulin-à-Vent), Poncereau (A.C. Beaujolais Cru Fleurie).

Jaegermeister (Ger) a dark red liqueur with digestive and tonic characteristics. See also Jägermeister. Produced by Mast.

Jaén (Sp) a province of Andalucía, home to the Vino Comarcal area of Lopera and Vino de Mesa areas of Bailén and Torreperogil.

Jaén (Sp) a white grape variety grown in Rioja, also known as the Cagazal, Calagrao, Jairia and the Navés. No relation to the Jaén varieties grown in the rest of Spain.

Jaén Blanco (Sp) a white grape variety once used to produce Málaga.

Jaén Doradillo (Sp) a white grape variety once used to produce Málaga.

Jaén Tinto (Sp) a red grape variety once used to produce Málaga.

Jaffelin Frères (Fr) a Burgundy négociant-éleveur. (Add): Caves du Chapitre, 2 Rue de Japitre, Beaune, Côte de Beaune, Burgundy (owned by Boisset).

Jagd Kümmel (Ger) a caraway-flavoured liqueur sold in stone jars 50% alc by vol.

J

Jäger (Aus) a winery based in the Wachau. (Add): 3610 Weissenkirchen 1. Grape varieties: Chardonnay, Grüner veltliner, Müller-Thurgau, Pinot gris, Riesling. Produces a range of dry and sweet (botrytised) wines.

Jager Lager (Eng) a bottled and canned lager 1032 O.G. brewed by the Davenports Brewery, Birmingham.

Jägermeister (Ger) a dark-red herb liqueur. *see* Jaegermeister.

Jaggery (Ind) palm juice from the palmyra tree which is left to evaporate, leaving a sugary brown syrup. *see* Jaggery Coffee.

Jaggery Coffee (Ind) made from unrefined palm sugar (jaggery) boiled with coffee and water. Is drunk black or with milk, the only food before morning prayers.

Jago (It) a single vineyard wine produced by Bolla, has 2–2½ years ageing in wood.

Jago's Love Cream liqueur (Scot) a 17% alc by vol. Scottish cream, vodka and vanilla liqueur produced by the Blackwood Distillery. When bottle is at the correct temperature the label's colour changes.

Jago's Vanilla Vodka Cream liqueur (Scot) a 17% alc by vol. Scottish cream, vodka and vanilla cream liqueur produced by the Blackwood Distillery.

Jagst [River] (Ger) a tributary of the river Neckar in Württemberg, has soil of shell limestone.

Jagter's Port (S.Afr) the label for a Port-style red wine (Cabernet sauvignon) produced by the Wamakersvallei Winery, Wellington, Western Cape.

Jahrgang (Ger) vintage/year.

Jahrgangsjuwel (It) lit: 'jewel of the year', a wine made in the Trentino-Alto Adige from old vines (over 70 years) of the Vernatsch grape.

Jaii (Eng) a vodka, lemon and green tea bottled drink 5% alc by vol. produced by the Independent Distillers Company.

Jail Ale (Eng) a 4.8% alc by vol. bottled ale brewed by the Princetown Breweries, Devon..

Jailleu (Fr) a vineyard based in the Grésivaudan Valley, Vienne département. Produces red wines.

Jaina (Sp) a white grape variety grown in the Rioja, also known as the Cagazal, Calagraño, Jaén and Navés.

Jakobus Mineralbrunnen (Ger) a natural spring mineral water from Jakobus Quelle, Trappenkamp. Mineral contents (milligrammes per litre): Sodium 13mg/l, Calcium 66mg/l, Magnesium 3mg/l, Bicarbonates 165mg/l, Chlorides 24mg/l, Sulphates 41mg/l.

Jalon (Fr) the old sixteenth century word for gallon. *See also* Galon.

Jamaica Babie (Cktl) 1 measure dark rum, ½ measure Tia Maria, ½ measure crème de noyau, ½ measure orange juice. Shake over ice, strain into a cocktail glass, add a dash of grenadine and a little grated nutmeg.

Jamaica Coffee (Eng) black coffee topped with whipped cream and grated nutmeg. *See also* Jamaican Coffee.

Jamaica Collins (Cktl) add to a highball glass containing a large piece of ice: 1 dash Angostura, juice ¾ lemon or lime, 1 teaspoon powdered sugar, 1 measure Jamaican rum. Top with soda water and stir and serve with straws.

Jamaica Dust (Cktl) 1 measure white rum, 1 measure coconut liqueur, 1 measure pineapple juice, mix together, stir and pour into a shot glass then top with powdered cinnamon.

Jamaica Hop (Cktl) ⅓ measure Tia Maria, ⅓ measure crème de cacao (white), ⅓ measure cream. Shake over ice and strain into a cocktail glass.

Jamaica Jake (Cktl) ½ measure dark rum, ½ measure Tia Maria, ½ measure apricot brandy, ½ measure pineapple juice. Shake over ice, strain into a cocktail glass, add a dash of grenadine and a little grated nutmeg.

Jamaica Joe (Cktl) ⅓ measure Tia Maria, ⅓ measure advocaat, ⅓ measure Jamaican rum, dash grenadine. Shake altogether over ice except grenadine. Strain into a cocktail glass, add grenadine and sprinkle with grated nutmeg.

Jamaica Mountain Cooler (Cktl) 300mls (½ pint) cold black coffee, 2 tots dark rum, 1 tot lime cordial, sugar to taste, orange soda, 1 banana, 1 orange. Chill all liquid ingredients, mix well over ice, strain into a highball glass, decorate with sliced banana and an orange slice.

Jamaican Coffee (W.Ind) considered to be some of the worlds' finest coffee. The best being Blue Mountain from the parishes of St. Andrew, St. Thomas and Portland. Other noted coffees are High Mountain Supreme and Prime Jamaica Washed. Produce a full-flavoured, good acidity, smooth and full-bodied coffee with a nutty flavour. *See also* Red Mountain and High Mountain.

Jamaican Coffee (Liq.Coffee) produced with a measure of dark rum.

Jamaican Cow (Cktl) 1 egg, 200mls (7fl.ozs) cold milk, 25mls (⅕ gill) Tia Maria. Shake well over ice, strain into an ice-filled highball glass and serve with straws.

Jamaican Glow (Cktl) 25mls (⅕ gill) gin, 15mls (⅛ gill) red bordeaux, 15mls (⅛ gill) orange juice, 3 dashes Jamaican rum. Shake over ice and strain into a cocktail glass.

Jamaican Lager (W.Ind) a lager beer 4.7% alc by vol. brewed by the Red Stripe Brewery, Kingston, Jamaica. Brewed in the U.K. under license by the Charles Wells Brewery.

Jamaican Granito (Cktl) 1 measure brandy, ½ measure Cointreau, ½ scoop orange water ice, ½ scoop lemon water ice. Blend altogether, pour into a highball glass, top with soda and grated nutmeg.

Jamaican Wonder Highball (Cktl) 25mls (1fl.oz) each of Lemon Hart Rum, Tia Maria, lime juice, 1 dash bitters. Place some ice in a highball glass with a twist and slice of lemon. Add ingredients, stir and top up with ginger ale.

Jamaica Old Fashioned (Cktl) place 1 lump sugar (which has 3 drops of Angostura soaked in) into an old-fashioned glass. Crush, add a lump of ice, a thick slice of orange and add 1½ measures of Jamaica rum.

Jamaica Orange Cocktail (Cktl) ½ measure Jamaica rum, ¼ measure dry vermouth, ¼ measure orange juice. Shake well with ice and strain into a cocktail glass.

Jamaica Punch (Punch) 60mls (2½ fl.ozs) Jamaican rum, 60mls (2½ fl.ozs) water, 300mls (½ pint) sweet cider, juice of 2 lemons, 1 finely-chopped and peeled apple, 60grms (2½ ozs) dried fruit. Heat fruit and water for 15 minutes, add remaining ingredients and reheat, stir, strain and serve.

Jamaica Rum (W.Ind) a rich, dark, full-bodied, pungent rum made from molasses, pot-stilled and cask matured.

Jamaica Rum Cocktail (Cktl) ⅚ measure Jamaica rum, ⅙ measure gomme syrup, dash Angostura. Stir over ice and strain into a cocktail glass.

Jamaica Rum Verschnitt (Ger) a verschnitt produced from Jamaican rum and spirit by the Schönauer C°.

Jamek (Aus) a winery (25ha) based in the Wachau. (Add): Joching, 3610 Weissenkirchen. Grape varieties: Chardonnay, Grüner veltliner, Muskateller, Pinot blanc, Riesling. Produces a range of dry and sweet (botrytised) wines.

James (USA) ***Vitis rotundifolia*** a wild black grape variety, known as Muscadines.

James Beam Distilling C°. (USA) a noted distillery. (Add): Clermont-Beam, Kentucky. Distillers of Jim Beam Sour Mash Kentucky Bourbon Whiskey.

James Boag & Son Brewery (Austr) an independent brewery (established 1881) based in Launceston, Tasmania. Brews: James Boag's Premium Lager.

James Boag's Premium (Austr) a 5% alc by vol. straw coloured, bottled lager brewed by James Boag & Son Brewery, Launceston, Tasmania.

James Bond Cocktail (Cktl) into a Champagne flute place a cube of sugar soaked with Angostura bitters. Add a spoon of crushed ice, 25mls (⅕ gill) vodka and top with iced Champagne and a spiral of lemon peel.

James Sedgwick Distillery (S.Afr) a distillery (established 1886) based in Wellington, Western Cape. Produces Three Ships single malt whiskey and a 5 y.o. version.

James E Pepper (USA) the brand-name of a well-known Bourbon whiskey from Kentucky.

James Foxe (Can) the brand-name for a Canadian whisky produced by Seagram.

James Haselgrove (Austr) a noted winery based in Coonawarra, South Australia.

James Martin (Scot) the label of a 20 year old lowland malt whisky.

Jameson (Ire) a whiskey distiller who produces a blend of pot-still whiskies matured in American oak.

Jameson Crested Ten (Ire) a blend of older pot-still whiskies which are matured in Sherry casks. Produced by Jameson.

Jameson Fifteen (Ire) a blend of pot-stilled whiskies. Produced by Jameson.

Jameson 1780 (Ire) a 12 year old single malt Irish whiskey produced by John Jameson 40% alc by vol.

Jamesons Irish Velvet (Ire) a liqueur produced from Jameson's Irish whiskey, coffee and sugar. Designed as a base for Irish coffee (boiling water and cream only needed) 20% alc by vol.

James Paine (Eng) *see* Paine.

James Parker (Scotland) Ltd (Eng) a distillery (established 1950). (Add): 79 Marylebone Lane, London W1U 2PU. Produces a range of whiskies and spirits. Website: http://www.angusdundee.co.uk 'E'mail: sales@angusdundee.co.uk

James Real Ale (Eng) *see* JRA.

Jamestown Julep (Cktl) a cocktail made with very dry rum over ice in an old-fashioned glass.

James White Suffolk Cider (Eng) (Add): Whites Fruit Farm, Ashbocking, Ipswich. 2 versions produced: Dry at 8% alc by vol and Medium 6% alc by vol.

Jammin (Eng) a 5.5% alc by vol. Caribbean crush cocktail fruit drink from Spilt Drinks, Exeter. Also Cherry Rum, Jammin' Black, Mellow Yellow, Perfect Pair, Peach Paradise, Space Doubt.

Jammin' Black (Eng) a 5.5% alc by vol. blackcurrant-flavoured fruit drink from Spilt Drinks, Exeter. Also Cherry Rum, Jammin, Mellow Yellow, Perfect Pair, Peach Paradise, Space Doubt.

Jammy (Eng) a term used to describe a fat, rich, fruity red wine.

Jamnica [1] (Cro) a sparkling natural spring mineral water (established 1828) from Jamnica Kiselica. Mineral contents (milligrammes per litre): Sodium 936.1mg/l, Calcium 112.5mg/l, Magnesium 36.5mg/l, Potassium 31.8mg/l, Bicarbonates 2422.9mg/l, Chlorides 269.8mg/l, Sulphates 134.9mg/l, Fluorides 0.9mg/l.

Jamnica [2] (Cro) a still natural spring mineral water (established 1828) from Jamnica Kiselica. Mineral contents (milligrammes per litre): Sodium 168.3mg/l, Calcium 78.7mg/l, Magnesium 31mg/l, Potassium 30.6mg/l, Bicarbonates 726.3mg/l, Chlorides 58.9mg/l, Sulphates 26.3mg/l.

Jampal (Port) a white grape variety grown in the Alenquer region.

Jamsheed (USA) the label for a red wine (Pinot noir) produced by the Maysara Estate, McMinnville, Oregon.

Jan (Pol) a sparkling natural spring mineral water. Mineral contents (milligrammes per litre): Sodium 13.3mg/l, Calcium 115.8mg/l, Magnesium 19.5mg/l, Potassium 1.9mg/l, Bicarbonates 418.6mg/l, Chlorides 21.3mg/l, Sulphates 50.7mg/l, Iron 3.9mg/l, Silicates 14mg/l.

Jana (Cro) a still natural spring mineral water (established 2002) from St. Jana. Mineral contents (milligrammes per litre): Sodium 2.2mg/l, Calcium 63mg/l, Magnesium 32.5mg/l, Potassium 0.8mg/l, Bicarbonates 354.7mg/l,

Chlorides 1.1mg/l, Sulphates 5.7mg/l, Fluorides 0.1mg/l, Silicates 4.2mg/l.

J & B (Scot) *abbr:* Justerini & Brooks.

J & B -6°C (Scot) a pale blended Scotch whisky which has been chill-filtered at -6°Celsius produced by Justerini and Brooks Ltd.

J and B Rare (Scot) a blended Scotch whisky produced by Justerini and Brooks Ltd. Part of International Distillers and Vintners Group 40% alc by vol.

Jane Brook Estate (Austr) a vineyard. (Add): Lot 19, Toodyay Road, Middle Swan, Western Australia, 6056. 15ha. Grape varieties: Cabernet franc, Cabernet sauvignon, Chardonnay, Chenin blanc, Grenache, Muscadelle, Pedro ximénez, Sauvignon blanc, Sémillon and Shiraz.

Janéza Private Cellar (S.Afr) a winery (established 2000) based in Robertson, Western Cape. 18ha. Grape varieties: Cabernet sauvignon, Chardonnay, Merlot, Sauvignon blanc, Shiraz. Label: Tresuva. Website: http://www.janeza.co.za

Janisson-Baradon et Fils (Fr) a Champagne producer (established 1922). (Add): 2, Rue des Vignerons, 51200 Épernay. 9ha. Propriétaire-Récoltant. Produces vintage and non-vintage wines. Vintages: 1995, 1996, 1997, 1999, 2000. A member of the Club Tresors de Champagne. Labels: Cuvée 'Special Club' Millésimée (100% Chardonnay), Cuvée Georges Baradon. Website: http://www.champagne-janisson.com

Janneau Cuvée Anniversaire (Fr) a special 25 year old Armagnac produced by Janneau Fils et Cie. to celebrate their 150th anniversary. Aged for 2 years in Sherry butts it is limited to 3000 bottles.

Janneau Fils et Cie (Fr) an Armagnac producer. (Add): 50 Ave. d'Aquitaine, 32100 Condom, Ténarèze. Produces 5, 8 year old and VSOP Armagnacs, also produced Janneau Cuvée Anniversaire, Tres Vieille Reserve. Firm taven over by Giovenetti (Italy) in 1993.

Janneau Tradition (Fr) a 5 year old Armagnac produced by Grand Armagnac Janneau.

Janneke (Hol) a 5.4% alc by vol. bottled special beer brewed by the Arcen Bier Brouwerij, Arcen.

Janner's Bitter (Eng) a cask-conditioned bitter 1038 O.G. brewed by the Mill Brewery in Newton Abbot, Devon.

Janot (Fr) an aniseed pastis produced by Janot, Aubagne, Provence.

Jansen (Hol) a liqueur producer based in Schiedam.

Jantara (S.Afr) the label for a range of wines produced by the Cape Vineyards winery, Rawsonville, Western Cape.

Jantjes Bier Brouwerij (Hol) a brewery (established 1994) based in Uden. Brews: Bedafse Vreugde, Jantjes Zomerbier.

Jantjes Zomerbier (Hol) a 5% alc by vol. bottle-conditioned special beer brewed by Jantjes Bier Brouwerij, Uden.

January Sale (Eng) a cask ale brewed by the Usher Brewery.

Jan van Gent (Bel) a 5.5% alc by vol. unfiltered,

unpasteurised beer brewed by Liefmans Brasserie, Oudenaarde.

Janvry (Fr) a Cru Champagne village in the Canton de Ville-en-Tardenois. District: Reims.

Japan (Jap) a country that produces many styles of alcoholic beverages: saké, lager-style beers, spirits are the main types with a small wine industry. Wine regions: Nagano, Okayama, Osaka, Yamagata and Yamanashi are the main producers of wines for the domestic market (made from American and European vines). *see* Suntory.

Japanese Beetles (USA) a vine pest that attacks American vine stock especially in the southern States.

Japanese Cocktail (Cktl) an alternative name for Mikado Cocktail.

Japanese Fizz (Cktl) 25mls (⅛ gill) whisky, juice ½ lemon, 15mls (⅛ gill) port wine, 1 teaspoon powdered sugar, 1 egg white. Shake over ice, strain into an ice-filled highball glass, top with soda and a cube of pineapple.

Japanese Green Tea Liqueur (Jap) a liqueur based on tea and grape brandy. Fairly rare outside Japan.

Japanese Rice Wine (Jap) saké.

Japanese Whiskey (Jap) a pot distilled and blended with Scottish malt whisky. *see* Suntory.

Jar (Eng) a slang term used in the north of England for a glass of beer.

Jarana (Cktl) 50mls (2fl.ozs) tequila, 50gms (2ozs) powdered sugar. Mix together and place in a highball with ice and top with pineapple juice.

Jarandilla (Sp) a wine-producing area in the Extremadura.

Jardin [René] (Fr) a Champagne producer. (Add): 3 Rue Charpentier Laurain, B.P. 8, 51190 Mesnil-sur-Oger. 16ha. Produces vintage and non-vintage wines including a blanc de blancs and Grande Réserve. Vintages: 1995, 1996, 1997, 1998, 1999, 2000.

Jardinage (Fr) a method of allowing vines to live to their maximum age and then replacing them individually.

Jardin de la France (Fr) a Vin de Pays area in the Cher département in central France. Regions Cher, Deux-Sèvres, Haute Vienne, Indre, Indre-et-Loire, Loire-Atlantique, Loiret, Loire-et-Cher, Maine-et-Loire, Vendée and Vienne.

Jardins [Les] (Fr) a vineyard in the A.C. commune of Montagny, Côte Chalonnaise, Burgundy.

Jarnac (Fr) a town within the Charente département where Cognac is made.

Jarnac-Champagne (Fr) a commune in the Charente-Maritime département whose grapes are used in the production of Cognac brandy.

Jarolières [Les] (Fr) a Premier Cru vineyard in the A.C. commune of Pommard, Côte de Beaune, Burgundy. 3.2ha. Also spelt Garollières (les) and Jarollières (les).

Jarollières [Les] (Fr) *see* Jarolières (Les).

Jarosov (Czec) an old established brewery based in central-southern Czec.

Jarra (Sp) a jar/pitcher of varying sizes (11½–12½ litres) used in Sherry blending.

J

Jarrah Ridge (Austr) a winery based in South-Eastern Australia. Produces: Chardonnay.

Jarro (Sp) water jug/pitcher.

Jarrons [Les] (Fr) an A.C. Brouilly produced and bottled by Thorins.

Jarrons [Les] (Fr) a Premier Cru vineyard in the A.C. commune of Savigny-lès-Beaune, Côte de Beaune, Burgundy.

Jarrow Brewery (Eng) a brewery (established 2002). (Add): Robin Hood, Primrose Hill, Jarrow, Tyne & Wear NE32 5UB. Brews: Jarrow Bitter 3.8% alc by vol., Jobling's Swinging Gibbet 4.1% alc by vol., Old Cornelius 4.8% alc by vol., Red Ellen 4.4% alc by vol., Riley's Army Bitter 4.3% alc by vol., Rivet Catcher 4% alc by vol., Venerable Bede 4.5% alc by vol. 'E'mail: jarrowbrewery@btconnect.com

Jarry [Daniel] (Fr) a propriétaire-récoltant based in Vouvray, Touraine, Loire. Produces fine Vouvray wines. (Add): La Vallée Coquette, 37210 Vouvray.

Jarzebiak (Pol) a dry vodka flavoured with rowan berries picked in the autumn 40% alc by vol. see Polmos.

Jasi (Rum) a wine-producing area, noted for white wines.

Jasmine Tea (Chi) a blend of teas from the Kwangtung Province, a large leaf, exotic tea, scented with Jasmine flowers.

Jasne (Pol) a low-alcohol lager beer with a good bitter flavour.

Jasnières (Fr) an A.C. medium-dry, white wine from the Chenin blanc grape in the Touraine district, Sarthe département in the Loire. Minimum alc by vol 10%.

Jason's Hill Private Cellar (S.Afr) a winery (established 2001) based in Slanghoek, Worcester, Western Cape. 100ha. Grape varieties: Cabernet sauvignon, Chardonnay, Chenin blanc, Merlot, Muscat d'Alsace, Pinotage, Sauvignon blanc, Sémillon. Label: Ivy du Toit. Website: http://www.jasonhill.com

Jasper Hill Vineyard (Austr) a winery (established 1975). (Add): Drummond's Lane, Off Northern Highway, Heathcote, 3523 Victoria. Grape varieties: Rhine riesling, Shiraz. Label: Georgia's Paddock. Website: http://www.jasperhill.com

Jasper Long Vineyards (USA) see Long Vineyards.

Jas Summer Ale (Eng) a 3.9% alc by vol. ale brewed by the Facers Brewery, Greater Manchester.

Jàszberényi Rizling (Hun) a light, medium-dry, white wine produced in the Jàszberény region.

Jau (Fr) a commune in the Bas Médoc, north-western Bordeaux.

Jaume Serra (Sp) a winery based in Catalonia, Penedés. Produce a range of white wines from Macabeo, Parellada. Also red reserva wines.

Jaune (Fr) a malady of white wines when they turn yellow. Treated either with sulphuric acid or fining agents. Not to be confused with Vins Jaune.

Java Coffee (E.Ind) an Indonesian coffee, produces a mellow but full aroma. Regions: Batavia, Buitenzorg, Cheribon and Preanger.

Java Rum (E.Ind) a medium-dark rum which is popular in Scandinavia.

Javrezac (Fr) a commune in the Borderies area of the Charente-Maritime département, Cognac.

Jaw Breaker (Eng) a 4% alc by vol. light bitter ale produced by Bateman's Brewery, Lincolnshire.

Jawhara (Iraq) a lager beer 12.5° Balling produced by the state-owned brewery based in Baghdad.

Jaworowy Zdroj (Pol) a natural spring mineral water from Swietej Jadwica. Mineral contents (milligrammes per litre): Sodium 17.8mg/l, Calcium 57.48mg/l, Magnesium 18.16mg/l, Potassium 2.7mg/l, Bicarbonates 116.58mg/l, Chlorides 39.01mg/l, Sulphates 115.2mg/l, Fluorides 0.1mg/l.

Jax (USA) a malt beer brewed by the Pearl Brewery in San Antonio, Texas.

Jane's Vineyard (USA) the label for a red wine (Pinot noir) produced by the Rodney Strong winery, Russian River Valley, California.

Jazz Jamboree (Pol) a 40% alc by vol. vodka from Polmos Starogard Gd.

J.B.A. (Eng) a bitter beer originally brewed in Wigan, Lancashire but now brewed by the Burtonwood Brewery in Staffordshire.

J. Bavet Fine Brandy (USA) the brand-name of a brandy produced by the Schenley Distillers, California.

J. Boag & Son Brewery (Austr) a brewery. (Add): 21 Shields Street, Lanceston, Tasmania 7250. Brews lager beers. Website: http://www.boags.com.au 'E'mail: info@boags.com.au

JC (Indo) a natural spring mineral water from Pandaan. Mineral contents (milligrammes per litre): Sodium 0.1mg/l, Calcium 21mg/l, Potassium 0.1mg/l, Bicarbonates 134mg/l, Chlorides 5mg/l, Sulphates 5.6mg/l. pH 7.0

J.C.B. (Eng) abbr: a 4.7% alc by vol. bitter ale brewed by Wadworth in Wiltshire, named after the grandson of the co-founder John Cairns Bartholomew.

J.C.B. (Eng) abbr: see Jolly's Centenary Bitter.

JC Blue (S.Afr) the label for a sparkling wine produced by the JC le Roux winery, Stellenbosch, Western Cape.

J.C. le Roux (S.Afr) a winery (27ha) that specialises in sparkling Cap Classique wines, based in Stellenbosch, Western Cape. Grape varieties: Chardonnay, Chenin blanc, Muscat, Pinot gris, Pinot noir, Sauvignon blanc. Label: JC Blue, La Chanson, La Vallée, Le Domaine, Scintilla. Owned by Die Bergkelder. Website: http://www.jcleroux.co.za

J.D. Dry Hop (Eng) a beer brewed by the Cornish Brewery C°. Devon.

Jean (Sp) a white grape variety grown in the Central Spanish regions

Jean Lafitte (Cktl) ½ measure dry gin, ¼ measure Cointreau, ¼ measure Pernod, 1 egg yolk, 2 dashes gomme syrup. Shake over ice and strain into a cocktail glass.

Jean le Long (S.Afr) the label for a white wine (Sauvignon blanc) named after the Hugeonot founder and produced by the Boschendal Wines winery, Franschhoek, Western Cape.

J

Jeanmaire (Fr) a Champagne producer. (Add): 12 Rue Godart-Roger, B.P. 256, 51207 Épernay. Négociant-manipulant. 80ha. Labels include Cuvée Elysée Millésimé.

Jean-Marc Brocard (Fr) a noted producer based in Chablis, northern Burgundy. (Add): Préhy, 89800 Chablis. Website: http://www.brocard.fr

Jean Daneel Wines (S.Afr) a winery (established 1997) based in Napier Southern Cape. 3.5ha. Grape varieties: Cabernet sauvignon, Chardonnay, Chenin blanc, Merlot, Sauvignon blanc. Label: Initial, Signature.

Jeanne d'Arc Brasserie (Fr) a brewery based at Ronchin. Brews: Ambré des Flandres, Belzebuth, Grain d'Orge, Scotch Triumph.

Jeannot (Fr) a noted brand of pastis.

Jean Perico (Sp) a dry sparkling wine made by the cava method by Gonzalez Byass (Gonzalez y Dubose) in Penedés.

Jean Robert (USA) the brand-name of a brandy produced by the Schenley Distillers at the Number One Distilling Cº., California.

Jean Taillefert (S.Afr) the label for a red wine (Shiraz) produced by the Laborie winery, Suider Paarl, Western Cape.

Jean Voisin (Fr) the second wine of Château Jean Voisin, Grand Cru A.C. Saint-Émilion, Saint-Émilion, eastern Bordeaux.

Jebenhauser (Ger) a natural spring mineral water. Mineral contents (milligrammes per litre): Sodium 21.5mg/l, Calcium 329mg/l, Magnesium 19mg/l, Bicarbonates 1080mg/l, Chlorides 14.8mg/l, Sulphates 40mg/l.

Jeber (Arab) a nineth century alchemist who is regarded as the father of distillation.

Jechtingen (Ger) village (Anb): Baden. (Ber): Kaiserstuhl-Tuniberg. (Gro): Vulkanfelsen. (Vins): Eichert, Enselberg, Gestühl, Hochberg, Steingrube.

Jeeper (Fr) a Champagne producer. (Add): 8 Rue Georges-Clemenceau, B.P. 119, 51480 Damery. Produces vintage and non-vintage wines. The 5 styles include Cuvée Ducale, Millésime, Domaine Grossard, Brut rosé and Grand Réserve. Website: http://www.champagne-jeeper.com 'E'mail: info@champagne-jeeper.com

Jefferson and Wine (USA) the Vinifera Wine Growers Association, The Plains, Virginia. Formed 1976.

Jefferson Vineyards (USA) vineyards based in Virginia in A.V.A. of Monticello. Noted for Chardonnay wines.

Jehan de Massol (Fr) a vineyard part of Santenots, A.C. Volnay, Côte de Beaune, Burgundy (owned by the Hospices de Beaune).

Jehan Humblot (Fr) a cuvée in the vineyard of Poruzots, A.C. Meursault, Côte de Beaune, Burgundy (owned by the Hospices de Beaune).

Jekel Vineyard (USA) a winery (58ha) based in Salinas Valley, Monterey, California. Grape varieties: Cabernet sauvignon, Chardonnay, Gamay and Johannisberg riesling. Produces varietal wines.

Jektiss (Tun) a natural spring mineral water. Mineral contents (milligrammes per litre): Sodium 69.19mg/l, Calcium 31.9mg/l, Magnesium 14.1mg/l, Bicarbonates 50.5mg/l, Chlorides 72.17mg/l, Sulphates 115.65mg/l. pH 7.14

Jekyll's Gold (Eng) a 4.3% alc by vol. traditional ale brewed by Hydes Brewery, 46 Moss Lane, West Manchester, Lancashire.

Jellab (M.East) a non-alcoholic beverage consisting of fresh date juice flavoured with rose water.

Jelly Bag (Eng) a fine cloth bag used for separating the fruit pulp from the juice in home wine-making.

Jemrose Vineyard (USA) the label for a red wine (Pinot noir) produced by the Deerfield Ranch Winery, Bennett Valley, Sonoma County, California.

Jenever (Hol) gin. Also spelt Genever.

Jenks Cocktail (Cktl) ½ measure dry gin, ½ measure dry vermouth, dash Bénédictine. Shake over ice and strain into a cocktail glass.

Jenlain (Fr) a 6.5% alc by vol. bière de garde brewed in Jenlain near Valenciennes in northern France by the Brasseries Duyck. Top fermented and unpasteurised.

Jenlain Bière Blonde (Fr) a 6% alc by vol blonde bière bottled in a Champagne-style bottle and cork and brewed in Jenlain near Valenciennes in northern France by the Brasseries Duyck.

Jenlain Bière de Luxe (Fr) a beer brewed by the Duyck Brasserie. Is presented in a wire-top bottle and is deep bronze in colour, it is matured for 1 month, filtered and unpasteurised.

Jennelotte [La] (Fr) a Premier Cru vineyard in the commune of Blagny, A.C. Meursault, Côte de Beaune, Burgundy 4.5ha.

Jennings Bitter (Eng) a dark malty bitter brewed by Jennings Brothers in Cocklemouth, Cumbria.

Jennings Brothers (Eng) a brewery (established 1828). (Add): Castle Brewery, Cockermouth, Cumbria. CA13 9NE. Brew: a sharp cask-conditioned Bitter, Jennings Bitter, Castle Keg Mild 1033 O.G. Cumbrian Ale 4.2% alc by vol. John Jennings Millennium Mash 5% alc by vol. Cumberland Ale 1040 O.G. Fell Runner 4.3% alc by vol. La'al Cockle Warmer, Sneck Lifter, Stage Struck, Oatmeal Stout. Website: http://www.jenningsbrewery.co.uk 'E'mail: plaws@jenningbrewery.co.uk

Jerepigo (S.Afr) see Hanepoot Jeripigo

Jerepiko (S.Afr) a wine fortified with brandy (grape spirit).

Jerevan (Arm) a wine-producing region in Armenia.

Jerez (Sp) see Jerez de la Frontera.

Jerezaños (Sp) the name given to a Coñac (Spanish brandy), also known as Jerinacs.

Jerezaños (Sp) a person who lives in Jerez, Andalusia.

Jerezaños Tres Estrellas (Sp) a solera brandy produced by Gil Galan.

Jerez Cocktail (Cktl) 50mls (2fl.ozs) dry Sherry, dash orange bitters, dash peach bitters, stir well together over ice and strain into a cocktail glass.

Jerez Cortado Hidalgo (Sp) a brand of Sherry

produced by Vinícola Hildalgo in Sanlúcar de Barrameda.

Jerez de la Frontera (Sp) a town in Andalucía which gives its name to Sherry, the main Sherry port.

Jerez Lustau (Sp) the brand-name of a range of Sherries produced by Lustau in Jerez.

Jerez-Quina (Sp) a quinine-based white wine or Sherry blended with the bitter skins from Seville oranges and macerated Cinchona bark.

Jerez Supérieur (Sp) consists of the districts Chiclana, Chipiona, Labrija, Puerto de Santa Maria, Puerto Real, Sanlúcar de Barrameda, Trebujena and town of Jerez de la Frontera.

Jerez-Xérès-Sherry y Manzanilla Sanlúcar de Barrameda (Sp) official D.O. wines produced in Jerez de la Frontera.

Jeriñac (Sp) the brand-name for the brandies produced in Jerez de la Frontera, Andalusia. Also spelt Cherinac, Xereñac. *See also* Jerezanos and Coñac.

Jeripegos (S.Afr) the name given to the fortified grape juice at about 32° proof (17% alc by vol.) used for dessert wines.

Jermuk (Arm) a natural spring mineral water (established 1999) from Jermuk Springs.

Jeroboam (Fr) a large bottle, holds 4 standard bottles, used mainly in Champagne.

Jéroboam (Fr) a large bottle of (3litres) 4 standard bottles capacity used in the Champagne region. *see* Champagne Bottle Sizes. (Eng) = jeroboam, (Ger) = doppelmagnum.

Jeroboam (USA) a bottle holding 101.44 USfl.ozs (3litres).

Jerome Quiot (Fr) a large producer of A.C. Châteauneuf-du-Pape wines. Labels: Les Combes d'Arnevel, Les Gemarelles.

Jeropiga (Port) boiled down grape juice used to sweeten wines. *see* Geropiga.

Jerry's Joy (Cktl) ⅓ measure Cointreau, ⅓ measure vodka, ⅓ measure Lillet, dash orange bitters, dash egg white, shake over ice, strain into a cocktail glass and add a cherry.

Jersey (Ch.Isles) the largest of the Channel Islands. Has several commercial vineyards. *see* Clos de la Mare, Château Catillon and Perquages (Les).

Jersey Brewery (Ch. Isles) the new name for the Ann Street Brewery. Brews: Force 135.

Jersey Cocktail (Cktl) 300mls (½ pint) dry still cider, 1 teaspoon sugar, 3 dashes Angostura. Shake over ice, strain into a cocktail glass and decorate with a strip of lemon peel.

Jersey Cocktail (Cktl)(Non-alc) 125mls (5fl.ozs) non-alcoholic cider, 2 dashes Angostura, 2 dashes gomme syrup. Stir well over ice, strain into a wine glass, add a cherry and squeeze of lemon juice on top.

Jersey Cream Liqueur (Ch.Isles) also known as Tipple. A blend of Jersey cream, French brandy with a dash of amaretto. *See also* Guernsey Cream Liqueur.

Jersey Lightning (USA) another name for Apple Jack Brandy.

Jersey Lightning Cocktail (Cktl) ¾ measure applejack brandy, ¼ measure sweet vermouth, juice of a small lime. Shake over ice and strain into a cocktail glass.

Jersey Lily (Pousse Café) equal parts of yellow Chartreuse and old Cognac in that order.

Jerte (Sp) a wine-producing area in Càceres, south-western Spain.

Jerusalem (Cro) a Lutomer vineyard noted for aromatic white wines.

Jerusalem Environs (Isr) a new wine-producing region which produces both red and white wines.

Jerzynowka (Pol) a liqueur made from the maceration of blackberries 30% alc by vol. Also spelt Jerzyvowka. Known in Germany as Kroatzbeerlikoer.

Jesses Vineyard (Eng) a vineyard (established 1977) based at Snow Hill, Dinton, near Salisbury, Wiltshire. 0.25ha. Grape varieties: Madeleine angevine, Müller-Thurgau and Triomphe d'Alsace.

Jester (Eng) a 3.5% alc by vol. ale brewed by the Butts Brewery Ltd., Berkshire.

Jester (Austr) a vineyard based in Mitolo, McLaren Vale, South Australia.

Jester Ale (Eng) the label of a 3.8% alc by vol. ale brewed by Charles Wells of Bedford at their Cox's Yard micro-brewery, Stratford upon Avon.

Jesuitenberg (Ger) vineyard (Anb): Franken. (Ber): Mainviereck. (Gro): Not yet assigned. (Vil): Rück.

Jesuitenberg (Ger) vineyard (Anb): Mosel-Saar-Ruwer. (Ber): Saar-Ruwer. (Gro): Scharzberg. (Vil): Wawern.

Jesuitengarten (Ger) vineyard (Anb): Ahr. (Ber): Walporzheim/Ahrtal. (Gro): Klosterberg. (Vil): Marienthal.

Jesuitengarten (Ger) vineyard (Anb): Mosel-Saar-Ruwer. (Ber): Saar-Ruwer. (Gro): Römerlay. (Vil): Waldrach.

Jesuitengarten (Ger) vineyard (Anb): Mosel-Saar-Ruwer. (Ber): Saar-Ruwer. (Gro): Scharzberg. (Vil): Pellingen.

Jesuitengarten (Ger) vineyard (Anb): Rheingau. (Ber): Johannisberg. (Gro): Honigberg. (Vil): Winkel.

Jesuitengarten (Ger) vineyard (Anb): Pfalz. (Ber): Mittelhaardt-Deutsche Weinstrasse. (Gro): Mariengarten. (Vil): Forst.

Jesuitengarten (Ger) vineyard (Anb): Pfalz. (Ber): Mittelhaardt-Deutsche Weinstrasse. (Gro): Meerspinne. (Vil): Königsbach.

Jesuitengarten (Ger) a vineyard within the village of Winkel, 31.2ha (83.3%) of which is proposed to be classified as Erstes Gewächs.

Jesuitenhofgarten (Ger) vineyard (Anb): Pfalz. (Ber): Mittelhaardt-Deutsche Weinstrasse. (Gro): Schwarzerde. (Vil): Dirmstein.

Jesuitenschloss (Ger) vineyard (Anb): Baden. (Ber): Markgräflerland. (Gro): Lorettoberg. (Vil): Freiburg.

Jesuitenschloss (Ger) vineyard (Anb): Baden. (Ber): Markgräflerland. (Gro): Lorettoberg. (Vil): Merzhausen.

J

Jesuitenwingert (Ger) vineyard (Anb): Mosel-Saar-Ruwer. (Ber): Saar-Ruwer. (Gro): Römerlay. (Vil): Trier.

Jet (Bel) a natural spring mineral water from Jet Moorsele.

Jeune (Fr) yound (wine).

Jever Light (Ger) a 2.7% alc by vol. bottled light pilsner brewed by the Friesischen Bräuhaus, Jever.

Jever Pilsener (Ger) a 4.9% alc by vol. bottled pilsener brewed by the Friesischen Bräuhaus, Jever. Imported into U.K. by the Ruddles Brewery. 1046 O.G.

Jevícko Brewery (Czec) a brewery based in central Czec, noted for pilsener-style beers.

Jewel Cocktail (Cktl) ⅓ measure dry gin, ⅓ measure green Chartreuse, ⅓ measure Italian vermouth, dash orange bitters. Shake over ice, strain into a cocktail glass and top with a cherry.

Jewel Collection (USA) a winery based in the Lodi, San Joaquin County, California. Grape varieties: Cabernet sauvignon.

Jewel of the Breede River (S.Afr) a winery (established 2004) based in Robertson, Western Cape. 26ha. Grape varieties: Chardonnay, Chenin blanc, Colombard, Ruby cabernet, Shiraz. Website: http://www.kingsriver-estate.com

Jeykell's Gold (Eng) a 4.3% alc by vol. traditional light-coloured, premium ale brewed by Hydes, 46 Moss Lane, West Manchester.

Jeyplak (Cktl) ⅔ measure dry gin, ⅓ measure Italian vermouth, 2 dashes Pernod. Stir over ice, strain into a cocktail glass and top with a cherry.

Jezebel (Austr) a red (Cabernet sauvignon and Merlot blend) wine produced by the Sinclair Estate, Western Australia.

Jezek 10% (Czec) lit: 'hedgehog'. 4.2% alc by vol. bottled lager beer from the Jihlava Brewery, Jihlava.

Jezek 11% (Czec) lit: 'hedgehog'. 4.9% alc by vol. straw coloured, bottled lager beer from the Jihlava Brewery, Jihlava.

Jezek 12% (Czec) lit: 'hedgehog'. 5.2% alc by vol. bottled lager beer from the Jihlava Brewery, Jihlava.

JFJ Bronco Winery (USA) a large winery based near Modesto, Stanislaus, California. Wines sold under many labels (mainly ordinary table wines), best known CC and JFJ.

JHB (Eng) a 3.8% alc by vol. bitter ale brewed by Oakham Ales, Cambridgeshire.

JH Pacas & C° (S.Afr) the label for a range of wines produced by the Bernheim Wines winery, Nooder-Paarl, Western Cape.

Jiangsu (Chi) a noted wine-producing province in northern China.

Jicara (Sp) a cup for chocolate.

Jidvei (Rum) an important wine-producing area, a part of the Tirnave Vineyard.

Jidvei Winery (Rum) a 600ha vineyard and winery based in the Tirnave, Transylvania.

Jigger (USA) a spirit measure mainly used for cocktails, size: 1½ fl.ozs, also in 1fl.oz and 2fl.oz versions

Jigsaw (Eng) a 4.8% alc by vol. dark wheat beer brewed by the Salopian Brewing Company, Shrewsbury.

Jihlava Brewery (Czec) a brewery (established 1860) based in Jihlava, Central Czec (originally founded as Iglau 'hedgehog' in 1860). Taken over by Zwettl in 1995. Noted for Jezek Lager beers.

Jil's Dune (S.Afr) the label for a white wine (Chenin blanc) produced by the Springfontein winery, Walker Bay, Western Cape.

Jim Barry (Austr) a winery based in the Clare Valley, South Australia. Labels: First XI and Lodge Hill.

Jim Beam (USA) the brand-name of a Sour Mash Kentucky Bourbon whiskey distilled by the James Beam Distilling C°., Clermont-Beam, Kentucky. 40% alc by vol. Also an 8 year old Black Label version. Other labels include Baker's, Basil Hayden's, Booker's, Knob Creek.

Jimmy's Bitter (Ch.Isles) an ale brewed by the Tipsy Toad Town House, St. Helier, Jersey.

Jimmy Woodser (Austr) a slang term for a man who drinks by himself.

Jin (Wal) gin.

Jindalee (Austr) a winery based in South-Eastern Saustralia.

Jingle Knockers (Eng) a 5.5% alc by vol. ale brewed by the Skinner's Brewery C°. Ltd., Cornwall.

Jingle Knockers (Eng) an ale brewed by Wychwood Brewery at Eagle Maltings, Witney, Oxfordshire.

Jinro (E.Asia) noted producers of Gingseng Ju in Seoul, South Korea.

Jin Sha Hotel (Chi) a natural spring mineral water brand.

Jinzu (Eng) a 5.4% alc by vol. RTD drink produced by Matthew Clark from a blend of Japanese saké, ginger and lemon soda.

Jirkov Brewery (Czec) an old established brewery based at Jirkov in north-west Czec.

Jiskra (Czec) lit: 'the spark', a full-flavoured lager beer brewed by the Hradec Kràlové Brewery in eastern Bohemia.

Jiu (Chi) the general description of wine, includes both distilled and fermented beverages (alcoholic beverages).

Jiuba (Chi) bar.

Jiubajian Zhaodaiyuan (Chi) bartender.

Jiuchang (Chi) winery.

Jiufeng (Chi) a natural spring mineral water. Mineral contents (milligrammes per litre): Silicates 32.8mg/l. pH 7.1

Jiulong (Chi) a natural spring mineral water. Mineral contents (milligrammes per litre): Calcium 33.8mg/l, Potassium 0.8mg/l, Bicarbonates 576mg/l, Silicates 26.8mg/l.

Jiweijiu (Chi) cocktail.

J.J. and S. Liqueur (Ire) an Irish whiskey and John Jameson blend 50% alc by vol., distilled and bottled by Jameson.

J.J.McWilliams (Austr) a label of the McWilliams winery, New South Wales.

J.J. Murphy Cocktail (Cktl) 15mls (⅛ gill) each of gin, Italian vermouth, French vermouth, dash

724

Bénédictine, dash lemon peel juice. Stir over ice, strain into a cocktail glass and serve with a cherry.

J.K. (Eng) *abbr*: **J**ames **K**ing a sweet bottled stout 1034 O.G. brewed by the King and Barnes Brewery in Sussex. Stands for James King the brewery founder, uses German bottom-fermented yeasts.

J. Lohr (USA) a winery based in the Napa Valley, California. (Add): 6169 Airport Road, Paso Robles, CA 93446. Also has vineyards in other districts of California. Grape varieties: Cabernet sauvignon. Also the label used by Turgeon and Lohr for their range of table wines. Vineyard: Carol's Vineyard, Seven Oaks. Website: http://www.jlohr.com

J.N.V. (Port) *abbr*: **J**unta **N**acional do **V**inho.

Joannes Seyve (USA) a series of hybrid grapes varieties related to the Seyval Blanc.

João de Santarém (Port) a red grape variety used in Ribatejo and Bairrada. Also known as Castelao Francês, Periquita.

Jobling's Swinging Gibbet (Eng) a 4.1% alc by vol. ale brewed by the Jarrow Brewery, Tyne & Wear.

Jo'burg (S.Afr) the brand-name of an apéritif similar in style to vermouth.

Joch (Aus) a vineyard site based on the banks of the River Kamp situated in the Kamptal region.

Jochinger (Aus) a vineyard site on the banks of the River Danube situated in the Wachau region, Niederösterreich.

Jockey Club (Cktl) 1 measure dry gin, juice ¼ lemon, 2 dashes (white) crème de menthe, dash Angostura. Shake over ice and strain into a cocktail glass.

Jockey Club Cocktail (Cktl) 25mls (⅕ gill) gin, 15mls (⅛ gill) white crème de noyau, juice ½ lemon, 2 dashes orange bitters, 2 dashes Angostura. Shake over ice and strain into a cocktail glass.

Jocose Julep (Cktl) ⅚ measure Bourbon whiskey, ⅙ measure (green) crème de menthe, juice ¼ lime, 3 dashes gomme syrup, 6 mint leaves. Blend altogether with a scoop of crushed ice, pour into a highball glass, top with soda and a sprig of mint.

Jodicum (Hun) a still natural spring mineral water (established 2000). Mineral contents (milligrammes per litre): Sodium 15mg/l, Calcium 78mg/l, Magnesium 28.6mg/l, Fluorides 0.12mg/l.

Jogger [The] (Cktl) 2 parts Johnny Walker Red Label, 1 part Cointreau, 1 part amaretto, 6 parts lemonade. Stir together, strain into an ice-filled highball, decorate with a slice of orange and cucumber peel.

Johanisquelle (Ger) a natural spring mineral water from Bad Dürrheim. Mineral contents (milligrammes per litre): Sodium 13mg/l, Calcium 289mg/l, Magnesium 50mg/l, Bicarbonates 384mg/l, Chlorides 70mg/l, Sulphates 610mg/l.

Johannesberg (Ger) vineyard (Anb): Nahe. (Ber): Schloss Böckelheim. (Gro): Paradiesgarten. (Vil): Sobernheim-Steinhardt.

Johannesberg (Ger) vineyard (Anb): Nahe. (Ber): Schloss Böckelheim. (Gro): Paradiesgarten. (Vil): Waldböckelheim.

Johannesberg (Ger) vineyard (Anb): Rheinhessen. (Ber): Bingen. (Gro): Abtey. (Vil): Gau-Augesheim.

Johanneshof (Aus) a winery (25ha) based in Tattendorf, Thermenregion. (Add): Johannes Reinisch, Im Weingarten 1, 2523 Tattendorf. Grape varieties: Cabernet sauvignon, Chardonnay, Merlot, Pinot blanc, Pinot noir, Riesling, St. Laurent, Sauvignon blanc, Zweigelt. Produces a range of dry and sweet wines.

Johann Graue (S.Afr) a wine estate based in Paarl, Western Cape.

Johannis (Ger) a still mineral water of the Johannis spring in the Ahrweiler/Rhineland.

Johannisbeerlikoer (Ger) a blackcurrant liqueur.

Johannisberg (Ger) bereich (Anb): Rheingau. (Gros): Burgweg, Daubhaus, Deutelsberg, Erntebringer, Gottesthal, Heiligenstock, Honigberg, Mehrhölzchen, Landkreis Melsungen, Steil, Steinmächer.

Johannisberg (Ger) village (Anb): Rheingau. (Ber): Johannisberg. (Gro): Erntebringer. (Vins): Goldatzel, Hansenberg, Hölle, Mittelhölle.

Johannisberg (Ger) vineyard (Anb): Franken. (Ber): Maindreieck. (Gro): Ravensburg. (Vil): Thüngersheim.

Johannisberg (Ger) vineyard (Anb): Franken. (Ber): Mainviereck. (Gro): Not yet assigned. (Vil): Rück.

Johannisberg (Ger) vineyard (Anb): Mosel-Saar-Ruwer. (Ber): Bernkastel. (Gro): Schwarzlay. (Vil): Dreis.

Johannisberg (Ger) vineyard (Anb): Mosel-Saar-Ruwer. (Ber): Saar-Ruwer. (Gro): Römerlay. (Vil): Franzenheim.

Johannisberg (Ger) vineyard (Anb): Mosel-Saar-Ruwer. (Ber): Saar-Ruwer. (Gro): Römerlay. (Vil): Mertesdorf.

Johannisberg (Ger) vineyard (Anb): Nahe. (Ber): Kreuznach. (Gro): Pfarrgarten. (Vil): Wallhausen.

Johannisberg (Ger) vineyard (Anb): Nahe. (Ber): Kreuznach. (Gro): Schlosskapelle. (Vil): Burg Layen.

Johannisberg (Ger) vineyard (Anb): Nahe. (Ber): Kreuznach. (Gro): Schlosskapelle. (Vil): Rümmelsheim.

Johannisberg (Ger) vineyard (Anb): Rheinhessen. (Ber): Bingen. (Gro): Sankt Rochuskapelle. (Vil): Aspisheim.

Johannisberg (Ger) vineyard (Anb): Rheinhessen. (Ber): Bingen. (Gro): Sankt Rochuskapelle. (Vil): Zotzenheim.

Johannisberg (Ger) vineyard (Anb): Rheinhessen. (Ber): Nierstein. (Gro): Sankt Alban. (Vil): Mainz.

Johannisberg (Switz) a name for the Sylvaner grape.

Johannisberg (Switz) a white wine made from the Johannisberg grape (Sylvaner). Is similar in style to a Rhine wine.

Johannisberger (Ger) a dry white wine from the Johannisberg vineyards in the Rheingau.

Johannisberger (S.Afr) the label for a red and white wine range produced by the Douglas Wine Cellar winery, Douglas, Northern Cape.

Johannisberger (S.Afr) the label for a white wine (Chenin blanc, Hanepoot and Muscadel blend) produced by the Simonsvlei International winery, Suider-Paarl, Western Cape.

Johannisberg Feuergold (Switz) a white wine produced from the Sylvaner grape by Les Fils Maye in Riddes, Valais.

Johannisberg Riesling (USA) a name for the true Riesling grape, named after the great Schloss Johannisberg in Germany.

Johannisbrünnchen (Ger) vineyard (Anb): Mosel-Saar-Ruwer. (Ber): Bernkastel. (Gro): Kurfürstlay. (Vil): Bernkastel-Kues.

Johanniskirchel (Ger) vineyard (Anb): Pfalz. (Ber): Mittelhaardt-Deutsche Weinstrasse. (Gro): Rebstöckel. (Vil): Diedesfeld.

Johanniswein (Ger) lit: 'St.John's wine', was drunk by St. John at the Last Supper (said to be poisoned but he suffered no affects). Is now often drunk as a Loving Cup as considered to bring peace and to benefit health.

Johannitergarten (Ger) vineyard (Anb): Pfalz. (Ber): Mittelhaardt-Deutsche Weinstrasse. (Gro): Meerspinne. (Vil): Mussbach.

Johanniter Quelle (Ger) a still natural spring mineral water. Mineral contents (milligrammes per litre): Sodium 98mg/l, Calcium 264mg/l, Magnesium 94mg/l, Bicarbonates 1207mg/l, Chlorides 80mg/l, Sulphates 188mg/l. Website: http://www.hassia.com

Johannserberg (Aus) a vineyard site on the banks of the River Danube situated in the Wachau region, Niederösterreich.

Johan van Zyl Wines (S.Afr) a winery (50ha) based in Citrusdal, Swartland, Western Cape. Grape varieties: Cabernet sauvignon, Chardonnay, Cinsaut, Grenache, Pinotage, Tempranillo.

John Arkell Bitter (Eng) see Arkell Bitter 1033 O.G.

John baker Original (Eng) a 4.8% alc by vol. bitter ale brewed by the Brandy Cask Pub & Brewery, Worcestershire.

John Baker's Private Blend (Austr) a fine red wine from the John Baker Vineyards in Coolawin, South Australia. Grape varieties: Cabernet 20%, Malbec 60% and Shiraz 20%.

John Barleycorn (Eng) an old eighteenth and nineteenth century nickname for beer.

John Barleycorn Bitter (Eng) a bitter beer brewed by the Pollards Brewery in Stockport.

John Barr (Scot) a blended Scotch whisky produced by George Cowie and Sons Ltd., Mortlach, Dufftown.

John Baxter's Bitter (Eng) a bitter beer 1030–1034 O.G. brewed by the Watney Mann Brewery.

John Begg (Scot) a Scotch whisky and malt whisky producer owned by DCL. Brands include: John Begg's Bluecap and Lochnagar.

John Begg's Bluecap (Scot) a blended Scotch whisky produced by John Begg Distillery (part of DCL) 40% alc by vol.

John Bewsher's Bitter (Eng) a bitter brewed by the Tirril Brewery, Cumbria.

John Brown Ale (Eng) a bottled brown ale 1031 O.G. brewed by the Hall and Woodhouse Brewery in Dorset.

John Brown Ale (Wal) a bottled brown ale 1032 O.G. brewed by the Felinfoel Brewery in Llanelli, South Wales.

John Brown's Special (Scot) the brand-name of a blended Scotch whisky 40% alc by vol.

John Bull Bitter (Eng) a keg bitter beer 1036 O.G. brewed by the Ind Coope Brewery in Romford, Essex. Bottled version is 4.5% alc by vol.

John Bull Export Bitter (Eng) an export bitter 1053 O.G. brewed by the Ind Coope Brewery in Burton-on-Trent, Staffordshire.

John Christ Winery (USA) a winery based in Avon Lake, Ohio. Produces mainly varietal wines from the Concord grape.

John Collins (Cktl) 50mls (2fl.ozs) Hollands gin, juice ½ lemon, 1 teaspoon sugar. Shake together with ice, strain into an ice-filled highball glass, top with soda water and a slice of lemon.

John Courage Ale (Eng) a keg and bottle pale ale 1042 O.G. brewed by Courage Breweries.

John Cunningham Night Fighter (Eng) a 4% alc by vol. ale brewed by the Potton Brewery Cº. Ltd., Bedfordshire.

John Davey (Eng) a 4.8% alc by vol. premium Cornish bitter brewed by Redruth Brewery in Cornwall.

John Devenish Bitter (Eng) a cask-conditioned bitter 1032 O.G. brewed by the Cornish Brewery Cº. in Dorchester, Dorset.

John Dockery's Winery (USA) a small winery based in Rockingham, North Carolina. Produces Scuppernong wines.

John Dowland's Greensleeves (Eng) a mint-flavoured brandy and cream liqueur produced in London by John Dowland 17% alc by vol.

John Groves Bitter (Eng) a keg bitter 1034 O.G. brewed by the Cornish Brewery Cº. in Dorchester, Dorset.

John Hampden's Ale (Eng) a 4.8% alc by vol. ale brewed using fuggles hops by the Chiltern Brewery in Bucks.

John Handons (Eng) a 4.8% alc by vol. ale brewed by The Chiltern Brewery, Buckinghamshire.

John Harvey (Sp) a brand of Sherry produced by Harvey of Bristol. Now known as Isis.

John Hop (Eng) a low alcohol beer (less than 1% alc by vol.) from Harveys of Lewes, East Sussex.

John Jameson Special Irish Whiskey (Ire) a 12 year old pure pot-still whiskey aged at least 12 years in Sherry casks. Also a Very Special Old whiskey aged for a minimum of 15 years in Sherry casks.

John Jennings Millennium Mash (Eng) a 5% cask and bottled ale produced by the Jennings Brothers at the Castle Brewery, Cockermouth, Cumbria (a limited edition named after the founder).

John Marston (Eng) a keg version 1043 O.G. of the Marston Brewery's Pedigree Bitter.

John Martin Brasserie Lessee (Bel) a brewery (established 1993) based in Genval. Brews: John Martin's.

John Martin's (Bel) a 5.8% alc by vol. amber coloured special beer brewed by John Martin Brasserie Lessee, Genval.

John McMullen (Eng) a special reserve cask ale from the McMullen Brewery in Hertfordshire. Brewed to celebrate the retirement of John McMullen after 40 years in business.

Johnnie Cocktail (Cktl) ¾ measure sloe gin, ¼ measure Curaçao, 2 dashes anisette. Shake over ice and strain into a cocktail glass.

Johnnie Walker Black Label (Scot) a de luxe blended Scotch whisky produced by John Walker and Sons Ltd., Kilmarnock, Ayrshire 43% alc by vol.

Johnnie Walker Green Label (Scot) a blended malt (4 different malts) whisky produced by John Walker & Sons Ltd.

Johnnie Walker 150 (Scot) a special blend of Scotch whiskies produced during Walker's 150th anniversary year (1970) laid down to mature for 15 years. Packaged in an oak travelling case and presented with its own crystal decanter.

Johnnie Walker Premier (Scot) a blend of old, mature malt and grain whiskies produced by John Walker and Sons Ltd., Kilmarnock, Ayrshire. Is presented in a decanter bottle and each bottle numbered to guarantee authenticity 43% alc by vol.

Johnnie Walker Pure Malt (Scot) a 15 year old highland malt whisky produced by John Walker and Sons Ltd., Kilmarnock, Ayrshire 43% alc by vol.

Johnnie Walker Red Label (Scot) a blended Scotch whisky produced by John Walker and Sons Ltd., Kilmarnock, Ayrshire.

Johnnie Walker Swing (Scot) a de luxe blended Scotch whisky produced by John Walker and Sons, Kilmarnock, Ayrshire 43% alc by vol.

Johnny Drum (USA) a 12 year old Kentucky straight bourbon whiskey. 43% alc by vol. Also 6 and 15 year old versions.

John Paul Jones (Eng) a 4% alc by vol. ale brewed by the Sulwath Brewers Ltd., Kirkcudbrightshire.

John Peel Bitter (Eng) a cask-conditioned bitter 1040 O.G. brewed by the Matthew Brown Brewery in Blackburn, Lancashire. Also a keg version.

John Peel Lager (Eng) a lager beer 1060 O.G. exported to the USA.

John Simon (Cktl) ¼ measure dry gin, ¼ measure Grand Marnier, ¼ measure crème de noyeau, ¼ measure orange squash, dash Angostura. Shake well over ice and strain into a cocktail glass.

John's Judicious Juice (Eng) one of a three-pack of bottled beers brewed by the great Stour Brewery, Canterbury. Name after the then Prime Minister: John Major.

John Smith's Bitter (Eng) a 4% alc by vol. dark, amber-coloured bitter beer brewed by John Smith Brewery, Tadcaster, North Yorkshire.

John Smiths LA (Eng) a low alcohol beer 0.9% alc by vol. from Scottish Courage.

Johnson County (USA) a wine-producing region in Arkansas. French and hybrid wines produced.

Johnson Estate Winery (USA) *see* Frederick Johnson Winery, Westfield.

Johnson's of Alexander Valley (USA) a small winery based in Alexander Valley, Sonoma County, California. 19ha. Grape varieties: Cabernet sauvignon, Chenin blanc, Johannisberg riesling, Pinot blanc and Zinfandel. Produces varietal wines.

Johnson-Turnbull Vineyards (USA) a small winery based in Rutherford, Napa Valley, California. 8.5ha. Grape variety: Cabernet sauvignon. Produces varietal wines.

John Thompson Pub (Eng) a home-brew public house in Ingleby, Derbyshire. Produces JTS XXXX bitter. *see* Lloyd's Country Bitter.

John Willie's Champion Beer (Eng) a 5% alc by vol. autumn ale brewed by J.W Lees, Middleton, Manchester, Lancashire (available September and October).

John Young London Lager (Eng) a lager beer 1037 O.G. brewed by the Youngs Brewery in London (named after the Chairman of the Brewery).

Joigny (Fr) an old town in the Yonne département, producing Chablis-style white wines.

Jolabrugg (Eng) a 5.2% alc by vol. ale brewed by the Bartrums Brewery, Suffolk.

Jolla [La] (Cktl) ¾ measure grappa, ¼ measure crème de banane, juice of ¼ lemon, 2 dashes orange juice. Shake over ice and strain into a cocktail glass.

Jolly Boat Brewery (Bideford) Ltd (Eng) a brewery (established 1995). (Add): 4 Buttgarden Street, Bideford, Devon EX39 2AU. Brews: Freebooter 4% alc by vol., Mainbrace Bitter 4.2% alc by vol., Plunder 4.8% alc by vol., Privateer 4.8% alc by vol.

Jolly Fenman (Eng) a home-brew public house based in Sidcup, Devon. Is owned by Clifton Inns. Noted for cask-conditioned Blackfen Bitter 1037 O.G. and Fenman Fortune 1047 O.G.

Jolly Ploughman (Eng) a 5% alc by vol. ruby red bitter from the Highwood Brewery, Barnetby, Lincolnshire.

Jolly Roger Bitter (Eng) *see* Jolly Roger Brewery.

Jolly Roger Brewery (Eng) a brewery based at the Old Anchor, Upton-on-Severn, Worcestershire. Is noted for cask-conditioned Severn Bore 1045 O.G. Old Anchor Ale 1060 O.G. Jolly Roger Bitter 1035 O.G. Old Lowesmore Bitter, Winter Wobbler.

Jolly's Centenary Bitter (Eng) *abbr*: J.C.B. 4.5% alc by vol. cask bitter from micro-brewery Mildmay Brewery, Holbeton, near Plymouth.

Jolly's Conquest (Eng) a cask-conditioned ale brewed in October 1998 to commemorate the Battle of Hastings in October 1066 by Batemans Brewery, Lincolnshire.

Jolly's Dome (Eng) a cask-conditioned ale brewed in December 1998 as a countdown to the millennium by Batemans Salem Bridge Brewery, Wainfleet, Skegness, Lincolnshire.

J

Jolly's Frolicking Reaper (Eng) a 4% alc by vol. ale brewed by Batemans Brewery, Lincolnshire.

Jolly's Giant Step (Eng) a cask-conditioned ale brewed in July 1998 to celebrate the first man on the moon in July 1969 by Batemans Brewery, Lincolnshire.

Jolly's Megabyte (Eng) a cask-conditioned ale brewed in February 1998 to celebrate the building of the first computer in February 1951 by Batemans Brewery, Lincolnshire.

Jolly's Yuletide Bash (Eng) a 4.4% alc by vol. bitter brewed by Batemans Brewery, Lincolnshire.

Jonathan's Coffee House (Eng) a seventeenth century coffee house based in Change Alley, London. Was a meeting place for stockbrokers that led to the formation of the London Stock Exchange.

Jonathon's Ridge (S.Afr) the label for a red wine (Pinotage) produced by the Springfontein winery, Walker Bay, Western Cape.

Jones Brewery (USA) a brewery based in Smithton, Pennsylvania (noted for Stoney's beer).

Jones's Ale (Eng) a cask-conditioned bitter brewed by the Penhros Court Brewery in Kingston, Herefordshire.

Jones Family (USA) a winery based in the Napa Valley, California. Grape varieties include: Cabernet sauvignon.

Jones Winery (Austr) a winery. (Add): Jones Road, Rutherglen, Victoria. Grape varieties: Riesling, Shiraz.

Jongeberg (Lux) a vineyard site in the village of Remerschen.

Jonge Genever (Hol) young Dutch gin.

Jongieux (Fr) a Cru village of A.C. Vin de Savoie. Based west of the Lac du Bourget. Grape varieties: Pinot noir, Gamay, Mondeuse, Jacquère

Jonicole Vineyards (USA) a vineyard based in Umpqua River Valley, Oregon. Produce vinifera wines at their Roseburg Winery.

Jonkheer Farmers' Winery (S.Afr) a co-operative winery (established 1912) based in the Breede River, Robertson, Western Cape. 185ha. (Add): Box 13, Bonnivale 6730. Grape varieties: Cabernet sauvignon, Chardonnay, Chenin blanc, Merlot, Muscadel, Muscat de frontignan, Muscat perlé, Red muscadel, Pinotage, Sauvignon blanc, Shiraz, Touriga nacional. Labels: Bakenskop, Buccanheer, Dead Frogge, Family Reserve, Muscatheer Family Reserve, Roothman Cape. Website: http://www.jonkheer.co.za

Jonquery (Fr) a Cru Champagne village in the Canton de Châtillon-sur-Marne. District: Reims.

Jonzac (Fr) a commune in the Charente-Maritime département. Grapes are used in the making of Cognac brandy.

Jooseu (Kor) juice/fruit juice.

Joostenberg Wines (S.Afr) a winery (established 1999) based in Elsenburg, Paarl, Western Cape. 33ha. Grape varieties: Cabernet sauvignon, Chenin blanc, Merlot, Shiraz, Viognier. Label: Bakermat, Fairhead. Website: http://www.joostenberg.co.za

Jopen (Hol) a 6.5% alc by vol. unpasteurised, unfiltered, bottle-conditioned special beer brewed by De Halve Maan Brouwerij, Hulst.

Jordan (M.East) a country that now produces only a little wine. Most grapes grown are used for the table. Arrack is now the main alcoholic beverage.

Jordan Valley (Isr) a natural spring mineral water (established 1997) from Ein Gedi Source, Jordan Valley.

Jordanka (Pol) a sparkling natural spring mineral water from Jordanow. Mineral contents (milligrammes per litre): Sodium 5mg/l, Calcium 38mg/l, Magnesium 27.8mg/l, Potassium 0.7mg/l, Bicarbonates 228.2mg/l, Chlorides 8mg/l, Sulphates 28.2mg/l, Fluorides 0.15mg/l, Iron 1.9mg/l.

Jordan Vineyard and Winery (USA) a large winery based in the Alexander Valley, Sonoma County, California. 125ha. Grape varieties: Cabernet sauvignon, Chardonnay and Merlot. Produces varietal wines.

Jordan Vineyards (S.Afr) a winery 105ha. (Add): P.O. Box 94, Vlottenburg 7604, Stellenbosch. Grape varieties: Cabernet franc, Cabernet sauvignon, Chardonnay, Chenin blanc, Merlot, Riesling, Sauvignon blanc, Syrah. Labels: Bradgate, Chameleon, Cobbler's Hill, Mellifera, Nine Yards. Website: http://www.jordanwines.com

Jordan Winery (Can) a winery based at Twenty Mile Creek, Niagara. Has an adjoining wine museum.

Jorgen B. Lysholm Distillery (Nor) a large distillery based in Trondheim. Is under the control of the A/S Vinmonopolet.

Jorum (Eng) an old drinking vessel of 300mls (½ pint) capacity or more usually used for punch. i.e. "A Jorum of punch".

José Michel et Fils (Fr) a Champagne producer (established 1847). (Add): 14, Rue Prélot, B.P. 16, 51530 Moussy. 21ha. Produces vintage and non-vintage wines. Vintages: 1995, 1996, 1997, 1999. A member of the Club Tresors de Champagne. Labels: Cuvée 'Special Club' Millésimée (Chardonnay 50% Petit meunier 50%).

Joseph (S.Afr) a 5 year old pot-stilled brandy produced by the Barrydale Wine Cellars, Little Karoo.

Joseph Cartron (Fr) a distillery based in the Burgundy region. (Add): 25, Rue du Dr. Legrand, 21700 Nuits-Saint-Georges. Produces a range of eaux-de-vies and spirits. Website: http://www.cartron.fr 'E'mail: cartron@cartron.fr

Joséphine (Fr) the label of a prestige cuvée Champagne of Champagne Perrier.

Josephine Grimbley (Eng) part of a range of ales brewed by the Charles Wells Brewery in Bedford, Bedfordshire.

Joseph Phelps Vineyard (USA) a leading Napa Valley winery in California. Grape varieties include: Cabernet sauvignon. Label: Bacchus Vineyard, Insignia. *see* Phelps Vineyard. Website: http://www.jpvwines.com 'E' mail: jpvwines@aol.com

Josephsberg (Ger) village (Anb): Baden. (Ber): Ortenau. (Gro): Fürsteneck. (Vil): Durbach.

Joseph's Hat (S.Afr) a red wine (Merlot 30% and Pinotage 70%) from the Concept Wines range produced by the Ashanti winery, Paarl, Western Cape.

Josephshöfer (Ger) vineyard (Anb): Mosel-Saar-Ruwer. (Ber): Bernkastel. (Gro): Münzlay. (Vil): Graach.

Joseph Swan Vineyard (USA) *see* Swan Vineyards.

Joseph Torrès (Fr) the label of a red (Syrah, Grenache) or white (Roussanne) wine produced in the A.C. Costières de Nîmes, Languedoc-Roussillon by Château de Nages.

Josephus Mayr (It) a winery based at Unterganzenerhof in the DOC Trentino-Alte-Adige, northern Italy. Grape variety: Lagrein.

José S. Ferrer (USA) the label for a red wine (Pinot noir) produced by the Gloria Ferrer winery, Carneros, California.

Joshua Privett (Eng) a cask-conditioned bitter 1043 O.G. brewed by the Pig and Whistle Home-brew public house in London.

Josko Gravner (It) a winery based in Oslavia in the Friuli-Venezia-Guilia region.

Jostr (Scan) the old Norse name for yeast.

Joubert [Claude et Michel] (Fr) a Beaujolais producer. (Add): Landigni, 69430 Beaujeau. Produces Juliénas and Beaujolais-Villages wines.

Joubertin (Fr) a red grape variety originally grown in Savoie.

Joubert-Tradauw Private Cellar (S.Afr) a winery (established 1999) based in Barrydale, Tradauw, Little Karoo. 30ha. Grape varieties: Cabernet sauvignon, Chardonnay, Merlot, Syrah. Label: R62. Website: http://www.joubert-tradauw.co.za

Jouffreau et Fils (Fr) a négociant-éleveur based in A.C. Cahors.

Joules Bitter (Eng) a bitter beer brewed by the Bass Worthington Brewery in Burton-on-Trent.

Joulouville Cocktail (Cktl) 25mls (⅕ gill) gin, 15mls (⅛ gill) sweet vermouth, juice ¼ lemon, 2 dashes Calvados, 2 dashes grenadine. Shake over ice and strain into a cocktail glass.

Journal (Fr) a land measure used in Burgundy ⅓ ha (⅚ acre).

Journalist Cocktail (Cktl) ⅔ measure dry gin, 20mls (⅙ gill) Italian vermouth, 20mls (⅙ gill) French vermouth, 2 dashes lemon juice, 2 dashes Triple Sec, dash Angostura. Shake over ice and strain into a cocktail glass.

Journaux (Fr) plural of Journal.

Journey's End (S.Afr) a red wine (Cabernet sauvignon) produced under the Kumala label, Stellenbosch.

Jouster (Eng) a 4% alc by vol. tawny coloured ale brewed by Goff's Brewery, Winchcombe, Gloucestershire.

Jouy-lès-Reims (Fr) a Cru Champagne village in the Canton de Ville-en-Tardenois. District: Reims.

Joven [1] (Sp) young (wine).

Joven [2] (Sp) a classification for the red wines of Rioja which is drunk usually within the first year after vinification, has no oak (cask) aging.

Joven (Mex) a brand-name for a local tequila.

Jovian Bitter (Eng) a 4.4% alc by vol. hoppy bitter from the Phoenix micro-brewery, Heywood, near Bury.

Joyau de France (Fr) a vintage de luxe cuvée Champagne produced by Boizel from 35% Chardonnay and 65% Pinot noir grapes.

Joy Bringer (Eng) a 6% alc by vol. strong ale brewed by Hanby Ales Ltd., Shropshire.

Joyous Garde Vineyard (Eng) a vineyard (established 1977). (Add): Crazies Hill, Wargrove, Berkshire. 1.25ha. Produces Crazies white wine. Grape varieties: Bacchus 50%, Huxelrebe 1%, Müller-Thurgau 49%.

JP Bredell (S.Afr) a winery (established 1991) based in Stellenbosch, Western Cape. 95ha. Grape varieties: Cabernet sauvignon, Merlot, Shiraz. Label: Bredell's CWG Auction, Cape Vintage, De Rigueur, Vineyard Collection. Website: http://www.bredellwines.co.za

JRA (Eng) *abbr*: **J**ames' **R**eal **A**le a 3.6% alc by vol. cask ale brewed by Arkells Kingsdown Brewery, Swindon, Wiltshire to celebrate managing director James Arkells' 50th birthday. Brewed using dry hops.

JSX (Eng) a 4.6% alc by vol. cask-conditioned ale brewed at John Smith's plant at Tadcaster (part of Scottish Courage).

J_2O (Eng) a range of non-alcoholic bottled fruit juice drinks from Britvic. Range includes: apple & mango, apple & raspberry, orange & passionfruit, orange & cranberry, apple & melon.

J. Tiefenbrunner-Schlosskellerei Turmhof (It) a noted winery based at Entiklar, Südtirol.

JTS. XXX Special Bitter (Eng) a bitter beer 1045 O.G. brewed by the John Thompsom Pub, Ingleby, Derbyshire.

Juan Cedron (S.Am) a priest who in 1556 crossed the Andes from Chile with vines to plant the first vineyards in Argentina.

Juan Garcia (Sp) a red grape variety grown in Toro.

Juan Ibañez (Sp) a red grape variety used for the production of heavy red wines in Cariñena. Known as Miguel del Arco in Calatayud.

Juanico (S.Am) a winery based in the southern region of Canelones, Uruguay. Produces Don Pascual Reserve Tannat and a Merlot/Tannat blend.

Juanito Cocktail (Cktl) ⅓ measure Pernod, ⅓ measure lime juice, ⅓ measure soda water. Stir over ice, strain into a Champagne saucer and add a cherry.

Juan's Grasshopper Cocktail (Cktl) ⅕ measure brandy, ⅕ measure white Curaçao, ⅕ measure Crème de Menthe, ⅖ measure cream. Shake with ice, strain into a cocktail glass and sprinkle with cinnamon.

Jubilation (Eng) a 4% alc by vol. ale brewed by the Goddards Brewery, Isle of Wight.

Jubilator (Fr) a 6.8% alc by vol. bottom-fermented, bottled, double bock beer brewed by the Schutzenberger Brasserie in Schiltigheim.

J

Jubiläumsrebe (Aus) a white grape variety cross between the black Portugieser and the black Blaufränkischer.

Jubilee (Sri.L) a top-fermented ale 1060 O.G. brewed by the Ceylon Breweries.

Jubilee Ale (Eng) a bottled ale brewed by the Harvey's Brewery in Lewes, Sussex to commemorate the Silver Jubilee of the Sussex University.

Jubilee Ale (Ch.Isles) a special ale brewed by the Guernsey Brewery, St. Peter Port, Guernsey to commemorate the silver jubilee of H.M. the Queen being on the throne (1952–1977).

Jubilee Bitter (Eng) a bottled strong ale 1049 O.G. brewed by the Hook Norton Brewery.

Jubilee Bitter (Eng) a full-flavoured bitter ale brewed by the Gibbs Mew Brewery in Salisbury.

Jubilee Cocktail (Cktl) a ¼ measure Van der Hum, ½ measure dry gin, ¼ measure lime juice, dash gomme syrup. Shake with ice and strain into a cocktail glass.

Jubilee Guinness (Eng) a special Guinness 1050 O.G. brewed at the Park Royal Brewery in London in 1986 (to the 1936 gravity) to commemorate the Brewery. 6000 bottles only produced.

Jubilee Juggin [The] (Wal) the name given to a whiskey produced in Bala, Montgomeryshire (Powys) in the nineteenth century (now no longer produced).

Jubilee Lager (Ch.Isles) a bottled strong lager beer 1064 O.G. brewed by the Jersey Brewery in St. Helier, Jersey.

Jubilee Lager (Ind) a premium lager beer 1052 O.G. brewed by the United Breweries in Bangalore.

Jubilee Stout (Eng) a bottled sweet stout 1040 O.G. brewed by the Bass Breweries.

Jubileums Akvavit (Den) a dill-flavoured akvavit.

Jucalette (Eng) Samuel Pepys' spelling of chocolate (drink) in the eighteenth century.

Jückemäller (Ger) a steinhäger producer, sold under the same name.

Judaczar (Eng) a vodka distilled from Jamaican molasses, distilled and bottled in Hull.

Judas (Bel) an 8.5% alc by vol. bottle-conditioned straw-coloured special beer brewed by Alken-Maes Brasserie, Jumet.

Juden Gaisberg (Aus) a vineyard site on the banks of the River Danube in the Kremstal region.

Judenkirch (Ger) vineyard (Anb): Rheingau. (Ber): Johannisberg. (Gro): Steinmäcker. (Vil): Dotzheim.

Judex Provisional Judgement (S.Afr) the label for a red wine (Merlot, Cabernet sauvignon, Ruby cabernet and Shiraz blend) produced by the Domaine Brahms Wineries, Paarl, Western Cape.

Judge Jr. (Cktl) ½ measure dry gin, ½ measure Bacardi, dash gomme syrup, dash grenadine, juice ¼ lemon. Shake over ice and strain into a cocktail glass.

Judges Brewery (Eng) a micro-brewery based in Rugby, Warwickshire. Brews: Barristers Bitter, Solicitor's Ruin 5.6% alc by vol.

Judgette Cocktail (Cktl) ⅓ measure dry gin, ⅓ measure peach brandy, ⅓ measure French vermouth, juice ½ lime. Shake over ice, strain into a cocktail glass and top with a cherry.

Juffer (Ger) vineyard (Anb): Mosel-Saar-Ruwer. (Ber): Bernkastel. (Gro): Kurfürstlay. (Vil): Braneberg.

Juffermauer (Ger) vineyard (Anb): Mosel-Saar-Ruwer. (Ber): Zell/Mosel. (Gro): Goldbäumchen. (Vil): Treis-Karden.

Juffer-Sonnenuhr (Ger) vineyard (Anb): Mosel-Saar-Ruwer. (Ber): Bernkastel. (Gro): Kurfürstlay. (Vil): Braneberg.

Jug (Austr) kettle.

Jug (USA) pitcher/urn.

Jug and Bottle (Eng) a name from the times when draught beer was served in jugs or bottles to take home. *'off-sales'*.

Jugenheim (Ger) village (Anb): Rheinhessen. (Ber): Bingen. (Gro): Kaiserpfalz. (Vins): Goldberg, Hasensprung, Heiligenhäuschen, St. Georgenberg.

Jug Method (Eng) a method of brewing coffee. The grinds are placed into a jug, boiling water poured onto them, allowed to infuse to required strength, strained and served.

Jugo (Sp) juice.

Jugo de Naranja (Sp) orange juice.

Jug of Beer (Eng) a slang term used for a glass of beer in the north of England.

Jug Wine (USA) wine slang for house-wine or ordinary table wines.

Jugy (Fr) a commune in the Mâconnais whose grapes can be used in the production of Mâcon Supérieur.

Juhfark (Hun) lit: 'lamb's (or sheep's) tail', the name for the Furmint grape in the Somoló region.

Juhfark (Hun) lit: 'lamb's tail', a medium white wine from Somoló region near Lake Balatòn. Made from the Juhfark grape.

Juice (Eng) the liquid content of the fruit (or vegetable). *See also* Must. (Arab) = asseer, (Aus) = saft, (Chi) = guozhi, (Cro) = sok, (Den) = juice, (Fr) = jus, (Ger) = saft, (Gre) = chimos, (Hol) = sap, (Indo) = sari buah, (Ire) = sú súlach, (Isr) = mitz, (It) = succo/succo di frutta, (Jap) = jyuusu/juusu, (Kor) = jyuseo/juuseu, (Lat) = sucus, (Pol) = sok, (Port) = sugo, (Rus) = sok, (Sp) = jugo, (Thai) = nampolamai, (Tur) = meyva suyu, (Wal) = nodd/sudd.

Juiced (USA) a slang term for drunk.

Juiced Up (Eng) a slang term to denote a drunken person.

Juice Extractor (Eng) an implement used to extract the juice from fruits either mechanically or by hand. Also called a Juicer.

Juice Glass (USA) another name for the Delmonico glass.

Juice of the Barley (Ire)(Scot) the nickname for whisky, whiskey (also used for beer).

Juice of the Fruit (Eng) the nickname often used for wine or brandy.

Juice of the Grape (Eng) the nickname for brandy (or sometimes wine).

J

Juicer (Eng) an alternative name for a juice extractor.

Juice Up (USA) a slang term for a drinks party.

Juicy (Eng) a term to describe wines that have a pleasant, fruity, fresh acid taste. (Fr) = juteaux.

Juigné-sur-Loire (Fr) a commune in the A.C. Coteaux de l'Aubance in Anjou-Saumur, Loire.

Juillac-le-Coq (Fr) a commune in the Grande Champagne district, Charente-Maritime. Grapes used for the finest Cognac brandies.

Juillet-Lallement (Fr) a Champagne producer. (Add): 30, Rue Carnot, 51380 Verzy. 4ha. Récoltant-Manipulant. Produces vintage and non-vintage wines. Vintages: 1990, 1995, 1996, 1997, 1999. A member of the Club Tresors de Champagne. Labels: Cuvée 'Special Club' Millésimée (Chardonnay 60% Pinot noir 40%).

Jule (Nor) a 1058 O.G. dry malty beer from the Aass Brewery in Drammen.

Julebryg (Den) a Christmas beer 5.3% alc by vol. brewed by the Albani Brewery in Odense.

Jule Øl (Den) a low-alcohol, tax-free beer brewed by the Albani Brewery in Odense.

Jule Øl (Nor) a Christmas beer 6% alc by vol. brewed by the Aass Brewery in Drammen.

Julep (Cktl) a long drink of spirit, sugar and mint served in a tankard or frosted glass with shaved ice.

Jules Planquette Cognac (Fr) the brand-name of a Cognac 40% alc by vol. selected for B. Grant & Cº. Ltd., Burton-on-Trent, Staffordshire.

Julia (Fr) a natural spring mineral water from Saint-Alban-les-Eaux.

Julia (It) the brand-name of a grappa.

Juliana (Euro) a still natural spring mineral water from Juliana, Hrusiski Peak, Karavanke, Slovenia. Mineral contents (milligrammes per litre): Sodium 0.7mg/l, Calcium 38mg/l, Magnesium 21mg/l, Potassium 0.3mg/l, Bicarbonates 189mg/l, Chlorides 0.5mg/l, Sulphates 8mg/l, Nitrates 2mg/l. pH 7.8

Juliana Blue Cocktail (Cktl) ½ measure dry gin, 1 measure coconut cream, 1 measure pineapple juice, ¼ measure blue Curaçao, 2 dashes lime juice. Blend altogether with a scoop of crushed ice. Strain into an ice-filled highball glass, decorate with a cherry, slice of pineapple and serve with straws.

Julia Reserve [Avondale] (S.Afr) a light red blend wine produced by the Avondale winery, Paarl, Western Cape.

Julia's Vineyard (USA) the label for a red wine (Pinot noir) produced by the Cambria winery, Santa Maria Valley, Santa Barbara County, California.

Julie Marie (Cktl) ⅓ measure Bacardi, ⅙ measure arum, ⅙ measure Brontë Liqueur, ⅓ measure orange squash, 1 egg white. Shake over ice and strain into a cocktail glass.

Juliénas (Fr) an A.C. Cru Beaujolais-Villages, Burgundy, 510ha under vines.

Julius (Bel) an 8.8% alc by vol. gold-straw, top-fermented, bottle-conditioned special beer brewed by De Kluis Brasserie, Hoegaarden.

Julius (It) an I.G.T. red wine produced by Fattoria Ormanni in Poggibonsi, Tuscany from 50% Sangiovese, 45% Merlot and 5% Syrah grapes.

Julius-Echter-Berg (Ger) vineyard (Anb): Franken. (Ber): Steigerwald. (Gro): Burgweg. (Vil): Iphofen.

Juliusspital (Ger) the Julius Hospice founded in the sixteenth century at Würzberg in Franconia. Wines are dry and bottled in bocksbeutels, owns its own vineyards. Proceeds from wine sales are held for the upkeep of the hospital.

Jullié (Fr) a commune in the Beaujolais. Has A.C. Beaujolais-Villages or Beaujolais-Jullié status.

Jully-lès-Buxy (Fr) a wine-producing town in the commune of A.C. Montagny, Côte Chalonnaise, Burgundy.

Julöl (Swe) a Christmas beer 3.5% alc by vol. brewed by the Pripps Brewery.

Jumbo Cocktail (Cktl) ¼ measure Cognac, ¼ measure Caperitif, ¼ measure French vermouth, ¼ measure Italian vermouth, dash pastis, dash Campari. Shake over ice and strain into a cocktail glass.

Jumelles [Les] (Fr) a vineyard in the A.C. Côte Rôtie, northern Rhône.

Jumilla (Sp) a Denominación de Origen wine region of Murcia, south-eastern Spain. 42,841ha. D.O. covers red, white, Doble Pasta and a sweet red wine. Grape varieties: mainly Monastrell plus Aíren, Cencibel, Garnacha tintorera, Merseguera, Pedro ximénez.

Junction Bitter (Eng) a 4.1% alc by vol. bitter ale brewed by the Thomas McGuinness Brewing Company, Lancashire.

Junen (Chi) a natural spring mineral water brand.

Jung (Ger) young wine/immature wine.

Jung [Carl] (Ger) a winery based at Rüdesheim, noted for alcohol-free, low calorie wines. De-alcoholised in a special still, Rotlack: red, Roselack: rosé, Weisslack: white. Also produces Schloss Boosenburg (a sparkling variety).

Jungbrunnen (Ger) vineyard (Anb): Nahe. (Ber): Kreuznach. (Gro): Schlosskapelle. (Vil): Dorsheim.

Jungfer (Ger) vineyard (Anb): Rheingau. (Ber): Johannisberg. (Gro): Mehrhölzchen. (Vil): Hallgarten.

Jungfer (Ger) vineyard (Anb): Württemberg. (Ber): Württembergisch Unterland. (Gro): Kirchenweinberg. (Vil): Lauffen.

Jungfernberg (Ger) vineyard (Anb): Mosel-Saar-Ruwer. (Ber): Saar-Ruwer. (Gro): Römerlay. (Vil): Waldrach.

Jungfernwein (Ger) lit: 'virgin wine', applies to the first wine made from new vineyards (usually in its 3rd year).

Jungferstieg (Ger) vineyard (Anb): Baden. (Ber): Bodensee. (Gro): Sonnenufer. (Vil): Meersburg.

Jungle Juice [1] (Cktl) 10mls (½ fl.oz) mandarine liqueur, 35mls (1½ fl.ozs) Pisang Ambon Henkes, 20mls (¾ fl.oz) gin, 3 dashes lemon juice, 75mls (3fl.ozs) orange juice. Stir over ice, strain into a highball glass, dress with a slice of pineapple and a cherry.

Jungle Juice [2] (Cktl) ½ measure gin, ½ measure lime juice. Shake over ice, strain into a highball glass and top with ginger beer.

Jungle Juice (Eng) a slang term for alcoholic liquor.

Jung [Roger] (Fr) a winery (15ha) based in the A.C. Alsace. (Add): 23, Rue de la Première Armée, 68340 Riquewihr. Grape varieties include: Gewurztraminer, Muscat, Pinot gris, Rielsing, Sylvaner. Produces a range of Grand Cru (Schoenenbourg) and A.C. Alsace wines. 'E'mail: rjung@terre-net.fr

Jung's Non-Alcoholic Wines (Ger) see Jung (Carl).

Jung's Roselack (Ger) a low-alcohol rosé wine from Carl Jung, Rüdesheim, western Germany.

Jung's Rotlack (Ger) a low-alcohol red wine from Carl Jung, Rüdesheim, western Germany.

Jung's Weisslack (Ger) a low-alcohol white wine from Carl Jung, Rüdesheim, western Germany.

Junin (Arg) a wine-producing area in the Mendoza region.

Juniper (Eng) berries used to flavour gin, from where gin gets its name. see Genièvre.

Juniper Estate (Austr) a winery based in the Margaret River region of Western Australia. Grape varieties include: Cabernet sauvignon.

Juniper Green (Eng) an organic London dry gin produced by the Organic Spirits Company.

Juniper Wine (Fr) a Middle-Ages drink of wine flavoured with Juniper berries to hide the off-flavours of the wine.

Junker (Ger) vineyard (Anb): Nahe. (Ber): Kreuznach. (Gro): Kronenberg. (Vil): Bad Kreuznach (ortsteil Ippesheim).

Junker (Ger) vineyard (Anb): Nahe. (Ber): Kreuznach. (Gro): Schlosskapelle. (Vil): Laubenheim.

Junmai Dai-Ginjo (Jap) pure rice saké produced by Hokusetsu (a small brewery).

Junot (Sp) a delicate, fruit-flavoured, white wine produced by Jaime Lluch Casanallas.

Juno Wine Company (S.Afr) a winery based in the Paarl region in the Western Cape. Grape varieties include: Chardonnay, Shiraz. Label: Cape Maiden's. Website: http://www.junowines.com

Junta Nacional do Vinho (Port) a government sponsored body (established 1937) for brandy distillers of Portugal. Also has control of Madeira.

Junta Provincial de Bodegas Cooperativas del Campo (Sp) a large co-operative winery that is one of the main wine-producers in Rioja.

Jupiter (Eng) a 3.5% alc by vol. ale brewed by the Milton Brewery Cambridge Ltd., Cambridgeshire.

Jupiter (Gre) a noted brandy producer.

Jupiter (Lat) the father of Bacchus.

Jupiterberg (Ger) vineyard (Anb): Württemberg. (Ber): Württembergisch Unterland. (Gro): Heuchelberg. (Vil): Hausen/Z.

Jupiter Brasserie (Bel) a brewery based near Liège, is noted for pilsener-style lager beers. Produces Jupiter and Lamot.

Jura (Fr) an A.C. wine area of central eastern France noted for Vins de Paille. see Château Chalon. Also produces red, rosé and Vin Jaune white wines. See

also Arbois and Étoile. Grape varieties: Gros noiren, Melon d'Arbois, Pinot blanc, Poulsard, Savagnin and Trousseau.

Jurade de Saint-Émilion (Fr) a wine brotherhood for the producers of Saint-Émilion in Bordeaux. Promotes the wines of Saint-Émilion. Responsible for the Cru Classé system in Saint-Émilion.

Juraiska (Pol) a sparkling natural spring mineral water. Mineral contents (milligrammes per litre): Sodium 9.5mg/l, Calcium 36.69mg/l, Magnesium 33.64mg/l, Potassium 2.5mg/l, Bicarbonates 339.9mg/l, Chlorides 10.64mg/l, Sulphates 35mg/l, Fluorides 0.34mg/l.

Jurançon (Fr) an amber-coloured dessert wine produced from vines grown near Pau. Minimum alc by vol. of 11%, vines are trained by 'en Hautains' system.

Jurançon (Fr) a grape variety used in the making of Armagnac.

Jurançon (Fr) an A.C. wine region of south-west France. Produces mainly dry and sweet white wines from Gros manseng and Petit manseng grapes. Minimum alc by vol. of 12.5%.

Jurançon Blanc (Fr) a white grape variety used in the making of Cognac.

Jurançon Noir (Fr) one of the grapes used in A.C. Cahors wine along with Malbec, Merlot and Tannat.

Jurignac (Fr) a commune in the Charente-Maritime département whose grapes are classed Petite Champagne (Cognac).

Juris Winery (Aus) a winery (11ha) based in Gols, Neusiedlersee. (Add): Untere Hauptstrasse 60, 7122 Gols. Grape varieties: Cabernet sauvignon, Chardonnay, Pinot blanc, Pinot noir, St. Laurent, Welschriesling, Zweigelt. Produces: Juris Saint Georg from a blend of Pinot noir and St-Laurent grapes.

Jurrestic (Eng) a 4.7% alc by vol. ale brewed by the Dorset Brewing Company Ltd., Dorset.

Jus (Fr) juice.

Jus de Chapeau (Fr) a term used in northern France for poorly-made coffee.

Jus de Goutte (Fr) the name used in the Beaujolais region for the partially fermented juice obtained from the macération carbonique fermentation.

Jus de Raisins (Fr) grape juice.

Jus d'Orange (Fr) orange juice.

Jusoda Orange (Scot) the brand-name of a soft drink produced by Barr (A.G.). See also Strike Cola, Tizer, Irn Bru.

Justa Spring Water (Can) a natural spring mineral water. Mineral contents (milligrammes per litre): Sodium 3.27mg/l, Calcium 4.2mg/l, Magnesium 1.49mg/l, Potassium 0.52mg/l, Bicarbonates 14.2mg/l, Chlorides 3.3mg/l, Sulphates 3.64mg/l. pH 6.54

Justerini and Brooks (Scot) wine merchants and Scotch whisky producers (part of International Distillers and Vintners). Brands include: Knockando, J & B Rare, J & B Reserve (15 year old), J & B -6°C.

J

Justices Licences (Eng) a licence issued by the Courts to enable a person to sell alcoholic beverages to the public. *see* Brewster Sessions.

Justification (USA) a red wine produced from Cabernet franc and Merlot grapes by Justin Vineyards and Winery, 11680 Chimney Rock Road, Paso Robles, California.

Justinho (Mad) a Funchal-based Madeira shipper.

Justin Vineyards and Winery (USA) a winery (established 1982). (Add): 11680 Chimney Rock Road, Paso Robles, California. Produces Isoscelas, Justification, Obtuse wines. Website: http://www.justinwine.com

Just Juice (Eng) a brand of pure fruit juices from Adams Foods, Leek, Staffordshire.

Juteaux (Fr) juicy.

Juusu (Jap) juice.

Juvé y Camps (Sp) a wine-producer based in San Sadurní de Noya, Barcelona. Produces Ermita d'Espiells.

Juvina (Aus) a sparkling natural spring mineral water from Juvinaquelle, Deutschkreubad. Mineral contents (milligrammes per litre): Sodium 333.9mg/l, Calcium 239.7mg/l, Magnesium 50.9mg/l, Potassium 16.9mg/l, Bicarbonates 1695mg/l, Chlorides 62mg/l, Sulphates 81mg/l, Fluorides 0.3mg/l, Nitrates 0.32mg/l, Ammonium 1.14mg/l.

Jewel (Ger) a still natural mineral water from the Teutoburger Wald. (Add): Teutoburger Mineralbrunnen, GmbH & Cº. 33649 Bielefeld. Mineral contents (grammes per litre): Sodium 0.13g/l, Calcium 0.013g/l, Magnesium 0.006g/l, Bicarbonates 0.244g/l, Chlorides 0.071g/l, Nitrates 0.001g/l.

Juwel (Ger) a natural spring mineral water from Bielefeld. Mineral contents (milligrammes per litre): Sodium 130mg/l, Calcium 13mg/l, Magnesium 5.8mg/l, Potassium 0.7mg/l, Chlorides 70.7mg/l, Fluorides 1.1mg/l.

Juwel (Ger) a white grape variety grown in the Rheinhessen.

Juzishui (Chi) orange juice.

J.V. (Sp) a solera gran reserva brandy produced by Juan Vincente Vergara.

J. Vineyards & Winery (USA) a winery based in the Russian River Valley, Sonoma County, California. (Add): PO Box 6009, Healdsburg, CA95448. Grape variety: Pinot noir. Label: Nicole's Vineyard. Website: http://www.jwine.com

J.W. Dant (USA) the brand-name of a noted Bourbon whiskey.

JWL (S.Afr) the label for a red wine (Shiraz) produced by the Terroir Wines of SA winery, Stellenbosch, Western Cape.

Jyuseo (Kor) juice.

Jyuusu (Jap) juice.

K

K (Eng) a premium bottled cider 8.4% alc by vol. sold in a matt black bottle. Produced by Matthew Clark. Replaced by K6. *See also* K. Neon.

KA (Eng) a range of canned/bottled soft drinks from Barr Soft Drinks, flavours include: Black grape, Pineapple, Kola, Shampane, Strawberry, Mango.

Kaaimansgat (S.Afr) the label for a white wine (Chardonnay) produced by the Bouchard Finlayson winery, Walker Bay, Western Cape.

Kaapse (S.Afr) a label for red and white wines from Zidela Wines, Stellenbosch. *see* Suikerbosch.

Kaapse Smaak (S.Afr) lit: 'cape taste', an early version of marc brandy, also spelt Cape Smaak.

Kaapse Vonkel (S.Afr) an extraordinary wine made by the méthode Cap Classique with the Steen grape (plus Chardonnay and Pinot noir) by the Simonsig Estate in Stellenbosch.

Kaapslig (S.Afr) the label for a range of wines Daglig (Chardonnay 40% Chenin blanc 60%), Naglig (Cinsaut 60% Ruby cabernet 40%), Keteka, Kleinbok and Welgedacht produced by the Dominion Wine Company winery, Stellenbosch, Western Cape.

Kaapzicht Estate (S.Afr) a winery (established 1946) based in Bottelay, Koelenhof, Stellenbosch. (Add): Steytdal Farm, (Pty) Ltd., Box 5, Sanlamhof 7532. 146ha. Grape varieties: Cabernet sauvignon, Chenin blanc, Hanepoot jerepigo, Merlot, Pinotage, Rhine Riesling, Sauvignon blanc, Shiraz. Labels: Bin-3, Cape View Classic, Combination, Steytler, Vision. Website: http://www.kaapzicht-wines.com

Kaapzicht Weisser Riesling (S.Afr) a white wine from the Rhine riesling grape produced by the Kaapzicht Estate.

Kab (Isr) an old Hebrew measure of approximately 4pints (2.3litres). *See also* Cab.

Kabänes (Ger) a medium-bitter herb liqueur produced in Cologne 26% alc by vol.

Kabarcik (Tur) a red grape variety.

Kaberne (Rus) a red wine (Cabernet) from the Moldavia region.

Kabernett (Slov) an alternative spelling of the Cabernet grape.

Kabinett (Aus) a qualitätswein with a minimum must weight of 17° KMW and residual sugar maximum of 9g/l. Can not be chaptalised and must have a maximum of 12.7% alc by vol.

Kabinett (Ger) the label description of a wine which is of QmP. quality and one grade up. Has no added sugar, an Oeschle reading of 67°–85° and is estate bottled. *see* Cabinet.

Kabinettwein (Ger) an old term used to identify selected barrels of the vineyard owner or special reserve.

Kachelberg (Ger) vineyard (Anb): Rheinhessen. (Ber): Bingen. (Gro): Adelberg. (Vil): Ensheim.

Kachelberg (Ger) vineyard (Anb): Rheinhessen. (Ber): Bingen. (Gro): Adelberg. (Vil): Wörrstadt.

Kadarka (Hun) a red grape variety used in the making of Bull's Blood (Egri Bikavér) together with the Kékfrankos and Médoc noir grapes varieties. Is also grown in the Banat region of Rumania. In Bulgaria is known as the Gamza.

Kadarka de Banat (Rum) a red wine produced in the Banat region from the Kadarka grape.

Kadeh (Tur) a glass, also word for a goblet, cup or any other drinking receptacle.

Kadette (S.Afr) the label for a red wine (Cabernet sauvignon 25%, Pinotage 55% and Merlot 20%) produced by the Kanonkop Estate winery, Stellenbosch, Western Cape.

Kaefferkopf (Fr) an A.C. Alsace Grand Cru vineyard in Ammerschwihr, Haut-Rhin 60ha.

Kærnemælk (Den) buttermilk.

Kærspringeren (Den) a natural spring mineral water from Artesisk Boring, Vinten-Kilden.

Kafa (Euro) the Serbo-Croatian word for coffee.

Kafe (E.Asia) the name for coffee in Laos.

Kafé (E.Asia) the Thai word for coffee.

Kafe (Fr) the Breton word for coffee.

Kafeguan (Chi) café.

Kafeh (Rus) coffee.

Kafei (Chi) coffee.

Kafels (Ger) vineyard (Anb): Nahe. (Ber): Schloss Böckelheim. (Gro): Burgweg. (Vil): Norheim.

Kafenion (Gre) a café serving coffee or alcoholic beverages which is used by males only.

Kafeo (Gre) coffee.

Käferberg (Aus) a vineyard site based on the banks of the River Kamp situated in the Kamptal region.

Kafes (Gre) coffee.

Kafeteria (Gre) café.

Kafe Yen (E.Asia) the name in Laos for iced coffee.

Kaffa (Afr) part of Ethiopia from which coffee is supposed to have originated and from which the name derives.

Kaffa (Arab) wine. *see* Wine of Araby.

Kaffe (Den) coffee.

Kaffé (Nor) coffee.

Kaffee (Aus)(Ger) coffee.

Kaffee (Isr) coffee. Also spelt Kavah.

Kaffee Hafooch (Isr) lit: 'upside down coffee', half fill a cup with milk and top with coffee.

Kaffeeklatsch (Ger) lit: 'coffee and gossip', afternoon coffee.

Kaffelstein (Ger) vineyard (Anb): Franken. (Ber): Mainviereck. (Gro): Not yet assigned. (Vil): Kreuzwertheim.

Kaffe med Fløde (Den) coffee with cream.

Kaffe med Mælk (Den) coffee with milk.

Kaffe Uden Fløde (Den) lit: 'coffee without cream', black coffee.

Kaffia (Sp) the Basque word for coffee.

Kaffia (Rus) a sparkling wine from the Crimea.

Kaffir Beer (Afr) a beer made from sorghum (kaffir corn) or from millet grain.

Kafir (Rus) an alcoholic beverage produced in the Caucasian mountains from fermented cow's milk and Kefir grain. Also spelt Kefir and Kephir. *See also* Koumiss.

Kafo (Esp) the Esperanto word for coffee.

Kafye (Rus) café.

Kaggi (Scan) the old norse name for a cask.

Kagor (Alb) a sweet, red dessert wine produced in the Sarandë region of southern Albania.

Kahawa (Afr) the Swahili word for coffee.

Kahisakan (Jap) the name given to tea/coffee houses.

Kahlberg (Ger) vineyard (Anb): Baden. (Ber): Badische Bergstrasse/Kraichgau. (Gro): Rittersberg. (Vil): Leutershausen.

Kahlenberg (Aus) a noted vineyard area in the Wien region.

Kahlenberg (Aus) a wine village near Vienna that is noted for white 'Heurige' wines.

Kahlenberg (Ger) vineyard (Anb): Nahe. (Ber): Kreuznach. (Gro): Kronenberg. (Vil): Bad Kreuznach.

Kahlenberg (Ger) vineyard (Anb): Nahe. (Ber): Schloss Böckelheim. (Gro): Paradiesgarten. (Vil): Feilbingert.

Kahlenberg (Ger) vineyard (Anb): Pfalz. (Ber): Südliche Weinstrasse. (Gro): Trappenberg. (Vil): Ottersheim.

Kahlenberger Jungherrn (Aus) a white wine made from the Müller-Thurgau grape produced by the Augustine Monks at Klosterneuburg, Vienna.

Kahlenberger Weisse (Aus) an old white grape variety that is little used nowadays.

Kahllay (Ger) vineyard (Anb): Mosel-Saar-Ruwer. (Ber): Zell/Mosel. (Gro): Weinhex. (Vil): Niederfell.

Kahlúa (Mex) a coffee-flavoured liqueur 26% alc by vol.

Kahlúa Alexander (Cktl) 25mls (1fl.oz) each of Kahlúa, gin and cream, shake over ice and strain into a cocktail glass.

Kahlúa Cocktail (Cktl) ½ measure Kahlúa liqueur, ½ measure Cognac, stir gently over ice and strain into a cocktail glass.

Kahlúa Java (Punch) 1.1ltrs (2pints) hot strong coffee, 1.1ltrs. (2pints) hot cocoa, 125mls (1gill) Kahlúa, heat together and serve in toddy glasses with a marshmallow on top.

Kahmig (Ger) ropy, a wine that has been attacked by bacteria, *see* Rope.

Kahouri (Geo) a white grape variety grown in Georgia. Produces dry white wines.

Kahuah (Tur) the old name for coffee.

Kahve (Tur) coffee.

Kahveci (Tur) a coffee house owner.

Kahvehane (Tur) a coffee-shop (bar) café.

Kahvi (Fin) coffee.

Kahwa (Afr) *see* Kahweh.

Kahweh (Afr) the old Arab name for coffee, denotes invigorating or stimulating, also spelt Kahwa and Quawah.

Kaifei (Chi) coffee.

Kaiken (Arg) a winery based in Mendoza. Grape varieties include: Malbec.

Kailberg (Ger) vineyard (Anb): Baden. (Ber): Badische Frankenland. (Gro): Tauberklinge. (Vil): Sachsenflur.

Kairi (W.Ind) a brand of dark rum produced by the Trinidad Distillers Ltd. in Trinidad.

Kaiserberg (Aus) a vineyard site on the banks of the River Danube situated in the Wachau region, Niederösterreich.

Kaiserberg (Ger) lit: 'emperor's hill', a popular name for vineyards in Germany. There are 12 separate vineyards holding this name.

Kaiserberg (Ger) vineyard (Anb): Baden. (Ber): Breisgau. (Gro): Burg Lichteneck. (Vil): Altdorf.

Kaiserberg (Ger) vineyard (Anb): Baden. (Ber): Breisgau. (Gro): Burg Lichteneck. (Vil): Bleichheim.

Kaiserberg (Ger) vineyard (Anb): Baden. (Ber): Breisgau. (Gro): Burg Lichteneck. (Vil): Broggingen.

Kaiserberg (Ger) vineyard (Anb): Baden. (Ber): Breisgau. (Gro): Burg Lichteneck. (Vil): Ettenheim.

Kaiserberg (Ger) vineyard (Anb): Baden. (Ber): Breisgau. (Gro): Burg Lichteneck. (Vil): Herbolzheim.

Kaiserberg (Ger) vineyard (Anb): Baden. (Ber): Breisgau. (Gro): Burg Lichteneck. (Vil): Ringsheim.

Kaiserberg (Ger) vineyard (Anb): Baden. (Ber): Breisgau. (Gro): Burg Lichteneck. (Vil): Tutschfelden.

Kaiserberg (Ger) vineyard (Anb): Nahe. (Ber): Schloss Böckelheim. (Gro): Burgweg. (Vil): Duchroth.

Kaiserberg (Ger) vineyard (Anb): Pfalz. (Ber): Südliche Weinstrasse. (Gro): Bischofskreuz. (Vil): Nussdorf.

Kaiserberg (Ger) vineyard (Anb): Pfalz. (Ber): Südliche Weinstrasse. (Gro): Herrlich. (Vil): Göcklingen.

Kaiserberg (Ger) vineyard (Anb): Württemberg. (Ber): Württembergisch Unterland. (Gro): Heuchelberg. (Vil): Frauenzimmern.

Kaiserberg (Ger) vineyard (Anb): Württemberg. (Ber): Württembergisch Unterland. (Gro): Heuchelberg. (Vil): Güglingen.

Kaiser Bier (Aus) a lager beer brewed by the Österreichische Bräu.

Kaiser Bill (Cktl) 1 measure schnapps, juice of a lime, shake over ice, strain into an ice-filled highball glass, top with soda water, dress with a slice of lime and serve with straws.

Kaiserbirnlikor (Aus) a lemon-flavoured liqueur.

Kaiserdom (Ger) based at Speyer, Pfalz, a museum which houses 2000 years of winemaking history, including an amphora of Roman origin that still holds the original wine.

Kaiserdom Brauerei (Ger) a Bavarian brewery in Ramburg that is noted for rauchbier (smoked beer).

Kaiser Festbock (Aus) a pale bock bier brewed by Bräu A.G. 6.7% alc by vol.

Kaiser Friedrich Heilquelle (Ger) a natural spring mineral water. Mineral contents (milligrammes per litre): Sodium 1390mg/l, Calcium 5mg/l, Magnesium 3.7mg/l, Potassium 17.3mg/l, Bicarbonates 2044mg/l, Chlorides 754.8mg/l, Sulphates 336.4mg/l, Silicates 10mg/l.

Kaiser Friedrich Heil-Quelle-N (Ger) a natural spring mineral water (established 1774) from Roisdorfer Quelle. Mineral contents (milligrammes per litre): Sodium 985mg/l, Calcium 129mg/l, Magnesium 89mg/l, Potassium 30mg/l, Bicarbonates 1504mg/l, Chlorides 916mg/l, Sulphates 343mg/l, Fluorides 0.5mg/l.

Kaiser Friedrich Quelle (Ger) a natural spring mineral water (established 1774) from Roisdorfer Quelle. Mineral contents (milligrammes per litre): Sodium 1020mg/l, Calcium 131mg/l, Magnesium 91mg/l, Potassium 30mg/l, Bicarbonates 1560mg/l, Chlorides 1034mg/l, Sulphates 362mg/l.

Kaisergarten (Ger) vineyard (Anb): Rheinhessen. (Ber): Bingen. (Gro): Kurfürstenstück. (Vil): Gau-Weinheim.

Kaiser Karl (Ger) vineyard (Anb): Franken. (Ber): Maindreieck. (Gro): Hofrat. (Vil): Repperndorf.

Kaiserpfalz (Ger) grosslage (Anb): Rheinhessen. (Ber): Bingen. (Vils): Bubenheim, Engelstadt, Gross-Winternheim, Heidesheim, Ingelheim, Jugenheim, Schwabenheim, Wackernheim.

Kaiser Pilsener (Ger) a well-known pilsner lager 4.8% alc by vol. brewed by the Henninger Brauerei in Frankfurt. Has a long lagering of 6–9 weeks.

Kaiserstuhl (Ger) vineyard (Anb): Pfalz. (Ber): Mittelhaardt-Deutsche Weinstrasse. (Gro): Rebstöckel. (Vil): Hambach.

Kaiserstuhl Rosé (Austr) a rosé wine produced in the Barossa Valley by the co-operative winery of same name (part of Penfolds).

Kaiserstuhl-Tuniberg (Ger) bereich (Gros): Attilafelsen, Vulkanfelsen.

Kaiserstuhl-Tuniberg Weinfest (Ger) a Baden wine festival held in Breisach in September.

Kaiserwasser (It) a natural spring mineral water from Innichen, S. Candido, Bozen. Mineral contents (milligrammes per litre): Sodium 1.2mg/l, Calcium 164mg/l, Magnesium 39.6mg/l, Potassium 0.51mg/l, Bicarbonates 224mg/l, Chlorides 0.4mg/l, Sulphates 366mg/l, Fluorides 0.82mg/l, Strontium 1.86mg/l, Silicates 5.88mg/l.

Kaituna Valley (N.Z) a winery. (Add): 150 Old Tai Tapu Road, Halswell, Canterbury. Specialises in Pinot noir.

Kajol (S.Afr) a white blend of Colombard, Hanepoot, Raisin blanc and Sultana grapes, a medium-sweet wine.

Kakabeka (Can) a cream lager beer brewed by the Doran Brewery.

Kakao (Aus)(Cro)(Ger)(Pol) cocoa.

Kakeil (Kor) cocktail.

Kakhetia (Geo) a large earthenware wine storage jar used in the Georgia region.

Kaktyeel (Rus) cocktail.

Kakubin (Jap) the brand-name of a blended whiskey produced by the Suntory Distillery.

Kakuteru (Jap) cocktail.

Kalary (Bra) a natural spring mineral water from Porto Velho, Sao Paolo. Mineral contents (milligrammes per litre): Sodium 0.18mg/l, Calcium 0.59mg/l, Potassium 0.88mg/l, Bicarbonates 2.83mg/l, Nitrates 0.93mg/l.

Kalashnikov Vodka (Eng) an 82° US Proof vodka produced by the Kalashnikov Joint Vodka Company, now known as General Kalashnikov's Vodka.

Kalavryta (Gre) a red wine produced in Morea.

Kalb (Ger) vineyard (Anb): Franken. (Ber): Steigerwald. (Gro): Burgweg. (Vil): Iphofen.

Kalbenstein (Ger) vineyard (Anb): Franken. (Ber): Maindreieck. (Gro): Rosstal. (Vil): Gambach.

Kaldi (Arab) a ninth century Arabian goatherd who is reputed to have discovered coffee through the antics of his goats after they had eaten the coffee cherries (berries). He told his discovery to the nearby priests who then brewed a beverage from the fruit so as to keep themselves awake through their long prayers.

Kalebag (Tur) the state monopoly-approved name for red and white wines from Ankara.

Kalecik Karasi (Tur) a white grape variety grown in central Anatolia.

Kaliber (Ire) a low-alcohol lager brewed by the Guinness Brewery at 0.5% alc by vol.

Kalimna (Austr) a winery based north of Nurioatpa, South Australia.

Kalimna (Austr) the name given to a full-bodied dry red wine produced by Penfolds from Shiraz grapes, aged in American oak.

Kalin Cellars (USA) a winery based in San Rafael, Marin, California. Grape varieties: Cabernet sauvignon, Chardonnay, Johannisberg riesling, Sémillon and Zinfandel. Produces varietal and some botrytised wines.

Kalkberg (Ger) vineyard (Anb): Pfalz. (Ber): Mittelhaardt-Deutsche Weinstrasse. (Gro): Pfaffengrund. (Vil): Duttweiler.

Kalkgasse (Ger) vineyard (Anb): Hessiche Bergstrasse. (Ber): Starkenburg. (Gro): Wolfsmagen. (Vil): Bernsheim.

K

Kalkgrube (Ger) vineyard (Anb): Pfalz. (Ber): Südliche Weinstrasse. (Gro): Königsgarten. (Vil): Frankweiler.

Kalkofen (Aus) a vineyard site on the banks of the River Danube situated in the Wachau region, Niederösterreich.

Kalkofen (Ger) village (Anb): Nahe. (Ber): Schloss Böckelheim. (Gro): Paradiesgarten. (Vin): Graukatz.

Kalkofen (Ger) vineyard (Anb): Pfalz. (Ber): Mittelhaardt-Deutsche Weinstrasse. (Gro): Kobnert. (Vil): Leistadt.

Kalkofen (Ger) vineyard (Anb): Pfalz. (Ber): Mittelhaardt-Deutsche Weinstrasse. (Gro): Mariengarten. (Vil): Deidesheim.

Kalkveld (S.Afr) a label for a range of wines (Shiraz) including Kalkveld Hill of Eon from the Zandvliet Estate, Roberstson.

Kallenberg (Ger) vineyard (Anb): Rheinhessen. (Ber): Bingen. (Gro): Kaiserpfalz. (Vil): Bubenheim.

Kallie's Dream (S.Afr) an oaked, dry white wine (Chardonnay 23%, Sauvignon blanc 30%, Sémillon 12%, Viognier 35%) produced by the Akkerdal Estate winery, Franschhoek, Western Cape.

Kalligas (Gre) a noted wine-merchant who specialises in Kephalonian wines.

Kallister (S.Afr) the label for a red wine (Merlot, Cabernet franc and Cabernet sauvignon blend) produced by the Vriesenhof Vineyards winery, Stellenbosch, Western Cape.

Kallmuth (Ger) vineyard (Anb): Franken. (Ber): Maindreieck. (Gro): Not yet assigned. (Vil): Homburg.

Kallskål (Swe) lit: 'cool tankard', nowadays denotes a fruit cup or other cold refreshing drink.

Kallstadt (Ger) village (Anb): Pfalz. (Ber): Mittelhaardt-Deutsche Weinstrasse. (Gro): Feuerberg. (Vins): Annaberg, Kreidkeller.

Kallstadt (Ger) village (Anb): Pfalz. (Ber): Mittelhaardt-Deutsche Weinstrasse. (Gro): Kobnert. (Vins): Kronenberg, Steinacker.

Kallstadt (Ger) village (Anb): Pfalz. (Ber): Mittelhaardt-Deutsche Weinstrasse. (Gro): Saumagen. (Vil): Horn, Kirchenstück, Nill.

Källvatten Mörarp (Swe) a natural spring mineral water.

Kalokhorio (Cyp) a village where the grapes for Commandaria are grown, based in the south-east of the island.

Kalopanayotis (Cyp) a wine village on the north-western slopes of the Troodos Mountains in the Marathassa region.

Kalta Katchka (USA) Kosher Cold Duck. *see* Cold Duck.

Kalte Ente [1] (Ger) lit: 'cold duck' a sparkling red wine. *see* Cold Duck.

Kalte Ente [2] (Ger) a white wine mixed half and half with soda water (or cold water).

Kaltenberg (Ger) a bottled pilsener lager 1047 O.G. brewed under licence by Whitbread.

Kaltenberg Hell (Eng) a 4.1% alc by vol. lager beer brewed under licence by the Thwaites Brewery.

Kaltenberg Castle Brauerei (Ger) a brewery based in Fürstenfeldbruck. Brews: Prinzregent Luitpold Weissbier, Prinzregent Luitpold Weissbier Dunkel.

Kalterberg (Ger) vineyard (Anb): Württemberg. (Ber): Württembergisch Unterland. (Gro): Schalkstein. (Vil): Rielinghausen.

Kalterersee (It) also known as Lago di Caldaro. Is a wine from the Trentino-Alto Adige, produced on the shore of the little lake Caldaro near Ora.

Kalt Pilsener (Eng) a pilsner-style lager beer brewed by Hydes Brewery, Moss Side, Manchester.

Kalyani Export Special (Ind) a 4.8% alc by vol. lager brewed and bottled by United Breweries in Calcutta.

Kamen Estate (USA) a winery based on the Mayacamas range, Sonoma County, California.

Kamikaze (Eng) a 5% alc by vol. ale brewed by the Dent Brewery, Cumbria.

Kammer (Ger) vineyard (Anb): Mosel-Saar-Ruwer. (Ber): Bernkastel. (Gro): Kurfürstlay. (Vil): Brauneberg.

Kammer Distillery (Ger) a noted liqueur producing company based in Kammer, western Germany.

Kammerforst (Ger) village (Anb): Franken. (Ber): Steigerwald. (Gro): Not yet assigned. (Vin): Teufel.

Kamok (Fr) a coffee-flavoured liqueur.

Kamos (Rus) a natural spring mineral water from Stavropol Territory, Northern Caucasus. Mineral contents (milligrammes per litre): Sodium <100mg/l, Calcium 20-150mg/l, Potassium <100mg/l, Bicarbonates 150-350mg/l, Chlorides <100mg/l, Sulphates <100mg/l.

Kamos Tselebnaya (Rus) a natural spring mineral water from Stavropol Territory, Northern Caucusus. Mineral contents (milligrammes per litre): Sodium 500-900mg/l, Calcium 100-350mg/l, Magnesium 30-150mg/l, Potassium 500-900mg/l, Bicarbonates 1000-1500mg/l, Chlorides 500-850mg/l, Sulphates 150-350mg/l.

Kamp (Aus) a tributary of the river Danube. It gives its name to the wines produced in its valley. Noted for wines from Veltliner and Riesling grapes.

Kampai (Chi)(Jap) a toast to guests, denotes '*good health*', '*cheers*'.

Kampai (Eng) a 5% alc by vol. premium fruit drink from Spilt Drinks, Exeter. Ingredients include guarana. Sold in 275mls silver bottles.

Kamp-Bornhofen-Kestert (Ger) village (Anb): Mittelrhein. (Ber): Rheinburgengau. (Gro): Loreleyfelsen. (Vins): Liebenstein-Sterrenberg, Pilgerpfad.

Kamptal (Aus) a wine district of (4200ha) that runs along the banks of the river Kamp. Soil: loess, loam, rock and slate, Main grape varieties: white (Chardonnay, Grüner veltliner, Pinot blanc and Riesling) red (Cabernet sauvignon, Merlot, Pinot noir, Zweigelt). **Villages**: Altenhof, Elsarn,

K

Engabrunn, Etsdorf, Gobelsburg, Hadersdorf, Langenlois, Lengenfeld, Mollands, Reith, Obernholz, Oberreith, Reith, Schiltern, Schönberg, Schönberg-Neustift, See, Seftenberg, Sittendorf, Stiefern, Strass, Stratzing, Walkersdorf, Zeiselberg, Zöbling. **Vineyard Sites**: Absdorf, Antenau, Auf der Setz, Badfeld, Berntal, Bleckenweg, Brunader, Brunngasse, Dorner, Eichberg, Eichelberg, Fahnbach, Fahnberg, Friesenrock, Fuchsloch, Gaisberg, Galgenberg, Gautscher, Geltsfreund, Geppling, Gerichtstal, Gleisseln, Gobelsberger Haide, Groisl, Grosses Stangl, Grub, Gsellgericht, Gugge, Haid (2), Hassel, Heiligenstein, Hintenaus, Hochstrasse, Hofstadt, Hofstatt (3), Hoheneck, Hohlenstein, Holzeg, Hund, Hüttbühel, Hutweg, Im Renner, In der Eben, Irrbling, Joch, Käferberg, Karl, Katl, Kiesling, Kirchengrund, Kirchholz, Kittmannsberg, Kleines Stangl, Kleinstein, Kogelberg, Kohlberg, Kremsfeld (2), Kremstal, Ladner, Laiser Haide, Lamm, Lammberg, Landstrass, Lauser, Leimer, Letten, Liss, Loischl, Loiser Berg, Merschein, Narerwiesen, Nesselthal, Neuberg, Obergugen, Oberhasel, Ober Mitterhassel, Obritzberg, Offenberg, Panzuan, Pfeifenberg, Placher, Point, Praidl, Rasstadt, Redling, Reising, Reith, Riedel, Rigerin, Rotbichel, Sachsenberg, Sand, Sanfgrube, Satzen (2), Saubaad, Sauberg, Saugraben, Sauzaggl, Schenkenbichl, Schnauterin, Schöntal, Schreckenberg, Schütt, Seeberg, Senthal, Soos, Spiegel, Spiess, Steinfeld, Steinhaus, Steinmassl, Steinsatz, Steinwand, Strobel, Tagler, Teller, Untergugen, Unter Mitterhasel, Vögerl Haseln, Wechselberg (2), Weinträgerin, Wiege, Wohra, Wolfsgruben (2), Zeiselberg.

Kamptal Klassik (Aus) a large marketing association based in the Kamptal region created to promote the wines of the region and traditional Austrian wine-making methods.

Kamtchatka Watky (Jap) a spirit made from rice.

Kamzík (Czec) a lager beer brewed by the Poprad Brewery.

Kanaka (Arab) the Arabian name for the Ibrik (Turkish) coffee boiler.

Kandeel (Hol) an old Dutch liqueur. A Cognac, cloves, vanilla and cinnamon liqueur produced only by Van Zuylekom Distillery in Amsterdam.

Kandel (Ger) village (Anb): Pfalz. (Ber): Südliche Weinstrasse. (Gro): Guttenberg. (Vin): Galgenberg.

Kangaroo Cocktail (Cktl) ¾ measure vodka, ¼ measure French vermouth. Shake over ice, strain into a cocktail glass and top with a twist of lemon peel juice.

Kangaroo Jump Cocktail (Cktl) 10mls (½ fl.oz) dry gin, 25mls (1 fl.oz) lemon juice, 5mls (¼ fl.oz) maraschino, dash gomme syrup. Shake over ice and strain into an ice-filled highball glass. Top with soda, add 2 dashes crème de menthe (green), 1 dash blue Curaçao, decorate with a spiral of lemon peel and serve with straws.

Kanga Rouge (Austr) a red wine made from 100% Hermitage grapes.

Kango Co-operative (S.Afr) a co-operative winery (established 1976) based in Oudtshoorn, Klein Karoo. 295ha. (Add): Box 46, Oudtshoorn 6620. Grape varieties: Cabernet sauvignon, Chardonnay, Merlot, Morio Muscat, Pinotage, Sauvignon blanc, Shiraz. Labels: Golden Jerepiko, Hanepoot golden dessert wine, Herfsgoud, Premier blanc, Red Jerepiko, Rijckshof claret, Rozelle and many varietals together with a range of brandies. Website: http://www.kangowines.com

Kang Xi (Chi) a natural spring mineral water. Mineral contents (milligrammes per litre): Sodium 9mg/l, Calcium 51.5mg/l, Magnesium 22.5mg/l, Potassium 0.6mg/l, Bicarbonates 237mg/l, Chlorides 6.2mg/l, Sulphates 4.1mg/l, Nitrates 15.6mg/l, Silicates 25.4mg/l. pH 8.1

Kannaland (S.Afr) the label for a red (Cabernet sauvignon & Merlot blend) white (Chardonnay & Sémillon) wines produced by the Domein Doornkraal winery, Little Karoo.

Kanneken (Hol) a metal drinking vessel used in the sixteenth and seventeenth centuries.

Kanokomet (Egy) an ancient wine from the vineyards of Rameses III (1198–1167 B.C).

Kanonkop Estate (S.Afr) a top winery (established 1910) based on the Elsenburg, Stellenbosch. 100ha. (Add): P.O. Muldersvlei 7606. Famous for its Pinotage wines it also produces Paul Sauer Fleur and many Varietals. Grape varieties include: Cabernet franc, Cabernet sauvignon, Chardonnay, Chenin blanc, Merlot, Pinotage. Label: Kadette, Paul Sauer. Website: http://www.kanonkop.co.za

Kanpai (Jap) cheers!

Kanta (Gre) a dry white wine, elegant in style.

Kantator (Fr) the brand-name of a beer brewed in Alsace.

Kanterbräu (Fr) an Alsatian beer.

Kantharos (Gre) a two-handled ladling cup used in ancient Greece to serve wines from amphora.

Kanuka Forest Wines (N.Z) a winery. (Add): Moore Road, Thornton, Whakatane. 3ha. Grape varieties: Cabernet sauvignon, Chardonnay, Merlot, Sauvignon blanc.

Kanu Winery (S.Afr) a winery (established 1998) based in Stellenbosch, Western Cape. 54ha. Grape varieties: Cabernet sauvignon, Chardonnay, Chenin blanc, Cinsaut, Merlot, Sauvignon blanc, Shiraz. Labels: Escape, Keystone, Kia-Ora, Limited Release, Rockwood. Website: http://www.kanu.co.za

Kanyak (Tur) brandy. See also Konyak.

Kanzem (Ger) village (Anb): Mosel-Saar-Ruwer. (Ber): Saar-Ruwer. (Gro): Scharzberg. (Vins): Altenberg, Hörecker, Schlossberg, Sonnenberg.

Kanzemer (Ger) a rare red wine from the Mosel-Saar-Ruwer.

Kanzler (Ger) a white grape variety, a cross between the Müller-Thurgau and the Silvaner. Produces good quality, full-bodied wines.

Kanzlerberg (Fr) an A.C. Alsace Grand Cru vineyard at Bergheim, Haut-Rhin 3.23ha.

Kaoliang Chiew (Chi) a medicinal tonic 12% alc by vol.

K

Kaoliang Wine (Chi) a spirit distilled from the kaoliang (a sorghum-like grain).

Kapé (Afr) the North-African name for coffee.

Kapellchen (Ger) vineyard (Anb): Mosel-Saar-Ruwer. (Ber): Bernkastel. (Gro): Michelsberg. (Vil): Minheim.

Kapelle (Ger) vineyard (Anb): Rheinhessen. (Ber): Bingen. (Gro): Kurfürstenstück. (Vil): Gau-Bickelheim.

Kapelle (Ger) vineyard (Anb): Rheinhessen. (Ber): Nierstein. (Gro): Sankt Alban. (Vil): Bodenheim.

Kapelle (Ger) vineyard (Anb): Pfalz. (Ber): Südliche Weinstrasse. (Gro): Ordensgut. (Vil): Hainfeld.

Kapellenberg (Ger) lit: 'church hill', the name used for many vineyards (28 in all) in Germany. Derived from when the vineyards were owned by the Church.

Kapellenberg (Ger) grosslage (Anb): Franken. (Ber): Steigerwald. (Vils): Schmachtenberg, Steinbach, Zeil, Ziegelanger.

Kapellenberg (Ger) vineyard (Anb): Ahr. (Ber): Walporzheim/Ahrtal. (Gro): Klosterberg. (Vil): Heimersheim.

Kapellenberg (Ger) vineyard (Anb): Baden. (Ber): Badische Bergstrasse/Kraichgau. (Gro): Stiftsberg. (Vil): Eichelberg.

Kapellenberg (Ger) vineyard (Anb): Baden. (Ber): Bodensee. (Gro): Not yet assigned. (Vil): Klettau (ortsteil Erzingen).

Kapellenberg (Ger) vineyard (Anb): Baden. (Ber): Bodensee. (Gro): Not yet assigned. (Vil): Klettau (ortsteil Rechberg).

Kapellenberg (Ger) vineyard (Anb): Baden. (Ber): Kaiserstuhl-Tuniberg. (Gro): Attilafelsen. (Vil): Munzingen.

Kapellenberg (Ger) vineyard (Anb): Baden. (Ber): Markgräflerland. (Gro): Vogtei Rötteln. (Vil): Bamlach.

Kapellenberg (Ger) vineyard (Anb): Baden. (Ber): Markgräflerland. (Gro): Vogtei Rötteln. (Vil): Rheinweiler.

Kapellenberg (Ger) vineyard (Anb): Baden. (Ber): Ortenau. (Gro): Fürsteneck. (Vil): Durbach.

Kapellenberg (Ger) vineyard (Anb): Franken. (Ber): Maindreieck. (Gro): Not yet assigned. (Vil): Eibelstadt.

Kapellenberg (Ger) vineyard (Anb): Franken. (Ber): Maindreieck. (Gro): Not yet assigned. (Vil): Frickenhausen am Main.

Kapellenberg (Ger) vineyard (Anb): Mosel-Saar-Ruwer. (Ber): Obermosel. (Gro): Gipfel. (Vil): Helfant-Esingen.

Kapellenberg (Ger) vineyard (Anb): Mosel-Saar-Ruwer. (Ber): Obermosel. (Gro): Gipfel. (Vil): Rehlingen.

Kapellenberg (Ger) vineyard (Anb): Mosel-Saar-Ruwer. (Ber): Zell/Mosel. (Gro): Grafschaft. (Vil): Alf.

Kapellenberg (Ger) vineyard (Anb): Mosel-Saar-Ruwer. (Ber): Zell/Mosel. (Gro): Rosenhang. (Vil): Briedern.

Kapellenberg (Ger) vineyard (Anb): Mosel-Saar-Ruwer. (Ber): Zell/Mosel. (Gro): Rosenhang. (Vil): Bruttig-Fankel.

Kapellenberg (Ger) vineyard (Anb): Mosel-Saar-Ruwer. (Ber): Zell/Mosel. (Gro): Rosenhang. (Vil): Treis-Karden.

Kapellenberg (Ger) vineyard (Anb): Nahe. (Ber): Kreuznach. (Gro): Schlosskapelle. (Vil): Münster-Sarmsheim.

Kapellenberg (Ger) vineyard (Anb): Nahe. (Ber): Schloss Böckelheim. (Gro): Paradiesgarten. (Vil): Odernheim.

Kapellenberg (Ger) vineyard (Anb): Rheingau. (Ber): Johannisberg. (Gro): Burgweg. (Vil): Lorch.

Kapellenberg (Ger) vineyard (Anb): Rheinhessen. (Ber): Bingen. (Gro): Rheingrafenstein. (Vil): Fürfeld.

Kapellenberg (Ger) vineyard (Anb): Rheinhessen. (Ber): Bingen. (Gro): Sankt Rochuskapelle. (Vil): Bingen.

Kapellenberg (Ger) vineyard (Anb): Rheinhessen. (Ber): Bingen. (Gro): Sankt Rochuskapelle. (Vil): Dromersheim.

Kapellenberg (Ger) vineyard (Anb): Rheinhessen. (Ber): Nierstein. (Gro): Domherr. (Vil): Ober-Olm.

Kapellenberg (Ger) vineyard (Anb): Rheinhessen. (Ber): Wonnegau. (Gro): Sybillenstein. (Vil): Alzey.

Kapellenberg (Ger) vineyard (Anb): Rheinhessen. (Ber): Wonnegau. (Gro): Sybillenstein. (Vil): Weinheim.

Kapellenberg (Ger) vineyard (Anb): Pfalz. (Ber): Mittelhaardt-Deutsche Weinstrasse. (Gro): Meerspinne. (Vil): Gimmeldingen.

Kapellenberg (Ger) vineyard (Anb): Pfalz. (Ber): Südliche Weinstrasse. (Gro): Mandelhöhe. (Vil): Maikammer-Alsterweiler.

Kapellenberg (Ger) a vineyard within the village of Lorch, 56.9ha (31.5%) of which is proposed to be classifed as Erstes Gewächs.

Kapellen-Drusweiler (Ger) village (Anb): Pfalz. (Ber): Südliche Weinstrasse. (Gro): Kloster Liebfrauenberg. (Vin): Rosengarten.

Kapellengarten (Ger) vineyard (Anb): Pfalz. (Ber): Mittelhaardt-Deutsche Weinstrasse. (Gro): Kobnert. (Vil): Dackenheim.

Kapellenpfad (Ger) vineyard (Anb): Nahe. (Ber): Kreuznach. (Gro): Kronenberg. (Vil): Bad Kreuznach.

Kapellenstück (Ger) vineyard (Anb): Rheinhessen. (Ber): Wonnegau. (Gro): Liebfrauenmorgen. (Vil): Worms.

Kapfontein (S.Afr) the brand-name for a range of wines from Pinotage or Chenin blanc grapes grown in the Coastal region.

Kapitein Kok (Cktl) 20mls (¾ fl.oz) tequila, 35mls (1½ fl.ozs) Fraises de Bois Dolphi. Build into an ice-filled highball glass, top up with bitter orange and add a slice of orange.

Käppele (Ger) vineyard (Anb): Württemberg. (Ber): Remstal-Stuttgart. (Gro): Wartbühl. (Vil): Beutelsbach.

K

Kappelrodeck (Ger) village (Anb): Baden. (Ber): Ortenau. (Gro): Schloss Rodeck. (Vin): Hex vom Dasenstein.

Kappishäusern (Ger) village (Anb): Württemberg. (Ber): Remstal-Stuttgart. (Gro): Hohenneuffen. (Vin): Schlossteige.

Kap Sekt (S.Afr) a brut sparkling wine produced by the Nederburg Estate from the Riesling and Rhine riesling grapes.

Kapsreiter (Aus) a lager beer brewed by the Kapsreiter Brauerei in Schärding near Linz.

Kapsreiter Brauerei (Aus) a brewery based in Schärding near Linz.

Kapsweyher (Ger) village (Anb): Pfalz. (Ber): Südliche Weinstrasse. (Gro): Guttenberg. (Vin): Lerchenberg.

Kaptein (S.Afr) the label from a range of wines (military names) produced by the Domein Doornkraal winery, Little Karoo.

Kaptenlojtnant (Swe) a blend of Bénédictine and grape brandy produced by Aktiebolaget Vin & Spritcentralem.

Kapucín (Czec) a lager beer brewed by the Vratislavice Brewery.

Kapuzinerbuck (Ger) vineyard (Anb): Baden. (Ber): Markgräflerland. (Gro): Lorettoberg. (Vil): Wittnau.

Kapuzinerlikoer (Ger) a brown-coloured Capuchin liqueur based on oils of celeriac, cinnamon, sweet oranges, cumin, fennel and mace with brandy.

Karabounar (Bul) see Karabunar.

Karabunar (Bul) a red grape variety grown in central-western Bulgaria.

Karabunar (Bul) a red wine produced in the town of same name near Plovdiv, central-western Bulgaria.

Karabunar (Bul) a noted wine-producing area in central-western Bulgaria, also spelt Karabounar.

Kara Chanakh (Rus) a dessert wine produced in Baku.

Karajorje (Euro) a natural spring mineral water from Serbia and Montenegro.

Karaf (Hol) decanter.

Karageorge (Slo) the brand-name of a slightly sparkling mineral water.

Kara-Isium (Rus) a dessert wine produced in Turkmenistan.

Karalâhana (Tur) a white grape variety grown in Thrace and Marmara.

Karamalz (Ger) a malzbier brewed by the Henninger Brauerei in Frankfurt.

Karat (Ger) a natural spring mineral water from Naturpark, Teutoburger Wald. Mineral contents (milligrammes per litre): Sodium 13.2mg/l, Calcium 110mg/l, Magnesium 8mg/l, Potassium 1.5mg/l, Bicarbonates 262mg/l, Chlorides 33.2mg/l, Sulphates 74mg/l, Fluorides 0.12mg/l.

Kara-Tachanakh (Asia) a white grape variety grown in the Azerbaijan region to produce dessert wines.

Karbacher Brauerei (Switz) an independent brewery based in Schönenwerd.

Karbonat (Tur) a drink charged with CO_2 gas (carbonated).

Karchesia Goblet (It) a large Roman drinking vessel, similar in shape to the modern Elgin glass.

Kardinalsberg (Ger) vineyard (Anb): Mosel-Saar-Ruwer. (Ber): Bernkastel. (Gro): Kurfürstlay. (Vil): Bernkastel-Kues.

Kardomah (Eng) the brand-name of a range of coffees produced specifically for the caterer. Produced by Premier Foodservice.

Karel Lager (Czec) a lager beer brewed in the Karlovy Vary Brewery.

Karien (S.Afr) the label for a white wine (Chenin blanc 85% and Sémillon 15% blend) part of the Jacques de Savoy range produced by the Vrede en Lust Wine Farm winery, Paarl, Western Cape.

Karina Vineyard (Austr) a vineyard (established 1984). (Add): Harrison's Road, Dromana, Victoria. Grape varieties: Riesling, Sauvignon blanc, Cabernet sauvignon.

Karl (Aus) a vineyard site based on the banks of the River Kamp situated in the Kamptal region.

Karlburg (Ger) village (Anb): Franken. (Ber): Maindreieck. (Gro): Rosstal. (Vins): Assorted parts of vineyards.

Karl Lawrence (USA) a winery based in the Napa Valley, California. Grape varieties include: Cabernet sauvignon.

Karloff (Eng) a proprietary brand of vodka 40% alc by vol.

Karlovac (Cro) a lager-style beer brewed in Croatia from south of the same city.

Karlovo (Bul) a delimited area in the southern region that is noted for white Misket wine.

Karlov White Muscatel (Bul) a straw coloured dry white wine with a bouquet of roses.

Karlovy Vary Brewery (Czec) a noted brewery based in north-western Czec, noted for Karel Lager.

Karlsberg (Austr) a winery based in the Barossa Valley, South Australia.

Karlsberg (Ger) vineyard (Anb): Mosel-Saar-Ruwer. (Ber): Saar-Ruwer. (Gro): Scharzberg. (Vil): Oberemmel.

Karlsberg (Ger) vineyard (Anb): Württemberg. (Ber): Kocher-Jagst-Tauber. (Gro): Tauberberg. (Vil): Weikersheim.

Karlsfelsen (Ger) vineyard (Anb): Mosel-Saar-Ruwer. (Ber): Obermosel. (Gro): Gipfel. (Vil): Palzem.

Karlskopf (Ger) vineyard (Anb): Ahr. (Ber): Walporzheim/Ahrtal. (Gro): Klosterberg. (Vil): Bachem.

Karlsquelle Heilwasser (Ger) a natural spring mineral water. Mineral contents (milligrammes per litre): Sodium 4795mg/l, Calcium 782mg/l, Magnesium 389mg/l, Potassium 113mg/l, Chlorides 6382mg/l, Sulphates 3860mg/l, Fluorides 0.27mg/l, Iron 3.65mg/l.

Karlsruhe-Durlach (Ger) village (Anb): Baden. (Ber): Badische Bergstrasse/Kraichgau. (Gro): Hohenberg. (Vin): Turmberg.

Karlsson (Swe) a natural spring mineral water from Assarebokällan.

Karlstadt (Ger) village (Anb): Franken. (Ber): Maindreieck. (Gro): Rosstal. (Vin): Im Stein.

K

Karmeliterlikoer (Ger) a yellow-green herb-based liqueur.

Karmen (Tur) the name used by the Diren Winery for a dry red wine and a reserve red wine.

Karmosyn (S.Afr) the label for a red wine (Shiraz) produced by the Terroir Wines of SA winery, Stellenbosch, Western Cape.

Karnemelk (Hol) buttermilk.

Karoo (S.Afr) a natural spring mineral water from Noblesfontein, Karoo Highlands, Paarl, Western Cape. Mineral contents (milligrammes per litre): Sodium 39mg/l, Calcium 79.5mg/l, Magnesium 28mg/l, Potassium 2mg/l, Bicarbonates 316mg/l, Chlorides 29mg/l, Sulphates 43mg/l, Fluorides 0.9mg/l, Nitrates 5.86mg/l. pH 7.2 Also known as Karoo Full Moon when bottled outdoors during a full moon! Now known as Cape Karoo.

Karoo Full Moon (S.Afr) see Karoo.

Karpi (Fin) a liqueur made by Lignell and Piispanen from cranberries and other fruits 29% alc by vol.

Karrapappas (Gre) lit: 'black priest' a dark grape variety.

Karrawirra (Austr) a winery based in the Barossa Valley, South Australia.

Karridale (Austr) a district in the Margaret River region of Western Australia.

Kartaeuserlikoer (Ger) a herb liqueur similar in style to Chartreuse. See also Karthauser.

Karthauser (Ger) another name for the liqueur Kartaeuserlikoer.

Karthäuser (Ger) vineyard (Anb): Franken. (Ber): Maindreieck. (Gro): Kirchberg. (Vil): Astheim.

Karthäuser (Ger) vineyard (Anb): Nahe. (Ber): Kreuznach. (Gro): Schlosskapelle. (Vil): Laubenheim.

Karthäuserhofberg Burgberg (Ger) vineyard (Anb): Mosel-Saar-Ruwer. (Ber): Saar-Ruwer. (Gro): Römerlay. (Vil): Trier.

Karthäuserhofberg Kronenberg (Ger) vineyard (Anb): Mosel-Saar-Ruwer. (Ber): Saar-Ruwer. (Gro): Römerlay. (Vil): Trier.

Karthäuserhofberg Orthsberg (Ger) vineyard (Anb): Mosel-Saar-Ruwer. (Ber): Saar-Ruwer. (Gro): Römerlay. (Vil): Trier.

Karthäuserhofberg Sang (Ger) vineyard (Anb): Mosel-Saar-Ruwer. (Ber): Saar-Ruwer. (Gro): Römerlay. (Vil): Trier.

Karthäuserhofberg Stirn (Ger) vineyard (Anb): Mosel-Saar-Ruwer. (Ber): Saar-Ruwer. (Gro): Römerlay. (Vil): Trier.

Karthuizer Dubbel (Hol) a 6.5% alc by vol. light-brown, bottle-conditioned double beer brewed by De Drie Kruizen Brouwerij, Westmaas.

Karukera (Cktl) 1.5cls Cointreau, 3cls white rum, 1 teaspoon orange flower water, 1 teaspoon liquid honey. Shake over ice, strain into an old-fashioned glass and decorate with a rondal of orange and rondal of lime.

Karusa Vineyards (S.Afr) a winery (established 2004) based in Robertson, Western Cape. Grape varieties: Shiraz, Viognier. Label: The Fifth Element.

Kasanje (S.Afr) the label for a white wine (Chenin blanc, Sauvignon blanc and Sémillon blend) produced by the La Chataigne winery, Franschhoek, Western Cape.

Kasbach (Ger) village (Anb): Mittelrhein. (Ber): Rheinburgengau. (Gro): Burg Hammerstein. (Vin): Stehlerberg.

Käsberg (Ger) vineyard (Anb): Württemberg. (Ber): Württembergisch Unterland. (Gro): Schalkstein. (Vil): Hessigheim.

Käsberg (Ger) vineyard (Anb): Württemberg. (Ber): Württembergisch Unterland. (Gro): Schalkstein. (Vil): Mundelsheim.

Kas Bitters De Luxe (Sp) a non-alcoholic bitters apéritif which is imported into the U.K. by Leisure Drinks of Derby.

Kasel (Ger) village (Anb): Mosel-Saar-Ruwer. (Ber): Saar-Ruwer. (Gro): Römerlay. (Vins): Dominikanerberg, Herrenberg, Hitzlay, Kehrnagel, Nieschen, Paulinsberg, Timpert.

Kashmiri Tea (Ind) a blend of 3 parts green tea to 1 part Darjeeling tea per pint of boiling water. Is then mixed with nuts and spices, strained and served with milk and brown sugar.

Kashmir Natural Spring Water (Pak) a natural spring mineral water (established 2001). Mineral contents (milligrammes per litre): Calcium 22mg/l, Magnesium 11mg/l, Potassium 2mg/l, Bicarbonates 190mg/l, Chlorides 38mg/l. pH 7.0

Kaskade (Eng) a species of barley malt from the Golden Promise variety that gives medium sugar yields.

Kasket Karl (Den) a light-coloured lager beer 10.7% alc by vol. brewed by the Thor Brewery.

Käsleberg (Ger) vineyard (Anb): Baden. (Ber): Kaiserstuhl-Tuniberg. (Gro): Vulkanfelsen. (Vil): Oberrotweil.

Kasselberg (Ger) vineyard (Anb): Baden. (Ber): Ortenau. (Gro): Fürsteneck. (Vil): Durbach.

Kastania (USA) the label for a red wine (Pinot noir) produced by the Landmark winery, Sonoma Coast, Sonoma County, California.

Kastanienbusch (Ger) vineyard (Anb): Pfalz. (Ber): Südliche Weinstrasse. (Gro): Königsgarten. (Vil): Birkweiler.

Kastaniengarten (Ger) vineyard (Anb): Pfalz. (Ber): Südliche Weinstrasse. (Gro): Schloss Ludwigshöhe. (Vil): Edenkoben.

Kasteelbier Ingelmunster (Bel) a 11% alc by vol. barley wine brewed by Van Honsebrouck Brasserie, Ingelmunster.

Kasteelbier Ingelmunster Triple Gold (Bel) a 11% alc by vol. special triple beer brewed by Van Honsebrouck Brasserie, Ingelmunster.

Kasteel Cru (Eng) a 5% alc by vol. lager beer brewed with Champagne yeast by Bass in Burton-on-Trent.

Kastel (N.Z) a former brand-name used by the Penfolds Winery for a selection of their wines.

Kastel (Rus) a red muscat dessert wine from the southern Crimea.

Kastel (Euro) a wine-producing region on the Dalmatian coast.

K

Kastelberg (Fr) an A.C. Alsace Grand Cru vineyard in Andlau, Bas-Rhin 5.82ha.

Kastell (Ger) vineyard (Anb): Nahe. (Ber): Schloss Böckelheim. (Gro): Paradiesgarten. (Vil): Boos.

Kastell (Ger) vineyard (Anb): Nahe. (Ber): Schloss Böckelheim. (Gro): Paradiesgarten. (Vil): Waldböckelheim.

Kastel-Staadt (Ger) village (Anb): Mosel-Saar-Ruwer. (Ber): Saar-Ruwer. (Gro): Scharzberg. (Vins): König Johann Berg, Maximin Staadt.

Kat (Arab) an alternative spelling of Khat.

Katabatic Winds (Eng) these occur in regions close to mountains holding glacial snows. Heavy cold air flows down the valleys attaining speeds of 60–80 knots. Examples are the Mistral in France, the Bora in Italy and the El Seré in Spain.

Katadin (C.Am) a natural spring mineral water from Barva, Costa Rica. Mineral contents (milligrammes per litre): Sodium 2.7mg/l, Calcium 17.5mg/l, Magnesium 7.7mg/l, Potassium 2.7mg/l, Sulphates 13.1mg/l, Fluorides 0.25mg/l. pH 6.8

Katbakkies Wine (S.Afr) a winery based in Cederberg, Western Cape. 2.8ha. Grape varieties: Cabernet sauvignon, Chenin blanc, Shiraz, Viognier. Produces varietal wines.

Kater (Hol) lit: 'cat', a slang term used for a hangover.

Katergrube (Ger) vineyard (Anb): Nahe. (Ber): Schloss Böckelheim. (Gro): Rosengarten. (Vil): Weinsheim.

Katheryn Kennedy (USA) a winery based in the Santa Cruz Mountains, California. Grape varieties include: Cabernet sauvingnon.

Kathryn Hall Winery (USA) a winery based in Rutherford, Napa Valley, California. Grape varieties include: Cabernet sauvignon. Label: Sacrashe Vineyard.

Katinka (Cktl) 1 measure vodka, ½ measure cherry brandy, juice ¼ lemon, shaken over ice, strain into a cocktail glass and dress with a slice of lemon.

Katl (Aus) a vineyard site based on the banks of the River Kamp situated in the Kamptal region.

Katnook Estate (Austr) a winery based at Penola Road, Coonawarra, South Australia. Produces varietal wines including Founder's Block and Odyssey. Grape varieties: Cabernet sauvignon, Chardonnay, Riesling, Sauvignon blanc.

Katnook [Sartori] (USA) a Japanese gentleman who is reputed to have invented instant coffee in Chicago in 1801.

Katsunuma Winery (Jap) vineyards based in the village of Katsunuma, Yamanashi. Sold under Sapporo wine label.

Kattell-Roc (Fr) a range of low-alcohol drinks (vermouth, pastis and bitter-sweet) with an alcoholic content of 1% by vol. or less. Bacarat (a red vermouth), Aperitivo (bitters and herbs), Anise (aniseed) are distributed by Brooke Bond C°.

Kattenes (Ger) village (Anb): Mosel-Saar-Ruwer. (Ber): Zell/Mosel. (Gro): Weinhex. (Vins): Fahrberg, Steinchen.

Kattengraben (Aus) a vineyard site on the banks of the River Danube in the Kremstal region.

Kattus (Aus) a famous winery based in the Wien region. (Add): Am Hof 8, 1011 Wien. Grape varieties include: Chardonnay, Grüner veltliner, Müller-Thurgau, Pinot gris, Riesling, Welschriesling. Produces a range of wine styles and is a leading producer of Austrian sekt (Alte Reserve, Grosser Jahrang and Hochriegel).

Katy (Eng) a single variety sparkling medium-dry cider from Thatcher's in Somerset 7.4% alc by vol.

Kätzchen (Ger) vineyard (Anb): Mosel-Saar-Ruwer. (Ber): Bernkastel. (Gro): Kurfürstlay. (Vil): Osann-Monzel.

Katzebuckel (Ger) vineyard (Anb): Rheinhessen. (Ber): Wonnegau. (Gro): Burg Rodenstein. (Vil): Mörstadt.

Ka-tzefet (Isr) cream.

Katzenbeisser (Ger) vineyard (Anb): Württemberg. (Ber): Württembergisch Unterland. (Gro): Kirchenweinberg. (Vil): Lauffen.

Katzenberg (Ger) vineyard (Anb): Baden. (Ber): Badische Bergstrasse/Kraichgau. (Gro): Hohenberg. (Vil): Weingarten.

Katzenhölle (Ger) vineyard (Anb): Nahe. (Ber): Kreuznach. (Gro): Kronenberg. (Vil): Bad Kreuznach (ortsteil Planig).

Katzenjammer (Ger) lit: 'cats crying', a slang term for a hangover.

Katzenkopf (Ger) vineyard (Anb): Franken. (Ber): Maindreieck. (Gro): Kirchberg. (Vil): Sommerach.

Katzenkopf (Ger) vineyard (Anb): Mosel-Saar-Ruwer. (Ber): Zell/Mosel. (Gro): Grafschaft. (Vil): Alf.

Katzenöhrle (Ger) vineyard (Anb): Württemberg. (Ber): Württembergisch Unterland. (Gro): Heuchelberg. (Vil): Meimsheim.

Katzenöhrle (Ger) vineyard (Anb): Württemberg. (Ber): Württembergisch Unterland. (Gro): Schalkstein. (Vil): Besigheim.

Katzenöhrle (Ger) vineyard (Anb): Württemberg. (Ber): Württembergisch Unterland. (Gro): Schalkstein. (Vil): Hessigheim.

Katzenöhrle (Ger) vineyard (Anb): Württemberg. (Ber): Württembergisch Unterland. (Gro): Schalkstein. (Vil): Mundelsheim.

Katzenstein (Ger) vineyard (Anb): Pfalz. (Ber): Mittelhaardt-Deutsche Weinstrasse. (Gro): Grafenstück. (Vil): Kindenheim.

Kaub (Ger) village (Anb): Mittelrhein. (Ber): Rheinburgengau. (Gro): Herrenberg. (Vins): Backofen, Blüchertal, Burg Gutenfels, Pfalzgrafenstein, Rauschelay, Rosstein.

Kaufee (Can) the Eskimo word for coffee.

Kaulenberg (Ger) vineyard (Anb): Nahe. (Ber): Schloss Böckelheim. (Gro): Paradiesgarten. (Vil): Auen.

Kautzenburg (S.Afr) a winery (established 2000) based in Stellenbosch, Western Cape. 5ha. Grape varieties: Pinotage.

Kautz Vineyards (USA) vineyards based at Murphys, California. Own Ironstone Vineyards, Calaveras

County, Sierra Foothills. Grapes include Cabernet franc.

Kauzenberg in der Mauern (Ger) vineyard (Anb): Nahe. (Ber): Kreuznach. (Gro): Kronenberg. (Vil): Bad Kreuznach.

Kauzenberg-Oranienberg (Ger) vineyard (Anb): Nahe. (Ber): Kreuznach. (Gro): Kronenberg. (Vil): Bad Kreuznach.

Kauzenberg-Rosenhügel (Ger) vineyard (Anb): Nahe. (Ber): Kreuznach. (Gro): Kronenberg. (Vil): Bad Kreuznach.

Kava (Cro) coffee.

Kava (Czec) the Bohemian name for coffee.

Kava (USA) a strong hallucinogenic drink made from the root of the pepper plant (many sub-species producing various strengths of kava) in Hawaii and other Pacific islands, can be made by either chewing the root or beating it between stones and then soaking in water. It is also known as Ava-Ava. Shrub botanical name is **Piper methysticum**.

Kava Bowl (Punch) 200mls (⅓ pint) light rum, 20mls (⅙ gill) each of golden rum, gomme syrup, grenadine, 125mls (1gill) orange juice, 125mls (1gill) lemon juice. Blend altogether with 300mls (½ pint) of crushed ice, pour into a punch bowl and decorate with lemon and orange slices.

Kavadarka (Ser) a wine-producing region in southern Macedonia.

Kavah (Isr) the old Hebrew word for coffee, *See also* Kaffee.

Kavaklidere (Tur) a large private wine-producing firm based in Anatolia that produces a large range of wines from both French and local grape varieties. Website: http://www.kavaklidare.com

Kavé (Hun) the Hebrew word for coffee in Hungary.

Kaveh (Tur) the old Turkish word for coffee.

Kaveh Kanes (Afr) the name given to the ancient coffee houses that were first frequented by men only.

Kawa (S.Asia) the Malayan word for coffee, also Koppi.

Kawa (Pol) coffee.

Kawarau Estate (N.Z) a winery. (Add): Box 1217, Queenstown, Central Otago. 5ha. Grape varieties: Cabernet franc, Chardonnay, Gewürztraminer, Malbec, Merlot, Pinot noir, Sauvignon blanc.

Kawther (Jor) a natural spring mineral water from Amman. Mineral contents (milligrammes per litre): Sodium 73mg/l, Calcium 46mg/l, Magnesium 48mg/l, Potassium 9mg/l, Bicarbonates 102mg/l, Chlorides 150mg/l, Sulphates 190mg/l, Fluorides 0.8mg/l. pH 8.2

Kaya (S.Afr) the label for a range of wines produced by the Coppoolse Finlayson Winery, Stellenbosch, Western Cape. Includes: Kaya Cape Vineyards (red and white), Kaya Traditional-Nandi (a dry white), Kaya Traditional-Shaka (Cabernet franc, Cinsaut and Pinotage blend).

Kayberg (Ger) vineyard (Anb): Württemberg. (Ber): Württembergisch Unterland. (Gro): Staufenberg. (Vil): Erlenbach.

Kayberg (Ger) vineyard (Anb): Württemberg. (Ber):

Württembergisch Unterland. (Gro): Staufenberg. (Vil): Oedheim.

Kaylined (Eng) a slang term for a person being drunk and incapable.

Kaymagh (Arab) lit: 'coffee cream', the name for the froth on the top of a cup of Turkish coffee.

Kaymak (Tur) cream.

Kayserberg (Fr) a commune in Alsace.

Kazakhstan (Rus) a wine-producing area in Armenia that runs from Mongolia to the Caspian Sea.

Kazakhstan (Rus) a white grape variety grown in the Kazakhstan area, used mainly for brandy production.

K.B. (Austr) *abbr*: Kent Brewery a lager beer 3.76% alc by vol. brewed by Tooth's Brewery and named after their Kent Brewery.

KC (S.Afr) the label for red wine blend (Cabernet sauvignon, Merlot, Pinot noir and Shiraz) produced by the Klein Constantia Estate winery, Constantia, Western Cape.

K.C.B. (Cktl) ¾ measure dry gin, ¼ measure kirsch, dash apricot brandy, dash lemon juice. Mix with ice, strain into a cocktail glass and top with a squeeze of lemon peel juice.

KC Bitter (Eng) a cask-conditioned bitter 1038 O.G. brewed by the Royal Clarence home-brew public house at Burnham-on-Sea, Somerset.

Keates Drift (S.Afr) the label for a wine produced by the Franschhoek Vineyards winery, Franschhoek, Western Cape.

Kecskemét (Hun) an ancient wine-producing area at Alföld in the Great Plain. Produces mainly white wines and fruit liqueurs.

Kecskeméti Barack (Hun) an apricot brandy produced in the Kecskemét region.

Kedai Kopi (Indo) café.

Keedorf (Aus) a vineyard site on the banks of the River Danube in the Kremstal region.

Keefersteiner (Switz) a medium-dry, white wine produced in the Stein-am-Rhein area.

Keel Over (Eng) a 4.2% alc by vol. ale brewed by the Skinner's Brewery Cº. Ltd., Cornwall.

Keelplate (Cktl)(Non-alc) 25mls (1fl.oz) clam juice, 50mls (2fl.ozs) tomato juice, 2 dashes Worcester sauce, 2 dashes celery salt. Shake over ice and strain into 125mls (5fl.oz) wine glass.

Keemun (Chi) a blend of tea, has a delicate flavour with a slight scent of orchids, originally a black tea, is now a green tea.

Keenan Winery (USA) a 19ha winery based near St. Helena, Napa Valley, California. Grape varieties: Cabernet sauvignon, Merlot and Chardonnay. Produces varietal wines.

Keene Dimick Vineyard (USA) a small vineyard based in the Napa Valley, California. Grape variety: Chardonnay.

Keeper Springs (USA) a natural spring mineral water. Mineral contents (milligrammes per litre): Sodium 2.5mg/l, Calcium 49mg/l, Magnesium 5.6mg/l, Potassium 1.1mg/l, Bicarbonates 110mg/l, Chlorides 3.4mg/l, Sulphates 14mg/l, Nitrates 1.4mg/l. pH 7.39

Keersmaeker (Bel) brewers of fruit flavoured lambic beers under Mort Subite label. Flavours include: framboise, pêche, cassis 4% alc by vol. Also Kriek (cherry) 4.5% alc by vol. and Gueuze 4.5% alc by vol.

Keerweder (S.Afr) a winery (established 1692) based in Franschhoek, Western Cape. 15ha. Grape varieties: Cabernet sauvignon, Merlot, Petit verdot, Pinotage, Shiraz. Website: http://www.keerweder.co.za

Keeskemeter Riesling (Ger) a varietal name for the grape cross between the Weisser pressburger and the Langsteiler.

Keeve (Scot) the name for a 36 gallon barrel.

Keewi (Eng) a crushed kiwi fruit drink from James White Juice Company.

Kefir (Geo) a drink made from fermented cows milk (in the Caucases). Is dried into pellets and then reconstituted with a little water and sugar. Also spelt Kafir and Kephir.

Kefraya (M.East) a 300ha wine estate in the village of Kefraya, Lebanon. Produces Château Kefraya Rosé (Carignan, Cinsaut, Grenache), Château Kefraya (70% Cabernet sauvignon plus Mourvèdre, Syrah, Grenache), Comte de M (Cabernet sauvignon and Syrah blend), Rouge de Kefraya (Cinsaut, Carignan), Nectar de Kefraya (a Mistelle).

Keg (Eng) a cask of various sizes for holding brewery conditioned beers, usually of cylindrical shape, also in metric sizes of 25litres, 50litres and 100litres. see Pin, Firkin, Kilderkin and Barrel.

Keg Beer (Eng) pressurised, processed or brewery-conditioned beer that is normally pasteurised.

Keg Buster (Eng) created by the famous British cartoonist Bill Tidy, is a cartoon character that represents the spirit of the British beer drinker.

Kegelbrau (USA) a premium beer 5% alc by vol. brewed by the Cold Spring Brewery, Cold Spring, Minnesota.

Kegging (Eng) a brewery term for the placing of beer into kegs.

Keglevich (It) the brand-name for a range of four flavoured vodkas: lemon 32% alc by vol. melon, peach, pear all 25% alc by vol. Produced by Stock in Trieste.

Kehr (Ger) vineyard (Anb): Rheinhessen. (Ber): Nierstein. (Gro): Gutes Domtal. (Vil): Weinolsheim.

Kehrberg (Ger) vineyard (Anb): Mosel-Saar-Ruwer. (Ber): Zell/Mosel. (Gro): Weinhex. (Vil): Kobern-Gondorf.

Kehrenberg (Ger) vineyard (Anb): Nahe. (Ber): Schloss Böckelheim. (Gro): Burgweg. (Vil): Altenbamberg.

Kehrnagel (Ger) vineyard (Anb): Mosel-Saar-Ruwer. (Ber): Saar-Ruwer. (Gro): Römerlay. (Vil): Kasel.

Keisseskraal Vineyards (S.Afr) a winery (established 2004) based in Bot River, Walker Bay, Western Cape. 2ha. Grape varieties: Cabernet sauvignon, Malbec, Merlot, Petit verdot, Shiraz, Viognier. Label: Galantskloof.

Keizerbitter (Hol) a brand of aromatic bitters.

Keizersberg (Bel) a 9% alc by vol. top-fermented, bottle-conditioned, abbaye beer brewed by Van Steenberge Brasserie, Ertvelde.

Kékfrankos (Hun) the local name for the Blaufränkisch grape. See also Nagyburgundi.

Kekkuti (Hun) a natural spring mineral water from Kekkut. Mineral contents (milligrammes per litre): Sodium 40mg/l, Calcium 242mg/l, Magnesium 68mg/l, Potassium 9.6mg/l, Bicarbonates 1804.3mg/l, Chlorides 16mg/l, Sulphates 50mg/l, Fluorides 0.98mg/l, Iron 1mg/l, Silicates 12mg/l.

Kéknyelü (Hun) a white grape variety grown around Lake Balatòn, Badacsonyi area. Produces a sweetish wine.

Kékoportó (Hun) a red grape variety grown in Villàny, the local name for the Blauer Portugieser. Produces good colour. Known as Oporto in Romania.

Kekre (Tur) sour. See also Eksi.

Kelburn Brewing C° (Scot) a brewery (established 2002). (Add): 10 Muriel Lane, Barrhead, Lanarkshire G78 1QB. Brews: Cart Blanche 5% alc by vol., Dark Moor 4.5% alc by vol., Goldihops 3.8% alc by vol., Red Smiddy 4.1% alc by vol. Website: http://www.kelburnbrewery.com 'E'mail: info@kelburnbrewery.com

Kelch (Ger) goblet/cup/chalice.

Kelder (Hol) cellar.

Kelders (S.Afr) cellars.

Kele (Chi) cola.

Kelechin (Ukr) a sparkling natural spring mineral water. Mineral contents (milligrammes per litre): Sodium 68mg/l, Calcium 275mg/l, Magnesium 41mg/l, Bicarbonates 1249mg/l, Chlorides 13mg/l, Sulphates 4mg/l, Fluorides 0.2mg/l, Silicates 25mg/l, Iron 22mg/l. pH 6.0

Kelham Gold (Eng) a 3.8% alc by vol. golden ale brewed by the Kelham Island Brewery, South Yorkshire.

Kelham Island Brewery (Eng) a brewery (established 1990). (Add): 23 Alma Street, Sheffield, South Yorkshire S3 8SA. Brews: Easy Rider 4.3% alc by vol., K I Bitter 3.8% alc by vol., Kelham Gold 3.8% alc by vol., Kelham Island Record Breaker, Pale Rider 5.2% alc by vol., Sheffield Cathedral Ale, Ale for Nigel. Website: http://www.kelhambrewery.co.uk 'E'mail: enquiries@kelhambrewery.co.uk

Kelham Island Record Breaker (Eng) a strong ale 1159 O.G. brewed by the Kelham Island Brewery in Sheffield, Yorkshire.

Kélibia (Afr) a co-operative based in Tunisia. Belongs to the UCCVT. Produces Muscat and Mistelle wines.

Kelk (Hol) cup/chalice.

Kelkierooi (S.Afr) the label for a red wine (Cabernet sauvignon, Cinsaut and Ruby cabernet blend) produced by the Bonnievale Cellar winery, Robertson, Western Cape.

Kelkiewit (S.Afr) the label for a white wine (Chenin blanc and Colombard blend) produced by the Bonnievale Cellar winery, Robertson, Western Cape.

K

Kella Distillers (I.O.M.) produce Glen Kella–a single malt white whiskey.

Kellar Lager (Eng) a light lager 1033 O.G. brewed by the Arkell Brewery in Swindon, Wiltshire.

Keller (Ger) cellar.

Kellerabfüllung (Ger) bottled in the Estate's own cellars.

Kellerabzug (Ger) lit: 'cellar proof', bottled at the cellar of estate/grower/shipper, etc.

Kelleramt Göttweig (Aus) a winery (38ha) based in the Kremstal region. (Add): Kirchengasse 14, 3511 Furth bei Göttweig. Grape varieties: Chardonnay, Grüner veltliner, Malvasier, Müller-Thurgau, Neuburger, Riesling, Zweigelt. Produces a range of wine styles.

Kellerberg (Aus) a vineyard site on the banks of the River Danube situated in the Wachau region, Niederösterreich.

Kellerberg (Ger) vineyard (Anb): Nahe. (Ber): Schloss Böckelheim. (Gro): Rosengarten. (Vil): Weinsheim.

Kellerbier (Ger) the term for an unfiltered lager.

Kellerbrau Lager (Eng) a lager beer 1034 O.G. brewed by the Charles Wells Brewery in Bedford.

Kellerei (Ger) cellars.

Kellerei Bozen (It) a co-operative winery based near Bozen in the Trentino-Alte-Adige (Südtirol). Grape varieties include: Lagrein. Label: St. Magdalena-Gries (rosé).

Keller Estate (USA) a winery based in the Sonoma Coast, Sonoma County, California. Grape variety: Pinot noir. Label: La Cruz Vineyard.

Kellergassen (Aus) lit: 'cellar streets', streets in the Austrian wine towns lined with wine cellars (especially in the Weinviertel region).

Kellerlokales (Aus) wine cellars/bars.

Kellermeister (Ger) cellar master/butler.

Kellerprinz Wines (S.Afr) produced by the SFW. Produce Amoroso, Grand Cru, Kellerprinz Stein, Late Harvest and Rosanne. *see* S.F.W.

Kellersberg (Ger) vineyard (Anb): Rheinhessen. (Ber): Nierstein. (Gro): Sankt Alban. (Vil): Gau-Bischofsheim.

Kellerwald (Ger) a natural spring mineral water from Bad Zwesten. Mineral contents (milligrammes per litre): Sodium 359mg/l, Calcium 173mg/l, Magnesium 79mg/l, Potassium 7mg/l, Chlorides 509mg/l, Fluorides 1mg/l.

Kellerwegfest (Ger) a Rheinhessen wine festival held in Guntersblum in August.

Kellerweingärten (Aus) a vineyard site on the banks of the River Danube situated in the Wachau region, Niederösterreich.

Kelley Creek Vineyard (USA) a small vineyard based in Lower Dry Creek, Sonoma County, California. 2.5ha. Grape variety: Zinfandel.

Kellner (Ger) barman/waiter/butler.

Kells Edge (Eng) a 5.5% alc by vol. cider from Gaymer. *See also* Fatboys, Ice Dragon.

Kellybrook Winery (Austr) a winery. (Add): Fulford Road, Wonga Park, Victoria 3115. 7ha. Grape varieties: Cabernet sauvignon, Chardonnay, Riesling and Shiraz. Also produces a fine cider.

Kelly's Lager (Eng) a 4.1% alc by vol. lager brewed to an Irish recipe from Federation Brewery, Tyneside.

Kelpie (Scot) a 4.4% alc by vol. ale brewed by Heather Ales Ltd., Lanarkshire.

Kelsale (Eng) a vineyard. (Add): Near Saxmundham, Suffolk. 1ha. Soil: clay, loam and flint. Grape varieties: Müller-Thurgau 66% and Seyval blanc 33%. Vinified at Pulham Market Vineyard.

Keltek Brewing C° Ltd (Eng) a brewery (established 1997). (Add): Unit 3, Restormel Ind Estate, Liddicoat Road, Lostwithiel, Cornwall PL22 0GH. Brews: 4K Mild 3.8% alc by vol., Golden Lance 3.8% alc by vol., King 5.1% alc by vol., Magik 4.2% alc by vol., Revenge 7% alc by vol.

Kelter (Ger) vineyard (Anb): Franken. (Ber): Maindreieck. (Gro): Rosstal. (Vil): Himmelstadt.

Kelter (Ger) wine-press.

Kelterberg (Ger) vineyard (Anb): Württemberg. (Ber): Württembergisch Unterland. (Gro): Schalkstein. (Vil): Kirchberg.

Kelterberg (Ger) vineyard (Anb): Württemberg. (Ber): Württembergisch Unterland. (Gro): Schalkstein. (Vil): Kleinaspach.

Kelterberg (Lux) a vineyard site in the village of Ehnen.

Keltern (Ger) to press the grapes.

Kelvin Sixty six [66] (Cktl) ¼ measure aquavit, ¼ measure Dubonnet, ¼ measure orange squash, ¼ measure Grand Marnier. Shake over ice, strain into a cocktail glass and add a cherry.

Kembach (Ger) village (Anb): Baden. (Ber): Badische Frankenland. (Gro): Tauberklinge. (Vin): Sonnenberg.

Kemblefield Estate Winery (N.Z) a winery (established 1993). (Add): Aorangi Road, RD 1, Hastings 44ha.

Kemelrain (Ger). Vineyard (Anb): Baden. (Ber): Badische Frankenland. (Gro): Tauberklinge. (Vil): Höhefeld.

Kemelrain (Ger) vineyard (Anb): Baden. (Ber): Badische Frankenland. (Gro): Tauberklinge. (Vil): Reicholzheim.

Kemptown (Eng) a 4% alc by vol. bitter beer brewed by the Kemptown Brewery, East Sussex.

Kemptown Brewery C° (Eng) a brewery (established 1985). (Add): 33 Upper St. James Street, Kemptown, Brighton, East Sussex BN2 1JN. Brews: Dragons Blood 5.2% alc by vol., Kemptown 4% alc by vol., Old Grumpy 5.2% alc by vol., Sid 5.2% alc by vol., Ye Old Trout 4.5% alc by vol. 'E'mail: ktb@keptownbreweryltd.co.uk

Kenbar (Ind) a natural spring mineral water (established 1991) from New Delhi.

Kenco Coffee (Eng) a range of fine coffees from the Kenco Coffee Company Ltd.

Kenco Coffee Company Ltd. (Eng) a noted coffee producing company based at Strathville Road, London SW18 4QY. *see* Kenco-Typhoo.

Kenco-Typhoo (Eng) a company formed by the merger of the Kenco Coffee C°. and Cadbury

Typhoo. (Add): Catering Services, P.O. Box 171, Franklin House, Bournville, Birmingham B30 2NA. Produces a vast range of fine coffee and tea products.

Kendall-Jackson (USA) a winery (established 1982) based in Lake County, California. Grape varieties: Cabernet sauvignon, Chardonnay, Merlot, Pinot noir, Riesling, Sauvignon blanc, Syrah, Zinfandel. Wines are sold under Vintners Reserve, Proprietors Reserve, Cambria labels. Part of Artisans & Estates. Website: http://www.kj.com

Kendermann (Ger) a winery based in Bingen-am-Rhein. (Add): Kendermann GmbH Weinkellerei, Postfach 1444, D-55384. Noted for dry Riesling wines.

Kenefick Ranch (USA) a red wine (Cabernet sauvignon) produced by the Behrens & Hitchcock winery, Napa Valley, California.

Ken Forrester Wines (S.Afr) a winery (established 1993) based in Stellenbosch, Western Cape. 33ha. Grape varieties: Chenin blanc, Grenache, Pinotage, Sauvignon blanc, Shiraz, Syrah. Label: FMC, Gypsy, Petit, T. Website: http://www.kenforresterwines.com

Kenn (Ger) village (Anb): Mosel-Saar-Ruwer. (Ber): Bernkastel. (Gro): Probstberg. (Vins): Held, Maximiner-Hofgarten.

Kennedy Wine (USA) a small winery based in Saratoga, Santa Clara, California. Grape variety: Cabernet sauvignon. Also known as the Kathryn Kennedy Wine.

Kentish Ales (Eng) a small Kent brewery re-established in 1984. Noted for cask-conditioned Royal Porter 1050 O.G. Royal Sovereign 1040 O.G. and Royal Pale 1035 O.G.

Kentish Gold (Eng) a 5% alc by vol. ale brewed by the Swale Brewery, Sittingbourne.

Kentish Gold Bitter (Eng) a cask-conditioned bitter 1035 O.G. brewed by the Ashford Brewery, Ashford, Kent.

Kentish Hills (Eng) a bottled spring water from Kent. Source is Scords Farm, Toys Hill. Still or carbonated.

Kentish Pride (Eng) a 3.8% alc by vol. cask ale brewed by the Swale Brewery, Sittingbourne.

Kentish Sovereign (Eng) a brand-name for wines produced by the Cherry Hill Vineyards, Nettleshead, Kent.

Kent's Best Invicta Ale (Eng) a 4.1% alc by vol. best bitter brewed by Shepherd Neame, Kent.

Kentucky [1] (USA) where Bourbon whiskey was originally made, now home to approximately 50% of all the Bourbon distilleries in the USA.

Kentucky [2] (USA) a wine-producing state (250ha planted–2006) based around towns of Lexington and Louisville. Was a major grape producer before Prohibition. Regions include: Bluegrass and Lexington. Soils: calcerous shale, clay and limestone. *see* Kentucky Grape and Wine Council.

Kentucky Black (USA) a lager and Bourbon whiskey mix.

Kentucky Cocktail (Cktl) ⅔ measure Bourbon whiskey, ⅓ measure pineapple juice. Shake over ice and strain into a cocktail glass.

Kentucky Coffee (USA) a coffee substitute made from the seeds of the Kentucky Coffee Tree. Botanical name is ***Gymnocladus dioica***. Produced the same way as for coffee beans.

Kentucky Colonel (Cktl) ¾ measure Bourbon whiskey, ¼ measure Bénédictine. Stir over ice, strain into a cocktail glass and top with twist of lemon peel.

Kentucky Gentleman Bittersweet (Cktl) 35mls (1½ fl.ozs) Kentucky Gentleman Bourbon whiskey, juice 1 orange, 2 dashes Angostura, ½ teaspoon powdered sugar. Shake over ice, strain and serve onto ice cubes in a stemmed glass.

Kentucky Grape and Wine Council (USA), a body set up in the state of Kentucky to develop its vineyards and wine production.

Kentucky River (USA) a Bourbon whiskey distillery based south-east of Frankfort in Kentucky.

Kentucky River Products Winery (USA) a small winery based near Frankfort, Kentucky. Produces wines mainly from French hybrid vines.

Kentucky Straight (USA) the brand-name for a Bourbon whiskey produced by the Medley Distillery, Kentucky.

Kentucky Straight Bourbon Whiskey (USA) the name given for any straight whiskey produced in Bourbon County, Kentucky.

Kentucky Sunset (Cktl) ⅗ measure Bourbon whiskey, ⅕ measure anisette, ⅕ measure Strega. Stir over ice, strain into a cocktail glass and add a twist of orange.

Kentucky Tavern (USA) a premium straight Bourbon whiskey 43% alc by vol. Produced by the Glenmore Distilleries C°. Louisville, Kentucky.

Kentucky Whiskey (USA) the name for a blend of straight whiskies that have been distilled in Kentucky.

Kentumi Cocktail (Cktl)(Non-alc) 25mls (⅕ gill) passion fruit syrup, 3 dashes lime juice, scoop vanilla ice cream. Blend well together in a blender. Pour into a large goblet, top with soda water and a cherry.

Kentwood Springs (USA) a natural spring mineral water from Atlanta, Georgia.

Kenwood (USA) a noted wine town, home of many wineries based in northern County, California.

Kenwood [Family] Vineyards (USA) a small winery based in Kenwood, Sonoma County, California. (Add): 9592 Sonoma Highway, P.O. Box 447 Kenwood California 95452. 8.5ha. Grape varieties: Cabernet sauvignon, Chardonnay, Chenin blanc, Johannisberg riesling, Pinot noir and Zinfandel. Produces varietal wines incl. Jack London. Website: http://www.kenwoodvineyards.com

Kenworth Vineyards (USA) a small winery based in Shenandoah Valley, Amador, California. Grape varieties: Cabernet sauvignon, Chardonnay and Zinfandel. Produce varietal wines.

Kenyan Coffee (Afr) some of the finest coffees, a coffee with a high acidity which is smooth and full flavoured arabica.

K

Kenyan Elephant Ears (Afr) a large grade of arabica coffee bean.

Kenyan Gold (Afr) a light-styled, spirit-based coffee liqueur.

Kenyan Teas (Afr) teas used mainly in blending.

Kenzingen (Ger) village (Anb): Baden. (Ber): Breisgau. (Gro): Burg Lichteneck. (Vins): Hummelberg, Roter Berg.

Keo (Cyp) the largest wine and brewing firm in the island. Produces fine wines, beers and spirits. Based in Limassol and Paphos. Labels include: Aphrodite, Alkion, Bellapais, Othello, Thisbe, Saint Panteleimon. Also produces a lager beer.

Keo Beer (Cyp) a pilsener-style beer (draught & bottled versions) brewed by Keo Ltd. of Limassol. 4.5% alc by vol.

Keoghan's Ale (Eng). 4.7% alc by vol. beer from the Federation Brewery, Tyneside.

Keopi (Kor) coffee.

Keopyung (S.Kor) a natural spring mineral water. Mineral contents (milligrammes per litre): Sodium 9.2mg/l, Calcium 21.5mg/l, Magnesium 3.8mg/l, Potassium 0.6mg/l, Fluorides 0.3mg/l.

Keosoe (Gre) the Central Union of Wine Producing Co-operatives of Greece. The union of wine co-operatives, 95% of all the co-ops in Greece are members.

Kephalonia (Gre) an Ionian island that is noted for Mavrodaphne and Robola wines.

Kephesia (Gre) a wine-producing district of Attica. Produces red and white wines.

Kephir (Rus) an alternative spelling of Kefir.

Keppoch (Austr) an area north of Coonawarra, South Australia. Is noted for Chardonnay and Pinot noir sparkling wines.

Kerah (Isr) ice.

Kerala (Ind) a tea-producing region of southern India.

Kerschbaum (Aus) a vineyard site on the banks of the River Danube in the Kremstal region.

Kerschbaum (Aus) a winery based in Horitschon, Mittel-Burgenland. (Add): Hauptstrasse 37, 7312 Horitschon. Grape varieties: Blaufränkisch, Cabernet sauvignon, Pinot blanc, Zweigelt.

Keringet (Afr) a natural spring mineral water from Molo, Keringet, Kenya. Mineral contents (milligrammes per litre): Sodium 34mg/l, Calcium 1.9mg/l, Magnesium 0.02mg/l, Bicarbonates 12.4mg/l, Chlorides 12.4mg/l, Sulphates 80mg/l, Fluorides 1.7mg/l, Nitrates 0.27mg/l.

Kermann (Fr) a herb liqueur both green (dry) and yellow (sweet) versions are produced. Produced by Cazanove 43% alc by vol.

Kern (USA) a wine district within the Great Central Valley of California. Produces sweet dessert wines.

Kernen [ortsteil Stetten i.R] (Ger) village (Anb): Württemberg. (Ber): Remstal-Stuttgart. (Gro): Sonnenbühl. (Vins): Mönchberg, Mönchhalde.

Kerner (Ger) a white grape variety used to replace the Riesling in Switzerland, a cross between the Trollinger and the Riesling, has a high sugar content.

Kerngeschmack (Ger) describes a white wine with a flavour of grape pips (left in contact with the must too long).

Kernig (Ger) firm wine.

Kernling (Ger) a red skinned grape with white flesh, a relative to the Kerner and Riesling.

Kernobstbranntwein (Ger) the collective name for fruit brandies based on apples or pears.

Kernow Noweth (Eng) a wine produced by Camel Valley Vineyard at Little Denby Farm, Nanstallon, near Bodmin. Bottled in early November as a 'nouveau-style' wine.

Kerry Cooler (Cktl) 40mls (⅓ gill) Irish whiskey, 20mls (⅙ gill) dry Sherry, 3 dashes gomme syrup, juice ¼ lemon. Shake well over ice, strain into an ice-filled collins glass, top with soda and a slice of lemon.

Kerry Spring (Ire) a still natural spring mineral water from Dingle, county Kerry. Mineral contents (milligrammes per litre): Sodium 23.9mg/l, Calcium 68.8mg/l, Magnesium 9.7mg/l, Potassium 2.2mg/l, Bicarbonates 228mg/l, Chlorides 49.9mg/l, Sulphates 10.8mg/l, Nitrates 14mg/l. pH 6.9

Kerstbier (Hol) a 10% alc by vol. bottle-conditioned Christmas beer brewed by De Gans Bier Brouwerij, Goes. Brewed with hop flowers, coriander, orange peel and grains of paradise.

Kerstmis (Bel) a 7.2% alc by vol. straw-coloured beer brewed especially for Christmas by Verhaeghe Brouwerij, Vichte.

Kertz (Ger) vineyard (Anb): Nahe. (Ber): Schloss Böckelheim. (Gro): Burgweg. (Vil): Niederhausen an der Nahe.

Kerzenheim (Ger) village (Anb): Pfalz. (Ber): Mittelhaardt-Deutsche Weinstrasse. (Gro): Schnepfenflug vom Kellertal. (Vin): Esper.

Kesan (Chi) a natural spring mineral water. Mineral contents (milligrammes per litre): Calcium 59.4mg/l, Magnesium 26.2mg/l, Bicarbonates 238mg/l, Silicates 34.6mg/l.

Kesselfeld (Ger) village (Anb): Württemberg. (Ber): Württembergisch Unterland. (Gro): Lindelberg. (Vin): Schwobajörgle.

Kessler (Fr) an A.C. Alsace Grand Cru vineyard in Guebwiller, Haut-Rhin 28.5ha.

Kessler (Ger) a large, noted producer of Deutscher Sekt.

Kessler (USA) the brand-name of a blended whiskey bottled by the Kessler Cº., Lawrenceburg, Dundalk, San Francisco 40% alc by vol.

Kestelberg (Ger) vineyard (Anb): Baden. (Ber): Ortenau. (Gro): Schloss Rodeck. (Vil): Weisenbach.

Kesten (Ger) village (Anb): Mosel-Saar-Ruwer. (Ber): Bernkastel. (Gro): Kurfürstlay. (Vins): Herrenberg, Paulinsberg, Paulinushofberger.

Kestenholz (Ger) the German name for the Alsace town of Chatenois.

Kestrel Lager (Scot) a lager beer 1032 O.G. brewed by the Younger Brewery (Scottish and Newcastle).

Kestrel Super Strength (Eng) a lager beer 1080–1088 O.G. brewed by the Scottish and Newcastle Breweries (Younger Brewery).

Ketel (Hol) kettle.

Ketel One Vodka (Hol) a 40% alc by vol. vodka produced from wheat, pot-distilled by the Nolet family in Schiedam.

Ketje (Bel) a top-fermented beer brewed by the Artois Brasserie in Louvain.

Kettle [1] (Eng) a vessel used for boiling water to make tea.

Kettle [2] (Eng) the vessel used for boiling the wort into which is added the hops, also known as the Copper.

Kettmeir (It) noted wine producers based in the Trentino-Alto Adige region. Produces dry white, light red and sparkling (cuve close) wines.

Kett's Rebellion (Eng) a 3.6% alc by vol. ale brewed by Woodeforde's Ltd., Norfolk.

Keuck (Ger) a noted liqueur distillery of Western Germany.

Keuka (USA) a region within the Finger Lakes, New York State.

Keukenhof Wines (S.Afr) a winery (65ha) based in Olifants River, Western Cape. Grape varieties: Cabernet sauvignon, Chardonnay, Chenin blanc, Colombard, Merlot, Sauvignon blanc.

Keulebuckel (Ger) vineyard (Anb): Baden. (Ber): Badische Bergstrasse/Kraichgau. (Gro): Hohenberg. (Vil): Dietlingen.

Keulebuckel (Ger) vineyard (Anb): Baden. (Ber): Badische Bergstrasse/Kraichgau. (Gro): Hohenberg. (Vil): Ellmendingen.

Keuper (Ger) a soil of mixed clay, chalk or gypsum found in Franken.

Keurfontein (S.Afr) the export label for a range of wines produced by the Viljoendrift wines winery, Robertson, Western Cape.

Kevedinka (Ser) a white grape variety grown in the regions of Subotica, Pescara and Vojvodina. Also spelt Kóvidinka, Dinka.

Kevin Arnold (S.Afr) the label for a red wine (Shiraz) produced by the Waterford Estate winery, Stellenbosch, Western Cape.

Keystone (Eng) used when dealing with cask beers. A wooden bung which has the centre partially bored through to enable the tap to be driven through the keystone into the cask to let the beer be drawn off.

Keystone (S.Afr) the label for a red wine (Cabernet sauvignon 91% and Merlot 9% blend) produced by the Kanu Wines winery, Stellenbosch, Western Cape.

Keystone Burgundy (Austr) the brand-label for the wines of the Tatachilla Vineyard.

K Frost (Eng) a limited edition cider from Matthew Clark Gaymer 8.4% alc by vol.

KGB (Cktl) equal quantities of Kahlúa, Galliano and Baileys.

Khaheti (Rus) the process of allowing grape skins to lie on the must for a full month before filtering.

Khal (Arab) vinegar.

Khalokhorio (Cyp) a major wine-producing village for commandaria (made from the Xynisteri grape).

Khamar (Isr) see Khemer.

Khan Krum (Bul) a D.G.O. area in the east region of Bulgaria. Noted for Gewürztraminer and Chardonnay.

Khan Tengri (Asia) a natural spring mineral water from Khan Tengri, Kazakhstan. Mineral contents (milligrammes per litre): Calcium 63mg/l, Bicarbonates 82mg/l. pH 8.1

Khanya (S.Afr) the label for an export range of wines produced by the Havana Hills winery, Philadelphia, Western Cape.

Khat (Arab) *Catha edulis* the leaves of a shrub which are brewed as a 'tea' which is drunk for its narcotic effect. Also known as African Tea, Arabian Tea, Cat, Kat, Qat, Quat.

Khatura Cooler (Cktl) ½ measure French vermouth, ½ measure Italian vermouth, ½ measure dry gin, 500mls (1 pint) soda water, 2 dashes Angostura. Stir gently with ice and serve in highball glasses.

Khemer (Isr) a white wine mentioned in the Bible. Also spelt Khamar.

Kheteteli (Rus) a white grape variety.

Khios (Gre) an island in the Aegean Islands in Eastern Greece. Produces mainly dessert wines.

Khledia (Afr) a large co-operative based in Tunisia. Owned by the UCCVT.

Khoday Breweries (Ind) a brewery group based in India. Brews: Lady Bird Bio Beer.

Khometz (Isr) a white wine mentioned in the Bible, described as being similar to vinegar in taste.

Khorasan (Iran) a noted wine region of northern Iran that produces a red wine of the same name from the Shiraz grape.

Khristianssand Brewery (Nor) a noted brewery based in Khristianssand, southern Norway.

Kia-Fey (Chi) the name for coffee in Cantonese.

Kiana (USA) the label for a red wine (pinot noir) produced by the Willakenzie Estate winery, Willamette Valley, Oregon.

Kian Dian Cong Lu (Chi) a Rémy Martin supervised wine farm in the Tianjin region near Beijing-Peking. Produces Dynasty (a dry white wine).

Kia-Ora (Eng) a brand of low-sugar squashes produced by Schweppes.

Kia-Ora (S.Afr) the label for a noble late harvest white wine (Chenin blanc) produced by the Kanu Wines winery, Stellenbosch, Western Cape.

Kibo Chagga (Afr) the finest coffee (arabica) produced in Tanzania on the slopes of Mount Kilimanjaro by the Chagga tribe. Has fine acidity and body. See also Kilimanjaro Coffee.

Kibowi (Hol) a kiwi fruit liqueur produced in Amsterdam 20% alc by vol.

Kick (Eng) a slang term given to some spirits with a high alcohol or fierce alcohol taste that 'hits' the stomach.

Kick (Eng) a small indent at the base of early glass bottles, as the bottles became more onion shaped so the 'kicks' became larger.

K

Kickelskopf (Ger) vineyard (Anb): Nahe. (Ber): Schloss Böckelheim. (Gro): Burgweg. (Vil): Traisen.

Kick Off (Eng) a seasonal ale brewed by Ridleys of Essex which is available each August.

Kid (Eng) a small wooden barrel used for spirits in the home in the eighteenth century.

Kid & Bard (Eng) a 3.5% alc by vol. ale brewed by the Weltons Brewery, West Sussex.

Kiddush (S.Afr) the label for a sweet red sacramental wine (Cinsaut, Shiraz and Ruby cabernet blend) wines produced by the Eshkol Kosher Winery, Wellington, Western Cape.

Kiddush (S.Afr) the label for a naturally sweet red sacramental wine (Cinsaut) produced by the Klein Draken winery, Paarl, Western Cape.

Kidman (Austr) a noted winery based in the Coonawarra district of South Australia.

Kidonitsa (Gre) lit: 'little quince', a local grape variety.

Kiechlinsbergen (Ger) village (Anb): Baden. (Ber): Kaiserstuhl-Tuniberg. (Gro): Vulkanfelsen. (Vins): Ölberg, Teufelsberg.

Kiedrich (Ger) village (Anb): Rheingau. (Ber): Johannisberg. (Gro): Heiligenstock. (Vils): Gräfenberg, Klosterberg, Sandgrub, Wasseros.

Kieler Brauerei am Alten Markt (Ger) a brewery. (Add): Alter Markt 9, Kiel D-24103. Brews beers and lagers. Website: http://www.kieler-brauerei.de

Kientzler [André] (Fr) an Alsace wine producer. (Add): 50 Route de Bergheim, 68150 Ribeauvillé.

Kierlinger (Aus) a winery based in the Wien region. (Add): Kahlenbergerstrasse 20, 1190 Wien. Grape varieties: Grüner veltliner, Müller-Thurgau, Pinot blanc, Riesling, Welschriesling, Zweigelt. Produces a range of wine styles and is a noted Heurige producer.

Kiernberg (Aus) a vineyard site on the banks of the River Danube situated in the Wachau region, Niederösterreich.

Kieselberg (Ger) vineyard (Anb): Nahe. (Ber): Schloss Böckelheim. (Gro): Burgweg. (Vil): Oberhausen an der Nahe.

Kieselberg (Ger) vineyard (Anb): Rheinhessen. (Ber): Bingen. (Gro): Sankt Rochuskapelle. (Vil): Biebelsheim.

Kieselberg (Ger) vineyard (Anb): Pfalz. (Ber): Mittelhaardt-Deutsche Weinstrasse. (Gro): Feuerberg. (Vil): Bobenheim am Berg.

Kieselberg (Ger) vineyard (Anb): Pfalz. (Ber): Mittelhaardt-Deutsche Weinstrasse. (Gro): Höllenpfad. (Vil): Kleinkarlbach.

Kieselberg (Ger) vineyard (Anb): Pfalz. (Ber): Mittelhaardt-Deutsche Weinstrasse. (Gro): Mariengarten. (Vil): Deidesheim.

Kieselberg (Ger) vineyard (Anb): Pfalz. (Ber): Mittelhaardt-Deutsche Weinstrasse. (Gro): Rosenbühl. (Vil): Erpolzheim.

Kieselguhr (Ger) a diatomaceous earth used for initial rough filtration of wines and beers. See also Bentonite, Montmorillonite.

Kiesling (Aus) a vineyard site based on the banks of the River Kamp situated in the Kamptal region.

Kievska (Ukr) a natural spring mineral water from Kiev.

Kijotschevaja Woda (Rus) a natural spring mineral water. Mineral contents (milligrammes per litre): Sodium 40-80mg/l, Calcium <20mg/l, Magnesium <15mg/l, Bicarbonates 100-200mg/l, Chlorides <80mg/l, Sulphates <25mg/l.

Kiko Masamune Saké (Jap) a popular brand of saké.

Kikusui (Jap) a term used to describe a sweet style saké. See also Sasaiwai.

Kilbeggan (Ire) an Irish whiskey distilled by Locke & C°., Kilbeggan Offaly. Produced a Vintage 1946 (39 dozen) bottled after 34 years in cask.

Kilbeggan (Ire) a blended double distilled whiskey from the Cooley Distillery in Dundalk.

Kilderkin (Eng) a beer barrel holding 18 gallons.

Kiliansberg (Ger) vineyard (Anb): Franken. (Ber): Steigerwald. (Gro): Schlossberg. (Vil): Grosslangheim.

Kilikanoon (Austr) a winery based in the Clare Valley and Barossa Valley, South Australia. Grape varieties: Cabernet sauvignon, Shiraz. Labels: Blocks Road, Oracle, Parable and Secret Places.

Kilimanjaro (Afr) a natural mineral water from Kenya.

Kilimanjaro (Afr) a natural spring mineral water from Tanzania. Mineral contents (milligrammes per litre): Sodium 15.5mg/l, Potassium 5.2mg/l, Chlorides 35.5mg/l, Fluorides 0.1mg/l.

Kilimanjaro Coffee (Afr) also known as Kibo Chagga, produced on the slopes of Mount Kilimanjaro in Tanzania by the Chagga tribe.

Kilimanjaro Lager (Afr) a full-flavoured lager beer brewed by the Tanzania Breweries Ltd. in Tanzania.

Kilkenny Irish Beer (Ire) a premium draught keg ale 5% alc by vol. from St. Francis Abbey Brewery, Kilkenny, Leinster. The oldest brewery (established 1710) in Ireland, brewed by Guinness, there is also a canned version.

Killawarra (Austr) a noted winery based in the Adelaide Hills, South Australia.

Killawarra Selection Chardonnay (Austr) a fine white wine from the Wynvale Winery, New South Wales.

Kill-Devil (Eng) the anglo-saxon name for aguardiente, is drawn from the distillation of sugar that is extracted from sugar cane after having left it to ferment.

Kill-Devil (W.Ind) one of the first names applied to rum in the British West Indies.

Killellan (Scot) a 3.7% alc by vol. ale brewed by the Houston Brewing C°., Renfrewshire.

Killer Bee (Eng) a 6% alc by vol. bottle conditioned beer made with honey from the Darwin Brewery (a micro-brewery) in Sunderland, Tyne and Wear.

Killer Bull (Eng) a 6% alc by vol. ale brewed by the Blanchfield Brewery, Essex.

Killian (Ire) George Killian's Irish Red Ale brewed by Pelford in France as Bière Rousse and by Coors in USA. Brewed under licence from the Letts Brewery.

Kiln (Eng) a building where germinating barley after malting is dried.

Kilned (Eng) denotes dried malt that has been dried in a kiln.

Kilning (Scot) the drying of the green malt (malted barley) for whisky production, dried over a peat fire to impart the smoky flavour (peet reek).

Kiló (It) a dark, inky red wine made from partially dried Cabernet sauvignon grapes by the Cantina Beato Bartolomeo co-operative, Breganze, Veneto.

Kilsern Distillers (Eng) a distillery based in Leicester. Produces Feeney's (an Irish cream liqueur) and their own brand spirits: Rostov Imperial Vodka, Marlborough London Dry Gin, Macintyre Blended Whisky, Gentilhomme (Le), Club 19, Raffles, Ron Briganti.

Kilzberg (Ger) vineyard (Anb): Rheingau. (Ber): Johannisberg. (Gro): Erntebringer. (Vil): Geisenheim.

Kimberley Ales (Eng) beers brewed by the Hardys and Hansons Brewery in Nottingham, Notts.

Kimberley Best Bitter (Eng) a 4.2% alc by vol. bitter beer brewed by Hardys and Hansons, Nottinghamshire.

Kimërt Bor (Hun) ordinary wine.

Kimmeridge Clay (Eng) the name for a bituminous clay first discovered around the village of Kimmeridge in Devon. Found in many areas i.e. Chablis (Burgundy) and Quincy (Loire).

Kina (Fr) a brand of French apéritif wine.

Kina [1] (Cktl) ¾ measure dry gin, ¼ measure Campari Reed Onion. Stir over ice and strain into a cocktail glass.

Kina [2] (Cktl) ½ measure Plymouth gin, ¼ measure Lillet, ¼ measure sweet vermouth. Shake over ice and strain into a cocktail glass.

Kina-Citron (Cktl) 60mls (½ gill) Kina, 20mls (⅙ gill) sirop de citron, soda water. Stir over ice and strain into a tall glass with ice.

Kinclaith (Scot) a single malt whisky distillery based on the outskirts of Glasgow, owned by Long John, a lowland malt 40% alc by vol.

Kindale Wines (N.Z) a winery. (Add): Falveys Road, Omaka Valley, RD 2, Blenheim, Marlborough. 14ha. Grape varieties: Chardonnay, Müller-Thurgau, Pinot noir. Label: Willowbrook.

Kindenheim (Ger) village (Anb): Pfalz. (Ber): Mittelhaardt-Deutsche Weinstrasse. (Gro): Grafenstück. (Vins): Burgweg, Katzenstein, Sonnenberg, Vogelsang.

Kinder Croft (Eng) a 4% alc by vol. ale brewed by the Edale Brewery C°., Derbyshire.

Kinder Downfall (Eng) a 5% alc by vol. ale brewed by the Edale Brewery C°., Derbyshire.

Kinder Right to Toam (Eng) a 3.9% alc by vol. bitter ale brewed by the Edale Brewery C°., Derbyshire.

Kinder Tresspass (Eng) a 4% alc by vol. ale brewed by the Edale Brewery C°., Derbyshire.

Kindilan (Austr) a '*nouveau*' wine produced by the Quelltaler Springvale Vineyards from Merlot and Shiraz grapes harvested in Clare Watervale, South Australia.

Kindl Brauerei (Ger) a famous brewery based in West Berlin which is noted for Weiss Bier.

Kindzma-Aruli (Rus) the alternative spelling of Kindzmaraouli.

Kindzmaraouli (Geo) a red grape variety grown in Georgia to produce red dessert wines. *See also* Kindzma-Aruli.

King (Eng) a 5.1% alc by vol. ale brewed by the Keltek Brewing C°. Ltd., Cornwall.

King Alfonse (Cktl) ¾ measure Kahlúa, ¼ measure cream, float cream on top of Kahlúa in a liqueur glass.

King Alfred Strong Best Bitter (Eng) a 3.8% alc by vol. strong best bitter ale from the Hampshire Brewery, Andover.

King and Barnes Brewery (Eng) a brewery. (Add): Horsham Brewery, 18 Bishopric, Horsham, West Sussex. Noted for cask-conditioned Sussex Mild 1034 O.G. Draught Festive 1050 O.G. Sussex Bitter 1034 O.G. J.K. Stout 1034 O.G. and Golding 1075 O.G. Broadwood Cream 4.2% alc by vol. Corn Beer 6.5% alc by vol. Harvest Ale 4.5% alc by vol. Oatmeal Stout 4.5% alc by vol. Rye Beer 5.5% alc by vol. Challenger Ale 4.7% alc by vol. Summer Ale 3.8% alc by vol. Sussex Best 3.5% alc by vol. Valentine Ale 4% alc by vol. Wheat Mash 4.3% alc by vol. Old Porter 5.5% alc by vol.

King Arthur (USA) a major brand of dry gin produced by Seagram.

King Barley (Can) a 6 year old pot still whisky from Tesetice, Moravia.

King Billy (Eng) a 3.6% alc by vol. ale brewed by the Cropton Brewery, Pickering, North Yorkshire.

King Cobra (Eng) a double-fermented, naturally carbonated, lager beer 8% alc by vol. (bottled in Champagne-style bottle with cork and cage) brewed by Cobra Beer Ltd., London.

King Cole (Cktl) 25mls (⅕ gill) Bourbon whiskey, 2 dashes gomme syrup, 20mls (⅙ gill) orange juice, slice of pineapple. Blend altogether with a scoop of ice and pour into a flute glass.

Kingdom Bitter (Eng) a 4.5% alc by vol. bitter beer brewed by the Dunn Plowman Brewery, Herefordshire.

King Duncan (Eng) the brand-name of a British wine and Scotch whisky drink.

King Edward The First (Scot) a blended Scotch whisky from the Scotch Whisky Association. Distilled by William Lawson.

King Estate (USA) a 14.5ha. winery at Lorane Valley, Oregon. Grape varieties: Chardonnay, Pinot gris, Pinot noir.

King Fergus Mac (Eng) the brand-name of a ginger wine and Scotch whisky drink.

Kingfisher Lager (Ind) a 4.8% alc by vol. bottled lager beer brewed by the United Breweries in Bangalore.

Kingfisher Stout (Ind) a bitter stout 1046 O.G. brewed by the United Breweries in Bangalore.

King George (Cktl) ¼ measure Plymouth gin, ¼ measure sweet vermouth, ¼ measure Bénédictine, ¼ measure Caperatif and dash of pastis. Shake over ice and strain into a cocktail glass.

K

King George Fourth (Scot) a blended Scotch whisky produced by the Distillers Agency Ltd. (Part of the DCL group).

King George Fourth Cocktail (Cktl) ¼ measure gin, ¼ measure Scotch whisky, ¼ measure Cointreau, ¼ measure lemon juice. Shake over ice and strain into a cocktail glass.

Kinghorn (Eng) a 5% alc by vol. ale from Tiger Top Brewery in Ossett (a micro-brewery).

King Keg Bitter (Eng) a keg bitter 1038 O.G. brewed by the Greene King Brewery in East Anglia.

King of Alsace (Fr) an accolade given to the Riesling grape.

King Offa (Eng) a cider brandy laid down in oak for 3 years, produced by Bulmers in Hereford.

King of Wines (Eng) a title sometimes used for Châteauneuf-du-Pape as the area was the founder of the modern A.O.C. system. *see* Baron le Roy and Château Fortia.

King Peter (Cktl) ⅓ measure Peter Heering, ⅓ measure tonic water, dash lemon juice. Build into an ice-filled highball glass.

Kingpin Mild (Eng) a dark keg mild ale brewed by Ansells Brewery.

Kings (USA) a wine district within the Great Central Valley of California. Produces sweet dessert wines.

Kings Acre (Eng) the brand-name of a premium cider produced by the Gloucestershire Cider Company (owned by Bulmers).

King's Ale (Eng) a strong bottled ale 1060 O.G. brewed by Matthew Brown of Blackburn, Lancashire.

King's Arms (Eng) a home-brew public house in Bishop Auckland, County Durham. Noted for cask-conditioned Weardale Bitter 1038 O.G.

Kings County (USA) a small wine-producing county in San Joaquin (between Tular and Fresno counties), California.

King's Court (Eng) a range of ales produced by Greene King. Includes Mad Judge (infused with cranberry juice).

Kings Creek Vineyard (Austr) a vineyard (established 1981). (Add): 237 Myers Road, Bittern, Victoria. Grape varieties: Cabernet sauvignon, Pinot noir, Chardonnay.

Kings Daiquiri (Cktl) 35mls (1½ fl.ozs) white rum, 10mls (½ fl.oz) parfait amour, 10mls (½ fl.oz) lime juice, ¼ teaspoon sugar, 1 dash egg white. Blend together with crushed ice and pour into a Champagne saucer.

Kingsdown Ale (Eng) a draught and bottled bitter 5% alc by vol (1050 O.G) brewed by Arkells in Stratton St. Margaret, near Swindon, Wiltshire.

King's Ginger Liqueur [The] (Hol) a liqueur produced from the root of the ginger plant. Produced in Amsterdam for Berry Bros. and Rudd of London 40% alc by vol.

Kings Green Vineyard (Eng) a vineyard based at Bouton, Gillingham, Dorset. 2.3ha. Grape varieties: Chardonnay, Gamay noir, Gewürztraminer, Müller-Thurgau, Pinot noir and Zweigeltrebe.

Kings Head (Eng) the name used by Vine Products Ltd. for their Fortified British Wine.

Kingshill Forest Glade (Scot) a slightly acidic natural spring mineral water. (Add): Kingshill Plantation, Brown Farm, Newmains, Lanarkshire. Mineral contents (milligrammes per litre): Sodium 9.9mg/l, Calcium 9.9mg/l, Magnesium 3.8mg/l, Bicarbonates 3.7mg/l, Chlorides 35.5mg/l, Fluorides <1.5mg/l, Nitrates <0.1mg/l. pH 4.6

Kingsland Wines & Spirits (Eng) a distillery and wine merchant (established 1965). (Add): The Winery, Fairhills Road, Irlam, Manchester, Greater Manchester M44 6BD. Produces a range of spirits. Website: http://www.kingsland-wines.com 'E'mail: info@kingsland-wines.com

Kingsley (Austr) a winery (established 1983). (Add): 50 Bancroft Street, Portland, Victoria. Grape varieties: Rhine riesling, Cabernet sauvignon.

Kings Old Ale (Eng) a 4.5% alc by vol. ale brewed by King WJ & C°., West Sussex.

King Solomon (S.Afr) the label for a range of white (Chardonnay/Chenin blanc) wines produced by the Eshkol Kosher Winery, Wellington, Western Cape.

King's Ransom (Scot) a 12 year old blended Scotch whisky produced by William Whiteley & C°., Pitlochry. 43% alc by vol (now owned by Pernod Ricard).

Kings River (S.Afr) the label for a white wine (Chardonnay) produced by the Robertson Co-operative Winery, Robertson, Western Cape.

King's Royal (Scot) a blended Scotch whisky produced by Clyde Distillers of Glasgow 43% alc by vol.

King's Screw (Eng) a patented 'rack and pinion' corkscrew produced in the eighteenth century.

Kings Shillin (Eng) a 4.5% alc by vol. ale brewed by the George Wright Brewing C°., Merseyside.

Kings Shilling (Eng) a 3.8% alc by vol. ale brewed by the Cannon Royall Brewery Ltd., Worcestershire.

Kingston (Fr) a 7.9% alc by vol. bottom-fermented, special beer brewed by the Fischer Brasserie, Schiltigheim, aromatised with rum.

Kingston (Port) vintage Port shippers. Vintages: 1922, 1924, 1927.

Kingston Black (Eng) a variety of cider apple of good quality, high in sugar and low in acidity.

Kingston Black (Eng) a blend of cider brandy and partly fermented cider made from Kingston Black apples by a Somerset farm. *See also* Stoke Red.

Kingston Black (Eng) a 7.2% alc by vol. smokey black cider produced by Sheppy's at Bradford-on-Tone, Somerset.

Kingston Cocktail [1] (Cktl) 1 measure Jamaican rum, ¼ measure kümmel, ¼ measure orange juice, dash pimento liqueur. Shake over ice and strain into a cocktail glass.

Kingston Cocktail [2] (Cktl) ⅓ measure Bacardi rum, ⅓ measure Cointreau, ⅙ measure crème de banane, ⅙ measure pineapple juice, dash blue Curaçao. Shake over ice, strain into a cocktail glass and top with a slice of lime.

Kingston Estate (Austr) a winery based in South Eastern Australia. Grape varieties include:

K

Cabernet sauvignon, Chardonnay, Petit Verdot, Syrah, Verdelho.

Kingston Topaz (Eng) a 4.2% alc by vol. ale brewed by the Newby Wyke Brewery, Lincolnshire.

King's Vat (Scot) a blended Scotch whisky produced by Sandeman & Son, Dundee, Perthshire. 40% alc by vol.

Kings Winter Ale (Eng) made by blending a dry light beer with St. Edmund and Five X. 1057–1063 O.G. Brewed by Greene King.

Kingswood Ale (Eng) a light coloured bitter 1035 O.G. from Clarks of Wakefield. Brewed to mark the Merrie City Beer Festival.

King's Wood Bitter (Eng) a keg bitter 1039 O.G. brewed by the New Forest Brewery in Hampshire.

King [W.J] & C° (Eng) a brewery (established 2001). (Add): 3–5 Jubilee Estate, Horsham, West Sussex RH13 5SU. Brews: Horsham Best bitter 3.8% alc by vol., Kings Old Ale 4.5% alc by vol., Red River 4.8% alc by vol., Summer Ale 4% alc by vol. Website: http://www.kingfamilybrewers.co.uk 'E'mail: sales@kingfamilybrewers.co.uk

Kinheim (Ger) village (Anb): Mosel-Saar-Ruwer. (Ber): Bernkastel. (Gro): Schwarzlay. (Vins): Hubertuslay, Rosenberg.

Kinik (Tur) a sparkling natural spring mineral water. Mineral contents (milligrammes per litre): Sodium 1216.17mg/l, Calcium 184.36mg/l, Magnesium 126.42mg/l, Bicarbonates 2940.2mg/l, Chlorides 42.6mg/l, Sulphates 87.6mg/l, Nitrates 2.23mg/l, Aluminium 1.045mg/l. pH 6.29

Kinine (Hol) quinine.

Kininvie (Scot) a highland malt whisky distillery owned by William Grant & Sons.

Kinizsi (Hun) a lager-style beer 3.5% alc by vol.

Kinley (Ind) a natural spring mineral water.

Kinnie (Euro) a branded soft drink produced on the island of Malta.

Kinnie Winnie (Cktl) 25mls (1 fl.oz) each of brandy, Grand Marnier, orange juice. Pour into a ice-filled highball glass and top with Kinnie.

Kinross Ale (Eng) a bottled Scotch ale 1064 O.G. brewed for export by the Paines Brewery in Cambridgeshire.

Kinsale Brewing Company (Ire) a brewery. (Add): The Glen, Kinsale, Cork, County Cork. Brews a variety of beers, stout and lager. Website: http://www.kinsalebrewing.com 'E'mail: info@kinsalebrewing.com

Kintyre (Scot) a peninsular on the west coast of Scotland where the Campbeltown whiskies are produced, also called the Mull of Kintyre.

Kinver Brewery (Eng) a brewery (established 2004). (Add): Unit 2, Fairfield Drive, Kinver, Stourbridge, West Midlands DY7 6EW. Brews: Caveman 5% alc by vol., Kinver Edge 4.2% alc by vol., Over the Edge 7.6% alc by vol. Website: http://www.kinverbrewery.co.uk 'E'mail: info@kinverbrewery.co.uk

Kinver Edge (Eng) a 4.2% alc by vol. ale brewed by the Kinver Brewery, West Midlands.

Kinver House (Eng) a vineyard (established 1973) based at Dunsley House, Kinver, Worcestershire. 1ha. Grape varieties: Auxerrois, Bacchus, Madeleine angevine, Müller-Thurgau, Pinot noir and others.

Kinzigtäler (Ger) vineyard (Anb): Baden. (Ber): Ortenau. (Gro): Fürsteneck. (Vil): Berghaupten.

Kinzigtäler (Ger) vineyard (Anb): Baden. (Ber): Ortenau. (Gro): Fürsteneck. (Vil): Bermersbach.

Kinzigtäler (Ger) vineyard (Anb): Baden. (Ber): Ortenau. (Gro): Fürsteneck. (Vil): Diersburg.

Kinzigtäler (Ger) vineyard (Anb): Baden. (Ber): Ortenau. (Gro): Fürsteneck. (Vil): Gengenbach.

Kinzigtäler (Ger) vineyard (Anb): Baden. (Ber): Ortenau. (Gro): Fürsteneck. (Vil): Hofweier.

Kinzigtäler (Ger) vineyard (Anb): Baden. (Ber): Ortenau. (Gro): Fürsteneck. (Vil): Niederschopfheim.

Kinzigtäler (Ger) vineyard (Anb): Baden. (Ber): Ortenau. (Gro): Fürsteneck. (Vil): Ohlsbach.

Kinzigtäler (Ger) vineyard (Anb): Baden. (Ber): Ortenau. (Gro): Fürsteneck. (Vil): Reichenbach.

Kinzigtäler (Ger) vineyard (Anb): Baden. (Ber): Ortenau. (Gro): Fürsteneck. (Vil): Zunsweier.

Kiola (It) producers of Moscato d'Asti based in the Piemonte region,

Kiona Vineyards Winery (USA) a winery based at West Richland, Yakima Valley, Washington. Varietal wines include Cabernet sauvignon, Riesling, Red lemberger.

Kippe (Hol) the eighteenth century name for a common ale house.

Kippenhausen (Ger) village (Anb): Baden. (Ber): Bodensee. (Gro): Sonnenufer. (Vin): Burgstall.

Kippenheim (Ger) village (Anb): Baden. (Ber): Breisgau. (Gro): Schutterlindenberg. (Vin): Haselstaude.

Kipperlé (Fr) the alternative spelling for the white Knipperlé grape.

Kir (Fr) a Burgundian apéritif of dry white Burgundy wine (Aligoté) and a dash of cassis. Named after Canon Kir the Mayor of Dijon. See also Kir Royale, Cardinal and Communiste.

Kiraathane (Tur) a coffee house/café (eastern-style).

Király Furmint (Hun) an approved clone of the Furmint grape. See also Nemes Furmint.

Királyleányka (Hun) the local name for Feteasca reagala grape grown in Romania.

Királyudvar (Hun) a wine estate based in Tarcal, Tokaji. Owns 100ha. of top vineyard sites.

Kirchardt [ortsteil Berwangen] (Ger) village (Anb): Baden. (Ber): Badische Bergstrasse/Kraichgau. (Gro): Stiftsberg. (Vin): Vogelsang.

Kirchberg (Ger) lit: 'church hill', a popular name for vineyards in Germany. No less than 49 have the name plus a grosslage and 2 villages.

Kirchberg (Ger) grosslage (Anb): Franken. (Ber): Maindreieck. (Vils): Astheim, Escherndorf, Fahr, Köhler, Krautheim, Neuses, Neusetz, Nordheim, Obereisenheim, Obervolkach, Sommerach, Stammheim, Untereisenheim, Volkach, Wipfeld.

Kirchberg (Ger) village (Anb): Baden. (Ber): Bodensee. see Salem.

K

Kirchberg (Ger) village (Anb): Württemberg. (Ber): Württembergisch Unterland. (Gro): Schalkstein. (Vin): Kelterberg.

Kirchberg (Ger) vineyard (Anb): Baden. (Ber): Badische Bergstrasse/Kraichgau. (Gro): Mannaberg. (Vil): Kraichtal (stadtteil Oberöwisheim, stadtteil Unteröwisheim).

Kirchberg (Ger) vineyard (Anb): Baden. (Ber): Badische Frankenland. (Gro): Tauberklinge. (Vil): Beckstein.

Kirchberg (Ger) vineyard (Anb): Baden. (Ber): Badische Frankenland. (Gro): Tauberklinge. (Vil): Königheim.

Kirchberg (Ger) vineyard (Anb): Baden. (Ber): Badische Frankenland. (Gro): Tauberklinge. (Vil): Königshofen.

Kirchberg (Ger) vineyard (Anb): Baden. (Ber): Breisgau. (Gro): Schutterlindenberg. (Vil): Ettenheim (ortsteil Wallburg).

Kirchberg (Ger) vineyard (Anb): Baden. (Ber): Breisgau. (Gro): Schutterlindenberg. (Vil): Münchweiler.

Kirchberg (Ger) vineyard (Anb): Baden. (Ber): Breisgau. (Gro): Schutterlindenberg. (Vil): Schmieheim.

Kirchberg (Ger) vineyard (Anb): Baden. (Ber): Kaiserstuhl-Tuniberg. (Gro): Attilafelsen. (Vil): Gottenheim.

Kirchberg (Ger) vineyard (Anb): Baden. (Ber): Kaiserstuhl-Tuniberg. (Gro): Vulkanfelsen. (Vil): Oberrotweil.

Kirchberg (Ger) vineyard (Anb): Baden. (Ber): Kaiserstuhl-Tuniberg. (Gro): Vulkanfelsen. (Vil): Schelingen.

Kirchberg (Ger) vineyard (Anb): Baden. (Ber): Markgräflerland. (Gro): Burg Neuenfels. (Vil): Lipburg.

Kirchberg (Ger) vineyard (Anb): Baden. (Ber): Markgräflerland. (Gro): Lorettoberg. (Vil): Kirchhofen.

Kirchberg (Ger) vineyard (Anb): Baden. (Ber): Markgräflerland. (Gro): Vogtei Rötteln. (Vil): Efringen-Kirchen.

Kirchberg (Ger) vineyard (Anb): Baden. (Ber): Markgräflerland. (Gro): Vogtei Rötteln. (Vil): Huttingen.

Kirchberg (Ger) vineyard (Anb): Baden. (Ber): Markgräflerland. (Gro): Vogtei Rötteln. (Vil): Istein.

Kirchberg (Ger) vineyard (Anb): Franken. (Ber): Maindreieck. (Gro): Not yet assigned. (Vil): Würzberg.

Kirchberg (Ger) vineyard (Anb): Franken. (Ber): Steigerwald. (Gro): Herrenberg. (Vil): Castell.

Kirchberg (Ger) vineyard (Anb): Franken. (Ber): Steigerwald. (Gro): Schild. (Vil): Castell.

Kirchberg (Ger) vineyard (Anb): Hessische Bergstrasse. (Ber): Starkenburg. (Gro): Wolfsmagen. (Vil): Bensheim.

Kirchberg (Ger) vineyard (Anb): Mosel-Saar-Ruwer. (Ber): Bernkastel. (Gro): Kurfürstlay. (Vil): Burgen.

Kirchberg (Ger) vineyard (Anb): Mosel-Saar-Ruwer. (Ber): Bernkastel. (Gro): Kurfürstlay. (Vil): Maring-Noviand.

Kirchberg (Ger) vineyard (Anb): Mosel-Saar-Ruwer. (Ber): Bernkastel. (Gro): Kurfürstlay. (Vil): Veldenz.

Kirchberg (Ger) vineyard (Anb): Mosel-Saar-Ruwer. (Ber): Saar-Ruwer. (Gro): Scharzberg. (Vil): Könen.

Kirchberg (Ger) vineyard (Anb): Mosel-Saar-Ruwer. (Ber): Zell/Mosel. (Gro): Goldbäumchen. (Vil): Moselkern.

Kirchberg (Ger) vineyard (Anb): Mosel-Saar-Ruwer. (Ber): Zell/Mosel. (Gro): Weinhex. (Vil): Hatzenport.

Kirchberg (Ger) vineyard (Anb): Nahe. (Ber): Schloss Böckelheim. (Gro): Burgweg. (Vil): Waldböckelheim.

Kirchberg (Ger) vineyard (Anb): Rheinhessen. (Ber): Bingen. (Gro): Rheingrafenstein. (Vil): Eckelsheim.

Kirchberg (Ger) vineyard (Anb): Rheinhessen. (Ber): Bingen. (Gro): Rheingrafenstein. (Vil): Frei-Laubersheim.

Kirchberg (Ger) vineyard (Anb): Rheinhessen. (Ber): Bingen. (Gro): Rheingrafenstein. (Vil): Hackenheim.

Kirchberg (Ger) vineyard (Anb): Rheinhessen. (Ber): Bingen. (Gro): Sankt Rochuskapelle. (Vil): Bingen.

Kirchberg (Ger) vineyard (Anb): Rheinhessen. (Ber): Nierstein. (Gro): Domherr. (Vil): Gabsheim.

Kirchberg (Ger) vineyard (Anb): Rheinhessen. (Ber): Nierstein. (Gro): Domherr. (Vil): Udenheim.

Kirchberg (Ger) vineyard (Anb): Rheinhessen. (Ber): Wonnegau. (Gro): Pilgerpfad. (Vil): Osthofen.

Kirchberg (Ger) vineyard (Anb): Pfalz. (Ber): Mittelhaardt-Deutsche Weinstrasse. (Gro): Rebstöckel. (Vil): Hambach.

Kirchberg (Ger) vineyard (Anb): Pfalz. (Ber): Südliche Weinstrasse. (Gro): Kloster Liebfrauenberg. (Vil): Barbelroth.

Kirchberg (Ger) vineyard (Anb): Pfalz. (Ber): Südliche Weinstrasse. (Gro): Kloster Liebfrauenberg. (Vil): Gleiszellen-Gleishorbach.

Kirchberg (Ger) vineyard (Anb): Pfalz. (Ber): Südliche Weinstrasse. (Gro): Königsgarten. (Vil): Albersweiler.

Kirchberg (Ger) vineyard (Anb): Pfalz. (Ber): Südliche Weinstrasse. (Gro): Schloss Ludwigshöhe. (Vil): Edenkoben.

Kirchberg (Ger) vineyard (Anb): Pfalz. (Ber): Südliche Weinstrasse. (Gro): Schloss Ludwigshöhe. (Vil): St. Martin.

Kirchberg (Ger) vineyard (Anb): Pfalz. (Ber): Südliche Weinstrasse. (Gro): Trappenberg. (Vil): Gross-und Kleinfischlingen.

Kirchberg (Ger) vineyard (Anb): Württemberg. (Ber): Remstal-Stuttgart. (Gro): Weinsteige. (Vil): Esslingen.

Kirchberg (Ger) vineyard (Anb): Württemberg. (Ber): Remstal-Stuttgart. (Gro): Weinsteige. (Vil): Stuttgart (ortsteil Obertürkheim).

K

Kirchberg (Ger) vineyard (Anb): Württemberg. (Ber): Württembergisch Unterland. (Gro): Stromberg. (Vil): Bönnigheim.

Kirchberg (Ger) vineyard (Anb): Württemberg. (Ber): Württembergisch Unterland. (Gro): Stromberg. (Vil): Freudental.

Kirchberg (Ger) vineyard (Anb): Württemberg. (Ber): Württembergisch Unterland. (Gro): Stromberg. (Vil): Hohenhaslach.

Kirchberg (Ger) vineyard (Anb): Württemberg. (Ber): Württembergisch Unterland. (Gro): Stromberg. (Vil): Hohenstein.

Kirchberg (Ger) vineyard (Anb): Württemberg. (Ber): Württembergisch Unterland. (Gro): Stromberg. (Vil): Kirchheim.

Kirchberg (Ger) vineyard (Anb): Württemberg. (Ber): Württembergisch Unterland. (Gro): Stromberg. (Vil): Kleinsachsenheim.

Kirchberg (Ger) vineyard (Anb): Württemberg. (Ber): Württembergisch Unterland. (Gro): Stromberg. (Vil): Riet.

Kirchberg de Barr (Fr) an A.C. Alsace Grand Cru vineyard at Barr, Bas-Rhin 40ha.

Kirchberg de Ribeauvillé (Fr) an A.C. Alsace Grand Cru vineyard at Ribeauvillé, Haut-Rhin 11.4ha.

Kirche (Ger) church.

Kirchengrund (Aus) a vineyard site based on the banks of the River Kamp situated in the Kamptal region.

Kirchenpfad (Ger) vineyard (Anb): Rheingau. (Ber): Johannisberg. (Gro): Burgweg. (Vil): Rüdesheim.

Kirchenstück (Ger) vineyard (Anb): Rheingau. (Ber): Johannisberg. (Gro): Daubhaus. (Vil): Hochheim.

Kirchenstück (Ger) vineyard (Anb): Rheinhessen. (Ber): Bingen. (Gro): Adelberg. (Vil): Bornheim.

Kirchenstück (Ger) vineyard (Anb): Rheinhessen. (Ber): Bingen. (Gro): Kaiserpfalz. (Vil): Ingelheim.

Kirchenstück (Ger) vineyard (Anb): Rheinhessen. (Ber): Nierstein. (Gro): Sankt Alban. (Vil): Mainz.

Kirchenstück (Ger) vineyard (Anb): Rheinhessen. (Ber): Wonnegau. (Gro): Domblick. (Vil): Hohen-Sülzen.

Kirchenstück (Ger) vineyard (Anb): Rheinhessen. (Ber): Wonnegau. (Gro): Sybillenstein. (Vil): Weinheim.

Kirchenstück (Ger) vineyard (Anb): Pfalz. (Ber): Mittelhaardt-Deutsche Weinstrasse. (Gro): Hofstück. (Vil): Ellerstedt.

Kirchenstück (Ger) vineyard (Anb): Pfalz. (Ber): Mittelhaardt-Deutsche Weinstrasse. (Gro): Kobnert. (Vil): Herxheim/Berg.

Kirchenstück (Ger) vineyard (Anb): Pfalz. (Ber): Mittelhaardt-Deutsche Weinstrasse. (Gro): Kobnert. (Vil): Leistadt.

Kirchenstück (Ger) vineyard (Anb): Pfalz. (Ber): Mittelhaardt-Deutsche Weinstrasse. (Gro): Mariengarten. (Vil): Forst.

Kirchenstück (Ger) vineyard (Anb): Pfalz. (Ber): Mittelhaardt-Deutsche Weinstrasse. (Gro): Saumagen. (Vil): Kallstadt.

Kirchenstück (Ger) vineyard (Anb): Pfalz. (Ber): Sudliche Weinstrasse. (Gro): Bischofskreuz. (Vil): Nussdorf.

Kirchenstück (Ger) vineyard (Anb): Pfalz. (Ber): Südliche Weinstrasse. (Gro): Mandelhöhe. (Vil): Maikammer.

Kirchenstück (Ger) vineyard (Anb): Pfalz. (Ber): Südliche Weinstrasse. (Gro): Ordensgut. (Vil): Hainfeld.

Kirchenstück (Ger) a vineyard within the village of Hochheim, 15.1ha. (84.8%) of which is proposed to be classified as Erstes Gewächs.

Kirchenweinberg (Ger) grosslage (Anb): Württemberg. (Ber): Württembergisch Unterland. (Vils): Flein, Heilbronn, Ilsfeld (ortsteil Schozach), Lauffen, Neckarwestheim, Talheim, Untergruppenbach.

Kirchgärtchen (Ger) vineyard (Anb): Rheinhessen. (Ber): Bingen. (Gro): Sankt Rochuskapelle. (Vil): Welgesheim.

Kirchgarten (Ger) vineyard (Anb): Pfalz. (Ber): Mittelhaardt-Deutsche Weinstrasse. (Gro): Schwarzerde. (Vil): Laumersheim.

Kirchhalde (Ger) vineyard (Anb): Baden. (Ber): Bodensee. (Gro): Sonnenufer. (Vil): Oberruhldingen.

Kirchheim (Ger) village (Anb): Pfalz. (Ber): Mittelhaardt-Deutsche Weinstrasse. (Gro): Schwarzerde. (Vins): Geisskopf, Kreuz, Römerstrasse, Steinacker.

Kirchheim (Ger) village (Anb): Württemberg. (Ber): Württembergisch Unterland. (Gro): Stromberg. (Vin): Kirchberg.

Kirchheimbolanden (Ger) village (Anb): Pfalz. (Ber): Mittelhaardt-Deutsche Weinstrasse. (Gro): Schnepfenflug vom Kellertal. (Vin): Schlossgarten.

Kirchhofen (Ger) village (Anb): Baden. (Ber): Markgräflerland. (Gro): Lorettoberg. (Vins): Batzenberg, Höllhagen, Kirchberg.

Kirchhöh (Ger) vineyard (Anb): Pfalz. (Ber): Südliche Weinstrasse. (Gro): Guttenberg. (Vil): Dierbach.

Kirchholz (Aus) a vineyard site based on the banks of the River Kamp situated in the Kamptal region.

Kirchlay (Ger) vineyard (Anb): Mosel-Saar-Ruwer. (Ber): Bernkastel. (Gro): Nacktarsch. (Vil): Kröv.

Kirchlay (Ger) vineyard (Anb): Mosel-Saar-Ruwer. (Ber): Bernkastel. (Gro): Kurfürstlay. (Vil): Osann-Monzel.

Kirchlay (Ger) vineyard (Anb): Mosel-Saar-Ruwer. (Ber): Zell/Mosel. (Gro): Goldbäumchen. (Vil): Ernst.

Kirchmayer (Aus) a noted winery based in the Kampstal region. (Add): 3351 Weistrach 123. Grape varieties: Chardonnay, Grüner veltliner, Merlot, Pinot blanc, Pinot noir, Riesling, Sauvignon blanc, Zweigelt. Also owns vineyards in a number of Austrian regions including: Burgenland, Kremstal, Wachau and Weinviertel. 'E'mail: kirchmayer@wein-erlebnis.at

Kirchplatte (Ger) vineyard (Anb): Rheinhessen. (Ber): Nierstein. (Gro): Spiegelberg. (Vil): Nierstein.

K

Kirchspiel (Ger) vineyard (Anb): Rheinhessen. (Ber): Wonnegau. (Gro): Bergkloster. (Vil): Westhofen.

Kirchtürmchen (Ger) vineyard (Anb): Ahr. (Ber): Walporzheim/Ahrtal. (Gro): Klosterberg. (Vil): Bad Neuenahr.

Kirchweg (Aus) a vineyard site on the banks of the River Danube situated in the Wachau region, Niederösterreich.

Kirchweih (Ger) a bier of 13.9° brewed specially for the Bergkirchweih festival.

Kirchweinberg (Ger) vineyard (Anb): Baden. (Ber): Badische Bergstrasse/Kraichgau. (Gro): Stiftsberg. (Vil): Hassmersheim.

Kirchweinberg (Ger) vineyard (Anb): Baden. (Ber): Badische Bergstrasse/Kraichgau. (Gro): Stiftsberg. (Vil): Neckarzimmern.

Kirchweingarten (Ger) vineyard (Anb): Mosel-Saar-Ruwer. (Ber): Zell/Mosel. (Gro): Grafschaft. (Vil): Bullay.

Kirchwingert (Ger) vineyard (Anb): Rheinhessen. (Ber): Bingen. (Gro): Rheingrafenstein. (Vil): Neu-Bamberg.

Kirf (Ger) village (Anb): Mosel-Saar-Ruwer. (Ber): Obermosel. (Gro): Gipfel. (Vins): Sites not yet chosen.

Kir Gallique (Fr) a brand-name of bottled kir.

Kirghizia (Rus) a wine-producing region in southern Russia. Produces red and white dessert wines.

Kiri (Eng) a sparkling non-alcoholic apple juice drink produced by Bulmers of Hereford, Herefordshire.

Kirigin Cellars (USA) a large winery based near the Hecker Pass district, Santa Clara, California. 19ha. Grape varieties: Pinot noir and Zinfandel. Produces varietal wines.

Kirin Australia Pty Ltd (Austr) a brewery. (Add): 47 McDowell Street, Welshpool, 6106. Brews: Kirin beer. Website: http://www.kirinaustralia.com.au 'E'mail: reception@kirinaustralia.com.au

Kirin Beer (Jap) a 4.8%–5% alc by vol. bottled, premium lager beer brewed by the Kirin Brewery, Tokyo using spring water, rice, barley, malt, maize, yeast and hops.

Kirin Beer (Eng) a 5% alc by vol draught Kirin Ichiban beer brewed by the Charles Wells Brewery, Bedford.

Kirin Brewery (Jap) a brewery (established 1870) based in Yokohama. Now a large brewery based in Tokyo. Produces beers and stout of same name. see Ichiban Shibori, See also Namcha.

Kirkeler Wald-Quelle (Ger) a sparkling natural spring mineral water. Mineral contents (milligrammes per litre): Sodium 3mg/l, Calcium 5mg/l, Magnesium 1mg/l, Potassium 2mg/l, Bicarbonates 15mg/l, Chlorides 8mg/l, Sulphates 3mg/l, Fluorides 0.007mg/l.

Kirkham Winery (USA) a small winery based near St. Helena, Napa Valley, California. 5ha. Grape varieties: Chenin blanc and Gray riesling. Produces varietal wines.

Kirner (Ger) a brewery. (Add): Kallenfelser Strasse 2-4, 55606 Kimoder Postfach 151, Kirn D-55606. Brews a variety of beers and lager. Website: http://www.kirner.de 'E'mail: Brauerei@kirner.de

Kirovabad (Rus) a major wine-producing centre in Azerbaijan.

Kir Rouge (Fr) a crème de cassis and a dry red Burgundy wine such as Passe-Tout-Grains.

Kir Royale (Fr) 20mls (⅛ gill) crème de cassis topped with chilled brut Champagne.

Kirrweiler (Ger) village (Anb): Pfalz. (Ber): Südliche Weinstrasse. (Gro): Mandelhöhe. (Vins): Mandelberg, Oberschloss, Römerweg.

Kirsbaer (Den) a cherry brandy.

Kirsberry (Den) a cherry liqueur.

Kirsch (Ger) a clear cherry-flavoured liqueur made with the cherry kernels. Is matured in earthenware or paraffin-lined casks so absorbs no colour 43% alc by vol.

Kirsch and Cassis Cocktail (Cktl) ⅓ measure kirsch, ⅔ measure crème de cassis. Shake over ice, strain into an ice-filled highball glass and top with soda.

Kirschböck (Aus) a vineyard site on the banks of the River Danube situated in the Wachau region, Niederösterreich.

Kirschbühel (Aus) a vineyard site on the banks of the River Danube in the Kremstal region.

Kirsch de Zoug (Switz) a cherry brandy made in Zug.

Kirschgarten (Ger) vineyard (Anb): Pfalz. (Ber): Mittelhaardt-Deutsche Weinstrasse. (Gro): Kobnert. (Vil): Erpolzheim.

Kirsch-Gewuerzlikoer (Ger) a liqueur made from cherries and herbal essences.

Kirschheck (Ger) vineyard (Anb): Nahe. (Ber): Kreuznach. (Gro): Pfarrgarten. (Vil): Wallhausen.

Kirschheck (Ger) vineyard (Anb): Nahe. (Ber): Schloss Böckelheim. (Gro): Burgweg. (Vil): Norheim.

Kirsch mit Whisky (Ger) a fruit liqueur based on neutral spirits and whisky as opposed to grape brandy. 34.5%–40% alc by vol. e.g. Aprikose mit Whisky.

Kirsch Peureux (Fr) a colourless cherry liqueur 40% alc by vol.

Kirschroth (Ger) village (Anb): Nahe. (Ber): Schloss Böckelheim. (Gro): Paradiesgarten. (Vins): Lump, Wildgrafenberg.

Kirschwasser (Ger) a Black Forest clear cherry brandy.

Kirsebaerlikoer (Mex) a fiery spirit produced from cacti.

Kirseboer Liqueur (Den) the name given to Peter Heering's Cherry Liqueur.

Kishbaba (Iran) a seedless white grape variety.

Kishinev (Rus) a dry white table wine produced in the Moldavia region.

Kishmish (Iran) a white grape variety grown in the Ispahan region. see Kismis.

Kiskadee (Ire) a white rum made by the Irish Distillers C°.

Kis-Kesay (Cktl) ½ measure white rum, ¼ measure

755

crème de cacao, ⅛ measure lime juice, ⅛ measure blackcurrant juice. Stir together over ice, strain into an ice-filled highball, top with orange cream and a twist of orange peel.

Kislav (Rus) a spirit made from water melons.

Kisling (Aus) a vineyard site on the banks of the River Danube in the Kremstal region.

Kislingbury Bitter (Eng) a 4% alc by vol. bitter beer brewed by Hoggleys, Northamptonshire.

Kismet (Ind) a 5% alc by vol. premium lager.

Kismis (M.East) an alternative name for the Sultana grape variety. Also known as Kishmish.

Kiss & Tell Reserve (S.Afr) the label for a red wine (Merlot 45%, Mourvèdre 10% and Shiraz 45% blend) produced by the Leopard Frog Vineyards winery, Stellenbosch, Western Cape.

Kissaten (Jap) café.

Kissingen Wasser (Ger) a natural sparkling spring saline water from Bavaria. Reputed to have medicinal properties.

Kissinger Bitterwasser Heilwasser (Ger) a natural spring mineral water. Mineral contents (milligrammes per litre): Sodium 4690mg/l, Calcium 539mg/l, Magnesium 4196mg/l, Potassium 92mg/l, Chlorides 3739mg/l, Sulphates 21634mg/l, Fluorides 0.09mg/l.

Kiss in the Dark (Cktl) ⅓ measure gin, ⅓ measure French vermouth, ⅓ measure cherry brandy. Stir over ice and strain into a cocktail glass.

Kisslegger (Ger) a still and sparkling natural spring mineral water. Mineral contents (milligrammes per litre): Sodium 188mg/l, Calcium 2.2mg/l, Magnesium 0.5mg/l, Potassium 1.2mg/l, Bicarbonates 479mg/l, Chlorides 9.4mg/l, Sulphates 7mg/l, Fluorides 2.1mg/l, Nitrates <0.1mg/l.

Kiss Me Quick (Cktl) 35mls (1½ fl.ozs) Pernod, 4 dashes Cointreau, 2 dashes Angostura. Shake with ice, strain into a highball glass, add ice and top up with soda.

Kiss Me Quick (Eng) an ale brewed by Bateman's of Lincolnshire to celebrate Valentine's Day. Part of the Jolly's range.

Kiss the Boys Goodbye (Cktl) 20mls (⅙ gill) sloe gin, 20mls (⅙ gill) Cognac, juice of small lemon, ½ egg white. Shake well over ice and strain into a cocktail glass.

Kiss With Love (Ger) a 'double bottle' that consists of hazelnut and chocolate liqueur one side 26% alc by vol. and blackberry liqueur the other side 30% alc by vol. Produced by Thienelt in Kaarst.

Kistler Vineyards (USA) a large winery based between the Napa and Sonoma Valleys. 16ha. Grape varieties: Cabernet sauvignon, Chardonnay and Pinot noir. Produces varietal wines.

Kite Bitter (Eng) *see* Ancient Druids.

Kite Mild (Eng) a 3.2% alc by vol. mild ale brewed by the Loddon Brewery, Berkshire.

Kitron (Gre) a liqueur made from the leaves of lemon trees distilled with grape brandy and sweetened.

Kitterlé (Fr) an A.C. Alsace Grand Cru vineyard in Guebwiller, Haut-Rhin 25.79ha.

Kittmannsberg (Aus) a vineyard site based on the banks of the River Kamp situated in the Kamptal region.

Kitty Highball (Cktl) ½ measure claret, ½ measure ginger ale. Mix well together and serve on ice.

Kitty Love (Cktl) ⅓ measure kirsch, ⅓ measure Carpano, ⅓ measure Cointreau, 2 dashes orange juice. Shake with ice, strain into a cocktail glass and garnish with orange zest.

Kitzeck (Aus) a wine district within the Styria region. Main vineyards: Altenberg, Annaberg, Einöd, Gauitsch, Langriegel, Trebien. Grape varieties: Pinot blanc, Pinot gris, Riesling, Welschriesling.

Kitzingen (Ger) village (Anb): Franken. (Ber): Maindreieck. (Gro): Hofrat. (Vin): Wilhelmsberg.

Kitzmann Bräu KG (Ger) a brewery. (Add): Südliche Stadtmauerstrasse 25, Erlangen D-91054. Brews beers and lagers. Website: http://www.kitzmann.de

Kivu (Afr) a major-coffee producing region in Zaire.

Kivu Coffee (Afr) a coffee bean with a high acidity used mainly for blending from the Kivu region in Zaire.

Kiwi Blue (N.Z) a natural spring mineral water from East Tamaki. Mineral contents (milligrammes per litre): Calcium 18mg/l, Magnesium 4mg/l, Potassium 8.4mg/l.

Kiwi Cuvée (Fr) a Vin du Pays du Jardin de la France produced by Lachéteau, Doué-la-Fontaine, Anjou-Saumur. Grape: Sauvignon blanc.

Kiwi Liqueur (N.Z) a golden green, kiwi fruit liqueur 40% alc by vol.

Kiwi Source (Eng) a 5.3% alc by vol. sparkling kiwi fruit and vodka-based drink from Whitbread. *See also* Vodka Source, Passion Fruit Source.

Kizilay (Tur) a natural spring mineral water from Gazligol. Mineral contents (milligrammes per litre): Sodium 842.12mg/l, Calcium 46.09mg/l, Magnesium 37.44mg/l, Potassium 16.2mg/l, Bicarbonates 2409.5mg/l, Chlorides 109.13mg/l, Fluorides 1.35mg/l, Nitrates 10.1mg/l, Silicates 1mg/l. pH 7.12

Kizlarskoye (Rus) a dessert wine produced near Machackala in eastern Russia.

K.K. (Eng) *abbr*: **K**ing **K**eg a cask-conditioned light mild 1031 O.G. brewed by the Greene King Brewery in East Anglia.

K.K.W. (S.Afr) *abbr*: **K**lawer **K**oöperatiewe **W**ynkelders. *see* Klawer Co-operative.

Klabauter Man (Cktl) 50mls (⅜ gill) arak, 250mls (2 gills) Port wine, 20mls (⅙ gill) lemon juice. Heat together slowly and pour into mugs adding sugar to taste.

Klager [Leopold] (Aus) a winery based in the Wien region. (Add): Stammersdorfer Straase 18, 1210 Wien. Grape varieties: Chardonnay, Gemischter satz, Grüner veltliner, Müller-Thurgau, Riesling, Welschriesling, Zweigelt. Produces a range of wine styles.

Klamm (Ger) vineyard (Anb): Nahe. (Ber): Schloss Böckelheim. (Gro): Burgweg. (Vil): Niederhausen an der Nahe.

K

Klapmuts (S.Afr) vineyards which produce fine red wines.

Klapotetzen (Aus) wooden 'rattles' to scare the birds away from the ripe grapes around harvest time.

Klarer (Ger) a term used to denote clear schnapps (corn), gin (steinhäger).

Klassiek Droë (S.Afr) classic dry. *See also* Klassiek Droog.

Klassiek Droog (S.Afr) classic dry. *See also* Klassiek Droë.

Klassischer Ausbau (Aus) the process of aging wines in small oak casks (around 220-225 litres) to give the wines more character. *See also* Ausbau.

Klassisches Ursprungsgebiet (It) a German term used in the Südtirol. *see* Classico.

Klàšter Hradište Brewery (Czec) an old brewery based in north-western Czec. Noted for lager-style beers.

Klastorna (Euro) a sparkling natural spring mineral water from Malej, Slovak Republic. Mineral contents (milligrammes per litre): Sodium 71mg/l, Calcium 290.5mg/l, Magnesium 74.1mg/l, Potassium 15.6mg/l, Bicarbonates 1340.5mg/l, Chlorides 14.5mg/l, Sulphates 88.5mg/l, Nitrates 0.5mg/l.

Klaus (Aus) a vineyard site on the banks of the River Danube situated in the Wachau region, Niederösterreich.

Klaus (Ger) vineyard (Anb): Rheingau. (Ber): Johannisberg. (Gro): Erntebringer. (Vil): Geisenheim.

Klaus (Ger) vineyard (Anb): Rheingau. (Ber): Johannisberg. (Gro): Honigberg. (Vil): Winkel.

Klaus (Ger) a vineyard within the village of Johannisberg, 2ha (100%) of which is proposed to be classified as Erstes Gewächs.

Klausenberg (Ger) vineyard (Anb): Rheinhessen. (Ber): Wonnegau. (Gro): Liebfrauenmorgen. (Vil): Worms.

Kläuserweg (Ger) vineyard (Anb): Rheingau. (Ber): Johannisberg. (Gro): Erntebringer. (Vil): Geisenheim.

Kläuserweg (Ger) a vineyard within the village of Geisenheim, 57.6ha. (24.8%) of which is proposed to be classified as Erstes Gewächs.

Klawer Co-operative (S.Afr) a co-operative winery (established 1956) based in Klawer, Olifants River, Western Cape. (Add): Klawer Koöperatiewe Wynkelders, Box 8, Klawer 8145. Grape varieties: Chardonnay, Chenin blanc, Hanepoot, Merlot, Muscadel, Pinotage, Shiraz. Labels: Birdfield, Halfsoet, Michelle. Website: http://www.wine.co.za

Klawervlei Wine Estate (S.Afr) a winery (established 1994) based in Stellenbosch, Western Cape. 20ha. (Add): P.O. Box 144, Koelenhof 7605, Stellenbosch. Grape varieties: Cabernet sauvignon, Chenin blanc, Merlot, Pinotage. Website: http://www.klawervlei.com

Klearly Kids (Eng) the brand-name given to a range of spring waters with fruit flavours: apple, orange, raspberry or blackberry.

Klein (Ger) small.

Klein [René et Fils] (Fr) a wine producer based in Alsace. (Add): Rue du Haut-Koenigsbourg, 68590 St-Hippolyte.

Kleinaspach (Ger) village (Anb): Württemberg. (Ber): Württembergisch Unterland. (Gro): Schalkstein. (Vin): Kelterberg.

Klein Babylonstoren (S.Afr) the label for a red wine (Cabernet sauvignon and Merlot blend) oak-aged for 16 months and produced by the Backsberg Cellars winery, Suider-Paarl, Western Cape.

Kleinberger (USA) a white grape variety used in California to make white table wines. Known as the Knipperlé and Elbling in Europe.

Kleinbosch (S.Afr) lit: 'small bush', a range of wines from five of Paarl's leading wine cellars: Boland, Bovlei, Cape Coastal Vintners, Wamakersvallei, Wellington. Grape varieties include Cabernet sauvignon, Pinotage, Merlot, Chardonnay, Sauvignon blanc, Steen, Dry Muscat.

Kleinbottwar (Ger) village (Anb): Württemberg. (Ber): Württembergisch Unterland. (Gro): Wunnenstein. (Vins): Götzenberg, Lichtenberg, Obererberg, Sussmund.

Klein Constantia Estate (S.Afr) a winery (established 1823) based in Constantia, Western Cape. 82ha. (Add): P.O. Box 375, Constantia. Grape varieties: Cabernet franc, Cabernet sauvignon, Chardonnay, Merlot, Muscat de frontignan, Rhine riesling, Sauvignon blanc, Shiraz. Labels: Danford's, High Gables, KC, Marlbrook, Mme Marlbrook, Perdeblokke, Vin de Constance. Website: http://www.kleinconstantia.com

Klein DasBosch (S.Afr) a winery (5.5ha) based in Stellenbosch, Western Cape. Grape varieties: Chardonnay, Merlot, Pinotage. Website: http://www.kleindabosch.com

Kleine Draken (S.Afr) a winery (established 1988) based in Paarl, Western Cape. 9ha. Grape varieties: Cabernet franc, Cabernet sauvignon, Cinsaut, Malbec, Merlot, Pinotage, Sauvignon blanc. Label: Kiddush. Website: http://www.kosherwines.co.za

Kleine Hazen (S.Afr) the label for a range of wines produced by the Hazendal winery, Stellenbosch, Western Cape. *see* Konynwijn.

Kleinelbling (Ger) an alternative name for the Elbling grape. *See also* Knipperlé.

Kleiner Feigling (Eng) a vodka-based, schnapps-style, drink from Fun Drinks in Derbyshire.

Kleinergelber (Fr) an alternative name for the white Knipperlé grape.

Kleiner Räuschling (Fr) an alternative name for the white Knipperlé grape.

Kleiner Reuschling (Fr) an alternative name for the white Knipperlé grape.

Kleiner Riesling (Ger) an erroneous varietal name for the Ortlieber (Knipperlé). Also Briesgauer riesling.

Kleines Stangl (Aus) a vineyard site based on the banks of the River Kamp situated in the Kamptal region.

Kleine Zalze Wines (S.Afr) a winery (60ha) based in Stellenbosch, Western Cape. Grape varieties:

K

Cabernet sauvignon, Chardonnay, Chenin blanc, Gamay noir, Merlot, Pinotage, Shiraz. Labels: Cellar Selection, Family Reserve, Foot of Africa, Vineyard Selection. Website: http://www.kleinezalze.com

Kleingartach (Ger) village (Anb): Württemberg. (Ber): Württembergisch Unterland. (Gro): Heuchelberg. (Vins): Grafenberg, Vogelsang.

Klein Gustrouw Estate (S.Afr) a winery (established 1817) based in Stellenbosch, Western Cape. 16ha. Grape varieties: Cabernet sauvignon, Merlot.

Kleinheppach (Ger) village (Anb): Württemberg. (Ber): Remstal-Stuttgart. (Gro): Kopf. (Vin): Greiner.

Kleinheppach (Ger) village (Anb): Württemberg. (Ber): Remstal-Stuttgart. (Gro): Wartbühl. (Vins): Sonnenberg, Steingrüble.

Klein-Höflein (Aus) a wine-producing area in the Eisenstadt district.

Kleiningersheim (Ger) village (Anb): Württemberg. (Ber): Württembergisch Unterland. (Gro): Schalkstein. (Vin): Schlossberg.

Kleinkarlbach (Ger) village (Anb): Pfalz. (Ber): Mittelhaardt-Deutsche Weinstrasse. (Gro): Höllenpfad. (Vins): Frauenlandchen, Herrenberg, Herrgottsacker, Kieselberg, Senn.

Klein Karoo (S.Afr) a demarcated wine district east of Montagu in Cape Province. See also Little Karoo.

Kleinkems (Ger) village (Anb): Baden. (Ber): Markgräflerland. (Gro): Vogtei Rötteln. (Vin): Wolfer.

Kleinlangheim (Ger) village (Anb): Franken. (Ber): Steigerwald. (Gro): Not yet assigned. (Vin): Wutschenberg.

Kleinniedesheim (Ger) village (Anb): Pfalz. (Ber): Mittelhaardt-Deutsche Weinstrasse. (Gro): Schwarzerde. (Vins): Schlossgarten, Vorderberg.

Kleinood (S.Afr) a winery (established 2000) based in Stellenbosch, Western Cape. 9.6ha. Grape varieties: Mourvèdre, Shiraz, Viognier. Label: Tamboerskloof.

Klein Optenhorst (S.Afr) a winery (established 2001) based in Wellington, Western Cape. Grape varieties: Merlot, Pinot noir. Label: Knife's Edge.

Kleinoscheck (Aus) one of the leading sparkling wine producers of Austria.

Klein Parys Vineyards (S.Afr) a winery (established 1692) based in Suider-Paarl, Western Cape. 48ha. Grape varieties: Cabernet sauvignon, Chenin blanc, Pinotage, Sauvignon blanc, Shiraz. Labels: Beatrix Selection, Classic Red, Cuvée Brut, Golden Vintage, Miller's Mile.

Kleinpereich (Ger) an alternative name for the Elbling grape.

Kleinsachsenheim (Ger) village (Anb): Württemberg. (Ber): Württembergisch Unterland. (Gro): Stromberg. (Vin): Kirchberg.

Klein Schwechat (Aus) see Schwechat.

Kleinstein (Aus) a vineyard site based on the banks of the River Kamp situated in the Kamptal region.

Kleintje (Hol) lit: 'baby', a term used to describe a small glass of drink.

Klein-Umstadt (Ger) village (Anb): Hessische Bergstrasse. (Ber): Umstadt. (Gro): Not yet assigned. (Vin): Stachelberg.

Kleinvallei Winery (S.Afr) a winery (established 2000) based in Klein Drakenstein, Paarl, Western Cape. 10ha. Grape varieties: Cabernet sauvignon, Chardonnay, Malbec, Merlot, Petit verdot, Pinotage, Shiraz. Label: Bel Canto. Website: http://www.kleinvallei.co.za

Kleinvernatsch (It) the German name for the red Schiava piccola grape in the Südtirol.

Kleinweiss (Ger) a white grape variety also known as the Budaer Riesling.

Klein-Winternheim (Ger) village (Anb): Rheinhessen. (Ber): Nierstein. (Gro): Domherr. (Vins): Geiershöll, Herrgottshaus, Villenkeller.

Klein Zalze Estate (S.Afr) vineyards sited in Stellenbosch. (Add): C/o Gilbeys, P.O. Box 137, Stellenbosch 7600 (owned by Gilbeys). Produces: Rare Late Vintage and varietals. Grape varieties include: Cabernet sauvignon, Chardonnay.

Klekovaça (Slo) see Klevovka.

Klekowatsch (Euro) a Balkan juniper berry flavoured gin 38% alc by vol.

Klenk (Ger) a method of red wine fermentation which is similar to maceration carbonique. See also Lidy.

Klepberg (Ger) vineyard (Anb): Baden. (Ber): Badische Bergstrasse/Kraichgau. (Gro): Hohenberg. (Vil): Bilfingen.

Klepberg (Ger) vineyard (Anb): Baden. (Ber): Badische Bergstrasse/Kraichgau. (Gro): Hohenberg. (Vil): Eisingen.

Klepberg (Ger) vineyard (Anb): Baden. (Ber): Badische Bergstrasse/Kraichgau. (Gro): Hohenberg. (Vil): Ersingen.

Klepberg (Ger) vineyard (Anb): Baden. (Ber): Badische Bergstrasse/Kraichgau. (Gro): Hohenberg. (Vil): Dietlingen.

Kletswater (Eng) a 4% alc by vol. ale brewed by the Anglo Dutch Brewery, West Yorkshire.

Kletterberg (Ger) vineyard (Anb): Rheinhessen. (Ber): Bingen. (Gro): Rheingrafenstein. (Vil): Neu-Bamberg.

Klettgau [ortsteil Erzingen] (Ger) village (Anb): Baden. (Ber): Bodensee. (Gro): Not yet assigned. (Vin): Kapellenberg.

Klettgau [ortsteil Rechberg] (Ger) village (Anb): Baden. (Ber): Bodensee. (Gro): Not yet assigned. (Vin): Kapellenberg.

Klevener (Switz) a local name for the Pinot Noir grape. Also spelt Clevener.

Klevner (Aus) an alternative name for the Pinot Blanc. Is also a local name for the red Pinot Noir.

Klevner (Fr) another name for the Pinot Blanc grape of Alsace. See also Clevner and Muscadet.

Klevner d'Heiligenstein (Fr) an alternative name for the Traminer grape in Alsace.

Klevovka (Slo) the distillation of juniper berries or plums. Also called Klekovaça (slivovitz = juniper berries).

Klicanje (Cro) cheers!

Klingelberger (Ger) the Baden region name for the Riesling grape.

Klingenberg (Ger) village (Anb): Franken. (Ber): Mainviereck. (Gro): Not yet assigned. (Vins): Hochberg, Schlossberg.

Klingenberg (Ger) village (Anb): Württemberg. (Ber): Württembergisch Unterland. (Gro): Heuchelberg. *see* Heilbronn.

Klingenmünster (Ger) village (Anb): Pfalz. (Ber): Südliche Weinstrasse. (Gro): Kloster Liebfrauenberg. (Vin): Maria Magdalena.

Klingle (Ger) vineyard (Anb): Württemberg. (Ber): Remstal-Stuttgart. (Gro): Wartbühl. (Vil): Grunbach.

Klingshirn Winery (USA) a winery based in Avon Lake, Ohio. Produces mainly Concord wines.

Klinos (Gre) a natural spring mineral water from Kalambaka. Mineral contents (milligrammes per litre): Sodium 2.1mg/l, Calcium 37.7mg/l, Magnesium 2.2mg/l, Potassium 0.4mg/l, Bicarbonates 122mg/l, Chlorides 3.5mg/l, Sulphates 2.4mg/l. pH 7.6

Klinto (It) a name given to a strawberry tasting red wine produced in the Treviso region (vino rosso).

Klipdrift (S.Afr) the brand-name for a brandy 43% alc by vol. produced by J.P. Marais, Robertson Valley.

Klipdrift Gold (S.Afr) the brand-name for a blended superior brandy 43% alc by vol. pot-stilled (up to 21 y.o.) produced by J.P. Marais, Robertson Valley.

Klipfel (Fr) a crèmant d'Alsace producer based at Barr in Alsace.

Kloane [S] Brauhaus (Aus) a brewery. (Add): Schallmooser Hauptstrasse 27, Salzburg A-5020. Brews beers and lagers. Website: http://www.brauhaus-austria.com

Kloch–Ost–Steiermark (Aus) a wine district within the region of Steiermark (Styria). Produces mainly white wines.

Kloeckera apiculata (Lat) one of the prolific 'wild yeasts' found in grape bloom.

Klondyke Cocktail (Cktl) 30mls (¼ gill) applejack, ¼ measure French vermouth, 3 dashes orange bitters. Stir over ice, strain into a cocktail glass, add a small olive and a squeeze of lemon peel juice on top.

Klondyke Cooler (Cktl) as for Gin Cooler using Bourbon whiskey instead of gin.

Kloovenburg Vineyards (S.Afr) a winery (established 1704) based in the Swartland, Western Cape. 130ha. Grape varieties: Cabernet sauvignon, Chardonnay, Merlot, Sauvignon blanc, Shiraz. Website: http://www.kloovenburg.com

Kloppberg (Ger) vineyard (Anb): Rheinhessen. (Ber): Wonnegau. (Gro): Pilgerpfad. (Vil): Dittelsheim-Hessloch.

Kloppenberg (Ger) vineyard (Anb): Rheinhessen. (Ber): Nierstein. (Gro): Gutes Domtal. (Vil): Mommenheim.

Kloster (Ger) monastery.

Kloster (Ger) vineyard (Anb): Nahe. (Ber): Schloss Böckelheim. (Gro): Paradiesgarten. (Vil): Odernheim.

Kloster Andechs Brauerei (Ger) a large monastery brewery based in Bavaria, Germany. Beers brewed by the monks.

Kloster Beer (E.Asia) a lager beer brewed in Kuala Lumpar, Malaya.

Klosterberg (Ger) lit; 'monastery hill', a popular name for vineyards in Germany. Named after the days when vineyards were owned by the church. There are 24 individual sites with this name. Also a grosslage.

Klosterberg (Ger) grosslage (Anb): Ahr. (Ber): Walporzheim/Ahrtal. (Vils): Ahrweiler, Altenahr, Bachem, Bad Neuenahr, Dernau, Heimersheim, Heppingen, Marienthal, Mayschoss, Rech, Walporzheim.

Klosterberg (Ger) vineyard (Anb): Baden. (Ber): Badische Bergstrasse/Kraichgau. (Gro): Mannaberg. (Vil): Bruchsal.

Klosterberg (Ger) vineyard (Anb): Mittelrhein. (Ber): Bacharach. (Gro): Schloss Reichenstein. (Vil): Oberheimbach.

Klosterberg (Ger) vineyard (Anb): Mosel-Saar-Ruwer. (Ber): Bernkastel. (Gro): Kurfürstlay. (Vil): Maring-Noviand.

Klosterberg (Ger) vineyard (Anb): Mosel-Saar-Ruwer. (Ber): Bernkastel. (Gro): Münzlay. (Vil): Wehlen.

Klosterberg (Ger) vineyard (Anb): Mosel-Saar-Ruwer. (Ber): Bernkastel. (Gro): Sankt Michael. (Vil): Schleich.

Klosterberg (Ger) vineyard (Anb): Mosel-Saar-Ruwer. (Ber): Bernkastel. (Gro): Schwarzlay. (Vil): Platten.

Klosterberg (Ger) vineyard (Anb): Mosel-Saar-Ruwer. (Ber): Bernkastel. (Gro): Schwarzlay. (Vil): Traben-Trarbach (ortsteil Wolf).

Klosterberg (Ger) vineyard (Anb): Mosel-Saar-Ruwer. (Ber): Saar-Ruwer. (Gro): Scharzberg. (Vil): Konz.

Klosterberg (Ger) vineyard (Anb): Mosel-Saar-Ruwer. (Ber): Saar-Ruwer. (Gro): Scharzberg. (Vil): Saarburg.

Klosterberg (Ger) vineyard (Anb): Mosel-Saar-Ruwer. (Ber): Saar-Ruwer. (Gro): Scharzberg. (Vil): Wiltingen.

Klosterberg (Ger) vineyard (Anb): Mosel-Saar-Ruwer. (Ber): Zell/Mosel. (Gro): Schwarze Katz. (Vil): Zell-Merl.

Klosterberg (Ger) vineyard (Anb): Mosel-Saar-Ruwer. (Ber): Zell/Mosel. (Gro): Weinhex. (Vil): Lehmen.

Klosterberg (Ger) vineyard (Anb): Nahe. (Ber): Schloss Böckelheim. (Gro): Burgweg. (Vil): Norheim.

Klosterberg (Ger) vineyard (Anb): Rheingau. (Ber): Johannisberg. (Gro): Burgweg. (Vil): Rüdesheim.

Klosterberg (Ger) vineyard (Anb): Rheingau. (Ber): Johannisberg. (Gro): Gottesthal. (Vil): Östrich.

Klosterberg (Ger) vineyard (Anb): Rheingau. (Ber): Johannisberg. (Gro): Heiligenstock. (Vil): Kiedrich.

Klosterberg (Ger) vineyard (Anb): Rheingau. (Ber):

K

Johannisberg. (Gro): Mehrholzchen. (Vil): Östrich.

Klosterberg (Ger) vineyard (Anb): Rheinhessen. (Ber): Bingen. (Gro): Adelberg. (Vil): Bermersheim v.d.H.

Klosterberg (Ger) vineyard (Anb): Rheinhessen. (Ber): Nierstein. (Gro): Gutes Domtal. (Vil): Nieder-Olm.

Klosterberg (Ger) vineyard (Anb): Rheinhessen. (Ber): Nierstein. (Gro): Petersberg. (Vil): Bechtolsheim.

Klosterberg (Ger) vineyard (Anb): Rheinhessen. (Ber): Nierstein. (Gro): Sankt Alban. (Vil): Mainz.

Klosterberg (Ger) vineyard (Anb): Rheinhessen. (Ber): Wonnegau. (Gro): Pilgerpfad. (Vil): Osthofen.

Klosterberg (Ger) vineyard (Anb): Württemberg. (Ber): Württembergisch Unterland. (Gro): Stromberg. (Vil): Hohenhaslach.

Klosterberg (Ger) vineyard (Anb): Württemberg. (Ber): Württembergisch Unterland. (Gro): Stromberg. (Vil): Horrheim.

Klosterberg (Ger) a herb liqueur produced by the Eckes Distillery.

Klosterbergfelsen (Ger) vineyard (Anb): Baden. (Ber): Ortenau. (Gro): Schloss Rodeck. (Vil): Varnhalt.

Kloster Bier (Ger) a 'cloister' beer produced in a monastery or convent.

Klosterbitter (Ger) a bitter digestive.

Klosterbock Dunkel (Ger) a dark, long-lagered beer produced by the Külmbacher Mönschof Brauerei in Bavaria.

Klosterbräu (Aus)(Ger) a Trappiste-style beer brewed mainly in Austria.

Klosterbräu Bamberg (Ger) a brewery (established 1533). (Add): Obere Muhlbrucke 1-3, Bamberg D-96049. Brews beers and lager. Website: http://www.klosterbraeu.de

Klosterbrauerei Neuzelle GmbH (Ger) a brewery. (Add): Brauhausplatz 1, 14898ftsführer, Helmu. Brews a variety of beers and lager. Website: http://www.klosterbauerei.com 'E'mail: info@neuzeller-bier.de

Klosterbräu Golden Pils (Ger) a pilsner lager 5% alc by vol. Brewed by the Klosterbräu Bamnberg brewery.

Klosterbruder (Ger) vineyard (Anb): Rheinhessen. (Ber): Bingen. (Gro): Kaiserpfalz. (Vil): Gross-Winternheim.

Kloster Eberbach (Ger) a Cistercian monastery at Steinberg, on the Rhine. Estates became part of the state domain.

Kloster Fürstental (Ger) vineyard (Anb): Mittelrhein. (Ber): Bacharach. (Gro): Schloss Stahleck. (Vil): Bacharach.

Klostergarten (Aus) a red wine made from the St. Laurent grape by the Augustine monks at Klosterneuburg, Vienna.

Klostergarten (Ger) lit: 'monastery garden', the name used for the old monastery vineyards now privately owned. There are 23 individual sites with this name in Germany.

Klostergarten (Ger) vineyard (Anb): Ahr. (Ber): Warporzheim/Ahrtal. (Gro): Klosterberg. (Vil): Marienthal.

Klostergarten (Ger) vineyard (Anb): Franken. (Ber): Mainviereck. (Gro): Not yet assigned. (Vil): Engelsberg.

Klostergarten (Ger) vineyard (Anb): Mosel-Saar-Ruwer. (Ber): Bernkastel. (Gro): Kurfürstlay. (Vil): Brauneberg.

Klostergarten (Ger) vineyard (Anb): Mosel-Saar-Ruwer. (Ber): Bernkastel. (Gro): Sankt Michael. (Vil): Leiwen.

Klostergarten (Ger) vineyard (Anb): Mosel-Saar-Ruwer. (Ber): Zell/Mosel. (Gro): Goldbäumchen. (Vil): Cochem.

Klostergarten (Ger) vineyard (Anb): Nahe. (Ber): Kreuznach. (Gro): Schlosskapelle. (Vil): Bingen-Bingerbrück.

Klostergarten (Ger) vineyard (Anb): Nahe. (Ber): Kreuznach. (Gro): Schlosskapelle. (Vil): Weiler.

Klostergarten (Ger) vineyard (Anb): Nahe. (Ber): Schloss Böckelheim. (Gro): Rosengarten. (Vil): Sponheim.

Klostergarten (Ger) vineyard (Anb): Nahe. (Ber): Schloss Böckelheim. (Gro): Rosengarten. (Vil): St. Katharien.

Klostergarten (Ger) vineyard (Anb): Rheinhessen. (Ber): Bingen. (Gro): Abtey. (Vil): Sankt Johann.

Klostergarten (Ger) vineyard (Anb): Rheinhessen. (Ber): Bingen. (Gro): Abtey. (Vil): Sprendlingen.

Klostergarten (Ger) vineyard (Anb): Rheinhessen. (Ber): Bingen. (Gro): Adelberg. (Vil): Flonheim.

Klostergarten (Ger) vineyard (Anb): Rheinhessen. (Ber): Bingen. (Gro): Kaiserpfalz. (Vil): Schwabenheim.

Klostergarten (Ger) vineyard (Anb): Rheinhessen. (Ber): Bingen. (Gro): Rheingrafenstein. (Vil): Hackenheim.

Klostergarten (Ger) vineyard (Anb): Rheinhessen. (Ber): Bingen. (Gro): Sankt Rochuskapelle. (Vil): Zotzenheim.

Klostergarten (Ger) vineyard (Anb): Rheinhessen. (Ber): Nierstein. (Gro): Spiegelberg. (Vil): Nierstein.

Klostergarten (Ger) vineyard (Anb): Pfalz. (Ber): Mittelhaardt-Deutsche Weinstrasse. (Gro): Hofstück. (Vil): Gönnheim.

Klostergarten (Ger) vineyard (Anb): Pfalz. (Ber): Mittelhaardt-Deutsche Weinstrasse. (Gro): Hofstück. (Vil): Niederkirchen.

Klostergarten (Ger) vineyard (Anb): Pfalz. (Ber): Mittelhaardt-Deutsche Weinstrasse. (Gro): Höllenpfad. (Vil): Grünstadt.

Klostergarten (Ger) vineyard (Anb): Pfalz. (Ber): Südliche Weinstrasse. (Gro): Königsgarten. (Vil): Godramstein.

Klostergarten (Ger) vineyard (Anb): Pfalz. (Ber): Südliche Weinstrasse. (Gro): Trappenberg. (Vil): Lustadt.

Klostergarten (Ger) vineyard (Anb): Pfalz. (Ber): Südliche Weinstrasse. (Gro): Trappenberg. (Vil): Zeiskam.

Klostergarten (Ger) vineyard (Anb): Pfalz. (Ber): Südliche Weinstrasse. (Gro): Schloss Ludwigshöhe. (Vil): Edenkoben.

Klostergut (Ger) vineyard (Anb): Baden. (Ber): Ortenau. (Gro): Schloss Rodeck. (Vil): Sinzheim.

Klostergut Schelzberg (Ger) vineyard (Anb): Baden. (Ber): Ortenau. (Gro): Schloss Rodeck. (Vil): Sasbackwalden.

Klosterkammer (Ger) vineyard (Anb): Mosel-Saar-Ruwer. (Ber): Zell/Mosel. (Gro): Grafschaft. (Vil): St. Aldegund.

Klosterkeller (Bul) a dry, full-bodied white wine made from the Sylvaner grape for the German market.

Klosterkellerei (It) a sparkling (cuve close) wine producer based in the Trentino-Alto Adige region.

Klosterkeller Siegendorf (Aus) a noted wine estate in Burgenland.

Klosterlay (Ger) vineyard (Anb): Rheingau. (Ber): Johannisberg. (Gro): Burgweg. (Vil): Rüdesheim.

Kloster Liebfrauenberg (Ger) grosslage (Anb): Pfalz. (Ber): Südliche Weinstrasse. (Vils): Bade Bergzabern. Barbelroth, Billigheim-Ingenheim, Gleiszellen-Gleishorbach, Göcklingen, Hergersweiler, Heuchelheim-Klingen, Kapellen-Drusweiler, Klingenmünster, Niederhorbach. Oberhausen, Pleisweiler-Oberhofen, Rohrbach, Steinweiler, Winden.

Klosterlikoer (Ger) a sweet digestive liqueur.

Kloster-Mitterfeldsatz (Aus) a vineyard site on the banks of the River Danube situated in the Wachau region, Niederösterreich.

Klosterneuburg (Aus) a wine district in the region of Niederösterreich that produces mainly white wines. The Augustine Monastery is the main producer and owns many of Austria's vineyards. *see* Höhere Bundeslehranstalt und Bundesamt für Wein und Obstbau.

Klosterneuburger (Aus) a white wine that comes from the old monastery vineyards on the Danube. A fruity medium sweet wine with a good bouquet.

Klosterneuburger Mostwaage (Aus) *abbr:* KMW a measurement for Specific Gravity. Approximate conversion to Oechsle by multiplying KMW x 5 (minimum KMW levels for Austrian wines are: Tafelwein = $10.6°$ KMW/Landwein = $14°$ KMW/Qualitätswein = $15°$ KMW/Kabinett = $17°$ KMW/Spätlese = $19°$ KMW/Auslese = $21°$ KMW/Beerenauslese $25°$ KMW/Ausbruch = $27°$KMW/Trockenbeerenauslese = $30°$ KMW/Eiswein = $25°$ KMW/Strohwein = $25°$ KMW).

Klosterpfad (Ger) vineyard (Anb): Nahe. (Ber): Kreuznach. (Gro): Schlosskapelle. (Vil): Dorsheim.

Klosterpfad (Ger) vineyard (Anb): Pfalz. (Ber): Südliche Weinstrasse. (Gro): Ordensgut. (Vil): Rhodt.

Klosterschaffnerei (Ger) vineyard (Anb): Pfalz. (Ber): Mittelhaardt-Deutsche Weinstrasse. (Gro): Grafenstück. (Vil): Bockenheim.

Kloster Schwarz (Ger) a dark, full-bodied beer

brewed by the Kulmbacher Mönschof Brauerei in Bavaria 4.9% alc by vol.

Klostersekt (Aus) a sparkling wine produced by the Augustine monks at Klosterneuburg, Vienna.

Kloster Stuben (Ger) vineyard (Anb): Mosel-Saar-Ruwer. (Ber): Zell/Mosel. (Gro): Rosenhang. (Vil): Bremm.

Klosterstüch (Ger) vineyard (Anb): Pfalz. (Ber): Mittelhaardt-Deutsche Weinstrasse. (Gro): Schnepfenflug vom Kellertal. (Vil): Einselthum.

Klosterstück (Ger) vineyard (Anb): Pfalz. (Ber): Mittelhaardt-Deutsche Weinstrasse. (Gro): Schnepfenflug vom Zellertal. (Vil): Zell.

Klosterweg (Ger) vineyard (Anb): Mosel-Saar-Ruwer. (Ber): Bernkastel. (Gro): Schwarzlay. (Vil): Hupperath.

Klosterweg (Ger) vineyard (Anb): Mosel-Saar-Ruwer. (Ber): Bernkastel. (Gro): Schwarzlay. (Vil): Wittlich.

Klosterweg (Ger) vineyard (Anb): Rheinhessen. (Ber): Bingen. (Gro): Sankt Rochuskapelle. (Vil): Dromersheim.

Klosterweg (Ger) vineyard (Anb): Rheinhessen. (Ber): Bingen. (Gro): Sankt Rochuskapelle. (Vil): Ockenheim.

Klosterweg (Ger) vineyard (Anb): Pfalz. (Ber): Mittelhaardt-Deutsche Weinstrasse. (Gro): Schwarzerde. (Vil): Gerolsheim.

Klotten (Ger) village (Anb): Mosel-Saar-Ruwer. (Ber): Zell/Mosel. (Gro): Goldbäumchen. (Vins): Branneberg, Burg Coreidelsteiner, Rosenberg, Sonnengold.

Klotzberg (Ger) vineyard (Anb): Baden. (Ber): Ortenau. (Gro): Schloss Rodeck. (Vil): Bühlertal.

Kluflaske (Den) decanter.

Klug (Ger) a lager-style beer 5.2% alc by vol.

Klüsserath (Ger) village (Anb): Mosel-Saar-Ruwer. (Ber): Bernkastel. (Gro): Sankt Michael. (Vins): Bruderschaft, Königsberg.

KMW (Aus) *abbr: see* Klosterneuberger Mostwaage. *See also* KNW.

Knappogue Castle (Ire) a triple distilled dated Irish whiskey 40% alc by vol. aged for 36 months in Sherry casks, distilled by the B. Daly Distillery in Tullamore.

Knappstein Estate (Austr) a winery based in the Clare Valley, South Australia. Labels include: Knappstein Three, Knappstein Single Vineyard. Grape varieties: Cabernet sauvignon, Gewurztraminer, Pinot gris, Riesling.

Kneipe (Ger) an old student drinking school, now denotes a friendly meeting place/bar.

K. Neon (Eng) a premium cider 8.4% alc by vol. produced by Showerings. Production of 2 million bottles sold in fluorescent electric blue bottles. *See also* K.

Kneitinger (Ger) a brewery. (Add): Kreuzgasse 7, D-93047. Brews a variety of beers and lagers. Website: http://www.kneitinger.de 'E'mail: info@kneitinger.de

Knickerbein (Pousse Café) pour into a tall glass in order- yolk of egg, 20mls (⅙ gill) Curaçao, 20mls (⅙ gill) kümmel, 2 dashes Angostura.

Knickerbocker [1] (Cktl) 1 measure dark rum, ½ measure Curaçao, ½ measure orange juice or lemon juice, dash grenadine. Shake over ice, strain into a cocktail glass and serve with a chunk of pineapple.

Knickerbocker [2] (Cktl) 1 measure dry gin, ½ measure French vermouth, dash Italian vermouth. Shake over ice, strain into a cocktail glass and top with a squeeze lemon peel juice.

Knickerbocker Special (Cktl) 50mls (2fl.ozs) dark rum, 2 dashes Cointreau, 5mls (¼ fl.oz) raspberry syrup, 5mls (¼ fl.oz) orange juice and lemon juice. Shake over ice, strain into a cocktail glass and top with a slice of pineapple.

Knicker Dropper Glory (Eng) a 5.5% alc by vol. ale brewed by the South Hams Brewery, Devon.

Knife's Edge (S.Afr) the label for a red wine (Merlot and Pinot noir blend) produced by the Klein Optenhorst winery, Wellington, Western Cape.

Knight's Granite Hills (Austr) a winery based at Burke and Wills Track, Victoria. Grape varieties: Cabernet sauvignon, Chardonnay, Riesling, Shiraz.

Knights Valley (USA) a small wine-producing area in Sonoma County, California.

Knights Valley Estates (USA) a small winery based in Knights Valley, Sonoma County, California. Grape variety: Johannisberg riesling. Noted for late harvest wines.

Knipperlé (Fr) a white grape variety once grown in Alsace (now banned). Also known as the Kleiner räuschling, Kleingelber, Kipperlé, Elbling.

Knittelsheim (Ger) village (Anb): Pfalz. (Ber): Südliche Weinstrasse. (Gro): Trappenberg. (Vin): Gollenberg.

Knittlingen (Ger) village (Anb): Württemberg. (Ber): Württembergisch Unterland. (Gro): Stromberg. (Vin): Reichshalde.

Knjaz Milos (Euro) a sparkling natural spring mineral water from Knjaz Milos Spring. Mineral contents (milligrammes per litre): Sodium 282.1mg/l, Calcium 107.3mg/l, Magnesium 44.96mg/l, Potassium 17.5mg/l, Bicarbonates 1256mg/l, Chlorides 13.01mg/l, Sulphates 39.04mg/l, Fluorides 1.71mg/l.

Knob Creek (USA) 100° US proof (50% alc by vol.) 9 year old Bourbon whiskey from Beam (James) Distilling Cº. Clermont-Beam, Kentucky.

Knockando (Scot) a single 15 year old malt whisky distillery on the Spey in Morayshire. Owned by Justerini and Brooks. A highland malt whisky 43% alc by vol. Also as an X.O.

Knockdhu (Scot) a single malt whisky distillery based east of Keith, Buchan. A highland malt whisky 40% alc by vol.

Knockendoch (Scot) a 5% alc by vol. ale brewed by Sulwath Brewers Ltd., Kirkcudbrightshire.

Knock it Back (Eng) an informal request to consume a drink quickly (usually to allow for another drink in the glass).

Knockout Box (Eng) the name for the container used in an espresso machine to hold the spent coffee grinds (after perculation). The spent grinds are 'knocked out' into the box.

Knockout Cocktail (Cktl) 20mls (⅛ gill) dry gin, 20mls (⅛ gill) dry vermouth, 2 dashes Pernod, 4 dashes (white) crème de menthe. Stir over ice, strain into a cocktail glass and top with a cherry.

Knoll (Aus) a winery (11ha) based in the Wachau. (Add): 3101 Unterloiben 10. Grape varieties: Chardonnay, Grüner veltliner, Muskateller, Riesling. Produces a range of dry and sweet (botrytised) wines.

Knoll Street Porter (Eng) a 5.2% alc by vol. porter brewed by the Bazens Brewery, Greater Manchester.

Knopf (Ger) vineyard (Anb): Rheinhessen. (Ber): Nierstein. (Gro): Gutes Domtal. (Vil): Friesenheim.

Knopf (Ger) vineyard (Anb): Rheinhessen. (Ber): Nierstein. (Gro): Gutes Domtal. (Vil): Hahnheim.

Knops (Eng) the name given to the turned elements in the stem of drinking glasses. i.e. baluster stems.

Knorhoek (S.Afr) a winery (established 1827) based in Koelenhof, Stellenbosch, Western Cape. 105ha. Grape varieties: Cabernet sauvignon, Chenin blanc, Merlot, Pinotage, Sauvignon blanc, Shiraz. Labels: Reserve, Two Cubs. Website: http://www.knorhoek.co.za

Knöringen (Ger) village (Anb): Pfalz. (Ber): Südliche Weinstrasse. (Gro): Bischofskreuz. (Vin): Hohenrain.

Knowle Hill (Eng) a vineyard (established 1970). (Add): Knowle Hill Farm, Ulcombe, Maidstone, Kent. 1ha. Grape varieties: Müller-Thurgau and Pinot noir.

Knox Alexander (USA) the label for a red wine (Pinot noir) produced by the Au Bon Climat winery, Santa Barbara County, California.

Knudsen Erath Winery (USA) a large vineyard based in Dundee, Willamette Valley, Oregon. 38ha. Grape varieties: Chardonnay, Pinot noir and Riesling. Produces varietal wines.

Knutwiler (Switz) a sparkling natural spring mineral water (established 1461) from Bad Knutwil. (blue label: sparkling/green label: light gas). Mineral contents (milligrammes per litre): Sodium 5mg/l, Calcium 88mg/l, Magnesium 24mg/l, Bicarbonates 371mg/l, Chlorides 5.9mg/l, Sulphates 22mg/l, Fluorides 0.12mg/l, Nitrates <0.1mg/l, Silicates 17mg/l. pH 7.7 Website: http://www.knutwiler.ch

KNW (Aus) *abbr*: an alternative initials used for KMW.

Koala Blue (Austr) a natural spring mineral water brand.

Köbànya Brewery (Hun) a brewery based in Budapest, noted for Rocky Cellar, Bak Beer and Hungària (a strong, pale beer).

Kobarn (Rus) a full-bodied red wine produced in the Crimea.

Kobern-Gondorf (Ger) village (Anb): Mosel-Saar-Ruwer. (Ber): Zell/Mosel. (Gro): Weinhex. (Vins): Fahrberg, Fuchshöhe, Gäns, Kehrberg, Schlossberg, Uhlen, Weissenberg.

Kobersberg (Ger) vineyard (Anb): Franken. (Ber): Maindreieck. (Gro): Not yet assigned. (Vil): Rimpar.

Kobes (Ger) the name given to the waiters in the tavern of Cölner Hofbräu in Cologne. They wear blue pullovers and leather aprons as their uniforms.

Kobl (Aus) a vineyard site on the banks of the River Danube in the Kremstal region.

Koblenz-Ehrenbreitstein (Ger) village (Anb): Mittelrhein. (Ber): Rheinburgengau. (Gro): Marksburg. (Vin): Kreuzberg.

Koblenz [ortsteil Lay] (Ger) village (Anb): Mosel-Saar-Ruwer. (Ber): Zell/Mosel. (Gro): Weinhex. (Vin): Hubertsborn.

Koblenz [ortsteil Moselweiss] (Ger) village (Anb): Mosel-Saar-Ruwer. (Ber): Zell/Mosel. (Gro): Weinhex. (Vin): Hamm.

Kobnert (Ger) grosslage (Anb): Pfalz. (Ber): Mittelhaardt-Deutsche Weinstrasse. (Vils): Dackenheim, Erpolzheim, Freinsheim, Herxheim/Berg, Kallstadt, Leistadt, Ungstein, Weisenheim am Berg.

Kochberg (Ger) vineyard (Anb): Baden. (Ber): Ortenau. (Gro): Fürsteneck. (Vil): Durbach.

Koch Brewery (USA) a brewery based in Dunkirk, New York, noted for Black Horse Ale (a bottom-fermented beer).

Kocher [River] (Ger) a tributary of the river Neckar in Württemberg. Soil: shell limestone.

Kocherberg (Ger) grosslage (Anb): Württemberg. (Ber): Kocher-Jagst-Tauber. (Vils): Belsenberg, Bieringen, Beutelsbach, Schnait i. R, Endersbach, Rommelshausen, Stetten i. R, Strümpfelbach.

Kocher-Jagst-Tauber (Ger) bereich (Anb): Württemberg. (Gros): Kocherberg, Tauberberg.

Kochgeschmack (Ger) describes a wine that has a 'cooked' flavour from the over-heating of the wine.

Kociokwik (Pol) lit: 'cats crying', a slang term for a hangover.

Kodaikanal (Ind) a wine-producing area in northern India.

Kodiak Gold (Eng) a 4% alc by vol. golden ale brewed by the Beartown Brewery, Cheshire.

Koelenhofer (S.Afr) a dry white wine made from the Steen grape by the Koelenhof Koöperatiewe.

Koelenhof Koöperatiewe Wynkelder (S.Afr) a co-operative winery (established 1941) based in Stellenbosch, Western Cape. (Add): Box 1, Koelenhof 7605. Grape varieties: Cabernet sauvignon, Chardonnay, Chenin blanc, Gewürztraminer, Jerepigo, Merlot, Pinotage, Sauvignon blanc, Shiraz. Labels: Bukettraube, Koelenbosch, Koelenhofer, Koelnektar, Pino Porto, Soet Hanepoot.

Koelfontein (S.Afr) a winery (established 1832) based in Ceres, Western Cape. 19ha. Grape varieties: Cabernet sauvignon, Chardonnay, Colombard, Merlot, Shiraz.

Koepp (Lux) see Koeppechen.

Koeppechen (Lux) a vineyard site in the village of Wormeldange. Also known as Koepp.

Koerner Distillery (Ger) a noted distillery based at Die Stonsdorferei that produces Enzian.

Kofé (Rus) coffee.

Koff Brewery (Fin) a brewery based in Helsinki, noted for Koff Finnish Beer 5.4% alc by vol. and Koff Imperial Stout 7% alc by vol (a top-fermented beer).

Koffeinfri (Den) de-caffeinated coffee.

Koffie (Hol) coffee.

Koffiekan (Hol) coffeepot.

Koffietavel (Hol) a luncheon of coffee, cold meats, cheeses, bread and cakes.

Kofu Valley (Jap) a top wine-producing district in the Yamanashi region.

Kofye (Rus) coffee.

Kogl (Aus) vineyard sites (2) on the banks of the River Danube in the Kremstal region.

Kögl (Aus) a vineyard site on the banks of the River Danube in the Kremstal region.

Kohala (Ind) a spirit made from barley which often has a slight whisky taste.

Kohlberg (Ger) village (Anb): Württemberg. (Ber): Remstal-Stuttgart. (Gro): Hohenneuffen. (Vin): Schlossteige.

Köhler (Ger) village (Anb): Franken. (Ber): Maindreieck. (Gro): Kirchberg. (Vins): Assorted parts of vineyards.

Köhler-Köpfchen (Ger) vineyard (Anb): Nahe. (Ber): Schloss Böckelheim. (Gro): Burgweg. (Vil): Bad Münster a. St. Ebernburg.

Koicha (Jap) one of the stages of 'chanoyu', the resulting tea is thick in consistency and has a bitter taste (a 'kneaded' tea).

Koji (Jap) 'steamed rice' to which is added koji mould for making saké.

Koji Mold (USA) the alternative spelling of Koji Mould.

Koji Mould (Jap) Apergillus aryzae' a strain of yeast used in the making of saké, converts starch into sugar.

Kokeicha (Jap) green tea. See also Sencha Genmaicha and Sencha Fukujyu.

Kokkineli (Cyp) a deep rosé, very dry table wine, high in alcohol.

Kokkineli (Gre) a dark rosé, dry, slightly resinated wine.

Koko Kanu (W.Ind.) a 40% alc by vol. coconut rum from the Rum Company in Jamaica.

Kokshetau Mineral Water (Asia) a sparkling natural spring mineral water (established 1991) from Turan, Kazakhstan. Mineral contents (milligrammes per litre): Sodium 15mg/l, Calcium 40mg/l, Magnesium 10mg/l, Potassium 0.4mg/l, Bicarbonates 122mg/l, Chlorides 25mg/l, Sulphates 36mg/l, Fluorides 0.6mg/l, Hydrobromide 1.2mg/l, Silicates 66mg/l, Oxygen 9.8mg/l.

Kokteil (Gre) cocktail.

Koktel (Cro) cocktail.

Koktem (Asia) a natural spring mineral water from Alamaty, Kazakhstan. Mineral contents (milligrammes per litre): Sodium 91mg/l, Calcium 8mg/l, Magnesium 2mg/l, Bicarbonates 10mg/l, Chlorides 26mg/l, Sulphates 54.5mg/l, Fluorides 10mg/l.

Kokteyl (Tur) cocktail.

K

Kokur Niznegorsky (Rus) a dry white wine from the Crimean Peninsular.

Kola (Rus) cola.

Kola (S.Am) another spelling of Cola.

Kola Liqueurs (Afr) liqueurs made from lemon and orange peel, kolanuts, vanilla and spices.

Kold Punch (Den) cup/fruit cup (cocktail).

Koelenbosch (S.Afr) the label for a range of red and white wines produced by the Koelenhof Winery, Stellenbosch, Western Cape.

Koelenhoffer (S.Afr) the label for a white wine (Sauvignon blanc) produced by the Koelenhof Winery, Stellenbosch, Western Cape.

Koelnektar (S.Afr) the label for a semi-sweet white wine (Gewürztraminer) produced by the Koelenhof Winery, Stellenbosch, Western Cape.

Kogelberg (Aus) a vineyard site based on the banks of the River Kamp situated in the Kamptal region.

Kohlberg (Aus) a vineyard site based on the banks of the River Kamp situated in the Kamptal region.

Kolin Brewery (Czec) an old brewery based in western Czec. Noted for lager-style beers.

Kolkmann (Aus) a winery based in Fels am Wagram, Donauland. (Add): Flugplattzstrasse 12, 3481 Fels am Wagram. Grape varieties: Grüner veltliner, Neuburger, Pinot blanc, Riesling, Zweigelt. Produces a range of dry and sweet wines.

Kollektsionye (Rus) a term used for wines that are matured in cask and bottle.

Köllig (Ger). Village. (Anb): Mosel-Saar-Ruwer. (Ber): Obermosel. (Gro): Gipfel. (Vin): Rochusfels.

Kollmitz (Aus) a vineyard site on the banks of the River Danube situated in the Wachau region, Niederösterreich.

Kollmûtz (Aus) a vineyard site on the banks of the River Danube situated in the Wachau region, Niederösterreich.

Kolln Vineyards (USA) vineyards based in Bellefonte, central Pennsylvania. Produce French hybrid wines.

Kölner (Ger) the name for a person who drinks Kölsch beer.

Kolor (Ger) a red grape variety, a cross between the Spätburgunder and the Teinturier. Produces a good colour blending wine.

Kolossi (Cyp) the brand-name used by SODAP for their red and white table wines and Sherry. Named after the castle of the Knights Templar of same name on south-eastern coast of island.

Kölsch (Ger) lit: 'from Cologne' the shortened name for Kölschbier.

Kölschbier (Ger) a top-fermented light beer 4.6%–5.5% alc by vol. brewed in Cologne and Bonn. Name protected by law, low in carbonation (a digestif beer), traditionaly served in a Stangen glass held in a Kranz holder.

Kolsch Style (Eng) a 4.8% alc by vol. kolshbier style beer brewed by the Grand Union Brewery, Middlesex.

Kolteschberg (Lux) a vineyard site in the village of Schwebsingen.

Kolz Estate (Austr) a winery based in the McClaren Vale, South Australia. Grape varieties include: Cabernet sauvignon. Label: The Carbine.

Kometenwein (Ger) a wine produced to commemorate the appearance of a comet (i.e. Haley's comet).

Komovica (Slo) a brandy distilled from the residue of grape pressings after wine production.

Kompania Piwowarska SA (Pol) a brewery. (Add): Szwajcarska 11 st, 61-285 Poznan. Brews beers and lagers. Website: http://www.kp.pl 'E'mail: poctza@kp.pl

Kona Coffee (USA) a Hawaiian coffee from the west volcanic slopes of the island. Does not usually need blending and produces a smooth, mild, buttery taste and aroma.

Kondrauer Antonien-Quelle (Ger) a natural mineral water (established 1973) from Antonien-Quelle, Waldsassen.

Kondrauer Bayern-Quelle (Ger) a natural spring mineral water (established 1968) from Bayern-Quelle, Waldsassen.

Kondrauer Diepold-Quelle (Ger) a natural spring mineral water (established 1992) from Diepold-Quelle, Waldsassen. Mineral contents (milligrammes per litre): Sodium 96mg/l, Calcium 103mg/l, Magnesium 26mg/l, Potassium 12mg/l, Bicarbonates 595mg/l, Chlorides 39mg/l, Sulphates 45mg/l.

Kondrauer Gerwig-Quelle (Ger) a natural spring mineral water (established 1989) from Gerwig-Quelle, Waldsassen.

Kondrauer Heilwasser Prinz-Ludwig-Quelle (Ger) a natural spring mineral water (established 1910) from Prinz-Ludwig-Quelle, Waldsassen. Mineral contents (milligrammes per litre): Sodium 77mg/l, Calcium 51mg/l, Magnesium 19mg/l, Potassium 11mg/l, Bicarbonates 324mg/l, Chlorides 41mg/l, Sulphates 54mg/l.

Köndringen (Ger) village (Anb): Baden. (Ber): Breisgau. (Gro): Burg Lichteneck. (Vin): Alte Burg.

K I Bitter (Eng) abbr: Kelham Island bitter a 3.8% alc by vol. bitter ale brewed by the Kelham Island Brewery, South Yorkshire.

Könen (Ger) village (Anb): Mosel-Saar-Ruwer. (Ber): Saar-Ruwer. (Gro): Scharzberg. (Vins): Fels, Kirchberg.

Köngernheim (Ger) village (Anb): Rheinhessen. (Ber): Nierstein. (Gro): Gutes Domtal. (Vin): Goldgrube.

Kong Hu Te (Chi) lit: 'tea prepared with care'. e.g. Congou Black Tea, an eighteenth century tea drink.

Koniak (Bul) brandy.

Koniak (Gre) the name for a grape brandy distilled around Piraeus.

König (Ger) vineyard (Anb): Württemberg. (Ber): Württembergisch Unterland. (Gro): Stromberg. (Vil): Diefenbach.

König (Ger) vineyard (Anb): Württemberg. (Ber): Württembergisch Unterland. (Gro): Stromberg. (Vil): Sternenfels.

König (Ger) a producer of steinhäger, sold under the same name.

König Brauerei (Ger) a brewery based in Duisburg. Noted for pilsener-style beer.

Königheim (Ger) village (Anb): Baden. (Ber): Badische Frankenland. (Gro): Tauberklinge. (Vin): Kirchberg.

Königin (Ger) vineyard (Anb): Franken. (Ber): Maindreieck. (Gro): Not yet assigned. (Vil): Tauberrettersheim.

Königin Viktoriaberg (Ger) vineyard (Anb): Rheingau. (Ber): Johannisberg. (Gro): Daubhaus. (Vil): Hochheim.

Königin Viktoriaberg (Ger) a vineyard within the village of Geisenheim, 4.7ha (100%) of which is proposed to be classified as Erstes Gewächs.

König Johann Berg (Ger) vineyard (Anb): Mosel-Saar-Ruwer. (Ber): Saar-Ruwer. (Gro): Scharzberg. (Vil): Kastel-Staadt.

König Johann Berg (Ger) vineyard (Anb): Mosel-Saar-Ruwer. (Ber): Saar-Ruwer. (Gro): Scharzberg. (Vil): Serrig.

König Ludwig International GmbH & C° KG (Ger) a brewery. (Add): Augsburger Strasse 41, Fürstenfeldbruck D-82256. Brews a variety of beers and lagers. Website: http://www.koenig-ludwig.com

König Otto-Sprudel (Ger) a still and sparkling natural spring mineral water from Wiesau. (forte: sparkling/andante: light gas/piano: still). Mineral contents (milligrammes per litre): Sodium 15mg/l, Calcium 7mg/l, Magnesium 11mg/l, Potassium 4.5mg/l, Bicarbonates 80mg/l, Chlorides 6.8mg/l, Sulphates 15mg/l, Fluorides 0.42mg/l, Nitrates 1.6mg/l, Silicates 69.5mg/l.

König-Pilsener (Ger) a pilsener beer brewed by the König Brauerei in Duisburg 4.9% alc by vol.

Königsbach (Ger) village (Anb): Pfalz. (Ber): Mittelhaardt-Deutsche Weinstrasse. (Gro): Meerspinne. (Vins): Idig, Jesuitengarten, Ölberg, Reiterpfad.

Königsbecher (Ger) vineyard (Anb): Baden. (Ber): Badische Bergstrasse/Kraichgau. (Gro): Stiftsberg. (Vil): Odenheim.

Königsberg (Ger) grosslage (Anb): Mosel-Saar-Ruwer. (Ber): Obermosel. (Vils): Edingen, Godendorf, Grewenich, Igel, Langsur, Liersberg, Mesenich, Metzdorf, Ralingen, Wintersdorf

Königsberg (Ger) vineyard (Anb): Mosel-Saar-Ruwer. (Ber): Bernkastel. (Gro): Sankt Michael. (Vil): Klüsserath.

Königsberg (Ger) vineyard (Anb): Mosel-Saar-Ruwer. (Ber): Bernkastel. (Gro): Schwarzlay. (Vil): Traben-Trarbach.

Königsberg (Ger) vineyard (Anb): Württemberg. (Ber): Württembergisch Unterland. (Gro): Schalkstein. (Vil): Höpfigheim.

Königsburg (Ger) a fruity 3% alc by vol. wine from the Morio-muscat grape.

Königschaffhausen (Ger) village (Anb): Baden. (Ber): Kaiserstuhl-Tuniberg. (Gro): Vulkanfelsen. (Vins): Hasenberg, Steingrüble

Königsfels (Ger) vineyard (Anb): Mosel-Saar-Ruwer. (Ber): Zell/Mosel. (Gro): Weinhex. (Vil): Güls.

Königsfels (Ger) vineyard (Anb): Nahe. (Ber): Schloss Böckelheim. (Gro): Burgweg. (Vil): Duchroth.

Königsfels (Ger) vineyard (Anb): Nahe. (Ber): Schloss Böckelheim. (Gro): Burgweg. (Vil): Schlossböckelheim.

Königsgarten (Ger) grosslage (Anb): Pfalz. (Ber): Südliche Weinstrasse. (Vils): Albersweiler, Arzheim, Birkweiler, Frankweiler, Godramstein, Landau, Ranschbach, Siebeldingen.

Königsgarten (Ger) vineyard (Anb): Nahe. (Ber): Schloss Böckelheim. (Gro): Burgweg. (Vil): Bad Münster a St-Ebernburg.

Königsgarten (Ger) vineyard (Anb): Nahe. (Ber): Schloss Böckelheim. (Gro): Paradiesgarten. (Vil): Feilbingert.

Königshofen (Ger) village (Anb): Baden. (Ber): Badische Frankenland. (Gro): Tauberklinge. (Vins): Kirchberg, Turmberg, Walterstal.

Königslay-Terrassen (Ger) vineyard (Anb): Mosel-Saar-Ruwer. (Ber): Zell/Mosel. (Gro): Schwarze Katz. (Vil): Zell-Merl.

Königsschild (Ger) vineyard (Anb): Nahe. (Ber): Kreuznach. (Gro): Sonnenborn. (Vil): Langenlonsheim.

Königsschloss (Ger) vineyard (Anb): Nahe. (Ber): Kreuznach. (Gro): Schlosskapelle. (Vil): Münster-Sarmsheim.

Königsteiner Raderheck-Quelle-Heilwasser (Ger) a natural spring mineral water. Mineral contents (milligrammes per litre): Sodium 8.4mg/l, Calcium 18.6mg/l, Magnesium 9.6mg/l, Potassium 0.9mg/l, Chlorides 19.38mg/l, Sulphates 13.32mg/l, Fluorides 0.08mg/l.

Königstuhl (Ger) vineyard (Anb): Rheinhessen. (Ber): Nierstein. (Gro): Gutes Domtal. (Vil): Lörzweiler.

Königstuhl (Ger) vineyard (Anb): Rheinhessen. (Ber): Wonnegau. (Gro): Bergkloster. (Vil): Gundersheim.

Königsweg (Ger) vineyard (Anb): Pfalz. (Ber): Mittelhaardt-Deutsche Weinstrasse. (Gro): Schnepfenflug vom Kellertal. (Vil): Niefernheim.

Königsweg (Ger) vineyard (Anb): Pfalz. (Ber): Mittelhaardt-Deutsche Weinstrasse. (Gro): Schnepfenflug vom Zellertal. (Vil): Zell.

Königswein (Aus) lit: 'royal wine', is found on the labels of the top wines. Made only from Neuberger, Rotgipfler and Zierfandler grapes and submitted to a tasting committee.

Königsweingarten (Ger) vineyard (Anb): Baden. (Ber): Bodensee. (Gro): Sonnenufer. (Vil): Bodman.

Königswingert (Ger) vineyard (Anb): Pfalz. (Ber): Mittelhaardt-Deutsche Weinstrasse. (Gro): Schenkenböhl. (Vil): Wachenheim.

Königswinter (Ger) village (Anb): Mittelrhein. (Ber): Siebengebirge. (Gro): Petersberg. (Vin): Drachenfels.

König Wenzel (Ger) vineyard (Anb): Mittelrhein.

(Ber): Rheinbergengau. (Gro): Gedeonseck. (Vil): Rhens.

König Wilhelmsberg (Ger) vineyard (Anb): Rheingau. (Ber): Johannisberg. (Gro): Daubhaus. (Vil): Wicker.

Koningsbrunnen (Bel) a natural spring mineral water from Koning, Brakel.

Koningsrivier Wines (S.Afr) a winery (established 2002) based in Robertson, Western Cape. 9ha. Grape varieties: Cabernet sauvignon, Shiraz.

Koninklijke Nederlandse Gist en Spiritusfabriek (Bel) a large distillery based in Bruges.

Konocti Cellars (USA) a grower-owned winery based near Kelseyville, Lake County, California. Grape varieties: Cabernet sauvignon, Cabernet franc, Gamay, Sauvignon blanc, White riesling and Zinfandel. Produces varietal wines.

Konpasomkruangdum (Thai) bartender.

Konsel (Czec) a special beer 14° brewed by the Litomerice Brewery in northern Bohemia.

Konstanz (Ger) village (Anb): Baden. (Ber): Bodensee. (Gro): Sonnenufer. (Vin): Sonnenhalde.

Konsumwein (Ger) the German equivalent of red vin ordinaire, an everyday drinking wine.

Kontiki (Hol) a tropical citrus liqueur 19.5% alc by vol.

Kontinentalna Hrvatska (Cro) a wine producing area inland, home to the Laski rizling in Croatia. Vineyards are on terraces between rivers Drava and Sava.

Kontuszowka (Pol) a liqueur flavoured with the oil of lavender.

Konya (Tur) a wine-producing region in southern Turkey. Produces mainly dry white wines.

Konyak (Alb)(Tur) an Armenian name for brandy.

Konynwijn (S.Afr) the label for a semi-sweet white wine (Chenin blanc) from the Kleine Hazen range produced by the Hazendal winery, Stellenbosch, Western Cape.

Konz (Ger) village (Anb): Mosel-Saar-Ruwer. (Ber): Saar-Ruwer. (Gro): Scharzberg. (Vins): Auf der Kupp, Brauneberg, Euchariusberg, Falkensteiner, Hofberg, Klosterberg, Sprung.

Konzelmann Vineyards (Can) vineyards based in Niagara, noted for ice wine (a sweet dessert wine).

Koohii (Jap) coffee.

Koohyar (Iran) a natural spring mineral water brand.

Koombahla Cabernet Sauvignon (Austr) a full-flavoured red wine from the Brown Brothers Koombahla Estate in Milawa, Victoria 1.5ha.

Koonunga Hill (Austr) a red wine produced by the Penfolds Estate from Cabernet sauvignon and Shiraz grapes.

Koöperatiewe Wijnbouwers Vereniging (S.Afr) *abbr*: K.W.V. A wine farmer's Association founded in 1916.

Kooperatif (Tur) co-operative (winery).

Koopmanskloof Estate (S.Afr) vineyards based in Stellenbosch. (Add): Koopmanskloof Landgoed, Kuils River 7580. Produces varietal wines including Blanc de Marbonne.

Koora (Jap) cola.

Koori (Jap) ice.

Koorianda Vineyard (Austr) a vineyard based in the Barossa Valley. Is owned by the Hill-Smith Estates 10.5ha. Grape variety: Sémillon.

Kooriander (Austr) part of the Hill-Smith Estate in South Australia. Grows mainly Sémillon grapes.

Kootenay Springs (Can) a natural spring mineral water from Cranbrook, British Columbia. Mineral contents (milligrammes per litre): Sodium 41mg/l, Calcium 94mg/l, Magnesium 35mg/l, Potassium 0.4mg/l, Fluorides 0.44mg/l. pH 7.5

Kop (Den) cup.

Kopé (USA) the name for coffee in Hawaii.

Kope (E.Ind) the name for coffee in Indonesia.

Koper (Slov) a winery based in Koper, on the Adriatic, Slovenia. Noted for Cabernet sauvignon, Merlot, Pinot gris, dry Malvasia wines.

Kopetdague (Rus) a white grape variety grown in Turkmenistania. Used to produce fortified wines.

Kopf (Ger) grosslage (Anb): Württemberg. (Ber): Remstal-Stuttgart. (Vils): Beinstein, Breuningsweiler, Bürg, Grossheppach, Grunbach, Hanweiler, Kleinheppach, Korb, Neustadt, Schorndorf, Waiblingen, Winnenden, Winterbach.

Kopf (Ger) the name of the local red wine from Korb in Württemberg.

Kopi (Indo) coffee.

Kopi (Sing) a black coffee poured over sweetened condensed milk placed in the bottom of the cup. Coffee is then stirred to make it sweeter it required.

Kopiaste (Cyp) the Turkish Cypriot custom of inviting people in to their house to join them for a cup of coffee.

Kopje (Hol) cup.

Kopke (Port) vintage Port shipper controlled by Barros. Vintages: 1870, 1872, 1873, 1875, 1878, 1881, 1884, 1887, 1890, 1892, 1894, 1896, 1897, 1900, 1904, 1908, 1912, 1917, 1919, 1920, 1922, 1927, 1935, 1945, 1948, 1950, 1952, 1955, 1958, 1960, 1963, 1966, 1970, 1974, 1975, 1977, 1978, 1979, 1980, 1982, 1983, 1985, 1987, 1989, 1991, 1994, 1997, 2003. Also produces brandies. *See also* Quinta St. Luiz (a single quinta vintage Port). Supposedly the oldest Port house.

Kopparbergs Bryggeri (Swe) a brewery. (Add): 7412 82 Kopparberg. Produces top-fermented beers, lagers and flavoured ciders. 'E'mail: konsumentkontakt@kopparberbs.se

Kopparbergs Cranberry Cider (Swe) a flavoured cider produced by Kopparbergs Brewery, central Sweden.

Kopparbergs Golden Pear Cider (Swe) a flavoured cider produced by Kopparbergs Brewery, central Sweden.

Koppelstein (Ger) vineyard (Anb): Mittelrhein. (Ber): Rheinburgengau. (Gro): Marksburg. (Vil): Braubach.

Koppelstein (Ger) vineyard (Anb): Mittelrhein. (Ber): Rheinburgengau. (Gro): Marksburg. (Vil): Lahnstein.

Koppi (E.Ind) the Malayan name for coffee. *See also* Kawa.

Koppig (Hol) heady.

Koppu (Jap) cup.

Köpük (Tur) beer head/frothy foam.

Köpüren (Tur) effervescent/sparkling/fizzy.

Korb (Ger) village (Anb): Württemberg. (Ber): Remstal-Stuttgart. (Gro): Kopf. (Vins): Berg, Hörnle, Sommerhalde.

Korb (Ger) village (Anb): Württemberg. (Ber): Remstal-Stuttgart. (Gro): Wartbühl. (Vin): Steingrüble.

Korbell Bros (USA) a vineyard and winery in Sonoma, California. Famous for its sparkling wines from a blend of Chardonnay and Pinot noir grapes.

Korcula (Euro) a wine-producing island off the Dalmatian coast. Noted for Grk, Maraština, Plavina and Pošip wines.

Korenjenever (Hol) a style of jenever.

Korenwijn (Hol) a moutwijn distilled without the addition of juniper.

Korepo (N.Z) a small winery near Blenheim at Ruby Bay, Nelson.

Korersbier (Fr) a 4.4% alc by vol Alsace lager beer.

Korinthiaki (Gre) a black grape variety grown in Patras. Used in Mavrodaphne of Patras.

Korkbrand (Ger) a branded cork.

Korken-Geschmack (Ger) denotes a corky, musky, mouldy wine with a taste of tannin.

Korkenzieher (Aus)(Ger) corkscrew.

Korlingen (Ger) village (Anb): Mosel-Saar-Ruwer. (Ber): Saar-Ruwer. (Gro): Römerlay. (Vin): Laykaul.

Korma (Fr) lit: 'beer of the Gauls', a 5.9% alc by vol. amber coloured, top-fermented, bottle-conditioned bière de garde brewed by Bénifontaine Brasserie, Bénifontaine. Brewed using seven malts.

Korn (Ger) *abbr*: **Korn**branntwein, a clear grain spirit 35% alc by vol. pot-stilled, and cask-aged (originally produced in the Harz 'mountains). *See also* Kornbrannt.

Kornbrannt (Ger) *see* Kornbranntwein.

Kornbranntwein (Ger) lit: 'corn whiskey', the equivalent for rye whiskey.

Kornbrennerei Schönau GmbH (Ger) a noted producer of kornbranntwein based in Friedrichsruh, Sachsenwald, Germany. Sold under the Schänauer label. Also Boonekamp.

Kornell Champagne Cellars (USA) a winery based in the Napa Valley, California. Noted for sparkling wines made by méthode traditionelle.

Korn-Genever (Ger) a kornbranntwein flavoured with juniper.

Kornschnapps (Ger) a schnapps made from corn only.

Korn-Wacholder (Ger) a kornbranntwein flavoured with juniper essence.

Koroglu (Tur) the brand-name for a white wine.

Körper (Ger) body.

Körperarm (Ger) of poor body.

Korpi (Gre) a natural spring mineral water. Mineral contents (milligrammes per litre): Sodium 4.7mg/l, Calcium 101.2mg/l, Magnesium 21mg/l, Potassium 0.8mg/l, Bicarbonates 305.5mg/l, Chlorides 10.2mg/l, Sulphates 4.3mg/l, Nitrates mg/l. pH 7.3

Korten (Bul) a D.G.O. area of the Southern Basic region noted for Cabernet sauvignon reserve wines.

Koruk (Tur) unripe grapes.

Koruku Nuki (Jap) corkscrew.

Korunni (Czec) a natural spring mineral water (established 1878) from Korunni. Mineral contents (milligrammes per litre): Sodium 103.2mg/l, Calcium 78.02mg/l, Magnesium 30.48mg/l, Potassium 25.46mg/l, Bicarbonates 615.6mg/l, Chlorides 10.33mg/l, Sulphates 60.39mg/l, Fluorides 0.82mg/l, Nitrates 40.67mg/l.

Korytnica (Euro) a sparkling natural spring mineral water (established circa 1500) from Mount Prasivio, Lower Tatras, Slovak Republic. Mineral contents (milligrammes per litre): Sodium 2.25mg/l, Calcium 8.02mg/l, Magnesium 1.22mg/l, Potassium 0.5mg/l, Bicarbonates 27.5mg/l, Chlorides 0.5mg/l, Sulphates 5.75mg/l, Fluorides 0.05mg/l.

Kos (Gre) an island which produces both red and white wines.

Kosher Cold Duck (USA) *see* Kalta Katchka.

Kosher Pilsner (Ger) a 4.9% alc by vol top quality kosher pilsener brewed from barley left untouched during the passover by the Herrenhäuser Brauerei, western Germany.

Kosher Rebeka (Pol) a natural spring mineral water from Kunice.

Kosher Vodka (USA) a neutral spirit produced under rabbinical supervision which meets all Talmudic stipulations.

Kosher Wine (Isr) produced under rabbinical supervision and meets all Talmudic stipulations. *See also* Vin Cacher and Shomrim.

Koshu (Jap) a native white grape variety.

Kosice Brewery (Czec) a brewery based in eastern Czec, noted for Cassovar Lager.

Kosie Möller Wines (S.Afr) a winery (established 2000) based in Suider-Paarl, Western Cape. 52ha. Grape varieties: Cabernet sauvignon, Chardonnay, Chenin blanc, Sémillon, Viognier. *see* Cru Wines and Klein Parys.

Koskenkorva (Fin) a sweet vodka.

Kosmet (Ser) a province of Serbia near Macedonia and Albania, noted for full-bodied red wines.

Kosnatural Mineral Water (Chi) a natural spring mineral water. Mineral contents (milligrammes per litre): Sodium 8.9mg/l, Calcium 38.1mg/l, Magnesium 5.5mg/l, Potassium 0.8mg/l, Bicarbonates 183mg/l, Silicates 38.5mg/l.

Kosovo (Ser) a key wine region in South Serbia near the Albanian border. Main wines are from the Cabernet franc, Gamay, Smederevka and Spätburgunder.

K

Kostas Lazaridis (Gre) a winery that produces Château Julia Assyrtiko white wine, plus Amethystos cava red wine from old vine Cabernet sauvignon grapes.

Kostelbräu (Czec) a 5% alc by vol. pilsener beer brand.

Kostelec Nad Cernymi Lesy (Czec) an old established brewery based in western Czec.

Kostheim (Ger) village (Anb): Rheingau. (Ber): Johannisberg. (Gro): Daubhaus. (Vins): Berg, Reichesthal, Steig, Weiss Erd.

Köstritzer Edel Pils (Ger) a 4.8% alc by vol. bottled pilsener brewed by the Köstritzer Schwarzbier Brauerei, Bad Köstritz.

Köstritzer Schwarzbier Brauerei (Ger) a brewery based in Bad Köstritx. Brews: Köstritzer Schwarzbier and Edel Pils.

Köstritzer Schwarz Pils (Ger) a 4.8% alc by vol. canned schwarzbier (black pilsener) brewed with malt extract by the Köstritzer Schwarzbier Brauerei, Bad Köstritz, Thuringia. Brewed using top-fermented lager yeasts. Served mixed with pale beers or drunk as a tonic in eastern Germany.

Köthener Brauerei (Ger) a brewery based in Köthen, brews Sachsen Krone.

Kotsifali (Gre) a red grape variety used in the production of Peza and Archanes wines.

Kottabos (Gre) a game played in ancient Greece after dinner where a plate was balanced on a pole and the dregs of wine in a glass were thrown at it. In modern times to swirl dregs around a glass or cup and then to fling them out to hit a predetermined spot on the table or floor.

Koumis (Asia) an alternative spelling of Koumiss.

Koumiss (Asia) fermented sour camel or mare's milk, made by the Tartars. See also Arjan, Kumiss, Koumis and Koumyss.

Koumyss (Asia) an alternative spelling of Koumiss. See also Koumiss, Kumiss and Arjan.

Kouros (Gre) the brand-name for a range of red and white wines produced by Kourtakis S.A.

Kourschels (Lux) a vineyard site in the village of Wellenstein.

Kourtakis S.A. [D.] (Gre) a winery based at 19003 Markopoulo, Attica. Produces Kouros (a range of red and white wines).

Kövidinka (Hun) a medium dry, white wine produced in south-western Hungary from grape of the same name. Also known as Dinka.

Köwerich (Ger) village (Anb): Mosel-Saar-Ruwer. (Ber): Bernkastel. (Gro): Sankt Michael. (Vins): Held, Laurentiuslay.

Kozel 14% (Czec) a dark special beer 14° balling brewed by the Velké Popovice Brewery.

Kozel Dark 10% (Czec) a 3.8% alc by vol. dark, malty bottled lager brewed by the Velké Popovice Brewery.

Kozel Straw 10% (Czec) a 4% alc by vol. gold coloured, bottled lager brewed by the Velké Popovice Brewery.

Kozel Straw 12% (Czec) a 5% alc by vol. straw coloured, bottled lager brewed by the Velké Popovice Brewery.

Kozjak (Slo) a white wine produced in Slovenia.

Kozuvcanka (Euro) a natural spring mineral water (established 1993) from Mrezicko, Macedonia. Mineral contents (milligrammes per litre): Sodium 44.7mg/l, Calcium 302mg/l, Magnesium 69.4mg/l, Bicarbonates 1083mg/l, Chlorides 10mg/l, Sulphates 55.38mg/l, Fluorides 0.9mg/l. pH 6.5

KPA (Eng) abbr: Keg Pale Ale 1035 O.G. brewed by the Brakspear Brewery, Henley-on-Thames, Berkshire.

Kraamanis (Hol) a liqueur produced by Van Zuylekom of Amsterdam.

Krabask Bitters (Den) an alcoholic bitters.

Kracher (Aus) an alternative name for the Blauer Wildbacher grape variety.

Kracher [Alois] (Aus) a wine producer. See also Weinlaubenhof.

Krachtig (Hol) potent/strong.

Kräftig (Ger) robust/rich in alcohol.

Krähenberg (Ger) vineyard (Anb): Württemberg. (Ber): Württembergisch Unterland. (Gro): Heuchelberg. (Vil): Massenbachhausen.

Krähenschnabel (Ger) vineyard (Anb): Franken. (Ber): Maindreieck. (Gro): Not yet assigned. (Vil): Rerlenbach bei Marktheidenfeld.

Krähenwinkler (Ger) the brand-name of a weizenkorn produced by August Schmidt Gutsbrennerein, Krähenwinkler, Hannover.

Kraichgau (Ger) a district within the Baden region. see Badische Bergstrasse/Kraichgau.

Kraichtal [stadtteil Bahnbrucker, Gochsheim and Oberacker] (Ger) village (Anb): Baden. (Ber): Badische Bergstrasse/Kraichgau. (Gro): Stiftsberg. (Vin): Lerchenberg.

Kraichtal [stadtteil Landshausen and Menzingen] (Ger) village (Anb): Baden. (Ber): Badische Bergstrasse/Kraichgau. (Gro): Stiftsberg, Spiegelberg.

Kraichtal [stadtteil Neuenbürg, Menzingen and Münzesheim] (Ger) village (Anb): Baden. (Ber): Badische Bergstrasse/Kraichgau. (Gro): Stiftsberg. (Vin): Silberberg.

Kraichtal [stadtteil Oberöwisheim, stadtteil Unteröwisheim] (Ger) village (Anb): Baden. (Ber): Badische Bergstrasse/Kraichgau. (Gro): Mannaberg. (Vin): Kirchberg.

Kraipale (Gre) drunkenness.

Krajina (Ser) a wine region that borders Bulgaria and Rumania. Produces mainly red wines from the Prokupac, Skadarka and Zacinka grapes. Also noted for Bagrina (a dry white wine from grape of same name).

Krakonose (Czec) a beer 14° brewed by the Trotnov Brewery in eastern Bohemia. Has a strong hop flavour and aroma.

Krakowianka (Pol) a natural spring mineral water. Mineral contents (milligrammes per litre): Sodium 457mg/l, Calcium 220.4mg/l, Magnesium 127.7mg/l, Bicarbonates 336mg/l,

Chlorides 398.9mg/l, Sulphates 1173.9mg/l, Fluorides 0.6mg/l.

Krakus (Pol) said to be the ladies favourite vodka. 40% alc by vol. Produced from rye by Polmos.

Krakus (Pol) a premium lager 5.2% alc by vol. from the Zywiec Brewery.

Královsky Pipovar Krušovice (Czec) the Royal Krušovice Brewery (established 1581) based in Rakovnik. Brews: Krušovice Cerné 10%, Krušovice Lezák 12%.

Kralupy nad Vltavou Brewery (Czec) a brewery based in northern Czec.

Krambamuli (Ger) a liqueur flavoured with angelica and violet extract and produced in eastern Germany.

Krampeln (Aus) denotes an empty, lifeless wine that has a rough, biting flavour.

Krampen (Ger) a section of wineland around Cochem on the lower Mosel. So called because of the shape of the bend (or cramp) in the river, it produces poor wines because of the hardness of the soil.

Kranawitter (It) a gin from juniper berries made in the Südtirol (Trentino-Alto Adige) 38% alc by vol.

Krans Estate [Die] (S.Afr) a wine estate based in Klein Karoo. (Add): Box 28, Calitzdorp 6660. Produces varietal wines. Was originally known as the Hoë Krans Wynmakery.

Kranskop Estate (S.Afr) a winery (established 2001) based in Robertson, Western Cape. 40ha. Grape varieties: Cabernet sauvignon, Chardonnay, Merlot, Shiraz. W.O. Klaasvoogds. Website: http://www.kranskopwines.co.za

Kranz (Ger) lit: 'crown', the name for a round holder that is made for the Stangen glass to prevent it from being accidentally knocked over. see Kölsch beer.

Kranz (Ger) a liqueur producer based in Zusenhofen, Schwarzwald.

Kranzberg (Ger) vineyard (Anb): Rheinhessen. (Ber): Nierstein. (Gro): Auflangen. (Vil): Nierstein.

Kranzberg (Ger) vineyard (Anb): Rheinhessen. (Ber): Nierstein. (Gro): Gutes Domtal. (Vil): Dalheim.

Krapfenberg (Ger) vineyard (Anb): Pfalz. (Ber): Südliche Weinstrasse. (Gro): Guttenberg. (Vil): Vollmersweiler.

Krasi (Gre) wine.

Kraskiteran (Slo) a robust red wine (high in iron and tannin) produced in the Slovenia region.

Krasnodar (Geo) the Crimean 'Champagne', produced between the Anapa and Gelendshik regions, is a wine region and city in own right.

Krasnoe Vino (Rus) a local red wine produced in the river Don area.

Krasnotop (Rus) a white grape variety grown in the river Don area.

Krasnyi Kamenj (Geo) a white table wine produced near Krasnodar.

Krassato (Gre) a red grape variety used for making dry red wines in northern Greece.

Krater (Gre) a wide round bowl that was used to combine wine and water in ancient Greece.

Krater (Ser) a red wine produced in south-eastern Macedonia.

Krating (Thai) a pilsner-style lager brewed by the Amant Brewery in Thailand.

Kratosija (Slo) a red wine produced in southern Macedonia from grape of the same name.

Krätzer (Aus) an alternative name for the Blauer wildbacher grape variety.

Kratzig (Ger) denotes a pétillant, bubbly wine.

Krauel [Carlos J.] (Sp) a noted producer and exporter of Málaga

Krausen (USA) unfermented wort added to the beer to produce a second fermentation to carbonate the beer.

Krausening (USA) a process of adding krausen to the beer.

Kräuterberg (Ger) vineyard (Anb): Ahr. (Ber): Walporzheim/Ahrtal. (Gro): Klosterberg. (Vil): Walporzheim.

Kräuterberg (Ger) vineyard (Anb): Mittelrhein. (Ber): Bacharach. (Gro): Schloss Stahleck. (Vil): Oberdiebach.

Kräuterhaus (Ger) vineyard (Anb): Mosel-Saar-Ruwer. (Ber): Bernkastel. (Gro): Schwarzlay. (Vil): Traben-Trarbach.

Krauterlikor (Ger) a herb-flavoured liqueur.

Krautheim (Ger) village (Anb): Baden. (Ber): Badische Frankenland. (Gro): Tauberklinge. (Vin): Heiligenberg.

Krautheim (Ger) village (Anb): Franken. (Ber): Maindreieck. (Gro): Kirchberg. (Vin): Sonnenleite.

Krautheim [stadtteil Klepsau] (Ger) village (Anb): Baden. (Ber): Badische Frankenland. (Gro): Tauberklinge. (Vin): Heiligenberg.

Kraxen (Aus) a vineyard site on the banks of the River Danube in the Kremstal region.

Kreaca (Rum) a white grape variety, also known as Banater riesling, Zokkelweiss, Kriacza and Creaca.

Kreidkeller (Ger) vineyard (Anb): Pfalz. (Ber): Mittelhaardt-Deutsche Weinstrasse. (Gro): Feuerberg. (Vil): Kallstadt.

Kreigsberg (Ger) vineyard (Anb): Württemberg. (Ber): Remstal-Stuttgart. (Gro): Weinsteige. (Vil): Stuttgart.

Kreimel [Herbert] (Aus) a winery based in Traisen, Traisental. (Add): Bäckergasse 2, 3130 Herzogenburg, St. Andräl/Traisen. Grape varieties include: Grüner veltliner, Muller-Thurgau, Pinot blanc, Riesling. Labels include: PI.NO.VI.TA.

Kreitzberg (Lux) a vineyard site in the village of Remerschen.

Krema Galaktos (Gre) cream.

Kremer [Louis] (Fr) a Champagne producer. (Add): B.P. 149, 51200 Épernay. Produces vintage and non-vintage wines. Vintages: 1971, 1973, 1975, 1976, 1978, 1979, 1980, 1982, 1983, 1988, 1990, 1995, 1996, 1998, 1999, 2000.

Kremlyovskaya (Rus) a 40% alc by vol. triple distilled vodka. Available in natural blackcurrant, pepper, chocolate and lemon flavours from Anopino distillers in Vladimir.

Krems (Aus) a wine town and district within the region of Niederösterreich, produces both red and white wines. *see* Kremstal.

Kremser (Aus) a vineyard site on the banks of the River Danube in the Kremstal region.

Kremser (Aus) a white, fruity wine from Krems district.

Kremser Kogl (Aus) a vineyard site on the banks of the River Danube in the Kremstal region.

Kremsfeld (Aus) vineyard sites (2) based on the banks of the River Kamp situated in the Kamptal region.

Kremsleiten (Aus) a vineyard site on the banks of the River Danube in the Kremstal region.

Kremsmünsterhof (Aus) a winery based in Gumpoldskirchen, Thermenregion. (Add): Badener Strasse 11, 2352 Gumpoldskirchen. Grape varieties: Chardonnay, Riesling, Rotgipfler, Zierfandler, Zweigelt. Produces a range of dry and botrytised sweet wines.

Kremstal (Aus) a wine-producing region (2450ha) situated around the city of Krems on the banks of the River Danube (Donau). Soil: gravel, loess, rock and sand. Main grape varieties: white (Chardonnay, Grüner veltliner, Müller-Thurgau, Neuburger, Riesling, Roter veltliner) red (Pinot noir, Zweigelt). Villages: Furth, Gedersdorf, Gneixendorf, Imbach, Krustetten, Mautern, Palt, Paudorf, Rehberg, Rohrendorf, Senftenberg, Stratzing. Vineyards: Acker Leithen, Altenburg, Am Sand, Auf der Hald, Auf der Höhe, Birbaum, Braunsdorf, Brunnfeld, Brunngraben, Brunnleiten, Danzern Grillenparz, Eben, Ebritzstein, Ehrenfels, Eichbühel, Eisfeld, Emerlingtal, Erdschüssl, Faucha, Frauenbach, Frauengrund, Frechau, Fröllern, Furthner Steig, Gaisberg, Ganshalt, Gartl, Gärtling, Gebling, Goldberg (2), Goldbühel, Gottschelle, Gross Gebirg, Hadratstall, Hausbergen, Herrentrost, Himmelreich, Hintere Pointen, Hinters Kirchel, Hochäck, Hochrain, Hochsatze, Hohenäcker, Hoher Rain, Höhlgraben (2), Hollenburgern, Holzäcker, Holzgasse, Hopfengrund, Im Berg, Im Grossen Feld, Im Innern Thalland, Im Paschingerin (2), Im Saherken, Im Talheim, In der Gais, Innausen, In Schiefern, In Schrötten, Juden Gaisberg, Kattengraben, Keedorf, Kerschbaum, Kirchbühel, Kisling, Kobl, Kogl (2), Kögl, Kraxen, Kremser, Kremser Kogl, Kremsleiten, Kreuzschragen, Kühberg, Landwig, Langen-Hadlinger, Langstampf Satzen, Langstampf Steiner, Leimern, Leisern, Leiten, Lilienfeldberg, Limberg, Lusthausberg, Marchgasse, Maring, Marthal, Meiseläckern, Mitterweg, Mosburgerin, Mugeln, Neuberg, Neubergen, Neubergern, Neusiedeln, Neu Vierteln, Obere Pointen, Oberer Weinzierlberg, Obere Ziestel, Oberfeld, Partschen, Paschingerin, Pellinger, Pfennigberg, Pitschental, Point (2), Pulferturm, Rammeln, Reisenthal, Richtern, Rohrendorfer Gebling, Sandgrube, Scheibelberg, Schlucht, Schreck (Steiner), Schweren Zapfen, Seebodenberg, Silberbügel, Sommerleithen, Spickenberg, Spiegel, Spiegeln, Spitaller, Sprinzenberg, Steinbühel, Steiner Pfaffenberg, Steingraten Tiefenthal, Steinhagen, Steinling, Thalland, Tiefenthal, Trenzen, Untere Ziestel, Vorden Berg, Wachtberg, Weinzierlberg, Weitgasse, Wendlstatt, Wieden, Wieland, Windleiten, Wolfsberg, Zasen, Zaum, Zehetnerin.

Kremstal (Aus) a vineyard site based on the banks of the River Kamp situated in the Kamptal region.

Kreos (It) the label for a rosé wine produced by the Castello Monaci winery in the Puglia region.

Krepkaya (Rus) a vodka of high proof (56% alc by vol). Is fined, filtered through charcoal and polished in a bed of quartz.

Kressbronn am Bodensee Tubingen [ortsteil Hirschau, Unterjesingen] (Ger) village (Anb): Württemberg. (Ber): Kocher-Jagst-Tauber. (Gro): Not yet assigned. (Vin): Sonnenhalden.

Kressmann (Fr) an Armagnac producer.

Kressmann La Tour (Fr) *see* Château La Tour Martillac.

Kreszenz (Ger) a word which denotes a wine grower/vineyard owner.

Kretchma (Cktl) ½ measure vodka, ½ measure (white) crème de menthe, juice ¼ lemon, dash grenadine. Shake over ice and strain into a cocktail glass.

Kretikos (Gre) the brand-name of a white Vin de Pays wine made from the Vilana grape from the Boutari winery, Crete.

Kretzer (It) a rosato wine produced in the Südtirol (Trentino-Alto Adige) region.

Kreusenbier (Ger) a yeasty sediment beer produced by the Haake-Beck Brauerei of Bremen.

Kreutles (Aus) a vineyard site on the banks of the River Danube situated in the Wachau region, Niederösterreich.

Kreuz (Ger) cross.

Kreuz (Ger) vineyard (Anb): Rheinhessen. (Ber): Bingen. (Gro): Sankt Rochuskapelle. (Vil): Ockenheim.

Kreuz (Ger) vineyard (Anb): Rheinhessen. (Ber): Nierstein. (Gro): Güldenmorgen. (Vil): Dienheim.

Kreuz (Ger) vineyard (Anb): Rheinhessen. (Ber): Nierstein. (Gro): Güldenmorgen. (Vil): Oppenheim.

Kreuz (Ger) vineyard (Anb): Pfalz. (Ber): Mittelhaardt-Deutsche Weinstrasse. (Gro): Schnepfenflug an der Weinstrasse. (Vil): Friedelsheim.

Kreuz (Ger) vineyard (Anb): Pfalz. (Ber): Mittelhaardt-Deutsche Weinstrasse. (Gro): Schwarzerde. (Vil): Kirchheim.

Kreuzberg (Aus) a vineyard site on the banks of the River Danube situated in the Wachau region, Niederösterreich.

Kreuzberg (Ger) vineyard (Anb): Baden. (Ber): Ortenau. (Gro): Fürsteneck. (Vil): Rammersweier.

Kreuzberg (Ger) vineyard (Anb): Baden. (Ber): Ortenau. (Gro): Schloss Rodeck. (Vil): Mösbach.

Kreuzberg (Ger) vineyard (Anb): Baden. (Ber): Ortenau. (Gro): Schloss Rodeck. (Vil): Renchen.

K

Kreuzberg (Ger) vineyard (Anb): Baden. (Ber): Ortenau. (Gro): Schloss Rodeck. (Vil): Waldulm.

Kreuzberg (Ger) vineyard (Anb): Franken. (Ber): Maindreieck. (Gro): Kirchberg. (Vil): Nordheim.

Kreuzberg (Ger) vineyard (Anb): Mittelrhein. (Ber): Rheinburgengau. (Gro): Marksberg. (Vil): Koblenz-Ehrenbreitstein.

Kreuzberg (Ger) vineyard (Anb): Mosel-Saar-Ruwer. (Ber): Bernkastel. (Gro): Schwarzlay. (Vil): Traben-Trarbach.

Kreuzberg (Ger) vineyard (Anb): Rheinhessen. (Ber): Nierstein. (Gro): Krötenbrunnen. (Vil): Dolgesheim.

Kreuzberg (Ger) vineyard (Anb): Rheinhessen. (Ber): Nierstein. (Gro): Sankt Alban. (Vil): Bodenheim.

Kreuzberg (Ger) vineyard (Anb): Pfalz. (Ber): Mittelhaardt-Deutsche Weinstrasse. (Gro): Pfaffengrund. (Vil): Dutweiler.

Kreuzberg (Ger) vineyard (Anb): Pfalz. (Ber): Mittelhaardt-Deutsche Weinstrasse. (Gro): Schnepfenflug vom Kellertal. (Vil): Einselthum.

Kreuzberg (Ger) vineyard (Anb): Pfalz. (Ber): Mittelhaardt-Deutsche Weinstrasse. (Gro): Schnepfenflug vom Kellertal. (Vil): Niefernheim.

Kreuzberg (Ger) vineyard (Anb): Pfalz. (Ber): Mittelhaardt-Deutsche Weinstrasse. (Gro): Schnepfenflug vom Zellertal. (Vil): Zell.

Kreuzblick (Ger) vineyard (Anb): Rheinhessen. (Ber): Wonnegau. (Gro): Liebfrauenmorgen. (Vil): Worms.

Kreuzhalde (Ger) vineyard (Anb): Baden. (Ber): Kaiserstuhl-Tuniberg. (Gro): Vulkanfelsen. (Vil): Ihringen.

Kreuzhalde (Ger) vineyard (Anb): Baden. (Ber): Kaiserstuhl-Tuniberg. (Gro): Vulkanfelsen. (Vil): Wasenweiler.

Kreuzkapelle (Ger) vineyard (Anb): Rheinhessen. (Ber): Nierstein. (Gro): Vogelsgärten. (Vil): Guntersblum.

Kreuzlay (Ger) vineyard (Anb): Mosel-Saar-Ruwer. (Ber): Zell/Mosel. (Gro): Schwarze Katz. (Vil): Zell.

Kreuznach (Ger) bereich (Anb): Nahe. (Gros): Kronenberg, Schlosskapelle, Sonnenborn, Pfarrgarten.

Kreuzschragen (Aus) a vineyard site on the banks of the River Danube in the Kremstal region.

Kreuzweg (Ger) vineyard (Anb): Baden. (Ber): Badische Bergstrasse/Kraichgau. (Gro): Mannaberg. (Vil): Leimen.

Kreuzweg (Ger) vineyard (Anb): Rheinhessen. (Ber): Nierstein. (Gro): Petersberg. (Vil): Framersheim.

Kreuzweiler (Ger) village (Anb): Mosel-Saar-Ruwer. (Ber): Obermosel. (Gro): Gipfel. (Vin): Schloss Thorner Kupp.

Kreuzwertheim (Ger) village (Anb): Franken. (Ber): Mainviereck. (Gro): Not yet assigned. (Vin): Kaffelstein.

Kriacza (Rum) a white grape variety also known as Banater riesling, Zakkelweiss, Kreaca, Creaca.

Kriek (Bel) a lambic beer 5%–7% alc by vol. which

has cherries added to produce a new fermentation for 4–8 months.

Kriekenbier (Bel) a cherry beer brewed without the use of lambic beer.

Krieken Lambic (Bel) *see* Kriek.

Krim (Indo)(Kor) cream.

Krim-Sekt (Rus) a sparkling (méthode traditionelle) wine, the first to be produced in Russia (circa 1779).

Kriska (Afr) a potent palm wine produced in western Africa.

Kriss Cocktail (Cktl) 20mls (⅙ gill) Cognac, 15mls (⅛ gill) dry vermouth, 15mls (⅛ gill) amaretto, juice ¼ lemon, dash gomme syrup. Stir over ice, strain into an ice-filled highball glass, top with tonic water, a cherry and a lemon slice.

Kristal (Rus) a brand of vodka 40% alc by vol. distilled in Riga.

Kristaliczna Woda (Pol) a still natural spring mineral water. Mineral contents (milligrammes per litre): Sodium 4.7mg/l, Calcium 30.93mg/l, Magnesium 27.21mg/l, Potassium 0.88mg/l, Bicarbonates 180.07mg/l, Chlorides 8.87mg/l, Sulphates 33.54mg/l.

Kristal-Liköre (Ger) indicates visible sugar crystals in a liqueur.

Kristal Weizen (Ger) a wheat beer brewed by the Erdinger Brauerei.

Kristalyviz (Hun) a sparkling natural spring mineral water from Budapest. Mineral contents (milligrammes per litre): Sodium 154mg/l, Calcium 150mg/l, Magnesium 40.8mg/l, Bicarbonates 560mg/l, Chlorides 166mg/l, Sulphates 201mg/l, Fluorides 2.4mg/l, Silicates 46.9mg/l.

Kristina (Cro) a sparkling natural spring mineral water from Lipik. Mineral contents (milligrammes per litre): Sodium 814.96mg/l, Calcium 40.44mg/l, Magnesium 16.58mg/l, Potassium 90.81mg/l, Bicarbonates 1506.65mg/l, Chlorides 395.67mg/l, Sulphates 242.22mg/l, Fluorides 10.06mg/l.

Kristina Still (Cro) a still natural spring mineral water from Veliko Vrilo, Kijevo. Mineral contents (milligrammes per litre): Sodium 4.8mg/l, Calcium 58.4mg/l, Magnesium 14.2mg/l, Bicarbonates 107mg/l, Chlorides 12mg/l, Sulphates 14.3mg/l.

Kristin Hill Winery (USA) a winery (established 1985) based in Willamette Valley, Oregon. Grape varieties: Chardonnay, Gewürztraminer, Müller-Thurgau, Pinot gris, Pinot noir, Riesling.

Kriter (Fr) a sparkling wine made by the transfer method. Produced from the Aligoté grape by Patriache Pére et Fils, Burgundy.

Kroatenpfad (Ger) vineyard (Anb): Pfalz. (Ber): Mittelhaardt-Deutsche Weinstrasse. (Gro): Pfaffengrund. (Vil): Lachen-Speyerdorf.

Kroatzbeere (Pol) a blackberry brandy produced from wild blackberries 30% alc by vol. *See also* Jerzyrowka.

Kroatzbeerlikoer (Ger) blackberry brandy. (Fr) =

eau-de-vie-de-mûre, (Pol) = jerzyrowka/ kroatzbeerlikor.

Kroeg (Hol) tavern/public-house/pub.

Kroegje (Hol) a street-corner local drinking place.

Kroes (Hol) cup/mug.

Kroger Drinking Water (USA) a still natural spring mineral water brand from Richmond.

Kroger Spring Water (USA) a natural spring mineral water from Richmond. Mineral contents (milligrammes per litre): Fluorides 0.06mg/l.

Krohn (Port) vintage Port producers. Vintages: 1957, 1958, 1960, 1961, 1963, 1965, 1967, 1968, 1970, 1975, 1978, 1982, 1984, 1985, 1991, 1994, 1997, 2003.

Krombacher Brauerei (Ger) a brewery based at Kreuztal-Krombach. Brews: Fairlight, Krombacher Pils.

Kromeríz Brewery (Czec) one of the countries oldest breweries based in Kromeríz, central Czec.

Kronberg (Ger) vineyard (Anb): Franken. (Ber): Steigerwald. (Gro): Kapellenberg. (Vil): Zeil.

Kronberger Brauhaus (Ger) a brewery. (Add): Katharinenstrasse 4, D-61476 Kronberg im Taunus. Brews a variety of beers and lager. Website: http://www.kronberger-brauhaus.de 'E'mail: brauhaus@kronberger-brauhaus.de

Krondorf (Austr) a winery. (Add): 19 North Street, Adelaide, South Australia 5000. 91.5ha. in Barossa Valley, Lyndoch and McLaren Vale. Grape varieties: Cabernet franc, Cabernet sauvignon, Chardonnay, Frontignan, Rhine riesling, Sémillon, Shiraz.

Krone (Aus) a dry, golden-coloured beer 12.5° brewed by the Schwechat Brauerei.

Krone (Ger) vineyard (Anb): Mosel-Saar-Ruwer. (Ber): Saar-Ruwer. (Gro): Römerlay. (Vil): Waldrach.

Krone (Ger) vineyard (Anb): Nahe. (Ber): Kreuznach. (Gro): Schlosskapelle. (Vil): Laubenheim.

Krone (Ger) vineyard (Anb): Rheingau. (Ber): Johannisberg. (Gro): Burgweg. (Vil): Lorch.

Krone (Ger) a vineyard within the village of Lorch, 14.5ha. (51.7%) of which is proposed to be classified as Erstes Gewächs.

Krone-Balm of the Night (S.Afr) the label for a fortified white wine (Muscat de frontignan) produced by the Twee Jongegezellen Estate winery, Tulbagh, Western Cape.

Kroneberg (Ger) vineyard (Anb): Mosel-Saar-Ruwer. (Ber): Zell/Mosel. (Gro): Grafschaft. (Vil): Bullay.

Krone Borealis (S.Afr) a sparkling wine from the slopes of the Obliqua Mountains in the Coastal Region. Made on the Twee Jonge Gezellen Estate.

Kronenberg (Ger) grosslage (Anb): Nahe. (Ber): Kreuznach. (Vils): Bad Kreuznach, Winzenheim, Bosenheim, Ippesheim, Planig, Bretzenheim, Hargesheim.

Kronenberg (Ger) vineyard (Anb): Mosel-Saar-Ruwer. (Ber): Zell/Mosel. (Gro): Grafschaft. (Vil): Alf.

Kronenberg (Ger) vineyard (Anb): Pfalz. (Ber): Mittelhaardt-Deutsche Weinstrasse. (Gro): Kobnert. (Vil): Kallstadt.

Kronenbourg 1664 (Fr) a lager beer 5% alc by vol. 1046 O.G. brewed under licence by Harp and Courage Breweries from the Kronenbourg Brasserie based in Strasbourg, Alsace.

Kronenbourg Blanc (Eng) an imported weisbier brewed by the Kronenbourg Brauerei for the the British market.

Kronenbrau 1308 (Afr) a lager beer brewed under licence by the Intercontinental Breweries.

Kronen Brauerei (Ger) is Dortmund's oldest brewery (circa 1430). Brews: Kronen Classic, Kronen Export, Kronen Premium Pilsner, Kronenbourg Blanc.

Kronenbühl (Ger) vineyard (Anb): Baden. (Ber): Breisgau. (Gro): Schutterlindenberg. (Vil): Friesenheim.

Kronenbühl (Ger) vineyard (Anb): Baden. (Ber): Breisgau. (Gro): Schutterlindenberg. (Vil): Heiligenzell.

Kronenbühl (Ger) vineyard (Anb): Baden. (Ber): Breisgau. (Gro): Schutterlindenberg. (Vil): Hugsweier.

Kronenbühl (Ger) vineyard (Anb): Baden. (Ber): Breisgau. (Gro): Schutterlindenberg. (Vil): Lahr.

Kronenbühl (Ger) vineyard (Anb): Baden. (Ber): Breisgau. (Gro): Schutterlindenberg. (Vil): Mietersheim.

Kronenbühl (Ger) vineyard (Anb): Baden. (Ber): Breisgau. (Gro): Schutterlindenberg. (Vil): Oberschopfheim.

Kronenbühl (Ger) vineyard (Anb): Baden. (Ber): Breisgau. (Gro): Schutterlindenberg. (Vil): Oberweier.

Kronen Classic (Ger) a 5% alc by vol. bottled pilsener brewed by the Kronen Brauerei, Dortmund.

Kronen Export (Ger) a 5.5% alc by vol. bottled dortmunder brewed by the Kronen Brauerei, Dortmund.

Kronenfels (Ger) vineyard (Anb): Nahe. (Ber): Schloss Böckelheim. (Gro): Burgweg. (Vil): Waldböckelheim.

Kronen Premium Pilsner (Ger) a 4.8% alc by vol. bottled pilsener brewed by the Kronen Brauerei, Dortmund.

Kronia Quelle (Ger) a still and sparkling natural spring mineral water (established 1911) from Bad Vilbel. (blue label: sparkling/green label: still). Mineral contents (milligrammes per litre): Sodium 128mg/l, Calcium 255mg/l, Magnesium 32mg/l, Potassium 13mg/l, Bicarbonates 971mg/l, Chlorides 156mg/l, Sulphates 29mg/l.

Krönleins Bryggeri (Swe) a brewery. (Add): Bryggaregatan 7–9, Hamlstad S-302 43. Brews a range of beers and lagers including Original Crocodile 5.2% alc by vol. 'E'mail: info@kroenleins.se

Kronsberg (Ger) vineyard (Anb): Franken. (Ber): Steigerwald. (Gro): Burgweg. (Vil): Iphofen.

Kronsteiner Felsenquelle (Ger) a natural spring mineral water. Mineral contents (milligrammes per litre): Sodium 37.5mg/l, Calcium 62mg/l,

K

Magnesium 9mg/l, Potassium 4.3mg/l, Bicarbonates 310mg/l, Chlorides 9.6mg/l, Sulphates 13.6mg/l, Nitrates 0.27mg/l.

Kronthaler (Ger) a natural spring mineral water. Mineral contents (milligrammes per litre): Sodium 535mg/l, Calcium 118mg/l, Magnesium 19mg/l, Potassium 23mg/l, Chlorides 805mg/l, Fluorides 0.8mg/l.

Kron Vodka (Den) the brand-name of a noted local vodka.

Kroon (S.Afr) the label for a red wine (Cinsaut, Grenache, Pinotage and Shiraz blend) produced by the Darling Cellars, Swartland, Western Cape.

Kroon Pilsener (Hol) see De Kroon Brouwerij.

Krötenbrunnen (Ger) grosslage (Anb): Rheinhessen. (Ber): Nierstein. (Vils): Alsheim, Dienheim, Dolgesheim, Eich, Eimsheim, Gimsheim, Guntersblum, Hillesheim, Ludwigshöhe, Mettenheim, Oppenheim, Ülversheim, Wintersheim.

Krötenpfuhl (Ger) vineyard (Anb): Nahe. (Ber): Kreuzbach. (Gro): Kronenberg. (Vil): Bad Kreuznach.

Kröv (Ger) village (Anb): Mosel-Saar-Ruwer. (Ber): Bernkastel. (Gro): Nacktarsch. (Vins): Burglay, Herrenberg, Kirchlay, Letterlay, Paradies, Steffensberg.

Krown (Ind) a strong lager beer 1048 O.G. brewed by the Mohan Meakin Brewery, Simla Hills, Solan.

Kruangdeum (Thai) beverage/drink/cocktail.

Krug (Fr) a Champagne producer. (Add): 5 Rue Coquebert, 51100 Reims. Grande Marque. 20ha. Produces vintage and non-vintage wines. Vintages: 1900, 1904, 1906, 1911, 1914, 1915, 1918, 1920, 1921, 1926, 1928, 1934, 1937, 1941, 1942, 1943, 1945, 1949, 1952, 1953, 1955, 1959, 1961, 1964, 1966, 1969, 1971, 1973, 1975, 1976, 1979, 1981, 1982, 1983, 1985, 1988, 1989, 1990, 1993, 1995, 1996, 1998, 1999, 2000, 2001. See Clos du Mesnil. Website: http://www.krug.com 'E'mail: krug@krug.fr

Krug (Ger) pitcher.

Krug Clos du Mesnil (Fr) See Clos du Mesnil.

Krug Collection (Fr) a cuvée vintage Champagne produced by Krug. Aged in Krug cellars. Vintages: 1947, 1953, 1961, 1964, 1966, 1969, 1973.

Kruger (Bel) the brand-name for a full-flavoured, strong-hopped, pilsener-style lager beer.

Kruger's Winery (USA) a medium-sized winery based in Nelson, Missouri. Produces French hybrid wines.

Krug Winery [Charles] (USA) a winery based in the Napa Valley, California. 500ha. Grape varieties: Cabernet sauvignon, Chenin blanc, Gewürztraminer and Johannisberg riesling. Produces varietal wines.

Kruidenbier (Bel) a Flemish term for a spiced beer.

Kruik (Hol) jug/pitcher.

Krumbach [1] (Ger) a still and sparkling natural spring mineral water from Kisslegg, Algäu. (red

label: sparkling/blue label: light gas/green label: still). Mineral contents (milligrammes per litre): Sodium 7.8mg/l, Calcium 104.2mg/l, Magnesium 21.9mg/l, Potassium 3.1mg/l, Bicarbonates 402.6mg/l, Chlorides 12mg/l, Sulphates 23.7mg/l, Fluorides 0.1mg/l, Nitrates <0.1mg/l.

Krumbach [2] (Ger) a still and sparkling natural spring mineral water from Kisslegg, Algäu. (red label: sparkling/blue label: still). Mineral contents (milligrammes per litre): Sodium 9.1mg/l, Calcium 87mg/l, Magnesium 23.3mg/l, Potassium 2.3mg/l, Bicarbonates 381mg/l, Chlorides 6.4mg/l, Sulphates 19mg/l, Fluorides 0.14mg/l, Nitrates <0.3mg/l.

Krupnik (Pol) a honey-flavoured vodka (liqueur) 40% alc by vol.

Kruse Winery (USA) a small winery based in the Hecker Pass, Santa Clara, California. Grape varieties: Cabernet sauvignon, Colombard, Sauvignon blanc and Zinfandel. Produces varietal wines.

Kruškovac (Pol) a pear liqueur produced in Maraska 43% alc by vol.

Krušovice Brewery (Czec) a noted old established brewery based in Krušovice, north-western Czec. Produces fine lager beers.

Krušovice Cerné 10% (Czec) a 3.8% alc by vol. dark, bottled lager brewed by Královský Pipovar Krušovice (Royal Krušovice Brewery), Rakovnik.

Krušovice Lezák 12% (Czec) a 5% alc by vol. dark, bottled lager brewed by Královský Pipovar Krušovice (Royal Krušovice Brewery), Rakovnik.

Krutzler (Aus) a winery (6.5ha) based in Deutsch-Schützen, Süd-Burgenland. (Add): Hauptstrasse 84, 7474 Deutsch-Schützen. Grape varieties: Blauburger, Blaufränkisch, Cabernet sauvignon, Zweigelt. Labels: Alter Weingarten, Perwolff.

Kryniczanka (Pol) a sparkling natural spring mineral water from Krynica. Mineral contents (milligrammes per litre): Sodium 59.5mg/l, Calcium 550.1mg/l, Magnesium 33mg/l, Potassium 6.5mg/l, Bicarbonates 2053.2mg/l, Chlorides 10.3mg/l, Sulphates 6.2mg/l, Fluorides 0.1mg/l.

Krynka (Pol) a natural spring mineral water from Krynki. Mineral contents (milligrammes per litre): Sodium 4.5mg/l, Calcium 65mg/l, Magnesium 18mg/l, Potassium 2mg/l, Bicarbonates 267mg/l, Chlorides 7mg/l, Sulphates 18mg/l, Fluorides 0.3mg/l, Silicates 10.6mg/l.

Krypton (Eng) an 8.4% alc by vol. cider from Matthew Clark Gaymer Group.

Krystal (Eng) a 3.7% alc by vol. bitter ale brewed by the Ossett Brewing C°. Ltd., West Yorkshire.

Krystal (Ger) a clear, filtered sediment-free löwen weisse wheat beer from Löwenbräu. See also Löwen Weisse, Hefe Weisse.

Krystal Lite (Eng) a low-calorie keg and bottled beer

K

1030 O.G. brewed by the Burtonwood Brewery in Cheshire.

Krystynka (Pol) a natural spring mineral water from Ciechocinek.

Ksara (Leb) a noted wine-producer who produces fine red wines from Aramon, Carignan and Cinsault grapes. Also produces Coteaux de Ksara (a dry white wine).

K Six [6] (Eng) a 6% alc by vol. cider produced by Matthew Clark Gaymer Group. Replaces K at 8.4% alc by vol.

Ksour (Tun) a natural spring mineral water. Mineral contents (milligrammes per litre): Sodium 10mg/l, Calcium 68mg/l, Magnesium 6mg/l, Potassium 1mg/l, Bicarbonates 207mg/l, Chlorides 28mg/l, Sulphates 10mg/l, Nitrates 23mg/l. pH 7.0

Ktima Kyr-Yanni (Gre) a winery that produces a Merlot (vin de pays) and Ramnista from Xinomavro grapes.

Ktima Papaioannou (Gre) a Cabernet franc wine produced by Papaioannou in Nemea.

K Two [2] (Eng) a lager beer brewed by the Fullers Brewery in Chiswick, West London to commemorate the climbing of K2 (a Himalayan mountain).

Kuad (Thai) bottle.

Kuangquanshui (Chi) mineral water.

Kubanskaya (Rus) a vodka flavoured with citrus peel and slightly sweetened 40% alc by vol.

Kuban Valley (Geo) a wine-producing area in Krasnodar which is noted for dessert and fortified wines.

Küchelberger (It) a red table wine produced from the Schiave grape near Merano, Trentino-Alto Adige.

Küchenmeister (Ger) vineyard (Anb): Franken. (Ber): Steigerwald. (Gro): Schlossberg. (Vil): Rödelsee.

Kuchlbauer Aloysius (Ger) a strong wheat beer 7.2% alc by vol. from the Kuchlbauer Brauerei. *See also* Kuchlbauer Weisse.

Kuchlbauer Brauerei (Ger) a brewery based in Abensberg. Brews: Kuchlbauer Aloysius, Kuchlbauer Weisse.

Kuchlbauer Weisse (Ger) an unfiltered wheat beer 5.5% alc by vol. from the Kuchlbauer Brauerei, Abensberg. *See also* Kuchlbauer Aloysius

Kuchuk-Lambat (Rus) a red Muscat dessert wine from the Southern Crimea.

Kuchuk-Uzen (Rus) a red grape variety grown in the Crimea. Produces Madeira-style dessert wines.

Kuehn [René] (Fr) a wine producer based in Ammerschwihr, Alsace.

Kuentz-Bas (Fr) an Alsace wine producer. (Add): 68420 Husseren-lès-Châteaux. 12.5ha. Website: http://www.kuentz-bas.fr

Kues (Ger) vineyards facing Bernkastel on the Mosel (sometimes spelt Cues).

Küf (Tur) mildew.

Küfelik (Tur) very drunk/highly intoxicated.

Kugelspiel (Ger) vineyard (Anb): Franken. (Ber): Steigerwald. (Gro): Herrenberg. (Vil): Castell.

Kühberg (Aus) a vineyard site on the banks of the River Danube in the Kremstal region.

Kuhberg (Ger) vineyard (Anb): Baden. (Ber): Badische Bergstrasse/Kraichgau. (Gro): Rittersberg. (Vil): Schriesheim.

Kuhlman-Oberlin (Fr) a famous French hybridiser.

Kuhnchen (Ger) vineyard (Anb): Mosel-Saar-Ruwer. (Ber): Saar-Ruwer. (Gro): Römerlay. (Vil): Riveris.

Kuhrmana (Iraq) a lager beer 13.5° balling brewed by the state-owned brewery based in Baghdad.

Kuhstall (Ger) vineyard (Anb): Mittelrhein. (Ber): Rheinburgengau. (Gro): Burg Rheinfels. (Vil): St. Goar-Werlau.

Kuierwyn (S.Afr) the label for a range of wines (dry and naturally sweet whites) produced by the Domein Doornkraal winery, Little Karoo.

Kuip (Hol) vat/barrel/tub.

Kuip & Clay (S.Afr) the label for a red wine (Cabernet sauvignon 35%, Merlot 35%, Touriga 30%) produced by the Boplaas Family Vineyards winery, Calitzdorp, Western Cape.

Kuipe (S.Afr) fermentation vat.

Kuiper (Hol) cooper.

Kuiperij (Hol) coopery.

Kujundzusa (Ser) a dry white wine produced by Dalmaciajavino at Split on the Dalmatian coast.

Kula Mineral Water (Tur) a natural spring mineral water (established 1970) from Manisa, Kula. Mineral contents (milligrammes per litre): Fluorides 0.54mg/l, Nitrates 3.96mg/l, Silicates 3mg/l, Oxygen 1.4mg/l.

Kuleto Estate (USA) a winery (40ha) based in the Pritchard Hill, Napa Valley, California. (Add): 2470 Sage Canyon Road, St. Helena, California 94574. Grape varieties include: Cabernet sauvignon, Syrah. Website: http://www.kuletoestate.com

Kulgan (Ukr) a strong vodka, flavoured with ginseng root and produced in the Ukraine.

Kulmbacher Kommunbräu (Ger) a brewery. (Add): Grünwehr 17, Kulmbach D-95326. Brews a range of beers and lagers. Website: http://www.kommunbraeu.de 'E'mail: info@ kommunbraeu.de

Kulmbacher Mönschof Brauerei (Ger) a brewery based in Kulmbach, Bavaria. Brews: full-bodied Maingold Lager 5.3% alc by vol. Kloster Schwarz 4.9% alc by vol. and Klosterbock Dunkel 6.4% alc by vol.

Kulminator (Ger) a very strong beer with an original gravity of 28%. *see* EKU.

Kulminator Dunkles Starkbier (Ger) a dark strong beer from the EKU Brauerei of Kulmbach, Bavaria. 7.6% alc by vol.

Kulminator 28 Urtyp Hell (Ger) a strong, slow-lagered beer from the EKU Brauerei in Kulmbach, Bavaria. The 28 denotes the O.G., the beer goes through the freezing process (see Eisbock) to raise its alcoholic strength.

Különleges (Hun) a wine classification which denotes a wine of distinction similar to Qmp in Germany and Austria.

K

Külsheim (Ger) village (Anb): Baden. (Ber): Badische Frankenland. (Gro): Tauberklinge. (Vin): Höher Herrgott.

Kulta (Fin) a pilsener lager 5.3% alc by vol. from the Hartwall Brewery.

K Ultraviolet Cider (Eng) an 8.4% alc by vol. cider from the Gaymer Group.

Kultur Brauerei Actiengesellschaft (Ger) a brewery. (Add): Leyergasse 6, Heidelberg D-69117. Brews beers and lagers. Website: http://www.heidelberger-kulturbrauerei.de 'E'mail: kulturbrauerei.ag@t-online.de

Kulturny (Rus) cultured.

Kumala (S.Afr) the export label for a range of wines produced by the Porterville Cellars winery, Swartland, Western Cape.

Kumala (S.Afr) a winery and branded wine range from the Stellenbosch region, Western Cape. Grape varieties include: Cabernet sauvignon. Labels include: Journey's End and Lounge Lizard.

Kumasi Brewery (Afr) a noted brewery based in Ghana which brews Star Lager and Gulder Lager.

Kumeu-Huapi-Waimauku (N.Z) a sub-region of Auckland (sited north-west of the city).

Kumeu River (N.Z) a winery based at 2 Highway 16, Kumeu, Auckland. Grape varieties: Cabernet sauvignon, Chardonnay, Merlot, Sauvignon blanc.

Kumeu River Wines (N.Z) a winery. (Add): 550 Highway 16, Kumeu, Auckland. 20ha. Grape variety: Chardonnay. *See also* Family of Twelve.

Kumis (Chi) fermented mare's milk, made by the tribesmen in the north-west of China for ceremonial occasions.

Kumiss (Asia) an alternative spelling of Koumiss, *See also* Koumiss, Koumyss,

Kümme (Ger) kümmel.

Kümmel (Hol) a clear white spirit/liqueur made from grain and flavoured with caraway seeds, has various alcoholic strengths.

Kümmel Crystallizé (USA) a kümmel which has crystallised sugar in it (in the bottle).

Kummel della val d'Aosta (It) a noted monastery herb liqueur produced in north-western Italy.

Kumquat (Gre) a liqueur produced from the miniature Japanese kumquat oranges.

Kumsu (Tur) a still natural spring mineral water (established 1980) from Kemerbutgazö, Istanbul. Mineral contents (milligrammes per litre): Calcium 20mg/l, Magnesium 2.67mg/l, Chlorides 29.29mg/l, Sulphates 13.1mg/l, Fluorides 0.15mg/l, Nitrates 1.62mg/l, Nitrite 1mg/l. pH 6.8

Kumys (Rus) the name used in the sixteenth century for koumiss made in south-eastern Russia.

Kumyz (Asia) the tartar's spelling of koumiss in the middle ages.

Kuncle Estate Winery [The] (USA) a 312.5ha winery in Sonoma Valley. Noted for Chardonnay. Sells most of the grapes.

Kunde Estate (USA) a winery (established 1904) based in Napa Valley, California. Produces three single vineyard wines from Chardonnay, Cabernet sauvignon and Zinfandel grapes. Label: Century Vines.

Künstlewr [Gunter] (Ger) a winery based in Hochheim, Rheingau. Grape varieties include: Riesling. Produces a range of wine styles.

Kunstrum (Aus) a neutral spirit distilled from potatoes (the flavour of rum is produced using chemicals).

Kuntra (Tur) a white grape variety grown in Marmara and Thrace.

Künzelsau (Ger) village (Anb): Württemberg. (Ber): Kocher-Jagst-Tauber. (Gro): Kocherberg. (Vin): Hoher Berg.

Kup (Kor) cup.

Kupelwieser [Fritz] (It) an old established winery based in Salurn, Südtirol (Trentino-Alto Adige).

Kuperflöz (Ger) vineyard (Anb): Mittelrhein. (Ber): Rheinburgengau. (Gro): Herrenberg. (Vil): Dörscheid.

Kupferberg (Ger) a famous sekt producer who uses the transfer method.

Kupferberger Auslese (S.Afr) an auslese-style wine made from the Steen grape (28 grammes of sugar per litre). Produced by the Bergkelder C°.

Kupfergrube (Ger) vineyard (Anb): Nahe. (Ber): Schloss Böckelheim. (Gro): Burgweg. (Vil): Schlossböckelheim.

Kupferhalde (Ger) vineyard (Anb): Württemberg. (Ber): Württembergisch Unterland. (Gro): Stromberg. (Vil): Obererdingen.

Kupferstube (Ger) a malty, bottom-fermented beer brewed by the Mailaender Bergbräu concern of Fürth. Is copper-red in colour.

Kupp (Ger) vineyard (Anb): Mosel-Saar-Ruwer. (Ber): Bernkastel. (Gro): Schwarzlay. (Vil): Wittlich.

Kupp (Ger) vineyard (Anb): Mosel-Saar-Ruwer. (Ber): Saar-Ruwer. (Gro): Römerlay. (Vil): Trier.

Kupp (Ger) vineyard (Anb): Mosel-Saar-Ruwer. (Ber): Saar-Ruwer. (Gro): Scharzberg. (Vil): Ayl.

Kupp (Ger) vineyard (Anb): Mosel-Saar-Ruwer. (Ber): Saar-Ruwer. (Gro): Scharzberg. (Vil): Ockfen.

Kupp (Ger) vineyard (Anb): Mosel-Saar-Ruwer. (Ber): Saar-Ruwer. (Gro): Scharzberg. (Vil): Saarburg.

Kupp (Ger) vineyard (Anb): Mosel-Saar-Ruwer. (Ber): Saar-Ruwer. (Gro): Scharzberg. (Vil): Serrig.

Kupp (Ger) vineyard (Anb): Mosel-Saar-Ruwer. (Ber): Saar-Ruwer. (Gro): Scharzberg. (Vil): Wiltingen.

Küppers Brauerei (Ger) a brewery (established 1893) based in Cologne (the largest kölsch brewery).

Küppers Kölsch (Ger) a kölschbier which is exported mainly to the USA. 4.8% alc by vol. Brewed by the Küppers Brauerei in Cologne.

Kup's Indispensable (Cktl) $\frac{3}{5}$ measure dry gin, $\frac{1}{5}$ measure sweet vermouth, $\frac{1}{5}$ measure dry vermouth, dash Angostura. Stir over ice and strain into a cocktail glass.

Kurant (Swe) a blackcurrant flavoured vodka from Absolut.

K

Kurbag Cocktail (Cktl) another name for the Whip Cocktail.

Kurdamir (Rus) a red grape variety grown in the Kurdamirsk area of Azerbaijan. Produces red dessert wines.

Kurdamirsk (Rus) one of the major wine-producing areas of Azerbaijan, noted for dessert wines.

Kurfürst (Ger) a natural spring mineral water. Mineral contents (milligrammes per litre): Sodium 98mg/l, Calcium 43mg/l, Magnesium 5.1mg/l, Potassium 2.3mg/l, Chlorides 72.2mg/l, Fluorides 1.3mg/l.

Kurfürst (Ger) vineyard (Anb): Mosel-Saar-Ruwer. (Ber): Zell/Mosel. (Gro): Goldbäumchen. (Vil): Ellenz-Poltersdorf.

Kurfürst (Ger) vineyard (Anb): Pfalz. (Ber): Mittelhaardt-Deutsche Weinstrasse. (Gro): Meerspinne. (Vil): Mussbach.

Kurfürstenberg (Ger) vineyard (Anb): Mosel-Saar-Ruwer. (Ber): Saar-Ruwer. (Gro): Römerlay. (Vil): Waldrach.

Kurfürstenbrunn-Quelle (Ger) a natural spring mineral water from Kurfürstbrunn-Quelle. Mineral contents (milligrammes per litre): Sodium 15.9mg/l, Calcium 43.3mg/l, Magnesium 4.5mg/l, Potassium 2.7mg/l, Bicarbonates 170mg/l, Chlorides 9.6mg/l, Fluorides 0.09mg/l.

Kurfürstenhofberg (Ger) vineyard (Anb): Mosel-Saar-Ruwer. (Ber): Saar-Ruwer. (Gro): Römerlay. (Vil): Trier.

Kurfürstenstück (Ger) grosslage (Anb): Rheinhessen. (Ber): Bingen. (Vils): Gau-Bickelheim, Gau-Weinheim, Gumbsheim, Vendersheim, Wallertheim.

Kurfürstlay (Ger) grosslage (Anb): Mosel-Saar-Ruwer. (Ber): Bernkastel. (Vils): Andel, Bernkastel-Kues, Brauneberg, Burgen, Kestern, Lieser, Maring-Noviand, Mulheim, Osann-Monzel, Veldenz, Wintrich.

Kuriimu (Jap) cream.

Kurk (Hol) cork.

Kurketrekker (Hol) corkscrew.

Kürnbach (Ger) village (Anb): Baden. (Ber): Badische Bergstrasse/Kraichgau. (Gro): Stiftsberg. (Vin): Lerchenberg.

Kurpfälzisches Winzerfest (Ger) a Baden wine festival held at Wiesloch in August-September.

Kursaal Cocktail (Cktl) 30mls (¼ gill) brandy, 15mls (⅛ gill) cherry brandy, 15mls (⅛ gill) French vermouth, dash absinthe, dash Angostura, dash orange bitters, 1 teaspoon plain syrup. Shake over ice, strain into a 125mls (5fl.oz) wine glass, serve with a cherry and squeeze lemon peel juice.

Kurselter Heilwasser (Ger) a natural spring mineral water. Mineral contents (milligrammes per litre): Sodium 504mg/l, Calcium 79.2mg/l, Magnesium 30mg/l, Potassium 12.8mg/l, Bicarbonates 840mg/l, Chlorides 506mg/l, Sulphates 27.3mg/l, Fluorides 0.58mg/l.

Kurvaka (Rus) a natural spring mineral water. Mineral contents (milligrammes per litre): Sodium mg/l, Calcium mg/l, Magnesium mg/l, Potassium mg/l, Bicarbonates mg/l, Chlorides mg/l, Sulphates mg/l, Fluorides mg/l, Nitrates mg/l, Silicates mg/l. pH 7.0

Kurvand (Den) a natural spring mineral water from Arnakke Kilde.

Kurz (Ger) lit: 'short', denotes very little flavour or aroma.

Küss den Pfennig (Aus) a vineyard site on the banks of the River Danube situated in the Wachau region, Niederösterreich.

Kuss mit Liebe (Ger) a unique bottle with two separate liqueurs: Kroatzbeere (blackberry brandy) and Kakao (coffee liqueur) produced by Thienelt near Düsseldorf. The coffee liqueur is poured gently on top of the blackberry brandy.

Kusuda (N.Z) a vineyard based in the Martinborough region of the North Island. Grape varieties: Cabernet sauvignon, Pinot noir, Syrah. Labels: G (Pinot Noir).

Kutjevo (Cro) a noted wine-producing town in Croatia.

Kutnà Hora Brewery (Czec) an old brewery based in western Czec.

Kutscher Alt (Ger) a bronze-red ale 5% alc by vol. from Binding.

Kuvaka (Rus) a natural spring mineral water. Mineral contents (milligrammes per litre): Sodium 6.5mg/l, Calcium 104mg/l, Magnesium 4.8mg/l, Potassium 0.8mg/l, Bicarbonates 317mg/l, Chlorides 6.7mg/l, Sulphates 21mg/l, Fluorides 0.725mg/l, Nitrates 0.01mg/l, Silicates 35mg/l. pH 7.0

Kuyalnick (Ukr) a natural spring mineral water from Odessa. Mineral contents (milligrammes per litre): Sodium 1100mg/l, Calcium 50mg/l, Magnesium 10mg/l, Bicarbonates 450mg/l, Chlorides 1450mg/l, Sulphates 330mg/l.

Kvalitetno Vino (Slo) a Q.W.P.S.R. a quality wine. See also Cuveno Vino, Vrhunsko Vino.

Kvasi (Euro) the Slavic name for yeast.

Kvass [1] (Rus) a light, carbonated beer made from malted rye and barley, is often flavoured with juniper, mint or cranberries. see Quass.

Kvass [2] (Rus) a low-alcohol, sweet drink made by the fermentation of bread.

K.Vintners (USA) a winery based in the Columbia Valley, Washington State. Grape varieties include: Syrah. Label: Morrison Lane.

Kwaliteitsmerk (Hol) a natural spring mineral water from Baarle-Nassau. Mineral contents (milligrammes per litre): Sodium 8.5mg/l, Calcium 64mg/l, Magnesium 9.7mg/l, Bicarbonates 250mg/l, Chlorides 11mg/l, Sulphates 28mg/l.

Kwangsi (Chi) a branch of the China National Cereals, Oils and Foodstuffs Import and Export Corporation.

Kwangtung (Chi) a branch of the China National Cereals, Oils and Foodstuffs Import and Export Corporation. Uses the Pearl River brand for their rum.

Kwartier na Vijven (Hol) lit: 'quarter past five', a liqueur produced by Van Zuylekom of Amsterdam.

K

Kwas (Rus) a liqueur made from rye.

Kweichow (Chi) a province in south-western China that is noted for Mao-t'ai (a grain spirit made from wheat and millet).

Kwevris (Geo) large earthenware pots that are buried under ground and used for fermenting wines.

K.W.V. International (S.Afr) *abbr*: Koöperatiewe Wijnbouwers Vereniging Van Zuid-Afrika. (Add): P.O. Box 528, Suider-Paarl. A large co-operative winery (established 1916–registered 1918). Is the Wine Farmers' Association that produces most styles of wines, varietal, fortified wines and brandies. Grape varieties: Cabernet sauvignon, Chardonnay, Chenin blanc (Steen), Cinsaut, Merlot, Muscadel, Pinotage, Red Muscadel, Sauvignon blanc, Shiraz, Souzão, Tinta. Wines include Bonne Esperance, Blanc de Noir, Cape Bouquet, Cape Forêt, Cathedral Cellars, Laborie, Millennium Port, Noble Late Harvest, Pearly Bay, Robert's Rock and Roodeberg. Website: http://www.kwv-international.com

Kykko (Cyp) the brand-name used by the Loel C°. for a range of their wines.

Kylian (Hol) a 6.5% alc by vol. top-fermented, amber-coloured bottled special beer brewed by Heineken Netherlands Brouwerij.

Kylix (Gre) a two-handled drinking vessel, often decorated with mythological scenes, similar to a large Champagne saucer.

Kylix (S.Afr) the label for a red wine (Cabernet sauvignon and Shiraz blend) produced by the Somerbosch Wines winery, Stellenbosch, Western Cape.

Kym (Eng) a species of barley from the Golden Promise variety which gives medium sugar yields.

Kyr-Yianni (Gre) a winery that is a part of The General Wine Company. 28ha Grape varieties: Merlot, Syrah, Xinomavro. *See also* Vergoritis.

L

Laacherberg (Ger) vineyard (Anb): Ahr. (Ber): Walporzheim/Ahrtal. (Gro): Klosterberg. (Vil): Mayschoss.

La'al Cockle Warmer (Eng) a 6.5% alc by vol. winter warmer ale brewed by Jennings Brewery, Cockermouth, Cumbria. Cask and bottled versions.

Laatoes (S.Afr) a white wine blend of Hanepoot and Steen grapes from the Nuwehoop Wynkelder.

Laatoes (S.Afr) a fruity, medium-sweet, white wine made from the Steen grape by Louwshoek Voorsorg Co-operative.

Laat-Oes (S.Afr) late-harvested.

Laat Oes [1] (S.Afr) a medium-sweet, white, fruity wine made from the Colombard grape by the Lutzville Co-operative.

Laat Oes Steen (S.Afr) a full-bodied, white, medium-sweet wine made from the Steen grape by the McGregor Co-operative.

Laban (Arab) cream.

Labarde (Fr) a commune within the district of Médoc in north-western Bordeaux.

Labastida (Sp) a noted wine village in the district of Rioja Alavesa, produces mainly red wines.

La Bastille (Cktl) 1 measure Campari poured over ice in a highball glass, top with soda (over a spoon), gently add 1 measure blue Curaçao, add slice of lime and serve with straws.

Labatt Ale (Can) a famous ale exported from the Labatt Brewery in Ontario.

Labatt Brewery (Can) a large brewery (established 1828) in Ontario. now taken over by Interbrew of Belgium. Produces: Labatt Ale, Labatt Ice and Blue (a sweet pilsner). Also brews under licence Budweiser, Guinness and Skol.

Labatt Ice (Can) a 5.6% alc by vol. bottled ice beer from the Labatt Brewery, Ontario.

Label (Eng) the identification mark on a drinks bottle, can be made of paper or a simple paint mark (Port wine bottle). Usually contains the name of wine, shipper, quality, alcohol content, capacity, origin, alcohol by volume depending on the laws of each country. e.g. E.C. *See also* Bottle Ticket, Bottle Label and Flash Mark.

Label Normandie (Fr) a label guarantee found on Normandy cider bottles to guarantee the quality of contents through analysis.

Label'O (Fr) a natural spring mineral water. Mineral contents (milligrammes per litre): Sodium 4.7mg/l, Calcium 98mg/l, Magnesium 1.4mg/l, Potassium 0.5mg/l, Bicarbonates 276.94mg/l, Chlorides 7.5mg/l, Sulphates 14mg/l.

Laberstall (Ger) vineyard (Anb): Rheinhessen. (Ber): Bingen. (Gro): Sankt Rochuskapelle. (Vil): Ockenheim.

Labertaler Sebastiani Brunnen (Ger) a natural spring mineral water (established 1997). Mineral contents (milligrammes per litre): Sodium 113mg/l, Calcium 46.9mg/l, Magnesium 20.7mg/l, Potassium 13.3mg/l, Bicarbonates 451mg/l, Chlorides 62.7mg/l, Sulphates 1.7mg/l, Fluorides 2.3mg/l, Strontium 1mg/l, Ammonium 1mg/l, Silicates 23.9mg/l.

Labertaler Stephanie Brunnen (Ger) a still and sparkling natural spring mineral water (established 1986). Mineral contents (milligrammes per litre): Sodium 5.8mg/l, Calcium 68.9mg/l, Magnesium 33.8mg/l, Potassium 1.8mg/l, Bicarbonates 390mg/l, Chlorides 0.6mg/l, Sulphates 7.6mg/l, Fluorides 0.13mg/l, Nitrates <0.3mg/l, Silicates 17.4mg/l.

La Beryl (S.Afr) the label for a red straw wine (Shiraz) and white air-dried (Chenin blanc and Sémillon) wines produced by the Fairview winery, Suider-Paarl, Western Cape.

Labicanum (It) a red wine produced in central-western Italy in Roman times.

Labologist (Eng) a collector of beer bottle labels, a society was formed in 1959.

La Bonne Vigne (S.Afr) the label for a dry white wine (Sauvignon blanc) produced by The Marais Family winery, Robertson, Western Cape.

Laborie (S.Afr) a winery (established 1691) based in Suider-Paarl, Western Cape. 39ha. (owned by KWV). Grape varieties: Cabernet sauvignon, Chardonnay, Merlot, Pinotage, Pinot noir, Sauvignon blanc, Shiraz. Labels: Jean Taillefert, Pineau de Laborie. Website: http://www.kwv-international.com

Labottière (Fr) the name given to red and white wines produced by Cordier A.C. Bordeaux.

Labouré Gontard (Fr) a noted négociant-éleveur based in Nuits-Saint-Georges, Burgundy. Produces many fine Burgundies and Comtesse de Roseval (a Crèmant de Bourgogne).

Labouré-Roi (Fr) a Burgundy négociant-éleveur (established 1832) based in Nuits-Saint-Georges, Côte de Nuits, Burgundy. Has many fine cuvées. Also produces A.C. Chablis Premier Cru Mont de Milieu.

Labrador (Can) a natural spring mineral water. Mineral contents (milligrammes per litre): Sodium 20mg/l, Calcium 42mg/l, Magnesium

21mg/l, Potassium 3mg/l, Bicarbonates 234mg/l, Chlorides 13mg/l, Sulphates 24mg/l, Fluorides 0.2mg/l, Nitrates 1.33mg/l, Silicates 15mg/l.

La Brasserie Balzane (Fr) a brewery. (Add): 10 Ter Avenue, Ox and Bucke, St. Arnoult ZA, F-14800. Brews a variety of beers and lager. Website: http://www.balzane.com 'E'mail: contact@balzane.com

La Brasserie Sancerroise (Fr) a brewery. (Add): Au 258 Route, F-18300 Sancerre. Brews a variety of beers and lager. Website: http://www.brasserie-sancerroise.com 'E'mail: info@brasserie-sancerroise.com

La Bri (S.Afr) a winery based in Franschhoek, Western Cape. 18ha. Grape varieties: Cabernet sauvignon, Chardonnay, Merlot. Labels: Affinity, Limited Release.

Labrija (Sp) an area in the Jerez Supérieur district of south-western Spain.

Labrum (Lat) vat/tub.

Labrusca (USA) see **Vitis labrusca**.

Lac (Lat) milk. See also Lactis.

La Cabane du Brasseur (Fr) a brewery. (Add): 21 Place du Marché, Découvert F-54000 Nancy. Brews beers and lagers.

La Cadène (Fr) the label for an A.C. Côtes-du-Rhône-Villages Vinsobres (red) from Domaine Chaume Arnaud, Vinsobres, Vaucluse.

La Cascade (S.Pac) a natural spring mineral water from Togo. Mineral contents (milligrammes per litre): Sodium 5.1mg/l, Calcium 8.8mg/l, Magnesium 5mg/l, Potassium 10mg/l, Bicarbonates 69.5mg/l, Chlorides 2mg/l, Sulphates 1mg/l, Nitrates 2.4mg/l. pH 6.11

La Castellana (It) a natural spring mineral water brand.

Lacasy (Chi) a natural spring mineral water. Mineral contents (milligrammes per litre): Sodium 6.9mg/l, Calcium 8.9mg/l, Magnesium 2.3mg/l, Potassium 1.2mg/l, Silicates 21.5mg/l.

La Cave (S.Afr) the label for a red wine (Cabernet sauvignon, Merlot, Pinotage and Shiraz blend) produced by the Wamakersvallei Winery, Wellington, Western Cape.

Lacchus (Lat) one of the words used for Bacchus. See also Bassareus, Bromius, Dionysus, Eleleus, Euan, Euhan, Euhius, Euius, Lyaeus and Thyoneus.

Lac des Roches (Gre) a full-bodied, deep-flavoured, white wine from Boutari in Crete and the Dodecanese Islands.

Lace (Eng) to add a measure of alcohol (usually spirits) to a drink to give it a 'kick', may be done with or without the consumer's knowledge.

L.A.Cetto (Mex) a label for a range of wines produced by Vinicola L.A. Cetto, Baja California.

Laceyts Real Lager (Eng) a 5.2% alc by vol. strong lager brewed by the Country Life Brewery, Devon.

La Chablisienne (Fr) a wine co-operative based in Chablis, northern Burgundy. (Add): 8, Boulevard Pasteur, B.P. N°14, 89800 Chablis. Has 280 members owning 1150ha [includes: 13ha A.C. Grand Cru Chablis, 150ha A.C. Premier Cru Chablis (Fourchaume and Montmains), 600ha A.C. Chablis 150ha A.C. Petit Chablis].

Lachaise (Fr) a commune of the Charente département whose grapes are classed Petite Champagne (Cognac).

La Chanson (S.Afr) the label for a sparkling wine produced by the JC le Roux winery, Stellenbosch, Western Cape.

La Chapelle (Fr) a natural spring mineral water from Saint Maurice sur Allier, Auvergne. Mineral contents (milligrammes per litre): Sodium 400mg/l, Calcium 200mg/l, Magnesium 133mg/l, Potassium 41mg/l, Bicarbonates 1380mg/l, Chlorides 379mg/l, Sulphates 173mg/l, Nitrates 8mg/l. pH 5.8

La Chataigne (S.Afr) a winery (established 1972) based in Franschhoek, Western Cape. 15ha. Grape varieties: Cabernet sauvignon, Chenin blanc, Merlot, Pinotage, Sauvignon blanc, Sémillon, Shiraz. Labels: Kasanje, Marron. Website: http://www.lachat.co.za

La Chaumiere Estate (S.Afr) a winery (established 2001) based in Franschhoek, Western Cape. 3.6ha. Grape varieties: Chardonnay, Shiraz.

Lache (Ch.Isles) a tot or small measure of drink. See also Feis.

Lachen-Speyerdorf (Ger) village (Anb): Pfalz. (Ber): Mittelhaardt-Deutsche Weinstrasse. (Gro): Pfaffengrund. (Vins): Kroatenpfad, Langenstein, Lerchenböhl.

Lachini Vineyard (USA) a winery based in the Dundee Hills, Oregon. Also has vineyards in the Willamette Valley. Grape variety: Pinot noir. Label: Ana Vineyard. Website: http://www.lachinivineyards.com

Lachlan Valley Vineyard (Austr) a vineyard based at Cowra, Central New South Wales. Part of the Rothbury Estate.

Lachryma di Morro (It) an alternative spelling of Lacrima di Morro.

Lackner-Tinnacker (Aus) a winery (13ha) based in Gamlitz, Süd-Steiermark. (Add): Steinbach 12, 8462 Gamlitz. Grape varieties: Chardonnay, Gewürztraminer, Muskateller, Pinot blanc, Pinot gris, Sauvignon blanc, Traminer, Zweigelt. Produces a range of dry and sweet wines and fruit-based schnapps.

La Clape (Fr) a new (1998) sub-region A.C. within the A.C. Coteaux du Languedoc based on its climate and soil (also Quatourze).

Lacons (Eng) the brand-name of a lager and lime drink 3.8% alc by vol. 1030–1034 O.G. (sold in cans only).

La Coromoto (Ven) a natural spring mineral water. Mineral contents (milligrammes per litre): Bicarbonates 24mg/l. pH 6.8

L.A.C.O.S. (Eng) abbr: Liqueur and Cocktail Orientated Seminars.

La Cotte (S.Afr) see Cellar Series.

La Couronne Estate (S.Afr) a winery (established 1999) based in Franschhoek, Western Cape. 21ha. Grape varieties: Cabernet sauvignon, Chardonnay, Chenin blanc, Malbec, Merlot, Sauvignon blanc,

L

Shiraz. Labels: Cevennes, Ménage à Trois, Mereaux, Rogues Rouge, 277. Website: http://www.lacouronne.co.za

Lacourte-Godbillon (Fr) a Premier Cru Champagne producer. (Add): 51500 Ecueil, France.

Lacourtoisie [Claude] (Fr) an Armagnac producer. (Add): Domaine de la Coste, 40240 Labastide d'Armagnac. 10ha. in the Bas Armagnac. Produces brandies aged for at least 5 years.

L'Acqua dei Giunchi (It) a natural spring mineral water from Agnana Calabra, Reggio Calabria.

La Crema (USA) a winery based in the Russian River Valley, Sonoma County, California. Also has vineyards in Anderson Valley, Mendocino County. Grape variety: Pinot noir. Label: Nine Barrel.

Lacre Oro (Sp) a solera reserva brandy produced by Garvey. See also Gran Garvey, Rango.

Lacre Violeta (Sp) a sweet, golden-coloured, dessert wine produced in Alella, near Barcelona, eastern Spain 14% alc by vol. and cask aged.

Lacrima (Sp) a class of Málaga (equals sweet).

Lacrima Christi (It) lit: 'tears of Christ', a delicate, medium dry white wine from the Campania region, produced on the slopes of Vesuvius, a non D.O.C. there is also a red and rosé.

Lacrima d'Abeto (It) lit: 'tears of the pine', a green pine-needle flavoured liqueur made by the Camaldolese order of monks in the Castentino Mountains.

Lacrima di Castrovillari (It) a red vino da tavola wine produced in Castrovillari, southern Italy.

Lacrima di Morro (It) a fast maturing red grape variety grown in the Marche. Also spelt Lachryma di Morro.

Lacrima di Morro d'Alba (It) a D.O.C. wine producing zone of the Marche.

Lacrima Nera (It) the local name for the red Gaglioppo grape in Pollino, Calabria.

La Croix des Grives (Fr) an A.C. Côtes-du-Rhône from Charpoutier, Tain.

Lacroix Triaulaire (Fr) a Champagne producer (established 1972). (Add):10110 Merrey Arce. 2.2ha. Produces vintage and non-vintage Champagnes and Marc de Champagne. Vintages: 1995, 1996, 1999, 2000, 2001, 2002.

La Cruz Vineyard (USA) the label for a red wine (Pinot noir) produced by the Keller Estate winery, Sonoma Coast, Sonoma County, California.

Lacryma Christi del Vesuvio (It). see Lacrima Christi, an alternative spelling of.

Lacteo (Port) milky.

Lactic Acid (Eng) $CH_3CH(OH)COOH$ found in wine, produced during malo-lactic fermentation by *Lactobacillus*, is also found in milk. (Fr) = acide lactique.

Lactic Taint (Eng) a wine malady, wine has a mousey smell, prevented by SO_2 and sterile bottling. Caused by a rod bacteria, See also Amertume, Graisse, Tourne.

Lactis (Lat) milk. See also Lac.

Lactobacillus (Lat) in the absence of air produces Lactic acid and CO_2 from Malic acid.

Lactose (Eng) milk sugar, not fermentable by wine yeasts.

Lacy Stagger (Eng) a cider cocktail produced by the Symonds Cider Cº. in Hereford, made from cider, English wine, vodka and orange juice.

Lad Anzebadi (Egy) a style of fermented milk (koumiss).

Ladaux (Fr) a commune in the Haut-Benauge, Entre-Deux-Mers, central Bordeaux.

Lade Inn & Trossachs Craft Brewery [The] (Scot) a brewery (established 2004). (Add): Kilmahog, Callander, Perthshire FK17 8HD. Brews a range of beers and lager. Website: http://www.theladeinn.com 'E'mail: steve@theladeinn.com

Ladeira de Envendos (Port) a slightly acidic natural spring mineral water from Ladeira de Envendos. Mineral contents (milligrammes per litre): Sodium 3.9mg/l, Calcium 1.1mg/l, Bicarbonates 1.7mg/l, Chlorides 6.8mg/l, Silicates 10.9mg/l. pH 5.0

Ladies Cocktail [1] (Cktl) ¾ measure Bourbon whiskey, ¼ measure anisette, 2 dashes Angostura. Stir over ice, strain into a cocktail glass and top with a pineapple cube.

Ladies Cocktail [2] (Cktl) 25mls (1fl.oz) rye whiskey, 2 dashes Pernod, 2 dashes anisette, dash Angostura. Stir over ice, strain into a cocktail glass and top with a grapefruit segment.

Ladismith Co-op Winery (S.Afr) a co-operative winery (established 1939) based in Little Karoo. 600ha. Grape varieties: Chardonnay, Ruby cabernet. Amalgamated with Barrydale in 2005 (now known as the Southern Cape Vineyards).

Ladiville (Fr) a commune in the Charente département in Petite Champagne, Cognac.

Ladner (Aus) a vineyard site based on the banks of the River Kamp situated in the Kamptal region.

Lado (Sp) a white grape variety grown in Ribeiro and Galicia, north-western Spain that is high in acidity.

Ladoix-Serrigny (Fr) an A.C. of the 2 villages near Beaune in the Côte de Beaune. Has the Premier Cru vineyards: Basses-Mourettes, La Contière, La Toppe-au-Vert, Les Grandes-Lolières, Les Maréchaudes and Les Petites-Lolières. Produces red and white wines.

Ladoucette [Baron de] (Fr) the owner of Château de Nozet, who produces a fine Pouilly Fumé under the name Baron de L'.

Ladroncillo (Sp) the name given to the metal pipe that transfers the wine from one cask to another.

Lady Amber (Cktl) 1 measure gin, ½ measure passion fruit juice, ½ measure kirsch, dash egg white. Shake over ice, strain into a cocktail glass and add a cherry.

Lady Anne Barnard (S.Afr) a label for a range of red and white varietal wines from African Pride Wines Constantia, Western Cape.

Lady Be Good Cocktail (Cktl) ¾ measure Cognac, ¼ measure (white) crème de menthe, 2 dashes sweet vermouth. Shake over ice and strain into a cocktail glass.

780

L

Lady Bird Bio Beer (Ind) a 5% alc by vol. lager beer flavoured with aloe vera and brewed by the Khoday Breweries.

Ladyburn (Scot) a single malt whisky distillery (established 1966) based at Girvan, Ayrshire. Owned by William Grant and Sons (a lowland malt). Produces a 14 year old malt whisky 43% alc by vol. and a 1973 vintage single cask malt.

Lady Finger Cocktail (Cktl) ⅓ measure dry gin, ⅓ measure cherry brandy, ⅓ measure kirsch. Shake over ice, strain into a cocktail glass and top with a cherry.

Lady Killer (Cktl) 20mls (⅙ gill) gin, juice of lime, dash cherry brandy, 2 dashes orgeat. Shake over ice, strain into an ice-filled highball glass, top with tonic water, a cherry and a slice of lime.

Lady Londonderry (Eng) an old eighteenth century tea blend.

Lady Love Fizz (Cktl) 25mls (⅕ gill) dry gin, 1 teaspoon powdered sugar, juice ½ lemon, 1 egg white, 20mls (⅙ gill) cream. Shake over ice, strain into an ice-filled highball glass and top with iced Champagne.

Lady Lyssa (Cktl) 1 part Cointreau, 5 parts dry gin, 1 part apricot brandy. Shake over ice, strain into a cocktail glass, add orange zest and a cherry.

Lady of the Lake (Eng) a 4.2% alc by vol. ale brewed by Glastonbury Ales, Somerset.

Lady Palmer (Fr) the new name for Cuvée Amazone, a Champagne produced by Palmer from 50% each of Pinot noir and Chardonnay.

Lady's Dream (Cktl) ⅓ measure Bourbon whiskey, ⅓ measure Curaçao, ⅓ measure crème de fraises, dash cream. Shake over ice and strain into a cocktail glass.

Lady's Finger (Eng) a variety of cider apple.

Ladysmith (S.Afr) a brandy and table wine-producing area in Klein Karoo (Little Karoo).

Ladysmith Koöperatiewe Wynmakery (S.Afr) a co-operative winery based in Klein Karoo. (Add): Box 56, Ladismith 6885. Produces: Towerkop Cinsault and Swartberg Aristaat.

Ladysmith-Oudtshoorn (S.Afr) a district in Klein Karoo noted for Sherry-style wines.

Lady Susan (Eng) a style of turntable combined in a tea-service/breakfast-service used with Crown Derbyware in the nineteenth century.

Lady's Wines (Eng) the name given to sweet white wines such as Sauternes, Barsac etc. *See also* Girl's Wines.

Laetitia (Fr) a medium dry white wine from Ajaccio in Corsica.

Latitia Vineyard & Winery (USA) a winery based in Paso Robles, San Luis Obispo County, California. (Add): 453 Laetitia Vineyard Drive, Arroyo Grande CA 93420. Website: http://www.laetitiawine.com

Laevulose (Eng) another name for Fructose.

Lafaurie-Peyraguey (Fr) *see* Château Lafaurie-Peyraguey.

Lafayette Punch (Cktl) 1 bottle Pimms N°1, 6 sliced oranges, 50grms (2ozs) sugar, 4 bottles sparkling wine, mix Pimms, oranges and sugar together,

stand 1 hour, add wine with plenty of ice and serve.

La Fée (Fr) the original French absinthe 68% alc. by vol. known as 'la fée verte' (the green fairy), it was banned in 1914 and relaunched in 2000. *see* Absinthe.

Laffay [Thierry] (Fr) a winery based in the A.C. Chablis, Burgundy. Produces a range of Chablis wines including Premier Crus Mont de Milieu and Vaillons.

Lafitte [Charles] (Fr) a Champagne producer (established 1976). (Add): 39 Rue de Général Leclerc, 51130 Vertes. Produces vintage and non-vintage wines.

Lafnetscha (Switz) a local name used in Valais for the white Completer grape variety.

Lafoes (Port) a DOC wine-producing region between the Dão and Vinho Verde regions, produces red and white wines.

Lafontan (Fr) an Armagnac producer. (Add): Societé Distillerie des Coteaux de Gascogne, B.P. 3, 32440 Castelnau d'Auzan. 65ha. in Bas Armagnac. Produces Doyen d'Âge 20–30 years old.

Lafont de Saint-Preuil (Fr) a Cognac producer. (Add): Daniel Bouju, 16130 Segonzac. Owns 20ha. in the Grande Champagne. Produces Tradition, Empéreur and V.S.O.P.

Lafont [Jean-Marc] (Fr) a winery based in Côte du Py in the A.C. Beaujolais Cru Morgon, southern Burgundy. Also produces: La Madone (A.C. Beaujolais Cru Fleurie).

La Forge Estate (Fr) a label used by the Domaines Paul Mas for its Vin de Pays d'Oc wines.

La Française (Fr) a natural spring mineral water. Mineral contents (milligrammes per litre): Sodium 653mg/l, Calcium 354mg/l, Magnesium 82mg/l, Potassium 22mg/l, Bicarbonates 1055mg/l, Sulphates 982mg/l, Nitrates 1mg/l.

La Francesca (It) a sparkling natural spring mineral water from La Francesca. Mineral contents (milligrammes per litre): Sodium 80.15mg/l, Calcium 56mg/l, Magnesium 13.84mg/l, Potassium 30mg/l, Bicarbonates 329mg/l, Chlorides 38mg/l, Sulphates 64.1mg/l, Fluorides 0.85mg/l, Nitrates 27.8mg/l, Silicates 84.7mg/l. pH 5.8

Lagache-Lecourt (Fr) a Champagne producer. (Add): 29, Rue du Maréchal Juin, 51530 Chavot. Produces: Brut Sélection, Blanc de Blancs Brut, Le Chambecy Brut Millésimé, Brut Rosé and Ratafia.

Lagar de Fornelos (Sp) a winery with vineyards in O Rosal, Rías Baixas, D.O. Galicia. Produces Lagar de Cervela.

Lagarde-sur-le-Né (Fr) a commune in the Charente département whose grapes are classed Petite Champagne (Cognac).

Lagare Cape Vintage (S.Afr) the label for a red wine (Touriga and Shiraz blend) produced by the Beyerskloof winery, Stellenbosch, Western Cape.

Lagares (Sp) used in Jerez, wooden troughs where grapes are placed to be pressed.

Lagariavini (It) a producer of sparkling (metodo

tradizionale) wines based in the Trentino-Alto Adige. Labels include Brut di Concilio.

Lagarino Rosato (It) a light red/rosé wine produced from the Lagrein grape, was formerly known as Lagreinkretzer.

Lagaritanum (It) a red wine produced in south-eastern Italy during Roman times.

Lagars (Port) wooden or concrete troughs used for the treading of the grapes in the production of Port.

Lagavulin (Scot) a single malt whisky distillery on the eastern side of the Isle of Islay overlooking Port Ellen (owned by the White Horse Distillers Ltd), an Islay malt. Produce a 12 and 16 year old malt at 43% alc by vol. also Lagavulin Bonded 1909.

Lagbi (Afr) a non-alcoholic drink made from the juice of grapes in Libya.

Lage (Ger) a specific named vineyard. *see* Einzellage and Grosslage.

Lageos (Lat) a red grape variety grown in Greece in Roman times.

Lager (Ger) lit: 'store/stock', a name for the beer produced by bottom fermentation during which it is 'lagered' for long periods to complete fermentation before it is bottled. *see* Dreher Brauerei. (Den) = øl af pilsnertype.

Lagerbier (Ger) lit: 'beer for storing', the nineteenth century term for lager.

Lagering (Ger) a method of storing new beer (lager) at very low temperatures so that the yeasts and other solids precipitate out naturally. During this period the flavour improves. Up to 3 months.

Lager Malt (Eng) a lightly kilned barley malt that gives less pronounced flavours to the lager beers.

Lagerøl (Den) dark coloured lager beer.

Lager-Weisse (Ger) a bottom-fermented wheat beer.

Lagery (Fr) a Cru Champagne village in the Canton de Ville-en-Tardenois. District: Reims.

Lager Yeasts (Eng) *Saccharomyces carlsbergensis* the name for yeasts that fall through the liquid and work on the sugar at the bottom of fermenting vessel.

Lagler [Karl] (Aus) a winery (8ha) based in the Wachau. (Add): Rote Tor Gasse 10, 3620 Spitz an der Donau. Grape varieties: Chardonnay, Grüner veltliner, Neuburger, Pinot blanc, Riesling, Sauvignon blanc. Produces a range of dry and sweet (botrytised) wines.

Lagni (Alg) palm milk.

Lagoa (Port) a DOC wine area based in the Algarve, southern Portugal.

Lagoa (Port) one of five co-operatives based in the DOC area of same name along the Algarve coast.

Lago di Caldaro (It) a D.O.C. red wine from the Trentino-Alto Adige. Made from 85%–100% Lagrein and Pinot nero grapes. Classico if grapes grown from specific communes, Superiore if min. alc. content 10.5% by vol. Scelto or Selezionato if from selected grapes and of 11% alc by vol. minimum. Also known as Kalterer or Kalterersee.

Lagoena (Lat) decanter.

Lagonda IPA (Eng) a 5% alc by vol. India pale ale brewed by Marble Beer, Greater Manchester.

Lagoon (S.Afr) the label for a rosé wine (Pinotage) produced by the Darling Cellars winery, Swartland.

Lagorthi (Gre) a rare white grape variety with tiny berries that matures with difficulty, noted for its elegance.

Lagos (Port) a DOC wine area based in the Algarve region of southern Portugal.

Lagosta (Port) the brand-name of a Vinho Verde from Real Companhía Vinícola do Norte de Portugal.

Lag Phase (Eng) a term for the period of time taken by active yeast to multiply (Binary Fission) and build a colony concentrated enough to start of visible fermentation in the beer, cider, wine, etc.

Lagrein (It) a red grape variety grown in the Trentino-Alto Adige (Südtirol).

Lagrein del Trentino (It) a D.O.C. red wine produced in the Trentino-Alto Adige from the Lagrein grape 12% alc by vol.

Lagrein di Gries (It) wines: Lagrein Rosato and Alto-Adige Lagrein Scuro are entitled to specification if produced in commune of Bolzano in the Trentino-Alto Adige.

Lagrein Dunkel (It) a German name for the red grape variety Lagrein scuro in the Südtirol (Trentino-Alto Adige). *See also* Lagrein Scuro.

Lagrein Kretzer (It) a German name for the red grape variety Lagrein rosato in the Südtirol (Trentino-Alto Adige). Also name for a local rosé wine produced in the region.

Lagrein Rosato (It) a red grape variety used in the Trentino-Alto Adige region, also a wine of same name. *see* Lagrein Kretzer.

Lagrein Scuro (It) a red grape variety used in the Trentino-Alto Adige region, also for a wine of same name. *See also* Lagrein Dunkel.

Lágrima (Port) the natural grape sugar in must.

Lágrima (Sp) the finest of the Málagas, not often shipped abroad, it is produced without using mechanical pressing. Made from the free-run must, it is light in colour, aroma and alcohol.

Lag Screw (Eng) a wooden screw with a square head used to fasten cask staves together in the seventeenth and eighteenth centuries.

Laguardim (Sp) a noted wine-producing village in the Rioja Alavesa.

La Guita (Sp) the brand-name of a Manzanilla Sherry produced by Sanchez de Alba.

Laguna Cocktail (Cktl) 40mls (⅓ gill) grappa, 20mls (⅙ gill) vodka, 20mls (⅙ gill) sweet white (bianco) vermouth, 3 dashes Campari. Shake well over ice, strain into a cocktail glass and top with a cherry.

Laguna-Verde (Cktl) ½ measure vodka, ¼ measure Galliano, ¼ measure French vermouth, 2 dashes blue Curaçao. Stir over ice, strain into a cocktail glass and add a cherry.

Lagunilla (Sp) a red and white wine produced by Bodegas Lagunilla, both are oak matured. Valle

Tinto is from the Tempranillo grape and Valle Blanco from Viura grape.

Lahnfelsquelle (Ger) a natural spring mineral water. Mineral contents (milligrammes per litre): Sodium 188mg/l, Calcium 186mg/l, Magnesium 79.3mg/l, Potassium 7.8mg/l, Bicarbonates 1019mg/l, Chlorides 2874mg/l, Sulphates 21.6mg/l, Fluorides 0.45mg/l, Silicates 16.5mg/l.

Lahnperle (Ger) a natural spring mineral water brand.

Lahnstein (Ger) village (Anb): Mittelrhein. (Ber): Rheinburgengau. (Gro): Marksburg. (Vin): Koppelstein.

Lahnsteiner (Ger) a still and sparkling natural spring mineral water (established 1989) from Lahnstein-Quelle. Mineral contents (milligrammes per litre): Sodium 211mg/l, Calcium 45mg/l, Magnesium 19mg/l, Potassium 9mg/l, Bicarbonates 456mg/l, Chlorides 124mg/l, Sulphates 111mg/l. Website: http://www.lahnsteiner.de

Lahntal (Ger) grosslage (Anb): Mittelrhein. (Ber): Rheinburgengau. (Vils): Bad Ems, Dausenau, Fachbach, Nassau, Obernhof, Weinähr.

Lahr (Ger) village (Anb): Baden. (Ber): Breisgau. (Gro): Schutterlindenberg. (Vins): Herrentisch, Kronenbühl.

Laibach Vineyards (S.Afr) a winery (established 1994) based in Stellenbosch, Western Cape. 42ha. Grape varieties: Cabernet franc, Cabernet sauvignon, Chardonnay, Chenin blanc, Merlot, Petit verdot, Pinotage, Sauvignon blanc, Shiraz. Labels: Friedrich Laibach, Inkawu, Special Selection, The Dogleg, The Ladybird. Website: http://www.laibach.co.za

Laid Back Wines (Eng) a term used to describe wines that are easy to drink. e.g. Californian wines.

La Ideal [1] (Sp) a still natural spring mineral water from Firgas, Canary Islands. Mineral contents (milligrammes per litre): Sodium 61mg/l, Calcium 82.6mg/l, Magnesium 39.9mg/l, Potassium 10.1mg/l, Chlorides 40.7mg/l, Sulphates 27.8mg/l, Fluorides 0.3mg/l.

La Ideal [2] (Sp) a still natural spring mineral water from Firgas, Canary Islands. Mineral contents (milligrammes per litre): Sodium 58.8mg/l, Calcium 76.2mg/l, Magnesium 39.4mg/l, Potassium 8.7mg/l, Bicarbonates 503.5mg/l, Chlorides 44mg/l, Sulphates 19.9mg/l, Silicates 112mg/l.

La Ideal [3] (Sp) a still and sparkling natural spring mineral water from Firgas, Canary Islands. (blue label: light gas/red label: still). Mineral contents (milligrammes per litre): Sodium 40.9mg/l, Calcium 59.3mg/l, Magnesium 32.6mg/l, Potassium 9.5mg/l, Bicarbonates 403.2mg/l, Chlorides 23.9mg/l, Sulphates 7.8mg/l, Fluorides 0.2mg/l, Nitrates 16.6mg/l.

Laila (It) a winery in the D.O.C. Verdicchio dei Castelli di Jesi, Marches region. Label: Ekiewktikus.

Laine Vineyards and Winery (USA) a winery based in Fulton, Kentucky. Produces French hybrid wines.

Laira (Austr) a winery. (Add): Main Pendar, Naracoorte Highway, (P.O. Box 18), Coonawarra, South Australia 5263. 28ha. Grape varieties: Cabernet sauvignon, Malbec, Merlot and Shiraz.

Laird o' Logan (Scot) see Logan (the original name for Logan Whisky).

Laireen (Sp) another spelling of Lairén.

Lairén (Sp) a white grape variety grown in southern Spain to produce medium white wines including Montilla-Moriles. Also known as Airén.

Laiser Haide (Aus) a vineyard site based on the banks of the River Kamp situated in the Kamptal region.

Lait (Fr) milk.

Lait [Au] (Fr) lit: 'with milk'. e.g. café au lait (coffee with milk).

Lait Condensé (Fr) condensed milk.

Lait de Coco (Fr) coconut milk, is used in some cocktail recipes. (W.Ind) = caraïbos.

Lait de Poule (Cktl) the famous French egg nogg. 2 egg yolks, castor sugar to taste. Beat up with boiling milk and add 60mls (½ gill) brandy.

Lait Desséchés (Fr) dried milk.

Lait Écrôimai (Ch.Isles) skimmed milk.

Laiteux (Fr) milky.

Lait Fermentés (Fr) fermented milk.

Laitiat (Fr) a non-alcoholic drink of whey which has had fruit infused in it, favoured in the Franche-Comté region.

Laives (Fr) a commune in the A.C. Mâcon where the grapes may be used for Mâcon Supérieur.

Laizé (Fr) a producer of A.C. Calvados. Based in Sourdeval (Manche). Produces Vieille Réserve, Cordon Jaune, Cordon Rouge.

Lajita (Mex) a 40% alc by vol Mezcal tequila with the agave worm in the bottle, produced by Licores Veracruz, S.A. de C.V.

La Jota Vineyard (USA) a winery based in the Howell Mountain, Napa Valley, California. Grape varieties: Cabernet sauvignon. Label: 21st Anniversary Release.

La Karnel (S.Afr) the label for a range of wines produced by the Crows Nest winery, Paarl, Western Cape.

Lake Balatòn (Hun) a vineyard region in western Hungary. Produces good white wines from the Furmint and Riesling grape.

Lake Chalice Wines (N.Z) a winery. (Add): Vintage Lane, P.O. Box 66, Renwick, Marlborough. 11.5ha. Grape varieties: Riesling, Cabernet sauvignon, Sauvignon blanc, Chardonnay, Merlot, Cabernet franc.

Lake County (USA) a wine-producing county on the northern coast of California.

Lake District (Aus) a noted wine-producing area in western Austria which is protected by the Leitha mountains. Produces fine white wines.

Lake Erie (USA) the second of the Great Lakes which has the districts of New York, Pennsylvania and Ohio.

Lake Fly (Eng) the name of an Oloroso Sherry from Findlater.

Lake Hayes (N.Z) a vineyard based in Otago, linked with Chard Farm that produces Lady of the Lake sparking wine.

Lake Keuka Wine C°. (USA) a winery based in the Finger Lakes region. Produces hybrid and American vine wines.

Lakeland Spring Water (Eng) a natural spring mineral water from Cleator Moor. Mineral contents (milligrammes per litre): Sodium 6mg/l, Calcium 1.2mg/l, Magnesium 1.2mg/l, Potassium 0.5mg/l, Bicarbonates 3.5mg/l, Chlorides 12mg/l, Sulphates 1mg/l, Fluorides 0.1mg/l, Nitrates 1mg/l. pH 6.3

Lakeland Willow Water (Eng) a natural spring mineral water (established circa 1200) from Cartmel Valley, Lake District, Cumbria.

Lake Osoyoos Vineyard (Can) a vineyard based in the Okanagan Valley, British Columbia. Produces: Osoyoos Larose.

Lake's Folly (Austr) a vineyard (13.2ha). (Add): Broke Road, Pokolbin, New South Wales 2321. Grape varieties: Cabernet sauvignon, Chardonnay, Hermitage, Malbec and Petit verdot.

Lakeside Winery (USA) a winery based in Harbert, Michigan. Produces French hybrid wines.

Lake Sylvia Vineyard (USA) a bonded winery based in Minnesota. 3ha. Produces hybrid wines.

Lakewood Vineyards (USA) a winery based in the Finger Lakes, New York State. Grape variety: Pinot noir.

Lakka (Fin) a liqueur with a bitter-sweet tang of cloudberries that are grown only in the Arctic. Also known as Suomurrain. Is produced by Chymos 29% alc by vol.

Lalande de Pomerol (Fr) an A.C. sub-district (1106ha) of Pomerol in eastern Bordeaux (10.5–13.5% alc by vol).

La Landonne (Fr) a vineyard (1.8ha) in Côte Rôtie, Côtes du Rhône, owned by Guigal 100% Syrah. See also Mouline (La) and Turque (La).

Laligant-Chameroy (Fr) a Burgundy négociant-éleveur based at Beaune, Côte de Beaune, Burgundy.

Lallier (Fr) a Champagne producer. Vintage: 1999.

Lal Toofan (Eng) a beer brewed under licence by Refresh UK plc., Oxfordshire.

Lal Toofan (Ind) lit: 'red storm', a 4.6% alc by vol. bottled straw coloured pilsner brewed by Shaw Wallace & C°. in Calcutta using basmati rice.

Lal Toofan Beer (Ind) a pilsner beer from Shaw Wallace Overseas, brewed in the U.K. by Ushers.

Lamarque (Fr) a commune of the Haut-Médoc, Bordeaux.

Lamb and Watt (Eng) a producer of a range of spirits and a sloe gin under the Mauget label. Also Vine Leaf Sherry.

Lambanog (E.Ind) a distilled tuba wine from the Philippines.

Lamberhurst Priory (Eng) see Ridge Farm, Kent.

Lambert Bridge (USA) a winery (33ha) based in Dry Creek Valley, Sonoma County, California. Grape varieties: Cabernet sauvignon, Chardonnay and Johannisberg riesling. Produces varietal wines.

Lamberti (It) wine producers east of Lake Garda, produces Bardolino, Soave and Valpolicella wines.

Lambic Beer (Bel) a wheat beer (average 5% alc by vol) with one or more fruits added (to the wort) for flavour, top fermented, which uses the natural wild yeasts to ferment the brew. 4.5% alc by vol. produced in the river Senne region they are often matured for a minimum of nine months. See **Brettanomyces bruxelliensis** and **Brettanomyces lambicus.**

Lambiek Beer (Bel) an alternative spelling of lambic beer.

Lamblin et Fils (Fr) a small Burgundy négociant-éleveur based at Maligny, Chablis, Burgundy. Produces a range of Chablis wines including Premier Crus Beauroy and Fourchaume.

Lambrini (Eng) the brand name for a range of flavoured (cherry, perry), sparkling bottled drinks 7.5% alc by vol. produced by Halewood International Ltd. Also produce an Orange Bucks Fizz 5.5% alc by vol. Website: http://www.lambrini.co.uk

Lambrusco (It) a red grape variety grown in the Po valley in north-eastern Italy. Produces classic red and sparkling red wines.

Lambrusco a Foglia Frastagliata (It) a red grape variety renamed Enantio.

Lambrusco di Salamino (It) a red grape variety used in the Emilia-Romagna region.

Lambrusco di Sorbara (It) a red grape variety used in the Emilia-Romagna region.

Lambrusco di Sorbara (It) a D.O.C. red wine made from 60% Lambrusco di sorbara and 40% Lambrusco di salamino grapes. Vinification can take place in Bologna, Modena, Parma and Reggio Emilia subject to Ministry approval. Vinificato fuori zona (vinified outside production area) must be on label.

Lambrusco Grappa Rossa (It) is similar to Lambrusco di Sorbara but thinner and darker.

Lambrusco Grasparossa (It) a red grape variety used in the Emilia-Romagna region.

Lambrusco Grasparossa di Castelvetro (It) a D.O.C. red wine made from 85% Lambrusco grasparossa and 15% Lambruso varieties/Uva d'oro grapes. Secco or amabile. Vinification can take place in Modena. Vinificato Fuori Zona (vinified outside production area) must appear on the label.

Lambrusco Maesini (Arg) a red grape variety.

Lambrusco Maestri (It) a red grape variety used in the Emilia-Romagna region.

Lambrusco Marani (It) a red grape variety used in the Emilia-Romagna region.

Lambrusco Montericco (It) a red grape variety used in the Emilia-Romagna region.

Lambrusco Reggiano (It) a D.O.C. red or rosé wine made from a variety of Lambrusco grapes. Vinification can also take place in Mantova, Modena and Parma. Vinficato fuori zona (vinified outside production area) must appear on the label.

Lambrusco Salamino (It) see Lambrusco di Salamino.

Lambrusco Salamino di Santa Croce (It) a D.O.C. red wine made from Lambrusco di Salamino grapes grown in the province of Moderna. Vinification can take place in Moderna but can be extended with permission. If so then Vinificato Fuori Zona (vinified outside production area) must appear on the label.

Lambrusco Varietus (It) a red grape variety used in the Emilia-Romagna region.

Lambsheim (Ger) village (Anb): Pfalz. (Ber): Mittelhaardt-Deutsche Weinstrasse. (Gro): Rosenbühl. (Vin): Burgweg.

Lamb's Navy Rum (Eng) the brand-name for a dark rum from the West Indies matured in England by United Rum Merchants.

Lamb's Wool (Cktl) into a large saucepan pour 2 bottles old strong ale, 500mls (1pint) white wine, 1 teaspoon nutmeg, 2 teaspoons mixed spices, brown sugar to sweeten. Mix together, add 6 cored and roasted apples (sugared and spiced before roasting), simmer and serve in mugs.

Lambton's (Eng) a smooth brew bitter 3.8% alc by vol. brewed by Vaux Breweries, Sunderland, a nitrokeg or canned ale.

Lamb Winery (USA) a small winery based in Santa Clara County, California. Grape varieties: Chardonnay, Chenin blanc, Gamay and Zinfandel. Produce varietal wines.

Lamego (Port) a district in the Douro that produces red, white and sparkling wines.

Lamiable Frères (Fr) a Champagne producer 6ha of Grand Cru vineyards. (Add): 8 Rempart Est, 51150 Tours sur Marne. Récoltant-manipulants. Produces vintage and non-vintage wines. Vintages: 1971, 1975, 1976, 1979, 1982, 1983, 1985, 1988, 1990, 1995, 1996, 1997, 1998, 1999, 2001. A member of the Club Tresors de Champagne. Labels: Cuvée Les Meslaines Grand Cru, Cuvée 'Special Club' Millésimée (Chardonnay 60% Pinot noir 40%). Website: http://www.champagnelamiable.com 'E'mail: lamiable@champagnelamiable.com

L'Ami Simon (S.Afr) the label for a red wine (Cabernet franc, Cabernet sauvignon, Merlot and Pinotage blend) produced by the L'Avenir Estate winery, Stellenbosch, Western Cape.

La Mitrale (Fr) the name given to the new (2002) bottle for the Châteauneuf-du-Pape wines by SIDOVAC.

Lamm (Aus) loam (soil).

Lamm (Aus) a vineyard site based on the banks of the River Kamp situated in the Kamptal region.

Lammberg (Aus) a vineyard site based on the banks of the River Kamp situated in the Kamptal region.

Lammerlaw (N.Z) the name of a single malt whiskey produced near Dunedin.

Lammershoek Winery (S.Afr) a winery (established 1999) based in Malmesbury, Swartland, Western Cape. 130ha. Grape varieties: Carignan, Chardonnay, Chenin blanc, Grenache, Hárslevelü, Pinotage, Shiraz, Tinta barocca, Viognier, Zinfandel. Labels: Aprilskloof, Cape Ruby, Pinodoux, Red-Red, Roulette. Website: http://www.lammershoek.co.za

Lämmler (Ger) vineyard (Anb): Württemberg. (Ber): Remstal-Stuttgart. (Gro): Weinsteige. (Vil): Fellbach.

Lamole di Lamole (It) a 45ha vineyard based in Tuscany. Owned by the Santa Margherita Group. Range of wines include Chianti Classico, Chianti Classico Riserva, Vin Santo.

La Monacesca (It) a winery in the D.O.C. Verdicchio di Matelica, Marches region. Label: Mirum.

Lamonts Winery (Austr) a winery. (Add): Bisdee Road, Millendon, Western Australia 6056. 3ha. Grape varieties: Cabernet sauvignon, Muscadelle, Sémillon, Shiraz and Verdelho.

Lamont Winery (USA) a large winery based in Delano, Kern County, California. Grape varieties: Colombard and Zinfandel. Produces varietal and dessert wines under Gold Peak, Mountain Gold and Lamont labels. Was originally known as Bear Mountain Winery.

La Mormoraia (It) a winery based in the DOCG Vernaccia di San Gimignano in the Tuscany region.

Lamot (Bel) a brewery producing a bottled pilsener lager 1045 O.G. imported by Bass.

La Motte (S.Afr) a winery (established 1984) based in the Franschhoek, Western Cape. 108ha. Grape varieties: Cabernet franc, Cabernet sauvignon, Chardonnay, Malbec, Sauvignon blanc, Shiraz, Viognier. Labels: Millenium, Pierneef Collection, Schoone Gevel. Website: http://www.la-motte.com

L'Amour Toujours (S.Afr) a red wine (Cabernet sauvignon and Merlot blend) produced by the Allée Bleu winery, Franschhoek, Western Cape.

Lampée (Fr) a slang word for swig.

Lampia (It) a sub-species of the Nebbiolo grape.

Lamplighter Gin (Eng) see Nicholson.

Lamp Oil (Eng) a 5% alc by vol. dark bitter ale brewed by the Aspinall Cambrinus Craft Brewery, Knowsley, Merseyside.

Lampons (Fr) lit: 'let us drink', a term used in the seventeenth century in verse.

Lancashire Strong Brown Ale (Eng) a 5% alc by vol. bottled brown ale brewed by Daniel Thwaites Brewery, Blackburn, Lancashire.

Lancaster Bomber (Eng) a 4.4% alc by vol. ale from Mitchells of Lancaster.

Lancaster Bomber (Eng) a 4.4% alc by vol. premium cask-conditioned ale from Thwaites Brewery, Blackburn

Lancaster County Winery (USA) a winery based in Willow Street, Pennsylvania. Produces French hybrid wines.

Lancaster Estate (USA) a 21ha winery (established 1994) based in the Alexander Valley, Sonoma County, California. Label: Nicole's.

Lancefield Winery (Austr) a winery (established 1983) based at Woodend Road, Lancefield, Victoria. Grape varieties: Chardonnay, Gewürztraminer, Cabernet sauvignon, Merlot, Pinot noir. Produces Rutherglen fortified, still and sparkling wines.

Lancer (Ire) a strong bottled Lager brewed by Harp.

Lancers (Port) a sweet carbonated rosé wine, sold in

L

a distinctively shaped bottle from J.M. da Fonseca. Also a red and a white version produced.

Lanchester (Eng) a firm based in Durham that produces a range of ciders. Labels include: Brambledown, Electric White, Zodiac.

Lancié (Fr) a commune in the Beaujolais. Has A.C. Beaujolais-Villages or Beaujolais-Lancié status.

Lancorta (Sp) a red wine produced by Bodegas Landalan, Alta region in Rioja. Oak and bottle matured. Also a white wine under same name from Viura grape.

Lancut (Pol) producers of Wyborowa Vodka 37.5% alc by vol.

Landalan (Sp) *see* Bodegas Landalan.

Landau (Ger) village (Anb): Pfalz. (Ber): Südliche Weinstrasse. (Gro): Königsgarten. (Vin): Altes Löhl.

Landau (S.Afr) the label for a range of wines produced by the Blaauwklippen Agricultural Estate winery, Stellenbosch, Western Cape.

Landau du Val (S.Afr) a winery based in Franschhoek, Western Cape. Grape varieties: Sauvignon blanc, Sémillon.

Landauer (Aus) a winery based in Rust, Neusiedlersee-Hügelland, Burgenland. (Add): Haydngasse 5, 7071 Rust. Grape varieties include: Pinot noir, Welschriesling.

Landbrauerei mit Braustube & Biergarten (Ger) a brewery. (Add): Bahnhofstrasse 40, Nalbach-Körprich D-66809. Brews a range of beers and lager. Website: http://www.landbrauerei.de

Landes (Fr) a Vin de Pays area in south-western France.

Landespreismünze (Ger) an award given for quality at a Federal state level to wines.

Landesregierungen (Ger) the governments of the wine growing Federal states, who determine legislation for the new (1971) wine law.

Landesverordnung Rheinland-Pfalz (Ger) a decree for the Federal state of the Rheinish Palatinate 12 August 1971 article [4] governs the production of Liebfrauenmilch/Liebfraumilch.

Landewein (Ger) *see* Landwein.

Landfall Wines (N.Z) an 8ha winery. (Add): SH2, Manutuke, Gisborne.

Landing (USA) applied to Champagne. Denotes the length of time the Champagne has been in the country. i.e. Champagne that has been in the country for 1 year is said to have 1 years landing.

Landiras (Fr) a commune in the A.C. Graves region of south-western Bordeaux.

Landkreis (Ger) parish.

Landlord (Eng) the name given to the publican/licensee.

Landlord (Eng) a strong cask-conditioned or bottled bitter 1042 O.G. brewed by Taylor (Timothy) at The Knowle Spring Brewery in Keighley, West Yorkshire.

Landlord Pale Ale (Eng) a 4.1% alc by vol. pale ale brewed by Taylor (Timothy) at The Knowle Spring Brewery in Keighley, West Yorkshire.

Landlords Choice (Eng) a 4.6% alc by vol. ale brewed by the Wylam Brewery Ltd., Tyne & Wear.

Landmark Vineyards (USA) a winery based in Windsor, Russian River Valley, Sonoma County, California. 33ha. Grape varieties: Cabernet sauvignon, Chardonnay, Chenin blanc, Gewürztraminer, Johannisberg riesling and Pinot noir. Produces varietal wines. Vineyards also in Sonoma and Alexander Valleys. Labels include: Grand Detour, Kastania.

Landot (Fr) a famous hybridiser.

Landry (Fr) a Cognac producer (established 1972). (Add): Logis de Beaulieu, 17520 Germignac. Owns 19ha. in the Petite Champagne. Produces Hors d'Age (a 17 year old Cognac).

Landscape (S.Afr) a winery based in Stellenbosch. Grapes varieties: Cabernet, Chenin blanc, Cinsaut, Merlot.

Landsdorf (Eng) a fine, non-pasteurised, filtered, draught lager beer 1034 O.G. brewed by the Hardington Brewery, Somerset.

Land's End Wines (S.Afr) a winery based in Simondium, Elim, Southern Cape. 35ha. Grape varieties: Cabernet sauvignon, Merlot, Sauvignon blanc, Sémillon, Shiraz.

Landshausen (Ger) *see* Kraichtal.

Landsker (Wal) an off-dry white wine produced by Cwm Deri Vineyard, Martletwy, Pembrokeshire from Madeleine angevine and Gewürztraminer grapes.

Landsknecht (Ger) vineyard (Anb): Franken. (Ber): Mainsdreieck. (Gro): Kirchberg. (Vil): Obervolkach.

Landskrone (Ger) vineyard (Anb): Ahr. (Ber): Walporzheim/Ahrtal. (Gro): Klosterberg. (Vil): Heimersheim.

Landskroon Wine Estate (S.Afr) a large winery (established 1874) based in Suider-Paarl, Western Cape. (Add): P.O. Box 519, Suider-Paarl 7624. 270ha. Grape varieties: Cabernet franc, Cabernet sauvignon, Chardonnay, Chenin blanc, Cinsaut, Gewürztraminer, Hanepoot, Jerepigo, Merlot, Morio muscat, Pinotage, Red jerepigo, Shiraz, Tinta barocca, Touriga. Labels: Blanc de noir, Bouquet blanc, Bouquet rouge, Paul de Villiers, Tinta Barocca and many varietals plus a Port-type wine. Website: http://www.landskroonwines.com

Landstrass (Aus) a vineyard site based on the banks of the River Kamp situated in the Kamptal region.

Landwein (Aus) a tafelwein from specific wine growing area and produced from legally recognised grape varieties with a maximum yield of 9000kgs/ha and a minimum of 14° KMW.

Landwein (Ger) from 1982, a new designation of Deutsche Tafelwein of E.C. 17 zones called Landweingebiet. Either Trocken or Halbtrocken with not more than 18 grammes/litre of residual sugar. *See also* Zones.

Landwein der Mosel (Ger) one of seventeen Deutsche Tafelwein zones.

Landwein der Saar (Ger) one of seventeen Deutsche Tafelwein zones.

Landweingebiete (Ger) the name for the wine zones (17) are equivalent to the French Vin de Pays.

Landwig (Aus) a vineyard site on the banks of the River Danube in the Kremstal region.

Landy Frères (It) a producer of Dubac brandy.

Landzicht GWK Wines (S.Afr) a winery (established 1976) based in Jacobsdal, Northern Cape. 300ha. Grape varieties: Cabernet sauvignon, Chardonnay, Chenin blanc, Colombard, Gewürztraminer, Hanepoot, Jerepigo, Muscadel, Pinotage, Red muscadel, Shiraz. Labels: Blümchen, Rosenblümchen.

La Neblina (USA) the label for a red wine (Pinot noir) produced by the Radio-Coteau Wine Cellars winery, Sonoma County, California.

Lang (Aus) a winery (12ha) based in Illmitz, Burgenland. (Add): Quergasse 5, 7142 Illmitz. Grape varieties: Blaufränkisch, Chardonnay, Gewürztraminer, Grüner veltliner, Pinot blanc, Pinot noir, Sauvignon blanc, Zweigelt. Produces a range of sweet wines.

Langa Antica (It) the brand-name for a grappa.

Langa Nebbiolo (It) the new name for Nebbiolo delle Langhe.

Lang-Biemont (Fr) a Champagne producer (established 1875). (Add): 26, Rue Pasteur, 51190 Avize. 30ha. Produces vintage and non-vintage wines. Vintages: 1971, 1973, 1974, 1976, 1977, 1979, 1980, 1982, 1983, 1985, 1988, 1990, 1995, 1998, 1999, 2000. De Luxe vintage cuvée: Cuvée d'Exception. Cuvée III is a blanc de blancs. Website: http://www.lang-biemont.com 'E'mail: info@ lang-biemont.com

Lang Brothers (Scot) distillers of Scotch whisky based at Glengoyne. A subsidiary of Robertson and Baxter. Produces Langs Supreme.

Langdale Wine Estate (N.Z) a winery. (Add): Langdales Road, West Melton, Christchurch. 4.5ha. Grape varieties: Breidecker, Cabernet sauvignon, Chardonnay, Merlot, Pinot noir, Riesling.

Langdons (Eng) a cider-producing firm based at Hewish, near Weston-Super-Mare, Avon. Noted for West Country Cider.

Lange Els (Ger) vineyard (Anb): Pfalz. (Ber): Mittelhaardt-Deutsche Weinstrasse. (Gro): Schwarzerde. (Vil): Hessheim.

Lange Favorita (It) a white D.O.C. wine made in Piemonte from Favorita grape.

Langenbach (Ger) a wine merchant and shipper based in Worms in the Rheinhessen. Produces Liebfraumilch under the brand-name of Crown of Crowns.

Langenberg (Ger) vineyard (Anb): Franken. (Ber): Maindreieck. (Gro): Rosstal. (Vil): Retzstadt.

Langenberg (Ger) vineyard (Anb): Rheingau. (Ber): Johannisberg. (Gro): Steinmacker. (Vil): Martinsthal.

Langenberg (Ger) a vineyard within the village of Martinsthal, 18.5ha. (43.8%) of which is proposed to be classified as Erstes Gewächs.

Langenbeutingen (Ger) village (Anb): Württemberg. (Ber): Württembergisch Unterland. (Gro): Lindelberg. (Vin): Himmelreich.

Langen-Hadlinger (Aus) a vineyard site on the banks of the River Danube in the Kremstal region.

Langenlois (Aus) a wine-producing town of same name that produces mainly white wines.

Langenlonsheim (Ger) village (Anb): Nahe. (Ber): Kreuznach. (Gro): Sonnenborn. (Vins): Bergborn, Königsschild, Lauerweg, Lohrer Berg, Rothenberg, St. Antoniusberg, Steinchen.

Langenmorgen (Ger) vineyard (Anb): Pfalz. (Ber): Mittelhaardt-Deutsche Weinstrasse. (Gro): Mariengarten. (Vil): Deidesheim.

Langenstein (Ger) vineyard (Anb): Franken. (Ber): Steigerwald. (Gro): Not yet assigned. (Vil): Martinsheim.

Langenstein (Ger) vineyard (Anb): Pfalz. (Ber): Mittelhaardt-Deutsche Weinstrasse. (Gro): Pfaffengrund. (Vil): Lachen-Speyerdorf.

Langenstück (Ger) vineyard (Anb): Rheingau. (Ber): Johannisberg. (Gro): Steinmäcker. (Vil): Eltville.

Langenstück (Ger) vineyard (Anb): Rheingau. (Ber): Johannisberg. (Gro): Steinmäcker. (Vil): Oberwalluf.

Langenstück (Ger) vineyard (Anb): Rheingau. (Ber): Johannisberg. (Gro): Steinmäcker. (Vil): Rauenthal.

Langenthal Brauerei (Switz) a brewery based in Langenthal. Part of the Interbera group.

Langenweine (Aus) a term used to describe single vineyard wines.

Langenzügen (Aus) a vineyard site on the banks of the River Danube situated in the Wachau region, Niederösterreich.

Langeskov Cherries (Den) used in the making of cherry wine.

Lange Winery (USA) a winery (established 1987) based in Dundee, Oregon. Grape varieties: Chardonnay, Pinot gris, Pinot noir.

Langgarten (Ger) vineyard (Anb): Mittelrhein. (Ber): Bacharach. (Gro): Schloss Stahleck. (Vil): Manubach.

Langham Vineyard (Eng) a vineyard based at Langham, near Colchester, Essex. 1.6ha. Grape variety: Müller-Thurgau.

Langhe (It) the name for the clay soil in the Barolo district of the Piemonte region.

Lang [Helmut] (Aus) a wine producer (12 ha) based in Neusielersee (Add): Quergasse 5, 7142 Illmitz. Grape varieties: Blaufränkisch, Chardonnay, Gewürztraminer, Grüner veltliner, Pinot blanc, Pinot noir, Sauvignon blanc, Scheurebe, Welschriesling, Zweigelt. Produces white, sweet white and red wines.

Langhölle (Ger) vineyard (Anb): Nahe. (Ber): Schloss Böckelheim. (Gro): Paradiesgarten. (Vil): Obermoschel.

Langhorne Creek (Austr) a wine-producing area in South Australia, east of Adelaide. Produces full-bodied red wines.

Lán Gloine (Ire) glassful.

Langlois-Château (Fr) a winery based in the Anjou-Saumur region of the Loire Valley. (Add): 3, Rue Léopold Palustre, 49400 Saint Hilaire Florent.

Produces a range of A.C. regional wines including sparkling, white, rosé and red varieties. Labels include: La Bretonnière. Website: http://www.langlois-chateau.fr 'E'mail: contact@langlois-chateau.fr

Langoed (S.Afr) estate.

Langoiran (Fr) a commune in the A.C. Premières Côtes de Bordeaux, central Bordeaux.

Langon (Fr) a commune in the A.C. Graves region in south-western Bordeaux.

Langriegel (Aus) a vineyard area based in the Kitzeck district of Süd-Steirmark.

Langscheid (Ger) village (Anb): Mittelrhein. (Ber): Rheinburgengau. (Gro): Schloss Schönburg. (Vin): Hundert.

Langs Supreme (Scot) a blended Scotch whisky produced by the Lang Brothers Ltd. 40% alc by vol. see Lang Brothers.

Langstampf Satzen (Aus) a vineyard site on the banks of the River Danube in the Kremstal region.

Langstampf Steiner (Aus) a vineyard site on the banks of the River Danube in the Kremstal region.

Langstieler (Ger) a lesser white grape variety.

Langsur (Ger) village (Anb): Mosel-Saar-Ruwer. (Ber): Obermosel. (Gro): Königsberg. (Vin): Brüderberg.

Langton Brewery (Eng) a brewery (established 1993). (Add): The Bell Inn, East Langton, Market Harborough, Leicestershire LE16 7TW. Brews bitter beers. Website: http://www.thebellinn.co.uk

Langton's (Austr) a noted wine auctioneer based in Sydney that has produced an un-official but respected classification (first list 1991) of Australia's finest (and rarest) wines. The classification (2005) lists: Exceptional (11), Outstanding (22), Excellent (34) and Distinguished (34).

Langtry (USA) the label used by Guenoc Estate in California for a top of the range red and white wine.

Languedoc (Fr) a wine area within the Midi in south-western France. Produces: white, rosé, red, sparkling, vin de liqueurs and vin doux naturels. Usually grouped together with the region of Roussillon. The Languedoc **A.O.C.'s**: Coteaux du Languedoc, Clairette du Languedoc, Corbières, Faugères, Limoux, Minervois, Minervois la Livinière, Frontignan, Mireval, Lunel, St. Jean de Minervois, Fitou, St.-Chinian, Cabardès, Malepère. Principal grape varieties: **white**: Bourboulenc, Grenache blanc, Maccabeu, Marsanne and Roussanne. **red**: Carignan, Cinsault, Grenache noir, Mourvèdre and Syrah. Website: http://www.languedoc-wines.com

Languedoc-Roussillon (Fr) a region of south-western France. Has the départements of Aude, Gard, Hérault, Lozère and Pyrénées-Orientales in its boundaries, a mountainous region with coastal plains. All styles of wines produced. **Vin de Pays regions**: Catalan/de Bessan/de Cassan/de Caux/de Cessenon/de Cucugnan/de la Cité de Carcassonne/de la Haute-Vallée de l'Aude/de la Haute-Vallée de l'Orb/de l'Ardailhou/de la Bénovie/de la Côte Vermeille/de la Vallée du Paradis/de la Vaunage/de la Vicomté d'Aumelas de la Vistrenque/de Pézenas/des Cévennes/des Cévennes 'Mont-Bouquet'/des Collines de la Moure/des Coteaux Cévenois/des Coteaux de Bessilles/des Coteaux de Cèze/des Coteaux d'Enserune/des Coteaux de Fenouillèdes/des Coteaux de Fontcaude/des Coteaux de la Cabrerisse/des Coteaux de Laurens/des Coteaux du Libron/des Coteaux du Littoral Audois/des Coteaux de Miramont /des Coteaux de Murviel/des Coteaux de Narbonne/des Coteaux de Peyriac/des Coteaux du Pont-du-Gard/des Coteaux du Salagou/des Côtes du Brian/des Côtes Catalanes/des Côtes du Céressou/des Côtes de Lastours/des Côtes de Pérignan/des Côtes de Prouille/des Côtes de Thau/des Côtes de Thongue/des Côtes du Vidourle/des Gorges de l'Hérault/des Hautes de Badens/des Monts de la Grage/des Sables-du-Golfe-du-Lion/des Vals d'Agly/d'Hauterive/d'Hauterive 'Coteaux du Termènès'/d'Hauterive 'Côtes de Lézignan'/d'Hauterive 'Val d'Orbieu'/du Bérange/du Duché d'Uzès/du Mont-Baudile/du Torgan/du Val de Cesse/du Val de Dagne/du Val de Montferrand/d'Oc. Many grape varieties including: Carignan, Cinsault, Grenache, Mourvèdre, Syrah.

Langverwacht Co-operative (S.Afr) a wine co-operative (established 1956) based in the Boesmans River, Bonnievale, Breede River and Robertson areas. 600ha. (Add): Box 87, Bonnievale 6730. Grape varieties: Cabernet sauvignon, Chardonnay, Chenin blanc, Colombard, Ruby cabernet, Shiraz. Produces varietal wines.

Lania (Cyp) a village on the south-east side of the Island that produces the grapes for Commandaria.

Lanjarón Fonte Forte (Sp) a sparkling natural spring mineral water from Lanjarón, Granada. Mineral contents (milligrammes per litre): Sodium 108.5mg/l, Calcium 80.6mg/l, Magnesium 19.9mg/l, Potassium 14.5mg/l, Bicarbonates 675mg/l, Chlorides 236mg/l, Sulphates 37.4mg/l, Fluorides 0.3mg/l, Nitrates 1mg/l.

Lanjarón Salud (Sp) a still natural spring mineral water from Lanjarón, Granada. Mineral contents (milligrammes per litre): Sodium 6.8mg/l, Calcium 38.1mg/l, Magnesium 11.4mg/l, Potassium 0.8mg/l, Bicarbonates 145.8mg/l, Chlorides 3.9mg/l, Sulphates 25.9mg/l, Fluorides 0.2mg/l, Nitrates 5.8mg/l. pH 6.77

Lanolin (Eng) a description that is often used to describe wines made with the Sémillon grape. i.e. white Bordeaux, denotes a soft fragrance.

Lanoy (S.Afr) a red wine blend of Shiraz, Merlot and Cabernet grapes from the Boschendal Estate in Paarl.

Lansdowne Lady (Cktl) 1 part gin, 2 parts dry Sherry, 1 part orange squash. Shake well over ice, strain into a cocktail glass and add a cherry.

Lanskroun Brewery (Czec) a brewery (established 1700) based in northern Czec.

Lanson (Fr) a Champagne producer (established 1760). (Add): 12 Boulevard Lundy, B.P. 163, 51100 Reims. A Grande Marque. Produces vintage and non-vintage wines. Vintages: 1900, 1904, 1906, 1911, 1914, 1915, 1918, 1920, 1921, 1926, 1928, 1934, 1937, 1941, 1942, 1943, 1945, 1949, 1952, 1953, 1955, 1959, 1961, 1964, 1966, 1969, 1971, 1975, 1976, 1979, 1981, 1982, 1983, 1985, 1988, 1989, 1990, 1995, 1996, 1998, 1999, 2001. De Luxe vintage cuvées: Noble Cuvée Millesimé and 225 Anniversary Cuvée. *See also* Colligny Père et Fils. Website: http://www.lanson.fr

Lanvin [H.] (Fr) the label used by Société Anonyme de Magneta for their vintage cuvée.

Lanzarote (Sp) one of three islands that make up Las Palmas de Gran Canaria, Canarias. *see* Fuerteventura and Gran Canaria. D.O. on the Canary Islands. Main style of wine produced is Vin de Licor from Malvasía and Listán, plus light red wines. Grape varieties: Listán negra, Malvasía, Negramoll, Burrablanca, Breval, Diego, Listán blanca, Malvasia, Moscatel, Pedro ximénez.

Lanzerac (S.Afr) the name used for export wines by the Stellenbosch Farmers' Winery. Produce a fine rosé wine under this label. Grape varieties: Cabernet sauvignon.

Lanzerac Wines (S.Afr) a winery (established 1991) based in Stellenbosch, Western Cape. 50 ha. Grape varieties: Cabernet sauvignon, Chardonnay, Merlot, Pinotage, Sauvignon blanc, Shiraz. Label: Classic (Cabernet sauvignon 53% and Merlot 47%). Website: http://www.lanzeracwines.co.za

Laochiu (Chi) drink of wine.

Laona (Cyp) the brand-name of a wine range from the Arsos winery.

Laoshan (Chi) a natural spring mineral water from Laoshan, Qingdao. Mineral contents (milligrammes per litre): Sodium 105mg/l, Calcium 114mg/l, Magnesium 22mg/l, Bicarbonates 286mg/l, Silicates 21.5mg/l.

Laowine (Thai) grape wine.

Lap (USA) chorus girls' slang for gin.

Lapalme (Fr) one of nine wine communes in the Fitou region, southern France.

La Paz (Sp) a still, natural spring mineral water from Marmolejo. Mineral contents (milligrammes per litre): Sodium 9.4mg/l, Calcium 103.4mg/l, Magnesium 14.9mg/l, Potassium 1.6mg/l, Chlorides 21.1mg/l, Sulphates 21.3mg/l, Fluorides 0.2mg/l, Nitrates 34.3mg/l.

La Petite Ferme (S.Afr) a winery (established 1996) based in Franschhoek, Western Cape. 8ha. Grape varieties: Cabernet sauvignon, Chardonnay, Merlot, Muscat, Pinotage, Sauvignon blanc, Sémillon, Shiraz. Labels: La Petite Sieste, Nectar du Val.

La Petite Sieste (S.Afr) the label for a straw wine (Sémillon 75% plus Chenin blanc and Muscat blend) produced by the La Petite Ferme winery, Franschhoek, Western Cape.

Laphroaig (Scot) a single malt whisky distillery on the eastern side of the Isle of Islay (owned by Long John Distilleries). An Islay malt, produce 10 and 15 year old malts 40% alc by vol.

Lapic Winery (USA) a winery based at New Brighton, south-western Pennsylvania. Produces French hybrid wines.

Lapierre [Hubert] (Fr) a winery (7.5ha) based in the A.C. Beaujolais Cru Moulin-á-Vent, southern Burgundy. Also produces A.C. Cru Beaujolais Chénas.

Lapin Kulta (Fin) a lager from the Tornio Brewery on Tornio river, northern Finland. 3 versions: 1020 O.G. (home market), 1030 O.G. (Swedish market), 1040 O.G. (U.K. market).

Lap it up (Eng) a term used to denote that a person is enjoying their beverage or food.

La Platina (Sp) a still natural spring mineral water from Salamanca. Mineral contents (milligrammes per litre): Sodium 9.8mg/l, Calcium 17.2mg/l, Magnesium 15.1mg/l, Potassium 0.8mg/l, Bicarbonates 150mg/l, Chlorides 11.9mg/l, Sulphates 20.2mg/l, Fluorides 0.2mg/l, Nitrates 31mg/l.

La Pleiade (Austr) a winery based in Heathcote, Victoria. Is a joint venture between Chapoutier of the Rhône Valley (France) and Ron Laughton. Grape varieties: 50% Shiraz/50% Syrah. Is biodynamic and uses no irrigation.

La Poja (It) a Cru vineyard (2.65ha) based in Verona, Veneto region that produces a red wine of same name. Grape variety: Corvina. Owned by the Allegrini winery it has calcerous soil.

La Ponce (Fr) the label for an A.C. Côtes-du-Rhône-Villages Rasteau (red) from Domaine des Escaravailles, Rasteau, Vaucluse.

Lapponia (Fin) loganberry liqueur.

La Provençale (Fr) a natural spring mineral water brand.

La Providence (S.Afr) a winery (established 2001) based in Franschhoek, Western Cape. 2.2ha. Grape varieties: Cabernet sauvignon. Website: http://www.laprovidence.co.za

Lapsang Souchong (Chi) a blend of teas from the Fukien Province. Has a pungent, smoky flavour and large leaf.

Lapuebla de Labarca (Sp) a noted wine-producing village in the Rioja Alavesa.

L'Aqua (It) a sparkling natural spring mineral water. Mineral contents (milligrammes per litre): Sodium 15mg/l, Calcium 61.7mg/l, Magnesium 18mg/l, Potassium 2.2mg/l, Bicarbonates 266.6mg/l, Chlorides 10.6mg/l, Sulphates 23.9mg/l, Nitrates 2.2mg/l, Silicates 12.4mg/l. pH 7.5

Lar (Sp) the name of a white wine produced by Bodega Co-operative de Ribeiro.

Laranjada (Port) orangeade.

Larate (S.Am) a well-known brand of pisco produced in Peru.

L'Argentière (Fr) the label for an A.C. Côtes-du-Rhône-Villages Visan (red) from Domaine de Coste Chaude, Visan, Vaucluse.

La Riada (Sp) a winery based in the D.O. Campo de Borja. Grape varieties include: Garnacha, Tempranillo. Label: Old Vines Garnacha.

La Riconada Vineyard (USA) the label for a red wine

(Pinot noir) produced by the Sanford winery, Santa Rita Hills, Santa Barbara County, California.

Lario (Sp) the brand-name of a gin.

La Rioja (Arg) a sub-region (8192ha) in the Cuyo region, central Argentina. Main grape varieties: Chardonnay, Malbec, Syrah, Torrontés.

LA RIOJANA Cooperativa Vitivinifruticola de La Rioja Ltda (Arg) a co-operative winery (established 1940) based in the La Rioja district, Cuyo region, central Argentina. Has 600 members (a member of the Fair Trade organisation). Labels: Nacari, Santa Florentina, Neo, Pircas Negras (organic), Raza Argentina, Viñas Riojanas. Website: http://www.lariojana.com.ar 'E'mail: scream@lariojana.com.ar

Larios (Sp) a producer of Málaga wine, brandy and other spirits based in Málaga, southern Spain.

Lark (Cktl) ½ measure Nassau orange liqueur, ¼ measure *** Cognac, ¼ measure lemon squash. Shake well with ice, strain into a cocktail glass and serve with a cherry.

Larkin's Best (Eng) a 1045 O.G./4.4% alc by vol. bitter ale brewed by Larkin's Brewery at Larkin's Farm, Chiddingstone, Kent.

Larkin's Brewery (Eng) a brewery (established 1986). (Add): Larkin's Farm, Chiddingstone, Edenbridge, Kent TN8 7BB. Brews: Chiddingstone 4% alc by vol. Sovereign, Traditional 3.4% alc by vol. Best Bitter 4.4% alc by vol. and a Porter 1053 O.G. (from October–March).

Larkin's Traditional (Eng) a 3.4% alc by vol. ale from Larkin's Brewery, Chiddingstone, Kent.

Larmandier-Bernier (Fr) a Champagne producer. (Add): 43 Rue du 28 Août, 51130 Vertus. 11ha. Récoltant-manipulants. Produces: vintage and non-vintage wines. A member of the C.V.C. Vintages: 1971, 1975, 1976, 1979, 1982, 1983, 1985, 1988, 1990, 1995, 1996, 1997, 1998, 1999, 2000, 2001.

Larmandier Père et Fils (Fr) a Champagne producer (established 1872). (Add): B.P. 4, 51530 Cramant. Produces vintage and non-vintage wines. Vintages: 1995, 1996, 1997, 1999, 2000. A member of the Club Tresors de Champagne. Labels: Cramant Grand Cru, Cuvée 'Special Club' Millésimée (Chardonnay 100%), Perle de Lamandier. 'E'mail: champagne.larmandier@wanadoo.fr

La Rocaille (Fr) the label for an A.C. Côtes-du-Rhône-Villages Visan (red) from Domaine de Coste Chaude, Visan, Vaucluse.

La Rocca (It) a Cru vineyard (5ha) based in the DOC Soave Classico, Veneto. Owned by the Pieropan winery.

La Roche aux Fées Buissonnière (Fr) a brewery. (Add): La Landelle, F-35134 Sainte-Colombe. Brews beers and lager. Website: http://www.roche-aux-fees.com

Laroche [Michel] (Fr) a noted négociant with 95ha. of vines based in Chablis, Burgundy. *See also* Domaine Laroche. Website: http://www.michellaroche.com 'E' mail: info@michellaroche.com

La Rosa (Chile) a winery based in the Cachapoal Valley, Central Chile.

La Rouget de Lisle (Fr) a brewery. (Add): La Brasserie, Rue des Vernes, F-39140 Bleterrans. Brews beers and lager.

Larressingle (Fr) the brand-name of an Armagnac produced by Ets. Papelorey S.A., Rue des Carmes, 32100 Condom 40% alc by vol.

Larsen (Fr) a Cognac producer. (Add): Larsen SA, 54 Boulevard de Paris, 16102 Cognac. Produces T.V.F.C. Fine Champagne 5 year old, Extra 35 year old and Fines Champagnes.

L'Aries (Fr) a natural spring mineral water from Source la Prime. Mineral contents (milligrammes per litre): Sodium 1.8mg/l, Calcium 3.7mg/l, Magnesium 0.58mg/l, Potassium 0.5mg/l, Bicarbonates 6.7mg/l, Chlorides 0.8mg/l, Sulphates 8mg/l. pH 6.5

Larmandier-Bernier (Fr) a Champagne producer based in Vertus. Produces vintage and non-vintage Champagnes. Vintages: 1995, 1996, 1997, 1998, 1999, 2000.

Larums (Sp) a red wine produced by Bodegas Bardón from the Garnacha grape (plus other varieties) in Ribera Baja.

Las [Les] (Fr) a vineyard in the A.C. commune of Montagny, Côte Chalonnaise, Burgundy.

Las Aberturas (Sp) a wine-producing area north of Valdepeñas, central Spain.

La Saint Amand (Fr) a natural spring mineral water from St. Alix. Mineral contents (milligrammes per litre): Sodium 28mg/l, Calcium 176mg/l, Magnesium 46mg/l, Potassium 2mg/l, Bicarbonates 312mg/l, Sulphates 372mg/l, Iron 2mg/l.

Las Alturas Vineyard (USA) the label for a red wine (Pinot noir) produced by the Belle Glos winery, Monterey County, California.

La Salvetat (Fr) a natural spring mineral water. Mineral contents (milligrammes per litre): Sodium 7mg/l, Calcium 253mg/l, Magnesium 11mg/l, Potassium 3mg/l, Bicarbonates 820mg/l, Chlorides 4mg/l, Sulphates 25mg/l, Nitrates 1mg/l. pH 6.0

La Sauvageonne (Fr) a vineyard based in the A.C. Terrasses du Larzac, Coteaux du Languedoc. Label: Les Ruffes.

Las Brisas (USA) the label for a red wine (Pinot noir) produced by the Mahoney Vineyards, Carneros, California.

Lasenberg (Ger) vineyard (Anb): Baden. (Ber): Kaiserstuhl-Tuniberg. (Gro): Vulkanfelsen. (Vil): Bötzingen.

Lasendal (Sp) the label for a red wine (Garnacha 100%) produced by the Capçanes wine co-operative, Montsant, Tarragona, Cataluña.

Laser (Eng) an 8.2% alc by vol. strong white cider from Cellars International.

La Siesta (S.Afr) the label for a range of wines produced by the Signal Hill winery, Cape Town, Western Cape.

La Sirena (USA) a winery based in the Napa Valley, California. Grape varieties include: Cabernet sauvignon.

L

Laski Riesling (Slo) a medium-dry white wine produced by Cloberg in the Podravski region of north-east Slovenia. Now known as Laski Rizling to comply with E.C. rules.

Laski Rizling (Ser) a name used in Lutomer, Slovenia, Podrava and Vojvodina for the white grape variety Welschriesling. *See also* Olasz Rizling, Riesling Italico.

Lasky Cocktail (Cktl) ⅓ measure Swedish Punsch, ⅓ measure gin, ⅓ measure grapefruit juice. Shake over ice and strain into cocktail glass.

Lassaigne-Berlot [Christian] (Fr) a Champagne producer (established 1964). (Add): 12, Rue de Troyes, 10300 Montgueux. Produces vintage and non-vintage Champagnes. Vintages: 1995, 1996, 1998, 2000. 5.5ha.

Lasselle [J] (Fr) a Champagne producer (established 1942). (Add): 21, Rue du Châtaignier, B.P. 5, 51500 Chigny-les-Roses. 11ha. Produces vintage and non-vintage wines. Vintages: 1995, 1996, 1997, 1999. A member of the Club Tresors de Champagne. Labels: Cuvée Angéline, Cuvée Préférence, Cuvée 'Special Club' Millésimée (Chardonnay 60% Pinot noir 40%). 'E'mail: champagne.j.lasselle@wanadoo.fr

Lassem [1] (Iran) a still natural spring mineral water (established 2002). Mineral contents (milligrammes per litre): Sodium 3mg/l, Calcium 35mg/l, Magnesium 5.8mg/l, Potassium 2mg/l, Chlorides 6mg/l, Sulphates 14mg/l, Nitrates 3.8mg/l, Silicates 4mg/l. pH 8.1

Lassem [2] (Iran) a still natural spring mineral water (established 2002). Mineral contents (milligrammes per litre): Sodium 3mg/l, Calcium 48mg/l, Magnesium 4.8mg/l, Potassium 2mg/l, Chlorides 6mg/l, Sulphates 15mg/l, Nitrates 5.4mg/l, Silicates 2mg/l. pH 8.3

Lassere (W.Ind) a noted rum distillery on the island of Guadeloupe.

Lasserre [Paul] (Fr) an Armagnac producer. (Add): Hontanx, 40190 Villeneuve de Marsan.

Lassi (Ind) a style of refreshing yoghurt 'milk shake' served with either salt or sugar and usually drunk either with or after a fiery hot curry (or similar dish).

Lass O'Gowrie (Eng) a Whitbread home-brew public house in Manchester. Produces cask-conditioned beers using malt extract.

Last Drop Bitter (Eng) a 4.5% alc by vol. bitter beer brewed by the York Brewery Company Ltd., North Yorkshire.

Lastingham Brewery (Eng) a brewery based at Lastingham, near Pickering, North Yorkshire. Brews: Amen 4.3% alc by vol. Prince of Ales 4.5% alc by vol. Church Bitter 3.7% alc by vol. Curate's Downfall 4.3% alc by vol.

Last Order Cocktail (Cktl) 175mls (6fl.ozs) brown ale, ½ measure brandy, 12 raisins, piece stem ginger. Heat gently until nearly boiling and serve in mugs with a cinnamon stick.

Last Orders (Eng) a term called on licensed premises by the landlord to announce that customers may purchase one more round of drinks before the licensing hours cease. Removed with new laws (2006). *See also* Drinking-Up Time.

Lastovo (Euro) a major wine-producing region in Dalmatia.

Last Resort (Eng) a 4.3% alc by vol. ale brewed by the Willy's Brewery, South Humberside.

Las Vegas (Chile) a wine-producing area in the Aconcagua province.

Latadas (Port) a method of growing the grapes on the lattice-work trellises on tall granite columns high above the ground.

La Tarnaise (Fr) a natural spring mineral water from Fontaine de la Reine, Castelnau de Brassac, Tarn. Mineral contents (milligrammes per litre): Sodium 2.8mg/l, Calcium 3.2mg/l, Magnesium 0.4mg/l, Potassium 0.35mg/l, Bicarbonates 7.5mg/l, Chlorides 3mg/l, Sulphates 1mg/l, Nitrates 5.5mg/l. pH 6.1

Late Bottled Vintage (Port) *abbr*: LBV, a Port wine from a single year (blend) which has been matured in cask 4–5 years then bottled. Has no sediment (unless stored in bottle for over 5 years when a light sediment may form).

Late Burgundy (Ger) the English name for the Spätburgunder grape.

Lateganskop Winery (S.Afr) a winery (established 1969) based in Breërivier, Worcester, Western Cape. 238ha. Grape varieties: Cabernet sauvignon, Ruby cabernet, Sauvignon blanc. Labels: Lion's Drift, Twin Peaks.

Late Gathered (Ger) spätlese.

Late Harvest (S.Afr) denotes grapes gathered after the commencement of the harvest date to produce a sweeter wine. *see* Edeloes.

Late Night Final (Eng) an egg-based drink produced by Townend of Hull, Humberside.

Late Red Autumn Ale (Eng) a 4.5% alc by vol. ale brewed by Shepherd Neame, Kent.

Lateron [Michel] (Fr) a crémant de Loire producer based at Amboise, Touraine, Loire.

La Terre (Fr) a Grand Cru vintage Champagne from the Mailly-Champagne co-operative.

Lates (Eng) a slang term for drinks that are sold after the permitted hours of opening.

Late Vintage (S.Afr) wines made of spätlese or auslese style.

Late Vintage (USA) late picked grapes, makes spätlese-style wines.

Latex (Lat) the word used to describe water or other liquids.

Latex (S.Am) a milky white sap of certain plants which is fermented into an alcoholic drink.

Lateyron (Fr) a producer of A.C. Bordeaux Mousseux based in the Saint-Émilion region of eastern Bordeaux.

Lathophora williamsi (Mex) the botanical name for the mezcal cactus used in the making of mezcal and tequila.

Latigné (Fr) a commune in the Beaujolais. Has A.C. Beaujolais-Villages or Beaujolais-Latigné status.

Latino do Brasil (Bra) a brewery that brews Carioca lager beer.

Latin Quarter (Cktl) ⅔ measure Dubonnet, ⅓ measure Amer Picon, dash Cointreau, shake over ice and strain into a cocktail glass.

Latisana (It) a locality on the river Tagliamento 50 miles north-east of Venice in the Friuli-Venezia Giulia region. Gives its name to wines of that region from certain communes.

Latisana (It) a D.O.C. red and white wines of Friuli-Venezia-Giulia. Name followed by a specific grape variety. 3 red: Latisana Cabernet, Merlot and Refosco. 4 white: Latisana Friulano, Pinot bianco, Pinot grigio and Verduzzo friulano. Vinification can occur in the province of Udine.

Latitude (Scot) a 3.6% alc by vol. ale brewed by the Atlas Brewery, Argyll.

Latium (It) a region in West-central Italy, south-west of Umbria. Famous for Frascati and Est! Est!! Est!!! Home to five I.G.T.'s: Civitella d'Agliano, Colli Cimini, Frusinate, Nettuno, Lazio. *see* Lazio.

Latour (Fr) *see* Château Latour.

Latour [F. and Cº.] (Fr) a Cognac producer. (Add): SARL Cognac, Beausdeil, 34 Rue de Ségonzac, 16140 Cognac.

Latour [Louis] (Fr) a famous Burgundy négociant-éleveur (established 1797) based in Beaune, Côte de Beaune, Burgundy. (Add): 18 Rue des Tonneliers, 21204 Beaune. One of the best known and respected of all the Burgundy shippers, has many cuvées in the region. Website: http://www.louislatour.com

Latour de France (Fr) an A.C. red wine in the Côtes du Roussillon, south-western France.

Latricières-Chambertin (Fr) a Grand Cru in the A.C. commune of Gevrey-Chambertin, Côte de Nuits, Burgundy 6.23ha.

Latrobe Brewery (USA) *see* Old Latrobe.

La Tropical Brewing Cº LLC (USA) a brewery. (Add): 1825 Ponce de Leon Blvd, Coral Gables, Florida 33134. Brews a range of beers and lager. Website: http://www.cervezatropical.com 'E'mail: madae@cervezatropical.com

Latt (Ger) vineyard (Anb): Pfalz. (Ber): Südliche Weinstrasse. (Gro): Königsgarten. (Vil): Albersweiler.

Lattacinio Glass (It) the name for Venetian glass that is worked with buds of opaque white or with ribbing and stringing.

Latte (Fr) boards used to separate the bottles in Champagne whilst they are under-going second fermentation. *see* Sur-Lattes.

Latte (It) milk.

Latteria (It) dairy.

Lattiera (It) milk jug.

Lattivéndolo (It) milkman.

Lattöl (Swe) lit: 'a small beer', a mildly-hopped, light-coloured lager.

Latzenbier (Ger) a name given to a strong version of altbier of Düsseldorf 7.5% alc by vol. brewed in March or September. It is also known as Sticke Alt.

Laubenheim (Ger) village (Anb): Nahe. (Ber): Kreuznach. (Gro): Schlosskapelle. (Vins): Fuchsen, Hörnchen, Junker, Karthäuser, Krone, St. Remigiusberg, Vogelsang.

L'Auberge du Paysan (S.Afr) a winery (established 1995) based in Somerset West, Stellenbosch, Western Cape. 3.5ha. Grape varieties: Merlot, Pinotage.

Lauchstädter Heilbrunnen (Ger) a sparkling natural spring mineral water (established 1710) from Bad Lauchstädt. Mineral contents (milligrammes per litre): Sodium 58.2mg/l, Calcium 112mg/l, Magnesium 44.2mg/l, Potassium 22.3mg/l, Bicarbonates 325mg/l, Chlorides 37mg/l, Sulphates 287mg/l, Nitrates 0.71mg/l, Silicates 13.8mg/l.

Lauda (Ger) village (Anb): Baden. (Ber): Badische Frankenland. (Gro): Tauberklinge. (Vins): Altenberg, Frankenberg, Nonnenberg.

Laudamusberg (Ger) vineyard (Anb): Mosel-Saar-Ruwer. (Ber): Bernkastel. (Gro): Michelsberg. (Vil): Neumagen-Dhron.

Laudatio (Aus) a sekt produced by the Kremser Winzergenossenschaft at Krems.

Laudenbach (Ger) village (Anb): Baden. (Ber): Badische Bergstrasse/Kraichgau. (Gro): Rittersberg. (Vin): Sonnberg.

Laudenbach (Ger) village (Anb): Franken. (Ber): Maindreieck. (Gro): Rosstal. (Vins): Assorted parts of vineyards.

Laudenbach (Ger) village (Anb): Württemberg. (Ber): Kocher-Jagst-Tauber. (Gro): Tauberberg. (Vin): Schafsteige.

Laudun (Fr) an A.C. region within the south-western Rhône. (Coms): Laudun, St. Victor, La Coste and Tresques. Red, rosé and white wines are produced. An A.C. Côtes-du-Rhône-Villages.

Lauerweg (Ger) vineyard (Anb): Nahe. (Ber): Kreuznach. (Gro): Sonnenborn. (Vil): Langenlonsheim.

Lauf (Ger) village (Anb): Baden. (Ber): Ortenau. (Gro): Schloss Rodeck. (Vins): Alter Gott, Gut Alsenhof, Schloss Neu-Windeck.

Laufen (Ger) village (Anb): Baden. (Ber): Markgräflerland. (Gro): Burg Neuenfels. (Vin): Altenberg.

Lauffen (Ger) village (Anb): Württemberg. (Ber): Württembergisch Unterland. (Gro): Kirchenweinberg. (Vins): Jungfer, Katzenbeisser, Nonnenberg, Riedersbückele.

Laugel (Fr) a famous Alsace wine producer. (Add): 67520 Marlenheim, one of the largest producers owns 5ha of vineyards. *see* Pichet d'Alsace.

Laughing Leprechaun Stout (Eng) a 4.5% alc by vol. stout brewed by the Hampshire Brewery, Hampshire.

Laughing Magpie [The] (Austr) a rich red wine produced from a blend of Shiraz and white Viognier grapes from D'Arenberg.

Laujar (Sp) a Vino Comarcal of Almería in Andalucía.

Laumersheim (Ger) village (Anb): Pfalz. (Ber): Mittelhaardt-Deutsche Weinstrasse. (Gro): Schwarzerde. (Vins): Kirchgarten, Mandelberg, Sonnengarten.

Launois Père et Fils (Fr) a Champagne producer (established 1872). (Add): 2, Avenue Eugène

Guillaume, Le Mesnil-sur-Oger. 20ha. Récoltants-manipulants. Produce vintage and non-vintage wines. A member of C.V.C. Vintages: 1971, 1975, 1976, 1979, 1982, 1983, 1985, 1988, 1990, 1995, 1996, 1997, 1998, 1999, 2000. A member of the Club Tresors de Champagne. Labels: Cuvée 'Special Club' Millésimée (Chardonnay 100%). Have a wine museum on site. Website: http://www.champagne-launois.fr 'E'mail: info@champagne-launois.fr

Lauréat (S.Afr) a fine red wine (Cabernet sauvignon 40%, Merlot 35% and Shiraz 25%) from the Zonnebloem winery, Stellenbosch.

Laurel Glen Vineyard (USA) a 15ha vineyard based in Hopland, Sonoma Mountain, California. Labels include Terra Rossa and Counterpoint (second label).

Laurel Light (Eng) a special bottled pale ale 6% alc by vol. brewed to commemorate the birth of Stan Laurel (comedian). Brewed in the Kings Arms (a Manchester pub) in Chorlton-on-Medlock.

Laurel Ridge Winery (USA) a winery based in Forest Grove, Oregon. Produces still and sparkling wines. Grape varieties: Gewürztraminer, Pinot noir, Riesling, Sémillon, Sylvaner.

Laurène (USA) the label for a red wine (Pinot noir) produced by Domaine Drouhin, Oregon.

Laurent (S.Am) a natural spring mineral water from Costa Rica.

Laurentina (It) a sparkling natural spring mineral water from Laurentina. Mineral contents (milligrammes per litre): Sodium 98mg/l, Calcium 230.5mg/l, Magnesium 36.5mg/l, Potassium 142.5mg/l, Bicarbonates 1140.7mg/l, Chlorides 35.5mg/l, Sulphates 124.4mg/l, Fluorides 0.12mg/l, Nitrates 0.1mg/l, Silicates 53.5mg/l. pH 6.35

Laurenti Père et Fils (Fr) a Champagne producer. (Add): 5 Rue de la Contrescarpe, Haut-Rive, 10340 Lès Riceys.

Laurentiusberg (Ger) vineyard (Anb): Mosel-Saar-Ruwer. (Ber): Saar-Ruwer. (Gro): Petersberg. (Vil): Oberdollendorf.

Laurentiusberg (Ger) vineyard (Anb): Mosel-Saar-Ruwer. (Ber): Saar-Ruwer. (Gro): Römerlay. (Vil): Waldrach.

Laurentiusberg (Ger) vineyard (Anb): Mosel-Saar-Ruwer. (Ber): Saar-Ruwer. (Gro): Scharzberg. (Vil): Saarburg.

Laurentiusberg (Ger) vineyard (Anb): Mosel-Saar-Ruwer. (Ber): Zell/Mosel. (Gro): Grafschaft. (Vil): Bremm.

Laurentiusberg (Ger) vineyard (Anb): Nahe. (Ber): Kreuznach. (Gro): Pfarrgarten. (Vil): Wallhausen.

Laurentiusberg (Ger) vineyard (Anb): Nahe. (Ber): Schloss Böckelheim. (Gro): Burgweg. (Vil): Altenbamberg.

Laurentiuslay (Ger) vineyard (Anb): Mosel-Saar-Ruwer. (Ber): Bernkastel. (Gro): Sankt Michael. (Vil): Köwerich.

Laurentiuslay (Ger) vineyard (Anb): Mosel-Saar-Ruwer. (Ber): Bernkastel. (Gro): Sankt Michael. (Vil): Leiwen.

Laurentius Schwarzwald Quirli (Ger) a natural spring mineral water brand.

Laurent-Perrier (Fr) a Champagne producer. (Add): Domaine Tours-sur-Marne, B.P. 3, 51150 Tours-sur-Marne. A Grande Marque. 105ha. Produces vintage and non-vintage wines. Vintages: 1904, 1906, 1911, 1914, 1919, 1921, 1926, 1928, 1934, 1937, 1941, 1943, 1945, 1947, 1949, 1952, 1953, 1955, 1959, 1961, 1962, 1964, 1966, 1969, 1970, 1973, 1975, 1976, 1978, 1979, 1982, 1983, 1985, 1988, 1990, 1996, 1997, 1998, 1999, 2001. Prestige cuvées: Cuvée Alexandra Rosé, Millésime Rare Brut, Grand Siècle Alexandra. Website: http://www.laurent-perrier.fr

Laurent Perrier (USA) a winery based in Almaden, California. Grape variety: Chardonnay. Produces sparkling wines, is linked to the Champagne firm of same name in France.

Laurenziweg (Ger) vineyard (Anb): Nahe. (Ber): Kreuznach. (Gro): Schlosskapelle. (Vil): Dorsheim.

Lauré Pristine Spring Water (USA) a natural spring mineral water from the Smoky Mountains. Mineral contents (milligrammes per litre): Calcium 12mg/l, Magnesium 10mg/l, Potassium 1.3mg/l, Fluorides 0.1mg/l, Nitrates 0.1mg/l. pH 7.6

Laure Spring Water (USA) a natural spring mineral water from Unicoi, Tennessee.

Lauretana (It) a sparkling natural spring mineral water from Caruzza. Mineral contents (milligrammes per litre): Sodium 1.08mg/l, Calcium 1.1mg/l, Magnesium 0.3mg/l, Potassium 0.32mg/l, Bicarbonates 4mg/l, Chlorides 0.53mg/l, Sulphates 1.55mg/l, Nitrates 1.4mg/l, Silicates 5.3mg/l. pH 5.75

Lauric Acid (Eng) $C_{11}H_{23}COOH$ an acid found in wine in minute traces.

Laurier (Fr) a natural spring mineral water from 77, Neufmoutiers. Mineral contents (milligrammes per litre): Sodium 9mg/l, Calcium 64mg/l, Magnesium 4mg/l, Potassium 2mg/l, Bicarbonates 186mg/l, Chlorides 16mg/l, Sulphates 10mg/l, Nitrates 1mg/l. pH 7.6

Lausannois (Switz) the local name for the Fendant Vert grape. Also known as White Valette.

Lauschied (Ger) village (Anb): Nahe. (Ber): Schloss Böckelheim. (Gro): Paradiesgarten. (Vin): Edelberg.

Lauser (Aus) a vineyard site based on the banks of the River Kamp situated in the Kamptal region.

Lausitzer Stille Quelle (Ger) a sparkling natural spring mineral water from Lausitzer-Quelle, Bad Liebenwerda. Mineral contents (milligrammes per litre): Sodium 4.2mg/l, Calcium 12.1mg/l, Magnesium 2mg/l, Potassium 1.1mg/l, Bicarbonates 57mg/l, Chlorides 3.4mg/l, Nitrates <0.5mg/l.

Lautenbach (Ger) village (Anb): Baden. (Ber): Ortenau. (Gro): Fürsteneck. (Vin): Renchtäler.

Lauter Tub (USA) see Lauter Tun.

Lauter Tun (Eng) a copper or stainless steel vessel containing a false bottom and series of movable

L

racks, used to filter the mash and draw off the wort in brewing.

L'Authentique Delubac (Fr) the label for an A.C. Côtes-du-Rhône-Villages Cairanne (red) from Domaine Delubac, Cairanne, Vaucluse.

Lauzet (Fr) a white grape variety grown in the Bergerac and Jurançon regions.

Lavagello (It) a natural spring mineral water from Lavagello.

La Vallée (S.Afr) the label for a white wine (Pinot gris) produced by the JC le Roux winery, Stellenbosch, Western Cape.

La Valoise (Fr) a natural spring mineral water. Mineral contents (milligrammes per litre): Sodium 16mg/l, Calcium 112mg/l, Magnesium 22mg/l, Potassium 2mg/l, Bicarbonates 332mg/l, Chlorides 19mg/l, Sulphates 86mg/l, Nitrates 10mg/l.

Lavan (Isr) a brand of dry red or white table wines produced by Carmel.

Lavaredo (It) a natural spring mineral water from Fonti san Candido, Merano. Mineral contents (milligrammes per litre): Sodium 2.4mg/l, Calcium 320mg/l, Magnesium 72mg/l, Potassium 0.7mg/l, Bicarbonates 231mg/l, Chlorides 0.6mg/l, Sulphates 860mg/l, Fluorides 1.6mg/l, Oxygen 4.4mg/l, Silicates 7.55mg/l, Strontium 5.5mg/l. pH 7.4

Lavaut (Fr) a Premier Cru vineyard in the A.C. commune of Gevrey-Chambertin, Côte de Nuits, Burgundy 9.43ha.

Lavaux (Switz) a sub-region of the Canton of Vaud. Produces white wines from the Chasselas grape.

L'Avella (Sp) a still natural spring mineral water. Mineral contents (milligrammes per litre): Sodium 2.6mg/l, Calcium 73.7mg/l, Magnesium 7.8mg/l, Potassium 0.4mg/l, Chlorides 6.9mg/l, Sulphates 14.4mg/l, Fluorides 0.1mg/l, Nitrates 5.3mg/l.

LaVelle Vineyards (USA) a 6.5ha vineyard based at Sheffler Road, Elmira, Oregon.

La Vena d'Oro (It) a sparkling natural spring mineral water (established 1800) from Ponte Nelle Alpi, Belluno. Mineral contents (milligrammes per litre): Sodium 1.15mg/l, Calcium 62.5mg/l, Magnesium 8.2mg/l, Potassium 0.95mg/l, Bicarbonates 232.4mg/l, Chlorides 1.21mg/l, Sulphates 5.14mg/l, Fluorides 0.06mg/l, Nitrates 0.7mg/l, Silicates 5.1mg/l. pH 7.7

L'Avenir Estate (S.Afr) a winery (established 1992) based in Stellenbosch, Western Cape. 53ha. Grape varieties: Cabernet franc, Cabernet sauvignon, Chardonnay, Chenin blanc, Cinsaut, Clairette, Colombard, Crouchen, Merlot, Pinotage, Riesling, Sauvignon blanc. Labels: Black Label Reserve, L'Ami Simon, Maison, Vin de Meurveur, Vin d'Erstelle. Website: http://www.lavenir.co.za

L'Aventure (USA) a winery based in the Paso Robles, San Luis Obispo, California. Grape varieties: Cabernet sauvignon, Pinot noir, Syrah.

Laverna (It) a bitter apéritif wine produced in Sicily.

La Vernière (Fr) a natural spring mineral water brand.

La Vie (Viet) a natural spring mineral water (established 1994) from Khang Hau. Mineral contents (milligrammes per litre): Sodium 60mg/l, Calcium 23mg/l, Magnesium 8mg/l, Potassium 4mg/l, Bicarbonates 251mg/l, Fluorides 0.2mg/l, Nitrates <1mg/l. pH 7.6

La Vie de Luc (S.Afr) a slightly acidic still and sparkling natural spring mineral water. Mineral contents (milligrammes per litre): Sodium 8mg/l, Calcium <1mg/l, Magnesium 1mg/l, Potassium <1mg/l, Chlorides 12mg/l, Sulphates <5mg/l, Fluorides 0.3mg/l, Nitrates <0.2mg/l. pH 5.3

Lavières [Les] (Fr) a Premier Cru vineyard in the A.C. commune of Savigny-lès-Beaune, Côte de Beaune, Burgundy.

La Ville (Viet) a natural spring mineral water from Hanoi.

Lavilledieu (Fr) an 80ha V.D.Q.S. wine-producing area in Tarn-et-Garonne, south-western France. Grape varieties: Cabernet franc, Cabernet sauvignon, Gamay, Négrette, Syrah, Tannat. Produces red and rosé wines.

Lavischio (It) fragrant red Merlot wine produced by Biondi Santi in Montalcino, Tuscany.

La Vita (S.Afr) a natural spring mineral water from Nholasane Mountain Range, Natal. Mineral contents (milligrammes per litre): Sodium 3.3mg/l, Calcium 4mg/l, Magnesium 2.2mg/l, Potassium <1mg/l, Chlorides 1.58mg/l, Sulphates 0.35mg/l, Nitrates 0.25mg/l. pH 6.74

La Vittoria (It) a natural spring mineral water from La Vittoria.

Lavrottes [Les] (Fr) a Premier Cru vineyard in the A.C. commune of Chambolle-Musigny, Côte de Nuits, Burgundy 1ha.

Lawhill Cocktail (Cktl) ⅔ measure Bourbon whiskey, ⅓ measure dry vermouth, 2 dashes absinthe, 2 dashes maraschino, 1 dash Angostura. Stir over ice and strain into a cocktail glass.

Lawrence Winery (USA) a large winery based in the Edna Valley, San Luis Obispo, California. Grape varieties: Cabernet sauvignon, Chardonnay, Chenin blanc, Gewürztraminer, Johannisberg riesling, Pinot noir and Zinfandel. Produces varietal wines.

Law's Cocktail (Cktl) *see* Coffee Cocktail.

Laws of Hammurabi (Arab) the first Licensing Laws! 2100 B.C. Written by a Babylonian king and mentioned rules for drinking which included loss of liberty for permitting riotous drinking on the premises and methods of viniculture.

Lawson (Jap) a natural spring mineral water. Mineral contents (milligrammes per litre): Sodium 10mg/l, Calcium 4.9mg/l, Magnesium 2mg/l, Potassium 1.4mg/l. pH 7.3

Lawson (William) Distillers (Scot) a Scotch whisky producer based at Coatbridge, Glasgow and MᵃᶜDuff, Banffshire (owned by Martini and Rossi). Produces Glendeveron–a 12 year old highland malt 43% alc by vol. and blended Scotch whiskies.

L

Lawson's Dry Hills Wines (N.Z) a winery. (Add): Alabama Road, P.O. Box 4020, Blenheim. Grape varieties: Riesling, Sauvignon blanc. *See also* Family of Twelve.

Laws Peach Bitters (Eng) a brand of flavouring bitters.

Laxton's Honey Beer (Eng) a bottled beer brewed by Ruddles Brewery, Leicester (part of their Ruddles Character Ale range).

Lay (Ger) lit: 'slate or rock', when placed at the end of a name denotes slatey soil. i.e. Burglay, Fässerlay, etc.

Lay (Ger) vineyard (Anb): Mosel-Saar-Ruwer. (Ber): Bernkastel. (Gro): Badstube. (Vil): Bernkastel-Kues.

Lay (Ger) vineyard (Anb): Mosel-Saar-Ruwer. (Ber): Bernkastel. (Gro): Schwarzlay. (Vil): Wittlich.

Lay (Ger) vineyard (Anb): Mosel-Saar-Ruwer. (Ber): Obermosel. (Gro): Gipfel. (Vil): Palzem.

Lay (Ger) vineyard (Anb): Mosel-Saar-Ruwer. (Ber): Zell/Mosel. (Gro): Not yet assigned. (Vil): Senheim.

Lay (Ger) vineyard (Anb): Mosel-Saar-Ruwer. (Ber): Zell/Mosel. (Gro): Weinhex. (Vil): Lehmen.

Layenberg (Ger) vineyard (Anb): Mosel-Saar-Ruwer. (Ber): Zell/Mosel. (Gro): Rosenhang. (Vil): Bruttig-Fankel.

Layenberg (Ger) vineyard (Anb): Nahe. (Ber): Schloss Böckelheim. (Gro): Paradiesgarten. (Vil): Niedermoschel.

Layering Technique (Eng) a method of growing vines freely and close to the ground and without training. When pruned, one small branch is buried in the ground to produce the next years growth. This was originally practiced in the Champagne region and the Champagne house of Bollinger still grows its vines (Pinot noir) in this style for its famous Vieille Vignes Françaises.

Laying Down (Eng) the action of cellaring bottles of wines on their sides to mature, this applies mainly to red wines and vintage Port but many fine white wines need this period of maturation. *see* Bin and Investment.

Laykaul (Ger) vineyard (Anb): Mosel-Saar-Ruwer. (Ber): Saar-Ruwer. (Gro): Römerlay. (Vil): Korlingen.

Layon [River] (Fr) a tributary of the river Loire in the Anjou-Saumur district, A.C. Coteaux du Layon. Produces fine sweet, botrytis-attacked wines. *see* Coteaux du Layon.

La Zaragozana Brewery (Sp) a brewery based in Aragón that is noted for its Ambar lager beer 5.2% alc by vol.

Lazarillo (Sp) a medium-dry, white wine produced by Nuestro Padre Jesus del Perdon.

La Zarza (Sp) a natural spring mineral water from Aliaga, Teruel. Mineral contents (milligrammes per litre): Sodium 3.9mg/l, Calcium 104.2mg/l, Magnesium 34.4mg/l, Potassium 0.8mg/l, Bicarbonates 250.1mg/l, Chlorides 13.5mg/l, Sulphates 100mg/l, Fluorides 0.6mg/l, Nitrates 4mg/l.

Lazio (It) the other name for the Latium region which includes Rome.

Lazio (It) an I.G.T. of Latium.

Lazy Creek Vineyards (USA) a winery based in the Anderson Valley, Mendocino County, California. Grape variety: Pinot noir.

Lazy Daze (Eng) a 4.6% alc by vol. summer ale brewed by Everards, Castle Acres, Narborough, Leicester.

Lazy Susan (Eng) a revolving tea carousel for tea pot, milk jug, sugar, cups etc. from the 18th–19th century, an alternative name for the Lady Susan.

Lazzaroni (It) a noted producer of Amaretto di Saronno in Milan.

L.B. (Eng) *abbr*: Light Bitter 1030 O.G. brewed by the Burt Brewery in Ventor, Isle of Wight.

L.B. (Eng) *abbr*: London Bottled, was found on a wine list.

L.B. (Port) *abbr*: Late Bottled, applies to Port wines.

LBA (Ch.Isles) *abbr*: a draught mild 1037.7 O.G. originally brewed by the Guernsey Brewery 1920 Ltd. in St. Peter Port, Guernsey. Initials stand for the ex-name of the Channel Isle C°. London Brewery Ale.

L.B.V. (Port) *abbr*: Late Bottled Vintage, applied to Ports of a single year that have been matured in cask 4–5 years then bottled. Has no sediment (crust).

L.C.B.O. (Can) *abbr*: Liquor Control Board of Ontario.

LCL Pils (Eng) a keg lager processed beer 1036 O.G. produced at the Dunston plant of the Northern Clubs Federation Brewery.

Lda. (Port) *abbr*: Limitada (Limited).

L de La Louvière (Fr) the second wine of Château La Louvière. Red A.C. Pessac-Léognan. 48ha. 70% Cabernet sauvignon, 30% Merlot. Aged for 1 year in oak. First vintage was in 1988.

Leabhar Tae (Ire) herbal tea/tisane.

Leabrook Estate (Austr) a winery (established 1998) based in the Adelaide Hills. 3ha. Grape varieties: Cabernet sauvignon, Pinot gris, Pinot noir and Merlot. Produces: Three Regions Shiraz. Website: http://wwwleabrookestate.com

Leac (Ire) ice.

Leacock (Mad) a producer and shipper of Madeira. Sold under the St. John Reserve label. Sercial, Verdelho, Bual and Special Reserve Malmsey.

Leadboiler (Eng) a cask-conditioned bitter ale 1063 O.G. brewed by the home-brew Sair public house in Linthwaite, Huddersfield.

Lead Crystal (Eng) a type of glass made from silica, sand and red lead-oxide. Has a maximum of 33.3% lead content. *see* Waterford Crystal.

Lead-oxide (Eng) used in glass making.

Leaf Roll (N.Z)(USA) a virus that is recognised by the downward roll of the margins on the vine leaf. The leaves also have premature autumn colouring.

Leaguer (S.Afr) cask (capacity 127 gallons).

Leaker (Eng) a term used to describe a bottle with wine leaking from the cork. This means air has come into contact with the wine which has either started to spoil or soon will. Usually caused by a poor cork or through great age.

Le Altanza (Sp) a rosé wine produced by Bodegas Altanza, Rioja.

Leamington Spa (Eng) an aperient still mineral water from central England.

Leamóg (Ire) alembic.

Leaning Glass (Switz) a specially-designed wine glass for the '*Glacier Express*' to allow for the steep gradients the train has to travel along during the journey. The stem is at an angle to keep the contents level.

Leann (Ire) ale.

Leann Gealbhui (Ire) pale ale.

Leann Úll Ceirtlis (Ire) cider.

Leànyka (Hun) a white grape variety which produces dry average wines. (Rum) = Feteasca alba. (Bul) = Fetiaska.

Leànyka Edes (Hun) a sweet white wine from the Eger region made from the Leànyka grape.

Leànyka Szaraz (Hun) a dry white wine from the Eger region made from the Leànyka grape.

Leap Frog Highball (Cktl) 25mls (⅕ gill) gin, juice ½ lemon. Place in an ice-filled highball glass and top with ginger ale.

Leap Year [1] (Cktl) ⅔ measure dry gin, ⅙ measure Grand Marnier, ⅙ measure Italian vermouth. Shake over ice, strain into a cocktail glass and serve with a cherry.

Leap Year [2] (Cktl) ⅗ measure dry gin, ⅕ measure orange gin, ⅕ measure sweet vermouth, 2 dashes lemon juice. Shake over ice and strain into a cocktail glass.

Leasingham (Austr) a winery. (Add): 7 Dominic Street, Clare, South Australia/P.O. Box. 56, Dandenong,3175, Victoria. 612ha. in Clare Valley. Grape varieties: Cabernet sauvignon, Chardonnay, Malbec, Rhine riesling and Shiraz.

Leatherbritches Brewery (Eng) a brewery. (Add): Bentley Brook Inn, Brewery Yard, Fenny Bentley, near Ashbourne, Derbyshire DE6 1LF. Brews: Druids Ale. Website: http://www.bentleybrookinn.co.uk 'E'mail: all@bentleybrookinn.co.uk

Leatico (It) an alternative name for the Aleatico grape.

Leatherwood (S.Afr) the label for a range of wines (Cabernet sauvignon/Shiraz and Viognier) produced by the Prospect 1870 winery, Robertson, Western Cape.

Leave It To Me [1] (Cktl) juice ½ lemon, teaspoon raspberry syrup, 60mls (½ gill) dry gin. Shake well over ice, strain into a 125mls (5fl.oz) wine glass and add dash soda water.

Leave It To Me [2] (Cktl) ⅗ measure dry gin, ⅕ measure dry vermouth, ⅕ measure apricot brandy, 2 dashes lemon juice, 2 dashes grenadine. Shake over ice and strain into a cocktail glass.

Leavening (Eng) the old name for yeast.

Le Baladin (It) a brewery. (Add): Birra Artigianale, Piazza V Luglio, Piozzo ZN 15 – 12060. Brews beers and lagers. Website: http://www.lebaladin.it 'E'mail: baladin@bierria.com

Leban (Afr) the whey left over from cheese production, used as a non-alcoholic beverage.

Lebanon (M.East) an old wine-producing country of 1400ha of vineyards, main wine producing region is the Bekaa Valley. 3 noted wine producers are: Châteaux Musar, Kefraya and Ksara.

Lebelin (Fr) a cuvée in the A.C. Duresses, Monthélie, Côte de Beaune, Burgundy (owned by the Hospices de Beaune).

Lebendig (Ger) a wine with a fresh, racy flavour.

Lebensraum Estate (S.Afr) a vineyard sited near Worcester on the Breed River. (Add): Lebensraum Landgoed, P.O. Box 36, Rawsonville 6845. Produces varietal wines.

Léberg (Bel) a natural spring mineral water from Léberg, Roosdaal. Mineral contents (milligrammes per litre): Sodium 10mg/l, Calcium 112mg/l, Magnesium 47mg/l, Potassium 2.7mg/l, Chlorides 47mg/l.

Leberl (Aus) a winery based in Grosshöflein, Neusiedlersee-Hügelland, Burgenland. (Add): Hauptstrasse 91, 7051 Grosshöflein. Grape varieties include: Blaufränkisch, Sauvignon blanc.

Le Berlou (Fr) a natural spring mineral water from Fontaine de la Reine, Monts de Lacaume, Haut Languedoc. Mineral contents (milligrammes per litre): Sodium 2.8mg/l, Calcium 3.2mg/l, Magnesium 0.4mg/l, Potassium 0.35mg/l, Bicarbonates 7.5mg/l, Chlorides 3mg/l, Sulphates 1mg/l, Nitrates 5.5mg/l. pH 6.1

Leberzipf (Aus) a winery (2ha) based in the Wachau. (Add): Unterloiben 11, 3601 Dürnstein. Grape varieties: Grüner veltliner, Pinot blanc, Riesling. Produces a range of dry and sweet (botrytised) wines.

Leblond-Lenoir [Pascal] (Fr) a Champagne producer. (Add): 49, Grande Rue, 10110 Buxeuil. Produces vintage and non-vintage Champagnes. Vintages: 1995, 1996, 1999, 2000. 'E'mail: pascal.leblond-lenoir@libertysurf.fr

Le Bonheur (S.Afr) a winery based in Langoed, Stellenbosch, Western Cape. Grape varieties: Cabernet sauvignon, Chardonnay, Merlot, Sauvignon blanc. Label: Prima. Website: http://www.lebonheur.co.za

Le Brewery (Fr) a brewery. (Add): La Poelerie F-61320 Joué-du-Bois. Brews beers and lager. Website: http://www.le-brewery.com

Lebrija (Sp) a Vino Comarcal of Sevilla in Andalucía.

Le Butts Biére (Eng) a 5% alc by vol. beer brewed by the Butts Brewery Ltd., Berkshire.

Le Castellada (It) a winery based in Oslavia in the Friuli-Venezia-Guilia region.

Lech (Pol) a 5.3% alc by vol. lager from Wielropolski S.A. Browary.

Leche (Sp) milk.

Lechinta (Rum) a wine-producing region noted for medium-dry white wines.

Leckerberg (Ger) vineyard (Anb): Rheinhessen. (Ber): Bingen. (Gro): Adelberg. (Vil): Armsheim.

Leckerberg (Ger) vineyard (Anb): Rheinhessen. (Ber): Wonnegau. (Gro): Pilgerpfad. (Vil): Dittelsheim-Hessloch.

L

Leckmauer (Ger) vineyard (Anb): Mosel-Saar-Ruwer. (Ber): Zell/Mosel. (Gro): Goldbäumchen. (Vil): Müden.

Leckzapfen (Ger) vineyard (Anb): Rheinhessen. (Ber): Wonnegau. (Gro): Gotteshilfe. (Vil): Otshofen.

Leclerc Briant (Fr) a Champagne producer. (Add): 67 Rue Chaude Ruelle, B.P. 108, Cumierès, 51204 Épernay Cedex. Récoltants-manipulants. Own 30ha. Produces vintage and non-vintage wines. A member of C.V.C. Vintages: 1971, 1973, 1976, 1979, 1982, 1983, 1985, 1989, 1990, 1995, 1998, 2000. Labels include: Les Authentiques. De Luxe vintage cuvée is Special Club Brut. Three single vineyard Champagnes: Les Chèvres Pirreuses, Les Clos des Champions, Les Crayères.

Le Clos de Madame (Fr) a red wine (50% Grenache & 50% Syrah) produced by Château Rasque, A.C. Côte de Provence.

Le Clos Jordan (Can) a 36ha vineyard based on the Niagara Peninsula.

L'Ecole N° 41 (USA) a winery based in the Columbia Valley, Washington State. (Add): PO Box 111, 41 Lowden School Road, Lowden, Washington 99 360. Grape varieties include: Merlot and Syrah. Labels: Columbia Valley, Seven Hills Vineyard Estate (Walla Walla). Website: http://www.lecole.com

Lecomte Père et Fils (Fr) a Champagne producer (established 1859). Produces non-vintage wines including Brut, Vieille Réserve, Demi-Sec, Sec and Génération. (Add): 7, Rue de Champagne, 51530 Vinay. Récoltants-manipulants. 'E' Mail: Champagne.lecomte@club-internet.fr

Leconfield (Austr) a winery based in Coonawarra, South Australia. Produces mainly Cabernet and Riesling-based wines.

Le Consulat de la Vinée (Fr) the wine brotherhood of the Bergerac region.

Ledaig (Scot) a single malt whisky from Tobermory Distillers on the Isle of Mull, a highland malt. 40% alc by vol. also a 1973 vintage at 43% alc by vol. and a 1974 vintage (bottled in 1992).

Ledbury Brewery Company (Eng) a micro-brewery based in Herefordshire. Brews: Black John, Challenger, Northdown, Pioneer and a 5.7% alc by vol. winter warmer.

Lederer Brauerei (Ger) a brewery that is part of the Nürnberg's Patrizer group.

Ledge Shiraz (Austr) a full-bodied red wine produced by the Chain of Ponds vineyard, Adelaide Hills.

Le Domaine (S.Afr) the label for a sparkling wine produced by the JC le Roux winery, Stellenbosch, Western Cape.

Ledru [Marie-Noëlle] (Fr) a Champagne producer. (Add): 5, Place de la Croix, 51150 Ambonnay. 6ha. Grand Cru. Vintages: 1996, 1998. Produces Cuvée du Goulté.

Le Due Terre (It) a winery based in Dolegnano in the Friuli-Venezia-Guilia region.

Leeds Castle (Eng) a winery based in Maidstone, Kent.

Leeds Summer Heritage Festival Ale (Eng) a 4.4% alc by vol. ale brewed to commemorate Allied Domecq's sponsorship of Leeds city's fifth summer heritage.

Leef op Hoop (S.Afr) the label for a red wine range produced by the Le Riche Wines winery, Stellenbosch, Western Cape.

Lee Poo Yee (Fr) a white table wine (vin de table) produced by the Caves de la Loire for Chinese restaurants.

Leer (Ger) thin/lacking in character.

Lees (Eng) a heavy sediment which is thrown by young wines in cask after fining and before racking. (Aus) = hefetrub, (Fr) = lie, (Ger) = hefetrub, (Hol) = drab.

Lees [J.W.] (Eng) a brewery based in Middleton, Manchester, Lancashire. Brews: cask-conditioned Moonracker 1074 O.G. Edelbräu 1052 O.G. Archer Stout 4.8% alc by vol. Jumbo Bitter, Tulip Lager 1034 O.G. Harvest Ale 11.5% alc by vol. Festive Ale, Fudger Cream Ale, John Willie's Champion Beer 5% alc by vol. Malted Mayhem 4.5% alc by vol., Number 15 Ale 3.5% alc by vol., Plum Pudding 4.8% alc by vol. Scorcher Summer Ale 4.2% alc by vol. Sloeberry Fruit Beer, White Bear 4.2% alc by vol. Golden Original (superseded Lees pilsner, Edelbräu Lite). http://www.jwlees.co.uk

Leeuw Bockbier (Hol) a 6.5% alc by vol. bottled, ruby-red, unpasteurised bock beer brewed by De Leeuw Bier Brouwerij, Valkenburg. *see* De Leeuw Brouwerij.

Leeuw Dortmunder (Hol) a 6.5% alc by vol. bottled unpasteurised straw Dortmunder brewed by De Leeuw Bier Brouwerij, Valkenburg. *see* De Leeuw Brouwerij.

Leeuwin Estate (Austr) a winery on the Margaret River region, Western Australia. (Add): P.O. Box 7196, Cloisters Square, Perth, Western Australia. 90ha. Grape varieties: Cabernet sauvignon, Chardonnay, Gewürztraminer, Merlot, Pinot noir, Rhine riesling, Sauvignon blanc. Produces varietal wines. Labels: Art Series, Prelude Vineyards

Leeuw Pilsener (Hol) a 5% alc by vol. bottled unpasteurised pilsener lager brewed by De Leeuw Bier Brouwerij, Valkenburg. *see* De Leeuw Brouwerij.

Leeuw Valkenburgs Witbier (Hol) a 4.8% alc by vol. bottled unfiltered wheat beer brewed by De Leeuw Bier Brouwerij, Valkenburg. *see* De Leeuw Brouwerij.

Leeuw Winter Wit (Hol) a 5.8% alc by vol. bottled unfiltered wheat beer brewed by De Leeuw Bier Brouwerij, Valkenburg. *see* De Leeuw Brouwerij.

Leeward Winery (USA) a winery based on the Camarillo coast, Ventura, California. Grape varieties: Cabernet sauvignon, Chardonnay and Zinfandel. Produces varietal wines.

Lefèbvre Brouwerij (Bel) a brewery (established 1876) based in Quenast. Brews abbaye-style beers, *see* Abbaye de Bonne Espérance, Barbãr, Floreffe Blond, Floreffe Double, Floreffe Triple, Floreffe la Meilleure, Moeder Overste, Newton.

L

Le Fer (Fr) the label for an A.C Saint-Émilion Grand Cru. *see* Mahler-Bresse. The second wine of Château Cheval Noir. Website: http://www.mahler-bresse.com 'E'mail: contact@mahler-bresse.com

Leffe Blond (Bel) a 6.6% alc by vol. top-fermented special abbaye beer brewed by St. Guilbert Brasserie, Mont-Saint-Guilbert.

Leffe Brasserie (Bel) an abbaye brewery based at Mont-Saint-Guilbert in southern Belgium. Also known as the Saint Guilbert Brasserie. Brews: Leffe Blond, Leffe Radieuse.

Leffe Radieuse (Bel) an 8.2% alc by vol. fruity special dark brune abbaye beer brewed by St. Guilbert Brasserie, Mont-Saint-Guilbert.

Leffe Triple (Bel) a blonde beer 6.8% alc by vol brewed by the Leffe Brasserie.

Lefkàs (Gre) a red wine-producing island in the Aegean sea. Also spelt Levkas.

Legacy (Eng) a 5% alc by vol. ale brewed by the Merlin Brewery, Lancashire.

Legacy (Scot) a blended Scotch whisky produced by MᶜKinlay (now owned by Scottish and Newcastle Breweries) 43% alc by vol.

Lega di Chianti (It) a dry white wine produced from Malvasia and Trebbiano grapes in Tuscany.

Legend (Eng) a cask-conditioned bitter beer brewed by the North Cornwall Brewers (Min Pin Inn home-brew public house) in Tintagel, north Cornwall.

Legend (Eng) a 4% alc by vol. ale brewed by the Nottingham Brewery, Nottinghamshire.

Legend (Eng) the information on a bottle label.

Legend LA (Eng) a draught, low-alcohol ale brewed by the Federation Brewery 1.2% alc by vol.

Léger (Fr) light wine.

Le Gera (It) a natural spring mineral water brand.

Légèrement Doux (Switz) a label term for wines with a residual sugar.

Legg Cutter Machine (Eng) a machine used in the production of tea, used for cutting leaves that have not been 'withered'.

Leggera (It) a natural spring mineral water from Monticchio, Bagni. Mineral contents (milligrammes per litre): Calcium 37mg/l, Potassium 28mg/l, Bicarbonates 268mg/l, Chlorides 25mg/l, Sulphates 16mg/l, Nitrates 3mg/l, Silicates 102mg/l.

Leggermente Appassite (It) an alternative name for Rigoverno.

Legion (Eng) a 3.5% alc by vol. beer from the micro-brewery Rose and Crown, Stelling Minnis, near Canterbury.

Legion (Eng) a 4.2% alc by vol. ale brewed by the Hadrian & Border Brewery, Tyne & Wear.

Legion's Choice (Eng) a 4.6% alc by vol. ale from Smiles Brewery, Bristol to commemorate 50 years of peace since the 1939–1945 war.

Legislador (Sp) a solera reserva brandy produced by Gil Galan. *See also* Condestable, Formidable, Romancero.

Le Grand Chasseur Estate (S.Afr) a winery (established 1881) based in Robertson, Western Cape. 250ha. Grape varieties: Cabernet sauvignon, Chardonnay, Pinotage, Ruby cabernet, Sauvignon blanc, Shiraz. Label: LGC. Also known as the Le Grand 1881 Estate. Website: http://www.lgc.co.za

Legras [R.L.] (Fr) a Champagne producer. (Add): Caves de la Madelaine, Chouilly. 22ha. Produces vintage and non-vintage wines. Blanc de blancs cuvée: St. Vincent.

Le Grazie (It) a natural spring mineral water from Primavera.

Legs (Eng) a term used to describe the ethyl alcohol and glycerine lines which run down the glass after the drink has been swirled round the glass. Also known as 'tears'.

Lehen (Ger) village (Anb): Baden. (Ber): Breisgau. (Gro): Burg Zähringen. (Vin): Bergle.

Lehensteiner (Aus) a winery based in the Wachau. (Add): 3610 Weissenkirchen 7. Grape varieties include: Grüner veltliner, Riesling. Produces a range of dry and sweet (botrytised) wines.

Lehmann [Peter] (Austr) a noted winery based at P.O. Box 315, Tanunda, 5352 South Australia. Grape varieties: Cabernet sauvignon, Shiraz, Chardonnay, Sémillon. Produces: The Futures Shiraz. Website: http://www.peterlehmannwines.com.au

Lehmen (Ger) village (Anb): Mosel-Saar-Ruwer. (Ber): Zell/Mosel. (Gro): Weinhex. (Vins): Ausoniusstein, Klostergarten, Lay, Wurzlay.

Lehrensteinsfeld (Ger) village (Anb): Württemberg. (Ber): Württembergisch Unterland. (Gro): Salzberg. (Vins): Althälde, Frauenzimmer, Steinacker.

Lehrner (Aus) a winery based in Horitschon, Mittel-Burgenland. (Add): Hauptstrasse 56, 7312 Horitschon. Grape varieties: Blaufränkisch, Cabernet sauvignon, Pinot blanc, Zweigelt. Label: Cuvée Paulus.

Leicester Brewery (Eng) a brewery (established 1983) based in Syston, Leicestershire. Produces Keg Old John 1036 O.G. and Sport Lager 1036 O.G.

Leidersburg Vineyards (S.Afr) a winery (established 1996) based in the Paarl, Western Cape. 6ha. Grape varieties: Cabernet sauvignon, Merlot, Pinotage, Sauvignon blanc, Shiraz. Labels: Migration-Serengeti, Vintners Reserve.

Leidhecke (Ger) vineyard (Anb): Rheinhessen. (Ber): Nierstein. (Gro): Sankt Alban. (Vil): Bodenheim.

Leiersberg (Ger) vineyard (Anb): Württemberg. (Ber): Württembergisch Unterland. (Gro): Heuchelberg. (Vil): Leingarten.

Leikaul (Ger) vineyard (Anb): Mosel-Saar-Ruwer. (Ber): Saar-Ruwer. (Gro): Römerlay. (Vil): Trier.

Leilani (USA) a noted rum produced in Hawaii by Seagram.

Leimen (Ger) village (Anb): Baden. (Ber): Badische Bergstrasse/Kraichgau. (Gro): Mannaberg. (Vins): Herrenberg, Kreuzweg.

Leimer (Aus) a vineyard site based on the banks of the River Kamp situated in the Kamptal region.

Leimern (Aus) a vineyard site on the banks of the River Danube in the Kremstal region.

L

Leinenkugel Brewery (USA) a brewery based in Chippewa Falls, Wisconsin that is noted for Chippewa Pride and Leinenkugel's.

Leingarten (Ger) village (Anb): Württemberg. (Ber): Württembergisch Unterland. (Gro): Heuchelberg. (Vins): Grafenberg, Leiersberg, Vogelsang.

Leinhöhle (Ger) vineyard (Anb): Pfalz. (Ber): Mittelhaardt-Deutsche Weinstrasse. (Gro): Mariengarten. (Vil): Deidesheim.

Leinsweiler (Ger) village (Anb): Pfalz. (Ber): Südliche Weinstrasse. (Gro): Herrlich. (Vin): Sonnenberg.

Leiselheim (Ger) village (Anb): Baden. (Ber): Kaiserstuhl-Tuniberg. (Gro): Vulkanfelsen. (Vin): Gestühl.

Leisern (Aus) a vineyard site on the banks of the River Danube in the Kremstal region.

Leisslinger (Ger) a natural spring mineral water from Naturpark, Saale-Unstrut-Triasland. Mineral contents (milligrammes per litre): Sodium 7.7mg/l, Calcium 92.8mg/l, Magnesium 23.3mg/l, Potassium 3.3mg/l, Bicarbonates 390mg/l, Chlorides mg/l, Fluorides 0.57mg/l.

Leistadt (Ger) village (Anb): Pfalz. (Ber): Mittelhaardt-Deutsche Weinstrasse. (Gro): Kobnert. (Vins): Herzfeld, Kalkofen, Kirchenstück.

Leistenberg (Ger) vineyard (Anb): Nahe. (Ber): Schloss Böckelheim. (Gro): Burgweg. (Vil): Oberhausen an der Nahe.

Leisure Drinks (Eng) based in Derby, a company that specialises in non-alcoholic drinks. (Add): 24, Willow Road, Trent Lane, Castle Donnington, Derbyshire. *see* Jung (Carl).

Leisure Time (USA) a natural spring mineral water brand.

Leitacher (It) red and white table wines produced in Bolzana, Südtirol (Trentino-Alto Adige). Sold in Italy as Guistina-Leitach or Santa Giustina. Also sold in Austria.

Leitaria (Port) dairy.

Leite (Port) milk.

Leiten (Aus) a vineyard site on the banks of the River Danube in the Kremstal region.

Leiterchen (Ger) vineyard (Anb): Mosel-Saar-Ruwer. (Ber): Bernkastel. (Gro): Michelsberg. (Vil): Trittenheim.

Leiterchen (Ger) vineyard (Anb): Mosel-Saar-Ruwer. (Ber): Obermosel. (Gro): Gipfel. (Vil): Nittel.

Leiter Pils (Eng) a 5% alc by vol. lager from the Vaux Brewery sold in 500mls cans.

Leith Brewery (Scot) *see* Argyle Brewery.

Leithner (Aus) a winery based in the Kampstal region. (Add): Walterstrasse 46, 3550 Langenlois. Grape varieties: Chardonnay, Grüner veltliner, Pinot blanc, Riesling, Traminer, Zweigelt. Produces a variety of wine styles.

Leiwen (Ger) village (Anb): Mosel-Saar-Ruwer. (Ber): Bernkastel. (Gro): Sankt Michael. (Vins): Klostergarten, Laurentiuslay.

Le Jardin (S.Afr) the label for a white wine (Chardonnay 30% and Chenin blanc 70% blend) produced by the Mountain Oaks Winery, Worcester, Western Cape.

Lejay-Lagoute (Fr) a large liqueur producer (established 1841) based in Dijon, Burgundy. Labels include: Tutti Cassis and Sisca.

Lejon (USA) the label used by United Vintners in California for their vermouths, brandies and sparkling wines.

Lekhayyim (Gre) cheers/good health. (Ger) = prost, (It) = cin-cin/salute, (Nor) = skol, (Scot) = slàinte mhath, (Wal) = lechyd dda.

Lekkerwijn (S.Afr) the label for a red wine (Grenache noir, Mourvèdre and Viognier blend) produced by the Solms-Delta winery, Franschhoek, Western Cape.

Lemberger (Ger) a lesser used red grape variety, also known as the Blaufränkisch. Is also an alternative spelling of Limberger.

Lemaire-Rasselet (Fr) a Champagne producer. (Add): 5, Rue de la Croix St. Jean, 51480 Boursault-Villesaint. Produce non-vintage Champagnes. 'E'mail: champ.lemaire.rasselet@wanadoo.fr

Le Manoir de Brendal (S.Afr) a winery 50 ha. Grape varieties: Cabernet sauvignon, Chardonnay, Chenin blanc, Merlot, Pinotage, Sauvignon blanc, Sémillon, Shiraz. Label: Wine 4U. Website: http://www.le-manoir-de-brendal.com

Lemberger (N.Am) the name used for the Blaufränkisch grape.

Lemberg Estate (S.Afr) a winery based in Tulbagh, Western Cape. 4ha. (Add): P.O. Box 108, Tulbagh 6820. Grape varieties: Pinot noir, Pinotage, Sauvignon blanc. Produces varietal wines.

Lembo Vineyards (USA) vineyards based in Lewistown, central Pennsylvania. Produces French hybrid wines.

Lembras (Fr) a commune in the A.C. district of Pécharmant in northern Bergerac (red wines).

Lemelson Vineyards (USA) a winery based in the Willamette Valley, Oregon. Grape variety: Pinot noir. Labels: Six Vineyards, Thea's Selection.

Lemnos (Gre) *see* Limnos.

Lemoine [J] (Fr) a Champagne producer. (Add): Rue de Chigny, B.P. 7, 51500 Rilly-la-Montagne. Négociant-manipulant. Produces vintage and non-vintage wines.

Lemonade (Eng) produced at home or commercially, a non-alcoholic, lemon-flavoured soft drink consisting of lemon juice, water and sugar. (Aus) = limonade, (Cro) = limunada, (Den) = citronvand, (Fr) = limonade, (Ger) = limonade, (Hol) = limonade, (It) = limonata, (Port) = limonada, (Sp) = limonada, (Tur) = limonata, (Wal) = diod lemon.

Lemonade (Cktl) 50mls (2fl.ozs) lemon juice, 1½ teaspoons sugar. Fill a tumbler ½ full with cracked ice, stir. Fill up with water, add a slice of lemon on top and serve with straws.

Lemon and Ginger Ale (Eng) a cask or bottled spiced ale brewed by the St. Peter's Brewery, St. Peter's Hall, South Elmham St. Peter, near Bungay, Suffolk.

799

Lemon Barley Water (Eng) a commercially produced concentrated non-alcoholic drink made by Robinsons.

Lemon Breeze (S.Afr) a brand of lemon-flavoured cane spirit.

Lemon Dream (Eng) a 4.5% alc by vol. ale brewed by the Salopian Brewing C°. Ltd., Shropshire.

Lemon Flip (Cktl)(Non-alc) 1 egg yolk, sugar syrup to taste, 60mls (½ gill) lemon juice. Shake well over ice, strain into 125mls (5fl.oz) goblet and top with grated nutmeg.

Lemon Frosted Iced Tea (Cktl) 1.1lts (2pints) cold tea, 500mls (1pint) lemon sorbet. Whisk well together until frothy and serve with lemon slices.

Lemon Gin (Eng) a gin flavoured with lemon (as opposed to juniper), the peel is steeped in the gin for 8–10 weeks.

Lemon Hart Rum (Eng) a famous rum brand (established 1804) by Mr. Lemon Hart, now a brand used by United Rum Merchants.

Lemonhead (Eng) an alcoholic lemon drink from Carlsberg-Tetley 4.9% alc by vol.

Lemonique (Hol) a lemon-flavoured liqueur from De Kuyper 35% alc by vol.

Lemon Jag (Eng) a 5.3% alc by vol RTD lemon flavoured drink from Whitbread Beer C°. under the Shott's Alcoholic Seltzer label. Re-named Hoopers Hooch.

Lemon Liqueurs (USA) a lemon-flavoured and scented liqueurs.

Lemon Ranch (USA) a small vineyard based near St. Helena, Napa Valley, California. 7.5ha. Grape variety: Cabernet sauvignon. Owned by Beringer Vineyards.

Lemon Shandy (Eng) beer and lemonade mixed half and half.

Lemon Squash (Eng) a concentrated cordial made with lemon and sugar produced commercially to be diluted with water.

Lemon Squash (USA) into a tumbler place ice, juice of a lemon (strained), add sugar syrup to taste, top up with soda water, stir and add a slice of lemon.

Lemon Tango (Eng) a lemon-flavoured version of orange Tango produced by Britvic Corona.

Lemon Tea (Eng) an alternative name for Russian tea (tea with a slice of lemon and no milk).

Lemon Tea (Sri L) a blend of high grown (Ceylon) teas, medium sized leaf. Has a scent of lemon.

Lemon Twist (Eng) a small spiral of lemon peel (zest) which is rubbed on the rim of the glass, twisted to release oils, then placed in the cocktail.

Lemon Verbena (Eng) a herbal tea with strong sedative properties.

Lemon White (Eng) a lemon-flavoured cider from Strongbow (Bulmers), Hereford.

Lemps (Fr) a commune in the A.C. Saint-Joseph region of the central Rhône.

Lena (Cktl) ⁹⁄₁₉ measure Bourbon whiskey, ⁷⁄₁₀ measure sweet vermouth, ¹⁄₁₀ measure dry vermouth, ¹⁄₁₀ measure Galliano, ¹⁄₁₀ measure Campari. Shake over ice, strain into a cocktail glass and add a cherry.

Le-Natures Water (USA) a natural spring mineral water from Latrobe, Pennsylvania.

Lenchen (Ger) vineyard (Anb): Rheingau. (Ber): Johannisberg. (Gro): Gottesthal. (Vil): Östrich.

Lenchen (Ger) vineyard (Anb): Rheinhessen. (Ber): Nierstein. (Gro): Domherr. (Vil): Stadecken-Elsheim.

Lenchen (Ger) a vineyard within the village of Östrich, 130.6ha. 27.4% of which is proposed to be classifed as Erstes Gewächs.

L'Enclos du Château Lezongars (Fr) an A.C. Premières Côtes de Bordeaux. Grape varieties: Cabernet franc 32%, Merlot 68%.

L'En de l'El (Fr) a white grape variety grown in the Gaillac region of south-western France.

Lendos (Gre) a dry white wine.

Lengfurt (Ger) village (Anb): Franken. (Ber): Maindreieck. (Gro): Not yet assigned. (Vins): Alter Berg, Oberrot.

Length (Eng) the term which describes a wine where the flavour lingers in the mouth for a long time after it has been swallowed.

Leningrad Cocktail (Cktl) 1 measure vodka, 1 measure Verveine du Vélay, stir over crushed ice in an old-fashioned glass and dress with a yellow cherry.

Lennenborn (Ger) vineyard (Anb): Mittelrhein. (Ber): Bacharach. (Gro): Schloss Stahleck. (Vil): Bacharach/Steeg.

Lenoble [A.R] (Fr) a Champagne producer. (Add): 35 Rue Douce, B.P. 6, 51480 Damery. 18ha. Négociant-manipulant. Produces vintage and non-vintage wines including a blanc de blancs and rosé. Vintages: 1995, 1998, 2001.

Lenoir (USA) a black grape variety little used now.

Lenora Cocktail (Cktl) 1 measure dry gin, ½ measure orange juice, ½ measure raspberry syrup. Shake well over ice and strain into a cocktail glass.

Lonotti (It) a winery based in the D.O.C. Bardolino, Veneto.

Lenswood (Austr) a sub-region of the Adelaide Hills, South Australia.

Lenta (Sp) the name given to the second fermentation which is much slower than the first.

Lenta's (Gre) a natural spring mineral water. Mineral contents (milligrammes per litre): Sodium 27.8mg/l, Calcium 56.1mg/l, Magnesium 24.4mg/l, Potassium 1.8mg/l, Bicarbonates 240.2mg/l, Chlorides 28.7mg/l, Sulphates 41.8mg/l, Nitrates <5mg/l.

Lente Bok (Hol) a 6% alc by vol. crisp, fresh, golden seasonal blond beer brewed by Grolsch at Enschede-Groenlo, Gelderland (available in the spring).

Lenton Brae (Austr) a winery based in the Margaret River region of Western Australia. Grape varieties include: Cabernet sauvignon.

Lentula (It) a sparkling natural spring mineral water from Cantagallo (FI), Tuscany. Mineral contents (milligrammes per litre): Sodium 4.1mg/l, Calcium 63.9mg/l, Magnesium 15.9mg/l, Potassium 1.1mg/l, Bicarbonates 232mg/l,

Chlorides 4.5mg/l, Sulphates 39mg/l, Nitrates 0.8mg/l, Silicates 7.4mg/l. pH 7.8

Lenzenberg (Ger) vineyard (Anb): Württemberg. (Ber): Remstal-Stuttgart. (Gro): Weinsteige. (Vil): Stuttgart (ortsteil Hedelfingen).

Lenzenberg (Ger) vineyard (Anb): Württemberg. (Ber): Remstal-Stuttgart. (Gro): Weinsteige. (Vil): Stuttgart (ortsteil Rohracker).

Lenz M. Moser (Aus) a winery (5ha) based in the Kremstal region. (Add): Lenz-Moser-Strasse 1, 3495 Rohrendorf. Grape varieties include: Grüner veltliner, Müller-Thurgau, Riesling, Neuberger, Zweigelt. Buys in grapes from a large number of growers. Produces a large range of wine styles.

Lenz-Moser [Dr.] (Aus) a wine grower and professor who discovered (in the 1950's) that there was no drop in yield if the vines were planted wide apart (3.5 metres) and having higher vine 'trunks' (1.3 metres) allowing machinery to be used for much of the old manual jobs. i.e. pruning and picking. This system reduces rot and frost damage, increases yields and produces fine wines with no lowering of quality.

Leo Buring (Austr) a winery at Para Road, Tanunda, South Australia. Grape varieties: Chardonnay, Sémillon, Shiraz. *See also* Château Leonay.

Léognan (Fr) a commune within the A.C. Graves district of south-western Bordeaux which has been granted its own A.C. status.

León (Sp) a wine region in north-western Spain. Rueda is the Denominación de Origen of the region.

Leona (It) a natural spring mineral water from Arezzo, Tuscany. pH 7.0

Leonardo (It) a sparkling natural spring mineral water from Leonardo. Mineral contents (milligrammes per litre): Sodium 2.5mg/l, Calcium 12.3mg/l, Magnesium 2.6mg/l, Potassium 0.6mg/l, Bicarbonates 41.6mg/l, Chlorides 0.9mg/l, Sulphates 10.1mg/l, Nitrates 2.5mg/l, Silicates 8.7mg/l. pH 7.9

León [Jean] S.A. (Sp) a small American-owned firm in Catalonia that produces red and white wines from mainly the Cabernet and Chardonnay grapes.

Leone (It) a winery based on the island of Sicily.

Leonetti Cellar (USA) a winery based near Walla Walla Valley, Washington. Produces Cabernet, Merlot and Riesling varietal wines.

Léon Millot (USA) a red hybrid grape variety.

Leon Negra (Mex) a dark beer brewed by the Yucateca Brewery.

Leonora (Sp) a dry white wine produced by Bodegas La Rioja Alta.

Leopard (N.Z) the smallest of 3 brewing groups, jointly owned by the Heineken and Malayan Breweries.

Leopard Frog Vineyards (S.Afr) a winery based in Stellenbosch, Western Cape. Grape varieties: Merlot, Mourvèdre, Shiraz. Label: Kiss & Tell Reserve. Website: http://www.leopard-frog.com

Leopard's Head (Eng) a 4.2% alc by vol. cask hopped

ale brewed under licence by Tring Brewery in Hertfordshire for The Vintage Hallmark Ale Company in Norwich.

Leopard's Leap Wines (S.Afr) a winery (established 2000) based in Franschhoek, Western Cape. Grape varieties: Cabernet sauvignon, Chardonnay, Chenin blanc, Merlot, Nebbiolo, Pinotage, Sauvignon blanc, Sémillon, Shiraz, Viognier. Label: The Lookout Cape Mountain.

Leopoldsberg (Ger) vineyard (Anb): Baden. (Ber): Bodensee. (Gro): Sonnenufer. (Vil): Bermatingen.

Leopoldsquelle (Ger) a sparkling natural spring mineral water from Rippoldsauer Mineral quellen. Mineral contents (milligrammes per litre): Sodium 153mg/l, Calcium 200mg/l, Magnesium 32mg/l, Potassium 7.8mg/l, Bicarbonates 650mg/l, Chlorides 22.3mg/l, Sulphates 384mg/l, Fluorides 1.2mg/l, Nitrates 2mg/l, Silicates 32.5mg/l, Strontium 1.26mg/l.

Léoville (Fr) formerly one of the largest estates in the Médoc, the property was divided during the French revolution into Châteaux: Las-Cases, Barton and Poyferré.

Lepanto (Sp) a solera gran reserva brandy of more than 15 years old produced by Gonzalez Byass.

Le Pavillon (S.Afr) the label for a range of wines produced by the Boschendal Wines winery, Franschhoek, Western Cape. Also Le Grand Pavillion Cap Classique.

Lepe (Sp) a noted wine-producing town on the coast west of Huelva.

Le Phantom (S.Afr) the label for a methode cap classique brut sparkling wine produced by the Saxenberg winery, Stellenbosch, Western Cape.

Le Phare de Verzenay en Champagne (Fr) a wine museum based in Verzenay. (Add): 51360 Verzenay. Open: 12 February to 23 December. Website: http://www.lepharedeverzenay.com 'E'mail: musee@lepharedeverzenay.com

Le Pigeoulet (Fr) a vineyard (10ha) based in the Vin de Pays Vaucluse, Rhône Valley. Owned by Domaine du Vieux Télégraphe, Châteauneuf-du-Pape.

Lepitre [Abel] (Fr) a Champagne producer. (Add): B.P. 124, Ave. du Général Giraud, 51055 Reims. Produces vintage and non-vintage wines. Vintages: 1926, 1928, 1934, 1937, 1941, 1943, 1945, 1947, 1949, 1952, 1953, 1955, 1959, 1961, 1962, 1964, 1966, 1969, 1970, 1971, 1973, 1974, 1975, 1976, 1978, 1979, 1980, 1981, 1982, 1983, 1986, 1988, 1989, 1990, 1995, 1996, 1997, 1998, 1999, 2000, 2001. De Luxe Cuvée: Prince A. de Bourbon-Parme.

Le Pommier Fine Wines (S.Afr) a winery (established 2002) based in Stellenbosch, Western Cape. (owned by Zorgvliet). Grape varieties: Cabernet franc, Cabernet sauvignon, Sauvignon blanc, Sémillon, Shiraz. Website: http://www.zorgvliet.com

Leprechaun [The] (Cktl) 1 part Irish whiskey, 2 parts tonic water. Mix over ice in a highball glass and add a twist of lemon peel.

Lerchenberg (Ger) vineyard (Anb): Baden. (Ber): Bodensee. (Gro): Sonnenufer. (Vil): Meersburg.

L

Lerchenberg (Ger) vineyard (Anb): Baden. (Ber): Bodensee. (Gro): Sonnenufer. (Vil): Stetten.

Lerchenberg (Ger) vineyard (Anb): Baden. (Ber): Badische Bergstrasse/Kraichgau. (Gro): Stiftsberg. (Vil): Bauerbach.

Lerchenberg (Ger) vineyard (Anb): Baden. (Ber): Badische Bergstrasse/Kraichgau. (Gro): Stiftsberg. (Vil): Eppingen.

Lerchenberg (Ger) vineyard (Anb): Baden. (Ber): Badische Bergstrasse/Kraichgau. (Gro): Stiftsberg. (Vil): Flehingen.

Lerchenberg (Ger) vineyard (Anb): Baden. (Ber): Badische Bergstrasse/Kraichgau. (Gro): Stiftsberg. (Vil): Kraichtal (stadtteil Bahnbruchen, Gochsheim and Oberacker).

Lerchenberg (Ger) vineyard (Anb): Baden. (Ber): Badische Bergstrasse/Kraichgau. (Gro): Stiftsberg. (Vil): Kürnbach.

Lerchenberg (Ger) vineyard (Anb): Baden. (Ber): Badische Bergstrasse/Kraichgau. (Gro): Stiftsberg. (Vil): Mühlberg.

Lerchenberg (Ger) vineyard (Anb): Baden. (Ber): Badische Bergstrasse/Kraichgau. (Gro): Stiftsberg. (Vil): Rohrbach a Gr.

Lerchenberg (Ger) vineyard (Anb): Baden. (Ber): Badische Bergstrasse/Kraichgau. (Gro): Stiftsberg. (Vil): Sulzfeld.

Lerchenberg (Ger) vineyard (Anb): Baden. (Ber): Badische Bergstrasse/Kraichgau. (Gro): Stiftsberg. (Vil): Zaisenhausen.

Lerchenberg (Ger) vineyard (Anb): Baden. Kaiserstuhl-Tuniberg. (Gro): Vulkanfelsen. (Vil): Eichstetten.

Lerchenberg (Ger) vineyard (Anb): Rheinhessen. (Ber): Wonnegau. (Gro): Liebfrauenmorgen. (Vil): Worms.

Lerchenberg (Ger) vineyard (Anb): Pfalz. (Ber): Südliche Weinstrasse. (Gro): Guttenberg. (Vil): Kapsweyher.

Lerchenberg (Ger) vineyard (Anb): Württemberg. (Ber): Remstal-Stuttgart. (Gro): Weinsteige. (Vil): Esslingen.

Lerchenberg (Ger) vineyard (Anb): Württemberg. (Ber): Württembergisch Unterland. (Gro): Stromberg. (Vil): Erligheim.

Lerchenberg (Ger) vineyard (Anb): Württemberg. (Ber): Württembergisch Unterland. (Gro): Stromberg. (Vil): Hofen.

Lerchenböhl (Ger) vineyard (Anb): Pfalz. (Ber): Mittelhaardt-Deutsche Weinstrasse. (Gro): Pfaffengrund. (Vil): Lachen-Speyerdorf.

Lerchenspiel (Ger) vineyard (Anb): Pfalz. (Ber): Mittelhaardt-Deutsche Weinstrasse. (Gro): Schwarzerde. (Vil): Gerolsheim.

Le Rêve de Saxenbourg (S.Afr) the label for a natural sweet wine produced by the Saxenberg winery, Stellenbosch, Western Cape.

Le Riche Wines (S.Afr) a winery (established 1996) based in Stellenbosch, Western Cape. Grape varieties: Cabernet sauvignon, Merlot. Label: Leef op Hoop. Website: http://www.leriche.co.za

Lérida (Sp) a province of Catalonia that borders Aragón, home to the Raimat Bodega.

Lerin (Sp) one of 3 sub-regions in western Ribera-Alta, is bordered by the Rioja Baja.

Lérina (Fr) a Cistercian liqueur, herb distillation, both green and yellow produced in the Abbaye de Lérius off the French coast at Marseilles.

Leroux (Aus) a noted liqueur distiller.

Le Roux (S.Afr) the label for a red wine (Merlot, Cabernet sauvignon and Cabernet franc blend) produced by the Verdôme winery, Paarl, Western Cape.

Leroux (USA) a famous liqueur producer (a subsidiary of Seagram).

Leroux [Patrice] (Fr) a Champagne producer. (Add): 12 Rue Georges, Legros, B.P. 2, 51500 Chigny-lès-Roses. Récoltants-manipulants. Produces vintage and non-vintage wines. Vintages: 1971, 1973, 1975, 1976, 1979, 1982, 1983, 1985, 1989, 1990, 1995, 1996, 1998, 2000.

Leroy (Fr) a Burgundy shipper based at Auxey-Duresses in the Côte de Beaune.

Lès (Fr) near or by. e.g: Chorey-lès-Beaune. Not to be confused with 'les' meaning 'the'.

Lesage Natural Wells (USA) a natural spring mineral water from Lesae, West Virginia.

Les Ailes de Berliquet (Fr) the second wine of Château Berliquet Grand Cru A.C. Saint-Émilion, Bordeaux.

Les Argiles Bleues (Fr) the label for an A.C. Côtes-du-Rhône-Villages Rasteau (red) from Domaine de Beaurenard, Châteauneuf-du-Pape, Vaucluse.

Les Auzines (Fr) a vineyard in the A.C. Corbières, south-western France. Labels: Cuvée des Roches and Fleurs des Garrigues.

Lesbian (Gre) a sweet white wine produced in ancient Greece from the isle of Lesbos.

Lesbos (Gre) an island in the Aegean islands in eastern Greece, produces mainly dessert wines. See also Lesbian.

Les Brasseurs de Gayant (Fr) a brewery. (Add): Douai Cedex F-59502. Brews a variety of beers and lager. Website: http://www.brasseurs-gayant.com 'E'mail: contact@brasseurs-gayant.com

Les Brasseurs de Lorraine (Fr) a brewery. (Add): 3 Rue de Lorraine, F-54700 Pont a Mousson. Brews beers and lager.

Les Brasseurs du Forez (Fr) a brewery. (Add): La Bruyère, F-42600 Verrières en Forez. Brews beers and lager. Website: http://www.brue.free.fr

Les Bruneau (Fr) the label for an A.C. Côtes-du-Rhône-Villages Cairanne (red) from Domaine Delubac, Cairanne, Vaucluse.

Les Celliers Saint Martin (Fr) a co-operative winery based in the A.C. Corbières, Languedoc-Roussillon. (Add): SVC 11540 Roquefort des Corbières. Produces: white, rosé and red wines. Labels: Roche Grise (rosé). Website: http://www.celliers-saintmartin.com 'E'mail: contact@celliers-saintmartin.com

Les Chanvrières (Fr) an A.C. Sancerre white wine from Fournier Père et Fils.

Les Cinc [5] (Fr) a group of five family Bordeaux château owners who have joined forces to market their wines and their quality. Châteaux are: Branaire-Ducru, Canon-la-Gaffelière, Gazin, Pontet-Canet and Smith Haut Lafite.

Les Coteaux (S.Afr) the label for a range of wines produced by the Mont du Toit Kelder winery, Wellington, Western Cape.

Les Creus (Sp) a natural spring mineral water (established 1955) from Maçanet de Cabrenys, Girona. Mineral contents (milligrammes per litre): Sodium 11.7mg/l, Calcium 28mg/l, Magnesium 7.3mg/l, Potassium 1mg/l, Bicarbonates 119mg/l, Chlorides 5.3mg/l, Sulphates 12.3mg/l, Fluorides 0.2mg/l, Nitrates <1mg/l, Silicates 23.6mg/l. pH 7.0

Les Échansons (Fr) a Grand Cru vintage Champagne from the Mailly-Champagne co-operative.

Lesegut-Aufbesserung (Aus) a method of increasing the alcohol content by the addition of sugar to the fermenting must. (Fr) = chaptalisation, (Ger) = anreicherung.

Les Entonneurs Rabelaisiens de Chinon (Fr) a wine brotherhood (established 30th September 1961) based in Chinon, Loire valley to promote the wines and food of the region. Website: http://www.entonneursrabelaisiens.com

Les Grandes Vignes du Roy (Fr) a winery based in the A.C. Côtes-du-Rhône-Villages Rasteau, Vaucluse.

Les Grands Chais de France (Eng) a winery. (Add): 7 Breweeke Drive, winchester, Hampshire SO22 6BH. Produces a range of red, rosé and white wines.

Les Grands Jours de Bougogne (Fr) a bi-annual (even number calender years) wine tasting and related events for wine professionals held in the spring in the five areas of the Burgundy region. 'E'mail: grands.jours.bourgogne@bivb.com

Les Jeannettes (Fr) a rosé wine produced by the Henri Bourgeois winery, Sancerre, Loire Valley.

Leskovac (Ser) an A.C. wine producing region in Serbia noted for white wines produced from the Sauvignon blanc grape.

Les Lauzes (Fr) the label for an A.C. Côtes-du-Rhône-Villages Laudun (red) from Domaine de Pont-le-Voy, Laudun, Vaucluse.

Lesmona (Ger) a still and sparkling natural spring mineral water from Kiians-Quelle, Lüdge. Mineral contents (milligrammes per litre): Sodium 216mg/l, Calcium 128mg/l, Magnesium 40mg/l, Bicarbonates 420mg/l, Chlorides 181mg/l, Sulphates 340mg/l.

Les Murailles (Fr) an A.C. Alsace Riesling from Château de Riquewihr.

Les Pleurs (S.Afr) a red wine (Syrah and Merlot blend) produced by the Avondale winery, Paarl, Western Cape.

Les Riceys (Fr) a commune (870ha) within the Côte des Bar, Champagne. (Add): 3, Place des Héros de la Résistance, 10340 Les Riceys. *see* A.C. Rosé des Riceys. Website: http://www.les-riceys-champagne.com 'E'mail: ot.lesriceys@wanadoo.fr

Les Sens de Syrah (Fr) a full-bodied red wine (Syrah and Grenache) produced by Château Beauchêne, A.C. Côtes-du-Rhône.

L'Espirit du Vin (Fr) lit: 'the wine's life', denotes the wine-maker's understanding of the wine as a living thing and its needs.

L'Espirit Vigne (Fr) lit: 'the vine's life', denotes a vine-grower's understanding of his/her vines and their needs.

Les Sommets de Rasteau (Fr) the label for an A.C. Côtes-du-Rhône-Villages Rasteau (red) from Domaine Martin, Rasteau, Vaucluse.

Lessona (It) a D.O.C. red wine from the Piemonte region made from the Nebbiolo grape.

L'Estaminet (Fr) a brewery. (Add): 45 Rue des Rouyers, F-55100 Verdun. Brews a variety of beers and lager. Website: http://www.brasserie-de-verdun.com 'E'mail: lestam@wanadoo.fr

Les Trois [3] Brasseurs (Fr) a brewery. (Add): Centre Commerciale, F-14120 Mondeville. Brews beers and lager. Website: http://www.les3brasseurs.fr

Lesumer (Ger) a natural spring mineral water from Bremen Lesum. Mineral contents (milligrammes per litre): Sodium 19mg/l, Calcium 302mg/l, Magnesium 10mg/l, Bicarbonates 235mg/l, Chlorides 16mg/l, Sulphates 640mg/l.

Les Vergers de la Morinière (Fr) the label for a dated Calvados Pays d'Auge produced by Michel Hubert, La Fresnaie-Fyel.

Les Vignerons de la Méditerranée (Fr) a winery based in the A.C. Corbières, south-western France. Label: Cuvée Mythique.

Les Vignerons de Laudun (Fr) a co-operative winery based in Laudun, Côtes-du-Rhône-Villages, Vaucluse. Label: Moment d'Exception.

Les Vignerons de Tavel (Fr) a co-operative winery based in the A.C. Tavel, southern Rhône.

Les Vignobles Mireille Petit-Roudil (Fr) a co-operative winery based in the A.C. Tavel, southern Rhône.

Lete (It) a sparkling natural spring mineral water (established 1893) from Lete. Mineral contents (milligrammes per litre): Sodium 5.1mg/l, Calcium 321mg/l, Magnesium 17.5mg/l, Potassium 2.23mg/l, Bicarbonates 1055.3mg/l, Chlorides 7.64mg/l, Sulphates 8.65mg/l, Fluorides 0.4mg/l, Nitrates 4.2mg/l, Silicates 16.4mg/l. pH 6.09

Letermago (S.Afr) an oak-aged, white (Chardonnay and Sauvignon blanc blend) wine produced by Ant Hill Wines, Somerset West, Western Cape.

Leth [Franz] (Aus) a winery (33ha) based in Fels am Wagram, Donauland. (Add): Kirchengasse 6, 3481 Fels am Wagram. Grape varieties: Cabernet sauvignon, Grüner veltliner, Riesling, Roter veltliner, Sauvignon blanc, Traminer, Zweigelt. Produces a range of dry and sweet wines.

Letmælk (Den) partially skimmed milk.

Let Pilsener (Den) a 'light' ale.

Letscheberg (Lux) a vineyard site in the village of Schwebsingen.

Letten (Aus) a vineyard site based on the banks of the River Kamp situated in the Kamptal region.

L

Letten (Ger) vineyard (Anb): Baden. (Ber): Markgräflerland. (Gro): Burg Neuenfels. (Vil): Auggen.

Letten (Ger) vineyard (Anb): Pfalz. (Ber): Mittelhaardt-Deutsche Weinstrasse. (Gro): Schnepfenflug an der Weinstrasse. (Vil): Deidesheim.

Letten (Ger) vineyard (Anb): Pfalz. (Ber): Südliche Weinstrasse. (Gro): Ordensgut. (Vil): Hainfeld.

Letterlay (Ger) vineyard (Anb): Mosel-Saar-Ruwer. (Ber): Bernkastel. (Gro): Nacktarsch. (Vil): Kröv.

Letts Brewery (Ire) a brewery based in Enniscorthy, Wexford which stopped production in 1956. Licenses Coors Brewery of the USA and Pelforth Brewery of France to brew its Ruby Ale as Irish Red Ale (USA) and George Killian's Bière (Fr).

Lettweiler (Ger) village (Anb): Nahe. (Ber): Schloss Böckelheim. (Gro): Paradiesgarten. (Vins): Inkelhöll, Rheingasse.

Leubsdorf (Ger) village (Anb): Mittelrhein. (Ber): Rheinburgengau. (Gro): Burg Hammerstein. (Vin): Weisses Kreuz.

Leucate (Fr) one of nine wine-producing communes in the Fitou region in southern France.

Leucine (Eng) an amino acid found in wine, formed by the yeasts.

Leuconostoc (USA) a cultured bacteria that causes malo-lactic fermentation.

Leutershausen (Ger) village (Anb): Baden. (Ber): Badische Bergstrasse/Kraichgau. (Gro): Rittersberg. (Vins): Kahlberg, Standenberg.

Leutesdorf (Ger) village (Anb): Mittelrhein. (Ber): Rheinburgengau. (Gro): Burg Hammerstein. (Vins): Forstberg, Gartenlay, Rosenberg.

Leutschach (Aus) a wine-producing region in the Südsteiermark.

Leuvense Wit (Bel) a white wheat beer.

Leuvrigny (Fr) a Cru Champagne village in the Canton de Dormans. District: Épernay.

Leuwenblanc (S.Afr) a white wine (Chenin blanc) produced by the Seidelberg Estate, Paarl, Western Cape.

Levada (Mad) a type of aqueduct used for irrigation in Madeira.

Levadura (Sp) yeast.

Levanan (Isr) a dry white table wine.

Levante (Sp) the hot winds in the Sherry district which blow from the east in winter, blows from the Gulf of Lions.

Levante (Sp) a wine-producing area in eastern Spain that contains the Denominación de Origens of Alicante, Jumilla, Utiel-Requena and Valencia-Yecla.

Levedura (Port) yeast.

Level (Swe) a premium brand vodka distilled by Absolut Spirits.

Level Best (Eng) a 4% alc by vol. ale brewed by Rother Valley Brewery, Sussex using yeoman hops.

Le Ventabren (Fr) the label for an A.C. Côtes-du-Rhône-Villages Cairanne (red) from Domaine des Escaravailles, Cairanne, Vaucluse.

Leventhorpe Vineyard (Eng) a 2.6ha vineyard (established 1984) near Woodlesford, south-east of Leeds. Produces red and white wines.

Leverano (It) a D.O.C. wine producing region in Southern Puglia. Red wines are produced from Negroamaro grapes.

Le Verre I.N.A.O. (Fr) a wine tasting glass created 1971.

Levert (Hol) a small distilling company that produces Jenevers.

Levia (It) a sparkling natural spring mineral water from Levia. Mineral contents (milligrammes per litre): Sodium 46.1mg/l, Calcium 18mg/l, Magnesium 15.8mg/l, Potassium 1.8mg/l, Bicarbonates 130.1mg/l, Chlorides 69.8mg/l, Sulphates 20.9mg/l, Fluorides 0.5mg/l, Nitrates 0.1mg/l, Silicates 14.1mg/l. pH 6.91

Leviathan (Cktl) ½ measure brandy, ¼ measure sweet vermouth, ¼ measure orange juice. Shake over ice and strain into a cocktail glass.

Levico Casara (It) a natural spring mineral water from Levico Casara. Mineral contents (milligrammes per litre): Sodium 1.3mg/l, Calcium 6.6mg/l, Magnesium 1.8mg/l, Potassium 0.5mg/l, Bicarbonates 25.2mg/l, Chlorides 0.4mg/l, Sulphates 12mg/l, Nitrates 0.7mg/l, Silicates 4.9mg/l. pH 6.4

Levico Forte (It) a natural spring mineral water from levico Forte.

Le Vigne di Zamò (It) a winery based in Manzano in the Friuli-Venezia-Guilia region.

Levissima (Bra) a natural spring mineral water from Santa Terezinha. Mineral contents (milligrammes per litre): Sodium 1.83mg/l, Calcium 0.57mg/l, Magnesium 0.35mg/l, Potassium 0.7mg/l, Bicarbonates 6.04mg/l, Chlorides 8.68mg/l, Sulphates 0.5mg/l, Fluorides 0.04mg/l. pH 6.5

Levissima (It) a still and sparkling natural spring mineral water from Levissima, Valdisotto. Mineral contents (milligrammes per litre): Sodium 1.8mg/l, Calcium 19.5mg/l, Magnesium 1.7mg/l, Potassium 1.7mg/l, Bicarbonates 56.8mg/l, Chlorides 0.3mg/l, Sulphates 13.7mg/l, Fluorides 0.2mg/l, Nitrates 1.6mg/l, Silicates 5.7mg/l. pH 7.8

Levkas (Gre) an island in the Ionian Islands of western Greece. Produces mainly country wines for local consumption. Also spelt Lefkàs.

Levogyrous Sugar (Eng) a sugar found in dried grapes.

Levulose (Eng) fermentable sugar (fructose).

Levurage (Fr) in Champagne the addition of Liqueur de Tirage.

Levure (Fr) the introduction of non-natural yeasts strains to start fermentation.

Lewis Estate (USA) a winery based in the Napa Valley, California. Grape varieties include: Cabernet sauvignon. Label: Cuvée 'L'.

Lex Domitiana (It) a Roman wine law A.D.91 relating to modern day Germany.

Lexham Hall (Eng) a 3.5ha vineyard (established 1975). (Add): Kings Lynn, Norfolk. Grape varieties: Madeleine angevine, Müller-Thurgau, Reichensteiner and Scheurebe.

Lexia (Austr) a white grape variety grown in Victoria.

Also known as Muscat of Alexandria. *See also* Muscat Gordo Blanco.

Lexia-Gordo Blanco (Austr) a name for the Muscat of Alexandria grape used for the early brandies of Australia.

Lexias (Sp) the name given to raisins that have been steeped in lye in Màlaga.

Leyda (Chile) a wine district with the San Antonio region.

Leyden Brewery (Eng) a brewery (established 2000). (Add): The Lord Raglan Hotel, Mount Pleasant, Nangreaves, Bury, Lancashire BL9 6SP. Brews: Crowning Glory 6.8% alc by vol., Light Brigade 4.2% alc by vol., Nanny Flier 3.8% alc by vol. Website: http://www.leydenbrewery.com 'E'mail: info@leydenbrewery.com

Leyenda (Sp) a solera reserva brandy produced by Gil Luque.

Leygues (Fr) a noted wine-producing area near Puy-l'Evêque in Cahors, south-western France.

Leyland Brewery (Eng) a small brewery based in Leyland, Lancashire. Produces cask-conditioned Tiger Ale 1038 O.G. from malt extract.

Leynes (Fr) a commune in the Beaujolais. Has A.C. Beaujolais-Villages or Beaujolais-Leynes status. Also as Mâconnais Blanc.

Leyrat [Edgard] (Fr) a Cognac producer. (Add): Domaine de Chez Maillard, 16440 Claix-Blanzac. 50ha. in the Fins Bois. Produces: Brut de Futs Hors d'Age, Napoléon and Vieille Réserve.

LGC (S.Afr) the label for a red wine (Cabernet sauvignon 50% and Ruby cabernet 50%) produced by the Le Grand Chasseur Estate winery, Robertson, Western Cape.

Li (Chi) the old Chinese word for wine. *See also* Chang and Chiu.

Lian (It) a natural spring mineral water brand. pH 7.61

Lias (Sp) wine lees.

Lia Sail (Scot) a 4.7% alc by vol. ale brewed by the Inveralmond Brewery Ltd., Perthshire.

Liason Cocktail (Cktl) 20mls (⅙ gill) Cognac, 15mls (⅛ gill) Cointreau, 1 teaspoon coconut cream, 2 dashes Angostura. Shake well over ice and strain into an ice-filled highball glass.

Liatiko (Gre) a red grape variety used for both dry and dessert wines, especially on the Isle of Crete.

Libanos (S.Am) a noted coffee-producing region of Colombia.

Libare (Lat) to pour an offering drink.

Libarna (It) a noted brand-name of grappa.

Libatio (Lat) a drink poured out to honour a God.

Libation (Eng) an alcoholic beverage poured out as an offering to honour a God. (Lat) = libato.

Libby (Eng) a firm who produce a wide range of fruit juices.

Libby's Moon Shine (Eng) a mixed berry drink from the Libby Company.

Libella Sveikas (Euro) a natural spring mineral water from Vilnius, Lithuania. Mineral contents (milligrammes per litre): Sodium 6-7mg/l, Calcium 92-98mg/l, Magnesium 36-38mg/l, Potassium 0.6-0.9mg/l, Bicarbonates 380-394mg/l, Chlorides 10-12mg/l, Sulphates 11-52mg/l, Fluorides 0.14-0.2mg/l.

Liberal (Cktl) ½ measure Canadian whisky, ½ measure sweet vermouth, 3 dashes Amer Picon, dash orange bitters. Stir over ice and strain into a cocktail glass.

Liberation Ale (Scot) a medium-bodied, bottled ale brewed by the Harviestoun brewery.

Liberation Rum (Ch.Isles) bottled by Bucktrout and C°. Ltd., St.Peter Port, Guernsey. A rum shipped during World War II and bottled in 1985 for the liberation celebration. 500 numbered bottles only.

Libertas (S.Afr) the label for a range of W.O. red and white wines produced by Distell, Western Cape.

Liberty (USA) a fruity variety of hop.

Liberty (Eng) a single varietal ale 4.2% alc by vol. brewed by Wadworth & C°. Ltd., Northgate Brewery in Devizes, Wiltshire between 28th June and 9th July.

Liberty (S.Afr) the label for a red wine (Cabernet sauvignon, Pinotage and Syrah blend) produced by the Freedom Hills Wines winery, Paarl, Western Cape.

Liberty Ale (USA) an ale 5.6% alc by vol. from the Anchor Brewery.

Liberty Bell (Cktl) 25mls (1fl.oz) Southern Comfort, 25mls (1fl.oz) Royal Mint Choc.Liqueur, 100mls (4fl.ozs) fresh orange juice, 1 egg white. Shake over ice, strain into a goblet and dress with an orange segment.

Liberty Cocktail (Cktl) ⅓ measure white rum, ⅔ measure applejack brandy, dash gomme syrup. Stir over ice and strain into cocktail glass.

Liberty School (USA) the label used by Caymus Vineyards for their range of varietal wines.

Libourne (Fr) an old city on the right side bank of the river Dordogne, once an important market for Pomerol and Fronsac wines.

Librandi (It) a 220ha winery based at Cirò Marina in Calabria. Grape varieties: Magliocco (Gaglioppo), Cabernet sauvignon, Chardonnay, Sauvignon blanc. Produces Magno Megonia, Duca Sanfelice, Cirò Riserva, Gravello, I.G.T. Critone.

Licensed Trade Charity (Eng) a charity (established 1793) to help those who have worked in the licensed drinks trade. (Add): Heatherly, London Road, Ascot, Berkshire SL5 8DR. Previously known as Licensed Victuallers National Homes, Society of Licensed Victuallers. Website: http://www.licensedtradecharity.org.uk 'E'mail: info@licensedtradecharity.org.uk

Licensed Victuallers Association (Eng) *see* L.V.A.

Licensed Victuallers [Wales] Ltd (Wal) an organisation. (Add): 2 Derwen Deg, Station Road, Govilon, Abergavenny, Monmouthshire NP7 9RG.

Licensee (Eng) a person who holds the Justices licence to sell alcoholic liquor.

Licensee (The) and Morning Advertiser (Eng) originally called the Morning Advertiser, this newspaper is printed weekly for the licensed trade.

Licensing Justices (Eng) a body of Lay Magistrates who deal with all licence applications and renewals for the selling of alcoholic beverages. *see* Brewster Sessions and Occasional Licenses.

Lichee (Cktl) equal parts of dry gin, dry vermouth and lychee syrup, 3 dashes Angostura. Shake over ice, strain into a cocktail glass and serve with canned lychees on a cocktail stick.

Lichenstein (Aus) a vineyard site on the banks of the River Danube situated in the Wachau region, Niederösterreich.

Licher Brauerei (Ger) a brewery (established 1854) based in Lich. Brews: Licher Ice beer, Licher Pilsner.

Licher Ice Beer (Ger) a 5.1% alc by vol. bottled ice beer brewed by the Licher Brauerei, Lich.

Licher Pilsner (Ger) a 4.9% alc by vol. bottled pilsner brewed by the Licher Brauerei, Lich.

Lichfield Gin (Scot) a gin produced by Grant (William and C°.) from natural botanicals.

Lichine [Alexis] (Fr) late famous, wine author, château owner, négociant and an esteemed authority on wine.

Lichtenauer (Ger) a natural spring mineral water from Niederlichtenau. Mineral contents (milligrammes per litre): Sodium 11.9mg/l, Calcium 69.5mg/l, Magnesium 10.8mg/l, Potassium 1.7mg/l, Bicarbonates 165mg/l, Chlorides 19.6mg/l, Sulphates 80.3mg/l, Fluorides 0.18mg/l. Website: http://www.hassia.com

Lichtenberg (Ger) vineyard (Anb): Baden. (Ber): Badische Bergstrasse/Kraichgau. (Gro): Hohenberg. (Vil): Grötzingen.

Lichtenberg (Ger) vineyard (Anb): Württemberg. (Ber): Remstal-Stuttgart. (Gro): Wartbühl. (Vil): Geradstetten.

Lichtenberg (Ger) vineyard (Anb): Württemberg. (Ber): Remstal-Stuttgart. (Gro): Wartbühl. (Vil): Hebsack.

Lichtenberg (Ger) vineyard (Anb): Württemberg. (Ber): Württembergisch Unterland. (Gro): Stromberg. (Vil): Illingen.

Lichtenberg (Ger) vineyard (Anb): Württemberg. (Ber): Württembergisch Unterland. (Gro): Stromberg. (Vil): Rosswag.

Lichtenberg (Ger) vineyard (Anb): Württemberg. (Ber): Württembergisch Unterland. (Gro): Wunnenstein. (Vil): Hof und Lembach.

Lichtenberg (Ger) vineyard (Anb): Württemberg. (Ber): Württembergisch Unterland. (Gro): Wunnenstein. (Vil): Grossbottwar.

Lichtenberg (Ger) vineyard (Anb): Württemberg. (Ber): Württembergisch Unterland. (Gro): Wunnenstein. (Vil): Ilsfeld.

Lichtenberg (Ger) vineyard (Anb): Württemberg. (Ber): Württembergisch Unterland. (Gro): Wunnenstein. (Vil): Kleinbottwar.

Lichtenberg (Ger) vineyard (Anb): Württemberg. (Ber): Württembergisch Unterland. (Gro): Wunnenstein. (Vil): Oberstenfeld.

Lichtenberg (Ger) vineyard (Anb): Württemberg. (Ber): Württembergisch Unterland. (Gro): Wunnenstein. (Vil): Steinhelm.

Lichtenberg (Ger) vineyard (Anb): Württemberg. (Ber): Württembergisch Unterland. (Gro): Wunnenstein. (Vil): Winzerhausen.

Lichtgartl (Aus) a vineyard site on the banks of the River Danube situated in the Wachau region, Niederösterreich.

Licht van Troost (Hol) an 8.5% alc by vol. bottle-conditioned tripel beer brewed by the Texel Bier Brouwerij, Oudeschild.

Licor (Port) liquid/liquor/liqueur.

Licor (Sp) alcoholic beverages.

Licor Cobana (Sp) a banana liqueur produced in the Canary Isles by Cocal S.A. in Telde.

Licor de Expedición (Sp) the dose of old wine (and sugar) after the cava wines have been disgorged. (Fr) = liqueur d'expédition.

Licor de Miel (Sp) a honey liqueur produced in the Canary Isles by Cocal S.A. in Telde.

Licor de Platano (Sp) banana liqueur.

Licor de Tiraje (Sp) the dosage of yeast and grape sugar to cava wines prior to the second fermentation in bottle. (Fr) = liqueur de tirage.

Licores (Sp) liqueurs.

Licor 43 (Sp) the alternative name for Cuarenta y Tres.

Licoroso (Port)(Sp) a rich, sweet, fortified wine.

Licoroso Dulce (Sp) a sweet white wine of the Cariñena region.

Liddington (Eng) beer wholesalers in the East Midlands who, in 1984, took over Litchborough and moved the plant to their Rugby depot. Produce: cask-conditioned Litchborough Bitter 1036 O.G. and Tudor Ale 1044 O.G.

Lidia [La] (Sp) a fine Manzanilla Sherry produced by Garvey in Jerez de la Frontera.

Lidio Carrero (Bra) a winery based in the Vale dos Vinhedos region. Grape varieties include: Cabernet sauvignon, Malbec, Merlot, Nebbiolo, Tannat, Tempranillo.

Lido Cocktail (Cktl) 30mls (¼ gill) Gin, 30mls (¼ gill) French vermouth, 2 dashes apricot brandy. Stir over ice, strain into a cocktail glass and top with a cherry.

Lidy (Gre) a method of red wine fermentation that occurs under pressure. *See also* Klenk.

Lie (Fr) lees. *see* Sur Lie.

Lie [La] (Fr) a distillation produced from the residue of the grapes after the final pressing in the Savoie region, south-eastern France.

Lieb (Eng) a wine trade's slang term for Liebfraumilch.

Liébana (Sp) a Vino de Mesa of Cantabria, north-central Spain.

Liebehöll (Ger) vineyard (Anb): Nahe. (Ber): Kreuznach. (Gro): Schlosskapelle. (Vil): Münster-Sarmsheim.

Liebenberg (Aus) a vineyard site on the banks of the River Danube situated in the Wachau region, Niederösterreich.

Liebenberg (Ger) vineyard (Anb): Rheinhessen. (Ber): Wonnegau. (Gro): Pilgerpfad. (Vil): Osthofen.

Liebenberg (Ger) vineyard (Anb): Württemberg. (Ber): Württembergisch Unterland. (Gro): Stromberg. (Vil): Ochsenbach.

Liebenberg (Ger) vineyard (Anb): Württemberg. (Ber): Württembergisch Unterland. (Gro): Stromberg. (Vil): Spielberg.

Liebeneck-Sonnenlay (Ger) vineyard (Anb): Mittelrhein. (Ber): Rheinburgengau. (Gro): Marksburg. (Vil): Osterpai.

Lieben-Frauen-Milch (Ger) the eighteenth century spelling of Liebfraumilch.

Lieben Frawenstift (Ger) the mid-sixteenth century spelling of Liebfraumilch.

Liebenstein-Sterrenberg (Ger) vineyard (Anb): Mittelrhein. (Ber): Rheinburgengau. (Gro): Loreleyfelsen. (Vil): Kamp-Bornhofen-Kestert.

Lieberstein (S.Afr) a semi-sweet white wine made from a blend of Steen and Clairette blanche grape varieties. Made by the SFW.

Liebesbrunnen (Ger) vineyard (Anb): Nahe. (Ber): Schloss Böckelheim. (Gro): Paradiesgarten. (Vil): Hochstätten.

Liebesbrunnen (Ger) vineyard (Anb): Pfalz. (Ber): Mittelhaardt-Deutsche Weinstrasse. (Gro): Kobnert. (Vil): Dackenheim.

Liebestraum (N.Z) a dry white wine produced by Corbans in Henderson Valley, North Island.

Liebfrau (Ger) vineyard (Anb): Rheinhessen. (Ber): Bingen. (Gro): Rheingrafenstein. (Vil): Volxheim.

Liebfrauenberg (Ger) vineyard (Anb): Mosel-Saar-Ruwer. (Ber): Saar-Ruwer. (Gro): Scharzberg. (Vil): Filzen.

Liebfrauenberg (Ger) vineyard (Anb): Nahe. (Ber): Schloss Böckelheim. (Gro): Paradiesgarten. (Vil): Meddersheim.

Liebfrauenberg (Ger) vineyard (Anb): Rheinhessen. (Ber): Wonnegau. (Gro): Pilgerpfad. (Vil): Dittelsheim-Hessloch.

Liebfrauenkirche (Ger) lit: 'the church of our lady', in the city of Worms, has its own vineyard the Liebfrauenstifte.

Liebfrauenmorgen (Ger) grosslage (Anb): Rheinhessen. (Ber): Wonnegau. (Vil): Worms.

Liebfrauenstifte (Ger) the wine of the Liebfrauenkirche vineyards Worms in the Rheinhessen. In latter days was the original Liebfraumilch. Known as Liebfrauenstiftwein.

Liebfrauenstift-Kirchenstück (Ger) vineyard (Anb): Rheinhessen. (Ber): Wonnegau. (Gro): Liebfrauenmorgen. (Vil): Worms.

Liebfrauenstiftwein (Ger) the original name for Liebfraumilch, now no longer used.

Liebfrauenthal (Ger) vineyard (Anb): Rheinhessen. (Ber): Nierstein. (Gro): Krötenbrunnen. (Vil): Gimbsheim.

Liebfraumilch (Ger) must be QbA wine and come only from one of the following four 'quality wine' regions (Rheinhessen, Rheingau, Pfalz and Nahe), minimum 51% of either Silvaner, Riesling or Müller-Thurgau and 49% of any permitted grape variety.

Liebfrauminch (Ger) an old spelling of Liebfraumilch.

Lieblich (Aus) a classification denoting sweet wines which can have up to 45g/l of residual sugar. See also Suss (Süß).

Lieblich (Ger) pleasant light wine.

Liebling (Ger) a brand of liebfraumilch produced by Deinhard in Koblenz.

Liebotschaner (USA) the brand-name used by the Lion Brewery in Wilkes-Barre, Pennsylvania for their range of beers.

Liechtenstein (Euro) lit: 'light coloured stone', a tiny country between Austria and Switzerland. Produces wines on a style between German and Austrian in character. 42 square miles (soil mainly limestone).

Liefmans Brasserie (Bel) a brewery based in Oudenaarde owned by Vaux of Sunderland. Produces Goudenband Special Provisie in litre bottles, Jan van Gent and Liefman's Kriek 6.5% alc by vol.

Liefman's Kriek (Bel) a 6.5% alc by vol. kriek beer brewed by Liefmans Brasserie, Oudenaarde.

Liège (Fr) cork. See also Bouchon.

Liel (Ger) village (Anb): Baden. (Ber): Markgräflerland. (Gro): Burg Neuenfels. (Vin): Sonnenstück.

Lienzingen (Ger) village (Anb): Württemberg. (Ber): Württembergisch Unterland. (Gro): Stromberg. (Vin): Eichelberg.

Liersberg (Ger) village (Anb): Mosel-Saar-Ruwer. (Ber): Obermosel. (Gro): Königsberg. (Vin): Pilgerberg.

Liesberg (Ger) vineyard (Anb): Nahe. (Ber): Kreuznach. (Gro): Schlosskapelle. (Vil): Waldlaubersheim.

Lieser (Ger) village (Anb): Mosel-Saar-Ruwer. (Ber): Bernkastel. (Gro): Beerenlay. (Vins): Niederberg-Helden, Rosenlay, Sussenberg.

Lieser (Ger) village (Anb): Mosel-Saar-Ruwer. (Ber): Bernkastel. (Gro): Kurfürstlay. (Vin): Schlossberg.

Lieshan (Chi) a natural spring mineral water. Mineral contents (milligrammes per litre): Calcium 57.1mg/l, Bicarbonates 370.8mg/l, Silicates 62.2mg/l. pH 7.2

Lieth (Ger) vineyard (Anb): Rheinhessen. (Ber): Nierstein. (Gro): Sankt Alban. (Vil): Harxheim.

Lieutenant Commander (Cktl) half Cognac half Bénédictine.

Lieux-Dits (Fr) describes the 50 specified vineyard sites permitted in the A.C. of Alsace Grand Cru.

Lieve Royale (Hol) a 6% alc by vol. top-fermented special beer brewed by the Arcen Brouwerij, Arcen.

Lievito (It) yeast.

Lievland (S.Afr) a winery (established 1982) in Stellenbosch-Simonsberg, Western Cape. 50ha. (Add): Box 66, Klapmuts 7625. Grape varieties: Cabernet franc, Cabernet sauvignon, Chardonnay, Chenin blanc, Cinsaut, Petit verdot, Riesling, Ruby cabernet, Sauvignon blanc, Sémillon, Shiraz, Weisser riesling. Produces: Chéandrie, Huiswyn, Rood and many varietals.

Lifeboat (Eng) a beer brewed by Titanic (an

independent brewery) in Burslem, Stoke-on-Trent. *See also* Valiant Stout.

Lifebuoy Beer (Eng) a cask-conditioned ale 1075 O.G. brewed by the two home-brew public houses of Pier Hotel, Gravesend and the Southeastern in Strood. Both in Kent.

Life Force (Austr) a natural spring mineral water from Mena Creek. Mineral contents (milligrammes per litre): Sodium 1.9mg/l, Calcium 0.2mg/l, Magnesium <0.1mg/l, Potassium <0.5mg/l, Bicarbonates 3.8mg/l, Chlorides 2.3mg/l.

Life From Stone (S.Afr) the label for a white wine (Sauvignon blanc) produced by the Springfield Estate winery, Robertson, Western Cape.

Life O2 (USA) a natural spring mineral water brand.

Lifestyle (S.Afr) the label for a red wine (Cabernet sauvignon, Merlot, Pinotage and Shiraz blend) produced by the Simonsvlei International winery, Suider-Paarl, Western Cape.

Lifestyle-Duet (S.Afr) the label for a soft, red wine made from (Cabernet sauvignon 45% and Pinotage 55%) produced by the Nederburg Estate, Wellington, Western Cape.

Liger (Fr) the old French name for the Loire.

Ligero (Sp) denotes a light Sherry.

Light (Eng) a term for wine which lacks body or is low in alcohol.

Light Ale (Eng) a low-gravity bottled ale, light in body but not in colour.

Light Ale (Euro) describes ales (beers) which are light in colour. *See also* Lite Beer.

Light and Bitter (Eng) half bottled light ale and half draught bitter ale.

Light and Dark (Eng) a mixture of half Guinness and half light ale.

Light Beer (USA) a low calorie lager-type beer 3.5%–4% alc by vol.

Light Beverage (USA) a name for natural still wine.

Light-Bodied Rums (USA) the name given to white rums and light-coloured rums. Has only a light molasses flavour: Cuban, Dominican Republic, Haitian, Hawaiian, Mexican, Philippine, Puerto Rican, Venezuelan and Virgin Isles.

Light Brigade (Eng) a 4.2% alc by vol. ale brewed by the Leyden Brewery, Lancashire.

Light Dinner Ale (Austr) a green-labelled, low-gravity ale 3.8% alc by vol. brewed by the Cooper's Brewery in South Australia.

Lightfoot (Eng) a 3.7% alc by vol. pale coloured ale from Theakston, Masham, Ripon, North Yorkshire. Bottled version is 5.2% alc by vol.

Light Hart Rum (Jam) a brand-name rum 40% alc by vol.

Lighthouse (Eng) a middle gravity beer brewed by Burt's Brewery, Ventnor, Isle of Wight. *See also* Yachtsman, Needles Bitter, VPA.

Lighthouse (Eng) a 4% alc by vol seasonal ale from the Robinsons Brewery, Cheshire.

Light Muscat (USA) *see* California Light Muscat.

Light Oxford (Eng) a bottled light ale 1032 O.G. brewed by the Morrell Brewery of Oxford.

Light Rum (W.Ind) denotes rums which are light in body as opposed to colour. May be white to silver/gold and aged 3 years or more. Coloured with caramel and pot-stilled. i.e. Cuban, Puerto Rican and Virgin Isles.

Light Summer Beer (Eng) a 5% alc by vol. bottle conditioned wheat beer brewed by St. Austell Brewery, Cornwall.

Light Whiskey (USA) a whiskey produced in USA of 160°–189° US proof on or after 26th January 1968. Stored in used or uncharred new oak containers and also includes mixtures of such whiskies.

Light Wines (Eng) a term which indicates wines of table wine strength not more than 14% alc by vol. A heavy wine duty does not have to be paid.

Light Year (Eng) a 3.9% alc by vol. ale brewed by the Glentworth Brewery, South Yorkshire.

Ligist (Aus) a wine-producing area in the Weststeiermark.

Lignell and Piispanen (Fin) a noted distilling company that produces Karpi, Mesimarja, Suomurrain and Tapio liqueurs.

Lignes (Fr) cork measure (24 lignes = 54 centimetres).

Lignières-Sonneville (Fr) a commune in the Charente département whose grapes are classed Grande Champagne (Cognac).

Lignification (Eng) the name given to the maturing of the wood on the vine.

Lignins (Eng) obtained from the wooden barrels into wine, soluble in ethanol.

Lignorelles (Fr) a commune in the A.C. Chablis, Burgundy.

Ligny-le-Châtel (Fr) a commune in the A.C. Chablis, Burgundy.

Ligte Droë (S.Afr) light dry.

Liguria (It) the smallest region, it borders France, Piemonte, Emilia-Romagna and Tuscany. To south is the Tyrrhenian sea. The Cinque Terre is part of it. Wines are Cinqueterre, Cinqueterre Sciacchetra, Coronata, Dolceacqua, Polcevera, Rossese di Dolceaqua and Vermentino Ligure.

Likendeeler Spreewald Bitter (Ger) a herbal digestif liqueur made from roots, berries, herbs, spices by Cottbus Spirituosen Spezialitäten in Cottbus, Brandenburg 22% alc by vol.

Likeur (Hol) liqueur.

Likier (Pol) liqueur.

Likier Ziolowy (Pol) a herb liqueur produced by Polmos.

Likør (Den) liqueur/cordial.

Likör (Tur) liqueur.

Likor Kohz Bouchinot (Fr) a sweet, grapey, green liqueur, mainly sold and consumed in Brittany.

Likörwein (Ger) a term for dessert wines. e.g. Trockenbeerenauslese.

Lilac Seal (Ger) a brand of Bernkasteler QbA. wine produced by Deinhard in Koblenz.

Lilalack (Ger) an auslesen wine from the 'Herrgottströpfchen' range of wines of Jakob Gerhardt, Nierstein.

Lilbert [Georges et Fils] (Fr) a Champagne

producer. (Add): 51200 Épernay. Produces vintage and non-vintage wines.

Lilibet's Best (Eng) a 4.5% alc by vol. best bitter beer brewed by the Belvoir Brewery, Leicestershire.

Lilienfeldberg (Aus) a vineyard site on the banks of the River Danube in the Kremstal region.

Lillehammer Brewery (Nor) a noted brewery based in central Norway.

Lillet (Fr) an apéritif wine, (red or white) fortified with Armagnac, herbs, fruit and white Bordeaux wine. Produced in Bordeaux 17% alc by vol. and matured in Slav oak.

Lillet-Citron (Cktl) 60mls (½ gill) Lillet (blanc), 20mls (⅙ gill) sirop de citron, soda water. Stir over ice and strain into a highball glass with ice.

Lillet Cocktail (Cktl) ⅔ measure Lillet (rouge), ⅓ measure gin. Stir over ice, strain into a cocktail glass and top with a twist of lemon peel juice.

Lillibrooke Manor (Eng) wine estate in Berkshire noted for Ehrenfelser.

Lillydale Vineyards (Austr) a winery. (Add): Davross Court, Seville Off Warburton Highway, Yarra Valley. Grape varieties: Chardonnay, Cabernet sauvignon, Merlot, Noble riesling, Pinot noir, Traminer. Website: http://www.mcwilliams.com.au

Lillypilly Estate (Austr) a winery based in Riverina, New South Wales.

Lil Naue Cocktail (Cktl) ½ measure brandy, ¼ measure Port, ¼ measure apricot brandy, dash gomme syrup, 1 egg yolk. Shake well over ice, strain into a 125mls (5fl.oz) goblet and top with powdered cinnamon.

Lilt (Eng) a sparkling non-alcoholic pineapple and grapefruit drink produced by the C.C.S.B. Also a diet version produced.

Lily Cocktail (Cktl) ½ measure dry gin, ½ measure Lillet, ⅓ measure crème de noyau, dash lemon juice. Shake over ice and strain into a cocktail glass.

Lima (Port) a wine district of the Entre Minho e Douro region. Produces both red and white wines of the Vinho Verde style.

Limarí Valley (Chile) a wine district based in northern Chile.

Limassol (Cyp) the main wine town. Situated in the south-east of the island and is Greek-Cypriot controlled. Most of the Island's wineries are based there. Keo, Sodap, Haggipavlo, Etko.

Limberg (Aus) a vineyard site on the banks of the River Danube in the Kremstal region.

Limberger (Ger) a red grape variety also grown in most western European countries. Known as the Blauer Limberger and Blaufränkirsch. Lemberger is an alternative spelling used in Washington State.

Limbo (Cktl) 25mls (1fl.oz) peach brandy, 100mls (4fl.ozs) pineapple juice. Serve over ice in a highball glass.

Limbo (S.Afr) a brand of cane spirit flavoured with lemon juice, is produced under licence from König of Western Germany.

Limbo Cooler (Cktl) 25mls (1fl.oz) dark rum, 20mls (¾ fl.oz) Amer Picon, 50mls (2fl.ozs) lemon juice, 3 dashes grenadine. Shake over ice with an orange slice, strain into a goblet filled with crushed ice, stir in 7-UP, decorate with an orange slice, cherry and stirrer.

Limbo Drummer (W.Ind) a brand of rum produced in Trinidad by the Trinidad Distillers Ltd.

Limburg (Ger) vineyard (Anb): Baden. (Ber): Kaiserstuhl-Tuniberg. (Gro): Vulkanfelsen. (Vil): Sasbach.

Lime (Eng) *Citrus aurantifolia* a major fruit variety, the juice of which is used in many cocktails. Has a green skin (zest). (Den) = grøn citron/lime, (Fr) = citron vert.

Limeade (USA) a non-alcoholic drink made from sweetened lime juice and carbonated water.

Limeade (USA) 3 teaspoons sugar, juice of 4 limes. Dissolve in a highball glass, fill with ice and top with soda water, top with a slice of lime and a cherry and serve with straws.

Lime Blossom Tea (Eng) a herbal tea which is good for colds.

Limeburners Bay Vineyards (N.Z) a 12ha vineyard. (Add): 112 Hobsonville Road, Hobsonville. Noted for dessert Cabernet sauvignon.

Lime Cordial (Eng) a preparation of concentrated lime juice and sugar of which the Rose's brand is the most famous.

Lime Giant Cocktail (Cktl) 25mls (⅛ gill) vodka, 20mls (⅙ gill) lime cordial, juice of a lime. Shake over ice, strain into an ice-filled highball glass, top with soda water and a slice of lime.

Lime Juice (Eng) the juice of fresh limes used as a flavouring in drinks and cocktails. (Den) = saft af lime, (Fr) = jus de citron vert .

Lime Juicer (Eng) a nineteenth century nickname for British sailors because they had to drink lime juice to ward off scurvy, the American term 'Limey' derives from this.

Lime Lager (USA) a lager beer flavoured with lime and brewed by the Lone Star Brewery, San Antonio, Texas.

Lime Lite (W.Ind) a lime-flavoured diet lager 3.5% alc by vol. brewed in Barbados.

Limerick (S.Afr) the label for a white wine (Chenin blanc & Sauvignon blanc blend) produced by the Bottelary Hills Wine winery, Stellenbosch, Western Cape.

Lime Road 1481 (S.Afr) the label for a red wine (Cabernet sauvignon, Merlot and Shiraz blend) produced by the Havana Hills winery, Philadelphia, Western Cape.

Lime Rose (Cktl)(Non-alc) ⅓ egg white, ½ measure lemon cordial, 1 measure lime juice cordial. Shake well over ice and strain into a cocktail glass.

Limestone (Eng) *see* Soils.

Limestone (USA) a flavoured apéritif produced by the Enz Vineyards in San Benito, California.

Limestone Cocktail (Cktl) 1 measure Bourbon whiskey, ¼ measure dry gin, 2 dashes gomme syrup, juice ½ lemon. Shake over ice, strain into an ice-filled highball glass, top with soda and squeeze of lemon peel juice.

Limestone Hill (S.Afr) the label for a white wine (Chardonnay) produced by the De Wetshof Estate winery, Robertson, Western Cape.

Limestone Ridge Vineyard (Austr) a part of the Lindemans Vineyards. New South Wales. 22ha. planted Shiraz, 2ha. planted Cabernet.

Limey (Cktl)(Non-alc) 25mls (1fl.oz) lime juice, 10mls (½ fl.oz) lemon juice, ½ egg white. Shake with ice and strain into a cocktail glass.

Limey (USA) the nickname given to Englishmen because they used lime juice with their gin. *See also* Lime Juicer.

Limey Cocktail (Cktl) ⅖ measure white rum, ⅖ measure lime cordial, ⅕ measure Cointreau, juice of a lime. Blend together with scoop of crushed ice, pour into a flute glass and top with a twist of lime peel juice.

Limings (W.Ind) the name given to the scum that forms on the surface of the molasses during sugar extraction in rum production.

Limited Release (S.Afr) the label for a range of wines produced by the La Bri winery, Franschhoek, Western Cape.

Limited Release (S.Afr) the label for a range of wines produced by the Kanu Wines winery, Stellenbosch, Western Cape.

Limited Release (S.Afr) the label for a white wine (Gewürztraminer) from the Isabela range produced by the Thirtytwo [32] South Ltd winery, Stellenbosch, Western Cape.

Limnio (Gre) a dark skinned grape variety grown on the Halkidiki Peninsula, Macedonia and on Limnos.

Limnos (Gre) an island in the Aegean Islands of eastern Greece. Produces A.O.Q.S. dry white wine, plus A.O.C. dessert wines. Both from Muscat d'Alexandrie grape. Also spelt Lemnos.

Limoensap (Hol) lime juice.

Limon (Eng) a carbonated, lemon-flavoured, low calorie soft drink produced by Schweppes.

Limonada (Port)(Sp) lemonade.

Limonade (Aus)(Fr)(Ger)(Hol) lemonade.

Limonade Gazeuse (Fr) fizzy (sparkling) lemonade.

Limonadier (Fr) a mediaeval seller of non-alcoholic drinks.

Limonata (It)(Tur) lemonade.

Limoncini (Fr) a 25% alc by vol. lemon liqueur produced by Marie Brizzard, Bordeaux.

Limone (It) flavour of lemon.

Limonesco (It) light sparkling Sicilian lemon and grape drink 4% alc by vol.

Limonnaya (Rus) a vodka infused with lemon peel 40% alc by vol.

Limosin (S.Afr) the brand-name of a brandy produced by Castle Wine and Green.

Limounade (Ch.Isles) lemonade.

Limousin (Fr) a special oak from the Limousin forests that is used to make the casks for maturing Cognac.

Limoux (Fr) an A.C. sparkling wine from the Gaillac, Languedoc region.

Limpas (It) a natural spring mineral water from Limpas, Sardinia.

Limpia (It) a sparkling natural spring mineral water from Limpia, San Pellegrino Terme. Mineral contents (milligrammes per litre): Sodium 0.42mg/l, Calcium 48mg/l, Magnesium 23.3mg/l, Potassium 0.09mg/l, Bicarbonates 244mg/l, Chlorides 0.78mg/l, Sulphates 9.4mg/l, Nitrates 4.2mg/l, Silicates 1.2mg/l. pH 7.79

Limpid (Eng) a term used to describe a wine with a clear appearance.

Limpidity (Eng) a description of sight in wine tasting, denotes outstanding brightness and clarity.

Limpio (Sp) describes a clean Sherry.

Limunada (Cro) lemonade/lemon squash.

Linarelle (It) a natural spring mineral water from Vernoli, Lecce.

Lincoln College (N.Z) a research college based at Canterbury, South Island that produces experimental wines.

Lincoln Green (Scot) a canned lager brewed entirely without additives using specially malted barley and organically grown German hops. 4.5% alc by vol. Brewed at the Belhaven Brewery, Dunbar, East Lothian. Canned by Thwaites.

Lincolnshire Hot Stuff (Eng) a cask ale brewed by Bateman's Brewery, Wainfleet, Lincolnshire.

Lincoln Winery (N.Z) a winery. (Add): 130 Lincoln Road, Henderson, North Island. 35ha. Grape varieties: Cabernet sauvignon, Chardonnay, Chenin blanc, Merlot, Riesling, Sauvignon blanc. Noted for dry Sherry-style wine. Also has 18ha. at Riverlea.

Lincourt (USA) a winery based in the Santa Barbara County, California. Grape variety: Pinot noir.

Linda (Cktl) ¼ measure gin, ¼ measure crème de cassis, ¼ measure crème de banane, measure lemon juice. Shake over ice and strain into a cocktail glass.

Linda (It) a carbonated natural mineral water. (Add): Tavina S.p.A. Nello Stabilimento di Salò, Brescia. Mineral contents (milligrammes per litre): Sodium 9.5mg/l, Calcium 84.8mg/l, Magnesium 25.3mg/l, Potassium 2.1mg/l, Bicarbonates 366mg/l, Chlorides 8.3mg/l, Sulphates 26.5mg/l, Silicate 15.8mg/l. pH 7.2

Linda And Stephen Wedding Ale (Eng) a commemorative ale brewed by the Heritage Brewery at Burton-on-Trent.

Lindau (Ger) an untergebiete of the Bayern district.

Lindauer (N.Z) the brand-name used by Montana wines for their bottle-fermented, sparkling wines using Chardonnay, Chenin blanc, Pinotage and Pinot noir grapes (brut or sec/white/rosé).

Lindeboom Bierouwerij BV (Hol) a brewery. (Add): Engelmanstraat 54, Postbus 54, 6086 ZG Neer. Brews a variety of beers including Lindeboom Lente Bock 6.5% alc by vol. Website: http://www.lindeboom.nl

Lindeboom Lente Bock (Hol) a 6.5% alc by vol. bottled bock beer brewed by De Lindeboom Brouwerij, Neer, Limburg.

L

Lindelbach (Ger) village (Anb): Baden. (Ber): Badische Frankenland. (Gro): Tauberklinge. (Vin): Ebenrain.

Lindelberg (Ger) grosslage (Anb): Württemberg. (Ber): Württembergisch Unterland. (Vils): Adolzfurt, Bretzfeld, Dimbach, Eschelbach, Geddelsbach, Harsberg (ortsteil Neuholz), Kesselfeld, Langenbeutingen, Maienfels, Michelbach a. W., Obersöllbach, Pfedelbach, Siebeneich, Schwabbach, Unterheimbach, Untersteinbach, Verrenberg, Waldbach, Windischenbach.

Lindemans (Austr) a winery. (Add): 31 Nyrang Street, Lidcombe, New South Wales 2141. 900ha. in Hunter River Valley, Padthaway, Coonawarra and Karadoc areas. Grape varieties: Cabernet sauvignon, Chardonnay, Shiraz. See also Pyrus.

Lindeman's Brasserie (Bel) a farmhouse brewery at Vlezenbeek. Produces wild lambic beers, usually exported to France and USA.

Lindeman's Cream (Austr) a fortified wine, a sweet Sherry-type made at Corowa on the river Murray.

Lindeman's Karadoc (Austr) a winery (established 1974). (Add): Karadoc Road, Karadoc, Victoria. Produces red, white and fortified wines.

Lindenblättriger (Aus) an ancient white grape variety that is rarely grown nowadays.

Lindenblättriger (Ger) an alternative name for the Hárslevelü.

Lindener Gilde-Bräu (Ger) a bottled diät pils 1050 O.G. brewed by the Lindener-Gilde Brauerei in Hanover and imported into the U.K. by the Thwaites Brewery, Blackburn, Lancashire.

Lindener-Gilde Brauerei (Ger) a brewery based in Hanover. Noted for malty beers, especially Brozhan Alt, a beer named after a famous Hanover brewmaster of the sixteenth century. Also Ratskeller Edel Pils.

Linden Estate Winery (N.Z) a winery. (Add): SH5, Napier/Taupo Highway, Eskdale, Napier. 21ha. Grape varieties: Cabernet sauvignon, Sauvignon blanc, Chardonnay, Gewürztraminer, Merlot.

Lindenfest (Ger) a Rheingau wine festival held at Geisenheim in July.

Linde Vineyards (S.Afr) a winery (established 1998) based in Tulbagh, Western Cape. 14ha. Grape varieties: Cabernet sauvignon, Chardonnay, Merlot, Shiraz.

Lindhorst Wines (S.Afr) a winery (established 1996) based in Suider-Paarl, Western Cape. 18ha. Grape varieties: Cabernet sauvignon, Merlot, Pinotage, Shiraz. Labels: Maz's Shiraz, Statement. Website: http://www.lindhorstwines.com

Lindisfarne (Eng) a whisky-based honey liqueur produced in Northumberland, north-eastern England.

Lindisfarne (Eng) the name given to a range of fruit-flavoured wines from Lanchester Wine Cellars, Durham. 14.4% alc by vol. Flavours include: apricot, blackberry, cherry, cowslip.

Lindisfarne Ltd (Eng) a distillery and winery (established 1968). (Add): St. Aidan's Winery, Holy Island, Northumberland TD15 2RX.

Produces liqueurs, gin, mead and fruit wines. Website: http://www.lindisfarne-mead.co.uk

Lindiwe Wines (S.Afr) a winery based in Paarl, Western Cape. Grape varieties: Cabernet sauvignon, Chardonnay, Chenin blanc, Merlot, Pinotage, Sauvignon blanc, Shiraz.

Lindóia Bio Leve (Bra) a natural spring mineral water brand.

Lindóia Premium (Bra) a natural spring mineral water (established 1999) from Água de Lindóia. Mineral contents (milligrammes per litre): Sodium 32mg/l, Calcium 17.23mg/l, Magnesium 3.64mg/l, Potassium 4mg/l, Bicarbonates 139.69mg/l, Chlorides 4.11mg/l, Sulphates 6.18mg/l, Fluorides 0.43mg/l, Silicates 19.4mg/l. pH 8.16

Lindores Abbey Malt (Scot) a malt whisky produced in Fife, Scotland. The first recorded reference to the Scottish national drink (a percentage of the profit will go towards the preservation of the Lindores Abbey).

Lindos (Gre) a dry white wine from Rhodes.

Lindóya Fonte Vida (Bra) a natural spring mineral water from Lindóia, San Paolo. Mineral contents (milligrammes per litre): Sodium 5.8mg/l, Calcium 10.6mg/l, Magnesium 5.6mg/l, Potassium 2.2mg/l, Bicarbonates 42.2mg/l, Nitrates 1mg/l. pH 6.3

Lindóya Verão (Bra) a natural spring mineral water from Fonte São José. Mineral contents (milligrammes per litre): Sodium 7.92mg/l, Calcium 16.6mg/l, Magnesium 5.56mg/l, Potassium 2.6mg/l, Bicarbonates 91.97mg/l, Chlorides 4.01mg/l, Sulphates 1.38mg/l, Fluorides 0.045mg/l, Nitrates 8.2mg/l. pH 6.33

Lindridge Ale (Eng) a 4.5% alc by vol. ale brewed by Bank's Brewery, Wolverhampton.

Lindsay's Wimsy (S.Afr) a red wine (Cabernet sauvignon & Pinotage) produced by the Slaley Estate, Stellenbosch, Western Cape.

Line Brandy (USA) a brandy glass which has a line marked on it to show the amount to pour.

Linfit Brewery (Eng) a brewery (established 1982). (Add): Sair Inn, Lane Top, Linthwaite, Huddersfield, West Yorkshire HD7 5SG. Brews a variety of beers including Linfit Mild 1032 O.G.

Linfit Mild (Eng) a cask-conditioned ale 1032 O.G. brewed by the Sair Inn home-brew public house in Linthwaite, Huddersfield, West Yorkshire.

Linfood Cash and Carry (Eng) a company based in Northamptonshire that produces many own-label brands of wines, vermouths and spirits.

Lingen's Blond (Hol) a 2% alc by vol. bottled, low-alcohol mild ale brewed by Heineken Netherlands Brouwerij, Zoeterwoude.

Lingering (Eng) a term used to describe the length of finish of a wine in the mouth.

Lingestière (Fr) a wine-producing district in the A.C. Bellet, Provence, south-eastern France.

Linhälder (Ger) vineyard (Anb): Württemberg. (Ber): Remstal-Stuttgart. (Gro): Wartbühl. (Vil): Stetten i R.

Linie Akvavit (Nor) a brand of Norwegian akvavit produced by A/S Vinmonopolet.

Linkwood (Scot) a single malt whisky distillery based south of Elgin in Speyside. Owned by John McEwan and C°. Ltd. A highland malt. Produces a 12 year old malt 43% alc by vol. 15 year old malt 40% alc by vol (part of the DCL group).

Linsenbusch (Ger) vineyard (Anb): Pfalz. (Ber): Mittelhaardt-Deutsche Weinstrasse. (Gro): Hofstück. (Vil): Ruppertsberg.

Linsenhofen (Ger) village (Anb): Württemberg. (Ber): Remstal-Stuttgart. (Gro): Hohenneuffen. (Vin): Schlossteige.

Linstead (Cktl) ½ measure Scotch whisky, 1 dash pastis, ½ measure pineapple juice. Shake over ice, strain into a cocktail glass and add a twist of lemon peel juice.

Linstead Cocktail (Cktl) 25mls (1fl.oz) Scotch whisky, 25mls (1fl.oz) grapefruit juice, dash absinthe. Shake over ice, strain into a club goblet, add a dash of lemon peel juice and a spiral of peel.

L'Intemporelle (Fr) a Grand Cru vintage Champagne from the Mailly-Champagne co-operative.

Linton Park (Austr) a natural spring mineral water from Upper Yarra Valley. Mineral contents (milligrammes per litre): Sodium 7.8mg/l, Calcium 1.2mg/l, Magnesium 0.84mg/l, Potassium 1.4mg/l, Fluorides <0.1mg/l. pH 6.3

Linton Park Wines (S.Afr) a winery (established 1995) based in Wellington, Western Cape. 89ha. Grape variety: Cabernet sauvignon, Chardonnay, Merlot, Shiraz. Labels: Capell's Court, De Groene Heuvel. Website: http://www.lintonparkwines.co.za

Lintz Estate (N.Z) a 9ha winery. (Add): Kitchener Street, P.O. Box 177, Martinborough. Grape varieties: Merlot, Cabernet sauvignon, Cabernet franc, Syrah, Pinot noir, Gewürztraminer, Chardonnay, Riesling, Optima, Scheurebe.

Linz (Ger) village (Anb): Mittelrhein. (Ber): Rheinburgengau. (Gro): Burg Hammerstein. (Vin): Rheinhöller.

Lion Ale (Afr) a top-fermented, sweet, copper-brown ale brewed by the South African Breweries.

Lion Ales (Eng) a keg bitter 1037 O.G. and Mild 1035 O.G. brewed by the Banks Brewery in Wolverhampton, Staffs.

Lion Ales (Eng) beers brewed by Matthew Brown's Brewery in Blackburn, Lancashire. see Lion Bitter and Lion Mild.

Lion Ales (N.Z) the name of the biggest brewing group in the country.

Lion Beer (Ind) a lager beer 1046 O.G. brewed by the Mohan Meakin Brewery in Simla Hills, Solan.

Lion Beer (N.Z) a beer brewed by the New Zealand Breweries.

Lion Bitter (Eng) a keg bitter beer 1037 O.G. brewed by the Banks Brewery, Wolverhampton, Staffs.

Lion Bitter (Eng) a cask-conditioned bitter 1036 O.G. brewed by Camerons Brewery in Hartlepool.

Lion Bitter (Eng) a bitter ale 1036 O.G. brewed by Matthew Brown's Brewery, Blackburn, Lancashire.

Lion Breweries Auckland (N.Z) a brewery. (Add): 111 Carlton Gore Road, P.O. Box 23, Newmarket, Auckland. Brews a variety of beers and lagers Lion Brown 1036 O.G., Lion red 1036 O.G. Website: http://www.lion-nathan.com

Lion Brewery (Eng) see Camerons Brewery.

Lion Brewery (USA) a brewery based in Wilkes-Barre, Pennsylvania. Brews under the Bartels, Gibbons and Liebotschaner labels.

Lion Brown/Red Beer (N.Z) copper-coloured, sweet beers 1036 O.G. highly carbonated beers brewed by the New Zealand Breweries.

Lionel Bruck (Fr) a Burgundy négociant based in Nuits-Saint-Georges, Côte de Nuits, Burgundy. (Add): 6, Quai Dumorey, 21700 Nuits-Saint-Georges.

Lion Cub (Eng) a 4.1% alc by vol. ale brewed by Bobs Brewing Company Ltd., West Yorkshire.

Lionheart (Eng) a 4.5% alc by vol. ale brewed by the Hampshire Brewery, Andover, Hampshire.

Lionheart (Eng) a 4.3% alc by vol. ale brewed by Greene King.

Lion Lager (Afr) a sweet lager beer brewed by the South African Breweries.

Lion Lager (Sri.L) a lager beer 1042 O.G. brewed by the Ceylon Brewery.

Lion Mild (Eng) a keg mild beer 1035 O.G. brewed by the Banks Brewery, Wolverhampton, Staffs.

Lion Mild (Eng) a mild ale 1031 O.G. brewed by Matthew Brown's Brewery, Blackburn, Lancashire.

Lion Nathan (Austr) a brewery based in Sydney. Brews Hahn Premium Lager. Part of New Zealand Breweries in New Zealand, brews Steinlager.

Lions' Drift (S.Afr) the label for a pair of wines (Cabernet sauvignon) and (Ruby cabernet) produced by the Lateganskop Winery, Worcester, Western Cape.

Lion Slayer (Scot) a 4.2% alc by vol. ale brewed by the Fyfe Brewing C°., Fife.

Lion's Pride (Cktl) 1 measure advocaat, ½ measure crème de banane, ½ measure lemon juice, dash crème de cacao, dash egg white. Shake well over ice, strain into a flute glass and top with iced Champagne.

Lions Pride (Eng) a 3.9% alc by vol. ale brewed by the Milestone Brewery C°., Nottinghamshire.

Lion Stout (Sri L) a premium stout 7.5% alc by vol. from the Ceylon Brewery.

Lion Super (N.Z) a strong, hoppy, golden lager beer 1045 O.G. brewed by the New Zealand Breweries.

Liosta Fionta (Ire) wine list.

Lipari Islands (It) see Aeolian Islands.

Lipburg (Ger) village (Anb): Baden. (Ber): Markgräflerland. (Gro): Burg Neuenfels. (Vin): Kirchberg.

Lipova (Rum) a natural spring mineral water from Lippa/Lipova, Transylvania.

Lipovina (Czec) a white grape variety used in the making of Czec 'Tokay'. (Hun) = Hárslevelü.

Lipovitan B3 (Jap) an energy drink produced using taurine, caffeine, triple vitamin B complex and royal jelly extract by Taisho Pharmaceutical.

L

Liquefacere (Lat) lit: 'to make liquid' or 'dissolve', from which the word 'liqueur' derives.

Liqueur (Eng) an alcoholic beverage made from either distilled fruit wines, flavoured spirits (herbs, spices, fruits), sweetened and used as a cocktail additive or digestif. *See also* Sweetened Spirits. (Den) = likør, (Fr) = liqueur/digestif, (It) = liquore, (Port) = licor, (Sp) = licore, (USA) = cordial.

Liqueur (Eng) a bottled barley wine 1072 O.G. brewed by the Castletown Brewery, Isle of Man.

Liqueur (Fr) cordial/liqueur.

Liqueur and Cocktail Orientated Seminars (Eng) *abbr:* L.A.C.O.S. Training sessions held by the De Kuyper Cº. to promote and improve knowledge of liqueurs and cocktails.

Liqueur aux Fraises (Bel) a liqueur made from Wépion strawberries by Distilleries Associées Belges at Jumet.

Liqueur Coffee (Eng) 1 measure of spirit or liqueur, 1 cube of sugar to taste, hot freshly brewed black coffee, cream. Place a teaspoon into a large paris goblet, add sugar if required. Pour in coffee (¾ full) and stir to dissolve sugar if used. Is best if stirred clockwise 6 times, then once anti-clockwise this prevents causing a whirl-pool in the glass. Add spirit/liqueur then pour in cream (lightly whipped helps it to float) into the '**bowl**' of teaspoon placed over the coffee. *see* Café Amaretto.

Liqueur d'Angélique (Fr) a liqueur made with Cognac and angelica.

Liqueur de Château (Swe) a liqueur that contains some of the élixir made at Grenoble by Chartreuse. Produced by Aktiebolaget Vin & Spritcentralem.

Liqueur de Citron (Fr) lemon liqueur (see Limoncini).

Liqueur de Frère Jean (Fr) *see* Aiguebelle.

Liqueur de Gentiane Sauvage (Fr) a green-coloured bitter aperitif 16% alc by vol. produced from wild gentiane. (Add): Route de Paris 14120 Mondeville.

Liqueur de Grand Saint Bernard (Switz) a pale green, honey liqueur which is flavoured with local seeds and flowers.

Liqueur de Jus de Noix Vertes (Fr) a green, walnut-based liqueur produced by Denoix of Brive.

Liqueur de Sapins (Fr) a spicey liqueur made in Pontarlier in the Jura flavoured with pine needle extract.

Liqueur des Moines (Fr) a liqueur made from aromatic plants and Cognac, yellow in colour.

Liqueur des Pins (Fr) *see* Sapindor.

Liqueur de Tirage (Fr) another name for Dosage, a sugar syrup added to Champagne before it is bottled for its second fermentation in bottle (has the potential to produce 1.5% alc. by vol).

Liqueur d'Expédition (Fr) the sugar and old wine that is added to Champagne after dégorgement. *see* Brut, Demi-Sec, Sec and Doux.

Liqueur d'Hendaye (Fr) a herbal liqueur produced near Bayonne, south-western France.

Liqueur d'Or (Fr) a lemon-flavoured clear liqueur with a slight herb flavour that has gold flakes floating in it 43% alc by vol. *see* Goldwasser.

Liqueur Frappé (Cktl) a measure of liqueur of choice, poured into a cocktail glass over shaved ice and served with small straws.

Liqueur Jaune (Fr) a yellow herbal liqueur produced in north-eastern France.

Liqueur Rum (W.Ind) a term given to rum that has been aged for over six years. *see* Vieux Rum.

Liqueur Sandalera (Austr) a sweet, white, wood-aged liqueur-style dessert wine produced by Sandalford, Western Australia.

Liqueur Scotch Whisky (Scot) a blended aged Scotch whisky with a high proportion of malts in its blend.

Liqueurs Jaunes (Fr) yellow liqueurs, herb-flavoured and sweet. e.g. Chartreuse. *See also* Liqueurs Vertes.

Liqueur Stomachique (Fr) a brand of élixir produced by Picard et Cazot Fils in Lyon, central-eastern France.

Liqueurs Vertes (Fr) green liqueurs, herb-flavoured, usually dry. e.g. Bénédictine, Chartreuse and Vieille Cure. *See also* Liqueurs Jaunes.

Liqueur Teas (Eng) a tea that is blended with the aroma of a fine liqueur Cognac, kirsch, orange brandy, rum, whisky or cream Sherry produced by Frametime of London.

Liqueur Verdelho (Austr) an aged Madeira-style fortified wine (approx. 18 years old) from the Jane Brook Estate, Western Australia.

Liqueur Watermelon (Fr) a watermelon-flavoured liqueur 18% alc by vol produced by Joseph Cartron. Website: http://www.cartron.fr

Liqueur Wines (E.C) the name for fortified wines.

Liquid Bread (Euro) the name given to beer by monks during the period of Lent during the Middle Ages.

Liquid Coffee (Eng) the name given to the water-soluble solids derived from roasted coffee.

Liquid Gold (Eng) a 4.1% alc by vol. ale contained in a golden cask, brewed by Belvoir Brewery, Leicester for Nottingham Campaign for Real Ale festival.

Liquid Gold (Eng) the nickname given to bottled mineral waters by the licensed trade because of its high selling price.

Liquid Lobotomy Stout (Eng) an 8% alc by vol. strong stout brewed by the Garton Brewery, East Yorkshire.

Liquid Lunch (Eng) a 4.6% alc by vol. bitter beer brewed by the Barum Brewery, Devon.

Liquidus (Lat) liquid.

Liqui Fruit (S.Afr) a 100% fruit juice blend, available as blackcurrant, mango, orange and other fruits also strawberry and other fruits. Produced by Liqui Fruit, Gillooly's View, Osbourne Lane, Bedfordview.

Liqui Spritz (S.Afr) a mix of 15% fruit juice and purified sparkling water. Available as: ruby grapefruit, tropical kiwi and strawberry. Produced by Liqui Fruit, Gillooly's View, Osbourne Lane,

Bedfordview.

Liquor (Eng) alcoholic beverages. (Aus) = spirituosen, (Fr) = boisson alcoolique, (Ger) = spirituosen, (Sp) = licor.

Liquor (Eng) the name for water used in the brewing process.

Liquor (Den) spirits.

Liquor Beirao (Port) a medicinal (herb) liqueur from J. Carranca Redonda Lda. of Lousan. 29% alc by vol.

Liquor Bernardinus (Fr) an old herb liqueur produced by the Cistercian monks at Citeaux in the seventeenth century (now no longer produced).

Liquor Boys (S.Afr) the label for a range of wines produced by the Oranjerivier Wine Cellars winery, Lower Orange, Northern Cape.

Liquor Control Board of Ontario (Can) *abbr:* L.C.B.O. a rare wines and spirits shop. All wines and spirits in Canada are sold by the Government monopoly (wineries can sell direct).

Liquor de Yervas (Sp) a green herbal liqueur made in the Balearic Islands.

Liquore (It) liqueur.

Liquore Carthusia (It) a liqueur made in Capri by Carthusian monks flavoured with herbs.

Liquore di Limone (It) lemon liqueur.

Liquore Galliano (It) *see* Galliano.

Liquore Santa Vittoria (It) a herb liqueur.

Liquoreux (Fr) a term to describe a sweet fortified wine which has retained much of its natural sugar. Such a wine would be 3° Baumé or more.

Liquore Vallombrosa (It) a herb liqueur.

Liquoroso Dolce Naturale (It) fortified, naturally sweet wine.

Liquoroso Secco (It) fortified dry wine.

Liquors C°. of America (USA) bottlers of Gecht (A) de luxe brandy.

Liquor Up (USA) a slang term for '*to be drunk*'.

Liquoureux (Fr) a wine which is rich and sweet.

Lirac (Fr) an A.C. district in the Rhône. Produces red, rosé and white wines. (Coms): St. Laurent des Arbres, St. Genies-de-Comolas, Roquemaure. Minimum alc by vol. 11%.

Lirac Rouge Classique (Fr) a red A.C. Lirac produced on the Garrigues by J.C. Assmat of Roquemaure, Gard. Grape varieties: Cinsault, Grenache.

Lirralirra Estate (Austr) a winery (established 1981) based at Paynes Road, Lilydale, Yarra Valley. Grape varieties: Cabernet sauvignon, Sauvignon blanc, Sémillon.

Lisbon (Port) a region where the vines are ungrafted. Famous for Setúbal.

Lisbon Port (Port) a Port-style wine produced in Lisbon. Now no longer allowed due to the Portuguese wine laws introduced in the early 1900's.

Lisbon Wine (USA) denotes Portuguese wines that are shipped from Lisbon in Portugal.

Lisiel (It) a natural spring mineral water from Crodo, Verbania.

Lisini Estate (It) a winery based in Montalcino,

Tuscany. Noted for its Prefillossero.

Lis Neris (It) a winery based in San Lorenzo Isontino in the Friuli-Venezia-Guilia region. Grape varieties include: Chardonnay, Pinot grigio, Riesling, Sauvignon blanc, Traminer. Labels: Gris, Jurosa, Lis. Website: http://www.lisneris.it

Lison Pramaggiore (It) a D.O.C. wine producing area in north-eastern Veneto.

Liss (Aus) a vineyard site based on the banks of the River Kamp situated in the Kamptal region.

Lissa (It) a natural spring mineral water (established 1973) from Posina. Mineral contents (milligrammes per litre): Sodium 0.9mg/l, Calcium 36mg/l, Magnesium 19mg/l, Potassium 0.5mg/l, Bicarbonates 189mg/l, Chlorides 1mg/l, Sulphates 15mg/l.

Listán Negro (Sp) a red grape variety grown in Lacoronte-Acentejo (an island off Tenerife), Canary Islands. Also known as Almuñeco.

Listán Palomino (Sp) a white grape used in the making of Sherry. Parent of Chasan.

Listel (Fr) a large Camargue estate in the Midi owned by Salins du Midi. Produces red, rosé and dry white wines. *see* Listel Gris.

Listel Gris (Fr) a Vin des Sables du Golfe du Lion rosé wine produced by the Salins du Midi.

Listofka (Rus) a blackcurrant-flavoured apéritif.

Listrac (Fr) an A.C. commune in the Haut-Médoc, north-western Bordeaux.

Listrao (Mad) a white grape variety used in the making of Madeira.

Litana (Aus) a winery based in Gösing, Donauland. (Add): Berggasse 1, 3482 Gösing. Grape varieties include: Grüner veltliner, Riesling, Welschriesling, Zweigelt. Produces a range of dry and sweet red and white wines.

Litchborough (Eng) *see* Liddington.

Litcheur (Ch.Isles) alcoholic liquor. *See also* Beuv'rie.

Lite Beer (USA) a beer that has a lower calorie content than normal beers. *See also* Light Ale.

Liter (USA) the American spelling of litre (0.26417 US gallon).

Literninum (It) a red wine produced in central-western Italy in Roman times.

Lithgow Valley (Austr) a natural spring mineral water (established 1893). Mineral contents (milligrammes per litre): Sodium 2.3mg/l, Calcium 0.39mg/l, Magnesium 0.65mg/l, Potassium 0.61mg/l, Bicarbonates <6mg/l, Chlorides 4mg/l, Sulphates 3mg/l, Fluorides <0.1mg/l.

Lithiated Water (Eng) a water rich in lithia salts. e.g. Baden-Baden, Carsbad, St. Marco, Salvator.

Lithinia (Rum) a still and sparkling natural spring mineral water (established 1890) from Tamaseu-Pahida, Transylvania. Mineral contents (milligrammes per litre): Sodium 166mg/l, Calcium 53.7mg/l, Magnesium 15.7mg/l, Potassium 1.3mg/l, Bicarbonates 673mg/l, Chlorides 9mg/l, Sulphates <1mg/l, Fluorides 0.33mg/l, Nitrates 0.4mg/l, Lithium 1.2mg/l. pH 7.1

Litomerice (Czec) a wine-producing town near

L

Prague on the river Elbe.

Litomerice Brewery (Czec) an old brewery based in Litomerice, northern Czec.

Litoral (Arg) a wine region that joins the provinces of Santa Fe and Buenos Aires.

Litovel Brewery (Czec) a brewery based in northern Czec.

Litr (Wal) litre.

Litre (Euro) liquid metric measure 1.76 pints. (USA) = liter, (Wal) = litr.

Litres of Absolute Alcohol (Eng) *abbr*: L.P.A. An expression used for measuring a given quantity of alcohol in a given quantity of spirit. Also seen as H.L.P.A.

Litron (Fr) an old measure of approximately 0.8 litre.

Little Boy (Eng) a special ale brewed to commemorate VJ day (named after the atom bomb) by the Steampacket Brewery, West Yorkshire.

Liitle Creatures Brewing (Austr) a brewery. (Add): 40 mews Road, Fremantle 6160. Brews a range of beers. Website: http://www.littlecreatures.com.au 'E'mail: email@littlecreatures.com.au

Little Devil (Cktl) ⅔ measure Cointreau, ⅓ measure Bacardi White Label, ⅓ measure dry gin, juice ¼ lemon. Shake over ice and strain into a cocktail glass.

Little Jem (Eng) a cask-conditioned ale brewed by the Six Bells Brewery, Bishop's Castle, Shropshire.

Little John (Eng) a bottled strong ale 1070 O.G. brewed by the Home Brewery, Nottingham.

Little John Myth (Eng) the name for a beer brewed by the Alcazar Brewery, Nottinghamshire.

Little Karoo (S.Afr) a major wine-producing area which stretches from Drakenstein to the Swartberg mountains. Produces mainly sweet Muscatel wines and brandy. Also called Klein Karoo.

Little Kings Cream Ale (USA) a 5% alc by vol. bottom-fermented, golden yellow, bottled mild ale brewed by The Schoenling Brewery, Cincinnatti.

Little Lambswick (Eng) a cask-conditioned ale from Marston's Head Brewers' Choice.

Little Lumphammer (Eng) a standard cask ale brewed by Allied Breweries.

Littlemill (Scot) a single lowland malt whisky distillery near Bowling in Dumbartonshire. Owned by Barton Distilling C°. Produces an 8 year old malt. 43% alc by vol. Part of Amalgamated Distilled Products.

Little Nigel (Eng) a local cider with an alc by vol. of 7.5%–8.5% produced by home-brew pub the Swan, Aston Munslow.

Little Pook Hill (Eng) a vineyard (established 1971) based at Burwash Weald, Sussex. 1.9ha. Grape varieties: Müller-Thurgau, Reichensteiner and others.

Little Princess (Cktl) ½ measure white rum, ½ measure sweet vermouth. Stir over ice and strain into a cocktail glass.

Little River (S.Afr) the label for a red wine (Cabernet sauvignon and Shiraz blend) produced by the De Meye Wines winery, Stellenbosch, Western Cape.

Little Scotney Ale (Eng) a 4% alc by vol. ale brewed by the Westerham Brewery C°. Ltd., Kent.

Little Wine (Ger) carafe wine.

Littorai (USA) a winery based in the Anderson Valley, Mendocino County, California. Also vineyards in Sonoma Coast. Grape variety: Pinot noir. Label: Hirsch Vineyard, Savoy Vineyard.

Littoral Orb-Hérault (Fr) a Vin de Pays area in the Hérault département, southern France. Produces red, rosé and dry white wines.

Liulang (Chi) a natural spring mineral water. Mineral contents (milligrammes per litre): Sodium 21.9mg/l, Calcium 54.3mg/l, Potassium 11.7mg/l, Chlorides 17.7mg/l, Sulphates 42.2mg/l, Silicates 19.6mg/l. pH 8.0

Liulong (Chi) a natural spring mineral water. Mineral contents (milligrammes per litre): Sodium 91.8mg/l, Calcium 35.1mg/l, Magnesium 20.4mg/l, Potassium 1.8mg/l, Silicates 19.8mg/l. pH 7.7

Livadia (Geo) a white muscat dessert wine from the southern Crimea. Also the name of a red wine made from the Cabernet grape.

Live-A-Little (S.Afr) the label for range of a wines produced by the Stellar Winery, Olifants River, Western Cape.

Lively (Eng) the name given to a wine that stimulates the palate with a pleasant acidity and freshness.

Livener Cocktail (Cktl) 25mls (1fl.oz) brandy, 75mls (3fl.ozs) Champagne, 1 teaspoon raspberry syrup, 2 dashes Angostura or lemon juice and stir well in a highball glass with ice.

Live Oaks (USA) a winery based at Hecker Pass, Santa Clara, California. Produces table wines.

Live Organic (Eng) a 4.6% alc by vol. bottle-conditioned organic ale brewed by Brakspear at the Griffith Brewery, Chiswick in London.

Livermore Valley (USA) wine-producing area east of San Francisco in the North Central Coast region. Has gravel soil and produces soft red wines, excellent white wines and sweet dessert wines.

Livernana (It) a red wine produced by Azienda Agricola Livernano in Radda, Tuscany from Merlot, Cabernet, Sangiovese and Carmenère grapes.

Livesey [Joseph] (Eng) the founder of the Temperance Seven in Lancashire in the nineteenth century. Original Pledge signed in Preston.

Liviana (Fr) a natural spring mineral water. Mineral contents (milligrammes per litre): Sodium 0.8mg/l, Calcium 64.9mg/l, Magnesium 17mg/l, Potassium 0.5mg/l, Bicarbonates 252.6mg/l, Chlorides 1.8mg/l, Sulphates 19.5mg/l, Silicates 3.4mg/l.

Livinière [La] (Fr) a village in Minervois awarded A.C. status in 1999. Group of 6 communes. Grape varieties: Syrah, Grenache, Mourvèdre (these equal 60% of planting). Yield: 45 hl/ha. Minimum of 15 months ageing in oak. Wines sold under Cru Livinière.

Livio Felluga (It) a sparkling (metodo tradizionale)

wine producer using Pinot grapes based in Brazzano in the Colli Orientali district of the Friuli-Venezia-Giulia region 135ha.

Livon (It) a winery based in San Giovanni al Natisone in the Friuli-Venezia-Guilia region.

Livre de Cave (Fr) cellar record (stock) book.

Livres (Fr) money used in the eighteenth and nineteenth century often mentioned in old books (wine ledgers, etc.).

Lizard Ales Ltd (Eng) a brewery (established 2004). (Add): Unit 2a, Treskewes Ind Estate, St. Keverne, Helston, Cornwall TR12 6PE. Brews: Bitter 4.2% alc by vol.

Lizard Point (Eng) a 4% alc by vol. organic ale brewed by the Organic Brewery, Cornwall.

Lizas (Gre) a light-coloured, dry brandy.

Lizzano (It) a D.O.C. wine producing region in Southern Puglia. Red wines are produced from 80% Negroamaro grapes.

Lizzarda (It) a natural spring mineral water from Lizzarda.

Ljutomer (Slo) see Lutomer-Ormoz.

Lladoner Pelut (Sp) the Catalonian name for the Grenache, Grenache Poilu or Grenache Velu grape. Also called Tinto Aragonés. see Lledoner Pelut.

Llaeth (Wal) milk.

Llaethferch (Wal) milkmaid.

Llaethwr (Wal) milkman.

Llanerch Vineyard (Wal) a top Welsh vineyard (established 1986). (Add): Hensol, Pendoylan, Vale of Glamorgan. 2.8ha. Produces a variety of wines under the Cariad label. Grape varieties: Bacchus, Huxelrebe, Kernling, Seyval blanc, Reichensteiner, Triomphe d'Alsace.

Llanllyr Water Company (Wal) a natural spring mineral water (established 1999). (Add): Llanllyr, Talsarn, Lampeter, Ceridigion, Dyfed SA48 8QD. Website: http://www.llanllyrwater.com 'E'mail: patrick@llanllyrwater.com

Llano del Maipo (Chile) a central region which produces most of Chile's wines.

Llano Estacado (USA) a small vineyard based in Lubbock, western Texas. 6ha. Produces many grape varieties.

Llanrhystud Vineyard (Wal) a vineyard (established 1973) based at Llanrhystud, Dyfed. 0.3ha. Grape varieties: Madeleine-angevine 10%, Müller-Thurgau 30%, Reichensteiner 10%, Seyval blanc 10% plus others.

Llansoy (Wal) see Brecon Court.

Llava Brewery (Czec) an old brewery based in eastern Czec.

Llebeig (Sp) a south-western wind that blows through the Penedés region in the summer. Also known as the Garbi (a warm wind).

Lledoner Pelut (Fr) a red grape variety grown in the Côtes du Roussillon, south-western France. (Sp) = Lladoner pelut.

Lleno (Sp) describes a Sherry with a foul-smelling bouquet.

Lliber-Jávea (Sp) a Vino Comarcal wine from the province of Alicante in Valencia.

Llicorella (Sp) reddish slate soil found in Tarragona and Priorato which contains small particles of mica/quartzite.

Llords and Elwood Winery (USA) a winery based in Alameda and Santa Clara, California. (H/Q in Los Angeles). Produces most styles of wine.

Lloyd and Trouncer (Wal) a subsidiary company of Ansells set up in 1981. Named after Lloyd, Newport and Trouncer of Shrewsbury.

Lloyd Light (Austr) a noted winery based in Southern Vales, South Australia.

Lloyd's Country Bitter (Eng) see Thompson (John).

Llwncdestun (Wal) a toast.

Llwydni (Wal) mildew.

Llymeltiwr (Wal) drinker of alcoholic beverages/a tippler.

Llyn (Lat) liquor.

Loam Soil (Eng) rich, fertile soil consisting of a mixture of sand, clay and decaying organic material. (Aus) = lamm.

Lobe (Eng) part of a leaf, a vine leaf has five lobes or divisions.

Lobkov (Czec) a 5% alc by vol. beer brewed at the Lobkowicz family brewery in Vysocky Chlumec (120 miles south of Prague). Produced using Bohemian barley, Hallertauer hops and artesian well water.

Lobster Cocktail (Cktl)(Non-alc) make a sauce of tomato juice, grape juice and lemon juice. Add salt, paprika and Worcestershire sauce. Stir over ice, strain and decorate with pieces of lobster in a sherbet glass.

Loburg (Bel) a bottled pilsner lager 5.7% alc by vol. or 1051 O.G. brewed by the Artois Louvain Brasserie.

Loca Blanca (Chile) a local variety of white grape which produces medium white table wines.

Lo-Cal (N.Z) a low-calorie beer 1036 O.G. brewed by the Leopard Brewery.

Local [The] (Eng) a slang term for the nearest public house to a person's home that is used regularly.

Local Bitter (Ch.Isles) a bitter ale 1036 O.G. brewed by the Randall Vautier Brewery in St. Helier, Jersey.

Local Bitter (Eng) a bitter ale 1038 O.G. brewed by the Greenall Whitley Brewery in Warrington, Lancashire.

Local Bitter (Eng) a bitter ale 1037 O.G. brewed by the Shipstone Brewery in Nottingham.

Local Bitter (Eng) a bitter ale 1037 O.G. brewed by the Tisbury Brewery in Wiltshire.

Località (It) the equivalent of the French Cru.

Local Licensing Justices (Eng) see Licensing Justices.

Local Line (Eng) a cask-conditioned ale 1038 O.G. brewed by the Chudley Brewery in London.

Locarnese (Switz) a noted vineyard based in the Sopra Cenevi, Ticino.

L'Occitaine (Fr) a natural spring mineral water from Fontaine de la Reine, Monts de Lacaume, Haut Languedoc. Mineral contents (milligrammes per litre): Sodium 2.8mg/l, Calcium 3.2mg/l, Magnesium 0.4mg/l, Potassium 0.35mg/l, Bicarbonates 7.5mg/l, Chlorides 3mg/l, Sulphates 1mg/l, Nitrates 5.5mg/l. pH 6.1

Lochan Ora (Scot) a 35% alc by vol. liqueur based on Scotch whisky and honey (owned by Seagram).

Loch Dhu (Scot) a 10 year old speyside black single malt whisky aged in double charred bourbon casks.

Loché (Fr) a commune in the Mâconnais, Burgundy.

Locher Brauerei (Switz) an independent brewery based in Appenzell and Buchs.

Löchgau (Ger) village (Anb): Württemberg. (Ber): Württembergisch Unterland. (Gro): Schalkstein. (Vin): Neckarberg.

Lochindaal (Scot) a 1983 single Islay malt whisky bottled in 1994 43% alc by vol.

Lochindaal 43 (Scot) a 10 year old single Islay malt whisky 43% alc by vol.

Loch Lomond (Scot) a single highland malt whisky distillery based north-west of Glasgow 40% alc by vol.

Loch Lomond Cocktail (Cktl) 1½ measures Scotch whisky, 1 measure gomme syrup, 3 dashes Angostura. Shake over ice and strain into an ice-filled old-fashioned glass.

Lochmühlerley (Ger) vineyard (Anb): Ahr. (Ber): Walporzheim/Arhtal. (Gro): Klosterberg. (Vil): Mayschoss.

Lochnagar (Scot) a single highland malt whisky distillery near Balmoral, west of the Spey in Aberdeenshire. Operated by John Begg Ltd. (part of the DCL group). Produces a 12 year old malt 43% alc by vol.

Lochside (Scot) a grain whisky distillery based near Montrose.

Lochside (Scot) a single highland malt whisky distillery near Montrose. Produces a vintage 1965 malt 43% alc by vol.

Lochvie Wines (Austr) winery (established 1987). (Add): 28 Lavender Park Road, Eltham, Yarra Valley. Grape varieties: Cabernet sauvignon, Merlot.

Lockal Brewery (Bra) a brewery which produces a bottled lager beer 4.7% alc by vol.

Locke and Company (Ire) a distillery based at Kilbeggan which closed down in 1952. The last whiskey produced is now sold as Locke's Kilbeggan (a 1946 Irish Whiskey).

Locke's (Ire) a blended whiskey from the Cooley Distillery in Dundalk.

Locke's Kilbeggan (Ire) a 'vintage' Irish whiskey from the last production of the Locke Distillery. see Locke and Company.

Lock Forty seven [47] (Eng) a mild ale brewed by micro-brewery Prince of Wales, Foxfields, near Broughton, Cumbria. See also Axeman's Wheat Mild.

Lock, Stock & Barrel (Eng) part of a range of ales brewed by the Charles Wells Brewery in Bedford, Bedfordshire.

Locorotondo (It) a D.O.C. white wine from Puglia. Made from Verdeca, Bianco d'alessano and Fiano grapes. Production area is the commune of Locorotondo and Cisterino plus part of commune of Fasano. D.O.C. also applies to naturally sparkling wines. See also Castel del Monte, San Severo.

Locret-Lachaud (Fr) a Champagne producer. (Add): 40 Rue Saint Vincent, 51160 Hautvillers. Récoltants-manipulants. Produces vintage and non-vintage wines. Vintages: 1971, 1976, 1979, 1982, 1983, 1985, 1990, 1996, 1998, 2001.

Loddiswell Vineyard (Eng) a vineyard (established 1977). (Add): Lilwell, Loddiswell, Kingsbridge, South Devon. Grape varieties: Bacchus, Huxelrebe, Müller-Thurgau, Reichensteiner and Siegerrebe.

Loddon Brewery (Eng) a brewery. (Add): Dunsden Reed Farm, Church farm, Reading, Berkshire RG4 9QT. Brews: Bamboozle 4.8% alc by vol., Ferrymans Gold 4.4% alc by vol., Hoppit classic Bitter 3.5% alc by vol., Hullabaloo Best 4.2% alc by vol., Kite Mild 3.2% alc by vol. Website: http://www.loddonbrewery.com 'E'mail: info@loddonbrewery.com

Lodge (Mad) a building where Madeira is matured.

Lodge (Port) a building in Vila Nova de Gaia where Port is matured. See also Loja.

Lodge Lot Cask (Port) a cask for maturing Port. Holds approximately 630litres.

Lodi (USA) abbr: **Lodi**-Sacramento. A.V.A. northern region of the Great Central Valley in California. Produces fortified, dessert and table wines. Home to Mondavi, Ravenswood, Kenwood Vineyards and Turley Cellars. Grape varieties include Zinfandel, Chardonnay, Sauvignon blanc.

Loel (Cyp) a large wine and spirits producer, sells under the labels of Amathus, Commandaria and Kykko.

Loëlla (Fr) a slightly acidic natural spring mineral water from Ogeu les Bains. Mineral contents (milligrammes per litre): Sodium 31mg/l, Calcium 48mg/l, Magnesium 11mg/l, Potassium 1mg/l, Bicarbonates 183mg/l, Chlorides 44mg/l, Sulphates 16mg/l, Nitrates 3mg/l. pH 5.3

Loess (Eng) a light-coloured, sand-based granular loam soil. An accumulation of sand, clay and silt particles, wind deposited.

Loevi Cocktail (Cktl) 1 measure dry gin, ½ measure orange gin, ½ measure French vermouth. Shake over ice, strain into an ice-filled highball glass and serve with straws.

Löf (Ger) village (Anb): Mosel-Saar-Ruwer. (Ber): Zell/Mosel. (Gro): Weinhex. (Vins): Goldblume, Sonnenring.

Loft Withering (Asia) an old method of drying tea where the tealeaf was placed on racks to dry, the process is little used now.

Logado (Gre) a grapey, straw-gold, white wine from Crete. Made with the Sultana and Villane grapes.

Logan De Luxe Scotch Whisky (Scot) a de luxe blended Scotch whisky formerly called Laird O Logan. Premium brand of White Horse Distillers Ltd 40% alc by vol.

Loge aux Moines [La] (Fr) an old historical vineyard of Pouilly-sur-Loire in the Central Vineyards, Loire. Produces a fine, excellent A.C. Pouilly-Fumé.

Loges [Les] (Fr) a vineyard in the A.C. Pouilly-Fumé, Central Vineyards, Loire 8ha.

Logis (Fr) a 5 year old Cognac produced by Jean Guerbé.

Logis de la Montagne (Fr) a Cognac producer. (Add): Paul Bonnin, Logis de la Montagne, Challignac, 16300. 30ha. in the Fins Bois. Produces: Extra Hors d'Age 20 year old, Pineau de Charente, Le Sauté Montagne and Vicomte Stephane de Castelbajac.

Logroño (Sp) the centre of the Rioja wine region in the Rioja Alta.

Logwood (Mex) see Campeaching Wood.

Lohberger Hang (Ger) vineyard (Anb): Rheingau. (Ber): Johannisberg. (Gro): Not yet assigned. (Vil): Frankfurt/Main.

Löhrer Berg (Ger) vineyard (Anb): Nahe. (Ber): Kreuznach. (Gro): Sonnenborn. (Vil): Langenlonsheim.

Lohr.J. Estates (USA) a winery based in Monterey (vineyards include Riverstone). Grape varieties: Chardonnay. Label: Arroyo Seco (Chardonnay). Website: http://www.jlohr.com

Loiben (Aus) a wine district within the Wachau region, western Austria.

Loibenberg (Aus) a vineyard site on the banks of the River Danube situated in the Wachau region, Niederösterreich.

Loibener (Aus) a light dry white wine from the Wachau region.

Loi Colbert (Fr) a decree which recommends that for every oak tree felled for making into casks a new oak should be planted to replace it.

Loimer (Aus) a winery (17ha) based in the Kampstal region. (Add): Rudolfstrasse 37-39, 3550 Langenlois. Grape varieties: Cabernet sauvignon, Chardonnay, Grüner veltliner, Pinot blanc, Pinot noir, Riesling. Produces a range of wine styles.

Loin d'Oeil (Fr) an alternative name for the Muscadelle grape.

Loire [River] (Fr) the longest river in France, runs from south-east to the north-west coast. Has four wine districts within the region: Nantais, Anjou-Saumur, Touraine and the Central Vineyards.

Loire-Atlantique (Fr) a département in western France in the Pays de la Loire. Has the Muscadet wine region (Nantais) in its boundaries.

Loiret (Fr) a Vin de Pays area in the Loiret département, central France (part of the Jardine de la France). Produces red, rosé, gris and dry white wines.

Loir-et-Cher (Fr) a Vin de Pays area in the Loir-et-Cher département of north-western France (part of the Jardine de la France). Produces red, rosé, gris and dry white wines.

Loischl (Aus) a vineyard site based on the banks of the River Kamp situated in the Kamptal region.

L'Oiselle (Fr) a natural spring mineral water. Mineral contents (milligrammes per litre): Sodium 86mg/l, Calcium 164mg/l, Magnesium 79mg/l, Potassium 22mg/l, Bicarbonates 312mg/l, Chlorides 144mg/l, Sulphates 430mg/l, Fluorides 1mg/l, Nitrates 1mg/l, Silicates 6mg/l.

Loiser Berg (Aus) a vineyard site based on the banks of the River Kamp situated in the Kamptal region.

Loisy-en-Brie (Fr) a Cru Champagne village in the Canton de Vertus. District: Châlons.

Loiten (Nor) the brand-name of an aquavit produced by A/S Vinmonopolet. Has a slight Sherry taste.

Loiten Braenderis-Destillation (Nor) a large distilling company based in Kristiania under the control of A/S Vinmonopolet. Produces Aquavit.

Loja (Port) a lodge or warehouse in Vila Nova de Gaia where Port is matured.

Lokal (Bra) a 4.7% alc by vol pilsener-style lager beer brewed by the Teresópolis Brewery.

Lokal (Tur) a dry rosé wine produced by Diren, Tokat.

Lokoya (USA) a winery based in the Napa Valley, California. Grape varieties include: Cabernet sauvignon. Labels: Diamond Mountain District, Howell Mountain, Mount Veeder.

Lolland-Falsters Brewery (Den) a small brewery in Nykobing. Noted for pilsener-style lager beer 4.5% alc by vol.

Lolle (Sp) a black grape variety grown in the Canary Isles.

Lolly Water (Austr) the nickname given to any coloured soft (non-alcoholic) drink. i.e. cherryade, orangeade, etc.

Lolly Water (Eng) nickname given to the mass German cheap sweet wines of the 1970's, 80's and 90's because they were favoured by the young wine drinkers.

Lolly-Water (N.Z) the nickname given to thin rosé wines that have been sweetened with cane sugar.

Lolonis Vineyard (USA) a vineyard based in Redwood Valley, Mendocino County, California. 41.5ha. Grape varieties: Cabernet sauvignon, Zinfandel.

Lombadas (Port) a natural spring mineral water. Mineral contents (milligrammes per litre): Sodium 22mg/l, Calcium 15mg/l, Magnesium 1mg/l, Bicarbonates 72mg/l.

Lombardia (It) see Lombardy.

Lombardi Wines (N.Z) a family-owned vineyard. (Add): 294 Te Mata Road, RD12, Havelock North, Hawkes Bay, North Island. 3ha. Specialises in Cabernet sauvignon plus dessert Cabernet sauvignon, liqueurs, vermouths, oak-aged Port-styles and sherries.

Lombard's Hanepoot (S.Afr) an average sweet fortified wine.

Lombardy (It) the third largest region in Italy. Borders Switzerland to the north, Veneto to the east, Piemonte to the west and Emilia-Romagna to the south.

Lomelino (Mad) the brand-name of producers Tarquinio T. da Camara Lomelino. Produces: Lomelino Imperial Sercial, Verdelho, Bual and Rare old Malmsey. Also Tarquino Sercial, Bual and Malmsey.

Lomond (S.Afr) a winery (established 1999) based in Cape Agulhas, Southern Cape. 100ha. Grape varieties: Merlot, Sauvignon blanc, Sémillon, Shiraz. Labels: Block 3, Block 5.

Lomond (Scot) a single malt whisky distillery based north of the river Clyde. A lowland malt whisky 40% alc by vol.

Lomond Gold Blond Ale (Scot) the name for an ale brewed by the Bridge of Allan Brewery, Stirlingshire.

Lomond Spring (Scot) a natural spring mineral water from Hangingmygre Farm, Fife.

Lomza Brewery (Pol) a brewery. (Add): Ul Poznanska 121, 18-402 Lomza. Brews a variety of beers and lager. Website: http://www.browarlomza.pl 'E'mail: browar@browarlomza.pl

Loncomilla Valley (Chile) a wine-producing district based in the Maule Valley. Home to Viña Tabontinaja and to Balduzzi in San Javier.

London (Can) a wine district between Niagara and Crystal Beach.

London (Cktl) ¾ measure London dry gin, dash gomme syrup, dash maraschino, dash Angostura. Stir well over ice, strain into a cocktail glass and dress with a spiral lemon peel.

London Bitter (Eng) a cask-conditioned bitter 1037 O.G. brewed by the Watney Brewery in London.

London Buck Cocktail (Cktl) 25mls (⅓ gill) dry gin, juice ½ lemon. Shake over ice, strain into an ice-filled highball glass and top with ginger ale.

London Cocktail (Cktl) 60mls (½ gill) London dry gin, 2 dashes absinthe, 2 dashes orange bitters, 2 dashes gomme syrup. Stir over ice, strain into a cocktail glass, add an olive and squeeze of lemon peel juice on top.

London Coffee Information Centre (Eng) based at 21 Berner's Street, London W1P 4DD. Centre originally run by the International Coffee Organisation to promote the drinking of coffee.

London Dock Rum (W.Ind) a Jamaican rum bottled in London and stored in bonded warehouses in London's docks.

London Dry Gin (Eng) a gin originally produced near or in London. Now denotes a very dry gin produced any where.

Londoner (Cktl) 35mls (1½ fl.ozs) dry gin, 10mls (½ fl.oz) each of rose hip syrup, dry vermouth, juice ½ lemon. Pour over ice in a highball glass, stir, top with soda water and a slice of lemon.

London Fog (Cktl) ½ measure anisette, ½ measure white crème de menthe, dash Angostura. Shake over ice and strain into a cocktail glass.

London Gin (Eng) *see* London Dry Gin.

London Lager (Eng) *see* John Young's London Lager.

London Market (Mad) the quality name sometimes seen on bottles of Madeira. This is a '*Lot*' name.

London Particular (Mad) the quality name sometimes seen on bottles of Madeira. This is a '*Lot*' name.

London Pilsener Brewery (Ind) a brewery based in Bangalore, India. Produces London Stout and Maharajah Lager, is India's largest brewery.

London Pride (Eng) a bitter beer 1041.5 O.G. brewed by the Fuller, Smith and Turner Brewery of Chiswick. Also a bottled version 1045 O.G.

London Special (Cktl) place a sugar cube soaked in orange bitters in a flute glass, top with iced Champagne and a twist of orange peel juice.

London Stout (Can) a sweet stout brewed by the Moosehead Brewery.

London Stout (Ind) a medium stout brewed by the London Pilsener Brewery, Bangalore.

London Stout (Ind) a bitter stout 1046 O.G. brewed by the United Breweries in Bangalore.

London Stout (USA) the name given to stouts produced outside of U.K.

London Tap Water (Eng) a bottled drinking water produced by Sodastream, available as still-filtered, unfiltered and carbonated.

London Vineyard (USA) a small vineyard based at Glen Ellen, west of Sonoma Valley, California. Grape varieties: Cabernet sauvignon and Pinot noir.

Lonehill (S.Afr) the label for a white wine (Chardonnay) produced by the Graham Beck Wines winery, Franschhoek, Western Cape.

Lone Star Beer (USA) a beer brewed by the Lone Star Brewery in San Antonio, Texas 1036–1040 O.G.

Lone Star Brewery (USA) a Texas Brewery and beer from San Antonio. Owned by Olympia in Washington.

Lone Tree (Cktl) ⅓ measure dry gin, ⅓ measure Italian vermouth, ⅓ measure French vermouth, 2 dashes orange bitters. Shake over ice and strain into a cocktail glass.

Lone Tree Cocktail (Cktl) ⅔ measure dry gin, ⅓ measure sweet vermouth. Stir over ice and strain into a cocktail glass.

Long (Eng) a term used to describe a long, lingering flavour (after-taste) in a wine, is often a sign of fine quality.

Longae Vitae (Hol) a brand of herb bitters.

Long Anis Cocktail (Cktl) place 25mls (⅓ gill) anisette and a dash lemon juice in an ice-filled highball glass, stir and top with soda water.

Longberry Harar (Afr) a style of coffee produced in Ethiopia that resembles mocha.

Long Blonde (Cktl) 25mls (⅓ gill) Dubonnet Blonde, 25mls (⅓ gill) dry gin. Stir over ice in a highball glass and top with soda water.

Long Bush Wines (N.Z) a winery. (Add): 265 Lytton Road, P.O. Box 1323, Gisborne. 8ha. Grape varieties: Pinot noir, Chardonnay, Müller-Thurgau, Merlot, late-harvest Riesling.

Long Drink (Eng) a large drink of non-alcoholic beverage. i.e. water, squash, lemonade, etc.

Longen (Ger) village (Anb): Mosel-Saar-Ruwer. (Ber): Bernkastel. (Gro): Sankt Michael. (Vins): Goldkupp, Zellerberg.

Longenburgerberg (Ger) vineyard (Anb): Mittelrhein. (Ber): Siebengebirge. (Gro): Petersberg. (Vil): Niederdollendorf.

Long Flat Red (Austr) a vintage red wine from the Tyrrell's Winery in New South Wales.

Long Glen (Cktl) 25mls (1fl.oz) gin or vodka, 25mls (1fl.oz) Cointreau. Pour over ice cubes in a highball glass, stir and add bitter lemon to taste.

Long Green Cocktail (Cktl) place 3 ice cubes in a

L

highball glass. Add 25mls (1fl.oz) green crème de menthe and top with soda water, decorate with a mint sprig and serve with straws.

Long Gully Estate (Austr) a winery (established 1982) based at Long Gully Road, Healsville, Off Healsville-Yarra Glen Road, Yarra Valley. Grape varieties: Cabernet sauvignon, Merlot, Pinot noir, Shiraz, Chardonnay, Riesling, Sauvignon blanc, Sémillon.

Longhi-de Carli (It) a wine producer in Franciacorta, Lombardy.

Long Island Tea (Cktl) 10mls (½ fl.oz) each of light rum, vodka, gin, 25mls (1fl.oz) cold weak tea. Build into ice-filled highball glass, stir in cola, decorate with a lemon slice and sprig of mint.

Longitude (S.Afr) the label for a blended red wine produced by the Flagstone Winery, Somerset West, Western Cape.

Long John (Scot) a blended Scotch whisky from the Long John M°Donald Distilleries, Glasgow 40% alc by vol (also a de luxe blended Scotch whisky 12 year old 40% alc by vol).

Long John International (Scot) a major Highland, Islay and Scotch whisky distillers (part of Whitbread). Whiskies include Laphroaig, Long John and Tormore. *See also* Long John M°Donald Distilleries.

Long John M°Donald Distilleries (Scot) distilleries based in Glasgow (part of Long John International).

Longleat Winery (Austr) a winery (established 1975). (Add): Old Weir Road, Murchison, Victoria. Grape varieties: Cabernet sauvignon, Merlot, Shiraz, Chardonnay, Sauvignon blanc, Sémillon.

Long Life (Aus) a sparkling natural spring mineral water from Stadtquelle, Bad Radkersburg. (red label: sparkling/blue label: light gas). Mineral contents (milligrammes per litre): Sodium 115mg/l, Calcium 263mg/l, Magnesium 206mg/l, Potassium 8.2mg/l, Bicarbonates 2100mg/l, Chlorides 33mg/l, Sulphates 4mg/l, Fluorides 0.05mg/l, Nitrates 0.5mg/l, Silicates 43mg/l, Iron 2.6mg/l.

Long Life (Eng) a keg bitter 1040 O.G. brewed by Allied Breweries, Wrexham. Also an Export version 1046 O.G.

Longman (Scot) a keg lager beer 1040 O.G. brewed by the Alice Brewery in Inverness.

Longman Premium Cider [The] (Eng) a 6% alc by vol. premium quality draught-style cider from Merrydown in Sussex.

Long Meadow Ranch Winery (USA) a winery. Website: http://www.longmeadowranch.com

Longmenshan (Chi) a natural spring mineral water. Mineral contents (milligrammes per litre): Sodium 60mg/l, Potassium 17.3mg/l, Bicarbonates 237mg/l, Silicates 38.5mg/l. pH 7.5

Longmorn-Glenlivet (Scot) a single highland malt whisky distillery near Longmorn. Now part of The Glenlivet Distillers Ltd. (part of the Seagram group). Produces 12 year old, 15 year old 45%

alc by vol. and a vintage 1957 malt 43% alc by vol.

Long Mountain Wines (S.Afr) a winery (established 1994) based in Stellenbosch, Western Cape. (Add): P.O. Box 1324, Stellenbosch 7599 (owned by Pernod-Ricard). Grape varieties: Cabernet sauvignon, Chardonnay, Chenin blanc, Merlot, Pinotage, Pinot noir, Riesling, Ruby cabernet, Sauvignon blanc, Sémillon, Shiraz. Produces a wide range of wines. Website: http://www.longmountain.co.za

Long Paddock (Austr) a Cabernet and Merlot blended wine produced by the Redbank Winery in Victoria. *See also* Sally's Paddock.

Long Pond (W.Ind) a noted rum distillery based in Jamaica, produces a 20 year old.

Long Pull (Eng) an illegal act, by the serving over a prescribed measure, a old Licensing Act offence (unfair competition).

Longridge Winery (S.Afr) a winery (established 1994) based in Stellenbosch, Western Cape. 60ha. (Add): P.O. Box 1435, Stellenbosch 7599 (owned by Winecorp). Grape varieties: Cabernet sauvignon, Chardonnay, Chenin blanc, Merlot, Pinotage, Pinot noir, Sauvignon blanc. Label: Bay View plus varietal and cap classique wines. Website: http://www.longridge.co.za

Longrow (Scot) a 12 year old, double-distilled, Campbeltown malt whisky produced by Mitchell and C°. 45% alc by vol. Also a 16 year old version.

Long Shadows (USA) a winery based in the Columbia Valley, Washington State. Grape varieties include: Syrah. Label: Sequel.

Long Tail (Eng) the term used to denote the finish in the mouth of a wine, a long after-taste.

Long Thirst (USA) the alternative nick-name for the Prohibition.

Longue Attente [La] (Fr) in Cognac the waiting period for the new brandy to mature in the oak casks.

Longueteau (W.Ind) a noted rum distillery based in Guadeloupe.

Longueville House (Ire) a vineyard (established 1972) based at Mallow, County Cork, Eire. 1.6ha. Grape varieties: Müller-Thurgau and Reichensteiner.

Longuich (Ger) village (Anb): Mosel-Saar-Ruwer. (Ber): Bernkastel. (Gro): Probstberg. (Vins): Hirschlay, Maximiner, Herrenberg.

Longview Estate (N.Z) a 5ha winery. (Add): SH1, Otaika, P.O. Box 6041, Whangarei. Grape varieties: Cabernet sauvignon, Merlot, Pinot noir, Chardonnay, Gewürztraminer, Müller-Thurgau.

Longview Vineyard (Austr) a vineyard (established 1997) based in the Adelaide Hills, South Australia. 70ha. Grape varieties: Cabernet sauvignon, Chardonnay, Riesling, Sauvignon blanc, Shiraz, Viognier. Labels: Beau Sea (Viognier), Iron Knob (Riesling) and Yakka (Shiraz). Website: http://www.longviewvineyard.com.au

Long Vineyards (USA) a small winery based near Rutherford, Napa Valley, California. 8.5ha. Grape varieties: Chardonnay and Johannisberg riesling. Produce varietal wines.

Long Vineyards (USA) also known as the Jasper Long Vineyards. Based in Dry Creek Valley, Sonoma County, California. Grape variety: Merlot.

Long Whistle (Cktl) 90mls (¾ gill) brandy or whisky, sugar syrup to taste, hot or cold milk and grated nutmeg on top.

Longyon (Chi) *see* Loong Yan.

Lonsdale Northern (I.O.M) the brand-name of a dry gin produced by Glen Kella Distillery, Sulby. *See also* Glen Kella, Troyka Black Bear.

Lonsheim (Ger) village (Anb): Rheinhessen. (Ber): Bingen. (Gro): Adelberg. (Vins): Mandelberg, Schönberg.

Lonton (Fr) a 40% alc by vol. white rum from the Savanna distillery, La Réunion.

Lontué (Chile) a wine region of central Chile. Produces sound table wines.

Lonz (USA) a winery based in Middle Bass Island, Ohio. Produces French hybrid wines.

Lonzac (Fr) a commune in the Charente-Maritime département. Grapes are used for Cognac.

Looby's Lust (Eng) a dark old mild ale 5% alc by vol. brewed by the Raisdale Sparging and Brewing Company.

Look Out Below (Cktl) 1 measure Pussers 100° Proof Navy rum, juice ½ lime, 1 teaspoon Grenadine. Shake over ice and strain into an ice-filled old-fashioned glass.

Loon County (USA) a natural spring mineral water. Mineral contents (milligrammes per litre): Calcium 26mg/l, Magnesium 15mg/l, Potassium 0.88mg/l, Chlorides 0.8mg/l, Sulphates 9.1mg/l. pH 8.05

Loong Ching (Chi) a green tea, rolled into pellets. Produced in Canton.

Loong Yan (Chi) the ancient name for the white grape variety Dragon's Eye.

Looped (USA) a slang term for under the influence of alcohol.

Loose Head (Eng) *see* Head.

Loosen [Ernst] (Ger) *see* Dr. Loosen [Ernst].

Lopera (Sp) a Vino Comarcal of Jaén in Andalucía.

López de Heredia (Sp) a noted wine-producer based at Avenida de Vizcaya 3 and 5, Haro, Rioja Alta. 170ha. in the Rioja Alta. Produces: Viña Bosconia, Viña Cubillo Viña Gravonia and Viña Tondonia (red and white). Grape varieties: Garnacha, Graciano, Mazuelo, Tempranillo.

López Hermanos (Sp) a noted producer and exporter of Málaga.

López Tello (Sp) an old-established bodega based in Valdepeñas, central Spain.

Lopo (Hun) a larger version of a pipette/valenche, a hollow rod with a bulbous head for drawing wine out of the cask. Holds the equivalent of one bottle.

Loppin (Fr) a vineyard in the A.C. Meursault, Côte de Beaune (owned by the Hospices de Beaune).

L'Ora di Recoaro (It) a sparkling natural mineral water from L'Ora, Recoaro. Mineral contents (milligrammes per litre): Sodium 1.4mg/l, Calcium 36.8mg/l, Magnesium 15.6mg/l,

Potassium 0.3mg/l, Bicarbonates 160.8mg/l, Chlorides 0.8mg/l, Sulphates 19.9mg/l, Fluorides 0.08mg/l, Silicate 1.7mg/l, Nitrate 4.2mg/l, Strontium 0.2mg/l. pH 8.0

Lorch (Ger) village (Anb): Rheingau. (Ber): Johannisberg. (Gro): Burgweg. (Vins): Bodental-Steinberg, Kapellenberg, Krone, Pfaffenweis, Schlossberg.

Lorchhausen (Ger) village (Anb): Rheingau. (Ber): Johannisberg. (Gro): Burgweg. (Vins): Rosenberg, Seligmacher.

Lord (Pol) a natural spring mineral water from Pomiechowek. Mineral contents (milligrammes per litre): Sodium 34.8mg/l, Calcium 102mg/l, Magnesium 20.2mg/l, Potassium 3.2mg/l, Bicarbonates 230mg/l, Chlorides 34.4mg/l, Sulphates 62.2mg/l.

Lord Anson's Ale (Eng) an ale brewed at the Shugborough Estate in Staffordshire (home to Lord Lichfield).

Lord Calvert Canadian (Can) a blend of Canadian whiskies 40% alc by vol. produced by Canadian Distillers Ltd. (a subsidiary of Seagram).

Lord Chesterfield (USA) a top-fermented, sweet, well-hopped ale brewed by the Yuengling Brewery in Pottsville.

Lord Ducane (Eng) the brand-name used by Vine Products Ltd. for their British Sherry.

Lord George Port (Port) the brand-name of a Port shipped by Taylor, Fladgate and Yeatman.

Lord Lieutenant's Ale (Eng) a 6% alc by vol. strong ale brewed by The Chiltern Brewery, Buckinghamshire.

Lord Neethlingshof-Laurentius (S.Afr) the label for a red wine (Cabernet sauvignon, Cabernet franc, Merlot and Shiraz blend) produced by the Neethlingshof Estate, Stellenbosch, Western Cape.

Lord Raglan (Eng) a micro-brewery based at Nangreave near Bury. Brews: Brendan's Birthday Beer, Nanny Flyer.

Lord's Ale (Eng) a strong ale 1048 O.G. brewed by the Chudley Brewery in London.

Lord Wisdom (Sp) a solera reserva brandy from Wisdom and Warter Ltd. in Jerez. 36% alc by vol. Aged minimum 1 year.

Lorelei (Ger) added to the Mittelrhein as a third Bereich from the 1990 vintage onwards.

Loreley-Edel (Ger) vineyard (Anb): Mittelrhein. (Ber): Rheinburgengau. (Gro): Loreleyfelsen. (Vil): St. Goarshausen.

Loreleyfelsen (Ger) grosslage (Anb): Mittelrhein. (Ber): Rheinburgengau. (Vils): Bornich, Kamp-Bornhofen-Kestert, Nochern, Patersberg, St. Goarshausen.

Lorentz [Gustave] (Fr) an Alsace wine producer. (Add): 35 Grand-Rue, 68750 Bergheim 31ha.

Lorestan (Iran) a wine-producing province in northern Iran.

Lorettoberg (Ger) grosslage (Anb): Baden. (Ber): Markgräflerland. (Vils): Bad Krotzingen, Biengen, Bollschweil, Buggingen, Ebringen, Ehrenstetten, Eschbach, Freiburg i. Br., Grunern, Heitersheim, Kirchhofen, Mengen, Merzhausen, Norsingen,

Pfaffenweiler, Schallstadt-Wolfenweile, Scherzingen, Schlatt, Seefelden, Staufen, Staufen (ortsteil Wettelbrunn), Tunsel, Wittnau.

Lorgues (Fr) a wine-producing village in the Côtes de Provence.

L'Origin (Chi) a natural spring mineral water (established 1992). Mineral contents (milligrammes per litre): Sodium 0.62-0.7mg/l, Calcium 36.3-39.6mg/l, Magnesium 9.31-9.61mg/l, Potassium 0.49-0.52mg/l, Bicarbonates 152.55-153.77mg/l, Chlorides 2.86-3.31mg/l, Sulphates 12.3-13.2mg/l. pH 7.7

Lorimars IPA (Scot) a 5.2% alc by vol. India pale ale brewed by The Caledonian Brewing C°. Ltd., Midlothian.

Lorimer and Clark Brewery (Scot) a brewery based in Edinburgh taken over by the Vaux Brewery of Sunderland in 1964. Noted for cask-conditioned 70/- Ale 1036 O.G. (known as Best Scotch in Vaux houses) and Caledonian Strong 1077 O.G.

L'Ormarins Private Cellar (S.Afr) a winery (established 1965) based in the Franschhoek Valley, Western Cape. 90ha. Grape varieties: Cabernet sauvignon, Chardonnay, Merlot, Pinot grigio, Sangiovese, Sauvignon blanc. Labels: Optima, Terra del Capo. Website: http://www.lormarins.com

Lorna Hughes (S.Afr) a winery (established 1990) based in Stellenbosch, Western Cape. 3.2ha. Grape varieties: Cabernet sauvignon, Shiraz. Label: Stonehill Bristle.

Loron et Fils (Fr) a Burgundy négociant based at Pontanevaux 71570 La Chapelle-de-Guinchay, Burgundy.

Lörrach (Ger) village (Anb): Baden. (Ber): Markgräflerland. (Gro): Vogtei Rötteln. (Vin): Sonnenbrunnen.

Lorraine (Fr) a wine province of north-eastern France, red, rosé and white plus Vin gris are produced V.D.Q.S. quality. Two areas: Vins de la Moselle and Côtes de Toul.

Lorraine Private Cellar (S.Afr) a winery (established 1875) based in Goudinin, Worcester, Western Cape. 150ha. Grape varieties: Cabernet franc, Cabernet sauvignon, Chardonnay, Chenin blanc, Merlot, Petit verdot, Pinotage, Ruby cabernet, Sauvignon blanc, Shiraz, Viognier. Label: Cape Harmony. Website: http://www.lorraine-wines.com

Lörsch (Ger) village (Anb): Mosel-Saar-Ruwer. (Ber): Bernkastel. (Gro): Sankt Michael. (Vins): Goldkupp, Zellerberg

Lörzweiler (Ger) village (Anb): Rheinhessen. (Ber): Nierstein. (Gro): Gutes Domtal. (Vin): Königstuhl.

Lörzweiler (Ger) village (Anb): Rheinhessen. (Ber): Nierstein. (Gro): Sankt Alban. (Vins): Hohberg, Ölgild.

Los Alamos Vineyards (USA) a small winery based near Los Alamos, Santa Barbara, California. Grape varieties: Chardonnay and Zinfandel. Produce varietal wines.

Los Angeles (Cktl) 25mls (⅛ gill) Bourbon whiskey, 1 egg, dash sweet vermouth, 1 teaspoon powdered sugar. Shake over ice and strain into a flute glass.

Los Angeles (USA) a Californian wine district within the region of Cucamonga. Produces table and dessert wines.

Los Angeles Cocktail (Cktl) ⅔ measure Scotch whisky, ⅓ measure lemon juice, 1 egg, dash sweet vermouth. Shake over ice and strain into a large cocktail glass.

Los Cerros de San Juan (S.Am) a vineyard (established 1854). 100ha. Grape varieties: Tannat, Tempranillo, Merlot.

Los Gatos (USA) a town in Santa Clara County, California, home to three wineries.

Los Hermanos (USA) the label used by Beringer Vineyards for a range of their generic and varietal wines.

Lositza (Bul) a vineyard area in Northern Basic region.

Los Llanos (Sp) a wine-producing area west of Valdepeñas, central Spain.

Los Monteros (Sp) a full-bodied red wine produced by Schenk in Valencia from 100% Monastrell grapes.

Lösnich (Ger) village (Anb): Mosel-Saar-Ruwer. (Ber): Bernkastel. (Gro): Schwarzlay. (Vins): Burgberg, Försterlay.

Los Niños (USA) a vineyard based near Yountville, Napa Valley, California. Grape variety: Chardonnay. Grapes vinified at the Con Creek Winery.

Los Olivos (USA) a wine-producing town near Santa Ynez Valley, Santa Barbara, California.

Los Olivos Vineyard (USA) a winery based in Santa Ynez Valley, Santa Barbara, California. Grape variety: Chardonnay.

Los Palacios (Sp) a Vino Comarcal of Sevilla in Andalucía.

Los Ranchos (S.Am) a noted wine-producer in Uruguay based in Rio Negro.

Los Reyes (Mex) the label used by Luis Cetto Vineyards in Guadaloupe, Baja California for a range of their wines.

Los Teques (Ven) a natural spring mineral water from Los Teques. Mineral contents (milligrammes per litre): Calcium 26mg/l, Magnesium 10mg/l, Potassium 34mg/l, Bicarbonates 35mg/l, Chlorides 30mg/l, Sulphates 80mg/l.

Los Tercios (Sp) an area within Andalusia whose vineyards produce the grapes for Sherry.

Lost Horizons (S.Afr) the export label for a range of wines produced by the Lost Horizons Premium Wines winery, Suider-Paarl, Western Cape.

Lost Horizons Premium Wines (S.Afr) a winery (established 1995) based in Suider-Paarl, Western Cape. Grape varieties: Cabernet sauvignon, Chardonnay, Chenin blanc, Merlot, Petit verdot, Pinotage, Ruby cabernet, Sauvignon blanc. Label: Classic Ruby, Guardian (discontinued), Panorama, Quantum, St. Dalfour. Website: http://www.losthorizons.co.za

Lost Lake (Austr) a winery based in Pemberton, Western Australia. Grape varieties: Merlot, Pinot noir, Shiraz, Chardonnay, Sauvignon blanc.

L

Lostorfer (Switz) a still and sparkling natural spring mineral water from Lostorf. (red label: sparkling/green label: light gas/blue label: still). Mineral contents (milligrammes per litre): Sodium 4.2mg/l, Calcium 279mg/l, Magnesium 78mg/l, Sulphates 780mg/l, Fluorides 2mg/l, Nitrates <0.1mg/l.

Lot (Fr) a département south-east of the Gironde. Famous for the red Cahors wines. Contains the areas: Coteaux de Glanes and Coteaux du Quercy.

Lot (Port) the designation given to a parcel of Port wine before it is blended.

Lota (Port) the process of racking the new Ports and topping up with brandy to bring up to strength at the end of the first year (November).

Lotberg (Ger) vineyard (Anb): Baden. (Ber): Kaiserstuhl-Tuniberg. (Gro): Vulkanfelsen. (Vil): Wasenweiler.

Lote (Mad) a collection of pipes or vats containing wines with different characteristics. It is from these that shippers create their brands.

Lote (Port) an amount of Port used for blending.

Lot-et-Garonne (Fr) a Vin de Pays area in the Lot-et-Garonne département, south-western France. Consists of the areas L'Agenais, Côtes de Brulhois and Côtes du Tarn.

Lotte Chilsung Beverage Company (Kor) produces a range of whiskies. Range consists of: Scotch Blue International (premium blend), Scotch Blue 21 year old (super deluxe blend).

Lottenstück (Ger) vineyard (Anb): Rheinhessen. (Ber): Bingen. (Gro): Kaiserpfalz. (Vil): Ingelheim.

Lottstetten [ortsteil Nack] (Ger) village (Anb): Baden. (Ber): Bodensee. (Gro): Not yet assigned. (Vin): Steinler.

Lotterbad (It) a natural spring mineral water from Lotterbad, St. Walburg, Ulten, Bozen. Mineral contents (milligrammes per litre): Sodium 4.7mg/l, Calcium 19.9mg/l, Magnesium 4.2mg/l, Potassium 2.5mg/l, Bicarbonates 39mg/l, Sulphates 48mg/l, Fluorides 0.4mg/l, Iron 2.25mg/l, Silicates 11.8mg/l.

Lotus (Eng) an orange or tropical-flavoured wine produced by Vine Products. Low in alcohol.

Lotus Flower (Eng) a lotus blossom-flavoured tea produced by Whittards of Chelsea C°. in London.

Loubère (Fr) an Armagnac producer. (Add): 40240 Labastide d'Armagnac. 15ha. in the Bas Armagnac.

Loubiere (W.Ind) a natural spring mineral water from Loubiere Springs, Dominica. Mineral contents (milligrammes per litre): Sodium 13mg/l, Calcium 12mg/l, Magnesium 4.5mg/l, Potassium 2.6mg/l, Bicarbonates 7.6mg/l, Chlorides 8.5mg/l, Sulphates 3mg/l, Nitrates 2.3mg/l.

Louche (Fr) cloudy/no longer clear, a term used for wine that has turned cloudy through age or disease.

Louiesenhof Stellenbosch Wines (S.Afr) a winery (established 1992) based in Stellenbosch, Western Cape. 120ha. (Add): P.O. Box 2013, Stellenbosch

7601. Grape varieties: Cabernet sauvignon, Chardonnay, Chenin blanc, Merlot, Pinotage, Pinot gris, Sauvignon blanc, Tinta barocca, Zinfandel. Produces: Marbonne (brandy), Cape LBV Port (Tinta barocca) and Cape Perroquet (tawny Port). Website: http://www.louiesenhof.co.za

Louis Adam (Fr) the label of a prestige cuvée Champagne produced by Adam Garnotel, Rilly-la-Montagne.

Louis' Block (Austr) a red (Cabernet sauvignon) wine produced by the Poacher's Ridge, Western Australia.

Louis California Brandy (USA) a brandy produced by Schenley Distillers at Number One Distilling C°., California.

Louis de Vernier (Sp) a brand of sparkling wine produced by Casa Masachs (white and rosé).

Louise Pommery (Fr) a de luxe vintage cuvée Champagne produced by Pommery et Gréno from 60% Chardonnay and 40% Pinot noir grapes.

Louise Vineyard (USA) a part of the Cristom Estate, Willamette Valley, Oregon.

Louis Guntrum (Ger) a well-known estate in the Rheinhessen, has vineyards in Dienheim, Nierstein and Oppenheim. Grape varieties: Bacchus, Kerner and Rieslaner.

Louisiana Clay (USA) bentonite.

Louisiana Lullaby (Cktl) 40mls (⅓ gill) Jamaican rum, 15mls (⅛ gill) red Dubonnet, 3 dashes Grand Marnier. Stir over ice, strain into a cocktail glass and add a slice of lemon.

Louis Martini (USA) a 1300ha winery in Napa, Sonoma and Lake County. Grape varieties: Sauvignon blanc, Cabernet sauvignon, Chardonnay, Pinot noir, Merlot, Petite sirah.

Louis Philippe (Fr) an 1840 distilled Cognac produced by A.E. Dor in Jarnac 34% alc by vol.

Louisvale Wines Stellenbosch (Pty) Ltd. (S.Afr) a winery (established 1989) based in Stellenbosch, Western Cape. 23ha. (Add): P.O. Box 542, Stellenbosch 7599. Grape varieties: Cabernet franc, Cabernet sauvignon, Chardonnay, Merlot. Labels: Chavant, Dominique. Website: http://www.louisvale.com

Louisville (USA) a town based in north Kentucky on the Indiana border. Is the home to many Bourbon whiskey distilleries.

Louis V (USA) the brand-name for a brandy produced by the Franzia Brothers, Ripon, California.

Louis XIII de Rémy Martin (Fr) a 50 year old Grande Champagne Cognac produced by Rémy Martin.

Louis XIV (S.Afr) the brand-name of a brandy produced by Oude Meester.

Lounge (Eng) a comfortably furnished room in a public house where the drinks are at a slightly higher price than in the public bar.

Lounge Lizard (S.Afr) the brand label for a red (Pinotage/Shiraz), rosé and white (Colombard/Sauvignon blanc) wine from the Kumala stable.

Louny Brewery (Czec) a brewery based in Louny, northern Czec. Brews: Fürst van Louny.

Loupiac (Fr) an A.C. commune in Bordeaux which produces sweet white wines. 12.5% alc by vol. minimum.

Lourd (Fr) denotes a dull, unbalanced wine.

Loureira (Sp) a white grape variety grown in Rias Baixas of Galicia. *see* Loureiro.

Loureiro (Port) a white grape variety used in the making of Vinhos Verdes. (Sp) = Loureira, Marqués.

Lourensford (S.Afr) a winery (established 1999) based in Stellenbosch, Western Cape. 285ha. Grape varieties: Cabernet sauvignon, Merlot, Sauvignon blanc, Sémillon, Shiraz, Viognier. Label: Seventeen Hundred. Website: http://www.lourensford.com

Lourens River Valley (S.Afr) the label for a red wine (Merlot 55% plus Cabernet sauvignon and Cabernet franc blend) produced by the Morgenster Estate winery, Stellenbosch, Western Cape.

Lourinha (Port) a DOC area based in the Estremadura region of central Portugal.

Loutraki (Gre) a natural spring mineral water from Loutraki. Mineral contents (milligrammes per litre): Sodium 13.2mg/l, Calcium 2.5mg/l, Magnesium 84mg/l, Potassium 0.7mg/l, Bicarbonates 450mg/l, Chlorides 14mg/l, Nitrates 9.87mg/l, Silicates 25mg/l. pH 8.31

Louvée [La] (Fr) an A.C. Cornas wine produced by Colombo (Jean Luc), La Roche, Tain l'Hermitage.

Louvois (Fr) a Premier Cru Champagne village in the Canton d'Aÿ. District: Reims.

Louwaege Brewery (Bel) a brewery (established 1877) based in Kortemark. Brews: Hapkin.

Louwshoek Voorsorg Co-operative (S.Afr) a co-operative winery based in the Breede River region. 890ha. (Add): P.O. Voorsorg 6860. Produces Laatoes and varietal wines. *See also* Daschbosch Wine Cellar.

Louzac (Fr) a commune in the Borderies (Charente-Maritime département) in the Cognac region.

Lovage (Eng) a low-alcohol, herbal beverage used as a digestive.

Lovage (Eng) a flavoured alcoholic cordial produced by Phillips of Bristol.

Lovat (Eng) a natural spring mineral water from Lovat Springs, Fanellan, Kiltarlity, Beauly, Inverness-shire.

Love Byte (Eng) the brand-name of a wine cocktail consisting of passion fruit and blood oranges 5.5% alc by vol.

Love Cocktail (Cktl) 50mls (2fl.ozs) gin, 2 dashes lemon juice, 2 dashes grenadine, 1 egg white. Shake over ice and strain into a cocktail glass.

Lovedale (Austr) an estate belonging to McWilliams in Hunter Valley, New South Wales.

Lovegrove (Austr) a winery (established 1988) based at 1420 Heidelberg-Kinglake Road, Cottles Bridge, Yarra Valley. Grape varieties: Cabernet sauvignon, Merlot, Chardonnay. Produce wines under the Dunmoochin label.

Lovelight (Cktl)(Non-alc) 25mls (⅛ gill) strawberry syrup, 25mls (⅛ gill) cream, 2 dashes lemon juice. Shake well over ice, strain into a wine goblet, top with alcohol-free wine and a lemon slice.

Lovely Jubbely (I.O.M) a Christmas ale brewed by Bushy's.

Love Potion (Eng) a drink that is supposed to arouse sexual stimulation in the person who drinks it. Some old liqueurs were based on this idea.

Löver (Hun) a lager beer brewed by the Sopron Brewery.

Lover's Dream (Cktl) a lemon flip filled up with ginger ale, also known as a Glasgow flip.

Lover's Livener (Eng) a 4.4% alc by vol. ale (with a secret aphrodisiac additive) for Valentines Day from the Newport Brewery, Isle of Wight.

Lovico Suhindol (Bul) a winery and independent co-operative with its own vineyards, the first co-op in Bulgaria (1909), and the first to be privatised (1992).

Loving Cup (Eng) a style of two handled glass/drinking vessel of which people take turns to drink out of it, especially at banquets. *See also* Johanniswein.

Loving Cup Cocktail (Cktl) pour into an ice-filled jug 50mls (2fl.ozs) brandy, 25mls (1fl.oz) Curaçao, 100mls (4fl.ozs) gomme syrup, 1 bottle claret, 1 small soda water, stir, decorate with fruit in season, mint and cucumber.

Lovin' Sup (Eng) a 4.5% alc by vol. seasonal ale brewed for Valentines brewed by Wadworth Brewery, Devizes, Wiltshire using malted oats and amber barley malt.

Low C (Eng) a bottled/keg low carbohydrate ale 1030 O.G./4.2% alc by vol. brewed by Marstons Brewery, fermented twice to convert more of the sugar to alcohol.

Low C (Eng) a low alcohol lager 1% alc by vol. from Hardy's and Hanson's in Nottinghamshire.

Lowden Hills Winery (USA) a winery based near Walla Walla Valley, Washington. Grape variety: Merlot.

Löwenbräu Brauerei (Ger) a brewery based in Munich. Brews: Hefe Weissbier, Ice Beer, Kristallweizen. Beers brewed under licence by Allied Breweries in U.K. Produces Keg 1041 O.G. (brewed by the Wrexham Brewery). Bottled Special Export 1051 O.G. and Pils 1047 O.G. are imported by Allied Breweries. In the USA is licensed by Miller.

Löwenbräu Brauerei (Switz) a brewery based in Zürich. Part of the Interbeva group.

Löwenbräu Hefe Weissbier (Ger) a 5.1% alc by vol. bottle-conditioned wheat beer brewed by the Löwenbräu Brauerei, Munich.

Löwenbräu Ice Beer (Ger) a 4.9% alc by vol. bottled ice beer brewed by the Löwenbräu Brauerei, Munich.

Löwenbräu Kristallweizen (Ger) a 4.9% alc by vol. bottled, filtered wheat beer brewed by the Löwenbräu Brauerei, Münich.

L

Löwengarten Brauerei (Switz) a brewery based in Rorschach, a part of the Interbeva group.

Löwenstein (Ger) village (Anb): Württemberg. (Ber): Württembergisch Unterland. (Gro): Salzberg. (Vins): Altenberg, Nonnenrain, Wohlfahrtsberg.

Löwenstein (Ger) village (Anb): Württemberg. (Ber): Württembergisch Unterland. (Gro): Schozachtal. (Vin): Sommerberg.

Löwenstein [ortsteil Hösslinsülz] (Ger) village (Anb): Württemberg. (Ber): Württembergisch Unterland. (Gro): Salzberg. (Vins): Dieblesberg, Zeilberg.

Löwen Weisse (Ger) a 5% alc by vol. wheat beer (cloudy or clear) from Löwenbräu, top-fermented but from lager malts. see Krystal, Hefe Weisse.

Lower Austria (Aus) a wine region, sub-divided into 8 districts. Wine towns: Retz, Krems and Lanenlois. see Niederösterreich.

Lower Corgo (Port) a district on the Douro river where the grapes are grown for Port. See also Upper Corgo.

Lower Hunter (Austr) part of the Hunter Valley wine region. Home to McWilliams, Mount Pleasant, Ladies Folley, Lindemans, Tyrrells, Rothbury. see Upper Hunter.

Lower Lake Winery (USA) a bonded winery based in Lake County, California. Grape varieties: Cabernet sauvignon and Fumé blanc. Produces varietal wines.

Lowes (Eng) a 1% alc by vol. low alcohol bottled bitter from Greene King.

Lowes Arms Brewery (Eng) a brewery (established 2001). (Add): The Lowes arms, 301 Hyde Road, Denton, Manchester, Greater Manchester M31 3FF. Brews a variety of beers. Website: http://www.lowesarms.co.uk 'E'mail: info@lowesarms.co.uk

Lowland (Scot) a classification of Scotch Malt Whisky.

Lowland Glen (Scot) a natural spring mineral water. Mineral contents (milligrammes per litre): Sodium 5.8mg/l, Calcium 6.8mg/l, Magnesium 9.7mg/l, Potassium 7mg/l, Bicarbonates 126.5mg/l, Chlorides 10mg/l, Sulphates 10mg/l, Nitrates 4mg/l.

Lowland Malt (Scot) the general term for malt whiskies produced south of the line between Dundee to Greenock. see Auchentoschan, Lowland and Rosebank.

Low Wines (W.Ind) the rum after the first distillation, has to go through a second distillation.

Low Wines (Scot) the malt whisky (at approx 21% alc by vol) after its first distillation, has to go through a second distillation. See also Strongs.

Loxarel (Sp) a noted producer of cava wines in the Penedés.

Loxley Ale (Eng) a 4.2% alc by vol. ale brewed by the Milestone Brewery C°., Nottinghamshire.

Loxley Gold (Eng) a 4.5% alc by vol. golden ale brewed by the Edale Brewery C°., Derbyshire.

Loyal Toast (Ch.Isles) brewed by Randalls Vauxlaurens Brewery in St. Peter Port, Guernsey to commemorate the visit of H.M. Queen Elizabeth II in May 1989.

Lozère (Fr) a département in Languedoc-Roussillon on the southern slopes of the Massif Central.

Lozia (Bul) vineyards.

Lozova Prachka (Bul) a red grape variety.

L.P.A. (Eng) abbr: Litres of (Pure) Absolute Alcohol.

LRN 150 (Eng) beer brewed to mark the 150th anniversary of Lowestoft-Reedham-Norwich railway line. Produced by Chalk Hill Brewery, Norwich and Green Jack Brewery, Oulton Broad (from same mash).

Luaka (Sri.L) de-caffeinated.

Lubovnianka (Slo) a sparkling natural spring mineral water from Lubovnianka, Levocske Hills, Presov, Stara Lubovna. Mineral contents (milligrammes per litre): Sodium 243.6mg/l, Calcium 213mg/l, Magnesium 204.6mg/l, Potassium 9.3mg/l, Bicarbonates 2323.6mg/l, Chlorides 15.9mg/l, Sulphates 8.14mg/l, Fluorides 0.32mg/l, Nitrates 0.65mg/l, Silicates 46.15mg/l. pH 6.25

Luca Vineyard (Arg) a vineyard belonging to the Cantena Alta Winery, Mendosa. Grape variety: Chardonnay.

Lucas Winery (USA) a small winery based west of Lodi, San Joaquin, California. 12.5ha. Grape variety: Zinfandel.

Luce (It) a sparkling natural spring mineral water from Siliqua, Cagliari. Mineral contents (milligrammes per litre): Sodium 52.8mg/l, Calcium 42.6mg/l, Magnesium 14.7mg/l, Potassium 3.1mg/l, Bicarbonates 216mg/l, Chlorides 68.5mg/l, Sulphates 31.3mg/l, Fluorides 0.5mg/l, Nitrates 0.4mg/l, Silicates 21.7mg/l. pH 7.66

Luce della Vita (It) a red wine produced jointly by Robert Mondavi and Marchesi de'Frescobaldi from 50% Sangiovese and 50% Merlot grapes. Aged in French oak and produced on a 40ha estate at Castelgiocondo. First vintage was in 1993.

Lucena (Sp) a wine town based in Montilla-Moriles, home to many wine producers.

Lucey (Fr) a commune in the Côtes de Toul, Lorraine. Produces Vins gris.

Luchon (Fr) a natural spring mineral water from the Pyrénées. (Add): SEML. 22, Avenue de Toulouse, 31110 Bagneres de Luchon. Mineral contents (milligrammes per litre): Sodium 0.8mg/l, Calcium 26.5mg/l, Magnesium 1mg/l, Potassium 0.2mg/l, Bicarbonates 78.1mg/l, Chlorides 8.2mg/l, Sulphates 2.3mg/l, Nitrates 1.8mg/l. pH 8.0

Lucido (It) a white grape variety grown in Sicily that is related to the Catarratto grape.

Lucifer (Bel) an 8% alc by vol. bottle-conditioned special Duvel beer brewed by the Riva Brasserie, Dentergem.

Lucifer Pilsner (Eng) a pilsner lager 4% alc by vol. brewed by the Raisdale Sparging and Brewing Company.

825

Lucka (Slo) a sparkling natural spring mineral water from Sachor (blue label (perliva): sparkling/green label (jemne perliva): light gas). Mineral contents (milligrammes per litre): Sodium 1.5mg/l, Calcium 62.3mg/l, Magnesium 35.2mg/l, Sulphates 13.2mg/l, Fluorides 0.15mg/l, Nitrates 5.2mg/l.

Luckens (Fr) an alternative name for the Malbec grape.

Lucky (Cktl) 10mls (½ fl.oz) Mandarine Napoléon, 25mls (1fl.oz) Cognac, 10mls (½ fl.oz) Irish Liqueur, dash pineapple syrup. Shake well over ice, strain into a highball glass, top up with tonic water and serve with a twist of lemon.

Lucky Dip (Cktl) ½ measure vodka, ¼ measure crème de banane, ¼ measure lemon squash, 1 egg white. Shake over ice and strain into a cocktail glass.

Lucky Jim (Cktl) 20mls (⅙ gill) vodka, 4 dashes French vermouth, 1 dash cucumber juice. Shake over ice and strain into a cocktail glass.

Lucky Summer (Cktl) 20mls each of Grand Marnier, Scotch whisky, lemon juice, 2 dashes grenadine. Shake with ice, strain and decorate with a cherry and slice of orange.

Lucozade (Eng) a sparkling orange and barley flavoured or natural glucose-flavoured sparkling drink produced by Smithkline Beecham Products in Middlesex. Also available are Lucozade low calorie and Sport versions.

Luddite (S.Afr) a winery (5.5ha) based in Bot River, Walker Bay, Western Cape. Grape varieties: Cabernet sauvignon, Mourvèdre, Shiraz. Labels: Barton, Hidden Valley, Iona, Niels Verburg.

Ludes (Fr) a Grand Cru Champagne village in the Canton de Verzy. District: Reims.

Ludon (Fr) a commune in the A.C. Haut-Médoc, north-western Bordeaux. Famous for Château La Lagune.

Ludovicus (Slo) a sparkling natural spring mineral water from Cigelka, Bardejov. Mineral contents (milligrammes per litre): Sodium 2.47mg/l, Calcium 35.32mg/l, Magnesium 5.6mg/l, Potassium 0.81mg/l, Bicarbonates 89.97mg/l, Chlorides 4.06mg/l, Sulphates 24.8mg/l, Fluorides 0.1mg/l, Nitrates 12.4mg/l. pH 7.82

Ludwig I Quelle (Ger) a slightly acidic natural spring mineral water. Mineral contents (milligrammes per litre): Sodium 2.84mg/l, Calcium 70.2mg/l, Magnesium 27.6mg/l, Potassium 11.2mg/l, Bicarbonates 210mg/l, Chlorides 2.28mg/l, Sulphates 122.5mg/l, Fluorides 0.3mg/l, Nitrates <0.1mg/l, Silicates 14.74mg/l. pH 4.99 Website: http://www.badbrueckenauer.de

Ludwigsburg [ortsteil Hoheneck] (Ger) village (Anb): Württemberg. (Ber): Württembergisch Unterland. (Gro): Schalkstein. (Vin): Neckarhälde.

Ludwigsburg [ortsteil Hoheneck] (Ger) village (Anb): Württemberg. (Ber): Württembergisch Unterland. (Gro): Wunnenstein. (Vin): Oberer Berg.

Ludwigshöhe (Ger) village (Anb): Rheinhessen. (Ber): Nierstein. (Gro): Krötenbrunnen. (Vin): Honigberg.

Ludwigshöhe (Ger) village (Anb): Rheinhessen. (Ber): Nierstein. (Gro): Vogelsgärten. (Vin): Teufelskopf.

Luftgeschmack (Ger) denotes wines that have been in contact with the air and have developed an unpleasant taste.

Lugana (It) a small district near the southern end of Lake Garda in the Lombardy region of northern Italy.

Lugana (It) a D.O.C. white wine from the Lombardy region. Made from the Trebbiano di lugana grape. Vinification can take place in Brescia and Verona. Still or sparkling.

Luganese (Switz) a noted vineyard based in the Sotto Ceneri, Ticino.

Lugger Cocktail (Cktl) ½ measure Cognac, ½ measure Calvados, 1 dash apricot brandy. Shake over ice and strain into a cocktail glass.

Luginsland (Ger) vineyard (Anb): Pfalz. (Ber): Mittelhaardt-Deutsche Weinstrasse. (Gro): Schnepfenflug an der Weinstrasse. (Vil): Wachenheim.

Luginsland (Ger) vineyard (Anb): Württemberg. (Ber): Remstal-Stuttgart. (Gro): Wartbühl. (Vil): Aichelberg.

Luglianca Bianca (It) a white grape variety. Also known as the Egri Leànyka in Hungary.

Luigi Bosca (Arg) a winery based in the Lujan de Cuyo and Maipú districts of the Mendoza region, eastern Argentina. Grape varieties include: Bonarda, Cabernet sauvignon, Chardonnay, Malbec, Merlot, Syrah, Torrontes. Labels: Finca la Linda and Luxury Collection. Website: http://www.luigibosca.com.ar 'E'mail: luigibosca@luigibosca.com.ar

Luigi Cocktail (Cktl) 60mls (½ gill) gin, 30mls (¼ gill) French vermouth, 1 teaspoon grenadine, 1 dash Cointreau, juice ½ tangerine. Shake over ice and strain into a cocktail glass.

Luigi Coppo e Figli (It) a winery. (Add): Via Alba 66, 14053 Canelli (Asti), produces: Barbera d'Asti, Freisa, Chardonnay, Gavi, Moscato d'Asti and Cabernet sauvignon wines.

Luigi Maffini (It) a winery based in the Avellino district in the Campania region. Produces: Kratos (IGT Paestum).

Luins (Switz). A wine-producing village in La Côte.

Luipaardsberg (S.Afr) the label for a red wine (Merlot) produced by the Du Preez Estate winery, Worcester, Western Cape.

Luisa (Cktl) ⁴⁄₁₀ measure Bacardi rum, ³⁄₁₀ measure parfait amour, ³⁄₁₀ measure fresh apple juice, dash egg white. Shake over ice, strain into a cocktail glass, top with a ½ slice of lemon and a cherry on the rim of the glass.

Luis Cetto Vineyards (Mex) a large winery based in Guadalupe, Baja California. Produces wines under the Calafia and Los Reyes labels.

Luisen (Ger) a natural spring mineral water. Mineral contents (milligrammes per litre): Sodium

L

240mg/l, Calcium 347mg/l, Magnesium 44.2mg/l, Potassium 20.3mg/l, Bicarbonates 1336mg/l, Chlorides 319mg/l, Sulphates 45mg/l. Website: http://www.hassia.com

Luisengarten (Ger) vineyard (Anb): Schloss Böckelheim. (Gro): Burgweg. (Vil): Bad Münster a. St-Ebernburg.

Luitenant (S.Afr) the label for a range of wines (military names) produced by the Domein Doornkraal winery, Little Karoo.

Luján (Arg) a wine-producing area in the Mendoza region.

Luján de Cuyo (Arg) one of three Denominaciónes de Origen of Mendoza. *see* Maipú, San Rafael.

Luksusowa (Pol) a highly refined (in a technical sense) clear vodka 44.5% alc by vol. Is rectified 3 times from potatoes. *see* Polmos.

Lumberjack's Martini (USA) the nickname for whiskey.

Lumiar (Bra) a natural spring mineral water from Rio Bonito de Lumiar, Nova Friburgo. Mineral contents (milligrammes per litre): Sodium 2.5mg/l, Calcium 1.98mg/l, Magnesium 0.57mg/l, Potassium 0.98mg/l, Bicarbonates 12.72mg/l, Chlorides 1.47mg/l, Sulphates 0.4mg/l, Fluorides 0.02mg/l, Nitrates 1.3mg/l. pH 6.01 Website: http://www.aguanovafriburgo.com.br

Lumley Old Ale (Eng) a dark winter ale 1050 O.G. brewed by the Hermitage Brewery of West Sussex.

Lump (Ger) vineyard (Anb): Franken. (Ber): Maindreieck. (Gro): Kirchberg. (Vil): Escherndorf.

Lump (Ger) vineyard (Anb): Nahe. (Ber): Schloss Böckelheim. (Gro): Paradiesgarten. (Vil): Kirschroth.

Lumumba (W.Ind) a nightcap made from a hot cocoa drink with a tot of dark rum added.

Luna (It) a sparkling natural spring mineral water from Luna, Lecco. Mineral contents (milligrammes per litre): Sodium 4.4mg/l, Calcium 44.2mg/l, Magnesium 15.7mg/l, Potassium 1.9mg/l, Bicarbonates 159.9mg/l, Chlorides 5.4mg/l, Sulphates 40.5mg/l, Nitrates 12.3mg/l, Silicates 8.5mg/l. pH 7.7

Luna de Miel (S.Afr) a barrel-fermented Chardonnay wine produced by the Avontuur Estate, Somerset West, Western Cape.

Luna [La] (Sp) a pale, dry Manzanilla Sherry from Findlaters.

Lunaie (It) an I.G.T. Chardonnay de Venezia wine (part of the Gamma range) from Bolla.

Lunares (Sp) a still natural spring mineral water from Lunares – El Cañar, Jaraba, Zaragoza. Mineral contents (milligrammes per litre): Sodium 39.5mg/l, Calcium 102.7mg/l, Magnesium 36.7mg/l, Potassium 2.7mg/l, Bicarbonates 296.3mg/l, Chlorides 58.8mg/l, Sulphates 138mg/l, Fluorides 0.3mg/l, Nitrates 14.9mg/l.

Luncheon Ale (Eng) a bitter ale 1034 O.G. brewed by the Home Brewery in Nottingham.

Luncheon Ale (Eng) a 2.5% alc by vol. bitter ale brewed by the Marston Brewery.

Luncheon Dry (Sp) a very pale, dry, Fino Sherry

from Harvey in Jerez de la Frontera. Now re-named Dune. *see* Harvey's of Bristol.

Lunchtime Special (Eng) a 2.5% alc by vol. light bitter ale brewed by Stonehenge Ales (Bunces Brewery) Ltd., Wiltshire.

Lundetangen Brewery (Nor) a noted brewery based in Skien, southern Norway.

Lundy Old Light (Eng) a cask-conditioned beer produced by a pub (Marisco Tavern) on the island of Lundy in the Bristol Channel.

Lunel (Fr) an A.C. vin doux naturel from the Hérault département of the Languedoc-Roussillon in southern France. Produced from the Muscat grape. Also produce a VdL from same grape variety.

Lunel (Hun) the name used in Tokaji for the yellow-berried version of Muscat blanc à petits grains.

Lunense (It) a white wine produced in north-western Italy in Roman times.

Lungarotti (It) a winery based at Torgiano, Umbria. 260ha. Noted for Rubesco Torgiano Riserva D.O.C.G (a single vineyard cru).

Lungo Coffee (It) a weak version of espresso coffee. *See also* Ristretto Coffee.

Lung Yen Vineyard (Chi) a white wine-producing vineyard based in Peking.

Luofushan (Chi) a natural spring mineral water. Mineral contents (milligrammes per litre): Sodium 4.81mg/l, Bicarbonates 61.63mg/l, Silicates 37.56mg/l. pH 7.0

Lupé-Cholet et Cie (Fr) a négociant-éleveur based in Nuits-Saint-Georges, Côte de Nuits, Burgundy.

Lupicaia (It) an oak aged red I.G.T. wine produced from Cabernet sauvignon and Merlot grapes by Tenuta del Terriccio in Tuscany.

Lupo Brauerei (Switz) a small brewery based in Hochdorf.

Luppolo (It) hop.

Lupulin (Eng) the name given to the sticky yellow powder in the hop cone, gives the bitter and preserving power to the hop.

Lúpulo (Port) (Sp) hop.

Lurets [Les] (Fr) a Premier Cru vineyard [part] in the A.C. commune of Volnay, Côte de Beaune, Burgundy.

Lurgashall Winery (Eng) a winery (established 1984). (Add): Dial Green, Lurgashall, Petworth, West Sussex GU28 9HA. Produces a range of wines including, white, red, sparkling, fruit and low-alcoholic. Website: http://www.lurgashall.co.uk 'E'mail: sales@lurgashall.co.uk

Lurisia (It) a sparkling natural spring mineral water from Fonte S. Barbara di Lurisia. Mineral contents (milligrammes per litre): Sodium 2.7mg/l, Magnesium <0.5mg/l, Potassium 1mg/l, Bicarbonates 14.9mg/l, Silicates 15.2mg/l. pH 6.9

Lurton [André] (Fr) a noted négociant-éleveur based in Léognan, A.C. Pessac-Léognan, south-western Bordeaux.

Lusan Premium Wines (S.Afr) the name for a group of Stellenbosch wineries: Alto, Flat Roof Manor, Hill & Dale, Le Bonheur, Neethlingshof,

Stellenzicht and Uitkyk who are marketed by Cape Legends.

Luscious (Eng) describes sweet, very rich and full-flavoured wines.

L'ush (Eng) a range of vodka-based RTD's 5.4% alc by vol.

Lush (USA) a slang term for a heavy drinker especially a female one (an alcoholic).

Lush (USA) the slang name given to the contraband liquor that was shipped to the USA during the Prohibition.

Lushai (Ind) a hardy variety of the Assam tea bush, noted for its large leaves.

Lu Shan Botanic Garden (Chi) based in the Szechwan province, it produces 'Cloud Mist' tea which originally was solely for the Emperor. Now served to Western V.I.P's.

Lushof Estate (S.Afr) a winery (established 1997) based in Stellenbosch, Western Cape. 12.5ha. Grape varieties: Cabernet sauvignon, Chardonnay, Merlot, Sauvignon blanc, Shiraz. Label: Signet. Website: http://www.lushof.co.za

Lusitania (Cktl) 1 measure dry vermouth, ½ measure brandy, dash Pernod, dash orange bitters. Shake over ice and strain into a cocktail glass.

Luso (Port) a slightly acidic natural spring mineral water from Luso 1. Mineral contents (milligrammes per litre): Sodium 6.9mg/l, Calcium 0.6mg/l, Magnesium 1.6mg/l, Potassium 0.8mg/l, Bicarbonates 11mg/l, Chlorides 8.2mg/l, Sulphates 1.3mg/l, Fluorides <0.06mg/l, Nitrates 1.8mg/l, Silicates 14.2mg/l. pH 5.6

Lussac-Saint-Émilion (Fr) a famous A.C. commune in eastern Bordeaux.

Lustadt (Ger) village (Anb): Pfalz. (Ber): Südliche Weinstrasse. (Gro): Trappenberg. (Vin): Klostergarten.

Lustau (Sp) a noted family-owned Sherry house in Jerez. (Add): Plaza del Cubo 4, Apartado 193, Jerez de la Frontera. Range includes Oloroso Muy Viejo, Otaolaurruchi and bottled Almacenista Sherries. *See also* Lustau (Emilio).

Lustau [Emilio] (Sp) a brandy producer. Produces Señor Lustau. Also produces a fine range of Sherries in Jerez de la Frontera under the Lustau label. Website: http://www.emilio-lustau.com 'E'mail: mail@emilio-lustau.com

Lusthausberg (Aus) a vineyard site on the banks of the River Danube in the Kremstal region.

Lustrillo (Sp) a style of Albariza soil in the Jerez region. Is slightly red due to the presence of iron oxide. Is known as Polvillejo in Sanlúcar de Barrameda.

Lusty Brew (Eng) denotes a strong beer or drink.

Lutèce (Fr) a brewery based in Paris that brews Lutèce–a bottom-fermented, all-malt bière de garde at 6.4% alc by vol. *see* Nouvelle de Lutèce Brasserie.

Luter (Fr) a term used in the Champenois 'To drink well/To enjoy a drink'.

Lutherwein (Aus) the nickname given to the sweet (botrytised) wines produced in the seventeenth century by the Protestant wine makers of Donnerskirchen by their Catholic neighbours.

Lutmannburg (Aus) a wine-producing area in the Mattersburg district.

Lutomer Estate (Slo) a wine producing area based in Slovenia. Grape varieties grown include Laski Rizling, Chardonnay, Pinot blanc, Gewürztraminer. Noted for the wine Ranina Radogan (Tiger's Milk).

Lutomer Fruit Cup (Cup) 1 bottle Lutomer Riesling, 500mls (1pint) soda water, fruit in season. Place fruit in the wine, chill down and add soda water prior to service.

Lutomer-Ormoz (Slo) a town and area of the Slovenia region. Welschriesling and Lutjomer riesling are best known wines. Also spelt Ljutomer-Ormoz.

Lutry (Switz) a wine-producing district near Lavaux in central Vaud.

Lutte (Fr) lit: 'the struggle', the term used to describe the fight against disease and parasites the vignéron has in his/her vineyards. Classed as *Lutte Intégrée* (natural methods – purely using organic and nature), *Lutte Raisonnée* (sensible methods – mixture of natural and precautionary methods), *Lutte d'Assurance* (precautions taken whether required or not).

Luttenberger (Ger) the name used for Lutomer produced in Slovenia (former Yugoslavia) before the First World War.

Lüttertaler (Ger) a natural spring mineral water. Mineral contents (milligrammes per litre): Sodium 5.8mg/l, Calcium 30mg/l, Magnesium 16.7mg/l, Potassium 0.5mg/l, Chlorides 8.6mg/l, Fluorides 0.3mg/l.

Lüttje Lage (Ger) lit; 'little one', a small beer accompanied by a korn (schnapps), the customary drink served at Schützenfest (is drunk simultaneously).

Lütz Bier (Switz) a 5% alc by vol. beer brewed with a light taste by the Feldschlösschen Brauerei in Brunswick.

Lützelberg (Ger) vineyard (Anb): Baden. (Ber): Kaiserstuhl-Tuniberg. (Gro): Vulkanfelsen. (Vil): Sasbach.

Lützelsachsen (Ger) village (Anb): Baden. (Ber): Badische Bergstrasse/Kraichgau. (Gro): Rittersberg. (Vin): Stephausberg.

Lützeltalerberg (Ger) vineyard (Anb): Franken. (Ber): Mainviereck. (Gro): Not yet assigned. (Vil): Grosswallstadt.

Lutzville Cape Diamond Vineyards (S.Afr) the name for the Lutzville Co-operative Winery.

Lutzville Co-operative (S.Afr) a co-operative winery (established 1961) based in Lutzville, Oliphants River, Western Cape. 2100ha. (Add): Box 50, Lutzville 8165 (also known as the Lutzville Cape Diamond Vineyards). Grape varieties: Cabernet sauvignon, Chardonnay, Chenin blanc, Merlot, Muscadel, Pinotage, Ruby cabernet, Sauvignon blanc, Shiraz. Produces: Bat's Rock, Laat Oes and varietal wines. Website: http://www.lutzvillevineyards.com

Luxardo (It) a famous liqueur producer noted for

L

maraschino based in Padua. Range also includes Passione liqueurs with a Sambuca base.

Luxator (Lux) a dark beer brewed by the Clausen Brasserie in Mousel.

Luxembourg (Lux) a small country whose small wine region follows the banks of the river Moselle. Main grape variety: Rivaner. Produces light, dry white wines that undergo taste tests. (**Marque Nationale** 12/20 in tasting, **Vin Classé** 14/20. **Premier Cru** 16/20, **Grand Premier Cru** 18/20). *see* Appellation Complète, Marque Nationale. Also produces fine Eaux-de-vies.

Luxembourgeois Moselle (Lux) a very light, sharp, often pétillant wine, almost colourless. It is light and has a cider (apple) scent.

Luxury Cocktail (Cktl) ⅓ measure gin, ⅙ measure each of banana liqueur, vermouth, Pimm's N°1, lime cordial, 1 dash Angostura. Shake over ice and strain into a cocktail glass.

Luxury Cocktail (Cktl) 40mls (⅓ gill) Cognac, 2 dashes orange bitters. Pour into a Champagne saucer glass and top with iced Champagne.

Luxury Double (Eng) the label of an ale brewed by Youngs of London.

Luxury Wine (Eng) a liqueur wine. i.e. Vin doux naturel and Vin de Liqueur.

Luzech (Fr) a wine-producing area in central Cahors, south-western France.

Luzhanka (Ukr) a natural spring mineral water (established 1994) from Svalyana, Transcarpathian. Mineral contents (milligrammes per litre): Sodium 900mg/l, Calcium 50-200mg/l, Magnesium <25mg/l, Potassium 900mg/l, Bicarbonates >2000mg/l, Chlorides <100mg/l, Sulphates <50mg/l.

L.V.A. (Eng) *abbr:* Licensed Vituallers Association a national body of Landlords (full On-licence holders) who wish to promote the interests of the '*Licensed trade*'.

L.V.K. Tagovischte (Bul) privatised winery that buys in its own grapes.

Lyaeus (Lat) a word used for Bacchus. *See also* Bassareus, Bromius, Dionysus, Eleleus, Euan, Euhius, Euius, Lacchus and Thyoneus.

Lyaskovetz (Bul) a vineyard area based in the foothills of the Balkans in Northern Basic region. Grape varieties include Cabernet sauvignon, Merlot.

Lychee (Cktl) *see* Lichee.

Lychee Chiew (Chi) a lychee-flavoured wine. It has a strength and taste similar to sweet Sherry.

Lydda (Isr) a white Palestinian wine written about by the Romans.

Lyde (It) a natural spring mineral water from Lyde.

Lying-Arm (Ire) *see* Lyne Arm.

Lymington Vineyard (Eng) a vineyard based at Furzay Cottage, Wainsford, Lymington, Hampshire. Grape varieties: Gutenborner, Huxelrebe, Müller-Thurgau and Schönburger.

Lympha (Lat) water.

Lynch-Bages (Fr) *see* Château Lynch-Bages. The property gets its name from having once belonged to an Irishman called Lynch, Mayor of Bordeaux. Today it belongs to the Cazes family.

Lynchet (Eng) an old English name for the terrace on which vines were grown to get the best sun in England.

Lynch Meritage (Arg) the label for a Bordeaux-style red wine produced by Bodegas Benegas, Mendoza.

Lynch-Moussas (Fr) *see* Château Lynch-Moussas. The property gets its name from having once belonged to an Irishman called Lynch, Mayor of Bordeaux.

Lyndale (Austr) a brand of white (Riesling) wine produced by Orlando Winery.

Lyne Arm (Ire) part of the pot-still, a long, horizontal portion of the still-head in which it lies submerged in a shallow trough filled with water, between the still-head and the condenser. Also known as the Lying-arm.

Lyne Down Farm (Eng) cider and perry producers based at Much Marcle, Herefordshire. Noted for Mothers Special.

Lyne Down Perry (Eng) a perry produced at Lyne Down Farm, Much Marcle, Herefordshire.

Lynesack Porter (Eng) a 5% alc by vol. porter from the Butterknowle Brewery, Lynesack, near Bishop Auckland.

Lynfred Winery (USA) a winery based in Roselle, Illinois. Produces French hybrid, vinifera and native grape wines.

Lyngrove (S.Afr) a winery (established 2000) based in Stellenbosch, Western Cape. 76ha. Grape varieties: Cabernet sauvignon, Chardonnay, Chenin blanc, Merlot, Pinotage, Sauvignon blanc, Shiraz. Labels: Platinum, Reserve. (Wines are included in the Baarsma Wine Group). Website: http://www.lyngrove.co.za

Lynmar (USA) a winery based in the Russian River Valley, Sonoma County, California. Grape variety: Pinot noir. Label: Quail Hill Vineyard.

Lynx (It) a sparkling natural spring mineral water from Fonti di San Fermo, Monte Pelpi, Masanti of Bedonia, Parma. Mineral contents (milligrammes per litre): Sodium 2.4mg/l, Calcium 51.4mg/l, Magnesium 4.8mg/l, Bicarbonates 165mg/l, Chlorides 4.05mg/l, Sulphates 12.4mg/l, Oxygen 7.6mg/l, Silicates 4.5mg/l. pH 7.45

Lynx Lager (Eng) an '*own label*' canned lager beer from the Booker Cash and Carry. (Add): Malt House, P.O. Box 65, Field End, Eastcote, Ruislip, Middlesex HA4 9LA.

Lynx Wines (S.Afr) a winery (established 2002) based in Franschhoek, Western Cape. 11ha. Grape varieties: Cabernet franc, Cabernet sauvignon, Merlot, Tinto, Shiraz, Viognier. Label: Xanache. Website: http://www.lynxwines.co.za

Lyonnaise Blanche (Fr) an alternative name for the Muscadet grape in south-eastern France.

Lyons Tetley (Eng) a famous firm noted for their wide range of teas and coffees.

Lyophilization (Eng) a method of freeze-drying freshly brewed coffee to make instant coffee.

L

Lyot (Rus) ice.

Lyre [En] (Fr) a highly, work-intensive, wide, high, v-shaped vine-training method developed by Dr. Alain Carbonneau which allows more leaves on the vine to photosynthesise whilst leaving the grapes to still be exposed to the sun's rays. System is used in the Hautes-Côtes, Burgundy and other countries.

Lyric (S.Afr) the label for a white wine (Chardonnay, Chenin blanc and Sauvignon blanc blend) produced by the Nederburg Estate, Wellington, Western Cape.

Lys (Den) light-coloured beer.

Lys [Les] (Fr) a Premier Cru A.C. Chablis often reclassified as the Premier Cru Vaillons.

Lysander (Cyp) the brand-name of a medium-sweet Cyprus Sherry.

Lysholm Aquavit (Nor) a light, delicate brand of aquavit which is matured in new Sherry casks. Produced by Vinmonopolet.

Lysine (Eng) an amino acid found in wines, formed by the yeasts.

Lyst Øl (Den) light beer.

Lytton Springs Winery (USA) a winery based near Healdsburg, Sonoma County, California. Grape variety: Zinfandel. Valley Vista is its home vineyard.

Lyttos (Gre) a natural spring mineral water. Mineral contents (milligrammes per litre): Sodium 16mg/l, Calcium 50.5mg/l, Magnesium 11.3mg/l, Potassium 0.8mg/l, Bicarbonates 199.9mg/l, Chlorides 24.2mg/l, Sulphates 6.3mg/l, Nitrates 4mg/l. pH 7.7

M

M.A. (Fr) *abbr*: Marque Anonyme, Marque Autorisée, Marque Auxiliaire, Marque d'Acheteur. Denotes any subsidiary name belonging to an establishment responsible for marketing Champagne that has been made by another producer, or made by a grower registered by C.I.V.C.

MA (Wal) a mixture of SA and Dark. Produced by the Brain's Brewery in Cardiff for The Crown public house in Skewen, near Swansea.

Ma'a (Arab) water.

Ma'a Ma'adani (Arab) mineral water.

Maankloof (S.Afr) the label for a range of wines (white, rosé and red) produced by the Mountain River Wines winery, Paarl, Western Cape.

Maarum (Den) a sparkling natural spring mineral water (established 1934) from Maarum, Gribskov. Mineral contents (milligrammes per litre): Sodium 400mg/l, Calcium 30mg/l, Magnesium 20mg/l, Potassium 10mg/l, Bicarbonates 1100mg/l, Chlorides 200mg/l, Fluorides 2mg/l, Nitrates <1mg/l.

Maasland Brouwerij (Hol) a brewery based in Oss, Brabant. Range includes D'n Schele Os, Witte Wieven Wirbier, Super Strongbock, Mallemok Amber.

Mabille (Fr) the name for the Horizontal Press.

Maborange (Fr) an orange liqueur produced by Intermarque.

Macabeo (Fr) a white grape variety grown in the south of Spain. Is also known as Alcañol, Alcanón and Viura. Also spelt Maccabéo, Maccabeu.

Macacauba (Port) the Brazilian mahogany from which Port wine vats are made (together with oak and chestnut).

Macaco (Port) lit: 'monkey', it is a wooden contrivance used to keep the must moving up and down in the lagares.

Macallan [The] (Scot) a single highland malt whisky distillery (established 1824). (Add): Easter Elchies, Craigellachie, Aberlour, Banffshire AB38 9RX. Produces 10 year old, 15 year old, 18 year old 43% alc by vol. (distilled 1973, bottled 1991). Vintage 1938, 1950, 1963 at 43% alc by vol. Produces:–10 y.o., 12 y.o., 15 y.o., 18 y.o., 25 y.o., 30 y.o., 1946, 1948, 1951, 1961 single malts, Cask Reserve, Millenium Decanter, 1861 Replica and Vintage Travel Range. Also produced for the Royal Wedding a blend of 1948 and 1961 single malts (birth years), plus Elegancia, The Macallan 60 year old (the most expensive malt whisky) and The Macallan Rare Reserved Distilled 1886. Website: http://www.themacallan.com

Macallan [The] (60 year old) (Scot) as yet the world's most expensive whisky produced by Macallan. Sold in a specially designed box of glass and brass (spirit safe shaped). Limited quantities.

Macallan [The] 1861 Replica (Scot) a single malt whisky 47.2% alc by vol. limited edition presented in a replica of the bottle type of the period.

Macallan-Glenlivet (Scot) a single malt highland whisky distillery based west of Rothes, Morayshire. A highland malt. Produces Macallan 80°, also a 10 year old, 18 year old, 45% alc by vol. and a 25 year old 45% alc by vol.

Macardles Brewery (Ire) a brewery based in Dundalk. Is part of Guinness-controlled Irish Ale Breweries. Produces keg and bottled ales.

Macaroni Cocktail (Cktl) ⅔ measure pastis, ⅓ measure sweet vermouth. Shake over ice and strain into a cocktail glass.

MᵃᶜArthurs (Scot) a selected blended Scotch whisky from Airdrie, Lanarkshire 40% alc by vol. Produced by Inver House Distillers.

Macau (Fr) a commune within the A.C. Haut-Médoc in north-western Bordeaux.

Maccabee (Isr) a sharp, bitter, straw coloured, bottled lager beer (1045 O.G) 4.9% alc by vol. brewed by Tempo Beer Industries, Netanya. Israel's sole producer of beer.

Maccabéo (Fr) the alternative spelling of Macabeo used in south-western France.

Maccabeu (Fr) an alternative spelling of Macabeo.

Macca Cocktail (Cktl) ⅓ measure dry gin, ⅓ measure dry vermouth, ⅓ measure sweet vermouth, 2 dashes crème de cassis. Stir over ice, strain into an ice-filled highball glass, top with soda water, dash of lemon peel juice and a lemon peel spiral.

Macchialupa (It) a vineyard in the DOCG Fiano di Avellino, Campania. Grape variety: Fiano di Avellino.

Macchinetta da Caffè (It) coffee mill.

Macchiole [Le] (It) a wine estate based in Bolgheri, Tuscany. Grape varieties: Cabernet franc, Merlot, Cabernet sauvignon, Sangiovese. Produces Messorio, Paléo Rosso wines.

MᵃᶜDonald and Muir (Scot) are highland malt whisky distillers based near Tain. Own Glenmorangie and Glenmoray-Glenlivet Distilleries. Brands include: Highland Queen, Muirheads, Glenmoray and Glenmorangie.

M

M^{ac}**Donald Greenlees** (Scot) a Scotch whisky distiller based at Leith, Midlothian. Produces Old Parr, 43% alc by vol (part of DCL). Glendullan Distillery still is licensed to M^{ac}Donald Greenlees.

M^{ac}**Duff** (Scot) a single highland malt whisky distillery in Banffshire. Produces a vintage 1963. Sometimes sold under the name of Glendeveron 40% alc by vol.

Macedonia (Gre) a wine region of northern Greece. Has O.P.A.P. regions of Amindeo, Naoussa, Goumenissa, Côtes de Meliton. T.O. region of Drama, Macedonia.

Macedonia (Ser) *see* Makedonija.

Maceracíon Semicarbónica (Sp) a method of fermentation. *see* Intercellular Fermentation.

Maceratino (It) a white grape variety grown in the Marches region.

Maceration (Eng) used in the making of aromatised wines and liqueurs. Herbs etc. are steeped in the wine/spirit to extract the flavour. (Fr) = macération.

Macération (Fr) maceration.

Macération Carbonique (Fr) a method of fermentation (at 30°C to 32°C) where the whole grapes are placed into large sealed vats under a slight pressure and allowed to ferment for 4 days before pressing, (fermentation at 20°C is then completed). This method produces light wines with plenty of colour and fruit without the tannin. i.e. Beaujolais Nouveau. *see* Dufays [Doctor].

Macération Pelliculaire (Fr) a term used to denote extended skin contact time during vinification. Adds richness and extract.

Macération Préfermentaire (Fr) a term to denote fermentation of must on skins

Macération Préfermentaire à Chaud (Fr) *abbr*: M.P.C. A technique that involves heating the grape must at the pre-fermentation stage before cooling it gradually to a temperature of 25°C (77°F). Leads to extraction of aromas and development of tannin structure, colour and taste of wine.

Macération Semi-Carbonique (Fr) *see* Intercellular Fermentation.

Macere (It) a natural spring mineral water from Matelica, Macerata.

Mace Sparkling Irish Spring water (Ire) a sparkling natural spring mineral water. Mineral contents (milligrammes per litre): Sodium 31mg/l, Calcium 8mg/l, Magnesium 8mg/l, Potassium 0.3mg/l, Bicarbonates 95.7mg/l, Chlorides 26mg/l, Sulphates 5mg/l, Nitrates mg/l. pH 7.6

Machackala (Rus) a wine region based in eastern Russia that produces mainly dessert wines.

Machanudo Fino Inocente (Sp) a brand of Fino Sherry produced by Valdespino in Jerez de la Frontera.

Macharnudo (Sp) chalk soil, an area of Andalusia. *See also* Marchanudo.

Machatten (Cktl) 35mls (1½ fl.ozs) Scotch whisky, 25mls (1fl.oz) sweet Martini, 10mls (½ fl.oz) Glayva, dash Angostura. Stir over ice, strain into an old-fashioned glass and add a cherry.

Mâché (Fr) lit: 'mashed', denotes a disturbed, unsettled wine.

Macherelles [Les] (Fr) a Premier Cru vineyard [part] in the A.C. commune of Chassagne-Montrachet, Côte de Beaune, Burgundy. 8.01ha (red and white).

Machiavelli (It) a vineyard (60ha). (Add): Villa Belvedere, 37010 Calmasino, Verona. Produces Chianti Classico plus Riserva, also Ser Niccolò (oak aged Cabernet sauvignon), Il Piano (white wine from red Canaiolo grapes).

Machinetta (It) the alternative name for the Neapolitain Pot coffee-making method.

Machtum (Lux) a wine village on the river Moselle. Sites are Ongkaf and Gollebour.

Macintyre (Scot) a blended whisky distributed by Kilsern Distillers, Leicester. *See also* Feeny's, Rostov Imperial Vodka, Marlborough London Dry.

Mack Brewery (Nor) a noted brewery based in Tromso. Is the most northerly brewery in the world!

Mackenzie (Port) vintage Port shippers. Vintages: 1870, 1873, 1875, 1878, 1881, 1884, 1887, 1890, 1896, 1900, 1904, 1908, 1912, 1919, 1920, 1922, 1927, 1935, 1945, 1947, 1948, 1950, 1952, 1954, 1955, 1957, 1958, 1960, 1963, 1966.

Mackenzie (Scot) a blended Scotch whisky 40% alc by vol.

MacKenzie's (Sp) a solera gran reserva brandy produced by John Harvey & Sons.

Mackeson's Brewery (Eng) a brewery (established 1669) was originally based in Hythe, Kent, now the famous milk stout is owned and brewed by Whitbread Breweries.

Mackeson's Stout (Eng) a bottled sweet stout 1042 O.G. created in 1910 by the Mackeson's Brewery but now brewed by Whitbread.

Mackinlay and C°. [Charles] (Scot) a fine whisky producer now owned by Invergordon Distillers. Produces highland malts and blended Scotch whiskies. These include Glenallachie, Isle of Jura, Legacy and The Original M^{ac}kinlay.

M^{ac}**kinlay-McPherson** (W.Ind) a distiller based in Jamaica. Produces Windjammer (a dark, navy rum).

M^{ac}**Kinlay's** (Scot) a blended Scotch whisky produced by Charles M^{ac}Kinlay and C°. Now owned by Invergordon Distillers.

M^{ac}**Kinlay's Legacy** (Scot) a 12 year old de luxe blended Scotch whisky blended by Donald M^{ac}Kinlay. 40% alc by vol. Produced by Charles M^{ac}Kinlay and C°. Now owned by Invergordon Distillers.

M^{ac}**Kinlay's Vatted Old Ben Vorlich** (Scot) the first proprietary brand of Scotch whisky produced by Charles M^{ac}Kinlay and C°. Now owned by Invergordon Distillers.

Mackintosh [The] (Scot) the brand-name for a blended Scotch whisky produced by Hiram Walker 40% alc by vol.

Maclay Brewery (Scot) a brewery based in Alloa.

Produces cask-conditioned keg and bottled ales. Noted for Imperial Pale 1030 O.G. Scotch Ale 5% alc by vol. Eighty Shilling Export Ale 4% alc by vol. Also Black Jock, Full Malty, HopScotch, Ruadh, Thrapple Warmer.

Macleod's (Scot) producers of Isle of Skye, an 8 year old Scotch whisky 40% alc by vol. Based in Edinburgh.

MᵃᶜMillan Wines (N.Z) a winery based in Nelson that owns no vineyards. Produce Chardonnay and botrytised Chardonnay.

Mac'n Ernie's Alco-Cola (Eng) a 4% alc by vol. micro-brewed cola with a real head on the top.

Mâcon (Fr) a district within the Burgundy region. Produces classic white wines and some red. (Coms): Boyer, Bresse-sur-Grosne, Champagny-sous-Uxelles, Champlieu, Etringy, Jugy, Laives, Mancey, Montceaux-Ragny, Nanton, Sennecey-le-Grand (Vers). *See also* Pouilly Fuissé, Pouilly-Loché, Pouilly-Vinzelles and Saint-Véran.

Mâconnais Blanc (Fr) an A.C. white wine from the Mâcon district in the Burgundy region. Minimum alc by vol. 10%.

Mâconnaise (Fr) an 800mls bottle (1.825pints) used in the Mâconnais region.

Mâconnaise (Fr) a wine cask of 212litres (58gallons) used in the Mâconnais region.

Mâcon-Rouge (Fr) an A.C. red wine from the Mâconnais region of southern Burgundy. Minimum alc by vol. 9%.

Mâcon Supérieur (Fr) a red and white A.C. wines from the Saône-et-Loire in the Mâconnais district in Burgundy.

Mâcon Villages (Fr) an A.C. commune within the district of Mâconnais in Burgundy. The name of the commune may replace name of village.

Mâcon-Viré (Fr) *see* Viré.

Macphail's (Scot) a highland malt whisky produced by Gordon & Macphail in Elgin. 10 year old, 43% alc by vol.

MᵃᶜQueens Nessie Whisky (Aus) a red beer produced by Eggenberger Brauerei using imported Scotch whisky malt. *see* Urbock 23°.

Macro-Climate (Eng) a term used by winemakers to describe a regional climate. *see* Meso-climate, Micro-climate.

Mac's Brown Ale (Eng) a bottled brown ale 1031 O.G. brewed by the MᶜMullen Brewery of Hertford.

Mac's Folly (Cktl) pour into a large jug 1 bottle gin, 1 measure dry vermouth, add plenty of ice, stir and serve.

Mac's N°1 (Eng) a keg/bottled ale 1036 O.G. brewed by the MᶜMullens Brewery in Hertford.

Maculan (It) a winery based at Breganze in Veneto. 11ha. Grape varieties include: Moscato. Also buys in grapes. Wines sold under Breganze and Dindarello labels.

Macvin (Fr) a liqueur from the Jura, consists of newly fermented red wine mixed with marc, cinnamon and coriander. Also spelt Maquevin.

Màd (Hun) a wine-producing village in the southern foothills.

Madame Goupil (Fr) a noted wine-producer based at Dampierre-sur-Loire, Saumur, Anjou-Saumur, Loire. Noted for Saumur Mousseux.

Madargues (Fr) a sub-appellation of V.D.Q.S. Côtes d'Auvergne region.

Mädchentraube (Aus) a red grape variety rarely grown now. Also known as the Feteasca.

Madder-Wort (Eng) *see* Garance.

Mad Dog (Eng) a 4.4% alc by vol. ale brewed by Elgood & Sons Ltd., Cambridgeshire.

Madeira (Mad) lit: 'wood', a DOC wine-producing island in the Atlantic ocean off the north-western coast of Africa. Belonging to Portugal, it is noted for fine fortified wines. *see* Estufado, Zarco (João Gonçalves). *See also* Tossed Wines.

Madeira (Mad) a fortified wine from the island of Madeira. Produced by the Estufado method and Solera system of blending. *see* Cubas de Calor, Sercial, Verdelho, Bual, Malmsey. (Fr) = Madère, (Hol) = Madera.

Madeira (USA) *see* California Madeira.

Madeira Cake (Eng) a British invention, cake eaten with Madeira wine. Does not contain Madeira wine in the recipe and is not from the island of Madeira.

Madeira Cup (Cktl) into a large jug place some ice, juice of a lemon, 60mls (½ gill) mandarine liqueur, 1 bottle Sercial Madeira, 1 bottle soda water. Stir well and decorate with slices of lemon and borage.

Madeira Guinada (Mad) a style of Madeira, laced with quinine that was originally sold to the British army in the nineteenth century.

Madeira Mint Flip (Cktl) 40mls (⅓ gill) Bual Madeira, 15mls (⅛ gill) Royal Mint Chocolate Liqueur, 3 dashes gomme syrup, 1 egg. Shake well over ice, strain into a large cocktail glass, top with grated nutmeg and chocolate.

Madeira Wine Company (Mad) a group of 27 major Madeira producers (established 1913) who joined forces to market Madeira wine.

Madeira Wine Institute (Mad) known as the I.V.M. Formed in 1979. Fixes the dates for start of harvest, banned the use of hybrid direct producer grapes for use in Madeira. Grant's 'Selo de Garantia', runs laboratory tests. *see* Instituto do Vinho da Madeira.

Madeleine Angevine (Ger) a white grape variety. Also known as Angevine.

Madeleine Collignon (Fr) a cuvée in the vineyard of Mazis-Chambertin, Grand Cru A.C. Gevrey-Chambertin, Côte de Nuits, Burgundy. 1.5ha (owned by the Hospices de Beaune).

Madera (Hol) Madeira.

Madera (USA) a wine district within the Great Central Valley that produces sweet dessert wines.

Madère (Fr) Madeira.

Mader et Fils (Fr) an Armagnac producer based in Ténarèze. (Add): Chemin de Ronde, 32190-Vic-Fezensac.

M

Maderisé (Fr) the term for white or rosé wines that have begun to spoil. It is caused by the wines contact with heat, oxygen or air. Makes the wine taste unpleasant, flat and musty. Not to be confused with Madeira.

Maderization (Eng) *see* Maderisé.

Maderize (Eng) *see* Maderisé.

Maderizzato (It) wines that have taken on a flavour reminiscent of Madeira due to oxidation. Not desirable in table wines, only in dessert wines.

Made-Wines (USA) wines made from preserved musts or dried raisins and not from freshly gathered grapes. *See also* British Wine.

Mad Ferret (Eng) a 4.3% alc by vol. seasonal ale brewed in May and June by Hydes Anvil, Manchester.

Madfish (Austr) a label of the Howard Park Winery, Western Australia. Grape varieties include: Cabernet sauvignon, Merlot.

Madhulika (Ind) a spirit made from wheat.

Madhvi (Sri.L) the name given to an arrack made from mahua flowers, also called Daru spirit.

Madilla (W.Ind) the middle part of the distillation of rum (the heart of the spirit). *See also* Aguardiente.

Madiran (Fr) an A.C. red wine of the Béarn, Basses Pyrénées département. A little white Madiran is also made. Grape varieties: Acheria rouge, Cabernet franc, Cabernet sauvignon, Fer and Tannat (up to 60%). Minimum alc by vol. 11%.

Mad Judge (Eng) a beer infused with cranberry juice. Brewed by Greene King. Part of their King's Court range.

Mad M^{ac}Cauley (Eng) the name of a 5% alc by vol. lemonade from Malt House Vintners.

Madone [La] (Fr) a fine vineyard in the A.C. Fleurie Cru Beaujolais-Villages.

Madonna Alta (It) a winery in the DOCG Sagrantino di Montefalco, Umbria region.

Madonna della Guardia (It) a sparkling natural spring mineral water from Madonna della guardia. Mineral contents (milligrammes per litre): Sodium 6.5mg/l, Calcium 20.5mg/l, Magnesium 4.3mg/l, Potassium 0.22mg/l, Bicarbonates 72.7mg/l, Chlorides 10.3mg/l, Sulphates 14.9mg/l, Nitrates 4.8mg/l, Silicates 11.6mg/l. pH 7.78

Madonna dell'Ambro (It) a sparkling natural spring mineral water from Fonti Gallo, Ascoli Piceno. Mineral contents (milligrammes per litre): Sodium 12.2mg/l, Calcium 82.96mg/l, Magnesium 33.6mg/l, Potassium 2.4mg/l, Bicarbonates 396.62mg/l, Chlorides 12.5mg/l, Sulphates 30.09mg/l, Fluorides 0.25mg/l, Nitrates 2.05mg/l, Silicates 14.5mg/l, Oxygen 7.99mg/l. pH 7.4

Madonna della Mercede (It) a natural spring mineral water from Madonna della Mercede. Mineral contents (milligrammes per litre): Sodium 48.4mg/l, Calcium 106.1mg/l, Magnesium 44.2mg/l, Potassium 3.6mg/l, Bicarbonates 475mg/l, Chlorides 39.3mg/l, Sulphates 86.4mg/l, Nitrates 28.6mg/l, Silicates 15.3mg/l. pH 7.2

Madonnenberg (Ger) vineyard (Anb): Baden. (Ber): Badische Bergstrasse/Kraichgau. (Gro): Rittersberg. (Vil): Schriesheim.

Madonnina della Calabria (It) a sparkling natural spring mineral water. Mineral contents (milligrammes per litre): Sodium 10mg/l, Calcium 9.2mg/l, Magnesium 4.1mg/l, Potassium 1.5mg/l, Bicarbonates 33.9mg/l, Chlorides 18.7mg/l, Sulphates 4.9mg/l, Oxygen 6.2mg/l, Silicates 13.5mg/l. pH 7.35

Madre (It) the name given to the wine kept in the cask from the previous bottling to which the next Vin Santo is added.

Madre (Sp) bunch of grapes.

Madrear (Sp) a term denoting the throwing of the complete bunch of grapes into the wine that has fermented to create a second fermentation.

Madre Pulque (Mex) lit: 'mother pulque', the fermentation of pulques after 10 days of slow fermentation.

Madre Vinho (Port) used to sweeten dessert wines, new must boiled to a syrup consistency.

Madre Vino (It) used to sweeten dessert wines, new must boiled to a syrup consistency.

Madrid (Sp) a city that was created a D.O. wine zone in 1990. Home to the D.O. Vinos de Madrid.

Madrid Pact (Sp) *see* Protection of Names.

Madrigal (Ger) bottle size. 35cls (¾ pint).

Madroñales (Sp) an area within Andalusia. Vineyards produce the grapes for Sherry.

Madrona Ranch Vineyards (USA) a vineyard based in the Sierra Foothills, California. Grape varieties: Cabernet sauvignon and Zinfandel. Produce varietal wines.

Madulsa (Lat) drunkard.

Madura (W.Ind) an orange liqueur made in Martinique. Also spelt Maduva.

Maduro (Port) an old or matured wine.

Maduva (W.Ind) an orange-flavoured spirit drink produced on the island of Martinique.

Ma-eem (Isr) water.

Ma-eem Mineralim (Isr) mineral water.

Maekjoo (Kor) beer.

Mælk (Den) milk.

Maes Cool (Bel) a 5.7% alc by vol. bottom fermented ice beer produced by the Alken-Maes Brasserie, Alken.

Maese Joan Sdad. Coop. Ltda. (Sp) a winery. (Add): Camino Santa Lucia, s/n 01320 Oyon, Alava. 175ha. Wines include Viñalzada, Armorial, Maese Joan.

Maestro (Swe) a sparkling natural spring mineral water (established 1996) from Helsingborg. Mineral contents (milligrammes per litre): Sodium 54mg/l, Calcium 55mg/l, Magnesium 5.3mg/l, Potassium 3mg/l, Bicarbonates 180mg/l, Chlorides 34mg/l, Sulphates 70mg/l, Fluorides 0.25mg/l, Nitrates <1mg/l.

Maestro [El] (Sp) the name given to a large cask known in the nineteenth century as El Cristo.

Maestro Lorenzo (Eng) the brand-name of a dark espresso coffee produced by Jacobs-Suchard. Available as beans or in ground form.

M

Maestro Vino (Sp) lit: 'master wine', used for adding colour to Málaga wine.

Maeve's Crystal Wheat (Ire) a 4.7% alc by vol. medium bodied wheat beer brewed by the Dublin Brewing Company in Dublin.

Magaratch Bastardo (Rus) a red grape variety produced by crossing Portugieser x Saperavi by the Magaratch Research Institute.

Magaratch Research Centre (Rus) an experimental station based at Yalta in the Crimea that tries to improve the quality of wines.

Magaratch Ruby (Rus) a red grape variety produced by crossing Cabernet sauvignon x Saperavi at the Magaratch Research Institute.

Magazzin (It) a noted distiller of maraschino and other liqueurs.

Magdala (Chile) a soft red wine produced by Torres mainly from the Pinot noir grape.

Magdalen (Eng) a white table wine produced by the Pulham Vineyards in Diss, Norfolk.

Magdalenenkreuz (Ger) vineyard (Anb): Rheingau. (Ber): Johannisberg. (Gro): Burgweg. (Vil): Rüdesheim.

Magdelaine (Fr) see Château Magdelaine.

Magdelen Rivaner (Eng) a white wine made from the Müller-Thurgau grape produced by the Pulham Vineyards in Norfolk.

Mager (Ger) thin, lacking in body, an undistinguished wine.

Maggi (It) a sparkling (metodo tradizionale) wine producer based in Lombardy. Labels include: Cristal Pinot Brut.

Maggs Mild (Eng) a 3.8% alc by vol. mild ale brewed by the West Berkshire Brewery C°. Ltd., Berkshire.

Magia (S.Afr) the label for a red wine (Cabernet franc 35%, Cabernet sauvignon 42% and Merlot 23% blend) produced by the Môreson winery, Franschhoek, Western Cape.

Magic (Swe) a non-alcoholic energy drink produced with guarana, ginseng and fructose.

Magical (Sp) the brand-name for a range of Sherries produced by the Bodegas Magical in Jerez de la Frontera.

Magic Mushroom (Eng) a 3.8% alc by vol. mild ale brewed by Whim Ales Ltd., Hartington, near Buxton, Derbyshire.

Magic Trace (Cktl) ⁵/₁₀ measure Bourbon whiskey, ¹/₁₀ measure lemon juice, ¹/₁₀ measure orange juice, ¹/₁₀ measure dry vermouth, ²/₁₀ measure Drambuie. Shake over ice and strain into a cocktail glass.

Magie (Eng) a species of barley (malt) from the Golden Promise variety. Gives medium sugar yields.

Magik (Eng) a 4.2% alc by vol. ale brewed by the Keltek Brewing C°. Ltd., Cornwall.

Magill Estate [The] (Austr) the name given to a red wine produced by Penfolds matured in French/American oak.

Magistral Etiqueta Negra (Sp) a solera reserva brandy produced by Emilio Hidalgo.

Magistral Etiqueta Roja (Sp) a solera brandy produced by Emilio Hidalgo.

Maglieri (Austr) a winery noted for Shiraz wines. (Add): Douglas Gully Road, M°Laren Flat, M°Laren Vale, South Australia.

Magliocco Canino (It) a red grape variety grown in Calabria. The local name for the Gaglioppo grape.

Magma (Eng) a schnapps-based liqueur drink 24% alc by vol. flavoured with cinnamon and chilli and produced by Allied-Domecq.

Magna (Bra) a natural spring mineral water. Mineral contents (milligrammes per litre): Sodium 4.1mg/l, Calcium 3.46mg/l, Magnesium 1.14mg/l, Potassium 3mg/l, Bicarbonates 23.36mg/l, Chlorides 1.84mg/l, Sulphates 1.8mg/l, Fluorides 0.07mg/l. pH 5.76

Magners (Ire) a noted cider producer based in Clonmel, produces a range of ciders including a bottled cider 4.5% alc by vol. Website: Http://www.magnerscider.com

Magnesia (Czec) a sparkling natural spring mineral water from Karlovarské/Carlsbad. Mineral contents (milligrammes per litre): Sodium 5mg/l, Calcium 36.59mg/l, Magnesium 236.3mg/l, Potassium 2.039mg/l, Bicarbonates 1292mg/l, Chlorides 3.949mg/l, Sulphates 25mg/l, Fluorides 0.134mg/l, Silicates 71.1mg/l.

Magnet Beer (Eng) the name given to the keg bitter 1040 O.G. bottled pale ale 1040 O.G. and the old ale 1070 O.G. brewed by the John Smith's Brewery, Tadcaster, Yorkshire.

Magnificat (Eng) a 6.5% alc by vol. strong ale brewed by The Durham Brewery Ltd., County Durham.

Magnificat (Port) a natural spring mineral water from Serra do Trigo-Ilha de S. Miguel-Açores.

Magnifico (It) a slightly bulbous-shaped bottle used by Ruffino in the Chianti region which is capable of improving the maturing of the wine.

Magno (Sp) a 5 year old, solera reserve, dark, sweet brandy produced by Osborne.

Magnolia (Cktl) 60mls (½ gill) brandy, 1 tablespoon Curaçao, yolk of egg, 1 tablespoon sugar syrup. Shake well over ice, strain into a highball glass and top with iced Champagne.

Magnolia Pub & Brewery (USA) a brewery. (Add): 1398 Haight Street, San Francisco, California CA94117. Brews a range of beers and lager. Website: http://www.magnoliapub.com 'E'mail: beer@magnoliapub.com

Magno Megonia (It) a red wine produced by Librandi in Calabria from 100% Magliocco grapes.

Magnotta Brewery (Can) a brewery. (Add): 271 Chrislea Road, Vaughan, Ontario L4L 8N6. Brews beers and lager. Website: http://www.magnotta.com 'E'mail: mailbox@magnotta.com

Magnum (Fr) a double bottle used in Burgundy: 52fl.ozs Bordeaux: 48fl.ozs

Magnum [2] (Fr) a large bottle of (1.5litres) 2 standard bottles capacity used in the Champagne region. see Champagne Bottle Sizes.

Magnum (USA) bottle 1.5litres (50.72 USfl.ozs)

M

Magnus (Hol) a trappiste double-style beer 6.5% alc by vol. brewed by the Arcen Brouwerij in Arcen, Limburg.

Magnusquelle (Ger) a natural spring mineral water from Norderstedt. Mineral contents (milligrammes per litre): Sodium 9.7mg/l, Calcium 59mg/l, Magnesium 4.4mg/l, Potassium 0.8mg/l, Bicarbonates 114mg/l, Chlorides 37mg/l, Sulphates 40mg/l.

Mago (Afr) a noted ancient Tunisian author who wrote a manual for wine-growers in the fourth century B.C.

Magor Brewery (Wal) a Whitbread brewery based in South Wales. Celebrated the 20th birthday with Whitbread Magor Celebration Ale. A limited edition ale. 5.2% alc by vol (800 cases produced).

Magpie (Eng) a chestnut-coloured bitter brewed by Cotleigh Brewery, Wiveliscombe, Somerset. Brewed as the 1500th different beer sold by wholesaler East West Ales.

Magpie Estate (Austr) a winery based in Nurioopta, South Australia. Grape varieties include Mourvèdre and Shiraz.

Magret (Fr) an alternative name for the Malbec grape.

Magrico (Port) the name for a dry white Vinho Verde from Minho.

Maguey Cactus (Mex) an alternative name for the Agave Cactus.

Maguey Worm (Mex) an alternative name for the Agave Worm. *See also* Gusano.

Magus (Eng) a 3.8% alc by vol. ale brewed by The Durham Brewery Ltd., County Durham.

Magyar Állami Pincegazdasàg (Hun) the Hungarian State Cellars.

Magyar Rosé (Hun) a very light rosé wine from the Pécs-Villàny region.

Mahewu (Afr) a thick fermented mealie-meal (fine ground maize) porridge drink. Is drunk as a stimulant.

Mahia (Afr) an eau-de-vie made from figs and served as an apéritif in Tunisia. Also known as Boukha.

Mahina Coco (Fr) a coconut liqueur 20% alc by vol. produced by Clémant in Martinique.

Mahlberg (Ger) village (Anb): Baden. (Ber): Breisgau. (Gro): Schutterlindenberg. (Vin): Haselstaude.

Mähler-Besse (Fr) a Dutch wine négociant-éleveur based in Bordeaux. Part owner of Château Palmer. (Add): 49 Rue Camille Godard, 33026 Bordeaux. Also owns: Château la Couronne, E Fer and Cheval Noir. Website: http://www.mahler-bresse.com 'E'mail: contact@mahler-bresse.com

Mahogany (Cktl) 1 measure Bols crème de cacao over ice, top with Coca Cola.

Mahogany (Cktl) ⅓ measure treacle, ⅓ measure dry gin, stir until dissolved.

Mahoney Vineyards (USA) a winery based in the Carneros, California. (Add): 1285 Dealy Lane, Napa, CA 94559. Grape variety: Pinot noir. Label: Las Brisas Vineyard. Website: http://www.mahoneyvineyards.com

Mahou (Sp) the name of a lager beer produced in Madrid.

Mährisch (Aus) a red grape variety grown in the Thermenregion.

Mahui Fizz (Cktl) 35mls (1½ fl.ozs) white rum, 1 egg, 100mls (4fl.ozs) pineapple juice, 10mls (½ fl.oz) gomme syrup. Blend altogether with a scoop of crushed ice, pour into a Champagne saucer, dress with a cherry and a pineapple cube and serve with straws.

Mahzen (Tur) cellar.

Maia (Slo) (Bul) (Gre) a name given in the Balkans to milk that has been soured before fermentation.

Maiberg (Ger) vineyard (Anb): Hessische Bergstrasse. (Ber): Starkenburg. (Gro): Schlossberg. (Vil): Heppenheim including Erbach and Hambach.

Maibock (Ger) a Bavarian bock beer developed by the Hofbräuhaus. Is brewed to celebrate Maytime celebrations.

Maiden Oak Brewery (Ire) a brewery (established 1985) based in Londonderry, Northern Ireland.

Maiden's Blush [1] (Cktl) 60mls (½ gill) gin, 2 dashes Oxygénée, 1 tablespoon grenadine. Shake over ice and strain into a 125mls (5fl.oz) wine goblet.

Maiden's Blush [2] (Cktl) ½ measure Pernod, 1 measure dry gin, ½ measure lemon juice, dash grenadine, dash gomme syrup. Shake over ice and strain into a cocktail glass.

Maidens Magic (Eng) the name for a beer brewed by the Alcazar Brewery, Nottinghamshire.

Maiden's Prayer (Cktl) ⅜ measure dry gin, ⅜ measure Cointreau, ⅛ measure orange juice, ⅛ measure lemon juice. Shake over ice and strain into a cocktail glass.

Maiden's Prayer (S.Afr) the label for a range of un-oaked varietal wines produced by the Diemersfontein Wines winery, Wellington, Western Cape.

Maidens Ruin (Eng) a 6% alc by vol. strong ale brewed by Enville Ales Ltd., West Midlands.

Maiden Voyage (Eng) a 4% alc by vol. ale brewed by the Ales of Scilly Brewery, Isles of Scilly.

Maiden Wine Cellars (S.Afr) a winery (established 1995) based in Gordon's Bay, Western Cape. Grape varieties: Cabernet sauvignon, Pinotage, Shiraz. Website: http://www.maidenwines.com

Maid of Erin Cocktail (Cktl) ⅓ measure brandy, ⅓ measure Royal Mint Chocolate Liqueur, ⅓ measure cream. Shake over ice and strain into a cocktail glass.

Maidstone Ale (Eng) a best bitter 1040 O.G. brewed by the Goacher Brewery in Maidstone, Kent.

Maidstone Light Ale (Eng) a light ale 1036 O.G. brewed by the Goacher Brewery in Maidstone, Kent.

Maie (Fr) a name given to the traditional Champagne press.

Maien (Ger) vineyard (Anb): Württemberg. (Ber): Remstal-Stuttgart. (Gro): Wartbühl. (Vil): Hanweiler.

M

Maienfels (Ger) village (Anb): Württemberg. (Ber): Württembergisch Unterland. (Gro): Lindelberg. (Vin): Schneckenhof.

Maigre (Fr) a term to denote a thin, feeble wine.

Maikammer (Ger) village (Anb): Pfalz. (Ber): Südliche Weinstrasse. (Gro): Mandelhöhe. (Vins): Heiligenberg, Immengarten, Kirchenstück.

Maikammer-Alsterweiler (Ger) village (Anb): Pfalz. (Ber): Südliche Weinstrasse. (Gro): Mandelhöhe. (Vin): Kapellenberg.

Mailaender Bergbräu Brauerei (Ger) a brewery based in Fürth which brews a copper-red beer known as Kupferstube (a malty bottom-fermented beer, coloured with smokey, roasted malts).

Mailberg (Aus) a village which gives its name to a light wine from the district of Weinviertel. Also the home to Malteser, a wine produced by Lenz Moser.

Mailly-Champagne (Fr) a Grand Cru Champagne village in the Canton de Verzy. District: Reims. (Add): 28, Rue de la Libération, 51500 Mailly Champagne. Has a large co-operative producing wines under the Mailly name. Produces: Brut Réserve, Brut Milléséme, Brut Rosé, Demi-Sec, Extra Brut, Blanc de Noirs, La Terre, L'Intemporelle and Les Échansons. (70 growers own 70ha. in Grand Cru of Mailly). Vintages: 1928, 1929, 1932, 1934, 1936, 1945, 1948, 1950, 1955, 1960, 1961, 1966, 1969, 1970, 1973, 1975, 1976, 1979, 1982, 1983, 1985, 1988, 1990, 1996, 1999. *see* Champagne Société de Producteurs Mailly-Champagne. Website: http://www.Champagne-mailly.com 'E' Mail: contact@Champagne-mailly.com

Mailly Rosé (Fr) a non-vintage brut rosé Champagne produced by Champagne Société de Producteurs, Mailly-Champagne from 100% Pinot noir grapes.

Main (Ger) an untergebiete of the Bayern district.

Mainbrace (Cktl) ⅓ measure gin, ⅓ measure Cointreau, ⅓ measure grapefruit juice. Shake over ice and strain into a cocktail glass.

Mainbrace (Eng) a 4.2% alc by vol. ale brewed by the Jolly Boat Brewery (Bideford) Ltd., Devon.

Mainbrace (W.Ind) the brand-name of a demerara rum matured by Allied Breweries in England.

Mainbrace Bitter (Eng) a 4.2% alc by vol. bitter brewed by the Jollyboat Brewery, Bideford, Devon.

Maindreieck (Ger) lit: 'main triangle', a bereich within the region of Franconia. Soil of coarse limestone with some over-lay of loess.

Maindreieck (Ger) bereich (Anb): Franken. (Gros): Burg, Ewig Leben, Hofrat, Honigberg, Kirchberg, Ravensburg, Rosstal. With some vineyards that have not yet been assigned Grosslagen.

Maine-et-Loire (Fr) a Vin de Pays area in the Maine-et-Loire département, western France (part of the Jardine de la France). Produces red, rosé and dry white wines.

Maingold (Ger) a full-bodied lager beer 5.3% alc by vol. brewed by the Kulmbacher Mönschof Brauerei in Bavaria.

Mainhölle (Ger) vineyard (Anb): Franken. (Ber): Mainviereck. (Gro): Not yet assigned. (Vil): Bürgstadt.

Mainleite (Ger) vineyard (Anb): Franken. (Ber): Maindreieck. (Gro): Not yet assigned. (Vil): Schweinfurt.

Main Ridge Estate (Austr) a winery (established 1975) at William Road, Red Hill, Victoria. Grape varieties: Chardonnay, Cabernet sauvignon, Pinot noir.

Main-Riesling (Ger) a white grape variety grown in Franconia. A cross between the Rhein riesling and the Sylvaner. Also known as the Rieslaner.

Mainstay (S.Afr) the brand-name of a leading double-distilled cane spirit.

Mainstockheim (Ger) village (Anb): Franken. (Ber): Maindreieck. (Gro): Hofrat. (Vin): Hofstück.

Main Street Winery (S.Afr) a winery (established 1999) based in Paarl, Western Cape. Grape varieties: Chardonnay, Chenin blanc, Merlot, Pinotage, Ruby cabernet, Sauvignon blanc, Shiraz. Label: Stoep.

Mainviereck (Ger) lit: 'main rectangle', a bereich within the region of Franconia. Has a sandstone soil.

Mainviereck (Ger) bereich (Anb): Franken. (Gros): Heiligenthal, Reuschberg.

Mainxe (Fr) a commune in the Charente département whose grapes are classed Grande Champagne (Cognac).

Mainz (Ger) village (Anb): Rheinhessen. (Ber): Nierstein. (Gro): Sankt Alban. (Vins): Edelmann, Hüttberg, Johannisberg, Kirchenstück, Klosterberg, Sand, Weinkeller.

Mainz-Drais (Ger) village (Anb): Rheinhessen. (Ber): Nierstein. (Gro): Domherr. (Vins): Sites not yet chosen.

Mainzerweg (Ger) vineyard (Anb): Rheinhessen. (Ber): Bingen. (Gro): Sankt Rochuskapelle. (Vil): Dromersheim.

Mainzer Weinmarkt (Ger) a Rheinhessen wine festival held in Mainz in August-September.

Mainz-Finthen (Ger) village (Anb): Rheinhessen. (Ber): Nierstein. (Gro): Domherr. (Vins): Sites not yet chosen.

Maipo Valley (Chile) a principal wine region of Central Chile. 697ha. Produces good, sound table wines from a variety of grapes. Santiago is situated in the Maipo Valley. Home to Cousiño Macul.

Maipú (Arg) one of three Denominaciónes de Origen of Mendoza. *See also* Lujàn de Cuyo, San Rafael.

Maïre (Ch.Isles) lees.

Maire [Henri] (Fr) a négociant-éleveur based in the Jura region of eastern France.

Maire et Fils (Fr) a négociant-éleveur based in Beaune, Côte de Beaune, Burgundy. Owns Domaine de Château de la Tour.

Maische (Ger) grape pulp.

Maisdon (Fr) a village in the central area of A.C. Muscadet Sèvre et Maine, Nantais, Loire. Produces some of the finest wines of the region.

Maisel Brothers (Ger) a brewery (established 1887) based at Bayreuth. Brews: wheat beers. Bottled Edelhopfen, Weisse, Weizen Bock.

Maisel's Edelhopfen (Ger) a bottled diet pilsner 4.9% alc by vol. brewed by Maisel Brothers Brauerei at Bayreuth.

Maisel's Weisse (Ger) a 5.7% alc by vol. wheat beer brewed by Maisel Brothers Brauerei at Bayreuth. Also Weisse Kristallklar, Light and Dunkel versions.

Maisel's Weizen Bock (Ger) 7.2% alc by vol. dark, unfiltered, bottle-conditioned wheat beer brewed by Maisel Brothers Brauerei at Bayreuth.

Maison (S.Afr) the label for a range of wines produced by the L'Avenir Estate winery, Stellenbosch, Western Cape.

Maison Albert Bichot (Fr) *see* Bichot (Albert et Cie).

Maison-Blanche (Fr) a vineyard in the A.C. Hermitage, northern Rhône.

Maison-Brûlée (Fr) a Premier Cru vineyard in the A.C. commune of Morey-Saint-Denis, Côte de Nuits, Burgundy.

Maison des Vins de Châteauneuf-du-Pape (Fr) a wine library of the wines of Châteauneuf-du-Pape with well over 250 varieties available for tasting and purchase and operated by the producer's federation. (Add): Vinedea 8, Rue Maréchel Foch, BP 68 84232 Châteauneuf-du-Pape. Website: http://www.chateauneufdupape.com 'E'mail: fedepapes@pacwan.fr

Maison du Vin, Allée Marine (Fr) one of four Maisons du Vin in Bordeaux. Based in Blaye.

Maison du Vin, Château des Ducs d'Epernon (Fr) one of four Maisons du Vin in Bordeaux. Based in Cadillac.

Maison du Vin d'Anjou (Fr) based at Boulevard Foch, Anger in the Loire and provides a full history of wine production.

Maison du Vin de Bordeaux (Fr) one of four Maisons du Vin in Bordeaux. Based in Bordeaux. Is also the home of the C.I.V.B. Bordeaux.

Maison du Vin, Quai Ferchaud (Fr) one of four Maisons du Vin in Bordeaux. Based at Pauillac.

Maisons (Fr) a Champagne shipper's name for their office-cum-cellars-cum-factory.

Maisons Marques et Domaines (Eng) a new U.K. company created by Louis Roederer (Champagne) and Bouchard Père et Fils (Burgundy).

Mai Tai [1] (Cktl) 25mls (1fl.oz) white rum, 10mls (½fl.oz) each of Curaçao, orgeat, lime juice, ½ teaspoon sugar, 25mls (1fl.oz) grenadine. Shake over ice, strain into a large cocktail glass 'on the rocks', dress with fresh pineapple and a maraschino cherry.

Mai-Tai [2] (Cktl) 300mls (½ pint) orange juice, 3 dashes Angostura, 2 dashes almond essence, 225mls (8fl.ozs) gomme syrup, blended together, it is used as an ingredient for certain cocktails.

Maitina (W.Ind) an orange-flavoured spirit drink produced on the island of Martinique.

Maitrank (Ger) a drink made in the spring from white wine, brandy and woodruff.

Maître D (Fr) a range of French vins de table wines (white, rosé and red) from Les Caves Saint-Arnoud, Saint-Martin-au-Laert.

Maître de Chai (Fr) cellar-master.

Maître de Chais (Fr) a red wine produced by Domaine la Tourmone from 85% Grenache, 10% Mouvedre and 5% Syrah.

Maître des Échansons (Fr) a wine society based in Reuilly, Loire.

Maître Sommelier (Fr) head wine-waiter.

Maitz [Wolfgang] (Aus) a winery (6.5ha) based in Ehrenhausen, Süd-Steiermark. (Add): Ratch an der Weinstrasse, 8461 Ehrenhausen. Grape varieties: Chardonnay, Gewürztraminer, Muskateller, Pinot blanc, Pinot gris, Sauvignon blanc, Traminer, Zweigelt. Produces a wide range of dry and sweet wines.

Maiwein (Ger) an aromatised wine made with sweet woodruff flowers (**Galum odoratum**) in May, it is normally made in German households.

Majaela (Sp) a red grape variety grown in the Navarra region, north-eastern Spain.

Majan (Arab) a natural spring mineral water (established 2000) from Nakhal, Oman. Mineral contents (milligrammes per litre): Sodium 12mg/l, Calcium 15.6mg/l, Magnesium 5.7mg/l, Potassium 1.4mg/l, Bicarbonates 42mg/l, Chlorides 23mg/l, Sulphates 32mg/l, Fluorides 0.6mg/l.

Majarca Alba (Rum) a white grape variety grown in Banat vineyard for production of white wines in Teremia Mare and Tomnatec.

Majella (Austr) a winery based in the Coonawarra, South Australia.

Majestic (Austr) a red wine (Cabernet sauvignon) from the Ferngrove Vineyard Estate, Western Australia.

Majestic (Eng) a large retail wine warehouse with nine outlets.

Majnoni-Guicciardini (It) a producer of Chianti Putto in Tuscany.

Majoor (S.Afr) the label for a range of wines (military names) produced by the Domein Doornkraal winery, Little Karoo.

Major Bailey Cocktail (Cktl) place 12 mint leaves in an old-fashioned glass with ½ teaspoon sugar, juice ¼ lime and ¼ lemon, muddle well, add ice and 25mls (⅛ gill) gin, dress with mint leaves and serve with straws.

Majorca (Sp) an island off the Catalonian coast that produces average drinking wines. Part of the Balearic Islands. Has 2000ha under vine. D.O. regions of Binissalem-Mallorca and Pla í Llevant.

Major P.R. Reid's (Scot) a single malt whisky distilled at the Glen Mhor Distillery. A highland malt. 14 year old 45.8% alc by vol.

Major's Hill Estate (S.Afr) a winery (established 2002) based in Robertson, Western Cape. 52ha. Grape varieties: Cabernet sauvignon, Chardonnay, Merlot, Pinotage, Sauvignon blanc, Shiraz. Website: http://www.majorshill.co.za

Major Slump Ale (Eng) a 4.2% alc by vol. bitter ale.

M

Majuelo (Sp) the name given to wine pressed from grapes grown on young vines.

Makana (S.Afr) the label for a range of wines produced by the Cape First Wines winery, Stellenbosch, Western Cape.

Makanissa (Afr) a winery based in northern Ethiopia.

Make Believe (Cktl) 10mls (½ fl.oz) marasquin, 5mls (¼ fl.oz) each of white rum, framboise, pineapple juice. Shake over ice, strain into a cocktail glass and top with a cherry.

Makedonija (Ser) a high mountainous region of in the south. Produces mainly red wines from Prokupac and Vranac grapes, plus a small proportion of white and rosé. Main production area is Povardarje.

Makelaar (Hol) wine-broker.

Maker's Mark (USA) the brand-name of a Bourbon whiskey 50% alc by vol. produced by the Star Hill Distillery in Loretta, Kentucky. Also a 9 year old Black Seal, Red Seal and Gold Seal.

Makers Mark (Eng) a 3.8% alc by vol. cask bitter brewed under licence by Tring Brewery in Hertfordshire for The Vintage Hallmark Ale Company in Norwich.

Makheras (Cyp) a region on the eastern side of the Troodos mountain range that produces fine wines.

Makler (Eng) a premium lager 4.5% alc by vol (1042 O.G) produced by McEwans.

Mako (N.Z) 2.5% alc by vol. light, brown coloured, bottom fermented, canned lager beer brewed by DB Breweries, Auckland.

Makro (Hol) the brand label used by a cash and carry store for spirits, wine, lager and bitter.

Malabar (S.Afr) the label for a red wine (Shiraz, Pinotage, Mourvèdre, Grenache and Viognier blend) produced by the Spice Route Wine Company, Swartland, Western Cape.

Malabor (Ind) a coffee-producing region in northern India.

Malacate (Sp) an old method of soil preparation using mules which turn a Noria wheel attached to a cable which in turn pulls a large plough. Still used in Jerez.

Malade de Mise (Fr) bottle sickness, a short lived period after bottling where the wine does not taste true to form. The wine is in shock and needs to rest.

Maladière [La] (Fr) a Premier Cru vineyard in the A.C. commune of Santenay, Côte de Beaune, Burgundy.

Maladies Cryptogamiques (Fr) the general term for fungal vine diseases such as black rot, oiidium, mildew, grey rot, etc.

Mala Dinka (Bul) the local name used for the Gewürztraminer grape.

Málaga (Sp) a coastal Denominación de Origen wine region in southern Spain. A province of Andalucía. Produces sweet, dark, fortified dessert wines from the Pedro Ximénez and Moscatel grapes. *see* Axarquía, Lágrima, Malligo, Mountain and Zareas-Antequera.

Malaga (USA) a red grape variety used in the making of dessert wines in California. Also known as the Cinsault and related to the Sémillon.

Malaga (USA) *see* California Malaga.

Málaga Abocado (Sp) fully fermented grape must with a residual sugar content of less than 5g/l. and dry in style. *See also* Málaga Semiseco.

Málaga Blanc (N.Am) a white grape variety used in the making of white sweet (fortified) wines.

Málaga Blanco Dulce (Sp) a golden yellow, sweet style of Málaga.

Málaga Blanco Seco (Sp) a pale gold, dry style of Málaga.

Málaga Dulce Color (Sp) an extremely dark, sweet style of Málaga. Sugar content is approximately 600g/l.

Málaga Dulce Lágrima (Sp) as for Málaga Dulce but made from free-run must.

Málaga Golden White (Sp) a light-coloured, sweet style of Málaga.

Málaga Lágrima (Sp) a dark gold, very sweet style of Málaga.

Málaga Moscatel (Sp) an amber-coloured, sweet style of Málaga.

Málaga Negro (Sp) a very dark, sweet style of Málaga.

Málaga Pajarete (Sp) a strong, amber-coloured, sweet style of Málaga.

Málaga Rome (Sp) a strong red (or golden white) medium-dry style of Málaga.

Málaga Seco (Sp) fully fermented grape must with a residual sugar content of less than 5g/l. Dry in style.

Málaga Semi-Dulce (Sp) a yellow (or red) sweet style of Málaga.

Málaga Semiseco (Sp) part fermented wines with more than 5g/l and up to 50g/l of sugar. *See also* Málaga Abocado.

Malagasy (Afr) the old name for the island of Madagascar off the south-west coast. Produces average white and red wines.

Malagousia (Gre) a white grape variety that produces good quality perfumed wines. Low in acidity, with a white peach and mint taste.

Malaka (Sp) the Phoenician name for Málaga.

Malamed's Brandy (S.Afr) the brand-name for a Kosher brandy produced by Gilbey's S.A. under strict Rabbinical supervision of the Cape Beth Din.

Malamed's Wines (S.Afr) are Kosher wines made by Gilbeys, produced under strict Rabbinical supervision of the Cape Beth Din. Are varietal wines.

Malat (Aus) a winery (30ha) based in the Kremstal region. (Add): 3511 Furth-Palt/Krems. Grape varieties: Cabernet sauvignon, Chardonnay, Grüner veltliner, Merlot, Müller-Thurgau, Pinot blanc, Pinot noir, Riesling, St. Laurent, Zweigelt. Produces a range of dry and sweet (botrytised) wines.

Malatya (Tur) a red and white wine-producing region in eastern Turkey.

Malavella (Sp) a still natural spring mineral water from Caldes de Malavella, Girona.

Malaville (Fr) a commune in the Charente département whose grapes are classed Grande Champagne (Cognac).

Malawi Carlsberg Lager (Afr) a lager beer 10.9° Plato produced by the Carlsberg Brewery in association with the Malawi Government.

Malawi Teas (Afr) are African teas used mainly for blending.

Malayan Breweries (Asia) a brewery based in Singapore which is noted for Tiger Beers (lager and stout).

Malbec (Fr) a red grape variety grown in Bordeaux, a small percentage planted in a vineyard has been found beneficial if blended with Cabernet and Merlot. Produces aromas and flavours of blackberried fruits, spice and earthy/rustic tones. Known as the Noir de pressac (or Pressac) in Pomerol. Is also known as Auxerrois, Cahors, Côt, Malbeck, Magret, Pied noir, Pied rouge, Prèchet, Séme and Uva francesa. *See also* Uva Argentina.

Malbeck (Arg) the name used for the Malbec grape variety grown in Mendoza.

Malbeck (It) a red grape variety used in Puglia. (Fr) = Malbec.

Maldano Egg Flip (Eng) an egg-based drink produced by Townend of Hull, Humberside.

Måleenhed (Den) quart (measure).

Malenchini (It) a winery based in the Tuscany region. Produces IGT Super Tuscan wines. Label: Bruzzico.

Malepère (Fr) an A.C. district within the Languedoc-Roussillon region of southern France.

Mâles [Les] (Fr) a vineyard in the A.C. commune of Montagny, Côte Chalonnaise, Burgundy.

Malescot-Saint-Exupéry (Fr) *see* Château Malescot-Saint-Exupéry.

Malessere (It) hangover.

Malheur (Bel) a brewery. (Add): Mandekensstraat 179, Buggenhout. Brews a range of beers and lager. Website: http://www.malheur.be 'E'mail: info@malheur.be

Malibu (Eng) a Jamaican white rum-based coconut-flavoured liqueur produced by the Twelve Islands Shipping C°. Ltd. Originally 28% alc by vol. now 24% alc by vol. Also produce a pineapple-flavoured version.

Malibu Beach Cocktail (Cktl) 2 measures orange juice, ½ measure vodka, dash grenadine, dash lemon juice, dash egg white. Shake over ice, strain into a cocktail glass, dress with a slice of lemon and orange.

Malibu Caribbean Cocktails (Eng) a range of 5.5% alc by vol. mixed drinks from I.D.V. sold in 200mls bottles. Flavours include orange spice, pineapple spice, tropical quencher, citrus twist.

Malibu Cocktail (Cktl) 40mls (⅓ gill) gin, 20mls (⅙ gill) French vermouth, 1 teaspoon absinthe, 1 teaspoon Angostura. Stir over ice, strain into cocktail glass, decorate with an olive and dash lemon peel juice.

Malic (Eng) a term used for an appley-flavoured wine.

Malic Acid (Eng) $HOOCCH_2CH(OH)COOH$ an acid found in fruits (especially apples) and unripe grapes. Is destroyed as the fruit matures. *see* Malo-Lactic Fermentation. (Fr) = acide malique.

Maligny (Fr) a commune in the A.C. Chablis, northern Burgundy.

Malinda's Vineyard (USA) a vineyard based in Ocala, Florida. Produces mainly Muscadine wines.

Maliniak (Pol) a honey and raspberry juice mead. Dark amber in colour, it is sold in bottles and earthenware jars.

Mali Plavac (Slo) a red grape variety that produces wines high in tannin and alcohol. *see* Postup, Dingac.

Malki (Rus) a sparkling natural spring mineral water (established 1998) from Kamachatka. Mineral contents (milligrammes per litre): Sodium 1200mg/l, Calcium 350mg/l, Magnesium 120mg/l, Potassium 100mg/l, Bicarbonates 2700mg/l, Chlorides 700mg/l, Sulphates 8mg/l, Fluorides 1mg/l, Iron 30mg/l, Silicates 140mg/l, Lithium 5mg/l, Barium 1mg/l, Hydrobromide 3mg/l, Iodine 1mg/l, Strontium 3mg/l, Ammonium 6mg/l. pH 6.8

Mallac Blanca (Sp) a solera brandy produced by De Terry.

Malla Dorada (Sp) a solera reserva brandy produced by De Terry.

Mallard Brewery (Eng) a brewery (established 1995). (Add): 15 Hartington Avenue, Carlton, Nottingham, Nottinghamshire NG4 3NR. Brews: Duck & Dive 3.7% alc by vol., Duckling Bitter 4.2% alc by vol., Feather Light 4.1% alc by vol., Quaka Jack 4% alc by vol. and Waddlers Mild. Website: http://www.mallard-brewery.co.uk 'E'mail: phil@mallard-brewery.co.uk

Mallasjuoma Breweries (Fin) the largest brewers in Finland. Has breweries in Oulu (northern Finland) and in Heinola and Lahti (southern Finland).

Malleret (Fr) a Bordeaux Mousseux producer based in Saint-Émilion, eastern Bordeaux.

Mallersdorfer Klosterbrauerei (Ger) a noted brewery based in Bavaria.

Mallet Decanter (Eng) *see* Mallet Shape.

Mallet Shape (Eng) a style of decanter, has six or eight sides and is shaped like a mallet. Popular in the eighteenth century, was used for Port wines.

Malliac (Fr) an Armagnac producer.(Add): Sté. Fermière du Château de Malliac, Montréal du Gers.

Malligo Sack (Sp) an old name for Málaga wine.

Mallorca [1] (Cktl) ½ measure white rum, ⅙ measure Drambuie, ⅙ measure dry vermouth, ⅙ measure crème de banane. Stir over ice and strain into a cocktail glass.

Mallorca [2] (Cktl) ½ measure vodka, ¼ measure Grand Marnier, ¼ measure pineapple juice. Shake over ice, strain into a cocktail glass, decorate with pieces of cherry, orange and lemon.

M

Malmaison Cocktail (Cktl. 25mls (⅙ gill) white rum, juice ½ lemon, 10mls (⅛ gill) sweet Sherry. Shake well over ice, strain into a cocktail glass which is sugar-rimmed with anisette.

Malmberg Original Water (Swe) a natural spring mineral water (established 1990) from Yngslö. Mineral contents (milligrammes per litre): Sodium 5mg/l, Calcium 63mg/l, Magnesium 4.2mg/l, Potassium 2.4mg/l, Bicarbonates 200mg/l, Chlorides 7.7mg/l, Sulphates 6.3mg/l, Fluorides 0.18mg/l. pH 7.9 Website: http://www.malmbergoriginal.se

Malmesbury (S.Afr) a wine-producing centre of Swartland. Is noted for dry white wines and distilleries.

Malmesey (Eng) the sixteenth century spelling of Malmsey.

Malmsey (Mad) the sweetest of the Madeira wines. Is dark brown with a powerful bouquet and a honied, luscious taste. A true dessert wine. Made with the Malvoisie (Pinot gris) grape.

Malmsey (Mad)(Port) an alternative name for the Malvoisie (Pinot gris) grape.

Malmslay (Eng) an old seventeenth century spelling of Malmsey.

Malmsly (Eng) an old seventeenth century spelling of Malmsey.

Malm Soil (Eng) a soft limestone soil with some clay.

Maloko (Rus) milk.

Malo-Lactic Bacteria (Eng) see Leuconostoc.

Malo-Lactic Fermentation (Eng) the conversion of malic acid into lactic acid which takes place after the normal fermentation. Usually takes place before wine is bottled but for some wines i.e. Vinho Verde is allowed to take place in bottle to give wine some pétillance. In most wine though has an adverse effect. Helps to reduce acidity in wine.

Malsch (Ger) village (Anb): Baden. (Ber): Badische Bergstrasse/Kraichgau. (Gro): Mannaberg. (Vins): Ölbaum, Rotsteig.

Malschenberg (Ger) village (Anb): Baden. (Ber): Badische Bergstrasse/Kraichgau. (Gro): Mannaberg. (Vin): Ölbaum.

Malsters Ale (Eng) a 5% alc by vol. bitter beer brewed by the Teignworthy Brewery in Newton Abbot using Regina malt.

Malt (Eng) barley corns which have been germinated and through enzyme action had the starch converted into maltose. Used in brewing and whisky production. Gives body, flavour and if roasted adds colour to beer. see Ale Malt, Black Malt, Chocolate Malt, Crystal Malt, Lager Malt. See also Roasted Barley. (Hol) = mout.

Malta (Euro) an island in the central Mediterranean sea. Has approx. 2000ha. under vines. Grape varieties: Dun Tumas, Gannaru, Gellewza and Nigruwa. Produces ordinary wines for mainly home consumption.

Malt and Hops (Eng) a 4.5% fresh harvest ale made to mark the end of the hop picking season. A green hop beer from unkilned new season green hops brewed by Wadworth Brewery, Devizes, Wiltshire.

Malt Cellar Range (Scot) six malt whiskies packaged together. Includes four Highlands (Linkwood, Lochnager, Strathconnan vatted malt and Talisker), one Lowland (Rosebank) and one Islay (Lagavulin).

Malt Culms (Scot) the alternative name given to the rootlets on the malting barley grains. Spent culms go for cattle food in whisky production.

Malt Duck (USA) a strong beer flavoured with grape concentrate from the National Brewing C°. of Baltimore (owned by Carling).

Malte (Port) malt.

Malted Barley (Eng) barley soaked in water, allowed to germinate and convert, through enzyme action, the starch into maltose, also known as Barley Malt. see Malt.

Malted Mayhem (Eng) a 4.5% alc by vol. cereal beer brewed by J.W. Lees, Middleton, Manchester, Lancashire (available March and April).

Malted Milk (Eng) a soluble powder made from dehydrated milk and malted cereals. A hot or cold drink is made from this. see Horlicks™ (most famous brand).

Malted Rice Fungus (Jap) see Aspergillus oryzae.

Malterdingen (Ger) village (Anb): Baden. (Ber): Breisgau. (Gro): Burg Lichteneck. (Vin): Bienenberg.

Malteser (Aus) the brand-name of a wine produced by Lenz Moser in Mailberg.

Maltesergarten (Ger) vineyard (Anb): Baden. (Ber): Markgräflerland. (Gro): Lorettoberg. (Vil): Biengen.

Maltesergarten (Ger) vineyard (Anb): Baden. (Ber): Markgräflerland. (Gro): Lorettoberg. (Vil): Buggingen.

Maltesergarten (Ger) vineyard (Anb): Baden. (Ber): Markgräflerland. (Gro): Lorettoberg. (Vil): Eschbach.

Maltesergarten (Ger) vineyard (Anb): Baden. (Ber): Markgräflerland. (Gro): Lorettoberg. (Vil): Heitersheim.

Maltesergarten (Ger) vineyard (Anb): Baden. (Ber): Markgräflerland. (Gro): Lorettoberg. (Vil): Schlatt.

Maltesergarten (Ger) vineyard (Anb): Baden. (Ber): Markgräflerland. (Gro): Lorettoberg. (Vil): Seefelden.

Maltesergarten (Ger) vineyard (Anb): Baden. (Ber): Markgräflerland. (Gro): Lorettoberg. (Vil): Staufen (ortsteil Wetttelbrunn).

Maltesergarten (Ger) vineyard (Anb): Baden. (Ber): Markgräflerland. (Gro): Lorettoberg. (Vil): Tunsel.

Malteserkreuz (Den) the brand-name for an akvavit produced by DDS 43% alc by vol.

Malt Extract (Eng) produced when the wort has been boiled under a very low pressure. The water content evaporates leaving a syrup containing the sugars extracted from the malt. Is used in the brewing process in place of barley malt. (Fr) = extrait de malt.

Maltezer (Bel) a Dortmunder-style beer 6.25% alc by vol. brewed by the De Ridder Brouwerij in Maastricht, Limburg.

Malt House (Eng)(Scot) the name for the building or room where the barley is turned into malt. (Hol) = mouterij.

Malthouse (Eng) a keg/canned ale 1033 O.G. brewed by the Hall and Woodhouse Brewery of Dorset.

Maltice (Czec) a wine district within the region of Bohemia. Produces some of the best wines of the region.

Malting[s] (Eng) a building where the malting of the barley takes place.

Maltivita (Eng) a commercially prepared powdered malt food drink from Cadbury's (part of Kenco-Typhoo). See also Bournvita.

Malt Liquor (USA) an American beer that varies greatly between each producer from light pale beers to dark hoppy beers, usually high in alcohol. Breaker and Colt are brands sold in G.B.

Malton Brewery (Eng) a brewery (established 1985). (Add): Malton, North Yorkshire. Noted for cask-conditioned Double Chance Bitter 1039 O.G., Owd Bob.

Maltose (Eng) a fermentable sugar produced in germinated barley used for beer and whisky production. see Malt.

Malpica de Tajo (Sp) a Vino de Mesa wine area in the province Toledo, Castilla-La Mancha.

Maltroie [La] (Fr) a Premier Cru vineyard [part] in the A.C. commune of Chassagne-Montrachet, Côte de Beaune, Burgundy. 8.9ha (red and white).

Malts (Scot) a Scotch whisky made entirely from malted barley.

Malt Shovel (Scot) a wooden shovel used to turn the germinating barley at floor maltings. Also used in England.

Malt Shovel Brewery (Austr) a brewery. (Add): 99 Pymont Bridge Road, Camperdown, Sydney, New South Wales 2050. Brews a variety of beers. Website: http://www.malt-shovel.com.au 'E'mail: goodbrew@malt-shovel.com.au

Malt Shovel Mild (Eng) a 3.8% alc by vol. mild ale brewed by the Fernanders Brewery, West Yorkshire.

Maltster (Eng)(Scot) an official who oversees the malting process.

Malt Stout (Eng) a bottled stout 1042 O.G. brewed by the Morrell's Brewery in Oxford.

Malt Syrup (Eng) a concentrated malt extract used in the mash to convert the grain, called copper syrup when used in the copper to extend brew length or adjust the gravity.

Malt Tax (Eng) a tax collected by the government until 1880 when beer duty was introduced.

Malt Vinegar (Eng) Alegar produced from a malt brew (less hops) which has been attacked by Acetobacter.

Malt Whisky (Scot) a whisky made from malted barley, water and yeast only. see Single Malt Whisky, Highland, Lowland, Islay, Campbeltown.

Malt Wine (Hol) the second distillate of Hollands Gin at a strength of between 50%–55% alc by vol.

Malty Towers (Eng) a 4.4% alc by vol. malt ale brewed by the Tower Brewery, Staffordshire.

Malvagia (Euro) another name for the Pinot gris grape. See also Malmsey, Malvasia and Malvoisie.

Malvar (Sp) a white grape variety grown in the central areas of Spain especially in D.O. Vinos de Madrid.

Malvasia (Euro) a famous ancient white grape from Greece, now grown in most other wine-producing countries. Has many clones throughout the World. Originally known as the Monemvasia. (Fr) = Pinot gris.

Malvasia Babosa (Mad) a white noble grape used in Malmsey production along with Malvasia candida and Malvasiao.

Malvasia Bianca (USA) a white grape variety used in the making of dessert wines in California.

Malvasia Bianca di Candia (It) a white grape variety grown in the Tuscany region.

Malvasia Bianca Toscana (It) a white grape variety grown in the Tuscany region.

Malvasia Branca (Port) a white grape variety used in the making of Port wine.

Malvasia Candiae (It) the old name for the wines of Crete in the thirteenth century. see Candia.

Malvasia Candida (Mad) a white noble grape variety used in Malmsey production along with Malvasia Babosa and Malvasiao.

Malvasia Corada (Port) an alternative spelling of Malvasia Corado.

Malvasia Corado (Port) a white grape variety used in the making of Port wine. Used because of its high sugar content. Also known as Vital.

Malvasia del Chianti (It) a white grape variety grown in the Tuscany region.

Malvasia del Lazio (It) a white grape variety used in Latium.

Malvasia delle Lipari (It) a D.O.C. white wine from the Aeolian Isles. north of Sicily. Made from the Corinto nero and Malvasia di Lipari grapes. Also a Passito type made which must have a minimum alc. content of 18% by vol. and 6° natural sugar.

Malvasia delle Lipari Liquoroso (It) a fortified wine produced on the Aeolian Isles north of Sicily. Produced by partially drying the grapes to produce a maximum of 60% of wine to be fortified. The finished product must have a minimum alc. content of 20% by vol. of which 16% is natural and at least 6% residual sugar. Wine aged for a minimum of 6 months.

Malvasia de Sitges (Sp) a sweet white wine produced around the little port of Sitges in the Penedés district of Cataluña in south-eastern Spain.

Malvasia di Bosa (It) a D.O.C. white wine from Sardinia. Made from the Malvasia di sardegna grapes. Cannot be sold to consumer before 2 years old. Four types produced are Secco, Dolce naturale, Liquoroso dolce naturale, Liquoroso secco.

Malvasia di Cagliari (It) a D.O.C. white wine from Sardinia. Made from the Malvasia di sardegna grape within the entire province of Cagliari. 4 types: Secco, Dolce naturale, Liquoroso secco and Liquoroso dolce naturale. Last two are entitled to the designation Riserva if aged 2 years (1 year in wooden casks). The ageing period commences from the date of fortification.

Malvasia di Candia (It) a white grape variety grown in the Emilia-Romagna region.

Malvasia di Casorzo (It) a red grape variety grown in the Piemonte region to make a wine of same name.

Malvasia di Casorzo d'Asti (It) a D.O.C. red and rosé wines from Piemonte. Made from 10% Barbera, Freisa and Grignolino and 90% Malvasia di casorzo grapes. The D.O.C. also applies to the sparkling wine made from musts or wines obtained from grapes in the production area.

Malvasia di Castelnuovo Don Bosco (It) a D.O.C. red wine from Piemonte region. Made from the Malvasia di schierano grape plus 15% of Freisa. D.O.C. also applies to fully sparkling wines with a minimum alc. content of 11% by vol.

Malvasia di Chianti (It) a red grape variety grown in the Tuscany region.

Malvasia di Lipari (It) a white grape variety grown in Sicily.

Malvasia di Lipari (It) a rich fortified dessert wine produced in Sicily from a grape of the same name.

Malvasia di Nus (It) a dry white alpine wine produced from the Malvasia grape in Valle d'Aosta.

Malvasia di Sardegna (It) a white grape variety grown in Sardinia.

Malvasia di Schierano (It) a red grape variety grown mainly in the Piemonte region.

Malvasia Fina (Port) a white grape variety used in the making of Port wine. Also known as the Arinto do Dão and Assario Branco.

Malvasia Istriana (It) a white grape variety grown in Collio.

Malvasia Nera di Lece (It) a red grape variety grown in the Alto Adige and Puglia regions.

Malvasiao (Mad) a rosé noble grape variety used for Malmsey production along with the Malvasia babosa and Malvasia candida grapes.

Malvasia Preta (Port) a black grape variety used in the making of Port wine, gives good colour, sugar and is resistant to heat. Also known as the Moreto do Dão.

Malvasia Puntinata (It) a white grape variety grown in the Latium region.

Malvasia Quinada (Cktl) a cocktail of Malmsey and quinine.

Malvasia Rei (Port) a white grape variety used in the production of Port.

Malvasía Riojana (Sp) the name used in the Rioja region for the local Malvasia grape. Also known as the Rojal blanco and Subirat.

Malvasia Rossa (It) a red grape variety grown in the Latium region.

Malvasia Roxa (Mad) a black grape variety used in the production of Madeira wine.

Malvasia Toscana (It) a white grape variety grown in most regions.

Malvasier (It) the German name for the Malvasia grape in the Süd-Tirol.

Malvasier (Ger) an erroneous varietal name for the Trollinger grape.

Malvazia (Mad) another spelling of Malvoisie.

Malvazia (Slo) an alternative spelling of the Malvazija grape.

Malvasier (Aus) an alternative name for the Frühroter veltliner.

Malvazija (Slo) the local spelling of the Malvasia grape grown in the north-west of the country

Malvedos Port (Port) a vintage Port shipped by Grahams. *see* Quinta dos Malvedos.

Malvern Hills Brewery (Eng) a brewery (established 1998). (Add): 15 West Malvern Road, Malvern, Worcestershire WR14 4ND. Brews: Black Country Wobble 4.5% alc by vol., Black Pear Premium Bitter 4.4% alc by vol., Doctor Gullys Winter Ale 5.2% alc by vol., Malvern Hills Bitter 3.9% alc by vol., Red Earl 3.7% alc by vol., Worcestershire Whym 4.2% alc by vol. Website: http://www.malvernhillsbrewery.co.uk 'E'mail: mbh.ales@tiscali.co.uk

Malvern Water (Eng) a still or carbonated mineral water from the Malvern hills, Derbyshire. (Add): Coca-Cola Enterprises Ltd., Uxbridge. UB8 1EZ. Mineral contents (milligrammes per litre): Sodium 15mg/l, Calcium 35mg/l, Magnesium 19mg/l, Potassium 1mg/l, Bicarbonates 123mg/l, Chlorides 39mg/l, Sulphates 35mg/l, Nitrates 8mg/l. pH 8.0

Malvesia Fina (Port) *see* Malvasia Fina.

Malvia (Port) an old name for the Malvasia grape. *See also* Malvoeira.

Malvina (Sp) the red colouring matter present in wines that originate from American root stock. Some countries forbid the importation of wines with malvina.

Malvoeira (Port) an old name for the Malvasia grape. *See also* Malvia.

Malvoisie (Fr) same as Malvasia. Also known as the Auxerrois gris, Fauvet, Pinot beurot, Pinot gris, Malmsey, Ruländer.

Malvoisie (Switz) a white dessert wine produced from late-gathered grapes.

Malvoisie de Corse (Fr) an alternative name for the Vermentino grape.

Malvoisie du Valais (Fr) an alternative name used in Aude for Macabeo, Languedoc for Bourboulenc, Roussillon for Torbato.

Malvoisie du Valais (Switz) an alternative name used for Pinot gris.

Malvoisie Noire (Fr) the local name used in the Lot, southern France for the Trousseau grape.

Malvoisie Rouge (Fr) the local name used in Savoie for Frühroter veltliner grape.

Malwa (Afr) a beer brewed in Uganda from fermented millet.

Malwenn (S.Afr) the label for a red wine (Pinotage) produced by the Signal Hill winery, Cape Town, Western Cape.

Maly Rohozec Brewery (Czec) a brewery based in northern Czec.

M

Malz (Ger) an alcohol-free beer from the Steffens Brauerei, St. Severinsberg.

Malzbier (Ger) a low alcohol, dark, sweet, malty beer produced from dark-roasted malt.

Mambourg (Fr) an A.C. Alsace Grand Cru vineyard at Sigolsheim, Haut-Rhin 65ha.

Mamertine (It) a light, red wine produced near Messina, Calabria and drunk by Caesar in 46BC. Also spelt Mamertinum.

Mamertino (It) a white wine from Sicily which was favoured by Julius Caesar. Made from the Catarrato and Grillo grapes in Messina, it is still produced today.

Mamertinum (Lat) *see* Mamertine.

Mamie Gilroy Cocktail (Cktl) 50mls (2fl.ozs) Scotch whisky, juice ½ lime, dash Angostura. Shake over ice, strain into an ice-filled highball and top with soda water and stir.

Mamie's Sister (Cktl) place 50mls (2fl.ozs) dry gin into an ice-filled highball glass with the juice of a small lime, top with ginger ale, stir and add a twist of lime peel.

Mamie Taylor (Cktl) 50mls (2fl.ozs) Scotch whisky, juice ½ lime. Shake over ice, strain into an ice-filled highball glass, top with ginger ale and stir.

Mammolo (It) a lesser red grape variety used in Chianti production.

Mammon (Eng) a 7% alc by vol. strong ale brewed by the Milton Brewery Cambridge Ltd., Cambridgeshire.

Mampe (Ger) a noted liqueur producer based in Berlin.

Mampe Bitter Drops (Ger) a type of aromatic bitters.

Mampoer (S.Afr) a spirit that was distilled from moepals and maroelas fruits and the berries of the kareeboom tree (now no longer made).

Mamreweg Wynkelders Koöperatief (S.Afr) a co-operative winery based in Groenkloof. (Add): P.O. Box 114, Darling 7345. Produces varietal wines under the Groenkloof label.

MAN (Aus) the label for a red wine (Cabernet sauvignon and Merlot blend) produced by the Schlossweingut Graf Hardegg winery, Weinviertel.

Mana (Cyp) a large earthenware jar used in Commandaria production.

Mana (Cyp) lit: 'mother', a system developed in the production of Commandaria. Is similar to the Spanish solera system but using earthenware jars instead of casks. A system of fractional blending.

Manchuela (Sp) a Denominación de Origen based in central Spain near the Mediterranean coast.

Manacor (Sp) one of the main wine-producing areas on Majorca in the Balearic Islands.

Manatiak (S.Am) a natural spring mineral from Colombia.

Manatial (Sp) spring (water) *see* Agua de Manatial.

Manatial Canario (Sp) a natural spring mineral water from Ingenio, Gran Canaria.

Mancey (Fr) a commune in the Mâcon region, Burgundy. Wines sold under A.C. Mâcon Mancey. Grapes may be used for A.C. Mâcon Supérieur.

Mancha [La] (Sp) the largest Denominación de Origen in Spain, based in Castilla-La Mancha near the Valdepeñas region. Produces red, rosado, white and sparkling wines in an extreme continental climate. The hot dry climate repels insects and diseases. Main grape variety is Airén, plus Cabernet sauvignon, Cencibel (Tempranillo), Garnacha, Macabeo, Moravia, Merlot, Pardilla, Verdoncho.

Manchega [a la] (Sp) a term used to denote the 'spur' or 'head' pruning. Is similar to 'en vaso' pruning method. Used in La Mancha.

Manchester Bitter (Eng) a bitter ale brewed by Lees Brewery in Manchester, sold in 440mls cans.

Manchester Bitter (Eng) a 4.2% alc by vol. bitter beer brewed by Marble Beer, Greater Manchester.

Manchester Dry (Eng) a brand of gin 40% alc by vol. produced by Willoughbys Ltd. in Manchester.

Manchester Gold (Eng) a 4.8% alc by vol. canned ale from Boddington Brewery, Manchester.

Manchuela (Sp) a Denominación de Origen region in La Mancha, central Spain. Became DO in 1982. Main grape varieties are Albillo, Bobal, Cencibel, Monastrell, Macabeo, plus Airén, Coloraillo, Pardillo and Moravia.

Mancy (Fr) a Cru Champagne village in the Canton d'Avize. District: Épernay.

Mandarin (Chi) a scented rice wine.

Mandarin (Hol) an orange coloured, orange-flavoured apéritif.

Mandarine (USA) a liqueur made from the dried peel of mandarine (tangerine) oranges 30% alc by vol.

Mandarine Napoléon (Bel) an orange and brandy liqueur made from the common tangerine (the rarest of tangerines). Dried skins are macerated in grape brandy 40% alc by vol.

Mandarine Sour [1] (Cktl) ½ measure Mandarine Napoléon, juice of ½ lemon. Shake together over ice, strain into a tulip glass, decorate with a cherry and slice of tangerine.

Mandarine Sour [2] (Cktl) 35mls (1½ fl.ozs) Mandarine Napoléon, 35mls (1½ fl.ozs) lemon juice, 2 dashes Angostura, 1 dash egg white. Shake over ice, strain into a wine glass and decorate with a slice of orange.

Mandarine Sunrise (Cktl) 10mls (½ fl.oz) Mandarine Napoléon, 25mls (1fl.oz) tequila, dash grenadine. Shake well over ice, strain into a highball glass, add ice and top up with orange juice.

Mandarine Tonic (Cktl) 1 measure Mandarine Napoléon. Top up with tonic water and serve 'on the rocks' with a slice of orange.

Mandarinette (Hol) a mandarine-flavoured liqueur produced by De Kuyper 30% alc by vol.

Mandarinetto (It) a tangerine liqueur.

Mandarin Imperiale (Fr) a brand of mandarin liqueur made from brandy and tangerine peel.

M and B (Eng) *abbr*: Mitchells and Butler.

Mandel (Ger) village (Anb): Nahe. (Ber): Schloss Böckelheim. (Gro): Rosengarten. (Vins): Alte Römerstrasse, Becherbrunnen, Dellchan, Palmengarten, Schlossberg.

M

Mandelaria (Gre) a red grape variety grown on the islands of Crete, Paros, Rhodes, Santorini. Also spelt Mandilaria.

Mandelbaum (Ger) vineyard (Anb): Rheinhessen. (Ber): Bingen. (Gro): Sankt Rochuskapelle. (Vil): Pfaffen-Schwabenheim.

Mandelberg (Ger) vineyard (Anb): Baden. (Ber): Badische Frankenland. (Gro): Tauberklinge. (Vil): Dertingen.

Mandelberg (Ger) vineyard (Anb): Rheinhessen. (Ber): Bingen. (Gro): Adelberg. (Vil): Lonsheim.

Mandelberg (Ger) vineyard (Anb): Rheinhessen. (Ber): Wonnegau. (Gro): Sybillenstein. (Vil): Offenheim.

Mandelberg (Ger) vineyard (Anb): Rheinhessen. (Ber): Wonnegau. (Gro): Sybillenstein. (Vil): Weinheim.

Mandelberg (Ger) vineyard (Anb): Pfalz. (Ber): Mittelhaardt-Deutsche Weinstrasse. (Gro): Pfaffengrund. (Vil): Duttweiler.

Mandelberg (Ger) vineyard (Anb): Pfalz. (Ber): Mittelhaardt-Deutsche Weinstrasse. (Gro): Schwarzerde. (Vil): Laumersheim.

Mandelberg (Ger) vineyard (Anb): Pfalz. (Ber): Südliche Weinstrasse. (Gro): Königsgarten. (Vil): Birkweiler.

Mandelberg (Ger) vineyard (Anb): Pfalz. (Ber): Südliche Weinstrasse. (Gro): Mandelhöhe. (Vil): Kirrweiler.

Mandelberg (Fr) an A.C. Alsace Grand Cru vineyard at Mittelwihr, Haut-Rhin 12ha.

Mandel Bitter (Ger) a wine that has a taste of bitter almonds.

Mandelbrunnen (Ger) vineyard (Anb): Rheinhessen. (Ber): Wonnegau. (Gro): Bergkloster. (Vil): Gundheim.

Mandelgarten (Ger) vineyard (Anb): Pfalz. (Ber): Mittelhaardt-Deutsche Weinstrasse. (Gro): Hofstück. (Vil): Gönnheim.

Mandelgarten (Ger) vineyard (Anb): Pfalz. (Ber): Mittelhaardt-Deutsche Weinstrasse. (Gro): Kobnert. (Vil): Weisenheim am Berg.

Mandelgarten (Ger) vineyard (Anb): Pfalz. (Ber): Mittelhaardt-Deutsche Weinstrasse. (Gro): Meerspinne. (Vil): Gimmeldingen.

Mandelgraben (Ger) vineyard (Anb): Mosel-Saar-Ruwer. (Ber): Bernkastel. (Gro): Kurfürstlay. (Vil): Braunerberg.

Mandelhang (Ger) vineyard (Anb): Pfalz. (Ber): Südliche Weinstrasse. (Gro): Ordensgut. (Vil): Edesheim.

Mandelhöhe (Ger) grosslage (Anb): Pfalz. (Ber): Südliche Weinstrasse. (Vils): Kirrweiler, Maikammer, Maikammer-Alsterweiler.

Mandelpfad (Ger) vineyard (Anb): Pfalz. (Ber): Mittelhaardt-Deutsche Weinstrasse. (Gro): Grafenstück. (Vil): Obrigheim.

Mandelpfad (Ger) vineyard (Anb): Pfalz. (Ber): Mittelhaardt-Deutsche Weinstrasse. (Gro): Schwarzerde. (Vil): Dirmstein.

Mandelpfad (Ger) vineyard (Anb): Pfalz. (Ber): Südliche Weinstrasse. (Gro): Kloster Liebfrauenberg. (Vil): Billigheim-Ingenheim.

Mandelpfad (Ger) vineyard (Anb): Pfalz. (Ber): Südliche Weinstrasse. (Gro): Kloster Liebfrauenberg. (Vil): Rohrbach.

Mandelring (Ger) vineyard (Anb): Pfalz. (Ber): Mittelhaardt-Deutsche Weinstrasse. (Gro): Meerspinne. (Vil): Haardt.

Mandelröth (Ger) vineyard (Anb): Pfalz. (Ber): Mittelhaardt-Deutsche Weinstrasse. (Gro): Kobnert. (Vil): Dackenheim.

Mandelstein (Ger) vineyard (Anb): Mittelrhein. (Ber): Rheinburgengau. (Gro): Gedeonseck. (Vil): Boppard.

Mandement (Switz) a wine region on the west side of Lake Geneva. Produces red and white wines.

Mandeville Cocktail (Cktl) ⅗ measure white rum, ⅖ measure dark rum, juice ¼ lemon, 10mls (⅛ gill) Coca Cola, 3 dashes Pernod, 2 dashes grenadine. Shake over ice and strain into an ice-filled old-fashioned glass.

Mandheling Coffee (E.Ind) a coffee from Sumatra that has a mellow flavour with a good strong aroma.

Mandilaria (Gre) an alternative spelling of Mandelaria.

Mandingo (It) a tangerine-flavoured liqueur.

Mandira (Tur) a dairy farm.

Mandis [Chevalier de] (Fr) an Armagnac producer. (Add): Cazanove S.A. 47600 Nérac.

M and M Punch (Cktl). ⅔ measure dark rum, ⅙ measure blackcurrant syrup, ⅙ measure lemon syrup. Add boiling water, stir and add slice of lemon.

Mandois [Michel et Claude] (Fr) a Champagne producer. (Add): Pierry, 51200 Épernay. Récoltants-manipulants. Produces vintage and non-vintage wines. Vintages: 1971, 1973, 1976, 1979, 1982, 1983, 1985, 1988, 1990, 1995, 1996, 1997, 1998, 1999, 2001. Label: Henri Mandois.

Mandora (Eng) the Mansfield Brewery's soft drinks subsidiary. Has the Rimark and St. Clements range of soft drinks.

Mandorla (It) an almond-flavoured liqueur produced by Francoli.

Manduria (It) a strong red wine from Puglia, may be fortified.

Maneblussertje (Hol) a 6.5% alc by vol. bottle-conditioned special beer brewed by De Gans Brouwerij, Goes.

Manègue (W.Ind) a noted distillery based in Haiti. Produces Rhum Tropical.

Manera (Arg) a natural spring mineral water. Mineral contents (milligrammes per litre): Sodium 128mg/l, Calcium 5mg/l, Magnesium 3mg/l, Potassium 5mg/l, Chlorides 63mg/l, Sulphates 8mg/l, Fluorides 1.3mg/l, Nitrates 60mg/l.

Manfred Vierthaler Winery (USA) a winery based in Sumner, Puyallup River Valley, western Washington. 12ha. Produces dry white, German-style wines.

Mangali (Euro) a natural spring mineral water from Latvia. Mineral contents (milligrammes per litre):

Sodium 60–95mg/l, Calcium 40–75mg/l, Magnesium 20–40mg/l, Potassium 4–15mg/l, Bicarbonates 140–210mg/l, Chlorides 130–245mg/l, Sulphates 55–129mg/l.

Manganese (Eng) a mineral found in the pips of grapes, therefore usually found in higher quantities in red wines than white.

Mangiatorella (It) a sparkling natural spring mineral water (established 1904) from Mangiatorella, Mount Pecoraro, Reggio Calabria. Mineral contents (milligrammes per litre): Sodium 9.8mg/l, Calcium 5.8mg/l, Magnesium 1.4mg/l, Potassium 0.8mg/l, Bicarbonates 26.5mg/l, Chlorides 12mg/l, Sulphates 4.5mg/l, Oxygen 11.5mg/l, Silicates 15.8mg/l. pH 6.0

Manglam (Ire) cocktail.

Mango Indica (Eng) a mango blossom flavoured tea produced by Whittards of Chelsea.

Mangra (Port) mildew. *See also* Mildio.

Mangualde (Port) a noted co-operative (1 of 10) in the Dão region.

Manhasset Cocktail (Cktl) ⅔ measure Bourbon whiskey, ⅙ measure Italian vermouth, ⅙ measure French vermouth, juice ¼ lemon. Shake over ice and strain into a cocktail glass.

Manhattan [1] (Cktl)(*sweet*) 1½ measures rye whiskey, ½ measure Italian vermouth, dash Angostura. Stir over ice, strain into a cocktail glass and add a cherry.

Manhattan Cocktail [2] (Cktl)(*sweet*) 30mls (¼ gill) Canadian Club whisky, 30mls (¼ gill) Italian vermouth, 2 dashes brown Curaçao, dash absinthe, dash Angostura. Stir over ice, strain into a cocktail glass, add cherry and piece of orange peel on top.

Manhattan Cocktail [3] (Cktl)(*medium*) 30mls (¼ gill) Canadian Club whisky, 15mls (⅛ gill) French vermouth, 15mls (⅛ gill) Italian vermouth, dash Angostura. Stir over ice, strain into a cocktail glass and add a cherry.

Manhattan Cocktail [4] (Cktl)(*dry*) 30mls (¼ gill) rye whiskey, 30mls (¼ gill) dry vermouth, dash Angostura. Stir over ice, strain into a cocktail glass and add a cherry.

Manhattan Cooler (Cktl) 50mls (2fl.ozs) claret, 3 dashes dark rum, juice ½ lemon, 2 tablespoons powdered sugar. Stir well with ice, strain into a medium-sized goblet and decorate with fruit in season.

Manhattan Perfect (Cktl) ⅓ measure rye whiskey, ⅓ measure dry vermouth, ⅓ measure sweet vermouth. Stir over ice and strain into a cocktail glass.

Manhattan Skyscraper (Cktl) in a highball glass containing ice pour 50mls (2fl.ozs) Bourbon whiskey, 25mls (1fl.oz) dry vermouth, dash Angostura and top with dry ginger ale.

Manicle (Fr) the name for a white grape variety grown in Bugey (near Savoie).

Manila (E.Ind) a leading brand of rum produced on the Philippine Islands by La Tondeña.

Manila Fizz (Cktl) 50mls (2fl.ozs) dry gin, 1 teaspoon powdered sugar, 1 egg, 50mls (2fl.ozs) Sarsaparilla, juice of a lime, shake over ice, strain into an ice-filled highball glass.

Manila Flame (Cktl) 1 measure Manila rum, ½ measure cranberry juice, ½ measure passion fruit juice, ¼ measure pineapple juice, juice ½ lime. Shake over ice and strain into a flute glass.

Manipuri (Ind) a hardy variety of the Assam tea bush.

Manisa-Izmir (Tur) a vineyard in the Aegean region that produces both red and white wines.

Manitoba Distillery (Can) a noted producer of Canadian whiskies.

Manitou Mineral Water (USA) a natural spring mineral water (established 1872) from Manitou Springs, Colorado. Mineral contents (milligrammes per litre): Sodium 150mg/l, Calcium 290mg/l, Magnesium 43mg/l, Potassium 23mg/l, Bicarbonates 1200mg/l, Chlorides 120mg/l, Sulphates 120mg/l, Fluorides 2.2mg/l, Nitrates 2.2mg/l. pH 7.0

Maniva (It) a sparkling natural spring mineral water from Maniva. Mineral contents (milligrammes per litre): Sodium 1.7mg/l, Calcium 36.9mg/l, Magnesium 4.3mg/l, Potassium 1.1mg/l, Bicarbonates 131.7mg/l, Chlorides 1mg/l, Sulphates 4.8mg/l, Fluorides 0.07mg/l, Nitrates 4.2mg/l, Silicates 6.5mg/l. pH 7.5

Manizales (S.Am) a fine coffee-producing region in Colombia.

Manjimup (Austr) a wine sub-region of Western Australia.

Mankazana (S.Afr) the label for a white wine (Sauvignon blanc) produced by the Ross Gower Wines winery, Elgin, Western Cape.

Manley Private Cellar (S.Afr) a winery (established 2002) based in Paarl, Western Cape. 8ha. Grape varieties: Cabernet sauvignon, Merlot, Pinotage, Sauvignon blanc, Shiraz. Website: http://www.manleywines.co.za

Mannaberg (Ger) grosslage (Anb): Baden. (Ber): Badische Bergstrasse/Kraichgau. (Vils): Bad Mingolsheim-Langenbrücken (ortsteil Bad Langenbrücken, ortsteil Bad Mingolsheim), Bruchsal (stadtteil Obergrombach), Bruchsal, Bruschal (stadtteil Untergrombach), Dielheim, Heidelberg, Heidelsheim, Helmsheim, Horrenberg, Kraichtal (stadtteil Oberöwisheim, stadtteil Unteröwisheim), Leimen, Malsch, Malschenberg, Mühlhausen, Nussloch, Östringen, Rauenberg, Rettigheim, Rotenberg, Tairnbach, Ubstadt-Weiher (ortsteil Stettfeld), Ubstadt-Weiher (ortsteil Ubstadt), Wiesloch, Zeutern.

Mannberg (Ger) vineyard (Anb): Rheingau. (Ber): Johannisberg. (Gro): Deutelsberg. (Vil): Hattenheim.

Mannberg (Ger) a vineyard within the village of Hattenheim, 8.1ha. (100%) of which is proposed to be classified as Erstes Gewächs.

Mannequines (Fr) the willow baskets used in Champagne to carry grapes 150lbs–175lbs (68kgs–79kgs) grapes can be held in each. *See also* Caques.

M

Mannite (Sp) a Sherry disease. Results in the formation of Mannitol.

Mannitic Fermentation (Eng) caused by the bacteria *Mannitopoen* that attacks at high temperatures the fructose in low-acid wines to produce Mannitol, ethanoic acid, lactic acid and CO_2. The wine throws a deposit and has a 'mousy' taste.

Mannitol (Eng) *see* Mannitic Fermentation, recognised by its acrid nose and palate. Sugar is produced when low-acid, sweet wines are attacked by lactic acid bacteria which reduces fructose to mannitol. *see* Mannite.

Mannochmore (Scot) a single highland malt whisky distillery based north of Rothes, Morayshire 40% alc by vol.

Mann of Norfolk (Eng) a 4.2% alc by vol. ale brewed by the Iceni Brewery, Norfolk.

Mann Ranch (USA) a small vineyard based in Anderson Valley, Mendocino, California. Grape variety: Chardonnay.

Manns (Eng) the Watney's East Midland Company, based in Northampton, the beers are brewed in London or Manchester. Produces all types of beers.

Mann's (Jap) one of the countries main wine-producers based in Katsunuma.

Mann's Brown (Eng) a famous brown ale 1034–1025 O.G. brewed by the Watney Mann Brewery in London.

Mann's Wine et Cie (Jap) *see* Mann's.

Mannweiler-Coelln (Ger) village (Anb): Nahe. (Ber): Schloss Böckelheim. (Gro): Paradiesgarten. (Vins): Rosenberg, Schloss Randeck, Seidenberg, Weissenstein.

Manoir du Kinkiz (Fr) a cider, cider brandy and pomeau producer. (Add): 75, Chemin du Quinquis, 29000 Quimper, Bretagne.

Manon (Fr) a natural spring mineral water from Vals les Bains. Mineral contents (milligrammes per litre): Sodium 579mg/l, Calcium 73mg/l, Magnesium 36mg/l, Potassium 44mg/l, Bicarbonates 1838mg/l, Chlorides 24mg/l, Sulphates 30mg/l. pH 6.14

Mansart-Baillet (Fr) a Champagne producer. (Add): 14 Rue Chaude Ruelle, B.P. 187, 51206 Épernay. 17ha.

Manseng (Fr) a white grape variety grown in south-western France in the regions of Madiran, Jurançon and Tursan. *see* Gros Manseng, Petit Manseng.

Mansfield Bitter (Eng) a classic bitter 3.9% alc by vol. brewed by Mansfield Brewery from a recipe dating back to 1855. *see* Riding Bitter, Riding Traditional Mild.

Mansfield Brewery (Eng) a brewery based in Littleworth, Mansfield, Notts. Noted for Mansfield Dark Smooth, Mansfield Mild, Mansfield Bitter 3.9% alc by vol. Old Baily Bitter, Red Admiral, Royal Stag, White Rabbit, Wild Boar, Marksman Lager 1039 O.G. Wicket & Willow, Riding Mild, Bitter and Traditional Mild. Took over the North Country Breweries in Hull in 1985. Also produce a range of bitter ales under the Chadburns label. *See also* Drayman's Choice.

Mansfield Dark Smooth (Eng) a 3.5% alc by vol. ale brewed by Mansfield Brewery, Littleworth, Mansfield, Notts.

Mansfield Winery (Austr) a winery based in Mudgee, New South Wales.

Mansikka (Fin) a strawberry liqueur.

Mansios (Fr) a red grape variety grown in the Côtes de Saint-Mont in the Gers département.

Manso de Velasco (Chile) a Cabernet sauvignon wine produced from very old vines by Torres.

Manstree (Eng) a vineyard based at New Barn Farm, Shillingford St. George, Exeter, Devon. Produces white and sparkling wines. Main Grape variety: Madeleine-Angevine.

Mans Wine (Jap) *see* Mann's.

Manta (Port) a method of pushing down the crust of the grape pulp in Port production when fermentation begins, wooden paddles are used.

Mantanegra (Sp) a Vino de la Tierra wine producing area in the province of Badajoz, Extremadura. 8000ha. Most widely planted grape is the Beba (table grape). Grape varieties: Cayetana, Eva, Pardina, Borba, Pedro ximénez, Borba, Alarije (white), Cencibel, Garnacha (red). Red, white and rosado wines are produced.

Manta Preta (Port) a red wine produced by DFJ Vinhos from Touriga nacional and Tinta roriz grapes grown in the Alentejo.

Mantar (Tur) cork (mushroom-shaped) i.e. a Champagne cork or stopper cork.

Mantel (Sp) the name used by Bodegas Alavez in La Rueda for a range of their white wines.

Manteúdo (Port) a white grape variety grown in Alentejo.

Mantey's Vineyard (USA) a winery based in Sandusky, Ohio. Produces vinifera and French-American hybrid wines.

Mantiko (Gre) a deep ruby red wine from the Isle of Crete. Aged for 1 year in cask.

Mantiniea (Gre) an A.O.Q.S. dry white wine from the Peloponnese made with the Moschofilero grape. Produced by Cambas.

Mantlerhof (Aus) a winery based in the Kremstal region. (Add): Hauptstrasse 50, 3494 Brunn im Felde. Grape varieties: Grüner veltliner, Müller-Thurgau, Pinot blanc, Riesling, Roter veltliner, Zweigelt. Produces a range of wine styles.

Manto Negro (Sp) a red grape variety grown in the Balearic Islands.

Mantonica (It) a dry red fortified wine from the Calabrian region.

Mantonico Bianco (It) a white grape variety grown in Calabria.

Mantonico Nero (It) the Calabrian name for the red grape Gaglioppo.

Mantúa (Sp) a white grape variety grown in the Huelva region, south-western Spain and the Extremadura. Also known as Montúa

Mantúo Castellano (Sp) a lesser white grape variety used in Sherry production.

M

Mantúo de Pila (Sp) a lesser white grape variety used in Sherry production. Also known as the Gabriela and Mantúo de Rey.

Mantúo de Rey (Sp) an alternative name for the Mantúo de Pila.

Mantúo de Sanlúcar (Sp) a white grape variety grown in the south-western regions.

Manubach (Ger) village (Anb): Mittelrhein. (Ber): Bacharach. (Gro): Schloss Stahleck. (Vins): Heilgarten, Langgarten, Mönchwingert, St. Oswald.

Manuel (S.Afr) the label for a red wine (Cabernet sauvignon 65% and Merlot 35% blend) produced by the Saxenberg winery, Stellenbosch, Western Cape.

MAN Vintners (S.Afr) a winery (established 2001) based in Agter-Paarl, Western Cape. Grape varieties: Cabernet sauvignon, Chardonnay, Chenin blanc, Merlot, Pinotage, Sauvignon blanc, Shiraz. Label: Sénga. Website: http://www.manvintners.co.za

Manwood Wines (Eng) a noted wholesale wine and spirit merchant based in Knutsford, Cheshire.

Manx Pure Beer Act (I.O.M) introduced in 1874 it decreed that only malt, hops, yeast and sugar shall be used to brew beer.

Manzana Verde (Sp) a green apple liqueur at 20% alc by vol.

Manzanarès (Sp) an important wine vineyard for the wines of Valdepeñas in the La Mancha region of central Spain.

Manzaneque (Sp) a winery based in Albacete, Castilla-La Mancha. Likely to apply for Castilla-La Mancha private D.O. status. *See also* Calzadilla, Sandoval, Dehesa del Carrizal, Valdepusa, Vallegarcía, Aalto, Mauro, San Román.

Manzanilla (Sp) a Fino Sherry that is matured on the coast at Sanlúcar de Barrameda, the flor yeast grows all year round and is thicker than on Jerez Sherries, develops a salty tang.

Manzanilla Amontillado (Sp) a very rare, old, matured wine from Sanlúcar de Barrameda.

Manzanilla de Sanlúcar (Sp) a fine, dry, Manzanilla Sherry produced by Antonio Barbadillo in Jerez.

Manzanilla Fina (Sp) the Fino version of Manzanilla.

Manzanilla Oloroso (Sp) an Oloroso version of Manzanilla Sherry.

Manzanilla Pasada (Sp) a well-aged Manzanilla Sherry.

Manzanita (Fr) a 25% alc by vol. green-apple flavoured liqueur produced by Marie Brizzard, Bordeaux.

Manzoni (It) a red grape variety, a cross between the Cabernet and the Prosecco. Yields a big dark red wine. Grown in the Treviso region.

Mao-t'ai (Chi) a grain spirit produced in Mao-t'ai, Kweichow province, south-western China. Made from wheat and millet 26% alc by vol.

Ma Pardoes (Eng) a home-brew public house in Netherton, near Dudley. Known also as the Old Swan. Produces a cask-conditioned bitter 1034 O.G.

Mà Partilha (Port) a 100% Merlot wine produced at João Pires.

Maple Leaf (Cktl) ⅔ measure Bourbon whiskey, ⅓ measure lemon juice, dash maple syrup. Shake over ice and strain into a cocktail glass.

Maple Leaf (Eng) a home-brew public house in Newark, Notts. Owned by Ind Coope. Produces cask-conditioned ales.

Maple Moon (Eng) a bottled ale brewed by the Holts Brewery, Manchester.

Maple Spring (Eng) a natural spring mineral water from Maple Spring Borehole 4, Burntwood, Staffordshire.

Maqha (Arab) café.

Maqintosh (Ind) a whiskey made up of a 5 year old Indian malt, neutral spirit and an imported Scotch pre-blended malts and grains whisky.

Maqua 2000 (Ind) a natural spring mineral water. Mineral contents (milligrammes per litre): Calcium 2mg/l, Chlorides 25mg/l, Sulphates 35a natural spring mineral water from. Mineral contents (milligrammes per litre): Sodium mg/l, Calcium mg/l, Magnesium mg/l, Potassium mg/l, Bicarbonates mg/l, Chlorides mg/l, Sulphates mg/l, Fluorides mg/l, Nitrates mg/l, Silicates 7.0mg/l. pH 7.3

Maquevin (Fr) *see* Macvin.

Maquey Aloe (Mex) used to make the spirit aquadiente and pulque.

Maquisards [Les] (Fr) a vineyard of Dopff & Irion in Alsace. Produces Gewurztraminer.

Maraca (W.Ind) the brand-name of a light rum produced in Puerto Rico.

Maracibos Coffee (S.Am) a variety of pure coffee produced in Venezuela.

Maracuja (Bra) a passion fruit-flavoured liqueur.

Maragopipe (S.Am) a large mutant variety of the arabica coffee bean.

Marais [Les] (Fr) a vineyard in the A.C. commune of Montagny, Côte Chalonnaise, Burgundy.

Marais Viljoen (S.Afr) the label for varietal red wines (Pinotage & Shiraz) produced by the Drakensig Wines winery, Paarl, Western Cape.

Maranges [Les] (Fr) a Premier Cru vineyard [part] in the commune of Cheilly-lès-Maranges, A.C. Santenay, Côte de Beaune, Burgundy.

Maranges [Les] (Fr) a Premier Cru vineyard [part] in the commune of Dezize-lès-Maranges, A.C. Santenay, Côte de Beaune, Burgundy.

Maranges [Les] (Fr) a Premier Cru vineyard [part] in the commune of Sampigny-lès-Maranges, A.C. Santenay, Côte de Beaune, Burgundy.

Marao (Cktl) ⅓ measure Port, ⅓ measure anis, ⅓ measure advocaat. Shake over ice and strain into a cocktail glass.

Maraschino (It) a clear cherry liqueur made from maraska cherries including the crushed kernels 30% alc by vol.

Maraschino Cherries (It) bright red dyed cherries preserved in maraschino and used for cocktail decoration.

Maraska (Slo) a cherry brandy from Zadar.

Maraska Cherries (Euro) a cherry used in the making of maraschino and cherry brandy.

M

Marasquin (Hol) a cherry-flavoured liqueur produced by De Kuyper from the distillation of green cherry kernels 30% alc by vol.

Marastina (Cro) a dry white wine from Croatia. Has an extra dry finish, is high in alcohol, not unlike a dry Sherry.

Marathassa (Cyp) the north-west region of the Troodos mountains. Produces fine wines.

Maratheftiko (Cyp) a red grape variety named after the region (Marathessa) it is grown in.

Marathon Ale (Eng) a 4% alc by vol. cask-conditioned ale brewed by the Six Bells Brewery, Bishop's Castle, Shropshire.

Marathon Challenger (Eng) a draught beer brewed by Wood's Brewery, Wistanstow, Shropshire.

Marbach (Ger) village (Anb): Baden. (Ber): Badische Frankenland. (Gro): Tauberklinge. (Vin): Frankenberg.

Marbach (Ger) vineyard (Anb): Nahe. (Ber): Schloss Böckelheim. (Gro): Paradiesgarten. (Vil): Sobernheim.

Marbach (Ger) village (Anb): Württemberg. (Ber): Württembergisch Unterland. (Gro): Schalkstein. (Vin): Neckarhälde.

Marbaix Brasserie (Bel) a brewery based in Charleroi. Brews: Gauloise and a Christmas Ale.

Marble Bitter (Eng) a seasonal bitter brewed by Marble Brewery.

Marble Brewery (Eng) a brewery (established 2004). (Add): Marble Arch Pub, 73 Rochdale Road, Ancoats, Manchester, Greater Manchester M4 4HY. Brews: Chocolate Heavy 5.5% alc by vol., Ginger Marble 4.5% alc by vol., Lagonda IPA 5% alc by vol., Manchester Bitter 4.2% alc by vol., Marble Bitter 3.9% alc by vol., Totally Marbled, Dobber 6.5% alc by vol. Website: http://www.marblebeers.co.uk 'E'mail: enquiries@marblebeers.co.uk

Marble Spa (Austr) a natural spring mineral water brand.

Marbonne (S.Afr) a 16 y.o. pot-stilled brandy produced by the Louiesenhof Winery, Stellenbosch, Western cape.

Marc (Fr) a brandy from the 3rd and 4th pressing of the grapes. Known as Eau-de-Vie-de-Marc. (Ger) = tresterbranntwein, (It) = vinaccio/grappa, (Lat) = vinacea, (S.Afr) – dop-brandy, (Ser) = vinjak, (Sp) = orujo.

Marc (Fr) the grape pulp, from which marc brandy gets its name, the wine made from the spent pulp (marc) is watered, repressed and the resulting fermented wine distilled into marc (brandy).

Marcación (Sp) a method of vine planting in which the rows are separated by 1.2 metres, although now tends to be 2.4 metres to allow for mechanical harvesting for example.

Marc Chauvet (Fr) a Champagne producer (established 1529). (Add): 3, Rue de la Liberté, 51500 Rilly-la-Montagne. Propriétaire-Récoltant. 13ha. Produces vintage and non-vintage wines. Vintages: 1995, 1996, 1997, 1998, 1999, 2002. A member of the Club Tresors de Champagne. Label: Club de Viticulteurs, Cuvée Rubis 'Brut Rosé',

Cuvée 'Special Club' Millésimée. Website: http://www.cha.npagne-marc-chauvet.com

Marc de Bourgogne (Fr) a marc brandy made in Burgundy from a distillation of the skins, pips and stems of the grapes left in the bottom of the casks after the wines have been racked off.

Marc de Café (Fr) coffee grounds.

Marc de Champagne (Fr) one of the lightest marcs available, made from the residue pulp. *see* Rebêche.

Marc de Hospices de Beaune (Fr) a marc brandy reserved and sold for the famous annual charity held in Beaune, Burgundy.

Marc du Valais (Switz) a marc brandy produced in the Valais Canton.

Marcel Contreras Brasserie (Bel) a brewery based at Gavere in eastern Flanders. Brews golden-coloured, abbaye-style beers.

Marcel de Reuck (S.Afr) the label for a range of wines produced by the Crows Nest winery, Paarl, Western Cape.

Marcella (Eng) the old eighteenth century spelling of Marsala.

Marcel's Cup (Cktl) ⅓ measure brandy, ⅓ measure rosé wine, ⅓ measure Bénédictine. Stir with ice in a large jug. Add slices of orange, cucumber peel and mint sprigs and top with soda water.

Marchampt (Fr) a commune in the Beaujolais. Has A.C. Beaujolais-Villages or Beaujolais-Marchampt status.

Marchànd à Vin (Ch.Isles) wine merchant.

Marchand de Vins (Fr) vintner.

Marchanudo (Sp) a district within Andalusia where the Sherry vineyards are based. Has chalky soil. *See also* Macharnudo.

March Beer (Eng) a very strong beer brewed in the spring in medieval times.

March Brown (Eng) a brown Sherry produced by Findlater's.

Marche (It) a wine region on the Adriatic coast. Noted for Verdicchio.

Marc Hebrart (Fr) a Champagne producer (established 1955). (Add): 18-20, Rue du Pont, 51160 Mareuil-sur-Aÿ. 13ha. Propriètaire-Récoltant. Produces vintage and non-vintage wines. Vintages: 1995, 1996, 1997, 1999. A member of the Club Tresors de Champagne. Labels: Cuvée 'Special Club' Millésimée Premier Cru (Chardonnay 40% Pinot noir 60%), Mareuil Rouge Premier Cru.

Marcher Lager (Eng) a lager beer 1034 O.G. brewed for their Border Brewery subsidiary in North Wales. *see* Border Brewery.

Marches [The] (It) a predominantly mountainous region which borders the Adriatic coast to the west of Umbria. Noted for D.O.C. Rosso Conero, Rosso Piceno, Verdicchio dei Castelli di Jesi wines.

Marches Ales (Eng) a brewery. (Add): Unit 6, western Close, Southern avenue Ind Estate, Leominster, Herefordshire HR6 0GD. Brews beers and lager. Website: http://www.beerinabox.co.uk 'E'mail: info@beerinabox.co.uk

M

Marches de Bretagne (Fr) a Vin de Pays area in the Loire Atlantique département in western France. Produces red, rosé and dry white wines.

Marchese di Vallamarina (It) a vineyard based in Sicily. Also a wine produced from 100% Cabernet sauvignon grapes by Sella and Mosca from estate grown grapes.

Marchesi di Barolo (It) a noted winery based in Barolo, Piemonte.

Marchgasse (Aus) a vineyard site on the banks of the River Danube in the Kremstal region.

March Hare (Eng) a 4% alc by vol. ale brewed by Smiles Brewery in Bristol.

Marchier (Fr) the old term for the treading of the grapes.

Marchio Depositato (It) trade-mark or registered brand-name.

March Vineyard (USA) a vineyard based in Potter Valley, Mendocino, California. Grape variety: Johannisberg riesling.

Marcile Lorraine (USA) the label for a red wine (Pinot noir) produced by the Broadley Vineyards winery, Willamette Valley, Oregon.

Marcilla (Sp) one of 3 sub-zones in the Ribera Alta based in the south of the region. Produces mainly rosado wines.

Marcillac (Fr) an A.C. red wine from the Côtes de Saint-Mont in the Gers département. Made from the Mansios grape (A.C. in 1990).

Marcilly Frères (Fr) a négociant-éleveur based in Beaune, Côte de Beaune, Burgundy.

Marciume Nobile (It) the local (Latium) term for *botrytis cinerea*. *See also Muffa nobile.*

Marckrain (Fr) an A.C. Alsace Grand Cru vineyard in Bennwihr and Sigolsheim, Haut-Rhin 45ha.

Marcle Orchard (Eng) a low-alcohol cider 1.2% alc by vol. from Westons in Herefordshire.

Marcobrunn (Ger) vineyard (Anb): Rheingau. (Ber): Johannisberg. (Gro): Deutelsberg. (Vil): Erbach.

Marcobrunn (Ger) a vineyard within the village of Erbach, 5.2ha. (100%) of which is proposed to be classified as Erstes Gewächs.

Marco de Bartoli (It) *see* De Bartoli.

Marco Felluga (It) a winery based in the Friuli-Venezia-Guilia region. Produces DOC Sauvignon del Collio. Label: Russiz. Website: http://www.marcofelluga.it

Marconi (Cktl) 2 parts dry gin, 1 part sweet vermouth, 2 dashes Angostura. Stir well with ice and strain into a cocktail glass.

Marconi (It) a winery in the D.O.C. Verdicchio dei Castelli di Jesi, Marches region. Label: Black Label.

Marconi Cocktail (Cktl) ½ measure sweet vermouth, ½ measure Calvados. Stir over ice and strain into a cocktail glass.

Marconnets [Les] (Fr) a Premier Cru vineyard in the A.C. commune of Beaune, Côte de Beaune, Burgundy 8.81ha.

Marconnets [Les] (Fr) a Premier Cru vineyard in the A.C. commune of Savigny-lès-Beaune, Côte de Beaune, Burgundy.

Marco Polo [1] (Cktl) 1½ measures brandy, 1½ measures Port, 1 measure fresh lime or lemon juice. Shake over ice, strain into a wine goblet, top with soda water and add straws.

Marco Polo [2] (Cktl) 1 bottle Verdelho Madeira, 100grms (¼ lb) sugar, 125mls (5fl.ozs) Cognac, 5 cinnamon sticks, 5 slices lemon, 6 cloves. Heat slowly, strain and serve.

Marco Real (Sp) an old way of planting vines in the Sherry region, 1.5metres apart. Now planted hedge-style (*see* Hedging) at 1metre apart.

Marcottage (Fr) the traditional layering method used to propagate vines. Permits the shoots to obtain roots of their own before being pruned from the vine.

Marcques [Les] (Fr) a vineyard in the A.C. commune of Montagny, Côte Chalonnaise, Burgundy.

Mar del Plata (Cktl) ½ measure dry gin, ⅛ measure Bénédictine, ⅜ measure dry vermouth, dash Grand Marnier. Stir over ice, strain into a cocktail glass and add a twist of lemon peel.

Mardeuil (Fr) a Cru Champagne village in the Canton de Montmort. District: Épernay.

Mardi Gras (Eng) the brand-name of a drink made from vodka, passion fruit and soda water 18% alc by vol.

Mardle Ale (Eng) a 5.5% alc by vol. ale brewed by a home-brew pub in Tivetshall St. Mary, Norfolk. *See also* Mardle Bitter, Mardle Strong Ale.

Mardle Bitter (Eng) a 4.5% alc by vol. bitter ale brewed by a home-brew pub in Tivetshall St. Mary, Norfolk. *See also* Mardle Ale, Mardle Strong Ale.

Mardler (Eng) a mild ale brewed by Woodforde's Brewery in Norwich.

Mardler's (Eng) a 3.5% alc by vol. ale brewed by Woodforde's Ltd., Norfolk.

Mardle Strong Ale (Eng) a 6.5% alc by vol. ale brewed by a home-brew pub in Tivetshall St. Mary, Norfolk. *See also* Mardle Ale, Mardle Bitter.

Mareb (Arab) a natural spring mineral water from Mareb Spring, Yemen. Mineral contents (milligrammes per litre): Sodium 80.3mg/l, Calcium 47.7mg/l, Magnesium 22.1mg/l, Bicarbonates 215.9mg/l, Sulphates 95mg/l.

Maréchal Foch (Can) a red French hybrid grape variety, a cross between a *Riparia rupestris* and Gold Riesling. Is grown in Ontario.

Maréchaudes [Les] (Fr) a Premier Cru vineyard [part] in the A.C. commune of Aloxe-Corton, Côte de Beaune, Burgundy.

Maréchaudes [Les] (Fr) a Premier Cru vineyard [part] in the commune of Ladoix-Serrigny, A.C. Aloxe-Corton, Côte de Beaune, Burgundy.

Maredsous (Bel) a top-fermented, bottle-conditioned abbaye beer brewed by the Moortgat and Duvel Brasseries for the Maredsous Abbaye. 2 versions: 8% alc by vol and 10% alc by vol.

Maredsous Abbaye (Bel) an abbey in southern Belgium whose ruby and amber beers are now brewed by the Duvel and Moortgat Brasseries.

Mare Nostrum Brasseur du Sud (Fr) a brewery. (Add): F-06500 Castillon-Menton. Brews beers and lager. Website: http://www.marenostrum.com

M

Mareotic (Egy) an ancient light, sweet white wine with a fragrant aroma produced near Alexandria at Marea on the banks of Lake Mareotis.

Maréotis (Fr) the label for an A.C. Côtes-du-Rhône-Villages St-Maurice (red) from Domaine Viret, St-Maurice, Vaucluse.

Mares (Fr) the name given to the clay layer under the alluvial galet stones in the Gard département.

Maresca (Hol) a natural spring mineral water from Maresca-1, Maarheeze.

Maresme (Sp) a district of Alella.

Marestel (Fr) a V.D.Q.S. vineyard on the bank of the river Rhône in the Savoie region.

Mareuil-le-Port (Fr) a Cru Champagne village in the Canton de Dormans. District: Épernay.

Mareuil-sur-Ay (Fr) a Premier Cru Champagne village in the Canton d'Aÿ. District: Reims.

Marfaux (Fr) a cru Champagne village in the Canton de Ville-en-Tardenois. District: Reims.

Marfil (Sp) a brand-name used by the Alella Co-operative in Catalonia for a range of their wines.

Marfil (Sp) lit: 'ivory', a white grape variety grown in Cáceres, south-western Spain.

Marfil Blanco (Sp) a white grape variety grown in Alella and Catalonia. Produces soft, fruity wines.

Margaine [A] (Fr) a Champagne producer. (Add): 3, Avenue de Champagne, 51380 Villiers Marmery. Produces vintage and non-vintage wines. Vintages: 1995, 1996, 1997, 1999. A member of the Club Tresors de Champagne. Labels: Cuvée Rosée, Cuvée 'Special Club' Millésimée (Chardonnay 100%). 'E'mail: champagne-margaine@terre-net.fr

Margan Family (Austr) a winery based in the Hunter Valley, New South Wales.

Margarete (Ger) vineyard (Anb): Württemberg. (Ber): Württembergisch Unterland. (Gro): Lindelberg. (Vil): Michelbach a.W.

Margarete (Ger) vineyard (Anb): Württemberg. (Ber): Württembergisch Unterland. (Gro): Lindelberg. (Vil): Obersöllbach.

Margaret River (Austr) a wine region in the province of Western Australia having a medium to warm 'seaside' climate and gravely loam soils. Part of Sandalford. Districts: Carbonup, Karridale, Treeton, Wallcliffe, Willyabrup, Yallingup. Grape varieties: Cabernet sauvignon, Merlot, Chardonnay, Sauvignon blanc, Sémillon. Wineries include Leeuwin Estate, Evans & Tate, Cullens, Cape Mentelle Vineyards.

Margaret River Winery (Austr) see Château Xanadu.

Margaret Rose (Cktl) ½ measure gin, ⅙ measure Calvados, ⅙ measure Cointreau, ⅙ measure lemon juice, dash grenadine. Shake over ice and strain into a cocktail glass.

Margarita (Cktl) a blend of tequila, lime juice and Cointreau. Shake over ice, strain and serve in a salt-rimmed glass. Named after Marjorie King in the 19th Century by a Mexican barman called Carlos Herrera. Majorie was allergic to all spirits except tequila!

Margaux (Fr) an A.C. commune in the Haut-Médoc, Bordeaux. 1232ha. under vine (59% Cru Classé) 21 Cru Classés. see Châteaux: Margaux, Brane-Cantenac, Durfort-Vivens, Lascombes, Rauzan-Gassies, Rauzan-Ségla, Boyd-Cantenac, Cantenac-Brown, Desmirail, Ferrière, Giscours, d'Issan, Kirwan, Malescot Saint-Expuéry, Marquis d'Alesme-Becker, Palmer, Pouget, Marquis de Terme, Prieuré-Lichine, Dauzac, du Tertre.

Margaux (Fr) see Château Margaux.

Margherita dells Sila (It) a natural spring mineral water from Spezzano della Sila, Cosenza.

Margnissen Estates Winery (Can) a winery based in Niagara-on-the-Lake, Ontario. Noted for Cabernet sauvignon and Ice wine.

Margonwasser (Ger) a natural spring mineral water (established 1903) from Burkhardwalde. Mineral contents (milligrammes per litre): Sodium 23.7mg/l, Calcium 90.8mg/l, Magnesium 19.9mg/l, Potassium 1mg/l, Bicarbonates 215mg/l, Chlorides 31mg/l, Sulphates 132mg/l.

Margoo (Eng) the eighteenth century spelling of Margaux.

Margoty (Fr) a vineyard in the A.C. commune of Montagny, Côte Chalonnaise, Burgundy.

Margrain Estate (N.Z) a vineyard based in the Martinborough region of the North Island.

Marguerite (S.Afr) the label for a white wine (Chardonnay) part of the Jacques de Savoy range produced by the Vrede en Lust Wine Farm winery, Paarl, Western Cape.

Marguerite (Fr) a natural spring mineral water from La Chapelle St. Laurice es Allier 63. Mineral contents (milligrammes per litre): Sodium 302mg/l, Calcium 71mg/l, Magnesium 40mg/l, Potassium 33mg/l, Bicarbonates 812mg/l, Chlorides 230mg/l, Sulphates 59mg/l.

Marguerite (S.Afr) the label for a semi-dry white wine (Chenin blanc and Muscat d'alexandrie blend) from the Nelson's Creek range produced by the Nelson Estate winery, Paarl, Western Cape.

Marguerite Cristel (Fr) the label used by the Société Anonyme de Magenta for their non-vintage and rosé Champagnes.

Marguet-Bonnerave (Fr) a Champagne producer. (Add): 14 Rue de Bouzy, 51150 Ambonnay.

Maria Ardoña (Sp) a black grape variety grown in Valdeorras.

Mariabader Original Excelsior (Czec) a sparkling natural spring mineral water from BJ6 Mariánské Lázni. Mineral contents (milligrammes per litre): Sodium 22.16mg/l, Calcium 25.49mg/l, Magnesium 15.64mg/l, Potassium 2.827mg/l, Bicarbonates 99.42mg/l, Chlorides 36.8mg/l, Sulphates 47.92mg/l, Fluorides 0.115mg/l, Nitrates 1.21mg/l, Silicates 34.5mg/l, Manganese 1.264mg/l.

Maria Bonita Cocktail (Cktl) 35mls (1½fl.ozs) white rum, ¼ measure Curaçao, 75mls (3fl.ozs) pineapple juice. Stir over ice, strain into a flute glass. Top with a cherry and pineapple cube.

M

Mariacron (Ger) the brand-name of a brandy produced by the Peter Eckes Distillery. Sold in frosted bottles.

Mariafelder (Ger) a Spätburgunder 'clone' grown mainly in southern Germany.

Mariage Frères (Fr) a Paris tea company that specialies in China teas. (Add): 70, Avenue des Terroirs de France, 75012 Paris. Website: http://www.mariagefreres.com

Maria Gomes (Port) a white grape variety grown in the Bairrada region. Also known as Fernão Pires.

Maria Magdalena (Ger) vineyard (Anb): Pfalz. (Ber): Südliche Weinstrasse. (Gro): Kloster Liebfrauenberg. (Vil): Klingenmünster.

Marianum (It) an ancient red wine produced in south-western Italy in Roman times.

Maria Ordoña (Sp) an alternative name for Merenzao.

Maria Theresa Cocktail (Cktl) 1½ measures tequila, ¾ measure lime juice, ¾ measure bilberry juice. Shake over ice and strain into a Champagne saucer.

Maribo Brewery (Den) a brewery based in the town of Maribo.

Maribor (Slo) a region of Slovenia. Produces mainly white wines from the Sylvaner, Traminer and Sauvignon grapes.

Marie Antoinette (Cktl) 35mls (1½fl.ozs) dry gin, 20mls (¾fl.oz) blue Curaçao, 25mls (1fl.oz) lemon juice, 10mls (½fl.oz) gomme syrup, shake over ice, strain into a cocktail glass (rim dipped in grenadine and castor sugar) and top with cherry.

Marie Brizard (Fr) a liqueur company that makes a wide range of liqueurs. Based in the western France. (Add): BP 557, 33000 Bordeaux. Produces: Limoncini, Manzanita, Melocotón.

Marie Colas (W.Ind) a rum distillery based at Port au Prince, Haiti. Produces Rhum Citadelle.

Marie Jeanne (Fr) a demi-john used in Bordeaux (2.5litres).

Marienberg (Austr) a vineyard. (Add): Black Road, Coromandel Valley, South Australia 5051. 23ha. Grape varieties: Cabernet sauvignon, Gewürztraminer, Rhine riesling, Sémillon, Shiraz.

Marienberg (Ger) vineyard (Anb): Mosel-Saar-Ruwer. (Ber): Zell/Mosel. (Gro): Weinhex. (Vil): Güls.

Marien Brunnen (Ger) a natural spring mineral water. Mineral contents (milligrammes per litre): Sodium 550mg/l, Calcium 119mg/l, Magnesium 6.9mg/l, Potassium 8.4mg/l, Bicarbonates 534mg/l, Chlorides 680mg/l, Sulphates 128mg/l, Fluorides 0.44mg/l, Silicates 11.2mg/l.

Marienburg (Ger) vineyard (Anb): Mosel-Saar-Ruwer. (Ber): Bernkastel. (Gro): Vom Heissen Stein. (Vil): Pünderich.

Marienburger (Ger) vineyard (Anb): Mosel-Saar-Ruwer. (Ber): Zell/Mosel. (Gro): Schwarze Katz. (Vil): Zell-Kaint.

Marienfeld (Aus) a vineyard site on the banks of the River Danube situated in the Wachau region, Niederösterreich.

Mariengarten (Ger) grosslage (Anb): Pfalz. (Ber): Mittelhaardt-Deutsche Weinstrasse. (Vils): Deidesheim, Forst, Wachenheim.

Marienholz (Ger) vineyard (Anb): Mosel-Saar-Ruwer. (Ber): Saar-Ruwer. (Gro): Römerlay. (Vil): Trier.

Marienpforter Klosterberg (Ger) vineyard (Anb): Nahe. (Ber): Schloss Böckelheim. (Gro): Burgweg. (Vil): Waldböckelheim.

Marienriesling (Ger) a white grape variety, a cross between the White riesling and the St. Laurent.

Mariensteiner (Ger) a white grape variety, a cross between the Silvaner and the Rieslaner.

Mariental (Aus) the label for a red wine (Blaufränkisch) produced by the Triebaumer [Ernst] winery, Rust, Burgenland.

Marienthal (Ger) village (Anb): Ahr. (Ber): Walporzheim/Ahrtal. (Gro): Klosterberg. (Vins): Jesuitengarten, Klostergarten, Rosenberg, Stiftsberg, Trotzenberg.

Marie Stuart (Fr) a Champagne producer. (Add): B.P. 268, Place de la République, 51109 Reims Cedex. Produces vintage and non-vintage wines. Vintages: 1973, 1975, 1976, 1979, 1981, 1985, 1988, 1990, 1995, 1998, 2000. Blanc de blancs cuvée (Cuvée R.G). See also Cuvée de la Reine.

Mariette (Cktl) 25mls (1fl.oz) white rum, 10mls (½fl.oz) each of Amaretto di Saronno, Cointreau. Build into an ice-filled highball glass, top with Kinnie, decorate with a slice of orange, apple and a cherry.

Marignan (Fr) a dry white wine from Sciez in the Savoie region.

Marillenbrand (Ger) an apricot brandy.

Marillen Likor (Ger) an apricot-flavoured brandy.

Marimar Torres Estate (USA) a 23ha. winery based in Cristina, Russian River Valley, Sonoma County. (Add): Don Miguel Vineyard, 11400 Graton Road, Sebastopol CA 95472. Produces a Chardonnay wine that is barrel fermented. Aged in 228litre Burgundian oak casks. Also noted for Pinot noir. Website: http://www.marimarestate.com

Mari Mayans (Sp) a 50% alc by vol. and 70% alc by vol. fluorescent green coloured absinthes from Ibiza.

Marimba (S.Afr) the label for a range of wines produced by the Overhex Private Cellar winery, Worcester, Western Cape.

Marimba (S.Afr) the label for a range of wines produced by the Southern Sky Wines winery, Paarl, Western Cape.

Marin (Fr) small Cru near the spa town of Evian. A.C. Savoie. Wines are produced from Chasselas grapes.

Marin (USA) a small wine-producing area across the Golden Gate from San Francisco, California.

Marina Cvetic (It) the label for red and white wines from the Azienda Agricola Masciarelli based in the Abruzzo region.

Marinaro (Arg) a natural spring mineral water from Jujuy. Mineral contents (milligrammes per litre): Sodium 22mg/l, Calcium 23.8mg/l, Potassium 2.2mg/l, Bicarbonates 81.2mg/l.

M

Marin County all Natural (USA) a natural spring mineral water (established 1903) from Marin County, CA.

Marinella (Fin) a fruit-based bitters produced by Marli.

Maring (Aus) a vineyard site on the banks of the River Danube in the Kremstal region.

Maring-Noviand (Ger) village (Anb): Mosel-Saar-Ruwer. (Ber): Bernkastel. (Gro): Kurfürstlay. (Vins): Honigberg, Kirchberg, Klosterberg, Romerpfad, Sonnenuhr.

Marinissmo (Liq.Coffee) put a teaspoonful of castor sugar in a wine goblet. Add hot coffee, stir, add 1 measure of Grand Marnier and float thick fresh cream on top.

Marin-Lasnier (Fr) a Champagne producer. (Add): Hameau de Bellevue, 10110 Celles sur Ource. Produces non-vintage Champagnes.

Marino (It) a D.O.C. white wine from Latium (from town of same name). Made from the Bonvino, Cacchione, Giallo, Malvasia del lazio, Malvasia rosso, Trebbiano toscano and Trebbiano verde grapes, grown in the commune of Marino and part of the communes of Rome and Castelgandolfo. Is classed Superiore if total alc. content is 12.% by vol. D.O.C. also applies to naturally sparkling wines.

Marionette (Cktl) ¼ measure each of apricot brandy, Dry Sack Sherry, Cherry Heering and white rum. Shake well over ice, strain into a cocktail glass and dress with a cherry.

Mariotte Margaux [La] (Fr) the second wine of Château Marquis-de-Terme, [Grand Cru Classé Margaux (4th)].

Mariposa (Mex) the brand-name of a popular tequila.

Mariposa Cocktail (Cktl) 1 measure white rum, ½ measure brandy, ⅙ measure lemon juice, ⅙ measure orange juice, 1 dash grenadine. Shake over ice and strain into a cocktail glass.

Mariscal (Eng) the brand-name for a range of Sherries from Tanner's of Shrewsbury, Shropshire.

Marisco Tavern (G.B) a Lundy Island home-brew public house which is noted for Puffin Bitter 1040 O.G. using malt extract.

Maris Gold (Eng) a 4% alc by vol. seasonal ale brewed in July and August by Hydes Anvil, Manchester.

Marismeño (Sp) a light, pale, dry Fino Sherry produced by Romate.

Maris Otter (Eng) a strain of barley grown in England and Wales.

Marisson (Fr) a vineyard in the A.C. commune of Rully, Côte Chalonnaise, Burgundy.

Maritsa Valley (Bul) a vineyard region in the southern half of the country. Produces the red wine Mavrud.

Marjorie Vineyard (USA) the label for a red wine (Pinot noir) produced by the Cristom winery, Willamette Valley, Oregon.

Markdorf (Ger) village (Anb): Baden. (Ber): Bodensee. (Gro): Sonnenufer. (Vins): Burgstall, Sängerhalde.

Markelsheim (Ger) village (Anb): Württemberg. (Ber): Kocher-Jagst-Tauber. (Gro): Tauberberg. (Vins): Mönchsberg, Probstberg.

Market (Eng) the buying and selling of wines and spirits etc.

Market Brewery (Eng) a Market Porter home-brew public house in Southwark, London. Noted for cask-conditioned Beach's Borough Bitter 1038 O.G.

Market Charter 700 (Eng) a 4.3% alc by vol. bitter ale from Moorhouses in Burnley, Lancashire. Brewed to commemorate the towns 700th anniversary.

Market Extension (Eng) an extension of normal licensing hours made under an order of Special Exemption which allows public houses to open outside of licensing hours on market days.

Markev (Scot) the label of a vodka sold in a frosted glass bottle. Produced in Cupar, Fife.

Markgraeflerland (Ger) lit: 'land of Margraves', a district of Baden. Near Loerrach on the German-Swiss border. Produces light, piquant table wines. Also spelt Markgräflerland.

Markgraf Babenberg (Ger) vineyard (Anb): Franken. (Ber): Maindreieck. (Gro): Not yet assigned. (Vil): Frickenwinheim am Main.

Markgraf Karl Friedrich (Ger) a person who planted vines in the Bereich Markgräflerland in the late eighteenth century, the bereich was named after him.

Markgräfler (Ger) an alternative name for the Gutedel grape variety.

Markgräflerland (Ger) bereich (Anb): Baden. (Gros): Burg Neuenfels, Lorettoberg, Vogtei Rotteln.

Markgräfschaft (Ger) another name for Markgräflerland.

Markgräningen (Ger) village (Anb): Württemberg. (Ber): Württembergisch Unterland. (Gro): Schalkstein. (Vins): Berg, Sankt Johännser.

Markham Vineyard (USA) a large winery based near St. Helena, Napa Valley, California. 125ha. Grape varieties: Cabernet sauvignon, Chardonnay, Chenin blanc, Gamay, Gray riesling, Johannisberg riesling and Muscat de frontignan. Produces varietal wines under the Vinmark and Markham labels. Website: http://www.markhamvineyards.com

Märkischer Mineralbrunnen (Ger) a natural spring mineral water. Mineral contents (milligrammes per litre): Sodium 58mg/l, Calcium 44mg/l, Magnesium 7mg/l, Potassium 2mg/l, Bicarbonates 317mg/l, Chlorides 15mg/l.

Märkisch Kristall (Ger) a sparkling natural spring mineral water. Mineral contents (milligrammes per litre): Sodium 29.2mg/l, Calcium 113mg/l, Magnesium 11.3mg/l, Potassium 2.4mg/l, Bicarbonates 366mg/l.

Marklew Family Wines (S.Afr) a winery (45ha) based in Esenburg, Stellenbosch, Western Cape. Grape varieties: Cabernet sauvignon, Chardonnay, Merlot, Pinotage. Label: Capensis Reserve. Website: http://www.marklew.co.za

M

Markko (USA) a small winery based in Conneaut, Ohio. 4ha. Grape varieties: Cabernet sauvignon, Chardonnay and Riesling. Produces varietal wines.

Marko (Gre) a dry white wine.

Markobrunn (Ger) see Marcobrunn.

Markovina (N.Z) a small winery based at Old Railway Road, Kumeu area. Has Grk vines.

Markowitsch (Aus) a winery (12ha) based in Göttlesbrunn, Carnumtum. (Add): Pfarrgasse 6 & 8, 2464 Göttlesbrunn. Grape varieties: Blaufränkisch, Cabernet sauvignon, Chardonnay, Grüner veltliner, Merlot, Pinot blanc, Pinot noir, Zweigelt. Labels: Redmont, Rubin.

Marksburg (Ger) grosslage (Anb): Mittelrhein. (Ber): Rheinburgengau. (Vils): Braubach, Filsen, Koblenz-Ehrenbreitstein, Lahnstein, Osterspai, Urbai, Vallendar.

Marksman Lager (Eng) a keg lager beer 1039 O.G. brewed by the Mansfield Brewery in Nottinghamshire.

Marktbreit (Ger) village (Anb): Franken. (Ber): Maindreieck. (Gro): Hofrat. (Vin): Sonnenberg.

Markt Einersheim (Ger). Village. (Anb): Franken. (Ber): Steigerwald. (Gro): Burgweg. (Vin): Vogelsang.

Mark Up (Eng) the price above cost, charged for wines and spirits etc. in hotels, restaurants, public houses.

Markus Brunnen Klassisch (Ger) a natural spring mineral water (established 1985) from Rosbach v. d. Höhe. Mineral contents (milligrammes per litre): Sodium 45mg/l, Calcium 89mg/l, Magnesium 34mg/l, Potassium 3mg/l, Bicarbonates 411mg/l, Chlorides 90mg/l, Sulphates 10mg/l.

Markus Brunnen Medium (Ger) a natural spring mineral water (established 1972) from Bornheim-Roisdorf. Mineral contents (milligrammes per litre): Sodium 480mg/l, Calcium 130mg/l, Magnesium 50mg/l, Potassium 20mg/l, Bicarbonates 900mg/l, Chlorides 400mg/l, Sulphates 280mg/l.

Markus Brunnen Quellfrisch (Ger) a natural spring mineral water (established 1972) from Bornheim-Roisdorf. Mineral contents (milligrammes per litre): Sodium 480mg/l, Calcium 130mg/l, Magnesium 50mg/l, Potassium 20mg/l, Bicarbonates 900mg/l, Chlorides 400mg/l, Sulphates 280mg/l.

Markus Brunnen Still (Ger) a natural spring mineral water (established 1985) from Rosbach v. d. Höhe. Mineral contents (milligrammes per litre): Sodium 45mg/l, Calcium 89mg/l, Magnesium 34mg/l, Potassium 3mg/l, Bicarbonates 411mg/l, Chlorides 90mg/l, Sulphates 10mg/l.

Markus Quelle (Aus) a natural spring mineral water. Mineral contents (milligrammes per litre): Sodium 44mg/l, Calcium 94.6mg/l, Magnesium 38.9mg/l, Potassium 5.2mg/l, Bicarbonates 465mg/l, Fluorides 0.14mg/l.

Mark West Vineyards (USA) a large winery based in the lower Russian River Valley, California. 15ha.

Grape varieties: Chardonnay, Gewürztraminer, Johannisberg riesling, Pinot noir and Zinfandel. Produces varietal wines.

Markwood Estate (Austr) a winery (established 1971). (Add): Morris Lane, Markwood via Milawa, Victoria. Grape varieties: Cabernet sauvignon, Chardonnay.

Marlboro Champagne Cellars (USA) a small estate winery based in Hudson Valley, eastern America.

Marlborough (N.Z) an area on the northern tip of the South Island. Home to Hunters, Cloudy Bay, Grove Mill, Montana, Te Whare Ra, Highfield Estate.

Marlborough London Dry (Eng) a brand of gin produced by Kilsern Distillers in Leicester. See also Feeny's Macintyre, Rostov Imperial Vodka.

Marlbrook (S.Afr) the label for red wine (Cabernet sauvignon 50% plus Merlot and Cabernet franc) produced by the Klein Constantia Estate winery, Constantia, Western Cape.

Marlen (Sp) a lager brewed at La Zaragozana, Aragón. See also Ambar.

Marli Distillery (Fin) a distillery based in Marli. Produces liqueurs, fruit bitters and cider.

Mar Lodge (Scot) a blended malt produced by Findlater, Mackie Todd and C°. Ltd. 8 years old 43% alc by vol.

Marl Soil (Eng) calcerous-clay, a sedimentary soil consisting of clay minerals, calcite or aragonite and silt. Is ideal for red wines. (Fr) = marne.

Marlstone (USA) the label for a red wine (Cabernet franc 1.5%, Cabernet sauvignon 75%, Malbec 8.5%, Merlot 14%, Petit verdot 1%) produced by the Clos du Bois winery, Alexander Valley, Sonoma County.

Marmara (Tur) a wine-producing area in eastern Turkey which produces still and sparkling wines.

Marmari (Gre) a dry white wine from Marmarion, south Euboea.

Marmertino (It) a white table wine produced in Sicily.

Marmolejo (Sp) a natural spring mineral water from Marmolejo, Jaén. Mineral contents (milligrammes per litre): Sodium 36mg/l, Calcium 130.6mg/l, Magnesium 58mg/l, Potassium 3.8mg/l, Bicarbonates 796mg/l.

Marmorberg (Ger) vineyard (Anb): Mittelrhein. (Ber): Rheinburgengau. (Gro): Marksburg. (Vil): Braubach.

Marne (Fr) a Cru Champagne village in the Canton de Suippes. District: Châlons.

Marne (Fr) marl (soil).

Marne [River] (Fr) a river that runs through the Champagne region (a tributary of the river Seine).

Marne & Champagne (Fr) a Champagne house. (Add): 22 Rue Maurice-Cerveaux, B.P. 138, 51205 Épernay. Prestige cuvée is Rothschild Grand Trianon Brut.

Marnier-Lapostolle (Fr) a Cognac and Armagnac producer. Also produces Grand Marnier.

M

Marnier Tonic (Cktl) fill a highball glass with ice, add a measure of Grand Marnier and a slice of lemon, stir and top up with tonic.

Marnique (Austr) a liqueur based on Australian brandy and tangerines. Produced by Beri Estates in South Australia.

Marniquet [J.P.] (Fr) a Champagne producer. Vintage: 1995.

Marnissimo (Cktl) *see* Marinissimo.

Maronean (Gre) a dark coloured wine which was usually drunk watered down in ancient Greece.

Maroto (Mad) a minor grape variety grown in Madeira.

Marquam Hill Vineyards (USA) a winery. (Add): 35803 So Highway 213, Molalla. Oregon. Grape varieties: Pinot noir, Chardonnay, Riesling, Gewürztraminer, Müller-Thurgau.

Marque (Fr) a Champagne houses' blend of wines. *See also* Grandes Marques.

Marque [La] (S.Afr). *see* Twee Jonge Gezellen Estate.

Marque Anonyme (Fr) *see* M.A.

Marque Autorisée (Fr) *see* M.A.

Marque Auxiliare (Fr) *see* M.A.

Marque d'Acheteur (Fr) *see* M.A.

Marque Déposée (Fr) trade mark.

Marque Nationale (Lux) the classification of wines. Certified by a small label on bottle-neck. Q.W.P.S.R. as Vin Classé, Premier Cru or Grand Premier Cru.

Marqués (Sp) an alternative name for the Loureiro grape.

Marqués de Alella (Sp) a dry white wine produced by Alta Alella from 60% Pansa and 40% Xarello grapes.

Marqués de Cáceres (Sp) *see* Bodegas Marqués de Cáceres.

Marqués de Casa Concha (Chile) the brand-name of a wine produced by Concha y Toro in the Maipo Valley. The red is produced from 100% Cabernet sauvignon and oak matured 3–4 years and 1–2 years bottle.

Marqués de Ciria (Sp) a winery based in Rioja. Owned by Savin who also own Campo Viejo (share a bodega).

Marqués de Domecq (Sp) the brand-name of a solera gran reserva brandy produced by Domecq.

Marqués de Figueroa (Sp) a bodega based in Zona del Albariño, north-western Spain. Is noted for Fefiñanes Palacio (a white oak-aged wine).

Marqués de Gastanga (Sp) a medium-dry white wine produced from 100% Cencibel grapes by Luis Megía in Valdepeñas.

Marqués de Gelida Brut Nature (Sp) the name of a cava wine aged for 3 years produced by El Cep in Sant Sadurní d'Anoia.

Marques de Griñón (Arg) a winery based in Mendoza. Grape varieties: Chenin blanc, Malbec.

Marqués de Griñón (Sp) a dry white wine produced by Bodegas de Crianza Castilla la Vieja in Rueda from must from the first pressing.

Marqués del Puerto (Sp) a red wine produced by Bodegas Lopez-Agos. Made from 20% Garnacha and 80% Tempranillo. Oak matured for 2 years and for 4 years in bottle.

Marqués del Real Tesoro (Sp) a Jerez de la Fontera Sherry shipper.

Marqués de Merito (Sp) a solera reserva brandy produced by Diez Merito.

Marqués de Misa (Sp) a Sherry bodega based in Jerez de la Frontera. Was once part of Rumasa. Labels include Amontillado Abolengo, Fino Chiquilla, Misa and Oloroso la Novia.

Marqués de Monistrol (Sp) a white/rosé sparkling wine made by the cava method in San Sadurní de Noya. 11.5% alc by vol. Owned by Martini and Rossi.

Marqués de Murrieta (Sp) wines produced by Bodegas Marqués de Murrieta, Rioja. Many grades are produced. Prado Lagar Reserva Especial is from 90% Tempranillo and 10% Mazuelo grapes, Dalmau comes from three separate vineyards (Altos de Tocatas, Canajas, Valsalado) using 85% Tempranillo, 10% Cabernet sauvignon, 5% Graciano grapes

Marqués de Riscal (Sp) a red wine produced by Vinos de Los Herederos del Marqués de Riscal, Rioja. Made from Tempranillo 90%, Mazuela and Graciano 10% grapes. Matured in oak for 3 years. Website: http://www.marquesderiscal.com

Marqués de Romeral (Sp) a red wine produced by A.G.E. Bodegas Unidas, S.A. Made from 30% Garnacha, 10% Graciano and 60% Tempranillo grapes. Oak matured for 3 years and for 2 years in bottle.

Marqués de Saporta (Fr) a rosé wine from the A.C. Coteaux d'Aix-en-Provence, south-eastern France.

Marqués de Vargas (Sp) a winery based in Rioja.

Marqués de Villamagna Gran Reserva (Sp) a red wine produced by Bodegas Campo Viejo, Rioja. Aged in Limousin oak for 5 years and a further 4 years in bottle. Made from 10% Graciano, 5% Mazuelo and 85% Tempranillo.

Marqués Real Tesoro (Sp) a solera gran reserva brandy produced by Real Tesoro.

Marquette (Cktl) 1 measure dry gin, ½ measure Italian vermouth, dash crème de noyau. Shake over ice and strain into a cocktail glass.

Marquis (Eng) a 3.8% alc by vol. ale brewed by the Brewster Brewing C°. Ltd., Leicestershire.

Marquis d'Alesme-Becker (Fr) *see* Château Marquis d'Alesme-Becker.

Marquis d'Angerville (Fr) a négociant-éleveur based in Volnay, Côte de Beaune, Burgundy.

Marquis de Bessac (Fr) a V.S.O.P. Armagnac produced by St. Maure de Peyriac in Ténarèze 40% alc by vol.

Marquis de Caussade (Fr) the brand-name for an Armagnac brandy. Sold by UCVA in Gers. Is blended from Aignan, Cazaubon, Eauze and Panjas distilleries.

Marquis de Goulaine (Fr) a noted vineyard in the A.C. Muscadet Sèvre et Maine, Nantais, Loire. Sur Lie wines. *See also* Chevaliers Bretvins.

Marquis de Maniban (Fr) Cognac brandies: V.S.O.P. 5

M

year old and Napoléon 9 year old produced by Château du Busca.

Marquis de Montesquiou (Fr) an Armagnac produced by Société des Produits d'Armagnac.

Marquis de Sade (Fr) a blanc de blancs Champagne.

Marquis de Saint-Estèphe (Fr) an A.C. Saint-Estèphe. (Com): Saint-Estèphe. 350ha. Grape varieties: Cabernet franc, Cabernet sauvignon, Malbec, Merlot and Petit verdot.

Marquis des Beys (Leb) a red wine (Cabernet sauvignon and Syrah blend) produced by the Domaine des Tourelles vineyard, Bekka Valley.

Marquis de Terme (Fr) *see* Château Marquis de Terme.

Marquise de Pompadour (Ind) a demi-sec sparkling (méthode traditionelle) wine produced by Narayangaon from Chardonnay grapes in Western Maharashka.

Marquises [Les] (Fr) a vineyard in the A.C. Bourgueil, Touraine, Loire.

Marquista (Sp) describes a merchant who exports wines under his own label but who has no separate bodega.

Marrakech (Afr) a major wine-producing region in Morocco.

Marrebæk Brewery (Den) a brewery based in Væggersløse.

Marriage Hill (Eng) a vineyard (established 1972). (Add): Marriage Farm, Wye, Ashford, Kent. 0.75ha. Grape varieties: Müller-Thurgau, Reichensteiner and Scheurebe.

Marriqcron (Ger) a weinbrand produced at Oppenheim on the upper Rhine.

Marris Otter [Pale Ale] (Eng) a brand of malted barley used by the Lees Brewery in Manchester.

Marron (S.Afr) the label for a red wine (Cabernet sauvignon, Merlot and Pinotage blend) produced by the La Chataigne winery, Franschhoek, Western Cape.

Marotti Campi (It) a winery based in the Marche region. Produces: DOC Lacrima di Morro d'Alba. Label: Rùbico.

Marrying (Eng) the blending of malt whiskies of different years to produce a blend. Also applies to blended Scotch whisky, after blending the whiskies are allowed to 'marry' in cask before being bottled.

Marsaglia (It) a vineyard. (Add): Via Mussone 2, 12050 Castellinaldo (CN). 15ha. vineyard that produces Roero Arneis, Roero, Nebbiolo d'Alba, Barbera d'Alba.

Marsala (It) a D.O.C. fortified wine from Sicily (created in 1773 by John Woodhouse). Types Ambra (amber) and Oro (gold) are made from Catarratto, Damaschino, Grillo and Inzolia grapes. Rubino (ruby) made from Calabrese, Nerello mascalese, Nero d'Avola and Pignatello grapes. Approved vineyards are in the province of Trapani (excluding Alcamo), plus Islands of Favignana, Levanzo, Pantelleria and Marettimo. Boiled must (calamich), concentrated must and mistella (sifone) have to come from the defined area and mentioned grape varieties. Base wine has a straw

yellow colour. Base wine min. alc by vol. is 12%. Main styles are Fine (17% alc by vol. aged min. 1 year), Superiore (18% alc by vol. aged 2+ years), Superiore Riserva (18% alc by vol. aged min. 4 years), Vergine Soleras (18% alc by vol. dry, 5+ years), Soleras Riserva (18% alc by vol. aged min. 10 years), plus Speciali. Must be bottled within the zone. *See also* Stravecchio, I.P., G.D. *see* Marsh el Allah.

Marsala (USA) *see* California Marsala.

Marsala all'Uovo (It) Marsala mixed with eggs and bottled.

Marsala Fine (It) has a minimum content of 17% alc by vol. and cannot be sold with less than 12 months of age. Tastes vary from dry to sweet.

Marsala Speciali (It) various flavours include egg, almond. Have the basic characteristics of Superiore. *See* Marsala all'Uovo.

Marsala Superiore (It) known also as L.P., S.O.M., G.D. and O.P. Must age for a minimum of 2 years. Minimum alc. content 18% by vol. Taste varies from dry to sweet. Superiore Riserva is aged for 4 years. No boiled must added to ruby and gold varieties.

Marsalato (It) wines that have taken on a flavour reminiscent of Marsala due to oxidation. Desirable in some dessert wines but not in table wines.

Marsala Vergine Soleras (It) has to age at least 5 years. Minimum alc. content is 18% by vol. Produced without the addition of 'cooked' must, concentrated must or Sifone. Taste is dry. Vergine Riserva/Stravecchio is aged for 10 years.

Marsalla (Eng) the eighteenth century spelling of Marsala.

Marsannay-la-Côte (Fr) the most northerly commune in the Côte de Nuits and Côte d'Or. Produces Rosé Bourgogne and Rosé de Marsannay which is the only rosé made in the Côte d'Or.

Marsanne (Fr) a white grape variety traditionally grown in the Rhône that produces wines with aromas and flavours of peaches, apricots, orange blossom, tropical fruits, toffee, nuts, marzipan, herbs, glue aroma (and lime marmalade in new world). Used in the making of white Hermitage and sparkling St. Péray. Known as Ermitage blanc in Switzerland.

Marsaxlokk (Euro) a vineyard estate owned by Marsovin, Malta.

Marsberg (Ger) vineyard (Anb): Franken. (Ber): Maindreieck. (Gro): Ewig Leben. (Vil): Randersacker.

Marschall (Ger) vineyard (Anb): Rheingau. (Ber): Johannisberg. (Gro): Steinmacher. (Vil): Frauenstein.

Marsden [Reverend Samuel] (N.Z) the man who introduced the first vines to New Zealand in 1819.

Marseillan (Fr) the alternative name for Pelure d'Oignon (onion skin wine).

Marselan (Sp) an old variety of red grape originally grown in north-eastern Spain.

Marsella (Eng) the eighteenth century spelling of Marsala.

M

Marsh el Allah (Arab) lit: 'port of God', the name given to a town in Sicily from which Marsala gets its name.

Marshmallow Coffee (Eng) milk and coffee in a goblet, topped with a pink and a white marshmallow.

Marsini Estate (Euro) a vineyard owned by Marsovin, Malta.

Mars Magic (Eng) a 4.6% alc by vol. ale brewed by the Wold Top Brewery, East Yorkshire.

Marsovin (Euro) the largest wine-producing firm on the island of Malta. (Add): Marsa, Malta. Grape varieties include: Cabernet franc, Cabernet sauvignon, Gellewza, Girgentina and Merlot. Label: Antonin.

Marston Brewery (Eng) a brewery based at Shobnall Road, Burton-on-Trent, Staffordshire DE14 2BW. Took over the Border Brewery in Wrexham in 1984. Taken over by Wolverhampton & Dudley in 1999. Noted for cask-conditioned Capital 1030 O.G., Dragon's Tale 4.5% alc by vol., Mercian Mild 1032 O.G. Merrie Monk 1043 O.G. Pedigree Bitter 1043 O.G. 4.5% alc by vol. Owd Rodger 1080 O.G. Albion Keg Mild 1030 O.G. and John Marston 1043 O.G. Chestnut Ale, FC, Luncheon Ale, Pradwood, Old Empire I.P.A., Regimental Ale, Resolution, Yuletide Ale. Has the Head Brewers Choice- a range that includes India Export Ale, Oyster Stout, Albion Porter, Burton Strong. Was also known as Marston, Thompson and Evershed. See Burton Union System. Website: http://.www.marstonsdontcompromise.co.uk

Marston Moor Brewery (Eng) a brewery (established 1984) based in York. Noted for cask-conditioned Cromwell Bitter 1037 O.G.

Marston, Thompson and Evershed (Eng) see Marston Brewery.

Marsum (It) an ancient red wine produced in central Italy in Roman times.

Martàgua (Port) a red grape variety grown in Lafoes.

Marta's Vineyard Ltd (Arg) a winery based in the Mendoza region, eastern Argentina. Website: http://www.martasvineyard.com 'E'mail: marta@martasvineyard.com

Martayrol (Fr) a Cognac producer. (Add): 137 Avenue du President Wilson, 93210 Saint-Denis-la-Plaine. Owns no vineyards or distilleries. Produces Chauffe Coeur and Chauffe Coeur Napoléon.

Martel [G.H.] (Fr) a Champagne producer. (Add): 69 Ave. du Champagne, B.P. 1011, 51318 Épernay Cedex. Négociant-manipulant. 50ha. Deluxe cuvée: Champagne Cuvée Victoire.

Martell (Fr) a Cognac producer. (Add): B.P. 21, 16100 Cognac. 455ha. in Grande Champagne 20%, Petite Champagne 30%, Borderies 38% and Fines Bois 12%. Produces: Medaillon V.S.O.P. Cordon Bleu, Cordon Argent Extra, Cordon Noir, Cordon Rubis and Réserve du Fondateur. Owned by Seagram.

Martell [Jean] (Fr) originally from Jersey in the Channel Islands in 1715. Traded in Cognac and

made his fortune. Founder of the Martell Cognac house in Cognac.

Marthal (Aus) a vineyard site on the banks of the River Danube in the Kremstal region.

Martha May's (USA) see Heitz Vineyards.

Martha's Vineyard Island (USA) an island that comes under the jurisdiction of Massachusetts. Is the base for several small wineries.

Martian Lady (Cktl) 1 measure gin, 1 measure lemon juice, ½ measure Cherry brandy, ½ egg white. Shake over ice and strain into a Champagne flute.

Martillac (Fr) a commune in the A.C. Graves district of south-western Bordeaux.

Martin [John] (Bel) an importer based in Antwerp. Imports Courage's Bulldog Ale and sells it as Martin's Pale Ale.

Martina (It) see Martina Franca.

Martina Franca (It) a D.O.C. white wine from Puglia. Made from the Bianco d'alessano, Fiano, Bombino, Malvasia toscana and Verdeca grapes. D.O.C. also applies to the naturally sparkling wine produced with wine/must obtained within specific area.

Martin & Weyrich (USA) a winery based in the Paso Robles, San Luis Obispo County, California. (Add): 2610 Buena Vista Drive, Paso Robles, CA 93446. Grape varieties: Cabernet sauvignon, Nebbiolo, Sangiovese, Zinfandel. Website: http://www.martinweyrich.com

Martinborough (N.Z) wine district (600ha) based north of Wellington on the North Island. With around 40 producers, it has gravel soil and is noted for its Chardonnay, Pinot gris, Pinot noir, Riesling and Sauvignon blanc. Sub-district: Te Muna.

Martinborough Vineyard (N.Z) a vineyard. (Add): Princess Street, Martinborough. 10ha. Produces varietal wines from Chardonnay, Pinot noir, Riesling, Sauvignon blanc.

Martin Brewery (Czec) a brewery based in eastern Czec.

Martin Brewery (Eng) a brewery (established 1984) based near Dover. Produces cask-conditioned Martin Ale 1040 O.G.

Martín Codax (Sp) a white wine produced by Bodegas Vilariño-Cambados in Val do Salnés, Rías Baixas, D.O. Galicia.

Martiner (Fr) the local (Touraine, Loire) term for 'to have a drink' (of wine).

Martiner le Vin (Fr) denotes the tapping of a cask of wine in the Touraine district of the Loire region.

Martinetti [Franco] (It) a winery based in Piemonte. Produces D.O.C. Barbera d'Asti wines. Labels include Bric dei Banditi, Montruc and Sulbric.

Martinez (USA) a wine town in Contra Costa County near San Francisco, California. Home to two small wineries.

Martinez [Gassiot] (Port) Vintage Port shippers. Vintages: 1870, 1872, 1873, 1874, 1875, 1878, 1880, 1881, 1884, 1885, 1886, 1887, 1890,

1892, 1894, 1896, 1897, 1900, 1904, 1908, 1911, 1912, 1919, 1922, 1927, 1931, 1934, 1945, 1955, 1958, 1960, 1963, 1967, 1970, 1975, 1977, 1980, 1982, 1985, 1987, 1991, 1994, 1997, 2003.

Martinez Cocktail [1] (Cktl) the original recipe from Prof. Jerry Thomas. 1 dash bitters, 2 dashes maraschino, 1 pony Old Tom Gin, 1 wine glass dry vermouth, 2 ice cubes. Shake, strain into a cocktail glass and add a slice of lemon. For sweet Martinez add 2 dashes of gomme syrup.

Martinez Cocktail [2] (Cktl) (*sweet*) 30mls (¼ gill) dry gin, 30mls (¼ gill) Italian vermouth, dash Angostura. Stir over ice, strain into a cocktail glass, serve with a cherry and dash lemon peel juice.

Martinez Cocktail [3] (Cktl) (*medium*) 30mls (¼ gill) gin, 15mls (⅛ gill) Italian vermouth, 15mls (⅛ gill) French vermouth, dash Angostura. Stir over ice, strain into a cocktail glass, serve with a cherry or olive and dash lemon peel juice.

Martinez Cocktail [4] (Cktl) (*dry*) ¼ measure dry gin, ¾ measure French vermouth, dash Angostura. Stir over ice, strain into a cocktail glass, serve with an olive and dash of lemon peel juice.

Martinez Lacuesta (Sp) a winery. (Add): Calle la Ventilla, N°71, Haro, Rioja. Holds no vineyards and buys in wine. 80% red, 5% rosé and 15% white.

Martinez Special Cocktail (Cktl) 30mls (¼ gill) dry gin, 20mls (⅙ gill) French vermouth, 6 dashes orange bitters, 1½ teaspoons maraschino, 4 dashes Angostura. Shake over ice, strain into a cocktail glass, serve with a cherry or olive and a dash of orange peel juice.

Martini (Cktl) *see* Martini Cocktail.

Martini [Louis] (USA) a family owned winery in Napa Valley, California. 353ha. Grape varieties: Barbera, Cabernet sauvignon, Gewürztraminer, Pinot noir, Petite sirah and Zinfandel. Produces varietal and dessert wines.

Martini and Prati (USA) a winery based near Santa Rosa, Sonoma County, California. Grape variety is mainly Cabernet sauvignon. Varietal wines sold under the Fountaingrove label.

Martini and Rossi (It) a famous company that produces all types of vermouth based in Turin. Also produces sparkling (metodo tradizionale) wines. Labels include: Riserva di Montelera Brut and cuve close wines. Also has many holdings in wines and spirit houses world-wide.

Martini Cocktail [1] (Cktl) (*sweet*) 40mls (⅓ gill) gin, 20mls (⅙ gill) Italian vermouth, dash orange bitters. Stir over ice, strain into a cocktail glass and add a squeeze of lemon peel juice on top.

Martini Cocktail [2] (Cktl) (*medium*) 30mls (¼ gill) dry gin, 15mls (⅛ gill) Italian vermouth, 15mls (⅛ gill) French vermouth. Stir over ice, strain into a cocktail glass and serve with a dash of lemon peel juice on top.

Martini Cocktail [3] (Cktl) (*dry*) 30mls (¼ gill) dry gin, 30mls (¼ gill) French vermouth. Stir over ice, strain into a cocktail glass and serve with a dash lemon peel juice.

Martini Cocktail [4] (Cktl) (*dry*) 1 measure dry gin, ¼ measure French vermouth, 2 dashes Pernod. Stir over ice, strain into a cocktail glass and decorate with an onion.

Martini Glass (USA) a stemmed, cone-shaped glass of various sizes (from 4fl.ozs to 12fl.ozs).

Martini Medium (Cktl) *see* Martini Cocktail (2).

Martini Metz (It) a 5.4% alc by vol. chill-filtered schnapps-based drink produced by Martini. Sold in 275mls bottles.

Martinique (Ch.Isles) a liqueur produced from a mixture of Jersey cream and West Indian rum.

Martinique Coffee (W.Ind) the largest grade of coffee seed (bean), green in colour. Grown on the island of Martinique. *see* De Clieu (Captain).

Martinique Rhum (W.Ind) a dark, full-bodied rum which has a dry, full, burnt flavour. Pot-stilled cane juice. 40% alc by vol. *see* St. James.

Martinique Rum (W.Ind) *see* Martinique Rhum.

Martini Special Cocktail (Cktl) 25mls (⅕ gill) dry gin, 15mls (⅛ gill) Italian vermouth, ½ teaspoon each of maraschino, absinthe and raspberry syrup. Shake over ice, strain into a cocktail glass and serve with a dash of lemon peel juice.

Martin Miller's Gin (Eng) a quality London dry gin brand at 45.2% alc by vol. blended with Icelandic water.

Martino Tea (Punch) 300mls (½ pint) hot mint tea, 1 teaspoon honey, 60mls (½ gill) arak. Stir altogether in a warmed mug and add sugar to taste.

Martin [Ray] Winery (USA) a winery based near Saratoga, Santa Clara, California. Grape varieties: Cabernet sauvignon, Chardonnay and Pinot noir. La Montaña is the second label.

Martinsberg (Ger) vineyard (Anb): Rheinhessen. (Ber): Bingen. (Gro): Rheingrafenstein. (Vil): Siefersheim.

Martinsborn (Ger) vineyard (Anb): Mosel-Saar-Ruwer. (Ber): Zell/Mosel. (Gro): Rosenhang. (Vil): Bruttig-Fankel.

Martinsheim (Ger) village (Anb): Franken. (Ber): Steigerwald. (Gro): Not yet assigned. (Vin): Langenstein.

Martinshöhe (Ger) vineyard (Anb): Pfalz. (Ber): Mittelhaardt-Deutsche Weinstrasse. (Gro): Feuerberg. (Vil): Gönnheim.

Martinsky Porter (Czec) the strongest beer in Czechoslovakia, at 20° Balling, from the Michalovce Brewery.

Martin's Pale Ale (Eng) an ale brewed by Courage 1068 O.G. known as Bulldog in Britain. Is bottled by the John Martin C°. in Antwerp for sale in Belgium.

Martinstein (Ger) village (Anb): Nahe. (Ber): Schloss Böckelheim. (Gro): Paradiesgarten. (Vin): Schlossberg.

Martinsthal (Ger) village (Anb): Rheingau. (Ber): Johannisberg. (Gro): Steinmacker. (Vins): Langenberg, Rödchen, Wildsau.

Martin Tesch (Ger) a winery based in the village of

Laubenheim, Nahe. Grape varieties include: Riesling. Produces a range of wine styles.

Martin Weyrich (USA) a winery based in the Napa Valley, California (also has vineyards in Paso Robles, San Luis Obispo). Grape varieties: Cabernet sauvignon.

Martinybrunnen (Ger) a natural spring mineral water. Mineral contents (milligrammes per litre): Sodium 380mg/l, Calcium 30mg/l, Potassium 20mg/l, Chlorides 480mg/l.

Marufo (Port) a red grape variety grown in the Beiras region.

Maruja Fino (Sp) a pale, light, Fino Sherry produced by Terry in Jerez de la Frontera.

Marumba Cocktail (Cktl) 1 measure Jamaican rum, 1 measure Mandarine Napoléon, juice ½ lemon. Shake over ice, strain into a goblet and dress with an orange slice.

Marvo (USA) an egg and Marsala trade-name drink. Similar to Marsala all'Uovo.

Marvol (S.Afr) the label for a red wine (Pinotage) produced by the Hazendal winery, Stellenbosch, Western Cape.

Marwa (Tun) a natural spring mineral water from Ain El Hammem Sidi Nsir. Mineral contents (milligrammes per litre): Sodium 37mg/l, Calcium 80mg/l, Magnesium 10mg/l, Potassium 2mg/l, Bicarbonates 244mg/l, Chlorides 64mg/l, Sulphates 24mg/l, Fluorides 0.2mg/l, Nitrates 3mg/l.

Mary Ann (Ch.Isles) the label used by the Jersey Brewery in St. Helier, Jersey (formerly known as Ann Street Brewery).

Mary Ann (Ch.Isles) a cask-conditioned bitter ale 1042 O.G. brewed by the Jersey Brewery, St. Helier, Jersey.

Mary Cruz (Sp) a solera brandy produced by Bodegas 501.

Mary Garden Cocktail (Cktl) ⅔ measure Dubonnet, ⅓ measure dry vermouth. Stir over ice and strain into a cocktail glass.

Maryland (USA) an eastern American wine district in the state of Maryland.

Mary le Bow (S.Afr) the label for a red wine (Cabernet sauvignon, Merlot and Shiraz blend) produced by the Flagstone Winery, Somerset West, Western Cape.

Mary Pickford (Cktl) ½ measure white rum, ½ measure unsweetened pineapple juice, dash grenadine, dash maraschino. Shake over ice and strain into a cocktail glass.

Mary Rose (Cktl) ½ measure Kirsch de Zoug, ¼ measure Manzanilla, ¼ measure apricot brandy. Stir with ice, strain, add zest of an orange and a cherry.

Mary Rose Champagne (Eng) a non-vintage Champagne produced by De Courcy et Fils for the Mary Rose Trust in Portsmouth to raise funds for the Mary Rose Trust. (Towards the raising and restoration of Henry VIII's flagship: the Mary Rose in 1983). Made from 25% Chardonnay and 75% Pinot noir.

Maryroy Vineyard (USA) a noted small winery based near Calistoga, California. 4.5ha. Grape varieties: Chenin blanc and Petite sirah. Produces varietal wines.

Maryville Vineyard (Ire) a vineyard based near Cork. (Add): Kilworth, County Cork. Produces dry white wines.

Marzelle [La] (Fr) see Château Lamarzelle.

Marzemina Bianca (It) the southern Italian name for the Chasselas grape.

Marzemino (It) a red grape variety grown in Lombardy and Trentino. Also used to make red wines in California.

Märzenbier (Ger) a specialty beer served at the Oktoberfest, a dark, strong, slightly sour beer.

Marzia (It) a natural spring mineral water from Marzia.

Mas (Fr) the name used in Roman times for the stone walls that surrounded the small terraced vineyards in Hermitage, Côtes du Rhône.

Masachs (Sp) a brand of sparkling wine produced by Casa Masachs (rosé and white).

Masada Kosher Wines (S.Afr) are Kosher wines produced under strict Rabbinical supervision. Varietals made by Charles Back, Fairview Estate, Box 583, Suider Paarl 7625.

Masafi (UAE) a natural spring mineral water. Mineral contents (milligrammes per litre): Sodium 14mg/l, Calcium 4.5mg/l, Magnesium 21.5mg/l, Potassium 1mg/l, Bicarbonates 70mg/l.

Masaglio (Fr) a dry white wine produced in Sicily.

Masaguera (Sp) a white grape variety grown in the southern region of Spain.

Mas Amiel (Fr) a 130ha vineyard that produces Maury (15 year old and vintaged).

Masberg Mansion (Euro) a vineyard based at Nauvoo, Liechtenstein. Produces white wines.

Mas Borras (Sp) a single vineyard 10ha. red wine produced from 100% Pinot noir grapes by Torres, Penedés.

Masbout (Egy) coffee.

Mas Bruguière (Fr) a 10ha vineyard based in Valflaunes. A.C. Pic-Saint-Loup, Coteaux du Languedoc. Grape varieties: Grenache, Syrah, Mourvèdre, Roussanne. Produces Cuvée Vinum de Calcadis, Cuvée Classique, Cuvée en Fûts de Chêne, La Grenadière, L'Arbouse.

Mascara (Afr) the centre of wine production in Algeria.

Mascarello [Giuseppe] (It) a winery based in Monchiero, a district of Barolo, Piemonte.

Mas Carlot (Fr) a 72ha domaine in the A.C. Costières de Nîmes, Languedoc-Roussillon. Produces Costières Mas Carlot from Grenache and Syrah grapes and Château Paul Blanc from Syrah grapes. Also some white wines.

Mascaró (Sp) a brandy and wine producer. (Add): Carbonell del Casal 9, Vilafranca del Penedés, Barcelona. Source of base wines is Penedés. All brandies Charentais pot-stilled. Produces: 3 y.o. V.O. Estilo fine Marivaux, 5 y.o. Narciso Etiqueta Azul, 8 y.o. Don Narciso and Viña Fresco.

Mascaron Rouge (Fr) the label for an A.C. Bordeaux red wine. Grape varieties: Cabernet franc 15%, Cabernet sauvignon 5%, Merlot 80%.

Maschio (It) a sparkling (metodo tradizionale) wine producer based in Veneto. Produces Prosecco di Conegliano-Valdobbiadene.

Masciarelli (It) a winery based in the Abruzzo. Produces: DOC Trebbiano d'Abruzzo. Label: Marina Cvetic.

Mas Collet (Sp) the label for a red wine (Cariñena, Grenacha and Tempranillo blend) produced by the Capçanes winery, Montsant, Cataluña.

Mas de Boislauzon (Fr) the label of a Châteauneuf-du-Pape produced by Chaussy (Jacky) at Quartier Boislauzon, Rte. D68, 84100 Orange, southern Rhône.

Mas de Bossard (Fr) the name for the granite soil on the slope of l'Hermitage in the northern Rhône.

Mas de Cadenet (Fr) a vineyard within A.C. Côtes de Provence that produces red and rosé wines. Ste-Victoire is a noted Cru.

Mas de Daumas Gassac (Fr) a famous estate in the Languedoc-Roussillon. Produces Vin de Pays de l'Hérault red wines. Planted with 18ha. of Cabernet franc, Merlot, Malbec, Syrah, Tannat, Pinot noir, Nebbiolo, Dolcetto. White wines from Viognier, Chardonnay, Petit manseng, Viognier. Produces: Cuvée Emile Peynaud.

Mas de Gourgonnier (Fr) an A.C. vineyard in the Coteaux-des-Baux-en-Provence. (Add): Le Destet, 13890 Mouriès.

Mas de Greffieux (Fr) clay soil on the slopes of l'Hermitage in the northern Rhône.

Mas de la Dame (Fr) an A.C. vineyard in the Coteaux-des-Baux-en-Provence. (Add): Les Baux-Route de Saint-Rémy, 13520 Maussane-lès-Alpilles.

Mas de la Rouvière (Fr) a vineyard in the A.C. Bandol, Provence.

Mas de l'Ecriture [Le] (Fr) a vineyard based in the A.C. Terrasses du Larzac, Coteaux du Languedoc. Label: Les Pensées.

Mas de Masos (Sp) a red wine produced by Capafons-Ossó, Falset from 45 year old Garnacha plus Cariñena grapes. Part of the Tarragona D.O.

Mas de Méal (Fr) the alluvial soil on the slopes of l'Hermitage in the northern Rhône.

Mas de Mortiès (Fr) a vineyard based in Pic-Saint-Loup in the Coteaux du Languedoc. Grape varieties include: Rolle, Roussanne, Viognier.

Mas des Bressandes (Fr) a 22ha domaine in the A.C. Costières de Nîmes, Languedoc-Roussillon. Produces a Vin de Pays du Gard from Cabernet sauvignon and Syrah grapes. A.C. Costières de Nîmes Tradition from 50% Syrah and 50% Grenache grapes and Tradition white from Grenache blanc, also a white wine from Roussanne grapes.

Mas de Tourelles (Fr) a winery near Beaucaire, southern France. Produces: Mulsum, Turriculae.

Masdeu (Fr) the name given to fortified red wines of the Roussillon, southern France. Originally spelt Masdieu and Masdu.

Masdieu (Fr) an old spelling of Masdeu.

Masdu (Fr) an old spelling of Masdeu.

Mas du Cellier (Fr) an A.C. vineyard in the Coteaux-des-Baux-en-Provence. (Add): La Haute Craline, 13210 Saint-Rémy-de-Provence.

Mash (Eng) the mixture of barley grist or other cereal and water (liquor) before fermentation in beer and whisky production.

Masham (Eng) an ale brewed by Theakston in Masham, Ripon, North Yorkshire.

Mash and Air (Eng) a micro-brewery based in Manchester. Brews: Mash Beer 4.7% alc by vol. Peach Beer 5% alc by vol. Black Porter 5.3% alc by vol. *See also* Mash to Measure.

Mash Beer (Eng) a 4.7% alc by vol. beer brewed by micro-brewery Mash and Air, Manchester.

Mash Beer (Eng) a 4.8 alc by vol. London brew made in the pilsner style by the Oliver Peyton micro-brewery.

Mashing (Eng) a northern England slang term for brewing tea.

Mashing (Eng) the extraction of the maltose from the milled, malted grain 'grist' (by mixing with hot water at 63.5°C) into a fermentable liquid (wort).

Mashke (Isr) beverage/drink.

Mash the Tea (Eng) a north of England term for making a pot (brew) of tea.

Mash to Measure (Eng) the name given to the monthly guest beer in the Mash and Air public house, Manchester.

Mash Tub (Scot) *see* Mash Tun.

Mash Tun (Eng) a squat cylindrical-shaped vessel where the mash infuses. Has a false floor to retain the spent grains as the wort is run off. Also known as the Mash Tub.

Mash Tun Mild (Eng) a 3.5% alc by vol. traditional mild brewed by Arkell's Brewery, Wiltshire.

Masi (It) a large producer of Veneto wines, noted for their Soave and Valpolicella. Website: http://www.masi.it

Masía Bach (Sp) a Catalan estate. Produces: Extrísimo, Masía Bach, Tinto and Vallformosa.

Masía Barril (Sp) a winery based in Priorato. Grape varieties: Garnacha, Cariñena. Produces Tipico a 15% alc by vol. inky wine with intense blackcurrant fruit flavours.

Mas Jullien (Fr) a 15ha vineyard based in Jonquières. A.C. Terrasses du Larzac, Coteaux du Languedoc-Montpeyroux. Grape varieties: Carignan, Grenache, Syrah, Mourvèdre, Cinsaut. Wines include: Les Cailloutis, Les Depierre, Les Etats d'Ame. Also produces Vin de Pays wines.

Mas la Plana (Sp) the new name for the Torres wine Gran Coronas Black Label. Cabernet sauvignon 100%.

Màslàs (Hun) *see* Tokaji Màslàs.

Mas Lumen (Fr) a vineyard (6ha) based in Gabian in the A.C. Pézenas, Coteaux du Languedoc. Label: La Sylve, Prélude.

Masna'a Khumur (Arab) winery.

Maso (It) estate. *See also* Fattoria, Masseria, Tenuta.

Mason Arms (Eng) a home brew public house based

M

at South Leigh, near Whitney, Oxfordshire. Produces a dark malty bitter.

Mason's Hill (S.Afr) a winery (established 2001) based in Suider-Paarl, Western Cape. Grape variety: Shiraz.

Masrapa (Tur) a metal drinking cup, tankard.

Massadah (Isr) a dry white, table wine.

Mas Sainte Berthe (Fr) an A.C. vineyard in the Coteaux-des-Baux-en-Provence. (Add): Les Baux, 13520, Maussane-lès-Alpilles.

Mas Saint Louis (Fr) the label of a Châteauneuf-du-Pape produced by Geniest (Louis), Ave. Baron le Roy, 84230 Châteauneuf-du-Pape, southern Rhône.

Massaly (Eng) the eighteenth century spelling of Marsala.

Massandra (Rus) a white Muscat dessert wine from Massandra in the southern Crimea produced from the Massandra muscatel. Also the name for red and dry white wines.

Massandra Muscatel (Rus) a rich, sweet dessert wine from the Crimea.

Massapes (Mad) the name for the clay soil found on Madeira.

Massenbachhausen (Ger) village (Anb): Württemberg. (Ber): Württembergisch Unterland. (Gro): Heuchelberg. (Vin): Krähenberg.

Massenez [G.E.] (Fr) an eau-de-vie distiller. (Add): Dieffenbach-au-Val, 67220 Villé.

Massé Père et Fils (Fr) a Grande Marque Champagne house based in Reims (part of Lanson).

Masseria (It) estate. *See also* Fattoria, Maso, Tenuta.

Masseria del Feudo Grottarossa (It) a winery based on the island of Sicily.

Masseto (It) a 100% Merlot wine produced in Tuscany at Tenuta dell'Ornellaia.

Massic (It) a dry white wine produced in central Italy during Roman times.

Massif (Fr) a large mountain range running north-south through central-southern France. The river Loire rises in them.

Massif Central (Fr) *see* Massif.

Massif d'Uchaux (Fr) a village in the A.C. Côtes du Rhône-Villages (awarded 2004). Produces mainly red wines (with a little rosé and white wine).

Masson [Paul] (USA) a large well-known wine producer of California. *see* Paul Masson Vineyards.

Massoni Main Creek Vineyard (Austr) a winery (established 1984). (Add): RMB 6580, Mornington-Finders Road, Red Hill, Victoria. Grape varieties include: Chardonnay and Pinot noir.

Masson Light (USA) a medium dry, white, low-alcohol 0.5% by vol. wine from the Paul Masson Vineyards in California.

Massougues (Fr) a Cognac producer famous for its vintage Cognacs.

Massum (It) a red wine produced in central-western Italy in Roman times.

Mastantuono Winery (USA) a winery based in San Luis Obispo, California Grape variety: Zinfandel.

Master Ale (Eng) a bottled old ale 1080 O.G. brewed by the Holden Brewery in Dudley, Worcs.

Master Blend (Eng) the brand-name of an instant coffee with added fresh coffee grounds produced by General Foods in Oxon.

Master Brew (Eng) the brand-name for Shepherd Neame's Beers: dark cask Mild 1031 O.G. Bitter 1036 O.G. and a keg Light Mild XX 1033 O.G.

Master Brew Ltd (Eng) *see* Miko Coffee Ltd.

Master Brew Smooth (Eng) a 3.7% alc by vol. nitrokeg beer brewed by Shepherd Neame, Kent. *see* Casey's Cream, Bishop's Cream.

Master Cellar Wine Warehouses [The] (Eng) a wine-warehouse operation based in Aberdeen Road, Croydon, London. Launched by Davidsons.

Master Lager (Eng) an 8% alc by vol. lager brewed by Harp Lager Company.

Masteroast Coffee Company (Eng) a coffee manufacturer (established 1981). (Add): 50–54 Ivatt Way, Westwood Ind Estate, Peterborough, Cambridgeshire PE3 7PN. Produces coffee, tea, cocoa and dinking chocolate. Website: http://www.masteroast.co.uk 'E'mail: info@masteroast.co.uk

Master of the Malt (Scot) an annual competition run by Invergordon Distillers at their Tamnavulin Distillery in Glenlivet.

Master of Wine (Eng) the highest qualification in the British wine trade. Obtained through a series of blind tastings and written examinations. Holders have M.W. after their names.

Masterpiece (Can) a Canadian whisky produced by Seagram 43% alc by vol.

Masterpiece (Eng) a 5.4% alc by vol. bottled beer from the Museum Brewing C°. in the Bass Museum, Burton-on-Trent.

Masterton (Austr) a winery. (Add): P.O. Box 255. Seven Hills, South Australia. Owns no vineyards and buys in Cabernet sauvignon, Rhine riesling, Sémillon and Shiraz grapes.

Mastic (Gre) the resin from the lentisk tree (turpentine tree) used to flavour raki. *see* Mastika.

Mastic (USA) another name for Mastikha 45%–46% alc by vol.

Masticha (Gre) an alternative spelling of Mastika.

Mastika (Gre) an arrack brandy with resin added, made from the gum of the mastikha plant and aniseed. *see* Mastic, Masticha and Mastikha.

Mastikha (Gre) an alternative spelling of Mastika.

Mastrasa (Rus) a red table wine produced in Baku.

Mastroberardino (It) a winery based at Atripalda in Campania. Produces: Naturalis Historia (from a blend of 85% Aglianico and 15% Piedirosso grapes fermented in oak), Novaserra (DOC Greco di Tufo) and DOC Sannio (Flanghina).

Mata-Bicho (Port) lit: 'a drop', denotes a tot of spirit.

Matador (Sp) the brand-label used by Valdespino for a range of their Sherries.

Matador Cocktail (Cktl) 35mls (1½fl.ozs) tequila, 2 dashes lemon juice. Shake over crushed ice, strain into an ice-filled highball and top with lemonade.

Matahiwi (N.Z) a winery based in Wairarapa. Grape varieties: Pinot noir and Sauvignon blanc.

Matakana (N.Z) a red wine produced from 70% Merlot, 20% Cabernet franc and 10% Malbec grapes by Providence Vineyard, Matakana, near Warkworth, Northland.

Matanzas (W.Ind) a major rum producer on the island of Cuba now State owned.

Matanzas Creek (USA) a winery based near Santa Rosa, Sonoma County, California. 111acres (50.45ha). Grape varieties: Cabernet sauvignon, Chardonnay, Gewürztraminer, Merlot, Pinot blanc and Pinot noir. Produce varietal wines.

Matar (Port) to quench one's thirst.

Matara (Tur) flask, a metal water bottle used by soldiers.

Mataro (Austr)(Sp)(USA) a red grape variety, also known as Carignan or Mourvèdre.

Matataki (Eng) a soft drink of oriental fruits and carbonated water with a hint of saké produced by J.N. Nichols in Manchester.

Matawhero Winery (N.Z) a winery. (Add): Riverpoint Road, RD1, Gisborne. 30ha. Grape varieties: Chardonnay, Chenin blanc, Gewürztraminer, Riesling-Sylvaner, Sauvignon blanc.

Maté (S.Am) *Ilex paraguariensis* a herbal tea containing caffeine from Paraguay. *see* Yerba Maté.

Máté Lacko Sepsi (Hun) the Private Secretary to Zsuzsanna Lorantffy, widow of Gyorgy Rakoczi 11 Prince of Transylvania who decided to postpone the vintage because of the threat of war, so creating Aszú berries that had shrivelled in the warm Autumn weather. *see* Tokai Aszú.

Mateppe Vineyards (Afr) a wine estate based near Marandellas, Salisbury, Zimbabwe. Grape varieties: Cabernet sauvignon, Chenin blanc, Cinsault, Clairette blanche, Hanepoot and Pinotage tinta (red and white).

Mater (Bel) a brown ale brewed by the Roman Brasserie in Mater near Oudenaarde.

Mated Brewery (N.Z) a brewery. (Add): 42 Holden Street, P.O. Box 3153, Onekawa, Napier. Brews beers and lager. Website: http://www.matesbeer.co.nz 'E'mail: info@matesbeer.co.nz

Mateus Mule (Cktl) 125mls (5fl.ozs). Mateus rosé, ¼ measure brandy, dash lemon juice. Place into a large goblet, stir, add a cube of ice and a twist of orange.

Mateus Rosé (Port) a famous pétillant rosé wine sold in a bocksbeutel in most countries of the world. Produced by SOGRAPE at Vila Real. *see* Mateus White. Website: http://www.casademateus.com

Mateus White (Port) a pétillant white wine sold in a bocksbeutel. Produced by SOGRAPE at Vila Real. *see* Mateus Rosé.

Mathäser Bierstadt (Ger) a famous beerhall in Bayerstrasse. Serves Löwenbrau beer.

Matheisbildchen (Ger) vineyard (Anb): Mosel-Saar-Ruwer. (Ber): Bernkastel. (Gro): Badstube. (Vil): Bernkastel-Kues.

Mather (Eng) a wines and spirits group owned mainly by the Matthew Clark Brewery. Produces Black Beer.

Mathews Napa Valley Winery (USA) an old-time winery in Napa City, Napa Valley, California. Still retains a few Port wines.

Mathias Weingarten (Ger) vineyard (Anb): Mittelrhein. (Ber): Bacharach. (Gro): Schloss Stahleck. (Vil): Bacharach.

Mathieu [Serge] (Fr) a Champagne producer. (Add): Avirey-Lingey, 10340 Les Riceys. Récoltants-manipulants. Produce vintage and non-vintage wines. Website: http://www.Champagne-serge-mathieu.com

Mathilde Aszú (S.Afr) the label for a sweet botrytised white '6 puttonyos' wine (Furmint and Sauvignon blanc blend) produced by the Signal Hill winery, Cape Town, Western Cape.

Matho (Fr) the brand-name of a wine-based apéritif.

Mathon Goldings (Eng) a variety of hop used in the production of ale. *See also* Bird Holdings.

Mathusalem (Fr) a large bottle of (6litres) 8 standard bottles capacity used in the Champagne region. *see* Champagne Bottle Sizes. (Eng) = methuselah.

Màti (S.Am) the old name for maté from the Quechua Màti gourd (from which the herbal tea maté is drunk).

Matild (Rum) a natural spring mineral water from Bodok-Szeklerland, Transylvania.

Matilda Bay (Austr) a cooler, a mixture of tropical fruit flavours and Australian wine 4% alc by vol.

Matilda Bay Brewing Company Ltd. (Austr) a brewery (established 1984) based in Perth. (Add): 130 Stirling Highway, Fremantle, Western Australia. Part of CUB. Beers include Brass Monkey Stout, Red Back, Dogbolter, Fremantle Bitter Ale.

Matilde Rosé (Austr) a dry, full-flavoured rosé wine produced by the Sandalford in Western Australia from the Cabernet sauvignon grape.

Matino (It) a D.O.C. red or rosé wine from Puglia. Made from the Malvasia, Negroamaro and Sangiovese grapes in the province of Lecce and part of Murge Salentine. 2 types produced: Rosso and Rosato.

Matlock Spring (Eng) a natural spring mineral water from Matlock, Derbyshire.

Matouba (W.Id) a natural spring mineral water from Guadaloupe. Mineral contents (milligrammes per litre): Sodium 7.7mg/l, Calcium 6.7mg/l, Magnesium 1.6mg/l, Potassium 0.5mg/l, Bicarbonates 30.5mg/l, Chlorides 6.2mg/l, Sulphates 5.83mg/l. pH 6.8

Màtraalya (Hun) a wine district in the Màtra Hills, northern Hungary. Includes areas of Debrö and Eger. Is noted for its fine white wines.

Matrassa (Rus) a red grape variety grown in Azerbaijan. Also known as Kara Shirai, Kara Shirei.

Matt (Ger) a flat, insipid wine.

Matt Brewing C° [The] (USA) a brewery based in Utica, New York. Noted for lager and ale beers. See *also* West End Brewing C°. Website: http://www.saranac.com 'E'mail: info@saranac.com

Mattersburg District (Aus) a wine-producing district at the foothills of Rosalien mountains.

M

Matthew Algie & C° Ltd (Scot) a coffee manufacturer (established 1864). (Add): 16 Lawmoor Road, Glasgow, Lanarkshire G5 0UL. Produces coffee, tea, cocoa and drinking chocolate. Website: http://www.matthewalgie.com 'E'mail: sales@matthewalgie.com

Matthew Brown (Eng) *see* Brown.

Matthew Brown Lancashire Bitter (Eng) a bitter ale brewed by the Matthew Brown Brewery Blackburn, Lancashire.

Matthew Clark (Eng) a drinks company that took over the Gaymer Group in 1994. Brands include: Babycham, Olde English and K Ciders, County Manor, Diamond Red, QC. Now known as Matthew Clark Brands and Matthew Clark Wholesale since 1997.

Matthew Clark Brands (Eng) *see* Matthew Clark Taunton Ltd.

Matthew Clark Gaymer (Eng) the new name for Matthew Clark after the take-over of the Gaymer Group in 1994. Taken over itself by Matthew Clark Taunton Ltd. in 1995.

Matthew Clark Taunton Ltd. (Eng) the new name for Matthew Clark Gaymer after the take-over of the Taunton Cider Company in 1995. Brands include: Dry Blackthorn, Taunton/Olde English, Diamond White, Gaymer, Red C. Renamed Matthew Clark Brands in May 1997. See *also* Matthew Clark.

Matthew Clark Wholesale (Eng) formed in 1993 by combination of Freetraders, Grants of St. James, Griersons, Dunn and Moore.

Matthieu [Louis] (Fr) a Champagne producer based at Reims.

Mattingly and Moore (USA) the brand-name of a straight Bourbon whiskey distilled by Calvert Distillers C°., Lawrenceberg 40% alc by vol.

Mattock (Fr) a hand tool for tilling the soil in the vineyards, is similar to a pick.

Mattoni (Czec) a natural spring mineral water from Karlovy Vary/Carlsbad. Mineral contents (milligrammes per litre): Sodium 61.4-62.4mg/l, Calcium 96.7-98.7mg/l, Magnesium 18-25.2mg/l, Chlorides 4.72-12.9mg/l, Sulphates 26.5-51.7mg/l, Fluorides 0.52-1.9mg/l.

Matt's Premium (USA) an all-malt lager beer brewed with imported hops by the West End Brewing C°. in Utica, New York.

Matty's Light Beer (Eng) a light keg beer 1033 O.G. brewed by the Matthew Brown Brewery in Blackburn, Lancashire.

Matua Valley Winery (N.Z) a winery. (Add): Waikoukou Road, Waimauku, Auckland. 25ha. Grape varieties: Breidecker, Cabernet sauvignon, Chardonnay, Flora, Grey riesling, Merlot, Muscat blanc, Pinot noir, Sauvignon blanc and Sémillon.

Matuba Premium Select (S.Afr) the label for a range of wines produced by the Cape Coastal Vintners winery, Paarl, Western Cape.

Maturana (Sp) a white grape variety grown in the Rioja region of north-east Spain.

Maturana Tinta (Sp) a black grape variety grown in Rioja.

Maturation (Eng) the time given to beer, wines or spirits in cask or bottle for improving the quality and allowing the impurities to settle out.

Matusalem (Sp) a methuselah bottle (equals 8 standard bottles) used for cava wines.

Matusalem (Sp) a sweet Oloroso Sherry produced by Gonzalez Byass in Jerez de la Frontera, Cadiz. Aged for 30 years. Part of their Rare Old Solera range.

Matuschka-Greiffenclau (Ger) family-owners of Schloss Vollrads.

Matyas Sor (Hun) a beer brewed by the Kobnya Brewery.

Matys (S.Afr) the label for a red wine (Pinotage 51% plus Merlot and Shiraz blend) produced by the Diemersdal Estate winery, Durbanville, Western Cape.

Matzen (Aus) part of the Weinviertel which is divided into Matzen, Retz and Falkenstein.

Matzikama Organic Cellar (S.Afr) an organic winery (established 1999) based in Mount Maskam, Olifants River, Western Cape. 4ha. Website: http://www.matzikamawyn.co.za

Mauchamps [Les] (Fr) a Premier Cru vineyard in the A.C. commune of Morey-Saint-Denis, Côte de Nuits, Burgundy.

Mauchen (Ger) village (Anb): Baden. (Ber): Markgräflerland. (Gro): Burg Neuenfels. (Vins): Frauenberg, Sonnenstück.

Mauchenheim (Ger) village (Anb): Rheinhessen. (Ber): Wonnegau. (Gro): Sybillenstein. (Vin): Sioner Klosterberg.

Maudite (Can) lit: 'devil', an 8% alc by vol. bottle-conditioned special beer brewed by the Unibroue Brewery, Chambly, Quebec.

Mauerberg (Ger) vineyard (Anb): Baden. (Ber): Ortenau. (Gro): Schloss Rodeck. (Vil): Neuweier.

Mäuerchen (Ger) vineyard (Anb): Mosel-Saar-Ruwer. (Ber): Saar-Ruwer. (Gro): Römerlay. (Vil): Mertesdorf.

Mäuerchen (Ger) vineyard (Anb): Rheingau. (Ber): Johannisberg. (Gro): Burgweg. (Vil): Geisenheim.

Mäuerchen (Ger) a vineyard within the village of Geisenheim, 32.6ha. (11%) of which is proposed to be classified as Erstes Gewächs.

Mauer Wines (Ger) wines from Baden which are, with certain wines from Franken, allowed to be sold in bocksbeutel.

Maufoux (Fr) family merchants based in Santenay, Beaune, Burgundy (owned by the Prieur de la Tour family).

Mauget (Eng) the brand-name for a range of fruit spirits (sloe gin, cherry brandy, cherry whisky, etc.) produced by Lamb and Watt of Liverpool, Lancashire.

Maugham's Brewery (S.E.Asia) a noted brewery based in Singapore that produces fine lagers.

Maui Blush (USA) a dry rosé wine produced on the island of Maui, Hawaii by Tedeschi Vineyard.

Maui Lager (USA) a lager beer of German bock-style brewed on the island Maui, Hawaii by the Pacific Brewing C°. Inc.

M

Maui Nouveau (USA) a white wine produced by the Tedeschi Vineyard on the island of Maui, Hawaii.

Maulbronn (Ger) village (Anb): Württemberg. (Ber): Württembergisch Unterland. (Gro): Stromberg. (Vins): Eilfingerberg, Klosterstück, Reichshalde.

Mauldon's Brewery (Eng) a brewery (revived in 1982 and 2000). (Add): 13 Churchfield Road, Sudbury, Suffolk CO10 2YA. Brews: BAH Humbug 4.9% alc by vol., Black Adder 5.3% alc by vol., Broomstick 4% alc by vol., Christmas Reserve 6.6% alc by vol (1065 O.G)., Cuckoo 4.3% alc by vol., Dickens 4% alc by vol., Eatanswill Old 4% alc by vol., George's Best 4.4% alc by vol., Mauldon's Bitter 3.6% alc by vol., Mauldon's Moletrap 3.8% alc by vol., May Bee 3.9% alc by vol., Mid-Autumn Gold 4.2% alc by vol., Mid-Summer Gold 4% alc by vol., Mid-Winter Gold 4.5% alc by vol., Peggotty's Porter 4.1% alc by vol., Pickwick Bitter 4.2% alc by vol., Ploughmans 4.3% alc by vol., Suffolk Pride 4.8% alc by vol., White Adder 5.3% alc by vol., Winter Gold 4.5% alc by vol. Website: http://www.maldons.co.uk 'E'mail: sims@maldons.co.uk

Mauler et Cie (Switz) wine producer. (Add): Le Prieur, Saint-Pierre, Motiers, Neuchâtel. Producers of vin mousseux and méthode traditionelle wines.

Maule Valley (Chile) a 697ha wine-producing region that encompasses the Claro and Loncomilla Valleys. Tutuven Valley is situated at the most southerly part of the Maule Valley.

Mauny [La] (W.Ind) a very popular brand of rum produced on the island of Martinique by Bellonie, Bourdillon et Cie.

Maureen (Cktl) 1 measure brandy, ½ measure Tia Maria, ½ measure cream. Shake over ice and strain into a cocktail glass.

Maures (Fr) a Vin de Pays area in south-western France. Produces red, rosé and dry white wines.

Maures [Les] (Fr) a Vin de Pays area in the Var département in south-eastern France.

Mauresque Cocktail (Cktl) 1 measure Pernod, ⅓ measure orgeat. Place in a highball, top with iced water and stir.

Maurice Cocktail (Cktl). ½ measure dry gin, ¼ measure Italian vermouth, ¼ measure French vermouth, juice ¼ orange, dash Angostura. Shake over ice and strain into a cocktail glass.

Maurice Drouhin (Fr) a cuvée in the Premier Cru vineyard Champs-Pimont, A.C. Beaune, Côte de Beaune, Burgundy (owned by the Hospices de Beaune).

Mauritius Breweries Limited (Afr) *see* Mauritius Brewery.

Mauritius Brewery (Afr) a brewery based on the island of Mauritius on the east coast of Africa. Brews local beers plus F.E.S. and Stella Pilsener Lager under licence.

Mauro (Sp) a Vino de la Tierra wine from Valladolid, Castilla-Léon. See *also* San Román, Aalto.

Mauro Mascarello (It) a winery based in the DOCG Barolo, Piemonte. Label: Monprivato.

Mauroma Winery (S.Afr) a winery based in Stanford, Walker Bay, Western Cape. Now known as Stanford Hills Winery.

Maury (Fr) the name for a yeast strain found in Maury near the Pyrénées. Is an excellent yeast for fermenting a honey solution into a sweet mead.

Maury (Fr) an A.C. red Vin Doux Naturel from Roussillon in south-eastern France. Made from the Grenache grape. Minimum age 2 years.

Mausac (Fr) a red grape variety grown in the southern Rhône that produces wines with an aromatic and dried apple aroma and flavour.

Mausat (Fr) an alternative name for the Malbec grape.

Mauseln (Ger) denotes a recognisable smell of mice in the wine.

Mäushöhle (Ger) vineyard (Anb): Pfalz. (Ber): Mittelhaardt-Deutsche Weinstrasse. (Gro): Mariengarten. (Vil): Deidesheim.

Maustal (Ger) vineyard (Anb): Franken. (Ber): Maindreieck. (Gro): Hofrat. (Vil): Sulzfeld.

Mautner Markoff (Aus) one of the leading sparkling wine producers in Austria.

Mauves (Fr) an A.C. commune of Saint-Joseph in the Rhône.

Mauzac (Fr) a white grape variety grown in Armagnac, Gaillac, the Rhône and Languedoc. Used in the making of Blanquette de Limoux (sparkling). Also known as the Blanquette.

Maverick (Bel) a premium lager brewed in Limburg.

Maverick (S.Afr) the label for a range of wines produced by the Bellingham winery, Wellington, Western Cape.

Maverick (Scot) a 4.2% alc by vol. ale brewed by Fyne Ales Ltd., Argyll.

Mavis Delight (Cktl) ⅔ measure Cordial Médoc, ⅓ measure Scotch whisky. Stir together over ice in a highball glass and top with lemonade.

Mavro (Gre) lit: 'black', used to describe dark, red wines.

Mavrodaphne (Gre) a red grape variety grown in Greece to produce sweet, fortified, dessert wines.

Mavrodaphne (Gre) a sweet, red, fortified dessert wine similar in taste to Verdelho.

Mavrodaphne de Cephalonia (Gre) a red dessert wine from the Isle of Cephalonia in the Ionian Islands in western Greece.

Mavrodaphne de Patras (Gre) an A.O.C. fine liqueur red dessert (fortified) wine from the Peloponnese.

Mavrodi (Gre) a dark red wine produced in Delphi from the Mavroutis grape.

Mavro Kalpaki (Gre) a red wine produced on the island of Limnos.

Mavron (Cyp) a red grape variety from Cyprus and Greece used in the making of the rosé wine Kokkineli.

Mavro Naoussis (Gre) a dry red wine from the Naoussa district in central Macedonia.

Mavro Nemeas (Gre) an alternative name for the Aghiorghitiko.

Mavro Romeiko (Gre) a dry red wine made in Crete from grape of the same name.

Mavroudi (Gre) a rare red grape variety thought to be Mavrud.

Mavroutis (Gre) a red mountain grape variety used to produce the robust red wines of rural Greece.

Mavrud (Bul) a thick skinned, dark red grape variety which produces a full, soft wine on the sweet side with little acidity and strong tannins. From the Maritsa Valley.

Mawby Vineyards (USA) a winery based at Sutton's Bay, Michigan. Produces hybrid wines.

Mawmesey (Eng) the Elizabethan (seventeenth century) spelling of Malmsey.

Max (Eng) a bottled strong dry white cider 8.2% alc by vol. from Bulmers, Hereford. Also a draught version 6% alc by vol.

Maxim (S.Afr) the label for a red wine (Cabernet sauvignon) produced by the Goedverwacht Estate winery, Robertson, Western Cape.

Maxima (Ger) a brand of de-caffeinated coffee.

Maximator (Ger) a doppelbock beer, brewed by the Augustiner Brauerei in Munich.

Maxim Cocktail (Cktl) ⅗ measure dry gin, ⅖ measure dry vermouth, dash (white) crème de menthe. Shake over ice and strain into a cocktail glass.

Maxime (Cktl) ⅗ measure vodka, ⅕ measure Campari, 3 dashes cherry brandy, ⅕ measure bianco vermouth. Stir with ice, strain into a cocktail glass, add a twist of lemon and a cherry.

Maximes Frères (Fr) a noted producer of brandy 40% alc by vol. of same name.

Maximiner (Ger) vineyard (Anb): Mosel-Saar-Ruwer. (Ber): Saar-Ruwer. (Gro): Römerlay. (Vil): Trier.

Maximiner Burgberg (Ger) vineyard (Anb): Mosel-Saar-Ruwer. (Ber): Bernkastel. (Gro): Probstberg. (Vil): Fell.

Maximiner Herrenberg (Ger) vineyard (Anb): Mosel-Saar-Ruwer. (Ber): Bernkastel. (Gro): Probstberg. (Vil): Longuich.

Maximiner Hofgarten (Ger) vineyard (Anb): Mosel-Saar-Ruwer. (Ber): Bernkastel. (Gro): Probstberg. (Vil): Kenn.

Maximiner Klosterlay (Ger) vineyard (Anb): Mosel-Saar-Ruwer. (Ber): Bernkastel. (Gro): Sankt Michael. (Vil): Detzem.

Maximin Grünhaus (Ger) a famous wine-producer based in the Mosel-Saar-Ruwer region.

Maximin Staadt (Ger) vineyard (Anb): Mosel-Saar-Ruwer. (Ber): Saar-Ruwer. (Gro): Scharzberg. (Vil): Kastel-Staadt.

Maxim Light (Eng) a 0.9% alc by vol. beer produced by Vaux Breweries Ltd., Sunderland.

Maxim's (It) a sparkling natural spring mineral water from Sita, Arezzo. Mineral contents (milligrammes per litre): Sodium 3.9mg/l, Calcium 20.2mg/l, Magnesium 1.59mg/l, Potassium 0.47mg/l, Bicarbonates 53.1mg/l, Chlorides 7mg/l, Sulphates 7.7mg/l, Nitrates 5mg/l, Silicates 3.7mg/l. pH 7.1

Maxim's Cuvée Réservée (Fr) a dry Champagne produced for Maxim's restaurant in Paris.

Maxim's de Paris (Fr) the name for a range of Cognacs produced by Château de la Grange. Available as V.S.O.P. (10 years old), Napoléon (20–30 years old) and X.O. (over 35 years old).

Maximus Super (USA) a strong beer brewed by the West End Brewing C°. in Utica, New York.

Max [Louis] (Fr) a winery based in the A.C. Chablis, Burgundy. Produces a range of Chablis wines including Premier Cru Fourchaume.

Max Rosé Pas Dosé (It) a sparkling (metodo tradizionale) wine produced by Marco Berlucchi in Lombardy.

Max's Shiraz (S.Afr) the label for a red wine (Shiraz 100%) produced by the Linhorst Wines winery, Suider-Paarl, Western Cape.

Maxwell House (Eng) a famous brand of instant coffee produced by General Foods in Oxon.

Maxwell Wines (Austr) a winery. (Add): 24 Kangarilla Road, McLaren Vale, South Australia 5171. Has no vineyards. Buys in Cabernet sauvignon, Merlot, Sémillon and Shiraz.

Maxxima (Bul) the label for a range of wines produced in a variety of Bulgarian vineyard sites.

Maya (S.Afr) the label for a red wine (Ruby cabernet and Shiraz blend) produced by the Rose Garden Vineyards winery, Paarl, Western Cape.

Maya (Tur) yeast.

Mayabe Brewery (S.Am) a brewery based at Holguin, Cuba. Brews: Hatvey Lager Beer.

Mayacamas (USA) a vineyard in the Napa Valley, California. Grape varieties: Cabernet sauvignon and Chardonnay. Produces varietal wines.

Maya Cocktail (Cktl) 35mls (1½fl.ozs) white rum, 10mls (½fl.oz) golden rum, 50mls (2fl.ozs) pineapple juice, 3 dashes Curaçao, 2 dashes gomme syrup. Blend altogether with a scoop of crushed ice in a blender. Strain into an old-fashioned glass, dress with a cherry, mint sprig and pineapple cube.

Mayalamak (Tur) fermentation.

Mayan Whore Cocktail (Cktl) place 25mls (⅕ gill) tequila into a flute glass, add 40mls (⅓ gill) pineapple juice (do not stir). Top with soda and then layer 1 measure of Kahlúa on top and serve with straws.

May Bee (Eng) a 3.9% alc by vol. ale brewed by Mauldon's Ltd., Suffolk.

Mayblossom Brandy (Eng) ¾ fill bottles with picked mayblossom (not leaves or stems). Top up with brandy, cork and seal. Store 4–6 weeks, strain off brandy, rebottle, seal then use as required.

May Blossom Fizz (Cktl) 50mls (2fl.ozs) Swedish Punsch, 20mls (¾fl.oz) lemon juice, 2 dashes grenadine. Shake over ice, strain into a highball glass containing ice, top with soda water, serve with a muddler and straws.

May Day (Eng) a strong straw-coloured summer ale 5% alc by vol. brewed by Adnams in East Anglia.

Maye [Les Fils] (Switz) wine-producers based in Riddes, Valais. Are noted for their Johannisberg Feuergold.

Mayer am Pfarrplatz (Aus) a winery based in the Wien region. (Add): Beethovenhaus, Pfarrplatz 2, 1190 Wien. Grape varieties: Chardonnay, Gelber

M

muskateller, Grüner veltliner, Müller-Thurgau, Pinot noir, Riesling, Traminer. Produces a range of wine styles.

Mayers (Afr) a natural spring mineral water from Kenya.

Mayetiola Destructor (Lat) *see* Hessian Fly.

Mayfair Cocktail (Cktl) ¼ measure gin, ¼ measure orange juice, 2 dashes apricot syrup, 2 dashes clove syrup. Shake well over ice and strain into a cocktail glass.

Mayfair Vineyards (N.Z) a winery based in Sturges Road, Henderson, North Island. Noted for fortified wines and Blackberry Nip.

Mayflower (Eng) a 4.5% alc by vol. ale brewed by Robert Cain in Liverpool with the addition of elderflowers.

Mayflower Brewery (Eng) a brewery (established 2002). (Add): Mayflower House, 15 longendale Road, Standish, Wigan, Lancashire WN6 0UE. Brews a variety of beers and ales. Website: http://www.mayflowerbrewery.co.uk 'E'mail: info@mayflowerbrewery.co.uk

Mayflower Special (Cktl) 25mls (1fl.oz) Mandarine Napoléon, 10mls (⅓ fl.oz) Angostura, ½ teaspoon powdered sugar. Shake well with ice, strain into a highball glass and top up with soda water.

May Fly (Eng) a light Oloroso Sherry produced by Findlater's.

Mayl (Tur) liquid.

Mayo (Afr) a still natural spring mineral water (established 1973) from Pointe Noir, Republic of Congo. Mineral contents (milligrammes per litre): Sodium 1.4mg/l, Calcium 33mg/l, Magnesium 22mg/l, Potassium 5.1mg/l, Bicarbonates 202mg/l, Chlorides 3mg/l, Sulphates 8mg/l, Fluorides 0.15mg/l, Nitrates <0.2mg/l, Silicates 20mg/l. pH 7.75 Website: http://www.sourcemayo.com

Mayoral (Eng) the term used to describe an experienced grape picker.

Mayorazgo (Sp) a solera brandy produced by Diez Merito, Bodegas Internacionales.

Mayor Cuerpo (Sp) describes a Sherry with a lesser body.

Maypole Mild (Eng) a 3.8% alc by vol. mild ale brewed by the Oakleaf Brewing C°. Ltd., Hampshire.

Maysara Estate (USA) a winery based in the McMinnville, Oregon. Grape variety: Pinot noir. Label: Jamsheed.

Mayschoss (Ger) village (Anb): Ahr. (Ber): Walporzheim/Ahrtal. (Gro): Klosterberg. (Vins): Burgberg, Laacherberg, Lochmuhlerley, Mönchberg, Schieferley, Silberberg.

Mayson Ridge (S.Afr) a winery based in the Paarl, Western Cape. Grape varieties include: Cabernet sauvignon.

Maysons Premier (Eng) an ale brewed by the Hart Brewery, Little Eccleston, Preston, Lancashire.

May Wine (Ger) the traditional preparation of a light Rhine wine into which the aromatic leaves of the herb waldmeister (woodruff) have been infused. May wine is served chilled and ladled from a bowl usually with strawberries or other fruit floating in it.

Mazagran (Arab) describes hot or cold coffee that is served in a glass.

Mazandaran (Iran) a famous red wine of ancient times produced in the then northern Persia.

Mazandaran (Iran) a natural spring mineral water brand.

Mazard (Eng) mazer. *see* Mazzard.

Mazarin (Fr) a light brown liqueur similar to Bénédictine.

Mazato of Pérou (S.Am) a drink made from boiled maize and sugar water in Peru.

Mazbout (Tur) medium sweet Turkish coffee.

Mazer (Eng) a drinking vessel, usually of wood, bound and mounted with silver or other metal. The Scottish type is also mounted on a stem as well. Vessels were often covered and used for the drinking of mead in mediaeval times. Also spelt Mazard and Mazzard.

Mazères (Fr) a commune within the A.C. Graves district of south-western Bordeaux.

Mazion (Fr) a commune within the A.C. Côtes de Blaye district of north-eastern Bordeaux.

Mazis-Chambertin (Fr) a Grand Cru vineyard in the A.C. commune of Gevrey-Chambertin, Côte de Nuits, Burgundy. Also spelt Mazys or Mazy 12.6ha.

Mazowszanka (Pol) a natural spring mineral water from Mazowsze. Mineral contents (milligrammes per litre): Sodium 114mg/l, Calcium 38.48mg/l, Magnesium 14.58mg/l, Potassium 10.9mg/l, Bicarbonates 378.31mg/l, Chlorides 72.68mg/l, Fluorides 0.42mg/l.

Mazoyères-Chambertin (Fr) a Grand Cru vineyard in the A.C. commune Gevrey-Chambertin, Côte de Nuits, Burgundy. 19.5ha. Is often sold as Charmes-Chambertin which it adjoins because of it not being so well known.

Mazuelo (Sp) a red grape variety grown in the Rioja, north-eastern Spain. Also known as the Carignan and Cariñena.

Mazuran Vineyard (N.Z) a winery based at 225 Lincoln Road, Henderson, North Island. 3ha. Grape varieties: Hamburgh, Merlot, Muscat alexandria, Palomino, Seibels. Noted for Port and Sherry-style wines.

Mazy-Chambertin (Fr) *see* Mazis-Chambertin.

Mazyn (Tur) a type of fermented milk from Armenia.

Mazys-Chambertin (Fr) *see* Mazis-Chambertin.

Mazza [Ilse] (Aus) a winery based in the Wachau. (Add): 3610 Joching 124. Grape varieties: Grüner veltliner, Pinot gris, Riesling, Zweigelt. Produces a range of dry and sweet wines, also a noted Heurige.

Mazzard (Eng) *see* Mazer.

Mazza Vineyards (USA) a winery based in Erie County, Pennsylvannia. Produces French hybrid, native American and Vinifera wines.

Mazzo (It) bouquet.

M

Mazzocco Vineyard (USA) a winery. (Add): 1400 Lytton Springs Road, P.O. Box 49, Healdsburg, Sonoma County, California. Grape variety: Zinfandel.

MBudget (Switz) a slightly acidic, sparkling natural spring mineral water from Aven. Mineral contents (milligrammes per litre): Sodium 8mg/l, Calcium 125mg/l, Magnesium 25mg/l, Potassium 2mg/l, Bicarbonates 155mg/l, Chlorides 12mg/l, Sulphates 250mg/l, Nitrates 4mg/l, Silicates 3mg/l, Strontium 2mg/l. pH 5.0

Mbuni (Afr) an east African coffee made from the whole dried coffee cherry (fruit), has a bitter taste.

M.C. (Eng) abbr: on a wine-list denotes Mise en bouteille au Château.

McAndrews (Scot) a blended Scotch whisky produced by Stewart and Son 40% alc by vol.

McAuslan Brewing (Can) a brewery. (Add): 5080 St-Ambroise, Montreal, Quebec H4C 2G1. Brews beers, stout and cider. Website: http://www.mcauslan.com 'E'mail: info@mcauslan.com

M.C.B. (Eng) abbr: Measuring Container Bottle.

McCallum [Duncan and John] (Scot) a Scotch whisky distillers.

McCallum Breweries (Sri.L) a brewery based in Meegoda, Colombo. Brews: Sando, Three Coins and Pilsener beers.

McClelland Cocktail (Cktl) ⅔ measure sloe gin, ¼ measure Cointreau, dash orange bitters. Shake over ice and strain into a cocktail glass.

McCormick Distilling (USA) a winery based in Kansas City, Missouri.

McCoys [The] (USA) the term given for the '*real stuff*'. Scotch whisky etc. that was bought in by the rum runners during the Prohibition 1919–1933. see Real McCoy (The).

McCrea (USA) a winery based in the Columbia Valley, Washington State. Grape varieties include: Syrah. Label: Cuvée Orleans.

McCrea Vineyard (USA) a small vineyard based near Healdsburg, Sonoma County, California. Grape variety: Chardonnay.

McDonald [C. & J.] (Scot) a subsidiary blend of Arthur Bell and Sons 40% alc by vol.

McDonald Winery (N.Z) part of Montana Wines, 150 Church Road, P.O. Box 7095, Taradale. 242ha. Grape varieties include: Cabernet sauvignon, Chardonnay, Pinot noir. Produces still and sparkling wines.

McDowell Valley Vineyards (USA) a large winery based near Hopland, Mendocino County, California. 150ha. Grape varieties: Cabernet sauvignon, Chardonnay, Chenin blanc, Colombard, Grenache, Petite sirah, Sauvignon blanc and Zinfandel. Produces varietal wines. Is a member of the Coro Mendocino (Zinfandel) wine group of Mendocino wineries.

McEwan (Scot) see Scottish and Newcastle.

McEwan and C°. (Scot) a highland and Scotch whisky distillery based in Perthshire. Part of DCL. Linkwood Distillery is under licence to McEwan.

Brands include Abbots Choice, Chequeurs and Linkwood.

McEwans LA (Scot) a low alcohol lager 0.9% alc by vol. from McEwans.

McEwan's Strong Ale (W.Ind) a bitter ale 1086 O.G. brewed by the Guinness Brewery in Jamaica in association with Scottish and Newcastle Breweries.

McEwan-Younger (Eng) the Scottish and Newcastle's north-west England, Yorkshire and North Wales marketing company.

McFadden Ranch (USA) a small vineyard based in Potter Valley, Mendocino, California. Grape variety: Sauvignon blanc.

McGregor Co-operative (S.Afr) a wine co-operative (established 1948) based in McGregor, Western Cape. 700ha. (Add): P.O. Box 519, McGregor, Robertson 6705. Has 42 members. Grape varieties: Cabernet sauvignon, Chardonnay, Chenin blanc, Colombard, Merlot, Pinotage, Sauvignon blanc, Shiraz. Produces: After Five, Edel Laat Oes Superior, Groot Toren, Laat Oes Steen, Late Bottled Cape Vintage Port, Winemaker's Reserve and many varietals. Website: http://www.mcgregorwinery.co.za

McGregor Late Bottled Cape Vintage Port (S.Afr) a port-style fortified wine produced from Ruby cabernet grapes. Aged for 3 years in 225litres French oak casks by the McGregor Co-operative.

McGuigan Brothers (Austr) a winery in the Hunter Valley. Grape varieties: Shiraz, Merlot, Cabernet sauvignon, Chardonnay, Sémillon.

McGuinness Beers (Eng) see Thomas McGuinness Brewing Company.

McGuinness Distillers (Can) distillers of Canadian whisky.

McHenry (Cktl) ½ measure dry gin, ½ measure Italian vermouth, dash apricot brandy. Shake over ice and strain into a cocktail glass.

McHenry Hohnen Vintners (Austr) a winery based in the Margaret River district of Western Australia. Grape varieties include: Cabernet sauvignon, Chardonnay, Grenache, Graciano, Marsanne, Mataro, Shiraz, Tempranillo, Viognier, Zinfandel. Label: 3 Amigos.

McIvor Creek Wines (Austr) a winery (established 1973). (Add): South of Heathcote, Victoria. Produces a wide range of dry and sweet white wines plus dry red and fortified wines.

McKenzie Mist (USA) a natural spring mineral water from Blue River, Oregon.

McKesson Liquor C°. (USA) major importers of Inca pisco from Casa Ranuzzi in Lima, Peru.

McLains Whisky (Eng) the brand-name of a Scotch whisky bottled by Linfood Cash and Carry, Northamptonshire.

McLaren Vale (Austr) a fertile valley and wine region based in South Australia, south of Adelaide. Has a warm Mediterranean climate and a variety of soils including sand, clay, clay loam, stony and black crackling clays. Wineries include Hardys, Jester, Marienberg, Reynella, Taticilla and Seaview.

M

McManis Family Vineyards (USA) a winery based in the San Jocquin Valley, California. Grape varieties include: Cabernet sauvignon.

McManus Winery (Austr) a winery based in Riverina, New South Wales.

McMullen Brewery (Eng) a brewery (established 1827). (Add): 26 Old Cross Road, Hertford, Hertfordshire SG14 1RD. Brews: Baroosh, (cask-conditioned) Country Best Bitter 4.3 Mid-Summer Gold 4% alc. by vol (1041 O.G.)., Christmas Ale 1071 O.G. Mac's N°1 Keg 1036 O.G. Hartsman Lager 1035 O.G. Farmer's Ale 1036 O.G. Gladstone, Golden Mild, Olde Time 1070 O.G. Original AK 3.8 Mid-Summer Gold 4% alc by vol., Steingold Lager 1042 O.G. and bottled Mac's Brown 1031 O.G. Website: http://www.mcmullens.co.uk 'E'mail: sgill@mcmullens.co.uk

McNab Ridge Winery (USA) a winery based in the Mendocino County, California. Is a member of the Coro Mendocino (Zinfandel) wine group of Mendocino wineries.

McNish [Robert and C°. Ltd.] (Scot) a blended Scotch whisky producer based at Glasgow.

McPherson Wines (Austr) a winery based in Murray Darling, Western Australia. Website: http://www.mcphersonwines.com

McSorley's (USA) a bottom-fermented malt beer brewed by the Schmidt Brewery in Philadelphia, Pennsylvania.

MC Square (S.Afr) a winery (established 1996) based in Somerset West, Western Cape. Grape varieties: Chardonnay. Produces sparkling (Méthode Cap Classique) wines.

McWilliams (Austr) a winery. (Add): P.O. Box 41, Pyrmont, New South Wales. 2009. Vineyards at Mount Pleasant in the Hunter Valley and in the M.I.A. Grapes are also purchased in large quantities from other growers' vineyards at Lovedale, Mount Pleasant and Rosehill. Grape varieties include Chardonnay, Riesling, Cabernet sauvignon, Shiraz. See also Hanwood. Labels include: J.J. McWilliams. Website: http://www.mcwilliams.com.au

McWilliams Dry Friar (Austr) a dry Australian Sherry produced by the McWilliams Winery in New South Wales.

McWilliams Oakville Vineyard (USA) a red wine (Cabernet sauvignon) produced by the Plumpjack winery, Napa Valley, California.

McWilliams Wines (N.Z) a winery. (Add): Church Road, Taradale, Hawkes Bay. 360ha. Grape varieties: Cabernet sauvignon, Gamay, Müller-Thurgau, Palomino. Noted for fortified wines.

M.D. (Eng) abbr: if found on a wine-list denotes Mise en bouteille au Domaine.

MD 20/20 (USA) the name for a range of wine-based drinks produced by the 20/20 Wine C°., Westfield, New York. Peach or mango and lime flavours, both at 13.5% alc by vol.

MDV (Sp) a dry Oloroso Sherry produced by Domecq in Jerez de la Frontera.

Mead (Eng) fermented honey, water and herbs which is historically the oldest drink known to man. 8% alc by vol. See also Methaglin, Tej. (Lat) = muslum/hydromel, (Swe) = mjöd, (Wal) = medd.

Meadowbrook (USA) the brand-name of a noted rye whiskey.

Meadow Creek (Austr) part of the Brown Brothers Estate in Victoria.

Mead Ranch (USA) a winery based in Atlas Peak, Napa Valley, California. 16.5ha. Grape variety: Zinfandel.

Meagers Distillery (Can) a noted Canadian whisky distillers.

Meal (Scot) another name for the ground malted grain also known as Grist.

Méal [Le] (Fr) a vineyard in the A.C. Hermitage, northern Rhône.

Mealie Beer (Afr) an alcoholic grain-based drink produced in southern Africa.

Meal Moth (Eng) the alternative name for the pyralis moth.

Mealt (Eng) the mediaeval name for malt.

Meander (S.Afr) the label for a range of wines (Crisp Dry/Fruity Red/Fruity White) produced by the Groot Eiland Winery, Worcester, Western Cape.

Meão (Port) a noted wine town based in the upper Douro. Its grapes are used for making Port.

Measure (Eng) an implement for measuring spirits etc.

Measuring Container Bottles (Eng) enables the contents in a bottle to be measured externally by means of a template embossed with a reverse epsilon together with the capacity if it is a MCB.

Measuring Jigger (USA) see Jigger.

Meaty (Eng) a term used to describe a wine rich in tannin and body, a chewy wine.

Mecedor (Sp) a spiked pole used to break up the cap (sombrero) of skins etc. on the fermenting wine. Also known as Basqueadores.

Méchage (Fr) fumigation (of casks, vats, etc.).

Mechín (Sp) a black grape variety grown in Rioja. Also known as the Monastel, Monastrel, Moraster, Ministrel, Negralejo and Valcarcelia. Grown also in Aragón and Catalonia.

Meckenheim (Ger) village (Anb): Pfalz. (Ber): Mittelhaardt-Deutsche Weinstrasse. (Gro): Hofstück. (Vins): Neuberg, Spielberg, Wolfsdarm.

Mecsek (Hun) a district producing white wines. Includes the areas of Pécs and Vilány.

Mecvini (It) a winery based in the Marches. Noted for Verdicchio dei Castelli di Jesi.

Meda (Port) a wine-producing area north of Beira Alta.

Medaillon (Fr) the brand-name for a V.S.O.P. Liqueur Cognac from Martell.

Medalla Real (S.Am) a 100% Cabernet sauvignon or Chardonnay wine from Santa Rita in Chile. 10% aged in French oak.

Medalla Reserva (S.Am) a 100% Cabernet sauvignon wine produced by Santa Rita in Chile.

Medallion Lager (Eng) a keg lager beer 1036 O.G. brewed by the Federation Brewery in Newcastle, Northumberland.

M

Med Breexe (Cyp) a méthode traditionelle special reserve wine produced by Loël.

Medd (Wal) mead.

Meddersheim (Ger) village (Anb): Nahe. (Ber): Schloss Böckelheim. (Gro): Paradiesgarten. (Vins): Altenberg, Edelberg, Präsent, Liebfrauenberg, Rheingrafenberg.

Meddw (Wal) drunk/intoxicated.

Meddwdod (Wal) drunkeness.

Meddwyn (Wal) an alcoholic/a drunkard.

Meddyglyn (Wal) metheglin (spiced mead).

Médéa (Alg) a wine area in Alger which produces dry rosé, white and full-bodied red wines.

Medellin Excelso (S.Am) a full-bodied, pure coffee from Colombia.

Meder Distillery (Hol) a noted distillery owned by Heineken. Produces many liqueurs and spirits.

Medford Rum (USA) the old general name for rum produced in colonial America.

Media (It) a variety of the red Schiave gentile grape.

Media (Sp) a hogshead or half-butt. see Media Bota.

Media Bocoy (Sp) a 76gallons (350litres) chestnut cask used for shipping wines. Also known as a Half-bocoy.

Media Bota (Sp) a 56gallons (250litres) wine cask also known as a Half Bota.

Medias (Rum) an important wine-producing area. Part of the Tirnave Vineyard.

Medicinal (Eng) applied to wines and spirits etc. that have a taste of medicine. e.g. Islay malt whiskies, vermouths, bitters and herb liqueurs.

Medicinal Compounds (USA) may contain up to 40% by vol. of alcohol but not classed as alcoholic beverages therefore not taxed.

Medina (Sp) a solera reserva brandy produced by Perez Megia.

Medine Distillery (Afr) a rum distillery based at Bambous on the island of Mauritius.

Mediona (Sp) a red wine from Cataluña.

Medio y Corazón (Sp) the name given to the grape must obtained by treading and further fermentation.

Mediterranean Cocktail (Cktl) 25mls (1fl.oz) gin, 10mls (½fl.oz) blue Curaçao. Pour gin and Curaçao over ice in a highball glass and top up with lemonade.

Médium (Fr) a small bottle of (60cls) capacity used in the Champagne region. see Champagne Bottle Sizes.

Medium (Ire) a term for a half-pint of draught Guinness.

Medium-High Culture (Aus) see Mittelhochkultur (a vine cultivation system).

Medium Spingo (Eng) a cask-conditioned ale 5% alc by vol. from the Blue Anchor Brewery.

Medjidieh (Iran) a dark-brown pilsener lager 11° Balling brewed in Tehran by a brewery backed by the Board for the Protection of Industries, now closed since the overthrow of the Shah.

Medjugorica (Cro) a wine-producing area in Croatia.

Medley Distillery (USA) a Bourbon whiskey distillery based near the Indiana border in Kentucky. See also Mellow Corn.

Médoc (Fr) the top wine district of the Bordeaux region on the west bank of the river Gironde. Made up of the Bas Médoc and the Haut-Médoc (finest).

Médoc Maritime (Fr) the old name for the Bas Médoc.

Médoc Noir (Hun) the Hungarian name for the Merlot (also used at times for the Cabernet sauvignon).

Medra (Wal) a 4% alc by vol. ale brewed by Bragdy Ynys Mon, Gwynedd.

Meeboulong (Cktl) 30mls (¼ gill) sloe gin, 15mls (⅛ gill) French vermouth, 15mls (⅛ gill) Italian vermouth, dash orange bitters. Stir over ice, strain into a cocktail glass and add a squeeze of lemon peel juice on top.

Meenyeralnaya Vada (Rus) mineral water.

Meerendal Estate (S.Afr) a winery (established 1702) based in Durbanville, Western Cape. 142ha. (Add): Meerendal Wynlandgoed, Durbanville 7550. Grape varieties: Cabernet sauvignon, Chardonnay, Gewürztraminer, Merlot, Pinotage, Shiraz. Produces varietal wines. Website: http://www.meerendal.co.za

Meerhof Winery (S.Afr) a winery (established 2000) based in Swartland, Western Cape. 65ha. Grape varieties: Cabernet sauvignon, Chardonnay, Merlot, Pinotage, Shiraz. Website: http://www.meerhof.co.za

Meerlust Estate (S.Afr) a winery (established 1693) based in Stellenbosch, Western Cape. 110ha. (Add): P.O. Box 15, Faure 7131. Produces Rubicon and varietal wines from Cabernet sauvignon, Chardonnay, Merlot, Pinot noir. Website: http://www.meerlust.co.za

Meersburg (Ger) village (Anb): Baden. (Ber): Bodensee. (Gro): Sonnenufer. (Vins): Bengel, Chorherrnhalde, Fohrenberg, Haltnau, Jungfernstieg, Lerchenberg, Rieschen, Sängerhalde.

Meerspinne (Ger) grosslage (Anb): Pfalz. (Ber): Mittelhaardt-Deutsche Weinstrasse. (Vils): Gimmeldingen, Haardt, Königsbach, Mussbach, Neustadt an der Weinstrasse.

Meester (S.Afr) the brand-name of a famous brandy. See also Oude Meester.

Mega Bottle (Fr) the biggest Bordeaux bottle in the world (1981), comes from négociants Cruse et Fils Frères. It contains the equivalent of 36 standard bottles, stands 3 feet 6 inches tall and weighs 6 stones (38kgs) when full.

Megakeggery (Eng) the nickname sometimes used for processed-beer factories built by the large national brewers.

Megapanos [Alexandros] (Gre) a winery based in Nemea. Grape varieties include: Agiorgitiko.

Megía [Luis] (Sp) a large Bodega based in the Valdepeñas district of central Spain. Produces Marqués de Gastanga (100% Cencibel).

Mehaletz (Isr) corkscrew.

M

Mehana (Rum) the brand-name for a range of wines shipped to the U.K.

Mehedinti (Rum) a red and white wine-producing area.

Mehrhölzchen (Ger) grosslage (Anb): Rheingau. (Ber): Johannisberg. (Vils): Hallgarten, Östrich.

Mehring (Ger) village (Anb): Mosel-Saar-Ruwer. (Ber): Bernkastel. (Gro): Probstberg. (Vins): On the right side of the Mosel.

Mehring (Ger) village (Anb): Mosel-Saar-Ruwer. (Ber): Bernkastel. (Gro): Sankt Michael. (Vins): Blattenberg, Goldkupp, Zellerberg.

Meia Encosta (Port) a fruity dry white wine from Borges and Irmao, Dão.

Meibok (Hol) a 6.5% alc by vol. bottle-conditioned bock beer brewed by De Drie Ringen Amersfoort Bier Brouwerij, Amersfoort. Top-fermented.

Meibock Moerenburg (Hol) a 5.8% alc by vol. bottle-conditioned bock beer brewed by the Moerenburg Bier Brouwerij, Tilburg. Top-fermented.

Meiers Wines Cellars (USA) a firm with wineries in Silverton and Sansky, Ohio. Has vineyards at New Richmond.

Meifort (S.Afr) the label for a red wine (Cabernet sauvignon 68% plus Cabernet franc and Merlot blend) produced by the Buitenverwachting, Constantia, Western Cape.

Meikles of Scotland (Scot) a distillery (established 1989). (Add): Station Road, Newtonmore, Inverness PH20 1AS. Produces whiskies and liqueurs. 'E'mail: stagsbreath@newtonmore.com

Meilen (Switz) a principal vineyard near Zürich.

Meimsheim (Ger) village (Anb): Württemberg. (Ber): Württembergisch Unterland. (Gro): Heuchelberg. (Vin): Katzenöhrle.

Mein Bräu (Jap) a premium lager beer 6.4% alc by vol. brewed by the Kirin Brewery in Tokyo.

Meiner (Cktl) 25mls (1fl.oz) gin, 20mls (¾ fl.oz) Campari. Build into an ice-filled highball glass. Stir in orange juice and decorate with a slice of orange.

Meinert Wines (S.Afr) a winery (established 1987) based in Stellenbosch, Western Cape. 13.5 Grape varieties: Cabernet sauvignon, Merlot, Pinotage. Labels: Devon Crest, Synchronicity. Website: http://www.meinert.co.za

Meinl (Aus) a leading producer of sparkling wines in Austria.

Meio Doce (Port) medium-sweet.

Meio Seco (Port) medium-dry.

Meireles (Port) a brand of Vinho Verde.

Meiron Bitter (Wal) a bitter ale brewed by a micro-brewery based near Shrewsbury (formerly Snowdonia Brewery at Bryn Arms, Gellilydan, Gwynedd).

Meiseläckern (Aus) a vineyard site on the banks of the River Danube in the Kremstal region.

Meisenberg (Ger) vineyard (Anb): Mosel-Saar-Ruwer. (Ber): Saar-Ruwer. (Gro): Römerlay. (Vil): Waldrach.

Meisenheim (Ger) village (Anb): Nahe. (Ber):

Schloss Böckelheim. (Gro): Paradiesgarten. (Vin): Obere Heimbach.

Meister Pils (Ger) a pilsener lager brewed by the D.A.B. Brauerei of Dortmund Westphalia. Is a full-bodied beer.

Meix [Les] (Fr) a Premier Cru vineyard [part] in the A.C. commune of Aloxe-Corton, Côte de Beaune, Burgundy.

Meix-Bas [Les] (Fr) a Premier Cru vineyard in the A.C. commune of Fixin, Côte de Nuits, Burgundy 1.88ha.

Meix-Bataille [Le] (Fr) a Premier Cru vineyard in the A.C. commune of Monthélie, Côte de Beaune, Burgundy 2.4ha.

Meix-Caillet (Fr) a vineyard in the A.C. commune of Rully, Côte Chalonnaise, Burgundy.

Meix-Rentiers (Fr) a Premier Cru vineyard in the A.C. commune of Morey-Saint-Denis, Côte de Nuits, Burgundy 1.2ha.

Meixue Natural Mineral Water (Chi) a natural spring mineral water. Mineral contents (milligrammes per litre): Sodium 168mg/l, Calcium 42.7mg/l, Magnesium 19.4mg/l, Potassium 3.1mg/l, Bicarbonates 433mg/l, Chlorides 159mg/l, Silicates 18mg/l.

Mekinzie Ridge (USA) a winery based in the Willamette Valley, Oregon. Grape variety: Pinot noir.

Meknès-Fez (Afr) a noted vineyard planted with imported vitis vinifera vines in the region of same name in Morocco. Contains A.O.G. areas: Beni M'Tir, Beni Sadden, Guerrouane, Saïs and Zerhoun.

Meko Natural Mineral Water (Chi) a natural spring mineral water. Mineral contents (milligrammes per litre): Sodium 5-15mg/l, Calcium 5-15mg/l, Magnesium 1-2.5mg/l, Potassium 2-3mg/l, Chlorides 5-9mg/l, Sulphates 0.5-5mg/l, Silicates 30-50mg/l. pH 6-pH 7.5

Mélange (Eng) a mixture, often a cocktail is referred to as 'a mixture of drinks'.

Mélange (Fr) blend (refers to Champagne).

Melanie (Eng) a winter malting barley. See also Optic.

Melaza (Sp) the name given to the sweet dregs of the residue in the sugar making process (inverting). (Fr) = miel.

Melba (Eng) a peach liqueur from Harvey's of Bristol.

Melbourne Bitter (Austr) a dry lager beer brewed by the Carlton and United Brewery in Melbourne.

Melbourne Brewery (Eng) an old brewery based in Stamford, Lincolnshire that now no longer brews beer but is a Museum, still has some 38 public houses.

Melbourne STA (Eng) a fictional Australian brand of lager adopted by the BBC TV soap opera 'East Enders' pub 'The Queen Vic'.

Melcan Distillery (Can) a distiller of Canadian whisky.

Melchers (Hol) a noted producer of advocaat and jenevers based in Schiedam.

Melchisedec (Fr) a large bottle of (30litres) 40

standard bottles capacity used in the Champagne region. *see* Champagne Bottle Sizes.

Melck's Red (S.Afr) the label for a red wine (Merlot 40% and Shiraz 60%) produced by the Muratie Estate winery, Stellenbosch, Western Cape.

Melen Winery (Tur) a large winery based in Thrace that produces a range of wines from local and French grape varieties.

Melesconera (N.Z) a light, sharp, fruity red wine once produced by Villa Maria in South Auckland.

Meleto (It) a Ricasoli-produced Chianti Classico.

Melette (It) an anisette produced in Ascoli Pinceno.

Melgaço [1] (Port) a natural spring mineral water from the Fonte Nova.

Melgaço [2] (Port) a natural spring mineral water from the Fonte Principal.

Melini (It) a large Chianti Classico producer. (Add): Villa Belvedere, 37010 Calmasino (VR). 145ha.

Mélinots (Fr) a Premier Cru vineyard of A.C. Chablis. Often has the Premier Crus of Roncières and Les Épinottes reclassified as the wines of this vineyard.

Melior (Ger) the brand-name of a coffee '*plunger*' system.

Melipilla (Chile) a wine-producing area near Santiago.

Melissa (It) a noted wine-producing commune in Calabria. Noted for red, rosé and white Ciró wines.

Melissa Cordial (Fr) *see* Eau de Mélisse.

Mélisse (Fr) a Carthusian green liqueur made from balm-mint in the nineteenth century.

Melk (Hol) milk.

Melkinrichting (Hol) dairy.

Mellars [John] of Great Barrier Island (N.Z) a vineayard based at Okupu Beach, Great Barrier Island. Nearly 1ha. Grape varieties: Cabernet sauvignon, Merlot.

Mellasat (S.Afr) a winery (established 1996) based in Paarl, Western Cape. 8ha. Grape varieties: Cabernet sauvignon, Chenin blanc, Pinotage, Shiraz. Labels: Dekker's Valley, Revelation, Tuin Wyn. Website: http://www.mellasat.com

Mellifera (S.Afr) a noble late harvest from botrytised Riesling grapes produced by the Jordan Vineyards, Stellenbosch.

Mellow (Eng) a term used to describe a wine which is at its peak of maturity.

Mellow Bird's (Eng) the brand-name of a mild instant coffee produced by General Foods in Oxon.

Mellow Corn (USA) the brand-name of a corn whiskey produced by the Medley Distillery in Kentucky.

Mellow Mild (Eng) a keg mild 1032 O.G. brewed by the Elgood Brewery in Wisbech, Cambridgeshire.

Mellow Red (S.Afr) the label for red wine (Ruby cabernet) produced by the Cape Bay winery, Walker Bay, Western Cape.

Mellow-Wood (S.Afr) the label of a pot-stilled brandy (established 1915) produced from Barrydale grapes and matured (solera-style) in wood for 5 years. Produced by Mellow-Wood Brandy C°., Stellenbosch 43% alc by vol.

Mellow Yellow (Eng) an alcoholic banana and mango-flavoured Caribbean Crush produced by Spilt Drinks, Exeter.

Mellow Yellow (Eng) a 4.5% alc by vol. ale brewed by the Ossett Brewing C°. Ltd., West Yorkshire.

Melnik (Bul) a red grape variety that produces dark, tannic, heavy wines. Produced in the city of Melnik in the South-Western region. Full name: Shiroka Melnishka Losa.

Melník (Czec) a wine-producing area of Bohemia.

Melnotte et Fils (Fr) a Champagne producer. (Add): 14 Rue de Bernon, 51200 Épernay.

Melocotón (Fr) a 25% alc by vol. peach-flavoured liqueur produced by Marie Brizzard, Bordeaux.

Melomel (Eng) a mead produced from fruit juices or fruit and honey.

Melon (USA) a white grape variety used in the making of white wines in California.

Melonball (Cktl) 1 measure vodka, 1 measure Midori. Stir in an ice-filled highball glass and top with orange juice.

Melon Blanc (Fr) a lesser name for the Chardonnay grape.

Meloncholly (Eng) a 4.1% alc by vol. ale brewed by the Belvoir Brewery, Leicestershire.

Melon Cocktail (Cktl) 25mls (⅙ gill) gin, 2 dashes maraschino, 2 dashes lemon juice. Shake over ice, strain into a cocktail glass and top with a cherry.

Melon d'Arbois (Fr) the local name for the Chardonnay grape in the Jura region.

Melon de Bourgogne (Fr) a white grape variety known as Muscadet in the Loire. Produces wines with an aroma and flavour of green apples, pears, lemon and lime juice, pineapple and yeast (sur-lie). Also known as Clevner, Gamay à Feuille Ronde, Gros Auxerrois, Klevener, Pinot bianco, Pinot blanc, Lyonnaise blanche, Muscadet, Pourrisseux and Weissburgunder.

Melon Driver (Cktl) 25mls (⅛ gill) Midori, 25mls (⅛ gill) orange juice. Pour into an ice-filled highball glass and dress with a slice of orange.

Melotti Brewery (Afr) a brewery based in Asmara, Ethiopia. Produces Melotti Lager 11.7° Plato and a sweet Stout 12° Plato.

Melroses (Scot) an Edinburgh-based tea company (established 1812). Produces a wide range of fine teas including Assam, Ceylon, Darjeeling, Earl Grey.

Melrose Vineyard (USA) a small winery based in Middleburg, Virginia. 18ha. Produces hybrid wines.

Melsungen (Ger) landkries (Anb): Rheingau. (Ber): Johannisberg. (Vil): Böddiger. (Vin): Berg.

Melton [Charles] (USA) a winery in the Barossa Valley that produces Nine Popes and Rose of Virginia wines.

Mel-Y-Moelwyn Bitter (Wal) lit: 'honey of the mountain', a lightly hopped bitter beer 1038 O.G. brewed by a micro-brewery based near Shrewsbury. (Formerly Snowdonia Brewery at

Bryn Arms, Gellilydan, Gwynedd). Water used comes from Snowdonia.

Membrane Filters (Eng) made from porous plastic sheeting folded into cartridge form. An absolute filter. Used as a final filter for wines that are already filtered to a high standard.

Memel Oak (Port) the best oak used for maturing Port wine.

Memorable (Sp) a solera brandy produced by Gil Luque.

Memphis Mist (Eng) a 5% alc by vol. flavoured fruit drink from Matthew Clark, Somerset.

Menabrea (It) a brewery (established 1846) based in Biella. Brews: Minabrea Birra.

Menabrea Birra (It) a 4.8% alc by vol. straw coloured, bottled export lager brewed by Menabrea S.p.A., Biella.

Menacing Dennis (Eng) a 4.5% alc by vol. ale brewed by the Summerskills Brewery, Devon.

Ménage à Troi (S.Afr) the label for a red wine (Cabernet sauvignon, Merlot and Shiraz blend) produced by the La Couronne Estate winery, Franschhoek, Western Cape.

Menard (Fr) a Cognac producer. (Add): J-P Menard et Fils, 16720 Saint Merne-lès-Carrieres. 80ha. in the Grande Champagne. Produces Traditional Imperiale 20–25 year old, Vieille Réserve Extra 35 year old, Grande Fine Ancestrale 45 year old.

Mencía (Sp) a red grape variety grown in El Bierzo, Léon, Rias Baixas, Ribeira Sacra, Valdeorras. Also known as the Tintorera.

Mendip Magic (Eng) a cider produced by Thatcher's in Somerset.

Mendocino County (USA) a north Californian district that produces mainly table and sparkling wines. Contains the A.V.A. districts of Anderson Valley, Mendocino Ridge, Redwood Valley and Ukiah Valley.

Mendocino Ridge (USA) a new A.V.A. region in the Napa Valley, California on western edge of Anderson Valley. Consists of ridge top land in Mendocino County. Grape varieties: Cabernet sauvignon, Merlot, Zinfandel. Established vineyards include Greenwood Ridge, DuPratt Vineyards, Fetzer Vineyards, Zeni, Ciapusci, Mariah and Alden.

Mendoza (Arg) a major wine-producing region 140000ha in the foothills of the Andes Mountains in central Argentina, divided into the Northern (Guaymallen, Las Heras, Lavalle and San Martin), Central (Uco Valley), Eastern (Junin, Rivadavia, San Martin and Santa Rosa) and southern (Cuadro Nacional and Las Parades) sub-regions. Home of the Uco Valley (south-western Mendoza).

Mendoza Vineyards S.A (Arg) a winery based in the Mendoza region, eastern Argentina. Website: http://www.mendozavineyards.com 'E'mail: info@mendozavineyards.com

Mendrisiotto (Switz) a vineyard based in the Sotto Ceneri area of Ticino, southern Switzerland.

Menea (Gre) a wine region based south-west of Corinth. Is noted for red wines produced from the Agiorghitico grape.

Menesi Rozsa (Rum) the rosé of Menes, the best rosé wine of Rumania, a full, fruity bouquet and body with a deep rose colour.

Ménétou-Salon (Fr) an A.C. red, rosé and white wines from the west of Sancerre in the Central Vineyards, Loire, made from the Pinot noir (red & rosé) and Sauvignon (white).

Menetrières (Fr) a vineyard in the commune of Fuissé in A.C. Pouilly-Fuissé, Mâcon, Burgundy.

Mengen (Ger) village (Anb): Baden. (Ber): Markgräflerland. (Gro): Lorettoberg. (Vin): Alemannenbuck.

Menir (It) a Trebbiano d'Abruzzo wine produced by the Cantina Tollo co-operative.

Meniscus (Eng) the line between the air and the must in the fermenting vat. Also used in wine-tasting the line where the wine touches the glass.

Meniscus (Eng) in glass production, crescent shaped.

Mennig (Ger) village (Anb): Mosel-Saar-Ruwer. (Ber): Saar-Ruwer. (Gro): Scharzberg. (Vins): Altenberg, Euchariusberg, Herrenberg, Sonnenberg.

Menor Cuerpo (Sp) describes a Sherry with a very full body.

Menta (It) an alternative name for the liqueur Mentuccia.

Menthe Pastille (Fr) a white crème de menthe liqueur produced in Angers, Loire 28% alc by vol.

Méntrida (Sp) a Denominación de Origen of Castilla-La Mancha near Madrid. Produces red (minimum of 12% alc by vol) and rosado (minimum of 11.5% alc by vol) wines. Grape varieties: Cencibel, Garnacha, Tinto madrid.

Mentuccia (It) a herb-flavoured liqueur made from 100 different herbs produced in the Abruzzi mountains, central-eastern Italy. Also known as Centerbe, Menta and Silvestro.

Menuet (Fr) a Cognac producer based in the Grande Champagne district, Charente.

Mentzendorf (Hol) a producer of a kümmel liqueur based in Amsterdam 39% alc by vol.

Menu Pineau (Fr) an alternative name for the Arbois grape.

Menzingen (Ger) *see* Kraichtal.

Meodu (Eng) the mediaeval name for mead.

Meon Valley (Eng) a vineyard based in Hampshire that produces wines under the Cellar Selection label.

Meraner (It) *see* Meranese di Collina.

Meraner Hugel (It) *see* Meranese di Collina.

Meranese (It) *see* Meranese di Collina.

Meranese di Collina (It) a D.O.C. red wine from the Trentino-Alto-Adige. Made from the Schiava grossa, Schiava grigia, Schiava media, Schiava piccolo and Tschaggele grapes. Additional specifications of Burgravio if wine obtained in land of former County of Tyrol.

Mercaptan (Fr) mercaptopentanone.

Mercaptopentanone (Eng) denotes the smell of grass, nettles, asparagus and fresh herbs, often

M

associated with the Sauvignon blanc grape. (Fr) = mercaptan.

Merced (USA) a county within the Great Central Valley. Produce sweet dessert wines. Climate is hot and dry.

Merced [La] (Sp) a brand of deep-brown, cream Sherry produced by Bobadilla in Sanlúcar de Barrameda.

Merchant (Eng) a trader. (Fr) = négociant.

Merchants Bay Blanc (Fr) the label for an A.C. Bordeaux Blanc Sec, Bordeaux. Grape varieties: Sauvignon blanc 60% and Sémillon 40%.

Mercian (Jap) a major wine-producer in southern Japan.

Mercian Mild (Eng) a cask-conditioned mild 1032 O.G. brewed by the Marston Brewery in Burton-on-Trent, Staffordshire.

Mercier (Fr) a Champagne producer (established 1858). (Add): 68-70 Avenue de Champagne, B.P. 143 51333 Épernay. 225ha. A Grande Marque. Produces vintage and non-vintage wines. Produces: Brut, Brut Rosé, Demi-Sec, Demi-Sec Rosé, Vendange and Cuvée Eugène Mercier. Vintages: 1900, 1904, 1906, 1911, 1914, 1921, 1923, 1926, 1928, 1929, 1933, 1934, 1937, 1941, 1943, 1945, 1947, 1949, 1952, 1953, 1955, 1959, 1961, 1962, 1964, 1966, 1969, 1970, 1971, 1973, 1975, 1976, 1978, 1980, 1982, 1983, 1985, 1988, 1990, 1995, 1996, 1998, 2001. see Réserve de l'Empereur. Website: http://www.Champagnemercier.fr

Merck Toch Hoe Sterck (Hol) an 8.5% alc by vol. bottle-conditioned special beer brewed by De Schelde Brouwerij-Gravenpolder. Unpasteurised and top-fermented with spices.

Mercurey (Fr) an A.C. wine commune (563ha) in the Côte Chalonnaise, Burgundy. Minimum alc by vol. 10.5%. Produces red and dry white wines.

Mercouri (Gre) a winery based at Korakochori, 271 00 Pyrgos. 8ha. vineyard region is in Western Peloponnese. Wine: Vin de Pays des Letrinon. Grape varieties: 85% Refosco, 15% Mavrodaphne.

Mercurol (Fr) a noted village in the Rhône valley.

Mercury Mineral Water (Rus) a natural spring mineral water (established 1995) from Cerkessek. Mineral contents (milligrammes per litre): Calcium 50-150mg/l, Magnesium <100mg/l, Bicarbonates 300-650mg/l, Chlorides 300-900mg/l, Sulphates 800-1400mg/l. Website: http://www.mercury.com.ru

Merdingen (Ger) village (Anb): Baden. (Ber): Kaiserstuhl-Tuniberg. (Gro): Attilafelsen. (Vin): Bühl.

Mereaux (S.Afr) the label for a red wine (Malbec, Merlot and Shiraz blend) produced by the La Couronne Estate winery, Franschhoek, Western Cape. Originally known as Rogues Rouge.

Mère de Vinaigre (Fr) see Mother of Vinegar.

Meredyth Vineyard (USA) a small vineyard based in Middleburg, Virginia. 18ha. that produces French hybrid and vinifera wines.

Mère Goutte (Fr) the name given to a wine produced from first crushing of the grapes prior to pressing.

Merenzao (Sp) a black grape variety grown in Valdeorras.

Merfy (Fr) a Cru Champagne village in the Canton de Bourgogne. District: Reims.

Merican (USA) the label of a red wine produced from Cabernet franc, Cabernet sauvignon and Merlot grapes by Chaddsford in Brandywine Valley, Pennsylvania.

Meridas Coffee (S.Am) a variety of pure coffee produced in Venezuela.

Meridian Vineyards (USA) the name given to the Estrella River Winery which Nestlé purchased in 1988. Has 225ha. in San Luis Obispo and Central Coast. (Add): 7000 Highway 46 East, P.O. Box 3289, Paso Robles, CA 93447. Grape varieties: Cabernet sauvignon, Syrah, Chardonnay, Sauvignon blanc. see Domaine Beringer Blass. Website: http://www.meridianvineyards.com

Merienda (Sp) an Amontillado Sherry from Harvey's of Bristol.

Mérignac (Fr) a commune in the A.C. Graves district of south-western Bordeaux.

Merille (Fr) a red grape variety grown in south west France (not permitted for A.C. wine production).

Meritage (USA) a generic wine term given to a group of people who make wines using Bordeaux Grape varieties (St. Macaire, Carmenir, Muscadelle) in California.

Merito (W.Ind) the brand-name of a Puerto Rican rum usually sold for export.

Merit Selection Merite (Can) a still natural spring mineral water from Athelstan, Hinchinbrooke Country, Quebec. Mineral contents (milligrammes per litre): Sodium 2mg/l, Calcium 36mg/l, Magnesium 8mg/l, Potassium 2mg/l, Bicarbonates 130mg/l, Chlorides 3mg/l, Sulphates 26mg/l, Fluorides 0.1mg/l.

Merjestic (Eng) a 4.2% alc by vol. ale brewed by the White Star Brewery, Hampshire.

Merkur Classic (Ger) a sparkling natural spring mineral water from Hecklingen. Mineral contents (milligrammes per litre): Sodium 44mg/l, Calcium 208mg/l, Magnesium 80.5mg/l, Potassium 6.2mg/l, Bicarbonates 329mg/l, Chlorides 197mg/l, Sulphates 396mg/l, Nitrates <1mg/l.

Merkus Classic (Ger) a sparkling natural spring mineral water from Vitus-Quelle, Bielefeld. Mineral contents (milligrammes per litre): Sodium 77.4mg/l, Calcium 188mg/l, Magnesium 46.3mg/l, Potassium 1.7mg/l, Bicarbonates 387mg/l, Chlorides 100mg/l, Sulphates 339mg/l, Silicates 11.2mg/l.

Merlan (Fr) another name for the Merlot grape in Bordeaux.

Merlen Wines (N.Z) a winery. (Add): Vintage Lane, P.O. Box 8, Renwick, Marlborough. 5ha. Grape varieties: Riesling, Sauvignon blanc, Gewürztraminer, Sémillon, Chardonnay, Morio-Muskat.

M

Merlin Ale (Wal) a cask-conditioned bitter beer 1032 O.G. brewed by the Usher Brewery in South Wales.

Merlin Brewery (Eng) a brewery (established 2004). (Add): Unit 12, Victoria Street Ind Estate, Victoria Street, Leigh, Lancashire WN7 5SE. Brews: Astley Gold 3.8% alc by vol., Cannon Ball 5% alc by vol., Legacy 5% alc by vol., Vision 4.2% alc by vol.

Merlin's Ale (Scot) a 4.2% alc by vol. ale brewed by the Broughton Brewery near Biggar, Lanarkshire.

Merlins Magic (Eng) a 5% alc by vol. ale brewed by the Hampshire Brewery, Hampshire.

Merlins Magic (Eng) a 4.3% alc by vol. ale brewed by the Moor Beer Company, Somerset.

Merlin's Oak (Wal) a 4.3% alc by vol. seasonal ale brewed by Brain Crown Buckley.

Merlin Stout (Wal) a 4.2% alc by vol. stout brewed by the Hurns Brewing C°., West Glamorgan.

Merlot (Fr) a prolific early-ripening red wine grape of Bordeaux next in importance to the Cabernet. Used extensively in Saint-Émilion and now planted throughout the world. Produces wines with an aroma and flavour of blackberries, blackcurrants, fruit cake, plums, violets, roses and spice. Also known as Bigney, Crabutet noir, Médoc noir, Petite merle, Sémillon noir and Vitraille.

Merlot Blanc (Fr) a white wine grape used in small quantities in the Sauternes district of Bordeaux.

Merlot del Piave Vecchio (It) see Piave Merlot.

Merlot di Aprilia (It) a D.O.C. red wine from Latium. Wine named after the main grape variety. See also Sangiovese di Aprilia and Trebbiano di Aprilia.

Merlot di Pramaggiore (It) a D.O.C. red wine from Veneto. Made from the Merlot plus 10% Cabernet grapes. If aged for 3 years and has alc. content of 12% by vol. then called Riserva.

Merlyn (Wal) a Welsh cream and whisky liqueur produced by the Brecon Brewery C°., Mid-Wales.

Merman XXX (Scot) a 4.8% alc by vol. ale brewed by Caledonian Brewery based in Edinburgh.

Merpins (Fr) a commune in the Charente département whose grapes are used for Grande Champagne Cognac.

Merrain (Fr) a split-oak cask used in the Médoc.

Merret Belgravia (Eng) a non-vintage sparkling wine produced from Chardonnay 40%, Pinot noir 48% and Pinot meunier 12% from the Ridgeview vineyard.

Merret Fitzrovia (Eng) a vintage rosé sparkling wine produced from Chardonnay 80%, Pinot noir 12% and Pinot meunier 8% from the Ridgeview vineyard. Vintages: 2002.

Merret Grosvenor (Eng) a 'blanc de blanc' vintage sparkling wine produced from 100% Chardonnay by the Ridgeway vineyard. Vintages: 2001.

Merriam Vineyards (USA) a winery based in the Dry Creek Valley, Sonoma County, California. Grape varieties: Cabernet sauvignon. Website: http://www.merriamvineyards.com

Merribrook Wines (Austr) a winery based in the Frankland River region of Western Australia. Grape varieties include: Cabernet sauvignon, Malbec, Merlot.

Merricks Estate (Austr) winery (established 1978). (Add): End of Thompson's Lane, Merricks, Victoria. Grape varieties: Chardonnay, Cabernet sauvignon, Shiraz.

Merrie Monk Mild (Eng) the strongest mild beer 1043 O.G. in the country. Brewed by the Marston's Brewery in Burton-on-Trent, Staffordshire.

Merrill [Geoff] (Austr) see Mount Hurtle.

Merry (Eng) a slang term to denote a person who is partially drunk (not incoherently) and happy.

Merrydown plc (Eng) a cider producer (established 1946). (Add): Castle Court, 41 London Road, Reigate, Surrey RH2 9RJ. Noted for cider, meads, fruit-based wines and carbonated drinks. Website: http://www.merrydownplc.co.uk 'E'mail: phillip.baines@merrydownplc.co.uk

Merry K (Cktl) ⅔ measure Bourbon whiskey, ⅓ measure orange Curaçao. Stir over ice, strain into a cocktail glass and add a twist of lemon.

Merry Man's Mild (Eng) brewed by Whitby's Own Brewery, Whitby, North Yorkshire.

Merry Sour (Cktl) 2 measures brandy, 4 measures dry cider, juice of a lemon. Stir over ice in a tall glass and dress with a lemon peel spiral.

Merryvale (USA) a winery based in the Starmont, Napa Valley, California. Grape varieties: Cabernet sauvignon. Website: http://www.Merryvale.com

Merry Widow [1] (Cktl) ½ measure Dubonnet, ½ measure Noilly Prat, dash Amer Picon. Stir over ice, strain into a cocktail glass and top with twist of lemon peel.

Merry Widow [2] (Cktl) ½ measure cherry brandy, ½ measure maraschino. Shake over ice, strain into a cocktail glass and top with a cherry.

Merry Widow [3] (Cktl) 1 measure brandy, 4 measures redcurrant wine, dash crème de cassis. Stir together over ice in a highball glass and top with a spiral of lemon peel.

Merry Widow Cocktail [1] (Cktl) 35mls (1½fl.ozs) Byrrh, 35mls (1½fl.ozs) dry gin. Stir over ice and strain into a cocktail glass.

Merry Widow Cocktail [2] (Cktl) ½ measure Bénédictine, ½ measure dry gin, 2 dashes Pernod, 2 dashes Campari. Stir over ice, strain into a cocktail glass and top with a twist of lemon peel.

Merry Widower (Cktl) ½ measure dry gin, ½ measure French vermouth, 2 dashes Pernod, 2 dashes Bénédictine, dash Angostura. Shake over ice, strain into a cocktail glass and top with a twist of lemon peel juice.

Merry Widow Fizz [1] (Cktl) 2 measures Dubonnet, 1 measure lemon juice, 1 measure orange juice, 1 egg white. Shake over ice, strain into an ice-filled highball glass, top up with soda water, serve with a muddler and straws.

Merry Widow Fizz [2] (Cktl) 25mls (⅛ gill) sloe gin, 1 teaspoon powdered sugar, juice ½ orange, juice ½ lemon, 1 egg white. Shake over ice, strain into an ice-filled highball glass and top with soda water.

M

Merschein (Aus) a vineyard site based on the banks of the River Kamp situated in the Kamptal region.

Merseguera (Sp) a large berried, white grape variety grown in the Penedés region of south-eastern Spain. Also known as the Escanyavella, Exquitxagos and Verdosilla.

Mersin (Tur) an orange liqueur similar to Curaçao.

Mertesdorf (Ger) village (Anb): Mosel-Saar-Ruwer. (Ber): Saar-Ruwer. (Gro): Römerlay. (Vins): Felslay, Johannisberg, Mäuerchen.

Mertesdorf [ortsteil Maximin Grünhaus] (Ger) village (Anb): Mosel-Saar-Ruwer. (Ber): Saar-Ruwer. (Gro): Römerlay. (Vins): Abstberg, Bruderberg, Herrenberg.

Mertesheim (Ger) village (Anb): Pfalz. (Ber): Mittelhaardt-Deutsche Weinstrasse. (Gro): Höllenpfad. (Vin): St. Martinskeuz.

Merum (Lat) wine. See also Vinum.

Merus (USA) a winery based in the Napa Valley, California. Grape varieties include: Cabernet sauvignon.

Merweh (Leb) a native white grape variety thought to be the Sauvignon blanc.

Merwespont Koöperatiewe Wynmakery (S.Afr) a co-operative winery (established 1956) based at Bonnievale, Western Cape. 568ha. (Add): Box 68, Bonnievale 6730. Grape varieties: Cabernet sauvignon, Chenin blanc, Colombard, Pinotage, Ruby cabernet, Sauvignon blanc, Shiraz. Labels: Agulhas, Ferry and varietal wines.

Merwida Koöperatiewe Wynkelder (S.Afr) a winery based at Worcester. (Add): Box 4, Rawsonville 6845. Produces varietal wines.

Merxheim (Ger) village (Anb): Nahe. (Ber): Schloss Böckelheim. (Gro): Paradiesgarten. (Vins): Hunolsteiner, Römerberg, Vogelsang.

Merz [Christian] Brauerei (Ger) a brewery based in Bamburg that specialises in bottom-fermentation rauchbier.

Merzeguera (Sp) a white grape variety grown in Alicante.

Merzhausen (Ger) village (Anb): Baden. (Ber): Markgräflerland. (Gro): Lorettoberg. (Vin): Jesuitenschloss.

Mesa (Port) table wine.

Mesa Verde Vineyards (USA) a winery based in Temecula, California. 61ha. Grape varieties: Cabernet sauvignon, Chardonnay, Gamay and Johannisberg riesling. Produce varietal wines.

Mescal (USA) the spelling of Mezcal.

Mescalin (Mex) a rough, potent spirit produced from the Peyote cactus.

Mescans Porter (Eng) a 4.3% alc by vol. porter brewed by The Moorcock Brewing C°., Cumbria.

Méscita (It) wine bar/public house.

Mese (Tur) oak.

Mesech (Isr) a 'Bible wine', word derives from the Hebrew for mixture of water and wine.

Meseg (Isr) the old Hebrew (Bible) word for mixed wines.

Mesenich (Ger) village (Anb): Mosel-Saar-Ruwer.

(Ber): Obermosel. (Gro): Königsberg. (Vin): Held.

Mesenich (Ger) village (Anb): Mosel-Saar-Ruwer. (Ber): Zell/Mosel. (Gro): Rosenhang. (Vins): Abteiberg, Deuslay, Goldgrübchen.

Mesilla Valley (USA) an A.V.A. area of New Mexico. Situated near the Mexican border.

Mesimarja (Fin) a liqueur made from arctic brambles. Produced by Lignell and Piispanen. Ruby red in colour 29% alc by vol.

Mesland (Fr) a commune in the A.C. Touraine district of the Loire. Is allowed to use its name in the A.C. Touraine.

Meslier St. Francois (Fr) a lesser white grape variety grown in the Loir-et-Cher département. Also used in the making of Champagne and Armagnac.

Mesneux [Les] (Fr) a Premier Cru Champagne village in the Canton de Ville-en-Tardenois. District: Reims.

Mesnil-le-Hutier [Le] (Fr) a Cru Champagne village in the Canton de Dormans. District: Épernay.

Mesnil-sur-Oger [Le] (Fr) a Grand Cru Champagne village in the Canton d'Avize. District: Épernay. Reclassified in 1985.

Meso-climate (Eng) a term used by wine makers to describe a site climate. See also Macro-climate, Micro-climate.

Meso-Inistol (Eng) a vitamin needed by yeast which is found in malt. Usually a solution of malt extract is used in yeast starter bottles.

Mesopotamium (It) a red wine produced in Sicily in Roman times.

Mesrubat (Tur) drinks.

Messager (Fr) a producer of A.C. Bordeaux Mousseux based in Saint-Émilion, eastern Bordeaux.

Messamins (USA) the name used for North American native grape varieties in early times. A large, juicy grape, so named by the American Indians.

Messenia (Gre) a red, rosé and dry white wine-producing area.

Messias (Port) a Bairrada wine firm (established 1928), produce Vinhos Verdes, brandy and garrafeiras (red and white).

Messias (Port) a vintage Port shipper. Vintages: 1975, 1982, 1983, 1985, 1991, 1994, 1997, 2003. Also produces red and white wines. Website: http://www.cavesmessias.pt

Messica (W.Ind) an orange-flavoured spirit drink produced on the island of Martinique.

Messina (It) a noted wine-producing district in north-eastern Sicily.

Messina (It) a brand of beer brewed in Sicily.

Messo in Bottiglia (It) estate bottled.

Messorio (It) a 100% Merlot wine aged in new oak. Produced by Le Macchiole in Bolgheri, Tuscany.

Mest (Tur) drunk (consumed).

Mešt'an Brewery (Czec) a brewery (established 1895) based in Prague. Brews: Mešt'an Dark 11%, Mešt'an Straw 10%.

Mešt'an Dark 11% (Czec) a 4.1% alc by vol. bottled dark lager brewed by the Mešt'an Brewery in Prague.

Mešt'an Straw 10% (Czec) a 4% alc by vol. straw coloured, bottled lager brewed by Mešt'an Brewery in Prague.

Mestres (Sp) a sparkling (cava) wine produced by Cavas Mestres in San Sadurní de Noya, south-eastern Spain.

Mestres Sagues [Antonio] (Sp) a noted cava wine producer based in south-western Spain.

Mestres Tastaires du Languedoc (Fr) a wine brotherhood in the Languedoc region for the promotion of the wines of the region.

Mestsky Pivovar Nova Paka a.s. (Czec) a brewery. (Add): Pivovarska 400, 509 01 Nova Paka. Brews beers and lagers. Website: http://www.pivovar.novapaka.cz 'E'mail: broucek@novopaka.cz

Meta Brewery (Afr) a brewery based in Addis Ababa, Ethiopia. Brews a lager beer at 11° Plato.

Métaireau [Louis] (Fr) a noted Muscadet négociant. (Add): La Févrie, 44690 Maisdon-sur-Sèvre, Loire Atlantique.

Metala (Austr) a wine producer based in Langhorne Creek, South Australia.

Metall-Geschmack (Ger) denotes a metallic taste caused by the use of poorly cleaned tools.

Metallic (Eng) a taste that some wines gain from fungicidal spraying. Can be treated with Blue finings (Potassium ferrocyanide).

Metal Strainer (Cktl) see Hawthorne Strainer.

Metamorphosis (Eng) the term given to the changing of shape or form. Applies to the flowers changing into grapes and to insects in their change from grub to adult.

Metatartaric Acid (Eng) $C_8H_8O_{10}$ Cologel (a wine additive), prevents tartrate crystalisation for a limited period only.

Metaxa (Gre) a well-known brand of brandy, range of star rating which gives a star for every year of ageing. Also produces V.S.O.P. Grade Fine 40 year old. and a Grade Fine dry 50 year old.

Metaxa Puff (Cktl) 1 measure Metaxa brandy, 1 measure milk. Place ice cubes into a highball glass. Add ingredients, stir gently and top up with Perrier or other sparkling mineral water.

Métayage (Fr) a feudal practice (which still occurs in Burgundy) where an owner passes his vines onto a farmer or tenant when he no longer wishes to tend them.

Metbrew (USA) a beer which has survived from the days of Prohibition, brewed by the Champale Brewery.

Methanoic Acid (Eng) HCOOH a volatile acid found in wine.

Methanol (Eng) CH_3OH a poisonous higher alcohol (fusel oil) which can be removed during distillation because of its lower boiling point. Boiling temperature 66°C (150.8°F). see Methyl Alcohol.

Metheglin (Wal) a type of mead flavoured with herbs and spices, derives from the old Welsh word 'healing liquor' or 'spiced drink'.

Methionine (Eng) an amino acid found in wine formed by the yeasts.

Méthode Ancienne (Fr) old methods of viticulture and viniculture which are still used. see Château Simone.

Méthode Ancienne (S.Afr) the label for a red wine (Cabernet sauvignon) produced by the Springfield Estate winery, Robertson, Western Cape.

Méthode Beaujolaise (Fr) denotes the carbonic maceration method used in Beaujolais where no extra CO_2 is added.

Méthode Cap Classique (S.Afr) a term used to replace méthode champenoise on local sparkling wine labels.

Méthode Champenoise (Fr) the process of producing a second fermentation in the bottle, remuage and dégorgement. The term is no longer used on any sparkling wine label (except Champagne) since 1994. New French term is now Méthode Traditionelle. (Eng) = champagne method, (It) = metodo tradizionale/talento metodo classico, (S.Afr) = méthode cap classique, (Sp) = cava, (Port) = espumantes naturais, (N.Am) = champagne method.

Méthode Champenoise Cider (Austr) a magnificent old gold cider, rich, oak aged using traditional European varieties of apples. Made by the Kellybrook Winery in Victoria.

Méthode Cuve Close (Fr) denotes producing sparkling wine by the tank method.

Méthode Dioise (Fr) the local name used in Clairette de Die for the production of Clairette de Die Mousseux. Is similar to the Transfer method but no Liqueur de tirage and no Liqueur d'expédition are added. Dégorgement occurs. Also known as Méthode Rurale.

Méthode Gaillaçoise (Fr) a variation of the Méthode Traditionelle way of fermentation. Is similar to Méthode Dioise but no filtration or transfer bottling occurs. Used in the Côtes du Jura Mousseux and Gaillac Mousseux production.

Méthode Rurale (Fr) a method for making a semi-sparkling wine from the Languedoc-Roussillon called Vin de Blanquette. The wine is filtered before it has completely finished its normal (first) fermentation and is then bottled. The remaining fermentation is sufficient to give a slight sparkle without creating enough sediment to require removal. See also Méthode Dioise.

Methode Traditionell (Ger) méthode traditionelle.

Méthode Traditionnelle (Fr) the new designation for non-Champagne sparkling wines that are made by the traditional Champagne method. (Ger) = methode traditionell, (It) = metodo tradizionale/metodo classico, (Sp) = metodo tradicional.

Methoxpyrazines (Bio) a group of chemicals found in Sauvignon blanc wine that give a strong green capsicum/canned asparagus flavour/aroma.

Methu (Gre) mead.

Methuein (Gre) an old Greek word to denote making a person drunk, to make intoxicated.

Methuen [John] (Port) the English ambassador to

M

Portugal who drew up the treaty between the 2 countries that was named after him. *see* Methuen Treaty.

Methuen Treaty (Eng)(Port) a treaty signed in 1703 giving the wines of Portugal preferential taxation than that for French wines. *see* Methuen (John).

Methusalem (Fr) *see* Methuselah.

Methusalem (Sp) the brand-name for a Sherry produced by Gonzalez Byass.

Methuselah (Eng) a bottle size equivalent of 8 standard bottles. Used in Champagne. Also called a Methusalem. (Fr) = mathusalem.

Methyl Alcohol (Eng) CH_3OH a higher alcohol (fusel oil), highly toxic, the simplest alcohol. When distilled is known as Methanol.

Methylated Spirits (Eng) alcohol that has been denatured by the addition of Methanol, Naphtha and Pyridine. Used to test for pectin haze in a sample of hazy wine, a purple dye is also added to identify the Methylated spirit.

Methyl ethylketone (Eng) an aldehyde formed by the oxidation of alcohols which is found in wine in small traces that contributes to the bouquet.

Methyl isothiocyanate (Eng) an anti-mould chemical that was found in higher than permitted levels in some Veneto wines in 1991/1992. Used as an anti-fermentation and as a component in certain vine sprays. *abbr*: M.I.T.

Métis (Fr) an intraspecific cross red grape variety.

Metodo Champenois (It) the Champagne method, now replaced by metodo tradizionale or Talento.

Metodo Charmat (It) the tank method of sparkling wine production. *See also* Cuve Close.

Metodo Classico (It) a local name in eastern Italy for metodo tradizionale.

Método Industrial (Sp) a term used to describe the commercial method of vinification.

Método Rural o a la Española (Sp) a term used to describe whole-grape fermentation (used only by a few of the smaller growers).

Metodo Tradicional (Sp) refers to the cava wines produced by the traditional method in the regions of Alava, Barcelona, Gerona, Lérida, Navarra, Rioja, Tarragona and Zaragoya.

Metodo Tradizionale (It) the name for the traditional method production of sparkling wines. *See also* Metodo Classico, Talento.

Metro Golden (Cktl) 1 part Glayva, top up with English cider in a highball glass over ice and dress with half a lemon slice.

Metropole Extra (Sp) a dry white wine produced by Bodegas La Rioja Alta.

Metropolitain (Cktl) ½ measure brandy, ½ measure Italian vermouth, 2 dashes gomme, dash Angostura. Shake over ice and strain into a cocktail glass.

Metsovo (Gre) a red table wine made from the Cabernet sauvignon and Agiorgitiko grapes produced in the Ipiros (Epirus) region.

Mettenheim (Ger) village (Anb): Rheinhessen. (Ber): Nierstein. (Gro): Krötenbrunnen. (Vin): Goldberg.

Mettenheim (Ger) village (Anb): Rheinhessen. (Ber): Nierstein. (Gro): Rheinblick. (Vins): Michelsberg, Schlossberg.

Metternich-Sàndor (Aus) a winery based in the Kampstal region. (Add): Talstrasse 162, 3491 Strass im Strassertal. Grape varieties: Grüner veltliner, Pinot blanc, Pinot noir, Riesling, Sauvignon blanc, Zweigelt. Produces a range of wine styles.

Metternich'sche Weingüter (Aus) a noted wine-producer based in Krems.

Mettre en Perce (Fr) beer cask tap.

Metu (Ger) the old German word for mead.

Metz (Fr) a wine-producing area in the Vins de la Moselle, Lorraine. Produces mainly rosé wines: Clairet de Moselle.

Metz (W.Ind) mixed bottled drink containing Bacardi white rum from Bacardi-Martini Ltd. *See also* Still Metz, Black Metz.

Metzdorf (Ger) village (Anb): Mosel-Saar-Ruwer. (Ber): Obermosel. (Gro): Königsberg. (Vins): Sites not yet chosen.

Metz Forty 40 (W.Ind) a 40% alc by vol. chilled and triple filtered schnapps with a twist of citrus essence from Bacardi-Martini Ltd.

Metzingen (Ger) village (Anb): Württemberg. (Ber): Remstal-Stuttgart. (Gro): Hohennenffen. (Vins): Hofsteige, Schlossteige.

Meung (Fr) a red wine from Orleans, central France.

Meunier (Fr) a red grape variety used in Champagne production, a probable mutation of Pinot noir. (Ger) = Müllerrebe, Schwarzriesling. *see* Pinot Meunier.

Meurgis (Fr) the name of a Crémant de Bourgogne produced by the Caves de Bailly.

Meurich (Ger) village (Anb): Mosel-Saar-Ruwer. (Ber): Obermosel. (Gro): Gipfel. (Vins): Sites not yet chosen.

Meursault (Fr) a commune in the Côte de Beaune. Produces Premier Cru white wines from the Chardonnay grape. Premier Cru vineyards: Clos des Perrières, La Goutte d'Or, Le Porusot, Le Porusot-Dessus, Les Bouchères, Les Caillerets, Les Charmes-Dessous, Les Charmes-Dessus, Les Cras, Les Genevrières-Dessous, Les Genevrières-Dessus, Les Perrières, Les Petures, Les Santenots-Blancs and Les Santenots du Milieu. 99.45ha. Also Premier Cru vineyards in Blagny of La Jennelotte, La Pièce-Sous-le-Bois and Sous le Dos d'Ane. 21.3ha.

Meuse (Fr) a district of the Lorraine in north-eastern France. Produces Vins de Table.

Meuse Brasserie (Fr) a brewery based in Champigneulles, Lorraine.

Meux (Fr) a commune in the Charente-Maritime Département whose grapes are classed Petite Champagne (Cognac).

Mev (USA) the brand-name used by Mt. Eden Vineyards for their Chardonnay wines made from Ventana Vineyard purchased grapes.

Mexcalli (Mex) the old Indian word for Mezcal.

Mexicana Cocktail (Cktl) ½ measure tequila silver, ¼

M

measure lemon juice, ⅙ measure pineapple juice, 4 dashes grenadine. Shake over ice and strain into a cocktail glass.

Mexican Century (Mex) the alternative name for the Maguey cactus.

Mexican Coffee (Liq.Coffee) using a measure of Kahlúa as the liqueur.

Mexican Coffee (Mex) a mild coffee with a dry aftertaste that can be drunk on its own, but is often blended with other South American coffees. Has good acidity and body. Produced in Coatepec, Huatusco, Orizaba and Pueblo Hills.

Mexican Dream (Cktl) 25mls (⅛ gill) tequila gold, 25mls (⅛ gill) Malibu, dash Sirop de Fraises, 1 scoop strawberry ice cream. Blend in a blender with a scoop of crushed ice and serve in a flute glass with a fresh strawberry.

Mexico (C.Am) a country that produces mainly spirits (notably tequila) with a small number of vineyards planted in the north (49200ha. of vines). The law prevents wineries owning vineyards. Regions: Aguascalientes, Baja California, Chihuahua (Delicías), Coahuila (Parras and Saltillo), Durango, Hidalgo, Laguna, Querétaro, San Juan del Rio, San Luis Potosi, Sonora (Hermosillo), Tlaxcala and Zacatecas. 10%–15% of crop is made into wine, the rest is distilled into brandy or sold as table grapes.

Mexicola Cocktail (Cktl) 50mls (2fl.ozs) tequila silver, juice ½ lime. Place in an ice-filled highball glass and top with Coca Cola.

Mexico y España (Cktl) 35mls (1½fl.ozs) tequila, 35mls (1½fl.ozs) Amontillado Sherry. Stir over ice, strain into a cocktail glass and decorate with a green olive.

Meyblum S.A. (Fr) a noted eau-de-vie producer based in Alb'e par Villé, (Bas-Rhin), Alsace.

Meyer [José et Fils] (Fr) an Alsace wine producer. (Add): 72 Rue Clénenceau, Wintzenheim, 68000 Colmar.

Meyre (Fr) a vineyard in the commune of Avensan. A.C. Médoc, Bordeaux. Cru Bourgeois Supérieur.

Meyva Suyu (Tur) juice/fruit juice. See also Özsu.

Mezcal (Mex) the early distillation from the Blue Maguey cactus from which tequila originated 40%–44.5% alc by vol.

Mezcal Azul (Mex) **Lathophora williamsi** the Blue Maguey cactus from which tequila is made.

Mezcal Con Gusano (Mex) a tequila produced by Monte Alban 38% alc by vol.

Mezcal Wine (USA) the old name for tequila.

Mezclar (Sp) to mix or blend.

Mézesfehér (Hun) lit: 'honey white', a white grape variety grown in south-western Hungary.

Mezes Maly Aszú (Hun) a 6 puttonyos Tokaji wine from the Royal Tokaji Wine Company.

Mezquita [La] (Sp) lit: 'the Mosque', the largest brandy bodega in Spain. Belongs to Domecq. Produces Fundador, Carlos I and Carlos III brandies.

Mezzo (It) denotes half a litre of wine.

Mezzofiasco (It) see Fiasco.

M'Hudi Wines (S.Afr) a winery (established 2003) based in Koelenhof, Stellenbosch, Western Cape. Grape varieties: Chenin blanc, Pinotage, Sauvignon blanc. Produces varietal wines. Website: http://www.villiera.com

M.I.A. (Austr) abbr: Murrumbidgee Irrigation Area.

Mia (It) a natural spring mineral water from Mia.

Mia Bira (Gre) a request for a beer.

Miajados (Sp) a wine-producing area in Cáceres near Guadalupe, south-western Spain.

Miamba (Austr) a brand of soft red wine produced by Orlando in the Barossa Valley.

Miami (Cktl) ¾ measure white rum, ¼ measure (white) crème de menthe, dash lemon juice. Shake over ice and strain into a cocktail glass.

Mia Mia Vineyard (Austr) a winery. (Add): Rutherglen, Victoria 3685. 80ha. Grape varieties: Brown muscat, Cabernet sauvignon, Cinsault, Durif, Hermitage, Muscadelle, Palomino, Sémillon and Shiraz.

Miami Beach (Cktl) ⅓ measure Scotch whisky, ⅓ measure grapefruit juice, ⅓ measure French vermouth. Shake over ice and strain into a cocktail glass.

Miami Cocktail (Cktl) 1 part Dubonnet, 1 part dry Sherry, 2 dashes orange bitters. Shake well over ice, strain into a cocktail glass, add twist of orange peel and a cherry.

Mibram (Arab) corkscrew.

Michael (Cktl) ⅗ measure Scotch whisky, ⅕ measure anis, ⅕ measure orange juice. Shake over ice, strain into a cocktail glass and add a cherry.

Michael Cocktail (Cktl) 10mls (½fl.oz) dry gin, 25mls (1fl.oz) lime liqueur, dash crème de fraises. Stir over ice, strain into a cocktail glass and top with a spiral of lemon peel.

Michaeliskapelle (Ger) vineyard (Anb): Nahe. (Ber): Schloss Böckelheim. (Gro): Rosengarten. (Vil): Braunweiler.

Michael Juillot (Fr) a négociant-éleveur based in the Côte Chalonnaise, Burgundy.

Michaelsberg (Ger) vineyard (Anb): Baden. (Ber): Badische Bergstrasse/Kraichgau. (Gro): Mannaberg. (Vil): Bruchsal (ortsteil Untergrombach).

Michaelsberg (Ger) vineyard (Anb): Württemberg. (Ber): Württembergisch Unterland. (Gro): Heuchelberg. (Vil): Cleebronn.

Michaelsberg (Ger) vineyard (Anb): Württemberg. (Ber): Württembergisch Unterland. (Gro): Heuchelberg. (Vil): Eibensbach.

Michaelsberg (Ger) vineyard (Anb): Württemberg. (Ber): Württembergisch Unterland. (Gro): Heuchelberg. (Vil): Frauenzimmern.

Michaelsberg (Ger) vineyard (Anb): Württemberg. (Ber): Württembergisch Unterland. (Gro): Heuchelberg. (Vil): Güglingen.

Michalovce (Czec) a brewery in an eastern Czec town of same name that produces fine beers. Noted for Siravar (a malty dark lager), was known as Micholup.

Michaud [Alain] (Fr) a winery (13ha) based in Saint-Léger, Beaujolais, southern Burgundy. Produces A.C. Beaujolais Cru Brouilly.

M

Michel [José] (Fr) a Champagne producer. (Add): B.P. 16, Moussy, 51200 Épernay. Récoltants-manipulants. Produces vintage and non-vintage wines. Vintages: 1971, 1973, 1975, 1976, 1982, 1983, 1985, 1988, 1990, 1995, 1998, 1999, 2001.

Michelau i. Steigerwald (Ger) village (Anb): Franken. (Ber): Steigerwald. (Gro): Not yet assigned. (Vin): Vollburg.

Michelbach (Ger) village (Anb): Franken. (Ber): Mainviereck. (Gro): Not yet assigned. (Vins): Apostelgarten, Steinberg.

Michelbach a. W (Ger) village (Anb): Württemberg. (Ber): Württembergisch Unterland. (Gro): Lindelberg. (Vins): Deuhsteiger, Margarete.

Michele (S.Afr) the label for a red wine (Cabernet sauvignon, Cabernet franc and Merlot blend) produced by the Horse Mountain Wines winery, Paarl, Western Cape.

Michele (S.Afr) the label for a sparkling rosé wine (Red muscadel) produced by the Klawer Co-operative Cellars winery, Olifants River, Western Cape.

Michèle Aubéry-Laurent (Fr) a winery based in the A.C. Côtes-du-Rhône-Villages Vinsobres, Vaucluse. Label: Les Hauts de Gramenon.

Michele Laluce (It) a winery (established 2000) based in Ginestra, Basilicata region. Produces: D.O.C. Aglianico del Vulture.

Michelfeld (Ger) village (Anb): Baden. (Ber): Badische Bergstrasse/Kraichgau. (Gro): Stiftsberg. (Vins): Himmelberg, Sonnenberg.

Michel Forgeron (Fr) a Cognac producer based in the Grande Champagne district, Charente.

Michelin (Eng) a variety of cider apple.

Michel [Jean et Olivier] (Fr) a Champagne producer (12ha). (Add): 15, Rue Jean Jaurès, 51530 Moussy. Produces vintage and non-vintage Champagnes. Vintages: 1995, 1996, 1998, 1999. Label: Cuvée Les Mulottes.

Michel Lenique (Fr) a Champagne producer (established 1768). (Add): 20, Rue du Général de Gaulle, 51530 Pierry. Produces: Blanc de Blancs, Le Brut Selection, Le Millesime and Rosé. Vintages: 1989. 'E'mail: Champagne.Michel.Lenique@wanadoo.fr

Michel Loriot (Fr) a Champagne producer. Label: Cuvée Marie Léopold 100 Centenary Sec.

Michelmark (Ger) vineyard (Anb): Rheingau. (Ber): Johannisberg. (Gro): Deutelsberg. (Vil): Erbach.

Michelob (USA) a 5% alc by vol. bottled lager beer brewed by Anheuser-Busch in St. Louis. Has a higher gravity than Budweiser, contains less rice.

Michelob Golden (USA) a 5% alc by vol. light yellow coloured, bottled lager beer brewed by Anheuser-Busch in St. Louis.

Michelsberg (Ger) grosslage (Anb): Mosel-Saar-Ruwer. (Ber): Bernkastel. (Vils): Hetzerath, Minheim, Neumagen-Dhron, Piesport, Rivenich, Sehlem, Trittenheim.

Michelsberg (Ger) vineyard (Anb): Rheinhessen. (Ber): Nierstein. (Gro): Rheinblick. (Vil): Mettenheim.

Michelsberg (Ger) vineyard (Anb): Pfalz. (Ber): Mittelhaardt-Deutsche Weinstrasse. (Gro): Hochmess. (Vil): Bad Dürkheim.

Michelsberg (Ger) vineyard (Anb): Pfalz. (Ber): Mittelhaardt-Deutsche Weinstrasse. (Gro): Hochmess. (Vil): Ungstein.

Michelsberg (Ger) vineyard (Anb): Pfalz. (Ber): Südliche Weinstrasse. (Gro): Ordensgut. (Vil): Weyher.

Michel Torino (Arg) a winery based in the Salta region, northern Argentina. Website: http://www.micheltorino.com.ar

Michet (It) a sub-species of the Nebbiolo grape.

Michielon [Luiz] S.A. (Bra) one of Brazil's leading wine-producing companies.

Michigan (USA) a wine region on the edge of Lake Michigan. Best parts are Benton Harbor and Paw Paw. Concorde, Catawba and Delaware are most used vines. Cold Duck is produced here.

Micholup (Czec) see Michalovce.

Mickey (USA) see Mickey Finn.

Mickey Finn (Eng) a 5.5% alc by vol. New Year beer brewed by the Hull Brewery. See also Old Acquaintance (a Christmas beer).

Mickey Finn (USA) a drink into which has been added a drug to render the consumer unconscious.

Mickey's (USA) a strong bottled lager 5.6% alc by vol. brewed by the Heileman Brewery, La Crosse, Wisconsin.

Mick The Tick's 10000th Brew (Eng) a special beer brewed by Canuck Brewery, Rowley Regis, West Midlands.

Micro-Brasserie Biéres Artisanales (Fr) a brewery. (Add): 34 Place des Marias, F-69400 Villefranche-sur-Saône. Brews beers and lager.

Micro-Brewery (Eng) a small independent brewery, sometimes within a public house. Brews on a small scale, usually cask-conditioned ales.

Microbullage (Fr) the injecting of oxygen into tanks of wine to stimulate the slow oxidative maturation that occurs in barrels and which adds structure, complexity and colour to the wines.

Microclimat (Fr) micro-climate.

Micro-Climate (Eng) individual climatic conditions of areas within a country. Effects of winds, sun, frosts, mists, fogs etc. Also used to describe the climate within the vine canopy. see Macro-climate, Meso-climate. (Fr) = microclimat.

Micro-Flora (Eng) yeasts, bacteria and moulds.

Micro-Oxygenation (Eng) a term used in wine production to denote a regular supply of tiny bubbles purified air into fermenting wine in order to enhance the fruit and soften the tannins.

Micro Vinification (Eng) production of a wine from a single vine to test for the vines' suitability for wine making. Used to improve cloning.

Mid-Autumn Gold (Eng) a 4.2% alc by vol. golden ale brewed by Mauldon's Ltd., Suffolk.

Middelpos (S.Afr) a winery (established 1978) based in Swartland, Western Cape. 57ha. Grape varieties: Pinotage.

M

Middelvlei Estate (S.Afr) vineyards (established 1919) based in Stellenbosch, Western Cape. 130ha. (Add): P.O. Stellenbosch 7600. Grape varieties: Cabernet sauvignon, Chardonnay, Merlot, Pinotage, Shiraz, Tinta. Produces: Hagelsberg, Robyn and varietal wines. Website: http://www.middelvlei.co.za

Middle (Eng) a 5% alc by vol. ale brewed by the Blue Anchor Brewery, Cornwall.

Middle Rhine (Ger) the Mittelrhein.

Middle Rio Grande (USA) an A.V.A. area of New Mexico based near Alberquerque.

Middle Stave (Eng) the centre piece at the end of a cask in which the keystone (tap hole) is sited.

Middleton's Brewery (Eng) a brewery based at St. Helen Auckland, County Durham. Brews: Stainton Bitter 4.4% alc by vol.

Middle Wicket (Eng) a 4.2% alc by vol. cask-conditioned summer ale (part of Tapster's Choice range from Carlsberg-Tetley) available in June.

Middy (Austr) the term used in New South Wales for a 300mls (10fl.ozs) glass and in Western Australia for a 200mls (7fl.ozs) glass.

Midhurst Mild (Eng) a mild ale brewed by Ballard's Brewery Ltd., Hampshire.

Midi (Fr) a large wine area of south-west France. Contains the region of Roussillon and Languedoc, and the départements of Aude, Gard and Hérault. see Midi-Pyrénées.

Midi-Pyrénées (Fr) the full name of the Midi region of south-western France from the Pyrénées to the Massif Central.

Midi Vineyards (USA) a winery based in Lone Jack on the western border of Missouri. Produces hybrid wines.

Midland Craft Brewers Association (Eng) a group of 7 breweries: Warwickshire, Judges, Belvoir, Lloyds Country Beers, Lichfield, Church End, Shardlow (formed to promote quality cask-conditioned ales).

Midlands Licensed Victuallers Association (Eng) an organisation (established 1998). (Add): Larkfield, Ashlawn Road, Rugby, Warwickshire CV22 5QE.

Midlands Mild (Eng) a keg mild 1036 O.G. brewed by the John Smith Brewery for the West Midlands.

Midleton Distillery (Ire) a distillery based in southern Ireland which has pot and patent stills. Produces Redbreast.

Midnight (Cktl) ⅔ measure apricot brandy, ⅓ measure Cointreau, juice ¼ lemon. Shake over ice and strain into a cocktail glass.

Midnight Cocktail (Cktl) ¼ measure dry gin, ⅙ measure French vermouth, ⅙ measure Italian vermouth, dash Angostura, juice ¼ orange. Shake well over ice and strain into a cocktail glass. Also known as a Minnehaha cocktail.

Midnight Madness (Eng) a millennium ale brewed by the Saint Austell Brewery, Cornwall.

Midori (Jap) a musk melon liqueur made by the Suntory C°. 30% alc by vol. bright green in colour.

Midori Dawn (Cktl) 1 part Midori, 1 part vodka. Stir over ice in a highball glass and top with tonic water.

Midori Sharp (Cktl) 1 part Midori, 5 parts grapefruit juice. Serve in a highball glass over ice.

Midori Sour (Cktl) 3 parts Midori, 2 parts lemon juice, 1 egg white, ½ teaspoon castor sugar. Shake well over ice, strain into a cocktail glass and dress with a cherry.

Mid-Summer Gold (Eng) a summer ale 4% alc by vol. brewed by the Mauldons Brewery, Suffolk.

Midulla Vineyards (USA) a vineyard based north of Tampa, Florida. Produces American wines.

Mid-Winter Gold (Eng) a 4.5% alc by vol. golden ale brewed by Mauldon's Ltd., Suffolk.

Miel (Fr) lit: 'honey', the name given to invert sugar. See also Melaza.

Mié-r'lévaîe (Ch.Isles) teabreak.

Miers (Fr) a natural spring mineral water. Mineral contents (milligrammes per litre): Sodium 447mg/l, Calcium 430mg/l, Magnesium 253mg/l, Potassium 9.3mg/l, Bicarbonates 209.8mg/l, Sulphates 2790mg/l.

Mietersheim (Ger) village (Anb): Baden. (Ber): Breisgau. (Gro): Schutterlindenberg. (Vin): Kronenbühl.

Migdali (Gre) lit: 'almond-shaped', a clone of the Rhoditis grape.

Mighty Oak brewing C° (Eng) a brewery (established 1996). (Add): 14b West Station Yard, Spital Road, Maldon, Essex CM9 6TW. Brews: Burntwood Bitter 4% alc by vol., Mildon Gold 4.8% alc by vol. Website: http://www.mightyoakbrewery.co.uk 'E'mail: info@mightyoakbrewery.co.uk

Migliarini Wines (S.Afr) a winery (established 2002) based in Stellenbosch, Western Cape. Grape variety: Shiraz. Website: http://www.migliarini.co.za

Mignard (Fr) the brand-name of a sparkling white grape juice made by Cidréries Mignard, Bellot, 77510.

Mignon [Jules] (Fr) a Champagne producer based at Aÿ, Reims.

Mignotte [La] (Fr) a Premier Cru vineyard in the A.C. commune of Beaune, Côte de Beaune, Burgundy 2.41ha.

Migraine (Fr) the local name used for wine produced in Auxerre, north-central France.

Migration (USA) the label used by Duckhorn Vineyards for a red wine (Pinot noir) produced from grapes grown in the Anderson Valley, Mendocino County, California. see Goldeneye Vineyards.

Migration-Serengeti (S.Afr) the label for a range of wines produced by the Leidersburg Vineyards winery, Paarl, Western Cape.

Migration-Serengeti (S.Afr) a winery based in Stellenbosch, Western Cape. Grape varieties: Cabernet sauvignon, Merlot, Pinotage, Sauvignon blanc, Shiraz. Produces varietal wines.

Miguel del Arco (Sp) a black grape variety grown in Aragón, Rioja and Valencia.

Miguel Torres (Sp) a 12 year old brandy produced by Torres in Penedés.

M

Miguel Torres Special Reserve (Sp) a pot-stilled brandy aged 1 year in new oak then 10 years in cask by Torres in Penedés.

Mihalkovo (Bul) a natural spring mineral water. Mineral contents (milligrammes per litre): Sodium 436.3mg/l, Calcium 218mg/l, Magnesium 43.7mg/l, Potassium 21mg/l, Bicarbonates 1641.4mg/l, Chlorides 50.7mg/l, Fluorides 3.2mg/l. pH 6.5

Mijar (Mex) a term used to describe the cutting off of the growing spikes on the agave plant in order to obtain bigger hearts.

Mijn-Burg Wines (S.Afr) a winery (established 1999) based in Klapmuts, Paarl, Western Cape 130ha.

Mikado Cocktail (Cktl) 60mls (½ gill) Cognac, 2 dashes each of Angostura, orgeat, Curaçao and Noyau. Stir well over ice, strain into a cocktail glass, add a cherry and squeeze of lemon peel juice. Also known as Japanese Cocktail.

Mike's Red (S.Afr) a red wine (Cabernet sauvignon 79% and Cinsaut 21%) produced by Agterplaas Wines, Stellenbosch, Western Cape.

Miko Coffee Ltd (Eng) a coffee manufacturer (established 1982). (Add): Beverages House, 7 Ember Centre, Hersham Trading Estate, Hersham, Surrey KT12 3PU. Produces coffee, tea, cocoa and drinking chocolate. Owned by Miko NV (Belgium), originally known as Master Brew. Website: http://www.miko.co.uk 'E'mail: info@miko.co.uk

Mikulov (Czec) a wine district within the region of Bohemia. Produces some of the regions best white wines.

Mikve Israel (Isr) a dry full-bodied wine sold on the USA market.

Mil (Rus) a dessert wine produced in Baku.

Milano Winery (USA) a winery based in Mendocino County, California. Grape varieties: Cabernet sauvignon, Chardonnay, Gamay and Zinfandel. Produces varietal wines.

Milan Wines (USA) a winery based in Detroit, Michigan. Produces hybrid wines.

Mi Lao Chiu (Chi) a noted brand of rice wine produced in Shantung province from yellow rice. *See also* Shaoh-Sing Rice Wine.

Milawa Estate (Austr) a 60ha estate part of the Brown Brothers in Milawa, Victoria. Produce varietal wines.

Milch (Aus)(Ger) milk.

Mild (Eng) a dark, low-alcohol beer, brewed mainly in the Midlands and North. Usually darker than bitter due to the higher roasting of the malt and to caramel (also a light version made).

Mildara Blass (Austr) a winery at Wentworth Road, Merbein, Victoria. Owns the Beringer Group of Vineyards. Produces a range of Mildara, Wolf Blass, Yellowglen wines. *see* Domaine Beringer Blass.

Mildara Wines (Austr) a winery. (Add): Main Road, Coonawarra, South Australia. Vineyards at Coonawarra, Eden Valley and the Murray River in Victoria. Grape varieties: Cabernet sauvignon, Chardonnay, Riesling, Shiraz. Also specialise in Sherry and brandy.

Milde (Ger) pleasantly soft but undistinguished wine.

Mildew (Eng) a fungus which withers the leaves and berries of the vine, particularly in wet weather. Copper sulphate, quicklime and water are used to treat it. *see* Alforra, Oïidium and Peronospera. (Fr) = mildiou, (Port) = mildio/alforra.

Mildio (Port) mildew. *See also* Mangra.

Mildiou (Fr) mildew.

Mild Manners (Eng) a 3.8% alc by vol. rich dark full-bodied mild ale brewed by Ridleys Hartford End Brewery, Chelmsford, Essex.

Mildmay Brewery (Eng) a micro-brewery at Holbeton near Plymouth. Brews: Jolly's Centenary Bitter (J.C.B.), bottle-conditioned Original Old Horsewhip, Colour's Best, 50-1, Tipster, Patrick's Cream Stout 4.2% alc by vol.

Mildon Gold (Eng) a 4.8% alc by vol. golden ale brewed by the Mighty Oak Brewing C°. Ltd., Essex.

Mildstedter Urquelle (Ger) a natural spring mineral water from Mildstedt. Mineral contents (milligrammes per litre): Sodium 17mg/l, Calcium 75mg/l, Magnesium 3.3mg/l, Potassium 1.1mg/l, Bicarbonates 214mg/l, Chlorides 32.8mg/l, Sulphates 22mg/l, Fluorides 0.11mg/l, Silicates 26.3mg/l.

Mildura (Austr) a New South Wales district that produces good quality wines.

Mileranio (Sp) a solera gran reserva brandy produced by Luis Caballero.

Miles Mossop Wines (S.Afr) a winery (established 2004) based in Stellenbosch, Western Cape. Grape varieties: Cabernet sauvignon, Chenin blanc, Merlot, Petit verdot, Viognier. Label: Bordeaux Blend.

Milestone (USA) a Merlot and Cabernet blend red wine from Columbia Winery, Woodinville, Washington State.

Milestone Brewery C° (Eng) a brewery (established 2004). (Add): Great North Road, Cromwell, Newark, Nottinghamshire NG23 6JE. Brews: Black Pearl 4.3% alc by vol., Crusader 4.4% alc by vol., Lions Pride 3.9% alc by vol., Loxley Ale 4.2% alc by vol., Milestone IPA 4.1% alc by vol., Rich Ruby 4.5% alc by vol. Website: http://www.milestonebrewery.co.uk 'E'mail: sales@milestonebrewery.co.uk

Milgranet (Fr) a rare red grape variety grown in vineyards north-west of Toulouse.

Milk (Eng) a white fluid from the mammary glands of animals, a highly nutritional food of vitamins, fats, calcium (1200mg/l) and minerals, proteins (30g/l), lipides (35g/l), glucides 45g/l), sugar and water (86%–88%) and energy (2570kj/l–620kcal/l). (Arab) = haleeb, (Aus) = milch, (Chi) = niunai, (Cro) = mlijeko, (Czec) = milch, (Den) = mælk, (Fr) = lait, (Ger) = milch, (Gre) = gala, (Hol) = melk, (Hun) = toj, (Indo) = susu, (Ire) = crúim, (Isr) = halav, (It) = latte,

(Jap) = gyuu/nyuu, (Kor) = wooyu, (Lat) = lac, (Port) = leite, (Rus) = maloko, (Sp) = leche, (Swe) = mjölk, (Thai) = namnom, (Wal) = llaeth.

Milk-e-Pan'tch (Ch.Isles) a milk punch made either of rum or brandy, eggs and milk. Nutmeg or cinnamon sprinkled on top. Some have lime or lemon juice in. *See also* Milk o' Punch.

Milk of Amnesia (Eng) a nickname for beer in northern England.

Milk of the Aged (Fr) the term given to wine in France.

Milk o'Punch (Ch.Isles) eggs, sugar, milk and rum served in the Isle of Alderney on the first Sunday in May. The first drink a customer receives (free) on entering a bar.

Milk Punch (Cktl) 30mls (¼ gill) rum, 60mls (½ gill) brandy, milk, loaf sugar and lemon juice. Is bottled and will keep for long periods. Served with grated nutmeg. *See also* Milk o'Punch.

Milk Shake (Eng) a non-alcoholic cocktail of milk, fruit juices, syrups or cordials and sugar to taste. Usually blended. Ice cream is optional.

Milk Sherry (Eng) a style of Oloroso Sherry which has been sweetened and coloured (between Cream and Brown Sherries). Now called Bristol Milk (cannot be called Milk Sherry because of Trades Description Act).

Milk Stout (Eng) is now known as sweet stout due to the Trades Description Act (no milk in stout). Alternative name for English stout. Only the Guernsey Brewery bottle Milk Stout 1042 O.G. (was allowed to be called such – as outside U.K. legislation).

Milk Street Brewery (Eng) a brewery (established 1999). (Add): The Griffin, Milk Street, Frome, somerset BA11 3DB. Brews: B4 4% alc by vol., Beer 5% alc by vol., Gulp! 3.5% alc by vol., Nature Ale 3.8% alc by vol., Zig Zag Stout 4.5% alc by vol.

Mill (S.Afr) the label for a range of wine, red (Shiraz, Cinsaut and Cabernet franc blend) and late harvest white (Chenin blanc 90% and Muscadel 10%) produced by the Windmeul Co-operative Cellar, Paarl, Western Cape.

Millaman Estate (Chile) a winery based in the Central Valley. Grape variety: Zinfandel.

Millandes [Les] (Fr) a Premier Cru vineyard in the A.C. commune of Morey-Saint-Denis, Côte de Nuits, Burgundy 4.3ha.

Millardet de Grasset (Sp) root stock, a cross of *Vitis chasselas* and *Vitis berlandieri*. Grown in Valdepeñas, central Spain.

Millars (Ire) the label of a double distilled whiskey produced by the Cooley Distillery.

Millberg (S.Afr) the label for a range of wines produced by the Franschhoek Vineyards, Franschhoek, Western Cape.

Mill Brewery (Eng) a brewery (established 1983) based in Newton Abbot, Devon. Produces: cask-conditioned Janner's Ale 1038 O.G. and Devon Special 1043 O.G.

Millbrook (USA) a winery based in the Hudson River Region, New York State. Grape variety: Pinot noir. Label: Proprietor's Special Reserve.

Millbrook Estate (Austr) a winery based in Western Australia. Grape varieties include: Cabernet sauvignon, Merlot.

Millburn (Scot) a single malt whisky distillery based near Inverness, Nairnshire. A highland malt. Produces a vintage 1966 malt 43% alc by vol.

Mill Creek Vineyards (USA) a winery based in the Russian River Valley, Sonoma County, California. 27ha. Grape varieties: Cabernet sauvignon, Chardonnay, Gewürztraminer and Merlot. Produce varietal wines.

Mill Down (Eng) a vineyard (established 1951). (Add): Hambledon, Portsmouth, Hampshire. 2ha. Soil: chalk. Grape varieties: Auxerrois, Chardonnay, Pinot meunier, Pinot noir and Seyval blanc.

Millefiori (It) a herb liqueur on the style of Fior d'Alpi 40% alc by vol.

Millennium (Pol) a honey and strawberry juice-flavoured mead, amber in colour, sold in double-handled flasks.

Millenium (S.Afr) the label for a red wine (Cabernet sauvignon 53%, Cabernet franc, Malbec and Merlot blend) produced by the La Motte winery, Franschhoek, Western Cape.

Millennium Ale (Eng) an ale brewed by Gales Brewery, Horndean, Hampshire. The ale was stored in tank from April 1997 until 1998 when it will be bottled, ready for the year 2000.

Millennium Ale (Eng) a 9.5% alc by vol. ale brewed by King & Barnes Brewery, Horsham, West Sussex.

Millennium Ale (Eng) an 8.5% alc by vol. ale brewed by Mansfield Brewery, Littleworth, Mansfield, Notts (sold in numbered bottles).

Millennium Ale (Eng) a 4% alc by vol. cask-conditioned winter ale. Part of the Tapster's Choice range from Carlsberg-Tetley (was available in December 1999).

Millennium Ale (Eng) a 4% alc by vol. strong ale brewed by Ridleys Hartford End Brewery, Chelmsford, Essex.

Millennium Bridge Ale (Eng) a 3.8% alc by vol. brewed by the Mordue Brewery Ltd., Tyne & Wear.

Millennium Mayor's Ale (Eng) a 4% alc by vol. ale brewed by Photographer & Firkin micro-brewery in Ealing.

Millennium 2000 (Eng) a 10.5% alc by vol. bottled ale from Pitfield, north London.

Millerandage (Fr) grape clusters which do not ripen evenly and which contain some quasi-raisins which remain small, hard and green. Caused by lack of water and poor climatic conditions.

Miller Brewing Company (USA) a large brewery (established 1855) based in Milwaukee. Brews: Miller beers plus Löwenbräu under licence. Owned by Phillip Morris. *see* Miller Lite.

Miller Genuine Draft (USA) cold filtered bottled draught lager beer (un-pasteurised) 4.7% alc by vol. brewed by the Miller Brewing Company, Milwaukee.

M

Miller Lite (USA) a lightly hopped lager 1030–1034 O.G. brewed under licence by the Courage Brewery in Reading. Now known as Miller Pilsner.

Miller Pilsner (USA) the new name for Miller Lite. Brewed under licence by the Courage Brewery in Reading.

Millers Burgundy (Austr) the name used for the Pinot meunier.

Miller's Mile (S.Afr) the label for a range of red wines produced by the Klein Parys Vineyards winery, Suider-Paarl, Western Cape.

Millesimato (It) vintage.

Millésime (Fr) vintage date, year of manufacture.

Millésime Exceptionnel (Fr) a very fine vintage, an exceptional vintage, one that will be long lived (fine wines).

Millésimé Rare Brut (Fr) the label of a prestige cuvée Champagne produced by Laurent-Perrier.

Millesimes (Fr) an Armagnac produced by Damblat.

Milligan's Mist (Eng) a 3.8% alc by vol. mixed gas dispense smooth Irish Bitter produced by Ushers of Trowbridge.

Milliliter (USA) 1/1000 part of a liter (litre).

Millilitre (Euro) 1/1000 part of a litre.

Milling (USA) the first stage of the process of making whiskey, the breaking up of the grain kernel (70% grist, 20% husk and 10% flour) to release the starch in the mashing and cooking which follows.

Millionaire [1] (Cktl) 7/10 measure brandy, 1/10 measure orgeat, 1/10 measure orange Curaçao, 1/10 measure crème de noyeau, 2 dashes Angostura. Shake over ice and strain into a cocktail glass.

Millionaire [2] (Cktl) 40mls (1/3 gill) rye whiskey, 20mls (1/6 gill) grenadine, 2 dashes Curaçao, egg white. Shake well over ice, strain into a 125mls (5fl.oz) wine glass and add a dash of Pernod.

Millionaire [3] (Cktl) 1/3 measure apricot brandy, 1/3 measure sloe gin, 1/3 measure Jamaican rum, dash grenadine, juice of 1/2 lime or lemon. Shake over ice and strain into a cocktail glass.

Millionaire Cocktail (Cktl) 2/3 measure Bourbon whiskey, 1/3 measure Cointreau, 2 dashes grenadine, 1 egg white. Shake over ice and strain into a cocktail glass.

Million Dollar Cocktail (Cktl) 1 1/2 measures gin, 1/2 measure sweet vermouth, 2 teaspoons cream, 1 teaspoon lemon juice, 2 teaspoons pineapple juice, 1/2 egg white. Shake well over ice and strain into a Champagne flute.

Million Dollars (Cktl) 1/2 measure dry gin, 1/4 measure Cointreau, 1/4 measure Calvados. Shake over ice and strain into a cocktail glass.

Millipore Process (Eng) describes the special process of rinsing and sterilising the empty bottles before being filled and corked.

Mill Lane Mild (Eng) a 4% alc by vol. mild ale brewed by Hoggleys, Northamptonshire.

Mill Race Red (S.Afr) the label for a red wine produced by the Vergelegen winery, Stellenbosch, Western Cape.

Millram Ale (Eng) a dark ale brewed by Hardy and Hansons in Kimberley, Nottinghamshire.

Mills Reef Winery (N.Z) a winery. (Add): Moffat Road, Bethlehem, Tauranga. 8ha. Grape varieties: Chardonnay, Sauvignon blanc, Riesling, Cabernet sauvignon, Merlot.

Mill Station (S.Afr) the label for a range of wines (Chardonnay-Chenin blanc and Pinotage-Shiraz) produced by the Cape First Wines winery, Stellenbosch, Western Cape.

Millstone (Eng) the name used for the original grinding stone used to crack the malted barley into grist before the start of the brewing process. Also name for the stone used to 'mill' cider apples in a cider mill.

Millstone (S.Afr) the label for a red wine (Pinotage) produced by the Stettyn Winery, Worcester, Western Cape.

Millstone Brewery (Eng) a brewery. (Add): Unit 4 Vale Mill, Mossley, Ashton-under-Lyne, Lancashire OL5 9JL. Brews: A Millers Ale 3.8% alc by vol., Autumn Leaves 4.3% alc by vol., Christmas Ruby 4.7% alc by vol., Grain Storm 4.2% alc by vol., Millstone Edge 4.4% alc by vol., Summer Daze 4.1% alc by vol., Three Shires Bitter 4% alc by vol., Windy Miller 4.1% alc by vol. Website: http://www.millstonebrewery.co.uk 'E'mail: info@millstonebrewery.co.uk

Millstone Edge (Eng) a 4.4% alc by vol. ale brewed by the Millstone Brewery, Lancashire.

Millton Vineyard (N.Z) a bio-dynamic vineyard based at Papatu Road, Manatuke, Gisborne, North Island. 20ha. Grape varieties: Chardonnay, Riesling, Sémillon and a barrel fermented Chenin blanc.

Mill Valley (Can) a natural spring mineral water from Baltimore, Ontario.

Millwood Whiskey Cream (Hol) a coco liqueur, Dutch cream and Irish whiskey based liqueur produced by Koninklijke Cooymans B.V. S'Hertogenbosch 14.9% alc by vol.

Milly (Fr) a commune in the A.C. Chablis, Burgundy.

Milmanda (Sp) a single vineyard 15ha. Chardonnay produced by Torres in Penedés. Fermented and aged in small casks of Limousin oak.

Milroy's Malt Whisky (Scot) an 8 year old single malt whisky made by the Tullibardine distillery for Milroy's, Soho Wine Market, Greek Street, London. A highland malt 40% alc by vol.

Milsch Glass Tankard (Ger) a large glass beer tankard produced in the eighteenth century. Was highly decorated with a milk-white coloured background (often had a lid).

Miltenberg (Ger) village (Anb): Franken. (Ber): Mainviereck. (Gro): Not yet assigned. (Vin): Steingrübler.

Miltenberg Classic (Eng) a strong draught lager from the Dorset brewer Eldridge Pope.

Milton Brewery Cambridge Ltd (Eng) a brewery (established 1999). (Add): Unit 111, Norman Ind Estate, Cambridge Road, Cambridge, Cambridgeshire CB4 6AT. Brews: Cyclops 5.3% alc by vol., Electra 4.5% alc by vol., Jupiter 3.5% alc by vol., Mammon 7% alc by vol., Minotaur 3.3% alc by vol., Neptune

3.8% alc by vol., Pegasus 4.1% alc by vol. Website: http://www.miltonbrewery.co.uk 'E'mail: enquiries@miltonbrewery.co.uk

Milton-Duff Glenlivet (Scot) a single malt whisky distillery based west of Elgin in the Speyside. Owned by George Ballantine and Son Ltd. (part of the Hiram Walker group). A highland malt. Produces a 12 year old malt 40% alc by vol.

Milton Grove (S.Afr) a red wine (Shiraz) produced by the African Terroir winery, Paarl, Western Cape.

Milvea Cocktail (Cktl) 25mls (1fl.oz) dry gin, 10mls (½fl.oz) crème de banane, 10mls (½fl.oz) St. Raphaël, dash cream. Shake over ice, strain into a cocktail glass and top with a cherry.

Mimbres Valley (USA) an A.V.A. area of New Mexico based in the south-west.

Mimosa (Cktl) a dash of orange Curaçao, orange juice and Champagne. Fill a Champagne flute ⅓ full of orange juice, add Curaçao and top up with iced Champagne.

Mimsach (Isr) a 'Bible wine' described as being similar in character to a Port wine or liqueur.

Minalba (Bra) a natural spring mineral water. Mineral contents (milligrammes per litre): Sodium 1.2mg/l, Calcium 16.4mg/l, Magnesium 8.34mg/l, Potassium 0.8mg/l, Bicarbonates 95.44mg/l, Chlorides 0.21mg/l, Nitrates 0.6mg/l. pH 7.6

Minaqua (Euro) a natural spring mineral water (established 1908) from Fruskogorski Izvori, Serbia and Montenegro. Mineral contents (milligrammes per litre): Sodium 335mg/l, Calcium 24.8mg/l, Magnesium 23.1mg/l, Potassium 7.75mg/l, Bicarbonates 640mg/l, Chlorides 300.5mg/l. pH 5.91

Minas Gerais (Bra) a noted wine-producing estate in southern Brazil.

Minchinbury (Austr) a district in New South Wales. Noted for sparkling wines made by the méthode traditionelle.

Minchinbury Estate (Austr) a non-producing estate owned by Penfolds Winery. Sometimes used on their wine labels.

Mine Beer (Eng) a 4.2% alc by vol. bitter beer brewed by the Blindmans Brewery, Ltd., Somerset.

Minella Bianca (It) a white wine grape grown in Sicily.

Minéneral (Thai) a natural spring mineral water from Bangkok. Mineral contents (milligrammes per litre): Sodium 56mg/l, Calcium 30.4mg/l, Magnesium 11.6mg/l, Potassium 2.5mg/l, Bicarbonates 68.32mg/l, Chlorides 92mg/l, Sulphates 40mg/l, Silicates 13mg/l.

Mineraal Water (Hol) mineral water.

Minera Brewery (Wal) a brewery run by Lloyd and Trouncer in North Wales at the City Arms, Minera, Wrexham. Produces cask-conditioned ales.

Minéral (Fr) mineral.

Mineral Finings (USA) diatomaceous earth (i.e. bentonite).

Mineralised Water (Eng) a term used for bottled waters that have had minerals added to them to improve flavour and mineral content.

Mineral Natural Drink Water (Egy) a natural spring mineral water. Mineral contents (milligrammes per litre): Sodium 56mg/l, Calcium 30.4mg/l, Magnesium 11.6mg/l, Potassium 2.5mg/l, Bicarbonates 68.32mg/l, Chlorides 92mg/l, Sulphates 40mg/l, Fluorides 0.4mg/l, Silicates 13mg/l.

Mineralna Woda Jurajska (Pol) a natural spring mineral water. Mineral contents (milligrammes per litre): Sodium 2.3mg/l, Calcium 92.18mg/l, Magnesium 7.3mg/l, Potassium 0.65mg/l, Bicarbonates 225.77mg/l, Chlorides 37.28mg/l, Sulphates 14.8mg/l.

Mineral Neri (It) a sparkling natural spring mineral water from Fonte delle Rocche, Viterbo. Mineral contents (milligrammes per litre): Sodium 20.22mg/l, Calcium 33.2mg/l, Magnesium 10.23mg/l, Potassium 22.61mg/l, Bicarbonates 119.1mg/l, Chlorides 31.9mg/l, Sulphates 11.02mg/l, Fluorides 0.82mg/l, Nitrates 19.81mg/l, Silicates 68.6mg/l. pH 6.78

Mineral Plus (Pak) a still natural spring mineral water (established 2000) from Karachi. Mineral contents (milligrammes per litre): Sodium 8mg/l, Calcium 27mg/l, Potassium 2mg/l, Chlorides 43mg/l, Sulphates 25mg/l. pH 7.4

Minerals (Eng) substances found in the soil, sub-soil and in wine, such as iron, magnesium and calcium.

Mineralvand (Den) mineral water.

Mineralwasser (Aus)(Ger) mineral water.

Mineralwasser (Ger) a natural spring mineral water from Alwaris-Quelle, Sachsenheim. Mineral contents (milligrammes per litre): Sodium 68mg/l, Calcium 522mg/l, Magnesium 92mg/l, Bicarbonates 311mg/l, Chlorides 47mg/l, Sulphates 1490mg/l, Nitrates 1.7mg/l.

Mineral Water (Bra) a still natural spring mineral water (established 2000). Mineral contents (milligrammes per litre): Sodium 27.5mg/l, Calcium 47.8mg/l, Magnesium 5.81mg/l, Potassium 5.72mg/l, Bicarbonates 204.5mg/l, Chlorides 20.93mg/l, Sulphates 11.8mg/l, Fluorides 0.1mg/l, Nitrates 1.7mg/l. pH 7.67

Mineral Water (Eng) still or sparkling natural spring water that is rich in minerals. Each country has its own regulations. Strict E.U. regulations govern the use of the name Natural Mineral Water within the E.U. including maximum quanties of certain minerals such as Nitrates. e.g: Apollinaris, Brecon, Buxton, Malvern Perrier, Vichy, etc. *See also* Spring Water. (Arab) = ma'a ma'adani, (Aus) = mineralwasser/sprudel, (Chi) = kuangquanshui, (Den) = mineralvand/ dansk vand, (Fr) = eau minérale, (Ger) = mineralwasser/heilwasser/sprudel, (Gre) = nero bukaliou, (Hol) = mineraal water/spa water, (Indo) = air mineral, (Ire) = uisce mianra, (Isr) = ma-eem mineralim, (It) = acqua minerale, (Jap) = mineraru uootaa, (Kor) = gwangchunsoo, (Pol) = woda mineralna, (Port) = água mineral, (Rus) = meenyeralnaya vada, (Sp) = agua mineral, (Thai) = namrae. Website: http://www.mineralwaters.org

M

Mineraru Uootaa (Jap) mineral water.

Minéré (Thai) a natural spring mineral water from Pho Sam Ion and produced by Nestlé. Mineral contents (milligrammes per litre): Sodium 115.5mg/l, Calcium 22mg/l, Magnesium 7.7mg/l, Potassium 1.61mg/l, Bicarbonates 219mg/l, Chlorides 55.5mg/l, Sulphates 68mg/l, Fluorides 0.47mg/l. pH 7.8

Miners Arms (Eng) a home-brew public house (established 1981) based in Somerset. Produces cask-conditioned and bottled beers.

Miner Valley Vineyards (USA) a winery based in the Napa Valley, California. Label: Simpson Vineyard. Grape variety: Viognier.

Minervois (Fr) an A.C. (1985) wine-producing district in the Languedoc-Roussillon, Midi. Produces red (90%–95%), rosé and white wines. Minimum alc by vol. 11%.

Minervois la Livinière (Fr) a new AC. (1998) within the Minervois region in the Languedoc-Roussillon. 165ha. of Grenache, Mourvèdre and Syrah grapes. A 65% minimum Grenache, Mouvèdre and Syrah content, 15 month aging period before bottling, quality tasting before and after bottling, 12% alc by vol. minimum are all a part of the strict A.C. regulations for its wines.

Minfeld (Ger) village (Anb): Pfalz. (Ber): Südliche Weinstrasse. (Gro): Guttenberg. (Vin): Herrenberg.

Mingolsheim und Langenbrücken (Ger) village (Anb): Baden. (Ber): Badische Bergstrasse/Kraichgau. (Gro): Mannaberg. (Vin): Goldberg.

Minhão (Port) *see* Minho. Alternative spelling.

Minheim (Ger) village (Anb): Mosel-Saar-Ruwer. (Ber): Bernkastel. (Gro): Michelsberg. (Vins): Burglay, Günterslay, Kapellchen, Rosenberg.

Minho (Port) a wine region of north-west Portugal that contains the DOC Vinho Verde. Vinho Verde wines can be red, rosé or white and the 'green' refers to the wine's age, the wines tend to be pétillant from the malo-lactic fermentation that takes place in bottle or more commonly now from CO_2 injection.

Minho [River] (Port) a river that runs through the Vinho Verde region.

Miniature [Nip] (USA) a small measure 1.6fl.ozs (45mls) used as a measure for cocktails.

Minicellar (Eng) a large range of mini scewcapped bottles of most popular world brands marketed by Read's World of Wine Ltd (Add): 48, Broadway, Maidenhead, Berkshire SL6 1PW. Website: http://www.readswow.com

Minieri (It) a natural spring mineral water from Santo Stefano, Lanterria.

Minifundio (Sp) a process of land division into small plots given to each peasant to farm. In wine areas the grapes produced on the plots are usually vinified in co-operatives.

Minis (Rum) a red wine-producing area, part of the Banat Vineyard. Grape varieties: Cabernet and Kardarka. *see* Kardarka de Banat.

Ministrel (Sp) a black grape variety grown in the Aragón, Rioja Baja and Catalonia. *see* Monastel.

Minke Wines (S.Afr) a winery based in Stellenbosch, Western Cape. Grape variety: Pinot noir.

Minkowitsch (Aus) a winery based in Mannersdorf an der March, Weinviertel. (Add): 2261 Mannersdorf an der March 64. Grape varieties: Chardonnay, Gewürztraminer, Riesling, Welschriesling. Produces a range of dry and sweet wines.

Minnehaha Cocktail (Cktl) same as a Midnight Cocktail.

Minnis Ale (Eng) a 4.5% alc by vol. malty beer from the Rose and Crown (a micro-brewery), Stelling Minnis, near Canterbury. *See also* Legion, Withey's Warmer.

Minorca (Sp) part of the Balearic Islands off the south coast of Spain. Two main producers are Alayor and San Luis.

Minos (Gre) the brand-name for a red wine produced on the island of Crete.

Minöségi Bor (Hun) best quality wine. Equivalent to Q.W.P.S.R. in the E.C. *See also* Asztali Bor.

Minotaur (Eng) a 3.3% alc by vol. light ale brewed by the Milton Brewery Cambridge Ltd., Cambridgeshire.

Min Pin Inn (Eng) a home-brew public house based in Tintagel, north Cornwall. Brews: cask-conditioned Legend and Brown Willy.

Minra (Pak) a natural spring mineral water brand.

Minskaya 4 (Euro) a natural spring mineral water from Minsk, Belarus.

Minsterley Ale (Eng) a 4.5% alc by vol. amber-coloured, bottle-conditioned bitter beer brewed by the Salopian Brewing Company Ltd. (Add): 67 Mytton Oak Road, Shrewsbury, Shropshire.

Minstrel Mac (Eng) the brand-name of a whisky and ginger wine drink.

Mint Cocktail (Cktl) 60mls (½ gill) crème de menthe, 60mls (½ gill) lime juice, dash Angostura. Stir in a highball glass with ice, top up with soda water, serve with slices of fruit and fresh mint on top.

Mint Coffee (Cktl) 4 parts hot coffee, 1 part crème de menthe, 1 part crème de cacao. Heat coffee and liqueurs, place in a glass and top with cream.

Mint Collins (Cktl) 1 measure dry gin, ½ measure crème de menthe, juice ½ lemon, 6 mint leaves. Shake over ice, strain into an ice-filled highball glass, top with soda water, a slice of lemon and a sprig of mint and serve with straws.

Mint Cooler (Cktl) 1 dash crème de menthe, 300mls (½ pint) ginger ale, 2–3 sprigs of mint. Squash mint in a highball glass, add other ingredients and ice cubes, stir well and decorate with mint sprigs.

Mint Highball (Cktl) place 25mls (⅕ gill) crème de menthe into a highball glass, top with ginger ale and dress with a sprig of mint.

Mint Julep [1] (Cktl) dissolve 5 sprigs of mint in sugar and a little hot water until flavour is extracted. Strain into a bar glass, add ice and 90mls (¾ gill) old Cognac, stir well, strain into a julep glass and top with a dash of rum. The glass

M

is decorated with mint leaves dipped in icing sugar.

Mint Julep [2] (Cktl) 1 measure Bourbon whiskey, 1 tablespoon hot water, 1 tablespoon castor sugar. Put 4–5 mint leaves into a highball glass, crush with the sugar and water. Add whiskey and fill with crushed ice, stir until outside of glass is frosted, decorate with sprigs of mint and serve with straws.

Mint Julep Glass (USA) a large glass shaped like bowl 300mls (10fl.ozs) capacity.

Minton Spring Water (Eng) a spring water from Devon, bottled at source in the Dartmoor Valley (still or carbonated).

Mint on the Rocks (Cktl) 1 measure crème de menthe served over ice in an old-fashioned glass.

Mint Royal Cocktail (Cktl) ⅓ measure Royal Mint Chocolate Liqueur, ⅓ measure brandy, ⅓ measure lemon juice, 1 egg white. Shake over ice and strain into a cocktail glass.

Minuet (S.Afr) a medium dry white wine made from the Steen grape with 13% of Muscat d'Alexandria and 5% Gewürztraminer added. Made by the Villiera Estate, Paarl.

Minuman (Indo) beverage/drink.

Minya Vineyard and Winery (Austr) a winery (established 1974). (Add): Minya Lane, Coonawarra, Victoria. Grape varieties: Cabernet sauvignon, Gewürztraminer, Grenache, Merlot, Shiraz.

Mionetto Spumanti (It) a winery based in Cartizze. Produces Grappa and Prosecco sparkling wines.

Miousap (Fr) a rare white grape variety grown in Gascony.

Mira (Hun) a natural spring mineral water. Mineral contents (milligrammes per litre): Sodium 4800mg/l, Calcium 230mg/l, Magnesium 496mg/l, Bicarbonates 1226mg/l, Chlorides 2700mg/l, Sulphates 8060mg/l.

Mira (Pol) a natural spring mineral water from Miroslawiec. Mineral contents (milligrammes per litre): Sodium 4.5mg/l, Calcium 58.6mg/l, Magnesium 11.1mg/l, Potassium 1.9mg/l, Bicarbonates 208mg/l, Chlorides 4.3mg/l, Sulphates 24.3mg/l.

Mirabelle (Fr) a plum brandy made from cherry plums, an alcool blanc 43%–45% alc by vol.

Mirabelle de Lorraine (Fr) a plum brandy made from cherry plums in Lorraine north-eastern France.

Mirabelle Fine du Val de Metz (Fr) a fine plum brandy from north-eastern France that is fermented with special yeasts, wood-aged 2 months and double-distilled.

Miracle (Pak) a sparkling natural spring mineral water. Mineral contents (milligrammes per litre): Sodium 16mg/l, Calcium 14mg/l, Magnesium 11mg/l, Potassium 0.7mg/l, Chlorides 36mg/l, Sulphates 29mg/l. pH 7.3

Miracle of Carna (Isr) the miracle of Christ turning water into wine.

Mirador [Le] (S.Afr) a dry white wine with a touch

of pink made from the Cabernet grape by Boschendal Estate in Paarl.

Miraflores (Sp) an area within Andalusia near Sanlúcar where vineyards of Sherry grapes are grown.

Mirage (Eng) a citrus fruit, white wine and vodka-based drink 14.9% alc by vol. produced by William Grant and Bulmer (joint) subsidiary companies.

Miramar Vineyard (Austr) a vineyard. (Add): Henry Lawson Drive, Eurunderee, Via Mudgee, New South Wales 2850. 20ha. Grape varieties: Cabernet sauvignon, Chardonnay, Rhine riesling, Sémillon and Shiraz.

Miranda (Sp) a low alcohol sangría 5% alc by vol. red and white styles produced.

Miranda Brothers (Austr) a winery (established 1938). (Add): Irrigation Way, Griffith, New South Wales 2680. Grape varieties: Cabernet sauvignon, Sauvignon blanc, Sémillon, Shiraz. Produces still and sparkling wines, vermouth, Marsala and cocktail nips.

Mirande Distillery (S.Am) a noted white rum distillery based in Guyana.

Mirassou Winery (USA) a winery based in Monterey County, California. 208ha. Grape varieties: Cabernet sauvignon, Chardonnay, Gewürztraminer, Pinot noir and Zinfandel. Produces sparkling and varietal wines.

Mireval (Fr) an A.C district within the Languedoc-Roussillon region of southern France.

Mirgorodska (Ukr) a natural spring mineral water from Mirgorod. Mineral contents (milligrammes per litre): Sodium 1050mg/l, Calcium 50mg/l, Magnesium 25mg/l, Bicarbonates 350mg/l, Chlorides 1400mg/l, Sulphates 275mg/l.

Mirin (Jap) a sweet saké, usually used in cooking.

Mirita (Port) a brand of Vinho Verde from Aliança.

Mirlo (Sp) a white wine produced by Bodegas Ayuso in La Mancha.

Miroir (Fr) the name given to the lower half of the Champagne cork that is in contact with the wine, consists of 2–3 discs of cork. *See also* Agglomeré.

Miron Spring (Isr) a natural spring mineral water from Miron. Mineral contents (milligrammes per litre): Sodium 12mg/l, Calcium 90mg/l, Magnesium 10mg/l, Potassium 2mg/l, Bicarbonates 260mg/l, Chlorides 29mg/l, Sulphates 9mg/l, Nitrates 19mg/l. pH 7.4

Mirum (It) a 100% Verdicchio I.G.T. wine produced by Fattoria La Monacesca in the Marche.

Miru Miru (N.Z) a sparkling wine made using the traditional method in Marlborough by Hunters.

Misa (Sp) the brand-name for a range of Sherries produced by Marqués de Misa in Jerez de la Frontera.

Mis au Domaine (Fr) bottled at the vineyard.

Mischa Estate (S.Afr) a winery based in the Wellington. Grape varieties include: Cabernet sauvignon.

Misch (USA) a black grape variety of the wild vine **Vitis rotundifolia** known as a Muscadine.

Mischa Estate (S.Afr) a winery (established 1999)

M

based in Wellington, Western Cape. 40ha. Grape varieties: Cabernet sauvignon, Merlot, Shiraz, Viognier. Label: The Eventide. Website: http://www.mischa.co.za

Mischlultur Gemischter Satz (Aus) the process of growing a selection of grape varieties in the same vineyard, harvesting them together and making a single wine from them.

Miscible (Eng) to be capable of mixing, drinks must be this for use in cocktails (some are not).

Mise dans nos Caves (Fr) bottled in our cellars, not necessarily those of the grower.

Mise d'Origine (Fr) bottled at the place of origin.

Mise du Château (Fr) bottled at the Château.

Mise du Domaine (Fr) bottled at the property where it is made in Bordeaux, bottled by the owner in Burgundy.

Mise en Bouteille par les Producteurs Réunis (Fr) on a bottle label denotes 'bottled by a co-operative'.

Mise en Bouteilles à la Propriété (Fr) bottled by the proprietor.

Mise en Bouteilles au Domaine (Fr) domaine bottled.

Mise en Bouteilles au Gare (Fr) bottled at the station (plant).

Mise en Bouteilles aux Réflets (Fr) bottled by the union of the leading proprietors of Châteauneuf-du-Pape. Only found on the finest wines' labels.

Mise en Bouteilles dans nos Caves (Fr) bottled by ourselves in our cellars.

Mise en Bouteilles dans nos Chais (Fr) bottled by ourselves in our warehouses.

Mise en Bouteilles en France (Fr) bottled in France/French bottled.

Mise en Bouteilles par le Propriétaire (Fr) bottled by the Proprietor.

Mise en Masse (Fr) the stacking of the bottles in Champagne upside down in the cellars with the neck of one resting in the punt of the other (sur point) after remuage. Allows the wine to age.

Mise-en-Place (Fr) getting everything ready before mixing a cocktail, decanting wines etc.

Mis en Bouteille (Fr) bottled.

Mis en Bouteilles au Château (Fr) château bottled.

Mis en Cave (Fr) a term used on Champagne labels by Charles Heidsieck to inform when the bottle was laid down in the cellar, introduced in 1992 for their non-vintage Brut Réserve.

Mise par le Propriétaire (Fr) bottled by the growers.

Mise Sur Lie (Fr) bottled off its lees. *see* Sur Lie.

Mise Sur Point (Fr) a term used during Champagne remuage, refers to the gradual turning upside down of the bottles on the pupître.

Misia (It) a sparkling natural spring mineral water from Misia, Perugia. Mineral contents (milligrammes per litre): Sodium 3.3mg/l, Calcium 67mg/l, Magnesium 3.2mg/l, Potassium 0.79mg/l, Bicarbonates 195mg/l, Chlorides 5.9mg/l, Sulphates 18mg/l, Nitrates 1.5mg/l, Silicates 6.8mg/l. pH 7.72

Misiones de Rengo (Chile) a winery based in the Cachapoal Valley, Central Chile.

Misket (Bul) a white grape variety which produces dry, fruity wines, produced as a result of crossing Dimiat x Riesling.

Misket de Karlovo (Bul) a dry white wine from the Misket grape.

Misket Karlova (Bul) *see* Misket de Karlovo.

Misleidende Reklame (Hol) the Dutch Trade Description Act.

Missery et Frère (Fr) a Burgundy négociant based at Nuits-Saint-Georges, Côte de Nuits, Burgundy.

Mission (USA) a name given to an early Spanish variety taken to America by Franciscan friars (1520) into California. So called because it was planted at their missions. Known as País in Chile. Possibly the same as Monica in Spain and Sardinia.

Mission Haut Brion [La] (Fr) *see* Château la Mission Haut Brion.

Mission Hill (Can) a winery based at Mission Hill 49 North, Okanagan Valley, British Columbia. Grape varieties: Bacchus, Chardonnay, Pinot noir, Riesling.

Mission San Jose (USA) a wine-producing town near the south boundary of Alameda County, California.

Missionvale (S.Afr) the label for a white wine (Chardonnay) produced by the Bouchard Finlayson winery, Walker Bay, Western Cape.

Mission Vineyard (N.Z) a winery based in Green Meadows, Taradale, Hawkes Bay, North Island. 45ha. Grape varieties: Cabernet sauvignon, Chardonnay, Chasselas, Gewürztraminer, Merlot, Müller-Thurgau, Pinot gris, Rhine riesling, Sauvignon blanc and Sémillon. Produces varietal and table wines.

Mississippi Planters Punch (Cktl) ½ measure brandy, ¼ measure white rum, ¼ measure Bourbon whiskey, juice of a lemon, sugar syrup to taste. Shake over ice, strain into an ice-filled collins glass, top with soda water and stir.

Mississippi Steamer (Eng) a brand drink made from a blend of dark fine old Bourbon with citrus lemon and orange flavours.

Missouri (USA) a white grape variety, a cross between the *Vitis labrusca* and the *Vitis riparia*.

Missouri (USA) a wine region in north-western USA. Produces wine in the Missouri River Valley and Ozark mountains in the southern part of the state. It was granted the first appellation of America by the B.A.T.F. in 1980.

Missouri Riesling (USA) a white grape variety, a cross between the *Vitis riparia* and the *Vitis labrusca*.

Missouri River Valley (USA) a wine district within the Missouri region of north-western USA.

Miss Prettyman (Scot) the name given to a small whisky flask of salt-glazed stoneware 6 inches (15cms) high and embossed with a lady. Made in circa 1846 by Doulton and Watts.

Miss Saucy (Eng) a 4.3% alc by vol. ale brewed by George Bateman & Son Ltd., Lincolnshire.

Mis Sur Point (Fr) the turning of the bottle in Champagne by the Remueur. (*See* Mise Sur Point).

M

Miss Whiplash (Eng) a summer ale brewed by Batemans, Salem Bridge Brewery, Wainfleet, Skegness, Lincolnshire.

Mist (Eng) a range of sparkling flavoured English spring waters from Britvic. Flavours include: apple, damson and raspberry.

Mistela (Port)(Sp) grape juice that has been fortified with brandy to prevent fermentation (used to sweeten fortified wines).

Mistelas (Sp) see Mistela.

Mistelas (Sp) sweet red, rosé or white 'muté' wines 14%–17% alc by vol. (Fr) = vin doux naturel.

Mistelas Moscatel (Sp) a sweet, golden-coloured wine 17% alc by vol.

Mistelas Rosé (Sp) medium-sweet, fortified wines 14%–17% alc by vol.

Mistella (It) fortified grape juice used for sweetening fortified wines and vermouths.

Mistelle (Fr) fortified grape juice (must and brandy) used for the sweetening of vermouths and fortified wines. Term also applies to local muted wine musts such as Pineau des Charentes (Cognac). (It) = mistella, (Port) = mistela, (Sp) = mistela.

Mistletoe Mull (Cktl) 550mls (1pint) water, 1 bottle red Burgundy, 4 cloves, 2 lemons, 200grms (½ lb) granulated sugar, 1 stick cinnamon. Boil water with sugar and spices for 5 minutes, add thinly sliced lemon, infuse 10 minutes, add wine and serve very hot.

Mistra (Fr) an aniseed-flavoured spirit (pastis).

Mistral (Fr) a violent, cold dry katabatic wind that blows down the Rhône Valley. Helps to clean the vines of aphids and diseases.

Mistral Special (Cktl) 35mls (1½fl.ozs) cherry whisky liqueur, 20mls (¾ fl.oz) Scotch whisky, 20mls (¾ fl.oz) Vieille Cure, dash lime juice. Shake over ice, strain into an ice-filled highball glass and top with bitter orange.

Misty (Cktl) ⅓ measure Cointreau, ⅓ measure vodka, ⅓ measure apricot brandy, dash lemon juice, dash crème de banane. Shake over ice, strain into a highball glass, decorate with a slice of orange, cherry and straws.

Misty (Hol) a dairy-based, tropical fruit-flavoured liqueur 14.9% alc by vol.

Misty Cooler (Cktl) 25mls (1fl.oz) Irish Mist, 50mls (2fl.ozs) lemon juice, dash grenadine, dash egg white. Shake over ice, strain into a highball glass with ice and top with soda water.

Misty Mountain Springs (Austr) a still natural spring mineral water (established 1996) from Wyndham, New South Wales. Mineral contents (milligrammes per litre): Sodium 18mg/l, Calcium 5.2mg/l, Magnesium 2.7mg/l, Potassium <1mg/l, Bicarbonates 38mg/l, Chlorides 13mg/l. pH 6.8

Misty Point (S.Afr) the label for a white (Chenin blanc, Gewürztraminer and Chardonnay blend) and red (Merlot and Ruby cabernet blend) produced by the Southern Cape Vineyards winery, Barrydale, Little Karoo

M.I.T. (Eng) abbr: Methyl isothiocyanate.

Mitad y Mitad (Sp) the name given to equal quantities of mature Sherry and alcohol used in the fortification of Sherry. See also Combinado, Mistela, Miteado and Paxarete.

Mitans [Les] (Fr) a Premier Cru vineyard in the A.C. commune of Volnay, Côte de Beaune, Burgundy 4ha.

Mitarbi (Geo) a natural spring mineral water brand.

Mitchell and Cº. (Scot) are Campbeltown whisky distillers based at Springbank. Produce a 12 year old deluxe blended whisky at 43% alc by vol. Brands include Longrow and Springbank.

Mitchell [Edgar] Distillery (Afr) a distillery owned by Leroy Francis in Liberia. Produces a large range of spirits.

Mitchells and Butlers (Eng) a company owned by Bass. Breweries are the Highgate Brewery in Walsall, Staffordshire, Cape Hill, Birmingham and the Springfield Brewery in Wolverhampton, Staffordshire. Noted for their cask-conditioned Brew X1 1040 O.G. Keg DPA 1033 O.G. bottled Sam Brown 1035 O.G. and Allbright 1040 O.G.

Mitchells Brewery (Eng) a brewery based at 11 Moor Lane, Lancaster. Brews: Mitchells Bitter, Dark Mild, ESB (Bitter), Bomber, Christmas Cracker, Fortress, Guy Fawkes, Old Faithful (autumn ale), Priory Porter, Scarecrow Bitter, Single Malt (winter warmer cask ale).

Mitchells Winery (Austr) a small winery based in the Clare Valley, South Australia. Grape varieties: Cabernet sauvignon and Riesling. Produce varietal wines. Labels: Peppertree Vineyard, Sevenhill Vineyard.

Mitchelton Winery (Austr) a winery. (Add) Nagambie, Victoria 3608. 100ha. Grape varieties: Cabernet sauvignon, Chardonnay, Marsanne, Rhine riesling, Sémillon and Trebbiano. Noted for a wood-aged Marsanne and a botrytised Riesling.

Miteado (Sp) the alternative name for Mitad y Mitad.

Mit Hefe (Ger) lit: 'with yeast', refers to the weizenbiers which have a sediment and the customer requests to have the sediment served with the beer.

Mitigation (Eng) a 4.2% alc by vol. ale brewed by the Edale Brewery Cº., Derbyshire.

Mitolo (Austr) a winery based in the McLaren Vale, Soiuth Australia. Labels: Reiver and Savitar.

Mitsikeli (Gre) a natural spring mineral water from Ioannina. Mineral contents (milligrammes per litre): Sodium 2.3mg/l, Calcium 96.4mg/l, Magnesium 3.5mg/l, Potassium 0.4mg/l, Bicarbonates 297mg/l, Chlorides 8.4mg/l, Sulphates 2.4mg/l, Nitrates 5mg/l.

Mitsuko's Vineyard (USA) the label for a white wine (Chardonnay) produced by the Clos Pegase Winery, St. Helena, Napa, California.

Mittelbach (Aus) a winery based in the Wachau. (Add): Unterloiben 12, 3601 Loiben. Grape varieties: Feinburgunder, Grüner veltliner, Pinot gris, Riesling. Produces a range of dry and sweet (botrytised) wines.

M

Mittelberg (Ger) vineyard (Anb): Nahe. (Ber): Schloss Böckelheim. (Gro): Paradiesgarten. (Vil): Bayerfeld-Steckweiler.

Mittel-Burgenland (Aus) a sub-wine region of Burgenland (2107ha) based near Lake Neusiedl. Main Cru districts: Deutschkreuz, Gfanger, Hochberg, Horitschon. Soil: basalt, crystalline, gravel, loam, marl and sand. Main grape varieties are white (30%): Pinot blanc, Welschriesling, red (70%): Blaufränkisch, Cabernet sauvignon, Zweigelt.

Mittelhaardt (Ger) a vineyard area of the Pfalz in that section of the Weinstrasse which lies between Bad Dürkheim in the north and Rupertsberg in the south. Soils: basalt, loam, loess, limestone and sandstone.

Mittelheim (Ger) village (Anb): Rheingau. (Ber): Johannisberg. (Gro): Erntebringer. (Vins): Edelmann, Goldberg, St. Nikolaus.

Mittelheim (Ger) village (Anb): Rheingau. (Ber): Johannisberg. (Gro): Honigberg. (Vins): Edelmann, St. Nikolaus.

Mittelhochkultur (Aus) medium-high culture, a method of vine cultivation.

Mittelhölle (Ger) vineyard (Anb): Rheingau. (Ber): Johannisberg. (Gro): Erntebringer. (Vil): Johannisberg.

Mittelhölle (Ger) a vineyard within the village of Johannisberg, 6.5ha. (100%) of which is proposed to be classified as Erstes Gewächs.

Mittelmosel (Ger) the middle section of the Mosel.

Mittelrhein (Ger) anbaugebiet (Bers): Bacharach, Lorelei, Rheinburgengau.

Mittelrhein Wine Festivals (Ger) see Weinblütenfest, Weinlesefest, Weinwoche and Weinfest.

Mittelwihr (Fr) a commune of the Haut-Rhin in Alsace.

Mitterbad (It) a natural spring mineral water from Mitterbad, St. Pankraz, Bozen. Mineral contents (milligrammes per litre): Sodium 15.3mg/l, Calcium 120mg/l, Magnesium 13mg/l, Potassium 14.3mg/l, Chlorides 1.6mg/l, Sulphates 418mg/l, Fluorides 3.4mg/l, Manganese 1.97mg/l, Aluminium 2.12mg/l, Silicates 22mg/l.

Mittervernatsch (It) the German name for the red grape variety from the Südtirol. Known as the Schiava media in Italian.

Mitterweg (Aus) a vineyard site on the banks of the River Danube in the Kremstal region.

Mitz (Isr) juice/fruit juice.

Mitz Tapuzeem (Isr) orange juice.

Mit Zugestzter Kohlensaeure (Ger) when found on a wine label denotes 'with added carbonic acid'.

Mivela (Euro) a natural spring mineral water (established 1901) from Veluce, Serbia and Montenegro. Mineral contents (milligrammes per litre): Sodium 123mg/l, Calcium 26.9mg/l, Magnesium 347mg/l, Potassium 9.8mg/l, Bicarbonates 2111mg/l, Chlorides 12.6mg/l, Sulphates 10mg/l, Fluorides 0.41mg/l, Nitrates 15mg/l.

Mix (Cktl) place ingredients in the cone of electric drink blender, add crushed ice, mix, pour or strain into chosen glass.

Mixed Case (Eng) a wine merchants' term for a case (12 bottles) of wine that is not all of the same kind.

Mixed Drink (Eng) a combination of more than one beverage whether they be alcoholic or non-alcoholic. i.e. cocktails.

Mixers (USA) non-alcoholic drinks that make up the bulk of a long cocktail. i.e. mineral water, soda, tonic, ginger ale etc.

Mixing Glass (Eng) a glass jug for the mixing (stirring) of cocktails that has no handle.

Mixing Spoon (Eng) a spoon holding about the same amount as a teaspoon but with a very long handle for stirring. May also have a muddlers disc on base. Also called a Barspoon.

Mixologist (USA) the nickname for a cocktail barman.

Mizu (Jap) water.

Mizzen Mast (Eng) a 4.4% alc by vol. ale brewed by the George Wright Brewing C°., Merseyside.

Mjöd (Swe) mead.

M J Special (Cktl) ¼ measure Cognac brandy, ¼ measure Dubonnet, ¼ measure apricot brandy, ¼ measure orange squash, 1 egg white, dash grenadine. Shake over ice and strain into a cocktail glass.

Mlynsky (Czec) a natural spring mineral water. Mineral contents (milligrammes per litre): Sodium 1682mg/l, Magnesium 43.54mg/l, Potassium 93.04mg/l, Bicarbonates 2019mg/l, Chlorides 591.1mg/l, Sulphates 1579mg/l, Fluorides 7.02mg/l, Lithium 2.746mg/l, Silicates 73.7mg/l.

MM (Eng) the name for the millennium celebration ale brewed by Adnams Sole Bay Brewery, Southwald, Suffolk.

Mme Marlbrook (S.Afr) the label for white wine (50% Sémillon plus Chardonnay, Muscat de Frontignon and Sauvignon blanc blend) produced by the Klein Constantia Estate winery, Constantia, Western Cape.

MM Millennium ale (Eng) a 4.7% alc by vol. seasonal ale brewed by J.W. Lees of Manchester.

M.O. (Eng) abbr: on a wine-list denotes Mise d'Origine.

Mobbie (W.Ind) a spirit produced from potatoes on the island of Barbados.

Mocasina (It) a variety of the red grape Groppello.

Moc-Baril (Fr) a producer of Touraine rosé pétillant based at Saumur, Loire.

Mocca (Eng) a term used to describe the taste of Tokaji Azsú.

Mocha Coffee (Arab) a fine coffee from Arabia (now Yemen) that has a winey flavour, beans are yellowish in colour, often produced as for Ethiopean Coffee. Was named after city first grown in. Also a pure coffee of Ethiopia.

Mocha Ice Cream Soda (Cktl) place a portion of ice cream into a highball glass, add a tot of liqueur or

M

coffee essence, top up with soda water and serve with straws.

Mocha Mint [1] (Cktl) ⅓ measure Kahlúa, ⅓ measure crème de cacao, ⅓ measure (white) crème de menthe. Shake over ice and strain into an ice-filled highball glass.

Mocha Mint [2] (Cktl) ½ measure Tia Maria, ½ measure (white) crème de menthe. Shake over ice, strain into an ice-filled (crushed ice) highball glass and serve with straws.

Mockingbird (Cktl) 1 measure tequila, 75mls (3fl.ozs) grapefruit juice, dash lime juice. Fill an old-fashioned glass with ice cubes, add ingredients, stir and garnish with a cherry.

Möckmühl (Ger) village (Anb): Württemberg. (Ber): Kocher-Jagst-Tauber. (Gro): Kocherberg. (Vins): Ammerlauden, Hofberg.

Mock Orange (Cktl) 1 measure gin, 4 measures apple wine, 3 measures orange wine. Stir together with ice and strain into an ice-filled highball glass.

Mocktails (Eng) a slang term for non-alcoholic 'cocktails'.

Moco Moresque (Fr) a ready-mixed pastis with a small amount of fruit flavouring.

Moco Perroquet (Fr) a ready-mixed pastis with a small amount of fruit flavouring.

Moco Tomate (Fr) a ready-mixed pastis that has a small amount of tomato flavouring.

Moctezuma Brewery (Mex) a brewery based in Monterrey which brews Nochebuena (Christmas Eve), Sol and Dos Equis.

Modelo Brewery (Mex) a brewery based in Mexico City. Noted for Corona Extra, Negra Modelo, Victoria beer.

Modena (It) a province of Emilia-Romagna from which Lambrusco di Sorbara is best known wine.

Modern Cocktail (Cktl) ⅔ measure Scotch whisky, ⅓ measure lemon juice, 2 dashes Pernod, 2 dashes Jamaican rum, dash Campari. Shake over ice, strain into a cocktail glass and top with a cherry.

Modesto (USA) the central region of the Central River Valley in California. Produces dessert and table wines.

Modification (Eng) in brewing, the germination stage of the malting process, when the barley sprouts shoot and chemical changes occur.

Modolet Brut (It) a sparkling (bottle-fermented) wine produced by Angons in the Friuli-Venezia-Giulia region.

Modra (Czec) a noted wine-producing region, has a high wine output.

Modri (Cro) when found on a wine label denotes 'black'.

Modri Burgundac (Cro) the Pinot noir grape.

Modus M (S.Afr) a red wine (Cabernet sauvignon 55%, Merlot 40%, Petit verdot 5%) produced by the Adler winery, Wellington, Western Cape.

Moeder Overste (Bel) lit: 'Mother Superior', an 8% alc by vol. amber-coloured, top-fermented, bottle-conditioned special beer brewed by Lefèbvre Brouwerij, Quenast.

Moelleux (Fr) a term used to denote sweet, sparkling wines (12g/l to 45g/l).

Moelleux (Fr) velvety, rich and smooth.

Moel! Moel! (Eng) a 6% alc by vol. ale originally named XB. Brewed by Moles of Melksham, Wiltshire. See also Moles Brew 97.

Moenchberg (Fr) an A.C. Alsace Grand Cru vineyard in Andlau and Eichhoffen 11.83ha.

Moerenburg Bier Brouwerij (Hol) a brewery (established 1922) based in Tilburg. Brews: Meibok Moerenburg.

Moët et Chandon (Fr) a Champagne producer. (Add): 18-20 Ave. de Champagne, 51200 Épernay. Grande Marque. 547ha. Produces vintage and non-vintage wines. Dom Pérignon (Brut/Rosé), Brut Impérial (Premier Cru/Rosé), Nectar Impérial. Vintages: 1900, 1904, 1906, 1911, 1914, 1921, 1923, 1928, 1929, 1933, 1934, 1937, 1938, 1941, 1943, 1945, 1947, 1949, 1952, 1953, 1955, 1959, 1961, 1962, 1964, 1966, 1969, 1970, 1971, 1973, 1975, 1976, 1978, 1980, 1981, 1982, 1983, 1985, 1986, 1988, 1990, 1998, 1999, 2000, 2001. The largest Champagne house. Has interests in Chandon (Arg), Provifin (Bra), Chandon GmBH (Ger), Green Point (USA), Torre de Gall (Sp). See also Dom Pérignon and Chandon (M). Website: http://www.moet.com

Moët Hennessey UK Ltd (Eng) Champagne and Cognac producer (established 1941). (Add): 13 Grosvenor Crescent, London SW1X 7EE. Produces Champagne, Cognac, spirits, liqueurs and wines. Website: http://www.moet.co.uk

Moezelwijn (Hol) Moselle (Mosel) wine.

Moffat (Scot) a single malt whisky distillery based to the east of Glasgow. A Lowland malt whisky. 40% alc by vol. Also produces a grain whisky.

Moflete (Sp) a name given to the process in the Sherry region where a vine in the last year of its useful life is allowed to grow as many buds as it can to get maximum production and so exhaust the vine.

Mog (Eng) an alcoholic cream soda 4% alc by vol. from Burton-on-Trent based Marston's company: Shack Beverage Company.

Mogen David Corporation (USA) producers of sweet sacramental wines based in Illinois (owned by the Coca Cola Bottling C°. in New York).

Mogue à Iaoue (Ch.Isles) water jug.

Mogue à Lait (Ch.Isles) milk jug.

Mohan Meakin Brewery (Ind) a brewery based in the Simla Hills, Solan. Produces: Baller Beer 1040 O.G. Golden Eagle 1050 O.G. Gymkhana 1045 O.G. Krown 1048 O.G. and Lion 1046 O.G.

Moho (Sp) mildew.

Mohoso (Sp) mildewed.

Moillard-Grivot (Fr) a Burgundy négociant-éleveur (established 1850) based at Nuits-Saint-Georges. (Add): 2 Rue F. Mignotte, 21700 Nuits-Saint-Georges, Burgundy. Has 40ha. of vineyards.

Moimento da Beira (Port) a white grape variety grown in the Dão region.

890

M

Moingeon-Gueneau Frères (Fr) a producer of Crèmant de Bourgogne based in Nuits-Saint-Georges, Burgundy.

Moings (Fr) a commune in the Charente-Maritime département whose grapes are classed Petite Champagne (Cognac).

Mojito (Cktl) 35mls (1½fl.ozs) golden rum, juice ½ lime, 2 dashes gomme syrup, sugar, 6 mint leaves. Squeeze lime juice into a highball glass, add spent lime shell, sugar and mint leaves. Stir, fill glass with shaved ice, add rum and stir, add dash soda water and decorate with mint and straws.

Mojo (Eng) a 5% alc by vol. premium lager beer brewed with caffeine, guarana and damiana by Bass in Burton-on-Trent.

Moka Coffee (Arab) also known as Yemen coffee, a grade of coffee seed (bean). Has small irregular rounded seeds of yellow appearance. See also Mocha Coffee.

Moka Express (USA) the name given to the household espresso coffee machine.

Moka Helado (Cktl)(Non-alc) 150mls (¼ pint) iced coffee, 1 scoop vanilla ice cream, 1 teaspoon of chocolate powder slaked down with a little water. Blend altogether in a blender and serve in highball glasses with straws.

Moka Ris (Eng) an espresso blend of coffee from Kenco Coffee.

Mokha (Arab) an alternative spelling of Mocha. See also Moka Coffee.

Mokka mit Sahne (Ger) a liqueur made with coffee and cream.

Molasse (Fr) sedimentary sub-soil found in the town in Saint-Émilion.

Molasses (W.Ind) the liquid from cane sugar from which after fermentation is distilled into rum.

Molasses Act (W.Ind) an act passed in 1973 which levied duty on rum and also on molasses if they were bought from anywhere other than the British West Indies.

Molassique (Fr) lumpy, rocky soil.

Moldova (Rus) a wine region bordering Rumania (once belonging to Rumania) between the rivers Dnieper and Danube. Main Grape varieties: Feteasc Alba, Feteasca Regala, Rkatsiteli, Saperavi. Main wines are Negru de Purkur (Saperavi and Cabernet blend), Rochu de Purkar (Cabernet, Merlot and Malbec blend). see Bessarabia.

Moledora (Sp) a process of passing the grapes through rubber rollers in the Sherry region to lightly press them before they go into the vaslin press.

Molegrip (Eng) a 4.3% alc by vol. ale brewed by the Moles Brewery, Wiltshire.

Molennium (Eng) a 4.5% alc by vol. ale brewed by the Moles Brewery, Wiltshire.

Moles Brewery (Eng) a brewery (established 1982). (Add): 5 Merlin Way, Bowerhill, Melksham, Wiltshire SN12 6TJ. Brews: Barleymole 4.2% alc by vol., Holy Moley 4.7% alc by vol., Moél Moél 6% alc by vol., Mole Catcher 5% alc by vol., Molegrip 4.3% alc by vol., Molennium 4.5% alc

by vol., (cask-conditioned) Moles Best Bitter 4% alc by vol (1040 O.G)., Moles Landlord's Choice 4.5% alc by vol., Moles Tap Bitter 3.5% alc by vol. Also Moles Brew 97 5% alc by vol., Moles XB 6% alc by vol. Black Rat Cider 6% alc by vol. Website: http://www.molesbrewery.com 'E'mail: moles-cascade@talk21.com

Moles Brew 97 (Eng) a 5% alc by vol. ale from Moles of Melksham, Wiltshire.

Molette (Fr) a white grape variety grown in Bugey and Seyssel to produce sparkling wines.

Molinara (It) a red grape variety grown in the Veneto region. Used in the making of light red wines. see Rosana.

Molinara (It) the Lombardy region name for the red Rossanella grape.

Molino di Grace (It) a vineyard based in the D.O.C.G. Chianti Classico, Tuscany. Website: http://www.ilmolinodigrace.com

Molisia (It) a natural spring mineral water from Sant'Elena, Sannitra, Isernia.

Moll (Sp) a white grape variety grown on the island of Majorca. Also known as Prensal.

Mollar (Sp) a white grape variety grown in southern Spain. Also known as the Cañocazo.

Mollenbrunnen (Ger) vineyard (Anb): Nahe. (Ber): Kreuznach. (Gro): Kronenberg. (Vil): Bad Kreuznach.

Mollenbrunnen (Ger) vineyard (Anb): Nahe. (Ber): Kreuznach. (Gro): Kronenberg. (Vil): Hargesheim.

Mölsheim (Ger) village (Anb): Rheinhessen. (Ber): Wonnegau. (Gro): Domblick. (Vins): Silberberg, Zellerweg am Scwarzen, Herrgott.

Molson Canada (Can) a group of large breweries (of the 'Big Two' breweries, based in Toronto since 1786, originally the 'Big Three' but Molson and Carling have now merged). (Add): 33 Carlingview Drive, Toronto, Ontario M9W 5EA. Noted for a range of lager and ice beers. See also Labatt. Website: http://www.molson.com

Molson Dry (Can) a 5% alc by vol. bottled premium lager brewed by Molson Breweries in Toronto.

Molson Special Dry (Can) a premium packaged lager 5.5% alc by vol. produced by Molson Breweries in Toronto.

Mombasa (Afr) a natural spring mineral water from Mombasa, Kenya.

Mombrier (Fr) a commune in the A.C. Côtes de Bourg, north-eastern Bordeaux.

Moment d'Exception (Fr) the label for an A.C. Côtes-du-Rhône-Villages Laudun (red) from the Les Vignerons de Laudun, Laudun, Vaucluse.

Mominette (Fr) the working-class name for an Absinthe-Swiss Style when sweetened with plain syrup.

Mommenheim (Ger) village (Anb): Rheinhessen. (Ber): Nierstein. (Gro): Gutes Domtal. (Vins): Kloppenberg, Osterberg, Silbergrube.

Mommessin (Fr) a négociant-éleveur based at Charnay lès Mâcon, Mâcon, Burgundy. Owns the Grand Cru Clos de Tart vineyard in the Côte de

Nuits. Labels include: Grande Exception (A.C. Beaujolais Cru Morgon), La Cerisaie (A.C. Beaujolais Cru Fleurie), Les Grumières (A.C. Beaujolais Cru Brouill), Javernières Grande Exception (A.C. Beaujolais Cru Morgon), Les Griottes (A.C. Beaujolais Cru Morgon), Réserve du Domaine de Champ de Cour (A.C. Beaujolais Cru Moulin-à-Vent), Réserve Fleurie (A.C. Beaujolais Cru Fleurie).Owned by Boisset.

Momokawa Sake Brewery (USA) noted for Japanese saké, now based at 820 Elm Street, Forest Grove, Oregon.

Monagri (Cyp) a village on the south-east side of the Island that produces grapes for Commandaria.

Mona Lisa (Cktl) ⅓ measure Bénédictine, ⅓ measure Amer Picon, ⅓ measure orange Curaçao, barspoon of double cream. Shake over ice, strain into a cocktail glass and sprinkle cinnamon on top.

Mona Lisa Cocktail (Cktl) place ½ measure dry gin, ½ measure Campari, 1¼ measures orange Chartreuse in an ice-filled highball glass, stir. Top with ginger ale, decorate with a slice of orange and a lemon spiral and serve with straws.

Mona Medium (Ger) a sparkling natural spring mineral water. Mineral contents (milligrammes per litre): Sodium 16.7mg/l, Calcium 83.7mg/l, Magnesium 4.5mg/l, Potassium 1.1mg/l, Bicarbonates 189mg/l, Chlorides 44.3mg/l, Sulphates 58.4mg/l.

Monarch Ale (Eng) a bottled bitter beer 1065 O.G. brewed by the Morland Brewery in Abingdon, Oxfordshire.

Monarch Wine Company (USA) a winery based in Atlanta, Georgia. Produces mainly brandy and peach wines.

Monashee (Can) a natural spring mineral water. Mineral contents (milligrammes per litre): Sodium 3mg/l, Calcium 23.4mg/l, Magnesium 6.4mg/l, Potassium 10.9mg/l, Bicarbonates 89.8mg/l, Chlorides 0.4mg/l. pH 7.57

Monastel (Sp) see Monastrel.

Monastère (Bel) the brand-name of a bottled mineral water.

Monasterio de Tentudia (Sp) a winery based in the VdT region of Extremadura. Label: Tradición.

Monastery Brandy (USA) the brand-name of a brandy produced by the Schenley Distillers.

Monastery Types (USA) modern liqueurs that are produced as copies of old herbal liqueurs which were produced by monks in the Middle Ages.

Monastico (Port) a herb and brandy based liqueur produced by Neto Casta.

Monastrel (Sp) a black grape variety grown in the Aragón, Catalonia, Penedés and Rioja regions. Also known as the Alcayata, Mataro, Mechín, Ministrel, Monastell, Moraster, Mourvèdre, Negralejo and Valcarcelica.

Monastrell (Sp) see Monastrel.

Monbazillac (Fr) an A.C. sweet white wine from Bergerac. Produced by the same method as Sauternes with the grapes attacked by **Botrytis cinerea**. (Coms): Colombier, Monbazillac,

Pomport, Rouffignac and Saint-Laurent-des-Vignes. Minimum alc by vol. of 13%.

Monbrison (Fr) a vineyard in the commune of Arsac. A.C. Médoc, Bordeaux. Cru Bourgeois Supérieur.

Monçao (Port) the northern district of the Entre Minho e Douro. Produces both red and white Vinhos Verdes. Reds are dark coloured.

Moncaro (It) a winery based in the Marche region that produces a range of wines including Verdicchio dei Castelli di Jesi. Label: Le Vele. Website: http://www.moncaro.com

Mönchbäumchen (Ger) vineyard (Anb): Rheinhessen. (Ber): Nierstein. (Gro): Gutes Domtal. (Vil): Zornheim.

Mönchberg (Ger) vineyard (Anb): Ahr. (Ber): Walporzheim/Arhtal. (Gro): Klosterberg. (Vil): Mayschoss.

Mönchberg (Ger) vineyard (Anb): Nahe. (Ber): Kreuznach. (Gro): Kronenberg. (Vil): Bad Kreuznach.

Mönchberg (Ger) vineyard (Anb): Nahe. (Ber): Kreuznach. (Gro): Kronenberg. (Vil): Bad Kreuznach.

Mönchberg (Ger) vineyard (Anb): Nahe. (Ber): Kreuznach. (Gro): Pfarrgarten. (Vil): Hergenfeld.

Mönchberg (Ger) vineyard (Anb): Nahe. (Ber): Schloss Böckelheim. (Gro): Rosengarten. (Vil): Hüffelsheim.

Mönchberg (Ger) vineyard (Anb): Rheinhessen. (Ber): Bingen. (Gro): Rheingrafenstein. (Vil): Volxheim.

Mönchberg (Ger) vineyard (Anb): Württemberg. (Ber): Remstal-Stuttgart. (Gro): Sonnenbühl. (Vil): Weinstadt (ortsteil Rommelshausen), also Mönchhalde.

Mönchberg (Ger) vineyard (Anb): Württemberg. (Ber): Remstal-Stuttgart. (Gro): Sonnenbühl. (Vil): Weinstadt (ortsteil Stetten i. R.), also Mönchhalde.

Mönchberg (Ger) vineyard (Anb): Württemberg. (Ber): Remstal-Stuttgart. (Gro): Weinsteige. (Vil): Fellbach.

Mönchberg (Ger) vineyard (Anb): Württemberg. (Ber): Remstal-Stuttgart. (Gro): Weinsteige. (Vil): Stuttgart.

Mönchberg (Ger) vineyard (Anb): Württemberg. (Ber): Remstal-Stuttgart. (Gro): Weinsteige. (Vil): Stuttgart (ortsteil Cannstatt).

Mönchberg (Ger) vineyard (Anb): Württemberg. (Ber): Remstal-Stuttgart. (Gro): Weinsteige. (Vil): Stuttgart (ortsteil Untertürkheim).

Mönchgarten (Ger) vineyard (Anb): Pfalz. (Ber): Mittelhaardt-Deutsche Weinstrasse. (Gro): Meerspinne. (Vil): Neustadt an der Weinstrasse.

Mönchhalde (Ger) vineyard (Anb): Württemberg. (Ber): Remstal-Stuttgart. (Gro): Sonnenbühl. (Vil): Weinstadt (ortsteil Rommelshausen), also Mönchberg.

Mönchhalde (Ger) vineyard (Anb): Württemberg. (Ber): Remstal-Stuttgart. (Gro): Sonnenbühl. (Vil): Weinstadt (ortsteil Stetten i. R.). also Mönchberg.

Mönchhalde (Ger) vineyard (Anb): Württemberg.

M

(Ber): Remstal-Stuttgart. (Gro): Weinsteige. (Vil): Stuttgart.

Mönchhalde (Ger) vineyard (Anb): Württemberg. (Ber): Remstal-Stuttgart. (Gro): Weinsteige. (Vil): Stuttgart (ortsteil Bad Cannstatt).

Monchhof (Aus) the name given to a medium-dry white wine from the Burgenland.

Mönchhube (Ger) vineyard (Anb): Rheinhessen. (Ber): Wonnegau. (Gro): Pilgerpfad. (Vil): Dittelsheim-Hessloch.

Monchique (Port) a slightly alkaline natural spring mineral water from Pancadas 1 e 2, Monchique. Mineral contents (milligrammes per litre): Sodium 105mg/l, Calcium 1.08mg/l, Magnesium 0.044mg/l, Potassium 2mg/l, Bicarbonates 106mg/l, Chlorides 39.6mg/l, Sulphates 59mg/l, Fluorides 1.2mg/l, Nitrates <0.03mg/l, Silicates 13.2mg/l. pH 9.5

Mönchpforte (Ger) vineyard (Anb): Rheinhessen. (Ber): Bingen. (Gro): Abtey. (Vil): Ober-Hilbersheim.

Mönchsberg (Ger) vineyard (Anb): Württemberg. (Ber): Kocher-Jagst-Tauber. (Gro): Tauberberg. (Vil): Markelsheim.

Mönchsberg (Ger) vineyard (Anb): Württemberg. (Ber): Kocher-Jagst-Tauber. (Gro): Tauberberg. (Vil): Elpersheim.

Mönchsberg (Ger) vineyard (Anb): Württemberg. (Ber): Württembergisch Unterland. (Gro): Heuchelberg. (Vil): Brackenheim.

Mönchsberg (Ger) vineyard (Anb): Württemberg. (Ber): Württembergisch Unterland. (Gro): Heuchelberg. (Vil): Dürrenzimmern.

Mönchsbrunnen (Ger) a sparkling natural spring mineral water from Bad Vilbel. Mineral contents (milligrammes per litre): Sodium 115mg/l, Calcium 124mg/l, Magnesium 27.1mg/l, Potassium 17.4mg/l, Bicarbonates 598mg/l, Chlorides 122mg/l, Sulphates 43mg/l.

Mönchshang (Ger) vineyard (Anb): Franken. (Ber): Steigerwald. (Gro): Not yet assigned. (Vil): Zeil a Main.

Mönchsleite (Ger) vineyard (Anb): Franken. (Ber): Maindreieck. (Gro): Not yet assigned. (Vil): Eibelstadt.

Mönchspfad (Ger) vineyard (Anb): Rheingau. (Ber): Johannisberg. (Gro): Burgweg. (Vil): Geisenheim.

Mönchspfad (Ger) vineyard (Anb): Rheinhessen. (Ber): Nierstein. (Gro): Domherr. (Vil): Schornsheim.

Mönchspfad (Ger) vineyard (Anb): Rheinhessen. (Ber): Nierstein. (Gro): Sankt Alban. (Vil): Bodenheim.

Mönchspfad (Ger) vineyard (Anb): Pfalz. (Ber): Südliche Weinstrasse. (Gro): Königsgarten. (Vil): Siebeldingen.

Mönchwingert (Ger) vineyard (Anb): Mittelrhein. (Ber): Bacharach. (Gro): Schloss Stahleck. (Vil): Manubach.

Moncreiffe (Scot) an 8 year old blended de luxe Scotch whisky (Sir Ian Moncreiffe) produced by Moncreiffe and Cº. Ltd. of Perth 43% alc by vol.

Moncuit (Fr) a Champagne producer based in Mesnil-sur-Ogier. Produces vintage and non-vintage wines. Vintage: 1995, 1996, 2000. Label: Cuvée Nicole Moncuit Vieille Vignes. Website: http://www.Champagnerobertmoncuit.com

Mondariz (Sp) a still natural spring mineral water from La Estrella 2, Mondariz, Pontevedra, Galicia. Mineral contents (milligrammes per litre): Sodium 50.5mg/l, Calcium 9.2mg/l, Magnesium 4.9mg/l, Potassium 5.1mg/l, Bicarbonates 163.4mg/l, Chlorides 17.9mg/l, Sulphates 1.5mg/l, Fluorides 0.4mg/l, Nitrates 1.9mg/l. pH 6.59

Mondavi [Robert] (USA) a large winery in the Napa Valley, California. Owned by Robert Mondavi. 260ha. Grape varieties: Cabernet sauvignon, Chardonnay, Chenin blanc, Johannisberg riesling and Pinot noir. Produce varietal wines. Label: To Kalon Vineyard Reserve.

Mondego [River] (Port) a river of which the river Dão is a tributary.

Mondeuse Blanche (Fr) a white grape variety used in the wines of Savoie and Bugey.

Mondeuse Noire (Fr) an old red grape variety used in the making of red wines in Savoie. Also known as the Refosco and Dongine.

Mon Don (S.Afr) a small winery in Robertson making varietal wines.

Mondotte [La] (Fr) a vineyard. (Add): Saint Laurent des Combes, 33330 Saint-Émilion. Grand Cru. A.C. Saint-Émilion. (Com): Saint Laurent des Combes. 4.3ha. Grape varieties: 75% Merlot, 25% Cabernet franc. Originally known as Château Mondotte.

Mondragone (It) one of the areas of Campania where Falerno wine is produced.

Mondschein (Ger) vineyard (Anb): Rheinhessen. (Ber): Wonnegau. (Gro): Pilgerpfad. (Vil): Dittelsheim-Hessloch.

Monee Thompson Vineyard (USA) a winery based near Chicago, Illinois. Noted for sparkling wines made by the traditional method (white and rosé).

Monemvasia (Gre) the Peloponnesian town which is the origination of the Malvasia grape variety.

Monferrato (It) a new D.O.C. wine produced in Piedmont.

Monfort (Ger) vineyard (Anb): Nahe. (Ber): Schloss Böckelheim. (Gro): Paradiesgarten. (Vil): Odernheim.

Mongueux (Fr) a blanc de blancs Champagne made from Chardonnay grapes grown in the Aube region.

Monhard (Ger) vineyard (Anb): Nahe. (Ber): Kreuznach. (Gro): Kronenberg. (Vil): Bad Kreuznach.

Monica (It) a red grape variety grown in Sardinia. Produces soft red velvety wines. Possibly the Mission grape.

Monica di Cagliari (It) a D.O.C. red wine from Sardinia. Made from the Monica grape in the province of Cagliari. Grapes can be dried on vine or frames. 4 types: Dolce Naturale, Secco,

Liquoroso Secco and Liquoroso Dolce Naturale. Liquoroso Dolce and Secco if aged 2 years (1 year in oak/chestnut casks) classed Riserva.

Monica di Sardegna (It) a D.O.C. red wine from Sardinia. Made from the Monica, Carignano, Bovale grande, Bovale sardo and Pascale di caligari grapes. If aged 1 year and minimum alc. content of 13% by vol. then classed Superiore. Made near Cagliari.

Monichino Winery (Austr) a small winery (established 1962) based at Berry's Road, Katunga, central Victoria.

Moniga-del-Garda (It) a red wine produced in the Lombardy region on the southern shores of Lake Garda.

Monilio Javanica (E.Ind) Batavian arak.

Monimpex (Hun) the state export monopoly that has wine cellars near Budapest.

Monin (Fr) a famous firm (established 1912). Produce a wide range of non-alcoholic syrups plus a liqueur made from brandy and lemon peel 33% alc by vol.

Monis Wines (S.Afr) a winery (established 1906) based in Paarl, Western Cape. Produces dessert and fortified wines from the SFW (Distell). Website: http://www.distell.co.za

Monitor (Arg) the brand-name of a sparkling wine produced by the cuve close method.

Monje de Autor (Sp) a red wine produced from Listán blanco, Listán negro and Negramoll grapes by Bodegas Monje, Tenerife.

Monk Cocktail (Cktl) ¼ measure Bénédictine, ½ measure dry gin, ¼ measure lemon juice. Shake over ice and strain into a cocktail glass.

Monk Export (Ire) the name for canned MᶜEwan's Export 1042 O.G. sold in Northern Ireland.

Monkey (Port) see Macaco.

Monkey (Sp) a small bottle on the end of a piece of string used by the Sherry workers to poach Sherry from the casks whilst the foreman is not looking.

Monkey Back (Scot) a condition of malt whisky workers who turn the germinating barley over (a back strain). See also Monkey Shoulder.

Monkey Bottle (Ger) see Affenflasche.

Monkey Gland [1] (Cktl) 1½ measures gin, ½ measure orange juice, 2 dashes grenadine, 2 dashes Pernod. Shake over ice, strain into a cocktail glass and add a dash of orange peel juice on top.

Monkey Gland [2] (Cktl) 25mls (⅙ gill) gin, 20mls (⅙ gill) Bénédictine, 20mls (⅙ gill) orange juice, 2 dashes grenadine. Stir over ice and strain into an ice-filled old-fashioned glass.

Monkey Magic (Eng) a 3.4% alc by vol. ale brewed by The Eccleshall Brewing Cᵒ. Ltd., Staffordshire.

Monkeys (Port) long poles with heavy end pieces which are used to push the skins down into the must.

Monkey's Fist (Eng) a strong beer brewed by the Cotswold Brewing Company in Cirencester, Gloucester. Sold in a Champagne-style bottle with a cork and wire top.

Monkey Shoulder (Scot) the nickname for a condition that maltsters develop after many years of turning the germinating barley grains. See also Monkey Back.

Monkey Shoulder (Scot) a blended (vatted) malt whisky (3 malts: Balvenie, Glenfiddich and Kininvie) produced by William Grant & Sons 40% alc by vol.

Monkey Wrench (Eng) a 5.3% alc by vol. bottled strong ale brewed by the Daleside Brewery in Harrogate, North Yorkshire.

Monkmans Slaughter (Eng) a 6% alc by vol. strong ale brewed by the Cropton Brewery, Pickering, North Yorkshire

Monks Coffee (Liq.Coffee) using a measure of Bénédictine.

Monks Comfort (Liq.Coffee) same as Monks Coffee.

Monkscroft House Ale (Scot) a bottled ale 1070 O.G. brewed for Export to Italy by the Belhaven Brewery.

Monk's Habit (Eng) an ale brewed by the Marston Brewery, Burton-on-Trent.

Monlezun Oak (Fr) *Quercus pedonculus albus* a black oak used for the making of casks for Armagnac brandy.

Monlouis (N.Z) the brand-name used by the Pacific Vineyards in Henderson, North Island for a range of their wines.

Monmousseau (Fr) the name given to the sparkling wines made by the méthode traditionelle in Monmousseau, Touraine, Loire. Owned by Taittinger.

Monmouth Brewery (Wal) a brewery based at the Queen's Head in Monmouth. Noted for cask-conditioned Ten Thirty Five 1035 O.G. and Piston 1045 O.G.

Monnet (Fr) a Cognac producer. (Add): J.G. Monnet and Cᵒ., P.O. Box 22, 52 Avenue Paul-Firno, 16101 Cognac. Produces Anniversaire Très Ancienne Sélection, Extra Belle Réserve.

Monnières (Fr) a village in the central part of the A.C. Muscadet Sèvre et Maine. Produces some of the finest wines.

Monnow Valley (Wal) a 1.6ha vineyard based at Great Osbaston Farm, Monmouth. Produces still and sparkling wines from Huxelrebe, Madeleine angevine, Seyval blanc grapes.

Mono-Cru (Fr) denotes single wines sold by the growers in Champagne.

Mononga Cobbler (Cktl) 35mls (1½fl.ozs) Bourbon whiskey, 1 teaspoon icing sugar, dash lemon juice. Shake well over ice, strain into an ice-filled (crushed ice) highball glass. Dress with a slice of orange and lemon and serve with straws.

Monopole (Fr) on an Armagnac brandy label indicates a minimum age of one year.

Monopole (Fr) denotes that the whole of the vineyard named belongs to the same proprietor.

Monopole (Sp) a dry, white wine produced by the C.V.N.E. in the Rioja Alta.

Monopole Labelling (USA) brand labelling.

Monosaccharides (Eng) unfermentable sugars that

M

cannot be converted by yeast enzymes and remain in the wine (pentose, arabinose, xylose and ribose for example).

Monos'Ló (Hun) a small wine-producing village in Transdanubia near Lake Balatòn. Noted for sweet wines.

Monro (S.Afr) the label for a dry sparkling white (Chardonnay) wine and flagship red (Cabernet sauvignon and Merlot blend) produced by the Villiera Wines winery, Stellenbosch, Western Cape.

Monsanto (It) a noted Chianti Classico producer based in Tuscany.

Monsedro (Port) a red grape variety grown in the Algarve.

Monsenor (Sp) a solera reserva brandy produced by Sanchez Romate.

Monsheim (Ger) village (Anb): Rheinhessen. (Ber): Wonnegau. (Gro): Domblick. (Vins): Rosengarten, Silberberg.

Monsieur Pastis (Fr) the nickname given to Paul Ricard.

Monsoon (Eng) low calorie, lightly sparkling, flavoured spring water range from Orchid Drinks. Flavours include: kiwi & lime, orange & passion fruit, elderflower & lemon.

Monsoon Coffee (Ind) the name given to coffee produced during the monsoon period. Has a full aroma and flavour.

Monsoon Valley (Thai) a premium white wine produced from Malaga blanc grapes grown in the floating vineyards north of the Gulf of Thai in the Chao Phraya delta.

Mons Ruber (S.Afr) a winery and distillery (established 1850) based near De Rust, Little Karoo. 38ha. Grape varieties: Cabernet sauvignon, Chardonnay, Hanepoot, Jerepigo, Muscadel, Sultana. Labels: Conari, Regalis, Vino. Also produces a range of brandies including an estate brandy distilled over an open fire dating back to 1936. Website: http://www.geocities.com

Monstelo (Sp) a red grape variety grown in the Galicia region.

Monsupello (It) a noted wine-producer based in Oltrepo Pavese, Lombardy.

Mont [Le] (Fr) a vineyard in the A.C. Vouvray, Touraine, Loire.

Montado (Sp) a solera brandy produced by Wisdom & Warter.

Montagna (Ger) a cross grape variety between the Rieslaner and Müller-Thurgau.

Montagne de Reims (Fr) a vineyard region of Champagne, grows mainly black grapes.

Montagne Estate (S.Afr) a large vineyard based in Stellenbosch. 133ha. Grape varieties: Cabernet sauvignon and Shiraz. Produce varietal wines made by the Gilbey C°.

Montagne-Saint-Émilion (Fr) an A.C. commune within the Saint-Émilion district in eastern Bordeaux.

Montagnes d'Arrée (Fr) a natural spring mineral water from Bassin Armorique, Brittany. Mineral contents (milligrammes per litre): Sodium 6.7mg/l, Calcium 0.8mg/l, Magnesium 1mg/l, Potassium 0.2mg/l, Bicarbonates 3.6mg/l, Chlorides 14mg/l, Sulphates 2mg/l, Nitrates 1.6mg/l.

Montagnes d'Auvergnes (Fr) a natural spring mineral water from Creteil, Auvergnes. Mineral contents (milligrammes per litre): Sodium 3.6mg/l, Calcium 3.6mg/l, Magnesium 1.8mg/l, Potassium 0.6mg/l, Bicarbonates 24.4mg/l, Chlorides 0.9mg/l, Sulphates 1.2mg/l, Nitrates 0.5mg/l, Silicates 23mg/l. pH 6.9

Montagny (Fr) an A.C. commune (301ha) of the Côte Chalonnaise in southern Burgundy (white wines).

Montagu (S.Afr) a district in the Klein Karoo noted for Sherry-type wines.

Montagu (S.Afr) the label for a range of wines produced by the Rietrivier Winery, Little Karoo.

Montagu Muskadel Boere Co-operative (S.Afr) a co-operative winery (established 1941) based in Klein Karoo. 660ha. (Add): Box 29, Montagu 6720. Grape varieties: Cabernet sauvignon, Chardonnay, Chenin blanc, Colombard, Merlot, Muscadel, Shiraz. Produces Volsoet Rooi Muskadel and varietal wines.

Montalbano Spalletti (It) a noted Chianti Classico producer based in Tuscany.

Montana (Cktl) ½ measure brandy, ½ measure dry vermouth, 2 dashes Port, 2 dashes anisette, 2 dashes Angostura. Stir over ice and strain into a cocktail glass.

Montaña (Sp) a district of the Navarra region in north-eastern Spain.

Montaña de León (Sp) a natural spring mineral water brand from Montaña, Navarra.

Montana [La] (USA) the brand-label used by Martin Ray Vineyards, Santa Clara, California.

Montana Wines (N.Z) a large winery and noted wine-producing company (produces over 50% of New Zealand's wines). (Add): 171 Pilkington Road, Glen Innes, Aukland. Vineyards at Gisborne 80ha. Hawkes Bay 240ha. Marlborough 580ha. Grape varieties: Cabernet sauvignon, Chardonnay, Gewürztraminer, Merlot, Pinotage, Pinot noir, Rhine riesling, Riesling-Sylvaner, Sauvignon blanc, Sémillon. Labels include Deutz Wines, East Coast Rosé, Terrace. Owned by Pernod-Ricard.

Montánchez (Sp) a Vino de la Tierra wine-producing village near to Mérida in the province of Cáceres, Extremadura, south-western Spain. 4000ha. Grape varieties: Borba, Alarije, Cayetana (white), Pedro ximénez Cencibel, Garnacha (red). Produces heavily-coloured, white, strong (14% alc by vol) flor-attacked wines often aged in tinajas, plus red wines (some of which are also flor-attacked).

Montanha (Port) a winery based in Bairrada. Produces mainly red wines.

Montara (Austr) a noted winery (established 1970) based in Great Western, Victoria. Grape varieties: Chardonnay, Riesling, Ondenc, Chasselas, Cabernet sauvignon, Pinot noir, Shiraz.

Montarcy Vieux (Fr) the brand-name of a Calvados distributed by the Merrydown C°. in the U.K.

Montaudon (Fr) a Champagne producer. (Add): 6 Rue Ponsardin, 51100 Reims. 35ha. Produces vintage and non-vintage wines. Vintages: 1970, 1971, 1973, 1975, 1976, 1979, 1982, 1983, 1985, 1990, 1995, 1998, 2000, 2001.

Montauzier [Pierre] (Fr) a Cognac producer. (Add): Bors-de-Montmoreau, 16190 Montmoreau-Saint-Cybard. 5ha. in the Bons Bois. Produces Vieille Réserve Napoléon (average age 15 years).

Mont Baudile (Fr) a Vin de Pays area of the Hérault département in southern France.

Mont-Bellet (Fr) a wine-producing district in Bellet, Provence.

Mont Blem (Isr) a brand of dry white wine.

Mont Blois (S.Afr) a wine estate based in Robertson. (Add): P.O. Robertson 6705. Produce varietal wines.

Mont Bouquet (Fr) a Vin de Pays area of the Gard département in south-west France.

Montbray Wine Cellars (USA) a small winery based in Maryland that produce hybrid wines.

Montbré (Fr) a Premier Cru Champagne village in the Canton de Verzy. District: Reims.

Montcalm (Fr) a natural spring mineral water from Captage La Prime Vallée d'Auzat Ariège, Pyrénées. Mineral contents (milligrammes per litre): Sodium 1.5mg/l, Calcium 3mg/l, Magnesium 0.6mg/l, Potassium 0.4mg/l, Bicarbonates 5.2mg/l, Chlorides 0.6mg/l, Sulphates 8.7mg/l, Nitrates <1mg/l, Silicates 7.5mg/l. pH 6.8

Mont Caume (Fr) a Vin de Pays area of the Var département in south-eastern France. Produces red and rosé wines.

Montceaux-Ragny (Fr) a commune in the A.C. Mâcon, the grapes of which may be used for Mâcon Supérieur.

Montchaude (Fr) a commune in the Charente département whose grapes are used for Petite Champagne Cognac.

Montchern (Fr) a vineyard in the Yonne département that produces red and white wines.

Montclair (Can) a natural spring mineral water. Mineral contents (milligrammes per litre): Sodium 475mg/l, Calcium 8mg/l, Magnesium 12mg/l, Potassium 13mg/l, Bicarbonates 890mg/l, Chlorides 230mg/l, Sulphates 39mg/l, Fluorides 1mg/l.

Montclair Winery (USA) a small winery based opposite the Bay of San Francisco, Alameda, California. Grape varieties: Cabernet sauvignon, Colombard and Zinfandel. Produces varietal wines.

Montclar (Fr) a natural spring mineral water from Source de l'Adoux/Source du Col St. Jean Montclar. Mineral contents (milligrammes per litre): Sodium 2mg/l, Calcium 41mg/l, Magnesium 3mg/l, Bicarbonates 134mg/l, Chlorides 3mg/l, Sulphates 2mg/l, Nitrates 3mg/l. pH 8.0

Mont Cole (Can) a natural spring mineral water. Mineral contents (milligrammes per litre): Sodium 2mg/l, Calcium 38mg/l, Magnesium 8mg/l, Potassium 2mg/l, Bicarbonates 130mg/l, Chlorides 3mg/l, Sulphates 26mg/l.

Montcuchots [Les] (Fr) a vineyard in the A.C. commune of Montagny, Côte Chalonnaise, Burgundy.

Mont de Milieu Beauroy (Fr) a Premier Cru vineyard of A.C. Chablis, Burgundy.

Mont Destin (S.Afr) a winery (established 1998) based in Paarl, Western Cape. 7ha. Grape varieties: Cabernet sauvignon, Chenin blanc, Merlot, Shiraz. Labels: Destiny, 1482. Website: http://www.montdestin.co.za

Mont d'Or (Switz) a brand of dry white wine produced in the Sion district of the Valais region.

Mont Dore (Fr) a natural spring mineral water from Grand Barbier, Puy de Dôme. Mineral contents (milligrammes per litre): Sodium 2.7mg/l, Calcium 4.1mg/l, Magnesium 1.7mg/l, Potassium 0.9mg/l, Bicarbonates 25.8mg/l, Chlorides 0.9mg/l, Sulphates 1.1mg/l, Nitrates 0.8mg/l, Silicates 32.7mg/l. pH 7.3

Mont du Toit Kelder (S.Afr) a winery (established 1996) based in Wellington, Western Cape. 26ha. Grape varieties: Alicante bouchet, Cabernet franc, Cabernet sauvignon, Merlot, Mourvèdre, Petit verdot, Shiraz, Tinta roriz. Labels: Hawequas, Les Coteaux, Le Sommet, Mont du Toit (Cabernet franc, Cabernet sauvignon, Merlot and Shiraz blend). A joint venture with Germany. Website: http://www.montdutoit.co.za

Monteagudo (Sp) a solera brandy produced by Delgado Zuleta.

Monte Aguila (W.Ind) a spicey digestive liqueur based on pimento produced on the island of Jamaica.

Montebello (Fr) a Champagne (the second wine of Ayala).

Monte Bello (USA) the label for a red wine (Cabernet sauvignon 56%, Merlot 36%, Petit verdot 8% blend) produced by the Ridge Vineyards winery, Cupertino, California.

Montebello Vineyard (USA) a small vineyard in Santa Clara, California. Grape variety: Cabernet sauvignon. Part of the Ridge Vineyards.

Monte Bernardi (It) a 5.5ha estate in Panzano Produces D.O.C.G. Chianti Classico, I.G.T. Sa'etta, and Bordeaux blend Tsingana.

Monte Bianco (It) a sparkling natural spring mineral water from Fonte Mont Blanc, Courmayeugr, Aosta. Mineral contents (milligrammes per litre): Sodium 1.2mg/l, Calcium 31.1mg/l, Magnesium 2.4mg/l, Potassium 1.9mg/l, Bicarbonates 67.1mg/l, Sulphates 36.3mg/l. pH 7.9

Monteblanco (S.Am) a natural spring mineral water from San Jose, Guatamala.

Monte Bove (It) a natural spring mineral water from Ussita, Macerata.

Montecappone (It) a winery in the D.O.C. Verdicchio dei Castelli di Jesi, Marches region. Label: Riserva Utopia.

Montecarlo (It) a D.O.C. white wine from Tuscany. Made from the Pinot bianco, Pinot gris, Roussanne, Sauvignon, Sémillon, Trebbiano

M

toscano, Verminto grapes. Vinification can occur in each of the communes Montecarlo, Maginone and Altopascio.

Monte Carlo Imperial Highball (Cktl) ⅔ measure gin, ⅓ measure (white) crème de menthe, juice ¼ lemon. Shake over ice, strain into an ice-filled highball and top with iced Champagne.

Montecatini Terme (It) a noted wine-producer based in the north of the Tuscany region. Produces Montecarlo white wine.

Montechiaro (It) a natural spring mineral water from Conversano, Bari.

Montecillo Rosé (Sp) a red wine produced by the Bodegas El Montecillo Alta Region, Rioja. Made from the Garnacha grape.

Monte Cimone (It) a sparkling natural spring mineral water from Monte Cimone, Fanano, Modena. Mineral contents (milligrammes per litre): Sodium 2.48mg/l, Calcium 32.4mg/l, Magnesium 6.47mg/l, Potassium 0.7mg/l, Bicarbonates 116mg/l, Chlorides 3.3mg/l, Sulphates 12.6mg/l, Fluorides <0.2mg/l, Nitrates 2mg/l, Silicates 4.2mg/l. pH 7.8

Monte Coman (Arg) a wine-producing area in southern Argentina.

Montecompatri-Colonna (It) a D.O.C. white wine from Latium. Made from the Bellone, Bonvino, Malvasia and Trebbiano grapes from the commune of Colonna and part of Montecompatri, Roccapriora and Zagarolo communes. If total alc. content is 12.5% by vol. can be classed Riserva.

Monte Crasto (Port) a noted producer of red and white wines based in the Bairrada region.

Montecristo (Sp) a wine-producing company in Montilla-Moriles. Was part of the Rumasa group.

Monte da Casta (Port) see Quinta da Lagoalva.

Montée de Tonerre (Fr) a Premier Cru vineyard of Chablis. Often has the Premier Crus Chapelot and Pied-d'Aloup reclassified as its vintages.

Montée-Rouge (Fr) a vineyard [part] in the A.C. commune of Beaune, Côte de Beaune, Burgundy.

Montefalco Bianco (It) a white wine produced from 50%–80% Grechetto grapes in Umbria.

Montefalco Rosso (It) a red wine produced from 60%–70% Sangiovese, 10%–15% Sagrantino grapes, plus 15%–30% other authorised varieties (usually Merlot).

Montefalco Sagrantino (It) a D.O.C.G. red (dry or sweet) wines from Montefalco in the Umbria. Produced from the Sagrantino grape. Secco: 30 months age (12 in wood), Passito: 30 months age (12 in wood), Riserva: 42 months age (18 in wood). Also written Sagrantino di Montefalco.

Montefaro (Port) a Vinho Verde producer based at the Quinta da Seara, Palmeira, 4740 Esposende.

Monteferrante (It) a natural spring mineral water from san Giovanni.

Montefiascone (It) see Est! Est!! Est!!!

Monteforte (It) a sparkling natural spring mineral water from Monteforte, Modena. Mineral contents (milligrammes per litre): Sodium 4.1mg/l, Calcium 108mg/l, Magnesium 15.4mg/l, Potassium 1.4mg/l, Bicarbonates 360mg/l, Chlorides 4.8mg/l, Sulphates 22.7mg/l, Boronioxyde 1.85mg/l, Nitrates 9.8mg/l, Silicates 14mg/l. pH 7.3

Montegiachi (It) a D.O.C.G. Chianti Classico produced by Agricoltori dei Chianti Geografico, Tuscany.

Monteith (Eng) a large ornamental bowl used for cooling wine glasses which are suspended from a notched rim.

Monteith's Brewing Cº. Ltd. (N.Z) a craft brewery (established 1858) based in Greymouth on the West Coast. Brews: Nugget Golden Lager.

Montejo (Mex) a pale beer brewed by the Yucateca Brewery.

Monte Jup (Ger) vineyard (Anb): Mittelrhein. (Ber): Rheinburgengau. (Gro): Burg Hammerstein. (Vil): Rheinbrohl.

Monteliana e dei Colli Ascolani [La] (It) a sparkling (metodo tradizionale) wine producer based in the Veneto region.

Montélis (Fr) a still natural spring mineral water (established 1590 & 1995) from Montélis. Mineral contents (milligrammes per litre): Sodium 3mg/l, Calcium 2mg/l, Magnesium 0.5mg/l, Potassium 4mg/l, Bicarbonates 8mg/l, Chlorides 1.6mg/l, Sulphates 5.5mg/l, Nitrates 0.9mg/l, Silicates 14mg/l. pH 6.5 Website: http://www.montelismineralwater.com

Monte Llano (Sp) a red wine produced by the Bodegas Ramón Bilbao. Matured in oak for 1 year.

Montelle Vineyards (USA) a winery based in Augusta, Missouri. Produces almost 40 styles of American and European hybrid wines.

Montellier (Can) a natural spring mineral water from Saint-Luc, Quebec. Mineral contents (milligrammes per litre): Sodium 3.4mg/l, Calcium 3mg/l, Magnesium 3.3mg/l, Potassium 5mg/l, Bicarbonates 902mg/l, Chlorides 26mg/l, Sulphates 1.5mg/l, Nitrates 0.04mg/l.

Montello e Colli Asolani (It) a D.O.C. wine producing area in north-eastern Veneto.

Montellori (It) a noted Chianti Putto producer based in Tuscany.

Monte Mario (Bra) a slightly acidic natural spring mineral water from Fonte Monte Libano, Rio Branco. Mineral contents (milligrammes per litre): Sodium 3mg/l, Calcium 4mg/l, Magnesium 5mg/l, Potassium 3mg/l, Bicarbonates 8mg/l, Chlorides 3mg/l, Nitrates 0.6mg/l. pH 5.4

Montenegro (Euro) a small wine-producing district in south-eastern Slovinia. Red wines produced from Prokupac, Vranac.

Monteneubel (Ger) vineyard (Anb): Mosel-Saar-Ruwer. (Ber): Bernkastel. (Gro): Scwarzlay. (Vil): Enkirch.

Montenuevo (Chile) the brand-name for a Sauvignon blanc wine produced by Vinícola Mondragon in the Maipo.

Montepaldi (It) a noted Chianti Classico producer based in Tuscany.

M

Monte Pinos (Sp) a still natural spring mineral water from Almazan, Soria. Mineral contents (milligrammes per litre): Sodium 1.8mg/l, Calcium 93.8mg/l, Magnesium 3.4mg/l, Bicarbonates 298mg/l, Chlorides 3.6mg/l, Sulphates 1.6mg/l. pH 7.44

Montepulciano (It) a red grape variety grown in Abruzzi, Apulia, Molise and also the Marches. Also known as Cordisco, Morellone, Primaticcio, Uva Abruzzi.

Montepulciano d'Abruzzo (It) a D.O.C. red wine from Abruzzi. Made from the Montepulciano and Sangiovese grapes. If skins are left in during fermentation to obtain a cherry red colour then the term Cerasuolo can be added to label. If aged 2 years then the term Vecchio can also appear on the label.

Monte Real Tinto (Sp) a red wine from the Bodegas Riojanas SA, Rioja. Made from 10% Graciano, 10% Garnacha and 80% Tempranillo grapes. Oak-matured for 3 years and bottle aged for 2 years.

Monterei (Sp) see Val de Monterrei.

Monterey County (USA) an A.V.A. wine area situated south of San Francisco, California and containing the Carmel Valley. Produces table, dessert and sparkling wines from Chardonnay, Sauvignon blanc, Pinot blanc, Pinot noir. Home to Morgan Vineyards, Lockwood, Lohr Winery, Jekel, Monterey Vineyard. See also Almaden.

Monterey Peninsula Winery (USA) a small winery based in Monterey, California. Grape varieties: Cabernet sauvignon, Chardonnay, Petite sirah, Pinot noir and Zinfandel.

Monterey Riesling (USA) an alternative name for the Green sylvaner grape.

Monterey Vineyard (USA) a winery based in the Upper Salinas Valley, Monterey County, California. Grape varieties: Gewürztraminer, Johannisberg riesling, Sauvignon blanc and Zinfandel (owned by Seagram). Produces varietal and noble rot wines.

Monterez (Eng) the brand-name of a drink of brandy, white wine and orange. Can de drunk straight or used as a mixer. Distributed by Harvey's of Bristol in the U.K. Produced by Monterez C°., 28, St. James Square, London. Also a lemon version called Monterez Citron.

Monterez Citron (Eng) the lemon-flavoured version of Monterez.

Monterez Peach (Eng) the peach flavoured version of Monterez.

Monteriggioni (It) a commune of Chianti Classico Riserva.

Monterminod (Fr) a V.D.Q.S. vineyard on the bank of lake Bourget in the Savoie region.

Monte Rossa (It) a sparkling (bottle-fermented) wine producer based in Lombardy.

Monterosso (It) one of the five towns in Cinque Terre, Liguria.

Monterosso Estate (S.Afr) a winery (established 2000) based in Stellenbosch, Western Cape. 68ha. Grape varieties: Cabernet sauvignon, Chenin blanc, Merlot, Sangiovese, Sauvignon blanc. Labels: Old Bush Vine, Socrate.

Monterosso Val d'Arda (It) a D.O.C. white wine from Emilia-Romagna. Made from the Malvasia di candia, Moscato bianco, Ortrugo, Trebbiano romagnolo grapes. The D.O.C. also applies to naturally sparkling wine obtained from musts and wines made according to the current regulations.

Monterrey (Sp) a Denominación de Origen wine-producing region in Galicia. Produces mainly red wines.

Montes (Aus) a natural spring mineral water (established 1990). Mineral contents (milligrammes per litre): Sodium 7mg/l, Calcium 78mg/l, Magnesium 30mg/l, Potassium 2mg/l, Bicarbonates 274mg/l, Chlorides 7mg/l, Sulphates 92mg/l.

Montes (Chile) a 104ha winery estate at Curicó. (Add): Vina Montes S.A. Santiago. Also has holdings in the Colchagua Valley (Apalta vineyard). Produces a range of wines from Cabernet sauvignon, Merlot, Chardonnay, Sauvignon blanc, Syrah. Labels include: Montes Alpha. Website: http://www.monteswines.com 'E'mail: montes@monteswines.com

Monteschiavo (It) a sparkling (cuve close) and still wine (D.O.C. Verdicchio dei Castelli di Jesi) producer based in the Marche region. Labels include: Le Giuncare. Website: http://www.monteschiavo.com 'E'mail: info@monteschiavo.it

Montescudaio Rosso (It) a D.O.C. red wine from the Tuscany region. Produced from the Sangiovese grape.

Monte Seco (Sp) a red wine made by Bodegas Ramón Bilbao SA, Rioja. Matured 2–4 years in oak and for 1–10 years in bottle.

Montes Folly (Chile) a winery based in the Apalta Valley.

Montetusa (It) a D.O.C. barrique-aged Barbera d'Asti wine produced by De Bertelli in Piemonte.

Monte Velaz (Sp) the name given to a range of two red wines produced by Bodegas Velazquez.

Monteverde (It) a natural spring mineral water from Monteverde Valley, Green Mountains, Pistoia. Mineral contents (milligrammes per litre): Sodium 6.1mg/l, Calcium 27.8mg/l, Magnesium 7.5mg/l, Potassium 0.7mg/l, Bicarbonates 98mg/l, Chlorides 4.7mg/l, Sulphates 25.3mg/l, Nitrates 1.6mg/l, Silicates 9mg/l. pH 7.7

Monteverde Spring Water (It) a natural spring mineral water from Monteverde Valley, Green Mountains, Pistoia. Mineral contents (milligrammes per litre): Sodium 25mg/l, Calcium 19.5mg/l, Magnesium 7mg/l, Potassium 18mg/l, Bicarbonates 139.5mg/l, Chlorides 12mg/l, Sulphates 7.3mg/l, Fluorides 0.86mg/l, Nitrates 25mg/l, Silicates 64mg/l. pH 6.7

Monteverdi (It) a low-alcohol white wine produced by European Vintners from mainly the Moscato grape 3% alc by vol.

Monteviejo (Arg) a winery based in the Mendoza region, eastern Argentina. Website:

http://www.monteviejo.com 'E'mail: mapeller@ciudad.com.ar

Monteviña Winery (USA) a winery based in the Shenandoah Valley, Amador County, California. Grape varieties: Barbera, Cabernet sauvignon, Sauvignon blanc and Zinfandel. Produces varietal wines.

Montevista Wines (S.Afr) the brand-name used by the Mooiuitsig Wynkelders for a range of their wines.

Monte Xanic (Mex) a winery based in Baja. Grape varieties include: Cabernet sauvignon, Merlot, Cabernet franc, Petit verdot, Malbec, Sauvignon blanc, Chenin blanc, Sémillon, Chardonnay.

Montezuma Blue (USA) a 38% alc by vol. tequila-based spirit.

Montezuma Cocktail (Cktl) ⅓ measure silver tequila, ⅓ measure verdelho Madeira, 1 egg yolk. Blend altogether with a scoop of crushed ice in a blender and pour into a flute glass.

Montezuma Silver (Mex) a clear tequila with a slight herb flavour.

Mont Fleur (Thai) a natural spring mineral water from Phob Phra Source, Northern Thailand. Mineral contents (milligrammes per litre): Sodium 68.8mg/l, Calcium 36mg/l, Magnesium 17.2mg/l, Potassium 0.9mg/l, Bicarbonates 363.07mg/l, Chlorides 1.2mg/l, Sulphates 5.9mg/l, Fluorides 0.36mg/l, Nitrates 0.1mg/l, Silicates 40.2mg/l, Oxygen 8.8mg/l. pH 7.35

Mont Fleuri (Switz) a dry white produced in the Sion district of the Valais region from the Riesling grape.

Montfras (Fr) a natural spring mineral water from Montfras. Mineral contents (milligrammes per litre): Sodium 10.6mg/l, Calcium 96mg/l, Magnesium 6.1mg/l, Potassium 3.7mg/l, Bicarbonates 297.7mg/l, Chlorides 22.6mg/l, Sulphates 9.3mg/l, Fluorides 0.18mg/l, Silicates 36.2mg/l. pH 7.3

Montgomery Ale (Eng) a 3.9% alc by vol. limited edition ale from the Theakston Brewery, Masham, North Yorkshire.

Montgomery Spring (Wal) a spring mineral water from Churchstoke, Powys.

Montgras Vineyards (Chile) vineyards based at Colchagua. 100ha. Grape varieties: Cabernet sauvignon, Merlot.

Montgros Blanc (Sp) a grapey white wine produced in the Penedés region by Aquila Rossa.

Montgueux (Fr) a Cru Champagne village in the Canton de l'Aube. District: Château Thierry.

Monthélie (Fr) an A.C. wine village (commune) in the Côte de Beaune. Has ten Premier Cru vineyards: Duresse, La Taupine, Le Cas-Rougeot, Le Château-Gaillard, Le Clos-Gauthey, Le Meix-Bataille, Les Champs-Fulliot, Les Riottes, Les Vignes Rondes and Sur la Velle. 100ha.

Monthélie-Côte de Beaune (Fr) the alternative A.C. classification of Monthélie wines.

Monthélie-Côte de Beaune-Villages (Fr) the alternative A.C. classification of Monthélie wines.

Monthelon (Fr) a Cru Champagne village in the Canton d'Avize. District: Épernay.

Montherminod (Fr) a noted wine-producing village of Roussette in the Savoie region, south-eastern France.

Monthoux (Fr) a V.D.Q.S. vineyard based on the left bank of the river Rhône in the Savoie region.

Montialbero S.A. (Sp) a noted producer of Montilla wines based in Montilla-Moriles.

Monticcello (Mex) a natural spring mineral water from Reynosa.

Monticello (It) a natural spring mineral water from Monticello.

Monticello (USA) an A.V.A. area of Virginia. Based near Charlottesville on eastern slopes of Blue Ridge Mountains. Home to vineyards of Barboursville, Horton Vineyards, Jefferson Vineyards.

Monticello Cellars (USA) a winery based near Trefethen, Napa Valley, California. Grape varieties: Cabernet sauvignon, Chardonnay, Gewürztraminer and Sauvignon blanc. Produce varietal wines.

Monticola (USA) an American vine species used for grafting in the Rhône in France.

Montigny-Sous-Châtillon (Fr) a Cru Champagne village in the Canton de Châtillon-sur-Marne. District: Reims.

Montilla (Sp) *see* Montilla-Moriles.

Montilla-Moriles (Sp) a D.O. wine region in southern Spain. Soil: alberos and ruedos. Produces wines similar in style to Sherry, but not always fortified. Wines are attacked by flor to produce Finos. Kept for 6–12 months in Tinajas. Matured in criaderas and soleras. Grape varieties: Baladí, Lairén, Moscatel, Pedro Ximénez, Torrontés. *see* A la Ciega, Afritado, Vinos Generosos. Three styles of wine produced: Vinos Jóvenes Afrutados from 100% Pedro ximénez or it is blended with other varieties. Solera white wines of natural strength (13%–15% alc by vol.) with one year in oak, sold as Pale Dry, Medium Dry, Medium Sweet, Pale Cream, Cream. Vinos Generosos or fortified wines between 15%–22% alc by vol. Fino at 15% min. alc by vol., Amontillado at 16% min. alc by vol., Olorosos at 16% min. alc by vol.

Montilla Sierra (Sp) a fine Montilla (of Fino Sherry quality).

Montilleros (Sp) Montilla wines.

Montils (Fr) a commune in the Charente-Maritime département whose grapes are used in the production of Cognac (grown in the Bois Ordinaires area). Also the local name for a white grape variety.

Montini (Mex) a noted liqueur producer. Produces Camino Real (a coffee-flavoured liqueur) and Xanath (a vanilla-flavoured liqueur).

Montino (S.Afr) the label for a petillant light white wine produced by the Riebeek Cellars winery, Swartland, Western Cape.

Montinore Vineyards (USA) vineyards based at Forest Road, Oregon. Grape varieties: Pinot noir, Pinot gris, Chardonnay, Riesling, Gewürztraminer, Müller-Thurgau.

M

Montinverno (It) a still and sparkling natural spring mineral water from Montinverno, Parma. (blue label: sparkling/green label: still). Mineral contents (milligrammes per litre): Sodium 17.5mg/l, Calcium 132.8mg/l, Magnesium 38.9mg/l, Potassium 2.8mg/l, Bicarbonates 401mg/l, Chlorides 7.1mg/l, Sulphates 183.5mg/l, Fluorides 0.2mg/l, Iron 815mg/l, Silicates 25mg/l. pH 7.2

Montisol S.A. (Sp) a producer of Montilla based in Montilla-Moriles.

Montjean (Fr) a commune in the A.C. Savennières, Anjou-Saumur, Loire.

Montjoie (Fr) a natural spring mineral water from Cairanne, Vaucluse. Mineral contents (milligrammes per litre): Sodium 32mg/l, Calcium 44mg/l, Magnesium 24mg/l, Potassium 2mg/l, Bicarbonates 287mg/l, Chlorides 5mg/l, Sulphates 3mg/l, Nitrates 1mg/l. pH 7.6

Mont Josephine (Sey) a natural spring mineral water from the Seychelles.

Mont la Salle (USA) part of the Napa Valley, California where the vineyards of the Christian Brothers are situated.

Mont-Laurent [Le] (Fr) a vineyard in the A.C. commune of Montagny, Côte Chalonnaise, Burgundy.

Mont 'Les Pierrailles' (Switz) a white wine produced in Rolle, La Côte, western Switzerland by Hammel.

Mont-le-Vignoble (Fr) a commune in the Côtes de Toul, Lorraine. Produces Vins gris.

Montlouis (Fr) an A.C. white wine produced in the Touraine district in the Central Loire. Produced from the Chenin blanc grape.

Montlouis Mousseux (Fr) an A.C. sparkling white wine from the Touraine district in the Loire.

Montlouis Pétillant (Fr) an A.C. white wine from the Touraine distict in the Loire.

Montloup (Fr) the brand-name for a red A.C. Coteaux du Languedoc wine and a white A.C. Touraine wine produced near Montpellier.

Montmains (Fr) a Premier Cru vineyard of Chablis. Often has the Premier Crus of Forêts and Butteaux used as its vintage.

Mont-Marçal (Sp) a fine wine-producer based in the Penedés region. Produces Blanco Añada, Primer Vi Novell and a Gran Reserva Cava (Parellada, Xarel-lo, Macabeo).

Montmartre (Cktl) ¾ measure dry gin, ⅛ measure Italian vermouth, ⅛ measure Curaçao. Stir over ice, strain into a cocktail glass and top with a cherry.

Montmélas-Saint-Sorlin (Fr) a commune in the A.C. Beaujolais-Villages or Beaujolais-Montmélas-Saint-Sorlin status.

Montmélian (Fr) a red wine from the Savoie in south-eastern France. Made with the Mondeuse grape.

Montmirail (Fr) an aperient mineral water.

Montmort (Fr) a canton in the district of Épernay, Champagne. Has the Cru villages of Baye, Beaunay, Broyes, Coizard-Joches, Congy, Courjeonnet, Étoges, Fèrebrianges, Oyes, Talus-Saint-Prix and Villevenard.

Montmurat (Fr) a red wine of the Cantal département.

Montner (Fr) a red wine produced in the Côtes du Roussillon-Villages.

Montonec (Sp) an alternative name for the Parellada grape.

Montonega (Sp) an aromatic Parellada clone developed at Agro 2001 (bio-technologic research station at Codorníu).

Montonel (Sp) an alternative name for the Parellada grape.

Mont-Palais (Fr) a vineyard in the A.C. commune of Rully, Côte Chalonnaise, Burgundy.

Montpellier de Tulbagh (S.Afr) *see* Montpellier du Sud.

Montpellier du Sud (S.Afr) a winery (established 1965) based in Tulbagh, Western Cape. 35ha. Grape varieties: Chenin blanc, Merlot, Pinot noir, Weisser riesling. Produces varietal and sparkling wines. Originally known as Constantia de Tulbagh then Montpellier de Tulbagh. Website: http://www.montpellier.co.za

Montpellier Estate (S.Afr) a winery (established 1968) based in Tulbagh, Western Cape. (Add): Box 24, Tulbagh 6820. Grape varieties: Cabernet sauvignon, Chardonnay, Chenin blanc, Colombard, Gewürztraminer, Pinot blanc, Pinot noir, Weisser riesling. Produce varietal and sparkling wines including Tuinwingerd. Website: http://www.montpellierwines.co.za

Montpeyroux (Fr) a sub-area of the A.C. Coteaux du Languedoc-Montpeyroux in the Hérault département, southern France.

Mont-Près-Chambord-Cour-Cheverny (Fr) a V.D.Q.S. white wine from the Loire. Is often shortened to Cheverny.

Montrachet [Le] (Fr) a Grand Cru vineyard between the communes of Bâtard-Montrachet, Chassagne-Montrachet, Chevalier-Montrachet, Criot-Bâtard-Montrachet and Puligny-Montrachet in the Côtes de Beaune 7.7ha. White wine made with the Chardonnay grape.

Montrachets [Les] (Fr) a Grand Cru vineyard in the A.C. commune of Montrachet, Côte de Beaune, Burgundy.

Montravel (Fr) an A.C. district of the Bergerac region. Produces dry, semi-dry and sweet white wines. *See also* Haut Montravel and Côtes de Montravel. Minimum alc by vol. 11%.

Montreal Club Bouncer (Cktl) 25mls (⅙ gill) dry gin, 2 dashes Pernod. Stir over ice in an old-fashioned glass.

Montreal Gin Sour (Cktl) ½ measure in, ½ measure lemon juice, ½ egg white. Shake over ice, strain into a sour glass and top with a slice of lemon.

Montredon (Fr) part of the Châteauneuf-du-Pape area of the southern Rhône.

Montregio di Massa Marittima (It) a new D.O.C. located in Tuscany.

M

Montrevenots [Les] (Fr) a Premier Cru vineyard [part] in the A.C. commune of Beaune, Côte de Beaune, Burgundy 8.28ha.

Mont Rochelle Mountain Vineyards (S.Afr) a winery (19ha) based in Franschhoek, Western Cape. Grape varieties: Cabernet franc, Cabernet sauvignon, Chardonnay, Merlot, Pinotage, Sauvignon blanc, Shiraz, Syrah. Label: Alchemy. Website: http://www.montrochelle.co.za

Montrolland (Afr) a natural spring mineral water from Senegal. Mineral contents (milligrammes per litre): Sodium 69mg/l, Calcium 64mg/l, Magnesium 9.7mg/l, Potassium 4.2mg/l, Bicarbonates 219mg/l, Chlorides 121mg/l, Sulphates 24.5mg/l, Nitrates 0.1mg/l.

Montrose Vineyard (Austr) a winery based at Henry Lawson Drive, Mudgee, New South Wales. Grape varieties: Chardonnay, Sémillon, Cabernet sauvignon, Malbec, Shiraz. Labels include Poet's Corner.

Montrose Whisky Company (Scot) a whisky blending company (established 1973) that buys in and then blends to its own labels. Labels include: Double Q, Old Montrose and Pipe Major.

Mont Rouge (Isr) a semi-dry red table wine.

Mont Rouscous [1] (Fr) a natural spring mineral water from Lacaune. (Add): Société des Eaux de Mont Rouscous, 81230 Laucaune les Bains. Mineral contents (milligrammes per litre): Sodium 2.8mg/l, Calcium 1.2mg/l, Magnesium 0.2mg/l, Potassium 0.4mg/l, Bicarbonates 4.9mg/l, Chlorides 3.2mg/l, Sulphates 3.3mg/l, Nitrates 2.3mg/l, Silicates 6.9mg/l. pH 6.0 Website: http://www.mont-roucous.com 'E'mail: mont-roucous@wanadoo.fr

Mont Rouscous [2] (Fr) a natural spring mineral water from Lacaune. (Add): Société des Eaux de Mont Rouscous, 81230 Laucaune les Bains. Mineral contents (milligrammes per litre): Sodium 2.9mg/l, Calcium 0.46mg/l, Magnesium 0.28mg/l, Potassium 0.39mg/l, Bicarbonates 7.32mg/l, Chlorides 2.85mg/l, Sulphates 3.3mg/l, Nitrates 7.04mg/l. pH 6.12 Website: http://www.mont-roucous.com 'E'mail: mont-roucous@wanadoo.fr

Montruc (It) a D.O.C. Barbera d'Asti wine produced by Martinetti (Franco) in Piemonte from low yielding 50 year old vines. Aged in barrique.

Montsant (Sp) a Denominación de Origen region created in 2002 based in the lower Priorato mountains of Tarragona.

Monts Damnes [Les] (Fr) a vineyard in the commune of Chavignol, A.C. Sancerre. Central Vineyards, Loire.

Monts de la Grage (Fr) a Vin de Pays area in the Saint-Chinian region in the Hérault département, southern France. Produces red, rosé and dry white wines.

Monts de Milieu (Fr) a Premier Cru vineyard of Chablis, Burgundy.

Monts du Tessalah (Alg) a wine-producing area in the Oran département. Produces red, rosé and white wines.

Montserrat Cocktail (Cktl) 40mls (⅓ gill) dry gin, 2 teaspoons lime juice, 1 teaspoon grenadine, 2 dashes absinthe. Shake over ice, strain into a cocktail glass and serve with a cherry.

Monts-Luisants (Fr) a Premier Cru vineyard in the A.C. commune of Morey-Saint-Denis, Côte de Nuits, Burgundy.

Montsoreau (Fr) a white wine of Saumur in the Anjou-Saumur district of the Loire.

Mont St. John Cellars (USA) a winery based in Carneros, Napa Valley, California. Grape varieties: Cabernet sauvignon, Chardonnay, Gewürztraminer, Johannisberg riesling, Pinot noir and Zinfandel. Produce varietal wines.

Mont-sur-Rolle (Switz) a wine-producing village in La Côte. Sometimes abbreviated to Rolle.

Mont Tauch (Fr) a wine co-operative based in the A.C. Fitou, Languedoc-Roussillon. Has 200 members owning 1850ha. Label: Les Gueches

Montù (It) a red grape variety grown in Emilia. Also spelt Montuni.

Montúa (Sp) a white grape variety grown in Extremadura. Also known as Mantúa.

Montulia S.A. (Sp) a producer of Montilla based in Montilla-Moriles.

Montuni (It) an alternative spelling of Montù.

Montys Python's Holy (Gr)ail (Eng) a 4.7% alc by vol. bottled beer. Brewed to mark the 30th anniversary celebrations of Monty Python by the Black Sheep Brewery, Masham, North Yorkshire.

Montys Revenge (Eng) a 4.1% alc by vol. ale brewed to commemorate V.E. day.

Monvedro (Port) a black grape variety grown in the Alentejo region.

Monviso (It) a sparkling natural spring mineral water from Fucine Luserna, San Giovanni, Torino. Mineral contents (milligrammes per litre): Sodium 1.1mg/l, Magnesium 0.5mg/l, Potassium 0.3mg/l, Chlorides 0.6mg/l, Sulphates 4.8mg/l. pH 7.9

Monymusk Distillery (W.Ind) a rum distillery based on the island of Jamaica.

Monzernheim (Ger) village (Anb): Rheinhessen. (Ber): Wonnegau. (Gro): Pilgerpfad. (Vins): Goldberg, Steinböhl.

Monzingen (Ger) village (Anb): Nahe. (Ber): Schloss Böckelheim. (Gro): Paradiesgarten. (Vins): Frühlingsplätzchen, Halenberg, Rosenberg.

Moodemere Red (Austr) a red wine from the Gracerray vineyards. Made from the Cabernet sauvignon, Shiraz and Durif grapes.

Moodies Mild (Eng) a 6% alc by vol. strong mild ale brewed by the Fernanders Brewery, West Yorkshire.

Mooi Bly Winery (S.Afr) a winery (established 2003) based in Huguenot, Paarl, Western Cape. 19ha. Grape varieties: Cabernet franc, Cabernet sauvignon, Chardonnay, Chenin blanc, Malbec, Petit verdot, Tannat. Website: http://www.moibly.com

Mooiplaas Estate (S.Afr) a winery (established 1963) based in Koelenhof, Stellenbosch, Western Cape. 120ha. Grape varieties: Cabernet sauvignon,

Merlot, Pinotage, Sauvignon blanc, Shiraz. Sells its wines in bulk to the SFW. Website: http://www.moiplaas.co.za

Mooiuitsig Wynkelders (S.Afr) a large winery (established 1947) based in Bonnievale, Western Cape. (Add): Box 15, Bonnievale 6730. Grape varieties: Cabernet sauvignon, Chardonnay, Chenin blanc, Hanepoot, Merlot, Muscadel, Pinotage, Shiraz. Labels: African Wine Adventure, Bonwin, Clemence Creek, (no longer produced), Nagmaalwyn, Oude Rust, Oulap Se Rooi, Overberger, Ptjie Effe Droog. Also produces a large number of fortified and varietal wines. Website: http://www.mooiuitsig.co.za

Mool (Kor) water.

Moomba Cocktail (Cktl) 20mls (¾ fl.oz) Bacardi rum, 20mls (¾ fl.oz) Grand Marnier, 10mls (½ fl.oz) orange juice, 5mls (¼ fl.oz) lemon juice, dash grenadine. Shake over ice, strain into a cocktail glass and add a twist of orange peel on top.

Moondah Brook (Austr) part of the Houghton Vineyards in Western Australia. 84ha. Grape varieties: Cabernet sauvignon, Chardonnay, Chenin blanc and Verdelho.

Moondance (Eng) a 3.8% alc by vol. bitter ale brewed by the Four Rivers Brewery, Newcastle-on-Tyne.

Moondance (Eng) a 4.2% alc by vol. ale brewed by the Triple FFF Brewery, Four Marks, near Alton, Hampshire.

Moonlight Cocktail (Cktl) 50mls (2fl.ozs) Calvados, juice of a lemon, 2 dashes gomme syrup. Shake over ice and strain into an ice-filled old-fashioned glass.

Moonlighter Cocktail (Cktl) ⅖ measure Mandarine Napoléon, ⅕ measure white rum, ⅖ measure pineapple juice, dash egg white. Shake over ice, strain into an ice-filled highball glass, dress with a pineapple cube and cherry.

Moonlight Mouse (Eng) the label of a seasonal ale brewed by Vaux Breweries.

Moonquake Cocktail (Cktl) ⅗ measure Jamaican rum, ⅖ measure Tia Maria, juice ¼ lemon. Shake over ice and strain into a cocktail glass.

Moonraker Brown Ale (Eng) a bottled brown ale 1032 O.G. brewed by the Gibbs Mew Brewery in Salisbury, Wiltshire.

Moonraker Strong Ale (Eng) a rich, dark, sweet ale 1047 O.G. brewed by the Lees Brewery in Middleton, Greater Manchester.

Moon River (Cktl) ¼ measure gin, ¼ measure Cointreau, ¼ measure apricot brandy, ⅛ measure Galliano, ⅛ measure lime juice. Stir over ice, strain into a cocktail glass and add a cherry.

Moon Rocket (Cktl) 1 measure kirsch, ½ measure apricot brandy, ½ measure orange juice, shake over ice, strain into a cocktail glass and finally add ⅓ barspoon grenadine.

Moonshine (Eng) a 4.3% alc by vol. ale brewed by the Abbeydale Brewery Ltd., South Yorkshire.

Moonshine (USA) the nickname of illegally distilled whiskey. Came about because of the 1791 Excise Tax of USA. *see* Whiskey Rebellion, Bushie and Poteen.

Moonshiner (USA) a person who makes and deals with Moonshine.

Moonstone (Eng) an extra strong bottled white cider from Matthew Clark, Somerset.

Moor Beer Company (Eng) a brewery (established 1996). (Add): Whitley Farm, Ashcott, Polden Hills, Bridgewater, Somerset TA7 9QW. Brews: Avalon Springtime 4% alc by vol., Merlins Magic 4.3% alc by vol., Old Freddy Walker 7.3% alc by vol., Peat Porter 4.5% alc by vol., Santa Moors 4.8% alc by vol., Withy Cutter 3.8% alc by vol. Website: http://www.moorbeer.co.uk 'E'mail: info@moorbeer.co.uk

Moorcock Brewing C° [The] (Eng) a brewery. (Add): The Moorcock Inn, Garsdalke Head, Sedbergh, Cumbria LA10 5PU. Brews: Mescans Porter 4.3% alc by vol., Mild 3.2% alc by vol., Oakley Pale Ale 3.8% alc by vol., Old Pa Porter 3.8% alc by vol. Website: http://www.moorcockinn.com 'E'mail: info@moorcockinn.com

Moore's Creek (Austr) a vineyard in the Hunter Valley (part of the Tyrrells vineyards). Produces: Chardonnay.

Moore's Diamond (USA) a white American grape variety grown in New York State. Produce neutral dry wines.

Moorgat Brasserie (Bel) a brewery (established 1871) based at Breendonk-Puurs. Brews: Duvel.

Moorhouses Brewery [Burnley] Ltd (Eng) a brewery (established 1865). (Add): The Brewery, 4 Moorhouse Street, Burnley, Lancashire BB11 5EN. Taken over by Apollo Leisure of Oxford (1979). Brews: Black Cat 3.4% alc by vol., Black Panther, Blondwitch, Broomstick Bitter, Owd Ale, 6% alc by vol., Noted for cask-conditioned Pendle Witches Brew 1050 O.G. (5.1% alc. By vol)., Premium Bitter, Pride of Pendle, Reinbeers Revenge, Witches Cauldron, Witchfinder General. Website: Http://www.moorhouses.co.uk 'E'mail: info@moorhouses.co.uk

Moorilla Estate (Austr) a vineyard. (Add): 655 Main Road, Berriedale, Tasmania 7011. 9ha. Grape varieties: Cabernet sauvignon, Chardonnay, Gewürztraminer, Rhine riesling and Pinot noir. Produce varietal wines.

Moorland Arms Bitter (Eng) a 3.3% alc by vol. bitter ale from Moorlands Arms in Romford, Essex.

Moorlynch (Eng) the label used by the Spring Farm Vineyard in Somerset for their white and sparkling wines. Grape varieties: Faber, Schönburger, Würzer.

Moorooduc Estate Vineyard (Austr) a winery (established 1983). (Add): Derril Road, Moorooduc, Victoria. Grape varieties: Chardonnay, Cabernet sauvignon, Pinot noir.

Moosberg (Ger) vineyard (Anb): Rheinhessen. (Ber): Nierstein. (Gro): Gutes Domtal. (Vil): Hahnheim.

Moosberg (Ger) vineyard (Anb): Rheinhessen. (Ber): Nierstein. (Gro): Gutes Domtal. (Vil): Sörgenloch.

M

Moosehead Brewery (Can) a famous independent brewery (established 1867) in Saint John, New Brunswick and Dartmouth. Originally started as the 'Army & Navy Brewery'. In 1877 known as 'S. Oland, Sons & Cº.' Produces a range of lagers, ales and an ice beer.

Moosehead Beer (Can) a 5% alc by vol. bottled lager brewed by the Moosehead Brewery, Saint John, New Brunswick and Dartmouth.

Moosehead Canadian Ice (Can) bottled ice beer brewed by the Moosehead Brewery, Saint John, New Brunswick and Dartmouth.

Moosehead Canadian Lager (Can) bottled lager brewed by the Moosehead Brewery, Saint John, New Brunswick and Dartmouth for the international market.

Moosehead Canadian Light (Can) bottled light lager brewed by the Moosehead Brewery, Saint John, New Brunswick and Dartmouth for the American market.

Mooser Dunkel (Ger) a red lager 5.2% alc by vol. from Arcobräu Brauerei in Bavaria.

Mooser Hell (Ger) a pale lager 4.8% alc by vol. from Arcobräu Brauerei in Bavaria.

Moose Valley Vineyard (USA) a red wine (Cabernet sauvignon) produced by the D.R. Stephens winery, Napa Valley, California.

Moot (Ger) must.

Moquega (S.Am) a vineyard area based in southern Peru.

Mór (Hun) a wine region 80kms west of Budapest. One of the few European wine regions that did not succumb to Phylloxera. Ezerjó is the main grape variety and Móri Ezerjó the best wine.

Moracia (Sp) a red grape variety grown in the La Mancha region.

Morafeitl Selektion (Aus) the label for a range of white wines (Morillon) and (Sauvignon blanc) produced by the Neumeister winery, Süd-Oststeiermark.

Morand (Switz) an eau-de-vie distillery based at Martigny, Valais. Produces: Williamine, Reine-Claude, Marc de Dôle, Vieille Lie du Valais, Grand-Saint-Bernard liqueur, Bon Valaisan.

Morandé Winery (Chile) a winery based in the Cachapoal Valley, Central Chile. Produces a range of varietal wines.

Morandell (Aus) a well-known wine merchants based in the Burgenland, Gumpoldskirchen and Vienna.

Morangie Water (Scot) a natural spring mineral water from Fuaran Nan Slainte, Glen Morangie.

Morangis (Fr) a Cru Champagne village in the Canton d'Avize. District: Épernay.

Morastell (Sp) a white grape variety used in the south-eastern area of Spain for sparkling wines.

Moraster (Sp) a black grape variety grown in Aragón, Penedés, Rioja and Catalonia. *see* Monastrel.

Moravia (Sp) a red grape variety grown in central and southern Spain.

Moravia-Pils (Ger) an outstanding pilsener lager 4.9% alc by vol. from the Moravia Brauerei in Lüheburg (a subsidiary of Holsten).

Mörbisch (Aus) a wine-village in the Burgenland. Produces fine sweet white wines plus some dry white and red wines.

Mór-Csàszàr (Hun) a wine-producing district in northern Transdanubia.

Mordant (Eng) a term given to wines with excess tannin/acid so that they taste sharp and astringent.

Morddré (S.Afr) a medium-sweet, dessert wine made from the Hanepoot grape.

Mordue Brewery (Eng) a brewery (established 1995). (Add): 21a Oak Road, West Chirton North Ind Estate, New York, North Shields, Tyne and Wear NE29 8SF. Brews: Al' Wheat Pet 4.1% alc by vol., Autumn Tyne 4% alc by vol., Five Bridge Bitter 3.8% alc by vol., Geordie Pride 4.2% alc by vol., Headmaster 5.2% alc by vol., India Pale Ale 5.1% alc by vol., India Pale Ale 5.5% alc by vol., Millennium Bridge Ale 3.8% alc by vol., Radgie Gadgie 4.8% alc by vol (brewed with American hops), Sprint Tyne 4% alc by vol., Summer Tyne 3.6% alc by vol., Workie Ticket 4.5% alc by vol. Website: http://www.morduebrewery.com 'E'mail: enquiries@morduebrewery.com

More (Tai) a natural spring mineral water from Taiwan.

Moreau & Fils [J.] (Fr) a Burgundy négociant-éleveur based at Chablis (owned by Boisset), a large producer of Chablis wines. (Add): Route d'Auxerre, 89800 Chablis. Range includes: Chablis Grand Cru Les Clos, Premier Cru Mont de Milieu, Montmains and Vaillon, Chablis, Petit Chablis. Also Pouilly Fuissé, Côte de Beaune-Villages, Bourgogne Pinot noir, Bourgogne Blanc, Sancerre, Muscadet, Vin de Pays d'Oc Chardonnay and Merlot.

Moreeke (Hol) a 5% alc by vol. bottled special beer brewed by the Bavaria Bier Brouwerij, Lieshout.

Morein (Fr) a Premier Cru vineyard of A.C. Chablis. Is often re-classified as the Premier Cru vineyard Les Fourneaux.

Morellino (It) the local name used in Grosetto for a red grape variety (a sub-variety of the Sangiovese).

Morellino de Scansano (It) a D.O.C. red wine from Tuscany. Produced from the Morellino (Sangiovese) grape plus up to 15% of other varieties.

Morellone (It) an alternative name for Montepulciano.

Moreno S.A. (Sp) a noted producer of Montilla. Based in Montilla-Moriles.

Möreson Wine Farm (S.Afr) a winery (established 1986) based in Franschhoek, Western Cape. 18ha. (Add): Box 114, Franshhoeck 7690. Grape varieties: Cabernet sauvignon, Chardonnay, Chenin blanc, Merlot, Pinotage, Sauvignon blanc. Labels: Cuvée Cape, Magia, Pinehurst, Soleil du Matin. Website: http://www.moreson.co.za

M

Moreto (Port) a black grape variety grown in Alentejo and Bairrada regions.

Moreto do Dão (Port) an alternative name for the Malvasia Preta in the Douro region.

Moretti Breweries (It) a brewing company with two breweries.

Morewag (S.Afr) a winery (established 1995) based in Klapmiuts, Stellenbosch, Western Cape. Grape variety: Pinotage.

Morey [André] (Fr) a noted négociant based in Beaune, Côte de Beaune, Burgundy.

Morey et Fils [Albert] (Fr) a négociant based in Chassagne-Montrachet and Meursault, Côte de Beaune, Burgundy.

Morey-Rocault [Bernard] (Fr) a noted négociant-éleveur based at Meursault, Côte de Beaune, Burgundy.

Morey-Saint-Denis (Fr) a commune within the Côte de Nuits between the communes of Gevrey-Chambertin and Chambolle-Musigny. Has 5 Grand Crus: Bonne Mares, Clos de la Roche, Clos des Lambrays, Clos de Tart and Clos Saint-Denis. 31.9ha. and 26 Premier Crus: Aux Charmes, Aux Cheseaux, Calouères, Chabiots, Clos Baulet, Clos Bussière, Clos Sorbet, Côte Rôtie, La Riotte, Le Clos des Ormes, Les Blanchards, Les Bouchots, Les Chaffots, Les Charnières, Les Chénevery, Les Faconnières, Les Fremières, Les Genevrières, Les Gruenchers, Les Millandes, Les Ruchots, Les Sorbet, Maison Brûlée, Meix-Rentiers, Monts-Luisants. 60.5ha.

Morgadio de Torre (Port) a Vinho Verde produced by SOGRAPE from the Alvarinho grape.

Morgan (Port) Vintage Port shippers. Vintages: 1870, 1872, 1873, 1875, 1878, 1881, 1884, 1887, 1890, 1894, 1896, 1900, 1904, 1908, 1912, 1920, 1922, 1924, 1927, 1942, 1948, 1950, 1955, 1960, 1963, 1966, 1970, 1977, 1982, 1985, 1991, 1994, 1997, 2003. (a subsidiary of Croft).

Morgan Estate (USA) a winery based in the Santa Lucia Highlands, Monterey County, California. Grape variety: Pinot noir. Labels: Double L. Vineyard, Twelve Clones.

Morgan Hill (USA) a wine town in Santa Clara County, California.

Morgan's Mellow Spiced (W.Ind) a blend of golden rums and spices from Captain Morgan in Jamaica (the word 'Captain' has been dropped).

Morgante (It) a winery based on the island of Sicily.

Morgan Vineyards (Austr) a winery based in Seville, Yarra Valley, Victoria. (Add): Davross Court, Seville, Victoria. Website: http://www.morganvineyards.com.au

Morgarinha-Bagaceira do Minho (Port) an aguardente produced by Joaquin Miranda Campelo & Filhos. 43% alc by vol.

Morgen (Ger) a land measure 0.25ha (0.6acre).

Morgenbachtahler (Ger) vineyard (Anb): Mittelrhein. (Ber): Bacharach. (Gro): Schloss Reichenstein. (Vil): Trechtingshausen.

Morgenhof Estate (S.Afr) a winery (established 1692) based in Simonsberg, Stellenbosch, Western Cape. 70ha. Grape Varieties include: Cabernet franc, Cabernet sauvignon, Chardonnay, Chenin blanc, Malbec, Merlot, Pinotage, Pinot noir, Sauvignon blanc, Shiraz. Labels: Fantail, Première Selection, Vineyards Red. Website: http://www.morgenhof.com

Morgenster Estate (S.Afr) a winery (established 1993) based in the Somerset West Valley, Stellenbosch, Western Cape. 40ha. Grape varieties: Cabernet franc, Cabernet sauvignon, Merlot, Petit verdot. Labels: Lourens River Valley, Third Wine. Website: http://www.morgenster.co.za

Morgeot (Fr) a Premier Cru vineyard [part] in the A.C. commune of Chassagne-Montrachet, Côte de Beaune, Burgundy 3.94ha.

Morgon (Fr) an A.C. Cru Beaujolais-Villages, Burgundy, 1120ha under vines.

Moriah (Isr) a sweet dessert wine.

Moriau Brasserie (Bel) a brewery based near Lot in central Belgium.

Moriers [Les] (Fr) a vineyard in the A.C. Fleurie Cru Beaujolais-Villages, Burgundy.

Móri Ezerjó (Hun) a dry golden wine from the Mór region. Made with the Ezerjó grape.

Moriles Alto (Sp) part of the Montilla-Moriles where the finest grapes are grown for Montilla wines.

Morillon (Fr) the local name for Pinot noir in Champagne region.

Morillon Blanc (Aus) a local name in Styria for the Chardonnay grape. See also Feinburgunder.

Morillon Taconé (Fr) an alternative name for the Pinot meunier grape in eastern France.

Morin (Fr) a producer of fine Calvados based in Ivry-la-Bataille, (Eure-et-Loir département).

Morio [Herren] (Ger) a German viticulturist who has produced many crossbred grape varieties. e.g. Morio-muscat.

Morio-Muskat (Ger) a white grape variety, a cross between Silvaner and Pinot blanc. Has a strong fruity flavour.

Morisca (Sp) a red grape variety grown in western Spain. Produces good red wines.

Morisfarms (It) a winery based in the Tuscany region. Label: Avvoltore.

Morisoli Vineyard (USA) a red wine (Cabernet sauvignon) produced by the Galleron winery, Napa Valley, California.

Moristel (Sp) a red grape variety grown in Somontano.

Moritz Fiege Brauerei (Ger) see Fiege Brauerei (Moritz).

Moritz Fiege Pils (Ger) a 4.9% alc by vol. bottled pilsner brewed by Moritz Fiege Brauerei, Bochum.

Moritz Thienelt (Ger) a noted liqueur producer based in Düsseldorf.

Morjuce (Eng) the brand-name for frozen fruit juices (un-sweetened) from the McCain Cº.

Mork and Mindy (Cktl) 1 part Royal Irish Chocolate Mint Liqueur, 2 parts Tia Maria, 3 parts Cognac. Shake over ice, strain into a large cocktail glass and float cream on top.

Morkel (S.Afr) the label for a red wine (Pinotage) produced by the Bellevue Estate, Stellenbosch, Western Cape. Also produces PK Morkel (Pinotage single vineyard and 50% oak-aging).

Mørkt (Den) dark brewed beer (bottom-fermented), also word for porter.

Mörkt (Swe) dark brewed beer (bottom-fermented).

Mørkt Øl (Den) dark beer.

Morland Brewery (Eng) a brewery. (Add): The Brewery, Ock Street, Abingdon, Oxfordshire. Noted for cask-conditioned Artist's Ale 1032 O.G. Viking Pale 1042 O.G. Old Speckled Hen 1050 O.G. Monarch 1065 O.G. Hen's Tooth, Original Bitter, Old Masters, Revival. Owns Ruddles.

Morland Old Masters (Eng) a premium cask bitter from the Morland Brewery, Abingdon.

Morland Vineyard (USA) a winery based near King George, Virginia. Produces French hybrid and vinifera wines.

Mormónta (Ire) wormwood.

Mormoreto (It) a red I.G.T. wine produced from 85% Cabernet sauvignon and 15% Cabernet franc grapes by Marchesi de' Frescobaldi in Tuscany.

Mornag (Afr) a co-operative based in Tunisia. Owned by the UCCVT.

Morning Advertiser (Eng) a newspaper once printed Monday-Thursday for the licensed trade. The L.V.A. journal. Now renamed The Licensee (and Morning Advertiser). Printed Thursdays. Websites: http://www.william-reed.co.uk/ http://www.MorningAdvertiser.co.uk

Morning Advertiser Gin (Eng) *see* Gin City.

Morning Cocktail (Cktl) 30mls (¼ gill) brandy, 30mls (¼ gill) French brandy, 2 dashes absinthe, orange bitters, Curaçao and maraschino. Stir well over ice, strain into a cocktail glass, add a cherry and a twist of lemon peel juice on top.

Morning Dew (Cktl) ½ measure Irish whiskey, ¾ measure grapefruit juice, ¼ measure crème de banane, dash blue Curaçao, 1 egg white. Shake over ice, strain into a cocktail glass, dress with a cherry and orange slice.

Morning Egg Nogg (Cktl) 80mls (⅔ gill) brandy, 20mls (⅙ gill) yellow Chartreuse, 1 egg, 1 teaspoon sugar, 80mls (⅔ gill) milk. Shake over ice, strain into a highball glass and add a dash of nutmeg on top.

Morning Glory Cocktail [1] (Cktl) ½ measure brandy, ¼ measure orange Curaçao, ¼ measure lemon juice, 2 dashes Pastis, 2 dashes Angostura. Shake over ice, strain into a cocktail glass and top with a twist of lemon peel.

Morning Glory Cocktail [2] (Cktl) 35mls (1½fl.ozs) Scotch whisky, 1 egg white, 1 teaspoon sugar. Shake over ice, strain into an ice-filled highball glass and top with soda water.

Morning Glory Daisy (Cktl) 60mls (½ gill) of spirit, juice of ½ lemon, 1 egg white, 1 teaspoon sugar syrup, 3 dashes absinthe. Shake well over ice and strain into a highball glass filled with ice.

Morning Glory Fizz (Cktl) 90mls (¾ gill) spirit, juice ½ lemon (or lime), 3 dashes Pernod, white of egg, sugar syrup to taste. Shake well over ice, strain into a highball glass and top with soda water.

Morning Mashie [The] (Cktl) ⅓ measure dry gin, ½ measure anisette, ⅓ measure lemon squash, 1 teaspoon Pernod, dash Angostura, ½ egg white, juice ½ lemon. Shake well over ice and strain into a 125mls (5fl.oz) goblet.

Mornington Vineyards (Austr) a winery (established 1988) based in Moorooduc, South Victoria. Grape varieties include Chardonnay, Pinot noir.

Moroccan Tea (Afr) 850mls (1½ pints) freshly made tea, few dashes peppermint essence and sugar to taste. Cool quickly and serve on crushed ice with mint leaves.

Morocco (N.Afr) a wine-producing country that produces most styles of wines. The red wines which are robust and high in alcohol are the most popular and by law must have a minimum alcohol content of 11% by vol. Main regions: Casablanca, Fez, Marrakech, Meknès, Oujda and Rabat-Rharb.

Morocco Ale (Eng) a 5.5% alc by vol. bottled dark ale brewed by the Daleside Brewery in Harrogate to an Elizabethan recipe.

Morón [Manuel Pancheco] (Sp) a producer and exporter of Málaga.

Morozkaraso (Tur) a red grape variety grown in eastern Turkey.

Morphett Vale (Austr) a region of South Australia which produces good red wines.

Morra [La] (It) a commune in the Barolo district of Piemonte, north-western Italy.

Morrastel (Fr) a red grape variety. (Sp) = Graciano. (Also known as Monastrell or Mourvèdre in parts of Spain).

Morrastel Bouschet (Fr) a red grape variety produced by crossing Morrastel x Petit Bouschet. Grown in the départements of Aude and Hérault.

Morrell's Brewery (Eng) a brewery based in Oxford. Noted for cask-conditioned Varsity 1041 O.G./4.3% alc by vol. College Ale 1073 O.G. Oxford Blue, Oxford Graduate 5.2% alc by vol. Oxford Mild, Oxford Bitter 3.7% alc by vol. Scorcher 4% alc by vol. plus keg Friars Ale 1036 O.G. Brewery Gate Bitter, Grumpy Cow Bitter, Advent, Colonel's Choice, bottled Light Oxford 1032 O.G. Brown Oxford 1032 O.G. and Castle Ale 1041 O.G. Website: http://www.morrellsofoxford.co.uk

Morre's Diamond (USA) a hybrid white grape variety grown in the New York State region.

Morris of Rutherglen (Austr) *see* Mia Mia Vineyard.

Morrison [Stanley P.] (Scot) known as Morrison Bowmore Distillers since 1988.

Morrison Bowmore Distillers (Scot) a company that owns the Auchentoshan (Lowland malt), Bowmore (Islay malt) and Glen Garioch (Highland malt) distilleries. Brand-name blended whiskies include Rob Roy. Originally known as Morrison (Stanley P.) (Add): Springburn Bond,, Carlisle Street, Glasgow, Lanarkshire G21 1EQ. Website: http://www.morrisonbowmore.co.uk 'E'mail: info@morrisonbowmore.co.uk

Morrison Fairlie Distillery C° (Scot) a distillery. (Add): Woodend House, Craigmill, Stirling, Stirlingshire FK9 5PP. Produces whiskies (malt and Scotch). 'E'mail: pjmfairlie@aol.com

Morrison's Carbonated Spring Water (Eng) a sparkling spring water from Shepley, Yorkshire. Mineral contents (milligrammes per litre): Sodium 88mg/l, Calcium 34mg/l, Magnesium 16mg/l, Potassium 4mg/l, Bicarbonates 378mg/l, Chlorides 19mg/l, Sulphates 1.7mg/l, Nitrates <1mg/l. pH 8.1

Morris Winery (USA) a winery based at Emeryville, Alameda, California. Grape varieties: Cabernet sauvignon, Chardonnay, Pinot noir, Sauvignon blanc and Zinfandel. Produce varietal and dessert wines.

Morris Wines (Austr) a winery based at Mia Mia Road, near Rutherglen, Victoria. Produces dry white and red wines.

Morrocco Ale (Eng) a 5.5% alc by vol. dry ale brewed by the Daleside Brewery, Harrogate, North Yorkshire.

Morro Cocktail (Cktl) ⅔ measure dry gin, ⅓ measure light rum, juice ¼ lemon, ⅛ measure pineapple juice, 2 dashes gomme syrup. Shake over ice and strain into a sugar-rimmed, ice-filled goblet.

Morscheid (Ger) village (Anb): Mosel-Saar-Ruwer. (Ber): Saar-Ruwer. (Gro): Römerlay. (Vins): Dominikanerberg, Heiligenhäuschen.

Morschheim (Ger) village (Anb): Pfalz. (Ber): Mittelhaardt-Deutsche Weinstrasse. (Gro): Schnepfenflug vom Kellertal. (Vin): Im Heubusch.

Morshinska (Ukr) a natural spring mineral water from Morshin, Lviv Region.

Mörstadt (Ger) village (Anb): Rheinhessen. (Ber): Wonnegau. (Gro): Burg Rodenstein. (Vins): Katzebuckel, Nonnengarten.

Morstein (Ger) vineyard (Anb): Rheinhessen. (Ber): Wonnegau. (Gro): Bergkloster. (Vil): Westhofen.

Mortágua (Port) a red grape variety grown in the Bucelas and Dão regions. Known as Touriga Nacional in Ribatejo, also Castelão Francês, Espadeiro and Trincadeira.

Mortalled (Eng) the Cockney slang for someone who is drunk (intoxicated).

Morterille Noire (Fr) the local name in southern France for the Cinsault grape.

Mortlach (Scot) a single highland malt whisky distillery sited just outside Dufftown in the Spey. Owned by George Cowie and Son Ltd. Produce a 12 and 13 year old malt, 16 year old at 43% alc by vol., a 1936 and 1965 vintage and a 1984 Centenary.

Morton [George] Ltd. (Scot) a leading rum producer based in Montrose, Angus. Produces OVD (Old Vatted Demerara) rum.

Morton Estate (N.Z) a winery. (Add): RD2, Kati Kati, Bay of Plenty. 100ha. Grape varieties: Cabernet sauvignon, Chardonnay, Chenin blanc, Gewürztraminer, Merlot, Müller-Thurgau, Pinot noir, Sauvignon blanc. Produces varietal wines.

Mort Subite (Bel) lit: 'sudden death', the nickname given to a style of lambic beer from De Keersmaeker Brasserie. However it is no stronger than other lambic beers.

Mort Subite Cassis Lambic (Bel) a 4% alc by vol. bottled blackcurrant lambic beer brewed by De Keersmaeker Lambic Brasserie, Koddegem. Matured in oak casks.

Mort Subite Gueuze Lambic (Bel) a 4.3% alc by vol. bottled amber-coloured gueuze lambic beer brewed by De Keersmaeker Lambic Brasserie, Koddegem. Matured in oak casks.

Mort Subite Kriek Lambic (Bel) a 4.3% alc by vol. bottled, red-coloured (cherry) kriek lambic beer brewed by De Keersmaeker Lambic Brasserie, Koddegem. Matured in oak casks.

Mort Subite Pêche (Bel) a 4.3% alc by vol. bottled straw-coloured peach lambic beer brewed by De Keersmaeker Lambic Brasserie, Koddegem. Matured in oak casks.

Mortuaries (Port) a name given to the old terraces by the vineyard workers in the Douro region because it is easier to plant new terraces than save the old.

Mory [Juan] & Cia (Sp) a producer and exporter of Málaga wines.

Mörzheim (Ger) village (Anb): Pfalz. (Ber): Südliche Weinstrasse. (Gro): Herrlich. (Vin): Pfaffenberg.

Mosaic (Cyp) a brand of Cream Sherry produced by Keo in Limassol.

Mösbach (Ger) village (Anb): Baden. (Ber): Ortenau. (Gro): Schloss Rodeck. (Vin): Kreuzberg.

Mosburgerin (Aus) a vineyard site on the banks of the River Danube in the Kremstal region.

Mosca (It) lit: 'flies', the name given to the coffee beans that are floated on top of Sambuca.

Mosca (Port) an aguardente produced by J.M. da Fonseca.

Moscadel (Fr) the old French spelling of the Muscatel grape. *See also* Muscadel and Muscadelle.

Moscadelleto (It) *see* Moscadello.

Moscadello (It) a white grape variety, a strain of the Moscato bianco. Also known as Moscadelleto.

Moscata Bianca (It) an alternative name for the Muscat blanc à petits grains grape.

Moscatel (Mad) a white grape variety grown on Porto Santo. Produces good sugar, used in Madeira production.

Moscatel (Sp) the sweet fortified wine which is used to sweeten sherries. 2 kinds: Jerez and Chipiona, the former being the sweeter.

Moscatel (Sp) a white grape variety. Also known as Muscat of Alexandria.

Moscatel a Grano Menudo (Sp) an alternative name for Muscat blanc à petits grains

Moscatel Branco (Port) a white grape variety used in the making of white Port.

Moscatel de Alejandría (Sp) an alternative name for Muscat of Alexandria.

Moscatel de Austria (S.Am) a white grape variety grown in Chile. (Arg) = Torrontés sanjuanino.

Moscatel de España (Sp) an alternative name for Muscat of Alexandria.

Moscatel de Frontignan (Sp) an alternative name for Muscat blanc à petits grains.

Moscatel de Grano Menudo (Sp) a white grape variety grown in the Navarra region. Also known as Muscat blanc à petits grains.

Moscatel de Málaga (Sp) an alternative name for Muscat of Alexandria.

Moscatel de Málaga (Sp) a light coloured and light bodied wine. Very sweet, is produced in Málaga from grapes dried in the sun. Made from the Muscat grape. Served as a dessert wine.

Moscatel de Setúbal (Sp) an alternative name for Muscat of Alexandria, also known as the Moscatel Graúdo.

Moscatel de Setúbal (Port) now known as Setúbal.

Moscatel de Valencia (Sp) a sweet white wine (may be fortified) produced in the D.O. region of Valencia.

Moscatel Galego Branco (Port) a local name in the Douro for the Muscat Blanc à Petits Grains.

Moscatel Galego Roxo (Port) a pink-skinned close relative of the Muscat Blanc à Petits Grains.

Moscatel Gordo (Sp) an alternative name for Moscatel de Setúbal and Muscat of Alexandria.

Moscatel Graúdo (Port) lit: 'great muscat', a local name for the Muscat of Alexandria in Setúbal.

Moscatella (It) a white grape variety grown in Sicily.

Moscatello (It) an alternative name for the Muscat blanc à petit grains.

Moscatello Giallo (It) the name given to the Moscato bianco grape in the commune of Siracusa, Sicily.

Moscatellone (It) the name given to the white grape variety Zibibbo on the island of Pantelleria of the coast of Sicily.

Moscatel Morisco (Sp) a white grape variety once used in the production of Málaga.

Moscatelo (It) the wine of Montefiascone in Latium. Usually known as Est! Est!! Est!!!

Moscatel Oro (Sp) sweet white wine (vino de licor) produced by Torres.

Moscatel Romano (It) an alternative name for the Muscat of Alexandria grape.

Moscatel Rosado (S.Am) a white grape variety grown in Argentina.

Moscatel Roxo (Port) a black grape variety grown in Setúbal. Also the name of sweet dessert wine.

Moscati di Trani (It) a sweet aromatic white wine made from the Muscat blanc grape in the province of Apulia.

Moscato (It) a white grape variety with many varietals including the Muscat blanc à petits grains.

Moscato Amabile (USA) a white grape variety similar to the Muscat blanc. Produces a light, often pétillant wine.

Moscato Bianco (It) a white grape variety grown in northern Italy. Also known as Moscato di Canelli, Muscat blanc à petits grains.

Moscato d'Asti (It) a D.O.C.G. white sparkling wine from Piemonte. Made from the Moscato bianco (Moscato naturale d'Asti) grape. Natural fermentation with no artificial carbonation allowed (only fermented once). A sweet wine, originally known as Asti Spumante, now known as Asti. Minimum alc by vol. 11.5%.

Moscato d'Asti Spumante (It) see Moscato d'Asti and Asti.

Moscato del Salento (It) a D.O.C. sweet red or white wine produced from the Muscat grape in the Apulia region.

Moscato del Tempio (It) a white dessert wine of grapey character made in Sardinia.

Moscato di Cagliari (It) a D.O.C. white wine from the Cagliari region. Made from the Moscato grape from within the Cagliari province. 2 types: Dolce Naturale and Liquoroso Dolce Naturale. If aged 1 year after fortification can be classed Riserva.

Moscato di Calabria (It) a D.O.C. white wine from the Calabria region. Is produced from dried Moscato grapes. Also known as Moscato di Cosenza.

Moscato di Canelli (It) a white grape variety used in the Veneto. The local name for the Moscato bianco.

Moscato di Casteggio (It) a sweet Muscat wine produced in Frecciarossa, Lombardy.

Moscato di Casteggio Spumante (It) a sweet sparkling wine produced from the Muscat grape in Frecciarossa, Lombardy.

Moscato di Cosenza (It) see Moscato di Calabria.

Moscato di Noto (It) a D.O.C. white wine from Sicily. Made from the Moscato bianco and a variety of grapes grown in the communes of Noto, Avola, Pachino and Rosolini. D.O.C. also applies to the sparkling wines and to the fortified wines obtained according to regulations.

Moscato di Noto Liquoroso (It) a D.O.C. fortified wine from Sicily. Made from Moscato bianco and other selected grapes giving a minimum natural total alc. content of 13% by vol. Fermentation continues to October when minimum alc. content is 16.5% by vol. Fortification then follows.

Moscato di Noto Naturale (It) also known as Moscato di Noto.

Moscato di Noto Spumante (It) a D.O.C. sparkling wine of Sicily. Made from the Moscato bianco grapes grown in the communes of Noto, Avola, Pachino and Rosolini.

Moscato di Pantelleria (It) a rich white wine produced on the small island of Pantelleria between Sicily and Africa. see Moscato di Pantelleria Naturale.

Moscato di Pantelleria Naturale (It) a D.O.C. white wine from Pantelleria. Made from the Zibibbo (Moscatellone) grape. Can be classified as Vino Naturalmente Dolce when total alc. content is not less than 17.5% by vol. of which 13% alc by vol. is obtained by using partially dried grapes. D.O.C. also applies to naturally sparkling and fortified wines. Spumante or Liquoroso follow the D.O.C. on the label.

Moscato di Salento (It) a rich, sweet white wine from the Moscato bianco grape made in the Apulia province. Also known as Salento bianco liquoroso.

Moscato di Sardegna (It) a D.O.C. white wine from Sardinia. Produced from the Moscato grape.

Moscato di Siracusa (It) a D.O.C. white wine from Sicily. Made from the Moscato bianco grapes grown in the commune of Siracusa in south-east Sicily (limited production).

Moscato di Sorso-Sennori (It) a D.O.C. sweet white wine from Sardinia. Made from Moscato bianco grapes with up to 5% of other varieties in the communes of Sorso and Sennori. A Liquoroso Dolce style can be produced with the addition of alcohol from wine.

Moscato di Trani (It) the local name in the Puglia region for the Moscato bianco grape. Used to make wine of same name.

Moscato di Trani (It) a D.O.C. white wine from the Puglia. Made from the Moscato bianco and other Muscat varieties. 2 styles: Dolce Naturale and Liquoroso.

Moscato d'Oro (USA) a white grape variety similar to the Muscat blanc.

Moscato-Fior d'Arancio (It) a sweet white dessert wine from Calabria in Sicily. Has a scent of orange blossom (Fior d'Arancio means flowers of orange).

Moscato Fior d'Arancio (It) a single varietal scented grappa produced by Fratelli Brunello in Vicenza.

Moscato Giallo (It) the name for the Moscato bianco grape in the Trentino-Alto-Adige region. (Goldenmuskateller in German).

Moscato Gordo Blanco (Sp) a white grape variety.

Moscato Naturale d'Asti (It) a D.O.C. still white wine from the Piemonte region. Made from the Moscato bianco grape.

Moscato Nero (It) a red grape variety.

Moscato Passito di Pantelleria (It) a D.O.C. sweet white wine from the isle of Pantelleria. Made from the Zibibbo grape. D.O.C. also applies to fortified wine (has Liquoroso on the label). Extra appears on label when aged for a minimum of 1 year and minimum alc. content 23.9% by vol. of which at least 15.5% alc by vol. is from natural fermentation.

Moscato Reale (It) a local name in the Puglia region for the Moscato bianco grape. Also known as the Moscato di Trani in the region.

Moscato Rosa (It) a red grape variety grown in the Trentino-Alto-Adige region (Rosenmuskateller in German). Used in the making of rosé wines.

Moscato Semplice di Canelli (It) a white dessert wine produced from the Moscato di Canelli grape in the Asti district of the Piemonte region.

Moscato Zibibbo (It) a name of the Moscato bianco (Moscatellone) in the isle of Pantelleria.

Moscato Zucco (It) a rich, dark, mellow white wine produced from the Zibibbo grape in Palermo on the isle of Sicily.

Moschofilero (Gre) a white grape variety which produces dry white wines in the Peloponnese. *see* Mantinia.

Moscophilero (Gre) an alternative spelling of Moschofilero.

Moscow (Rus) a beer 13° Balling made with rice as opposed to corn. Brewed by the Yantar Brewery.

Moscow Mule (Cktl) ginger beer, lime juice and vodka, mixed over ice, strained into a cocktail glass with a twist of lime.

Mosel (Ger) an untergebiet of the Rhein und Mosel district.

Mosel [River] (Ger) a tributary of the river Rhine. Runs south to north and has the rivers Saar and Ruwer as its tributaries. *see* Mosel-Saar-Ruwer. Rises in France and flows through Luxembourg before it enters Germany.

Moselblümchen (Ger) lit: 'little flower of the Mosel', the Mosel-Saar-Ruwer equivalent of Liebfraumilch. *See also* Moseltaler.

Mosele S.A. (Bra) a leading wine-producer based in southern Brazil.

Moselkern (Ger) village (Anb): Mosel-Saar-Ruwer. (Ber): Zell/Mosel. (Gro): Goldbäumchen. (Vins): Kirchberg, Rosenberg, Übereltzer.

Moselland (Ger) a winzergenossenschaft. (Add): D-54470 Bernkastel-Kues, Germany. Website: http://www.Mosselland.de 'E'mail: info@mosselland.de

Moselle (Fr) the French spelling of the river Mosel (German) also of Luxembourg. Often used in the U.K. and USA to denote the wines of the Mosel-Saar-Ruwer.

Moselle Cobbler (Cktl) 125mls (1gill) Mosel wine, 1 dash lemon juice, 2 dashes old brandy, 3–4 dashes plain syrup. Stir over ice, strain into a highball half filled with crushed ice, serve with a dash of lemon peel juice, 2 slices of lemon and straws.

Moselle Cup (Cktl) 1 bottle Mosel wine, 60mls (½ gill) brandy, 40mls (⅓ gill) yellow Chartreuse, 30mls (¼ gill) maraschino, 30mls (¼ gill) kümmel, 550mls (1 pint) soda water. Stir in a bowl with ice, strain into highball glasses with orange and lemon slices, fruit and mint.

Mosel-Saar-Ruwer (Ger) anbaugebiet (Bers): Bernkastel, Obermosel, Saar-Ruwer, Zell/Mosel. Grape varieties: Elbling 9%, Kerner 3%, Müller-Thurgau 21%, Optima 6% and Riesling 61%. 12,900ha. Wines are bottled in green bottles.

Mosel-Saar-Ruwer Wine Festivals (Ger) *see* Mosel-Wein-Woche, Saarweinfest and the Weinfest der Mittelmosel.

Moselsürsch (Ger) village (Anb): Mosel-Saar-Ruwer. (Ber): Zell/Mosel. (Gro): Weinhex. (Vin): Fahrberg.

Moseltaler (Ger) the Mosel-Saar-Ruwer local version of a medium-sweet white wine (similar to Liebfraumilch). *see* Moselblümchen, Nahesteiner, Rheinhess.

Moselwein (Ger) a wine from the Mosel-Saar-Ruwer.

Mosel-Wein-Woche (Ger) a Mosel-Saar-Ruwer wine festival held at Cochem in June.

Mosen Cleto (Sp) a red wine produced by Vincente Suso y Perez in Cariñena, north-eastern Spain. Is aged 4 years in oak. Made from the Garnacha grape.

M

Moser [Sepp] (Aus) a winery (50ha) based in the Kremstal region. (Add): Untere Wiener Strasse 1, 3495 Rohrendorf bei Krems. Grape varieties: Cabernet franc, Cabernet sauvignon, Chardonnay, Grüner veltliner, Pinot blanc, Pinot noir, Riesling, Sauvignon blanc, Zweigelt. Produces a range of dry and sweet (botrytised) wines.

Moshofileros (Gre) a white grape variety grown on the Peloponnese.

Moskovskaya (Rus) a Russian vodka, straight, low strength, made from grain and flavouring herbs 37.5% alc by vol.

Moslem Prohibition (Arab) followers of Islam are forbidden to touch any form of alcoholic beverage.

Mosler (Aus) an alternative name for the Furmint grape.

Mosler (Slo) an alternative name for the Sipón (Furmint) grape.

Möslinger Fining (Ger) an alternative name for Blue Finings.

Moslins (Fr) a Cru Champagne village in the Canton d'Avize. District: Épernay.

Mosnac (Fr) a commune in the Charente département whose grapes are used for Petite Champagne (Cognac).

Mosnier [Sylvain] (Fr) a winery based in the A.C. Chablis, Burgundy. Produces a range of Chablis wines including Premier Crus Beauroy and Côte de Léchet.

Moss (Scot) the name used in the Orkneys to describe the third layer of peat. Only the top layer is used in malt whisky production. *See also* Frog, Yarpie.

Moss Brewery (Nor) a small brewery based in Moss, south-eastern Norway.

Mosselman's Brasserie (Bel) a noted brewery based in Dworp, central Belgium.

Moss Wood Vineyard (Austr) a vineyard. (Add): Metricup Road, Willyabrup, Western Australia. 10ha. Grape varieties: Cabernet sauvignon, Chardonnay, Merlot, Pinot noir and Sémillon. Labels: Ribbon Vale Vineyard, The Amy's Blend. Website: http://www.mosswood.com.au

Most (Ger)(It)(Port)(Sp) unfermented grape juice. (Eng) = must, (Fr) = moût.

Mostaganem-Kenenda (Alg) a wine-producing area of the Oran département. Produces red, rosé and white wines.

Mostar Blatina (Slo) medium bodied red wine from Bosnia-Hercegovina.

Mostarska Zilavka (Slo) a dry white wine from Croatia around the town of Mostar. Made with the Zilavka grape.

Moster (Aus) a local name for the Chasselas grape.

Mostertsdrift Noble Wines (S.Afr) a winery (established 2001) based in Stellenbosch, Western Cape. 7.5ha. Grape varieties: Cabernet sauvignon, Chenin blanc, Cinsaut, Merlot, Sauvignon blanc. Label: Ané Rouge.

Mostgewicht (Ger) the measuring of the sugar content in the must/wine, measured in degrees Oechsle.

Mostini (Czec) a sparkling natural spring mineral water from Horni Mostenice. Mineral contents (milligrammes per litre): Sodium 412.4mg/l, Calcium 185.2mg/l, Magnesium 107.1mg/l, Bicarbonates 2058mg/l, Chlorides 144.2mg/l, Sulphates 0.185mg/l, Fluorides 0.63mg/l, Iron 2.45mg/l. pH 6.42

Mosto (It)(Port)(Sp) grape juice/must.

Mosto Concentrato Retificato (It) concentrated rectified grape must.

Mosto Cotto (It) boiled grape must used as a sweetening agent in the production of Marsala-type wines.

Mosto Parzialmente Fermentato (It) partially fermented grape must. (Fr) = mutage.

Mosttraube (Aus) the alternative name for the Chasselas grape.

Mostwager (Aus) must weigher.

Moterist Beer (Swe) a low-alcohol beer brewed for the motorist in Sweden 2.8% alc by vol.

Motette (It) a sparkling natural spring mineral water from Motette, Perugia. Mineral contents (milligrammes per litre): Sodium 5.5mg/l, Calcium 55mg/l, Magnesium 1.3mg/l, Potassium 0.6mg/l, Bicarbonates 160mg/l, Chlorides 9.8mg/l, Sulphates 8.9mg/l, Fluorides 0.05mg/l, Silicates 5mg/l. pH 7.9

Mother Clone (USA) the label for a red wine (Zinfandel) produced by the Pedroncelli winery, Dry Creek Valley, California.

Mother Cognac (Fr) the name for old Cognac at Rémy Martin used in fine blends.

Mother in Law (Eng) a 4.2% alc by vol. ale brewed by the Wizard Brewery, Warwickshire.

Mother-in-Law (Eng) the cockney slang for a bitter ale and stout mix.

Mother is Watching (Cktl)(Non-alc) juice ½ grapefruit and 1 orange, 2 dashes Angostura. Shake over ice, strain into a highball glass, top with Perrier water and a slice of orange.

Mother of Vinegar (USA) the nickname for *Mycrodermae aceti* (acetobacter). (Fr) = mère de vinaigre.

Mother of Wine (Sp) a term in the Sherry region when the Flor sinks to the bottom of the cask.

Mother's Cellar Winery (N.Z) a small winery based in Henderson, North Island. Produces varietal wines and All Black Port (a Port-style wine).

Mother's Ruin (Eng) a slang term or gin.

Mother Wine (Eng) boiling a wine to make it concentrated, used to strengthen young wines.

Moto (Jap) the next stage of the koji (steamed rice) when it is added to a thin paste of boiled starch in a vat and it is then allowed to ferment.

Motte [La] (S.Afr) a vineyard (established 1983) based in Franschhoek, produces varietal wines. Noted for Shiraz wines.

Motte Cordonnier Brasserie (Fr) a noted brewery (part of the Artois Brasserie of Belgium).

Mou (Fr) a flabby wine, lacking in character.

Mouchão (Port) a vineyard estate based in the DOC Alejento.

M

Moueix et Fils (Fr) a famous négociant-éleveur of Bordeaux based in Pomerol and Saint-Émilion. (Add): Taillefer 33500, Libourne.

Mouillage (Fr) the addition of water to alcoholic drinks to weaken their strength.

Mouillé (Fr) watered.

Mouillière [La] (Fr) a vineyard in the A.C. commune of Montagny, Côte Chalonnaise, Burgundy.

Mouldy (Eng) a term used to describe a wine that has an off-flavour. May have originated from stale, dirty casks, rotten grapes or from the wine coming into contact with verdigris from the capsule when being decanted.

Moulesne (Fr) a vineyard in the A.C. commune of Rully, Côte Chalonnaise, Burgundy.

Moulettes (Fr) a natural spring mineral water from Hautes-Alpes. Mineral contents (milligrammes per litre): Sodium 1.4mg/l, Calcium 63mg/l, Magnesium 10.2mg/l, Potassium 0.4mg/l, Bicarbonates 173.2mg/l, Chlorides 1mg/l, Sulphates 51.3mg/l, Nitrates 2mg/l. pH 7.6

Mouleydier (Fr) a commune within the A.C. district of Pécharmant in northern Bergerac (red wines).

Moulin à Café (Fr) coffee mill.

Moulin-à-Vent (Fr) an A.C. Cru Villages Beaujolais, Burgundy. 650ha. under vines.

Moulin Brewery (Scot) a brewery. (Add): The Old Coach house, Balemund Road, Moulin, Pitlochry, Perthshire PH16 5EW. Brews a range of ales and beers. Website: http://www.moulinhotel.co.uk 'E'mail: enquiries@moulinhotel.co.uk

Moulin de Café (Fr) coffee grinder/coffee mill.

Moulin de la Gravelle (Fr) an A.C. Muscadet Sèvre et Maine. (Add): Saint-Fiacre-sur-Maine, Gorges 12ha.

Moulin de la Pitance (Fr) a vineyard in the commune of St-Girons, A.C. Côtes de Blaye, north-eastern Bordeaux.

Moulin des Carruades (Fr) a wine made in certain good years from Château Lafite vineyards and of the second pressings. Entitled to the A.C. Pauillac if reaches the requirements of the appellation. Always Château bottled. Second wine of Château Lafite-Rothschild.

Moulin des Costes (Fr) a vineyard in the A.C. Bandol, Provence 45ha.

Moulin Desoubeyran (Fr) a vineyard in the commune of Le Pian. A.C. Haut-Médoc, Bordeaux. Cru Bourgeois.

Moulin-du-Cadet (Fr) Grands Crus Classés of Côtes Saint-Émilion.

Mouline [La] (Fr) property on the Côte Blonde. Has 11% Viognier in the Côte Rôtie, Rhône. Owned by Guigal. *See also* Lalandonne (La), Turque (La).

Moulinneuf Distillerie (Fr) a Cognac distillery based near Jarnac. Owned by Martell.

Moulin Rouge (Cktl) 10mls (½ fl.oz) brandy, 50mls (2fl.ozs) pineapple juice. Stir over ice, strain into a highball glass half-filled with ice, top up with dry sparkling wine, decorate with a cherry, slice of pineapple and orange.

Moulin Rouge Cocktail (Cktl) ⅔ measure sloe gin, ⅓ measure Italian vermouth, dash Angostura. Stir over ice and strain into a cocktail glass.

Moulin Saint-Georges (Fr) a vineyard. (Add): 33330, Saint-Émilion. A.C. Saint-Émilion. (Com): Saint-Émilion.

Moulis (Fr) an A.C. commune within the southern part of the Haut-Médoc. Some wines are sold under the adjoining A.C. Listrac.

Moullay-Hofberg (Ger) vineyard (Anb): Mosel-Saar-Ruwer. (Ber): Bernkastel. (Gro): Vom Heissen Stein. (Vil): Reil.

Mounié [Denis] (Fr) a Cognac producer. (Add): B.P. 14, 16200 Jarnac. Produces Edouard VII Grand Réserve Fine Champagne. Owns no vineyards (part of Hine).

Mounier (Fr) a lesser black grape variety grown in the Champagne region.

Mountadam Winery (Austr) a winery. (Add): High Eden Road, High Eden Ridge, South Australia. Produces varietal wines. Grape varieties: Cabernet sauvignon, Pinot noir, Chardonnay, Riesling.

Mountain (Sp) a classification of Málaga, a medium sweet wine.

Mountain Cocktail (Cktl) 1 measure Bourbon whiskey, 2 dashes Italian vermouth, 2 dashes French vermouth, 2 dashes lemon juice, 1 egg white. Shake over ice and strain into a cocktail glass.

Mountain Creek Vineyard (Austr) a winery (established 1973). (Add): Mountain Creek Road, Moonambel, Victoria. Grape varieties: Cabernet sauvignon, Sauvignon blanc.

Mountain Dew (Eng) a blend of citrus flavours with a bright neon colour. Regular or diet versions available from Britvic Soft Drinks, Chelmsford.

Mountaineer Pure (USA) a natural spring mineral water from Charleston, West Virginia.

Mountain Forest Spring Water (USA) a natural spring mineral water from Unicoi, Tennessee.

Mountain Goat Beer Pty Ltd (Austr) a brewery. (Add): Warehouse 1, 18 river street, Richmond, Victoria 3121. Brews a variety of beers. Website: http://www.goatbeer.com.au

Mountain Gold (USA) the label used by the Lamont Winery for their generic wines.

Mountain Lite (Can) a natural spring mineral water from Alberta Rockies. Mineral contents (milligrammes per litre): Sodium <1mg/l, Calcium 58.7mg/l, Magnesium 11.5mg/l, Potassium 1mg/l, Fluorides 0.2mg/l. pH 8.1

Mountain Mist (Scot) a natural spring mineral water brand.

Mountain Oaks Winery (S.Afr) a winery (established 2003) based in Rawsonville, Worcester, Western Cape. 20ha. W.O. Slangheok. Grape varieties: Cabernet franc, Cabernet sauvignon, Chardonnay, Chenin blanc, Mourvèdre, Pinotage, Shiraz. Label: Le Jardin.

Mountain Oyster (Cktl) another name for a Prairie Oyster.

Mountain Range (S.Afr) a winery based in Oranjezicht, Western Cape. Grape varieties: Cabernet sauvignon,

Chardonnay, Chenin blanc, Merlot, Sauvignon blanc, Shiraz. Labels: Table Red, Table White. Website: http://www.mountainrange.co.za

Mountain Red (USA) the generic name used for inexpensive dry red wines.

Mountain Ridge (S.Afr) the label for a range of red and white wines produced by the Romansrivier Cellar winery, Wellington, Western Cape.

Mountain River Wines (S.Afr) a winery (established 1993) based in Paarl, Western Cape. W.O. Olifants River. Grape varieties: Cabernet sauvignon, Chardonnay, Chenin blanc, Merlot, Pinotage, Sauvignon blanc, Shiraz. Labels: Estuary, Maankloof, Zaràfa. Website: http://www.mountainriverwines.co.za

Mountainside (S.Afr) the label for a range of wines white (Chenin blanc and Colombard blend), red (Merlot), pink (Pinotage) and gold (Chenin blanc and Colombard blend) produced by the Ruitersvlei Wines winery, Suider-Paarl, Western Cape.

Mountainside (USA) the label used by Château Chevalier for their wines produced from purchased grapes.

Mountain Skier (Cktl) 2 parts Johnnie Walker Red Label, 2 parts Drambuie, 5 parts lemon squash, 1 part lemonade, dash Angostura, dash egg white. Shake all over ice except lemonade. Strain into a highball glass, top with the lemonade and decorate with beaten egg white and a slice of lemon.

Mountain Spring (Scot) a natural spring mineral water from Blackford, Perthshire. Mineral contents (milligrammes per litre): Sodium 6mg/l, Calcium 27mg/l, Magnesium 9mg/l, Potassium 0.6mg/l, Bicarbonates 124mg/l, Chlorides 7mg/l, Sulphates 9mg/l, Fluorides 0.06mg/l, Nitrates 1.5mg/l.

Mountain Valley (USA) a still natural spring mineral water from Glazypeau, Hot Springs, Kansas. Mineral contents (milligrammes per litre): Sodium 2.8mg/l, Calcium 68mg/l, Magnesium 8mg/l, Potassium 1mg/l, Bicarbonates 238.05mg/l, Sulphates 9.72mg/l, Fluorides 0.25mg/l. pH 7.8

Mountain White (USA) the generic name used for inexpensive dry white wines.

Mount Aitken Estate (Austr) a winery (established 1974). (Add): Calder Highway, Gisborne South, Victoria. Produces a large range of light wines plus Port and Sherry styles.

Mount Alexander Winery (Austr) winery (established 1987). (Add): Calder Highway, Harcourt, Victoria. Produces a large range of table wines, mead and cider.

Mountarrow Wines (Austr) a winery. (Add): Arrowfield Vineyard, Denman Road, Jerry's Plains, New South Wales. Grape varieties: Chardonnay, Sémillon, Shiraz.

Mount Augustin (Austr) a winery based in Western Australia. Grape varieties include: Cabernet sauvignon, Shiraz.

Mount Avoca Winery (Austr) a winery. (Add): Moates Lane, Avoca, Victoria 3467. 20ha. Grape varieties: Cabernet sauvignon, Shiraz, Chardonnay, Sauvignon blanc, Sémillon.

Mount Barker (Austr) a wine sub-region in Western Australia.

Mount Barker (Austr) a brand-name for the Jane Brook Estate in Western Australia.

Mount Bethel (USA) a winery based in Altus.

Mount Claire Mountain Red (S.Afr) the label for red wine (Merlot & Shiraz blend) produced by the Cordoba Winery, Stellenbosch, Western Cape.

Mount Edelstone (USA) a famous vineyard owned by Henschke. Based in the Eden Valley. Noted for Shiraz grapes. *See also* Hill of Grace.

Mount Eden Vineyards (USA) a small winery based near Saratoga, Santa Clara, California. 9.5ha. Grape varieties: Cabernet sauvignon, Chardonnay and Pinot noir. Produce varietal wines.

Mount Elise Vineyards (USA) a small vineyard based in Bingen, South Washington. 12ha. Produces vinifera wines. Originally known as the Bingen Wine Cellars.

Mount Franklin (Austr) a still natural spring mineral water from Mount Franklin. Mineral contents (milligrammes per litre): Sodium 14mg/l, Calcium 3mg/l, Magnesium 5mg/l, Potassium 1mg/l, Bicarbonates 2mg/l, Chlorides 20mg/l.

Mount Fuji (Cktl) blend a scoop of crushed ice, 20mls (⅙ gill) light rum, 20mls (⅙ gill) applejack brandy, 15mls (⅛ gill) Southern Comfort, 25grms (1oz) castor sugar and the juice of ½ lime. Pour into an old-fashioned glass, top with ½ lime shell filled with 151° US Proof rum, ignite and as the ice melts, serve (with straws).

Mount Gay Distillery (W.Ind) the world's oldest and noted rum distillery (established 1703) in Barbados. (Add): Prince Wm. Henry Street, Bridgetown. Part of Rémy Martin. Produces a variety of rums (including flavoured rums) and labels include: Extra Old, Eclipse.

Mount Helen (Austr) a red grape variety.

Mount Helen (Austr) part of the Tisdall Estate, 50ha. in Victoria. Grape varieties: Cabernet sauvignon, Merlot, Pinot noir, Chardonnay, Gewürztraminer, Rhine riesling, Sauvignon blanc.

Mount Hood Mild (Eng) a 3.4% alc by vol. single varietal ale brewed by Wadworth & C°. Ltd., Northgate Brewery in Devizes, Wiltshire between 3rd and 14th May.

Mount Horrocks (Austr) a winery in Clare Valley with vineyards in the Watervale. Noted for Riesling wines.

Mount Hurtle (Austr) a winery at Pimpala and Byards Road, Reynella, South Australia. Wines are sometimes sold under the Geoff Merrill label. Grape varieties: Cabernet sauvignon, Grenache, Chardonnay, Sauvignon blanc.

Mount Langi Ghiran Vineyards (Austr) a winery. (Add): Vine Road, Buangor, Victoria. Grape varieties: Cabernet sauvignon, Shiraz, Chardonnay, Riesling.

M

Mount Lindsey (Austr) a winery based in Western Australia. Grape varieties include: Cabernet sauvignon, Shiraz.

Mount Linton (N.Z) a 20ha winery based in Marlborough. Grape varieties: Chardonnay, Sauvignon blanc.

Mount Martha Vineyard (Austr) a winery (established 1985). (Add): Range Road, Mount Martha, Victoria. Grape varieties: Cabernet sauvignon, Chardonnay, Sauvignon blanc.

Mount Mary Winery (Austr) a winery. (Add): Coldstream, West Road, Lilydale, Victoria 3140. 7.5ha. Grape varieties: Cabernet franc, Cabernet sauvignon, Chardonnay, Malbec, Merlot, Muscadelle, Pinot noir, Sauvignon blanc and Sémillon.

Mount Murray Brewing C° [Bushys] (I.O.M) a brewery (established 1985). (Add): Mount Murray, Braddan, Isle of Man IM4 1JE. Brews: Bushys Bitter 3.8% alc by vol., Old Bushy Tail 4.5% alc by vol., Oyster Stout 4.2% alc by vol., Ruby 1874 Mild 3.5% alc by vol. Website: http://www.bushys.com 'E'mail: bushys@manx.com

Mount Olympus (USA) a natural spring mineral water (established 1899) from Neff's Canyon, Mount Olympus, Salt Lake City. Mineral contents (milligrammes per litre): Sodium 3.4mg/l, Calcium 7.9mg/l, Magnesium 2.4mg/l, Potassium 0.48mg/l, Chlorides 5.9mg/l, Sulphates 8.8mg/l. pH 7.24

Mount Palomar Winery (USA) a large winery based near Temecula, southern California. 60ha. Grape varieties: Cabernet sauvignon, Petite sirah and Sauvignon blanc. Produces varietal wines.

Mount Pleasant Hunter Vineyards (Austr) part of the McWilliams Estate in New South Wales. 115ha. Grape varieties: Chardonnay, Hermitage and Sémillon.

Mount Pleasant Vineyards (USA) a small winery based in Augusta, Missouri. Produce native American and French hybrid wines.

Mount Prior (Austr) a winery at Howlong Road, near Rutherglen, Victoria. Grape varieties: Cabernet sauvignon, Durif, Merlot, Chardonnay, botrytised Riesling.

Mount Richmond (USA) the label for a red wine (Pinot noir) produced by the Elk Cove Vineyards, Willamette Valley, Oregon.

Mount Rozier (S.Afr) a winery (established 1997) based in Stellenbosch, Western Cape. 45ha. Grape varieties: Cabernet sauvignon, Chardonnay, Merlot, Pinotage, Ruby cabernet, Sauvignon blanc, Shiraz. Labels: Cuvée Burr, Red Reef, Rozier Bay, Rozier Reef. Website: http://www.mountrozier.co.za

Mount Rufus Port (Austr) a vintage tawny Port-style wine produced by the Seppelts Winery.

Mount Seaview Spring Water (Austr) a natural spring mineral water (established 1996) from New South Wales. Mineral contents (milligrammes per litre): Sodium 59mg/l, Calcium 17mg/l, Magnesium 11mg/l, Potassium 1.4mg/l, Bicarbonates 150mg/l, Chlorides 73mg/l, Sulphates 11.5mg/l, Fluorides 0.2mg/l, Nitrates 0.07mg/l, Silicates 53mg/l. pH 8.5

Mount Tivy Winery (USA) a winery owned by the Christian Brothers, Napa Valley, California. Produces and ages brandies.

Mount Veeder Vineyard (USA) an A.V.A. of Napa Valley, California since 1990. 405ha. Grape varieties include Cabernet sauvignon, Chardonnay, Merlot, Zinfandel. Main wineries: Hess, Maycamas, Mount Veeder.

Mount Vernon Farm (S.Afr) a winery (established 2003) based in Klapmuts, Paarl, Western Cape. 28ha. Grape varieties: Cabernet sauvignon, Chenin blanc, Malbec, Merlot, Petit verdot, Pinotage, Shiraz. Label: Three Peaks.

Mount William Winery (Austr) a winery. (Add): End of Mount William Road, Lancefield, Victoria. Grape varieties: Cabernet franc, Pinot noir, Sémillon.

Moura (Port) an I.P.R. wine produced within the Alentejo region.

Moura Basto (Port) a brand of Vinho Verde made from the Azal grape. Produced in Basto and Amarante.

Mourane (Fr) an alternative name for the Malbec grape.

Mouraton (Sp) a red grape variety grown in the Galicia region.

Mourens (Fr) a commune in the Haut-Benauge, Entre-Deux-Mers, central Burgundy.

Mourestel (USA) a red grape variety grown in California, used for making red wines.

Mourisco (Port) a red grape variety used in the making of Port wine which gives good fruit flavours.

Mourisco Branco (Port) a white grape variety used in the making of white Port.

Mourisco de Semente (Port) a red grape variety used in the making of Port.

Mourisco Preto (USA) a white grape variety used in the making of dessert wines.

Mourisco Semente (Port) *see* Mourisco de Semente.

Mournier (Aus) a noted sparkling wine producer.

Mourvèdre (Fr) a red grape variety grown in the southern Rhône and Provence that produces wines of high alcohol with an aroma and flavour of blackberry, tannin, leather, animal game, tobacco. Also known as Beni Carlo, Catalan, Espar, Mataró, Monastrell, Morrastel, Négron and Tinto.

Mousel et Clausen Basserie (Lux) a brewery noted for Luxator 13° Balling and Royal Altmunster 13° Balling.

Mousey (Eng) *see* Mousy.

Mousquetaires d'Armagnac (Fr) a body of Armagnac lovers.

Mousse (Fr) the foam or sparkle of Champagne or sparkling wines.

Mousserende Vin (Den) sparkling wine.

Mousset [Louis] (Fr) a wine producer based in Châteauneuf-du-Pape, southern Rhône. Also produces Côtes du Rhône wines.

M

Mousseux (Fr) foaming/sparkling. *See also* Vin Mousseux.

Mousseux de Savoie (Fr) also known as Vin de Savoie Mousseux. An A.C. sparkling (méthode traditionelle or méthode gaillaçoise) wine from the Savoie region.

Mousseux de Savoie-Ayze (Fr) also known as Vin de Savoie-Ayze Mousseux. An A.C. sparkling (méthode traditionelle or méthode gaillaçoise) wine from the Savoie region. Grape varieties: Altesse, Gringet and Roussette d'Ayze.

Mousseux du Bugey (Fr) also known as Vin du Bugey Mousseux. An A.C. sparkling (méthode traditionelle or méthode gaillaçoise) wine from the Savoie region.

Mousseux Naturel (Fr) a sweet white sparkling wine. e.g. Clairette de Die, Demi-Sec.

Moussierend (Ger) sparkling.

Moussy (Fr) a Cru Champagne village in the Canton d'Épernay. District: Épernay.

Moustère (Fr) the alternative name for the Malbec grape.

Moustillants (Switz) sparkling.

Moustille (Fr) *see* Semi-Sparkling.

Moustrou (Fr) an alternative name for the Tannat grape.

Mousy (Eng) an offensive odour and taste in wine due to the presence of an infection caused by lactic acid bacteria. Occurs in wines that are not regularly racked. Also spelt Mousey.

Moût (Fr) unfermented grape juice.

Mout (Hol) an old Dutch word for malt.

Mou-Tai Chiew (Chi) a spirit made from fermented millet and wheat which is stored in cellars before bottling to give it a characteristic taste. Produced by the Mou-Tai Distillery in Kweichow. *See also* Mow Toy Wine.

Mou-Tai Distillery (Chi) a noted distillery based in Kweichow.

Moutard-Diligent (Fr) a Champagne producer. (Add): Buxeuil, 10110 Bar-sur-Seine. 20ha. Récoltants-manipulants. Produces vintage and non-vintage wines. Labels include Moutard Père et Fils, Francois Diligent.

Moutardier [Jean] (Fr) a Champagne producer. (Add): Le Breuil, 51210 Montmirail. Récoltants-manipulants. Produce vintage and non-vintage wines. Vintages: 1971, 1973, 1975, 1976, 1979, 1982, 1983, 1985, 1988, 1990, 1995, 1998, 2000.

Moutard Père et Fils (Fr) the label of a Champagne produced by Moutard-Diligent.

Moût de Goutte (Fr) free-run wine.

Moutere Reserve (N.Z) a medium-dry white wine made from a blend of Gewürztraminer, Rhine riesling, Chenin blanc and Chardonnay grapes. Produced by Weingut Seifried in Nelson.

Mouterij (Hol) malting house.

Mouterij-Branderij de Koning BV (Hol) a large moutwijn producer (a subsidiary of Bols).

Mouth-Filling (Eng) a term used in wine tasting to describe a wine with a high alcohol content.

Mouton-Cadet (Fr) a famous red, rosé and white blended vintage wines, A.C. Bordeaux, from the stable of Baron Philippe de Rothschild. Also a Réserve red (A.C. Médoc).

Mouton d'Armailhacq (Fr) formerly Château Baron Philippe (name changed in 1956). Now known as Château d'Armailhacq.

Mouton Rothschild (Fr) *see* Château Mouton Rothschild.

Moutwijn (Hol) lit: 'malt wine', a name given to the distillate before rectification and flavouring of Gin.

Moutwijnjenever (Hol) the name given to jenever that is redistilled twice.

Mouvedre (N.Z) a red grape variety. *see* Mourvèdre.

MouVin (Fr) lifeless wine.

Mouyssaguès (Fr) an ancient red vine of Aveyron in south-western France. Produces dark, tannic wines.

Mouzillon (Fr) a wine village in the Muscadet Sèvre et Maine region, Nantais, Loire Atlantique.

Movia (Slo) a winery based in Primorska, Slovenia. Noted for Tocai, Chardonnay, Pinot noir and Merlot wines.

Movimosto (Port) a machine which pumps and sprays the must over the '*cap*' in the fermentation vat, superceeded by autovinificators.

Mow Toy Wine (Chi) a clear spirit 40% alc by vol. made from kaoliang, a sorghum-like grain. *See also* Mou Tai.

Moxie (Eng) the trade mark of a soft drink.

Moya (N.Z) the alternative name for the black hybrid grape variety Seibel 5455.

Moyer Vineyards (USA) a winery based on the right bank of the Ohio river, Ohio. Produces hybrid and sparkling wines.

Moyey [Ets] (Fr) a Cognac producer. (Add): 62 Rue de L'Industrie, 16104 Cognac. Owns no vineyards. Produces many styles of Cognacs.

Moyle (Eng) an old English cider-making apple.

Moza Fresca (Sp) the local name used in Valdeorras for Doña Blanca.

Mozambique Teas (Afr) teas used mainly for blending.

Mozart Liqueur (Aus) a chocolate, kirsch, cream and nougat liqueur 20% alc by vol. produced in Salzburg.

Mozartquelle (Ger) a natural spring mineral water from Augsburger Hochterasse. Mineral contents (milligrammes per litre): Sodium 27mg/l, Calcium 25mg/l, Magnesium 17mg/l, Potassium 1mg/l, Bicarbonates 222mg/l, Chlorides 1mg/l, Sulphates 11mg/l.

Mozé (Fr) an A.C. commune in the Coteaux de l'Aubance in Anjou-Saumur, Loire.

Mozeg (Isr) bartender/barman.

M.P. (Eng) *abbr*: On a wine list denotes **M**ise en bouteilles par la **P**ropriétaire.

M.P.C. (Fr) *abbr*: **M**acération **P**réfermentaire à **C**haud.

Mr. and Mrs. Caudle (Scot) a famous salt-glazed stoneware whisky flask. 17.5cms (7½ ins.) high made by Doulton and Watts circa 1846, decorated

M

with an embossed man and woman under bed cloths and inscribed.

Mr. Cherrys (Eng) a home-brew public house in St. Leonards, Sussex. Noted for Mak's Special Beer 1050 O.G.

Mr. Chubbs Lunchtime Bitter (Eng) a 3.7% alc by vol. bitter ale brewed by the West Berkshire Brewery C°. Ltd., Berkshire.

Mr. George's Unique Flavours (Eng) a range of beers produced by Batemans, Lincolnshire. *see* Waynflete Hedgerows.

Mr. Harry (Eng) a 4.8% alc by vol. winter ale from Fuller Smith and Turner.

Mrira (Afr) a co-operative winery in Tunisia. Is owned by the UCCVT.

Mr. Manhattan (Cktl) muddle 4 sprigs of mint with juice of ¼ orange and 2 dashes lemon juice, add 50mls (2fl.ozs) gin, shake over ice and strain into a cocktail glass.

Mr. Perretts (Eng) a 5.9% alc by vol. ale brewed by the Wickwar Brewing C°. Ltd., Gloucestershire.

Mr. Shepherds Crook (Eng) a 4.7% alc by vol. ale brewed by the Exe Valley Brewery, Devon.

Mrs. McGillvray's Scotch Apple Liqueur (Scot) an apple and Scotch whisky based liqueur 25% alc by vol.

Mrs. Pucker's Alcoholic Cola (Eng) a 5.3% alc by vol. cola produced by Bulmers of Hereford. *See also* Skinny Pucker's.

Mrs. Pucker's Alcoholic Lemonade (Eng) a 5.5% alc by vol. lemonade produced by Bulmers of Hereford. *See also* Skinny Pucker's.

Mrs. Pucker's Alcoholic Orangeade (Eng) a 5.5% alc by vol. orangeade produced by Bulmers of Hereford. *See also* Skinny Pucker's.

Mrs. Pucker's Alcoholic Strawberryade (Eng) a 5.5% alc by vol. strawberryade produced by Bulmers of Hereford. *See also* Skinny Pucker's.

Mrs. Walker's Drumgray Highland Cream (Scot) a 17% alc by vol. Scotch whisky liqueur.

M.S.B. (Eng) *abbr*: Mark's Special Beer 1050 O.G. brewed by the Pensans Brewery in Penzance, Cornwall.

Mt. Anakie (Austr) a winery (established 1968) at 130 Staughton Vale Road, Anakie, Victoria. Grape varieties: Chardonnay, Riesling, Sémillon, Cabernet sauvignon, Cabernet franc, Dolcetto, Shiraz.

Mt. Avoca (Austr) a noted winery based in Pyrenees, Victoria.

Mt. Dangar (Austr) a winery based in the Hunter Valley, New South Wales. Produces varietal wines.

Mt. Erin Müller-Thurgau (N.Z) the brand-name of a fruity, medium-dry, white wine produced by Vidal Wine Products in Hawkes Bay.

Mt. Gay Distilleries (W.Ind) a large rum distillery based in Barbados.

Mt. Hood (Eng) a 4% alc by vol. ale brewed by the York Brewery Company Ltd., North Yorkshire.

Mt. Hope Estate (USA) a winery based in Cornwall, Pennsylvania. Produces hybrid wines.

M3 Vineyard (Austr) a white (Chardonnay) wine produced by the Shaw and Smith winery, Adelaide Hills, South Australia.

Mt. Jefferson Cuvée (USA) the label for a red wine (Pinot noir) produced by the Cristom winery, Willamette Valley, Oregon.

Mt. Kenya (Afr) a natural spring mineral water from Mount Kenya, Kenya.

Mt. McKinley Clear (USA) a natural spring mineral water from Hatcher Pass, Alaska.

Mt. Rufur Port (Austr) a traditional fortified port-type wine from the Seppelts vineyard in South Australia.

M Twenty three [23] (S.Afr) the label for a range of wines produced by the Bottelary Hill Wine winery, Stellenbosch, Western Cape.

Mtzvane (Rus) the alternative spelling of Mzvane.

Muaga Vineyards (N.Z) an old established vineyard based at Henderson, North Island.

Mucaro Cocktail (Cktl) 25mls (1fl.oz) golden rum, 25mls (1fl.oz) Tia Maria, 50mls (2fl.ozs) cream. Shake over ice, strain into a cocktail glass, dress with powdered cinnamon and a cinnamon stick.

Mucilage (Eng) a substance present in vegetable organisms which help to give body to a wine (in small quantities only).

Muckerhölle (Ger) vineyard (Anb): Nahe. (Ber): Schloss Böckelheim. (Gro): Burgweg. (Vil): Waldböckelheim.

Mucky Duck (Eng) an ale 4.5% alc by vol. brewed by the Buffy's Brewery Ltd., Norfolk.

Mud (USA) a slang term for wine lees.

Muddler (USA) a special wooden implement with a flat head used to mix and crush such items as sugar, mint etc. in liquids in the bottom of a glass or jug.

Muddler Spoon (Eng) a barspoon with a flat disc at its base which acts as a muddler.

Muddy (Eng) a term used to describe cloudy drinks i.e. red wine which has had the sediment (lees) disturbed, or beer (cask-conditioned) that has a haze or its sediment (lees) disturbed. Can also be caused by dirty pipes/casks.

Müden (Ger) village (Anb): Mosel-Saar-Ruwer. (Ber): Zell/Mosel. (Gro): Goldbäumchen. (Vins): Funkenberg, Grosslay, Leckmauer, St. Castorhöhle, Sonnenring.

Mudge (Eng) a Midlands term to denote the crushing of the hops to help extract the oil in brewing.

Mudgee (Austr) a wine region in New South Wales. Estate wineries include Augustine, Craigmoor, Huntington, Montrose.

Mud House Winery (N.Z) a winery based in Marlborough, South Island. Produces white and red wines. Grape varieties: Chardonnay, Merlot, Pinot noir, Sauvignon blanc. Labels: Le Grys and Black Swan. Website: http://www.mudhouse.co.nz

Mud Puppy (Eng) a 4.2% alc by vol. ale brewed by the Salamander Brewing Company Ltd., West Yorkshire.

Mudshake (Eng) *see* Vodka Mudshake.

M

Muehlhausen (Fr) the German name for the district of Mulhouse in Alsace.

Mueller-Thurgau (Eng) the English spelling of Müller-Thurgau.

Muenchberg (Fr) an A.C. Alsace Grand Cru vineyard at Nothalten, Bas-Rhin 18ha.

Muerza (Sp) see Bodegas Muerza S.A.

Muffa Nobile (It) *Botrytis cinerea* (noble rot).

Mufti of Aden (Arab) a fifteenth century Arab who is purported to have discovered coffee. *See also* Kaldi.

Mug (Eng) the name for a beer glass with a handle. *see* Dimple Mug.

Muga (Sp) a red wine produced by the Bodegas Muga, Rioja. Made from Garnacha tinto, Mazuelo and Viura grapes. Matured for 1 year in oak vats of 18000litres and for 2 years in oak Barricas. Also produce white wines. Website: http://www.bodegasmuga.com

Mugamart (Sp) the brand-name of a fruity sparkling wine produced by the Bodegas Muga, Rioja.

Mugeln (Aus) a vineyard site on the banks of the River Danube in the Kremstal region.

Mugneret [René] (Fr) a négociant-éleveur based in the Côte d'Or. (Add): 21670 Vosne-Romanée, Burgundy.

Mugwort (Eng) an aromatic plant also known as tansy used in the flavouring of ale in mediaeval times. (Fr) = barbotine (herbe aux vers).

Mühlbach (Ger) village (Anb): Baden. (Ber): Badische Bergstrasse/Kraichgau. (Gro): Stiftsberg. (Vin): Lerchenberg.

Mühlbach (Ger) village (Anb): Franken. (Ber): Maindreieck. (Gro): Rosstal. (Vins): Assorted parts of vineyards.

Mühlbacher (Ger) vineyard (Anb): Württemberg. (Ber): Württembergisch Unterland. (Gro): Schalkstein. (Vil): Mundelsheim.

Mühlberg (Aus) a vineyard site on the banks of the River Danube situated in the Wachau region, Niederösterreich.

Mühlberg (Ger) vineyard (Anb): Baden. (Ber): Badische Frankenland. (Gro): Tauberklinge. (Vil): Boxberg (stadtteil Unterschüpf).

Mühlberg (Ger) vineyard (Anb): Mittelrhein. (Ber): Rheinburgengau. (Gro): Marksburg. (Vil): Braubach.

Mühlberg (Ger) vineyard (Anb): Mosel-Saar-Ruwer. (Ber): Bernkastel. (Gro): Kurfürstlay. (Vil): Veldenz.

Mühlberg (Ger) vineyard (Anb): Nahe. (Ber): Schloss Böckelheim. (Gro): Burgweg. (Vil): Schlossböckelheim.

Mühlberg (Ger) vineyard (Anb): Nahe. (Ber): Schloss Böckelheim. (Gro): Burgweg. (Vil): Waldböckelheim.

Mühlberg (Ger) vineyard (Anb): Nahe. (Ber): Schloss Böckelheim. (Gro): Rosengarten. (Vil): Sponheim.

Mühlberg (Ger) vineyard (Anb): Pfalz. (Ber): Südliche Weinstrasse. (Gro): Schloss Ludwigshöhe. (Vil): Edenkoben.

Mühlberg (Ger) vineyard (Anb): Württemberg. (Ber): Württembergisch Unterland. (Gro): Kirchenweinberg. (Vil): Ilsfeld (ortsteil Schozach).

Mühlenberg (Ger) vineyard (Anb): Mosel-Saar-Ruwer. (Ber): Bernkastel. (Gro): Sankt Michael. (Vil): Ensch.

Mühlenberg (Ger) vineyard (Anb): Nahe. (Ber): Kreuznach. (Gro): Pfarrgarten. (Vil): Wallhausen.

Mühlenberg (Ger) vineyard (Anb): Nahe. (Ber): Schloss Böckelheim. (Gro): Rosengarten. (Vil): Roxheim.

Mühlgassner (Aus) a winery (1.2ha) based in Eisenstadt, Neusiedlersee-Hügelland, Burgenland. (Add): Dreifaltigkeitsstrasse 72, 7000 Eisenstadt. Grape variety; Blaufränkisch. Produces red and rosé wines.

Mühlhausen (Ger) vineyard (Anb): Baden. (Ber): Badische Bergstrasse/Kraichgau. (Gro): Mannaberg. (Vil): Heilgenstein.

Mühlhausen (Ger) village (Anb): Württemberg. (Ber): Remstal-Stuttgart. (Gro): Weinsteige. see Stuttgart.

Mühlhausen (Ger) village (Anb): Württemberg. (Ber): Württembergisch Unterland. (Gro): Stromberg. (Vin): Halde.

Mühlpoint (Aus) a vineyard site on the banks of the River Danube situated in the Wachau region, Niederösterreich.

Mühringer (Ger) a sparkling natural spring mineral water. (red label: sparkling/blue label: light gas). Mineral contents (milligrammes per litre): Sodium 65.5mg/l, Calcium 307mg/l, Magnesium 52.7mg/l, Potassium 5.6mg/l, Bicarbonates 708mg/l, Chlorides 69.7mg/l, Sulphates 445mg/l, Fluorides 0.3mg/l, Nitrates 0.4mg/l.

Mühringer Heilwasser (Ger) a sparkling natural spring mineral water. Mineral contents (milligrammes per litre): Sodium 137mg/l, Calcium 369mg/l, Magnesium 55.9mg/l, Potassium 14.7mg/l, Bicarbonates 1053mg/l, Chlorides 91mg/l, Sulphates 458mg/l, Fluorides 0.2mg/l, Nitrates <0.1mg/l.

Mui Kive Lu (Chi) a clear spirit distilled from Kaoliang, a Sorghum-like grain 40% alc by vol.

Muirheads (Scot) a blended Scotch whisky produced by MᵃᶜDonald and Muir 40% alc by vol.

Muirlea Rise (N.Z.) a winery based at 50 Princess Street, Martinborough. 1.9ha. Grape variety: Pinot noir.

Múisiúnta (Ire) musty.

Múisiúntacht (Ire) mustiness.

Mukuzani (Geo) a red grape variety grown in Georgia.

Mukuzani (Geo) a full red wine from the Georgia region (Tiflis district) 14% alc by vol. Produced from a grape of the same name.

Mulata (Cktl) 25mls (1fl.oz) Bacardi Elixir, juice ½ lime, 25mls (1fl.oz) Bacardi White Label, ½ teaspoon sugar. Shake well over ice and strain into a cocktail glass.

Mulberry Tree (Eng) a 5% alc by vol. ale brewed by HB Clark & C°. Ltd., West Yorkshire.

Mulch (Eng) rotting vegetation, wood chips, etc. to prevent soil erosion and enrichment. *See also* Crushed Glass.

Mulderboch Vineyards (S.Afr) a winery (established 1989) based in Stellenbosch, Western Cape. 27ha. Grape varieties: Cabernet franc, Cabernet sauvignon, Chardonnay, Malbec, Merlot, Petit verdot, Sauvignon blanc, Shiraz. Labels: Beta Centauri, Faithful Hound, Stee-op-Hout. Website: http://www.mulderbosch.co.za

Mülheim (Ger) village (Anb): Mosel-Saar-Ruwer. (Ber): Bernkastel. (Gro): Kurfürstlay. (Vins): Amtsgarten, Elisenberg, Helenenkloster, Sonnenlay.

Mülhoff (Ger) a producer of liqueurs and wheat-based whiskey. (Add): Spirituosenfabrik 418 Goch.

Mulhouse (Fr) a town and district of Alsace. (Ger) = Muehlhausen.

Mull (Eng) a seventeenth century practice of heating drinks of wine or ale that have been flavoured with spices, lemon and beaten egg. The method of heating was usually done with a red hot poker (never boiled).

Mulled (Eng) hot drinks, usually served from a silver jug with a lid.

Mulled Cider (Cktl) 1200mls (2pints) cider, 75mls (3fl.ozs) brandy, 1 tablespoon brown sugar, 6 cloves, ¼ teaspoon ginger and cinnamon. Mix spice, sugar and cider, heat slowly until nearly boiling, add brandy, serve in warmed glasses with a slice of orange.

Mulled Claret (Cktl) 1 bottle claret, 1 wine glass port, 150mls (¼ pint) water, tablespoon sugar, rind of ½ lemon, 12 cloves, pinch nutmeg. Simmer spices with water, strain, add wine, Port and sugar, heat and serve very hot with thin slices of lemon rind.

Mulled Red Wine (Cktl) 1 bottle claret or Burgundy, 2 lemons, 200mls (⅓ pint) water, 100gms (4ozs) sugar, 4 cinnamon sticks, 4 cloves. Boil water, sugar and spices for 5 minutes, add thinly sliced lemons, infuse 10 minutes, add wine, heat slowly and serve.

Mulled Spiced Ale (Cktl) 1 teaspoon powdered sugar in 300mls (½ pint) tankard, add pinch cinnamon, top with strong dark beer and heat by inserting a hot poker.

Mulled Wine (Eng) wine (mainly red) which has been heated and flavoured with spices and fruits. Usually served at Christmas time. (Den) = gløgg, (Fr) = vin chaud, (Ger) = glühwein.

Müller [Matheus] (Ger) a large producer of fine Deutscher Sekt.

Müller Brauerei (Switz) an independent brewery based in Baden.

Müller Brauerei (Switz) a brewery based in Neuchâtel, part of the Feldschlösschen group.

Müllerrebe (Ger) a red grape variety known also as the Schwarzriesling and Pinot Meunier. Also spelt Müller Rebe.

Müller-Scharzhofberg [Egon] (Ger) a large wine-producing company based in Wiltingen, Mosel-Saar-Ruwer.

Müller-Schwarzriesling (Ger) see Müllerrebe.

Müller-Thurgau (Ger) a white grape variety (early ripener and high yielder). Thought to be a cross between Riesling/Silvaner x Rivaner, created by Hermann Müller at the Geisenheim viticultural research station in the 1882. Named after the Swiss Canton (Thurgau) he came from. Produces perfumed wines with an aroma and flavour of elderflower, privet, flowering currant, apricot and apple. (Hun) = rizlingszilvani, (Lux) = rivaner. Now generally reckoned to be Riesling x Riesling.

Müllheim (Ger) village (Anb): Baden. (Ber): Markgräflerland. (Gro): Burg Neuenfels. (Vins): Pfaffenstück, Reggenhag, Sonnhalde.

Mulligan (Ire) an Irish whiskey and fruit-flavoured liqueur produced in Ballinaneashagh, Waterford 40% alc by vol.

Mull of Kintyre (Cktl) 1 part Glayva in a highball glass, top up with ice, cola and a twist of lemon peel and serve with straws.

Mulsum (Lat) mead.

Mulsum (Fr) a red wine with honey and cinnamon produced by Mas de Tourelles, near Beaucaire, southern France. See also Turriculae.

Mulsus (Lat) mead.

Multaner (Ger) a white grape variety, a cross between the Riesling and the Silvaner. Only good for wine making if very ripe.

Multidestilada (Sp) multi-distilled.

Multivita Blue Label (Pol) a sparkling natural spring mineral water from Krynica-Tylicz. Mineral contents (milligrammes per litre): Sodium 154.5mg/l, Calcium 226mg/l, Magnesium 48.23mg/l, Potassium 10.3mg/l, Bicarbonates 1311.8mg/l, Chlorides 14.18mg/l, Sulphates 18.75mg/l, Fluorides 0.183mg/l.

Multivita Green Label (Pol) a sparkling natural spring mineral water from Krynica-Tylicz. Mineral contents (milligrammes per litre): Sodium 4.93mg/l, Calcium 72.14mg/l, Magnesium 24.36mg/l, Potassium 1.55mg/l, Bicarbonates 305.09mg/l, Chlorides 10.6mg/l, Sulphates 28.5mg/l, Fluorides 0.136mg/l.

Multivita Red Label (Pol) a still natural spring mineral water from Krynica-Tylicz. Mineral contents (milligrammes per litre): Sodium 26.37mg/l, Calcium 46.09mg/l, Magnesium 19.46mg/l, Potassium 2.01mg/l, Bicarbonates 259.33mg/l, Chlorides 3.55mg/l, Sulphates 38.54mg/l, Fluorides 0.034mg/l.

Mum (Eng) a type of beer brewed in the seventeenth century from cereals and beans.

Mumford's Vineyard (Eng) a vineyard based at Shockerwick Lane, Bannerdown, Bath. Produces white, rosé and red wines. Grapes include: Kerner, Madeleine-Angevine.

Mumm [G.H.] (Fr) a Champagne producer. (Add): 29 Rue de Champ de Mars, 51053 Reims. A Grande Marque. 340ha. Produces vintage and non-vintage wines. Vintages: 1900, 1904, 1906, 1911, 1913, 1920, 1921, 1923, 1926, 1928, 1929, 1933, 1934, 1937, 1941, 1943, 1945, 1947, 1949, 1952, 1953, 1955, 1958, 1959,

1961, 1962, 1964, 1966, 1969, 1971, 1973, 1975, 1976, 1982, 1983, 1985, 1988, 1990, 1995, 1996, 1998, 1999. *See also* René Lalou, Cordon Rouge, Cordon Rosé, Cordon Verte. De Luxe vintage cuvée is Grand Cordon. This replaced Mumm de Mumm in 1985. Mumm de Mumm replaced Mumm Cuvée Presidente René Lalou in 1982. Controls Heidsieck Monopole and Perrier Jouët. *See also* Cuvée Napa. Website: http://www.mumm.com

Mumma (Swe) a mixture of porter, ale and sweetened soda water often with gin added.

Mumm Cognac (USA) a Cognac brandy produced by Seagram for the USA market.

Mumm Cuvée Presidente René Lalou (Fr) a de luxe vintage cuvée Champagne produced by G.H. Mumm from 50% Chardonnay and 50% Pinot noir. It was also known as René Lalou. Now replaced by Mumm de Mumm.

Mumm de Mumm (Fr) a prestige cuvée from G.H. Mumm. Produced from a blend of Pinot noir (from Ambonnay, Aÿ and Verzenay) and Chardonnay (from Avize and Cramant). Replaces René Lalou.

Mumme (Ger) a non-fermented malt extract beer from Braunschweig. Served as a tonic or mixed with pale beers.

Münchner (Ger) a dark, brown, malty, bottom-fermented beer 4.3% alc by vol. Originates from Munich.

Münchner Kindl Weissbier (Ger) a 5.1% alc by vol. bottle-conditioned white wheat beer brewed by Hofbräu Münchnen, Munich.

Münchweiler (Ger) village (Anb): Baden. (Ber): Breisgau. (Gro): Schutterlindenberg. (Vin): Kirchberg.

Mundelsheim (Ger) village (Anb): Württemberg. (Ber): Württembergisch Unterland. (Gro): Schalkstein. (Vins): Käsberg, Katzenöhrle, Mühlbächer, Rozenberg.

Mundend (Ger) denotes a tasty, pleasant wine.

Mundenhamer (Aus) a bock beer brewed by the brewery of same name.

Mundenhamer Brauerei (Aus) a brewery noted for bock beers.

Mundingen (Ger) village (Anb): Baden. (Ber): Breisgau. (Gro): Burg Lichteneck. (Vin): Alte Burg.

Mundklingen (Ger) vineyard (Anb): Hessische Bergstrasse. (Ber): Starkenburg. (Gro): Not yet assigned. (Vil): Seeheim.

Muniesa (Sp) a Vino Comarcal of Teruel in Aragón.

Munkekilden (Den) a natural spring mineral water from Munkekilden.

Munkeln (Aus) denotes a wine with the taste of a dirty cask.

Munson (USA) a vine hybridiser who developed the red Delicatessen.

Münster (Ger) village (Anb): Württemberg. (Ber): Remstal-Stuttgart. (Gro): Weinsteige. *see* Stuttgart.

Münsterappel (Ger) village (Anb): Nahe. (Ber): Schloss Böckelheim. (Gro): Paradiesgarten. (Vin): Graukatz.

Münsterberg (Ger) vineyard (Anb): Mosel-Saar-Ruwer. (Ber): Zell/Mosel. (Gro): Goldbäumchen. (Vil): Treis-Karden.

Münster-Sarmsheim (Ger) village (Anb): Nahe. (Ber): Kreuznach. (Gro): Schlosskapelle. (Vins): Dautenpflänzer, Kapellenberg, Konigsschloss, Liebenhöll, Pittersberg, Rheinberg, Römerberg, Steinkopf, Trollberg.

Münsterstatt (Ger) vineyard (Anb): Mosel-Saar-Ruwer. (Ber): Obermosel. (Gro): Gipfel. (Vil): Temmels.

Münzberg (Ger) vineyard (Anb): Pfalz. (Ber): Südliche Weinstrasse. (Gro): Königsgarten. (Vil): Godramstein.

Münzesheim (Ger) *see* Kraichtal.

Munzingen (Ger) village (Anb): Baden. (Ber): Kaiserstuhl-Tuniberg. (Gro): Attilafelsen. (Vin): Kapellenberg.

Münzlay (Ger) grosslage (Anb): Mosel-Saar-Ruwer. (Ber): Bernkastel. (Vils): Graach, Wehlen, Zeltingen-Rachtig.

Mûr (Fr) ripe.

Murailles [Les] (Fr) a vineyard of Dopff & Irion in Alsace. Produces Riesling wines.

Muralles (Sp) *see* Grans Muralles.

Muratie Wine Estate (S.Afr) a winery (established 1685) based in the Koelenhof, Stellenbosch, Western Cape. 46ha. (Add): P.O. Box 133, Koelenhof 7605. Grape varieties: Cabernet sauvignon, Chardonnay, Merlot, Muscat d'Alsace, Pinot noir, Shiraz, Tinta barocca, Tinta roriz, Tinta souzão. Labels: Amber Forever, Ansela, Cape Vintage (Port), Isabella, Melck's Red. Website: http://www.muratie.co.za

Murcia (Sp) a wine producing area in the Levante. Home to the province of Murcia. Has the D.O.'s Bullas, Jumilla, Yecla and Alicante (part). Vinos de la Tierra of Abanilla, Campo de Cartagena. Vino de Mesa of Espinardo.

Mûre (Fr) a blackberry and mulberry spirit liqueur.

Muré (Fr) an Alsace wine-producer. (Add): 68250 Rouffach 19ha.

Mureck (Aus) a wine-producing area in Klöch, southern Austria.

Muree Beer (Pak) a 4.5% alc by vol. beer brewed by the Rawalpindi Brewery.

Mürefte (Tur) a wine-producing region in southern Turkey.

Mûre Sauvage (Fr) a brandy-based liqueur flavoured with blackberries.

Mureto (Port) a red grape variety sometimes used in Bairrada production.

Murets de Sion [Les] (Switz) a white wine from the Valais produced from the Fendant grape.

Murettes [Les] (Fr) a vineyard of Château de l'Hermitage, northern Rhône (white wine).

Murfatlar (Rum) a fine dessert wine which has a faint bouquet of orange blossoms. Produced near the region of Focsani from the vineyard of the same name in Dobrudja.

Murfatler Hills (Rum) an area near the wine region of Focsani. Noted for dessert wines.

M

Murganheira (Port) a winery 47ha that specialises in sparkling wines based in Távora-Varosa south of the Doura. Grape varieties: Cerceal, Chardonnay, Gouveio, Malvasia fina, Pinot noir. Also buys in grapes.

Murgers-des-Dents-de-Chien [Les] (Fr) a Premier Cru vineyard in the A.C. commune of Saint Aubin, Côte de Beaune, Burgundy.

Murgeys (Fr) another name for Cheys.

Múrice (Sp) the label of a D.O.Ca. Rioja produced by Viña Ijalba in Logroño from 90% Tempranillo, 5% Graciano, 5% Mazuelo grapes.

Muri-Gries (It) a vineyard based in the DOC Trentino-Alto-Adige, northern Italy. Grape variety: Lagrein. Label: Riserva Abtei Muri. Website: http://www.muri-gries.com 'E'mail: muri-gries-kg@muri-gries.com

Murillo (Sp) a Zona de Crianza in the Rioja Baja.

Muristellu (It) a name used in Sardinia for the red Bovale sardo grape.

Murmurer Cocktail (Cktl) 30mls (¼ gill) Sherry, 30mls (¼ gill) gin, ¼ teaspoon lime juice, ½ teaspoon Angostura. Stir over ice, strain into a cocktail glass and serve with a dash of lemon peel juice on top.

Muroto (Jap) a natural spring mineral water brand.

Murphy Brewery (Ire) a brewery based in Cork (owned by Heineken of Holland), noted for stout.

Murphy-Goode (USA) a winery based in the Alexander Valley, Sonoma County, California. Grape varieties: Cabernet sauvignon, Fumé-blanc, Zinfandel.

Murphy's (Ire) a second blend of Middleton light pot-still and grain whiskies, matured in charred barrels.

Murphy's Irish Red (Ire) a 5% alc by vol. keg/bottled ale brewed by the Murphy Brewery in Cork.

Murr (Ger) village (Anb): Württemberg. (Ber): Württembergisch Unterland. (Gro): Schalkstein. (Vin): Neckarhälde.

Murr [River] (Ger) a tributary of the river Neckar in Württemberg. Soil: red marl.

Murra Coffee (Tur) the name given to unsweetened Turkish coffee.

Murrao (Port) a white grape variety grown in Peñafiel (a sub-region of Vinho Verde).

Murray [River] (Austr) a wine region of South Australia. Main estates are Angoves, Brown Brothers and Thomas Hardy. Noted for Port-style wines and brandies.

Murree Brewery (Pak) a brewery based in Rawalpindi which produces London Lager 10.4° Balling, Export 11.4° Balling and a bottom-fermented, medium Stout 14.2° Balling.

Murrina (Lat) myrrh wine.

Murrumbidgee Irrigation Area (Austr) *abbr*: M.I.A. A wine region of New South Wales. Main estates are De Bortoli, Seppelts, McWilliams, Penfolds, Rooty Hill.

Mûrs (Fr) an A.C. commune in the Coteaux de l'Aubance district of the Anjou-Saumur, Loire. Produces light, white wines.

Mus (Tur) a banana liqueur.

Musaafi (Pak) a natural spring mineral water (established 2004). Mineral contents (milligrammes per litre): Calcium 52mg/l, Magnesium 82mg/l, Chlorides 55mg/l, Sulphates 490mg/l. pH 7.8

Musanté (S.Afr) a sweet, sparkling white wine from the Muscat grape made by the K.W.V.

Muscach (Ire) musky.

Muscade (Fr) an alternative name for the Muscadelle grape.

Muscadel (Eng) an old name for Muscatel wine.

Muscadel (USA) the term for a Port-style fortified wine made with the Muscat grape.

Muscadelle (Austr) a white grape variety also known as the Tokay.

Muscadelle (Fr) a white grape variety grown in Bordeaux. Cultivated in small portions with the Sémillon and Sauvignon blanc. It gives a faint Muscat flavour to the wine. Also known as the Angelicant, Auvernat blanc, Catape, Collemusquette, Douzanelle, Guépie, Guillan, Guillan musqué, Loin d'Oeuil, Muscade, Muscat fou, Musquette, Resinotte, Sauvignon vert.

Muscadelle du Bordelais (USA) a white grape variety grown in California to make white table wines.

Muscadet (Fr) the local Loire name for the white grape variety Melon de Bourgogne (also known as the Lyonnaise blanche).

Muscadet (Fr) an A.C. classification of wines produced south of Nantes in the Nantais. Overall designation but accounts for only 10% of the Muscadet produced. 1,754ha. Minimum alc by vol. 9.5%.

Muscadet Coteaux de la Loire (Fr) an A.C. category of Muscadet wines. From the east of Nantes. Includes the districts: Ancenis, Carquefou, Champtoceaux, Ligné, Saint-Florent-le-Vieil, Varades. Produces about 5% of Muscadet A.C. wines. 354ha. Minimum alc by vol. 10%.

Muscadet Côtes de Grand Lieu (Fr) a new appellation granted in 1994. Produced in Herbauges, Logne, Boulogne areas (districts of St. Philbert-de-Grand-Lieu and neighbouring parishes). 205ha. *See also* Muscadet Sur Lie, Muscadet Sèvre et Maine.

Muscadet de Dieppe (Fr) a noted cider apple grown in the Normandy region. Has good acidity and produces dry ciders.

Muscadet des Coteaux de la Loire (Fr) *see* Muscadet Coteaux de la Loire.

Muscadet de Sèvre et Maine (Fr) *see* Muscadet Sèvre et Maine.

Muscadet Saint-Clément (Fr) the name that the wines of Château la Berrière are sold under.

Muscadet Sèvre et Maine (Fr) the finest of the A.C. Muscadets, accounts for 85% of production. Produced in an area south of Nantes around and between the rivers Sèvre and Maine in the districts: Aigrefeuille, Clisson, Le Loroux-Bottereau, Vallet, Vertou. 10392ha. Often produced Sur Lie. Originally known as Muscadet de Sèvre et Maine.

Muscadet Sur Lie (Fr) from the 1994 vintage the wine must be bottled where it was made directly from the lees. Can be bottled only from 1st March to 30th June, 15th October to 30th November for this designation.

Muscadet Troisième Niveau (Fr) lit: 'third level Muscadet', a proposed new grading (2006) of Muscadet by allowing it to spend at least 18 months on its lees (will not allowed to be designated Sur-Lie).

Muscadines (USA) members of the *Vitis rotundifolia* American vine species. 3 types: Sappenog (white), James (black) and Misch (black), also known as the Scuppernong or Bullace grape.

Muscardin (Fr) a red grape variety grown in the southern Rhône for the making of Châteauneuf-du-Pape.

Muscat (Euro) a wine and table grape with varieties ranging from pale yellow to blue-black. In wine it produces a very distinctive bouquet and flavour of honey, fruit, grapey, aromatic spice, orange blossom, roses, sweet spice, musk, raisin, apricot. Grown in most wine districts that have plenty of sunshine.

Muscat à Petit Grains Rouge (Fr) a red-skinned Muscat grape variety, also known as the Brown Frontignac in Australia.

Muscat Aigre (Fr) the lesser name for the Ugni blanc.

Muscat Alexandria (USA) *see* Muscat of Alexandria.

Muscat Baily A (USA) a white American hybrid grape used in Japan.

Muscat Blanc (USA) the alternative name for the Muscat of canelli and the Muscat of frontignan. Known as Tamîioasa alba in Romania.

Muscat Blanc à Petits Grains (Fr) the local Rhône name for the Muscat d'Alexandria grape in the Clairette de Die, also in Alsace. Black and white varieties. Also known as Brown muscat, Gelber muscateller, Moscatello galego branco, Moscatello galego roxo, Moscato, Moscato bianco, Moscato branco, Muscat d'alsace, Muscat lunel, Muscat rosé à petits grains d'Alsace, Muscatel, Muscatel branco, Muskat, Muskotàly, Muskateller, Muskuti, Sargamuskotaly, White frontignan, Zutimuscat.

Muscat Brandy (USA) *see* California Brandy.

Muscat Courtillier (Fr) a relation of the Muscat grape. Also known as the Coutillier musqué and Muscat precoce de courtillier.

Muscat d'Alexandria (S.Afr) a white grape variety known as the Muscadelle in Europe.

Muscat d'Alsace (Fr) an A.C. dry white, perfumed wine made from the Muscat grape in Alsace. *see* Muscat Blanc à Petits Grains, Muscat d'Ottonel and Muscat Rosé à Petits Grains.

Muscat de Beaumes de Venise (Fr) an A.C. Vin Doux Naturel from the Côtes du Rhône Villages. Made from the Muscat grape, it has a powerful muscat 'honied' aroma.

Muscat de Cephalonia (Gre) a dessert wine from the Island of Cephalonia in the Ionian Isles, western Greece. Made from the Muscat grape.

Muscat de Chypre (Cyp) a fine Muscat dessert wine sold on the USA market.

Muscat de Frontignan (Fr) an A.C. VdN dessert wine produced in the Midi region. Made from the Muscat blanc à petits grains.

Muscat de Grain Touge (Austr) a red grape variety grown in Victoria.

Muscat de Hambourg (Chi) a white Muscat grape variety grown in the Tianjin region.

Muscat de Kéliba (Afr) the name given to a white A.O.C. wine from Tunisia (dry and sweet versions) produced by UCCVT.

Muscat de Lemnos (Gre) a sweet dessert wine from the Muscat d'Alexandria made on the island of Lemnos in the Aegean Isles, eastern Greece.

Muscat de Lunel (Fr) a Vin Doux Naturel from the Hérault département in the Midi region (white).

Muscat de Miréval (Fr) a VdN dessert wine produced in Montpellier (white). Made from the Muscat blanc à petits grains.

Muscat de Patras (Gre) an A.O.C. fine white liqueur dessert wine from the Peloponnese.

Muscat de Rhodes (Gre) a naturally sweet dessert wine made from the Muscat and Muscat de Trani grape varieties. Produced on the Rhodes Islands in the Dodecanese Isles, south-eastern Greece.

Muscat de Rivesaltes (Fr) an A.C. Vin Doux Naturel from near Perpignan in the Roussillon region (white). 100% Muscat (Muscat Blanc à Petits Grains/Muscat d'alexandrie).

Muscat de Saint-Jean-de-Minervois (Fr) a VdN dessert wine produced in the Midi region (white).

Muscat de Samos (Gre) an A.O.C. sweet white dessert wine from the island of in the Aegean Islands, eastern Greece.

Muscat de Setúbal (Port) a D.O.C. sweet fortified wine produced in southern Portugal around the Port of Setúbal. When the required balance is achieved during fermentation it is fortified with grape spirit. Muscatel grape skins are added and allowed to macerate with the wine until the following spring. It is then racked and matured for several years before sale. 6 and 20 year old versions are produced as well as vintage. Renamed Setúbal.

Muscat de Terracina (Tun) a white grape variety that produces medium-sweet perfumed wines.

Muscat de Trani (Gre) a white grape variety grown mainly in southern Greece to produce naturally **sweet wines.**

Muscat Doré de Frontignan (Fr) an alternative name for the Muscat blanc à petits grains.

Muscat d'Ottonel (Fr) a white grape variety of Muscat grown in the Alsace region.

Muscat du Cap Corse (Fr) an A.C. of Corsica.

Muscat du Moulin [Couderc 19] (Fr) a cross grape variety between the Pedro Ximénez and C603.

Muscatel (Austr) *see* Muscat Gordo Blanco and Muscat Blanc à Petits Grains.

M

Muscatel (Isr) a sweet, dessert, Port-style wine.

Muscatel Branco (Port) a white grape variety used in the making of white Port. Also known as the Muscat blanc à petits grains.

Muscateller (Euro) an alternative name for the Muscat blanc à petits grains.

Muscateller Ottonel (Aus) an alternative name for the Muscat ottonel.

Muscat Fou (Fr) an alternative name for the Muscadelle grape.

Muscat Frontignan (USA) see Muscat of Frontignan.

Muscat Gamburgski (Euro) an alternative name for the Muscat of Hamburg.

Muscat Gordo Blanco (Austr) a white grape variety of the Muscat family. Also known as the Muscat of Alexandria, Muscatel and Lexia.

Muscat Hamburg (USA) see Muscat of Hamburg.

Muscat-Hamburg (Ser) a red wine produced in southern Macedonia from the grape of same name.

Muscatheer Family Reserve (S.Afr) the label for a range of white (Muscat de Frontignan) and red (Pinotage) wines produced by the Jonkeer winery, Robertson, Western Cape.

Muscat Italia (It) a relation of the Muscat grape, a cross between the Bicane and the Muscat of Hamburg.

Muscat Lunel (Aus) an alternative name for the Muskateller. See also Gelber Muskateller.

Muscat Lunel (Hun) the local name used in the Tokaji district for Muscat blanc à petits grains.

Muscat Massandra (Rus) a medium-dry white wine produced near Simferopol in the Ukraine.

Muscato di Amburgo (It) an alternative name for the Muscat of Hamburg.

Muscat of Alexandria (Austr) see Muscat Gordo Blanco.

Muscat of Alexandria (S.Afr) a white grape variety. Also known as the Hanepoot, Iskendiriye, Lexia, Moscatel de España, Moscatel de Málaga, Moscatel graúdo, Moscatel romano, Muscat d'Alexandrie, Muscat gordo blanco, Muscat romain, Panse musquée, White hanepoot and Zibibbo.

Muscat of Alexandria (USA) a white grape variety used in the making of dessert wines in California.

Muscat of Canelli (USA) a white grape variety used in the making of dessert wines in California. Also known as the Muscat de Frontignan and Muscat blanc à petits grains.

Muscat of Frontignan (USA) a white grape variety used in the making of white and dessert wines in California.

Muscat of Hamburg (USA) a black grape variety used in the making of dessert wines in California. Also known as the Black muscat, Black of Alexandria, Muscat gamburgski, Muscato di Amburgo and Tamaiîoasa Hamburg.

Muscat of Kirghiz (Rus) a white dessert grape variety grown in the Kirghizian region.

Muscat of Lemnos (Gre) a sweet white wine produced on the Aegean Island of Lemnos from the Muscat grape.

Muscat of Rhodes (Gre) a sweet white wine produced on the Aegean Island of Rhodes from the Muscat grape.

Muscat of Samos (Gre) a sweet white wine produced on the Aegean Island of Samos from the Muscat grape.

Muscat of St. Laurent (USA) a red grape variety used in the making of dessert wines in California.

Muscat Ottonel (Fr) a white grape variety grown in Alsace. Also known as Muscateller ottonel, Muskat ottonel and Muskateller ottonel. Found in Austria, Hungary and Romania.

Muscat Ottonel (Rum) a highly flavoured dessert wine from the Valea Calugareasca region.

Muscat Précoce de Courtiller (Fr) a white grape variety grown in the Midi region. Also known as the Muscat courtillier.

Muscat Reine des Vignes (Hun) a Muscat cross which gives strong scented wines.

Muscat Riesling (Ger) a white grape variety, a cross between the White riesling and the Muscat St. Laurent.

Muscat Rion de Patras (Gre) a fine O.P.E. white dessert liqueur wine from Peloponnese.

Muscat Romain (It) an alternative name for the Muscat of Alexandria.

Muscat Rosé à Petits Grains (Fr) a red skinned grape variety also known as the Muscat d'alsace, Muscat rosé à petits grains d'alsace, Rotter muscateller and Rottermuskateller.

Muscat Rosé à Petits Grains d'Alsace (Fr) see Muscat Rosé à Petits Grains.

Muscat Sàrgamuskot ly (Hun) a white grape variety, a variety of the Muscat family.

Muscat St. Laurent (Fr) a red grape variety.

Muscat-Sylvaner (Fr) a white grape variety known as the Sauvignon in Germany.

Muscat Violet (Rus) a white grape variety used in the production of dessert wines in the regions of Kazakhstan and Kirghizian.

Muscavado (Sp) the name given to the evaporated liquid derived from sugar cane, the Arabs call it Sukkar.

Muscel (Rum) a noted white wine-producing vineyard.

Muschekalk (Ger) a name for the soil of shell-lime in Franconia.

Muscovital (Cktl) 25mls (1fl.oz) Campari, 25mls (1fl.oz) vodka, 50mls (2fl.ozs) Green's Ginger Wine. Mix over ice in a highball and serve with a cherry.

Musée de la Brasserie (Fr) a brewery. (Add): Rue Charles Courtois, F-54210 Saint-Nicolas-de-Port. Brews beers and lagers. Website: http://www.passionbrasserie.com 'E'mail: mfb@passionbrasserie.com

Musée de la Vigne et du Vin (Fr) a wine museum based in Champagne. (Add): 2, Avenue Eugène Guillaume, B.P. 7, 51190 Le Mesnil-sur-Oger. Website: http://www.champagne-launois.fr 'E'mail: info@champagne-launois.fr

Musée du Cidre (Fr) a working cider museum based

M

in the village of Eau-Puiseaux, Pays d'Othe (open 1st May to 30th September).

Musée du Vin de Bourgogne (Fr) a museum which has displays of wine and the vine based at the former Hôtel des Ducs de Bourgogne.

Musée du Vin de Champagne (Fr) a museum based at Épernay. Shows the Champagne process including a model of the abbey at Hautvillers.

Muselage (Fr) lit: 'muzzling', the wiring of the clamps onto Champagne bottles.

Muselet (Fr) the wire cage that is placed over the corks on Champagne and sparkling wine bottles.

Muselet de Fil de Fer (Fr) the name for the wire muzzle used to hold the cork down in a bottle of sparkling wine.

Musenhang (Ger) vineyard (Anb): Pfalz. (Ber): Mittelhaardt-Deutsche Weinstrasse. (Gro): Mariengarten. (Vil): Forst.

Museum Ale (Eng) a standard draught bitter from Smith (Samuel) in Tadcaster, North Yorkshire.

Musigny (Fr) a Grand Cru vineyard in the A.C. commune of Chambolle-Musigny, Côte de Nuits, Burgundy. 10.7ha. owned by 6 owners of various-sized plots. Also known as Les Musigny.

Musigny Blanc (Fr) a rare white wine made by the Comte de Vogue from the Chardonnay grape that is produced in the Musigny vineyard in the Chambolle-Musigny commune. In many years none is produced so it is expensive. About 2000 bottles produced.

Musika (Bul) a premium red wine produced by the B.V.C. See also Azbuka.

Musikantenbuckel (Ger) vineyard (Anb): Pfalz. (Ber): Mittelhaardt-Deutsche Weinstrasse. (Gro): Kobnert. (Vil): Freinsheim.

Muskadel (S.Afr) an alternative name for Muscat blanc à petits grains.

Muskat (Aus) an alternative name for the Muscat blanc à petits grains.

Muskat Crveni (Cro) a red grape variety grown in Croatia.

Muskateller (Aus) a white grape variety which produces low acid wines. Also known as the Gelber muskateller and Muscat-Lunel. See also Muscat Blanc à Petits Grains.

Muskat-Ottonel (Aus)(Ger) a white grape variety which produces wines of intense bouquet. see Muscat Ottonel.

Muskat-Sylvaner (Aus) a white grape variety, also known as Sauvignon blanc.

Muskotàly (Hun) a white grape variety, a species of the Moscatel used in the making of Tokaji wines. Also the name of a fortified wine with an intense Muscat flavour. see Muscat Blanc à Petits Grains.

Muskuti (Rum) an alternative name for the Muscat blanc à petits grains.

Musky (Eng) a description of the smell of wines made from the Muscat grape. A pronounced smell of musk. (Ire) = muscach.

Muslim (Arab) the Islamic religion that forbids alcoholic consumption, therefore promotes coffee drinking.

Muslin Madeira (Eng) the nineteenth century name of Madeira marketed in London.

Musqué (Fr) a term used to describe a strongly perfumed grape (musky).

Musquette (Fr) an alternative name for the Muscadelle grape.

Mussbach (Ger) village (Anb): Pfalz. (Ber): Mittelhaardt-Deutsche Weinstrasse. (Gro): Meerspinne. (Vins): Bischofsweg, Eselshaut, Glockenzehnt, Johannitergarten, Kurfürst, Spiegel.

Must (Eng) an 8.5% alc by vol. lager brewed by Morrells, Oxford.

Must (Eng) unfermented grape juice. (Fr) = moût, (Ger) = moot/most, (It) = most/mosto, (Port) = most/mosto, (Sp) = most/mosto.

Mustang (Eng) a 4% alc by vol. ale produced with Phoenix hops by Hambleton Brewery, Holme-on-Swale, North Yorkshire. See also Nightmare, Stallion, Stud.

Mustimètre (Fr) a device for measuring the specific gravity of grape juice (must). Also known as the Oechsle, Babo, Baumé and Areometer.

Mustiness (Eng) the odour that occurs in vessels that have been put away damp (carafes, coffee pots, decanters, jugs, tea pots, etc.) enabling fungi to develop and produce a musty smell. (Ire) = múisiúntacht.

Mustoasa (Rum) a white wine produced near Arad in eastern Rumania.

Mustometer (Eng) see Mustimetre.

Must Weight (Eng) the specific gravity of the grape must, measured on the mustimetre to give the amount of natural sugar in the must.

Musty (Eng) a term for a wine that has a mouldy, damp room smell and taste. The condition is usually obtained through bad cellaring. (Ire) = múisiúnta.

Muswellbrook (Austr) a wine-producing region based north of Sydney in New South Wales.

Muszyna Zdroj (Pol) a natural spring mineral water. Mineral contents (milligrammes per litre): Sodium 65.7mg/l, Calcium 242.88mg/l, Magnesium 48.64mg/l, Potassium 11.8mg/l, Bicarbonates 1159.34mg/l, Chlorides 3.55mg/l, Sulphates 10.95mg/l, Fluorides 0.16mg/l, Iron 6.16mg/l.

Mut (Fr) balanced.

Mutage (Fr) the arresting of the fermentation by the addition of alcohol.

Mutage sur Grains (Fr) the addition of alcohol to macerating grapes. Occurs in the production of VdN wines. See also Mutage sur Moût.

Mutage sur Moût (Fr) describes the fortification of the fermenting must once it has been pressed. Used in VdN production. See also Mutage sur Grains.

Muté (Fr) mistelle or sweet wine whose fermentation has been inhibited by the addition of brandy.

Muted Wine (Eng) a wine which has had brandy added during fermentation. A fortified wine i.e. Port, Pineau des Charentes, Ratafia.

921

M

Mutigny (Fr) a Premier Cru Champagne village in the Canton d'Aÿ. District: Reims.

Mutinense (It) a red wine produced in northern Italy in Roman times.

Mutleys Old Oak Meal Stout (Eng) a 4.4% alc by vol. stout brewed by the Spinning Dog Brewery, Herefordshire.

Mutleys Pit Stop (Eng) a 4% alc by vol. ale brewed by the Spinning Dog Brewery, Herefordshire.

Mütterle (Ger) vineyard (Anb): Pfalz. (Ber): Südliche Weinstrasse. (Gro): Herrlich. (Vil): Wollmesheim.

Mutterweinberge (Aus) a vine nursery based in Vöslau.

Mutto Quellwasser (Ger) a still natural spring mineral water from Bispingen. Mineral contents (milligrammes per litre): Sodium 6.45mg/l, Calcium 28.5mg/l, Magnesium 2.22mg/l, Potassium 0.83mg/l, Bicarbonates 97.6mg/l, Chlorides 5.06mg/l, Sulphates 7.83mg/l, Nitrates <0.1mg/l, Oxygen 6mg/l. pH 6.5

Mutts Nutts (Eng) a 5% alc by vol. ale brewed by the Spinning Dog Brewery, Herefordshire.

Mutzig (Fr) the brand-name used by the Albra Brauerei in Alsace.

Muzzle Loader (Eng) a 4.2% alc by vol. ale brewed by the Cannon Royall Brewery Ltd., Worcestershire.

Muzzling (Eng) see Muselage.

M.W. (Eng) abbr: Master of Wine, the highest award in the British Wines and Spirits Trade.

Myanmar Brewery (Asia) a brewery based in Yangon, Burma that brews beers and lagers.

Mycodermae aceti (Lat) vinegar yeasts.

Mycodermae vini (Lat) the yeast responsible for vineous fermentation. see Voile, Flor and Fleurs de Vin.

My Eie Keur (S.Afr) the label for a sweet white wine (Chardonnay 50% and Sémillon 50%) produced by the My Wyn winery, Franschhoek, Western Cape.

Myer's Rum (W.Ind) the brand-name of a rum 40% alc by vol. distilled in Jamaica by Myers Distillery.

My Fair Lady (Cktl) 25mls (1fl.oz) dry gin, 10mls (½fl.oz) lemon juice, 10mls (½fl.oz) orange juice, 1 teaspoon fraise liqueur, 1 egg white. Shake well over ice and strain into a cocktail glass.

My Huiswyn (S.Afr) the label for a red wine (Cabernet sauvignon 15% and Shiraz 85%) produced by the My Wyn winery, Franschhoek, Western Cape.

Mymering (S.Afr) the brand-name for a South African Sherry.

Mynydd Da (Wal) lit: 'black mountain', see Black Mountain Liqueur.

Myohyansan (N.Kor) a natural spring mineral water from Mount Myohtang, North Korea. Mineral contents (milligrammes per litre): Sodium 1mg/l, Calcium 5.88mg/l, Magnesium 2.88mg/l, Bicarbonates 19.2mg/l, Sulphates 1mg/l.

Myr (Fr) chilled dry white wine and crème de myrtilles.

Myriad (S.Afr) the label for a fortified red wine (Merlot and Pinot noir blend) produced by the BWC Wines, Stellenbosch, Western Cape.

Myrrhy Christmas Ale (Eng) a 5% alc by vol. limited cask-conditioned bitter beer from Castle Eden Brewery, Durham. Contains spices, liquorice, hops, coriander, nutmeg, mace, clove, cinnamon, caraway and cardamon.

Myrtille (Fr) a bilberry-flavoured brandy. see Crème de Myrtilles.

Myrto (It) a Sardinian myrtle liqueur.

Myshako Riesling (Geo) a white table wine from the Georgia region.

My Shout (Eng) see Shout.

Mysliwska (Pol) lit: 'hunter's vodka', a vodka flavoured with juniper berries. see Polmos.

Mysore (Ind) a coffee and tea-producing area of southern India.

Mysterytor (Eng) a 3.8% alc by vol. ale brewed by Glastonbury Ales, Somerset.

Mystic Brew (Eng) a range of 12 cask ales each based on a star sign. e.g. Aries Aphrodisiac Ale, Taurus Ale, Gemini Double Trouble, Pisces Fishing Tackle Ale.

Mystic Park (Austr) a vineyard 60ha. on the shores of Lake Kangaroo. Part of the Brown Brothers Estate in Victoria.

Mythos Brewery (Gre) a brewery. (Add): VI PE Sindou, 570 22 Sindos Thessaloniki. Brews a range of beers and lager. Website: http://www.mythgosbrewery.gr 'E'mail: info@mythosbrewery.gr

My Wyn (S.Afr) a winery (established 2001) based in Franschhoek, Western Cape. Grape varieties: Cabernet sauvignon, Chardonnay, Sémillon, Shiraz, Viognier. Labels: My Eie Keur, My Huiswyn. Also produces Méthode Cap Classique sparkling wines.

Mzvane (Geo) a full-bodied red wine from the Tamada region. Also spelt Mtzvane.

N

Nabana (Fr) a banana liqueur produced by Cazanove.

Nabay (Can) a natural spring mineral water from Keewatin, Ontario.

Nabeeth (Arab) grape wine.

Nabeghlavi (Geo) a natural spring mineral water (established 1948). Mineral contents (milligrammes per litre): Sodium 1250mg/l, Calcium 139mg/l, Magnesium 125mg/l, Potassium 5.5mg/l, Bicarbonates 4210mg/l, Chlorides 83mg/l, Sulphates 143mg/l, Strontium 1.51mg/l, Nitrates 1.2mg/l. Website: http://www.nabeghlavi.ch

Nabeul (Afr) a wine-producing region situated on the tip of Cap Bon in Tunisia. Noted for dry and sweet Muscat wines.

NABLAB (Eng) describes lagers and beers that contain little or no alcohol.

Nabuchodonoser (Fr) a large bottle of (15litres) 20 standard bottles capacity used in the Champagne region. *see* Champagne Bottle Sizes. (Eng) = nebuchadezzar.

Nabygelen Private Cellar (S.Afr) a winery (established 1712) based in Wellington, Western Cape. 18ha. Grape varieties: Cabernet sauvignon, Chenin blanc, Merlot, Petit verdot, Sauvignon blanc, Tempranillo. Labels: At The Limiet, Scaramanga. Website: http://www.nabygelegen.co.za

Náchod Brewery (Czec) a brewery based in northern Czec.

Nacional (Port) a term used to refer to un-grafted vine stocks in the Douro region.

Nacional de Cerveza Brewery (Peru) a brewery based in Callao. Brews: Pilsen Callao.

Nack (Ger) village (Anb): Baden. (Ber): Bodensee. *see* Lottstetten.

Nack (Ger) village (Anb): Rheinhessen. (Ber): Bingen. (Gro): Adelberg. (Vin): Ahrenberg.

Nackenheim (Ger) village (Anb): Rheinhessen. (Ber): Nierstein. (Gro): Gutes Domtal. (Vin): Schmittskapellche.

Nackenheim (Ger) village (Anb): Rheinhessen. (Ber): Nierstein. (Gro): Rehbach. (Vin): Rothenberg.

Nackenheim (Ger) village (Anb): Rheinhessen. (Ber): Nierstein. (Gro): Spiegelberg. (Vin): Engelsberg.

Nacktarsch (Ger) grosslage (Anb): Mosel-Saar-Ruwer. (Ber): Bernkastel. (Vil): Kröv.

Nadal Cava (Sp) a 120ha winery at El Pla del Penedés, Barcelona. Produces Nadal Brut Salvatage (a vintage cava with 5 years of age).

Nadder Bite (Eng) a 7.5% alc by vol. cider produced by Nadder Valley Cider in Downton, Devon.

Nadderjack (Eng) an ale brewed by the Tisbury Brewery, in Tisbury, Wiltshire from a single hop variety.

Nadder Valley Cider (Eng) a cider producer based in Downton. Produces Ambush and Nadder Bite.

Naddniprjanske (Ukr) a white table wine produced near Cherson in the Ukraine.

Nadrosyanska (Ukr) a natural spring mineral water from Korsun-Shevchenkovsky. Mineral contents (milligrammes per litre): Sodium 21.4mg/l, Calcium 96mg/l, Magnesium 36.5mg/l, Bicarbonates 420.9mg/l, Chlorides 30.1mg/l, Sulphates 47.3mg/l.

Nadwislanski (Pol) a cherry and honey mead, clear and red in colour, it is sold in earthenware jars.

Nafree (Sp) a natural spring mineral water from Lorquí, Murcia.

Nagambie (Austr) a vineyard producing fine Cabernet sauvignon wines. Part of the College winery in Victoria.

Nagambie Cabernet Sauvignon (Austr) a varietal red wine from the Redbank Winery in Victoria.

Nagano (Jap) a wine-producing region in southern Japan.

Nagmaalwyn (S.Afr) the label for a sacramental wine produced by the Mooiuitsig Wine Cellars winery, Robertson, Western Cape.

Nagutskaya (Rus) a natural spring mineral water brand.

Nàgyburgundi (Hun) an alternative name for the Blaufränkisch grape. *See also* Kékfrankos.

Nagykanizsa Brewery (Hun) a brewery based in south-western Hungary. Noted for Göcseji Barna and Siràly beer.

Nahe (Ger) anbaugebiet (Bers): Kreuznach, Schloss Böckelheim. Produces 90% white wine. Grape varieties: Müller-Thurgau 30%, Riesling 22%, Scheurebe 5% and Silvaner 23%.

Nahe [River] (Ger) a tributary of the river Rhine, its banks make up the anbaugebiet of same name.

Nahegau (Ger) another name used for the Nahe.

Nahegauer Landwein (Ger) one of the fifteen Deutsche Tafelwein zones.

Nahesteiner (Ger) a generic wine from the Nahe (their own version of liebfraumilch). *See also* Moselblümchen, Moseltaler, Rheinhess.

Naheweinstrasse (Ger) the Nahe wine road route.

Nahe Wine Festival (Ger) a wine festival known as

the Rund um die Naheweinstrasse, held in late August.

Nahli (Afr) a co-operative winery based in Tunisia, owned by the UCCVT.

Nail Brewing Australia (Austr) a brewery. (Add): P.O. Box 610, Applecross 6153. Brews a range of beers and stout. 'E'mail: brewer@nailbrewing.com

Nailmaker Mild (Eng) a 4% alc by vol. mild ale brewed by Enville Ales Ltd., West Midlands.

Nairi (Arm) a white grape variety grown in Armenia, used in the production of brandy.

Naissance (S.Afr) the label for a red wine (Cabernet sauvignon) produced by the De Wetshof Estate winery, Robertson, Western Cape.

Naiyou (Chi) cream.

Naked Merry Widow (Cktl) *see* Mary Garden Cocktail.

Naked Truth (S.Afr) the label for a range of wines marketed by the Picardi Rebel drinks chain, Western Cape.

Nakshatra (Ind) a natural spring mineral water (established 2002) from Chennai. Mineral contents (milligrammes per litre): Calcium 13.6mg/l, Magnesium 7.6mg/l, Bicarbonates 28mg/l, Chlorides 12mg/l, Sulphates 9.24mg/l, Nitrates 2mg/l.

Nalagenia (Isr) a Málaga-style, sweet, dessert wine.

Naleczowianka (Pol) a natural spring mineral water from Naleczow. Mineral contents (milligrammes per litre): Sodium 13mg/l, Calcium 115mg/l, Magnesium 23mg/l, Potassium 5mg/l, Bicarbonates 497mg/l, Chlorides 9mg/l, Sulphates 32mg/l, Fluorides 0.27mg/l, Silicates 32.2mg/l. pH 7.2

Nalevka (Pol) the name given to a fine, first infusion vodka that is usually kept for guests.

NALHM (Eng) *abbr*: The National Association of Licensed House Managers, the trade union for public house and club managers.

Nalle Winery (USA) a winery based at Dry Creek Valley, Napa, California. (Add): 2383 Dry Creek Road, P.O. Box 454, Healdburg, CA 95448. Grape varieties: Alicante bouschet, Cabernet sauvignon, Carignan, Gamay, Petite sirah, Pinot noir, Syrah, Zinfandel. Website: http://www.nallewinery.com

Nam (Thai) water.

Nama (Cyp) the ancient name for Commandaria.

Namaka (S.Afr) the label for a range of boxed wines produced by the WestCorp International, Olifants River, Western Cape.

Namasté Vineyards (USA) a winery based in the Willamette Valley, Oregon. Grape variety: Pinot noir. Labels: Abundance Vineyard, Prosperity Vineyard.

Namazake (Jap) an unpasteurised draft saké produced by the Gekkeikan Brewery, near Kyoto.

Namcha (Jap) a branded, bottled cold non-alcoholic, green tea from the Kirin Brewery.

Namcha (Thai) tea.

Namkaeng (Thai) ice.

Nampolamai (Thai) juice/fruit juice.

Namrae (Thai) mineral water.

Namsom (Thai) orange juice.

Namyslow Brewery (Pol) a brewery based in south-west Poland that brews Zamkowe Jasne 5.5% alc by vol.

Nancy's Fancy (Punch) 1 bottle apple wine, juice 1 lemon and 3 oranges, 2 teaspoons of sugar. Blend in a punch bowl over ice, add a syphon of soda and orange and lemon slices.

Nandilari (Gre) a white grape variety grown on the island of Crete for the production of Peza and Archanes wines.

Namnom (Thai) milk.

Namsomsaichoo (Thai) vinegar.

Nana (Cro) a still natural spring mineral water from Babotok. Mineral contents (milligrammes per litre): Sodium 7.8mg/l, Calcium 68.99mg/l, Magnesium 22.79mg/l, Potassium 1.06mg/l, Chlorides 2.77mg/l, Sulphates 5.34mg/l, Fluorides 0.15mg/l, Nitrates 1.19mg/l.

Nanny Flyer (Eng) a 3.8% alc by vol. ale brewed by micro-brewery Lord Raglan, Nangreave, near Bury.

Nanok (Den) a polar beer 6.5% alc by vol. a strong lager beer brewed by the Wiibroe Brewery.

Nantaise Bottle (Fr) a long-necked dump bottle used in the Nantais district mainly for Muscadet wines.

Nantes (Fr) the principal city in the Loire region. Sited in the Nantais in the western Loire on the river's estuary. Noted mainly for Muscadet and Gros Plant wines.

Nantillais [La] (Fr) a non-alcoholic mixer produced using sugar, citrus fruits and ginger. Sold in 50cls bottles. (Add): Route de Sables, Les Granges, 44840 Les Sorinières.

Nanton (Fr) a commune in the A.C. Mâcon whose grapes may be used to produce Mâcon Supérieur.

Nanton Edge-of-the-Rockies Water (Can) a natural spring mineral water (established 1950) from Nanton, Alberta. Mineral contents (milligrammes per litre): Calcium 36.7mg/l, Magnesium 48.6mg/l, Potassium 7.5mg/l, Chlorides 4mg/l, Fluorides 0.5mg/l, Oxygen 23mg/l.

Nantz (Fr) the name given to a brandy produced in Nantes, Loire-Atlantique.

Naoussa (Gre) an A.O.Q.S. full-bodied, cask-aged red wine from the mountains near Salonica, Macedonia. Made from the Xynomavro grape by the Boutari winery.

Napa Creek (USA) a label used for cheap red and white wines produced from grapes (Chardonnay and Merlot) grown in the Central Valley, California by Bronco Wines.

Napa Gamay (USA) a red grape variety. *see* California Gamay and Gamay Noir à Jus Blanc.

Napareuli (Rus) a medium-dry, white wine produced in the Caucasian mountains, also spelt Napuréouli. Also a red variety produced.

Napa Ridge (USA) a label used for cheap red and white wines produced from grapes (Chardonnay and Merlot) grown in the Central Valley, California by Bronco Wines.

Napa Valley (USA) a famous wine district in northern California. Contains the sub A.V.A.'s of: Atlas Peak, Carneros, Howell Mountain, Mount Veeder, Oakville and Rutherford, Saint Helena, Spring Mountain District, Stags Leap District, Wild Horse Valley. Produces many fine table and dessert wines and has a climate similar to that of Burgundy.

Napa Valley Co-operative Winery (USA) a large winery based near St. Helena, Napa Valley, California. Produces varietal and table wines.

Napa Valley Vintners Association (USA) a group of wine producers who have joined together. *abbr*: N.V.V.A. Website: http://www.napavintners.com

Napa Vintners (USA) a winery based in the Napa Valley, California. Grape varieties: Cabernet sauvignon, Chardonnay and Zinfandel. Produces varietal wines.

Napa Vista (USA) a label of the Peter Mondavi Family wines. Produces Cabernet sauvignon. Website: http://www.napavista.com

Napa Wine Cellars (USA) a winery based north of Yountville in the Napa Valley, California. Grape varieties: Cabernet sauvignon, Chardonnay, Gewürztraminer and Zinfandel. Produces varietal wines.

Nap Frappé (Cktl) ⅓ measure brandy, ⅓ measure kümmel, ⅓ measure Green Chartreuse. Mix over ice, strain into a large cocktail glass containing crushed ice and serve with straws.

Napier Vacuum Pump (Scot) the first fully developed filtration system for coffee, named after inventor Robert Napier circa 1840.

Napier Winery (S.Afr) a winery (established 1993) based in Wellington, Western Cape. 34ha. (Add): P.O.Box 138, Wellington 7654. Grape varieties: Cabernet franc, Cabernet sauvignon, Chardonnay, Merlot. Produces a range of varital wines (Labels: Greenstone, Red Medallion, Saint Catherine) and brandies including Sir George Brandy. Website: http://www.napierwinery.co.za

Napoléon (Bel) an 8% alc by vol. top-fermented, bottle-conditioned, red coloured special beer brewed by De Smedt Brouwerij, Opwijk.

Napoléon (Cktl) 1 measure V.S.O.P. Armagnac, ¼ measure Noilly Prat, 1 dash gomme syrup. Stir over ice, strain into a flute glass and top with iced Champagne.

Napoléon (Fr) a Champagne producer. (Add): 2 Rue de Villiers-aux-Bois, 51130 Vertus. Owns no vineyards. Produces vintage and non-vintage wines. Vintages: 1970, 1971, 1973, 1975, 1976, 1978, 1979, 1980, 1982, 1983, 1985, 1988, 1990, 1995, 1996, 1998, 1999, 2000. Carte Verte (non-vintage) and Carte Orange (non-vintage).

Napoléon (Fr) a marque for Cognac to indicate a minimum of six years in barrels. *see* Napoléon Brandy.

Napoléon (Fr) on an Armagnac label indicated a minimum age of five years.

Napoléon (Fr) the alternative name for the Bicane Chasselas grape.

Napoleon (Sp) an 1830 vintage Sherry produced by Domecq in Jerez de la Frontera 21% alc by vol.

Napoléon Aigle d'Or (Fr) a 25–30 year old Cognac produced by Brugerolle.

Napoléon Aigle Rouge (Fr) a 10 year old Cognac produced by Brugerolle.

Napoléon Brandy (Fr) a name which does not denote, as is often thought, a brandy of long age. For most brandies it is no more than a gimmick. *see* Napoléon.

Napoléon Cocktail (Cktl) ⅒ measure Fernet Branca, ⁷⁄₁₀ measure dry gin, ¹⁄₁₀ measure orange Curaçao, ¹⁄₁₀ measure Dubonnet. Stir over ice, strain into a cocktail glass and add a twist of lemon peel.

Napoléon III Empéreur (Fr) a fine, 1858 distilled Cognac produced by A.E. Dor in Jarnac 37% alc by vol.

Napolitana Pot (It) a coffee-making unit, known as the Flip Pot or Machinetta. Has a built-in filter. Two containers separated by a filter. Cold water is placed in lower container, top unit is screwed on. The unit is then placed on heat, brought to the boil then flipped over so that the hot water passes through the coffee to the bottom unit. *See also* Neapolitain Flip-Over Pot.

Nappo (It) the name given to a goblet, drinking cup or glass.

Napuréouli (Geo) a white, medium-dry table wine from Takhetia in the Georgia region, also spelt Napareuli.

Naranča Sok (Cro) orange juice.

Naranja (Sp) orange.

Naranjada (Sp) orangeade.

Naranjo [El] (Sp) a noted vineyard in the Moriles area of Montilla-Moriles, southern Spain.

Narayangaon (Ind) the town where India's first sparkling wine was made. *see* Omar Khayyam, Marquise de Pompadour and Royal Mousseux.

Narbag (Tur) a fine white wine produced in the Anatolia region.

Narbantons [Les] (Fr) a Premier Cru vineyard in the A.C. commune of Savigny-lès-Beaune, Côte de Beaune, Burgundy.

Narciso Etiqueta Azul (Sp) a 5 year old brandy produced by Mascaró.

Nardi-Dei (It) a Chianti putto producer based in Tuscany.

Nardini (It) the brand-name of a grappa.

Nardò (It) a D.O.C. wine producing area in Southern Puglia, red wines are produced from Negroamaro grapes.

Nardo (It) an I.G.T. red wine produced from a blend of Sangiovese and Cabernet grapes by Villa Monte Rico, Suvereto, Maremma, Tuscany.

Narelle 1 (Pol) a natural spring mineral water from Ozarow, Mazowiecki. Mineral contents (milligrammes per litre): Sodium 19mg/l, Calcium 142mg/l, Magnesium 15.5mg/l, Potassium 1.4mg/l, Sulphates 208mg/l, Fluorides 0.2mg/l, Nitrates 1.9mg/l.

Narelle 2 (Pol) a natural spring mineral water from Ozaow, Mazowiecki. Mineral contents (milligrammes per litre): Sodium 67mg/l, Calcium 46.6mg/l, Magnesium 17.9mg/l, Potassium 9mg/l, Bicarbonates 343mg/l, Chlorides 42.9mg/l, Sulphates 1mg/l, Fluorides 0.5mg/l, Nitrates 0.9mg/l.

Narerwiesen (Aus) a vineyard site based on the banks of the River Kamp situated in the Kamptal region.

Narince (Tur) a local white grape variety that produces crisp, white wines.

Naroc (Rum) cheers/good health.

Narranga Cocktail (Cktl) ¾ measure Bourbon whiskey, ¼ measure Italian vermouth, dash anisette, stir over ice, strain into a cocktail glass and top with a twist of lemon peel juice.

Narrenberg (Ger) vineyard (Anb): Pfalz. (Ber): Südliche Weinstrasse. (Gro): Kloster Liebfrauenberg. (Vil): Winden.

Narrenberg (Ger) vineyard (Anb): Pfalz. (Ber): Südliche Weinstrasse. (Gro): Kloster Liebfrauenberg. (Vil): Hergersweiler.

Narrenberg (Ger) vineyard (Anb): Pfalz. (Ber): Südliche Weinstrasse. (Gro): Trappenberg. (Vil): Römerberg.

Narrenkappe (Ger) vineyard (Anb): Nahe. (Ber): Kreuznach. (Gro): Kronenberg. (Vil): Bad Kreuznach.

Narzan (Rus) a natural spring mineral water (established 1894) from Kislovodsk. Mineral contents (milligrammes per litre): Sodium 130–200mg/l, Calcium 300–400mg/l, Magnesium 80–120mg/l, Bicarbonates 1000–1500mg/l, Sulphates 300–500mg/l.

Nascente do Alardo (Port) a natural spring mineral water from Nascente do Alardo.

Nascente Salutis (Port) an acidic-tasting natural spring mineral water from Ferreira-Parede de Coura. Mineral contents (milligrammes per litre): Sodium 5.6mg/l, Calcium 1.1mg/l, Potassium 0.82mg/l, Bicarbonates 3.1mg/l, Chlorides 8.4mg/l, Silicates 6.5mg/l. pH 4.75

Nasco (It) a white grape variety grown in Sardinia. Produces both yellow, delicate table wines and fortified dessert wines.

Nasco di Cagliari (It) a D.O.C. white wine from Sardinia. Made from the Nasco grape in the province of Cagliari. 4 styles: Dolce Naturale, Secco, Liquoroso Dolce Naturale and Liquoroso Secco. Liquoroso Dolce and Liquoroso Secco with a minimum age of 2 years in wooden casks can be classified Riserva.

N.A.S.D.M. (Eng) abbr: National Association of Soft Drink Manufacturers.

Nasha Marka (Rus) a sparkling natural spring mineral water. Mineral contents (milligrammes per litre): Sodium 198.6mg/l, Magnesium 3692.4mg/l, Potassium 97.6mg/l, Bicarbonates 943mg/l, Chlorides 16.5mg/l, Sulphates 459.3mg/l, Fluorides 1592mg/l, Nitrates 333.3mg/l, Silicates 2mg/l, Cobalt 7.1mg/l, Thallium 5.6mg/l, Boration 2.2mg/l, Hydrogene-phosphate 22.7mg/l. pH 7.5

Nashoba Valley Winery (USA) a winery based at Somerville, Massachusetts. Produces mainly hybrid wines.

Nash's Mineral Water (Ire) a natural spring mineral water from Newcastle West, County Limerick. Mineral contents (milligrammes per litre): Sodium 22mg/l, Calcium 101mg/l, Magnesium 25mg/l, Potassium 2.3mg/l, Bicarbonates 436mg/l, Chlorides 32mg/l, Sulphates 9.2mg/l. pH 7.2

Nashville Egg Nogg (Cktl) 300mls (¼ pint) brandy, 300mls (½ pint) golden rum, 550mls (1 pint) Bourbon whiskey, 9 eggs, 1650mls (3pints) double cream, 200grms (½ lb) sugar. Blend together over ice, strain into small wine goblets and top with grated nutmeg.

Nash Vineyard (Eng) a vineyard (established 1974) based at Nash, Stoywing, Sussex. 0.6ha. Grape varieties: Madeleine angevine 10%, Müller-Thurgau 50%, Seyve villard 20% and others.

Nassau (Ger) village (Anb): Mittelrhein. (Ber): Rheinburgengau. (Gro): Lahntal. (Vin): Schlossberg.

Nassau Nº1 (Cktl) 5 parts Nassau Orange liqueur, 1 part rum, 2 parts lemon juice, 1 teaspoon sugar. Shake well over ice, strain into a cocktail glass and add a slice of lemon.

Nassau Orange (Hol) a pale gold liqueur with a flavour of bitter oranges. Also known as Pimpeltjens Liqueur.

Nassau Orange Tonic (Cktl) 25mls Nassau Orange Liqueur, pour over ice cubes in a highball glass, fill with tonic water and garnish with a slice lemon.

Nässjö Brewery (Swe) a small brewery based in Nässjö, south-eastern Sweden.

Nastoika (Rus) a term used to describe heavily-flavoured vodkas that are almost like liqueurs.

Nastro Azzurro (It) a bottled export lager brewed by the Birra Peroni Brewery in Rome 5.2% alc by vol.

Nata (Port) cream. See also Crème.

Natalija (Rus) a natural spring mineral water St. Petersburg. Mineral contents (milligrammes per litre): Sodium <20mg/l, Calcium 60-100mg/l, Magnesium 15-25mg/l, Potassium <20mg/l, Bicarbonates 200-400mg/l, Chlorides <30mg/l, Sulphates <40mg/l.

Natasha (Fr) a species of barley malt from the Triumph variety that gives a good sugar yield.

Natch (Eng) a strong dry cider from Matthew Clark Taunton (abbr: for natural dry).

Nathaniel Johnston et Fils (Fr) an old established firm of wine négociants in Bordeaux. Specialise in the wines of the Graves and Médoc.

Natia (It) a sparkling natural spring mineral water from Natia, Caserta. Mineral contents (milligrammes per litre): Sodium 30mg/l, Calcium 32mg/l, Magnesium 7mg/l, Potassium 28mg/l, Bicarbonates 189mg/l, Chlorides 18mg/l, Sulphates 5mg/l, Fluorides 1mg/l, Nitrates 8mg/l, Silicates 51mg/l. pH 6.3

Nation [Carrie] (USA) a notorious Kansas lady who used to enter saloons and smash liquor contents up to, and during the American Prohibition period.

National Association of Cider Makers (Eng) an organisation. (Add): 6 Catherine Street, London WC2B 5JJ. Website: http://www.cideruk.com 'E'mail: bob.price@fdf.org.uk

National Association of Licensed House Managers (Eng) *abbr*: N.A.L.H.M. the trade union (established 1969) for public house and club managers. (Add): Transport House, Merchants Quay, Salford Quays, Manchester, Greater Manchester M5 2SG. 'E'mail: plove@tng.org.uk

National Association of Soft Drink Manufacturers (Eng) *abbr*: N.A.S.D.M. a body that monitors the sales of soft drinks. *See also* B.S.D.A.

National Breweries (Afr) a brewery based in Harare, Zimbabwe. Brews: Zambezi.

National Distillers (Isr) a leading wine and spirits producer based in Israel.

National Distillery (USA) a Bourbon whiskey distillery based in Frankfort and Louisville, Kentucky.

National Hop Association (Eng) *abbr*: N.H.A. an organisation (established 1987) that campaigns to promote the hop.

National Institute for the Protection of Denomination of Origin (It) *see* the Istituzione del Comitato Nazionale per la Tutela delle Denominazioni di Origine.

National Union of Licensed Victuallers (Eng) *see* N.U.L.V.

National Wine Buying Group (Eng) an organisation (established 1974). (Add): Vintage House, St. Nicholas Street, Coventry, West Midlands CV1 4BG. Website: http://www.nwbg.co.uk 'E'mail: nwbg@mooreswines.co.uk

National Yeast Bank (Eng) a 'library' of yeast strains based in Norwich, having yeasts (deposited by brewers nationwide) for reference, etc.

Nativa (Chile) a winery based in the Valle de Maipo. Grape variety: Cabernet sauvignon.

Natrone Spring (Egy) a natural spring mineral water from the Natrone Valley.

Natte (Hol) a 6.5% alc by vol. top-fermented, bottle-conditioned, double special beer brewed by 't IJ Brouwerij, Amsterdam.

Natterjack (Eng) a 4.8% alc by vol. ale brewed by the Frog Island Brewery, Northamptonshire.

Natterjack (Eng) a 4.3% alc by vol. ale brewed by the South Port Brewery, Merseyside.

Natural Beauty (Eng) a 4.2% alc by vol. ale brewed by the Ales of Scilly Brewery, Scilly Isles.

Natural Icelandic Mineral water (Ice) a natural spring mineral water from Akureyyeri. Mineral contents (milligrammes per litre): Sodium 4mg/l, Calcium 5.7mg/l, Magnesium 1.5mg/l, Potassium 0.5mg/l, Bicarbonates 18mg/l, Chlorides 7.1mg/l, Sulphates 5mg/l, Fluorides 0.25mg/l. pH 7.4

Natual Mineral Water of Patagonia (Arg) a natural spring mineral water from Patagonia. Mineral contents (milligrammes per litre): Sodium <4mg/l, Potassium 0.4mg/l, Bicarbonates 70mg/l, Chlorides 5.2mg/l, Sulphates 24mg/l. pH 7.58

Natu Nobilis (Bra) a whiskey produced by Seagram from imported malts and local grain spirits.

Natur (Fr) a wine with no sugar added/a natural wine.

Naturagua (Bol) a natural spring mineral water from Pojpocollo, Cochabamba, Bolivia. pH 7.3

Natural (USA) denotes a sparkling wine that has been made without the addition of dosage. Also spelt Naturel.

Natural Light (S.Afr) the label for a range of dry white, rosé and red wines (7.5% to 9.5% alc by vol) produced by the Robertson Co-operative Winery, Robertson, Western Cape.

Naturalis Historia (It) a red wine produced by Mastroberardino in Campania from a blend of 85% Aglianico and 15% Piedirosso grapes fermented in oak.

Naturalle Mountain Spring Water (USA) a natural spring mineral water. Mineral contents (milligrammes per litre): Chlorides 1.2mg/l. pH 8.1

Naturally-Conditioned (Eng) a term used to describe beer which continues to mature in cask or bottle. *see* Cask-Conditioned.

Naturally Dutch (Cktl) 1 measure advocaat, ½ measure cherry brandy, dash grenadine. Shake over ice, strain into a flute glass, top with Champagne and serve with a cherry.

Natural Mineral Waters and Bottled Waters Association (Eng) *abbr*: N.M.W.B.W.A. Association formed to represent the interests of packers and importers who bottle natural mineral waters. *See also* B.S.D.A.

Naturalno (Bul) natural (wine).

Natural Production (Eng) denotes viniculture without the addition of chemical insecticides or fertilizers.

Natural Sediment (Eng) the sediment that falls from wine without the aid of a fining agent.

Natural Spring Water (Eng) the name for a water flow that is sourced naturally from an under ground water table. Spring waters are usually high in dissolved minerals (Bicarbonate, Calcium, Fluoride, Iodine, Magnesium, Oxygen, Potassium, Sodium, Zinc, etc.) and may contain other harmful minerals (Nitrate, strontium, etc.). Most natural spring waters that are sold as bottled waters are tested for mineral contents. These waters are often naturally 'sparkling' due to the depth of the water source when gasses are absorbed due to the underground pressures. *see* Mineral Waters.

Natural Spring (Mal) a still natural spring mineral water from Negeri Sembilan. Mineral contents (milligrammes per litre): Sodium 4mg/l, Calcium 29mg/l, Magnesium 1mg/l, Potassium 2mg/l, Chlorides 10mg/l, Sulphates 1mg/l, Fluorides 1mg/l. pH 7.4

Natural Wine (Eng) an unadulterated wine, has not had anything added to alter the strength or taste.

Naturbelassen (Aus) not sweetened (wine).

Nature (Fr) applied to Champagne, the driest, no sweetening added. *see* Brut Zero.

Nature Ale (Eng) a 3.8% alc by vol. ale brewed by the Milk Street Brewery, Somerset.

Nature in Concert (S.Afr) the label for a range of sur-lie wines (Chardonnay and Pinot noir) produced by the De Wetshof Estate winery, Robertson, Western Cape.

Naturel (Fr) when seen on a kirsch label indicates natural distillation from cherries with no additives.

Naturel (USA) *see* Natural.

Nature Pac (Can) a natural spring mineral water from Waterloo, Ontario. Mineral contents (milligrammes per litre): Sodium 4.7mg/l, Calcium 86.2mg/l, Magnesium 25mg/l, Potassium 1.3mg/l, Bicarbonates 104mg/l, Chlorides 4.8mg/l, Sulphates 37.5mg/l, Nitrates 0.18mg/l.

Natures Spring (E.Ind) a natural spring mineral water from Philippines. Mineral contents (milligrammes per litre): Calcium 9.5mg/l, Magnesium 15mg/l, Chlorides 10mg/l, Nitrates 2mg/l. pH 7.0

Nature's Wine (Eng) a nickname for water.

Natureza (Bra) a natural spring mineral water (established 1954). Mineral contents (milligrammes per litre): Sodium 59.85mg/l, Calcium 37.61mg/l, Potassium 4.35mg/l, Bicarbonates 5.17mg/l, Chlorides 5.13mg/l, Sulphates 11.72mg/l. pH 7.2

Naturnah (Aus) denotes wines that have been made as natural as possible (no chemical fertilisers, pesticides or sugaring of the grape must).

Naturrein (Ger) natural and pure.

Natürsüsse (Aus) on a wine bottle label indicates that the wine has been naturally sweetened.

Naturwein (Ger) a wine with no added sugar, a natural wine.

Naturweinversteigerer (Ger) *see* Prädikatsweinversteigerer.

Naughty Boys Bitter (Eng) a 4.8% alc by vol. bitter ale brewed by the Blencoe Brewing C°., Rutland.

Naughty French Wine Coolers (Fr) a range of wine-based drinks (red and white) with fruit juices 5% alc by vol. distributed in the U.K. by Cambrian Soft Drinks.

Nautico (Austr) a company based in South Australia that produces infused wines including: Chardonnay (infused with citrus and peach concentrates), Sauvignon blanc/Sémillon (infused with tropical fruit concentrates) and Shiraz (infused with wild berries and vanilla concentrates).

Nautilus (N.Z) a winery based in Blicks Road, Renwick, Auckland 11ha. Grape varieties: Chardonnay, Sauvignon blanc, Cabernet franc, Cabernet sauvignon and Merlot. Produces Cuvée Marlborough (méthode traditionelle wine). *See also* Family of Twelve.

Naughton's Flight (S.Afr) the brand-name for a red wine (Shiraz) produced in the W.O. Paarl, Western Cape.

Nauvoo State Historic Site and Park Vineyard (USA) a winery based in Nauvoo, Illinois on the Mississippi River.

Navalle (USA) the label used by the Inglenook Winery for a range of varietal and generic table wines made from a blend of San Joaquin and Coastal grapes.

Navarra (Sp) a Denominación de Origen wine region (17335ha) of northern Spain, situated north-east of Rioja. 13097ha. Has 5 districts: Montaña, Ribera Alta, Ribera Baja, Tierra Estella and Valdizarbe. The D.O. applies to red, rosé and white wines. Grape varieties: Cabernet sauvignon, Chardonnay, Garnacha blanca, Garnacha tinta, Graciano, Tempranillo, Majaela, Malvasía riojana, Merlot, Moscatel de grano menudo, Palomino and Viura. *See also* EVENA.

Navarre (Sp) an alternative spelling of Navarra.

Navarrete (Sp) a noted wine-producing village in the Rioja Alta.

Navarro Vineyards (USA) a winery based in the Anderson Valley, Mendocino County, California. Grape varieties: Cabernet sauvignon, Gewürztraminer and Johannisberg riesling. Produce varietal wines.

Navazza (Switz) a noted wine and spirit importation company founded in 1856.

Naveltje Bloot (Hol) lit: 'bare navel', a liqueur on the old Dutch style produced by Van Zuylekom.

Navés (Sp) a white grape variety grown in the Rioja. Is also known as the Cagazal, Calagraño, Jaén and Jaina.

Navigation Ale (Eng) an ale brewed by Bridgewater Ales in Salford.

Navip (Ser) a grower's co-operative based at Serbia. The headquarters are in Belgrade. Also produces a slivovitz of same name which is popular in Greece.

Navy Mixture (Cktl) 1 measure rum, ½ measure lemon juice, ½ measure dry vermouth, dash cherry brandy. Shake over ice and strain into a cocktail glass.

Navy Rum (Eng) old name, also known as Grog. 1 part dark rum, 3 parts water.

Navy Rum (W.Ind) a style of dark rum, very pungent.

Naxos (Gre) an island in the southern Aegean sea. The largest of the Cyclades Islands. Was the ancient centre for the worship of Dionysius.

Naya [1] (Can) a natural spring mineral water (established 1986) from Mirabel, Quebec. Mineral contents (milligrammes per litre): Sodium 6mg/l, Calcium 45mg/l, Magnesium 22mg/l, Potassium 2mg/l, Bicarbonates 134mg/l, Chlorides 1mg/l, Sulphates 17mg/l, Fluorides 0.2mg/l, Nitrates <0.5mg/l, Silicates 7mg/l. pH 7.5

Naya [2] (Can) a natural spring mineral water (established 1995) from Revelstoke, British

Columbia. Mineral contents (milligrammes per litre): Sodium 1mg/l, Calcium 50mg/l, Magnesium 18mg/l, Potassium <1mg/l, Chlorides <1mg/l, Sulphates 42mg/l, Fluorides 0.2mg/l, Nitrates <0.5mg/l. pH 7.8

Naya [3] (Can) a natural spring mineral water from St. André Est, Quebec. Mineral contents (milligrammes per litre): Sodium 24mg/l, Calcium 42mg/l, Magnesium 21mg/l, Potassium 3mg/l, Chlorides 21mg/l, Sulphates 23mg/l, Fluorides 0.2mg/l, Nitrates <0.5mg/l. pH 7.7

Naylor Wine Cellars (USA) based in York, Pennsylvania.

Nazdarovye (Rus) cheers!/good health.

Na Zdrowie (Pol) lit: 'your health'.

Nazionale Brauerei (Switz) an independent brewery based in Locarno-Muralto.

Ndovu Lager (Afr) a lager beer brewed by the Tanzania Breweries in Tanzania.

Néac (Fr) a region north of Saint-Émilion producing red wines, has now merged with the A.C. Lalande de Pomerol.

Neapolitan Flip-Over Pot (It) a method of making filter coffee. It has two pots with the coffee grounds placed between, when the water boils, pots are turned over and boiling water passes through coffee into lower pot. Is also known as the Machinetta. *See also* Napolitana Pot.

Near Beer (Switz) a beer-style, alcohol-free lager, brands include Ex-Beer and Birell.

Near Beer (USA) a beer surviving from the prohibition days, brewed by the Pearl Brewing C°.

Near Wine (USA) sugar and water added to grape skins and pulp etc. Fermentation is then induced, the acids and other substances remaining in the skins are released and the resulting liquid is marketed usually as Jug wine (sold by the 2½ litres (½ gallon) or multiples of.)

Neat (Eng) a term to denote having a drink (usually spirits) without anything added.

Nebbiola (USA) a white grape variety used to produce white table wines in California.

Nebbiolo (It) a red grape of outstanding quality, is at its best in the Piemonte and Lombardy regions where it produces full-bodied, long-lived wines of high alcohol. Name derives from the Italian word Nebbia meaning fog (because the grapes mature late and so are often gathered in foggy conditions). Produces wines with aromas and flavours of violets, pitch, raisins, chocolate, prunes, blackberries and liquorice. Is also known as Chiavennasca, Nebbiolo lampia, Nebbiolo michet, Nebbiolo rosé, Nebbiolo-spanna, Picoutener, Picutener, Pugnet, Spanna and Spauna.

Nebbiolo (Switz) a smooth, fruity, red wine from the Ticino region.

Nebbiolo d'Alba (It) a D.O.C. red wine from the Piemonte region. Made from the Nebbiolo grape grown in the communes of Alba and Cuneo. Must be aged 1 year. D.O.C. also applies to the sparkling wine obtained from grapes grown within the defined area. *see* Roero.

Nebbiolo delle Langhe (It) *see* Langa Nebbiolo.

Nebbiolo Lampia (It) a local name used for the Nebbiolo grape in the Barbaresco district of Piemonte, a sub-variety of the Nebbiolo.

Nebbiolo Michet (It) a local name used for the Nebbiolo grape in the Barbaresco district of Barbaresco, a sub-variety of the Nebbiolo grape.

Nebbiolo Rosé (It) a local name for the Nebbiolo grape in the Barbaresco district of Piemonte, a sub-variety of the Nebbiolo grape.

Nebbiolo-Spanna (It) an alternative name for the Nebbiolo grape in the Piemonte region.

Nebbiolo Spumante (It) a red sparkling wine made from the Nebbiolo grape in the Piemonte region.

Nebenführ (Aus) a winery based in Mitterretzbach, Weinviertel. (Add): 2070 Mitterretzbach 64. Grape varieties: Grüner veltliner, Gewürztraminer, Pinot blanc, Sauvignon blanc, Welschriesling.

Nebiker (Switz) an eau-de-vie distillery based in Sissach, northern Switzerland. Produces a kirsch under the General Sutter label.

Nebuchadnezzar (Fr) the largest of the wine bottles (20 standard bottles). *See also* Mega Bottle and Champagne Bottle Sizes. (Fr) = nabuchodonosor.

Neckar [River] (Ger) a tributary of the river Rhine. Runs through the Württemberg Anbaugebiete.

Neckarberg (Ger) vineyard (Anb): Württemberg. (Ber): Württembergisch Unterland. (Gro): Schalkstein. (Vil): Besigheim.

Neckarberg (Ger) vineyard (Anb): Württemberg. (Ber): Württembergisch Unterland. (Gro): Schalkstein. (Vil): Bietigheim.

Neckarberg (Ger) vineyard (Anb): Württemberg. (Ber): Württembergisch Unterland. (Gro): Schalkstein. (Vil): Bissingen.

Neckarberg (Ger) vineyard (Anb): Württemberg. (Ber): Württembergisch Unterland. (Gro): Schalkstein. (Vil): Gemmrigheim.

Neckarberg (Ger) vineyard (Anb): Württemberg. (Ber): Württembergisch Unterland. (Gro): Schalkstein. (Vil): Löchgau.

Neckarberg (Ger) vineyard (Anb): Württemberg. (Ber): Württembergisch Unterland. (Gro): Schalkstein. (Vil): Walheim.

Neckarhälde (Ger) vineyard (Anb): Württemberg. (Ber): Württembergisch Unterland. (Gro): Schalkstein. (Vil): Affalterbach.

Neckarhälde (Ger) vineyard (Anb): Württemberg. (Ber): Württembergisch Unterland. (Gro): Schalkstein. (Vil): Bietigheim.

Neckarhälde (Ger) vineyard (Anb): Württemberg. (Ber): Württembergisch Unterland. (Gro): Schalkstein. (Vil): Benningen.

Neckarhälde (Ger) vineyard (Anb): Württemberg. (Ber): Württembergisch Unterland. (Gro): Schalkstein. (Vil): Erdmannhausen.

Neckarhälde (Ger) vineyard (Anb): Württemberg. (Ber): Württembergisch Unterland. (Gro): Schalkstein. (Vil): Ludwigsburg (ortsteil Hoheneck).

Neckarhälde (Ger) vineyard (Anb): Württemberg. (Ber): Württembergisch Unterland. (Gro): Schalkstein. (Vil): Marbach.

Neckarhälde (Ger) vineyard (Anb): Württemberg. (Ber): Württembergisch Unterland. (Gro): Schalkstein. (Vil): Murr.

Neckarhälde (Ger) vineyard (Anb): Württemberg. (Ber): Württembergisch Unterland. (Gro): Schalkstein. (Vil): Neckarweihingen.

Neckarhälde (Ger) vineyard (Anb): Württemberg. (Ber): Württembergisch Unterland. (Gro): Schalkstein. (Vil): Poppenweiler.

Neckarmühlbach (Ger) village (Anb): Baden. (Ber): Badische Bergstrasse/Kraichgau. (Gro): Stiftsberg. (Vin): Hohberg.

Neckarsulm (Ger) village (Anb): Württemberg. (Ber): Württembergisch Unterland. (Gro): Staufenberg. (Vin): Scheuerberg.

Neckarweihingen (Ger) village (Anb): Württemberg. (Ber): Württembergisch Unterland. (Gro): Schalkstein. (Vin): Neckarhälde.

Neckarwein (Ger) the name given to wines produced around the river Neckar in the Württemberg Anbaugebiet.

Neckarwestheim (Ger) village (Anb): Württemberg. (Ber): Württembergisch Unterland. (Gro): Kirchenweinberg. (Vin): Herrlesberg.

Neckarzimmern (Ger) village (Anb): Baden. (Ber): Badische Bergstrasse/Kraichgau. (Gro): Stiftsberg. (Vins): Götzhalde, Kirchweinerg, Wallmauer.

Neckenmarkt (Aus) a wine-producing area in the Mattersburg district.

Nectar (Eng) a 4.5% alc by vol. light straw-coloured, cask-conditioned ale brewed using Scottish honey. Part of the Tapster's Choice range from Carlsberg-Tetley (available in August).

Nectar (Gre) the wine of the Greek Gods on Mount Olympus in Ancient Greece.

Nectar (Gre) a Muscat dessert wine produced by a co-operative winery on the island of Samos.

Nectar Cream (Sp) a full-flavoured, rich Oloroso Sherry produced by Gonzalez Byass in Jerez de la Frontera.

Nectar de Kefraya (Leb) mistelle wine produced by the Kefraya estate in Lebanon.

Nectar des Dieux (Fr) lit: 'nectar of the Gods', the designation King Louis XIV gave to the wines of Saint-Émilion.

Nectar du Val (S.Afr) the label for a white sweet wine (Muscat and Sauvignon blanc blend) produced by the La Petite Ferme winery, Franschhoek, Western Cape.

Nector (Eng) a 5.2% alc by vol. ale brewed by the Roosters Brewing C°. Ltd., North Yorkshire.

Ned Belcher's Bitter (Eng) a bitter beer 1040 O.G. brewed by the Priory Brewery in Nottinghamshire.

Nederburg 'Auction' Wines (S.Afr) varietal wines sold at the annual Nederburg wine auction of the Nederburg Estate. Instituted by the S.F.W.

Nederberg Estate (S.Afr) a large wine estate (established 1792) based in Paarl, Western Cape. (Add): Ernst le Roux, Nederburg, P.O. Box 46, Paarl 7645. Grape varieties: Cabernet sauvignon, Chardonnay, Chenin blanc, Gewürztramner, Merlot, Muscat, Pinotage, Riesling, Sauvignon blanc, Shiraz. Produces a vast range of famous wines including 'Private bin' and 'Auction' wines, Baronne, Edelrood, Edeltropfen, Fonternel, Kap Sekt and varietals. Operated by the SFW. Labels include: Manor House Collection. Website: http://www.nederburg.co.za

Nederburg 'Private Bin' Wines (S.Afr) specially selected blended wines sold at the annual Nederburg wine auctions of the Nederburg estate. Made by Günter Brözel. i.e. Private Bin S312 the (S = sweet, D = dry, R = red).

Ned Kelly (Austr) the brand-name of an Australian whiskey.

Needles Bitter (Eng) a bitter beer 1049 O.G. brewed by Burt's Brewery at Ventnor, Isle of Wight. *See also* Lighthouse, Yachtsman VPA.

Needle's Eye (Eng) a 3.5% alc by vol. ale brewed by the Wentworth Brewery, South Yorkshire.

Neef (Ger) village (Anb): Mosel-Saar-Ruwer. (Ber): Zell/Mosel. (Gro): Grafschaft. (Vins): Frauenberg, Petersberg, Rosenberg.

Neerslag (Hol) sediment.

Neethlingshof Estate (S.Afr) a winery (established 1692) based in Stellenbosch, Western Cape. 210ha. (Add): P.O. Box 104, Stellenbosch 7599. Grape varieties: Cabernet franc, Cabernet sauvignon, Chardonnay, Chenin blanc, Gewürztraminer, Gamay, Merlot, Pinotage, Pinot noir, Rhine riesling, Sauvignon blanc, Sémillon, Shiraz, Weisser riesling. Labels: Lord Neethlingshof-Lauhrentius, Standard, plus a range of varietal wines. Website: http://www.neethlingshof.co.za

Nefeli (Cyp) the label for a dry white wine produced by the Keo Company, Limassol.

Negev (Isr) a newly planted wine-producing region in southern Israel that is noted for fine white wines.

Négociant (Fr) a wine shipper-merchant, one who buys the wines off the producer and then sells them either in bulk or bottle. (It) = negoziante.

Négociant-Embouteilleur (Fr) a wine merchant who bottles purchased bulk wines.

Négociant-Distributeur (Fr) in Burgundy, a négociant who acts as an intermediate for the sale of bottles of wine for a vineyard

Négociant-Éleveur (Fr) a merchant and grower, one who makes wine and then sells it.

Négociant Manipulant (Fr) found on a Champagne wine label, denotes the actual maker. *see* N.M.

Negociants UK Ltd (Eng) alcoholic drinks manufacturer (established 1990). (Add): Davenport House, Bowers Way, Harpenden, Hertfordshire AL5 4EW. Produces a range of wine and alcohol-based drinks. Website: http://www.negociantsuk.com 'E'mail: neguk@negociants.com

Negoska (Gre) a red grape variety used in the production of Goumenissa wine.

Negoziante (It) merchant/shipper. (Fr) = négociant.

Negra Corriente (S.Am) a white grape variety grown in Peru, also known as Criolla Chica in Argentina.

Negra de Madrid (Sp) an alternative name for the Garnacha (Grenache) in Madrid.

Negralejo (Sp) a black Riojan grape variety also known as the Mechín, Monastel, Monastrel, Moraster and Valcarcelia. Also grown in Aragón, Catalonia and Penedés.

Negra Modelo (S.Am) a 5.3% alc by vol. red-brown, bottled lager beer brewed by the Cerveceria Modelo, Mexico City, Mexico.

Negra Mole (Port) a black grape variety grown in the Algarve.

Negrara (It) a red grape variety used in the making of Valpolicella and Bardolino.

Negrara Gattinara (USA) a white grape variety grown in California to make white table wines.

Negrara Trentina (It) a red grape variety grown in north-east Italy. *see* Negrara.

Negrette (Fr) a red grape variety grown in southern France between the Garonne and Tarn départements. Produces full-bodied and alcoholic wines.

Negri (It) a wine producer based in Moniga del Garda near Verona.

Negri (It) a fine producer of Valtellina D.O.C. and Sfursat wines in Lombardy.

Negri (Rus) the Russian name for the Malbec grape.

Negri de Purkar (Rus) a light, slightly sweet and scented red wine of Moldavia. Has a taste and scent of blackcurrants. Made from the Cabernet, Rara-njagra and Sapanis grapes.

Negrita (W.Ind) the brand-name of a dark rum produced on the island of Martinique. Produced by Bardinet in north-west Martinique.

Negroamaro (It) a red grape variety grown in the Puglia region. Sometimes spelt Negro Amaro. Is the principal black grape of the region.

Négron (Fr) a red grape variety also known as the Mourvèdre.

Negroni (Cktl) ⅓ measure gin, ⅓ measure sweet vermouth, ⅓ measure Campari. Shake well with ice, strain into a cocktail glass and add a twist of lemon.

Negru de Purkar (Rus) a red grape variety.

Negru de Purkar (Rus) a dry, fruity, red wine from the grape of same name produced in Moldavia.

Negus (Cktl) 1 bottle Sherry, 1.1lts (2pints) boiling water, 60mls (2½ fl.ozs) brandy, sugar, nutmeg, 1 lemon. Warm the wine in a pan, add sliced lemon, water, finally add brandy and grated nutmeg (makes 18 glasses). Port can be used in place of Sherry. The drink is named after Colonel Francis Negus its inventor in the eighteenth century.

Neherleschol (M.East) an ancient white grape variety, has recently been planted in Languedoc, southern France.

Nehren (Ger) village (Anb): Mosel-Saar-Ruwer. (Ber): Zell/Mosel. (Gro): Grafschaft. (Vin): Römerberg.

Neige (Eng) an iced cider 12% alc by vol. produced by the Blackwood Distillers.

Neil Ellis Estate (S.Afr) a winery based in Groenekloof, Paarl, Western Cape. Grape varieties include: Sauvignon blanc.

Neil Ellis Meyer-Näkel (S.Afr) a winery (established 1998) based in Stellenbosch, Western Cape. 10ha. Grape varieties: Cabernet sauvignon and Merlot. Label: Zwalu. A joint venture between Neil Ellis and Werner Näkel of the Ahr, Germany.

Neil Ellis Wines (S.Afr) a winery (established 1984) based in Stellenbosch, Western Cape. (Add): P.O. Box 917, Stellenbosch 7599. Buys in grapes. Varietal wines include: Cabernet sauvignon, Chardonnay, Chenin blanc, Merlot, Pinotage, Sauvignon blanc, Syrah. Labels include: Aenigma, Elgin, Groenekloof, Jonjershoek Vineyard, Stellenbosch, Vineyard Selection. Website: http://www.neilellis.com

Neipperg (Ger) village (Anb): Württemberg. (Ber): Württembergisch Unterland. (Gro): Heuchelberg. (Vins): Grafenberg, Schlossberg, Steingrube, Vogelsang.

Neive (It) a noted wine commune in Barbaresco.

Nekowitsch (Aus) a vineyard (4ha) based in Illmitz, Burgenland. (Add): Schrändlgasse 2, 7142 Illmitz. Grape varieties: Blaufränkisch, Grüner veltliner, Müller-Thurgau, Scheurebe, Traminer, Welschriesling, Zweigelt. Produces a range of sweet wines.

Nelas (Port) a noted co-operative based in the Dão region.

Nellie Dean (Eng) a 3.5% alc by vol. ale from Old Mill Brewery, Snaith, North Yorkshire.

Nello Stabilimento (It) on a label denotes '*at the producers' premises*'.

Nel'Origine (It) estate bottled.

Nel's Best (Eng) a 4.2% alc by vol. best bitter ale brewed by the High House Farm Brewery, Tyne & Wear.

Nelson (N.Z) a wine-producing area on the north coast of the South Island.

Nelson (Sp) a rare, fine, old, Palo Cortado Sherry produced by Domecq in Jerez de la Frontera.

Nelson Brewing Company (Eng) a brewery (established 2003). (Add): Unit 2, Building 64, The Historic Dockyard, Chatham, Kent ME4 4TE. Brews a variety of beers. The new name for the Flagship brewery.

Nelson Decanter (Eng) similar in style to a Royal Decanter but with only one ring around the neck (circa 1820).

Nelson Estate (S.Afr) a winery (established 1993) based in Windmeul, Paarl, Western Cape. 60ha. Grape varieties: Cabernet sauvignon, Chardonnay, Chenin blanc, Cinsaut, Merlot, Muscat d'Alexandrie, Pinotage, Sauvignon blanc, Sémillon, Shiraz. Labels: Albenet, Marguerite, Nelson's Creek, Triple Creek. Website: http://www.nelsoncreek.co.za

Nelson's Blood (Eng) a term used for dark rum.

Nelson's Revenge (Eng) a 4.5% alc by vol. ale brewed by Woodforde's Ltd., Norfolk.

Nemea (Gre) a A.O.Q.S. dry red table wine from the Tsamtali winery, Peloponnese. Made from the Agiorgitako grape.

Nemes Furmint (Hun) approved clone of the Furmint grape. *See also* Király Furmint.

N

Nemes Kadar (Hun) an unusual rosé wine with a garnet colour made from the Kardarka grape. Has good body and sweetness.

Nemo (It) a red I.G.T. wine produced from 100% Cabernet sauvignon grapes by Castello di Monsanto in Tuscany.

Nendaz (Switz) a still and sparkling natural spring mineral water from Nendaz. (green label: sparkling/blue label: still). Mineral contents (milligrammes per litre): Sodium 2mg/l, Calcium 84mg/l, Magnesium 20mg/l, Potassium 1mg/l, Bicarbonates 103mg/l, Chlorides 2mg/l, Sulphates 190mg/l, Strontium 1mg/l, Nitrates 1mg/l, Silicates 6mg/l.

Neoplanta (Ser) a white grape variety grown in Vojvodina.

Nepente di Oliena (It) this can appear on the label of Cannonau di Sardegna if grapes used for the wine are produced in Oliena.

Nephritis (Lat) a disease of the kidneys caused through chronic alcoholism.

Nepi (It) a natural spring mineral water from Nepi.

Neptunas (Euro) a natural spring mineral water from Varena, Lithuania. Mineral contents (milligrammes per litre): Sodium 19.8mg/l, Calcium 50mg/l, Magnesium 18.3mg/l, Bicarbonates 202mg/l, Chlorides 24.9mg/l, Sulphates 24mg/l.

Neptun Brewery (Den) a brewery based in North Jutland, owned by the United Breweries.

Netpune (Eng) a 3.8% alc by vol. ale brewed by the Milton Brewery Cambridge Ltd., Cambridgeshire.

Neptune (UK) Ltd (Eng) a mineral water producer (established 1993). (Add): Westmead House, 123 Westmead Road, Sutton, Surrey SM1 4JH. Produces mineral and spring waters. Website: http://www.neptunewater.co.uk 'E'mail: neptuneukltd@btinternet.com

Nera (It) a fine producer of Valtellina D.O.C. and Sforzato wines in Lombardy.

Nerea (It) a sparkling natural spring mineral water from Nerea Fonte degli Uccelli, Castelsantangelo sul Nera, Macerata (MC), Marche. Mineral contents (milligrammes per litre): Sodium 1.9mg/l, Calcium 52.8mg/l, Magnesium 0.6mg/l, Potassium 0.4mg/l, Bicarbonates 189.1mg/l, Chlorides 3.5mg/l, Sulphates 2mg/l, Nitrates 1.2mg/l, Silicates 5.8mg/l. pH 7.5

Nerello (It) a red grape variety grown in Sicily and Calabria. see Nerello Mascalese and Nerello Mantellata.

Nerello Cappuccio (It) the local name (Etna district) for the Nerello Mantellata grape in Sicily.

Nerello Mantellata (It) a red grape variety grown in Sicily.

Nerello Mascalese (It) a red grape variety grown in Sicily used mainly for rosé wines.

Nerino (It) the name used in the province of Arezzo for the Sangiovese Piccolo grape.

Nero (Gre) water.

Nero (It) a black or deep red wine.

Neroberg (Ger) a vineyard within the village of Wiesbaden, 4.9ha (100%) of which is proposed to be classified as Erstes Gewächs.

Nero Bukaliou (Gre) mineral water.

Nero Buono di Cori (It) a red grape variety grown in the Latium.

Nero d'Avola (It) a red grape variety grown in Sicily. Prone to rot, it has a spicy, blackberry and plum aroma and flavour. Also known as the Calabrese. See also Pachino.

Nero di Troia (It) an alternative name for the Uva di Troia.

Néron Distillery (W.Ind) a rum distillery based in Guadeloupe.

Nertert (Lux) a wine village on the river Moselle. Vineyard sites are Syrberg, Herrenberg.

Nerthe [La] (Fr) part of the Châteauneuf-du-Pape area in the southern Rhône. See also Château La Nerthe.

Nerthe [Marquis de] (Fr) a wine maker of the nineteenth century who gave the name to Châteauneuf-du-Pape, originally (circa 1850), it was known as Châteauneuf Calcernier.

Nerveaux (Fr) a strong full-bodied wine.

Nervig (Ger) a good, full-bodied wine.

Nervo Winery (USA) a small winery based in the Russian River Valley, California. Produces varietal wines.

Nescafé (Eng) the brand-name™ used by Nestlé Foodservice for a range of instant coffees. The top-selling U.K. brand.

Nesher Lager (Isr) a lager beer 10° Balling brewed by a Canadian-financed brewery.

Nesle-le-Repons (Fr) a Cru Champagne village in the Canton de Dormans. District: Épernay.

Nessel (Fr) a natural spring mineral water from Soultzmatt

Nesselried (Ger) village. (Anb): Baden. (Ber): Ortenau. (Gro): Fürsteneck. (Vins): Renchtäler, Schlossberg.

Nesselthal (Aus) a vineyard site based on the banks of the River Kamp situated in the Kamptal region.

Nessie (Aus) see MᵃᶜQueens Nessie Whiskey.

Nest Egg (Austr) a wine label of the Bird in Hand winery, Adelaide Hills.

Nestlé Foodservice (Eng) (Add): St. George's House, Croydon, Surrey CR9 1NR. A famous coffee-producing company. Brands include: Blend 37, Gold Blend, Nescafé and Santa Rica. Also owns Aquarel and Ashbourne mineral water.

Nestlé Pure Life (Bra) a still natural spring mineral water from the Nestlé company.

Nestlé Pure Life (Ind) a natural spring mineral water from the Nestlé company. Mineral contents (milligrammes per litre): Sodium 21mg/l, Calcium 51mg/l, Magnesium 6mg/l, Bicarbonates 53mg/l, Chlorides 99mg/l, Sulphates 10mg/l, Fluorides 0.3mg/l.

Nes-Ziona (Isr) a viticultural centre of Israel which produces most styles of wines.

Nethergate Holdings Ltd (Eng) a brewery (established 1982). (Add): 11-13 High Street, Clare, Sudbury, Suffolk CO10 8NY. Brews:

N

Augustinian Ale 4.5% alc by vol., IPA 3.6% alc by vol., Old Growler 5% alc by vol (1055 O.G)., Priory Mild 3.6% alc by vol., Suffolk County Best Bitter 4% alc by vol., Umbel Ale 3.8% alc by vol., Umbel Magna 5% alc by vol. also Old Newgate Bitter. Website: http://www.nethergate.co.uk 'E'mail: orders@nethergate.co.uk

Netherlands (Cktl) 25mls (1fl.oz) brandy, 10mls (½ fl.oz) Cointreau, dash range bitters. Stir with ice and strain into a cocktail glass.

Netherlands Wijnmuseum (Hol) a wine museum based at Velperweg 23, 6824 BC Arnhem. Has a comprehensive range of wine artefacts from the family firm of Robbers en Van den Hoogen B.V.

Neto Costa (Port) a noted wine-producer in the Bairrada region. Produces fine still and sparkling wines, brandies and liqueurs. Uses the labels of Monastico, Choupal. Also produces Tijuana Coffee liqueur.

Nettlethrasher (Eng) a 4.4% alc by vol. dark ale brewed by Eastwood & Sanders Ltd (Fine Ales), Elland, West Yorkshire.

Nettuno (It) an I.G.T. of Latium.

Neu-Bamberg (Ger) village (Anb): Rheinhessen. (Ber): Bingen. (Gro): Rheingrafenstein. (Vins): Eichelberg, Heerkretz, Kirschwingert, Kletterberg.

Neuberg (Aus) a vineyard site on the banks of the River Danube in the Kremstal region.

Neuberg (Aus) a vineyard site based on the banks of the River Kamp situated in the Kamptal region.

Neuberg (Ger) vineyard (Anb): Rheinhessen. (Ber): Wonnegau. (Gro): Gotteshilfe. (Vil): Osthofen.

Neuberg (Ger) vineyard (Anb): Pfalz. (Ber): Mittelhaardt-Deutsche Weinstrasse. (Gro): Hofstück. (Vil): Meckenheim.

Neuberg (Ger) vineyard (Anb): Pfalz. (Ber): Südliche Weinstrasse. (Gro): Trappenberg. (Vil): Bornheim.

Neubergen (Aus) a vineyard site on the banks of the River Danube in the Kremstal region.

Neuberger (Aus) a white early-ripening grape variety grown in the Burgenland, Krems and Langenlois, the result of a cross between Weissburgunder x Silvaner. Also known as the Grüner Burgunder.

Neubergern (Aus) a vineyard site on the banks of the River Danube in the Kremstal region.

Neuberger Sylvaner (Czec) a white grape variety.

Neuchâtel (Switz) a wine area which produces good white wines. Also famous for Cortaillod Oeil de Perdrix (pink wine). Grape varieties: Chasselas and Pinot noir.

Neudenau (Ger) village (Anb): Baden. (Ber): Badische Bergstrasse/Kraichgau. (Gro): Stiftsberg. (Vin): Berg.

Neudorf (N.Z) a small winery near Blenheim at Upper Moutere, Nelson. 5ha. Grape varieties: Chardonnay, Pinot noir, Riesling, Sauvignon blanc, Sémillon. Produces varietal wines. *See also* Family of Twelve.

Neuenbürg (Ger) *see* Kraichtal.

Neue Otto-Quelle (Ger) a natural spring mineral water. Mineral contents (milligrammes per litre):

Sodium 43mg/l, Calcium 18.8mg/l, Magnesium 43mg/l, Potassium 11.6mg/l, Chlorides 4.2mg/l, Sulphates 9.7mg/l, Fluorides 0.42mg/l, Silicates 93mg/l.

Neuerl (Aus) denotes a taste of cask/a woody taste that results from wood resin.

Neuershausen (Ger) village (Anb): Baden. (Ber): Kaiserstuhl-Tuniberg. (Gro): Vulkanfelsen. (Vin): Steingrube.

Neuselters (Ger) a natural spring mineral water from Löhnberg, Selters. Mineral contents (milligrammes per litre): Sodium 90mg/l, Calcium 100mg/l, Magnesium 27mg/l, Potassium 6mg/l, Bicarbonates 570mg/l, Chlorides 60mg/l, Sulphates 6mg/l.

Neuffen (Ger) village (Anb): Württemberg. (Ber): Remstal-Stuttgart. (Gro): Hohennenffen. (Vin): Schlossteige.

Neuholz (Ger) village (Anb): Württemberg. (Ber): Württembergisch Unterland. (Gro): Lindelberg. *see* Harsberg.

Neuillac (Fr) a commune in the Charente-Maritime département whose grapes are classed Petite Champagne (Cognac).

Neuleiningen (Ger) village (Anb): Pfalz. (Ber): Mittelhaardt-Deutsche Weinstrasse. (Gro): Höllenpfad. (Vins): Feuermännchen, Schlossberg, Sonnenberg.

Neulles (Fr) a commune in the Charente-Maritime département whose grapes are classed Petite Champagne (Cognac).

Neumagen-Dhron (Ger) village (Anb): Mosel-Saar-Ruwer. (Ber): Bernkastel. (Gro): Michelsberg. (Vins): Engelgrube, Grafenberg, Grosser Hengelberg, Hofberger, Laudamusberg, Rosengärtchen, Roterd, Sonnenuhr.

Neumayer [Ludwig] (Aus) a noted winery (8ha) based in Herzogenburg, Traisental. (Add): Inzersdorf ob der Traisen 22, 3130 Herzogenburg. Grape varieties include: Chardonnay, Grüner veltliner, Pinot blanc, Pinot noir, Riesling, St. Laurent, Zweigelt. Produces a range of dry and sweet wines.

Neumeister (Aus) a winery (13.5ha) based in Straden, Süd-Oststeiermark. (Add): 8345 Straden 42. Grape varieties: Blauburger, Morillon, Muskateller, Pinot blanc, Pinot gris, Traminer, Sauvignon blanc, Zweigelt. Labels: Morafeitl Selektion, Saziani Selektion.

Neuquén (Arg) a sub-region (1050ha) in the Patagonia region, southern Argentina. Main grape varieties: Cabernet sauvignon, Chardonnay, Malbec, Merlot, Pinot noir, Sauvignon blanc, Sémillon.

Neuritis (Eng) a disease of the nervous system caused through chronic alcoholism.

Neusatz (Ger) village (Anb): Baden. *see* Bühl.

Neuses (Ger) village (Anb): Franken. (Ber): Maindreieck. (Gro): Kirchberg. (Vin): Glatzen.

Neusetz (Ger) village (Anb): Franken. (Ber): Maindreieck. (Gro): Kirchberg. (Vins): Assorted parts of vineyards.

933

Neusiedeln (Aus) a vineyard site on the banks of the River Danube in the Kremstal region.

Neusiedlersee (Aus) a wine region (10387ha.) in eastern Burgenland. (Vils): Apetlon, Frauenkirchen, Gols, Halbturn, Illmitz, Mönchef, Neusiedl, Pamhagen, Podersdorf, St. Andrâ, Wallern, Weiden. Main grape varieties: white (Bouvier, Chardonnay, Grüner Veltliner, Muskat-Ottenel, Neuburger, Scheurebe, Traminer, Welschriesling) red (Blaufränkisch, Caernet Sauvignon, Pinot Noir, St. Laurent, Zweigelt). Is also known as Seewinkel.

Neusiedlersee-Hügelland (Aus) a wine region (6264ha.) in eastern Burgenland, (Vils): Breitenbrunn, Donnerskirchen, Eisenstadt (town), Grosshöflein, Mattersburg, Oggau, Pöttelsdorf, Purbach, Rust, Schützen, Siegendorf. Has a variety of soils including: black earth, chalk, crystalline slate, loam, loess, marl and sand. Main grape varieties: white 75% (Chardonnay, Neuburger, Pinot Blanc, Welschriesling) red 25% (Blaufränkisch, Caernet Sauvignon, Pinot Noir, St. Laurent, Zweigelt). Noted for Ruster Ausbruch.

Neustadt (Ger) village (Anb): Württemberg. (Ber): Remstal-Stuttgart. (Gro): Kopf. (Vin): Söhrenberg.

Neustadt an der Weinstrasse (Ger) village (Anb): Pfalz. (Ber): Mittelhaardt-Deutsche Weinstrasse. (Gro): Meerspinne. (Vin): Mönchgarten.

Neustadt an der Weinstrasse (Ger) village (Anb): Pfalz. (Ber): Mittelhaardt-Deutsche Weinstrasse. (Gro): Rebstöckel. (Vins): Erkenbrecht, Grain.

Neutral (Eng) a term that describes a wine as having virtually no positive flavour. Often denotes that the wine is blended.

Neutral Brandy (Eng) a brandy (wine distillate) distilled to 100% alc by vol. has no characteristics. Rectified, produced in a Patent still.

Neutral Grain Spirit (Eng) alcohol produced from cereals, has no flavour. Rectified, produced in a Patent still.

Neutral Spirits (USA) spirits that are pure and have no flavour. Made from potatoes, grain etc. 190° US proof (95% alc by vol).

Neutral Vodka (Eng) distilled from grain or molasses, rectified, filtered and diluted to required strength.

Neu Vierteln (Aus) a vineyard site on the banks of the River Danube in the Kremstal region.

Neuville (Switz) a wine village in the Berne canton.

Neuville-aux-Larris [La] (Fr) a Cru Champagne village in the Canton de Châtillons-sur-Marne. District: Reims.

Neuville-sur-Seine (Fr) a Cru Champage village in the Canton de l'Aube. District: Château Thierry.

Neuweier (Ger) village (Anb): Baden. (Ber): Ortenau. (Gro): Schloss Rodeck. (Vins): Altenberg, Gänsberg, Heiligenstein, Mauerberg, Schlossberg.

Neuweiler's Cream Ale (USA) a light malt beer brewed by the Ortlieb Brewery in Philadelphia.

Neuwies (Ger) vineyard (Anb): Mosel-Saar-Ruwer. (Ber): Saar-Ruwer. (Gro): Scharzberg. (Vil): Ockfen.

Neuzüchtungen (Ger) a term used for the man-made grape varieties. e.g. Scheurebe.

Nevada (Ven) a natural spring mineral water from Venezuela.

Nevada Cocktail (Cktl) ⅓ measure dark rum, ⅓ measure lime juice, ⅓ measure grapefruit juice, ⅙ measure gomme syrup. Shake over ice and strain into a cocktail glass.

Neval (Sp) a natural spring mineral water from Moratalla, Murcia.

Nevards Vineyard (Eng) a vineyard (established 1977) based at Boxted, Colchester, Essex. 0.45ha. Grape varieties: Huxelrebe and Reichensteiner.

Neve (It) a natural spring mineral water from Cadorgo, Como.

Neverfail Spring Water (Austr) a natural spring mineral water. Mineral contents (milligrammes per litre): Sodium 12mg/l, Calcium 0.33mg/l, Magnesium 2.8mg/l, Potassium 0.36mg/l, Chlorides <0.05mg/l, Fluorides <0.1mg/l, Nitrates 3.1mg/l.

Nevers Oak (Fr) French oak used for wine casks in Burgundy.

Nevins Cocktail (Cktl) ½ measure Bourbon whiskey, ½ measure apricot brandy, 5mls (¼ fl.oz) grapefruit juice, 10mls (½fl.oz) lemon juice, dash Angostura. Shake over ice and strain into a cocktail glass.

Neviot (Isr) a natural spring mineral water from Ein Zahav. Mineral contents (milligrammes per litre): Sodium 9mg/l, Calcium 70mg/l, Magnesium 16mg/l, Potassium 0.8mg/l, Bicarbonates 260mg/l, Chlorides 25mg/l, Sulphates 7mg/l, Nitrates 17mg/l, Silicates 11mg/l. pH 7.5

Nevis Bluf (N.Z) a vineyard (established 1998) based in the Central Otago region of the South Island. Grape varieties: Pinot gris and Pinot noir.

Nevoeira (Port) lit: 'fog', the name for grapes grown before phylloxera in the Douro. Found only in small quantities.

Nevsehir-Kayseri-Nigde (Tur) a red and white wine-producing vineyard based in the Middle Anatolia region.

New Albion Brewery (USA) a brewery based in Sonoma, California. Noted for top-fermented ales at 5.2% alc by vol.

New Amsterdam Amber (USA) a beer 4.8% alc by vol (1048 O.G) sold in a long neck bottle. Brewed in New York and imported by Continental Lager Distillers.

Newark Castle Brown (Eng) a 5% alc by vol. brown ale brewed by the Springhead Brewery, Nottinghamshire.

New Beginnings Wines (S.Afr) a winery (established 1997) based in Windmeul, Paarl, Western Cape. Grape varieties: Cabernet sauvignon, Chardonnay, Pinotage. Produces varietal wines.

New Brunswick (Can) a small wine-producing region based in south-eastern Canada.

Newby Wyke Brewery (Eng) a brewery (established 2001). (Add): Willoughby Arms Cottages, Little Bytham, Grantham, Lincolnshire NG33 4RA.

Brews: Bear Island 4.6% alc by vol., Chesapeake 5.5% alc by vol., Kingston Topaz 4.2% alc by vol., White Scroll 4.8% alc by vol., White Sea 5.2% alc by vol. Website: http://www.newbywyke.co.uk 'E'mail: newbywyke.brewery@btopenworld.com

New Cape Wines (S.Afr) a winery (established 2000) based in Worcester, Western Cape. Grape varieties: Cabernet sauvignon, Chardonnay, Chenin blanc, Merlot, Pinotage, Sauvignon blanc, Shiraz, Viognier. Labels: Dwyka Hills, Eagles' Cliff. Website: http://www.newcapewines.co.za

Newcastle (Eng) a brewery that is part of Scottish and Newcastle Breweries. Brews: cask-conditioned/keg Exhibition 1042 O.G. keg IPA 1032 O.G. and bottled Amber 1033 O.G. Brown 1045 O.G.

Newcastle Brown Ale (Eng) a famous English brown ale 1045 O.G. brewed by the Scottish and Newcastle Breweries. Sold in clear-glass 33cls beer bottles (also canned), first brewed in 1927.

New England Rum (USA) a term given to American rum of the eighteenth century shipped to Europe and Africa. Made from Indian molasses (now no longer recognised).

New Feeling (Chi) a natural spring mineral water brand.

Newe Timer (Eng) a 4.6% alc by vol. winter warmer ale brewed by Hall and Woodhouse, Dorset. Available from November 1999 until February 2000.

New Fashion Cocktail (Cktl) ⅔ measure dry Sherry, ⅙ measure Grand Marnier, ⅙ measure Cognac, dash Angostura. Shake over ice, strain into a cocktail glass and add a pineapple cube.

New Fashioned Cocktail (Cktl) 1¼ measures Cognac, dash Angostura, sugar cube. Place in an old-fashioned glass with ice, add a dash of soda, slice of orange and lemon.

New Fermor Arms (Eng) a home-brew public house in Rufford, Lancashire noted for cask-conditioned Blezards Bitter 1039 O.G.

New Forest (Eng) based at the Hollybush Vineyard in Hampshire. Grape variety: Pinot blanc.

New Forest Brewery (Eng) a brewery (established 1980) based in Cadnam, Hampshire. Brews: cask-conditioned New Forest Real Ale 1036 O.G. keg Forest Lager 1038 O.G. King's Wood 1039 O.G. Woodsman Mild 1034 O.G. and Old Evel 1048 O.G.

New Forest Spring Water (Eng) a natural spring mineral water from the New Forest, Hampshire.

New Generation (Hun) a rosé wine (Cabernet sauvignon) produced by the Figula winery, Balatonfüred.

New Hall (Eng) a vineyard (Add): Chelmsford Road, Purleigh, Chelmsford, Essex (12.5ha). Soil: heavy London clay. Grape varieties: Huxelrebe, Müller-Thurgau, Pinot noir, Reichensteiner, Ruländer and Würtzburger perle.

New Imperial (Eng) a 4.6% alc by vol. ale brewed by The Concertina Brewery, South Yorkshire.

New Inn (Eng) a home-brew public house owned by Tetley in Harrogate, Yorkshire. Noted for cask-conditioned Gate Ale 1045 O.G.

New Jersey (USA) a wine district of the Eastern States, vines are grown around Egg Harbor near Atlantic City.

New Jersey Champagne (USA) made in the nineteenth century from turnip juice, brandy and honey.

Newkie Broon (Eng) a slang term for Newcastle Brown Ale.

New Make (Scot) the name for the spirit from the second distillation in malt whisk production. Also known as Clearick or Spirit.

Newman Brewery (USA) a brewery (established 1981) in Albany, New York. Brews a naturally conditioned draught beer called Newman's Pale Ale.

Newmans Brewery (Eng) a brewery (established 2003). (Add): Meadow Court, Wolvershill Road, Banwell, Avon BS29 6DT. Brews: Bite IPA 4.6% alc by vol., Cave Bear Stout 4% alc by vol., Red Stag Bitter 3.6% alc by vol., Wolvers Ale 4.1% alc by vol., Woolly Mammothweis 4.5% alc by vol. Website: http://www.newmansbrewery.com 'E'mail: sales@newmansbrewery.com

New Mexico (USA) a wine region that has three A.V.A areas: Middle Rio Grande (near Alberquerque), Mimbres Valley (in south-west), Mesilla valley (near Mexican border).

New Orleans Best (USA) a beer 1039 O.G. brewed by the Royal Brewing Company in New Orleans.

New Orleans Buck (Cktl) ¾ measure white rum, ¼ measure orange juice, 4 dashes lemon juice. Stir over ice in a highball glass and top with ginger ale.

New Orleans Fizz (Cktl) 1 large measure gin, 10mls (½ fl.oz) lime juice, 10mls (½ fl.oz) lemon juice, 3 dashes orange flower water, 2 dashes gomme syrup, 1 dessertspoon cream. Shake well over ice, strain into a highball glass containing ice, top with soda water, serve with a muddler and straws.

New Orleans Gin Fizz (Cktl) 1½ measures dry gin, 1½ measures cream, 1 teaspoon sugar, juice ½ lemon, 1 teaspoon kirsch, ½ egg white. Shake over ice, strain into a highball glass, top with soda water and serve with straws.

Newport Best Bitter (Eng) 1045 O.G. cask bitter brewed by Hartridge's Island Brewery, Newport on the Isle of Wight.

Newquay Real Steam (Eng) the name given to a range of beers produced by the Cornish Brewery Cᵒ. Ltd., Redruth, Cornwall. Bitter 5.6% alc by vol. Brown 5.7% alc by vol. Lager 9% alc by vol. Stout 1064–1068 O.G. Sold in flip-top bottles.

Newquay Steam (Eng) the brand-name for a cider, bitter or lager beer brewed by Whitbread.

News Centenary Ale (Eng) a special ale brewed by the Druids pub in Cambridge to mark 100 years of the towns evening newspaper.

New Season Ale (Eng) a seasonal ale brewed by Jennings of Cocklemouth.

New South Wales (Austr) a wine state, the second

largest area of production in Australia. Best areas: Hunter Valley (split into the upper and lower), Mudgee, Murrumbidgee Irrigation Area (Riverina). Main Grape varieties: Sémillon, Shiraz in Lower Hunter, Chardonnay in Upper Hunter, Chardonnay and Merlot in Mudgee, Shiraz, Trebbiano and Sémillon in M.I.A.

New Special Draught (Austr) a golden-coloured, lager-type beer brewed by Toohey's Brewery in New South Wales.

New Special Monthly (Eng) the name for a beer brewed by the West Berkshire Brewery C°. Ltd., Berkshire.

New Strathmore Spring (Scot) a natural spring mineral water brand.

New Summer Peach (Eng) a 5.3% alc by vol. cocktail. Part of Woody's World of Cocktails. Others include Sea Breeze, Margarita, Pina Colada, Bellini, Blue Lagoon, Pineapple Daiquiri.

Newt 'N' Wriggly (Eng) a 4.6% alc by vol. bitter ale brewed by the Burrington Brewery, Devon.

Newton and Ridley (Eng) a fictitious brewery name used for the television series Coronation Street (Granada T.V.). *See also* The Rovers Return.

Newton Johnson Wines (S.Afr) a winery (established 1996) based in the Walker Bay, Western Cape. 8ha. Grape varieties include: Cabernet sauvignon, Chardonnay, Mourvèdre, Pinot noir, Sauvignon blanc, Sémillon, Shiraz. Labels: Felicité, Pour Mes Amis. Website: http://www.newtonjohnson.com

Newton's Ale (Eng) a keg bitter 1032 O.G. brewed by the Devenish Brewery, Weymouth, Dorset.

Newton's Ale (Eng) a keg bitter 1032 O.G. brewed by the Wilson's Brewery, Manchester.

Newton's Drop (Eng) a 4.1% alc by vol. ale brewed by Oldershaw Brewery in Lincolnshire.

Newton Vineyard (USA) a winery at St. Helena, Napa Valley, California. Produces varietal wines from Cabernet sauvignon, Merlot, Chardonnay and Viognier grapes.

New World (Eng) a general term used for the wine-producing countries of the Americas (north and south), Australia, New Zealand and South Africa.

New World (S.Afr) the label for a range of wines (Cabernet sauvignon-Merlot/Shiraz/Shiraz-Pinotage/Sauvignon blanc/Sémillon-Chardonnay) produced by The Winery, Stellenbosch, Western Cape.

New Yarmouth Distillery (W.Ind) a rum distillery based on the island of Jamaica. Produces dark rums.

New York (USA) a wine region of Eastern America. Contains the districts: Five Finger Lakes, Long Island, Westfield-Fredonia, Lake Erie, Hudson Valley, Highland in Sullivan County, Chautauqua, Niagara County. Hybrid native varieties, French hybrids such as Seyval blanc, Baco noir, Marechal foch plus Chardonnay and Riesling are planted.

New York Cocktail (Cktl) as for New York Cooler.

New York Cooler (Cktl) 60mls (½ gill) Canadian Club whisky, 30mls (¼ gill) lemon juice, 3 dashes grenadine. Stir well with ice in a highball glass. Fill up with soda water, stir, serve with a dash of lemon peel juice and a slice of lemon.

New York Market (Mad) the old name given to a style of Madeira wine that was shipped to the USA.

New York Seltzer (USA) *see* Original New York Seltzer.

New York Sour (Cktl) 50mls (2fl.ozs) Bourbon whiskey, juice ½ lemon, teaspoon powdered sugar. Shake over ice, strain into a sour glass, float 10mls (½ fl.oz) claret wine on top, add a cherry and slice of lemon.

New Zealand (N.Z) a country (wine-producing from 37°S to 45°S) producing mainly white and fortified wines. (Add): New Zealand Wine Growers, Level 2, 52 Symonds Street, Auckland City, P.O. Box 90276, Auckland Mail Centre, New Zealand. Famous for Sauvignon blanc, Pinot gris, Pinot noir and sparkling wines. Main regions are North Island: (Auckland, Gisborne, Hawkes Bay, Martinborough and Waikato). South Island: (Canterbury, Marlborough, Otago and Nelson). Climate is akin to Germany. *See also* Gimblett Gravels. Website: http://www.nzwine.com 'E'mail: info@winz.org.nz

New Zealand Breweries (N.Z) a large brewing concern that has many plants (based in Wellington). Brews: Lion beers and Steinlager.

New Zealand Crew (N.Z) a natural spring mineral water from Canterbury Plains, South Island. Mineral contents (milligrammes per litre): Sodium 6.9mg/l, Calcium 12mg/l, Magnesium 1.9mg/l, Potassium 0.7mg/l, Chlorides 3.9mg/l, Sulphates 3.6mg/l, Nitrates 0.26mg/l, Silicates 18mg/l. pH 7.9

New Zealand Nouveau (N.Z) the first wine of the new vintage (March–April) which is shipped to U.K.

New Zealand Viticultural Association (N.Z) an organisation that is now no longer in existence.

Neyen Estate (Chile) a winery based in the Apalta Valley, Colchagua Valley, Central Chile. Grape varieties include: Cabernet sauvignon, Carmenère.

Neyret (It) a red grape variety grown in Valle d'Aosta.

Nez du Vin [Le] (Fr) a patented cabinet with small phials of '*aromas*' plus reference cards on the bouquets found in wines (from 12 to 54 phials).

Nezhinskaya Ryafina (Rus) a liqueur made from rowanberries and spirit.

Ngatarawa Winery (N.Z) a winery based at Bridge Pa, Hawkes Bay, North Island. 10.5ha. Grape varieties: Cabernet sauvignon, Chardonnay, Merlot, Rhine riesling and Sauvignon blanc. Produce varietal and table wines.

Nga Waka Vineyard (N.Z.) a vineyard (Add): Kitchener Street, P.O. Box 128, Martinborough. 4ha. Grape varieties: Chardonnay, Riesling, Sauvignon blanc.

N

N.H.A. (Eng) *abbr*: National Hop Association.

Niagara (Pol) a natural spring mineral water from Tarczyn. Mineral contents (milligrammes per litre): Calcium 72.1mg/l, Magnesium 15.6mg/l, Bicarbonates 305.1mg/l, Fluorides 0.2mg/l.

Niagara (USA) a white grape variety, one of the first hybrids, a cross (Concord and Cassady), can withstand very cold winters. Used for still white wines. Also planted in Brazil.

Niagara (USA) a wine region of Eastern America between Lake Erie and Ontario on both sides of the river. Produces good quality wines.

Niagara (USA) a non-alcoholic, sparkling, blue coloured drink supplied by Wycoff Coffee House and Candy Company in Arkansas. Is claimed to be an aphrodisiac.

Niagara [Le] (Fr) an early nineteenth century inventor who invented a metallic tower, 70 feet in height, with copper rods on top to try and stop hailstorms.

Niagara Escarpment (Can) a wine sub-region.

Niagara Falls (Can) a wine region of Eastern Canada.

Niagara Wine Cellars (USA) a winery based in Lewiston, Niagara, Eastern America. Produces American native wines.

Nib (Eng) the edible part of the cocoa bean after the shell has been removed from which the cocoa is obtained.

Nicaragua (C.Am) a country in Central America that produces coffee beans for blending (mainly Robustas).

Nicasio Winery (USA) a winery based in Santa Cruz, California. Produces varietal wines.

Nice Try Ian (Eng) a 5% alc by vol. lager brewed by Somerset's Ash Vine Brewery for an Oxford pub.

Nichelini Vineyards (USA) a winery based near Rutherford, Napa Valley, California. Grape varieties: Cabernet sauvignon and Zinfandel. Produces varietal wines.

Nicholas Cocktail (Cktl) ½ measure sloe gin, ½ measure orange gin. Shake over ice and strain into a cocktail glass.

Nicholoff Red Vodka (Eng) a British-made, red-coloured spirit with a base of Dutch vodka 40% alc by vol.

Nichols [Austin] Distilling C°. (USA) a distillery based in Kentucky. Noted for 8 year old Wild Turkey Bourbon 53% alc by vol.

Nicholson Distillery (Eng) a noted distillery based in London. Produces a fine range of gins and vodka. Gin sold under the Lamplighter label. J.& W. Nicholson & C°. Ltd.

Nick & Forti's Wines (S.Afr) a winery (established 2004) based in Wellington, Western Cape. Grape varieties: Cabernet sauvignon, Malbec, Merlot, Petit verdot, Shiraz. Label: Epicentre.

Nickel & Nickel (USA) a winery based in the Napa Valley, California. Noted for Napa Valley Merlot and Russian River Valley Zinfandel varietal wines. Label: Sterling Vineyard.

Nick's Own Cocktail (Cktl) 30mls (¼ gill) Cognac, 30mls (¼ gill) Italian vermouth, 1 dash Angostura, 1 dash absinthe. Stir well over ice, strain into a cocktail glass, add a cherry and lemon peel juice on top.

Nicolas [Ets] (Fr) a famous Paris-based wine wholesalers and retailing merchants.

Nicolaska (Cktl) 1 measure brandy in a 125mls (5fl.oz) goblet. Place a slice of peeled lemon on rim of glass. Sprinkle liberally with powdered sugar and finely ground coffee. To drink: place lemon with the coating on in mouth and drink brandy through it.

Nicolauswein (Ger) a wine made from grapes gathered on Saint Nicholas day (6th December).

Nicole's (USA) a red wine (Cabernet sauvignon) produced by the Lancaster Estate winery, Alexander Valley, California.

Nicole's Hat (S.Afr) a white wine (Chardonnay 50% and Chenin blanc 50%) from the Concept Wines range produced by the Ashanti winery, Paarl, Western Cape.

Nicole's Vineyard (USA) the label for a red wine (Pinot noir) produced by the J Vineyards & Winery, Russian River Valley, Sonoma County, California.

Nicoresti (Rum) a wine area which produces good red wines. *see* Babeasca.

Nicotinic Acid (Eng) vitamin B (a vitamin found in wine).

Nico van der Merwe Wines (S.Afr) a winery (established 1999) based in Stellenbosch, Western Cape. Grape varieties: Cabernet sauvignon, Merlot, Sauvignon blanc, Sémillon, Shiraz. Labels: Mas Nicolas, Robert Alexander.

Nico Vermeulen Wines (S.Afr) a winery (established 2003) based in Paarl, Western Cape. Grape varieties: Cabernet sauvignon, Merlot, Sauvignon blanc, Sémillon. Labels: The Right Two (Reds & Whites).

Niebaum-Coppola Estates (USA) a winery based at St. Helena Highway, Rutherford, Napa Valley, California. 67ha. Grape varieties: Cabernet sauvignon and Chardonnay. Produces varietal wines. Label: Rubicon.

Nieder-Alteich (Aus) a monastery that also owns vineyards near Krems.

Niederberg (Ger) vineyard (Anb): Mosel-Saar-Ruwer. (Ber): Bernkastel. (Gro): Michelsberg. (Vil): Rivenich.

Niederberg-Helden (Ger) vineyard (Anb): Mosel-Saar-Ruwer. (Ber): Bernkastel. (Gro): Beerenlay. (Vil): Lieser.

Niederburg (Ger) village (Anb): Mittelrhein. (Ber): Rheinburgengau. (Gro): Schloss Schönburg. (Vins): Bienenberg, Rheingoldberg.

Niederdollendorf (Ger) village (Anb): Mittelrhein. (Ber): Siebengebirge. (Gro): Petersberg. (Vins): Goldfusschen, Longenburgerberg, Heisterberg.

Niedereggenen (Ger) village (Anb): Baden. (Ber): Markgräflerland. (Gro): Burg Neuenfels. (Vins): Röthen, Sonnenstück.

Niederfell (Ger) village (Anb): Mosel-Saar-Ruwer. (Ber): Zell/Mosel. (Gro): Weinhex. (Vins): Fächern, Goldlay, Kahllay.

Niederhausen an der Nahe (Ger) village (Anb): Nahe. (Ber): Schloss Böckelheim. (Gro): Burgweg. (Vins): Felsensteyer, Hermannsberg, Hermannshöhle, Kertz, Klamm, Pfaffenstein, Pflingstweide, Rosenberg, Rosenheck, Steinberg, Steinwingert, Stollenberg.

Niederhausen an der Nahe (Ger) village (Anb): Nahe. (Ber): Schloss Böckelheim. (Gro): Paradiesgarten. (Vin): Graukatz.

Niederheimbach (Ger) village (Anb): Mittelrhein. (Ber): Bacharach. (Gro): Schloss Reichenstein. (Vins): Froher Weingarten, Reiferslay, Schloss Hohneck, Sooonecker Schlossberg.

Nieder-Hilbersheim (Ger) village (Anb): Rheinhessen. (Ber): Bingen. (Gro): Abtey. (Vins): Honigberg, Steinacker.

Niederhofen (Ger) village (Anb): Württemberg. (Ber): Württembergisch Unterland. (Gro): Heuchelberg. (Vins): Grafenberg, Vogelsang.

Niederhorbach (Ger) village (Anb): Pfalz. (Ber): Südliche Weinstrasse. (Gro): Kloster Liebfrauenberg. (Vin): Silberberg.

Niederkirchen (Ger) village (Anb): Pfalz. (Ber): Mittelhaardt-Deutsche Weinstrasse. (Gro): Hofstück. (Vins): Klostergarten, Osterbrunnen, Schlossberg.

Niedermayr [Josef] (It) a noted small winery based in Jesuheimstr, Südtirol.

Niedermoschel (Ger) village (Anb): Nahe. (Ber): Schloss Böckelheim. (Gro): Paradiesgarten. (Vins): Geissenkopf, Hahnhölle, Layenberg, Silberberg.

Niedernhall (Ger) village (Anb): Württemberg. (Ber): Kocher-Jagst-Tauber. (Gro): Kocherberg. (Vins): Burgstall, Engweg, Hoher Berg.

Nieder-Olm (Ger) village (Anb): Rheinhessen. (Ber): Nierstein. (Gro): Gutes Domtal. (Vins): Goldberg, Klosterberg, Sonnenberg.

Niederösterreich (Aus) lower Austria, a wine region in the north of the country that produces most of its wines. Sub-regions: Kamptal-Donauland, Krems, Thermenregion, Wachau, Weinviertel. Noted areas: Falkenstein, Gumpoldskirchen, Klosterneuburg, Langenlois, Retz, Voslau.

Niederotterbach (Ger) village (Anb): Pfalz. (Ber): Südliche Weinstrasse. (Gro): Guttenberg. (Vin): Eselsbuckel.

Niederrhein Alt (Ger) a 4.7% alc by vol. bottled alt beer brewed by the Bolten Brauerei, Korschenbroich.

Niederrimsingen (Ger) village (Anb): Baden. (Ber): Kaiserstuhl-Tuniberg. (Gro): Attilafelsen. (Vin): Rotgrund.

Niederschopfheim (Ger) village (Anb): Baden. (Ber): Ortenau. (Gro): Fürsteneck. (Vin): Kinzigtäler.

Niederstetten (Ger) village (Anb): Württemberg. (Ber): Kocher-Jagst-Tauber. (Gro): Tauberberg. (Vin): Schafsteige.

Niederwalluf (Ger) village (Anb): Rheingau. (Ber): Johannisberg. (Gro): Steinmacher. (Vins): Berg Bildstock, Oberberg, Walkenberg.

Niederweiler (Ger) village (Anb): Baden. (Ber): Markgräflerland. (Gro): Burg Neuenfels. (Vin): Römerberg.

Nieder-Weisen (Ger) village (Anb): Rheinhessen. (Ber): Bingen. (Gro): Adelberg. (Vin): Wingertsberg.

Niefernheim (Ger) village (Anb): Pfalz. (Ber): Mittelhaardt-Deutsche Weinstrasse. (Gro): Schnepfenflug vom Kellertal. (Vins): Königsweg, Kreuzberg.

Niehaus [Dr. Charles] (S.Afr) discovered the indigenous flor yeast in the Cape vineyards in 1935.

Niel Joubert Wines (S.Afr) a winery (established 1898) based in Paarl, Western Cape. 350ha. (Add): P.O. Box 17, Klapmuts 7625, Paarl. Grape varieties: Cabernet sauvignon, Chardonnay, Chenin blanc, Merlot, Pinotage, Sauvignon blanc, Viognier. Produces varietal wines. Website: http://www.nieljoubert.co.za

Nielka Cocktail (Cktl) ¾ measure vodka, ¼ measure French vermouth, ½ measure orange juice. Stir over ice and strain into a cocktail glass.

Nielluccio (Fr) a local red grape variety grown in Corsica. (It) = Sangiovese.

Niels Verburg (S.Afr) the export label for range of wines produced by the Luddite Wines winery, Walker Bay, Western Cape.

Niepoort (Port) Vintage Port shippers. Vintages: 1927, 1945, 1955, 1960, 1963, 1966, 1970, 1975, 1977, 1978, 1980, 1982, 1983, 1985, 1987, 1991, 1992, 1994, 1997, 1998, 2000, 2003. Also produces: Charme (still red), Redoma (rosé).

Nierstein (Ger) bereich (Anb): Rheinhessen. (Gros): Auflangen, Domherr, Güldenmorgen, Gutes Domtal, Krötenbrunnen, Petersberg, Rehbach, Rheinblick, Sankt Alban, Spiegelberg, Vogelsgärten.

Nierstein (Ger) village (Anb): Rheinhessen. (Ber): Nierstein. (Gro): Auflangen. (Vins): Bergkirche, Glöck, Heiligenbaum, Kranzberg, Ölberg, Orbel, Schloss Schwabsburg, Zehnmorgen.

Nierstein (Ger) village (Anb): Rheinhessen. (Ber): Nierstein. (Gro): Gutes Domtal. (Vin): Pfaffenkappe.

Nierstein (Ger) village (Anb): Rheinhessen. (Ber): Nierstein. (Gro): Rehberg. (Vins): Brudersberg, Goldene Luft, Hipping, Pettenthal.

Nierstein (Ger) village (Anb): Rheinhessen. (Ber): Nierstein. (Gro): Spiegelberg. (Vins): Bildstock, Brückchen, Ebersberg, Findling, Hölle, Kirchplatte, Klostergarten, Paterberg, Rosenberg, Schloss Hohenrechen.

Niersteiner Domtal (Ger) an old Germanic name now no longer allowed, now known as Niersteiner Gutes Domtal.

Niersteiner Gutes Domtal (Ger) the name for wine from the grosslagen of Gutes Domtal in the Bereich of Nierstein.

Nieschen (Ger) vineyard (Anb): Mosel-Saar-Ruwer. (Ber): Saar-Ruwer. (Gro): Römerlay. (Vil): Kasel.

Nietvoorbij (S.Afr) abbr: V.O.R.I. see South African Viticultural and Oenological Research Institute.

Nietvoorbij Wine Callar (S.Afr) a winery (established 1963) based in Stellenbosch, Western Cape. 32ha. Grape varieties: Cabernet franc, Cabernet sauvignon, Chardonnay, Chenin blanc, Gewürztraminer, Pinotage, Ruby cabernet. Produces varietal wines. Website: http://www.heritagegarden.co.za

Nieuwedrift Vineyards (S.Afr) a winery (established 1996) based in Swartland, Western Cape. 29ha. Grape varieties: Chardonnay, Chenin blanc, Colombard, Shiraz. Produces varietal wines.

Nièvre (Fr) a Vin de Pays area in the Nièvre département, central France. Produces red, rosé and dry white wines.

Nig (Eng) the Victorian name for the metal tag around glass decanter necks (bottle ticket).

Nig (USA) the American Negro slang term for gin.

Nigerian Breweries Limited (Afr) a noted brewery based in Nigeria which produces Star and Gulder Lagers at 1047 O.G.

Night (Eng) a 4.5% alc by vol. ale brewed by Wilds Brewery Ltd., Herefordshire.

Night and Day (Eng) the name given to a water-decaffeinated coffee from Jacobs Suchard.

Night Cap (Eng) a pre-bedtime drink. May be either hot or cold, alcoholic or not.

Night Cap [1] (Cktl) 50mls (2fl.ozs) Jamaican rum, 2 dashes gomme syrup. Place into a mug, top with warm milk and nutmeg.

Night Cap [2] (Cktl) heat 500mls (1pint) light ale, 2 teaspoons cocoa powder and 75mls (3fl.ozs) Scotch whisky slowly until nearly boiling, pour slowly over 3 egg yolks (beaten with 4 teaspoons sugar), stir and serve in mugs with a pinch of cinnamon.

Night Cap [3] (Cktl) heat a bottle of red wine with a thickly-sliced lemon, 3 cloves, cinnamon stick and sugar to taste, strain and serve very hot in mugs.

Night Cap Cocktail (Cktl) ⅓ measure Cognac, ⅓ measure Grand Marnier, ⅓ measure anisette, yolk of an egg. Shake well over ice and strain into a cocktail glass.

Night Cap Flip (Cktl) 30mls (¼ gill) each of brandy, anisette, Curaçao, yolk of egg. Shake well over ice and strain into a cocktail glass.

Night Light (Cktl) ⅓ measure Grand Marnier, ⅔ measure dark rum, 1 egg yolk. Shake over ice and strain into a large cocktail glass.

Night Light (Punch) boil the zest of an orange and lemon with a teaspoon of mixed spice and 50 grms (2ozs) sugar in 200mls (⅓ pint) of water for 5 minutes. Add 1 bottle full-bodied red wine, bring almost to the boil, strain and serve.

Nightmare Cocktail (Cktl) ⅜ measure gin, ⅛ measure Boal Madeira, ⅛ measure cherry brandy, 4 dashes orange juice. Shake over ice, strain into a cocktail glass and top with a squeeze of orange peel juice.

Nightmare Stout (Eng) a 5% alc by vol. 'winter warmer' stout brewed by Hambleton Ales in North Yorkshire.

Nightporters (Eng) 5.2% alc by vol. ale produced in South Devon.

Night Shade Cocktail (Cktl) ½ measure Bourbon whiskey, ¼ measure sweet vermouth, ¼ measure orange juice, dash yellow Chartreuse. Shake over ice and strain into a cocktail glass.

Nigl [Martin] (Aus) a winery (15ha) based in the Kremstal region. (Add): Priel 7, 3541 Senftenberg. Grape varieties: Chardonnay, Grüner veltliner, Müller-Thurgau, Riesling, Sauvignon blanc. Produces a range of wine styles.

Nigrara (It) a red grape used in the making of Bardolino.

Nigruwa (Euro) a red grape variety grown on the island of Malta in the Mediterranean.

Nihonsakari (Jap) the term used for a sweet saké. Also Ozeki.

Nikela (S.Afr) the label for a red wine (50% Cabernet sauvignon plus Merlot and Pinotage blend) produced by the Grangehurst Winery, Stellenbosch, Western Cape.

Nikita (Eng) a mild vodka 20% alc by vol. produced by Gilbert and John Greenall Ltd., Warrington, Lancashire.

Nikita (Fr) the Beaujolais version of vin blanc cassis using red wine.

Nikita Twenty 20 (Eng) a mild vodka produced by Vladivar in Warrington, Cheshire.

Nikka Distilleries (Jap) a whiskey distillery. Produces: Black Nikka, G & G, High Nikka, Super Nikka, All Malt (vatted), Corn Base, Rye Base, Hokkaido (single malt), Pure Malt White (Islay-style) whiskies.

Nikolai (USA) a vodka 40% alc by vol. produced by the General Wine and Spirits C° (a subsidiary of Seagram).

Nikolaihof (Aus) a winery based in the Wachau. (Add): Nikolaigasse 3, 3512 Mautern. Grape varieties: Chardonnay, Grüner veltliner, Neuburger, Riesling. Produces a range of dry and sweet (botrytised) wines.

Nikolausberg (Ger) vineyard (Anb): Mosel-Saar-Ruwer. (Ber): Zell/Mosel. (Gro): Rosenhang. (Vil): Cochem.

Nikolayev (Ukr) a wine-producing centre in the Ukraine on the Black Sea.

Niksar (Tur) a natural spring mineral water. Mineral contents (milligrammes per litre): Calcium 2.5mg/l, Magnesium 0.3mg/l, Potassium 0.45mg/l, Nitrates 0.4mg/l.

Niksic (Ser) a full-bodied beer brewed by the Niksic Brewery in Montenegro.

Niksic Brewery (Ser) a brewery based in Montenegro in the south-west.

Nile Breweries (Afr) a noted brewery based in Jinja, Uganda. Noted for Source of the Nile Ale 1042 O.G. (top-fermented).

Nilgiri (Ind) a coffee and tea-producing region of southern India.

Nill (Ger) vineyard (Anb): Pfalz. (Ber): Mittelhaardt-Deutsche Weinstrasse. (Gro): Saumagen. (Vil): Kallstadt.

Nimburg (Ger) village (Anb): Baden. (Ber): Kaiserstuhl-Tuniberg. (Gro): Vulkanfelsen. (Vin): Steingrube.

N

Nimbus (Scot) a 5% alc by vol. ale brewed by the Atlas Brewery, Argyll.

Nimbus Brewing C° (USA) a brewery. (Add): 3850E 44th Street, Suite 138, Tucson, Arizona 85713. Brews a range of beers and lager. Website: http://www.nimbusbeer.com 'E'mail: thegeneral@nimbusbeer.com

Nimmo's XXXX (Eng) 4.4% alc by vol. ale brewed by Castle Eden Brewery, County Durham. Nicknamed the 'Golden Oldie' due to the colour, also available in bottle.

Nimrod (Port) the name of a fine Tawny Port produced by the Warre's Port shippers.

Nina (Cktl) 25mls (1fl.oz) each of Bacardi rum, Vaapukka liqueur, lime juice cordial. Build into an ice-filled highball glass, stir in ginger ale, garnish with a cherry and slice of orange.

Nincusa (Euro) a minor red grape variety grown on the Dalamtian coast.

Nine Altars (Eng) a 5.2% alc by vol. ale brewed by The Durham Brewery Ltd., County Durham.

Nine Barrel (USA) the label for a red wine (Pinot noir) produced by the La Crema winery, Russian River Valley, Sonoma County, California.

Nine Dragon Mountail Mineral Spring (Chi) a natural spring mineral water. Mineral contents (milligrammes per litre): Sodium 20.9mg/l, Calcium 95.2mg/l, Magnesium 24.9mg/l, Potassium 0.8mg/l, Bicarbonates 274.6mg/l, Chlorides 37.2mg/l, Sulphates 75.1mg/l, Silicates 21mg/l. pH 7.5

Nine Lives (Eng) a 3.6% alc by vol. ale brewed by the Whittington Brewery, Gloucestershire.

Nine-O-Nine [909] (Can) a Canadian whisky produced by the Canadian Gibson Distilleries.

Nine Popes (Austr) a Grenache, Shiraz and Mataro blended red wine produced by Melton in the Barossa. See also Rose of Virginia.

Nineteen Forty Five [1945] Ale (Eng) a 5.1% alc by vol. fruity bottled beer brewed by World War II veteran Colin Jones at Bass Breweries.

Nineteen Hundred [1900] Lefébvre (Bel) a beer brewed by the Dupont Brasserie in Tourpes.

Nineteenth Hole (Cktl) ⅓ measure Scotch whisky, ⅓ measure sweet vermouth, ⅓ measure dry Sherry. Shake over ice and strain into a cocktail glass.

Nineteenth [19th] Hole (Eng) the nickname for the club bar at a golf club.

Nineteenth [19th] Meeting Cabernet Sauvignon (Austr) a full-bodied red wine produced by The Lane vineyard, Adelaide Hills.

Ninety Seven [97] (Eng) a cask-conditioned bitter 1048 O.G. brewed by the Moles Brewery in Melksham, Wiltshire (also known as Moles 97).

Ninety Shilling Ales [90/-] (Scot) a term for strong ales. See also Shilling System.

Nine [9] X (Eng) a specially produced super strength export ale brewed by Cain (Robert) in Liverpool.

Nine Yards (S.Afr) a reserve Chardonnay wine from the Jordan Winery, Stellenbosch.

Ninfa (It) a natural spring mineral water from Ninfa. Mineral contents (milligrammes per litre):

Sodium 41.1mg/l, Calcium 32.2mg/l, Magnesium 8.7mg/l, Potassium 25.2mg/l, Bicarbonates 219mg/l, Chlorides 23.5mg/l, Sulphates 13.8mg/l, Nitrates 2.8mg/l, Silicates 100mg/l. pH 5.76

Ninja Beer (Eng) a 5% alc by vol. beer brewed by Summerskill Brewery, Devon.

Ninotchka (Cktl) ¾ measure vodka, ¼ measure (white) crème de cacao, juice ¼ lemon. Shake over ice and strain into a cocktail glass.

Nip (Eng) a very small bottle of barley wine, Champagne or spirits 175mls (6fl.ozs)

Nip (USA) a cocktail measure (1.6fl.ozs).

Nipa (Asia) an alcoholic beverage made in Malaysia from the sap of the Nipa tree (Nipa fructicans).

Nipah (Asia) see Nipa (the alternative spelling).

Nipozzano (It) a Chianti estate near Florence (outside the Classico area).

Nipper (Eng) a cask-conditioned ale (1038 O.G). brewed by Hartridges Island Brewery, Newport, Isle of Wight. See also Newport Best Bitter, Wight Winter Warmer.

Nipperkin (Eng) an eighteenth century vessel holding approximately 250mls (½ pint).

Nissen (Ger) a brand of rum produced by Hansen in Flensburg.

Nissley Vineyards (USA) a small winery based in Bainbridge, Pennsylvania. 11ha. Produces French hybrid wines.

Nitida Cellars (S.Afr) a winery (established 1992) based in Durbanville, Western Cape. 15ha. (Add): P.O. Box 1423, C/o Maaspruit Farm, Durbanville 7550. Grape varieties: Cabernet franc, Cabernet sauvignon, Chardonnay, Merlot, Sauvignon blanc, Sémillon, Shiraz. Labels: Calligraphy, Club Select. Website: http://www.nitida.co.za

Nitra Brewery (Czec) a brewery based in south-eastern Czec. Produces fine lager-style beers.

Nitrogen (Eng) found in grape must, the yeasts build the protein they need from the nitrogen. If the grape must is nitrogen deficient the yeast obtains it from dead yeast cells and then produces Fusel oils.

Nitro-keg (Eng) a special pressurised keg that contains beer, ready to dispense, no separate gas cylinder required. Method of delivery ensures ale poured has a creamy head.

Nittel (Ger) village (Anb): Mosel-Saar-Ruwer. (Ber): Obermosel. (Gro): Gipfel. (Vins): Blümchen, Hubertusberg, Leiterchen, Rochusfels.

Nittnaus [Hans & Anita] (Aus) a winery (10ha) based in Gols, Burgenland. (Add): Untere Hauptstrasse 49, 7122 Gols. Grape varieties: Blaufränkisch, Cabernet sauvignon, Chardonnay, Merlot, Sauvignon blanc, St. Laurent, Welschriesling. Produces a variety of wines.

Niunai [1] (Chi) milk.

Niunai [2] (Chi) the ancient name for the red grape variety now known as the 'cow's nipple'.

Niva (It) a natural spring mineral water from Pian della Mussa, Torino.

Nivernaise (Fr) a district in the Central Vineyards

(Pouilly-sur-Loire). Mainly dry white wines are produced.

Nix (Cktl) ⅓ measure brandy, ⅓ measure Port, ⅓ measure lime juice. Shake over ice, strain into an ice-filled highball glass and top with cola.

Nixenberg (Ger) vineyard (Anb): Nahe. (Ber): Kreuznach. (Gro): Schlosskapelle. (Vil): Dorsheim.

Nix Wincott Brewery (Eng) a brewery based at Ye Three Fyshes, Turvey near Bedford. Brews: Two Henrys (a malty bitter) 1040 O.G.

Nizerand [River] (Fr) a small river in the Beaujolais region of Burgundy that separates the Haut-Beaujolais from the Bas-Beaujolais (a tributary of the Saône).

Njalo (S.Afr) the label for a red wine (Shiraz, Merlot and Pinotage blend) produced by the Umkhulu Wines winery, Stellenbosch, Western Cape.

N.M. (Fr) *abbr*: Négociant Manipulant on a Champagne wine label that is followed by a number denotes the registered name of the wine by the C.I.V.C.

N.M.D. (Eng) the name for a beer brewed by Ballard's Brewery Ltd., Hampshire.

N.M.W.B.W.A. (Eng) *abbr*: Natural Mineral Waters and Bottled Waters Association.

Noah (Isr) the Hebrews say he introduced wine to civilisation.

Noah (USA) a white grape variety now little used.

Noah's California Spring Water (USA) a slightly alkaline natural spring mineral water from San Antonio Valley, California. Mineral contents (milligrammes per litre): Sodium 6.3mg/l, Calcium 4.4mg/l, Magnesium 110mg/l, Bicarbonates 529mg/l, Chlorides 6mg/l, Sulphates 13mg/l, Nitrates 3.1mg/l. pH 8.7

Noah's Mill (USA) a straight Bourbon whiskey from Willetts, Bardstown, Kentucky 57% alc by vol.

No Angel (Eng) a 4% alc by vol. ale brewed by HB Clark & C°. Ltd., West Yorkshire.

Nobilo Winery (N.Z) a winery. (Add): Station Road, Huapai, Auckland. 30ha. Grape varieties: Cabernet sauvignon, Merlot, Muscat, Pinotage, Pinot noir, Sauvignon blanc and grapes bought in from Gisborne. (Chardonnay, Gewürztraminer and Müller-Thurgau).

Noble (Fr) a term used for certain grape varieties, certain vineyards and certain wines which are inherently superior to other grapes, vineyards and wines.

Noble (Fr) a red grape variety of the Touraine in the Loire.

Noble Bitter (Eng) a bitter ale brewed by the Beowulf Brewery, Yardley, Birmingham.

Noblé Cuvée Millesimé (Fr) a de luxe vintage cuvée Champagne produced by Lanson from 57% Chardonnay and 43% Pinot noir grapes.

Noble Experiment (USA) the name given for the Prohibition of 1919–1933.

Noble Hill (S.Afr) the label for red wine (Cabernet sauvignon-Merlot) produced by the Cowlin Wines winery, Paarl, Western Cape.

Noblejas (Sp) the name given to the wines originating from Toledo.

Noble Late Harvest (S.Afr) a superior classification for wines with over 50g/l of residual sugar. Must show **Botrytis cinerea** (a dessert wine).

Noble Mold (USA) *Botrytis cinerea*. Also spelt Noble Mould.

Noble Mould (USA) *Botrytis cinerea*. Also spelt Noble Mold.

Noble One (Austr) a dessert wine produced by De Bortoli, New South Wales from Sémillon grapes.

Noble Rot (Eng) *Botrytis cinerea*.

Noblessa (Ger) a white grape variety, a cross between Madeleine angevine and Silvaner. Gives very high sugar.

Noblesse (Can) a Canadian whisky produced by the Canadian Gibson Distilleries.

Noblige (Fr) a light style of Cognac produced by Martell that is picked between V.S.O.P. and Cordon Bleu 40% alc by vol.

Nobling (Ger) a white grape variety, a cross between Silvaner and Gutedel, used mainly in Baden it gives high sugar and balance.

Nocello (It) a walnut-flavoured liqueur produced by Toschi.

Nocera Umbra (It) a natural spring mineral water brand.

Noces de Diamant (Fr) a Grande Champagne Cognac produced by Hardy.

Noceto Michelotti (It) a winery based in Castelboglione, Piemonte. Produces Barbera d'Asti.

Nochebuena (Mex) lit: 'Christmas Eve', a dark beer brewed by the Moctezuma Brewery in Monterrey.

Nochera (It) a red grape variety grown in Sicily.

Nochern (Ger) village (Anb): Mittelrhein. (Ber): Rheinburgengau. (Gro): Loreleyfelsen. (Vin): Brünnchen.

Noches de Maquieta (Cktl) 50mls (2 fl.ozs) golden rum, 1 teaspoon sugar, dash Angostura, 6 dashes crème de cacao, lemon peel, place sugar, lemon peel, bitters and a dash of soda in an old-fashioned glass. Mix well with ice, add rest of ingredients and decorate with an orange slice, cherry and straws.

Nocino (It) a herb liqueur made from nut husks and green walnuts macerated in spirit and sugar for 1 year before being bottled by Trappist monks 30% alc by vol.

Nocino (It) a home-made liqueur obtained by steeping hazelnuts or walnuts in sugar and water and letting it ferment in the sun, the fermentation is then arrested by the addition of alcohol.

Noctuelles (Fr) the name given (by the vignérons) to the various catipillars that come out at night and eat the young shoots, flower buds, etc. in the vineyard during the year.

Nodd (Wal) juice. *See also* Sudd.

Noe (Sp) a Pedro ximénez Sherry produced by Gonzalez Byass in Jerez de la Frontera, Cadiz. Aged for 30 years, it is a part of their Rare Old Solera range.

N

Noël (Eng) a 5.5% alc by vol. winter ale brewed by Arkell's Brewery, Kingsdown, Swindon using 90% malt from winter barley (bottled or draught).

Noëllat [Charles] (Fr) a négociant-éleveur of fine wines based in Nuits-Saint-Georges, Côte de Nuits, Burgundy.

No Eye Deer (Eng) a 4% alc by vol. ale brewed by the Goose Eye Brewery Ltd., West Yorkshire.

Nog (Cktl) a filling drink based on eggs served hot or cold in a large bowl or individual mug.

Nogent-l'Abbesse (Fr) a Cru Champagne village in the Canton de Beine. District: Reims.

Nogg (Eng) the East Anglian nickname for strong beer produced locally.

Noggin [1] (Eng) a liquid measure equal to a gill of 5fl.ozs (125mls).

Noggin [2] (Eng) the old English term for a small mug (1gill/125mls capacity).

Noggin (Eng) a slang term for a drink (usually of beer). i.e. *"Would you like a noggin?"*.

Noggin Warming Winter Ale (Eng) a full-flavoured malt ale 5% alc by vol. brewed by the Charles Wells Brewery in Bedford, Bedfordshire.

Nogueira do Cravo (Port) a co-operative winery based in the Dão region.

No Heel Taps (Eng) *see* Heel Tap.

Noilly [Louis] (Fr) an inventor of the dry vermouth Noilly Prat around circa 1813.

Noilly Prat (Fr) a famous French vermouth made from 40 herbs. 17% alc by vol. (Add): 2BD Anatole de la Forge, Marseille (founded in circa 1813).

Noir de Pressac (Fr) the Pomerol name for the Malbec grape.

Noir Doux (Fr) an alternative name for the Malbec grape.

Noiren (Fr) an old spelling for the Noirien (Pinot noir).

Noirien (Fr) an alternative name for the Pinot noir grape in the Burgundy region. Also spelt Noiren.

Noirien Blanc (Fr) an alternative name for the Chardonnay grape.

Noirot [Michel] (Fr) a Champagne producer. (Add): Le Clos Saint-Rich, 10340 Lès Riceys.

Noirots [Les] (Fr) a Premier Cru vineyard in the A.C. commune of Chambolle-Musigny, Côte de Nuits, Burgundy 2.9ha.

Noisettia (Fr) a hazelnut liqueur produced by Berger under the Fournier label.

Noizai (Fr) a commune in Vouvray, Touraine district in the Loire.

Nolet (Hol) a small Schiedam company. Produces a Korenjenever called Proosje Van Schiedam.

Nollenköpfle (Ger) vineyard (Anb): Baden. (Ber): Ortenau. (Gro): Fürsteneck. (Vil): Gengenbach.

Nomentane (Gre) a variety of red grape grown in ancient Greece. Had red-tinged stems.

Nomentanum (It) a red wine produced in central western Italy in Roman times.

Nomimono (Jap) beverage/drink.

Nominal Volume (Euro) the bottle contents, amount is shown on label (E.C. regulation).

Nominé-Renard (Fr) a Champagne producer. (Add): 12, Rue Vigne'l'Abbesse, 51270 Villevenard. 20ha. Récoltants-manipulants. Produces vintage and non-vintage wines. Vintages: 1995, 1996, 1997, 1999. A member of the Club Tresors de Champagne. Labels: Cuvée 'Special Club' Millésimée (Chardonnay 70% and Pinot noir 30%). 'E'mail: nominee-renard@wanadoo.fr

Non-Alcoholic Egg Nogg (Cktl) 300mls (½ pint) milk, 1 egg, teaspoon castor sugar. Shake well over ice, strain into a large tumbler and top with grated nutmeg.

Nonaville (Fr) a commune in the Charente département whose grapes are used in Petite Champagne (Cognac).

Non-Combustible Matter (Eng) in vinification the ash residue (potassium, sodium, calcium, magnesium, iron, manganese, phosphorus, aluminium, iodine, sulphur and trace elements).

Non Dilué (Fr) undiluted. Also Pur.

Non Dosé (Fr) a term to denote a completely dry Champagne with only 3 grammes of sugar or less. Also known as Brut Nature and Dosage Zéro.

Nonee (Mal) a natural spring mineral water brand.

Nongfu Shanquan (Chi) a natural spring mineral water brand.

Nonic Glass (Eng) a straight 'sleeve' glass with an outward protruding rim near the lip.

Nonini Winery (USA) a winery based near Fresno City, California. 83ha. Grape varieties: Barbera, Grenache and Zinfandel. Produces varietal wines.

Nonnberg (Ger) vineyard (Anb): Rheingau. (Ber): Johannisberg. (Gro): Daubhaus. (Vil): Wicker.

Nonnenberg (Ger) vineyard (Anb): Baden. (Ber): Badische Frankenland. (Gro): Tauberklinge. (Vil): Beckstein.

Nonnenberg (Ger) vineyard (Anb): Baden. (Ber): Badische Frankenland. (Gro): Tauberklinge. (Vil): Lauda.

Nonnenberg (Ger) vineyard (Anb): Franken. (Ber): Steigerwald. (Gro): Kapellenberg. (Vil): Steinbach.

Nonnenberg (Ger) vineyard (Anb): Mosel-Saar-Ruwer. (Ber): Bernkastel. (Gro): Münzlay. (Vil): Wehlen.

Nonnenberg (Ger) vineyard (Anb): Rheingau. (Ber): Johannisberg. (Gro): Steinmacker. (Vil): Rauenthal.

Nonnenberg (Ger) vineyard (Anb): Württemberg. (Ber): Remstal-Stuttgart. (Gro): Wartbühl. (Vil): Strümpfelbach.

Nonnenberg (Ger) vineyard (Anb): Württemberg. (Ber): Württembergisch Unterland. (Gro): Kirchenweinberg. (Vil): Lauffen.

Nonnenberg (Ger) a vineyard within the village of Rauenthal, 5.7ha. (36.8%) of which is proposed to be classified as Erstes Gewächs.

Nonnengarten (Ger) vineyard (Anb): Mosel-Saar-Ruwer. (Ber): Bernkastel. (Gro): Vom Heissen Stein. (Vil): Breidel.

Nonnengarten (Ger) vineyard (Anb): Mosel-Saar-Ruwer. (Ber): Bernkastel. (Gro): Vom Heissen Stein. (Vil): Pünderich.

Nonnengarten (Ger) vineyard (Anb): Nahe. (Ber): Kreuznach. (Gro): Kronenberg. (Vil): Bad Kreuznach (ortsteil Planig).

Nonnengarten (Ger) vineyard (Anb): Nahe. (Ber): Schloss Böckelheim. (Gro): Burgweg. (Vil): Traisen.

Nonnengarten (Ger) vineyard (Anb): Rheinhessen. (Ber): Wonnegau. (Gro): Burg Rodenstein. (Vil): Mörstadt.

Nonnengarten (Ger) vineyard (Anb): Pfalz. (Ber): Mittelhaardt-Deutsche Weinstrasse. (Gro): Feuerberg. (Vil): Bad Dürkheim.

Nonnenhorn (Ger) village (Anb): Franken. (Ber): Bayer. Bodensee. (Gro): Lindauer Seegarten. (Vins): Seehalde, Sonnenbückel.

Nonnenrain (Ger) vineyard (Anb): Württemberg. (Ber): Württembergisch Unterland. (Gro): Salzberg. (Vil): Löwenstein.

Nonnenstück (Ger) vineyard (Anb): Pfalz. (Ber): Mittelhaardt-Deutsche Weinstrasse. (Gro): Hofstück. (Vil): Deidesheim.

Nonnenwingert (Ger) vineyard (Anb): Rheinhessen. (Ber): Wonnegau. (Gro): Liebfrauengarten. (Vil): Worms.

Non Plus Ultra (Sp) a dry-style sparkling (cava) wine produced by Cordorníu in San Sadurní de Noya, Penedés, the top cuvée of Cordorníu.

Non Plus Ultra (Sp) a solera gran reserva brandy produced by Sanchez Romate.

Non Plus Ultra (USA) a red wine (Cabernet sauvignon) produced by the Paoletti winery, Napa Valley, California.

Non-Returnable (Eng) on a container (bottle, can, etc.) denotes that no deposit on the container has been made and it is not needed for recycling (refilling).

Non-Vintage (Eng) a wine blended from wines made from grapes of more than one year, not of a single year. (Fr) = sans année.

Noon Gun (S.Afr) the label for a white wine (Sauvignon blanc based blend) produced by the Flagstone Winery, Somerset West, Western Cape.

Noon Winery (Austr) a winery (established 1973) based in McLaren Vale, also has vineyards in Langhorne Creek, South Australia. Produces full-bodied reds, rosés and Port-style wines. Grape varieties: Grenache, Shiraz, Cabernet.

Noppingerbräu (Aus) a beer range brewed by the Noppinger Brauerei.

Noppinger Brauerei (Aus) a brewery (established 1630) based in Oberndorf near Salzburg.

NORA (Eng) abbr: Northern Real Ale Agency.

Norachéne (Arm) a red grape variety grown in Armenia.

Norda (It) still or sparkling mineral water from Sorgente Daggio, Introbio.

Nordale Co-operative (S.Afr) a co-operative winery (established 1950) based in Robertson, Western Cape. 500ha. (Add): Box 105, Bonnievale 6730. Grape varieties: Cabernet sauvignon, Chardonnay, Chenin blanc, Merlot, Red muscadel, Ruby cabernet, Sauvignon blanc, Shiraz. Labels: Captain's Drift, Double Cabernet, Rocco Bay, Tabiso. Also produces varietal wines. Website: http://www.nordale.co.za

Nordexpress (Cktl) ⅓ measure rye whiskey, ⅓ measure Cinzano dry vermouth, ⅓ measure Cordial Médoc. Shake over ice and strain into a cocktail glass.

Nordhausen (Ger) village (Anb): Württemberg. (Ber): Württembergisch Unterland. (Gro): Heuchelberg. (Vin): Sonntagsberg.

Nordheim (Ger) village (Anb): Franken. (Ber): Maindreieck. (Gro): Kirchberg. (Vins): Kreuznach, Vögelein.

Nordheim (Ger) village (Anb): Württemberg. (Ber): Württembergisch Unterland. (Gro): Heuchelberg. (Vins): Grafenberg, Gräfenberg, Ruthe, Sonntagsberg.

Nordic Express (Cktl) 1 part Cordial Médoc, 1 part rye whiskey, 1 part dry vermouth. Stir well over ice and strain into a cocktail glass.

Nordoff (Ire) a brand of vodka 40% alc by vol. produced by the Irish Distillers Group.

Nord Water (Fin) a natural spring mineral water from Lake Päijänne. Mineral contents (milligrammes per litre): Sodium 6.2mg/l, Calcium 21mg/l, Magnesium 1.5mg/l, Bicarbonates 50mg/l, Chlorides 5.7mg/l, Fluorides 0.1mg/l, Nitrates 0.23mg/l. pH 8.5 Website: http://www.nordwater.fi

Nordweil (Ger) village (Anb): Baden. (Ber): Breisgau. (Gro): Burg Lichteneck. (Vin): Herrenberg.

Norfolk Cottage Brewing (Eng) a brewery. (Add): 22 The Green North Burlingham, Norwich, Norfolk NR13 3DJ. Brews: Norfolk Cottage Bitter 4% alc by vol., Setters Retreat 4% alc by vol.

Norfolk Dry (Eng) the brand-name of a dry cider produced by the Showerings C° (part of Allied-Domecq).

Norfolk Nip (Eng) a bottled beer first brewed in 1929 (production stopped in 1960's), now brewed by the Woodforde Brewery, Norwich 8.5% alc by vol (1080–1085 O.G).

Norfolk Nog (Eng) a 4.6% alc by vol. dark ale brewed by Woodeforde Brewery, Norfolk.

Norfolk Porter (Eng) a cask-conditioned ale 1041 O.G. brewed by the Woodforde Brewery in Norwich.

Norfolk Pride (Eng) a cask-conditioned bitter 1036 O.G. brewed by the Woodforde Brewery in Norwich.

Norfolk Punch (Eng) a drink made from honey, lemon, herbs, spices and well-water. Made at Welle Manor Hall, Upwell, Norfolk.

Norheim (Ger) village (Anb): Nahe. (Ber): Schloss Böckelheim. (Gro): Burgweg. (Vins): Dellchen, Götzenfels, Kafels, Kirschheck, Klosterberg, Oberberg, Onkelchen, Sonnenberg.

Noria (Sp) the name given to the large wheel in the malacate method of ploughing the vineyards in the Jerez region.

Normale (It) a non-riserva wine.

Normandie (S.Afr) a natural spring mineral water from Groot Drakenstein Mountains. Mineral contents (milligrammes per litre): Sodium 9.2mg/l, Calcium 1.6mg/l, Magnesium 0.6mg/l, Potassium 1.8mg/l, Bicarbonates 11mg/l, Chlorides 13mg/l, Sulphates 1mg/l, Fluorides <0.2mg/l, Nitrates 0.27mg/l. pH 5.9

Normandin-Mercier (Fr) a Cognac producer. (Add): Château de la Péraudière, 17139 Dompierre. S.M. Owns no vineyards. Produces a wide range of Cognacs.

Normandy Coffee (Liq.Coffee) using a measure of Calvados.

Normandy Golden Dawn Cocktail (Cktl) ¼ measure Calvados, ¼ measure apricot brandy, ¼ measure orange juice, dash grenadine. Shake over ice, strain into a cocktail glass and dress with a slice of orange.

Normandy Rose (Cktl) ¼ measure Calvados, ¼ measure Dubonnet, ¼ measure rye whiskey, ¼ measure apricot brandy. Shake over ice and strain into a cocktail glass.

Norman's (Austr) a winery at Grants Gully Road, Clarendon, South Australia. Grape varieties: Chenin blanc, Colombard, Sémillon, Shiraz. Produces Conquest (a sparkling wine).

Normans Conquest (Eng) a 5% alc by vol. (1066 O.G.) barley wine from Cottage Brewing C°., West Lydford, Somerset.

Norman's Conquest (Cktl) 1 measure brandy, 3 measures mead. Stir well together, strain into a goblet, add ice cube and a cherry.

Normans Pride (Eng) a 4.3% alc by vol. ale brewed by the Corvedale Brewery, Shropshire.

NORMAS (Mex) each distiller of tequila is assigned an official number by the Norma Oficial Mexicana.

Norseman Lager (Eng) a lager that used to be brewed by the Vaux Brewery in Sunderland (now no longer produced).

Norse Necta (Eng) a beer brewed by the Rudgate Brewery, Tockwith, North Yorkshire.

Norsingen (Ger) village (Anb): Baden. (Ber): Markgräflerland. (Gro): Lorettoberg. (Vin): Batzenberg.

Norte (Arg) a wine region that joins Jujvy and Salta.

Northamptonshire Bitter (Eng) a 4% alc by vol. ale brewed by Hoggleys, Northamptonshire.

Northamptonshire Bitter (Eng) a bitter beer brewed by the Litchborough Brewery in Northamptonshire.

North Brink Porter (Eng) a 5% alc by vol. porter brewed by Elgood & Sons Ltd., Cambridgeshire.

North British (Scot) a grain whisky distillery based near Edinburgh.

Northbrook Springs (Eng) a 6.25ha vineyard (established 1991) with Bacchus, Huxelrebe, Kerner, Reichensteiner, Schönburger.

North Carolina (USA) a small wine-producing state that produces wines made mainly from the Scuppernong grape.

North Coast Brewing C°. (USA) a brewery (established 1987) based in Fort Bragg, Mendocino County, California. Brews: Acme Pale Ale, Old N° 38 Stout, Red Seal Ale.

North Coast Counties (USA) refers to the counties of Mendocino, Napa and Sonoma.

North Cornwall Brewers (Eng) a small brewery based in Tintagel. North Cornwall. Brews: Legend and Brown Willy.

North Country Brewery (Eng) the former name of the Hull Brewery in Yorkshire. Was taken over by the Mansfield Brewery in 1985. Brews: cask-conditioned Riding Bitter 1038 O.G. and keg Anchor Export 1048 O.G. Hopfenperle Lager 1038 O.G. and Old Tradition Mild 1033 O.G.

North County (Eng) the brand-name for bitter and mild beers brewed in the Kings Arms (a pub), Brunswick, Manchester. *See also* West Coast Brewing Company.

Northdown (Eng) a full-flavoured variety of English hop used to brew ales.

Northdown (Eng) a cask-conditioned ale brewed using a single hop variety of same name by Ledbury Brewery Company, Herefordshire.

North Downs Spring Water (Eng) a natural spring mineral water from Silver Spring Source. Mineral contents (milligrammes per litre): Sodium 16mg/l, Calcium 103mg/l, Magnesium 3mg/l, Potassium 2mg/l, Bicarbonates 292mg/l, Chlorides 26mg/l, Sulphates 20mg/l, Nitrates 21mg/l. pH 7.5

North Eastern Bitter (Eng) a keg bitter 1032 O.G. brewed by the Bass Brewery in the north-east of England.

Northeast Vineyards (USA) a winery based in the Hudson Valley, New York. Noted for hybrid wines.

Northern Brewer (Eng) an intensely flavoured and bitter hop variety.

Northern Brewing (Eng) a brewery (established 2004). (Add): 1 Cormorant Centre, Cormorant Drive, Runcorn, Cheshire WA7 4NQ. Brews: All Nigter 3.8% alc by vol., Dancer 4.2% alc by vol., Northern 45 4.5% alc by vol., Northern Star 4.3% alc by vol., Spell Binder 4.1% alc by vol. Website: http://www.norbrew.co.uk 'E'mail: sales@norbrew.com

Northern Clubs' Federation Brewery (Eng) *see* Federation Brewery.

Northern Counties (Eng) labelling designation for English wine. Now replaced by English Vineyards, Welsh Vineyards.

Northern Crystal (Can) a natural spring mineral water from Piedmont, Quebec. Mineral contents (milligrammes per litre): Sodium 13mg/l, Calcium 20mg/l, Magnesium 7mg/l, Potassium 1mg/l, Bicarbonates 46mg/l, Chlorides 44mg/l, Sulphates 13mg/l, Fluorides 0.4mg/l, Nitrates 1mg/l. pH 7.3

Northerner Ale (Eng) a bottled dark ale 1033 O.G. brewed by the Timothy Taylor Brewery in Keithley, Yorkshire.

Northern Light (Scot) a 4% alc by vol. light ale brewed by The Orkney Brewery Ltd., Orkney.

N

Northern Lights (Cktl) 2 parts Glayva, 1 part orange juice, 1 part lemon juice. Build into a slim jim glass (Glayva, lemon juice and ice), add orange juice and top with soda water.

Northern Pride (Eng) a 4.2% alc by vol. cask ale brewed by the Hull Brewery.

Northern Real Ale Agency (Eng) formed in 1969 as a wholesaler and off-licence to supply polypins and firkins of cask-conditioned ales. *abbr:* NORA.

Northern Region (Bul) has the key D.G.O. regions of Russe, Suhindol, Svischtov. Grapes are predominantly Cabernet sauvignon.

Northern Source (Can) a natural spring mineral water. Mineral contents (milligrammes per litre): Sodium 5.1mg/l, Calcium 75mg/l, Magnesium 19mg/l, Potassium 1.1mg/l, Bicarbonates 202mg/l, Chlorides 9.4mg/l.

Northgate Bitter (Eng) a keg bitter 1036 O.G. brewed by the Wadworth Brewery in Wiltshire.

Northland (N.Z) a vine growing area on the north-west coast of the North Island.

Northminster Winery (USA) a winery based in Wilmington, Delaware. Produces hybrid wines.

North Para (Austr) a winery based near Seppeltsfield, Barossa Valley, South Australia. Produces varietal wines.

North Pole Cocktail (Cktl) ½ measure dry gin, ¼ measure lemon juice, ¼ measure maraschino, 1 egg white. Shake over ice, strain into a cocktail glass and top with whipped, sweetened cream.

North Port (Scot) a single malt whisky distillery in Brechin, Angus-shire. Owned by James Munro and Sons Ltd. (a highland malt). Produces a 15 year old malt 45% alc by vol.

North Queensland (Austr) *see* N.Q.

North Region (Arg) wine-producing region. Has the sub-regions of: Salta, Tucumán and Catamarca.

North Salem Vineyards (USA) a winery based in North Salem, Hudson Valley, New York. Produces hybrid wines.

North Star (Eng) a keg bitter 1036 O.G. brewed by the Arkell Brewery in Swindon, Wiltshire.

North Star (Eng) a 3.6% alc by vol. ale brewed by the Spectrum Brewery, Norfolk.

Northstar Winery (USA) a winery based near Walla Walla Valley, Washington. Grape variety: Merlot.

Northumberland Best Bitter (Eng) a 4.5% alc by vol. bitter brewed by the Northumberland Brewery, Ashington.

Northumberland Brewery (Eng) a brewery. (Add): On Earth Balance, Bomarsund, Bedlington, Northumberland NE22 7AD. Brews: Northumberland Best Bitter 4.5% alc by vol., Northumberland Castles Bitter 3.7% alc by vol., Duke of Northumberland 5% alc by vol. Website: http://www.northumberlandbrewery.co.uk 'E'mail: dave@northumberlandbrewery.co.uk

Northumberland Castles Bitter (Eng) a 3.7% alc by vol. bitter brewed by the Northumberland Brewery, Ashington.

Northumbrian Spring (Eng) a natural spring mineral water from Broken Scar, Darlington.

North Western Wine Merchant's Wines (S.Afr) the name for the Olifantsriver Co-operative.

North Yorkshire Brewery C° **[The]** (Eng) a brewery. (Add): Pinchinthorpe Hall, Pinchinthorpe, Guisborough, Cleveland TS14 8HG. Brews Xmas Herbert, a seasonal Ale. Website: http://www.pinchinthorpehall.co.uk 'E'mail: nyb@pinchinthorpehall.freeserve.co.uk

Norton (Sp) the brand-name for a sparkling wine produced by the Bodegas Norton.

Norton (USA) a black grape variety that is little used now, also known as Cynthiana.

Norton Ale (Eng) a 3.5% alc by vol. ale brewed by the Shoes Brewery, Herefordshire.

Norton Wines (S.Afr) a winery (established 2002) based in Stellenbosch, Western Cape. Grape varieties: Merlot.

Norwater (Nor) a natural spring mineral water from Imsdalen. Mineral contents (milligrammes per litre): Sodium 1mg/l, Calcium 12mg/l, Bicarbonates 37mg/l, Sulphates mg/l. pH 7.0

Norwegian Blue (Eng) a 4.9% alc by vol. ale brewed by the Buffy's Brewery, Norfolk.

Norwegian Fizz (Cktl) 1 measure kümmel, 1 measure cream, dash lemon juice, dash egg white. Shake well over ice, strain into an ice-filled highball glass and top with sparkling wine.

Norwegian Gin (Nor) a strong-flavoured dry gin.

Norwegian Punch (Nor) a sweet liqueur with a batavian arrack base. Produced by A/S Vinmonopolet 27% alc by vol.

Norwegian Spring Water (Nor) a natural spring mineral water. Mineral contents (milligrammes per litre): Sodium 2.2mg/l, Calcium 60mg/l, Magnesium 3.8mg/l, Potassium 4.3mg/l, Chlorides 2.3mg/l, Sulphates 36.2mg/l, Fluorides <0.1mg/l, Nitrates 0.2mg/l. pH 7.8

Norwich Brewery (Eng) a Watney's brewery which has now closed down. Beers are now brewed in London and Manchester. Anchor Bitter 1034 O.G. Anglian Strong Ale 1048 O.G. Bullards Old Ale 1057 O.G. Norwich Bitter 1034 O.G. and cask-conditioned S & P Bitter 1038 O.G.

Norwich Terrier (Eng) a 3.6% alc by vol. ale brewed by the Buffy's Brewery, Norfolk.

Nose (Eng) the bouquet or aroma of a wine or spirit.

Nose [The] (Sp) the nickname of Don José Ignacio Domecq, a top Sherry maker. *see* Domecq.

Nosing Glass (Eng) a balloon glass usually used for the drinking of brandy in U.K. and USA. In France used for testing the bouquet of young wines whilst maturing.

Nosiola (It) a white grape variety grown in the Trentino-Alto-Adige.

Nosovice Brewery (Czec) a large modern brewery based in eastern Czec.

Nostalgie (Fr) the prestige label of Champagne Beaumont des Crayères.

Notios (Gre) a winery based in the Peloponnese. Grape varieties include: Agiorgitiko, Moshofilero, Rhoditis. Label: Gaia Estate.

Nostrano (Switz) a smooth, fruity red wine from the Ticino region.

Notables [The] (Ger) a name for the members of the International Beer Convention.

Notar Domenico (It) a red grape variety grown in the Puglia region.

Notiose (Gre) a red wine produced by Yannis Paraskevopolous at the Gaia Winery, Nemea from Aghiorgitiko grapes.

Notley Ale (Eng) a 3.3% alc by vol. ale brewed by the Vale Brewery, Haddenham, Buckinghamshire.

Noto (It) a Muscat wine from Sicily.

Notre-Dame du Raisin (Fr) lit: 'our lady of the grape', a religious shrine built in the nineteenth century on the Mont de Brouilly in the hope of ridding the Beaujolais region of Oïdium.

Nottage Hill Claret (Austr) a red wine produced by the Old Mill Winery in South Australia.

Nottingham Brewery (Eng) a brewery (established 2000). (Add): 17 St. Peters Street, Radford, Nottingham, Nottinghamshire NG7 3EN. Brews: Bullion 4.7% alc by vol., Cock & Hoop 4.3% alc by vol., Dreadnought 4.5% alc by vol., Extra Pale Ale 4.2% alc by vol., Legend 4% alc by vol., Nottingham Supreme 5.2% alc by vol., Rock Bitter 3.8% alc by vol., Rock Mild 3.8% alc by vol., Sooty Oatmeal Stout 4.8% alc by vol. Website: http://www.nottinghambrewery.com 'E'mail: philipdarby@nottinghambrewery.com

Nottingham Dark Stout (Eng) a 4.5% alc by vol. stout brewed by the Castle Rock Brewery, Nottinghamshire.

Nottingham Gold (Eng) a 3.5% alc by vol. golden ale brewed by the Castle Rock Brewery, Nottinghamshire.

Nottingham Pale Ale (Eng) abbr: N.P.A. 3.6% alc by vol. ale brewed by Castle Rock Brewery, Nottinghamshire.

Not Tonight (Cktl) ½ measure Bacardi White Label, ⅙ measure blue Curaçao, ⅙ measure Mandarine Napoléon, ⅙ measure crème de banane. Stir over ice, strain into a cocktail glass, top with a cherry and banana slice.

Not Tonight Josephine (Cktl) 1 measure Mandarine Napoléon, 4 drops Malibu coconut liqueur, 4 drops cherry brandy, juice of an orange. Shake with ice and strain into a highball glass filled with ice.

Nouaison (Fr) lit: 'fruit set', denotes when the fruit forms just after the vine has flowered.

Nourishing Stout (Eng) a bottled stout 1034 O.G. brewed by the Gales brewery in Horndean, Hampshire.

Nourishing Stout (Eng) a bottled stout 1050 O.G. brewed by the Samuel Smith brewery in Tadcaster, Yorkshire.

Nourish Pure Distilled Water (Chi) a bottled water brand.

Nouveau [Le] (Fr) the French equivalent (Alsace) of Federweisser (a drink of still-fermenting wine).

Nouveau Rouge (S.Afr) a copy of the Beaujolais Nouveau first started by the SFW in 1982.

Nouvelle (S.Afr) a white grape cross (Sémillon x Crouchen).

Nouvelle de Lutèce (Fr) a brewery based at Bonneuil, Paris. Brews: Lutèce (a bière de garde).

Nouvelle Église [La] (Fr) the label of a Châteauneuf-du-Pape produced by the négociant Coste at St.-Felix-de-Lodez.

Nouvel Ordre Hospitalier (Fr) a wine society based in Paris.

Nova Fonte di Crodo (It) a sparkling natural spring mineral water from Sorgente Cesa, Crodo, Verbania. Mineral contents (milligrammes per litre): Sodium 5.3mg/l, Calcium 31.5mg/l, Magnesium 4.7mg/l, Potassium 5.5mg/l, Bicarbonates 113mg/l, Chlorides 2.1mg/l, Sulphates 14.3mg/l, Fluorides 0.1mg/l, Nitrates 7.3mg/l, Silicates 13.8mg/l. pH 7.6

Nova Friburgo (Bra) an acidic natural spring mineral water from Rio Bonito de Lumiar, Nova Friburgo. Mineral contents (milligrammes per litre): Sodium 1.89mg/l, Calcium 0.81mg/l, Magnesium 0.56mg/l, Potassium 1.07mg/l, Bicarbonates 7.05mg/l, Chlorides 1.55mg/l, Sulphates 0.3mg/l, Fluorides 0.01mg/l, Nitrates 1.9mg/l. pH 5.04 Website: http://www.aguanovafriburgo.com.br

Nova Friburgo Plus (Bra) an acidic natural spring mineral water from Rio Bonito de Lumiar, Nova Friburgo. Mineral contents (milligrammes per litre): Sodium 1.88mg/l, Calcium 0.61mg/l, Magnesium 0.29mg/l, Potassium 0.7mg/l, Bicarbonates 2.95mg/l, Chlorides 1.64mg/l, Sulphates 0.4mg/l, Nitrates 3.2mg/l. pH 4.8 Website: http://www.aguanovafriburgo.com.br

Noval (Port) see Quinta do Noval.

Novalja (Euro) a red wine produced on the island of Pag off the north-west Dalmatian coast.

Novà Paka Brewery (Czec) a brewery based in northern Czec.

Nova Schin (Bra) a 4.7% alc by vol. bottled lager beer brewed by the Schincariol Brewery.

Nova Scotia (Can) a small wine region.

November Fifteenth (Fr) the old date for the release of Beaujolais Nouveau (since 1985 changed to the third Thursday in November).

Novi Pazar (Bul) a State winery that produces a noted Chardonnay white wine.

Novi Sad (Ser) a wine-producing area in the north-east. Produces mainly white wines.

Novitiate Winery (USA) a winery based in Los Gatos, California. Grape varieties: Cabernet sauvignon, Chenin blanc, Johannisberg riesling, Petite sirah and Pinot blanc. Owned by Jesuit monks, produces Altar wines 18% alc by vol. see L'Admirable and Vin Doré.

Novocherkassk (Rus) a wine-producing centre in the River Don area. Produces mainly white wines.

Novo Cocktail (Cktl) 1 measure Strega, 1 egg yolk, dash lime juice. Shake over ice, strain into a flute glass, top with lemonade and a cherry and serve with straws.

Novo Mundo (Port) a Dão wine produced by the Caves Acàcio.

Novo Selo (Bul) a delimited wine-producing area

based in the northern region of Bulgaria. Main grape varieties: Gamza and Pinot noir.

Noyau (Fr) a pale pinkish-yellow liqueur made from peach and apricot kernels 30% alc by vol. *See also* Crème de Noyau.

Noyau Rose (Cktl) *see* Cocktail Mixer.

Noyaux (Fr) a liqueur produced from a selection of nuts and fruit kernels.

Noyeau (Fr) *see* Crème de Noyeau.

Nozze d'Oro (It) a white wine produced by Regaleali winery from Inzolio and Tasca grapes in Sicily.

Nozzole (It) an estate in the Chianti Classico region.

N.P.A. (Eng) *abbr:* Nottingham Pale Ale.

N.P.U. Amontillado (Sp) a very dry, unblended solera Amontillado Sherry produced by Romate.

N.Q. (Austr) *abbr:* North Queensland, a lager beer brewed by the CUB Brewery.

N.R.B. (Eng) *abbr:* Non-Returnable Bottles. Found on a wine and beer merchants' list, denotes that these bottles cannot be returned for a credit.

nt (Eng) dt plus vodka. 5.5% alc by vol. stimulating drink containing vodka, taurine, caffeine, ginseng and vitamins from Virgin. Available in 3 versions: blue: mixed fruits, green: ice lemon, purple: sea breeze (cranberry and grapefruit). Also produce a non-alcoholic version. *see* dt.

Nu (Fr) bare, the cost of wine without its overheads (cask, bottles etc.).

Nuance (Eng) describes a wine as having a specific smell. i.e. of almonds or flint.

Nuance (S.Afr) the label for a white wine (Muscadel and Crouchen blend) produced by the Seidelberg Estate, Paarl, Western Cape.

Nube (Fr) cloudiness.

Nubia (Egy) a natural spring mineral water brand.

Nubian Gin (Afr) an east African illegally distilled spirit. Is similar to the USA 'Moonshine'.

Nuchter (Hol) sober.

Nuclear Brown Ale (Eng) a cask beer from the Hull brewery, Kingston-Upon-Hull.

Nudes (USA) the name (in 1983) for cans of beer that had pictures of near naked women on the sides. The clothes can be removed by rubbing with a coin which reveals the lady naked underneath. Were also called Nudies.

Nudies (USA) *see* Nudes.

Nuestra Señora de la Paz (Sp) a natural spring mineral water from El Ecijano, Marmolejo, Jaén.

Nuestro Padre Jesus del Perdon (Sp) a co-operative winery based in La Mancha. Labels include Lazarillo and Yuntero.

Nugget Golden Lager (N.Z) a 5% alc by vol. full-bodied, premium, bottled lager brewed by Monteith's Brewing Company (DB), Greymouth.

Nuit d'Or (Fr) brand label of Champagne Beaumont des Crayères.

Nuits-Saint-Georges (Fr) an A.C. commune in the Côte de Nuits, Burgundy. Although it has no Grand Crus it has 39 Premier Cru vineyards including those of the village of Premeaux. Vineyards: Nuits-Saint-Georges, Aux Argillats, Aux Boudots, Aux Bousselots, Aux Chaignots, Aux Champs-Perdrix, Aux Cras, Aux Crots, Aux Damodes, Aux Murgers, Aux Thorey, Aux Vignerondes, En la Chaine-Carteau, En la Perrière-Noblet, La Richemone, La Roncière, La Perrière, Les Argillats, Les Cailles, Les Chaboeufs, Les Hauts-Pruliers, Les Pourrets, Les Poulettes, Les Procès, Les Pruliers, Les Saint-Georges, Les Valleros, Les Vaucrains, Rue-de-Chaux. 129.5ha. Premeaux: Aux Perdrix, Clos de la Maréchale, Clos des Argillières, Clos des Arlots, Clos des Corvées, Clos des Forêts, Clos des Grandes-Vignes, Les Clos Saint-Marc, Les Corvées-Paget, Les Didiers. 40.3ha.

N.U.L.V. (Eng) *abbr:* National Union of Licensed Vituallers, the union for public house licensees.

Numancia (Sp) the brand-name for a brandy produced by Pemartin in Jerez.

Numbered Bottles (Eng) used extensively in Italy but also in many other countries which is used for various reasons. e.g. to tell which cask a particular wine came from, when bottled, amount bottled etc.

Number Eight (Can) a blended Canadian rye whisky produced by Gilbey Canada Ltd. 40% alc by vol.

Number 15 Ale (Eng) a limited edition (2006) 3.5% alc by vol. bottled ale brewed by J W Lees of Manchester in honour of Nemanja Vidic (a Manchester United Football team player who's squad number is 15).

Number Nine [N°9] (Eng) a cask-conditioned bitter 1043 O.G. brewed by the Bodicote brewery in Oxon.

Number Nine [N°9] (Eng) a 4.2% alc by vol. nitrokeg bitter brewed by Wolverhampton & Dudley.

Number One [N°1] (Eng) a keg/bottled pale ale 1036 O.G. brewed by the McMullen Brewery in Hertford.

Number One [N°1] (I.O.M) a barley wine 1070 O.G. brewed by the Okell Brewery in Douglas.

Number One [N°1] (Eng) a 4% alc by vol (1039 O.G) naturally conditioned bottled ale brewed by the Selby (Middlesborough) Brewery Ltd., North Yorkshire.

Number One [N°1] Consitution Road (S.Afr) the label for a red wine (Shiraz) produced by the Robertson Co-operative Winery, Robertson, Western Cape.

Number One Distilling Company (USA) a distillery belonging to the Schenley Distillers C°.

Number 7 (Eng) a 4.2% alc by vol. beer brewed by the Bristol Beer Factory, Avon.

Number 7 (Eng) a 6% alc by vol. cider produced by Bulmers of Hereford. Part of their Heritage range.

Number Three [N°3] (Eng) a 4% alc by vol. ale brewed by the Selby (Middlesborough) Brewery Ltd., North Yorkshire.

Number Three [N°3] (Eng) a 4.5% alc by vol. ruby coloured ale brewed by Younger's (William).

Number Three [N°3] (Scot) a cask-conditioned ale 1043 O.G. brewed by the Youngers brewery in Edinburgh.

Nuova Augusta (It) a natural spring mineral water from Fornace.

Nuova Cutolo Rionero (It) a natural spring mineral water from Nuova Cutolo Rionero.

Nuova Dolomiti (It) a natural spring mineral water from Dolomiti 2.

Nuova Gareisa (It) a sparkling natural spring mineral water from Nuova Gareisa, Cueno. Mineral contents (milligrammes per litre): Sodium 12mg/l, Calcium 32mg/l, Magnesium 3mg/l, Potassium 2mg/l, Bicarbonates 106mg/l, Chlorides 1.9mg/l, Sulphates 18mg/l, Nitrates 5.1mg/l, Silicates 24.5mg/l, Oxygen 9.5mg/l. pH 7.3

Nuova Santa Vittoria (It) a natural spring mineral water from Fontana Fredda.

Nuova Traficante (It) a natural spring mineral water from Nuova Traficante.

Nuptu Ale (Eng) a 4.2% alc by vol. ale brewed by the Oakleaf brewing C°. Ltd., Hampshire.

Nuragus (It) a white grape variety grown in Sardinia. Produces the oldest wine in Sardinia (Campidano district). Also known as Campidano bianco.

Nuragus (It) an alternative name for the white wine Campidano bianco in Sardinia.

Nuragus di Cagliari (It) a D.O.C. white wine from Sardinia. Made from the Nuragus, Clairette, Semidano, Trebbiano romagnolo, Trebbiano toscano and Vermentino grapes. Area of production is entire province of Cagliari plus other communes.

Nürburgquelle (Ger) a sparkling natural spring mineral water from Dreis, Vulkaneiffel. Mineral contents (milligrammes per litre): Sodium 365mg/l, Calcium 232mg/l, Magnesium 337mg/l, Potassium 43.5mg/l, Bicarbonates 3388mg/l, Chlorides 20.7mg/l, Sulphates 22.8mg/l, Fluorides 0.31mg/l, Ammonium 3.4mg/l.

Nuriootpa (Austr) a wine-producing area in the Barossa Valley, South Australia.

Nuriootpa Winery (Austr) a winery based in Nuriootpa, Barossa Valley, South Australia. Produces varietal wines.

Nürnberger Altstadthof (Ger) a brewery. (Add): Bergstrasse 19-21, Nürnberg D-90403. Brews beers and lagers. Website: http://www.altstadthof.de 'E'mail: info@altstadthof.de

Nursery Brewery (Eng) a new brewery (established 2001) based in Keynsham, near Bristol. Brews: Georgie Porgie 3.7% alc by vol. Three Blind Mice 4.2% alc by vol. Hey Diddle Diddle 4.7% alc by vol. Old Mother Hubbard 5.2% alc by vol. Oat King Cole 6% alc by vol.

Nursery Vineyard (Austr) part of the Lindemans winery in New South Wales. 35ha. Grape variety: Rhine riesling.

Nursing (Eng) the careful care and attention lavished on some wines during their production and maturation. e.g. clarets.

Nussbach (Ger) village (Anb): Baden. (Ber): Ortenau. (Gro): Fürsteneck. (Vin): Renchtäler.

Nussbaum (Ger) village (Anb): Nahe. (Ber): Schloss Böckelheim. (Gro): Paradiesgarten. (Vins): Höllenberg, Rotfeld, Sonnenberg.

Nussbaum (Lux) a vineyard site in the village of Wormeldange.

Nussberg (Aus) a noted vineyard area in the Wien region.

Nussberg (Ger) vineyard (Anb): Mosel-Saar-Ruwer. (Ber): Zell/Mosel. (Gro): Schwarze Katz. (Vil): Zell.

Nussbien (Ger) vineyard (Anb): Pfalz. (Ber): Mittelhaardt-Deutsche Weinstrasse. (Gro): Hofstück. (Vil): Ruppertsberg.

Nussbrunnen (Ger) vineyard (Anb): Rheingau. (Ber): Johannisberg. (Gro): Deutelsberg. (Vil): Hattenheim.

Nussbrunnen (Ger) a vineyard (10.8ha) within the village of Hattenheim, (100%) of which is proposed to be classified as Erstes Gewächs.

Nussdorf (Aus) a famous white wine from Vienna.

Nussdorf (Ger) village (Anb): Pfalz. (Ber): Südliche Weinstrasse. (Gro): Bischofskreuz. (Vins): Herrenberg, Kaiserberg, Kirchenstück.

Nussloch (Ger) village (Anb): Baden. (Ber): Badische Bergstrasse/Kraichgau. (Gro): Mannaberg. (Vin): Wilhelmsberg.

Nussriegel (Ger) vineyard (Anb): Pfalz. (Ber): Mittelhaardt-Deutsche Weinstrasse. (Gro): Honigsäckel. (Vil): Ungstein.

Nutbourne Manor (Eng) a vineyard based in Sussex.

Nut Brown (Eng) a name often used by brewers for bottled brown ales.

Nut Brown Ale (Eng) a 5% alc by vol. bottled ale brewed by the Samuel Smith Brewery in Tadcaster, Yorkshire.

Nutcracker (Eng) a cask-conditioned ale 1036 O.G. brewed by the Cotleigh Brewery in Somerset.

Nutcracker (Eng) a 5% alc by vol. draught traditional winter ale with a reddish hue and fruity character. Brewed by Everards in Leicester.

Nutcracker (Eng) a 6% alc by vol. strong ale brewed by Hanby Ales Ltd., Shropshire.

Nuthouse (USA) the label for a white (Chardonnay) wine produced by the Argle winery, Dundee Hills, Oregon.

Nutty (Eng) usually applied to Sherries to describe a flavour which is reminiscent of walnuts and hazel nuts.

Nuwara Eliya (Sri.L) a tea producing region in the high region. Teas of the same name have a light, delicate flavour.

Nuwehoop Co-operative (S.Afr) a co-operative winery based in Goudini. (Add): Nuwehoop Wynkelder, Box 100, Rawsonville 6845. Produces Laatoes and varietal wines.

Nuwehoop Wynkelder (S.Afr) *see* Nuwehoop Co-operative.

Nuy Wynkelder Koöperatiewe (S.Afr) a co-operative (established 1963) winery based in Nuy, Worcester, Western Cape. (Add): Bpk., P.O. Nuy 6700. Grape varieties: Cabernet sauvignon, Chardonnay, Chenin blanc, Colombard, Fernão pires, Hanepoot, Muscadel, Red muscadel, Sauvignon blanc. Labels: Chant de Nuy, Rouge de Nuy and varietal wines.

N.V.V.A. (USA) *abbr:* Napa Valley Vintners Association.

Nycteri (Gre) a white wine, high in alcohol from Thira Isle in the Cyclades Isles in Southern Greece. From the Assyrtiko grape.

Nyetimber Vineyard (Eng) a noted sparkling wine vineyard (established 1994) based at Ridgeway Vineyard, Gay Street, Pulborough, West Chiltington, West Sussex. Produces a vintage traditional method sparkling wine from Chardonnay, Pinot meunier and Pinot noir grapes under the Merret Bloomsbury label. Has recently been sold (2006) and is due to be expanded. Website: http://www.ridgeview.co.uk

Nyköpings Brannvin (Den) the brand-name of an akvavit flavoured with aniseed, caraway, fennel and other herbs.

Nylon Powder (USA) used for fining wines.

Nymburk Brewery (Czec) a brewery based in north-western Czec. Is noted for lager-style beers.

Nyon (Switz) a wine-producing area of the Vaud Canton. Produces mainly light red wines from the Gamay grape.

Nyuu (Jap) milk. Also spelt Gyuu.

NZNatural (N.Z) a natural spring mineral water from Kaiapoi. Mineral contents (milligrammes per litre): Sodium 12.5mg/l, Potassium 1mg/l, Chlorides 6.5mg/l.

O (N.Z) a white wine produced from the Chardonnay grape by Montana Wines in the Ormond sub-region.

Oak (Eng) *Quercus* the best wood for making and maturing wines. American, Argonne, Dalmatian, Limousin, Memel, Monlezun and Tronçais are considered to be the best. Methyloctolactone is the chemical precusor of the water-soluble vanillin that percolates out into the wine. The oak with the highest level of methyloctolactone is *Quercus alba* (American), followed by *Quercus petraea* (Sessile). *Quercus robur* (English common oak) is the main material used for French barrels. (Fr) = chêne, (Ger) = eiche, (Hol) = eik, (It) = quercia, (Lat) = quercus, (Port) = carvalho, (Sp) = roble, (Tur) = mese, (Wal) = derwen.

Oak (Eng) a 4% alc by vol. ale brewed by the Bowland Beer Company Ltd., Lancashire.

Oak-Aged Ale (Scot) a 6.6% alc by vol. ale brewed then matured for 77 days (30 days in lightly toasted American oak casks) by the Innis & Gunn brewery. The casks are then used by William Grant & Sons to mature their Ale Cask Reserve Scotch Whisky.

Oak Barrel Winery (USA) a winery based in Berkley, Alameda, California. Grape varieties: Cabernet sauvignon, Chardonnay, Muscat and Zinfandel. Produces varietal wines.

Oak Cask Chardonnay (Austr) a fruity white wine from the Wyndham estate in New South Wales.

Oak Cheshire (Eng) a brewery (established 1982) in Ellesmere Port, Cheshire. Noted for cask-conditioned Old Oak 1044 O.G. and Double Dagger 1050 O.G.

Oak Chips (Eng) a practice of adding oak chips to wines (usually red) to give a 'cask mature' flavour although wines are in stainless steel vats. Used in Australia, USA, etc. and is banned in many E.C. countries.

Oak Extract (Eng) methyloctolactone added to wines in New World wine-producing countries to give wines an 'oak' flavour.

Oakham Ales (Eng) a brewery (established 1995). (Add): 80 Westgate, Peterborough, Cambridgeshire PE1 2AA. Brews: Bishops Farewell 4.6% alc by vol., JHB 3.8% alc by vol., White Dwarf 4.3% alc by vol. Website: http://www.oakham-ales.co.uk 'E'mail: oakhamales@aol.com

Oakhill Brewery (Eng) a brewery (established 1984), originally opened as the Beacon Brewery in 1981 in Bath. (Add): The Old Maltings, Oakhill, Bath, Avon BA3 5BX. Brews: cask-conditioned Farmer's Ale 1038 O.G. and Oakhill Stout 1045 O.G. Website: http://www.oakhillbrewery.co.uk 'E'mail: gary@oakhillbrewery.co.uk

Oakhill Stout (Eng) a bottled stout 1045 O.G. brewed by the Oakhill Brewery in Bath.

Oak Knoll (USA) a wine district of the Napa Valley, California.

Oak Knoll Winery (USA) a winery based in Hillsboro, Willamette Valley, Oregon. Produces varietal, fruit and berry wines. *see* Frambrosia. Grape varieties include: Chardonnay, Pinot gris, Pinot noir, Riesling.

Oaklands Wine Exporters (S.Afr) a negociant company (established 2002) based in the Western Cape that exports to many countries. Labels include: Boschenmeer, Deza Collection, Ukusa. Website: http://www.deza.co.za

Oakleaf Brewing C° Ltd (Eng) a brewery (established 2000). (Add): Unit 7, Mumby Road, Clarence Wharf Ind Estate, Gosport, Hampshire PO12 1AJ. Brews: Blake's Gosport Bitter 5.2% alc by vol., Blake's Heaven 7% alc by vol., Farmhouse Ale 3.5% alc by vol., Green Gold 4.3% alc by vol., Heart of Oak 4.5% alc by vol., Hole Hearted 4.7% alc by vol., India Pale Ale 5.5% alc by vol., It's Not Bitter 4.9% alc by vol., Maypole Mild 3.8% alc by vol., Nuptu Ale 4.2% alc by vol., Oakleaf Bitter 3.8% alc by vol., Piston Porter 4.6% alc by vol., Reindeer's Delight 4.5% alc by vol., Stokers Stout 5% alc by vol. Website: http://www.oakleafbrewing.co.uk 'E'mail: info@oakleafbrewing.co.uk

Oakleigh Burgundy (N.Z) a slightly sweet, red wine produced by the Ormond Vineyards.

Oakley Pale Ale (Eng) a 3.8% alc by vol. pale ale brewed by The Moorcock Brewing C°., Cumbria.

Oakridge Estate (Austr) a winery (established 1978) based at Aitken Road, Seville, Yarra Valley. Grape varieties: Cabernet franc, Cabernet sauvignon.

Oak Staves (Austr) a cheaper form of adding oak flavour to wines than using oak casks. The staves are hung in the wine in stainless steel vats until the right degree of flavour is achieved before removing.

Oakvale Winery (Austr) a winery based at Braye Road, Pokolbin, New South Wales. Grape varieties: Chardonnay, Sémillon, Shiraz. Part of the Elliot Vineyards.

Oak Valley Wines (S.Afr) a winery (established 1898)

based in Elgin, Walker Bay, Western Cape. 35ha. Grape varieties: Cabernet franc, Cabernet sauvignon, Chardonnay, Merlot, Pinot noir, Sauvignon blanc. Website: http://www.oakvalleywines.com

Oakview Plantations (USA) a large (148ha) winery based in Woodruff, South Carolina. Grape varieties: Catawba, Concord and Muscadine.

Oak Village (S.Afr) the name given to a range of varietal wines from Stellenbosch that include Cabernet sauvignon, Chardonnay, Chenin blanc, Pinotage, Sauvignon blanc.

Oakville (USA) an Approved Viticultural Area between Yountville and Rutherford, Napa Valley, California. *See also* Rutherford.

Oakville Ranch (USA) a winery based in the Oakville, Napa Valley, California. Grape varieties: Cabernet sauvignon.

Oakville Vineyards (USA) a label used by the Robert Mondavi Winery for varietal and non-vintage wines. Was once the name of a winery.

Oakwell Brewery (Eng) a brewery (established 1997). (Add): Pontefract Road, Barnsley, South Yorkshire S71 1HS. Brews: Oakwell Bitter 3.8% alc by vol. Acorn Lager 3.8% alc by vol. Old Tom 3.4% alc by vol.

Oakwood Draught Cider (Eng) a cider produced by Sheppy's of Bradford-on-Tone, Somerset.

Oaky (Eng) a taste in wine, obtained from wines stored in new oak casks.

Oasis (Afr) a natural spring mineral water brand from Omaruru, Namibia.

Oasis (Eng) the name for a range of sparkling water and fruit drinks available in three flavours from the CCSB.

Oasis (USA) a natural spring mineral water (established 1946).

Oast House (Eng) a kiln where the malted barley is heated to arrest germination.

Oat King Cole (Eng) a 6% alc by vol. oatmeal porter brewed by the Nursery Brewery, Keynsham, near Bristol.

Oatley Vineyard (Eng) a vineyard based at Oatley, Cannington, Bridgwater, Somerset. Produces white wines.

Oatmeal Ale (Eng) a 5% alc by vol. ale brewed by McMullens, Hertfordshire for the American market. Sold in 500mls bottles.

Oatmeal Stout (Eng) a beer which is made from malted oats as well as malted barley.

Oatmeal Stout (Eng) a cask stout brewed by Jennings at Castle Brewery, Cockermouth, Cumbria.

Oatmeal Stout (Wal) a 4.4% alc by vol. stout brewed by Granny's, Aberystwyth.

Oatmeal Stout (Eng) a 4.5% seasonal (March) stout produced by King & Barnes, Horsham, West Sussex.

Oatmeal Stout (Eng) a 5% alc by vol. bottled stout brewed by Samuel Smith in Tadcaster.

Oatmeal Stout (Eng) a 4.8% alc by vol. stout brewed by the Wentworth Brewery, South Yorkshire.

Oatmeal Stout (Eng) a 5% alc by vol. bottled stout

brewed by the Young Brewery, Wandsworth, London.

Oaza Tesanj (Bos) a natural spring mineral water from Tesanj, Bosnia and Herzegovina.

O.B. (Eng) *abbr*: **O**ldham **B**rewery Lancashire beers have these initials on the side of a bell.

O.B. (E.Asia) *abbr*: **O**riental **B**rewery, lager beer brewed in Seoul, South Korea.

Obaideh (Leb) a native white grape variety thought to be Chardonnay.

Oban (Scot) a single highland malt whisky distillery at Argyll on the western coast. Owned by John Hopkins Ltd. (Part of DCL group). Produces 12 year old malt at 40% alc by vol. and 14 year old malt at 43% alc by vol.

O.B.B. (Eng) *abbr*: **O**ld **B**rewery **B**itter a 1039 O.G. brewed by the Samuel Smith Brewery in Tadcaster, Yorkshire.

'O' Be Joyful (Eng) a 4.8% alc by vol. ale brewed by Brakspear, Henley-on-Thames, Oxon using roasted malts and brown sugars blended to produce citrus and dried fruit aromas. Part of the Brewers Selection range.

Ober (Ger) lit: 'upper or higher', denotes villages or vineyards that are situated above a town, village, church, etc.

Oberachem (Ger) village (Anb): Baden. *see* Achern.

Oberacker (Ger) *see* Kraichtal.

Oberberg (Ger) vineyard (Anb): Nahe. (Ber): Schloss Böckelheim. (Gro): Burgweg. (Vil): Norheim.

Oberberg (Ger) vineyard (Anb): Rheingau. (Ber): Johannisberg. (Gro): Steinmacher. (Vil): Niederwalluf.

Oberbergen (Ger) village (Anb): Baden. (Ber): Kaiserstuhl-Tuniberg. (Gro): Vulkanfelsen. (Vins): Bassgeige, Pulverbuck.

Oberbillig (Ger) village (Anb): Mosel-Saar-Ruwer. (Ber): Obermosel. (Gro): Gipfel. (Vins): Hirtengarten, Römerberg.

Oberdiebach (Ger) village (Anb): Mittelrhein. (Ber): Bacharach. (Gro): Schloss Stahleck. (Vins): Bischofshub, Fürstenberg, Kräuterberg, Rheinberg.

Oberdollendorf (Ger) village (Anb): Mittelrhein. (Ber): Siebengebirge. (Gro): Petersberg. (Vins): Rosenhügel, Laurentiusberg, Sülzenberg.

Oberdorfer Weissbier (Ger) a bottle-conditioned wheat beer brewed by the Franz Joseph Sailer Brauerei, Marktoberdorf. Two versions – Dunkel (dark), Helles (light), both 4.8% alc by vol.

Oberdürrenberg (Ger) vineyard (Anb): Baden. (Ber): Markgräflerland. (Gro): Lorettoberg. (Vil): Pfaffenweiler.

Obereggenen (Ger) village (Anb): Baden. (Ber): Markgräflerland. (Gro): Burg Neuenfels. (Vin): Röthen.

Obere Heimbach (Ger) vineyard (Anb): Nahe. (Ber): Schloss Böckelheim. (Gro): Paradiesgarten. (Vil): Meisenheim.

Oberehnheim (Fr) the German name for the village of Obernai in Alsace.

Obereisenheim (Ger) village (Anb): Franken. (Ber): Maindreieck. (Gro): Kirchberg. (Vin): Höll.

Oberemmel (Ger) village (Anb): Mosel-Saar-Ruwer. (Ber): Saar-Ruwer. (Gro): Scharzberg. (Vins): Agritiusberg, Altenberg, Hütte, Karlsberg, Raul, Rosenberg.

Obere Pointen (Aus) a vineyard site on the banks of the River Danube in the Kremstal region.

Oberer Berg (Ger) vineyard (Anb): Württemberg. (Ber): Württembergisch Unterland. (Gro): Wunnenstein. (Vil): Kleinbottwar.

Oberer Berg (Ger) vineyard (Anb): Württemberg. (Ber): Württembergisch Unterland. (Gro): Wunnenstein. (Vil): Ludwigsburg, (ortsteil Hoheneck).

Obererdingen (Ger) village (Anb): Württemberg. (Ber): Württembergisch Unterland. (Gro): Stromberg. (Vin): Kupferhalde.

Oberer Weinzierlberg (Aus) a vineyard site on the banks of the River Danube in the Kremstal region.

Obere Ziestel (Aus) a vineyard site on the banks of the River Danube in the Kremstal region.

Oberfeld (Aus) a vineyard site on the banks of the River Danube in the Kremstal region.

Oberfell (Ger) village (Anb): Mosel-Saar-Ruwer. (Ber): Zell/Mosel. (Gro): Weinhex. (Vins): Brauneberg, Goldlay, Rosenberg.

Ober-Flörsheim (Ger) village (Anb): Rheinhessen. (Ber): Wonnegau. (Gro): Burg Rodenstein. (Vins): Blucherpfad, Herrenberg.

Obergugen (Aus) a vineyard site based on the banks of the River Kamp situated in the Kamptal region.

Oberhasel (Aus) a vineyard site based on the banks of the River Kamp situated in the Kamptal region.

Oberhausen (Ger) village (Anb): Pfalz. (Ber): Südliche Weinstrasse. (Gro): Kloster Liebfrauenberg. (Vin): Frohnwingert.

Oberhausen an der Nahe (Ger) village (Anb): Nahe. (Ber): Schloss Böckelheim. (Gro): Burgweg. (Vins): Felsenberg, Kieselberg, Leistenberg, Rotenberg.

Oberhausen an der Nahe (Ger) village (Anb): Nahe. (Ber): Schloss Böckelheim. (Gro): Paradiesgarten. (Vin): Graukatz.

Oberhauser (Aus) a vineyard site on the banks of the River Danube situated in the Wachau region, Niederösterreich.

Oberheimbach (Ger) village (Anb): Mittelrhein. (Ber): Bacharach. (Gro): Schloss Reichenstein. (Vins): Klosterberg, Römerberg, Sonne, Wahrheit.

Ober-Hilbersheim (Ger) village (Anb): Rheinhessen. (Ber): Bingen. (Gro): Abtey. (Vin): Mönchpforte.

Oberkirch (Ger) village (Anb): Baden. (Ber): Ortenau. (Gro): Fürsteneck. (Vin): Renchtäler.

Oberkirch [ortsteil Haslach] (Ger) village (Anb): Baden. (Ber): Ortenau. (Gro): Fürsteneck. (Vin): Renchtäler.

Oberlauda (Ger) village (Anb): Baden. (Ber): Badische Frankenland. (Gro): Tauberklinge. (Vins): Altenberg, Steinlinge.

Oberlin Wine Research Institute (Fr) founded in 1874 in Colmar, Alsace. Carries out research in clonal selection, crossing, pest control etc.

Ober Mitterhassel (Aus) a vineyard site based on the banks of the River Kamp situated in the Kamptal region.

Obermoschel (Ger) village (Anb): Nahe. (Ber): Schloss Böckelheim. (Gro): Paradiesgarten. (Vins): Geissenkopf, Langhölle, Schlossberg, Silberberg, Sonnenplätzchen.

Obermosel (Ger) bereich (Anb): Mosel-Saar-Ruwer. (Gros): Gipfel, Konigsberg.

Obernai (Fr) a wine village of the Bas-Rhin in Alsace. (Ger) = Oberehnheim.

Obernai Mini Fût (Fr) a beer sold in a small barrel with a re-sealable tap.

Oberndorf (Ger) village (Anb): Nahe. (Ber): Schloss Böckelheim. (Gro): Paradiesgarten. (Vins): Aspenberg, Beutelstein, Feuersteinrossel, Weissenstein.

Odernheim (Ger) village (Anb): Nahe. (Ber): Schloss Böckelheim. (Gro): Paradiesgarten. (Vins): Disibodenberg, Hessweg, Kapellenberg, Kloster, Monfort, Weinsack.

Obernhof (Ger) village (Anb): Mittelrhein. (Ber): Rheinburgengau. (Gro): Lahntal. (Vin): Goetheberg.

Ober-Olm (Ger) village (Anb): Rheinhessen. (Ber): Nierstein. (Gro): Donmherr. (Vin): Kapellenberg.

Oberon (Eng) a seasonal ale brewed by Wychwood Brewery, at Eagle Maltings, Witney, Oxfordshire. Available in June.

Oberotterbach (Ger) village (Anb): Pfalz. (Ber): Südliche Weinstrasse. (Gro): Guttenberg. (Vin): Sonnenberg.

Oberöwisheim (Ger) *see* Kraichtal.

Oberrhein (Ger) a Deutscher Tafelwein region. Has two untergebiete: Burgengau and Romertor.

Oberrimsingen (Ger) village (Anb): Baden. (Ber): Kaiserstuhl-Tuniberg. (Gro): Attilafelsen. (Vin): Franziskaner.

Oberrot (Ger) vineyard (Anb): Franken. (Ber): Maindreieck. (Gro): Not yet assigned. (Vil): Lengfust.

Oberrotweil (Ger) village (Anb): Baden. (Ber): Kaiserstuhl-Tuniberg. (Gro): Vulkanfelsen. (Vins): Eichberg, Henkenberg, Käsleberg, Kirchberg, Schlossberg.

Obersasbach (Ger) village (Anb): Baden. (Ber): Ortenau. (Gro): Schloss Rodeck. (Vins): Alter Gott, Eichwäldele.

Obersätzen (Aus) a vineyard site on the banks of the River Danube situated in the Wachau region, Niederösterreich.

Oberschloss (Ger) vineyard (Anb): Pfalz. (Ber): Südliche Weinstrasse. (Gro): Mandelhöhe. (Vil): Kirrweiler.

Oberschopfheim (Ger) village (Anb): Baden. (Ber): Breisgau. (Gro): Schutterlindenberg. (Vin): Kronenbühl.

Oberschüpf (Ger) village (Anb): Baden. (Ber): Badische Frankenland. (Gro): Tauberklinge. (Vins): Altenberg, Herrenberg.

Oberschwarzach (Ger) village (Anb): Franken. (Ber): Steigerwald. (Gro): Not yet assigned. (Vin): Herrenberg.

Oberselters (Ger) a natural spring mineral water (established 1731) from Bad Camberd, Oberselters. Mineral contents (milligrammes per litre): Sodium 622mg/l, Calcium 94.7mg/l, Magnesium 36.5mg/l, Potassium 16.2mg/l, Bicarbonates 991mg/l, Chlorides 658mg/l, Sulphates 29mg/l, Fluorides 0.67mg/l.

Obersöllbach (Ger) village (Anb): Württemberg. (Ber): Württembergisch Unterland. (Gro): Lindelberg. (Vin): Margarete.

Oberstenfeld (Ger) village (Anb): Württemberg. (Ber): Württembergisch Unterland. (Gro): Wunnenstein. (Vins): Forstberg, Harzberg, Lichtenberg.

Oberstetten (Ger) village (Anb): Württemberg. (Ber): Kocher-Jagst-Tauber. (Gro): Tauberberg. (Vin): Shafsteige.

Oberstreit (Ger) village (Anb): Nahe. (Ber): Schloss Böckelheim. (Gro): Paradiesgarten. (Vin): Auf dem Zimmerberg.

Obersulm [ortsteil Affaltrach] (Ger) village (Anb): Württemberg. (Ber): Württembergisch Unterland. (Gro): Salzberg. (Vins): Dieblesberg, Zeilberg.

Obersulm [ortsteil Eichelberg] (Ger) village (Anb): Württemberg. (Ber): Württembergisch Unterland. (Gro): Salzberg. (Vin): Hundsberg.

Obersulm [ortsteil Eschenau] (Ger) village (Anb): Württemberg. (Ber): Württembergisch Unterland. (Gro): Salzberg. (Vin): Paradies.

Obersulm [ortsteil Sülzbach] (Ger) village (Anb): Württemberg. (Ber): Württembergisch Unterland. (Gro): Salzberg. (Vin): Altenberg.

Obersulm [ortsteil Weiler] (Ger) village (Anb): Württemberg. (Ber): Württembergisch Unterland. (Gro): Salzberg. (Vins): Hundsberg, Schlierbach.

Obersulm [ortsteil Willsbach] (Ger) village (Anb): Württemberg. (Ber): Württembergisch Unterland. (Gro): Salzberg. (Vins): Dieblesberg, Zeilberg.

Obersülzen (Ger) village (Anb): Pfalz. (Ber): Mittelhaardt-Deutsche Weinstrasse. (Gro): Scwarzerde. (Vin): Schnepp.

Obertsrot (Ger) village (Anb): Baden. (Ber): Ortenau. (Gro): Schloss Rodeck. (Vin): Grafensprung.

Obertürkheim (Ger) village (Anb): Württemberg. (Ber): Remstal-Stuttgart. (Gro): Weinsteige. *see* Stuttgart.

Oberuhldingen (Ger) village (Anb): Baden. (Ber): Bodensee. (Gro): Sonnenufer. (Vin): Kirchhalde.

Obervolkach (Ger) village (Anb): Franken. (Ber): Maindreick. (Gro): Kirchberg. (Vin): Landsknecht.

Oberwalluf (Ger) village (Anb): Rheingau. (Ber): Johannisberg. (Gro): Steinmacher. (Vins): Fitusberg, Langenstück.

Oberweier (Ger) village (Anb): Baden. (Ber): Breisgau. (Gro): Schutterlindenberg. (Vin): Kronenbühl.

Oberwessel (Ger) village (Anb): Mittelrhein. (Ber): Rheinburgengau. (Gro): Schloss Schönburg. (Vins): Bernstein, Bienenberg, Goldemund, Ölsberg, Römerkrug, St. Martinsberg, Sieben Jungfrauen.

Obester Winery (USA) a small winery based in San Mateo, California. Grape varieties: Cabernet sauvignon, Johannisberg riesling and Sauvignon blanc. Produces varietal wines.

O.B.I. (Hun) *abbr*: Orszàgos Borminósitó Intézet.

Obidos (Port) a DOC wine area within the region of Estremadura.

Obikwa (S.Afr) the export brand label for varietal wines produced by Distell, Western Cape. Grape varieties include: Cabernet sauvignon, Chardonnay, Chenin blanc, Merlot, Pinotage and Shiraz.

Obj Zulol (Asia) a natural spring mineral water brand from Tajikistan.

O Bolo (Sp) a Vino Comarcal wine from the province of Ourense in Galicia.

Obolonskaya (Ukr) a natural spring mineral water from Kiev.

Obregon (Sp) a solera brandy produced by José Gonzalez Obregon.

Obrigheim (Ger) village (Anb): Pfalz. (Ber): Mittelhaardt-Deutsche Weinstrasse. (Gro): Grafenstück. (Vins): Benn, Hochgericht, Mandelpfad, Rosengarten, Schloss, Sonnenberg.

Obritzberg (Aus) a vineyard site based on the banks of the River Kamp situated in the Kamptal region.

Obscuration (Eng) the amount of false reading on a hydrometer caused by impurities (mainly sugar in the alcohol).

Observatoire de la Qualité (Fr) monitoring unit set up by B.I.V.B. to test the quality of Burgundy wines as they pass from retailer to the consumer, it is performed anonymously.

Obstbranntwein (Ger) the term for fruit brandies, also called obstwasser, brandy must be produced without the addition of sweetening, alcohol or colour.

Obstwasser (Aus) fruit brandies, most famous is Wacholderbranntweine. *see* Obstbranntwein.

Obstwasser (Ger) *see* Obstbranntwein.

Obtuse (USA) a Port-style wine produced by Justin Vineyards and Winery, 11680 Chimney Rock Road, Paso Robles, California.

Obudai (Hun) a natural spring mineral water from Budapest.

Occasional Licence (Eng) the licence given to a full-on licence holder to run a licensed bar in un-licensed premises.

Occasional Permissions (Eng) licenses granted for up to 24 hours to sell alcoholic liquor (usually at an outside bar). 4 licenses per year may be granted.

Occhio di Pernice (It) a red grape variety grown in Tuscany.

Occidente (Arg) a wine region that joins Catamarca and La Rioja.

Occitane (Fr) the name for the dumpy bottle used in the Languedoc region of south-western France.

OCE (Afr) a State body in Morocco responsible for the monitoring and exporting of Moroccan wines. Analyses and tastes the wines and selects wines to be bottled under OCE names.

O

Ocean [The] (Port) a name given to the area around the estuary of the river Tejo in the Estremadura region. Noted for wind breaks of reeds to protect the vines from the Atlantic winds.

Ocean Boulevard (Eng) a label for an Argentina wine from Chalié Richards company.

Ocean Point (Eng) a label for an Australian white wine (Chardonnay) from Chalié Richards company.

Ocet (Pol) vinegar.

Ocha (Jap) tea. *See also* O-Cha.

O-Cha (Jap) a liqueur made from essence of Matcha, powdered tea and Gyokuro rolled tea. Also written Ocha.

Ochavico Dry Oloroso (Sp) a brand of Oloroso Sherry produced by Garvey's in Jerez de la Frontera.

Ochoa (Sp) a noted family winery based in the Navarra region. Grape varieties include: Garnacha, Tempranillo. Produces red, rosé and white wines.

Ochsenbach (Ger) village (Anb): Württemberg. (Ber): Württembergisch Unterland. (Gro): Stromberg. (Vin): Liebenberg.

Ochsenberg (Ger) vineyard (Anb): Württemberg. (Ber): Württembergisch Unterland. (Gro): Heuchelberg. (Vil): Brackenheim (ortsteil Botenheim).

Öchsle (Ger) *see* Oechsle.

Ochtinskaja (Rus) a natural spring mineral water from St. Petersburg. Mineral contents (milligrammes per litre): Sodium 1300–1600mg/l, Calcium 80–160mg/l, Magnesium <100mg/l, Bicarbonates 150–190mg/l, Chlorides 2370-2900mg/l, Sulphates <100mg/l.

Ockenheim (Ger) village (Anb): Rheinhessen. (Ber): Bingen. (Gro): Sankt Rochuskapelle. (Vins): Hockenmühle, Klosterweg, Kreuz, Laberstall, St. Jakobsberg, Schönhölle.

Ockfen (Ger) village (Anb): Mosel-Saar-Ruwer. (Ber): Saar-Ruwer. (Gro): Scharzberg. (Vins): Bockstein, Geisberg, Heppenstein, Herrenberg, Kupp, Neuwies, Zickelgarten.

Ocsidio (Wal) oxidise.

Octave (Eng) a cask, ⅛ of a pipe, butt or cask (16½ gallons approx).

Octave (Eng) an old-fashioned term used as a request for Sherry. Eight different Sherries would be presented from very dry to sweet in range.

Octavilla (Sp) an ⅛ of a Sherry cask (16½ gallons). *see* Octave.

Octavius (Austr) the name for an old vine Shiraz matured in Missouri oak octaves from Yalumba Vineyards, Barossa Valley, South Australia.

Oculus (S.Afr) the label for a dry white wine produced by the Ouoin Rock Winery, Stellenbosch, Western Cape.

Oda (Slo) a natural spring mineral water brand. Mineral contents (milligrammes per litre): Sodium 1mg/l, Calcium 50mg/l, Magnesium 30mg/l, Potassium 0.2mg/l, Bicarbonates 292.8mg/l, Chlorides 6mg/l, Sulphates 45.6mg/l, Nitrates 4.87mg/l.

Odaesan Water (S.Kor) a natural spring mineral water brand.

O'Darby (Ire) a cream liqueur with a chocolate and Irish whiskey base 17% alc by vol. Produced in Cork.

Ödårka Taffel Aquavit (Swe) a caraway, coriander, cumin and fennel-flavoured aquavit.

Oddbins (Eng) a large retail wines, beers and spirits chain owned by Seagram Distillers PLC.

Odéis (Fr) a natural spring mineral water from Source des Moulettes. Mineral contents (milligrammes per litre): Sodium 173.2mg/l, Calcium 63mg/l, Magnesium 10.2mg/l, Potassium 0.4mg/l, Bicarbonates 51.3mg/l, Sulphates 1mg/l, Nitrates 2mg/l. pH 7.8

Odenas (Fr) a commune in the Beaujolais. Has A.C. Beaujolais-Villages or Beaujolais-Odenas status.

Odenheim (Ger) village (Anb): Baden. (Ber): Badische Bergstrasse/Kraichgau. (Gro): Stiftsberg. (Vin): Königsbecher.

Odenwald Mountains (Ger) the slopes on which the vines grow in the Hessische Bergstrasse anbaugebiet. Also protects the Rheinhessen from easterly winds.

Odenwald Quelle (Ger) a natural spring mineral water (established 1932) from the Odenwald Mountains. Mineral contents (milligrammes per litre): Sodium 370mg/l, Calcium 170mg/l, Magnesium 20mg/l, Potassium 20mg/l, Bicarbonates 300mg/l, Chlorides 760mg/l, Sulphates 30mg/l.

Odessa (Ukr) a wine-producing centre on the Black Sea in the Ukraine.

Odeur (Fr) the smell of (wine, yeast, cork, etc).

Odfjell (Chile) a winery based in the Maule Valley. Grape variety: Carignan. Website: http://www.odfjellvineyards.cl

Odilienberg (Fr) the German name for the wine village of Sainte-Odile in the Bas-Rhin, Alsace.

Odin Brewery (Den) a noted brewery based in Viborg, North Jutland.

Odine St. Benoit (Fr) a natural spring mineral water from St. Martin d'Abbat. Mineral contents (milligrammes per litre): Sodium 6.5mg/l, Calcium 47.5mg/l, Magnesium 4.3mg/l, Potassium 3mg/l, Bicarbonates 172mg/l, Chlorides 8mg/l, Sulphates 9mg/l. pH 7.6

Odinstal (Ger) vineyard (Anb): Pfalz. (Ber): Mittelhaardt-Deutsche Weinstrasse. (Gro): Schenkenböhl. (Vil): Wachenheim.

Odobesti (Rum) a wine-producing area in central Foçsani, noted for white wines produced from the Feteasca and Riesling grapes.

Odour (Eng) a pleasant or an unpleasant smell, also referred to as the bouquet. (Fr) = odeur.

Odre (Port)(Sp) a wine bag made from animal skin.

Ödsbach (Ger) village (Anb): Baden. (Ber): Ortenau. (Gro): Fürsteneck. (Vin): Renchtäler.

Odwalla (USA) a still natural spring mineral water (established 1980) from the Sierra Nevada Mountains, California. Mineral contents (milligrammes per litre): Calcium 12mg/l, Magnesium 3.8mg/l.

Odyssey (S.Afr) a label for a range of naturally sweet wines produced by the Robertson Winery (now no longer produced).

Odyssey 2001 (Eng) a cask-conditioned ale specially brewed to celebrate the 250th anniversary of St. Austell Brewery, Cornwall.

O.E. (Gre) abbr: Oínos Epitrapézios.

°Oe (Ger) abbr: Degree Oechsle.

Oechsle (Ger) scale of sugar density of grape musts. Recorded as °O. i.e. 82°O = 1082 gravity.

Oechsle [Ferdinand] (Ger) 1774 – 1852, a chemist of Pforzheim who devised a hydrometer to measure the sugar content of grape must. see Oechsle.

Oechsle [German Wine Ratings] (Ger) QbA = 57°Oe–72°Oe. QmP = 65°Oe–72°Oe. Kabinett = 67°Oe–85°Oe. Spätlese = 79°Oe–95°Oe. Auslese = 83°Oe–105°Oe. Beerenauslese = 110°Oe–128°Oe. Trockenbeerenauslese = 150°Oe minimum.

Oedheim (Ger) village (Anb): Württemberg. (Ber): Württembergisch Unterland. (Gro): Staufenberg. (Vin): Kayberg.

Oeil de Perdrix (Fr) lit: 'partridge eye', a tawny pink colour given to certain rosé wines. i.e. sparkling Burgundy. Produced from the Pinot noir.

Oeillade (Fr) a red grape variety from the A.C. Cassis in southern France. Produces high alcohol. Also known as Cinsaut.

Oeiras (Port) a district in the Carcavelos region which is allowed to use that designation.

Oelberg (Ger) vineyard (Anb): Baden. (Ber): Markgräflerland. (Gro): Lorettoberg. (Vil): Ehrenstetten.

Oelberg (Ger) vineyard (Anb): Baden. (Ber): Markgräflerland. (Gro): Vogtei Rötteln. (Vil): Efringen-Kirchen.

Oelig (Ger) a wine of high consistency that gives the impression of being oily as it is poured. Has viscosity.

Oenin (USA) a newly discovered compound of wine by Dr. Leo McCluskey PhD. owner of the Felton-Empire Winery in Santa Cruz, Mid-California. Is a secret chemical that has been christened 'Oenin'.

Oenobilia (Eng) wine artifacts. i.e. coasters, corkscrews, decanters, wine funnels, glasses, etc.

Oenoforos Winery (Gre) a winery based at Selinous 25100, Aegio. V.Q.P.R.D: Patras. Vineyard region is in Côtes d'Agion. Produces Asprolithi from Rhoditis grapes.

Oenological Amelioration (N.Z) the term given to the practice of adding water to wine to help improve the quality.

Oenologist (Eng) a specialist in the study of winemaking.

Oenology (Eng) the study of wine from a scientific point of view.

Oenomel (Eng) an old English drink of wine and honey.

Oenoparagogos (Gre) wine producer. Also spelt Oinoparagogas.

Oenophile (Eng) a person who enjoys and loves wine and who also wishes to learn more about wine.

Oenopoyeyon (Gre) winery. Also spelt Oinopoieion.

Oenos (Gre) wine. Also spelt Oínos.

Oenos Erythros (Gre) red wine. See also Oenos Mowros and Oínos Erythros.

Oenos Lewkos (Gre) white wine. See also Oínos Lefkos.

Oenos Mowros (Gre) red wine. See also Oenos Erythros and Oínos Erythros.

Oenothèque (Fr) a vintage Champagne from Cuvée Dom Pérignon Oenothèque. Three releases of each vintage – as usual, 12–20 years later, then between 20 and 35 years. Launched June 2000.

Oenotria (Gre) lit: 'the land of wine', the ancient Greek name for Italy.

Oenoxidase (Eng) an enzyme found in grape pips which causes a brown stain to occur in white wines if they are not removed before fermentation.

Oeral (Bel) a 6% alc by vol. top-fermented, bottled bitter brewed by De Dolle Brouwers, Esen-Diksmuiden.

Oerbier (Bel) a 7.5% alc by vol. dark brown, top-fermented bottle-conditioned special beer brewed by De Dolle Brouwers, Esen-Diksmuiden. Unfiltered and unpasteurised.

Oesjaar (S.Afr) vintage.

Oesterreicher (Aus)(Ger) another name for the white grape variety Sylvaner.

Oesterreichische Weinguetesiegel (Aus) the official seal for Austrian wine.

Oestrich (Ger) village see Östrich.

Oetis (Gre) a natural spring mineral water from Thessaloniki. Mineral contents (milligrammes per litre): Sodium 18.4mg/l, Calcium 38mg/l, Magnesium 34mg/l, Potassium 1.2mg/l, Bicarbonates 281.9mg/l, Chlorides 17.7mg/l, Sulphates 14.9mg/l, Nitrates 4.3mg/l.

Oettingen (Ger) see Bräuhaus Oettingen.

Oeuil de Perdrix (Fr)(Switz) see Oeil de Perdrix (mis-spelling of).

Oeuilly (Fr) a Cru Champagne village in the Canton de Dormans. District: Épernay.

Oewerzicht Private Cellar (S.Afr) a winery (established 2002) based in Greyton, Overberg, Western Cape. 3ha. Grape varieties: Cabernet sauvignon.

Oeybad-Quelle (Switz) a sparkling natural spring mineral water from Adelboden. Mineral contents (milligrammes per litre): Sodium 6mg/l, Calcium 532mg/l, Magnesium 32mg/l, Bicarbonates 245mg/l, Sulphates 1190mg/l, Fluorides 0.2mg/l, Nitrates 0.18mg/l.

OFC (Can) a Canadian rye whisky produced by the Canadian Schenley Distilleries Ltd. 40% alc by vol.

Off (Eng) a term that when applied to a beverage denotes it is un-drinkable through some malady.

Offa's Vineyard (Wal) a 1.1ha vineyard based at the Old Rectory, Llanvihangel-Ystern-Llewern, Monmouth. Produces red and white wines from Cabernet sauvignon, Merlot, Bacchus, Faber and Schönburger grapes.

Off-Dry (Eng) see Semi-Dry.

Offenau (Ger) village (Anb): Württemberg. (Ber): Württembergisch Unterland. (Gro): Staufenberg. (Vin): Schön.

Offenberg (Aus) a vineyard site on the banks of the River Danube situated in the Wachau region, Niederösterreich.

Offenberg (Aus) a vineyard site based on the banks of the River Kamp situated in the Kamptal region.

Offenburg [ortsteil Fessenbach] (Ger) village (Anb): Baden. (Ber): Ortenau. (Gro): Fürsteneck. (Vins): Bergle, Franzensberger.

Offenburg [ortsteil Zell-Weierbach] (Ger) village (Anb): Baden. (Ber): Ortenau. (Gro): Fürsteneck. (Vin): Abtsberg.

Öffener Wein (Aus) carafe wine.

Öffener Wein (Ger) wine sold by the glass.

Offenheim (Ger) village (Anb): Rheinhessen. (Ber): Wonnegau. (Gro): Sybillenstein. (Vin): Mandelberg.

Offertory (Eng) a term which refers to the wine etc, which is offered during religious ceremonies. i.e. The Eucharist.

Off-flavour (Eng) unwanted flavours found in wine, many causes, the main one being due to careless or bad wine making.

Office International du Vin (Fr) a working group of legislators and wine growers who assess other countries production.

Office National de Comercialisation des Produits Viti-Vinicoles (Alg) *abbr:* O.N.C.V. a state body established in 1968 to supervise the quality, production and distribution of wines.

Office National Interprofessionnel des Vins de Table (Fr) *abbr:* O.N.I.V.I.T. a body formed in 1973 to help control the quality of Vin de Table wines.

Offley Forrester Boa Vista (Port) Vintage Port shippers. Vintages- 1870, 1872, 1873, 1874, 1875, 1878, 1881, 1884, 1885, 1887, 1888, 1890, 1892, 1894, 1896, 1897, 1900, 1902, 1904, 1908, 1910, 1912, 1919, 1920, 1922, 1924, 1925, 1927, 1929, 1935, 1950, 1954, 1960, 1962, 1963, 1966, 1967, 1970, 1972, 1975, 1977, 1980, 1982, 1983, 1985, 1987, 1991, 1994, 1995, 1997, 2003. Grape varieties used are Barroca, João de santarém, Malvasia pieta, Rufete, Tinta amarela, Touriga francesa and Touriga nacional.

Off-Licence (Eng) a special licence issued to a shop, supermarket etc. which permits the sale of alcoholic beverages between 8.30 a.m. and 10.30 p.m. It does not permit alcoholic beverages consumed on the premises.

Off Premise (USA) off licence. i.e. the sale of alcoholic liquor for consumption off the premises.

Offstein (Ger) village (Anb): Rheinhessen. (Ber): Wonnegau. (Gro): Domblick. (Vins): Engelsberg, Schlossgarten.

Off-Vintages (Eng) denotes great wines in a poor year which are quite drinkable but not great. Other lesser wines of that year would be poor.

Ofique (Sp) a type of refrigeration used to prevent the wine from turning cloudy.

O.G. (Eng) *abbr: see* Original Gravity.

Oger (Fr) a Grand Cru Champagne village in the Canton d'Avize. District: Épernay. Re-classified in 1985.

Ogeu (Fr) a natural sparkling mineral water from the Pyrénées. (Add): Société des Eaux Minérales d'Ogeu, 64680 Ogeu-les-Bains. Mineral contents (milligrammes per litre): Sodium 31mg/l, Calcium 48mg/l, Magnesium 12mg/l, Potassium 1mg/l, Bicarbonates 183mg/l, Chlorides 48mg/l, Sulphates 18mg/l, Nitrates 5mg/l.

Oggau (Aus) a wine region of the Burgenland.

O'Hanlon's Brewing C°. (Eng) a brewery (established 1995). (Add): Great Barton Farm, Whimple, Devon EX5 2NY. Brews: Dry Stout 4.2% alc by vol., Firefly 3.7% alc by vol., The Original Port Stout 4.8% alc by vol., Thomas Hardy 11.5% alc by vol., Wheat Beer 4% alc by vol., Yellowhammer 4.2% alc by vol. Website: http://www.ohanlons.co.uk 'E'mail: info@ohanlons.co.uk

Oh Be Joyful (Eng) a barley wine brewed by the Whitbread Brewery in Blackburn, Lancashire.

O'Higgins (Chile) a red wine region south of Santiago.

Ohinemuri Estate (N.Z) a winery. (Add): Morestby Street, Karangahake, (P.O. Box 137), Paeroa, Waikato.

Ohio (USA) a wine region of the eastern States, has vineyards from Cleveland to Sandistay along Lake Erie.

Ohio Cocktail (Cktl) ½ measure sweet vermouth, ½ measure Scotch whisky, 3 dashes orange bitters. Shake well with ice and strain into a cocktail glass.

Ohlenberg (Ger) vineyard (Anb): Mittelrhein. (Ber): Rheinburgengau. (Gro): Gedeonseck. (Vil): Boppard.

Ohligpfad (Ger) vineyard (Anb): Pfalz. (Ber): Mittelhaardt-Deutsche Weinstrasse. (Gro): Feuerberg. (Vil): Bobenheim am Berg.

Ohligsberg (Ger) vineyard (Anb): Mosel-Saar-Ruwer. (Ber): Bernkastel. (Gro): Kurfürstlay. (Vil): Wintrich.

Ohlsbach (Ger) village (Anb): Baden. (Ber): Ortenau. (Gro): Fürsteneck. (Vin): Kinzigtäler.

Ohm (Ger) a wine cask of approximately 160 litres.

O'Hooligan's Revolt (Eng) a bottle-conditioned stout 6% alc by vol. brewed by the Raisdale Sparging and Brewing Company, Penarth.

Ohrid (Ser) a wine-producing area in Macedonia.

Oïdium Tuckerii (Fr) *see* Oiidium tuckerii.

Oiidium Tuckerii (Lat) *Uncinula necator* powdery mildew, a fungal vine disease, also spelt **Oïdium tuckerii**.

Oiliness (Eng) a wine malady, should disappear on its own, but if persistent in a wine, treatment by 'airing' (decanting from one cask to another) will help. Then it should be filtered.

O.I.M.L. (Euro) *abbr:* Organisation Internationale de Métrologie Légale a measurement of alcohol by hydrometer at 20° Celcius (pure water 0% and pure alcohol 100%). *See also* Gay Lussac and Sykes Hydrometer.

Oinochoikos (Gre) a young wine waiter in ancient Greecian times.

Oinoparagogas (Gre) wine-producer. Also spelt Oenoparagogos.

Oinophoros (Gre) a wine butler in ancient Greecian times.

Oinopoieion (Gre) winery. Also spelt Oenopoyeyon.

Oínos (Gre) wine. Also spelt Oenos.

Oínos Epitrapézios (Gre) *abbr*: O.E. a table wine. *see* Tópikos Oínos, Onom sia Proelésios Anóteras Poiotútos, Onom sia Proelésios Elechoméni.

Oínos Erythros (Gre) red wine. *See also* Oenos Erythros.

Oínos Lefkos (Gre) white wine. *see* Oenos Lefkos.

O-i Ocha (Jap) a branded, bottled, non-alcoholic green tea produced by the Ito-En Brewery.

Oirschots Witbier (Hol) a 5% alc by vol. unfiltered, top-fermented bottled cloudy wheat beer brewed by De Kroon Bier Brouwerij, Oirschot.

Oiry (Fr) a Grand Cru Champagne village in the Canton d'Avize. District: Épernay. Re-classified in 1985.

Oja [River] (Sp) a river of northern Spain on which the Rioja wine region is situated and from where it gets its name.

O'Jaffa (Isr) a liqueur made from jaffa oranges, tangerines and grapefruit.

Ojen (Sp) a dry high-proof anis, made from star aniseed in the town of Ojen in southern Spain. 42.5% alc by vol.

Ojo de Gallo (Sp) lit: 'partridge eye', applied to the rosé wines of Navarra in north-eastern Spain.

Ojo de Liebre (Sp) lit: 'eye of the hare', a red grape variety grown in Cataluña, Penedés, also the Cataluña name for the Tempranillo.

O.K. (Isr) a pilsener-style beer at 11.5° Balling produced by a Canadian-financed brewery.

Okahu Estate (N.Z) a winery. (Add): Cnr. Okahu Road/Main Highway to Ahipara. 2.2ha. Grape varieties: Cabernet sauvignon, Merlot, Shiraz, Chardonnay, Sémillon.

Okanagan (Can) a white grape variety grown in the Okanagan Valley, British Columbia.

Okanagan Valley (Can) a wine-producing region in British Columbia, accounts for 95% of grape production.

Okayama (Jap) a wine-producing region.

O.K. Distillery (Afr) a rum distillery based on the island of Mauritius in the Indian Ocean.

Oke (USA) the Hawaiian name for the spirit drink Okolehao.

O'Keefe (Can) *see* Carling O'Keefe.

Okell & Sons Ltd (I.O.M) a brewery (established 1850). (Add): Falcon Brewery, Kewaigue, Douglas, Isle of Man IM2 1QG (also known as the Isle of Man Breweries). Brews: Dr Okells IPA 4.5% alc by vol., Okells (nitra keg) Bitter 3.7% alc by vol., Okells Maclir 4.4% alc by vol., Okells Mild 3.4% alc by vol (1035 O.G)., Pure Brewed., St. Nicks 4.5% alc by vol., Summer Storm 4.2% alc by vol., also Barley Wine 1070 O.G. Old Skipper, Cooil (pilsener). *See also* Castledown Bitter.

Website: http://www.okells.co.uk 'E'mail: mac@okells.co.uk

Okells 45 (I.O.M) a 1045 O.G. cask-conditioned beer brewed by the Isle of Man Breweries.

Okells TT 90 (I.O.M) a 4.2% alc by vol. cask-conditioned ale brewed by Isle of Man Breweries to mark 90th anniversary of TT races.

Okertaler Quelle (Ger) a natural spring mineral water from Goslar, Harz. Mineral contents (milligrammes per litre): Sodium 320mg/l, Calcium 33.5mg/l, Magnesium 5.2mg/l, Potassium 3.9mg/l, Bicarbonates 128mg/l, Chlorides 470mg/l, Sulphates 57.6mg/l.

Okhotnichya (Rus) a hunters' vodka 44% alc by vol. flavoured with botanicals, honey, spices, peppers, fruit peel and coffee.

Oklahoma Cocktail (Cktl) ⅓ measure Jamaican rum, ⅓ measure dry vermouth, ⅓ measure dry gin, shake well with ice and strain into a cocktail glass.

Okoboji Winery (USA) a winery based in Okoboji, Iowa, produces mainly French hybrid wines.

Okocim (Pol) a major brewing town in Poland.

Öko Krone (Ger) a 5% alc by vol. organic beer.

Okolehao (USA) a spirit made in Hawaii from roots of the ti plant, molasses and rice lees, also known as Oke.

Okolehao Cocktail (Cktl) 1 measure Oke, ½ measure lime juice, 1 measure pineapple juice, shake well over ice and strain into a cocktail glass.

Okowita (Pol) the old Polish name for aqua vitae.

Oksamit Ukraine (Ukr) a white table wine produced near Cherson in the Ukraine.

Oktemberian (USA) a wine-producing centre in Armenia.

Oktoberfest (Can) a beer festival held by the Mennonites in their county at Niagara.

Oktober Fest (Ger) the Munich beer festival, held annually for a week in October.

Okura (Jap) a company who, along with Takara Shuzo, has taken over the Scottish distillery of Tomatin in 1986.

Öküzgözü (Tur) a red grape variety.

Öl (Scan) the old Norse word for ale (beer).

Ol (Nor) ale/beer.

Olarra (Sp) a red wine produced by the Bodegas Olarra S.A. Made from the Garnacha, Graciano, Mazuelo and Tempranillo grapes.

Olasrisling (Hun) *see* Olasz Rizling.

Olaszliszka (Hun) a noted wine-producing village in the southern foothills.

Olasz Rizling (Hun) a white grape variety grown in Pécs. Also known as the Riesling Italico, Laski Rizling, Welschriesling. Sometimes spelt Olasrisling.

Ölbaum (Ger) vineyard (Anb): Baden. (Ber): Badische Bergstrasse/Kraichgau. (Gro): Mannaberg. (Vil): Malsch.

Ölbaum (Ger) vineyard (Anb): Baden. (Ber): Badische Bergstrasse/Kraichgau. (Gro): Mannaberg. (Vil): Malschenberg.

Ölbaum (Ger) vineyard (Anb): Baden. (Ber): Badische Bergstrasse/Kraichgau. (Gro): Mannaberg. (Vil): Rettigheim.

Ölberg (Ger) vineyard (Anb): Baden. (Ber): Badische Bergstrasse/Kraichgau. (Gro): Rittersberg. (Vil): Dossenheim.

Ölberg (Ger) vineyard (Anb): Baden. (Ber): Kaiserstuhl-Tuniberg. (Gro): Vulkanfelsen. (Vil): Kiechlinsbergen.

Ölberg (Ger) vineyard (Anb): Baden. (Ber): Ortenau. (Gro): Fürsteneck. (Vil): Durbach.

Ölberg (Ger) vineyard (Anb): Rheinhessen. (Ber): Bingen. (Gro): Rheingrafenstein. (Vil): Wöllstein.

Ölberg (Ger) vineyard (Anb): Rheinhessen. (Ber): Bingen. (Gro): Sankt Rochuskapelle. (Vil): Grolsheim.

Ölberg (Ger) vineyard (Anb): Rheinhessen. (Ber): Nierstein. (Gro): Auflangen. (Vil): Nierstein.

Ölberg (Ger) vineyard (Anb): Rheinhessen. (Ber): Nierstein. (Gro): Petersberg. (Vil): Gau-Odernheim.

Ölberg (Ger) vineyard (Anb): Pfalz. (Ber): Mittelhaardt-Deutsche Weinstrasse. (Gro): Meerspinne. (Vil): Königsbach.

Old Acquaintance (Eng) a Christmas beer brewed by the Hull Brewery. *See also* Mickey Finn.

Oldacre's (Fr) the brand-name of a 4% alc by vol. Chardonnay or Sauvignon blanc spritzer.

Old Ale (Eng) a rich, dark, high-gravity draught ale with good body. Sold usually between November and March (a 'winter ale').

Old Ale (Eng) a 3.6% alc by vol. ale brewed by Harvey's, Lewes, East Sussex.

Old Ale (Eng) a 4.5% alc by vol. dark winter warmer brewed with chocolate malt by King and Barnes (bought out by Hall and Woodhouse in 2000).

Old Ale Winter Warmer (Eng) a 5.35% alc by vol. ale brewed by the Highgate Brewery Ltd., West Midlands.

Old Anchor Ale (Eng) a strong cask-conditioned ale 1060 O.G. brewed by the Jolly Roger Brewery in Upton-on-Severn, Worcestershire.

Old Appledore (Eng) a 3.7% alc by vol. ale brewed by the Country Life Brewery, Devon.

Old Baily (Eng) a smooth premium cask-conditioned bitter from Mansfield Brewery. Named after the founder William Baily. Originally 4.8% alc by vol. now reduced to 4.3% alc by vol.

Old Bank Street (Eng) a home-brew public house in Manchester. Noted for cask-conditioned Old Bank Street Bitter 1043 O.G. brewed from malt extract.

Old Bardstown (USA) a 6 year old Kentucky straight Bourbon whiskey. Also a 10 year old at 101° US proof/50.5% alc by vol.

Old Bear Brewery (Eng) a brewery. (Add): 6 Keighly Road, Cross Hills, Keightly, West Yorkshire BD20 7RN. Brews bears and lager. Website: http://www.oldbearbrewery.com 'E'mail: sales@oldbearbrewery.com

Old Bedford (Eng) a bottled barley wine 1078 O.G. brewed by the Charles Wells Brewery in Bedford.

Old Ben (Eng) a 4.3% alc by vol. ale brewed by the Red Rose Brewery, Lancashire.

Old Bill (Eng) a cask-conditioned ale 1065–1071 O.G. brewed by the Everards Brewery, Leicester, Leicestershire.

Old Bismark (Port) a vintage character Port shipped by Yates Bros.

Old Black Shuck (Eng) a 4.5% alc by vol. cask-conditioned stout from the Elgood & Sons Ltd. (Northbrink Brewery), Wisbech, Cambridgeshire.

Old Block Vines (Austr) vieille vignes.

Old Block (S.Afr) the label for a red wine (Pinotage) produced by the Darling Cellars winery, Swartland.

Old Bob Ale (Eng) a bottled strong pale ale 5.1% alc by vol (1050 O.G) brewed by the TD Ridley & Sons Ltd., brewery in Chelmsford, Essex.

Old Boone Distillery (USA) a Bourbon whiskey distillery based in Louisville, Kentucky.

Old Borer (Austr) a red wine from the Bonnonee Winery, Victoria.

Old Bosham Bitter (Eng) a cask-conditioned bitter 1044 O.G. brewed by the Bosham Brewery in Bosham, West Sussex.

Old Boy (Eng) a 4.8% alc by vol. ale brewed by Oldershaw Brewery, Lincolnshire.

Old Brewery Bitter (Eng) a cask-conditioned and keg bitter 1039 O.G. brewed by the Samuel Smith Brewery in Tadcaster, Yorkshire.

Old Brewery Pale Ale (Eng) a 5% alc by vol. bottled pale ale brewed by the Samuel Smith Brewery in Tadcaster, Yorkshire.

Old Bridge (Eng) a 3.8% alc by vol. bitter brewed by the Fernandes Brewery, Kirkgate, Wakefield, West Yorkshire.

Old Bridge Wines (S.Afr) a negociant company based in the Western Cape that exports to many countries. Labels include: African Gold Collection, Big Six Collection and Old Bridge.

Old Buck (S.Afr) a brand of medium Sherry.

Old Buffer Dark Mild (Eng) a 4.5% alc by vol. dark mild ale brewed by the Garton Brewery, East Yorkshire.

Old Burton Brewery (Eng) a museum. *see* Everards.

Old Bushmills (Ire) a single malt whiskey from the famous distillery of Bushmills. An Irish whiskey 43% alc by vol.

Old Bushmills Black Bush (Ire) a premium blend of Old Bushmills pot-still whiskies matured in Sherry casks for a minimum of 7 years and lightened slightly with a dash of Coleraine grain whiskey 43% alc by vol.

Old Bushmills Distillery C° (Ire) a distillery (established 1608). (Add): 2 Distillery Road, Bushmills, County Antrim, Northern Ireland BT57 8XH. Produces a range of Irish whiskies. Owned by Irish Distillers Group plc. Website: http://www.whiskytours.ie

Old Bush Vine (S.Afr) the label for a white wine (Pinotage) produced by the Monterosso Estate winery, Stellenbosch, Western Cape.

Old Bush Vines (S.Afr) vieille vignes.

Old Bush Vines (S.Afr) the label for a red wine (Pinotage plus Cabernet sauvignon and Merlot blend) produced by the Warwick Estate winery, Stellenbosch, Western Cape.

Old Bushy Tail (I.O.M) a 4.5% alc by vol. ale brewed by the Mount Murray Brewery C°., Isle of Man.

O

· ·

Old Buzzard (Eng) a 4.8% alc by vol (1048 O.G) winter brew brewed by the Cotleigh Brewery in Wiveliscombe, Somerset.

Old Cameron Brig (Scot) a famous straight grain whisky from the Cameron Brig distillery. The only single grain whisky sold as a single grain in bottle 43% alc by vol. *see* Cameronbridge.

Old Cannon Brewery (Eng) a brewery (established 1999). (Add): 86 Cannon Street, Bury St. Edmunds, Suffolk IP33 1JR. Brews beers and lager. Website: http://www.oldcannon.co.uk

Old Cape Colony (S.Afr) the label for a vintage Port-style wine produced by the Vergenoegd Estate winery, Stellenbosch, Western Cape.

Old Carrock (Eng) a 6.5% alc by vol (1060 O.G) traditional strong ale brewed at a small brewery behind the Old Crown Inn (pub), Heskett Newmarket in Cumbria.

Old Cask (N.Afr) the brand-name of a dark rum distilled, blended and bottled by Caroni (1975) in Trinidad.

Old Chalet (S.Afr) a brand of brandy produced by Uniewyn.

Old Chapel (S.Afr) the label for a red wine (Merlot and Ruby cabernet blend) produced by the Robertson Co-operative Winery, Robertson, Western Cape.

Old Charlie (W.Ind) the brand-name of a dark rum produced on the island of Jamaica.

Old Charter Distillery C°. (USA) a Bourbon whiskey distillery based in Louisville, Kentucky. Produces a Bourbon whiskey of same name 40% alc by vol.

Old Chester Ale (Eng) a bottled dark ale 1067 O.G. brewed by the Greenall Whitley Brewery in Warrington. Exported under the names of Warrington Brown, Ebony and Chester Brown.

Old Chicago (USA) a 4.8% alc by vol. beer brewed by Joseph Huber Brewing C°. in Monroe, Wisconsin.

Old Chimneys Brewery (Eng) a brewery. (Add): Market Western, Diss, Norfolk IP22 2NZ. Brews beers and lager.

Old Cocky (Eng) a 4.3% alc by vol. ale brewed by the Weltons Brewery, West Sussex.

Old Codswallop (Eng) a 4.2% alc by vol. ale brewed by Cask & Codpiece, Sandtown, Isle of Wight.

Old Colonial Ale (Austr) a full-bodied, well-matured beer brewed by the Courage Brewery in Victoria.

Old Cornelius (Eng) a 4.8% alc by vol. ale brewed by the Jarrow Brewery, Tyne & Wear.

Old Coronation Ruby (Port) a fine ruby Port (brand-name) from the da Silva Port shippers.

Old Country Cider (Eng) a canned cider from Nurdin & Peacock.

Old Croak Beer (Eng) a cask-conditioned ale 1035 O.G. brewed by the Frog and Parrot home-brew public house, Sheffield, Yorkshire.

Old Crofter (Eng) *see* David's Old Crofter's Bitter.

Old Crow Bourbon (USA) the oldest Bourbon whiskey brand from the Old Crow distillery started by Dr. James Crow. Now owned by the National Distillers.

Old Crow Distillery (USA) *see* Old Crow Bourbon.

Old Curiosity (Eng) a 4.5% alc by vol. ale from the Old Mill Brewery, Snaith, North Yorkshire.

Old Custom House Extra Special Pale (Mad) a brand of Madeira produced by Rutherford and Miles.

Old Dalby Ale (Eng) a 5.1% alc by vol. ale brewed by the Belvoir Brewery, Leicestershire.

Old Dan Ale (Eng) a bottled brown ale 1075 O.G. brewed by the Daniel Thwaites Brewery in Blackburn, Lancashire.

Old Dark Attic (Eng) a 4% alc by vol. ale brewed by The Concertina Brewery, South Yorkshire.

Old Deadly's White Cider (Eng) a 6.9% alc by vol. white cider from Aston Manor, Birmingham.

Old Devil (Eng) a strong ale 1060 O.G. brewed by the Wiltshire Brewery C°. in Tisbury, Wiltshire.

Old Devil (Eng) a 4.7% alc by vol. amber-coloured ale brewed by Wychwood Brewery, Witney.

Old Dick (Eng) a 5.2% alc by vol. ale brewed by the Swale Brewery, Sittingbourne.

Old Dray (Eng) a 4.4% alc by vol. beer brewed by the Worldham Brewery, near Alton, Hampshire. *see* Barbarian.

Old Duque de Sevilla (Sp) a cask-aged brandy produced by Vincente Suso y Perez in Cariñena, north-eastern Spain.

Old Dutch Liqueurs (Hol) these are traditional-styled drinks that are closely associated with domestic life.

Old East India (Eng) an old English grade of Sherry. An old Oloroso with a natural sweet taste. Named by the practice of taking Olorosos on voyages to India. Similar to Madeiras.

Old Ebeneezer (Eng) an 8% alc by vol. winter warmer barley wine from the Butterknowle Brewery. *See also* Banner Bitter.

Olde Emplor IPA (Eng) a 5.5% alc by vol. India pale ale brewed by the Red Rose Brewery, Lancashire.

Olde English Cyder (Eng) *see* Gaymers Olde English Cyder.

Olde English 800 (USA) is America's strongest natually fermented beer 7.5% alc by vol. brewed by the Blitz-Weinhard Brewery in Portland, Oregon.

Old Eli (Eng) a cask-conditioned ale 1050 O.G. brewed by the Sair home-brew public house in Linthwaite, Huddersfield, Yorkshire.

Old Empire (Eng) an I.P.A. brewed by the Marstons Brewery.

Olden (Nor) a still natural spring mineral water from Blafjellskilden. Mineral contents (milligrammes per litre): Sodium 1.89mg/l, Calcium 4.4mg/l, Magnesium 0.31mg/l, Potassium 0.32mg/l, Chlorides <2mg/l, Sulphates <10mg/l, Fluorides 0.3mg/l, Nitrates 0.1mg/l, Silicates 4.5mg/l. pH 6.8

Old Engine Oil (Scot) a 4.4% alc by vol. ale brewed by the Harviestoun Brewery, Clackmannanshire.

Old England (Eng) the brand-name of a range of fortified British wines produced by Mather & Sons (Matthew Clark).

Old English Advocaat (Eng) an advocaat produced by Townend and Sons of Hull under the name of Keelings. Made from fortified wine and eggs.

Old English Mead (Eng) 2 cups clear honey, 4½ litres (4quarts) spring water, 75grms (3ozs) brown sugar, juice of a lemon, 2 egg whites, 25grms (1oz) yeast. Simmer honey, water, sugar and eggs, add lemon, cool, add yeast, stand in a warm cupboard, bottle.

Olde Norfolk Punch (Eng) a monastic herbal drink produced by Welle Manor Hall in Upwell. Contains various herbs.

Oldershaw Brewery (Eng) a brewery. (Add): 12 Harrowby Hall, Grantham, Lincolnshire NG31 9HB. Brews: Ahtanum Gold 4.3% alc by vol., Caskade 4.2% alc by vol., Ermine Ale 4.2% alc by vol., Grantham Stout 4.3% alc by vol., High Dyke 3.9% alc by vol., Newton's Drop 4.1% alc by vol., Old Boy 4.8% alc by vol., Regal Blonde Lager 4.4% alc by vol. Website: http://www.oldershawbrewery.com 'E'mail: goldbrew@btconnect.com

Oldesloer Fruit Schnapps (Ger) pure fruit blended with natural wheat-based schnapps 15% alc by vol. 6 flavours: apple, plum, pineapple, blackberry, peach, grenadine.

Oldest [The] (Fr) an 1805 distilled Cognac 30% alc by vol. produced by A.E. Dor in Jarnac.

Oldest-Ally (Port) a 25 year old tawny Port from Warre.

Olde Stoker (Eng) a winter ale from Branscombe Vale. *See also* Summa'That.

Olde Swannie (Eng) a 4.3% alc by vol. best bitter from Welton's of Dorking. Brewed using Sussex Bramling Cross hops.

Olde Time Ale (Eng) a bottled strong ale 1070 O.G. brewed by the McMullen's Brewery in Hertford.

Old Etonian (Cktl) ½ measure Lillet, ½ measure gin, 2 dashes orange bitters, 2 dashes crème de noyau. Stir over ice, strain into a cocktail glass and add a twist of orange peel.

Old Etonian Cocktail (Cktl) ½ measure dry gin, ½ measure Lillet, 2 dashes Amer Picon, 2 dashes crème de noyau. Shake over ice and strain into a cocktail glass.

Old Evan Williams Distillery (USA) an 8 year old Bourbon whisky producer from Bardstown, Kentucky.

Old Evel (Eng) a cask-conditioned ale 1048 O.G. brewed by the New Forest Brewery, Hampshire.

Old Expensive Ale (Eng) a strong winter ale 1065 O.G. brewed by the Burton Bridge Brewery, Burton-on-Trent, Staffordshire.

Old Faithful (Eng) a 5.2% alc by vol. autumn ale brewed by Mitchells Brewery, 11 Moor Lane, Lancaster.

Old Faithful (Eng) a 4% alc by vol. ale brewed by the Tirril Brewery, Cumbria.

Old Farm (Scot) a premium blended Scotch whisky from Glenmoriston Estates, Glenmoriston 40% alc by vol.

Old Farnes (Eng) an ale brewed by the micro-brewery Pett Brewing Company in Hastings.

Old Fart (Eng) a 5% alc by vol. bottled dark ale brewed by Merrimans, Hunslet, West Yorkshire.

Old Fashioned (Cktl) into a heavy tumbler place 1 lump of sugar, moisten with Angostura. Crush, add an ice cube and a slice of orange, add 2 measures of Bourbon whiskey, stir and serve with a spoon.

Old Fashioned Cocktail (Cktl) 1 sugar cube, 60mls (½ gill) Bénédictine, 1 teaspoon orange bitters, 1 teaspoon Angostura. Place sugar in wine glass, add 1½ tablespoons water and crush. Add an ice cube and rest of ingredients, stir well and serve with a dash of lemon peel juice on top.

Old-Fashioned Glass (Eng) a squat, straight-sided tumbler of 200mls (⅓ pint) capacity used for drinks served 'on the rocks'. Also known as an 'on-the-rocks' glass.

Old Fettercairn (Scot) a single highland malt whisky distillery in Kincardineshire. Owned by Whyte and Mackay Ltd. Produces an 8 year old malt 40% alc by vol. 10 year old 43% alc by vol.

Old Fitzgerald (USA) an 8 or 12 year old Bourbon whiskey 40% alc by vol. produced in Louisville by Heaven Hill Distillers.

Old 5X (Eng) a 12% alc by vol. oak matured, barley wine brewed by Greene King at the Westgate Brewery, Bury St. Edmunds, Suffolk. Not available comercially as used as a blending base for other beers.

Old Forester (USA) a brand of Kentucky Bourbon whiskey produced by the Brown-Forman Distillers in Louisville, Kentucky.

Old Fort Brewery (Can) a brewery based in British Columbia. Noted for Pacific Gold and Yukon Gold (both pilsener-style lager beers).

Old Freckled Ken (Eng) a 4.5% alc by vol. ale from Cottage Brewing Company, West Lydford, near Yeovil, Somerset.

Old Freddy Walker (Eng) a 7.3% alc by vol. old-style strong ale brewed by Moor Brewery at Ashcolt, Polden Hills.

Old Genie Ale (Eng) a naturally-conditioned bottled strong ale 1070 O.G. brewed by the Big Lamp Brewery in Newcastle-on-Tyne.

Old Georgia Cola (Eng) produced from Crystal Drinks, West Yorkshire. Made with kola nut and coca leaf extract.

Old Georgia Julep (Cktl) dissolve a little sugar in some water in a tumbler. Add 60mls (½ gill) brandy, 60mls (½ gill) peach brandy, a few sprigs of mint and ice, stir and serve. Also known as a Southern Julep.

Old German Beer (USA) a beer brewed by the Yuengling Brewery in Pottsville.

Old Git (Fr) the label for a Côtes de Ventoux red wine.

Old Gloag (Scot) a 60 year old Scotch whisky produced by Mathew Gloag & Sons.

Old Glory (Cktl) 3 parts Zwacks Viennese Apricot, 2 parts lemon juice, 2 parts orange juice, 1 part Barack Palinka, dash egg white. Shake over ice and strain into a cocktail glass.

Old Glory (Eng) a 4.5% alc by vol. ale brewed by the Butterknowle Brewery, Lynesack, Durham.

Old Glory (Eng) a medium strength bitter produced by the Old Washford Mill home-brew public house at Redditch New Town.

Old Glory Ale (Eng) a bottled pale ale 1074 O.G. brewed by the Greenall Whitley Brewery in Warrington, Lancashire. Exported as Old Chester Gold or Chester Gold.

Old Gold (Can) a Canadian whisky produced by Gilbey Canada Ltd.

Old Gold (Cktl) fill a brandy balloon half-full of golden tequila, add a few drops of Maggi sauce to give a rich golden colour, add 8 drops lime juice, stir and top with ice.

Old Gold (Swe) a lager beer 5% alc by vol. from Spendrups.

Old Gold Beer (Eng) a cask-conditioned ale 1047 O.G. brewed by the Ashford Brewery in Ashford, Kent.

Old Granary Bitter (Eng) a 4.2% alc by vol. bitter ale brewed by the Butlers Brewery C°. Ltd., Berkshire.

Old Grand-Dad (USA) a famous old Bourbon whiskey from Kentucky (1880) commonly known as the 'Head of the Bourbon family'. Produced by a distillery of same name 40% alc by vol.

Old Grog (Eng) a range of alcoholic lemonade or alcoholic orange 4% alc by vol. from Nurdin & Peacock.

Old Growler (Eng) a 5% alc by vol (1055 O.G) rich, dark malty old-fashioned porter. Brewed by Nethergate Brewery in Clare, Suffolk. Produced from a mid eighteenth century recipe. *See also* Old Nethergate.

Old Groyne (Eng) a 6.2% alc by vol. strong ale brewed by the Willy's Brewery, South Humberside.

Old Grumble Ale (Eng) a cask-conditioned, kegged and bottled ale 1060 O.G. brewed by the Tisbury Brewery in Wiltshire.

Old Grumpy (Eng) a 5.2% alc by vol. ale brewed by the Kemptown Brewery C°. Ltd., East Sussex.

Old Gurner's Ale (Eng) a 5% alc by vol. ale brewed by the Ossett Brewing C°. Ltd., West Yorkshire.

Oldham Brewery (Eng) a brewery that was taken over by the Boddington Brewery in 1982. Brews a variety of beers.

Old Harbour (S.Afr) the label for a red wine (Merlot, Cabernet sauvignon and Shiraz blend) produced by the Whalehaven Wines, Hermanus, Western Cape.

Old Harmany (Scot) a blended Scotch whisky produced exclusively for the Japanese market by John Walker and Son.

Old Henry (Eng) a 5.2% alc by vol. ale brewed by the Malvern Hills Brewery, Worcestershire.

Old Hereford Cider (Eng) a 7.3% alc by vol. slightly cloudy cider produced in Hereford for the Sainsbury Supermarkets.

Old Hickory (USA) a brand of Bourbon whiskey produced in Illinois 40% alc by vol.

Old Highland Blend (Scot) a brand of blended Scotch whisky bottled by Eldridge Pope and C°. Ltd. in Dorset 40% alc by vol.

Old Hill Vineyard (USA) a small vineyard based near Glen Ellen, Sonoma Valley, California. Grape variety: Zinfandel.

Old Hock (Eng) an eighteenth century term found on bottle tickets to define the finer German wines.

Old Hoffman Distillery (USA) a Bourbon whiskey distillery based near Frankfort, Kentucky. Produces a Bourbon whiskey of same name 40% alc by vol.

Old Hooky (Eng) a dark winter ale 4.6% alc by vol. brewed by the Hook Norton Brewery in Oxfordshire.

Old Horizontal Ale (Eng) a strong ale 1054 O.G. brewed by the Stocks Brewery in Doncaster, Yorkshire.

Old Horny (Eng) a 4.2% alc by vol. light coloured, cask-conditioned ale brewed by Greene King, Bury St. Edmunds for Valentine's Day.

Old Horsewhip (Eng) an ale brewed by the Mildmay Brewery, Holbeton, near Plymouth.

Old Humbug (Eng) a 5.5% alc by vol. ale brewed by the Hexhamshire Brewery, Northumberland.

Old Intentional (Eng) a 5% alc by vol. ale brewed by The Derby Brewing C°. Ltd., Derbyshire.

Old Ivory (Eng) a lager brewed by the Original Brewing Company in Hertfordshire.

Old Izaak (Eng) a 4.8% alc by vol. beer brewed by Whim Ales, Hartington, near Buxton, Derbyshire.

Old Jack (S.Am) the brand-name of a demerara rum from British Guyana.

Old Jamaica Ginger Beer (Eng) a ginger beer made from Jamaican root ginger by Suncharm Ltd., Queen's Square, Honley, Huddersfield.

Old Jock Ale (Scot) a 6.7% alc by vol (1070 O.G) bottled strong ale brewed by the Broughton Brewery near Biggar. *see* Greenmantle, Scottish Oatmeal Stout.

Old John Bitter (Eng) a keg bitter 1036 O.G. brewed by the Leicester Brewery, Leicester.

Old Jones (Eng) a Christmas ale produced by the British Oak Brewery.

Old Kentucky (USA) a brand of Kentucky Bourbon whiskey produced in Louisville, Kentucky.

Old Kim (Eng) an ale brewed by Hardy and Hansons in Kimberley, Nottinghamshire.

Old Knucker (Eng) a 5.5% alc by vol. ale brewed by the Arundel Brewery Ltd., West Sussex.

Old Knucklehead (USA) a barley wine brewed by the Bridgeport Brewing Company, Portland, Oregon.

Old Landed (Eng) the alternative name for British Bonded. Derives from the fact that the Cognac is landed before being put into bottle.

Old Latrobe (USA) a brewery based in Latrobe, Pennsylvania. Brews: Rolling Rock Lager.

Old Laxey Brewing Company (I.O.M) a micro-brewery based at the Shore Inn. Brews: Bosun Bitter.

Old Legover (Eng) a 4.1% alc by vol. ale brewed by the Daleside Brewery Ltd., North Yorkshire.

Old Lodge (Port) the brand-name of a fine old Tawny Port produced by the Smith Woodhouse Port shippers.

Old Lowesmoor (Eng) an ale brewed by the Jolly Roger Brewery in Worcester, Worcestershire.

Old Lubrication (Eng) a 4.1% alc by vol. ale brewed by the Daleside Brewery Ltd., North Yorkshire.

Old Luxters Barn Ale (Eng) a soft sweet ale from Chiltern Valley Wines in Hambledon, Oxfordshire.

Old Luxters Brewery (Eng) a brewery (established 1991). (Add): Chiltern Valley Vineyard, Hambleden, Henley-on-Thames, Oxfordshire RG9 6JW. Brews: Barn Ale Bitter (bottled) 5.4% alc by vol., Barn Ale Bitter (cask) 4% alc by vol., Dark Roast 5% alc by vol., Gold Ale 5% alc by vol., Special (cask) 4% alc by vol., Winter Warmer 6% alc by vol. Website: http://www.chilternvalley.co.uk 'E'mail: enquiries@chilternvalley.co.uk

Old Man Ale (Eng) a 4.2% alc by vol. ale brewed by the Corniston Brewing Company Ltd., Cumbria.

Old Manor Porter (Eng) a 4.4% alc by vol. porter brewed by the Acorn Brewery, South Yorkshire.

Old Man's Blend (S.Afr) the label for a red (Cabernet sauvignon, Merlot, Pinot noir and Shiraz blend) and white (40% Chenin blanc and 60% Sauvignon blanc) wines produced by the Groote Post Vineyards winery, Darling, Western Cape.

Old Master Ale (Eng) a strong ale 1060 O.G. brewed by the Raven Brewery in Brighton.

Old Masters (Eng) a cask-conditioned bitter 4.6% alc by vol. from the Morland Brewery, Oxfordshire.

Old Masters Cream Sherry [The] (N.Z) a brand of sweet Sherry produced by the Villa Maria Winery in South Auckland.

Old Mill Bitter (Eng) a 3.9% alc by vol. bitter brewed by the Mill Brewery, Snaith, Humberside.

Old Mill Brewery (Eng) a brewery (established 1983). (Add): Mill Street, Snaith, Goole, East Yorkshire DN14 9HU. Brews: cask-conditioned and keg beers. Old Mill Bitter 3.9% alc by vol. Bullion 4.7% alc by vol. Mild 3.5% alc by vol. Nellie Dean 3.5% alc by vol. Old Curiosity 5% alc by vol. Porter 5% alc by vol. Website: http://www.oldmillbrewery.co.uk 'E'mail: oldmillbrewery@demon.co.uk

Old Millennium (Eng) a 4.1% alc by vol. ale from the Hull Brewery, North Humberside.

Old Mill Special Reserve (Scot) a special reserve highland malt whisky (vintage 1968) from the Tamnavulin-Glenlivet Distillery 43% alc by vol.

Old Mill Winery [The] (Austr) a winery. (Add): Willunga Road, McLaren Vale, South Australia. Vineyards at Barossa Valley, Tintara in the McLaren Vale and in Waikerie. Winery- Siegersdorf Winery.

Old Moggie (Eng) a 4.4% alc by vol. ale brewed by the Teignworthy Brewery Ltd., Devon.

Old Montrose (Scot) a de luxe blended Scotch whisky blended and distributed by the Montrose Whisky Company.

Old Mother Hubbard (Eng) a 5.2% alc by vol. conditioned ale brewed by the Nursery Brewery, Keynsham, near Bristol.

Old Mr. Boston (USA) a large noted distilling company based in Boston, Massachusetts. Produces most styles of spirits and liqueurs.

Old Mull (Scot) a blended Scotch whisky from John Hopkins and C°. Ltd. in Glasgow (part of DCL).

Old Mulled Ale (Eng) a 4.5% alc by vol. rich ruby coloured cask ale brewed by the Tisbury Brewery, in Tisbury, Wiltshire.

Old Navy (W.Ind) the brand-name of a dark rum sold by Seagram U.K.

Old Needles Eye (Eng) a cask beer formerly brewed at the Unicorn, a home-brew pub in Shropshire.

Old Nethergate (Eng) a special bitter 4% alc by vol. from the Nethergate Brewery, Clare, Suffolk. See also Old Growler.

Old Nick (Cktl) ¼ measure Drambuie, ½ measure rye whiskey, ⅛ measure orange juice, ⅛ measure lemon juice, 2 dashes orange bitters. Shake over ice, strain into a cocktail glass and top with a cherry.

Old Nick (Eng) a 7.2% alc by vol. strong ale brewed by the George Gale Brewery, Hampshire.

Old Nick (Eng) a barley wine 6.8% alc by vol (1084 O.G) brewed by the Young & C°., The Ram Brewery, Wandsworth, London.

Old Nick (W.Ind) the brand-name of a white rum produced by Bardinet on the island of Martinique.

Old Nigel Ale (Eng) a winter ale 1060 O.G. brewed by the Hoskins Brewery in Leicester.

Old Norfolk Ale (Eng) a winter ale 1043 O.G. brewed by the Woodforde Brewery in Norfolk.

Old Number 7 (USA) the brand-name of a sour-mash whiskey produced by the Jack Daniel Distillery, Tennessee 39% alc by vol.

Old Number 38 Stout (USA) a 5.7% alc by vol. bottled, fruity, chocolate, dry stout brewed by North Coast Brewing C°. in Fort Bragg, California.

Old Oak (W.Ind) a brand of rum produced on the island of Trinidad by the Trinidad Distillers Ltd.

Old Oak Ale (Eng) a cask-conditioned ale 1044 O.G. brewed by the Oak Brewery in Ellesmere Port, Cheshire.

Old Oporto (Port) the brand-name of a rich old vintage character Port produced by Smith Woodhouse Port shippers, produced in 1984 to celebrate their centenary.

Old Original (Eng) a strong cask-conditioned bitter 1050 O.G. brewed by the Everards Brewery in Leicester.

Old Overholt (USA) the brand-name of a rye whiskey 40% alc by vol.

Old Pal (Cktl) ⅓ measure Campari, ⅓ measure rye whiskey, ⅓ measure dry vermouth. Stir over ice and strain into a cocktail glass.

Old Pa Porter (Eng) a 3.8% alc by vol. porter brewed by The Moorcock Brewing C°., Cumbria.

Old Parr (Scot) a 12 year old de luxe blended Scotch whisky produced by MacDonald Greenlees in Leith, Edinburgh 43% alc by vol.

Old Particular (It) see O.P.

Old Peculier (Eng) a famous strong ale 1058.5 O.G. brewed by Theakston, in Marsham, Ripon, Yorkshire, named after the town's ancient Ecclesiastical court, (Peculier of Marsham) hence

O

the peculiar spelling. Also a variety is exported to Holland at 1066 O.G. bottled version is 5.6% alc by vol.

Old Pledge (USA) see O.P.

Old Pomfretian (Eng) a 4.3% alc by vol. malty ale brewed at the Old Castle Brewery, Yorkshire.

Old Porter (Eng) a 4.5% alc by vol. porter brewed by Enville Ales Ltd., West Midlands.

Old Porter (Eng) a 1040 O.G. beer brewed by the Wortley Brewery at Wortley, near Barnsley, South Yorkshire. see Brewer's Best Bitter, Wortley Best Bitter.

Old Porter (Eng) a 5.5% alc by vol. dark, sweet bottle-conditioned porter brewed by King & Barnes, Horsham, West Sussex.

Old Post Office Tree (S.Afr) a still and sparkling natural spring mineral water (established 1488) from Mossel Bay. Mineral contents (milligrammes per litre): Calcium <16mg/l, Magnesium <6mg/l, Bicarbonates <1mg/l, Chlorides <0.2mg/l, Sulphates <0.5mg/l.

Old Prentice Distillery (USA) a Kentucky Bourbon whiskey distillery based in Lawrenceburg, Kentucky. Produces Eagle Rare.

Old Priory Vintage Character (Port) a full-bodied, ruby Port produced by Smith Woodhouse Port shippers.

Old Pulteney (Scot) a single highland malt whisky distillery based in Wick, Caithness (owned by the Hiram Walker Group). Produces 8 and 12 year old Malts. 40% alc by vol. Also Old Pulteney Malt Liqueur at 30% alc by vol. Website: http://www.oldpulteney.com

Old Raby Ale (Eng) an ale brewed by the Hambleton Brewery, near Thirsk, Yorkshire. See also Bull, Stallion, White Boar Bitter.

Old Railway (N.Z) the brand-name used by the Pechar's Vineyards for their wines.

Old Rarity (Scot) a blended Scotch whisky produced by Bulloch, Lade and Cº. Ltd. of Glasgow. 40% alc by vol. Also a 12 year old de luxe blended Scotch whisky 43% alc by vol.

Old Rascal (Eng) a 6% alc by vol. bottled cider produced by Thatcher's, Somerset.

Old Recumbent (Eng) a 5.2% alc by vol. cask-conditioned ale brewed by the Six Bells Brewery, Bishop's Castle, Shropshire.

Old Red Fox (USA) the brand-name of a Kentucky Bourbon whiskey produced by the Old Red Fox Bourbon Whiskey Cº. of Louisville, Kentucky. 8 years old, it is aged in charred oak 40% alc by vol.

Old Red Fox Kentucky Bourbon Whiskey Cº. (USA) a distillery based in Louisville, Kentucky. see Old Red Fox.

Old Rio (Cktl) 1 measure Batida de Coco, 1 measure Scotch whisky. Shake well over crushed ice, strain into a cocktail glass and dress with a cherry.

Old Rosie Scrumpy (Eng) a 7.3% alc by vol. cider from Westons of Much Marcle, Hereford.

Old Rott (Eng) an ale brewed by the Quay Brewery, Hope Square, Weymouth.

Old Ruby (Eng) a 4.2% alc by vol. ale produced by the Allsopp Brewery.

Old Ruby Bitter (Eng) the name for a bitter ale brewed by the Ventnor Brewery Ltd., Ise of Wight.

Old Rummy (Eng) the name given to Admiral Vernon 1745 who used rum to end scurvy on ships from which the drink gets its name. see Rumbustion and Rumbullion.

Old Santa Beer (Eng) a cask-conditioned bitter 1066 O.G. brewed by the Bridgewater Arms, a home-brew public house in Little Gaddesden, Hertfordshire.

Old Schiedam (Hol) a brand of Dutch gin. see Schiedam Gin.

Old Schmidt (Ger) a brand of rum produced by Hansen in Flensburg.

Old Screse (Eng) a 6% alc by vol. strong ale brewed by the Three Tuns Brewery, Shropshire.

Old Scrum (Eng) a 4.1% alc by vol. ale brewed by the Hidden Brewery Ltd., Wiltshire.

Old Shields Vineyard (Eng) a vineyard (established 1971). (Add): Ardleigh, Essex. 1ha. Grape varieties: Müller-Thurgau, Pinot gris.

Old Shrimper (Eng) a 5.5% alc by vol. ale brewed by the South Port Brewery, Merseyside.

Old Skipper (I.O.M) a 4.5% alc by vol. cask-conditioned ale brewed by Okell's at their Kewaigue Brewery, near Douglas for the Peel Boat Weekend.

Old Slapper (Eng) a 4.2% alc by vol. ale brewed by the Bank Top Brewery Ltd., Lancashire.

Old Slug (Eng) a 4.5% alc by vol. draught or bottle conditioned nutty porter brewed by RCH Brewery, West Hewish, Weston Super Mare, Avon.

Old Smiley (Eng) a rich, dark ale based on a traditional whisky nose, (roasted over peat-fired kilns). Produced by Whitbread, brewed at Flowers Brewery, Cheltenham.

Old Smokey (Eng) a 5% alc by vol. beer brewed by Bunce's Brewery, Netheravon, near Salisbury, Wiltshire. See also Famous Pigswill (The), Benchmark.

Old Smoothie Bitter Fenman (Eng) a 3.8% alc by vol. nitrokeg bitter and mild brewed by Elgood & Sons Ltd., Cambridgeshire.

Old Smoothie Mild (Eng) a 3.6% alc by vol. mild ale brewed by Elgood & Sons Ltd., Cambridgeshire.

Old Smuggler (Scot) a blended Scotch whisky from the Hiram Walker group 40% alc by vol.

Old Smuggler (Scot) a brand of Scotch whisky now managed by Stewart & Son of Dundee (since February 1989).

Old Snowy Ale (Eng) a cask-conditioned winter ale 1054 O.G. brewed by the Alexandra Brewery in Brighton.

Old Socks (Eng) a wine tasting term often used to describe young white Burgundy and oak-aged Chardonnay that shows promise after sufficient bottle aging.

Old Southside (Eng) the old name for blended Madeira wines in London.

Old South Winery (USA) a small winery based in

963

Natchez, Mississippi. 5.5ha. Produces Muscadine wines.

Old Speckled Hen (Eng) a bottled strong pale ale 1050 O.G./5.2% alc by vol. Brewed by the Morland Brewery in Abingdon, Oxfordshire to commemmorate the 50th anniversary opening the M.G. car plant. Website: http://www.oldspeckledhen.co.uk

Old Spot Prize Ale (Eng) a strong ale brewed by the Uley Brewery in Gloucestershire.

Old Stables Brewing Company (Eng) a brewery (established 2002). (Add): 38 The Avenue, Sandy, Bedfordshire SG19 1ER. Brews: Black Beauty Stout 4.4% alc by vol., Pallomino Pale Ale 4.2% alc by vol., Sir William Peel Best Bitter 4.8% alc by vol. 'E'mail: bob.trenhome@btinternet.com

Old Stagg (USA) the brand-name of a Bourbon whiskey produced in Kentucky 40% alc by vol.

Old St. Andrews (Scot) a brand of a premium blended Scotch whisky.

Old Stanley Distillery (USA) a Bourbon whiskey distillery based in Kentucky. Produces Bourbon whiskey of same name 40% alc by vol.

Old St. Croix (W.Ind) the brand-name of a rum produced by the Virgin Islands Rum Industries Ltd.

Old Stockport (Eng) a 3.5% alc by vol. light golden ale brewed by Robinson Ltd., Unicorn Brewery, Stockport, Cheshire.

Old Stonehenge Bitter (Eng) a bitter beer 1041 O.G. brewed by the Wiltshire Brewery Company, Tisbury, Wiltshire.

Old Strong Porter (Eng) a bottled winter ale 1046 O.G. brewed by the Tolly Cobbold Brewery in Ipswich.

Old Style (USA) a sweet, full-bodied beer brewed by the Heileman Brewery in La Crosse, Wisconsin.

Old Sunnybrook (USA) the brand-name of a Bourbon whiskey produced in Kentucky 40% alc by vol.

Old Suntory (Jap) the brand-name of a mature blended whiskey produced by the Suntory Distilling C°.

Old Swan (Eng) see Ma Pardoes.

Old Swan (Eng) a Whitbread home-brew public house in Cheltenham. Produces cask-conditioned beers from malt extract.

Old Swan Brewery (Eng) a brewery. (Add): 87-89 Halesowen Road, Netherton, Dudley, west Midlands DY2 9PY. Brews a range of ales and beers. Website: http://www.oldswanbrewery.co.uk

Old Tankard (USA) a nationally distributed beer brewed by the Pabst Brewery.

Old Tap (USA) a lager beer brewed by the Pabst Brewery.

Old Tart (Fr) the label for a vintage Vin de Pays d'Oc white and rosé (Syrah) wines.

Old Taylor Bourbon (USA) a famous Bourbon whiskey (established circa 1882) of Kentucky founded by Col. E.H. Taylor 43% alc by vol.

Old Telegram (USA) the brand-name of a wine produced by Bonny Doon Winery in California. Produced from Rhône grape varieties only in best years.

Old Thumper (Eng) a 5.6% alc by vol (1060 O.G) cask-conditioned and bottled bitter brewed by the Ringwood Brewery, Hampshire.

Old Timber (Eng) a 4.5% alc by vol. dark amber malty ale brewed by the Highwood Brewery, Lincolnshire.

Oldtimer [The] (Hol) a 7.5% alc by vol. unfiltered, unpasteurised, bottled special triple beer brewed by Maasland Brouwerij, Oss (contains spices).

Old Timer Ale (Eng) a 5.8% alc by vol. winter ale brewed by the Wadworth Brewery in Devizes, Wiltshire. Available in December, a bottled version 6% alc by vol. is also produced.

Old Tom (Eng) a 3.4% alc by vol. ale brewed by the Oakwell Brewery, Barnsley.

Old Tom (Eng) a 6.5% alc by vol. strong ale brewed by the Selby (Middlesborough) Brewery Ltd., North Yorkshire.

Old Tom Ale (Eng) a bottled ale 1065 O.G. brewed by the Oldham Brewery in Lancashire.

Old Tom Ale (Eng) a keg bitter 1037 O.G. brewed by the John Smith Brewery in East Midlands.

Old Tom Ale (Eng) a strong dark ale 8.5% alc by vol brewed by Robinson Ltd., Unicorn Brewery, Stockport, Greater Manchester.

Old Tom Gin (USA) a sweetened gin (originally created in the 1820's) used mainly for cocktails.

Old Tongham Tasty (Eng) a strong ale brewed by the Hog's Back Brewery at Tongham, near Guilford, Surrey.

Old Tosser (Eng) an ale brewed by Smiles Brewery, Bristol.

Old Tradition (Eng) a bitter beer 1038 O.G. and a mild ale 1033 O.G. brewed by the North County Breweries in Hull, Yorkshire.

Old Triangle Vineyard (Austr) part of the Hill-Smith Estate in the Barossa Valley. 20ha of mainly Chardonnay, Rhine riesling, Schreube, Sémillon and Shiraz grapes.

Old Trinity House Bual (Mad) a medium sweet Madeira produced by Rutherford and Miles.

Old Vectis Venum (Eng) a beer brewed by Burt's Brewery, Isle of Wight.

Old Vic (Eng) 4.2% alc by vol. smooth cask-conditioned ale, a part of the Tapster's Choice range from Carlsberg-Tetley, available in July.

Old Vienna (Can) a lager beer brewed by the Carling O'Keefe Brewery.

Old Vines (Eng) old vines produce grapes of fine quality and balanced, concentrated flavours that improve with each following year (although they produce less grapes − eventually making it uneconomic − or they die). The term can range between vines of 12 years old and 60+ years! (Austr) = old block, (Fr) = vieilles vignes, (Ger) = alte reben, (Sp) = viñas viejas.

Old Vines Cellars (S.Afr) a winery (established 1995) based in Cape Town, Western Cape. (Add): 50 Liesbeek Road, Rosebank, Cape Town 7700. Grape varieties: Cabernet sauvignon, Chenin blanc, Merlot, Sauvignon blanc, Shiraz. Labels: Baron von Holt, Blue White, Spring Valley, Stein

Select. Also produces Cap Classique (Chenin blanc). Website: http://www.oldvines.co.za

Old Vintage (Fr) a blend of very old Grande Champagne Cognac (over 30 years) produced by Hine.

Old Wagg (Eng) a 4% alc by vol. ale brewed by Elgood & Sons Ltd., Cambridgeshire.

Old Wardour (Eng) a 4.8% alc by vol. ale brewed by the Tisbury Brewery, Tisbury, Wiltshire.

Old Washford Mill (Eng) a home-brew public house in Redditch New Town. Brews a medium strength bitter ale called Old Glory.

Old Wemian (Eng) a 4.9% alc by vol. ale brewed by Hanby Ales Ltd., Shropshire.

Old Winery Vineyard (Austr) part of the Hill-Smith Estate in the Barossa Valley 4ha.

Old Winter Ale (Eng) a winter warmer ale from Fuller, London. Draught 4.8% alc by vol. bottled 5.3% alc by vol.

Old XL (Eng) a strong bottled ale from Holden's in Dudley.

Oleron's Disease (Eng) a vine bacterial blight, stains appear on the leaves and flowers and destroy the cell walls. Copper sprays have almost erradicated it from Europe.

Olevano Romano (It) *see* Cesanese di Olevano Romano.

Olfaction (Eng) the technical term for smell. e.g. to smell a wine.

Olgaberg (Ger) vineyard (Anb): Baden. (Ber): Bodensee. (Gro): Sonnenufer. (Vil): Singen.

Ölgässel (Ger) vineyard (Anb): Pfalz. (Ber): Mittelhaardt-Deutsche Weinstrasse. (Gro): Rebstöckel. (Vil): Diedesfeld.

Ölgild (Ger) vineyard (Anb): Rheinhessen. (Ber): Nierstein. (Gro): Sankt Alban. (Vil): Lörzweiler.

Oliang (Thai) a hot, thick, black coffee served with sugar in glasses with tinned cream in Thailand. If cream is omitted is called Café-Oh.

Oliena (It) the label term for the wine Cannonau di Sardegna if the grapes used for making the wine are produced in this commune.

Oliena (It) a sweet heavy red wine of Sardinia.

Olifant (Hol) a jenever produced by Allied Breweries.

Olifants River (S.Afr) a wine region based in the north-western Cape province.

Olifantsrivier Koöperatiewe Wynkelders (S.Afr) a co-operative winery based in Olifants River. (Add): Box 75, Vredendal 8160. North Western Wine Merchants Wines. Produces Varietal wines.

Oligocen (Pol) a natural spring mineral water from Warsaw. Mineral contents (milligrammes per litre): Sodium 4.5mg/l, Calcium 150mg/l, Magnesium 30mg/l, Potassium 0.5mg/l, Bicarbonates 134mg/l, Chlorides 10mg/l, Sulphates 23mg/l, Nitrates 1.2mg/l. pH 7.9

Oligocene (It) sandstone.

Oligominerale (It) natural mineral water.

Olimpia (It) a natural spring mineral water from Pomezia, Rome.

Olimpia Brewery (USA) a brewery based in St. Paul.

Olite (Sp) one of three sub-zones in the Ribera Alta. Based in the north of the region, it produces the best wines. Grape varieties: Garnacha and Tempranillo.

Olivar (Sp) a straw-coloured fino Sherry produced by Wisdom and Warter in Jerez de la Frontera.

Olivares Dulce Monastrell (Sp) the label for a red wine from a 275ha wine estate based in Jumilla. Grape varieties include: Merlot, Monastrell, Tempranillo, Syrah.

Oliveira Ferrari (Sp) a cava now owned by Cavas del Ampurdán. Is based in Vilafranca del Penedés.

Olivella (It) a red grape variety grown in Campania.

Olive Oil (Euro) used in ancient times before the invention of the cork to keep the air from the wine by floating it on top. *see* Amphora.

Oliver's Army (Eng) a 4.4% alc by vol. ale brewed by the Springhead Brewery, Nottinghamshire.

Olivers Nectar (Eng) a 5.2% alc by vol. ale brewed by the Clearwater Brewery, Devon.

Oliver Winery (USA) a winery based in Bloomington, Indiana. Has vineyards in Kentucky.

Olivet Grange Vineyard (USA) the label for a red wine (Pinot noir) produced by the Inman Family winery, Russian River Valley, Sonoma County, California.

Olivette Cocktail [1] (Cktl) 60mls (½ gill) Plymouth gin, 2 dashes gomme syrup, 2 dashes absinthe, 2 dashes orange bitters. Stir over ice, strain into a cocktail glass, add an olive and squeeze of lemon juice on top.

Olivette Cocktail [2] (Cktl) 30mls (¼ gill) dry gin, 30mls (¼ gill) French vermouth, 2 dashes absinthe, 2 dashes plain syrup, 2 dashes Angostura, 2 dashes orange bitters. Stir over ice, strain into a 125mls (5fl.oz) wine glass, serve with an olive and dash of lemon peel juice on top.

Olivier (Fr) *see* Château Olivier.

Olivier Leflaive (Fr) a noted producteur-négociant based in the A.C. Puligny-Montrachet, Côte d'Or. Has a range of red Côte de Beaune reds together with holdings in the Montrachet Grand Crus. Also produces A.C. Chablis Premier Crus Côte de Lêchet and Fourchaume.

Oliviers (Fr) a natural spring mineral water. Mineral contents (milligrammes per litre): Sodium 14.6mg/l, Calcium 164mg/l, Magnesium 22mg/l, Potassium 1.6mg/l, Bicarbonates 371mg/l, Chlorides 50mg/l, Sulphates 158mg/l, Nitrates 3.8mg/l. pH 7.1

Olivin (Aus) the local name in south-east Styria for the red wines produced in the Winzerkogel vineyards.

Olizy-Violaine (Fr) a Cru Champagne village in the Canton de Châtillon-sur-Marne. District: Reims.

Ollauri (Sp) a noted wine-producing village in the Rioja Alta.

Olle Cocktail (Cktl) into a Champagne saucer put an ice cube, 1½ tablespoons dry gin, 1½ tablespoons Cointreau. Stir and fill up with iced Champagne.

Ollioules (Fr) a commune in the A.C. Bandol, Provence, south-eastern France.

Ollon (Switz) a wine-producing village in the Chablais, Vaud Canton.

Ollwiller (Fr) an A.C. Alsace Grand Cru vineyard in Wuenheim, Haut-Rhin 35.86ha.

Olmeca (Mex) a brand-name of tequila.

Olmega Tequila (Mex) a tequila available as añejo (gold) oak aged for 1 year or blanco (silver), produced by Seagram (both are 38% alc by vol).

Olmeto (Fr) a wine-producing region of south-western Corsica. Produces full-flavoured wines.

Olmo's Reward (Austr) a red (Cabernet sauvignon) wine produced by the Frankland Estate, Western Australia.

Olof Bergh (S.Afr) a 43% alc by vol. solera-aged brandy, enters the solera at 3 y.o. and blended for 3 years. Distilled by Goudini, Worcester, Western Cape.

Olomouc Brewery (Czec) a brewery based in north-eastern Czec.

Oloroso (Port) denotes fragrant, scented.

Oloroso (Sp) heavy golden Sherries which are dry in their natural state, usually sweetened for the U.K. market. *see* Cream, Milk and Brown Sherries.

Oloroso Dona Juana (Sp) a brand of Oloroso Sherry produced by Sanchez Romate in Jerez.

Oloroso la Novia (Sp) a brand of Oloroso Sherry produced by Marqués de Misa.

Oloroso Muy Viejo (Sp) an Almacenista Sherry bottled by Lustau in Jerez de la Frontera.

Oloroso Sangre y Trabajadero (Sp) a brand of dry Oloroso Sherry produced by Cuvillo at Puerto de Santa Maria.

Ölsberg (Ger) vineyard (Anb): Mittelrhein. (Ber): Rheinburgengau. (Gro): Schloss Schonburg. (Vil): Oberwessel.

Ölschnabel (Ger) vineyard (Anb): Franken. (Ber): Steigerwald. (Gro): Kapellenberg. (Vil): Ziegelanger.

Olsen Wines (S.Afr) a winery (established 2002) based in the Du Toitskloof Mountains, Paarl, Western Cape. 30ha. Grape varieties: Cabernet sauvignon, Chardonnay, Pinotage, Shiraz.

Olson Vineyards (USA) a winery. (Add): Redwood Valley, Mendocino County, California. 14acres (6.6ha). Grape varieties: Chardonnay, Colombard, Sauvignon blanc, Cabernet/Merlot blends, Petite Sirah, Zinfandel.

Oltravianello (It) an alternative name for the Cinsault grape grown in Puglia.

Oltrepó Barbera (It) a D.O.C. red wine from Lombardy. Made from the Barbera grape 90%–100%, Uva rara and Croatina 10% grapes.

Oltrepó Bonarda (It) a D.O.C. red wine from Lombardy. Made from the Croatina, Barbera and Uva rara grapes.

Oltrepó Cortese (It) a D.O.C. white wine from Lombardy. Made from 100% Cortese grapes.

Oltrepó Moscato (It) a D.O.C. white wine from Lombardy. Made from 100% Moscato bianco grapes. The D.O.C. can also be used for the sparkling wines produced in accordance with regulations in the region.

Oltrepó Pavese (It) an area in the province of Pavia in Lombardy. 20 miles south of Milan, south of the bank of the river Pó.

Oltrepó Pavese (It) a D.O.C. red wine from Lombardy. Made from the Barbera 65%, Croatina 25% and Uva rara and Ughetta 45% grapes. The D.O.C. can also be used to describe the sparkling wine produced in accordance with regulations in the region.

Oltrepó Pinot (It) a red, rosé or white wine from Lombardy. Style depends on grape variety and vinification method. Pinot grigio and Pinot nero are used. D.O.C. can also be used to describe the sparkling wines produced in accordance with regulations in the region.

Oltrepó Riesling (It) a D.O.C. white wine from Lombardy. Made from the Riesling italico and Renano grapes. D.O.C. can also be used to describe the sparkling wines produced in accordance with the regulations in the region.

Olvi Brewery plc (Fin) a brewery. (Add): Olvitie I-IV, 74100 Iisalmi. Brews beers and lager. Website: http://www.virallinenolvi.fi

Olympia (Gre) a wine-producing region in north-eastern Greece. Produces red, rosé and white wines.

Olympia (USA) a light beer brewed by the Olympia Brewery in Washington.

Olympia Brewing (USA) a brewery based in Olympia, Washington.

Olympia Cocktail (Cktl) 40mls (⅓ gill) dark rum, juice ½ lime, 2 dashes cherry brandy. Stir over ice and strain into a cocktail glass.

Olympian (USA) a style of wine glass of various sizes made by the Libbey Company.

Olympic (Cktl) ⅓ measure brandy, ⅓ measure orange Curaçao, ⅓ measure orange juice. Shake well over ice and strain into a cocktail glass.

Olympic Gold Premium (Eng) the brand-name of a bottled lager 1045 O.G. brewed by Cameron Brewery, Hartlepool, Yorkshire.

Olympic Gold Premium (Eng) the name of a bitter 1047 O.G. brewed by Tolly Cobbold Brewery in Suffolk.

Olympus (Cyp) a dry red wine produced by Etko Ltd., Limassol.

Olyvenbosch Vineyards (S.Afr) a winery (established 1990) based in Wellington, Western Cape. 20ha. Grape varieties: Cabernet sauvignon and Merlot.

Omaka Springs Estate (N.Z) a winery. (Add): Kennedy's Road, RD 2, Blenheim. 58ha. Grape varieties: Chardonnay, Merlot, Pinot noir, Riesling, Sauvignon blanc, Sémillon. Produces still and traditional method wines.

Omarama Vineyard (N.Z) a winery. (Add): Omarama Ave., (P.O. Box 57), Omarama, North Otago. 3ha. Grape varieties: Morio-Muscat, Müller-Thurgau, Pinot gris.

Omar Khayyam (Egy) a full red wine with the lightest flavour of dates.

Omar Khayyam (Ind) a dry sparkling (traditional

O

method) wine produced from Chardonnay grapes at Narayangaon, Western Maharashka.

Ombretta (It) the name used in Venice for a barely sparkling Prosecco. *See also* Bianchetta.

Omega (Ger) a method of bench grafting developed at the Geisenheim Research Institute using a machine which cuts an Omega [Ω] cut into the root-stock with the scion cut so as to slot into the root-cut.

Omihi Hills Vineyard (N.Z) a winery. (Add): Reeces Road, Omihi Valley, Waipara. 7.5ha. Grape varieties: Chardonnay, Chenin blanc, Pinot blanc, Pinot noir.

Omnia Cocktail (Cktl) ½ measure brandy, ½ measure vodka, 2 dashes each of sweet vermouth, maraschino and Grand Marnier. Stir over ice, strain into a cocktail glass and top with a cherry.

Omnia Wines (S.Afr) a winery (established 2004) by a merger of Vinfruco and Stellenbosch Vineyards based in Stellenbosch, Western Cape. Labels include: Arniston Bay, Credo, Inglewood, Kumkani-JJJ, Lanner Hill, Shamwari, Versus, VVS, Welmoed. Website: http://www.omniawines.co.za

Omphacium (Lat) the juice of unripe grapes.

Omrah (Austr) a red (Cabernet sauvignon) wine produced by the Plantagenet Estate, Western Australia.

Onctueuse Cuvée (Fr) a rosé Champagne produced by Jacquart.

Onctueux (Fr) a fat, rich, full-bodied wine.

O.N.C.V. (Alg) *abbr: see* Office National de Commercialisation des Produits Viti-Vinicoles.

Ondaàš (Czec) a dark, special beer 16° Balling brewed in north Moravia.

Ondarrabi Beltza (Sp) a red grape variety grown in Chacolí. Also spelt Hondarrabi Beltza.

Ondarrabi Zuria (Sp) a white grape variety grown in Chacolí. Is also known as the Courbut blanc. Also spelt Hondarrabi Zuria.

Ondenc (Fr) a white grape variety grown in Gaillac, Bergerac and the Côtes de Duras.

Onderkloof (S.Afr) a winery (established 1998) based in Stellenbosch, Western Cape. 25ha. Grape varieties: Cabernet sauvignon, Chardonnay, Chenin blanc, Crouchen, Malbec, Merlot, Muscat, Pinotage, Sauvignon blanc. Label: Floreal. Website: http://www.onderkloofwines.co.za

Ondine (S.Afr) the export label for a range of wines produced by the Ormonde Vineyards winery, Swartland, Western Cape.

Ondine Cristal Roc (Fr) a natural spring mineral water. Mineral contents (milligrammes per litre): Sodium 10.5mg/l, Calcium 73.6mg/l, Magnesium 2.2mg/l, Potassium 1.8mg/l, Bicarbonates 198.5mg/l, Chlorides 18.5mg/l, Sulphates 19.5mg/l, Nitrates 2mg/l.

Ondine Eau de Source (Fr) a natural spring mineral water from St. Benoit, 45110 St. Martin d'Abbat. Mineral contents (milligrammes per litre): Sodium 6.3mg/l, Calcium 46.1mg/l, Magnesium 4.3mg/l, Potassium 3.5mg/l, Bicarbonates 163.5mg/l, Chlorides 3.5mg/l, Sulphates 9mg/l. pH 7.65

Ondrasovka (Czec) a sparkling natural spring mineral water from Ondrasov. Mineral contents (milligrammes per litre): Sodium 29.6mg/l, Calcium 184mg/l, Magnesium 19.56mg/l, Potassium 1.582mg/l, Bicarbonates 706.2mg/l, Chlorides 5.46mg/l, Sulphates 15.38mg/l, Fluorides 1.17mg/l, Nitrates 0.41mg/l.

Ondrinkbaar (Hol) undrinkable.

O'Neale (Sp) a Sherry producer based in Jerez de la Frontera.

One Eight 18 Organic Water (Austr) a natural spring mineral water brand. Mineral contents (milligrammes per litre): Sodium 0.05mg/l, Calcium 0.005mg/l, Magnesium 0.05mg/l, Potassium 0.66mg/l, Chlorides 1.2mg/l.

One For The Toad (Eng) a 4% alc by vol. ale brewed by the Wizard Brewery, Warwickshire.

One Hundred & Eighty [180] (USA) a lightly carbonated, orange citrus, energy drink that contains Viatmins B6, B12, C plus guarana. Produced by Anheuser-Busch, St. Louis, Missouri.

One Hundred and Five [105] (Scot) a natural strength Glenfarclas (highland) malt whisky 60% alc by vol. bottled straight from the cask, allows the customer to dilute it as required.

One Hundred & One [101] Ale (Eng). 4.8% alc by vol. draught or bottled dark, hoppy ale. brewed by Branscombe Brewery in Devon.

One Hundred & Three [103] White Label (Sp) the brand-name of a brandy from Bobadilla in Andalusia, is almost colourless.

One Hundred [100] Pipers (Scot) the brand-name for a de luxe blended Scotch whisky from Seagram 43% alc by vol.

One Ireland Cocktail (Cktl) 25mls (⅛ gill) Irish whiskey, 2 dashes (green) crème de menthe. Blend with a scoop of vanilla ice cream in a blender. Pour into a champagne saucer, dress with a cherry and serve with straws.

One [1]-Two (Eng) a 5% alc by vol. premium bottled lager from 21st Century Drinks, Exeter.

One Yard of Flannel (Cktl) *see* Ale Flip.

Ongakushu (Jap) a 10 year old saké, 16% alc by vol. produced by Hokusetsu (a small brewery).

Ongkaf (Lux) a vineyard site in the village of Machtum.

Onion Shape (Eng) a bottle shape (circa 1670–1720), made of glass, it was the most associated shape of early glass bottles.

Onion Skin (Eng) a description of the colour of certain rosé wines. e.g. Vin Gris of the Jura and Tavel of the Rhône.

O.N.I.V.I.T. (Fr) *abbr: see* Office National Interprofessionnel des Vins de Table.

Onkelchen (Ger) vineyard (Anb): Nahe. (Ber): Schloss Böckelheim. (Gro): Burgweg. (Vil): Norheim.

On Licence (Eng) a licence issued by the Licensing Justices for the sale of alcoholic beverages. *see* Full-On Licence.

Onomasía Proelesías Anotéras Piotítos (Gre) *abbr*: O.P.A.P. Controlled Appellation of Superior

O

Quality. Equivalent to French V.D.Q.S. *see* O.E., T.O., O.P.E. Also spelt Onomasias Proelefseos Anoteras Piotitas.

Onomasía Proelesías Eleikhómeni (Gre) *abbr*: O.P.E. Controlled Appellation of Origin. Equivalent to French A.O.C. *see* O.E., T.O., O.P.A.P.

Onomasias Proelefseos Anoteras Piotitas (Gre) *see* Onomasía Proelesías Anotéras Piotítos

On Premise (USA) on licence. i.e. bar/restaurant/ hotel/etc. for the consumption of alcohol on the premises of sale.

Onsdorf (Ger) village (Anb): Mosel-Saar-Ruwer. (Ber): Obermosel. (Gro): Gipfel. (Vin): Hubertusberg.

Ontario (Can) a lager 5% alc by vol. from the Lakeport Brewery.

Ontario (USA) a little used white cross grape variety.

Ontario (USA) a wine district of southern California. Produces dessert, table and sparkling wines.

Ontario Department of Agriculture Experimental Station (Can) based at Vineland, Ontario. A research station that tests vines to establish their wine-making qualities.

On The Hop (Eng) the name of a beer brewed by the Ballard's Brewery Ltd., Hampshire.

On The House (Eng) a term used by the management of a hostelry for free drinks given by them to celebrate an occasion or for some other reason.

On The Nose (Eng) a term given to the art of judging a wine's qualities for blending without tasing, only by smell. Used in brandy, Port and Sherry production etc.

On The Rocks (USA) served with ice, usually straight spirits in a tumbler with plenty of ice.

On-The-Rocks Glass (USA) a name for the 'old-fashioned' glass.

On The Waggon (Eng) denotes a person that has 'given up' or is being 'taken off' alcoholic drinks due to ill health or other reasons. i.e. financial, family etc. *See also* Cold Turkey and Waggon (Off the).

Onthouding (Hol) abstinence from alcohol.

Ontkurken (Hol) uncork.

Onyx Range (S.Afr) the label for a range of wines produced by the Darling Cellars winery, Swartland.

Ooksoos (Rus) vinegar.

Oolitic Chalk (Fr) the chalk soil of Champagne.

Oolong Tea (Tai) a designation for semi-fermented whole leaf tea from Taiwan, drunk without milk, *See also* Black Tea and Green Tea.

Oom Tas (S.Afr) a white, dry wine made by the Stellenbosch Farmers' Winery from the white Cinsault and Muscat d'Alexandria grapes.

Oorsprong (S.Afr) origin.

007 (Eng) *see* Double Zero Seven (007).

O.P. (Asia) *abbr*: Orange Pekoe a black tea grade.

O.P. (It) *abbr*: Old Particular, an old style name given to Marsala, denotes 2 years ageing at 18% alc by vol.

O.P. (USA) *abbr*: Old Pledge, a pledge taken by people in the nineteenth century to drink only moderately.

Opal Cocktail [1] (Cktl) ¾ measure dry gin, ¼ measure crème de banane, dash blue Curaçao, dash lemon juice, teaspoon powdered sugar. Shake well over ice, strain into a cocktail glass (frosted with blue castor sugar) and dress with a slice of lime.

Opal Cocktail [2] (Cktl) 1 measure dry gin, ½ measure triple sec, ½ measure orange juice, 2 dashes orange flower water, 2 dashes gomme syrup. Shake over ice and strain into a cocktail glass.

Opal Nera (It) a black-style Sambuca produced from a beet molasses-based neutral spirit. Produced by the House of Fratelli Francoli Spa 40% alc by vol.

O.P. Anderson (Swe) a brand of aniseed, caraway, cumin and fennel-flavoured akvavit. Is light yellow in colour.

O.P.A.P. (Gre) *abbr*: *see* Onomasía Proelesías Anotéras Piotítos.

Opava Brewery (Czec) a brewery based in north-eastern Czec.

O.P.B. (It) *abbr*: *see* Opera Pia Barolo.

O.P.E. (Gre) *abbr*: *see* Onomasía Proelesías Eleikhómeni.

Open Fermenter (USA) the name given to an open fermentation vat for beer or wine.

Opening Cocktail (Cktl) ½ measure rye whiskey, ¼ measure sweet vermouth, ¼ measure grenadine. Stir over ice and strain into a cocktail glass.

Opening Times (Eng) these are the fixed times that licensed premises are allowed to open. Times (up to 24 hours) may vary from region to region and public house to public house (from 2006).

Openknit (Eng) a term used to describe an open and enjoyable nose or palate on a wine.

Open Sky (S.Afr) the label for a range of wines marketed by the Premium Cape Wines company, Stellenbosch, Western Cape.

Opera (Cktl) ⅔ measure dry gin, ⅙ measure Dubonnet, ⅙ measure maraschino. Stir over ice, strain and add a squeeze of orange peel juice on top.

Opera (It) a natural spring mineral water from Cottorella, Rieti. Mineral contents (milligrammes per litre): Sodium 4.3mg/l.

Opera Pia Barolo (It) stands for the 'Good works of Barolo', a family named Falletti, the Marchesi of Barolo, were vineyard owners who did much to popularise the wines of Barolo. The last Marchesia, a charitable woman, devoted both time and money to the poor and her activities were known as O.P.B.

Operette (S.Afr) a fresh, dry white wine produced by the Villiera Estate.

Opfingen (Ger) village (Anb): Baden. (Ber): Kaiserstuhl-Tuniberg. (Gro): Attilafelsen. (Vin): Sonnenberg.

Ophélia (Fr) a bière brewed by the Ricour Brasserie in Cappel.

Opici Winery (USA) a small winery based in Cucamonga, California. Produces varietal wines.

Opimian (It) a white wine produced in Falernum in

Roman times, made from very ripe grapes, also known as Falerian Opimian.

Opitz [Willi] (Aus) a famous wine maker based in Neusiedlersee 5ha. (Add): Quergasse 11, 7142 Illmitz. Grape varieties: Blauburgunder, Gewürztraminer, Grüner veltliner, Muscat ottonel, Pinot blanc, Scheurebe, St. Laurent, Welschriesling, Weissburgunder, Zweigelt. Produces a range of dry and sweet (botrytised) wines..

Oplenac (Ser) a key wine region in Serbia. Main grape is the Cabernet sauvignon.

Oplenacka Ruzica (Ser) a rosé wine produced near Split and Sibenik in Oplenac, northern Serbia.

Opol (Euro) a dark coloured, medium-dry, rosé made from the Plavac grape in Dalmatia.

Oporto (Hun) a red grape variety grown in central Hungary. Also known as the Kékoporto, Portugieser and the Bastardo in Portugal.

Oporto (Port) a wine port on the mouth of the river Douro. Is the centre of the Port wine trade. *See also* Vila Nova de Gaia.

Oppacher (Ger) a natural spring mineral water brand. Mineral contents (milligrammes per litre): Sodium 10mg/l, Calcium 30mg/l, Magnesium 6mg/l, Potassium 2mg/l, Bicarbonates 46mg/l, Chlorides 13mg/l, Sulphates 71mg/l.

Oppenheim (Ger) village (Anb): Rheinhessen. (Ber): Nierstein. (Gro): Güldenmorgen. (Vins): Daubhaus, Gutlenthaus, Herrenberg, Kreuz.

Oppenheim (Ger) village (Anb): Rheinhessen. (Ber): Nierstein. (Gro): Krötenbrunnen. (Vins): Herrengarten, Paterhof, Schloss, Schlossberg.

Oppenheimer Goldberg (Ger) an old Germanic name for the wines from around Oppenheim town and vineyards up to 30kms in area (now no longer allowed to be used).

Oppigärds Bryggeri AB (Swe) a brewery. (Add): Smedjegatan 14, 776 93 Hedemora. Brews beers and lagers. 'E'mail: info@oppigards.com

Opstal Estate (S.Afr) a winery (established 1950) based in Slanghoek, Worcester, Western Cape. 103ha. (Add): Slanghoek, Rawsonville 6845. Grape varieties: Cabernet sauvignon, Chardonnay, Chenin blanc, Merlot, Pinotage, Ruby cabernet, Sauvignon blanc, Shiraz. Labels: Carl Everson, Droë Wit and varietal wines. Website: http://www.opstal.co.za

Opthalmo (Cyp) an oval-shaped white grape variety.

Optic (Eng) a spring malting barley. *See also* Melanie.

Optic (Eng) the name given to the visual measure which is automatic and gives a pre-set measure and are sealed by the Government. Pre-metric sizes were ⅓, ¼, ⅕ and ⅙ gill. New (metric) sizes are 25mls, 35mls and 50mls.

Optic Goblet (USA) an alternative name for the Club goblet.

Optima (Ger) a white grape variety, a cross between Silvaner X Riesling with Müller-Thurgau. High sugar, early ripener.

Optima (S.Afr) the label for a red wine (Cabernet sauvignon 70% and Merlot 30%) produced by the L'Ormarins Private Cellar winery, Franschhoek, Western Cape.

Optimator (Ger) a doppelbock beer brewed by the Spatenbräu Brauerei in Munich.

Opulent (Eng) a term used to describe a rich, luxurious bouquet and palate, usually from a recognised grape variety. i.e. Pinot noir, Riesling, Sauvignon, etc.

Opus Eximium (Aus) the label for a red wine (Cabernet sauvignon, Pinot noir and St. Laurent blend) produced by the Gesellmann winery, Mittel-Burgenland.

Opus One (USA) the name of a rich, red wine produced jointly by Baron Philippe de Rothschild and Robert Mondavi in the Napa Valley, California. 108acres (49ha). Grape varieties: Cabernet sauvignon, Cabernet franc, Merlot. First vintage in 1979 was made at the Mondavi Winery.

Oracle (S.Afr) the export brand-name for a range of W.O. Coastal wines produced by the Distell winery, Western Cape. Range includes: Cabernet sauvignon, Chardonnay, Pinotage, Sauvignon blanc and Shiraz.

Oracle Oaks Winery (USA) a winery based in the Mendocino County, California. Is a member of the Coro Mendocino (Zinfandel) wine group of Mendocino wineries.

Oradea (Rum) a wine-producing area of north-western Rumania. Produces mainly medium-dry, white wines.

Ora del Garda (It) a spring wind that blows through vineyards around Lake Garda, Trentino.

Oragnac (Hol) a Cognac and Triple Sec-flavoured liqueur produced by the Bols Company.

Oráiste sú Súlach (Ire) orange juice.

Oran (Alg) a mainly red wine-producing region based in western Algeria. The wines are low in acid and strong in alcohol. Principle areas: Coteaux de Tlemcen, Coteaux du Mascara, Dahra and Monts du Tessalah.

Orange (Austr) a wine producing district 200kms west of Sydney. Soils: gravel over clay, limestone, basaltic. Home to Rosemount, Reynolds.

Orange (Eng) a home-brew public house in Pimlico, London. Owned by the Clifton Inns. Brews: cask-conditioned SW1 1040 O.G. and SW2 1050 O.G. Chelsea Blossom.

Orangeade (Eng) a non-alcoholic carbonated orange drink.

Orangeade (USA) orange juice, sugar syrup, soda water, orange slices. Served in tall glasses over crushed ice.

Orange Bitters (Euro) used widely in cocktails, especially gin based. Has tonic and digestive properties. *see* Amer Picon, Campari and Seville Orange Bitters.

Orange Bloom (Cktl) ¼ measure gin, ¼ measure Cointreau, ¼ measure sweet vermouth. Stir over ice, strain into a cocktail glass and add a cherry.

Orange Blossom (Cktl) 1 jigger dry gin, 25mls (1fl.oz) orange juice, 1 teaspoon sugar. Shake over ice, strain into a cocktail glass and top with a squeeze of orange peel juice.

Orange Brandy (Eng) made from Seville oranges steeped in brandy with lemons and sugar.

Orange Buck (Cktl) ¾ measure dry gin, ¼ measure orange juice, juice ¼ lime. Shake over ice, strain into an ice-filled highball glass. Top with ginger ale.

Orange Cadillac (Cktl) 25mls (1fl.oz) Galliano, 20mls (¾ fl.oz) white crème de cacao, 5mls (¼ fl.oz) fresh orange juice, 25mls (1fl.oz) cream, 1 scoop of crushed ice. Blend all together in a blender and serve in a small wine goblet.

Orange Chartreuse (Fr) a new version to the Chartreuse family of fine liqueurs that is flavoured with fresh orange juice.

Orange Cup (Cktl)(Non-alc) into a large jug place some ice, 500mls (1pint) orange juice, juice of a lemon, 60mls (½ gill) gomme syrup, 60mls (½ gill) apricot syrup. Stir, top with soda water and decorate with orange slices.

Orange Curaçao (W.Ind) originally made from oranges from the island of Curaçao. Now made from oranges from most countries and made in many styles. *see* Curaçao.

Orange Daiquiri (Cktl) 35mls (1½ fl.ozs) white rum, 35mls (1½ fl.ozs) orange juice, 10mls (½ fl.oz) lemon juice, 10mls (½fl.oz) gomme syrup. Blend together with a scoop of crushed ice, pour into a Champagne saucer and dress with a slice of orange.

Orange Fizz (Cktl) 90mls (¾ gill) dry gin, juice of an orange, 1 teaspoon gomme syrup. Shake well over ice, strain into a highball glass and top with soda water. Sometimes it is then topped with a dash of Cointreau.

Orange Flower Water (Fr) a non-alcoholic, distilled infusion of orange blossoms, used in some cocktails.

Orange Gin (Eng) orange peel steeped in gin for 8–10 weeks. Strained and bottled (may be sweetened).

Orangehead (Eng) a 4.9% alc by vol. orange-flavoured alcopop from Carlsberg-Tetley.

Orange Juice (Eng) the strained juice of the orange fruit. (Arab) = asseer burtuqal, (Aus) = orangensaft, (Chi) = juzishui, (Cro) = naranča sok, (Den) = appelsinjuice, (Fr) = jus d'orange, (Ger) = orangensaft, (Gre) = portokalatha, (Hol) = sinasappelsap, (Indo) = sari buah jeruk, (Ire) = oráiste sú súlach, (Isr) = mitz tapuzeem, (It) = succo d'arancia, (Jap) = orenji jyuusu, (Kor) = orenjii jyuseo, (Port) = suco de laranja, (Rus) = apyel'seenaviysok, (Sp) = jugo de naranja, (Thai) = namsom, (Wal) = oren sudd.

Orange Liqueurs (Euro) a spirit-based, orange-flavoured liqueurs which vary in strength, colour and flavour. *see* Grand Marnier, Cointreau, Pimpleltjens, Triple Sec, Curaçao etc. Produced in most other countries.

Orange Lotus Light (Eng) an orange-flavoured 'cooler' produced from a blend of British wine and sparkling water 4.5% alc by vol.

Orange Muscat (USA) a white grape variety used in the making of dessert wines in California.

Orangentraube (Aus) a lesser white grape variety grown in northern Austria.

Orange Oasis (Cktl) ¾ measure dry gin, ¼ measure cherry brandy, juice 2 oranges. Shake well over ice, strain into an ice-filled highball glass and top with ginger ale.

Orange Pekoe (Sri.L) *abbr*: OP a blend of high grown unbroken black teas, made from the end bud youngest first leaf, long and wiry in appearance. Has a light and delicate flavour.

Orange-Peppermint Shake (Cktl)(Non-alc) 2 mint sprigs, 2 teaspoons powdered sugar, 1 egg white. Blend with a scoop of crushed ice for two minutes, add 200mls (⅓ pint) orange juice. Pour into a highball glass, dress with an orange slice and mint sprig and serve with straws.

Orange Smile (Cktl)(Non-alc) 1 egg, juice of an orange, 20mls (⅙ gill) grenadine. Shake well over ice and strain into a 125mls (5fl.oz) goblet.

Orange Squash (USA) into a tumbler place juice of 1 orange (strained), add ice, sugar syrup to taste. Top with soda water and slice of lemon.

Orange Street (Eng) a label for a South African red wine (Ruby cabernet and Merlot blend) from Chalié Richards company.

Orange Tea (Eng) pour a little barley water over a slice of orange in a cup or glass, top with fresh brewed tea, stir with stick of cinnamon.

Orangetise (Eng) a sparkling orange flavoured drink from C.C.S.B. *See also* Appletise.

Orangette (Cktl)(Non-alc) juice of an orange, ½ beaten egg, sugar to taste, water. Shake over ice, strain into a cocktail glass and add a slice of orange.

Orange Wine (Bra) an orange-flavoured wine produced from fermented orange juice.

Orangina (Fr) a non-alcoholic, sparkling orange juice containing natural fruit pulp. Owned by Pernod-Ricard. Is distributed in the U.K. by Bulmers of Hereford.

Oranjebitter (Hol) a liqueur usually drunk to toast the Dutch Royal family.

Oranjeboom (Hol) taken over by Allied Breweries in 1967 (part of Breda). Brews: Oranjeboom Oud Bruin, Oranjeboom Premium Malt, Oranjeboom Premium Pilsener. Lager brewed by Wrexham Breweries at 1033 O.G. Bottled Oranjeboom 1045 O.G. is imported into G.B. by Allied Breweries in Rotterdam.

Oranjeboom Oud Bruin (Hol) a 2.5% alc by vol. deep-brown, bottled old brown beer brewed by Oranjeboom.

Oranjeboom Premium Malt (Hol) a 0.1% alc by vol. bottled, straw-coloured beer brewed by Oranjeboom.

Oranjeboom Premium Pilsener (Hol) a 5% alc by vol. bottled pilsener brewed by Oranjeboom.

Oranjegenever (Hol) an orange-flavoured jenever.

Oranjerivier Wynkelders (S.Afr) a co-operative winery (established 1965) based in the Benede Oranje, Lower Orange, Northern Cape. (Add): Box 544, Upington 800. 332837ha. Grape varieties: Cabernet sauvignon, Chardonnay, Chenin blanc, Colombard, Hanepoot, Jerepigo, Muscadel, Red muscadel, Pinotage, Ruby cabernet, Shiraz. Labels: Cape Fest, Liquor Boys, River's Tale, Vineyard Collection and varietal wines. Website: http://www.owk.co.za

Oran Mor (Scot) a liqueur based on 12 year old malt whisky, herbs and honey, produced near Edinburgh.

O Rasal (Sp) a sub-zone in D.O. Rías Baixas. Produces mainly white wines from 86% Albariño, 4% Treixadura, 2% Caiño Blanco grapes.

O Rayas (Sp) hieroglyphic-type markings used in the Sherry region to denote a young Oloroso style wine.

Orbæk Bryggeri (Den) a brewery. (Add): Assensvej 38, Orbæk 5853. Brews beers and lager. Website: http://www.oerbaek-bryggeri.nu

Orb Ale (Eng) a special ale at 4.3% alc by vol. brewed by the Potton Brewing Company for the Golden Jubilee of Queen Elizabeth 2nd in 2002.

Orbe (Switz) a wine-producing area in the northern Vaud Canton. Produces red and white wines.

Orbel (Ger) vineyard (Anb): Rheinhessen. (Ber): Nierstein. (Gro): Auflangen. (Vil): Nierstein.

Orbey (Fr) a district in Alsace. (Ger) = Urbeis.

Orbit (Cktl) ⅓ measure rye whiskey, ⅓ measure yellow Chartreuse, ⅓ measure Dubonnet, ⅓ measure Cinzano bianco. Stir over ice, strain into a cocktail glass and add a cherry.

Orchard Heights Winery (USA) a winery. (Add): Orchard Heights Road NW, Salem, Oregon. Noted for Gewürztraminer wines.

Orchard Mill (Eng) a strong dry bottled cider, amber in colour 5% alc by vol.

Orchata (Sp) a drink made from tiger nuts which are crushed and soaked in water for hours, strained and served sweetened and chilled. Is milky in appearance and popular in Valencia.

Orchid (Cktl) 1 measure dry gin, ½ measure pink crème de noyau, ½ measure lemon juice, dash crème de violette. Shake over ice and strain into a sugar frosted cocktail glass.

Orchid Cocktail (Cktl) 40mls (⅓ gill) dry gin, dash Crème Yvette, 1 egg white. Shake over ice and strain into a cocktail glass.

Orchid Fruits (Eng) cherry, peach and raspberry flavoured waters from Orchid Drinks.

Ord (Scot) a single highland malt whisky distillery at the Muir of Ord, Inverness-shire. Owned by Peter Dawson Ltd. Glasgow. Produces a 12 year old malt 40% alc by vol (part of the DCL group).

Ordal (Bel) a natural spring mineral water from Ordal, Ranst. Mineral contents (milligrammes per litre): Sodium 11mg/l, Calcium 112mg/l, Magnesium 11mg/l, Potassium 6mg/l, Bicarbonates 282mg/l, Chlorides 44mg/l, Sulphates 80mg/l, Nitrates 0.5mg/l.

Ordensgut (Ger) grosslage (Anb): Pfalz. (Ber): Südliche Weinstrasse. (Vils): Edesheim, Hainfeld, Rhodt, Weyher.

Order of Merit (Can) a Canadian rye whisky produced by the Canadian Schenley Distilleries Ltd.

Ordinaire (Fr) a term applied to a beverage wine of no stated origin. Sold in France simply as Vin Rouge, Vin Blanc or Vin Rosé.

Ordinaire [Dr. Pierre] (Fr) the creator of the spirit absinthe in the eighteenth century.

Ordinary (Eng) the name used for a standard bitters.

Ordinary el Dorado (S.Am) a brand of rum produced in Guyana by the Guyana Distilleries Ltd.

Ordination Ale (Eng) a 1066 O.G. ale brewed by Harvey & Son, Bridge Wharf Brewery, Lewes.

Ordonnac (Fr) a commune in the Bas-Médoc, north-western Bordeaux. Wines have A.C. Médoc status. Also known as Ordonnac-et-Potensac.

Ordonnac-et-Potensac (Fr) see Ordonnac.

Ordre de la Boisson de la Stricte Observance des Costières du Gard (Fr) a wine society based in the Midi.

Ordre de la Channe (Switz) a wine society.

Ordre de la Dive Bouteille et Confrérie Albigeoise de Rabelais (Fr) a wine brotherhood based in Gaillac.

Ordre des Chevaliers Bretvins [L'] (Fr) see Chevaliers Bretvins.

Ordre des Chevaliers du Cep (Fr) a wine brotherhood based in Montpellier.

Ordre des Compagnons du Beaujolais (Fr) the wine brotherhood of Beaujolais.

Ordre des Coteaux Commanderie de Champagne (Fr) a wine brotherhood of Champagne.

Ordre des Fins Palais de Saint Pourçain et Bourbonnais (Fr) a wine brotherhood based in Côtes d'Auvergne.

Ordre Illustre des Chevaliers de Méduse (Fr) a wine brotherhood based in Côtes de Provence.

Orée du Bois (Fr) a natural spring mineral water from Saint Amand les Eaux. Mineral contents (milligrammes per litre): Sodium 43mg/l, Calcium 234mg/l, Magnesium 70mg/l, Potassium 9mg/l, Bicarbonates 292mg/l, Sulphates 635mg/l, Fluorides 2.1mg/l.

Oregon (USA) a wine-producing area in the Pacific North-West. 4045ha. (2001) vineyards sited mainly around the north Willamette Valley plus Rogue River and Umpqua Valleys. First planted in the 1960's with Vitis vinefera, Oregon wines must contain minimum of 90% of stated variety (except for Cabernet sauvignon which is 75%). See also Columbia Valley and Walla Walla Valley.

Oregon Amber (Eng) an ale brewed by Youngs (part of the Tapster's Choice range from Carlsberg-Tetley).

Orémus (Hun) a white grape variety, a small amount of which is used in the production of Tokaji wines. A cross between Furmint x Bouvier.

Orendain (Mex) the producers of a tequila of same name.

Orengensaft (Aus)(Ger) orange juice.

Oregun (Eng) a 4.7% alc by vol. ale brewed by the Ossett Brewing C°. Ltd., West Yorkshire.

Orenji Jyuseo (Kor) orange juice.

Orenji Jyuusu (Jap) orange juice.

Orense (Sp) a principal wine-producing area in Galicia.

Oren Sudd (Wal) orange juice.

Orezza (Fr) a natural spring mineral water from Rappagio, Corsica. Mineral contents (milligrammes per litre): Sodium 5.7mg/l, Calcium 200mg/l, Magnesium 20mg/l, Potassium 1.9mg/l, Bicarbonates 731mg/l, Chlorides 7.6mg/l, Sulphates 12mg/l, Fluorides 0.17mg/l.

Orfila [José] (Arg) a bodega based at St. Martin, Mendoza. Noted for Cautivo (Cabernet and Pinot blanc based wines).

Organic (Eng) grown without any artificial help (chemical fertilisers, pesticides, etc.). (Fr) = biologique.

Organic Acids (Eng) acids produced by plants.

Organic Best Ale (Eng) a 5% alc by vol. organic ale brewed by Samuel Smith of Tadcaster.

Organic Brewery (Eng) a brewery (established 2000). (Add): Unit 1, Rural Workshops, Higher Bochym, Curry Cross Lanes, Helston, Cornwall TR12 7AZ. Brews: Black Rock Stout 4.7% alc by vol., Lizzard Point 4% alc by vol., Serpentine Dark Ale 4.5% alc by vol. 'E'mail: a.hamer@btclick.com

Organic Catalysts (Eng) enzymes responsible for the fermentation, spoilage and instability of wine. Excreted by micro-organisms.

Organic Honey Dew (Eng) a 5% alc by vol. bottled or 4.3% alc by vol. cask-conditioned golden organic honey ale brewed by Fuller's at their Griffith Brewery, Chiswick in London. Replaces Honey Dew.

Organic Lager (Eng) a 5% alc by vol. lager beer brewed by Bath Ales Ltd., Avon.

Organic Spirits Company [The] (Eng) a distillery. (Add): Meadow View House, Tannery Lane, Bramley, Guilford, Surrey GU5 0AB. Produces a range of spirits including Highland Harvest and Juniper Green. 'E'mail: office@londonandscottish.co.uk

Organic Viticulture (Eng) growing grapes on land that is free of chemicals. (Fr) = lutte raisonée.

Organic Wines (Euro) light table wines made without the use of any chemicals either during viticulture or viniculture.

Organic 'Yella' Belly (Eng) see Yella Belly.

Organisation Internationale de Métrologie Légale (Euro) abbr: see O.I.M.L.

Organistrum (Sp) a white wine produced by Bodegas de Vilariño-Cambados in Val do Salnés, Rías Baixas, D.O. Galicia. Barrel fermented in French oak.

Organoleptic Examination (Eng) the only known method of judging the quality of wines, spirits or beers is by the human organs of sight, smell and taste.

Organoleptic Judgment (Eng) see Organoleptic Examination.

Org de Rac Domain (S.Afr) a winery (established 2004) based in Piketberg, Swartland, Western Cape. 42ha. Grape varieties: Cabernet sauvignon, Merlot, Shiraz. Website: http://www.orgderac.com

Orgeat (Fr) a non-alcoholic, almond-flavoured syrup used in cocktails.

Orgeat Cocktail (Cktl) ½ measure dry gin, ¼ measure orgeat syrup, ¼ measure lemon juice, teaspoon sugar. Shake well over ice and strain into a cocktail glass.

Orgle (Fr) barley.

Oriachovitza (Bul) a D.G.O. area of the Southern Basic Region. Noted for Cabernet sauvignon reserve wines.

Orianda (Rus) a dry white wine from the Crimea.

Orianna (It) a sparkling natural spring mineral water from Carignano di Fano, Pesaro. Mineral contents (milligrammes per litre): Sodium 3mg/l, Calcium 103mg/l, Magnesium 32mg/l, Potassium 13mg/l, Bicarbonates 412mg/l, Chlorides 52mg/l, Sulphates 65mg/l, Fluorides 0.22mg/l, Silicates 7.8mg/l. pH 7.23

Oridenc (Fr) a white grape variety grown in Gaillac.

Oriental (Cktl) ⅜ measure rye whiskey, ⅛ measure white Curaçao, ⅓ measure sweet vermouth, ⅓ measure lime juice. Shake over ice and strain into a cocktail glass.

Oriental Brewery (E.Asia) a brewery based in Seoul, South Korea which produces O.B. and Crown beers.

Oriental Tea Punch (Cktl) 1.1ltrs (2pints) fresh tea, 2 tots brandy or rum, honey to taste, chopped raisins and almonds. Heat all together, strain and top with anise.

Orientation (Sp) in viticulture, the training of the vines on wires (usually three wires).

Original (Eng) a 4.4% alc by vol. bitter beer brewed by the Barum Brewery, Devon.

Original (Eng) a premium cask-conditioned bitter 1945 O.G. brewed by Greenall Whitley.

Original (Eng) a 4.4% alc by vol. bitter ale brewed by The Eccleshall Brewing C°. Ltd., Staffordshire.

Original-Abfüllung (Ger) the term used to indicate that the wine is estate bottled by the producer (now forbidden). Also known as Originalabzug.

Originalabzug (Ger) see Original-Abfüllung.

Original AK (Eng) a 3.8% alc by vol. standard draught bitter ale brewed by McMullen & Sons Ltd., Hertfordshire.

Original Bitter (Eng) a 3.8% alc by vol. bitter ale brewed by the Blackthorn Brewery, Cornwall.

Original Bitter (Eng) a 3.9% alc by vol. bitter ale brewed by the Willy's Brewery, South Humberside.

Original Brewing Company (Eng) a micro-brewery in Hertfordshire. Produces two lagers: Hellanbach and Old Ivory, two bitters: Disciples Brew and V.S.P.

Original Brown (Eng) a bottled brown ale 1032 O.G. brewed by the Matthew Brown Brewery in Blackburn, Lancashire.

Original Canton [The] (Chi) a 20% alc by vol. ginger liqueur produced by Doumen Canton Liqueur C°. Ltd., Jin an Town, Doumen, Guandong.

Original Coffee (Eng) a term used to describe unblended coffee. Is also known as Pure Coffee.

Original Distillation (USA) after '*direct*' distillation in gin production the resulting vapours are condensed to complete the '*original*' distillation.

Original Fountain of Youth (USA) a sparkling natural spring mineral water (established 1956) from The Springs, Florida. Mineral contents (milligrammes per litre): Sodium 4973mg/l, Calcium 512mg/l, Magnesium 609mg/l, Potassium 189mg/l, Bicarbonates 167mg/l, Chlorides 9300mg/l, Sulphates 1667mg/l, Nitrates <0.001mg/l, Silicates 6mg/l, Oxygen 1mg/l. pH 6.94

Original Gerstacker Glühwein (Ger) a brand name for a ready-mixed mulled wine cup. Imported into U.K. by H. Sichel and Sons.

Original Glenshiel [The] (Scot) a 12 year old single malt whisky produced at the Loch Lomond distillery in Dumbartonshire. Launched by Landmark.

Original Grand Cru (Bel) a natural spring mineral water (established 1991) from Hotton sur Ourthe les Bains. (Add): Industries, Brukskensweg 70, 3800 St. Truiden. a natural spring mineral water from. Mineral contents (milligrammes per litre): Sodium 6.6mg/l, Calcium 101mg/l, Magnesium 7.9mg/l, Potassium 2.8mg/l, Bicarbonates 306mg/l, Chlorides 18.1mg/l, Sulphates 31mg/l, Nitrates <10mg/l.

Original Gravity (Eng) *abbr*: O.G. a term used to express beer strength. Pure water is measured as 1000. The density of the wort is then measured by the Customs and Excise officer to assess Excise duty payable by the brewery. The measurement i.e. 1043 gives the amount of fermentable and unfermentable matter plus water in the wort. Originally was displayed on beer labels, can, etc. [now superseded by alcohol by volume (alc by vol) as required by law in the 1990's as the actual alcohol content of the finished beer depended on the brewer with each brew].

Original Gravity (Eng) an ale brewed in the memory of Sir Isaac Newton by Hardy and Hansons, Kimberley, Nottingham.

Original Green Ginger Wine (USA) a ginger-flavoured currant wine, made in the U.K. for the USA market 19.5% alc by vol.

Original Grenn (Mal) a natural spring mineral water from Johore. Mineral contents (milligrammes per litre): Sodium 0.5mg/l, Calcium 4.6mg/l, Magnesium 2.9mg/l, Potassium 0.7mg/l, Chlorides 10.8mg/l, Sulphates 1.9mg/l, Nitrates 1.4mg/l. pH 7.4

Original HB München (Ger) a 5.1% alc by vol. bottled lager brewed by the Hofbräuhaus München, Munich.

Original Light Beer (Scot) a dark keg ale 1032 O.G. brewed by the Alloa Brewery.

Original London Porter (Eng) a 1058 O.G. porter brewed by the Pitfield Brewery. Sold in 33cls bottles.

Original Mackinlay [The] (Scot) a blended Scotch whisky produced by Charles Mackinlay & Cº 40% alc by vol.

Original Mackinlay Legacy De Luxe [The] (Scot) a 12 year old blended de luxe Scotch whisky produced by Charles Mackinlay & Cº 43% alc by vol.

Original Münchner Dunkel (Ger) a 5% alc by vol. bottled dark lager brewed by the Paulaner Brauerei, Munich.

Original New York Seltzer (USA) a carbonated soft drink available in six flavours (black cherry, blueberry, concord grape, lemon, lime, raspberry and vanilla). Sold in 250mls bottles (has no added colours or flavours).

Original Norfolk Punch (Eng) a non-alcoholic drink produced in Upwell, Norfolk.

Original Oettinger Alt (Ger) a 4.9% alc by vol. bottled medium-brown alt beer brewed by the Gotha Brauerei, Gotha.

Original Oettinger Dunkels Hefeweizen (Ger) a 4.9% alc by vol. cloudy, medium-brown, bottle-conditioned wheat beer brewed by the Gotha Brauerei, Gotha.

Original Oettinger Hefeweissbier (Ger) a 4.9% alc by vol. cloudy, bottle-conditioned wheat beer brewed by the Gotha Brauerei, Gotha.

Original Oettinger Kristall Weizen (Ger) a 4.9% alc by vol. filtered, bottled wheat beer brewed by the Gotha Brauerei, Gotha.

Original Oettinger Pils (Ger) a 4.7% alc by vol. bottled pilsner brewed by the Gotha Brauerei, Gotha.

Original Oettinger Schwarzbier (Ger) a 4.9% alc by vol. bottled schwarzbier (black beer) brewed by the Oettingen Brauerei, Oettingen.

Original Old Horsewhip (Eng) a bottle-conditioned beer brewed by Mildmay (a micro-brewery), at Holbeton, near Plymouth.

Original Paarl Perlé (S.Afr) a medium-sweet, pétillant wine made from the Steen grape in the Paarl, Western Cape.

Original Pale Ale (Eng) a keg and canned light ale 1032 O.G. brewed by the Vaux Brewery in Sunderland.

Original Pale Ale (Scot) a keg and canned light ale 1032 O.G. brewed by the Alloa Brewery.

Original Peachtree Liqueur (Hol) a clear, peach-flavoured liqueur produced by De Kuyper 24% alc by vol.

Original Schlichte (Ger) the oldest brand of steinhäger produced by Schlichte.

Originalwein (Ger) original wine (an old term now no longer allowed).

Original Wood (Wal) a 5.2% alc by vol. ale brewed by the Swansea Brewing Cº., West Glamorgan.

Original Zurzacher (Switz) a still and sparkling natural spring mineral water from Zurzach. Mineral contents (milligrammes per litre): Sodium 283mg/l, Calcium 15mg/l, Magnesium 0.3mg/l, Potassium 7.3mg/l, Bicarbonates 306mg/l, Chlorides 131mg/l, Sulphates 247mg/l, Fluorides 3.4mg/l, Nitrates <0.5mg/l.

Originel (Fr) a blanc de blancs Champagne vinified in oak casks. Produced by Cheurlin & Fils.

Origin Napa (USA) a winery based in the Napa Valley, northern California. Grape varieties include: Cabernet sauvignon. *see* Family Home Estate. Website: http://www.originnapa.com

Origin Wine (S.Afr) a winery (established 2002) based in Stellenbosch, Western Cape. Labels include: African Horizon, Cape Nature Organic, Cape Original, Cape 1652, Evolution, Fair Hills, Kaap Hollands, Lion's Gate, Noble Cape, Palm Grove, South Point, Sunbird.

Orinico Flavius Fly (Euro) the cork fly, an insect that lays its eggs on cork and whose grubs eat the cork.

Oriol (Fr) a natural spring mineral water from Cornillon en Trièves, Les Alpes du Dauphiné. Mineral contents (milligrammes per litre): Sodium 26.1mg/l, Magnesium 23mg/l, Potassium 2.9mg/l, Bicarbonates 1030.9mg/l, Chlorides 13.2mg/l, Sulphates 32.3mg/l, Fluorides 0.27mg/l, Nitrates 2.5mg/l.

Orion (Eng) a white grape variety grown in parts of England. Parent is Seyval blanc.

Orion (S.Afr) the label for a red wine (Cabernet sauvignon 64% plus Cabernet franc and Merlot blend) produced by the Stellekaya Winery, Stellenbosch, Western Cape.

Orion Brewery (E.Ind) a large brewery based on the island of Okinawa. Produces Orion Premium (5% alc by vol).

Oristano (It) a commune in Sardinia in the valley of the Tirso river. Noted for Venaccia.

Orizaba (Mex) a coffee-producing region in southern Mexico.

Orkney Brewery Ltd [The] (Scot) a brewery (established 1988). (Add): Quoyloo, Sandwick, Orkney Islands KW16 3LT. Brews: Dark Island Ale 4.6% alc by vol., Dragonhead Stout 4% alc by vol., Northern Light 4% alc by vol., Raven Ale 3.8% alc by vol., Red M^{ac}Gregor 4% alc by vol., Skullsplitter 8.5% alc by vol., Skullplitter. Website: http://www.orkneybrewery.co.uk 'E'mail: Karen@hibreweries.com

Orkney Dark Island (Scot) *see* Dark Island Ale.

Orkney Islands (Scot) noted for two malt whiskies: Highland Park and Scapa. Both are classed as highland malts, they are between a highland malt and an Islay malt in flavour.

Orkney Isle (Scot) a natural spring mineral water from St. Magnus Cistern, Wellpark, Kirkwall, Orkney.

Orlando Wyndham (Austr) a large winery. (Add): Stuart Highway, Rowland Flat, South Australia. 420ha. at Rowland Flat, Eden Valley and Riverland. Grape varieties include: Cabernet sauvignon, Chardonnay, Riesling, Shiraz. Noted for Coolabah, Jacob's Creek and Miamba (label) wines.

Orleance (Eng) an old sixteenth century name for the wines of Orléans, Central Vineyards, Loire.

Orleanian (Cktl) 25mls (⅕ gill) rye whiskey, 15mls (⅛ gill) gomme syrup, 3 dashes absinthe, 2 dashes Angostura. Shake over ice, strain into a cocktail glass and dress with a lemon peel spiral.

Orlenberg (Ger) vineyard (Anb): Pfalz. (Ber): Mittelhaardt-Deutsche Weinstrasse. (Gro): Schwarzerde. (Vil): Bisserheim.

Orloff (Eng) a British vodka produced by Seagrams.

Ormanni (It) *see* Fattoria Ormanni.

Ormarins Estate [L'] (S.Afr) a winery based in Franschhoek. (Add): P/Bag Suider, Paarl 7624. Produces varietal wines from Chardonnay, Sauvignon blanc grapes.

Ormeasco (It) a local name used in north-west Italy for Dolcetto.

Ormes (Fr) a Cru Champagne village in the Canton de Reims. District: Reims.

Ormonde (S.Afr) the label for a range of white (Chardonnay and Chenin blanc) and red (Cabernet sauvignon and Merlot) wines produced by the Ormonde Vineyards winery, Swartland, Western Cape.

Ormond Estate (N.Z) a label used by Montana Wines, Marlborough for a Chardonnay. *See also* Brancott Estate, Renwick Estate.

Ormonde Vineyards (S.Afr) a winery (established 1999) based in Darling, Swartland, Western Cape. 400ha. Grape varieties: Cabernet sauvignon, Chardonnay, Chenin blanc, Merlot, Sauvignon blanc. Labels: Alexanderfontein, Ondine, Westerland. Website: http://www.ormonde.co.za

Ormond Vineyard (N.Z) part of Montana Wines. The name used for their everyday drinking wines. *see* Waihirere Winery.

Ormoz (Slo) a white wine produced in Slovenia.

Ornellaia (It) a Super Tuscan red wine made from up to 25% Merlot plus Cabernets. A Vino da Tavola produced by Bolgheri at Tenuta deil'Ornellaia, Tuscany (similar to Sassicaia).

Oro (It) a style of Marsala from Sicily. *See also* Ambra and Rubino.

Oro (It) a mellow 7 year old brandy produced by Vecchia Romagna. *see* Etichette Nera.

Oro (Sp) a solera gran reserva brandy produced by Bodegas 501.

Orobianco (USA) the brand-name of a dry, fragrant, white wine produced by Villa Armando in Alameda, California 14% alc by vol.

Oribica (It) a sparkling natural spring mineral water from Orobica. Mineral contents (milligrammes per litre): Sodium 17.1mg/l, Calcium 89.6mg/l, Magnesium 22.4mg/l, Potassium 1.4mg/l, Bicarbonates 323.4mg/l, Chlorides 14.7mg/l, Sulphates 55.1mg/l, Nitrates 9.5mg/l, Silicates 10.8mg/l. pH 7.46

Oro del Rhin (Arg) a brand of dry white wine produced by Greco Hermanos in Mendoza.

Oro del Rhin (Chile) a medium-dry, white wine blend of Moscatel and Sauvignon blanc. Produced by Concha y Toro.

Oropa (It) a natural spring mineral water from Oropa.

O

Oro Penedés (Sp) a white wine produced by Cavas Hill in Moja-Alt, Penedés.

Oro Pilla (It) a noted brandy producer.

O Rosal (Sp) one of four sub-regions of Rías Baixas, Galicia. *See also* Condado do Tea, Sotomayor, Val do Salnés.

O Rosal (Sp) a white wine produced from Albariño and Treixadura grapes by Albariño Santiago Ruíz in Sotomayor, Rías Baixas, D.O. Galicia.

Orotana (Sp) a still natural spring mineral water from Artana, Castelló. Mineral contents (milligrammes per litre): Sodium 8mg/l, Calcium 24mg/l, Magnesium 21mg/l, Potassium 2mg/l, Bicarbonates 174mg/l, Chlorides 8.5mg/l, Sulphates 5mg/l, Fluorides 0.2mg/l. Website: http://www.afuensanta.com

Orotava (Sp) a medium-dry, white wine produced on the Canary Islands.

Orris (It) the root of the Iris, was used in Chianti by putting a piece in the vats of maturing wine to give bouquet (not now practiced).

Orris Root (It) *see* Orris.

Orsinella (It) a natural spring mineral water from Poggiorsini, Bari.

Orszàgos Borminósitó Intézet (Hun) *abbr*: O.B.I. Based in Budapest where the Tokaji aszú wines are analysed and taste tested. Issues certificate of export.

Ortega (Ger) a white grape variety, a cross between (Müller-Thurgau and Siegerrebe), gives good sugar and bouquet.

Ortelberg (Ger) vineyard (Anb): Pfalz. (Ber): Südliche Weinstrasse. (Gro): Trappenberg. (Vil): Böbingen.

Ortenau (Ger) a district within the area of Baden, situated in the foothills of the Black Forest. Produces fine wines. Also has the unique right to bottle their product in bocksbeutels which is, by law, reserved for Franconian wines.

Ortenau (Ger) bereich (Anb): Baden. (Gros): Fürsteneck, Schloss Rodeck.

Ortenberg (Ger) village (Anb): Baden. (Ber): Ortenau. (Gro): Fürsteneck. (Vin): Andreasberg, Franzensberger, Freudental, Schlossberg.

Orthophosphoric (Eng) a permitted bacteriacide used in wine-production.

Ortlieb (USA) a beer brewed by the Schmidt Brewery in Philadelphia, Pennsylvania.

Ortlieber (Ger) a white grape variety also known as the Knipperlé, Briergauer riesling and Kleiner riesling.

Ortman Winery (USA) a winery based in Napa Valley, California. Grapes from St. Clement and Spring Mountain Vineyards. Also has vineyards in the Santa Rita Hills, Santa Barbara County and Willamette Valley, Oregon. Labels include: Fiddlestix Vineyard.

Ortrugo (It) a white grape variety grown in the Emilia-Romagna region.

Ortsteil (Ger) lit: 'suburb of/part of'.

Orucoglu (Tur) a natural spring mineral water (established 1998) from Orucoglu. Mineral contents (milligrammes per litre): Sodium 4.5mg/l, Calcium 21.5mg/l, Magnesium 5.2mg/l, Potassium 3.6mg/l, Chlorides 8.73mg/l, Sulphates 13mg/l, Fluorides 0.35mg/l, Nitrates 6.6mg/l. pH 7.2

Orujo (Sp) the Spanish equivalent of French marc, the grape pips, skins, etc. which are fermented and distilled into brandy.

Orval (Bel) a 6.2% alc by vol. amber coloured, triple-fermented trappist ale brewed by the Abbaye of Orval, Villers-devant-Orval, sold in skittle-shaped bottles that contain yeast which continues to act for 8 to 9 months.

Orvian (W.Ind) a natural spring mineral water from Costa Rica.

Orvieto (It) a D.O.C. white wine from Umbria. Made from 50%–65% Trebbiano toscano plus Drupeggio, Grechetto, Malvasia toscano and Verdello grapes. Secco and Abboccato produced. Orvieto Superiore D.O.C. has maximum yield of 60 hl/ha. Also an Orvieto Classico. Minimum alc. = 11.5% by vol. *see* Classico.

Orzechowka (Pol) a vodka flavoured with green walnuts that give it a bitter, nutty taste. Produced by Polmos 45% alc by vol.

Orzo (It) barley.

Osaka (Jap) a small wine-producing province.

Osann-Monzel (Ger) village (Anb): Mosel-Saar-Ruwer. (Ber): Bernkastel. (Gro): Kurfürstlay. (Vins): Kätzchen, Kirchlay, Paulinslay, Rosenberg.

Osborne (Port) a Sherry house in Cadiz that also produces Port. Vintages: 1985, 1991, 1994, 1995, 1997, 2003.

Osborne (Sp) a Sherry and brandy producer. (Add): Osborne y Ca, Fernan Caballero S/N, Puerto de Santa Maria, Cadiz. Base wine for brandy from La Mancha. Produces Conde de Osborne 20 year old, Veterano Brandy. Owns Duff Gordon. Range of Sherries includes Coquinero, Fino Quinta and P▲P Palo Cortado.

Oschelkopf (Ger) vineyard (Anb): Pfalz. (Ber): Mittelhaardt-Deutsche Weinstrasse. (Gro): Kobnert. (Vil): Freinsheim.

Oscura (Mex) a Münchener-style beer.

Oseleta (It) a low-yielding, red grape variety giving deep colour and fresh tannins used in Valpolicella wines.

Osey (Eng) the old English word (mediaeval) for the wines from around the river Rhine in Alsace. Usually sweet. *see* Aussay and Osaye. Word also sometimes referred to naturally sweet Iberian wines of that era.

Oshakan (Arm) a dessert wine produced in Armenia.

Osicka (Austr) a winery. (Add): Off Heathcote, Nagambie, Central Victoria. Produces varietal and vintage Port-style wines. Grape varieties: Cabernet sauvignon, Chardonnay, Hermitage.

Osier Cutter (Eng) a 4.2% alc by vol. ale brewed by the Fenland Brewery Ltd., Cambridgeshire.

Osijek (Cro) a beer brewed in Croatia from north of Zagreb.

O

Osiris (Egy) the ancient Egyptian God of wine.

Osiris (Ger) a white grape variety, a cross between Riesling and Rieslaner, gives good sugar and Riesling bouquet.

Osmosis (Eng) the method of perculation of fluids through porous partitions, used in filtering.

Osmotic Pressure (Eng) created by high concentrations of sugar, slows down the yeast activity. i.e. Sauternes, Trockenbeerenauslese.

Osoye (Eng) *see* Aussay.

Osoyoos Larose (Can) a red (Merlot-based) wine from the Lake Osoyoos vineyards in the Okanagan Valley, British Columbia, named after the joint venture between the vineyard and Château Gruaud-Larose (St.-Julien).

Ossett Brewing C° Ltd (Eng) a brewery (established 1998). (Add): Kings Yard, Low Mill Road, Ossett, West Yorkshire WF5 8ND. Brews: Black Bull Bitter 3.9% alc by vol., Dazzler 4.5% alc by vol., Excelsior 5.2% alc by vol., Falstaff Pale 4% alc by vol., Fine Fettle 4.8% alc by vol., Krystal 3.7% alc by vol., Mellow Yellow 4.5% alc by vol., Old Gurner's Ale 5% alc by vol., Oregun 4.7% alc by vol., Pale Gold 3.8% alc by vol., Santiam 4.3% alc by vol., Silver Fox 4.1% alc by vol., Silver King 4.3% alc by vol., Silver Link 4.6% alc by vol., Silver Shadow 3.9% alc by vol. Website: http://www.ossett-brewery.co.uk 'E'mail: brewery@ossett.co.uk

Ossian (Scot) a 4.1% alc by vol. golden ale brewed by Inveralmond Brewery, Perth, Perthshire.

Osterberg (Fr) an A.C. Alsace Grand Cru vineyard at Ribeauvillé, Haut-Rhin (approx 24ha).

Osterberg (Ger) vineyard (Anb): Baden. (Ber): Badische Bergstrasse/Kraichgau. (Gro): Mannaberg. (Vil): Horrenberg.

Osterberg (Ger) vineyard (Anb): Rheinhessen. (Ber): Bingen. (Gro): Abtey. (Vil): Wolfsheim.

Osterberg (Ger) vineyard (Anb): Rheinhessen. (Ber): Bingen. (Gro): Sankt Rochuskapelle. (Vil): Bingen.

Osterberg (Ger) vineyard (Anb): Rheinhessen. (Ber): Nierstein. (Gro): Gutes Domtal. (Vil): Mommenheim.

Osterberg (Ger) vineyard (Anb): Rheinhessen. (Ber): Nierstein. (Gro): Gutes Domtal. (Vil): Selzen.

Osterberg (Ger) vineyard (Anb): Rheinhessen. (Ber): Nierstein. (Gro): Petersberg. (Vil): Spiesheim.

Osterberg (Ger) vineyard (Anb): Pfalz. (Ber): Mittelhaardt-Deutsche Weinstrasse. (Gro): Kobnert. (Vil): Ungstein.

Osterberg (Ger) vineyard (Anb): Pfalz. (Ber): Mittelhaardt-Deutsche Weinstrasse. (Gro): Schwarzerde. (Vil): Grosskarlbach.

Osterberg (Ger) vineyard (Anb): Pfalz. (Ber): Südliche Weinstrasse. (Gro): Trappenberg. (Vil): Essingen.

Osterbrunnen (Ger) vineyard (Anb): Pfalz. (Ber): Mittelhaardt-Deutsche Weinstrasse. (Gro): Hofstück. (Vil): Niederkirchen.

Osterhöll (Ger) vineyard (Anb): Nahe. (Ber): Kreuznach. (Gro): Kronenberg. (Vil): Bad Kreuznach.

Osteria (It) inn.

Osterizer (USA) a brand of electric bar mixing machine.

Osterlämmchen (Ger) vineyard (Anb): Mosel-Saar-Ruwer. (Ber): Zell/Mosel. (Gro): Grafschaft. (Vil): Ediger-Eller.

Osterpai (Ger) village (Anb): Mittelrhein. (Ber): Rheinburgengau. (Gro): Marksburg. (Vin): Liebeneck-Sonnenlay.

Österreicher (Ger) lit: 'Austrian', a name often used for the Silvaner grape as it is said to have originated in Austria.

Österreichische Bräu (Aus) the largest brewery in Austria based in Linz. Has seven breweries based throughout Austria. Brews: Kaiser beer.

Öesterreichisches Weingutesiegel (Aus) *abbr*: W.G.S, the Austrian wine quality seal.

Österreichmarke (Aus) the old Austrian wine trademark, consisting of a wine glass (roemer) surrounded by a triangle, was found on all of the Austrian quality wines.

Ostessa (It) lit: 'mine host', the name for an Inn's landlady.

Osthofen (Ger) village (Anb): Rheinhessen. (Ber): Wonnegau. (Gro): Gotteshilfe. (Vins): Goldberg, Hasenbiss, Leckzapfen, Neuberg.

Osthofen (Ger) village (Anb): Rheinhessen. (Ber): Wonnegau. (Gro): Pilgerpfad. (Vins): Kirchberg, Klosterberg, Liebenberg, Rheinberg.

Ostlers Cider (Eng) a cider producer (established 1989). (Add): Eastacott Lane, Norleigh Hill, Goodleigh, Barnstable, Devon EX32 7NF. Produces a range of ciders. Website: http://www.ostlerscidermill.co.uk 'E'mail: ostelerscidermill@hotmail.com

Ostlers Summer Ale (Eng) a 4% alc by vol. ale brewed by the Coach House Brewing C°. Ltd., Cheshire.

Östra Brewery (Swe) a small brewery based in Halmstead, southern Sweden.

Ostravar Brewery (Czec) a brewery based in north-eastern Czec. that brews a premium beer of same name 5% alc by vol.

Ostreicher (Ger) *see* Österreicher, the alternative spelling of.

Östrich (Ger) village (Anb): Rheingau. (Ber): Johannisberg. (Gro): Gottesthal. (Vins): Doosberg, Klosterberg, Lenchen.

Östrich (Ger) village (Anb): Rheingau. (Ber): Johannisberg. (Gro): Mehrholzchen. (Vin): Klosterberg.

Östringen (Ger) village (Anb): Baden. (Ber): Badische Bergstrasse/Kraichgau. (Gro): Mannaberg. (Vins): Hummelberg, Rosenkranzweg, Ulrichsberg.

Ostroh Brewery (Czec) an old established brewery based in southern Czec.

Ostuni Ottavianello (It) a D.O.C. red wine from Puglia. Made from the Ottavianello, Malvasia nera, Negro amaro, Notar domenico and Sassumariello grapes.

Osu (Jap) vinegar.

Otago (N.Z) the most southerly of the country's

O

wine-growing regions. Produces mainly Sauvignon blanc and some Pinot noir wines.

Otaika Vineyards (N.Z) the name of vineyards belonging to Continental Wines.

Otaolaurruchi (Sp) a mature Manzanilla Sherry produced by Lustau in Jerez de la Frontera.

Otard (Fr) a Cognac producer. (Add): Château de Cognac, B.P. 3, 16101 Cognac. Produces Baron Otard V.S.O.P. Fine Champagne 8 year old, Prince de Cognac 15 year old, X.O. average age of 35 years.

Othalmo (Cyp) a black grape variety.

Othello (Cyp) a full-bodied dry red wine made by the Keo Cº. in the Limassol region of south-eastern Cyprus.

Otin Fiorin Piè Franco (It) a DOCG Barolo (first produced 1994) from ungrafted, phylloxera-free vines by Teobaldo Cappellano in Serralunga d'Alba, Langhe, Piemonte.

Otley Brewing Company (Wal) a micro-brewery (established 2005) based at the Bunch of Grapes public house, Pontypridd, Mid-Glamorgan.

Ötisheim (Ger) village (Anb): Württemberg. (Ber): Württembergisch Unterland. (Gro): Stromberg. (Vin): Sauberg.

Ötlingen (Ger) village (Anb): Baden. (Ber): Markgräflerland. (Gro): Vogtei Rötteln. (Vins): Sonnhohle, Steige.

Otras Comarcas con Derecha a la Utilización de Mención Geogrífica en Vinos de Mesa (Sp) the equivalent to the French Vin de Pays. Table wine with geographical area stated. Shortened to Vino Comarcal.

Otra Vida (Arg) lit: 'the other life', the brand label for a white Chardonnay) and red (Malbec) range of wines from the Concha y Toro vineyards, Mendoza.

OTT (Eng) a 6% alc by vol. strong ale brewed by the Hogs Back Brewery Ltd., Surrey.

Ottakringer Harmer Brauerei (Aus) a family-owned brewery based in Vienna. Brews under the Goldfassl label.

Ottavianello (It) a red grape variety grown in the Puglia to make wines of the same name. (Fr) = Cinsaut.

Ottavianello di Ostuni (It) see Ostuni Ottavianello.

Otter Ale (Eng) the name of a small micro-brewery based in Devon. Brews: Otter Ale, Otter Bitter, Otter Bright 4.3% alc by vol. Otter Head 5.8% alc by vol.

Otterberg (Ger) vineyard (Anb): Nahe. (Ber): Kreuznach. (Gro): Schlosskapelle. (Vil): Waldlaubersheim.

Otter Brewery (Eng) a brewery (established 1990). (Add): Mathayes, Luppitt, Honiton, Devon EX14 4SA. Brews: Otter Ale 4.5% alc by vol., Otter Bitter 3.6% alc by vol. Website: http://www.otterbrewery.com 'E'mail: info@otterbrewery.com

Otter Bright (Eng) a 4.3% alc by vol. bottled ale. see Otter Ale.

Otter Creek Brewing (USA) a brewery. (Add): 793 Exchange Street, Middlebury, Vermont 05753.

Brews a range of beers and lager. Website: http://www.ottercreekbrewing.com 'E'mail: info@ottercreekbrewing.com

Otter Head (Eng) a 5.8% alc by vol. bottled ale. see Otter Ale.

Ottersheim (Ger) village (Anb): Pfalz. (Ber): Südliche Weinstrasse. (Gro): Trappenberg. (Vin): Kahlenberg.

Ottersheim/Zellerthal (Ger) village (Anb): Pfalz. (Ber): Mittelhaardt-Deutsche Weinstrasse. (Gro): Schnepfenflug vom Kellertal. (Vin): Bräunersberg.

Ottersweier (Ger) village (Anb): Baden. (Ber): Ortenau. (Gro): Schloss Rodeck. (Vins): Althof, Wolfhag.

Ottonese (It) a white grape variety grown in Latium, also known as the Bombino bianco.

Oubenheim Estate (S.Afr) a winery (established 2002) based in Olifants River, Western Cape. Grape varieties: Chenin blanc, Merlot, Pinotage, Sauvignon blanc, Shiraz.

Oud and Cº. (Hol) a noted producer of advocaat based in Haarlem.

Oudart [Pierre] (Fr) see Dom Oudart.

Oud Bruin (Hol) old brown beer.

Oude Beersel Brasserie (Bel) a fine brewery based in Beersel, central Belgium.

Oude Compagnies Post (S.Afr) a winery (established 1699) based in Tulbagh, Western Cape. 18ha. Grape varieties: Cabernet sauvignon, Merlot, Pinotage, Shiraz.

Oude Denneboom (S.Afr) a winery (established 2003) based in Windmeul, Paarl, Western Cape. 39ha. Grape varieties: Cabernet sauvignon, Mourvèdre, Pinotage, Shiraz, Viognier.

Oude Genever (Hol) old gin, drunk neat from a small glass before dinner, often followed by a beer chaser.

Oude Heerengracht (S.Afr) a selection of fine quality dessert wines by Union Wines Limited of Wellington. Also the name of a ginger liqueur from same company.

Oude Kaap (S.Afr) a range of W.O. Western Cape wines produced by DGB for export. Labels include: Elegant Wit (Chenin blanc & Colombard), Klassiek Rood (Cinsaut & Ruby cabernet), Klassiek Wit (Muscat).

Oude Klaren (Hol) a slang term for gin.

Oudekloof Private Cellar (S.Afr) a winery (established 1752) based in Tulbagh, Western Cape. 22ha. Grape varieties: Cabernet sauvignon, Chardonnay, Chenin blanc, Shiraz.

Oude Libertas (S.Afr) varietal wines made by the Stellenbosch Farmers' Winery.

Oude Meester Group (S.Afr) wine-producers and spirit distillers based in Stellenbosch. Formed in 1970 by a merger of South African Distillers & Wines and some old established wine producers. Is also known as the Distillers Corporation. The wine arm is known as Die Bergkelder. Produces: Oude Meester 43% alc by vol. 12 y.o. pot-stilled liqueur brandy and Oude Meester Souverain 38% alc by vol. 12 y.o. brandy from Distell, Stellenbosch.

Oude Molen [De] (S.Afr) a brandy distillery based in Stellenbosch, Western Cape. Produces: 100 Reserve 40% alc by vol. pot-stilled 8 y.o. vintage., VOV 38% alc by vol. 14 y.o. vintage and a 10–15 year old brandy. Owned by Gilbeys.

Oudenaarde Brasserie (Bel) a brewery based in Oudenaarde, northern Belgium. Noted for dark brown ales and kriek 7% alc by vol.

Oudenaarde Special (Bel) a bottle-conditioned ale 5.2% alc by vol. Brewed by the Oudenaarde Brasserie.

Oude Nektar Estate (S.Afr) a winery based in Stellenbosch. (Add): Box 389, Stellenbosch 7600. Produces varietal wines. Grape varieties include Cabernet sauvignon, Pinotage.

Oude Pruim Brasserie (Bel) a brewery based in Beersel, central Belgium.

Oude Rust Wines (S.Afr) *see* Mooi Uitsig Wynkelders.

Oude Wellington Estate (S.Afr) a winery (13ha) based in Wellington, Western Cape. Grape varieties: Cabernet sauvignon, Chardonnay, Chenin blanc, Ruby cabernet, Shiraz. Label: Currant Abbey. Website: http://www.kapwein.com

Oude Weltevreden (S.Afr) the label for a red wine (Merlot and Cabernet sauvignon blend) produced by the Weltevrede Estate winery, Robertson Western Cape.

Oudinot-Jeanmarie (Fr) a Champagne producer. (Add): 12 Rue Godart Roger, B.P. 256, 51207 Épernay Cedex. 80ha. Produces vintage and non-vintage wines. Vintage: 1971, 1973, 1975, 1976, 1979, 1981, 1985, 1989, 1990, 1993, 1995, 1996, 1997, 1998, 1999, 2000. De Luxe vintage cuvée is Cuvée Elysée.

Oud Limburgs (Hol) a copper-coloured beer 5.5% alc by vol. brewed by the Arcen Brouwerij in Arcen, Limburg.

Oud Piro (Bel) a beer brewed by the Bevernagie Brasserie in Lichtervelde, western Flanders (a red beer).

Oudtshoorn (S.Afr) a wine-producing district in Klein Karoo.

Oud-Zottegems Bier (Bel) a 6.5% alc by vol. amber-coloured, bottled Flanders brown beer brewed by the Crombé Brouwerij in Zottegem.

Oued-Imbert (Alg) a wine-producing area in the Oran département. Produces red, rosé and white wines.

Ouillage (Fr) the regular topping up of the barrels with the same wine to keep out the air.

Ouimet Canyon Springs (Can) a natural spring mineral water from Dorion, Ontario.

Oujda (Afr) a wine-producing region of Morocco.

Oujda-Taza (Afr) a noted vineyard in the Oujda region that is planted with vinifera vines.

Oulap se Rooi (S.Afr) the label for a red wine (Cabernet sauvignon, Merlot and Pinotage blend) produced by the Mooiuitsig Wine Cellars winery, Robertson, Western Cape.

Oulmes (Mor) a natural spring mineral water from Oulmes, Casablanca. Mineral contents (milligrammes per litre): Sodium 252mg/l, Calcium 171.3mg/l, Magnesium 52.3mg/l, Potassium 27.3mg/l, Bicarbonates 994mg/l, Chlorides 294.2mg/l, Sulphates 16mg/l, Silicates 34.8mg/l.

Oulton Ales Ltd (Eng) a brewery. (Add): Oulton Broad, Lowestoft, Suffolk NR32 3LZ. Brews bitter beers. Website: http://www.oultonales.co.uk 'E'mail: rose@oultonales.co.uk

Ouma se Wyn (S.Afr) the label for a sweet white wine (Muscat de frontignan) produced by the Weltevrede Estate winery, Robertson, Western Cape.

Oupa se Wyn (S.Afr) the label for a sweet white wine (Red muscadel, and Muscat de hambourg blend) produced by the Weltevrede Estate winery, Robertson, Western Cape (exported under the Cape Muscat label).

Ouras (Fr) a red grape variety grown in the Gaillac region of south-west France.

Our Compliments Pure Spring Water (Can) a natural spring mineral water from Water Valley, Alberta. Mineral contents (milligrammes per litre): Sodium 4.2mg/l, Calcium 68mg/l, Magnesium 14.8mg/l, Potassium 1.3mg/l, Fluorides 0.52mg/l.

Our Founders (S.Afr) the label for a range of wines produced by the Bellingham winery, Wellington, Western Cape.

Ourika (Afr) a full-bodied, red wine produced in the Beni Amar Vineyard in Zenatas, Morocco. Grape varieties: Alicante, Cinsault and Grenache.

Our Lady of the Grape (Fr) *see* Notre Dame du Raisin.

Ouro Fino (Bra) a sparkling natural spring mineral water (established 1946) from Ouro Fino, Campo Largo, Paraná. Mineral contents (milligrammes per litre): Sodium 1.2mg/l, Calcium 32.06mg/l, Magnesium 12.15mg/l, Potassium 0.4mg/l, Bicarbonates 161.21mg/l, Chlorides 0.32mg/l. pH 7.8

Our Special Ale (USA) a draught and bottled ale from the Anchor Steam Brewery in San Francisco. Brewed from a blend of spices, hops and roasted malt.

Ousahelohouri (Geo) a white grape variety grown in Georgia to produce white dessert wines.

Oustalet (Afr) a dry white wine produced in Morocco.

Out of Africa (S.Afr) a label for a range of varietal wines from African Terroir winery, Paarl, Western Cape.

Outrigger Cocktail (Cktl) ¼ measure each of vodka, peach brandy, lime cordial and pineapple juice. Shake over ice and strain into an ice-filled highball glass.

Ouverture des Vendanges (Fr) in the Champagne region the announcement of the date that the grape harvest may commence.

Ouvrée (Fr) a land measure used in the Burgundy region one twentyfourth of a hectare (one tenth of an acre).

Ouzeri (Gre) a small café that specialises in serving ouzo.

Ouzo (Gre) a clear, aniseed-flavoured liqueur distilled from grapes with aromatic herbs. 37%–40% alc by vol. Drunk with water.

Ovation (S.Afr) the label for a white wine (Rhine riesling) produced by the Weltevrede Estate winery, Robertson, Western Cape.

O.V.D. (Scot) *abbr*: **O**ld **V**atted **D**emerara, a dark rum bottled by George Montrose.

Ovens Valley Shiraz (Austr) a red wine produced by the Wynns Vineyard, Coonawarra, South Australia.

Over & Stout (Eng) a 5.2% alc by vol. stout brewed by the Goose Eye Brewery Ltd., West Yorkshire.

Overberg (S.Afr) a wine district that surrounds the town of Caledon.

Overberg Aqua (S.Afr) a still natural spring mineral water from Western Cape. Mineral contents (milligrammes per litre): Sodium 5.9mg/l, Calcium 0.5mg/l, Magnesium 0.3mg/l, Potassium 0.7mg/l, Chlorides 8mg/l, Sulphates 0.6mg/l, Fluorides <0.1mg/l, Nitrates <0.1mg/l. pH 6.4

Overberg Co-operative (S.Afr) *see* Mooi Uitsig Wynkelders.

Overdraught (Eng) a 5.2% alc by vol. ale brewed by a micro-brewery in Sutton (part of Grosvenor Inns).

Over-fining (Eng) the term used for wines that have been excessively fined using too much fining agent, often having little taste.

Overgaauw Estate (S.Afr) a winery (established 1905) based in Stellenbosch, Western Cape. 75ha. (Add): P.O. Box 3, Vlottenburg 7604. Grape varieties: Cabernet franc, Cabernet sauvignon, Chardonnay, Merlot, Sauvignon blanc, Shiraz, Sylvaner. Labels: Overtinto, Tria Corda and varietal wines. Website: http://www.overgaauw.co.za

Overhex Private Cellars (S.Afr) a winery (established 2002) based in Worcester, Western Cape. Grape varieties: Cabernet sauvignon, Chenin blanc, Colombard, Hanepoot, Merlot, Muscadel, Muscat d'Alexandrie, Pinotage, Red muscadel, Sauvignon blanc, Shiraz. Labels: Balance, Cape Mist, Country Cellars, Five Senses, Soulo (Lavida Cape), Marimba, Thorntree, Yammé. Website: http://www.overhex.com

Overhex Koöpertiewe Wynkelders (S.Afr) a co-operative winery based in Worcester, Western Cape. (Add): Box 139, Worcester 6850. Produces varietal wines.

Overmeer (S.Afr) a range of boxed wines produced by Distell, Western Cape. Labels include: Grand Cru, Late Harvest, Selected Red and Stein.

Over Proof (Eng) *see* Proof Testing.

Over Ripe (Ger) a condition of the grapes suitable for the making of sweet white wines. i.e. Auslese.

Överste Brännvin (Swe) a light, spicy (cumin-flavoured) brand of brandy.

Overstone Pale Ale (Eng) a 4.1% alc by vol. pale ale brewed by the Hawkshead Brewery Ltd., Cumbria.

Over the Edge (Eng) a 7.6% alc by vol. strong ale brewed by the Kinver Brewery, West Midlands.

Over the Top (Eng) a wine past its best. Not a clear statement, but is applied to wines that should be drunk young i.e. Beaujolais Nouveau, Vinho Verde or to very old wines that have '*passed it*'.

Overtinto (S.Afr) a red wine made from the Tinta barocca and other Portuguese grape varieties. Made in the Overgaauw Estate.

Overtone (Eng) the term used to describe the dominating element of nose or palate. i.e. oak.

Overture (S.Afr) the label for a red wine (Cabernet sauvignon 45%, Merlot 30% and Shiraz 25%) produced by the Bonfoi Estate, Stellenbosch, Western Cape.

Overvaal Wines (S.Afr) *see* Vaalharts Co-operative.

OVS (Fr) a new company (2006) formed by recruiting seven of France's largest wine companies to group together and produce French wines under the Chamarre label to compete with cheap New World wines.

Owd Ale (Eng) a 6% alc by vol. winter warmer ale from Moorhouses, Burnley, Lancashire.

Owd Bob (Eng) a Christmas ale from Malton Brewery in North Yorkshire.

Owd Roger (Eng) a sweet and heavy barley wine first brewed at the Royal Standard of England at Forty Green in Buckinghamshire. Is now brewed by the Marston's Brewery in Burton-on-Trent, Staffordshire.

Owens (Wal) a cider produced in Botneuydd, North Wales.

O Wine Tumbler [The] (Aus) a stemless, large tulip-bowled glass produced by the Reidel glass company. Website: http://www.riedel.com 'E'mail: info@riedelcrystal.co.uk

Owlcotes Special Ale (Eng) a 3.9% alc by vol. seasonal ale brewed by Green Bottle Ltd., Worth Brewery, Keighley, Yorkshire.

Own Ale (Eng) a cask-conditioned bitter 1040 O.G. brewed by the Miners Arms home-brew public house in Westbury-sub-Mendip, Somerset.

Oxblood (Eng) used as a fining agent for wines, a little wine is mixed with the blood and then it is poured on top of the wine. As it sinks through the wine it takes the impurities with it. Used in the Sauternes district.

Oxford Bitter (Eng) a 3.7% alc by vol. bitter brewed by Morrells Brewery, Oxford.

Oxford Blue (Eng) a seasonal cask ale brewed by Morrells Brewery, Oxford.

Oxford Brew House (Eng) a home-brew public house that brews beer and also bakes bread.

Oxford Graduate (Eng) a 5.2% alc by vol. ale brewed by Morrells Brewery, Oxford.

Oxford Varsity (Eng) a 4.3% alc by vol. premium bitter brewed by Morrells Brewery, Oxford.

Oxfordshire Bitter (Eng) a 3.7% alc by vol. bitter ale brewed by the White Horse Brewery C°. Ltd., Oxfordshire.

Oxhoft (Scan) a liquid measure. 56–58 imperial gallons (67–69 US. gallons/254–264 litres).

Oxidasic Casse (Eng) a wine malady, caused by the enzyme polyphenoloxidase which causes the wine to turn cloudy on contact with air and a deposit to form, occurs in wines made from mouldy or overipe grapes. Is cured by adding ascorbic acid or SO_2 to wine, also by heating the musts or adding bentonite.

Oxidation (Eng) exposure to air through faulty corking, at worst leads to an unpleasant smell and colour darkening.

Oxidised (Eng) a wine that has started to spoil through too much contact with the air. White wines go flat and brown and smell musty. see Maderised.

Oxidised Wines (Eng) wines of a style similar to Sherry that have been subjected to oxidation without being spoilt.

Oxjen (Sp) see Ojen.

Oxyder (Fr) oxidise.

Oxfordshire Bitter (Eng) a 3.7% alc by vol. bitter beer brewed by the Butlers Brewery C°. Ltd., Berkshire.

Oxygen (Eng) needed for wine to mature, also can destroy wine. When added to wine in the micro-oxygenation process it can change the wine's structure. see Oxidation.

Oxygene (USA) see Oxygénée.

Oxygénée (USA) an aniseed-flavoured absinthe substitute 40% alc by vol.

Oxygizer (Aus) a natural spring mineral water. Mineral contents (milligrammes per litre): Sodium 1.2mg/l, Calcium 180mg/l, Magnesium 41mg/l, Potassium 0.58mg/l, Bicarbonates 230mg/l, Chlorides 0.6mg/l, Sulphates 400mg/l, Fluorides 0.8mg/l, Nitrates 1mg/l. pH 7.52 Website: http://www.oxygizer.co

Oxymel (Eng) a British Pharmacopoeia name for the drink of vinegar and honey known as Honegar, an old fourteenth century remedy.

Oy Alko Ab (Fin) the State monopoly that controls all retailing and domestic spirits production. Has 3 distilling plants at Koskenkorva, Salmivaara and Rajamaki.

Oyes (Fr) a Cru Champagne village in the Canton de Montmort. District: Épernay.

Oyón (Sp) a noted wine-producing village in the Rioja Alavesa.

Oyster Bay (N.Z) a famous winery based in Marlborough. Noted for Sauvignon blanc and Chardonnay wines.

Oyster Bay Cocktail (Cktl) ½ measure gin, ½ measure orange Curaçao. Shake over ice and strain into a cocktail glass.

Oyster Stout (Eng) a 4.3% alc by vol. stout brewed by Adnams Sole Bay Brewery, Southwold, Suffolk.

Oyster Stout (I.O.M) a 4.2% alc by vol. stout once produced by the Castletown Brewery, made from real oysters, now produced by the Mount Murray Brewery C°.

Oyster Stout (Eng) a 4.5% alc by vol. bottle conditioned ale from Marston's, Burton-on-Trent. Part of their range of 4 Head Brewers Choice Beers.

Oyster Stout (Eng) a 4.3% alc by vol. stout brewed by the Roosters Brewing C°. Ltd., North Yorkshire.

Oyster Stout (Eng) a 5% alc by vol. stout brewed by the Ventnor Brewery Ltd., Isle of Wight.

Oy Suomen Marjat (Fin) a company that produces liqueurs sold under the Tyrni brand-name.

Oyzo (Gre) an alternative spelling of Ouzo.

Ozardar (USA) a natural spring mineral water from Texas. Mineral contents (milligrammes per litre): Sodium 2.1mg/l, Calcium 1.1mg/l, Magnesium 0.8mg/l, Potassium 0.5mg/l, Bicarbonates 306mg/l, Chlorides 3mg/l, Sulphates 1mg/l, Silicates 6.2mg/l. pH 5.7

Ozarka (USA) a natural spring mineral water (established 1905) from Texas. Mineral contents (milligrammes per litre): Sodium 2.3mg/l, Calcium 2mg/l, Magnesium 1.2mg/l, Bicarbonates 4.9mg/l, Chlorides 3.5mg/l, Sulphates 2.1mg/l. pH 6.56

Ozark Mountains (USA) the southern region of the Missouri district in north-western America.

Ozark Vineyards (USA) a winery based in Cuba, Missouri. Produces French-American hybrid wines.

Ozeki (Jap) a popular brand-name of saké. See also Nihonsakari.

Özkaynak (Tur) a sparkling natural spring mineral water. Mineral contents (milligrammes per litre): Sodium 51.725mg/l, Calcium 96.192mg/l, Magnesium 87.516mg/l, Bicarbonates 834.053mg/l, Chlorides 21.837mg/l, Sulphates 9.25mg/l, Fluorides 0.72mg/l, Silicates 35mg/l. pH 6.5

Ozon (Indo) a natural spring mineral water (established 1995) from Slawi.

Özpinar (Tur) a natural spring mineral water from Istanbul Bodazköy Forest. Mineral contents (milligrammes per litre): Calcium 13.2mg/l, Magnesium 2.4mg/l, Chlorides 40mg/l, Sulphates 23.6mg/l, Fluorides 0.05mg/l, Nitrates 1mg/l. pH 7.68

Özsu (Tur) juice. See also Meyva Suyu.

P

P.A. (Eng) *abbr:* **P**ale **A**le the initials used for a variety of light bitter beers and ales from the West Country.

P.A. (Eng) *abbr:* **P**ale **A**le a cask-conditioned bitter 1034 O.G. brewed by the Ridley Brewery in Chelmsford, Essex.

Paantsch (Ind) the Hindi word for 5 from which 'punch' derives. *see* Punch.

Paarl (S.Afr) a wine region which produces fine white and red wines. The KWV headquarters is based in Paarl.

Paarl Cinsault (S.Afr) a red grape variety of the Cinsault strain.

Paarl Height (S.Afr) the label for a wine produced by the False Bay Vineyards winery, Wellington, Western Cape.

Paarl Perlé (S.Afr) *see* Union Wines.

Paarl Riesling (S.Afr) an alternative name for the Crouchen grape of France.

Paarl Riesling (S.Afr) a Rhine-style wine produced from the Riesling grape variety from the Paarl Vineyards.

Paarl Rock (S.Afr) a 5 y.o. superior brandy distilled by the Paarl Wine and Brandy Company.

Paarl Rock 7 (S.Afr) a 38% alc by vol. 7 y.o. superior brandy distilled from Hanepoot grape wine by Paarl Wine and Brandy Company.

Paarl Rock 21 (S.Afr) a 38% alc by vol. 7 y.o. superior brandy distilled by Paarl Wine and Brandy Company.

Paarl Roodeberg (S.Afr) a Burgundy-style red wine from the Paarl Vineyards.

Paarlsack (S.Afr) a South African Sherry range made by the KWV at Paarl.

Paarl Valais Rouge (S.Afr) *see* Douglas Green.

Paarl Vallei Co-operative (S.Afr) *see* Bolandse Co-operative (the two have now merged).

Paarl Wine and Brandy Company (S.Afr) a winery and distillery (established 1856). (Add): Paarl, West Cape. Produces: Paarl Rock brandies 5 y.o., 7 y.o. and 21 y.o.

Paarl Wine Company (S.Afr) wine wholesalers based in Paarl, Western Cape. Owns Casa Potuguesa range, Fairbridge and Spenser's Creek.

Paaske Øl (Den) an ale brewed by the Wiibroe Brewery in Elsinore.

Pabrik Anggur (Indo) winery.

Pabst Breweries (USA) breweries based in Los Angeles, Newark, Pabst, Peoria and Milwaukee. Brews: Andeker, Blue Ribbon and Old Tap 4.6% alc by vol.

Pacaret (Sp) *see* Paxarete.

Pacheco Ranch Winery (USA) a small winery based in San Rafael, Marin, California. Grape variety: Cabernet sauvignon.

Pacheran Aralar (Sp) a liqueur flavoured with sloe berries produced in the Balearic Islands.

Pachérenc (Fr) a local name for the white Manseng grape in Madiran south-west France.

Pachérenc du Vic-Bihl (Fr) an A.C. sweet white wine from Pachérenc in the Pyrénées. Adjoins Armagnac. Grape varieties: Courbu, Manseng, Ruffiac, Sauvignon blanc and Sémillon. Mimimum alc by vol. 12%. Vines trained in Pachets-en-rang.

Pachets-en-Rang (Fr) the local name used in Pachérenc du Vic Bihl for piquets-en-rang (posts in a line used for vines).

Pachino (It) the old name for the black grape Nero d'Avola.

Paciencia (Port) the name for the train that carries the Port wine from Pinhao (upper Douro) to Oporto.

Pacific (Fr) a non-alcoholic Ricard substitute produced by Pernod-Ricard.

Pacific Bitter (Eng) a 3.8% alc by vol. bitter ale brewed by the Bazens Brewery, Greater Manchester.

Pacific Brewery C°. Inc. (USA) a brewery based on the island of Maui in Hawaii. Brews: Maui Lager.

Pacific Gem (Eng) a single varietal ale brewed by Wadworth & C°. Ltd., Northgate Brewery in Devizes, Wiltshire between 6th and 13th September.

Pacific Gold (Can) a pilsener-style lager beer brewed by the Old Fort Brewery, British Columbia.

Pacifico Brewery (S.Am) a brewery (established 1900) by Jacob Scheule in Mazatalán, Sinaloa, Mexico. Brews: Pacifico Clara.

Pacifico Clara (S.Am) a 4.5% straw coloured bottled lager beer brewed by the Pacifico Brewery, Mazatalán, Sinaloa, Mexico.

Pacific Star Winery (USA) a winery based in the Mendocino County, California. Is a member of the Coro Mendocino (Zinfandel) wine group of Mendocino wineries.

Pacific Vineyards (N.Z) a winery at 90 McLeod Road, Henderson, North Island. 4ha. Produces wines under the Saint Stefan and Montlouis labels. Noted for fortified wines. Grape varieties: Cabernet sauvignon, Chardonnay, Gewürztraminer, Merlot.

Pacific Western Brewing C°. (Can) a brewery based

P

in Vancouver. Brews: Ironhorse, a 5.7% alc by vol. malt liquor.

Pacini Vineyard (USA) a small vineyard based near Ukiah, Mendocino County, California. Grape variety: Zinfandel.

Packaged Premium Lager (Eng) *abbr*: P.P.L.

Package Store (USA) a store where alcoholic beverages are sold for consumption off the premises. *See also* Liquor Store. (U.K.) = off-licence.

Pack o' Cards Pub (Eng) a public house based in Coome Martin, Devon. Is built in the shape of a *'pack of cards house'*. Has 52 windows and 4 floors. The pub was originally built because of a bet.

Paço d'Anha (Port) a producer of Vinho Verde. (Add): Anha, 4900 Vana do Castelo. Grape varieties mainly Loureiro and Trajadura.

Paço Teixeiró (Port) a producer of Vinho Verde. (Add): Cidadelhe, 5050 Peso da Regua. Grape variety: mainly Avesso.

Padapoot (S.Afr) the label for a white (Hanepoot) wine produced by the Paddagang Wines winery, Tulbagh, Western Cape.

Padarotti (S.Afr) the label for a red (Cabernet sauvignon 40% and Shiraz 60% blend) wine produced by the Paddagang Wines winery, Tulbagh, Western Cape.

Paddadundee (S.Afr) the label for a white (Chardonnay) wine produced by the Paddagang Wines winery, Tulbagh, Western Cape.

Paddagang Wines (S.Afr) a winery (established 1987) based in Tulbagh, Western Cape. Grape varieties: Cabernet sauvignon, Chardonnay, Hanepoot, Pinotage, Ruby cabernet, Sauvignon blanc, Shiraz. Labels: Brulpadda Cape, Padapoot, Padarotti, Paddadundee, Paddajolyt, Paddasang. Website: http://www.tulbagh.net

Paddajolyt (S.Afr) the label for a red (Pinotage 50% and Ruby cabernet 50% blend) wine produced by the Paddagang Wines winery, Tulbagh, Western Cape.

Paddasang (S.Afr) the label for a white (Sauvignon blanc) wine produced by the Paddagang Wines winery, Tulbagh, Western Cape.

Paddle Steamer (Cktl) 1 measure Southern Comfort, 1 measure vodka, 2 measures orange juice. Serve in an ice-filled highball glass, top with ginger ale and decorate with an orange peel spiral.

Paddock (S.Afr) the label for a red (Shiraz) and white (Viognier) wine produced by the Excelsior Estate winery, Paarl, Western Cape.

Paddy (Ire) the second largest selling whiskey in Ireland. Blended from 3 whiskey types: a straight pot-still malt, a pot-still barley malt and a grain whiskey. Distilled in Cork 40% alc by vol.

Paddy Cocktail (Cktl) 1½ measures Irish whiskey, ½ measure sweet vermouth, dash Angostura. Shake over ice and strain into a cocktail glass.

Paddy's Proportional Pint (Eng) one of a 3-pack of bottled beers brewed by the Great Stour Brewery in Canterbury, Kent. Named after the politician Paddy Ashdown the then leader of the Liberal party.

Padeiro (Port) a red grape variety grown in the Vinho Verde region.

Paderborner Brauerei (Ger) a brewery based in Paderborn. Brews: Paderborner Pilsner.

Paderborner Pilsner (Ger) a 4.9% alc by vol. bottled pilsner brewed by the Paderborner Brauerei, Paderborn.

Paderna (Port) a white grape variety, known as Arinto in Vinho Verde.

Padova (It) a province of the Veneto region. Produces white and red wines, notably Colli Euganei from the Euganean hills.

Padova Cooler (Cktl) 40mls Luxardo Passione Rossa, 70mls apple juice served in a tall glass with lemonade and ice.

Padre Junipero Serra (USA) a Franciscan missionary who, with settlers from Mexico, established a mission in San Diego which became the first known vineyard site there.

Padthaway (Austr) a key wine district in South Australia, 100kms north of Coonawarra. Dominated by 3 companies: Hardys, Lindemans, Seppelts. Grapes include Chardonnay, Pinot noir, Riesling, Sauvignon blanc.

Paelignum (It) a red wine produced in central-eastern Italy in Roman times.

Paf (Fr) a slang term for soused/sozzled (heavily drunk/intoxicated). *See also* Ivrogne and Poivrot.

Pägen Brauerei (Ger) a small brewery in Cologne (Friesenstrasse). Noted for Kölschbier.

Pagadebit (It) a white grape variety grown in the Emilia Romagna region. Also used in California for making dessert wines. Also known as Bombino Bianco, Debit.

Pagadebit (It) a D.O.C. white wine made from a grape of the same name in Emilia-Romagna.

Pagan (Eng) a 4.8% alc by vol. ale brewed by the Durham Brewery, Bowburn, County Durham.

Pagani (Lat) the monastic name for the peasants that worked around the abbeys in early times. This was specially used for those that worked in the abbey's vineyards. They were paid for their labours in grapes, food or wine.

Pageant Ale (Eng) a 4.3% alc by vol. ale from Elgood's, North Brink Brewery. Brewed to celebrate the bi-centenary (1795–1995) of brewing here.

Page Mill Winery (USA) a winery based in the Santa Cruz Mountains, Santa Clara, California. Grape varieties: Cabernet sauvignon, Chardonnay and Chenin blanc. Produces varietal wines.

Pages (Fr) a large liqueur producer based in Le Pay en Vélay in the Auvergne. Produces Verveine du Vélay (a digestif).

Pagliarese (It) a Chianti Classico producer based in San Gusme, Siena, Tuscany.

Paglieri [I.] (It) a major wine producer of Barbaresco in Piemonte.

Pagney-Derrière-Barine (Fr) a commune in the Côtes de Toul, Lorraine. Produces Vins gris.

Pago (Eng) a range of eleven premium natural bottled fruit juices.

P

Pago (Sp) a vineyard area, on a label describes wines produced from a single vineyard.

Pagodas (Scot) a name given to the kilns of the whisky distilleries.

Pago de los Capellanes (Sp) a red wine produced by a 70ha vineyard in D.O. Ribera del Duero from 80% Tinto fino and 10% each of Cabernet sauvignon and Merlot grapes.

Pago Fruit Juices UK Ltd (Eng) fruit and vegetable juice producers (established 1998). (Add): Jakob House, 6 Alfred Court, Saxon Business Park, Stoke Prior, Bromsgrove, Worcestershire B60 4AD. Produces a range of fruit and vegetable juices. Website: http://www.pago.cc 'E'mail: email@pago.cc

Pago La Negralada (Sp) a red wine produced from 100% Tempranillo grapes by Abadía Retuerta in Ribera del Duero, aged in Bertranges oak for 2 years.

Pagos (Gre) ice.

Pagos (Sp) district.

Pagosa Springs (USA) a natural spring mineral water. Mineral contents (milligrammes per litre): Sodium 790mg/l, Magnesium 25mg/l, Potassium 90mg/l, Bicarbonates 8.55mg/l, Chlorides 180mg/l, Sulphates 1400mg/l, Fluorides 4.3mg/l, Boron 1.8mg/l, Silicates 54mg/l. pH 6.5

Pagos de Noblejas (Sp) a red Vino de la Tierra de Castilla wine produced from the Tempranillo grape.

Pago Valdebellón (Sp) a red wine produced by Abadía Retuerta in Ribera del Duero from 100% Cabernet grapes. Spends 20 months in Tronçais oak.

Pahlmeyer (USA) a winery based in the Napa Valley, California. Grape varieties: Cabernet sauvignon. Label: Proprietary Reserve.

Pahrump Valley Vineyards (USA) a winery based in Nevada, 60 miles west of Las Vegas. Produces red and white wines.

Pai Chiu (Chi) a term used to describe grain spirits.

Paicines (USA) a wine-producing region in the central coastal county of San Benito, California.

Paico (S.Am) the brand-name of an aguardiente from Ecuador.

Païen (Switz) the Valais name for the Traminer grape. *See also* Savagnin, Heida.

Paigny-lès-Reims (Fr) a Cru Champagne village in the Canton de Ville-en-Tardenois. District: Reims.

Paillard [Bruno] (Fr) a Champagne producer. (Add): Ave. du Champagne, 51100 Reims. Produces vintage and non-vintage wines. Vintages: 1976, 1979, 1982, 1985, 1989, 1990, 1995, 1996, 1997, 1998, 1999, 2000, 2001.

Paine (Chile) a wine-producing area based near Santiago.

Paine Brewery (Eng) a brewery based in St. Neots, Cambridgeshire. Brews: cask-conditioned St. Neots Bitter 1041 O.G. EG 1047 O.G. For export Cambridge Pale Ale 1052 O.G. Kinross 1064 O.G. Royal Stag 1052 O.G. and Special Red 1052 O.G.

Painel (Port) a Dão wine produced by the Caves Império.

Pairie des Grands Vins de France (Fr) the wine brotherhood of the Jura region.

País (Chile) a white grape variety that originated from Spain. Known locally in Bío Bío and Maule as Negra Peruana. Also as Criolla Chica in Argentina and Mission in California.

Paisaje de Tupungato (Arg) the label for a red wine (Cabernet sauvignon, Malbec and Merlot blend) produced by the Finca Flichman winery in the Mendoza region.

Paisley Martini (Cktl) ⅔ measure dry gin, ⅙ measure French vermouth, 3 dashes Scotch whisky. Stir in an ice-filled old-fashioned glass and top with a twist of lemon peel juice.

País Vasco (Sp) situated in the north-west. Known as Euskadi in Basque. Home to D.O.'s: Cava, Chacolí de Guetaria, Chacolí de Vizcaya, Getariako Txakolina, Rioja. Grape varieties: Hondarrabi Beltza, Hondarrabi Zuri.

Pajarete (Sp) the Andalusian spelling of Paxarette, a wine from Bornos not far from Arcos de la Fronteira. *See also* Paxerete.

Pajarete (Sp) the term used to describe a semi-sweet Málaga wine.

Pajarete (Sp) a white grape variety grown in southern Spain.

Pajarilla (Sp) a medium white wine produced in the Cariñena region.

Pajuela (Sp) a small insect that weaves a nest around the vine flowers. It eats the shoots and destroys the young branches.

Pak Aqua (Pak) a natural spring mineral water (established 2004) from Musaafi. Mineral contents (milligrammes per litre): Calcium 52mg/l, Magnesium 82mg/l, Chlorides 55mg/l, Sulphates 490mg/l. pH 7.8

Pakhuis [T] (Bel) a brewery. (Add):Vlaamse Kaai 76, Antwerpen B-2000. Brews beers and lagers. Website: http://www.pakhuis.info 'E'mail: pakhuis@pandora.be

Palace (Eng) the brand-name of a coffee blend of 100% arabica beans, lightly roasted. The coffee has a low acidity and full body. Produced by the Lyons C°.

Palace Hill Ranch (USA) a vineyard based in Dry Creek Valley, California. Grape variety: Zinfandel.

Palace Premier (Eng) a special beer brewed by Crouch Vale in Essex for the Palace Theatre, Southend.

Palàcio de Brejoeira (Port) a Vinho Verde produced from the Alvarinho grape fermented at 18°C. (Add): Pinheiros, 4590 Moncao.

Palacio de Cirat (Sp) an oak-aged red reserva D.O. Almansa wine 13.5% alc by vol. from Bodegas Piqueras S.A. produced from Garnacha and Tempranillo grapes.

Palacio de Guzmàn (Sp) a light, dry, fruity white wine produced by VILE in León.

Palacio de la Vega (Sp) a winery based in Discastillo, Tierra Estella in the D.O.C. Navarra, north-eastern Spain (owned by Pernod Ricard).

Palackozott (Hun) bottled.

Palagrello Nero (It) a red grape variety from the Campagnia.

Palaion (Gre) old wine.

Palandri Estate (Austr) a winery based in the Margaret River region of Western Australia. Grape varieties include: Cabernet sauvignon.

Palari (It) a winery based on the island of Sicily. Label: Faro.

Palate (Eng) the area of the mouth where the wine tastes are pronounced and experienced. Used to describe the taste of a beverage.

Palatinate (Ger) the other name for the Rheinpfalz (now Pfalz) anbaugebiet.

Palatinate (Eng) a 3% alc by vol. ale from the Durham Brewery, Bowburn, County Durham. *See also* Celtic, Sanctuary.

Palatinate Cherry Brandy (Eng) a company that also makes other fine liqueurs under this brand name. A British cherry liqueur made by Lamb and Watt of Liverpool, Lancashire.

Palatine (Eng) a 4% alc by vol. ale from the Durham Brewery, Bowburn, County Durham. *See also* Celtic, County Durham.

Palatino (Sp) a solera reserva brandy produced by José de Soto.

Palava (Czec) a local white grape variety grown in Pavlov and Satov.

Pale Ale (Eng) a bottled ale of medium gravity, a strong pale ale would be 1045–1050 O.G. In the south-west of England pale ales are low-gravity draught beers.

Pale Eighty (Scot) an 80/- cask-conditioned ale 1042 O.G. brewed by the Devanha Brewery in north-east Scotland.

Pale Gold (Eng) a 3.8% alc by vol. golden ale brewed by the Ossett Brewing C°. Ltd., West Yorkshire.

Pale Gold (Eng) the brand-name of a light-style rum produced by URM (not white, golden or dark).

Pale Malt (Eng) the term used in brewing for ale malts.

Palenque (Mex) an organic coffee grown in the Chiapas Highlands and sold under the Fairtrade organisation. Website: http://www.cafedirect.co.uk/palenque

Palepuntz (Hol) derives from the English word Belleponge.

Palermo (Fr) an alcohol-free vermouth-style drink (red and white versions) imported into the U.K. by Leisure Drinks of Derby.

Paléo Rosso (It) a red wine produced from Cabernet sauvignon, Cabernet franc and Sangiovese grapes by Le Macchiole, Bolgheri, Tuscany.

Pale Rider (Eng) 5.2% alc by vol. ale brewed by the Kelham Island Brewery, South Yorkshire.

Palette d'Aix (Fr) an A.C. wine of the Côtes de Provence. *see* Château Simone. Made from Carignan, Grenache and Mourvèdre grapes.

Pálido (Sp) a vino de licor, flor-attacked white wine, rich, honey-coloured with a hint of almonds. Produced in D.O. Rueda. 15% alc by vol. it must be aged for a minimum of three years in oak before release.

Palina (It) a sparkling natural spring mineral water. Mineral contents (milligrammes per litre): Sodium 7.3mg/l, Calcium 45.4mg/l, Magnesium 5mg/l, Potassium 1mg/l, Bicarbonates 143mg/l, Chlorides 10.3mg/l, Sulphates 17.9mg/l, Fluorides 0.06mg/l, Nitrates 0.8mg/l, Silicates 8.5mg/l. pH 7.8

Palinkas (Hun) fruit brandies.

Palisades Cocktail (Cktl) ½ measure dry gin, ½ measure dry cider, 2 dashes Angostura. Shake with ice and strain into a cocktail glass.

Palissage (Fr) a method of vine training in Alsace, vines are trained on high trellises of poles and wires about 2 metres high to afford better elevation above the frosts.

Palladius (S.Afr) the label for a white wine (Chardonnay, Chenin blanc, Grenache blanc and Viognier blend) produced by the Sadie Family winery, Swartland, Western Cape.

Pallars (Sp) a still natural spring mineral water from Rialp, Lleida. Mineral contents (milligrammes per litre): Sodium 45.5mg/l, Calcium 44.5mg/l, Magnesium 6.1mg/l, Bicarbonates 94.6mg/l, Chlorides 70.9mg/l, Sulphates 56.1mg/l, Fluorides 0.2mg/l, Nitrates 3mg/l.

Pallas S.A. [San Gill] (Fr) an Armagnac producer. (Add): Domaine de Cassanel, 47600 Nérac.

Pallet (Eng) a portable wooden platform used for moving goods i.e. beer crates, wine/spirit boxes. Is slatted and lifted by fork-lift trucks (a pallet of beer).

Pallet [Le] (Fr) a noted village in the A.C. Muscadet Sèvre et Maine district, Nantais, Loire Atlantique département.

Pallini (Gre) a dry white wine.

Palliser Distillery (Can) a Canadian whisky distillery (part of Gilbey Canada Ltd).

Palliser Estate (N.Z) a winery. (Add): Kitchener Street, Martinborough, North Island. 18ha. Grape varieties: Chardonnay, Pinot noir, Riesling, Sauvignon blanc. Label: Pencarrow. *See also* Family of Twelve.

Pall Mall (Cktl) ⅓ measure dry gin, ⅓ measure French vermouth, ⅓ measure Italian vermouth, 2 dashes orange bitters, 1 teaspoon (white) crème de menthe. Stir over ice and strain into a cocktail glass.

Pallomino Pale Ale (Eng) a 4.2% alc by vol. pale ale brewed by the Old Stables Brewing Company, Bedfordshire.

Pallye [Le] (Fr) a vineyard in the A.C. commune of Montagny, Côte Chalonnaise, Burgundy.

Palma (Sp) a classification of young Fino Sherries. Marks are placed on casks of original Rayas to denote quality and age of the Sherry. In a style of hieroglyphics.

Palma [La] (Sp) an island in the Canary Islands. D.O. Palma. 3 zones: Hoya de Mazo, Fuencaliente and the north. The three areas produce Vinos del Tea. Grape varieties include Bermejuela, Bujariego, Gual, Sabro, Listàn, Malvasia, Negramoll, Almuñeco.

P

Palma Cortada (Sp) denotes a Fino Sherry that is almost similar in style to an Amontillado Sherry.

Palma de Mallorca (Sp) consists of four islands: Mallorca, Menorca, Ibiza (Eivissa), Formentura. *see* Balearic Islands (The).

Palmarès (Fr) lit: 'prize list', the list of Cru Bourgeois of the Bordeaux region.

Palma Sack (Sp) a dry white wine produced in Las Palmas, Gran Canaria.

Palmas de Gran Canaria [Las] (Sp) a province of the Canary Islands (Canarias). Comprises of the islands of Lanzarote, Fuerteventura and Gran Canaria.

Palm Beach (Cktl) 4⁄6 measure dry gin, 1⁄6 measure sweet vermouth, 1⁄6 measure grapefruit juice. Shake over ice and strain into a cocktail glass.

Palm Beach Coolers (Eng) a range of low-alcohol, sparkling, wine-based drinks (tropical fruit blend of passion fruit and grapes with white wine) and a summer fruit drink with a base of red and white wine. From Bonlouis U.K.

Palmberg (Ger) vineyard (Anb): Mosel-Saar-Ruwer. (Ber): Zell/Mosel. (Gro): Rosenhang. (Vil): Valwig.

Palmberg (Lux) a vineyard site in the village of Ahn.

Palmberg-Terrassen (Ger) vineyard (Anb): Mosel-Saar-Ruwer. (Ber): Zell/Mosel. (Gro): Grafschaft. (Vil): St. Aldegund.

Palm Brasserie (Bel) a brewery (established 1747). (Add): Steenhuffeldrop 3, Steenhuffel, B-1840. Brews: Aerts 1900, Palm Speciale, Steendonk Brabants Witbier. Website: http://www.palm.be 'E'mail: info@palm.be

Palm Speciale (Bel) a 5.1% alc by vol. bottled, top fermented ale brewed by the Palm Brasserie, Steenhuffel.

Palm Breeze (Cktl) ⅓ measure yellow Chartreuse, ½ measure dark rum, 1⁄6 measure crème de cacao, juice ½ lime, dash grenadine. Shake over ice and strain into a cocktail glass.

Palmela (Port) a DOC region situated between Lisbon and Setúbal. Produces mainly rosé and red Periquita.

Palmengarten (Ger) vineyard (Anb): Nahe. (Ber): Schloss Böckelheim. (Gro): Rosengarten. (Vil): Mandel.

Palmense del Piceno (It) a still and sparkling natural spring mineral water (established 1930/1968) from Palmense del Piceno. Mineral contents (milligrammes per litre): Sodium 35.5mg/l, Calcium 120mg/l, Magnesium 21.5mg/l, Potassium 2mg/l, Bicarbonates 323mg/l, Chlorides 81mg/l, Sulphates 39.5mg/l, Fluorides 0.55mg/l, Silicates 9.8mg/l. pH 7.2

Palmenstein (Ger) vineyard (Anb): Rheinhessen. (Ber): Bingen. (Gro): Sankt Rochuskapelle. (Vil): Sponsheim.

Palmer and C°. (Fr) a Champagne producers (established 1984). (Add): 67 Rue Jacquart, 51100 Reims. 200ha (founded by a group of wine-lovers in Avize). Produces vintage and non-vintage wines. De Luxe vintage cuvées- Cuvée Amazone and Cuvée Rubis (rosé).

Palmer [JC & RH] (Eng) a brewery (established 1794). (Add): The Old Brewery, West Bay Road, Bridport, Dorset DT6 4JA. Brews: Dorset Gold 4.5% alc by vol., IPA 4.4% alc by vol., Palmer 200 Premium Ale 5% alc by vol., Palmers Best Bitter 4.2% alc by vol., Palmers Copper Ale 3.7% alc by vol., Tally Ho! 5.5% alc by vol (1046 O.G). also cask-conditioned IPA Bitter 1039.5 O.G. and B.B. Bitter 1030.4 O.G. Also Golden Cap (a blended Scotch whisky). Website: http://www.palmersbrewery.com 'E'mail: enquiries@palmersbrewery.com

Palmer Cocktail (Cktl) 40mls (⅓ gill) Bourbon whiskey, dash Angostura, 2 dashes lemon juice. Stir over ice and strain into a cocktail glass.

Palmer Creek Vineyard (USA) the label for a red wine (Pinot noir) produced by the Et Fille winery, Oregon.

Palmers Poison (Eng) a 4.4% alc by vol. ale brewed by the Blythe Brewery, Staffordshire.

Palmer 200 (Eng) a 5% alc by vol. ale from the Palmer Brewery, Bridport, Dorset.

Palmer Vineyards (USA) a winery. (Add): Aquebogue, Long Island. Grape varieties: Chardonnay, Gewürztraminer, Merlot.

Palme 70 (Cktl) ⅓ measure Extra Bitter Badel, ⅓ measure Vinjak Cezar, ⅓ measure Stari Granciar, dash strawberry juice. Stir over ice, strain into a cocktail glass and add a cherry.

Palmetto (Cktl) ½ measure white rum, ½ measure French vermouth, 2 dashes Angostura. Stir over ice and strain into a cocktail glass.

Palm Spring (Chi) a natural spring mineral water. Mineral contents (milligrammes per litre): Sodium 5.34–5.39mg/l, Calcium 30–31.5mg/l, Magnesium 2.64–2.88mg/l, Potassium 2.34–2.36mg/l, Chlorides 5mg/l, Sulphates 11–12mg/l.

Palmspring Mineral Water (Ind) a natural spring mineral water brand (established 1998).

Palm Wine (Afr) an alcoholic beverage produced from the fermented sap of the palm tree.

Palm Wine (USA) a name used to describe alcoholic drinks made from the sap of tropical palm trees through fermentation. e.g. coconut and date palms.

Palo Cortado (Sp) a classification of Sherry between an Amontillado and Oloroso. Classed as: Un Cortado, Dos Cortados, Tres Cortados, Cuatro Cortados, etc.

Palomar Mountain Spring Water (USA) a natural spring mineral water (established 1989) from Palomar Mountain, Southern California. Mineral contents (milligrammes per litre): Sodium 9.3mg/l, Calcium 15.1mg/l, Magnesium 5.3mg/l, Potassium 3.4mg/l, Bicarbonates 80mg/l, Chlorides 6.8mg/l, Sulphates 9mg/l, Fluorides 0.1mg/l, Nitrates 0.69mg/l, Silicates 26.9mg/l. pH 7.4

Paloma (Cktl) a measure of Sauza Hacienda Reposado and citrus juice over ice in a highball glass.

Paloma Wines (USA) a winery (established 1984). Grape varieties: Cabernet, Merlot.

P

Palombina (It) an alternative name for Piedirosso.
Palomino (Sp) the best known and most widely used grape variety in the Jerez region for Sherry production. *see* Palomino de Jerez and Palomino Fino. Also known as the Albán, Chasselas doré, Fransdruif, Horgazuela, Listán, Paulo, Perrum and Sweetwater.
Palomino Basto (Sp) *see* Palomino de Jerez.
Palomino de Jerez (Sp) also known as Palomino Basto. A white grape variety that is now being replaced by the Palomino Fino in Sherry production.
Palomino Fino (Sp) a white grape variety (a clone) that is now replacing Palomino de Jerez for Sherry production.
Palomino y Vergara (Sp) Sherry shippers based in Jerez. Was part of the Rumasa group. Now owned by Harveys of Bristol. Sherry brands include Tio Mateo, brandies includes Fabuloso.
Palo Viejo (W.Ind) the brand-name of a rum produced by Marquis and C°. on the island of Puerto Rico.
Palud (Fr) a lesser district of Bordeaux.
Paluel-Marmont (Fr) an Armagnac produced by Esprit de France, Domaine de Taulet, 32330 Gondrin, Ténarèze. Also produce Des Seigneurs (a 3 year old).
Palumbo (It) a white grape variety grown in the Puglia region.
Palus (Fr) rich alluvial soil (often near or along a river bank), unsuitable to grow those grapes that are to be made into fine wines.
Palwin (Isr) the name given to a range of rich, red, dessert wines produced by Carmel.
Palzem (Ger) village (Anb): Mosel-Saar-Ruwer. (Ber): Obermosel. (Gro): Gipfel. (Vins): Karlsfelsen, Lay.
Pamelita [La] (Sp) a sparkling red wine from Monastrell grapes by Bodegas Castaño, Yecla.
Pamid (Bul). A red grape variety. Produces sweet, low acid, light coloured wines. (Hun) = Piros szlanka, (Rom) = Rosioara.
P-Aminobenzoic Acid (Eng) a vitamin that is found in minute traces in wines.
Pamirswater (Chi) a natural spring mineral water from Xinjiang.
Pampanino (It) a white grape variety grown in the Puglia region. Also known as the Pampanuto.
Pâmpano (Port) a vine-shoot.
Pampanuto (It) *see* Pampanino.
Pampara (Fr) a still natural spring mineral water (Add): GTA – BP 363, 40108 Dax cedex. Mineral contents (milligrammes per litre): Sodium 19.5mg/l, Calcium 65.4mg/l, Magnesium 5.2mg/l, Bicarbonates 223mg/l, Chlorides 19mg/l, Sulphates 24.6mg/l, Nitrates 0mg/l. pH 7.4
Pampas (Arg) a white wine from the Mendoza region.
Pampinus (Lat) vine-shoots.
Pan (Tur) a natural spring mineral water (established 1998). Mineral contents (milligrammes per litre): Sodium 1.6mg/l, Calcium 18.04mg/l, Magnesium 18.23mg/l, Potassium 0.9mg/l, Chlorides 12.87mg/l, Fluorides 0.17mg/l, Nitrates 5.4mg/l. pH 7.2
Panaché (Fr) a shandy (½ beer, ½ lemonade).
Panaché Cocktail (Cktl) ½ measure vodka, ½ measure Noilly Prat, dash of cherry brandy. Stir over ice, strain into a cocktail glass and top with a cherry.
Panache d'Or (Fr) a 3*** and V.S.O.P. Armagnacs produced by Carrère.
Panadés (Sp) *see* Penedés (the old spelling).
Panama Cocktail (Cktl) ⁴⁄₁₀ measure brandy, ³⁄₁₀ measure crème de cacao, ³⁄₁₀ measure sweetened cream. Shake well with ice and strain into a cocktail glass.
Pan American Cocktail (Cktl) 25mls (⅕ gill) rye whiskey, 2 dashes gomme syrup, juice ½ lemon. Stir over ice in an old-fashioned glass.
Panch (Ind) *see* Paantsch.
Pancho Cocktail (Cktl) 1 measure Pimpeltjens, 1 measure crème de café. Stir over ice and strain into a cocktail glass.
Pancho Villa (Cktl) 1 measure tequila, ½ measure Tia Maria, dash Cointreau. Shake over ice, strain into a cocktail glass, dress with a lemon slice and coffee bean.
Pancho Villa Cocktail (Cktl) ½ measure Campari, ½ measure tequila. Shake over ice, strain into a cocktail glass and decorate with a cocktail onion.
Panciu (Rum) white table wines from Focsani.
Pandars [Les] (Fr) a vineyard in the A.C. commune of Montagny, Côte Chalonnaise, Burgundy.
Panda Pops (Eng) a range of carbonated drinks produced by Popzone (set up by Hall & Woodhouse Beverage Division). Flavours include: cola, lemonade, sherbert lemon, blue raspberryade, strawberry jelly, ice cream.
Panda Soft Drinks (Eng) a large soft drinks manufacturer based in Dorset. Produces a wide range of soft drinks.
Panda Still Pops (Eng) a range of soft drinks produced by Popzone (set up by Hall & Woodhouse Beverage Division). Flavours include: orange, pineapple, blackcurrant, raspberry.
Pandemonium (Eng) a 4.8% alc by vol. ale brewed by the South Hams Brewery, Devon.
Pandilla (Sp) a white grape variety grown in La Mancha.
Pando (Sp) a full, fine, Fino Sherry produced by Williams & Humbert.
Pandur Heilwasser (Ger) a natural spring mineral water (established 2001). Mineral contents (milligrammes per litre): Sodium 2815mg/l, Calcium 569mg/l, Magnesium 191.5mg/l, Potassium 102mg/l, Chlorides 4389mg/l, Sulphates 999mg/l, Fluorides 0.29mg/l.
Panelenbier (Hol) a 5% alc by vol. top-fermented, bottle-conditioned special beer brewed by De Drie Ringen Amersfoort Brauerei, Amersfoort.
Pangkarra (Austr) the aboriginal word used for the composition, structure and nature of the soil. (Fr) = terroir.
Pangolin (S.Afr) a winery based in the Western Cape. Grape varieties include: Cabernet sauvignon.

Panier (Fr) the name of the basket used for gathering the grapes in the Champagne region.

Panimoravintola Koulu (Fin) a brewery. (Add): Eerikinkatu 18, Fin-20100 Turku. Brews a range of beers and lagers. Website: http://www.panimoravintolakoulu.fi 'E'mail: mypa@panimoravintolakoulu.fi

Panizzi (It) a winery based in the DOCG Vernaccia di San Gimignano in the Tuscany region.

Panj (Iran) an old Persian word for punch (drink).

Panna (It) cream.

Panna (It) a still natural mineral water (established 1927) from Florence. (Add): Panna Springs, Scarperia (Florence), Italy. Mineral contents (milligrammes per litre): Sodium 6.2mg/l, Calcium 32.5mg/l, Magnesium 7mg/l, Potassium 1.1mg/l, Bicarbonates 107mg/l, Chlorides 7.1mg/l, Sulphates 24.5mg/l, Fluride 0.04mg/l, Nitrates 6mg/l, Silcates 7.4, Strontium 0.2mg/l. Part of the Sanpellegrino group.

Pannier (Fr) a Champagne producer. (Add): 23 Rue Roger Catillon, B.P. 55, 02400 Château Thierry. Produces vintage and non-vintage wines. Vintages: 1970, 1975, 1979, 1981, 1983, 1985, 1987, 1988, 1990, 1995, 1996, 1998. Prestige cuvée: Cuvée Louis Eugène Pannier, Egérie de Pannier.

Pannier [Rémy] (Fr) wine merchants based in Saumur in the Anjou-Saumur district of the Loire.

Pannikin (Eng) a small metal cup used in the nineteenth century.

Pannobile (Aus) the name adopted by local growers for those top wine made from Austrian grapes.

Pannonia (Lat) the Roman name for Austria (around lake Neusiedl) that was a prime Roman wine-growning area.

Pannonia Winery (USA) a winery based in the Napa Valley, California. 14ha. Grape varieties: Chardonnay, Pinot noir and Sauvignon blanc. Produces varietal wines.

Panorama (S.Afr) the export label for a range of wines produced by the Lost Horizons Premium Wines winery, Suider-Paarl, Western Cape.

Panorama Vineyards (N.Z) a small winery based at Awaroa Road, Henderson, North Island. 3ha. Grape varieties: Cabernet sauvignon, Chardonnay, Gewürztraminer, Palomino and Pinotage. Produces varietal wines.

Panquehua (Arg) the brand-name of a white wine produced by Bodegas Gonzales Videla.

Pansa Blanca (Sp) a white grape variety grown in the Alella district. Also known as the Xarel-lo.

Pansa Rosado (Sp) a red grape variety grown in the Alella.

Panse Musquée (Sp) an alternative name for the Muscat of Alexandria.

Pansgue (S.Am) a rum-based cordial flavoured with cherry juice that is produced in Venezuela.

Panstwowy Monopol Spirytusowy (Pol) the Polish State vodka producer. Polmos (short name). Wyborowa is the principal brand.

Pansu (Tur) a natural spring mineral water (established 2001) from Kayseri. Mineral contents (milligrammes per litre): Sodium 18.5mg/l, Calcium 19.2mg/l, Magnesium 11.9mg/l, Potassium 7.6mg/l, Sulphates 20.8mg/l, Fluorides 0.05mg/l, Nitrates 15mg/l. pH 7.5

Pantelleria (It) a small island of volcanic origin, part of the province of Trapani, a town in western Sicily. Better known wines are Moscato and Moscato Passito.

Pantelleria (It) the name of a Muscat dessert wine made from sun-dried grapes on the island of same name.

Pantera Cocktail (Cktl) ⅓ measure dry Sherry, ⅓ measure dry gin, ⅓ measure red Curaçao. Stir with ice, strain into a cocktail glass and add a sprig of mint.

Panther (Aus) a premium lager beer 5.4% alc by vol. brewed by the Reininghaus Brauerei in Graz.

Panther Creek (USA) a natural spring mineral water (established 1999). Mineral contents (milligrammes per litre): Sodium 0.5mg/l, Calcium 10.5mg/l, Magnesium 0.05mg/l, Potassium 1mg/l, Fluorides 0.2mg/l.

Panther Creek Cellars (USA) a winery based at McMinnville, Willamette Valley, Oregon. Grape varieties: Chardonnay, Melon de Bourgogne, Pinot noir.

Panther Malta (Fr) a rich, dark, malty, non-alcoholic bière brewed by Union de Brasseries, 33 Ave. de Wagram, 75017 Paris.

Panticosa (Sp) a still natural spring mineral water from San Augustin, Balneario de Panticosa, Huesca. Mineral contents (milligrammes per litre): Sodium 17.9mg/l, Calcium 5.7mg/l, Magnesium 0.1mg/l, Potassium 0.4mg/l, Bicarbonates 24.2mg/l, Chlorides 3mg/l, Sulphates 18.1mg/l, Fluorides 0.6mg/l, Nitrates 1mg/l.

Pantothenic Acid (Eng) a vitamin that is present in wine in minute traces.

Pany Rum (E.Ind) a leading rum brand produced in the Philippine Islands.

Panzuan (Aus) a vineyard site based on the banks of the River Kamp situated in the Kamptal region.

Paoletti (USA) a winery based in the Napa Valley, California. Grape varieties include: Cabernet sauvignon. Label: Non Plus Extra.

Paolo Scavino (It) a winery based in the DOCG Barolo, Piemonte. Label: Carobric.

Papagni Vineyards (USA) a winery based in Madera County, San Joaquin Valley, California. Grape varieties: Alicanté bouschet, Barbera, Chenin blanc and Zinfandel. Produce varietal wines.

Papaioannou (Gre) a winery based in Nemea. Produces Ktima Papaioannou from Cabernet franc grapes.

Papa Luna (Sp) a red wine produced in Calatayud from a blend of Garnacha, Mazuelo, Monastrell and Tempranillo grapes. Named after the fourteenth century Pope Benedict XIII (Pedro Martinez de Luna).

Papapietro Perry (USA) a winery based in the Russian River Valley, Sonoma County, California. Grape variety: Pinot noir.

P

Papaya Royal Cocktail (Cktl) 25mls (⅕ gill) white rum, 75mls (⅗ gill) milk, 300grms (12ozs) papaya pulp, 2 dashes gomme syrup. Blend altogether with a scoop of crushed ice, pour into the hollowed-out papaya and serve with straws.

Papaya Sling (Cktl) 1 measure dry gin, juice of a lime, 10mls (½ fl.oz) papaya syrup, dash Angostura. Shake well over ice, strain into an ice-filled highball glass, top with soda and a pineapple cube.

Papazkarasi (Tur) a white grape variety grown in Marmara and Thrace.

Pape Clément (Fr) see Château Pape Clément.

Papelory [Ets] (Fr) an Armagnac producer based in Ténarèze. (Add): Rue des Carmes, 32100 Condom. Noted for Laressingle brand.

Paphos (Cyp) a wine area and town in the south-east of the island.

Papillon (S.Afr) the label for a carbonated white wine produced by the Van Loveren Private Cellar winery, Robertson, Western Cape.

Papillon (USA) a winery based in the Willamette Valley, Oregon. Grape variety: Pinot noir.

Papua New Guinea (E.Ind) a coffee-producing country. Produce a soft, full-flavoured coffee.

Paquereau (Fr) a Cognac producer. (Add): B.P. N°4, Chez Perruchon, 16250 Blanzac. 9.3ha. in the Fins Bois. Produces a range of fine Cognacs.

Paracelhaus (Aus) a noted Austrian beer.

Paracelsus (Aus) a dark, Münchner-style beer brewed by the Stiegl Brauerei in Salzburg 4.4% alc by vol.

Paracelsus-Quelle Heilwasser (Ger) a natural spring mineral water (established 1926) from Paracelsus-Quelle. Mineral contents (milligrammes per litre): Sodium 314mg/l, Calcium 40mg/l, Magnesium 5mg/l, Potassium 20mg/l, Bicarbonates 336mg/l, Chlorides 362mg/l, Sulphates 61mg/l.

Parachute (Eng) a funnel-shaped piece of equipment, used in brewing to draw off excess yeast as it spills over in the fermenting vessel.

Paradella (Sp) a red grape variety which produces rich, red, fruity wines.

Parádi (Hun) a natural spring mineral water from Paradsasvar. Mineral contents (milligrammes per litre): Sodium 154mg/l, Calcium 139mg/l, Magnesium 33mg/l, Bicarbonates 903mg/l.

Paradies (Ger) vineyard (Anb): Baden. (Ber): Markgräflerland. (Gro): Burg Neuenfels. (Vil): Feldberg.

Paradies (Ger) vineyard (Anb): Franken. (Ber): Steigerwald. (Gro): Schlossstück. (Vil): Bullenheim.

Paradies (Ger) vineyard (Anb): Mosel-Saar-Ruwer. (Ber): Bernkastel. (Gro): Nacktarsch. (Vil): Kröv.

Paradies (Ger) vineyard (Anb): Nahe. (Ber): Kreuznach. (Gro): Kronenberg. (Vil): Bad Kreuznach (ortsteil Bosenheim).

Paradies (Ger) vineyard (Anb): Pfalz. (Ber): Mittelhaardt-Deutsche Weinstrasse. (Gro): Rebstöckel. (Vil): Diedesfeld.

Paradies (Ger) vineyard (Anb): Württemberg. (Ber):

Württembergisch Unterland. (Gro): Salzberg. (Vil): Eschenau.

Paradiesgarten (Ger) grosslage (Anb): Nahe. (Ber): Schloss Böckelheim. (Vils): Alsenz, Auen, Bayerfeld-Steckweiler, Boos, Desloch, Feilbingert, Gaugrehweiler, Hochstätten, Kalkofen, Kirschroth, Lauschied, Lettweiler, Mannweiler-Coelln, Martinstein, Meddersheim, Meisenheim, Merxheim, Monzingen, Münsterappel, Niederhausen an der Nahe, Niedermoschel, Nussbaum, Oberhausen an der Nahe, Obermoschel, Oberndorf, Oberstreit, Odernheim, Raumbach, Rehborn, Sobernheim, Sobernheim-Steinhardt, Staudernheim, Unkenbach, Waldböckelheim, Weiler bei Monzingen, Winterborn.

Paradiesgarten (Ger) vineyard (Anb): Pfalz. (Ber): Mittelhaardt-Deutsche Weinstrasse. (Gro): Mariengarten. (Vil): Deidesheim.

Paradis (Fr) the name used in the Beaujolais for the juice from the first pressing of the grape pulp after macération carbonique.

Paradis (Fr) a warehouse where old and fine Cognacs are stored. Also the name given to certain fine old Cognacs.

Paradis (USA) a dry white wine produced from the Pinot noir grape by the Alatera Vineyards in the Napa Valley, California.

Paradise (Austr) a natural spring mineral water from Winnellie. Mineral contents (milligrammes per litre): Sodium 9mg/l, Calcium 2mg/l, Magnesium 3mg/l, Potassium 1mg/l, Bicarbonates 210mg/l, Chlorides 40mg/l, Sulphates 9mg/l, Nitrates 15mg/l.

Paradise [1] (Cktl) ⅔ measure dry gin, ⅓ measure apricot brandy, ⅓ measure orange juice or lemon juice. Shake over ice and strain into a cocktail glass.

Paradise [2] (Cktl) 8 parts Bacardi, 1 part apricot brandy, 2 parts orange juice. Shake over crushed ice, strain into a cocktail glass and add a twist of lemon peel juice.

Paradise Brewery (Eng) a brewery (established 1981) based in Hayle, Cornwall. Noted for cask-conditioned Artists Ale 1055 O.G. and Victory Ale 1070 O.G.

Paradise Hill Vineyard (USA) a red wine (Cabernet sauvignon) produced by the Blanklet Estate winery, Napa Valley, California.

Paradise Lost Cocktail (Cktl)(Non-alc) ½ measure lime juice, ½ measure peppermint cordial, 3 dashes Angostura. Shake over ice, strain into an ice-filled highball glass and top with soda water.

Paradisi (Hol) a grapefruit-flavoured liqueur 26% alc by vol.

Paradisiaque (Cktl) 50mls (2fl.ozs) dark rum, 25mls (1fl.oz) Mandarine Napoléon, 10mls (½ fl.oz) syrup of ginger, 10mls (½ fl.oz) passion fruit juice, 25mls (1fl.oz) lime juice, 50mls (2fl.ozs) orange juice. Shake over ice, strain into a large highball glass with ice, decorate with a mint sprig and 2 cherries.

Paradiso Cocktail (Cktl) ¾ measure white rum, ¼

measure apricot brandy. Shake over ice and strain into a cocktail glass.

Parador (Sp) the brand-name of a 10 year old, full-bodied red wine produced by Julián Chivite in the Navarra region.

Paraduux (USA) a red wine from Duckthorn Vineyards in the Napa Valley, California. Grape varieties: Cabernet sauvignon, Merlot, Petite sirah, Zinfandel.

Paradyskloof (S.Afr) the second label of Vriesenhof Vineyard that includes a range of wines.

Paraflow (Eng) in the brewing process the heat-exchanger that cools the wort as it leaves the Copper from near boiling point down to fermenting temperature.

Paragogay ky Euphialosis (Gre) produced and bottled by. See also Paragogi ke Emfialosis.

Paragogi ke Emfialosis (Gre) produced and bottled by. See also Paragogay ky Euphialosis.

Paraguay Ta (S.Am) the nickname for maté.

Para Liqueur Port (Austr) a dark, Tawny Port-style wine made by Seppelts in South Australia.

Parallèle 45 (Fr) an A.C. Côtes du Rhône from Paul Jaboulet Aîné.

Paralytic (Eng) lit: 'paralysed', i.e. incapable through drink, drunk and incapable.

Paramount Choice (Port) a full, Tawny Port produced by Delaforce Port shippers.

Paranoia Green (Bel) a 6.2% alc by vol. top-fermented, bottled special beer brewed by the Villers Brasserie, Liezele-Puurs. The label depicts a pink and green hippopotamus and has a green neck foil.

Paranoia Pink (Bel) a 7% alc by vol. top-fermented, bottled special beer brewed by the Villers Brasserie, Liezele-Puurs. The label depicts a pink and green hippopotamus and has a pink neck foil.

Para River (Austr) the label for a red wine (Shiraz) produced by the Inghams winery, Barossa Valley, south Australia.

Paraskevopolous [Yannis] (Gre) based at Gaia Winery, Nemea. Noted for: 14h –18h a light rosé wine produced from Aghiorgitiko grapes. (Spends 14–18 hours on the skins). Also Notiose.

Para Springs (Indo) a natural spring mineral water from Para, Suriname. Mineral contents (milligrammes per litre): Calcium 16mg/l, Magnesium 0.9mg/l, Potassium 0.7mg/l, Bicarbonates 70mg/l, Chlorides 8mg/l, Sulphates <5mg/l. pH 7.5

Paraviso (It) a carbonated natural mineral water. (Add): Lanzo d'Intelvi (Como), Italy. Mineral contents (milligrammes per litre): Sodium 1.5mg/l, Calcium 72.78mg/l, Magnesium 9.45mg/l, Potassium 0.38mg/l, Bicarbonates 244mg/l, Chlorides 3.4mg/l, Sulphates 8.31mg/l, Fluoride 0.1mg/l, Silicates 6.1mg/l, Nitrates 13.26mg/l, Strontium 0.15mg/l. pH 7.55

Paravita (It) a natural spring mineral water from Sorgente della Coltura. Mineral contents (milligrammes per litre): Sodium 70.2mg/l,

Calcium 106.7mg/l, Magnesium 38.7mg/l, Potassium 1.8mg/l, Bicarbonates 446mg/l, Chlorides 120mg/l, Sulphates 42.2mg/l, Fluorides 0.1mg/l, Nitrates 25.7mg/l, Silicates 19mg/l. pH 7.63

Parcay-Meslay (Fr) a commune in the Loire Valley part of which is in Vouvray in the Touraine district.

Parcel [Land] (Fr) lit: 'a piece of land', applied to the vineyards, (especially in Burgundy) which were divided amongst the citoyens after the French Revolution.

Parcel [Merchant] (Eng) applies to cases of wine a wine merchant may offer for sale.

Parcel [Wine] (Eng) the name given to bulk wines which are normally blended with other 'parcels' to produce an acceptable wine.

Parchment Skin (Eng) the name given to the thin outer skin on a coffee cherry which covers the seeds. See also Endocarp.

Parde (Fr) an alternative name for the Malbec grape.

Parde de Haut-Bailly [La] (Fr) the second wine of Château Haut-Bailly Grand Cru Classé A.C. Graves.

Pardella (Sp) see Pardillo.

Pardilla (Sp) see Pardillo.

Pardillo (Sp) a white grape variety grown in the central regions. Also known as the Pardella, Pardillo, Pardina.

Pardina (Sp) an alternative for Pardillo grape.

Pardoemps (S.Afr) the label for a red wine (50% Pinot noir and other grapes blend) produced by the Goedevertrouw Estate winery, Walker Bay, Western Cape.

Pardubicky Brewery (Czec) a brewery based in northern Czec.

Pardubicky Porter (Czec) a porter-style beer, 19° Balling. Brewed by the Pardubicky Brewery at Christmas time.

Parducci Wine Cellar (USA) a large winery (166ha) based in Mendocino County, California. Grape varieties: Barbera, Cabernet sauvignon, Chenin blanc, Flora, French colombard, Johannisberg riesling, Petite sirah, Pinot noir. Produces varietal and table wines. Is a member of the Coro Mendocino (Zinfandel) wine group of Mendocino wineries. Website: http://www.mendocinowineco.com

Parel (Hol) a straw, top-fermented ale 6% alc by vol. brewed by the Budelse Brouwerij, Budel. see Budels Alt, Capucijn.

Parellada (Sp) a white grape variety grown in the Penedés region. Also known as the Montonel.

Parempuyre (Fr) a commune in the A.C. Haut-Médoc, north-western Bordeaux.

Pares (Ger) vineyard (Anb): Rheinhessen. (Ber): Bingen. (Gro): Kaiserpfalz. (Vil): Ingelheim.

Par Excellence (S.Afr) the label for a Bordeaux-style red wine produced by the Daview Vineyards winery, Nooder-Paarl, Western Cape.

Parfait Amour (Fr) a lilac-coloured, Curaçao-flavoured liqueur with rose petals, vanilla pods and almonds 30% alc by vol.

Parfait Amour (USA) a liqueur of purple shade, derived from lemon, citron, coriander, sugar and alcohol 30% alc by vol.

Parfum (Fr) the fragrance of perfume in a wine.

Pargetters Mild (Eng) a 3.6% alc by vol. mild ale brewed by the Buntingford Brewery, Hertfordshire.

Pariah Arrack (Ind) a spirit distilled from Toddy (palm juice).

Parigot et Richard (Fr) a producer of Crèmant de Bourgogne based at Savigny-lès-Beaune, Burgundy.

Parilla (Sp) the mark on a Sherry butt, three lines crossed by another three. Denotes the wine is to be distilled and not used for Sherry.

Paringa Estate (Austr) a winery (established 1985) based at 44 Paringa Road, Red Hill, South Victoria. Grape varieties: Chardonnay, Cabernet sauvignon, Pinot noir, Shiraz.

Pariscot et Cie (Fr) a small négociant based in Beaune, Côte de Beaune, Burgundy.

Paris Goblet (Eng) a round bowled, stemmed glass which is the most common of all glasses used for wines and spirits. Popular sizes range from 25mls (⅙ gill) for liqueurs to 300mls (12fl.ozs) for beers. (Fr) = ballon.

Parish Bitter (Eng) a cask-conditioned bitter 1040 O.G. brewed by the Woods Brewery in Shropshire.

Parish Brewery (Eng) a micro-brewery based in Somerby, Leicestershire. Brews Baz's Bonce, Baz's Super Brew.

Parisian (Cktl) ⅖ measure gin, ⅖ measure dry vermouth, ⅕ measure crème de cassis. Stir over ice and strain into a cocktail glass.

Parisian Blonde Cocktail (Cktl) ⅓ measure Jamaican rum, ⅓ measure Curaçao, ⅓ measure cream. Shake over ice and strain into a cocktail glass.

Parisien (Liq.Coffee) using a measure of Cointreau.

Parisienne (Cktl). 2 parts Warninks advocaat, 3 parts bitter lemon. Mix together with ice and decorate with a cherry.

Paris Peacock (Cktl) ½ measure Cognac, ½ measure (green) crème de menthe. Shake well over ice, strain into a Champagne flute and top with dry Champagne, dress with a mint sprig and a cherry.

Park and Tilford Brandy (USA) the brand-name of a brandy produced by the Schenley Distillers in California.

Park Avenue (Cktl) ⅔ measure dry gin, ⅓ measure Italian vermouth, 10mls (½ fl.oz) pineapple juice. Stir over ice and strain into a cocktail glass.

Park Lane Special (Cktl) ⅗ measure dry gin, ⅕ measure apricot brandy, juice ½ orange, dash grenadine, ½ egg white. Shake over ice and strain into a cocktail glass.

Park Méthode Champenoise (N.Z) a winery. (Add): 24 Banks Street, P.O. Box 572, Gisborne. Noted for sparkling wines. Grape varieties: Chenin blanc, Chardonnay, Pinot noir, Pinotage, Sémillon.

Park Royal Brewery (Eng) the Guinness Brewery in London (opened on Feb. 21st 1936), supplies London and southern England.

Parley's Canyon (USA) a natural spring mineral water from Park City, Utah. Mineral contents (milligrammes per litre): Sodium 22.01mg/l, Calcium 156mg/l, Magnesium 37.5mg/l, Potassium 2mg/l, Bicarbonates 10.4mg/l, Chlorides 23.3mg/l, Sulphates 68.1mg/l, Fluorides 0.46mg/l, Nitrates 0.5mg/l, Silicates 14mg/l. pH 7.0

Parliamentary Brandy (Eng) the name given to poor quality, unflavoured spirit that was sold as it was, outside the scope of the tax put on gin in 1729. In 1733 an Act was passed forbidding the sale.

Parlour (Eng) a term for the invitation by the public house landlord into his private quarters (rare now).

Parmalat (It) a still natural spring mineral water. Mineral contents (milligrammes per litre): Sodium 1.5mg/l, Calcium 40mg/l, Magnesium 21mg/l, Potassium 36mg/l, Bicarbonates 57mg/l.

Parmelia Moselle (Austr) a fresh, slightly pétillant white wine produced by Sandalford.

Parnay (Fr) a commune in Saumur in the Anjou-Saumur region of the Loire.

Paroisse [La] (Fr) a vineyard. (Add): Saint Seurin de Cadourne, Gironde. A.C. Haut-Médoc. (Com): Saint Seurin de Cadourne. 122ha. Grape varieties: Cabernet franc, Cabernet sauvignon, Merlot.

Paros (Gre) an island in the Cyclades group of islands in southern Greece. Produces mistelles for the making of vermouth. Also a red A.O.Q.S. wine of the same name from Monemvassia and Mandilaria grapes.

Parot (Fr) a sparkling natural spring mineral water (established 1894). (Add): S.E.M.N. St-Romain-Le-Puy Parot S.A. B.P.2, 42610 Saint-Romain-Le-Puy. Mineral contents (milligrammes per litre): Sodium 905mg/l, Calcium 94mg/l, Magnesium 83.5mg/l, Potassium 116mg/l, Bicarbonates 3204.77mg/l, Chlorides 80mg/l, Sulphates 25mg/l, Nitrates <1mg/l, Fluride 1.5mg/l. pH 6.45 Website: http://www.parot.fr

Parparoussis (Gre) a 4ha winery based at Parparoussis Achilleos, 1 Proastio, 26442 Patras. Grape varieties: Athiri, Assyrtiko. Produces: Drosallis Patras V.Q.P.R.D. Oenari Nemea V.Q.P.R.D. Muscat Rion Patras A.C. Lyrikos Oenos, Ta Dora Tou Dionysou.

Parra (Port) vine-leaf.

Parra (Sp) grapevine.

Parral Training (Chile) a method training vines on high trellises.

Parras de la Fuente (Mex) lit: 'vine trellises viticulture', a centre in the Coahuila region where the first vineyard was planted with Don Francisco grapes.

Parreira (Port) denotes a trellis-grown vine.

Parrina (It) a D.O.C. red and white wines from Tuscany. Made from the Ansonica, Malvasia del chianti and Trebbiano toscano grapes for the white wines and the Canaiolo nero, Colorino, Montepulciano and Sangiovese grapes for the red wines. Produced only in Orbetello (part of the Grosseto province).

Parrina Bianco (It) *see* Parrina.

Parrina Rosso (It) *see* Parrina.

Parrot Cocktail (Cktl) 25mls (⅓ gill) Pernod, 3 dashes mint syrup. Stir over ice in a highball glass, top with water and dress with sliced cucumber and a sprig of mint.

Parry's Porter (Eng) a bottled beer brewed by Ruddles Brewery, Leicester. Part of their Ruddles Character Ale range.

Parsac-Saint-Émilion (Fr) an A.C. commune within the Saint-Émilion district of eastern Bordeaux.

Parsons Creek (USA) a winery based near Ukiah, Mendocino County, California. Grape varieties: Chardonnay, Gewürztraminer and Johannisberg riesling. Produces varietal wines.

Parson's Particular (Cktl)(Non-alc) 25mls (1fl.oz) lemon juice, 1 egg yolk, 50mls (2fl.ozs) orange juice, 4 dashes grenadine. Shake over ice and strain into a large cocktail glass.

Parson's Special (Cktl)(Non-alc) 50mls (2fl.ozs) orange juice, 1 egg yolk, 4 dashes grenadine. Shake over ice, strain into an ice-filled highball glass and top with soda water.

Parsons Winery (USA) a small winery based in Soquel, Santa Cruz, California. Grape variety: Cabernet sauvignon.

Part des Anges [La] (Fr) the Angel's Share (*see*).

Partenheim (Ger) village (Anb): Rheinhessen. (Ber): Bingen. (Gro): Abtey. (Vins): Sankt Georgen, Steinberg.

Partial Root-zone Drying (Austr) *see* P.R.D.

Parti-Gyling (Eng) a slang term for describing the action of a brewery making a large batch of ale and changing it's character by adding hops, colour, etc. to produce different beers and ales.

Partners (Port) a full ruby Port produced by Sandeman Port shippers.

Partners Choice (USA) the brand-name of a single whiskey.

Partom (Isr) a sweet, full-bodied, Port-style red wine produced for the USA market by Carmel.

Partridge Eye (Eng) *see* Oeil de Perdrix. The name given to the sparkling Burgundy that has the colour of a partridge's eye.

Partschen (Aus) a vineyard site on the banks of the River Danube in the Kremstal region.

Parxet (Sp) a cava producer based at Tiana, Barcelona. Grape varieties include Xarel-lo, Parellada, Macabeo, Chardonnay.

Pasada (Sp) very old Manzanilla Sherry, can also be used to describe delicate Fino Sherries.

Pascal Blanc (Fr) a white grape variety grown in southern France (Rhône and Provence).

Pascale di Cagliari (It) a red grape variety grown in Sardinia.

Pascalle (Fr) a 3.5% alc by vol. wine from the south of France.

Pascarete (Sp) a local spelling of Paxarette. Also known as Pacaret.

Paschingerin (Aus) a vineyard site on the banks of the River Danube in the Kremstal region.

Pas de Deux (Fr) a red wine produced by Val d'Orbieu from Merlot and Syrah grapes in the Languedoc-Roussillon.

Pas Dosé (It) extremely dry (refers to sparkling wines).

Pasha (Tur) a coffee-flavoured liqueur 25% alc by vol. Produced by Seagram.

Påskebryg (Den) denotes a beer with a high alcoholic content which is usually brewed at Easter time.

Påske Bryg (Den) an Easter beer 7.75% alc by vol. brewed by the Albani Brewery in Odense.

Påskebryg (Den) an Easter beer 6.2% alc by vol. brewed by the Tuborg Brewery.

Pasmados (Port) a red wine produced from a blend of Alentejo grapes by J.M. Fonseca in Azeitao.

Paso Fino (W.Ind) a rum liqueur produced in Puerto Rico 31% alc by vol.

Pasolini dall'Onda (It) a vineyard. (Add): Piazza Mazzini 10, 50021 Barberino Val d'Elsa (FI). Winery noted for Badia a Sicelle Chianti Classico D.O.C.G. Also produces Chianti Riserva wines.

Paso Robles (USA) an A.V.A. wine-producing town based in Luis Obispo County, California. 4,858ha. Noted for red wines produced from Cabernet franc, Cabernet sauvignon, Pinot noir, Syrah, Zinfandel. Home to over 40 wineries including: Wild Horse Winery, Lohr Winery, Meridian Vineyards, Tablas Creek, Eberle Winery. Website: http://www.pasowine.com

Pasqua (It) a vineyard and winery (established 1925) based in Verona. Produce a range of two white wines: Soave Superiore D.O.C. and Pinot Grigio delle Venezia I.G.T. and two red wines: Valpolicella D.O.C. and Merlot delle Venezia I.G.T. Also a producer of sparkling (cuve close) wines. Website: http://www.pasqua.it 'E'mail: info@pasqua.it

Pasquier-Desvignes (Fr) a noted winery and wine merchants based in Brouilly, Beaujolais in Burgundy. (Add): St-Leger, 69220 Belleville.

Pasquiers [Les] (Fr) a vineyard in the A.C. commune of Montagny, Côte Chalonnaise, Burgundy.

Passadouro (Port) a brand-name of a vintage Port.

Passarelle (Fr) the name for dried Muscatel grapes in the Frontignan region, produces sweet, non-brotrytised wines. The process is known as Passarillage or Passerillage.

Passarillage (Fr) a method whereby the grape stalks are pinched just above the clusters prior to harvesting. This prevents sap travelling down the stalk. The grapes ripen and dry out since no sap gets through to them. Rich in natural sugar. *see* Passarelle. Also the name used in the Béarn region for *Botrytis cinerea* attacked grapes used for the wines of Portet.

Passaro (It) a moscato spumante producer based in Piemonte.

Passat (Cktl) 25mls (1fl.oz) peach brandy, 25mls (1fl.oz) orange Curaçao, 50mls (2fl.ozs) passion fruit juice, 5mls (¼fl.oz) gomme syrup, 5mls (¼fl.oz) lime cordial. Shake over ice, strain into a Champagne flute, top up with iced Champagne and decorate with a cherry.

Passé (Fr) applied to wine that is *'over the top'*, one that has passed its best.

Passeretta (It) lit: 'shrivelled or dried', a white grape used to add flavour to sweet dessert Moscato wines.

Passerillage (Fr) *see* Passarelle.

Passerillé (Sp) Pedro Ximénez grapes that are put outside under cover to partially dry out. Produces a very sweet wine which is rich in alcohol.

Passerina (It) a white grape variety grown in the Marches region. Also known as Biancame.

Passes (Fr) the name for a small label carrying information other than the label on the body or neck of the bottle.

Passe-Temps [Le] (Fr) a Premier Cru vineyard in the A.C. commune of Santenay, Côte de Beaune, Burgundy.

Passe-Tout-Grains (Fr) an A.C. red wine of Burgundy, made from a blend of ⅓ Pinot noir and ⅔ Gamay grapes.

Passing Cloud (Austr) a noted winery (established 1974) based in central Victoria. Grape varieties: Cabernet sauvignon, Pinot noir, Shiraz, Chardonnay.

Passion (Eng) a 4.5% alc by vol. ale brewed by Banks's Brewery.

Passion (S.Afr) the label for a red (Malbec, Mourvèdre, Pinotage and Shiraz) and white (25% each of Chardonnay, Sauvignon blanc, Sémillon and Viognier) wine produced by the Akkerdal Estate, Franschhoek, Western Cape.

Passion Ale (Eng) a 4.3% alc by vol. ale brewed by the Fruit & Firkin, Bracknell.

Passionate Yellow (Cktl) a 25mls each of Galliano, Passoã and vodka. Shake well with ice cubes. Strain into a chilled highball glass containing ice cubes and top with apple juice.

Passione (It) a range of sambuca-based liqueurs (Ambra: cinnamon-flavoured/Nera/Rossa: cranberry-flavoured) produced by the Luxardo distillery, Padua.

Passion Fruit (Austr) a sweet citrus-based liqueur.

Passion Fruit Cocktail (Cktl) ⅓ measure passion fruit, ⅓ measure gin, ⅓ measure dry vermouth. Shake over ice and strain into a cocktail glass.

Passion Fruit Daiquiri (Cktl) ¾ measure white rum, ¼ measure passion fruit juice, juice of a lime, 2 dashes gomme syrup. Shake over ice and strain into a cocktail glass.

Passion Fruit Source (Eng) a 5.3% alc by vol. sparkling passion fruit and vodka-based drink from Whitbread. *See also* Vodka Source and Kiwi Source.

Passionola (USA) a non-alcoholic cordial produced from passion flowers.

Passion Splitz (USA) a brand of sparkling cooler produced from fruit juices and white wine 1.2% alc by vol.

Passionwine (Austr) a sparkling passion fruit-flavoured wine produced by the Berri Estates in South Australia.

Passiti (It) the Tuscany name for the vino passito

wines, grapes have to dry before being made into wine.

Passito (It) a wine made from dried grapes, once made, the wine has to age until June 1st following the vintage (pl): passiti.

Passito di Pantelleria (It) *see* Moscato Passito di Pantelleria.

Passoã (W.Ind) a passion fruit liqueur.

Passover Slivovitz (Pol) a vodka-flavoured plum spirit, matured in oak casks, bottled at natural strength 75% alc by vol. Produced by Polmos.

Passover Wine (USA) a Jewish wine produced especially for the religious ceremony in the USA. Made from the Concord grape.

Passport (Scot) a blended Scotch whisky 40% alc by vol. produced by Seagram.

Passport Decanter (Eng) a patented Port decanter with a round base and stand, designed so that the decanter cannot be placed on the table but must be passed round all the guests until it is back on its base. (Add): Le Talbooth, Dedham, Colchester, Essex.

Passport Varieties (Eng) a term to denote non-indigenous grape varieties allowed into a country 'under license' for experimentation to see if the grapes will improve the quality of the local wines (e.g. Cabernet sauvignon in Italy, Spain, Portugal, etc.).

Passugger (Switz) a sparkling natural spring mineral water (established 1562) from Passugg. Mineral contents (milligrammes per litre): Sodium 39.9mg/l, Calcium 211.5mg/l, Magnesium 24.6mg/l, Potassium 2.2mg/l, Bicarbonates 769.8mg/l, Chlorides 15mg/l, Sulphates 56.8mg/l, Fluorides 0.12mg/l, Nitrates 0.6mg/l, Strontium 2mg/l.

Passulated Grapes (Eng) partially dried grapes either on the vine or on the ground. i.e. grapes used for Vin de Paille.

Passum (Lat) raisin-wine.

Passy (Fr) a Chalybeate mineral water.

Passy-Grigny (Fr) a Cru Champagne village in the Canton de Châtillon-sur-Marne. District: Reims.

Passy-sur-Marne (Fr) a Cru Champagne village in the Canton de Condé-en-Brie. District: Château Thierry.

Pasteur [Louis] (Fr) a nineteenth century scientist from the Jura who discovered that yeast causes fermentation and invented the process of Pasteurisation. Also completed many experiments on the effects of oxidation.

Pasteurisation (Fr) the process of heating wines and beers to destroy micro-organisms which would be harmful to the liquid, also used to prevent further fermentation. Temperature is strictly controlled 55°C–60°C (131°F–140°F) to prevent off-flavours (although it does give beer a biscuity flavour). System was pioneered by Louis Pasteur. For wines: 82°C (179.6°F).

Pasteurisation Tang (Eng) the term given to some beers that after pasteurisation obtain a stale taste.

Pastiche (Fr) pastis, the true name of pastis,

introduced when absinthe was banned because of its poisoning and social effect.

Pastis (Fr) lit: 'mixture', brandy, aniseed, liquorice and wild herbs, the French name for an aniseed-flavoured apéritif 45% alc by vol. *see* Pastiche

Pastis de Marseilles (Fr) an aniseed-flavoured spirit from southern France. *see* Pastis.

Pastis 51 (Fr) a brand of pastis 40% alc by vol produced in Marseilles. Also a lemon-flavoured version.

Pastizarra (Cktl) 1 part Yellow Izarra, 1 part Pernod, 3 parts water. Shake over ice and strain into a cocktail glass.

Pastor Ale (Fr) a 6.4% alc by vol. bottom-fermented, non-pasteurised, straw coloured-bottled bière de garde brewed by D'Annoeulin Brasserie, Annoeulin.

Pastorei (Ger) vineyard (Anb): Nahe. (Ber): Kreuznach. (Gro): Kronenberg. (Vil): Bretzenheim.

Pastorenberg (Ger) vineyard (Anb): Nahe. (Ber): Kreuznach. (Gro): Pfarrgarten. (Vil): Wallhausen.

Pastori Winery (USA) a small winery based in the Russian River Valley, Sonoma County, California. Grape varieties: Cabernet sauvignon and Zinfandel. Produces varietal wines.

Pastoso (It) off-dry, hint of sweetness.

Pasubio (It) a sparkling natural spring mineral water from Pasubio. Mineral contents (milligrammes per litre): Sodium 1.4mg/l, Calcium 53.5mg/l, Magnesium 28.7mg/l, Potassium 1.1mg/l, Bicarbonates 244.5mg/l, Chlorides 1.7mg/l, Sulphates 52.8mg/l, Nitrates 5mg/l, Silicates 6.7mg/l. pH 7.7

Patacas (Mad) coins of Madeira which were minted for the firm of Cossart Gordon and Cº. and paid to their workers for carting the wine. Workers could redeem them at the company shop for goods.

Patagonia (Arg) a wine-producing region of southern Argentina. Has the sub-regions of: Neuquén, Rio Negro and La Pampa. Main grape varieties: Cabernet sauvignon, Chardonnay, Malbec, Merlot, Pinot noir, Sauvignon blanc, Sémillon, Syrah.

Patagonia Mineral (Arg) a natural spring mineral water from Patagonia.

Patamares (Port) round terraced vineyards (2 metres wide).

Patavinum (It) a white wine produced in north-eastern Italy in Roman times.

Patent Apéritif (Fr) similar to vermouth, either based on wine or spirits.

Patent Still (Scot) invented by Robert Stein (circa 1826) and improved by an Irish Excise man called Aeneas Coffey in 1832, a continuous still.

Pater (Bel) *see* Abt.

Paterberg (Ger) vineyard (Anb): Rheinhessen. (Ber): Nierstein. (Gro): Spiegelberg. (Vil): Nierstein.

Paterhof (Ger) vineyard (Anb): Rheinhessen. (Ber): Nierstein. (Gro): Krötenbrunnen. (Vil): Dienheim.

Paterhof (Ger) vineyard (Anb): Rheinhessen. (Ber): Nierstein. (Gro): Krötenbrunnen. (Vil): Oppenheim.

Paternoster (It) a winery (established 1925) based in Barlie, Basilicata region. Produces: D.O.C. Aglianico del Vulture.. Top wines are Don Anselmo, Rotondo.

Patersberg (Ger) village (Anb): Mittelrhein. (Ber): Rheinburgengau. (Gro): Loreleyfelsen. (Vin): Teufelstein.

Pâteux (Fr) a term denoting a thick, syrupy consistency.

Patina (Eng) the name given to the hardening process that a cork of a sparkling wine bottle goes through during its time in the bottle under pressure. Goes from a soft, spongy appearance to a hard woody appearance over a period of years.

Pat O'Brians (USA) claimed as being America's largest pub based in New Orleans. Open 20 hours per day, has the longest bar in the world. Noted for Hurricane Cocktail.

Patois (Ch.Isles) a 5% alc by vol. cask ale brewed by Randall Ltd., Vauxlaurens Brewery, St. Juliens Avenue, St. Peter Port, Guernsey.

Patras (Gre) a still white wine produced in the Peloponnese.

Patriarche Père et Fils (Fr) a Burgundy négociant-éleveur based in Beaune, Côte de Beaune. Produces Kriter sparkling wines.

Patriator (Fr) a 6.8% alc by vol. brown, bottom-fermented, double bock beer brewed by Schutzenberger in Schiltigheim.

Patricia (Cktl) ⅓ measure Italian vermouth, ⅓ measure vodka, ⅓ measure orange Curaçao. Stir over ice, strain into a cocktail glass and add a twist of lemon.

Patricia (Fr) a natural spring mineral water from Arcens. Mineral contents (milligrammes per litre): Sodium 170mg/l, Calcium 7.3mg/l, Magnesium 9.6mg/l, Potassium 4.2mg/l, Bicarbonates 517mg/l, Chlorides 9.6mg/l, Sulphates 9.6mg/l, Fluorides 1.19mg/l, Nitrates 0.1mg/l, Silicates 40mg/l. pH 6.9

Patrick's Cream Stout (Eng) a 4.2% alc by vol. bottled stout brewed by Mildmay (a micro-brewery), Holbeton, near Plymouth.

Patrimoire (Fr) a non-vintage Champagne produced by Canard-Duchêne from 30% Chardonnay, 10% Pinot meunier and 60% Pinot noir grapes.

Patrimonio (Fr) the name given to A.C. red, rosé and white wines produced near the town of Bastia in Corsica.

Patriti Winery (Austr) a winery based near Adelaide, Southern Vales, South Australia. Produces varietal wines.

Patrizier-Bräu AG (Ger) a brewery based in Nurnberg. Brews: Albrecht Dürer Pils, Edelhell Export Beer.

Patron Blanco (Mex) a 40% alc by vol smooth silver tequila.

Pattes-de-Lièvre (Fr) lit: 'hare's feet', the local Touraine name given to the Chenin blanc grape (Pineau de la Loire).

Patxaran (Sp) a Basque sloe-flavoured liqueur.

Patz & Hall (USA) a winery based in the Sonoma Coast AVA, Sonoma County, California. Grape varieties include: Pinot noir.

Patzimaro Vineyard (USA) a red wine (Cabernet sauvignon) produced by the Duckhorn winery, Napa Valley, California.

Pau Ferro (Port) a red grape variety grown in the Algarve.

Pauillac (Fr) an A.C. commune in the Haut-Médoc. Many rate as the finest of all the communes. Châteaux Lafite, Latour and Mouton Rothschild are all within the commune. 1049ha. (81% Cru Classé).

Paulaner Brauerei (Ger) a brewery (established 1634) based in Munich. Brews: the Doppelbock beer known as Salvator, Hefe Weissbier. Also Münchner Hell 4.8% alc by vol. Münchner Dunkel 5% alc by vol. and Urtyp 5.5% alc by vol (lager beers).

Paulaner Hefe Weissbier (Ger) a 5.5% alc by vol. cloudy, unfiltered, bottle-conditioned wheat beer brewed by the Paulaner Brauerei, Munich.

Paulaner Hefe Weissbier Dunkel (Ger) a 5.3% alc by vol. dark, bottle-conditioned wheat beer brewed by the Paulaner Brauerei, Munich.

Paulaner Weissbier Kristallklar (Ger) a 5.5% alc by vol. clear bottled wheat beer brewed by the Paulaner Brauerei, Munich.

Paul-Bara (Fr) a Champagne producer. (Add): 4 Rue Yvonnet, 51150 Bouzy. Récoltants-manipulants. Produces vintage and non- vintage wines. A member of the Club Tresors de Champagne. Vintages: 1970, 1971, 1973, 1975, 1976, 1979, 1982, 1983, 1985, 1988, 1990, 1995, 1996, 1997, 1998, 1999, 2000, 2001. Labels: Cuvée Brut Millésime, Cuvée Brut Réserve, Cuvée Comtesse Marie de France, Cuvée Grand Rosé de Bouzy, Cuvée 'Spécial Club' Millésimée.

Paul Chanson (Fr) a cuvée based in the Premier Cru vineyard of Corton-Vergennes, Côte de Beaune, Burgundy (owned by the Hospices de Beaune).

Paul Clouet (Fr) a Champagne producer. (Add): 10, Rue Jeanne d'Arc, 51150 Bouzy. Produces non-vintage wines.

Paul Cluver (S.Afr) a winery (established 1859) based in Elgin, Western Cape. 100ha. Grape varieties: Cabernet sauvignon, Chardonnay, Gewürztraminer, Merlot, Pinot noir, Sauvignon blanc, Weisser riesling. Website: http://www.cluver.com

Paulée de Meursault (Fr) a luncheon held on the Monday after the wine sales of the Hospices de Beaune at mid-day. Each guest brings wine to accompany the meal. *see* Chevalier du Tastevin.

Paul de Villiars (S.Afr) the label for a red reserve wine (Shiraz 40%, Merlot 30%, Pinotage 30% plus Touriga nacional blend) also a red (Shiraz) wine produced by the Landskroon winery, Suider-Paarl, Western Cape.

Paul Gauguin (S.Pac) a natural spring mineral water from Te Vai Arii, French Polynesia. Mineral contents (milligrammes per litre): Sodium 48.7mg/l, Calcium 13mg/l, Magnesium 5.8mg/l, Potassium 4.5mg/l, Bicarbonates 69.5mg/l, Chlorides 67mg/l, Sulphates 5mg/l, Nitrates 0.9mg/l.

Paulhan (Fr) a wine-producing commune in the Clairette du Languedoc, southern France.

Paul Hobbs (USA) a winery based in the Napa Valley, California. Grape varieties include: Cabernet sauvignon. Label: Beckstoffer Tokalon.

Paulinas Drift (S.Afr) a winery (established 1797) based in Franschhoek, Western Cape. Labels include: Paulinas Reserve and Rickety Bridge Vineyards. Now known as Rickety Bridge Winery since 2001.

Paulinas Reserve (S.Afr) the label for a red wine (Cabernet sauvignon, Merlot, Cabernet franc and Malbec blend) matured in new 225litres American and French oak casks for 18 months and produced by the Rickety Bridge winery, Franschhoek, Western Cape.

Paulinsberg (Ger) vineyard (Anb): Mosel-Saar-Ruwer. (Ber): Bernkastel. (Gro): Kurfürstlay. (Vil): Kesten.

Paulinsberg (Ger) vineyard (Anb): Mosel-Saar-Ruwer. (Ber): Saar-Ruwer. (Gro): Römerlay. (Vil): Kasel.

Paulinslay (Ger) vineyard (Anb): Mosel-Saar-Ruwer. (Ber): Bernkastel. (Gro): Kurfürstlay. (Vil): Osann-Monzel.

Paulinushofberger (Ger) vineyard (Anb): Mosel-Saar-Ruwer. (Ber): Bernkastel. (Gro): Kurfürstlay. (Vil): Kesten.

Paul Jones (USA) the brand-name of a blended whiskey bottled by the Paul Jones Distilling C°., Louisville, Kentucky 40% alc by vol.

Paul Masson Light (USA) a de-alcoholised, slightly sparkling, white wine 0.5% alc by vol. Produced by Paul Masson from Chenin blanc and Colombard grapes plus wine grape juice. The alcohol is removed by centrifuge.

Paul Masson Vineyards (USA) a large winery based in Monterey County, California and San Joaquin Valley, California. 1872ha. Grape varieties: Chardonnay, Fumé blanc, Gewürztraminer, Johannisberg riesling, Zinfandel. Produces most styles of wines.

Paulo (Austr) an alternative name for the Palomino grape.

Paul Robert (Alg) a wine producing area in north-western Algeria. Produces mainly red wines.

Paul Sauer (S.Afr) the label for a red wine (Cabernet franc 18%, Cabernet sauvignon 64% and Merlot 18%) produced by the Kanonkop Estate winery, Stellenbosch, Western Cape.

Paulsen Vineyard (USA) a vineyard based near Cloverdale, Russian River Valley, Sonoma County, California. Main grape is Sauvignon blanc. Vinified at Château St. Jean.

Paulus (Ger) vineyard (Anb): Hessiche Bergstrasse. (Ber): Starkenburg. (Gro): Wolfsmagen. (Vil): Bensheim.

Paul Wallace Wines (S.Afr) a winery based in Elgin,

P

Western Cape. Grape variety: Malbec (from the Paarl region).

Pause-Thé (Fr) tea break.

Pauvre (Fr) poor, describes a wine without charm.

Pauwel Kwak (Bel) an 8% alc by vol. top-fermented, amber coloured, bottled barley wine brewed by Bosteels Brasserie, Buggenhout.

Pavia (It) a province of Lombardy in northern Italy. Produces mainly red wines, the most famous being Oltrepo Pavese.

Pavillion Beast (Eng) a 6% alc by vol. ale from the Dark Star Brewery, Brighton.

Pavillon [Le] (S.Afr) a dry white wine produced by the Boschendal Estate from Chenin blanc, Clairette blanche and Colombard grapes.

Pavillon Blanc du Château Margaux (Fr) a white wine made in part of Château Margaux (Premier Grand Cru Classé) vineyard in the commune of Margaux, Haut-Médoc, Bordeaux. Sold as A.C. Bordeaux Blanc.

Pavillon Cardinal (Fr) a red A.C. Bordeaux wine.

Pavillon de Bellvue (Fr) vineyard. (Add): Ordonnac, 33340 Lesparre Médoc. A.C. Médoc. (Com): Ordonnac. 210ha. Grape varieties: Cabernet franc, Cabernet sauvignon, Merlot.

Pavillon des Connétables (Fr) an A.C. Saint-Julien, Bordeaux red wine.

Pavillion Pale Ale (Eng) a 4.5% alc by vol. pale ale brewed by the Bank Top Brewery Ltd., Lancashire.

Pavillon Rouge du Château Margaux (Fr) an A.C. Margaux. A red wine made in part of the Château Margaux (Premier Grand Cru Classé) vineyard in the commune of Margaux, Haut-Médoc, Bordeaux.

Pavlikeni (Bul) a D.G.O. wine-producing area in the Northern Region. Produces Cabernet, Gamza and Pinot noir grapes.

Pavlos (Gre) a red wine grape variety grown in Zakynthos.

Paw Paw (USA) a wine-producing area in Michigan. Produces Catawba, Concord and Delaware grapes.

Paxarete (Sp) an alternative spelling of Paxarette.

Paxarette (Sp) a sweetening and colouring wine made from the Pedro Ximénez grape. Used also to colour whisky. Also spelt Pacaret, Pajarete, Paxerette, Paxarete, Paxerete, Paxorotta.

Paxerete (Sp) an alternative spelling of Paxarette.

Paxerette (Sp) an alternative spelling of Paxarette.

Paxorotta (Eng) the spelling of Paxarette in the eighteenth century when sold as a wine.

Pax Verbatim Vineyards (S.Afr) a winery (established 2004) based in Stellenbosch, Western Cape. Grape varieties: Syrah. Label: Blazing Hill. Website: http://www.paxverbatim.co.za

Paya (S.Am) a beer made from sweet potatoes in Guyana.

Paychaud Bitters (USA) an aromatic bitters used for cocktails.

Pays Catalan (Fr) a Vin de Pays area in the Pyrénées-Orientales département in south-western France.

Pays d'Auge (Fr) an area in which the Appellation Calvados Contrôlée exists, the finest of the Calvados.

Pays d'Othew (Fr) an A.O.C. cider region based in northern Burgundy. Villages: Aix-en-Othe, Boeurs-en-Othe, Chaource, Eaux-Puiseaux, Mayraye-en-Othe, Paisy-Cosdon, Palis, Saint-Mards-en-Othe, Vulaines, Vaujurennes. Has a working cider museum in Eaux-Puiseaux.

Pays de Retz (Fr) a Vin de Pays area in the Loire-Atlantique département in western France.

Pays Nantais (Fr) a wine area within the Loire region. Situated on the west coast around the mouth of the river. In this area Muscadet and Gros plant are produced. Now known as Nantais.

Paz (Tur) a sparkling natural spring mineral water (established 1967) from Beypazari. Mineral contents (milligrammes per litre): Sodium 7.22mg/l, Calcium 226.45mg/l, Magnesium 164.84mg/l, Potassium 55.9mg/l, Bicarbonates 2732.8mg/l, Chlorides 80.23mg/l, Sulphates 112.22mg/l, Boration 1.32mg/l, Nitrite 1mg/l. pH 6.33

Pazardjik (Bul) a demarcated area based in the Southern Region.

Paziols (Fr) a commune in the A.C. Fitou region of southern France.

Pazo (Sp) the brand-name used by Bodegas Cooperativa de Ribeiro for a range of red, rosé and white wines. Produced from selected grapes.

Pazo de Barrantes (Sp) a winery with vineyards based in Val do Salnés, north of Rías Baixas. (Add): 36636 Barrantes, Ribadumia. Produce one white wine from Albariño grapes.

Pazo de Señorans (Sp) a winery with vineyards based in Val do Salnés, in north of Rías Baixas. (Add): Vilanoviña, 36637 Meís.

Pazo San Mauro (Sp) a winery based in Condado do Tea, Rías Baixas. (Add): Porto, 36770 Salvatierra de Miño. Produce two wines: Condado and Pazo San Mauro.

PBD (Eng) abbr: Progressive Beer Duty.

P.D. (Fr) abbr: Producteurs Directs.

Peaberries (Eng) the name given to the individual coffee bean before it is roasted. Also known as Caracol.

Peace Cup (Cup) crush 4 slices fresh pineapple, 30 strawberries and 25grms (1oz) castor sugar with a little iced water. Strain into a large jug and add 1 bottle of dry Champagne, 60mls (½ gill) maraschino and 1 bottle soda water. Stir, decorate with slices of pineapple and strawberries.

Peaceful Bend Vineyards (USA) a winery based in Steelville near St. James, Missouri. Produces French-American hybrid wines.

Peach Beer (Eng) a 5% alc by vol. beer from the micro-brewery Mash & Ale, Manchester.

Peach Bitters (Eng) prepared from extract of peach kernels and other flavourings.

Peach Blossom (Cktl) 50mls (2fl.ozs) dry gin, juice ¼ lemon, 2 dashes gomme syrup, ½ ripe peach. Blend with a scoop of crushed ice, pour into a highball glass, top with soda water and dress with a peach slice.

Peach Blow Fizz (Cktl) 50mls (2fl.ozs) gin, juice ½

lemon, 25mls (1fl.oz) cream, ¼ fresh peach, 2 dashes gomme. Shake over ice, strain into an ice-filled highball glass and top with soda.

Peach Boy (Fr) a peach liqueur 24% alc by vol. produced by Cusenier.

Peach Brandy (Fr) a liqueur made from ripe peaches and extract of kernels. Medium alc. strength of 30% by vol. May have a small amount of fruit spirit added to improve flavour.

Peach Brandy Mint Julep (Cktl) 1 teaspoon sugar and water to make a smooth paste in a julep glass. Add 2–3 sprigs mint. Rub mint leaves along inside of glass. Add ice, 1½ measures Cognac, 1 measure Peach brandy. Stir, garnish with mint sprigs and a peach slice and serve with straws.

Peach Bunny (Cktl) ⅓ measure peach brandy, ⅓ measure (white) crème de cacao, ⅓ measure cream. Shake over ice and strain into a cocktail glass.

Peach County Schnapps (Can) a clear peach-flavoured schnapps from Archers 23% alc by vol.

Peach Daiquiri (Cktl) 35mls (1½fl.ozs) white rum, 10mls (½fl.oz) peach brandy, juice ½ lime, ⅓ skinned fresh peach. Blend on high speed with 2 scoops crushed ice, pour into a glass, serve with short straws and wedge of peach.

Peach Fizz (Cktl) place 50mls (2fl.ozs) Peach County Schnapps into an ice-filled highball glass and top with a dash of soda water.

Peach Flavoured Brandy (USA) a brandy-based liqueur infused with fresh peaches.

Peach Liqueur (USA) a peach-flavoured liqueur made from fresh and dried peaches 30% alc by vol.

Peach Paradise (Eng) a 5.5% alc by vol. flavoured, bottled drink produced by Spilt Drinks Company, Exeter, Devon.

Peach Sangaree (Cktl) place a measure of peach brandy into an ice-filled highball glass, top with soda water and float 25mls (1fl.oz) Port on top.

Peachtree Liqueur (Eng) see Original Peachtree Liqueur.

Peach West Indies Cocktail (Cktl) 25mls (⅕ gill) golden rum, ¼ fresh peach, juice ½ lime, 3 dashes maraschino. Blend together with scoop of crushed ice and strain into a flute glass.

Peachy Canyon (USA) a winery based in the Paso Robles, San Luis Obispo, California. (Add): 1480 North Bethel Road, Templeton, CA 93465. Grape varieties: Cabernet sauvignon, Zinfandel. Label: De Vine. Website: http://www.peachycanyon.com

Peacock Ridge (S.Afr) the label for a wine produced by the False Bay Vineyards winery, Wellington, Western Cape.

Peacock's Glory (Eng) a 4.7% alc by vol. ale brewed by the Belvoir Brewery, Leicestershire.

Peacock Spreading (Eng) a tea brand of green and white teas hand-tied to resemble a bird.

Peacock's Tail Character (Eng) describes a wine whose flavour opens out in the mouth. The explosion of flavour that increases with every second the wine is held in the mouth.

Peak (Eng) the term used to describe the peak in maturity of a wine (usually a personal view).

Peak Perfection (Eng) a dark cask ale brewed by Hardy and Hansons Brewery based in Kimberley, Nottinghamshire.

Peardrax (Eng) a sparkling, non-alcoholic pear drink produced by Whiteways.

Pear Drop (Eng) a term used to describe the aroma of wines made using the macération carbonique method. The aroma is due to increased ethyl acetate produced by this method.

Pearl (Austr) the brand-name of a well-known 'bag-in-the-box' wine.

Pearl (Eng) a carbonated, non-alcoholic, vanilla and orange drink made with skimmed-milk.

Pearl (Eng) a strain of barley used in the brewing industry for ales.

Pearl (N.Z) a sparkling wine produced by Montana Wines.

Pearl Brewery (USA) a brewery based in San Antonio, Texas. Noted for Jax and Pearl beers.

Pearl of Carmel (Isr) the name given to a sparkling wine made using the traditional method by Carmel.

Pearl of Lake (Cktl) ⅓ measure Scotch whisky, ⅓ measure Bols Gold Liqueur, ⅓ measure lime juice. Shake over ice and strain into a cocktail glass.

Pearl Spring (Chi) a natural spring mineral water. Mineral contents (milligrammes per litre): Sodium 5mg/l, Calcium 132mg/l, Magnesium 44mg/l, Potassium 0.9mg/l, Bicarbonates 365mg/l, Silicates 16.2mg/l.

Pearl Tea (Chi) another name for Green Gunpowder tea in China.

Pearly (Afr) a natural spring mineral water from Kenya.

Pearmain (Eng) an old English cider apple.

Pear Soup (Cktl) 4 parts Zwacks Viennese pear, 2 parts rum, 2 parts lemon juice. Shake well over ice with a sprig of mint and fresh parsley and strain into a cocktail glass.

Peasant's Run (S.Afr) the label for a white wine (Sauvignon blanc) produced by the Graham Beck Wines winery, Franschhoek, Western Cape.

Peasant Wine (Eng) the name given to locally produced and consumed wine, usually sold from the cask.

Peat (Scot) a decomposed vegetable substance found in bogs, turfs of it are used for fuel (after drying) to fire malting kilns in Scotch whisky production. see Peating, Peat Reek.

Peating (Scot) the use of peat on the kiln fires of the malt whisky distilleries, the amount of peat used will determine the 'peat reek' of the finished product.

Peatling and Cawdron (Eng) a chain of 35 wine shops (part of Greene King and Son).

Peat Monster (Scot) a 46% alc by vol blended malt whisky blended by Compass Box company. Website: http://www.compassboxwhisky.com

Peat Porter (Eng) a 4.5% alc by vol. porter brewed by the Moor Beer Company, Somerset.

Peat Reek (Scot) the aroma from the burning peat smoke used to heat the kiln in the malting of the barley in Scotch 'malt' whisky, Islay malts have the strongest peat reek.

Peats Ridge (Austr) a natural spring mineral water from Peats Ridge. Mineral contents (milligrammes per litre): Sodium 10mg/l, Calcium 2mg/l, Magnesium 2.8mg/l, Potassium 64mg/l, Bicarbonates 0.6mg/l, Chlorides 18mg/l.

Peaux (Fr) a commune in the Charente-Maritime département whose grapes are classed Petite Champagne (Cognac).

Pebbling (Aus)(Ger) the habit of adding pebbles to the wine casks as the wine evaporates to ensure the casks are always full.

Pec (Fr) a brand Pastis label.

Pecan Stream (S.Afr) the label for a red (Cabernet sauvignon) and white (Chenin blanc) produced by the Waterford Estate winery, Stellenbosch, Western Cape.

Pécharmant (Fr) an A.C. district of northern Bergerac in south-west France. (Coms): Creysse, Lembras, Mouleydier and Saint-Sauveur. Produces medium-style red wines. Minimum alc by vol. 11%.

Pechar's Vineyards (N.Z) a small winery based in Valley Road, Henderson, North Island. 4ha. Produces hybrid wines under the Old Railway label.

Pêche (Fr) the name for peach liqueurs.

Pechgeschmack (Ger) taste of tar, occurs in wines that have come into contact with the aroma of tar. i.e. freshly tarred roads.

Pechstein (Ger) vineyard (Anb): Pfalz. (Ber): Mittelhaardt-Deutsche Weinstrasse. (Gro): Mariengarten. (Vil): Forst.

Pécket (Bel) a local sparkling gin made from corn.

Peck Ranch (USA) a small vineyard based in San Luis Obispo County, California. Grape variety: Sauvignon blanc.

Pecorella (It) a red grape variety grown in Calabria.

Pecorino (It) a white grape variety grown in The Marche and Calabria regions.

Pecota Winery (USA) a winery based near Calistoga, Napa Valley, California. 16.5ha. Grape varieties: Cabernet sauvignon, Colombard, Flora, Gamay and Sauvignon blanc. Produces varietal wines.

Pécoui-Touar (Fr) a red grape variety grown in the A.C. Bandol, Provence.

Pécs (Hun) a white wine made from the Olasz rizling grape around the town of Pécs in the Mecsek Hills.

Pécs Brewery (Hun) a noted brewery based in south-western Hungary.

Pecsenyibór (Hun) a term that denotes dessert wine on a label.

Pécs Riesling (Hun) a sweet, white wine from the Pécs-Villány region made from the Welschriesling grape.

Pécs-Villàny (Hun) vineyards sited near the southern frontier on the right bank of the river Danube.

Pectic Enzymes (Eng) enzymes found naturally in fruits which degrade pectin.

Pectin (Eng) a soluble substance found in ripe fruits that can cause hazy wine (home-made fruit wines). Is removed by using pectic enzymes.

Pectin-Methyl-Esterase (Bio) an enzyme that reduces pectin haze in wines. Known as P.M.E.

Pectinolytic Enzymes (Bio) enzymes added to wines musts to aid extraction.

Peddler's Pride (Eng) a 4.3% alc by vol. cask-conditioned ale brewed in April and May by Hardy and Hansons at their Kimberley Brewery, Nottingham (part of the Cellarmans cask range).

Pedernã (Port) a white grape variety grown in the Vinho Verde region. Also known as the Arinto in Bucelas, Estramadura and Ribatejo.

Pedhoullas (Cyp) a wine village in the Troodos mountains on the north-west side in the region of Marathassa.

Pedicle (Eng) the name for the grape stem, contains tannin.

Pedigree Bitter (Eng) a malty bitter beer 1043 O.G. 4.5% alc by vol. the flagship beer of the Marston Brewery in Burton-on-Trent, Staffordshire.

Pedigreed Brewer's Yeast (USA) a yeast which is most suitable to the brewer to produce beer. The best strain to convert the wort sugars into alcohol.

Pediococcus (Lat) the alternative name for the lactobacillus.

Pedology (Eng) the study of the soil and classification type, age and origin.

Pedras do Monte (Port) a Vinho Regional Terras do Sado produced by DFJ Vinhos in the Ribatejo from Castelão grapes.

Pedras Salgadas (Port) a natural spring mineral water from Pedras Salgadas. Mineral contents (milligrammes per litre): Sodium 533mg/l, Calcium 175mg/l, Bicarbonates 2003mg/l, Fluorides 2.5mg/l. pH 6.2

Pedras Salgadas 12 (Port) a natural spring mineral water from Pedras Salgadas 12.

Pedras Salgadas 13 (Port) a natural spring mineral water from Pedras Salgadas 13.

Pedras Salgadas 17 (Port) a natural spring mineral water from Pedras Salgadas 17.

Pedrizzetti Winery (USA) a winery based near Morgan Hill, Santa Clara, California. Grape varieties: Barbera, Chenin blanc, Colombard, Petite sirah and Zinfandel. Produces varietal wines.

Pedro II [Dom] (Port) signed the Methuen Treaty in 1703 on behalf of Portugal.

Pedro Domecq (Sp) see Domecq.

Pedro Giménez (Arg) a widely planted white grape variety.

Pedro Jiménez (Sp) an alternative spelling for the Pedro Ximénez grape.

Pedro Luis (Sp) a white grape variety grown in the Huelva region of south-western Spain. Also known as False Pedro.

Pedro Mole (Mad) decomposed, yellow tufa soil found on Madeira.

Pedroncelli (USA) a winery in the Alexander Valley, Sonoma County, California. 56ha. (Add): 1220 Canyon Road, Geyserville, CA 95441. Grape varieties: Cabernet sauvignon, Chardonnay, Chenin blanc, Fumé blanc, Gewürztraminer, Pinot noir, Merlot, Zinfandel. Produces varietal wines. Label: Mother Clone (Zinfandel). Website: http://www.pedroncelli.com

Pedro Rodriguez (Sp) the brand-name of a range of young Sherries from Barbadillo in Sanlúcar de Barrameda.

Pedro Ximen (Sp) the local Málaga name for the Pedro Ximénez grape.

Pedro Ximénez (Sp) also known as the P.X. A red grape variety grown in south-western Spain. Used in the making of Sherry, Málaga and Montilla wines. Also known in Germany, Alsace and Austria as the Elbling, Knipperlé, Räuschling and Grossriesling. Also spelt Pedro Jimenez, Pedro Ximen, Pedro Ximinez.

Pedro Ximinez (USA) an alternative spelling of Pedro Ximénez.

Peduncles (Lat) the flower/fruit stalk.

Pedwar Bawd (Wal) a 4.8% alc by vol. ale from the Bragdy Dyffryn Brewery, Denbigh. *See also* Cysur Bitter, Castle Bitter, Cwrw Derwydd.

Peek Performance (Eng) a non-alcoholic, high-energy, glucose-rich, fruit and tropical fruit drink produced by Nabisco Food Service. Still and carbonated versions.

Peel Estate Winery (Austr) a winery based in Peel. (Add): Fletcher Road, Baldivis, P.O. Box 37, Mandurah 6210 Western Australia. 12.6ha. Grape varieties: Cabernet sauvignon, Chardonnay, Chenin blanc, Sauvignon blanc, Shiraz, Verdelho and Zinfandel.

Peeterman Artois (Bel) an 4% alc by vol white wheat beer once brewed by Stella Artois Brasserie (now owned by Inbev). *See also* Hoegaards Wit.

Peg (Eng) in early times drinking vessels would have small studs (pegs) on the inside which were used as measure marks. A customer would ask for a peg, two pegs etc. *See also* 'to drink a peg'. *See also* Chotapeg.

Pegasus (Aus) the label for a red (Syrah 80% plus Cabernet sauvignon and Zweigelt blend) wine produced by the Pitnauer winery, Göttlesbrunn, Carnuntum.

Pegasus (Eng) a 4.1% alc by vol. ale brewed by the Milton Brewery Cambridge Ltd., Cambridgeshire.

Pegasus Bay (N.Z) a winery (phylloxera-free). (Add): Stockgrove Road, RD 2, Amberley, Waipara. 22ha. Grape varieties: Sémillon/Sauvignon blanc, Chardonnay, Riesling, Pinot noir, Cabernet sauvignon/Merlot. *See also* Family of Twelve.

Peggotty's Porter (Eng) a porter 4.1% alc by vol. brewed using roasted rye malt and Fuggles hops by the Mauldon Brewery, Suffolk.

Peggy Cocktail (Cktl) ⅔ measure dry gin, ⅓ measure dry vermouth, 2 dashes Ricard, 2 dashes Dubonnet. Stir over ice and strain into a cocktail glass.

Pegleg (S.Afr) the label for a red wine (Carignan) produced by the Fairview winery, Suider-Paarl, Western Cape.

Pegões Claros (Port) a winery (80ha) based in the Palmela region. Grape variety: Castelão.

Pehu-Simonet (Fr) a Champagne producer. (Add): 7, Rue de la Gare, 51360 Verzenay. Produces both vintage and non-vintage Champagnes.

Peissy (Switz) a wine-producing area in Geneva.

Pejo Fonte Alpina (It) a sparkling natural spring mineral water from Fonte Alpina, Stelvio National Parc. Mineral contents (milligrammes per litre): Sodium 2mg/l, Calcium 17mg/l, Magnesium 3.5mg/l, Potassium 1.5mg/l, Bicarbonates 51.5mg/l, Chlorides 0.6mg/l, Sulphates 18.5mg/l, Nitrates 2.7mg/l, Silicates 7mg/l. pH 6.8

Peju Province (USA) a winery based in the Napa Valley, California. Grape varieties: Cabernet sauvignon.

Peké (Eng) *abbr*: Pekoe, tea grade.

Peket (Bel) the alternative name for Jenever.

Pek Ho (Chi) lit: 'white hair', refers to the tip of the tea bush. *see* Pekoe. Also spelt Pak Ho.

Peking (Chi) a base for a branch of the China National Cereals, Oils and Foodstuffs Import and Export Corp. Produces a sparkling wine and a brandy.

Peking Beer (Chi) a beer brewed by the Peking Brewery, eastern China.

Peking Brewery (Chi) a noted brewery based in Peking, eastern China.

Pekko (Fin) the ancient god of beer and barley.

Pekoe (Asia) tea grade, a large black leaf with twist, derived from the Chinese Pak Ho (white hairs) describes the fine downy hairs on the young tea buds. *see* Orange Pekoe, Pekoe Souchong. *See also* Pek Ho.

Pekoe Souchong (Asia) a grade of unbroken tea leaf, irregular in shape and smaller than Souchong.

Pelago (It) a red I.G.T. wine produced by Umani Ronchi in the Marche from 50% Cabernet sauvignon, 40% Montepulciano and 10% Merlot grapes.

Pelagonia (Euro) a natural spring mineral water from Macedonia.

Pelargonic Acid (Eng) an ester found in wines in small quantities.

Pelaverga (It) a pale red grape variety grown in Piemonte.

Pelee Island Winery (Can) a 200ha winery based on Pelee Island, Ontario. Grape variety: Pinot noir.

Pelequen (Chile) a wine-producing area near Santiago.

Pelforth Brasserie (Fr) a famous brewery owned by Heineken in Lille. Brews: Bière Brune (Pelforth Brune) at 6.5% alc by vol. (1069 O.G.), Bière Blonde d'Abbaye (Afflingem Bière de l'Abbaye) at 6.7% alc by vol., Bière Blanche (Wieckse Witte) at 4.5% alc by vol., a top-fermented brown ale 6.5% alc by vol. and Bière Ambrée (George Killian's Irish Red–Bière Rousse) 6.5% alc by vol. which is brewed under licence. Website: http://www.culturebiere.com

Pelham Ale (Eng) a bottled pale ale 1031 O.G. brewed by the Greene King Brewery in Bedford.

Pelhrimov Brewery (Czec) an old established brewery based in central-southern Czec.

Pelican Export (Fr) a lager beer brewed by the Pelforth Brasserie in Lille.

Pelin (Bul) a style of bitters made from alcohol, herbs, quinces, apples, grapes and old wine.

Pelin (Rum) a herb-infused wine usually served 'iced'.

Pelisterka (Euro) a sparkling natural spring mineral water (established 1954) from Medzitlija, Macedonia. Mineral contents (milligrammes per litre): Sodium 139mg/l, Calcium 140mg/l, Magnesium 68mg/l, Potassium 7.9mg/l, Chlorides 108mg/l, Sulphates 190mg/l, Fluorides 0.22mg/l, Nitrates 0.7mg/l, Manganese 1.28mg/l.

Peljesac (Cro) a small wine-producing area at Croatia on the Dalmatian coast. Noted for Postup (dry red wine), Peljesac (off-dry red wine).

Pella Wines (S.Afr) a winery (established 2004) based in Vlottenburg, Stellenbosch, Western Cape. Grape varieties: Shiraz. Label: Hoogland.

Pellegrino (It) a carbonated, natural mineral water from Milan.

Pellejo (Sp) wine skin/bag.

Pellicle (Eng) a membrane, film or skin that forms on a wine's surface.

Pellingen (Ger) village (Anb): Mosel-Saar-Ruwer. (Ber): Saar-Ruwer. (Gro): Scharzberg. (Vins): Herrgottsrock, Jesuitengarten.

Pellinger (Aus) a vineyard site on the banks of the River Danube in the Kremstal region.

Pelne (Pol) a well-hopped, dry pale lager beer (a pilsner beer).

Pelo (Fr) a top cuvée A.C. Saumur-Champigny wine produced from old vines grown on tuffeau soil produced by Château Yvonne, Saumur-Champigny.

Peloponnese (Gre) the largest and most important region of wine production in Greece. Phylloxera free. Key A.O.C. wines are Muscat de Patras, Mavrodaphne de Patras. A.O.Q.S. wines are Mantineia, Nemea.

Peloponnesiaskos Topikos (Gre) a white wine produced by Achaia Clauss from a blend of 70% Rhoditis, plus Chardonnay, Ugni blanc and Moscophilero.

Pelorus (N.Z) a traditional method wine produced by Cloudy Bay. 40% is oak fermented. Has 9 months on lees before the second fermentation. Further 3 years on lees before disgorging.

Pelorus Vineyard (N.Z) a winery. (Add): Patons Road, RD 1, Richmond, Nelson. 3ha. Grape varieties: Chardonnay, Riesling, Pinot noir, Cabernet sauvignon/Merlot, Sauvignon blanc.

Peloursin (Fr) a rare red grape variety.

Peloux [Les] (Fr) a wine producing village in the commune of Solutré-Pouilly in A.C. Pouilly-Fuissé, Mâcon, Burgundy.

Pelure d'Oignon (Fr) colour of onion skin, applied to certain rosé and red wines as they gradually take on the colour due to their age.

Pelzerberger (Ger) vineyard (Anb): Mosel-Saar-Ruwer. (Ber): Zell/Mosel. (Gro): Grafschaft. (Vil): Beuren.

Pemartin (Sp) a noted bodega based in Jerez. Was part of the Rumasa group. Also produces brandy.

Pemberley (Eng) a natural spring water from the Penwith Hills in Cornwall. Produces both still and sparkling varieties.

Pemberton (Austr) one of five sub-regions of Western Australia.

Pemboa Vineyard (Eng) a vineyard based at Mellangoose Mill, Pemboa, Helston, Cornwall. Produces white wines.

Peñaclara (Sp) a still natural spring mineral water from Torrecilla en Cameros, Rioja. Mineral contents (milligrammes per litre): Sodium 13.9mg/l, Calcium 141mg/l, Magnesium 28.2mg/l, Potassium 1.3mg/l, Bicarbonates 226.7mg/l, Chlorides 15.2mg/l, Sulphates 273.3mg/l, Fluorides 0.8mg/l, Nitrates 1.5mg/l.

Penadés (Sp) *see* Penedés, an alternative spelling.

Penafiel (Mex) a slightly acidic natural spring mineral water (established 1928) from Tehuacan. Mineral contents (milligrammes per litre): Sodium 159mg/l, Calcium 131mg/l, Magnesium 41mg/l, Potassium 11mg/l, Chlorides 131mg/l, Sulphates 130mg/l, Fluorides 0.51mg/l. pH 5.28

Peñafiel (Port) a wine district of the Entre e Douro region. Produces both red and white Vinhos Verdes.

Peñaflor (Arg) the largest Argentinian wine company, based in the Mendoza region. Deals with bulk wines and Tio Quinto (a Sherry-style wine for export).

Penalva do Castelo (Port) a large co-operative based in the Dão region.

Peñascal Rosado (Sp) a semi-dry (semi-seco) rosé wine from the Castille-Leon region produced from Garnacha and Tempranillo grapes. Has a light pétillance due to the fermentation process being frozen at -4°C for 10 days.

Peña Vieja (Sp) the name of a Riojan wine produced by Bodega San Miguel in Ausejo, Rioja.

Pencabut Gabus Botol (Indo) corkscrew.

Pendant (Eng) a blended wine produced by the Elham Valley Vineyards in Barham, Kent.

Pendeli (Gre) a dry red table wine produced in Attica by Cambas.

Pendennis (Cktl) 25mls (⅛ gill) dry gin, 15mls (⅛ gill) apricot brandy, juice ¼ lime, 2 dashes Peychaud bitters. Shake over ice and strain into a cocktail glass.

Pendennis Toddy (Cktl) dissolve a sugar cube in a little water in a sour glass. Add 50mls (2fl.ozs) Bourbon whiskey, stir, add ice and a slice of lemon.

Penderyn (Wal) a single malt Welsh whiskey at 46% alc by vol. matured in Bourbon whiskey casks and produced by The Welsh Whisky Company.

Pendlebogen (Ger) a version of the guyot system, a two-arm replacement-cane system. Vines are planted at 1.4 metre intervals in rows 2 metres

P

apart. They are trained up a 2 metre post and wire trellis, system is also used in England.

Pendleton Winery (USA) a winery based in San Jose, Santa Clara, California. Grape varieties: Cabernet sauvignon, Chardonnay, Chenin blanc, Pinot noir and Zinfandel. Produces varietal wines.

Pendle Witches Brew (Eng) a 5.1% alc by vol (1050 O.G) cask-conditioned ale brewed by the Moorhouse Brewery in Burnley, Lancashire.

Pendragon (Eng) a 4.8% alc by vol. ale from the Hampshire Brewery, Hampshire.

Pendura (Port) a white grape variety grown in the Alentejo region.

Penedés (Sp) a wine region of south-eastern Spain. Part of Cataluña. 26418ha. Has 3 sub-regions: Alto Penedés, Bajo Penedés and the Medio Penedés. Produces red, rosé and white wines, also Cava and Rancio wines. Main Grape varieties: Cariñena (Mazuelo), Garnacha tinta, Macabeo, Monastrell (Alcayata), Parellada, Samsó, Subirat-Parent, Tempranillo and Xarel-lo (Pansa blanca). Permitted varieties also include: Cabernet franc, Merlot, Pinot noir, Chardonnay, Chenin blanc, Gewürztraminer, Muscat d'Alsace, Riesling, Sauvignon blanc. *See also* Torres.

Pénétrant (Fr) a treatment product that penetrates the vines capillary system. Not a surface or contact product that can be washed off.

Penetrating (Eng) a term used to describe a powerful wine with a strong bouquet. Is usually high in alcohol.

Penfolds (Austr) a famous vineyard and winery. (Add): 634 Prince's Highway, Tempe, New South Wales 2004. 650ha. in the Barossa Valley, Clare, Coonawarra and Morgon. Grape varieties: Cabernet sauvignon, Chardonnay, Muscat gordo, Rhine riesling, Shiraz and Traminer. Has wineries at Eden Vale, Barossa Valley and McLaren Vale Vineyard (New South Wales), Murrumbidgee Irrigation Area, plus Auldana near Magill, Modbuny and Kalimma in the Barossa Valley. Produces: Great Western Sparkling, Penfolds Grange, Rawsons Retreat, St. Henri and a range of '**bin**' numbered wines.

Penfolds (N.Z) a winery. (Add): 190 Lincoln Road, Henderson, Auckland. No vineyards, grapes bought in from Blenheim, Gisborne and Hawkes Bay. Grape varieties: Cabernet sauvignon, Chardonnay, Chenin blanc, Gewürztraminer, Müller-Thurgau, Rhine riesling, Sauvignon blanc.

Penfolds Grandfather (Austr) the brand-name of a Port-style wine produced by the Penfolds Winery.

Penguin Cocktail (Cktl) ⅓ measure Cointreau, ⅙ measure Cognac, ⅙ measure lemon juice, ⅙ measure orange juice, dash grenadine. Stir well over ice, strain into an ice-filled balloon glass, dress with a slice of orange, lemon and cherry.

Penguine Brewery (S.Am) a brewery based in Stanley in the Falkland Islands owned by Everards. Brews traditional cask-conditioned ales and lager beer.

Penguin Porter (Eng) a porter brewed by the Ash Vine Brewery, Trudoxhill, near Frome, Somerset.

Penguin Stout (Eng) a 4.2% alc by vol. stout from the Dark Star Brewery in Brighton under the Skinners brand label.

Península de Morrazo (Sp) a Vino de Mesa wine from the province of Pontevedra in Galicia.

Peninsula Estate (Austr) a winery (established 1985) based at Red Hill Road, Red Hill, near Red Hill Market, Victoria. Grape varieties: Chardonnay, Riesling, Sauvignon blanc, Sémillon, Cabernet sauvignon, Pinot noir.

Peninsula Estate (N.Z) a winery. (Add): 52a Korora Road, Onera, Waiheke Island. 5ha. Produces Cabernet, Malbec Merlot blends, Syrah plus Chardonnay.

Pennine Bitter (Eng) a keg bitter 1037 O.G. brewed by the Webster Brewery in Halifax, Yorkshire.

Pennine Gold (Eng) a 3.9% alc by vol. golden ale brewed by the Goldcar Brewery, West Yorkshire.

Pennine Spring Water (Eng) a sparkling natural spring mineral water from Holme Valley, West Yorkshire. Mineral contents (milligrammes per litre): Sodium 34mg/l, Calcium 64mg/l, Magnesium 23mg/l, Potassium 5mg/l, Bicarbonates 319mg/l, Chlorides 51mg/l, Sulphates 27mg/l, Nitrates 2mg/l.

Penn's Ale (Eng) a cask-conditioned bitter 1045 O.G. brewed by the Hoskins Brewery in Leicester.

Penn Shore Vineyards (USA) a winery based in Erie County, north-east Pennsylvania. Produces Concord and American wines.

Pennsylvania Punch (Cktl) 1.1ltrs (1quart) water, juice of 12 lemons, 150 grms (6ozs) powdered sugar, ½ bottle peach brandy, 1 bottle brandy, 1 bottle Bourbon whiskey. Stir all together with ice in a punch bowl and garnish with orange slices.

Penny Black (Mad) a noted brand of Malmsey produced by Leacock.

Penny Black (S.Afr) the label for a red wine (Merlot 32%, Shiraz 32% plus Cabernet sauvignon and Petit verdot blend) produced by the Post House Cellar winery, Stellenbosch, Western Cape.

Penny Black Porter (Eng) a 4.5% alc by vol. porter brewed by the Hapshire Brewery, Hampshire.

Penny Universities (Eng) the nickname for the first coffee houses in the late seventeenth century that stemmed from the habit of discussing business over coffee. Most of these coffee houses became the business institutions of the present day i.e. The Stock Exchange and Lloyds of London.

Penrhos Court (Eng) a small brewery based near Kington in Herefordshire. Brews: cask-conditioned Penrhos Bitter, Jones's Ale and an original Porter.

Pensans Brewery (Eng) a brewery based in Penzance, Cornwall. Noted for cask-conditioned MSB 1050 O.G. and Caref Ertach Pensans 1055 O.G.

Penshaws Pint (Eng) a 4.1% alc by vol. bitter ale brewed by the Darwin Brewery, Tyne & Wear.

Penshurst Vineyards (Eng) a small vineyard (established 1972) based at Grove Road, Penshurst, Kent. 5ha. Grape varieties: Müller-Thurgau, Reichensteiner and Seyval blanc.

Penta (USA) a natural spring mineral water brand.

Pentagel (Eng) 4.6% alc by vol. ale bottled for the American market. Brewed by Gales Brewery, Horndean, Hampshire. Known as HSB in England.

Pentaploa (Gre) an ancient drink consisting of five ingredients (cheese, flour, honey, oil and wine).

Pentes (Fr) lit: 'slopes', a term found on a wine label from Cahors, from the red soil slopes near the river Lot.

Pentland Beer (Scot) a cask-conditioned heavy ale 1036 O.G. brewed by the Drybrough Brewery in Edinburgh.

Pentland Fizz (Cktl) 50mls (2fl.ozs) orange juice, 25mls (1fl.oz) Glayva. Mix together in an ice-filled highball glass and top up with iced Champagne.

Pentose (Eng) a monosaccharide found in wines.

Pentre Nant (Wal) a still and sparkling natural spring mineral water from the Kerry Hills, Montgomeryshire (Powys).

Penukanda (Ind) a wine-producing area.

Penwith Hills (Eng) a natural spring mineral water from St. Ives.

People's Pub Company (Wal) *see* People's Unity Bitter.

People's Unity Bitter (Wal) a cask ale brewed by the People's Pub Company (PPC) based in Rhondda and Pontypool to help rural communities afffected by the foot and mouth crisis (1980s).

PEOS Estate (Austr) a winery based in the Manjimup region of Western Australia. Grape varieties include: Cabernet sauvignon.

Pepi (It) a Chianti Classico producer based in Tuscany.

Pepi Winery (USA) a winery based between Yountville and Oakville in the Napa Valley, California. Grape variety: Sauvignon blanc.

Peplina Stepu (Ukr) a table wine produced near Cherson in the Ukraine.

Pepper Bridge Winery (USA) a winery based in the Walla Walla Valley, Washington State.

Peppermint Get (Fr) alt spelling of Pippermint Get.

Peppermint Iceberg (Cktl) ¾ measure vodka, ¼measure peppermint cordial. Mix together in an ice-filled highball and dress with a sprig of mint.

Peppermint Paddy (Cktl) ⅓ measure peppermint cordial, ⅓ measure Bourbon whiskey, ⅓ measure cream. Shake over ice and strain into a cocktail glass.

Peppermint Park (Cktl) 40mls (⅓ gill) dry gin, 20mls (⅙ gill) lemon juice, dash gomme syrup. Shake over ice, strain into a Champagne saucer, top with iced Champagne and serve with straws.

Peppermint Pastille (Fr) a green crème de menthe liqueur 28% alc by vol.

Peppermint Pattie (Cktl) ½ measure (white) crème de menthe, ½ measure (white) crème de cacao. Shake over ice and strain into an ice-filled old-fashioned glass.

Peppermint Pick Me Up (Cktl) add 25mls (⅕ gill) crème de menthe to a glass of hot, strong, black coffee. Stir, top with whipped cream and a few dashes of crème de menthe.

Peppermint Schnapps (USA) a mint liqueur, lighter in body than crème de menthe 30% alc by vol.

Peppermint Stick (Cktl) ⅖ measure (white) crème de cacao, ⅕ measure vodka, ⅕ measure cream, ⅕ measure peppermint cordial. Shake over ice and strain into a cocktail glass.

Peppermint Tea (Eng) a herbal tea which helps settle the stomach and aids digestion.

Pepper Vodka (Rus) *see* Okhotnichaya.

Pepperwood Grove (USA) a label for the Don Sebastiani winery, Sonoma Country, California.

Peppery (Eng) a term used to describe the aroma and flavour of the Grenache-based wines of southern France. Also to young wines that are fierce and prickly on the nose.

Pepsi-Cola (USA) a famous brand-name for a carbonated soft cola drink, red-brown in colour, it is produced by Pepsi-Cola Worldwide Beverages and drunk world-wide. Diet version also available. *See also* Diet Pepsi. Website: http://www.pepsico.com

Pepsi-Cola Worldwide Beverages (USA) a large company that produces Pepsi-Cola. Partly owns Britvic Corona.

Pepsi Max (USA) the name for a carbonated soft cola drink that contains no sugar. Produced by Pepsi-Cola Worldwide Beverages.

Pequea Valley Winery (USA) a large winery based in Willow Street, Pennsylvania. Produces hybrid wines.

Pera Manca (Port) a red wine produced in Alentejo by Eugénio de Almeida. Now known as Cartuxa Evura.

Perbibere (Lat) drink up.

Perchaud [C] (Fr) a winery based in the A.C. Chablis, Burgundy. Produces a range of Chablis wines including Premier Cru Fourchaume.

Percolate (Eng) the action of wines and spirits as they are passed through herbs to extract flavours for vermouths and liqueurs. Also applies to coffee when hot water is passed through the coffee grounds to extract colour and flavour.

Percolateur (Fr) percolator.

Percolation (Eng) is '*intensive maceration*', where pure spirit is continuously passed through botanicals to extract flavours for liqueurs.

Percolator (Eng) a unit used in the making of coffee. Either automatic or manual. Near boiling water is passed over the grounds to extract the flavour and colour.

Percy Fox & C° (Eng) a drinks manufacturer and supplier (established 1886). (Add): Unit C, Woodside, Dunmow Road, Bishops Storford, Essex CM23 5RG. Produces a range of wines. Part of Diago Group. Website: http://www.percyfox.com

Perdeberg Wynboere Koöperatiewe (S.Afr) a co-operative winery (established 1941) based in Paarl, Western Cape. 3000ha. (Add): Box 214, Paarl 7621. Grape varieties: Cabernet sauvignon, Chenin blanc, Cinsaut, Merlot, Pinotage, Shiraz. Produces varietal wines. Website: http://www.perdeberg.co.za

Perdeblokke (S.Afr) the label wine produced by the Klein Constantia Estate winery, Constantia, Western Cape.

Perdido Vineyard (USA) a bonded winery based in Alabama. Wines are produced mainly from the Muscadine grape.

Perdiz (Sp) a white grape variety grown in the León region.

Perdriel (Arg) the brand-name used by Bodegas Norton for their premium wines.

Père Anselme (Fr) the label of a Châteauneuf-du-Pape produced by Brotte in Châteauneuf-du-Pape, southern Rhône. *See also* Flascoulet (Le), Fiole du Pape (La).

Père Blanc (Lux) a herb-flavoured liqueur.

Pere'e Palummo (It) an alternative name for Piedirosso.

Père et Fils (Fr) father and sons.

Père Hennepin (USA) a sparkling wine produced by the Thompson Winery in Michigan.

Perelada (Sp) a sparkling wine (cava) producer in Penedés, Alto Ampurdàn on the Costa Brava. Produces wines by the méthode traditionelle. Gran Claustro is their top named wine.

Perelli-Minetti Winery (USA) a large winery based at Delano, Kern County, California. Produces most styles of wines under the California Wine Association C°. (Ambassador, Greystone, Guasti and Perelli-Minetti).

Père Magloire (Fr) an A.C. V.S.O.P. Calvados marketed by Debrise-Dulac. Aged in Limousin oak.

Père Marquete (USA) a sparkling wine produced by the Thompson Winery in Michigan.

Peré Palummo (It) lit: 'pigeon foot', refers to colour of the Piedirosso grape variety grown in the Campania region.

Perera Quelle (Ger) a natural spring mineral water from Werder.

Pères Blancs (W.Ind) a rum distillery based on the island of Guadeloupe.

Péret (Fr) a wine-producing commune in Clairette du Languedoc, southern France.

Pérez Barquero S.A. (Sp) a producer of Montilla wines based in Córdoba (was part of Rumasa).

Pérez Cruz (Chile) a winery based in the Maipo Valley. Grape varieties: Cabernet franc, Cabernet sauvignon, Carmenère, Syrah. Website: http://www.perezcruz.com

Pérez Martin (Sp) a Sherry bodega based in Sanlúcar de Barrameda.

Pérez Texeira (Sp) a producer and exporter of Málaga.

Perfect Affinity Cocktail (Cktl) ½ measure Scotch whisky, ¼ measure Italian vermouth, ¼ measure French vermouth, 2 dashes Angostura. Shake over ice, strain into a cocktail glass and decorate with a spiral of lemon peel.

Perfect Cocktail [1] (Cktl) ½ measure dry gin, ¼ measure dry vermouth, ¼ measure sweet vermouth, dash Angostura. Stir with ice, strain into a cocktail glass and add a twist of orange peel.

Perfect Cocktail [2] (Cktl) 60mls (½ gill) gin, 20mls (⅙ gill) French vermouth, 20mls (⅙ gill) Italian vermouth, dash absinthe. Shake over ice, strain into a wine glass, serve with a slice of lemon and dash of lemon peel juice on top.

Perfection (Fr) a limited edition Cognac of 300 exclusively numbered bottles from Hardy. Sold in a crystal decanter.

Perfection Pale (Eng) a medium-dry Sherry from Peter Dominic Wine Shops.

Perfect Lady (Cktl) ½ measure dry gin, ¼ measure lemon juice, ¼ measure peach brandy, 1 egg white. Shake over ice and strain into a cocktail glass.

Perfect Love (Cktl) place 25mls Parfait Amour liqueur into a Champagne flute and top up with iced Champagne.

Perfectly Pure (S.Afr) a natural spring mineral water. Mineral contents (milligrammes per litre): Sodium 15mg/l, Calcium 24mg/l, Potassium <2mg/l, Chlorides 9.5mg/l, Sulphates 0.9mg/l, Fluorides 0.4mg/l, Nitrates 1.5mg/l. pH 6.5

Perfect Martini (Cktl) ⅔ measure gin, ⅙ measure dry vermouth, ⅙ measure sweet vermouth. Stir over ice, strain into a cocktail glass and add twist of lemon.

Perfect Match (Cktl) ½ measure Glayva, ¼ measure cherry brandy, ¼ measure lemon juice, egg white. Shake over ice and strain into a cocktail glass.

Perfect Pair (Eng) a 5.5% alc by vol. flavoured, bottled drink from Spilt Drinks Company, Exeter, Devon.

Perfect Rob Roy (Cktl) ½ measure Scotch whisky, ¼ measure dry vermouth, ¼ measure sweet vermouth. Stir over ice, strain into a cocktail glass and dress with a lemon peel spiral.

Perfume (Eng) description of the bouquet of a wine when it has a flowery scent. i.e. violets in Clarets.

Perfik (Eng) a spring ale brewed by Everards at Castle Acres, Narborough, Leicester.

Pergola (Port) a method of training vines to grow from a single trunk and trained on trellises with other crops underneath. Also used in Italy, Greece, Spain etc.

Pergola Torte (It) a red Vino da Tavola made from the Sangiovese grape in central-western Italy.

Pérignac-de-Pons (Fr) a commune in the Charente-Maritime département whose grapes are classed Petite Champagne (Cognac).

Pérignon [Pierre] (Fr) the name of Dom Pérignon before he took the monastic orders in 1658.

Pergoli di Tobiano (It) a natural spring mineral water from Pergoli. Mineral contents (milligrammes per litre): Sodium 69mg/l, Calcium 680mg/l, Magnesium 54mg/l, Potassium 3.8mg/l, Bicarbonates 520mg/l, Chlorides 77mg/l, Sulphates 1455mg/l, Fluorides 0.5mg/l, Silicates 50mg/l. pH 6.4

Perigord (Fr) a red grape variety grown in the Bergerac region.

Perikum-Snaps (Den) the brand-name of an aquavit.

Perino (Bra) a spirit produced by the Indians from cassavy root (the root is poisonous to eat).

P

Perino (Eng) the brand-name given to a range of drinks produced from red and white Italian wine, spring water and fruit flavours. 5% alc by vol. from Goldwell (part of Allied-Domecq).

Periquita (Port) an alternative name for Castelao Francês or Trincadeira red grape variety.

Periquita (Port) a strong red wine produced in Azeitao and Palmela districts in the Estremadura, and in the Algarve. Grape varieties: Aragonez, Castelão, Trincadeira. Also known as João de Santarém. Website: http://www.jmf.pt

Perisco (Hol) a peach-flavoured bitters liqueur.

Perla (Czec) lit: 'pearl', a special pale ale brewed by the Ilava Brewery.

Perla de Tîrnave (Rum) a well-balanced, light, slightly sweet, blended wine from the Tîrnave region on the river Tîrnave. Is produced from the Feteasca, Muskat-ottonel and Riesling grapes.

Perla Harghitei (Rum) a sparkling natural spring mineral water (established 1974) from Sancraieni Harghita. Mineral contents (milligrammes per litre): Sodium 58.5mg/l, Calcium 142.02mg/l, Magnesium 59.8mg/l, Potassium 13.6mg/l, Bicarbonates 994.21mg/l, Chlorides 17.7mg/l, Sulphates 5.3mg/l. pH 5.9

Perla Lublin Breweries (Pol) a brewery. (Add): Ul Bernardynska 15, 20-950 Lubin. Brews beers and lager. Website: http://www.perla.pl 'E'mail: perla@perla.pl

Perlan (Switz) the generic name given to the white wines produced in Geneva from the Chasselas grape. Also known as Dorin, Fendant.

Perlant (Fr) the term for very slightly sparkling wines.

Perlant Perlé (S.Afr) pétillant.

Perlato del Bosco (It) an I.G.T. 100% Sangiovese wine with 33% aged in new oak. Produced by Tua Rita, Maremma, Tuscany.

Perlé (Fr) beaded/light sparkle/pétillant.

Perle (Ger) a white grape variety, a cross between the Gewürztraminer and the Müller-Thurgau. Gives light fruity wines and resists low temperatures -30°C (-22°F) in Winter and -5°C (23°F) in the Spring.

Perles Joyeuses (Fr) a special promotional label of sparkling mineral water produced by Badoit for the 2000/2001 festive season.

Perling (Ger) a natural spring mineral water from Rhens. Mineral contents (milligrammes per litre): Sodium 852mg/l, Calcium 113mg/l, Magnesium 57mg/l, Potassium 13mg/l, Bicarbonates 1321mg/l, Chlorides 575mg/l, Sulphates 468mg/l, Fluorides 0.7mg/l.

Perlino Perlé (S.Afr) a slightly sparkling medium-sweet white wine made by the Stellenbosch Farmers' Winery from the Clairette blanche, Muscat d'alexandrie and Steen grapes.

Perlivá (Czec) a natural spring mineral water. Mineral contents (milligrammes per litre): Sodium 10mg/l, Calcium 6.6mg/l, Magnesium 9mg/l, Potassium 10.6mg/l, Bicarbonates 109.9mg/l, Chlorides 2.8mg/l, Sulphates 4.8mg/l, Fluorides 0.7mg/l, Nitrates 0.1mg/l.

Perlwein (Ger) a term for light sparkling wines. carbonic acid pressure must not be more than 2.5 atmospheres to qualify.

Perlwein (Lux) a term for a pétillant wines (slightly sparkling).

Perlweizen (Ger) a well-matured pale wheat beer 5% alc by vol. Produced by the Riegele Brauerei in Augsburg.

Permezzo (Cktl) 25mls (1fl.oz) red Dubonnet, 25mls (1fl.oz) dry Dubonnet. Place in an old-fashioned glass and serve 'on the rocks' with a slice of lemon.

Permitted Hours (Eng) the hours for which a person can consume alcoholic beverages on licensed premises, can be 24 hours but vary from district to district and pub to pub. See also Drinking-Up Time.

Pernod (Fr) an un-sweetened aniseed-flavoured famous branded pastis 45% alc by vol produced by Pernod-Ricard. See also Ricard.

Pernod and Clementine (Cktl) 1 part Pernod, 1 part orange juice. Stir with ice in a highball glass and top with bitter lemon.

Pernod Caribbean (Cktl) 1 part Pernod, 1 part Malibu, 3 parts pineapple juice. Stir with ice in a highball glass and top with soda water.

Pernod Cocktail (Cktl) 1 measure Pernod, 1 measure water, dash gomme syrup, dash Angostura. Shake over ice and strain into a cocktail glass.

Pernod Drip (Cktl) pour 1 measure of Pernod onto a lump of ice in a small tumbler. Place 1 sugar lump on a French drip spoon, rest on the rim of the glass and slowly pour cold water over the sugar lump until dissolved.

Pernod Hex (Fr) a sparkling blackcurrant and lime juice or lime and cola-flavoured pre-mix Pernod drink. 5.5% alc by vol. from Pernod-Ricard.

Pernod Jelly Bean (Cktl) 1 measure Pernod, 1 measure vodka, 1 measure blackcurrant syrup. Stir into a highball glass with ice and top with lemonade.

Pernod Oriental (Cktl) 1 measure Pernod, ½ measure Midori, dash lime juice. Stir with ice into a highball glass and top with soda water.

Pernod-Ricard (Fr) a large company (merger of Pernod and Ricard Pastis companies 1985). Produces Alize, Pernod and Ricard (pastis). Owns the highland malt whiskies The Glenlivet, Aberlour-Glenlivet and Edradour. Also owns Besserat de Bellefron Champagne, Chivas Regal Scotch Whisky, Gecko Ridge Winery, Havana Club Rum, Heidsieck Monopole Champagne, Jacob's Creek Winery, Jameson Irish Whiskey, Long Mountain Wine Company, Martell Cognac, Montana, Olmeca Tequilla, OVD Rum, Stolichnaya Vodka, White Satin Gin, Tia Lusso. Website: http://www.pernod-ricard.com 'E'mail: general@pernodricard-uk.com

Pernod-Ricard Pacific (Fr) a branch of the Pernod-Ricard group consisting of Montana Wines (New Zealand) and Orlando Wyndham (Australia). A part of Pernod-Ricard Asia.

P

Pernod Riviera (Cktl) ⅔ measure Pernod, ⅓ measure dry gin, dash Angostura. Place into an ice-filled highball glass, top with lemonade and a slice of lemon.

Perold (S.Afr) the name of a wine produced by KWV from 100% Shiraz grapes grown on old vines in Paarl, aged for 2 years in 300hls hogshead casks.

Peroni Beer (It) an Italian brewed beer exported to the USA.

Peroni Brewery (It) a large brewing company (established 1846) that has eight breweries in Italy. Website: http://www.peroniitaly.com

Peroni Nastri Azzuro (It) a 5.1% alc by vol (1055 O.G) beer brewed by Peroni Brewery.

Peronospora (Lat) downy mildew, a vine disease, treated with copper sulphate.

Perpetua (It) a dessert wine produced by the Villa Fontna Winery in the Cerasuola di Vittoria, south-eastern Sicily.

Perpotare (Lat) to drink continuously.

Perpotatio (Lat) a heavy drinking bout.

Perquages [Les] (Ch.Isles) a 1.2ha vineyard (established 1980) based at Les Perquages Cottage, Mount Remon, St. Peter, Jersey. Grape varieties: Blauberger 20%, Regner 30%, plus others.

Perréon [Le] (Fr) a commune in the Beaujolais. Has A.C. Beaujolais-Villages or Beaujolais-Le-Perréon status.

Perricone (It) a black grape variety grown in Sicily. Is also known as the Piedirosso and Pignatello.

Perrier (Fr) a slightly acidic sparkling natural spring mineral water (established 1863) from 30310 Vergése, Gard. Mineral contents (milligrammes per litre): Sodium 11.5mg/l, Calcium 149mg/l, Magnesium 7mg/l, Potassium 0.6mg/l, Bicarbonates 420mg/l, Chlorides 23mg/l, Sulphates 42mg/l, Fluorides 0.12mg/l, Nitrates 18mg/l. pH 5.46. It is also available in lemon, lime and orange flavours.

Perrier [Joseph et Fils] (Fr) a Champagne producer. (Add): 69 Avenue de Paris, B.P. 31, 51016 Châlons-sur-Marne. 20ha. A Grande Marque. Produces vintage and non-vintage wines. Vintages: 1900, 1904, 1906, 1911, 1914, 1915, 1921, 1926, 1928, 1929, 1933, 1934, 1937, 1938, 1942, 1943, 1945, 1947, 1949, 1959, 1961, 1962, 1964, 1966, 1969, 1971, 1973, 1975, 1976, 1979, 1982, 1983, 1985, 1989, 1995, 1996, 1997, 1998, 1999, 2000, 2001. Prestige cuvees: Belle Epoque, Cuvée Cinquantenaire, Cuvée Royale 1995 (Chardonnay 50%, Pinot noir 45%, Pinot meunier 5%) and Joséphine.

Perrier Champagne (Fr) three separate Champagne houses. *see* Laurent-Perrier, Perrier (Joseph et Fils), Perrier-Jouët & C°.

Perrière [La] (Fr) a Premier Cru vineyard [part] in the A.C. commune of Fixin, Côte de Nuits, Burgundy. 6.53ha. Part also in Gevrey-Chambertin. Also known as Clos de la Perrière.

Perrière [La] (Fr) a Premier Cru vineyard [part] in the A.C. commune of Gevrey-Chambertin, Côte de Nuits, Burgundy. 2.47ha. Part also in Fixin.

Perrière [La] (Fr) a Premier Cru vineyard in the A.C. commune of Nuits-Saint-Georges, Côte de Nuits, Burgundy 4ha.

Perrière-Noblet (Fr) Premier Cru vineyard [part] in the A.C. commune of Nuits-Saint-Georges, Côte de Nuits, Burgundy 2.2ha.

Perrières [Les] (Fr) a Premier Cru vineyard in the A.C. commune of Beaune, Côte de Beaune, Burgundy 3.18ha.

Perrières [Les] (Fr) a wine producing village in the commune of Fuissé, in A.C. Pouilly-Fuissé, Mâcon, Burgundy.

Perrières [Les] (Fr) a Premier Cru vineyard in the A.C. commune of Meursault, Côte de Beaune, Burgundy 17.8ha.

Perrières [Les] (Fr) a vineyard in the A.C. commune of Montagny, Côte Chalonnaise, Burgundy.

Perrier-Jouët & C°. (Fr) a Champagne producer established 1811. (Add): 26-28 Ave. de Champagne, B.P. 31, 51200 Épernay. 108ha. A Grande Marque. Produces vintage and non-vintage wines. Produces: Le Grand Brut, Le Grand Brut Millésimé, Le Blason Rosé, La Cuvée Belle Epoque Millésimée La Cuvé Belle Epoque Rosé Millésimé. Vintages: 1901, 1904, 1911, 1913, 1914, 1919, 1921, 1923, 1926, 1928, 1934, 1937, 1942, 1943, 1946, 1947, 1949, 1950, 1952, 1953, 1955, 1959, 1961, 1964, 1966, 1969, 1971, 1973, 1975, 1976, 1979, 1982, 1983, 1985, 1988, 1989, 1990, 1993, 1995, 1996, 1997, 1998, 1999, 2000, 2002. Part of G.H. Mumm. De Luxe vintage cuvée is Belle Epoque. Also produces Blason de France Rosé (a non-vintage rosé). Website: http://www.perrier-jouet.com 'E'mail: Frederique_Baveret@perrier-jouet.fr

Perrier-Jouët Belle Epoque, Fleur de Champagne (Fr) the Perrier-Jouët houses' top of the range Champagne. Vintages: 1966, 1969, 1971, 1973, 1975, 1976, 1979, 1982, 1983, 1985, 1988, 1989, 1990, 1995. 40%–45% Chardonnay and 55%–60% Pinot noir grapes. A blanc de blancs version is also produced.

Perrier Water (Fr) *see* Perrier.

Perrize (Eng) the brand-name for a sparkling perry from Showerings.

Perroquet Bleu (Fr) a blue coloured mint-flavoured '*menthe bleu*' 21% alc by vol. produced by the R.R. & C°.

Perroquet Cape Tawny (S.Afr) the label for a tawny Port-style wine (Tinta barroca) produced by the Louiesenhof Wines winery, Stellenbosch, Western Cape.

Perroud (Fr) a noted producer of Beaujolais wine based in Lantignié. *see* Château du Basty.

Perroy (Switz) a wine-producing area in La Côte on the west bank of Lake Geneva.

Perrum (Port) a white grape variety grown in the Algarve region, also known as the Palomino. Has a neutral flavour.

Perruno (Sp) a white grape variety grown in the Vino de la Tierra areas of Cádiz and Contraviesa-Alpujarra, Andalucía.

Perry (Eng) an alcoholic beverage made from pear

P

juice, either still or sparkling and usually slightly sweet.

Perrys (Ire) a keg beer brewed by the Irish Ale Breweries.

Persan (Fr) a rare red grape variety formerly grown in Savoie.

Perscheid (Ger) village (Anb): Mittelrhein. (Ber): Rheinburgengau. (Gro): Schloss Schönburg. (Vin): Rosental.

Perseval [Julien] (Fr) Champagne producer. (Add): Jouy-les-Reims, 51390. Produces: Demi-Sec (Premier Cru).

Persico (Hol) a brandy-based liqueur produced from almonds, peach stones, sugar and spices 30% alc by vol. Also known as Persicot.

Persicot (Hol) *see* Persico.

Persigny de Bergerac (Fr) the Méhler-Besse Bordeaux négociant-éleveurs' label for their A.C. Bergerac wines sold in the U.K.

Personalidad (Sp) a term that denotes a wine of character and of breeding.

Pertaringa (Austr) lit: 'belonging to the hills', a winery based at Corner of Hunt and Rifle Range Roads, McLaren Vale, South Australia. Grape varieties include: Cabernet sauvignon, Muscat blanc à petits grains. Label: Full Fronti.

Perth Hills (Austr) a wine area in West Australia.

Perthshire Mountain Spring (Scot) a natural spring mineral water from Blackford, Perthshire. Mineral contents (milligrammes per litre): Sodium 12mg/l, Calcium 35mg/l, Magnesium 15mg/l, Potassium 1.3mg/l, Bicarbonates 179mg/l, Chlorides 10mg/l, Sulphates 6mg/l, Fluorides <0.2mg/l, Nitrates 1.5mg/l.

Perthuis [Le] (Fr) a vineyard in the A.C. commune of Montagny, Côte Chalonnaise, Burgundy.

Pertois-Lebrun (Fr) a Champagne producer. (Add): 399 Rue de la Liberation, Cramant, 51200 Épernay. Récoltants-manipulants. Produces vintage and non-vintage wines. Vintages: 1971, 1973, 1975, 1976, 1979, 1982, 1983, 1985, 1988, 1990, 1995, 1996, 1998 1999, 2000.

Pertsovaka (Rus) a dark brown pepper-flavoured vodka. Has a pleasant aroma and burning taste. Made from an infusion of capsicum, cayenne and cubeb. 35% alc by vol. Also spelt Pertsovka.

Pertsovka (Rus) *see* Pertsovaka.

Pertuisots [Les] (Fr) a Premier Cru vineyard in the A.C. commune of Beaune, Côte de Beaune, Burgundy. 5.16ha. Also spelt Les Pertuizots.

Pertuizots [Les] (Fr) *see* Pertuisots (Les).

Peru Gold (Peru) a 5% alc by vol. premium lager from Compania Cervecera.

Perushtitza (Bul) a State wine co-operative.

Peruvian Coffee (Peru) a light bodied, mild-flavoured coffee from Peru. Used mainly for blending with strong coffees as it is low in acidity.

Perwolff (Aus) the label for an oak-aged red wine (Blaufränkisch, Cabernet sauvignon and Zweigelt blend) produced by the Krutzler winery, Süd-Burgenland.

Pescador (Sp) a sparkling wine produced using the cuve close method by Cavas del Ampurdón.

Pesenti Winery (USA) a winery based in Templeton, San Luis Obispo County, California. 27ha. Grape varieties: mainly Zinfandel.

Pesquera (Sp) a crianza Ribero del Duero wine.

Pessac-Léognan (Fr) a commune within the A.C. Graves district that has been granted its own A.C. (in 1988). Has the Premier Grand Cru Château Haut Brion within its boundaries.

Pessah [Le] (Fr) the Château Pommery Grand Cru Kosher wine made under Rabbinical supervision.

Pests (Eng) insects which attack the vine and its fruit. Phylloxera, Red spider, Cochylis etc.

Petake Cocktail (Cktl) 50mls (2fl.ozs) golden rum, 25mls (1fl.oz) Cointreau, dash Van der Hum, dash pineapple juice, dash papaya juice, dash lime juice. Shake over ice and strain into a cocktail glass.

Petalon (Austr) a winery based in the Margaret River region of Western Australia. Grape varieties include: Cabernet sauvignon. Label: Hocus Pocus.

Petaluma (Austr) vineyard. (Add): Spring Gully Road, Piccadilly, South Australia. Vineyards in Coonawarra, Hanlin Hill at Clare and Piccadilly. Also own Old Bridgewater Mill. Grape varieties: Cabernet sauvignon, Chardonnay and Riesling. Produces varietal wines. Labels include Croser.

Pet Bottle (Eng) a moulded™ plastic bottle made from Polyethylene terephthalate by the Metal Box C°. Ltd.

Petenara (Sp) a light, dry, Manzanilla Sherry produced by Romate.

Peter Austin's Original Formula (Eng) a 4% alc by vol. bitter from Tisbury Brewery, Tisbury, Wiltshire.

Peter Barlow (S.Afr) a red wine (Cabernet sauvignon) produced by the Rustenberg Estate, Stellenbosch, Western Cape.

Peter Bayly (S.Afr) a winery (established 2002) based in Calitzdorp, Little Karoo. 1.2ha. Grape varieties: Souzão, Tinta barocca, Touriga. Produces Cape Vintage Port.

Peter Crau (Fr) a Vin de Pays area of the Bouches du Rhône département, south-eastern France.

Peter Dominic (Eng) part of IDV Ltd. under the Grand Metropolitain umbrella with a large chain of off-licences around the U.K. Took over the Bottoms Up group. Then was acquired by Whitbread in 1992.

Peter Lehmann Winery (Austr) a winery based in the Barossa Velley, South Australia. (Add): Off Para Road, Tanunda SA 5352, P.O. Box 315. Grape varieties: Cabernet sauvignon, Chardonnay, Grenache, Merlot, Mourvèdre, Riesling, Sauvignon blanc, Sémillon, Shiraz, Weighbridge. Labels: Clancy's, Mentor, Seven Surveys, Stonewell, Wildcard Reserve. Website: http://www.peterlehmannwines.com.au

Peter Michael Winery (USA) a winery based in Calistoga, Knights Valley, Napa Valley, California. Produces varietal wines including Clos du Ciel

(Chardonnay), Le Moulin Roubge (Pinot noir), Les Pavots (Cabernet sauvignon).

Peter Pan (Cktl) ⅓ measure dry gin, ⅓ measure French vermouth, ⅓ measure orange juice, 2 dashes Angostura. Shake over ice and strain into a cocktail glass.

Peter Piper (Eng) a 4.3% alc by vol. beer brewed by Hanby Ales of Wem, Shropshire.

Peterquelle (Aus) a sparkling natural spring mineral water. Mineral contents (milligrammes per litre): Sodium 532mg/l, Calcium 159mg/l, Magnesium 39mg/l, Bicarbonates 1788mg/l, Chlorides 208mg/l.

Petersberg (Ger) grosslage (Anb): Mittelrhein. (Ber): Siebengebirge. (Vils): Oberdollendorf, Niederdollendorf, Königswinter, Rhondorf.

Petersberg (Ger) grosslage (Anb): Rheinhessen. (Ber): Nierstein. (Vils): Albig, Bechtolsheim, Biebelnheim, Framersheim, Gau-Heppenheim, Gau-Odernheim, Spiesheim.

Petersberg (Ger) vineyard (Anb): Baden. (Ber): Badische Bergstrasse/Kraichgau. (Gro): Hohenberg. (Vil): Weingarten.

Petersberg (Ger) vineyard (Anb): Mosel-Saar-Ruwer. (Ber): Zell/Mosel. (Gro): Grafschaft. (Vil): Neef.

Petersborn–Kabertchen (Ger) vineyard (Anb): Mosel-Saar-Ruwer. (Ber): Zell/Mosel. (Gro): Schwarze Katz. (Vil): Zell.

Peter's Brandy Sour (Eng) brandy, sparkling water, cherry and lemon crush sold in aluminum cans. Produced by Flaggl (Peter) in Camberley, Surrey.

Peter's Porter (Eng) a 4.8% alc by vol. porter brewed by Arkells in Stratton St. Margaret, near Swindon, Wiltshire.

Peterstaler Mineralwasser (Ger) a still natural spring mineral water from Bad Perterstal in the Black Forest. (blue label; sparkling/green label: light gas/light blue label: still). Mineral contents (milligrammes per litre): Sodium 170mg/l, Calcium 140mg/l, Magnesium 30mg/l, Potassium 10mg/l, Bicarbonates 820mg/l, Chlorides 20mg/l, Sulphates 170mg/l, Fluorides <2mg/l. Website: http://www.peterstaler.de

Peterstaler Mineralwasser (Ger) a sparkling natural spring mineral water from Bad Peterstal in the Black Forest. Mineral contents (milligrammes per litre): Sodium 17mg/l, Calcium 11mg/l, Magnesium 0.2mg/l, Potassium 0.1mg/l, Bicarbonates 700mg/l, Chlorides 0.1mg/l, Sulphates 14mg/l. Website: http://www.peterstaler.de

Peterstirn (Ger) vineyard (Anb): Franken. (Ber): Maindreieck. (Gro): Not yet assigned. (Vil): Schweinfurt.

Peters Val (Ger) a naturally sparkling spring water from the Black Forest mountains, bottled at source.

Peter Thompson [Perth] Limited (Scot) producers of the blended Scotch whisky Beneagles. (Add): Box 22, Crieff Road, Perth.

Peter Yates 1884 Bitter (Eng) a 4.1% alc by vol. hoppy ale brewed by Moorhouses (named after the man who founded the Peter Yates public house chain more than 120 years ago).

Pete's Brewing Company (USA) a micro-brewery (established 1986) based in Palo Alto, California. Brews over 12 beers including: Ale, Amber Ale, Pale Ale, Summer Brew, Winter Brew, Oktoberfest, Honey Wheat Beer, Strawberry Beer, plus a Bohemian Pilsner. All are marketed under 'Pete's Wicked' label.

Pete's Wicked Ale (USA) a 5% alc by vol. copper coloured, top-fermented, bottled brown ale brewed by Pete's Brewing Company, Palo Alto, California.

Pete's Wicked Bohemian Pilsner (USA) a 4.9% alc by vol. hoppy dark lager brewed by Pete's Brewing Company, Palo Alto, California.

Pete's Wicked Honey Wheat (USA) a delicately malted beer flavoured with clover honey, Tettnang and Cascade hops brewed by Pete's Brewing Company, Palo Alto, California.

Pete's Wicked Springfest (USA) a 7% alc by vol. ale brewed by Pete's Brewing Company, Palo Alto, California.

Pete's Wicked Summer Brew (USA) a 4.8% alc by vol. pale summer ale with a hint of lemon brewed by Pete's Brewing Company, Palo Alto, California.

Pete's Wicked Winter Brew (USA) a winter ale flavoured with raspberry and nutmeg brewed by Pete's Brewing Company, Palo Alto, California.

Pétillant (Fr) the term for slightly sparkling wines, especially those that have had a malo-lactic fermentation in the bottle.

Pétillant de Listel (Eng) a clear, slightly sparkling low-alcohol wine produced from musts of fresh grapes which have been partially fermented. 2%–3% alc by vol. Produced by Listel.

Pétillant de Savoie (Fr) *see* Vin de Savoie Pétillant.

Pétillant de Savoie-Ayze (Fr) *see* Vin de Savoie-Ayze Pétillant.

Pétillant du Bugey (Fr) *see* Vin du Bugey Pétillant.

Pétillant Fronté (S.Afr) the label for a light (8% alc by vol) medium-sweet wine (Muscat de frontignan) produced by the De Wet Co-operative winery, Worcester, Western Cape.

Pétiller (Fr) to sparkle/fizz. *see* Pétillant.

Petit (Fr) small.

Petit (S.Afr) the label for a range of wines red (Pinotage) white (Chenin blanc) produced by the Ken Forrester Wines winery, Stellenbosch, Western Cape.

Petit Bouschet (Afr) a local name for the Alicante bouschet in Tunisia. A cross between the Teinturier and the Aramon.

Petit Cabernet (Fr) the local Bordeaux name for the Cabernet Sauvignon.

Petit Calva [Un] (Fr) the slang term for a small Calvados drunk in the morning as a pick-me-up.

Petit Chablis (Fr) the lowest grade of the Chablis wines. A.C. it is much lighter than the Premier Crus. Minimum alc by vol. of 9.5%. *see* Chablis.

Petit Château (Fr) the name given to the lesser châteaux that are not included in the Cru Classés.

Petit Cheval [Le] (Fr) the second wine of Château Cheval Blanc.

Petit Clos de Brouard (Fr) a vineyard in the commune of Lalande de Pomerol. A.C. Lalande de Pomerol, Bordeaux.

Petit Clos Figeac (Fr) a vineyard in the commune of Saint-Émilion. A.C. Saint-Émilion, Bordeaux 3ha.

Petit Courbu (Fr) a white grape variety grown in Gascony. Used in Pacherenc du Vic Bilh production.

Petite Arvine (Switz) a white grape variety grown in the Valais.

Petite Blanc (S.Afr) the label for a white wine (Chardonnay, Colombard and Sauvignon blanc blend) produced by the Rietrivier Winery, Little Karoo.

Petite Bouschet (USA) a white grape variety grown in California for the production of dessert wines.

Petite Champagne (Fr) the second Cru of Cognac only to Grande Champagne. 14.7% of district. Jarnac is best known town. (Coms): [Charente département] Angeac-Charente, Ars, Barbezieux, Barret, Birac, Bourg-Charente, Châteauneuf, Graves, Guimps, Jurignac, Lachaise, Ladiville, Lagarde-sur-le-Né, Montchaude, Mosnac, Nonaville, Saint-Amant-de-Graves, Saint-Bonnet, Saint-Hilaire-de-Barbezieux, Saint-Médard-de-Barbezieux, Saint-Palais-du-Né, Salles-de-Barbezieux and Vignolles. [Charente-Maritime département] Allas-Champagne, Archiac, Arthenac, Biron, Bougneau, Brie-sous-Archiac, Brives-sur-Charente, Celles, Chadenac, Champagnac, Cierzac, Coulonges, Clam, Échebrune, Germignac, Jarnac-Champagne, Jonzac, Lonzac, Meux, Moings, Montils, Neuillac, Neulles, Perignac-de-Pons, Saint-Germain-de-Lusignan, Saint-Germain-de-Vibrac, Saint-Martial-de-Coculet, Saint-Martial-de-Vitaterne, Saint-Maurice-de-Tavernolles, Saint-Lheurine, Saint-Seurin-de-Palenne, Saint-Sever, Salignac-de-Pons.

Petite Chapelle (Fr) see Champitonnois.

Petite Crau (Fr) a red, rosé and dry white wine-producing area in the north of Bouches du Rhône.

Petite Dôle (Switz) a red wine from the Valais canton. Made from the Pinot noir grape.

Petite-Fer (Fr) the local name for Cabernet franc in southern France.

Petite Ferme (S.Afr) the name for wines produced by Dendy-Young at La Petite Ferme Cellar in Franschhoeck. Grape varieties include Shiraz, Merlot, Pinotage, Chardonnay.

Petite Flandre de Médoc (Fr) a lesser district of Bordeaux.

Petite Fleur (Cktl) ⅓ measure Cointreau, ⅓ measure white rum, ⅓ measure fresh grapefruit juice. Shake over ice and strain into a cocktail glass.

Petite Liquorelle (Fr) a pétillant rich dessert and sparkling wine made with old Cognac produced by Moët and Chandon 18% alc by vol.

Petite Rouge (S.Afr) the label for a red wine (Pinotage and Ruby cabernet blend) produced by the Rietrivier Winery, Little Karoo.

Petite-Sainte-Marie (Fr) the local name used in the Savoie region for the Chardonnay grape.

Petite Sirah (Fr) another name for the Syrah grape. (Austr) = durif.

Petite Sirah (USA) see California Petite Sirah.

Petites-Lolières [Les] (Fr) a Premier Cru vineyard in the commune of Ladoix-Serrigny, A.C. Aloxe-Corton, Côte de Beaune, Burgundy.

Petites Marques (Fr) a term used in Champagne for the lesser known brands. See also Grandes Marques.

Petite Syrah (USA) an alternative spelling of Petite sirah.

Petit Flute Cocktail (Cktl) ½ measure Bacardi White Label, ¼ measure dry Martini vermouth, ¼ measure passion fruit liqueur, 2 dashes sweet Martini vermouth. Shake over ice, strain into a cocktail glass, dress with mint and a spiral of lemon peel.

Petit Gamai (Fr) an alternative name for the Gamay noir à jus blanc.

Petit Manseng (Fr) a white grape variety grown in the Jurançon that produces wines with an aroma and flavour of quince, grapefruit and honey. When the grapes are left to dry on the vines to make sweet wines it has an aroma and flavour of honey, dried apricots, quince, cinnamon and candied orange peel.

Petit Merle (Fr) an alternative name for the Merlot grape.

Petit Meslier (Fr) a white grape variety grown in Champagne. Related to the Sémillon, produces a wine of great bouquet.

Petit Mouton de Mouton-Rothschild [Le] (Fr) the second wine of Château Mouton-Rothschild, Pauillac.

Petit Musigny (Fr) an old division together with Grand Musigny which divided the Grand Cru vineyard of Musigny in the commune of Chambolle-Musigny.

Petit Pineau (Fr) an alternative name for the Arbois grape.

Petit Propriétaires (Fr) small vineyard owners.

Petit Rhin (Switz) the local name for the Riesling grape.

Petit-Rouge (It) a red grape variety grown in the Valle d'Aosta.

Petit St. Vincent [Le] (Fr) a 12ha vineyard in A.C. Saumur Champigny, Anjou-Saumur, Loire. Noted for Pelo: top cuvée produced from vines grown on tuffeau soil.

Petits Châteaux (Fr) see Petit Château.

Petits-Épenots [Les] (Fr) a Premier Cru vineyard in the A.C. commune of Pommard, Côte de Beaune, Burgundy 20.2ha.

Petits-Godeaux [Les] (Fr) a Premier Cru vineyard [part] in the A.C. commune of Savigny-lès-Beaune, Côte de Beaune, Burgundy.

Petits-Monts [Les] (Fr) a Premier Cru vineyard in the A.C. commune of Vosne-Romanée, Côte de Beaune, Burgundy 3.7ha.

Petits Vins Sucrés (Fr) a French description of the lesser German wines that have been sweetened with süssreserve.

Petits-Vougeots [Les] (Fr) a Premier Cru vineyard in

the A.C. commune of Vougeot, Côte de Nuits, Burgundy 5.8ha.

Petit Verdot (Fr) a red grape variety grown in Bordeaux.

Petit Vidure (Fr) a local name for the Cabernet sauvignon in Bordeaux.

Petra Pertusa (It) a natural spring mineral water from Metaura. Mineral contents (milligrammes per litre): Sodium 12mg/l, Calcium 88mg/l, Magnesium 2.5mg/l, Bicarbonates 253mg/l, Chlorides 20mg/l, Sulphates 12mg/l, Nitrates 12mg/l, Silicates 5.5mg/l.

Petri Brandy (USA) the brand-name of a brandy produced by the United Vintners, Lodi, California.

Petrich Damianitza (Bul) a D.G.O. area of South Western region. Main grape is Cabernet sauvignon.

Petrol (Eng) a wine term used to describe the aroma of mature Riesling wines (especially from Alsace and Germany).

Petropolis Paulista (Bra) a natural spring mineral water from Sao Joao de Petropolis. Mineral contents (milligrammes per litre): Sodium 2.2mg/l, Calcium 3.49mg/l, Magnesium 1.78mg/l, Potassium 0.55mg/l, Bicarbonates 12.61mg/l, Chlorides 3.38mg/l, Nitrates 0.3mg/l. pH 6.3

Petrovskaya (Rus) the method of distilling vodka until it becomes a spirit (either pot or continuous still or both).

Petrus Boonkamp (Hol) the full name of Boonkamp bitters.

Petrus Triple (Bel) a 7.5% alc by vol. straw, top-fermented bottle-conditioned triple beer brewed by the Bavik Braserie, Bavikhove.

Pett Brewing Company (Eng) a micro-brewery based in Hastings. Produces: Brothers Best Bitter 3.9% alc by vol. Pett Progress 4.6% alc by vol. Old Farnes.

Pettenthal (Ger) vineyard (Anb): Rheinhessen. (Ber): Nierstein. (Gro): Rehbach. (Vil): Nierstein.

Pett Progress (Eng) a 4.6% alc by vol. ale brewed by the micro-brewery Pett Brewing Company in Hastings.

Petures [Les] (Fr) a Premier Cru vineyard in the A.C. commune of Meursault, Côte de Beaune, Burgundy 11ha.

Petures [Les] (Fr) a Premier Cru vineyard in the A.C. commune of Volnay, Côte de Beaune, Burgundy.

Peuillets [Les] (Fr) a Premier Cru vineyard [part] in the A.C. commune of Savigny-lès-Beaune, Côte de Beaune, Burgundy.

Peumo (Chile) a sub-district within the Cachapoal Valley. Main grape variety: Carmenère.

Peureux (Fr) a firm in the Haute-Savoie that produces fine fruit liqueurs.

Peverella (USA) a white grape variety grown in the San Joaquin Valley, California.

Pévy (Fr) a Cru Champagne village in the Canton de Fismes. District: Reims.

Pewsey Vale Rhine Riesling (Austr) a white wine produced by the Yalumba vineyard in South Australia.

Pewter (Eng) an alloy of tin, lead and copper used to make the pewter pot-drinking vessels which are now illegal as they are not Government stamped.

Pewter (Eng) the old name for the draining board behind the bar in a public house.

Pewter Tankard (Eng) see Pewter.

Pexém (Port) a red grape variety grown in the Algarve region.

Péychaud's Bitters (USA) aromatic bitters produced in New Orleans.

Peyote (Mex) the old local name for the Mescal cactus.

Peyote Cactus (Mex) the name for the small buds from the Mescal catus. The source of Mescalin.

Peza (Gre) an A.O.Q.S. wine region on the island of Crete. Produces a dry red and white wines from Kotsifeli, Mandelari and Vilana grapes.

Peza Winery (Gre) a large co-operative winery on the island of Crete.

Pézenas (Fr) a new (2006) sub-region A.C. within the A.C. Coteaux du Languedoc based on its climate and soil (also Cabrières).

Pezerolles [Les] (Fr) a Premier Cru vineyard in the A.C. commune of Pommard, Côte de Beaune, Burgundy 7.3ha.

Pezinok (Czec) a wine-producing area which, together with the Modra area has the highest concentration of vines in the country.

Pezsgö (Hun) sparkling.

Pezsgö (Hun) a méthode classique traditional wine from Leitner Wise, Pécs.

Pfaffenberg (Ger) vineyard (Anb): Ahr. (Ber): Walporzheim/Ahrtal. (Gro): Klosterberg. (Vil): Walporzheim.

Pfaffenberg (Ger) vineyard (Anb): Franken. (Ber): Maindreieck. (Gro): Not yet assigned. (Vil): Würzburg.

Pfaffenberg (Ger) vineyard (Anb): Mosel-Saar-Ruwer. (Ber): Zell/Mosel. (Gro): Grafschaft. (Vil): Ediger-Eller.

Pfaffenberg (Ger) vineyard (Anb): Nahe. (Ber): Schloss Böckelheim. (Gro): Rosengarten. (Vil): Burgsponheim.

Pfaffenberg (Ger) vineyard (Anb): Rheingau. (Ber): Johannisberg. (Gro): Deutelsberg. (Vil): Hattenheim.

Pfaffenberg (Ger) vineyard (Anb): Rheinhessen. (Ber): Bingen. (Gro): Adelberg. (Vil): Flonheim.

Pfaffenberg (Ger) vineyard (Anb): Pfalz. (Ber): Südliche Weinstrasse. (Gro): Herrlich. (Vil): Mörzheim.

Pfaffenberg (Ger) vineyard (Anb): Pfalz. (Ber): Südliche Weinstrasse. (Gro): Kloster Liebfrauenberg. (Vil): Billigheim-Ingenheim.

Pfaffenberg (Ger) a vineyard within the village of Hattenheim, 6.6ha. (100%) of which is proposed to be classified as Erstes Gewächs.

Pfaffengarten (Ger) vineyard (Anb): Rheinhessen. (Ber): Nierstein. (Gro): Domherr. (Vil): Saulheim.

Pfaffengrund (Ger) grosslage (Anb): Pfalz. (Ber): Mittelhaardt-Deutsche Weinstrasse. (Vils): Diedesfeld, Duttweiler, Geinsheim, Hambach, Lachen-Speyerdorf.

P

Pfaffenhalde (Ger) vineyard (Anb): Rheinhessen. (Ber): Wonnegau. (Gro): Sybillenstein. (Vil): Alzey.

Pfaffenhofen (Ger) village (Anb): Württemberg. (Ber): Württembergisch Unterland. (Gro): Heuchelberg. (Vin): Hohenberg.

Pfaffenkappe (Ger) vineyard (Anb): Rheinhessen. (Ber): Nierstein. (Gro): Gutes Domtal. (Vil): Nierstein.

Pfaffenmütze (Ger) vineyard (Anb): Rheinhessen. (Ber): Wonnegau. (Gro): Pilgerpfad. (Vil): Dittelsheim-Hessloch.

Pfaffenpfad (Ger) vineyard (Anb): Nahe. (Ber): Schloss Böckelheim. (Gro): Paradiesgarten. (Vil): Alsenz.

Pfaffen-Schwabenheim (Ger) village (Anb): Rheinhessen. (Ber): Bingen. (Gro): Sankt Rochuskapelle. (Vins): Hölle, Mandelbaum, Sonnenberg.

Pfaffensteig (Ger) vineyard (Anb): Franken. (Ber): Maindreieck. (Gro): Hofrat. (Vil): Segnitz.

Pfaffenstein (Ger) vineyard (Anb): Nahe. (Ber): Schloss Böckelheim. (Gro): Burgweg. (Vil): Niederhausen an der Nahe.

Pfaffenstück (Ger) vineyard (Anb): Baden. (Ber): Markgräflerland. (Gro): Burg Neuenfels. (Vil): Müllheim.

Pfaffenthal (Aus) a vineyard site on the banks of the River Danube situated in the Wachau region, Niederösterreich.

Pfaffenweg (Ger) vineyard (Anb): Rheinhessen. (Ber): Nierstein. (Gro): Sankt Alban. (Vil): Gau-Bischofsheim.

Pfaffenweiler (Ger) village (Anb): Baden. (Ber): Markgräflerland. (Gro): Lorettoberg. (Vins): Batzenberg, Oderdürrenberg.

Pfaffenwies (Ger) vineyard (Anb): Rheingau. (Ber): Johannisberg. (Gro): Burgweg. (Vil): Lorch.

Pfaffl (Aus) a winery (25ha) based in Stetten, Weinviertel. (Add): Hauptstrasse 24, 2100 Stetten. Grape varieties: Cabernet sauvignon, Chardonnay, Gewürztraminer, Grüner veltliner, Riesling, Sauvignon blanc, Welschriesling, Zweigelt. Produces a range of dry and sweet wines.

Pfahlkultur (Aus) stake culture, a cultivation system.

Pfalz (Ger) lit: 'palatinate', anbaugebiet (Bers): Mittelhaardt-Deutsche Weinstrasse, Südliche Weinstrasse. Main grape varieties are Müller-Thurgau, Portugieser, Riesling and Silvaner. The new name for the Rheinpfalz.

Pfälzer Landwein (Ger) one of the fifteen Deutsche Tafelwein zones.

Pfalzgrafenstein (Ger) vineyard (Anb): Mittelrhein. (Ber): Rheinburgengau. (Gro): Herrenberg. (Vil): Kaub.

Pfarrberg (Ger) vineyard (Anb): Baden. (Ber): Ortenau. (Gro): Schloss Rodeck. (Vil): Waldulm.

Pfarrgarten (Ger) grosslage (Anb): Nahe. (Ber): Kreuznach. (Vils): Schoneberg, Spabrücken, Dalberg, Hergenfeld, Walhausen, Sommerloch, Gutenberg.

Pfarrgarten (Ger) vineyard (Anb): Mittelrhein. (Ber): Rheinburgengau. (Gro): Marksberg. (Vil): Filsen.

Pfarrgarten (Ger) vineyard (Anb): Mosel-Saar-Ruwer. (Ber): Zell/Mosel. (Gro): Rosenhang. (Vil): Bruttig-Fankel.

Pfarrgarten (Ger) vineyard (Anb): Rheinhessen. (Ber): Bingen. (Gro): Sankt Rochuskapelle. (Vil): Bingen.

Pfarrgarten (Ger) vineyard (Anb): Rheinhessen. (Ber): Nierstein. (Gro): Petersberg. (Vil): Gau-Heppenheim.

Pfarrgut (Ger) a vineyard owned by the church whose product is given to the priest, parson etc. as part of his renumeration.

Pfarrwingert (Ger) vineyard (Anb): Ahr. (Ber): Walporzheim/Ahrtal. (Gro): Klosterberg. (Vil): Dernau.

Pfedelbach (Ger) village (Anb): Württemberg. (Ber): Württembergisch Unterland. (Gro): Lindelberg. (Vin): Goldberg.

Pfeffrig (Aus) denotes a wine with a peppery taste.

Pfeifenberg (Aus) a vineyard site based on the banks of the River Kamp situated in the Kamptal region.

Pfeiffer Wines (Austr) a winery (established 1984). (Add): Distillery Road, Wahgunyah, near Rutherglen, Victoria. Grape varieties: Chardonnay, Riesling, Cabernet sauvignon, Gamay, Pinot noir.

Pfennigberg (Aus) a vineyard site on the banks of the River Danube in the Kremstal region.

Pfersigberg (Fr) an A.C. Alsace grand Cru vineyard at Eguisheim, Haut-Rhin 56ha.

Pfingstberg (Fr) an A.C. Alsace grand Cru vineyard at Orschwihr and Kintzheim, Haut-Rhin 28ha.

Pfirsichgarten (Ger) vineyard (Anb): Mosel-Saar-Ruwer. (Ber): Zell/Mosel. (Gro): Grafschaft. (Vil): Ediger-Eller.

Pflingstweide (Ger) vineyard (Anb): Nahe. (Ber): Schloss Böckelheim. (Gro): Burgweg. (Vil): Niederhausen an der Nahe.

Pfülben (Ger) vineyard (Anb): Franken. (Ber): Maindreieck. (Gro): Ewig Leben. (Vil): Randersacker.

Pfungstädter Eddel Pils (Ger) a 4.7% alc by vol. bottled pilsner brewed by the Hildebrand Brauerei, Pfungstadt.

P.G. (Eng) abbr: Polygalacturonase.

PG Steam (Eng) a 3.9% alc by vol. ale brewed by the RCH Brewery, West Hewish, near Weston-Super-Mare, Somerset.

P.G. Tips (Eng) the famous brand-name for a tea produced by the Brooke Bond Oxo Ltd. Often called the 'monkey tea' due to the use of chimpanzees in their advertising.

pH (Bio) abbr: potential of Hydrogen, the measurement of acidity and alkalinity in a substance on a scale of 1 (acid) to 14 (alkaline) with 7 (neutral). A litmus paper test turns red when acid is present and blue when alkaline is present.

Phalanx (Eng) a 4.3% alc by vol. ale brewed by the Feast & Firkin in Leeds.

Phanto Ridge (S.Afr) the label for a red wine

(Pinotage) produced by the Robertson Co-operative Winery, Robertson, Western Cape.

Pharma.O (Can) a purified spring water brand.

Pharoah and Firkin (Eng) a micro-brew pub in Fulham, London. Brews: Hard Tackle.

Pheasant and Firkin (Eng) a home-brew public house in London. Noted for cask-conditioned Pheasant Bitter 1036 O.G. Barbarian 1045 O.G. and Dogbolter 1060 O.G.

Phellos (Gre) cork.

Phelps Vineyard (USA) a small winery based in the Napa Valley, California. 83ha. Grape varieties: Cabernet sauvignon, Gewürztraminer, Johannisberg riesling and Syrah. Produces varietal wines under the Le Fleuron label.

Phénix (Fr) a noted bière brand.

Phenols (Scot) flavouring chemicals derived from the smoking of the barley during the malting process for whisky.

Phenylalanine (Eng) an amino acid found in small traces in wine, formed by the yeasts.

Phileri (Gre) a red grape variety grown in Peloponnese.

Philip Jonker (S.Afr) the label for a methode cap classique white sparkling wine (Chardonnay) produced by the Weltevrede Estate winery, Robertson Western Cape.

Philip Jordan Wines (S.Afr) a winery (established 1998) based in Rawsonville, Western Cape. 1ha. Grape varieties: Cabernet franc.

Philippe Guillet Grande Fine Champagne (Fr) an 80 year old Cognac produced by Rouyer.

Philippe le Bon (Fr) part of the vineyard Genevrières in the A.C. commune of Meursault, Côte de Beaune, Burgundy (owned by the Hospices de Beaune).

Philipponnat (Fr) a Champagne producer. (Add): 13 Rue du Pont, Mareuil-sur-Aÿ, 51160 Aÿ. 16ha. Produces vintage and non-vintage wines. Produces: Royal Réserve Brut. Vintages: 1971, 1973, 1975, 1976, 1979, 1980, 1982, 1986, 1988, 1989, 1990, 1995, 1996, 1997, 1998, 1999, 2000, 2001. Owned by Gosset. De Luxe vintage cuvee: Clos des Goisses and also Royal Réserve (non-vintage).

Philip Togni Vineyard (USA) a winery (established 1983). Grape varieties include Cabernet franc, Cabernet sauvignon, Merlot, Sauvignon blanc.

Philizot & Fils (Fr) a Champagne producer. (Add): 49, Grande Rue, 51480 Reuil. Produces vintage and non-vintage wines. Labels: Brut Plaisir, Cuvée Alequente. 'E'mail: sphilizot@hotmail.com

Phillipine Ron (E.Ind) rum.

Phillips [Captain Arthur R.N.] (Eng) a naval officer who introduced vines to Australia in 1788. Vines were probably from South America and of Cabernet sauvignon variety.

Phillips Brewery (Eng) a home-brew public house brewery in the Greyhound at Marsh Gibbon near Bicester, Buckinghamshire. Noted for cask-conditioned Heritage Bitter 1036 O.G. Ailric's Old Me 1045 O.G. and keg Hallerbrau Lager 1042 O.G.

Phillip the Bold (Fr) the fourteenth century Duke of Burgundy who, because he was keen on wine-making, could be claimed as being responsible for its vineyards of today.

Philo (USA) a wine-producing area in the Anderson Valley, Mendocino County, California.

Philosopher's Stone (S.Afr) the label for red wine (Merlot and Shiraz blend) produced by the Camberley Wines winery, Stellenbosch, Western Cape.

Philter (USA) see Philtre.

Philtre (Eng) a drink produced in the sixteenth and seventeenth centuries which was supposed to arouse sexual desire, love, etc. (USA) = philter.

Phlegm Cutters (USA) an early American slang term for cider or beer.

Phoebe Snow Cocktail (Cktl) ½ measure Cognac, ½ measure Dubonnet, 2 dashes Pernod. Stir over ice and strain into a cocktail glass.

Phoenix (Eng) a hop variety developed by scientists at the Horticultural Research Institute at Wye College, Ashford, Kent. Resists fungal diseases especially Wilt.

Phoenix (Eng) a Watney owned company based in Brighton, Sussex. Tamplins Bitter 1038 O.G. is brewed for it in London.

Phoenix (Eng) a white grape variety produced by crossing Seyval blanc x Bacchus. Resistant to fungal diseases.

Phoenix and Firkin (Eng) a home-brew public house in London. Noted for cask-conditioned Rail Ale 1036 O.G.

Phoenix Beer (Afr) a pilsener-style beer brewed in Mauritius by the Mauritius Brewery.

Phoenix Bitter (Ire) a keg bitter brewed by the Irish Ale Breweries.

Phoenix Gin Sling (Cktl) place ½ measure gin, ½ measure Cherry Heering, 2 dashes lemon juice, 2 dashes gomme syrup in an ice-filled highball glass. Stir, decorate with a cherry and slice of lemon.

Phoenix Indian Pale Ale (Eng) a 4.8% alc by vol. India pale ale brewed by Enville Ales Ltd., West Midlands.

Phonicin 47 (Cktl) ½ measure vodka, ¼ measure Mandarine Napoléon, ½ measure sweet vermouth, dash lemon juice. Stir over ice in a highball glass and decorate with slices of lemon, orange and a cherry.

Phosphotage (Fr) the addition of phosphate of lime to wines to increase the acidity. As for Gypsum.

Photographer & Firkin (Eng) a micro-brewery based in Ealing. Brews Millennium Mayor's Ale.

Phyllocoptes Vitis (Lat) the grape rust mite. See also Calepitrimerus vitis and Acariosis.

Phylloxera vastatrix (Lat) a vine louse from America which devastated the European vineyards from 1863–1890. Attacks the roots of the vine. Treatment by grafting Vitis vinifera scions onto American vines root stock which is the only known cure in Europe. (It) = fillossero.

Physiological Maturity (USA) the point at which the

P

grapes have reach perfect ripeness (skins, flesh, tannins and pips).

Physiological Ripening (USA) an alternative term for Hang Time.

Piagge del Prete (It) a natural spring mineral water from Piagge del Prete.

Pianoalto (It) a D.O.C. Barbera d'Asti wine aged in new 1500litres casks by Bava (Roberto) in Piedmont.

Pianalto Mirandés (Port) an I.P.R. wine from the Trás-os-Montes.

Pian dei Susini (It) a white wine produced from 80% Trebbiano and 20% Sauvignon blanc grapes by Tenuta dell'Ornellaia in Bolgheri, Tuscany.

Pian della Mussa (It) a sparkling natural spring mineral water from Fonte Sauzè. Mineral contents (milligrammes per litre): Sodium 0.75mg/l, Calcium 6.1mg/l, Magnesium 3mg/l, Potassium 0.25mg/l, Bicarbonates 24.1mg/l, Chlorides 0.15mg/l, Sulphates 6.1mg/l, Fluorides 0.018mg/l, Nitrates 2.2mg/l, Silicates 7.3mg/l. pH 6.86

Piano [Il] (It) a white wine produced by Machiavelli in Villa Belvedere, 37010 Calmasino, Verona from red Canaiolo grapes.

Piast (Pol) the label for a range of beers including a pils and strong dark ale.

Piat (Fr) a measure of wine, now only associated with the Beaujolais. The bottle resembles an Indian club in shape and holds approximately 50cls (500mls)

Piat d'Or (Fr) a popular brand (in the U.K) of red and white wine produced by Piat Père et Fils.

Piat Père et Fils (Fr) négociants-éleveurs of Mâcon and Beaujolais wines in Burgundy. (Add): La Chapelle-de-Guinchay.

Piave Cabernet (It) a D.O.C. red wine from Veneto. Made with the Cabernet grape. If minimum alc. content 12.5% by vol. and 3 years of age can be classed Riserva.

Piave Merlot (It) a D.O.C. red wine from Veneto. Made from the Merlot and 10% Cabernet franc/Cabernet sauvignon grape. If minimum alc. content 12% by vol. and aged 2 years can be classed Vecchio.

Piave Tocai (It) a D.O.C. white wine from Veneto. Made from the Tocai grape.

Piave Verduzzo (It) a D.O.C. white wine from Veneto. Made from the Verduzzo grape.

Pic (It) a sparkling natural spring mineral water from Pic, Vaie, Torino. Mineral contents (milligrammes per litre): Sodium 2.9mg/l, Calcium 42mg/l, Magnesium 13.2mg/l, Potassium 1.8mg/l, Chlorides 1.5mg/l, Sulphates 18mg/l, Nitrates 2.8mg/l, Silicates 10.7mg/l. pH 8.0

Pic [Le] (Fr) the name given to a range of red and white wines from UCOVIP. Sold in 75cls bottles plus 3, 5, 10 litre boxes.

Picador Cocktail (Cktl) 1½ measures Kahlúa, 1½ measures tequila. Stir over ice, strain into a cocktail glass and dress with a spiral of lemon peel.

Picamoll (Sp) a white grape variety grown in the Alella region of north-eastern Spain.

Picapoll (Sp) a red grape variety grown in the Tarragona region of south-eastern Spain. *see* Picapoll Blanco. (Fr) = Picpoul.

Picapoll Blanco (Sp) a white grape variety grown in the Tarragona region of south-eastern Spain. Also known as Folle blanche.

Pic à Pou (Fr) a local wine from the Pyrénées in south-east France.

Picarda (Fr) a red grape variety grown in the southern Rhône.

Picard et Cazot Fils (Fr) major distillers of élixers based in Lyon.

Picardie (S.Afr) a slightly acidic natural spring mineral water from Picardie Farm, Suider-Paarl, Western Cape. Mineral contents (milligrammes per litre): Sodium 33mg/l, Calcium 2.7mg/l, Magnesium 4.5mg/l, Potassium 3.2mg/l, Chlorides 52mg/l, Sulphates 5mg/l, Fluorides <0.1mg/l, Nitrates 3.6mg/l. pH 5.3

Picardin (Fr) a white grape variety grown in the southern Rhône.

Picardin Noir (Fr) the alternative name for the Cinsault grape.

Picardi Rebel (S.Afr) a national drinks chain (established 1994). Labels include: Coast, Naked Truth. Also boxed wines from the Roberson Winery, Western Cape.

Picard Père et Fils (Fr) a Burgundy négociant based at Chagny.

Picardy Estate (Austr) a winery based in Pemberton, Western Australia. Grape varieties include: Cabernet franc, Cabernet sauvignon, Merlot.

Picata (It) a black grape variety grown in Roman times. Produced a wine called Vinum Picatum which had a taste of pitch.

Picca (Cktl) 25mls (1fl.oz) Scotch whisky, 10mls (½ fl.oz) Punt-e-Mes, 10mls (½ fl.oz) Galliano. Stir over ice, strain into a cocktail glass and decorate with a cherry.

Piccadilly (Cktl) ⅔ measure dry gin, ⅓ measure dry vermouth, dash pastis, dash grenadine. Stir over ice and strain into a cocktail glass.

Picens (It) a white wine produced in eastern Italy in Roman times.

Pichet (Fr) an earthenware jug that hold half a litre/pitcher.

Pichet d'Alsace (Fr) a popular edelzwicker produced by Laugel. Grape varieties: 5% Gewurztraminer, 85% Pinot noir and 10% Riesling.

Pichia membranaefaciens (Lat) a prolific 'wild yeast' found on the grape bloom.

Pichler [Franz & Maria] (Aus) a winery (established 1982) based in the Wachau. (Add): 3610 Wösendorf 68. Grape varieties: Blauer portugieser, Feinburgunder, Grüner veltliner, Pinot noir, Riesling, Sauvignon blanc. Produces a range of dry and sweet wines.

Pichler [Franz X] (Aus) a winery (8ha) based in the Wachau. (Add): 3601 Oberloiben 27. Grape varieties: Chardonnay, Grüner veltliner,

Muskateller, Riesling, Sauvignon blanc. Produces a range of dry and sweet (botrytised) wines. Labels: Arachon, M.

Pichler [Rudi] (Aus) a winery (5.5ha) based in the Wachau. (Add): Wösendorf 38, 3610 Weissenkirchen. Grape varieties: Grüner veltliner, Muskateller, Pinot blanc, Riesling, Zweigelt. Produces a range of dry and sweet wines.

Pichlpoint (Aus) a vineyard site on the banks of the River Danube situated in the Wachau region, Niederösterreich.

Pick'n'Pay (S.Afr) a supermarket chain that sells its own label boxed wines (3 and 5 litres) produced by the Robertson Winery, Western Cape. Website: http://www.picknpay.co.za

Pickett Brewery (USA) a brewery based in Dubuque, Iowa. Noted for Dubuque Star and Edelweiss beers.

Pickled (Eng) a slang term for intoxicated, very drunk.

Pickled Pam (Eng) a 7.2% alc by vol: beer brewed by Hanby Ales of Wem, Shropshire.

Pick Me Up (Eng) a tonic, a drink to settle the stomach. Can be either alcoholic or non-alcoholic.

Pick-Me-Up [1] (Cktl) ⅓ measure pastis, ⅓ measure Cognac, ⅓ measure dry vermouth. Stir over ice and strain into a 125mls (5fl.oz) wine glass.

Pick-Me-Up [2] (Cktl) 1 measure brandy, 100mls (4fl.ozs) milk, 1 teaspoon sugar, dash Angostura. Shake over ice, strain into a highball glass and add soda water.

Pick-Me-Up [3] (Cktl) ¾ measure Cognac, ¼ measure Grand Marnier, juice ½ orange, dash grenadine. Shake over ice, strain into a balloon glass. Top with dry Champagne and decorate with a slice of orange, lemon and a cherry and serve with straws.

Pick-Me-Up [4] (Cktl) (Non-alc) to settle the stomach. Juice of half lemon, 2 teaspoons Worcestershire sauce. Mix with ice in a highball glass and top up with soda water.

Pick'n Pay Mineral Water (S.Afr) a still natural spring mineral water. Mineral contents (milligrammes per litre): Sodium 5mg/l, Calcium 41.9mg/l, Magnesium 23.5mg/l, Chlorides <5mg/l, Sulphates 6mg/l, Fluorides 0.08mg/l, Nitrates 1.4mg/l. pH 7.8

Pick'nWyntjie (S.Afr) the label for a late-havested white wine (Chenin blanc) produced by the Bonnievale Cellar winery, Robertson, Western Cape.

Pickwick Bitter (Eng) a 4.2% alc by vol. bitter ale brewed by Mauldon's Ltd., Suffolk.

Pico (Port) a D.O.C. wine region on the island of Pico in the Azores.

Pico (Port) an I.P.R. wine produced in the Terras do Sado.

Pico (Port) a vineyard based in the Azores that once produced wines under the Fayal label.

Picolit (It) a white grape variety grown in the Colli Orientali del Fruili (Udine district of the Friuli-Venezia-Giulia region). Produces rich, sweet, botrytised wines. 13%–15% alc by vol.

Picon (Fr) *see* Amer Picon.

Picon [1] (Cktl) 50mls (2fl.ozs) Amer Picon in a highball with ice and top up with 100mls (4fl.ozs) soda water.

Picon [2] (Cktl) ½ measure Amer Picon, ½ measure sweet vermouth. Stir over ice and strain into a cocktail glass.

Picon-Grenadine (Cktl) 60mls (½ gill) Amer Picon, 20mls (⅙ gill) grenadine. Stir over ice in a highball glass and top up with soda water.

Picon Punch (Cktl) place some ice in a club goblet, add 35mls (1½fl.ozs) Amer Picon. Fill with soda water, top with a twist of lemon peel and stir. Often has dash of brandy on top.

Picotin (Cktl) ½ measure Vodka 72, ¼ measure Liquore Santa Vittoria, ¼ measure Cinzano Bianco, dash lemon juice. Stir over ice, strain into an ice-filled highball glass and add a twist orange peel.

Picoutener (It) the local name for the Nebbiolo grape in the Val d'Aosta region. Also spelt Picutener pugnet.

Picpouille (Fr) the alternative spelling of Picpoul.

Picpoul (Fr) the name given to the Folle blanche grape grown in the Armagnac and Cognac regions. It gives thin acid wine, but makes an outstanding brandy. *See also* Gros Plant, Picpouille and Piquepoul. (Sp) = Picapoll.

Picpoul Blanc (Fr) a white grape variety grown in the Languedoc.

Picpoul Noir (Fr) a red grape variety grown in southern France.

Picpoul-de-Pinet (Fr) a dry, white V.D.Q.S. wine produced in the Languedoc region of southern France.

Picq [Didier et Pascal] (Fr) a winery based in the A.C. Chablis, Burgundy. Produces a range of Chablis wines including Premier Cru Vosgros.

Picquepoul (Fr) an alternative spelling of Picpoul.

Picquepoul du Gers (Fr) the local Armagnac name for the Folle blanche grape.

Picquepoul du Pays (Fr) a white grape variety grown in the Armagnac region.

Pic-Saint-Loup (Fr) a red and rosé A.C wine-producing region in the Hérault département in southern France. Minimum vine age of 6 years, maximum yield of 50hl/ha. and a minimum alcohol of 11.5% alc by vol. For red wines a maximum of 10% Cinsault and Carignan grapes, plus 90% of any combination of Grenache, Syrah and Mourvèdre grapes. White wines are known as Coteaux du Languedoc. Awarded A.C. status 1994.

Pictish Brewing C° (Eng) a brewery (established 2000). (Add): Unit 9, Canalside Ind Estate, Woodbine Street East, Rochdale, Lancashire OL16 5LB. Produces bitter beers. Website: http://www.pictish-brewing.co.uk

Picutener Pugnet (It) an alternative spelling of the Picoutener.

Pidans [Les] (Fr) a vineyard in the commune of Montagny, Côte Chalonnaise, Burgundy.

P

Piddle in the Hole (Eng) a bottled beer produced by the Wyre Piddle Brewery in Worcestershire.

Pie (Eng) a term sometimes used for the pulp left after the first pressing of the grapes.

Pièce (Fr) a hogshead, cask. Also known as a Fût. Côte d'Or: 228litres, southern Burgundy: 216litres, Bordeaux: 225litres.

Pièce de Vin (Fr) cask of wine.

Pièce Noble (Fr) a red wine (50% Grenache & 50% Syrah) produced by Château Rasque, A.C. Côtes de Provence.

Pièce Sous le Bois [La] (Fr) a Premier Cru vineyard in the commune of Blagny, A.C. Meursault, Côte de Beaune, Burgundy.

Pied (Fr) a single vine stock.

Pied-d'Aloup (Fr) an A.C. Premier Cru Chablis. Sometimes reclassified as the Premier Cru Monée de Tonerre.

Pied de Cuve (Fr) the bottom of the vat (the lees) after the décuvage, often used as a yeast starter.

Pied de Pedrix (Fr) an alternative name for the Malbec grape in southern France.

Piede di Palumbo (It) a red grape variety grown in Gragnano in the Campania region to produce a young red wine of the same name.

Piedirosso (It) lit: 'red foot', a red grape variety (so named because the vine's stems look like a pigeon's foot) grown in the Campania region that is noted for its acidity and firm tannins. *See also* Palombina, Pere'e Palummo, Perricone.

Piedmont (It) the American spelling of Piemonte.

Piedmonte (It) the English spelling of Piemonte.

Piedmont Vineyard (USA) a small winery based in Middleburg, Virginia. 10ha. Grape varieties: Chardonnay and Sémillon. Produces varietal wines.

Pied Noir (Fr) an alternative name for the Malbec grape.

Pied Rouge (Fr) an alternative name for the Malbec grape.

Pied-Tendre (Fr) a white grape variety grown in the Charente region in western France. *See also* Bon Blanc, Blanquette and the Colombard.

Piemonte (It) lit: 'at the foot of the mountain'. famous Italian wine region. Pennine, Graian, Cottian and Maritime Alps surround it to the north and south. East is the Po valley. Wines include Barbaresco, Barolo, Gattinara (all D.O.C.G.). *See also* Piedmont, Piedmonte.

Piemontello (It) a slightly sparkling wine made from the Moscato grape in Piemonte.

Pieprozwka (Pol) a pepper-flavoured vodka produced by Wodka Wyttrawna 45% alc by vol.

Pierce's Disease (USA) a major incurable vine disease that occurs in California. Bacteria (*Xylella fastidiosa*) are spread by an insect: the blue-green sharpshooter (leaf hopper) onto the grape leaves, these become yellow along the veins, fruit wilts and dwarf shoots appear. The vine usually dies within 2–5 years. First noted in 1880. Prefers hot climates to cool climates.

Pierelle [La] (Fr) a vineyard in the A.C. Hermitage, northern Rhône.

Pierlant Imperial (Fr) a lightly sparkling, medium-dry, white wine produced by Moët et Chandon from grapes grown in 9 different regions of France 9.2% alc by vol.

Pierlot [Jules] (Fr) a Champagne producer. (Add): 15 Rue Henry Martin, B.P. 129, 51200 Épernay. Produces vintage and non-vintage wines. Vintages: 1971, 1973, 1975, 1976, 1979, 1982, 1983, 1985, 1988, 1990, 1995, 1996, 1997, 1998, 1999, 2000, 2002.

Piermont (Eng) an apple-juice and natural water drink made by the Tauton Cider C°. Ltd. Also a blackcurrant and apple version.

Pierneef Collection (S.Afr) the label for a range of wines red (Shiraz and Viognier blend), white (Sauvignon blanc) produced by the La Motte winery, Franschhoek, Western Cape.

Pierre-à-Fusil (Fr) gun flint, describes flinty wines.

Pierrefeu (Fr) a wine-producing village in the Côtes de Provence. Produces fine rosé wines.

Pierre Jourdan (S.Afr) the label for a range of cap classique wines: blanc de blancs, brut sauvage, cuvee Belle Rose (Pinot noir 100%) and cuvee reserve (Chardonnay 60%, Pinot noir 40%) produced by the Cabrière Estate winery, Franschhoek, Western Cape.

Pierre Leon (USA) the label for a red wine (Pinot noir) produced by the Willakenzie Estate winery, Willamette Valley, Oregon.

Pierre Mignon (Fr) a Champagne producer. (Add): 5, Rue des Grappes d'Or, 51210 Le Breuil. Produces both vintage and non-vintage Champagnes. Vintages: 1995, 1998, 2001. Website: http://www.pierre-mignon.com 'E'mail: p.mignon@voila.fr

Pierres (Fr) stones (soil).

Pierres [Les] (Fr) a vineyard in the A.C. commune of Rully, Côte Chalonnaise, Burgundy.

Pierres Dorées (Fr) an area where most of the Beaujolais Nouveau is produced.

Pierrevert (Fr) the new A.C. Collective name for 11 villages based in the Alpes de Provence. 450ha. Wine production is 60% red, 10% white, 30% rosé. Grape varieties are as for Provence and southern Rhône.

Pierre Winery (N.Z) a small winery based in Waikanae, Wellington, North Island. 3ha. Grape varieties: Cabernet sauvignon, Chardonnay, Chenin blanc, Merlot, Müller-Thurgau and Pinot noir. Produces varietal wines.

Pierro Estate (Austr) a winery based in the Margaret River region of Western Australia. Grape varieties include: Cabernet sauvignon, Merlot.

Pierry (Fr) a Premier Cru Champagne village in the Canton d'Épernay. District: Épernay.

Piersanti (It) a sparkling natural spring mineral water from Collesalvetti, Livorno. Mineral contents (milligrammes per litre): Sodium 210mg/l, Calcium 457mg/l, Magnesium 117.8mg/l, Potassium 13.8mg/l, Bicarbonates 1598mg/l, Chlorides 283mg/l, Sulphates 379mg/l, Fluorides 0.2mg/l, Strontium 1.8mg/l, Silicates 55.2mg/l. pH 6.0

Pierval (Fr) a still natural spring mineral water from the River Andelle, Pont St. Pierre. Mineral contents (milligrammes per litre): Sodium 8mg/l, Calcium 104mg/l, Magnesium 4mg/l, Potassium 0.8mg/l, Bicarbonates 314mg/l, Chlorides 13.6mg/l, Sulphates 8mg/l, Nitrates 12mg/l.

Piesport (Ger) village (Anb): Mosel-Saar-Ruwer. (Ber): Bernkastel. (Gro): Michelsberg. (Vins): Domherr, Falkenberg, Gärtchen, Goldtröpfchen, Gunterslay, Schubertslay, Treppchen.

Piestinger GmbH (Aus) a brewery. (Add): Gutensteiner Strasse 48, A-2753 Markt Piesting. Produces beers and lagers. Website: http://www.piestinger.at 'E'mail: bier@brauerei-piesting.at

Pieter Cruythoff (S.Afr) *see* Riebeek Wynboere Koöperatiewe.

Pietra (Fr) a 6% alc by vol. amber coloured, top-fermented, bottled beer brewed by the Pietra Brasserie, Corsica. Made using chestnuts picked in the Castagniccia forest. *See also* Colomba.

Pietra Brasserie (Fr) a brewery base in Furiani, Corsica. Brews: Pietra.

Pietracupa (It) a vino da tavloa red wine produced from 60% Sangiovese and 40% Cabernet sauvignon grapes by Fattoria di Montecchio, Tuscany.

Pietramarina (It) a white wine from the Carricante grape produced by Tenuta di Castiglione on Mount Etna.

Pietroasele (Rum) a wine-producing area, part of the Dealul-Mare vineyard.

Pieve (It) a sparkling natural spring mineral water from Pieve. Mineral contents (milligrammes per litre): Sodium 26.7mg/l, Calcium 26.9mg/l, Magnesium 15.8mg/l, Potassium 6.9mg/l, Bicarbonates 112.8mg/l, Chlorides 46.1mg/l, Sulphates 16.2mg/l, Fluorides 0.13mg/l, Nitrates 32.5mg/l, Silicates 12.3mg/l. pH 6.6

Pig and Whistle (Eng) a home-brew public house at Privett, Hampshire. Noted for cask-conditioned BDS 1055 O.G. and Joshua Privett 1043 O.G.

Pig and Whistle (Scot) a home-brew public house in the Gorbals, Glasgow. Noted for cask-conditioned Pig Brew 1040 O.G. and Pig Light 1035 O.G.

Piganot (Switz) a red wine made from the Savagnin grape in the Vaud Canton.

Pigato (It) a rare white grape variety grown in Liguria.

Pigeage (Fr) the treading (and pumping) down of the cap in Burgundy, also known as foulage.

Pigeoulet [Le] (Fr) a red vin de pays produced by Domaine la Rocqette, Châteauneuf-du-Pape. Grape varieties: Cabernet sauvignon, Cinsault and Syrah.

Pigeon Holes (Fr) the term used in Armagnac for the resting of the casks in such a way that they do not touch one another, but rest in '*pigeon holes*'.

Piggin (Eng) a cask of 2 gallons capacity (rare now).

Piglio (It) a commune 40 miles from Rome in Latium, which gives its name to two types of red wine. *see* Cesanese del Piglio.

Pigment (Eng) the colouring matter in the skins of red grapes.

Pignan (Fr) the second label of Château Rayas in Châteauneuf-du-Pape, southern Rhône (white and red).

Pignatello (It) a black grape variety grown in Sicily. Used in the production of Marsala. Also known as the Perricone and Piedirosso.

Pignerol (Fr) a white grape variety grown in Bellet, Provence.

Pignola Valtellinese (It) a red grape variety from northern Italy.

Pignoletto (It) an alternative name for the Italian rizling and Welschriesling grapes.

Pignolo (It) a red grape variety grown in Friuli and Colli Orientali.

Pig Rye (Eng) a 5% alc by vol. premium bottled rye mash lager brewed by King and Barnes of Horsham.

Pig's Ear (Eng) a Cockney rhyming slang term for beer.

Pig's Eye (USA) a pilsner lager beer produced by a 137 year old brewery in St. Paul, Minnesota.

Pig's Nose (Eng) a brand of blended Scotch whisky blended and bottled by M.J. Dowdeswell & Cº. Ltd., Oldbury-on-Severn, Gloucestershire. *See also* Sheep Dip.

Pigswill (Eng) a 4% alc by vol. ale brewed by the Stonehenge Ales (Bunces Brewery) Ltd., Wiltshire.

Pihlajanmarja (Fin) a rowanberry liqueur.

Pijiu (Chi) beer.

Pikant (Ger) denotes an attractive, intriguing wine.

Pikantus Weizenbock (Ger) a wheat beer brewed by the Erdinger Brauerei.

Pike & Joyce Vineyard (Austr) a winery (established 1998) based in Lenswood, Adelaide Hills, South Australia. 18ha. Grape varieties: Chardonnay, Pinot gris, Pinot noir and Sauvignon blanc. Website: http://www.pikeswines.com.au

Pike's Peak Cooler (Cktl) 1 egg, 1 teaspoon powdered sugar, juice ½ lemon. Shake over ice, strain into an ice-filled highball glass. Top with dry cider, stir, dress with an orange peel spiral.

Piketberg (S.Afr) a wine district of the west coast. Produces mainly dry white and dessert wines.

Pilarita Fino (Sp) a brand of Fino Sherry produced by Lustau in Jerez de la Frontera.

Piledriver (Eng) a 5.3% alc by vol. ale brewed by the Sawbridge Worth Brewery, Hertfordshire.

Pilgerberg (Ger) vineyard (Anb): Mosel-Saar-Ruwer. (Ber): Obermosel. (Gro): Königsberg. (Vil): Liersberg.

Pilgerpfad (Ger) grosslage (Anb): Rheinhessen. (Ber): Wonnegau. (Vils): Bechtheim, Dittelsheim-Hessloch, Frettenheim, Monzernheim, Osthofen.

Pilgerpfad (Ger) vineyard (Anb): Mittelrhein. (Ber): Rheinburgengau. (Gro): Loreleyfelsen. (Vil): Kamp-Bornhofen-Kestert.

Pilgerstein (Ger) vineyard (Anb): Rheinhessen. (Ber): Nierstein. (Gro): Petersberg. (Vil): Biebelnheim.

Pilgerweg (Ger) vineyard (Anb): Rheinhessen. (Ber): Nierstein. (Gro): Gutes Domtal. (Vil): Zornheim.

Pilgrim (USA) a brand of light rum produced by Felton and Son in New England 40% alc by vol.

Pilgrim Brewery (Eng) a brewery (established 1982). (Add) The Old Brewery, 11C West Street, Reigate, Surrey RH2 9BL. Brews: Crusader Premium Bitter 4.9% alc by vol., Progress Best Bitter 4% alc by vol (1042 O.G)., cask-conditioned Surrey Bitter 3.7% alc by vol (1038 O.G)., Talisman 5% alc by vol (1048 O.G). Website: http://www.pilgrim.co.uk 'E'mail: pilgrimbrewery@hotmail.co.uk

Pilgrims (Eng) a low-alcohol bitter 0.9% alc by vol. brewed by Shepherd Neame. Sold in 275mls (½ pint) bottles.

Pilgrims Cyder (Eng) a cider made by Badgers Farm in Chilham near Canterbury, Kent. Made from Kentish dessert and cider apples.

Pilgrims Progress (Eng) a 4.2% alc by vol. ale brewed by the Three Rivers Brewing C°. Ltd., Cheshire.

Piliers Chablisiens (Fr) a wine brotherhood of the Chablis, Burgundy.

Pillar Tap (Scot) see Tall Fount.

Pillar Rock (USA) a winery based in the Stag's Leap District, Napa Valley, California. Grape varieties include: Cabernet sauvignon.

Pillot (Fr) a vineyard in the A.C. commune of Rully, Côte Chalonnaise, Burgundy.

Pilon [Le] (Fr) a wine-producing district in A.C. Bellet, Provence.

Pilongo (Port) an alternative name for the Alvarelhao grape.

Pils (Ger) short for pilsener, a strong bottled lager beer.

Pilsator (Ger) a premium beer brewed without the use of additives.

Pilsen (Czec) a town in Bohemia from which pilsener lager gets its name, the German spelling. see Plzen.

Pilsen Callao (Peru) a 5% alc by vol. bottled lager beer brewed by the Nacional de Cerveza Brewery, Callao.

Pilsener (Euro) the name given to lager beers on the style of the original beer from Plzen (Pilsen). see Pilsner Urquell.

Pilsener Glass (Ger) a tall, slim glass which is 'waisted' in the centre and opens out at the top.

Pils-Krone (Ger) a fine pilsener beer, light and delicate, with a malty flavour, brewed by the Dortmunder Kronen Brauerei in Dortmund, Westphalia.

Pilsner (Czec) other spelling of Pilsen. see Pilsner Urquell.

Pilsner (Den) lager beer/light beer.

Pilsner (Eng) the English spelling of pilsener.

Pilsner (Ger) a full-bodied Bavarian made 'hoppy' beer, now made much lighter.

Pilsner Urquell (Czec) a famous brewery (founded in 1842). (Add): U Prazdroje 7, Pilzen 304 97. Established when a group of Czech brewers founded the Citizen's Brewery. Known as Plzensky Prazdroj, it is the largest brewing group. Brews Gambrinus range of beers, plus Pilsner Urquell and Primus Straw 10%. Website: http://www.prazdroi.cz

Pilsner Urquell 10% (Czec) a 3.3% alc by vol. light straw coloured, bottled lager brewed by Plzensky Prazdroj Brewery, Plzen.

Pilsner Urquell 12% (Czec) a 4.4% alc by vol. straw coloured, bottled lager brewed by Plzensky Prazdroj Brewery, Plzen.

Pils 27 (Afr) a lager beer brewed in Benin 11.2° Plato.

Pilton Manor de Marsac (Eng) a sparkling wine made by traditional methods from 66% Müller-Thurgau and 34% Seyval blanc grapes. Produced by the Pilton Manor Vineyard.

Pilton Manor Vineyard (Eng) a vineyard and distillers (established 1966). (Add): The Manor House, Pilton, near Shepton Mallet, Somerset. 2.7ha. Soil: stoney marl overlying rock, clay, limestone and blue lias. Grape varieties: Müller-Thurgau, Seyval blanc (5276), Bacchus, Huxelrebe, Schônburger. Also distilled the first Single Cask British brandy in 1992.

Piment (Fr) see Vin Piment.

Pimento (W.Ind) a liqueur made from dried, aromatic berries.

Pimento Dram (W.Ind) a dark red liqueur made by steeping green, ripe pimento berries in rum. Made by the Caribbean Indians.

Piments (Eng) the name given to the flavourings used in wines in the Middle Ages (herbs and spices).

Pimms (Eng) a famous branded cocktail-type mix. Spirit based. 6 varieties: N°1 gin, N°2 whisky, N°3 brandy, N°4 rum, N°5 Bourbon whiskey, N°6 vodka. Only N°1 is now produced. 31% alc by vol. Owned by the DCL group. See also Pimm's N°3 Winter.

Pimm's Royal (Cktl) 1 measure Pimms N°1. 4 measures iced Champagne. Stir lightly together in a highball over ice.

Pimm's N°3 Winter (Eng) the relaunch of the original Pimm's N°3.

Pimm's Winter Warmer (Punch) 200mls Pimm's N°3 Winter Brandy Cup, 600mls clear apple juice. Mix ingredients together, gently warm (approx 45°C) in a saucepan, pour into a pitcher with sliced fresh fruits and serve in old-fashioned glasses.

Pimpeltjens (Hol) an orange Curaçao with selected herbs. see Nassau Orange. Produced by De Kuyper, Schiedam. 40% alc by vol.

Pimpinella anisum (Lat) the botanical name for the anise plant used in the making of Pastis.

Pin (Eng) a beer cask/keg 4½ gallons capacity.

Pin [Le] (Fr) a famous and expensive 1.95ha vineyard based in Pomerol. A.C. Pomerol. Grape varieties: 90% Merlot, 10% Cabernet franc.

Piña (Mex) lit: 'pineapple', the name given to the bulbous core in the centre of the Maguey cactus. Weighs 80–175 lbs. Take 8–10 years to mature. Cooked in an Adobe oven.

Pina Colada [1] (Cktl) 25mls (1fl.oz) coconut

cream, 35mls (1½fl.ozs) white rum, 50mls (2fl.ozs) pineapple juice, 2 scoops crushed ice, blend altogether and pour into a large-bowled glass. Decorate with a slice of pineapple and a cherry and serve with straws.

Pina Colada [2] (Cktl) 3 tots Malibu liqueur, a dash lemon juice. Top up with chilled pineapple juice, mix well in blender, pour into a large-bowled glass and serve with straws.

Pina Colada Glass (Eng) a stemmed, large, round-bowled glass with a curved (outwards) rim.

Pinalito (Sp) a natural spring mineral water from Vilaflor, Tenerife. Mineral contents (milligrammes per litre): Sodium 294mg/l, Calcium 19.2mg/l, Potassium 16.4mg/l, Bicarbonates 887.6mg/l, Chlorides 5.2mg/l, Fluorides 2.3mg/l, Silicates 135mg/l.

Pinard (Fr) the French army name for Vin Ordinaire, also the name for their wine ration.

Pinar Madran (Tur) a natural spring mineral water. Mineral contents (milligrammes per litre): Sodium 2.48mg/l, Calcium 2.6mg/l, Magnesium 1.4mg/l, Potassium 2mg/l, Bicarbonates 22mg/l, Chlorides 8.4mg/l, Fluorides 0.25mg/l. pH 7.0

Pinar Sasal (Tur) a natural spring mineral water from Izmir. Mineral contents (milligrammes per litre): Sodium 23mg/l, Calcium 6mg/l, Magnesium 1mg/l, Potassium 2mg/l, Bicarbonates 43mg/l, Chlorides 20mg/l, Sulphates 0.1mg/l.

Pince à Champagne (Fr) the Champagne cork pliers used for the removal of any tight-fitting corks from sparkling wine bottles.

Pinceszet (Hun) the name given to the cellars used for the storage and maturation of Tokaji aszú (in lava rock).

Pinchbottle (USA) the slang name for Haig's Dimple De Luxe Scotch Whisky. Refers to the bottle shape which is 3 cornered.

Pinching Back (Eng) the pruning or topping off of the ends of the leafy branches of the plant. Usually done by machine nowadays.

Pîncota (Rum) a wine-producing area, part of the Banât vineyard.

Pineapple Cobbler (Cktl)(Non-alc) 200mls pineapple juice, dash lime juice, 5 dashes Angostura. Shake well over ice, strain into a highball glass, top with bitter lemon, cherry and a pineapple cube and serve with straws.

Pineapple Cocktail (Cktl) 35mls (1½fl.ozs) white rum, 20mls (¾fl.oz) pineapple juice, ½ teaspoon lime juice. Shake over ice and strain into a cocktail glass.

Pineapple Cooler [1] (Cktl) place 50mls (2fl.ozs) pineapple juice, ½ teaspoon powdered sugar and 50mls (2fl.ozs) soda water into a collins glass. Stir, add ice, top with 50mls (2fl.ozs) dry white wine, soda and an orange spiral.

Pineapple Cooler [2] (Cktl)(Non-alc) 200mls (8fl.ozs) pineapple juice, 10mls (½fl.oz) lime juice, 75mls (3fl.ozs) bitter lemon, 5 dashes Angostura. Stir over ice, strain into an ice-filled

highball glass, dress with a pineapple cube, cherry and serve with straws.

Pineapple Fizz (Cktl) 50mls (2fl.ozs) light rum, 35mls (1½fl.ozs) pineapple juice, 1 teaspoon gomme syrup. Shake over ice, strain into an ice-filled highball glass, top up with soda and lemonade, serve with a muddler and straws.

Pineapple Liqueur (Fr) see Crème d'Ananas.

Pineapple Sparkle (Cktl) 35mls (1½fl.ozs) dry Sherry, 75mls (3fl.ozs) sweet vermouth, 125mls (1gill) each of pineapple juice and soda water, 300mls (½ pint) sparkling cider. Stir altogether in a large jug with ice, add 300mls (½ pint) soda water prior to service.

Pineau (Fr) an alternative name for the Pinot noir grape.

Pineau (Fr) an apéritif (muted wine), wine fortified with brandy made from grapes grown in the A.C. Cognac area. Minimum strength of 60% alc by vol. The proportion of grape must to Cognac is 3–1. No chaptalisation allowed. Must and Cognac aged on lees for 1 year. After ageing reduced to 16%–22% alc by vol. see Pineau des Charentes.

Pineau Blanc de la Loire (USA) the name for the Chenin blanc white grape variety.

Pineau d'Aunis (Fr) a red grape variety grown in the Anjou district of the Loire. Sometimes known as Chenin noir.

Pineau de Laborie (S.Afr) the label for a pineau wine produced by the Laborie winery, Suider-Paarl, Western Cape.

Pineau de la Loire (Fr) the local (Loire) name for the Chenin blanc grape variety.

Pineau de Loire (Fr) see Pineau de la Loire.

Pineau des Charentes (Fr) local A.C. Charente wines blended with Cognac to produce a sweet apéritif wine (A.C. created 1945) 16%–22% alc by vol. Matured 1 year in oak cask. White, rosé and red produced, must be made with grapes from the départements of Charente and Charente-Maritime. White: Colombard, Blanc ramé, Folle blanche, Jurançon blanc, Merlot blanc, Montils, Sauvignon blanc, Sémillon and Ugni blanc. rosé & red: Cabernet franc, Cabernet sauvignon, Malbec and Merlot.

Pineau Meunier (Fr) a red grape variety, also known in Germany as the Müllerrebe and Schwarzriesling. See also Wrotham Pinot.

Pine Barrens (USA) a natural spring mineral water from Long Island Pine Barrens.

Pinehurst (S.Afr) the label for a range of red wines produced by the Môreson winery, Franschhoek, Western Cape.

Pinehurst Estate (S.Afr) a vineyard based in the Coastal Region. Grape variety: Chardonnay.

Pinella (It) a white grape variety grown in the Veneto region.

Pinenc (Fr) a red grape variety grown in the Pyrénées, used in the production of Madiran, also known as Fer Servadou.

Pineo (Sp) a sparkling natural spring mineral water from Pyrenees. Mineral contents (milligrammes per litre): Sodium 1.2mg/l, Calcium 80.9mg/l, Magnesium 3.4mg/l, Potassium 0.5mg/l, Bicarbonates 245mg/l, Chlorides 1.7mg/l, Sulphates 7.9mg/l, Fluorides 0.1mg/l, Nitrates 1.6mg/l.

Pine Ridge Vineyard (Eng) a vineyard (established 1979) based at Staplecross, Robertsbridge, East Sussex. Grape varieties: Gutenborner, Huxelrebe, Kerner, Müller-Thurgau, Reichensteiner [50%] and Scheurebe.

Pine Ridge Winery (USA) a winery based in the Stag's Leap district, near Yountville, Napa Valley, California. (Add): 5901 Siverado Trail, Napa. CA 94558. Grape varieties: Cabernet sauvignon and Chardonnay. Produces varietal wines. Website: http://www.pineridgewinery.com

Pineta (It) a sparkling natural spring mineral water from Sorgente Sales, Pineta, Clusone (BG), Lombardy. Mineral contents (milligrammes per litre): Sodium 0.43mg/l, Calcium 59.2mg/l, Magnesium 10.2mg/l, Potassium 0.21mg/l, Bicarbonates 213.6mg/l, Chlorides 0.75mg/l, Sulphates 5.8mg/l, Fluorides 0.12mg/l, Nitrates 5.7mg/l, Silicates 3.4mg/l. pH 7.98

Ping (Chi) bottle.

Pinga (Bra) a fiery spirit produced from molasses.

Pinga (Port) denotes a drop of wine (or other drink).

Ping Pong (Cktl) ½ measure sloe gin, ½ measure Crème Yvette, 1 egg white, juice ¼ lemon. Shake over ice and strain into a cocktail glass.

Ping Pong Cocktail (Cktl) 30mls (¼ gill) sloe gin, 30mls (¼ gill) italian vermouth, 2 dashes Angostura, 2 dashes gomme syrup. Stir over ice, strain into a cocktail glass, add a cherry and a squeeze lemon peel juice on top.

Pingsaizuan (Chi) corkscrew.

Pingus (Sp) the label name of Dominio de Pingus a 4.5ha. vineyard in D.O. Ribera del Duero. Produces wines from Tinto fino grapes and uses French oak.

Pin Head (Asia) the name given to the small grade of green gunpowder teas.

Pinhel (Port) an I.P.R. district in the central-east that produces light pleasant wines including rosé. *see* Beira Interior.

Pin-Hi (Eng) the brand-name for a range of soft drinks from the Nicholas group.

Pink Camellia (Cktl) 3⁄10 measure dry gin, 2⁄10 measure apricot brandy, 1⁄10 measure Campari, 2⁄10 measure orange juice, 2⁄10 measure lemon juice, dash egg white, shake well over ice and strain into a cocktail glass.

Pink Celebration (Cktl) 1 measure rosé Cinzano, 1 dash fresh lime juice. Serve in an ice-filled highball glass and top with sparkling wine.

Pink Chablis (USA) a generic term used on labels to denote an off-dry, rosé wine.

Pink Champagne (Cktl) iced Champagne with a dash of Angostura bitters added. Not to be confused with rosé Champagne.

Pink Champagne (USA) a generic term used on labels to denote sweet, rosé, sparkling wines. (Den) = rosa Champagne.

Pink Cloves (Eng) an alcoholic cordial produced by Phillips, Avonmouth Way, Bristol 6% alc by vol.

Pink Creole Cocktail (Cktl) ½ measure white rum, ⅙ measure lime juice, ⅙ measure grenadine, ⅙ measure cream. Shake over ice, strain into a cocktail glass and add a black cherry soaked in rum.

Pinkers (Eng) the slang name given by the Royal Navy Officers for a Pink Gin.

Pink Explosion (Cktl) ½ measure Grand Marnier, ½ measure French vermouth, ⅙ measure Pernod, dash Angostura, dash grenadine, 1 measure cream. Shake well over ice, strain into a Champagne saucer and dress with a fresh strawberry.

Pink Gin (Cktl) a drink invented by Royal Naval Surgeons as a medicine. 1½ measures Plymouth gin, 2 dashes Angostura. The modern method is to rinse a club goblet out with a few dashes of Angostura bitters, empty and add a measure of Plymouth (or London Dry) gin with an ice cube.

Pink Grapefruit (Cktl) ⅓ measure Malibu, ⅔ measure grapefruit juice. Pour over crushed ice in an old-fashioned glass, add dash of Campari and cherry.

Pink Ice (USA) ice cubes which have had Angostura bitters dripped onto them, used in the making of cocktails.

Pink Killer (Bel) a wheat beer flavoured with grapefruit juice and brewed by the Silly Brasserie.

Pink Lady (Cktl) 20mls (¾fl.oz) dry gin, 1 egg white, 10mls (½fl.oz) grenadine, dash lemon juice. Shake well over ice and strain into a cocktail glass.

Pink Lady (Eng) a brand of sparkling perry made by the Goldwell C°.

Pink Lady Cocktail (Cktl) as for a Pink Lady but with the addition of 10mls (½ fl.oz) of cream.

Pink Melon Delight (Cktl) blend a scoop of orange sorbet, 150grms (6ozs) honeydew melon, 10 fresh strawberries together in a blender. Pour into a highball glass, top with ginger ale and decorate with a strawberry and melon cube.

Pink Muscat (Rus) a red grape variety used to produce dessert wines in the Crimea.

Pink Panther (Cktl) ½ measure Pernod, ½ measure vodka. Shake over ice, strain into an ice-filled highball and top with lemonade.

Pink Panther (Wal) a 4.5% alc by vol. ale brewed by the Cwmbran Brewery, Gwent.

Pink Panther Flip (Cktl)(Non-alc) 20mls (⅙ gill) grenadine, 1 egg yolk, 2 dashes Angostura, 200mls (⅓ pint) orange juice. Blend together with a scoop of crushed ice in a blender, pour into a tulip glass and dress with a cherry.

Pink Pearl (Cktl) 1 measure Dry Cane rum, 1 measure Cinzano bianco, ½ measure lemon juice, dash grenadine, dash egg white. Shake well over ice, strain into a cocktail glass, serve with a cherry and a slice of lemon.

Pink Pearl (Cktl)(Non-alc) 1 part grenadine, 4 parts

fresh grapefruit juice, 1 part lemon juice, 1 egg white. Shake over ice and strain into a wine glass.

Pink Pussy (Cktl) 25mls (1fl.oz) Campari, 10mls (½fl.oz) peach brandy, dash egg white. Shake over ice, strain into an ice-filled highball glass and top with bitter lemon.

Pink Pussy Cat (Cktl) 1 measure vodka, 2 measures grapefruit juice, ¼ measure grenadine. Shake over ice and strain into an ice-filled highball glass.

Pink Rose Fizz (Cktl) 25mls (⅕ gill) dry gin, 20mls (⅙ gill) cream, 1 egg white, juice ¼ lemon, 2 dashes gomme syrup. Shake over ice, strain into an ice-filled highball and top with soda water.

Pink Squirrel (Cktl) 25mls (1fl.oz) crème d'amande, 10mls (½fl.oz) crème de cacao (white), 25mls (1fl.oz) light cream. Shake well over ice and strain into a cocktail glass.

Pink Tonic (Cktl)(Non-alc) place the juice of ½ a lemon and three dashes Angostura bitters in an ice-filled highball glass, top with tonic water and a lemon slice.

Pinkus Alt (Ger) a well-known altbier from the Pinkus Müller Brauerei of Münster. Light in colour 4.9% alc by vol.

Pinkus Müller Brauerei (Ger) a famous brewery based in Münster in western Germany. Produces a famous pale altbier and exports to USA. *see* Pinkus Weizen, Alt and Pils.

Pinkus Pils (Ger) a fine pilsner lager beer from the Pinkus Müller Brauerei of Münster 4.9% alc by vol.

Pinkus Weizen (Ger) a top fermented beer from the Pinkus Müller Brauerei of Münster 4.9% alc by vol.

Pinnacle Selection (Austr) the brand-name for a range of wines produced by the Saltram Winery in the Barossa Valley.

Pinnacles Ranches (USA) the label for a red wine (Pinot noir) produced by the Estancia winery, Monterey County, California.

Pinneau (S.Afr) the label for a white un-fermented, fortified wine (Sémillon) produced by the Backsberg Cellars winery, Suider-Paarl, Western Cape.

Pinnerkreuzberg (Ger) vineyard (Anb): Mosel-Saar-Ruwer. (Ber): Zell/Mosel. (Gro): Goldbäumchen. (Vil): Cochem.

Pinno (S.Afr) the label for a red and rosé wine (Pinotage) produced by the Graham Beck Wines winery, Franschhoek, Western Cape.

Pino (Fr) a full-bodied, red wine from St. Florent, Corsica.

Pinodoux (S.Afr) the label for a fortified red wine (Pinotage) produced by the Lammershoek Winery, Swartland, Western Cape.

Pinon [Claude] (Fr) a producer of A.C. Vouvray in the Touraine district of the Loire. Usually pétillant.

Pino Porto (S.Afr) the label for a red wine (Pinotage) produced by the Koelenhof Winery, Stellenbosch, Western Cape.

Pinord (Sp) a winery based in the Penedés region. Produces white, red and cava wines. Website: http://www.pinord.es

Pinot (Fr) one of the most distinguished of the wine grape families. Pinot chardonnay, Pinot gris, Pinot meunier and Pinot noir.

Pinotage (S.Afr) a red grape variety, a hybrid cross (circa 1920) between the Pinot noir and Cinsaut (Hermitage). Produces wines with aromas and flavours of bramble jelly, banana, raspberries, plums, smoke, soot and tar.

Pinot Auxerrois (Fr) another name for the Auxerrois blanc in Alsace.

Pinot Beurot (Fr) a white grape variety, also known as the Pinot gris. Grown in the Côte de Beaune in the production of Hautes-Côtes de Beaune and Bourgogne blanc. (Ger) = Ruländer, (It) = Pinot Grigio.

Pinot Bianco (It) a white grape variety grown in the Veneto and Lombardy regions. Also known in Germany as the Weissburgunder.

Pinot Blanc (Fr) a white grape variety that produces an apple, butter and sappy flavours, also known as the Pinot chardonnay. (Aus) = Weissburgunder/Weisser burgunder/Klevner, (Ger) = Weisser burgunder, (It) = Pinot bianco. In Alsace it is also known as the Clevner.

Pinot Blanc (S.Am) an alternative name of the Pinot Chardonnay grape.

Pinot Blanc (USA) *see* California Pinot Blanc.

Pinot Blanc Chardonnay (USA) the alternative name for the Chardonnay grape.

Pinot Blanche de Loire (USA) the Californian name for the Chenin blanc grape.

Pinot Blanc Vrai Clevner (Fr) an alternative name for the Pinot blanc grape.

Pinot Chardonnay (Fr) an alternative name for a white grape variety, more correctly known as Pinot Blanc.

Pinot-Chardonnay-Mâcon (Fr) dry white wines that are produced from Chardonnay or Pinot blanc grapes. May use this A.C. or just A.C. Mâcon.

Pinot de Juillet (Fr) a red grape variety (relation of the Pinot noir). Grown by Moët et Chandon, it is an early ripener.

Pinot de la Loire (Fr) a white grape variety also known as the Chenin blanc.

Pinot de Loire (Fr) *see* Pinot de la Loire.

Pinot Grigio (It) a white grape variety grown in northern Italy. Produces wines of varying colours due to the copper pigment in the skin. Also known as the Ruländer in Germany and the Südtirol. (Fr) = Pinot gris.

Pinot Gris (Fr) a white grape variety, a member of the Pinot family, produces a spicy, perfumed (musk, smoke) aroma with a flavour of spice, honey, nuts and nougat. (Aus) = Grauer burgunder/Grauburgunder/Ruländer, (Ger) = Ruländer, (It) = Pinot grigio, (Hun) = Szürkebaràt, (Slo) = Tocai. Is also known as the Tokay d'Alsace in Alsace. Also known as Auxerrois Gris, Fauret, Grey Pinot, Malmsey, Malvoisie, Malvasia, Pinot beurot.

Pinot Liébault (Fr) a black grape variety. Is closely related to the Pinot noir.

P

Pinot Maltais (Euro) a red grape variety grown on Malta which was grown in France in the middle ages. Also known as the Pinot morgeot.

Pinot Meslier (Fr) a red grape variety grown in the Burgundy region. Same as Pinot noir.

Pinot Meunier (Fr) a black grape variety grown in the Champagne region. Not as fine as the Pinot noir, but ripens later, therefore good assurance against frost. Related to the Gris meunier. Also known as the Auvernat gris, Blanche feuille, Dusty miller, Goujan, Morillon taconé, Müllerrebe, Müller schwarzriesling, Plant de brie, Schwarzriesling and Wrotham pinot.

Pinot Morgeot (Euro) see Pinot Maltais.

Pinot Negro (Arg) a local name for Pinot noir.

Pinot Nero (It) the black Pinot noir in Italy. Known as the Blauburgunder in the Südtirol.

Pinot Noir (Fr) the classical black grape of Burgundy and Champagne, one of the greatest red wine grapes. Produces wines with complex aromas and flavours of roses, raspberries, strawberries, cherries, cranberries, black and redcurrants, violets, boiled beetroot, farmyard, cabbage, vegetal, spices and game. Known as the Pinot negro, Pinot nero, Pinot vérot, Blauer burgunder, Blauburgunder, Blauer spätburgunder, Klevner, Nàgyburgundi, Noirien, Pineau and Sauvignon noir.

Pinot Noir (USA) see California Pinot Noir.

Pinot Noir Rosé d'Alsace (Fr) a rosé wine of Alsace, drunk locally. Known as schillerwein by the German speaking locals.

Pinot Oltrepo Pavese (It) a D.O.C. white wine from the Pinot grigio and Pinot nero grapes in north-western Italy.

Pinot St. George (USA) a red grape variety grown in California to make red table wines.

Pinot St. Laurent (Aus) an alternative name for the St. Laurent red grape variety.

Pinot 2 (S.Afr) the label for a non-vintage sparkling (carbonated) white wine produced by the Riebeek Cellars winery, Swartland, Western Cape.

Pinot Vérot (Fr) another name for the Pinot noir grape.

PI.NO.VI.TA (Aus) the label for a white (Grüner veltliner and Pinot blanc blend) wine produced by the Kreinel winery, Traisendal.

Pint (Eng) measure 20fl.ozs.1.76pints=1litre=⅛ gallon=0.568litre. (Den) = ca, (Fr) = pinte.

Pint (USA) 16fl.ozs (0.473 litre).

Pinta (Eng) a slang term for a pint of milk.

Pinta (S.Afr) the label for a red wine (Jerepigo from Pinotage, Tinta and Touriga nacional) produced by the Domein Doornkraal winery, Little Karoo.

Pintail Ale (USA) an ale brewed by the Bridgeport Brewing Company, Portland, Oregon.

Pinte (Fr) pint.

Pinte (Ger) denotes a rough, drinking place.

Pintia (Port) a red wine (Tempranillo) produced from un-grafted, phylloxera-free vines by Bodegas Pintia, DO Toro Ribera del Duero. Owned by Vega Sicilia.

Pintos dos Santos [A.] (Port) Vintage Port shippers. Vintages: 1955, 1957, 1958, 1960, 1963, 1970, 1974, 1975, 1977, 1978, 1979, 1980.

Pinwinnie (Scot) a de luxe blended Scotch whisky 43% alc by vol. Produced by Inver House Distillers in Aidrie, Lanarkshire.

Pio-Cesare (It) a noted winery based in Alba, Piemonte. Owns vineyards in Barbaresco and Barolo.

Pioda (It) a still natural spring mineral water from Pioda. Mineral contents (milligrammes per litre): Sodium 0.95mg/l, Calcium 34.4mg/l, Magnesium 14.8mg/l, Potassium 0.47mg/l, Bicarbonates 161.7mg/l, Sulphates 9.6mg/l, Nitrates 6mg/l, Silicates 3.4mg/l. pH 8.0

Pioneer (Eng) a new variety of dwarf hop. See also First Gold, Herald.

Pioneer (Eng) a cask ale brewed using a single hop variety by Ledbury Brewery Company, Herefordshire.

Pioneer Cocktail (Cktl) ⅓ measure Drambuie, ⅓ measure vodka, ⅓ measure orange Curaçao. Shake over ice, strain into an ice-filled highball glass and serve with straws.

Pioule (Fr) a natural spring mineral water (established 1884) from Le Luc en Provence. Mineral contents (milligrammes per litre): Sodium 33.5mg/l, Calcium 140.8mg/l, Magnesium 11.4mg/l, Potassium 1.1mg/l, Bicarbonates 351mg/l, Chlorides 38.2mg/l, Sulphates 117.7mg/l, Silicates 37mg/l. pH 7.3

Pipa (Port)(Sp) butt or pipe (cask) of wine.

Pipe (Mad) a cask of wine 92 gallons.

Pipe (Port) a cask of Port between 500litres–595litres depending from which area it originates. 115gallons (522.5litres) approximately. Douro pipe: 550litres, Vila Nova de Gaia pipe: 547litres and a Shipping pipe: 534litres.

Pipe (Sp) a cask of wine in Marsala 93gallons (424litres).

Pipe Major (Scot) a blended Scotch whisky distributed by the Montrose Whisky Cº. Ltd. Also De Luxe 12, 21 and 24 year old versions 43% alc by vol.

Piper (Scot) a fine keg Scotch ale 1036 O.G. brewed by the Tennent Caledonian Brewery in Glasgow. Also produce a Piper Export 1042 O.G.

Piperdy (Fr) an alternative name for the Malbec grape.

Piper Export (Scot) see Piper.

Piper-Heidsieck (Fr) a Champagne producer. (Add): 51 Boulevard Henri Vasnier, 51100 Reims. A Grande Marque. Produces vintage and non-vintage wines. Vintages: 1902, 1906, 1910, 1912, 1916, 1918, 1921, 1926, 1929, 1933, 1937, 1943, 1947, 1949, 1952, 1953, 1955, 1957, 1959, 1961, 1963, 1967, 1969, 1971, 1973, 1975, 1976, 1979, 1982, 1983, 1985, 1990, 1995, 1996, 1997, 1998, 1999, 2000, 2002. De Luxe vintage cuvée; Champagne Rare. Prestige cuvée: Florens-Louis Brut. Now owns the Dolbec Champagne house.

P

Pipers (Scot) a blended Scotch whisky produced by Seagram 40% alc by vol.

Piper's Brook (Austr) one of five main wine-producing areas in Tasmania. Accounts for 52% of production. Grape varieties include: Chardonnay, Riesling, Sauvignon blanc.

Piper's Brook Winery (Austr) a winery based near Launceston, Tamar Valley, Tasmania. Grape varieties: Chardonnay, Gewürztraminer, Riesling and Pinot noir. Produces varietal wines.

Pipers Gold (Scot) a 3.8% alc by vol. golden ale brewed by Fyne Ales Ltd., Argyll.

Piper-Sonoma (USA) a sparkling (traditional method) wine produced jointly by Piper Heidsieck of Champagne, France and Sonoma Vineyards, California.

Pipette (Eng) a long glass tube, narrowed at one end which is used to extract wine from the cask for testing during its maturation period.

Pipette (Pol) a drinking glass with a long narrow neck and a small bulb at the bottom. Used for drinking vodka.

Pipkin (Eng) a species of barley malt from the Golden Promise variety. Gives medium sugar yields.

Pipkin (Eng) a cask-conditioned ale brewed by Bank's Brewery.

Pipkin Cider (Eng) a 5.5%–6.5% alc by vol. cider produced in the Yorkshire Dales at a cottage in Masham, North Yorkshire.

Pipoli (It) an aged D.O.C. Aglianico del Vulture wine produced by Basilium in Basilicata. Aged for 12 months in oak.

Pippermint Get (Fr) a peppermint liqueur produced by the Bénédictine company of monks. 28% alc by vol. See also Peppermint Get.

Pippin Cocktail (Cktl) ½ measure Calvados, ½ measure apricot brandy, juice ½ orange, ½ egg white. Shake well over ice, strain into a highball glass and top with lemonade.

Pippins (Eng) an old English cider-making apple.

Pips (Eng) the seeds of the grapes, contain unwanted tannins and bitter oils.

Pipz (Eng) an alcoholic apple drink 4% alc by vol. from Showerings (has added apple flavouring).

Piquant (Fr) a sharp-tasting wine.

Piqué (Fr) pricked, pétillant wine, can also be used to describe a wine with a slightly vinegary taste.

Piquepouls de Pays (Fr) in Armagnac the alternative name for Baco 22A. See also Plant de Grèce.

Piquepoult (Fr) the name given to wine produced in the Gers département that is distilled into Armagnac.

Piquetberg (S.Afr) see Piketberg.

Piquets-en-Rang (Fr) a method of vine training where posts 'in line' are used to train the vines up to two metres above the ground. See also Pachets-en-Rang.

Piquette (Fr) a common, ordinary wine used in certain parts of France. Is made from a fermentation of the marc from the 2nd or 3rd pressing and water.

Piqûre (Fr) wine malady. see Acescence, Piqué.

Piraat (Bel) a 10.5% alc by vol. top-fermented, bottle-conditioned barley wine brewed by Van Steenberge Brasserie, Ertevelde.

Piranha (Cktl) 1 measure Bols crème de cacao, 1 measure vodka. Stir over ice and strain into a cocktail glass.

Pirate Porter Beer (Eng) a cask-conditioned ale 1036 O.G. brewed by the home-brew public house at the Pier Hotel, Gravesend, Kent.

Pirate Porter Beer (Eng) a cask-conditioned ale 1036 O.G. brewed by the home-brew public house at the South-eastern Hotel, Strood, Kent.

Pirie (Austr) a sparkling wine produced in Tasmania by Pipers Brook from 70% Pinot noir, 30% Chardonnay grapes.

Pirin (Bul) a still natural spring mineral water from Pirin Mountains. Mineral contents (milligrammes per litre): Sodium 2.7mg/l, Magnesium 2.8mg/l, Potassium 0.6mg/l, Manganese 2.8mg/l, Silicates 4mg/l. pH 7.7

Piros Cirfandli (Hun) a white grape variety.

Piros Szlanka (Hun) the local name for the Pamid grape.

Pirque (Chile) a wine-producing area.

Pirramimma Winery (Austr) a winery based in the McLaren Vale, Southern Vales, South Australia. Produces varietal wines.

Pirrone Winery (USA) a winery based in the Central Valley, California. Produces varietal wines.

Pisa (Sp) the name given to a small cistern into which Vino de Lágrima was run during the production of Málaga.

Pisador (Sp) a person who treads the grapes in the Sherry region.

Pisano (S.Am) a 30ha wine estate in Uruguay. Noted for Gewürztraminer and Tannat.

Pisco (S.Am) a brandy made from Muscat wine, is colourless, with a slight oily consistency. Produced in Argentina, Bolivia, Chile and Peru 45% alc by vol. See also Pisquero.

Pisco Aba (Chile) a pisco brandy produced from Muscat grapes.

Pisco Control (Chile) a 40% alc by vol. brandy, distilled and bottled in Valley of Elqui by Cooperativa Agrícola Control Pisquero de Elqui y Limarí Ltda.

Pisco Punch (Cktl) a 50mls (2fl.ozs) pisco, 25mls (1fl.oz) lime juice, 25mls (1fl.oz) fresh pineapple juice, 2 dashes maraschino, 2 dashes gomme syrup. Shake over ice and strain into 125mls (5fl.oz) goblet.

Pisco Sour (Cktl) a 60mls (2½fl.ozs) lime juice, 35mls (1½fl.ozs) Pisco, 5mls (¼fl.oz) gomme syrup, 2 dashes Angostura, dash egg white. Shake well over ice, strain into 125mls (5fl.oz) goblet and top with dash bitters.

Pisquero (Chile) a pot-still used in the production of Pisco.

Piss (Austr) a slang unsavoury term for beer.

Piss Artist (Eng) a slang unsavoury term for a habitual drunkard.

Pissed (Eng) a slang unsavoury term for drunk, intoxicated.

Piss Up (Eng) a slang unsavoury term for a heavy drinking bout.

Piston Bitter (Eng) a 4.8% alc by vol. bitter ale brewed by the Beer Engine, Devon.

Piston Porter (Eng) a 4.6% alc by vol. porter brewed by the Oakleaf Brewing C°. Ltd., Hampshire.

Pitcher (Eng) a container for water or wine. Made of clay, stone or glass. (Aus) = krug, (Fr) = pichet, (Ger) = krug, (Sp) = jarra.

Pitchfork Ale (Eng) a 4.3% alc by vol. bottle-conditioned bitter ale brewed by the RCH Brewery, West Hewish, Weston-Super-Mare (bottled with the yeast).

Pitching (Eng) a name given to the adding of yeast to the cooled wort to start the fermentation in brewing.

Pitesti (Rum) a wine-producing area in southern Rumania. Produces red and white wines.

Pitfield Bitter (Eng) a 3.6% alc by vol. bitter brewed by the Pitfield Brewery, Shoreditch, London.

Pitfield Brewery [London] Ltd (Eng) a brewery (established 1981). (Add): 14 Pitfield Street, Hoxon, London N1 6EY. Brews: cask-conditioned Amber Ale 4.2% alc by vol., Black Eagle 5% alc by vol., East Kent Goldings 4.2% alc by vol., Eco Warrier 4.5% alc by vol., Hoxton Best Bitter, Hoxton Heavy 4.8% alc by vol. Dark Star 1050 O.G. Jack Frost, Pitfield Original Bitter 3.7% alc by vol. Pumpkin Porter, Shoreditch Stout 4% alc by vol. Singhboulton 4.7% alc by vol. Valentine Ale 5% alc by vol. Eco Warrier 4.5% alc by vol. Website: http://www.pitfieldbeershop.co.uk 'E'mail: sales@pitfieldbeershop.co.uk

Pithoi (Gre) the name given to ancient fermenting jars.

Pitnauer [Hans] (Aus) a winery based in Göttlesbrunn, Carnuntum. (Add): Weinbergstrasse 4-6, 2464 Göttlesbrunn. Grape varieties: Cabernet sauvignon, Chardonnay, Pinot blanc, St. Laurent, Syrah, Zweigelt. Label: Pegasus.

Pitovske Plaze (Euro) a wine-producing region in Dalmatia.

Pits (Sri.L) a pilsener-style beer 12.25° Balling brewed by the McCallum Brewery in Colombo.

Pitschental (Aus) a vineyard site on the banks of the River Danube in the Kremstal region.

Pitsilia (Cyp) a district in the north-west Troodos mountain range.

Pittara (Fr) a noted brand of Basque cider produced in the Pyrénées.

Pittermännchen (Ger) vineyard (Anb): Nahe. (Ber): Kreuznach. (Gro): Schlosskapelle. (Vil): Dorsheim.

Pittersberg (Ger) vineyard (Anb): Nahe. (Ber): Kreuznach. (Gro): Schlosskapelle. (Vil): Münster-Sarmsheim.

Pittsburgh Brewing C°. (USA) a noted brewery based in Pittsburgh, Pennsylvania.

Pittyvaich-Glenlivet (Scot) a single highland malt whisky distillery based west of Dufftown, Banffshire 43% alc by vol.

Pitú (Bra) a well-known brand of cachaça.

Pitures-Dessus [Les] (Fr) a Premier Cru vineyard in the A.C. commune of Volnay, Côte de Beaune, Burgundy.

Pivare (Slo) a tavern specifically designed for beer drinking.

Pivnita (Rum) cellar.

Pivo Niksic (Ser) a beer brewed by the Niksic Brewery, Montenegro. 1048 O.G.

Pivovar Benesov s.r.o (Czec) a brewery. (Add): Táborská 306, 256 31 Benesov u Prahy. Brews a range of beers and lagers. Website: http://www.pivovarbenosov.cz 'E'mail: ferdinand@pivovarbenosov.cz

Pivovar Cerná Hora s.a (Czec) a brewery. (Add): 679 27 Cerná Krumlov 381 01. Brews a range of beers and lagers. Website: http://www.pivovarch.cz 'E'mail: pivovarch@pivovarch.cz

Pivovar Eggenberg a.s (Czec) a brewery. (Add): Latrán 27, Cesky Krumlov 381 01. Brews a variety of beers and lagers. Website: http://www.eggenberg.cz 'E'mail: info@eggenberg.cz

Pivovar Nymburk spol s.r.o (Czec) a brewery. (Add): Prazská 581, 288 25 Nymburk. Brews a variety of beers and lagers. Website: http://www.postriziny.cz 'E'mail: nymburk@postriziny.cz

Pivovarská Basta s.r.o (Czec) a brewery. (Add): Horská 198, 543 02 Vrchlabi. Brews a varety of beers and lagers. Website: http://www.hotelbasta.cz 'E'mail: hotelbasta@hotelbasta.cz

Pivrnec (Czec) a 4.55% alc by vol. gold-yellow, 11% Balling, bottled lager brewed by Radegast Sedlec Brewery, Sedlec.

Piwniczanka (Pol) a natural spring mineral water. Mineral contents (milligrammes per litre): Sodium 148mg/l, Calcium 277mg/l, Magnesium 136mg/l, Potassium 200.3mg/l, Bicarbonates 1861mg/l, Chlorides 21.2mg/l, Sulphates 32.9mg/l, Fluorides 0.23mg/l.

Piwo (Port) beer/ale.

Pixilated (Eng) a slang term for drunk/intoxicated.

Pizarra (Sp) slate (soil).

Pizões (Port) a natural spring mineral water (established 1919) from Nascente 7, Moura. Mineral contents (milligrammes per litre): Sodium 34mg/l, Calcium 118mg/l, Magnesium 29.2mg/l, Bicarbonates 383.1mg/l, Chlorides 103.7mg/l, Sulphates 17.8mg/l. pH 7.2

Pjolter (Nor) grog.

PK Morkel (S.Afr) see Morkel.

Placer County (USA) a wine-producing county in the Sierra foothills, California.

Placerville (USA) a noted wine-producing town in Eldorado County, California.

Placher (Aus) a vineyard site based on the banks of the River Kamp situated in the Kamptal region.

Plà de Bages (Sp) a Denominación de Origen of Cataluña. Produces light white Joven wines. Grape varieties include: Cabernet sauvignon, Chardonnay and Tempranillo.

Plafond Limité de Classement (Fr) abbr: P.L.C. 'Ceiling yield' the maximum amount of wine which producers can produce for a single A.C. classification.

P

Pla í Llevant de Mallorca (Sp) a new D.O. area of Mallorca, Balearic Islands.

Plain (Ire) word for porter (beer).

Plaine de L'Aude (Fr) a wine area within the département of Aude of the Languedoc-Roussillon.

Plaine du Vidourle (Fr) a wine area within the département of Gard of the Languedoc-Roussillon.

Plaine du Vistre (Fr) a wine area within the département of Gard of the Languedoc-Roussillon.

Plaisir de Merle Vineyard (S.Afr) a vineyard based in Paarl. Grape varieties includes: Cabernet sauvignon, Chardonnay.

Plaize (Fr) a Cognac producer. (Add): Denis Plaize et Fils, 17150 Mirambeau. 30ha. in the Fins Bois.

Planalto (Port) a white reserve wine produced by SOGRAPE from Viosinho, Malvasia fina and Gouveio grapes in the Douro.

Planalto Mirandes (Port) a DOC region in the Douro.

Planat (Fr) a Cognac producer. Produces Prestige V.S. and V.S.O.P., Premier Cru Grande Champagne.

Planche à Égoutter (Fr) a draining board used for the cleaning of bottles. Made of metal, it has spikes so as to allow the placing of the necks of the bottles over the spikes so they can drain after cleaning.

Plancoët (Fr) a naturel mineral water from Brittany, north-western France. (Add): Source Saasay, 22130 Plancoët. Mineral contents (milligrammes per litre): Sodium 24mg/l, Calcium 56mg/l, Magnesium 10.5mg/l, Potassium 3mg/l, Bicarbonates 220mg/l, Chlorides 28mg/l, Sulphates 18mg/l, Nitrates 0mg/l.

Planda Tae (Ire) tea plant/tea bush.

Plan de Dieu (Fr) a village in the A.C. Côtes du Rhône-Villages. Produces mainly red wines (with a little rosé and white wine).

Planeta (It) a noted winery based in Sicily. Produces Alastro and La Segreta Bianco from Greciano and Chardonnay grapes, La Segreta Rosso from Nero d'Avola, Cabernet and Merlot grapes. Also produces: Cerasuolo di Vittoria. Website: http://www.planeta.it

Plane Tree Estate (N.Z) a winery based in Marlborough, South Island. Grape varieties include: Sauvignon blanc.

Planèzes (Fr) a noted wine-producing village in the Côtes du Roussillon.

Planococcus ficus (USA) see Vine Mealybug.

Planque (S.Afr) a range of wines (Cabernet sauvignon & Pinotage) produced by the Slaley Estate, Stellenbosch, Western Cape.

Planta de Elaboración y Ebotellado de Vinos (Sp) see VILE. Label Catedral de León. A modern winery based in León. Main grape varieties are the Picudo, Prieto, Mencia, Tempranillo and Verdejo.

Planta de Pedralba (Sp) an alternative name for the Planta fina grape.

Planta Fina (Sp) a white grape variety grown in southern Spain. Also known as the Planta de pedralba.

Plantagenet Winery (Austr) a winery based in Great Southern region. (Add): Lot 46, Albany Hwy., Mount Barker, Western Australia. Produces varietal wines. Grape varieties: Cabernet sauvignon, Shiraz, Chardonnay. Label: Omrah.

Planta Nova (Sp) a white grape variety grown in southern Spain. Also known as the Tardania.

Plant d'Arles (Fr) the southern Rhône name for the Cinsault grape.

Plant de Brie (Fr) an alternative name for the Pinot meunier.

Plant de Grèce (Fr) a white grape variety grown if the Gers département. Also known as Piquepouls de Pays.

Plant Doré (Fr) an alternative name for the Pinot noir.

Planter's (Cktl) 1 measure Jamaican rum, juice ½ lemon, 1 teaspoon gomme syrup, dash Angostura. Shake over ice, strain into a cocktail glass and top with grated nutmeg.

Planter's Punch [1] (Cktl) 25mls (1fl.oz) lime juice, 1 teaspoon sugar, 50mls (2fl.ozs) Jamaican rum. Dissolve sugar in lime juice. Shake rum over ice and strain into a highball glass with ice, sugar and lime juice. Decorate with pineapple, cherry, sliced orange and mint and serve with straws.

Planter's Punch [2] (Cktl) 35mls (1½fl.ozs) lemon or lime juice, 35mls (1½fl.ozs) dark rum, 2 barspoons grenadine, dash Angostura. Build into an ice-filled highball glass. Stir with soda water added, decorate with a slice of orange and lemon.

Planter's Punch [3] (Cktl) put some ice into a highball glass, add 1 teaspoon orange Curaçao, 1 measure Jamaican rum, 2 dashes Angostura, juice 1½ limes or lemons, 1 teaspoon grenadine. Stir well, decorate with an orange slice, cherry and serve with straws.

Planter's Punch [4] (Cktl) 25mls (1fl.oz) Bacardi White Label, juice ½ lemon, dash Curaçao, dash maraschino, 2 dashes pineapple juice. Stir altogether in an ice-filled highball glass, dress with a pineapple cube and a cherry soaked in white rum.

Planter's Tea (Cktl) 2 parts strong tea, 1 part dark rum, 300mls (½ pint) orange juice, 125mls (¼ pint) lemon juice. Heat, sweeten with sugar syrup, decorate with slices of orange and lemon.

Planter's Tea Punch (Punch) as for Planter's Tea using Assam tea.

Plantes [Les] (Fr) a Premier Cru vineyard in the A.C. commune of Chambolle-Musigny, Côte de Nuits, Burgundy 2.6ha.

Plantes-de-Maranges [Les] (Fr) a Premier Cru vineyard [part] in the commune of Cheilly-lès-Maranges, A.C. Santenay, Côte de Beaune, Burgundy.

Plantet (Fr) a popular red hybrid grape variety grown in Loire.

Plantin [Carl G.] & Cº. (Nor) a producer of aquavit under the control of A/S Vinmonopolet.

Plant Liqueurs (USA) liqueurs produced by either

percolation or by distillation of the base spirit and plants.

Plant Médoc (Fr) another name for the Merlot grape.

Plant Noble (Port) noble grape (species)/noble vine.

Plaque [La] (Fr) the metal disc on the top of the Champagne or other sparkling wine bottle to stop the wire cage cutting the cork. Also known as Planque de Muselet.

Plaque de Muslelet (Fr) see La Plaque.

Plasmopara Viticola (Lat) formerly known as Peronospora Viticola.

Plassac (Fr) a commune in the A.C. Côtes de Blaye, north-eastern Bordeaux.

Plassey Bitter (Wal) a bitter brewed by the Plassey Brewery, Eyton, near Wrexham, Clwyd.

Plassey Brewery (Wal) a brewery (established 1985). (Add): Eyton, Wrexham, Clwyd LL13 0SP. Brews: Cwrw Tudno 5% alc by vol. Dragon's Breath 6% alc by vol. Farmhouse Bitter 1039 O.G., Royal Welsh Fusilier 4.5% alc by vol., Special 1050 O.G. Extra Special 1059 O.G., Plassey Bitter 4% alc by vol., Vale Ale 4.1% alc by vol. Website: http://www.web-nexus.com/plassey 'E'mail: plassey@globalnet.co.uk

Plastered (Eng) a slang term for drunk and incapable, very intoxicated.

Plastering (Sp) the adding of gypsum (calcium sulphate) to grape must to increase the acidity. Was especially used in Sherry production. (Fr) = plâtrage.

Plat (Fr) flat or a dull wine.

Platan 11% (Czec) a 4.5% alc by vol. gold-yellow, bottled lager beer from the South Bohemian Brewery Group in Protivín.

Platan 10% (Czec) a 3.9% alc by vol. bottled lager beer from the South Bohemian Brewery Group in Protivín.

Plateau Calcaire [Le] (Fr) lit: 'limestone plateau', a zone of production in Saint-Émilion, east Bordeaux.

Platière [La] (Fr) a Premier Cru vineyard in the A.C. commune of Pommard, Côte de Beaune, Burgundy 5.8ha.

Platin Extra Fin (Swe) a Swedish Punsch 26% alc by vol. produced by Aktiebolaget Vin & Spritcentralem.

Platinum Blonde Cocktail (Cktl) 25mls (1fl.oz) Jamaican rum, 25mls (1fl.oz) Grand Marnier, 10mls (½ fl.oz) cream. Shake over ice, strain into a cocktail glass and dress with a slice of orange.

Plato (Euro) a measure used in beer production (1 degree Plato = 4.08 degrees of gravity).

Plâtrage (Fr) plastering, the addition of gypsum to the grape must to increase acidity.

Platres (Cyp) a wine village on the south-eastern slopes of the Troodos mountain in the Makheras region. Produce some of the islands' finest red wines from the Mavron grape.

Platten (Ger) village (Anb): Mosel-Saar-Ruwer. (Ber): Bernkastel. (Gro): Schwarzlay. (Vins): Klosterberg, Rotlay.

Plattensee (Hun) another name for Lake Balatòn.

Platzer [Manfred] (Aus) a winery based in Tieschen, Süd-Steiermark. (Add): Pichla 25, 8355 Tieschen. Grape varieties: Gewürztraminer, Pinot blanc, Pinot gris, Sauvignon blanc, Traminer, Welschriesling, Zweigelt. Produces a range of dry and sweet wines. Also has vineyards in the Süd-Oststeiermark

Platzl Special (Ger) a sweet, full-bodied beer, light in colour 5% alc by vol. brewed by the Aying Brauerei in Bavaria.

Plauelrain (Ger) vineyard (Anb): Baden. (Ber): Ortenau. (Gro): Fürsteneck. (Vil): Durbach.

Plavac Beli (Cro) a local white grape variety.

Plavac Mali (Cro) a red grape variety (Dobricic x Zinfandel) grown in Croatia and the Dalmatian Isles. Produces full-bodied and distinctive wines. See also Plavina.

Plavai (Euro) late-ripening white grape variety native to Moldova where it is also known as Belan, Plakun. (Aus) = Plavez gelber, (Hun) = Melvais, (Rom) = Palvana, (Rus) = Ardanski/Bila muska/Oliver.

Plavina (Euro) the name given to light red wines produced on the Dalmatian coast. Also known as Brajdica, Plavac Mali.

Plavka (Ser) a red wine produced in Montenegro.

Plaxtol (Eng) a vineyard based in Kent. Grape varieties: Seyval blanc, Schönburger.

Playa Delight (Cktl) ½ measure dry gin, ½ measure white rum, juice ¼ lime, 1 measure orange juice. Shake over ice, strain into a cocktail glass, dress with slice of lime and serve with straws.

Playmate (Cktl) ¼ measure Grand Marnier, ¼ measure apricot brandy, ¼ measure brandy, ¼ measure orange squash, 1 egg white, dash Angostura. Shake over ice, strain into a cocktail glass and add a twist of orange peel.

Playtime (Cktl) ⅓ measure Grand Marnier, ⅓ measure apricot brandy, ⅓ measure orange juice, dash egg white. Shake over ice, strain into a cocktail glass, dress with a spiral of lemon and a cherry.

Plaza Cocktail (Cktl) 30mls (¼ gill) dry gin, 15mls (⅛ gill) Italian vermouth, 15mls (⅛ gill) French vermouth. Shake over ice, strain into a cocktail glass and serve with a thin slice of pineapple on top.

P.L.C. (Fr) abbr: see Plafond Limité de Classement.

Pleasanton (USA) a wine-producing town based in Alameda County, California.

Pleasant Valley Wine Company (USA) a leading wine producer of the Finger Lakes region of New York district. Lake Keuka. Produces fine sparkling wines under the Great Western label.

Pleasant Valley Winery (N.Z) a winery based at 322 Henderson Valley Road, Henderson, North Island. 7ha. Grape varieties: Baco N°1, Baco 22A, Müller-Thurgau, Niagara, Palomino and Pinotage. Produces wines under the Château Yelas label.

Pleil (Aus) a winery based in Wolkersdorf, Weinviertel. (Add): Aldergasse 32, 2120 Wolkersdorf. Grape varieties: Gewürztraminer, Grüner veltliner, Riesling, Welschriesling. Produces a range of wine styles.

Plein (Fr) a frank, forward, full-bodied wine.

Pleisweiler-Oberhofen (Ger) village (Anb): Pfalz. (Ber): Südliche Weinstrasse. (Gro): Kloster Liebfrauenberg. (Vin): Schlossberg.

Pleitersheim (Ger) village (Anb): Rheinhessen. (Ber): Bingen. (Gro): Rheingrafenstein. (Vin): Sternberg.

Plemenka (Ser) a red wine from the Vojvodina region in northern Serbia. Made from the Bouvier (red and white) grapes.

Plemenka Ruzica (Cro) a rosé wine produced near Kutjevo in eastern Croatia.

Plenio (It) a D.O.C. Verdicchio dei Castelli di Jesi Classico Riserva wine produced by Umani Ronchi in Osimo, Marche.

Plensky Prazdroj (Czec) a golden beer brewed by a brewery of the same name.

Plessac et Cie (Fr) a noted nineteenth century Cognac producer.

Pletchistik (Rus) a white grape variety grown in the river Don area.

Pleudihen (Fr) a noted cider from Brittany, north-western France.

Pleven (Bul) a demarcated wine-producing area of northern Bulgaria. Produces mainly red wines.

Plevna (Bul) the brand-name of a red wine from Pleven.

Plinque (S.Afr) a rosé wine (Pinotage) produced by the Slaley Estate, Stellenbosch, Western Cape.

Pliny the Elder (Gre) an author who wrote a book devoted to a variety of wines and vines. AD23–AD79.

Pliska (Bul) the trade-name used for brandy produced in Preslav in the Balkan mountains for export.

PLJ (Eng) abbr: Pure Lemon Juice a brand™ of bottled lemon juice used as a flavouring in food and drinks.

Pljesevica (Cro) a wine-producing area based in Croatia.

P.L.O (Austr) abbr: Penfolds, Lindemans and Orlando.

Plod (Eng) a 4.5% alc by vol. traditional light brew from Arundel Brewery, West Sussex. 400 gallons brewed to honour P.C. Tony Gilks retirement.

Plonk (Eng) a slang word which now denotes cheap ordinary wine, derived from the English 'Tommies' (foot soldiers) in the First World War who could not pronounce 'blanc' (white wine).

Plonko (Austr) slang term for an alcoholic who drinks mainly wine.

Plose (It) a sparkling natural spring mineral water from Plose, Merano, Südtirol. Mineral contents (milligrammes per litre): Sodium 1.3mg/l, Calcium 2.5mg/l, Magnesium 2mg/l, Potassium 0.3mg/l, Bicarbonates 15mg/l, Sulphates 2.7mg/l, Nitrates 2.1mg/l, Silicates 6.7mg/l. pH 6.6

Ploughbottles (Eng) wooden casks used by farmworkers to carry their daily ration of ale to the fields. Mainly in the Midlands.

Plough Inn & Leith Hill Brewery (Eng) a brewery (established 1980). (Add): Coldharbour Lane, Coldharbour, Dorking, Surrey RH5 6HD. Brews a range of beers and lager. Website: http://www.ploughinn.com

Ploughmans (Eng) a 4.3% alc by vol. bitter ale brewed by Mauldon's Ltd., Suffolk.

Ploughman's Ale (Eng) a bottled XXX bitter ale 1049 O.G. brewed by the Bateman Brewery in Wainfleet, Lincolnshire (also an Export 1060 O.G. version).

Ploughman's Bitter (Eng) a canned bitter 1032 O.G. brewed by the Watneys Brewery.

Ploughman's Lunch (Eng) a snack consisting of a pint of bitter ale, bread, cheese, pickles and fruit (usually apples).

Ploughmans Punch (Eng) a 4.5% alc by vol. ale brewed by the Hampshire Brewery, Hampshire.

Ploughman's Scrumpy (Eng) a dry cider produced by Countryman in Devon.

Plovdina (Ser) a red grape variety grown in Macedonia.

Plovdiv (Bul) a wine-producing region based in the Southern Basic Region. Produces mainly red wines.

Ployez-Jacquemart (Fr) a Champagne producer. (Add): 8 Rue Astoin, 51500 Ludes. Produces vintage and non-vintage wines. Vintages: 1971, 1973, 1975, 1976, 1978, 1979, 1982, 1985, 1988, 1989, 1990, 1995, 1996, 1997, 1998, 1999. The de luxe vintage cuvée: Cuvée Liesse d'Harbonville.

Plumage Archer (Eng) a barley strain which is ideal for brewing giving beers a rich depth of flavour.

Plum Brandy (Euro) a colourless eau-de-vie produced from a variety of plums.

Plume d'Ange (Fr) a white wine produced from Sauvignon blanc grapes by Domaine les Cailloux du Paradis, Loire.

Plummer (W.Ind) a style of rum produced in Jamaica. Also known as Wedderburn. see Grand Arôme.

Plummer Type (W.Ind) a Jamaican rum using dunder in the process. see Grand Arôme.

Plummy (Eng) a term used to describe wines that are rich and flavoursome.

Plump Jack Winery (USA) a 21ha. winery (established 1985) based near Oakville, Napa Valley, California. Grape varieties include Chardonnay, Cabernet sauvignon, Merlot. Noted for Cabernet sauvignon Reserve wines. Label: McWilliams Oakville Vineyard.

Plum Pudding (Eng) a 4.8% rich dark beer brewed by J.W. Lees, Middleton, Manchester, Lancashire. Available November and December.

Plum Shake (Cktl)(Non-alc) 75mls (3fl.ozs) orange juice, 125mls (5fl.ozs) plum juice, 2 scoops vanilla ice cream. Blend together in a blender. Pour into a large club goblet and serve with straws.

Plunder (Eng) a 4.8% alc by vol. beer from the Jollyboat Brewery (Bideford) Ltd., Devon.

Plunger Coffee (Eng) a name given to the cafetière method of coffee-making.

Plunkett Wines (Austr) a winery (established 1992). (Add): Cnr. Lambing Gully Road and Hume Freeway, Avenel, Victoria. Grape varieties: Chardonnay, Rhine riesling, Sauvignon blanc, Traminer, Cabernet sauvignon, Merlot.

Plus (W.Ind) a non-alcoholic drink produced in Barbados by Banks. Is rich in vitamin C, fructose and amino acids. Its make-up is similar to honey.

Plymouth (USA) a wine-producing town based in Amador County, California.

Plymouth Gin (Eng) a 40% alc by vol. and 41.2% alc by vol. gins distilled in Plymouth. *see* Blackfriars Distillery. *See also* Gurgling Jug.

Plymouth Heavy (Eng) a mild ale 1032 O.G. brewed by the Courage Brewery.

Plymouth Navy Strength (Eng) a 57% alc by vol. gin from the Blackfriars Distillery, Plymouth.

Plymouth Pride (Eng) a 3.8% alc by vol. bitter ale brewed by the South Hams Brewery, Devon.

Plympton Brewery (Eng) a brewery based in Plymouth, Devon. (Halls Brewery). Noted for Plympton Pride 1045 O.G. and Plympton Best 1039 O.G.

Plzen (Czec) the Czec. spelling of the town of Pilsen (the German spelling).

Plzen (Hol) a 5% alc by vol. bottle-conditioned pilsner brewed by 't IJ Brouwerij, Amsterdam.

Plzensky Prazdroi (Czec) the Czec. spelling of the Pilsner Urquell Brewery in Pilzen.

PM (Can) the brand-name of a Canadian whiskey produced by Canadian Gibson Distilleries 40% alc by vol.

PM Blended (USA) the brand-name of a blended whiskey 40% alc by vol.

P.M.E. (Eng) *abbr*: Pecti-Methyl-Esterase.

Pneumatic Press (Ger) consists of cylinder into which the grapes are placed. A deflated plastic or synthetic rubber bag is placed in the cylinder then inflated, pressing the grapes against the slatted sides of the drum.

Po [River] (It) a major river that flows from the west of Turin to the Adriatic south of Venice.

Poacher Bitter (Eng) a keg bitter 1032 O.G. brewed by Whitbread.

Poachers Brewery (Eng) a brewery. (Add): Unit 4, Swinderby Ind Park, Swinderby, Lincoln, Lincolnshire LN6 9TW. Brews bitter beers. Website: http://www.poachersbrewery.co.uk 'E'mail: george@poachersbrewery.co.uk

Poacher's Ridge (Austr) a winery based in the Great Southern region of Western Australia. Grape varieties include: Cabernet sauvignon. Label: Louis' Block.

Pocas Junior (Port) vintage Port shippers. Vintages: 1960, 1963, 1967, 1970, 1975, 1977, 1978, 1980, 1985, 1991, 1994, 1997, 2000, 2003. L.B.V. 1998.

Pocholoa Manzanilla (Sp) a fine, pale, dry Manzanilla Sherry from Domecq.

Pochon (Fr) a bottle-shaped bag/pouch made from either cardboard, plasic or cloth with a string-tie neck band, used to carry wine bottles. Usually has the producer's name embossed on the side.

Pocillum (Lat) small cup.

Pocket (Eng) a sack used to pack hops in for delivery to the brewery 166lbs (77.72 kgs).

Pöckl (Aus) a winery (11ha) based in Mönchhof, Burgenland. (Add): Baumschulgasse 12, 7123 Mönchhof. Grape varieties: Blaufränkisch, Cabernet franc, Cabernet sauvignon, Chardonnay, Merlot, Pinot noir, St. Laurent, Welschriesling, Zweigelt. Label: Admiral.

Pocnhka (Rus) a natural spring mineral water. Mineral contents (milligrammes per litre): Sodium 12mg/l, Calcium 22mg/l, Magnesium 8mg/l, Potassium 4mg/l, Bicarbonates 122mg/l, Chlorides 24mg/l, Sulphates 3mg/l. pH 8.0

Pocono Springs Pure Mountain Spring Water (USA) a natural spring mineral water from Pennsylvania.

Pocullum (Lat) cup. *See also* Cymbium.

Poculum (Lat) goblet. *See also* Cullulus.

Poda en Vaso (Sp) low pruning of the vines. i.e. Goblet shaped. *See also* En Vaso.

Podar (Port) to prune (the vine).

Podebradka (Czec) a sparkling natural spring mineral water (established 1905) from Podebrady. Mineral contents (milligrammes per litre): Sodium 354.6mg/l, Calcium 144mg/l, Magnesium 47.5mg/l, Potassium 49.3mg/l, Bicarbonates 955.5mg/l, Chlorides 373.3mg/l, Sulphates 76.8mg/l, Fluorides 1.3mg/l.

Podensac (Fr) a commune within the district of A.C. Cérons in south-western Bordeaux. Produces sweet white wines.

Podensac (Fr) a commune within the district of A.C. Graves in south-western Bordeaux. Produces mainly dry white wines.

Podere (It) farm/estate.

Podere Aldo Conterno (It) a winery based in the DOCG Barolo. Label: Vigna Cicala.

Podere Collelungo (It) an 8ha. wine estate in Castellina. Produces D.O.C.G. Chianti Classico Riserva and Roveto (a selected vineyard Chianti).

Podere di Cignano (It) a noted Chianti Putto producer based in the Tuscany region.

Podere Rocche dei Manzoni (It) a noted wine producer based in Monforte d'Alba, Piemonte. Produces sparkling (metodo tradizionale) wines. Labels includes Valentino Brut.

Podere Terrano alla Via della Volpaia (It) a 3.5ha vineyard. (Add): 53017 Radda in Chianti (SI). Noted for Chianti Classico.

Poderi Alasia (It) describes a range of wines produced by Araldici Vini Piemontesi at 14040 Castelboglione (AT). Range includes Roleto, Sorilaria, Renero, Rive, Castellero, Il Cascione.

Poderi Aldo Conterno (It) based in the DOCG Barolo. Produces: Barolo Cicala. Website: http://www.poderialdoconterno.com

Poderi e Cantine Fratelli Oddero (It) based in the DOCG Barolo. Produces: Vigna Rionda Barolo DOCG. Website: http://www.odderofratelli.it

Poderi Marcarini (It) a noted winery based in La Morra (district of Barolo) in Piemonte.

Podersdorf (Aus) a wine-producing area in the Eisenstadt district.

Podium (It) a D.O.C. Verdicchio dei Castelli dei Jesi Classico Superiore wine from Garofoli in the Marche.

Podkovàn Brewery (Czec) a very old brewery (circa 1434) in northern Czec.

Podo (Kor) grape.

Podowon (Kor) winery.

Podravje (Ser) key region on the banks of the river Drava, near the town of Maribor. Grape varieties: Sauvignon blanc, Rhine riesling, Traminer, Laski Rizling. Home to the Haloze winery.

Poeirinha (Port) an alternative name for the Baga grape.

Poema (N.Z) the name of an old vine Garnacha wine produced by Montana at 171 Pilkington Road, Glen Innes, Aukland. *See also* Timara.

Poesia Estate (Chile) a 13ha winery (established 1935) based in Luján de Cuyo, Mendoza. Grape varieties: Cabernet sauvignon 40% and Malbec 60%. Produces: Poesia Duena H. Garcin.

Poesia S.A (Arg) a winery based in the Mendoza region, eastern Argentina. Website: http://www.bodegapoesia.com 'E'mail: poesia@uolsinectis.com.ar

Poetry (USA) a winery based in the Stags Leap District, Napa Valley, California. Grape varieties: Cabernet sauvignon.

Poet's Corner (Austr) the label used by Montrose in New South Wales for a white Sémillon and Chardonnay wine and a red from a blend of Shiraz, Cabernet and Malbec grapes.

Poet's Prayer (S.Afr) the label for a white wine (Chardonnay) produced by the Weltevrede Estate winery, Robertson Western Cape.

Pogada (Eng) a 3.8% alc by vol. ale brewed by the Battersea Brewery C°. Ltd., London.

Poggibonsi (It) a commune of the Chianti Classico Riserva in Tuscany.

Poggio Alle Gazze (It) a 100% Sauvignon blanc wine produced at Tenuta dell'Ornellaia, Bolgheri, Tuscany.

Poggio Guiseppe (It) a 3ha winery based at Roccagrimalda, Piemonte.

Poggio Reale (It) a Chianti Putto produced by Spalletti in Tuscany.

Poggio Romita (It) a Chianti Putto producer based in Tuscany.

Poggio Valente (It) a D.O.C. Cru Morellino di Scansano wine produced by Le Pupille in Maremma, Tuscany.

Pohorje (Slo) a wine produced in Slovenia.

Poiane [Le] (It) a D.O.C. Valpolicella Classico. Made using the 'ripasso' method by Bolla from Corvina, Rondinella and Molinara grapes. matured for 2 years in oak and several months in bottle.

Poiana Negri (Rum) a natural spring mineral water from Dorna. Mineral contents (milligrammes per litre): Sodium 209mg/l, Calcium 264mg/l, Magnesium 47mg/l, Potassium 22mg/l, Bicarbonates 2000mg/l, Chlorides 50.1mg/l. pH 6.0

Poigen (Aus) a vineyard site on the banks of the River Danube situated in the Wachau region, Niederösterreich.

Poignettage (Fr) the gentle shaking of the bottles in Champagne, given to those that have received their dosage (to mix the contents).

Poilly (Fr) a Cru Champagne village in the Canton de Ville-en-Tardenois. District: Reims.

Poilly-sur-Serein (Fr) a commune in the A.C. Chablis, Burgundy.

Poinchy (Fr) a commune in the A.C. Chablis, Burgundy.

Poin de Pétillance (Fr) lit: 'a hint of pétillance', very slightly sparkling

Poinsettia (Cktl) a cocktail of cranberry juice and Curaçao, topped with Champagne.

Point (Aus) vineyard sites (2) on the banks of the River Danube in the Kremstal region.

Point (Aus) a vineyard site based on the banks of the River Kamp situated in the Kamptal region.

Point (Eng) the acidity in coffee.

Point [à] (Fr) a term used to describe a wine which is ready for drinking, is at its peak.

Point Brewery (USA) a brewery based in Stevens Point, Wisconsin. Brews beers under the Point label.

Point d'Angles (Fr) a Premier Cru vineyard in the A.C. commune of Volnay, Côte de Beaune, Burgundy. 1.5ha. Also known as Les Point d'Angles.

Pointe (Aus) a vineyard site on the banks of the River Danube situated in the Wachau region, Niederösterreich.

Pointe (Fr) punt, the depression in the bottom of most red wine bottles and some whites. Helps stacking, decanting (some red wines). *see* Sur Pointe.

Pointe de Fraîcheur (Fr) an Alsatian term for a wine with a 'slight prickle' on the palate.

Point Five (Can) a low alcohol lager 0.5% alc by vol. brewed by Labatts.

Pointouille (Fr) a term that denotes a wine with only a hint of oak from a short cask ageing.

Poio (Port) terrace.

Poire au Cognac (Fr) a blend of natural extract of Poire Williams and Eau-de-vie-de-Cognac produced by Brillet 30% alc by vol.

Poire de Fer (Fr) a variety of pear used in the production of Calvados.

Poire de Grise (Fr) a variety of pear used in the production of Calvados.

Poire Williams (It) a pear spirit liqueur, usually has a pear which is grown in the bottle from bud (the bottle is tied over the set bud on the tree) 43% alc by vol. *see* Williamine.

Poiron [Jean et Fils] (Fr) an A.C. Muscadet Sèvre et Maine producer from 44690 Château-Thébaud.

Poirot et Fils (Fr) a Champagne producer. (Add): Rue Pernet, 51130 Bergères-les-Vertus. Produces vintage and non-vintage Champagnes (Blanc de Blancs, Rosé, Brut Tradition, Vintage). 'E'mail: Champagnepoirot@terre-net.fr

Poissenot (Fr) a Premier Cru vineyard in the A.C.

commune Gevrey-Chambertin, Côte de Nuits, Burgundy 2.19ha.

Poit Dhubh (Scot) lit: 'black pot', malt whisky produced in parish of Sleat, Isle of Orinsay (south of Skye) by Pràban na Linne. Owner is Mr. Noble. 12 year old Black Label 40% alc by vol., 12 year old Green Label 40% alc by vol.

Poitin (Ire) an alternative name for potcheen (legalised in March 1998), now produced under licence. *see* Hackler Poitín, Bunratty Poteen.

Poivrot (Fr) a slang term for soused (heavily drunk/intoxicated). *See also* Ivrogne and Paf.

Pojer e Sandri (It) a small winery based at Faedo near San Michele all'Adige in the Trentino-Alto Adige region. Produces mainly white wines and sparkling (metodo tradizionale) wine plus grappa.

Pokal (Ger) a rotund ¼ litre, green-stemmed glass.

Pokale (Ger) a thick trunked glass used to serve tafelwein in the Haardt region, close to the border with Alsace in France.

Pokal Wine (Ger) tafelwein.

Poker (Cktl) ½ measure Bacardi White Label, ½ measure Italian vermouth. Stir over ice and strain into a cocktail glass.

Polaire (Jap) a brand-name wine of Sapporo Wines Ltd.

Poland (Pol) a country in north-west Europe noted for vodka and plum brandies. Has no wines of note. *See also* Slivovitch.

Poland Spring (USA) a natural spring mineral water (established 1845) from Maine. Mineral contents (milligrammes per litre): Sodium 1.5mg/l, Calcium 4.1mg/l, Magnesium 1mg/l, Potassium 0.5mg/l, Bicarbonates 396.5mg/l, Chlorides 1.6mg/l, Sulphates 5.3mg/l, Silicates 1.7mg/l. pH 6.5

Polar (Fin) a cranberry liqueur produced by Chymos, red in colour 29% alc by vol.

Polar (Ger) a brand of rum produced at Hockheim. (Part of Seagram).

Polar Beer (Ice) a beer brewed by the Egill Skallagrimsson Brewery Ltd.

Polar Eclipse (Eng) a 4.8% alc by vol. ale brewed by the Beartown Brewery, Cheshire.

Polar Ice Vodka (Can) a 40% alc by vol. quadruple distilled, triple filtered vodka.

Polaris Water (Can) a natural spring mineral water (established 1991) from Coastal Mountains, British Columbia.

Pol Carson (Fr) a B.O.B. Champagne.

Polcevera (It) a white wine from Liguria. Made from the Bianchetta and Vermentino grapes.

Pol d'Argent (USA) a sparkling wine produced by Robin Fils in eastern America.

Pol Dubreuil (Fr) a B.O.B. Champagne.

Polgazao (Port) a white grape variety grown in the Lafoes region.

Pol Gessner (Fr) a Champagne producer based in Épernay. Wines sold only at Selfridges in London.

Policalpo (It) a D.O.C. Barbera del Monferrato wine produced by Cascina Castlèt in Piedmont. Contains up to 20% Cabernet sauvignon grapes.

Policella (It) a 1970's U.K. promotional name for basic Valpolicella wines (sold in 2litres screwcap bottles) which was promoted as Mr. & Mrs. Policella and their daughter Val.

Pölich (Ger) village (Anb): Mosel-Saar-Ruwer. (Ber): Bernkastel. (Gro): Sankt Michael. (Vins): Held, Südlay.

Polichinelle (Cktl) 60mls (½ gill) cassis de Dijon, 20mls (⅙ gill) kirsch, soda water. Stir over ice and strain into a highball glass on ice. Also known as Cassis-Kirsch.

Policka Brewery (Czec) a brewery based in central Czec.

Polignac [Prince Hubert de] (Fr) a Cognac producer. (Add): Unico-op, 49 Rue Lohmeyer, 16102 Cognac. 5200ha. in the co-operative, 49% sited in the Fins Bois, 36% in the Bons Bois. Produces Dinasty Grande Champagne.

Poligny (Fr) a commune of the Jura département, eastern France.

Polish (Eng) a brewery term used for the fine filtering of light-coloured beers to make them crystal clear, before bottling or kegging.

Polish Filtration (USA) the final filtration of wines, beers, etc. to give clarity prior to bottling.

Polish Hill (Austr) the label for a white wine (Riesling) produced by the Grosset winery, Clare Valley, South Australia.

Polish Hill River Vineyard (Austr) a range of wines from the Quelltaler Estate, Clare Valley, South Australia. Originally called Spring Vale. Noted for Riesling wines.

Polish White Spirit (Pol) a potent vodka-type spirit 80% alc by vol.

Polisy (Fr) a Cru Champagne village in the Canton de l'Aube. District: Château Thierry.

Polito Vineyard (USA) a winery based in Vincentown, New Jersey.

Polja (Euro) a wine-producing area in Dalmatia.

Poljana (Ukr) a natural spring mineral water from Svalyava, Transcarpathia. Mineral contents (milligrammes per litre): Sodium 2500mg/l, Calcium 125mg/l, Magnesium 50mg/l, Bicarbonates 6250mg/l, Chlorides 450mg/l, Sulphates 50mg/l.

Poljana Kupel (Ukr) a natural spring mineral water (established 1994) from Svalyava, Transcarpathia. Mineral contents (milligrammes per litre): Sodium 2000mg/l, Calcium 50-125mg/l, Magnesium <50mg/l, Potassium 2000mg/l, Bicarbonates 4500-7000mg/l, Chlorides 200-600mg/l, Sulphates <25mg/l, Boration 100-125mg/l.

Poljana Podilska (Ukr) a natural spring mineral water from Slavuta.

Poljoprivredne Zadruge (Cro) (Slo) lit: 'made in the co-operative cellars of the place named'.

Poljustrovo (Rus) a natural spring mineral water (established 1718) from St. Petersburg. Mineral contents (milligrammes per litre): Sodium <100mg/l, Calcium <50mg/l, Magnesium <50mg/l, Bicarbonates 80-150mg/l, Chlorides

<150mg/l, Sulphates <350mg/l, Iron 40-70mg/l.

Polla (Pol) a natural spring mineral water from Wiazowna. Mineral contents (milligrammes per litre): Sodium 35mg/l, Calcium 65.7mg/l, Magnesium 17.1mg/l, Potassium 3mg/l, Bicarbonates 372mg/l, Chlorides 3.7mg/l, Sulphates 7.2mg/l, Fluorides 0.4mg/l.

Pollard's Brewery (Eng) a brewery based in Stockport, Cheshire. Brews: John Barleycorn Bitter.

Polla's Red (S.Afr) the label for a red wine (Pinotage, Petit verdot, Ruby cabernet and Shiraz blend) produced by the Du Preez Estate winery, Worcester, Western Cape.

Pollera Nera (It) a red grape variety grown in Liguria and Tuscany.

Pollino (It) a D.O.C. red wine from Calabria. Made from the Gaglioppo, Greco nero, Guarnaccia bianca, Malvasia bianca and Montonico grapes. If minimum total alc. is 12.5% by vol. and aged 2 years then classed Superiore.

Polluted (USA) a slang term for intoxicated, drunk.

Polly (Eng) the nickname for Apollinaris mineral water. i.e. Scotch and Polly.

Pollyanna (Cktl) crush 2 slices of fresh pineapple with 50mls (2fl.ozs) dry gin. Add 10mls (½fl.oz) Italian vermouth, 2 dashes grenadine, juice ½ orange. Shake over ice and strain into a large cocktail glass.

Polly's Folly (Eng) a bitter ale 4.3% alc by vol. brewed by the Buffy's brewery, Norfolk.

Polmassick Vineyard (Eng) a vineyard (established 1976). (Add): Polmassick, St. Ewe, St. Austell, Cornwall PL26 6HA. 0.65ha. Grape varieties: Müller-Thurgau and Seyve villard. 'E'mail: musgrave@polmassick.fsnet.co.uk

Polmos (Pol) short for Panstwowy Monopol Spirytusowy. Polish State vodka producers. Principal brand is Wyborowa.

Polnic (Cktl) 25mls (1fl.oz) Polar liqueur, 25mls (1fl.oz) gin. Pour into an ice-filled highball glass and stir in tonic water.

Polo Cocktail (Cktl) ⅗ measure dry gin, ⅕ measure lemon juice, ⅕ measure orange juice. Shake over ice and strain into a cocktail glass.

Polonaise Cocktail (Cktl) ⅗ measure brandy, ⅕ measure dry Sherry, ⅕ measure blackberry brandy, dash lemon juice. Shake over ice and strain into an ice-filled old-fashioned glass.

Pol Roger (Fr) a Champagne producer (established 1849). (Add): 1 Rue Henri Lelarge, 51200 Épernay. 1.8ha. A Grande Marque. Produces vintage and non-vintage wines. Produces : Cuvée Winston Churchill, Extra Cuvée de Réserve (Brut Réserve, Rich), Brut Vintage, Chardonnay Vintage, Rosé VintageVintages: 1906, 1909, 1911, 1914, 1915, 1919, 1921, 1923, 1926, 1928, 1929, 1933, 1934, 1937, 1942, 1943, 1945, 1947, 1949, 1952, 1953, 1955, 1959, 1961, 1962, 1964, 1966, 1969, 1971, 1973, 1975, 1976, 1979, 1982, 1983, 1985, 1986, 1988, 1989, 1990, 1995, 1996, 1997, 1998, 1999, 2000. *See also* Cuvée Sir Winston Churchill. Website: http://www.polroger.com 'E'mail: polroger@polroger.fr

Polsuho (Slav) medium dry.

Pölstar Cucumber Vodka (Ice) a 37.5% alc by vol. cucumber-flavoured vodka.

Polvillejo (Sp) the alternative name used in Sanlúcar de Barrameda for Lustrillo.

Polychrosis viteana (Lat) a strain of the grape berry moth that produces larvae which feed on bunches of grapes leaving them susceptible to disease, especially rot.

Polyculture (Port) mixed cropping. i.e. vines grown on high trellises with vegetables grown underneath.

Polyethylene Terephthalate (Eng) *see* Pet Bottle.

Polygalacturonase (Lat) *abbr*: P.G. a yeast enzyme that reduces pectic acid. Cleans wines that have a pectin haze.

Polynesian Cocktail (Cktl) ⅔ measure vodka, ⅓ measure cherry brandy, juice of a lime. Shake over ice, strain into a sugar (lime) rimmed cocktail glass and top with a twist of lime peel juice.

Polynnaia (Rus) a wormwood whiskey made around Odessa.

Poly Parrot (Cktl) 1 measure (green) crème de menthe, dash lime juice. Shake over ice, strain into a cocktail glass and float double cream on top coloured with 4 dashes of grenadine.

Polyphenols (Eng) the substances that cause browning (tannins).

Polypin (Eng) a plastic insert inside a rigid cardboard container. Holds 4½ gallons of beer.

Polythene Drums (Eng) containers of 240litres capacity for transporting wine, can often give the wines a slight plastic taint.

Polyvinylpyorolidone (Eng) *abbr*: P.V.P. a substance used to help stabilize wines and prevent them turning brown, precipitates with excess tannin.

Polz [Erich & Walter] (Aus) a winery (45ha) based in Spielfeld, Süd-Steiermark. (Add): Grassnitzberg 54a, 8471 Spielfeld. Grape varieties: Cabernet sauvignon, Chardonnay, Pinot gris, Sauvignon blanc, Traminer, Welschriesling, Zweigelt. Produces a range of dry and sweet wines.

Pomace (Eng) the residue from apples after the juice has been extracted for cider. Pectin is then extracted from it, then it is used for cattle feed.

Pomace Brandy (USA) *see* California Brandy.

Pomagne (Eng) a brand-name sparkling cider made by Bulmers in Hereford. Allowed to ferment twice naturally.

Pombal [Marquis de] (Port) the man to whom is attributed the starting of the Port wine district in the Douro.

Pombe (Afr) an east African beer made from millet which has been germinated and roasted, then mixed with posho (maize flour) and fermented. Is usually drunk through tubes (high in alcohol). *See also* Pombo.

Pombo (Afr) the Bantu name for Pombe.

Pomegranate Wine Company [The] (Austr) a

P

winery based in McLaren Vale, South Australia. Grape varieties include: Cabernet sauvignon, Shiraz. Labels: Bylines (25% Cabernet sauvignon & 75% Shiraz), Songlines (5% Cabernet sauvignon & 95% Shiraz).

Pomegreat (Eng) the brand name for a non-alcoholic pomegranate drink.

Pomeral (Fr) an old, established Cognac house who, with Antier, united in 1949 to form the house of Gaston de Lagrange.

Pomerans (Swe) bitter orange used in the production of liqueurs.

Pomeranz (Ger) *see* Pomeranzen Bitters.

Pomeranzen Bitters (Ger)(Hol) flavoured orange bitters made from unripe oranges.

Pomeranzen Liqueurs (Austr) based on Pomeranzen oranges both green and orange coloured.

Pomeranzen Liqueurs (Ger) a Curaçao-type liqueur, green-gold in colour made on a base of unripe Pomeranzen oranges.

Pomerol (Fr) an area within the region of Bordeaux, on the east of the town of Libourne and Saint-Émilion. Produces fine red wines from a high percentage of Merlot and Cabernet franc grapes. Top growth is Château Pétrus. *See also* Le Pin.

Pomino Bianco (It) a D.O.C. dry, white wine from Tuscany. Produced from the Pinot bianco, Pinot grigio and Chardonnay grapes.

Pomino Rosso (It) a D.O.C. red wine from Frescobaldi in Tuscany. Produced from 60% Sangioveto, 20% Cabernet sauvignon, 10% Pinot nero, 10% Merlot. 12–15 months in barrique.

Pommard (Fr) an A.C. village and commune of the Côte de Beaune, Burgundy. 300ha. Has 27 Premier Cru vineyards: Clos de la Commaraine, Clos des Épenots, Clos du Verger, Derrière Saint-Jean, La Chanière, La Platière, La Refène, Le Clos Blanc, Le Clos Micot, Les Argillières, Les Arvelets, Les Bertins, Les Boucherottes, Les Chanlins-Bas, Les Chaponnières, Les Charmots, Les Combes-Dessus, Les Croix-Noires, Les Épenots, Les Fremiers, Les Jarollières, Les Petits-Épenots, Les Pézerolles, Les Poutures, Les Rugiens-Bas, Les Rugiens-Haut, Les Saussilles. 141.43ha.

Pommeau (Fr) a northern French drink of apple juice muted with Calvados to produce a sweet, fortified beverage 17% alc by vol.

Pomme Prisonière [La] (Fr) the imprisoning of apples in flasks, then filling with Calvados du Pays d'Auge. By Drouin (Christian), La Distillerie des Fiefs Sainte-Anne, Normandy. *See also* Coeur de Lion.

Pommeraie Vineyards (USA) a small winery based near Sebastopol, Sonoma County, California. Grape varieties: Cabernet sauvignon and Chardonnay. Produces varietal wines.

Pommeranzen Bitters (Ger)(Hol) the alternative spelling of Pomeranzen Bitters.

Pommeraye [La] (Fr) a commune in the A.C. Savennières, Anjou-Saumur, Loire.

Pommerell (Ger) vineyard (Anb): Mosel-Saar-Ruwer. (Ber): Zell/Mosel. (Gro): Schwarze Katz. (Vil): Zell.

Pommern (Ger) village (Anb): Mosel-Saar-Ruwer. (Ber): Zell/Mosel. (Gro): Goldbäumchen. (Vins): Goldberg, Rosenberg, Sonnenuhr, Zeisel.

Pommery (Fr) the new name for the old firm of Pommery et Gréno.

Pommery et Gréno (Fr) a Champagne producer. (Add): 5 Place du Général Gouraud, P.O. Box B7, 51100 Reims. A Grande Marque. 307ha. Produces vintage and non-vintage wines. Vintages: 1904, 1906, 1911, 1915, 1921, 1926, 1928, 1929, 1934, 1937, 1941, 1943, 1947, 1949, 1952, 1953, 1955, 1959, 1961, 1962, 1964, 1966, 1969, 1973, 1975, 1976, 1978, 1979, 1980, 1981, 1982, 1985, 1987, 1988, 1989, 1990, 1995, 1996, 1997, 1998, 1999, 2001. Their de luxe vintage cuvée is Louis Pommery. Labels include: Cuvée Louise (vintage). *See also* Pommery.

Pommier [Isabelle & Denis] (Fr) a winery based in the A.C. Chablis, Burgundy. Produces a range of Chablis wines including Premier Crus Beauroy and Côte de Léchet.

Pommie's Revenge (Eng) a 5.2% alc by vol (1060 O.G) cask-conditioned ale brewed by the Goose Eye Brewery in Yorkshire.

Pommy (Eng) a local Somerset word for the milled apple pulp before it is pressed. Short for Pomace.

Pomona Ridge Vineyard (N.Z.) a vineyard. (Add): Pomona Road, Ruby Bay, Nelson. 1.5ha. Specialises in Pinot noir.

Pomorosso (It) a D.O.C. Barbera d'Asti wine made from 60 year old vines and aged in new barriques by Coppo (Luigi) in Piemonte.

Pompango Cocktail (Cktl) ½ measure dry gin, ½ measure grapefruit juice, 2 dashes dry vermouth. Shake over ice and strain into a cocktail glass.

Pompejaner (Ger) vineyard (Anb): Franken. (Ber): Mainviereck. (Gro): Not yet assigned. (Vil): Aschaffenburg.

Pomperjanum (It) a red wine produced in central-western Italy in Roman times.

Pompey Royal (Eng) a cask-conditioned bitter ale 1043 O.G. brewed by the Whitbread Brewery at Cheltenham for Wessex.

Pompier Daisy Cocktail (Cktl) 1 measure crème de cassis, 1½ measures Noilly Prat. Stir over ice, strain into an old-fashioned glass and top with soda water.

Pompier Highball (Cktl) ½ measure crème de cassis, ½ measure French vermouth stirred over cracked ice in a highball glass.

Pomponette (Fr) a tall thin glass used for tasting and testing Champagnes.

Pomport (Fr) a commune in the A.C. Monbazillac in Bergerac. Produces sweet white (botrytised) wines.

Ponce (It) punch (drink).

Poncello (Sp) a ponche orange and brandy liqueur produced by the Caballero C°.

Ponche de Crema (S.Am) a drink, rum-based with eggs, milk and sugar Produced in Venezuela.

Ponches (Sp) a liqueur digestive that is brandy based (a punch-type).

1029

Ponches (Sp) liqueur Sherries.
Ponché Soto (Sp) a famous liqueur sold in a silver bottle, a blend of herbs, old Sherries and brandy. Produced by José de Soto in Jerez de la Frontera 21% alc by vol.
Ponder Estate Wines (N.Z) a winery. (Add): New Renwick Road, P.O. Box 215, Blenheim. 60ha. Grape varieties: Chardonnay, Riesling, Sauvignon blanc.
Ponferrada (Sp) a wine-producing area in the Galicia region. Produces red and white wines.
Pongràcz (S.Afr) a méthode cap classique wine produced from a blend of Pinot noir and Chardonnay grapes by Die Bergkelder (Distell), Stellenbosch, Western Cape. Labels include: Desiderius.
Poniatowski [Prince] (Fr) a noted producer of A.C. Vouvray in Touraine, Loire.
Poniente (Sp) a cool, humid wind, not very strong, that tends to bring on mildew in the Sherry region.
Ponnelle [Pierre] (Fr) a famous Burgundy négociant based in Beaune, Côte de Beaune. (Now part of Boisset).
Ponoma Valley Claret (N.Z) a full-bodied red wine produced by Abel and C°. in Kumeu.
Ponsigue (S.Am) a rum-based cordial flavoured with ponsigue cherries. Produced in Venezuela.
Pontac (Eng)(Fr) the general name used in the seventeenth century for claret (red Bordeaux) wines of good quality. Derives from the name of the owner of many early château in the region.
Pontac (S.Afr) a red grape variety.
Pont d'Avignon (Fr) a brand name for a French wine produced by E & J Gallo (France) for the American market. The name designed to appeal to the Americans in place of the complicated French label names!
Ponte da Barca (Port) an aguardente produced by Adega Cooperativa de Ponte da Barca.
Pontet [Le] (Fr) a vineyard in the commune of St-Médard-d'Eyrans. A.C. Graves, Bordeaux. 5ha (red).
Pontevedra (Sp) a wine-producing region in north-western Spain. Is noted for a '*green wine*' which is similar in style to the Vinhos Verdes of Portugal.
Pontil (Eng) an old name for the punt at the bottom of the bottle. *See also* Kick Up.
Pony (Eng) a brand-name cherry wine.
Pony (Eng) small bottle/glass ⅓ pint.
Pony (USA) a measure for cocktails (1fl.oz US).
Pony Ales (Ch.Isles) a cask-conditioned bitter ale 1035–1039 O.G. and mild ale 1037 O.G. brewed by the Guernsey Brewery 1920 Ltd. St. Peter Port, Guernsey (now no longer in production).
Pony Glass (USA) a small version of the flip glass. 2fl.ozs (flute-shaped).
Pony Punch (Cktl) 1 bottle dry white wine, juice 3 lemons, 300mls (½ pint) green tea, 1 teaspoon cinnamon oil, sugar syrup, 125mls (5fl.ozs) each of rum, brandy and arrack. Mix all well together, heat gently and serve hot.
Ponzi Vineyards (USA) a small vineyard (established 1970) based in the Willamette Valley, Oregon. Grape varieties: Arneis, Chardonnay, Pinot noir, Pinot gris.
Poodle (Cktl) 1 measure gin, 1 measure orange juice. Pour into an ice-filled highball glass, top with ginger ale and decorate with a slice of orange on rim.
Poodle's Passion (S.Afr) the label for white wine (Sauvignon blanc) produced by the Cowlin Wines winery, Paarl, Western Cape.
Pooh Beer (Eng) a 4.3% alc by vol. ale brewed by The Church End Brewery Ltd., Warwickshire.
Poole Brewery (Eng) a brewery (established 1981) in Poole, Dorset. Noted for cask-conditioned Dolphin Best 1038 O.G. Bedrock, Bosun Premium, Hedgehog, Holes Bay, Poole Best Bitter, Viagra. *See also* Brewhouse.
Pooles Best Bitter (Eng) a 3.8% alc by vol. cask-conditioned bitter ale brewed by Poole Brewery, Poole.
Poominator (Eng) a 4.8% alc by vol. ale brewed by the Darwin Brewery, Tyne & Wear.
Poop Deck (Cktl) ⅖ measure brandy, ⅖ measure Port wine, ⅕ measure blackberry brandy. Shake over ice and strain into a cocktail glass.
Poor (Eng) a term used to describe a wine that has little positive character or quality.
Poor Man's Champagne (S.Am) a term given to sparkling cider.
Poor Man's Drink (Eng) a drink produced by infusing pearl barley in water over heat with figs, raisins and liquorice.
Poort Winery [Die] (S.Afr) a winery based in Klein Karoo. (Add): P.O. Box 45, Albertina 6795. Produces varietal wines.
Pop (Eng) the slang name for any fizzy, non-alcoholic drink. i.e. coke, lemonade, 7-Up etc.
Pope (Cktl) tokaji wine heated with sugar and an orange studded with cloves.
Pope Clément V (Fr) *see* Clément V.
Poperings Hommelbier (Bel) a 7.5% alc by vol. top fermented, bottle-conditioned special beer brewed by Van Eecke Brasserie Watou.
Pope's 1880 (Eng) a keg/bottled ale 1041 O.G. brewed by the Eldridge Pope Brewery in Dorchester, Dorset.
Pope Valley Winery (USA) a winery based in the Napa Valley, California. Grape varieties: Cabernet sauvignon, Chardonnay, Chenin blanc, Johannisberg riesling, Petite sirah and Sauvignon blanc. Produces varietal wines.
Pop Festival (Punch) 3 sliced oranges, 1 part soda water, 1 part Monterez, 1 part Pimms, 2 parts lemonade. Mix altogether gently. May add sugar if required.
Popoff (Eng) a proprietary brand of vodka.
Po-Pomme Cocktail (Cktl) ⅔ measure cherry brandy, ⅓ measure Calvados, 2 dashes Angostura. Stir over ice, strain into a highball glass, top with dry cider, 2 ice cubes and an apple slice.
Popovice Brewery (Czec) a brewery based in western Czec.

Poppenweiler (Ger) village (Anb): Württemberg. (Ber): Württembergisch Unterland. (Gro): Schalkstein. (Vin): Neckarhälde.

Poppy Ale (Eng) a 4.2% alc by vol. ale brewed by the Skinner's Brewery C°. Ltd., Cornwall.

Poppy Ale (Eng) brewed by the Swale Brewery, Sittingbourne for the Royal British Legion for the 75th anniversary.

Poppy Ale Pride (Eng) a limited edition ale brewed by Tolly Cobbold, Suffolk to commemorate the Royal British Legion Poppy Appeal.

Poppy Cocktail (Cktl) ⅔ measure dry gin, ⅓ measure crème de cacao. Shake over ice and strain into a cocktail glass.

Poprad Brewery (Czec) a brewery based in eastern Czec. Brews: Tatran (a lager beer).

Popular Troubador (Eng) a brand of Sherry shipped by Saccone and Speed.

Pop Wines (Can) artificially carbonated wines, have a full sparkle.

Pop Wines (USA) natural wines which are flavoured with herbs, spices or fruit juices and other flavourings, most are sweet.

Popzone (Eng) developed by Hall & Woodhouse Beverage Division. Consists of The Simpsons, Panda Pops, Panda Still Pops.

Porcupine Ridge (S.Afr) a vineyard based within the Boekenhoutskloof Estate, Coastal Region. Grape varieties include: Cabernet sauvignon, Merlot and Sauvignon blanc..

Poretti Breweries (It) breweries (established 1877) based in northern Italy (owned by Carslberg). Brews a premium draught or bottled lager 5% alc by vol. Also Splügen Fumé (a red-brown beer). Website: http://www.poretti.co.uk

Porich'a (Kor) a non-alcoholic barley 'tea', light and dry in flavour.

Porkers Pride (Eng) a 3.8% alc by vol. ale brewed by the Ring 'O' Bells Brewery, Cornwall.

Porky & Best (Eng) a 4.5% alc by vol. best bitter ale brewed by the Hampshire Brewery, Hampshire.

Porous Peg (Eng) a soft wooden peg (spile) fitted into the shive to allow a cask to breath whilst it is working. See also Hard Spile (peg).

Porrets [Les] (Fr) a Premier Cru vineyard in the A.C. commune of Nuits-Saint-Georges, Côte de Nuits, Burgundy. 7ha. Also known as Porrets.

Porrón (Sp) a decanter/flask/bottle with two cross-over spouts, gives a stream of wine into the mouth.

Porsbrannvin (Den) a brand of akvavit flavoured with bog myrtle.

Port (Port) a fortified red wine produced in the upper Douro region of northern Portugal. Has many varieties including: Vintage, Crusted, L.B.V. Wood, Dated, Tawny and Ruby. See also Beneficio, Passport Decanter and White Port. (Den) = portvin, (Fr) = porto.

Porta Winery (Chile) a winery based in the Bío Bío Valley, southern Chile. Grape variety: Pinot noir. Also has vineyards in the Cachapoal Valley, Central Chile Website: http://www.portawinery.cl

Port à Binson (Fr) a Cru Champagne village in the Canton of Dormans. District: Épernay.

Portacask (Eng) a 2650litres container used for transporting wines. Made of fibre glass with a stainless steel liner.

Portador (Sp) describes the wooden container used to transport the grapes from the vineyard.

Portainjerto (Sp) a resistant root stock onto which the vine is then grafted.

Portalegre (Sp) one of five D.O.C. districts in Alentejo.

Portal (Port) a vintage Port producer. Vintages: 2003.

Portal de Fidalgo (Port) a D.O.C. Vinho Verde (Alvarhino) wine produced by the Provam co-operative.

Portali Aglianico (It) a D.O.C. wine produced by Basilium in Basilicata. Aged for 18 months in oak.

Portan (Fr) a red grape variety produced in the Languedoc by crossing Grenache noir x Portugais bleu. Permitted in Vin de Pays d'Oc production.

Port and Starboard (Pousse Café) ½ measure grenadine and ½ measure (green) crème de menthe.

Port Carras (Gre) a sweet red wine produced in Mount Vilia, Macedonia.

Portchester Brewery (Eng) a brewery (established 2000). (Add): 6 Audret Close, Portchester, Fareham, Hampshire PO16 9ER. Brews ales, beers and lager. Website: http://www.porchesterbrewery.co.uk 'E'mail: info@porchesterbrewery.co.uk

Port Cobbler (Cktl) 90mls (¾ gill) Port, 2 dashes brandy, 5 dashes plain syrup. Shake over ice, strain into a highball glass ½ full of crushed ice, serve with slices of fresh fruit and a dash of lemon peel juice.

Port Cocktail (Cktl) 50mls (2fl.ozs) Port wine, dash Cognac brandy. Stir over ice, strain into a cocktail glass and a squeeze of orange peel juice on top.

Port da Ravessa (Port) the brand-name of red and white V.Q.P.R.D. wines produced by the Adega Cooperativa de Redondo, Alentejo.

Port Dock Brewery Hotel (Austr) a brewery. (Add): 10 Todd Street, Port Adelaide 5015. Brews beers and stout. 'E'mail: admin@portdockbreweryhotel.com.au

Port Dundas (Scot) a malt and grain whisky distillery based near the mouth of the river Clyde, western Scotland. 10 year old malt whisky at 60% alc by vol.

Porte-Bouchon (Fr) cork-pin.

Porte-Fût (Fr) the name for the wooden trestles that support the wine casks.

Port Egg Nogg (Cktl) 90mls (¾ gill) Port, 30mls (¼ gill) brandy, 30mls (¼ gill) rum, 40mls (⅓ gill) milk, 1 egg, 1 teaspoon sugar. Shake over ice, strain into a tumbler and serve with a dash of nutmeg on top.

Porte-Hotte (Fr) a Bordeaux hod carrier.

Port Ellen (Scot) a single malt whisky distillery based on the Isle of Islay, western Scotland. An Islay malt whisky. 43% alc by vol. Also a 22 year old (60.5% alc by vol.), a 1974 plus a 1980 vintage at 64.7% alc by vol. cask strength (part of the DCL group).

Porter (Den) stout.

Porter (Eng) a beer made from roasted unmalted barley. High hopping, very bitter, was popular in the seventeenth and eighteenth century. *see* Guinness. (Den) = mørkt/bittert øl.

Porter Brewing C° (Eng) a brewery (established 1994). (Add): 84-86 Hud Rake, Haslingden, Rossendale, Lancashire BB4 5AF. Brews a range of beers.

Porter Gaff (Austr) a South Australian mixture of stout and lemonade.

Porterhouse (Eng) an eighteenth century ale house where only porter was served.

Porterhouse Brewing Company [The] (Ire) a brewery. (Add): 16–18 Parliament Street, Dublin 2, Republic of Ireland. Brews a range of beers and lager. Website: http://www.porterhousebrewco.com 'E'mail: info@porterhousebrewco.co.uk

Porter Mill Station (S.Afr) a red wine (Cabernet sauvignon) produced by the Porterville Cellars winery, Swartland, Western Cape.

Porter's (Eng) a light or brown ale from Gibbs Mew, Salisbury, Wiltshire.

Porter's Perfection (Eng) a cider made from an old Somerset apple of the same name near Yeovil, Somerset.

Porter 39 (Fr) a sweetish, dark, stout-style beer 6.9% alc by vol. brewed by the '33' Brasserie in the north of Maubeuge (part of the Union de Brasseries group).

Porter un Toast (Fr) a toast.

Porterville (S.Afr) a wine and brandy-producing region based north of Tulbagh.

Porterville Koöperatiewe Keldermaatskappy (S.Afr) a co-operative winery (established 1941) based in Piketberg, Swartland, Western Cape. 1380ha. (Add): Box 52, Porterville 6810. Grape varieties: Cabernet sauvignon, Chardonnay, Chenin blanc, Cinsaut, Colombard, Golden jerepigo, Grenache, Hanepoot, Merlot, Pinotage, Sauvignon blanc, Shiraz. Labels include: Disa, Black Eagle, Kumala, Porter Mill Station, Snakebite, Visage. Website: http://www.portervillecellars.co.za

Porter XXXX (Eng) a 1048 O.G. winter warmer ale brewed by the Ringwood Brewery, Ringwood, Hampshire.

Portes-Greffes (Fr) lit: 'carry grafting', describes American vine stocks that are resistant to phylloxera on which European stock is now grafted as a remedy against the pest.

Portet (Fr) a sweet (or dry) white wine from the Béarn region of south-western France. Grapes are often attacked by botrytis (known as Passerillage locally) in good years.

Portets (Fr) a commune in the A.C. Graves in south-western Bordeaux.

Porte Vecchio (Fr) an A.C. sub-region in southern Corsica.

Port Flip (Cktl) 35mls (1½fl.ozs) port, 10mls (½fl.oz) brandy, 1 egg yolk, 1 teaspoon sugar. Shake over ice, strain into a cocktail glass and top with grated nutmeg.

Port-Greffes (Fr) *see* Portes-Greffes.

Port Highball (Cktl) as for Gin Highball, substituting Port for gin.

Porticus (Aust) a red wine produced by Schloss Hardegg in the Weinviertel from Syrah grapes.

Portimao (Port) a co-operative based in the Algarve.

Portimao (Port) a DOC wine region based in the Algarve region, southern Portugal.

Portinhola (Port) a narrow entrance at the base of the head of the vat in which one can put one's head to smell that the inside is clean and sweet smelling.

Portland (USA) a white grape variety, a Labrusca cross (little used now).

Port Light Cocktail (Cktl) 25mls (1fl.oz) Bourbon whiskey, 10mls (½fl.oz) lemon juice, 1 egg white, 2 teaspoons clear honey. Blend together with crushed ice in a blender, pour into a highball glass and dress with a sprig of mint.

Port Mahon Brewery (Eng) a brewery (established 2000). (Add): Cask and Cutler, 1 Henry Street, Sheffied, South Yorkshire S3 7EQ. Brews: Black Pearl 5% alc by vol., Herald Bitter 4.2% alc by vol.

Port Milk Punch (Cktl) 125mls (1 gill) milk, 40mls (⅓ gill) Port. Shake over ice, strain into a collins glass and top with grated nutmeg.

Portnersberg (Ger) vineyard (Anb): Mosel-Saar-Ruwer. (Ber): Bernkastel. (Gro): Schwarzlay. (Vil): Wittlich.

Porto (Fr) the French for Port wine.

Porto/Douro (Port) a DOC wine region based in northern Portugal on the river Douro.

Porto (Port) the Portuguese pronunciation of Oporto, the town situated on the mouth of the river Douro (north bank) from where Port gets its name. *see* Portus Cale.

Porto dos Cavaleiros (Port) a Dão red wine produced by Caves Sao João.

Portofino (It) a dry white wine from Liguria, yellow in colour, 10%–11% alc by vol.

Port of Leith [The] (Port) a vintage character Port produced by Churchill Graham Lda, Vila Nova de Gaia.

Portokalatha (Gre) orange juice.

Portos (USA) the American for Port wines.

Porto-Vecchio (Fr) a wine-producing region in southern Corsica. Produces full-flavoured wines.

Port Phillip (Austr) the old name for Melbourne (where the first Australian wines were shipped from).

Port Phillip Estate (Austr) a winery (established 1987) based at 261 Red Hill Road, Red Hill South, Victoria. Grape varieties: Chardonnay, Pinot noir, Shiraz.

Portrait of a Winegrower (It) a famous eighteenth century painting by Girlamo Forabosco (circa 1700).

Portree Vineyard (Austr) a winery (established 1983). (Add): Off Mount William Road, Lancefield, Victoria. Grape varieties: Cabernet franc, Chardonnay.

Port Royal (N.Am) a draught pilsner sold in a long-necked bottle. Produced in the Honduras 1045 O.G.

Port Stout (Eng) a cask-conditioned ale brewed by O'Hanlons Brewery, Devon.

Port Tilter (Eng) another name for a mechanical decanter cradle made of brass or silver.

Port Tongs (Eng) an instrument to remove the neck and cork off old bottles of Port. The tongs are heated then applied to the neck. A wet feather is then used over the heated part to create a break.

Port Type (S.Afr) a designation given to fortified wines that are similar in style to Port.

Portugais Bleu (Fr) the local name in south-western France for the Blauer Portugieser grape. Parent of Portan.

Portugais Rouge (Fr) a red grape variety also known as the Limburger.

Portugal (Port) a wine-producing country on the west coast of the Iberian peninsular. Regions: Alentejano, Algarve, Beiras, Estramadura, Minho, Ribatejano, Terras do Sado, Tras-os-Montes. D.O.C. regions: Alcobaça, Alenouer, Alentejo, Algarve, Arruda, Baira Interior, Bairrada, Biscontos, Borba, Bucelas, Carcavelos, Chaves, Colares, Dão, Douro/Porto, Encostas de Aire, Graciosa, Lafoes, Lagoa, Lagos, Louriha, Madeira, Obidos, Palmela, Pico, Planalto Mirandes, Portalegre, Portimao, Redondo, Reguengos, Ribatejo, Setúbal, Tavira, Tavora-Varosa, Torres Vedras, Valpaços, Vidigueira, Vinho Verde. Noted for Periquita, Port wines. *See also* I.P.R. Website: http://www.viniportugal.pt

Portugaljka (Cro) the local name used for the Portugieser grape. *see* Portugizac crni.

Portugieser (Ger) a red grape variety. Produces light red wines. Known in (Cro) = Portugizac crni, Portugaljka, (Fr) = Autrichen/Portugais bleu, (Hun) = Kékoporto, (Rum) = Kékoporto. Also known as the Blauer Portugieser.

Portugizac Crni (Cro) the name given to the Portugieser grape in Croatia. *See also* Portugaljka.

Portuguese Cork Association (Port) *abbr*: APCOR. Website: http://www.corkmasters.com

Portuguese Espresso Coffee (Port) *see* Uma Bica.

Portus Cale (Lat) the Roman name for the old port on the river Douro. Was the centre of life and trade of ancient Lusitania. Gave its name to Portugal's Port wine.

Port-Vendres (Fr) a commune in the A.C. Banyuls, south-western France.

Portvin (Den) Port (wine).

Portwein (Ger) the German for Port wine.

Portwijn (Hol) the Dutch for Port wine.

Port Wine (Cktl) ⅔ measure port, ⅓ measure brandy. Stir over ice, strain into a cocktail glass and add a twist of orange peel.

Port Wine Cobbler (Cktl) dissolve a teaspoon of sugar in a little water in a highball glass. Add ice, 75mls (3fl.ozs) Port, top with fruit in season and serve with straws.

Port Wine Eggnog (Cktl) 1 egg, 125mls (1gill) milk, 75mls (3fl.ozs) Port, 2 dashes gomme syrup. Shake well over ice, strain into a collins glass and top with grated nutmeg.

Port Wine Flip (Cktl) 100mls (4fl.ozs) Port, 1 egg yolk, 1 teaspoon powdered sugar. Shake well with ice, strain into a small tumbler and top with grated cinnamon.

Port Wine Institute (Port) a body that governs the Port trade, decides how much grape must may be made.

Port Wine Negus (Cktl) pour 75mls (3fl.ozs) of hot water onto a sugar cube in an old-fashioned glass. Add 50mls (2fl.ozs) Port and top with grated nutmeg.

Port Wine Sangaree (Cktl) 55mls (2¼ fl.ozs) Port, 10mls (½fl.oz) syrup. Stir with crushed ice, strain into a highball glass filled with ice and add grated nutmeg.

Portwyn (S.Afr) the South African for Port-style wine.

Portz (Ger) village (Anb): Mosel-Saar-Ruwer. (Ber): Obermosel. (Gro): Gipfel. (Vins): Sites not yet chosen.

Porusots [Le] (Fr) *see* Poruzots (Le).

Porusots-Dessus [Le] (Fr) *see* Poruzots-Dessus (Le).

Poruzots [Le] (Fr) a Premier Cru vineyard in the A.C. commune of Meursault, Côte de Beaune, Burgundy. 1.6ha. Also known as Le Porusots.

Poruzots-Dessus [Le] (Fr) a Premier Cru vineyard in the A.C. commune of Meursault, Côte de Beaune, Burgundy. 1.8ha. Also known as Le Porusots-Dessus.

Posada (Sp) inn/tavern.

Posavje (Slo) a wine region in Slovenia. Grape varieties: Chardonnay, Modra frankija (Blaufränkisch), Pinot grigio, Riesling, Traminer, Neuburger, Yellow Muscatel. Home to Cvicek (light red wine).

Posca (Lat) a cheap wine carried by the Roman soldiers.

Posho (Afr) maize flour used in the making of pombe beer.

Poshoote (Eng) the fifteenth and sixteenth century name for Posset.

Pošip (Euro) a white grape variety grown in Dalmatia.

Positano (It) a bitter-sweet apéritif wine.

Poso (Sp) sediment/lees.

Possenheim (Ger) village (Anb): Franken. (Ber): Steigerwald. (Gro): Burgweg. (Vins): Assorted parts of vineyards.

Posset (Eng) a middle ages drink of hot curdled milk with ale or wine and flavoured with spices, sugar and honey.

Posset Pot (Eng) an early eighteenth century large double handled bottle with a flat cover. Drink was sucked through the spout Held approximately 2pints (1litre).

Possonnière [La] (Fr) a commune in the A.C. Savennières, Anjou-Saumur, Loire.

Posta Arignano (It) a D.O.C. wine produced by d'Alfonso del Sordo in San Severo, Puglia. White is produced from Bombino, Trebbiano and Malvasia grapes, rosé from 100% Montepulciano grapes.

Postaller (Aus) a vineyard site on the banks of the

River Danube situated in the Wachau region, Niederösterreich.

Postel Brasserie (Bel) an abbaye brewery based in north-eastern Belgium.

Posten (Ger) vineyard (Anb): Mittelrhein. (Ber): Bacharach. (Gro): Schloss Stahleck. (Vil): Bacharach.

Post Horn Premium Ale (Eng) a 5% alc by vol. ale brewed by the Coach House Brewing C°. Ltd., Cheshire.

Post House Cellar (S.Afr) a winery (established 1997) based in Stellenbosch, Western Cape. 37ha. Grape varieties: Cabernet sauvignon, Chenin blanc, Merlot, Petit verdot, Shiraz. Label: Penny Black. Website: http://www.posthousewines.co.za

Post Mix (Eng) the name given to concentrated syrups dispensed at the bar with water at ratios of (5:1 to 7:1). Concentrates are of cola, lemonade, soda, tonic, etc.

Postnoff (Rus) a smooth vodka 40% alc by vol. Quadruple distilled and produced by Wimpex Ltd.

Post Stones (S.Afr) the label for a wine produced by the False Bay Vineyards winery, Wellington, Western Cape.

Postup (Cro) a dry red wine from the Croatia region. Made from the Plavac grape, is high in alcohol and full-bodied.

Post Winery (USA) a small winery based in Altus.

Posum Trot Vineyards (USA) a small vineyard based in Unionville, Indiana. 2.5ha. Produces French hybrid wines.

Pot (Eng) a slang name given to a pint tankard/mug.

Pot (Eng) a slang term used to denote that a customer has a drink bought for him by another customer in a public house which is 'in the pot' (held in stock) for him.

Pot (Fr) a specially shaped bottle containing 50cls peculiar to the Burgundy region especially in the Beaujolais district.

Pot (Fr) jug/tankard.

Pot (Fr) an old wine measure now no longer used.

Pot à Bière (Fr) beer tankard.

Potabilis (Lat) drinkable (potus: a drink).

Potable (Fr) drinkable/fit to drink.

Potable Spirits (Eng) drinkable spirits.

Potable Strength (Eng) the name given to spirits that passed the gunpowder proofing test in the olden days. see Proof.

Pot Ale (Scot) the spent wash in malt whisky production.

Pot Ale (Ire) the religious establishments' barley-based spirit, earliest record of spirit in the British Isles.

Potash Salts (Eng) used in the rectification of spirits (purifying).

Potassium Bitartrate (Sp) a deposit sometimes found in bottles of Sherry which the wine naturally contains. Is removed by storage at low temperatures then filtering. Also used as a preservative in wines (aids in stabillising the wine). Another name for Potassium Hydrogen Tartrate.

Potassium Carbonate (Eng) K_2CO_3 used to reduce the acidity (pH) of wines that contain a high amount of tartaric acid.

Potassium Ferrocyanide (Eng) $K_4Fe(CN)6.3H_2O$ known as blue finings. Used to clear an excess of metallic salts from the wine. If these salts were left they would tend to oxidise with the air, leaving the wine cloudy and bitter. Must be used with caution.

Potassium Hydrogen Tartrate (Eng) $KHC_4H_4O_6$ forms tartrate crystals which show when the wine is chilled to low temperatures. Are harmless and can be decanted off or will disappear when the wine is warmed. Also known as Potassium Bitartrate.

Potassium Metabisulphide (Eng) $K_3S_2O_5$ also known as campden tablets. Is added to the grape must or wine to inhibit the growth of micro-organisms.

Pot à Thée (Ch.Isles) teapot.

Potatio (Lat) a drinking bout.

Potation (Eng) the fifteenth and sixteenth century term for the drinking of alcoholic beverages.

Potatory (Eng) an old fifteenth century word to denote a person who has succumbed to alcoholic drink.

Potàvel (Port) drinkable.

Potàvel Agua (Port) drinking water.

Potbelly Brewery Ltd (Eng) a brewery (established 2005). (Add): Sydney Street, Kettering, Northamptonshire NN16 0HY. Brews: Aisling 4% alc by vol., Red Wing 4.8% alc by vol. Website: http://www.potbelly-brewery.co.uk 'E'mail: toni@potbelly-brewery.co.uk

Pot Boy (Austr) barman. See also Potman.

Pot de Vin (Fr) see Vin du Marche.

Poteen (Ire) an illegal spirit made from either grain or potatoes (legalised in March 1998). see Poitin and Potscheen.

Potel (Wal) bottle.

Potell (Eng) the old middle ages spelling of bottle.

Potensac (Fr) a commune in the Bas-Médoc, north-western Bordeaux. Has A.C. Médoc status.

Potential Alcohol (Eng) the amount of alcohol that could be produced by fermentation from a certain amount of sugar. see Actual Alcohol, Total Alcohol.

Poterium (Lat) goblet. See also Culullus.

Potferré (Fr) an Armagnac producer. (Add): Domaine de Jouanda de Jean du Haut, 40190 Arthez d'Armagnac, Villeneuve de Marsan. 38ha. in the Bas Armagnac.

Pot Gascon (Fr) the traditional bottle used for Armagnac. Also called a Basquaise.

Potheen (Ire) see Poteen.

Potio (Lat) drink.

Potion (Eng) an old word for a drink. i.e. "*Take a potion with me*", usually spirits.

Potion (Eng) a drink made from a mixture of drinks, herbs and flavourings that was used as a medicine or élixer in the Middle Ages.

Potitare (Lat) to drink more.

Potitianum (It) a red wine produced in Sicily in Roman times.

Potjie Effe Droog (S.Afr) the label for a white blend wine produced by the Mooiuitsig Wine Cellars winery, Robertson, Western Cape.

Potman (Austr)(Eng) barman. *See also* Pot Boy.

Potor (Lat) a drinker (of alcohol).

Potosi (Mex) the name given to a range of rums (Anejo, Blanco and Oro) produced by Destileria Huasteca.

Potrix (Lat) a female drinker.

Pots Ale (Eng) a 3.8% alc by vol. ale brewed by The Cheriton Brewhouse, Hampshire.

Potscheen (USA) a legal version (legalised in March 1998) of the illegal Irish whiskey (Poteen). *See also* Poitin.

Pot Still (Scot) a copper still used for the distillation of malt whisky. Also used in Ireland. *see* Cognac, rum and Bergstrom. Also Alambic Armagnaçais, Alambic Charentais and Proquero.

Pott (Ger) a large rum distiller based at Rinteln. Produces rum under the Pott label.

Pöttelsdorf (Aus) a wine-producing area in the Mattersburg district.

Potter Distillery (Can) a distillery based in British Columbia. Produces Canadian whiskies.

Potter Drainer (USA) equipment that drains the must through fine screens inside a tank, resulting in free-run juice.

Potting (Eng) an old slang seventeenth century term for going on a drinking 'binge', the pot was the name used for a beer tankard. *see* Pot.

Pöttinger (Aus) a vineyard site on the banks of the River Danube situated in the Wachau region, Niederösterreich.

Pottle (Eng) a fourteenth century wine measure of half a gallon capacity.

Potton Brewing Company (Eng) a brewery (established 1997). (Add): 10 Shannon Place, Potton, Sandy, Bedfordshire SG19 2SP. Brewed a ranges of beers for the 2002 Golden Jubilee of Queen Elizabeth Second. Besides being sold on draught, the beers were sold in 4 bottle packs and each pack contained one each of the Crown Ale at 5.5% alc by vol./Sceptre Ale at 4.8% alc by vol./Orb Ale at 4.3% alc by vol./Throne Ale at 4.1% alc by vol. Brews: John Cunningham Night Fighter 4% alc by vol., Potton Gold 4.1% alc by vol., Shambles Bitter 4.3% alc by vol., Shannon IPA 3.6% alc by vol., The Village Bike 4.3% alc by vol. Also produces Potton Mixed Devon Cider 6% alc by vol. Website: http://www.potton-brewery.co.uk 'E'mail: info@potton-brewery.co.uk

Potton Mixed Devon Cider (Eng) a 6% alc by vol. cider produced by the Potton Brewing Company, Devon.

Pott's Brauerei (Ger) a brewery based in Oelde. Brews: Pott's Landbier, Pott's Pilsener.

Pott's Landbier (Ger) a 4.8% alc by vol. bottled lager brewed by Pott's Brauerei, Oelde.

Pott's Pilsener (Ger) a 4.8% alc by vol. bottled pilsner brewed by Pott's Brauerei, Oelde.

Pottsville Porter (USA) the Yuengling of Pennsylvania's dark 'roasted beer' 5% alc by vol.

Potulentus (Lat) drinkable.

Potus (Lat) a drink (potare: to drink), also denotes a drunken person. *See also* Vinolentus.

Pouançay (Fr) a commune in the Vienne département. Has A.C. Saumur status.

Pougeoise [Charles] (Fr) récoltants-manipulants in Champagne. (Add): 21-23 Boulevard Paul Goerg, 51130 Vertus. Produces vintage and non-vintage wines.

Pouhon de Bande (Bel) a natural spring mineral water from Pouhon de Bande.

Pouillon (Fr) a Cru Champagne village in the Canton de Bourgogne. District: Reims.

Pouilly Blanc Fumé (Fr) an A.C. dry white wine from the Central Vineyards of the Loire. Made with Sauvignon blanc.

Pouilly Fuissé (Fr) an A.C. dry white wine from the Mâconnais in the southern Burgundy. Made from the Chardonnay grape. Minimum alc by vol. 11%.

Pouilly Fumé (Fr) an A.C. dry white wine from the Central Vineyards of the Loire. Made from the Sauvignon blanc grape.

Pouilly-Loché (Fr) an A.C. dry white wine from the Mâconnais in the southern Burgundy. Made from the Chardonnay grape from around the town of Loché.

Pouilly-sur-Loire (Fr) a commune in the Central Vineyards of the Loire. Produces a wine of the same name from the Chasselas grape.

Pouilly-Vinzelles (Fr) an A.C. white wine from the Mâconnais in the southern Burgundy. Made from the Chardonnay grape from around the town of Vinzelles.

Poulet Père et Fils (Fr) an old established Burgundy négociant based at 12 Rue Chaumergy, 21200 Beaune. Noted for their heavy-styled wines.

Poulet Poulet (N.Z) a sparkling wine produced by Montana Wines.

Poulettes [Les] (Fr) a Premier Cru vineyard in the A.C. commune of Nuits-Saint-Georges, Côte de Nuits, Burgundy 2.4ha.

Poulsard (Fr) a black grape variety grown in the Jura. Used to make the local Vin Gris of same name (a variety of the Pinot).

Poulsart (Fr) a white grape variety grown in the Jura.

Poulsen and C°'s Destillation (Nor) a producer of aquavits under the control of A/S Vinmonopolet.

Pouparae Park (N.Z) a winery. (Add): Bushmere Road, P.O. Box 419, Gisborne. Grape varieties: Chardonnay, Riesling, Sauvignon blanc, Pinotage.

Pour [to] (Eng) the process of transferring liquids from one container to another e.g. to pour wine from a bottle to a glass. (Aus) = giessen, (Fr) = verser, (Ger) = giessen, (Hol) = gieten, (Sp) = echar.

Pourcy (Fr) a Cru Champagne village in the Canton de Châtillon-sur-Marne. District: Reims.

Pour Mes Amis (S.Afr) the label for a white wine (Sauvignon blanc 75% and Sémillon blend 25%)

produced by the Newton Johnson Wines winery, Walker Bay, Western Cape.

Pourridié (Lat) a family of fungi that attacks the vine roots. *see* Armillaria Root-Rot.

Pourrisseux (Fr) an alternative name for the Melon de Bourgogne grape.

Pourriture aigre (Fr) bitter rot, occurs in sweet white wine-producing areas.

Pourriture gris (Fr) grey rot, is *Botrytis cinerea* (pourriture noble) in red wine areas, attacks the skin colour and bouquet (aroma) of grapes and wines.

Pourriture noble (Fr) noble rot *Botrytis cinerea*.

Pourriture vulgaire (Fr) describes both *Aspergillus* and Penicillium mould. Similar to Pourriture Aigre (bitter rot) that occurs in sweet white wine-producing areas.

Pourshins (Wal) a natural spring mineral water from Trofarth, Conway. Mineral contents (milligrammes per litre): Sodium 7.7mg/l, Calcium 10.6mg/l, Magnesium 4.8mg/l, Potassium 0.6mg/l, Bicarbonates 46mg/l, Chlorides 11mg/l, Sulphates 17.5mg/l, Fluorides 0.1mg/l, Nitrates 1mg/l. pH 6.8

Pousada (Port) an inn/hotel.

Pousse (Fr) a malady of wine caused by a bacteria which attacks the tartaric acid in wine causing a brown deposit to appear, treated with tartaric acid and bisulphates.

Pousse Café (Cktl) these are cocktails made up of layers of different coloured liquids and of different densities which are gently floated on top of each other with the aid of a barspoon. Known in the USA as floated liqueurs. *See*: Albermarle Fancy Free, Angel's Delight, Angel's Dream, Angel's Kiss, Angel's Tit, Angel's Wing, Aunt Jemima , Bacardi Elixer Pousse, B52, Champerelle, Fifth Avenue Cocktail, French Pousse Café, Golden Slipper, Irish Nigger, Jersey Lily, Knickerbein, Port and Starboard, Pousse Café, Pousse Café American, Pousse Café 81, Pousse Café Parisien, Pousse l'Amour, Princess Pousse Café, Rainbow Cocktail, Santini, Stars and Stripes, Union Jack, Welsh Connection, Yuma Jana Cocktail, Xochimilco. *See also* Stirring Rod. (USA) = floated liqueurs.

Pousse Café [1] (Pousse Café) place in layers as above in the following order equal quantities of grenadine, yellow Chartreuse, crème Yvette, white crème de menthe, green Chartreuse and Cognac.

Pousse Café [2] (Pousse Café) place in layers as above in the following order. ⅙ each of grenadine, brown crème de cacao, maraschino, orange Curaçao, green crème de menthe, parfait amour, liqueur Cognac.

Pousse Café American (Pousse Café) place in order in a pousse café glass. 1 teaspoon raspberry syrup, ⅙ each of maraschino, crème vanille, Curaçao, yellow Chartreuse and liqueur brandy. Also known as the Rainbow.

Pousse Café 81 (Pousse Café) equal quantities of the following poured gently on top of each other in

the following order. grenadine, crème de menthe, Galliano, kümmel and brandy.

Pousse Café Glass (Fr) a thin narrow glass specially designed for pousse cafés 50mls (⅜ gill) in capacity. Similar in style to an Elgin.

Pousse Café Parisien (Pousse Café) place into a pousse café glass gently in the following order ⅕ glass sirop de framboise, Marasquin de Zara, red Curaçao, Yellow Chartreuse and Champagne.

Pousse l'Amour [1] (Pousse Café) into a pousse café glass pour in order 3–4 dashes grenadine, yolk of an egg, 20mls (⅙ gill) maraschino, 20mls (⅙ gill) Champagne. Do not stir. Drink in one gulp.

Pousse l'Amour [2] (Pousse Café) into a pousse café glass pour in order ¼ measure maraschino, egg yolk, Bénédictine and Cognac.

Pousse Rapière (Cktl) 25mls (1fl.oz) Armagnac topped up with vin sauvage. Serve chilled. Originates from the Pyrénées.

Poutures [Les] (Fr) a Premier Cru vineyard in the A.C. commune of Pommard, Côte de Beaune, Burgundy 4.2ha.

Povardarje (Ser) main area of production in Makedonija. Produces predominantly red wines.

Poverella (Bra) a red grape variety.

Poverty Bay (N.Z) a wine area of the central eastern part of the North Island.

Powdery Mildew (Eng) *Oidium tuckerii*.

Powell (Wal) a beer, wines and spirits wholesaler based in Newtown, Powys, Mid-Wales. Operates under the name of Eagle Brewery. Took over the Powys Brewery in Newtown in 1983. Brews Samuel Powell's Traditional Bitter 1040 O.G. Bitter now brewed by Woods Brewery, Shropshire.

Power Drury Lda (Mad) a shipping company (established 1888), now part of the Madeira Wine Association (since 1925).

Powerful (Eng) a term that describes a red wine that has a forceful bouquet and flavour.

Powerhouse (Eng) a strong cask-conditioned bitter ale 1050 O.G. brewed by the Battersea Brewery in London.

Power's Distillery (Ire) a noted distiller based in Dublin. Produces Power's Gold Label (part of the Irish Distillers Group).

Powers Gold Label (Ire) a leading brand of Irish whiskey, a blend of Power's Pot-still whiskey and Grain whiskey.

Power's Special Dry (Ire) a brand of dry gin distilled by the Power's Distillery in Dublin.

Power Station Porter (Eng) a 4.9% alc by vol. porter brewed by the Battersea Brewery C°. Ltd., London.

Powwow (Eng) the label for a bottled mineral water produced in large formats for offices, canteens, factories, etc.

Poysdorf (Aus) a wine area in the Weinviertel. Produces red and white wines.

Pozohondo (Sp) a Vino de la Tierra of La Mancha, 30kms south of the province Albacete. Grape varieties include: Monastrell and Airén. Produce red and white wines.

Pozzillo (It) a sparkling natural spring mineral water

P

from Pozzillo. Mineral contents (milligrammes per litre): Sodium 252.1mg/l, Calcium 82.1mg/l, Magnesium 75mg/l, Potassium 36.8mg/l, Chlorides 294mg/l, Sulphates 220mg/l, Fluorides 0.51mg/l, Nitrates 43mg/l, Silicates 27.7mg/l. pH 6.75

P.P.L. (Eng) *abbr*: Packaged Premium Lager.

P.P.S. (Eng) *abbr*: Premium Packaged Spirit.

P▲P Palo Cortado (Sp) a rare Sherry (250litres per year) from a solera started in 1921 (from original Sherries of 1911) by Osborne. Has sun-dried Palomino grapes added.

Prában na Linne (Scot) a Gaelic whisky company at Eilean Larmain, Isle of Skye. Produces a 21 year old Gaelic vatted malt of the same name, plus 12 year old Poit Dhubh.

Pracastello (It) a sparkling natural spring mineral water from S. Pellegrino Terme (BG), Lombardy. Mineral contents (milligrammes per litre): Sodium 29.4mg/l, Calcium 168mg/l, Magnesium 48.6mg/l, Potassium 2.2mg/l, Bicarbonates 241mg/l, Chlorides 50.4mg/l, Sulphates 408.4mg/l, Fluorides 0.62mg/l, Nitrates 1.9mg/l. pH 7.37

Pradel (Fr) a wine from the Côtes de Provence.

Pradicino-Rio delle Ghiaie (It) a natural spring mineral water from Pradicino.

Prädikatssekt (Ger) a grade of sekt which must contain at least 60% of German wine.

Prädikatssekt mit Geographischer Bezeichung (Ger) the top appellation of sekt, only a limited amount made. e.g. Kupferberg Herringer.

Prädikatsweine (Aus) also known as Qualitätswein Besonderer Reife und Leseart. Law requires that residual sugar achieved only through the interruption of fermentation/minimum alc by vol. 5%/harvested grapes have to be presented to the official controller/neither the must or the wine is permitted to be chaptalised (sugared)/a maximum yield of 9000kgs of grapes per hectare (6750litres of wine maximum)/harvesting by machines not permitted (exemptions for spätlese and eisweine)/sales of wines may not commence until 1st May of following year (1st March for spätlese)/bottling has be completed in Austria/exportation of wine only in bottles. *see* Spälese/Auslese/Eiswein/Strohwein/Beerenausles e/Ausbruch/Trockenbeerenauslese.

Prädikatsweine (Ger) quality wine.

Prädikatsweinversteigerer (Ger) the name given to growers who sell their natural wine by auction, formally known as Naturweinversteigerer.

Pradis (It) a natural spring mineral water from Clauzetto, Pordenone, Friuli. Mineral contents (milligrammes per litre): Sodium 0.59mg/l, Calcium 30.8mg/l, Magnesium 16.7mg/l, Potassium 0.1mg/l, Chlorides 1.2mg/l, Sulphates 5mg/l, Nitrates 5mg/l. pH 8.2

Prado [El] (Sp) a Sherry producer based in Jerez.

Prado Cocktail (Cktl) ⅔ measure tequila silver, ⅓ measure lemon juice, 10mls (½ fl.oz) Maraschino, 3 dashes grenadine, ½ egg white, shake over ice, strain into a sour glass, top with a slice of lemon and a cherry.

Prado Enea (Sp) a red wine produced by the Bodegas Muga S.A. Rioja. Made from 20%–30% Garnacha, 10% Mazuelo and 60% Tempranillo. Aged for 1 year in oak vats of 18000litres and for 4 years in Barricas, then aged 2 years minimum in bottle.

Prado Lagar Reserva Especial (Sp) *see* Bodegas Marqués de Murrieta.

Pradwood (Eng) a 4.2% alc by vol. ale brewed by Marston's, Burton-on-Trent using goldings hops.

Praelatenberg (Fr) an A.C. Alsace Grand Cru vineyard in Orschwiller and Kintzheim, Bas-Rhin 12ha.

Praenestinum (It) a red wine produced in central-western Italy in Roman times.

Praetutium (It) a white wine produced in north-eastern Italy in Roman times.

Praga (Czech) a 5% alc by vol. bottled premium lager beer.

Prager (Aus) a winery (13ha) based in the Wachau. (Add): Toni Bodenstein, 3610 Weissenkirchen 48. Grape varieties: Chardonnay, Grüner veltliner, Muskateller, Riesling, Sauvignon blanc, Zweigelt. Produces a range of dry and sweet (botrytised) wines.

Prager Winery and Port Works (USA) a winery based near St. Helena, Napa Valley, California. Grape varieties: Cabernet sauvignon and Chardonnay. Produces varietal and dessert wines.

Prague Breweries (Czec) formed by a merger in 1992 of three of the four Prague breweries. The third largest brewery in Czech Republic. Mestan, (established 1895) as Prvni Prazsky Mestansky Pipover) is based in Holesovice. Staropramen (established 1869) is based in Prague. Braník (established 1900) is the youngest member.

Praidl (Aus) a vineyard site based on the banks of the River Kamp situated in the Kamptal region.

Prairie (Eng) a 5% alc by vol. ale brewed by the Wolf Brewery, Ltd., Norfolk.

Prairie Chicken (Cktl) 20mls (⅙ gill) dry gin, 1 egg, pepper and salt. Place the egg in a wine glass (yolk unbroken), add gin, pepper and salt.

Prairie Crystal Spring Water (Can) a natural spring mineral water from Marchand, Manitoba.

Prairie Oyster (Cktl) (Non-alc) equal measures of Worcestershire sauce, vinegar and tomato sauce (ketchup). Mix well together, add yolk of egg (unbroken) and red pepper (do not stir). Also known as a Mountain Oyster.

Prairie Oyster Cocktail (Cktl) as for Prairie Oyster with the addition of 25mls (⅛ gill) brandy added and top with cayenne pepper.

P.R.D. (Austr) *abbr*: Partial Root-zone Drying, where one side of the vine is allowed to dry out and stress slightly whilst the other side is watered. Used in the Riverland. *See also* R.D.I.

Prélat (Ger) vineyard (Anb): Mosel-Saar-Ruwer. (Ber): Bernkastel. (Gro): Schwarzlay. (Vil): Erden.

Prelude Vineyard (Austr) a vineyard which is a part of the Leeuwin Estate, Western Australia.

Pramnian Wine (Gre) a sweet, dessert wine produced in ancient Greece in Homer's time.

P

Prandell (It) a producer of sparkling (metodo tradizionale) wines based in Lombardy.

Prâs [Les] (Fr) a wine-producing village in the commune of Solutré-Pouilly in A.C. Pouilly Fuissé, Mâcon, Burgundy.

Präsent (Ger) vineyard (Anb): Nahe. (Ber): Schloss Böckelheim. (Gro): Paradiesgarten. (Vil): Meddersheim.

Prata (Bra) a natural spring mineral water from Prata. Mineral contents (milligrammes per litre): Sodium 2.11mg/l, Calcium 8.53mg/l, Magnesium 4.71mg/l, Potassium 3mg/l, Bicarbonates 51.36mg/l, Sulphates 2.91mg/l, Fluorides 0.22mg/l, Nitrates 2.42mg/l. pH 6.29

Prata (It) a sparkling natural spring mineral water from Pratella, Caserta. Mineral contents (milligrammes per litre): Sodium 3.9mg/l, Calcium 162.4mg/l, Magnesium 12.2mg/l, Potassium 2.9mg/l, Bicarbonates 512.4mg/l, Chlorides 6.1mg/l, Sulphates 4.5mg/l, Fluorides 0.1mg/l, Nitrates 5.1mg/l, Silicates 4.3mg/l, Oxygen 7.3mg/l. pH 6.76

Prata do Vale (Bra) an acidic natural spring mineral water. Mineral contents (milligrammes per litre): Sodium 6mg/l, Calcium 1mg/l, Magnesium 0.48mg/l, Potassium 0.7mg/l, Bicarbonates 1.22mg/l, Chlorides 9.78mg/l, Sulphates 3.2mg/l, Nitrates 0.4mg/l. pH 4.5

Prava (Slo) a natural spring mineral water brand.

Praxxan (Sp) a spirit-based drink made from aromatic herbs and berries. 21.5% alc by vol. Also known as 22 (this is the twentysecond blend).

Prayssac (Fr) a wine-producing area in northern Cahors, south-western France (red wines).

Prazanka (Czec) a dark, draught beer brewed by the Holesovice Brewery in Prague.

Preakness Cocktail (Cktl) ⅔ measure Bourbon whiskey, ⅓ measure Italian vermouth, dash Angostura, 2 dashes Bénédictine. Stir over ice, strain into a cocktail glass and top with a twist of lemon peel juice.

Prealpi (It) a sparkling natural spring mineral water from Monte dei Giubilini. Mineral contents (milligrammes per litre): Sodium 30.8mg/l, Calcium 70.4mg/l, Magnesium 19.4mg/l, Potassium 1.6mg/l, Bicarbonates 311.2mg/l, Chlorides 12.8mg/l, Sulphates 43.8mg/l, Nitrates 7mg/l, Silicates 11.4mg/l. pH 7.98

Preanger (E.Ind) a noted coffee-producing area in Java.

Préau (Fr) a vineyard in the A.C. commune of Rully, Côte Chalonnaise, Burgundy.

Preblauer (Aus) a sparkling natural spring mineral water. Mineral contents (milligrammes per litre): Sodium 646mg/l, Calcium 177mg/l, Magnesium 25mg/l, Potassium 42mg/l, Bicarbonates 2212mg/l, Chlorides 52mg/l, Sulphates 105mg/l, Fluorides 0.2mg/l, Boron 9mg/l, Silicates 67mg/l.

Prèchet (Fr) an alternative name for the Malbec grape.

Precipitated Chalk (USA) used to cut down the acitity in grape must.

Precipitation (Eng) the action of tartrates forming crystals through exposure of the wine to low temperatures. Encouraged in some wines especially in Germany before the wine is bottled to remove excess acidity.

Précoce (Fr) a wine which has come forward too early, a precocious wine.

Précoce de Malingre (Fr) a lesser white grape variety.

Predicati (It) the name of an unofficial joint brand-name as opposed to an individual brand-name. e.g. Sassicaia, Tignanello.

Predicato del Muschio (It) a Chardonnay and Pinot bianco wine produced in Tuscany. A private classification wine from Terra Capitolari Hills (1 of 4).

Predicato del Selvante (It) a 100% Pinot bianco wine produced in Tuscany. A private classification wine from Terra Capitolari Hills (1 of 4).

Predicato di Bitriàca (It) a wine produced from a blend of Sangiovese plus a minimum of 30% Cabernet sauvignon produced in Tuscany. A private classification wine from Terra Capitolari Hills (1 of 4).

Predicato di Cardisco (It) a 100% Sangiovese wine produced in Tuscany. A private classification wine from Terra Capitolari Hills (1 of 4).

Predigtstuhl (Ger) vineyard (Anb): Franken. (Ber): Mainviereck. (Gro): Not yet assigned. (Vil): Dorfprozelten.

Preferido (Sp) a red wine produced by the Bodegas Berberana S.A. Rioja. Produced from 80% minimum Tempranillo and has no ageing.

Prefillossero (It) lit: 'pre-phylloxera', a wine produced by the Lisini Estate in Montalcino, Tuscany. The wine is produced from ungrafted vines.

Préhy (Fr) a commune in the A.C. Chablis, northern Burgundy.

Preignac (Fr) a commune within the Sauternes district in south-western Bordeaux.

Preiselbeerlikoer (Ger) a cranberry liqueur.

Preiss Henny (Fr) an Alsace producer. (Add): 68630 Mittelwhir 33ha.

Preiss Zimmer (Fr) a wine merchant based in Riquewihr, Alsace.

Prélèvement (Fr) the practice of randomly sampling grapes to determine the correct time to harvest.

Prelude Cocktail (Cktl) ½ measure Noilly Prat, ¼ measure peach liqueur, ¼ measure peach juice, 2 dashes dry gin, dash crème de framboise, ½ teaspoon clear honey. Shake well over ice, strain into a cocktail glass, dress with a slice of peach and mint sprig.

Prelum (Lat) wine press.

Prémeaux (Fr) a wine village within the A.C. commune of Nuits-Saint-Georges, Côte de Nuits. Its vineyards are all classed **Premier Cru** (10 in all): Aux Perdrix, Clos de la Maréchale, Clos des Argillières, Clos des Arlots, Clos des Corvées, Clos des Forêts, Clos des Grandes-Vignes, Les Clos Saint-Marc, Les Corvées-Paget, Les Didiers. 40.3ha.

Premiat (Rum) the brand-name of high-quality wines that are produced for export.

Premier Beverages (Eng) a large company that is responsible for Kenco-Typhoo. Brand-names include: Bournvita, Cadbury, Cocoa, Fresh Brew, Marvel, Q.T., Suprema. (Add): Pasture Road, Moreton, Wirral.

Premier Côtes de Gaillac (Fr) the designation for wines from Gaillac that have attained 12% alc by vol.

Premier Crew (Eng) a 4.3% alc by vol. ale brewed by Tarka Ales Ltd., Devon.

Premier Cru (Fr) the second classification in Burgundy, next to the Grand Cru.

Premier Cru (Fr) refers to Champagne, approximately 40 villages have this second designation. 90%–99%. *see* Échelle des Crus, Grand Cru.

Premier Cru (Fr) a 6% alc by vol. premium beer brewed by the Kronenbourg 1664 Brewery, Strasbourg.

Premier Cru Classé Sauternes (Fr) the top wine classification of sweet white wines in Sauternes and Barsac. There are 12 châteaux so classified: Château d'Yquem (Premier Grand Cru Classé), Château Climens, Château Coutet, Château de Rayne-Vigneau, Château Guiraud, Château Haut-Peyraguey, Château Lafaurie-Peyraguey, Château la Tour Blanche, Château Rabaud-Promis, Château Rieussec, Château Siglas-Rabaud, Château Suduiraut.

Première (Fr) a demi-sec perry blended from French and Belgian products. Sold in a Champagne-style bottle.

Première Chauffe (Fr) the first distillate of Cognac.

Premier Écoulage (Fr) the first racking when wine is taken off the skins, pips etc. (this residue is then used as Vin de Presse).

Premières Côtes de Blaye (Fr) an A.C. wine-producing region based in north-eastern Bordeaux. (Red, demi-sec, sweet and dry white wines). Soil: clay and sand on top, limestone sub-soil. Grape varieties: Cabernet franc, Cabernet sauvignon, Colombard, Malbec, Merlot, Muscadelle, Sauvignon blanc, Sémillon. *See also* Blaye.

Premières Côtes de Bordeaux (Fr) a commune on the eastern bank of the river Garonne. Commences from opposite the town of Bordeaux to the Sauternes. Produces sweet white wines.

Premières Côtes de Gaillac (Fr) the designation for wines from Gaillac that have attained 12% alc by vol.

Première Taille (Fr) the second pressing of the Champagne grapes.

Premier Grand Cru (S.Afr) the makers top classification for white wines only (not an official classification).

Premier Grand Cru Classé (Fr) the top classification of the wines of the Médoc from the 1855 classification. Château Lafite, Château Latour, Château Margaux, Château Haut Brion (Graves) and in 1973 Mouton Rothschild. Also Château Y'Quem in Sauternes.

Premier Grand Cru (S.Afr) the label for a white wine (Chenin blanc, Colombard and Sauvignon blanc blend) produced by the Bellingham winery, Wellington, Western Cape.

Premiers Grands Crus (Fr) a classification of Pomerol wines in Bordeaux.

Premio Uropeo Mercurio d'Oro (It) an award presented for beers (first presented in 1970).

Premium-Aenigma (S.Afr) the label for a white wine (Chardonnay) produced by the Neil Ellis Wines, Stellenbosch, Western Cape.

Premium Bier (Ger) a 5% alc by vol. draught, canned or bottled lager brewed by Lowenbräu. Name replaces Lowenbräu.

Premium Bitter (Eng) a cask-conditioned bitter 1039 O.G. brewed by the Gibbs Mew Brewery in Salisbury, Wiltshire.

Premium Bitter (Eng) a cask-conditioned bitter 1036 O.G. brewed by the Moorhouses Brewery of Burnley.

Premium Cape Wines (S.Afr) a négociant company (established 2003) based in Stellenbosch, Western Cape. Labels include: De Sonnenberg, Imvelo, Open Sky, Uhambo.

Premium Scottish Export (Scot) a 3.9% alc by vol. beer from Belhaven Brewery, Spott Road, Dunbar, Lothian.

Premium Verum Lager (Ger) a classification for a fine lager (no additives or chemicals).

Prendiville (Austr) a red (Cabernet sauvignon) wine produced by the Sandalford Estate, Western Australia.

Prensa (Sp). The third pressing of the grapes in Jerez. The wine produced from this is usually made into brandy or vinegar. The pressing is usually done by hydraulic press. *See also* Espirraque.

Prensa de Lagar (Port) wine press.

Prensal (Sp) an alternative name for the white Moll grape variety.

Prensar (Port) to press/to squeeze.

Prepared Cocktails (USA) these are cocktails that can be made and kept without losing their flavour or crystallising. Only certain cocktails will stand up to this. Usually finished by adding ice and a sparkling liquid (tonic, soda, Champagne, lemonade).

Prepecenica (Pol) *see* Slivovitz.

Pre-Prandials (Eng) another name for apéritif.

Prerov Brewery (Czec) a noted brewery based in central Czec.

Près (Fr) near. i.e. Près Reims (near Reims).

Preša za Vino (Cro) wine press.

Presby (Bel) a natural spring mineral water from Yvoir. Mineral contents (milligrammes per litre): Sodium 7mg/l, Calcium 84mg/l, Magnesium 11mg/l, Potassium 1.5mg/l, Bicarbonates 250mg/l, Chlorides 15mg/l, Sulphates 34mg/l, Nitrates 14mg/l, Silicates 14mg/l.

Presbyterian (Cktl) place 1 measure rye whiskey, dash Angostura into a tumbler, add ice and top up with ½ soda water, ½ ginger ale.

Président (Ger) the brand-name for a rum produced by Hansen in Flensburg.

President (Switz) the brand-name of a beer used by Feldschlösschen and Haldengut.

President Brut (It) a sparkling (cuve close) wine produced by Riccadonna in the Piemonte region.

President Cocktail (Cktl) 1 measure pineapple juice, 1 measure rum, dash grenadine. Shake over ice and strain into a cocktail glass.

Presidente [1] (Cktl) 35mls (1½ fl.ozs) Bacardi White Label, 35mls (1½ fl.ozs) red vermouth. Stir over ice, strain into a cocktail glass and serve with a twist of orange peel.

Presidente [2] (Cktl) 50mls (2fl.ozs) Bacardi Gold Label, 25mls (1fl.oz) dry vermouth, dash grenadine. Stir together over ice, strain into a cocktail glass, add a twist of orange peel and cherry.

Presidente (Mex) the brand-name of a noted Mexican brandy.

President's Ale (Eng) a limited edition ale (121 bottles) produced by the Truman brewery.

President's Choice (Can) a sparkling natural spring mineral water. Mineral contents (milligrammes per litre): Sodium 20mg/l, Calcium 132mg/l, Magnesium 41mg/l, Potassium 1mg/l, Bicarbonates 256mg/l, Chlorides 32mg/l, Sulphates 278mg/l, Fluorides 0.4mg/l.

President's Sparkling Wines [The] (Isr) the brand-name of a sparkling wine produced using traditional methods by Carmel in Richon-le-Zion and Zichron-Zacob.

Presolana (It) a sparkling natural spring mineral water from Presolans. Mineral contents (milligrammes per litre): Sodium 0.83mg/l, Calcium 48.8mg/l, Magnesium 17.5mg/l, Potassium 0.25mg/l, Bicarbonates 228.8mg/l, Chlorides 9.7mg/l, Sulphates 6.1mg/l, Nitrates 2.8mg/l, Silicates 4.2mg/l. pH 7.9

Presque Isle Wine Cellars (USA) a winery based near Erie County, north-eastern Pennsylvania. Produces hybrid and vinifera wines.

Pressac (Fr) an alternative name for the Malbec grape.

Pressac-Malbec (Fr) a red grape variety (strain of the Malbec) in the Saint-Émilion district of Bordeaux.

Pressburg (Czec) an old wine region in the Bratislava, produces mainly light, pleasant white wines.

Press Cake (Eng) after the first pressing of the grapes (the skins, pips and stalks), usually used to make vin de presse.

Pressed Rat & Warthog (Eng) a 3.8% alc by vol. mild ale brewed by Triple FFF Brewery, Four Marks, near Alton, Hampshire.

Pressoir (Fr) press house.

Pressurage (Fr) the pressing of the marc to produce vin de presse.

Pressure (Eng) the pressure inside a Champagne bottle measured in atmospheres (ats). 1 ats = 15 lbs. per sq. inch. The pressure of a bottle of Champagne is approximately 5.5 ats.

Pressurised Extractive Distillation (Eng) the removal of microscopic impurities during vodka production.

Press Wine (Fr) the wine made from the press cake which has water added, is re-pressed and fermented. Either drunk locally or distilled.

Prestige (Fr) a de luxe vintage cuvée Champagne produced by Roland Fliniaux.

Prestige (S.Afr) the label for a red wine (Cabernet sauvignon 33% and Ruby cabernet 66%) produced by the Thelma Mountain Vineyards winery, Stellenbosch, Western Cape.

Prestige Brut (Fr) a non-vintage Champagne produced by Cheurlin et Fils from 25% Chardonnay and 75% Pinot noir grapes.

Prestige Cuvée (Fr) in Champagne usually a high quality vintage wine from the top villages. Produced by many Champagne houses.

Prestige d'Argent (Fr) the label of a Champagne produced by St-Reol, Ambonnay.

Prestige du Médoc (Fr) a vineyard. (Add): Gaillan en Médoc, 33340 Lesparre. A.C. Médoc. (Com): Gaillan. Grape varieties: Cabernet sauvignon 50% and Merlot 50%.

Presto Cocktail (Cktl) 1 measure brandy, ⅓ measure Italian vermouth, juice ¼ lemon, 2 dashes Pernod. Shake over ice and strain into a cocktail glass.

Preston Brewing C°. (Eng) a micro-brewery based in Lancashire. Brews: Pride Ale 3.8% alc by vol. Pride Dark Mild 3.6% alc by vol., Atlas Really Strong Export 6.5% alc by vol.

Preston Wine Cellars (USA) a winery based in Yakima Valley, Washington. 80ha. Grape varieties: Chardonnay and Fumé blanc. Produces varietal wines.

Preston Winery (USA) a small winery based at Dry Creek Valley, Sonoma County, California. 33ha. Grape varieties: Sauvignon blanc and Zinfandel. Produces varietal wines.

Pret (Wal) a natural spring mineral water from south Wales.

Preta (Port) a Münchener-style dark beer brewed by S.C.C.

Preto Martinho (Port) a red grape variety grown in Ribatejo.

Preto Mortàgua (Port) a red grape variety grown in the Dão region. Used to make medium red wines.

Pretti (It) the infant Bacchus. i.e. The emblem on the Chianti Putto label.

Pretty Perrier (Cktl)(Non-alc) ⅓ measure raspberry syrup, juice ½ lemon, shake well over ice, strain into an ice-filled highball glass, top with iced Perrier water, a cherry and a lemon peel spiral.

Preuses [Les] (Fr) a Grand Cru vineyard of A.C. Chablis, Burgundy.

Preuve (Fr) a small clear glass vessel on the end of a chain which is lowered into Cognac barrels in order to test the liquor. Also called a Taupette.

Preuze (Fr) a Premier Cru vineyard in the A.C. commune of Chablis, Burgundy.

Preview (S.Afr) the label for a red wine (Pinot noir)

produced by the Hoopenburg Wines winery, Stellenbosch, Western Cape.

Preview Ale (Eng) a 5.6% alc by vol. ale from the Black Sheep Brewery in Marsham, North Yorkshire.

Prévot (S.Am) one of two rum distilleries based in French Guyana.

Prevoteau [Patrice] (Fr) a Champagne producer. (Add): 15 Rue A. Maginot, Damery, 51200 Épernay. Récoltants-manipulants. Produces vintage and non-vintage wines. Vintages: 1971, 1973, 1975, 1976, 1979, 1982, 1983, 1985, 1989, 1990, 1996, 1999, 2000.

Preziosa (It) a natural spring mineral water from Preziosa.

Priapus (Lat) the classical God of vineyards.

Price Coffees (Eng) the bulk of the coffee produced especially from Brazil that are used to make cheap blends.

Pricked (Eng) a term to denote excessive volatile acidity.

Pricked Wine (Eng) the same as pique, a wine which has started to turn to vinegar.

Prickle (Eng) the term given to describe the sensation on the tongue from wines which are pétillant, spritzig, etc.

Pride Ale (Eng) a 3.8% alc by vol. ale brewed by the micro-brewery Preston Brewing C°. in Lancashire.

Pride & Joy (Eng) a 2.8% alc by vol. light ale brewed by the Weltons Brewery, West Sussex.

Pride Dark Mild (Eng) a 3.6% alc by vol. mild brewed by the micro-brewery Preston Brewing C°. in Lancashire.

Pride Mountain Vineyards (USA) vineyards based in the Napa Valley, California. Grape varieties include Cabernet sauvignon, Chardonnay, Merlot, Viognier. Label: Claret Reserve.

Pride of England (Eng) a 4% alc by vol. ale brewed by the Daleside Brewery Ltd., North Yorkshire.

Pride of Pendle (Eng) the name for a beer brewed by the Moorhouses Brewery (Burnley) Ltd., Lancashire.

Pride of Romsey (Eng) a 5% alc by vol. ale brewed by the Hampshire Brewery, Hampshire.

Pride of the Islay (Scot) a 12 year old 40% alc by vol. Islay whisky from Gordon & MacPhail.

Pride of the Lowlands (Scot) a 12 year old 40% alc by vol. Islay whisky from Gordon & MacPhail.

Pride of the Orkney (Scot) a 12 year old 40% alc by vol. Orkney whisky from Gordon & MacPhail.

Pride of the Strathspey (Scot) a 12 year old 40% alc by vol. Strathspey whisky from Gordon & MacPhail.

Prieler (Aus) a winery based in Schützen am Gebirge, Neusiedlersee-Hügelland, Burgenland. (Add): Hauptstrasse 181, 7081 Schützen am Gebirge. Grape varieties: Blaufränkisch, Cabernet sauvignon, Chardonnay, Pinot blanc, Pinot gris. Produces a range of wines including Ausbruch.

Prieto Picudo (Sp) a black grape variety grown in the Léon region.

Prieur [Ch. and A.] (Fr) a Champagne producer. (Add): 2 Rue de Villers-aux-Bois, 51130 Vertus.

Produces vintage and non-vintage wines. *See* Napoléon

Prieuré de Cénac (Fr) a 34ha vineyard in Cahors.

Prieuré de Meyney (Fr) the second wine of Château Meyney, Cru Grand Bourgeois Exceptionnel, A.C. Saint-Estèphe.

Prieuré de Montézargues (Fr) a winery based in the A.C. Tavel, southern Rhône. (Add): Route de Rochefort du Gard, 30126 Tavel.

Prieuré de Saint-Amand [Le] (Fr) a wine producing domaine in Château Corbières, Languedoc, southern France.

Prieuré de Saint-Jean-de-Bebian (Fr) a 32ha vineyard. A.C. Pézenas, Coteaux du Languedoc-Cabrières Pézenas. Produces red wines from Grenache, Syrah and Mourvèdre grapes. Second wine is La Chapelle de Bébian.

Prignac (Fr) a commune in the Bas-Médoc. Has A.C. Médoc status.

Prignac-Marcamps (Fr) a commune in the A.C. Côtes de Bourg, north-eastern Bordeaux.

Prikkelbaar (Hol) pétillant/prickling.

Prima (S.Afr) the label for a red wine (Cabernet sauvignon 25% and Merlot 75%) produced by the Le Bonheur Estate winery, Stellenbosch, Western Cape.

Prima Goccia (It) a white wine produced by Corvo in Sicily. *See also* Colomba Platino.

Primary Fermentation (Eng) the main fermentation of all beers in the fermentation vessels.

Primary Rock (It) a natural spring mineral water brand.

Primato (Fr) a large bottle of (27litres) 36 standard bottles capacity used in the Champagne region. *see* Champagne Bottle Sizes.

Primatticio (It) an alternative name for the Montepulciano grape variety.

Primavera (Cktl) 1 part dry gin, 1 part orange juice. Shake well over ice, strain into a cocktail glass, add a dash of orange cordial and a twist of orange peel juice.

Primavera del Prosecco (It) a wine festival period of tastings and events held in the Prosecco region of Veneto, northern Italy. 'E'mail: info@primaveraprosecco.it

Primavera (Pol) a natural spring mineral water. Mineral contents (milligrammes per litre): Calcium 46.2mg/l, Magnesium 7mg/l, Potassium 1.3mg/l, Bicarbonates 156.9mg/l, Chlorides 7.1mg/l, Sulphates 7.4mg/l.

Prime (Eng) *see* Priming.

Prime Jamaica Washed (W.Ind) one of three grades of coffee produced on the island of Jamaica. Has fine body and acidity.

Primerberg (Lux) a vineyard site in the village of Remich.

Primerberg (Lux) a vineyard site in the village of Stadtbredimus.

Primer vi Novell (Sp) a light, fruity, white wine produced by Mont-Marça in the Penedés region.

Primes d'Arrachage (Fr) subsidies paid to vignerons by the French government and Brussels to pull up their vines.

Primeur (Fr) a term used to denote an early wine usually of Beaujolais origin, that can be drunk young.

Primia (It) a natural spring mineral water from Primia.

Primicia (Sp) a red wine produced by Abadía Retuerta in Ribera del Duero using Tempranillo, Cabernet and Merlot grapes using ⅓ maceration carbonique.

Primings (Eng) a sugar and yeast solution added to cask-conditioned ales to encourage a secondary fermentation in the cask (or tank if brewery conditioned). Usually has some dry hops added. *see* Dry Hopping and St. Martin.

Primitivo (It) a red grape variety grown in the Puglia region to produce a red wine of same name.

Primitivo di Manduria (It) a D.O.C. red wine from Puglia. Made from the Primitivo grape grown in the commune of Manduria and others in the province of Taranto. Grapes are slightly dried. 3 types made are: Dolce Naturale, Liquoroso Dolce Naturale and Liquoroso Secco. Liquoroso must be aged for a minimum of 2 years from time of fortification.

Primo (S.Afr) the label for a red wine (Pinotage) produced by the Fairview winery, Suider-Paarl, Western Cape.

Primo (USA) a beer brewed in Hawaii by the Schlitz Brewing C°. in Honolulu.

Primo Estate (Austr) a winery based in Adelaide Hills. Grape varieties include Colombard, Muscat and Sauvignon blanc. Produces fortified liqueur wines under the 'The Fronti III' and The Fronti IV' labels.

Primoldial (Sp) a solera gran reserva brandy produced by John Harvey and Sons.

Primor (Isr) a dry, red table wine of Burgundy style.

Primorska Hrvatska (Cro) coastal Croatia. Includes area of Istria. Grape varieties: Tocai friulano, Pinot gris, Chardonnay, Merlot, Cabernet sauvignon, Rafosk, Plavac mali. Home to the Movia winery. Wines include Dingac, Faros, Postup, Peljesac, Prosek.

Primosic Gmajne (It) a wine producer based in the D.O.C. Collio in the Friuli-Venezia Giulia. Grape variety: Ribolla gialla. Website: http://www.primosic.com

Primula (It) a sparkling natural spring mineral water from Primula. Mineral contents (milligrammes per litre): Sodium 8.9mg/l, Calcium 91.2mg/l, Magnesium 32.1mg/l, Potassium 0.76mg/l, Bicarbonates 353.9mg/l, Chlorides 3.9mg/l, Sulphates 77.1mg/l, Fluorides 0.35mg/l, Nitrates 2.7mg/l, Silicates 9.3mg/l. pH 7.38

Primus (Afr) a beer brand brewed in Zaire with the technical assistance of Heineken. Is also brewed in Rwanda and Burundi.

Primus straw 10% (Czec) a 3.3% alc by vol. bottled pilsner brewed by Plzensky Prazdroj (Gambrinus) in Plzen.

Princ (Asia) the local name for the Traminer grape variety.

Prince (Chi) a natural spring mineral water. Mineral contents (milligrammes per litre): Sodium 6.2mg/l, Calcium 53.7mg/l, Magnesium 21mg/l, Potassium 2.43mg/l, Bicarbonates 274mg/l, Chlorides 6mg/l, Sulphates 1.92mg/l. pH 7.1

Prince A. de Bourbon Parme (Fr) a de luxe vintage cuvée Champagne produced by Abel Lepitre from 87% Chardonnay and 13% Pinot noir grapes.

Prince Albert (Fr) an 1834 distilled Cognac produced by A.E. Dor in Jarnac 30% alc by vol.

Prince Albert Vineyard (Austr) vineyard. (Add): Waurn Ponds, Victoria 3221. 2ha. Grape variety: Pinot noir.

Prince Beer (Fr) a bière brewed by the Sedan Brasserie in Lorraine.

Prince Bishop Ale (Eng) a straw coloured beer 1044 O.G. brewed by the Big Lamp Brewery, Tyneside.

Prince Charles (Cktl) ⅓ measure Drambuie, ⅓ measure Cognac, ⅓ measure lemon juice. Shake over ice and strain into a cocktail glass.

Prince Charles Coffee (Liq.Coffee) using a measure of Drambuie. *See also* Highland Coffee.

Prince Charles Edward's Liqueur (Scot) the old name for Drambuie.

Prince Cocktail (Cktl) ⅓ measure gin, ⅓ measure Italian vermouth, ⅓ measure (white) crème de menthe. Shake over ice and strain into a cocktail glass.

Prince Consort (Eng) the brand-name given to a range of spirits from Landmark Wholesale Cash & Carry.

Prince de Cognac (Fr) a Cognac produced by Otard in Cognac 40% alc by vol.

Prince Hill (USA) the label for a red wine (Pinot noir) produced by the Heath winery, Willamette Valley, Oregon.

Prince Imperial (Fr) an 1875 distilled Cognac produced by A.E. Dor in Jarnac 36% alc by vol.

Prince Noir (Fr) a natural spring mineral water from Prince Noir. Mineral contents (milligrammes per litre): Sodium 9mg/l, Calcium 528mg/l, Magnesium 78mg/l, Potassium 3mg/l, Bicarbonates 329mg/l, Chlorides 9mg/l, Sulphates 1342mg/l, Nitrates 1.3mg/l.

Prince of Ales (Eng) a 4.5% alc by vol. beer brewed with American hops by the Lastingham Brewery, near Pickering, North Yorkshire.

Prince of Wales (Chi) a blend of tea from the Anhei province. Exclusive to the Twinings company. Full-flavoured and light coloured, it is one of the best teas.

Prince of Wales (Eng) a micro-brewery at Foxfields, near Broughton, Cumbria. Brews: Lock 47, Axeman's Wheat Mild.

Prince of Wales (Wal) a 10 year old Scottish malt whisky with herbs produced by the Brecon Brewery in Powys.

Prince of Wales (Wal) a single vatted Welsh whisky produced by the Welsh Whisky company, Brecon, Powys 40% alc by vol.

Prince's Ale (Eng) a strong beer 1100 O.G. that was

brewed and bottled by the St. Austell Brewery, Cornwall. Produced to celebrate Prince Charles' 21st birthday.

Prince's Punch (Cktl)(Non-alc) boil a cinnamon stick, 6 cloves and a piece of ginger together with a little water and sugar syrup for 5 minutes. Cool, add juice of 1 lemon and 2 oranges. Shake over ice with sprigs of mint. Strain into a highball glass and decorate with mint, slices of fruit in season and serve with a spoon.

Princess Cocktail (Cktl) ⅔ measure gin, ⅓ measure crème de cacao, ⅔ measure cream. Shake over ice and strain into a cocktail glass.

Princess Dania (Cktl) ⅓ measure Mandarine Napoléon, ⅓ measure vodka, ⅓ measure iced Champagne, dash lime juice. Shake spirits and juice together, strain into a Champagne flute and add Champagne.

Princesse d'Isenbourg (Fr) a Champagne producer. (Add): 13 Rue Pont, B.P. 2, 51160 Mareuil-sur-Aÿ.

Princess Jaulke (Ind) a traditional method sparkling wine from Pimpane Coop. India Ltd., Mahnashtra.

Princess Mary Cocktail (Cktl) 20mls (⅙ gill) each of dry gin, crème de cacao, fresh cream. Shake well over ice and strain into a cocktail glass.

Prince's Smile (Cktl) ½ measure gin, ¼ measure Calvados, ¼ measure apricot brandy, 2 dashes lemon juice. Shake over ice and strain into a cocktail glass.

Princes Soft Drinks Group (Eng) a carbonated drinks manufacturer (established 1996). (Add): Weaverthorpe Road, Bradford, West Yorkshire BD4 6SX. Website: http://www.princes.co.uk

Princess Pippin (Eng) a vintage cider produced by the Symonds Cider Co. in Hereford.

Princess Pousse Café (Pousse Café) 1 measure of apricot brandy with a measure of cream on top.

Princess Pride (Cktl). 40mls (⅓ gill) Calvados, 20mls (⅙ gill) Dubonnet, 20mls (⅙ gill) Italian vermouth. Shake well over ice and strain into a cocktail glass.

Prince's Wedding Ale (Eng) a strong bottled ale from the Gibbs Mew Brewery.

Princeton (Cktl) ⅓ measure Port, ⅔ measure dry gin, dash orange bitters. Stir over ice, strain into a cocktail glass and add a twist of lemon peel juice.

Princeton Cocktail (Cktl) ½ measure dry gin, ½ measure dry vermouth, juice ½ lime. Stir over iceand strain into a cocktail glass.

Princetown Breweries Ltd (Eng) a brewery (established 1994). (Add): The Brewery, Tavistock Road, Princetown, Yelverton, Devon PL20 6QF. Brews: Dartmoor IPA 4% alc by vol., Jail Ale 4.8% alc by vol.

Principauté de Franc Pineau (Fr) a wine brotherhood based in Cognac.

Principauté d'Orange (Fr) a département in the southern Rhône. Communes of Bollerie, Orange, Vaison-la-Romaine and Valréas. Produces red and rosé wines.

Principe (Sp) the brand-name of a Manzanilla Sherry

produced by Barbıdillo in Sanlúcar de Barrameda. Is around 60 years old (solera).

Principe di Venosa (It) a wine-producer based in Latium. Noted for red wines.

Priniac (Eng) the seventeenth century spelling for **Preignac.**

Prinsen UK Ltd (Eng) a coffee manufacturer (established 1996). (Add): Mayfair House, 11 Lurke Street, Bedford, Bedfordshire MK40 3HZ. Produces a variety of coffee, cocoa, drinking chocolate and teas. Owned by Prinsen BV Netherlands. Website: http://www.prinsen.com 'E'mail: prinsenuk@prinsen.nl

Prinzbräu Brauerei (It) a brewery owned by the German Oetker group.

Prinzenburger Felsenquelle (Ger) a natural spring mineral water. Mineral contents (milligrammes per litre): Sodium 6.5mg/l, Calcium 57.1mg/l, Magnesium 5.8mg/l, Potassium 1.2mg/l, Chlorides 9.9mg/l, Fluorides 0.07mg/l.

Prinzenquelle Minaqua (Ger) a natural spring mineral water from Naila. Mineral contents (milligrammes per litre): Sodium 112mg/l, Calcium 2mg/l, Magnesium 1mg/l, Bicarbonates 278mg/l, Chlorides 2mg/l, Nitrates 0.5mg/l.

Prinzregent Luitpold Weissbier (Ger) a 5.5% alc by vol. bottled wheat beer brewed by Kaltenberg Castle Brauerei, Fürstenfeldbruck.

Prinzregent Luitpold Weissbier Dunkel (Ger) a 5.5% alc by vol. bottled dark wheat beer brewed by Kaltenberg Castle Brauerei, Fürstenfeldbruck.

Prior (Bel) see Abt.

Prior (USA) a dark beer brewed by the Prior Brewery based in Pennsylvania.

Priorato (Sp) a red wine from the banks of the river Ebro in the Catalonia region. Known in the USA as Tarragona Port. see Bombonas.

Priorato (Sp) a Denominación de Origen region of Catalonia, south-eastern Spain, just north of Tarragona. 1820ha. Grape varieties: 40% Garnacha tinta, Garnacha peluda, 54% Cariñena, Cabernet sauvignon, Garnacha blanca, Macabeo, Pedro ximénez, Chenin blanc. Home to Cartoixa Scala Dei from 100% Garnacha tinta. Red, white, rosé and rancio wines produced.

Prior Brewery (USA) a noted brewery based in Pennsylvania.

Priors Gold (Eng) a 4.5% alc by vol. ale brewed by The Durham Brewery Ltd., County Durham.

Priory Brewers (Eng) a brewery (established 1980) based in Newark-on-Trent, Nottinghamshire. Brews: Ned Belcher's Bitter 1040 O.G. and Priory Pride Bitter 1035 O.G.

Priory Mild (Eng) a 3.6% alc by vol. mild ale brewed by Nethergate Holdings Ltd., Suffolk.

Priory Porter (Eng) a cask porter from Mitchells Brewery in Lancaster.

Priory Pride (Eng) a bitter beer 1035 O.G. brewed by the Priory Brewers in Newark-on-Trent, Nottinghamshire.

Pripps Brewery (Swe) a famous Swedish brewery that exports to the USA. Has eight plants: Arboga,

Bromma, Gällivare, Grötebug, Mora, Sundsvall, Tingsyd and Torsby. Is Sweden's largest brewing company.

Pripps Energy (Scot) a light sparkling 'energy' drink produced in 3 natural flavours from A.G. Barr.

Prirodno (Slo) natural.

Pris de Boisson (Fr) under the influence of alcohol. Drunk/intoxicated.

Prise de Mousse (Fr) the second fermentation in the bottle in Champagne production.

Prissey (Fr) a commune which is part of the Côte de Nuits Villages. Is not allowed to use the commune's name as its A.C. About 12.5ha. of vineyards.

Pristine (Ind) a natural spring mineral water from Nilgiris. Mineral contents (milligrammes per litre): Sodium 5.1mg/l, Calcium 7mg/l, Magnesium 3.2mg/l, Potassium 0.2mg/l, Bicarbonates 24.4mg/l, Chlorides 10mg/l, Sulphates 2mg/l.

Pristine Peaks (USA) a natural spring mineral water from Appalachian Mountains, Blue Ridge Mountain District, Georgia.

Pritchard Hill (USA) a red wine (Cabernet sauvignon) produced by the Bryan Family winery, Napa Valley, California.

Privaatkeur (S.Afr) the label for a red wine (Cabernet sauvignon, Cabernet franc and Merlot blend) produced by the De Compagnie winery, Wellington, Western Cape.

Privada (Arg) a red wine produced by Bodegas Norton from Cabernet sauvignon, Malbec and Merlot.

Privatbrauerei Christian Fiedler (Ger) a brewery. (Add): Silberstrasse 28, Scheibenberg OT Oberscheibe D-09481. Brews beers and lagers. Website: http://www.brauerei-fiedler.de 'E'mail: info@brauerei-fiedler.de

Privatbrauerei Erdinger Weissbräu Werner Brombach GmbH (Ger) a brewery (established 1886). (Add): Lange Zeile fund 3, Erding D-85435. brews a variety of beers including bottle-conditioned. Website: http://www.erdinger.com 'E'mail: export@erdinger.de

Privatbrauerei M Ketterer GmbH & C° (Ger) a brewery. (Add): Frombachstrasse 27, Homberg D-78132. Brews a variety of beers and lagers. Website: http://www.kettererbier.de 'E'mail: info@kettererbier.de

Privatbrauerei Schweiger GmbH & C° KG (Ger) a brewery. (Add): Ebersberger St 25, Markt Schwaben bei München D-85570. Brews a variety of beers and lagers. Website: http://www.schweiger-bier.de 'E'mail: info@schweiger-bier.de

Private Collection (S.Afr) the label for a red wine (Cabernet sauvignon plus Cabernet franc, Merlot, Pinotage and Shiraz blend) produced by the Diemersdal Estate winery, Durbanville, Western Cape.

Private Collection (S.Afr) the label for a red wine (Pinotage) produced by the Goede Hope Estate winery, Stellenbosch, Western Cape.

Privateer (Eng) a 4.8% alc by vol. ale brewed by the Jolly Boat Brewery (Bideford) Ltd., Devon.

Private Hotel (Austr) a hotel that does not have a licence to sell alcoholic liquor.

Private Reserve (Scot) a bottled ale 1056 O.G. brewed by the Drybrough Brewery in Edinburgh.

Private Stock Winery (USA) a winery based in Boone, Iowa. Produces mainly French hybrid wines.

Privé de Bois (S.Afr) a wood-matured, dry white wine produced from a blend of Colombard and Steen grapes by the Weltevrede Estate in Robertson, Western Cape.

Privilège d'Alexandre Bisquit (Fr) one of the world's most expensive Cognacs. Produced by Bisquit and marketed by Saccone and Speed.

Privilegio (Sp) a red or dry white wine produced by SOGE-VIÑAS in the Rioja Alavesa.

Privilegio (Sp) a solera gran reserva brandy produced by Emilio Hidalgo.

Privilegio del Rey Sancho (Sp) a red wine from the Bodegas Domecq, S.A., Rioja. Made from the Tempranillo grape.

Privilegio Fiano di Avellino (It) a red wine produced by Feudi di San Gregorio in Campania.

Privnita (Rum) cellar.

Prix du Base (Fr) the basic or top price for grapes upon which the lower qualities are based.

Prix du Raisin (Fr) the name given to the list of graded prices which are to be paid for the varieties of grapes of a Champagne vintage.

Prize Brew (Eng) a keg light mild ale 1032 O.G. brewed by the Truman Brewery in London.

Prize Idiot (Cktl) 25mls (1fl.oz) vodka, 25mls (1fl.oz) crème de banane, dash grenadine, 2 dashes lemon juice. Pour into an ice-filled highball glass. Stir in Sinalco. Decorate with a green cherry, lemon wedge, serve with a spoon and straws.

Prize Medal (Eng) a bottled ale 1035 O.G. brewed by the Bass Charrington Brewery in London.

Prize Old Ale (Eng) a naturally-conditioned bottled ale 1095 O.G. (9% alc by vol.) brewed by the Gales Brewery in Horndean, Hampshire. Sold in a corked bottle, it will improve with age.

Probar (Sp) to taste wine/wine tasting.

Probstberg (Ger) grosslage (Anb): Mosel-Saar-Ruwer. (Ber): Bernkastel. (Vils): Fell, Kenn, Longuich, Mehring, Riol, Schweich.

Probstberg (Ger) vineyard (Anb): Württemberg. (Ber): Kocher-Jagst-Tauber. (Gro): Tauberberg. (Vil): Elpersheim.

Probstberg (Ger) vineyard (Anb): Württemberg. (Ber): Kocher-Jagst-Tauber. (Gro): Tauberberg. (Vil): Markelsheim.

Probsteiberg (Ger) vineyard (Anb): Mittelrhein. (Ber): Rheinburgengau. (Gro): Not yet assigned. (Vil): Hirzenach.

Probstey (Ger) vineyard (Anb): Rheinhessen. (Ber): Nierstein. (Gro): Domherr. (Vil): Saulheim.

Procanico (It) the local Tuscan name for the Trebbiano grape, also used in Elba.

P

Procedente (Sp) lit: 'originating from', found on a bottle label.

Procès [Les] (Fr) a Premier Cru vineyard in the A.C. commune of Nuits-Saint-Georges, Côte de Nuits, Burgundy 1.9ha.

Pro Cork (Euro) a new ™ natural wine cork that is sealed at one end (wine end) with five layers of membrane which prevents any taint coming into contact with the wine.

Proctor (Eng) a 5.8% alc by vol. dark tawny-coloured ale brewed by Morrells of Oxford.

Procurator (Fr) a name in the middle ages for an abbaye cellar master.

Prodromos (Cyp) a wine village in the north-west region of Marathassa in the Troodos mountains.

Producer (Eng) the maker/manufacturer. (Fr) = producteur, (It) = produttore.

Producteur (Fr) producer.

Producteurs de Blanquette de Limoux (Fr) a group of producers of over 80% of A.C. Blanquette de Limoux. Labels include Alderic, Fleur de Lys and Sieur de Limoux.

Producteurs de Plaimont (Fr) a wine co-operative based in the Gascony region. Has 1000 members. Labels include: St. Albert (A.C. Pacherenc de Vic Bihl).

Producteurs Directs (Fr) a term used to describe hybrid vines (banned in French A.C. areas).

Productos de Uva Aguascalientes (Mex) a co-operative winery based in Aguascalientes.

Productos Vinícola (Mex) a winery based in the Guadalupe area in the Baja California district. Produces wines under the Terrasda and Domecq (a division of the noted Sherry house).

Produit de Queue (Fr) the tailings, the end of the distillation in Cognac which is put back to be re-distilled. Only the heart, the 'brouillis' is retained.

Produit de Tête (Fr) the headings, the start of the distillation in Cognac which is drawn off before the 'brouillis' is collected. see Produit de Queue also.

Produttore (It) producer. (Fr) = producteur.

Produttori di Barbaresco (It) a co-operative winery (established 1968) in the Barbaresco, Piemonte region. Has 60 growers and 100ha of vineyards.

Produttori Santa Maddalena (It) a winery based in the DOC Trentino-Alto-Adige, northern Italy. Grape variety: Lagrein. Label: Lagrein Reserva Taber.

Proef Brouwerij (Bel) a brewery. (Add): Doornzelestraat 20, B-9080 Lochristi-Hijfte. Brews a variety of beers and lagers. Website: http://www.proefbrouwerij.com 'E'mail: info@proefbrouwerij.com

Proemio Wines (Arg) a winery based in the Mendoza region, eastern Argentina. Website: http://www.proemiowines.com 'E'mail: agallardo@proemiowines.com

Professor Black (S.Afr) the label for a white wine (Sauvignon blanc) produced by the Warwick Estate winery, Stellenbosch, Western Cape.

Profs Pint (Eng) a 4.8% alc by vol. ale brewed by the Darwin Brewery, Tyne & Wear.

Profumo (It) denotes a flowery bouquet.

Progress (Eng) the name of a hop variety used in brewing.

Progress (Eng) a 4% alc by vol. bitter ale brewed by the York Brewery Company Ltd., North Yorkshire.

Progress Best Bitter (Eng) a cask-conditioned best bitter 1042 O.G. brewed by the Pilgrim Brewery in Woldingham, Surrey.

Progressive Beer Duty (Eng) abbr: PBD the U.K. government's 50% tax break incentive (introduced 2001) for small brewers to develop new micro-breweries producing under 60000hl of beer annually. Has seen the introduction of numerous new brewery enterprises.

Prohibition (USA) the complete government ban on alcoholic drink between the years 1919 and 1933. See Noble Experiment.

Prohibition (Eng) a 0.6% alc by vol. low alcohol lager from the Cornish Brewery Company. Sold in flip-top bottles.

Prohibitionist (USA) the name for a person who favoured and supported the Prohibition.

Proidl (Aus) a winery (10ha) based in the Kremstal region. (Add): Oberer Markt 5, 3541 Senftenberg. Grape varieties: Cabernet sauvignon, Grüner veltliner, Müller-Thurgau, Riesling, St. Laurent, Zweigelt. Produces a range of wine styles.

Proizvedeno u Viastitoj Vinariji Poljoprivredne Zadruge (Ser) on a wine label denotes 'Made in the Co-operative cellars of the place named'.

Proizvedeno u Vinariji (Ser) produced at.

Project Burgundy (Fr) an initiative developed in 2001 by the B.I.V.B. to random test Burgundy wines already in retail outlets to assess quality.

Prokupac (Ser) a red grape variety grown in Makedonija and southern Serbia. Produces wines of the same name and Ruzica (a rosé wine).

Prokupac (Ser) a red wine from Montenegro, Makedonija and the Serbia region. Made from various grape varieties. A fresh fruity wine that needs to be drunk young.

Proline (Eng) an amino acid found in wines formed by the yeasts.

Prolom Voda (Ser) a natural spring mineral water from Serbia and Montenegro. Mineral contents (milligrammes per litre): Sodium 49.7mg/l, Calcium 2.2mg/l, Bicarbonates 92.72mg/l, Chlorides 7.5mg/l, Sulphates 1.6mg/l, Fluorides 0.12mg/l.

Pro Long (Eng) isotonic sports drink of orange, or lemon and lime flavours from Wells, Worcestershire. Sold in 500mls PET™ bottles.

Prolongeau (Fr) an alternative name for the Malbec grape.

Prolonged Fermentation (Eng) the addition of small quantities of sugar to fermenting wines to extend or prolong the fermentation to obtain a high alcohol level (especially in home-made 'fruit' wines).

Promiscua (It) a method of planting vines with other crops planted between them. Produces good wines but a poor yield.

Proof (Eng) the old British system of measuring alcohol content. Proof spirit contains 57.1% alcohol. A liquid containing less is deemed to be 'under-proof', if more then deemed 'over-proof'. Was tested in the Middle Ages with a pan and gunpowder. The more gunpowder that was needed then the less alcohol the spirit contained. See Sykes.

Proof Gallon (Eng) the term used to describe a gallon of spirit at 'proof' strength.

Proof Spirit (Eng) a 57.1% alc by vol (49.28% alc by weight) at 15.6°C (60°F). Range is 0° Proof (water)/175° Proof (pure alcohol). To caculate alcohol by volume: divide proof by 175 and multiply by 100.

Proof Spirit (USA) a 50% alc by vol. at 15.6°C (60°F). Range is 0° Proof (water)/200° Proof (pure alcohol). To caculate alcohol by volume: divide by 2.

Proosje Van Schiedam (Hol) a golden korenjenever produced by Nolet.

Proper Job (Eng) a 5.5% alc by vol. India pale ale produced by the St. Austell brewery, Cornwall.

Propiedad Grial, S.L. (Sp) a 20ha winery at Avda. Estación 28, 26360 Fuenmayor, Rioja. Main wine is Gribena.

Propional-Dehyde (Eng) an aldehyde found in wine which contributes to the bouquet and flavour of the wine.

Propionic Acid (Eng) an acid found in minute quantities.

Propriétaire-Récoltant (Fr) an independent wine grower, an owner-manager.

Proprietary Red (USA) a red wine (Cabernet sauvignon 10% and Merlot 90%) from the Hyde Vineyards, Napa Valley, California.

Proprietary Reserve (USA) a red wine (Cabernet sauvignon) produced by the Pahlmeyer winery, Napa Valley, California.

Proprietor's (S.Afr) the label for a range of varietal wines produced by the Avondale winery, Paarl, Western Cape.

Proptrækker (Den) corkscrew.

Propyl Alcohol (Eng) C₃H₇OH a higher alcohol. Part of the Fusil Oils.

Prosecco (It) a white grape variety, produces bitterish dry wines in the Treviso and Veneto regions.

Prosecco di Conegliano-Valdobbiadene (It) a D.O.C. white wine from Veneto. Made from the Prosecco grape and up to 10% of Verdiso grapes. If grown in the restricted area called Cartizze then entitled to the special specification Superiore di Cartizze. Both produced by natural re-fermentation-Frizzante and Spumante. Brut, dry and extra-dry versions.

Prosecco di Valdobbiadene (It) see Prosecco di Conegliano-Valdobbiadene.

Prosek Dioklecian (Euro) a medium-sweet dessert wine from raisined grapes. 15% alc by vol. from Dalmatia. Has unique aroma of ripe grapes.

Prosit (Ger) good health/cheers. See also Prost.

Prospect Hill (S.Afr) the label for a red wine (Cabernet sauvignon) produced by the Robertson Co-operative Winery, Robertson, Western Cape.

Prospect 1870 (S.Afr) a winery (established 1990) based in Robertson, Western Cape. 45ha. Grape varieties: Cabernet sauvignon, Chardonnay, Shiraz, Viognier. Label: Leatherwood. Website: http://www.prospectwines.com

Prospect Golden Cask Ale (Eng) a cask-conditioned ale 4.1% alc by vol. brewed by the Ridley's Brewery, Essex.

Prosperity Vineyard (USA) the label for a red wine (Pinot noir) produced by the Namasté winery, Willamette Valley, Oregon.

Prosper Maufoux (Fr) a Burgundy négociant-éleveur. (Add): 21590, Santenay. Noted for white wines.

Prost (Aus)(Ger) cheers/good health. See also Prosit.

Prostejov Brewery (Czec) a brewery based in central Czec.

Prostel (Ger) a type of low alcohol lager brewed by Burgenbräu Bamberg Worner 0.5% alc by vol.

Prost Lager (Eng) a canned lager beer 1031 O.G. brewed by the Higsons Brewery in Liverpool, Lancashire.

Protein Casse (Eng) a wine malady, a haze or brownish deposit. Unstable proteins in the wine. Cured by fining with Bentonite.

Protivín Brewery (Czec) a brewery based in south-western Czec.

Proton N°1 (Cktl) ⅓ measure triple sec, ⅓ measure vodka, ⅓ measure Galliano. Shake over ice and strain into a cocktail glass.

Protos (Sp) a 5 year old red wine produced by the Cooperativa de Ribero del Duero in Peñafiel.

Prouilly (Fr) a Cru Champagne village in the Canton de Fismes. District: Reims.

Provadya (Bul) a wine-producing area noted for white wines.

Provam (Port) a co-operative winery (established 1992) based at Monção in the D.O.C. Vinho Verde. Has 10 members and also buys in grapes. Labels: Côto de Mamoelas, Portal de Fidalgo, Varanda do Conde.

Provechon (Sp) a red grape variety grown in Aragón.

Provenance Vineyards (USA) a winery based in Rutherford, Napa Valley, California. Grape variety: Cabernet sauvignon.

Provence (Fr) a wine region in south-eastern France. Produces red, rosé and white wines both A.C. and V.D.Q.S. mainly from the Mourvèdre and Ugni blanc grapes but up to 30% Cabernet sauvignon is permitted. A.C. areas: Bandol, Bellet, Cassis, Côtes de Provence and Palette.

Provence [La] (S.Afr) a noted wine producing estate based in the Franschhoek district.

Provence et Corse (Fr) a vin de pays region in south-eastern France and the Island of Corsica, which contains the vins de pays districts: d'Aigues/d'Argens/de la Petite Crau/de la Principauté d'Orange/de l'Île de Beauté/des Maures/des Sables-du-Golfe-du-Lion/du Mont-Caume/Portes de Méditerranée.

Provenza Vineyards (USA) a small vineyard based in

Brookeville, Maryland. 6ha. Produces hybrid wines.

Providence Private Reserve (N.Z) a red wine produced from 66% Cabernet franc, 33% Merlot and 1% Malbec grapes, produced by Providence Vineyard, Matakana, near Warkworth, Northland.

Providence Vineyard (N.Z) a vineyard based at Matakana, near Warkworth, Northland. Produces Matakana and Providence Private Reserve wines.

Provifin Winery (Bra) a large winery based in Rio Grande do Sol. 70ha. A joint venture of Moët-Hennessy, Cinzano and Montero Aranha. Sparkling wines are produced under the Moët et Chandon label.

Provinage (Fr) the term given to the layering of vines so that over the years the roots contain the earth in a tangled mass. Used on hillside vineyards, prevents erosion.

Provinci (It) provinces, the equivalent of English counties.

Provins (Switz) a wine co-operative based in the Valais Canton.

Provisie (Bel) a beer made by Liefmans Brasserie that is classed as a vintage beer. Matures in the bottle in 2 years but will keep for 20 years plus.

Provisie (Bel) a top-fermented bière 6% alc by vol. brewed by the Oudenaarde Brasserie.

Prudence Island (USA) a wine-producing island based in the centre of the Naragansett Bay, Rhode Island. Produces Vinifera wines.

Prugna (It) a plum-based liqueur made by the Carmelite friars in Gethsemane.

Prugnolo Gentile (It) a red grape variety grown in central Italy, a species of the Sangiovese used for Chianti.

Pruht (W.Ind) a rum-based proprietary apéritif.

Pruimpje Prik In (Hol) a plum-based liqueur produced by Van Zuylekom Distillery, Amsterdam.

Pruliers [Les] (Fr) a Premier Cru vineyard in the A.C. commune of Nuits-Saint-Georges, Côte de Nuits, Burgundy 7ha.

Prune (Fr) plum brandy.

Prunelle (Fr) a plum-flavoured liqueur, purple in colour 40% alc by vol.

Prunelle (Fr) a green-coloured liqueur produced from sloe kernels by Garnier.

Prunelle Fine de Bourgogne (Fr) a plum brandy produced in the Burgundy region.

Prunelle Sauvage (Fr) an alcool blanc made from sloes.

Prunellia (Fr) a green-coloured liqueur produced from sloe kernels by Cusenier.

Prunier (Fr) a Cognac producer. (Add): Maison Prunier S.A., 16102.

Pruning (Eng) the process of cutting back the growth of a plant to encourage new growth and to prevent excessive foliage production so allowing better fruit.

Prunotto [Alfredo] (It) a winery based in Cassiano, Piemonte. Produces a D.O.C.G. Barolo that is aged for 24 months in 100hls and 50hls Slovenian and French oak barrels.

Prunt (Ger) the name given to the raised globules on the sides of a roemer glass stem and on the bowl of the glass.

Prünte (Aus) a winery based in Spielfeld, Süd-Steiermark. (Add): Grassnitzberg 14, 8471 Spielfeld. Grape varieties include: Muskateller, Pinot gris, Sauvignon blanc, Traminer.

Prussian-shaped (Eng) a decanter shape (circa 1780), is tapered similar to a barrel and has 3 neck rings to provide a safe grip.

Pruzilly (Fr) a commune in the Beaujolais region. Has A.C. Beaujolais-Villages or Beaujolais-Pruzilly status. Can also produce grapes for A.C. Mâconnais blanc.

Pr-vesi (Fin) a natural spring mineral water from Lempaala.

Prvni Prazsky Mestansky Pipover (Czec) *see* Prague Breweries.

Prysg (Wal) a carbonated natural mineral water bottled by Carmarthen Water in Mid-Wales. Bottled at Maesycrugiau, Dyfed. Still or carbonated.

Prystel (Fr) a still natural mineral water from the Vendée. (Add): 25 Bld de l'Industrie, La Roche sur Yon. Mineral contents (milligrammes per litre): Sodium 39.6mg/l, Calcium 36.3mg/l, Magnesium 10.9mg/l, Potassium 2.2mg/l, Bicarbonates 0mg/l, Chlorides 0mg/l, Sulphates 41.2mg/l, Nitrates 0mg/l, Fluoride 0.34. pH 7.4

P.S. (Asia) *abbr*: **P**ekoe **S**ouchong, a tea grade.

Pschitt (Fr) a fizzy fruit drink.

Pseudococcus (Lat) a yellow insect that attacks vines and is difficult to destroy. Hibernates underneath the bark of the vine. *see* Pulgón.

Pshenichnaya (Rus) a clean, pure wheat-distilled vodka 40% alc by vol.

Psou (Geo) a white grape variety grown in Georgia used to produce dessert wines.

Ptarmigan (Scot) a 4.5% alc by vol. ale brewed by the Harviestoun Brewery, Clackmannanshire.

P'tit Barri (Ch.Isles) keg. *See also* Fuste.

Ptolemées (Egy) *see* Cru des Ptolemées.

Ptolemy (Egy) a noted white wine-producing vineyard based in eastern Egypt.

Ptuj (Slo) a district of Slovenija region. Produces fine white wines.

Pub (Austr) a licensed hotel.

Pub (Eng) *abbr*: **Pub**lic House.

Pubbing (Austr) a slang term for a drinking bout. *See also* Pub Crawl (Eng).

Pubco (Eng) *abbr*: **Pub co**mpany – a non-brewing company that owns public houses and operates a 'free-house' system.

Pub Crawl (Eng) the term for a heavy drinking bout going from one public house (or hotel bar) to another and having a drink in each.

Pub Eighty [80] (Eng) a style of public house (circa 1984) that caters for the younger generation of drinkers.

Publican (Eng) the person (male or female) who

runs a public house, holds the Liquor Licence. Also called a Licensee, Landlord Landlady or Host/Hostess.

Public Bar (Eng) a room in an inn or hotel for selling drinks to the general public. i.e. non-residents.

Public House (Eng) a building designed for selling alcoholic and other cold beverages under strict licensing laws. *see* Pub.

Public House (USA) an inn/tavern or small hotel.

Publicker (USA) a Philadelphian straight whiskey distiller.

Publicker's White Duck (USA) the brand-name of a white whiskey produced by the Publicker Distillery in Philadelphia.

Pubwatch (Eng) a scheme that is operated by the publicans within a licenced area that collectively bans individuals (mainly for violent behaviour) in their public houses (either for a given period or for life). System operates with the local police force.

Púcaro (Port) mug (drinking).

Puck (Bel) a natural spring mineral water from Puck, Heule.

Pudding Stones (Fr) the stones of the southern Rhône area which store the heat given off by the sun during the day to give warmth to the grapes at night. Help to combat the coolness of the Mistral wind. *See also* Gros Galets.

Pudding Wines (Eng) a slang term used to describe sweet white wines (usually botrytised).

Puddled & Barmey (Eng) a 5.8% old ale brewed by Briscoe's in Otley, West Yorkshire.

Puddleduck Porter (Eng) a 4.5% alc by vol. porter brewed by the Westerham Brewery Cº. Ltd., Kent.

Pueblo Hills (Mex) a noted coffee-producing region.

Puelles (Sp) the label of a Rioja wine produced by Bodegas Puelles, Camino Los Molinos, s/n 26339 Abalos, Rioja 10ha.

Puente Viejo (Sp) the brand-name used by Bodegas García Carrión in Jumilla for a range of red, rosé and white wines.

Pu'er (Chi) the Cantonese for Bolay Tea.

Puerta Viesa Blanco (Sp) a white wine from the Bodegas Riojanas S.A. Rioja. Made from 100% Viura grapes and matured for 1 year in oak vats.

Puerto Apple (Cktl) ⅓ measure applejack brandy, ⅓ measure white rum, juice ¼ lime, 2 dashes orgeat syrup. Shake well over ice, strain into an ice-filled old-fashioned glass and top with a slice of lime.

Puerto Cabello (Fr) a Bordeaux-based liqueur-producing company.

Puerto de Santa Maria (Sp) the Sherry town which together with Jerez and Sanlúcar, make the triangle of towns in Andalusia which is the Sherry Supérieur area.

Puerto Fino (Sp) a very dry Sherry from Burdon in Puerto de Santa Maria 16.5% alc by vol.

Puerto Lucero (Sp) a solera brandy produced by Delgado Zuleta.

Puerto Real (Sp) an area in the Jerez Supérieur district.

Puerto Rican Coffee (W.Ind) a full-flavoured, low acidity, sweetish coffee. Produced in Puerto Rico.

Puerto Rican Don (W.Ind) a light rum.

Puerto Rican Rum (W.Ind) a light-bodied rum made by the patent still (a white rum), Bacardi is the best known brand.

Puerto Rico Distilleries (W.Ind) a white rum distillery based on the island of Puerto Rico.

Puff (USA) a drink consisting of brandy, fresh milk and Schweppes tonic water served in a highball with ice.

Puffin Bitter (Eng) a bitter beer 1040 O.G. brewed by the home-brew public house on Lundy Island using malt extract.

Puget Sound (USA) a wine district in the region of Washington.

Puget-Ville (Fr) a noted wine-producing village based in the Côtes de Provence.

Puglia (It) the 'heel' of Italy's boot, a region that produces the most wine in Italy. Over 100000ha. Some interesting D.O.C. wines now produced. Much of production was originally used for vermouths and blending with weaker wines of the E.C. to be sold as table wine. Also known as Apulia. Over 20 D.O.C.'s for red wines. D.O.C.'s in Southern Puglia include Alezio, Brindisi, Copertino, Leverano, Lizzano, Matino, Nardò, Salice Salentino, Squinzano. *see* Castel del Monte, Locorontondo, San Severo.

Pugnac (Fr) a commune in the A.C. Côtes de Bourg, north-eastern Bordeaux.

Púic Tae (Ire) tea cosy.

Puisieulx (Fr) a Grand Cru Champagne village in the Canton de Verzy. District: Reims.

Puissant (Fr) denotes a robust, powerful wine.

Puisseguin-Saint-Émilion (Fr) an A.C. commune in the Saint-Émilion region of eastern Bordeaux.

Puits St-Georges (Fr) a sparkling natural spring mineral water (established 1891) from Puits St. Georges, Saint-Romain-le-Puy. Mineral contents (milligrammes per litre): Sodium 430mg/l, Calcium 45mg/l, Magnesium 33mg/l, Potassium 18mg/l, Bicarbonates 1421mg/l, Chlorides 38mg/l, Sulphates 9mg/l, Fluorides 0.42mg/l, Nitrates 7.4mg/l, Silicates 38mg/l. pH 6.75

Pujols (Fr) a commune in the A.C. Graves region of south-western Bordeaux.

Pukhliakovski (Rus) a white grape variety grown in the river Don area.

Pulchen (Ger) vineyard (Anb): Mosel-Saar-Ruwer. (Ber): Saar-Ruwer. (Gro): Scharzberg. (Vil): Filzen.

Pulcianella (It) a 50cls straw covered flask. Much of the Orvieto wine is bottled in these.

Pulcinculo (It) a white grape variety grown in Tuscany. *See also* the Grechetto Bianco.

Pulenta Estate (Arg) a winery based in the Mendoza region, eastern Argentina. Website: http://www.pulentaestate.com 'E'mail: info@pulentaestate.com

Pulferturm (Aus) a vineyard site on the banks of the River Danube in the Kremstal region.

P

Pulgar (Sp) *see* Thumb.

Pulgón (Sp) a yellow-green, oval insect that emerges from the bark of the vine roots in the spring. The eggs hatch out on the vine and eat the tender leaves and shoots. *see* Pseudococcus.

Pulham Vineyard (Eng) a vineyard. (Add): Mill Lane, Pulham Market, Diss, Norfolk. 2.5ha. Soil: loam over clay. Grape varieties: Auxerrois, Bacchus, Cortaillod, Ebling, Kerner, Müller-Thurgau, Optima and Pinot noir. Wine sold under the Magdalen label.

Puligny Montrachet (Fr) an A.C. village and commune which has the Grand Cru vineyards of Bâtard-Montrachet [part], Bienvenues-Montrachet [part], Chevalier-Montrachet [part] and Montrachet [part] 14.4ha. plus the Premier Cru vineyards of Clovaillon, Garenne, Hameau de Blagny, Le Cailleret, Le Champ-Canet, Le Refert, Les Chalumeaux, Les Combettes, Les Folatières, Les Pucelles, Sous le Puits. 63.9ha. *see* Montrachet, Côte de Beaune, Burgundy and Chassagne-Montrachet.

Pulkau (Aus) a wine-producing district in Weinviertel. Noted for light-styled wines.

Pulliat (Fr) a Frenchman who developed the chart used to show the stages of grape maturation.

Pullman (Eng) a bottled beer 4.2% alc by vol. brewed by the Hepworth & C°. Brewery under their Beer Station label.

Pulmuone Saemmul (S.Kor) a natural spring mineral water. Mineral contents (milligrammes per litre): Sodium 16.6mg/l, Calcium 16.9mg/l, Magnesium 4.19mg/l, Potassium 0.78mg/l, Fluorides 0.33mg/l.

Pulp (Eng) a grape compound. 80% of the whole grape.

Pulp (Eng) the name for the flesh of the coffee cherry between the skin and the parchment.

Pulpito (Sp) a mechanical wine press.

Pulpit Rock Winery (S.Afr) a winery (established 2003) based in Swartland, Western Cape. 400ha. Grape varieties: Cabernet sauvignon, Chardonnay, Chenin blanc, Merlot, Pinotage, Shiraz. Label: Cape Heaven.

Pulque (Mex) a beery liquid made from the agave cactus from which tequila is distilled. *See also* Maguey Cactus.

Pulqueria (Mex) an old bar that sells pulque.

Pulse (Eng) the brand-name of a cider.

Pulse (USA) the alternative name for the Fever thermometer.

Pulteney (Scot) *see* Old Pulteney.

Pulverbuck (Ger) vineyard (Anb): Baden. (Ber): Kaiserstuhl-Tuniberg. (Gro): Vulkanfelsen. (Vil): Oberbergen.

Pulverised Coffee (Eng) a very fine ground coffee used to make Greek and Turkish coffees.

Pump (N.Z) a natural spring mineral water from Taupo.

Pumphouse (S.Afr) the label for an oak-aged red wine (Shiraz 95% and Malbec 5%) produced by the Backsberg Cellars, Suider-Paarl, Western Cape.

Pumping Over (Eng) the process of pumping the must over the '*cap*' to percolate through the cap and extract the colour from the skins in the cap.

Pumping Percolator (USA) the name used for the Percolator coffee making system.

Pumpkin Ale (Eng) a 4.4% alc by vol. draught ale brewed by Whitbread for Hallowe'en. Made from squashed pumpkins, malt and Golding hops.

Pumpkin Porter (Eng) a Hallowe'en ale brewed by the Pitfield Brewery, Shoreditch, London.

Punch (Cktl) *see* Paantsch, an alcoholic drink made up of a number of beverages. Originally five, now any number. Originated in India in the eighteenth century. Was originally rum-based.

Puncheon (Eng) a 72 gallon cask.

Puncheon (Fr) a cask for holding brandy. Size varies between 327litres–545litres.

Puncheon (W.Ind) a 110gallon cask used for holding rum.

Punching Down (Eng) a term used for pushing the '*cap*' of the fermenting grape must under the juice to aid extraction of colour.

Punch Martiniquais (W.Ind) a rum-based drink also containing cane-sugar syrup and sliced lemon peel.

Puncia (Fr) a wine-producing district in A.C. Bellet, Provence.

Pünderich (Ger) village (Anb): Mosel-Saar-Ruwer. (Ber): Bernkastel. (Gro): Vom Heissen Stein. (Vins): Goldlay, Marienburg, Nonnengarten, Rosenberg.

Pundy (Scot) a seventeenth century term for second mash, low-gravity beer. Now describes the free allowance of beer given to the brewery workers.

Pungent (Eng) a term used to describe a wine that is spicy, heavily-scented and powerful.

Punjéno u (Slo) bottled at.

Punsch (Swe) a rum-based drink served hot or cold.

Punt (Eng) the depression in the bottom of bottles, used for stacking by placing the neck of one into the punt of the other.

Punt e Mes (It) lit: 'point and a half', a delicious apéritif produced by Carpano of Turin. A bitter sweet vermouth flavoured with quinine. It is traditionally drunk with piece of chocolate 17% alc by vol.

Puntigam Bier (Aus) a beer brewed by the Reininghaus Brauerei for export to the USA.

Puntigam Märzen (Aus) a beer 5% alc by vol. brewed by the Reininghaus Brauerei in Graz.

Punty-Mark (Eng) this is left when the blown bottle is broken off the punty rod. The '*kick*' was introduced to ensure that the bottle stood even and steady. *see* Kick and Punty-Rod.

Punty-Rod (Eng) in early glass bottle making, a metal rod for carrying gathered glass at the tip, which was attached to the bottom of the bottle to enable the mouth to be reheated for shaping. This left a punty-mark or rough scar when the bottle was broken off.

Punzante (Sp) describes a Sherry with a sharp bouquet.

P

Pupille [Le] (It) the best known estate of D.O.C. Morellino di Scansano. Also producce a Morellino called Poggio Valente and a Bordeaux blend with Alicante grapes included called Saffredi.

Pupillin (Fr) a wine-producing village in the Jura. Produces a dry white wine of same name.

Pupimatic (Fr) an alternative word for the Gyropalette.

Pupistras (Sp) special racks to hold sparkling wines. see Pupîtres.

Pupîtres (Fr) lit: 'desks', special racks in which Champagne bottles are placed for turning by the remueurs before dégorgement. See also Crecelles, Gyropalettes and Riddling Frames.

Pur (Fr) unblended/undiluted.

Pur (Fr) a term applied to kirsch that is a natural distillation. Has no additives apart from cherries.

Pura (It) a sparkling natural spring mineral water from Cagliari, Sardinia. Mineral contents (milligrammes per litre): Sodium 42.7mg/l, Calcium 14.7mg/l, Magnesium 12.7mg/l, Potassium 1.4mg/l, Bicarbonates 84.1mg/l, Chlorides 66.6mg/l, Sulphates 18.9mg/l, Fluorides 0.1mg/l, Nitrates 1.8mg/l, Silicates 12.3mg/l. pH 6.84

Pura Bronnen (Bel) a natural spring mineral water from Hertog, Dikkelvenne.

Purborn (Ger) a natural spring mineral water. Mineral contents (milligrammes per litre): Sodium 8.6mg/l, Calcium 50.6mg/l, Magnesium 31.3mg/l, Potassium 8mg/l, Bicarbonates 313mg/l, Chlorides 5.3mg/l, Fluorides 0.14 mg/l.

Pure Alcohol (Eng) denotes alcohol at over 99% pure (distilled in a patent still) also known as rectified spirit. (Ire) = fioralcól.

Purebred (S.Afr) the label for a red wine (Shiraz, Cabernet sauvignon, Merlot blend) produced by the Excelsior Estate winery, Paarl, Western Cape.

Purdey's (Eng) a sparkling drink of multi-vitamins and herbs in a base of natural fruit juices and spring water. Produced by Callitheke, Upwell, Hartlepool.

Pure Brewed (I.O.M) the name for a draught bitter ale brewed by the Okells Brewery.

Pure Brewed Lager (Eng) a 5% alc by vol. lager brewed by Samuel Smith in Tadcaster.

Pure Coffee (Eng) unblended coffee beans from one area of a coffee-producing country. Is also known as Original Coffee.

Purée (Fr) another name for Absinthe Swiss-Style where grenadine is used instead of syrup to sweeten it. Also known as Tomate.

Pure Gold (Eng) a 4.8% alc by vol. golden ale brewed by the Itchen Valley Brewery, Hampshire.

Pure Lemon Juice (Eng) abbr: see PLJ.

Pure Lifekare (Ind) a natural spring mineral water. Mineral contents (milligrammes per litre): Sodium 4mg/l, Calcium 0.6mg/l, Magnesium 1.2mg/l, Bicarbonates 29mg/l, Chlorides 14mg/l. pH 7.2

Pure Lincoln County Corn Whiskey (USA) a 21 year old N°7 Whiskey produced by the Jack Daniel Distillery in Tennessee.

Pure Love (Cktl) 20mls (¾ fl.oz) framboise, 35mls (1½ fl.ozs) gin, 20mls (¾ fl.oz) lime juice. Shake over ice, strain into an ice-filled highball glass, stir in ginger ale and decorate with a slice of lime.

Pure Montana (USA) a natural spring mineral water from Giant Springs Heritage State Park, Great Falls, Montana. Mineral contents (milligrammes per litre): Calcium 88mg/l, Magnesium 31mg/l, Bicarbonates 246mg/l, Sulphates 148mg/l, Fluorides 0.6mg/l, Nitrates 0.5mg/l. pH 7.6

Pure Pride (USA) a natural spring mineral water from New Hope, Pensylvania.

Purely Scottish (Ch.Isles) the name of fruit flavoured still and sparkling Scottish waters from Purely Scottish. Bottled at Oldhamstocks on the Scottish borders. Called Scotty in France.

Purely Scottish (Scot) a natural spring mineral water from Lammermuir Hills. Mineral contents (milligrammes per litre): Sodium 16mg/l, Calcium 30mg/l, Potassium 3mg/l, Chlorides 29mg/l, Sulphatès 15mg/l, Nitrates 11mg/l.

Purely Sedona (USA) a natural spring mineral water (established circa 1800) from Oak Creek Canyon, Sedona, Arizona.

Pure Malt (Scot) an 8 y.o. vatted malt whisky 40% alc by vol. produced by Inver House Distillers Ltd. in Airdrie.

Pure Malt White (Jap) an Islay-style malt whiskey produced by Nikka.

Pure Six [6] (Eng) a 5.9% alc by vol. premium lager brewed and bottled by Holsten in Hamburg.

Pure Strain (Eng) the native grape/not a hybrid.

Pureza Aga (Mex) a natural spring mineral water from Ixtapaluca. Mineral contents (milligrammes per litre): Calcium 8mg/l, Magnesium 9mg/l, Bicarbonates 80mg/l, Chlorides 16mg/l, Sulphates 8mg/l.

Pureza Vital (Arg) a natural spring mineral water. Mineral contents (milligrammes per litre): Sodium 4.6mg/l, Calcium 51.5mg/l, Magnesium 5.2mg/l, Potassium 1.6mg/l, Bicarbonates 32.8mg/l, Chlorides 80.3mg/l, Sulphates 18.1mg/l, Fluorides 0.5mg/l.

Purification Fining (Eng) a term given to the use of a fining agent to remove taint, tannins or colour from wine.

Purificator (Eng) a white cloth used to wipe the chalice after Communion has been taken.

Purisima [La] (Sp) a large co-operative based in Yecla in the Levante. Produces wines under the Viña Montana label.

Purisima [La] (USA) a small winery based south of San Francisco, San Mateo, California. Grape varieties: Cabernet sauvignon, Pinot noir, Zinfandel. Produces varietal wines.

Puritans Porter (Eng) a 4% alc by vol. porter brewed by the Springhead Brewery, Nottinghamshire.

Purity Law (Ger) 1615. see Reinheitsgebot.

Pur Jus (Fr) pure juice.

Purl (Eng) an old-fashioned English drink of gin, hot ale and bitters.

Purosangue (It) a 100% Sangiovese red wine produced by Azienda Agricola Livernano in Radda, Tuscany.

Purple Abbot [The] (Fr) a famous ninth century monk of Angers who had a song written about his drinking habits saying that his skin was dyed with wine and his flesh became incorruptible through so much drink.

Purple Delight Cocktail (Cktl) ¼ measure gin, ½ measure Parfait Amour, ¼ measure lemon juice. Shake over ice and strain into a cocktail glass.

Purple Flag Winery (Austr) a winery based in Western Australia. Grape varieties include: Cabernet sauvignon.

Purple Heather (Cktl) 1 teaspoon cassis, 40mls whisky. Pour into an ice-filled highball glass, stir and top with soda water.

Purple Kiss (Cktl) 1 measure dry gin, ½ measure crème de noyau, ½ measure lemon juice, dash cherry brandy, dash egg white. Shake over ice and strain into a cocktail glass.

Purple Mask Cocktail (Cktl) ⅖ measure vodka, ⅖ measure grape juice, ⅕ measure (white) crème de cacao. Shake over ice and strain into a cocktail glass.

Purple Parrot (USA) a natural spring mineral water from Bear Hollow Springs, Florida. Mineral contents (milligrammes per litre): Fluorides 0.2mg/l.

Purple Passion (Eng) an alcoholic drink produced by Commercial Concepts in Brighton.

PurQuell (Ger) a natural spring mineral water from Dreis, Vulkaneifel. Mineral contents (milligrammes per litre): Sodium 9mg/l, Calcium 51mg/l, Magnesium 31mg/l, Potassium 8mg/l, Bicarbonates 313mg/l, Chlorides 5mg/l.

Puschkin Red (Eng) a vodka-based mixer drink from Berentzen Distillers, Hailsham, Sussex. *See also* Black Sun.

Pusser's (Eng) famous producers of British Navy rum 40% alc by vol. From the sale of which goes a donation to the Sailors fund.

Pussy Cat Cocktail (Cktl)(Non-alc) 50mls (2fl.ozs) each of pineapple juice, orange juice, 25mls (1fl.oz) grapefruit juice, 3 dashes grenadine. Shake over crushed ice, pour into a cocktail glass, top with a slice of orange and grapefruit.

Pussyfoot (Cktl) 35mls (1½fl.oz) each of white rum, cream, pineapple juice, lime juice, cherry juice. Blend in a blender with a scoop of crushed ice, pour into a collins glass, dress with a cherry and slice of orange.

Pussyfoot [1] (Cktl)(Non-alc) ⅓ measure lime juice, ⅓ measure orange juice, ⅓ measure lemon juice, dash grenadine. Shake over ice and strain into a large cocktail glass.

Pussyfoot [2] (Cktl)(Non-alc) juice of a lemon and an orange, 20mls (⅙ gill) apricot syrup, white of egg, sprig of mint. Shake well over ice and strain into a 125mls (5fl.oz) goblet.

Pussyfoot Cocktail (Cktl)(Non-alc) 50mls (2fl.ozs) each of lime juice, lemon juice, orange juice, 1 egg yolk, dash of grenadine. Shake over ice, strain into a tulip glass, dress with a cherry and slice of orange.

Putachieside (Scot) a de luxe vatted Scotch whisky. 12 years old. Produced by William Cadenhead in Aberdeen 43% alc by vol.

Putao (Chi) grapes (is often written Pu-Tao).

Putao Chiu (Chi) grape wine.

Putaojiu (Chi) wine. Also spelt Putao Chiu.

Putt (Hun) *see* Puttonyos.

Putto (It) the Tuscan dialect for the infant Bacchus. Used on the Chianti Putto neck label.

Puttony (Hun) *see* Puttonyos.

Puttonyos (Hun) a bucket for gathering grapes in the Tokaji region. Holds about 13.5kgs. Used to denote the sweetness and quality in Tokaji Aszú wines. Each puttonyos of botrytis affected grapes used is indicated on the bottle label (now measured in g/l).

Puvermächer (Ger) vineyard (Anb): Württemberg. (Ber): Remstal-Stuttgart. (Gro): Wartbühl. (Vil): Stetten i R.

Puy de Dôme (Fr) a Vin de Pays area in the Puy de Dôme département, central France. Is part of the Jardin de la France. Produces red, rosé and dry white wines (part of the Côte d'Auvergne region).

Puymeras (Fr) a village in the A.C. Côtes du Rhône-Villages. Produces mainly red wines (with a little rosé and white wine).

Puysegur [Marquis de] (Fr) an Armagnac distiller of Labastide d'Armagnac.

Puzzle (Eng) a 4.8% alc by vol. ale brewed by Salopian Brewing C°. Ltd., Shropshire.

Puzzle Jug (Eng) a joke jug, a jug/mug with many holes which tests the drinker as to which is the correct hole to drink out of and which holes to cover with the fingers.

P.V.P. (Eng) *abbr*: **P**oly**v**inyl**p**yorolidone.

P.X. (Sp) *abbr*: **P**edro **X**iménez.

Pyment (Eng) a mead made from honey and grape juice (similar to Madeira).

P.Y.N.C. (Sp) *abbr*: **P**enedés **y** **N**ort **C**ataluña.

Pynikki Brewery (Fin) a small family brewery based in Tampere, western Finland. Brews Admiral (labelled with a series of mariners from Nelson to Alfred Von Tirpitz).

Pyralis (Lat) the grape moth whose caterpillar attacks the spring buds on the vine and then the grapes. *See also* Cochylis, Eudemis.

Pyramus (Fr) a white wine produced from Rolle grapes in the A.C. Coteaux Varois by Château Routas.

Pyrazine (Bio) a compound found in under-ripe grapes that gives wines a '*green*', herbaceous aroma and flavour.

Pyrenäen (Fr) a natural spring mineral water from Montcalm, Captage, La Prime Vallée d'Auzat Ariège. Mineral contents (milligrammes per litre): Sodium 1.5mg/l, Calcium 3mg/l,

Magnesium 0.6mg/l, Potassium 0.4mg/l, Bicarbonates 5.2mg/l, Chlorides 0.6mg/l, Sulphates 8.7mg/l, Nitrates <1mg/l, Silicates 7.5mg/l. pH 6.8

Pyrenees (Austr) a light wine-producing area in Victoria where a winery of the same name is based that has a cool climate and stony quartz loam soil. Also known as Avoca.

Pyrénées (Fr) a large area in south-western France on the Spanish border. Made up of the Ariège, Basses Pyrénées, Hautes Pyrénées and Pyrénées-Orientales. Produces red, rosé, white and fortified (VdN) wines.

Pyrénées (Fr) a natural spring mineral water from Ogeu. Mineral contents (milligrammes per litre): Sodium 31mg/l, Calcium 48mg/l, Magnesium 12mg/l, Potassium 1mg/l, Bicarbonates 183mg/l, Chlorides 48mg/l, Sulphates 18mg/l, Nitrates 5mg/l.

Pyrénées Atlantiques (Fr) a Vin de Pays area in the Basse Pyrénées département, south-western France.

Pyrénées-Orientales (Fr) a département of the Languedoc-Roussillon. Based in the low valleys of rivers Agly and Tech.

Pyridine (Eng) the violet dye added to methanol to produce methylated spirits.

Pyridoxin (Eng) a vitamin found in wine in minute traces.

Pyrolysis (Lat) the chemical decomposition of sucrose in the coffee bean which is released when the bean is subjected to excessive heat (roasting). Occurs at 240°C (464°F).

Pyromucic Aldehyde (Lat) an aldehyde formed at the beginning of spirit distillation which gradually disappears as it matures in the cask.

Pyrus (Austr) a red wine produced by Lindemans in New South Wales.

Q (It) a quality award shown on Marsala labels, may be applied to all classifications.

Qahwa (Arab) coffee.

Qarabas (Iran) the name for the large wine jars used in Persian times.

Qat (Arab) an alternative name for Khat.

Q.b.A. (Ger) *abbr*: Qualitätswein bestimmter Anbaugebiete.

Q.b.U. (Ger) *abbr*: Qualitätswein Garantierten Ursprungs.

Q.C. British Fortified Wine (Eng) a brand-name wine made from imported concentrated grape must by Vine Products Ltd. Originally known as British Sherry.

Qenena (Arab) bottle.

Q Four Cocktail (Cktl) ¼ measure Scotch whisky, ¼ measure Chartreuse, ¼ measure Royal Mint Chocolate Liqueur, ¼ measure Cinzano bianco. Shake over ice and strain into a cocktail glass.

Qigh Chun Bao (Chi) a natural spring mineral water. Mineral contents (milligrammes per litre): Sodium 1.3mg/l, Calcium 2mg/l, Magnesium 2.5mg/l, Potassium 0.3mg/l, Silicates 10mg/l.

Q Marchia di Qualità (It) the quality seal found on the label of Sicilian wines that have passed strict analysis and tasting tests. Is above D.O.C.

Q Mark (It) *see* Q Marchia di Qualità.

Q.m.P. (Ger) *abbr*: Qualitätswein mit Prädikat.

Qt (Eng) *abbr*: Quart.

Q.T. (Eng) the brand-name of a tea produced by Premier Beverages.

Q2 (Ger) a natural spring mineral water from Rosendahl. Mineral contents (milligrammes per litre): Sodium 17.1mg/l, Calcium 77.4mg/l, Magnesium 3.2mg/l, Potassium 1.1mg/l, Chlorides 34.4mg/l, Sulphates 22mg/l.

Quacka Jack (Eng) a 4% alc by vol. ale brewed by the Mallard Brewery, Nottinghamshire.

Quady Winery (USA) a winery based in Madera, California. Grape varieties include: Zinfandel. Noted for Starboard (Port-style), Electra (California Orange muscat), Elysium (Black muscat) wines.

Quaff (Eng) to drink in large gulps.

Quaffing (Eng) drinking in large gulps, everyday drinking without care.

Quaffing Ale (Eng) a 3.8% alc by vol. ale brewed by the Red Rose Brewery, Lancashire.

Quagga Ridge (S.Afr) the label for a range of wines red (Cabernet sauvignon & Merlot), rosé (80% Pinotage plus Merlot) and white (Sauvignon blanc and Sémillon) produced by the Horse Mountain Wines winery, Paarl, Western Cape.

Quaich (Scot) Gaelic for cup, (cuach = cup), of highlands origin, it is like a small bowl with up to four handles on the sides, made of wood or metal.

Quai des Chatrons (Fr) area where the négociants have their headquarters in Bordeaux.

Quail Hill Vineyard (USA) the label for a red wine (Pinot noir) produced by the Lynmar winery, Russian River Valley, Sonoma County, California.

Quail Ridge Winery (USA) a winery based in the Napa Valley, California. Grape varieties: Cabernet sauvignon, Chardonnay. Produces varietal wines.

Quail's Gate Winery (Can) a winery based in British Columbia.

Quaker Bean (Eng) denotes from an immature or unripe coffee bean.

Quaker's Cocktail (Cktl) ½ measure white rum. ½ measure brandy, juice of a ¼ lemon, 2 dashes raspberry syrup. Shake over ice and strain into a cocktail glass.

Qualitätsprüfung (Ger) quality examination.

Qualitäts-Schaumwein (Aus) a sparkling wine produced by having the second fermentation in tank (or bottle then disgorged in tank). Also known as Qualitätssekt. Uses Austrian grapes only.

Qualitätsschaumwein (Ger) a classification of sekt which is above schaumwein it must be 10% alc by vol and have secondary fermentation, remain on the yeast for at least 21 days and mature for 9 months. Also referred to as Qualitätssekt.

Qualitäts-Sekt (Aus) *see* Qualitäts-Schaumwein.

Qualitätssekt (Ger) *see* Qualitätsschaumwein.

Qualitätswein (Aus) quality wine, subjected to strict conditions such as grapes used, quality and a minimum must weight of 15° KMW. May be chaptalised by up to 4.5kgs of sugar to 100litres of must (maximums: white wines 19° KMW and 9% alc by vol./red wines 20° KMW and 8.5% alc by vol.).

Qualitätswein (Ger) quality wine (quality controlled).

Qualitätswein Besonderer Reife und Leseart (Aus) also known as Prädikatswein, has 6 possible designations: spätlese, auslese, eiswein, beerenauslese, ausbruch and trockenbeerenauslese.

Qualitätswein Bestimmter Anbaugebiete (Ger) *abbr*: QbA quality wines from specific areas (13 anbaugebiete).

Qualitätswein Garantierten Ursprungs (Ger) *abbr*:

QbU a new designation since 1994, 100% of produce (wine and süssreserve) must come from the designated bereich, grosslage or einzellage.

Qualitätswein Kabinett (Aus) as for Qualitätswein but can be chaptalised or enriched and have a minimum must weight of 17° KMW.

Qualitätswein mit Prädikat (Ger) abbr: QmP, quality wine with predicate (distinction). i.e. made under superior quality control or specially harvested and quality controlled. see Kabinett, Spätlese, Auslese, Eiswein, Beerenauslese and Trockenbeerenauslese. See also Oechsle.

Qualitätsweinprufstelle (Ger) the official testing station where the A.P. number for quality control is awarded.

Qualité Anglaise (Fr) a name given to claret wine in the eighteenth and nineteenth centuries for Claret that had the qualities the English liked.

Qualité Recomponsée Chaque Année (Fr) quality re-assessed annually, found on a label or advert.

Quality Spirits UK Ltd (Scot) a distillery (established 2004). (Add): Strathclyde Business park, Phoenix Crescent, Motherwell, Lanarkshire ML4 3AN. Produces a range of spirits and vermouths. Part of William Grant & Sons Ltd. Website: http://www.wgrant.com 'E'mail: lynn.orwatt@wgrant.com

Quality Wine Produced in a Specific Region (E.C.) abbr: Q.W.P.S.R.

Quality Wine Scheme (Eng) abbr: Q.W.S. a pilot scheme from the 1991 harvest. Regulatory authority is the Wine Standards Board. All wines have to submit to a tasting panel.

Quancard (Fr) a Burgundy shipper based in Beaune in the Côte de Beaune.

Quando (S.Afr) a winery (established 2001) based in Bonnievale, Robertson, Western Cape. 80ha. Grape varieties include: Sauvignon blanc.

Quantum (S.Afr) the export label for a range of wines produced by the Lost Horizons Premium Wines winery, Suider-Paarl, Western Cape.

Quarles Harris (Port) vintage Port shippers. Vintages: 1927, 1934, 1945, 1947, 1950, 1955, 1958, 1960, 1963, 1966, 1970, 1975, 1977, 1980, 1983, 1985, 1991, 1994, 1995, 1997, 2003. Owned by Symingtons Family Estates.

Quarrelbrook (S.Afr) a natural spring mineral water (established 1996). Mineral contents (milligrammes per litre): Sodium 38mg/l, Calcium 52mg/l, Magnesium 44mg/l, Potassium 2.8mg/l, Chlorides 57mg/l, Sulphates 13mg/l, Nitrates 0.53mg/l. pH 7.4

Quart (Eng) abbr: **Qt**. 2pints (40fl.ozs). ¼ Gallon (1.136litres). 1.2009 USquarts. (Den) = måleenhed.

Quart (Fr) a small bottle of (18.75cls) capacity used in the Champagne region. see Champagne Bottle Sizes. See also Quarter Bottle.

Quart (USA) abbr: **Qt**. 2pints (0.946litres) 0.8326 UK quarts. (Den) = måleenhed.

Quart (USA) bottle size 32fl.ozs (¼ U.Sgallon).

Quartaut (Fr) a barrel holding about 56litres.

Quart de Chaume (Fr) see Quarts de Chaume.

Quarter (Eng) a measure of barley 448lbs (205kgs), each quarter yields about 336lbs (155kgs) of malt or 80lbs–100lbs (36kgs–45kgs.) of malt extract for the brewer.

Quarter Bottle (Eng) the alternative name for a Quart Champagne bottle.

Quarter Bottle (USA) a wine bottle containing 6fl.ozs–6½ fl.ozs (185mls) ½ of a standard wine bottle.

Quarter Cask (Port) a cask of 134litres capacity.

Quarter Cask (USA) in cases where the standard cask, pipe or butt is too large for a merchant, casks containing one fourth the original are used. Quarter casks vary in contents, depending on the wine region where they are used.

Quarter Deck (Cktl) ⅓ measure dry Sherry, ⅔ measure dark rum, dash lime cordial. Stir over ice and strain into a cocktail glass.

Quartern (Eng) also known as a noggin or a gill, a measure of 140mls (5fl.ozs ¼ pint).

Quarter Pipe (Port) a cask of 134litres capacity.

Quarter Round (Eng) an old-style spirits bottle (brandy) of quarter bottle size, discontinued in 1981 in favour of the flask (rectangular) bottle.

Quarters (Port) cask 28gallons (Port).

Quarters (Scot) cask 28gallons (whisky).

Quarters (Sp) cask 28gallons (Sherry).

Quartet (S.Afr) the label for a red wine (Merlot 50% plus Cabernet sauvignon, Pinotage and Shiraz blend) produced by the Domaine Brahms Wineries, Paarl, Western Cape.

Quartet (USA) a sparkling wine produced by Champagne Louis Roederer in Anderson Valley from a blend of 70% Chardonnay, 30% Pinot noir grapes.

Quartet (Eng) a mandarin orange liqueur 30% alc by vol.

Quartiers (Fr) plots (small vineyards) in the Rhône.

Quartino (It) a quarter litre of wine.

Quarts-de-Chaume (Fr) an A.C. wine made from the Chenin blanc grapes that have been attacked by *Botrytis cinerea* a sweet white wine from the Coteaux du Layon in the Anjou-Saumur district in the Loire region (4 vineyard sites).

Quasi-Raisins (Fr) grapes that do not ripen but appear like raisins, hard, small and green. see Millerandage.

Quass (Rus) a rye beer made from stale black bread. See also Kvass and Kvas.

Quassen (Ger) a seventeenth century term to denote excessive drinking.

Quat (Arab) an alternative name for Khat.

Qua-ter (Viet) a natural spring mineral water. Mineral contents (milligrammes per litre): Sodium 70mg/l, Calcium 32.9mg/l, Magnesium 4.2mg/l, Potassium 1.5mg/l, Bicarbonates 75.8mg/l, Chlorides 9.6mg/l, Fluorides 0.27mg/l. pH 7.0

Quatourze (Fr) an A.C. district of the Aude département in the Midi. Is classed as part of the Coteaux du Languedoc. Produces mainly red and dry white wines. Minimum alc by vol. of 11%.

Quatre Coteaux [Les] (Fr) an A.C. Côtes du Roussillon. A red wine by Les Grands Vignobles.

Quatrième Crus (Fr) the fourth growth Cru Classé of the Médoc of the 1855 classification. Chateaux: Beychevelle, Branaire-Duluc, Duhart-Milon, La Tour-Carnet, Marquis de Terme, Pouget, Prieuré-Lichine, Rochet, Saint-Pierre, Talbot.

Quawah (Afr) the old Arabic word used for coffee. *See also* Kahweh and Kahwa.

Quay Brewery (Eng) a brewery based in Hope Square, Weymouth. Brews: Weymouth Special Pale Ale, SOS, Weymouth JD 1742, Bombshell Bitter, Old Rott, Silent Knight, Groves Oatmeal Stout, Weymouth Organic Gold. Now known as the Dorset Brewing Company Ltd.

Qudengnima (Chi) a natural spring mineral water from Tibet. Mineral contents (milligrammes per litre): Sodium 1.05mg/l, Calcium 17.26mg/l, Magnesium 2.97mg/l, Potassium 1.57mg/l, Bicarbonates 59.07mg/l, Chlorides 1.7mg/l, Sulphates 9.87mg/l, Nitrates 0.16mg/l. pH 7.39

Quebec Cocktail (Cktl) 1 measure Canadian whisky, ¼ measure French vermouth, 2 dashes Amer Picon, 2 dashes maraschino. Shake over ice, strain into a cocktail glass and dress with a cherry.

Quebranta (S.Am) a grape used in the production of Pisco in Peru.

Queen Adelaide (Austr) the label used by the Woodleys Winery for their Claret.

Queen Anne (Scot) a blended Scotch whisky from Hill Thompson and C°. Ltd. Edinburgh (part of the Glenlivet Distillers Ltd).

Queen Bee (Cktl) ⅓ measure vodka, ⅓ measure Tia Maria, ⅙ measure lime juice, ⅙ measure sweet Sherry. Shake over ice and strain into a cocktail glass.

Queen Charlotte Cocktail (Cktl) ⅔ measure red wine, ⅓ measure grenadine. Stir over ice, strain into a highball glass and top with iced lemonade.

Queene Court Wine (Eng) a medium dry wine made from the Müller-Thurgau grapes. Produced at the Ospringe Vineyards near Faversham. Made by Shepherd Neame.

Queen Elizabeth [1] (Cktl) ¾ measure dry gin, ¼ measure dry vermouth, 2 dashes Bénédictine. Stir over ice and strain into a cocktail glass.

Queen Elizabeth [2] (Cktl) ½ measure Cognac, ½ measure sweet vermouth, dash Grand Marnier. Shake over ice, strain into a cocktail glass and top with a cherry.

Queen Isabella (Sp) a dry apéritif wine produced by the Bodegas Los Curros and bottled in Rueda.

Queen Mary (Ind) a blend of Darjeeling teas, made from fine Broken Orange Pekoe by Twinings for Queen Mary of England.

Queen of May (Eng) a 3.2% alc by vol. seasonal ale brewed by Green Bottle Ltd., Worth Brewery, Keighley, Yorkshire.

Queen's Cocktail (Cktl) 20 mls (⅙ gill) each of dry gin, French vermouth, Italian vermouth. Shake well over ice, strain into a cocktail glass. Decorate with a slice of orange and a piece of pineapple.

Queen's Head Brewery (Eng) a brewery based in Evesham, Worcestershire. Brews: Fat God's Mild.

Queen Victoria (Eng) a home-brew public house in London, noted for cask-conditioned Sidekick 1047 O.G. and County 1036 O.G.

Queijeira (Port) dairy.

Queimada (Sp) a drink made by pouring aguardiente into an earthenware bowl, adding lemon slices, coffee beans and maraschino cherries. The spirit is then set alight.

Quel (Sp) a Zona de Crianza in the Rioja Baja.

Quelle (Ger) spring (water).

Quelle Acht Bornheim (Ger) a natural spring mineral water from Bornheim. Mineral contents (milligrammes per litre): Sodium 99mg/l, Calcium 106mg/l, Magnesium 27mg/l, Bicarbonates 360mg/l, Chlorides 90mg/l, Sulphates 191mg/l, Fluorides 0.44mg/l.

Quelle Pur (Ger) a natural spring mineral water from Rottenburg, Obernau. Mineral contents (milligrammes per litre): Sodium 26.4mg/l, Calcium 625mg/l, Magnesium 87.5mg/l, Bicarbonates 1149mg/l, Chlorides 41mg/l, Sulphates 942mg/l.

Quelltaler Springvale Vineyard (Austr) a winery. (Add): Main Road (P.O. Box 10), Watervale, South Australia 5452. 265ha. Grape varieties: Chenin blanc, Rhine riesling, Sauvignon blanc, Sémillon and Traminer riesling. Noted for Granfiesta South African Sherry.

Quenard [André et Michel] (Fr) a 20ha wine estate on the Côteau de Torméry, Chignin. Produces Chignin-Bergeron Cuvée les Terrasses, Chignin Mondeuse Cuvée Vieilles Vignes.

Quench (Eng) to satisfy i.e. 'to quench one's thirst'.

Quench (Eng) the name of a range of fruit syrups from Brooke Bond Foodservice that need to be diluted with water.

Quench Dispensers Ltd (Eng) still water producers. (Add): Vale House, 100 Vale road, Windsor, Berkshire SL4 5JL. Produces still water (in dispensers). Website: http://www.quenchltd.co.uk 'E'mail: quench@btconnect.com

Querce Sola (It) a winery that produces Chianti Classico aged in oak. (Add): Via Quercesola 44, I-53011 Castellina in Chianti (FI).

Quercetin (Eng) *see* Flavenoids.

Quercia (It) oak.

Querciabella (It) a winery (26ha) in the DOCG Chianti Classico, Tuscany region. Grape varieties: Cabernet sauvignon, Merlot, Pinot blanc, Sangiovese, Syrah.

Quercus (Lat) oak.

Quercus alba (USA) a pale barked white American oak.

Quercus Gold (S.Afr) the label for a white wine (Chardonnay) produced by the Darling Cellars, Swartland.

Quercus pendonculus albus (Lat) Monlezun oak.

Quercus petraea (Euro) a brown oak from northern Europe.

Quercus suber (Lat) the name for the Cork Oak, the

Q

bark is used for bottle corks. Found in Portugal and Spain.

Quercus Vineyard (USA) a vineyard based in Lake County, California. Grape variety: Cabernet sauvignon. Vinified at the Carey Winery.

Quercy (Fr) an alternative name for the Malbec grape.

Querétaro (Mex) a wine-producing district that contains the Juan del Rîo area.

Quetsch (Fr) an alcool blanc made from switzen plums 43%–45% alc by vol.

Quetsch d'Alsace (Fr) a plum liqueur brandy made in Alsace.

Queue (Fr) a Burgundy cask holding 2 hogsheads.

Queue de Hareng (Fr) a vineyard in the commune of Brochon, Côte d'Or, Burgundy.

Queue de Renard (Fr) an alternative name for the Ugni blanc grape.

Queue Tendre (Fr) an alternative name for the Colombard grape. Also called the Queue verte.

Queue Verte (Fr) an alternative name for the Colombard grape. Also called the Queue tendre.

Queyrac (Fr) a commune in the Bas-Médoc, north-western Bordeaux.has A.C. Médoc status.

Quézac (Fr) a naturally carbonated mineral water from the Lozère, Loire Valley. (Add): S.E.M. Quézac, Molines, 48320 Ispagnac, Loire. Mineral contents (milligrammes per litre): Sodium 255mg/l, Calcium 241mg/l, Magnesium 95mg/l, Potassium 49.7mg/l, Bicarbonates 1685.4mg/l, Chlorides 38mg/l, Sulphates 143mg/l, Fluoride 2.1mg/l. pH 6.8

Quibell (USA) a sparkling natural spring mineral water from Martinsville, Virginia. Mineral contents (milligrammes per litre): Calcium 36.6mg/l, Magnesium 9.27mg/l.

Quick Brew (Eng) a famous tea blend produced by Lyons Tetley.

Quickie (Eng) a term which refers to an alcoholic drink (usually a tot of spirit or half pint [300mls] of beer) a quick drink drunk without any ceremony or conversation. Also called a Quick one.

Quick One (Eng) see Quickie.

Quiet Sunday (Cktl) 25mls (1fl.oz) vodka, 10mls (½fl.oz) amaretto, 100mls (4fl.ozs) fresh orange juice, 3 dashes grenadine. Shake over ice (all except grenadine), strain into ice-filled highball glass and add grenadine.

Quila (E.Ind) see Quilang.

Quilang (E.Ind) a spirit distilled from cane juice in the Philippines, also known as Quila.

Quilceda Creek Vintners (USA) a winery based in Oregon. Produces Quilceda from Cabernet sauvignon, Merlot and Cabernet franc grapes. Aged for 22 months in French oak.

Quillardet [Charles] (Fr) a négociant-éleveur. (Add): 18 Rte. de Dijon, 21200 Gevrey-Chambertin, Côte de Nuits, Burgundy.

Quilmes (Arg) a top-selling lager-style beer 4.9 alc by vol.

Quina Gris (Sp) lit: 'grey quinine', an ingredient used to produce Vinos Quinados.

Quina Roja (Sp) lit: 'red quinine', an ingredient used to produce Vinos Quinados.

Quincié (Fr) a commune in the Beaujolais region, has A.C. Beaujolais-Villages or Beaujolais-Quincié status.

Quincy (Fr) an A.C. wine area of the Central Vineyards district in the eastern Loire. Produces steely, dry, well-perfumed white wines from the Sauvignon blanc grape. Red and rosé wines from Pinot noir grapes. (Coms): Brinay and Quincy. Minimum alc by vol. 10.5%.

Quincy Vin Noble (Fr) an A.C. white dry wine from Quincy in the Central Vineyards district of the Loire.

Quindto's Port (Fr) the brand-name of a Port.

Quinine (Bot) $C_{20}H_{24}$ obtained from the chinchona bark N_2O_2 used in the making of vermouth, quinquina and Indian tonic water. (Hol) = kinine.

Quinine Wine (Fr) see Quinquina.

Quinn's (Eng) a 4% alc by vol pure fruit juice RTD produced by Diago G.B. Flavours include: Mango & Passionfruit/Orange & Tropical Fruits/Raspberry & Blueberry.

Quinn's Cooler (USA) a 'cooler' produced from red wine and natural citrus fruit 6% alc by vol. Also a white wine and natural citrus flavour 6% alc by vol.

Quinoa (S.Am) *Chenopodium quinoa* the seeds of a herbaceous plant used in the making of Chicha.

Quinquina (Fr) an apéritif wine, has a flavour of quinine and was given to the soldiers who were fighting in the tropics to fight malaria.

Quinquina Bourin (Fr) a proprietary apéritif with a quinine flavour.

Quinta (Port) lit: 'farm', a vineyard or estate. It includes the actual vineyards and buildings. see Vinha Vinhedo.

Quinta Amarela (Port) a noted Port wine quinta based south of the Vale de Mendiz in the Alto Douro.

Quinta Boa Vista (Port) a 250ha noted vineyard owned by Offley Forester, based north-east of Peso da Pegua in the Alto Douro. Wine often sold as a single quinta vintage Port. Vintages: 1900, 1904, 1908, 1910, 1912, 1919, 1920, 1922, 1924, 1925, 1927, 1929, 1935, 1947, 1950, 1954, 1955, 1960, 1962, 1963, 1966, 1967, 1970, 1972, 1975, 1977, 1980, 1982, 1983, 1985, 1991, 1994, 1995, 1997, 2000, 2003.

Quinta Crown (Port) a fine old Tawny Port from Balls Brothers of London.

Quinta D Carlos (Port) see Quinta De Pancas.

Quinta da Abelheira (Port) a vineyard estate based in the Douro (part of the Quinta do Portal group of vineyards).

Quinta da Agua Alta (Port) a single quinta vintage Port from Churchill Graham Lda. Based near Ferrao. Grape varieties: Tinta barroca, Tinta roriz and Touriga nacional.

Quinta da Aguieira (Port) a vineyard based in the northern Bairrada region 14ha. Produces garrafeira wines.

Q

Quinta da Alegria (Port) a '*Port-style*' wine vineyard based north-east of Sao João da Pesqueira in the Alto Douro.

Quinta da Alorna (Port) a winery based in Robatejano. Grape varieties include: Touriga nacional. Produces red white and rosé wines.

Quinta da Avelada (Port) a vineyard based in Peñafiel. 24ha. (Add): PO Box 77, 4560-730 Peñafiel, Portugal. Grape varieties: Loureiro, Pederna and Trajadura. Produces Avelada and Casal Garcia. Website: http://www.avelada.pt 'E'mail: info@avelada.pt

Quinta da Bacalhoa (Port) a vineyard based near Setúbal in the Estremadura owned by João Pires. Grape varieties: mainly Cabernet sauvignon, Merlot. Website: http://www.bacalhoa.com

Quinta da Baleira (Port) a Port-producing vineyard based north-east of Sao João de Pesqueira in the Alto Douro.

Quinta da Boa Vista (Port) a 150ha vineyard in the Estremadura. Light wines are bottled under Qunita da Espiga, Palha-Canas, Casa Santos Lima, Quinta de Setencostas labels.

Quinta da Cabana (Port) a Port-wine vineyard based east of Peso da Regua in the Alto Douro.

Quinta da Cachucha (Port) a Port wine vineyard based north of the river Douro in the Alto Douro.

Quinta da Carvalheira (Port) a Port wine vineyard based south-east of Pinhão in the Alto Douro.

Quinta da Cavadinha (Port) a single quinta Port vineyard owned by Warre. Vintages: 1978, 1982, 1984, 1991, 1994, 1997, 1998, 2003.

Quinta da Corte (Port) a vintage Port from Delaforce. Grape varieties: Malvasia preta, Rufete, Tinta amarela, Tinta cão, Tinta roriz, Touriga francesa and Touriga nacional. Vintages: 1978, 1980, 1984, 1987, 1991, 1994, 1997, 2003.

Quinta da Cortezia (Port) a winery based in the Estremadura. Noted for red wines produced from Touriga nacional, Tinta roriz and Merlot grapes.

Quinta da Costa (Port) a Port wine vineyard based north of the Vale de Mendiz in the Alto Douro.

Quinta da Costa de Bo (Port) a Port wine vineyard based north of the river Douro in the Alto Douro.

Quinta da Eira Velha (Port) a single quinta vineyard based near Pihão. The wine is produced by foot-treading in a lagar. Produced by Cockburn Smithies (was originally shipped as Tuke Holdsworth). Vintages: 1945, 1953, 1970, 1972, 1974, 1975, 1978, 1983, 1992, 1994, 1997, 1998, 2003.

Quinta da Ervamoira (Port) a 10 year old Tawny Port from Ramos Pinto. Also a vintage Port produced.

Quinta da Espiga (Port) *see* Quinta da Boavista.

Quinta da Ferrad (Port) a Port wine vineyard based south of the river Douro near Peso da Regua in the Alto Douro.

Quinta da Ferradosa (Port) a Port wine vineyard based east of Sao João da Pesqueira in the Alto Douro.

Quinta da Foz (Port) a Port wine vineyard based near Pinhão in the Alto Douro. Produces vintage Port,

owned by Cal'em. Grape varieties: Barroca, Tinta amarela, Tinta francisca, Tinta roriz, Touriga francesa and Touriga nacional. Vintages: 1927, 1931, 1934, 1935, 1938, 1949, 1954, 1955, 1958, 1960, 1963, 1966, 1970, 1975, 1977, 1978, 1980, 1982, 1985, 1991, 1994, 1995, 1997, 2000, 2003.

Quinta da Foz de Temjlobos (Port) a Port wine vineyard based south of the river Douro in the Alto Douro.

Quinta da Gaivosa (Port) a winery based in the Douro, noted for Touriga-based wines.

Quinta da Giesta (Port) a winery based in the Beiras, northern Portugal. Grape varieties include: Touriga nacional. Produces red rosé and white wines.

Quinta d'Aguieira (Port) noted wine-producers based in Agueda.

Quinta da Leda (Port) a new winery based in the upper Douro, owned by SOGRAPE.

Quinta da Lagoa Alta (Port) a Port wine vineyard based north of the river Douro in the Alto Douro.

Quinta da Lagoalva (Port) a winery based in the Ribatejo, southern Portugal. Produces white wines from Fernão pires and Chardonnay grapes together with reds from local grapes plus Syrah. Light wines are bottled under the Monte de Casta label.

Quinta da Malvedos (Port) *see* Quinta dos Malvedos.

Quinta da Moinha (Port) an 8ha vineyard (established 1993) based in the Algarve near Albufeira (owned by Sir Cliff Richard). Grape varieties: Aragonez and Shiraz.

Quinta da Pacheca (Port) a Port wine vineyard based south of Peso da Regua in the Alto Douro.

Quinta da Pilarrela (Port) a Port wine vineyard based near Santa Marta de Penaguiao in the Alto Douro.

Quinta da Poca (Port) a Port wine vineyard based north of the river Douro in the Alto Douro.

Quinta da Portela (Port) a Port wine vineyard based south of the river Douro near Peso da Regua in the Alto Douro.

Quinta da Portela (Port) a producer of Vinho Verde. (Add): Carreira, Barcelos.

Quinta da Quintao (Port) a noted producer of Vinho Verde wine from Loureiro and Trajadura grapes. (Add): S. Tome Negreios, 4780 Santa Tirso.

Quinta da Ribeira (Port) a Port wine vineyard based near Pinhão in the Alto Douro.

Quinta da Roeda (Port) a quinta that belongs to Crofts, based south of the Vale de Mendiz in the Alto Douro. Produces fine Ports.

Quinta da Romeira (Port) a large winery based in the DOC Bucelas.

Quinta da Romaneira (Port) a Colheita Port (tawny with vintage date).

Quinta da Sapa de B (Port) a Port wine vineyard based north of the river Douro in the Alto Douro.

Quinta das Baratas (Port) a Port wine vineyard based south of Pinhão in the Alto Douro.

Quinta das Bouças (Port) a vineyard based near Braga. Grape varieties: Loureiro and Trajadura.

Q

Quinta das Carvalhas [Royal Oporto] (Port) a Port wine vineyard based south of Pinhão in the Alto Douro. A single quinta vintage Port. Vintages: 1952, 1954, 1958, 1960, 1962, 1963, 1967, 1970, 1977, 1978, 1980, 1985, 1991, 1994, 1977, 2003. Owned by SOGRAPE.

Quinta da Senhora da Ribeira (Port) a 22ha single quinta Port wine vineyard based east of São João de Pesqueira in the Alto Douro (owned by Symington).

Quinta da Serra (Port) a Port wine vineyard based south-east of Pinhão in the Alto Douro.

Quinta das Lajes (Port) a Port wine vineyard based south-east of Pinhão in the Alto Douro.

Quinta das Maias (Port) a winery 35ha based near Gouveia in the D.O. Dão region. Grape varieties include: Barcelo, Malvasia fina. Labels: Jaen.

Quinta das Manuelas (Port) a Port wine vineyard based north of the Vale de Mendiz in the Alto Douro.

Quinta da Sta. Maria (Port) a single quinta estate that produces fine Vinho Verde wine.

Quinta da Teixeira (Port) a Port wine vineyard based east of Pinhão in the Alto Douro.

Quinta da Torre (Port) a Port wine vineyard based south-east of Peso da Regua in the Alto Douro.

Quinta da Urtiga (Port) a single vineyard Port from Ramos-Pinto.

Quinta da Vacaria (Port) a Port wine vineyard based east of Peso da Regua in the Alto Douro.

Quinta de Abrigada (Port) a winery based in Alenquer. Produces white wines from Vital and Arinto, red wines from Periquita.

Quinta de Azevedo (Port) a Vinho Verde produced by SOGRAPE from 70% Loureiro, 30% Paderna grapes.

Quinta de Baguste (Port) a Port wine vineyard based south-east of Peso da Regua in the Alto Douro.

Quinta de Cabriz (Port) a red and white wine vineyard based in Dão.

Quinta de Campanha (Port) a Port wine vineyard based north of Peso da Regua in the Alto Douro.

Quinta de Confradeiro (Port) a table wine produced by Sandeman in the Douro.

Quinta de Cruzeiro (Port) a Port vineyard owned by Fonseca 40ha.

Quinta de Cruzeiro (Port) a single vineyard estate that produces fine Vinho Verde wines.

Quinta de Curvos (Port) a brand of Vinho Verde (is domaine-bottled by Espasende).

Quinta de la Rosa (Port) a vintage Port, 1988 was the first vintage that the Bergquist family vinified themselves. Vintages: 1988, 1990, 1991, 1994, 1995, 1998, 2003.

Quinta de Nàpoles (Port) a Port wine vineyard based south of the river Douro in the Alto Douro.

Quinta de Pancas (Port) a winery based in Alenquer, Estremadura. Produces light red wines from Chardonnay, Cabernet sauvignon, Merlot, Syrah, Touriga nacional, Tinta roriz and Vital grapes. The white Arinto grape is bottled as Quinta D Carlos.

Quinta de Pecheca (Port) a vineyard estate based in Pemental in the Douro region. Produces red vintage wines.

Quinta de Romarigo (Port) a Port wine vineyard based south of Santa Marta de Penaguiao in the Alto Douro.

Quinta de Saes (Port) a winery in the DOC Dão region.

Quinta de Santa Barbara (Port) a Port wine vineyard based south-east of Peso da Regua in the Alto Douro.

Quinta de Santo André (Port) a winery based in the Ribatejo. Produces Horta de Nazure, a red wine from 50% Trincadeira and 50% Castelão pires grapes.

Quinta de São Claudio (Port) a famous Vinho Verde estate at Curvos, 4740 Esposende in Braga, Vinho Verde. 4ha. Grape variety: Loureiro.

Quinta de São Martinho (Port) a Port wine vineyard based north of São João de Pesqueira in the Alto Douro.

Quinta de Seara (Port) a Vinho Verde producer based in Esposende. Brand-names include Montefaro.

Quinta de Sentencostas (Port) see Quinta da Boavista.

Quinta de Soalheiro (Port) a vineyard based at Melgaço, Vinho Verde. Produces an unoaked Vinho Verde.

Quinta de Tamariz (Port) a winery based in the Vinho Verde. Grape varieties: Alvarinho and Loueiro.

Quinta de Terrafeita (Port) a Port vineyard based in the Pinhão Valley 88ha. Owned by Taylors.

Quinta de Tourais (Port) a Port wine vineyard based south of Peso da Regua in the Alto Douro.

Quinta de Vargellas (Port) a Port wine vineyard in the Alto Douro 100ha. Grape varieties: Tinto amarella, Tinta barroca, Tinto cão, Tinta roriz, Touriga francesa and Touriga nacional. Produces single vineyard vintage Ports. Owned by Taylors. Vintages: 1903, 1905, 1910, 1919, 1926, 1937, 1947, 1957, 1958, 1961, 1964, 1965, 1967, 1968, 1969, 1972, 1974, 1976, 1978, 1984, 1986, 1987, 1988, 1991, 1994, 1995, 1996, 1997, 1998, 2003.

Quinta de Ventozelo (Port) a Port wine vineyard based south-east of Pinhão in the Alto Douro.

Quinta de Vila Nova (Port) a single vineyard estate that produces Vinho Verde wines.

Quinta do Ameal (Port) a winery in the DOC Vinho Verde, northern Portugal. Grape varieties include: Alvarinho. Label: Escolha.

Quinta do Arnozelo (Port) a Port wine vineyard based east of the Vale de Figueira in the Alto Douro.

Quinta do Barao (Port) vineyards owned by Raul Ferreira and Filho Lda. in Carcavelos.

Quinta do Barrilario (Port) a Port wine vineyard based south of the river Douro, near Peso da Regua in the Alto Douro.

Quinta do Bibio (Port) a Port wine vineyard based near Castedo in the Alto Douro.

Quinta do Bom Dia (Port) a Port wine vineyard based north of the river Douro in the Alto Douro.

1058

Quinta do Bomfim (Port) a Port wine vineyard based south of the Vale de Mendiz in the Alto Douro (owned by Dow). Vintages: 1978, 1984, 1986, 1987, 1989, 1991, 1994, 1998, 2003.

Quinta do Bom Retiro (Port) a Port wine vineyard based south of Pinhão in the Alto Douro. Owned by Ramos Pinto. Also produces 20 year old Tawny Ports.

Quinta do Bragao (Port) a Port wine vineyard based north of São Cristovao do Douro in the Alto Douro.

Quinta do Cachào (Port) a single quinta vintage Port vineyard based at Ferradosa. Vintages: 1960, 1963, 1965, 1967, 1970, 1975, 1977, 1980, 1985, 1991, 1994, 2003 (owned by the Caves Messias).

Quinta do Canal (Port) a Port wine vineyard based near Peso da Regua in the Alto Douro.

Quinta do Carmo (Port) a wine estate near Borba. Grape varieties: Alicante bouschet, Trincadeira, Periquita, Aragonez (red), Roupeiro, Arinto, Fernão Pires, Perum (white). Two vineyards: Dom Martinho, Carvailhas.

Quinta do Carneiro (Port) a 50ha Port wine vineyard based near Peso da Regua, on the frontier of Alenquer and Ribatejo in Estremadura. Light red wines are produced from Castelão francês, Cabernet, Trincadeira and Tinta roriz grapes.

Quinta Casal Branco (Port) a winery based in the Ribatejo on the bank of the Tagus river. Produces the red wine Falcoaria from a blend of Trincadeira preta and Castelão francês grapes.

Quinta do Castelinho (Port) a Port wine vineyard based north of Sao João da Pesqueira in the Alto Douro.

Quinta do Castello Borges (Port) a Port wine vineyard based south of the river Douro in the Alto Douro.

Quinta do Cavalinho (Port) a single quinta Port produced by Warre.

Quinta do Charondo (Port) a Port wine vineyard based south-east of Pinhão in the Alto Douro.

Quinta do Cipreste (Port) a Port wine vineyard based east of Pinhão in the Alto Douro.

Quinta do Confradeiro (Port) a vineyard estate based in the Douro (part of the Quinta do Portal group of vineyards).

Quinta do Corval (Port) a vineyard based near Pinhão in Tràs-os-Montes. Produces light red wines.

Quinta do Côtto (Port) a single quinta vintage Port produced by Champalimaud at Cidadelhe near Régua. Also produces DOC red wines. 50ha. vineyard. Website: http://www.quinta-do-cotto.pt

Quinta do Crasto (Port) a Port wine vineyard based north of the river Douro in the Alto Douro. Part of Ferreira. Produces a still red wine: Vinha Maria Teresa, Vinha do Ponte.

Quinta do Crasto (Port) a Vinho Verde vineyard. (Add): Travanca, 4690 Cinfaes. Grape varieties: Avesso, Azal, Pederna plus others.

Quinta do Cruzeiro (Port) a Vinho Verde vineyard. (Add): Modelos, 4590 Pacos de Ferreira. Grape varieties: Avesso, Loureiro, Trajadura.

Quinta do Dr. Christiano (Port) a Port wine vineyard based south-east of Pinhão in the Alto Douro.

Quinta do Eiravelha (Port) see Quinta da Eira Velha.

Quinta do Fojo (Port) a Port wine vineyard based north of the Vale de Mendiz in the Alto Douro.

Quinta do Garcia (Port) a Port wine vineyard based south-east of Peso da Regua in the Alto Douro.

Quinta do Junco (Port) a Port wine vineyard based south of Sao Cristovao do Douro (near Pinhão) in the Alto Douro. Grape varieties are Bastardo 5%, Donzelinho 10%, Mourisco tinto 5%, Tinta amarela 20%, Tinta barroca 20%, Tinta roriz 20%, Touriga francesa 5%. Produced by Borges.

Quinta do Lelo (Port) a Port wine vineyard based south-east of Pinhão in the Alto Douro.

Quinta do Loreiro (Port) a 'vintage' Port of the nineteenth century bottled in 1971 by Cabral Port shippers. It is in fact a vintage 'Tawny' Port.

Quinta do Merouco (Port) a Port wine vineyard based south-east of the Vale de Mendiz in the Alto Douro.

Quinta do Minho (Port) a winery based in the DOC Vinho Verde. Grape varieties: Alvarhino, Vinhão. Also buys in grapes.

Quinta do Miogo (Port) a DOC Vinho Verde vineyard. (Add): Campelos, 4800 Guimaraes. Grape variety: Loureiro.

Quinta do Moinho (Port) a winery based in the Algarve. Grape varieties include: Aragonez, Mouvèdre, Syrah, Trincadeira. Label: Vida Nova. Owned by Sir Cliff Richard.

Quinta do Monte d'Oiro (Port) a winery (established 1992) based in the Estremadura. Noted for Syrah-based wines of same name that is aged for 15 months in new oak.

Quinta do Mouro (Port) a Port wine vineyard based near Peso da Regua in the Alto Douro.

Quinta do Nova de Nossa Senhora do Carmo (Port) a single quinta vintage Port bottled by Burmester. Vintages: 1992, 1995, 1997.

Quinta do Noval (Port) a Port wine vineyard based south of the Vale de Mendiz in the Alto Douro. A single vintage Port shipper. Single vineyard is Nacional. Vintages: 1896, 1900, 1904, 1908, 1912, 1917, 1919, 1920, 1923, 1927, 1931, 1934, 1941, 1942, 1945, 1947, 1948, 1950, 1955, 1958, 1960, 1962, 1963, 1964, 1966, 1967, 1970, 1975, 1978, 1980, 1982, 1985, 1987, 1991, 1994, 1995, 1997, 1998, 2000, 2003.

Quinta do Noval Nacional (Port) Vintages: 1960, 1963, 1964, 1966, 1967, 1970, 1975, 1978, 1980, 1982, 1985, 1987, 1991, 1994, 1996, 1997, 2000, 2003. Produced from phylloxera free, ungrafted vines. See also Quinta do Noval.

Quinta do Noval Silval (Port) a vintage Port that is produced from grapes grown from the quintas immediate boundaries including the Silval vineyards near the river Pinhão. Made to be drunk early.

Quinta do Outeiro de Baixo (Port) a Vinho Verde vineyard. (Add): S. Goncalo, 4600 Amarante. Grape varieties: Azal, Espadeiro and Pederna.

Quinta do Paço (Port) a single quinta estate that produces fine Vinho Verde wine.

Quinta do Panascal (Port) a Port wine vineyard based south of the river Douro in the Alto Douro. 80ha. Owned by Fonseca. Vintage: 1996.

Quinta do Passadoura (Port) a 25ha. Port wine vineyard based north of the Vale de Mendiz in the Alto Douro. Owned by Niepoort, a single quinta. Vines aged 30–60 years old. Vintages: 1992, 1994, 1995, 1998, 2000, 2003. Also produces red wines.

Quinta do Pedrogao (Port) a Port wine vineyard based south-east of Pinhão in the Alto Douro.

Quinta do Pego (Port) a Port wine vineyard based south of the river Douro in the Alto Douro.

Quinta do Peso (Port) a Port wine vineyard based east of Peso da Pegua in the Alto Douro.

Quinta do Poço do Lobo (Port) a Bairrada wine produced by Caves São João.

Quinta do Portal (Port) a Port winery 95ha (4 estates [Quintas]: da Abelheira, do Confradeiro, dos Muros and do Portal). Grape varieties include: Tinta roriz, Touriga franca, Touriga nacional. Produces both Ports and still wines. Website: http://www.quintadoportal.com

Quinta do Porto (Port) a 10 year old Tawny Port produced by A.A. Ferreira Port shippers.

Quinta do Roriz (Port) a Port wine vineyard based east of Pinhão in the Alto Douro.

Quinta do Sagrado (Port) a Port wine vineyard based near Pinhão in the Alto Douro.

Quinta dos Canais (Port) a Port wine vineyard based east of São João da Pesqueira in the Alto Douro.

Quinta dos Currais (Port) a Port wine vineyard based east of Peso da Regua in the Alto Douro.

Quinta do Seixo (Port) a vintage Port single vineyard in the Rio Torto Valley. Owned by Ferreira.

Quinta dos Frades (Port) a Port wine vineyard based south of the river Douro near Peso da Regua in the Alto Douro.

Quinta do Sibio (Port) a vintage Port shipper owned by Real Vinícola. Vintages: 1945, 1947, 1950, 1955, 1960.

Quinta do Silval (Port) a Port wine vineyard based north of the Vale de Mendiz in the Alto Douro. Second wine of Quinta do Noval.

Quinta dos Lagares (Port) a Port wine vineyard based north of the Vale de Mendiz in the Alto Douro.

Quinta dos Malvedos (Port) a Port wine vineyard based near the river Tua in the Alto Douro. 128ha. Grape varieties are Malvasia preta, Tinta barroca, Tinta roriz and Touriga nacional. Owned by Grahams. Vintages: 1954, 1957, 1958, 1961, 1962, 1964, 1965, 1968, 1982, 1985, 1991, 1994, 1996, 1998, 2003.

Quinta dos Muros (Port) a vineyard estate based in the Douro (part of the Quinta do Portal group of vineyards).

Quinta do Sol (Port) a Port wine vineyard based south of the river Douro in the Alto Douro.

Qunita dos Roques (Port) a winery in the DOC Dão that also produces the white Barcelo 40ha.

Qunita dos Rocques (Port) a winery in the Douro that is noted for Touriga-based wines.

Quinta do St. Antonio (Port) a Port vineyard owned by Taylors 12ha.

Quinta do Tamariz (Port) a noted Vinho Verde producer based at Barcelos. Run by the Soc. Agrícola da Quinta Santa Maria. Grape varieties: Loureiro and Trajadura.

Quinta do Tedo (Port) a Port wine vineyard based south of the river Douro in the Alto Douro. Still wine: Escada d'Oro.

Quinta do Tua (Port) a single quinta Port from Cockburn.

Quinta do Val de Figueira (Port) a Port wine vineyard based near Pinhão in the Alto Douro.

Quinta do Valdoeira (Port) a winery based in the DOC Bairrada. Owned by the Caves Messias.

Quinta do Vale de Dona Maria (Port) a single quinta Port vineyard owned by Smith Woodhouse.

Quinta do Vale de Sapos (Port) a Port wine vineyard based south of Peso da Regua in the Alto Douro.

Quinta do Vallado (Port) a vineyard based in the Douro. Produces grapes for Port wine production and produces own red wines.has 2ha of Syrah vines planted.

Quinta do Vale Meão (Port) a fine 65ha estate in the upper Douro. Produces grapes for Barca Velha. Still wine: Dona Maria

Quinta do Vau (Port) a 79ha. Port vineyard bought by Sandeman in 1988, bottled a small quantity as a single quinta in 1988. Vintages: 1988, 1997, 2000, 2003.

Quinta do Vesuvio (Port) a Port wine vineyard based east of the Vale de Figueira in the Alto Douro. Vintages: 1989, 1990, 1991, 1992, 1994, 1995, 1997, 1998, 1999, 2003. Owned by Symington Family Estates.

Quinta do Zambujal (Port) a Port wine vineyard based near Peso da Regua in the Alto Douro.

Quinta do Zimbro (Port) a Port wine vineyard based near Ribalonga in the Alto Douro.

Quinta Fonte Bela (Port) a winery based near Cartaxo in the Ribatejo. Now converted to a bottling centre. *see* DFJ Vinhos.

Quintal (Fr) liquid measure of cask 100kgs.

Quintal (Sp) liquid measure of cask 100lbs.

Quintal (It) an expression used for grape yields per hectare. Quintals x Resa/100 = hl/ha.

Quinta Malvedos (Port) *see* Quinta dos Malvedos.

Quinta Milieu (Port) a Port wine vineyard based east of Pinhão in the Alto Douro.

Quinta Nova do Roncao (Port) a Port wine vineyard based south of the Vale de Mendiz in the Alto Douro.

Quintarelli (It) a noted amarone wine-producer based in the north-east of Italy.

Q

Quintas (Port) vineyard and wineries.

Quinta St. Luiz (Port) a single quinta vintage Port produced by Kopke. Grape varieties: Tinta cao, Tinta roriz, Touriga francesa and Touriga nacional.

Quinta Velha (Port) a Port wine vineyard based east of Peso da Regua in the Alto Douro.

Quintessa (USA) a winery based in Rutherford, . Napa Valley, California. (Add): 1601 Silverado Trail, St. Helena CA 94574. Grape varieties include: Cabernet sauvignon, Merlot. Website: http://www.quintessa.com

Quintessence (Fr) a 21 year old Cognac produced by L. Gourmel with a flavour and aroma of grapes.

Quiriga (S.Afr) the label for two red wines (Merlot Reserve/Shiraz Reserve) produced by the Rietrivier Winery, Little Karoo.

Qui Sent le Bouchon (Fr) lit: 'corked'.

Quist Brouwerij (Hol) a brewery (established 1993) based in Ezinge. Brews: Borgenbier.

Quivira (USA) a winery (established 1986) based in California, main grapes are Sauvignon blanc and Zinfandel.

Quizzling Glass (Eng) a seventeenth century glass which is crazed to give a sparkle to the contents.

Quoin Rock Winery (S.Afr) an organic winery (established 2000) based in Stellenbosch, Western Cape. Grape varieties: Chardonnay, Merlot, Pinotage, Sauvignon blanc, Shiraz, Syrah, Viognier. Label: Cape Blend, Glenhurst, Oculus (oaked Sauvignon blanc), Vine Dried. Website: http://www.quoinrock.com

Quoique ce Soit (Fr) lit: 'whatever this may be', the name given to a nineteenth century French apéritif.

Quondyp Rhine Riesling (Austr) a fruity, aromatic wine from Château Barker in Western Australia.

Quorum (It) a D.O.C. barrique-aged Barbera d'Asti wine produced as a joint venture by Coppo, Bologna, Vietti, Prunotto and Chiarlo.

Quosh (Eng) the brand-name of a whole fruit, non-alcoholic drink produced by Beecham.

Qvarzia (It) a still and sparkling natural spring mineral water. Mineral contents (milligrammes per litre): Sodium 1.4mg/l, Calcium 68.8mg/l, Magnesium 7.9mg/l, Potassium 0.4mg/l, Chlorides 2.8mg/l, Sulphates 8.2mg/l, Silicates 7mg/l. pH 7.5

Q.W.P.S.R. (E.C.) abbr: Quality Wine Produced in a Specific Region, the E.C. classification for quality wines.

Q.W.S. (Eng) abbr: Quality Wine Scheme.

R

R (Aus) the middle ages cask brand for the ausruch wines from the Rust region.

Raats Family Wines (S.Afr) a winery (established 2000) based in Stellenbosch, Western Cape. 20ha. Grape varieties: Cabernet franc, Chenin blanc. Website: http://www.raats.co.za

Rabaja (It) a famous Cru vineyard (5ha) based in the DOCG Barbaresco in Piemonte. Grape variety: Nebbiolo. Has soils composed of limestone and sand and is owned by a number of growers.

Rabaner (Ger) a white grape variety, a cross between Riesling and a Riesling cross. Has a lower acidity than the true Riesling.

Rabassa Morta System (Sp) a system of land tenure, drawn up between a proprietor and farmer in the twelfth century. The landowner has the right to share the produce with the farmer who leased the land from him.

Rabat (Afr) a wine-producing area and capital of Morocco based on the west coast. Produces mainly red wines.

Rabat [José] (Chile) a noted wine exporter based in Santiago.

Rabat-Casablanca (Afr) a vineyard planted with imported vines in the Rabat area of Morocco.

Rabate Brandy (S.Afr) a brandy produced in South Africa.

Rabat-Rharb (Afr) a wine-producing region on the western coast of Morocco.

Rabaud-Promis (Fr) see Château Rabaud-Promis.

Rabaud-Sigalas (Fr) see Château Rabaud-Sigalas.

Rabbit (Fr) see French Rabbit.

Rabbit Poacher (Eng) a 3.8% alc by vol. ale brewed by the Fenland Brewery Ltd., Cambridgeshire.

Rabenkopf (Ger) vineyard (Anb): Rheinhessen. (Ber): Bingen. (Gro): Kaiserpfalz. (Vil) Ingelheim.

Rabenkopf (Ger) vineyard (Anb): Rheinhessen. (Ber): Bingen. (Gro): Kaiserpfalz. (Vil): Wackenheim.

Rabigato (Port) a white grape variety used in the production of white Port and Vinho Verdes.

Rabinowka (Rus) a pink liqueur flavoured with rowanberries, dry or sweet, it is also produced in other eastern European countries.

Rablay-sur-Layon (Fr) a commune of the Coteaux du Layon in the Anjou-Saumur district of the Loire. Has its own A.C.

Rabo de Ovelho (Port) an early ripening white grape variety used in the making of white Port and Bairrada wines, also written as Rabo d'Ovelha.

Rabo d'Ovelha (Port) see Rabo de Orvelho.

Rabosino (It) a dry white wine from the Piave Valley in Treviso, has a Riesling character.

Raboso (It) a D.O.C. red wine from the Treviso district of Veneto in the valley of the river Piave, a tough, tannic wine.

Raboso Piave (It) a red grape variety grown in the Veneto.

Raboso Piave (USA) a red grape variety grown in California. Used in the making of red table wines.

Raboso Veronese (It) a red grape variety grown in the Veneto.

Raboursay (Fr) a vineyard in the A.C. commune of Rully, Côte Chalonnaise, Burgundy.

Raca (Fr) the old word for the residue of grapes after they have been pressed in wine-making.

Racahout (Eng) a hot drink reconstituted with water, produced from rice flour, cocoa, potato flour, sugar, vanilla, acorn flour and salep.

R.A.C. Cocktail (Cktl) 30mls (¼ gill) gin, 15mls (⅛ gill) French vermouth, 15mls (⅛ gill) Italian vermouth, dash grenadine, dash orange bitters. Stir well over ice and strain into a cocktail glass, add a cherry and a squeeze of orange peel juice on top.

Race (Fr) breeding, a term to denote a wine of distinction.

Race [Denis] (Fr) a winery based in the A.C. Chablis, Burgundy. Produces a range of Chablis wines including Premier Cru Montmains.

Racemus (Lat) bunch of grapes.

Rachis (Eng) the branch of the vine onto which the bunch of grapes is attached. (Fr) = rafle.

Racimo (Sp) a bunch of grapes.

Racking (Eng) the changing of wine or beer from one cask to another, leaving the sediment (lees) behind in the old cask.

Raclet Festival (Fr) a festival celebrated in conjunction with the Beaujolais Nouveau, Mâcon and Beaujolais celebrations in Burgundy.

Raclot (Fr) a vineyard in the A.C. commune of Rully, Côte Chalonnaise, Burgundy.

Racodium cellare (Hun) a dry, springy black fungus found in Tokaji cellars.

Racy (Eng) the term used to describe wines made from the Riesling grape that are lively, full of vitality, with a fresh acidity.

Racy Rosé (Austr) a rosé wine produced by the Bremerton winery, Langhorne Creek, South Australia.

Rada (Ser) a natural spring mineral water from Serbia and Montenegro.

R

Radda (It) a commune of Chianti Classico Riserva.

Radeberger (Ger) a 4.8% alc by vol. bottled pilsener brewed at Radeberger Export Bier Brauerei, Radeberg near Dresden in eastern Germany.

Radeberger Brauerei (Ger) a brewery (established 1872) based at Radeberg near Dresden.

Radegast Dark (Czec) a 3.6% alc by vol. dark, 10° balling, bottled lager brewed and bottled by the Radegast Sedlec Brewery, Sedlec.

Radegast Premium (Czec) a 5.1% alc by vol. straw coloured, 12° balling, bottled lager brewed and bottled by the Radegast Sedlec Brewery, Nošovice.

Radegast Sedlec Brewery (Czec) the second largest brewery, based in Nošovice. Brews: Radegast Dark, Radegast Premium, Radegast Triumf and Pivrnec.

Radegast Triumf (Czec) a 3.9% alc by vol. straw coloured, 12° balling, bottled lager brewed and bottled by the Radegast Sedlec Brewery, Nošovice.

Radenska-Kraljevi Vrelec (Slo) a sparkling natural spring mineral water from Kraljevi Vrelec, Radenci. Mineral contents (milligrammes per litre): Sodium 490mg/l, Calcium 233mg/l, Magnesium 81mg/l, Potassium 75mg/l, Bicarbonates 2300mg/l, Chlorides 46mg/l, Fluorides 0.28mg/l, Nitrates 2.2mg/l.

Radenska-Vrelec Miral (Slo) sparkling a natural spring mineral water from Vrelec Miral, Radenci. Mineral contents (milligrammes per litre): Sodium 480mg/l, Calcium 126mg/l, Magnesium 61mg/l, Potassium 44mg/l, Bicarbonates 1960mg/l, Chlorides 74mg/l, Fluorides 1.4mg/l.

Radenska-Vrelec Radin (Slo) a still natural spring mineral water from Vrelev Radin, Radenci. Mineral contents (milligrammes per litre): Sodium 141mg/l, Calcium 106mg/l, Magnesium 37mg/l, Potassium 18mg/l, Bicarbonates 790mg/l, Chlorides 21mg/l, Fluorides 0.5mg/l.

Radford Dale-Gravity (S.Afr) the label for a red wine (Merlot, Shiraz and Cabernet sauvignon blend) produced by The Winery, Stellenbosch, Western Cape.

Radgie Gadgie (Eng) a 4.8% alc by vol. bitter ale brewed by the Mordue Brewery, North Shields, Tyne and Wear.

Radgona (Slo) a district within the region of Slovenija. Famous for its sweet white wine Radgona Ranina, better known as Tiger Milk.

Radgona Ranina (Slo) see Tiger Milk.

Radgie Gadgie (Eng) a 4.8% alc by vol. ale brewed by the Mordue Brewery Ltd., Tyne & Wear.

Radgonska Ranina (Slo) the alternative spelling of Radgona Ranina.

Radicosa (It) an IGT red wine made from Cabernet sauvignon and a variety of local Puglia grape varieties by the Tenuta Coppadoro vineyards.

Radio-Coteau Wine Cellars (USA) a winery based in the Sonoma County, California. Grape varieties include: Pinot noir, Syrah, Zinfandel. Label: La Neblina.

Radiosa (It) a natural spring mineral water from Radiosa.

Radis (It) a bitters apéritif made by the Stock C°.

Radkersburg (Aus) a wine-producing area in Klöch, southern Austria.

Radler (Ger) a bottled shandy beer from the Steffens Brauerei, St. Severinsberg.

Radlermass (Ger) lit: 'cyclists' beer', a mix of ordinary beer and lemonade, a shandy (half and half).

Radnor Hills (Wal) a natural spring mineral water (established 1988). (Add): Heartsease, Knighton, Radnorshire, Powys LD7 1LU. Mineral contents (milligrammes per litre): Sodium 28.3mg/l, Calcium 6.2mg/l, Magnesium 6.8mg/l, Potassium 1.6mg/l, Chlorides 1.4mg/l, Sulphates 10.9mg/l, Fluorides 0.09mg/l, Nitrates 12mg/l. Website: http://www.radnorhills.co.uk 'E'mail: sales@radnorhills.co.uk

Raeticum (It) a white wine produced in north-eastern Italy in Roman times.

Rafanelli Winery (USA) a winery based in Dry Creek Valley, Sonoma County, California. Grape varieties: Gamay and Zinfandel. Produces varietal wines.

Raffiat (Fr) an alternative name for the Arrufiac grape.

Raffles (Eng) the brand-name of a London Dry gin from Kilsern Distillers in Leicester 43% alc by vol (47% alc by vol. for export).

Raffles Bar Sling (Cktl) 50mls (2fl.ozs) gin, 25mls (1fl.oz) cherry brandy, juice half a lime, 2 dashes Angostura, 3 dashes Bénédictine. Put brandy and gin with the lime juice and bitters in an ice-filled highball glass, stir in ginger beer, top with Bénédictine and decorate with lime zest and some mint.

Rafle (Fr) see Rachis.

Rafle (Ger) a term used to denote a harsh, stemmy, green wine.

Rafosk (Euro) a local name for the Refosco or Teran grape in Istria.

Rafsi (Afr) a white grape variety grown in North Africa.

Ragazz (It) a pétillant, pale ruby red wine produced from Malvasia and Freisa grapes in north-west Italy. 4.5% alc by vol. Known by the term Filtrato Dolce.

Ragel (Sp) a solera reserva brandy produced by Bobadillo.

Ragi (E.Ind) the name given to compressed balls of rice that are added to fermenting juice to give extra alcohol to the end spirit.

Raging Bull Bitter (Eng) a 4.9% alc by vol. bitter ale brewed by the Blanchfield Brewery, Essex.

Raging Rooster (Eng) a 4.2% alc by vol. cask-conditioned, dark oak-coloured seasonal ale. Brewed by Hardy's and Hanson's, Kimberley, Nottingham under the Cellarman's Cask banner. Available April and May.

Ragnaud [Raymond] (Fr) a Cognac producer. (Add): Le Château Ambleville, 16300 Barbezieux. 50ha. in the Grande Champagne. Produces Cognacs under the Château Ambleville label.

Ragnaud Sabourin (Fr) a Cognac producer. (Add): S.A. Ragnaud Sabourin, Domaine de la Voute, Ambleville, 16300 Barbezieux. 50 ha in Grande Champagne. Produces: Grande Champagne Fontvieille 35 year old, Grande Champagne Heritage Gaston Briand 1925, Heritage Gaston Briand la Paradis 90 year old, Heritage Mme. Paul Ragnaud 1908.

Ragusa (It) a wine-producing area in Sicily.

Raiarngoon (Thai) winery.

Rail Ale (Eng) a 3.8% alc by vol. ale brewed by the Beer Engine brewery, Devon.

Rail Ale (Eng) a cask-conditioned ale 1036 O.G. brewed by a home-brew public house the Phoenix and Firkin in London.

Railroad Red (S.Afr) the label for a red wine (Cabernet sauvignon 40% and Shiraz 60%) produced by the Graham Beck Wines winery, Franschhoek, Western Cape.

Railway (Eng) a Whitbread home-brew public house in Burgess Hill, Sussex. Noted for cask-conditioned Burgess Best 1036 O.G. and Railway Special 1048 O.G. using malt extract.

Railway Cocktail (Eng) 1 measure dry gin, 1 measure orange juice, dash gomme syrup. Shake over ice, strain into an ice-filled highball glass, top with Ashbourne water and an orange slice.

Railway Special (Eng) see Railway.

Raimat (Sp) a bodega based in Lérida. Produces a full range of cava and table wines. Grape varieties: Cabernet sauvignon, Chardonnay, Chenin blanc, Colombard, Garnacha, Macabeo, Merlot, Parellada and Tempranillo. see Can Abadía, Can Casal, Can Clamor, Can Rius and Clos Casal.

Rain (Eng) moisture falling as drops of water from clouds through precipitation. Is free of any contamination except through air pollution or through pollution on contact with the earth. see Water, Mineral Water, Natural Spring Water.

Rain (Eng) organic grain vodka.

Rain (S.Afr) the label for a naturally sweet wine (Chenin blanc and Colombard blend) from the Elements range of wines produced by the Hartswater Wine Cellar winery, Hartswater, Northern Cape.

Rain (USA) an alkaline natural spring mineral water from Utah. Mineral contents (milligrammes per litre): Sodium <1mg/l. pH 9.0 Website: http://www.gonaturalnow.com

Rainbow (Cktl) see Pousse Café Américan.

Rainbow (Pak) a natural spring mineral water. Mineral contents (milligrammes per litre): Sodium 9mg/l, Calcium 61mg/l, Magnesium 5mg/l, Potassium 2.5mg/l, Bicarbonates 246mg/l, Chlorides 15mg/l, Sulphates 8mg/l, Nitrates 9mg/l.

Rainbow Chaser (Eng) a 4.3% alc by vol. ale brewed by Hanby Ales Ltd., Shropshire.

Rainbow Cocktail (Cktl) place 25mls (1fl.oz) advocaat and 3 dashes orange juice into an ice-filled Paris goblet. Stir, carefully add 10mls (½ fl.oz) cherry brandy, 10mls (½ fl.oz) blue Curaçao. Do not stir and serve with straws.

Rainbow Cocktail (Pousse Café) pour in order into a pousse café glass equal measures of grenadine, anisette, green crème de menthe, blue Curaçao, parfait amour, goldwasser and Cognac.

Rainbow's End Estate (S.Afr) a winery (established 1978) based in Stellenbosch, Western Cape. 23ha. Grape varieties: Cabernet franc, Cabernet sauvignon, Malbec, Merlot, Petit verdot, Shiraz.

Raindrops (Ind) a natural spring mineral water (established 2000) from Chennai. Mineral contents (milligrammes per litre): Sodium 10mg/l, Calcium 0.8mg/l, Magnesium 0.2mg/l, Chlorides 8.8mg/l, Sulphates <0.1mg/l, Fluorides 0.25mg/l, Nitrates <0.1mg/l. pH 6.76

Rain Farm (Austr) a natural spring mineral water. Mineral contents (milligrammes per litre): Sodium 0.2mg/l, Calcium 0.1mg/l, Magnesium 0.1mg/l, Potassium 0.5mg/l, Chlorides 2mg/l, Sulphates 2mg/l, Fluorides 0.1mg/l, Nitrates 0.5mg/l.

Rainha Santa (Port) vintage Port shippers based at Vila Nova de Gaia.

Rainier (USA) a beer 7.25% alc by vol. brewed in Seattle, Washington. Also known as Green Death (has a green label).

Rainier Brewery (USA) a brewery based in Seattle, Washington. see Green Death.

Rainmaker (Eng) a 4.1% alc by vol. ale brewed by the Bells Brewery, Leicestershire.

Rainoldi (It) a fine producer of D.O.C. Valtellina and Sfursat wines in Lombardy. Noted for sparkling (metodo tradizionale) wines.

Rainsong Vineyards Winery (USA) a winery. (Add): 92989 Goldson/Templeton Road, Cheshire, Oregon. Produces still and sparkling wines. Grape varieties: Pinot noir, Chardonnay, Pinot meunier, Pinot gris.

Rainstorm Cocktail (Cktl) 35mls (1½ fl.ozs) Beefeater gin, 10mls (½ fl.oz) Grand Marnier, 35mls (1½ fl.ozs) pineapple juice, 10mls (½ fl.oz) jus de citron, dash grenadine. Shake well over ice, strain into an ice-filled highball glass, top up with soda water and decorate with half a pineapple slice and a cherry.

Rain Vodka (USA) a wheat-based vodka produced in Kentucky 40% alc by vol.

Rainwater (Eng) the accumulation of rain.

Rainwater (Mad) the name given to blended Madeiras (Sercial and Verdelho) in the USA. So called because casks were stored outside like rainwater butts. First sold by a Mr. Habishan of Savannah in Georgia.

Raisin (Fr) grape.

Raisin Blanc (S.Afr) a white grape variety cultivar used in the production of Vins de Table (Vins Ordinaire) and in distilling. Also known as Servin Blanc.

Raisin Bleu de Frankenthal (Fr) the name given to the red grape variety Trollinger.

Raisins Secs (Fr) sun-dried grapes.

Rajika (Tur) the alternative spelling of Raki or Rakía.

Rajinski Rizling (Slo) the local name for the Rhine

R

riesling grape grown in Ljutomer-Ormoz. *See also* Renski Riesling.

Rajnai Rizling (Hun) an alternative name for Riesling.

Raka (S.Afr) a winery (established 2002) based in Caledon, Walker Bay, Western Cape. 62ha. Grape varieties: Cabernet franc, Cabernet sauvignon, Malbec, Merlot, Pinotage, Ruby cabernet, Sauvignon blanc, Sémillon, Shiraz., Labels: Best Barrique, Biography, Figurehead Cape Blend, Shannoneau, Spliced. Website: http://www.rakawine.co.za

Raker Bitter (Eng) a keg bitter 1030 O.G. brewed by the Wadworth Brewery in Devises, Wiltshire.

Raki (Tur) a spirit produced in the Balkans made from aniseed and liquorice (34.5%–40% alc by vol). *See also* Lion's Milk and Arrack. Also spelt Rajika and Rakía.

Rakía (Tur) the alternative spelling of Raki or Rajika.

Rakija (Bos)(Ser) the alternative name for slivovitz in Bosnia and Serbia.

Rakoczy Heilwasser (Ger) a natural spring mineral water. Mineral contents (milligrammes per litre): Sodium 2490mg/l, Calcium 518mg/l, Magnesium 170.9mg/l, Potassium 91.5mg/l, Chlorides 3850mg/l, Sulphates 853mg/l, Fluorides 0.27mg/l.

Rakovnik Brewery (Czec) an old (established 1454) brewery based in north-western Czec.

Rakwon Kumgangsan (N.Kor) a natural spring mineral water. Mineral contents (milligrammes per litre): Sodium 4.2mg/l, Calcium 4.8mg/l, Magnesium 1.2mg/l, Potassium 0.6mg/l, Nitrates 0.001mg/l. pH 7.1

Ralingen (Ger) village (Anb): Mosel-Saar-Ruwer. (Ber): Obermosel. (Gro): Königsberg. (Vins): Not yet chosen.

Rama (Port) a bamboo stick decorated with paper flowers which is presented to the lady of the quinta at the end of the harvest to celebrate the vintage.

Rama Caida (Arg) a wine-producing area in southern Argentina.

Ramadas (Port) tunnel trellises used to allow the growing grapes to be cooled by the winds.

Ramal Road Reserve (USA) the label for a red wine (Pinot noir) produced by Domaine Chandon, Carneros, California.

Ramandolo (It) a sweet version of the wine Colli Orientali Fruili Verduzzo.

Ramato (It) the name given to white wine from the Pinot grigio grapes. Its copper colour is due to a brief maceration on the skins.

Ramava (Latv) a natural spring mineral water from Latvia. Mineral contents (milligrammes per litre): Sodium 30–50mg/l, Calcium 50–100mg/l, Magnesium 15–40mg/l, Potassium 5–20mg/l, Bicarbonates 310–350mg/l, Sulphates 70–100mg/l.

Ramazzotti (It) a noted brandy producer based in Milan. Also produces Fior di Vite (grappa), Sambuca Ramazzotti.

Rambler (Eng) a 5% alc by vol. ale from the Furze and Firkin, Streatham High Road, London.

Ramblers Ruin (Wal) a 5% alc by vol. ale brewed by the Breconshire Brewery, Powys.

Rambooze (W.Ind) see Rumbooze.

Ram Cooler (Cktl) 25mls (⅛ gill) white rum, 15mls (⅛ gill) Galliano, 50mls (⅖ gill) lime juice. Shake over ice, strain into a cocktail glass, dress with cherry and slice of lime.

Ramé (It) pot-still.

Rameau (Fr) a commune in A.C. Chablis, Burgundy.

Rameau-Lamarosse (Fr) a cuvée in the Basses-Vergelesses vineyard in A.C. Pernand-Vergelesses, Côte de Beaune, Burgundy (owned by the Hospices de Beaune).

Ramey (USA) a winery in the Napa Valley, California with vineyards in Carneros.

Ramillete (Sp) bouquet.

Ramisco (Port) a red/black grape variety grown in 'the ocean' Colares district of the Estremadura. Used to make red and white wines but getting rare because of the difficulties experienced in planting. see Ocean (The).

Ramlösa (Swe) a carbonated natural spring mineral water from Ramlösa Hälsbronn, Helsingborg. Mineral contents (milligrammes per litre): Sodium 222mg/l, Calcium 2.2mg/l, Magnesium 0.5mg/l, Potassium 1.5mg/l, Bicarbonates 12mg/l, Chlorides 23mg/l, Sulphates 7.3mg/l, Fluorides 2.8mg/l. Scandinavia's leading natural mineral water.

Rammeln (Aus) a vineyard site on the banks of the River Danube in the Kremstal region.

Rammersweier (Ger) village (Anb): Baden. (Ber): Ortenau. (Gro): Fürsteneck. (Vin): Kreuzberg.

Ramonet-Prudhon (Fr) noted Burgundy growers.

Ramos Fizz (Cktl) 2 measures gin, 1 measure lemon juice, 3 dashes orange flower water, 1 egg white, 1 dash gomme syrup, 1 dessertspoon cream. Shake over ice, strain into an ice-filled highball glass, top with soda water, serve with straws and a muddler.

Ramos Pinto (Port) vintage Port shippers. Vintages: 1924, 1927, 1945, 1955, 1963, 1970, 1975, 1982, 1983, 1984, 1985, 1991, 1994, 1997, 2003. Plus single quinta: Quinta da Urtiga.

Rampant Gryphon (Eng) a 6.2% alc by vol. strong ale brewed by the Wentworth Brewery, South Yorkshire.

Rampant Ram (Eng) a 4.3% alc by vol. seasonal ale brewed by Hydes Anvil, Manchester.

Ram Rod Ale (Eng) a cask-conditioned and bottled bitter beer 1046 O.G. brewed by the Young Brewery in Wandsworth, London.

Ramsbottom (Eng) a 4.5% alc by vol. ale brewed by the Dent Brewery, Cumbria.

Ramsgate Brewery (Eng) a brewery (established 2002). (Add): 98 Harbour Parade, Ramsgate, Kent CT11 8LP. Brews: Gadd's Champion Mild Ale 4% alc by vol., Gadd's Dogbolter Winter Porter 5.6% alc by vol., Gadd's Dr Sunshine 4.2% alc by vol., Gadd's N°3 Ramsgate Pale Ale 5% alc by vol., Gadd's N°5 Ramsgate Best Bitter 4.4% alc by vol., Gadd's N°7 Ramsgate Bitter 3.8% alc by vol.,

Gadd's Old Pig Brown Ale 4.8% alc by vol. Website: http://www.ramsgatebrewery.co.uk 'E'mail: info@ramsgatebrewery.co.uk

Rams Revenge (Eng) a 4.6% alc by vol. ale brewed by HB Clark & C°. Ltd., West Yorkshire.

Ramsthal (Ger) village (Anb): Franken. (Ber): Maindreieck. (Gro): Burg. (Vin): St. Klausen.

Ram Tam (Eng) a winter ale 1043 O.G. brewed by the Timothy Taylor Brewery in Keighley, Yorkshire.

Ranch Series (USA) a winery based in Montery County, California. Grape varieties: Cabernet sauvignon. Label: Lawson Ranch.

Ranchita Oaks Winery (USA) a winery based near Paso Robles, San Luis Obispo County, California. Grape varieties: Cabernet sauvignon, Petite syrah, Zinfandel. Produces varietal wines.

Rancho Alto Vista (USA) a vineyard based in Sonoma Valley, California. *see* Château St. Jean.

Rancho de la Merced (Sp) an experimental station in Jerez, Andalucia where improvements to Sherry production are tested.

Rancho de Philo (USA) a small winery based in Cucamonga, California. Produces dessert wines.

Rancho dos Amigos (USA) a vineyard in Paso Robles, San Luis Obispo County, California. Produces grapes (Barbera bianca) for the Pedrizzetti Winery.

Rancho Santa Rosa (USA) the label for a red wine (Pinot noir) produced by the Foley winery, Santa Rita Hills, Santa Barbara County, California.

Rancho Sisquoc (USA) a winery (83ha) based in Santa Barbara, California. Grape varieties: Cabernet sauvignon, Franken riesling, White riesling. Produces varietal wines.

Rancho Viejo (Mex) a wine-producing region in Baja California.

Rancio (Eng) a special flavour of some wines (especially fortified wines) acquired as they age in wood. Also Cognac which has a 'burnt' flavour.

Rancio (Sp) rank or rancid, usually denotes a dessert wine that has been kept for a long time in the bottle. Is deep-golden in colour with an aroma similar to Sherry. Now very rare.

Rancio (Tun) a noted wine-producing area. Produces fortified wines.

Randall (R.W.) Ltd. (Ch.Isles) a family brewery (established 1868). (Add): Vauxlauren Brewery, St. Julian's Avenue, St. Peter Port, Guernsey GY1 3JG. Noted for VB Bobby cask-conditioned/keg beers. Bobby Ale 1036 O.G. Regal Lager 1045 O.G. canned bitter 5% alc by vol. bottled Clameur de Haro 3.6% alc by vol., Cynful Mild 3.5% alc by vol., Envy 4.8% alc by vol., Hop off the Press 4.5% alc by vol., India Pale Ale 3.8% alc by vol., Low Alcohol 1% alc by vol., Original V.B. 3.4% alc by vol., Patois 4.8% alc by vol., Stout 5.5% alc by vol. (now known as Guilty 5.2% alc by vol. in 2005) and Wycked 4.2% alc by vol. They are also agents for Breda Lager. Taken over by The Guernsey Pub Company Ltd and Wychwood Brewery (April 2006). Website: http://www.itsnotacyn.com 'E'mail: benrandall@rwrandall.co.uk

Randall's Bitter (Ch.Isles) a 5% alc by vol. bitter ale from R.W. Randall Ltd., Vauxlauren Brewery, St. Julians Avenue, St. Peter Port, Guernsey.

Randall's Real Ale (Ch.Isles) a strong cask-conditioned bitter brewed by the Randalls Vautier Brewery in St. Helier, Jersey.

Randall's Reserve (Ch.Isles) the brand-name of a blended Scotch whisky 40% alc by vol. from the R.W. Randall's Brewery, St. Peter Port, Guernsey.

Randalls Vautier (Ch.Isles) a brewery based in St. Helier, Jersey. Brews Top Island Keg Bitter 1042 O.G. Randall's Real Ale and produces Grünhalle Lager which it also licenses to the Devenish and Greenall Whitley Breweries in England.

R & B Brewing C° (Can) a brewery. (Add): 54 East, 4th avenue, Vancouver, British Columbia V5T 1E8. Brews a variety of beers. Website: http://www.r-and-b.com 'E'mail: ales@r-and-b.com

R and C Vintners (Eng) producers of Wincarnis (a beef and malt-based tonic wine) based in Carrow, Norwich, Norfolk 15% alc by vol.

Randegger Ottilien-Quelle (Ger) a sparkling natural spring mineral water from Randegger Ottilien-Quelle. Mineral contents (milligrammes per litre): Sodium 9.7mg/l, Calcium 88mg/l, Magnesium 31mg/l, Potassium 1.7mg/l, Bicarbonates 392mg/l, Chlorides 5.9mg/l, Sulphates 33mg/l, Fluorides 0.25mg/l, Nitrates <0.3mg/l, Silicates 20mg/l. pH 7.26 Website: http://www.randegger.de

Randersacker (Ger) village (Anb): Franken. (Ber): Maindreieck. (Gro): Ewig Leben. (Vins): Marsberg, Pfülben, Sonnenstuhl, Teufelskeller.

Randersacker (Ger) village (Anb): Franken. (Ber): Maindreieck. (Gro): Not yet assigned. (Vin): Dabug.

Randy Dandy (Eng) a mix of vodka, lime juice and dandelion and burdock (or sarsaparilla) drunk in the northern pubs. *See also* Temperence Bars.

Ranelagh (Eng) an eighteenth century tea garden.

Rabgauer Life Heilwasser (Ger) a natural spring mineral water. Mineral contents (milligrammes per litre): Sodium 325mg/l, Calcium 620mg/l, Magnesium 98.8mg/l, Potassium 21.3mg/l, Chlorides 481mg/l, Sulphates 1640mg/l, Fluorides 0.3mg/l.

Rangen (Fr) an A.C. Alsace Grand Cru vineyard in Thann and Vieux Thann, Haut-Rhin 18.81ha.

Rango (Sp) a solera reserva brandy produced by Garvey. *See also* Lacre Oro, Gran Garvey.

Rani (M.East) a mandarin orange juice produced by a process of removing the skin and pith leaving the fruit cells intact.

Ranina (Slav) a white grape variety grown in the Radogona district to produce Tiger's Milk, also known as the Bouvier.

Ranina Radgona (Slo) a sweet white wine also known as Tiger's Milk.

Ranin Brewery (Fin) a small brewery based in Kuopio, central Finland. Noted for alcohol-free beers.

Rankafae (Thai) café.

Ranschbach (Ger) village (Anb): Pfalz. (Ber):

Südliche Weinstrasse. (Gro): Königsgarten. (Vin): Seligmacher.

Ranton (Fr) a commune in the A.C. Saumur district of the Anjou-Saumur, Loire (Vienne département).

Ranzau (N.Z) a small vineyard based in Nelson, North Island. 1.5ha. Grape varieties: Cabernet sauvignon, Gamay, Gewürztraminer, Müller-Thurgau and Rhine riesling. Produces varietal and table wines.

Ranzenberg (Ger) vineyard (Anb): Württemberg. (Ber): Württembergisch Unterland. (Gro): Salzberg. (Vil): Ellhofen.

Ranzenberg (Ger) vineyard (Anb): Württemberg. (Ber): Württembergisch Unterland. (Gro): Salzberg. (Vil): Weinsberg.

Raoul's Old Basket Press Rustic Red (S.Afr) the label for an un-oaked red wine (Tinta) produced by the Beaumont Wines winery, Walker Bay, Western Cape.

Rapazzini Winery (USA) a winery based in Gilroy, Santa Clara, California. Produces varietal, sparkling and dessert wines.

Rape (Eng) the name for the skins and stalks of grapes left after wine-making in the seventeenth century. (Fr) = râpé.

Râpé (Fr) a name given to the pomace which is fermented and used for vinegar, also applied to the grapes removed during Triage in Châteauneuf-du-Pape that are used for the same purpose.

Rapel Valley (Chile) a 2041ha wine-producing area based in central Chile.

Rapet Père et Fils (Fr) a négociant-éleveur based in the Côte d'Or. (Add): Pernand-Vergelesses, 21420, Savigny-lès-Beaune.

Raphael Vineyard (USA) a vineyard (established 1996) based on Long Island. 148ha. Grape varieties: (white): Sauvignon blanc, (red): Cabernet franc, Cabernet sauvignon, Malbec, Merlot and Petit verdot.

Rapid Ageing (Eng) the art of attempting to quickly bring wine to the peak of maturation in order for the wine-maker to have a faster turnover and less money tied up in wine stocks.

Rapid Fermentation (W.Ind) a method used in rum production, takes a minimum of 12 hours to 1½ days. Produces light-styled rums.

Rapier Lager (Eng) a lager beer brewed in England and distributed by Linfood Cash and Carry, Northamptonshire.

Rapley Trail Vineyard (USA) the label for a red wine (Pinot noir) produced by the Thomas Fogarty winery, Santa Cruz Mountains, San Francisco Bay, California.

Raposeira (Port) a sparkling wine produced by the traditional method at Lamego, Beira Alta.

Rappe (Fr) a term used for the pulp left over after the first pressing of the grapes for Cognac. This is then pressed twice more and may be used for distillation.

Rappen (Ger) vineyard (Anb): Württemberg. (Ber): Württembergisch Unterland. (Gro): Schozachtal. (Vil): Ilsfeld.

Rappoltsweier (Fr) the German name for the town of Ribeauvillé in the Haut-Rhin, Alsace.

Rappu (Fr) a white VdN produced in Corsica from the Muscat grape.

Rapsani (Gre) an A.O.C. red wine produced in eastern Greece on the foothills of Mount Olympus. Grape varieties: Krassatio, Stavroto and Xynomavro. Soils: low zone is sandy/middle zone is loess/high zone rock, sand and loess.

Rapsani (Gre) an A.O.Q.S. dry red wine produced mainly from Xynomavro grape by Tsantalis, Agios Pavlos, Halkidiki. Bottled in their winery at Olympos.

Rapsig (Ger) the term to denote a stalky-taste in wines where the must has a taste of grape pips, skins and stalks.

Rapsini (Gre) a dry red table wine made from the Xynomavro, Krassato and Stavroto grapes. Produced in northern Greece.

Raquet Club (Cktl) ⅔ measure gin, ⅓ measure dry vermouth, dash Campari. Stir over ice and strain into a cocktail glass.

Rara-Njagra (Rus) a red grape variety grown in Moldavia around the river Dnieper (lower reaches).

Rare (Fr) *see* Champagne Rare.

Rare Breed (USA) a 109.6° US proof Bourbon whiskey produced by Wild Turkey Distillery, Lawrenceburg.

Rare Cabinet (S.Afr) a 20 year old aged brandy produced by Van Ryn in Vlottenburg near Stellenbosch, Western Cape.

Rare Old Highland (Scot) a brand of blended Scotch whisky produced by Hiram Walker 40% alc by vol.

Rasiguères (Fr) a red wine from the Côtes du Roussillon-Villages.

Rasillo (Sp) a red wine produced by Faustino Rivero Ulecia, S.A., Rioja. Made from Garnacha, Tempranillo and Viura grapes. Oak matured.

Raspail (Fr) a yellow liqueur made from herbs, invented by François Raspail in 1847.

Raspani (Gre) a red wine produced in Thessaly.

Raspberry Brandy (Euro) a fruit brandy made from raspberries in France, Germany and Switzerland.

Raspberry Cooler (Cktl) 30mls (¼ gill) dry gin, 30mls (¼ gill) raspberry syrup, 15mls (⅛ gill) lime juice, 2 dashes grenadine, 200mls (⅓ pint) ginger ale. Stir well in a highball glass with an ice cube and serve with a dash of grenadine.

Raspberry Highball (Cktl) 60mls (½ gill) raspberry syrup, dash lemon juice, soda water and stir in a highball glass with an ice cube.

Raspberry Leaf Tea (Eng) a herbal tea whose properties are as a settler of stomachs and labour soother in pregnancy. Has a light astringency.

Raspberry Smash Cooler (Cktl)(Non-alc) 30mls (¼ gill) raspberry syrup, 30mls (¼ gill) lemon juice, dash Angostura. Stir well over ice, strain into an ice-filled highball glass, top with soda water and serve with a few fresh raspberries.

Raspberry Wheat (Eng) a 4.5% alc by vol. wheat

beer brewed by the Downton Brewery C°., Wiltshire.

Raspberry Wheat (Eng) a 5% alc by vol. wheat beer brewed by the Iceni Brewery, Norfolk.

Raspon (Sp) vine stalk.

Rasputin's Revenge (Cktl) ½ measure Bols Blue Curaçao, ½ measure vodka. Stir over ice and strain into a cocktail glass.

Rassig (Ger) a wine with race and breeding.

Rasstadt (Aus) a vineyard site based on the banks of the River Kamp situated in the Kamptal region.

Rasteau (Fr) a village in the A.C. Côtes du Rhône-Villages. Noted for a Vin Doux Naturel made from the Grenache grape. Also produces red, rosé and white wines.

Rasteau Rancio (Fr) a special version of the vin doux naturel which has obtained bottle age and has a rancio taste.

Ratafee (Eng) the alternative spelling of ratafia in the eighteenth century.

Ratafia (Fr) a sweet apéritif wine made by adding brandy to grape juice (*see* Muted Wine), produced mainly in southern France and in the Champagne region.

Ratafia (Pol) a fruit-flavoured vodka produced by Polmos 25% alc by vol.

Ratafia de Bourgogne (Fr) a ratafia made in the Burgundy region.

Ratafia de Champagne (Fr) a sweet apéritif that originates from Champagne. ⅔ grape juice (must) and ⅓ brandy (marc de Champagne).

Rat & Ratchet Brewery (Eng) a brewery. (Add): 40 Chapel Hill, Huddersfield, West Yorkshire HD1 3EB. Brews bitter beers. Website: http://www.ratandratchet.co.uk 'E'mail: mail@ratandratchet.co.uk

Rat-Arsed (Eng) an unsavoury slang term for being drunk/inebriated.

Ratcliff Ale (Eng) an ale brewed by Bass on 16th December 1869 to celebrate the birth of Henry Ratcliff (1120 O.G.).

Rathausberg (Ger) vineyard (Anb): Mosel-Saar-Ruwer. (Ber): Zell/Mosel. (Gro): Rosenhang. (Vil): Bruttig-Fankel.

Rather Revealing (S.Afr) the label for a rosé wine (Shiraz) produced by the Stellar Winery, Olifants River, Western Cape.

Ratsch (Aus) a wine-producing town in Styria.

Ratsgrund (Ger) vineyard (Anb): Nahe. (Ber): Kreuznach. (Gro): Pfarrgarten. (Vil): Sommerloch.

Ratsherr (Ger) vineyard (Anb): Franken. (Ber): Maindreieck. (Gro): Kirchberg. (Vil): Volkach.

Ratskeller (Ger) a beer hall in a cellar/basement. The cellar is that of a town hall.

Ratskeller Edel-Pils (Ger) a bitter pilsener lager brewed by the Lindener-Gilde Brauerei in Hanover. Has a long lagering period 5.5% alc by vol.

Rattler (Eng) a 4.3% alc by vol. ale brewed by the Boat Brewery, West Yorkshire.

Rattle Skull (Cktl) ½ measure Cognac, ½ measure Port wine. Stir over ice in a highball glass and top with red wine.

Rattlesnake Cocktail (Cktl) 1½ measure Bourbon whiskey, 4 dashes lemon juice, 2 dashes gomme, 1 dash pastis, 1 egg white. Shake over ice and strain into a cocktail glass.

Rattlesnake Hill (USA) a red wine (Cabernet sauvignon) produced by the Barnett Estate winery, Napa Valley, California.

Rauchbiers (Ger) a smoked beer, made in much the same way as malt whisky through the smoking of the barley (*see* Peat Reek) but using wood smoke. Produced in Bamburg, Bavaria.

Rauenberg (Ger) village (Anb): Baden. (Ber): Badische Bergstrasse/Kraichgau. (Gro): Mannaberg. (Vin): Burggraf.

Rauenthal (Ger) village (Anb): Rheingau. (Ber): Johannisberg. (Gro): Steinmacher. (Vins): Baiken, Gehrn, Langenstück, Nonnenberg, Rothenberg, Wülfen.

Rauh (Ger) raw/harsh.

Rauhenneck (Aus) a vineyard site on the banks of the River Danube situated in the Wachau region, Niederösterreich.

Rauhreif (Cktl) ⅓ measure gin, ⅓ measure Curaçao, ⅓ measure Jamaican rum, 3 dashes grenadine, 4 dashes lemon juice. Shake over ice and strain into a cocktail glass.

Raul (Ger) vineyard (Anb): Mosel-Saar-Ruwer. (Ber): Saar-Ruwer. (Gro): Scharzberg. (Vil): Oberemmel.

Rauli (Chile) a local wood used for wine and spirit casks.

Raumbach (Ger) village (Anb): Nahe. (Ber): Schloss Böckelheim. (Gro): Paradiesgarten. (Vins): Schlossberg, Schwalbennest.

Rauner and Sons Winery (USA) a small winery based in South Bend, Indiana. 1.25ha. Produces hybrid wines.

Rausch (Ger) drunkenness.

Rausch (Ger) vineyard (Anb): Mosel-Saar-Ruwer. (Ber): Saar-Ruwer. (Gro): Scharzberg. (Vil): Saarburg.

Rauschelay (Ger) vineyard (Anb): Mittelrhein. (Ber): Rheinburgengau. (Gro): Herrenberg. (Vil): Kaub.

Räuschling (Ger) a white grape variety. Also known as the Elbling, Kleinberger and Knipperlé.

Ravager (Fr) one of the nicknames for phylloxera. *See also* Vastatrix.

Ravanello (Fr) a vanilla and coffee-flavoured liqueur produced by the Germain C°. in southern France.

Ravat (Fr) a famous hybridiser.

Ravel (Port) a Vinho Verde made at Farmalicao by Carvalho, Ribeiro and Ferreira in Ribatejo.

Ravello (It) a wine-producing area in Campania, southern Italy. Produces red, rosé and white wines.

Ravelsbach (Aus) a wine-producing district in the Weinviertel. Noted for light-styled white wines.

Raven Ale (Scot) a 3.8% alc by vol. seasonal ale brewed by The Orkney Brewery Ltd., Orkney..

Raven Brewery (Eng) a brewery based in Brighton,

R

Sussex (reopened in 1983). Noted for cask-conditioned Old Master 1060 O.G.

Ravenhead (Eng) famous glass producers based in Staines, Middlesex. Produce a fine, large range of beverage glassware.

Ravensburg (Ger) grosslage (Anb): Franken. (Ber): Maindreieck. (Vils): Erlabrunn, Güntersleben, Retzbach, Thüngersheim, Veitshöchheim.

Ravenscroft [George] (Eng) a glassmaker who invented 'glass of lead' in 1675 (lead crystal glass).

Ravenswood Winery (USA) a winery based in Sonoma County, California. Grape varieties: Cabernet sauvignon, Pinot noir, Zinfandel. Labels: Old Hill, Vintners Blend. A part of Icon Estates (Constellation Brands).

Raventós [Don José] (Sp) the first Spaniard to produce cava wines in Spain in 1872.

Rawalpindi Brewery (Pak) a brewery that produces 4.5% alc by vol Muree Beer.

Raw Passion (Wal) the name for a range of 3 exotic, vodka-based fruit cocktails: Caribbean, Tropical and Wild. Produced by Welsh Distillers. Sold in an aluminium screw-top bottle.

Rawson's (S.Afr) the label for red wine (Ruby cabernet-Merlot) produced by the Cape Vineyards winery, Rawsonville, Western Cape.

Raw Spirit (Eng) a 38% alc by vol. vodka sold in pure aluminium bottles. Chill-filtered five times, run through a honeycomb to give a hint of sweetness. From MDT International.

Raw Spirit Mix (Eng) a 5% alc by vol. vodka cocktail drink available in three flavours. Marketed by Imperial Drinks based in Bishops Stortford, in Hertfordshire.

Raw Spirits (Eng) undiluted spirits.

Raya (Sp) a system of classification of newly fermented wine for Sherry as a series of strokes (marks). 1 stroke denotes wines destined for Finos. See also Dos Rayas and Tres Rayas.

Raya Olorosa (Sp) a Sherry that has not quite made the grade of Oloroso.

Raya y Punto (Sp) a special mark on the side of a Sherry cask (one long stroke and one short stroke) which denotes that a new wine has not yet been finely classified. see Raya.

Ray Martin Winery (USA) a winery based near Saratoga, Santa Clara, California. Grape varieties: Cabernet sauvignon, Chardonnay, Pinot noir. Produces varietal wines. La Montaña is the second label.

Rayment Brewery (Eng) a brewery based in Furneaux Pelham, Hertfordshire. Is a subsidiary of the Greene King Brewery. Noted for cask-conditioned BBA 1036 O.G. and Pelham Ale 1031 O.G.

Rayments Special Bitter (Eng) a 4% alc by vol./1040 O.G. bitter from the Rayment Brewery.

Raymond Winery (USA) a vineyard and winery based near St. Helena, Napa Valley, California. 38ha. Grape varieties: Cabernet sauvignon, Chardonnay, Chenin blanc, Sauvignon blanc, Zinfandel. Produces varietal wines.

Rayyan (Arab) a natural spring mineral water from Ar Rayyan, Qatar. Mineral contents (milligrammes per litre): Sodium 9mg/l, Calcium 10mg/l, Magnesium 12mg/l, Potassium 6.2mg/l, Bicarbonates 55mg/l, Chlorides 20mg/l, Sulphates 39mg/l, Fluorides 0.7mg/l. pH 7.8

R.C. (Fr) abbr: Récoltant-Coopérateur. Indicates a co-operative produced Champagne.

R.C. (Wal) abbr: see Red Crown.

Rcakzitelli (Bul) a white grape variety which produces strong, full-bodied dry wines. Also spelt Rcatzitelli.

Rcatzitelli (Bul) an alternative spelling of Rcakzitelli.

RCH Brewery (Eng) a brewery (established 1984). (Add): West Hewish, Weston-Super-Mare, Avon BS24 6RR. Brews: Ale Mary 6% alc by vol., Double Header 5.3% alc by vol., East Stream Cream 5% alc by vol., Firebox Premium Bitter 6% alc by vol., Golding Years, Hewish IPA 3.6% alc by vol., Old Slug Porter 4.5% alc by vol., , PG Steam 3.9% alc by vol., Pitchfork Ale 4.3% alc by vol. Website: http://www.rchbrewery.com 'E'mail: rchbrew@aol.com

R. C. Iveson (Sp) a solera gran reserva brandy from Wisdom & Warter. See also Gran Reserva Wisdom.

R.D. (Fr) abbr: Récemment Dégorgé™ the brand-name of a wine which has recently been disgorged. Produced by Bollinger Champagne. Shows date of vintage and dégorgement.

R.D.I. (Austr) abbr: Regulated Deficit Irrigation, the use of soil moisture probes to detect when irrigation is required. Used in the Riverland region. See also P.R.D.

RDR (Eng) abbr: Responsible Drinks Retailing.

Read's (Austr) a winery (established 1972) based at Evan's Lane, Oxley via Milawa, Victoria. Grape varieties: Chardonnay, Sauvignon blanc, Riesling, Cabernet sauvignon, Pinot noir, Shiraz.

Ready Steady (S.Afr) the label for a range of wines (red is a blend) (white Chenin blanc and Chardonnay blend) produced by the Southern Sky Wines winery, Paarl, Western Cape.

Ready to Drink (Eng) abbr: RTD a collective name for bottled mixed drinks whick need no further additions or mixing (usually white spirit and fruit juices).

Real (Eng) the name given to a range of 6 fruit juices produced by St. Ivel.

Real Ale (Eng) the term used for cask-conditioned draught and bottle-conditioned beers. Cask ales dispensed with the natural CO_2 and has no additional CO_2 added, the CAMRA name for Traditional Ale.

Real Ale (Eng) a 4% alc by vol. cask-conditioned ale brewed by the Teignworthy Brewery, Tuckers Maltings, Newton Abbot.

Realbrut (It) a sparkling (metodo tradizionale) wine produced by Calissano in the Piemonte region.

Real Cave do Cedro (Port) the producer of sparkling wines made by the traditional method.

Real Companhía Vinícola do Norte de Portugal (Port) produces wines under the Lagosta label and Cabido (a Dão wine) plus a wide range of other wines.

1069

Reale di Tarsogno (It) a sparkling natural spring mineral water from Tarsogno, Parma. Mineral contents (milligrammes per litre): Sodium 2.8mg/l, Calcium 12.9mg/l, Magnesium 1.9mg/l, Potassium 0.5mg/l, Bicarbonates 39.5mg/l, Chlorides 4mg/l, Sulphates 7.1mg/l, Nitrates 2.1mg/l, Silicates 5.5mg/l. pH 7.7

Real é Insigne Iglesia Colegial (Sp) on the steps of this building, hundreds of homing pigeons are released to announce the start of the Sherry vintage festival. see Fiesta de la Vendimia.

Realengo (Sp) the brand-name of a full-bodied, medium-dry, Oloroso Sherry from the Diez Hermanos range produced by Diez Merito.

Real Junta, S.A. (Sp) a winery at San Cristobal 20-21, 26360 Fuenmayor, Rioja. Produces Rioja wines.

Real Lavrados (Port) the label of a red and white wine produced by Adego Cooperativa de Redondo in Alentejo.

Really Ravishing (S.Afr) the label for a red wine (Shiraz) produced by the Stellar Winery, Olifants River, Western Cape.

Real Mackay (Scot) a 3.8% alc by vol. ale brewed by the Far North Brewery, Caithness.

Real Mackenzie [The] (Scot) a blended Scotch whisky produced by P. Mackenzie and C° (part of Arthur Bell and Sons), Perth.

Real McCoy [The] (Scot) the brand-name of a Scotch whisky and ginger wine drink.

Real Oyster Stout (Eng) a 5% alc by vol. cask-conditioned stout brewed by Murphys using a third of a fresh oyster to every pint.

Real Vinicola (Port) vintage Port shippers based at Quinta do Sibio. Vintages: 1945, 1947, 1950, 1955, 1960.

Reaper's Reward (Eng) a 5% alc by vol. ale produced by W. H. Brakspear & Sons, Henley-on-Thames. Made using crystal rye.

Reaullt Hir (Wal) the monk who is purported to have introduced whiskey to Wales in the fourth century (on Bardsey Island), was used as a medicine (pain killer).

Rebate Brandy (S.Afr) the name given to 3 year old brandy that has been tasted by the Government Brandy Board. If acceptable will award a customs rebate to the distiller. Helps improve the quality of South African brandy.

Rebe (Ger) grape vine tendril.

Rebêche (Fr) the juice of the final pressing in Champagne. Used for the making of wine which is either distilled for marc or is consumed by the vineyard workers.

Rebel Charge (Cktl) ⅔ measure Bourbon whiskey, ⅓ measure triple sec, ½ measure orange juice, ½ measure lemon juice, ½ egg white. Shake over ice, strain into an ice-filled highball glass and top with a slice of orange.

Rebellion Beer C° (Eng) a brewery (established 1993). (Add): Bencombe Farm, Marlow Bottom, Marlow, Buckinghamshire SL7 3LT. Brews: Rebellion Blond3 4.3% alc by vol., Rebellion IPA 3.7% alc by vol., Rebellion Mutiny 4.5% alc by vol., Rebellion Red 4.5% alc by vol., Rebellion Smuggler 4.1% alc by vol., Rebellion White 4.5% alc by vol. Website: http://www.rebellionbeer.co.uk 'E'mail: info@rebellionbeer.co.uk

Rebello Valente (Port) vintage Port shippers. Vintages: 1870, 1875, 1878, 1881, 1884, 1887, 1890, 1892, 1894, 1896, 1897, 1900, 1904, 1908, 1911, 1912, 1917, 1920, 1922, 1924, 1927, 1931, 1935, 1942, 1955, 1960, 1963, 1966, 1967, 1970, 1972, 1975, 1977, 1980, 1983, 1985, 1991, 1994, 2003. Owned by Robertson.

Rebel Yell (USA) a Kentucky Bourbon 40% alc by vol. Produced since 1849 at Stitsle Weller Distillery in Louisville, originally sold in a plastic pint hip flask.

Rebholz Von Bunsanstein (Ger) a winery based in the Pfalz. Grape varieties: Gewürztraminer, Müller-Thurgau, Muskateller and Riesling.

Reblausgesetz (Ger) a Prussian law introduced on February 27th 1878 that was eventually extended in 1885. Contained procedures for destroying phylloxera-attacked vineyards. Was adopted by the whole of Germany in 1904.

Rebsorten (Ger) vine varieties.

Rebstöckel (Ger) grosslage (Anb): Pfalz. (Ber): Mittelhaardt-Deutsche Weinstrasse. (Vils): Diedesfeld, Hambach, Neustadt an der Weinstrasse.

Rebtal (Ger) vineyard (Anb): Baden. (Ber): Kaiserstuhl-Tuniberg. (Gro): Attilafelsen. (Vil): Tiengen.

Rebula (Slo) a red wine produced in Vipava in north-western Slovenia. also known as Ribolla.

Rebus (Iran) a natural spring mineral water (established 2000) from Golmakan. Mineral contents (milligrammes per litre): Sodium 51.98mg/l, Calcium 54.28mg/l, Magnesium 9.64mg/l, Bicarbonates 185.5mg/l, Chlorides 49.97mg/l, Sulphates 43.42mg/l, Fluorides 0.16mg/l, Nitrates 14.06mg/l. pH 7.5

Rebus (S.Afr) the label for a red wine (Cabernet franc and Cabernet sauvignon blend) produced by the Romond Vineyards winery, Stellenbosch, Western Cape.

Recas (Rum) a wine-producing area (part of the Banat Vineyard). Main red grape varieties are Cabernet sauvignon and Kadarka.

Recastra (Sp) the method of pruning in the Jerez district to remove any useless buds and so improve the chances of good buds on the vine.

Récemment Dégorgé (Fr) see R.D.

Recently Disgorged (Eng) see R.D.

Recession Beer (Eng) a 1032 O.G. beer brewed by Scotties Brewery in Lowestoft, Suffolk.

Rech (Ger) village (Anb): Ahr. (Ber): Walporzheim/Ahrtal. (Gro): Klosterberg. (Vins): Blume, Hardtberg, Herrenberg.

Recharge (Eng) a bottled energy drink that contains caffeine, taurine and added vitamins from Waters & Robson.

R

Rechböchel (Ger) vineyard (Anb): Pfalz. (Ber): Mittelhaardt-Deutsche Weinstrasse. (Gro): Mariengarten. (Vil): Wachenheim.

Rechberg (Ger) village (Anb): Baden. (Ber): Bodensee. *see* Klettgau.

Rechnitz (Aus) a wine-producing area in the district of south Burgenland.

Recia (It) ear. *see* Recie.

Recie (It) lit: 'ears', adapted to Valpolicella Recioto where only the outer bunches of grapes that have had the most sunshine are used. Also known as Recia, Recioto.

Recioto (It) *see* Recie.

Recioto Amarone Della Valpolicella (It) a D.O.C. red Valpolicella wine made in limited quantities from semi-dried grapes which are fully fermented resulting in a wine with a dry (bitter) finish. High in alcohol, up to 15½% by vol. *See also* Amarone, Recie, Recioto Della Valpolicella.

Recioto Della Valpolicella (It) a D.O.C. red wine from the Veneto. Made from the Barbera, Corvina veronese, Molinara, Rondinella and Rossignola negrara grapes which are semi-dried. Vinification can take place in Verona and the fermentation is stopped resulting in sweetness. The D.O.C. can also apply to sparkling wines vinified in Verona and also for fortified wines in Lombardy and Veneto.

Recioto di Gambellara (It) a D.O.C. white wine from Veneto. Made from the Garganega and Trebbiano nostrano grapes which are partially dried. D.O.C. also applies to the sparkling wines produced according to current regulations by natural fermentation within 4 specific communes.

Recioto di Soave (It) a D.O.C.G. white wine from Veneto. Made from the Garganega, may include 15% of Chardonnay/Trebbiano di soave. Grapes are partially dried. Wine has a slight taste of bitter almonds. D.O.C.G. in 1998. D.O.C. applies to sparkling wines and to fortified wines if the preparation takes place in Lombardy and Veneto.

Recioto Nobile (It) a recioto wine in which the grapes have been attacked by **Botrytis cinerea** (muffa nobile). It is a sweet, sparkling red wine.

Recked 'Em (Wal) a 5.2% alc by vol. ale brewed by Eric's Brewery, Pontypridd, Mid Glamorgan.

Réclame Trompeuse (Fr) lit: 'misleading advertisement' the French Trade Description Act.

Recolta (Rum) vintage.

Récoltant-Coopérateur (Fr) *abbr*: R.C. a grower who sells Champagne made for him or by him through a cooperative.

Récoltants-Manipulants (Fr) Champagne producers who make their own Champagne and sell direct to the customer.

Récolte (Fr) crop/vintage.

Record (Fr) a full-bodied beer brewed by the '33' Brasserie in Paris 7.5% alc by vol.

Re-Cork (Eng) many fine wines, after several years in the bottle, require their corks to be replaced with new ones. The wines are decanted and topped up with a sacrificial bottle of the same wine.

Recoulles [Les] (Fr) a vineyard of Coteaux de l'Hermitage, northern Rhône (white wine).

Rectified Spirits (Eng) purified spirits.

Rectifier (Eng) part of the continuous-still (Patent or Coffey still) which produces the pure spirit. Condenses a hot vapour (the spirits) to a liquid in distillation. *See also* Analyser.

Rectify (Eng) to change a natural spirit in some way, either by re-distilling or adding colour or flavourings. *see* Potash Salts.

Rectifying (Eng) the process of producing pure spirit. *see* Rectify.

Rector's Ruin (Eng) a limited edition ale brewed by Jennings Brewery, Cockermouth, Cumbria.

Red (Eng) a 5% alc by vol. vodka-based, bottled drink produced by Bass. Contains herbal extracts (also a blue version).

Red Admiral (Eng) a seasonal summer ale brewed by Mansfield Brewery, Littleworth, Mansfield, Notts.

Redalevn Liqueur (Eng) a liqueur made with a 100% Scotch whisky base. Produced by Savermo Ltd. of London. 40% alc by vol. Is sold only to the Manchester United Football club.

Red Apple Cocktail (Cktl) 20mls (⅛ gill) Smirnoff Blue Label, 20mls (⅛ gill) apple juice, 10mls (½ fl.oz) lemon juice, 2 dashes grenadine. Shake over ice and strain into a cocktail glass.

Redark (Bul) a label for a red wine (Cabernet sauvignon and Melot blend) from the Damianitza winery.

Red Azur (Cktl) ½ measure Cointreau, ¼ measure kirsch, ¼ measure dry vermouth, dash grenadine. Shake over ice and strain into a cocktail glass.

Redbach (Bel) a 4.1% alc by vol lager and cherry juice blended drink from the Rodenbach Brewery.

Red Back Beer Light (Austr) a 3.4% alc by vol. bottled wheat beer brewed by the Matilda Bay Brewing Company (C.U.B.), 130 Stirling Highway, Fremantle, Western Australia.

Red Band Export (N.Z) the brand-name used for a range of beers brewed by the New Zealand Breweries.

Red Bank Winery (Austr) a winery (established 1973). (Add): Redbank, Victoria 3467. 10ha. Grape varieties: Cabernet franc, Cabernet sauvignon, Malbec, Merlot, Pinot noir, Shiraz, Chardonnay. Labels include Long Paddock, Sally's Paddock.

Red Beer (Bel) a top-fermented beer-style. The brew is blended with beer which has been oak aged for at least 18 months. Barley, maize grits, caramel, Vienna malts are added. Lactic acid is formed during the brewing process which gives the beer a sharp acidic flavour.

Red Biddy (Eng) a slang term for cheap red wine usually fortified with methylated spirits.

Redbreast (Ire) a 12 year old pure pot-still whiskey produced from 55%–60% unmalted barley by Middleton.

Redbrook Estate (Austr) part of the Evans and Tate Vineyards in Western Australia 18ha.

Red Bull (Aus) a popular carbonated soft drink

(created in 1987 by Dietrich Mateschitz) that contains caffeine (80mgs per 250mls), sugar and taurine (an amino acid).

Red Bull C° Ltd (Eng) a carbonated drink producer (established 1995). (Add): 14 Soho Square, London W1D 3QG. Part of Red Bull Trading GmbH. Website: http://www.redbull.com/http://www.redbull.co.uk

Red Bullet Cocktail (Cktl) 1 measure gin, 2 measures redcurrant wine, 4 measures cider. Mix together, chill well down and serve in a highball glass with an apple slice.

Red Bull Trading GmbH. (Aus) produces Red Bull, factory based in the Volarlberg region. *See also* Red Bull C°. Ltd.

Red Bush (Ire) an alternative name for Bushmills White Label.

Red Bicyclette (Fr) a brand name for a French wine produced by E & J Gallo (France) for the American market. The name designed to appeal to the Americans in place of the complicated French label names!

Red C (Eng) a 4% alc by vol. draught sweet cider produced by Matthew Clark, replacing Blackthorn Sweet.

Red Cardinal Cup (Punch) 1 bottle claret, ½ bottle soda water, 1 sliced lemon, mix together with ice and serve.

Red Cloud Cocktail (Cktl) ¾ measure dry gin, ¼ measure apricot brandy, juice ¼ lemon, 2 dashes grenadine. Shake well over ice and strain into a cocktail glass.

Red Corner (Fr) a three star Cognac brandy produced by A. Hardy, average age of 3 years for Cognacs from Borderies.

Red Crown (Eng) a bottled pale ale 1034 O.G. brewed by the Everards Brewery, Leicester.

Red Crown [R.C.] (Wal) a dark cask-conditioned mild ale 1035 O.G. brewed by the Brains Brewery in Cardiff.

Red Delicious (Gre) a sweet red liqueur (version of Mavrodaphne of Patras) wine produced by Tsantali.

Red Devil (Scot) a 'red hot spirit' 40% alc by vol. that contains Bells 8 year old Scotch whisky plus herbs, spices and chilli peppers from United Distillers, Perth.

Red Dragon (Eng) a 4% alc by vol. bitter ale brewed by the Highgate Brewery Ltd., West Midlands.

Red Dragon (Wal) a 4.7% alc by vol. bitter ale brewed by the Breconshire Brewery, Powys.

Red Dragon (Wal) an ale brewed by S.A. Brain & C°. Ltd. in Cardiff.

Red Dragon (Wal) the brand-name of an own-label cider sold in 1 or 2litres PET bottles from Symonds of Hereford (plant based in Cardiff). *See also* Black Dragon, Gold Dragon, Silver Dragon.

Red Dust Bitter (Eng) a 4.5% alc by vol. bitter brewed by the Derwentrose Brewery in Consett, County Durham.

Red E (USA) an early instant coffee brand which had a poor taste.

Red Earl (Eng) a 3.7% alc by vol. ale brewed by the Malvern Hills Brewery, Worcestershire.

Red Edge (Austr) a winery based in Heathcote, Victoria. Grape varieties include: Shiraz.

Red Ellen (Eng) a 4.4% alc by vol. ale brewed by the Jarrow Brewery, Tyne & Wear.

Red Erik (Den) a 6.5% alc by vol. lager brewed by the Ceres Brewery, Aarhus.

Red Eye (Can) a drink of three parts beer and one part tomato juice.

Redeye (Eng) a 4.5% alc by vol. premium smooth ale from the Mansfield Brewery, Nottingham.

Red Eye (USA) a slang term for cheap whiskey.

Red Fox (Eng) a 4% alc by vol. ale brewed by the Butlers Brewery C°. Ltd., Berkshire.

Red Fox (Eng) a 4% alc by vol. seasonal ale brewed in October/November by Cain (Robert) Brewery, Liverpool. Ruby red in colour due to the addition of elderberry juice.

Redgate (Austr) a winery. (Add): P.O. Box 117, Margaret River, Off Boodiscup Road, Western Australia. 12ha. Grape varieties: Cabernet franc, Cabernet sauvignon, Chenin blanc, Riesling, Sauvignon blanc, Sémillon.

Red Hackle (Cktl) ¼ measure red Dubonnet, ¼ measure brandy, ¼ measure grenadine. Shake over ice and strain into a cocktail glass.

Red Hackle (Scot) a brand of blended Scotch whisky now owned by Highland Distilleries.

Red Hanepoot (S.Afr) a relative of the Muscat grape. *See also* Flame Muscat.

Redhawk Vineyard (USA) a vineyard (established 1979). (Add): Michigan City NW Salem, Oregon. Grape varieties: Pinot noir, Chardonnay, Merlot, Cabernet sauvignon, Cabernet franc.

Red Head (Cktl) a 3 parts Guinness and 1 part tomato juice.

Red Heart Rum (Eng) the brand-name for a rum produced by U.R.M. 40% alc by vol.

Red Hill Estate (Austr) a winery (established 1989) based at 53 Red Hill-Shoreham Road, Red Hill South, Victoria. Grape varieties: Cabernet sauvignon, Pinot noir, Chardonnay. Produces still and traditional method wines.

Red Hock (Eng) the eighteenth and nineteenth century name for German red wines.

Red Horse (Eng) the label of an extra strong beer.

Redigaffi (It) a red I.G.T. Merlot wine aged in new oak. Produced by Tua Rita, Suvereto, Maremma, Tuscany.

Red Light Cocktail (Cktl)(Non-alc) ¼ measure pineapple juice, ¼ measure orange juice, ¼ measure syrop de fraises, ¼ measure lemon juice, 2 dashes grenadine. Shake well over ice, strain into a cocktail glass and dress with a slice of orange.

Redling (Aus) a vineyard site based on the banks of the River Kamp situated in the Kamptal region.

Red Lion (Cktl) ⅓ measure dry gin, ⅓ measure Grand Marnier, ⅙ measure orange juice, ⅙ measure lemon juice. Shake well over ice and strain into a cocktail glass.

Red Lion Bitter (Eng) a bitter beer 1038 O.G. distributed by Linfood Cash and Carry, Northamptonshire.

Red Lion Punch (Eng) an eighteenth century recipe served hot or cold, made from calves-foot jelly, oranges, lemons, sugar syrup, gin and white wine heated together.

Red Lips (Cktl) 25mls (1fl.oz) vodka, 5mls (¼ fl.oz) Campari, 5mls (¼ fl.oz) Grand Marnier, 2 dashes egg white, dash Angostura. Shake over ice and strain into a cocktail glass.

Red MacGregor (Scot) a 4% alc by vol. ale brewed by The Orkney Brewery Ltd., Orkney.

Redman (Austr) a winery in Coonawarra, South Australia. Produces varietal wines.

Red Medallion (S.Afr) the label for a red wine (Cabernet franc 20%, Cabernet sauvignon 60% and Merlot 20% blend) produced by the Napier Winery, Wellington, Western Cape.

Red Misket (Bul) a red grape variety grown in northern Bulgaria.

Redmond (Austr) a winery. (Add): P.O. Box 433, Albany, Western Australia 6330. 4.4ha. Grape varieties: Cabernet sauvignon, Gewürztraminer, Rhine riesling, Sauvignon blanc. Produces varietal wines.

Redmont (Aus) the label for a red (Cabernet sauvignon and Zweigelt blend) wine produced by the Markowitsch winery, Göttlesbrunn, Carnuntum.

Red Mountain (USA) the new A.V.A. in Yakima Valley, Washington. The smallest to date with 1,400ha. Grape varieties include Cabernet sauvignon, Cabernet franc, Merlot, Syrah.

Red Mountain (Eng) the brand-name of a freeze-dried instant coffee produced by Brooke Bond Oxo Ltd.

Red Muscadel (S.Afr) a red grape variety.

Red Nose (Eng) a 1057 O.G. beer brewed by the Finnesko and Firkin Brewery in Derham Road, Norwich, Norfolk (formerly known as the Reindeer Brewery).

Red Nose Reindeer (Eng) a Christmas ale from Cotleigh Brewery in Wiveliscombe, Somerset.

Red October (Cktl) place 4cls vodka and 1cl crème de cassis over ice in a highball and top with 8cls Schweppes Indian tonic water.

Redoma (Port) a red D.O. Douro wine produced by Niepoort.

Redondo (Port) a DOC district within the Alentejo region. Produces mainly red wines.

Redondo (Sp) a round, well-balanced Sherry wine.

Redouellage (Fr) denotes the substitution of two new staves in old barrels.

Redox Reactions (Eng) the collective name for the reductive and oxygen reactions that occur in wines which help it to age.

Red Pinot (USA) see California Red Pinot.

Red Raider Cocktail (Cktl) ⅔ measure Bourbon whiskey, ⅙ measure lemon juice, ⅙ measure Grand Marnier, dash grenadine. Shake over ice and strain into a cocktail glass.

Red-Red (S.Afr) the label for a red wine (Cabernet sauvignon, Grenache, Merlot, Pinotage and Zinfandel blend) produced by the Lammershoek Winery, Swartland, Western Cape. Part of the Aprilskloof range.

Red Reef (S.Afr) the label of a red wine from the Mount Rozier Estate winery in Stellenbosch, Western Cape that is no longer produced.

Redrescuts (Fr) a Premier Cru vineyard [part] in the A.C. commune of Savigny-lès-Beaune, Côte de Beaune, Burgundy.

Red Riesling (USA) a lesser grape variety grown in western America.

Red River (Eng) a 4.8% alc by vol. ale brewed by King WJ & C°., West Sussex.

Red Rock (Eng) a lager brewed by the Cornish Brewery Company in Redruth, Cornwall.

Red Rock (Eng) the brand-name of a draught or bottled cider produced by the Taunton Cider Company.

Red Rock Terrace (USA) the brand-name used by the Diamond Creek Winery for a style of wine from a specific section of their vineyards.

Red Rose (Eng) a 4.3% alc by vol. ale from the Walker Brewery, Warrington, Cheshire.

Red Rose (W.Ind) a noted brand of Jamaican rum produced by the Wray and Nephew Group on the island of Jamaica.

Red Rose Brewery (Eng) a brewery (established 1994). (Add): Unit 4, Stanley Court, Alan Ramsbottom Way, Great Harwood, Blackburn, Lancashire BB6 7UR. Brews: Caretaker of History 6% alc by vol., Old Ben 4.3% alc by vol., Olde Emplor IPA 5.5% alc by vol., Quaffing Ale 3.8% alc by vol. Website: http://www.redrosebrewery.co.uk 'E'mail: beer@redrosebrewery.co.uk

Red Rose Stout (Eng) a bottled stout 1040 O.G. brewed by the Greenall Whitley Brewery in Warrington, Cheshire.

Redruth Brewery (Eng) a brewery based in Cornwall. Brews: Yixing beer licensed from Yixing Brewery, Jiangsu Province, China. Made using English malt, rice, Janjing hops, water and yeast. Also Cornish Rebellion, Crofty, Indianhead, John Davey, Rudolph the Redruth Rain Beer, Scream'n Beaver.

Red Santos (Bra) a grade of pure coffee produced in the Santos region of north-eastern Brazil.

Red Seal (S.Afr) the label for a range of wines produced by the Fairview winery, Suider-Paarl, Western Cape.

Red Seal Ale (I.O.M) a bottled pale ale 1036 O.G. brewed by the Castletown Brewery.

Red Seal Ale (Eng) a premium ale 1046–1052 O.G. from Scottish & Newcastle. Sold under the McEwan name.

Red Seal Ale (USA) a 5.6% alc by vol. top-fermented, amber coloured, bottled American ale brewed by the North Coast Brewing C°. in Fort Bragg, California.

Red Shed (Eng) a 3.8% alc by vol. ale brewed by the Bazens Brewery, Greater Manchester.

Red Smiddy (Scot) a 4.1% alc by vol. ale brewed by the Kelburn Brewing C°., Lanarkshire.

Red Snapper (Scot) a non-alcoholic canned energy drink containing caffeine and taurine.

Red Sombrero Cocktail (Cktl)(Non-alc) ⅓ measure

grenadine, ⅓ measure pineapple juice, ⅓ measure orange juice. Shake over ice, strain into an ice-filled highball glass, top with ginger ale, dress with a cherry and lemon slice and serve with straws.

Red Square Irn Bru (Eng) a bottled drink of vodka and Irn Bru from Halewood International. *See also* Cranberry Ice, Reloaded Red Square. Website: http://www.redsquareworld.com

Red Squirrel Brewery (Eng) a brewery. (Add): 14b Mimram Road, Hertford, Hertfordshire SG14 1NN. Brews bitter beers. Website: http://www.redsquirrelbrewery.co.uk 'E'mail: gary@redsquirrelbrewery.co.uk

Red Stag Bitter (Eng) a 3.6% alc by vol. bitter ale brewed by the Newmans Brewery, Avon.

Redstone (S.Afr) the label for a red wine (Bordeaux blend) produced by the Dreamview Hill winery, Somerset West, Western Cape.

Red Stone (S.Afr) the label for a red wine (Merlot, Petit verdot, Ruby cabernet and Shiraz blend) produced by the Du Preez Estate winery, Worcester, Western Cape.

Red Stone Reserve (S.Afr) the label for a red wine (Cabernet sauvignon 30% and Touriga nacional 70%) produced by the De Krans winery, Little Karoo.

Redstreak (Eng) a variety of cider apple.

Redstreak (Eng) a 6% alc by vol. cider from Perry's Cider Mills, Dowlish Wake, Illminster, Somerset.

Red Stripe Crucial Brew (W.Ind) a Jamaican lager 1080–1086 O.G. brewed with American yeast and hops to a Jamaican recipe by the Charles Wells Brewery, Bedford.

Red Stripe Lager (W.Ind) a 4.7% alc by vol. bottled lager beer brewed by Desnoes & Geddes Ltd., Kingston, Jamaica. Website: http://www.redstripe.net

Red Sumoll (Sp) a red grape variety grown in Conca de Barbera in the province of Tarragona.

Red Sunset (Cktl) ⅖ measure white rum, ⅖ measure Mansikka liqueur, ⅕ measure lemon liqueur, ⅕ measure lemon juice, shake over ice and strain into a cocktail glass.

Red Swizzle (Cktl) as for a Gin Swizzle adding 25mls (1fl.oz) grenadine.

Red Traminer (USA) the alternative name for the Gewürztraminer grape (so named due to the red blush of the grapes as they are ripening).

Red Triangle Beer (Eng) the old name for the sediment beer from the Worthington Brewery called White Shield.

Red Trollinger (Fr) an alternative name for the Trollinger grape.

Reducing (Eng) the term applied to the operation of lowering the alcoholic strength of a spirit by the addition of water.

Reduction (Eng) a wine fault caused by *Hydrogen sulphide* (H_2S) formed by yeast during fermentation that will normally bond with any oxygen available after fermentation. In an oxygen-free environment such as a bottle of wine, the H_2S (having no oxygen present) bonds with other chemicals to form off aromas and flavours. These aromas/flavours can be: sulphurous (burnt match), struck flint, rubber, cabbage or rotten eggs. Screwcap, Crown Cork and Selvin stoppers all produce an oxygen-free environment so wines in bottles using these stopper mediums should not be kept to mature for long periods. (Fr) = reduit.

Reductive Vinification (Eng) the modern process of wine fermentation by minimising the fermenting must's contact with air (in stainless steel tanks) which produces a fresher and fruitier wine.

Reduit (Fr) a term to denote a disagreeable smell that occurs due to the wine being stored in the absence of air, needs racking to eliminate this.

Red Velvet (Can) a Canadian whisky produced by Gilbey Canada Ltd.

Red Vermouth (It) the sweet-flavoured, fortified wine which is now also produced in France.

Red Viking (Cktl) ⅓ measure akvavit, ⅓ measure maraschino, ⅓ measure lime juice cordial. Stir over ice and strain into an ice-filled highball glass.

Red, White and Blue (USA) a lager beer brewed by the Pabst Brewery.

Red Wine (Eng) any wine which has the red colouring obtained from the pigment in the grape skins by natural extraction. This is usually extracted during the fermentation process when the skins are left in the fermenting must. (Den) = rødvin, (Fr) = vin rouge, (Ger) = rotwein, (Gre) = oinos erythros, (Hol) = rood wijn, (Ire) = fion dearg, (It) = vino rosso, (Port) = vinho tinto, (Sp) = vino tinto, (Wal) = gwin coch.

Red Wine Island (Ger) the name given to Assmanshausen in the Rheingau because the vineyards produce red wines (from the Spätburgunder grape) and are surrounded by white grape vineyards.

Red Wine Path (Ger) rotweinwanderweg: the wine road of the Ahr Valley.

Red Wine Punch (Cktl) 2 bottles red wine, 1 bottle Port, ½ bottle cherry brandy, juice of 6 oranges and 4 lemons, 100grms (4ozs) powdered sugar. Mix in a large bowl, add contents of a soda syphon and ice and decorate with sliced fruit in season.

Red Wing (Eng) a 4.8% alc by vol. ale brewed by the Potbelly Brewery Ltd., Northamptonshire.

Redwood Trail (USA) the label used by Sterling Vineyards, California. Wine range includes Chardonnay, Sauvignon blanc, Cabernet sauvignon, Pinot noir, red and rosé Zinfandel.

Redwood Valley (USA) an A.V.A. area of Mendocino.

Redwood Valley Estate (N.Z) a winery based in Nelson. Has 83.5ha. over five vineyards. Grape varieties: Chardonnay, Sauvignon blanc, Cabernet sauvignon.

Reebok Fitness Water (Can) a bottled mineral water brand.

Reef (Eng) a 5% alc by vol. RTD still orange and passion fruit/pineapple and citrus/mango and apple/red berry and kiwi drinks from Hooper's Hooch.

R

Reekin' (Scot) a slang term for *'smelling of drink'*.

Reel Ale (Eng) a 4% alc by vol. bitter ale brewed by the Teignworthy Brewery Ltd., Devon.

Reeling (Eng) a slang term used to denote being unsteady on one's feet through intoxication.

Reepham Brewery (Eng) a brewery (established 1983) based in Reepham, Norfolk. Noted for cask-conditioned Brewhouse Ale 1055 O.G. Granary Bitter 1038 O.G. Summer Velvet 1040 O.G. Velvet Stout.

Refène [La] (Fr) a Premier Cru vineyard in the A.C. commune of Pommard, Côte de Beaune, Burgundy 2.5ha.

Referencia (Sp) the name given to the sample of wine the shipper retains.

Refert [Le] (Fr) a Premier Cru vineyard in the A.C. commune of Puligny-Montrachet, Côte de Beaune, Burgundy 13.2ha.

Reflets (Fr) a union of proprietors.

Reflets de Châteauneuf-du-Pape (Fr) a union of the leading estate proprietors in Châteauneuf-du-Pape, southern Rhône (bottle wines under the Reflets label).

Reflux (Scot) during the distillation process of whisky, when the spirit rises up the neck as a vapour and fails to reach the top of the neck, falling back again. Repeated many times.

Reform Cocktail (Cktl) another name for the Bamboo Cocktail.

Reform Cordial (USA) a temperance name for gin. The gin was placed in unusual shaped bottles to hide the fact that the contents were gin.

Refosco (It) a red grape variety grown in the Aquileia region.

Refosco (USA) a red grape variety grown in California to make red table wines.

Refosco dal Penduncolo Rosso (It) a variety of the red Refosco grape variety grown in the Aquileia region.

Refosco Nostrano (It) a variety of the Refosco grape grown in the Aquileia region. Also the name of a red wine made from the same grape.

Refractometer (Eng) an instrument used to measure the sugar content of grape must. Measures the bending of light as it passes through the grape juice. One gram of sugar causes light to bend one degree Balling.

Refresco (Port) denotes a refreshing cool drink.

Refresh (Eng) a fruit juice drink from McDougalls Catering Foods. Four flavours: apple, orange, grapefruit, tropical.

Refresher (Eng) a cold drink, one that refreshes the thirst. i.e. iced lemonade, beer, water, etc.

Refresher Cocktail (Cktl) 200grms (½lb) fresh ripe strawberries, juice of a lemon, 50mls (2fl.ozs) water. Squeeze the juice from the fruit, mix with other ingredients over ice and strain into a highball glass. Other soft fruits may be substituted for strawberries.

Refreshing (Eng) the process of adding young wines to old to give added life to the old wine.

Refreshment of the Devil (Eng) the religious temperance movement's nickname for alcoholic drink.

Refresh UK plc (Eng) a brewery (established 2000). (Add): Wychwood Brewery, Eagle Maltings, The Crofts, Witney, Oxfordshire OX28 4DP. Brews: Bangla Beer, Brakspear, Coniston Bluebird, Fiddlers Elbow 4.5% alc by vol., Hobgoblin, Lal Toofan, Löwenbräu Original, Löwenbräu Pils. Website: http://www.refreshuk.com 'E'mail: info@refreshuk.com

Régab (Afr) a pilsener beer brewed by the Société des Brasseries du Haut Ogooué in Gabon.

Régalade (Fr) describes the art of drinking out of a bottle without the bottle touching the lips.

Regal Blonde Lager (Eng) a 4.4% alc by vol. lager beer brewed by the Oldershaw Brewery, Lincolnshire.

Regal Bräu (USA) a beer brewed by the Huber Brewery in Monroe, Wisconsin.

Regaleali (It) a region of Sicily producing red and white wines.

Regaleali Winery (It) a winery based in Regaleali, Sicily. Produce Nozze d'Oro and Rosso del Conte. Home to the Tasca grape.

Regal Fizz (Cktl) ½ measure Bols cherry brandy, ½measure kirsch. Shake over ice, strain into an ice-filled highball glass and top with Champagne.

Regal Flyer (Cktl) 1 measure each of gin, grenadine, egg white, 3 measures passion fruit juice. Shake over ice, strain into a tall glass, add 4 measures sparkling spring water, garnish with a lemon slice, strawberry and straws.

Regalis (S.Afr) the label for a fortified white wine (Muscadel) produced by the Mons Ruber Estate winery, Little Karoo.

Regal Lager (Ch.Isles) a lager-style beer 1045 O.G. brewed by R.W. Randalls Vauxlaurens Brewery in St. Peter Port, Guernsey.

Regal Lager (Eng) a lager beer 1039 O.G. brewed by the Holt Brewery in Manchester.

Regal Lager (Ind) a lager beer produced by the Vinedale Brewery in Hyderabad. 1042 O.G.

Regar (Port) drink with food/to wash down (the food) with a drink.

Regatta Ale (Eng) a 4.3% alc by vol. bitter brewed by Adnams, Suffolk.

Regency (Eng) a beer brewed by the Wiltshire Brewery Company in Tisbury, Wiltshire.

Regency (Ire) a label for cream liqueurs at 17% alc by vol. Styles include: Crème de Cognac (Cognac based) and Crème de Rhum (rum based).

Regency (Sp) a Sherry produced in Jerez de la Frontera.

Regency Brandy (Thai) a VSOP brandy distilled and bottled by the Suwannaphoome Distillery Company.

Regency Cask (Eng) a light bitter beer 1038 O.G. brewed by the Wiltshire Brewery Company in Tisbury, Wiltshire.

Regency Cocktail (Cktl) ½ measure dry gin, ½ measure Mandarine Napoléon, 2 dashes French vermouth, dash crème de banane. Stir over ice,

R

strain into a cocktail glass, top with a cherry and mint leaf.

Regency Star (Cktl) ¼ measure orange Curaçao, ½ measure dry gin, ⅛ measure passion fruit juice, ⅛ measure dry vermouth. Shake over ice and strain into a cocktail glass.

Regensburger Landwein (Ger) a new Deutsche Tafelwein zone.

Regensteiner Mineralbrunnen (Ger) a sparkling natural spring mineral water from Blankenburg. Mineral contents (milligrammes per litre): Sodium 7.8mg/l, Calcium 109mg/l, Magnesium 16.9mg/l, Bicarbonates 307mg/l.

Regent (Czec) a brewery (established 1379), moved to Trebon in 1698. Part of the South Bohemian Brewery Group. Brews: Regent 10% alc by vol, Regent 12% alc by vol.

Regent (Ger) a red grape cross Diana (Silvaner x Muller-Thurgau) x Chambourcin that is resistant to mildew. Produces full-bodied and deep-coloured wines. Close relation of the Diana grape.

Regenten Pils (Ger) a 4.8% alc by vol. canned pilsener brewed by the Lindener Brauerei, Unna.

Regent 10% (Czec) a 3.3% alc by vol. bottled lager brewed by the Regent Brewery, Trebon (part of the South Bohemian Brewery Group).

Regent 12% (Czec) a 4.9% alc by vol. pale straw coloured, bottled lager brewed by the Regent Brewery, Trebon (part of the South Bohemian Brewery Group).

Rege Wine C°. (USA) a winery based near Cloverdale, Sonoma County, California. Grape varieties: Barbera and Cabernet sauvignon. Produces varietal wines.

Rege Winery (USA) a winery based in the Russian River Valley, California.

Reggenhag (Ger) vineyard (Anb): Baden. (Ber): Markgräflerland. (Gro): Burg Neuenfels. (Vil): Müllheim.

Regiaes Demarcadas (Port) demarcated regions. Plural of Região Demarcada.

Reggiano (It) a D.O.C. wine area of Emilia-Romagna.

Região Demarcada (Port) demarcated area. There are ten in total: Algarve, Bairrada, Bucelas, Carcavelos, Colares, Dão, Douro, Madeira, Setúbal and Vinho Verde. Term is now being replaced by DOC.

Regilla (It) a sparkling natural spring mineral water from Rome. Mineral contents (milligrammes per litre): Sodium 7mg/l, Calcium 20mg/l, Magnesium 15mg/l, Potassium 8mg/l, Silicates 25mg/l. pH 7.6

Regimental Ale (Eng) a 5.5% alc by vol. I.P.A. with a dry nutty flavour. Cask matured for 2 weeks before sale by Marston's Brewery, Burton-on-Trent. Brewed in honour of the locally based Staffordshire Regiment under the Head Brewer's Choice banner. *see* Albion Porter, Union Mild.

Regimental Port (Austr) a Port-style wine from County Hamley in South Australia. Made from Cabernet sauvignon grapes and fortified with 2 year old brandy.

Regina Malt (Ger) a type of malt used in lager production.

Reginaris (Ger) a natural spring mineral water from Mendig. Mineral contents (milligrammes per litre): Sodium 300mg/l, Calcium 190mg/l, Magnesium 110mg/l, Potassium 20mg/l, Bicarbonates 1950mg/l, Chlorides 32mg/l, Sulphates 38mg/l.

Regina Staro (It) a natural spring mineral water from Fonte Regina Staro.

Reginum (It) a red wine produced in southern Italy in Roman times.

Regional (Eng) denotes that a beverage has been produced within a region as opposed to an individual village, district or vineyard.

Regional Bottling (Eng) on a label shows that the wines are made from grapes grown in the region named and are controlled by the local laws and customs.

Regional Designation (USA) in California, wines may obtain Regional Designation if at least 75% of the grapes are grown in that location. All the grapes though must be grown in California.

Regional Wine (Eng) a wine which takes its name from a district or region, not from a specific town or vineyard. Usually wines are blended.

Regione Siciliano (It) a Sicilian D.O.C. re-enforcement of their wines. Has a large Q encircling it. *see* Q Mark.

Régisseurs (Fr) managers.

Réglementation (Fr) the rules for wine production within the A.O.C. laws (from A.O.C. to Vins de pays). These rules govern such areas as minimum alcohol levels, grape varieties, maximum production, use of names (château/clos/domaine), etc. The higher the classification the more regulations apply.

Regnard [A. et Fils] (Fr) a Burgundy négociant-éleveur based in Chablis. Noted for Grand Cru and Premier Cru wines.

Regner (Ger) a white grape variety, a cross between the Siedentraube and the Gamay (produces high sugar).

Regnié (Fr) an A.C. Cru Beaujolais-Villages, Burgundy 580ha.

Regnier (Fr) a subsidiary of Cointreau. Produces a large range of liqueurs.

Reg's Tipple (Eng) a cask-conditioned ale brewed by the Gribble Inn, Oving, Chichester.

Régua (Port) a Port-producing town in the Douro region.

Reguengos (Port) a D.O.C. district within the Alentejo region. Produces full-bodied red wines.

Regulated Deficit Irrigation (Austr) *see* R.D.I.

Rehbach (Ger) grosslage (Anb): Rheinhessen. (Ber): Nierstein. (Vils): Nachenheim, Nierstein.

Rehborn (Ger) village (Anb): Nahe. (Ber): Schloss Böckelheim. (Gro): Paradiesgarten. (Vins): Hahn, Herrenberg, Schikanenbukel.

Rehlingen (Ger) village (Anb): Mosel-Saar-Ruwer. (Ber): Obermosel. (Gro): Gipfel. (Vin): Kapellenberg.

Réhoboam (Fr) a large bottle of (4.5litres) 6 standard bottles capacity used in the Champagne region. *see* Champagne Bottle Sizes. (Eng) = rehoboam.

Rei (Port) a variety of the white grape Malvasia used in the making of white Port.

Reichelberg (Ger) vineyard (Anb): Mosel-Saar-Ruwer. (Ber): Bernkastel. (Gro): Schwarzlay. (Vil): Flussbach.

Reichenau (Ger) village (Anb): Baden. (Ber): Bodensee. (Gro): Sonnenufer. (Vin): Hochwart.

Reichenbach (Ger) village (Anb): Baden. (Ber): Ortenau. (Gro): Fürsteneck. (Vins): Amselberg, Kinzigtäler.

Reichensteiner (Ger) a white grape variety, a cross between the Müller-Thurgau and the (Madeleine angevine X Calabresi fröhlich).

Reichenweir (Fr) the German name for the town of Riquewihr in Alsace.

Reichesthal (Ger) vineyard (Anb): Rheingau. (Ber): Johannisberg. (Gro): Daubhaus. (Vil): Hochheim.

Reichesthal (Ger) vineyard (Anb): Rheingau. (Ber): Johannisberg. (Gro): Daubhaus. (Vil): Kostheim.

Reicholzheim (Ger) village (Anb): Baden. (Ber): Badische Frankenland. (Gro): Tauberklinge. (Vins): First, Kemelrain, Satzenberg.

Reichshalde (Ger) vineyard (Anb): Württemberg. (Ber): Württembergisch Unterland. (Gro): Stromberg. (Vil): Freudenstein.

Reichshalde (Ger) vineyard (Anb): Württemberg. (Ber): Württembergisch Unterland. (Gro): Stromberg. (Vil): Knittlingen.

Reichshalde (Ger) vineyard (Anb): Württemberg. (Ber): Württembergisch Unterland. (Gro): Stromberg. (Vil): Maulbronn.

Reichskeller (Ger) vineyard (Anb): Rheinhessen. (Ber): Bingen. (Gro): Rheingrafenstein. (Vil): Frei-Laubersheim.

Reichsrebsortiment (Ger) the official Government list of vines.

Reichsritterstift (Ger) vineyard (Anb): Rheinhessen. (Ber): Nierstein. (Gro): Sankt Alban. (Vil): Bodenheim.

Reidel (Aus) famous crystal glass manufacturers who specialise in decanters, wine and drinking glasses. (Add): Riedel Glas, A-6330 Kufstein, Austria. Website: http://www.reidelcrystal.com

Reid Gertberg (Aus) the label for a cask-aged white wine (Chardonnay) produced by the Triebaumer [Paul] winery, Rust, Burgenland.

Reif (Ger) ripe, denotes a fine sweet wine.

Reifbräu Brauerei (Ger) a brewery owned by Patrizer.

Reifenbeisser (Aus) lit: 'hoop biter', the name given to the very poor 1456 wine vintage. Wine produced was so acid that it penetrated the wood and hoops of the cask.

Reifenstein (Ger) vineyard (Anb): Franken. (Ber): Maindreieck. (Gro): Not yet assigned. (Vil): Sommerhausen.

Reifersley (Ger) vineyard (Anb): Mittelrhein. (Ber): Bacharach. (Gro): Schloss Reichenstein. (Vil): Niederheimbach.

Reif Estate Winery (Can) a winery that is based in Ontario.

Reigate Bitter (Eng) *see* Reigate Brewery.

Reigate Brewery (Eng) a brewery in the John Landregan Off-Licence in Reigate, Surrey. Brews: cask-conditioned Reigate Bitter 1042 O.G. using malt extract.

Reignots [Les] (Fr) a Premier Cru vineyard in the A.C. commune of Vosne-Romanée, Côte de Nuits, Burgundy 1.7ha.

Reil (Ger) village (Anb): Mosel-Saar-Ruwer. (Ber): Bernkastel. (Gro): Vom Heissen Stein. (Vins): Falklay, Goldlay, Moullay-Hofberg, Sorentberg.

Reims (Fr) a major town in the Champagne region, has Cantons of: Aÿ, de Beine, de Bourgogne, de Reims, de Verzy, de Châtillon-sur-Marne, de Fismes and de Ville-en-Tardenois. *see* Montagne de Reims.

Rein (Aus)(Ger) pure/clean/natural.

Reina Verdelho [La] (Mad) a medium dry Madeira produced by Rutherford and Miles.

Reinbeer (Eng) a 5.9% alc by vol. light Christmas ale brewed by the Elgood Northbrink Brewery, Wisbech, Cambs.

Reinbeer Revenge (Eng) a 4.5% alc by vol. seasonal ale brewed by Moorhouses, Burnley, Lancashire.

Reindeer (Eng) a home-brew public house based at Derham Road, Norwich. Brews: cask-conditioned Bill's Bevy, Gnu Bru, Reindeer Bitter, Red Nose, Sanity Clause. Name changed in 1996 to Finnesko and Firkin.

Reindeer Bitter (Eng) a 1047 O.G. bitter brewed by the Finnesko and Firkin, Dereham Road, Norwich.

Reindeer's Delight (Eng) a 4.5% alc by vol. ale brewed by the Oakleaf Brewing C°. Ltd., Hampshire.

Reine [La] (S.Afr) an estate that produces varietal wines.

Reinecker (Ger) a specialist sekt winery based in Baden. (Add): Oberdorfstrasse 17, D-79424 Auggen. Produces a range of methode traditionell sparkling wines from a variety of grapes.

Reine-Claude (Fr) a greengage plum spirit produced in Alsace. Noted for its strong bouquet.

Reine Cléopatre (Egy) a fine, white, full-flavoured wine produced by the Gianaclis Vineyards at Abú-Hummus.

Reine des Basaltes (Fr) a natural spring mineral water from Asperjoc.

Reine Juliana (Cktl) 25mls (1fl.oz) Mandarine Napoléon, 40mls (1¼ fl.ozs) vodka, 25mls (1fl.oz) Sabra liqueur. Shake over ice and strain into an old-fashioned glass 'on the rocks'.

Reine Pédauque (Fr) a large wine-producer based in Aloxe-Corton, Côte de Beaune, Burgundy. (Add): Corgolin, 21700 Nuits-Saint-Georges.

Reinhards-Quelle Heilwasser (Ger) a natural spring mineral water. Mineral contents (milligrammes per litre): Sodium 13.4mg/l, Calcium 152.2mg/l, Magnesium 67.1mg/l, Potassium 2.64mg/l, Chlorides 11mg/l, Sulphates 33.9mg/l, Fluorides 0.1mg/l, Iron 4.44mg/l.

Reinheitsgebot (Ger) the oldest known food and drink law. The German Purity Law dated from 1516 to control the production of German beer (originally Bavarian beers but now amended to allow for wheat beers). Chemical additives and sugar are banned. Only pure water, hops, barley malt and yeast can be used in beer production.

Reinig auf der Burg (Ger) vineyard (Anb): Mosel-Saar-Ruwer. (Ber): Obermosel. (Gro): Gipfel. (Vil): Wasserliesch.

Reininghaus (Aus) a beer brewed by the brewery of same name based in Graz.

Reininghaus Brauerei (Aus) a noted brewery based in Graz. Brews under its own and the Puntigam label.

Reinprecht (Aus) a winery based in the Wien region. (Add): Cobenzlgasse 22, 1190 Wien. Grape varieties: Chardonnay, Gewürztraminer, Grüner veltliner, Müller-Thurgau, Pinot noir, Welschriesling. Produces a range of wine styles.

Reinsbronn (Ger) village (Anb): Württemberg. (Ber): Kocher-Jagst-Tauber. (Gro): Tauberberg. (Vin): Röde.

Reinsortig (Aus) lit: 'only this particular type'.

Reintönig (Ger) well-balanced/very good wine.

Reischklingeberg (Ger) vineyard (Anb): Franken. (Ber): Mainviereck. (Gro): Heiligenthal. (Vil): Grossostheim.

Reisenthal (Aus) a vineyard site on the banks of the River Danube in the Kremstal region.

Reishu (Jap) a melon liqueur.

Reising (Aus) a vineyard site based on the banks of the River Kamp situated in the Kamptal region.

Reissdorf Kölsch (Ger) a 4.8% alc by vol. bottled pale straw-coloured kölsch bier brewed by the Heinr. Reissdorfer Brauerei in Cologne.

Reiterpfad (Ger) vineyard (Anb): Pfalz. (Ber): Mittelhaardt-Deutsche Weinstrasse. (Gro): Hofstück. (Vil): Ruppertsberg.

Reiterpfad (Ger) vineyard (Anb): Pfalz. (Ber): Mittelhaardt-Deutsche Weinstrasse. (Gro): Meerspinne. (Vil): Königsbach.

Reith (Aus) a vineyard site based on the banks of the River Kamp situated in the Kamptal region.

Reitsteig (Ger) vineyard (Anb): Franken. (Ber): Steigerwald. (Gro): Herrenberg. (Vil): Castell.

Reiver IPA (Eng) a 4.4% alc by vol. India pale ale brewed by the Hadrian & Border Brewery, Tyne & Wear.

Rejoice (Wal) a 6% alc by vol. ale brewed by Eric's Brewery, Pontypridd, Mid Glamorgan.

Relevage (Fr) the moving of spreading vine shoots inside the horizontal wires to enable the sun to penetrate and permit tractors to pass.

Relève de Col (Fr) a term to denote the racking the wine clear of its fining.

Rélique Ancestrale (Fr) an Armagnac produced by Salamens in Laujuzan, Bas Armagnac. Contains 25% 1900 year old Armagnac and is sold as a 15 year old.

Relishing Red (S.Afr) the label for a red wine (Pinotage, Ruby cabernet and Merlot blend) produced by the De Krans winery, Little Karoo.

Reliz Creek Reserve (USA) the label for an Arroyo Seco red wine (Pinot noir) produced by the Wente winery, Monterey County, California.

Reloaded Red Square Irn Bru (Eng) a 5.5% alc by vol. vodka and Irn Bru drink that also contains ginger, caffeine and taurine. From Halewood International. *See also* Cranberry Ice, Red Square.

Remain Sober (Cktl)(Non-alc) in a highball glass place an ice-cube, 3 dashes Angostura, 1 wine glass lime juice cordial, stir and top up with soda water.

Remelluri (Sp) a red wine produced by La Granja Nuestra Señora de Remelluri from a single vineyard.

Remerschen (Lux) a wine co-operative. Part of Vinsmoselle.

Remerschen (Lux) a wine-producing village on the river Moselle. Vineyard sites- Kreitzberg, Jongeberg.

Remeyerhof (Ger) vineyard (Anb): Rheinhessen. (Ber): Wonnegau. (Gro): Liebfrauenmorgen. (Vil): Worms.

Remhoogte Estate (S.Afr) a winery (established 1994) based in Stellenbosch, Western Cape. 30ha. Grape varieties: Cabernet sauvignon, Merlot, Pinotage. Labels: Aigle Noir, Bonne Nouvelle, Estate Wine.

Remich (Lux) a wine-producing village on the river Moselle. Vineyard sites: Primerberg, Hôpertsbour. Has a marl and chalk soil.

Remi Landier et Fils (Fr) a Cognac brandy producer. (Add): GAEC Domaine du Carrefour, Cors, Foussignac, 162000 Jarnac. 50ha. in the Fins Bois.

Remírez de Ganuza (Sp) a wine produced in the D.O. Rioja Alavasa.

Remoissenet Père et Fils (Fr) a Burgundy négociant-éleveur based at Beaune, Côte de Beaune.

Remontage [1] (Fr) denotes the piping of the fermenting must over the cap of skins.

Remontage [2] (Fr) in the Burgundy and Champagne regions denotes the carrying of eroded soil back up the hill.

Remounting (Eng) pumping the fermenting must onto the cap of the must to extract the colour and break up the cap. (Fr) = remontage.

Remour (Fr) *see* Remueur (the mis-spelling of).

Removido (Sp) remuage.

Rems [River] (Ger) a tributary of the river Neckar in Württemberg. Has soil of red marl.

Remsen Cooler (Cktl) dissolve ½ teaspoon of sugar in 50mls (2fl.ozs) water in a highball glass. Add ice, 50mls (2fl.ozs) dry gin, top with ginger ale and a spiral of lemon peel over the rim of the glass.

Remstaler (Ger) a sparkling natural spring mineral water. (red label: sparkling/blue label: light gas). Mineral contents (milligrammes per litre): Sodium 230mg/l, Calcium 300mg/l, Magnesium 70mg/l, Potassium 20mg/l, Bicarbonates 640mg/l, Chlorides 300mg/l, Sulphates 570mg/l, Fluorides 0.7mg/l, Nitrates 0.3mg/l.

Remstal-Stuttgart (Ger) bereich (Anb):

R

Württemberg. (Gros): Hoheneneuffen, Kopf, Sonnenbühl, Wartbühl, Weinsteige.

Remuage (Fr) the process of guiding the sediment down (by agitation) to the neck of a Champagne bottle so that it settles on the cork ready for dégorgement. *see* Remueur and Pupîtres. *See also* Billes.

Remueur (Fr) the person who performs remuage in the méthode traditionelle sparkling wine production.

Rémy (Austr) the brand-name of a brandy locally blended by a Rémy Martin subsidiary. *see* Dynasty, Rémy Martin and C°.

Rémy Martin and C°. (Fr) a Cognac producer (established 1724). (Add): B.P. 37, 16102 Cognac. 150ha. in Grande Champagne. Produces only Fine Champagne Cognacs. Range includes: V.S.O.P., X.O. Special, Extra Perfection, Louis XIII. Also has interests in many countries. *See also* Dynasty.

Rémy Martin Extra (Fr) a Cognac made with mature eaux-de-vies (up to 50 years old) by Rémy Martin. Sold in a pebble-shaped bottle.

Rémy Martin 1738 Accord Royal (Fr) a 40% alc by vol. Cognac made with mature eaux-de-vies aged in Limousin oak (for up to 25 years old) by Rémy Martin.

Renacimiento (Sp) a solera gran reserva brandy from Garvey.

Renaissance (Eng) a 3.3% alc by vol. pale bitter brewed by the Aspinall Cambrinus Craft Brewery, Knowsley, Merseyside.

Renaissance (S.Afr) the label for a range of red wines (Cabernet sauvignon and Pinotage) produced by the Doolhof Estate winery, Wellington, Western Cape.

Renaissance Cocktail (Cktl) a ¼ measure dry gin, ¼ measure dry Sherry, 10mls (½ fl.oz) cream. Shake over ice and strain into a cocktail glass.

Renaissance Winery (USA) vineyards and winery based in the Sierra foothills, Sacramento, California. Grape varieties: Cabernet sauvignon, Johannisberg riesling. Produces mainly varietal wines.

Renaldo de Lucca (S.Am) a 40ha winery north of Montevideo. Wines are sold under the Preludio label. Grape varieties include: Chardonnay, Tannat, Viognier.

Renano (It) the northern Italian name for the Rhine riesling or True riesling.

Renarde [La] (Fr) a vineyard in the A.C. commune of Rully, Côte Chalonnaise, Burgundy.

Renat (Swe) local pure spirit (un-flavoured) made from potatoes.

Renata (Ger) a natural spring mineral water. Mineral contents (milligrammes per litre): Sodium 1.9mg/l, Calcium 7.1mg/l, Magnesium 0.8mg/l, Potassium 1.6mg/l, Chlorides 3.7mg/l.

Renaud [Michel] (Fr) an Armagnac producer. (Add): Domaines de Jeanton Tauzia, Route de Sentex, 32150 Cazaubon. 13ha. in the Bas Armagnac.

Renaudin [R.] (Fr) Champagne producer. (Add):

Domaine des Conardins, 51530 Moussy. Récoltants-manipulants. 24ha. Produce vintage and non-vintage wines. Vintages: 1973, 1974, 1975, 1976, 1978, 1981, 1983, 1985, 1990, 1995, 1996, 1998, 2000, 2001.

Renault (Alg) a wine-producing area in north-western Algeria, produces mainly red wines.

Renault Cognac (Fr) a Cognac producer. (Add): Castillon Renault S.A., 22 Rue du Port, 16101 Cognac. Produces Renault Carte Noire Extra 15–20 years old, Renault OVB 12–15 years old, Carte d'Argent Extra 35 years of ageing, Renault Age Unknown 40 years plus.

Renault Museum (USA) a wine-glass museum based at the Renault Winery in Egg Harbour, New Jersey.

Renault Winery (USA) a large winery based in Egg Harbour, New Jersey. 520ha. Produces hybrid, native and vinifera wines. Also noted for its wine-glass museum.

Renchen (Ger) village (Anb): Baden. (Ber): Ortenau. (Gro): Schloss Rodeck. (Vin): Kreuzberg.

Renchtäler (Ger) vineyard (Anb): Baden. (Ber): Ortenau. (Gro): Fürsteneck. (Vil): Bottenau.

Renchtäler (Ger) vineyard (Anb): Baden. (Ber): Ortenau. (Gro): Fürsteneck. (Vil): Erlach.

Renchtäler (Ger) vineyard (Anb): Baden. (Ber): Ortenau. (Gro): Fürsteneck. (Vil): Lautenbach.

Renchtäler (Ger) vineyard (Anb): Baden. (Ber): Ortenau. (Gro): Fürsteneck. (Vil): Nesselried.

Renchtäler (Ger) vineyard (Anb): Baden. (Ber): Ortenau. (Gro): Fürsteneck. (Vil): Nussbach.

Renchtäler (Ger) vineyard (Anb): Baden. (Ber): Ortenau. (Gro): Fürsteneck. (Vil): Oberkirch.

Renchtäler (Ger) vineyard (Anb): Baden. (Ber): Ortenau. (Gro): Fürsteneck. (Vil): Oberkirch (ortsteil Haslach).

Renchtäler (Ger) vineyard (Anb): Baden. (Ber): Ortenau. (Gro): Fürsteneck. (Vil): Ödsbach.

Renchtäler (Ger) vineyard (Anb): Baden. (Ber): Ortenau. (Gro): Fürsteneck. (Vil): Ringelbach.

Renchtäler (Ger) vineyard (Anb): Baden. (Ber): Ortenau. (Gro): Fürsteneck. (Vil): Stadelhofen.

Renchtäler (Ger) vineyard (Anb): Baden. (Ber): Ortenau. (Gro): Fürsteneck. (Vil): Tiergarten.

Renchtäler (Ger) vineyard (Anb): Baden. (Ber): Ortenau. (Gro): Fürsteneck. (Vil): Ulm.

Rendement Annuel (Fr) the yield set each year, may be above or below the Rendement de Base.

Rendement de Base (Fr) basic yield, the amount of wine allowed to be produced at base level. *See also* Plafond de Classement.

Rendements (Fr) the amount of wine that is produced from a given area.

Rene Briand SpA (It) a noted brandy producer.

René Lalou (Fr) top-of-the-range vintage Champagne from G.H. Mumm. Named after one of their first directors. Mumm de Mumm label replaced it in 1982. Grand Cordon replaced Mumm de Mumm in 1985.

Renero (It) a red wine produced from Pinot noir grapes by Araldici Vini Piemontesi, 14040 Castel Boglione. Part of the Poderi Alasia range.

R

Rengo (Chile) a wine-producing area near Santiago.

Renishaw Vineyard (Eng) a vineyard (established 1972) based at Renishaw Hall, near Sheffield, Yorkshire. 0.85ha. Grape varieties: Huxelrebe, Pinot meunier, Pinot noir, Reichensteiner, Schönburger and Seyval blanc.

Renmano Wines (Austr) a part of Berri Renmano, South Australia. (Add): Renmark Avenue, Renmark, South Australia 5341.

Renmark (Austr) a wine district in New South Wales. Produces fine quality wines.

Rennsteig Sprudel (Ger) a still and sparkling natural spring mineral water from Thüringer Wald. Mineral contents (milligrammes per litre): Sodium 12mg/l, Calcium 73mg/l, Magnesium 27mg/l, Potassium 4mg/l, Bicarbonates 186mg/l, Chlorides 15mg/l, Sulphates 141mg/l.

Reno (It) a D.O.C. wine area of Emilia-Romagna.

Renouard Larivière (Fr) a producer of Eau de Melisse des Carmes Boyer (an élixer) in Paris.

Renown Ale (Wal) a 4% alc by vol. ale brewed by Eric's Brewery, Pontpridd, Mid Glamorgan.

Renski Riesling (Slo) a white grape also known as the Rhine riesling and Rajinski rizling.

Rentamt (Ger) collecting office.

Renwick Estate (N.Z) a label used by Montana Wines of Marlborough for a Chardonnay wine. See also Brancott Ormond Estate.

Renyshe (Eng) the old sixteenth century name for Rhenish (Rhine) wines.

Renzo Tedeschi (It) a noted recioto and ripasso producer based in the Valpolicella region. Produces Ripasso [Capitel San Rocco Rosso] and Recioto [Cru Capitel Monte Fontana].

Repeal [The] (USA) the end of Prohibition 5th December 1933.

Repiquage (Fr) replanting only those individual vines that have died, not grubbing up the whole area.

Repisa (Mad) the second pressing of the grapes.

Reposado (Mex) the name given to a tequila that has been aged for 2–11 months. See also Añejo Tequila, Blanco Tequila.

Répouf et Fils (Fr) an Armagnac producer based in the Ténarèze. (Add): 'Notre Dame' 32190-Vic-Fesensac.

Repperndorf (Ger) village (Anb): Franken. (Ber): Maindreieck. (Gro): Hofrat. (Vin): Kaiser Karl.

Reputed Pint (Eng) a half-bottle, an imperial gallon contains 12 half-bottles.

Reputed Quart (Eng) 1.33 imperial pints or 26.66fl.ozs The normal British bottle size.

Requeno (Sp) an alternative name for the Bobal grape.

Resaca (Sp) a hangover.

Resan (Euro) a natural spring mineral water (established 1996) from Kishinev, Moldavia. Mineral contents (milligrammes per litre): Sodium 112.72mg/l, Calcium 62.1mg/l, Magnesium 132.5mg/l, Bicarbonates 530.9mg/l, Chlorides 58.8mg/l, Sulphates 391.1mg/l. pH 7.1

Resch's KB (Austr) a lager beer brewed by the Tooths Brewery in Sydney.

Reserva (Sp) mature quality wine. Red: aged in cask and bottle for a mimimum of 3 years (min. 12 months in oak). White & Rosé: aged 2 years (min. 6 months in oak).

Reservado (Chile) a wine that is 4 years old.

Reserva 904 (Sp) a red wine from La Rioja Alta.

Reserva Real (Sp) a red wine from Torres vineyards. Grape varieties: Cabernet franc, Cabernet sauvignon, Merlot.

Reservas (Port) the best wine from a particular year. See also Garrafeira (which is better).

Réserve (Fr) found on Armagnac and Cognac labels and denotes a minimum of 4 years of age.

Réserve (Lux) the second from top grade for wine (first: Grande Réserve).

Réserve Ancestrale (Fr) a 50 year old Cognac brandy produced by Pierre Ferrand. Only 22 bottles are produced per year.

Réserve Baron Philippe de Rothschild (Fr) a prestige cuvée Champagne produced by Henriot.

Réserve Belle Époque (Fr) a limited edition Champagne (2000 jeroboams) produced by Perrier-Jouët 1995 vintage.

Reserve Blend (S.Afr) the label for a barrel-aged red wine (Cabernet sauvignon, Merlot and Pinotage blend) produced by the Kaapzicht Estate winery, Stellenbosch, Western Cape.

Réserve de Fondateur (Fr) a blend of rare Cognacs produced by Martell in Cognac. Limit of 2160 bottles produced.

Réserve de la Comtesse (Fr) the second wine of Château Pichon-Longueville-Lalande [Grand Cru Classé (2nd), A.C. Pauillac].

Réserve de l'Empéreur (Fr) a de luxe cuvée Champagne produced by Mercier for the French market only.

Réserve des Ancestres (Fr) a 35 year old Cognac produced by Raymond Dudognon.

Réserve des Diacres (Fr) the label of a Châteauneuf-du-Pape produced by Chausse (Henri) at Terres Blanches, 84230 Châteauneuf-du-Pape, southern Rhône.

Réserve du Général (Fr) the second wine of Château Palmer. Now known as Alter Ego de Palmer.

Reserved for England (Fr) usually found on a Champagne label (denotes the wine is dry).

Réserve Exceptionelle (Fr) a qualification in Alsace, a phrase of quality used on some wines to denote a much better all round wine.

Reserve Madeira (Mad) blended Madeira. The youngest wine must be a minimum of 5 years old after estufagem. If the grape variety is stated it must contain 85% of named grape variety.

Réserve Mirabelle (Fr) a white A.C. Bergerac Sec wine from Château la Jaubertie (80% Sémillon, 20% Sauvignon blanc grapes).

Réserve Nouvelle (Fr) abbr: R.N. After 5 years in cask the marking Cognac obtains. It is then left until it is used (often stored in the Paradis).

Réserve Royale (Fr) a Cognac produced by Croizet.

R

Réserve Saint Landelin (Fr) a full-bodied beer brewed by the Rimaux Brasserie based near Valenciennes.

Réserve Spéciale (Fr) late gathered in Alsace, has the same meaning as spätlese in Germany. *See also* VendangeTardive.

Reserve 214 (S.Afr) the label for a red wine (Cabernet sauvignon 46%, Merlot and Shiraz blend) produced by the Vrendenheim Wines winery, Stellenbosch, Western Cape.

Residential Licence (Eng) the liquor licence issued to certain Hotels, Boarding houses and Guest houses which only allows the sale of alcoholic beverages to residents of the establishment and their guests (providing the residents pay for them also).

Residenz Quelle (Ger) a natural spring mineral water. Mineral contents (milligrammes per litre): Sodium 114mg/l, Calcium 567mg/l, Magnesium 88mg/l, Potassium 12mg/l, Bicarbonates 400mg/l, Chlorides 120mg/l, Sulphates 1485mg/l, Nitrates 1mg/l.

Residual Sugar (USA) the natural grape sugar that remains unfermented in a wine. Measured usually in degrees Brix (from 0.1° to 27° the sweetest).

Resinated Wine (Gre) *see* Retsina.

Resinotte (Fr) an alternative name for the Muscadelle grape.

Resolute (Cktl) 20mls (⅙ gill) dry gin, 15mls (⅛ gill) apricot brandy, 15mls (⅛ gill) lemon juice. Shake over ice and strain into a cocktail glass.

Resolution (Eng) a 4.4% alc by vol. ale brewed using toasted barley by Brakspear, Henley-on-Thames, Oxon. Part of the Brewers Selection range.

Resolution (Eng) a bottled ale brewed by the Marstons Brewery.

Resolution (Eng) a low-calorie, low carbohydrate beer brewed by WDB Brands.

Respetable (Sp) a solera brandy from Sanchez Romate. *See also* Abolengo, Cesar (El), Conquistador, Tres Espadas.

Responsible Drinks Retailing (Eng) *abbr:* RDR a drinks trade-sponsored promotion organised to demonstrate its social responsibility in the sale of intoxicating beverages. Supported by many organisations. Website: http://www.rdr05.co.uk 'E'mail: hazel.smith@william-reed.co.uk

Resposado (Mex) a term used to describe white or silver tequila that is aged for 2 months in oak barrels.

Resses [Les] (Fr) a vineyard in the A.C. commune of Montagny, Côte Chalonnaise, Burgundy.

Restanques (Fr) the name used in Bandol, Côtes de Provence for the terraced vineyards.

Restaurant Licence (Eng) a liquor licence issued to establishments to permit them to sell alcoholic beverages with a meal. Basic law allows 16–18 year olds to consume beer, cider or perry with a meal and the restaurant to be open during the afternoon (since May 1987). Drinking up time is 30 minutes. Opening hours differ from those of a full On licence. Scottish laws also differ slightly. New laws being introduced in 2006.

Restorance (Eng) a 3.6% alc by vol. pale bitter brewed by Aspinall Cambinus Craft Brewery, Knowsley, Merseyside.

Restoration (Wal) a 4.3% alc by vol. ale brewed by Eric's Brewery, Pontypridd, Mid Glamorgan.

Restorffs Bryggjari (Den) a brewery. (Add): Landavegur 32, FO-110 Torshavn, Faroe Islands. Brews a range of beers and lagers. Website: http://www.restorffs.fo 'E'mail: restorff@post.olivant.fo

Restsüsse (Ger) lit: 'residual sweetness', an old term, that denotes the unfermented grape sugar in the wine which the yeasts fail to ferment.

Restzuckerbegrenzungen (Ger) the laws governing unfermented sugar retention in wines.

Resveratrol (Eng) an antioxidant found in red wines (especially Pinot noir) which helps prevent the grapes being attacked by botrytis. *see* Flavenoids.

Reticent (Eng) a term used to describe wines that are holding back on the nose or palate due possibly to immaturity.

Retort (Eng) the name used for the base of a pot-still (the round tapering piece) that holds the liquid to be distilled.

Retour des Indes (Fr) a term used to describe the wines used as ballast (especially Madeira) in ships making the round trip to India and back during the eighteenth and nineteenth centuries. Ended soon after the Suez Canal was opened. *see* Estufada.

Retrate (Fr) the short spur found on the main arm of the Guyot method of vine training.

Retreat (S.Afr) the label for a white wine (Sauvignon blanc) produced by the Robertson Co-operative Winery, Robertson, Western Cape.

Retriever (Eng) a 3.9% alc by vol. ale brewed by The Dog House Brewery C°., Cornwall.

Retriever Legend (Eng) a 4.2% alc by vol. ale brewed by the Hart Brewery, Little Eccleston, Preston, Lancashire.

Retro (Eng) a non-alcoholic 'pick-me-up' soft drink from Britvic.

Retsina (Gre) red and white wines which have the resin of the Aleppo pine *Calitris quadrivalvis* added as a preservative and flavouring. One of the oldest methods of keeping wine. Grapes used are the Savatiano and Rhoditis. *see* T.A.

Rettigheim (Ger) village (Anb): Baden. (Ber): Badische Bergstrasse/Kraichgau. (Gro): Mannaberg. (Vin): Ölbaum.

Retz (Aus) a wine-growing district in the region of Niederösterreich. Produces mainly white wines from the Grüner veltliner grape. *See also* Weinviertel.

Retzbach (Ger) village (Anb): Franken. (Ber): Maindreieck. (Gro): Ravensburg. (Vin): Benediktusberg.

Retzl (Aus) a winery based in the Kampstal region. (Add): Heiligensteinerstrasse 9, 3561 Zöbling. Grape varieties: Grüner veltliner, Merlot, Pinot blanc, Pinot noir, Riesling, Sauvignon blanc, Welshriesling, Zweigelt. Produces a range of wine styles.

Retzstadt (Ger) village (Anb): Franken. (Ber): Maindreieck. (Gro): Rosstal. (Vin): Langenberg.

R

Reugne (Fr) a Premier Cru vineyard in the A.C. commune of Auxey-Duresses, Côte de Beaune, Burgundy. Also known as La Chapelle 7.8ha.

Reugny (Fr) a commune of Vouvray in the Touraine district of the Loire.

Reuil (Fr) a Cru Champagne village in the Canton de Châtillon-sur-Marne. District: Reims.

Reuilly (Fr) an A.C. area in the Central Vineyards district of the Loire. Produces a steely, dry, white wine made from the Sauvignon blanc grape variety.

Réunion Island (Afr) an island off the east coast of Africa (a département of France) that produces white rum plus a little cask aged rum. Also produces coffee.

Reunion Shiraz (Austr) a full-bodied red wine produced by The Lane vineyard, Adelaide Hills.

Reuschberg (Ger) grosslage (Anb): Franken. (Ber): Mainviereck. (Vil): Hörstein.

Reuter's Hill Vineyard (USA) a small vineyard based in Forest Grove, Oregon. 24ha. Produces vinifera wines. Owned by the Charles Coury Vineyards since 1928.

Reuze (Fr) a dortmunder-style beer 7% alc by vol. brewed by the Pelforth Brasserie in Lille.

Revat 51 (USA) a white hybrid grape variety.

Rêve de Carignan (Fr) lit: 'Carignan dream', a red wine produced by Domaine Borie de Maurel.

Revenge (Eng) a 7% alc by vol. strong ale brewed by the Keltek Brewing C°. Ltd., Cornwall.

Revenooers (USA) the name given to the revenue agents who sought out the moonshiners after the 1791 Excise Tax Act. see Whiskey Rebellion.

Reverend James Original Ale (Wal) a 1046 O.G. cask-conditioned ale brewed at Crown Buckley, Llanelli, Dyfed. Now brewed by S.A. Brain in Cardiff.

Reverend Samuel Marsden (N.Z) credited with making the first recorded planting of vines in Auckland in 1819. First wine was made by James Busby in 1833.

Reversées [Les] (Fr) a Premier Cru vineyard in the A.C. commune of Beaune, Côte de Beaune, Burgundy 4.97ha.

Reverse Osmosis (Eng) a method of removing alcohol (or acetic acid) by passing the beer, wine, etc. through porous partitions.

Revington Vineyard (N.Z) a vineyard. (Add): 110 Stout Street, Gisborne. 4.47ha. Grape varieties: Chardonnay, Gewürztraminer.

Revival (Eng) a standard keg mild from Morland Brewery in Abingdon. See also Old Speckled Hen, Morland Old Masters.

Rev. James [The] (Wal) a 4.5% alc by vol. ale brewed by S.A. Brain & C°. Ltd. Cardiff.

Revolve (Scot) the brand-name of a new 'vodka-style' Scotch whisky produced by Chivas Regal. Designed for the cocktail market as a cocktail ingredient it has a lighter taste than Scotch whisky.

Reward (Eng) a 4.2% alc by vol. bitter ale brewed by Daniel Thwaites, Lancashire.

Rex Hill Vineyards (USA) vineyards based in Oregon at Newberg, Willamette Valley, Oregon. Grape varieties: Chardonnay, Pinot blanc, Pinot gris, Pinot noir, Riesling, Sauvignon blanc.

Reyka Vodka (Ice) a distillery based in Borgarnes, produces a vodka 40% alc by vol (owned by William Grant & Sons Ltd).

Reyneke Wines (S.Afr) a winery (established 1863) based in Vlottenburg, Stellenbosch, Western Cape. 20ha. Grape varieties: Cabernet sauvignon, Merlot, Pinotage, Sauvignon blanc, Shiraz. Label: Cornerstone, Reyneke Reserve (Shiraz 100%). Website: http://www.reynekewines.co.za

Reynella (Austr) a region in Clare-Watervale, Southern Vales, South Australia. Noted for red table wines and brandies.

Reynella Flor (Austr) a fortified, pale, dry wine made by W. Reynell and Sons in South Australia.

Reynella Winery (Austr) a winery based in Reynella, Clare-Watervale, Southern Vales, South Australia. Produces varietal wines.

Reyniers (Eng) Eldridge Pope's Wine Library (established 1986) based in Fleet Street, London, where its customers may purchase and sample wines.

Rèze (Switz) a white grape variety used in the production of Vin du Glacier (rare nowadays).

RGB Coffee Ltd (Eng) a coffee manufacturer (established 1965). (Add): P.O. Box 2663, Imperial Way, Worton Grange, Reading, Berkshire RG2 0ZL. Produces a range of coffees (including Rombouts) and teas. Website: http://www.rombouts.co.uk 'E'mail: enquiries@rombouts.co.uk

Rhacodium cellare (Hun) a blue-grey velvety fungus that covers the walls of the cellars cut in the rocks to store Tokaji Azsú wines. Also found elsewhere. Also spelt Rhacodium celare. Aids the regulation of humidity.

Rhagoletis pomonella (Lat) the apple maggot, a fruit fly larvae that feeds (bores) on the fruit of the apple tree. Family = Trypetidae.

Rhapsody (S.Afr) the label for a red wine (Pinotage 53% and Shiraz 43% plus others) produced by the Stellenzicht Vineyards winery, Stellenbosch, Western Cape.

Rhapsody (S.Afr) the label for a red wine (Cabernet sauvignon, Cinsaut and Merlot blend) produced by the Bottelary Hills Wine winery, Stellenbosch, Western Cape.

Rhäzünser (Switz) a sparkling natural spring mineral water from Rhäzüns. Mineral contents (milligrammes per litre): Sodium 122.8mg/l, Calcium 210.2mg/l, Magnesium 44.1mg/l, Potassium 5.5mg/l, Bicarbonates 1071.5mg/l, Chlorides 17.6mg/l, Sulphates 120.4mg/l, Fluorides 0.8mg/l, Nitrates 0.26mg/l, Silicates 49.5mg/l.

Rhebokskloof Estate (S.Afr) a winery based on the slopes of Paarl Mountain, Paarl, Western Cape. 84ha. Grape varieties: Cabernet sauvignon, Chardonnay, Chenin blanc, Gamay, Hanepoot, Merlot, Riesling, Sauvignon blanc, Shiraz, Weisser riesling. Labels: Bouquet Blanc, Rhebok, Tamay. Website: http://www.rhebokskloof.co.za 'E'mail: info@rhebokskloof.co.za

Rheenen Vineyard (S.Afr) a small winery that sells its grapes to the Mooiuitsig Wynkelders.

Rheidol Reserve (Wal) an ale from the micro-brewery Tynllidiart Arms in Capel Bangor, Dyfed.

Rhein (Ger) an Untergebiet of the Rhein und Mosel district.

Rheinberg (Ger) vineyard (Anb): Mittelrhein. (Ber): Bacharach. (Gro): Schloss Stahleck. (Vil): Oberdiebach.

Rheinberg (Ger) vineyard (Anb): Nahe. (Ber): Kreuznach. (Gro): Schlosskapelle. (Vil): Münster-Sarmsheim.

Rheinberg (Ger) vineyard (Anb): Rheingau. (Ber): Johannisberg. (Gro): Steinmächer. (Vil): Eltville.

Rheinberg (Ger) vineyard (Anb): Rheinhessen. (Ber): Wonnegau. (Gro): Liebfrauenmorgen. (Vil): Worms.

Rheinberg (Ger) vineyard (Anb): Rheinhessen. (Ber): Wonnegau. (Gro): Pilgerpfad. (Vil): Osthofen.

Rheinblick (Ger) grosslage (Anb): Rheinhessen. (Ber): Nierstein. (Vils): Alsheim, Dorn-Dürkheim, Mettenheim.

Rheinbrohl (Ger) village (Anb): Mittelrhein. (Ber): Rheinburgengau. (Gro): Burg Hammerstein. (Vins): Monte Jup, Römerberg.

Rheinburgengau (Ger) bereich (Anb): Mittelrhein. (Gros): Burg Hammerstein, Burg Rheinfels, Gedeonseck, Herrenberg, Hahntal, Loreleyfelsen, Marksburg, Schloss Schönburg.

Rheinburger Landwein (Ger) one of 17 Deutsche Landwein zones.

Rheinfels Quelle (Ger) a natural spring mineral water from Walsum, Duisburg. Mineral contents (milligrammes per litre): Sodium 258mg/l, Calcium 1.8mg/l, Magnesium 0.6mg/l, Potassium 4.8mg/l, Bicarbonates 405mg/l, Chlorides 123mg/l, Sulphates 27mg/l, Fluorides 0.62mg/l.

Rheinfront (Ger) the finest part of the Rheinhessen that fringes the river Rhine on steep slopes. Has outcrops of sandstone.

Rheingasse (Ger) vineyard (Anb): Nahe. (Ber): Schloss Böckelheim. (Gro): Paradiesgarten. (Vil): Lettweiler.

Rheingau (Ger) anbaugebiet (Ber): Johannisberg. 3000ha. Main Grape varieties: Müller-Thurgau 10%, Riesling 75%, Silvaner 4%. (Plus others). Soil: slate, loam and loess. Wines are sold in brown bottles.

Rheingauer Riesling Route (Ger) a wine route through the Rheingau taking its name from the principal grape variety of the region.

Rheingau Information Service (Ger) Der 'Rheingau-Der Weingau', Im altern Rathaus, 6225 Johannisberg Rheingau, Germany.

Rheingau Wine Festivals (Ger) see Hilchenfest, Hochheimer Weinfest, Lindenfest, Weinfest-Rüdesheim, Weinfest-Hattenheim.

Rheingold (Fr) a full-bodied beer brewed by the Fischer-Pêcheur group at their Adelshoffen Brasserie.

Rheingoldberg (Ger) vineyard (Anb): Mittelrhein. (Ber): Rheinburgengau. (Gro): Schloss Schönburg. (Vil): Niederburg.

Rheingold Brewery (USA) a brewery based in Orange.

Rheingrafenberg (Ger) vineyard (Anb): Nahe. (Ber): Schloss Böckelheim. (Gro): Paradiesgarten. (Vil): Meddersheim.

Rheingrafenberg (Ger) vineyard (Anb): Rheinhessen. (Ber): Bingen. (Gro): Adelberg. (Vil): Wörrstadt.

Rheingrafenberg (Ger) vineyard (Anb): Rheinhessen. (Ber): Bingen. (Gro): Rheingrafenstein. (Vil): Frei-Laubersheim.

Rheingrafenstein (Ger) grosslage (Anb): Rheinhessen. (Ber): Bingen. (Vils): Eckelsheim, Frei-Laubersheim, Fürfeld, Hackenheim, Neu-Bamberg, Pleitersheim, Siefersheim, Stein-Bockenheim, Tiefenthal, Volxheim, Wöllstein, Wonsheim.

Rheinhess (Ger) own version of a medium-sweet white wine (similar to Liebfraumilch) from the Rheinhessen. See also Moselblümchen, Moseltaler, Nahesteiner.

Rheinhessen (Ger) anbaugebiet (Bers): Bingen, Nierstein, Wonnegau. 24900ha (largest region). Soil: mainly sand. Grape varieties mainly Müller-Thurgau, plus Silvaner. See also Liebfraumilch.

Rheinhessen Information Service (Ger) Rheinhessenweine e. V. 117er Ehrenhof 5, 6500 Mainz, Germany.

Rheinhessen Wine Festivals (Ger) see Winzerfest, Kellerwegfest, Bachfischfest, Mainzer Weinmarkt, Rotweinfest.

Rheinhöhe (Ger) vineyard (Anb): Rheinhessen. (Ber): Bingen. (Gro): Kaiserpfalz. (Vil): Ingelheim.

Rheinhöller (Ger) vineyard (Anb): Mittelrhein. (Ber): Rheinburgengau. (Gro): Burg Hammerstein. (Vil): Linz.

Rheinisch-Bergische Brauerei (Ger) a brewery (established 1887) based in Cologne. Brews: Wicküler.

Rheinischer Landwein (Ger) one of 17 Deutsche Landwein zones.

Rheinnieder (Ger) vineyard (Anb): Mittelrhein. (Ber): Rheinburgengau. (Gro): Marksburg. (Vil): Urbar.

Rheinnieder (Ger) vineyard (Anb): Mittelrhein. (Ber): Rheinburgengau. (Gro): Marksburg. (Vil): Vallendar.

Rheinpfalz (Ger) anbaugebiet (Bers): Mittelhaardt-Deutsche Weinstrasse, Südliche Weinstrasse. Main grape varieties: Müller-Thurgau, Portugieser, Riesling and Silvaner. Now known as the Pfalz.

Rheinpforte (Ger) vineyard (Anb): Rheinhessen. (Ber): Nierstein. (Gro): Gutes Domtal. (Vil): Selzen.

Rhein-Riesling (Aus) the name given to the Riesling

(white riesling) grape of Germany. Also known as the Riesling renano in the Süd-Tirol in Italy.

Rhein Terrasse (Ger) the name for the vineyards in the Rheinhessen, south of Mainz at Nierstein, Oppenheim and Dienheim.

Rhein und Mosel (Ger) a region which has three untergebiete (table wine sub-areas) of the Rhein, Mosel and Saar.

Rheinweiler (Ger) village (Anb): Baden. (Ber): Margräflerland. (Gro): Vogtei Rötteln. (Vin): Kapellenberg.

Rhenania Brauerei (Ger) an alt beer brewery based at Krefeld, near Düsseldorf.

Rhenish (Eng) an old name for Rhine wines, mostly the red wines at the time of Shakespeare in the sixteenth/seventeenth century.

Rhenish Hesse (Ger) the Rheinhessen (alternative name of).

Rhenish Palatinate (Ger) the Pfalz (alternative name of).

Rhens (Ger) village (Anb): Mittelrhein. (Ber): Rheinburgengau. (Gro): Gedeonseck. (Vins): König Wenzel, Sonnenlay.

Rhenser (Ger) a still and sparkling natural spring mineral water from Rhens. Mineral contents (milligrammes per litre): Sodium 80mg/l, Calcium 118mg/l, Magnesium 31mg/l, Potassium 3.5mg/l, Bicarbonates 396mg/l, Chlorides 120mg/l, Sulphates 94.2mg/l, Fluorides 0.5mg/l.

Rhine (USA) a term used to describe generic white wines that are off-dry to sweet.

Rhine [River] (Ger) is Germany's most famous river flows from the Bodensee in the south to Mainz in the north when it then flows east-west to the North Sea. Is the centre of its famous vineyards. Has the rivers: Ahr, Main, Mosel, Nahe and Neckar as its main tributaries.

Rhine Front [The] (Ger) an area of the Rheinhessen south of the Mainz-Nachenheim, Nierstein and Oppenheim where the Riesling grape is grown.

Rhinewine Cobbler (Cktl) place some ice into a large wine goblet. Add 4 dashes orange Curaçao, 1 teaspoon sugar syrup. Top up with a medium Rhine wine, stir and decorate with fruit in season and a sprig of mint and serve with straws.

Rhine Wine Cup (Cktl) 35mls (1½ fl.ozs) sugar, small soda water, 25mls (1fl.oz) Triple Sec, 50mls (2fl.ozs) brandy, 1 bottle Liebfraumilch. Stir altogether over ice, add fruits in season and mint sprigs.

Rhine Wines (Ger) the general term used to describe wines that are produced along the river Rhine. i.e. Rheinhessen, Pfalz, Mittelrhein and sold in brown coloured bottles.

Rhiwlas St. Beuno (Wal) a table water brand produced in the late nineteenth century.

Rhodes (Gre) the main wine-producing island of the Dodecanese group of islands. Produces mainly white wines with some sparkling.

Rhodesian Breweries Limited (Afr) a brewery based in Zimbabwe that brews under the Castle and Lion brands.

Rhoditis (Gre) a pink grape variety used in the making of Retsina and Anchialos wines together with the Savatiano grape. Clones include Alepou and Migdali.

Rhodius Fellbuhr-Quelle (Ger) a sparkling natural spring mineral water from Fellbuhrquelle, Vulkaneifel. Mineral contents (milligrammes per litre): Sodium 190mg/l, Calcium 111mg/l, Magnesium 150mg/l, Potassium 31mg/l, Bicarbonates 1452mg/l, Chlorides 45mg/l, Sulphates 49mg/l, Fluorides 0.32mg/l.

Rhodt (Ger) village (Anb): Pfalz. (Ber): Südliche Weinstrasse. (Gro): Ordensgut. (Vins): Klosterpfad, Rosengarten, Schlossberg.

Rhom (Ch.Isles) rum.

Rhona (S.Afr) the label for a white wine (Muscadel) produced by the Graham Beck Wines winery, Franschhoek, Western Cape.

Rhöndorf (Ger) village (Anb): Mittelrhein. (Ber): Siebengebirge. (Gro): Petersberg. (Vin): Drachenfels.

Rhône (Fr) a major wine region which extends from south of Lyons in eastern France, southwards down to Avignon. Vineyards are sited mainly along the banks of the river Rhône. Most styles of wines are produced. *see* Château Grillet, Châteauneuf-du-Pape, Condrieu, Cornas, Côte Rôtie, Côtes-du-Rhône, Côtes-du-Rhône-Villages, Crozes-Hermitage, Gigondas, Hermitage, Lirac, Muscat de Beaumes de Venise, St. Joseph, Tavel, Vacqueyras. Website: http://www.vins-rhone.com

Rhône [River] (Fr) a major river that runs through eastern France to the Mediterranean sea. Has the rivers Saône and Isère as its main tributaries. Runs through the northern and southern wine regions of the Rhône (Côtes du Rhône).

Rhône-Alpes (Fr) a vin de pays region situated in south-eastern France which contains the vin de pays districts of: d'Allobrogie/des Balmes Dauphinoises/des Colliones Rhodaniennes/des Comtés Rhodaniens/des Coteaux de l'Ardèche/des Coteaux des Baronnies/des Coteaux du Grésivaudan/du Comté de Grignan/d'Urfé.

Rhön Sprudel (Ger) a still and sparkling natural spring mineral water from Ebersburg. Mineral contents (milligrammes per litre): Sodium 3.2mg/l, Calcium 45.2mg/l, Magnesium 26mg/l, Potassium 16.6mg/l, Bicarbonates 302mg/l, Chlorides 8.5mg/l, Sulphates 17mg/l, Fluorides 0.6 mg/l.

R.H. Phillips (USA) a winery based in the Dunnigan Hills, Yolo County, California. Grape varieties: Cabernet sauvignon.

Rhubarb Rhubarb (Austr) a 5% alc by vol. rhubarb-based drink from Duncan MacGillivray.

Rhum (Fr) rum.

Rhum Barbancourt (W.Ind) a rum produced by the Damien Distillery in Haiti.

Rhum Black (Fr) rum producers based in Bordeaux, south-western France.

Rhum Blanc (Fr) white rum.

Rhum Champion (W.Ind) the brand-name of a rum produced by the Croix des Bouquets Distillery in Haiti.

Rhum Citadelle (W.Ind) a brand of rum produced at Port au Prince, Haiti by Marie Colas.

Rhum Clément (W.Ind) a fine, full rum from the Clément Distillery based in Martinique. Produces both white and golden varieties.

Rhum Duquesne (W.Ind) the name given to a white rum produced on the southern part of Martinique. Sold under the Genippa label or if is aged 3 years then Grand Case (silver label) or 10 years then Val d'Or (gold label).

Rhum Marie Colas (W.Ind) the brand-name of a rum produced in Haiti by the Cazeau Distillery.

Rhum Nazon (W.Ind) the brand-name of a rum produced on Haiti.

Rhum Negrita (W.Ind) a fine, full rum from Martinique.

Rhum Saint James (W.Ind) a fine, full rum from Martinique, made from cane juice syrup strengthened with dunder.

Rhum Tesserot (W.Ind) the brand-name of a rum produced on Haiti.

Rhum Tropical (W.Ind) the brand-name of a rum produced in Haiti by the Manègue Distillery.

Rhum Verschnitt (Ger) lit: 'rum sandwich', a blend of concentrated pot-stilled rums and local corn spirits.

Rhyls' Revenge (Wal) a dark ale 7% alc by vol. brewed by the Snowdonia Brewery, Shropshire (a micro-brewery).

Rhymney Brewery Ltd [The] (Wal) a brewery. (Add): Unit A2 Valleys, Enterprise Centre, Pant Ind Estate, Merthyr Tydfil, Mid Glamorgan CF48 2SR. Brews: Bevans Bitter 4.2% alc by vol., Celtic Pride 4.5% alc by vol., Centenary Ale 3.9% alc by vol., Christmas Special 5% alc by vol., Easter Ale 4.3% alc by vol. Website: http://www.rhymneybreweryltd.com 'E'mail: enquiries@rhymneybreweryltd.com

Rhyolite Rock (Hun) rock from which the cellars of Tokaji (for Azsú) are cut.

Rhyton (Gre) a drinking vessel used in ancient Greece. Was horn-shaped, the hole for drinking through being at the sharp (pointed) end.

Rialheim (S.Afr) see Clairvaux Koöperatiewe.

Rialto Cocktail (Cktl) 30mls (¼ gill) Calvados, 30mls (¼ gill) Italian vermouth, 2 dashes orange squash, 2 sugar cubes. Crush sugar with squash, add remaining ingredients, stir over ice, strain into a cocktail glass, top with mint and an orange slice.

Rialtococo (Cktl) ⅓ measure Campari, ⅓ measure dry gin, ⅓ measure Coconut cream, 1 scoop crushed ice. Blend all together and serve in a large wine goblet with straws.

Rías Baixas (Sp) a D.O. of Galicia in the province of Pontevedrain at the Atlantic Coast. 1978ha. Four sub-regions: Val do Salnés (north), Condado do Tea, O Rosal, Soutomaior (all south). D.O. recognises six types of wines- Val do Salnés (white from 70% Albariño), O Rosal (white from 70% Albariño or Loureiro or blend of both), Condado do Tea (white from 70% Albariño or Treixadura or blend of both), O Rosal (red), Albariño (100%), plus white varietals (minimum of 85% of named grape). Eleven varieties are permitted in D.O. Rías Baixas. (5 white, 6 red). 90% of vineyard area is Albariño grape. Other grape varieties include: Brancellao, Caiño blanco, Caiño tinto, Espadeiro, Loureiro blanca, Loureiro tinta, Mencía, Sousón, Torrontés, Treixadura. Wines are produced in 147 bodegas. D.O. in 1988.

Ribatejo (Port) a DOC wine district that straddles the banks of the Tagus river. Has the I.P.R. wines: Tomar, Santarém, Almeirim, Cartaxo, Chamusca, Coruche. Produces low acid, white wines and full-bodied, dark red wines with high alcohol.

Ribeauvillé (Fr) a wine town in the Haut-Rhin, Alsace. (Ger) = Rappoltsweiler.

Ribeira do Ulla (Sp) a Vino Comarcal wine from the provinces of Pontevedra/A Coruña in Galicia.

Ribeira Sacra (Sp) a D.O. in the province of Lugo, Galicia, north-west Spain. 13700 acres of vines. Sub-regions: Amandi, Ribeiras do Miño, Chantada, Quiroga, Ribeiras do Sil. White grapes: Doña branca, Torrontés, Godello, Albariño, Palomino, Loureiro. Red grapes: Brancellao, Garnacha, Negrada.

Ribeiro (Sp) a Denominación de Origen wine producing area on the Portuguese border of north-western Spain. 3100ha. 15 grape varieties are permitted (7 red, 8 white). Treixadura and Caiño are most important. Other permitted grape varieties include: Albariño, Albillo, Godello, Loureira, Macabeo, Palomino, Torrontés (white), Brancellao, Garnacha, Ferrón, Mencía, Souzón, Tempranillo (red). Produces red, white and enverado (under ripe) wines.

Ribeiro and Irmão (Port) producers of Ribeiros (a brand of Vinho Verde).

Ribeiros (Port) a brand of Vinho Verde produced by Ribeiro and Irmao.

Ribena (Eng) the brand-name used by Beecham Products, Brentford, Middlesex for their famous non-alcoholic blackcurrant drink.

Ribera Alta (Sp) one of five wine-producing districts in the Navarra region. Divided into three sub-zones: Lerin, Marcilla and Olite.

Ribera Alta del Guadiana (Sp) a Vino de la Tierra wine-producing area in the province of Badajoz, Extremadura. 8500ha. Main Grape varieties: Montúa, Pedro ximénez, Alarije, Borba, Pardina, Cayetana (white), Cencibel and Garnacha (red) plus Chardonnay, Cabernet sauvignon and Pinot noir experimentally. Red and white wines are produced.

Ribera Baja (Sp) one of five Denominación de Origen wine-producing districts in the Navarra region. A D.O. of Navarra.

Ribera Baja del Guadiana (Sp) a Vino de la Tierra wine-producing area in the province of Badajoz,

Extremadura. 7000ha. Main Grape varieties: Alarije, Cayetana, Pardina, Macabeo, Montúa, Pedro ximénez, Eva, Borba, (white), Cencibel and Garnacha (red). Red and white wines are produced.

Ribera de Ebro (Sp) one of three sub-zones in Tarragona. Grape varieties: Cariñena, Garnacha tinta, Tempranillo for red, Macabéo, Parellada, Garnacha and Xarello for white wines.

Ribera del Arlanza [La] (Sp) a Vino Comarcal wine of the province Burgos in Castilla-León.

Ribera del Cea [La] (Sp) a Vino de Mesa wine of the province León/Valladolid in Castilla-León.

Ribera del Duero (Sp) a Denominación de Origen (created in 1982) in the Douro Valley. 10357ha. Home to the famous wine Vega Sicilia. Grape varieties include 85% Tinto del país/Tinto fino (Tempranillo) plus Garnacha tinta, Albillo, Cabernet sauvignon, Malbec, Merlot. see Unico, Valbuena. Red and rosé wines are produced. Website: http://www.riberadelduero.es

Ribera del Guadiana (Sp) a Denominación de Origen based on the central-southern border with Portugal.

Ribera Sacra (Sp) a Denominación de Origen in Galicia (5546 ha). Contains the sub-zones: Amandi, Ribeiras do Miño, Ribeiras do Sil, Chantada, Quiroga-Bibei. Grape varieties include: Albariño, Loureiro, Godello, Doña lanca, Torrontés, Palomino (white), Mencía (25% of vineyard), Brancellao, Caiño, Loureiro tinta, Sousón, Merenzao, Ferrón, Espadeiro, Negrada, Garnacha (red).

Ribero (Sp) the alternative spelling of the river Ribeiro and the region.

Ribes (Sp) a still natural spring mineral water. Mineral contents (milligrammes per litre): Sodium 4.2mg/l, Calcium 54.1mg/l, Magnesium 8mg/l, Potassium 0.6mg/l, Bicarbonates 163.4mg/l, Chlorides 2mg/l, Sulphates 33.4mg/l, Fluorides 0.1mg/l, Nitrates 6.7mg/l.

Riboflavin (Eng) vitamin B$_2$ found in small traces in wines.

Ribolla (It) a white grape variety grown in north-eastern Italy. Produces dry white and sparkling wines. Full name is Ribolla Gialla in Friuli.

Ribolla Gialla (It) a variety of the white Ribolla grape grown in north-eastern Italy. see Ribolla.

Ribolla Nera (It) an alternative name for the Schioppettino grape.

Ribolla Verde (It) a white grape variety. Produces average wines.

Ribose (Eng) a Monosaccharide found in wine.

Ribote (Fr) a drunken bout/a booze-up.

Ricard (Fr) a famous French brand-name Pastis created by Paul Ricard 44.5% alc by vol. it is nearly colourless. see Monsieur Pastis.

Ricard-Bisquit Dubouché (Fr) a noted Cognac distillery based in Jarnac.

Ricardo (S.Afr) the brand-name of a dark rum.

Ricasoli (It) a famous Tuscan family, the originators of Chianti at Brolio.

Riccadonna (It) a brand-name Italian vermouth made by the Gancia C°. of Turin 15% alc by vol. Also produces sparkling wines by both metodo tradizionale and cuve close. see President Brut.

Ricciuti-Revolte (Fr) a Champagne producer. (Add): Avenay Val d'Or 51160 Aÿ. Récoltants-manipulants. Produces vintage and non-vintage wines.

Rice Beer (Chi)(Jap) saké, also known as Rice Wine.

Rice Water (Eng) a non-alcoholic convalescent drink. Wash 50grms (2ozs) rice and boil in 2¼ litres (4½ pints) water for 1½ hours. Add sugar to taste and grated nutmeg, strain and serve hot or cold.

Rice Wine (Chi)(Jap) saké (rice beer), is of a higher acoholic strength than rice beer. see Aspergillus oryzae. (Kor) = soju.

Riceys [Les] (Fr) a Cru Champagne village in the Canton de l'Aube. District: Château Thierry.

Rich (Eng) denotes a wine having a generous bouquet, flavour and fullness of body.

Richard Cobden Brewery [The] (Eng) a brewery based in Stockport, Cheshire. A micro-brewery that produces a premium bitter.

Richard Fryer (S.Afr) the label for a red wine (Cabernet sauvignon 50% and Merlot 50%) produced by the Fryer's Cove Vineyards winery, Stellenbosch, Western Cape.

Riche (Fr) a wine having a generous bouquet, flavour and fullness of body.

Richebourg (Fr) a Grand Cru vineyard in the A.C. commune of Vosne-Romanée, Côte de Nuits, Burgundy. 8ha. Also known as Les Richebourg.

Richegude (Fr) a village in the A.C. Côtes du Rhône-Villages, south-eastern Rhône.

Richelieu Cocktail (Cktl) 1 measure Dubonnet, 1 measure Bourbon whiskey, 2 dashes Vieille Cure. Shake over ice, strain into an old-fashioned glass, add a lemon peel spiral and an ice cube.

Richelieu's Infusion (Fr) a nickname given to Bordeaux wine in the eighteenth century after Cardinal Richelieu went to Aquitaine to retire after an active life. The wines of Bordeaux were said to have given him a new lease of life.

Richemone [La] (Fr) a Premier Cru vineyard in the A.C. commune of Nuits-Saint-Georges, Côte de Nuits, Burgundy 2.2ha.

Richemont (Fr) a commune in the Charente-Maritime département whose grapes are classed as Borderies.

Richeneau (S.Afr) a still and sparkling spring water from the Drakenstein Mountains, Franschhoek, Western Cape. (Add): Richeneau Water C°., Suite 3, Private Bag X15, Somerset West 7129. Mineral contents (milligrammes per litre): Sodium 12mg/l, Calcium 0.3mg/l, Magnesium 1.3mg/l, Potassium 0.2mg/l, Chlorides 21mg/l, Sulphates 2mg/l. pH 5.8

Richert Cellars (USA) a winery based in Santa Clara, California. Grape varieties: Cabernet sauvignon and Chardonnay. Produces varietal and dessert wines.

Richis (Rum) an important wine-producing area (part of the Tîrnave Vineyard).

Richlieu (S.Afr) the brand-name of a brandy produced by Oude Meester.

Richmodis Kölsch (Ger) a beer brewed by the Richmodis Brauerei based in Cologne.

Richmond Ale (Eng) a 4.8% alc by vol. draught or bottled double brown ale. Brewed by Darwin Brewery, Crook, County Durham.

Richmond Grove Vineyard (Austr) vineyard. (Add): Sandy Hollow, New South Wales, 2333. 150ha. Grape varieties: Cabernet sauvignon, Chardonnay, Gewürztraminer, Merlot, Sauvignon blanc and Sémillon.

Richon (Isr) a brand of medium-sweet white wine produced by Carmel.

Richon-le-Zion (Isr) lit: 'first in Zion', the most important centre for viticulture in Israel. Produces red, white and sparkling wines from French grape varieties.

Rich Ruby (Eng) a 4.5% alc by vol. ale brewed by the Milestone Brewery Ltd., Nottinghamshire.

Richtern (Aus) a vineyard site on the banks of the River Danube in the Kremstal region.

Richter 110 (Sp) a rootstock used in the regions of Alicante, Jumilla, Yecla and Tarragona. A cross between the *Vitis rupestris* and *Vitis berlandieri*.

Rick (USA) a constructed framework or rack in a warehouse in which barrels of distilled spirits are stored for ageing.

Ricketts [Thomas] (Eng) an early Bristol glassmaker who in 1811 patented a hinged butterfly mould which enabled bottles to be blown in one operation.

Rickety Bridge Winery (S.Afr) a winery based in Franschhoek, Western Cape. 16ha. (Add): P.O. Box 455, 7690 Franschhoek. Grape varieties: Cabernet franc 0.42ha, Cabernet sauvignon 3.88ha, Chardonnay 1.85ha, Chenin blanc 1.48ha, Malbec 0.17ha, Merlot 1.6ha, Sauvignon blanc 1.01ha, Semillon 0.6ha, Shiraz 1.63ha. Labels: Duncan's Creek, Paulinas Reserve. Owns Zonnenbloem Vineyards, Simondium. See also Cru Wines. Website: http://www.ricketybridgewinery.com 'E'mail: sales@ricketybridgewinery.com

Rickey (Cktl) a spirit, lime and soda water served in a tall glass with ice that is usually dry in taste. see Gin Rickey.

Ricking (USA) the process of stacking whiskey barrels on ricks.

Ricoliano Cocktail (Cktl) 30mls (1¼ fl.ozs) white rum, 10mls (½ fl.oz) lime juice, 5mls (¼ fl.oz) Galliano, dash gomme syrup. Stir over ice in a highball glass, top with soda water, dress with a cherry, orange slice and serve with straws.

Ricour Brasserie (Fr) a small family brewery based in St. Sylvestre Chappel. Brews: Du Moulin beers.

Riddar Cocktail (Cktl) 50mls (2fl.ozs) Mandarine Napoléon, 10mls (½ fl.oz) each of white rum, dry gin, 25mls (1fl.oz) pineapple juice, shake well with ice and strain into a cocktail glass.

Ridder Maltezer (Hol) a 6.5% alc by vol. bottled Dortmund beer brewed by De Ridder Stadsbrouwerij, Maastricht, South Limburg. see De Ridder.

Ridder Pilsener (Hol) a 5% alc by vol. bottled, unpasterised pilsner brewed by De Ridder Stadsbrouwerij, Maastricht, South Limburg. see De Ridder.

Ridder's Creek (S.Afr) a winery based in Wellington, Western Cape. Grape varieties: Cabernet sauvignon, Chardonnay, Sauvignon blanc, Shiraz. Website: http://www.ridderscreek.co.za

Riddling (Eng) see Remuage.

Riddling Bins (Eng) the name given to the automatic remueurs (crécelles) for sparkling wines.

Rider's Valley (S.Afr) the export label for a range of wines produced by the Ruitersvlei Wines winery, Suider-Paarl, Western Cape.

Ridgeback Wines (S.Afr) a winery (established 1997) based in Windmeul, Paarl, Western Cape. 35ha. Grape varieties: Cabernet franc, Chenin blanc, Cinsaut, Merlot, Sauvignon blanc, Shiraz, Viognier. Labels: His Master's Choice, Vansha. Website: http://www.ridgebackwines.co.za

Ridge Farm (Eng) a vineyard (established 1972). (Add): Lamberhurst, Kent. 16.5ha. Soil: clay on sandstone. Grape varieties: Müller-Thurgau, Ortega, Reichensteiner, Riesling, Schönburger, Seyvre villard. Wines sold under the Lamberhurst Priory label.

Ridgeview Wine Estate (Eng) a vineyard (established 1994) based in Ditchling Common, Surrey that specialises in sparking wines under the Nyetimber logo. Produces: Merret Belgravia N.V., Merret Bloomsbury vintage, Merret Grosvenor vintage and Merret Fitzrovia vintage rosé. Website: http://www.ridgeview.co.uk 'E'mail: ridgeviewestate@aol.com

Ridge Vineyards (USA) a winery based in Santa Cruz Mountains, Santa Clara, California. (Add): 17100 Monte Bello Road, Cupertino, CA 95014. Grape varieties: Cabernet sauvignon, Carignan, Chardonnay, Merlot, Petite syrah, Petit Verdot, Zinfandel. Labels: Geyserville, Monte Bello. Website: http://www.ridgewine.com 'E'mail: wine@ridgewine.com

Ridgeway Bitter (Eng) a bitter brewed by the Tring Brewery, Hertfordshire. 4% alc by vol (1039.5 O.G).

Ridgeway Brewing (Eng) a brewery (established 2002). (Add): Beer Counter Ltd, 6 Chapel Close, South Stoke, Reading, Berkshire RG8 0JW. Brews: Bad Elf 6% alc by vol., Ironman 4.8% alc by vol., Ivanhoe 5.2% alc by vol., Ridgeway Bitter 4% alc by vol., Ridgeway IPA 5.5% alc by vol., Ridgeway Organic 4.3% alc by vol. 'E'mail: sales@beercounter.co.uk

Ridgways (Eng) tea producers noted especially for their Imperial blend.

Ridgways Royal H.M.B. (Eng) a high grown Ceylon, Chinese and Formosa blend tea favoured by Queen Victoria and others. Produced by Ridgways.

Riding Bitter (Eng) a traditional bitter brewed by Mansfield Brewery 3.6% alc by vol.

Riding Brewery (Eng) originally part of North Country Breweries, Hull, Yorkshire. Taken over by Mansfield Brewery, Notts. Brews: cask-conditioned Riding Bitter 3.6% alc by vol. Riding Mild 3.5% alc by vol.

Riding Mild (Eng) a traditional mild brewed by Mansfield Brewery 3.5% alc by vol.

Ridley [T D] & Sons Ltd (Eng) a brewery (established 1842). (Add): Hatford End Brewery, Hartford End, Chelmsford, Essex CM3 1JZ. Noted for cask-conditioned HE Bitter 1045 O.G., Big Tackle 4.1% alc by vol., Bishops Ale 1080 O.G., Essex Ale 1030 O.G,. Finnegans 3.8% alc by vol. Fisherman's Whopper Ale 4.3% alc by vol., Five Rings 4.1% alc by vol., Hoppy Easter 4.3% alc by vol. Mild Manners 3.8% alc by vol. Millennium Ale 4% alc by vol. Old Bob 5.1 % alc by vol (1050 O.G.)., Ridley's IPA 4.3% alc by vol., Santa's Secret 4.8% alc by vol., Snow Joke 4.5% alc by vol. Stock Ale 1050 O.G. Spectator 4.6% alc by vol., Tolly Original 3.8% alc by vol., Valentine 3.9% alc by vol. Winter Winner 5.5% alc by vol., Witchfinder General, Prospect Golden Cask Ale 4.1% alc by vol. Y2K Also brew cask-conditioned Cheshire Cheese, Chester Rock, Greenalls Grand and Tatton Ale for Greenall retail outlets. Website: http://www.ridleys.co.uk 'E'mail: info@ridleys.co.uk

Riebeek-Wes (S.Afr) a table wine-producing region based west of Tulbagh.

Riebeek Wine Farmers' Co-operative (S.Afr) a co-operative winery (established 1941) based at Riebeek-Kasteel, Swartland, Western Cape. 1400ha. (Add): Riebeek Wynboere Koöperatiewe, Box 13, Riebeek-Kasteel, 6801. Grape varieties: Cabernet sauvignon, Chardonnay, Chenin blanc, Cinsaut, Merlot, Pinotage, Red jerepigo, Sauvignon blanc, Shiraz, Stein. Labels: A Few Good Men, Cape Table, Cellar Lite, Montino, Pinot 2. Also produces varietal wines. Website: http://www.riebeek.cellars.com

Riebeek Wynboere Koöperatiewe (S.Afr) see Riebeek Wine Farmers' Co-operative.

Riebeek Wine Cellars (S.Afr) a winery. (Add): P.O. Box 528, Southern Paarl 7624, Malmesbury. Grape varieties: Cabernet sauvignon, Chardonnay, Chenin blanc, Pinotage, Sauvignon blanc, Shiraz.

Riecine (It) a Chianti Classico producer based in Tuscany.

Ried (Aus) vineyard.

Riedel (Aus) a vineyard site based on the banks of the River Kamp situated in the Kamptal region.

Rieden (Aus) cru vineyards.

Riedersbückele (Ger) vineyard (Anb): Württemberg. (Ber): Württembergisch Unterland. (Gro): Kirchenweinberg. (Vil): Lauffen.

Riedlingen (Ger) village (Anb): Baden. (Ber): Markgräflerland. (Gro): Vogtei Rötteln. (Vin): Steingässle.

Rieffel [Lucas et André] (Fr) a winery based in Wiebelsberg, Alsace. Produces a variety of wines including Riesling Grand Cru. Label: Riesling Rieffel.

Rieffel [Pierre] (Fr) a noted eau-de-vie distiller based in Breitenbach, Bas Rhin, Alsace.

Riegel (Ger) village (Anb): Baden. (Ber): Kaiserstuhl-Tuniberg. (Gro): Vulkanfelsen. (Vin): St. Michaelsberg.

Riegele Brauerei (Ger) a brewery based in Augsburg. Noted for Perlweizen 5% alc by vol. and Hefeweizen 5% alc by vol. (both wheat beers), Spezi 5% alc by vol. (a malty lager beer) and Speziator 7.9% alc by vol.

Riegelfeld (Ger) vineyard (Anb): Ahr. (Ber): Walporzheim/Ahrtal. (Gro): Klosterberg. (Vil): Ahrweiler.

Riegelnegg (Aus) a winery based in Gamlitz, Süd-Steiermark. (Add): Olwitschhof, Steinbach 62, 8462 Gamlitz. Grape varieties: Chardonnay, Gewürztraminer, Muskateller, Pinot blanc, Pinot gris, Sauvignon blanc, Traminer. Produces a range of dry and sweet wines.

Rigerin (Aus) a vineyard site based on the banks of the River Kamp situated in the Kamptal region.

Reigersburg (Aus) a winery based in Leutschach, Süd-Oststeiermark. (Add): Glanz 75, 8463 Leutschach. Grape varieties: Blauburger, Chardonnay, Pinot blanc, Traminer, Zweigelt, Welschriesling.

Rieliel Distillerie (Fr) an eau-de-vie distillery based in Breitenbach, Bas-Rhin, Alsace.

Rielinghausen (Ger) village (Anb): Württemberg. (Ber): Württembergisch Unterland. (Gro): Schalkstein. (Vin): Kelterberg.

Riemerschmied (Ger) a liqueur made from figs.

Riemerschmied (Ger) a large distillery based in Munich noted for Enzian.

Rieschen (Ger) vineyard (Anb): Baden. (Ber): Bodensee. (Gro): Sonnenufer. (Vil): Meersburg.

Rieslaner (Ger) a white grape variety that produces fruity wines, a cross between the Silvaner and the Riesling. Is also known as the Main Riesling.

Riesler (Aus) a local name for the Welschriesling grape.

Riesling (Ger) one of the greatest white grape varieties, produces superior quality white wines with a petrol, floral, elderflower, walnut, apple, orange, lime and passion fruit aromas and flavours. Is ideal for **Botrytis cinerea** and produces exceptionally long-lived sweet white wines (with a peach and honey aroma and flavour). Known also as the Johannisberg riesling, Rhine riesling, Weisser riesling, White riesling, Riesling renano (no relation to the Welschriesling).

Riesling (USA) see California Riesling.

Riesling Cup (Cktl) 1 bottle riesling, ½ bottle dry cider, small bottle lemonade. Chill ingredients, stir all together, add slices of orange and lemon and a sprig of mint.

Riesling de Banat (Rum) see Creata.

Riesling de Caldas (Bra) see Duchesse.

Riesling de Dealulmare (Rum) a white wine from the Dealul Mare district.

Riesling de Italie (Rum) a name given to the white grape variety Welschriesling. see Riesling Italien (alternative spelling).

R

Riesling Doré (Fr) the name given to the Goldriesling of Germany.

Riesling-Italiano (It) *see* Riesling Italico.

Riesling Italico (It) a name given to the white grape variety Welschriesling in the Trentino-Alto Adige. *See also* Laski rizling, Olasz rizling.

Riesling Italien (Rum) *see* Riesling de Italie.

Riesling Massandra (Rus) a dry white wine from the Crimean Peninsular. Produced from the Riesling grape.

Riesling Renano (It) the name given to the true Riesling in the Trentino-Alto Adige region.

Riesling-Sylvaner (N.Z) the name used for the Müller-Thurgau grape.

Riesling Talianski (Czec) a name given to the white grape variety Welschriesling.

Riesling Tea (Eng) an eighteenth and nineteenth century nickname for the wines of the Mosel-Saar-Ruwer made from the Riesling grape because of the reputed health-giving properties of the wine.

Riesling X Sylvaner (It) the Trentino-Alto Adige name for the Müller-Thurgau white grape variety.

Riet (Ger) village (Anb): Württemberg. (Ber): Württembergisch Unterland. (Gro): Stromberg. (Vin): Kirchberg.

Rietenau (Ger) village (Anb): Württemberg. (Ber): Württembergisch Unterland. (Gro): Schalkstein. (Vin): Güldenkern.

Rietenauer (Ger) a natural spring mineral water (established 1262) from Dilleniusquelle. Mineral contents (milligrammes per litre): Calcium 567mg/l, Magnesium 88mg/l, Sulphates 1437mg/l.

Rietrivier Wynkelder Koöperatiewe (S.Afr) a co-operative winery (established 1965) based at Klein Karoo. 300ha. (Add): Box 144, Montagu 6720. Grape varieties: Chardonnay, Colombard, Hanepoot, Muscadel, Pinotage, Ruby cabernet, Sauvignon blanc, Shiraz. Labels: Chenel, Montague, Petite Blanc, Quiriga and varietal wines. Website: http://www.rietrivier.co.za

Rietvallei Estate (S.Afr) a winery based at Robertson. (Add): Box 368, Robertson, 6705. Grape varieties include: Cabernet sauvignon. Produces varietal and some fortified wines.

Rieux Light (Eng) a low alcohol wine produced by Greene King, has less than 3.5% alc by vol.

Riex (Switz) a noted vineyard based in Lavaux.

Riffault [Pierre et Étienne] (Fr) propriétaires-viticulteurs based at Verdigny-en-Sancerre, Cher.

Riga (Rus) a pilsener-style beer brewed at the Yantar Brewery.

Rigagno (It) a natural spring mineral water from Taceno, Como.

Riggwelter (Eng) a 5.9% alc by vol. ale from the Black Sheep Brewery, Masham, North Yorkshire. Was trialed in 1995 as Sheep Preview at 6.5% alc by vol.

Right Arm (Eng) a slang term "*To exercise my right arm*", to raise a glass of beer to the mouth.

Rignana (It) a Chianti Classico producer based in Tuscany.

Rigoverno (It) occurs in March–April, the second operation which is similar to the Governo process (which occurs in December), also known as Leggermente Appassite.

Rijckshof Wines (S.Afr) *see* Kango Co-operative.

Rijk's Private Cellar (S.Afr) a winery (established 1996) based in the Tulbagh, Stellenbosch, Western Cape. 28ha. Grape varieties: Cabernet sauvignon, Chardonnay, Chenin blanc, Merlot, Pinotage, Sauvignon blanc, Sémillon, Shiraz. Labels: Bravado, Private Cellar. Website: http://www.rijks.co.za

Rijnwijn (Hol) Hock/Rhine wine.

Rikyu (Jap) the tea master who conducts the Chanoyu tea ceremony.

Rilchinger (Ger) a natural spring mineral water. Mineral contents (milligrammes per litre): Sodium 226mg/l, Calcium 126mg/l, Magnesium 60mg/l, Potassium 6mg/l, Bicarbonates 278mg/l, Chlorides 390mg/l, Sulphates 271mg/l.

Riley's Army Bitter (Eng) a 4.3% alc by vol. bitter ale brewed by the Jarrow Brewery, Tyne & Wear.

Rilly-la-Montagne (Fr) a Premier Cru Champagne village in the Canton de Verzy. District: Reims.

Rimage (Fr) describes a vintage Banyuls that is bottled and drunk young.

Rimauresco (Fr) a rosé wine (Cinsault and Tibouren blend) produced by the Domaine de Rimauresq, A.C. Côtes de Provence.

Rimaux Brasserie (Fr) a family-run brewery based near Valenciennes. Was formerly an abbaye brewery. Brews: Réserve Saint Landelin.

Rimavsk Brewery (Czec) a brewery based in eastern Czec.

Rimontaggio (It) the name given to the process of extracting the colour in red wine using the maceration technique.

Rimpar (Ger) village (Anb): Franken. (Ber): Maindreieck. (Gro): Not yet assigned. (Vin): Kobersberg.

Rimski (Can) a brand of vodka produced by Hiram Walker 40% alc by vol.

Rinaldi [Guiseppe] (It) a small winery based in Barolo, Piemonte.

Rince Cochon (Fr) lit: 'pig's swill', the old slang name for Nikita.

Rince Gueule (Fr) lit; 'mouth rinse', refers to a light wine drunk before a meal to refresh the palate. i.e. Beaujolais.

Rinces [Les] (Fr) a wine-producing village in the commune of Solutré-Pouilly in A.C. Pouilly-Fuissé, Mâcon, Burgundy.

Ring Bolt (Austr) a winery based in the Margaret River region of Western Australia. Grape varieties include: Cabernet sauvignon.

Ringelbach (Ger) village (Anb): Baden. (Ber): Ortenau. (Gro): Fürsteneck. (Vin): Renchtäler.

Ringing Roger (Eng) a 6% alc by vol. strong ale brewed by the Edale Brewery Cº., Derbyshire.

Ringnes Brewery (Nor) a brewery based in Oslo, produces bock beers and Tuborg under licence. Exports to the USA.

Ringnes Lager (Nor) a 4.5% alc by vol. lager brewed by the Ringnes Brewery, Oslo.

Ring 'O' Bells Brewery (Eng) a brewery (established 1999). (Add): Pennygillam Way, Pennygillam Ind Estate, Launceston, Cornwall PL15 7ED. Brews: Bodmin Boar 4.3% alc by vol., Cornish Steamer 4% alc by vol., Dreckly 4.8% alc by vol., Porkers Pride 3.8% alc by vol., Sozzled Swine 5.5% alc by vol., Tipsy Trotter 5.1% alc by vol. Website: http://www.ringobellsbrewery.com 'E'mail: enquiries@ringobellsbrewery.com

Ring Pull (USA) *see* Cudzik [Daniel F].

Ringsheim (Ger) village (Anb): Baden. (Ber): Breisgau. (Gro): Burg Lichteneck. (Vin): Kaiserberg.

Ringtons Teas (Eng) an old established tea-blending company (1907) for the north-east of England based in Newcastle. Produces a fine range of teas.

Ringwood Best Bitter (Eng) a 1038 O.G. bitter brewed by the Ringwood Brewery, Ringwood, Hampshire.

Ringwood Brewery (Eng) a brewery (established 1978). (Add): 138 Christchurch Road, Ringwood, Hampshire BH24 2AP. Noted for cask-conditioned Best Bitter 3.8% alc by vol., Bold Forester 4.2% alc by vol., Boondoggle, Huffkin 4.4% alc by vol., True Glory 4.3% alc by vol., XXXX Porter 4.7% alc by vol., Forty Niner 4.9% alc by vol (1049 O.G)., Old Thumper 5.6% alc by vol (1060 O.G)., 21 Not Out 4.5% alc by vol. Website: http://www.ringwoodbrewery.co.uk 'E'mail: enq@ringwoodbrewery.co.uk

Rinquinquin (Fr) a peach-flavoured liqueur 14.8% alc by vol.

Rinsol (Sp) a dry white wine produced by Federico Paternina S.A. in Rioja, north-western Spain.

Rio (Eng) the name given to a range of sparkling spring water and exotic fruit juice drinks from Hall and Woodhouse. Flavours include Florida, Mediterranean, Oriental, Tropical.

Rio Bravo (Port) a natural spring mineral water from Agueda, Serra de Calamulu.

Rio de Janeiro (Bra) a noted wine-producing state in central-western Brazil.

Rio Grande (Mad) a *Vitis vinifera* cross white grape variety used in Madeira production.

Rio Grande do Sul (Bra) the main vineyard area in southern Brazil which borders Uruguay. Main Grape varieties: Barbera, Bonarda, Cabernet sauvignon, Chardonnay, Merlot, Pinot noir, Riesling, Sémillon.

Rioja (Sp) a Denominación de Origen Calificada (D.O.Ca.) region of north-western Spain around the banks of the river Ebro and the tributary river Oja from which the region takes its name. 49694ha. Produces most styles of wines (dry) and is the best known of all the Spanish table wines. Grape varieties: Garnacha, Garnacha blanca, Graciano, Malvasía riojana, Mazuelo, Tempranillo and Viura. Some Cabernet sauvignon is also permitted in older plantations. *see* Crianza, Vino Joven, Reserva, Rioja Alavesa, Rioja Alta, Rioja Baja, Grand Reserva.

Website: http://www.riojawine.com 'E'mail: info@riojawine.com

Rioja [La] (Arg) a wine-producing region north-west of Cordoba.

Rioja Alavesa (Sp) an area within the Rioja region of northern Spain. Lies north-west of the river Ebro. Soil: chalky. Main grape variety is Tempranillo.

Rioja Alta (Sp) an area within the Rioja region of northern Spain. Lies south-east of the river Ebro. Soil: clay. Main grape variety is Tempranillo.

Rioja Alta S.A. [La] (Sp) a winery. (Add): Avenida de Vizcays s/n, Haro (La Rioja). 120ha. Grape varieties: Garnacha, Graciano, Tempranillo, Viura. Wines: 96% red, 3% white, 1% rosé. Produce Viña Alberdi, Viña Ardanza, Reserva 904, Metropol Extra (white).

Rioja Baja (Sp) an area within the Rioja region of northern Spain. Lies south-east of river Ebro. Soil: clay. Main grape variety is Garnacha.

Rioja Blanco (Sp) a D.O.Ca. white wine that must attain 11.5% alc by vol. in Rioja Alavesa, Rioja Alta and Rioja Baja reions. *see* Rioja.

Rioja Bordon (Sp) a red wine from the Bodegas Franco-Españolas. Made from Garnacha 40%, Mazuelo 10% and Tempranillo 50% grapes. Matured in oak 2½ years and in bottle 1 year.

Rioja Ederra (Sp) a red wine produced by Bodegas Bilbainas, Haro, Rioja.

Rioja Mark (Sp) a complicated series of lines put onto a wine cask to denote the style of wine.

Rioja Rosado (Sp) a D.O.Ca. rosé wine that must attain 10.5% alc by vol. in Rioja Alavesa and Rioja Alta, 11.5% alc by vol. in Rioja Baja. *see* Rioja.

Riojanas S.A. (Sp) *see* Bodegas Riojanas.

Rioja Santiago (Sp) a firm that exports Yago wines to the USA and most other countries. *see* Bodegas Rioja Santiago.

Rioja Tinto (Sp) a D.O.Ca. red wine that must attain 11.5% alc by vol. in Rioja Alavesa and Rioja Alta, 12.5% alc by vol. in Rioja Baja. *see* Rioja.

Rioja Vega (Sp) red and white wines produced by the Bodegas Muerza S.A. Rioja.

Riol (Ger) village (Anb): Mosel-Saar-Ruwer. (Ber): Bernkastel. (Gro): Probstberg. (Vin): Römerberg.

Riomaggiore (It) one of five towns in the Cinque Terre, Liguria region.

Rio Negro (Arg) a wine-producing sub-region (2866ha) in the Patagonia region, southern Argentina. Main grape varieties: Cabernet franc, Merlot, Pinot noir, Sémillon.

Rions (Fr) a commune in the Gironde département. Produces red and white wines.

Rion Valley (Geo) a wine valley of the Georgia region. Noted for white wines.

Rio Oja (Sp) a small river (a tributary of the river Ebro) in the Rioja Alta near Haro where the region gets its name.

Rio Plata (Mex) the brand-name of a noted tequila.

Rio Segundo Beer (Arg) a beer brewed for export to the USA.

Riotte [La] (Fr) a Premier Cru vineyard in the A.C.

commune of Morey-Saint-Denis, Côte de Nuits, Burgundy 2.47ha.

Riottes [Les] (Fr) a Premier Cru vineyard in the A.C. commune of Monthélie, Côte de Beaune, Burgundy 0.7ha.

Rio Viejo (Sp) a brand of dry Oloroso Sherry produced by Domecq at Jerez de la Frontera.

Ripaille Blanc (Fr) a dry white wine produced in Savoie.

Riparia (USA) see Vitis riparia.

Riparia x Rupestris (Mad) a rootstock grown in Madeira.

Ripasso (It) a slow fermentation method used for wines similar in style to Valpolicella. The finished wine is refermented (passed over the lees) of Amarone or Recioto.

Ripasso Valpolicella (It) when on the label denotes that the wine has been subjected to the Ripasso process.

Ripe [1] (Eng) the balance between the point of sugar and acid content.

Ripe [2] (Eng) a term used to describe wines that have been made from ripe grapes (not necessarily mature).

Ripon Jewel (Eng) a 5.9% alc by vol. beer brewed by the Daleside Brewery based in Harrogate, North Yorkshire.

Ripley (USA) a white hybrid grape variety that produces dry white wines.

Ripped (USA) a slang term for drunk/intoxicated.

Rippon Vineyard (N.Z) a winery. (Add): Mount Aspiring Road, (P.O. Box 175), Wanaka. 12.8ha. Grape varieties: Chardonnay, Gamay rosé, Gewürztraminer, Merlot, Osteiner, Pinot noir, Riesling, Sauvignon blanc.

Rip Snorter (Eng) a 5% alc by vol. ale brewed by the Hogs Back Brewery Ltd., Surrey.

Riquewihr (Fr) a wine town in the Haut-Rhin in Alsace. (Ger) = Reichenweir.

Riserva (It) a wine aged for a statutory period in cask. (Usually 3–4 years).

Riserva Cambrugiano (It) a Verdicchio di Matelica wine (20% is aged in oak barrels), produced by Belisario, in Matelica.

Riserva del Granduca (It) a Chianti Putto produced by Artimino in Tuscany.

Riserva di Montelera Brut (It) a sparkling (metodo tradizionale) wine produced by Martini and Rossi in the Piemonte region.

Riserva Ducale Oro (It) a riserva Chianti Classico produced from Sangiovese grapes and produced in honour of the official certificate for quality of the Ruffino winery's wines by the Duke of Aosta in the nineteenth century.

Riserva Rara (It) a soft 15 year old brandy from Buton. see Vecchia Romagna.

Riserva Speciale (It) a wine aged for at least 5 years in cask.

Risingsbo Brewery (Swe) a brewery based in Smadjebacken in eastern Sweden.

Risling Italianski (Rus) the name given to the white grape Welschriesling.

Risorgimento (It) lit: 'rebirth', the term used for wine that has passito grapes added to the fermenting must.

Ristow Estate (USA) a winery based in the Napa Valley, California. Grape varieties include: Cabernet sauvignon. Vineyard: Quinta de Pedras.

Ristretto Coffee (It) very strong, black espresso coffee. See also Lungo Coffee.

Ritchie Creek (USA) a small winery (established 1974) based near St. Helena, Napa Valley, California. Grape varieties: Cabernet sauvignon, Chardonnay, Viognier.

Rite Flanker (Eng) a 4.3% alc by vol. ale brewed by the Wickwar Brewing C°. Ltd., Gloucestershire.

Ritsch (Ger) vineyard (Anb): Mosel-Saar-Ruwer. (Ber): Bernkastel. (Gro): Sankt Michael. (Vil): Thörinich.

Rittenhouse (USA) a brand of rye whiskey.

Ritterberg (Ger) vineyard (Anb): Rheinhessen. (Ber): Nierstein. (Gro): Domherr. (Vil): Schornsheim.

Ritter Brauerei (Ger) a brewery (established 1889) based in Dortmund. Brews: Ritter Export, Ritter First. see Dortmunder Ritter.

Ritter Export (Ger) a 5.3% alc by vol. bottled Dortmunder beer brewed by the Dortmunder Ritter Brauerei in Dortmund, Westphalia.

Ritter First (Ger) a 4.8% alc by vol. bottled pilsner brewed by the Dortmunder Ritter Brauerei in Dortmund, Westphalia.

Rittergarten (Ger) vineyard (Anb): Pfalz. (Ber): Mittelhaardt-Deutsche Weinstrasse. (Gro): Hochmess. (Vil): Bad Dürkheim.

Ritterhölle (Ger) vineyard (Anb): Nahe. (Ber): Kreuznach. (Gro): Pfarrgarten. (Vil): Dalberg.

Ritterpfad (Ger) vineyard (Anb): Mosel-Saar-Ruwer. (Ber): Saar-Ruwer. (Gro): Scharzberg. (Vil): Wawern.

Rittersberg (Ger) grosslage (Anb): Baden. (Ber): Badische Bergstrasse/Kraichgau. (Vils): Dossenheim, Grossachsen, Heidelberg, Hemsbach, Hohensachsen, Laudenbach, Leutershausen, Lützelsachsen, Schriesheim, Sulzbach, Weinheim.

Rittersberg (Ger) vineyard (Anb): Pfalz. (Ber): Südliche Weinstrasse. (Gro): Herrlich. (Vil): Ilbesheim.

Rittersheim (Ger) village (Anb): Pfalz. (Ber): Mittelhaardt-Deutsche Weinstrasse. (Gro): Schnepfenflug vom Zellertal. (Vin): Am Hohen Stein.

Ritter von Dürnstein Trocken (Aus) a brand of sekt produced by Inführ, from the Riesling grape.

Rittos, Irmaos. Lda. (Port) a wine producer of Dão wines.

Ritz (Ire) the brand-name of a perry produced by Showerings.

Ritz [The] (Eng) an old nineteenth century tea blend.

Ritz Fizz (Cktl) 1 dash blue Curaçao, 1 dash Amaretto, 1 dash PLJ. Place ingredients into a Champagne flute, stir, top up with iced Champagne and decorate with a rose petal.

Ritzling (Aus) a vineyard site on the banks of the River Danube situated in the Wachau region, Niederösterrich.

Riunite (It) the name of a growers' co-operative based in Emilia-Romagna that receives wine from other co-operatives then blends, matures and bottles it.

Riva [La] (It) a D.O.C. Barbera wine produced by Alfiero Boffa, San Marzano Oliveto, Piemonte. Grapes come from a 1.5ha. vineyard.

Riva [La] (Sp) Sherry shippers based in Jerez de la Frontera. Produce the Fino Sherry Tres Palmas. Other labels include Guadalupe and Royal Cream. Owned by Domecq.

Riva Blanche (Bel) a 5.2% alc by vol. wheat beer from the Riva Brasserie, Dentergem.

Riva Brasserie (Bel) a brewery (established 1896) based at Dentergem. Brews: Riva Blanche, Lucifer, Vondel.

Rivadavia (Arg) a wine-producing area based in the Mendoza region.

Rivaner (Lux) a local name given to the Müller-Thurgau white grape variety.

Rivarey (Sp) red and white wines produced by Bodegas Marqués de Cáceres S.A. Rioja. Red wines made from 85% Tempranillo plus 15% of Garnacha, Graciano, Mazuelo and Viura. Oak matured for 6–12 months and 6 months in bottle. White made from the Viura grape.

Rive (It) a D.O.C. Barbera d'Asti wine produced by Araldici Vini Piemontesi (Add): 14040 Castel Boglione (part of the Poderi Alasia range).

Rivenich (Ger) village (Anb): Mosel-Saar-Ruwer. (Ber): Bernkastel. (Gro): Michelsberg. (Vins): Brauneberg, Geisberg, Niederberg, Rosenberg.

River (Hol) a natural spring mineral water from Heerlen. Mineral contents (milligrammes per litre): Sodium 7mg/l, Calcium 16mg/l, Magnesium 4mg/l, Potassium 2.6mg/l, Bicarbonates 31mg/l, Chlorides 17mg/l, Sulphates 23mg/l, Nitrates 13mg/l, Silicates 3.2mg/l.

Rivera (It) a winery (established in 1950). (Add): SS 98 km. 19,800 Contrada Rivera, 70031 Andria (BA). 85ha. winery based in Puglia. Grape varieties include: Aglianico, Bombino negro, Montepulciano, Nero di troia. Produces wines under the Cappellaccio, Castel del Monte D.O.C. Rosé (from 100% Bombino nero grapes), Il Falcone (70% Nero di Troia, 30% Montepulciano grapes), Puer Apuliae, Triusco. Website: http://www.rivera.it 'E'mail: info@rivera.it

River City (USA) a 5% alc by vol. lager brewed by Evansville Brewery Company, Evansville, Indiana.

River City Brewery (USA) a brewery based in Sacramento, California. Noted for unpasteurised, dry-hopped lager River City Gold 4.8% alc by vol.

River City Gold (USA) see River City Brewery.

River Don (Rus) a wine-producing region based near the Sea of Azov. Contains centres of Constantinovka, Novocherkassk and Tsimliansa. Produces mainly white wines.

River East Vineyard (USA) a vineyard owned by Sonoma Vineyards. Produces Johannisberg riesling grapes.

Riverettes [Les] (Switz) a white wine produced from the Fendant grape in the Valais region.

River Fly (Eng) a light-bodied Fino Sherry from Findlater.

River Grandeur (S.Afr) the label for a range of wines produced by the Viljoendrift Wines winery, Robertson, Western Cape.

Riverhead Brewery Tap Ltd (Eng) a brewery (established 1995). (Add): 2 Peel Street, Marsden, Huddersfield, West Yorkshire HD7 6BR. Brews beers and stout. Website: http://www.riverheadbrewery.co.uk 'E'mail: info@riverheadbrewery.co.uk

Riverhead Estate (N.Z) a brewery. (Add): 1171 Coatesville, Riverhead Highway, RD2 Kumeu, Aukland. Brews a range of beers and lager. Website: http://www.riverhead-estate.co.nz 'E'mail: service@riverhead-estate.co.nz

Riverhead Wines Glenburn Limited (N.Z) the brand-name used by the Glenburn Winery in Riverhead for a range of their wines.

Riverina (Austr) a wine area surrounding the towns of Riverina and Griffith in New South Wales. Noted for white and botrytised sweet wines.

Riverina College Winery (Austr) see College Winery.

Riveris (Ger) village (Anb): Mosel-Saar-Ruwer. (Ber): Saar-Ruwer. (Gro): Römerlay. (Vins): Heiligenhäuschen, Kuhnchen.

Riverland (Austr) a wine area around the Murray Valley region in South Australia/Victoria border. The vineyards are irrigated.

Riverland Chardonnay (Austr) part of Orlando Wines.

Riverlands Winery (N.Z) part of Montana Wines.

Rivero (Sp) a Sherry house based in Jerez de la Frontera.

River Oaks Winery (USA) a winery based in the Alexander Valley, Sonoma County, California. 83ha. Grape varieties: Cabernet sauvignon, Chardonnay, Chenin blanc, Colombard, Gamay and Gewürztraminer. Produces varietal and table wines.

Riverain (S.Afr) the label for a white wine (Chardonnay) produced by the Van Zylshof Estate winery, Robertson, Western Cape.

River Road Winery (USA) a winery based in Forestville, Sonoma County, California. 50ha. Grape varieties: Chardonnay, Johannisberg riesling and Zinfandel. Produces varietal wines.

River Rock (Ire) a natural spring mineral water from The Green, Lambeg, Lisburn, County Antrim, Northern Ireland.

River Run Vintners (USA) a winery based near Watsonville, Monterey County, California. Grape varieties: Cabernet sauvignon, Pinot noir, White riesling and Zinfandel. Produces varietal wines.

River's Edge (S.Afr) the label for a white wine (Chardonnay, Colombard and Sauvignon blanc blend) produced by the Weltevrede Estate winery, Robertson Western Cape.

Riverside (USA) a Californian wine district within the region of Cucamonga. Produces table and dessert wines.

Riverside Wines (N.Z) a winery. (Add): 434 Dartmoor Road, Puketapu, Napier. (P.O. Box 7148, Taradale, Hawkes Bay). 20ha. Grape varieties: Chardonnay, Sauvignon blanc, Cabernet/Merlot.

River's Tale (S.Afr) the export label for a range of wines produced by the Oranjerivier Wine Cellars winery, Lower Orange, Northern Cape.

Riverstone Vineyards (S.Afr) a winery (established 1975) based in Rawsonville, Worcester, Western Cape. 630ha. Grape varieties: Barbera, Cabernet sauvignon, Chardonnay, Chenin blanc, Muscadel, Petit verdot, Sauvignon blanc, Shiraz, Viognier. Labels: Family Reserve, Heron. Website: http://www.merwida.com

River West Vineyard (USA) a vineyard owned by Sonoma Vineyards. Produces Chardonnay grapes.

River White (S.Afr) the label for a white wine (Colombard and Sauvignon blanc blend) produced by the Van Loveren Private Cellar winery, Robertson, Western Cape.

Rivesaltes (Fr) a fortified A.C. red or gold Vin Doux Naturel from the Midi region. Made from Grenache, Macabeo, Malvoisie, Muscat grapes. Minimum age 1 year.

Rivesaltes Ambré (Fr) a light red-brown coloured version of the VdN Rivesaltes.

Rivet Catcher (Eng) a 4% alc by vol. ale brewed by the Jarrow Brewery, Tyne & Wear.

Riviana (It) a natural sparkling mineral water from Riviana, Parma.

Riviera (Cktl) ¼ measure Regnier Framboise, ¼ measure Cointreau, ½ measure white rum. Mix in a tumbler with ice, top with bitter lemon and squeeze over with the juice of ¼ lemon.

Riviera Cocktail (Cktl) (Non-alc) 200mls (⅓ pint) orange juice, 15mls (⅛ gill) Angostura, 25mls (⅕ gill) blackcurrant syrup. Shake over ice, strain into an ice-filled highball glass, dress with an orange slice and serve with straws.

Riviera del Garda Chiaretto (It) a D.O.C. rosé wine from Lombardy. Made from the Barbera, Berzemino, Gropello and Sangiovese grapes.

Riviera del Garda Rosso (It) a D.O.C. red wine from Lombardy. Made from the Barbera, Berzemino, Gropello and Sangiovese grapes. If the minimum alc. content is 12% by vol. and aged 1 year can be classed Superiore.

Riviera Ligure di Ponente (It) a D.O.C. in Liguria which has 225ha. of Pigato planted.

Rivière [Roland] (Fr) a Cognac producer. (Add): Domaine de St-Pardon, Mortiers, 17500 Jarnac. 160ha. in the Fins Bois. Produces five different styles of Cognacs.

Rivivo (It) a natural spring mineral water from Pomerance, Pisa.

Rivola (Sp) a red wine produced by Abadía Retuerta in Ribera del Duero from 60% Tempranillo, 40% Cabernet grapes. 50% of wine is aged in new oak for 3 months.

Rivolet (Fr) a commune in the Beaujolais district. Has A.C. Beaujolais-Villages or Beaujolais-Rivolet status.

Rívolo (It) a white 100% Sauvignon blanc table wine produced by Biondi Santi in Tuscany.

Riwa (M.East) a natural spring mineral water from Syria. Mineral contents (milligrammes per litre): Sodium 2.3mg/l, Calcium 33mg/l, Magnesium 16mg/l, Potassium 0.3mg/l, Bicarbonates 150mg/l, Chlorides 7mg/l, Sulphates 12mg/l, Fluorides 0.1mg/l, Nitrates 1.5mg/l.

Rizling (Hun) riesling.

Rizling-Szemelt (Hun) a light, dry, white wine of Riesling character.

Rizlingszilvàni (Hun) a white grape variety, also known as the Müller-Thurgau. Permitted for retail sale within E.C.

Rizling Vlassky (Czec) lit: 'Riesling of Vlassos', a name for the white grape variety Welschriesling.

Rizvanec (Slo) the local name in Slovenia for the Müller-Thurgau grape.

Rkatsiteli (USA) a white grape variety originating in Georgia. (Chi) = Baiyu.

Rkatsiteli (Rus) a white grape variety. see Rka-ziteli.

Rka-ziteli (Geo) the name for a white grape variety grown in Georgia. See also Rkasiteli.

R.M. (Fr) abbr: Récoltant-Manipulant. Champagne label initials which are registered by the C.I.V.C. for the name belonging to the proprietor of a vineyard who makes and sell his own wines.

R.N. (Fr) abbr: Réserve Nouvelle. In Cognac production given to those Cognacs that had 5 years in cask.

Road House (Eng) a public house (pub) situated on a major highway. Usually incorporates a restaurant.

Road Runner (Cktl) 25mls (1fl.oz) vodka, 5mls (¼ fl.oz) amaretto, 5mls (¼ fl.oz) coconut milk. Shake over ice, strain into a cocktail glass and top with nutmeg.

Roadster (Cktl) ⅓ measure gin, ⅓ measure Grand Marnier, ⅓ measure orange juice. Shake over ice, strain into a cocktail glass and add a twist of lemon.

Road Tanker (Eng) 16000 litres containers usually of several compartments so that many different wines can be transported in bulk at the same time.

Road To Rome (Eng) a 5% alc by vol. premium ale brewed by the Hart Brewery at Little Eccleston, near Preston.

Roaillan (Fr) commune in the A.C. Graves district in the south-western Bordeaux.

Roaix (Fr) a village in the A.C. Côtes du Rhône-Villages. Produces mainly red wines (with a little rosé and white wine).

Roana (It) a sparkling natural spring mineral water from Panico, Massaa, Tuscany. Mineral contents (milligrammes per litre): Sodium 0.65mg/l, Calcium 38.72mg/l, Magnesium 1.09mg/l, Potassium 0.45mg/l, Bicarbonates 115.93mg/l, Chlorides 4.91mg/l, Sulphates 0.49mg/l, Silicates 1.18mg/l. pH 7.45

Roaring Meg (Eng) a pale-coloured cask-conditioned ale 5.5% alc by vol. brewed by the Springhead Brewery, Nottinghamshire.

Roast and Grinders (Eng) coffee trader's slang term for people who make and grind fresh coffee.

Roast and Post Coffee C° [The] (Eng) a coffee manufacturer (established 2002). (Add): Bridgeview House, Redhill Lane, Elberton, Bristol, Avon BS35 4AE. Produces a variety of coffees and teas. Website: http://www.realcoffee.co.uk 'E'mail: sales@realcoffee.co.uk

Roasted Barley (Eng) unmalted, kilned barley used to add colour to porter and stout beers.

Roasting (Eng) a process of heating the green coffee beans to 240°C (464°F) to colour and release chemicals which give the coffee aroma and flavour. *see* Pyrolysis.

Rob (Eng) describes a fruit juice that has been evaporated to a thick syrupy consistency.

Robardelle (Fr) a Premier Cru vineyard [part] in the A.C. commune of Volnay, Côte de Beaune, Burgundy.

Robart [Comte de] (Fr) a Champagne producer. (Add): 14-16 Rue de Bernon, 51200 Épernay.

Robe (Fr) the colour (purple) of wine.

Roberta (Cktl) ⅓ measure dry vermouth, ⅓ measure cherry brandy, ⅓ measure vodka, dash crème de banane, dash Campari. Shake over ice, strain into a cocktail glass and add zest of an orange.

Robert Alexander (S.Afr) the label for a range of red wine (Merlot/Shiraz) produced by the Nico van der Merwe Wines winery, Stellenbosch, Western Cape.

Robert-Allait (Fr) a Champagne producer. (Add): 6, Rue du Parc, 51700 Villers-sous-Chatillon. Produces vintage and non-vintage wines. Labels: Cuvée Brut Réserve, Cuvée Brut Rosé, Cuvée Jordan, Cuvée Prestige, Cuvée Stéphanie. Website: http://www.champagne-robert-allait.com 'E'mail: champagne.allait@wanadoo.fr

Roberta May (Cktl) ⅓ measure aurum, ⅓ measure vodka, ⅓ measure orange juice, dash egg white, shake and strain into a cocktail glass.

Robert Brown (Jap) a brand of whiskey produced by Seagram and the Kirin Brewery.

Robert Burns Cocktail (Cktl) 25mls (1fl.oz) Scotch whisky, 10mls (½ fl.oz) sweet vermouth, dash Pernod, dash Angostura. Stir over ice and strain into a cocktail glass.

Robert Burns Scottish Ale (Scot) a 4.2% alc by vol. ale from Tennent Caledonian.

Robert Cain Brewery (Eng) *see* Cain (Robert) Brewery. Website: http://www.cains.co.uk

Robert Craig (USA) a winery based in the Mount Veeder, Napa Valley, California. (Add): 625 Imperial Way, Suite One, Napa, CA 94559. Grape varieties: Cabernet sauvignon. Website: http://www.robertcraigwine.com

Robert E. Lee Cooler (Cktl) dissolve ½ teaspoon of sugar into juice of ½ a lime and a little water in a highball glass. Add ice, 50mls (2fl.ozs) gin and 2 dashes Pernod. Top with ginger ale and dress with a spiral of lemon peel.

Robert Foley (USA) a winery based in the Napa Valley, California. Grape varieties include: Cabernet sauvignon. Label: Claret.

Robert Keenan Winery (USA) *see* Keenan Winery.

Robert Mondavi Winery (USA) *see* Mondavi Winery.

Roberto Voerzio (It) a winery based in the DOCG Barolo, Piemonte. Label: Cerequio.

Robert Parker (USA) a famous wine commentator and assessor of quality of the world's wines who uses an assessment grading system of 100 points for a perfect wine. Website: http://www.erobertparker.com 'E'mail: info@erobertparker.com

Robert Pecota Winery (USA) *see* Pecota Winery.

Roberts (Eng) the trading name for a chain (229) of wine shops run by Imperial Retail Shops Ltd. (a division of Courage Ltd).

Robert Setrakian Vineyards (USA) *see* Setrakian Vineyards.

Robertson (S.Afr) a district in the Breede River Valley. Noted for Muscat dessert wines and brandy.

Robertson and Baxter (Scot) a company (established 1857), one of the Lang Brothers subsidiaries. Were originally whisky blenders.

Robertson Bros (Port) Vintage Port shippers. Vintages: 1942, 1945, 1947, 1955, 1963, 1966, 1967, 1970, 1972, 1975, 1977, 1980, 1983, 1985, 1991, 1994, 1997, 2003. Subsidiary of Sandemans. Ships Rebello Valente vintage port, also Gamebird Ruby and Tawny Ports.

Robertson Koöperatief Wynmakery (S.Afr) a co-operative winery (established 1941) based in Robertson, Western Cape. 190ha. (Add): Box 37, Robertson 6705. Grape varieties: Cabernet sauvignon, Chardonnay, Chenin blanc, Colombard, Gewürztraminer, Johannisberger riesling, Merlot, Muscadel, Pinotage, Ruby cabernet, Sauvignon blanc, Shiraz, Stein, Weisser riesling. Labels: Almond Grove, Beaukett, Kings River, Natural Light, N°1 Constitution Road, Old Chapel, Phanto Ridge, Prospect Hill, Robroi, Vineyard Selection, Wide River Reserve, Wolfkloof. Website: http://www.robertsonwinery.co.za

Robert's Pride (Eng) a winter ale brewed by Hall and Woodhouse Badger Brewery, Dorset.

Robert Stemmler Winery (USA) *see* Stemmler Winery.

Robert Weil (Ger) a winery based in the Rheingau (owned by Suntory since 1988).

Robert Young Vineyards (USA) *see* Young Vineyards.

Robespierre (Fr) a strong bière de garde from La Choulette 7.5% alc by vol.

Robigato (Port) a white grape variety used in the making of Port.

Robin (Eng) a seasonal ale brewed by Frederic Robinson Ltd., Unicorn Brewery, Stockport, Cheshire (available near Christmas).

Robin [Jules] (Fr) a Cognac producer. (Add): 36 Rue Gabriel Jaulin, 16103 Cognac (part of the Martell group).

Robin Fils (USA) producers of sparkling wines based near New York. Labels includes Pol d'Argent.

Robin Hood Ale (Eng) a bottled pale ale 1045 O.G. brewed by the Home Brewery, Nottingham.

Robino Bodegas y Viñedos (Arg) a winery based in the Mendoza region, eastern Argentina. Websites: http://www.bodegarobino.com/http://www.orbitasua.com 'E'mail: info@bodegarobino.com

Robin's Nest Cocktail (Cktl) ⅗ measure vodka, ⅗ measure cranberry juice, ⅕ measure (white) crème de menthe. Shake over ice and strain into a cocktail glass.

Robinson [Frederic] (Eng) a brewery. (Add): Frederic Robinson Ltd., Unicorn Brewery, Stockport, Cheshire SK1 1JJ. Noted for cask-conditioned Old Tom 8.5% alc by vol (1080 O.G),. Old Stockport 3.5% alc by vol. Hatter's Mild 3.3% alc by vol. Frederics 5% alc by vol. XB 4% alc by vol. Cock Robin 1035 O.G. Einhorn Lager 1035 O.G. Best Bitter 4.2% alc by vol. Lighthouse 4% alc by vol., Whistling Will 4% alc by vol. Coopers Bell, Double Hop Premium ale 5% alc by vol., Robin Bitter 4.5% alc by vol., Samuel Oldknow Bitter, Smooth Bitter 3.8% alc by vol. Sunny Jim 3.8% alc by vol. Unicorn Best Bitter 4.2% alc by vol., young Tom 4% alc by vol. Took over the Hartley Brewery in Cumbria in 1982. Website: http://www.frederick-robinson.co.uk 'E'mail: brewery@frederick-robinson.co.uk

Robinsons (Eng) the brand-name used by Colman's of Norwich, Norfolk for a range of non-alcoholic soft fruit drinks.

Robinsons Barley Water (Eng) a famous non-alcoholic fruit drink made from citrus juice, sugar and cooked barley flour by Colman's of Norwich, Norfolk.

Robinsons Family Vineyard (Austr) a winery. (Add): Lyra Church Road, Ballandean, Queensland. 18ha. Grape varieties: Cabernet sauvignon, Chardonnay, Gewürztraminer, Malbec, Merlot, Pinot noir, Sauvignon blanc, Shiraz.

Robinvale Winery (Austr) part of the McWilliams Vineyards in New South Wales. Bio-dynamic. Also a winery in Murray River, Victoria.

Robinwood Brewery (Eng) now no longer in existence. Originally brewed Old Fart in Todmorden, West Yorkshire. Now superseded by Merriman's Hunslet Brewery in Leeds.

Robiola (It) a white grape variety more commonly known as Ribolla.

Robka (Austr) the brand-name of an Australian vodka.

Roble (Chile) casks made from Chilian oak.

Roble (Sp) oak.

Robola (Gre) a white grape variety grown on the Isle of Cephalonia. Used to produce dry white wines of same name.

Robola (Gre) a dry, white A.O.Q.S. wine made on Cephalonia Island. Also spelt Rombola.

Robola de Cephalonia (Gre) *see* Robola.

Robroi (S.Afr) a full-bodied red wine made from Cabernet 85% and Tinta barocca 15% grape varieties. Oak matured, produced by the Robertson Koöperatiewe.

Rob Roy [1] (Cktl) 1½ measures Scotch whisky, ½ measure Italian vermouth, dash Angostura. Stir over ice and strain into a cocktail glass.

Rob Roy [2] (Cktl) 30mls (¼ gill) Scotch whisky, 90mls (¾ gill) French vermouth, 2 dashes Angostura, 2 dashes gomme syrup. Stir over ice, strain into a cocktail glass, add a cherry and a squeeze of lemon peel juice.

Rob Roy [3] (Cktl) 20mls (⅙ gill) French vermouth, 20mls (⅙ gill) Scotch whisky, 2 dashes Angostura, 1 dash orange bitters, 2 dashes brown Curaçao. Stir over ice, strain into a cocktail glass, serve with a cherry and dash of lemon peel juice.

Rob Roy (Scot) a blended Scotch whisky produced by Stanley P. Morrison 40% alc by vol.

Robson Cocktail (Cktl) 40mls (⅓ gill) Jamaican rum, 40mls (⅓ gill) orange juice, 4 dashes grenadine, 4 dashes lemon juice. Shake over ice and strain into a cocktail glass.

Robson Vineyard (Austr) a winery. (Add): Mount View, Hunter Valley, New South Wales. 5ha. Grape varieties: Cabernet sauvignon, Chardonnay, Hermitage, Malbec, Merlot, Pinot noir, Sauvignon blanc, Traminer.

Robust (Chi) a natural spring mineral water from Guangzhou. Mineral contents (milligrammes per litre): Sodium 1–20mg/l, Calcium 1–12mg/l, Magnesium 1–8mg/l, Potassium 0.05–5mg/l, Bicarbonates 20–100mg/l, Sulphates 0.1–8mg/l, Silicates >19.2mg/l. pH 6.0/pH 8.5

Robust (Eng) the term used by a wine taster to describe a sturdy, full-bodied wine.

Robusta Coffee (Afr) *see Coffea canephora.*

Robusto (S.Afr) the label for a white wine (Chenin blanc) produced by the Rudera Wines winery, Stellenbosch, Western Cape.

Robyn (S.Afr) the label for a red wine (Cabernet sauvignon, Pinotage, Shiraz and Tinta blend) produced by the Middelvlei Estate winery, Stellenbosch, Western Cape.

Roc (Fr) a proprietary apéritif.

Rocallaura (Sp) a natural spring mineral water from Vallbona de les Monges, Lleida.

Roc Amadour (Fr) a liqueur made from Armagnac and juniper berries made by Denoix of Brive.

Rocamar (Sp) the brand-name of a range of red, rosé and white wines from the D.O. Valencia region supplied in England by I.D.V.

Roc Blanquant (Fr) a vineyard. (Add): 33330 Saint-Émilion, (Com): Saint-Émilion. A.C. Saint-Émilion, Bordeaux.

Roc Blanquet (Fr) the second wine of Château Belair Grand Cru Classé A.C. Saint-Émilion, Bordeaux.

Rocca (It) an honoury title awarded to the best wines annually.

Rocca [La] (It) a Cru D.O.C. Soave produced by Pieropan from 100% Garganega grapes, fermented and matured in wood. *See also* Calvarino, Colombare Recioto di Soave Classico (Le).

Roccabianca (It) a sparkling natural spring mineral water from Messina, Sicily. Mineral contents (milligrammes per litre): Sodium 14.5mg/l, Calcium 22.9mg/l, Magnesium 10.6mg/l, Potassium 2.2mg/l, Bicarbonates 112.9mg/l, Chlorides 18.8mg/l, Sulphates 19.6mg/l, Fluorides 0.7mg/l, Nitrates 5.7mg/l, Silicates 9.2mg/l. pH 7.65

Rocca dei Giorgi (It) a sparkling (metodo tradizionale) wine produced by Gancia in the Piemonte region.

Rocca delle Macie (It) a winery in the DOCG Chianti Classico based in the Tuscany region.

Rocca di Montegrossi (It) a winery in the DOCG Chianti Classico, Tuscany region. Produces Chianti Classico Riserva. Label: San Marcellino.

Roccaforte (It) a natural spring mineral water (established 1965) from Roccaforte, Mondovi (CN).

Rocca Galgana (It) a sparkling natural spring mineral water from Parma. Mineral contents (milligrammes per litre): Sodium 7.1mg/l, Calcium 17.43mg/l, Magnesium 39.52mg/l, Potassium 0.36mg/l, Bicarbonates 176.29mg/l, Chlorides 5.03mg/l, Sulphates 60.98mg/l, Oxygen 7.71mg/l, Nitrates 2.89mg/l, Silicates 20.65mg/l. pH 7.85

Rocchetta (It) a still and sparkling natural spring mineral water from Rocchetta, Gualdo Tadino. Mineral contents (milligrammes per litre): Sodium 4.66mg/l, Calcium 57.12mg/l, Magnesium 3.48mg/l, Potassium 0.54mg/l, Bicarbonates 178.4mg/l, Chlorides 7.9mg/l, Sulphates 8.27mg/l, Fluorides 0.11mg/l, Nitrates 1.41mg/l, Silicates 5.37mg/l. pH 7.46

Rocco Bay (S.Afr) the label for a range of wines produced by the Bottelay Wine International winery, Stellenbosch, Western Cape.

Rocco Bay (S.Afr) the label for a range of wines for the Swedish market produced by the Nordale Winery, Robertson, Western Cape.

Roc des Cambes (Fr) a 10ha. A.C. Côtes de Bourg plus 4ha. sold as Domaine des Cambes A.C. Bordeaux (rouge). Grape varieties: 55% Merlot, 20% Cabernet sauvignon, 15% Cabernet franc, 10% Malbec.

Rocha (Port) a producer of vintage Port. Vintages: 1990, 1991, 1994, 2003.

Roche [La] (Ger) vineyard (Anb): Rheinhessen. (Ber): Bingen. (Gro): Adelberg. (Vil): Flonheim.

Roche (It) an alternative name for the Ruchè grape.

Roche-aux-Moines [La] (Fr) a famous vineyard in the A.C. Savennières, Anjou-Saumur district in the Loire. 25ha. Produces quality sweet and dry white wines from the Chenin blanc grape. *See also* Coulée de Serrant.

Roche Claire (Fr) a natural spring mineral water. Mineral contents (milligrammes per litre): Sodium 5mg/l, Calcium 55mg/l, Magnesium 24mg/l, Chlorides 5mg/l, Sulphates 10mg/l, Fluorides 0.15mg/l. pH 7.57

Rochecorbon (Fr) a commune in the A.C. Vouvray, Touraine district of the Loire.

Roche des Ecrins (Fr) a natural spring mineral water

from Chorges, Hautes Alpes. Mineral contents (milligrammes per litre): Sodium 1.4mg/l, Calcium 63mg/l, Magnesium 10.2mg/l, Potassium 0.6mg/l, Bicarbonates 173.2mg/l, Chlorides <1mg/l, Sulphates 51.3mg/l, Nitrates 2mg/l. pH 7.6

Rochefort Brasserie (Bel) a Trappist abbaye brewery based near Dinant in south-east Belgium. Produces copper-coloured, bottle-conditioned bières. *see* Rochefort Double, Rochefort Triple.

Rochefort Double (Bel) a strong dark Trappist ale 9.2% alc by vol. from the Rochefort Brasserie.

Rochefort-sur-Loire (Fr) a commune of the Coteaux du Layon, Anjou-Saumur district of the Loire. Sweet white wines.

Rochefort Triple (Bel) an extra-strong Trappist ale 11.3% alc by vol. from the Rochefort Brasserie.

Rochegude (Fr) a village in the A.C. Côtes du Rhône-Villages. Produces mainly red wines (with a little rosé and white wine).

Rochelle [La] (S.Afr) a wine and brandy company based in Bonnievale. Also noted for fortified wines.

Roche Pourrie (Fr) the name given to the disintegrating schist soil in the Mâcon district of Burgundy.

Roches [Les] (Fr) a vineyard in the A.C. Pouilly-Fumé, Central Vineyards, Loire. (Add): 58150 Pouilly-sur-Loire.

Rocheval (Fr) a natural spring mineral water from Source Aurele, Jandun. Mineral contents (milligrammes per litre): Sodium 4.1mg/l, Calcium 98mg/l, Magnesium 4mg/l, Potassium 1.9mg/l, Bicarbonates 269mg/l, Chlorides 3.6mg/l, Sulphates 43mg/l, Nitrates 2mg/l.

Rochford (Austr) a winery (established 1988) based at Romsey Park, Rochford, Victoria. Grape varieties: Cabernet sauvignon, Pinot noir, Riesling.

Rochusfels (Ger) vineyard (Anb): Mosel-Saar-Ruwer. (Ber): Obermosel. (Gro): Gipfel. (Vil): Köllig.

Rochusfels (Ger) vineyard (Anb): Mosel-Saar-Ruwer. (Ber): Obermosel. (Gro): Gipfel. (Vil): Nittel.

Rociador (Sp) the name for the perforated pipes used to refresh wine casks.

Rociar (Sp) to refresh an old solera with young new wine.

Rock [Hugh] (Eng) a wine-producer based at Loddon Park Farm, Twyford, Berkshire.

Rock and Rum (USA) a liqueur based as for Rock and Rye.

Rock and Rye (USA) a liqueur with a rye whiskey base, but including grain neutral spirits, rock candy syrup and fruits (lemons, oranges and cherries) the sugar crystallises inside the bottle.

Rock and Rye Cooler (Cktl) 75mls (⅔ gill) vodka, 50mls (⅓ gill) Rock and Rye, juice ¼ lime. Shake over ice, strain into an ice-filled highball glass, top with bitter lemon and a slice of lime.

Rock Bitter (Eng) a 3.8% alc by vol. bitter ale brewed by the Nottingham Brewery, Nottinghamshire.

Rock Crystal (Eng) a type of glass from Thomas Webb.

R

Rocket (Eng) a 3.5% alc by vol. ale from Firecracker and Firkin, Brighton Road, Crawley.

Rockfied (S.Afr) the label for a range of white wines produced by the Du Preez Estate winery, Worcester, Western Cape.

Rock Fish Grill & Anacortes Brewery (USA) a brewery. (Add): 320 Commercial avenue, Anacortes, Washington 98221. Brews beers and lager. Website: http://www.anacortesrockfish.com 'E'mail: info@anacortesrockfish.com

Rocket Fuel (Eng) a 5% alc by vol. seasonal ale brewed by Hydes at 46 Moss Lane, West Manchester, Lancashire, available November and December, part of their Craft Ale range.

Rockhead Spring (Eng) a natural spring mineral water from Buxton, Derbyshire.

Rock Hill Farm (USA) a 100° and 80° US proof single barrel Bourbon whiskies from Ancient Age in Leestown, Frankfort, Kentucky.

Rocking Robin (Eng) a summer ale brewed by the Hale and Hearty Brewery in Surrey using strawberry extract.

Rockingham Ales (Eng) a brewery (established 1997). (Add): C/o 25 Wansford Road, Elton, Peterborough, Cambridgeshire PE8 6RZ. Brews: A1 Amber Ale 4% alc by vol., Dark Forest 5% alc by vol., Fruits of the Forest 4.5% alc by vol., Hop Devil 3.9% alc by vol., Saxon Cross 4.1% alc by vol. Website: http://www.rockinghamales.co.uk 'E'mail: brian@rockinghamales.co.uk

Rocking Rudolph (Eng) a 5.5% alc by vol. cask-conditioned premium seasonal ale produced by Hardys and Hansons at their Kimberley Brewery, Nottingham under the Cellarman's Cask banner.

Rock Lodge Vineyard (Eng) a vineyard (established 1965). (Add): Scaynes Hill, Sussex. 14.5ha. Soil: sandy loam. Grape varieties: Müller-Thurgau, Ortega, Reichensteiner.

Rock Mild (Eng) a 3.8% alc by vol. mild ale brewed by the Nottingham Brewery, Nottinghamshire.

Rockpile (USA) a new A.V.A. in the Sonoma County, California.

Rock's Country Wines (Eng) a range of wines produced by Hugh Rock, Loddon Park Farm, Twyford, Berkshire.

Rocks Glass (USA) is similar in style to an old fashioned glass but has a slightly wider mouth than base.

Rockwood (S.Afr) the label for a red wine (Shiraz 49% plus Cabernet sauvignon and Merlot blend) produced by the Kanu Wines winery, Stellenbosch, Western Cape.

Rockwood Cellars (N.Z.) a winery. (Add): Omahu Road, Hastings. Grape varieties: Chardonnay, Sauvignon blanc, Sémillon, Cabernet/Merlot.

Rocky Cellar (Hun) the brand-name used for the pilsener-style beers in Dreher.

Rocky Grove (USA) a natural spring mineral water from Titusville, Pennsylvania.

Rocky Mountain Cooler (Cktl) shake together over ice 1 egg, juice of a lemon and gomme syrup to taste. Strain into a highball glass, top with iced cider and a little grated nutmeg.

Rocky Mountain Spring (Can) a natural spring mineral water from Hinton, Alabama. Mineral contents (milligrammes per litre): Sodium 3.7mg/l, Calcium 40.9mg/l, Magnesium 6.2mg/l, Potassium 1.1mg/l, Bicarbonates 161mg/l, Chlorides 1.4mg/l, Sulphates 5.8mg/l, Fluorides 0.19mg/l. pH 7.4

Rococo (Eng) a light and elegant glass (circa 1705–1745)

Rococo Cocktail (Cktl) ⅔ measure kirsch, ⅓ measure orange juice, ⅙ measure Triple Sec. Shake over ice and strain into a cocktail glass.

Rocoules [Les] (Fr) a vineyard in the A.C. Hermitage, northern Rhône.

Rocquette (Ch.Isles) a 6% alc by vol. traditional bottled dry cider produced by the Guernsey Cider Company.

Roc Vert (W.Afr) a natural spring mineral water from Bamako, Mali. Mineral contents (milligrammes per litre): Sodium 2.3mg/l, Calcium 17.6mg/l, Magnesium 46.5mg/l, Potassium 6.2mg/l, Bicarbonates 260mg/l, Chlorides 3mg/l, Nitrates 1mg/l.

Rocwell Spring (Ire) a natural spring mineral water from Pomeroy, County Tyrone, Northern Ireland. Mineral contents (milligrammes per litre): Sodium 10.9mg/l, Calcium 41.8mg/l, Magnesium 13.1mg/l, Potassium 2mg/l, Bicarbonates 202mg/l, Chlorides 12mg/l, Sulphates <10mg/l.

Rödchen (Ger) vineyard (Anb): Rheingau. (Ber): Johannisberg. (Gro): Steinmacher. (Vil): Martinsthal.

Roddis Cellars (USA) a small winery based near Calistoga, Napa Valley, California. Grape variety: Cabernet sauvignon.

Röde (Ger) vineyard (Anb): Württemberg. (Ber): Kocher-Jagst-Tauber. (Gro): Tauberberg. (Vil): Reinsbronn.

Rödelsee (Ger) village (Anb): Franken. (Ber): Steigerwald. (Gro): Schlossberg. (Vins): Küchenmeister, Schwanleite.

Rodenbach Alexander (Bel) a 6.5% alc by vol. red beer with the addition of cherry essence (Grand Cru plus essence). Brewed by the Rodenbach Brasserie.

Rodenbach Brasserie (Bel) a brewery (established 1836). (Add): Spanjestraat 133-141, Roeselare B-8800. Noted for Rodenbach (Grand Cru) 5.25% alc by vol light-hopped, sour beer matured 2 years in which time a lactic fermentation occurs and is blended with a younger version of Rodenbach. *See also* Alexander Rodenbach, Redbach and Rodenbach Classic. Website: http://www.rodenbach.be 'E'mail: visit.rodenbach@palmbreweries.com

Rodenbach Classic (Bel) a 5% alc by vol. bottled West Flanders brown beer with a sour fruity aroma, brewed by the Rodenbach Brasserie, Roeselare. A blend of 6 week old beer and 2 year old oak matured beer.

Rodenbach Grand Cru (Bel) a 6% alc by vol. light-hopped, top-fermented bottled West Flanders brown beer from the Rodenbach Brasserie, Roeselare. Matured in oak.

Rodeorm (Swe) a brand of mead produced by the Till Brewery.

Rödersheim-Gronau (Ger) village (Anb): Pfalz. (Ber): Mittelhaardt-Deutsche Weinstrasse. (Gro): Hofstück. (Vin): Fuchsloch.

Rodet [Antonin] (Fr) a négociant-eleveur based in Mercurey, Côte Chalonnaise, Burgundy.

Rodet [Jacques] (Fr) propriétaire-récoltant based in Tauriac, Gironde. Produces Château Brulesécaille.

Rode Wijn (Hol) claret.

Roditis (Gre) a grape variety used mainly in spirit production. *See also* Rhoditis.

Roditys (Gre) a fairly dry, fragrant rosé wine.

Rodney Decanter (Eng) the name given to the ship's decanter of the time of Admiral Rodney in the eighteenth century. Has a ringed neck.

Rodney Strong (USA) a winery (established 1961) based in the Russian River Valley, Sonoma County, California (also in Mendocino County). 2350ha. (Add): 11455 Old Redwood Hinghway, Healdsburg, CA 95448. Grape varieties include: Cabernet sauvignon, Pinot noir. Label: Jane's Vineyard. Website: http://www.rodneystrong.com

Rodriguez y Berger (Sp) noted wine-producers based in the La Mancha region.

Rod Tuborg (Den) a red label Tuborg lager produced by Carlsberg, a Münchener-style beer.

Rødvin (Den) red wine.

Roederer [Louis] (Fr) a Champagne producer. (Add): 21 Boulevard Lundy, B.P. 66, 51530 Reims Cedex. A Grande Marque. 190ha. Produces vintage and non-vintage wines. Vintages: 1900, 1904, 1906, 1911, 1913, 1914, 1915, 1919, 1921, 1923, 1926, 1928, 1929, 1932, 1933, 1934, 1935, 1937, 1938, 1941, 1942, 1943, 1945, 1947, 1948, 1949, 1952, 1953, 1955, 1959, 1960, 1961, 1962, 1963, 1964, 1966, 1967, 1969, 1971, 1973, 1974, 1975, 1976, 1979, 1980, 1982, 1983, 1985, 1986, 1988, 1989, 1990, 1991, 1995, 1996, 1998, 1999, 2001. Produces Cristal Brut (in a white glass bottle). Also Linked with Roederer Estate and produces Quartet in USA.

Roederer [Théophile] (Fr) a Champagne producer. (Add): 20 Rue Andrieux, B.P. 1214, 51058 Reims Cedex. Produces vintage and non-vintage wines.

Roederer Estate (USA) a winery. (Add): 4501 Highway, 128 Philo, California. Winery based in Anderson Valley, California. Produces traditional method wines from Chardonnay and Pinot noir. Labels include Quartet. Prestige cuvée: L'Hermitage.

Roemer (Ger) a medium-stemmed decorated glass used for German wines that has a tapered stem (brown or green). Not to be confused with the 'hock' glass used for Rhine wines. *see* Prunt.

Roemer (Hol) a toasting glass used in the nineteenth century. Was egg-shaped and short-stemmed. *See also* Rummer.

Roemerblut (Switz) a red (grand vin) produced by Martigny in the Valais from the Pinot noir.

Roero (It) a D.O.C. red wine (introduced 1985) in central Piemonte. Made from the Nebbiolo grape. Pre 1985 was known as Nebbiolo d'Alba.

Roeselare Brasserie (Bel) a brewery based in western Flanders that brews red beers.

Roetschelt (Lux) a vineyard site in the village of Bech-Kleinmacher.

Roeulx Brasserie (Bel) a brewery in central Belgium noted for St. Feuillion (a golden abbaye beer).

Roffignac [Comte Ferdinand de] (Fr) a Cognac producer. (Add): Château Chesnel, B.P. 113, 16104. 34ha. in Borderies. Produces Vieille Fine Champagne 20 years old, Extra Grande Champagne 25–30 years old.

Roga (Port) a band of pruners who cut back the vines in the Douro in the winter season.

Rogaska-Quell Heilwasser (Slo) a natural spring mineral water (established 1865). Mineral contents (milligrammes per litre): Sodium 1170mg/l, Calcium 398mg/l, Magnesium 859mg/l, Potassium 22mg/l, Bicarbonates 6605mg/l, Chlorides 51mg/l, Sulphates 1574mg/l.

Roger (Cktl) 35mls (1½ fl.ozs) each of gin, peach juice, orange juice, 2 dashes lemon juice. Shake over ice and strain into an ice-filled highball glass.

Roger & Out (Eng) a strong 16.9% alc by vol. beer brewed in Yorkshire (overtaken by Uncle Igor in strength).

Roger's Special Beer (Eng) a cask-conditioned ale 1065 O.G. brewed by the Frog and Parrot (Whitbread) home-brew public house in Sheffield, Yorkshire.

Rogge (Hol) rye.

Roggen (Ger) rye.

Rognage (Fr) describes the pruning of vine shoots to reduce the vegetation and force the sap to travel through the branches.

Rogues Rouge (S.Afr) *see* Mereaux.

Rogue Valley (USA) a 267ha. appellation south of Umpqua Valley, Oregon. Has the sub-regions: Illinois Valley, Applegate Valley, Rogue River Valley. Vineyards include: Bridge View, Foris, Valley View.

Rohrendorfer Gebling (Aus) a vineyard site on the banks of the River Danube in the Kremstal region.

Rohracker (Ger) village (Anb): Württemberg. (Ber): Remstal-Stuttgart. (Gro): Weinsteige. *see* Stuttgart.

Rohrbach (Ger) village (Anb): Pfalz. (Ber): Südliche Weinstrasse. (Gro): Herrlich. (Vin): Schäfergarten.

Rohrbach (Ger) village (Anb): Pfalz. (Ber): Südliche Weinstrasse. (Gro): Kloster Liebfrauenberg. (Vin): Mandelpfad.

Rohrbach a Gr (Ger) village (Anb): Baden. (Ber): Badische Bergstrasse/Kraichgau. (Gro): Stiftsberg. (Vil): Lerchenberg.

Roi de Rome (Fr) an 1811 distilled Cognac 31% alc by vol. produced by A.E. Dor in Jarnac.

Rois de France (Fr) a 30 year old Cognac produced by Rouyer.

Rojal Blanco (Sp) the alternative name used for Subirat and Malvasia riojana grape.

Rokko No Oishii Mizu (Jap) a natural spring mineral water (established 1983) from the Rokko Mountains. Mineral contents (milligrammes per litre): Sodium 18mg/l, Calcium 24mg/l, Magnesium 6mg/l, Potassium 0.3mg/l, Bicarbonates 83mg/l.

Roland Champion (Fr) a Champagne producer. (Add): 19, Grande Rue, 51530 Chouilly. 20ha. Produces vintage and non-vintage wines. Vintages: 1995, 1996, 1997, 1998, 2000. A member of the Club Tresors de Champagne. Labels: Cuvée Aramis, Cuvée 'Special Club' Millésimée.

Rolande [La] (Fr) a vineyard in the A.C. Châteauneuf-du-Pape, southern Rhône.

Roland's Reserve (S.Afr) a red wine (Cabernet sauvignon) produced by the Seidelberg Estate, Paarl, Western Cape.

Roleto (It) a barrique fermented Chardonnay produced by Araldici Vini Piemontesi, 14040 Castel Boglione. Part of the Poderi Alasia range of wines.

Roliand [Bernard] (Fr) récoltants-manipulants in Champagne. (Add): 21 Rue Corbier, Mareuil. Produces vintage and non-vintage wines.

Rolin [Nicolas] (Fr) the founder of the Hospices de Beaune, Beaune, Burgundy in 1443. Also the name for certain cuvées in En Genêt 0.4ha. Les Cents Vignes 1.5ha. and Les Grèves 0.8ha. (all Premier Cru Beaune vineyards which are owned by the Hospices de Beaune).

Rolinck [A.] Brauerei (Ger) a brewery based in Steinfurt. Brews: Rolinck Pilsener Premium.

Rolinck Pilsener Premium (Ger) a 4.7% alc by vol. bottled pilsener brewed by A. Rolinck Brauerei, Steinfurt.

Rolle (Fr) a white grape variety grown in A.C. Bellet, Provence.

Roller Disco (Cktl) place 25mls (⅕ gill) cherry brandy into an ice-filled highball glass and top with bitter lemon.

Rolling Hills (S.Afr) the label for a range of wines produced by the Doninion Wine Company winery, Stellenbosch, Western Cape.

Rolling Rock (USA) a 5% alc by vol. straw-coloured, green bottled premium lager. Brewed by the Old Latrobe Brewery in Pennsylvania.

Rolling Rock Extra Pale (USA) a 4.5% alc by vol. pale straw-coloured, green bottled lager. Brewed by the Pittsburgh Brewing Company, Pennsylvania

Rolls-Royce [1] (Cktl) ⅓ measure Cointreau, ⅓ measure brandy, ⅓ measure orange juice. Shake over ice and strain into a cocktail glass.

Rolls-Royce [2] (Cktl) ⅗ measure dry gin, ⅕ measure dry vermouth, ⅕ measure sweet vermouth, 2 dashes Bénédictine. Stir over ice and strain into a cocktail glass.

Rolly-Gassmann (Fr) a wine-producer based in Alsace. (Add): 1–2 Rue de l'Église, 68590 Rorschwihr.

Rom (Den) rum.

Roma (Austr) a wine-producing area based in Queensland.

Roma (USA) a label used by the Guild Wineries and Distilleries.

Roma Director's Choice Brandy (USA) the brand-name of a brandy bottled by the Guild of Wineries and Distilleries at Lodi, California.

Romagnano (It) a red wine produced by Bruno Colacicchi in the Latium region.

Romaine (Fr) a natural spring mineral water from Romaine, Montfras. Mineral contents (milligrammes per litre): Sodium 10.6mg/l, Calcium 96mg/l, Magnesium 6.1mg/l, Potassium 3.7mg/l, Bicarbonates 297.7mg/l, Chlorides 22.6mg/l, Sulphates 9.3mg/l, Silicates 30.8mg/l. pH 7.3

Roman (Bel) a natural spring mineral water from Roman, Oudenaarde.

Roman Brasserie (Bel) a brewery (established 1545) based near Oudenaarde-Mater. Produces: Sloeber (a Duvel beer), Mater (a brown ale named after the village), Brunor (a brown ale) and Dobbelen Bruinen (a double-brown ale).

Romancero (Sp) a solera reserva brandy from Gil Galan. See also Condestable, Formidable, Legislador.

Romance Royale (Cktl) into a large cocktail glass place some crushed ice, then pour in order, 10mls (½ fl.oz) Roses lime cordial, 10mls (½ fl.oz) Coco-Ribe and 25mls (1fl.oz) Bols Parfait Amour. Serve with straws.

Romanèche-Thorins (Fr) a commune in the Beaujolais district. Has A.C. Beaujolais-Villages or Beaujolais-Romanèche-Thorins status.

Romanée (Fr) a famous Grand Cru vineyard in the A.C. commune of Vosne-Romanée, Côte de Nuits, Burgundy. 0.83ha. Also known as La Romanée.

Romanée [La] (Fr) a famous Premier Cru vineyard [part] in the A.C. commune of Chassagne-Montrachet, Côte de Beaune, Burgundy 3.16ha.

Romanée-Conti (Fr) a famous Grand Cru vineyard in the A.C. commune of Vosne-Romanée, Côte de Nuits, Burgundy 1.87ha.

Romanée la Tâche (Fr) a famous Grand Cru vineyard in the A.C. commune of Vosne-Romanée, Côte de Nuits, Burgundy. Also known as La Tâche 6ha.

Romanée-Saint-Vivant (Fr) a Grand Cru vineyard in the A.C. commune of Vosne-Romanée, Côte de Nuits, Burgundy. 8.5ha. Also known as La Romanée-Saint-Vivant.

Romanesti (Mol) a red wine from Moldovia. Produced in the Bordeaux style from Malbec, Merlot and Cabernet sauvignon grapes.

Roman Glass (It) the Romans were producing a crude form of drinking glasses 100BC.

Romania (Rum) wine-producing country. Main regions: Cotnari, Dealul-Mare, Murfatler, Tîrnave. Produces red and white wines. Most esteemed wine is Cotnari, a white dessert wine.

Romano Cream (Sp) a brand of Cream Sherry produced by Gonzalez Byass in Jerez de la Frontera.

Romanoff (Cktl) ⅓ measure crème de fraise, ⅓ measure Cointreau, ⅓ measure cream, dash lemon juice, dash egg white. Shake well over ice, strain

R

into a flute glass, dress with a fresh strawberry and sprig of mint.

Romanoff (Eng) a brand-name, British-made vodka from Grants of St. James 40% alc by vol.

Romanoff Cocktail (Cktl)(Non-alc) ⅓ measure sirop de fraises, ⅓ measure orange juice, ⅓ measure cream, dash lemon juice, dash egg white. Shake well over ice, strain into a flute glass, dress with a fresh strawberry and mint sprig.

Roman Sling (Cktl) 35mls (1½ fl.ozs) dry gin, 5mls (¼ fl.oz) Grand Marnier, 10mls (½ fl.oz) orange juice, 10mls (½ fl.oz) lemon juice, 5mls (¼ fl.oz) brandy. Shake over ice, strain into an ice-filled highball glass, dress with an orange slice and a cherry.

Romansrivier Koöperatiewe (S.Afr) a co-operative winery (established 1949) based at Breede River, Wellington, Western Cape. 500ha. (Add): P.O. Box 108, Wolseley 6830. Grape varieties: Cabernet sauvignon, Chardonnay, Colombard, Malbec, Pinotage, Sauvignon blanc. Label: Mountain Ridge.

Romany (Eng) the old English name for the wines of Rumania. *See also* Rumney.

Romate (Sp) a brandy producer. (Add): Sanchez Romate Tlnos S.A., Lealas 26-28, P.O. Box 5, Jerez de la Frontera, Cadiz. Obtains wines from Jerez. Produces brandies under the labels of Cardenal Cisneros over 10 years old, Cardenal Mendoza over 10 years old. Also produces a range of Sherries including Don José, Iberia Cream, Marismeño, N.P.U. Amontillado, Petenara and La Sacristía de Romate.

Roma Wines (S.Afr) the label for wines produced by the Stellenbosch Farmers' Winery.

Rombola (Gre) *see* Robola.

Rombouts (Ger) a coffee-produced by the RGB Coffee Ltd. company that produced the first individual (primed with ground coffee) disposable one cup filters.

Rome (Sp) a red grape variety once used in Málaga production.

Rome Anglais (W.Ind) a spirit derived from sugar cane, is superior to guildhive. The name later altered to rum.

Romefort (Fr) a Bourgeois Supérieur A.C. Médoc, (Com): Avensan, north-western Bordeaux.

Romeiko (Gre) a red grape variety grown on the island of Crete.

Romeo (Eng) a cask ale brewed by the Wychwood Brewery, Eagle Maltings, Witney, Oxfordshire. Part of their Character Ale range.

Römer (Ger) a natural spring mineral water. Mineral contents (milligrammes per litre): Sodium 19.8mg/l, Calcium 601mg/l, Magnesium 43mg/l, Chlorides 28.5mg/l.

Romeral (Sp) a red wine produced by the A.G.E. Bodegas Unidas S.A, Rioja. Grape varieties: Garnacha 20%, Mazuelo 20% and Tempranillo 60%.

Römerberg (Ger) lit: 'Roman hill', a popular name for German vineyards. 23 individual sites have this name.

Römerberg (Ger) vineyard (Anb): Baden. (Ber): Markgräflerland. (Gro): Burg Neuenfels. (Vil): Badenweiler.

Römerberg (Ger) vineyard (Anb): Baden. (Ber): Markgräflerland. (Gro): Burg Neuenfels. (Vil): Niederweiler.

Römerberg (Ger) vineyard (Anb): Mittelrhein. (Ber): Bacharach. (Gro): Schloss Reichenstein. (Vil): Oberheimbach.

Römerberg (Ger) vineyard (Anb): Mittelrhein. (Ber): Bacharach. (Gro): Burg Hammerstein. (Vil): Rheinbrohl.

Römerberg (Ger) vineyard (Anb): Mosel-Saar-Ruwer. (Ber): Bernkastel. (Gro): Kurfürstlay. (Vil): Burgen.

Römerberg (Ger) vineyard (Anb): Mosel-Saar-Ruwer. (Ber): Bernkastel. (Gro): Probstberg. (Vil): Riol.

Römerberg (Ger) vineyard (Anb): Mosel-Saar-Ruwer. (Ber): Obermosel. (Gro): Gipfel. (Vil): Oberbillig.

Römerberg (Ger) vineyard (Anb): Mosel-Saar-Ruwer. (Ber): Zell/Mosel. (Gro): Grafschaft. (Vil): Nehren.

Römerberg (Ger) vineyard (Anb): Mosel-Saar-Ruwer. (Ber): Zell/Mosel. (Gro): Goldbäumchen. (Vil): Senheim.

Römerberg (Ger) vineyard (Anb): Nahe. (Ber): Kreuznach. (Gro): Pfarrgarten. (Vil): Gutenberg.

Römerberg (Ger) vineyard (Anb): Nahe. (Ber): Kreuznach. (Gro): Schlosskapelle. (Vil): Bingen-Bingerbrück.

Römerberg (Ger) vineyard (Anb): Nahe. (Ber): Kreuznach. (Gro): Schlosskapelle. (Vil): Münster-Sarmsheim.

Römerberg (Ger) vineyard (Anb): Nahe. (Ber): Kreuznach. (Gro): Schlosskapelle. (Vil): Weiler.

Römerberg (Ger) vineyard (Anb): Nahe. (Ber): Kreuznach. (Gro): Schlosskapelle. (Vil): Windesheim.

Römerberg (Ger) vineyard (Anb): Nahe. (Ber): Schloss Böckelheim. (Gro): Burgweg. (Vil): Waldböckelheim.

Römerberg (Ger) vineyard (Anb): Nahe. (Ber): Schloss Böckelheim. (Gro): Paradiesgarten. (Vil): Merxheim.

Römerberg (Ger) vineyard (Anb): Rheinhessen. (Ber): Bingen. (Gro): Kaiserpfalz. (Vil): Engelstadt.

Römerberg (Ger) vineyard (Anb): Rheinhessen. (Ber): Bingen. (Gro): Sankt Rochuskapelle. (Vil): Badenheim.

Römerberg (Ger) vineyard (Anb): Rheinhessen. (Ber): Nierstein. (Gro): Domherr. (Vil): Essenheim.

Römerberg (Ger) vineyard (Anb): Rheinhessen. (Ber): Nierstein. (Gro): Rheinblick. (Vil): Alsheim.

Römerberg (Ger) vineyard (Anb): Rheinhessen. (Ber): Nierstein. (Gro): Rheinblick. (Vil): Dorn-Dürkheim.

Römerberg (Ger) vineyard (Anb): Rheinhessen.

R

(Ber): Wonnegau. (Gro): Sybillenstein. (Vil): Alzey.

Römerberg (Ger) vineyard (Anb): Pfalz. (Ber): Südliche Weinstrasse. (Gro): Trappenberg. (Vins): Alter Berg, Narrenberg, Schlittberg.

Römerbrunnen (Ger) vineyard (Anb): Pfalz. (Ber): Mittelhaardt-Deutsche Weinstrasse. (Gro): Pfaffengrund. (Vil): Hambach.

Römer Brunnen Heilwasser (Ger) a sparkling natural spring mineral water from Rheinpfalz. Mineral contents (milligrammes per litre): Sodium 492mg/l, Calcium 506.7mg/l, Magnesium 72.5mg/l, Potassium 33.7mg/l, Bicarbonates 1903mg/l, Chlorides 773.4mg/l, Sulphates 48.4mg/l, Fluorides 0.36mg/l, Nitrates 0.11mg/l, Silicates 21.1mg/l, Boron 1.3mg/l, Strontium 5.45mg/l, Ammonium 1.4mg/l.

Römergarten (Ger) vineyard (Anb): Mosel-Saar-Ruwer. (Ber): Zell/Mosel. (Gro): Rosenhang. (Vil): Briedern.

Römerhalde (Ger) vineyard (Anb): Nahe. (Ber): Kreuznach. (Gro): Kronenberg. (Vil): Bad Kreuznach (ortsteil Planig).

Römerhof (Aus) an estate and winery (22.5ha) based in Grosshöflein, Burgenland. (Add): Hauptstrasse 120, 7051 Grosshöflein. Grape varieties: Blaufränkisch, Cabernet sauvignon, Chardonnay, Pinot blanc, Sauvignon blanc, Welschriesling, Zweigelt. Labels: Steinzeiler, Tatschler.

Römerkrug (Ger) vineyard (Anb): Mittelrhein. (Ber): Rheinburgengau. (Gro): Schloss Schönburg. (Vil): Dellhofen.

Römerkrug (Ger) vineyard (Anb): Mittelrhein. (Ber): Rheinburgengau. (Gro): Schloss Schönburg. (Vil): Oberwessel.

Römerlay (Ger) grosslage (Anb): Mosel-Saar-Ruwer. (Ber): Saar-Ruwer. (Vils): Franzenheim, Hockweiler, Kasel, Korlingen, Mertesdorf, Mertesdorf (ortsteil Maximin Grünhaus), Morscheid, Riveris, Sommerau, Trier, Waldrach.

Römerpfad (Ger) vineyard (Anb): Mosel-Saar-Ruwer. (Ber): Bernkastel. (Gro): Kurfüstlay. (Vil): Maring-Noviand.

Römerpfad (Ger) vineyard (Anb): Nahe. (Ber): Schloss Böckelheim. (Gro): Paradiesgarten. (Vil): Unkenbach.

Römerquelle (Aus) a sparkling natural spring mineral water from Edelstal. Mineral contents (milligrammes per litre): Sodium 13.9mg/l, Calcium 146mg/l, Magnesium 65.6mg/l, Potassium 2mg/l, Bicarbonates 421mg/l, Chlorides 8mg/l, Sulphates 298.6mg/l, Fluorides 0.33mg/l, Nitrates 0.5mg/l.

Römerquelle (Ger) a natural spring mineral water from Bad Niederauer. (Add): D-72108 Bad Niedernau. Mineral contents (milligrammes per litre): Sodium 12.4mg/l, Calcium 401mg/l, Magnesium 55.9mg/l, Bicarbonates 878mg/l, Chlorides 19.7mg/l, Sulphates 495mg/l, Fluorides 0.54mg/l, Nitrates 1mg/l, Strontium 1.7mg/l. pH 7.0

Römerquelle (Ger) vineyard (Anb): Mosel-Saar-Ruwer. (Ber): Zell/Mosel. (Gro): Schwarze Katz. (Vil): Zell-Kaimt.

Römerquelle Mainhardt Heilwasser (Ger) a natural spring mineral water. Mineral contents (milligrammes per litre): Sodium 19.2mg/l, Calcium 577mg/l, Magnesium 46.2mg/l, Potassium 3.7mg/l, Chlorides 5.6mg/l, Sulphates 1470mg/l, Fluorides 0.24mg/l.

Römerschanze (Ger) vineyard (Anb): Rheinhessen. (Ber): Nierstein. (Gro): Krötenbrunnen. (Vil): Eimsheim.

Römersprudel (Ger) a sparkling natural spring mineral water from Mainardter Wald, Schwäbisch-Fränkischer Wald. Mineral contents (milligrammes per litre): Sodium 20mg/l, Calcium 543mg/l, Magnesium 54mg/l, Bicarbonates 200mg/l, Chlorides 6mg/l, Sulphates 1420mg/l.

Römersteg (Ger) vineyard (Anb): Rheinhessen. (Ber): Wonnegau. (Gro): Liebfrauengarten. (Vil): Worms.

Römerstich (Ger) vineyard (Anb): Nahe. (Ber): Schloss Böckelheim. (Gro): Paradiesgarten. (Vil): Auen.

Römerstrasse (Ger) vineyard (Anb): Pfalz. (Ber): Mittelhaardt-Deutsche Weinstrasse. (Gro): Schwarzerde. (Vil): Kirchheim.

Römertor (Ger) an untergebiet of the Oberrhein district.

Römerwall Quelle (Ger) a natural spring mineral water from Walsum, Duisburg. Mineral contents (milligrammes per litre): Sodium 260mg/l, Calcium 1.4mg/l, Magnesium 0.58mg/l, Potassium 4.8mg/l, Bicarbonates 384mg/l, Chlorides 121mg/l, Sulphates 27mg/l, Fluorides 0.68mg/l.

Römerweg (Ger) vineyard (Anb): Pfalz. (Ber): Südliche Weinstrasse. (Gro): Mandelhöhe. (Vil): Kirrweiler.

Romery (Fr) a Cru Champagne village in the Canton d'Aÿ. District: Reims.

Romford Brewery (Eng) a large brewery based in London and owned by Allied Breweries. Closed 1992. Was noted for cask-conditioned Benskins Bitter 1037 O.G. Taylor Walker 1037 O.G. Friary Meux 1037 O.G. keg John Bull 1036 O.G. canned Falcon Lager 1032 O.G.

Romina (Ger) a natural spring mineral water. Mineral contents (milligrammes per litre): Sodium 8mg/l, Calcium 137mg/l, Magnesium 37mg/l, Potassium 4mg/l, Bicarbonates 350mg/l, Chlorides 3mg/l, Sulphates 202mg/l.

Rommelshausen (Ger) village (Anb): Württemberg. (Ber): Remstal-Stuttgart. *see* Kernen.

Rommelshausen (Ger) village (Anb): Württemberg. (Ber): Remstal-Stuttgart. (Gro): Wartbühl. (Vin): Häder.

Romond Vineyards (S.Afr) a winery (established 1993) based in Helderberg, Stellenbosch, Western Cape. Grape varieties: Cabernet franc, Cabernet sauvignon. Label: Rebus.

R

Romorantin (Fr) a white grape variety grown in the eastern Loire, named after the town lying on a tributary of the river Cher.

Rom Ponche (Cktl) 2 dashes Angostura, teaspoon grenadine, teaspoon sugar, juice of half a lemon. Build into an ice-filled highball glass. Fill with golden rum, decorate with an orange, lemon and apple slice and a cherry.

Romy (Bel) the brand-name of a well-hopped pilsener lager beer.

Ron (Sp) rum.

Ron (W.Ind) rum.

Ronald Lamb Winery (USA) *see* Lamb Winery.

Ron Anejo Cacique (W.Ind) a brand of rum produced in Costa Rica (part of Seagram).

Ronas Spring (Scot) a natural spring mineral water from Muckle Ballia Clett, Northmavine, Shetland Isles.

Ron Briganti (W.Ind) the label of de-luxe light and dark rums imported into the U.K. by Kilsern Distillers, Leicester.

Ronceret (Fr) a Premier Cru vineyard in the A.C. commune of Volnay, Côte de Beaune, Burgundy.

Roncière [La] (Fr) a Premier Cru vineyard in the A.C. commune of Nuits-Saint-Georges, Côte de Nuits, Burgundy 2.1ha.

Roncières (Fr) a Premier Cru A.C. Chablis often is re-classified as the Premier Cru vineyard Mélinots.

Ronco (It) the Italian version of the French 'Cru'.

Ronco dei Quattroventi (It) a red wine produced by Fattoria San Francesco in Cirò, Calabria. Aged for 14 months in oak.

Ronco del Gelso (It) a winery based in Cormons in the Friuli-Venezia-Guilia region. Produces Pinot Grigio sot lis Rivis. Website: http://www.libero.it 'E'mail: roncodelgelso@libero.it

Ronco delle Betulle (It) a vineyard based in the DOC Colli Orientali. Grape variety: Ribolla gialla. Website: http://www.roncodellebetulle.it 'E'mail: info@roncodellebetulle.191.it

Ron Con Agua de Coco (S.Am) a local drink produced in Colombia drunk straight from a fresh coconut to which has been added a tot of rum, crushed ice and sugar.

Roncus (It) a winery based in Capriva in the Friuli-Venezia-Guilia region.

Rond (Fr) denotes a full, supple, fleshy wine.

Rondeur (Fr) roundness, a wine that drinks easily.

Rondibús (Fr) a term used in the Champagne region for a drunken person.

Rondinaia (It) a white wine produced by Tenuta del Terriccio from Chardonnay and Sauvignon blanc grapes.

Rondinella (It) a red grape variety grown in the Veneto region. Used in the making of Bardolino.

Rong (Chi) a natural spring mineral water from Xian.

Rongopai (N.Z) a winery. (Add): 71 Waerenga Road, Te Kauwhata. 4ha. winery that produces Chardonnay and Riesling botrytis-attacked sweet wines.

Ron Guajiro (Sp) a brand of rum produced by Cocal in Telde, Canary Isles.

Ron Llave (W.Ind) a white rum produced in Puerto Rico and shipped for Seagram.

Ron Medellin (S.Am) the brand-name of a rum that has been aged in Colombia to obtain a dark or yellowish colour.

Ron Montilla (Arg) a brand of rum from Seagram.

Ronoro (W.Ind) a golden-coloured rum produced on the island of Cuba.

Ron Peloeon (Sp) lit: 'drink for sailors', a primitive rum-style liquor.

Ron Popular (S.Am) the brand-name of a rum produced in Colombia by the State-owned Industria Licorera de Bolivar from molasses that have been distilled only once.

Ronrico (W.Ind) a white rum shipped by Ronrico Rum C°. for Seagram.

Ron Viejo de Caldas (S.Am) the brand-name of a rum produced in Colombia that has been aged to give a dark or yellowish colour.

Roobernet (S.Afr) a local red grape variety from the Stellenbosch, Western Cape.

Rood (Hol) red.

Rood (S.Afr) a red wine blend of 80% Cabernet sauvignon and 20% Cinsaut grapes from the Lievland Estate.

Roodeberg (S.Afr) a red grape variety, a cross between Hermitage and Shiraz grapes.

Roodeberg (S.Afr) a full-bodied red wine made from Pinotage, Tinta barocca and Shiraz grapes. Made by the K.W.V.

Roodebloem (S.Afr) a smooth red wine made from the Cinsault based blended wine, produced by the Stellenryck Wines.

Roodehof (S.Afr) a red wine made from Pinotage grapes by the De Doorns co-operative winery Worcester, Western Cape.

Roode Huiswyn (S.Afr) a red wine made from 50% Cabernet sauvignon and 50% Tinta barocca grapes, produced by the Roodezandt Koöperatiewe.

Roodendal (S.Afr) a rich red wine made by the SFW from Cabernet sauvignon grapes.

Rooderust (S.Afr) a blended red wine made from the Cabernet sauvignon, Pinotage and Shiraz grapes by SFW.

Roodewagen (S.Afr) the label for a red wine (Pinotage and Cinsaut blend) produced by the Waboomsrivier Co-operative winery, Worcester, Western Cape.

Roodewyn (S.Afr) red wine.

Roodezandt Koöperatiewe Wynmakery (S.Afr) a co-operative winery (established 1953) based in Robertson, Western Cape. 1400ha. (Add): Box 164, Robertson 6705. Grape varieties: Cabernet sauvignon, Chardonnay, Chenin blanc, Merlot, Muscadel, Ruby cabernet, Sauvignon blanc. Labels: Balthazar Classic, The Keizer's Creek, The Red, The White. Website: http://www.roodezandt.co.za

Rooibergse Koöperatiewe Wynmakery (S.Afr) a co-operative winery (established 1964) based in Robertson, Western Cape (also vineyards in

Vinkrivier, Eilandia, Goree and Riverside). 600ha. (Add): P.O. Box 358, Robertson 6705. Produces a vast range of varietal wines. Grape varieties include: Cabernet sauvignon, Chardonnay, Chenin blanc, Colombard, Hanepoot, Jerepiko, Merlot, Pinotage, Red muscadel, Rhine riesling, Sauvignon blanc, Shiraz. Labels: African Collection, African Dawn, Amandalia, Cape Circle, De Sonnenberg, Flamingo, Goeie Tye, Signum, Umculi, Zebra Collection. Website: http://www.rooiberg.co.za

Rooibos Tea (S.Afr) a low tannin, caffeine-free tea made from the indigenous Rooibos herb *Aspalathus linearis.*

Rooiwyn (S.Afr) red wine.

Room (Hol) cream.

Room Temperature (Eng) the ideal temperature for red wines. 65°F to 68°F (18°C to 20°C). *See also* Chambré.

RO 15 4513 (Eng) a new drug that inhibits the intoxicating affect of alcohol (lasts approximately 30 minutes).

Roosje Zonder Doornen (Hol) lit: 'rose without thorns', a liqueur made from rose essence.

Roosters (Eng) a 4.7% alc by vol (1046 O.G) aromatic, fairly bitter beer brewed at Roosters Brewing, North Yorkshire. *See also* Yankee.

Roosters Brewing C° Ltd (Eng) a brewery (established 1992). (Add): Unit 3, Grimbald Park, Wetherby Road, Knaresborough, North Yorkshire HG5 8LJ. Also known as the Roosters Pioneer Brewery. Brews: Cream 4.7% alc by vol., Hooligan 4.3% alc by vol., Nector 5.2% alc by vol., Oyster Stout 4.3% alc by vol., Roosters (aromatic, fairly bitter beer) 4.7% alc by vol., Roosters 22 Carat, Special 3.9% alc by vol., Yankee (a soft pale ale) 4.3% alc by vol., YPA 4.3% alc by vol., also Seventh Heaven. Website: http://www.roosters.co.uk 'E'mail: sean@roosters.co.uk

Roosters 22 Carat (Eng) a fruity beer brewed by Roosters Brewing, North Yorkshire.

Root Beer (USA) a carbonated drink made from ginger and other roots and herbs.

Roothman Cape Red (S.Afr) the label for a red wine (Cabernet sauvignon, Merlot, Pinotage and Shiraz blend) produced by the Jonkeer winery, Robertson, Western Cape.

Rooty Hill (Austr) a vineyard based in the Murrumbidgee Irrigation Area, New South Wales.

Ropa (Gre) a red wine produced on the island of Corfu.

Rope (Eng) a bacterial infection that occurs in brewing. *Zymamonas* is an anaerobic bacteria that produces gelatinous threads in the beer, ruins a cask in a few hours. *see* Ropey Beer. Can also be found in wine.

Rope and Anchor (W.Ind) a demerara navy rum producer 40% alc by vol.

Rope of Sand (Scot) a 3.7% alc by vol. ale brewed by the Fyfe Brewing C°., Fife.

Ropewalk (USA) an ale brewed by the Bridgeport Brewing Company, Portland, Oregon.

Ropey Beer (Eng) a slang term for beer in a poor condition.

Ropiness (Eng) *see* Graisse des Vins.

Ropiteau-Frères (Fr) a Burgundy négociant-éleveur (established 1848) based at Meursault, Côte de Beaune. Noted for the wines of Meursault and Monthélie. Also produces A.C. Premier Cru Chablis Vaillons. Acquired by Boisset.

Ropley Vineyard (Eng) a vineyard (established 1979) based at Ent House, Court Lane, Ropley, Hampshire. 0.4ha. Grape varieties: Huxelrebe, Madeleine angevine, Müller-Thurgau, Reichensteiner.

Roquemaure (Fr) a commune of the A.C. Lirac in the southern Rhône. Produces white, rosé and red wines.

Roriz (Port) a red grape variety used in the making of Port, used for its good colour and sugar. Also known as Tinto roriz.

Rorke's Lager C°. (S.Afr) a brewery based in Liphook. Brews: Rorke's Real Lager.

Rorke's Real Lager (S.Afr) a 5% alc by vol. bottled lager brewed by the Rorke's Lager C°. in Liphook.

Rory O'More Cocktail (Cktl) ⅔ measure Bushmills Irish Whiskey, ⅓ measure Italian vermouth, dash orange bitters. Stir over ice and strain into a cocktail glass.

Rosa (Bul) a liqueur made from damascene rose petals.

Rosa (Ser) a still and sparkling natural spring mineral water from Izvor, Serbia. (pink label: still). Mineral contents (milligrammes per litre): Sodium 2.5mg/l, Calcium 5.9mg/l, Magnesium 0.43mg/l, Potassium 0.38mg/l, Bicarbonates 20.9mg/l, Chlorides 0.46mg/l, Sulphates 2.9mg/l, Nitrates 1.95mg/l, Silicates 13.7mg/l. pH 7.0

Rosabrook Estate (Austr) a winery based in the Margaret River region of Western Australia. Grape varieties: Cabernet sauvignon, Merlot. Label: Slaughterhouse Block.

Rosacker (Fr) an A.C. Alsace Grand Cru vineyard at Hunawihr, Haut-Rhin 26.18ha.

Rosacki (Gre) a pink-red table grape sometimes used for making dessert wines in Crete.

Rosa de Perú (Mex) a red grape variety grown in Baja California.

Rosado (Port)(Sp) rosé. (Fr) = rosé, (It) = rosato.

Rosado Fernandes (Port) a winery based in Reguengos, Alentejo. Produces red wines and pot-stilled brandies.

Rosales Distillery (Mex) a producer of tequila of same name.

Rosa Muskat (Aus) a red grape variety also known as the Schönburger.

Rosati Winery (USA) a winery based in St. James, Missouri. Produces many different wines mainly based on the Concord grape.

Rosato (It) pink/rosé wine. (Port) = rosado, (Sp) = rosado.

Rosato del Salento (It) a non-D.O.C. rosé wine from the Puglia region. Made from Negramaro and Malvasia grapes.

R

Rosato di Carmignano (It) a D.O.C. rosé wine (also known as Vin Ruspo). Produced from the same grapes as Carmignano. Must remains in contact with the skins for a maximum time of 12 hours. Fermented wine is aged in stainless steel over the winter only.

Rosbacher (Ger) a natural spring mineral water from Rosbach. Mineral contents (milligrammes per litre): Sodium 85mg/l, Calcium 209mg/l, Magnesium 93mg/l, Potassium 3.9mg/l, Bicarbonates 1079mg/l, Chlorides 141mg/l, Sulphates 12mg/l.

Rosbacher Gloria Quelle (Ger) a natural spring mineral water from Rosbach. Mineral contents (milligrammes per litre): Sodium 9mg/l, Calcium 93mg/l, Magnesium 16mg/l, Bicarbonates 368mg/l, Chlorides 9mg/l, Sulphates 6mg/l, Fluorides 0.1mg/l, Nitrates 1.9mg/l.

Rosbacher Ur-Quelle (Ger) a natural spring mineral water from Rosbach. Mineral contents (milligrammes per litre): Sodium 39.9mg/l, Calcium 261.6mg/l, Magnesium 131.4mg/l, Potassium 3.1mg/l, Bicarbonates 1477mg/l, Chlorides 50mg/l, Fluorides 0.05mg/l.

Rosbach Water (Fr) a naturally effervescent mineral water from Homburg.

Rosbercon (Austr) part of the Tisdall Estate in Victoria. 80ha. Grape varieties: Cabernet sauvignon, Malbec, Merlot, Shiraz, Chardonnay, Chenin blanc, Colombard, Rhine riesling, Sémillon, Sauvignon blanc.

Rosca (Port) the name for the spiral of a corkscrew. see Saca-Rolhas.

Roschbach (Ger) village (Anb): Pfalz. (Ber): Südliche Weinstrasse. (Gro): Bischofskreuz. (Vins): Rosenkränzel, Simonsgarten.

Roscoe's Red (USA) a 5% alc by vol. premium bottled lager brewed by Anheuser-Busch, Missouri from specially roasted barley that gives a chestnut-red colour.

Roscommon (Ire) a natural spring mineral water from Roscommon. Mineral contents (milligrammes per litre): Sodium 19.4mg/l, Calcium 209mg/l, Magnesium 37.9mg/l, Potassium 4.3mg/l, Bicarbonates 261mg/l, Chlorides 15mg/l, Sulphates 45mg/l.

Rosé (Fr) lit: 'rosy', the term to denote a pink wine. see Vin Rosé. (Gre) = roze, (Rum) = rozsa, (Tur) = roze.

Rosé (It) a sub-species of the Nebbiolo grape.

Rose and Crown (Eng) a Tetley Brewery home-brew public house in York. Noted for cask-conditioned Viking Bitter 1043 O.G.

Rosebank (Scot) a single malt distillery at Camelon near Falkirk, Stirlingshire. A Lowland malt, distilled three times. Produces an 8 year old malt 43% alc by vol. Also a 1983 and 1984 vintage at 40% alc by vol. Licence held by Distillers Agency Ltd.

Rosebank Estate (N.Z) a 0.5ha. winery. (Add): Corner of Johns Road and Groynes Drive, Belfast, Christchurch. Grape varieties: Chardonnay, Riesling, Sauvignon blanc, Cabernet sauvignon/Shiraz.

Rosebower Vineyard (USA) a small vineyard based in Hampton-Sydney, Virginia. 1ha. Produces French hybrid and vinifera wines.

Rose Cocktail [1] (Cktl) 30 ms (¼ gill) dry gin, 15mls (⅛ gill) French vermouth, 15mls (⅛ gill) Dubonnet, 3 dashes grenadine. Stir over ice, strain into a cocktail glass, add a cherry and a squeeze of lemon peel on top (orange peel can be used instead of lemon).

Rose Cocktail [2] (Cktl) ⅔ measure dry vermouth, ⅓ measure kirsch, teaspoon rose syrup. Stir over ice, strain into a cocktail glass and top with a cherry.

Rose Cocktail [3] (Cktl) ½ measure apricot brandy, 1 measure gin, ½ measure dry vermouth, dash lemon juice, 4 dashes grenadine. Shake over ice and strain into a cocktail glass.

Rose Cocktail [4] (Cktl) ⅔ measure dry gin, ⅙ measure orange juice, ⅙ measure grenadine. Shake over ice and strain into a cocktail glass.

Rose Cocktail [5] (Cktl) 25mls (1fl.oz) French vermouth, 5mls (¼fl.oz) cherry brandy, 5mls (¼ fl.oz) kirsch. Stir well over ice, strain into a cocktail glass and dress with a cherry.

Rose Cocktail [6] (Cktl)(Non-alc) 4 strawberries cut into pieces, ½ slice pineapple cut into pieces, juice ½ lemon, juice ½ orange, few dashes orange cordial, gomme syrup to taste. Shake all well over ice, strain into a 125mls (5fl.oz) wine glass and decorate with rose petals.

Rose Cocktail Number One (Cktl) 1 measure gin, ½ measure cherry brandy, ½ measure dry vermouth, stir over ice and strain into a cocktail glass.

Rose Cocktail Number Two (Cktl) 1 measure gin, ½ measure kirsch, ½ measure cherry brandy, stir over ice and strain into a cocktail glass.

Rosé d'Anjou (Fr) an A.C. rosé wine from the Anjou-Saumur district of the Loire. Made from the Cot, Gamay, Groslot, Noble and Pinot d'Aunis grapes.

Rosé de Béarn (Fr) a V.D.Q.S. rosé wine from the south-west tip of France. Made from various grapes. see Irouléguy.

Rosé de Cabernet Anjou (Fr) an A.C. rosé wine from the Anjou-Saumur district of the Loire. Made from the Cabernet franc grape.

Rose de Chambertin (Cktl) 35mls (1½ fl.ozs) gin, 10mls (½ fl.oz) crème de cassis, 10mls (½ fl.oz) lime juice, dash egg white. Shake over ice and strain into a frosted cocktail glass (crème de cassis and castor sugar).

Rosé de Gamay (Switz) a dry rosé wine from the cantons of Geneva and Valais, made from the Gamay grape.

Rosé de Loire (Fr) a recently created rosé wine of the Anjou-Saumur and the Touraine districts of the Loire. Has a minimum of 30% Cabernet grapes plus Gamay, Grolleau and Pineau d'Aunis.

Rosé de Marsannay (Fr) see Bourgogne Rosé de Marsannay.

Rosé de Riceys (Fr) a still rosé wine made in the Champagne region.

Rosé de Saignée (Fr) a vintage rosé Champagne made from 100% Pinot noir by the house of François Vallois.

Rosé de Saignée (S.Afr) the label for a rosé wine (Petit verdot) produced by the Signal Hill winery, Cape Town, Western Cape.

Rosé des Riceys (Fr) an A.C. Rosé Champagne (created February 1971) from the Côte des Bar, Champagne.

Rosé de Varsouie (Cktl) ⅙ measure Cointreau, ½ measure vodka, ⅓ measure cherry cordial, dash Angostura. Stir over ice, strain into an ice-filled highball glass and add a cherry.

Rosé d'Orches (Fr) an Appellation Grand Ordinaires from the village of Orches near Auxey-Duresses and produced by La Cave Coopérative des Hautes-Côtes, Burgundy.

Rosée de la Reine (Fr) a natural spring mineral water from Mont Rouscous. Mineral contents (milligrammes per litre): Sodium 2.9mg/l, Calcium 0.46mg/l, Magnesium 0.23mg/l, Potassium 0.39mg/l, Bicarbonates 7.32mg/l, Chlorides 2.85mg/l, Sulphates 2.4mg/l, Nitrates 1mg/l, Silicates 7.04mg/l. pH 6.12

Roseewein (Ger) a rosé wine made from a blend of more than one type of red grape variety.

Rose Garden Vineyards (S.Afr) a winery (established 1976) based in Windmeul, Paarl, Western Cape. 15ha. Grape varieties: Cabernet sauvignon, Chardonnay, Chenin blanc, Merlot, Pinotage, Pinot noir, Shiraz. Label: Maya's Red.

Rosé-Gris (Fr) a grade of rosé wine which is light and almost colourless.

Rosehill Vineyard (Austr) an estate belonging to the McWilliams Winery in Hunter Valley, New South Wales.

Rosehip Tea (Eng) a herbal tea rich in Vitamin C. Is sweet and astringent in taste.

Rosella (Cyp) a light, medium-dry, rosé wine produced by Keo in Limassol.

Rosellinia necatrix (Lat) a fungus (family **Pourridié**) that attacks the vine roots. see Armillaria Root-Rot.

Roselyn (Cktl) another name for the Rosington Cocktail.

Rosé Millésimé (Fr) a vintage Champagne produced by Besserat de Bellefon from 70% Pinot noir and 30% Chardonnay grapes.

Rosemount Estate (Austr) a winery. (Add): Rosemount Road, Denman, Hunter Valley, New South Wales. 400ha. in Coonawarra and Hunter Valley. Grape varieties include: Cabernet sauvignon, Chardonnay, Sauvignon blanc, Sémillon, Shiraz and Traminer (owned by FGL Wine Estates).

Rosenberg (Ger) lit: 'rosehill', a popular name for vineyards in Germany, 42 individual vineyard sites are so named.

Rosenberg (Ger) vineyard (Anb): Ahr. (Ber): Walporzheim/Ahrtal. (Gro): Klosterberg. (Vil): Marienthal.

Rosenberg (Ger) vineyard (Anb): Baden. (Ber): Badische Bergstrasse/Kraichgau. (Gro): Mannaberg. (Vil): Dielheim.

Rosenberg (Ger) vineyard (Anb): Baden. (Ber): Badische Bergstrasse/Kraichgau. (Gro): Mannaberg. (Vil): Tairnbach.

Rosenberg (Ger) vineyard (Anb): Baden. (Ber): Markgräflerland. (Gro): Burg Neuenfels. (Vil): Britzingen.

Rosenberg (Ger) vineyard (Anb): Baden. (Ber): Markgräflerland. (Gro): Burg Neuenfels. (Vil): Britzingen (ortsteil Dattingen).

Rosenberg (Ger) vineyard (Anb): Baden. (Ber): Markgräflerland. (Gro): Burg Neuenfels. (Vil): Zunzingen.

Rosenberg (Ger) vineyard (Anb): Baden. (Ber): Markgräflerland. (Gro): Lorettoberg. (Vil): Ehrenstetten.

Rosenberg (Ger) vineyard (Anb): Franken. (Ber): Maindreieck. (Gro): Kirchberg. (Vil): Sommerach.

Rosenberg (Ger) vineyard (Anb): Franken. (Ber): Maindreieck. (Gro): Not yet assigned. (Vil): Frankenwinheim.

Rosenberg (Ger) vineyard (Anb): Mittelrhein. (Ber): Rheinburgengau. (Gro): Burg Hammerstein. (Vil): Leutesdorf.

Rosenberg (Ger) vineyard (Anb): Mittelrhein. (Ber): Rheinburgengau. (Gro): Burg Rheinfels. (Vil): St. Goar-Werlau.

Rosenberg (Ger) vineyard (Anb): Mosel-Saar-Ruwer. (Ber): Bernkastel. (Gro): Kurfürstlay. (Vil): Bernkastel-Kues.

Rosenberg (Ger) vineyard (Anb): Mosel-Saar-Ruwer. (Ber): Bernkastel. (Gro): Kurfürstlay. (Vil): Osann-Monzel.

Rosenberg (Ger) vineyard (Anb): Mosel-Saar-Ruwer. (Ber): Bernkastel. (Gro): Michelsberg. (Vil): Minheim.

Rosenberg (Ger) vineyard (Anb): Mosel-Saar-Ruwer. (Ber): Bernkastel. (Gro): Michelsberg. (Vil): Rivenich.

Rosenberg (Ger) vineyard (Anb): Mosel-Saar-Ruwer. (Ber): Bernkastel. (Gro): Schwarzlay. (Vil): Kinheim.

Rosenberg (Ger) vineyard (Anb): Mosel-Saar-Ruwer. (Ber): Bernkastel. (Gro): Schwarzlay. (Vil): Wittlich.

Rosenberg (Ger) vineyard (Anb): Mosel-Saar-Ruwer. (Ber): Bernkastel. (Gro): Vom Heissen Stein. (Vil): Pünderich.

Rosenberg (Ger) vineyard (Anb): Mosel-Saar-Ruwer. (Ber): Obermosel. (Gro): Gipfel. (Vil): Wehr.

Rosenberg (Ger) vineyard (Anb): Mosel-Saar-Ruwer. (Ber): Saar-Ruwer. (Gro): Scharzberg. (Vil): Oberemmel.

Rosenberg (Ger) vineyard (Anb): Mosel-Saar-Ruwer. (Ber): Saar-Ruwer. (Gro): Scharzberg. (Vil): Wiltingen.

Rosenberg (Ger) vineyard (Anb): Mosel-Saar-Ruwer. (Ber): Zell/Mosel. (Gro): Goldbäumchen. (Vil): Klotten.

Rosenberg (Ger) vineyard (Anb): Mosel-Saar-Ruwer. (Ber): Zell/Mosel. (Gro): Goldbäumchen. (Vil): Moselkern.

Rosenberg (Ger) vineyard (Anb): Mosel-Saar-Ruwer.

R

(Ber): Zell/Mosel. (Gro): Goldbäumchen. (Vil): Pommern.

Rosenberg (Ger) vineyard (Anb): Mosel-Saar-Ruwer. (Ber): Zell/Mosel. (Gro): Grafschaft. (Vil): Neef.

Rosenberg (Ger) vineyard (Anb): Mosel-Saar-Ruwer. (Ber): Zell/Mosel. (Gro): Rosenhang. (Vil): Bruttig-Fankel.

Rosenberg (Ger) vineyard (Anb): Mosel-Saar-Ruwer. (Ber): Zell/Mosel. (Gro): Rosenhang. (Vil): Cochem.

Rosenberg (Ger) vineyard (Anb): Mosel-Saar-Ruwer. (Ber): Zell/Mosel. (Gro): Rosenhang. (Vil): Senheim.

Rosenberg (Ger) vineyard (Anb): Mosel-Saar-Ruwer. (Ber): Zell/Mosel. (Gro): Weinhex. (Vil): Oberfell.

Rosenberg (Ger) vineyard (Anb): Nahe. (Ber): Kreuznach. (Gro): Kronenberg. (Vil): Bad Kreuznach.

Rosenberg (Ger) vineyard (Anb): Nahe. (Ber): Kreuznach. (Gro): Schlosskapelle. (Vil): Windesheim.

Rosenberg (Ger) vineyard (Anb): Nahe. (Ber): Schloss Böckelheim. (Gro): Burgweg. (Vil): Niederhausen an der Nahe.

Rosenberg (Ger) vineyard (Anb): Nahe. (Ber): Schloss Böckelheim. (Gro): Paradiesgarten. (Vil): Mannweiler-Coelln.

Rosenberg (Ger) vineyard (Anb): Nahe. (Ber): Schloss Böckelheim. (Gro): Paradiesgarten. (Vil): Monzingen.

Rosenberg (Ger) vineyard (Anb): Rheingau. (Ber): Johannisberg. (Gro): Burgweg. (Vil): Lorchhausen.

Rosenberg (Ger) vineyard (Anb): Rheinhessen. (Ber): Nierstein. (Gro): Petersberg. (Vil): Biebelnheim.

Rosenberg (Ger) vineyard (Anb): Rheinhessen. (Ber): Nierstein. (Gro): Spiegelberg. (Vil): Nierstein.

Rosenberg (Ger) vineyard (Anb): Pfalz. (Ber): Südliche Weinstrasse. (Gro): Kloster Liebfrauenberg. (Vil): Billigheim-Ingenheim.

Rosenberg (Ger) vineyard (Anb): Pfalz. (Ber): Südliche Weinstrasse. (Gro): Kloster Liebfrauenberg. (Vil): Steinweiler.

Rosenberg (Ger) vineyard (Anb): Pfalz. (Ber): Südliche Weinstrasse. (Gro): Königsgarten. (Vil): Arzheim.

Rosenberg (Ger) vineyard (Anb): Pfalz. (Ber): Südliche Weinstrasse. (Gro): Königsgarten. (Vil): Birkweiler.

Rosenberg (Ger) vineyard (Anb): Pfalz. (Ber): Südliche Weinstrasse. (Gro): Königsgarten. (Vil): Siebeldingen.

Rosenberg (Lux) a vineyard site in the village of Grevenmacher.

Rosenblum Cellars (USA) a winery based in Oakland, Alameda County, California. Grape varieties: Cabernet sauvignon, Chardonnay, Johannisberg riesling, Petite syrah and Zinfandel. Produces varietal wines. Label: Rockpile Road (Zinfandel).

Rosenblümchen (S.Afr) the label for a naturally sweet rosé wine (Cabernet, Colombard and Hanepoot blend) produced by the Landzicht GWK Eines winery, Jacobsdal, Northern Cape.

Rosenbock (Ger) a bock beer brewed by the Rosenbrauerei based in Kaufbeuren, western Munich.

Rosenborn (Ger) vineyard (Anb): Mosel-Saar-Ruwer. (Ber): Zell/Mosel. (Gro): Schwarze Katz. (Vil): Zell-Kaimt.

Rosenbrauerei (Ger) a brewery based in Kaufbeuren, western Munich. Uses the symbol of a goat around the neck of the bottle. Brews: Rosenbock and Buronator.

Rosenbühl (Ger) grosslage (Anb): Pfalz. (Ber): Mittelhaardt-Deutsche Weinstrasse. (Vils): Erpolzheim, Freinsheim, Lambsheim, Weisenheim/Sand.

Rosengärtchen (Ger) vineyard (Anb): Mosel-Saar-Ruwer. (Ber): Bernkastel. (Gro): Michelsberg. (Vil): Neumagen-Dhron.

Rosengarten (Ger) lit: 'rose garden', a name used for vineyards in Germany. 13 individual vineyard sites are so named.

Rosengarten (Ger) grosslage (Anb): Nahe. (Ber): Schloss Böckelheim. (Vils): Bockenau, Braunweiler, Burgsponheim, Hüffelsheim, Mandel, Roxheim, Rüdesheim, St. Katharinen, Sponheim, Weinsheim.

Rosengarten (Ger) vineyard (Anb): Baden. (Ber): Badische Bergstrasse/Kraichgau. (Gro): Hohenberg. (Vil): Hohenwettersbach.

Rosengarten (Ger) vineyard (Anb): Mosel-Saar-Ruwer. (Ber): Bernkastel. (Gro): Schwarzlay. (Vil): Traben-Trarbach (ortsteil Starkenberg).

Rosengarten (Ger) vineyard (Anb): Rheingau. (Ber): Johannisberg. (Gro): Burgweg. (Vil): Rüdesheim.

Rosengarten (Ger) vineyard (Anb): Rheinhessen. (Ber): Bingen. (Gro): Sankt Rochuskapelle. (Vil): Bingen.

Rosengarten (Ger) vineyard (Anb): Rheinhessen. (Ber): Nierstein. (Gro): Domherr. (Vil): Gabsheim.

Rosengarten (Ger) vineyard (Anb): Rheinhessen. (Ber): Wonnegau. (Gro): Domblick. (Vil): Monsheim.

Rosengarten (Ger) vineyard (Anb): Rheinhessen. (Ber): Wonnegau. (Gro): Gotteshilfe. (Vil): Bechtheim.

Rosengarten (Ger) vineyard (Anb): Pfalz. (Ber): Mittelhaardt-Deutsche Weinstrasse. (Gro): Grafenstück. (Vil): Obrigheim.

Rosengarten (Ger) vineyard (Anb): Pfalz. (Ber): Mittelhaardt-Deutsche Weinstrasse. (Gro): Hofstück. (Vil): Freidelsheim.

Rosengarten (Ger) vineyard (Anb): Pfalz. (Ber): Südliche Weinstrasse. (Gro): Kloster Liebfrauenberg. (Vil): Kapellen-Drusweiler.

Rosengarten (Ger) vineyard (Anb): Pfalz. (Ber): Südliche Weinstrasse. (Gro): Ordensgut. (Vil): Edesheim.

Rosengarten (Ger) vineyard (Anb): Pfalz. (Ber):

Südliche Weinstrasse. (Gro): Ordensgut. (Vil): Rhodt.

Rosengarten Brauerei (Switz) an independent brewery based in Einsieden.

Rosenhang (Ger) grosslage (Anb): Mosel-Saar-Ruwer. (Ber): Zell/Mosel. (Vils): Beilstein, Bremm, Briedern, Bruttig-Fankel, Cochem, Ellenz-Poltersdorf, Mesenich, Senheim, Treis-Karden, Valwig.

Rosenheck (Ger) vineyard (Anb): Nahe. (Ber): Kreuznach. (Gro): Kronenberg. (Vil): Bad Kreuznach (ortsteil Winzenheim).

Rosenheck (Ger) vineyard (Anb): Nahe. (Ber): Schloss Böckelheim. (Gro): Burgweg. (Vil): Niederhausen an der Nahe.

Rosenhügel (Aus) a winery based in the Kampstal region. (Add): Heidler, Am Roselhügel 13, 3550 Langenlois. Grape varieties: Chardonnay, Grüner veltliner, Pinot blanc, Pinot noir, Riesling, Zweigelt. Produces a range of wine styles.

Rosenhügel (Ger) vineyard (Anb): Mittelrhein. (Ber): Siebengebirge. (Gro): Petersberg. (Vil): Oberdollendorf.

Rosenkranz (Ger) vineyard (Anb): Baden. (Ber): Kaiserstuhl-Tuniberg. (Gro): Vulkanfelsen. (Vil): Bischoffingen.

Rosenkranz (Ger) vineyard (Anb): Pfalz. (Ber): Südliche Weinstrasse. (Gro): Bischofskreuz. (Vil): Böchingen.

Rosenkränzel (Ger) vineyard (Anb): Pfalz. (Ber): Südliche Weinstrasse. (Gro): Bischofskreuz. (Vil): Roschbach.

Rosenkranzweg (Ger) vineyard (Anb): Baden. (Ber): Badische Bergstrasse/Kraichgau. (Gro): Mannaberg. (Vil): Östringen.

Rosenlay (Ger) vineyard (Anb): Mosel-Saar-Ruwer. (Ber): Bernkastel. (Gro): Beerenlay. (Vil): Lieser.

Rosenmuskateller (It) the German name for the Moscato rosa grape variety in the Trentino-Alto-Adige (Südtirol) region.

Rosental (Ger) vineyard (Anb): Mittelrhein. (Ber): Rheinburgengau. (Gro): Schloss Schonburg. (Vil): Perscheid.

Rosenteich (Ger) vineyard (Anb): Nahe. (Ber): Kreuznach. (Gro): Schlosskapelle. (Vil): Guldental.

Rosenthal (Ger) vineyard (Anb): Ahr. (Ber): Walporzheim/Ahrtal. (Gro): Klosterberg. (Vil): Ahrweiler.

Rosenthaler Riesling (Bul) a white wine produced from a blend of Riesling grapes grown in Karlovo.

Rosé of Cabernet Sauvignon (USA) the name given to a pink varietal wine made from the Cabernet sauvignon grape.

Rosé of Carmel (Isr) a semi-dry rosé wine produced for the USA market by the Carmel C°.

Rosé of Menes (Rum) *see* Menesi Rozsa.

Rosé of Pinot Noir (USA) the name given to a pink varietal wine made from Pinot noir grapes.

Rose of Virginia (Austr) a rosé wine from 100% Grenache grapes produced by Melton (Charles) in the Barossa Valley.

Rose of Warsaw (Ckd) 25mls (⅕ gill) vodka, 20mls (⅙ gill) Wisniak cherry liqueur, 3 dashes Cointreau, dash Angostura. Stir over ice and strain into a cocktail glass.

Rose Pauillac [La] (Fr) a vineyard in the commune of Pauillac, A.C. Pauillac, Haut-Médoc, Bordeaux.

Rose-Pauillac [La] (Fr) a blended wine from the Pauillac co-operative, Haut-Médoc, Bordeaux.

Rose Petal Tea (Eng) freshly brewed tea, 3 dashes Angostura per cup, decorate with rose petals and serve hot.

Rose Pouchong (Chi) a China tea flavoured with rose petals.

Roseraie de Gruaud Larose [La] (Fr) a wine of Château Gruaud Larose in St. Julien.

Rose's (Eng) the famous brand-name used by Schweppes for their famous lime juice cordial and High Juice orange squash.

Rose Street (Scot) a home-brew public house owned by the Alloa Brewery in Edinburgh. Noted for cask-conditioned Auld Reekie 1037 O.G.

Rosette (Fr) an A.C. district of the Bergerac region (is *not* a rosé), produces medium-sweet white wines.

Rosette (Fr) a hybrid red grape variety also known as Seibel 1000.

Rossetto's (Austr) a winery (established 1939) based in New South Wales.

Rosé Vermouth (It) a base of rosé wine flavoured with herbs and spices. Has a bitter-sweet flavour. Also produced by most major vermouth manufacturers.

Rose Water (Eng) a perfumed water (oil of roses and of petals) used in certain cocktails.

Rosewhite Vineyards (Austr) a winery (established 1983). (Add): Happy Valley Road, Rosewhite, Victoria. Grape varieties: Traminer, Chardonnay, Pinot noir, Cabernet sauvignon, Shiraz.

Rosey Nosey (Eng) a 4.9% alc by vol. seasonal ale brewed by Batemans Salem Bridge Brewery, Wainfleet, Skegness, Lincolnshire.

Rosie Lee (Eng) the Cockney rhyming slang for tea.

Rosington (Cktl) 40mls (⅓ gill) dry gin, 20mls (⅙ gill) Italian vermouth. Shake over ice with a piece of orange zest. Strain into a cocktail glass and top with a squeeze of orange peel juice. Also known as the Roselyn Cocktail.

Rosinka (Rus) a natural spring mineral water from St. Petersburg. Mineral contents (milligrammes per litre): Sodium 30-80mg/l, Calcium <25mg/l, Magnesium <20mg/l, Bicarbonates 100-200mg/l, Sulphates <30mg/l.

Rosioara (Rum) a local name for Pamid grape.

Rosita Cocktail (Cktl) ⅓ measure tequila, ⅓ measure Campari, ⅙ measure Italian vermouth, ⅙ measure French vermouth. Stir over ice, strain into an ice-filled highball glass, add a twist of lemon peel juice and serve with straws.

Rosley Beer (Eng) a 5% alc by vol. beer brewed by the Greenwich Meantime Brewing C°. Ltd., London.

Rosnay (Fr) a Cru Champagne village in the Canton de Ville-en-Tardenois. District: Reims.

R

Rosoglio (USA) *see* Rosolio.

Rosolio (USA) a liqueur made from red rose petals, orange blossom water, cinnamon, clove, jasmine, sundew plant, alcohol and sugar. Also known as Rosoglio, Rossoll and Rossolis.

Rosport (Lux) a still and sparkling natural spring mineral water from Rosport. (green label: sparkling/yellow label: light gas/blue label: still). Mineral contents (milligrammes per litre): Sodium 66.1mg/l, Calcium 295mg/l, Magnesium 119mg/l, Potassium 19.8mg/l, Bicarbonates 1043mg/l, Chlorides 76.1mg/l, Sulphates 405mg/l, Nitrates 0.3mg/l.

Ross (Can) the brand-name used by the Canadian Schenley Distilleries Ltd. for a range of liqueurs.

Rossanella (It) a red grape variety, also known in Lombardy as the Molinara.

Rossara (It) a red grape variety grown in the Lake Garda district.

Rossberg (Ger) vineyard (Anb): Hessische Bergstrasse. (Ber): Umstadt. (Gro): None. (Vil): Rossdorf.

Rossberg (Ger) vineyard (Anb): Pfalz. (Ber): Südliche Weinstrasse. (Gro): Trappenberg. (Vil): Essingen.

Rossberg (Ger) vineyard (Anb): Württemberg. (Ber): Remstal-Stuttgart. (Gro): Kopf. (Vil): Winnenden.

Ross Brewing Company (Eng) a brewery based in Bristol. Brews: 21% alc by vol. Uncle Igor beer. First produced at 17.3% alc by vol. Also Hartcliffe Bitter, Ross's Pale Ale.

Rossdorf (Ger) vineyard (Anb): Hessische Bergstrasse. (Ber): Umstadt. (Gro): None. (Vil): Rossberg.

Rossel (Ger) vineyard (Anb): Nahe. (Ber): Kreuznach. (Gro): Schlosskapelle. (Vil): Genheim.

Rosselli Mâté Rosso (S.Am) an apéritif, low in alcohol, made from Yerbe Mâté (a herbal tea).

Rossendale Wines (N.Z) a winery. (Add): 150 Old Tai Tapu Road, Christchurch. 4ha. Grape varieties: Chardonnay, Müller-Thurgau.

Rossese (It) a red grape variety grown in Liguria.

Rossese di Dolceacqua (It) a D.O.C. red wine from Liguria, made from the Rossese grape. If total alc. content is 13% by vol. and is 10–11 months old then classed Superiore.

Rossetto (It) the local name for the Trebbiano giallo grape in Latium region.

Ross Gower Wines (S.Afr) a winery (established 2003) based in Elgin, Walker Bay, Western Cape. 5ha. Grape varieties: Sauvignon blanc, Shiraz. Label: Mankazana.

Rossignol [Philippe] (Fr) a négociant-éleveur based at Gevrey-Chambertin, Nuits-Saint-Georges, Burgundy.

Rossignola (It) a red grape variety grown in the Veneto.

Rossiya (Rus) the name of a sparkling dry white wine.

Rosso (It) red wine.

Rosso Antico (It) an apéritif wine produced and bottled by Gio Buton and G.S.P.A. in Trieste.

Rosso Barletta (It) a D.O.C. red wine from Apulia. Made from the Uva di Troia grape 14% alc by vol.

Rosso Conero (It) a D.O.C. red wine from The Marches. Made from Montepulciano and Sangiovese grapes in an area in the province of Ancona. The Governo all'uso Toscano is recommended. Wine is named after Mount Conero.

Rosso del Conte (It) a red wine produced from a blend of 50% Nero d'avola and 50% Perricone grapes by Regaleali in Sicily.

Rosso della Quercia (It) a D.O.C. red wine from 100% Montepulciano d'Abruzzo grapes in the Chieti Hills.

Rosso delle Colline Lucchesi (It) a D.O.C. red wine from Tuscany. Made from the Sangiovese 40%–60% and Canaiolo, Ciliegiolo, Colorino, Malvasia, Trebbiano toscano and Verminto grapes.

Rosso di Barletta (It) a D.O.C. red wine produced from Uva di troia grapes in Southern Italy.

Rosso di Cerignola (It) a D.O.C. red wine from Puglia. Made from the Barbera, Malbeck, Montepulciano, Nero amaro, Sangiovese, Trebbiano toscano and Uva di troia grapes. If aged minimum 2 years in cask and has total minimum alc. content of 13% by vol. then classed Riserva.

Rosso di Montalcino (It) a D.O.C. red wine from Montalcino, Siena in Tuscany. Produced mainly from the Sangiovese grape.

Rossola (It) a white grape variety also known as the Ugni blanc.

Rosso La Fabriseria (It) the name of a red Vino da Tavola wine produced by Azienda Agricola Tedeschi, Verona. Grape varieties: Corvina, Rondinella, Molinara, Dindarella. Spends 1 year in oak, 6 months in bottle.

Rossolis (Fr) the French equivalent of Rosolio.

Rossoll (It) also known as Rosolio.

Rosso Piceno (It) a D.O.C. red wine from The Marches, made from 40% Montepulciano and 60% Sangiovese grapes. Vinification can occur within the whole area of Ancona, Ascoli Piceno and Macerata. If total alc. content is 11.5% by vol. and aged 1 year minimum then classed Superiore (also grapes must be grown in the restricted area).

Ross Royal (Cktl) ½ measure Royal Mint Chocolate Liqueur, ½ measure crème de banane, ½ measure brandy. Shake over ice and strain into a cocktail glass.

Rosstal (Ger) grosslage (Anb): Franken. (Ber): Maindreieck. (Vils): Arnstein, Eussenheim, Gambach, Gössenheim, Himmelstadt, Karlburg, Karlstadt, Laudenbach, Mühlbach, Retzstadt, Stetten.

Rosstein (Ger) vineyard (Anb): Mittelrhein. (Ber): Rheinburgengau. (Gro): Herrenberg. (Vil): Kaub.

Rosswag (Ger) village (Anb): Württemberg. (Ber): Württembergisch Unterland. (Gro): Stromberg. (Vins): Forstgrube, Halde, Lichtenberg.

Rostov Imperial Vodka (Eng) a brand of vodka from Kilsern Distillers in Leicester. *See also* Feeny's, Macintyre, Marlborough London Dry.

Rosy Cheeks (Cktl) 60mls (½ gill) Ashbourne

R

sparkling mineral water, 60mls (½ gill) dry white wine. Place with ice in a highball glass, add dash of grenadine, a slice of lime and serve with straws.

Rot (Ger) red.

Rota (Sp) part of the Jerez Supérieur region.

Rota (Sp) the name given to the wine produced in the north of Spain, usually used in blending.

Rotari Brut (It) a D.O.C. metodo classico wine produced by the Sociale Cooperativa di Mezzocorona, Trento from Chardonnay and Pinot noir grapes.

Rota Tent (Sp) see Tintilla de Rota.

Rotberger (Ger) an alternative name for the red grape variety Zweigelt. See also Blauer Zweigelt.

Rotbichel (Aus) a vineyard site based on the banks of the River Kamp situated in the Kamptal region.

Rot Blanc (Fr) a white rot that attacks the ripening berries and splits them. Is treated using a copper solution or sodium bisulphite.

Rotclevener (Fr) a red grape variety grown in Alsace, the local name for the Pinot noir.

Rotclevner (Switz) see Rotclevener.

Rote Halde (Ger) vineyard (Anb): Baden. (Ber): Kaiserstuhl-Tuniberg. (Gro): Vulkanfelsen. (Vil): Sasbach.

Rote Kirsch (Ger) a bitter-sweet, deep red, cherry liqueur, made by the Mampe Co.

Rotenberg (Ger) village (Anb): Baden. (Ber): Badische Bergstrasse/Kraichgau. (Gro): Mannaberg. (Vin): Schlossberg.

Rotenberg (Ger) vineyard (Anb): Nahe. (Ber): Schloss Böckelheim. (Gro): Burgweg. (Vil): Altenbamberg.

Rotenberg (Ger) vineyard (Anb): Nahe. (Ber): Schloss Böckelheim. (Gro): Burgweg. (Vil): Oberhausen an der Nahe.

Rotenberg (Ger) vineyard (Anb): Rheinhessen. (Ber): Wonnegau. (Gro): Domblick. (Vil): Wachenheim.

Rotenberg (Ger) vineyard (Anb): Pfalz. (Ber): Südliche Weinstrasse. (Gro): Trappenberg. (Vil): Hochstadt.

Rotenberg (Ger) village (Anb): Württemberg. (Ber): Remstal-Stuttgart. (Gro): Weinsteige. see Stuttgart.

Rotenbusch (Ger) vineyard (Anb): Baden. (Ber): Badische Bergstrasse/Kraichgau. (Gro): Hohenberg. (Vil): Söllingen.

Rotenfels (Ger) vineyard (Anb): Nahe. (Ber): Schloss Böckelheim. (Gro): Burgweg. (Vil): Traisen.

Rotenfels (Ger) vineyard (Anb): Rheinhessen. (Ber): Wonnegau. (Gro): Sybillenstein. (Vil): Alzey.

Rotenfelser im Winkel (Ger) vineyard (Anb): Nahe. (Ber): Schloss Böckelheim. (Gro): Burgweg. (Vil): Bad Münster a. St-Eburnburg.

Rotenpfad (Ger) vineyard (Anb): Rheinhessen. (Ber): Bingen. (Gro): Adelberg. (Vil): Flonheim.

Rotenstein (Ger) vineyard (Anb): Rheinhessen. (Ber): Wonnegau. (Gro): Bergkloster. (Vil): Westhofen.

Roter Berg (Ger) vineyard (Anb): Baden. (Ber): Breisgau. (Gro): Burg Lichteneck. (Vil): Kenzingen.

Roter Berg (Ger) vineyard (Anb): Franken. (Ber): Steigerwald. (Gro): Schlosstück. (Vil): Weimersheim.

Roter Berg (Ger) vineyard (Anb): Württemberg. (Ber): Württembergisch Unterland. (Gro): Kirchenweinberg. (Vil): Ilsfeld (ortsteil Schozach).

Roter Bur (Ger) vineyard (Anb): Baden. (Ber): Breisgau. (Gro): Burg Zähringen. (Vil): Glottertal.

Roterd (Ger) vineyard (Anb): Mosel-Saar-Ruwer. (Ber): Bernkastel. (Gro): Michelsberg. (Vil): Neumagen-Dhron.

Roter Muskateller (Aus) a white grape variety (mutation of the Grüner Veltliner) also known as the Roter Veltliner.

Röter Traminer (Aus)(It) a local clone in the Adige of the rosé grape variety Traminer.

Roter Veltliner (Aus) a white grape variety (mutation of the Grüner Veltliner) also known as the Roter Muskateller.

Rotes Haus (Euro) lit: 'red house', a wine from the Abtwingert vineyard in Liechtenstein.

Rotes Kreuz (Ger) vineyard (Anb): Rheinhessen. (Ber): Bingen. (Gro): Kaiserpfalz. (Vil): Ingelheim.

Rotes Tor (Aus) a vineyard site on the banks of the River Danube situated in the Wachau region, Niederösterreich.

Rotfeld (Ger) vineyard (Anb): Nahe. (Ber): Schloss Böckelheim. (Gro): Paradiesgarten. (Vil): Nussbaum.

Rotgipfler (Aus) a white grape variety grown in southern Austria, used for making Gumpoldskirchener.

Rotgrund (Ger) vineyard (Anb): Baden. (Ber): Kaiserstuhl-Tuniberg. (Gro): Attilafelsen. (Vil): Niederrimsingen.

Rot Gut (USA) a slang term for 'bath-tub gin' or any other cheap inferior liquor.

Röth (Ger) vineyard (Anb): Pfalz. (Ber): Mittelhaardt-Deutsche Weinstrasse. (Gro): Höllenpfad. (Vil): Grünstadt.

Rothbury Estate (Austr) a winery. (Add): Broke Road, Pokolbin, New South Wales 2321. 185ha. Grape varieties: Cabernet sauvignon, Chardonnay, Hermitage, Pinot noir, Sauvignon blanc and Sémillon. The second vineyard of Cowra.

Röthen (Ger) vineyard (Anb): Baden. (Ber): Markgräflerland. (Gro): Burg Neuenfels. (Vil): Niedereggenen.

Röthen (Ger) vineyard (Anb): Baden. (Ber): Markgräflerland. (Gro): Burg Neuenfels. (Vil): Obereggenen.

Rothenack (Ger) vineyard (Anb): Mittelrhein. (Ber): Rheinburgengau. (Gro): Loreleyfelsen. (Vil): Bornich.

Rothenberg (Aus) a vineyard site on the banks of the River Danube situated in the Wachau region, Niederösterreich.

Rothenberg (Ger) vineyard (Anb): Nahe. (Ber): Kreuznach. (Gro): Schlosskapelle. (Vil): Burg Layen.

Rothenberg (Ger) vineyard (Anb): Nahe. (Ber): Kreuznach. (Gro): Schlosskapelle. (Vil): Rümmelsheim.

Rothenberg (Ger) vineyard (Anb): Nahe. (Ber): Kreuznach. (Gro): Sonnenborn. (Vil): Langenlonsheim.

Rothenberg (Ger) vineyard (Anb): Nahe. (Ber): Schloss Böckelheim. (Gro): Burgweg. (Vil): Duchroth.

Rothenberg (Ger) vineyard (Anb): Rheingau. (Ber): Johannisberg. (Gro): Burgweg. (Vil): Geisenheim.

Rothenberg (Ger) a vineyard within the village of Geisenheim of which 26.8ha. (33.6%) is proposed to be classified as Erstes Gewächs.

Rothenberg (Ger) vineyard (Anb): Rheingau. (Ber): Johannisberg. (Gro): Steinmacher. (Vil): Rauenthal.

Rothenberg (Ger) a vineyard within the village of Rauenthal of which 22.1ha. (22.2%) is proposed to be classified as Erstes Gewächs.

Rothenberg (Ger) vineyard (Anb): Rheinhessen. (Ber): Bingen. (Gro): Abtey. (Vil): Gau-Algesheim.

Rothenberg (Ger) vineyard (Anb): Rheinhessen. (Ber): Nierstein. (Gro): Rehbach. (Vil): Nachenheim.

Rothenhof (Aus) a vineyard site on the banks of the River Danube situated in the Wachau region, Niederösterreich.

Rother Valley Brewing C° (Eng) a brewery (established 1993). (Add): Gate Court Farm, Station Road, Northiam, Rye, East Sussex TN31 6QT. Brews: Boadicea Ale 4.6% alc by vol., Hoppers Ale 4.4% alc by vol., Level Best 4% alc by vol., Smild 3.8% alc by vol., Wealden Bitter 3.7% alc by vol.

Rothschild [A. & C°.] (Fr) a Champagne producer based in Épernay. Produces: vintage and non-vintage wines. Vintages: 1900, 1904, 1906, 1911, 1914, 1921, 1926, 1928, 1934, 1937, 1941, 1943, 1945, 1947, 1952, 1953, 1955, 1959, 1961, 1962, 1964, 1966, 1969, 1970, 1971, 1975, 1976, 1979, 1982, 1983, 1985, 1990, 1995, 1996, 1997, 1998, 1999, 2001.

Rotlay (Ger) vineyard (Anb): Mosel-Saar-Ruwer. (Ber): Bernkastel. (Gro): Michelsberg. (Vil): Sehlem.

Rotlay (Ger) vineyard (Anb): Mosel-Saar-Ruwer. (Ber): Bernkastel. (Gro): Schwarzlay. (Vil): Platten.

Rotlay (Ger) vineyard (Anb): Mosel-Saar-Ruwer. (Ber): Saar-Ruwer. (Gro): Römerlay. (Vil): Trier.

Rotling (Ger) a pink wine made from red and white grapes mixed or musts, is not made from mixed wines (red and white).

Roto Fermenters (Eng) see Roto System.

Rotondo (It) a D.O.C. Aglianico del Vulture wine produced by Paternoster from Villa Rotondo (a 4.5ha. vineyard). Barrel aged for 14 months, plus 1 year in bottle.

Roto System (Aus) a method of red wine vinification, a rotating inner container extracts the juice from the grapes leaving the pomace behind. Also known as Roto Fermenters.

Rotspon (Aus) the label for a red wine (Merlot, Pinot noir and Zweigelt blend) produced by the Sonnhof winery, Kamptal.

Rotsteig (Ger) vineyard (Anb): Baden. (Ber): Badische Bergstrasse/Kraichgau. (Gro): Mannaberg. (Vil): Malsch.

Rott (Ger) grosslage (Anb): Hessische Bergstrasse. (Ber): Starkenburg. (Vils): Bensheim-Auerbach, Bensheim-Schönberg, Seeheim, Zwingenberg.

Rotten Egg Smell (Eng) see Hydrogen sulphide.

Rotten Wood (Fr) a cask sickness that sometimes befalls Armagnac brandy between 8–14 months, blending with older Armagnacs will hide this.

Rotter Muscateller (Ger) an alternative name for the Muscat rosé à petits grains grape variety.

Röttingen (Ger) village (Anb): Franken. (Ber): Maindreieck. (Gro): Not yet assigned. (Vin): Feuerstein.

Rottland (Ger) lit: 'red land', an old vineyard near the town of Rüdesheim in the Rheingau. Named after the colour of the schistous soil. see Berg Rottland.

Rotunda (Gre) the name used by Boutari for a range of their cheaper wines.

Rotwein (Ger) red wine.

Rotweinfest (Ger) the Rheinhessen wine festival held at Ingelheim in September.

Rotweinwanderweg (Ger) the Ahr red wine road route.

Rouchalin (Fr) an alternative name for the Chenin blanc grape in southern France.

Rouchet (It) red grape variety. Also known as Ruchè.

Roudey [Le] (Fr) an A.C. Saint-Émilion. (Com): Saint-Sulpice-de-Faylrens. 4.44ha.

Roudnice (Czec) a wine-producing town based near Prague on the river Elbe.

Roudnice nad Labem Brewery (Czec) a brewery in northern Czec. based near Prague on the river Elbe.

Roudon-Smith Vineyards (USA) a winery based in Santa Cruz, California. Grape varieties: Cabernet sauvignon, Chardonnay, Gewürztraminer, Petite syrah, Pinot blanc, Zinfandel. Produces varietal wines.

Rouffach (Fr) a wine town in the Haut-Rhin region, Alsace. Known in German as either Rufach or Ruffach.

Rouffiac (Fr) a commune in the Charente-Maritime département whose grapes are classed Petite Champagne (Cognac).

Rouffignac (Fr) a commune within the A.C. district of Monbazillac in Bergerac. Produces sweet (botrytis) white wines from Sémillon, Sauvignon blanc.

Rouge (Fr) red, see Vin Rouge (red wine).

Rouge (S.Afr) the label for a red wine (Merlot plus Cabernet sauvignon and Shiraz blend) produced by the Du Toitskloof Winery, Worcester, Western Cape.

Rougeau (Fr) lit: 'leaf reddening', is caused by a

R

wound in the plant stem that prevents the sap from rising from the roots. If it occurs above the ground the offending part is removed if possible.

Rouge de Nuy (S.Afr) the label for a red (Cabernet sauvignon and Merlot blend) wine produced by the Nuy Wine Cellar winery, Worcester, Western Cape.

Rouge d'Été (Fr) a brand label of J.C. Assemat in Roquemaure, Gard for a red A.C. Lirac produced by the semi-carbonique method from Cinsault and Grenache grapes.

Rouge Homme (Austr) a winery. (Add): Coonawarra, South Australia. 60ha. Grape varieties: Cabernet sauvignon, Chardonnay, Malbec, Pinot noir, Rhine riesling, Shiraz.

Rougemont Castle (Eng) a range of British wines from Whiteway's.

Rouge Noble (S.Afr) a red wine blend of (Cabernet franc, Cabernet sauvignon and Roobernet grapes) produced by the Audacia Wines Estate, Stellenbosch, Western Cape.

Rougeon (USA) a red grape variety also known as the Seibel 5898.

Rougeot (Fr) a fungus which causes sores to appear on the vines which eventually die and fall off. Not a regular hazard to vines, treated by spraying with copper solution.

Rouge Sega de Cor (Fr) a biodynamic wine from Domaine le Roc des Anges, Côtes du Roussillon-Villages.

Rougets (Fr) the name for the light red (rosé,) wines of the Anjou-Saumur district of the Loire.

Rough (Eng) a term used to describe a wine that is coarse and not balanced. Is heavy with tannin that will not soften with ageing.

Rough Elvot (Eng) an old cider apple variety. *See also* Elvot.

Rouissillón Tinto (Sp) an alternative name for the Garnacha grape.

Roujolais (S.Afr) a soft red wine produced from the Cinsault grape in the coastal regions.

Roulette (S.Afr) the label for a range of wines red (Syrah 66% plus Carignan, Grenache and Viognier blend) and white (Chardonnay, Chenin blanc, Hárslevelü and Viognier blend) produced by the Lammershoek Winery, Swartland, Western Cape.

Roullet et Fils (Fr) a Cognac producer. (Add): Le Goulet de Foussignac, 16200, Jarnac. 21ha. in the Fins Bois and 35ha. in the Borderies. Produces Amber Gold *** and a wide range of other Cognac styles.

Round [1] (Eng) a term used to describe drinks bought for those persons in drinking company. "*A round of drinks*", "*Whose round is it?*" "*My round*" are some expressions used.

Round [1] (Eng) a term used to describe a wine which is balanced and harmonious.

Roundheads Gold (Eng) a 4.2% alc by vol. golden ale brewed by the Springhead Brewery, Nottinghamshire.

Round Hill Winery (USA) a winery based near St. Helena, Napa Valley, California. Grape varieties: Cabernet sauvignon, Chardonnay, Gewürztraminer, Petite syrah, Zinfandel. Produces varietal wines.

Round the World (Cktl) 25mls (1fl.oz) gin, 60mls (2½ fl.ozs) pineapple juice, 35mls (1½ fl.ozs) crème de menthe. Shake over ice, strain into a large cocktail glass, decorate with a pineapple piece on a cocktail stick.

Roupeiro (Port) a white grape variety grown in the Alentejo region, is also known as Códega and Alva in Douro. Also known as the Síria.

Rousanne (Fr) *see* Roussanne and Ugni Blanc.

Rouse (Eng) a term used for a full measure of a drink (alcoholic) in the eighteenth century.

Rouse (Eng) a term used in brewing to describe the mixing of the wort with large wooden paddles, air injection or by recycling the wort by spraying it back across the yeast head.

Roussan (Fr) an alternative spelling of Roussanne.

Roussanne (Fr) a white grape variety grown in the Rhône that produces wines with a perfumed herb tea aroma and tropical fruits flavour. *See also* Ugni Blanc.

Rousseau-Deslandes (Fr) a cuvée in the Cent-Vignes vineyard in the A.C. commune of Beaune, Côte de Beaune, Burgundy (owned by the Hospices de Beaune).

Rousselet de Béarn (Fr) a V.D.Q.S. district of the Pyrénées.

Rousset-les-Vignes (Fr) a village in the A.C. Côtes du Rhône-Villages. Produces mainly red wines (with a little rosé and white wine).

Roussette (Fr) a white grape variety grown in the Bugey and Seyssel regions of eastern France. Also known as the Altesse.

Roussette d'Ayse (Fr) a white grape variety grown in the Ayse area of Savoie, south-eastern France.

Roussette de Bugey (Fr) a V.D.Q.S. wine-producing region. Produces wine of same name from the Altesse and Chardonnay grapes.

Roussette de Savoie (Fr) an A.C. of Savoie, south-eastern France. Includes the villages: Frangy, Marestel, Monterminod and Monthoux.

Roussile (Fr) a Cognac producer. (Add): Roussille, Linars, 16290 Hiersac. 35ha. in the Fins Bois. Produces a fine range of Cognac brandies. Also makes Pineau de Charentes.

Roussillon (Fr) a wine region of south-western France which together with the Languedoc makes up part of the Midi.

Roussillonen (Fr) an alternative name for the Carignan grape.

Roussillon Tinto (Sp) an alternative name for the Grenache grape.

Routa Distillery (W.Ind) a rum distillery based in Guadeloupe.

Route des Vins (Fr) the road that travels through a region's vineyards.

Rouvas (Gre) a natural spring mineral water from Gergeri, Crete. Mineral contents (milligrammes per litre): Sodium 7.7mg/l, Calcium 24.8mg/l, Magnesium 11.7mg/l, Potassium 0.4mg/l, Bicarbonates 113.5mg/l, Chlorides 17mg/l, Sulphates 1mg/l, Nitrates 7mg/l. pH 7.85

Rouvière (Fr) an A.C. Coteaux Varois rosé wine produced by Château Routas.

Rouvrettes [Les] (Fr) a Premier Cru vineyard [part] in the A.C. commune of Savigny-lès-Beaune, Côte de Beaune, Burgundy.

Roux Père et Fils (Fr) a winery based in the A.C. Chablis, Burgundy. Produces a range of Chablis wines including Premier Cru Montmains.

Rouyer (Fr) a Cognac producer. (Add): Rouyer Guillet S.A. Château de la Roche, 17100 Saintes, Cognac. 86ha. 42% in the Borderies and 58% in the Fins Bois. Produces Rois de France 30 year old, Philippe Guillet Grande Fine Champagne 80 year old.

Rovalley Winery (Austr) a winery based in the Barossa Valley, South Australia.

Rovellats S.A. (Sp) a vineyard at Pau Claris 136, Entlo. 2a, 08009 Barcelona. 210ha. Produces cava wines including a Brut Imperial that is aged for 3 years.

Roveto (It) a single vineyard selected D.O.C.G. Chianti produced by Podere Collelungo in Castellina.

Rovitello (It) a red wine produced from 80% Nerello mascalese and 20% Nerello cappuccio grapes by Tenuta di Castiglione on Mount Etna.

Rovral (Eng) a common fungicide used as a spray against grey mould.

Rowan (Eng) a 4.2% alc by vol. premium ale from Four Rivers Brewery, Newcastle-on-Tyne.

Rowan's Creek (USA) a 12 year old Bourbon bottled by Rowan's Creek Distillery, Bardstown, Kentucky 50.5% alc by vol.

Rowan Vineyard (USA) a vineyard based near Santa Maria, Santa Barbara County, California. Grape variety: Chardonnay.

Rowenden (Eng) a vineyard based in Kent. Grape varieties include Huxelrebe and Reichensteiner.

Rowney Vineyard (Eng) a vineyard (established 1978) based at Rowney Farm, Chaseways, Sawbridgeworth, Herts. 1ha. Grape varieties: Madeleine angevine, Müller-Thurgau and Seyval blanc.

Roxanaise (Fr) a natural spring mineral water from Cristal Roc. Mineral contents (milligrammes per litre): Sodium 10.5mg/l, Calcium 73.6mg/l, Magnesium 2.2mg/l, Potassium 1.8mg/l, Bicarbonates 198.5mg/l, Chlorides 18.6mg/l, Sulphates 19.5mg/l, Nitrates 2mg/l.

Roxane (Fr) a natural spring mineral water. Mineral contents (milligrammes per litre): Calcium 60mg/l, Magnesium 23mg/l.

Roxheim (Ger) village (Anb): Nahe. (Ber): Schloss Böckelheim. (Gro): Rosengarten. (Vins): Berg, Birkenberg, Höllenpfad, Hüttenberg, Mülhenberg, Sonnenberg.

Royal (Cktl) ⅓ measure dry gin, ⅓ measure Port, ⅓ measure Grand Marnier, dash Angostura. Stir over ice and strain into a cocktail glass.

Royal (Eng) a barley wine 1064 O.G. brewed by the Tolly Cobbold Brewery in Ipswich.

Royal (Jap) the brand-name for a whiskey produced by Suntory.

Royal (Port) the brand-name of a 10 year old Tawny Port from Seagram (a partner to 20 year old Imperial).

Royal Altmunster (Lux) a premium beer brewed by the Mousel et Clausen Brasserie.

Royal Ambassador Brut (It) a sparkling (metodo tradizionale) wine produced by G & L Fratelli in the Piemonte region.

Royal Amber (USA) a beer brewed by the Wiedemann Brewery based in Newport, Kentucky.

Royal Ambrosante (Sp) a Palo Cortado Sherry produced by Sandeman.

Royal and Ancient (Scot) the label of a blended Scotch whisky 40% alc by vol.

Royal Assent (Eng) an ale brewed by Branscombe Brewery, Devon to mark the Queen's visit to the 100th Devon County Show.

Royal Blanc (S.Afr) the label for white wine blend (for the Dutch market) produced by the Citrusdal Cellars winery, Swartland, Western Cape.

Royal Blanco (Sp) an alternative name for the Subirat-parent grape.

Royal Blend (It) a dry liqueur produced from imported Scottish malt whisky.

Royal Blush (Cktl) 1 measure vodka, ½ measure crème de framboise, ½ measure cream, dash grenadine. Shake over ice, strain into a 125mls (5fl.oz) goblet and serve with a cherry.

Royal Blush Cocktail (Cktl) ⅓ measure Topaz, ⅓ measure blackberry liqueur, ⅓ measure lemon juice. Stir over ice, strain into an ice-filled highball glass, top with iced Champagne and dash of French vermouth.

Royal Brackla (Scot) a single highland malt whisky distillery near Nairn in Morayshire. Produces a vintage 1969 malt 43% alc by vol.

Royal Brewery (Eng) a brewery based in Manchester. Owned by Scottish and Newcastle Breweries.

Royal Brewing Cº. (USA) a brewery based in New Orleans. Brews: New Orleans Best 1039 O.G.

Royal Bristol Brew (Eng) the name given to 250 numbered and boxed bottles produced to mark H.R.H. the Princess Anne's visit to the Courage Brewery in Bristol in February 1989.

Royal Bronx (Cktl) 1 measure dry gin, ½ measure dry vermouth, ½ measure sweet vermouth, 1 measure orange juice, dash dark rum, dash orange Curaçao. Shake over ice and strain into a Champagne flute.

Royal Buchanan (Cktl) ⅓ measure Royal Mint Chocolate liqueur, ⅓ measure Scotch whisky, ⅓ measure cream. Stir gently with ice and strain into a 125mls (5fl.oz) goblet.

Royal Canadian (Can) a blended Canadian whisky produced by Jas Barclay and Cº (a subsidiary of Hiram Walker).

Royal Carlton (Sp) the brand-name of a cava wine produced by the Bodegas Bilbainas.

Royal Charter (Can) a brand of Canadian whisky produced by the Hudson's Bay Cº (a subsidiary of Seagram).

Royal Cherry Chocolate (Eng) a cherry and chocolate-based liqueur from Hallgarten 30% alc by vol.

Royal Choice (Scot) a de luxe blended Scotch whisky from the Long John Distillery, Glasgow. 21 year old 43% alc by vol.

Royal Cider (Eng) a brew of cider distilled and often fortified with other spirits and sugar. Encouraged in 1703 to discourage smuggling.

Royal Clarence (Eng) a home-brew public house in Burnham-on-Sea, Somerset. Brews: cask-conditioned KC Bitter 1038 O.G.

Royal Clover Club Cocktail (Cktl) as for Clover Club Cocktail but with egg yolk instead of egg white.

Royal Cocktail [1] (Cktl) 40mls (⅓ gill) dry gin, 20mls (⅙ gill) Dubonnet, dash Angostura, dash orange bitters. Stir over ice, strain into a cocktail glass, add a cherry and squeeze of lemon peel juice on top.

Royal Cocktail [2] (Cktl) ¾ measure dry gin, ¼ measure lemon juice, 1 egg, 2 dashes gomme syrup. Shake over ice and strain into a cocktail glass.

Royal Coco (Cktl) ⅓ measure Kahlúa, ⅓ measure golden rum, ⅙ measure crème de cacao, ⅙ measure Cointreau, 2 dashes coconut cream. Shake over ice, strain into a flute glass, top with grated chocolate, a slice of lime and a cherry.

Royal Coconut Liqueur (Fr) a coconut, cacao beans, French milk and spirit-based liqueur produced by Peter Hallgarten in Bordeaux 21% alc by vol.

Royal Coffee (Liq.Coffee) *see* Café Royale.

Royal Colmbier (Fr) a herb liqueur produced in Nantes, north-western France.

Royal Command (Can) a Canadian rye whisky produced by Canadian Park and Tilford (a subsidiary of Canadian Schenley Distilleries Ltd).

Royal Concquidor (Sp) a brand of Oloroso Sherry produced by Sandeman in Jerez de la Frontera.

Royal Corregidor (Sp) a deep gold, old Oloroso Sherry produced by Sandeman.

Royal Coteau [Le] (Fr) a Champagne producer. (Add): Union de Proprietors, Rue de la Co-opérative Graves, 51190 Avize. Co-opérative-manipulant 83ha.

Royal Cream (Sp) a sweet, Cream Sherry produced by La Riva in Jerez de la Frontera.

Royal Culross (Scot) an 8 year old blended malt produced by A. Gillies and C°. Glasgow. 40% alc by vol. Part of Amalgamated Distilled Products.

Royal Decanter (Eng) a decanter of the 1820's named after George 1V.

Royal Denmark (Den) a strong ale 7.75% alc by vol. brewed by the Tuborg Brewery in Copenhagen. Also known as Fine Festival.

Royal Diana [The] (Cktl) ⅛ measure brandy, ⅛ measure De Kuyper Nassau Orange, ¾ measure Kriter sparkling wine. Stir Cognac and liqueur together over ice, strain into a Champagne flute, top up with sparkling wine and add a slice of orange.

Royal Divorce (Eng) a bottled ale from Buffy's Brewery, near Diss, Norfolk. Has two pictures on lable: one of the late Diana, Princess of Wales, one of H.R.H. Prince Charles.

Royal Dragon (Eng) 25% alc by vol. cranberry fruit vodka from Liquid Dragon in Suffolk.

Royal Dutch (Cktl) ⅓ measure Mandarine Napoléon, ⅓ measure white rum, ⅓ measure Cointreau, dash orange bitters, dash lemon juice. Stir together with ice and strain into a cocktail glass.

Royal Dutch Lager (Hol) a brand of lager beer 1030–1034 O.G. 2.8% alc by vol. brewed by the De Posthorn, Brouwerij, Breda.

Royale (S.Afr) the label for a red wine (Cabernet sauvignon plus Cabernet franc and Merlot blend) produced by the Vriesenhof Vineyards winery, Stellenbosch, Western Cape.

Royale Family Vineyards (S.Afr) a winery (established 2000) based in Klapmuts, Paarl, Western Cape. 45ha. Grape varieties: Cabernet sauvignon, Merlot, Mourvèdre, Pinotage, Ruby cabernet, Shiraz, Viognier. Website: http://www.royalewines.com

Royal Engagement (Cktl) ⅓ measure Scotch whisky, ⅓ measure Irish Mist, ⅓ measure Welsh cream, dash English mead. Shake over ice, strain into a blue-frosted cocktail glass and garnish with a cherry.

Royal Esmeralda (Sp) a fine Amontillado Sherry produced by Sandeman in Jerez de la Frontera.

Royal Export (Den) a premium lager 5.8% alc by vol. from Ceres Brewery in Aarhus.

Royal Fizz (Cktl) 90mls (¾ gill) dry gin, 1 whole egg, juice of a lemon, teaspoon grenadine. Shake well over ice, strain into a highball glass and top with soda water.

Royal Framboise (Fr) a méthode traditionelle raspberry apéritif with the addition of Cognac and fruit syrup produced by Gratien et Meyer 15.2% alc by vol.

Royal French Coffee-Chocolate Liqueur (Eng) a liqueur made from roasted coffee, chocolate and French milk by Hallgarten 30% alc by vol.

Royal Fruit and Nut Chocolate Liqueur (Eng) a fruit, nut and cocoa bean-based liqueur produced by Peter Hallgarten, London 30% alc by vol.

Royal Gin Fizz (Cktl) 40mls (⅓ gill) gin, 1 egg, juice ½ lemon, teaspoon powdered sugar. Shake over ice, strain into an ice-filled highball glass, top with soda water and a slice of lemon.

Royal Ginger Chocolate (Eng) a liqueur made from ginger and cocoa beans. Produced by Hallgartens 30% alc by vol.

Royal Gold (S.Am) a 5 year old demerara rum produced by Banks DIH Ltd. in Guyana.

Royal Gordon Perfection (Scot) a rare Scotch whisky thought to be more than 100 years old.

Royal Highland (Scot) a 12 year old whisky produced by William Teacher & Sons, Glasgow.

Royal Hofbräu (Ger) a premium Bavarian lager 4.8% alc by vol. brewed under licence by Hall and Woodhouse from the Hofbräuhaus.

Royal Host (USA) a label used by the East-Side

Winery, California for their table, dessert wines and brandies.

Royal Household (Scot) a 40% alc by vol. whisky originally created for the exclusive use of the Royal Family by Buchanan and Company (now available more widely).

Royal Inn (Eng) a home-brew public house in Horsebridge, Devon. Noted for cask-conditioned Tamar Bitter 1039 O.G. Heller 1060 O.G. and Horsebridge Best 1045 O.G.

Royal Irish Distilleries (Ire) was once one of the largest companies in Ireland (has been closed since 1936).

Royal Irish Liqueur C° (Ire) based under Tullamore centre. Makes advocaat, chocolate mint and coffee-flavoured liqueurs.

Royalist (Cktl) ¼ measure Bénédictine, ¼ measure Bourbon whiskey, ½ measure dry vermouth, dash peach bitters. Stir over ice and strain into a cocktail glass.

Royal King (S.Afr) a sweet amber wine made from white Cinsault and Hanepoot grapes by the SFW.

Royal King (Switz) the brand-name given to vin mousseux fruit-flavoured wines: mûres, cassis or white peach. Produced by Thiébaud & C°. Sparkling wines, Dôle.

Royal Krušovice Brewery (Czec) *see* Královská Pipovar Krušovice.

Royal Lemon Chocolate Liqueur (Eng) a lemon, cocoa bean-based liqueur produced by Peter Hallgarten, London 30% alc by vol.

Royal Liquid Gold (S.Am) a 10 year old demerara rum produced by Banks DIH Ltd. in Guyana.

Royal Lochnagar (Scot) a single malt whisky distillery based at Deeside, central-eastern Scotland. A highland malt whisky 43% alc by vol.

Royal Love (Cktl) ⅓ measure apricot brandy, ⅓ measure Mandarine Napoléon, ⅙ measure orange juice, ⅙ measure crème de cassis. Shake over ice, strain into a sugar-frosted (egg white and castor sugar) flute glass, top with iced Champagne.

Royal Mail (Cktl) ¼ measure Van der Hum, ¼ measure sloe gin, ¼ measure orange juice, ¼ measure lemon juice, dash Pernod. Shake over ice and strain into a cocktail glass.

Royal Médoc Mousseux (Fr) a dry sparkling wine produced by Château Dauzac in the Médoc, north-western Bordeaux.

Royal Mint Ball (Cktl) ½ measure Royal Mint Chocolate liqueur, ½ measure advocaat, 1½ measures lemonade. Stir over ice and strain into a 125mls (5fl.oz) goblet.

Royal Mint Chocolate Liqueur (Eng) a mint and chocolate liqueur made by Hallgartens 30% alc by vol.

Royal Mint Coffee (Liq.Coffee) using a measure of Royal Mint Chocolate liqueur.

Royal Misa (Sp) a solera brandy from Bodegas Internacionales. *See also* Baron de Brodzia, Mayorazgo, Pemartin.

Royal Mountain (Can) a natural spring mineral water from New Brunswick. Mineral contents

(milligrammes per litre): Fluorides <0.1mg/l. pH 6.9

Royal Mousseux (Ind) a sparkling wine made by the méthode traditionelle, south-east of Bombay in a new winery at Narayangaon. Made from Chardonnay, Pinot meunier and Pinot noir grapes.

Royal Muscadine (Fr) an alternative name for the white Chasselas grape.

Royal Nut Chocolate Liqueur (Eng) a nut and cocoa bean-based liqueur produced by Peter Hallgarten, London 30% alc by vol.

Royal Oak (Eng) a cask-conditioned ale 1048 O.G. brewed by the Eldridge Pope Brewery in Dorchester, Dorset.

Royal Oak (S.Afr) the brand-name of a brandy from Oude Meester.

Royal Oak Twelve (W.Ind) a 12 year old rum produced by Trinidad Distillers Ltd. on the island of Trinidad.

Royal Oporto Wine C°. (Port) vintage Port shippers. Vintages: 1934, 1945, 1952, 1953, 1954, 1955, 1958, 1960, 1961, 1962, 1963, 1965, 1967, 1970, 1975, 1977, 1980, 1983, 1985, 1987, 1991, 1994, 1997, 2003.

Royal Orange Chocolate (Eng) a liqueur made from orange oil and cocoa beans by Hallgarten 30% alc by vol.

Royal Orchard (Eng) the brand-name of a cider produced by the Weston's Cider C°. of Much Marcle, near Ledbury, Herefordshire.

Royal Palace (Sp) a brand-name of an Amontillado Sherry produced by Wisdom and Warter in Jerez de la Frontera.

Royal Pale (Eng) a cask-conditioned ale 1035 O.G. brewed by the Kentish Ales Brewery in Tunbridge Wells, Kent.

Royal Pemartin (Sp) a brand of Oloroso Sherry produced by Sandeman in Jerez de la Frontera.

Royal Pimms (Cktl) 1 part Pimm's N°1 and N°3 and 3 parts Champagne served over ice in a highball glass.

Royal Porter (Eng) a cask-conditioned ale 1050 O.G. brewed by the Kentish Ales Brewery in Tunbridge Wells, Kent.

Royal Punch (Cktl) 2 glasses calves foot jelly, 1 measure arrack, 1 measure Curaçao, 1 measure brandy, 550mls (1pint) boiling green tea, 12 sugar cubes rubbed into rind of 2 limes, 12 slices of lemon. Add all together, serve hot and garnished with the slices of lemon.

Royal Purple (Punch) place into a punch bowl some ice, 2 bottles claret, 1100mls (2pints) ginger ale, 1 sliced lemon and a whole lemon studded with 24 cloves, stand for 10 minutes and serve.

Royal Raspberry Chocolate Liqueur (Eng) a raspberry and chocolate-flavoured liqueur produced by Peter Hallgarten, London 30% alc by vol.

Royal Raven (Eng) a 4.5% alc by vol. cask-conditioned stout from Greene King, Suffolk.

Royal Réserve (Fr) the label used by Philiponnat for a range of vintage and non-vintage Champagnes (including a non-vintage rosé Champagne).

Royal Reserve (Scot) a 20 year old blended Scotch whisky produced by Bells.

Royal Romance (Cktl) ½ measure dry gin, ¼ measure Grand Marnier, ¼ measure passion fruit juice, dash grenadine. Shake over ice and strain into a cocktail glass.

Royal Russian Cocktail (Cktl) 25mls (1fl.oz) vodka, 25mls (1fl.oz) (white) crème de menthe, 10mls (½ fl.oz) cream, dash grenadine. Shake over ice, strain into a Champagne saucer and dress with a cherry.

Royal Salute (Scot) a 21 year old de luxe blended Scotch whisky from the Chivas Brothers (Seagram) 43% alc by vol.

Royal Shaker (Cktl) 300mls (½ pint) milk, 25mls (1fl.oz) Royal Mint Chocolate liqueur, 1 scoop ice cream. Mix in a blender and serve in a tumbler.

Royal Silk (Scot) label of a 40% alc by vol. blended Scotch whisky.

Royal Smile [1] (Cktl) 30mls (¼ gill) Calvados, 60mls (½ gill) dry gin, juice ½ lime (or lemon), 1 teaspoon grenadine. Shake over ice, strain into a 125mls (5fl.oz) goblet and top with a little cream.

Royal Smile [2] (Cktl) 3/10 measure Bell's whisky, ⅕ measure crème de cassis, ⅕ measure pineapple juice, ⅕ measure grapefruit juice, 1/10 measure coconut cream. Shake over ice, strain into a cocktail glass and dress with a cube of pineapple.

Royal Society of Harvesters of the Rioja (Sp) a society formed in 1790 to help improve viticulture and the developing market.

Royal Sovereign (Eng) a cask-conditioned best bitter 1040 O.G. brewed by the Kentish Ales Brewery in Tunbridge Wells, Kent.

Royal Stag (Eng) a seasonal autumn ale brewed by Mansfield Brewery, Littleworth, Mansfield, Notts.

Royal Stag Ale (Eng) a bottled strong ale 1052 O.G. brewed for export by the Paines Brewery in St. Neots, Cambridgeshire.

Royal Standard (Eng) a 4.3% alc by vol. ale brewed by the White Star Brewery, Hampshire.

Royal St-Émilion (Fr) a cave copérative with 775ha. in total under vines. Part of Côtes Rocheues.

Royal Stewart (Scot) a 12 year old de luxe blended Scotch whisky produced by Stewart and Son, Dundee.

Royal Stock (It) a brandy produced by the Stock C°.

Royal Stout (W.Ind) a sweet stout 1054 O.G. brewed by the Carib Brewery C°. in Trinidad.

Royal Tara Irish Cream Liqueur (Ire) an Irish whiskey and cream liqueur produced in Cork 17% alc by vol.

Royal Tawny (Port) a 10 year old dated tawny Port from Sandeman Port shippers.

Royal Taylor Wine Company (USA) a large producer of sparkling wines based near New York.

Royal Toast (Eng) a specially brewed barley wine 1086 O.G. brewed by the Mauldon Brewery in Suffolk to commemorate the engagement of H.R.H. Prince Andrew to Miss Sarah Ferguson in the Spring of 1986.

Royal Triple Sec (Swe) a white Curaçao líqueur produced by the Aktiebolaget Vin & Spritcentralem.

Royalty 1390 (USA) a red-fleshed hybrid grape variety introduced by University of California at Davis for use in dessert wines. A cross between the Alicante Ganzin x Trousseau.

Royal Victor (Cktl) ⅓ measure Liqueur d'Or, ⅓ measure lemon gin, ⅙ measure Cointreau, ⅙ measure lemon squash. Shake over ice, strain into a cocktail glass and add a cherry.

Royal Wedding (Cktl) ¼ measure kirsch, ¼ measure orange juice, ¼ measure peach brandy. Shake well with ice, strain into a large goblet and top with iced Champagne.

Royal Wedding Cocktail (Cktl) ⅖ measure Cointreau, ⅖ measure sirop de fraises, ⅕ measure Cognac. Stir over ice, strain into a flute glass and top with iced Champagne.

Royal Wedding Vintage Character Port (Eng) a vintage character Port introduced by Eldridge Pope to celebrate the wedding of the Prince of Wales in 1981.

Royal Welsh Fusilier (Wal) a 4.5% alc by vol. ale brewed by the Plassey Brewery, Clwyd.

Royal York (Eng) a 4% alc by vol. ale brewed by the York brewery Company Ltd., North Yorkshire.

Royat Cordon (Fr) one of the methods of pruning permitted in the Champagne region. *see* Taille Chablis.

Royé et Fils (Fr) a noted producer of Kosher Beaujolais-Villages wines 8ha. (Add): La Salle, Lantigni, Beaujolais, Burgundy.

Royer [Louis] (Fr) a Cognac producer. (Add): Cognac Louis Royer, B.P. 12, 16200 Jarnac. Noted for the single distilleries collection. *see* Distillerie: Chantal, d'Aumagne, de l'Ecole, les Magnolias, des Saules.

Royet [Bernard et Nicole] (Fr) a winery (13ha) based in Couches, Côtes de Chouchois. (Add): 71490 Couches. Produces: A.C. Maranges Premier Cru Clos Rosssots, A.C. Bourgogne-Côtes-du-Couchois, and other wines. Grape varieties: Aligoté, Chardonnay, Pinot noir.

Roy [René] (Fr) a Cognac producer. (Add): Le Mas, Juillac-le-Coq, 16130 Segonzac. 30ha in Grande Champagne.

Rozana (Fr) a sparkling natural spring mineral water from the Puy-de-Dôme. (Add): 63460 Beauregard, Vendon. Mineral contents (milligrammes per litre): Sodium 493mg/l, Calcium 301mg/l, Magnesium 160mg/l, Potassium 52mg/l, Bicarbonates 1837mg/l, Chlorides 649mg/l, Sulphates 230mg/l, Nitrates 1mg/l. pH 6.3

Rozanne (S.Afr) the label for a red wine (Merlot 59% plus Pinotage and Shiraz) produced by the Bellevue Estate, Stellenbosch, Western Cape.

Roze (Gre)(Tur) rosé.

Rozenberg (Ger) vineyard (Anb): Württemberg. (Ber): Württembergisch Unterland. (Gro): Schalkstein. (Vil): Mundelsheim.

Rozendal Farm (S.Afr) a winery (established 1983) based at Stellenbosch, Western Cape. 6ha. (Add): Box 160, Stellenbosch 7600. Grape varieties: Cabernet franc, Cabernet sauvignon, Merlot. Produces varietal wines.

Rozès (Port) a company owned by Moët-Hennessy Port shippers since 1978. Based in Vila Nova de Gaia. Vintages: 1963, 1967, 1977, 1978, 1981, 1983, 1985, 1987, 1991, 1994, 1997, 1998, 2003.

Rozier Bay (S.Afr) the label for a red wine range produced by the Mount Rozier Estate winery, Stellenbosch, Western Cape.

Rozier Reef (S.Afr) the label for a red wine range produced by the Mount Rozier Estate winery, Stellenbosch, Western Cape.

Rozova Dolina (Bul) a vineyard area in the west of the Sub-Balkan region. Mainly white wines produced.

Rozovoe Vino (Rus) rosé wine.

Rozsa (Rum) rosé.

RPB S.A (Arg) a winery based in the Mendoza region, eastern Argentina. Website: http://www.baggio.com.ar 'E'mail: jcaminos@baggio.com.ar

R62 (S.Afr) the label for a red wine (Cabernet sauvignon and Merlot blend) produced by the Joubert-Tradauw Private Cellar winery, Little Karro.

RSVP (Eng) the brand-name used by Vine Products Ltd. for a brand of their British Sherry.

RTD (Eng) abbr: see Ready To Drink.

Ruadh (Scot) a dry, spicy rye cask ale brewed by the Maclay Brewery of Alloa in April (Gaelic = red).

Rub-a-dub (Eng) a Cockney rhyming slang for a pub (public-house).

Rubber (Eng) an off-aroma found in some wines caused by reduction.

Rubberdy (Austr) a slang term for a pub. (from Rub-a-dub-dub), also pronounced Rubbity or Rubidy. Also spelt Rubbity and Rubidy.

Rubbity (Austr) see Rubberdy. Also spelt Rubidy.

Rubby (Can) a slang used to denote an old drunkard (a down and out).

Rubellite (S.Afr) the label for a sparkling Port-style wine produced by the Waboomsrivier Co-operative winery, Worcester, Western Cape.

Rubens Rood (Bel) a 4% alc by vol. bottle-conditioned special red beer brewed by Du Bocq Brasserie in Namur.

Rubér (S.Afr) the label for a red wine (Cabernet sauvignon and Merlot blend) produced by the Stonewall Wines winery, Stellenbosch, Western Cape.

Rüberberger Domherrenberg (Ger) vineyard (Anb): Mosel-Saar-Ruwer. (Ber): Zell/Mosel. (Gro): Goldbäumchen. (Vil): Briedern.

Rüberberger Domherrenberg (Ger) vineyard (Anb): Mosel-Saar-Ruwer. (Ber): Zell/Mosel. (Gro): Goldbäumchen. (Vil): Ellenz-Poltersdorf.

Rüberberger Domherrenberg (Ger) vineyard (Anb): Mosel-Saar-Ruwer. (Ber): Zell/Mosel. (Gro): Goldbäumchen. (Vil): Senheim.

Rüberberger Domherrenberg (Ger) vineyard (Anb): Mosel-Saar-Ruwer. (Ber): Zell/Mosel. (Gro): Schwarze Katz. (Vil): Senheim.

Rubesco Torgiano Riserva (It) a D.O.C.G. single vineyard red wine produced by Lungarotti in Umbria.

Rubicon (S.Afr) the label for a red wine (Cabernet franc 10%, Cabernet sauvignon 70% and Merlot 20% blend) produced by the Meerlust Estate winery, Stellenbosch, Western Cape.

Rubicon Estate (USA) a winery based in the Rutherford, Napa Valley, California. Grape varieties include: Cabernet sauvignon. Label: Cask Cabernet. Owned by the Nieubaum-Coppola estate.

Rubidy (Austr) see Rubberdy. Also spelt Rubbity.

Rubin (Aus) the label for a red (Zweigelt) wine produced by the Markowitsch winery, Göttlesbrunn, Carnuntum.

Rubin (Bul) a red grape variety cross (Nebbiolo x Syrah) first produced in the 1940's. Has low acidity with good colour, fruit and firm tannins.

Rubiner (S.Afr) a light red wine made from Cabernet grapes by the Villiera estate in Paarl, Western Cape.

Rubino (It) ruby.

Rubino (It) a rare style of Marsala from Perricone, Calabrese, Nerello mascalese plus up to 30% white grape varieties in Sicily. See also Ambra and Oro.

Rubino di Cantavenna (It) a D.O.C. red wine from Piemonte. Made from 75%–90% Barbera and up to 25% Grignolino/Fresia grapes.

Rubinosa (Nor) a sloe liqueur.

Rubion (USA) a hybrid red grape variety developed by the University of California. Is grown in the Paul Masson Vineyard.

Rubired (USA) a red-fleshed hybrid grape variety grown in California, produced by crossing (Alicante ganzin x Tinto cão).

Rubis Cocktail (Cktl) 1 measure Noilly Prat, 4 dashes Cherry Heering, 3 dashes lime juice, 4 dashes Bourbon whiskey. Stir over ice, strain into a cocktail glass, dress with a cherry and a slice of lime.

Ruby (Eng) the colour of certain red wines, denotes a deep purple/red colour typical of a young wine. (It) = rubino.

Ruby (Eng) a 3.9% alc by vol. ale brewed by Tarka Ales Ltd., Devon.

Ruby Ale (Eng) 6.2% alc by vol. bottled ale brewed by Usher of Trowbridge. Part of the Vintage Ale Collection. See also Tawny Ale, White Ale.

Ruby Bay Wines (N.Z) a 4.1ha. winery. (Add): Korepo Road, (RD 1), Upper Moutere, Nelson.

Ruby Cabernet (USA) a varietal red grape grown in the Napa Valley, California. Cross between Cariñena and Cabernet sauvignon.

Ruby Cocktail (Cktl) ½ measure dry vermouth, ½ measure sloe gin, 3 dashes raspberry syrup. Stir over ice and strain into a cocktail glass.

Ruby 1874 Mild (I.O.M) a 3.5% alc by vol. mild ale

R

brewed by the Mount Murray Brewery C°. (Bushys), Isle of Man.

Ruby Fizz (Cktl) 50mls (2fl.ozs) sloe gin, 1 egg white, juice ½ lemon, 3 dashes grenadine, 3 dashes gomme syrup. Shake over ice, strain into an ice-filled highball glass and top with soda water.

Ruby Jack (Eng) a limited edition ale brewed by the St. Austell Brewery, St. Austell, Cornwall (so called because it was the nickname of a famous Cornish fighter).

Ruby Mild (Eng) a 4.4% alc by vol. mild ale brewed by the Rudgate Brewery Ltd., North Yorkshire.

Ruby Newt (Eng) a 3.6% alc by vol. ale brewed by the Burrington Brewery, Devon.

Ruby Port (Port) a young deep red blended Port.

Ruby Ratchet's Porter (Eng) a 5.3% alc by vol. seasonal porter ale brewed by Hydes of Manchester in January and February.

Ruby Red Bitter (Eng) a bitter brewed by the Cameron Brewery, Hartlepool, Yorkshire.

Ruby's (Eng) a cranberry soda range of drinks containing sparkling water from Britvic. Flavours include: blueberry, raspberry, orange.

Ruby Wine (Eng) a British wine of a Port type (sweet and rich).

Ruchè (It) a red Piemonte grape variety. Also known as Roche, Rouchet.

Ruchets [Les] (Fr) an A.C. Cornas wine produced by Colombo (Jean Luc), La Roche, Tain l'Hermitage.

Ruchots [Les] (Fr) a Premier Cru vineyard in the A.C. commune of Morey-Saint-Denis, Côte de Nuits, Burgundy 2.6ha.

Ruchottes-Chambertin (Fr) a Grand Cru vineyard in the A.C. commune of Gevrey-Chambertin, Côte de Nuits, Burgundy 3.2ha.

Rück (Ger) village (Anb): Franken. (Ber): Mainviereck. (Gro): Not yet assigned. (Vins): Jesuitenberg, Johannisberg.

Rudd Estate (USA) a winery based in Oakville, Napa Valley, California that produces a cult red wine. (Add): 500 Oakville Crossroads, Oak ville, CA 94562. Grape varieties: Cabernet sauvignon. Labels: Cream Label, Oakville Estate, Orange Label. Website: http://www.ruddwines.com

Ruddles Brewery (Eng) a brewery based in Langham, Rutland (Leicestershire). Noted for cask-conditioned Rutland Bitter 1032 O.G. County 1050 O.G. Ruddles Best 1037 O.G. Barley Wine 1080 O.G. Also Ruddles Character Ale range. *see* Bob's Gold, Ebeneezer's Surprise, Laxton's Honey Beer, Parry's Porter.

Ruddles County (Eng) a 4.7% premium cask-conditioned ale from Ushers Brewery (Greene King). Now 4.3% alc by vol. Originally brewed by Rutland at 5% alc by vol.

Rude (Fr) astringent.

Rudera Wines (S.Afr) a winery (established 1999) based in Stellenbosch, Western Cape. 18ha. Grape varieties: Cabernet sauvignon, Chenin blanc, Shiraz, Label: Robusto. Website: http://www.rudera.co.za

Rüdesheim (Ger) village (Anb): Nahe. (Ber): Schloss Böckelheim. (Gro): Rosengarten. (Vins): Goldgrube, Wiesberg.

Rüdesheim (Ger) village (Anb): Rheingau. (Ber): Johannisberg. (Gro): Burgweg. (Vins): Berg Roseneck, Berg Rottland, Berg Schlossberg, Bischofsberg, Drachenstein, Kirchenpfad, Klosterberg, Klosterlay, Magdalenenkreuz, Rosengarten.

Rudezusa (Slo) a wine-producing area near the Dalmatian coast in the south.

Rudgate Brewery (Eng) brewery (established 1992). (Add): Unit 2, Centre Park, Marston Moor Business Park, Tockwith, York, North Yorkshire YO26 7QF. Brews: Battleaxe Best Bitter 4.2% alc by vol. Bernie's LXIV 4.5% alc by vol., Ruby Mild 4.4% alc by vol., Rudolf's Ruin 5.4% alc by vol., Special 4.5% alc by vol., Ideas of March 4.7% alc by vol., Norse Necta, Viking 3.8% alc by vol., Well Blathered 5% alc by vol. Website: http://www.rudgate-beers.co.uk 'E'mail: sales@rudgate-brewery.co.uk

Rudi Schulz Wines (S.Afr) a winery (established 2002) based in Stellenbosch, Western Cape. Grape varieties include: Syrah.

Rudolfinger Beerli (Switz) a red wine produced from Pinot noir grapes.

Rudolf Quelle (Czec) a natural spring mineral water from BJ37, Marienbad. Mineral contents (milligrammes per litre): Sodium 84.17mg/l, Calcium 276.7mg/l, Magnesium 136.2mg/l, Potassium 11.13mg/l, Bicarbonates 1581mg/l, Chlorides 45.32mg/l, Sulphates 122.7mg/l, Fluorides 0.103mg/l, Silicates 117.8mg/l.

Rudolfs Revenge (Eng) *see* Alford Arms.

Rudolph (Eng) a 5% alc by vol. ale brewed by the Stonehenge Ales (Bunces Brewery) Ltd., Wiltshire.

Rudolph's Revenge (Eng) a 4.6% alc by vol. ale brewed by the Cropton Brewery, North Yorkshire.

Rudolfs Ruin (Eng) a 5.4% alc by vol. ale brewed by Rudgate Brewery, Tockwith, North Yorkshire.

Rudolf Steiner (Aus) *see* Biodynamics.

Rudolfuv Pramen (Czec) a natural spring mineral water from Marienbad.

Rudolph the Redruth Brain Beer (Eng) a 3.5% alc by vol. cask-conditioned ale brewed by the Redruth Brewery, Cornwall.

Rueda (Sp) a Denominación de Origen district and wine town in the Valladolid region. Produces white Sherry-style wines (high in alcohol) and dry white wines. Grape varieties: Palomino, Sauvignon blanc, Verdejo blanco, Viura. Plus experimental varieties of Tempranillo, Cabernet sauvignon, Chardonnay. Verdejo must be present to 25% in Rueda and 85% in D.O. Rueda Superior. Rueda Espumoso, Rueda Pálido, Rueda Dorada also produced.

Rueda Dorada (Sp) a dry, Vino de Licor flor wine, rancio in style. 15% alc by vol. white wine aged for four years (two in oak). Produced in D.O. Rueda.

Rueda Espumoso (Sp) a sparkling wine made by the

1117

metodo tradicional in D.O. Rueda. Produced from a minimum of 85% Verdejo with a minimum of 9 months on the lees before disgorging. Must be between 11.5 and 13% alc by vol. and show a vintage on the label.

Rueda Pálido (Sp) a dry, Vino de Licor flor wine. 15% alc by vol. white wine aged in oak for a minimum of three years before release.

Rue-de-Chaux (Fr) a Premier Cru vineyard in the A.C. commune of Nuits-Saint-Georges, Côte de Nuits, Burgundy 3ha.

Ruedo (Sp) a dry, pale, light white wine at 14% alc by vol. produced in Montilla-Moriles (not a solera wine).

Ruedos (Sp) compact loam soil found in D.O. Montilla-Moriles. *See also* Alberos.

Ruelle-Pertois (Fr) a Champagne producer (6ha). (Add): 11, Rue de Champagne, 51350 Moussy. Produces vintage and non-vintage Champagnes.

Rue Royale (Cktl) 2 measures dry gin, 4 dashes anisette, ½ egg white, 4 dashes milk. Shake over ice and strain into a cocktail glass.

Rufach (Fr) the German name of the town of Rouffach in the Haut-Rhin in Alsace. *See also* Ruffach.

Rufete (Port) an early ripening red grape variety used in the making of Port. Also known as the Tinto pinheira.

Ruffach (Fr) the German name for the town of Rouffach in the Haut-Rhin in Alsace. *See also* Rufach.

Ruffiac (Fr) a white grape variety used in the production of A.C. Pachérenc du Vic Bihl in the Pyrénées. Also known as Arrufiac.

Ruffino (It) a famous Chianti producer who belongs to neither the Classico or Putto consorzio. *see* Riserva Ducale Oro.

Rufina (It) a commune of Chianti in Tuscany.

Rugenbräu Brauerei AG (Switz) a brewery. (Add): Wagnerenstrasse 40, 3800 Matten-Interlaken. Brews beers and lagers. Website: http://www.rugenbraeu.ch 'E'mail: office@rugenbraeu.ch

Ruggeri [L] (It) a sparkling (metodo tradizionale) wine producer based in the Veneto region.

Ruggie's Russet Nectar (Eng) a 7.6% alc by vol. seasonal ale brewed by Green Bottle Ltd., Worth Brewery, Keighley, Yorkshire.

Rugiada (It) a natural spring mineral water from Rugiada.

Rugiens-Bas [Les] (Fr) a Premier Cru vineyard in the A.C. commune of Pommard, Côte de Beaune, Burgundy 5.8ha.

Rugiens-Hauts [Les] (Fr) a Premier Cru vineyard in the A.C. commune of Pommard, Côte de Beaune, Burgundy 7.6ha.

Ruinart Père et Fils (Fr) a Champagne producer. (Add): 4 Rue des Crayères, 51100 Reims. A Grande Marque. Produces vintage and non-wines. Produces: Brut Rosé. Vintages: 1900, 1904, 1911, 1914, 1919, 1921, 1923, 1926, 1928, 1929, 1934, 1937, 1941, 1943, 1945, 1947, 1949, 1952, 1953, 1955, 1959, 1961, 1964, 1966, 1969, 1971, 1973, 1975, 1976, 1978, 1979, 1981, 1982, 1985, 1986, 1988, 1990, 1995, 1998, 1999, 2001. Website: http://www.ruinart.com

Ruins (S.Afr) the label for a range of wines produced by the Bon Cap winery, Robertson, Western Cape.

Ruitersvlei Estate (S.Afr) a 289ha winery (established 1692). (Add): P.O. Box 532, Suider Paarl 7624. Grape varieties: Cabernet sauvignon, Chardonnay, Chenin blanc, Colombard, Merlot, Pinotage, Sauvignon blanc, Shiraz. Labels: Four Sisters, Gold, Mountainside, Rider's Valley. Website: http://www.ruitersvlei.co.za

Ruiz (Mex) a well-known brand of tequila.

Ruiz (Sp) a solera brandy produced by José Esteve. *See also* Guadal, Sautu.

Ruiz [José Garijo] (Sp) a noted producer and exporter of Málaga.

Ruiz [Luis Ortiz] (Sp) a producer of Montilla-Moriles wines.

Ruiz Hermanos (Sp) a second range of Sherries produced by Ruiz Mateos.

Ruiz Mateos (Sp) a Sherry bodega and producer. Gives its name to the Rumasa group.

Ruju (It) red (Sardinia).

Ruländer (Ger) a white grape variety grown mainly in Baden and Franconia. Also known as the Auxerrois gris, Fauvet, Grauer riesling, Grey burgundy, Pinot grigio, Pinot gris, Tokayer, Grauburgunder, Grauer burgunder.

Rulany (Czec) the local name used for a grape related to the Ruländer.

Rule of Three (Eng) an unwritten rule that states that to be under the limit for the Drink Drive Laws (80 milligrammes of alcohol to 100 millilitres of blood), the average person can drink: 3 x glasses of table wine or 3 x ⅙ gill (20mls) spirits or 3 x ⅓ gill (40mls) Sherries or 3 x ½ pints (250mls) beer. *It is a dangerous rule to follow.*

Rully (Fr) a district (207ha) of the Côte Chalonnaise in southern Burgundy. Produces A.C. red, white and sparkling wines.

Rum (W.Ind) a spirit made from molasses distilled by the pot-still or patent-still methods. A light, clear spirit which is either matured in oak casks and coloured with caramel. i.e. Jamaican, Martinique. or left clear i.e. Cuban and Puerto Rican. *see* Dunder. (Den) = rom, (Fr) = rhum.

Rum Alexander Cocktail (Cktl) ⅓ measure crème de cacao, ⅓ measure rum, ⅓ measure cream. Shake well over ice and strain into a cocktail glass.

Rum and Rill Water (Cktl) an old name for the highball.

Rumania (Rum) a large wine-producing country in eastern Europe. Produces most styles of wines. Main regions: Banat, Cotnari, Dealul-Mare, Murfatler, Tîrnave and Vrancea. Local grapes include: Feteasca Alba, Francusa, Grasa, Murfatler, Tamîoasa. *See also* Romania.

Rumasa Group (Sp) was one of the largest Sherry producers in Spain. Run by the Government since 1983.

Rumbarricoe (Eng) a container (cask) for holding

rum on a ship, was guarded by an officer until rum rations were issued.

Rum Booze (Cktl) beat 4 egg yolks and 2 tablespoons sugar. Heat ½ bottle of Sherry, grated peel of ½ lemon, 1 teaspoon grated nutmeg, stick of cinammon. Bring to the boil, add 3 measures rum. Add to the egg yolks, stir well, serve in glasses with a drop of sweetened, beaten egg white on top.

Rumbooze (W.Ind) a term used to denote a good wine in Puerto Rico, also spelt Rambooze.

Rumbullion (Eng) a name given to the rum from which it gets its name in the seventeenth century. *See also* Rumbustion.

Rumbustion (Eng) *see* Rumbullion.

Rum Cobbler (Cktl) 1 measure dark rum, 1 barspoon sugar, 4 dashes orange Curaçao, fill a medium-sized goblet with ice, add the ingredients, stir, decorate with sliced fruit and a sprig of mint and serve with straws.

Rum Cocktail (Cktl) a 40mls (⅓ gill) rum, 2 dashes Angostura, dash brown Curaçao, stir over ice, strain into a cocktail glass, serve with a cherry and dash of lemon peel juice.

Rum Cola (Cktl) *see* Cuba Libra.

Rum Collins (Cktl) 90mls (¾ gill) rum, sugar syrup to taste, juice of ½ lemon, shake well together over ice, strain into an ice-filled highball and top with soda water.

Rum Company [Jamaica] Ltd. (W.Ind) a company (established 1943) by a Swiss firm on the island of Jamaica. Produces Coruba and Sugar Mill rums.

Rum Cooler (Cktl) 1 measure dark rum, 4 dashes Angostura, juice of lemon or lime. Shake over ice, strain into an ice-filled highball glass and fill with soda water.

Rum Corps [The] (Austr) an old nickname given to the police in New South Wales (also known as Corps) to help enforce a ban on rum distribution. They forced a strangle force on the rum trade.

Rum Daisy [1] (Cktl) 50mls (2fl.ozs) Bacardi White Label, ½ teaspoon yellow Chartreuse, juice ½ lime, dash Angostura, teaspoon gomme syrup. Stir well together over ice, strain into an ice-filled highball glass, garnish with mint, cherries and fruit in season.

Rum Daisy [2] (Cktl) 60mls (½ gill) rum, 2 dashes brown Curaçao, 15mls (⅛ gill) grenadine, 60mls (½ gill) lemon juice. Shake over ice, strain into a highball glass, top with soda, decorate with fresh fruit and a spoon.

Rum Domaci (Slo) a brand of rum produced by Badel-Vinoprodukt in Zagreb.

Rum Dubonnet (Cktl) ⅔ measure white rum, ⅓ measure Dubonnet, 2 dashes lemon juice. Shake over ice and strain into a cocktail glass.

Rum Egg Nogg (Cktl) 80mls (⅔ gill) rum, 1 egg, 90mls (¾ gill) milk, 1 teaspoon sugar. Shake over ice, strain into a tumbler and top with grated nutmeg.

Rum Egg Punch (Cktl) 12 beaten eggs, 1 bottle Jamaican rum, 300mls (½ pint) cream, ½ bottle brandy, sugar to taste. Stir well in a punch bowl and finish with grated nutmeg.

Rumeni Muskat (Slo) a medium-dry, white wine produced in north-east Slovenia.

Rum Fix (Cktl) ⅚ measure white rum, ⅙ measure lemon juice, 1 teaspoon powdered sugar. Stir over ice in a highball glass, top with soda water, slice of lemonand serve with straws.

Rum Fizz (Cktl) 2 measures white rum, juice of 2 lemons, 2 teaspoons sugar. Shake well over ice, strain into a highball glass and top with soda water.

Rum Flip (Eng) an old drink that consisted of ale, mulled rum, cream, spices and beaten eggs (mulled with a hot poker).

Rum Float (Cktl) 1 measure white rum, juice ½ lime, 1 teaspoon sugar. In an ice-filled highball glass mix the juice and sugar, top with soda, stir and pour rum in over the back of a spoon to float. Add slice of lime on rim of glass.

Rum Gimlet (Cktl) 25mls (1fl.oz) white rum, 10mls (½ fl.oz) lime juice, dash gomme syrup. Stir over ice, strain into a cocktail glass and dress with a slice of lime.

Rum Highball (Cktl) as for Gin Highball using rum.

Rum Hospital (Austr) the name given to a hospital building built by contractors who were granted a 45000 gallon monopoly to import rum over 3 years in lieu of cash for their work.

Rumi (Slo) a red grape variety.

Rum Julep (Cktl) as for Mint Julep but substitute dark rum for brandy.

Rum Mac (Cktl) ½ measure dark rum, ½ measure ginger wine. Stir over ice, strain into a small wine glass (can add a dash of water).

Rummager (Scot) four rotating arms carrying a copper mesh chain inside the wash-still in malt whisky production, used to prevent solid particles in the wash sticking and burning.

Rümmelsheim (Ger) village (Anb): Nahe. (Ber): Kreuznach. (Gro): Schlosskapelle. (Vins): Hölle, Johannisberg, Rothenberg, Schlossberg, Steinkopfchen.

Rummer (Eng) a name given to the roemer glass in the nineteenth century.

Rum Milk Punch (Cktl) 125mls (1gill) milk, 25mls (⅕ gill) Jamaican rum, dash gomme syrup, shake over ice, strain into a collins glass and top with nutmeg.

Rümmingen (Ger) village (Anb): Baden. (Ber): Markgräflerland. (Gro): Vogtei Rötteln. (Vin): Sonnhohle.

Rummy (USA) the nickname for an alcoholic who likes rum.

Rumney (Eng) the old Elizabethan name for Rumanian wines. *See also* Romany.

Rumona (W.Ind) a rum liqueur produced on the island of Jamaica.

Rumor (Sp) the name used for a range of red and white wines from San Isidro in Jumilla in the Levante.

Rum Orange Cocktail (Cktl) 25mls (1fl.oz) white

rum into an ice-filled highball glass. Top with orange juice and dress with orange slices.

Rumor-Bagaceira do Minho (Port) an aguardente produced by Caves Dom Teodósio.

Rum Punch (Cktl) 90mls (¾ gill) rum, 1 tablespoon gomme syrup, juice of ½ lemon, dash brandy, shake well over ice, strain into a 125mls (5fl.oz) wine glass and top with soda water.

Rumpus (Eng) a 4.5% alc by vol. ruby-coloured ale from the Ridley Brewery, Essex. Also available in bottle.

Rum Rickey (Cktl) ¾ measure Bacardi White Label, ¼ measure lime juice. Stir over ice in a highball glass, top with soda and a slice of lime.

Rum Runner (USA) a person who brought in spirits from his boat anchored outside the 3 mile limit during Prohibition 1919–1933.

Rum Runner Cocktail (Cktl) ⅗ measure dry gin, ⅖ measure pineapple juice, juice of a lime, dash Angostura, 2 dashes gomme syrup. Shake over ice and strain into a salt-rimmed cocktail glass.

Rum Screwdriver (Cktl) as for a Screwdriver Cocktail substituting white rum for the vodka.

Rum Shops (W.Ind) the nickname for Barbadian taverns that serve cheap rum (and groceries).

Rum Shrub (Eng) 1.1lts (2pints) dark rum, 400mls (¾ pint) orange juice, 100grms (¼ lb) loaf sugar, mix altogether, place in a covered container and rest for six weeks.

Rum Smash (Cktl) as for Gin Smash but substitute rum for gin.

Rum Sour (Cktl) 20mls (¾ fl.oz) lemon or lime juice, 35mls (1½ fl.ozs) white rum, 1 teaspoon powdered sugar, shake over ice, strain into an old-fashioned glass, add cherry and a slice of orange.

Rum Swizzle (Cktl) as for Gin Swizzle but using white rum in place of the gin.

Rum Toddy (Cktl) 1 cube sugar, 35mls (1½ fl.ozs) Jamaican rum, fill the glass with boiling water, rum and sugar, stir with cinnamon stick, garnish with lemon and 4 cloves and twist of lemon peel juice.

Rum Verschnitt (Ger) *see* Rhum Verschnitt.

Rumverschuitt (Ger) *see* Rhum Verschnitt.

Rund (Ger) round.

Run De Quan (Chi) a natural spring mineral water. Mineral contents (milligrammes per litre): Sodium 19.8mg/l, Calcium 48.7mg/l, Magnesium 21.9mg/l, Potassium 1.4mg/l, Bicarbonates 294.7mg/l, Silicates 13.7mg/l.

Rund um die Nahe-Weinstrasse (Ger) the Nahe region wine festival.

Runlet (Eng) a small cask used in mediaeval times for beer, wines and spirits.

Runnels (Fr) wooden troughs from which the grape juice runs from the presses to vats in Champagne.

Runners (Eng) the bands on wine casks that keep the main staves off the floor when the cask is being moved (rolled).

Running Wine (USA) *see* Free Run Wine.

Runnymede Island (N.Z) a brand label for a white (Sauvignon blanc) and red (Pinot noir) range of wines especially produced for the Shepherd Neame (wine & spirit division) by the Jackson Estate, Marlborough.

Rupert & Rothschild (S.Afr) a winery (established 1997) based in Simondium, Paarl, Western Cape. The wines produced are a joint venture between Anthonij Rupert and Benjamin Rothschild (owner of Château Clarke, Listrac). Range includes Baron Edmond (Cabernet and Merlot blend) and Classique (mainly Merlot), Baroness Nadine (Chardonnay). Website: http://www.rupert-rothschildvignerons.com

Rupert Group (S.Afr) a group that has links with the United Breweries of Denmark (Carlsberg and Tuborg) and Carling of Canada.

Rupert's Ruin (Eng) a 4.2% alc by vol. ale brewed by the Springhead Brewery, Nottinghamshire.

Rupestris du lot (Fr) American root stock used for grafting at Châteauneuf-du-Pape in the Rhône.

Rupestris martin (Mad) a rootstock found on Madeira.

Rupestris monticola (Mad) a rootstock found on Madeira.

Rupestris St.George (USA) the basic root stock used for grafting to fight off Phylloxera.

Rupestris x Berlandieri (Mad) a cross American rootstock found on Madeira. Likes clay soil.

Ruppert Brewery (USA) a brewery based in New Bedford.

Ruppertsberg (Ger) village (Anb): Pfalz. (Ber): Mittelhaardt-Deutsche Weinstrasse. (Gro): Hofstück. (Vins): Gaisböhl, Hoheburg, Linsenbusch, Nussbien, Reiterpfad, Spiess.

Rural-Method (Fr) *see* Méthode Rurale.

Rusa (Rom) a local name for the Gewürztraminer grape.

Rusalca (Sp) a brand of vodka produced by Campeny in Barcelona.

Ruscella (It) a natural spring mineral water from Modica, Ragusa.

RusdenDriftsand (Austr) a winery based in the Barossa Valley, South Australia. Grape varieties include: Grenache, Mourvèdre, Shiraz.

Russ (Ger) a drink made from a top-fermented beer mixed with lemonade half and half (a shandy).

Russe (Bul) a D.G.O. region in the Northern area. Produces red and white wines.

Russenski Briag (Bul) a vineyard area in the Northern Basic region.

Russet Ale (Eng) a bottled mild ale 1032 O.G. brewed by the Elgood Brewery in Wisbech, Cambridgeshire.

Russia [R.S.F.S.R.] (Rus) produces a range of spirits (especially vodka), beers and wines. The main regions are the Don Valley and the Krasnodar area. *See also* U.S.S.R.

Russian Bear (Cktl) ½ measure vodka, ¼ measure (white) crème de cacao, ¼ measure cream. Shake over ice and strain into a cocktail glass.

Russian Caravan (Chi) a blend of Anhwei province and Taiwan Oolong teas. Has excellent fragrance, named after the camel caravans that crossed Russia.

R

Russian Champagne (Rus) produced between Anapa and Gelendshipe districts. Has names such as Krasnodar, Tbilisi and Tsimlyanskoye.

Russian Cocktail (Cktl) ⅓ measure vodka, ⅓ measure gin, ⅓ measure crème de cacao. Shake over ice and strain into a cocktail glass.

Russian Coffee (Liq.Coffee) using a measure of vodka.

Russian Imperial (Eng) a bottled stout 1098 O.G. brewed by Courage.

Russian Method (Eng) *see* Continuous Method.

Russian River Valley (USA) an A.V.A. wine producing region north of San Francisco. Has 2 sub-regions, both A.V.A: Chalk Hill and Green Valley. Main Grape varieties: Chardonnay, Gewürztraminer, Sauvignon blanc, Cabernet sauvignon, Merlot, Pinot noir, Zinfandel. Wineries include Dry Creek, Korbel and Simi.

Russian River Vineyards (USA) a winery based in the Russian River Valley, California. Produces varietal wines.

Russian Rum (Rus) made from sugar cane grown around the area of Tashkent.

Russian Stout (Eng) an ale originally brewed for the Russian Imperial family. A strong, vintage stout which is well matured now brewed by Courage 1100 O.G. matured 1 year, sold in date-stamped nip size bottles.

Russian Tea (Rus) a tea served without milk in a glass seated in a two-handled silver holder. A slice of lemon is added and sugar to taste, also known in England as Lemon tea.

Russin (Switz) a wine-producing area in Geneva.

Rüssingen (Ger) village (Anb): Pfalz. (Ber): Mittelhaardt-Deutsche Weinstrasse. (Gro): Schnepfenflug vom Zellertal. (Vin): Breinsberg.

Russkaya (Rus) a clean, neutral vodka 37.5% alc by vol.

Russky Blazam (Rus) a bitter, spicy, dark brown Nastoika (high in alcohol).

Rüssling (Ger) an old eighteenth century German name for the Riesling grape.

Rust (Aus) a wine growing area in Burgenland that is noted for Ausbruch wines.

Rusted Soil (S.Afr) the label for a white wine (Chardonnay) produced by the Weltevrede Estate winery, Robertson Western Cape.

Rustenberg Estate (S.Afr) *see* Schoongezicht Estate.

Rustenberg Wines (S.Afr) red wines produced by the Schoongezicht Estate, P.O. Box 33, Stellenbosch 7599. Gape varieties include: Cabernet sauvignon, Chardonnay. Label: Five Soldiers. Website: http://www.rustenberg.co.za

Rust-en-Vrede (S.Afr) a winery (established 1694) based in Stellenbosch, Western Cape. 50ha. (Add): Box 473, Stellenbosch 7599. Grape varieties: Cabernet sauvignon, Merlot, Shiraz. Label: Peter Barlow. Website: http://www.rustenvrede.com

Ruster Ausbruch (Aus) a white wine produced from late-picked grapes in the Lake District, Burgenland.

Rusthof Wines (S.Afr) *see* Mooiuitsig Wynkelders, a brand-name for the varietals produced by them.

Rusticus Vintage Cellar (S.Afr) a winery (established 2001) based in Robertson, Western Cape. Grape varieties: Cabernet sauvignon, Merlot, Pinotage, Pinot noir, Ruby cabernet, Shiraz, Website: http://www.patbusch.co.za

Rust (Aus) a famous wine town noted for the production of ausbruch-style wines. *see* Ruster Ausbruch.

Rust Neusiedlersee (Aus) a wine district within the region of Burgenland. Produces mainly white wines.

Rusty Nail (Cktl) 1½ measures Scotch whisky, ½ measure Drambuie, stir '*on the rocks*' in an old-fashioned glass and add a twist of lemon.

Rutalian (Eng) a 4.8% alc by vol. ale brewed by the Brewster Brewing C°. Ltd., Leicestershire.

Ruthe (Ger) vineyard (Anb): Württemberg. (Ber): Württembergisch Unterland. (Gro): Heuchelberg. (Vil): Nordheim.

Ruthe (Ger) vineyard (Anb): Württemberg. (Ber): Württembergisch Unterland. (Gro): Heuchelberg. (Vil): Schwaigern.

Rutherford (USA) an A.V.A. wine-producing town based in the central Napa Valley, California. *See also* Oakville.

Rutherford and Miles (Mad) a Madeira producer. Produces Old Custom House Extra Pale Sercial, La Reina Verdelho, Old Trinity House Bual and Fine Old Malmsey.

Rutherford Grove Winery (USA) a winery based in Rutherford, Napa Valley, California. (Add): PO Box 552, Rutherford, CA 94573. Grape variety: Cabernet sauvignon. Website: http://www.rutherfordgrave.com 'E'mail: info@rutherfordgrove.com

Rutherford Hill Winery (USA) a winery based near Rutherford, Napa Valley, California. Grape varieties: Chardonnay, Gewürztraminer, Merlot, White riesling and Zinfandel. Produces varietal wines.

Rutherford Ranch (USA) a label owned by a Napa Valley grower in California.

Rutherford Vintners (USA) a winery based near Rutherford, Napa Valley, California. Grape varieties: Cabernet sauvignon, Johannisberg riesling and Pinot noir. Produces varietal wines.

Rutherglen (Austr) a large vineyard site in Victoria, based 200kms north of Melbourne. Famous for liqueur Muscats and Tokays produced on red loam soil.

Ruthven Brew (Scot) a 3.8% alc by vol. ale brewed by the Aviemore Brewery.

Rutin (Eng). *see* Flavenoids.

Rutini Wines (Arg) a winery based in the Mendoza region, eastern Argentina. Website: http://www.rutiniwines.com 'E'mail: exports@rutiniwines.com

Rutland Beast (Eng) a 5.3% alc by vol. bitter ale brewed by Davis'es Brewing C°. Ltd., Rutland.

Rutland Bitter (Eng) a cask-conditioned bitter 1032 O.G. brewed by the Ruddles Brewery in Rutland, Leicestershire.

Rutland Independence Ale (Eng) a 6.5% alc by vol. bottled ale brewed by Ruddles in Langham.

Rutland Panther (Eng) a 3.4% alc by vol. ale brewed by Davis'es Brewing C°. Ltd., Rutland.

Rutterkin (Eng) a 4.6% alc by vol. ale brewed by the Brewster Brewing C°. Ltd., Leicestershire.

Ruttgers (Ger) a large producer of Deutsche Sekt.

Ruwer [River] (Ger) a tributary of the river Mosel which joins it at the village of Ruwer in the upper Mosel.

Ruzica (Ser) lit: 'little rose', a rosé wine from the Serbia, also known as Dinka.

Rwanda Coffee (Afr) an arabica pure coffee grown on Rwanda, has good acidity and a full-flavour.

Rwenzori (Afr) a natural spring mineral water from Uganda.

RWT (Austr) a quality red wine (Shiraz) from the Penfolds winery now sealed with a scewcap top (from 2004 vintage).

Ryans Daughter (Cktl) 1 measure Irish Mist, ¾ measure crème de cacao. Pour into a small cocktail glass with crushed ice and float a little cream on top.

Ryan's Genuine Irish Cream Liqueur (Ire) a liqueur produced in Dublin from Irish cream and Irish whiskey (first produced in 1981).

Ryburn Brewery (Eng) a brewery based at Sowerby Bridge, near Halifax, West Yorkshire. Brews: Hair of the Dog 4.5% alc by vol.

Rydon Spring (Eng) a bottled still or sparkling spring water from a naturally occurring artesian well in Kingsteignton, Devon. Produced by Fairwater Trading Company.

Rye (USA) the earliest style of whiskey produced in America, must contain 51% of rye grain. *see* Rye Whiskey.

Rye and Dry (Cktl) 50mls (2fl.ozs) rye whiskey poured over ice into an old-fashioned glass and top with ginger ale.

Rye Base (Jap) a Canadian-style whiskey produced by Nikka. *See also* Corn Base.

Rye Beer (Eng) a 5.5% alc by vol. seasonal ale produced by King and Barnes, Horsham, West Sussex.

Rye Cocktail (Cktl) 25mls (1fl.oz) rye whiskey, 2 dashes Angostura, 1 teaspoon gomme syrup. Shake over ice and strain into a cocktail glass.

Rye Collins (Cktl) 25mls (1fl.oz) rye whiskey, 10mls (½ fl.oz) lemon juice, 1 teaspoon powdered sugar. Stir well over ice in a collins glass, top with soda water and a slice of lemon.

Ryecroft (Austr) a winery. (Add): Ingoldby Road, McLaren Flat, South Australia. Produces Shiraz Contemporary and Tradition wines.

Rye Fizz (Cktl) 60mls (½ gill) Canadian Club whisky, 1 teaspoon brown Curaçao, dash grenadine, 90mls (¾ gill) lemon juice, white of egg. Shake over ice, strain into a highball glass and fill with soda.

Rye Highball (Cktl) pour 1 measure rye whisky into an ice-filled highball glass. Stir in dry ginger ale or soda water and add a twist of lemon.

Rye Lane (Cktl) ⅓ measure rye whisky, ⅓ measure white Curaçao, ⅓ measure orange juice, 2 dashes crème de noyau. Shake over ice and strain into a cocktail glass.

Rye Malt Whiskey (USA) not exceeding 160° US proof from fermented mash of not less than 51% corn, rye, wheat, malted barley or malted rye grain respectively and stored at not more than 125° US Proof in new charred oak. May be a blend of same whiskies of same type.

Rye Sour (Cktl) 25mls (1fl.oz) rye whiskey, 10mls (½ fl.oz) lemon juice, 1 teaspoon sugar. Shake over ice, strain into a cocktail glass and dress with a cherry.

Rye Whiskey (USA) made from a mash containing not less than 51% rye and aged in new charred oak barrels.

Rye Whiskey Cocktail (Cktl) 40mls (⅓ gill) Canadian Club, 2 dashes gomme syrup, dash Angostura. Shake over ice, strain into a cocktail glass and top with a cherry.

Rye Whisky (Can) *see* Canadian Whisky.

Ryland River (Austr) a winery (established 1986) based at Lot 2, Main Creek Road, Main Ridge, Victoria. Grape varieties: Chardonnay, Sauvignon blanc, Sémillon, Cabernet sauvignon, Merlot, Shiraz.

Ryman's Revenge (Eng) a wheat beer brewed using lager yeast and Saaz hops at Castle Eden Brewery, County Durham.

Rymill Estate (Austr) a winery based in the Coonawarra, South Australia. Grape varieties include: Cabernet franc, Cabernet sauvignon, Merlot, Shiraz. Label: The Bee's Knees.

Ryst-Dupeyron (Fr) an Armagnac brandy producer. Noted for the Dupeyron brand range.

Ryst Sarl [Jacques] (Fr) an Armagnac producer based in Ténarèze. (Add): 25 Rue de la République, 32100 Condom.

S

SA (Wal) *abbr*: **S**ummer **A**le, a malty best bitter 1042 O.G./4.2% alc by vol. brewed by S.A. Brain in Cardiff. Is also known locally as *'Skull Attack'*.

Saaleck (Ger) vineyard (Anb): Franken. (Ber): Maindreieck. (Gro): Burg. (Vil): Schlossberg.

Saale-Unstrut (Ger) the most northerly anbaugebiet whose vineyards lie south-east of Leipzig in the valley of the rivers Saale and Unstrut. Produces mainly dry white wines from Müller-Thurgau, Silvaner, Weissburgunder. An original region of the old Eastern Germany. *See also* Sachsen.

Saar (Ger) an untergebiet of the Rhein und Mosel district.

Saar [River] (Ger) a tributary of the river Mosel. *see* Mosel-Saar-Ruwer.

Saarburg (Ger) village (Anb): Mosel-Saar-Ruwer. (Ber): Saar-Ruwer. (Gro): Scharzberg. (Vins): Antoniusbrunnen, Bergschlösschen, Fuchs, Klosterberg, Kupp, Rausch, Laurentiusberg, Schlossberg, Stirn.

Saarfeilser Marienberg (Ger) vineyard (Anb): Mosel-Saar-Ruwer. (Ber): Saar-Ruwer. (Gro): Scharzberg. (Vil): Schoden.

Saar-Ruwer (Ger) bereich (Anb): Mosel-Saar-Ruwer. (Gro): Römerlay, Scharzberg.

Saarweinfest (Ger) a Mosel-Saar-Ruwer wine festival held at Saarburg in September.

Saaz (Czec) a delicate strain of hops often used for *'dry-hopping'* as it gives an excellent bouquet.

S.A.B. (S.Afr) *abbr*: **S**outh **A**frican **B**reweries.

Saba (It) boiled down grape must that is used as a sweetening.

Sabai (Thai) a blend of white wine and the red fruit of the hibiscus tree bottled drink 5% alc by vol. produced by the Siam Winery.

Sabatacha (Sp) the name given to a range of mature wines from San Isidro in the Jumilla district of the Levante.

Sabathi (Aus) a winery (9ha) based in Leutschach, Süd-Steiermark. (Add): Pössnitz 48, 8463 Leutschach. Grape varieties: Chardonnay, Gewürztraminer, Muskateller, Pinot blanc, Pinot gris, Sauvignon blanc, Traminer. Produces a range of dry red, white and sweet wines.

Sabauda Riserva (It) a sparkling (metodo tradizionale) wine produced by Contratto in the Piemonte region.

Sabbath Cooler (Cktl) 20mls (⅙ gill) Cognac, 20mls (⅙ gill) French vermouth, juice ¼ lime. Stir over ice, strain into an ice-filled highball glass, top with soda and dress with a mint sprig.

Sabil (Leb) a natural spring mineral water. Mineral contents (milligrammes per litre): Sodium 6mg/l, Calcium 21mg/l, Magnesium 9mg/l, Potassium 1mg/l, Bicarbonates 81mg/l, Chlorides 9mg/l, Sulphates 4mg/l, Fluorides 0.6mg/l, Nitrates 4mg/l. pH 7.3

Sabinum (It) a white wine produced in central Italy during Roman times.

Sablant (Fr) a brand-name used for fine Crémant de Loire sparkling wines.

Sablant [En] (Fr) an old Loire custom of filtering wines through fine sand. Now wines of the Loire use the names Sablant and Crémant de Loire.

Sable (Fr) sand (soil).

Sables Anciens (Fr) sandy soil, applied to the Saint-Émilion district in eastern Bordeaux.

Sables du Golfe du Lion (Fr) a Vin de Pays area in the Languedoc-Roussillon region, southern France.

Sables du Golfe du Rhône (Fr) a Vin de Pays area of the Bouches du Rhône département in south-eastern France.

Sables-Saint-Émilion (Fr) a commune within the A.C. Saint-Émilion, south-eastern Bordeaux.

Sablet (Fr) a noted wine-village in A.C. Côtes du Rhône-Villages, Vacluse.

Sable View (S.Afr) the label for a range of wines produced by Distell (now no longer produced).

Sablo-Graveleux (Fr) a sandy, gravelly soil production zone in Saint-Émilion, eastern Bordeaux.

Sablon (Hol) a natural spring mineral water from Sittard. Mineral contents (milligrammes per litre): Sodium 4.9mg/l, Calcium 60mg/l, Magnesium 12mg/l, Potassium 2.2mg/l, Bicarbonates 250mg/l, Chlorides 9mg/l, Sulphates 9.5mg/l, Nitrates 0.2mg/l, Silicates 12mg/l.

SAB Miller International (Eng) a brewery. (Add): One Stanhope Gate, London W1K 1AF. Brews beers and lager. Website: http://www.sabmiller.com

Sabotée Sancerroise et Comité de Propagande des Vins A.O.C. de Sancerre (Fr) a wine brotherhood based in the Central Vineyards district of the Loire. Promotes and improves the wines of Sancerre.

Sabra (Isr) an orange and Swiss chocolate liqueur. 30% alc by vol. name is thought to derive from the sabra cactus. Produced by Seagram.

Sabrage (Fr) the decapitation of a Champagne bottle with a sabre.

Sabragia (USA) a winery based in the Howell

1123

Mountain, Napa Valley, California. (Add): 1083 Vine Street, 238 Healdsburg, California 95448. Grape varieties: Cabernet sauvignon. Label: Monte Rosso Vineyard, Rancho del Oso.

Sabra Sour (Cktl) 50mls (2fl.ozs) Sabra, 25mls (1fl.oz) lemon juice. Shake over ice and strain into a cocktail glass.

Sabre [Champagne] (Fr) a curved 'scimitar-style' sword used for cutting the top part of a Champagne bottle (un-opened with the glass top, foil, wire cage and cork still intact).

Sabre Cocktail (Cktl) ⅓ measure Sabra, ⅓ measure dry gin, ⅓ measure cream, dash syrop de framboises. Shake over ice and strain into a cocktail glass.

Sabrine (Tun) a natural spring mineral water. Mineral contents (milligrammes per litre): Sodium 24mg/l, Calcium 35mg/l, Magnesium 10mg/l, Potassium 4mg/l, Bicarbonates 170mg/l, Chlorides 3mg/l, Sulphates 14mg/l. pH 7.5

Sabrita (Cktl) 50mls (2fl.ozs) Sabra, 25mls (1fl.oz) brandy. Stir together with ice in a large balloon glass.

Sabro (Sp) the local grape variety grown on the island of La Palma in the Canary Islands.

Sabrosa (Mex) a natural spring mineral water from Merida.

Sabrosa (Port) a wine-producing area north of Pinhão in the Alto Douro.

S.A.B.V.A. (S.Afr) abbr: South African Black Vintners' Alliance.

Saca (Sp) lit: 'to draw out', wine for export is designated Saca. See also Sacar.

Saca Corcho (Sp) corkscrew.

Sacador (Sp) a worker who carries the grape baskets from the vineyard.

Sacar (Sp) lit: 'to draw out', is suggested that 'sack' derived from it. See also Vinos de Saca and Saca.

Saca-Rolhas (Port) corkscrew. See also Rolhas.

Sac-à-Vin (Fr) a term used for a drunk in the Champagne region.

Saccharine Method (USA) the term given to the process of converting starch into fermentable sugars.

Saccharometer (Eng) an instrument for measuring the sugar content in the wort for beer or the must for wine.

Saccharomyces (Lat) the botanical name for yeast.

Saccharomyces acidifaciens (Lat) a wine yeast.

Saccharomyces apiculatus (Lat) a wild wine yeast.

Saccharomyces baileii (Lat) a yeast that has a high alcohol tolerance and is highly resistant to SO$_2$.

Saccharomyces bayanus (Lat) a wine yeast used in eastern Bordeaux for Pomerol and Saint-Émilion wines. Is fairly resistant to alcohol and therefore produces high levels during fermentation. Also used in the Valpolicella region of Italy for amarone-style wines.

Saccharomyces beticus (Lat) see Saccharomyces ellipsoideus beticus.

Saccharomyces carlsbergensis (Lat) a bottom-fermenting yeast used in the making of lager beer. see Saccharomyces uvarum.

Saccharomyces cerevisiae (Lat) a wine yeast, also used as a top-fermenting wine yeast.

Saccharomyces ellipsoideus (Lat) a wine yeast, the bloom which settles on the grape skins and is used to convert grape sugar into CO$_2$ and alcohol when fermentation takes place.

Saccharomyces ellipsoideus beticus (Lat) flor, the yeast used in the making of Fino Sherries, vins de paille etc.

Saccharomyces oviformis (Lat) a yeast that has a high alcohol tolerance and is highly resistant to SO$_2$.

Saccharomyces pastovianus (Lat) a wild wine yeast.

Saccharomyces saké (Lat) a yeast strain used in the **brewing of saké.**

Saccharomyces uvarum (Lat) a bottom-fermenting lager yeast. see Saccharomyces carlsbergensis.

Saccharomyces vordermanni (Lat) a wild yeast used in the making of Batavian arak.

Saccharomycodes ludwigii (Lat) a true yeast, if found in wines can cause problems because it is highly resistant to SO$_2$ and can carry on fermenting if residual sugar is present.

Saccharose (Lat) the sugar obtained from sugar beet. Used for chaptalisation.

Saccharum officiarum (Lat) sugar cane from which rum is produced.

Sacco (It) a peppermint liqueur produced in Turin.

Saccone and Speed (Eng) a large wine and spirit shippers owned by Courage.

Saccone and Speed (N.Z) the brand-name used by McWilliams for their range of cask-aged, fortified wines.

Sacedón-Mondéjar (Sp) a Vino de la Tierra of La Mancha in the province of Guadaljara. Split into two sub-regions: Sacedón and Mondéjar. 2500ha of vines. Produces white, sweet white and red wines. Grape varieties include: Cencibel, Malvar, Torrontés, Airén, Garnacha tinta, Tinta madrid, Pedro ximénez and Jaén.

Sache (Fr) a white wine produced in the Touraine district of the Loire.

Sachet de Thé (Fr) tea bag.

Sachoonspruit (S.Afr) a natural spring mineral water. Mineral contents (milligrammes per litre): Sodium 5mg/l, Calcium 32.9mg/l, Magnesium 20.4mg/l, Potassium 1mg/l, Bicarbonates 163mg/l, Chlorides <5mg/l, Sulphates <5mg/l, Nitrates 1mg/l. pH 7.9

Sachsen (Ger) an anbaugebiet around the city of Dresden. Mainly dry white wines are produced from Müller-Thurgau, Traminer, Weissburgunder. An original region of the old Eastern Germany. See also Saale-Unstrut.

Sachsenberg (Aus) a vineyard site based on the banks of the River Kamp situated in the Kamptal region.

Sachsenflur (Ger) village (Anb): Baden. (Ber): Badische Frankenland. (Gro): Tauberklinge. (Vin): Kailberg.

Sachsen Krone (Ger) a 5.1% alc by vol. pilsner brewed by the Köthener Brauerei, Köthen.

Sack (Eng) the anglification of Spanish seco, a dry fortified still wine. see Sacar.

S

Sack (Eng) the brewers name for the hessian or plastic container used to package malt.

Sacke (Sp) Sherry. *see* Sack, as referred to in Pasquil's Palinodia in 1619.

Sack Mead (Eng) a sweet mead produced in the west country in the seventeenth and eighteenth centuries.

Sack Metheglin (Eng) a sweet metheglin-type mead produced in the seventeenth and eighteenth centuries.

Sacktträger (Ger) vineyard (Anb): Rheinhessen. (Ber): Bingen. (Gro): Sankt Rochuskapelle. (Vil): Zotzenheim.

Sacotte (Fr) a Champagne producer. (Add): 13 Rue de la Verrière, B.P. 1017, Épernay, 51318. Produces vintage wines.

Sacra (It) a natural spring mineral water from Sacra.

Sacramental Wine (Eng) an altar wine for the Eucharist that may be red or white and must be the natural grape juice.

Sacramento (USA) Lodi-Sacramento, a northern region of the Great Central Valley of California. Produces dessert and table wines.

Sacramora (It) a still and sparkling natural spring mineral water from Sacramora. (blue label: light gas/red label: still). Mineral contents (milligrammes per litre): Sodium 52mg/l, Calcium 114.5mg/l, Magnesium 24mg/l, Potassium 3.25mg/l, Bicarbonates 359mg/l, Chlorides 48.5mg/l, Sulphates 128mg/l, Silicates 8.7mg/l.

Sacrarios (Sp) a tenth century name used in Catalonia for the Bodega.

Sacrashe Vineyard (USA) the label for a red wine (Cabernet sauvignon) produced by the Kathryn Hall winery, Rutherford, Napa Valley, California.

Sacred Hill Winery (N.Z) a winery. (Add): Dartmoor Road, Puketapu RD 6, Napier. 20ha. Grape variety: Sauvignon blanc.

Sacristía (Sp) lit: 'The Chapel', a part of the Harvey old Bodega where old butts of unblended Sherry are assembled from the best vintages.

Sacristía de Romate [La] (Sp) a range of Sherries produced by Sánchez Romate Hnos. in Lealas 26, Jerez de la Frontera, Cádiz. Range includes Oloroso, Amontillado, Cream and Pedro Ximénez.

Sacromonte (It) a natural spring mineral water from Sacromonte, Varallo, Piemonte.

Sacy (Fr) a Premier Cru Champagne village in the Canton de Ville-en-Tardenois. District: Reims.

Sacy (Fr) a white grape variety grown in the Burgundy region (in the Yonne). Also known as the Tressalier.

Sadana (Sp) a pale Cream Sherry produced by Bobadilla in Jerez de la Frontera.

Saddlers Celebrated Premium Best (Eng) a 4% alc by vol. best bitter ale brewed by the Highgate & Walsall Brewing Company.

Saddleworth More (I.O.M) a 3.8% alc by vol. ale brewed by the Church Inn, Uppermill, near Saddleworth.

Sadie Family (S.Afr) a winery (established 1999) based in Malmesbury, Swartland, Western Cape. 7ha. Grape varieties: Chardonnay, Chenin blanc, Grenache, Grenache blanc, Mourvèdre, Shiraz, Viognier. Labels: Columella, Palladius.

Sadilly (Rus) a white table wine produced in Baku.

Sadova Rosé (Rum) a sweet rosé wine produced on the Danube plain.

Saegertown Beverage Eureka Springs (USA) a natural spring mineral water from Saegertown, Pennsylvania.

Saemling 88 (Ger) an alternative name for the Scheurebe grape.

Saering (Fr) an A.C. Alsace grand Cru vineyard in Guebwiller, Haut-Rhin 26.75ha.

Sa'ette (It) an I.G.T. Sangiovese barrique-aged wine produced by Monte Bernardi in Panzano, Tuscany.

Safa (Iran) a natural spring mineral water. Mineral contents (milligrammes per litre): Sodium 4.25mg/l, Calcium 56mg/l, Magnesium 12.96mg/l, Potassium 1.4mg/l, Bicarbonates 188mg/l, Chlorides 5mg/l, Sulphates 10mg/l, Fluorides 0.4mg/l. pH 8.0

Saffredi (It) a Bordeaux blend wine that also contains Alicante grapes produced by Le Pupille, Maremma, Tuscany.

Saffron Cider Company (Eng) a small family-run cider firm based at Radwinter, near Saffron Walden, Essex. Produces Saffy's West Country Scrumpy, Black Bull, Cripple Cock and Sherston Scorcher.

Saffy's West Country Scrumpy (Eng) the brand-name of a bottled medium-dry, slightly carbonated, extra strong cider produced by the Saffron Cider Company.

Safi (Egy) a natural spring mineral water from Siwa. Mineral contents (milligrammes per litre): Sodium 34mg/l, Calcium 7mg/l, Magnesium 8.3mg/l, Potassium 17mg/l, Bicarbonates 107.4mg/l, Chlorides 28mg/l, Sulphates 16.5mg/l, Fluorides 0.6mg/l, Silicates 14mg/l.

Safia (Tun) a natural spring mineral water. Mineral contents (milligrammes per litre): Sodium 10mg/l, Calcium 68mg/l, Magnesium 6mg/l, Potassium 1mg/l, Bicarbonates 207mg/l, Chlorides 28mg/l, Sulphates 10mg/l, Nitrates 23mg/l. pH 7.0

Safir (Bel) the brand-name of a well-hopped pilsner lager beer.

Safrap (Eng) a 2400litres mild steel containers lined with expoxy resin. They are used for the transportation of wines. If the lining is damaged iron contamination of the wine can occur.

Saft (Aus)(Den)(Ger) juice (fruit).

Saft af Lime (Den) lime juice.

Saftevand (Den) squash (fruit-flavoured drink).

Saftig (Ger) juicy, fine wine of character.

Sagatiba (Bra) a new branded multi-distilled cachaça 38% alc by vol. Website: http://www.sagatiba.com

Sage Canyon Winery (USA) a winery based at St. Helena, Napa Valley, California. Produces varietal wines.

Sagemoor Farms Vineyards (USA) a large vineyard

1125

based in the South Columbia River Basin, Washington. 200ha. Sells the grapes that it grows.

Sage's Milk (Eng) an old nineteenth century nickname for coffee.

Saget [Guy] (Fr) a wine producer at La Castille, 58150, Pouilly-sur-Loire. Owns vineyards in Touraine, Anjou and Montlouis.

Sage Tea (Eng) used in the old days to combat fever, place 10grms (½ oz) dried sage leaves in a jug or pot, add 1.1lts (1quart) of boiling water, sugar to taste and a dash of lemon juice. Infuse 5 minutes, strain and use as required.

Sagmak (Tur) milk.

Sagrantino (It) a black grape variety grown in the Umbria region. Used in the production of D.O.C.G. Sagrantino di Montefalco.

Sagrantino di Montefalco (It) a D.O.C.G. (awarded 1992) dry or sweet red wines produced in Umbria around the town of Montefalco 850ha (Coms): Bevagna, Castel Ritaldi, Giano dell'Umbria, Gualdo Cattaneo, Montefalco. Secco must have a min. of 13% alc by vol. and be aged for 30 months (12 months must be in wood). Riserva version is aged for 42 months (of which 18 must be in wood).

Sagrantino di Montefalco Passito (It) a sweet, tannic red wine produced from Sagrantino grapes in Umbria. Min. alc by vol. 14.5%, residual sugar no lower than 30g/l, aged for 30 months (12 months must be in wood).

Sagres (Port) a 5.1% alc by vol. straw coloured, bottled lager brewed by Central De Cervejas, Vialonga. *see* S.C.C.

Sahara Water (Can) a natural spring mineral water. Mineral contents (milligrammes per litre): Calcium 76mg/l, Magnesium 29mg/l, Fluorides 0.13mg/l, Nitrates 0.11mg/l.

Sahateni (Rum) a wine-producing area (part of the Dealul-Mare Vineyard).

Sahel (Afr) an A.O.G. area in the wine-producing region of Casablanca, western Morocco.

Sahne (Aus)(Ger) cream.

Sahti (Fin) a festival beverage produced by female home-brewers consisting of barley, rye, malt, hops, juniper berries/branches and straw (the branches act as a filter). Is fermented in milk churns.

Saibro (Mad) decomposed red tufa mixed with stones found on the island of Madeira.

Saignée (Fr) the name given to the first pressing of Cinsault and Grenache grapes for the Rhône rosé of Tricastin in the Côtes du Rhône. Is also used in Champagne and in Touraine, Loire.

Saigon Brewery (Viet) a brewery based in Ho Chi Minh City (was Saigon) Vietnam which brews Saigon Export Beer.

Saillans (Fr) a commune in the A.C. Côtes de Fronsac, eastern Bordeaux.

Sail les Bains (Fr) a natural spring mineral water brand.

Sainsbury's Scottish Caladonian (Scot) a natural spring mineral water from Beauly, Inverness.

Saint Alban (Fr) a natural spring mineral water from St. Alban-les-Eaux. Mineral contents (milligrammes per litre): Sodium 350mg/l, Calcium 220mg/l, Magnesium 70mg/l, Potassium 46mg/l, Bicarbonates 2000mg/l, Chlorides 21mg/l, Sulphates 6mg/l, Fluorides 2.45mg/l. pH 6.5

Saint Amand (Fr) a natural spring mineral water from 59230 Saint Amand les Eaux. Mineral contents (milligrammes per litre): Sodium 28mg/l, Calcium 176mg/l, Magnesium 46mg/l, Potassium 5mg/l, Bicarbonates 312mg/l, Chlorides 37mg/l, Sulphates 372mg/l, Fluorides 1.3mg/l. pH 7.2 Website: http://www.saint-amand.com

Saint Amand Vauban (Fr) a natural spring mineral water from Prince Noir, Saint-Antonin-Noble-Val.

Saint-Amant-de-Graves (Fr) a commune in the Charente département whose grapes are classed as Petite Champagne (Cognac).

Saint-Amour (Fr) an A.C. Cru Beaujolais-Villages, Burgundy. Has 240ha under vines.

Saint-Amour-de-Bellevue (Fr) a commune in the Beaujolais district. Has A.C. Beaujolais-Villages or Beaujolais-Saint-Amour-de-Bellevue status. Also as Mâconnais Blanc.

Saint Andelain (Fr) a commune in the Central Vineyards district of the Loire which produces A.C. Pouilly Fumé.

Saint-André (Fr) a commune in the Charente-Maritime département whose grapes are classed Borderies and used for Cognac.

Saint-Aubin (Fr) an A.C. commune in the Côte de Beaune, Burgundy. Is also known as Saint-Aubin-Côte de Beaune. Has 8 Grand Cru vineyards: Champlot, En Remilly, La Chatenière, Les Combes, Les Frionnes, Les Murgers-des-Dents-de-Chien, Sur Gamay and Sur-le-Sentier-du-Clou. 65ha (red and white).

Saint Aubin (Fr) a commune in the A.C. Médoc, north-western Bordeaux. Produces red and white wines 155ha.

Saint-Aubin-Côte de Beaune (Fr) *see* Saint Aubin.

Saint-Aubin-de-Luigné (Fr) an A.C. commune in the Coteaux du Layon in the Anjou-Saumur district of the Loire.

Saint-Avertin (Fr) a white wine produced in the Touraine district of the Loire.

Saint Barnabus (Cyp) the label of an A.O.C. Commandaria from SODAP.

Saint Benoit (Fr) a natural spring mineral water from St. Martin d'Abbat. Mineral contents (milligrammes per litre): Sodium 6.5mg/l, Calcium 47.5mg/l, Magnesium 4.3mg/l, Potassium 3mg/l, Bicarbonates 172mg/l, Chlorides 8mg/l, Sulphates 9mg/l. pH 7.6

Saint Boes (Fr) *see* St. Boes.

Saint-Bonnet (Fr) a commune in the Charente département whose grapes are classed as Petite Champagne (Cognac).

Saint Brendan's Irish Cream Liqueur (Eng) an Irish cream liqueur produced by the Saint Brendan's Irish Cream Liqueur Company, Leckpatrick.

S

Saint-Brice (Fr) a commune in the Charente département whose grapes are classed as Grande Champagne (Cognac).

Saint-Bris (Fr) a newly created A.C. 895ha. (promotion of the V.D.Q.S. Sauvignon de Saint-Bris) from 2001 harvest (maximum yield 58 hl/ha) and based in the Yonne (Burgundy). Soil: chalk-clay, minimum alc by vol 10%.

Saint-Catages [Les] (Fr) a vineyard in the A.C. commune of Montagny, Côte Chalonnaise, Burgundy.

Saint Chinian (Fr) an A.C. red wine from the Béziers region in the Hérault département.

Saint Christoly (Fr) a commune in the Bas-Médoc, A.C. Médoc, north western Bordeaux.

Saint Christophe (Fr) a natural spring mineral water brand.

Saint-Christophe-des-Bardes (Fr) a commune in the A.C. Saint-Émilion, eastern Bordeaux.

Saint-Ciers-Champagne (Fr) a commune in the Charente-Maritime département whose grapes are classed Petite Champagne (Cognac).

Saint Clair Estate Wines (N.Z) a winery. (Add): Vintech, Rapaura Road, (739 New Renwick Road, RD2), Blenheim, Marlborough, South Island. 49ha. Grape varieties: Chardonnay, Merlot, Riesling, Sauvignon blanc.

Saint-Cyprien (Afr) a noted wine-producing area in Tunisia.

Saint-Cyr-en-Bourg (Fr) a commune in the A.C. Saumur, Anjou-Saumur, Loire.

Saint-Cyr-sur-Mer (Fr) a commune in the Provence region of which Bandol is a part.

Saint-Didier-Parnac (Fr) a 70ha vineyard based in Cahors.

Saint Diéry (Fr) a natural sparkling mineral water (established 1872) from the d'Auverne. (Add): Source Rentaigue, 63320 Saint Diéry. Mineral contents (milligrammes per litre): Sodium 385mg/l, Calcium 85mg/l, Magnesium 80mg/l, Potassium 65mg/l, Bicarbonates 1350mg/l, Chlorides 285mg/l, Sulphates 25mg/l, Nitrates 1.9mg/l. ph 5.9

Saint-Drézery (Fr) a small A.C. wine-producing region in Languedoc near Pic-Saint-Loup. Minimum alc. 11% by vol. Grape variety is mainly Carignan.

Sainte Baume [La] (Fr) a pale green, Liqueur de Provence from Distillerie Janot. 43% alc by vol. it is an infusion of Provence herbs, sugar and honey.

Sainte-Chapelle Vineyards (USA) vineyards based near Caldwell, Idaho. 60ha. Grape varieties: Chardonnay and Riesling. Produces varietal wines.

Sainte-Croix-du-Mont (Fr) an A.C. commune producing sweet white wines in southern Bordeaux.

Saint Edmund (Eng) a vineyard based in Bury-St.-Edmunds, Suffolk. Grape variety: Huxelrebe.

Sainte-Euphraise (Fr) a Cru Champagne village in the Canton de Ville-en-Tardenois. District: Reims.

Sainte-Foy-Bordeaux (Fr) an A.C. commune in the south-eastern Bordeaux (south of the Entre-Deux-Mers). Produces sweet white wines plus a small amount of red wine.

Sainte-Gemme (Fr) a Cru Champagne village in the Canton de Châtillon-sur-Marne. District: Reims.

Sainte-Genevieve Vineyards (USA) a 240ha. estate based in Texas. Linked with Cordier of Bordeaux, France.

Sainte-Jeoire-Prieuré (Fr) a village in the A.C. Savoie region that may use its own name to sell wine.

Sainte Marguerite (Fr) a lightly sparkling natural spring mineral water from Sources la Chapelle, 63270 St. Maurice-les-Allier, Puy de Dôme. Mineral contents (milligrammes per litre): Sodium 302mg/l, Calcium 71mg/l, Magnesium 40mg/l, Potassium 33mg/l, Bicarbonates 812mg/l, Chlorides 230mg/l, Sulphates 59mg/l.

Sainte-Marie-d'Alloix (Fr) a village in the A.C. Savoie that may sell wines under its own name.

Saint-Émilion (Fr) an A.C. district in eastern Bordeaux. 5440ha. Produces fine red wines. (Classified in 1955 and reviewed every ten years). Has eight communes: Saint-Christophe-des-Bardes, Saint-Émilion, Saint-Étienne-de-Lisse, Saint-Hippolyte, Saint Laurent des Combes, Saint Pey d'Armens, Saint-Sulpice-de-Faleyrens and Vignonet, plus part of Libourne. See also St-Émilion and Saint-Émilion Classification.

Saint-Émilion (Fr) a white grape variety which is thick skinned and sturdy. Produces rather sour wines of about 8% alc by vol. It is a smooth maturer and does not rot. Now more than 80% of the total yield for Cognac is this grape variety. Also known as the Ugni Blanc.

Saint-Émilion Classification (Fr) wines were first classified in 1954/1955 and completed in 1958. Are reclassified every ten years 1969, 1988 (a dispute caused a delay of two years), 1996, 2006. Following the 2006 classification has 15 Premier Grand Cru Classé, 46 Grand Cru Classé, over 90 Grand Cru and numerous A.C. Saint-Émilion. The previous reclassification of 1986 was two years late because of a court case. The new classification was released in late 2006. Grape varieties: Cabernet franc 25%, Cabernet sauvignon 5%, Merlot 70%.

Saint-Émilion des Charentes (Fr) a white grape variety, see Saint-Émilion. Also known as the Trebbiano and Ugni blanc.

Saint-Émilion Grand Cru Classés Proprietors Association (Fr) the Association des Propriètaires de Grands Crus Classés de Saint-Émilion. (Add): Les Templiers, Rue Guadet B.P. 46, 33330 Saint-Émilion.

Saint-Émilion Soils (Fr) the soils are divided in 5 zones as derived by Professor Enjalbert with Féret (13th edition) Bordeaux et Ses Vins. They are: [1] Le Plateau Calcaire, [2] Côtes et "Pieds de Côtes", [3] Graves et Sables Anciens, [4] Sables Anciens, [5] Sablo-Graveleux.

Sainte-Odile (Fr) a wine village in the Bas-Rhin in Alsace. Known in German as Odilienberg.

Sainte Odile Distillerie (Fr) a liqueur producer based in Alsace. (Add): 3 Rue de la Gare, 67210 Obernai.

Sainte-Radegonde (Fr) a commune in the A.C. Vouvray, Touraine district of the Loire.

Saint-Estèphe (Fr) an A.C. commune in the Haut-Médoc in Bordeaux (wines come under the 1855 classification).

Saint-Estèphe [Marquis de] (Fr) a co-operative producing A.C. Saint-Estèphe. (Com): Saint-Estèphe. 350ha. Grape varieties: Cabernet franc, Cabernet sauvignon, Malbec, Merlot, Petit verdot.

Saint-Étienne-de-Lisse (Fr) a commune of A.C. Saint-Émilion in eastern Bordeaux.

Saint-Étienne-des-Ouillières (Fr) a commune in the Beaujolais district. Has A.C. Beaujolais-Villages or Beaujolais-Saint-Étienne-des-Ouillières status.

Saint-Étienne-la-Varenne (Fr) a commune in the Beaujolais district. Has A.C. Beaujolais-Villages or Beaujolais-Saint-Étienne-la-Varenne status.

Saint-Eugène (Fr) a commune in the Charente-Maritime département whose grapes are classed Petite Champagne (Cognac).

Saint-Féréon (Fr) a noted growth of cider produced in Brittany.

Saint-Fiacre sur Maine (Fr) a commune in the A.C. Muscadet district of Nantais, Loire.

Saint-Fort-sur-le-Né (Fr) a commune in the Charente département whose grapes are classed Grande Champagne (Cognac).

Saint Gall (Fr) a fortified apéritif red wine.

Saint Galmier (Fr) an alkaline mineral water bottled in a Burgundy-shaped, long-necked bottle.

Saint-Georges [Les] (Fr) a Premier Cru vineyard in the A.C. commune of Nuits-Saint-Georges, Côte de Nuits, Burgundy 7.5ha.

Saint-Georges [Les] (Fr) a commune in the Nuits-Saint-Georges, Côte de Nuits, Burgundy.

Saint-Georges-d'Orques (Fr) an A.C. red wine-producing area based near Montpellier in the Languedoc. Grape varieties: Carignan 50%, Cinsault 35% and Grenache 15%.

Saint-Georges-Saint-Émilion (Fr) an A.C. Bordeaux red wine from the Saint-Émilion district.

Saint-Georges-sur-Loire (Fr) a commune in the A.C. Savennières, Anjou-Saumur, Loire.

Saint Germain (Cktl) see St. Germain.

Saint-Germain-de-Lusignan (Fr) a commune in the Charente-Maritime département whose grapes are classed Petite Champagne (Cognac).

Saint-Germain-de-Vibrac (Fr) a commune in the Charente-Maritime département whose grapes are classed Petite Champagne (Cognac).

Saint-Gervais (Fr) a wine-producing village in the Gard département. Wines are of A.C. Côtes du Rhône-Villages.

Saint Ginés de la Jara (Sp) the patron saint of vintners. see Fiesta de la Vendimia.

Saint-Grégoire (Fr) a natural spring mineral water from Soultzmatt. Mineral contents (milligrammes per litre): Sodium 108mg/l, Calcium 84.1mg/l, Magnesium 35.3mg/l, Potassium 22.2mg/l, Bicarbonates 674mg/l, Chlorides 16.4mg/l, Sulphates 39.1mg/l, Fluorides 1.5mg/l.

Saint Helena (Fr) the patron saint of the Champagne vineyard workers.

Saint-Hilaire-de-Barbezieux (Fr) a commune in the Charente département whose grapes are classed Petite Champagne (Cognac).

Saint-Hippolyte (Fr) a wine town in the Bas-Rhin in Alsace. In German known as Sankt Pilt.

Saint-Jean-de-la-Porte (Fr) an A.C. vineyard on the right bank of the river Isère in Savoie. Produces mainly red wines from the Mondeuse grape.

Saint-Jean-des-Mauvrets (Fr) an A.C. commune in the Coteaux de l'Aubance in the Anjou-Saumur district of the Loire.

Saint-Jean-de-Trézy (Fr) a commune of A.C. Bourgogne Côtes du Couchois.

Saint-Joseph (Fr) an A.C. district in the northern Rhône, west of the Hermitage district. Produces red and white wines. (Coms): Glun, Lemps, Mauves, St. Jean-de-Muzels, Vion. Grape varieties: mainly the Syrah, plus Marsanne and Roussanne. In red wine production can add up to 10% white grapes if all are vinified together. Minimum alc. 10% by vol.

Saint-Julien (Fr) an A.C. commune in the Haut-Médoc in Bordeaux (wine comes under the 1855 classification) red wines only. Minimum alc. 10.5% by vol.

Saint-Julien-en-Montmélas (Fr) a commune in the Beaujolais district. Has A.C. Beaujolais-Villages or Beaujolais-Saint-Julien-en-Montmélas status.

Saint Justine (Can) a natural spring mineral water. Mineral contents (milligrammes per litre): Sodium 415mg/l, Calcium 7mg/l, Magnesium 6mg/l, Potassium 3mg/l, Bicarbonates 560mg/l, Chlorides 350mg/l.

Saint Lambert (Fr) a natural spring mineral water from Vallée de Chevreuse. Mineral contents (milligrammes per litre): Sodium 16.2mg/l, Calcium 63.2mg/l, Magnesium 7.5mg/l, Potassium 1.2mg/l, Bicarbonates 180mg/l, Chlorides 28mg/l, Sulphates 25mg/l.

Saint-Lambert-du-Lattay (Fr) a commune in the A.C. Coteaux du Layon in the Anjou-Saumur district of the Loire. Produces sweet white (botrytised) wines.

Saint Landelin Ambrée (Fr) a 6.8% alc by vol. tawny-coloured amber abbaye beer (Abbaye de Crespin).

Saint Landelin Blonde (Fr) a 5.9% alc by vol. pale abbaye beer (Abbaye de Cespin).

Saint Landelin Brasserie (Fr) a brewery based in Crespin. Brews: Ambrée, Blonde and Brune beers.

Saint Landelin Brune (Fr) a 6.2% alc by vol. top-fermented, brown, bottled abbaye ale (Abbaye de Crespin). Brewed by Enfants de Guyant, Douai.

Saint-Laurent (Aus) a red grape variety. Also grown in Czec where it is known as Svatovavrinecke and Vavrinecke.

Saint Laurent (Fr) a commune within the A.C. Médoc, Bordeaux.

Saint-Laurent-de-Cognac (Fr) a commune in the Charente-Maritime département whose grapes (classed Borderies) are used in Cognac production.

Saint Laurent des Arbes (Fr) a commune in the A.C. Lirac, southern Rhône.

Saint-Laurent-des-Vignes (Fr) a commune in the A.C. Monbazillac district of the Bergerac. Produces sweet (botrytised) wines.

Saint-Leger (Fr) a commune in the Beaujolais district. Has A.C. Beaujolais-Villages or Beaujolais-Saint-Leger status.

Saint-Léger (Fr) a natural spring mineral water from Pérenchies. Mineral contents (milligrammes per litre): Sodium 92mg/l, Calcium 60mg/l, Magnesium 23mg/l, Potassium 20mg/l, Bicarbonates 476mg/l, Chlorides 36mg/l, Sulphates 55mg/l.

Saint-Leger-de-Montbrillais (Fr) a commune in the A.C. Saumur, Anjou-Saumur, Vienne département, Loire.

Saint Lheurine (Fr) a commune in the Charente-Maritime département whose grapes are used in Cognac production.

Saint Marco (Fr) a brand of lithiated mineral water.

Saint Martial (Fr) a natural spring mineral water (established 1887). Mineral contents (milligrammes per litre): Sodium 4.8mg/l, Calcium 114mg/l, Magnesium 3mg/l, Potassium 0.4mg/l, Bicarbonates 356mg/l, Chlorides 11mg/l, Sulphates 6mg/l, Nitrates 1mg/l. pH 7.03

Saint Martial-Coustalou Lot (Fr) a natural spring mineral water. Mineral contents (milligrammes per litre): Sodium 5.4mg/l, Calcium 106mg/l, Magnesium 1.7mg/l, Potassium 1mg/l, Bicarbonates 327mg/l, Chlorides 8mg/l, Sulphates 6mg/l, Nitrates 3mg/l.

Saint-Martial-de-Coculet (Fr) a commune in the Charente-Maritime département whose grapes are classed Petite Champagne (Cognac).

Saint-Martial-de-Vitaterne (Fr) a commune in the Charente-Maritime département whose grapes are classed Petite Champagne (Cognac).

Saint Martin (Fr) the patron saint of wine in the Loire Valley. Discovered that vines flourished if they were pruned. *See also* St. Martin.

Saint Martin d'Abbat (Fr) a natural spring mineral water brand.

Saint-Martin-d'Ablois (Fr) a Cru Champagne village in the Canton d'Épernay. District: Épernay.

Saint Martin-le-Beau (Fr) a commune of A.C. Montlouis in the Touraine district of the Loire. Also spelt Saint Martin-les-Beaux.

Saint-Martin-sous-Montaigus (Fr) a commune in the A.C. Mercurey, Côte Chalonnaise, Burgundy.

Saint Maurice (Fr) a Champagne produced by Bruno Bocquet in Épernay. Part of the sales were donated to the British entry in the 1987 America's Cup race.

Saint Maurice (Fr) a Drôme vineyard of the A.C. Côtes du Rhône-Villages.

Saint-Maurice-de-Tavernolles (Fr) a commune in the Charente-Maritime département whose grapes are classed Petite Champagne (Cognac).

Saint-Maurice-les-Couches (Fr) a commune of A.C. Bourgogne Côtes du Couchois.

Saint-Médard-de-Barbieux (Fr) a commune in the Charente département whose grapes are classed Petite Champagne (Cognac).

Saint-Médard-en-Jalles (Fr) a commune in the A.C. Médoc, north-western Bordeaux.

Saint-Melaine (Fr) a commune in the A.C. Coteaux de l'Aubance in the Anjou-Saumur district of the Loire.

Saint-Même (Fr) a commune in the Charente département whose grapes are classed Grande Champagne (Cognac).

Saint Morille [Les] (Fr) a vineyard in the A.C. commune of Montagny, Côte Chalonnaise, Burgundy.

Saint Morillon (Fr) a commune in the A.C. Graves district of western Bordeaux. Produces red and white wines.

Saint Nectaire (Fr) a brand of chalybeate mineral water.

Saint Nicholas (Cyp) a still natural spring mineral water from Kakopetria. Mineral contents (milligrammes per litre): Sodium 18mg/l, Calcium 49mg/l, Magnesium 28mg/l, Bicarbonates 292mg/l, Chlorides 19mg/l, Sulphates 11mg/l.

Saint Nicolas de Bourgueil (Fr) an A.C. within the Touraine district of the Loire. Produces the finest red wines of the whole region from the Breton (Cabernet franc) grape. Also some rosé produced.

Saint-Palais-du-Né (Fr) a commune in the Charente département whose grapes are classed Petite Champagne (Cognac).

Saint Panteleimon (Cyp) a medium-sweet, white wine produced by Keo in Limassol.

Saint Pantéléon (Fr) a Drôme vineyard of the A.C. Côtes du Rhône-Villages.

Saint-Paul de Dominique (Fr) a Grand Cru vineyard in the A.C. Saint-Émilion, Bordeaux.

Saint-Péray (Fr) an A.C. district of the central western Rhône. Produces good sparkling and still white wines from the Roussanne and Marsanne grape varieties.

Saint-Péray Mousseux (Fr) an A.C. sparkling white wine produced in the Côtes du Rhône from Roussanne and Marsanne grapes. Produced by the méthode traditionelle, it is considered by many as second only to Champagne. Minimum alc by vol. 10%.

Saint Pey d'Armens (Fr) a commune of the A.C. Saint-Émilion in Bordeaux.

Saint-Pey-de-Langon (Fr) *see* Saint-Pierre-de-Mons.

Saint-Pierre-de-Bat (Fr) a commune in the Haut-Benauge, Entre-Deux-Mers, central Bordeaux.

Saint-Pierre-de-Mons (Fr) a commune in the A.C. Graves district (also known as Saint-Pey-de-Langon). Produces sweet white wines.

Saint-Pierre-Doré (Fr) a white grape variety grown in the Loire region to produce wines of St-Pourçain-sur-Sioule.

Saint Pourçain (Fr) *see* St-Pourçain-sur-Sioule.

Saint-Preuil (Fr) a commune in the Charente

S

département whose grapes are classed Grande Champagne (Cognac).

Saint Raphaël (Fr) *see* St. Raphaël.

Saint Romain (Fr) a small A.C. commune in the southern Côte de Beaune, Burgundy. 100ha. Produces red and white wines often sold as Côte de Beaune-Villages. Grape varieties: Chardonnay, Pinot blanc and Pinot noir.

Saint-Romain-de-Bellet (Fr) a wine-producing district in A.C. Bellet, Provence, south-eastern France.

Saints (Eng) there are a great number of Saints associated with the making of wines and spirits etc. some being general patrons whilst others being local associations. (Fr) = St. [Saint] (male) and Ste. [Sainte] (female), (Ger) = Sankt, (Hol) = Heilige, (It) = Santo, (Port) = Sao, (Sp) = Santa, (Tur) = Aziz.

Saint Saphorin (Switz) a Lavaux wine village. Produces dry white wines.

Saint-Sardon (Fr) a Vin de Pays area in the Tarn-et-Garonne département in central-southern France.

Saint Saturnin (Fr) a small A.C. red wine-producing area in the Languedoc, southern France. Also produces Vin d'Une Nuit.

Saint-Sauveur (Fr) a wine-producing district in the A.C. Bellet, Provence, south-eastern France.

Saint-Sauveur (Fr) a commune in the A.C. Pécharmant in northern Bergerac. Produces red wines.

Saintsbury (USA) a winery based in the Napa Valley, California. (Add): 1500 Los Carneros Avenue, Napa. CA 94559. Also has vineyards in Carneros. Grape varieties: Chardonnay, Sauvignon blanc, Cabernet sauvignon, Pinot noir. Produces varietal wines. Label: Garnet. Website: http://www.saintsbury.com

Saint Seurin-de-Cadourne (Fr) a commune within the A.C. Haut-Médoc, north-western Bordeaux.

Saint-Seurin-de-Palenne (Fr) a commune in the Charente-Maritime département whose grapes are classed Petite Champagne (Cognac).

Saint-Seurin-du-Plain (Fr) a commune of A.C. Bourgogne Côtes du Couchois.

Saint-Sever (Fr) a commune in the Charente-Maritime département whose grapes are classed Petite Champagne (Cognac).

Saint Simon (Fr) a non-vintage Champagne produced by the Le Crayère co-operative at Bethon in the southern Marne.

Saint's Sinner (Eng) a 4% alc by vol. cask ale from the Darwin Brewery, Crook, County Durham.

Saint Springs (Rus) a natural spring mineral water from Kostroma. Mineral contents (milligrammes per litre): Sodium 10.4mg/l, Calcium 48.2mg/l, Magnesium 12.2mg/l, Potassium 1mg/l, Bicarbonates 240mg/l, Fluorides 0.3mg/l. pH 7.1/pH 7.4

Saint Stefan (N.Z) the brand-name used by the Pacific Vineyards for their wines.

Saint Sulphice (Fr) a commune in the Charente-Maritime département whose grapes are classed Borderies (Cognac).

Saint-Sulpice-de-Faleyrens (Fr) an A.C. commune within the Saint-Émilion district of eastern Bordeaux.

Saint Supéry (USA) vineyards and winery at St. Helena Highway, Rutherford, Napa Valley, California. Grape varieties: Cabernet sauvignon, Chardonnay, Sauvignon blanc.

Saint-Symphorien-d'Ancelles (Fr) a commune in the Beaujolais district. Has A.C. Beaujolais-Villages or Beaujolais-Saint-Symphorien-d'Ancelles status.

Saint-Thierry (Fr) a Cru Champagne village in the Canton de Bourgogne. District: Reims.

Saint-Vallerin (Fr) a wine-producing town in the commune of A.C. Montagny, Côte Chalonnaise, Burgundy.

Saint-Véran (Fr) a commune in the Mâconnais district. Has A.C. Beaujolais-Villages or Beaujolais-Saint-Véran status (red wines). Also as A.C. Saint-Véran (white wine from the Chardonnay grape). Minimum alc. 11% by vol. and A.C. Mâconnais Blanc (white wines).

Saint Victor-la-Coste (Fr) a commune in the A.C. Lirac, southern Rhône.

Saint Vincent (Fr) the patron Saint of wine in Burgundy. A holiday on 22nd of January to celebrate his day (with processions). Also celebrated in other French wine regions.

Saint-Vivant (Fr) an Armagnac producer. (Add): Compagnie d'Armagnac, Saint Vivant, Rte. de Nerac, 32100 Condom. Produces Saint-Vivant ***, V.S.O.P. and X.O. Armagnacs.

Saint Vivien (Fr) a vineyard in the commune of Saint Vivien. A.C. Bourgeais et Blayais, Bordeaux.

Saint-Yzans (Fr) a commune in the Bas-Médoc. A.C. Médoc wines.

Saint-Yzans-de-Médoc (Fr) a noted cave coopérative based at Saint-Brice, Médoc, Bordeaux.

Saint Zeno (It) the patron Saint of wine producers.

Sair (Eng) a home-brew public house in Linthwaite, Huddersfield Yorkshire. Noted for cask-conditioned Linfit Mild 1032 O.G. Old Eli 1050 O.G. Leadboiler 1063 O.G. and Enoch's Hammer 1080 O.G.

Sairme (Geo) a natural spring mineral water from the Tsalabris Valley.

Saïs (Afr) an A.O.G. area in the wine-producing region of Meknès-Fez, Morocco.

Saison (Bel) a top-fermented bière from the French speaking region. Has a second fermentation in the bottle from a dosage of yeast. 5.6% alc by vol. Saison Régal is the most popular.

Saison de Silly (Bel) a bottle conditioned saison beer 5% alc by vol. from the Silly Brasserie. *See also* Double Enghien, Silly Scotch, Titje.

Saison Dupont (Bel) a saison bière brewed by the Dupont Brasserie in Tourpes.

Saison Régal (Bel) *see* Saison.

Saisons de Pipaix (Bel) a sharp saison bière brewed by the Dupont Brasserie in Tourpes.

Saix (Fr) a region in the Saumur area of the Anjou-Saumur district in the Loire.

Saka (Tur) a water carrier.

S

Saka (Tur) a spring mineral water from Istanbul. (Add): Kiskli Cad N°90 34662 Altunizade, Istanbul. Mineral contents (milligrammes per litre): Sodium 5.4mg/l, Calcium 28.4mg/l, Magnesium 3.73mg/l, Potassium 0.16mg/l, Bicarbonates 110mg/l, Chlorides 1.12mg/l, Sulphates 8.18mg/l. pH 8.1

Sakar (Bul) a D.G.O. area of the Southern Basic region. Noted for Merlot wines.

Sakazuki (Jap) a small porcelain bowl into which saké is poured from the Tokkuri. From this bowl the saké is sipped.

Saké (Jap) a beer made from rice, named after the town of Osaka from where it was first produced. Served with seaweed biscuits. *See also* Koji and Suk.

Saké Collins (Cktl) 50mls (2fl.ozs) saké, 25mls (1fl.oz) lemon juice, ½ teaspoon sugar. Mix juice and sugar together, add saké and shake well over ice, strain into a highball glass with ice, top up with soda and dress with fruit in season.

Saké Gozenshu (Jap) the brand-name of a popular saké.

Saké Manhattan (Cktl) 1 part saké, 2 parts rye whiskey. Stir well with ice, strain into a cocktail glass and top with a cherry.

Saké Martini (Cktl) 1 part saké, 3 parts gin. Stir well with ice, strain into a cocktail glass and top with an olive.

Saké Screwdriver (Cktl) place 2–3 ice cubes in a tumbler. Pour in 50mls (2fl.ozs) saké and 150mls (6 fl.oz) fresh orange juice, stir and decorate with a slice of orange.

Saké Sour (Cktl) 10mls (½ fl.oz) saké, 25mls (1fl.oz) lemon juice, 1 teaspoon sugar. Mix in a mixing glass, add ice, then shake well together, strain into a sour glass, add a dash of soda and a cherry.

Saké Tonic (Cktl) place 2–3 ice cubes into a highball glass. Pour 50mls (2fl.ozs) saké over the ice, top with tonic water.

Sakhre (Iran) a natural spring mineral water (established 2000) from Zagros. Mineral contents (milligrammes per litre): Sodium 0.9mg/l, Calcium 40mg/l, Magnesium 22mg/l, Potassium 1.3mg/l, Bicarbonates 183mg/l, Chlorides 7mg/l, Sulphates 7.5mg/l, Fluorides 0.12mg/l. pH 7.2

Saki (Arab) bartender.

Sakini (Cktl) 1 part saké, 3 parts gin. Stir over ice and serve 'on the rocks' with an olive.

Sakonnet Vineyards (USA) a winery based on Rhode Island. 14ha. Produces vinifera and varietal hybrid wines.

Saku Brewery Ltd (Est) a brewery. (Add): 75 701 Saku, Harju Maakond, Estonia. Brews beers and lagers. Website: http://www.saku.ee 'E'mail: saku@pruul.ee

Sakura Masamune (Jap) the brand-name of a popular brand of saké.

Salacia (Czec) a sparkling natural spring mineral water. Mineral contents (milligrammes per litre): Sodium 24.5mg/l, Calcium 245.1mg/l, Magnesium 33mg/l, Potassium 1.9mg/l, Bicarbonates 1005mg/l, Chlorides 4.6mg/l, Sulphates 16.7mg/l, Fluorides 1.1mg/l.

Saladin Box (Scot) a large uncovered, automated, open-ended, rectangular box used for modifying (germinating) barley during the malting process. For whisky and beer production. *See also* Wanderhaufen.

Salage (Fr) the adding of sea water to wines to increase the mineral content. Up to 1g/l is permitted.

Salamander Brewing Company Ltd (Eng) a brewery (established 2000). (Add): 22 Harry Street, Bradford, West Yorkshire BD4 9PH. Brews: Golden Salamander 4.5% alc by vol., Mud Puppy 4.2% alc by vol., Stout 4.5% alc by vol. Website: http://www.salamanderbrewing.com 'E'mail: salamanderbrewing@fsmail.net

Salamanzar (Fr) a large bottle of (9litres) 12 standard bottles capacity used in the Champagne region. *see* Champagne Bottle Sizes. (Eng) = salamanzar.

Salamanzar (Sp) a cava wine bottle that equals 12 standard bottles. (Fr) = salmanazar.

Salamis (Cyp) a dry red wine produced by SODAP wineries.

Salaparuta-Corvo (It) a producer of sparkling (cuve close) wines in Sicily.

Salcheto (It) a wine estate based in Montepulciano, Tuscany. Produces Salco Evolution.

Salco Evolution (It) a D.O.C.G. Vino Nobile di Montepulciano wine produced by the Salcheto winery.

Salem (Eng) a premium cask porter beer from Batemans in Lincolnshire. *See also* Victory Ale.

Salem [ortsteil Kirchberg] (Ger) village (Anb): Baden. (Ber): Bodensee. (Gro): Sonnenufer. (Vin): Schlossberg.

Salem Porter (Eng) a 4.7% alc by vol. porter brewed by George Bateman & Son Ltd., Lincolnshire.

Salento Bianco Liquoroso (It) *see* Moscato di Salento.

Salep (Eng) *see* Saloop.

Salia (Sp) a winery based in the D.O. Manchuela, Castilla-La Mancha. Grape varieties include: Monestrell, Syrah. Label: Sinca Sandoval.

Salice de Quincy (Fr) a 7ha wine estate in A.C. Quincy, Central Vineyards, Loire.

Salice Salentino Bianco (It) a D.O.C. white wine produced in Puglia from a minimum 70% Chardonnay grapes.

Salice Salentino Pinot Bianco (It) a D.O.C. white wine produced in Puglia from Pinot bianco grapes.

Salice Salentino Rosso (It) a D.O.C. red wine from Puglia. Produced mainly from the Negroamaro grape. Also made in rosato form.

Salignac (Fr) a Cognac producer. (Add): Domaine de Breuil, Rue Robert Daugas, 16100 Cognac. 7ha. in the Grande Champagne. Produces Très Vieille Grande Réserve 50 year old plus (part of the Hiram Walker group).

Salignac-de-Pons (Fr) a commune in the Charente-Maritime département whose grapes are classed Petite Champagne (Cognac).

S

Salinas (USA) a new wine district in Monterey County, California.

Salinger (Austr) a sparkling wine produced by the traditional method by Seppelt in South Australia.

Salins du Midi (Fr) a Vin de Pays region, has its own co-operative the Domaine Viticoles. Also has own gradings: Cuvée Regence, Cuvée Gastronomique and Cuvée Centenaire.

Salisbury Bitter (Eng) a cask-conditioned bitter 1042 O.G. brewed by the Gibbs Mew Brewery, Salisbury, Wiltshire.

Salisbury Estate (Austr) the name used by Alambie Wine Cº. in Victoria for a range of varietal wines. Grape varieties include: Chardonnay, Cabernet sauvignon, Sémillon.

Salishan Vineyards (USA) a vineyard based in La Centre, Washington. 5ha. Grape variety: mainly Pinot noir.

Salitage (Austr) a winery at Vase Highway, Pemberton, West Australia. Grape varieties: Chardonnay, Pinot noir.

Salkim (Tur) a bunch of grapes.

Salle de Bistro (Fr) tap-room.

Salles (Fr) a commune in the Beaujolais district. Has A.C. Beaujolais-Villages or Beaujolais-Salles status.

Salles-d'Angles (Fr) a commune in the Charente département whose grapes are classed Grande Champagne (Cognac).

Salles-de-Barbezieux (Fr) a commune in the Charente département whose grapes are classed Petite Champagne (Cognac).

Sally's Paddock (Austr) a blended wine mainly of Shiraz and Cabernet sauvignon grapes from the Redbank Estate, Victoria.

Salmanazar (Fr) a large bottle of (9litres) 12 standard bottles capacity used in the Champagne region. *see* Champagne Bottle Sizes.

Salm Braeu Vienna (Aus) a brewery. (Add): Rennweg 8, 3rd District, Vienna. Brews beers and lagers. Website: http://www.salmbraeu.com

Salmen Brauerei (Switz) a brewery based in Rheinfelden (part of the Sibra group [Cardinal] Breweries).

Salome (Cktl) ⅓ measure dry gin, ⅓ measure Dubonnet, ⅓ measure dry vermouth. Stir over ice and strain into a cocktail glass.

Salomon (Fr) a large Champagne bottle (18litres) consisting of 24 bottles produced by Gosset in 1986. *See also* Sovereign.

Salomon [Denis] (Fr) a récoltant-manipulant Champagne producer. (Add): 5, Rue Principale, 51700 Vandières. Produces vintage and non-vintage wines. Produces: Cuvée Elégance, Cuvée Prestige, Rosé de Saignée, Rosé Brut, Réserve Brut, Carte Noir (Brut/Demi-Sec) and Ratafia. Vintages: 1995, 1996, 1998, 1999, 2000, 2001, 2002. Website: http://www.Champagne-salomon.com 'E'mail: info@Champagne-salomon.com

Salomon [Josef] (Aus) a winery based in Falkenstein, Weinviertel. (Add): 2162 Falkenstewin 24. Grape varieties: Grüner veltliner, Riesling, Sylvaner.

Salon (Aus) an annual wine competition for Austrian growers. Wines are panel-tasted blind and those awarded with prizes can use the designation 'salon' on their winning wine's label.

Salon (Fr) a Champagne producer. (Add): B.P. 3, Le Mesnil-sur-Oger, 51190 Avize. 1ha. Grande Marque. Produces vintage and non-vintage wines. Vintages: 1911, 1914, 1915, 1917, 1921, 1923, 1928, 1929, 1932, 1934, 1937, 1942, 1943, 1945, 1947, 1949, 1950, 1952, 1953, 1955, 1959, 1961, 1964, 1966, 1967, 1969, 1971, 1973, 1976, 1979, 1982, 1983, 1985, 1988, 1990, 1995, 1996, 1997, 1998, 1999, 2001.

Salón Rioja (Chile) the name given to red and white wine produced by Concha y Toro.

Saloon (USA) an old bar, especially in the old 'wild west' (circa 1840 – 1910) era. Now the equivalent of a U.K. lounge bar.

Saloop (Eng) a mediaeval tonic drink made from herbs and plants. Also spelt Salep.

Salopian Brewing Company (Eng) a brewery (established 1995) (Add): The Brewery, 67 Mytton Oak Road, Shrewsbury, Shropshire SY3 8UQ. Brews: Gingersnap, Golden Thread 5% alc by vol., Heaven Sent 4.5% alc by vol., Icon 4.2% alc by vol., Ironbridge Stout, Lemon Dream 4.5% alc by vol., Minsterley Ale, Puzzle 4.8% alc by vol., Shropshire Gold 3.8% alc by vol., Wheat Beer.

Salopian Springs (Eng) a natural spring mineral water (established 2000) from Shropshire. Mineral contents (milligrammes per litre): Sodium 146mg/l, Calcium 71mg/l, Magnesium 47mg/l, Potassium 2.2mg/l, Fluorides 0.1mg/l, Nitrates 1mg/l.

Salta (Arg) the most northly wine-producing region 2000ha that has the districts of: Cafayate, Colchaqui and San Carlos. Main grape varieties: Cabernet sauvignon, Chardonnay, Chenin blanc, Malbec, Merlot, Sauvignon blanc, Syrah, Tannat, Torrontés. *see* Colomé.

Saltana (S.Afr) a white grape variety.

Saltare (S.Afr) a winery based in Stellenbosch, Western Cape. Produces a range of white, red and methode cap classique sparkling wines. W.O. Simonsberg-Paarl.

Salters Winery (Austr) a winery based in the Barossa Valley, South Australia. Produces varietal and table wines.

Saltillo (Mex) a wine-producing area in the Coahuila district at the base of Nazario Ortiz Garza. Produces wines and brandies.

Saltram Winery (Austr) a winery based in Southern Vales and Barossa Valley, South Australia (owned by Seagram). Grape varieties: Cabernet sauvignon, Shiraz, Chardonnay, Sauvignon blanc.

Salts (Eng) minerals that are found in wines. *see* Mineral Salts.

Salty Dog (Cktl) 35mls (1½ fl.oz) vodka, 85mls (3½ fl.ozs) grapefruit juice. Moisten and salt the rim of a large wine glass, fill with ice and add ingredients but do not stir.

Saluccio (It) a white barrique-fermented Chardonnay wine produced by Tenuta del Terriccio, 56040 Castellina Marittima (PI).

Salud (Sp) cheers!

Salus (S.Am) a natural spring mineral water from Minas, Uruguay. Mineral contents (milligrammes per litre): Sodium 7.2mg/l, Calcium 36mg/l, Magnesium 8.9mg/l, Potassium 0.71mg/l, Chlorides 7.1mg/l, Sulphates 5.7mg/l, Nitrates 0.7mg/l.

Salus Brewery (S.Am) a brewery based in Uruguay.

Salus-Vidago (Port) a natural spring mineral water from Fonte Salus.

Salus-Vidago 16 (Port) a natural spring mineral water from Vidago 16.

Salus-Vidago 18 (Port) a natural spring mineral water from Vidago 18.

Salute (It) cheers!/good health.

Salutus (Port) a natural spring mineral water from Ferreira.

Salva [La] (It) a producer of sparkling (cuve close) wines in the Lazio region.

Salvador (USA) a red-fleshed hybrid grape variety grown in California for the making of dessert wines.

Salvador Coffee (S.Am) produces mild, smooth coffees from high grade beans. Some of the coffees can be poor and thin and are used in blending. Grown in Salvador.

Salvador Poveda (Sp) a vineyard in Monóvar, Alicante. Produces 100% Monastrell wines. Fondillón is wood-aged for 15 years.

Salvagnin (Switz) a red wine from the Vaud, of guaranteed quality. Made from a blend of Salvagnin noir and Gamay grapes. Deep in colour and high in alcohol.

Salvagnin Noir (Fr) the local name used in the Jura for the Pinot noir grape.

Salvation (Eng) a 4.8% alc by vol. ale brewed by Abbey Ales Ltd., Avon.

Salvator (Ger) a brand of lithiated mineral water.

Salvator (Ger) the brand-name of a dopplebock beer brewed at the Paulaner-Thomas-Bräu Brauerei in Munich. See also St. Francis of Paula (the oldest doppelbock) 7.5% alc by vol.

Salvator (Slo) a sparkling natural spring mineral water (established 1794) from Lipovice. Mineral contents (milligrammes per litre): Sodium 270.1mg/l, Calcium 431.4mg/l, Magnesium 177.6mg/l, Potassium 36mg/l, Bicarbonates 2576.1mg/l, Chlorides 114.8mg/l, Sulphates 147.4mg/l, Ammonium 1.25mg/l.

Salvatore (Cktl) ⅓ measure Kirsch de Zoug, ⅓ measure vodka, ⅓ measure Cointreau, ⅓ measure grapefruit juice. Shake over ice, strain into a cocktail glass and add a cherry.

Salvavidas (S.Am) a natural spring mineral water from Guatemala.

Salvetat (Fr) a natural spring mineral water from Rieumajou. Mineral contents (milligrammes per litre): Sodium 7mg/l, Calcium 253mg/l, Magnesium 11mg/l, Potassium 3mg/l,

Bicarbonates 820mg/l, Chlorides 4mg/l, Sulphates 25mg/l, Nitrates 1mg/l, Silicates 72mg/l. pH 6.0

Salvus (Ger) a natural spring mineral water. Mineral contents (milligrammes per litre): Sodium 18.8mg/l, Calcium 97mg/l, Magnesium 4.9mg/l, Potassium 0.9mg/l, Bicarbonates 201.4mg/l, Chlorides 46.3mg/l, Sulphates 67.5mg/l.

Salzberg (Ger) grosslage (Anb): Württemberg. (Ber): Württembergisch Unterland. (Vils): Affaltrach, Eberstadt, Eichelberg, Ellhofen, Eschenau, Gellmersbach, Grantschen, Lehrensteinsfeld, Löwenstein, Löwenstein (ortsteil Hösslinsülz), Sulzbach, Weiler/Weinsberg, Weinsberg, Willsbach, Wimmental.

Salzberg (Fr) the German name for the wine town of Château-Salins in Alsace.

Sam Adams Summer Ale (USA) imported into the U.K. by Shepherd Neame. A seasonal summer ale that is brewed with lemon zest and grains of paradise spice.

Sámago (Sp) a virus that turns the stem of the vine spongy and so preventing the production of fruit, the vine then dies.

Samalens (Fr) a noted Armagnac producer based at Laujuzen, Bas Armagnac. Rélique Ancestrale is a 25% 1900 Armagnac. Sold as a 15 year old (youngest age).

Samaniego (Sp) a noted wine-producing village in the Rioja Alavesa.

Samaria (Gre) a natural spring mineral water from Stylos Chania. Mineral contents (milligrammes per litre): Sodium 6.9mg/l, Calcium 32.1mg/l, Magnesium 11.2mg/l, Potassium 0.4mg/l, Bicarbonates 142.8mg/l, Chlorides 14.2mg/l, Sulphates 4.8mg/l, Fluorides 0.11mg/l, Nitrates 0.05mg/l. pH 7.4

Samarkand (Iran) a luscious white grape variety.

Sam Brown (Eng) a brown ale 1035 O.G. brewed and bottled by the Mitchells and Butler Brewery in the Midlands.

Sam Brown (Eng) a brown ale 1034 O.G. brewed and bottled by the Webster Brewery in Halifax, Yorkshire.

Sambuca (It) a liqueur made from an infusion of witch elder bush and liquorice, traditionally served ignited with 3 coffee beans floating on top. 40% alc by vol. See also Sabucco (an alternative spelling). Now produced in a variety of flavours including: banana, coffee, liquorice, mandarin orange, raspberry and vanilla.

Sambuca Cocktail (Cktl) fill a liqueur glass with Sambuca, float 3 coffee beans (dark roasted) on top. Ignite, allow to burn for 30 seconds, douse and serve.

Sambuca Negra (It) a coffee-flavoured Sambuca liqueur 40% alc by vol.

Sambucco (It) a liqueur made from elderberry and liquorice. See also Sambuca.

Sam Da Doo (S.Kor) a natural spring mineral water from Cheju Island. Mineral contents (milligrammes per litre): Sodium 5.3mg/l, Calcium 2.9mg/l, Magnesium 2.1mg/l, Potassium 2.1mg/l.

Samichlaus (Switz) a beer brewed by the Hürlimann Brauerei, Zürich annually on Switzerland's traditional Santa Claus day (December 6). Lagered for 1 year it is purported to be the strongest beer in the world 13.94% alc by vol.

Sämling 88 (Aus) an alternative name for the Scheurebe grape.

Samogon (Rus) the name given to 'bootleg' vodka.

Samonac (Fr) a commune in the A.C. Côtes de Bourg in north-eastern Bordeaux.

Samora (Sp) a solera reserva brandy produced by Bodegas Internacionales.

Samorodno (Cro) a medium-dry, white wine produced in north-east near the Hungarian border.

Samos (Gre) an island in the Aegean Islands, eastern Greece. Produces mainly sweet, A.O.C. dessert wines. 3 types: Samos Doux (mistela), Samos Netar (from sun-dried grapes), Samos Vin Doux Naturel Grand Cru (mutage).

Samos Muscatel (Gre) a luscious dessert wine made from the Muscatel grape on the island of Samos.

Samotok (Ser) a white wine produced in southern Macedonia.

Samovar (Rus) an elaborate container used for the serving of tea.

Sampania (Gre) Champagne/sparkling wine.

Šampanjac (Cro) Champagne/sparkling wine.

Şampanya (Tur) Champagne/sparkling wine.

Sampigny-lès-Maranges (Fr) a vineyard in the A.C. commune of Sampigny, Côte de Beaune, Burgundy. 44ha. Wines may be sold as Sampigny-lès-Maranges or Côte de Beaune-Villages. Has two vineyards that can use their name: Clos du Roi and Les Maranges both prefixed with Sampigny-lès-Maranges.

Sam Powell Original (Eng) a 3.7% alc by vol. bitter ale brewed by The Wood Brewery Ltd., Shropshire.

Sampson Ale (Eng) a cask-conditioned ale 1055 O.G. brewed by the Truman Brewery in London.

Sam's (Eng) a 4.2% alc by vol. stout from the Allsopp Brewery C°.

Samshoo (Chi) a liqueur made from distilled rice wine.

Samshu (Chi) see Samshoo.

Samsó (Sp) a red grape variety grown in Catalonia. Known as Carignan in Penedés.

Samson Brewery (Czec) a brewery (established 1795) in the town of Ceské Budejovice. Noted for Dalila (a medium dark lager) and Samson Straw. Part of the South Bohemian Brewery Group.

Samson Smooth (Eng) a 4% alc by vol. beer brewed by Vaux. Available in cask, nitrokeg and can.

Samson Straw 10% (Czec) a 3.3% alc by vol. bottled straw lager brewed by Samson Brewery, Ceské Budejovice.

Samson Straw 12% (Czec) a 5% alc by vol. golden, bottled lager brewed by Samson Brewery, Ceské Budejovice.

Samson Strong Bitter (Eng) a bitter beer 1042 O.G. brewed by the Vaux Brewery in Sunderland.

Samtrot (Ger) lit: 'velvet red', a mutation of the red grape variety Schwarzriesling.

Samual Crompton Ale (Eng) a 4.2% alc by vol. ale brewed by the Bank Top Brewery Ltd., Lancashire.

Samuel Adams Boston Lager (USA) a 4.8% alc by vol. amber lager from the Boston Beer C°.

Samuel Allsopp Brewery (Eng) a micro-brewery within Carlsberg-Tetley. Brews: Brierley Court, Cobnut Ale, Cockle Pippin and Summer Golden Ale. All are part of the Tapster's Choice.

Samuel Berrys IPA (Eng) a 5.1% alc by vol. India pale ale brewed by the Edale Brewery C°., Derbyshire.

Samuel Oldknow (Eng) a bitter ale brewed by the Robinson Brewery.

Samuel Port (Austr) a Port-style wine from the Wynvale Vineyards, New South Wales.

Samuel Powell Traditional Bitter (Wal) see Powell.

Samuels [T.W.] (USA) a Bourbon whiskey distillery based south of Frankfort in Kentucky.

Samuel's Bay (Austr) the brand-name for a range of wines from the Barossa Valley produced by Wynn, Eden Valley South Australia. Grape varieties: Grenache, Riesling, Chardonnay, Malbec, Colombard.

Samuel Smith (Eng) the oldest brewery in Yorkshire based in Tadcaster. Still uses wooden casks. Noted for cask-conditioned ales.

Samuel Whitbread Bitter (Eng) a cask-conditioned bitter 1044 O.G. brewed by the Whitbread Brewery in London (also produced in kegs).

San Adrián (Sp) a Zona de Crianza in the Rioja Baja.

San Andrés (Sp) a natural spring mineral water from S. Andres de Rabanedo, Leon. Mineral contents (milligrammes per litre): Sodium 1mg/l, Calcium 17mg/l, Magnesium 7mg/l, Potassium 1mg/l, Bicarbonates 74mg/l, Chlorides 3mg/l, Sulphates 2mg/l, Fluorides <0.5mg/l, Silicates 8.3mg/l.

San Angelo (It) a Tuscan Pinot grigio wine produced by Castello Banfi, Montalcino, Siena.

San Angelo Medium Amontillado (Sp) a brand of Amontillado Sherry produced by Garvey's at Jerez de la Frontera.

San Anton (Sp) a still natural spring mineral water from Moya, Gran Canaria. Mineral contents (milligrammes per litre): Sodium 25.5mg/l, Calcium 10.6mg/l, Magnesium 7.9mg/l, Potassium 4.9mg/l, Bicarbonates 111.1mg/l, Chlorides 14.4mg/l, Sulphates 4mg/l, Fluorides <0.2mg/l, Nitrates 9.6mg/l.

San Antonio (Peru) a natural spring mineral water brand.

San Antonio Valley (Chile) a wine region based in central Chile.

San Antonio Winery (USA) a large winery based in Los Angeles, California. Produces table, sparkling and dessert wines.

Sanary (Fr) a commune in the Bandol district of Provence.

San Asensio (Sp) a wine-producing district in the Rioja Alta.

S

San Asensio (Sp) a red wine produced by Bodegas Campo Viejo in the district of same name in the Rioja Alta.

Sanatogen (Eng) a tonic wine from the Whiteway Company (original formula or added iron formula).

San Benedetto (Bel) a natural spring mineral water from Bonne Fontaine, Genval.

San Benedetto (It) a (still and carbonated) natural mineral water from Scorzé. (Add): S.p.A Sede e Stablimento Viale Kennedy, Scorzé (VE). Mineral contents (milligrammes per litre): Sodium 6.8mg/l, Calcium 46mg/l, Magnesium 30mg/l, Potassium 1.1mg/l, Bicarbonates 293mg/l, Chlorides 2.8mg/l, Sulphates 4.9mg/l, Silica 17mg/l, Fluorides <0.1mg/l, Oxygen 7.1mg/l. pH 7.68

San Benito Valley (USA) a new wine area of Central Coast, California. Produces table, dessert and sparkling wines. see Almaden.

San Bernardino (Switz) a slightly sparkling natural spring mineral water (established 1500/1998) from San Berardino. Mineral contents (milligrammes per litre): Sodium 10.2mg/l, Calcium 638.9mg/l, Magnesium 78mg/l, Potassium 6.2mg/l, Bicarbonates 995.5mg/l, Chlorides 4.65mg/l, Sulphates 1111.1mg/l, Fluorides 0.8mg/l, Nitrates 0.5mg/l, Silicates 26.8mg/l, Strontium 4.5mg/l. pH 6.22

San Bernardino (USA) a wine district within the region of Cucamonga, California. Produces table and dessert wines.

San Bernardino Winery (Austr) a winery based in Riverina, New South Wales.

San Bernardo (It) a natural spring mineral water (established 980) from San Bernardo. Mineral contents (milligrammes per litre): Sodium 0.5mg/l, Calcium 11.5mg/l, Magnesium 0.5mg/l, Potassium 0.4mg/l, Bicarbonates 35mg/l, Chlorides 0.6mg/l, Sulphates 2mg/l, Nitrates 1.3mg/l, Silicates 4.7mg/l. pH 7.28

San Bernardo Sorgente della Rocca (It) a slightly sparkling natural spring mineral water from Ormea, Cunea. Mineral contents (milligrammes per litre): Sodium 0.7mg/l, Calcium 46mg/l, Magnesium 0.4mg/l, Potassium 0.1mg/l, Bicarbonates 140mg/l, Chlorides 0.6mg/l, Sulphates 3.1mg/l, Nitrates 1.4mg/l, Silicates 2.5mg/l. pH 8.2

San Bernardo Sorgente Rocciaviva (It) a sparkling natural spring mineral water from Garesso, Cuneo. Mineral contents (milligrammes per litre): Sodium 0.6mg/l, Calcium 10mg/l, Magnesium 0.5mg/l, Potassium 0.7mg/l, Bicarbonates 30mg/l, Chlorides 0.9mg/l, Sulphates 2.8mg/l, Nitrates 1.8mg/l, Silicates 4.7mg/l. pH 7.4

San Carlo Fonte Aurelia (It) a sparkling natural spring mineral water from Fonte Aurelia, Massa, Massa Carrara. Mineral contents (milligrammes per litre): Sodium 10mg/l, Calcium 2.8mg/l, Magnesium 2.6mg/l, Potassium 0.32mg/l, Bicarbonates 10.8mg/l, Chlorides 14mg/l,

Sulphates 2.4mg/l, Nitrates 11.5mg/l, Silicates 9.6mg/l. pH 5.7

San Carlos (Arg) a wine-producing area in central Argentina.

San Carlo Spinone (It) a still and sparkling natural spring mineral water from Fonte Nuova, Bergamo. Mineral contents (milligrammes per litre): Sodium 6mg/l, Calcium 100.8mg/l, Magnesium 27.2mg/l, Potassium 0.8mg/l, Bicarbonates 360mg/l, Chlorides 4.1mg/l, Fluorides 0.3mg/l, Nitrates 5.4mg/l, Silicates 10mg/l, Strontium 3.3mg/l. pH 7.36

San Cascaino (It) a commune of Chianti Classico Riserva.

San Cassiano (It) a sparkling natural spring mineral water from Ancona. Mineral contents (milligrammes per litre): Sodium 6mg/l, Calcium 74mg/l, Magnesium 1.3mg/l, Bicarbonates 219mg/l, Chlorides 10mg/l, Sulphates 9mg/l, Nitrates 2.1mg/l, Silicates 5.5mg/l. pH 7.35

Sancerre (Fr) a noted A.C. dry white wine area within the Central Vineyards of the Loire. Soil types: silex (flint), terres blanches (clay/limestone), caillottes (chalky stone). White wines produced from the Sauvignon blanc 75%, red and rosé from Pinot noir 25%.

Sanchez de Alba (Sp) a Sherry producer based at Jerez de la Frontera. Labels include La Guita.

Sanchez-Romate (Sp) see Romate.

San Ciro (It) a sparkling natural spring mineral water from La Ferrina. Mineral contents (milligrammes per litre): Sodium 112.7mg/l, Calcium 55mg/l, Magnesium 78.2mg/l, Potassium 205.4mg/l, Bicarbonates 744mg/l, Fluorides 7.7mg/l, Oxygen 4mg/l. pH 6.61

San Clemente (Switz) a sparkling natural spring mineral water from Castascio. (blue label: sparkling/green label: light gas). Mineral contents (milligrammes per litre): Sodium 1.9mg/l, Calcium 8.2mg/l, Magnesium 1.6mg/l, Sulphates 8.2mg/l, Nitrates 4.7mg/l.

Sancocho (Sp) the action of boiling must down to one third of its volume. This is used to sweeten and colour Sherries. see Paxarete.

San Cosma (It) a Chianti Classico producer based in Tuscany.

San Costanza Nouveau (It) a young red wine produced by Castello Villa Banfi from the Brunello grape.

San Cristobal (Cktl) ¼ measure golden rum, ¼ measure grenadine, ¼ measure pineapple juice, ¼ measure orange juice, dash Angostura, 2 dashes lime juice. Shake well over ice, strain into an ice-filled collins glass, dress with a slice of orange and pineapple cube.

Sanctified Wine (USA) a wine for religious service.

Sanctuary (Eng) a 6% alc by vol. strong ale brewed by The Durham Brewery Ltd., County Durham.

Sanctum Wines (S.Afr) a winery (established 2002) based in Koelenhof, Stellenbosch, Western Cape. Grape varieties include: Shiraz. Website: http://www.sanctumwines.com

Sanct Zacharias (It) a natural spring mineral water from Sanct Zacharias, Brenner. Mineral contents (milligrammes per litre): Sodium 8.8mg/l, Calcium 100mg/l, Magnesium 11.5mg/l, Potassium 1.9mg/l, Bicarbonates 244mg/l, Chlorides 10mg/l, Sulphates 98mg/l, Fluorides mg/l.

Sanctuary (Eng) a 5% alc by vol. dark sweet ale from Durham Brewery in Bowburn, County Durham. *See also* Palatinate, Celtic.

Sand (Aus) a vineyard site based on the banks of the River Kamp situated in the Kamptal region.

Sand (Ger) vineyard (Anb): Rheinhessen. (Ber): Nierstein. (Gro): Sankt Alban. (Vil): Mainz.

Sand (Eng) soil that gives good drainage, is resistant to Phylloxera and is good for vine cultivation. Occurs in the Côtes du Rhône and Armagnac. (Fr) = sable.

Sandalera (Austr) a grape liqueur from the Sandalford winery in the Swan Valley, Western Australia. Made from the Pedro ximénez (P.X) grape. Has a raisiny flavour and aroma.

Sandalford Winery (Austr) a winery based in the Margaret River region. (Add): West Swan Road, Caversham, 6055, Western Australia. 175ha. in the Margaret River and Swan Valley. Grape varieties: Cabernet sauvignon, Chardonnay, Chenin blanc, Merlot, Verdelho, Pedro ximénez, Riesling, Sémillon and Shiraz. Labels: Element, Prendiville.

Sandalia (It) a sparkling natural spring mineral water from S'Acqua Cotta. Mineral contents (milligrammes per litre): Sodium 520mg/l, Calcium 35.7mg/l, Magnesium 9.24mg/l, Potassium 25mg/l, Bicarbonates 927mg/l, Chlorides 329mg/l, Sulphates 59.9mg/l, Fluorides 8.4mg/l, Silicates 42.7mg/l. pH 7.52

San Damiano (It) a natural spring mineral water from Sicily.

San Daniel (Sp) a natural spring mineral water from Fuente de la Pólvora, Girona.

San Daniele (It) a sparkling natural spring mineral water from Peschiere. Mineral contents (milligrammes per litre): Sodium 7.7mg/l, Calcium 59.2mg/l, Magnesium 7.2mg/l, Potassium 1.4mg/l, Bicarbonates 211.8mg/l, Chlorides 4.7mg/l, Sulphates 29.2mg/l, Nitrates 3.6mg/l, Silicates 3mg/l, Oxygen 8.99mg/l. pH 7.78

Sandberg (Ger) vineyard (Anb): Mosel-Saar-Ruwer. (Ber): Saar-Ruwer. (Gro): Scharzberg. (Vil): Wiltingen.

S and D (Eng) *abbr*: Somerset and Dorset a 4.4% alc by vol. ale brewed by the Cottage Brewing C°., Somerset.

Sand Creek Brewing C° [The] (USA) a brewery. (Add): 320 Pierce Street, P.O. Box 187, Black River Falls, Wisconsin W154615. Brews a variety of beers and lager. Website: http://www.sandcreekbrewing.com

Sandeman (Port) vintage Port shippers. Vintages: 1870, 1872, 1873, 1875, 1878, 1880, 1881, 1884, 1887, 1890, 1892, 1894, 1896, 1897, 1900, 1904, 1908, 1911, 1912, 1917, 1920, 1927, 1934, 1935, 1942, 1943, 1945, 1947, 1950, 1955, 1957, 1958, 1960, 1962, 1963, 1966, 1967, 1970, 1975, 1977, 1980, 1982, 1983, 1985, 1991, 1992, 1994, 1997, 2000, 2003. *see* Quinta do Vau.

Sandeman (Sp) a noted Sherry producer. (Add): Calle Pizarro 10, Jerez de la Frontera. Over 675ha. of vineyards. Sherry brands include Don Fino, Royal Ambrosante, Royal Corregidor, Royal Esmeralda. Also a noted Port producer. Famous for its 'Black Don' motif.

Sandeman and Son (Scot) a distillery based in Dundee, Perthshire. Produces King's Vat (a blended Scotch whisky) 40% alc by vol. Also ships Madeira wine.

Sandeman Jubilee Port (Port) a vintage 1977 Port bottled to celebrate H.R.H. Queen Elizabeth II's Silver Jubilee.

Sandeman Silver Jubilee Port (Port) a vintage 1935 Port bottled to celebrate H.R.H. King George V's Silver Jubilee.

Sanderson [William and Son] (Scot) a noted whisky distiller and blender based in Leith, Midlothian. Created the blend of VAT 69. Now part of DCL. Still hold the license of Glenesk Distillery Montrose.

Sandessano (It) a natural spring mineral water from Clusone. Mineral contents (milligrammes per litre): Sodium 0.43mg/l, Calcium 59.2mg/l, Magnesium 10.2mg/l, Potassium 0.21mg/l, Chlorides 0.75mg/l, Sulphates 5.8mg/l, Fluorides 0.12mg/l.

S & G (Sp) a white wine produced in La Mancha by the Vinícola de Castilla.

Sandgrounder Bitter (Eng) a 3.8% alc by vol. bitter ale brewed by the South Port Brewery, Merseyside.

Sandgrub (Ger) vineyard (Anb): Rheingau. (Ber): Johannisberg. (Gro): Heiligenstock. (Vil): Eltville.

Sandgrub (Ger) vineyard (Anb): Rheingau. (Ber): Johannisberg. (Gro): Heiligenstock. (Vil): Kiedrich.

Sandgrub (Ger) vineyard (Anb): Rheingau. (Ber): Johannisberg. (Gro): Steinmacher. (Vil): Eltville.

Sandgrube (Aus) a vineyard site on the banks of the River Danube in the Kremstal region.

Sandhurst Vineyards (Eng) a winery (established 1988). (Add): Hoads Farm, Sandhurst, Cranbrook, Kent TN18 5PA. Main grape variety is Ruländer which produces a dry white wine. Website: http://www.sandhurstvineyards.co.uk 'E'mail: ca.nicholas@btinternet.com

San Diego (USA) a wine district in southern California which produces table, sparkling and dessert wines.

Sandihurst Wines (N.Z) a winery. (Add): Main West Coast Road, West Melton, Canterbury. 16ha. Grape varieties: Breidecker, Chardonnay, Gewürztraminer, Pinot gris, Pinot noir, Riesling.

Sand Martin (Cktl) ⅔ measure dry gin, ⅓ measure Italian vermouth, ⅙ measure Green Chartreuse. Shake well over ice and strain into a cocktail glass.

Sando (Sri.L) a bitter stout 13.8° Balling brewed by the McCallum Brewery in Colombo.

San Domingo (Sp) a sweet, pale, Cream Sherry produced by Gonzalez Byass in Jerez de la Frontera.

San Donato (It) a sparkling natural spring mineral water from Pianura, Naples. Mineral contents (milligrammes per litre): Sodium 99.3mg/l, Calcium 66.4mg/l, Magnesium 8.2mg/l, Potassium 44.7mg/l, Bicarbonates 195.2mg/l, Chlorides 42.5mg/l, Sulphates 252mg/l, Fluorides 3.4mg/l, Nitrates 0.7mg/l, Silicates 34.2mg/l, Oxygen 2.3mg/l. pH 7.5

Sandoval (Sp) a winery based in Cuenca, Castilla-La Mancha. Likely to apply for Castilla-La Mancha private D.O. status. See also Calzadilla, Manzaneque, Dehesa del Carrizal, Sandoval, Vallegarcía, Aalto, Mauro, San Román.

S and P (Eng) a cask-conditioned bitter 1038 O.G. brewed by the Norwich Brewery, Norfolk.

Sandpitts Vineyard (Eng) a vineyard (established 1981) based near Gastard, Wiltshire. 0.25ha. Grape varieties: Chambourcin, Leon Millot and Zweigeltrebe.

Sandro (Cktl) 10mls (½ fl.oz) Campari, 10mls (½ fl.oz) Bacardi White Rum, 35mls (1½ fl.oz) Cinzano Rossi. Stir over ice, strain into a cocktail glass and add orange zest.

Sand Rock (Eng) a 5.6% alc by vol. ale brewed by the Ventnor Brewery Ltd., Isle of Wight.

Sandrocken (Ger) vineyard (Anb): Baden. (Ber): Badische Bergstrasse/Kraichgau. (Gro): Rittersberg. (Vil): Grossachsen.

Sandrone [Luciano] (It) a small grower based in Barolo, Piemonte.

Sandstone (Eng) a red sand-based soil that produces fine wines. see Coonawarra. (Fr) = grès, (It) = oligocene.

Sandstone Winery (USA) a winery based in Iowa. Produces mainly French hybrid wines.

Sandwald Weizen Krone (Ger) a wheat beer 5.1% alc by vol. brewed by the Dinkelacker Brauerei in Stuttgart.

Sandwalls Brewery (Swe) a brewery based in Boras, south-western Sweden.

Sandweine (Aus) the name given to wines of Burgenland grown on sandy soil (resistant to Phylloxera). see Winkel (seen on the label).

Sand Wines (Hun) the name given to the wines produced on the Transdanubian plain which has sandy soil.

Sandy Bottoms (Eng) a slang term used in the navy to obtain the rest of the rum offered by a mate from his mug.

Sandy MᵃᶜDonald (Scot) the label of a blended Scotch whisky 43% alc by vol.

Sandy Soil (Eng) see Sand.

Sanel Valley Vineyard (USA) a vineyard based near Hopland, Mendocino County, California. 42ha. Grape variety: Cabernet sauvignon. Vinified at the Milano Winery.

Sanfaustino (It) a sparkling natural spring mineral water from San Faustino. Mineral contents (milligrammes per litre): Sodium 17.4mg/l, Calcium 413.9mg/l, Magnesium 17.2mg/l, Potassium 2.5mg/l, Bicarbonates 1244.4mg/l, Chlorides 221mg/l, Sulphates 90.2mg/l, Fluorides 0.2mg/l, Nitrates 3.8mg/l, Silicates 15.2mg/l, Oxygen 2.6mg/l. pH 6.05

San Felice (It) a sparkling natural spring mineral water from San Felice. Mineral contents (milligrammes per litre): Sodium 8.8mg/l, Calcium 58.7mg/l, Magnesium 8.7mg/l, Potassium 1.1mg/l, Bicarbonates 200mg/l, Chlorides 9.5mg/l, Sulphates 15.8mg/l, Oxygen 7.5mg/l, Nitrates 13.3mg/l, Silicates 8.6mg/l. pH 7.38

San Felice (It) a wine-producer based at 53010 Castelnuovo Berardenga, Siena, Tuscany. Noted for Poggio Rosso Chianti Classico D.O.C.G. Riserva, Brunello di Montalcino, Campogiovanni, Vigorello, Belcaro, Ancherona Chardonnay.

San Felipe (Chile) a wine-producing area in the Aconcagua province.

San Félipe Bianco (Arg) a white wine produced in the Mendoza region from Pinot bianco and Riesling grapes.

San Félipe Traminer (Arg) an Alsace-type wine produced from the Traminer grape in the Mendoza region.

San Fernando (Chile) a wine-producing area in the Colchagua province.

Sanfgrube (Aus) a vineyard site based on the banks of the River Kamp situated in the Kamptal region.

Sanford, Sandford and Benedict Vineyards (USA) a winery (46ha) based near Buellton, Santa Rita Hills, Santa Barbara, California. Grape varieties: Chardonnay and Pinot noir. Produces varietal wines. Label: La Rinconada Vineyard.

San Francisco (Cktl) ⅓ measure sloe gin, ⅓ measure Italian vermouth, ⅓ measure French vermouth, dash Angostura, dash orange bitters. Shake over ice, strain into a cocktail glass and top with a cherry.

San Francisco Bay (USA) an A.V.A. that includes four counties surrounding the Bay as well as the City and County of San Francisco. A sub-region of Central Coast. 2500ha. of vineyards and over 40 wineries.

San Francisco Brandy (USA) the brand-name of a 10 year old brandy bottled by the Guild of Wineries and Distilleries in Lodi, California.

Sangarees (Cktl) spirit, lemon slice, sugar syrup, fruit and nutmeg served in a tall glass over cracked ice. Can also be made with beer or wine in place of the spirits. Is similar to Sangría.

Sang des Pierres [Le] (Fr) the label of a Châteauneuf-du-Pape négociant Andrée Amouroux. (Add): Ave. St. Joseph, 84230 Châteauneuf-du-Pape, southern Rhône. Other Châteauneuf-du-Pape labels include Domaine Amouroux.

S.Angelo (It) a sparkling natural spring mineral water from Siliqua (CA), Cagliari, Sardinia. Mineral contents (milligrammes per litre): Sodium 37.2mg/l, Calcium 12.9mg/l,

Magnesium 13.7mg/l, Potassium 1.6mg/l, Bicarbonates 74.9mg/l, Chlorides 68.1mg/l, Sulphates 36.6mg/l, Fluorides 0.3mg/l, Nitrates 0.6mg/l, Silicates 11.9mg/l. pH 6.65

Sangemini (It) a natural spring mineral water from Sangemini, Umbria. Mineral contents (milligrammes per litre): Sodium 19.67mg/l, Calcium 328.1mg/l, Magnesium 17.5mg/l, Potassium 3.65mg/l, Bicarbonates 1042.7mg/l, Chlorides 18.34mg/l, Sulphates 52.9mg/l, Fluorides 0.38mg/l, Nitrates 0.64mg/l, Silicates 23.81mg/l, Strontium 1.42mg/l. pH 6.26

Sanger (Fr) a Champagne producer. (Add): Coopérative des Anciens de la Viticulture, Lycée Viticole, 51190 Avize. Coopérative-manipulant.

Sängerhalde (Ger) vineyard (Anb): Baden. (Ber): Bodensee. (Gro): Sonnenufer. (Vil): Stetten.

Sängerhalde (Ger) vineyard (Anb): Baden. (Ber): Bodensee. (Gro): Sonnenufer. (Vil): Markdorf.

Sängerhalde (Ger) vineyard (Anb): Baden. (Ber): Bodensee. (Gro): Sonnenufer. (Vil): Meersburg.

Sangermano (It) a natural spring mineral water from Caserta.

Sanghioveto (It) an alternative name for Sangiovese.

San Giacomo (It) a sparkling natural spring mineral water from San Giacomo, Sarnano, Macerata. Mineral contents (milligrammes per litre): Sodium 25mg/l, Calcium 130mg/l, Magnesium 15.8mg/l, Potassium 1.8mg/l, Bicarbonates 443mg/l, Chlorides 27.5mg/l, Sulphates 43mg/l, Silicates 11.3mg/l. pH 6.99

San Giacomo di Roburent (It) a natural spring mineral water from San Giacomo di Roburent, Roburent, Cuneo.

San Gil (Fr) the brand-name of an Armagnac brandy produced by the Domaine de Cassanel in Nerac 40% alc by vol.

San Ginés de la Jara (Sp) see Saint Ginés de la Jara.

Sangineto (It) an alternative name for Sangiovese.

San Giocondo (It) a Tuscan 'Nouveau' wine produced by Antinori.

San Giorgio (It) a red Vino da Tavola wine from 80%–90% Sangiovese and 10%–30% Cabernet grapes. Produced in central Italy.

Sangiovese (It) a red grape variety grown mainly in the southern regions of Italy. Used in the making of full-bodied, well balanced wines giving an aroma and taste of bitter plums/cherries, violets, herbs, prunes, farmyard, leather, herbs and tobacco. e.g. Chianti. Sangiovese can be divided into two branches with many clones including: Sangiovese Grosso, Sangiovese Piccolo. See also Sanghioveto, Sangioveto, Sangineto, Sanvicetro, Brunello, Cardisco, Ingannacane, Morellino, Nerino, Prugnolo, Tignolo.

Sangiovese dei Colli Pesaresi (It) a D.O.C. red wine from The Marches. Made from the Sangiovese, Ciliegiolo and Montepulciano grapes. Produced in an area around Pesaro.

Sangiovese di Aprilia (It) see Merlot di Aprilia (pink with orange reflections).

Sangiovese di Romagna (It) a D.O.C. red wine from the Emilia-Romagna. Made from the Sangiovese grape. If aged minimum 2 years then classed Riserva. Cannot be sold to the consumer before 1st April following the vintage.

Sangiovese Grosso (It) a red grape variety grown in the Tuscany region for Chianti wines. Sangiovese can be divided into two main branches, the other being Sangiovese Piccolo. Grosso includes Brunello, Prugnolo, Sangioveto di Lamole, Sangiovese Romagnolo.

Sangiovese Piccolo (It) the Sangiovese vine variety can be divided into two main branches, the other being Sangiovese Grosso. Piccolo includes Nerino.

Sangiovese Romagnolo (It) an alternative name for Sangiovese Grosso grape.

Sangiovese Toscano (It) the local Tuscany name for a variety of the Sangiovese grape.

Sangioveto (It) an alternative name used for the Sangiovese grape used in the making of Chianti.

Sangioveto di Coltibuono (It) a red Vino da Tavola wine produced from 100% Sangiovese grapes by Badia a Coltibuono in Tuscany.

Sangioveto di Lamole (It) an alternative name for Sangiovese Grosso grape.

Sangiovetto di Coltibuono (It) a red Vino da Tavola wine produced from the Sangiovese grape in central-western Italy.

Sangiovetto Piccolo (Arg) a red grape variety grown in the Mendoza region.

Sangiuliano (It) a sparkling natural spring mineral water from Viserba Rimini (RN). Mineral contents (milligrammes per litre): Sodium 45mg/l, Calcium 113mg/l, Magnesium 23mg/l, Potassium 3.1mg/l, Bicarbonates 336mg/l, Chlorides 60mg/l, Sulphates 120mg/l, Fluorides 0.16mg/l, Nitrates 10.2mg/l, Silicates 9.4mg/l. pH 7.2

San Giuseppe (It) a natural spring mineral water brand.

San Grato (It) a natural spring mineral water from Cirie, Torino. Mineral contents (milligrammes per litre): Sodium 2.8mg/l, Calcium 13.8mg/l, Magnesium 14.9mg/l, Potassium 1.5mg/l, Bicarbonates 101mg/l, Chlorides 3.6mg/l, Sulphates 6.8mg/l, Oxygen 8.5mg/l, Nitrates 10.9mg/l, Silicates 23.1mg/l.

Sangre de Toro (Sp) the brand-name of an oak aged red wine produced by Torres in Penedés, Cataluña. Grape varieties: 60% Garnacha, 40% Cariñena. Now known as Tres Torres in U.K.

Sangri (Eng) a drink made with Madeira, sugar, water and grated nutmeg (served hot or cold).

Sangría (Sp) a wine cup made by adding fruit to red wine. 75grms (3ozs) sugar, 125mls (1gill) water, 1 sliced orange, 1 sliced lime, 1 bottle red wine. Make a syrup with the water and sugar, whilst still hot add the thinly sliced fruit. Marinade for 4 hours, then add ice and red wine, stir well and serve.

Sangria Punch (Cktl) 1 bottle dry red wine, 1 bottle apple juice, juice ½ small grapefruit, slices of orange, lemon, apple and pear, sugar syrup to taste. Combine all together, stand in a cool place for 24 hours and serve with ice.

Sangrita (Cktl) 1 measure tequila, 1 measure tomato juice. Shake over ice and strain into a cocktail glass.

Sangue de Boi (Bra) lit: 'bull's blood', a locally named wine. Has no association and bares little resemblance to the Hungarian variety.

Sangue di Giuda (It) a red wine from Lombardy.

San Isidro (Sp) a large co-operative based in the Jumilla district in the Levante. Produces wines under names of Rumor, Sabatacha and Zambra.

Sanity Clause (Eng) a winter warmer beer from Finnesko and Firkin Brewery, Derham Road, Norwich (formerly known as the Reindeer Brewery).

San Joaquin (Sp) a natural spring mineral water from San Joaquin de Huemos de Cañedo, Valdunciel, Salamanca.

San Joaquin Valley (USA) a Californian wine area in the Fresno-San Joaquin Valley. Southern part of the Great Valley in California. Produces most of California's dessert wines with some table and sparkling wines.

San José (USA) a large city in Santa Clara, California. Has many wineries based there.

San Juan (Arg) a large wine-producing region 47080ha based in the Cuyo region north of Mendoza. Districts: Calingasta Valley, Pendernal Valley, Tulum Valley, Ullum Valley and Zonda Valley. Main grape varieties: Bonarda, Cabernet sauvignon, Chardonnay, Malbec, Shiraz, Syrah, Tannat, Viognier.

San Juan del Río (Mex) a wine-producing region in the Querétaro district.

San Juan de Peteroa (Chile) a wine-producing area in central Chile.

Sanka (USA) a leading brand of de-caffeinated coffee.

Sankt (Ger) saint.

Sankt Alban (Ger) grosslage (Anb): Rheinhessen. (Ber): Nierstein. (Vils): Bodenheim, Gau-Bischofsheim, Harxheim, Lörzweiler, Mainz.

Sankt Annaberg (Ger) vineyard (Anb): Rheinhessen. (Ber): Wonnegau. (Gro): Liebfrauenmorgen. (Vil): Worms.

Sankt Conrad (Ger) a sparkling natural spring mineral water from Goslar, Harz. Mineral contents (milligrammes per litre): Sodium 306mg/l, Calcium 72.7mg/l, Magnesium 8.2mg/l, Potassium 3.3mg/l, Bicarbonates 69.6mg/l, Chlorides 492mg/l, Sulphates 144mg/l.

Sankt Georgen (Ger) vineyard (Anb): Rheinhessen. (Ber): Bingen. (Gro): Abtey. (Vil): Partenheim.

Sankt Johann (Ger) village (Anb): Rheinhessen. (Ber): Bingen. (Gro): Abtey. (Vins): Geyersberg, Klostergarten, Steinberg.

Sankt Johännser (Ger) vineyard (Anb): Württemberg. (Ber): Württembergisch Unterland. (Gro): Schalkstein. (Vil): Markgröningen.

Sankt Julianenbrunnen (Ger) vineyard (Anb): Rheinhessen. (Ber): Nierstein. (Gro): Krotenbrunnen. (Vil): Guntersblum.

Sankt Kathrin (Ger) vineyard (Anb): Rheinhessen. (Ber): Bingen. (Gro): Abtey. (Vil): Wolfsheim.

Sanktkönigsquele (Hun) a sparkling natural spring mineral water from Szentkirály. Mineral contents (milligrammes per litre): Sodium 19mg/l, Calcium 61mg/l, Magnesium 28mg/l, Bicarbonates 390cmg/l.

Sankt Laurent (Aus) an alternative spelling of the red grape variety St. Laurent. *See also* Pinot St. Laurent.

Sankt Margarethen (Aus) a Burgenland area which produces mainly white wines.

Sankt Martin (Ger) village (Anb): Pfalz. (Ber): Südliche Weinstrasse. (Gro): Schloss Ludwigshöhe. (Vins): Baron, Kirchberg, Zitadelle. (*See* St. Martin).

Sankt Michael (Ger) grosslage (Anb): Mosel-Saar-Ruwer. (Ber): Bernkastel. (Vils): Bekond, Detzem, Ensch, Klusserath, Köwerich, Leiwen, Longen, Lörsch, Mehring, Pölich, Schleich, Thörnich.

Sankt Pilt (Fr) the German name for the wine village of Saint-Hippolyte in the Bas-Rhin, Alsace.

Sankt Rochuskapelle (Ger) grosslage (Anb): Rheinhessen. (Ber): Bingen. (Vils): Aspisheim, Badenheim, Biebelsheim, Bingen, Dromersheim, Gensingen, Grolsheim, Ockenheim, Pfaffen-Schwabenheim, Sponsheim, Welgesheim, Zotzenheim.

San Leonino (It) a Chianti Classico producer based in Tuscany.

San Leopoldo (It) a sparkling natural spring mineral water from Sorgente del Riguado. Mineral contents (milligrammes per litre): Sodium 1340mg/l, Calcium 301.4mg/l, Magnesium 157.5mg/l, Potassium 26mg/l, Bicarbonates 3245.2mg/l, Chlorides 588.5mg/l, Sulphates 862.6mg/l, Nitrates 9.5mg/l, Silicates 30mg/l, Strontium 5.9mg/l, Oxygen 4.1mg/l. pH 6.87

San Leopoldo (It) a Super-Tuscan I.G.T. wine produced by Tenuta Il Poggione, Montalcino, Siena from 50% Sangiovese, 25% Cabernet sauvignon and 25% Cabernet franc grapes.

San Lorenzo (It) a sparkling natural spring mineral water from San Lorenzo, Marche. Mineral contents (milligrammes per litre): Sodium 136mg/l, Calcium 103mg/l, Magnesium 315mg/l, Potassium 13.2mg/l, Bicarbonates 1842mg/l, Chlorides 32.5mg/l, Sulphates 324mg/l, Fluorides 0.12mg/l, Nitrates 0.7mg/l, Silicates 59.8mg/l. pH 6.2

San Lorenzo (It) a D.O.C. Rosso Conero wine produced by Umani Ronchi in Osimo, Marche.

Sanlúcar de Barrameda (Sp) a sea port on the river Guadalquivir where Fino Sherries are brought to mature into Manzanilla. The climate is cooler so the flor remains active all year imparting a different character (slightly salty taste) to the Sherry. Part of the Jerez Supérieur region.

San Luigi (It) a sparkling natural spring mineral water from San Luigi. Mineral contents (milligrammes per litre): Sodium 0.9mg/l, Calcium 61.3mg/l, Magnesium 13.8mg/l, Bicarbonates 234.9mg/l, Chlorides 1.9mg/l,

Sulphates 14mg/l, Nitrates 7.5mg/l, Silicates 4.7 mg/l. pH 7.6

San Luis (Sp) a wine-producer based on Minorca in the Balearic Isles.

San Luis Obispo (USA) a wine-producing area in South Central Coast region, California.

San Luis Potosi (Mex) a wine-producing area in northern Mexico.

San Lunardo (It) a white grape variety grown on the island of Ischia.

San Marcellino (It) an IGT red wine (100% Sangiovese) produced by the Rocco di Montegrossi winery in the Tuscany region.

San Marco (It) a sparkling natural spring mineral water from Latina, Lazio. Mineral contents (milligrammes per litre): Sodium 20mg/l, Calcium 312mg/l, Magnesium 90.6mg/l, Potassium 45mg/l, Bicarbonates 1605mg/l, Chlorides 116.9mg/l, Sulphates 4mg/l, Silicates 58.3mg/l. pH 6.2

San Marino (It) a sparkling natural spring mineral water from Pesaro. Mineral contents (milligrammes per litre): Sodium 8.2mg/l, Calcium 110mg/l, Magnesium 8mg/l, Potassium 0.7mg/l, Bicarbonates 360mg/l, Chlorides 11mg/l, Sulphates 14mg/l, Fluorides 0.19mg/l, Nitrates 2.9mg/l, Silicates 5.8mg/l. pH 7.1

San Marino (N.Z) a winery. (Add): 2 Highway 16, Kumeu, Auckland. 32ha. at Kumeu, also grapes from Gisborne. Grape varieties: Cabernet franc, Cabernet sauvignon, Chardonnay, Gewürztraminer, Merlot, Müller-Thurgau, Pinot noir, Sauvignon blanc.

San Marino (S.Afr) a natural spring mineral water. Mineral contents (milligrammes per litre): Sodium 2mg/l, Calcium 6mg/l, Magnesium 5mg/l, Potassium <1mg/l, Chlorides <5mg/l, Sulphates <0.2mg/l, Fluorides <0.2mg/l, Nitrates 0.4mg/l. pH 6.5 Website: http://www.dominique.co.za

San Marino Della Battaglia (It) a D.O.C. dry white or liquoroso wine made from Friuli Tocai.

San Marino Trinity (N.Z) a slightly spicy wine made from a blend of Chardonnay, Gewürztraminer and Müller-Thurgau grapes by San Marino in Kumeu.

San Martin (Arg) a wine-producing area based in the Mendoza region.

San Martin Cocktail (Cktl) 30mls (¼ gill) gin, 30mls (¼ gill) Italian vermouth, 4 dashes Yellow Chartreuse. Shake well over ice, strain into a cocktail glass and add a squeeze of lemon peel juice on top.

San Martino (It) a sparkling natural spring mineral water from San Martino, Sassari. Mineral contents (milligrammes per litre): Sodium 670mg/l, Calcium 195mg/l, Magnesium 69mg/l, Potassium 89.5mg/l, Bicarbonates 2013.56mg/l, Chlorides 294.24mg/l, Sulphates 288.7mg/l, Fluorides 0.92mg/l, Nitrates 0.85mg/l, Silicates 20.2mg/l. pH 7.29

San Martino Della Battaglia (It) a small locality 2 miles south of Lake Garda in Lombardy. Tocai de San Martino della Battaglia is the white wine produced there.

San Martin Winery (USA) a winery based in Morgan Hill, Santa Clara, California. Grape varieties: Johannisberg riesling, Muscat and Petite syrah. Produces varietal wines.

San Mateo (Sp) a Vino Comarcal wine from the province of Castellón in Valencia.

San Mateo (USA) a small wine-producing county based near San Francisco, California.

San Matias (Mex) a producer of tequila sold under the same name.

San Matteo (It) a natural spring mineral water from Fonte della Salute, Forli.

San Michel (Euro) a natural spring mineral water from Valletta, Malta. pH 7.3

San Michele (Den) a tangerine-based liqueur produced by the Peter Heering Cº.

San Michele (It) a sparkling natural spring mineral water from Vaie. Mineral contents (milligrammes per litre): Sodium 2.1mg/l, Calcium 5.6mg/l, Magnesium 0.7mg/l, Potassium 0.7mg/l, Chlorides 0.4mg/l, Sulphates 4mg/l, Nitrates 2.6mg/l, Silicates 11mg/l. pH 7.3

San Miguel (Sp) a dry, pilsner-style beer 5% alc by vol–5.4% alc by vol. brewed by the San Miguel Brewery.

San Miguel Brewery (E.Ind) a brewery with a home-base in Manila which produces San Miguel lager beers. One of the largest brewing groups in Asia, also brew in China and other parts of Asia.

San Miguel Brewery (Sp) a major brewing company in Spain. Has three breweries in Burgos, Lérida and Málaga. Brews: San Miguel 5% alc by vol (1049-1055 O.G) and Selecta XV Lager beers.

San Narciso (Sp) a sparkling natural spring mineral water from Caldes de Malavella, Girona. Mineral contents (milligrammes per litre): Sodium 1138mg/l, Potassium 53.4mg/l, Chlorides 595.7mg/l, Sulphates 53.8mg/l, Fluorides 7.7mg/l.

San Nicodemo (It) a natural spring mineral water from Barillaro, Mammola, Reggio Calabria.

Sannine (Leb) a still natural spring mineral water from Liban-Bkaatouta. Mineral contents (milligrammes per litre): Sodium 10mg/l, Calcium 50mg/l, Magnesium 12mg/l, Potassium 2mg/l, Bicarbonates 230mg/l, Chlorides 10mg/l, Sulphates 40mg/l, Fluorides 0.25mg/l. pH 7.1

San Pancrazio (It) a natural spring mineral water from Bergamo. Mineral contents (milligrammes per litre): Sodium 569mg/l, Calcium 85.6mg/l, Magnesium 32.6mg/l, Potassium 31.4mg/l, Bicarbonates 280.6mg/l, Chlorides 859.3mg/l, Sulphates 91.1mg/l, Fluorides 0.55mg/l, Strontium 4.6mg/l, Silicates 9.4mg/l. pH 7.71

San Pantaleo (It) a sparkling natural spring mineral water from Olbia, Sassari. Mineral contents (milligrammes per litre): Sodium 108mg/l, Calcium 15mg/l, Magnesium 8.6mg/l, Potassium 2mg/l, Bicarbonates 154.07mg/l, Chlorides 110.22mg/l, Sulphates 23mg/l, Fluorides 3.75mg/l, Nitrates 0.18mg/l, Silicates 15.3mg/l. pH 7.39

S

San Paolo (It) a sparkling natural spring mineral water from Fonte San Paolo, Rome. Mineral contents (milligrammes per litre): Sodium 250mg/l, Calcium 306.3mg/l, Magnesium 77.4mg/l, Potassium 254mg/l, Bicarbonates 1953mg/l, Chlorides 46.3mg/l, Sulphates 256mg/l, Fluorides 2.4mg/l, Oxygen 1.28mg/l, Silicates 95mg/l. pH 6.2

San Pasqual Vineyards (USA) a winery based in Escondido, San Diego California. 42ha. Grape varieties: Gamay, Muscat canelli and Sauvignon blanc. Produces varietal and table wines.

San Patricio (Sp) a very dry, pale, Fino Sherry produced by Garvey in Jerez de la Frontera.

San Pedro Winery (Chile) a winery based in Talca province. Owned by Rumasa. Wines produced include red Gato Negro, white Gato Blanco.

San Pellegrino (It) a carbonated natural spring mineral water (established 1899) from the San Pellegrino Terme. Mineral contents (milligrammes per litre): Sodium 43.6mg/l, Calcium 208mg/l, Magnesium 55.9mg/l, Potassium 2.7mg/l, Bicarbonates 135.5mg/l, Chlorides 74.3mg/l, Sulphates 549.2mg/l, Fluorides 0.52mg/l, Nitrates 0.45mg/l, Silicates 9mg/l, Boration 1.2mg/l, Strontium 2.7mg/l. pH 7.7

San Pietro (It) a sparkling natural spring mineral water from San Pietro, Marino, Rome. Mineral contents (milligrammes per litre): Sodium 38.5mg/l, Calcium 106mg/l, Magnesium 34mg/l, Potassium 52.2mg/l, Bicarbonates 561.2mg/l, Chlorides 39.05mg/l, Sulphates 69.6mg/l, Fluorides 0.42mg/l, Strontium 1.3mg/l, Silicates 104mg/l. pH 6.2

San Quintin (Sp) a solera brandy produced by Domecq. See also Fundador, Hispano, Tres Cepas.

San Rafael (Arg) one of three Denominaciónes de Origen of Mendoza. See also Luján de Cuyo, Maipú.

San Rafael (USA) a wine town in Marin County, California. Has many wineries based there.

Sanraku Ocean (Jap) one of the largest whiskey and wine producers in Japan. Based in Yamanashi, Tokyo. Noted for Château Mercian (Grand Cru Classé) wine.

San Rocco (It) a sparkling natural spring mineral water from San Rocco. Mineral contents (milligrammes per litre): Sodium 5.5mg/l, Calcium 80mg/l, Magnesium 38mg/l, Potassium 0.65mg/l, Bicarbonates 393mg/l, Chlorides 53mg/l, Sulphates 28mg/l, Fluorides 0.18mg/l, Nitrates 10mg/l, Silicates 21.6mg/l. pH 7.6

San Román (Sp) a Vino de la Tierra wine from Zamora, Castilla-Léon. See also Mauro, Aalto.

San Roque (Sp) a natural spring mineral water from Valsequillo, Las Palmas de Gran Canaria.

San Sadurní de Noya (Sp) the Penedés town where the sparkling wines of the region are made and stored (spelt Sant Sadurni d'Anoia in Catalan).

Sans Année (Fr) non-vintage.

Sans Barrique (S.Afr) the label for an un-oaked white wine (Chardonnay) produced by the Bouchard Finlayson winery, Walker Bay, Western Cape.

Sans Culottes (Fr) a bottle conditioned ale 7% alc by vol. from La Choulette.

San Sebastian Cocktail (Cktl) ⅓ measure dry gin, ⅓ measure white rum, ⅓ measure triple sec, 10mls (½ fl.oz) grapefruit juice, 10mls (½ fl.oz) lemon juice. Shake over ice and strain into a cocktail glass.

San Severo Bianco (It) a D.O.C. white wine from the Puglia. Made from the Bombino bianco, Malvasia bianco, Trebbiano toscano and Verdeca grapes. The D.O.C. can also apply to naturally sparkling wines.

San Severo Rosato (It) a D.O.C. rosé wine from the Puglia region. Made from the Montepulciano di Abruzzo and Sangiovese grapes. D.O.C. can also apply to the naturally sparkling wines.

San Severo Rosso (It) a D.O.C. red wine from the Puglia region. Made from the Montepulciano di Abruzzo and Sangiovese grapes D.O.C. can also apply to the naturally sparkling wines.

San Silvestro (It) a liqueur said to contain 100 herbs produced in the Abruzzi mountains. Also called Centerbe or Mentuccia 40% alc by vol.

San Silvestro (It) a sparkling natural spring mineral water from San Silvestro, Angolo Terme, Brescia. Mineral contents (milligrammes per litre): Sodium 2.4mg/l, Calcium 288mg/l, Magnesium 80.2mg/l, Potassium 0.84mg/l, Bicarbonates 231.8mg/l, Chlorides 1.4mg/l, Sulphates 820.5mg/l, Fluorides 0.36mg/l, Nitrates 1.5mg/l, Silicates 8.5mg/l, Strontium 9.2mg/l. pH 7.39

San Simón (Sp) the brand-name used by Bodegas García Carrión in Jumilla for a range of their red, rosé and white wines.

San Souci (Cktl) ⅓ measure Tia Maria, ⅓ measure Jamaican rum, ⅓ measure Grand Marnier, 125mls (1gill) orange juice, 2 dashes lime juice. Stir over ice and strain into a highball glass.

Sans Thorn Rosé (Slo) a light, fragrant, rosé wine.

Sansu (S.Kor) a natural spring mineral water. Mineral contents (milligrammes per litre): Chlorides 2mg/l, Sulphates 7mg/l, Fluorides 0.5mg/l, Nitrates 1.5mg/l. pH 7.6

Sansuidokugen (Jap) a term used to describe a medium style saké. See also Shihizendokoro.

Santa (It) saint.

Santa (It) a natural spring mineral water from Santa, Chianciano, Siena.

Santa Amalia (Chile) a winery based in the Cachapoal Valley. Noted for Sauvignon blanc wines produced from old vines.

Santa Barbara (Bra) a natural spring mineral water (established 1981) from Fonte Santa Catarina, Santa Barbara, Sao Paulo. Mineral contents (milligrammes per litre): Sodium 8.29mg/l, Calcium 15.4mg/l, Magnesium 0.09mg/l, Potassium 2.49mg/l, Bicarbonates 72.96mg/l, Chlorides 0.048mg/l, Sulphates 0.03mg/l, Fluorides 0.36mg/l, Nitrates 0.148mg/l. pH 7.59

Santa Barbara (It) a winery in the D.O.C. Verdicchio dei Castelli di Jesi, Marches region. Label: Le Veglie.

S

Santa Barbara (USA) a wine-producing county on the central-southern coast of California.

Santa Barbara County Vintners' Association (USA) an association of Santa Barbara wineries (50 plus) to promote their wines. Website: http://www.sbcountywines.com

Santa Barbara Winery (USA) a small winery based near Buellton, Santa Barbara, California. 17ha. Produces varietal and generic wines.

Santa Brigida (It) a Super Tuscan barrique-aged red wine produced by Fattoria La Ripa from 50% Cabernet sauvignon and 50% Sangiovese grapes.

Santa Carolina (Chile) a vineyard and winery based in the Maipo Valley. Vineyards: Santa Rosa and Los Toros. Grape varieties: Cabernet sauvignon, Chardonnay, Gewürztraminer, Merlot, Pinot noir, Sauvignon blanc.

Santa Catarina (Bra) a wine-producing state in south-eastern Brazil.

Santa Christina (It) a Chianti Classico produced by Antinori in Tuscany.

Santa Clara (Bra) a slightly acidic natural spring mineral water from Santa Clara. Mineral contents (milligrammes per litre): Sodium 10.16mg/l, Calcium 0.61mg/l, Magnesium 1.63mg/l, Potassium 9.55mg/l, Bicarbonates 13.69mg/l, Chlorides 10.76mg/l, Sulphates 15.02mg/l, Silicates 24.13mg/l. pH 5.54

Santa Clara (It) a sparkling natural spring mineral water from Santa Clara, Borzonasca, Genova. Mineral contents (milligrammes per litre): Sodium 4mg/l, Calcium 37mg/l, Magnesium 4.5mg/l, Potassium 0.4mg/l, Bicarbonates 120mg/l, Chlorides 3.5mg/l, Sulphates 13mg/l, Nitrates 2.5mg/l, Silicates 4mg/l. pH 7.65

Santa Clara Oligomineral (W.Ind) a carbonated natural spring mineral water from the Dominican Republic. Mineral contents (milligrammes per litre): Sodium 7.3mg/l, Calcium 20mg/l, Magnesium 15mg/l, Potassium 0.3mg/l, Bicarbonates 158mg/l, Chlorides 6mg/l, Sulphates 5.5mg/l, Nitrates 1.2mg/l, Silicates 40mg/l. pH 6.7

Santa Clara Valley (USA) a Californian valley which produces fine red and white wines plus dessert and sparkling wines.

Santa Claudia (Bra) a natural spring mineral water from the Amazon.

Santa Claus (Eng) a 5% alc by vol. ale brewed by the Bank Top Brewery Ltd., Lancashire.

Santa Claus (Eng) a 5% alc by vol. ale brewed by Wychwood Brewery at Eagle Maltings, Witney, Oxfordshire.

Santa Claus (Fin) a still natural spring mineral water. Mineral contents (milligrammes per litre): Sodium 7.4mg/l, Calcium 10.1mg/l, Magnesium 4.7mg/l, Bicarbonates 31.7mg/l, Chlorides 9.1mg/l, Sulphates 15.5mg/l, Fluorides 0.1mg/l, Nitrates 16mg/l, Silicates 15.9mg/l. pH 6.5

Santa Corina (It) a still natural spring mineral water from Tavina, Salo, Lake Gardia. Mineral contents (milligrammes per litre): Sodium 10.6mg/l,

Calcium 83.2mg/l, Magnesium 25.8mg/l, Potassium 1.8mg/l, Bicarbonates 363mg/l, Chlorides 9.1mg/l, Sulphates 26.5mg/l, Nitrates 9.5mg/l, Silicates 14.2mg/l. pH 7.64

Santacroce (It) a red Vino da Tavola wine produced from 80% Sangiovese and 20% Cabernet sauvignon grapes by Castell'in Villa in Tuscany.

Santa Croce (It) a natural spring mineral water (established 1969) from Santa Croce, Canistro, L'Aquila. Mineral contents (milligrammes per litre): Sodium 1.23mg/l, Calcium 48.1mg/l, Magnesium 4.57mg/l, Potassium 0.4mg/l, Bicarbonates 195mg/l, Chlorides 7mg/l, Sulphates 1.3mg/l, Fluorides 0.002mg/l, Nitrates 1mg/l, Silicates 1.7mg/l. pH 7.84

Santa Croce (It) a small village in the commune of Carpi in Emilia-Romagna. Lends its name to a red wine Lambrusco Salamino di S. Croce.

Santa Cruz (USA) a wine district sited south of San Francisco which produces table, sparkling and dessert wines.

Santa Cruz de Tenerife (Sp) a wine province of the Canarias. Comprises of the islands: Tenerife, La Gomera, El Hierro, La Palma.

Santa Cruz Mountain Vineyard (USA) a winery based in Santa Cruz, California. 5ha. Grape varieties: Cabernet sauvignon and Pinot noir. Produces varietal wines.

Santa Daría (Sp) the brand-label for wines produced by the Co-operative Vinícola de Cenicero, Bodegas 'Santa Daría', Rioja.

Santa Digna (Chile) the name used by Torres of Spain for a Sauvignon blanc wine produced in Chile.

Santa Emiliana (Chile) the name given to a red wine made from the Cabernet sauvignon and a white wine made from a blend of Sémillon and Sauvignon blanc. Produced by Concha y Toro.

Santa Fiora (It) a natural spring mineral water from Santa Fiora.

Santa Giustina (It) see Leitacher.

Santa Helena (Chile) the brand-name of a range of wines produced in the Curicó Valley. Grape varieties: Cabernet sauvignon, Merlot.

Santa Helena (Gre) a silky dry white wine produced by the Achaia Claus winery of Patras.

Santa Julia (Arg) the label and winery based in Mendoza and owned by the Familia Zuccardi. Produces varietal wines including Bonarda, Cabernet sauvignon, Malbec, Chardonnay, Sangiovese, Syrah, Tempranillo, Torrontés, Viognier. Website: http://www.familiazuccardi.net

Santa Laura (Gre) a dry white wine.

Sant Alberico (It) a natural spring mineral water from Forli.

Santa Lucia (It) a Chianti Classico producer based in Tuscany.

Santa Lucia (It) a 15ha winery in Castel del Monte, Puglia. Grape varieties: Nero di Troia, Montepulciano, Malbec. Some wines are oak aged.

Santa Lucia (It) a sparkling natural spring mineral water from Sassari. Mineral contents

1142

(milligrammes per litre): Sodium 250mg/l, Calcium 105mg/l, Magnesium 66mg/l, Potassium 5.65mg/l, Bicarbonates 1159.32mg/l, Chlorides 70.9mg/l, Fluorides 1.54mg/l, Silicates 45mg/l. pH 6.6

Santa Lucia Highlands (USA) an A.V.A. region in Monterey County, California. Grape varieties include: Chardonnay, Pinot blanc. Home to Mondavi, Paraiso Springs, Morgan Winery, Pisoni Cellars.

Santa Maddalena (It) a D.O.C. red wine from the Trentino-Alto-Adige. Made from the Schiava grigia, Schiava grossa, Schiava media and the Tschaggele grapes in the province of Bolzano. Classico designation is reserved to wine produced in the restricted area delimited by Ministerial decree.

Santa Margherita di Portogruaro (It) a producer of sparkling (cuve close) wines based in Veneto.

Santa Maria (It) a natural spring mineral water from Modica, Ragusa. Mineral contents (milligrammes per litre): Sodium 16mg/l, Calcium 89.2mg/l, Magnesium 10.4mg/l, Potassium 3.05mg/l, Bicarbonates 273.5mg/l, Chlorides 35.7mg/l, Sulphates 12.2mg/l, Nitrates 27.1mg/l, Silicates 7.2mg/l. pH 7.3

Santa Maria (Sp) a Cream Sherry produced by Duff Gordon in Puerto de Santa Maria.

Santa Maria alle Capannelle (It) a natural spring mineral water from Santa Maria Capannelle, Rome. Mineral contents (milligrammes per litre): Sodium 39mg/l, Calcium 131.33mg/l, Magnesium 27.68mg/l, Potassium 61mg/l, Bicarbonates 603.9mg/l, Chlorides 31.91mg/l, Sulphates 20mg/l, Fluorides 1.05mg/l, Nitrates 40mg/l, Silicates 68.6mg/l, Strontium 2.4mg/l. pH 6.23

Santa Maria degli Angeli (It) a sparkling natural spring mineral water from Potenza. Mineral contents (milligrammes per litre): Sodium 24.2mg/l, Calcium 20mg/l, Magnesium 6.68mg/l, Potassium 17mg/l, Bicarbonates 125mg/l, Chlorides 12.4mg/l, Sulphates 7.2mg/l, Fluorides 0.7mg/l, Nitrates 27.5mg/l, Silicates 68.9mg/l. pH 6.6

Santa Maria della Versa (It) a producer of sparkling (cuve close) wines based in Lombardy.

Santa Maura (Gre) a wine-producing area noted for dark, red wines.

Santa Mavra (Gre) a red wine made from the Vertzami grape on the island of Levkas in the Ionian islands in western Greece.

Santa Moors (Eng) a 4.8% alc by vol. ale brewed by the Moor Beer Company, Somerset.

Sant Andrea (It) a natural spring mineral water from Parma. Mineral contents (milligrammes per litre): Sodium 73mg/l, Calcium 59.8mg/l, Magnesium 56mg/l, Potassium 3.9mg/l, Bicarbonates 457.5mg/l, Nitrates 5mg/l. pH 7.6

Santangel (Ven) a natural spring mineral water from Los Teques. Mineral contents (milligrammes per litre): Calcium 104mg/l, Magnesium 5mg/l,

Bicarbonates 190mg/l, Chlorides 30mg/l, Sulphates 138mg/l, Fluorides 0.08mg/l, Nitrates 0.1mg/l, Silicates 7mg/l. pH 7.4

Sant Aniol (Sp) a still and sparkling natural spring mineral water from Sant Aniol de Finestres, Girona. Mineral contents (milligrammes per litre): Sodium 6.8mg/l, Calcium 13.9mg/l, Magnesium 0.1mg/l, Potassium 1.5mg/l, Bicarbonates 344.8mg/l, Chlorides 4.3mg/l, Sulphates 93mg/l, Fluorides 0.2mg/l, Nitrates 1.5mg/l.

Sant Anna (It) a sparkling natural spring mineral water from Sant Anna di Vinadio, Vinadio, Cuneo. Mineral contents (milligrammes per litre): Sodium 1.1mg/l, Calcium 12mg/l, Bicarbonates 29mg/l, Sulphates 7.7mg/l, Oxygen 9.4mg/l, Silicates 6.2mg/l. pH 7.6

Sant Antonio (It) a sparkling natural spring mineral water from Sant Antonio, Sponga. Mineral contents (milligrammes per litre): Sodium 3.6mg/l, Calcium 33.5mg/l, Magnesium 5.4mg/l, Potassium 0.69mg/l, Bicarbonates 133mg/l, Chlorides 1.3mg/l, Sulphates 1.6mg/l, Nitrates 4.4mg/l, Silicates 16.7mg/l. pH 7.7

Santarém (Port) an I.P.R. region within I.P.R. Ribatejo.

Santarém (Port) an alternative name for the Castelão Francês grape.

Santarém-João Santarém (Port) a blue-black grape variety grown in Colares. see Santarém.

Santa Reparata (It) a natural spring mineral water from Teramo, Abruzzo. Mineral contents (milligrammes per litre): Sodium 11mg/l, Calcium 131mg/l, Magnesium 31mg/l, Potassium 11.5mg/l, Fluorides 0.18mg/l, Nitrates 46mg/l. pH 7.24

Santa Rica (Eng) a freeze-dried instant coffee from the Nestlé C°. Made from 100% arabica coffee beans.

Santa Rita (It) a natural spring mineral water from Genova. Mineral contents (milligrammes per litre): Sodium 4mg/l, Calcium 13mg/l, Magnesium 2.5mg/l, Potassium 0.2mg/l, Bicarbonates 50.5mg/l, Chlorides 4mg/l, Sulphates 4mg/l, Nitrates 0.65mg/l, Silicates 6mg/l. pH 8.0

Santa Rita Company (Chile) a wine-producing exporter of Santiago based at Casablanca in the Maipo Valley. Noted for Casa Reserve, Medalla Real wines. Grape varieties include Cabernet sauvignon, Merlot, Pinot noir, Chardonnay, Riesling, Sauvignon blanc.

Santa Rosa (USA) a wine-producing area in the Russian River Valley, Sonoma County, California.

Santa Sarah Estate (Bul) a winery based in Nova Zagora, southern Bulgaria. Grape varieties: Cabernet sauvignon, Mavrud, Merlot. Labels: Genowski, Privat.

Santa's Delight (Eng) a 4.2% alc by vol. seasonal ale brewed by the Wye Valley Brewery, Herefordshire.

Santa's Descent (Eng) a 5.8% alc by vol. seasonal ale brewed by Wye Valley as part of range of Dorothy Goodbody's seasonal ales.

S

Santas Reindeer (Eng) a 4.6% alc by vol. ale brewed by the Bazens Brewery, Greater Manchester.

Santa's Revenge (Eng) a bitter 1058 O.G. or 5.7% alc by vol. brewed by Crouch Vale Brewery, Essex.

Santa's Rocket Fuel (Eng) the label of an ale brewed by Burt's Brewery on the Isle of Wight. *See also* Haggis Ale.

Santa's Secret (Eng) a 4.8% alc by vol. dark bitter brewed by Ridleys Hartford End Brewery, Chelmsford, Essex (available in December).

Santa's Tipple (Wal) a 5% alc by vol. ale brewed by the Cwmbran Brewery, Gwent.

Santa's Wobble (Eng) a 7.5% alc by vol. strong Christmas ale brewed by the Hogs Back Brewery, Surrey.

Santa Teresa (Chile) a winery based in the Colchagu province. Wines are produces in Santiago.

Santa Tirso (Port) a small district of the Vinho Verde region that produces white Vinho Verde wines.

Santa Toss (Eng) an 8.1% alc by vol. seasonal ale brewed by Green Bottle Ltd., Worth Brewery, Keighley, Yorkshire.

Santa Vittoria (It) a natural spring mineral water from Imperia, Liguria. Mineral contents (milligrammes per litre): Sodium 2.1mg/l, Calcium 56mg/l, Magnesium 8mg/l, Potassium 0.4mg/l, Bicarbonates 185mg/l, Chlorides 1mg/l, Sulphates 19.5mg/l, Nitrates 2.5mg/l, Silicates 4.5mg/l. pH 7.99

Santa Ynez Valley (USA) an A.V.A. wine area in Santa Barbara, southern California. Wineries include: Firestone, Santa Ynez Valley Winery and Zaca Mesa.

Santa Ynez Valley Winery (USA) a small winery based near Solvang, Santa Barbara, California. Grape varieties: Cabernet sauvignon, Chardonnay, Gewürztraminer, White riesling and Sauvignon blanc. Produces varietal wines.

Sant Elena (It) a sparkling natural spring mineral water from Siena. Mineral contents (milligrammes per litre): Sodium 24.8mg/l, Calcium 123.7mg/l, Magnesium 13.6mg/l, Potassium 0.9mg/l, Bicarbonates 366mg/l, Chlorides 33.9mg/l, Sulphates 45mg/l, Fluorides 0.3mg/l, Nitrates 31.7mg/l, Silicates 17.1mg/l, Oxygen 8.6mg/l. pH 7.3

Santenay (Fr) an A.C. wine commune of the southern Côte de Beaune in the Burgundy region.

Santenots [Les] (Fr) a Premier Cru vineyard in the A.C. commune of Volnay, Côte de Beaune, Burgundy. Also known as Clos les Santenots.

Santenots-Blancs [Les] (Fr) a Premier Cru vineyard in the A.C. commune of Meursault, Côte de Beaune, Burgundy 2.95ha.

Santenots-du-Milieu [Les] (Fr) a Premier Cru vineyard in the A.C. commune of Meursault, Côte de Beaune, Burgundy 7.7ha.

Santhagens Original Cape Velvet Cream (S.Afr) a liqueur produced by Gilbey in Stellenbosch. Is similar in style to Baileys Cream.

Santhè (It) a natural spring mineral water from Pesaro, Marche.

Sant Hilari (Sp) a natural spring mineral water brand.

Santi (It) a D.O.C. white wine produced in Verona by a firm of the same name.

Santi [A.G.] (It) a noted producer of sparkling (metodo tradizionale) wines in the Veneto region. Labels include Durello Spumante Brut.

Santiago (Chile) a wine-producing area in the central zone.

Santiago (Cktl) 50mls (2fl.ozs) Bacardi White Label rum, juice of ½ a lime, 4 dashes red Curaçao, ½ teaspoon sugar, combine the juice and sugar, add other ingredients. Shake well with ice, and strain into a cocktail glass.

Santiago (W.Ind) the brand-name of a white rum produced by U.R.M.

Santiago Ruiz (Sp) a bodega based in El Rosal, Galicia. Produces mainly white wines.

Santiam (Eng) a 4.3% alc by vol. ale brewed by the Ossett Brewing C°. Ltd., West Yorkshire.

Santini (Pousse Café) pour into a slim liqueur glass an equal measure of the following in order: Cognac, maraschino, Grand Marnier and white rum.

Santino Winery (USA) a winery based in the Shenandoah Valley, Amador County, California. Grape varieties: Cabernet sauvignon and Zinfandel. Produces varietal wines.

Sant Manel Brut Nature (Sp) a cava wine produced by Cavas Hill. Has a flinty, earthy flavour.

Santola (Port) a dry Vinho Verde produced by Vinhos Messias in Beira Alta.

Santolin (Sp) a still natural spring mineral water. Mineral contents (milligrammes per litre): Sodium 2.6mg/l, Calcium 89.9mg/l, Magnesium 2.4mg/l, Chlorides 3.8mg/l, Sulphates 7.4mg/l.

S.Antonio (It) a sparkling natural spring mineral water from Sant' Antonio. Mineral contents (milligrammes per litre): Sodium 3.6mg/l, Calcium 33.5mg/l, Magnesium 5.4mg/l, Potassium 0.69mg/l, Bicarbonates 133mg/l, Chlorides 1.3mg/l, Sulphates 1.6mg/l, Nitrates 4.4mg/l, Silicates 16.7mg/l. pH 7.7

Santonja [Vincente Simó] (Sp) a producer of wines from Valencia. Noted for Foldillón (a fine red wine).

Santoraggio (It) a natural spring mineral water from Assisi.

Santorini (Gre) an A.O.Q.S. straw-coloured, dry white wine produced on the island of Santorini from the Assyrtiko grape.

Santorini (Gre) a phylloxera-free A.O.C. island that, along with Paros, forms part of the Cyclades. Has ash, pumice and stone-laden soils. Grape varieties include: Agiorgitiko, Aidani, Assyrtiko, Athiri, Mandilaria, Moschophilero, Roditis, Savatiano. Noted for Santorini and Vinsanto.

Santos (Bra) a mild smooth coffee which produces a mild soft flavour with little acidity. Is the major coffee bean of Brazil. *see* Bourbon Santos, Flat Bean Santos and Red Santos (all are pure coffees).

Santos Junior (Port) Vintage Port producers

controlled by Barros. Vintages: 1957, 1960, 1970, 1974, 1975, 1977, 1978, 1979, 1980, 1982, 1983, 1985, 1987, 1991, 1994, 1997, 2003.

Santo Stefano (It) a natural spring mineral water from Salerno, Campania. Mineral contents (milligrammes per litre): Sodium 4mg/l, Calcium 49.9mg/l, Magnesium 14.7mg/l, Potassium 1.4mg/l, Bicarbonates 237.9mg/l, Chlorides 8.86mg/l, Sulphates 3mg/l, Nitrates 6.3mg/l, Silicates 4.9mg/l. pH 6.95

Santo Stefano in Campo (It) a natural spring mineral water from Santo Stefano in Campo.

Santo Steffano (It) a red wine produced in the Apulia province that ages well.

Santo Tomàs (Mex) a wine-producing area in the Baja California.

Santo Tomàs (Mex) a winery (established 1888) based in Baja California. The oldest winery in Mexico. Produces a joint Bordeaux-style red wine with Wente in California.

Santovka (Slo) a natural spring mineral water. Mineral contents (milligrammes per litre): Sodium 343mg/l, Calcium 421.8mg/l, Magnesium 80.4mg/l, Potassium 40mg/l, Chlorides 252.5mg/l, Sulphates 329mg/l, Fluorides 1.5mg/l, Iron 1.5mg/l, Strontium 6.55mg/l, Lithium 1.5mg/l, Ammonium 1.3mg/l.

San Trocado (Sp) a white wine produced from Treixadura, Torrontés and Albariño grapes by Bodegas Alanís, Ribeiro.

Santys Port Wines (S.Afr) are Port-style wines produced by the Gilbeys Cº.

San Valentin (Sp) a semi-dry, white wine produced by Torres in the Penedés from the Parellada grape.

San Vigilio (It) a natural spring mineral water from Bagni dell'Orso, San Vigilio, Meran. Mineral contents (milligrammes per litre): Sodium 3.17mg/l, Calcium 4.1mg/l, Magnesium 0.76mg/l, Potassium 0.88mg/l, Bicarbonates 14mg/l, Chlorides 0.4mg/l, Sulphates 5.1mg/l, Fluorides 1.2mg/l, Silicates 6.1mg/l. pH 6.35

San Vincente (Sp) a still natural spring mineral water. Mineral contents (milligrammes per litre): Sodium 5.9mg/l, Calcium 22mg/l, Magnesium 7.3mg/l, Potassium 0.8mg/l, Bicarbonates 81.1mg/l, Chlorides 3.3mg/l, Sulphates 19.4mg/l, Fluorides 0.2mg/l, Nitrates 8.8mg/l.

San Vincente (Sp) a wine-producing district in the Rioja Alta, north-western Spain.

San Vincente Vineyard (USA) a vineyard based near Soledad, Salinas Valley, Monterey County, California. Grape variety: Cabernet sauvignon. Vinified at the Staiger Winery.

San Vincetro (It) an alternative name for the Sangiovese grape.

Sanvito (It) a natural spring mineral water from Sanvito.

San Vito di Canistro (It) a natural spring mineral water from San Vito.

San Vitro di Luzzi (It) a new D.O.C. found in Calabria. *See also* Scavigna.

Sanwald Brauerei (Ger) a brewery based in Stuttgart which is noted for top-fermented weizen beers. Owned by the Dinkelacker Cº.

San Zanobi Pasolini d'All Onda (It) a red wine produced in Tuscany from Sangiovese, Merlot and Cabernet sauvignon grapes. Aged for 12 months in 225litres oak casks, matured in Slovenian oak and released after 3 years.

Sanzay-le-Grand [Paul] (Fr) a wine producer based at Varrains, Saumur, Anjou-Saumur, Loire. Noted for Saumur Mousseux.

San Zeno d'Oro (It) the annual awards given to the best wine producers. Saint Zeno is the patron saint of wine producers.

San Zoveto (It) an early nineteenth century name for the Sangiovese grape.

São Cristóvão (Port) a still natural spring mineral water (established 1999) from Serra de Montemuro. Mineral contents (milligrammes per litre): Sodium 6.3mg/l, Calcium 3.11mg/l, Magnesium 0.83mg/l, Potassium 0.9mg/l, Bicarbonates 14.8mg/l, Chlorides 4.7mg/l, Sulphates 0.6mg/l, Silicates 17.9mg/l. pH 6.07 Website: http://www.aguasaocristovao.com

São Domingos (Port) an extra-dry, sparkling wine made using the traditional method by Caves Solar de São Domingos.

São Domingos (Port) the brand-name of an aguardente brandy produced by Caves Solar de São Domingos.

Sao Francisco (Bra) a local, well-known brand of cachaça.

Sao João (Mad) the name once given to a Madeira-style wine (the name is obtained from the district).

São Lourenco (Bra) a slightly acidic, sparkling natural spring mineral water (established 1890) from Fonte Oriente, Parque das Aguas, Sao Lourenco, Minas Gerais. Mineral contents (milligrammes per litre): Sodium 22.62mg/l, Calcium 14.63mg/l, Magnesium 6.04mg/l, Potassium 19.09mg/l, Bicarbonates 157.38mg/l, Chlorides 1.83mg/l, Sulphates 1.62mg/l, Fluorides 0.09mg/l. pH 5.29

Sao Lourenco (Port) a natural spring mineral water from Azeito. Mineral contents (milligrammes per litre): Sodium 20.2mg/l, Calcium 48mg/l, Bicarbonates 134.2mg/l, Chlorides 38.3mg/l. pH 6.6

Sao Martinho (Mad) the name once given to a Madeira style (the name obtained from district).

Sâone [River] (Fr) a river that runs through the Beaujolais in Burgundy to join the river Rhône.

Saône-et-Loire (Fr) a département between Mâcon and Chagny in the Burgundy region. Divided into Mercurey and Mâconnais.

Sao Rico (Eng) a soft drink produced from sparkling water, exotic fruits and spices by Bulmer (has a strong ginger taste).

Saothróir Finiuna (Ire) wine grower.

Saothru (Ire) wine growing.

Sap (Hol) *abbr*: juice. *see* **Sap**rijk.

Sapa (Lat) a word used to describe a new wine.

Sapan d'Or (Fr) a green liqueur similar in style to Bénédictine.

Saperavi (Asia) a red grape variety grown in Crimea, Georgia, Kazakhsran, Moldova, Tajikistan, Turkmenistan, Uzbekistan. Produces light, sweet wines. Parent of Magaratch Ruby.

Saperavi (Geo) a strong, dark red wine, high in alcohol 14% alc by vol. produced in the Tiflis district of Georgia.

Saperavi Massandra (Rus) a dry red wine from the Crimean peninsular.

Saphir (Fr) a brut méthode traditionelle wine produced by Bouvet-Ladubay from 80% Chenin blanc and 20% Chardonnay grapes.

Sapido (It) spicey, a term applied to wines such as the Gewürztraminer in the Südtirol.

Sapin (Fr) see Sapindor.

Sapindor (Fr) a herb liqueur made at Pontarlier in the Jura since 1825. Sold in tree-trunk shaped bottles. Has a pine-needle extract flavour. Also known as Liqueur des Pins, Sapin and Extrait des Pins.

Sapore (It) flavour.

Sapore di Toscana (It) a natural spring mineral water from Stia (AR), Tuscany. Mineral contents (milligrammes per litre): Sodium 4.2mg/l, Calcium 22.6mg/l, Potassium 0.6mg/l. pH 7.4

Sappig (Hol) juicy. See also Saprijk.

Sapporo Brewery (Jap) a brewery based in Sapporo. Brews: Black Beer, Lager and Yebisu.

Sapporo Dry (Jap) a cold filtration dry-style beer from the Sapporo Brewery.

Sapporo Wines Limited (Jap) see Katsunuma Winery.

Saprijk (Hol) abbr: Sap, juicy. See also Sappig.

Sapuwa (Viet) a natural spring mineral water. Mineral contents (milligrammes per litre): Chlorides 20mg/l, Sulphates 4.6mg/l. pH 7.0

Saquier (Fr) a wine-producing district in A.C. Bellet, Provence, south-eastern France.

Sarabi (Tur) the Turkish name for Sherry. See also Ispanyol Sarabi.

Sarah Hughes Brewery (Eng) a brewery based at Beacon Hotel, Sedgley, Wolverhampton, West Midlands. Brews: Dark Ruby Mild, Sedgley Surprise.

Sarah Hughes Ruby Mild (Eng) a cask mild brewed by the Sarah Hughes Brewery, Sedgley, Wolverhampton, West Midlands.

Sarah's Hop House (Eng) a micro-brewery based at the Railway, Golborne, near Wigan.

Sarah's Vineyard (USA) a winery based near Gilroy, Santa Clara, California. Grape varieties: Chardonnay, Chenin blanc, Petite syrah and Zinfandel. Produces varietal and table wines.

Sarajevska Voda (Bos) a still natural spring mineral water from Bosnia and Herzegovina. Mineral contents (milligrammes per litre): Sodium 414mg/l, Calcium 72.94mg/l, Magnesium 4.86mg/l, Potassium 11.73mg/l, Bicarbonates 272.33mg/l, Chlorides 17.75mg/l, Sulphates 64.5mg/l, Fluorides 0.04mg/l, Nitrates 7.53mg/l.

Sarajevski Kiseljak (Bos) a sparkling natural spring mineral water from Vrelo Park, Kiseljak, Bosnia and Herzegovina. Mineral contents (milligrammes per litre): Sodium 644mg/l, Calcium 236.5mg/l, Magnesium 48.6mg/l, Potassium 19.5mg/l, Bicarbonates 1805.6mg/l, Chlorides 86.7mg/l, Sulphates 600mg/l, Silicates 2.8mg/l. pH 6.5

Sarap (Tur) wine.

Sarap Beyaz (Tur) white wine.

Sarap Garson (Tur) wine waiter.

Sarap Gül (Tur) rosé wine.

Sarap Kirmizi (Tur) red wine.

Saratica (Czec) a natural spring mineral water from Moravsky Beroun. Mineral contents (milligrammes per litre): Sodium 2203mg/l, Calcium 219.7mg/l, Magnesium 943.8mg/l, Potassium 26.3mg/l, Bicarbonates 537.2mg/l, Chlorides 124.2mg/l, Sulphates 8141mg/l, Fluorides 1mg/l, Lithium 1.1mg/l.

Saratoga (USA) a city based in eastern Santa Clara County, California. Has a large number of wineries based there.

Saratoga Cocktail (Cktl) 25mls (1fl.oz) brandy, 10mls (½ fl.oz) lemon juice, 10mls (½ fl.oz) pineapple juice, 2 dashes maraschino, 2 dashes Angostura. Shake over ice and strain into a cocktail glass.

Saratoga Cooler (Cktl) (Non-alc) into a large tumbler place 2 ice cubes, juice of a lime, sugar syrup to taste. Top up with cold ginger ale, stir and serve.

Saratoga Spring (USA) a natural spring mineral water brand.

Sarbi-Afash (Asia) a natural spring mineral water from Kazakhstan. Mineral contents (milligrammes per litre): Sodium 240mg/l, Calcium 64mg/l, Magnesium 0.1mg/l, Potassium 2.9mg/l, Bicarbonates 390mg/l.

Sarbi-Arka (Asia) a natural spring mineral water from Chimkent, Kazakhstan. Mineral contents (milligrammes per litre): Sodium 253mg/l, Calcium 6mg/l, Magnesium 2mg/l, Bicarbonates 407mg/l, Chlorides 71mg/l, Sulphates 119.3mg/l, Fluorides 1.2mg/l, Silicates 17.8mg/l.

Sarcy (Fr) a Cru Champagne village in the Canton de Ville-en-Tardenois. District: Reims.

Sardegna (It) Sardinia.

Sardinia (It) the second largest island of Italy. Produces many fine wines. The **Vitis vinifera** is indigenous to the island. (It) = Sardegna.

Sárfehér (Hun) a white grape variety grown on the Great Plain for sparkling wine production.

Sárgamuskotály (Hun) a minor white grape variety used in the making of Tokaji wines. Also known as Muscat Blanc à Petits Grains.

Sarget de Gruaud-Larose (Fr) the second wine of Château Gruaud-Larose [Grand Cru Classé (4th), A.C. Saint-Julien], north-western Bordeaux.

Sarhos (Tur) a slang term for drunk/drink.

Sari Buah (Indo) juice.

Sari Buah Jeruk (Indo) orange juice.

S

Sarica (Rum) a wine-producing region in the Dobrudja district.

Sarmento (Port) vine-shoot.

Sarmientos (Sp) a term used to describe the two renewed spurs on the vine that will eventually bear grapes.

Saronno Cocktail (Cktl) 40mls (⅓ gill) Amaretto di Saronno, 125mls (1gill) milk, 10mls (½ fl.oz) Galliano. Blend together with a scoop of crushed ice in a blender and serve in a flute glass.

Saronno Sunset (Cktl) ⅙ measure Amaretto di Saronno, ⅙ measure Drambuie, ⅔ measure orange juice, dash grenadine. Shake over ice, strain into a cocktail glass, dress with a cherry and orange slice.

Saronsberg Cellar (S.Afr) a winery (established 2002) based in Tulbagh, Western Cape. 27ha. Grape varieties: Chardonnay, Mourvèdre, Muscat de frontignan, Sauvignon blanc, Shiraz, Viognier. Labels: Full Circle, Seismic. Website: http://www.saronsberg.com

Sàrospatak (Hun) a wine-producing area in the southern foothills.

Sarrau [Robert] (Fr) a Burgundy négociant-éleveur based at Saint Jean d'Ardières, Beaujolais.

Sarsaparilla (USA) *Smilacaceae* a prickly bush the dried roots made into flavouring for an old American non-alcoholic 'soda pop'. Was popular in the U.K. during the Temperance era. *See also* Sasparella.

Sartène (Fr) an A.C. red and rosé wine produced around the town of same name on the south-west of the island of Corsica.

Sarum Special (Eng) a pale ale 1048 O.G. brewed and bottled by the Gibbs Mew Brewery in Salisbury, Wiltshire.

Saryagach (Asia) a natural spring mineral water from Saryagach, Kazakhstan. Mineral contents (milligrammes per litre): Sodium 107mg/l, Calcium 39mg/l, Magnesium 14mg/l, Bicarbonates 219mg/l.

Saryagach Yassayi (Asia) a natural spring mineral water from Saryagach, Kazakhstan. Mineral contents (milligrammes per litre): Sodium 165mg/l, Calcium 8mg/l, Magnesium 6mg/l, Bicarbonates 268mg/l, Chlorides 64mg/l, Sulphates 85mg/l.

SAS (Eng) a cask-conditioned Stronger Anglian Special beer 1048 O.G. brewed by the Crouch Vale Brewery in Essex.

Sasaiwai (Jap) a term used to describe a sweet style saké. *See also* Kikusui.

Sásar (Ire) saucer.

Sasbach (Ger) village (Anb): Baden. (Ber): Kaiserstuhl-Tuniberg. (Gro): Vulkanfelsen. (Vins): Limburg, Lützelberg, Rote Halde, Sceibenbuck.

Sasbachwalden (Ger) village (Anb): Baden. (Ber): Ortenau. (Gro): Schloss Rodeck. (Vins): Alter Gott, Klostergut Schelzberg.

Saskatchewan (Can) a small wine region in central southern Canada.

Saskia (S.Afr) the label for a white wine (Chenin blanc and Viognier blend) produced by the Miles Mossop Wines winery, Stellenbosch, Western Cape.

Saskia Quelle (Ger) a natural spring mineral water from Leissling. Mineral contents (milligrammes per litre): Sodium 7.8mg/l, Calcium 90mg/l, Magnesium 21.4mg/l, Potassium 3mg/l, Bicarbonates 371mg/l, Fluorides 0.66mg/l.

Sasparella (USA) an alternative spelling of Sarsaparilla.

Sassella (It) a sub district of Lombardy in the foothills of the Alps in the Valtellina Valley. Produces red wines of the same name from the Nebbiolo grape.

Sassicaia (It) a famous red (super Tuscan) wine made from Cabernet franc and Cabernet sauvignon grapes (first planted 1944) in Bolgheri in the Tuscany region. 70ha. Owned by Antinori. Formerly Vino da Tavola (first released in 1968), it was awarded the D.O.C. from the 1994 vintage. Now known as Bolgheri-Sassicaia.

Sassoalloro (It) a red I.G.T. wine produced from 100% Sangiovese grosso grapes by Biondi Santi in Tuscany.

Sassovivo (It) a natural spring mineral water from Sassovivo. Mineral contents (milligrammes per litre): Sodium 3.7mg/l, Calcium 70mg/l, Magnesium 0.94mg/l, Potassium 0.46mg/l, Bicarbonates 205mg/l, Chlorides 10mg/l, Sulphates 5.6mg/l, Nitrates 0.49mg/l, Silicates 6mg/l. pH 7.59

Sassumariello (It) a red grape variety grown in the Puglia region.

Satan Gold (Bel) an 8% alc by vol. top-fermented, bottle-conditioned special beer brewed by De Block in Peizegem-Merchtem.

Satan Red (Bel) an 8% alc by vol. top-fermented, bottle-conditioned special double beer brewed by De Block in Peizegem-Merchtem.

Satan's Brew (M.East) early religious (Christian) nickname for coffee, because of its Islamic origins.

Satan's Whiskers (Cktl) ⅕ measure Grand Marnier, ⅕ measure gin, ⅕ measure dry vermouth, ⅕ measure sweet vermouth, ⅕ measure orange juice, dash orange bitters. Shake over ice and strain into a cocktail glass.

S.A.T. Arana (Sp) a winery at Vitgen de la Rioja, 3 26339 Abalos, Rioja. 28ha. Labels include Solana de Ramirez, Valsarte.

Satén (It) a term that is equivalent to D.O.C.G. Crémant, associated with Franciacorta. Made from white grapes only. 5 atmospheres of pressure.

Satigny (Switz) a wine-producing area in Geneva.

Satinela (Sp) a slightly sweet white wine from late-harvested Viura and Malvasia grapes by the Marqués de Cáceres, Rioja. *see* Antea.

Satoraljaujhely (Hun) a wine-producing town based in north-eastern Tokaji.

Sattai (It) a sparkling natural spring mineral water from Sardinia. Mineral contents (milligrammes per litre): Sodium 56mg/l, Calcium 21.24mg/l, Magnesium 11.18mg/l, Potassium 2.3mg/l,

Bicarbonates 75mg/l, Chlorides 88.24mg/l, Sulphates 23.06mg/l, Fluorides 0.24mg/l, Nitrates 16.08mg/l, Silicates 35.2mg/l. pH 6.51

Sattlerhof (Aus) a winery (13ha) based in Gamlitz, Süd-Steiermark. (Add): Sernau 2, 8462 Gamlitz. Grape varieties: Chardonnay, Gewürztraminer, Muskateller, Pinot blanc, Pinot gris, Sauvignon blanc, St. Laurent, Traminer, Welschriesling, Zweigelt. Produces a range of dry and sweet wines.

Sattui Winery (USA) a winery based near St. Helena, Napa Valley, California. Grape varieties: Cabernet sauvignon, Johannisberg riesling and Zinfandel. Produces varietal and dessert wines.

Satul Marc (Rum) a wine-producing region based in the Siebenbürgen district.

Saturnus (Cktl) ⅛ measure gin, ½ measure orange juice, ⅛ measure bianco vermouth, ¼ measure crème de banane. Pour ingredients into an ice-filled highball glass, stir and add a dash of iced Champagne.

Satyn Rooi (S.Afr) a red wine (Pinotage 50%, Ruby cabernet 50%) produced by the Ashton Winery, Robertson, Western Cape.

Satyr (Gre) the mythological goat-like man who drank and danced in Dionysus's train.

Satyr Play (Gre) an ancient Greek drama with a ribald flavour performed at a Dionysian festival (has a choir of Satyrs).

Satzen (Aus) vineyard sites (2) based on the banks of the River Kamp situated in the Kamptal region.

Satzenbräu (Ire) a bottled pils lager 1047 O.G. brewed by the Harp Brewery in Dundalk (also brewed in London).

Satzenheim (Ger) vineyard (Anb): Baden. (Ber): Badische Frankenland. (Gro): Tauberklinge. (Vil): Reicholzheim.

Sätzler (Ger) vineyard (Anb): Baden. (Ber): Ortenau. (Gro): Schloss Rodeck. (Vil): Baden-Baden.

Sätzler (Ger) vineyard (Anb): Baden. (Ber): Ortenau. (Gro): Schloss Rodeck. (Vil): Sinzheim.

Saubaad (Aus) a vineyard site based on the banks of the River Kamp situated in the Kamptal region.

Sauber (Ger) a clean, pure wine.

Sauberg (Aus) a vineyard site based on the banks of the River Kamp situated in the Kamptal region.

Sauberg (Ger) vineyard (Anb): Württemberg. (Ber): Württembergisch Unterland. (Gro): Stromberg. (Vil): Ötisheim.

Sauce (USA) a slang name for alcoholic liquor.

Saucer (Eng) a round, concave china receptacle with a flattened base onto which a teacup is placed for ease of carrying. (Ire) = sásar.

Saucer (Fr) the name given to the glass used for Champagne cocktails, said to be modelled on Marie Antoinette's breast. It is saucer-shaped on a thin stem and wide base and often used mistakenly as the correct glass for serving Champagne. *see* Champagne Flute.

Saucy Sue (Cktl) ⅓ measure Calvados, 2 dashes Pernod, 2 dashes apricot brandy. Stir over ice and strain into a cocktail glass.

Saudoy (Fr) a Cru Champagne village in the Canton de Sézanne. District: Épernay.

Saufen (Ger) heavy drinking/to swill.

Saugraben (Aus) a vineyard site based on the banks of the River Kamp situated in the Kamptal region.

Saukopf (Ger) vineyard (Anb): Nahe. (Ber): Bad Kreuznach. (Gro): Schlosskapelle. (Vil): Windesheim.

Saukopf (Ger) vineyard (Anb): Rheinhessen. (Ber): Bingen. (Gro): Kurfürstenstück. (Vil): Gau-Böckelheim.

Saulcet (Fr) a white wine from Allier département in central France. Usually uses the Saint Pourçain label.

Saulheim (Ger) village (Anb): Rheinhessen. (Ber): Nierstein. (Gro): Domherr. (Vins): Haubenberg, Heiligenhaus, Hölle, Pfaffengarten, Probstey, Schlossberg.

Saulo (Sp) the granitic soil based around Barcelona in the D.O. Alella.

Sauloch (Ger) vineyard (Anb): Rheinhessen. (Ber): Wonnegau. (Gro): Burg Rodenstein. (Vil): Flörsheim-Dalsheim.

Saulx [La] (Fr) a 7% alc by vol. deep-brown, top-fermented, bottle-conditioned special ale brewed by the Brasserie Henry, Baizincourt sur Saulx.

Saumagen (Ger) grosslage (Anb): Pfalz. (Ber): Mittelhaardt-Deutsche Weinstrasse. (Vil): Kallstadt.

Saumur (Fr) an A.C. wine area within the Anjou-Saumur district of the Loire. Produces red, rosé, white and sparkling wines.

Saumur-Champigny (Fr) an A.C. red wine area in the Anjou-Saumur district of the Loire. Wines made from the Cabernet franc.

Saumur-Mousseux (Fr) an A.C. sparkling wine from the Saumur area of the Anjou-Saumur district in the Loire. Is medium-sweet to dry.

Saumur Rosé de Cabernet (Fr) an A.C. rosé wine made from the Cabernet franc grape in the Saumur area of Anjou-Saumur district in the Loire. Now classed as Cabernet rosé.

Säure (Aus)(Ger) acid/acidic flavour.

Sausal-Leibnitz (Aus) a wine-producing area in Weststeiermark. Produces dark, spicy, fresh red wines.

Sausal Winery (USA) a winery based in Alexander Valley, Sonoma County, California. Grape varieties: Cabernet sauvignon, Chardonnay, Colombard and Zinfandel. Produces varietal wines.

Sauschwänzel (Ger) vineyard (Anb): Pfalz. (Ber): Südliche Weinstrasse. (Gro): Kloster Liebfrauenberg. (Vil): Billigheim-Ingenheim.

Saussiles [Les] (Fr) a Premier Cru vineyard in the A.C. commune of Pommard, Côte de Beaune, Burgundy 3.8ha.

Sauté Bouchon (Fr) lit: 'cork popper', this is the name given to old sparkling wines that blew their cork.

Sauté Montagne [Le] (Fr) an orange and Cognac liqueur made by Logis de la Montagne (Cognac producer).

Sauternais (Fr) the people of the Sauternes district, also to do with the Sauternes area.

Sauterne (USA) a californian dry white wine, if it has Haut-Sauterne then is medium-sweet.

Sauterne Cup (Cktl) 1 bottle Sauternes, 60mls (½ gill) brandy, 30mls (¼ gill) brown Curaçao, 500mls (1pint) soda water, 30mls (¼ gill) Bénédictine, 40mls (⅓ gill) Yellow Chartreuse, 60mls (½ gill) maraschino, 15mls (⅛ gill) grenadine, 60mls (½ gill) lemon juice. Stir in a bowl with ice, strain and serve with a slice of lemon, cucumber and fresh fruit.

Sauternes (Fr) an area of southern Bordeaux, west of the river Garonne. Produces sweet botrytis-attacked wines. (Coms): Barsac (also has separate A.C.), Bommes, Fargues and Preignac. All come under the A.C. Sauternes. Grape varieties: Sémillon 80%–85% (body and structure), Sauvignon blanc 10%–15% (fruitiness and acidity) and Muscadelle 5% (aromats). Wines must have a natural alcoholic content of 12.5% alc by vol. to be classed A.C. Sauternes and 221g/l of natural sugar (taking the grapes of approximately six vines to produce one bottle of Sauternes).

Sautomar (Port) an extra dry sparkling wine made by the traditional method. Produced by Real Cave do Cedro.

Sautu (Sp) a solera brandy produced by José Esteve. *See also* Guadal, Ruiz.

Sauvignon (Fr) an excellent white grape variety used in the making of dry white wines in western France, Bordeaux and the Central Vineyards in the Loire. Produces wines that have aromas and tastes of gooseberry, grassy, tinned asparagus, elderflower, nettles, basil, cats pee, tropical fruits (N.Z), flint (Pouilly Fumé). Is rich in sugar and extracts with moderate acidity. Also known as the Sauvignon blanc and Surin. *see* Methoxpyrazine. (Aus) = Muskat-sylvaner.

Sauvignonasse (Chile) an alternative name for the Sauvignon Vert.

Sauvignon Blanc (Fr) *see* Sauvignon.

Sauvignon Blanc (USA) a white grape variety grown in California to make dry white wines.

Sauvignon de Banat (Rum) a white wine from Banat Vineyards.

Sauvignon dei Colli Bolognesi (It) a D.O.C. dry, white wine from Bologna in Emilia Romagna. Produced from the Sauvignon and Trebbiano grapes.

Sauvignon de St. Bris (Fr) a V.D.Q.S. dry white wine from the Yonne département in northern Burgundy. Made from the Sauvignon blanc, minimum alc by vol. of 9.5%. Recently upgraded to A.O.C. and now known as A.C. Saint-Bris.

Sauvignon Vert (USA) a white grape variety grown in California to make dessert wines. Also known as the Colombard, Sauvignonasse.

Sauzaggl (Aus) a vineyard site based on the banks of the River Kamp situated in the Kamptal region.

Sauza Hornitos Reposado (Mex) a brand name of pure oak-aged (4 months) tequila produced by a distillery of same name. 38% alc by vol. Also a 51% alc by vol version.

Sauza Margarita (Cktl) 35mls (1½ fl.oz) Sauza tequila, 10mls (½ fl.oz) triple sec, 25mls (1fl.oz) lime/lemon juice. Shake over ice, strain into a cocktail glass that has been rimmed with salt and lime juice.

Sauza Sour (Cktl) ⅔ measure Sauza tequila, ⅓ measure lemon juice, 1 teaspoon powdered sugar. Shake over ice, strain into a cocktail glass, dress with a cherry and lemon slice.

Savages Winery (Austr) a winery based in Riverina, New South Wales.

Savagnin (Fr) a small white berried grape variety grown in the Jura that produces wines with aromas and flavours that are Sherry-like and of roasted nuts. Used in the production of the Vins Jaunes, (*see* Château Chalon) and the Vins Gris. Also known as Gringet, Savagnin Rosé Aromatique and Gelber Traminer in Austria.

Savagnin (Switz) the local name for the Traminer grape. *See also* Païen.

Savagnin Noir (Fr) an alternative name for the Pinot noir grape in the Jura.

Savagnin Noir Cortaillod (Fr) an alternative name in eastern France for the Pinot noir grape.

Savagnin Rosé Aromatique (Fr) the alternative name for the Gewurztraminer grape in Alsace.

Savanha Wine (Pty) Ltd. (S.Afr) winery based in the Western Cape (owned by Winecorp). 300ha. (Add): P.O. Box 15589, Vlaeberg 8018. Grape varieties: Cabernet sauvignon, Chardonnay, Chenin blanc, Merlot, Pinotage, Sauvignon blanc, Sémillon, Shiraz. Labels include Agulhas Bank, Benguela Current, Selunga (discontinued). Website: http://www.winecorp.co.za

Savanna (Afr) a natural spring mineral water from Kenya.

Savanna (Fr) a bottled 6% alc by vol. dry premium cider.

Savanna (W.Ind) a rum distillery based on the French island of La Réunion. Produces a variety of rums (including white and dark at 40% alc by vol.–45% alc by vol) which there are both oaked and un-oaked versions.

Savannaha (Eng) a brand of South African dry cider 6% alc by vol. (Add): Babco Ltd., The White House, Clifton Marine Parade, Gravesend, Kent. DA11 0DY. Website: http://www.babco.co.uk

Savannah Cocktail (Cktl) 25mls (⅕ gill) dry gin, juice ½ orange, 1 egg white, dash (white) crème de cacao. Shake over ice and strain into a cocktail glass.

Savannah Gold (Eng) a brand of smooth rum bottled by Saccone and Speed from Barbados rums.

Savary [Francine et Olivier] (Fr) a winery based in the A.C. Chablis, Burgundy. Produces a range of Chablis wines including Premier Cru Fourchaume.

Savatiano (Gre) a white grape variety used in the making of Retsina and Anchialos together with the Rhoditis.

Savatu (It) a D.O.C. wine from Calabria.

Savennières (Fr) an A.C. (130ha) dry white wine from the vineyards in the Coteaux de la Loire area of the Anjou-Saumur district of the Loire. Produces fragrant, dry white wines from the Chenin blanc grape. see Coulée de Serrant, Roche-aux-Moines (La).

Saveur (Fr) denotes a '*general taste*'.

Savidge Estates (N.Z) a winery. (Add): P.O. Box 1247, Gisborne. Grape varieties: Chardonnay, Chenin blanc, Sauvignon blanc.

Savigny-lès-Beaunes (Fr) an A.C. commune of the Côte de Beaune in the Burgundy region.

Savigny-sur-Ardre (Fr) a Cru Champagne village in the Canton de Ville-en-Tardenois. District: Reims.

Savin (Sp) a large, noted Bodega based in Jumilla. Produces wines mainly from the Monastrell grape. Owns Campo Viejo and has a major share in Vinícola Navarra.

Savion (Isr) a Tokaji-style, sweet, dessert wine.

Savoie (Fr) a wine region of eastern France. Produces A.C. red, rosé, white and sparkling wines. A.O.C's: Crépy, Roussette de Savoie, Seyssel, Seyssel Mousseux and Vins de Savoie. Cru villages: (Roussette de Savoie): Frangy, Marestel, Monterminod and Monthoux. (Vins de Savoie): Arbin, Abymes, Apremont, Ayze, Bergeron, Chantagne, Chaupignat, Chignin, Jongieux, Marignan, Montmélian, Ripaille, Saint Jeoire-Prieuré, Sante Marie d'Alloix and St. Jean-de-la-Porte. Also spelt Savoy.

Savoir Faire (Fr) the brand-name for a range of red and white table wines.

Savoy (Fr) an alternative spelling of Savoie.

Savoy Glasses (Eng) the brand-name for a range of glassware from the Dema Glass C°.

Savoy Ninety [90] (Cktl) ½ measure amaretto, ½ measure lime juice, dash orange flower water. Shake over ice, strain into a sugar-frosted tulip glass and top with iced Champagne.

Savoy Springbok (Cktl) ⅓ measure dry Sherry, ⅓ measure Lillet, ⅓ measure Van der Hum, 2 dashes orange bitters. Stir over ice and strain into a cocktail glass.

Savuti (S.Afr) a dry premium 6% alc by vol. bottled cider produced by the Stellenbosch Farmers Winery, Cape Town.

Savuto (It) a D.O.C. red or rosé wines from Calabria. Made from the Capuccio, Galioppo, Greco nero, Magliocco canino, Malvasia, Nerello, Percorino and Sangiovese grapes. Production area and vinification occur in 14 communes in provinces of Cosenza and Catanzaro. Classed Superiore if total alc by vol. is 12.5% and aged 2 years.

Savuto du Rogliano (It) a D.O.C. red wine of Calabria. see Savuto.

Sawanotsuru (Jap) a saké produced in Nada, 657, Japan 14.9% alc by vol.

Sawbridge Worth Brewery (Eng) a brewery (established 2000). (Add): The Gate, 81 London Road, Sawbridgeworth, Hertfordshire CM21 9JJ. Brews: Brooklands Express 4.6% alc by vol., Brown Bomber 3.8% alc by vol., Is it Yourself 4.2% alc by vol., Piledriver 5.3% alc by vol., Selhurst Park Flyer 3.7% alc by vol., Teflon 3.7% alc by vol. Website: http://www.the-gate-pub.co.uk 'E'mail: the.gate.pub@dial.pipex.com

Sawell (Ger) a sparkling natural spring mineral water (established 2002) from Sawell Brunnen. Mineral contents (milligrammes per litre): Sodium 24.7mg/l, Calcium 69.1mg/l, Magnesium 4.08mg/l, Bicarbonates 171mg/l, Chlorides 59.1mg/l, Sulphates 23.5mg/l.

Sawyer Cellars (USA) a winery based in the Rutherford, Napa Valley, California. Grape varieties include: Cabernet sauvignon.

S.A.W.F.A. (S.Afr) abbr: South African Wine Farmer's Association.

S.A.W.I.T. (S.Afr) abbr: South African Wine Industry Trust.

Sawley Tempted (Eng) a 3.7% alc by vol. ale brewed by the Bowland Beer Company Ltd., Lancashire.

Saxenburg Wine Farm (S.Afr) a winery (established 1693) based in Stellenbosch, Western Cape. 85ha. (Add): Box 171, Kuilsriver 7580, Stellenbosch. Grape varieties: Cabernet sauvignon, Chardonnay, Chenin blanc, Merlot, Pinotage, Sauvignon blanc, Shiraz. Labels: Adrianus and Fiona, Appollonia, Bosman's Hill, Concept, Guinea Fowl, Gwendolyn, Le Phantom, Le Rêve de Saxenbourg, Manuel, Selection Famille (also the producer of Buchu brandy). Website: http://www.saxenburg.com

Saxon Bitter (Eng) a keg bitter 1033 O.G. brewed by the Devenish Brewery in Cornwall.

Saxon Cocktail (Cktl) 25mls (⅛ gill) Bacardi White Label, juice ½ lime, 2 dashes grenadine. Shake over ice, strain into a cocktail glass and top with a twist of orange peel juice.

Saxon Cross (Eng) a 4.1% alc by vol. ale brewed by Rockingham Ales, Cambridgeshire.

Saxon Cross (Eng) the trade-name used by the Winkles Brewery in Buxton, Derbyshire for their beers.

Saxon Mead (Eng) place together 12gallons (54litres) spring water, 20lbs (9kgs) honey, 6 beaten egg whites, 1 teaspoon ginger, 1 teaspoon cinnamon, 1 teaspoon nutmeg, 1 sprig rosemary, 1oz (25gms) brewer's yeast. Mix egg white with water, add honey, boil 1 hour. Skim, add herb and spices, when cool add yeast, ferment and rack into bottles when fermentation has ceased then allow to stand 6 months.

Saxonvale Winery (Austr) a winery based in the Hunter Valley, New South Wales. Grape varieties: Cabernet, Chardonnay, Sémillon and the Shiraz. Produces varietal wines.

Sax Winery (USA) a winery based in Altus.

Say When (Eng) an informal request to say when a person should stop pouring one's measure of drink.

Sazerac (USA) a premium Bourbon producer. Labels include Eagle Rare 10 year old (50.5% alc by vol.) 101° US proof, Benchmark 7 year old 80° US proof.

S

Sazerac [1] (Cktl) add 1 sugar cube to a teaspoon of water, 2 dashes Angostura, 3 dashes Pernod. Mix together, add 35mls (1½ fl.oz) Bourbon whiskey, 1 ice cube, stir then strain into an old-fashioned glass and add a twist of lemon.

Sazerac [2] (Cktl) fill an old-fashioned glass with crushed ice and add a dash of absinthe. In a mixing glass place a teaspoon of gomme syrup, a dash each of Angostura bitters and Peyvhaud with 2 ice cubes. Add 50mls (2fl.ozs) Bourbon whiskey and stir. Empty the old-fashioned glass of its contents and strain into it the Bourbon mix, dress with a twist of lemon zest.

Saziani Selektion (Aus) the label for a white wine (Pinot gris) produced by the Neumeister winery, Süd-Oststeiermark.

SBA (Eng) abbr: Special Bitter Ale 1042 O.G. brewed by the Donnington Brewery in the Cotswolds.

Sbarra (It) bar.

SBB (Wal) abbr: Special Bitter Beer 1036 O.G. brewed by the Crown Brewery in Pontyclun, Mid-Glamorgan.

S.Bernardo Sorgente della Rocca (It) a natural spring mineral water from Sorgente della Rocca. Mineral contents (milligrammes per litre): Sodium 0.7mg/l, Calcium 46mg/l, Magnesium 0.4mg/l, Potassium 0.1mg/l, Bicarbonates 140mg/l, Chlorides 0.6mg/l, Sulphates 3.1mg/l, Nitrates 1.4mg/l, Silicates 2.5mg/l. pH 8.2

Sbornia (It) intoxication/drunkenness.

Sbragia Family Vineyards (USA) a winery based in the Dry Creek Valley, Sonoma County, California. Grape varieties include: Chardonnay, Merlot, Zinfandel. Also has holdings in the Napa Valley.

Scacciadiavoli (It) a winery in the DOCG Sagrantino di Montefalco, Umbria region. Also produces Passito.

Scacco Matto (It) lit: 'check mate' a D.O.C.G. Albana di Romagna Passito wine from Emilia-Romagna. Produced by Fattoria Zerbina, Mille Gusti.

Scaffa [The] (Cktl) ½ measure Cognac, ½ measure Green Chartreuse, 2 dashes Angostura. Shake over ice and strain into a cocktail glass.

Scaffeld Bond [Spring] (Eng) a 4% alc by vol. spring ale brewed by the Hesket Newmarket Brewery, Cumbria.

Scalabrone (It) a single vineyard rosé wine produced by Antinori.

Scala Dei (Sp) a winery in Priorato. Produces white wines from Garnacha blanco, Chenin blanc. Red wines from Garnacha.

Scales (Sp) part of the solera system for Sherry, each scale consists of those casks holding the same grades of wine.

Scali (S.Afr) a winery based in Nooder-Paarl, Western Cape. 70ha. Grape varieties: Cabernet sauvignon, Chardonnay, Chenin blanc, Merlot, Pinotage, Sauvignon blanc, Shiraz, Viognier. Website: http://www.scali.co.za

Scandia Special (Den) an extra strong lager beer 1078–1084 O.G. brewed exclusively for Cash & Carry outlets.

Scandinavian Akvavit (Scan) a caraway-flavoured akvavit.

Scandinavian Coffee (Liq.Coffee) using a measure of akvavit.

Scanex (Cktl) ¼ measure Polar liqueur, ¼ measure vodka, ¼ measure gomme syrup, ¼ measure lemon juice, dash grenadine. Shake over ice and strain into a cocktail glass.

Scansano (It) a co-operative with its own D.O.C. in Maremma.

Scantling (Fr) wooden beams to support the casks in the cellars.

Scantling Pipes (Mad) used for the storing of fine Madeira wines for estufagem and fermentation. 630litres–650litres.

Scapa (Scot) a single highland malt whisky distillery based in Kirkwall, in the Orkney Isles. Owned by the Hiram Walker Group. 40% alc by vol. Produces a 1985 vintage.

Scaramanga (S.Afr) the label for a red wine (Cabernet sauvignon, Malbec and Tempranillo blend) produced by the Nabygelegen Private Cellar winery, Wellington, Western Cape.

Scarecrow Bitter (Eng) a 4.5% alc by vol. bitter brewed by Mitchells Brewery, 11 Moor Lane, Lancaster to mark the Lancaster Wray Fayre.

Scarlet Fever (Eng) the name of a beer brewed by the Alcazar Brewery, Nottinghamshire.

Scarlet Lady [1] (Cktl) 1 part dry gin, 3 parts redcurrant wine. Stir together over ice and strain into a wine goblet.

Scarlet Lady [2] (Cktl) ¼ measure Mandarine liqueur, ¼ measure white rum, ¼ measure Campari, ¼ measure lemon juice, 2 barspoons maraschino. Shake over ice, strain into a cocktail glass and dress with a spiral of orange peel.

Scarlet Lady [3] (Cktl) ⅓ measure vodka, ⅓ measure cherry brandy, ⅓ measure Tia Maria. Shake over ice, strain into a cocktail glass, float a little cream on top and dress with a cherry and a slice of lemon.

Scarlet O'Hara Cocktail (Cktl) 25mls (1fl.oz) Southern Comfort, juice ½ lime, 10mls (½ fl.oz) bilberry juice. Shake over ice and strain into a flute glass.

Scattor Rock Brewery (Eng) a brewery (established 1998). (Add): 5 Gidley's Meadow, Christow, Exeter, Devon EX6 7QB. Brews a range of beers. Website: http://www.scattorrockbrewery.com 'E'mail: inquiries@scattorrockbrewery.com

Scavigna (It) a new D.O.C. found in Calabria. See also San Vito di Luzzi.

S.C.C. (Port) abbr: Sociedade Central de Cervejas. Brews Sagres.

Scelto (It) the Italian word for auslese in the Trentino-Alto-Adige. Also known as Selezionato.

Scented (Eng) the term used to describe a wine with a grapey, flowery bouquet.

Scented Teas (Eng) teas that have had flower scent added (either mixed in or impregnated). Such flowers as: rose, jasmine, strawberry, camomile, mango, etc. See also China Teas.

Sceptre Ale (Eng) a special ale at 4.8% alc by vol. brewed by the Potton Brewing Company for the Golden Jubilee of Queen Elizabeth 2nd in 2002.

Schaaner (Euro) the name given to the wines produced in Schaan, Liechtenstein.

Schaapenberg (S.Afr) the label for an oak-aged white wine (Sauvignon blanc) produced by the Vergelegen winery, Stellenbosch, Western Cape.

Schaapskooi Abbaye Brouwerij (Hol) lit: 'sheep pen', a Trappist brewery based near Tilburg, north Brabant. Produces La Trappe (a bottle-conditioned ale) 6.5% alc by vol. and a pilsener-style lager beer.

Schaefer Brewery (USA) a brewery based in Baltimore.

Schaefer Horlacher Brewery (USA) a brewery based in Allentown.

Schäf (Ger) vineyard (Anb): Baden. (Ber): Markgräflerland. (Gro): Burg Neuenfels. (Vil): Auggen.

Schäf (Ger) vineyard (Anb): Baden. (Ber): Markgräflerland. (Gro): Burg Neuenfels. (Vil): Steinenstadt.

Schafberg (Ger) vineyard (Anb): Pfalz. (Ber): Mittelhardt-Deutsche Weinstrasse. (Gro): Schwarzerde. (Vil): Grossniedesheim.

Schäfchen (Ger) vineyard (Anb): Nahe. (Ber): Kreuznach. (Gro): Schlosskapelle. (Vil): Windesheim.

Schäfergarten (Ger) vineyard (Anb): Pfalz. (Ber): Südliche Weinstrasse. (Gro): Herrlich. (Vil): Insheim.

Schäfergarten (Ger) vineyard (Anb): Pfalz. (Ber): Südliche Weinstrasse. (Gro): Herrlich. (Vil): Rohrbach.

Schäferlay (Ger) vineyard (Anb): Mosel-Saar-Ruwer. (Ber): Bernkastel. (Gro): Vom Heissen Stein. (Vil): Briedel.

Schäfersley (Ger) vineyard (Anb): Nahe. (Ber): Kreuznach. (Gro): Pfarrgarten. (Vil): Schöneberg.

Schäffbräu (Ger) a brewery based in Treuchtlingen, Bavaria. Brews: Schäff's Helle Weisse.

Schaffermahlzeit (Ger) a formal dinner/ceremony held on the second Friday of February (winter's end), traditionally to send the port's skippers off on a new season at sea. Drink Seefahrtbier.

Schaffhausen (Switz) a Swiss-German canton, wines are produced from the Klevner grape, the village of Hallau has the finest vineyards.

Schäff's Helle Weisse (Ger) a 5.4% alc by vol. wheat beer brewed by the Schäffbräu Brauerei, Treuchtlingen.

Schafft (Afr) a strong beer brewed by the South African Breweries.

Schafiser (Switz) the name given to a wine-producing area in Béarn and to a Chasselas-based wine (also known as Twanner).

Schaflerhof (Aus) a winery based in Traiskirchen, Thermenregion. (Add): Wiener Strasse 9-11, 2541 Traiskirchen. Grape varieties: Blauer portugieser, Chardonnay, Pinot noir, Rotgipfler, Zweigelt. Labels include: Grosser Wein.

Schafsteige (Ger) vineyard (Anb): Württemberg. (Ber): Kocher-Jagst-Tauber. (Gro): Tauberberg. (Vil): Haagen.

Schafsteige (Ger) vineyard (Anb): Württemberg. (Ber): Kocher-Jagst-Tauber. (Gro): Tauberberg. (Vil): Laudenbach.

Schafsteige (Ger) vineyard (Anb): Württemberg. (Ber): Kocher-Jagst-Tauber. (Gro): Tauberberg. (Vil): Niederstetten.

Schafsteige (Ger) vineyard (Anb): Württemberg. (Ber): Kocher-Jagst-Tauber. (Gro): Tauberberg. (Vil): Oberstetten.

Schafsteige (Ger) vineyard (Anb): Württemberg. (Ber): Kocher-Jagst-Tauber. (Gro): Tauberberg. (Vil): Vorbachzimmern.

Schafsteige (Ger) vineyard (Anb): Württemberg. (Ber): Kocher-Jagst-Tauber. (Gro): Tauberberg. (Vil): Wermutshausen.

Schaft (Ger) lit: 'stock', denotes the vineyards within the area (village).

Schal (Ger) musty/a tired wine.

Schalkenbosch Wines (S.Afr) a winery (established 1792) based in Tulbagh, Western Cape. 35ha. Grape varieties: Cabernet franc, Cabernet sauvignon, Chardonnay, Chenin blanc, Cinsaut, Hanepoot, Merlot, Ruby cabernet, Sauvignon blanc, Shiraz. Labels: Edenhof, Glen Rosa, Ibis. Website: http://www.schalkenbosch.co.za

Schalkstein (Ger) grosslage (Anb): Württemberg. (Ber): Württembergisch Unterland. (Vils): Affalterbach, Allmersbach a. W., Asperg, Beihingen, Benningen, Besigheim, Bietigheim, Bissingen, Ermannhausen, Gemmrigheim, Grossingersheim, Hessigheim, Höpfigheim, Kirchberg, Kleinaspach, Kleiningersheim, Löchgau, Ludwigsburg (ortsteil Hoheneck), Marbach, Markgröningen, Mundelsheim, Murr, Neckarweihingen, Poppenweiler, Rielinghausen, Rietenau, Steinheim/Murr, Walheim.

Schallbach (Ger) village (Anb): Baden. (Ber): Markgräflerland. (Gro): Vogtei Rötteln. (Vin): Sonnhohle.

Schallstadt-Wolfenweile (Ger) village (Anb): Baden. (Ber): Markgräflerland. (Gro): Lorettoberg. (Vins): Batzenberg, Durrenberg.

Schanderl (S.Afr) the label for a white wine (Muscat de frontignan 100%) produced by the Twee Jongegezellen Estate winery, Tulbagh, Western Cape.

Schandl (Aus) a winery based in Rust, Neusiedlersee-Hügelland, Burgenland. (Add): Haydngasse 3, 7071 Rust. Grape varieties: Blaufränkisch, Pinot blanc, Pinot gris. Produces a range of wines including Ausbruch (Pinot gris).

Schankbieres (Ger) low-gravity draught beers with an O.G. range of 7%–8% and 2%–3% alc. by weight.

Schanzreiter (Ger) vineyard (Anb): Württemberg. (Ber): Württembergisch Unterland. (Gro): Stromberg. (Vil): Ensingen.

Schanzreiter (Ger) vineyard (Anb): Württemberg. (Ber): Württembergisch Unterland. (Gro): Stromberg. (Vil): Illingen.

S

Scharf (Ger) fermentative, wines that contain too much carbonic acid or contain unfermented sugar and have a second fermentation.

Scharffenberger (USA) a winery based in Philo, California. Under the control of Veuve Clicquot. Produces sparkling wines from Pinot noir and Chardonnay grapes produced in Mendocino County. Styles include a blanc de blancs, rosé, brut, crémant.

Scharlachberg (Ger) lit: 'the scarlet mountain'.

Scharlachberg (Ger) a liqueur and weinbrand producer based in Bingen, western Germany.

Scharlachberg (Ger) vineyard (Anb): Franken. (Ber): Maindreieck. (Gro): Ravensburg. (Vil): Thüngersheim.

Scharlachberg (Ger) vineyard (Anb): Rheinhessen. (Ber): Bingen. (Gro): Sankt Rochuskapelle. (Vil): Bingen.

Scharlachberg Meisterbrand (Ger) a weinbrand produced by the Scharlachberg distillery in Bingen, Germany.

Scharrenberg (Ger) vineyard (Anb): Württemberg. (Ber): Remstal-Stuttgart. (Gro): Weinsteige. (Vil): Stuttgart. (ortsteil Degerloch).

Scharzberg (Ger) grosslage (Anb): Mosel-Saar-Ruwer. (Ber): Saar-Ruwer. (Vils): Ayl, Estate, Filzen, Hamm, Irsch, Kanzem, Kastel-Staadt, Könen, Konz, Mennig, Oberemmel, Ockfen, Pellingen, Saarburg, Schoden, Serrig, Wawern, Wiltingen.

Scharzhofberger (Ger) vineyard (Anb): Mosel-Saar-Ruwer. (Ber): Saar-Ruwer. (Gro): Scharzberg. (Vil): Estate.

Schatzgarten (Ger) vineyard (Anb): Mosel-Saar-Ruwer. (Ber): Bernkastel. (Gro): Schwarzlay. (Vil): Traben-Trarbach (ortsteil Wolf).

Schatzkammer (Ger) lit: 'treasure room', a cellar where old fine wines are kept in a winery or cellars.

Schaumwein (Ger) lit: 'foaming wine', the lowest level of German sparkling wine, either made by the cuve close method or by CO_2 injection. Uses cheap white wines from France, Italy etc.

Schaumwein mit Zugesetzter Kohlensaure (Ger) cheap wines given a sparkle by CO_2 injection.

Schäwer (Ger) vineyard (Anb): Pfalz. (Ber): Südliche Weinstrasse. (Gro): Bischofskreuz. (Vil): Burrweiler.

Schechar (Isr) a '*bible wine*', an ancient wine that is mentioned in the bible.

Scheibelberg (Aus) a vineyard site on the banks of the River Danube in the Kremstal region.

Scheibenbuck (Ger) vineyard (Anb): Baden. (Ber): Kaiserstuhl-Tuniberg. (Gro): Vulkanfelsen. (Vil): Sasbach.

Scheibental (Aus) a vineyard site on the banks of the River Danube situated in the Wachau region, Niederösterreich.

Scheibkuern (Aus) an ancient vine variety that is rarely grown nowadays.

Scheidterberger (Ger) vineyard (Anb): Mosel-Saar-Ruwer. (Ber): Saar-Ruwer. (Gro): Scharzberg. (Vil): Ayl.

Scheinberg (Ger) vineyard (Anb): Franken. (Ber): Maindreieck. (Gro): Burg. (Vil): Wirmsthal.

Schekar (Isr) the Hebrew word for the fermented drink from which cider originates.

Schelingen (Ger) village (Anb): Baden. (Ber): Kaiserstuhl-Tuniberg. (Gro): Vulkanfelsen. (Vin): Kirchberg.

Schell Brewery (USA) a brewery based in New Ulm, Minnesota. Noted for Schells and Ulmer ales.

Schellenbrunnen (Ger) vineyard (Anb): Baden. (Ber): Badische Bergstrasse/Kraichgau. (Gro): Stiftsberg. (Vil): Tiefenbach.

Schellmann (Aus) a winery based in Gumpoldskirchen, Thermenregion. (Add): Wiener Strasse 41, 2352 Gumpoldskirchen. Grape varieties: Chardonnay, Traminer, Zierfandler. Produces a range of dry and sweet wines.

Schelm (Ger) vineyard (Anb): Mosel-Saar-Ruwer. (Ber): Bernkastel. (Gro): Vom Heissen Stein. (Vil): Briedel.

Schelmen (Ger) vineyard (Anb): Rheinhessen. (Ber): Wonnegau. (Gro): Sybillenstein. (Vil): Wahlheim.

Schelmenklinge (Ger) vineyard (Anb): Württemberg. (Ber): Württembergisch Unterland. (Gro): Kirchenweinberg. (Vil): Ilsfeld (ortsteil Schozach).

Schelmenstück (Ger) vineyard (Anb): Rheinhessen. (Ber): Bingen. (Gro): Sankt Rochuskapelle. (Vil): Bingen.

Schelvispekel (Hol) a brandewijn liqueur flavoured with herbs and cinnamon, served only to Vlaardingen fishermen in southern Schiedam.

Schemelsberg (Ger) vineyard (Anb): Württemberg. (Ber): Württembergisch Unterland. (Gro): Salzberg. (Vil): Weinsberg.

Schench (Eng) the sixteenth century word for a drink.

Schengen (Lux) a wine village on the river Moselle.

Schenk (Sp) a Swiss-owned vineyard in Valencia, noted for Los Monteros (a red wine produced from the Monastrell grape).

Schenk (Switz) the largest wine-producing firm in the Vaud canton. Owns 237ha. of vineyards. Also owns vineyards in Valencia, Spain.

Schenkenberg (Ger) vineyard (Anb): Württemberg. (Ber): Remstal-Stuttgart. (Gro): Weinsteige. (Vil): Esslingen.

Schenkenbichl (Aus) a vineyard site based on the banks of the River Kamp situated in the Kamptal region.

Schenkenböhl (Ger) grosslage (Anb): Pfalz. (Ber): Mittelhaardt-Deutsche Weinstrasse. (Vils): Bad Dürkheim, Wachenheim.

Schenley Distillers (USA) distillers of brandies at their Number One Distilling Company in California.

Schenley Distillery (USA) Bourbon whiskey distilleries based in Louisville and Frankfort, Kentucky.

Scherdel (Ger) a brewery noted for Baux, Weizen Weisse Dunkel, Weisse Hell, Doppelbock and a premium Pilsner.

S

Scherdel Pilsner (Ger) a 4.7% alc by vol. premium pilsner brewed by Scherdel.

Scheris (Sp) the original Moors' name for Jerez.

Scherisch (Sp) the Moors' name for Sherry.

Scherisk (Arab) the Arabian spelling of Sherry.

Scherp Bier (Hol) bitter beer.

Scherrer Family Vineyards (USA) a winery based in the Alexander Valley, Sonoma County, California. Grape variety: Zinfandel.

Scherzingen (Ger) village (Anb): Baden. (Ber): Markgräflerland. (Gro): Lorettoberg. (Vin): Batzenberg.

Scheucher (Aus) a winery based in Süd-Steiermark. (Add): Labuttendorf 20, 8423 St. Veit a. V. Grape varieties: Muskateller, Pinot blanc, Pinot gris, Traminer, Zweigelt.

Scheuerberg (Ger) vineyard (Anb): Württemberg. (Ber): Württembergisch Unterland. (Gro): Staufenberg. (Vil): Neckarsulm.

Scheurebe (Ger) a white grape variety, a cross between the Silvaner and the Riesling, named after Herr Scheu (rebe is vine). Known as Sämling 88 in Austria.

Schiava (It) a red grape variety grown in the Trentino-Alto-Adige, known as the Vernatsch in Germany, also known as Schiave.

Schiava Gentile (It) a red grape variety also known as the Schiave piccola and Kleinvernatsch.

Schiava Grigia (It) a red grape variety grown in the Trentino-Alto-Adige, known as the Grauvernatsch in Germany.

Schiava Grossa (It) a red grape variety grown in the Trentino-Alto-Adige, known as the Grossvernatsch in Germany, also known as the Trollinger.

Schiava Media (It) a red grape variety grown in the Trentino-Alto-Adige. Known as the Mittervernatsch in Germany.

Schiava Piccola (It) a red grape variety grown in the Trentino-Alto-Adige. Known as the Kleinvernatsch in Germany. Also known as the Schiava gentile.

Schiave (It) see Schiava.

Schidione (It) a red Vino da Tavola wine produced from 40% Cabernet sauvignon, 40% Sangiovese grosso and 20% Merlot grapes by Biondi Santi in Tuscany. Fermented for 2 years in French barriques.

Schiedam (Hol) a gin distilling centre near Rotterdam.

Schiedam Gin (Hol) a very full-bodied gin with a clean but pronounced malty aroma and flavour.

Schiedamsch Provenier (Hol) a 5% alc by vol. bottle-conditioned special beer brewed at the De Halve Maan in Hulst by the Schiedam Bier Brouwerij, Schiedam.

Schiefer (Ger) the name for the fossilised slate and shale which makes up the majority of Mosel ground on which the vines grow.

Schieferley (Ger) vineyard (Anb): Ahr. (Ber): Walporzheim/Ahrtal. (Gro): Klosterberg. (Vil): Bad Neuenahr.

Schieferley (Ger) vineyard (Anb): Ahr. (Ber):

Schieferley (Ger) vineyard (Anb): Ahr. (Ber): Walporzheim/Ahrtal. (Gro): Klosterberg. (Vil): Mayschoss.

Schiehallion (Scot) a 4.8% alc by vol. bottled lager brewed by Harviestoun Brewery, Clackmannanshire.

Schiehallion Vineyards (USA) a vineyard based in Keysville, Virginia. Produces French hybrid and vinifera wines.

Schiergold (Eng) a premium lager 1043 O.G. brewed by Holden's in Dudley, West Midlands. Adheres to strict German purity laws.

Schierstein (Ger) village (Anb): Rheingau. (Ber): Johannisberg. (Gro): Steinmacher. (Vins): Dachsberg, Hölle.

Schikanenbuckel (Ger) vineyard (Anb): Nahe. (Ber): Schloss Böckelheim. (Gro): Paradiesgarten. (Vil): Rehborn.

Schilcher (Aus) the local name for the red grape variety (Blauer wildbacher) and acidic rosé wine of the Styria (west) region. Also spelt Schilder.

Schild (Ger) grosslage (Anb): Franken. (Ber): Steigerwald. (Vils): Abtswind, Castell, Greuth.

Schildberg (Ger) vineyard (Anb): Rheinhessen. (Ber): Bingen. (Gro): Adelberg. (Vil): Sulzheim.

Schilder (Aus) a dry acidic rosé wine from Blauer wildbacher grapes in Styria. Also spelt Schilcher.

Schildetaler (Ger) a natural spring mineral water from Mecklenburg Vorpommern. Mineral contents (milligrammes per litre): Sodium 29.3mg/l, Calcium 59mg/l, Magnesium 5mg/l, Potassium 2mg/l, Bicarbonates 150mg/l, Chlorides 45.4mg/l, Sulphates 27mg/l, Nitrates <1mg/l.

Schilfwein (Aus) lit: 'reed wine' similar to strohwein but using reeds instead of straw.

Schilfwein (Aus) a golden-coloured reed wine, a rich, intense sweet wine made from Sämling 88, Welschriesling, Grüner veltliner and Traminer/Müller-Thurgau grapes dried on reed mats in Neusiedlersee.

Schillerbrunnen Bad Lauchstädt (Ger) a natural spring mineral water (established 1992) from Bad Lauchstädt. Mineral contents (milligrammes per litre): Sodium 37mg/l, Calcium 152mg/l, Magnesium 39.7mg/l, Potassium 12.5mg/l, Bicarbonates 415mg/l, Chlorides 49.6mg/l, Sulphates 233mg/l, Fluorides <0.2mg/l, Nitrates <0.5mg/l.

Schiller [John] (Can) a Canadian who, in 1811, settled near Toronto, Ontario. Was a pioneer wine-producer in Canada.

Schillerfarbe (Ger) lit: 'iridescent or lustrous colour', used to describe the wines of Württemberg.

Schillerwein (Fr) the name given to the rosé wines of Alsace by the German speaking people of the region. Pinot noir rosé d'Alsace.

Schillerwein (Ger) the name given to a rosé wine made from a blend of red and white grapes in the Württemberg. Only QbA. and QmP. allowed.

Produced from grapes grown in same vineyard plot.

Schilling [Herbert] (Aus) a winery based in the Wien region. (Add): Langenzersdorffer Strasse 54, 1210 Wien-Strebersdorf. Grape varieties: Chardonnay, Grüner veltliner, Müller-Thurgau, Pinot blanc, Riesling, St. Laurent, Welschriesling. Produces a range of wine styles.

Schilscher (Aus) an alternative name for the Blauer Wildbacher grape. Also the name for the rosé wine made from the grape (in West Styria).

Schilscherwein (USA) the Austrian equivalent of the German Schillerwein.

Schimmel (Hol) mildew.

Schimmelig (Ger) denotes a wine that has a mouldy, musty smell.

Schincariol (Bra) a natural spring mineral water. Mineral contents (milligrammes per litre): Sodium 17.4mg/l, Calcium 29.9mg/l, Magnesium 12.9mg/l, Potassium 2.01mg/l, Bicarbonates 194.47mg/l, Chlorides 8.68mg/l, Sulphates 10.24mg/l, Fluorides 0.038mg/l, Nitrates 14.81mg/l. pH 7.59

Schincariol Brewery (Bra) a Brazilian large brewery company. Brews: Nova Schin lager.

Schinkenhäger (Ger) the brand-name used for a steinhäger produced by König.

Schinus Molle (Austr) the brand-name of a sparkling wine produced by Dromana Estate, Harrison's Road, Dromana, Victoria.

Schiopetto (It) a famous winery based at Capriva del Friuli in Friuli-Venezia-Guilia. Produces a range of white and red wines. Website: http://www.schiopetto.it

Schioppettino (It) a red grape variety grown only in the Prepotto commune, near Udine in Friuli-Venezia-Guilia.

Schiras (Euro) an alternative spelling of Syrah.

Schist (Eng)(Fr) a soil consisting of foliated rock with mineral layers. *see* Schistous Rock. Also known as Shale.

Schistous Rock (Eng) this is formed of thin plates, formed from the splitting of foliated rock consisting of layers of different materials.

Schitterend (Hol) brilliant/a brilliant wine.

Schizan (Eng) the brand-name of a sparkling fruit cooler from C.C.S.B.

Schladerer (Ger) a famous liqueur and spirits (eau-de-vie) producer based in the Schwarzwald.

Schladminger Brau GmbH (Aus) a brewery. (Add): Hammerfeldweg 183, 8970 Schladming. Brews beers and lagers.

Schlafly Tap Room (USA) a brewery. (Add): 2100 Locust Street, St. Louis, MO 63103. Brews beers and lager. Website: http://www.schlafly.com

Schläfrigkeit (Ger) *see* Sleepiness.

Schlagengraben (Ger) vineyard (Anb): Mosel-Saar-Ruwer. (Ber): Saar-Ruwer. (Gro): Scharzberg. (Vil): Estate.

Schlatt (Ger) village (Anb): Baden. (Ber): Markgräflerland. (Gro): Lorettoberg. (Vins): Maltesergarten, Steingrüble.

Schlehenschwarze (Aus) an ancient red vine variety now rarely grown.

Schleich (Ger) village (Anb): Mosel-Saar-Ruwer. (Ber): Bernkastel. (Gro): Sankt Michael. (Vins): Klosterberg, Sonnenberg.

Schleidberg (Ger) vineyard (Anb): Mosel-Saar-Ruwer. (Ber): Obermosel. (Gro): Gipfel. (Vil): Fellerich.

Schlemmertröpfchen (Ger) vineyard (Anb): Mosel-Saar-Ruwer. (Ber): Zell/Mosel. (Gro): Grafschaft. (Vil): Bremm.

Schlenkerla (Ger) a home-brew tavern in Bamberg, Bavaria. Produces Rauchbieres.

Schlettstadt (Fr) the German name for the town of Selestat in the Bas-Rhin in Alsace.

Schlichte Distillery (Ger) a steinhäger producer based in Steinhägen, Westphalia. Also producers of Alte Ernte (a kornbranntwein).

Schliengen (Ger) village (Anb): Baden. (Ber): Markgräflerland. (Gro): Burg Neuenfels. (Vin): Sonnenstück.

Schlierbach (Ger) vineyard (Anb): Württemberg. (Ber): Württembergisch Unterland. (Gro): Salzberg. (Vil): Weiler.

Schlipf (Ger) vineyard (Anb): Baden. (Ber): Markgräflerland. (Gro): Vogtei Rötteln. (Vil): Weil am Rhein.

Schlittberg (Ger) vineyard (Anb): Pfalz. (Ber): Südliche Weinstrasse. (Gro): Trappenberg. (Vil): Römerberg.

Schlitz (USA) a bottled lager 1044 O.G./5% alc by vol. brewed by the Stroh Brewery in Milwaukee.

Schlitz Brewery (USA) a former brewery based in Milwaukee, Wisconsin. Has been taken over by the Stroh Brewery of Detroit.

Schloss (Ger) castle.

Schloss (Ger) vineyard (Anb): Rheinhessen. (Ber): Nierstein. (Gro): Krötenbrunnen. (Vil): Dienheim.

Schloss (Ger) vineyard (Anb): Rheinhessen. (Ber): Nierstein. (Gro): Krötenbrunnen. (Vil): Oppenheim.

Schloss (Ger) vineyard (Anb): Rheinhessen. (Ber): Nierstein. (Gro): Krötenbrunnen. (Vil): Ülversheim.

Schloss (Ger) vineyard (Anb): Pfalz. (Ber): Mittelhaardt-Deutsche Weinstrasse. (Gro): Grafenstück. (Vil): Obrigheim.

Schloss (Ger) vineyard (Anb): Pfalz. (Ber): Mittelhaardt-Deutsche Weinstrasse. (Gro): Höllenpfad. (Vil): Grünstadt.

Schloss (Ger) vineyard (Anb): Pfalz. (Ber): Südliche Weinstrasse. (Gro): Ordensgut. (Vil): Edesheim.

Schlossabfüllung (Ger) estate bottled.

Schlossabzug (Ger) estate bottled.

Schlossberg (Fr) an A.C. Alsace Grand Cru vineyard at Kayserberg and Kientzheim, Haut-Rhin 80ha.

Schlossberg (Ger) lit: 'castle hill', a popular vineyard name used in Germany. There are 87 individual vineyard sites with this name plus 2 grosslagen.

Schlossberg (Ger) grosslage (Anb): Franken. (Ber): Steigerwald. (Vils): Grosslangheim, Rödelsee, Sickershausen, Wiesenbronn.

S

Schlossberg (Ger) grosslage (Anb): Hessische Bergstrasse. (Ber): Starkenberg. (Vil): Heppenheim (including Erbach and Hambach).

Schlossberg (Ger) vineyard (Anb): Baden. (Ber): Badische Bergstrasse/Kraichgau. (Gro): Mannaberg. (Vil): Rotenberg.

Schlossberg (Ger) vineyard (Anb): Baden. (Ber): Badische Bergstrasse/Kraichgau. (Gro): Rittersberg. (Vil): Schriesheim.

Schlossberg (Ger) vineyard (Anb): Baden. (Ber): Badische Frankenland. (Gro): Tauberklinge. (Vil): Wertheim.

Schlossberg (Ger) vineyard (Anb): Baden. (Ber): Bodensee. (Gro): Sonnenufer. (Vil): Salem (ortsteil Kirchberg).

Schlossberg (Ger) vineyard (Anb): Baden. (Ber): Breisgau. (Gro): Burg Lichteneck. (Vil): Hecklingen.

Schlossberg (Ger) vineyard (Anb): Baden. (Ber): Breisgau. (Gro): Burg Zähringen. (Vil): Freiburg i. Br.

Schlossberg (Ger) vineyard (Anb): Baden. (Ber): Kaiserstuhl-Tuniberg. (Gro): Vulkanfelsen. (Vil): Achkarren.

Schlossberg (Ger) vineyard (Anb): Baden. (Ber): Kaiserstuhl-Tuniberg. (Gro): Vulkanfelsen. (Vil): Ihringen.

Schlossberg (Ger) vineyard (Anb): Baden. (Ber): Kaiserstuhl-Tuniberg. (Gro): Vulkanfelsen. (Vil): Oberrotweil.

Schlossberg (Ger) vineyard (Anb): Baden. (Ber): Markgräflerland. (Gro): Lorettoberg. (Vil): Grunern.

Schlossberg (Ger) vineyard (Anb): Baden. (Ber): Markgräflerland. (Gro): Lorettoberg. (Vil): Staufen.

Schlossberg (Ger) vineyard (Anb): Baden. (Ber): Ortenau. (Gro): Fürsteneck. (Vil): Diersburg.

Schlossberg (Ger) vineyard (Anb): Baden. (Ber): Ortenau. (Gro): Fürsteneck. (Vil): Durbach.

Schlossberg (Ger) vineyard (Anb): Baden. (Ber): Ortenau. (Gro): Fürsteneck. (Vil): Nesselried.

Schlossberg (Ger) vineyard (Anb): Baden. (Ber): Ortenau. (Gro): Fürsteneck. (Vil): Ortenberg.

Schlossberg (Ger) vineyard (Anb): Baden. (Ber): Ortenau. (Gro): Schloss Rodeck. (Vil): Neuweier.

Schlossberg (Ger) vineyard (Anb): Franken. (Ber): Maindreieck. (Gro): Burg. (Vil): Saaleck.

Schlossberg (Ger) vineyard (Anb): Franken. (Ber): Maindreieck. (Gro): Not yet assigned. (Vil): Hallburg.

Schlossberg (Ger) vineyard (Anb): Franken. (Ber): Maindreieck. (Gro): Not yet assigned. (Vil): Würzburg.

Schlossberg (Ger) vineyard (Anb): Franken. (Ber): Mainviereck. (Gro): Not yet assigned. (Vil): Klingenberg.

Schlossberg (Ger) vineyard (Anb): Franken. (Ber): Mainviereck. (Gro): Not yet assigned. (Vil): Wasserlos.

Schlossberg (Ger) vineyard (Anb): Franken. (Ber): Seigerwald. (Gro): Herrenberg. (Vil): Castell.

Schlossberg (Ger) vineyard (Anb): Mittelrhein. (Ber): Rheinburgengau. (Gro): Burg Hammerstein. (Vil): Bad Hönningen.

Schlossberg (Ger) vineyard (Anb): Mittelrhein. (Ber): Rheinburgengau. (Gro): Burg Hammerstein. (Vil): Hammerstein.

Schlossberg (Ger) vineyard (Anb): Mittelrhein. (Ber): Rheinburgengau. (Gro): Lahntal. (Vil): Nassau.

Schlossberg (Ger) vineyard (Anb): Mosel-Saar-Ruwer. (Ber): Bernkastel. (Gro): Kurfürstlay. (Vil): Bernkastel-Kues.

Schlossberg (Ger) vineyard (Anb): Mosel-Saar-Ruwer. (Ber): Bernkastel. (Gro): Kurfürstlay. (Vil): Lieser.

Schlossberg (Ger) vineyard (Anb): Mosel-Saar-Ruwer. (Ber): Bernkastel. (Gro): Münzlay. (Vil): Zeltingen-Rachtig.

Schlossberg (Ger) vineyard (Anb): Mosel-Saar-Ruwer. (Ber): Bernkastel. (Gro): Sankt Michael. (Vil): Bekond.

Schlossberg (Ger) vineyard (Anb): Mosel-Saar-Ruwer. (Ber): Bernkastel. (Gro): Schwarzlay. (Vil): Burg.

Schlossberg (Ger) vineyard (Anb): Mosel-Saar-Ruwer. (Ber): Bernkastel. (Gro): Schwarzlay. (Vil): Traben-Trarbach.

Schlossberg (Ger) vineyard (Anb): Mosel-Saar-Ruwer. (Ber): Saar-Ruwer. (Gro): Römerlay. (Vil): Sommerau.

Schlossberg (Ger) vineyard (Anb): Mosel-Saar-Ruwer. (Ber): Saar-Ruwer. (Gro): Scharzberg. (Vil): Estate.

Schlossberg (Ger) vineyard (Anb): Mosel-Saar-Ruwer. (Ber): Saar-Ruwer. (Gro): Scharzberg. (Vil): Kanzem.

Schlossberg (Ger) vineyard (Anb): Mosel-Saar-Ruwer. (Ber): Saar-Ruwer. (Gro): Scharzberg. (Vil): Saarburg.

Schlossberg (Ger) vineyard (Anb): Mosel-Saar-Ruwer. (Ber): Zell/Mosel. (Gro): Goldbäumchen. (Vil): Cochem.

Schlossberg (Ger) vineyard (Anb): Mosel-Saar-Ruwer. (Ber): Zell/Mosel. (Gro): Rosenhang. (Vil): Beilstein.

Schlossberg (Ger) vineyard (Anb): Mosel-Saar-Ruwer. (Ber): Zell/Mosel. (Gro): Weinhex. (Vil): Kobern-Gondorf.

Schlossberg (Ger) vineyard (Anb): Nahe. (Ber): Kreuznach. (Gro): Pfarrgarten. (Vil): Dalberg.

Schlossberg (Ger) vineyard (Anb): Nahe. (Ber): Kreuznach. (Gro): Pfarrgarten. (Vil): Gutenberg.

Schlossberg (Ger) vineyard (Anb): Nahe. (Ber): Kreuznach. (Gro): Schlosskapelle. (Vil): Burg Layen.

Schlossberg (Ger) vineyard (Anb): Nahe. (Ber): Kreuznach. (Gro): Schlosskapelle. (Vil): Rümmelsheim.

Schlossberg (Ger) vineyard (Anb): Nahe. (Ber): Schloss Böckelheim. (Gro): Burgweg. (Vil): Altenbamberg.

Schlossberg (Ger) vineyard (Anb): Nahe. (Ber):

Schloss Böckelheim. (Gro): Burgweg. (Vil): Bad Münster a. St-Ebernburg.

Schlossberg (Ger) vineyard (Anb): Nahe. (Ber): Schloss Böckelheim. (Gro): Paradiesgarten. (Vil): Martinstein.

Schlossberg (Ger) vineyard (Anb): Nahe. (Ber): Schloss Böckelheim. (Gro): Paradiesgarten. (Vil): Obermoschel.

Schlossberg (Ger) vineyard (Anb): Nahe. (Ber): Schloss Böckelheim. (Gro): Paradiesgarten. (Vil): Raumbach.

Schlossberg (Ger) vineyard (Anb): Nahe. (Ber): Schloss Böckelheim. (Gro): Rosengarten. (Vil): Braunweiler.

Schlossberg (Ger) vineyard (Anb): Nahe. (Ber): Schloss Böckelheim. (Gro): Rosengarten. (Vil): Burgsponheim.

Schlossberg (Ger) vineyard (Anb): Nahe. (Ber): Schloss Böckelheim. (Gro): Rosengarten. (Vil): Mandel.

Schlossberg (Ger) vineyard (Anb): Rheingau. (Ber): Johannisberg. (Gro): Burgweg. (Vil): Lorch.

Schlossberg (Ger) vineyard (Anb): Rheingau. (Ber): Johannisberg. (Gro): Deutelsberg. (Vil): Erbach.

Schlossberg (Ger) vineyard (Anb): Rheingau. (Ber): Johannisberg. (Gro): Honigberg. (Vil): Winkel.

Schlossberg (Ger) vineyard (Anb): Rheinhessen. (Ber): Bingen. (Gro): Kaiserpfalz. (Vil): Gross-Winternheim.

Schlossberg (Ger) vineyard (Anb): Rheinhessen. (Ber): Bingen. (Gro): Kaiserpfalz. (Vil): Ingelheim.

Schlossberg (Ger) vineyard (Anb): Rheinhessen. (Ber): Bingen. (Gro): Kaiserpfalz. (Vil): Schwabenheim.

Schlossberg (Ger) vineyard (Anb): Rheinhessen. (Ber): Nierstein. (Gro): Domherr. (Vil): Saulheim.

Schlossberg (Ger) vineyard (Anb): Rheinhessen. (Ber): Nierstein. (Gro): Krötenbrunnen. (Vil): Oppenheim.

Schlossberg (Ger) vineyard (Anb): Rheinhessen. (Ber): Nierstein. (Gro): Petersberg. (Vil): Gau-Heppenheim.

Schlossberg (Ger) vineyard (Anb): Rheinhessen. (Ber): Nierstein. (Gro): Rheinblick. (Vil): Mettenheim.

Schlossberg (Ger) vineyard (Anb): Rheinhessen. (Ber): Nierstein. (Gro): Sankt Alban. (Vil): Harxheim.

Schlossberg (Ger) vineyard (Anb): Pfalz. (Ber): Mittelhaadt-Deutsche Weinstrasse. (Gro): Grafenstück. (Vil): Bockenheim.

Schlossberg (Ger) vineyard (Anb): Pfalz. (Ber): Mittelhaardt-Deutsche Weinstrasse. (Gro): Hofstück. (Vil): Niederkirchen.

Schlossberg (Ger) vineyard (Anb): Pfalz. (Ber): Mittelhaardt-Deutsche Weinstrasse. (Gro): Höllenpfad. (Vil): Battenberg.

Schlossberg (Ger) vineyard (Anb): Pfalz. (Ber): Mittelhaardt-Deutsche Weinstrasse. (Gro): Höllenpfad. (Vil): Neuleiningen.

Schlossberg (Ger) vineyard (Anb): Pfalz. (Ber): Mittelhaardt-Deutsche Weinstrasse. (Gro): Rebstöckel. (Vil): Hambach.

Schlossberg (Ger) vineyard (Anb): Pfalz. (Ber): Mittelhaardt-Deutsche Weinstrasse. (Gro): Schenkenböhl. (Vil): Wachenheim.

Schlossberg (Ger) vineyard (Anb): Pfalz. (Ber): Mittelhaardt-Deutsche Weinstrasse. (Gro): Schnepenflug vom Zellertal. (Vil): Bolanden.

Schlossberg (Ger) vineyard (Anb): Pfalz. (Ber): Südliche Weinstrasse. (Gro): Kloster Liebfrauenberg. (Vil): Pleisweiler-Oberhofen.

Schlossberg (Ger) vineyard (Anb): Pfalz. (Ber): Südliche Weinstrasse. (Gro): Ordensgut. (Vil): Rhodt.

Schlossberg (Ger) vineyard (Anb): Pfalz. (Ber): Südliche Weinstrasse. (Gro): Trappenberg. (Vil): Weingarten.

Schlossberg (Ger) vineyard (Anb): Württemberg. (Ber): Remstal-Stuttgart. (Gro): Kopf. (Vil): Bürg.

Schlossberg (Ger) vineyard (Anb): Württemberg. (Ber): Remstal-Stuttgart. (Gro): Weinsteige. (Vil): Stuttgart (ortsteil Rotenberg).

Schlossberg (Ger) vineyard (Anb): Württemberg. (Ber): Remstal-Stuttgart. (Gro): Weinsteige. (Vil): Stuttgart (ortsteil Uhlbach).

Schlossberg (Ger) vineyard (Anb): Württemberg. (Ber): Remstal-Stuttgart. (Gro): Weinsteige. (Vil): Stuttgart (ortsteil Untertürkheim).

Schlossberg (Ger) vineyard (Anb): Württemberg. (Ber): Württembergisch Unterland. (Gro): Heuchelberg. (Vil): Brackenheim.

Schlossberg (Ger) vineyard (Anb): Württemberg. (Ber): Württembergisch Unterland. (Gro): Heuchelberg. (Vil): Heilbronn (ortsteil Klingenberg).

Schlossberg (Ger) vineyard (Anb): Württemberg. (Ber): Württembergisch Unterland. (Gro): Heuchelberg. (Vil): Neipperg.

Schlossberg (Ger) vineyard (Anb): Württemberg. (Ber): Württembergisch Unterland. (Gro): Kirchenweinberg. (Vil): Talheim.

Schlossberg (Ger) vineyard (Anb): Württemberg. (Ber): Württembergisch Unterland. (Gro): Kirchenweinberg. (Vil): Untergrappenbach.

Schlossberg (Ger) vineyard (Anb): Württemberg. (Ber): Württembergisch Unterland. (Gro): Lindelberg. (Vil): Dimbach.

Schlossberg (Ger) vineyard (Anb): Württemberg. (Ber): Württembergisch Unterland. (Gro): Lindelberg. (Vil): Schwabbach.

Schlossberg (Ger) vineyard (Anb): Württemberg. (Ber): Württembergisch Unterland. (Gro): Lindelberg. (Vil): Siebeneich.

Schlossberg (Ger) vineyard (Anb): Württemberg. (Ber): Württembergisch Unterland. (Gro): Lindelberg. (Vil): Waldbach.

Schlossberg (Ger) vineyard (Anb): Württemberg. (Ber): Württembergisch Unterland. (Gro): Schalkstein. (Vil): Grossingersheim.

Schlossberg (Ger) vineyard (Anb): Württemberg. (Ber): Württembergisch Unterland. (Gro): Schalkstein. (Vil): Kleiningersheim.

Schlossberg (Ger) vineyard (Anb): Württemberg. (Ber): Württembergisch Unterland. (Gro): Schozachtal. (Vil): Auenstein.

Schlossberg (Ger) a vineyard within the village of Erbach, 5.7ha. (42.1%) of which is proposed to be classified as Erstes Gewächs.

Schlossberg-Schwätzerchen (Ger) vineyard (Anb): Rheinhessen. (Ber): Bingen. (Gro): Sankt Rochuskapelle. (Vil): Bingen.

Schloss Böckelheim (Ger) bereich (Anb): Nahe. (Gros): Burgweg, Paradiesgarten, Rosengarten.

Schlossböckelheim (Ger) village (Anb): Nahe. (Ber): Schloss Böckelheim. (Gro): Burgweg. (Vins): Felsenberg, Heimberg, Im den Felsen, Königsfels, Kupfergrube, Mühlberg.

Schloss Boosenburg (Ger) a sparkling alcohol-free wine from Rudesheim. Produced by Carl Jung. Imported into U.K. by Leisure Drinks of Derby.

Schlossbraeu (Aus) a brewery. (Add): Oberdorferstrasse 9, 6850 Dombirn. Brews beers and lagers. Website: http://www.schlossbraeu.at 'E'mail: office@schlossbraeu.at

Schlossbrauerei Friedenfels GmbH (Ger) a brewery. (Add): Gemmingenstrasse 33, Friedenfels D-95688. Brews a variety of beers and lagers. Website: http://www.schlossbrauerei-friedenfels.de

Schlössel (Ger) vineyard (Anb): Pfalz. (Ber): Mittelhaardt-Deutsche Weinstrasse. (Gro): Meerspinne. (Vil): Gimmeldingen.

Schloss Eltz (Ger) a noted Rheingau estate.

Schlösser Alt (Ger) a 4.8% alc by vol. altbier brewed by the Schlösser Brauerei in Düsseldorf.

Schlösser Brauerei (Ger) a brewery (established 1873) based in Düsseldorf. Noted for altbier.

Schlossgarten (Ger) vineyard (Anb): Baden. (Ber): Kaiserstuhl-Tuniberg. (Gro): Vulkanfelsen. (Vil): Burkheim.

Schlossgarten (Ger) vineyard (Anb): Baden. (Ber): Markgräflerland. (Gro): Burg Neuenfels. (Vil): Hügelheim.

Schlossgarten (Ger) vineyard (Anb): Nahe. (Ber): Kreuznach. (Gro): Kronenberg. (Vil): Bretzenheim.

Schlossgarten (Ger) vineyard (Anb): Nahe. (Ber): Kreuznach. (Gro): Schlosskapelle. (Vil): Schweppenhausen.

Schlossgarten (Ger) vineyard (Anb): Rheingau. (Ber): Johannisberg. (Gro): Erntebringer. (Vil): Geisenheim.

Schlossgarten (Ger) vineyard (Anb): Rheinhessen. (Ber): Wonnegau. (Gro): Domblick. (Vil): Offstein.

Schlossgarten (Ger) vineyard (Anb): Pfalz. (Ber): Mittelhaardt-Deutsche Weinstrasse. (Gro): Schnepfenflug an der Weinstrasse. (Vil): Friedelsheim.

Schlossgarten (Ger) vineyard (Anb): Pfalz. (Ber): Mittelhaardt-Deutsche Weinstrasse. (Gro): Schnepfenflug vom Kellertal. (Vil): Kirchheimbolanden.

Schlossgarten (Ger) vineyard (Anb): Pfalz. (Ber): Mittelhaardt-Deutsche Weinstrasse. (Gro): Schwarzerde. (Vil): Kleinniedesheim.

Schlossgarten (Ger) vineyard (Anb): Pfalz. (Ber): Südliche Weinstrasse. (Gro): Bischofskreuz. (Vil): Burrweiler.

Schloss Gobelsburg (Aus) a winery (32ha) based in the Kamptal region. (Add): Schlossstrasse 16, 3550 Gobelsburg. Grape varieties: Grüner veltliner, Merlot, Riesling, St. laurent, Zweigelt. Produces a range of red and white wines.

Schloss Grafenegg (Aus) a family-owned estate based near Krems. Noted for fine white wines.

Schloss Grohl (Ger) vineyard (Anb): Baden. (Ber): Ortenau. (Gro): Fürsteneck. (Vil): Durbach.

Schloss Gutenburg (Ger) vineyard (Anb): Nahe. (Ber): Kreuznach. (Gro): Pfarrgarten. (Vil): Gutenberg.

Schloss Hammerstein (Ger) vineyard (Anb): Rheinhessen. (Ber): Nierstein. (Gro): Petersberg. (Vil): Albig.

Schloss Hohenrechen (Ger) vineyard (Anb): Rheinhessen. (Ber): Nierstein. (Gro): Spiegelberg. (Vil): Nierstein.

Schloss Hohneck (Ger) vineyard (Anb): Mittelrhein. (Ber): Bacharach. (Gro): Schloss Reichenstein. (Vil): Niederheimbach.

Schlosshölle (Ger) vineyard (Anb): Rheinhessen. (Ber): Bingen. (Gro): Kurfürstenstück. (Vil): Gumbsheim.

Schloss Johannisberg (Ger) vineyard (Anb): Rheingau. (Ber): Johannisberg. (Gro): Erntebringer. (Vil): Estate.

Schloss Johannisberg (Ger) a vineyard within the village of Johannisberg, 21.9ha. (75.8%) of which is proposed to be classified as Erstes Gewächs.

Schloss Kaltenburg (Ger) a brewery based in a castle in Bavaria. Beer brewed by the Von Bayern royal family.

Schlosskapelle (Ger) grosslage (Anb): Nahe. (Ber): Kreuznach. (Vils): Bingen-Bingerbrück, Burg Layen, Dorsheim, Eckenroth, Genheim, Guldental, Laubenheim, Münster-Sarmsheim, Rümmelsheim, Schweppenhausen, Waldlaubersheim, Weiler, Windesheim.

Schloss Kauzenberg (Ger) vineyard (Anb): Nahe. (Ber): Kreuznach. (Gro): Kronenberg. (Vil): Bad Kreuznach.

Schlosskellerei Schwanburg (It) a noted winery based in Nals, Süd-Tirol (Trentino-Alto-Adige).

Schloss Ludwigshöhe (Ger) grosslage (Anb): Pfalz. (Ber): Südliche Weinstrasse. (Vils): Edenkoben, St. Martin.

Schloss Neu-Windeck (Ger) vineyard (Anb): Baden. (Ber): Ortenau. (Gro): Schloss Rodeck. (Vil): Lauf.

Schloss Quelle (Ger) a sparkling natural spring mineral water from Essen. Mineral contents (milligrammes per litre): Sodium 14.2mg/l, Calcium 127mg/l, Magnesium 23mg/l, Potassium 9.7mg/l, Bicarbonates 294mg/l, Chlorides 44mg/l, Sulphates 150mg/l, Fluorides 0.24mg/l.

S

Schlossquelle Friedrichsroda (Ger) a natural spring mineral water. Mineral contents (milligrammes per litre): Sodium 110mg/l, Calcium 296mg/l, Magnesium 106mg/l, Potassium 3mg/l, Bicarbonates 171mg/l, Chlorides 105mg/l, Sulphates 945mg/l, Fluorides 1.46mg/l. Website: http://www.hassia.com

Schloss Randeck (Ger) vineyard (Anb): Nahe. (Ber): Schloss Böckelheim. (Gro): Paradiesgarten. (Vil): Mannweiler-Coelln.

Schloss Reichenstein (Ger) grosslage (Anb): Mittelrhein. (Ber): Bacharach. (Vils): Neiderheimbach, Oberheimbach, Trechtingshausen.

Schloss Reinhartshausen (Ger) a noted wine-producing estate in the Rheingau.

Schloss Rodeck (Ger) grosslage (Anb): Baden. (Ber): Ortenau. (Vils): Achern (ortsteil Oberachem), Altschweier, Baden-Baden, Bühl (ortsteil Neusatz), Bühlertal, Eisental, Kappelrodeck, Lauf, Mösbach, Neuweier, Obersasbach, Obertsrot, Ottersweier, Renchen, Sasbachwalden, Sinzheim, Steinbach, Varnhalt, Waldulm, Weisenbach.

Schloss Saarfelser Schlossberg (Ger) vineyard (Anb): Mosel-Saar-Ruwer. (Ber): Saar-Ruwer. (Gro): Scharzberg. (Vil): Serrig.

Schloss Saarsteiner (Ger) vineyard (Anb): Mosel-Saar-Ruwer. (Ber): Saar-Ruwer. (Gro): Scharzberg. (Vil): Serrig.

Schloss Schönburg (Ger) grosslage (Anb): Mittelrhein. (Ber): Rheinburgengau. (Vils): Damscheid, Dellhofen, Langscheid, Niederburg, Oberwessel, Perscheid, Urbar b. St. Goar.

Schloss Schwabsburg (Ger) vineyard (Anb): Rheinhessen. (Ber): Nierstein. (Gro): Auflangen. (Vil): Nierstein.

Schloss Stahlberg (Ger) vineyard (Anb): Mittelrhein. (Ber): Bacharach. (Gro): Schloss Stahleck. (Vil): Bacharach/Steeg.

Schloss Stahleck (Ger) grosslage (Anb): Mittelrhein. (Ber): Bacharach. (Vils): Bacharach, Bacharach/Steeg, Mannbach, Oberdiebach.

Schloss Stolzenberg (Ger) vineyard (Anb): Nahe. (Ber): Schloss Böckelheim. (Gro): Paradiesgarten. (Vil): Bayerfeld-Steckweiler.

Schlossteige (Ger) vineyard (Anb): Württemberg. (Ber): Remstal-Stuttgart. (Gro): Hohenneuffen. (Vil): Beuren.

Schlossteige (Ger) vineyard (Anb): Württemberg. (Ber): Remstal-Stuttgart. (Gro): Hohenneuffen. (Vil): Frickenhausen.

Schlossteige (Ger) vineyard (Anb): Württemberg. (Ber): Remstal-Stuttgart. (Gro): Hohenneuffen. (Vil): Kappishäusern.

Schlossteige (Ger) vineyard (Anb): Württemberg. (Ber): Remstal-Stuttgart. (Gro): Hohenneuffen. (Vil): Kohlberg.

Schlossteige (Ger) vineyard (Anb): Württemberg. (Ber): Remstal-Stuttgart. (Gro): Hohenneuffen. (Vil): Linsenhofen.

Schlossteige (Ger) vineyard (Anb): Württemberg. (Ber): Remstal-Stuttgart. (Gro): Hohenneuffen. (Vil): Metzingen.

Schlossteige (Ger) vineyard (Anb): Württemberg. (Ber): Remstal-Stuttgart. (Gro): Hohenneuffen. (Vil): Neuffen.

Schlossteige (Ger) vineyard (Anb): Württemberg. (Ber): Remstal-Stuttgart. (Gro): Hohenneuffen. (Vil): Weilheim.

Schloss Thorner Kupp (Ger) vineyard (Anb): Mosel-Saar-Ruwer. (Ber): Obermosel. (Gro): Gipfel. (Vil): Kreuzweiler.

Schlosstück (Ger) grosslage (Anb): Franken. (Ber): Steigerwald. (Vils): Bullenheim, Ergersheim, Frankenberg, Hüttenheim, Ippesheim, Seinsheim, Weimersheim.

Schloss Turmhof (It) a winery based in Entiklar in the Trentino-Alto-Adige. 18ha. Produces mainly red wines.

Schloss Vollrads (Ger) vineyard (Anb): Rheingau. (Ber): Johannisberg. (Gro): Honigberg. (Vil): Estate.

Schloss Vollrads (Ger) a famous vineyard within the village of Winkel, 37.7ha. (39.8%) of which is proposed to be classified as Erstes Gewächs.

Schlossweingut Graf Hardegg (Aus) a winery (43ha) based in Seefeld-Kadolz, Weinviertel. (Add): 2026 Seefeld-Kadolz. Grape varieties: Blauer portugieser, Cabernet sauvignon, Grüner veltliner, Merlot, Pinot blanc, Riesling, Viognier, Zweigelt. Labels: MAX, Veltlinsky.

Schlosswengert (Ger) vineyard (Anb): Württemberg. (Ber): Württembergisch Unterland. (Gro): Wunnenstein. (Vil): Beilstein.

Schloss Westerhaus (Ger) vineyard (Anb): Rheinhessen. (Ber): Bingen. (Gro): Kaiserpfalz. (Vil): Ingelheim.

Schlucht (Aus) a vineyard site on the banks of the River Danube in the Kremstal region.

Schluck (Aus) lit: 'a drop of wine', the brand-name for a fresh, dry white wine from the Wachau district. Often spritzig. Made from the Grüner veltliner grape by Lenz Moser.

Schlumberger (Aus) a leading producer of sparkling (traditional method) wines based in Vöslau. Produces Goldeck.

Schlumberger et Cie (Fr) a négociant-éleveur based in Guebwiller in Alsace.

Schlürfen (Ger) to sip.

Schlüsselberg (Ger) vineyard (Anb): Württemberg. (Ber): Kocher-Jagst-Tauber. (Gro): Kocherberg. (Vil): Bieringen.

Schmachtenberg (Ger) village (Anb): Franken. (Ber): Steigerwald. (Gro): Kapellenberg. (Vin): Eulengrund.

Schmaranz Gut (Aus) a brewery. (Add): Wieden 52, A-5630 Bad, Hofgastein. Brews beers and lagers. Website: http://www.schmaranz.at 'E'mail: bio@schmaranz.at

Schmecker (Ger) vineyard (Anb): Württemberg. (Ber): Kocher-Jagst-Tauber. (Gro): Tauberberg. (Vil): Weikersheim.

Schmelz [Johann] (Aus) a winery (6ha) based in the Wachau. (Add): Joching 14, 3610 Weissenkirchen. Grape varieties: Feinburgunder,

1159

Grüner veltliner, Müller-Thurgau, Riesling. Produces a range of dry and sweet wines, is also a noted Heurige.

Schmidl (Aus) a winery based in the Wachau. (Add): 3601 Dürnstein 21. Grape varieties: Chardonnay, Grüner veltliner, Pinot blanc, Riesling, Sauvignon blanc. Produces a range of dry and sweet (botrytised) wines.

Schmidmayer Bräu (Ger) a brewery. (Add): Hopfenstrasse 3, Slegenburg D-93354. Brews a range of beers and lagers. Website: http://www.schmidmayer.de 'E'mail: info@schmidmayer.de

Schmidt (Aus) a winery based in the Wien region. (Add): Stammersdorfer Strasse 105, 1210 Wien. Grape varieties: Gemischter satz, Müller-Thurgau, Pinot blanc, Riesling, Sauvignon blanc, Welschriesling. Produces a range of wine styles.

Schmidt Brewery (USA) a brewery based in Philadelphia, Cleveland. Noted for McSorley's, Prior Double Dark Beers, Ortlieb, Rheingold and Tiger Head beers.

Schmidt [Josef] (Aus) a winery based in the Kremstal region. (Add): Obere Hauptstrasse 89, 3552 Stratzing bei Krems. Grape varieties: Chardonnay, Grüner veltliner, Müller-Thurgau, Riesling, Zweigelt. Produces a range of wine styles.

Schmidt Winery (Austr) a winery based in north-eastern Victoria. Produces varietal and table wines.

Schmieheim (Ger) village (Anb): Baden. (Ber): Breisgau. (Gro): Schutterlindenberg. (Vin): Kirchberg.

Schmittskapellchen (Ger) vineyard (Anb): Rheinhessen. (Ber): Nierstein. (Gro): Gutes Domtal. (Vil): Nackenheim.

Schmucker Brauerei (Ger) a brewery based in Ober-Mossau. Brews: Schmucker Hefe Weizen Dunkel.

Schmucker Hefe Weizen Dunkel (Ger) a 5% alc by vol. dark, bottle-conditioned wheat beer brewed by the Schmucker Brauerei, Ober-Mossau.

Schnait i. R (Ger) village (Anb): Württemberg. (Ber): Remstal-Stuttgart. (Gro): Wartbühl. (Vins): Altenberg, Sonnenberg.

Schnait i. R (Ger) village (Anb): Württemberg. (Ber): Remstal-Stuttgart. *see* Weinstaat.

Schnapps (Scan) *see* Schnaps.

Schnaps (Ger) spirits/liquor, a rectified spirit.

Schnapsteufel (Ger) lit: 'drink of the devil', a fifteenth century term to describe a corn-based spirit.

Schnauterin (Aus) a vineyard site based on the banks of the River Kamp situated in the Kamptal region.

Schneckenberg (Ger) vineyard (Anb): Rheinhessen. (Ber): Wonnegau. (Gro): Liebfrauenmorgen. (Vil): Worms.

Schneckenhof (Ger) vineyard (Anb): Württemberg. (Ber): Württembergisch Unterland. (Gro): Lindelberg. (Vil): Adolzfurt.

Schneckenhof (Ger) vineyard (Anb): Württemberg. (Ber): Württembergisch Unterland. (Gro): Lindelberg. (Vil): Geddelsbach.

Schneckenhof (Ger) vineyard (Anb): Württemberg. (Ber): Württembergisch Unterland. (Gro): Lindelberg. (Vil): Maienfels

Schneckenhof (Ger) vineyard (Anb): Württemberg. (Ber): Württembergisch Unterland. (Gro): Lindelberg. (Vil): Unterheimbach.

Schneewein (Ger) snow wine, another name for eiswein.

Schneeweiss (Aus) a winery based in the Wachau. (Add): 3610 Weissenkirchen 27. Grape varieties: Chardonnay, Grüner veltliner, Muskateller, Pinot blanc, Riesling, Zweigelt. Produces a range of dry and sweet (botrytised) wines.

Schneider (Aus) a winery based in the Kampstal region. (Add): Cobaneschof, Weinstrasse 37, 3550 Gobelsberg. Grape varieties: Grüner veltliner, Pinot blanc, Pinot noir, Riesling, Zweigelt.

Schneider Beers (Arg) major brewers in Argentina.

Schneider Brauerei (Ger) a family brewery (established 1872) based in Kelheim, Munich. Noted for Aventinus 7.8% alc by vol. Weisse 5.5% alc by vol. Weisse Kristall 5.3% alc by vol. (filtered), Weisse Light 3.3% alc by vol. Weisse Original 5.4% alc by vol. Weisse Weizenhell 4.9% alc by vol. (all unpasteurised, unfiltered).

Schneider Weisse (Ger)(Switz) a Berliner-style wheat beer brewed by the Hürlimann Brauerei 5.4% alc by vol.

Schneller (Ger) a seventeenth century drinking tankard, tall and tapered with a lid and usually heavily ornamented with a Coat of Arms etc.

Schnepfenflug an der Weinstrasse (Ger) grosslage (Anb): Pfalz. (Ber): Mittelhaardt-Deutsche Weinstrasse. (Vils): Deidesheim, Forst, Friedelsheim, Wachenheim.

Schnepfenflug vom Zellertal (Ger) grosslage (Anb): Pfalz. (Ber): Mittelhaardt-Deutsche Weinstrasse. (Vils): Albisheim, Bolanden, Bubenheim, Einselthum, Gauersheim, Immesheim, Kerzenheim, Kirchheimbolanden, Morschheim, Niefernheim, Ottersheim/Zellertal, Rittersheim, Rüssingen, Stetten, Zell.

Schnepp (Ger) vineyard (Anb): Pfalz. (Ber): Mittelhaardt-Deutsche Weinstrasse. (Gro): Schwarzerde. (Vil): Obersülzen.

Schnitzlbaumer KG (Ger) a brewery. (Add): Muhlenstrasse 8, Traunstein D-83278. Brews a range of beers and lagers. Website: http://www.schnitzlbaumer.de 'E'mail: Brauerei-schnitzlbaumer@t-online.de

Schoden (Ger) village (Anb): Mosel-Saar-Ruwer. (Ber): Saar-Ruwer. (Gro): Scharzberg. (Vins): Geisberg, Herrenberg, Saarfeilser, Marienberg.

Schoenenbourg (Fr) an A.C. Alsace Grand Cru vineyard at Riquewihr, Haut-Rhin 40ha.

Schoenling Brewery (USA) a brewery based in Cincinatti, Ohio. Brews: Top Hat beer, Little Kings Cream Ale.

Schöfferhofer (Ger) a brewery noted for weizen and hefeweizen beers.

Schoffit [Robert] (Fr) a wine producer based in

Alsace. (Add): 27 Rue des Aubépines, 6800 Colmar.

Schollerbuckel (Ger) vineyard (Anb): Baden. (Ber): Badische Bergstrasse/Kraichgau. (Gro): Stiftsberg. (Vil): Eberbach.

Scholtz Hermanos (Sp) dessert wine-makers based in Málaga, southern Spain.

Schön (Aus) a vineyard site on the banks of the River Danube situated in the Wachau region, Niederösterreich.

Schön (Ger) lit: 'lovely', a charming, pleasant, harmonious wine.

Schön (Ger) vineyard (Anb): Württemberg. (Ber): Württembergisch Unterland. (Gro): Staufenberg. (Vil): Duttenberg.

Schön (Ger) vineyard (Anb): Württemberg. (Ber): Württembergisch Unterland. (Gro): Staufenberg. (Vil): Offenau.

Schönauer (Ger) see Kornbrennerei Schönau GmbH.

Schönberg (Aus) a wine-producing area in the Klosterneuburg region.

Schönberg (Ger) vineyard (Anb): Rheinhessen. (Ber): Bingen. (Gro): Adelberg. (Vil): Bornheim.

Schönberg (Ger) vineyard (Anb): Rheinhessen. (Ber): Bingen. (Gro): Adelberg. (Vil): Lonsheim.

Schönbergquelle (Ger) a natural spring mineral water. Mineral contents (milligrammes per litre): Sodium 11.2mg/l, Calcium 192mg/l, Magnesium 22.3mg/l, Potassium 2.3mg/l, Bicarbonates 342mg/l, Chlorides 42.5mg/l, Sulphates 258mg/l, Fluorides 0.18mg/l, Nitrates 1mg/l.

Schönborn [Graf von] (Ger) an estate at Hattenheim in the Rheingau.

Schöntal (Aus) a vineyard site based on the banks of the River Kamp situated in the Kamptal region.

Schönburger (Ger) a pink berried grape variety, a cross between the Spätburgunder (Pinot noir) and the IP1 (Chasselas x Muscat Hamburg), also known as the Rosa muskat. Gives good bouquet and sugar.

Schöneberg (Ger) village (Anb): Nahe. (Ber): Kreuznach. (Gro): Pfarrgarten. (Vins): Schäferslay, Sonnenberg.

Schöne Blume (Ger) the name for the frothy head on a glass of beer or lager.

Schönhell (Ger) vineyard (Anb): Rheingau. (Ber): Johannisberg. (Gro): Mehrhölzchen. (Vil): Hallgarten.

Schönhell (Ger) a vineyard within the village of Hallgarten, 52.1ha. (36.3%) of which is proposed to be classified as Erstes Gewächs.

Schönhölle (Ger) vineyard (Anb): Rheinhessen. (Ber): Bingen. (Gro): Sankt Rochuskapelle. (Vil): Ockenheim.

Schools of the Wise (Tur) the general name used for coffee houses in the seventeenth century due to the fact that much could be learned there.

Schoonberg (S.Afr) a vineyard (17ha) based in Upper Langkloof, Oudtshoorn, Western Cape. Grape variety: Cabernet sauvignon. Wine vinified at Fairview. Website: http://www.schoonberg.co.za

Schooner (Austr) a large beer glass.

Schooner (Eng) a double elgin glass ⅔ gill (80mls) capacity.

Schooner (USA) a large beer glass.

Schooner Beer (Ire) a pale ale beer brewed by the Murphy & C°. Ltd. at their Ladywell Brewery, Cork.

Schoon Gevel (S.Afr) the export label for a range of wines produced by the La Motte winery, Franschhoek, Western Cape.

Schoongezicht Estate (S.Afr) a winery (established 1682) based in Stellenbosch, Western Cape. 150ha. (Add): P.O. Box 33, Stellenbosch 7600. Grape varieties: Cabernet franc, Cabernet sauvignon, Chardonnay, Merlot, Petit verdot, Roussanne, Sauvignon blanc, Shiraz. Labels: Brampton, Five Soldiers, Peter Barlow, John X Merriman, Old Vines, QF. White wines sold under the Rustenberg wines label. Produces varietal wines. Website: http://www.rustenberg.co.za

Schoppen (Ger) a style of glass which is covered with a metal top, used for drinking beer.

Schoppenwein (Ger) a term used to describe an everyday drinking wine.

Schoppenwein (Ger) a glass of wine (schoppen = glass, wein = wine).

Schoppenweine (Ger) lit: 'open wine', a new wine, drunk young from the Palatinate (sweet and heavy).

Schorle (Ger) a drink of half white table wine and half soda water. Also known as Spritzer.

Schorle-Morle (Ger) a mixture of ½ wine and ½ aerated mineral water.

Schörnbornquelle (Ger) a natural spring mineral water from Bruchsal. Mineral contents (milligrammes per litre): Sodium 14mg/l, Calcium 184mg/l, Magnesium 22mg/l, Potassium 1.2mg/l, Bicarbonates 343mg/l, Chlorides 59mg/l, Sulphates 213mg/l, Fluorides 0.17mg/l, Nitrates <1mg/l.

Schorndorf (Ger) village (Anb): Württemberg. (Ber): Remstal-Stuttgart. (Gro): Kopf. (Vin): Grafenberg.

Schornsheim (Ger) village (Anb): Rheinhessen. (Ber): Nierstein. (Gro): Domherr. (Vins): Mönchspfad, Ritterberg, Sonnenhang.

Schots (Hol) the Dutch name for Scotch (whisky).

Schou Brewery (Nor) a brewery based in Oslo. Produces bock beers and Tuborg brewed under licence.

Schouten Single Vineyard (USA) the label for red wine (Pinot noir) produced by the Amity Vineyards, Willamette Valley, Oregon.

Schozach (Ger) village (Anb): Württemberg. (Ber): Württembergisch Unterland. (Gro): Kirchenweinberg. see Ilsfeld.

Schozachtal (Ger) grosslage (Anb): Württemberg. (Ber): Württembergisch Unterland. (Vils): Abstatt, Auenstein, Ilsfeld, Löwenstein, Unterheinriet.

Schrader Estate (USA) a winery based in the Napa Valley, California. Grape varieties include: Cabernet sauvignon. Label: Beckstoffer.

Schramsberg (USA) a small winery based in the

S

Napa Valley, northern California. 17ha. Grape varieties: Chardonnay, Gamay, Muscat, Pinot noir and Pinot blanc. Noted for sparkling wines made by the traditional method.

Schreckenberg (Aus) a vineyard site based on the banks of the River Kamp situated in the Kamptal region.

Schreck [Steiner] (Aus) a vineyard site on the banks of the River Danube in the Kremstal region.

Schreiberberg (Aus) a vineyard site on the banks of the River Danube situated in the Wachau region, Niederösterreich.

Schremser Bier (Aus) a brewery. (Add): Niederschremsertr 1, A-3943 Schrems. Brews beers and lagers. Website: http://www.schremser.at 'E'mail: office@schremser.at

Schriesheim (Ger) village (Anb): Baden. (Ber): Badische Bergstrasse/Kraichgau. (Gro): Rittersberg. (Vins): Kuhberg, Madonnenberg, Schlossberg, Staudenberg.

Schröck [Heidi] (Aus) a winery based in Rust, Neusiedlersee-Hügelland, Burgenland. (Add): Rathausplatz 8, 7071 Rust. Grape varieties: Blaufränkisch, Muskateller, Pinot blanc, Welschriesling, Zweigelt. Produces a range of wines.

Schröder et Schyler (Fr) a famous négociant-éleveur of Bordeaux. Owns Château Kirwan.

Schubert Estate (N.Z) a vineyard based in the Martinborough region of the North Island.

Schubertslay (Ger) vineyard (Anb): Mosel-Saar-Ruwer. (Ber): Bernkastel. (Gro): Michelsberg. (Vil): Piesport.

Schuckert [Rainer] (Aus) a winery based in Poysdorf, Weinviertel. (Add): Wilhelmsdorferstrasse 40, 2170 Poysdorf. Grape varieties: Chardonnay, Grüner veltliner, Riesling, Welschriesling.

Schug Winery (USA) a winery based at Carneros, Sonoma Valley, California. Grape varieties include Chardonnay, Pinot noir and Bordeaux varieties. Is associated with Phelps Winery. Label: Heritage Reserve.

Schuigui (Afr) a co-operative winery based in Tunisia. Is owned by the UCCVT.

Schuim Manchet (Hol) the name for the creamy head on a beer or lager.

Schultheiss Brauerei (Ger) a major brewery (established 1842) based in Berlin that is noted for weisse (white) beers and pilsner 5% alc by vol.

Schulwein (Ger) the term parents use to threaten children with when they decide they don't want to attend school. They are given a dose of acidic wine.

Schumacher Altbier (Ger) a fine altbier produced by the Ferdinand Schumacher Brauerei in Düsseldorf. Pale in colour, it has a good malty flavour.

Schuss (Ger) the term for the dash of raspberry juice that is sometimes added to Berliner Weisse.

Schuster [John and Son] (USA) a winery based in Egg Harbour, New Jersey. Produces hybrid wines.

Schütt (Aus) a vineyard site on the banks of the River

Danube situated in the Wachau region, Niederösterreich.

Schütt (Aus) a vineyard site based on the banks of the River Kamp situated in the Kamptal region.

Schutterlindenberg (Ger) grosslage (Anb): Baden. (Ber): Breisgau. (Vils): Ettenheim (ortsteil Wallburg), Friesenheim, Heiligenzell, Hugsweier, Kippenheim, Lahr, Mahlberg, Mietersheim, Münchweiler, Oberschopfheim, Oberweier, Schmieheim, Sulz.

Schutzenberger (Fr) a brewery (established 1740) based in Schilitigheim. Brews: Copper (an amber malt beer), Jubilator and Patriator (double bock beers), Schutzenberger Tradition (lager), Tütz (ice beer).

Schützenfest (Austr) the name given to a beer produced annually for the German club of South Australia.

Schützenfest (Ger) a beer festival held in Hanover.

Schützengarten Brauerei (Switz) a brewery based in St. Gall. Is part of the Interbeva group. Brews: High Life beer.

Schützengarten Lagerbier (Switz) a 4.8% alc by vol. lager beer brewed by Brauerei Schützengarten AG, St. Gallen.

Schützengold Alcoholfrei (Switz) an alcohol-free beer brewed by Brauerei Schützengarten AG, St. Gallen.

Schützenhaus (Ger) vineyard (Anb): Rheingau. (Ber): Johannisberg. (Gro): Deutelsberg. (Vil): Hattenheim.

Schützenhütte (Ger) vineyard (Anb): Rheinhessen. (Ber): Bingen. (Gro): Sankt Rochuskapelle. (Vil): Zotzenheim.

Schützenhütte (Ger) vineyard (Anb): Rheinhessen. (Ber): Nierstein. (Gro): Krötenbrunnen. (Vil): Dolgesheim.

Schützenlay (Ger) vineyard (Anb): Mosel-Saar-Ruwer. (Ber): Zell/Mosel. (Gro): Grafschaft. (Vil): Ediger-Eller.

Schutz French Pils (Eng) a low alcohol lager (less than 1% alc by vol.) from Christopher Longman.

Schützingen (Ger) village (Anb): Württemberg. (Ber): Württembergisch Unterland. (Gro): Stromberg. (Vin): Heiligenberg.

Schwabbach (Ger) village (Anb): Württemberg. (Ber): Württembergisch Unterland. (Gro): Lindelberg. (Vin): Schlossberg.

Schwaben Brauerei (Ger) a brewery based at Rob. Leicht, Stuttgart. Brews: Schwaben Bräu Märzen seasonal beer, Schwaben Bräu Meister Weizen.

Schwaben Bräu Märzen (Ger) a 5.5% alc by vol. March beer brewed by the Schwaben Brauerei, Rob. Leicht, Stuttgart.

Schwaben Bräu Meister Weizen (Ger) a 5% alc by vol. bottle-conditioned wheat beer brewed by the Schwaben Brauerei, Rob. Leicht, Stuttgart.

Schwabenheim (Ger) village (Anb): Rheinhessen. (Ber): Bingen. (Gro): Kaiserpfalz. (Vins): Klostergarten, Schlossberg, Sonnenberg.

Schwabischer Landwein (Ger) one of seventeen Deutsche Landwein zones.

Schwäbische Weinstrasse (Ger) the wine route through the Württemberg Anbaugebiet. The Swabian wine route.

Schwabler (Ger) an alternative name for the Silvaner grape.

Schwaigern (Ger) village (Anb): Württemberg. (Ber): Württembergisch Unterland. (Gro): Heuchelberg. (Vins): Grafenberg, Ruthe, Sonnenberg, Vogelsang.

Schwalben (Ger) vineyard (Anb): Rheinhessen. (Ber): Bingen. (Gro): Kaiserpfalz. (Vil): Wackernheim.

Schwalbennest (Ger) vineyard (Anb): Nahe. (Ber): Schloss Böckelheim. (Gro): Paradiesgarten. (Vil): Raumbach.

Schwanleite (Ger) vineyard (Anb): Franken. (Ber): Steigerwald. (Gro): Schlossberg. (Vil): Rödelsee.

Schwarzböck (Aus) a winery based in Hagenbrunn, Weinviertel. (Add): Schlossgasse 21, 2102 Hagenbrunn. Grape varieties: Grüner veltliner, Riesling, Zweigelt.

Schwarze Katz (Ger) grosslage (Anb): Mosel-Saar-Ruwer. (Ber): Zell/Mosel. (Vils): Senheim, Zell, Zell-Kaimt, Zell-Merl.

Schwartzenstein (Ger) vineyard (Anb): Rheingau. (Ber): Johannisberg. (Gro): Erntebringer. (Vil): Estate.

Schwarzenberg (Ger) vineyard (Anb): Mosel-Saar-Ruwer. (Ber): Zell/Mosel. (Gro): Rosenhang. (Vil): Valwig.

Schwarzenberg (Ger) vineyard (Anb): Rheinhessen. (Ber): Bingen. (Gro): Sankt Rochuskapelle. (Vil): Bingen.

Schwarzer Bär Dunkelbier (Switz) a 5% alc by vol. dunkel bier brewed by Brauerei Schützengarten AG, St. Gallen.

Schwarzerde (Ger) grosslage (Anb): Pfalz. (Ber): Mittelhaardt-Deutsche Weinstrasse. (Vils): Bisserheim, Dirmstein, Gerolsheim, Grosskarlbach, Grossniedesheim, Hessheim, Heuchelheim/Frankenthal, Kirchheim, Kleinniedesheim, Laumersheim, Obersülzen.

Schwarzer Herrgott (Ger) vineyard (Anb): Pfalz. (Ber): Mittelhaardt-Deutsche Weinstrasse. (Gro): Schnepfenflug vom Zellertal. (Vil): Zell.

Schwarzer Letten (Ger) village (Anb): Pfalz. (Ber): Südliche Weinstrasse. (Gro): Schloss Ludwigshöhe. (Vin): Edenkoben.

Schwarzer Muskateller (Aus) a rosé-coloured grape variety now no longer grown.

Schwarzes Kreuz (Ger) vineyard (Anb): Pfalz. (Ber): Mittelhaardt-Deutsche Weinstrasse. (Gro): Kobnert. (Vil): Freinsheim.

Schwarze Weisse (Ger) a 5.1% alc by vol. dark, bottle-conditioned wheat beer brewed by State Court Brauerei, Munich.

Schwarzfränkisch (Aus) a red grape variety that used to be grown in the Thermenregion.

Schwarz Klevner (Ger) the local name for the Pinot noir grape.

Schwarzlay (Ger) grosslage (Anb): Mosel-Saar-Ruwer. (Ber): Bernkastel. (Vils): Bausendorf,

Bengel, Burg, Dreis, Enkirch, Erden, Flussbach, Hupperath, Kinheim, Lösnich, Platten, Traben-Trarbach, Traben-Trarbach (ortsteil Starkenburg), Traben-Trarbach (ortsteil Wolf), Urzig, Wittlich.

Schwarzquell Spezial (Aus) a sweet, dark-brown beer 13° Balling brewed by the Schwechat Brauerei.

Schwarzriesling (Ger) an erroneous varietal name of the red grape Müllerrebe. Also known as the Pinot meunier.

Schwarzwalder (Ger) a name for Kirsch or Kirschwasser.

Schwarzwald Kirschwasser (Ger) a cherry liqueur made with the fruit and crushed stones.

Schwarzwald Sprudel (Ger) a sparkling natural spring mineral water from Kniebis, Black Forest. (Add): Scharzwald-Sprudel GmbH & C° KG. Bad Griesbach/Schwarzwald. Mineral contents (milligrammes per litre): Sodium 126mg/l, Calcium 259mg/l, Magnesium 19mg/l, Potassium 7mg/l, Bicarbonates 729mg/l, Chlorides 13mg/l, Sulphates 334mg/l.

Schwebsingen (Lux) a wine village on the river Moselle. Vineyard sites: Kolteschberg and Letscheberg.

Schwechat Brauerei (Aus) a brewery (established 1632) based at Klein Schwechat near Vienna. Was the hub of the world's greatest brewing empire in the eighteenth century.

Schwechater (Aus) a noted lager beer brewed by the Schwechat Brauerei.

Schwedenwein (Ger) a wine produced in the year that Sweden invaded Europe.

Schwefel (Ger) a sulphur smell in the bouquet of the wine.

Schwefelddioxid (Ger) sulphur-dioxide.

Schwefelquelle Kastelruth (It) a natural spring mineral water (established 1715) from Bozen. Mineral contents (milligrammes per litre): Sodium 18.6mg/l, Calcium 56mg/l, Magnesium 25.6mg/l, Potassium 1.46mg/l, Bicarbonates 201mg/l, Chlorides 18mg/l, Sulphates 96mg/l, Fluorides 0.2mg/l, Silicates 4.7mg/l.

Schwefelquelle Wengen (It) a natural spring mineral water from Bozen. Mineral contents (milligrammes per litre): Sodium 30.6mg/l, Calcium 64.4mg/l, Magnesium 26.6mg/l, Potassium 2.4mg/l, Bicarbonates 231mg/l, Chlorides 7mg/l, Sulphates 150mg/l, Fluorides 0.35mg/l, Silicates 7.6mg/l.

Schwefelwasser Innichen (It) a natural spring mineral water from Bozen. Mineral contents (milligrammes per litre): Sodium 3mg/l, Calcium 445mg/l, Magnesium 87mg/l, Potassium 0.9mg/l, Bicarbonates 211mg/l, Sulphates 1280mg/l, Fluorides 2mg/l, Strontium 5.1mg/l, Silicates 6.4mg/l.

Schwegenheim (Ger) village (Anb): Pfalz. (Ber): Südliche Weinstrasse. (Gro): Trappenberg. (Vin): Bründelsberg.

Schweich (Ger) village (Anb): Mosel-Saar-Ruwer. (Ber): Bernkastel. (Gro): Probstberg. (Vins): Annaberg, Burgmauer, Herrenberg.

S

Schweigen-Rechtenbach (Ger) village (Anb): Pfalz. (Ber): Südliche Weinstrasse. (Gro): Guttenberg. (Vin): Sonnenberg.

Schweiger Vineyards (USA) a winery (established in 1994). Grape varieties include Chardonnay, Cabernet sauvignon, Merlot 13ha.

Schweighofen (Ger) village (Anb): Pfalz. (Ber): Südliche Weinstrasse. (Gro): Guttenberg. (Vins): Sonnenberg, Wolfsberg.

Schweinfurt (Ger) village (Anb): Franken. (Ber): Maindreieck. (Gro): Not yet assigned. (Vins): Mainleite, Peterstirn.

Schweppenhausen (Ger) village (Anb): Nahe. (Ber): Kreuznach. (Gro): Schlosskapelle. (Vins): Schlossgarten, Steyerberg.

Schweppervessence (Austr) a sparkling natural spring mineral water from Tullamarine, Victoria. Mineral contents (milligrammes per litre): Sodium 95mg/l, Calcium 50mg/l, Magnesium 45mg/l, Potassium 6mg/l, Bicarbonates 225mg/l, Chlorides 220mg/l.

Schweppes (Eng) a famous soft-drinks™ manufacturer (established in 1783 by Jakob Schweppe) based at St. Albans in Hertfordshire. Products include Malvern Water, Rose's Cordials, Slimline, Soda Water, Tonic Water, Tropical Spring. Merged with the Coca Cola C°. in January 1987 and now known as the 'Coca Cola and Schweppes Beverages Company'. *Abbr*: C.C.S.B.

Schweppes Green Ginger Wine (Eng) a Green Ginger Wine™ produced by the C.C.S.B.

Schweppes Italia (It) a brandy producer. Produces Cavallino Rosso.

Schweppes Mineral Water (Egy) a sparkling natural spring mineral water. Mineral contents (milligrammes per litre): Sodium 40mg/l, Calcium 26.8mg/l, Magnesium 12mg/l, Potassium 3.7mg/l, Bicarbonates 195.2mg/l, Chlorides 22.6mg/l, Sulphates 12mg/l, Silicates 12mg/l.

Schweppes Natural Mineral Water (Austr) a sparkling natural spring mineral water. Mineral contents (milligrammes per litre): Sodium 95mg/l, Calcium 50mg/l, Magnesium 45mg/l, Potassium 6mg/l, Bicarbonates 225mg/l, Chlorides 220mg/l. *See* Schweppervessence.

Schweren Zapfen (Aus) a vineyard site on the banks of the River Danube in the Kremstal region.

Schwithein-Bravarie (Ger) a producer of the low alcohol lager: Germania 0.9% alc by vol.

Schwobajörgle (Ger) vineyard (Anb): Württemberg. (Ber): Württembergisch Unterland. (Gro): Lindelberg. (Vil): Eschelbach.

Schwobajörgle (Ger) vineyard (Anb): Württemberg. (Ber): Württembergisch Unterland. (Gro): Lindelberg. (Vil): Kesselfeld.

Sciacarello (Fr) a red grape variety grown in Corsica.

Sciacchetrà (It) a D.O.C.G. passito dessert wine from the Liguria region at Cinqueterre. Produced by Riomaggiore co-op from Albarola, Bosca and Vermentino grapes.

Sciampagna (It) the Italian name for Champagne.

Sciascinoso (It) a red grape variety grown in Campania.

Scimitar (Eng) a 4.1% alc by vol. ale brewed by The Durham Brewery Ltd., County Durham.

Scintilla (S.Afr) the label for a sparkling Cap Classique wine (75% Chardonnay and 25% Pinot noir) produced by the JC le Roux winery, Stellenbosch, Western Cape.

Scion (Eng) the part of the vine shoot or cane used for grafting onto root-stock. i.e. *Vitis vinifera* scion onto *Vitis berlandieri* root-stock.

Sclafani (It) a wine co-operative based near Palermo in Sicily.

Scolca [La] (It) a producer of sparkling (metodo tradizionale) wines based in the Piemonte region, north-western Italy.

Sconce [The] (Eng) a university students' (Oxford and Cambridge) beer drinking challenge (to drink a large quantity in one go) because of a misdemeanor. Also the name for the large mug used for Sconcing.

Sconcing (Eng) the drinking of a large quantity of beer through a challenge by university students. *see* Sconce.

Scooter Cocktail (Cktl) ⅓ measure brandy, ⅓ measure amaretto, ⅓ measure cream. Shake over ice and strain into a cocktail glass.

Scopelo (Gre) an eastern Mediterranean island that produces wines similar to Malmsey.

Scorched (Eng) a term applied to white wines that are made from grapes that have had too much sun and too little rain.

Scorcher (Eng) a 4% alc by vol. seasonal malty ale from Morrells of Oxford.

Scorcher Summer Ale (Eng) a cask-conditioned seasonal ale 4.2% alc by vol. brewed by Lees (J.W.), Middleton, Manchester, Lancashire (available July and August).

Scoresby Rare (USA) a blended Scotch whisky bottled in America by Long John International.

Scoresby Stout (Eng) a 4.2% alc by vol. stout brewed by the Cropton Brewery, Pickering, North Yorkshire.

Scorpion (Cktl) 10mls (½ fl.oz) brandy, 35mls (1½ fl.oz) golden rum, 25mls (1fl.oz) each of orange juice, lemon juice, 2 dashes orgeat. Blend altogether with a scoop of crushed ice. Pour into a large old-fashioned glass filled with ice cubes, decorate with a slice of orange, sprig of mint and serve with straws.

Scorpion (Eng) a super strength bottled or canned lager 8.5% alc by vol. brewed by Vaux.

Scorpion Island Brewing Company Limited (Eng) a brewery that brews Scorpion Lager 5% alc by vol.

Scorpion Lager (Eng) a 5% alc by vol. lager brewed by the Scorpion Island Brewing Company Limited.

Scorpio Porter (Eng) a 4.5% alc by vol. porter brewed by Hanby Ales Ltd., Shropshire.

Scotch [1] (Eng) a slang term for Scottish whisky.

Scotch [2] (Eng) short for Scotch ale (a mild style of beer).

Scotch Ale (Bel) a term used for a strong, dark, bottled beer.

Scotch Ale (Eng) the term used in the north of England for heavy beers.

Scotch Ale (Scot) an export ale 1041 O.G. brewed and bottled by the Belhaven Brewery in Dunbar near Edinburgh. Produced for USA market.

Scotch Ale (Scot) a 5% alc by vol. ale from Maclay & C°. Thistle Brewery in Alloa. *See also* Export Ale.

Scotch Apple Liqueur (Scot) *see* Mrs. McGillvray's Scotch Apple Liqueur.

Scotch Bird Flyer (Cktl) ½ measure de luxe Scotch whisky, ⅙ measure Cointreau, ⅓ measure cream, 1 egg yolk. Shake well over ice and strain into a flute glass.

Scotch Bishop (Cktl) ½ measure Scotch whisky, ¼ measure dry vermouth, ¼ measure orange juice, 2 dashes Cointreau, 2 dashes gomme syrup. Shake over ice, strain into a cocktail glass and add a twist of lemon peel juice.

Scotch Blue (Kor) a whisky brand owned by the Lotte Chilsung Beverage Company. Range consists of Scotch Blue International (premium blend), Scotch Blue 21 year old (super deluxe blend).

Scotch Bounty (Cktl) 1 measure Malibu, 1 measure (white) crème de cacao, 1 measure Scotch whisky, 4 measures orange juice, dash egg white, dash grenadine. Shake well over ice, strain into a highball glass, add a slice of orange and serve with straws.

Scotch Coffee (Liq.Coffee) using a measure of Scotch whisky.

Scotch Collins (Cktl) 25mls (1fl.oz) each of Scotch whisky, lemon juice, 10mls (½ fl.oz) gomme syrup. Stir over ice in a highball glass, top with soda water and serve with straws.

Scotch Cooler (Cktl) 40mls (⅓ gill) Scotch whisky, 3 dashes (white) crème de menthe. Stir over ice in a highball glass and top with soda.

Scotch Fir (Scot) a brand of Sherry once produced by Arthur Bell and Sons.

Scotch Frappé (Cktl) place 35mls (1½ fl.oz) Bell's Scotch whisky in an old-fashioned glass filled with crushed ice and dress with a spiral of lemon peel.

Scotch Frog (Cktl) ¼ measure Galliano, ¼ measure Cointreau, ½ measure vodka, juice of a lime, dash Angostura, barspoon maraschino cherry juice. Shake over ice and strain into a cocktail glass.

Scotch Highball (Cktl) place some ice in a highball glass and add 90mls (¾ gill) Scotch whisky, fill with iced soda water and top with a dash of lemon juice.

Scotch Holiday Sour (Cktl) ⅜ measure Scotch whisky, ¼ measure cherry brandy, ¼ measure lemon juice, ⅛ measure Italian vermouth. Shake over ice, strain into an ice-filled old-fashioned glass and add a slice of lemon.

Scotch Malt (Scot) a malt whisky. *see* Malt Whisky.

Scotch Malt Whisky Society Ltd. (Scot) an organisation. (Add): The Vaults, 87 Giles Street, Leith, Edinburgh EWH6 6B7. a club that blends and bottles its own whiskies for its members.

Scotchman's Hill Vineyard (Austr) a winery (established 1982). (Add): Scotchman's Road, Drysdale, Victoria. Grape varieties: Chardonnay, Riesling, Cabernet sauvignon, Pinot noir.

Scotch Milk Punch (Cktl) 40mls (⅓ gill) Scotch whisky, 125mls (1gill) milk, 1 teaspoon gomme syrup. Shake well over ice, strain into a collins glass and top with grated nutmeg.

Scotch Mist (Cktl) place some shaved ice in an old-fashioned glass. Pour in 1 jigger of Scotch whisky and a twist of lemon peel juice.

Scotch Mist (Eng) 3 parts Ceylon tea and 2 parts Scotch whisky, heated together. Add honey to taste, pour into small coffee cups (demi-tasse) and float cream on top.

Scotch Mist (Scot) a natural spring mineral water brand™. Mineral contents (milligrammes per litre): Sodium 12.1mg/l, Calcium 55mg/l, Magnesium 20mg/l, Potassium 0.9mg/l, Bicarbonates 151mg/l, Chlorides 21mg/l, Sulphates 0.6mg/l.

Scotch Old Fashioned (Cktl) moisten a cube of sugar with 2 dashes Angostura in an old-fashioned glass. Add sufficient water to dissolve the sugar, add 2 ice cubes and 25mls (1fl.oz) Scotch whisky and stir.

Scotch on the Rocks (Cktl) a measure of Scotch whisky served over ice in an old-fashioned glass.

Scotch Rickey (Cktl) 25mls (⅕ gill) Scotch whisky, juice ½ lime. Stir over ice in a highball glass, top with soda and add a twist of lemon peel.

Scotch Sour [1] (Cktl) 1½ measures Scotch whisky, 20mls (¾ fl.oz) lemon or lime juice, 1 teaspoon powdered sugar. Shake over ice, strain into a cocktail glass, add a slice of orange and cherry.

Scotch Sour [2] (Cktl) 35mls (1½ fl.oz) Scotch whisky, 25mls (1fl.oz) lemon juice, 10mls (½ fl.oz) Gomme syrup, dash egg white. Shake over ice, strain into a large cocktail glass and decorate with lemon slice.

Scotch Stinger (Cktl) as for Stinger Cocktail using Scotch whisky in place of brandy.

Scotch Triumph (Fr) a 6% alc by vol. top-fermented, brown ale brewed by Jeanne d'Arc Brasserie, Ronchin.

Scotch Whisky (Scot) a blend of malt and grain whiskies. The proportion varies from blend to blend but is approximately 40% malts and 60% grain. *see* De Luxe Scotch Whisky. (Den) = skotsk whisky, (Hol) = schots.

Scotch Whisky Appreciation Society [The] (Scot) a society based at the Scotch Whisky Heritage Centre (*see*) in Edinburgh. Membership details from the Scotch Whisky Heritage Centre.

Scotch Whisky Association (Scot) an organisation (established 1942). (Add): 20 Atholl Crescent, Edinburgh, Midlothian EH3 8HF. Website: http://www.Scotch-whisky.org.uk 'E'mail: contact@swa.org.uk

Scotch Whisky Brands Limited (Scot) formed on the 1st April 1915 by the merger of Buchanan and Dewar. Name was then changed to Buchanan Dewar Ltd.

Scotch Whisky Heritage Centre [The] (Scot) based in Edinburgh below the castle it is an informative exhibition on the history and production of Scotch Whisky. Visitors can taste and purchase Scotch whiskies and join The Scotch Whisky Appreciation Society. (Add): The Scotch Whisky Heritage Society Ltd., 354, Castlehill, The Royal Mile, Edinburgh, Scotland. EH1 2NE. Website: http://www.whisky-heritage.co.uk 'E'mail: enquiry@whisky-heritage.co.uk

ScotCo (Eng) *abbr*: Scottish Courage.

Scotia Royale (Scot) a 12 year old de luxe blended Scotch whisky produced by Amalgamated Distillery Products.

Scots Dream (Scot) 1 measure Islay malt whisky, dash lime juice. Stir over ice, strain into a cocktail glass and float a teaspoon double cream on top.

Scots Grey (Scot) a de luxe blended Scotch whisky produced by Invergordon Distilleries.

Scott Henry Trellis (Eng) a vertically divided canopy held in place with foliage wires. Some shoots are trained down and others upward.

Scotties Brewery (Eng) a brewery based in Lowestoft, Suffolk. Brews: Recession Beer 1032 O.G.

Scottish and Newcastle Brewery (U.K.) have taken over Courage, now known as Scottish Courage. Decided to shut down Nottingham and Halifax. 4 breweries: Tyne in Newcastle, Royal in Manchester, Fountain and Holyrood in Edinburgh. Owns: Beamish & Crawford, Berkshire Brewery, John Smith's Ltd., Royal Brewery, Scottish & Newcastle Pub Enterprises, Scottish Courage Brands Ltd., T & R Theakson Ltd., Waverley TSB. Brews most styles of beer. *see* Scottish Brewers, Newcastle Brewery, Scottish Courage. Website: http://www.scottish-newcastle.com 'E'mail: enquiries@scottish-newcastle.com

Scottish Beer & Pub Association (Scot) an organisation. (Add): 6 St. Colme Street, Edinburgh, Midlothian EH3 6AD. Website: http://www.scottishpubs.co.uk

Scottish Border Springs (Scot) a natural spring mineral water brand.

Scottish Brewers (Scot) the Scottish part of the Scottish and Newcastle Brewery (formed in 1931). Noted for cask-conditioned McEwan 70/-1036.5 O.G. (also known as Younger's Scotch). keg Tartan Bitter 1036 O.G. Harp Lager 1032 O.G. Kestrel Lager 1032 O.G. and bottled Blue Label 1032 O.G. Double Century 1054 O.G. Also produces a canned Monk Export 1042 O.G.

Scottish Cordial (Scot) a nickname for whisky.

Scottish Courage (Eng) *abbr*: ScotCo a brewery and cider producer (established 1887). (Add): The Cider Mills, Plough Lane, Hereford, Herefordshire HR4 0LE. Originally known as Bulmers Cider. Produces lager and cider. Websites: http://www.bulmers.com/http://www.scottish-courage.co.uk

Scottish Courage (Scot) the new name formed as a

result of the merger between Scottish & Newcastle Brewery.

Scottish Courage Brands Ltd (Scot) a brewery (established 1995). (Add): Broadway Park, South Gyle Broadway, Edinburgh, Midlothian EH12 9JX. Part of Scottish & Newcastle and owns Waverley TSB. Brews a range of beers and lager. Website: http://www.scottish-newcastle.com 'E'mail: enquiries@scottish-newcastle.com

Scottish Hours (Scot) licensing hours of Scotland that vary within each region. Regular extension licenses may permit opening during the afternoon, prior to 11 a.m. and after 11 p.m. Differ from the hours in England and Wales.

Scottish Island Malt Whisky Liqueur (Scot) a honey and herb liqueur produced by the Melldalloch Liqueur Company, Tighnabruaich, Argyll 40% alc by vol.

Scottish Leader (Scot) a 40% alc by vol. blended Scotch whisky from Burn Stewart Distillers, Dumbarton.

Scottish Mineral Water (Scot) a natural spring mineral water brand.

Scottish Mountain Spring (Scot) a natural spring mineral water brand.

Scottish Oatmeal Stout (Eng) a 4.2% alc by vol. stout from Broughton Brewery, near Biggar. *see* Greenmantle Ale, Old Jock.

Scottish Pride (Scot) a canned lager beer 1032 O.G. brewed by the Drybrough Brewery in Edinburgh.

Scottish Spring (Scot) a natural spring mineral water brand.

Scottish Wine (Scot) a nickname for whisky.

Scott's Valley (USA) a small wine-producing area of Santa Cruz city, Santa Cruz, California. Has one winery sited there.

Scott [Allan] Wines & Estates (N.Z) a winery. (Add): Jacksons Road, Blenheim. 36ha. Grape varieties: Chardonnay, Riesling, Sauvignon blanc, late-harvest Riesling.

Screaming Eagle (USA) a famous winery based in Oakville, Napa Valley, California. A cult red wine of same name is produced from Cabernet sauvignon, Merlot and Cabernet franc grapes. First vintage was produced in 1992 (approximately 500 cases produced per year).

Scream'n Beaver (Eng) a 5% alc by vol. lager made with spring water by Redruth Brewery, Cornwall.

Screened (Eng) during the brewing process the term given to the removal of all impurities in the malted barley and to grade the corns into size.

Screwcap (Eng) a stelvin, a bottle closure. *See also* Reduction.

Screwdriver (Cktl) 1 measure vodka, 2 measures orange juice, shake well over ice and strain into a cocktail glass.

Screwed (Eng) a slang term for drunk/intoxicated.

Screwpool (Fr) *see* Screwpull.

Screwpull (Eng) a modern style of corkscrew that has two side-pieces that slip between the cork and the bottle-neck together with a conventional corkscrew.

Screw Top (Eng) invented by Dan Rylands in Barnsley (1889), the bottle capping of cheap, inexpensive wines. Uses a metal cap with screw which can be refitted to keep contents fresh. Wines of this nature are meant to be drunk young. Is also applied to beers and carbonated soft drinks. *See also* Reduction.

Scrumdown (Eng) a 4.5% alc by vol. ale brewed by the Belvoir Brewery, Leicestershire.

Scrumpy (Eng) a slang name for rough, draught cider.

Scrumpy Jack (Eng) a strong, clear, traditional cider produced by Symonds in Hereford. 6% alc by vol. (brand is owned by Bulmers).

Scrumpy Jack's Old Hazy (Eng) a cask-conditioned cider from Symonds, Herefordshire 5.5% alc by vol.

Scuddy (Eng) a thick and cloudy wine with a disturbed sediment.

Scummed (Eng) a slang term used to describe the foamy 'scum' appearance on the top of fermenting ales (from top-fermenting yeasts).

Scuppered (Eng) a 4.6% alc by vol. ale brewed by the Ales of Scilly Brewery Ltd., Scilly Isles.

Scuppernong (USA) a species of **Vitis rotundifolia** found along the Atlantic seaboard from Maryland to Florida. Gives sweet, rich white wines and is also known as the Muscadine grape.

Scurati (It) the label for a red wine (Cabernet sauvignon, Nero d'vola and Merlot blend) produced by the Ceuso winery, Sicily.

Scuttlebutt (Eng) an old eighteenth and nineteenth century cask of drinking water on a ship. Also the nickname for a modern drinking fountain.

Scyady (Arab) *see* Chadely.

Scyphus (Lat) wine-cup.

S. de Suduiraut (Fr) an oak-aged dry white wine produced from a blend of Sauvignon blanc 40% and Sémillon 60% grapes by Château Suduiraut, Sauternes, Bordeaux.

Seaboard Cocktail (Cktl) ½ measure Bourbon whiskey, ½ measure gin, 10mls (½ fl.oz) lemon juice, 2 dashes gomme syrup. Shake over ice, strain into an ice-filled highball glass and dress with a sprig of mint.

Sea Breeze [1] (Cktl) ½ measure vodka, ¼ measure blue Curaçao, ¼ measure dry vermouth, ¼ measure Galliano. Stir over ice, strain into an ice-filled goblet and add a twist of orange.

Sea Breeze [2] (Cktl) 1 measure vodka, 3 measures cranberry juice, 1 measure grapefruit juice. Shake over ice and strain into an ice-filled glass.

Seagavin (Austr) the brand-name of a raisin-flavoured dessert wine.

Seagers Egg Flip (Eng) a drink produced from egg yolks and British wine by Seagers Wines Ltd., Isleworth, Middlesex 17% alc by vol.

Seagram (Can) the world's largest alcoholic beverage producer. Has interests in most countries and produces most styles of beverages including many top brands such as: The Glenlivet, Glen Grant, Chivas Regal.

Seagrams Cooler (Cktl) 1 measure Bourbon whiskey, ¼ measure Martini vermouth, 3 dashes orange Curaçao, 1 dash Angostura. Place in an ice-filled tumbler with a slice of lemon and a strip of cucumber peel, stir and top with ginger ale.

Seagrams Distillery (USA) a Bourbon whiskey distillery based in Louisville and near Frankfort, Kentucky.

Seagrams V.O. (Can) a 6 year old blended Canadian whisky produced by Seagram 43% alc by vol.

Seaimpéin (Ire) Champagne.

Seal (Eng) an early identification mark of a bottle's owner. Put onto the bottle because of the bottles value (were re-used over and over), bottles were used to carry the wine from the merchant's cask to the household.

Sealed Bottle (Eng) a bottle that had the owner's seal stamped on the bottle's side, popular until 1850. *see* Seal.

Sealord Ale (Eng) a strong ale 1060 O.G. brewed by the Southsea Brewery near Portsmouth, Hampshire.

Searbhghás Carbónach (Ire) carbonic acid gas.

Sea Serpent Cocktail (Cktl) ½ measure vodka, ½ measure (green) crème de menthe, stir together in an ice-filled highball glass. Top with lemonade, dress with a slice of lemon and a cherry.

Sea Side Cooler (Cktl)(Non-alc) 35mls (1½ fl.oz) grenadine, 500mls (1pint) soda water, juice of a lime. Stir gently over ice in a jug and serve in highball glasses with a slice of lime.

Sea Smoke Winery (USA) a winery based in the Santa Rita Hills, Santa Barbara County, California. Grape variety: Pinot noir. Label: Southing.

Sea Tossed Wines (Eng) a name given to Madeiras and old East India Sherries.

Seau à Bouteille (Fr) wine cooler/wine bucket.

Seau à Glace (Fr) ice bucket.

Seaview (Austr) a winery. (Add): Chaffey's Road, McLaren Vale, South Australia. Vineyards in McLaren Vale and Willunga, Clare Watervale, Southern Vales, Adelaide Hills.

Sea Water (Eng) used to preserve and hide 'off' flavours in wine in the early ages.

Seaweed Extract (Eng) an ingredient of seaweed used to retain the 'head' on a glass of beer.

Seawitch (Cktl) 2 measures Strega, 1 measure blue Curaçao, 3 measures dry white wine. Stir over ice and strain into 125mls (5fl.ozs) goblet, add a lemon slice.

Sebastiaan (S.Afr) the label for a red wine (Cabernet franc and Cabernet sauvignon blend) produced by the High Constantia winery, Constantia, Western Cape.

Sebastiani (USA) a winery (established 1904) based in Sonoma Coast, Sonoma County, California. (Add): 389 Fourth Street East, Sonoma, California 95476. Grape varieties: Barbera, Chenin blanc, Gewürztraminer, Pinot noir and Zinfandel. Produces varietal and dessert wines.

Sebastopol (USA) a winery town in the western Russian River Valley, Sonoma County, California.

Sebor Absinth (Eng) distillers (established 1999). (Add): P.O. Box 1111, Kingston-on-Thames, Surrey KT1 4YX. Produces a range of spirits, liqueurs and cocktails. Website: http://www.seborabsinth.com 'E'mail: Jeremy@seborabsinth.com

Sebor Absinthe (Czec) a 55% alc by vol. and 70% alc by vol. deep green coloured absinthes produced by Mr. Sebor from Swiss and French recipes.

Sec (Fr) a term used to denote dry for still wines, when applied to Champagne it denotes not as dry as Brut.

Sec (Rum) dry.

Sec (S.Afr) dry.

Secano (Sp) a red grape variety grown in the Navarra region that produces light red wines, also known as Ojo de Gallo.

Secateurs (Fr) a pair of special, strong, curved bladed scissors to prune the vines and also used to remove the ripe grapes from the vine.

Seccarezze (It) a natural spring mineral water from Seccarezze.

Secco (It) dry.

Secentenario (It) a red wine produced by Antinori to commemorate the 600th anniversary. Produced from Cabernet sauvignon 30% and Sangiovese 70% grapes.

Séché (Fr) denotes a flat, harsh wine that has a sharp aftertaste. Also spelt Séchet.

Séché (Fr) a Premier Cru Chablis that is often reclassified as Premier Cru Vaillons.

Séchet (Fr) the alternative spelling of Séché.

Sechsamtertropfen (Ger) a herb liqueur produced by Eckes.

Secke (Eng) the sixteenth century spelling of Sack.

Seco (Sp) a medium-dry grading for sparkling wines.

Seco (Port) dry.

Secoffex Water Process (Switz) a patented process of removing the caffeine from coffee using water only.

Secondary Fermentation (Eng) the presence of bubbles, cloudiness, blown cork, nasty smell and taste (these are all signs of secondary fermentation). Caused by bacterial infection, early bottling etc. See also Second Fermentation and Malo-Lactic Fermentation.

Second Fermentation (Fr) a part of most sparkling wine production. The addition of yeast and grape must to new wine which is then bottled or sealed under pressure and allowed to ferment for a second time.

Second Fermentation (Scot) the term used in whisky production for the marrying of the malt and grain whiskies that occurs in the casks. Also known as the 'first marriage'. (the marrying of malts).

Second Growths (Fr) the classification of the Bordeaux Haut-Médoc wines. see Deuxièmes Crus.

Second Growths (Fr) the classification of the Bordeaux sweet wines of Sauternes and Barsac. see Deuxièmes Crus de Sauternes.

Second to None (Eng) a 4.6% alc by vol. ale brewed by the Stonehenge Ales (Bunces Brewery) Ltd., Wiltshire.

Second Wine (Fr) a wine produced by a top vineyard (classified crus). Usually produced from young vines or from grapes that are not up to the quality status for the vineyard's top wine.

Seco-Seco (Cktl) 1 measure Dubonnet, dash Roses lime juice. Serve 'on the rocks' in an old-fashioned glass, decorate with a slice of lime.

Sécrestat (Fr) bitters.

Sécrestat Curaçao (Cktl) ½ measure Sécrestat, ½ measure Curaçao, ice, soda water. Stir all together in a highball glass.

Secret Cellar Barrel (S.Afr) the label for a range of numbered wines from Ultra Liquors.

Secret Hope (Eng) a 4.5% alc by vol. ale brewed by the Corvedale Brewery, Shropshire.

Secret House Vineyards Winery (USA) a winery (established 1972) based in Willamette Valley, Oregon. Grape varieties: Pinot noir, Riesling, Chardonnay.

Secret Kingdom (Eng) a 4.3% alc by vol. ale brewed by the Hadrian & Border Brewery, Tyne & Wear.

Secret Love (Cktl) a Cherry 'B' and bitter lemon.

Secret Spring (Eng) a natural spring mineral water brand.

Secundo Año (Sp) bottled in the second year.

Sedgley Surprise (Eng) the label of a beer brewed by the Sarah Hughes Brewery at Sedgley, near Wolverhampton.

Sedgewick Taylor (S.Afr) a producer of a range of brandies.

Sedgwick's Old Brown Sherry (S.Afr) a 16.8% alc by vol Sherry-style wine produced by Distell from Jerepiko. Also a dry Sherry-style from Muscat and Chenin blanc (a percentage of the sales is donated to the World Wildlife Fund – South African Fish-Tagging project).

Sediento (Sp) thirsty.

Sediment (Eng) a deposit in wine or beer, caused through a secondary or other fermentation in bottle or for red wines the precipitation of colouring matter and tannins through age. (Fr) = depot.

Sediment Beer (Eng) a 'conditioned' beer sold either in cask or in bottle whilst still 'working'. Settles out by the addition of finings.

Sedimento (Sp) lees/sediment/dregs.

Sedlescombe Vineyard (Eng) a vineyard based at Robertsbridge, Sussex. Produces bottled organic cider at 7.5% alc by vol (dry and medium styles).

Sedlmayr [Gabriel] (Ger) the man who, in the nineteenth century, pioneered the use of steam power in breweries, also associated with Pasteur in the study of fermentation. Based at the Spätenbräu Brauerei in Munich.

Seduction (Eng) a 4.5% alc by vol. ale brewed by the Hampshire Brewery, Hampshire.

Séduction (Fr) a vintage cuvée Champagne produced by Ellner (Charles).

Seeberg (Aus) a vineyard site based on the banks of the River Kamp situated in the Kamptal region.

Seebodenberg (Aus) a vineyard site on the banks of the River Danube in the Kremstal region.

S

Seefahrtbier (Ger) a light, malty beer produced by the Haake-Beck Brauerei in Bremen. Originally brewed for seamen to take to sea which fermented in the bottle to be consumed later at sea. Now brewed for a maritime dinner in Bremen. *see* Schaffermahlzeit.

Seefelden (Ger) village (Anb): Baden. (Ber): Markgräflerland. (Gro): Lorettoberg. (Vin): Maltesergarten.

Seeforth Ale (Scot) a 4.2% alc by vol. ale brewed by the Hebridean Brewery C°., Isle of Lewis.

Seehalde (Ger) vineyard (Anb): Franken. (Ber): Bayer Bodensee. (Gro): Lindauer Seegarten. (Vil): Nonnenhorn.

Seeheim (Ger) village (Anb): Hessische Bergstrasse. (Ber): Starkenburg. (Gro): Not yet assigned. (Vin): Mundklingen.

See-it-Offers (Eng) a slang term used in the navy to empty the pot of rum.

Seewein (Ger) lit: 'lake wine', a wine named after the Lake Constance (Konstanz) in the Bodensee (Baden) area. The vines grow on the banks of the lake.

Seewinkel (Aus) on a label denotes that the vines have been grown in sandy soil (resistant to Phylloxera). *see* Sandweine. Is also the alternative name for the Neusiedlersee in Burgenland, eastern Austria.

Sefel (Isr) cup.

Ségalin (Fr) a red grape variety, produced by crossing Jurançon noir x Portugais bleu.

Segarcea Cabernet (Rum) a sweet, soft red wine produced in the Valea Calugareasca region.

Seghisio Family Vineyard (USA) a winery (established 1985) based in the Sonoma County, California. Grape varieties include: Zinfandel. Website: http://www.seghesio.com 'E'mail: E.seghesio@seghesio.com

Segnana (It) the brand-name of a noted Grappa.

Segnitz (Ger) village (Anb): Franken. (Ber): Maindreieck. (Gro): Hofrat. (Vins): Pfaffensteig, Zobelsberg.

Segonzac (Fr) a commune in the Charente département whose grapes are classed Grande Champagne (Cognac).

Segré Cidre (Fr) a fine cider produced in the Anjou-Saumur district of the Loire.

Seguin (Fr) a company producing a Fine Bretagne brandy 40% alc by vol. Based at Machecoul.

Seguin-Moreau (Fr) noted French oak cask makers. (Add): Z.I Merpins–B.P. 94 16103 Cognac. Website: http://www.seguinmoreau.com

Séguinot [Daniel] (Fr) a winery based in the A.C. Chablis, Burgundy. Produces a range of Chablis wines including Premier Cru Fourchaume.

Séguinot [Pierre et Gérard] (Fr) a Cognac producers. (Add): La Nerolle, B.P. N°21, 16130 Segonzac. 47ha. in the Grande Champagne. Produces a range of Cognacs including a Vieille Réserve.

Segura [Guillermo Rein] (Sp) a producer and exporter of Málaga.

Segura Viudas (Sp) a cava sparkling wine producer based in the Penedés. Labels include Aria.

Séguret (Fr) a village in the A.C. Côtes du Rhône-Villages. Produces mainly red wines (with a little rosé and white wine).

Sehlem (Ger) village (Anb): Mosel-Saar-Ruwer. (Ber): Bernkastel. (Gro): Michelsberg. (Vin): Rotlay.

Sehr Herb (Ger) very dry.

Seibel (Fr) *See also* Siebel.

Seibel 5279 (Fr) a white hybrid grape variety that produces light, pale wines.

Siebel 5437 (N.Z) a black hybrid grape variety also known as the Seibouchet and Tintara.

Seibel 5455 (N.Z) a black hybrid grape variety also known as Cinqua, Moya and Plantet.

Seibel 5898 (USA) a red grape variety also known as the Rougeon.

Seibel 7053 (USA) a red hybrid grape variety. Also known as the Chancellor.

Seibel 9110 (USA) a white hybrid grape variety which produces a lightly perfumed wine.

Seibel 13053 (USA) a red hybrid grape variety which produces good red and rosé wines.

Seibel Wines (N.Z) a winery. (Add): 113–117 Sturges Road, Henderson. 2ha. Grape varieties: Cabernet sauvignon, Chardonnay, Sauvignon blanc.

Seibouchet (N.Z) the local name for the Seibel 5437 black hybrid grape variety. Also known as the Tintara.

Seicentario (It) a limited edition anniversary red wine from Antinori.

Seidelberg Estate (S.Afr) a winery (established 1692) based in the Suider-Paarl, Western Cape. 110ha. Grape varieties: Cabernet franc, Cabernet sauvignon, Chardonnay, Chenin blanc, Crouchen, Merlot, Muscadel, Pinotage, Red muscadel, Sauvignon blanc, Shiraz, Viognier. Labels: De Leuwen Jagt, Leuwenblanc, Nuance, Roland's Reserve, Un Deux Trois. Website: http://www.seidelberg.co.za

Seidenberg (Ger) vineyard (Anb): Nahe. (Ber): Schloss Böckelheim. (Gro): Paradiesgarten. (Vil): Mannweiler-Coelln.

Seidl (USA) a style of glass used for drinking beer. *see* Beer Seidl.

Seidlitz (Ger) an aperient mineral water.

Seifried Estate (N.Z) a winery. (Add): Redwood Road, Appleby, Richmond, Nelson, South Island. 60ha. Noted for dry and sweet botrytised Riesling wines. Also: Cabernet sauvignon, Chardonnay, Pinot noir, Sauvignon blanc.

Seigle (Fr) rye.

Seigneur (Ger) the person who set the date for the harvest in feudal times. Also kept order in the vineyards so that no one pilfered another's grapes etc.

Seigneurs d'Aiguilhe (Fr) an A.C. Côtes de Castillon, Bordeaux. Grape varieties: Cabernet franc 15%, Merlot 85%.

Seigneur's Delight (Cktl) 1 measure fine old Cognac,

S

1 measure fresh babaco juice, dash lime juice. Shake over ice, strain into a cocktail glass and dress with a slice of lime.

Seilgarten (Ger) vineyard (Anb): Rheinhessen. (Ber): Wonnegau. (Gro): Burg Rodenstein. (Vil): Bermersheim/Worms.

Seine-et-Marne (Fr) a département in the Champagne region that adjoins the Marne département.

Seinsheim (Ger) village (Anb): Franken. (Ber): Steigerwald. (Gro): Schlosstück. (Vin): Hohenbühl.

Seiris (Ire) Sherry.

Seishu (Jap) a refined style of saké exported to Europe.

Seismic (S.Afr) the label for a red Bordeaux-blend wine produced by the Saronsberg Cellar winery, Tulbagh, Western Cape.

Seitsen (Fin) a natural spring mineral water from Seitsemisen Lähdevesi.

Sekhor (Isr) an old Hebrew (Bible) word for strong drink.

Sekt (Ger) a term for sparkling wine, derived from Sack of Fallstaff's (Shakespeare) German actor Ludwig Devriant. He drank German sparkling wine instead of the Sherry (Sack) that he was meant to (so the name stuck circa 1825).

Sekt (Ger) a sparkling wine that may be produced by the traditional method, cuve close or transfer method. The lower grades are now known as Schaumwein. May not be bottled in quantities larger than 3.2litres, the name 'sekt' is only allowed for special Qualitätsschaumwein.

Selaks Vineyard (N.Z) a vineyard. (Add): Old North Road, Kumeu, Auckland. 28ha. plus 34ha. under contract from Kumeu, Gisborne and Hawkes Bay. Grape varieties: Cabernet sauvignon, Chardonnay, Chenin blanc, Merlot, Müller-Thurgau, Pinot noir, Rhine riesling, Sauvignon blanc and Sémillon.

Selby [Middlesbrough] Brewery Ltd (Eng) a brewery (established 1870). (Add): 131 Millgate, Selby, North Yorkshire YO8 3LL. Brews: cask-conditioned Best Bitter 4% alc by vol (1039 O.G. which is bottled as N°1). N°3 4% alc by vol., Old Tom 6.5% alc by vol., also Brahm and Liszt (a special bottle-conditioned pale ale).

Selecta XV (Sp) a beer brewed by the San Miguel Brewery 5.1% alc by vol.

Selected Late-Gathered (Fr) an old auslesen grade in Alsace (now no longer used).

Selected Madeira (Mad) may use a brand-name or word 'Madeira' and a description e.g. dry, medium, but not the name of the grape. Must be a minimum age of 3 years after Estufagem.

Selection (Ger) a new term to describe top class, dry style wines from select sites. See also Classic.

Sélection Clonale (Fr) the selection of individual healthy vines by vignerons.

Sélection de Grains Nobles (Fr) late picked, botrytised, over-ripe berries, as for vendange tardive but must have a higher minimum sugar content. An official classification in Alsace and

often used in other regions to indicate wines made from botrytis-attacked grapes.

Sélection Deluxe (Fr) on an Armagnac label indicates a minimum age of 1 year old.

Sélection des Anges (Fr) a 25 year old Cognac produced by Pierre Ferrand.

Sélection Massale (Fr) still used by some vignerons before cloning. The selection of suitable wood/shoots from the healthiest vines.

Select Rosé (S.Afr) the label for a rosé wine (part of the Hemisphere range) produced by the Lost Horizons Premium Wines winery, Suider-Paarl, Western Cape.

Selenzhiz (Fr) an alternative name for the Sylvaner grape.

Selestat (Fr) a wine town in the Bas-Rhin in Alsace. Known in German as Schlettstadt.

Selezionato (It) the Italian for Auslese. Also Scelto.

Selezione (It) a wine made from very ripe grapes.

Self Whiskies (Scot) a term used in the Scotch whisky trade to denote a 'straight' or an unblended Scotch malt whisky.

Selhurst Park Flyer (Eng) a 3.7% alc by vol. ale brewed by the Sawbridge Worth Brewery, Hertfordshire.

Seligmacher (Ger) vineyard (Anb): Rheingau. (Ber): Johannisberg. (Gro): Burgweg. (Vil): Lorchheusen.

Seligmacher (Ger) vineyard (Anb): Pfalz. (Ber): Südliche Weinstrasse. (Gro): Königsgarten. (Vil): Arzheim.

Seligmacher (Ger) vineyard (Anb): Pfalz. (Ber): Südliche Weinstrasse. (Gro): Königsgarten. (Vil): Rauschbach.

Selinari (Gre) a natural spring mineral water from Vrakhasi, Crete. Mineral contents (milligrammes per litre): Sodium 8mg/l, Calcium 35.3mg/l, Magnesium 9.5mg/l, Potassium 0.4mg/l, Bicarbonates 131.8mg/l, Chlorides 19.5mg/l, Sulphates 5.8mg/l. pH 7.8

Sella e Mosca (It) a winery based at Alghero in Sardinia. Grape varieties include: Cabernet sauvignon, Cannonau. Label: Tanca Farra. Website: http://www.sellaemosca.com

Sellarin (Sp) a natural spring mineral water brand.

Selo de Guarantia (Port) a seal of guarantee for Portuguese wines and Madeiras.

Selo de Origem (Port) seal of origin, guarantees the authenticity of a demarcated wine. see D.O.C., I.P.R.

Selosse [Jacques] (Fr) a Champagne producer. (Add): Rue Ernest Vallée, 51190 Avize. 15ha. Récoltants-manipulants. Produce vintage and non-vintage wines. Vintages- 1970, 1971, 1973, 1975, 1976, 1979, 1981, 1983, 1985, 1986, 1988, 1989, 1990 1992, 1993, 1994, 1995, 1996, 1997, 1998, 1999, 2000. Prestige cuvée is Origine. Also produces a Blanc de Blancs and Extra Brut. Uses the solera system to replenish wines each year, increasing the complexity. Website: http://www.Champagne-selosse.com

Selters (Ger) a sparkling natural spring mineral

1170

S

water. (Add): Setlers Mineralquelle, 35792 Löhnberg-Selters. Mineral contents (grammes per litre): Sodium 299g/l, Calcium 110mg/l, Magnesium 38mg/l, Potassium 13mg/l, Bicarbonates 850mg/l, Chlorides 269mg/l, Fluoride 0.85gm/l, Sulphates 20mg/l, Nitrate 29mg/l. Website: http://www.selters.de

Seltzer (USA) a general term for sparkling non-alcoholic drinks.

Selvanella (It) a noted Chianti Classico producer based in Tuscany.

Selzen (Ger) village (Anb): Rheinhessen. (Ber): Nierstein. (Gro): Gutes Domtal. (Vins): Gottesgarten, Osterberg, Rheinpforte.

Semaphore (S.Afr) the label for a dry rosé wine produced by the Flagstone Winery, Somerset West, Western Cape.

Sembault Delange (Fr) a Champagne producer.

Séme (Fr) an alternative name for the Malbec grape.

Semele (Lat) the mother of Bacchus.

Semeli (Cyp) the name of a traditional red wine produced by the Haggipavlu Winery.

Semeli (Gre) a winery at Nemea, near Corinth. Produces Château Semeli (100% Cabernet sauvignon) aged for 24 months in new French oak barrels.

Semidano (It) a white grape variety grown in Sardinia.

Semi-Dry (S.Afr) a classification of sweetness in a wine 4–12 grammes per litre of grape sugar in the wine, also known as 'off-dry'.

Semi-Dulce (Sp) semi-sweet for sparkling wines.

Sémillante (Fr) a natural spring mineral water from Brasserie Milles, Toulouges. Mineral contents (milligrammes per litre): Sodium 17mg/l, Calcium 52mg/l, Magnesium 13.9mg/l, Potassium 1.13mg/l.

Sémillon (Fr) an excellent white grape variety grown mainly in Bordeaux in the Sauternes and Graves districts. Produces wines with aromas and flavours of lanolin, apricot, honey (noble rot), grassy, nettles and citrus fruits. Has a thin skin so suitable for *botrytis cinerea* attack. Is also known as the Blanc doux, Chevier, Chevrier, Colombier, Malaga and Cinsault riesling.

Sémillon du Soleil (USA) a white wine produced by the Stony Hill Vineyards, Napa Valley, California.

Sémillon Noir (Fr) the name for the Merlot grape in Bordeaux.

Sémillon Oreanda (Rus) a dry white wine from the Crimea Peninsular. Produced from the Sémillon grape.

Semi-Oscura (Mex) the name for Vienna-style beers.

Semisecco (It) medium-dry, usually applied to sparkling wines.

Semi Seco (Sp) a term for medium to sweet (semi-dry) sparkling wines.

Semi Soet (S.Afr) semi-sweet.

Semi-Sparkling (Eng) describes those wines that have traces of effervescence but are not quite sparkling. (Fr) = moustille.

Semi-Sweet (S.Afr) a classification of sweetness in a wine 4–30 grammes per litre of grape sugar in the wine.

Sempé (Fr) a famous Armagnac producer based at Aignan who uses single continuous stills. Releases a V.S.O.P. where the youngest in the blend is 6 years old.

Seña (Chile) a red wine produced by Robert Mondavi and two Chilean wine makers at Viña Errazuriz Don Maximiano Estate and Winery in Panquehue from Cabernet sauvignon, Merlot and Carmenère grapes.

Sénancole [La] (Fr) a Cistercian liqueur, yellow in colour made from assorted herbs in alcohol. Produced at the Abbey of Sénanque, Provence.

Senard [Daniel] (Fr) a négociant based in Aloxe-Corton, Côte de Beaune, Burgundy.

Sencha Fukujyu (Jap) a brand of green tea. *See also* Sencha Genmaicha and Kokeicha.

Sencha Genmaicha (Jap) a brand of green tea. *See also* Sencha Fukujyu and Kokeicha.

Senda do Vale (Port) a dry, spicy red Vinho Regional Ribatejano wine produced by DFJ Vinhos in the Ribatejo from Trincadeira and Cabernet sauvignon grapes on the Fonte Bela estate, Valada.

Seneca (USA) a region within the Finger Lakes, New York State.

Senez [Christian] (Fr) a Champagne producer. 32ha. (Add): Fontette, 10360 Essoys. Négociant-manipulant and récoltant-manipulant. Produces vintage and non-vintage wines. Vintages: 1973, 1974, 1977, 1978, 1979, 1988, 1989, 1990, 1993, 1995, 1996, 1997, 1998, 2000. Labels include Carte Blanche, Carte Verte, Cuvée Angélique, Grande Réserve.

Sénga (S.Afr) the label for a range of red wines produced by the MAN Vintners winery, Agter-Paarl, Western Cape.

Senheim (Ger) village (Anb): Mosel-Saar-Ruwer. (Ber): Zell/Mosel. (Gro): Goldbäumchen. (Vins): Römerberg, Rüberberger Domherrenberg.

Senheim (Ger) village (Anb): Mosel-Saar-Ruwer. (Ber): Zell/Mosel. (Gro): Not yet assigned. (Vin): Lay.

Senheim (Ger) village (Anb): Mosel-Saar-Ruwer. (Ber): Zell/Mosel. (Gro): Rosenhang. (Vins): Bienengarten, Rosenberg, Vogeilberg, Wahrsager.

Senheim (Ger) village (Anb): Mosel-Saar-Ruwer. (Ber): Zell/Mosel. (Gro): Schwarze Katz. (Vin): Rüberberger Domherrenberg.

Seniffeln (Aus) denotes a foul smell and taste. *See also* Böckser.

Senior Service (Eng) the brand-name of a dark rum bottled by Saccone and Speed 40% alc by vol.

Senn (Ger) vineyard (Anb): Pfalz. (Ber): Mittelhaardt-Deutsche Weinstrasse. (Gro): Höllenpfad. (Vil): Kleinkarlbach.

Sennecey-le-Grand (Fr) a commune in the A.C. Mâcon where Mâcon Supérieur may be produced.

Sennheim (Fr) the German name for the town of Cernay in southern Alsace.

Señor Fabbri (It) a brandy produced by the Fabbri Distillery.

Señorial (Sp) a solera gran reserva brandy produced by José de Soto.

Señorío Agos (Sp) a red wine produced by the Bodegas Lopez-Agos, Rioja. Made from 100% Tempranillo grapes. Oak matured for 2 years and 2 years in bottle.

Señorío Agos (Sp) a red wine produced by Bodegas Marqués del Puerto in Fuenmayor, Rioja. 12.5% alc by vol.

Señorío de Guadianeja (Sp) a perfumed white wine produced by the Vinícola de Castilla in La Mancha.

Señorío de Prayla (Sp) a red wine produced by the Bodegas Faustino Rivero Ulecia, S.A. Arnedo, Rioja. (Baja region). Made from Garnacha, Tempranillo and Viura grapes. Oak matured for 2 years then bottle matured.

Señorío de Saraía (Sp) a bodega based in Navarra. Grape varieties: Garnacha, Graciano, Mazuelo and Tempranillo. Noted for Ecoyen Tinto and Viña del Perdón.

Señor Lustau (Sp) a brandy produced by Emilio Lustau. (Add): Plaza de Cubo, Jerez de la Frontera. Base wine from Jerez.

Sensation Cocktail (Cktl) 20mls (⅙ gill) each of dry gin, lemon juice, 3 dashes maraschino, 3 sprigs fresh mint. Shake well over ice and strain into a cocktail glass.

Sensible Shoes (Eng) half Guinness and half brown ale mixed.

Sensoric Tasting (Eng) a tasting of liquids using the three senses (sight, smell and taste) and assessing the recorded results.

Senthal (Aus) a vineyard site based on the banks of the River Kamp situated in the Kamptal region.

Sentiers [Les] (Fr) a Premier Cru vineyard in the A.C. commune of Chambolle-Musigny, Côte de Nuits, Burgundy 4.8ha.

Sentinel Vineyards (S.Afr) a winery (23ha) based in Stellenbosch, Western Cape. Grape varieties: Cabernet sauvignon, Chardonnay, Merlot, Pinotage, Sauvignon blanc, Shiraz. Label: Cape Snort. Website: http://www.cfwines.co.za

Sentovrenka (Cro)(Slo) a local name for the St. Laurent red grape variety.

Séoules [Les] (Fr) a wine producing district in Bellet, Provence.

Sepidan (Iran) a natural spring mineral water from Sepidan. Mineral contents (milligrammes per litre): Sodium 2mg/l, Calcium 55mg/l, Magnesium 4mg/l, Potassium 0.4mg/l, Bicarbonates 171mg/l, Chlorides 8mg/l, Sulphates 6mg/l, Fluorides 0.5mg/l, Nitrates 6mg/l.

Sepinia (It) a sparkling natural spring mineral water from Campobasso. Mineral contents (milligrammes per litre): Sodium 4mg/l, Calcium 74.7mg/l, Magnesium 4.7mg/l, Potassium 1.3mg/l, Bicarbonates 264mg/l, Chlorides 4.5mg/l, Sulphates 3.2mg/l, Fluorides 0.1mg/l, Nitrates 1.8mg/l, Silicates 7.2mg/l, Oxygen 8.97mg/l. pH 7.75

Seppelts (Austr) a large winery. (Add): 181-187 Flinders Street, South Australia 5000. Has 870ha. at Barooga, Barossa, Coonawarra, Drumborg, Keppock, Mt. Pleasant, Qualco, Riverland, Western and Victoria. Grape varieties: Cabernet sauvignon, Chardonnay, Riesling, Shiraz. Produces varietal, sparkling and dessert wines.

Seppelt's Great Western Imperial Reserve (Austr) a sparkling wine made by the traditional method from the Seppelts estates.

Seppelt's Para Vintage Tawny (Austr) a Port-style dessert wine made by the Seppelts estates.

Seppelt's Spritzig Rosé (Austr) a pétillant rosé wine produced by the Seppelts estates.

Sepphöld Winery (Aus) a winery based at St. Georgen in Burgenland. Produces a wide range of wines (mainly white) including Grüner Husar, Habsburg-Husar and Weisser Husar.

September Morn (Cktl) 60mls (½ gill) Bacardi White Label, juice ½ lime, 4 dashes grenadine, white of egg. Shake well over ice and strain into a cocktail glass.

Septemvri (Bul) a State wine-co-operative.

Septimer (Ger) a white grape variety, a cross between the Gewürztraminer and the Müller-Thurgau. Ripens early, has high sugar and a strong bouquet.

Sequillo Cellars (S.Afr) a winery (established 2003) based in Malmesbury, Swartland, Western Cape. Grape varieties: Grenache, Mourvèdre, Shiraz. Website: http://www.sequillo.com

Sequoia Cellars (USA) a winery based in Woodland, Yolo, California. Grape varieties: Cabernet sauvignon, Carnelian, Gewürztraminer and Zinfandel. Produces varietal and table wines.

Sequoia Grove Vineyards (USA) a winery based between Rutherford and Oakville, Napa Valley, California. 9.5ha. Grape varieties: Cabernet sauvignon and Chardonnay. Produces varietal wines.

Serbia (Ser) largest of the republics in the Balkans. Key wine regions: Fruska Gora, Kosovo, Oplenac, Velika Morava, Vranje. Produces red and white wines from a wide range of grape varieties. Noted for Smederevka (white wine), Prokupac (red) and Ruzica (rosé).

Sercial (Mad) the driest of the Madeira dessert wines, made from the Sercial grape.

Sercial (Port) a white grape variety used in the production of Madeira. Originally known as Esgana Cão.

Seré (Sp) the local name for the Katabatic wind in Priorato.

Serègo Alighieri (It) a D.O.C. Valpolicella Classico produced by the Masi Winery 12.5% alc by vol.

Serein [River] (Fr) a river that runs through the district of Chablis in the Burgundy region (a tributary of the River Seine).

Serenata (It) a winery based on the island of Sicily. Grape varieties include: Grillo, Nero d'Avola.

Serendipity Cellars Winery (USA) a winery. (Add): 15275 Dunne Forest Road, Monmouth, Oregon.

S

Grape varieties: Zinfandel, Marchal foch, Chenin blanc, Müller-Thurgau, Riesling.

Serenissima (Cktl) 35mls (1½ fl.oz) vodka, 35mls (1½ fl.oz) grapefruit juice, dash Campari. Shake over ice and strain into an ice-filled goblet.

Serenissima (It) a natural spring mineral water from Treviso, Veneto.

Serenity (S.Afr) the label for a red wine (Cabernet sauvignon 40%, Merlot 30%, Cabernet franc 20% and Petit verdot blend) produced by the Viljoendrift wines winery, Robertson, Western Cape.

Sereno Winery (It) a winery based in Canelli. Produces vermouths and sparkling wines.

Seret (Eng) an old name for Sherry. Corruption of Ceret. i.e. Xera-Ceret-Seret.

Sergi Karasi (Tur) a white grape variety.

Series C (S.Afr) the label for a red wine (Cabernet sauvignon 82% plus Malbec, Merlot and Cabernet franc blend) produced by the Vilafonté winery, Paarl, Western Cape.

Series M (S.Afr) the label for a red wine (Cabernet sauvignon 39%, Malbec 41% plus Merlot and Cabernet franc blend) produced by the Vilafonté winery, Paarl, Western Cape.

Serimpi Brewery (E.Ind) a brewery based in Djakarta, Java which is noted for stout.

Serine (Eng) an amino acid found in minute traces in wines, formed by the yeast.

Sérine (Fr) a red grape variety also known as the Syrah. Used in the northern Rhône.

Seris (Eng) an old name for Sherry. From Xera (Greek). Progressed from Ceret-Seret-Seris. Pronounced Sheris.

Seritium (Eng) an ancient spelling of Sherry.

Sermiers (Fr) a Cru Champagne village in the Canton de Verzy. District: Reims.

Ser Niccolò (It) an oak aged Cabernet sauvignon wine produced by Machiavelli at Villa Belvedere, 37010 Calmasino, Verona.

Serpentin (Fr) the name of the spiral tube used to cool the Cognac vapour back into liquid form during distillation. see Serpentine.

Serpentine (Eng) the name for the copper spiral tube used for the condensing of the alcoholic vapour in an alambic distillerie. (Fr) = serpentin.

Serpentine Dark Ale (Eng) a 4.5% alc by vol. organic dark ale brewed by the Organic Brewery, Cornwall.

Serpent's Tooth (Cktl) 25mls (1fl.oz) Irish whiskey, 10mls (½ fl.oz) kümmel, 25mls (1fl.oz) lemon juice, 50mls (2fl.ozs) sweet vermouth, dash Angostura. Stir well over ice and strain into a wine glass.

Serpette (Fr) pruning knife.

Serpia [La] (Sp) a system of long wedge-shaped troughs in the Sherry region, made between the rows of vines to collect the rainfall in the winter to water vines and stop erosion. Also known as Serpias.

Serpias (Sp) see Serpia (La).

Serpico (It) a red wine produced from 60% Aglianico, 30% Piedirosso and 10% Sangiovese grapes by Feudi di San Gregorio in Campania.

Serprina (It) a white grape variety grown in northern Italy. Used for making grapey, medium wines with softness.

Serra [Friar Junipéro] (USA) a Franciscan who introduced wine-making to California.

Serra and Sons Ltd. (Port) a winery based in Lisbon. Produces red and white wines.

Serra da Estrela (Port) a natural spring mineral water from Gouveia. Mineral contents (milligrammes per litre): Sodium 2mg/l, Calcium 1mg/l, Magnesium 0.3mg/l, Potassium 0.4mg/l, Bicarbonates 9mg/l, Chlorides 2mg/l, Sulphates 0.5mg/l. pH 5.9

Serra da Penha (Port) a natural spring mineral water from Guimaraes. Mineral contents (milligrammes per litre): Sodium 8.6mg/l, Calcium 3.2mg/l, Magnesium 0.7mg/l, Potassium 0.67mg/l, Bicarbonates 21.4mg/l, Chlorides 8.2mg/l, Sulphates 0.4mg/l, Silicates 21.3mg/l. pH 6.3

Serradayres (Port) the brand-name for red and white wines produced by Carvalho, Ribeiro and Ferreira in Ribatejo (the red is cask matured).

Serra do Segreda (Bra) a slightly acidic natural spring mineral water. Mineral contents (milligrammes per litre): Sodium 20.34mg/l, Calcium 4.65mg/l, Magnesium 14.65mg/l, Potassium 2.56mg/l, Chlorides 15.61mg/l, Sulphates 8.33mg/l, Fluorides 0.18mg/l, Nitrates 0.55mg/l, Silicates 26.08mg/l. pH 5.6

Serra Gaúcha (Bra) a wine-producing region on the 29th parallel.

Serralles (W.Ind) a noted rum distillery based in Ponce, Puerto Rico. Produces Don Q (a popular local rum brand).

Serralunga d'Alba (It) a commune of Barolo in Piemonte.

Serralunga d'Alba (It) a D.O.C.G. Barolo produced by the Fontanafredda winery.

Serrana (Port) a slightly acidic natural spring mineral water from Cabril, Agueda. Mineral contents (milligrammes per litre): Sodium 7.2mg/l, Bicarbonates 12.8mg/l, Silicates 13.6mg/l. pH 5.6

Serra Negra (Bra) a natural spring mineral water brand.

Serre (Fr). High quality first pressing in Champagne. Vin de Cuvée.

Serre de Coiran (Fr) a Vin de Pays area of the Gard département in south-western France.

Serre de Prieur [La] (Fr) a vineyard in the Côtes du Rhône. A.C. Côtes du Rhône. (Add): Suze-la-Rousse, Drôme.

Serre-Long (Fr) a wine-producing district in A.C. Bellet, Provence, south-eastern France.

Serrenne (Fr) an alternative name for the Syrah grape.

Serres (Fr) a noted liqueur producer based in Toulouse. Produces Dojon, Eau de Noix Serres, Fine Pyrénées and Violette.

Serricella (It) a sparkling natural spring mineral

S

water from Vibo, Calabria. Mineral contents (milligrammes per litre): Sodium 10.47mg/l, Calcium 4.44mg/l, Magnesium 1.45mg/l, Potassium 0.7mg/l, Bicarbonates 26.16mg/l, Chlorides 10.14mg/l, Sulphates 9.02mg/l, Nitrates 5.2mg/l, Silicates 5.08mg/l. pH 6.9

Serrig (Ger) village (Anb): Mosel-Saar-Ruwer. (Ber): Saar-Ruwer. (Gro): Scharzberg. (Vins): Antoniusberg, Helligenborn, Herrenberg, Hoeppslei, König Johann Berg, Kupp, Schloss Saarfelser Schlossberg, Schloss Saarsteiner, Vogelsang, Würtzberg.

Serrigny (Fr) a commune in the Côte d'Or, Burgundy. Produces red wines.

Serrine (Fr) see Sérine.

Serschin Wodka (Ger) a silver vodka produced in Eastern Germany 37.5% alc by vol.

Servagnat [Henry] (Fr) an Armagnac producer and owner of Domaine de Toul at Dému in the Bas Armagnac.

Servanin (Fr) a rare red grape variety grown in the Isère département.

Servatiusberg (Ger) vineyard (Anb): Mosel-Saar-Ruwer. (Ber): Zell/Mosel. (Gro): Rosenhang. (Vil): Briedern.

Serveuse (Fr) barmaid.

Service à Thé (Fr) tea set/tea service.

Service de la Répression des Fraudes et du Contrôle de la Qualité (Fr) abbr: S.R.F.C.Q. a body that helps in controlling the quality of wines in France. May prosecute offending vintners.

Service des Contributions Indirectes (Fr) in Burgundy a body who have to be notified in advance by a written declaration prior to chaptalisation.

Serviços de Cadastro da Região dos Vinhos do Dão (Port) a body that keeps a detailed vineyard register. Works with the Federaçao in Dão.

Servin Blanc (S.Afr) an alternative name for the Raisin blanc.

Servir à Buffet (Fr) the serving of watered down wine. see Buffeter.

Servir Frais (Fr) serve cold/chilled.

Servir Gelado (Port) on a label denotes 'serve chilled'.

Servus (Austr) a dry white wine from Lenz Moser in Neusiedlersee-Hügelland, Burgenland. 11.5% alc by vol.

Serzy-et-Prin (Fr) a Cru Champagne village in the Canton de Ville-en-Tardenois. District: Reims.

Sessa Aurunca (It) one of the areas in Campania where Falerno wine is produced.

Session (Eng) a slang term for a heavy drinking bout.

Session (Eng) a light-style ale 3.6% alc by vol. from Worldham Brewery, Worldham, near Alton, Hampshire. see Barbarian, Old Dray.

Session Ale (Eng) a general term for a light style (3.5% alc by vol) draught ale for long drinking bouts. see Session.

Session Bitter (Eng) a cask-conditioned bitter 1038 O.G. brewed by Three Crowns in Ashurstwood, Sussex.

Setanta Vineyard (Austr) a vineyard (planted 1996 and named after an Irish mythological hero) and winery based in the Adelaide Hills, South Australia. Produces: Black Sanglain Cabernet Sauvignon, Cuchulain Shiraz, Emer Chardonnay, Speckled House Riesling. Grape varieties: Cabernet sauvignon, Chardonnay, Riesling, Shiraz. Website: http://www.setantawines.com.au

Setarah (Iran) a lager beer produced by Sarkissian and Sahakians Brewing Company in Tehran. 11° Balling.

Setefontes (Port) a natural spring mineral water from Covilha. Mineral contents (milligrammes per litre): Sodium 2.5mg/l, Calcium 0.7mg/l, Potassium 0.4mg/l, Bicarbonates 7.2mg/l, Sulphates 0.2mg/l, Silicates 9.5mg/l. pH 6.2

Setges (Sp) the alternative spelling of Sitges in south-eastern Spain.

Setine (It) a light red wine said to have been a favourite of Caesar. see Setinum.

Setinum (It) a red wine produced in central-western Italy during Roman times. see Setine.

Set Mash (Eng) occurs during the brewing process when the wort will not drain off properly due to a very sticky mash.

Setrakian Vineyards (USA) the brand-label produced at the California Growers Winery (owned by Setrakian) in Cutler, California.

Setters Retreat (Eng) a 4% alc by vol. ale brewed by Norfolk Cottage Brewing, Norfolk.

Settesóli (It) a wine co-operative based in Menfi, near Palermo, Sicily. Produces bianco, rosato and rosso wines.

Settler Vineyards and Winery (N.Z.) a winery. (Add): Crownthorpe, Settlement Road, RD 9, Hastings 2.5ha.

Settlings (Eng) a rare word used for the lees of wine or beer.

Setúbal (Port) a Port in southern Portugal where the D.O.C. wine Setúbal is made. A fortified sweet wine, it is produced by placing grape skins into the finished wine to obtain a strong Muscat aroma and flavour. Has a golden colour and is sold as a 6 year old vintage or at 20 years of age. Originally known as Moscatel de Setúbal (name dropped as less than 85% of Muscat grape used). See also Torna-Viagem.

Setzberg (Aus) a vineyard site on the banks of the River Danube situated in the Wachau region, Niederösterreich.

Setzer [Hans] (Aus) a winery based in Hohenwarth, Weinviertel. (Add): 3472 Hohenwarth 28. Grape varieties: Chardonnay, Grüner veltliner, Sauvignon blanc, Zweigelt.

Seuca (Rum) an important wine-producing area. Part of the Tîrnave Vineyard.

Seurey [Les] (Fr) a Premier Cru vineyard in the A.C. commune of Beaune, Côte de Beaune, Burgundy 1.23ha.

Sève (Fr) a brandy-based, orange-flavoured herbal liqueur.

Sève (Fr) refers to the strength and aroma when

being tasted in the mouth. Differs from bouquet in that it will indicate the presence of spirit, or a sappy, woody spirit/wine. Is also applied to a deep, rich Sauternes.

Sève de Sapin (Bel) a pine sap-flavoured liqueur produced by the Distilleries Associées Belges.

Sève Fournier (Fr) a Sève liqueur produced by the Fournier C°.

Seven Creeks Spring water (USA) a still natural spring mineral water (established 1998) from Ohio. Mineral contents (milligrammes per litre): Sodium 4.63mg/l, Calcium 39.7mg/l, Magnesium 9.61mg/l, Potassium 1.33mg/l, Sulphates 40.2mg/l, Nitrates 1mg/l. pH 7.78

Seven Crown (USA) a brand of single whiskey produced by Seagram. 40% alc by vol.

Seven Deadly Sins (Austr) the name given to a range of 150mls bottled wine drink produced by BRL Hardy. *see* Envy, Flirt, Greed.

Seven Falls (S.Afr) the label for a white (Muscadel) and red (Ruby muscadel) wine produced by the Southern Cape Vineyards winery, Barrydale, Little Karoo

Sevenhill Monastry Winery (Austr) a Jesuit winery based near Clare, South Australia. Produces table and Sacramental wines.

Seven Hills Winery (USA) a winery based in Walla Walla Valley, Oregon. Grape varieties: Merlot, Cabernet sauvignon, Pinot gris.

Seven Oaks (S.Afr) a winery (established 2003) based in Breerivier, Worcester, Western Cape. 26ha. Grape varieties: Cabernet sauvignon, Chenin blanc, Cinsaut, Pinotage, Ruby cabernet, Sauvignon blanc, Shiraz. Labels: United Bulk, Villa Verde. Website: http://www.sevenoaks.co.za

Sevenoaks Bitter 7X (Eng) a 4.8% alc by vol. bitter ale brewed by the Westerham Brewery C°. Ltd., Kent.

Sevenoaks Brewery (Eng) a home-brew brewery (established 1981) based at the Crown Point Inn, Seal Chart, Kent. Noted for cask-conditioned Crown Point B.B. 1038 O.G.

Seven Peaks (USA) a winery based in the Central Coast, California. Joint venture between Southcorp and California vineyard owners in Edna Valley. Noted for Cabernet sauvignon wines.

Seven Seas (S.Afr) a leading brand of double-distilled cane spirit.

Seven Springs (USA) the label for a red wine (Pinot noir) produced by the Et Fille winery, Oregon.

Seventeen Hundred (S.Afr) the label for a red wine (Cabernet sauvignon 75% plus Merlot and Shiraz blend) produced by the Lourensford winery, Stellenbosch, Western Cape.

Seventeen Hundred and Seven [1707] Reserve (S.Afr) the label for a red wine (Cabernet sauvignon 50% and Merlot 50% blend) produced by the Stellenbosch Hills winery, Stellenbosch, Western Cape.

Seventeen-Ninety-Six [1796] (Sp) the label used by Harveys for three Sherries: Rich Old Oloroso, Palo Cortado and Fine Old Amontillado. Date refers to

the year when the company was founded in Bristol.

Seventeen-Sixty-One [1761] London Dry gin (Eng) a fine, well-known dry gin produced by Greenalls of Warrington, Lancashire 40% alc by vol.

Seventeen-Twenty-Seven [1727] (Eng) the brand-name for a range of lightly sparkling ciders 8.3% alc by vol. from Symonds of Hereford. Medium-dry or medium-sweet in style.

Seventh Heaven (Eng) a 4.3% alc by vol. beer from Rooster Pioneer Brewery, Harrogate.

Seventh Heaven (Cktl) an 8 parts gin, 1 part maraschino, 2 parts grapefruit juice. Shake over ice, strain into a cocktail glass and add a twist of grapefruit peel.

Seventy-Five [75] (Cktl) 50mls (2fl.ozs) gin, juice of lemon, 1 teaspoon powdered sugar, 2 dashes Angostura. Shake over ice, strain into a flute glass and top with iced Champagne.

Seventy Five Cocktail [75 Cocktail] (Cktl) 40mls (⅓ gill) dry gin, 20mls (⅙ gill) Calvados, 4 dashes lemon juice, 2 dashes grenadine. Shake over ice and strain into a cocktail glass.

Seventy Shilling Ale [70/-] (Scot) a term used for medium gravity beers, light in colour. Synonymous with 'Heavy'. *see* Shilling System.

Seven-Up [7-Up] (USA) a brand of carbonated, clear, non-alcoholic soft drink. Produced by the 7-Up C°., St. Louis, Missouri. Also a 7-Up Light version (sugar-free).

Severe (Eng) a term used to describe hard, immature wines, usually high in tannin.

Severinquelle (Aus) a natural spring mineral water. Mineral contents (milligrammes per litre): Sodium 293.7mg/l, Calcium 112.6mg/l, Magnesium 30.6mg/l, Potassium 14.7mg/l, Chlorides 151.5mg/l, Fluorides 0.52mg/l.

Severn Bore (Eng) a best bitter beer 1045 O.G. brewed by the Jolly Roger Brewery in Upton-on-Severn, Worcs.

Severny (Rus) a red grape variety produced from Malengra and *Vitis amurensis*.

Sevilla (Sp) a province of Andalucía. Home to the Vino Comarcale areas: Aljarafe, Lebrija and Los Palacios.

Sevilla Cocktail (Cktl) 20mls (⅙ gill) white rum, 20mls (⅙ gill) Port wine, 1 egg, 2 dashes gomme syrup. Shake over ice and strain into a cocktail glass.

Seville (Cktl) 1 part Mandarine Napoléon, ½ part ginger wine, dash grenadine, dash egg white, juice of an orange. Shake over ice, strain into a 300mls (10 fl.oz) highball glass and add a slice of orange.

Seville Estate (Austr) a winery. (Add): Linwood Road, Seville, Victoria 3139. 3.1ha. Grape varieties: Cabernet sauvignon, Chardonnay, Merlot, Pinot noir, Rhine riesling and Shiraz.

Seville Orange Bitters (Sp) a strong, orange-flavoured bitters made with Seville oranges.

Sèvre-et-Maine (Fr) two rivers that are tributaries of the Loire. The best Muscadet is produced in the area. *see* Muscadet Sèvre et Maine.

Sexau (Ger) village (Anb): Baden. (Ber): Breisgau. (Gro): Burg Zähringen. (Vin): Sonnhalde.

Sextarius (Lat) a measurement of liquid (standard: hogshead/minor: half litre).

Sexual Wine (Fr) a brand name for a French wine produced by M. Charles Perrin and sold in 25cls screw cap bottles (complete with straw) for the American market. The name designed to appeal to the Americans in place of the complicated French label names!

Seyarua Cabernet (Rum) a rosé wine, sweet in taste produced on the Danube plain.

Seychelles Mountain Spring Water (S.Hem) a natural spring mineral water from the Seychelles.

Seymour Winery (Austr) a winery based in central Victoria. Produces fine varietal wines.

Seyssel (Fr) a wine-producing region in the upper Rhône Valley, Savoie in eastern France. Includes the communes of Corbonod and Seyssel (Ain département) and Seyssel (Haut-Savoie département). All are white wines (sparkling or still) made from the Roussette grape.

Seyssel Mousseux (Fr) an A.C. sparkling wine produced by a second fermentation in the bottle from Seyssel in Savoie, eastern France.

Seyval Blanc (Fr) a hardy white hybrid grape variety produced from Seibel 4995 x Seibel 4986. Also known as Seyval-Villard.

Seyve [Bertille] (Fr) a famous French hybridiser who has many grapes named after him.

Seyve [Joannes] (Fr) a famous French hybridiser.

Seyve-Villard (Fr) a famous hybridiser, noted for many new varieties especially N° 5276 (also known as the Seyval blanc).

Seyve Villard (Fr) see Seyval-Villard.

Sevye-Villard 5276 (USA) a white grape variety grown in the eastern USA and G.B.

Sézanne (Fr) a canton in the Épernay district. Villages of Barbonne Fayel, Fontaine Denis Nuisy, Saudoy, Sézanne and Vinedey.

Sézanne (Fr) a Cru Champagne village in the Canton de Sézanne. District: Épernay.

S.F.C. (Fr) abbr: In Cognac denotes a Supérieur Fine Cognac.

Sforzato (It) see Sfursat.

S.Francesco (It) a still and sparkling natural spring mineral water from San Francesco, Caslino al Piano di Cardorago, Como. Mineral contents (milligrammes per litre): Sodium 3.8mg/l, Calcium 35.6mg/l, Magnesium 4.9mg/l, Potassium 0.8mg/l, Bicarbonates 135.5mg/l, Chlorides 1.4mg/l, Sulphates 1.2mg/l, Nitrates 4.8mg/l, Silicates 14.3mg/l. pH 8.0

Sfursat (It) lit: 'strained', a strong red wine produced in the Valtellina. The grapes are hung to dry over the winter and so concentrate the sugar. It has a curious, intense flavour and is dry and high in alcohol. Also known as Sforzato.

S.F.W. (S.Afr) abbr: Stellenbosch Farmers' Winery.

S.G. (Eng) abbr: Specific Gravity.

S.Giorgio (It) a sparkling natural spring mineral water from Mitza Migheli. Mineral contents

(milligrammes per litre): Sodium 45.5mg/l, Calcium 23.3mg/l, Magnesium 16.7mg/l, Potassium 1.9mg/l, Bicarbonates 138.5mg/l, Chlorides 79mg/l, Sulphates 9.3mg/l, Fluorides 0.2mg/l, Nitrates 0.2mg/l, Silicates 28.7mg/l. pH 7.11

Sgt. Peppermint (Eng) a brand of peppermint-flavoured cream liqueur 15% alc by vol.

Shadow Creek (USA) a winery based in Carneros, Napa Valley, California. Produces traditional method sparkling wines. Linked with Moët et Chandon, France. see Torre del Gall.

Shadowfax Vineyard (Austr) a winery based in the Yarra Valley, Heathcote, Victoria. Labels: One Eye, Pink Cliffs.

Shady Grove Cooler (Cktl) 1 measure gin, juice ½ lemon, 1 teaspoon gomme syrup. Place in a highball with ice, stir and top with ginger beer.

Shafer Vineyard Cellars (USA) a winery. (Add): 6200 NW Gales Road, Forest Grove, Willamette Valley, Oregon. 27.5acres. Grape varieties: Cabernet sauvignon, Pinot noir, Chardonnay, Sauvignon blanc, Müller-Thurgau, White riesling, Gewürztraminer. Produces still and sparkling wines. Label: Hillside Select. Website: http://www.shafervineyards.com

Shafer Vineyards (USA) a winery based in the Stags Leap district near Yountville, Napa Valley, California. Grape varieties: Cabernet sauvignon, Chardonnay and Zinfandel. Produces varietal wines. Label: Hillside Select.

Shaft and Globe (Eng) the name given to a type of decanter (circa 1630 – 1675). Has a long neck and round bowl, the first bottle-shape of glass.

Shaftbender (I.O.M) a 5.4% alc by vol. ale brewed by the Old Church Inn, Uppermill, near Saddleworth.

Shahoni (Iran) known as the Royal grape, grown in the Cashbia region.

Shake a Drink (USA) a literal request for a shaken cocktail. To shake over ice and strain into the required glass.

Shakemantle (Eng) a 5% alc by vol. ale brewed by the Freeminer Brewery.

Shake Over Ice (Eng) see Shake a Drink.

Shaker (USA) two styles: Boston and Standard. Consists of 2 metal plated containers which fit one in the other. The unit is held in both hands and shaken up and down (filled with ice and the cocktail ingredients) until the cocktail is well chilled and mixed. see Hawthorn Strainer.

Shakers Smoovie (Eng) a 5.5% alc by vol. fruit drinks with either vodka or white rum base from Halewood International. Flavours include: orange and strawberry, tropical, blackcurrant and raspberry.

Shale (Eng) schist.

Shaler Vineyard Cellars (USA) a winery based in Tualatin Valley, Oregon. Produces vinifera wines.

Shalom Cocktail (Cktl) ⅔ measure Blue Label Smirnoff Vodka, ⅓ measure Madeira, 10mls (½ fl.oz) orange juice. Shake over ice, strain into an

S

ice-filled old-fashioned glass and add a slice of orange.

Shambania (Arab) Champagne/sparkling wine.

Shambles Bitter (Eng) a 4.3% alc by vol. bitter ale brewed by the Potton Brewery C°. Ltd., Bedfordshire.

Shamlan (Arab) a natural spring mineral water from the Yemen. Mineral contents (milligrammes per litre): Sodium 42mg/l, Calcium 46.6mg/l, Magnesium 17.93mg/l, Potassium 4.5mg/l, Bicarbonates 240mg/l. pH 7.5

Shampanskoye (Rus) Champagne/white sparkling wines made by the méthode traditionelle.

Shampein (Kor) Champagne/sparkling wine.

Shamrock (Cktl) ½ measure Irish whiskey, ½ measure dry vermouth, 3 dashes green Chartreuse, 3 dashes (green) crème de menthe. Stir over ice and strain into a cocktail glass.

Shams (Iran) a lager beer 11.5° Balling produced by the Sarkissian and Sahakians Brewery Company in Tehran.

Shandimac (Eng) a bottled shandy from McMullen in Hertford.

Shandong (Chi) a noted wine-producing province.

Shandy (Eng) equal quantities of bitter beer and lemonade, a bottled version is available which is non-alcoholic.

Shandy Bass (Eng) a famous (introduced 1972) non-alcoholic, bottled beer shandy produced by Bass. Now owned by Britvic & C°.

Shandy Gaff (Eng) equal parts of bitter beer and ginger ale.

Shanghai (Chi) a major Chinese city that has a branch of the China National Cereals, Oils and Foodstuffs Import and Export Corporation. Specialises in rice wines.

Shanghai [1] (Cktl) ½ measure dark rum, ⅛ measure pastis, ⅜ measure lemon juice, 2 dashes grenadine. Shake over ice and strain into a cocktail glass.

Shanghai [2] (Cktl) 25mls (1fl.oz) Jamaican rum, juice ¼ lemon, 3 dashes anisette, 2 dashes grenadine. Shake over ice and strain into a cocktail glass.

Shanghai Beer (Chi) a bottled lager-style beer 1043 O.G. brewed in Shanghai.

Shanghai Cocktail (Cktl) 40mls (⅓ gill) brandy, 1 teaspoon each of brown Curaçao, Angostura, gomme syrup and maraschino. Stir over ice, strain into a cocktail glass, serve with a dash of lemon peel juice and a cherry.

Shanghai Cossack Punch (Cktl) 500mls (1pint) dark rum, 1100mls (1quart) hot tea, zest of 2 lemons, 275mls (½ pint) Curaçao, strained juice of 4 lemons, 1½ teaspoons orgeat syrup or orange flower water. Bring slowly to the boil and strain into glasses.

Shanghai Gin Fizz (Cktl) 1 measure gin, ¼ measure Bénédictine, ¼ measure yellow Chartreuse. Shake over ice, strain into a large wine goblet and top with lemonade.

Shan Niang (Chi) a noted brand of rice wine. see Shaoh-Sing Rice Wine.

Shannon (Ire) a natural spring mineral water from Limerick. Mineral contents (milligrammes per litre): Sodium 10.5mg/l, Calcium 95mg/l, Magnesium 19mg/l, Potassium 1.5mg/l, Chlorides 21mg/l.

Shannoneau (S.Afr) the label for a white wine (Sauvignon blanc) produced by the Raka winery, Walker Bay, Western Cape.

Shannon IPA (Eng) a 3.6% alc by vol. India pale ale brewed by the Potton Brewery C°. Ltd., Bedfordshire.

Shannon Shandy (Cktl) 25mls (1fl.oz) Irish Mist, dash Angostura. Pour over ice into a highball glass and top with dry ginger ale.

Shan Pen (Jap) Champagne/sparkling wine.

Shantell Vineyard (Austr) a winery (established 1981). (Add): Near Melba Highway, Dixon's Creek, Yarra Valley. Grape varieties: Cabernet sauvignon, Chardonnay, Sémillon, Pinot noir.

Shantung (Chi) a major Chinese city that has a branch of the China National Cereals, Oils and Foodstuffs Import and Export Corporation. Sells gin, vodka and whiskey under the Sunflower label. Also produces a cider and brandy.

Shantung (Chi) a province that is noted for rice wines. see Shaoh-Hsing Rice Wine.

Shanxi (Chi) a wine-producing province in eastern China.

Shao Chiu (Chi) lit: 'burning spirits'.

Shao-Hsing Rice Wine (Chi) a generic rice wine made from glutinous rice, millet, yeast and spring water and aged for 10 years or more in earthenware urns. Amber in colour and of high alcoholic strength it resembles a medium-dry Sherry in character. Served at 37°C (98.6°F) in small cups. 11%–15% alc by vol. Also spelt Shaoxing. see Chia Fan, Hua Tiao and Yen Hung.

Shao-Hsing Shan Niang Chiew (Chi) a brand of rice wine produced in Shanghai by the C.N.C.O.F.I.E.C.

Sharab (Arab) beverage/drink/mixed drink.

Shariba (Arab) to drink/drinking.

Sharir (Isr) a semi-dry golden wine produced in the Sherry-style for the USA market. Produced by Carmel.

Shark Bite (Eng) the label of 4% alc by vol. lemonade and cola drinks produced by Spring Water Beverages in Leicester.

Shark's Tooth Cocktail [1] (Cktl) 1 measure golden rum, 3 dashes each of sloe gin, dry vermouth, lemon juice and passion fruit juice, 1 dash Angostura. Shake well over ice and strain into a cocktail glass.

Shark's Tooth Cocktail [2] (Cktl) 25mls (1fl.oz) golden rum, dash gomme, dash grenadine, juice ½ lime. Stir over ice in a highball glass, top with soda water and decorate with a slice of lime and mint sprig.

Sharpham Vineyard (Eng) a vineyard (established 1982) based at Sharpham House, Ashprington, Totnes, Devon. 1ha. Grape varieties: Huxelrebe, Madeleine angevine, Pinot noir and Reichensteiner.

Sharpness (Eng) describes a wine that has excessive acidity.

Sharpness (Switz) a quality peculiar to certain soils, giving the wine a much appreciated taste.

Sharp's Brewery (Eng) a brewery (established 1994). (Add): Rock, Cornwall PL27 6NU. Brews: Cornish Coaster 3.6% alc by vol., Doom Bar Bitter 4% alc by vol., Eden Pure Ale 4.4% alc by vol., Sharp's Own 4.4% alc by vol., Special Ale 5.2% alc by vol., Wills Resolve 4.6% alc by vol. Website: http://www.sharpsbrewery.co.uk 'E'mail: enquiries@sharpsbrewery.co.uk

Sharp's Own (Eng) a 4.4% alc by vol. ale brewed by Sharp's Brewery in Cornwall.

Shasha (Gro) a vodka produced in Georgia that is distilled from wine.

Shavetail Cocktail (Cktl) ⅖ measure vodka, ⅕ measure peppermint cordial, ⅕ measure pineapple juice, ⅕ measure cream. Shake over ice and strain into a cocktail glass.

Shaw and Smith (Austr) a winery based in the Adelaide Hills, South Australia. Grape varieties include: Cabernet sauvignon, Chardonnay, Shiraz.

Shawsgate Winery (Eng) a winery based in Suffolk. Grape variety: Müller-Thurgau.

Shaw Vineyards (USA) a winery based near St. Helena, Napa Valley, California. Grape varieties: Chenin blanc, Gamay and Sauvignon blanc. Produces varietal wines (Chenin blanc sold under the Bale Mill Cellars label). Labels include: M3 Vineyard.

Shaw Wallace & C°. (Ind) a brewery based in Calcutta. Brews: Lal Toofan.

Sheaf Stout (Austr) a sweet stout brewed by the Tooths Brewery in Sydney.

Shea Vineyards (USA) vineyard estate based in Willamette Valley, Oregon. Label: Belles Soeurs. *See also* Broadley Vineyards.

Shebean (USA) *see* Shebeen (alternative spelling).

Shebeen (Ire)(S.Afr)(Scot) a shop or bar where excise liquor is sold without a licence (illegally). Also in South Africa.

Shebeen (Ire)(USA) a nickname for weak beer.

Shebeen (S.Afr) the name for a place where black Africans drink together.

Shechem (Isr) a red Palestinian wine written about by the Romans.

Sheep Dip (Cktl) 25mls (1fl.oz) Tio Pepe, 50mls (2fl.ozs) gin, 125mls (5fl.ozs) sweet Merrydown cider. Shake over ice and strain into a large goblet.

Sheep Dip (Eng) an 8 year old highland malt whisky bottled by M.J. Dowdeswell and C°. Ltd. in Oldbury-on-Severn, Gloucestershire. 40% alc by vol. Known as 'The Original Oldbury Sheep Dip'. *See also* Pig's Nose.

Sheephaggers Gold (Scot) a 4.5% alc by vol. golden ale brewed by The Cairngorm Brewery C°. Ltd., Inverness.

Sheep Preview (Eng) a 6.5% alc by vol. cask beer. Now known as Riggwelter 7.

Sheep's Nose (Eng) a variety of cider apple.

Sheet Filters (Eng) sheets of filter medium used for the coarse filtration of wines and beers (*see* Kieselguhr).

Sheffield Best Bitter (Eng) a cask-conditioned bitter beer 1038 O.G. brewed by the Ward Brewery in Sheffield, Yorkshire. Also sold in a keg version.

Sheffield Cathedral Ale (Eng) a beer brewed by Kelham Island Brewery, Sheffield, Yorkshire.

Sheffield Stout (Eng) equal quantities of black beer and lemonade.

Sheffield Stout (Eng) an old English drink of mineral water or rum mixed with spruce beer.

Shefford Bitter (Eng) a 3.8% alc by vol (1038 O.G) cask-conditioned bitter brewed by the B & T Brewery, Bedfordshire.

Shefford Mild (Eng) a 3.8% alc by vol. mild ale brewed by the B & T Brewery, Bedfordshire.

Shefford Old Dark (Eng) a 5% alc by vol. dark ale brewed by the B & T Brewery, Bedfordshire.

Shefford Old Strong (Eng) *abbr*: S.O.S. a 5% alc by vol (1050 O.G) light-coloured strong ale brewed by the B & T Brewery, Bedfordshire.

Shefford Pale Ale (Eng) a 4.5% alc by vol. pale ale brewed by the B & T Brewery, Bedfordshire.

Shekhar (Isr) lit: 'strong drink'.

Shelf [Off The] (Eng) a term to denote a drink, usually bottled beer, that is not cold i.e. has not been in the cooler.

Shelf Life (Eng) a term to denote the length of time a product (wine, beer, etc.) will last before starting to deteriorate. *See also* Best Before Date.

Shell (USA) a style of beer glass. *see* Beer Shell.

Shell Creek Vineyards (USA) a winery based near Paso Robles, San Luis Obispo County, California. Grape varieties: Barbera, Cabernet sauvignon and Petite syrah. Produces varietal wines.

Shellisage (Fr) the illegal practice of adding glycerine to wines to improve the wine's body that is easily detected.

Shelmerdine (Austr) a winery based in Heathcote, Central Victoria. Grape varieties include: Shiraz. Website: http://www.shelmerdine.com.au

Shenandoah Spring Water (USA) a natural spring mineral water from California.

Shenandoah Valley (USA) a sub A.V.A. wine-producing region based in the Amador County, Sierra Foothills, California. Grapes: Barbera, Cabernet sauvignon, Chenin blanc, Marsanne, Mourvèdre, Roussanne, Syrah, Sangiovese and Zinfandel. Home to Montevińa Winery, Renwood Winery, Shenandoah Vineyards, Terre Rouge.

Shenandoah Vineyards (USA) a winery based in the Shenandoah Valley, Amador County, California. Grape varieties: Barbera, Cabernet sauvignon, Chenin blanc and Zinfandel. Produces varietal and dessert wines.

Shen Nung (Chi) an Emperor 2737BC who is often regarded as the founder of tea drinking.

Shepherd Neame Brewery (Eng) a brewery (established 1698). (Add): 17 Court Street, Faversham, Kent ME13 7AX. Brews: cask-conditioned Canterbury Jack 4.5% alc by vol. Master Brew Bitter 1036 O.G. Master Brew Mild

S

1031 O.G. Spitfire 4.7% alc by vol. Stock Ale 1036 O.G. Early Bird 4.3% alc by vol. Goldings Summer Hop Ale 4.7% alc by vol., Kent's Best Invicta Ale 4.1% alc by vol., 1698 Ale 4.5% alc by vol. Late Red Autumn Ale 4.5% alc by vol. Porter 5.2% alc by vol. Harvest Ale 5% alc by vol. Invicta Best Bitter 1044 O.G. keg Abbey 1039 O.G. Hurlimann Sternbräu Lager 1045 O.G. Bottled Bishop's Finger 1053 O.G. 1698 bottle-conditioned ale 6.5% alc by vol., Bourough Brown 1034 O.G. Harry Halfyard 4.5% alc by vol. Master Brew Smooth 3.7% alc by vol. Casey's Cream Ale 4.5% alc by vol., Whitstable Bay 4.1% alc by vol. Website: http://www.shepherdneame.co.uk

Shepherd's Creek Classic (S.Afr) the label for red wine (Cabernet sauvignon and Pinotage blend) produced by the Clos Malverne winery, Stellenbosch, Western Cape.

Shepherd's Delight (Cktl) 40mls (⅓ gill) red St. Raphaël, 1 small bitter lemon, dash Pernod. Stir in a highball with ice and decorate with a slice of orange.

Shepherd's Delight (Eng) a 4.3% alc by vol. seasonal ale brewed by the Highwood Brewery, Barnetby, Lincolnshire.

Shepherd's Delight (Eng) a 4.6% alc by vol. ale brewed by the Blackawton Brewery, Cornwall.

Shepley Spring (Eng) a still natural spring mineral water from Shepley Spring. Mineral contents (milligrammes per litre): Sodium 90mg/l, Calcium 32mg/l, Magnesium 11mg/l, Potassium 3mg/l, Bicarbonates 412mg/l, Chlorides 15mg/l, Sulphates 1.2mg/l, Nitrates 1mg/l. pH 7.8

Sheppy's (Eng) based at Bradford-on-Tone, Somerset. Produces: Oakwood draught cider, Kingston Black Cider, Organic Cider, Taylor Gold, Cider with Honey (each bottle contains a teaspoonful of clear honey).

Sherbet Glass (USA) a small tumbler holding ¾ gill (90mls).

Sheridan's (Eng) a liqueur with the bottle divided into two halves. Coffee and chocolate flavoured liqueur and vanilla cream. Served individually. 2 parts black (liqueur) : 1 part white (vanilla cream) over ice. From I.D.V.

Sheriffmuir (Scot) the name for an ale brewed by the Bridge of Allan Brewery Ltd., Stirlingshire.

Sheris (Sp) an old name and pronunciation of Seris (Sherry). From the Greek Xera (Jerez). Progressed from Ceret-Seret-Seris-Sheris.

Sherish (Sp) one of the many old Moorish names for Jerez that have been recorded.

Sherrill Cellars (USA) a small winery based near Saratoga, Santa Cruz Mountains, Santa Clara, California. Grape varieties: Cabernet sauvignon, Petite syrah and Zinfandel. Produces varietal wines.

Sherris Sack (Eng) the Shakespeare name for Sherry. *see* Sheris and Sack.

Sherry (Sp) the name given to the fortified wine produced in the Andalucía region of south eastern Spain. Name derives from the main town of Jerez

de la Frontera. The D.O. region lies in a triangle of Jerez and the towns of Sanlúcar de Barrameda and Puerto de Santa Maria. *see* Albariza, Amontillado, Arenas, Barros, Criadera, Flor, Manzanilla, Moscatel, Oloroso, Palo Cortado, Palomino, Pedro Ximénez, Rayas, Solera. (Ire) = seiris. Website: http://www.jerez.org

Sherry Butt (Sp) a 600litres capacity storage butt. The shipping butt contains 516litres.

Sherry Case (Sp) a lengthy court case in 1968 which decided that only the fortified wine from Andalusia could be called Sherry. All other copies were known as British Sherry, Australian Sherry, Cyprus Sherry etc. until January 1996. Now known as British (Cyprus) Fortified Wine.

Sherry Circle (Eng) a Sherry-producers body. (Add): 3–5 Duke Street, London W1M 6BA.

Sherry Cobbler [1] (Cktl) fill a 125mls (5fl.ozs) wine glass with ice, add dry Sherry until ½ full. Add 4 dashes Curaçao and 1 teaspoon gomme syrup, stir, decorate with fresh fruit and a sprig of mint and serve with straws.

Sherry Cobbler [2] (Cktl) half fill a tumbler with ice, add a dash of orange bitters, 1 teaspoon orange Curaçao, 1 teaspoon peach brandy, 100mls (4fl.ozs) dry Sherry. Stir gently and decorate with a piece of fresh pineapple.

Sherry Cobbler American Style (Cktl) 125mls (1gill) Sherry, 1 teaspoon pineapple syrup, 1 teaspoon sugar syrup. Shake well over ice, strain into an ice-filled highball glass. Decorate with fruit and top with a dash of Port, serve with a spoon and straws.

Sherry Cobbler French Style (Cktl) as for American Style but change the pineapple syrup to Curaçao.

Sherry Cocktail [1] (Cktl) 1 measure dry Sherry, 1 dash orange bitters, 2 dashes dry vermouth. Stir over ice and strain into a cocktail glass.

Sherry Cocktail [2] (Cktl) 40mls (⅓ gill) Sherry, 2 dashes Angostura, 2 dashes orange bitters. Stir over ice, strain into a cocktail glass, serve with a cherry and dash of orange peel juice on top.

Sherry Egg Nog (Cktl) 1 egg, 40mls (⅓ gill) sweet Sherry, teaspoon sugar. Shake over ice, strain into a collins glass, top with milk, stir and add grated nutmeg.

Sherry Exporters's Association (Sp) an association that includes producers and exporters of British firms.

Sherry Flip (Cktl) 1 egg, 1 teaspoon powdered sugar, 35mls (1½ fl.oz) Sherry. Shake over ice, strain into a small goblet and add grated nutmeg on top.

Sherry Glass (Eng) *see* Copita. (Ire) = gloine seirise.

Sherry Highball (Cktl) as for Gin Highball but using Sherry instead of gin.

Sherry Kina (Sp) a Sherry-flavoured, Spanish vermouth with quinine.

Sherry Milk Punch (Cktl) 40mls (⅓ gill) sweet Sherry, 275mls (½ pint) milk, 1 teaspoon powdered sugar. Stir well over ice, strain into a large highball glass and top with grated nutmeg.

Sherrys (Eng) the early English spelling of Jerez.

Sherry Sangaree (Cktl) 1 measure Sherry, barspoon sugar. Fill a glass with crushed ice, stir, sprinkle nutmeg on top and decorate with a slice of lemon.

Sherry Style (Eng) the designation given to wines which have a sweet taste and are dark in colour with high alcohol. Usually of USA, South African or Australian origin.

Sherry Twist (Cktl) ⅖ measure dry Sherry, ⅖ measure orange juice, ⅕ measure Scotch whisky, 2 dashes Cointreau. Shake over ice and strain into a cocktail glass.

Sherry Twist Cocktail (Cktl) ⅖ measure dry Sherry, ⅕ measure brandy, ⅕ measure French vermouth, ⅕ measure Cointreau, 2 dashes lemon juice. Shake over ice, strain into a cocktail glass, top with a twist of lemon peel juice and a pinch of cinnamon.

Sherry Type (Eng) *see* Sherry Style.

Sherrywijn (Hol) the Dutch name for Sherry.

Sherston Scorcher (Eng) the brand-name of a cider produced by the Saffron Cider Company, Radwinter, Essex.

Sherwood Estate Wines (N.Z) a winery. (Add): Weedons Ross Road, (RD5) Christchurch. 5ha. Grape varieties: Chardonnay, Müller-Thurgau, Riesling, Pinot noir.

Shetland Whisky (Scot) a Scotch whisky distilled by the Blackwood Distillers, Shetland Isles. Website: http://www.shetlandwhisky.com

Shevardnadze (Geo) a '*Peace Vodka*' from the Republic of Georgia.

Shibori (Jap) in the Japanese brewing process denotes the '*pressing*' of the ingredients to extract the malt sugars. *See also* Ichiban Shibori.

Shibul (S.Afr) the label for a range of wines produced by the Freedom Hill Wines winery, Paarl, Western Cape.

Shicker (Austr) a slang term for an alcoholic drink/strong liquor.

Shickered (Austr) a slang term for drunk/intoxicated.

Shiel (Scot) the wooden shovel used to turn the barley during the malting process.

Shihizendokoro (Jap) a term used to describe a medium-style saké. *See also* Sansuidokugen.

Shilling (Eng) a half-strength bitter ale produced by Younger's (draught or bottled). Alcohol is restricted during the brewing process after 1.6% alc by vol.

Shilling System (Scot) a method of grading beer in Scotland. Used (circa 1870) to indicate the level of original gravity. 70/-, 80/-, 90/-. Higher gravity beers have a higher beer duty (the higher the shilling mark the stronger the beer).

Shine (USA) *abbr*: for moonshine.

Shiner Premium Beer (USA) a beer brewed by the Spoetzl Brewery in Shiner, Texas.

Shiney Sheff Ale (Eng) a 4.5% alc by vol. limited edition ale from Ward's in Sheffield. Brewed to mark the visit of HMS Sheffield.

Shingle Peak (N.Z) a vineyard based in Matua, Marlborough, South Island. Grape variety: Pinot noir.

Shinjiro Torii (Jap) the founder (1899) of Suntory C° (the largest whiskey producer in Japan).

Shin-Neck Bottle (Fr) an old Champagne bottle with a thin, narrow neck.

Shipper (Eng) a person (company) that ships (imports) wines, spirits etc. from one country to another. May be in bulk or already bottled.

Shipper's Label (Eng) denotes wines (usually generic) that are bottled by the shipper. i.e. Médoc, Côtes du Rhône, etc.

Shipping Butt (Sp) a Sherry cask of 110gallons (516litres) for shipping Sherry. Used afterwards for malt whisky maturation.

Shipping Pipe (Port) a Port cask of 534litres used for the shipping of Port wine. *see* Pipe.

Ship's Decanter (Eng) originally designed to be used at sea. Has a large flat base and tapered neck to prevent it falling over.

Ship Sherry (S.Afr) a jerepigo-style wine produced by Distell from two Muscats and Chenin blanc grapes. 16.8% alc. by vol.

Shipstone Brewery (Eng) a brewery based in Shipstone Nottinghamshire. Taken over by Greenall Whitley, Warrington, Lancs. Noted for cask-conditioned and keg beers, bottled Gold Star 1034 O.G. Ship Stout 1042 O.G.

Ship Stout (Eng) a bottled stout 1042 O.G. brewed by the Shipstone Brewery in Nottinghamshire.

Shiraz (Austr)(S.Afr) the local name for the red Syrah grape variety.

Shiraz (Iran) the ancient city in south-western Iran. Gave its name to the wines of Persia. Also the name for one of the oldest grape varieties.

Shire Bitter (Eng) a 3.8% alc by vol. bitter ale brewed by the Hexhamshire Brewery, Northumberland.

Shirley Temple (Cktl)(Non-alc) top an ice-filled highball glass with ginger ale, Add a dash of grenadine, stir slightly and decorate with cherries.

Shiroka Melnishka Loza (Bul) lit: 'broad-leafed vine of Melnik', the full name for the Melnik grape.

Shive [1] (Eng) a flat cork used as a bung in a cask of wine.

Shive [2] (Eng) a wooden bung which plugs the beer cask where it has been filled. Has a central part (Tut) which is punched in when the cask of beer has been delivered to the public house and is vented. *see* Spile.

Shivowitza (Hun) a liqueur produced from the shiva plum 43% alc by vol.

Shloer (Eng) a non-alcoholic apple juice drink produced by Beecham Products, Brentford, Middlesex. Also available as a sparkling red or white grape juice. Plus white grape juice with raspberries and cranberries and white grape juice with elderflower.

Shochu (Jap) a white spirit distilled from rice wine or sweet potato. Is similar to vodka.

Shock (Eng) an 8.4% alc by vol. strong cider from Intercontinental Brands, Harrogate.

Shoemaker (Eng) a 4.2% alc by vol. ale brewed by the Frog Island Brewery, Northamptonshire.

Shoes Brewery (Eng) a brewery (established 1994). (Add): Three Horseshoes Inn, Norton Canon, Hereford, Herefordshire HR4 7BH. Brews: Cannon Bitter 4.2% alc by vol., Norton Ale 3.5% alc by vol.

Shomrim (Isr) the name for the Rabbi who presides over the production of Vin Cacher. *See also* Cachérisation.

Shomron (Isr) a wine-producing region in central Israel.

Shoot [The] (Cktl) ⅔ measure Scotch whisky, ⅓ measure Fino Sherry, ¹⁄₁₀ measure orange juice, ¹⁄₁₀ measure lemon juice, 2 dashes gomme syrup, shake over ice and strain into a cocktail glass.

Shooting Lodge (Scot) a brand of blended Scotch whisky sold through Peter Dominic stores 37.5% alc by vol.

Shop (Ger) a natural spring mineral water brand. Mineral contents (milligrammes per litre): Sodium 279mg/l, Calcium 110mg/l, Magnesium 20mg/l, Potassium 5mg/l, Bicarbonates 537mg/l, Chlorides 124mg/l, Sulphates 319mg/l.

Shoprite Checkers (S.Afr) the name for two national retail stores that have their own wine ranges: Oak Ridge (Cabernet franc, Cabernet sauvignon/ Cabernet sauvignon-Merlot-Cabernet franc/Merlot/ Pinotage/ Shiraz) and Oddbins Limited Edition (varietals that have the bin numbers changed with each batch. Grapes include: Cabernet sauvignon/ Chardonnay/ Chenin blanc/Merlot/ Pinotage/ Sauvignon blanc). Website: http://www.shoprite.co.za

Shoreditch Stout (Eng) a 5% alc by vol. stout brewed by the Pitfield Brewery, Shoreditch, London.

Short (Eng) the term used to describe a wine that has a good nose and flavour, but falls short on the finish (the taste disappears quickly).

Short Berries (Eng) the alternative name for millerandage. Describes the condition of the vine after coulure, the grapes vary in size and resemble buckshot.

Shortridge Lawton (Mad) a producer of fine Madeiras.

Shot (USA) a single measure of spirit, usually drunk neat and in one go often accompanying another drink such as beer. Modern shots are often flavoured spirits (with fruit juices aimed at the younger drinker). *See also* Slammer.

Shot Glass (USA) a small glass (of all shapes and sizes) that takes a single measure of spirits, designed so that the spirit must be drunk neat.

Shotted Bottles (Port) in olden days Port bottles were pitted with shot from a cartridge shaken by hand. They were used as the crust thrown by vintage Port was said to adhere more firmly to the uneven surface.

Shott's Alcoholic Seltzer (Eng) a 5.3% alc by vol. flavoured alcoholic beverages from the Whitbread Beer Company. Flavours include: Lemon Jag, Vanilla Heist, Cranberry Charge.

Shoulders (Eng) the point on a bottle where the neck joins the body of the bottle. Most pronounced on a Bordeaux bottle.

Shoulder Shape (Eng) a style of decanter developed from the mallet-shaped decanter. Has pronounced shoulders at the join of the neck and body. The body is straight sided.

Shout (Eng) a slang term to denote whose turn it is to buy the next round of drinks. i.e. '*Whose shout is it?*', "*Your shout*", "*My shout*", etc.

Showerings (Eng) a noted company based in Bristol, a subsidiary of Allied-Domecq. Products include: Babycham, Gaymer's Cider, Vine Products, Warninks Advocaat, Whiteways. Known as the Gaymer Group (taken over in 1992).

Shown and Sons (USA) a winery based near Rutherford, Napa Valley, California. 32ha. Grape varieties: Cabernet sauvignon, Chenin blanc and Johannisberg riesling. Produces varietal wines.

Shrapnel Corkscrew (Eng) a rare corkscrew produced in 1839 by Henry Shrapnel which was operated by a cranked handle to turn the screw into the cork. The handle is then turned in reverse to extract the cork.

Shrew Brew (Eng) a celebration ale to commemorate the Shrewsbury Town football club winning promotion from the 3rd to the 2nd division. Brewed by the Wood Brewery, Winstantow, Shropshire. *see* Shrewsbury Shield.

Shrewsbury [Earl of] (Eng) *see* Talbot (John).

Shrewsbury and Wem Brewery (Eng) *see* Wem.

Shrewsbury Shield (Eng) a celebration ale brewed to commemorate Shrewsbury Towns first visit to Wembley. Brewed by the Wood Brewery, Winstantow, Shropshire. *see* Shrew Brew.

Shrimpers (Eng) a 4.1% alc by vol. ale brewed by the Daleside Brewery Ltd., North Yorkshire.

Shriner Cocktail (Cktl) ½ measure brandy, ½ measure sloe gin, 2 dashes Angostura. Stir over ice, strain into a cocktail glass and top with a twist of lemon peel juice.

Shropshire Gold (Eng) a 3.8% alc by vol. golden ale brewed by the Salopian Brewing C°. Ltd., Shropshire.

Shropshire Lad Bitter (Eng) a springtime ale 4.5% alc by vol. draught bitter from the Wood Brewery, Winstantow, South Shropshire.

Shropshire Spring (Eng) a natural spring mineral water from Brockhurst (Source 6).

Shropshire Stout (Eng) a 4.4% alc by vol. stout brewed by Hanby Ales Ltd., Shropshire.

Shrub (Eng) an alcoholic cordial 9.5% alc by vol. produced by Phillips of Bristol.

Shrub (Eng) a mixed drink made of rum, sugar, spices and fruit juices.

Shrubs (USA) a special mixed drink made from spirits and fruit juices to special recipes. Mixed in jugs and served with ice. Often allowed to mature (can be alcoholic or non-alcoholic).

Shtopor (Rus) corkscrew.

Shui (Chi) water.

Shumen (Bul) a D.G.O. wine-producing region in eastern Bulgaria.

Shurb (Arab) drink.

Shy (Arab) tea.

Shypoo (Austr) a slang term for cheap, low quality liquor. Also slang name for public house that sells cheap liquor.

Shypoo Shanty (Austr) the nickname for a bar where poor quality drinks are sold. ·

Shyraz (Euro) an alternative name for the Syrah grape.

Siam Winery (Thai) a winery based in Bangtorud, Samut Sakhon. Grapes are grown on floating vineyards on the plains of the Chao Phraya delta and River Kwai valley. Label: Châtemp.

SIBA (Eng) *abbr*: **S**ociety of **I**ndependent **B**rewers.

Sibarita (Sp) an 1863 vintage Amontillado Sherry produced by Domecq.

Sibenik (Slav) a wine-producing area on the Dalmatian coast.

Siberia (Eng) a 4.7% alc by vol. ale brewed by the Blindmans Brewery Ltd., Somerset.

Sibilla (It) a natural spring mineral water from Scoglio della Volpe, Ascoli, Marche.

Sibin (Ire) the Gaelic for weak beer (low quality). *see* Shebeen.

Sibirskaya (Rus) a grain vodka produced in Siberia 45% alc by vol.

Sibras (Afr) a beer brewed by the Sibras Brewery in Senegal, West Africa.

S.I.C.A (Fr) *abbr*: **S**ociété d'**I**ntérêt **C**ollective **A**gricole. a local society based in the Languedoc. Interested in modernising equipment and technology.

Sica les Viticulteurs de Fort Médoc (Fr) a co-operative winery. (Add): Les Caperans, Cussac-Fort-Médoc. A.C. Haut-Médoc. (Com): Cussac-Fort-Médoc. 55ha. Grape varieties: Cabernet sauvignon 60% and Merlot 40%.

Sica Mouluc (Fr) a wine-producer based in Cognac in the Charente département. Produces méthode traditionelle wines. Noted for Vin sauvage.

Siccus (Lat) thirsty/dry.

Sicera (Isr) the fermented juice of apples from which the word cider derives. *See also* Schekar.

Sichel et Cie (Fr) famous wine merchants of Bordeaux and Burgundy.

Sicilia (It) the Italian spelling of Sicily.

Sicily (It) the largest island in the Mediterranean which, together with Puglia, is the largest wine-producing region in Italy (125000ha). Grape varieties include: Cataratto, Grillo, Nerello cappuccino, Nerello mascalese, Nero d'avola, Zibibbo moscato. Noted mainly for the fortified wine Marsala. *see* Woodhouse (John) and Q Mark.

Sick (Eng) the general term used to describe diseased wines that are unfit for drinking.

Sickershausen (Ger) village (Anb): Franken. (Ber): Steigerwald. (Gro): Schlossberg. (Vin): Storchenbrünnle.

Sid (Arab) *abbr*: the nickname for **Sid**iqi.

Sid (Eng) a 5.2% alc by vol. ale brewed by the Kemptown Brewery C°. Ltd., East Sussex.

Sidamo (Afr) a coffee-producing region in Ethiopia (a pure coffee).

Sidecar (Cktl) ⅓ measure Cognac brandy, ⅓ measure Cointreau, ⅓ measure lemon juice. Shake over ice and strain into a cocktail glass.

Sidecar Cocktail (Cktl) 15mls (⅛ gill) dry gin, 30mls (¼ gill) brandy, juice ¼ lemon. Shake over ice and strain into a cocktail glass.

Sidekick (Eng) 20% alc by vol. single serve fruit-flavoured schnapps sold in a plastic 30mls glass with a plastic lid from Bulmers in Hereford. Flavours include: sour apple, cranberry, grapefruit, vanilla.

Sidekick Beer (Eng) a cask-conditioned ale 1047 O.G. brewed by the home-brew public house The Queen Victoria in London.

Side Pocket for a Toad (Eng) a 3.6% alc by vol. ale brewed by the Tring Brewery C°. Ltd., Hertfordshire.

Sider (Eng) an old spelling of cider.

Sideritis (Gre) a white grape variety grown in Patras.

Sidhu (Ind) the name given to a drink produced from pure cane juice in ancient India.

Sidi Ali (Mor) a natural spring mineral water from Casablanca. Mineral contents (milligrammes per litre): Sodium 26.8mg/l, Calcium 22.4mg/l, Magnesium 7.3mg/l, Potassium 3.4mg/l, Bicarbonates 97.6mg/l, Chlorides 18.5mg/l, Sulphates 31.6mg/l, Nitrates 5.4mg/l, Silicates 14.5mg/l.

Sidi el Kebir (Alg) a natural spring mineral water. Mineral contents (milligrammes per litre): Sodium 34mg/l, Calcium 55mg/l, Magnesium 11mg/l, Bicarbonates 230mg/l, Chlorides 22mg/l, Sulphates 21mg/l, Nitrates 4.8mg/l, Silicates 10.9mg/l. pH 7.03

Sidi Harazem (Mor) a natural spring mineral water from Fès. Mineral contents (milligrammes per litre): Sodium 120mg/l, Calcium 70mg/l, Magnesium 40mg/l, Potassium 8mg/l, Bicarbonates 335mg/l, Chlorides 220mg/l, Sulphates 20mg/l, Nitrates 4mg/l.

Sidi Larbi (Afr) a wine-producing area based near Rabat in Morocco. Produces fine red wines.

Sidiqi (Arab) *abbr*: Sid, the illicitly distilled spirit produced in Saudi Arabia and drunk by the '*expat*' workers in the illegal bars on their domicile compounds. Also known as Sid.

Sidi Raïs (Afr) the brand-name of a rosé wine produced by the UCCVT in Takelsa, Tunisia.

Sidi Thabet (Afr) a large co-operative winery belonging to the UCCVT in Tunisia.

SIDOVAC (Fr) the group of Châteauneuf-du-Pape producers who are based around the town of Orange in the A.O.C. Châteauneuf-du-Pape. (Add): 2260, Route du Grès, 841000 Orange. *see* La Mitrale. 'E'mail: sidovac.chateauneuf@worldonline.fr

Sidra (Port) (Sp) cider.

Sidro (It) cider.

Siebel (USA) the American spelling of Seibel.

Siebel 1000 (USA) a red hybrid grape variety grown in eastern USA.

Siebel 5278 (USA) a white hybrid grape variety grown in eastern USA.

Siebel 5279 (USA) a white grape variety grown in the eastern USA. Also known as Aurora.

Siebel 5409 (USA) a red hybrid grape variety grown in the eastern USA. Also known as Cascade.

Siebel 8357 (USA) a red hybrid grape variety grown in the eastern USA. Also known as Colobel.

Siebel 9110 (USA) a white hybrid grape variety grown in the eastern USA. Also known as Verdlet.

Siebeldingen (Ger) village (Anb): Pfalz. (Ber): Südliche Weinstrasse. (Gro): Königsgarten. (Vins): Im Sonnenschein, Mönchspfad, Rosenberg.

Siebeneich (Ger) village (Anb): Württemberg. (Ber): Württembergisch Unterland. (Gro): Lindelberg. (Vins): Himmelreich, Schlossberg.

Siebengebirge (Ger) bereich (Anb): Mittelrhein. (Gro): Petersberg. (Vils): Königswinter, Niederdollendorf, Oberdollendorf, Rhöndorf.

Sieben Jungfrauen (Ger) vineyard (Anb): Mittelrhein. (Ber): Rheinburgengau. (Gro): Schloss Schönburg. (Vil): Oberwessel.

Siebers Quelle (Ger) a natural spring mineral water from Allgäu.

Siebers Quelle-Monte Classic (Ger) a natural spring mineral water from Allgäu.

Siefersheim (Ger) village (Anb): Rheinhessen. (Ber): Bingen. (Gro): Rheingrafenstein. (Vins): Goldenes Horn, Heerkretz, Höllberg, Martinsberg.

Siegast GmbH (Ger) a brewery. (Add): Holzgasse 37-39, Siegburg D-53721. Brews beers and lagers. Website: http://www.siegburger-brauhaus.de 'E'mail: service@siegberger-brauhaus.de

Siege Ale (Eng) a beer brewed to celebrate the 350th anniversary of the siege of Hereford City in September 1645. Brewed by the Wye Valley Brewery, Hereford. *See also* V.E. Day Ale, V.J. Day Ale.

Siegel Pils (Ger) a 4.8% alc by vol. pilsener brewed by the D.U.B. Brauerei of Dortmund, Westphalia (a dry pilsner lager with a light bitterness).

Siegelsberg (Ger) vineyard (Anb): Rheingau. (Ber): Johannisberg. (Gro): Deutelsberg. (Vil): Erbach.

Siegelsberg (Ger) a vineyard within the village of Erbach, 15.1ha. (90.7%) of which is proposed to be classified as Erstes Gewächs.

Siegerrebe (Ger) a white grape variety, a cross between the Riesling and the Traminer.

Siegersdorf Winery (Austr) a winery. (Add): Sturt Highway, Dorrien, Barossa Valley, South Australia. The winery is based in the McLaren Vale.

Siegert's Distillery (W.Ind) a rum distillery based on the island of Trinidad.

Sieges (Sp) an alternative spelling of Sitges in south-eastern Spain.

Siegsdorfer Petrusquelle (Ger) a sparkling natural spring mineral water (established 1864) from Hochfelln. Mineral contents (milligrammes per litre): Sodium 9mg/l, Calcium 92mg/l, Magnesium 24mg/l, Potassium 1mg/l, Bicarbonates 381mg/l, Chlorides 16mg/l, Sulphates 10mg/l.

Siemens [Peter] (Ger) a seventeenth-century German soldier reputed to have brought the Rhine riesling vine into Spain. Now known as the Pedro Ximénez.

Siena (It) a wine area in Tuscany that is outside Chianti Classico. A sub-area of Chianti Colli Senesi.

Sierk (Fr) a wine-producing area in the Vins de la Moselle district of Lorraine. Produces mainly white wines.

Sierra Alhamilla (Sp) a natural spring mineral water brand.

Sierra Bonela (Sp) a natural spring mineral water brand.

Sierra Cazorla (Sp) a still natural spring mineral water (established 1997) from Virgen de la Esperanza. Mineral contents (milligrammes per litre): Sodium 1.3mg/l, Calcium 77.8mg/l, Magnesium 37.1mg/l, Potassium 0.3mg/l, Bicarbonates 465.4mg/l, Chlorides 2.7mg/l, Sulphates 14.9mg/l, Silicates 7mg/l.

Sierra de Los Padres (Arg) a natural spring mineral water. Mineral contents (milligrammes per litre): Sodium 205mg/l, Calcium 13.5mg/l, Magnesium 4.5mg/l, Potassium 8mg/l, Chlorides 78mg/l, Sulphates 6mg/l, Fluorides <1.5mg/l, Nitrates 18mg/l, Silicates 61mg/l. pH 7.9

Sierra de Montilla (Sp) an area where the fine solera Montilla-Moriles are produced.

Sierra de Salamanca Valtiendas (Sp) a Vino Comarcal in the province of Segovia, Castilla-León.

Sierra Foothills (USA) a wine-producing district consisting of several sub A.V.A. areas within it. Includes: El Dorado, Fiddletown, Amador, Shenandoah Valley.

Sierra Fria (Sp) a natural spring mineral water from El Chumacero, Valencia de Alcántara, Cáceres.

Sierra Jardin (Sp) a natural spring mineral water from Paraje Rio Arquillo, Masegoso, Albacete.

Sierra Nevada Brewing C°. (USA) a brewery (established 1978), moved to new premises in 1989. (Add): 1075 East 20th Street, Chico, California, CA95928. Brews: Sierra Nevada Pale Ale, Sierra Nevada Porter, Sierra Nevada Stout. Website: http://www.sierranevada.com 'E'mail: info@sierranevada.com

Sierra Nevada Pale Ale (USA) a 5.6% alc by vol. top-fermented, bottled pale ale brewed by the Sierra Nevada Brewing C°. in Chico, California.

Sierra Nevada Porter (USA) a 5.9% alc by vol. top-fermented, full-bodied, bottled porter brewed by the Sierra Nevada Brewing C°. in Chico, California.

Sierra Nevada Stout (USA) a 6% alc by vol. top-fermented, bottled stout brewed by the Sierra Nevada Brewing C°. in Chico, California.

Sierras de Jaén (Sp) a still natural spring mineral water. Mineral contents (milligrammes per litre): Sodium 2.5mg/l, Calcium 48.2mg/l, Magnesium 14.6mg/l, Potassium 0.2mg/l, Bicarbonates 172.8mg/l, Chlorides 6.9mg/l, Sulphates 29.2mg/l, Nitrates 5.7mg/l.

Sierra Springs (USA) a natural spring mineral water brand.

Sierra Vista Winery (USA) a winery based in Placerville, Eldorado, California. Grape varieties: Cabernet sauvignon, Chardonnay, Sauvignon blanc and Zinfandel. Produces varietal wines.

Sierre (Switz) a Valais vineyard producing a vin de paille called Soleil de Sierre.

Siete Fuentes (It) a natural spring mineral water from Santulussurgiu (OR), Sardinia. Mineral contents (milligrammes per litre): Sodium 22.1mg/l, Calcium 6.5mg/l, Magnesium 5.5mg/l, Potassium 1.2mg/l, Bicarbonates 32mg/l, Chlorides 37.8mg/l, Sulphates 5.2mg/l, Fluorides 0.1mg/l, Nitrates 1.9mg/l, Silicates 18.8mg/l. pH 7.4

Sietges (Sp) an alternative spelling of Sitges in south-eastern Spain.

Sieur de Limoux (Fr) the name of a Blanquette de Limoux produced by Producteurs de Blanquette de Limoux.

Sievering (Aus) a famous white wine produced in the Vienna region.

Sifa (Tur) a natural spring mineral water (established 1985) from Cercin, Burdur. Mineral contents (milligrammes per litre): Sodium 147.752mg/l, Calcium 68.136mg/l, Magnesium 371.973mg/l, Sulphates 702.4mg/l, Iron 6.331mg/l, Aluminium 6.331mg/l. pH 5.55

Si Fen (Chi) a grain spirit produced in the Shensi province.

Sifi Flip (Cktl) 1 egg yolk, 25mls (1fl.oz) gin, 10mls (½ fl.oz) each of Cointreau, grenadine, lemon juice. Shake well over ice and strain into 125mls (5fl.oz) wine glass.

Sifon (Hol) siphon.

Sifone (It) a name used in Sicily for Mistella. Used in the making of Marsala.

Sifrés (Hol) a natural spring mineral water from Hoensbroek.

Sigerrebe (Ger) see Siegerrebe.

Siggiewi (Euro) a wine-producing area on the island Malta.

Sigille de la Confrérie St. Étienne (Fr) a red seal awarded to particularly good wines by the growers' promotional body in Alsace.

Sigl Brauerei (Aus) a brewery (established 1601) based in Obertrum. Noted for top-fermented Weizenbier.

Siglingen (Ger) village (Anb): Württemberg. (Ber): Kocher-Jagst-Tauber. (Gro): Kocherberg. (Vin): Hofberg.

Siglo Saco Red (Sp) a red wine produced by A.G.E. Bodegas Unidas S.A. Rioja. Made from 35% Garnacha, 15% Mazuelo and 50% Tempranillo grapes. Matured in oak for 2 years and bottle for 10 months. Sold in a hessian sacking-covered bottle (owned by Allied Domecq).

Siglo White (Sp) a dry white wine made by the A.G.E. Bodegas Unidas S.A. Rioja. 100% Viura grapes used (owned by Allied Domecq).

Signal Hill (S.Afr) an inner city winery (established 1997) based in Cape Town, Western Cape. 5ha. Grape varieties: Cabernet sauvignon, Chardonnay, Chenin blanc, Furmint, Grenache, Grenache blanc, Malbec, Muscat d'alexandrie, Petit verdot, Pinot noir, Pinotage, Pontac, Riesling, Shiraz, Tinta, Viognier. Labels: Antica MM, Argile Rouge, Climat de Corsaire, Clos de l'Orange, Crème de Tête, Grand Rouge de Constance, La Siesta, Malwenn, Mathilde, Rosé de Saignée, Straw Wine, Tête Blanche, Vin de Glacière, Vin de l'Empereur. Website: http://www.winery.co.za

Signatory Vintage Scotch Whisky C° Ltd (Scot) blenders (established 1988). (Add): 7-8 Elizafield, Bonnington Ind Estate, Newhaven Road, Edinburgh, Midlothian EH6 5PY. Produces a variety of malt and blended Scotch whiskies (a subsidiary of Edradour Distillery C° Ltd). 'E'mail: signatory@signatory.demon.co.uk

Signature (Fr) a Cognac brandy produced by Hine in Jarnac. Is of an average age of 5 years old.

Signature (Fr) a vintage de luxe cuvée Champagne produced by Jacquesson et Fils from 50% Chardonnay and 50% Pinot noir grapes.

Signature (USA) the American name used for the Japanese Imperial Whiskey produced by Suntory.

Signature (USA) a premium lager beer 1046 O.G. produced by the Stroh Brewery. Is imported into the U.K. by Bass.

Signature Reserve (S.Afr) the label for a red wine (Cabernet sauvignon and Shiraz blend) produced by the Stettyn Winery, Worcester, Western Cape.

Signatures (S.Afr) the label for a range of varietal white wines (Chardonnay and Sauvignon blanc) produced by the Doolhof Estate winery, Wellington, Western Cape.

Signature Series (S.Afr) the label for a range of wines produced by the Jean Daneel Wines winery, Napier, Southern Cape.

Signet (S.Afr) the label for a red wine (Cabernet sauvignon, Merlot and Shiraz blend) produced by the Lushof Estate winery, Stellenbosch, Western Cape.

Signinum (It) a red wine produced in central-western Italy in Roman times.

Sign of Spring (Eng) a 4.6% alc by vol. ale brewed by Bunce's Brewery, Netheravon, Wiltshire.

Signum (S.Afr) the export label for a range of wines produced by the Rooiberg Winery, Robertson, Western Cape.

Signum (Swe) a natural spring mineral water from Hellebrunn, Jeppetorp, Hällefors. Mineral contents (milligrammes per litre): Sodium 5mg/l, Calcium 15mg/l, Magnesium 3.5mg/l, Potassium 0.95mg/l, Bicarbonates 46mg/l, Chlorides 7mg/l, Sulphates 13mg/l, Fluorides 0.45mg/l.

Sign of Spring (Eng) a 4.6% alc by vol. ale brewed by the Stonehenge Ales (Bunces Brewery) Ltd., Wiltshire.

Sigtún Special (Cktl) ⅓ measure dry vermouth, ⅓ measure lemon gin, ⅓ measure Torres medium onion. Stir over ice and strain into a cocktail glass.

S

Sikcho (Kor) vinegar.

Sikera (Gre) strong drink (alcoholic).

Sikes (Eng) the alternative spelling of the name of a British inventor of the hydrometer used to ascertain the proof (alcohol content) of spirits. *see* Sykes Hydrometer.

Silana (It) a sparkling natural spring mineral water from Cosenza. Mineral contents (milligrammes per litre): Sodium 6.8mg/l, Calcium 16mg/l, Magnesium 4.86mg/l, Potassium 3.4mg/l, Bicarbonates 54.05mg/l, Chlorides 0.93mg/l, Sulphates 11.4mg/l, Nitrates 2.2mg/l, Silicates 17.4mg/l. pH 7.69

Silberberg (Aus) *see* Steiermärkisches Landesweingut Weinbauschule Silberberg.

Silberberg (Ger) vineyard (Anb): Ahr. (Ber): Walporzheim/Ahrtal. (Gro): Klosterberg. (Vil): Ahrweiler.

Silberberg (Ger) vineyard (Anb): Ahr. (Ber): Walporzheim/Ahrtal. (Gro): Klosterberg. (Vil): Mayschloss.

Silberberg (Ger) vineyard (Anb): Baden. (Ber): Badische Bergstrasse/Kraichgau. (Gro): Stiftsberg. (Vil): Kraichtal (stadtteil Neuenbürg, Menzingen and Münzesheim).

Silberberg (Ger) vineyard (Anb): Baden. (Ber): Kaiserstuhl-Tuniberg. (Gro): Vulkanfelsen. (Vil): Bahlingen.

Silberberg (Ger) vineyard (Anb): Mosel-Saar-Ruwer. (Ber): Zell/Mosel. (Gro): Rosenhang. (Vil): Ellenz-Poltersdorf.

Silberberg (Ger) vineyard (Anb): Nahe. (Ber): Schloss Böckelheim. (Gro): Paradiesgarten. (Vil): Niedermoschel.

Silberberg (Ger) vineyard (Anb): Nahe. (Ber): Schloss Böckelheim. (Gro): Paradiesgarten. (Vil): Obermoschel.

Silberberg (Ger) vineyard (Anb): Rheinhessen. (Ber): Nierstein. (Gro): Sankt Alban. (Vil): Bodenheim.

Silberberg (Ger) vineyard (Anb): Rheinhessen. (Ber): Wonnegau. (Gro): Domblick. (Vil): Mölsheim.

Silberberg (Ger) vineyard (Anb): Rheinhessen. (Ber): Wonnegau. (Gro): Domblick. (Vil): Monsheim.

Silberberg (Ger) vineyard (Anb): Pfalz. (Ber): Südliche Weinstrasse. (Gro): Bischofskreuz. (Vil): Walsheim.

Silberberg (Ger) vineyard (Anb): Pfalz. (Ber): Südliche Weinstrasse. (Gro): Kloster Liebfrauenberg. (Vil): Niederhorbach.

Silberbügel (Aus) a vineyard site on the banks of the River Danube in the Kremstal region.

Silberbühel (Aus) a vineyard site on the banks of the River Danube situated in the Wachau region, Niederösterreich.

Silbergrube (Ger) vineyard (Anb): Rheinhessen. (Ber): Nierstein. (Gro): Gutes Domtal. (Vil): Mommenheim.

Silbernagel Brauerei (Ger) a brewery based at Bellheim. Brews: Bellheimer Weiz'n Bräu Hefe-Weizen, Bellheimer Weiz'n Bräu Kristall.

Silberquell (Ger) a natural spring mineral water from Baden. Mineral contents (milligrammes per litre): Sodium 7.5mg/l, Calcium 214mg/l, Magnesium 41mg/l, Potassium 4mg/l, Bicarbonates 325mg/l, Chlorides 3.2mg/l, Sulphates 423mg/l, Fluorides 0.8mg/l.

Silberquell (Ger) vineyard (Anb): Baden. (Ber): Badische Frankenland. (Gro): Tauberklinge. (Vil): Tauberbischofsheim (ortsteil Impfingen).

Silberquelle (Aus) a natural spring mineral water from Silberquelle, Brixlegg. Mineral contents (milligrammes per litre): Sodium 6.9mg/l, Calcium 77.8mg/l, Magnesium 30mg/l, Potassium 1.7mg/l, Bicarbonates 273.6mg/l, Chlorides 6.9mg/l, Sulphates 91.8mg/l, Fluorides 0.24mg/l, Nitrates 4.5mg/l. pH 7.6

Silberwasser (Ger) *see* Silverwasser.

Silberweisse (Aus) a white grape variety now no longer grown.

Silbury Golden Organic Bitter (Eng) a 4.5% alc by vol. bitter brewed by Ushers Brewer, Trowbridge, Wiltshire.

Siléar Fiona (Ire) wine cellar.

Silenca Quelle (Ger) a natural spring mineral water. Mineral contents (milligrammes per litre): Sodium 6.4mg/l, Calcium 69mg/l, Magnesium 24mg/l, Potassium 1.1mg/l, Bicarbonates 335mg/l, Chlorides 3.2mg/l, Sulphates 7.1mg/l, Fluorides 0.09mg/l, Nitrates 0.18mg/l.

Silence (Eng) a 5.2% alc by vol. ale brewed by the Buntingford Brewery, Hertfordshire.

Sileni Estates (N.Z) a 100ha winery and estate based in Hawkes Bay, North Island. Grape varieties: Cabernet franc, Cabernet sauvignon, Merlot, Sauvignon blanc. Label: Cellar Selection Saignée.

Sileno (Port) a wine and spirit distributor based in Lisbon. Merged with IDV.

Silent Knight (Eng) a 3.9% alc by vol. cask or bottle conditioned ale brewed by the Dorset Brewing Company, Weymouth, Dorset. *See also* Summer Knight.

Silent Spirit (Eng) the name given to the colourless, odourless and tasteless rectified spirit used in spirit production, also called Neutral or Cologne spirit.

Silent Third (Cktl) ⅓ measure Scotch whisky, ⅓ measure Cointreau, ⅓ measure lemon juice. Shake over ice and strain into a cocktail glass.

Silesian Goblet (Ger) a fine eighteenth century bell-shaped, short knob-stemmed wine glass with a glass lid. Usually heavily engraved. *See also* Silesian Stem.

Silesian Stem (Eng) a pedestal-stemmed glass (circa 1715). *see* Silesian Goblet.

Silex (Fr) chalk and flint soil, found in the Sancerre area of the Central Vineyards in the eastern Loire valley.

Silex [Les] (Fr) the label used by Château Cabrières, in Châteauneuf-du-Pape, southern Rhône for export.

Silia (It) a natural spring mineral water from Silia. pH 7.12

Silicaceous Earth (Eng) a useful fining agent obtained from Spanish, American and South American soils.

Silic Acid (Ger) a compound used to help precipitate out the unwanted materials in wine.

Siliceous (Eng) a soil with a high quartz content. e.g. Sancerre in the Loire. (Fr) = silico.

Silico (Fr) silicon-based soil.

Silico-Calcaires (Fr) silicon and chalk soil.

Siliusbrunnen (Ger) vineyard (Anb): Rheinhessen. (Ber): Nierstein. (Gro): Güldenmorgen. (Vil): Dienheim.

Silk Stockings [1] (Cktl) 35mls (1½ fl.oz) tequila, 35mls (1½ fl.oz) cream, 25mls (1fl.oz) crème de cacao (white), dash grenadine. Blend with a scoop of ice and serve in a tulip glass, decorate with a cherry and a sprinkle of cinnamon on top and serve with straws.

Silk Stockings [2] (Cktl) 25mls (⅕ gill) tequila, 40mls (⅓ gill) evaporated milk, 20mls (⅙ gill) each of white crème de cacao, grenadine. Stir over ice, strain into a goblet, top with a cherry and powdered cinnamon.

Silk Stockings [3] (Cktl) 25mls (1fl.oz) tequila, 10mls (½ fl.oz) white crème de cacao, 10mls (½ fl.oz) grenadine, 2 teaspoons milk powder. Blend altogether with scoop of crushed ice in a blender, pour into a Paris goblet and top with a cherry and powdered cinnamon.

Siller (Hun) rosé or red wine.

Sillerwein (Ger) a deep rosé wine produced from red and white grapes that are mixed before vinification. The juice is only in contact with skins for a short length of time. See also Schillerwein and Schilscherwein.

Sillery (Fr) a Grand Cru Champagne village in the Canton de Verzy. District: Reims.

Sillery (Fr) a red wine produced in the Champagne region.

Sillery [Marquis de] (Fr) a seventeenth-century Champagne salesman who was the first to ship Champagne to London.

Silly Brasserie (Bel) a brewery named after the village based in southern Belgium, noted for Saison de Silly, Double Enghien 7.5% alc by vol., Pink Killer, Silly Scotch, Titje.

Silly Drinking (Eng) see Speed Drinking.

Silly Scotch (Bel) an 8% alc by vol. whiskey malt bottled beer from the Silly Brasserie. Has hops and chocolate aromas.

Silly Titje (Bel) a 5% alc by vol. beer brewed by Silly Brasserie, Silly.

Silva (It) a natural spring mineral water from Orticaia.

Silva and Cosens (Port) a family group who own Dow, Graham and Warre brands of Port.

Silval (Port) Port shippers. Vintages: 1997, 2000, 2003.

Silvana (It) a sparkling natural spring mineral water from Fonte Minerali di Romagna. Mineral contents (milligrammes per litre): Sodium 27.2mg/l, Calcium 85.9mg/l, Magnesium 27.4mg/l, Potassium 3.1mg/l, Bicarbonates 341.6mg/l, Chlorides 10.6mg/l, Sulphates 92.5mg/l, Fluorides 0.13mg/l, Nitrates 0.2mg/l, Silicates 6.7mg/l, Strontium 2.45mg/l. pH 7.38

Silvanaquelle Frankenbrunnen (Ger) a natural spring mineral water. Mineral contents (milligrammes per litre): Sodium 15.2mg/l, Calcium 14.2mg/l, Magnesium 11.2mg/l, Bicarbonates 105mg/l, Chlorides 1.77mg/l, Sulphates 9.79mg/l, Nitrates 0.23mg/l.

Silvaner (Ger) a white grape variety grown throughout Germany, an early ripener it produces wines with a floral and perfumed aroma and flavour. Parent to Bacchus, Ehrenfelser, Morio-Muskat, Optima, Rieslaner, Scheurebe. Known also as Österreicher. (Fr) = Sylvaner.

Silvaner Feodosüsky (Rus) a dry white wine from the Crimean Peninsular. Made from the Silvaner grape.

Silvan Ridge (USA) a winery based in Oregon. Noted for Pinot gris wines.

Silver (Afr) a natural spring mineral water from Kenya.

Silver Acquette (Eng) see Acquette d'Argent.

Silverado Brewing C° (USA) a brewery. (Add): 3020A North Street, Helena Highway, St. Helena, California CA94574. Brews a variety of beers and lager. Website: http://www.silveradobrewingcompany.com

Silverado Cellars (USA) a winery based in Yountville, Napa Valley, California. Grape varieties: Cabernet sauvignon, Chardonnay and Sauvignon blanc. Produces varietal wines.

Silver Bronx (Cktl) 1 measure dry gin, ½ measure dry vermouth, ½ measure sweet vermouth, juice ¼ measure orange, ¼ measure egg white. Shake well over ice and strain into a cocktail glass.

Silver Bullet [1] (Cktl) ½ measure dry gin, ¼ measure kümmel, ¼ measure lemon juice. Shake over ice and strain into a cocktail glass.

Silver Bullet [2] (Cktl) 25mls (1fl.oz) kümmel, 35mls (1½ fl.oz) vodka. Stir over ice and strain into a cocktail glass.

Silver Bullet (Eng) a 4.7% alc by vol. ale brewed by the Bobs Brewing Company Ltd., West Yorkshire.

Silver Cocktail [1] (Cktl) 40mls (⅓ gill) dry gin, 20mls (⅙ gill) bianco vermouth, 1 teaspoon maraschino, 1 teaspoon orange bitters. Shake over ice, strain into a cocktail glass, serve with a cherry and a squeeze of lemon peel juice.

Silver Cocktail [2] (Cktl) 30mls (¼ gill) gin, 30mls (¼ gill) French vermouth, 2 dashes orange bitters, 3 dashes maraschino. Stir over ice, strain into a cocktail glass and add a squeeze of lemon peel juice.

Silver Creek (USA) a natural spring mineral water (established 1952) from Century Springs, Waukesha County, Wisconsin.

Silver Creek Lager (Can) see Sleeman Silver Creek Lager.

Silver Crown (Ger) a Deutscher Sekt (produced by the cuve close method) from Langenbach as part of the Centenary celebrations of Stowells of Chelsea.

Silver Dragon (Wal) a vintage dry cider 7.5% alc by vol. sold in 1 and 2litres PET bottles. Produced by Symonds of Hereford (in Cardiff). *See also* Black Dragon, Gold Dragon, Red Dragon.

Silver Fizz (Cktl) juice ½ lemon, 25mls (⅕ gill) dry gin, 1 teaspoon sugar, 1 egg white. Shake over ice, strain into a highball glass, top with soda water and twist of lemon.

Silver Fox (Eng) a 4.1% alc by vol. ale brewed by the Ossett Brewing C°. Ltd., West Yorkshire.

Silverfresh (Can) a natural spring mineral water from Lake Huron.

Silver Jubilee (Cktl) ½ measure gin, ¼ measure cream, ¼ measure crème de banane. Shake over ice and strain into a cocktail glass.

Silver King (Cktl) ⅕ measure gin, juice ¼ lemon, 1 egg white, 2 dashes gomme syrup, 2 dashes Campari. Shake over ice and strain into a cocktail glass.

Silver King (Eng) a 4.3% alc by vol. ale brewed by the Ossett Brewing C°. Ltd., West Yorkshire.

Silver Lady (Eng) a medium-sweet sparkling perry produced by the Goldwells Company.

Silver Lining (Eng) a 4% alc by vol. bottled wheat beer brewed by the Butterknowle Brewery, Lynesack, Durham.

Silver Link (Eng) a 4.6% alc by vol. ale brewed by the Ossett Brewing C°. Ltd., West Yorkshire.

Silver Mountain Vineyards (USA) a winery based near Los Gatos, Santa Clara, California. Grape varieties: Chardonnay, Zinfandel. Produces varietal wines.

Silver Myn (S.Afr) a label for a range of red and white wines from Zorgvliet Wines, Stellenbosch.

Silver Needle Shou Mei (Chi) a style of Chinese tea.

Silver Oak Cellars (USA) a winery based near Yountville, Napa Valley, California. Grape varieties: Cabernet sauvignon, Chardonnay. Website: http://www.silveroak.com

Silver Peg (Scot) a brand of white rum bottled by Scottish and Newcastle.

Silver Shadow (Eng) a 3.9% alc by vol. bitter ale brewed by the Ossett Brewing C°. Ltd., West Yorkshire.

Silverskin (Eng) the inner skin of the coffee cherry which holds the beans (peaberries). Also known as the Testa.

Silver Snipe (Eng) a label used by the Snipe vineyard in Woodbridge, Suffolk for their wines.

Silver Source (S.Afr) a still natural spring mineral water (established 1999) from Silver Hills, Natal. Mineral contents (milligrammes per litre): Sodium 112mg/l, Magnesium 29mg/l, Potassium 3.9mg/l, Chlorides 165mg/l, Sulphates 74mg/l, Fluorides 1.2mg/l, Nitrates <0.1mg/l. pH 7.37

Silver Special Mild (Eng) a keg light mild 1030 O.G. brewed by the Charles Wells Brewery in Bedford.

Silver Spring (Eng) a still and carbonated natural spring mineral water brand (established 1870). (Add): Park Farm Ind Estate, Park Farm Road, Folkstone, Kent CT19 5EA. Website: http://www.silverspring.co.uk 'E'mail: sales@silverspring.co.uk

Silver Springs (Ven) a still natural spring mineral water (established 1996) from San Diego de Los Altos. Mineral contents (milligrammes per litre): Sodium 4.49mg/l, Calcium 67.2mg/l, Magnesium 7.7mg/l, Potassium 2.1mg/l, Bicarbonates 181mg/l, Chlorides 17.3mg/l, Sulphates 49mg/l, Barium 4.23mg/l, Silicates 4.23mg/l. pH 7.48

Silver Springs Aqua (Ind) a still natural spring mineral water (established 1994) from Gandipet. pH 7.2

Silver Stallion Fizz (Cktl) blend 1 scoop of vanilla ice cream with 40mls (⅓ gill) gin. Pour into a highball glass. Top with soda water, stir and serve with straws.

Silverstone (Cktl) equal amounts of white rum and dry Martini. Stir with ice, strain into a highball glass and add bitter lemon.

Silver Stone (Ire) a natural spring mineral water from Donegal. Mineral contents (milligrammes per litre): Sodium 15mg/l, Calcium 104mg/l, Magnesium 11mg/l, Potassium 1.1mg/l, Bicarbonates 334mg/l, Chlorides 32mg/l, Sulphates 22mg/l. pH 7.2

Silver Streak (Cktl) 1 measure kümmel, 1 measure dry gin. Pour the kümmel through the gin and drink straight.

Silverstream Vineyard (N.Z) a winery. (Add): Giles Road, Clarkville, (RD2) Kaiapoi. 4ha. Grape varieties: Pinot noir, Chardonnay.

Silver Sunset (Cktl) 25mls (1fl.oz) vodka, 10mls (½ fl.oz) apricot brandy, 10mls (½ fl.oz) lemon juice, 75mls (3fl.ozs) orange juice, dash Campari, dash egg white. Shake over ice and strain into an ice-filled highball glass. Top with a cherry and an orange slice and serve with straws.

Silver Tequila (Mex) young tequila not aged, light matured in wax-lined vats so remains colourless, bottled soon after distillation.

Silverthorne Brewery (Wal) a brewery (established 1981) based in Cwmbran, Gwent. Noted for cask-conditioned Druid's Ale 1072 O.G. Celtic Gold 1046 O.G. and keg Springvale Bitter 1033 O.G. The brewery was originally called the Gwent Brewery.

Silverwasser (Ger) a sweet, colourless liqueur, flavoured with aniseed and orange that has a small amount of silver flakes floating in it. *See also* Silberwasser.

Silvestro (It) *see* Mentuccia.

Simart-Moreau (Fr) a Grand Cru Champagne producer. (Add): 51530 Chouilly. Produces: Grande Réserve Brut (25% Chardonnay/75% Pinot noir).

Sîmburesti (Rum) a wine-producing vineyard noted for red wines. Also produces medium-dry white wines.

Simferopol (Ukr) a noted wine-producing area in the Ukraine.

Similan (Thai) the label for a range of rums at 40% alc by vol. produced and bottled by the Sang Som C°. Ltd. Also a Special Rum 80° Proof.

Similkameen Valley (Can) a designated wine region in British Columbia.

Simi Winery (USA) a winery based in the Alexander Valley, Sonoma County, California. Grape varieties: Cabernet sauvignon, Chardonnay, Muscat canelli and Zinfandel. Produces varietal wines.

Simkin (Ind) the Urdu corruption of Champagne (from 1863).

Simon [André] (Fr) a famous author, gourmet and wine entrepreneur 1877–1970.

Simon Brasserie (Lux) a small brewery based in Wiltz.

Simon Brauerei (Ger) a brewery based in Bitburg in the Palatinate. Brews: Bitburger Pils.

Simond (S.Afr) the label for a red wine (Shiraz, Cabernet sauvignon, Malbec and Pinotage blend) part of the Jacques de Savoy range produced by the Vrede en Lust Wine Farm winery, Paarl, Western Cape.

Simondium (S.Afr) a still natural spring mineral water from Franschhoek, Cape Town. Mineral contents (milligrammes per litre): Sodium 5.9mg/l, Calcium 0.5mg/l, Magnesium 0.3mg/l, Potassium 0.7mg/l, Chlorides 8mg/l, Sulphates 0.6mg/l, Fluorides <0.1mg/l, Nitrates <0.1mg/l. pH 6.4

Simonds Bitter (Eng) a keg light bitter 1032 O.G. brewed by the Courage Brewery in Southern England.

Simonds Farso (Malta) a brewery. (Add): The Brewery, Notabile Road, Mriehel BKR 01. Brews a range of beers and lager. Website: http://www.farsons.com 'E'mail: sfc@farsons.com

Simonds Farsons Cisk (Euro) see Farsons Brewery, Farsons Strong.

Simonnet (W.Ind) a producer of Grosse Montagne (a popular local rum brand) on the island of Guadeloupe.

Simonnet-Febvre (Fr) a producer of Crèmant de Bourgogne based at Chablis, Burgundy. (Add): 9 Ave. d'Oberwesel, 89800 Chablis. A négociant-éleveur. Also produces a range of Chablis wines including Premier Crus Fourchaume and Montmains.

Simonsay-Classic Red (S.Afr) the label for a red wine (Cinsaut blend) produced by the Simonsvlei International winery, Suider-Paarl, Western Cape.

Simonsblanc (S.Afr) the label for a white wine (Chenin blanc) produced by the Simonsvlei International winery, Suider-Paarl, Western Cape.

Simon-Selosse (Fr) a Champagne producer. (Add): 20, Rue d'Oger, 51190 Avize. Produces non-vintage wines. Website: http://www.champagne-online.com/simon-sellose 'E'mail: champ.simon-selosse@wanadoo.fr

Simonsgarten (Ger) vineyard (Anb): Pfalz. (Ber): Südliche Weinstrasse. (Gro): Bischofskreuz. (Vil): Roschbach.

Simonsig Wine Estate (S.Afr) a winery based in Stellenbosch. (Add): Box 6, Koelenhof 7605. Produces most styles of varietal wines including a sparkling wine made by the méthode cap classique. Grape varieties include: Cabernet sauvignon, Chardonnay.

Simonsrood (S.Afr) the label for a red wine (Cinsaut) produced by the Simonsvlei International winery, Suider-Paarl, Western Cape.

Simonsvlei Koöperatiewe Wynkelders (S.Afr) a co-operative winery (established 1947) based in Suider-Paarl, Western Cape. 1200ha. (Add): Box 584, Suider Paarl 7624. Grape varieties: Cabernet sauvignon, Chenin blanc, Cinsaut, Colombard, Crouchen, Hanepoot, Merlot, Muscadel, Pinotage, Red jerepigo, Sauvignon blanc, Sémillon, Shiraz. Labels: Extra-Light, Humbro, Johannisberger, Lifestyle, Premier, Simonay plus many varietal wines. Also known as Simonsvlei International. Website: http://www.simonsvlei.co.za

Simpkiss Brewery (Eng) a brewery based in Brierley Hill in the West Midlands. Noted for cask-conditioned AK 1036 O.G. Supreme 1043 O.G. TNT 1050 O.G. and bottled Black Country Old 1052 O.G.

Simply Irish (Eng) a 5.6% alc by vol. ale brewed by the Three Rivers Brewing C°. Ltd., Cheshire.

Simply Natural Canadian Spring Water (Can) a natural spring mineral water from Middlebro, Manitoba.

Simpsons [The] (Eng) a range of flavoured carbonated drinks and flavoured waters from Popzone (set up by Hall & Woodhouse Beverage Division).

Simpson Vineyard (USA) a vineyard within the Miner Valley Vineyards winery based in Madera in the Napa Valley, California. Grape variety: Viognier.

Simunye (S.Afr) the label for a wine that was a joint venture between Backsberg, South Africa and California (now no longer produced).

Sinasappelsap (Hol) orange juice.

Sinclair Estate (Austr) a winery based in the Manjimup region of Western Australia. Grape varieties include: Cabernet sauvignon. Labels: Giovanni, Jezebel.

Sin Crianza (Sp) lit: 'without ageing', applies to wines that may or may not have spent time in cask. Bottled the year following the vintage. Sometimes called Vino Joven. See also Vino de Crianza.

Sinday (Ind) a Hindustan wine made from the sap of palm trees.

Sindhu Safe Water (Ind) a natural spring mineral water brand.

Sinebrychoff Brewery (Fin) a brewery based in Kereva, western Finland and Helsinki in southern Finland. Noted for Sinebrychoff Porter 7.2% alc by vol.

Singapore Gin Sling (Cktl) place some ice in a tumbler. Add 1 measure of dry gin, juice of ½ lemon, 1 teaspoon sugar, dash Angostura. Fill ⅔ soda water, stir, add ¼ measure Curaçao, ¼ measure cherry brandy and decorate with an orange slice.

Singapore Sling [1] (Cktl) original. 50mls (2fl.ozs) gin, juice 1 lemon, 1 teaspoon powdered sugar. Pour over ice in a highball glass. Add soda water, 10mls (½ fl.oz) Cointreau, 10mls (½ fl.oz) cherry brandy, stir, decorate with a slice of lemon and serve with straws.

Singapore Sling [2] (Cktl) 50mls (2fl.ozs) dry gin, 25mls (1fl.oz) cherry liqueur, 2 tablespoons lime juice. Stir together, pour onto ice in a highball glass and add soda water.

Singapore Sling [3] (Cktl) ½ measure dry gin, ¼ measure cherry brandy, ¼ measure lemon juice, Stir over ice in a highball glass, top with soda water and a slice of orange.

Singapore Sling [4] (Cktl) ½ measure dry gin, ½ measure Cherry Heering, dash Bénédictine, dash lemon juice. Shake over ice, strain into a highball glass, top with soda water and slice of lemon.

Sing Beer (E.Ind) a strong malt beer brewed in Kuala Lumpur.

Singeing (Eng) an old method of roasting the coffee beans in which the beans are in direct contact with a naked flame.

Singen (Ger) village (Anb): Baden. (Ber): Bodensee. (Gro): Sonnenufer. (Vins): Elisabethenberg, Olgaberg.

Singerriedel (Aus) a vineyard site on the banks of the River Danube situated in the Wachau region, Niederösterrich.

Singha Drinking Water (Thai) a natural spring mineral water brand.

Singha Lager Beer (E.Asia) a lager beer brewed in Thailand by the Boon Rawd Brewery in Bangkok 6.2% alc by vol.

Singha Soda Water (Thai) a sparkling spring mineral water brand.

Singhboulton (Eng) a 4.7% alc by vol. dark-style organic bitter ale brewed by the Pitfield Brewery, London.

Singing Cups (Jap) *see* Singing Saké Cups.

Singing Ginger (Scot) a slang term for a Whisky Mac (also for ginger wine).

Singing Saké Cups (Jap) a special type of sakazuki cup which has a tube from which the saké is sipped. As you sip air is drawn in with the saké into your mouth to give a whistling sound.

Single (Eng) a request for a '*single*' measure of spirits: ⅙ or ⅕ gill (now 25mls). Usually denotes a whisky.

Single Harvest (Eng) an alternative term for vintage.

Single Malt (Scot) a malt whisky from one distillery.

Single Malt Winter Warmer (Eng) a strong dark golden winter ale from Mitchells Brewery, Lancaster, Lancs 7.5% alc by vol.

Singleton [The] (Scot) a speyside malt whisky from the Auchroisk Distillery (built in 1974). Matured in Sherry casks. Minimum of 10 years old, each bottle carries a vintage date to represent the year in which the malt whisky was filled into the oak casks.

Single Vineyard (S.Afr) the label for a range of wines produced by the Durbanville Hills winery, Durbanville, Western Cape.

Single Vineyard (USA) a term used on bottle labels to denote that the wine is produced from grapes grown in one vineyard area and not imported in from other locations.

Single Whisky (Scot) *see* Single Malt.

Singlings (Eng) the name given to brandy that has been distilled once and before its second distillation.

Siniya (Mor) a copper (or brass/silver) tray used for holding the tea utensils during the making (brewing) of the tea.

Sinker (Eng) the name given to the heavy perforated plate which is used for keeping the cap of the pulp and grape skins submerged below the must during fermentation.

Sinkiang (Chi) a wine-producing province.

Sino-Filipino (Chi) a natural spring mineral water. Mineral contents (milligrammes per litre): Sodium 26mg/l, Silicates 44.6mg/l.

Sinsheim [stadtteil Hilsbach] (Ger) village (Anb): Baden. (Ber): Badische Bergstrasse/Kraichgau. (Gro): Stiftsberg. (Vin): Eichelberg.

Sinsheim [stadtteil Weiler] (Ger) village (Anb): Baden. (Ber): Badische Bergstrasse/Kraichgau. (Gro): Stiftsberg. (Vins): Goldberg, Steinberg.

Sin-Yassus (Gre) cheers (a toast), your good health.

Sinzheim (Ger) village (Anb): Baden. (Ber): Ortenau. (Gro): Schloss Rodeck. (Vins): Frühmessler, Fremersberger, Feigenwäldchen, Klostergut, Sätzler, Sonnenberg.

Sinziger (Ger) a natural spring mineral water from Sinzig, Eifel. Mineral contents (milligrammes per litre): Sodium 140mg/l, Calcium 50mg/l, Magnesium 60mg/l, Potassium 10mg/l, Bicarbonates 650mg/l, Chlorides 70mg/l, Sulphates 50mg/l.

Sioma Natural Melted Drinking Water (Asia) a bottled spring water from Tajikistan.

Sion (Switz) centre of the Valais canton. Famous for Fendant.

Sion Brauerei (Ger) a brewery (established 1511) based in Cologne with its own tavern based at 5-12 Unter Taschen. Noted for Kölschbier. Full name is Joh. Sion Alstadt Bräu.

Sion Kölsch (Ger) a 4.8% alc by vol. kölsch beer brewed by the Joh. Sion Alstadt Bräu, Cologne.

Sioner Klosterberg (Ger) vineyard (Anb): Rheinhessen. (Ber): Wonnegau. (Gro): Sybillenstein. (Vil): Mauchenheim.

Sionon (Ger) a diabetic sekt from Sohnlein Rheingold cellars.

Sip (Eng) to drink a liquid by taking small mouthfuls.

Siphon Bottle (Eng) *see* Soda Syphon.

Siphon Vat (Port) a method of fermentation, once fermentation begins the self-circulation system of the syphon starts. Grape juice is forced up into an

S

open upper tank which, when full opens and lets fermenting juice fall back with considerable force on the 'manta', beating colour out of it (repeated many times). Also known as Autovinification.

Šipon (Slav) a white grape variety grown in the Maribor region, Slovenia. Known as the Furmint in Hungary. *See also* Mesler.

Sipp [Louis] (Fr) an Alsace wine producer. (Add): 68150 Ribeauvillé, Haut-Rhin.

Sippers (Eng) a slang term used in the navy to obtain a small sip of a shipmates' rum ration.

Sipping (Eng) drinking in small mouthfuls, daintily.

Sira (Tur) grape juice.

Sirac (Fr) an alternative spelling for the Syrah grape.

Sirah (S.Am) an alternative spelling of the Petite sirah grape.

Siràly (Hun) a strong, pale beer 6% alc by vol. brewed by the Nagykanizsa Brewery.

Siravar (Czec) a strong dark, malty lager beer brewed by the Michalovce Brewery.

Sir Benfro (Wal) a medium white wine produced by Cwm Deri Vineyard, Martletwy, Pembrokeshire.

Sire (It) a red wine produced by Azienda La Mea di Marco Maci, Brindisi, Puglia. *See also* Vita.

Sir Frederick's Wild Strawberry (Fr) a liqueur brandy base with fraises des bois, pink in colour, produced by Louis Baron 26% alc by vol.

Sir George Brandy (S.Afr) the label for a pot-stilled vintage brandy distilled from Chenin blanc grapes, produced by the Napier Winery, Wellington, Western Cape.

Sirgis (Fr) a sweet muscat wine produced in the Midi.

Siria (Rum) a wine-producing area, part of the Banat Vineyard.

Síria (Port) a white grape variety, also known as the Alva, Côdega and Roupeiro.

Sirius (Fr) an oak-matured A.C. Bordeaux wine produced by Peter Sichel (red and white). Grape varieties: Cabernet sauvignon 45%, Merlot 55%.

Sir James (Austr) the label of a sparkling traditional method wine produced by Hardy's Winery in South Australia.

Sirke (Tur) vinegar.

Sirma (Tur) a natural spring mineral water. Mineral contents (milligrammes per litre): Sodium 407.813mg/l, Calcium 304.608mg/l, Magnesium 106.972mg/l, Bicarbonates 2196mg/l, Chlorides 202.4mg/l, Nitrates 1.947mg/l, Silicates 36mg/l.

Sirop (Fr) syrup.

Sirop de Citron (Fr) a lemon syrup used for sweetening and flavouring (non-alcoholic).

Sirov Vodka (Hol) the brand-name of a vodka produced by De Kuyper 37.5% alc by vol.

Sirrac (Fr) another name for the red Syrah grape.

Sirrah (Fr) an alternative spelling of the Syrah grape.

Sirras (Fr) an alternative spelling of the Syrah grape.

Sir Robert Burnett and Cº. Ltd. (Eng) *see* Burnett gin.

Sir Rogers Porter (Eng) a 4.2% alc by vol. porter brewed by the Earl Soham Brewery, Suffolk.

Sirrus (Eng) a 5% alc by vol. smooth cider produced by Strongbow.

Sir Walter (Cktl) ½ measure Bacardi White Label, ½ measure old brandy, 3 dashes grenadine, 3 dashes Cointreau, 3 dashes lemon juice. Shake over ice and strain into a cocktail glass.

Sir Walt's Liqueur (Eng) a spicy sweet liqueur 40% alc by vol. with curry-style flavours produced by the Hayman Distillery.

Sir William Peel Best Bitter (Eng) a 4.8% alc by vol. best bitter ale brewed by the Old Stables Brewing Company, Bedfordshire.

Sir Winston Churchill (Fr) a de luxe vintage Champagne produced by Pol Roger. *see* Cuvée Sir Winston Churchill.

Sisca (Fr) the brand-name of a crème de cassis produced in Dijon by Lejay-Lagoute 26% alc by vol.

Sise (Tur) bottle/flask.

Sisi (Ger) a cross white grape variety, a cross between the Silvaner and Siegerrebe.

Sisies [Les] (Fr) a Premier Cru vineyard in the A.C. commune of Beaune, Côte de Beaune, Burgundy 8.5ha.

Siskiyou Vineyards (USA) a vineyard based near Siskiyou National Forest, Oregon. 5ha. Produces vinifera wines.

Sistowa (Bul) the brand-name of a local wine.

Sitges (Sp) an area on the coast of Cataluña, south-eastern Spain. Noted for Malvasia and Moscatel sweet, dessert wines.

Sitges (Sp) an eighteenth century sweet Muscatel wine produced in south-eastern Spain.

Sitia (Gre) a wine-producing region on the isle of Crete. Produces an A.O.Q.S. full, robust red wine from the Liatiko grape. Also an A.O.C. sweet version.

Siúcra Fionchaor (Ire) grape sugar.

Siwa (Egy) a natural spring mineral water from Siwa Oasis. Mineral contents (milligrammes per litre): Sodium 44mg/l, Calcium 7.5mg/l, Magnesium 8.7mg/l, Potassium 16.5mg/l, Bicarbonates 116.1mg/l, Chlorides 36mg/l, Sulphates 18mg/l, Fluorides 0.5mg/l, Silicates 11mg/l.

Six [VI] (Eng) a 4% alc by vol. amber malt beer brewed by the Hook Norton Brewery, using First Gold hops.

Six Bells (Cktl) ½ measure dark rum, ¼ measure orange juice, ¼ measure lime juice, dash gomme syrup, 2 dashes Angostura. Shake over ice and strain into a cocktail glass.

Six Bells Brewery (Eng) a brewery (established 1997). (Add): Church Street, Bishop's Castle, Shropshire SY9 4AA. Brews: cask-conditioned Bertie's Rocket Fuel, Big Nevs 3.8% alc by vol., Cloud Nine 4.2% alc by vol., Duck n Dive 4.6% alc by vol., Festival Pale, Little Jem, Marathon Ale 4% alc by vol., Old Recumbent. Website: http://www.bishops-castle.co.uk/SixBells/brewery.htm

Six [6] Dre (Fr) a 5% alc by vol sweet cider produced by Ciderie Bellot SA, Chaource.

Six Etoiles (Fr) a standard litre 'returnable' bottle

1190

(wine) used in France. Is distinguished by the 6 stars around the bottle's neck.

Sixex (Eng) a fine bottled barley wine 1064 O.G. brewed by the Holt Brewery in Manchester.

Six [6.0] (Eng) a 6% alc by vol. bottled beer brewed by Wood's Brewery, Wistanstow, Shropshire.

Six Nations (Scot) a 4.2% alc by vol. golden ale brewed by the Caledonian Brewing Company for the 2006 Six Nations rugby championships.

Six o'Clock Swill (Austr) the title given to the time when pubs close at 6p.m. The rush to drink from the time work closed (5p.m) until the pubs closed (6p.m) was hectic hence the name. Died out in the 1960's when laws changed.

Six Pack (USA) a slang term for the pack of six canned or bottled beers. *See also* Four Pack.

Six Row Barley (Eng) a strain of barley used in brewing that produces heavy beers. The name refers to the number of rows of grain per ear of corn. *See also* Two Row Barley, Four Row Barley.

Sixteenth (Port) a size of cask in the Port (Douro) region.

Sixteen Fortysix [1646] (Eng) a 4.8% alc by vol. bitter ale brewed by the Clearwater Brewery, Devon.

Sixteen Fortyeight [1648] Brewery Company (Eng) a brewery (established 2003) based in Mill Lane, East Hoathly, Lewes, East Sussex. BN8 6QB. Brews a variety of ales including: 1648 Festive 4.8% alc by vol., 1648 Honey Beer 4.1% alc by vol., Original 3.9% alc by vol., 1648 Signature 4.4% alc by vol., 1648 Warrant 4.8% alc by vol., 3 Threads 4.3% alc by vol., Armistice Ale 4.2% alc by vol. Website: http://www.1648brewing.co.uk 'E'mail: Brewmaster@1648brewing.co.uk

Sixteen Sixtyfour [1664] (Fr) a 6.3% alc by vol. light straw coloured, bottled lager brewed by Kronenbourg Brasserie in Strasbourg.

Sixteen Ninetyeight [1698] (Eng) a bottle-conditioned beer at 6.5% alc by vol. brewed by the Shepherd Neame Brewery, Faversham, Kent.

Sixteen Ninetyeight [1698] Ale (Eng) a 4.5% alc by vol. cask-conditioned ale brewed by Shepherd Neame in Kent using malted rye. Also a 6.5% alc by vol. bottled version.

Six Tonner (S.Afr) the label for a red wine (Merlot) produced by the Darling Cellars winery, Swartland.

Sixty Ale (Scot) a strong ale 1060 O.G. brewed by the Alice Brewery in Inverness.

Sixty Shilling Ale [60/-] (Scot) a term for mild beers, dark in colour 1030–1034 O.G. *see* Shilling System.

Sixty Shilling Light (Scot) a beer brewed by the Belhaven Brewery in Dunbar, East Lothian.

Six Vineyards (USA) the label for a red wine (Pinot noir) produced by the Lemelson Vineyards, Willamette Valley, Oregon.

Six X [XXXXXX] (Eng) a popular cask-conditioned bitter 1040 O.G. brewed by the Wadworth Brewery in Wiltshire.

Siyabonga (S.Afr) a winery (established 1998) based in Wellington, Western Cape. 15ha. Grape varieties: Cabernet sauvignon, Chenin blanc, Merlot, Pinotage, Sémillon. Label: Severney.

Sizer [La] (Fr) a vineyard in the A.C. Hermitage, Coteaux de l'Hermitage, northern Rhône.

Sizzano (It) a small town 12 miles north-west of Novarra in Piemonte. Noted for a red wine of the same name.

Sizzano (It) a D.O.C. red wine of Piemonte. Made from 40%–60% Nebbiolo, 15%–40% Vespolina and up to 25% Bonarda novarese grapes. Has to be aged 3 years of which 2 years must be in oak/chestnut cask.

Sizzerane [La] (Fr) the name given to a red A.C. Hermitage wine from the firm of Charpoutier in Tain, Côtes du Rhône.

Sjoes (Hol) a 4.5% alc by vol. bottled special beer brewed by the Gulpener Bier Brouwerij, Gulpen. Combination of Gulpener Pilsner and Old Brown.

Skaal (Scan) denotes 'good health', a toast. *See also* Skol.

Skadarka (Slo) a red grape variety.

Skadarlijska (Ser) a natural spring mineral water from Serbia and Montenegro.

Skaling (Den) the term used when drinking akvavit and a glass of ice cold lager beer.

Skåne Aquavit (Swe) an aquavit flavoured with aniseed, caraway, fennel and herbs.

Skerryvore (Scot) a blended Scotch whisky producd by Arthur Bell and Sons.

Skhou (Rus) the name given to a brand of koumiss that is distilled in Siberia. Also produced in the Caucasus.

Skibsol (Den) lit: 'ship's ale', a tax-free, low-alcohol beer, dark in colour brewed by the Tuborg Brewery 1.9% alc by vol.

Ski Bunny (Punch) heat 300mls (½ pint) beer, pinch of cardamom, cinnamon and ginger, 25mls (1fl.oz) gin, 10mls (½ fl.oz) dark rum until nearly boiling. Pour over 3 beaten egg yolks, whisking until smooth, serve in mugs with a cinnamon stick.

Skiddaw Special Bitter (Eng) a 3.5% alc by vol. bitter ale brewed by the Hesket Newmarket Brewery, Cumbria.

Skier's Smoothie (Cktl) 2 measures Galliano, 1 cup hot strong tea. Pour tea onto Galliano in a wine goblet and drink whilst hot.

Skillogalee Estate (Austr) a vineyard (68ha) based in Clare Valley, South Australia. Grape variety: Riesling.

Skim (Eng) in brewing, a term used for the removal of excess yeast from the top of the fermenting vessel (the best being reserved for the next brew). The surplus yeast is sold to make yeast products.

Skim (Eng) to remove the cream off the top of milk (or skin off the top of hot milk).

Skimmed Milk (Eng) milk (fresh) which has had the cream removed.

Skinful (Eng) a slang term to denote a large

S

consumption of alcoholic beverage. Also used to describe a drunken person.

Skinner's Brewery (Eng) a brewery (established 1997). (Add): Riverside, Newham Road, Newham, Truro, Cornwall TR1 2DP. (Label used by the Brighton Dark Star Brewery for Ale Trail Mild 3.5% alc by vol). Brews: Betty Stoggs 4% alc by vol., Brighton Rock 4% alc by vol., Cliffhanger Porter 5.5% alc by vol., Coastliner, Cornish Blonde 5% alc by vol., Cornish Knocker 4.5% alc by vol., Cornish Storm Lager, Figgy's Brew 4.5% alc by vol., Greenhop Ale 4.2% alc by vol., Heligan Honey 4% alc by vol., Jingle Knockers 5.5% alc by vol., Keel Over 4.2% alc by vol., Pavillion Beast 6% alc by vol., Penguin Stout 4.2% alc by vol., Poppy Ale 4.2% alc by vol., Spriggan Ale 3.8% alc by vol., St Pirans Ale 4.5% alc by vol., Who Put The Lights Out, Wobbly Dog. Website: http://www.skinnersbrewery.com 'E'mail: info@skinnersbrewery.com

Skinner's Old Strong (Eng) a 5.5% alc by vol. ale from the Bitter End Brewery, Cockermouth, Cumbria.

Skinny Pucker's (Eng) a diet RTD range of drinks. Flavours include lemonade and cola. *see* Mrs. Pucker's.

Skins (Eng) the skin of the grape, contains colour and tannin (red varieties).

Skipper Ale (Eng) a 4.2% alc by vol. ale brewed by Wye Valley Brewery, Herefordshire.

Skips (Scot) the alternative name for the long handled wooden shovels used to turn the barley during the malting process in whisky production.

Skiraz (Austr) another name for the red Sirah grape.

Ski Wasser Cocktail (Cktl)(Non-alc) 25mls (1fl.oz) raspberry juice, 25mls (1fl.oz) lemon juice. Pour into an ice-filled highball glass, top with soda water, dress with a slice of lemon and orange and serve with straws.

Skoff [Walter] (Aus) a winery based in Gamlitz, Styria. (Add): Eckberg 16 & 99, 8462 Gamlitz. Grape varieties include: Pinot blanc, Riesling, Traminer, Welschriesling, Zweigelt. Label: Edition.

Skokiaan (S.Afr) a highly alcoholic beverage which is consumed by the black Africans in their shebeens.

Skol (Nor) cheers/good health. *See also* Skaal.

Skol-Caracu (Bra) a brewing group linked with Labatt of Canada.

Skol Lager (Eng) first brewed in Holland in 1959 and now is brewed internationally. Owned by Allied Breweries who brew keg Skol 1037 O.G. in Alloa (Scot), Burton, Romford and Wrexham (Wal), bottled/canned 1035 O.G. Skol Special Strength 1046 O.G. and Extra Strength 1080 O.G.

Skona Lager (Eng) a canned lager beer 1032 O.G. brewed by the Hall and Woodhouse Brewery in Dorset.

Skopelos (Gre) an eastern Mediterranean island that produces wines similar to Malmsey.

Skopje (Ser) a wine-producing region in the south that produces mainly red wines.

Skopsko Export (Ser) the brand-name of a premium lager beer.

Skotsk Whisky (Den) Scotch whisky.

Skouras Winery (Gre) a winery based in Argos, Peloponnesos. Produces Megas Oenos from Aghiorghitiko and Cabernet sauvignon grapes.

Skull Attack (Wal) a cask-conditioned best bitter 1042 O.G. brewed by the Brains Brewery in Cardiff.

Skullcrusher (Eng) the brand-name of a cask-conditioned ale.

Skullsplitter (Scot) an 8.5% alc by vol. strong cask ale brewed by Orkney Brewery, Scottish Isles.

Skummetmælk (Den) skimmed milk.

Skunky (USA) a description of the odour that a beer may have when opened if it has been stored in strong sunlight.

Skurkerabt (Hun) a white grape variety used in Tokaji production.

Skuttlebutt (Austr) a winery based in the Margaret River region of Western Australia. Grape varieties include: Cabernet sauvignon, Merlot, Shiraz.

Skydew (Sing) a pure distilled drinking water pH 6.6–pH 7.2 from Super Coffeemix Manufacturing Ltd., (Add): 2, Senoka South Road, Super Industrial Building, Singapore 758096

Skylark (Eng) a 4% alc by vol. ale brewed by the Butlers Brewery C°. Ltd., Berkshire.

Skyscraper Cocktail (Cktl) ⅜ measure gin, ¼ measure dry vermouth, ⅛ measure orange Curaçao, ⅛ measure lemon juice, ⅛ measure grenadine, dash Angostura. Shake over ice and strain into a cocktail glass.

Sky Vineyards (USA) a winery based in the Sonoma County, California. Grape variety: Zinfandel.

Slack-my-Girdle (Eng) a variety of cider apple.

Sladko Vino (Bul) sweet wine.

Slåenlikør (Den) sloe gin.

Slaghmuylder Brouwerij (Bel) a brewery (established 1860) based in Ninove. Brews: Witkap Pater Dubbele Pater, Witkap Pater Stimulo, Witkap Pater Tripel.

Slàinte Mhath (Scot) the Gaelic for 'good health', traditionally used when drinking a toast with whisky.

Slake (Eng) to satisfy, i.e. 'to slake one's thirst'.

Slaley Estate (S.Afr) a winery (70ha) based in the Stellenbosch, Western Cape. Grape varieties include: Cabernet sauvignon, Chardonnay, Merlot, Pinotage, Savignon blanc, Shiraz. Labels include: Broken Stone, Hunting Family, Lindsay's Whimsy, Planque, Plinque. Website: http://www.slaley.co.za

Slalom (Cktl) ¼ measure Cointreau, ½ measure Bacardi White Label, ¼ measure lime juice. Shake over ice, strain into a cocktail glass and add an olive.

Slalom Lager (Eng) a lager beer 1036 O.G. brewed by Matthew Brown of Lakeland Lager Brewery in Workington, Cumbria. Produces: keg/bottled Slalom D. 1045 O.G. and Slalom International 1068 O.G.

Slammer (Eng) an iced short of neutral-flavoured

spirits (vodka, tequila, schnapps, etc, often flavoured with fruit juices) drunk in one go often accompanying another drink such as beer, lager or wine. *See also* Shot.

Slamnak (Slo) the name given to a late-harvested Riesling wine from a Lutomer estate, Slovenia.

Slane (Ire) the name given to the spade that is used to cut peat from the peat bogs. (Scot) = fal.

Slanghoek Koöperatiewe Wynkelder (S.Afr) a co-operative winery (established 1951) based in Slanghoek, Worcester, Western Cape. 1830ha. (Add): Box 75, Rawsonville 6845. Grape varieties: Cabernet sauvignon, Chardonnay, Chenin blanc, Hanepoot, Jerepigo, Malbec, Merlot, Muscadel, Pinotage, Shiraz, Touriga. Labels: Camera, Vinay, Zonneweelde also produces varietal wines. Website: http://www.slanghoek.co.za

Slankamenkarebe (Aus) an ancient red grape variety rarely grown nowadays.

Slantchev Birag (Bul) lit: 'sunshine coast', a basic dry white wine made from the Rcakztelli grape, is strong and full-bodied.

Slate (Eng) a slang term used for obtaining drinks without payment (on tick, to be paid for at a later date), an illegal practice under the licensing laws. The term derives from the nineteenth century when the debts would be chalked on a slate.

Slate (Eng) a soil style found in the Mosel Valley (Germany), Upper Douro (Portugal), Galicia (Spain). Produces fine wines. (Fr) = ardoise, (Sp) = pizarra.

Slaterand Scott's Grassy Green (Scot) a John Walker and Sons light, fresh blended Scotch whisky produced for the French market.

Slaters Bitter (Eng) a 3.6% alc by vol. bitter ale brewed by the Eccleshall Brewery, Staffordshire.

Slate Square (Eng) *see* Square.

Slatina (Slo) a natural spring mineral water from Levice District, Western Slovakia. Mineral contents (milligrammes per litre): Sodium 183mg/l, Calcium 136.3mg/l, Magnesium 36.5mg/l, Potassium 28.5mg/l, Bicarbonates 677mg/l, Chlorides 184mg/l, Sulphates 11.9mg/l, Fluorides 2.46mg/l, Nitrates 0.21mg/l, Iron 1.34mg/l, Ammonium 1mg/l.

Slatko (Slo) sweet.

Slate 20 (Eng) a 4.5% alc by vol. blended Bourbon mixed drink produced by the Slate Distilling Company (a subsidiary of the Diago group).

Slaughterhouse Block (Austr) a red (Cabernet sauvignon) wine produced by the Rosabrook Estate, Western Australia.

Slaughter House Brewery Cº (Eng) a brewery (established 2003). (Add): Bridge Street, Warwick, Warwickshire CV34 5PD. Brews: Hog Goblin 4.6% alc by vol., Hog Rider 4% alc by vol., Stout Snout 4.4% alc by vol., Summerdaze 3.9% alc by vol., Swillmore Original 4.2% alc by vol., Wild Boar 5.2% alc by vol. 'E'mail: slaughter@trgroup.co.uk

Slaughterhouse Cellars (USA) a winery based in the Rutherford, Napa Valley, California. Grape varieties: Cabernet sauvignon.

Slav (Euro) former Yugoslavia. *see* Slovenia, Croatia, Bosnia-Herzegovina, Serbia, Makedonija, Macedonia, Montenegro. *See also* Cuveno Vino, Kvalitetno Vino, Vrhunsko Vino.

Slavia (Fr) a bière brewed by the Union des Brasseries group.

Slaviantzi (Bul) a vineyard area in east part of Sub-Balkan region. Mainly white wines produced.

Slav Oak (USA) *abbr*: **Slav**inian **Oak**, cooperage from European grown oak.

Slavonski Brod (Cro) a wine-producing town based in northern Croatia.

Slavyanvskaya (Ukr) a natural spring mineral water from Slavyansk, Stavropol Territory, Northern Caucasus. Mineral contents (milligrammes per litre): Sodium 600-800mg/l, Calcium 250-350mg/l, Magnesium 21.9mg/l, Potassium 600-800mg/l, Bicarbonates 1200-1500mg/l, Chlorides 250-350mg/l, Sulphates 143.6mg/l.

Slavyanskoye (Rus) a heavily-hopped beer brewed by the Yantar Brewery.

Sleefkee (Rus) cream.

Sleeman Brewery (Can) a brewery. (Add): 551 Clair Road West, Guelph, Ontario N1L 1E9. Brews: Sleeman Silver Creek Lager 5% alc by vol., Cream Ale 5% alc by vol. and a range of other beers. Website: http://www.sleeman.com

Sleeman Silver Creek Lager (Can) a 5% alc by vol. pilsner-style lager brewed by the Sleeman Brewery, Ontario.

Sleeper (USA) the term given to a wine that is rather special but has not yet been fully recognised.

Sleeper Heavy (Eng) a 5.4% alc by vol. heavy bitter ale brewed by the Beer Engine, Devon.

Sleepiness (Ger) a term used to describe grapes attacked by *Botrytis cinerea*. (Ger) = schläfrigkeit.

Sleeping Draught (Eng) a slang term for a strong bedtime drink or for any drink that contains a drug that induces sleep.

Sleepy Hollow Vineyard (USA) the label for a red wine (Pinot noir) produced by the Barnett Vineyards winery, Santa Lucia Highland, Monterey County, California.

Sleeve (Eng) the name given to a straight glass with no handle.

Sleutel (Hol) *see* De Sleutel.

Sleutel Brouwerij (Hol) a brewery based at Dordrecht, southern Holland (now no longer brews). Owned by Heineken, the name is still used. *see* De Sleutel.

Sleutel Bokbier (Hol) a 6.5% alc by vol. ruby-red, bottled bock beer brewed by Heineken Netherlands Brouwerij, Zoeterwoude.

Slewed (Eng) a slang term for drunk/intoxicated.

Slibovitza (Rum) slivovitz (plum brandy).

Slibowitz (Ger) slivovitz.

Slim and Trim Cocktail (Cktl) 1½ measures dry gin, 4 measures grapefruit juice, artificial sweetener to taste. Shake over ice, strain into a scooped out grapefruit shell with crushed ice and serve with straws.

Slim Jane (Cktl)(Non-alc) equal quantities of orange

juice and tomato juice. Shake over ice with a dash of Worcestershire sauce and strain into a goblet.

Slim Jim (Cktl)(Non-alc) equal quantities of grapefruit juice and tomato juice. Shake over ice with a dash of Worcestershire sauce and strain into a goblet.

Slim Jim (USA) another name for a highball glass.

Slimline (Eng) a range of low-calorie, non-alcoholic, soft 'mixer' drinks from the Coca Cola and Schweppes Beverages Company.

Slimmer's Breakfast (Cktl) 1 egg, 200mls (⅓ pint) cold tea, 1 teaspoon honey. Shake over ice and strain into a goblet.

Slimsta (Eng) the name used by Britvic for a range of fruit crushes and mixers.

Slings (USA) spirit, fruit juice and cordials served in tall glasses with ice.

Slip Slop (Eng) a seventeenth century term for a poor quality, weak (unappetising) drink.

Slipstream (Cktl) ¼ measure brandy, ¼ measure Grand Marnier, ¼ measure Lillet, ¼ measure orange juice, 1 egg white, 2 dashes Angostura. Shake over ice and strain into a cocktail glass.

Slipway (Eng) a 4.2% alc by vol. ale brewed by the Captain Cook Brewery Ltd., Cleveland.

Sliva Plum (Pol) *Prunus domestica* the plum species from which the spirit slivovitz is made.

Sliven (Bul) a vineyard area in north part of Southern Basic region, noted for white wines.

Sliven Misket (Bul) a sub-variety of Red Misket. *See also* Varna Misket.

Slivovica (Slo) an alternative spelling of Sljivovica.

Slivovitz (Pol) a plum brandy made from the dark-blue sliva plum. Fermented, double-distilled and aged in oak. Either colourless or pale gold in colour. *see* Slivovica, Slibovitza, Sljivovica, also made from the Pozega plum 45% alc by vol.

Slivovitza (Slo) an alternative spelling of Sljivovica.

Slivovo (Hun) the local name given for plum brandy.

Slivovitz (Cro) an alternative spelling of Sljivovica.

Sliwowica (Pol) a potato vodka flavoured with plum spirit produced by Polmos 45% alc by vol.

Sljivovica (Ser) a single distilled plum brandy 26% alc by vol. Also spelt Slivovica, Slivowitz.

Sljivovica-Prepecenia (Ser) a double distilled plum brandy 40%–50% alc by vol.

Sloan Estate (USA) a red wine (Cabernet sauvignon) produced in the Napa Valley, California.

Slodowe (Pol) a low-alcohol, dark beer.

Sloeber (Bel) a 7.5% alc by vol. amber coloured, top-fermented, bottle-conditioned special Duvel beer brewed by the Roman Brasserie, Oudenaarde-Mater.

Sloeberry Cocktail (Cktl) 40mls (⅓ gill) sloe gin, 1 dash Angostura. Stir over ice and strain into a cocktail glass.

Sloeberry Fruit Beer (Eng) a seasonal cask-conditioned ale brewed by Lees (J.W.), Middleton, Manchester, Lancashire.

Sloe Comfortable Screw (Cktl) 10mls (½ fl.oz) each of sloe gin, Southern Comfort, 25mls (1fl.oz) vodka, 100mls (4fl.oz) orange juice. Pour

ingredients into an ice-filled highball glass. *See also* Slow Comfortable Screw.

Sloe Driver (Cktl) as for a Screwdriver but using a measure of sloe gin in place of the vodka.

Sloe Gin (Eng) a sloe-flavoured gin. Made by steeping ripe sloes that have been pricked with a pin in gin with sugar, matured for six months (some are left much longer) then strained and bottled. Traditional name is Stirrup cup 25% plus alc by vol. (Den) = slåenlikør.

Sloe Gin Cocktail (Cktl) ½ measure sloe gin, ¼ measure dry vermouth, ¼ measure sweet vermouth. Stir over ice and strain into a cocktail glass.

Sloe Gin Collins (Cktl) 40mls (⅓ gill) sloe gin, juice ½ lemon. Shake over ice, strain into an ice-filled collins glass, top with soda, decorate with a lemon slice, orange slice, cherry and serve with straws.

Sloe Gin Fizz (Cktl) 1 teaspoon powdered sugar, 35mls (1½ fl.oz) sloe gin. Shake over ice, strain into an ice-filled highball and top with soda water.

Sloe Gin Flip (Cktl) 1 egg, teaspoon sugar, 25mls (1fl.oz) sloe gin, 25mls (1fl.oz) cream. Shake over ice, strain into a flip glass and top with grated nutmeg.

Sloe Gin Rickey (Cktl) put 2 ice cubes into a highball glass. Add juice of ½ lime, 90mls (¾ gill) sloe gin. Stir and top with soda water.

Sloe Tequila Cocktail (Cktl) ⅔ measure tequila, ⅓ measure sloe gin, juice ¼ lime. Blend together with scoop of crushed ice in a blender, pour into an ice-filled old-fashioned glass and dress with sliced cucumber.

Sloe Vermouth (Cktl) ½ measure sloe gin, ½ measure French vermouth, 10mls (½ fl.oz) lemon juice. Shake over ice and strain into a cocktail glass.

Sloppen (Hol) to sip.

Sloppy Joe (Cktl) 25mls (1fl.oz) brandy, 50mls (2fl.ozs) pineapple juice, 25mls (1fl.oz) Port, 2 dashes Cointreau. Shake over ice and strain into a cocktail glass.

Sloppy Joe Cocktail (Cktl) 20mls (⅙ gill) Bacardi White Label, 20mls (⅙ gill) French vermouth, 2 dashes grenadine, 2 dashes Cointreau, juice of a lime. Shake over ice and strain into a cocktail glass.

Slops (Eng) denotes waste or spilt beer either from a drip trap sited below the beer tap or from half consumed glasses of beer.

Slops (Eng) a slang term for poor quality drink.

Slops (Scot) a term sometimes used for the residue in the pot-still after the first distillation.

Sloshed (Eng) a slang term for drunk/intoxicated.

Slotsmollen Brewery (Den) a brewery based in Kolding.

Slovenia (Slo) the home to three wine regions: Primorska, Posavje, Podravje. Grape varieties: Laski rizling, Chardonnay, Pinot blanc, Gewürztraminer, Ranina, Šipon. *see* Tiger Milk.

Slovenian Summer (Punch) 1 bottle Laski riesling, 3

measures Amontillado Sherry, 1 sliced lemon, borage. Mix altogether, chill down for 2 hours, add 550mls (1pint) soda water, stir and serve in highball glasses with ice.

Slovenija (Slo) an alternative spelling of Slovenia.

Slovenske (Slo) a wine produced in Slovenia.

Slovin (Slo) a popular brand of Slivovitz.

Slow Comfortable Screw (Cktl) ⅓ measure sloe gin, ⅓ measure Southern Comfort, ⅓ measure orange juice. Shake over ice and strain into a cocktail glass. See also Sloe Comfortable Screw.

Slow Fermentation (W.Ind) a method used in rum production that may take 12 days, dunder is included and produces a heavy-style rum.

Sludge Wines (Eng) a term given to denote blended wines with many varieties of wines contained in it which has little or no character or individuality. They are completely unmemorable and totally without personality.

Slug (Eng) a slang term for a drink of spirits.

Slug (USA) a slang term for a single measure of spirit, usually served in a very small glass and drunk in one mouthful.

Slug of Blue Fish-Hooks (USA) a slang term used in local inns for a measure of applejack.

Sluknov Brewery (Czec) an old brewery (established circa 1514) based in north-western Czec.

Slurp (Eng) to drink noisily.

Small Beer (Eng) see Strong Ale.

Small Beer (Eng) an ancient term for a weak, low quality beer.

Small Beer (Eng) a modern term for a half-pint of draught beer of a half-pint (250mls) bottle of beer.

Small Brewers Revenge (Eng) the brand-name of a draught beer 1134 O.G. produced by the Jolly Roger Brewery.

Small Bulls Bitter (Eng) a bitter beer brewed by the Mouldon's Brewery in Sudbury, Suffolk.

Small Independent Brewers Association (Eng) abbr: S.I.B.A. now renamed The Society. Set up by Peter Austin.

Smaragd (Aus) a term used in Wachau to describe wines of 12% alc by vol. with the highest level of ripeness (may reach 14% alc by vol. in best vintages). Minimum sugar level of 18.2° KMW. See also Steinfeder, Federspiel.

S.Maria degli Angeli (It) a natural spring mineral water from Regione Basilicata. Mineral contents (milligrammes per litre): Sodium 25mg/l, Calcium 19.5mg/l, Magnesium 7mg/l, Potassium 18mg/l, Bicarbonates 139.6mg/l, Chlorides 12mg/l, Sulphates 7.3mg/l, Fluorides 0.86mg/l, Nitrates 25mg/l, Silicates 64.7mg/l. pH 6.7

Smart Cool Purified Water (Chi) a bottled purified water brand.

Smash (Cktl) ¼ measure vodka, ¼ measure Mandarine Napoléon, ¼ measure blackberry liqueur, ¼ measure lemon juice. Shake over ice, strain into a cocktail glass and top with a twist of orange peel juice.

Smashed (Eng) a slang term to denote a very drunken person.

Smashes (USA) spirit, sugar cubes, mint and fruit served over ice in an old-fashioned glass.

Smederevka (Ser) a white wine from the Smederevo area of the Serbia region. Made from the Smederevka and Welschriesling grape. Is also produced in Macedonia.

Smederevo (Ser) a wine-producing region based on the south bank of the river Danube. Noted for white wines made from the Smerderevka and Welschriesling grapes.

Smeets Distillerie (Bel) a large distillery based in Hasselt which produces a fine range of jenevers, advocaat, cocktail and fruit liqueurs.

Smeralda (It) a natural spring mineral water from Endine.

Smeraldina (It) a natural spring mineral water from Smeraldina. Mineral contents (milligrammes per litre): Sodium 30.5mg/l, Calcium 13.1mg/l, Magnesium 7.9mg/l, Potassium 1.56mg/l, Bicarbonates 50.34mg/l, Chlorides 52.78mg/l, Sulphates 10.62mg/l, Fluorides 0.15mg/l, Nitrates 9.9mg/l, Silicates 10.99mg/l. pH 6.66

S.Michele (It) a natural spring mineral water from La Perle, Vaie. Mineral contents (milligrammes per litre): Sodium 2.1mg/l, Calcium 5.6mg/l, Magnesium 0.7mg/l, Potassium 0.7mg/l, Chlorides 0.4mg/l, Sulphates 4mg/l, Nitrates 2.6mg/l, Silicates 11mg/l.

Smild (Eng) a 3.8% alc by vol. ale brewed by the Rother Valley Brewing C°., East Sussex.

Smile Cocktail (Cktl) 20mls (⅙ gill) dry gin, 20mls (⅙ gill) grenadine, 2 dashes lemon juice. Shake over ice and strain into a cocktail glass.

Smiler (Cktl) ½ measure dry gin, ¼ measure Italian vermouth, ¼ measure French vermouth, dash Angostura, 2 dashes orange juice. Shake over ice and strain into a cocktail glass.

Smiles Brewery (Eng) a brewery based in Bristol. Noted for cask-conditioned Exhibition Bitter 1051 O.G. March Hare 4% alc by vol. Brewery Bitter 1036 O.G. and Whisky Ale.

Smiling Cocktail (Cktl) ⅔ measure dry white wine, ⅓ measure dry ginger ale, dash Cognac. Stir gently over ice, strain into a Champagne saucer and add a cherry and an orange slice.

Smiling Duchess (Cktl) ⅓ measure Lillet, ⅓ measure dry gin, ⅙ measure apricot brandy, ⅓ measure crème de noyeau. Stir over ice, strain into a cocktail glass and add a cherry.

Smiling Ivy (Cktl) ⅓ measure dark rum, ⅓ measure peach brandy, ⅓ measure pineapple juice, 1 egg white, dash lemon juice. Shake over ice and strain into a cocktail glass.

Smiling Through (Cktl) ⅓ measure Grand Marnier, ⅓ measure dark rum, ⅓ measure maraschino, dash lemon juice, dash grenadine. Shake over ice, strain into a cocktail glass and add a cherry.

Smirnoff (Pol) a vodka that is now produced in the U.K. and USA. Main styles: Red Label, White Label 37.5% alc by vol. Black Label 40% alc by vol. and Blue Label 43% alc by vol. Also available as a range of flavoured vodkas at 37.5% alc by vol.

S

Black 'n' Blue (crushed forest berries), Bloody (peppers, tomatoes and spices), Creamed (vanilla and burnt spices), Twisted (orange, lime, pink grapefruit). *See also* Appleback and Vodka Mudshake (part of the Diago group).

Smirnoff Ice (Pol) a triple distilled 5% alc by vol. Smirnoff vodka based mixed bottled drink that has a taste of lemon, red and black label varieties.

Smirnoff Mule (Pol) a Smirnoff Red Label vodka with the addition of lime and ginger, sold in a bronze coloured bottle.

Smirnovskaya (Rus) a sparkling natural spring mineral water from Stavropol Territory, Northern Caucasus. Mineral contents (milligrammes per litre): Sodium 600–800mg/l, Calcium 250–350mg/l, Magnesium <50mg/l, Potassium 600–800mg/l, Bicarbonates 1200–1500mg/l, Chlorides 250–350mg/l, Sulphates 800–1000mg/l, Fluorides 1.2mg/l, Iron 3.9mg/l, Silicates 43.6mg/l.

Smith (N.Z) a 3ha winery. (Add): 73 Princess Street, Martinborough, North Island.

Smith [George and J.G.] (Scot) a highland malt whisky distillers. The only distillers allowed to have exclusive use of The Glenlivet. Other distilleries may only hyphenate their name with Glenlivet. Part of Seagram. *see* Glenlivet (The).

Smith [John] (Eng) a brewery based in Tadcaster, Yorkshire. Taken over by Courage in 1970. Noted for cask-conditioned John Smith Bitter 1036 O.G. keg Chestnut 1033 O.G. Midland Mild 1036 O.G. Tawny Light 1032 O.G. Old Tom 1037 O.G. Magnet 1040 O.G. John Smith's Lager 1036 O.G. and bottled Double Brown 1041 O.G. Also cask-conditioned Yorkshire Bitter.

Smith [Samuel] (Eng) the oldest brewery in Yorkshire, based in Tadcaster. Still uses wooden casks. Noted for cask-conditioned ales.

Smith Bowman Distillery (USA) a Bourbon whiskey distillery based in Sunset Hills, Fairfax County, Virginia. Noted for fine Virginia Gentleman 45% alc by vol.

Smith-Madrone Vineyards (USA) a winery (established 1971) based near St. Helena, Napa Valley, California. Grape varieties: Cabernet sauvignon, Chardonnay, Johannisberg riesling and Pinot noir. Produces varietal wines.

Smithwicks AFB (Ire) an alcohol-free bitter from Guinness 0.05% alc by vol.

Smithwicks Ale (Ire) a keg/bottled ale 1036 O.G. brewed by the Irish Ale Brewery in Kilkenny.

Smith Woodhouse (Port) vintage Port shippers. Vintages: 1870, 1872, 1873, 1875, 1878, 1880, 1881, 1884, 1887, 1890, 1896, 1897, 1900, 1904, 1908, 1912, 1917, 1920, 1924, 1927, 1935, 1945, 1947, 1950, 1955, 1960, 1963, 1966, 1970, 1975, 1977, 1980, 1983, 1985, 1991, 1994, 1995, 1997, 1998, 2000, 2003. Owned by Symingtons Family Estates.

Smith Woodhouse Vale D. Maria (Port) a single quinta of Smith Woodhouse.

Smoke Cured (Scot) refers to the malted barley for malt whisky which is peat smoked as it is dried. *see* Peat Reek.

Smoked Beer (Ger) *see* Rauchbier.

Smoke-Room (Eng) originally a room in a public house where customers retired to smoke (now known as the lounge). Banned 2007.

Smoke Stack Lightning (Eng) a 5% alc by vol. ale brewed by the Bank Top Brewery Ltd., Lancashire.

Smoking Loon (USA) a label for the Don Sebastiani winery, Sonoma Country, California.

Smoky (Eng) a term used to describe the bouquet on some Chardonnay and Sauvignon blanc wines.

Smooch (Eng) a 5% alc by vol passion fruit-flavoured drink produced by Bass for Valentine's day. *see* Hoopers Hooch.

Smook [Anthony] (S.Afr) a winery (30ha) based in Norder-Paarl, Western Cape. Grape varieties: Cabernet sauvignon, Chardonnay, Merlot, Pinotage, Shiraz. Website: http://www.smookwines.co.za

Smooth (Eng) a term used to describe wines that are mature and have rounded off the tannin, acidity and extract especially on the finish on the palate.

Smooth Bitter (Eng) a 3% alc by vol. bitter from Burtonwood, Warrington, Cheshire.

Smoothie (Eng) a non-alcoholic drink of one or more fruit purées.

Smooth [Robinson's] (Eng) a bitter ale 3.8% alc by vol. brewed by the Robinson's Brewery.

Smothers Winery (USA) a winery based in Santa Cruz Mountains, Santa Cruz, California. Grape varieties: Cabernet sauvignon, Chardonnay, Gewürztraminer, Johannisberg riesling, Pinot noir and Zinfandel. Produces varietal and table wines.

Smouch (Eng) an old brew of ash tree leaves boiled in iron sulphate with sheep's dung for an imitation of black tea because true tea was so scarce. For green tea, elder buds were used. Produced mainly in the late eighteenth century (circa 1784).

Smudge Pots (Austr)(USA) stoves that are burned through the night to protect the vines against frost.

Smugglers (Eng) a dark barley wine 1070 O.G. brewed and bottled by the St. Austell Brewery in Cornwall.

Smugglers Grog (Eng) a 5.5% alc by vol. winter warmer ale with a dark creamy appearance. Brewed by Thwaites in Lancashire.

Smugglers Mild (Eng) a 4% alc by vol. mild ale brewed by the Darwin Brewery, Tyne & Wear.

Smugglers Tipple (Eng) a 5.5% alc by vol. rich amber winter warmer ale brewed by St. Austell Brewery in Cornwall (available December to March).

Snakebite (Austr) a half pint lager, half cider and 25mls blackcurrant cordial.

Snakebite (S.Afr) the label for a range of fortified wines (Golden jerepiko/Hanepoot) produced by the Porterville Cellars winery, Swartland, Western Cape.

Snake Bite (Eng) a ½ pint Guinness and ½ pint cider mixed.

Snake Bite (USA) a ½ pint lager and ½ pint cider mixed.

Snake Bite (Eng) a 5.5% alc by vol. cider and lager mix from the Aston Manor Brewery, Birmingham.

Snake-in-the-Grass (Cktl) ¼ measure dry vermouth, ¼ measure dry gin, ¼ measure Cointreau, ¼ measure lemon juice. Shake over ice and strain into a cocktail glass.

Snapdragon (Eng) a 4.5% alc by vol. bottle-conditioned ale enriched with Chinese five spices. Brewed by The Salopian Brewing Company, Shrewsbury, Shropshire.

Snaps (Den) an alternative spelling of Schnapps.

Snaps (Eng) an old slang name for a drink made from an equal quantity of gin and schnapps.

Snarlsberg Lager (Wal) a 4.5% alc by vol. lager beer brewed by SA Brain & C°. Ltd., South Glamorgan.

Sneck Lifter (Eng) a winter warmer beer brewed by Jennings in Castle Eden Brewery, Cockermouth, Cumbria 5.1% alc by vol.

Sneeuberg (S.Afr) a natural spring mineral water. Mineral contents (milligrammes per litre): Sodium 11mg/l, Calcium 23mg/l, Magnesium 89mg/l, Bicarbonates 122mg/l, Chlorides 15mg/l, Sulphates 25mg/l, Fluorides 1mg/l, Nitrates 4.4mg/l. pH 7.9

Snifter (Eng) a slang term for a quick drink.

Snifter (USA) a name given to the nosing glass (balloon glass).

Snipe Vineyard (Eng) a vineyard (established 1977) (Add): Snipe Farm Road, Clopton, Woodbridge, Suffolk. 0.65ha. Grape variety: Müller-Thurgau. Uses the Silver Snipe label.

Snob Screen (Eng) above the bar counter, a pivoted screen which allowed the upper classes to drink in private in the nineteenth century.

Snoozy Suzy (Eng) a 4.3% alc by vol. bitter ale brewed by The Dog House Brewery C°., Cornwall.

Snoqualmie Falls Brewing C° (USA) a brewery. (Add): 8032 Falls Avenue, S E Box 924, Snoqualmie WA98065. Brews beers and lager. Website: http://www.fallsbrew.com

Snowball (Cktl) 25mls (1fl.oz) advocaat, dash lime cordial. Shake well over ice, strain into an ice-filled highball glass, stir in lemonade, decorate with a cherry and orange slice and serve with straws.

Snowball (Eng) a commercially made bottled cocktail by the Goldwell C°. Contains advocaat, lime juice and lemonade.

Snowball Cocktail [1] (Cktl) ⅓ measure gin, ⅙ measure anisette, ⅙ measure (white) crème de menthe, ⅙ measure crème de violette, ⅙ measure sweetened cream. Shake over ice and strain into a cocktail glass.

Snowball Cocktail [2] (Cktl) ¾ measure gin, ¼ measure anisette, 25mls (1fl.oz) cream. Shake over ice and strain into a cocktail glass.

Snow Bird (USA) a natural spring mineral water brand.

Snow Cap Lager (Afr) a lager beer brewed by the Tanzania Breweries in Tanzania.

Snowdonia Brewery (Wal) a micro-brewery based near Shrewsbury. Formerly at Bryn Arms, Gellilydan, Gwynedd. Brews: Celt, Choir Porter, Gingersnap, Meiron Bitter, Mel-Y-Moelwyn Best Bitter, Rhyls' Revenge 7% alc by vol. and Snowdon Strong Bitter.

Snowdonia Park (Wal) a brewery. (Add): Waunfawr, Caernarfon, Gwynedd LL55 4AQ. Brews: Snowdonia Gold 4.7% alc by vol., Welsh Highland Bitter 5% alc by vol. Website: http://www.snowdonia-park.co.uk 'E'mail: info@snowdonia-park.co.uk

Snowdon Strong Bitter (Wal) a bitter brewed by Snowdonia Brewery near Shrewsbury.

Snowflake (Chi) the brand-name of a lager-style beer.

Snowflake Cocktail (Cktl) ⅖ measure vodka, ⅕ measure advocaat, ⅖ measure orange juice, 2 dashes Southern Comfort, 2 dashes Galliano. Shake over ice, strain into a highball glass, top with lemonade and a little cream, dress with a cherry and a slice of orange.

Snowhite (Eng) a 4.2% alc by vol. ale brewed by the Castle Rock brewery, Nottinghamshire.

Snow Joke (Eng) a 4.5% alc by vol. dark beer brewed by Ridleys Hartford End, Chelmsford, Essex.

Snow Line Natural Water (USA) a slightly acidic natural spring mineral water from DeBorgia, Montana. Mineral contents (milligrammes per litre): Sodium 2.3mg/l, Calcium 2.6mg/l, Magnesium 1.4mg/l, Potassium 0.07mg/l, Chlorides <1mg/l, Sulphates <1mg/l, Nitrates 0.07mg/l, Silicates <0.005mg/l. pH 5.2

Snowman's Revenge (Eng) a 4.4% alc by vol. cask beer produced by Whitbread at Castle Eden. Ingredients include spruce bark, juniper berries, satsuma oranges.

Snowpack (Afr) a natural spring mineral water from Kenya.

Snow Queen (Asia) a vodka brand distilled in Kazakhstan.

Snow Valley Mountain (USA) a slightly acidic natural spring mineral water (established 1973) from the Appalachian Mountains, Pennsylvania. Mineral contents (milligrammes per litre): Sodium 2.7mg/l, Chlorides 4.2mg/l, Sulphates 1mg/l, Nitrates 1.3mg/l. pH 5.44

Snowy Ale (Eng) a winter ale brewed by the Cotleigh Brewery, Wiveliscombe, Somerset.

Snowy Mountains Mineral Water (Austr) a natural spring mineral water brand.

SnoZone (N.Z) a still natural spring mineral water (established 2001) from Hihitahi. Mineral contents (milligrammes per litre): Sodium 5.21mg/l, Calcium 42.2mg/l, Magnesium 2.39mg/l, Potassium 0.9mg/l, Bicarbonates 135mg/l, Chlorides 6.1mg/l, Sulphates 4.6mg/l, Fluorides 0.07mg/l, Nitrates 0.184mg/l, Silicates 18.8mg/l. pH 8.0

Snug (Eng) a small room in a public house, usually used for private drinking.

Snyder Cocktail (Cktl) ¾ measure dry gin, ¼ measure

S

anisette, 25mls (1fl.oz) cream. Shake over ice and strain into cocktail glass.

SO₂ (Eng) *abbr:* Sulphur-dioxide.

Soak (Eng) a slang term for a person who is always intoxicated (drunk), who drinks excessively, who drinks continuously.

Soave (It) a small town 15 miles east of Verona in the Veneto. Name is given to famous dry white wine of region.

Soave (It) a D.O.C. white wine from Veneto. Made from 100% Garganega, may include up to 15% Chardonnay or other grapes including Trebbiano di Soave. D.O.C. also applies to sparkling wines. Also Soave Classico. (*See* Classico). Is classed Superiore if total alc. content is 11.5% by vol. Also a Recioto di Soave D.O.C G. (*See*).

Sober (Eng) having no alcohol in the body/not intoxicated. (Gre) = amethustos.

Soberano (Sp) a 2 year old solera brandy produced by Gonzalez Byass 38% alc by vol.

Soberba (Bra) a natural spring mineral water from Fonte Kátia. Mineral contents (milligrammes per litre): Sodium 41.59mg/l, Calcium 11.08mg/l, Magnesium 0.13mg/l, Potassium 0.62mg/l, Bicarbonates 98.48mg/l, Chlorides 10.56mg/l, Sulphates 31.3mg/l, Fluorides 0.23mg/l, Nitrates 0.1mg/l. pH 8.28

Soberbio (Sp) a solera brandy produced by Bodegas 501. *See also* Mary Cruz, 501 Etiqueta Amarilla.

Sobernheim (Ger) village (Anb): Nahe. (Ber): Schloss Böckelheim. (Gro): Paradiesgarten. (Vins): Domberg, Marbach.

Sobernheim-Steinhardt (Ger) village (Anb): Nahe. (Ber): Schloss Böckelheim. (Gro): Paradiesgarten. (Vins): Johannisberg, Spitalberg.

Sober Sundae (Cktl)(Non-alc) 200mls (⅓ pint) freshly brewed (iced) coffee, ¼ lemon, 1 scoop vanilla ice cream. Blend in a blender, pour into a highball glass, top with soda water and ground cinnamon.

Sobota Brewery (Czec) a brewery based in Eastern Czec.

Sobr (Wal) sober.

Sobre (Fr) sober.

Sobreira (Port) cork oak.

Sobrero (Port) oak.

Sobretabla (Sp) in the Sherry region new fortified racked wine which is placed into cleaned casks. Fortified on top of wood.

Soca (Eng) a golden rum and tropical fruit-flavoured drink.

Socalcos (Sp) the Galician name for vineyard terraces.

Sochu (Jap) a neutral spirit made from grain or sweet potatoes.

Sociale Cooperativa di Mezzocorona (It) a producer of sparkling wine made by the metodo tradizionale in Trentino-Alto-Adige. Labels include Rotari.

Social Wine (Eng) a term used for any wine that is drunk socially without food, i.e. Sherry and sparkling wine.

Sociedad Agrícola (Sp) a large co-operative winery

based in La Seca, Rueda. Is noted for Verdejo Palido (a light and fruity white wine).

Sociedade Agrícola da Quinta da Avelada (Port) a small winery based in northern Portugal. Produces Vinhos Verdes.

Sociedade Agrícola da Quinta de Santa Maria (Port) a large Vinho Verde producer. (Add): Carreira, 4750 Barcelos. Owns the Quinta do Tamariz and Quinta da Portela vineyards.

Sociedade Agrícola dos Vinhos Messias (Port) a noted Portuguese producer of a sparkling wine by the traditional method.

Sociedade Brasileira de Vinhos, Ltda. (Bra) a leading wine-producer in Brazil.

Sociedade Central de Cervejas (Port) *abbr:* S.C.C. a brewery group which has two thirds of the Portuguese market with their Preta and Sagres beers. Has plants at Coimbra and Vialonga.

Sociedade Com. Abel Pereira da Fonseca (Port) a winery based in the Dão region. Produces Viriatus (a Dão wine).

Sociedade Comercial dos Vinhos de Mesa de Portugal (Port) *abbr:* SOGRAPE. Largest wine producer. Includes Aveleda (Vinho Verde) and Mateus Rosé.

Sociedade Constantino (Port) Vintage Port shippers. Vintages: 1912, 1927, 1935, 1941, 1945, 1947, 1950, 1958, 1966.

Sociedade da Quinta da Aveleda (Port) *see* Quinta da **Aveleda.**

Sociedade dos Vinhos do Porto Constantino (Port) noted shippers of Dão wines in northern Portugal.

Sociedade dos Vinhos Vice-Rei (Port) a noted shipper of Dão wines in northern Portugal.

Sociedade Vinhos Unico, Ltda. (Bra) a leading wine-producer based in southern Brazil.

Sociedad General de Vinos (Sp) a bodega based in Elciego in the Rioja Alavesa.

Sociedad Vinícola Laserna (Sp) a winery (established 1974) by Viña Real S.A. (Add): Finca San Rafael, Laserna Laguardia, Alva. 59ha. in the Rioja Alavesa. Grape varieties: Garnacha 7%, Graciano 5%, Mazuela 5%, Tempranillo 70% and Viura 13%. Only red wine is produced. *see* Viñedos del Contino.

Société Anonyme de Magenta (Fr) a co-operative Champagne producer. Produces vintage and non-vintage wines sold under the Marguerite Christel label. Vintages: 1971, 1973, 1976, 1981, 1985, 1991, 1994, 1995, 1996, 1998, 1999, 2000, 2001.

Société Civile de La Romanée-Conti (Fr) a seal seen on the label and cork of all wines from the Romanée-Conti winery. The owners of La Romanée-Conti in Vosne-Romanée, Côte de Nuits, Burgundy. Also owns La Tâche, Côte de Nuits, Burgundy.

Société Coopérative de Saint Yzans de Médoc (Fr) a co-operative winery. (Add): 33340 St. Yzans de Médoc. A.C. Médoc. (Com): St. Yzans. Grape varieties: Cabernet 45% and Merlot 55%.

S

Société Coopérative Vigneronne des Grandes Caves Richon-le-Zion et Zikhron-Yaacv (Isr) a co-operative formed in the early 1900's. Produces 75% of Israel's wine under name of Carmel.

Société de Récoltants (Fr) *abbr*: S.R. a company created by wine growers in the Champagne region who share vinification equipment.

Société des Brasseries du Haut Ogooué (Afr) a brewery based in Gabon which brews a pilsener-style lager beer 6% alc by vol.

Société des Produits d'Armagnac [Marquis de Montesquiou] (Fr) an Armagnac producer. (Add): Route de Cazaubon, 32800 Eauze.

Société de Viticulture du Jura (Fr) a society for the information and promotion of Jura wines.

Société d'Intérêt Collective Agricole (Fr) *see* S.I.C.A.

Société Hellenique des Vins et Spiritueux (Gre) a large winery based in Greece.

Société Socovin (Afr) a winery based in Casablanca, Morocco. Is noted for Domaine de Ben Naceaur.

Société Vinicole de Perroy (Switz) a wine-producer based in the Vaud.

Society [The] (Eng) the original name for the Small Independent Brewers Association.

Society Cocktail (Cktl) ⅔ measure dry gin, ⅓ measure French vermouth, 2 dashes grenadine. Stir over ice and strain into a cocktail glass.

Society of Independent Brewers (Eng) *abbr*: SIBA. (Add): The Siba Office, P.O. Box 101, Thirsk, North Yokrkshire. YO7 4WA. Website: http://www.siba.co.uk 'E'mail: brewersenquiries@siba.co.uk

Socio (Sp) the name given to a partner in a co-operative winery.

Socosani (Peru) a natural spring mineral water from Socosani. Mineral contents (milligrammes per litre): Sodium 134.3mg/l, Calcium 91mg/l, Magnesium 69mg/l, Potassium 10.1mg/l, Bicarbonates 66mg/l.

Socrate (S.Afr) the label for a red wine produced by the Monterosso Estate winery, Stellenbosch, Western Cape.

Sød (Den) sweet (taste).

Soda Fountain (USA) the American name for a soda syphon.

Soda Fountain (USA) the service area in drug stores, etc. where soda water and carbonated drinks are dispensed.

Soda Jerk (USA) an old slang name for a person that serves at a soda fountain in a drug store.

SODAP (Cyp) the Vine Products Co-operative Marketing Union Ltd. (established 1947) based in Limassol and near Paphos, it works on behalf of the growers. Produces most styles of wines. Labels include Island Vines (a range of red and white wines).

Soda Pop (USA) the name given to any carbonated soft drink.

Soda Tonic (USA) tonic water.

Sodavand (Den) fruit-flavoured soda water.

Soda Water (Eng) a sparkling water containing the alkaline sodium bicarbonate. (Den) = danskvand,

(It) = acqua gassosa/acqua di seltz, (Pol) = woda sodowa.

Sodden (Eng) a slang term used to describe a person who is drunk (intoxicated). Usually a person who is perpetually drunk.

Sodium Benzoate (Eng) a form of benzoic acid which is used to stop a fermentation.

Sødmælk (Den) full milk/whole milk (un-skimmed).

Söderåsen (Swe) a natural spring mineral water from Söderåsens Källa.

Soest (Ger) village (Anb): Mosel-Saar-Ruwer. (Ber): Obermosel. (Gro): Gipfel. (Vins): Sites not yet chosen.

Soet Hanepoot (S.Afr) a sweet dessert, golden, honey-flavoured wine from the Koelenhof Koöperatiewe Wynkelder.

Soet Karoo (S.Afr) a winery (established 2000) based in Prince Albert, Western Cape. 0.6ha. Grape varieties: Muscat d'alexandrie, Petit verdot. Website: http://www.soetkaroo.co.za

Soetwynboere Koöperaise (S.Afr) a winery. (Add): Box 127, Montagu 6720. Produces varietal wines.

Sofi Mini Blanc de Blanc (USA) a canned wine (complete with drinking straw) produced by the Niebaum-Coppola winery in the Napa Valley from 10% Muscat cannelli, 70% Pinot blanc, 20% Sauvignon blanc.

Sofrino (Rus) a natural spring mineral water (established 2001). Mineral contents (milligrammes per litre): Sodium 64mg/l, Calcium <0.5mg/l, Magnesium <0.5mg/l, Potassium 5.6mg/l, Bicarbonates 122mg/l, Chlorides 1mg/l, Sulphates 38.4mg/l, Fluorides 0.4mg/l, Nitrates 1.1mg/l.

Soft (Eng) a term used to describe wines that have plenty of fruit on the palate. If wines are too soft they become weak and flabby.

Soft Drinks (Eng) a term given to non-alcoholic fruit drinks. i.e. lemonade, coca cola, squashes etc. (Den) = alkoholfri drik.

Softening Wine (Eng) a wine used to soften hard (tannic) wines so as to make them mature earlier.

Soft Water (Eng) a water that has a low mineral content. Whilst it is not ideal for brewing ales, tea and coffee infuse more easily (although some quality in the taste is lost).

Soft Wines (USA) wines that have a very low alcohol content.

Soge-Vinas (Sp) a large bodega in Rioja. Owned by Pedro Domecq. Has 571ha. in the Rioja Alavesa.

Sogno Uno (It) lit: 'dream one', a red wine produced for the American market in the Lazio region from Cesanese 70%, Sangiovese 20% and Montepulciano 10%. Is noted for its label depicting a semi-nude female.

SOGRAPE (Port) *abbr*: Sociedade Comercial dos Vinhos de Mesa de Portugal. Portugal's largest wine company that owns over 500ha. and has Barca Velha, Ferreira Wine and Port company, Mateus Rosé, Quinta da Leda, Quinta das Carvalhais, Qunita de Azevedo (Vinho Verde) and Vila Real within its portfolio.

S

Soha (Iran) a natural spring mineral water (established 1997) from Besh Ghardash Spring, Soha. Mineral contents (milligrammes per litre): Sodium 57mg/l, Calcium 53mg/l, Magnesium 28mg/l, Bicarbonates 204mg/l, Chlorides 67mg/l, Sulphates 116mg/l. pH 7.3

Sohat (Leb) a natural spring mineral water from Falougha, Lebanon. Mineral contents (milligrammes per litre): Sodium 3.5mg/l, Calcium 31.3mg/l, Magnesium 5.2mg/l, Potassium 0.5mg/l, Bicarbonates 105.2mg/l, Chlorides 5.1mg/l, Sulphates 10.9mg/l, Fluorides 0.01mg/l, Nitrates 1.8mg/l. pH 7.9

Sohlander Blauborn (Ger) a natural spring mineral water. Mineral contents (milligrammes per litre): Calcium 30.8mg/l, Magnesium 7.8mg/l, Bicarbonates 36.8mg/l, Sulphates 96mg/l.

Sohnlein (Ger) a noted producer of sekt by the cuve close method.

Soho (Eng) the name of a 24% alc by vol. lychee-based liqueur from J.R. Parkington (part of Pernod-Ricard).

Soho Drinks Ltd (Eng) distillers (established 2001). (Add): Hardres Court, Canterbugry, Kent CT4 6EN. Produces a wine range of spirits and alcohol-based drinks. Website: http://www.dillonsspirits.co.uk

Soho Brewing C°. (Eng) a brewery based in London. Brews: Pale Ale, U.S. Red Beer, London Porter and a Bavarian-style wheat beer.

Söhrenberg (Ger) vineyard (Anb): Württemberg. (Ber): Remstal-Stuttgart. (Gro): Kopf. (Vil): Neustadt.

Soif (Fr) thirst (avoir soif = 'to have thirst').

Soil (Eng) the general term for the top layer of earth (land surface) which is made up of disintegrated rock, humus, water and air. Plays an important part in grape production and other vegetation used in beverage production (cereals, hops, tea, coffee, etc.). see Alluvial Soil, Calcerous, Clay, Loam, Loess, Schist.

Soilly (Fr) a Cru Champagne village in the Canton de Dormans. District: Épernay.

Soir [Le] (Eng) the brand-name of up-market table wines from Grants of St. James.

Soju (Kor) a Korean rice wine, strong in alohol it is usually drunk as an apéritif.

Sojuzplodoimport (Rus) the old Soviet foreign trade organisation, established in 1966 it now no longer exists.

Sok (Cro)(Pol)(Rus) juice/fruit juice.

Soko (Ser) a natural spring mineral water brand from Serbia and Montenegro.

Sokol Blosser Winery (USA) a winery based in Dundee Hills, Willamette Valley, Oregon. Produces varietal wines. Grape varieties include: Pinot noir.

Sol (S.Am) a 4.5% alc by vol. straw coloured, bottled lager beer brewed by Cerveceria Moctezuma S.A., Monterrey, Mexico.

Solado (It) an orange-flavoured liqueur.

Solaia (It) a red I.G.T. wine produced by Antinori in the Chianti Classico region from 20% Cabernet franc and 80% Cabernet sauvignon grapes.

Solana De Ramirez (Sp) the label of a Riojan wine produced by S.A.T. Arana, Abalos, Rioja.

Solan de Cabras (Sp) a still natural spring mineral water from Beteta, Cuenca. Mineral contents (milligrammes per litre): Sodium 5mg/l, Calcium 59.3mg/l, Magnesium 25.8mg/l, Potassium 0.9mg/l, Bicarbonates 279.4mg/l, Chlorides 8.1mg/l, Sulphates 18mg/l, Fluorides 0.4mg/l, Nitrates 2.1mg/l, Silicates 7.2mg/l. pH 7.4

Solano Brewery (USA) a brewery based in Solano, California that is noted for steam beer.

Solano County (USA) a wine district in northern California. Produces most styles of wines.

Solanos (Sp) the name given to the warm winds from the east that blow over the Rioja region in the Spring.

Solar (Port) manor/manor house.

Solar (Sing) a natural mineral water produced by the Polar Water Distillery Pte Ltd. (Add): 371, Beach Road, Keypoint 16-02, Singapore 199597. Mineral contents (milligrammes per litre): Sodium 9.2mg/l, Calcium 18mg/l, Magnesium 4mg/l, Potassium 15mg/l, Bicarbonates 82mg/l, Chlorides 10mg/l, Sulphates 7.5mg/l. pH 7.4 Website: http://www.chateaudeloei.com

Solar das Bouças (Port) a Vinho Verde producer. (Add): Prozelo, 4720 Amares. Grape variety: Loureiro.

Solar de Francesas (Port) a winery based in Bairrada. Produces red and white wines.

Solar de Ribeiro (Port) a Vinho Verde producer. (Add): S. Lourenço do Douro, 4630 Marco de Canaveses.

Solar de Samaniego (Sp) from the Bodegas Alavesas S.A. in Rioja. All classes of wines are produced.

Solares (Sp) a natural spring mineral water from Solares, Cantabria. Mineral contents (milligrammes per litre): Sodium 89.3mg/l, Calcium 72.9mg/l, Magnesium 16.5mg/l, Potassium 1.8mg/l, Bicarbonates 251.9mg/l, Chlorides 148.9mg/l, Sulphates 33.6mg/l, Fluorides 0.1mg/l, Nitrates 3.5mg/l, Silicates 8.5mg/l.

Solbaerrom (Den) a fruity liqueur.

Sol de Mayo (Cktl) ½ measure Scotch whisky, ⅒ measure orange juice, ⅛ measure Cointreau. Shake over ice and strain into a cocktail glass.

Solé (It) a still and sparkling natural spring mineral water (established 1977) from Nuvolento (BS), Lombardy. Mineral contents (milligrammes per litre): Sodium 2.6mg/l, Calcium 108mg/l, Magnesium 31.1mg/l, Potassium 43mg/l, Bicarbonates 439.3mg/l, Chlorides 2.9mg/l, Sulphates 19.3mg/l, Fluorides 0.1mg/l, Nitrates 6.6mg/l, Silicates 6mg/l. pH 7.42 Website: http://www.solewater.com

Solear (Sp) a term meaning 'sunning', describes the exposure of the grapes to the sun (sol) for 24–48 hours in the Sherry region.

Soledad (USA) a noted wine town based in the Salinas Valley, Monterey, California.

Soleil de Sierra (Switz) a Vin de Paille wine from

1200

S

Sierre in Valais made from Fendant and Malvasia grapes.

Soleil du Valais (Switz) a white wine produced in Valais from the Fendant grape.

Soléo (Sp) a full-flavoured Fino Sherry from Sandeman in Jerez. *See also* Don Fino, Dry Seco.

Solera (Sp) a system of blending and maturing Sherry. Gives a consistent standard product. Consists of a series of casks from which a measured amount of wine (maximum 40%) is removed from one cask and is replaced by younger wine from another cask and so on. *see* Criadera.

Solera Brandy (Sp) a brandy de Jerez. D.O. rules were established in 1989. Solera: aged 6 months in butt, Solera Reserva: minimum 1 year in butt, Solera Gran Reserva: minimum 3 years in butt.

Solera Madeira (Mad) on a label the date must be the date of the original wine. May start drawing off 10% of wine after 5 years. Solera may exist for only 10 years, it must then all be bottled or returned to stock lotes.

Solera Manzanilla (Sp) a full, dry, Manzanilla Sherry produced by Antonio Barbadillo in Sanlúcar de Barrameda.

Solera Manzanilla Pasada (Sp) an old, pale, dry 20 year old Manzanilla Sherry produced by Antonio Barbadillo in Sanlúcar de Barrameda.

Solera Nineteen Hundred [1900] (Sp) a brandy produced by De Terry.

Solera Nineteen Fourteen [1914] (Sp) a fine, rare Amontillado Sherry produced by Berisfords.

Solera Privada (Sp) a solera gran reserva brandy produced by Croft.

Soleras (It) an alternative term used for Vergine Marsala even if a solera has not been used.

Solera Selecta Brandy (Sp) a brandy aged in American oak for 5 years. Produced by Torres in the Penedés region.

Solestice (Eng) a 4.7% alc by vol. ale brewed by the Three Tuns Brewery, Shropshire.

Solicchiato (It) a dessert wine produced at the Vila Fontana winery in Cerasuola di Vittoria in south-eastern Sicily.

Solicitor's Ruin (Eng) a 5.6% alc by vol. ale from Judges Brewery in Warwickshire.

Solide (Fr) denotes a full-bodied, well-balanced wine.

Solijans (N.Z) a 5ha winery based in 263 Lincoln Road, Henderson, North Island. Noted for Sherry-style wines. Grape varieties: Chardonnay, Gewürztraminer, Sauvignon blanc. Produces still and sparkling wines. Also has a vineyard at Riverlea.

Solimar (Sp) the name used by De Muller for their inexpensive range of table wines.

Solina (Fin) a natural spring mineral water brand.

Solitaire (Aus) the label for a red wine (Blaufränkisch, Cabernet sauvignon and Zweigelt blend) produced by the Feiler-Artinger winery, Rust, Burgenland.

Solitaire (Eng) a deep finger bowl with two lips used for inserting glasses in order to clean them or to chill them before use.

Solitude (S.Afr) the label for a red wine (Shiraz) produced by the Fairview winery, Suider-Paarl, Western Cape.

Söll (Aus) a winery based in Gamlitz, Styria. (Add): Sernau Steinbach 63a, 8462 Gamlitz. Grape varieties include: Gewürztraminer, Muskateller, Pinot blanc, Riesling. Produces a range of wines.

Sollar (Asia) a natural spring mineral water from Azerbaijan. Mineral contents (milligrammes per litre): Sodium 57.2mg/l, Calcium 65.8mg/l, Magnesium 34.5mg/l, Potassium 41mg/l, Chlorides 17.5mg/l, Sulphates 42mg/l, Nitrates 3mg/l. pH 7.6

Söllingen (Ger) village (Anb): Baden. (Ber): Badische Bergstrasse/Kraichgau. (Gro): Hohenberg. (Vin): Rotenbusch.

Solms–Delta (S.Afr) a winery (established 1690) based in Franschhoek, Western Cape. 12ha. Grape varieties: Carignan, Grenache blanc, Grenache noir, Mourvèdre, Shiraz, Viognier. Labels: Amalie, Hiervandaan, Lekkerwijn. Website: http://www.solms-delta.com

Solnechnaya Dolina (Rus) a sweet white, dessert wine from the Crimean Peninsular.

Solomon Cocktail (Cktl) ⅓ measure advocaat, ⅓ measure orange juice, dash Cointreau. Shake over ice, strain into a flute glass, top with iced Champagne and a cherry.

Solonis (Fr) an American vine used for grafting in the Rhône.

Solopaca Bianco (It) a D.O.C. white wine from Campania. Made from the Coda di volpe, Malvasia di candia, Malvasia toscana, Trebbiano toscano and Uva cerreto grapes grown in the commune of Solpaca plus 3 others in the province of Benevento.

Solopaca Rosso (It) a D.O.C. red wine from Campania. Made from the Aglianico, Piedirosso, Sangiovese and Sciascinoso grapes grown in the commune of Solpaca and part of 3 others in the province of Benevento.

Solotoje Polje (Ukr) a table wine produced near Cherson in the Ukraine.

Solstice (Eng) a 4% alc by vol. ale from the Dark Star Brewery in Brighton (under the Dark Star label). *see* Black Hole, Dark Star.

Solstice Stout (Eng) a 5% alc by vol. stout brewed by Hoggleys, Northamptonshire.

Solstis (Eng) a non-alcoholic 'energy drink' produced by Beecham Products in Middlesex.

Soluble Coffee (Eng) the old name for instant coffee.

Solubles (USA) the nickname for instant coffee.

Soluble Tea (Eng) *see* Instant Tea.

Soluble Tea (Jap) the alternative name for green tea powder.

Solutré-Pouilly (Fr) a town in the Mâconnais, southern Burgundy. Vineyards in the communes of Pouilly-Fuissé and Saint Véran.

Solway Mist [May-Oct] (Scot) a 5.5% alc by vol. summer ale brewed by the Sulwath Brewers Ltd., Kirkcudbrightshire.

Sol y Sombra (Sp) lit: 'sun and shadow', a drink

consisting of a half measure gin and half measure Spanish brandy. Drunk by Spanish sailors.

Sol y Sombra Cocktail (Cktl) ½ measure golden rum, ¾ measure apricot brandy, ¼ measure white rum, 1 measure pineapple juice, dash Angostura, juice ¼ lemon. Blend with a scoop of crushed ice in a blender, pour into a scooped out pineapple shell, replace the top and serve with straws pushed through the top.

S.O.M. (It) *abbr*: **S**uperior **O**ld **M**arsala. The old style name, denotes ageing for two years and 18% alc by vol.

Som (Rum) the local name for the Furmint grape.

Som (Thai) juice.

Soma (Ind) a potent alcoholic beverage prominently used in the (Vedu/Vedic) Hindu religious ceremonies. Made from various plants.

Sombra (Sp) the alternative name for the '*cap*' of skins that forms at the top of the fermenting vat.

Sombrero Cocktail (Cktl) 1 measure Kahlúa served frappé in a flute glass with fresh cream floated on top.

Somerbosch Wines (S.Afr) a winery (established 1950) based in Stellenbosch, Western Cape. 80ha. Grape varieties: Cabernet sauvignon, Chardonnay, Chenin blanc, Merlot, Pinotage, Sauvignon blanc, Shiraz. Label: Kylix. Website: http://www.somerbosch.co.za

Somerley (Eng) a natural spring mineral water from Ringwood, Hampshire. Mineral contents (milligrammes per litre): Sodium 1.8mg/l, Calcium 1mg/l, Magnesium 0.1mg/l, Potassium 0.7mg/l, Chlorides 5.7mg/l, Sulphates 2mg/l, Nitrates 0.1mg/l.

Somerlust (S.Afr) the export label for a range of wines produced by the Viljoendrift wines winery, Robertson, Western Cape.

Somers Distillers (W.Ind) a noted liqueur producer in Bermuda, noted for Bermuda Gold.

Somerset and Dorset (Eng) a 4.4% alc by vol. bitter ale brewed by the Cottage Brewing Company, West Lydford, near Yeovil, Somerset.

Somerset Cider (Eng) a medium-sweet cider produced by Showerings.

Somerset Cider Brandy C° Ltd (Eng) cider distillers (established 1989). (Add): Burrow Hill, Kingsbury Episkopi, Martock, Somerset TA12 5BU. Produces a range of ciders and applejack. Website: http://www.ciderbrandy.co.uk 'E'mail: apples@ciderbrandy.co.uk

Somerset Cooler (Cktl)(Non-alc) 40mls (⅓ gill) apple juice, 40mls (⅓ gill) Ceylon tea, dash lemon juice, dash gomme syrup. Stir over ice in a highball glass and top with a slice of lemon.

Somerset Crossing (Austr) a winery (established 1969). (Add): 1 Emily Street, Victoria. Grape varieties: Cabernet sauvignon, Chardonnay, Merlot, Riesling, Sauvignon blanc, Shiraz. Noted for late-harvest Riesling wines.

Somerset [Electric] Brewery (Eng) a brewery (established 2003). (Add): New Inn, Halse, Taunton, Somerset TA4 3AF. Brews: B.T.S. 4.3% alc by vol.,

Golden Age of Steam 4.2% alc by vol., Mark 1 3.9% alc by vol., Somerset Sunrise 4.8% alc by vol. Website: http://www.newinnhalse.co.uk 'E'mail: web@newinnhalse.co.uk

Somerset Red Streak (Eng) a 7.4% alc by vol. bottled cider from Thatcher's of Somerset.

Somerset Royal (Eng) a cider brandy distilled from cider made with Somerset apples by Pass Vale Farm Distillery 42% alc by vol.

Somerset Special (Eng) a cask-conditioned bitter ale1043 O.G. brewed by the Hardington Brewery in Somerset.

Somerset Spring (Eng) a natural spring water bottled for the East Indies market by a small family firm.

Somerset Sunrise (Eng) a 4.8% alc by vol. ale brewed by the Somerset (Electric) Brewery, Somerset.

Somerset West (S.Afr) a wine-producing area in the Cape province.

Something Special (Scot) a de luxe Scotch whisky produced by Hill Thompson and C°. in Edinburgh 40% alc by vol (part of Seagram).

Somlauer Auslese (Hun) the name used to market Somloi Furmint.

Somló (Hun) a small wine-producing district in north-eastern Hungary. Noted for quality dry, white wines produced from the Riesling and Furmint grapes. Also spelt Somlyó.

Somloi Furmint (Hun) a fragrant dry white wine produced in Somlyó on Lake Balaton. *see* Somlauer Auslese.

Somlyó (Hun) *see* Somló.

Sommelier (Fr) wine waiter, also the name of a style of corkscrew. *see* Waiter's Friend.

Sommelier Winery (USA) a winery based in Mountain View, Santa Clara, California. Grape varieties: Cabernet sauvignon, Chardonnay, Petite syrah and Zinfandel. Produces varietal wines.

Sommerach (Ger) village (Anb): Franken. (Ber): Maindreieck. (Gro): Kirchberg. (Vins): Katzenkopf, Rosenberg.

Sommerau (Ger) village (Anb): Mosel-Saar-Ruwer. (Ber): Saar-Ruwer. (Gro): Römerlay. (Vin): Schlossberg.

Sommerberg (Fr) an A.C. Alsace Grand Cru vineyard at Niedermorschwihr and Katzenthal, Haut-Rhin 28ha.

Sommerberg (Ger) vineyard (Anb): Baden. (Ber): Markgräflerland. (Gro): Lorettoberg. (Vil): Ebringen.

Sommerberg (Ger) vineyard (Anb): Württemberg. (Ber): Kocher-Jagst-Tauber. (Gro): Kocherberg. (Vil): Criesbach.

Sommerberg (Ger) vineyard (Anb): Württemberg. (Ber): Württembergisch Unterland. (Gro): Schozachtal. (Vil): Abstatt.

Sommerberg (Ger) vineyard (Anb): Württemberg. (Ber): Württembergisch Unterland. (Gro): Schozachtal. (Vil): Löwenstein.

Sommerberg (Ger) vineyard (Anb): Württemberg. (Ber): Württembergisch Unterland. (Gro): Schozachtal. (Vil): Unterheinriet.

S

Sommerhalde (Ger) vineyard (Anb): Baden. (Ber): Breisgau. (Gro): Burg Lichteneck. (Vil): Bombach.
Sommerhalde (Ger) vineyard (Anb): Baden. (Ber): Ortenau. (Gro): Schloss Rodeck. (Vil): Eisental.
Sommerhalde (Ger) vineyard (Anb): Württemberg. (Ber): Remstal-Stuttgart. (Gro): Kopf. (Vil): Korb.
Sommerhalde (Ger) vineyard (Anb): Württemberg. (Ber): Württembergisch Unterland. (Gro): Salzberg. (Vil): Eberstadt.
Sommerhausen (Ger) village (Anb): Franken. (Ber): Maindreieck. (Gro): Not yet assigned. (Vins): Reifenstein, Steinbach.
Sommerheil (Ger) vineyard (Anb): Rheingau. (Ber): Johannisberg. (Gro): Daubhaus. (Vil): Hochheim.
Sommerleithen (Aus) a vineyard site on the banks of the River Danube in the Kremstal region.
Sommerloch (Ger) village (Anb): Nahe. (Ber): Kreuznach. (Gro): Pfarrgarten. (Vins): Birkenberg, Ratsgrund, Sonnenberg, Steinrossel.
Sommerstuhl (Ger) vineyard (Anb): Franken. (Ber): Maindreieck. (Gro): Ravensburg. (Vil): Güntersleben.
Sommerwende (Ger) vineyard (Anb): Rheinhessen. (Ber): Wonnegau. (Gro): Bergkloster. (Vil): Hangen-Weisheim.
Sommet (S.Afr) the label for a red wine (Shiraz blend) produced by the Mont du Toit Kelder winery, Wellington, Western Cape.
Somontano (Sp) a Denominación de Origen based north of Zaragoza in the province of Hesca in the Pyrénées foothills. 2000ha. Most of the wine is red produced from Moristel, Garnacha tinta, Tempranillo, Parreleta and Cabernet sauvignon grapes. White wines from Alcanón, Garnacha blanca, Viura and Chardonnay. Rosé wine is also produced.
Somosierra (Sp) the name of a still mineral water sourced at La Cabrera in the Somosierra mountains, central Spain. Bottled by Fonsana.
Songlines (Austr) a red wine produced from 5% Cabernet sauvignon & 95% Shiraz by The Pomegranate Wine Company, South Australia.
Songloed (S.Afr) the label for a range of wines produced by the Coppoolse Finlayson Winery, Stellenbosch, Western Cape.
Songoularé Misket (Bul) a dry white wine from the Black Sea coast. Produced from the Misket grape.
Sonne (Ger) vineyard (Anb): Mittelrhein. (Ber): Bacharach. (Gro): Schloss Reichenstein. (Vil): Oberheimbach.
Sonneck (Ger) vineyard (Anb): Mosel-Saar-Ruwer. (Ber): Zell/Mosel. (Gro): Grafschaft. (Vil): Bullay.
Sonneck (Ger) vineyard (Anb): Mosel-Saar-Ruwer. (Ber): Zell/Mosel. (Gro): Schwarze Katz. (Vil): Zell-Merl.
Sonnelle (Fr) a producer of a popular range of canned wines.
Sonnema (Hol) a producer of Beerenburg, an aromatic bitters.
Sonnenberg (Ger) lit: 'sunny hill', a popular name for south facing vineyards in Germany. There are 71 individual sites within the wine regions.

Sonnenberg (Ger) vineyard (Anb): Ahr. (Ber): Walporzheim/Aartal. (Gro): Klosterberg. (Vil): Bad Neuenahr.
Sonnenberg (Ger) vineyard (Anb): Baden. (Ber): Badische Bergstrasse/Kraichgau. (Gro): Hohenberg. (Vil): Berghausen.
Sonnenberg (Ger) vineyard (Anb): Baden. (Ber): Badische Bergstrasse/Kraichgau. (Gro): Rittersberg. (Vil): Laudenbach.
Sonnenberg (Ger) vineyard (Anb): Baden. (Ber): Badische Bergstrasse/Kraichgau. (Gro): Stiftsberg. (Vil): Eichtersheim.
Sonnenberg (Ger) vineyard (Anb): Baden. (Ber): Badische Bergstrasse/Kraichgau. (Gro): Stiftsberg. (Vil): Eschelbach.
Sonnenberg (Ger) vineyard (Anb): Baden. (Ber): Badische Bergstrasse/Kraichgau. (Gro): Stiftsberg. (Vil): Michelfeld.
Sonnenberg (Ger) vineyard (Anb): Baden. (Ber): Badische Bergstrasse/Kraichgau. (Gro): Stiftsberg. (Vil): Waldangelloch.
Sonnenberg (Ger) vineyard (Anb): Baden. (Ber): Badische Frankenland. (Gro): Tauberklinge. (Vil): Dertingen.
Sonnenberg (Ger) vineyard (Anb): Baden. (Ber): Badische Frankenland. (Gro): Tauberklinge. (Vil): Kembach.
Sonnenberg (Ger) vineyard (Anb): Baden. (Ber): Breisgau. (Gro): Burg Zähringen. (Vil): Wildtal.
Sonnenberg (Ger) vineyard (Anb): Baden. (Ber): Kaiserstuhl-Tuniberg. (Gro): Attilafelsen. (Vil): Opfingen.
Sonnenberg (Ger) vineyard (Anb): Baden. (Ber): Ortenau. (Gro): Schloss Rodeck. (Vil): Sinzheim.
Sonnenberg (Ger) vineyard (Anb): Baden. (Ber): Ortenau. (Gro): Schloss Rodeck. (Vil): Varnhalt.
Sonnenberg (Ger) vineyard (Anb): Franken. (Ber): Maindreieck. (Gro): Hofrat. (Vil): Marktbreit.
Sonnenberg (Ger) vineyard (Anb): Franken. (Ber): Maindreieck. (Gro): Kirchberg. (Vil): Untereisenheim.
Sonnenberg (Ger) vineyard (Anb): Mittelrhein. (Ber): Rheinburgengau. (Gro): Burg Hammerstein. (Vil): Unkel.
Sonnenberg (Ger) vineyard (Anb): Mosel-Saar-Ruwer. (Ber): Bernkastel. (Gro): Sankt Michael. (Vil): Schleich.
Sonnenberg (Ger) vineyard (Anb): Mosel-Saar-Ruwer. (Ber): Saar-Ruwer. (Gro): Römerlay. (Vil): Trier.
Sonnenberg (Ger) vineyard (Anb): Mosel-Saar-Ruwer. (Ber): Saar-Ruwer. (Gro): Römerlay. (Vil): Waldrach.
Sonnenberg (Ger) vineyard (Anb): Mosel-Saar-Ruwer. (Ber): Saar-Ruwer. (Gro): Scharzberg. (Vil): Irsch.
Sonnenberg (Ger) vineyard (Anb): Mosel-Saar-Ruwer. (Ber): Saar-Ruwer. (Gro): Scharzberg. (Vil): Kanzem.
Sonnenberg (Ger) vineyard (Anb): Mosel-Saar-Ruwer. (Ber): Saar-Ruwer. (Gro): Scharzberg. (Vil): Mennig.

1203

Sonnenberg (Ger) vineyard (Anb): Mosel-Saar-Ruwer. (Ber): Zell/Mosel. (Gro): Goldbäumchen. (Vil): Cochem.

Sonnenberg (Ger) vineyard (Anb): Nahe. (Ber): Kreuznach. (Gro): Pfarrgarten. (Vil): Dalberg.

Sonnenberg (Ger) vineyard (Anb): Nahe. (Ber): Kreuznach. (Gro): Pfarrgarten. (Vil): Hergenfeld.

Sonnenberg (Ger) vineyard (Anb): Nahe. (Ber): Kreuznach. (Gro): Pfarrgarten. (Vil): Schöneberg.

Sonnenberg (Ger) vineyard (Anb): Nahe. (Ber): Kreuznach. (Gro): Pfarrgarten. (Vil): Sommerloch.

Sonnenberg (Ger) vineyard (Anb): Nahe. (Ber): Kreuznach. (Gro): Schlosskapelle. (Vil): Guldental.

Sonnenberg (Ger) vineyard (Anb): Nahe. (Ber): Schloss Böckelheim. (Gro): Burgweg. (Vil): Norheim.

Sonnenberg (Ger) vineyard (Anb): Nahe. (Ber): Schloss Böckelheim. (Gro): Paradiesgarten. (Vil): Nussbaum.

Sonnenberg (Ger) vineyard (Anb): Nahe. (Ber): Schloss Böckelheim. (Gro): Rosengarten. (Vil): Roxheim.

Sonnenberg (Ger) vineyard (Anb): Rheingau. (Ber): Johannisberg. (Gro): Steinmacher. (Vil): Eltville.

Sonnenberg (Ger) vineyard (Anb): Rheinhessen. (Ber): Bingen. (Gro): Abtey. (Vil): Sprendlingen.

Sonnenberg (Ger). vineyard. (Anb): Rheinhessen. (Ber): Bingen. (Gro): Kaiserpfalz. (Vil): Ingelheim.

Sonnenberg (Ger) vineyard (Anb): Rheinhessen. (Ber): Bingen. (Gro): Kaiserpfalz. (Vil): Schwabenheim.

Sonnenberg (Ger). vineyard. (Anb): Rheinhessen. (Ber): Bingen. (Gro): Kurfürstenstück. (Vil): Vendersheim.

Sonnenberg (Ger) vineyard (Anb): Rheinhessen. (Ber): Bingen. (Gro): Eheingrafenstein. (Vil): Hackenheim.

Sonnenberg (Ger) vineyard (Anb): Rheinhessen. (Ber): Bingen. (Gro): Rheingrafenstein. (Vil): Stein-Bockenheim.

Sonnenberg (Ger) vineyard (Anb): Rheinhessen. (Ber): Bingen. (Gro): Rheingrafenstein. (Vil): Wonsheim.

Sonnenberg (Ger) vineyard (Anb): Rheinhessen. (Ber): Bingen. (Gro): Sankt Rochuskapelle. (Vil): Aspisheim.

Sonnenberg (Ger) vineyard (Anb): Rheinhessen. (Ber): Bingen. (Gro): Sankt Rochuskapelle. (Vil): Pfaffen-Schwabenheim.

Sonnenberg (Ger) vineyard (Anb): Rheinhessen. (Ber): Nierstein. (Gro): Domherr. (Vil): Udenheim.

Sonnenberg (Ger) vineyard (Anb): Rheinhessen. (Ber): Nierstein. (Gro): Gutes Domtal. (Vil): Nieder-Olm.

Sonnenberg (Ger) vineyard (Anb): Rheinhessen. (Ber): Nierstein. (Gro): Krötenbrunnen. (Vil): Guntersblum.

Sonnenberg (Ger) vineyard (Anb): Rheinhessen.

Sonnenberg (Ger) vineyard (Anb): Rheinhessen. (Ber): Nierstein. (Gro): Petersberg. (Vil): Bechtolsheim.

Sonnenberg (Ger) vineyard (Anb): Rheinhessen. (Ber): Nierstein. (Gro): Rheinblick. (Vil): Alsheim.

Sonnenberg (Ger) vineyard (Anb): Rheinhessen. (Ber): Wonnegau. (Gro): Bergkloster. (Vil): Gundheim.

Sonnenberg (Ger) vineyard (Anb): Rheinhessen. (Ber): Wonnegau. (Gro): Domblick. (Vil): Hohen-Sülzen.

Sonnenberg (Ger) vineyard (Anb): Rheinhessen. (Ber): Wonnegau. (Gro): Sybillenstein. (Vil): Heimersheim.

Sonnenberg (Ger) vineyard (Anb): Pfalz. (Ber): Mittelhaardt-Deutsche Weinstrasse. (Gro): Feuerberg. (Vil): Ellerstadt.

Sonnenberg (Ger) vineyard (Anb): Pfalz. (Ber): Mittelhaardt-Deutsche Weinstrasse. (Gro): Grafenstück. (Vil): Bockenheim.

Sonnenberg (Ger) vineyard (Anb): Pfalz. (Ber): Mittelhaardt-Deutsche Weinstrasse. (Gro): Grafenstück. (Vil): Kindenheim.

Sonnenberg (Ger) vineyard (Anb): Pfalz. (Ber): Mittelhaardt-Deutsche Weinstrasse. (Gro): Grafenstück. (Vil): Obrigheim.

Sonnenberg (Ger) vineyard (Anb): Pfalz. (Ber): Mittelhaardt-Deutsche Weinstrasse. (Gro): Hofstück. (Vil): Gönnheim.

Sonnenberg (Ger) vineyard (Anb): Pfalz. (Ber): Mittelhaardt-Deutsche Weinstrasse. (Gro): Höllenpfad. (Vil): Neuleiningen.

Sonnenberg (Ger) vineyard (Anb): Pfalz. (Ber): Mittelhaardt-Deutsche Weinstrasse. (Gro): Kobnert. (Vil): Weisenheim am Berg.

Sonnenberg (Ger) vineyard (Anb): Pfalz. (Ber): Südliche Weinstrasse. (Gro): Guttenberg. (Vil): Oberotterbach.

Sonnenberg (Ger) vineyard (Anb): Pfalz. (Ber): Südliche Weinstrasse. (Gro): Guttenberg. (Vil): Schweigen-Rechtenbach.

Sonnenberg (Ger) vineyard (Anb): Pfalz. (Ber): Südliche Weinstrasse. (Gro): Guttenberg. (Vil): Schweighofen.

Sonnenberg (Ger) vineyard (Anb): Pfalz. (Ber): Südliche Weinstrasse. (Gro): Herrlich. (Vil): Leinsweiler.

Sonnenberg (Ger) vineyard (Anb): Pfalz. (Ber): Südliche Weinstrasse. (Gro): Trappenberg. (Vil): Essingen.

Sonnenberg (Ger) vineyard (Anb): Württemberg. (Ber): Remstal-Stuttgart. (Gro): Wartbühl. (Vil): Beutelsbach.

Sonnenberg (Ger) vineyard (Anb): Württemberg. (Ber): Remstal-Stuttgart. (Gro): Wartbühl. (Vil): Geradstetten.

Sonnenberg (Ger) vineyard (Anb): Württemberg. (Ber): Remstal-Stuttgart. (Gro): Wartbühl. (Vil): Kleinheppach.

Sonnenberg (Ger) vineyard (Anb): Württemberg. (Ber): Remstal-Stuttgart. (Gro): Wartbühl. (Vil): Schnait i. R.

S

Sonnenberg (Ger) vineyard (Anb): Württemberg. (Ber): Württembergisch Unterland. (Gro): Heuchelberg. (Vil): Schwaigern.

Sonnenberg (Ger) vineyard (Anb): Württemberg. (Ber): Württembergisch Unterland. (Gro): Heuchelberg. (Vil): Stetten a. H.

Sonnenberg (Ger) vineyard (Anb): Württemberg. (Ber): Württembergisch Unterland. (Gro): Kirchenweinberg. (Vil): Flein.

Sonnenberg (Ger) vineyard (Anb): Württemberg. (Ber): Württembergisch Unterland. (Gro): Kirchenweinberg. (Vil): Heilbronn.

Sonnenberg (Ger) vineyard (Anb): Württemberg. (Ber): Württembergisch Unterland. (Gro): Kirchenweinberg. (Vil): Talheim.

Sonnenberg (Ger) vineyard (Anb): Württemberg. (Ber): Württembergisch Unterland. (Gro): Stromberg. (Vil): Bönnigheim.

Sonnenberg (Ger) a vineyard within the village of Eltville, 68.3ha (44.5ha) of which is proposed to be classified as Erstes Gewächs.

Sonnenborn (Ger) grosslage (Anb): Nahe. (Ber): Kreuznach. (Vil): Langenlonsheim.

Sonnenbräu Brauerei (Switz) a brewery based in Rebstein (part of the Interbeva group).

Sonnenbrunnen (Ger). vineyard. (Anb): Baden. (Ber): Markgräflerland. (Gro): Vogtei Rötteln. (Vil): Lörrach.

Sonnenbückel (Ger) vineyard (Anb): Franken. (Ber): Bayer Bodensee. (Gro): Lindauer Seegarten. (Vil): Nonnenhorn.

Sonnenbühl (Ger) grosslage (Anb): Württemberg. (Ber): Remstal-Stuttgart. (Vils): Beutelsbach, Schnait i. R, Endersbach, Rommelshausen Stetten i. R, Strümpfelbach.

Sonnengarten (Ger) vineyard (Anb): Pfalz. (Ber): Mittelhaardt-Deutsche Weinstrasse. (Gro): Schwarzerde. (Vil): Laumersheim.

Sonnenglanz (Fr) an A.C. Alsace Grand Cru vineyard at Beblenheim, Haut-Rhin 32.8ha.

Sonnengold (Ger) vineyard (Anb): Mosel-Saar-Rower. (Ber): Zell/Mosel. (Gro): Goldbäumchen. (Vil): Klotten.

Sonnengold (N.Z) the brand-name of a Chasselas varietal wine produced by the Glenvale Winery, Hawkes Bay.

Sonnenhalde (Ger) vineyard (Anb): Baden. (Ber): Bodensee. (Gro): Sonnenufer. (Vil): Konstanz.

Sonnenhalden (Ger) vineyard (Anb): Württemberg. (Ber): Kocher-Jagst-Tauber. (Gro): Tauberberg. (Vil): Kressbronn am Bodensee Tubingen (ortsteil Hirschau, Unterjesingen).

Sonnenhang (Ger) vineyard (Anb): Rheinhessen. (Ber): Bingen. (Gro): Kaiserpfalz. (Vil): Ingelheim.

Sonnenhang (Ger) vineyard (Anb): Rheinhessen. (Ber): Nierstein. (Gro): Domherr. (Vil): Schornsheim.

Sonnenhang (Ger) vineyard (Anb): Rheinhessen. (Ber): Nierstein. (Gro): Krötenbrunnen. (Vil): Eimsheim.

Sonnenhang (Ger) vineyard (Anb): Rheinhessen.

(Ber): Nierstein. (Gro): Krötenbrunnen. (Vil): Guntersblum.

Sonnenköpfchen (Ger) vineyard (Anb): Rheinhessen. (Ber): Bingen. (Gro): Rheingrafenstein. (Vil): Eckelsheim.

Sonnenküste (Bul) the brand-name of a medium-sweet white wine produced from the Rcatzitelli grape that is sold in Germany.

Sonnenlauf (Ger) vineyard (Anb): Nahe. (Ber): Kreuznach. (Gro): Pfarrgarten. (Vil): Gutenberg.

Sonnenlay (Ger) vineyard (Anb): Mittelrhein. (Ber): Rheinburgengau. (Gro): Gedeonseck. (Vil): Rhens.

Sonnenlay (Ger) vineyard (Anb): Mosel-Saar-Ruwer. (Ber): Bernkastel. (Gro): Kurfürstlay. (Vil): Mülheim.

Sonnenlay (Ger) vineyard (Anb): Mosel-Saar-Ruwer. (Ber): Bernkastel. (Gro): Sankt Michael. (Vil): Ensch.

Sonnenlay (Ger) vineyard (Anb): Mosel-Saar-Ruwer. (Ber): Bernkastel. (Gro): Schwarzlay. (Vil): Traben-Trarbach (ortsteil Wolf).

Sonnenleite (Ger) vineyard (Anb): Franken. (Ber): Maindreieck. (Gro): Honigberg. (Vil): Dettelbach.

Sonnenleite (Ger) vineyard (Anb): Franken. (Ber): Maindreieck. (Gro): Kirchberg. (Vil): Krautheim.

Sonnenmorgen (Ger) vineyard (Anb): Nahe. (Ber): Kreuznach. (Gro): Schlosskapelle. (Vil): Windesheim.

Sonnenplätzchen (Ger) vineyard (Anb): Nahe. (Ber): Schloss Böckelheim. (Gro): Paradiesgarten. (Vil): Obermoschel.

Sonnenring (Ger) vineyard (Anb): Mosel-Saar-Ruwer. (Ber): Zell/Mosel. (Gro): Goldbäumchen. (Vil): Münden.

Sonnenring (Ger) vineyard (Anb): Mosel-Saar-Ruwer. (Ber): Zell/Mosel. (Gro): Weinhex. (Vil): Löf.

Sonnenschein (Ger) vineyard (Anb): Ahr. (Ber): Walporzheim/Ahrtal. (Gro): Klosterberg. (Vil): Bachem.

Sonnenschein (Ger) vineyard (Anb): Franken. (Ber): Maindreieck. (Gro): Not yet assigned. (Vil): Veitshöchheim.

Sonnenseite (Ger) vineyard (Anb): Mosel-Saar-Ruwer. (Ber): Bernkastel. (Gro): Kurfürstlay. (Vil): Wintrich.

Sonnenseite ob der Bruck (Ger) vineyard (Anb): Baden. (Ber): Badische Bergstrasse/Kraichgau. (Gro): Rittersberg. (Vil): Heidelberg.

Sonnenstück (Ger) vineyard (Anb): Mittelrhein. (Ber): Rheinburgengau. (Gro): Schloss Schönburg. (Vil): Damscheid.

Sonnenstück (Ger) vineyard (Anb): Baden. (Ber): Markgräflerland. (Gro): Burg Neuenfels. (Vil): Bad Bellingen.

Sonnenstück (Ger) vineyard (Anb): Baden. (Ber): Markgräflerland. (Gro): Burg Neuenfels. (Vil): Liel.

Sonnenstück (Ger) vineyard (Anb): Baden. (Ber): Markgräflerland. (Gro): Burg Neuenfels. (Vil): Mauchen.

Sonnenstück (Ger) vineyard (Anb): Baden. (Ber): Markgräflerland. (Gro): Burg Neuenfels. (Vil): Niedereggenen.

Sonnenstück (Ger) vineyard (Anb): Baden. (Ber): Markgräflerland. (Gro): Burg Neuenfels. (Vil): Schliengen.

Sonnenstück (Ger) vineyard (Anb): Baden. (Ber): Markgräflerland. (Gro): Burg Neuenfels. (Vil): Steinenstadt.

Sonnenstück (Ger) vineyard (Anb): Pfalz. (Ber): Mittelhaardt-Deutsche Weinstrasse. (Gro): Schnepfenflug vom Kellertal. (Vil): Immesheim.

Sonnenstuhl (Ger) vineyard (Anb): Franken. (Ber): Maindreieck. (Gro): Ewig Leben. (Vil): Randersacker.

Sonnenufer (Ger) grosslage (Anb): Baden. (Ber): Bodensee. (Vils): Bermatingen, Bodman, Hagnau, Hilzingen, Immenstaad, Kippenhausen, Konstanz, Markdorf, Meersburg, Oberuhldingen, Reichenau, Salem (ortsteil Kirchberg), Singen, Stetten, Überlingen.

Sonnenuhr (Ger) vineyard (Anb): Mosel-Saar-Ruwer. (Ber): Bernkastel. (Gro): Kurfürstlay. (Vil): Maring-Noviand.

Sonnenuhr (Ger) vineyard (Anb): Mosel-Saar-Ruwer. (Ber): Bernkastel. (Gro): Michelsberg. (Vil): Neumagen-Dhron.

Sonnenuhr (Ger) vineyard (Anb): Mosel-Saar-Ruwer. (Ber): Bernkastel. (Gro): Münzlay. (Vil): Wehlen.

Sonnenuhr (Ger) vineyard (Anb): Mosel-Saar-Ruwer. (Ber): Bernkastel. (Gro): Münzlay. (Vil): Zeltingen-Rachtig.

Sonnenuhr (Ger) vineyard (Anb): Mosel-Saar-Ruwer. (Ber): Zell/Mosel. (Gro): Goldbäumchen. (Vil): Pommern.

Sonnenweg (Ger) vineyard (Anb): Nahe. (Ber): Kreuznach. (Gro): Pfarrgarten. (Vil): Wallhausen.

Sonnenweg (Ger) vineyard (Anb): Rheinhessen. (Ber): Nierstein. (Gro): Krötenbrunnen. (Vil): Gimbsheim.

Sonnenwinkel (Ger) vineyard (Anb): Franken. (Ber): Steigerwald. (Gro): Not yet assigned. (Vil): Altmannsdorf.

Sonnet (S.Afr) the label for a white wine (Muscat ottonel and Chenin blanc blend) produced by the Villiera Wines winery, Stellenbosch, Western Cape.

Sonnhalde (Ger) vineyard (Anb): Baden. (Ber): Breisgau. (Gro): Burg Zähringen. (Vil): Buchholz.

Sonnhalde (Ger) vineyard (Anb): Baden. (Ber): Breisgau. (Gro): Burg Zähringen. (Vil): Denzlingen.

Sonnhalde (Ger) vineyard (Anb): Baden. (Ber): Breisgau. (Gro): Burg Zähringen. (Vil): Sexau.

Sonnhalde (Ger) vineyard (Anb): Baden. (Ber): Markgräflerland. (Gro): Burg Neuenfels. (Vil): Müllheim.

Sonnheil (Ger) vineyard (Anb): Rheinhessen. (Ber): Nierstein. (Gro): Krötenbrunnen. (Vil): Hillesheim.

Sonnhof (Aus) a winery (50ha) based in the Kampstal region. (Add): Rudolfstrasse 37-39, 3550 Langenlois. Grape varieties: Chardonnay, Grüner veltliner, Merlot, Pinot blanc, Pinot noir, Riesling, Sauvignon blanc, Zweigelt. Label: Rotspon.

Sonnhohle (Ger) vineyard (Anb): Baden. (Ber): Markgräflerland. (Gro): Burg Neuenfels. (Vil): Britzingen.

Sonnhohle (Ger) vineyard (Anb): Baden. (Ber): Markgräflerland. (Gro): Burg Neuenfels. (Vil): Britzingen (ortsteil Dattingen).

Sonnhohle (Ger) vineyard (Anb): Baden. (Ber): Markgräflerland. (Gro): Lorettoberg. (Vil): Heitersheim.

Sonnhohle (Ger) vineyard (Anb): Baden. (Ber): Markgräflerland. (Gro): Vogtei Rötteln. (Vil): Binzen.

Sonnhohle (Ger) vineyard (Anb): Baden. (Ber): Markgräflerland. (Gro): Vogtei Rötteln. (Vil): Sfringen-Kirchen.

Sonnhohle (Ger) vineyard (Anb): Baden. (Ber): Markgräflerland. (Gro): Vogtei Rötteln. (Vil): Egringen.

Sonnhohle (Ger) vineyard (Anb): Baden. (Ber): Markgräflerland. (Gro): Vogtei Rötteln. (Vil): Eimeldingen.

Sonnhohle (Ger) vineyard (Anb): Baden. (Ber): Markgräflerland. (Gro): Vogtei Rötteln. (Vil): Fischingen.

Sonnhohle (Ger) vineyard (Anb): Baden. (Ber): Markgräflerland. (Gro): Vogtei Rötteln. (Vil): Hertingen.

Sonnhohle (Ger) vineyard (Anb): Baden. (Ber): Markgräflerland. (Gro): Vogtei Rötteln. (Vil): Ötlingen.

Sonnhohle (Ger) vineyard (Anb): Baden. (Ber): Markgräflerland. (Gro): Vogtei Rötteln. (Vil): Rummingen.

Sonnhohle (Ger) vineyard (Anb): Baden. (Ber): Markgräflerland. (Gro): Vogtei Rötteln. (Vil): Schallbach.

Sonnleiten (Aus) a vineyard site on the banks of the River Danube situated in the Wachau region, Niederösterreich.

Sonntagsberg (Ger) vineyard (Anb): Württemberg. (Ber): Württembergisch Unterland. (Gro): Heuchelberg. (Vil): Heilbronn (ortsteil Klingenberg).

Sonntagsberg (Ger) vineyard (Anb): Württemberg. (Ber): Württembergisch Unterland. (Gro): Heuchelberg. (Vil): Nordhausen.

Sonntagsberg (Ger) vineyard (Anb): Württemberg. (Ber): Württembergisch Unterland. (Gro): Heuchelberg. (Vil): Nordheim.

Sonny Boy (Cktl) 10mls (⅓ fl.oz) orange Curaçao, 10mls (⅓ fl.oz) peach brandy, 2 dashes Angostura. Shake over ice, strain into a Champagne flute and fill with iced Champagne.

Son Of A Bitch (Wal) a 6.5% alc by vol. strong ale brewed by SA Brain & Cº. Ltd., South Glamorgan.

Son of a Bitch (Eng) a best bitter brewed by the Bullmastiff Brewery, Anchor Way, Penarth.

Sonoita Vineyards (USA) a winery. (Add): H.C.R., Box 33, Elgin, Arizona 85611. Grape varieties: Cabernet sauvignon, Chardonnay, Pinot noir.

Sonoma Coast (USA) an A.V.A. region within Sonoma Valley, California. Grape varieties include Chardonnay and Pinot noir. Home to Kistler Vineyards, Marcassin Vineyard & Winery, Marimar Torres Estates.

Sonoma County AVA's (USA) the A.V.A.'s are: Alexander Valley, Bennett Valley, Carneros, Dry Creek Valley, Green Valley, Knights Valley, North Coast, Rockpile, Russian River Valley, Sonoma County, Sonoma Valley.

Sonoma County Wineries Association (USA) an asssociation of Sonoma wine-produces (136 members). Website: http://www.sonomawine.com

Sonoma Creek (USA) a winery based in Sonoma county, California. Grape varieties include: Chardonnay, Pinot noir.

Sonoma-Cutrer Vineyards Inc. (USA) a specialist estate based in Sonoma County, California. Grape varieties: Cabernet sauvignon, Chardonnay and Colombard. Produces varietal and sparkling wines.

Sonoma Reserve (USA) the label for a red wine (Pinot noir) produced by the Gallo Family winery, Sonoma County, California.

Sonoma Riesling (USA) an alternative name for the Green sylvaner grape in California.

Sonoma Valley (USA) a county in northern California (24280ha and 200 wineries). Has 2 smaller A.V.A.'s: Sonoma Coast, Carneros. Fine, full-bodied red wines are produced from Cabernet sauvignon, Pinot noir and Zinfandel grapes, with the white wines from Chardonnay. Home to: Sebastiani Vineyards, Château St. Jean, Arrowood Winery, Kenwood, Carmenet, Buena Vista, Gundlach-Bundschu's Kunde Estate, Benziger, St. Francis, Laurel Glen Vineyards.

Sonoma Vineyards (USA) vineyards based in Sonoma County, California. Wines are produced from Cabernet sauvignon, Chardonnay and French colombard grapes. Owns Alexander's Crown, Baron Vineyard.

Sonop Organic (S.Afr) an organic range of red and white wines (15% French oak aged) produced by the African Terroir winery, Paarl, Western Cape.

Sonora (Mex) a district that contains the wine-producing area of Hermosillo.

Sonsón (Sp) a red grape variety grown in Galicia. Produces fine, perfumed wines.

Sool (Kor) wine.

Soonecker Schlossberg (Ger) vineyard (Anb): Mittelrhein. (Ber): Bacharach. (Gro): Schloss Reichenstein. (Vil): Niederheimbach.

Soonwald (Ger) a series of hills in the Nahe Anbaugebiet.

Soopjeshoogte (S.Afr) the label for a red wine (Cabernet franc, Cabernet sauvignon and Merlot blend) produced by the Welgemeend Estate winery, Suider-Paarl, Western Cape.

Soortelijk Gewicht (Hol) specific gravity. S.G.

Soos (Aus) a vineyard site based on the banks of the River Kamp situated in the Kamptal region.

Soother Cocktail (Cktl) ⅓ measure brandy, ⅓ measure Calvados, ⅓ measure Grand Marnier, juice ½ lemon, 2 dashes gomme syrup. Shake over ice and strain into a cocktail glass.

Sooty Oatmeal Stout (Eng) a 4.8% alc by vol. oatmeal stout brewed by the Nottingham Brewery, Nottinghamshire.

Sophenia Synthesis (Arg) the label for a red wine (Malbec, Merlot and Cabernet sauvignon blend) produced by the Finca Sophenia winery in the Mendoza region.

Sophie Charlotte (Ger) a natural spring mineral water from St. Georg Quelle, Norderstedt.

Sophiste [La] (USA) a white wine produced by Grahm at Bonny Doon, Santa Cruz from Marsanne and Roussanne grapes.

Sophistiquer (Fr) to falsify a wine or to ameliorate a defective wine with anything which will cover up its defects.

Soplica (Pol) a brandy and apple-flavoured vodka produced by Polmos 40% alc by vol.

Sopra Ceneri (Switz) a wine-producing area in Ticino. Includes the vineyards of Bellinzonese and Locarnese.

Sopron (Hun) a wine-producing district in north-western Hungary. Noted for red wines from the Gamay grape.

Sopron Brewery (Hun) a brewery based in north-western Hungary. Noted for Löver Lager.

Soquel (USA) a noted winery town based in Santa Cruz, California.

Sorbés [Les] (Fr) a Premier Cru vineyard in the A.C. commune of Morey-Saint-Denis, Côte de Nuits, Burgundy 3ha.

Sorbet and Tea Punch (Cktl) (Non-alc) 50mls (2fl.ozs) cold tea, 25mls (1fl.oz) orange juice, 5mls (¼ fl.oz) lemon juice, 10mls (½ fl.oz) gomme syrup, 2 scoops orange sorbet. Blend altogether in a blender and pour into a flute glass.

Sorbic Acid (Eng) an additive to wine, inhibits yeast, but does not kill it, has no effect on bacteria. Efficiency depends on the presence of alcohol and SO_2, a stabiliser. see Garlic.

Sorbino (Fin) a cherry-flavoured liqueur.

Sorbitio (Lat) a drink.

Sorbitol (Eng) a sugar that wine yeasts cannot ferment, a useful agent for sweetening home-made wines.

Sorcerer (Eng) a 4.3% alc by vol. ale brewed by the Wizard Brewery, Warwickshire.

Sorcerer [The] (Eng) a 4.5% alc by vol. seasonal amber cask ale from Greene King in East Anglia.

Sorcières [Les] (Fr) a vineyard of Dopff & Irion in Alsace. Named after the site where witches and unfaithful wives were burnt at the stake in the Middle Ages. Produces Gewurztraminer wines.

Sorelle (Eng) a sparkling herbal fruit drink from the London Herb & Spice Company. Made from passion fruit, Mediterranean peach, herbs and sparkling water.

Sorentberg (Ger) vineyard (Anb): Mosel-Saar-Ruwer. (Ber): Bernkastel. (Gro): Vom Heissen Stein. (Vil): Reil.

S

Sorgenbrecher (Ger) lit: 'breaker of cares', the local name for the red wine of Stumpfelbach in Württemberg.

Sörgenloch (Ger) vineyard (Anb): Rheinhessen. (Ber): Nierstein. (Gro): Gutes Domtal. (Vin): Moosberg.

Sorgente (It) spring. *See also* Acqua di Sorgente.

Sorgente Aurora (It) a natural spring mineral water from Alessandria, Piemonte. Mineral contents (milligrammes per litre): Sodium 5.4mg/l, Calcium 632mg/l, Magnesium 4.2mg/l, Potassium 3.3mg/l, Bicarbonates 423mg/l, Chlorides 6.3mg/l, Sulphates 1380mg/l, Fluorides 0.22mg/l, Silicates 32.5mg/l. pH 6.9

Sorgente Azzurra (It) a natural spring mineral water from Azzurra.

Sorgente degli Ontani (It) a natural spring mineral water from Grosseto, Tuscany.

Sorgente del Bucaneve (It) a natural spring mineral water from Scorze (VE). Mineral contents (milligrammes per litre): Sodium 4mg/l, Calcium 71mg/l, Magnesium 27mg/l, Potassium 1mg/l, Chlorides 6mg/l, Sulphates 46mg/l. pH 7.63

Sorgente del Cacciatore (It) a natural spring mineral water from Perugia, Umbria.

Sorgente del Grotto (It) a natural spring mineral water from Como, Lombardy.

Sorgente dell' Amore (It) a sparkling natural spring mineral water from Grimaldi, Cosenza. Mineral contents (milligrammes per litre): Sodium 10.3mg/l, Calcium 89.6mg/l, Magnesium 15.52mg/l, Potassium 1.55mg/l, Bicarbonates 320mg/l, Chlorides 8.51mg/l, Sulphates 22mg/l, Nitrates 2.5mg/l, Silicates 8.73mg/l. pH 7.37

Sorgente Flamina (It) a sparkling natural spring mineral water from Perugia, Umbria. Mineral contents (milligrammes per litre): Sodium 3.1mg/l, Calcium 72mg/l, Magnesium 1mg/l, Potassium 0.62mg/l, Bicarbonates 219mg/l, Chlorides 5.7mg/l, Sulphates 3.7mg/l, Nitrates 2.3mg/l, Silicates 6.5mg/l. pH 7.5

Sorgente Grigna (It) a sparkling natural spring mineral water from Lecco, Lombardy. Mineral contents (milligrammes per litre): Sodium 1.4mg/l, Calcium 52mg/l, Magnesium 14.5mg/l, Potassium 0.6mg/l, Bicarbonates 214.5mg/l, Chlorides 1.9mg/l, Sulphates 8.8mg/l, Nitrates 9.5mg/l, Silicates 5.2mg/l. pH 7.9

Sorgente Imperiale (It) a natural spring mineral water. Mineral contents (milligrammes per litre): Sodium 3.5mg/l, Calcium 12.8mg/l, Magnesium 1.8mg/l, Bicarbonates 40.7mg/l, Chlorides 3.6mg/l, Sulphates 7.4mg/l, Nitrates 2.8mg/l. pH 8.1

Sorgente Linda (It) a sparkling natural spring mineral water from Linda. Mineral contents (milligrammes per litre): Sodium 14.6mg/l, Calcium 89.6mg/l, Magnesium 27.2mg/l, Potassium 2.1mg/l, Bicarbonates 363.1mg/l, Chlorides 19.8mg/l, Sulphates 32.5mg/l, Nitrates 9.3mg/l, Silicates 14.1mg/l. pH 7.47

Sorgente Lissa (It) a natural spring mineral water from Lissa. Mineral contents (milligrammes per litre): Sodium 0.65mg/l, Calcium 35mg/l, Magnesium 19mg/l, Potassium 0.4mg/l, Bicarbonates 189mg/l, Chlorides 0.8mg/l, Sulphates 14.3mg/l, Nitrates 3.3mg/l. pH 8.04

Sorgente Moschetta (It) a sparkling natural spring mineral water from Moschetta. Mineral contents (milligrammes per litre): Sodium 9.8mg/l, Calcium 14.04mg/l, Magnesium 8.75mg/l, Potassium 1.9mg/l, Bicarbonates 90.25mg/l, Chlorides 18.89mg/l, Sulphates 8.21mg/l, Oxygen 7.8mg/l, Nitrates 5.22mg/l, Silicates 14.8mg/l. pH 6.95

Sorgente Oro – Alpi Cozie (It) a natural spring mineral water from Oro.

Sorgente Palina (It) a natural spring mineral water from Palina.

Sorgente Pura (It) a natural spring mineral water from Monte Orri, Sardinia. Mineral contents (milligrammes per litre): Sodium 42.7mg/l, Calcium 14.7mg/l, Magnesium 12.7mg/l, Potassium 1.4mg/l, Bicarbonates 84.1mg/l, Chlorides 66.6mg/l, Sulphates 18.9mg/l, Fluorides 0.1mg/l, Nitrates 1.8mg/l, Silicates 12.3mg/l. pH 6.84

Sorgente San Michele (It) a natural spring mineral water from Nettuno Uno, Celano, L'Aquila.

Sorgente Santa Lucia (It) a sparkling natural spring mineral water from Tolentino, Macerata MC. Mineral contents (milligrammes per litre): Sodium 44.9mg/l, Calcium 116mg/l, Magnesium 26.7mg/l, Potassium 4.1mg/l, Bicarbonates 447.7mg/l, Sulphates 11.5mg/l, Nitrates 19.7mg/l, Silicates 11.5mg/l. pH 7.5

Sorgente Serra Policaretto (It) a sparkling natural spring mineral water from Acri, Cosenza. Mineral contents (milligrammes per litre): Sodium 15.3mg/l, Calcium 9.2mg/l, Magnesium 7.03mg/l, Potassium 1.39mg/l, Bicarbonates 85.4mg/l, Chlorides 16.32mg/l, Sulphates 6.2mg/l, Fluorides 0.45mg/l, Nitrates 2.2mg/l, Silicates 16.7mg/l, Oxygen 9.52mg/l. pH 6.68

Sorgente Sovrana (It) a sparkling natural spring mineral water from Sovrana. Mineral contents (milligrammes per litre): Sodium 5.5mg/l, Magnesium 38mg/l, Potassium 0.7mg/l, Bicarbonates 370mg/l, Sulphates 15mg/l, Oxygen 8.7mg/l, Nitrates 5.7mg/l, Silicates 23.5mg/l. pH 7.7

Sorgente Tesorino (It) a natural spring mineral water from Tersorino. Mineral contents (milligrammes per litre): Sodium 36.8mg/l, Calcium 126.8mg/l, Magnesium 27.9mg/l, Potassium 1.6mg/l, Bicarbonates 359.9mg/l, Chlorides 36.6mg/l, Sulphates 159.4mg/l, Fluorides 0.2mg/l, Nitrates 0.8mg/l, Silicates 14.5mg/l. pH 7.18

Sorgente Tione (It) a sparkling natural spring mineral water from Terni, Umbria. Mineral contents (milligrammes per litre): Sodium 12.6mg/l, Calcium 14.9mg/l, Magnesium

5.1mg/l, Potassium 18.2mg/l, Bicarbonates 85.4mg/l, Chlorides 10.7mg/l, Sulphates 6.1mg/l, Fluorides 0.98mg/l, Nitrates 18.1mg/l, Silicates 50.2mg/l. pH 7.2

Sorghum (Afr) a brownish-pink beer with a slightly sour taste. 3% alc by vol. Made from sorghum, maize, malt and coarse oatmeal.

Sorgil (It) a natural spring mineral water brand.

Sorilaria (It) a wine produced from the Arneis grapes by Araldici Vini Piemontesi, 14040 Castel Boglione. Part of the Poderi Alasia range. A D.O.C. Roero Arneis wine.

Sorni (It) a D.O.C. red wine produced in Trentino-Alto-Adige. Made from the Lagrein, Schiava and Teroldego grapes.

Soroco (Euro) a natural spring mineral water (established 1998) from Moldavia. Mineral contents (milligrammes per litre): Sodium 1300mg/l, Calcium 36.1mg/l, Magnesium 8.5mg/l, Potassium 820.25mg/l, Bicarbonates 100-200mg/l, Chlorides 2211.6mg/l, Sulphates 125.9mg/l, Fluorides 4.9mg/l, Nitrates <0.1mg/l. pH 7.4

Soro de Leite (Port) buttermilk.

Sorrenberg Vineyard (Austr) a winery (established 1985). (Add): Alma Road, Beechworth, Victoria. Grape varieties: Chardonnay, Sauvignon blanc, Sémillon, Cabernet, Gamay.

Sorrentine (It) a red wine produced in Roman times from Minean grapes.

Sortilegio (Sp) a solera reserva brandy produced by Luis Caballero.

SOS (Eng) *abbr*: Shefford Old Strong 1050 O.G. brewed by the Banks and Taylor Brewery in Shefford, Bedfordshire.

SOS (Eng) an ale brewed by the Quay Brewery, Hope Square, Weymouth.

Sosban Fach (Wal) a 4.3% alc by vol. ale brewed by Bragdy Ynys Mon, Gwynedd.

Sot (Eng) a slang term for a person who is consistantly intoxicated (drunk).

Sotatachna Zahar (Bul) denotes semi-sweet with residual grape sugar.

Soto (Chi) a liqueur made from lychees and produced in Hong Kong.

Soto (Sp) the name given to a range of Sherries (Amontillado, Oloroso and Cream) produced by Sandeman.

Sotomayor (Sp) also spelt Soutomaior. One of four sub-zones in D.O. Rías Baixas in Galicia. *See also* Condado do Tea, O Rosal, Val do Salnés. Main grape variety is Albariño.

Sotoyome Winery (USA) a winery based in Healdsburg, Sonoma County, California. Grape varieties: Cabernet sauvignon, Petite syrah and Zinfandel. Produces varietal wines.

Sotto Ceneri (Switz) a wine-producing area in Ticino. Includes the vineyards of Luganese and Mendrisiotto.

Sottodenominazioni Geografiche (It) geographical sub-district names.

Sottosuolo (It) sub-soil.

Sottozona (It) denotes a single vineyard.

Souche (Fr) cep or vine root stock.

Souchong (Chi) comes from the Chinese 'sian ching' (little plant). Describes the size of tea bush. i.e. Pekoe Souchong, Lapsang Souchong etc. Large coarse leaf.

Soucoupe (Fr) saucer.

Sou-Dag (Rus) a white grape variety grown in the Crimea. Produces Port-style and red wines.

Soudak (Rus) an alternative spelling of Sou-Dag, a rich, red wine.

Soûl (Fr) a slang term for stoned (very drunk/intoxicated).

Soulaines (Fr) a commune in the A.C. Coteaux de l'Aubance in the Anjou-Saumur district of the Loire. Produces light red wines.

Soulières (Fr) a Cru Champagne village in the Canton de Vertus. District: Châlons.

Soulignac (Fr) a commune in the Haut-Benauge, Entre-Deux-Mers, central Bordeaux.

Soul Kiss (Cktl) 1 part French vermouth, 1 part Italian vermouth, 1 part Dubonnet, 2 teaspoons orange juice. Mix over ice and strain into an ice-filled highball glass.

Soul Kiss Cocktail (Cktl) 20mls (⅙ gill) French vermouth, 20mls (⅙ gill) Bourbon whiskey, 10mls (½ fl.oz) orange juice, 10mls (½ fl.oz) Dubonnet. Shake over ice and strain into a cocktail glass.

Soul of the Wine (Hol) the old Dutch description of brandy (Cognac) which was imported to Holland. Shipped to save freight charges that would have been levied if the wine had been shipped.

Soultz-les-Bains (Fr) a village in Alsace. Known as Sulzbach in German.

Soul Water (Can) a natural spring mineral water brand.

Soumoll (Sp) *see* Sumoll.

Sound (Eng) a wine tasting term for a wine which has no defects and shows no abnormal qualities.

Sound of Alps (Aus) a natural spring mineral water from Tirol. Mineral contents (milligrammes per litre): Calcium 243.69mg/l, Magnesium 37.21mg/l, Fluorides 0.16mg/l, Nitrates 2mg/l.

Souped-Up (Eng) a term used to describe a wine that has been blended with something more robust or richer (may be done legally) to improve the quality.

Souple (Fr) describes a supple, well-balanced wine, soft and easy to drink.

Sour (Cktl) 1 measure of desired spirit, juice ¼ lemon, 1 teaspoon castor sugar, dash Angostura, white of egg. Shake well over ice and strain into a small wine glass.

Sour (Eng) used to describe a wine which is spoiled and unfit to drink. Acidic, bitter or vinegary, it is usually caused through bacterial infection or too much acid. (Cro) = kiseo, (Den) = sur, (Sp) = agrio.

Source (Fr) spring (water).

Source aux Nymphes [La] (Fr) the label of a

Châteauneuf-du-Pape produced by Gonnet (J. et M.), 14 Impasse des Vignerons, 84370 Bédarrides, southern Rhône. Other label is Domaine Font de Michelle.

Source Caudana (It) a still and sparkling natural spring mineral water from Ivrea. (blue label: light gas/pink-blue label: still). Mineral contents (milligrammes per litre): Sodium 2.9mg/l, Calcium 11.2mg/l, Magnesium 5.3mg/l, Potassium 0.5mg/l, Bicarbonates 53.7mg/l, Chlorides 2.4mg/l, Sulphates 5.7mg/l, Fluorides 0.1mg/l. pH 7.4

Source de la Doye (Fr) a natural spring mineral water from De la Doye. Mineral contents (milligrammes per litre): Sodium 6mg/l, Calcium 64.2mg/l, Magnesium 3.3mg/l, Potassium 2mg/l, Bicarbonates 195mg/l, Chlorides 18mg/l, Sulphates 10mg/l, Nitrates 4mg/l, Silicates 2mg/l. pH 7.8

Source de la Prime (Fr) a natural spring mineral water. Mineral contents (milligrammes per litre): Sodium 1.8mg/l, Calcium 2.7mg/l, Magnesium 0.58mg/l, Potassium 0.5mg/l, Bicarbonates 6.7mg/l, Chlorides 0.8mg/l, Sulphates 8mg/l, Silicates 6.9mg/l. pH 6.5

Source de Pasquère (S.Hem) a natural spring mineral water from Praslin, Seychelles. Mineral contents (milligrammes per litre): Sodium 5mg/l, Calcium 1.53mg/l, Magnesium 0.62mg/l, Potassium 1.8mg/l. pH 6.5

Source d'Or (S.Hem) a natural spring mineral water from the Seychelles. Mineral contents (milligrammes per litre): Sodium 2.4mg/l, Calcium 26.85mg/l, Magnesium 14.25mg/l, Potassium 5.7mg/l, Chlorides 22mg/l, Sulphates 10mg/l. pH 6.8

Source of the Nile (Afr) a lager beer 1040 O.G. brewed by the Nile Breweries in Jinja, Uganda.

Source Serena (It) a sparkling natural spring mineral water from Serena, Oleggio, Castelle. Mineral contents (milligrammes per litre): Sodium 6.5mg/l, Calcium 31.2mg/l, Magnesium 11.9mg/l, Potassium 2.1mg/l, Bicarbonates 143mg/l, Chlorides 5.4mg/l, Sulphates 13.4mg/l, Nitrates 6.5mg/l, Silicates 14.6mg/l. pH 7.89

Source 7 (Eng) a natural spring mineral water from Church Stretton, Shropshire.

Sourcy (Eng) the label of a sparkling fruit-flavoured spring water.

Sourcy 1 (Hol) a natural spring mineral water from Bunnik. Mineral contents (milligrammes per litre): Sodium 10mg/l, Calcium 50mg/l, Magnesium 3.5mg/l, Potassium 0.9mg/l, Bicarbonates 150mg/l, Chlorides 12mg/l, Sulphates 3.7mg/l, Nitrates <0.6mg/l, Silicates 15mg/l.

Sourcy 2 (Hol) a natural spring mineral water from Bunnik. Mineral contents (milligrammes per litre): Sodium 10mg/l, Calcium 40mg/l, Magnesium 3.1mg/l, Potassium 0.8mg/l, Bicarbonates 135mg/l, Chlorides 12mg/l,

Sulphates 0.7mg/l, Nitrates 0.3mg/l, Silicates 15mg/l.

Sourire de Reims (Fr) a non-vintage Champagne produced by Abele from 10%–30% Chardonnay and 40%–70% Pinot noir grapes.

Sour Mash (USA) in whiskey production the adding of a quarter of the spent beer from previous fermentation to the fresh mash and fresh yeast.

Sourness (Eng) taste of sourness/like lemon or vinegar/tart. (Fr) = acitité, (Port) = ácido, (Sp) = ácido.

Souroti (Gre) a sparkling natural spring mineral water. Mineral contents (milligrammes per litre): Sodium 58.5mg/l, Calcium 168.5mg/l, Magnesium 52.5mg/l, Potassium 12.3mg/l, Bicarbonates 805.5mg/l, Chlorides 50.5mg/l, Sulphates 66.8mg/l, Fluorides 0.3mg/l, Nitrates 0.5mg/l, Silicates 88.5mg/l, Boron 1.5mg/l. pH 5.95

Sourteq (Cktl) 50mls (2fl.ozs) tequila, 25mls (1fl.oz) lemon juice, 2 dashes gomme syrup, dash egg white. Shake over ice, strain into a large cocktail glass, decorate with a lemon slice and a cherry.

Sourz Tower (Eng) a one metre tall 'tube' glass™ (which can hold two litres of liquid and a half litre of ice) for mixing the Sourz range of mixers into large cocktails for parties and large groups.

Sousan (Sp) a black grape variety grown in Ribeiro.

Sousão (Port) a red grape variety grown in the Douro for the production of Port. Used mainly for colour as it has red flesh and juice. Also known as the Vinhão

Sousas (Sp) a natural spring mineral water from Verin, Ourense, Galicia. Mineral contents (milligrammes per litre): Sodium 19.5mg/l, Calcium 6mg/l, Magnesium 0.7mg/l, Potassium 1.2mg/l, Bicarbonates 63mg/l, Chlorides 3.6mg/l, Fluorides 0.4mg/l, Oxygen 51.2mg/l. pH 7.52

Sous Bois (Fr) a term to describe a full oaky flavour behind the fruit and spice flavours in a full-bodied red wine.

Soused (Eng) a slang term for a person who is consistantly intoxicated (drunk). (Fr) = ivrogne/poivrot.

Sous-le-Dos-d'Ane (Fr) a Premier Cru vineyard in the commune of Blagny, A.C. Meursault, Côte de Beaune, Burgundy 5.6ha.

Sous le Puits (Fr) a Premier Cru vineyard in the A.C. commune of Puligny-Montrachet, Côte de Beaune, Burgundy 6.9ha.

Sous-lès-Roches (Fr) a vineyard in the A.C. commune of Montagny, Côte Chalonnaise, Burgundy.

Sous-Marques (Fr) the name given to the lesser wines of the Champagne houses.

Sous-Noms (Fr) under-names, names given to wines especially in Bordeaux to Châteaux that do not exist.

Sousón (Sp) a red grape variety grown in Galicia.

Soussans (Fr) a commune in the A.C. Haut-Médoc, north-western Bordeaux.

South Africa (S.Afr) a wine and brandy-producing country (100000ha) that was first planted with vines in 1654 by Jan Van Riebeck. Produces most styles of wines including fine fortified Port and Sherry-styles. Planted mainly with Vitis vinifera and Vitis vinifera crosses, the main regions are Western Cape/Coastal Area [Constantia Valley, Durbanville, Malmesbury, Paarl, Stellenbosch, Tulbagh and Wellington] and Klein Karoo [Breede River, Ladismith, Montagu, Oudtshoorn, Robertson and Worcester]. see SFW, KWV, Nederburg, Pinotage, Steen and Wine of Origin Superior.

South African Black Vintners' Alliance (S.Afr) abbr: S.A.B.V.A. A newly formed body (2005) to promote the interests of black-owned wine producers, wine companies, suppliers and marketers. Also known as the Black Vintners' Alliance.

South African Breweries (S.Afr) a brewery (established 1895) based in Johannesburg. Brews most styles of beer.

South African Fortified Wine (S.Afr) name supersedes South African Sherry.

South African Premium Wines (S.Afr) a winery (established 2003) based in Sandton, Western Cape. Grape varieties: Cabernet sauvignon, Chardonnay, Merlot, Shiraz. Label: Jabulani. Website: http://www.jabulani.com

South African Riesling (S.Afr) a lesser name for the Crouchon grape of France.

South African Sherry (S.Afr) Sherry-type wines made in most styles from Finos to Creams. Now known as South African Fortified Wine.

South African Viticultural and Oenological Research Institute (S.Afr) abbr: V.O.R.I. a body that conducts clonal experiments etc. Produces new grape varieties. Also referred to as the Nietvoorbij.

South African Wine Industry Trust (S.Afr) abbr: S.A.W.I.T.

Southard (Port) Vintage Port shippers. Vintages include 1927.

South Australia (Austr) a state that includes the wine regions of Adelaide Hills, Barossa Valley, Clare Watervale, Coonawarra, Keppoch Valley, McLaren Vale, Padthaway and Riverland. Two thirds of Australia's annual wine production comes from this state (phylloxera-free).

South Australian Brewing (Austr) a brewery based in Adelaide. Brews Southwark Bitter and uses the brand-name of Southwark. Is also noted for lager beers.

South Barrel Camber (S.Afr) the label for a white wine (Chardonnay) produced by the Hoopenburg Wines winery, Stellenbosch, Western Cape.

South Beara Vineyard (Eng) a vineyard based at South Beara, Chulmleigh, Devon. Produce red and white wines.

South Bohemian Brewing Group (Czec) an amalgamation of three breweries: Platan Brewery in Protivín (founded in 1598), Regent Brewery in Trebon (founded in 1379, moved to Trebon in 1698), Samson Brewery in Ceske Budejovické (founded in 1795, known as Samson in 1865).

South Burgenland (Aus) Süd-Burgenland a wine-producing district (457ha) the smallest in Burgenland. Soil: clay, loam, slate. Villages: Deutsch Schützen, Eberau, Eisenberg, Heiligenbrunn, Rechnitz. Main grape varieties: white 60% (Grüner veltliner, Muscat ottonel, Pinot blanc, Welschriesling) red 40% (Blaufränkisch, Cabernet sauvignon, Uhudler, Zweigelt). Produces maily soft red wines.

South Carolina (USA) a small wine-producing State. Produces mainly wines from the Catawba, Concord and Muscadine grapes.

Southcorp (Austr) now own Rosemount.

Southcott House (Eng) a vineyard. (Add): Pewsey, Wiltshire. 0.5ha. Grape varieties: Müller-Thurgau 80%, Ortega 10% and Septima 10%.

South County Vineyards (USA) a winery based in Slocum, Rhode Island. Produces Vinifera wines.

Southdown Bitter (Eng) a keg bitter 1040 O.G. brewed by the Gales Brewery in Horndean, Hampshire.

Southeast Block Reserve (USA) the label for a red wine (Pinot noir) produced by the Bethel Heights Vineyard winery, Willamette Valley, Oregon.

South-East English Wine Festival (Eng) a wine festival held annually in September in East Sussex.

South-Eastern Seaboard (USA) the wine region which stretches from Virginia to Florida along the coastal plain.

Southern Basic (Bul) a wine producing area that contains vineyard areas: Assenovgrad, Brestnik, Haskovo, Korten, Oriachovitza, Plovdiv, Sakar, Sliven, Stambolovo, Stara Zagora. Noted for red wines. Grape varieties: Cabernet sauvignon, Mavrud, Merlot.

Southern Belle (Cktl) 1 measure Southern Comfort, 1 measure lime. Pour into an ice-filled highball glass, top with soda water, stir gently and serve with tall straws.

Southern Belle Cocktail (Cktl) ½ measure Bourbon whiskey, ⅓ measure cream, dash (white) crème de cacao, dash (green) crème de menthe. Shake over ice and strain into a cocktail glass.

Southern Bitter (Eng) a 3.7% alc by vol. bitter from the Cottage Brewing Company, West Lydford, near Yeovil, Somerset.

Southern Bride (Cktl) ¾ measure dry gin, ¼ measure grapefruit juice, dash maraschino. Shake over ice and strain into a cocktail glass.

Southern California (USA) a general descriptive term used for the wine-producing districts based south and east of Los Angeles in California.

Southern Cape Vineyards (S.Afr) the name for the amalgamated vineyards of Barrydale (152ha) and the Ladismith Co-op Winery (600ha). Grape varieties: Cabernet sauvignon, Chardonnay, Chenin blanc, Colombard, Gewürztraminer, Hanepoot, Merlot, Muscadel, Pinotage, Pinot noir,

Ruby cabernet, Sauvignon blanc, Shiraz, Tinta. Labels: Amalienstein, Green Wine, Misty Point, Seven Falls, Towerkop, Towersoet, Tradouw. Website: http://www.kleinkaroowines.co.za

Southern Comfort (USA) an orange and peach-flavoured whiskey. Produced by the Southern Comfort Corporation 50% alc by vol.

Southern Counties (Eng) a quality designation used for English and Welsh wine. Replaced by English Vineyards, Welsh Vineyards from 1993 harvest.

Southern Gin Cocktail (Cktl) 40mls (⅓ gill) dry gin, 3 dashes Cointreau, 2 dashes Campari. Stir over ice, strain into a cocktail glass and top with a twist of lemon peel juice.

Southern Ginger Cocktail (Cktl) 25mls (1fl.oz) Bourbon whiskey, 10mls (½ fl.oz) lemon juice. Shake over ice, strain into an ice-filled highball glass and top with ginger ale.

Southern Liqueur Cº (S.Afr) a liqueur producing company. see Amarula.

Southern Mint Julep (Cktl) the same as an Old Georgia Julep but using liqueur brandy instead of brandy.

Southern Region (Bul) a wine district that produces mainly red wines from Cabernet sauvignon, Merlot, Mavrud. Key D.G.O.'s are: Assenovgrad, Korten, Oriachovitza, Plovdiv, Sakar, Stambolovo.

Southern Right (S.Afr) a winery (established 1994) based in Hemel-en-Aarde Valley, Western Cape. 13ha. Grape varieties: Pinotage, Sauvignon blanc. Label: Ashbourne.

Southern Sky Wines (S.Afr) a winery (established 2002) based in Paarl, Western Cape. Grape varieties: Cabernet sauvignon, Chardonnay, Chenin blanc, Colombard, Merlot, Sauvignon blanc, Sémillon, Shiraz. Labels: Marimba, Ready Steady, Tara Hill. Website: http://www.southernskywines.com

Southern Star (USA) high quality Kentucky Bourbon whiskey from the Southern Star Distillery in Bardstown, Kentucky. 6 year old at 45% alc by vol. 10 year old at 50.5% alc by vol.

Southern Style (Eng) a term used to describe a full-bodied, full-flavoured red wine with a peppery character from southern France. In white wines denotes a flabby wine with excess alcohol and too little acidity and freshness.

Southern Ukraine (Ukr) the main wine district north of the Black Sea.

Southern Vales (Austr) a wine area of South Australia that includes McLaren Vale. Home to many wineries including Château Reynella and Wirra Wirra.

Southern Vales Co-operative (Austr) a winery based in McLaren Vale in Southern Vales, South Australia. Produces varietal wines.

Southern Viking Cocktail (Cktl) ⅓ measure Kahlúa, ⅓ measure akvavit, ⅓ measure double cream. Shake over ice, strain into a cocktail glass and decorate with grated nutmeg on top.

Southfield Vineyard (Eng) a vineyard based at the Huntley Vineyard in Gloucestershire.

South Hams Brewery (Eng) a brewery (established 2003). (Add): Stokeley Barton, Stokenham, Kingsbridge, Devon TQ7 2SE. Brews: Eddystone 4.8% alc by vol., Knicker Dropper Glory 5.5% alc by vol., Pandemonium 4.8% alc by vol., Plymouth Pride 3.8% alc by vol., Sutton Comfort 4.5% alc by vol., Wild Blonde 4.4% alc by vol., XSB 4.2% alc by vol. Website: http://www.southhamsbrewery.co.uk 'E'mail: info@southhamsbrewery.co.uk

Southing (USA) the label for a red wine (Pinot noir) produced by the Sea Smoke Winery, Santa Barbara County, California.

South of the Border (Cktl) 25mls (1fl.oz) Kahlúa, 35mls (1½ fl.oz) gin, 25mls (1fl.oz) lemon juice, 1 egg white. Shake well over ice, strain into a cocktail glass and decorate with a cherry.

South of the Border Cocktail (Cktl) ½ measure tequila, ⅛ measure Tia Maria, juice ½ lime. Shake over ice, strain into a cocktail glass and top with a slice of lime.

South Pacific (Cktl) 25mls (1fl.oz) gin, 10mls (½ fl.oz) blue Curaçao, 10mls (½ fl.oz) Galliano. Pour gin and Galliano into an ice-filled highball glass and top with lemonade. Splash in the Curaçao, decorate with a slice of lemon and a cherry and serve with straws.

South Pacific (Eng) a limited edition beer brewed by the St. Austell Brewery, St. Austell, Cornwall to highlight the connection between St. Austell and New Zealand.

South Port Brewery (Eng) a brewery (established 2004). (Add): Unit 3, Southport Enterprise Business Park, Russell Road, Southport, Merseyside PR9 7RF. Brews: Carousel 4% alc by vol., Natterjack 4.3% alc by vol., Old Shrimper 5.5% alc by vol., Sandgrounder Bitter 3.8% alc by vol.

Southsea Brewery (Eng) a brewery (established 1982) based in the Old Lion Brewery in Portsmouth. Noted for cask-conditioned Bosun Dark 1032 O.G. Captain's Bitter 1037 O.G. Admiral's Ale 1048 O.G. and Sealord 1060 O.G.

Southside (Mad) a blend of Madeira (medium-sweet) sold in America.

South-Side Cocktail (Cktl) 25mls (⅓ gill) gin, juice ½ lemon, 2 dashes gomme syrup. Shake over ice, strain into a cocktail glass and top with a sprig of mint.

South-Side Fizz (Cktl) as for South-Side Cocktail but place in an ice-filled highball glass and top with soda.

South South West (S.Afr) abbr: S.S.W. the name given to a range of easy drinking wines produced by African Wine and Spirits sold in 1litre bottles. Varieties include: Chardonnay, Chenin blanc, Ruby cabernet, Shiraz.

South Tyrol (Aus) see Südtirol and Trentino-Alto-Adige.

South Wales Clubs (Wal) a brewery based in Pontyclun, Mid-Glamorgan. see CPA and SBB.

Southwark (Austr) the brand-name used by the

South Australian Brewing C°. for their range of beers.

Southwark Beer (Austr) a pasteurised, bottom-fermented bitter beer brewed by Cooper's Brewery in Southwark, South Australia.

South-West Breweries Limited (Afr) a brewery based in Windhoek, Namibia.

South West Coastal (Austr) an area in Western Australia, noted for tuart (the eucalyptus tree) and sand that the vines grow in.

South Western Region (Bul) a wine district that produces mainly red wines from Melnik and Cabernet sauvignon. Key D.G.O. areas are Melnik, Harsovo, Pétrich Damianitza.

South Yorkshire Brewery Company (Eng) a brewery. (Add): Elsecar, near Barnsley. Brews: Barnsley Bitter 3.8% alc by vol. IPA 4.2% alc by vol. Black Heart Stout 4.6% alc by vol.

Soutirage (Fr) racking, the drawing off of the wine from the lees.

Soutiran [A] (Fr) a Champagne producer. Label: Brut Perle Noir. Website: http://www.soutiran.com

Soutiran [Gérard et Fils] (Fr) a Champagne producer. (Add): Ambonnay, 51500 Tours-sur-Marne. Produces vintage and non-vintage wines.

Sourtiran [Patrick] (Fr) a Champagne producer (370ha). (Add): 3, Rue des Crayères, 51150 Ambonnay. Produces vintage and non-vintage wines. Vintages: 1990, 1995, 1996, 1998, 2000. Labels: Precieuse d'Argent. 'E'mail: Patrick.sourtiran@wanadoo.fr

Soutirer (Fr) to rack/to draw off wine.

Soutomaior (Sp) see Sotomayor.

Souto Vedro (Port) a brand of sharp, dry, pétillant Vinho Verde produced by Amarante.

Souverain (USA) a winery based in the Alexander Valley Sonoma County, California. Grape varieties: Cabernet sauvignon, Chardonnay, Chenin blanc, Colombard, Johannisberg riesling and Zinfandel. Produces varietal and table wines.

Souverain Cellars (USA) a winery based near Lake Henessey, Napa Valley, California. Produces varietal wines.

Souverain Vineyards (USA) a winery based in Geyersville, California. Grape varieties: Cabernet sauvignon and Chardonnay. Produces varietal wines.

Souza (Port) vintage Port shippers. Vintages: 1965, 1970, 1974, 1978, 1979, 1980, 1982, 1983, 1985, 1987, 1991, 1994, 1997, 2003. Controlled by Barros.

Souzao (S.Afr) a red grape variety used in the making of Port-type fortified wines.

Souzy-Champigny (Fr) a commune in the Saumur area of the Anjou-Saumur district, Loire region.

Soveh (Isr) a 'Bible wine'.

Sovelle (N.Z) a white, wood-treated, Burgundy-style wine produced by Montana Wines.

Sovereign (Eng) a beer 1040 O.G. brewed by the Larkins Brewery at Larkins Farm, Chiddingstone, Kent. Now known as Chiddingstone Bitter 4% alc by vol. See also Traditional Standard, Larkins Best.

Sovereign (Fr) a bottle size (35 bottles) of Champagne produced by Taittinger in 1988. Now no longer produced. See also Salomon.

Sovereign Bitter (Eng) a keg bitter 1037 O.G. brewed by the Samuel Smith Brewery in Tadcaster, Yorkshire.

Soviet Cocktail (Cktl) ¾ measure vodka, ¼ measure medium Sherry, ¼ measure dry vermouth. Shake over ice, strain into an ice-filled old-fashioned glass and top with a twist of lemon peel juice.

Sowman Estate (N.Z) a winery based in Marlborough, South Island.

Soyeux (Fr) denotes smooth, silky wine.

Soyhières (Fr) a district containing the oldest distilleries in the Jura area. Produces whiskey and damassine.

Sozzled (Eng) a slang term for drunk/intoxicated. (Fr) = paf.

Sozzled Swine (Eng) a 5.5% alc by vol. ale brewed by the Ring 'O' Bells Brewery, Cornwall.

Spa (Bel) a still and sparkling mineral water of Spa. Still comes from the Reine Springs in the Ardenne hills whilst the sparkling comes from the Marie-Henriette Springs.

Spa (Eng) a 3.7% alc by vol. ale brewed by Bath Ales Ltd., Avon.

SPA (Eng) abbr: Special Pale Ale 1041 O.G. brewed by the Wethered Brewery in Marlow, Buckinghamshire.

Spaa Aqua (Ind) a natural spring mineral water (established 1997) from Vijayawada. pH 7.0

Spa Barisart (Bel) a still and sparkling natural spring mineral water from Spadel, Ardennes. Mineral contents (milligrammes per litre): Sodium 5mg/l, Calcium 5.5mg/l, Magnesium 1.5mg/l, Potassium 0.5mg/l, Bicarbonates 18mg/l, Chlorides 5.5mg/l, Sulphates 7.5mg/l, Nitrates 1.5mg/l, Silicates 10mg/l. Distributed by Crombie Eustace.

SpA Birra Peroni (Eng) a brewery (established 1846). (Add): Wellington Building, 28-32 Wellington Road, St. John's Wood, London NW8 9SP. Brews lager beer. Website: http://www.birraperoni.co.uk 'E'mail: srucci@birraperoni.co.uk

Spabrücken (Ger) village (Anb): Nahe. (Ber): Kreuznach. (Gro): Pfarrgarten. (Vin): Höll.

Space Doubt (Eng) a 5.5% alc by vol. star fruit cocktail Caribbean crush drink from Spilt Drinks in Exeter.

Spaceman (Cktl) 1½ measures vodka, ½ measure dry vermouth, dash Pernod, dash grenadine. Stir over ice and strain into a cocktail glass.

Spade (Sp) a name given in the Sherry region to the long branch left during pruning together with the Thumb. Also known as the Espada.

Spadel (Bel) a mineral water bottler, bottles both still and sparkling (owns Brecon Beacons Natural Waters).

Spagnol (Fr) a rare white grape variety grown in Provence.

Spain (Sp) a large wine-producing country on the

Iberian peninsular with the world's largest area planted with vines. Produces most styles of wines and is noted for Sherry and cava wines. Regions are: Alella, Alicante, Ampurdán Costa Brava, Aragón, Arribes, Balearic Islands, Bullas, Campo de Borja, Canaries, Cariñena, Calatayud, Cataluña, Cheste, Cigales, Costers del Segre, Empordà-Costa Brava, Estremadura, Gandesa Terralta, Galicia, Getariako Txakolina, Huelva, Jerez, Jumilla, La Mancha, León, Levante, Málaga, Manchuela, Montilla-Moriles, Montsant, Navarra, Penedés, Pla de Bages, Priorato, Rias Baixas, Ribera del Duero, Ribera del Guadiana, Ribeiro, Rioja, Rueda, Somontano, Tarragona, Terra Alta, Toro, Utiel-Requena, Valencia, Valdeorras, Valdepeñas, Vinos de Madrid and Yecla. *See also* Demoninación de Origen, Cava, Vino de la Tierra. Website: http://www.winesfromspain.com

Spalato (It) the name given to red table and dessert wines from the vineyards of central Italy.

Spa Line (Aus) a natural spring mineral water (established circa 1800) from Aubad, Tirol. Mineral contents (milligrammes per litre): Sodium 4.4mg/l, Calcium 431.26mg/l, Magnesium 47.2mg/l, Potassium 2.05mg/l, Bicarbonates 242.62mg/l, Sulphates 1027.86mg/l, Nitrates 0.6mg/l.

Spalletti (It) a Chianti Putto producer based in Tuscany. *see* Poggio Reale.

Spalletti di Montalbano (It) a Chianti Putto producer based in Tuscany.

Spalliera (It) a method of vine training (similar to the Cordon system). *see* Alberello.

Spalt (Ger) a strain of hops that produces pronounced bitterness in beers.

Spa Marie Henriette (Bel) a sparkling natural spring mineral water from Spa, Ardennes. Mineral contents (milligrammes per litre): Sodium 10.5mg/l, Calcium 11mg/l, Magnesium 7mg/l, Potassium 1.3mg/l, Bicarbonates 75mg/l, Chlorides 9.5mg/l, Sulphates 6.5mg/l, Nitrates 0.5mg/l, Silicates 15mg/l.

Spa Mineral Water (Pak) a natural spring mineral water brand (established 2003).

Spanchevtzi (Bul) a still, slightly alkaline natural spring mineral water from Spanchevizi-Varshetz. Mineral contents (milligrammes per litre): Sodium 44.9mg/l, Calcium 7.2mg/l, Potassium 0.51mg/l, Bicarbonates 97.6mg/l, Chlorides 4.7mg/l, Sulphates 25.1mg/l, Fluorides 0.6mg/l, Nitrates 2mg/l. pH 8.8

Spanish Brandy (Sp) a pot-distilled brandy, distilled from the wines of La Mancha and Valdepeñas. Produced mainly in Jerez and Penedés

Spanish Captain (Cktl) ⅓ measure dry Sherry, ⅔ measure white rum, teaspoon lime juice. Shake over ice, strain into a cocktail glass and decorate with a cherry.

Spanish Cocktail (Cktl) 60mls (½ gill) Italian vermouth, 4 dashes Angostura, ½ egg white. Shake well over ice, strain into a cocktail glass, top with a twist of lemon peel juice. Also known as Spanish Delight.

Spanish Delight (Cktl) *see* Spanish Cocktail.

Spanish Earth (Sp) a diatomaceous soil found in Lebrija, northern Andalusia. Used to remove proteins etc. out of Sherry. *See also* Silicaceous Earth.

Spanish Fly (Eng) the name for any drink that has been laced with a soft drug (or with a very high alcohol content).

Spanish Oyster (Cktl) 1 egg yolk (unbroken) in a goblet, add 50mls (2fl.ozs) dry Sherry, salt and pepper. Do not stir.

Spanish Punch (Sp) an alternative name for sangria, based with wine and fruit.

Spanish Town (Cktl) 40mls (⅓ gill) white rum, 3 dashes triple sec. Stir over ice and strain into a cocktail glass.

Spanish Wax (Euro) wax mixed with a little fat, used to seal the corks in the bottles in the nineteenth and early twentieth centuries to prevent insects, etc. getting at the cork.

Spanna (It) another name used for the red Nebbiolo grape.

Spanna (It) a red wine from the Vercelli province in Piemonte, made from the Spanna (Nebbiolo) grape

Spano (It) a red wine from 90% Negroamaro and 10% Malvasia Nera grapes. 60% of wine aged one year in barriques, 40% in stainless steel. Produced by Calò (Michele) & Figli, Via Masseria Vecchia, 73058 Tuglie (LE).

Sparea (It) a sparkling natural spring mineral water from Sparea. Mineral contents (milligrammes per litre): Sodium 1.1mg/l, Calcium 2.8mg/l, Magnesium 1mg/l, Potassium 0.3mg/l, Chlorides 0.3mg/l, Sulphates 4mg/l, Nitrates 3.7mg/l. pH 6.8

Spa Reine (Bel) a still and sparkling natural spring mineral water (established 1583) from Spa, Ardennes. (red label: sparkling/cyan label: light gas/blue label: still). Mineral contents (milligrammes per litre): Sodium 3mg/l, Calcium 4.5mg/l, Magnesium 1.3mg/l, Potassium 0.5mg/l, Bicarbonates 15mg/l, Chlorides 5mg/l, Sulphates 4mg/l, Nitrates 1.9mg/l, Silicates 7mg/l. pH 6.0

Spa Family Value Still Spring Water (Ire) a still natural spring mineral water from Rathmolyon. Mineral contents (milligrammes per litre): Sodium 8mg/l, Calcium 150mg/l, Magnesium 9mg/l, Potassium 4mg/l, Bicarbonates 28mg/l, Chlorides 28mg/l, Sulphates 34mg/l, Nitrates 7mg/l. pH 7.1

Sparging (Eng) in brewing, the process of spraying (sparging) the grist with hot liquor to extract the sugar.

Sparkler (Cktl)(Non-alc) 2 dashes Angostura in an ice-filled highball glass. Top with mineral water and dress with a cherry.

Sparkler (Eng) a device attached to the beer engine outlet. The beer is forced through small holes to produce a head and to aerate it. This can be varied by altering the setting of the sparkler.

S

Sparkletts (Pak) a still natural spring mineral water (established 1991) from Hattar, N.W.F.P. Mineral contents (milligrammes per litre): Calcium 55mg/l, Magnesium 17mg/l, Bicarbonates 180mg/l, Chlorides 3mg/l, Sulphates 11mg/l, Fluorides 0.12mg/l. pH 7.7

Sparkletts (USA) a natural spring mineral water from California. Mineral contents (milligrammes per litre): Sodium 3.8mg/l, Calcium 1.3mg/l, Magnesium 0.6-1.2mg/l, Bicarbonates 5.8mg/l, Chlorides 3.5mg/l, Sulphates 3.4mg/l. pH 7.3

Sparkling (Chi) a sparkling natural spring mineral water from Shanghai.

Sparkling (Eng) a term to describe a beverage that contains gas under pressure (Champagne, bottled mineral waters, aeriated waters, etc.) and when the cap is removed the gas is released in the form of bubbles.

Sparkling Aerobic (Cktl) 2 parts Johnny Walker Red Label Scotch whisky, 1 part Cointreau, 1 part lime juice, 6 parts soda water. Mix over ice, strain into an ice-filled highball glass and add a slice of lemon or lime.

Sparkling Ale (Eng) an old term used by brewers to denote that their bottled ales have been filtered.

Sparkling Apple Juice (Eng) a new name of the sparkling apple juice drink Apple Spark. Produced by Merrydown.

Sparkling Bordeaux (Fr) usually white or rosé wines from vineyards in the Garonne.

Sparkling Burgundy (Fr) denotes red wine made from the Gamay grape and white wine from the Aligoté. see Bourgogne Mousseux.

Sparkling Burgundy (USA) see Californian Sparkling Burgundy.

Sparkling Cider (Eng) a still cider injected with CO_2 gas.

Sparkling Golden Lexia (Austr) a clean, Muscat-sweet, non-alcoholic grape juice from Bonnonee, Victoria.

Sparkling Kir (Cktl) in a highball glass place 20mls (⅙ gill) blackcurrant cordial, ice and top with 40mls (⅓ gill) each of white wine and Ashbourne mineral water.

Sparkling Malvasia Bianca (USA) see California Sparkling Malvasia Bianca.

Sparkling Mineral Water (Eng) bottled mineral waters that are aeriated naturally or artificially with CO_2 gas. (Fr) = eau gazeuse minerale, (It) = acqua minerale frizzante, (Port) = água sem gas.

Sparkling Moselle (USA) see California Sparkling Moselle.

Sparkling Muscat (USA) see California Sparkling Muscat.

Sparkling Sauterne (USA) see California Sparkling Sauterne.

Sparkling Spring Water (S.Afr) a sparkling natural spring mineral water brand from Franschhoek.

Sparkling Wines (Eng) wines that contain CO_2 gas which has been put in either by the traditional method, cuve close, Charmat or injection. (Den) = vin mousserende.

Sparkling Wit (Eng) a 4.5% alc by vol. ale brewed by the Fenland Brewery Ltd., Cambridgeshire.

Spark Lite (Mex) a natural spring mineral water. Mineral contents (milligrammes per litre): Sodium 15mg/l, Calcium 15mg/l, Magnesium 7.5mg/l, Bicarbonates 100mg/l, Chlorides 7.5mg/l, Sulphates 7.5mg/l, Nitrates 1mg/l. pH 7.0

Sparr (Fr) an Alsace wine-producer. (Add): 2 Rue de la Premier Armée, 68240 Sigolsheim.

Sparta (Can) a natural spring mineral water from Sparta, Ontario. Mineral contents (milligrammes per litre): Sodium 0.9mg/l, Calcium 21.6mg/l, Magnesium 6.6mg/l, Potassium 0.33mg/l, Bicarbonates 83.8mg/l, Chlorides 0.2mg/l, Sulphates 12.7mg/l, Nitrates 0.12mg/l.

Spartan (Eng) a 5.2% alc by vol. pale coloured cider produced by Thatchers Sandford, north Somerset. A single variety cider apple cider. See also Cox's Katy, Tremletts Bitter.

Spätburgunder (Ger) a red grape variety flourishing on the Rhine and the Ahr, also in Baden. It produces a dark, strong and finely spiced wine. Known in France as Pinot noir, in Italy as Pinot nero. See also Frühburgunder and Mariafelder.

Spaten Franziskaner Bräu GmbH (Ger) a large, noted brewery. (Add): Marketing Division, Marsstrasse 46-48, Munich D-80335. Brews a large range of beers and lagers including Spatengold. Website: http://www.franziskanerbraeu.com

Spatengold (Ger) a pale beer 5.4% alc by vol. brewed in Munich by the Spatenbräu Brauerei.

Spätlese (Aus) a wine made from grapes picked after the main harvest which are completely ripe. Minimum must weight of 19° KMW. Wine must be bottled in Austria and connot be sold before the 1st March of the following year. see Prädikatsweine.

Spätlese (Ger) lit: 'late-harvest', denotes a style of wine made from grapes gathered after the official harvest date. Have a higher sugar content, are made naturally without additives and are of QmP. quality. 76°Oe–95°Oe. (Aus) = spätlese, (Austr) = late-harvest, (Fr) = vendange tardive, (It) = vendemmia tardiva, (S.Afr) = edeloes.

Spätrot (Aus) see Zierfändler.

Spätrot-Rotgipfler (Aus) a wine produced from a blend of Rotgipfler and Zierfandler grapes.

Spatzendreck (S.Afr) the label for a late-harvest white wine (Chenin blanc and Pinot blanc blend) produced by the Delheim Wines winery, Stellenbosch, Western Cape..

Spaulding Vineyard (USA) a vineyard based in the Napa Valley, California. 8.5ha. Grape variety: Chardonnay. Also owns the Stonegate Vineyard.

Spauna (It) an alternative name for the Nebbiolo grape in northern Italy.

Spa Water (Bel) see Spa.

Spa Water (Hol) mineral water.

Spay (Ger) village (Anb): Mittelrhein. (Ber): Rheinburgengau. (Gro): Gedeonseck. (Vin): Engelstein.

Speakeasy (USA) an outlet for the sale of illicit beverages during the Prohibition period. Gets its name from the New York Irish saloon keepers who used to ask their clients to '*speak-easy*' when drinking after hours so as not to be heard by any passing police officers.

Special (Ch.Isles) a draught bitter 1045 O.G. brewed by the Guernsey Brewery, St. Peter Port, Guernsey. Originally named Captain. Now brewed on Jersey by the Mary Ann Brewery.

Special (Chile) denotes a wine that is 2 years old.

Special (Eng) a 6.6% alc by vol. strong ale brewed by the Blue Anchor Brewery, Cornwall.

Special (Eng) a 3.9% alc by vol. bitter ale brewed by the Roosters Brewing C°. Ltd., North Yorkshire.

Special (Eng) a 4.5% alc by vol. bitter ale brewed by the Rudgate Brewery Ltd., North Yorkshire.

Special (Eng) a term used to describe above average beers.

Special (Sp) a solera brandy produced by Osborne. *See also* Tres Ceros, Veterano.

Special Ale (Eng) a 4.4% alc by vol. bottled ale produced by the Black Sheep Brewery, Masham, North Yorkshire.

Special Ale (Eng) a 5.2% alc by vol. ale brewed by the Sharps Brewery, Cornwall.

Special Bitter (Eng) a traditional cask ale 1038 O.G. from Goddards Brewery, Ryde, Isle of Wight.

Special Chun Mee (Tai) *see* Chun Mee.

Special Club Brut (Fr) a vintage de luxe cuvée Champagne produced from 26% Chardonnay and 74% Pinot noir grapes by Henri Goutorbe.

Special d'Avignon (Bel) a dark, sweet ale brewed in Nismes, southern Belgium.

Special Dry (Can) a 5.5% alc by vol. dry lager produced by Molson. Process involves a longer fermentation time and more complete starch conversion.

Special Dutch (Hol) a sweet, premium beer brewed by a Stella Artois subsidiary brewery.

Speciale Aerts (Bel) a top-fermented beer traditionally sold in Burgundy bottles.

Special Late Harvest (S.Afr) a wine classification. Must have 20–50 grammes per litre of grape sugar. 22° Balling minimum.

Special London Ale (Eng) a 6.4% alc by vol. bottle conditioned ale brewed by Young's, Wandsworth, London. *See also* Ram Rod, Oatmeal Stout.

Special Marsala (It) an early Marsala of the twentieth century produced in northern Italy and abroad using additives, chemicals and colouring.

Special Old (Can) a blended Canadian whisky produced by Hiram Walker.

Special Quality Wine (Hun) a State wine seal is awarded to those wines made from grapes attacked by noble rot.

Special R (Eng) a range of non-alcoholic fruit drinks containing fruit and 'Nutrasweet'™ (an artificial sweetener) produced by Robinsons.

Special Red (Eng) a high strength white cider 8.4% alc by vol.

Special Red Ale (Eng) a strong bottled ale 1052 O.G.

brewed by the Paine Brewery, St. Neots, Cambridgeshire for export.

Special Rough Cocktail (Cktl) ½ measure Calvados, ½ measure Cognac, 2 dashes Pernod. Stir over ice and strain into a cocktail glass.

Special Select Dry (S.Afr) the label for a red wine (Merlot and Pinotage blend) produced by the Stellendrift winery, Stellenbosch, Western Cape.

Special Selection (S.Afr) the export label for a range of wines produced by the Laibach Vineyards winery, Stellenbosch, Western Cape.

Special Spingo (Eng) a cask-conditioned ale 6.6% alc by vol. from the Blue Anchor Brewery.

Special Variety Madeira (Mad) blended, the youngest wine must be a minimum of 10 years old after estufagem. If grape variety is stated then it must contain 85% of that named variety.

Special Vat (Eng) a draught premium cider from Taunton in Somerset.

Specific Gravity (Eng) *abbr*: S.G. The ratio of the density of a substance to that of still water (water being 1000). *See also* O.G. (the S.G. prior to fermentation) and Twadell Scale.

Speckled House Riesling (Austr) a dry white wine produced by the Setanta Vineyard, Adelaide Hills, South Australia.

Spectacular (Eng) a 4.6% alc by vol. light coloured seasonal ale brewed by Ridleys Hartford End Brewery, Chelmsford, Essex.

Spectre Special (Eng) a special ale brewed by Spinnaker for Hallowe'en.

Spectrum (USA) the brand-name for a range of red or white wine-based '*coolers*' in cans that are produced by Paul Masson in California. Flavours include: lemon, redcurrant, peach, strawberry, mango and orange juice. 6% alc by vol.

Spectrum Brewery (Eng) a brewery (established 2002). (Add): c/o Briton Way, Wymondham, Norfolk NR18 0TT. Brews: Bezzants Bitter 4% alc by vol., Black Buffle Stout 4.5% alc by vol., Don't Panic 4.2% alc by vol., 42 4.2% alc by vol., North Star 3.6% alc by vol., Spring Promise 4.5% alc by vol. Website: http://www.spectrumbrewery.co.uk 'E'mail: info@spectrumbrewery.co.uk

Speculation Ale (Eng) a 4.7% alc by vol. bottle-conditioned beer from the Freeminer Brewery, Sling, Coleford, Gloscestershire.

Speed Drinking (Eng) a slang term for the fast '*volumn*' drinking that often takes place during the '*happy hour*' pub/hotel bar drinking sessions. Also known as Silly Drinking.

Speight's (N.Z) the brand-name used by the New Zealand Breweries in Dunedin.

Spell Binder (Eng) a 4.1% alc by vol. ale brewed by Northern Brewing, Cheshire.

Spencer Cocktail (Cktl) ⅔ measure dry gin, ⅓ measure apricot brandy, 2 dashes orange juice, 1 dash Campari. Shake over ice, strain into a cocktail glass, top with a cherry and twist of orange peel juice.

Spencer Hill Estate (N.Z) a winery. (Add): Best Road, Upper Moutere, P.O. Box 3255, Richmond,

Nelson. 13ha. Grape varieties: Chardonnay, Sauvignon blanc, Pinot noir, Pinot gris, Merlot, Riesling, Gewürztraminer.

Spencer's Special (Eng) a limited edition beer label from the Federation Brewery to celebrate an employees 50 years service with the brewery.

Spence's Vineyard (N.Z) a former vineyard that has now been closed.

Spendrup's Brewery (Swe) a brewery based in Grängesberg that produces Old Gold Lager beer 5% alc by vol.

Spent Grains (Eng) in brewing the term for left-over malt grains after mashing, usually sold for cattle food.

Spent Liquor (Eng) a term used for the leftover residue after distillation has occurred.

Spergola (It) the name used in Emilia Romagna for the Sauvignon blanc grape, also known as the Spergolina.

Spergolina (It) see Spergola.

Sperone (It) a producer of Moscato spumante wines in Piemonte.

Sperr (Aus) a term that describes a wine that leaves a drying taste in the mouth. Caused by sulphur or woodiness.

Spessart (Ger) a natural spring mineral water. Mineral contents (milligrammes per litre): Calcium 60mg/l, Magnesium 30.7mg/l, Potassium 3.5mg/l, Chlorides 31mg/l.

Spetsat (Swe) a herb beer brewed by the Till Brewery.

Spey [River] (Scot) see Speyside.

Speyburn (Scot) a single malt whisky distillery based north of Inverness, a highland malt whisky 43% alc by vol.

Spey Cast (Scot) a de luxe blended Scotch whisky blended by Gordon and MᵃᶜPhail of Elgin 40% alc by vol.

Spey Royal (Scot) a blended Scotch whisky 40% alc by vol.

Speyside (Scot) a famous area of eastern Scotland on the river Spey which produces many of the highland malt whiskies.

Speyside Distillery Cº. [The] (Scot) a malt whisky distillery based on the river Spey. Produces a range of whiskies including an 8 year old single malt, Druniguisk, Speyside Millennium [The].

Speyside Millennium [The] (Scot) exclusive first distillation bottled from the first casks ever distilled at The Speyside Disitllery Cº. A limited edition of 2000 specially numbered bottles. Sold in a thistle shaped decanter in a lockable wooden tantalus.

Spezi (Ger) a malty, Bavarian lager beer 5% alc by vol. brewed by the Riegele Brauerei in Augsburg.

Spezia [La] (It) a coastal region of Liguria from which Cinque Terre is part. Many vineyards only accessible by boat as they rise straight out of the sea.

Speziator (Ger) a doppelbock beer 7.9% alc by vol. brewed by the Riegele Brauerei in Augsburg.

Sphinx (Cktl) 50mls (2fl.ozs) gin, 10mls (½ fl.oz) Italian vermouth, 10mls (½ fl.oz) French

vermouth. Stir over ice, strain into a cocktail glass and top with a slice of lemon.

Spiagga de Lesina (It) the name given to the white, dessert wines from Dalmatia.

Sphinx (Eng) a 6.5% alc by vol. cinnamon and apple spiced ale brewed by St. Peter's Brewery, St. Peter's Hall, South Elmham St. Peter, near Bungay, Suffolk. See also Winter Ale.

Spiced Tea (Sri.L) a blend of high grown Ceylon teas. Pekoe leaf, mixed with cloves and dried orange peel which gives a full, heady aroma.

Spiced Tea Punch (Cktl) 850mls (1½ pints) tea, juice of a lemon, 550mls (1 pint) red wine, 4 cloves, 1 cinnamon stick, sugar syrup. Heat together, strain and serve hot in glasses with a slice of lemon.

Spice Imperial (Eng) a clove and orange peel-flavoured tea produced by Whittards of Chelsea.

Spice Route Wine Company (S.Afr) a wine estate (established 1998) situated in Amoskuil near Malmesbury. 123ha. (part of the Fairview Winery) based in Malmesbury, Paarl, Western Cape. Grape varieties: Chenin blanc, Grenache, Merlot, Mourvèdre, Pinotage, Sauvignon blanc, Shiraz, Viognier. Labels: Flagship, Malabar.

Spickenberg (Aus) a vineyard site on the banks of the River Danube in the Kremstal region.

Spicy (Eng) the term used to describe a varietal characteristic i.e. Gewürztraminer, Scheurebe, or a complex bouquet or palate derived from cask and bottle ageing.

Spider Cocktail (Cktl) place 25mls (1fl.oz) crème de café in a highball glass, top with Coca Cola and a scoop of vanilla ice cream, stir and serve with straws.

Spider Mite (Eng) family: *Tetranychidae*. The vine pest (Lat) = *Panonychus ulmi*. see Red Spider.

Spiegel (Aus) a vineyard site on the banks of the River Danube in the Kremstal region.

Spiegel (Aus) a vineyard site based on the banks of the River Kamp situated in the Kamptal region.

Spiegel (Fr) an A.C. Grand Cru Alsace vineyard at Bergholtz and Guebwiller, Haut-Rhin 18.26ha.

Spiegel (Ger) vineyard (Anb): Pfalz. (Ber): Mittelhaardt-Deutsche Weinstrasse. (Gro): Meerspinne. (Vil): Mussbach.

Spiegel (Hol) glass.

Spiegelberg (Ger) grosslage (Anb): Rheinhessen. (Ber): Nierstein. (Vils): Nackenheim, Nierstein.

Spiegelberg (Ger) vineyard (Anb): Baden. (Ber): Badische Bergstrasse/Kraichgau. (Gro): Stiftsberg. (Vil): Elsenz.

Spiegelberg (Ger) vineyard (Anb): Baden. (Ber): Badische Bergstrasse/Kraichgau. (Gro): Stiftsberg. (Vil): Kraichtal (stadtteil Landshausen and Menzingen).

Spiegelberg (Ger) vineyard (Anb): Baden. (Ber): Badische Bergstrasse/Kraichgau. (Gro): Stiftsberg. (Vil): Tiefenbach.

Spiegeln (Aus) a vineyard site on the banks of the River Danube in the Kremstal region.

Spiel (Ger) denotes a balanced wine.

Spielberg (Ger) village (Anb): Württemberg. (Ber):

Württembergisch Unterland. (Gro): Stromberg. (Vin): Liebenberg.

Spielberg (Ger) vineyard (Anb): Pfalz. (Ber): Mittelhaardt-Deutsche Weinstrasse. (Gro): Hochmess. (Vil): Bad Dürkheim.

Spielberg (Ger) vineyard (Anb): Pfalz. (Ber): Mittelhaardt-Deutsche Weinstrasse. (Gro): Hofstück. (Vil): Meckenheim.

Spielbühl (Ger) vineyard (Anb): Württemberg. (Ber): Württembergisch Unterland. (Gro): Lindelberg. (Vil): Harsberg (ortsteil Neuholz).

Spier Estate (S.Afr) a famous winery (established 1767) based in Stellenbosch, Western Cape. 300ha. (Add): Box 28, Vlottenburg 7604. Part of Winecorp. Grape varieties: Cabernet sauvignon, Chardonnay, Chenin blanc, Colombard, Merlot, Pinotage, Riesling, Sauvignon blanc, Shiraz and Viognier. Labels: Discover, Private Collection, Vintage Selection and many varietal wines including Port-style wine. Websites: http://www.spier.co.za/http://www.winecorp.co.za

Spiesheim (Ger) village (Anb): Rheinhessen. (Ber): Nierstein. (Gro): Petersberg. (Vin): Osterberg.

Spiess (Aus) a vineyard site based on the banks of the River Kamp situated in the Kamptal region.

Spiess (Ger) vineyard (Anb): Pfalz. (Ber): Mittelhaardt-Deutsche Weinstrasse. (Gro): Hofstück. (Vil): Ruppertsberg.

S.Pietro (It) a natural spring mineral water from San Pietro.

Spigot (Eng) the cask bung hole, also the old name for a tap (cask).

Spigot (USA) the name for a cask tap.

Spike (Austr) a 5.5% alc by vol Australian white cider from Yates Brothers Ltd.

Spike a Drink (Eng) to lace a drink with a strong alcoholic liquor. Is usually done without the knowledge of the drinker!

Spiked (USA) a slang term similar to fortified, a drink that has had alcohol added to it. Especially in the Prohibition era.

Spiked Beer (USA) a glass of beer to which a measure of neutral spirits (vodka) has been added to it. Usually not to the knowledge of the drinker.

Spiked Lemonade (USA) lemonade with spirit (usually whiskey) added to it.

Spiked Wine (Sp) a wine that has been fermented with the mother stock.

Spike's on t'way (Eng) a 4.2% alc by vol. ale brewed by the Anglo Dutch Brewery, West Yorkshire.

Spile (Eng) a small wood/cane peg (hard/soft spile) which is inserted into the shive through the tut hole. Is used either to allow the escape of CO_2 gas (soft cane spile) or prevent the escape of CO_2 gas (hard wooden spile).

Spillare (It) to tap a cask or barrel.

Spilt Drinks (Eng) a drinks manufacturer based in Exeter. Produces: Jammin–a 5.5% alc by vol. pina colada-flavoured Caribbean crush. Also Mellow Yellow (banana and mango), Space Doubt (star fruit), Batida, Black Cherry Rum, Kampai.

Spin (Fr) a 7.9% alc by vol. bottled lager brewed by Heineken.

Spingo (Eng) an early Cornish word for strong ale.

Spingo (Eng) the collective name of Blue Anchor beers brewed by the Blue Anchor (Helston) Brewery in Cornwall.

Spinnaker Brewery (Eng) a brewery. (Add): The Brewery-on-the-Sea, Lancing, West Sussex. Brews: Mild 3.5% alc by vol., Bitter and London Porter.

Spinnaker Mild (Eng) a 3.5% alc by vol. mild brewed by micro-brewery The Brewery-on-Sea, Lancing, West Sussex.

Spinning Dog Brewery (Eng) a brewery (established 2000). (Add): 88 St. Owen Street, Hereford, Herefordshire HR1 2QD. Brews: Celtic Gold 4% alc by vol., Herefordshire Olde Bull 3.9% alc by vol., Mutleys Old Oak Meal Stout 4.4% alc by vol., Mutleys Pit Stop 4% alc by vol., Mutts Nutts 5% alc by vol. Website: http://www.spinningdogbrewery.co.uk 'E'mail: jfkenyon@aol.com

Spinona [La] (It) vineyard. (Add): Via Secondine 22, 1050 Barbaresco (CN). Noted for D.O.C.G. Barbaresco and Barolo, D.O.C. Barbera d'Alba, Dolcetto d'Alba, Nebbiolo, Chardonnay and Freisa wines.

Spinster's Dream (Cktl) 1 measure gin, ½ measure brandy, ½ measure passion fruit juice, 4 dashes orange Curaçao. Shake over ice and strain into a cocktail glass.

Spiral (Eng) for cocktails the complete peel of fruit cut in spiral fashion.

Spiral Cellar [The] (Eng) see Caves Harnois. (Add): 27 Grafton Park Road, Worcester Park, Surrey.

Spire (Eng) a high gravity bottled beer produced by Whitbread at Fremlins Brewery (23,000 pints only for Faversham Church Restoration Appeal, Kent).

Spire Ale (Eng) a 3.8% alc by vol. ale brewed by the Stonehenge (Bunces Brewery) Ltd., Wiltshire.

Spireite Special (Eng) an ale brewed by Ward's in Sheffield.

Spirit (Eng) the name given to the alcohol removed from a fermented beverage during distillation. see Rectified Spirit. (Den) = spiritus/liquor.

Spirit (Scot) the name for the spirit from the second distillation in malt whisk production. Also known as New Make or Clearick.

Spirit Beverages (USA) lit: 'the result from a pure distillation of fermented beverages'.

Spirit Caramel (Scot) a caramel colouring that can be used to colour malt whiskies that may lack colour through aging.

Spirit Frame (Eng) a Victorian silver or plate cruet stand type holder for spirit bottles.

Spirit of Freedom (Eng) a 4.3% alc by vol. ale brewed by the Belvoir Brewery, Leicestershire.

Spirit of Today (USA) the label of a 4 year old Bourbon whiskey.

Spirits (USA) the generic term for distilled liquors, neutral spirits and Cologne spirits, a spirit distilled out at 95% alc by vol. or more. Used for blending and the preparation of rectified products. (Den) = spiritus/liquor.

Spirit Safe (Scot) in malt whisky distilling, a Customs and Excise glass case where the new distillate passes through under lock and key. The distiller can separate the foreshots and feints by the operation of levers.

Spirits of Wine (Eng) the distillate from wine, eau-de-vie-de-vin (brandy).

Spirits Receiver (Scot) a container to receive the newly distilled spirit in malt whisky production.

Spirit Tyne (Eng) a 4% alc by vol. ale brewed by the Mordue Brewery Ltd., Tyne & Wear.

Spiritueux (Fr) spirity, a wine high in alcohol.

Spirituosen (Aus)(Ger) liquor/alcoholic beverages.

Spirituous (Eng) lit: 'containing alcohol', an alcoholic beverage.

Spiritus (Den) spirits.

Spiritus Vini de Gallice (Lat) the medical term for brandy used in England during Roman times.

Spirit Water (Can) a natural spring mineral water from Annacis Island, British Columbia.

Spirit Whiskey (USA) a mixture of neutral spirits and not less than 5% on a proof gallon (US) basis of whiskey, or straight whiskey and whiskey, if the straight whiskey component is less than 20% on a proof gallon (US) basis.

Spirity (Eng) a taste of spirits applied to wine especially a fortified wine. i.e. Port.

Spitalberg (Ger) vineyard (Anb): Nahe. (Ber): Schloss Böckelheim. (Gro): Paradiesgarten. (Vil): Sobernheim-Steinhardt.

Spitaller (Aus) a vineyard site on the banks of the River Danube in the Kremstal region.

Spitfire (Eng) a 4.7% alc by vol. amber cask or bottle conditioned bitter from Shepherd Neame, Faversham, Kent. See also Bishops Finger, Masterbrew.

Spittoon (Eng) a metal container used to spit/pour excess wine into during a wine tasting session. (Fr) = cracher du vin, (Ger) = spucknapf, (It) = spumare di vino, (Sp) = escupir el vino.

Spittoons (USA) a metal container (urn) used in the nineteenth century in saloon bars for customers to spit tobacco juice from the habit of chewing a tobacco plug.

Spitz (Ger) denotes a thin wine, deteriorating.

Spitz (S.Afr) the label for a range of wines produced by the Bellingham winery, Wellington, Western Cape.

Spitzberg (Ger) vineyard (Anb): Rheinhessen. (Ber): Nierstein. (Gro): Domherr. (Vil): Stadecken-Elsheim.

Spitzenberg (Ger) vineyard (Anb): Baden. (Ber): Badische Bergstrasse/Kraichgau. (Gro): Mannaberg. (Vil): Wiesloch.

Spitzengewächs (Ger) an old term used to denote best growths (now no longer used).

Spitzenlagen (Ger) peak growths, these vineyards almost always produce outstanding wines.

Spitzenweins (Aus)(Ger) lit: 'peak wines', the best wines, quality wines.

Splash (Eng) an informal request for a dash of one beverage into another. i.e. a 'splash' of soda into a measure of whisky.

Spliced (S.Afr) the label for a red wine (Cabernet sauvignon, Merlot, Ruby cabernet and Shiraz blend) produced by the Raka winery, Walker Bay, Western Cape.

Splice the Mainbrace (Eng) the term used in the Royal Navy for the issue of the crews' daily rum ration.

Split (USA) same as a quarter bottle 6fl.oz (U.S. 187mls).

Splitrock (Austr) a natural spring mineral water brand.

Splitstone Pale Ale (Scot) a 4.2% alc by vol. pale ale brewed by the Far North Brewery, Caithness.

Spoetzl Brewery (USA) a brewery based in Shiner, Texas. Brews: Shiner Premium Beer.

Spogna (It) a sparkling natural spring mineral water from Aquila, Abruzzo. Mineral contents (milligrammes per litre): Sodium 1.6mg/l, Calcium 50mg/l, Magnesium 5mg/l, Potassium 0.4mg/l, Bicarbonates 195mg/l, Chlorides 7mg/l, Sulphates 1.3mg/l, Nitrates 0.9mg/l, Silicates 1.7mg/l, Oxygen 7mg/l. pH 7.8

Spoiled Beer (Eng) a beer that has spoiled whilst at the brewery. Excise duty can be reclaimed.

Spoletinum (It) a red wine produced in central Italy in Roman times.

Sponheim (Ger) village (Anb): Nahe. (Ber): Schloss Böckelheim. (Gro): Rosengarten. (Vins): Abtei, Grafenberg, Klostergarten, Mühlberg.

Sponsheim (Ger) village (Anb): Rheinhessen. (Ber): Bingen. (Gro): Sankt Rochuskapelle. (Vin): Palmenstein.

Spontaneous Fermentation (W.Ind) wild fermentation in rum production.

Spontin (Bel) a natural spring mineral water from Spontin. Mineral contents (milligrammes per litre): Sodium 14mg/l, Calcium 38mg/l, Magnesium 15mg/l, Potassium 2.5mg/l, Bicarbonates 180mg/l, Chlorides 19mg/l, Sulphates 28mg/l, Nitrates 6.5mg/l, Silicates 19mg/l. pH 7.3

Spore (Eng) the condition a yeast cell (or certain bacteria cells) can adopt when deprived of moisture. Will lie dormant until moisture is restored i.e. dried yeast.

Sporen (Fr) an A.C. Alsace Grand Cru vineyard at Riquewihr, Haut-Rhin 22ha.

Sporen (Fr) a lesser white grape variety grown in eastern France.

Sporting House (Eng) an eighteenth and nineteenth century name for an inn or public house where gambling took place or sportsmen frequented.

Sport Lager (Eng) a keg lager beer 1036 O.G. brewed by the Leicester Brewery.

Sportsman Bitter (Eng) a cask-conditioned bitter from Ridleys in Chelmsford, Essex. See also Old Bob, Bishops Ale, Stock Ale.

Sportsman Lager (S.Afr) a lager beer brewed by Intercontinental Breweries

Spot (Eng) an informal request for a small amount of

S

one beverage to be added to the main drink. i.e. whisky and a 'spot' of soda. See also Dash and Splash.

Spots Farm (Eng) a vineyard, also known as the Tenterden Vineyards. (Add): Small Hythe, Tenterden, Kent. Grape varieties: Bacchus, Gutenborner, Müller-Thurgau, Reichensteiner, Seyval blanc and others.

Spottswoode Winery (USA) a winery based in St. Helena, Napa Valley, California. Produces varietal wines.

Spotykach (Rus) a cherry-based spirit.

Spraying (Eng) vines sprayed to protect against mildew, oiidium, insects, etc. see Bordeaux Mixture. Also with water to protect against frost in the Spring. see Aspersion.

Spread Eagle (Eng) a home-brew public house (established 1983) in Erpingham, Norfolk. Home of the Woodeforde Brewery. Brews: Spread Eagle Bitter.

Spread Eagle Bitter (Eng) a cask-conditioned Bitter 1036 O.G. brewed by the Spread Eagle public house in Woodeforde, Norfolk.

Spreequell (Ger) a natural spring mineral water from Berlin. Mineral contents (milligrammes per litre): Sodium 48mg/l, Calcium 208mg/l, Magnesium 22.8mg/l, Potassium 4.1mg/l, Bicarbonates 403mg/l, Chlorides 93.9mg/l, Sulphates 258mg/l.

Sprendlingen (Ger) village (Anb): Rheinhessen. (Ber): Bingen. (Gro): Abtey. (Vins): Hölle, Honigberg, Klostergarten, Sonnenberg, Wissberg.

Spriggan Ale (Eng) a 3.8% alc by vol. ale brewed by Skinner's Brewery, Truro, Cornwall.

Spring (Eng) the source of a natural outflow of ground water. (Fr) = source, (Ger) = quelle, (It) = sorgente, (Pol) = źródło, (Sp) = fuente/manatial.

Spring (Gre) a natural spring mineral water from Karouzanou Lyttos. Mineral contents (milligrammes per litre): Sodium 38.7mg/l, Calcium 72mg/l, Magnesium 17mg/l, Potassium 1.6mg/l, Bicarbonates 216mg/l, Chlorides 44mg/l, Sulphates 93.7mg/l. pH 8.0

Spring Ale [S] (Eng) a 3.8% alc by vol. spring ale brewed by the Wickwar Brewing C°. Ltd., Gloucestershire.

Springbank (Scot) a single malt whisky distillery in the centre of Campbeltown. Owned and operated by J. and A. Mitchell and C°. of Argyll. A Campbeltown malt. Produces a 12 year old Malt at 45% alc by vol. and 57% alc by vol. Also a 21 year old 46% alc by vol. and a 25 year old. Standard blend is Campbeltown Loch at 40% alc by vol.

Spring Beer (Eng) a 4.3% alc by vol. seasonal beer brewed by the Exe Valley Brewery, Silverton, Devon using Phoenix hops (available March to May).

Springberry Scottish (Scot) a natural spring mineral water from Gallaberry Estate, Kirkton, Dumfries.

Springbok [1] (Cktl) 1 measure white rum, 1

measure Van der Hum, 1 measure fresh cream. Shake well over ice, strain into a cocktail glass, Serve with straws and a twist of orange peel juice on top.

Springbok [2] (Cktl) ⅓ measure Van der Hum, ⅓ measure Lillet, ⅓ measure medium Sherry, 2 dashes orange bitters. Stir well over ice and strain into a cocktail glass.

Springbok Ale (Eng) a 5% alc by vol. light ale brewed in April and May by Cain Brewery Stanhope Street, Liverpool.

Spring Breeze (Eng) a 5% alc by vol. bottled pale ale brewed by George Bateman & Son Ltd., Lincolnshire.

Spring Call (Eng) a 4% alc by vol. ale brewed by the Hogs Back Brewery Ltd., Surrey.

Spring Clear (Eng) a natural lemon and lime fruit flavoured, low calorie sparkling spring water drink.

Springdale Winery (USA) a winery based in Granby, Connecticut. Produces mainly French hybrid wines.

Spring Duw (Wal) a natural spring mineral water (established 2002) from Gwynedd. Mineral contents (milligrammes per litre): Sodium 15mg/l, Calcium 1.4mg/l, Magnesium 1.1mg/l, Potassium 1mg/l, Chlorides 23mg/l, Sulphates 6mg/l, Nitrates 25.6mg/l. pH 6.0

Spring Farm Vineyard (Eng) a vineyard (established 1981) based at Moorlynch, Bridgewater, Somerset. 6.5ha. Grape varieties: Madeleine angevine 25%, Müller-Thurgau 20%, Seyval blanc 20%, Schönberger 10% and others. Sells wines under the Moorlynch label.

Spring Feeling (Cktl) ½ measure dry gin, ¼ measure lime juice, ¼ measure green Chartreuse. Shake over ice and strain into a cocktail glass.

Spring Fever (Eng) a draught seasonal ale 4% alc by vol. brewed with malted oats and ginseng from the Ushers Brewery in Trowbridge.

Springfield Bitter (Eng) a bitter beer 1036 O.G. brewed by Highgate and Walsall Brewery. (Formerly by Bass, Mitchells and Butlers in Wolverhampton, then in Birmingham).

Springfield Bitter (Eng) a bitter beer brewed by the White Swan, a home-brew public house in Netherton, Lancashire.

Springfield Brewery (Eng) a brewery formerly belonging to Bass, Mitchells and Butlers based in Wolverhampton, Staffs.

Springfield Estate (S.Afr) a winery (established 1995) based in Robertson, Western Cape. 150ha. (Add): P.O. Box 770, Robertson 6705. Grape varieties: Cabernet franc, Cabernet sauvignon, Chardonnay, Merlot, Petit verdot, Sauvignon blanc. Labels: Life From Stone, Methode Ancienne, Special Cuvée, The Work of Time, Whole Berry, Wild Yeast. Website: http://www.springfieldestate.com

Springfontein (S.Afr) a winery (established 1996) based in Walkerbay, Western Cape. 25ha. Grape varieties: Cabernet sauvignon, Chardonnay,

Chenin blanc, Merlot, Mourvèdre, Petit verdot, Pinotage, Sauvignon blanc, Sémillon, Shiraz. Labels: Ikhalezi, Jil's Dune, Jonathan's Ridge, Ulumbaza. Website: http://www.springfontein.co.za

Spring Fresh (Mal) a still natural spring mineral water from Bukit Raja. Mineral contents (milligrammes per litre): Sodium 4.94mg/l, Calcium 9.19mg/l, Magnesium 0.26mg/l, Potassium 0.33mg/l, Bicarbonates 5.3mg/l, Chlorides 4.97mg/l. pH 6.7

Spring Goddess (Eng) a 4.2% alc by vol bottled pale ale brewed by the Batemans Brewery, Skegness, Lincolnshire.

Spring Grove (S.Afr) a label for a red wine range (Cabernet sauvignon and Shiraz) from Zorgvliet Wines, Stellenbosch, Western Cape.

Springhead Bitter (Eng) a 4% alc by vol. bitter ale brewed by Springhead Brewery, Sutton on Trent, Nottinghamshire.

Springhead Brewery (Eng) a brewery (established 1990). (Add): Old Great North Road, Sutton on Trent, Newark, Nottinghamshire NG23 6QS. Brews: Barebones 4.7% alc by vol., Charlies Angel 4.5% alc by vol., Cromwell's Hat 6% alc by vol., Goodrich Castle 4.4% alc by vol., Newark Castle Brown 5% alc by vol., Oliver's Army 4.4% alc by vol., Puritans Porter 4% alc by vol., Roaring Meg 5.5% alc by vol., Roundheads Gold 4.2% alc by vol., Rupert's Ruin 4.2% alc by vol., Springhead Bitter 4% alc by vol., Surrender 1646 3.6% alc by vol., Sweetlips 4.6% alc by vol., The Leveller 4.8% alc by vol., Willy's Wheat Beer 5.3% alc by vol. Website: http://www.springhead.co.uk 'E'mail: info@springhead.co.uk

Springhill (Eng) a natural spring mineral water from North Yorkshire. Mineral contents (milligrammes per litre): Sodium 19.1mg/l, Calcium 22mg/l, Magnesium 6.4mg/l, Potassium 1mg/l, Chlorides 28.5mg/l, Sulphates 22mg/l, Nitrates 4.57mg/l. pH 7.8

Springhill Cellars (USA) a winery. (Add): 2920 NW Scenic Drive, Albany, Oregon. Grape varieties: Pinot noir, Pinot gris, Chardonnay, Riesling.

Spring Hop (Eng) an aromatic beer brewed by Hardy and Hansons Brewery based in Kimberley, Nottinghamshire.

Springland Wines (S.Afr) are varietal wines bottled by the Drop-Inn Group in Cape Town. (Add): 42 Main Road, Diep River 7800.

Spring Mist (Eng) spring water with a hint of fruit from Spring Mist Soft Drinks. Flavours include: apple, mango, guava, passion fruit, wild blackberry.

Spring Mountain (USA) an A.V.A. of Napa Valley, California since 1993. 162ha. Grape varieties include Chardonnay, Sauvignon blanc, Riesling, Syrah, Zinfandel.

Spring Mountain Vineyard (USA) a winery based in the Napa Valley, California. Grape varieties: Cabernet sauvignon. Label: Elivette Reserve.

Spring Promise (Eng) a 4.5% alc by vol. ale brewed by the Spectrum Brewery, Norfolk.

Spring Tide (Eng) a 4.3% alc by vol. ale brewed by the Teignworthy Brewery Ltd., Devon.

Springtime Bitter (Eng). a 1040 O.G./4% alc by vol. bitter from the Wye Valley Brewery, Hereford (available in April and May) Part of the Dorothy Goodbody's Seasonal Ale range.

Spring Time Cocktail (Cktl) 35mls (1½ fl.oz) vodka, 25mls (1fl.oz) orange juice, 10mls (½ fl.oz) Cointreau. Shake over ice, strain into an ice-filled highball glass, top with ginger ale, dress with lemon and orange peel spirals and a cherry and serve with straws.

Springtime Cocktail (Cktl) ⅔ measure Bacardi White Label rum, ⅓ measure (green) crème de menthe. Shake over ice, strain into an ice-filled highball glass, top with ginger ale and serve with straws.

Springvale (Austr) a dry white wine produced by the Berri Estates, South Australia.

Springvale Bitter (Wal) a keg bitter 1033 O.G. brewed by the Silverthorne Brewery in Cwmbran, Gwent.

Spring Valley (S.Afr) the label for a range of white wines (Chenin blanc/Sémillon) produced by the Old Vine Cellars winery, Cape Town, Western Cape.

Spring Water (Eng) a natural water obtained from underground springs. Bottled and sold as spring water. May be classed as a natural mineral water if meets E.C. minimum standards. (Fr) = eau de source, (Ire) = fioruisce, (It) = acqua di sorgente, (Pol) = źródło, (Sp) = agua fuente/agua de manatial.

Spring Water (Fr) a still natural spring mineral water from Normandy. Mineral contents (milligrammes per litre): Sodium 8mg/l, Calcium 104mg/l, Magnesium 4mg/l, Potassium 0.8mg/l, Bicarbonates 314mg/l, Chlorides 13.6mg/l, Sulphates 8mg/l, Nitrates 12mg/l.

Spring Water (N.Z) a natural spring mineral water from Auckland. Mineral contents (milligrammes per litre): Sodium 8.9mg/l, Calcium 2.31mg/l, Magnesium 1.42mg/l, Potassium 3.9mg/l.

Sprint Up (Ind) a natural spring mineral water (established 2002) from Chennai. Mineral contents (milligrammes per litre): Calcium 40mg/l, Magnesium 1.5mg/l, Chlorides 36mg/l. pH 7.36

Sprinzenberg (Aus) a vineyard site on the banks of the River Danube in the Kremstal region.

Sprite (USA) the brand-name of a lemon and lime carbonated soft drink with 5% lemon and lime juice produced by CCSB (also a diet version).

Spritz (Eng) a branded, bottled sparkling wine drink 5.5% alc by vol (low-carbohydrate version 1.2% alc by vol), also a rosé version 5.5% alc by vol. Website: http://www.spritz.com 'E'mail: info@spritz.com

Spritz (Switz) a pétillant wine, slightly sparkling.

Spritzer (Aus)(Ger) a drink of half white table wine, half soda water. Pour into an ice-filled highball glass and add a twist of lemon. Also known as a Schorle. Mineral water may be used in place of

S

soda water. *See also* Spritzer Highball and Tinto de Verano.

Spritzer (Mal) a natural spring mineral water from Taiping, Perak. Mineral contents (milligrammes per litre): Sodium 6mg/l, Calcium 12mg/l, Magnesium 1.6mg/l, Potassium 3.5mg/l, Bicarbonates 62mg/l, Chlorides <1mg/l, Sulphates <3mg/l, Silicates 4mg/l. pH 7.4

Spritzer (N.Z) a hock wine, lime juice and soda water drink once produced by Cooks, Te Kauwata.

Spritzer Highball (USA) the American name for Spritzer.

Spritzig (Ger) a term given to semi-sparkling wines. Wines which have a slight sparkle or prickle caused by a malo-lactic fermentation in the bottle. (Fr) = pétillant.

Spritzigkeit (Ger) the name given to German pétillant wines.

Spruce Beer (Eng) a black beer brewed from fermented spruce fir shoots, sugar and malted barley.

Sprudel (Aus)(Ger) mineral water.

Spruitdrift Koöperatiewe Wynkelders Bpk (S.Afr) a co-operative winery based in Spruitdrift. (Add): Box 129, Vredendal 8160. Produces varietal wines.

Sprung (Ger) vineyard (Anb): Mosel-Saar-Ruwer. (Ber): Saar-Ruwer. (Gro): Scharzberg. (Vil): Konz.

Spucknapf (Ger) spittoon.

Spuitwater (Hol) soda water.

Spuma (It) to sparkle or foam.

Spumante (It) sparkling, applied to a wine that is truly sparkling, Gran Spumante is made by the metodo tradizionale, others are made by the cuve close method. The name also used for Champagne. *see* Asti.

Spumante Naturale (It) the name for sparkling wines made by the metodo tradizionale. *See also* Gran Spumante.

Spumare (It) to sparkle or foam.

Spumos (Rum) sparkling.

Spumoso (Port) sparkling.

Sputacchiera (It) a spittoon.

Sputnik (Cktl). 1 measure vodka, 1 measure cream, 1 teaspoon maraschino. Shake over ice, strain into a cocktail glass and decorate with 2 cocktail sticks stuck crossways through a cherry.

Sputnik (Rus) a horseradish-flavoured grain vodka brand 40% alc by vol.

Spy Valley (N.Z) a vineyard 146ha (other name Waihopai) based in the Marlborough region of the South Island. Grape varieties: Cabernet sauvignon, Pinot noir, Riesling, Sauvignon blanc plus others.

Squadron (S.Afr) the brand-name of a rum marketed by Gilbeys.

Square (Eng) traditional form of fermenting vessel, square in shape, now made of stainless steel.

Square Barrel (Switz) created by the Cybox company as a better way of storing wines. 225litres in capacity.

Square Bottle (Hol) the early name for jenever (gin).

Squareface (Eng) the nickname given to the square bottles of Dutch geneva gin in the nineteenth century.

Squash (Eng) a fruit drink which is usually diluted with water to drink. Is non-alcoholic.

Squeeze (USA) another name for Red Eye.

Squiffy (Eng) a slang term used to denote a person who is partially intoxicated.

Squinzano (It) a D.O.C. red wine from the Puglia made from the Malvasia and Negroamaro grapes.

Squires (Eng) a session bitter brewed by Beowulf Brewery in Birmingham.

Squires Beer (Eng) a cask-conditioned bitter 1044 O.G. brewed by the Blackawton Brewery in Devon.

Squires Bitter (Eng) a traditional ale brewed by Mauldon's Brewery in Sudbury, Suffolk.

Squirrel's Hoard (Eng) an ale brewed by the Hart Brewery, Little Eccleston, Preston, Lancashire.

S.R. (Fr) *abbr*: **S**ociété de **R**écoltants.

Sremski Karlovici (Cro) a wine-producing area in Fruska Gora, Vojvodina. Noted for Carlowitz (a red full-bodied wine).

SRFCQ (Fr) *abbr*: **S**ervice de la **R**épression des **F**raudes et du **C**ontrôle de la **Q**ualité.

S.Silvestro (It) a natural spring mineral water from Angolo Terme (BG), Lombardy. Mineral contents (milligrammes per litre): Sodium 2.4mg/l, Calcium 288mg/l, Magnesium 80.2mg/l, Potassium 0.84mg/l, Bicarbonates 231.8mg/l, Chlorides 1.4mg/l, Sulphates 820.5mg/l, Fluorides 0.36mg/l, Nitrates 1.5mg/l, Silicates 8.5mg/l, Strontium 9mg/l. pH 7.39

SSS (Eng) *abbr*: **S**ubalterns' **S**oothing **S**yrup (an old military name used in England for Madeira wines).

SSW (S.Afr) *abbr*: **S**outh **S**outh **W**est.

Staatl. Bad Brückenauer (Ger) a slightly acidic sparkling natural spring mineral water Bad Brückenauer. Mineral contents (milligrammes per litre): Sodium 2.84mg/l, Calcium 70.2mg/l, Magnesium 27.6mg/l, Potassium 11.2mg/l, Bicarbonates 210mg/l, Chlorides 2.28mg/l, Sulphates 122.5mg/l, Fluorides 0.3mg/l, Nitrates 0.1mg/l, Silicates 14.74mg/l. pH 4.99 Website: http://www.badbruckenauer.de

Staatl. Bad Brückenauer Heilwasser (Ger) a still natural spring mineral water from Bad Brückenauer. Mineral contents (milligrammes per litre): Sodium 2.9mg/l, Calcium 16.9mg/l, Magnesium 7.2mg/l, Potassium 5.6mg/l, Chlorides 6.2mg/l, Sulphates 10.7mg/l, Fluorides 0.08mg/l. Website: http://www.badbruckenauer.de

Staaliche Domaene (Ger) are State-owned viticultural domaines.

Staatliche Hofkeller (Ger) a Bavarian State Domaine (119ha), vineyards based in Franken.

Staatliche Prüfnummer (Aus) an official analysed number given to a wine (except tafelweins and landweins) after it has been chemically analysed. The number is displayed on all bottles of wines (post 1995).

Staatliche Weinbaudomäne Rheinhessia (Ger) are state-owned vineyards based in the Rheinhessen. The wines are marketed by Jakob Gerhardt.

Staatlich Fachingen Classic (Ger) a still natural spring mineral water (established 1742) from D-65626 Fachingen. Mineral contents (milligrammes per litre): Sodium 574mg/l, Calcium 99mg/l, Magnesium 60.5mg/l, Potassium 14.5mg/l, Bicarbonates 1854mg/l, Chlorides 129mg/l, Sulphates 37mg/l, Fluorides 0.3mg/l, Silicates 40.2mg/l. Website: http://www.fachingen.de

Staatlich Fachingen Heilwasser (Ger) a sparkling natural spring mineral water (established 1746) from Lahntal. Mineral contents (milligrammes per litre): Sodium 602.5mg/l, Calcium 122mg/l, Magnesium 53.2mg/l, Potassium 28.1mg/l, Bicarbonates 1950mg/l, Chlorides 150.7mg/l, Sulphates 65.5mg/l, Fluorides 0.3mg/l, Iron 1.95mg/l, Ammonium 1.37mg/l. Website: http://www.fachingen.de

Staatsweingut (Ger) a vineyard owned by the State.

Staatsweinkellerei (Hun) State wine cellars.

Stabilise (Eng) wines are stabilised by passing them through filters to remove all the yeast cells or by pasteurisation.

Stabilisierungsfonds Für Wein (Ger) overseers for the promulgation of the 1971 German Wine Laws. A fund set up to help pay for flurbereinigung. Created by a per litre sales tax paid four times a year.

Stachelberg (Ger) vineyard (Anb): Hessische Bergstrasse. (Ber): Umstadt. (Gro): None. (Vil): Klein-Umstadt.

Stadecken-Elsheim (Ger) village (Anb): Rheinhessen. (Ber): Nierstein. (Gro): Domherr. (Vins): Blume, Bockstein, Lenchen, Spitzberg, Tempelchen.

Stadelhofen (Ger) village (Anb): Baden. (Ber): Ortenau. (Gro): Fürsteneck. (Vin): Renchtäler.

Stades Leicht (Ger) a 2.8% alc by vol. bottled pilsner brewed by D.U.B. in Dortmund.

Stadion (Ger) a natural spring mineral water. Mineral contents (milligrammes per litre): Sodium 178mg/l, Calcium 206mg/l, Magnesium 38mg/l, Potassium 9.7mg/l, Bicarbonates 720mg/l, Chlorides 83.4mg/l, Sulphates 350mg/l.

Stadler [Ferdinand] (Aus) a winery based in Grossweikersdorf, Donauland. Grape varieties: Grüner veltliner, Pinot blanc, Riesling, Zweigelt.

Stadlmann (Aus) a winery based in Traiskirchen, Thermenregion. (Add): Wiener Strasse 41, 2514 Traiskirchen. Grape varieties: Blauer portugieser, Riesling, Rotgipfler, Zierfandler, Zweigelt.

Stadtbrauerei Spalt (Ger) a brewery. (Add): Brauereigasse 3, Spalt D-91174. Brews a range of beers and lagers. Website: http://www.spalter-bier.de 'E'mail: info@spalter-bier.de

Stadtbredimus (Lux) a wine co-operative owned by Vinsmoselle.

Stadtbredimus (Lux) a wine village on the river Moselle. Vineyard sites: Primerberg, Dieffert.

Stadtbühl Brauerei (Switz) an independent brewery based in Gossau.

Stafili (Gre) grape(s).

Stag (Scot) a 4.1% alc by vol. ale brewed by The Cairngorm Brewery C°. Ltd., Inverness.

Stag (Scot) a cask-conditioned ale from Tomintoul Brewery.

Stag Beer (Eng) a cask-conditioned bitter 1044 O.G. brewed by the Watney Brewery. Named after their Stag Brewery in Mortlake. Also a canned version.

Stage Struck (Eng) a 4.5% alc by vol. cask-conditioned ale brewed by Jennings in Cocklemouth, Cumbria to commemorate the annual Keswick Beer Festival.

Staggers (Eng) a slang term to denote a person who is unsteady on their feet when under the influence of alcohol.

Stag Lager (Austr) a lager beer brewed by the Toohey's Brewery in New South Wales.

Staglin Winery (USA) a winery based in the Napa Valley, California. 20ha. Grape varieties: Cabernet franc, Cabernet sauvignon, Chardonnay, Petit verdot, Sangiovese.

St. Agnes (Austr) the brand-name of a brandy. Varieties: V.O. age not less than 20 years. Old brandy minimum age 5 year old, *** must be aged at least 2 years in wood.

Stag's Breath (Scot) a whisky and fermented comb honey liqueur from Meikles 20% alc by vol.

Stag's Leap (USA) an A.V.A. district in the Napa Valley, California since 1989. Home to Clos du Val, Pine Ridge, Stags Leap Wine Cellars, Shafer Vineyards, Silverado.

Stag's Leap Wine Cellars (USA) a winery based in Artemis, Napa Valley, California. Grape varieties: Cabernet sauvignon, Chardonnay, Johannisberg riesling and Merlot. Produces varietal wines. Label: Cask 23 (Cabernet sauvignon), Fay. Website: http://www.CASK23.com

Stags Leap Winery (USA) a winery and vineyard based in the Napa Valley, California. Grape varieties: Chenin blanc and Petite syrah. Produces varietal wines.

Stahlberg (Ger) vineyard (Anb): Baden. (Ber): Badische Frankenland. (Gro): Tauberklinge. (Vil): Uissigheim.

Stahlbühl (Ger) vineyard (Anb): Württemberg. (Ber): Württembergisch Unterland. (Gro): Staufenberg. (Vil): Heilbronn.

Stahlig (Ger) steely or sour lesser wines of the Mosel.

Stahlquelle Gris (It) a natural spring mineral water from Stahlquelle Gais, Bozen. Mineral contents (milligrammes per litre): Sodium 4.85mg/l, Calcium 3.25mg/l, Magnesium 0.35mg/l, Potassium 1.57mg/l, Bicarbonates 5mg/l, Chlorides 0.6mg/l, Sulphates 13.5mg/l, Fluorides 0.95mg/l, Silicates 2.6mg/l.

Staig (Ger) vineyard (Anb): Württemberg. (Ber): Württembergisch Unterland. (Gro): Heuchelberg. (Vil): Hausen/Z.

Staiger Winery (USA) a small winery based near

Boulder Creek, Santa Cruz, California 2.5ha. Grape varieties: Cabernet sauvignon, Chardonnay, Pinot noir and Zinfandel. Produces varietal wines.

St-Aignan (Fr) a commune in the A.C. Côtes de Fronsac, Bordeaux.

Stainless Dry (Cktl) ⅔ measure gin, ⅓ measure grapefruit juice. Pour over ice into a tall glass, add a teaspoon of Cointreau, a dash Angostura and top with lemonade.

Stainless Steel (Eng) used in the lining of vats especially for white wines to exclude air, fermenting vessels for beer are also made of this.

Stainton Bitter (Eng) a 4.4% alc by vol. bitter brewed by Middleton's Brewery C°. at Banard Castle in County Durham.

Stairway (Eng) a 4.6% alc by vol. ale brewed by the Triple FFF Brewery, Hampshire.

Stairway to Heaven (Eng) a 5% alc by vol. ale brewed by the Burton Bridge Brewery, Staffordshire.

Stake Culture (Aus) pfahlkultur, a cultivation system.

Staked Plains Winery (USA) a winery based in the South Plains, Lubbock, western Texas. Produces American and vinifera wines.

St. Albert (Fr) the label of an A.C. Pacherenc de Vic Bihl sweet (non-botrytised) white wine (Arrufiac, Colombard, Gros manseng, Petit manseng) produced by the Producteurs Plaimont Co-operative, Gascony.

St. Aldegund (Ger) village (Anb): Mosel-Saar-Ruwer. (Ber): Zell/Mosel. (Gro): Grafschaft. (Vins): Himmelreich, Klosterkammer, Palmberg-Terrassen.

St. Alix (Fr) a natural spring mineral water from Brittany. Mineral contents (milligrammes per litre): Sodium 33.3mg/l, Calcium 8mg/l, Magnesium 10.2mg/l, Potassium 4mg/l, Bicarbonates 84.2mg/l, Chlorides 37mg/l, Sulphates 20mg/l, Nitrates <0.5mg/l, Silicates 5mg/l.

Stalk (Eng) the stem of the grape, attaches the fruit to the plant, removed before the grapes are crushed as they contain tannin. *see* Égrappage and Pedicule.

Stalky (Eng) the term used to describe the characteristics of the Cabernet grapes. Can also apply to wines made where grapes were pressed with the stalks. May also indicate a corked wine.

Stallard (Port) a vintage Port shipper.

Stallion (Eng) a 4.2% alc by vol. beer brewed by Hambleton Brewery (a micro-brewery) at Holme-on-Swale, near Thirsk, North Yorkshire. Also brews Hambleton Best Bitter.

Stallion Bitter (Eng) *see* Stallion Brewery.

Stallion Brewery (Eng) a brewery based in Chippingham, Berkshire. Noted for cask-conditioned Barnstormer 1048 O.G. and Stallion Bitter 1037 O.G.

Stallion Stout (W.Ind) a stout brewed by Banks Brewery Ltd., St. Michael, Barbados. *See also* Ebony Lager.

St. Amant Vineyard (USA) an independent vineyard based in Amador County, California. Grape variety: Zinfandel.

Sta. Maria (Mex) a natural spring mineral water from Lomas de Chapultepec. Mineral contents (milligrammes per litre): Sodium 7.4mg/l, Calcium 5.7mg/l, Magnesium 4.5mg/l, Potassium 2.5mg/l, Bicarbonates 63mg/l, Sulphates 2.6mg/l. pH 7.2

Stambolovo (Bul) a D.G.O. area of the Southern Basic Region. Produces mainly Merlot wines.

Stammersdorf (Aus) a noted vineyard area in the Wien region.

Stammheim (Ger) village (Anb): Franken. (Ber): Maindreieck. (Gro): Kirchberg. (Vin): Eselsberg.

Stammtische (Ger) drinking tables found in weinstüben (bars). Are usually reserved for various drinking fraternities ritual drinking, the best table in the house.

Stamna (Gre) a natural spring mineral water from Heraklion, Crete. Mineral contents (milligrammes per litre): Sodium 12.6mg/l, Calcium 28.1mg/l, Magnesium 9.2mg/l, Potassium 0.4mg/l, Bicarbonates 173.3mg/l, Chlorides 21.3mg/l, Sulphates 9.6mg/l. pH 7.8

Stanbridge Estate (Austr) a winery based in Riverina, New South Wales. Produces varietal wines.

Standard (S.Afr) the label for a red wine range produced by the Neethlingshof Estate, Stellenbosch, Western Cape.

Standard Bitter (Wal) a cask-conditioned (and keg) bitter 1032 O.G. brewed by the Buckley Brewery in Llanelli.

Standard Collection (S.Afr) the label for a range of wines produced by the Fleur du Cap winery, Stellenbosch, Western Cape.

Standard Panel [The] (M.East) one of the earliest finds from Ur, depicts wine drinking and is dated from about 2500BC.

Standard Shaker (Eng) a 3 piece utensil, stainless steel or silver plate. Has a cone-shaped base, dumpy top and built in strainer with a fitted cap. *See also* Boston Shaker.

Standard Uiterwyk (S.Afr) the label for a red wine (Merlot & Shiraz blend) produced by the De Waal Wines winery, Stellenbosch, Western Cape.

Standfast (Scot) a blended Scotch whisky produced by Grant and Sons 40% alc by vol.

St-André-de-Cubzac (Fr) a town in eastern Bordeaux. Produces A.C. Bordeaux red and white wines.

St. Andrew (Slo) a sparkling natural spring mineral water (established 1876) from Baldovce. Mineral contents (milligrammes per litre): Sodium 81.3mg/l, Calcium 269.3mg/l, Magnesium 73.7mg/l, Potassium 18mg/l, Bicarbonates 1117.2mg/l, Chlorides 59mg/l, Sulphates 165mg/l, Fluorides 0.18mg/l, Nitrates 2.8mg/l.

St. Andrews (Eng) a 3.9% alc by vol. ale brewed by the Fenland Brewery Ltd., Cambridgeshire.

St. Andrews (USA) a small estate based near Napa City, Napa Valley, California. Noted for Chardonnay wines.

St. Andrews Ale (Scot) an ale brewed by the Belhaven Brewery.

St. Androny (Fr) a commune in the A.C. Côtes de Blaye, north-eastern Bordeaux.

Stanford Hills Winery (S.Afr) a winery (established 2002) based in Stanford Hills, Walker Bay, Western Cape. 4ha. Grape variety: Pinotage.

Stangeland Vineyards & Winery (USA) a winery (established 1978) based in Salem, Oregon. Grape varieties: Chardonnay, Gewürztraminer Pinot gris, Pinot noir.

Stangen (Ger) a narrow beer glass of 200mls (7.5fl.ozs) capacity used for serving kölsch beer in Cologne. Also known as a Rod. *See also* Kranz.

Stanislaus (USA) a wine-producing county in the San Joaquin Valley, California.

Stankov Brewery (Czec) a noted brewery based in western Czec.

Stanley Cocktail (Cktl) ¾ measure dry gin, ¼ measure Bacardi White Label, juice ¼ lemon, 3 dashes grenadine. Shake over ice and strain into a cocktail glass.

Stanley's Steamhammer (Eng) a special ale 7% alc by vol. brewed by the Raisdale Sparging and Brewing Company.

Stanley Wine Company (Austr) a winery in the Claire-Watervale district. Grape varieties: Cabernet and Rhine riesling. Sells wines under Leasingham label.

St. Annaberg (Ger) vineyard (Anb): Pfalz. (Ber): Südliche Weinstrasse. (Gro): Bischofskreuz. (Vil): Burrweiler.

St. Anna Heilwasser (Ger) a natural spring mineral water. Mineral contents (milligrammes per litre): Sodium 305mg/l, Calcium 304.3mg/l, Magnesium 84.9mg/l, Potassium 16.4mg/l, Chlorides 432mg/l, Sulphates 656mg/l, Fluorides 0.31mg/l.

St. Anna Schloss (S.Afr) a medium sweet, white wine made from the Steen and Sémillon grapes by the Douglas Green Cellars label of Paarl.

St. Anne's Vineyard (Eng) a vineyard (established 1979) based at Wainhouse, Oxenhall, Newent, Gloucestershire. 0.8ha. Grape varieties: Madeleine angevine 50%, Müller-Thurgau 25%, Triomphe d'alsace 30% and Wrotham pinot.

Stannington Stout (Eng) a 5% alc by vol. stout brewed by the Edale Brewery C°., Derbyshire.

Stansfield (S.Afr) the label for a red blend wine produced by the Warwick Estate winery, Stellenbosch, Western Cape.

St. Antoine Distillery (Afr) a rum distillery based at Goodlands on the island of Mauritius, western Africa.

Stanton and Killeen (Austr) a winery. (Add): Gracerray Vineyards, Rutherglen, Victoria 3685. 22ha. Grape varieties: Cabernet sauvignon, Durif, Frontignan rouge, Muscadelle and Touriga. Noted for Liqueur Muscat, Liqueur Tokay.

Stanton Estate (USA) a vineyard based near Rutherford, Napa Valley, California. Grape variety: Johannisberg riesling. Is owned jointly by the Phelps and Burgess Cellars.

St. Antonius Heilwasser (Ger) a natural spring mineral water. Mineral contents (milligrammes per litre): Sodium 374.2mg/l, Calcium 395.9mg/l, Magnesium 84.5mg/l, Potassium 14mg/l, Chlorides 808mg/l, Sulphates 459mg/l, Fluorides 0.38mg/l.

St. Antoniusweg (Ger) vineyard (Anb): Nahe. (Ber): Kreuznach. (Gro): Sonnenborn. (Vil): Langenlonsheim.

Stanway Brewery (Eng) a brewery (established 1993). (Add): Stanway, Cheltenham, Gloucestershire GL54 5PQ. Brews bitter beers. Website: http://www.stanwaybrewery.co.uk

Staple (Eng) a wine estate in Staple near Canterbury, Kent. Produces dry white wines from the Müller-Thurgau, Huxelrebe and Reichensteiner grapes. 3ha.

Staplecombe Vineyards (Eng) a vineyard (established 1981) based at Burlands Farm, Staplegrove, Taunton, Somerset. Produces white wines. 2ha. Grape varieties: Huxelrebe, Madeleine angevine, Reichensteiner, Siegerrebe, plus others.

Stappare (It) to uncork a bottle/cask.

Star [The] (Switz) a name the Swiss give to pétillant wines.

Stara Zagora (Bul) a delimited wine-producing area based in Southern Basic region. Produces mainly red wines from Cabernet sauvignon.

Stara Zagora (Bul) a privatised winery that buys in grapes.

Star Bitter (Eng) a 3.9% alc by vol. bitter ale brewed by the Belvoir Brewery, Leicestershire.

Star Bitter (Eng) a 3.9% alc by vol. bitter ale brewed by Star Brewery, Nottingham.

Starboard (USA) a Port-style wine from Quady, Madera, California. *See also* Electra, Elysium.

Starboard Light (Cktl) ½ measure dry gin, ¼ measure crème de menthe, ¼ measure lemon juice. Shake over ice and strain into a cocktail glass.

Star Brewery (Eng) a brewery based in Nottingham. Brews Star Bitter.

Star-Bright (Eng) a descriptive term used for beers and wines that are brilliantly clear.

Starbright IPA (Eng) a pale ale 1039 O.G. brewed and bottled by the Hardys and Hanson Brewery in Nottingham.

Starbucks (USA) a famous coffee company with coffee houses based world-wide. *See also* Frappuccino.

Starch (Eng) $C_6H_{10}O_5$ unfermentable by wine yeasts and may cause a haze in home-made wines.

Star Cocktail (Cktl) 30mls (¼ gill) apple brandy, 30mls (¼ gill) French vermouth, 3 dashes orange bitters, 3 dashes orange Curaçao. Stir over ice, strain into a cocktail glass, add an olive and a squeeze of lemon peel juice on top.

Star Daisy (Cktl) 25mls (1fl.oz) each of Calvados and gin, 10mls (½ fl.oz) lemon juice, ½ barspoon powdered sugar, 2 dashes grenadine. Shake well over ice, strain into a wine glass containing cracked ice, top with soda water and fresh fruit.

Star Hill (USA) a Bourbon whiskey distillery based in Loretta, south of Frankfort, Kentucky. Produces Maker's Mark. 50% alc by vol.

Starico (Cktl) ½ measure Puerto Rican rum, ⅕ measure apricot brandy, ⅕ measure pineapple juice, ⅒ measure blue Curaçao. Shake over ice and strain into a cocktail glass.

Stark (Eng) a term used to denote a strong, vigorous wine that is high in alcohol.

Stark (S.Afr) the label for a red wine (Cabernet sauvignon, Merlot and Syrah blend) produced by the Stark-Condé Wines winery, Stellenbosch, Western Cape.

Starka (Pol) a vodka aged 10 years in oak giving it a rich brown colour and a kick like a mule. Made with an infusion of leaves from the Crimean apple tree with Port, Malaga and brandy added. *see* Polmos.

Starkbieres (Ger)(Switz) strong beers with an O.G. of 18%–20%.

Stark-Condé Wines (S.Afr) a winery (established 1998) based in Stellenbosch, Western Cape. 40ha. Grape varieties: Cabernet sauvignon, Merlot, Syrah. Label: Condé. Website: http://www.stark-conde.co.za

Starkenburg (Ger) bereich (Anb): Hessische Bergstrasse. (Gros): Rott, Wolfsmagen, Schlossberg.

Starkenburg Brauerei (Aus) a small independent brewery based in the Tyrol.

Starkenburger Landwein (Ger) one of seventeen recognised zones.

Star Lager (Afr) a lager beer 1047 O.G. brewed by the Nigerian Breweries Limited in Nigeria. Is also brewed by the Kumasi Brewery in Ghana.

Starlette Rouge (S.Afr) a red wine (Cabernet sauvignon, Grenache, Merlot and Shiraz blend) produced by the Allée Bleu winery, Franschhoek, Western Cape.

Star Light (Eng) a 5% alc by vol. light ale brewed by the White Star Brewery, Hampshire.

Starlight Beer (Eng) a keg bitter 1033 O.G. brewed by the Watney Combe Reid Brewery in London.

Starlight Cocktail (Cktl) ⅓ measure dry gin, ⅓ measure apricot brandy, ⅓ measure French vermouth. Shake over ice, strain into an ice-filled highball glass and top with grapefruit juice.

Starobrno a.s. (Czec) a brewery (established 1872). (Add): Hlinky 160/12, 661 47 Brno. Taken over by Austrian Brau Union in 1994. Brews: a straw 8%, 10%, 12% and 14%, straw seasonal beer Drak, dark 10%, semi-dark 10% Rezák, Zlatý Trumf 10%. Website: http://www.starobrno.cz 'E'mail: starobrno@starobrno.cz

Starobrno Drak 14% (Czec) lit: 'dragon'. 5.7% alc by vol. straw coloured, seasonal lager brewed by Starobrno in Brno.

Starobrno Premium 12% (Czec) a 5.2% alc by vol. straw coloured, exclusive lager brewed by Starobrno in Brno.

Starobrno Rezák 10% (Czec) a 4.1% alc by vol. amber coloured, lager brewed by Starobrno in Brno.

Starobrno Tradicní Svetlé Pivo 10% (Czec) a 4.3% alc by vol. straw coloured, lager brewed by Starobrno in Brno.

Staropolanka (Pol) a natural spring mineral water from Polanica Zdroj. Mineral contents (milligrammes per litre): Sodium 44mg/l, Calcium 169mg/l, Magnesium 11.3mg/l, Potassium 24mg/l, Bicarbonates 674mg/l, Chlorides 10.5mg/l, Sulphates 26.5mg/l.

Staropolanka 2000 (Pol) a natural spring mineral water from Polanica Zdroj. Mineral contents (milligrammes per litre): Sodium 132mg/l, Calcium 360.5mg/l, Magnesium 65.9mg/l, Potassium 46mg/l, Bicarbonates 1804.5mg/l, Chlorides 10.6mg/l, Sulphates 27.2mg/l, Fluorides 0.5mg/l.

Staropolski (Pol) a blended-honey mead sold in earthenware jars.

Staropramen (Czec) a brewery (established 1869) based in the Prague district of Smichovis. The largest brewery in the Prague Breweries. Produces fine lager beers. *See also* Braník, Mestan.

Staropramen Dark 11% (Czec) a 4.6% alc by vol. bottled, dark lager brewed by Prague Breweries, Prague.

Staropramen Premium 10% (Czec) a 4.2% alc by vol. gold-yellow coloured, bottled, premium lager brewed by Prague Breweries, Prague.

Staropramen Premium 12% (Czec) a 5.2% alc by vol. bottled, premium lager brewed by Prague Breweries, Prague.

Starovar (Czec) lit: 'old brew', brewed by the Zatec Brewery.

Stars and Stripes (Pousse Café) pour in order into an elgin liqueur glass ⅓ measure grenadine, ⅓ measure cream and ⅓ measure Crème Yvette.

Star Stout (Eng) a 5% alc by vol. stout brewed by the Fernandes Brewery, Kirkgate, Wakefield, West Yorkshire.

Star System (Fr) an old system introduced by Maurice Hennessey in 1865 to show the ages of Cognac. *, **, ***, ****, ***** etc. which showed how many years brandy had spent in wood (now only the *** is used).

Starter (Eng) added to wine yeasts to start the must fermenting (a selected wine yeast).

Starters Orders (Cktl) 25mls (⅕ gill) Midori in an ice-filled highball glass and top with 125mls (1gill) sparkling wine.

Stassen Peach (Bel) a 4% alc by vol. light, dry, sparkling cider flavoured with peach juice.

State Domain (Ger) possesses important holdings, many are the top vineyards and it is the largest single owner of these famous vineyard properties. Headquarters are at Eltville.

Statement (S.Afr) the label for a red wine (Shiraz 62% and Merlot 48%) produced by the Linhorst Wines winery, Suider-Paarl, Western Cape.

Statianum (It) a red wine produced in central Italy in Roman times.

Station (Eng) a Tetley home-brew public house based in Guiseley, Leeds, Yorkshire. Noted for cask-

S

conditioned Guiseley Gyle 1045 O.G. using malt extract.

Station Hotel (Eng) a micro-brewery at Easingwold. Brews: Steamcock Bitter 3.8% alc by vol. Inspector's Ale 4.2% alc by vol.

Station Porter (Eng) a 6.1% alc by vol. strong porter brewed by the Wickwar Brewing C°. Ltd., Gloucestershire.

Staton Hills (USA) a winery. (Add): 71 Gangl Road, Wapato, Washington State 98951. Grape varieties: Cabernet sauvignon, Chardonnay, Fumé blanc, Merlot, Pinot noir.

Statti (It) a wine estate at Lamezia Terme, Calabria. 35ha. of vineyards. Produce I.G.T. red Cauro.

Statute of Vines, Wines and Spirits (Sp) are Spanish wine laws introduced in 1970 by the Ministerio de Agricultera. *see* Consejos.

St. Aubyns Claret (N.Z) a red wine from the Vidal winery, is full-flavoured and dry with a soft after-taste.

Staudenberg (Ger) vineyard (Anb): Baden. (Ber): Badische Bergstrasse/Kraichgau. (Gro): Rittersberg. (Vil): Leutershausen.

Staudenberg (Ger) vineyard (Anb): Baden. (Ber): Badische Bergstrasse/Kraichgau. (Gro): Rittersberg. (Vil): Schriesheim.

Stauder [Jacob] Brauerei (Ger) a brewery (established 1867) based in Essen. Noted for Stauder Premuim Pilsener Lager.

Staudernheim (Ger) village (Anb): Nahe. (Ber): Schloss Böckelheim. (Gro): Paradiesgarten. (Vins): Goldgrube, Herrenberg.

Stauder Premuim Pils (Ger) a 4.6% alc by vol. pilsner brewed by the Stauder [Jacob] Brauerei in Essen.

Staufen (Ger) village (Anb): Baden. (Ber): Markgräflerland. (Gro): Lorettoberg. (Vin): Schlossberg.

Staufenberg (Ger) grosslage (Anb): Württemberg. (Ber): Württembergish Unterland. (Vils): Brettach, Cleversulzbach, Duttenberg, Erlenbach, Gundelsheim, Heilbronn, Horkheim, Neckarsulm, Oedheim, Offenau,Talheim, Untereiseheim.

Staufen [ortsteil Wettelbrunn] (Ger) village (Anb): Baden. (Ber): Markgräflerland. (Gro): Lorettoberg. (Vin): Maltesergarten.

Staughton Vale Vineyard (Austr) a winery (established 1986) based at Anakie, Victoria. Grape varieties: Chardonnay, Riesling, Sauvignon blanc, Cabernet sauvignon, Pinot noir, Shiraz.

St. Augustine (S.Afr) a blended red wine from the Douglas Green Group in the Paarl, Western Cape. Made from the Cabernet sauvignon, Merlot, Pinotage, Shiraz and Tinta barocca grapes.

St. Austell Brewery (Eng) a brewery (established 1851). (Add): 63 Trevarthian Road, St. Austell, Cornwall PL25 4BY. Brews: Black Prince 4% alc by vol., Clouded Yellow Ale 4.8% alc by vol., Cornish Cream Ale 3.6% alc by vol., Dartmoor Best Bitter 3.9% alc by vol., Devon Cream Ale 3.6% alc by vol., Duchy Bitter 3.7% alc by vol., HSD 5% alc by vol., IPA 4.4% alc by vol., (cask-conditioned) Tinners Ale 3.7% alc by vol (1038 O.G)., Tribute 4.2% alc by vol., also brews Hicks Special 1050 O.G. keg Duchy 1037 O.G. and bottled Smugglers 1070 O.G. Prince's Ale 1100 O.G. Also brews Brass Monkey, Cousin Jack's, Crippledick, 1851, E.P. Hothouse Ale, Odyssey 2001, Proper Job IPA 5.5% alc by vol., Ruby Jack, South Pacific, Vanilla Ice, Wreckers. Also Castle d'Or Sherry 15% alc by vol. Website: http://www.staustellbrewery.co.uk 'E'mail: info@staustellbrewery.co.uk

St. Austell Clouded Yellow (Eng) a bottled conditioned beer brewed by the St. Austell Brewery in Cornwall using wheat flavoured with vanilla.

Staves (Eng) the side sections of a cask.

Stavropol (Rus) a wine-producing region based near the Caucasus mountains, produces dry white and dessert wines.

Stavroto (Gre) a red grape variety grown in northern Greece to make dry red wines.

St. Benoit Blonde (Bel) a lighter version of St. Benoit Brune. 7% alc by vol. from Du Bocq Brasserie. *See also* Saison Blanche de Namur, Triple Moine, La Gauloise.

St. Benoit Brune (Bel) a dark malt beer 7% alc by vol. from Du Bocq Brasserie. *See also* Saison Blanche de Namur, Triple Moine, La Gauloise.

St. Bernardus Abt 12 (Bel) a 10% alc by vol. bottled barley wine brewed by St. Bernadus Brasserie, Watou.

St. Bernardus Brouwerij (Bel) a brewery (established 1946) based in Watou. Brews: St. Bernadus Abt 12, St. Bernadus Prior 8, St. Bernadus Tripel, St. Bernadus Pater 6 (a dark-brown, strong, top-fermented, bottle-conditioned Trappist-style beer) for St. Sixtus to enable them to meet demands.

St. Bernardus Pater 6 (Bel) a 6.7% alc by vol. top-fermented, bottled special double beer brewed by St. Bernadus Brouwerij, Watou.

St. Bernardus Prior 8 (Bel) an 8% alc by vol. top-fermented, bottled double beer brewed by St. Bernardus Brouwerij, Watou.

St. Bernardus Tripel (Bel) a 7.5% alc by vol. top-fermented, bottled triple beer brewed by St. Bernadus Brouwerij, Watou.

St. Bernhard Bräu (Ger) a beer sold in a monk-shaped bottle 1045 O.G. brewed by St. Bernadus Brouwerij, Watou.

St. Blaise (Switz) a principal vineyard based in the Neuchâtel.

St. Boes (Fr) a sulphurous mineral water brand.

St. Bris (Fr) an A.C. dry white wine from the Yonne département in northern Burgundy. Made from the Sauvignon blanc. Minimum alc by vol. of 9.5%. Recently upgraded from V.D.Q.S. Formerly known as Sauvignon de St. Bris.

St-Bris-le-Vineux (Fr) a village near Irancy (Chablis) which produces dry, white wines from the Sauvignon grape and some minor red wines.

S

St. **Castorhöhle** (Ger) vineyard (Anb): Mosel-Saar-Ruwer. (Ber): Zell/Mosel. (Gro): Goldbäumchen. (Vil): Müden.

St. **Catherine** (S.Afr) the label for a white wine (barrel-fermented Chardonnay) produced by the Napier Winery, Wellington, Western Cape.

St. **Catherines** (Can) a wine district between Niagara and Crystal Beach.

St. **Cedd's Vineyard** (Austr) a part of the Lindemans estate, New South Wales. 24ha. of mixed grape varieties, mainly Gewürztraminer.

St. **Charle's Punch** (Cktl) 60mls (½ gill) port, 60mls (½ gill) brandy, juice ½ lemon, sugar syrup, 4 dashes Curaçao. Shake over ice, strain into an ice-filled highball glass, decorate with fruit and serve with straws.

St. **Chinian Berlou** (Fr) a new (2005) sub-region A.C. within the A.C. Coteaux du Languedoc based on its climate and soil.

St. **Chinian Roquebrun** (Fr) a new (2005) sub-region A.C. within the A.C. Coteaux du Languedoc based on its climate and soil.

St-**Christ-de-Blaye** (Fr) a commune in the A.C. Côtes de Blaye, north-eastern Bordeaux.

St. **Christoly** (Fr) see Saint Christoly.

St. **Christopher Lager** (Eng) an alcohol-free lager brewed and bottled by Allied Breweries 0.5% alc by vol.

St-**Ciers-de-Canesse** (Fr) a commune in the A.C. Côtes de Bourg, north-eastern Bordeaux.

St. **Clair Vineyard** (USA) the label for a red wine (Pinot noir) produced by the Acacia winery, Napa Valley, California.

St. **Clements** (Cktl) a mix of half orange juice and half lemonade over ice in a highball with a slice of orange and lemon.

St. **Clements** (Eng) a range of sparkling, non-alcoholic, soft drinks produced by Mandora (part of the Mansfield Brewery) available in a variety of flavours. Also a range of fruit squashes.

St. **Clement Vineyards** (USA) a winery based Oropas, near St. Helena, Napa Valley, California. Grape varieties: Cabernet sauvignon and Chardonnay. Produces varietal wines.

St. **Croix Rum** (USA) a light rum produced in the eastern states.

St. **Cyriakusstift** (Ger) vineyard (Anb): Rheinhessen. (Ber): Wonnegau. (Gro): Liebfrauenmorgen. (Vil): Worms.

St. **Dalfour** (S.Afr) the export label for wines produced by the Lost Horizons Premium Wines winery, Suider-Paarl, Western Cape.

St. **David's Day Ale** (Wal) a 4.1% alc by vol. seasonal ale brewed by S.A. Brain & C°. Ltd. in Cardiff.

St. **David's Porter** (Wal) a brown ale 1036 O.G. brewed and bottled by the Felinfoel Brewery for export to the USA.

St. **Diéry** (Fr) a natural spring mineral water from Renlaige, Puy de Dôme. Mineral contents (milligrammes per litre): Sodium 425mg/l, Calcium 90mg/l, Magnesium 90mg/l, Potassium 65mg/l, Bicarbonates 1450mg/l, Chlorides 300mg/l, Sulphates 30mg/l, Nitrates 1mg/l. pH 6.0

Steam (Eng) a seasonal ale brewed by the Hook Norton Brewery, Banbury in Oxfordshire.

Steam Beer (USA) a Californian method of brewing using bottom-fermenting yeasts at ale temperatures (rare). See Anchor Steam 5% alc by vol.

Steamcock (Eng) a 3.8% alc by vol. bitter ale from Station Hotel micro-brewery, Easingwold.

Steamin Billy (Eng) a 4.3% alc by vol. bitter ale brewed by Davis'es Brewing C°. Ltd., Rutland.

Steamin' Billy Brewing Company (Eng) brews Steamin' Billy Championship Bitter brewed in the Vaults, Leicester to celebrate Leicester county's success at cricket.

Steamin' Billy Championship Bitter (Eng) see Steamin' Billy Brewing Company.

Steaming (Scot) a slang term for very intoxicated (drunk).

Steaming Boggart (Eng) a 9% alc by vol. strong ale brewed by the Boggart Hole Clough Brewery Ltd., Greater Manchester.

Steaming Jack (Eng) a 5.5% alc by vol. ale brewed by the Hart Brewery, Little Eccleston, Preston, Lancashire.

Steaming On (Eng) a 4.4% alc by vol. ale brewed by the Hook Norton Brewery C°. Ltd., Oxfordshire.

Steampacket Brewery (Eng) a brewery based in Knottingley, West Yorkshire. Brews: Bitter Blow, Bit o Black (dark ale), Blue Rocket, Corn Rose, Happy Major, Little Boy, Giddy Ass (barley wine), Gamekeeper.

Steap (Eng) a mediaeval type of jug or flagon.

Ste. Cécile (Fr) a natural spring mineral water. Mineral contents (milligrammes per litre): Sodium 23mg/l, Calcium 44mg/l, Magnesium 24mg/l, Potassium 2mg/l, Bicarbonates 287mg/l, Chlorides 5mg/l, Sulphates 3mg/l, Nitrates 1mg/l. pH 7.3

Ste. Chapelle (USA) a major winery based in Idaho, Pacific North-West. see Sainte-Chapelle Vineyards.

Sté. Delord (Fr) an Armagnac producer. (Add): 32520 Lannepax.

St. **Edmund Original Strong Ale** (Eng) a 5.5% alc by vol. ale brewed by Greene King in Bury St. Edmunds, Suffolk to celebrate the life of St. Edmund.

St. **Edmunds Ale** (Eng) a bottled Ale 1060 O.G. Brewed by the Greene King Brewery in East Anglia to mark the anniversary of the martyrdom of Edmund Saxon, King of East Anglia.

Steel Coulson (Scot) a brewery. (Add): Greenhead Brewery, Glasgow. Taken over by Vaux in 1866. Brewed Double Brown Stout.

Steel's Masher (Eng) a rotary device which ensures a correct balance of liquor and grist and runs the mixture into the mash tun.

Steel Town Bitter (Eng) a 3.8% alc by vol. bitter brewed by the Derwentrose Brewery in Consett, County Durham.

Steely (Eng) a term to describe a wine that is hard, though not harsh (white wines).

S

Steen (S.Afr) a white grape variety. Known as the Chenin blanc in France. Also known as the Steendruif.

Steen & Groen (S.Afr) the label for a range of wines produced by the Dellrust Wines winery, Stellenbosch, Western Cape.

Steenberg Vineyards (S.Afr) a winery (established 1990) based in Constantia, Western Cape. 63ha. (Add): P.O. Box 10801, Steenberg Estate, Cape Town 7947. Grape varieties: Cabernet franc, Cabernet sauvignon, Chardonnay, Merlot, Nebbiolo, Pinotage, Pinot noir, Sauvignon blanc, Sémillon. Labels: Catharina, Steenberg 1682, CWG Auction Reserve. Website: http://www.steenberg-vineyards.co.za

Steenbrugge Dubbel (Bel) a 6.5% alc by vol. brown, top-fermented, bottle-conditioned special abbaye beer brewed by De Gouden Boom Brouwerij in Bruges.

Steenbrugge Tripel (Bel) an 8.5% alc by vol. straw coloured, top-fermented, bottle-conditioned special abbaye beer brewed by De Gouden Boom Brouwerij in Bruges.

Steendonk Brabants Witbier (Bel) a 4.5% alc by vol. unfiltered, top-fermented, bottled wheat beer brewed by the Palm Brasserie, Steenhuffel. Spiced with Curaçao and coriander.

Steendruif (S.Afr) *see* Steen.

Steen-op-Hout (S.Afr) the label for a white wine (Chenin blanc) produced by the Mulderbosch Vineyards winery, Stellenbosch, Western Cape.

Steep (Eng) lit: 'to soak', applied to barley that is soaked in water (known as the liquor) for germination. Also for solids to be steeped in liquids to extract flavour. i.e. tea, herbs in alcohol or wine, etc.

Steep (Scot) a stone trough in which the barley is soaked before being spread on the floor to germinate.

Steeped (Eng) the term used for soaking the barley in cold fresh water (up to 4 days in a minimum of 2 steepings) prior to the germination period.

Steeping (Scot) the soaking of the barley grain before the malting process begins.

Steeple Jack (Eng) a 4.6% alc by vol. ale brewed by Abbey Ales Ltd., Avon.

Steeps (Scot) tanks in which the grain (barley) is soaked before it is allowed to germinate for malt whisky production.

Stefanesti (Rum) a wine-producing area, produces mainly white wines.

Stefano Ferrucci (It) a winery based in Tuscany that is noted for its DOC Sangiovese di Romagna.

Stefansberg (Ger) vineyard (Anb): Mosel-Saar-Ruwer. (Ber): Zell/Mosel. (Gro): Schwarze Katz. (Vil): Zell-Merl.

Stefanslay (Ger) vineyard (Anb): Mosel-Saar-Ruwer. (Ber): Bernkastel. (Gro): Kurfürstlay. (Vil): Wintrich.

Sté. Fermière du Château de Malliac (Fr) an Armagnac producer. (Add): Château de Malliac, 32250 Montréal du Gers.

Steffens (Ger) a brewery. (Add): Privat-Brauerei Steffens, St.Severinsberg D-53542, Linz/Rhein. Brews: Alt, Braunbier, Funtasy, Kräusen, Malz, Radler, Steffens Pils and Steffi. Website: http://www.brauerei-steffens.de

Steffensberg (Ger) vineyard (Anb): Mosel-Saar-Ruwer. (Ber): Bernkastel. (Gro): Nacktarsch. (Vil): Kröv.

Steffensberg (Ger) vineyard (Anb): Mosel-Saar-Ruwer. (Ber): Bernkastel. (Gro): Schwarzlay. (Vil): Enkirch.

Steffl (Aus) the first lager beer ever brewed in 1841. Produced by Anton Dreher. Known generally as the original 'Vienna Lager'.

Steffl Export (Aus) a lager beer 5.4% alc by vol. brewed by the Schwechat Brauerei in Vienna. Conditioned for 3 months (part of Bräu A.G).

Sté-Foy-Bordeaux (Fr) an A.C. red and white wine commune in southern Bordeaux.

Stegbach-Quelle (Ger) a still and sparkling natural spring mineral water from Wallhausen. (green label: sparkling/red label: light gas/yellow label: still). Mineral contents (milligrammes per litre): Sodium 6.9mg/l, Calcium 100mg/l, Magnesium 42.3mg/l, Potassium 5.37mg/l, Bicarbonates 471mg/l, Chlorides 13.5mg/l, Sulphates 39.9mg/l, Fluorides 0.92mg/l, Nitrates <0.1mg/l.

Stehlerberg (Ger) vineyard (Anb): Mittelrhein. (Ber): Rheinburgengau. (Gro): Burg Hammerstein. (Vil): Kasbach.

Steichling (Ger) vineyard (Anb): Hessische Bergstrasse. (Ber): Starkenburg. (Gro): Wolfsmagen. (Vil): Bensheim.

Steierbräu AG (Aus) a brewery based in Graz. Brews Gösser.

Steiermärk (Aus) a wine region situated in the south-eastern corner of Austria which contains the districts of Südost-Steiermark, Südsteiermark and Weststeiermark 1900ha. Soil: marl, sand and slate. Main grape varieties: white (Chardonnay, Sauvignon blanc, Welschriesling), red (Uhudler, Zweigelt). Main villages: Czamillonberg, Ehrenhausen, Gamlitz, Glanz, Grassritzberg, Hochgrassritzberg, Karnerberg, Kitzeck, Kranachberg, Labitschberg, Leibnitz, Leutschach, Mitteregg, Obegg, Oberglanzberg, Ratsch, Seggauberg, Sernauberg, Spielfeld, St. Andrä, Sulztal, Wildon, Zieregg.

Steiermärkisches Landesweingut Weinbauschule Silberberg (Aus) a wine school based in Leibnitz that trains local wine makers in viticultural and vinicultural techniques. Have their own vineyards that assist in the costs of running the school.

Steig (Ger) vineyard (Anb): Baden. (Ber): Badische Bergstrasse/Kraichgau. (Gro): Hohenberg. (Vil): Eisingen.

Steig (Ger) vineyard (Anb): Rheingau. (Ber): Johannisberg. (Gro): Daubhaus. (Vil): Kostheim.

Steig (Ger) vineyard (Anb): Rheinhessen. (Ber): Wonnegau. (Gro): Burg Rodenstein. (Vil): Flörsheim-Dalsheim.

Steig (Ger) vineyard (Anb): Pfalz. (Ber): Mittelhaardt-Deutsche Weinstrasse. (Gro): Schwarzerde. (Vil): Bisserheim.

Steige (Ger) vineyard (Anb): Baden. (Ber): Markgräflerland. (Gro): Vogtei Rötteln. (Vil): Haltingen.

Steige (Ger) vineyard (Anb): Baden. (Ber): Markgräflerland. (Gro): Vogtei Rötteln. (Vil): Ötlingen.

Steige (Ger) vineyard (Anb): Rheinhessen. (Ber): Bingen. (Gro): Rheingrafenstein. (Vil): Fürfeld.

Steiger (Aus) a vineyard site on the banks of the River Danube situated in the Wachau region, Niederösterreich.

Steigerberg (Ger) vineyard (Anb): Rheinhessen. (Ber): Bingen. (Gro): Adelberg. (Vil): Wendelsheim.

Steigerdell (Ger) vineyard (Anb): Nahe. (Ber): Schloss Böckelheim. (Gro): Burgweg. (Vil): Bad Münster a. St-Ebernburg.

Steigerwald (Ger) bereich (Anb): Franken. (Gros): Burgweg, Herrenberg, Kapellenberg, Schild, Schlossberg, Schlosstück. Has a soil of marl which gives an earthy taste to the wines.

Steig-Terrassen (Ger) vineyard (Anb): Rheinhessen. (Ber): Nierstein. (Gro): Vogelsgärten. (Vil): Guntersblum.

Steil (Ger) grosslage (Anb): Rheingau. (Ber): Johannisberg. (Vils): Assmannshausen, Assmannshausen-Aulhausen.

Steillage (Ger) very steep-sloping vineyards.

Stein (Ger) a beer mug (earthenware) of between a ½ litre and 2litres capacity, often has a lid – to keep out the flies!

Stein (Ger) lit: 'stone'.

Stein (Ger) vineyard (Anb): Franken. (Ber): Maindreieck. (Gro): Not yet assigned. (Vil): Würzburg.

Stein (Ger) vineyard (Anb): Franken. (Ber): Maindreieck. (Gro): Rosstal. (Vil): Stetten.

Stein (Ger) vineyard (Anb): Rheingau. (Ber): Johannisberg. (Gro): Daubhaus. (Vil): Hochheim.

Stein (Ger) vineyard (Anb): Rheingau. (Ber): Johannisberg. (Gro): Daubhaus. (Vil): Wicker.

Stein (Ger) vineyard (Anb): Rheinhessen. (Ber): Wonnegau. (Gro): Gotteshilfe. (Vil): Bechtheim.

Stein (S.Afr) a medium-sweet wine produced from a blend of Steen and other white grape varieties.

Stein (S.Afr) the label for a special late harvest white wine made from (Chenin blanc, Gewürztraminer and Muscat blend) produced by the Nederburg Estate, Wellington, Western Cape.

Stein [Robert] (Scot) the pioneer and inventor of the continuous still which was perfected by Aeneas Coffey in 1826.

Steinacker (Ger) vineyard (Anb): Baden. (Ber): Markgräflerland. (Gro): Vogtei Rötteln. (Vil): Herten.

Steinacker (Ger) vineyard (Anb): Rheinhessen. (Ber): Bingen. (Gro): Abtey. (Vil): Nieder-Hilbersheim.

Steinacker (Ger) vineyard (Anb): Rheinhessen. (Ber): Bingen. (Gro): Kaiserpfalz. (Vil): Heidesheim.

Steinacker (Ger) vineyard (Anb): Rheinhessen. (Ber): Bingen. (Gro): Kaiserpfalz. (Vil): Ingelheim.

Steinacker (Ger) vineyard (Anb): Pfalz. (Ber): Mittelhaardt-Deutsche Weinstrasse. (Gro): Kobnert. (Vil): Kallstadt.

Steinacker (Ger) vineyard (Anb): Pfalz. (Ber): Mittelhaardt-Deutsche Weinstrasse. (Gro): Schwarzerde. (Vil): Kirchheim.

Steinacker (Ger) vineyard (Anb): Württemberg. (Ber): Württembergisch Unterland. (Gro): Salzberg. (Vil): Lehrensteinsfeld.

Stein am Rain (Aus) a vineyard site on the banks of the River Danube situated in the Wachau region, Niederösterreich.

Stein-am-Rhein (Switz) a wine-producing area based in Schauffhausen, northern Switzerland. Famous for white wines.

Steinbach (Ger) village (Anb): Baden. (Ber): Ortenau. (Gro): Schloss Rodeck. (Vins): Stich den Buben, Yburgberg.

Steinbach (Ger) village (Anb): Franken. (Ber): Steigerwald. (Gro): Kapellenberg. (Vin): Nonnenberg.

Steinbach (Ger) vineyard (Anb): Franken. (Ber): Maindreieck. (Gro): Not yet assigned. (Vil): Sommerhausen.

Steinbachhof (Ger) vineyard (Anb): Württemberg. (Ber): Württembergisch Unterland. (Gro): Stromberg. (Vil): Gründelbach.

Steinberg (Ger) vineyard (Anb): Baden. (Ber): Markgräflerland. (Gro): Lorettoberg. (Vil): Bollschweil.

Steinberg (Ger) vineyard (Anb): Baden. (Ber): Ortenau. (Gro): Fürsteneck. (Vil): Durbach.

Steinberg (Ger) vineyard (Anb): Franken. (Ber): Maindreieck. (Gro): Not yet assigned. (Vil): Michelbach.

Steinberg (Ger) vineyard (Anb): Nahe. (Ber): Kreuznach. (Gro): Kronenberg. (Vil): Bad Kreuznach.

Steinberg (Ger) vineyard (Anb): Nahe. (Ber): Schloss Böckelheim. (Gro): Burgweg. (Vil): Niederhausen an der Nahe.

Steinberg (Ger) vineyard (Anb): Rheingau. (Ber): Johannisberg. (Gro): Deutelsberg. (Vil): Estate.

Steinberg (Ger) vineyard (Anb): Rheinhessen. (Ber): Bingen. (Gro): Abtey. (Vil): Partenheim.

Steinberg (Ger) vineyard (Anb): Rheinhessen. (Ber): Bingen. (Gro): Abtey. (Vil): Sankt Johann.

Steinberg (Ger) vineyard (Anb): Rheinhessen. (Ber): Bingen. (Gro): Kaiserpfalz. (Vil): Wackernheim.

Steinberg (Ger) vineyard (Anb): Rheinhessen. (Ber): Nierstein. (Gro): Gutes Domtal. (Vil): Dalheim.

Steinberg (Ger) vineyard (Anb): Rheinhessen. (Ber): Nierstein. (Gro): Krötenbrunnen. (Vil): Guntersblum.

Steinberg (Ger) vineyard (Anb): Pfalz. (Ber): Mittelhaardt-Deutsche Weinstrasse. (Gro): Feuerberg. (Vil): Bad Dürkheim.

S

Steinberg (Ger) vineyard (Anb): Württemberg. (Ber): Württembergisch Unterland. (Gro): Wunnenstein. (Vil): Beilstein.

Steinberg (Ger) a vineyard within the village of Hattenheim, 36.7ha. (73.3%) of which is proposed to be classified as Erstes Gewächs.

Steinberger (Ger) vineyard (Anb): Mosel-Saar-Ruwer. (Ber): Saar-Ruwer. (Gro): Scharzberg. (Vil): Filzen.

Steinbier (Ger) a rauch beer with an intense smokey aroma from Rauchenfels. 3.5% alc by vol. *See also* Steinweizen.

Steinbock (Eng) a draught lager beer 1034 O.G. brewed by the Shepherd Neame Brewery in Faversham, Kent.

Stein-Bockenheim (Ger) village (Anb): Rheinhessen. (Ber): Bingen. (Gro): Rheingrafenstein. (Vin): Sonnenburg.

Steinbock Super (Eng) a pale coloured, light-flavoured lager from Shepherd Neame 9.1% alc by vol.

Steinböhl (Ger) vineyard (Anb): Rheinhessen. (Ber): Wonnegau. (Gro): Pilgerpfad. (Vil): Monzernheim.

Steinborz (Aus) a vineyard site on the banks of the River Danube situated in the Wachau region, Niederösterreich.

Steinbronn (Ger) a natural spring mineral water. Mineral contents (milligrammes per litre): Sodium 40mg/l, Calcium 219mg/l, Magnesium 27mg/l, Potassium 3mg/l, Bicarbonates 458mg/l, Chlorides 93mg/l, Sulphates 229mg/l, Silicates 31mg/l.

Steinbuck (Ger) vineyard (Anb): Baden. (Ber): Kaiserstuhl-Tuniberg. (Gro): Vulkanfelsen. (Vil): Bischoffingen.

Steinbühel (Aus) a vineyard site on the banks of the River Danube in the Kremstal region.

Steinchen (Ger) vineyard (Anb): Mosel-Saar-Ruwer. (Ber): Zell/Mosel. (Gro): Weinhex. (Vil): Kattenes.

Steinchen (Ger) vineyard (Anb): Nahe. (Ber): Kreuznach. (Gro): Sonnenborn. (Vil): Langenlonsheim.

Steinenstadt (Ger) village (Anb): Baden. (Ber): Markgräflerland. (Gro): Burg Neuenfels. (Vins): Schäf, Sonnenstück.

Steiner Hund (Aus) a dry white wine from the Wachau district, made from the Riesling grape.

Steiner Pfaffenberg (Aus) a vineyard site on the banks of the River Danube in the Kremstal region.

Steinert (Fr) an A.C. Alsace Grand Cru vineyard in Pfaffenheim, Haut-Rhin 38ha.

Steinert (Ger) vineyard (Anb): Rheinhessen. (Ber): Bingen. (Gro): Abtey. (Vil): Gau-Algesheim.

Steinertal (Aus) a vineyard site on the banks of the River Danube situated in the Wachau region, Niederösterreich.

Steiner Vineyard (USA) a vineyard based near Glen Ellen, Sonoma Valley, California. Grape variety: Cabernet sauvignon. *see* Crema Vinera (La).

Steinfeder (Aus) a term used in the Wachau to describe light wines with a maximum alc by vol. of 10.7% and minimum sugar level of 15° KMW. Known locally as 'stone feather'. *See also* Federspiel, Smaragd. *see* Vinea Wachau Nobilis Districtus.

Steinfeld (Aus) a vineyard site based on the banks of the River Kamp situated in the Kamptal region.

Steinfeld (Ger) village (Anb): Pfalz. (Ber): Südliche Weinstrasse. (Gro): Guttenberg. (Vin): Herrenwingert.

Steinfelsen (Ger) vineyard (Anb): Baden. (Ber): Kaiserstuhl-Tuniberg. (Gro): Vulkanfelsen. (Vil): Bickensohl.

Steinfelsen (Ger) vineyard (Anb): Baden. (Ber): Kaiserstuhl-Tuniberg. (Gro): Vulkanfelsen. (Vil): Ihringen.

Steingarten (Austr) the label used by the Orlando Winery in the Barossa Valley for their Riesling-based wines.

Steingässle (Ger) vineyard (Anb): Baden. (Ber): Markgräflerland. (Gro): Vogtei Rötteln. (Vil): Efringen-Kirchen.

Steingässle (Ger) vineyard (Anb): Baden. (Ber): Markgräflerland. (Gro): Vogtei Rötteln. (Vil): Feuerbach.

Steingässle (Ger) vineyard (Anb): Baden. (Ber): Markgräflerland. (Gro): Vogtei Rötteln. (Vil): Holzen.

Steingässle (Ger) vineyard (Anb): Baden. (Ber): Markgräflerland. (Gro): Vogtei Rötteln. (Vil): Riedlingen.

Steingässle (Ger) vineyard (Anb): Baden. (Ber): Markgräflerland. (Gro): Vogtei Rötteln. (Vil): Tannenkirch.

Steingässle (Ger) vineyard (Anb): Baden. (Ber): Markgräflerland. (Gro): Vogtei Rötteln. (Vil): Welmlingen.

Steingässle (Ger) vineyard (Anb): Baden. (Ber): Markgräflerland. (Gro): Vogtei Rötteln. (Vil): Wintersweiler.

Steingässle (Ger) vineyard (Anb): Baden. (Ber): Markgräflerland. (Gro): Vogtei Rötteln. (Vil): Wollbach.

Steingebiss (Ger) vineyard (Anb): Pfalz. (Ber): Südliche Weinstrasse. (Gro): Kloster Liebfrauenberg. (Vil): Billigheim-Ingenheim.

Steingeröll (Ger) vineyard (Anb): Hessische Bergstrasse. (Ber): Starkenburg. (Gro): Rott. (Vil): Zwingenberg.

Steingerück (Ger) vineyard (Anb): Hessische Bergstrasse. (Ber): Umstadt. (Gro): None. (Vil): Gross-Umstadt.

Steingold Lager (Eng) a lager beer 1042 O.G. brewed by the McMullen Brewery in Hertford.

Steingraten Tiefenthal (Aus) a vineyard site on the banks of the River Danube in the Kremstal region.

Steingrube (Ger) vineyard (Anb): Baden. (Ber): Kaiserstuhl-Tuniberg. (Gro): Vulkanfelsen. (Vil): Endingen.

Steingrube (Ger) vineyard (Anb): Baden. (Ber): Kaiserstuhl-Tuniberg. (Gro): Vulkanfelsen. (Vil): Jechtingen.

Steingrube (Ger) vineyard (Anb): Baden. (Ber):

1231

S

Kaiserstuhl-Tuniberg. (Gro): Vulkanfelsen. (Vil): Neuershausen.

Steingrube (Ger) vineyard (Anb): Baden. (Ber): Kaiserstuhl-Tuniberg. (Gro): Vulkanfelsen. (Vil): Nimburg.

Steingrube (Ger) vineyard (Anb): Rheinhessen. (Ber): Wonnegau. (Gro): Bergkloster. (Vil): Westhofen.

Steingrube (Ger) vineyard (Anb): Württemberg. (Ber): Remstal-Stuttgart. (Gro): Weinsteige. (Vil): Stuttgart (ortsteil Uhlbach).

Steingrube (Ger) vineyard (Anb): Württemberg. (Ber): Württembergisch Unterland. (Gro): Heuchelberg. (Vil): Neipperg.

Steingrüble (Ger) vineyard (Anb): Baden. (Ber): Markgräflerland. (Gro): Lorettoberg. (Vil): Bad Krotzingen.

Steingrüble (Ger) vineyard (Anb): Baden. (Ber): Markgräflerland. (Gro): Lorettoberg. (Vil): Schlatt.

Steingrüble (Ger) vineyard (Anb): Baden. (Ber): Kaiserstuhl-Tuniberg. (Gro): Vulkanfelsen. (Vil): Königschaffhausen.

Steingrüble (Ger) vineyard (Anb): Württemberg. (Ber): Remstal-Stuttgart. (Gro): Wartbühl. (Vil): Grossheppach.

Steingrüble (Ger) vineyard (Anb): Württemberg. (Ber): Remstal-Stuttgart. (Gro): Wartbühl. (Vil): Kleinheppach.

Steingrüble (Ger) vineyard (Anb): Württemberg. (Ber): Remstal-Stuttgart. (Gro): Wartbühl. (Vil): Korb.

Steingrüble (Ger) vineyard (Anb): Württemberg. (Ber): Remstal-Stuttgart. (Gro): Wartbühl. (Vil): Waiblingen.

Steingrubler (Fr) an A.C. Alsace Grand Cru vineyard in Wettolsheim, Haut-Rhin 19ha.

Steingrübler (Ger) vineyard (Anb): Baden. (Ber): Ortenau. (Gro): Schloss Rodeck. (Vil): Varnhalt.

Steingrübler (Ger) vineyard (Anb): Franken. (Ber): Mainviereck. (Gro): Not yet assigned. (Vil): Miltenberg.

Steinhaeger (Ger) a gin, colourless and juniper-flavoured, sold in stone jars and produced in Steinhägen, Westphalia 38% alc by vol. Also spelt Steinhaeger.

Steinhagen (Aus) a vineyard site on the banks of the River Danube in the Kremstal region.

Steinhäger (Ger) see Steinhaeger.

Steinhalde (Ger) vineyard (Anb): Baden. (Ber): Kaiserstuhl-Tuniberg. (Gro): Vulkanfelsen. (Vil): Amoltern.

Steinhalde (Ger) vineyard (Anb): Württemberg. (Ber): Remstal-Stuttgart. (Gro): Weinsteige. (Vil): Stuttgart (ortsteil Cannstatt).

Steinhalde (Ger) vineyard (Anb): Württemberg. (Ber): Remstal-Stuttgart. (Gro): Weinsteige. (Vil): Stuttgart (ortsteil Mühlhausen).

Steinhalde (Ger) vineyard (Anb): Württemberg. (Ber): Remstal-Stuttgart. (Gro): Weinsteige. (Vil): Stuttgart (ortsteil Münster).

Stein/Harfe (Ger) vineyard (Anb): Franken. (Ber):

Maindreieck. (Gro): Not yet assigned. (Vil): Würzburg.

Steinhaus (Aus) a vineyard site based on the banks of the River Kamp situated in the Kamptal region.

Steinhaus (USA) the brand-name used by Schell Brewery in New Ulm, Minnesota for their range of light-style beers.

Steinheim (Ger) village (Anb): Württemberg. (Ber): Württembergisch Unterland. (Gro): Schalkstein. (Vin): Burgberg.

Steinheim (Ger) village (Anb): Württemberg. (Ber): Württembergisch Unterland. (Gro): Wunnenstein. (Vin): Lichtenberg.

Steinie (N.Z) abbr: Steinlager.

Steinkaul (Ger) vineyard (Anb): Ahr. (Ber): Walporzheim/Ahrtal. (Gro): Klosterberg. (Vil): Bachem.

Steinkaut (Ger) vineyard (Anb): Nahe. (Ber): Schloss Böckelheim. (Gro): Rosengarten. (Vil): Weinsheim.

Steinklinge (Ger) vineyard (Anb): Baden. (Ber): Badische Frankenland. (Gro): Tauberklinge. (Vil): Oberlauda.

Steinklotz (Fr) an A.C. Alsace Grand Cru vineyard in Marlenheim, Bas-Rhin 24ha.

Steinkopf (Ger) a vineyard. (Anb): Hessische Bergstrasse. (Ber): Starkenburg. (Gro): Schlossberg. (Vil): Heppenheim including Erbach and Hambach.

Steinkopf (Ger) vineyard (Anb): Nahe. (Ber): Kreuznach. (Gro): Schlosskapelle. (Vil): Münster-Sarmsheim.

Steinkopf (Ger) vineyard (Anb): Pfalz. (Ber): Mittelhaardt-Deutsche Weinstrasse. (Gro): Schwarzerde. (Vil): Heuchelheim/Frankenthal.

Steinköpfchen (Ger) vineyard (Anb): Nahe. (Ber): Kreuznach. (Gro): Schlosskapelle. (Vil): Rümmelsheim.

Steinkreuz (Ger) vineyard (Anb): Nahe. (Ber): Schloss Böckelheim. (Gro): Rosengarten. (Vil): St. Katharinen.

Stein Lager (Ch.Isles) a lager beer 1048 O.G. brewed by the Guernsey Brewery 1920 Ltd., St. Peter Port, Guernsey. Previously known as Hi-Bräu (now no longer produced).

Stein Lager (Eng) a lager beer 1036 O.G. brewed by the Thwaites Brewery in Blackburn, Lancashire.

Steinlager (N.Z) abbr: Steinie, a full-bodied, bottled, premium lager beer 1045 O.G./5% alc by vol. brewed by the New Zealand Breweries.

Steinler (Ger) vineyard (Anb): Baden. (Ber): Bodensee. (Gro): Not yet assigned. (Vil): Lottstetten (ortsteil Nack).

Steinler (Ger) vineyard (Anb): Baden. (Ber): Markgräflerland. (Gro): Lorettoberg. (Vil): Freiburg.

Steinling (Aus) a vineyard site on the banks of the River Danube in the Kremstal region.

Steinmächer (Ger) grosslage (Anb): Rheingau. (Ber): Johannisberg. (Vils): Dotzheim, Eltville, Frauenstein, Martinsthal, Niederwalluf, Oberwalluf, Rauenthal, Schierstein.

Steinmassl (Aus) a vineyard site based on the banks of the River Kamp situated in the Kamptal region.

Steinmauer (Ger) vineyard (Anb): Baden. (Ber): Kaiserstuhl-Tuniberg. (Gro): Attilafelsen. (Vil): Waltershofen.

Steinmorgen (Ger) vineyard (Anb): Rheingau. (Ber): Johannisberg. (Gro): Deutelsberg. (Vil): Erbach.

Steinmorgen (Ger) a vineyard within the village of Erbach, 28.2ha. (30.5%) of which is proposed to be classified as Erstes Gewächs.

Steinriedl (Aus) a vineyard site on the banks of the River Danube situated in the Wachau region, Niederösterreich.

Steinriegel (Aus) the label for a white wine (Chardonnay) produced by the Gesellmann winery, Mittel-Burgenland.

Steinrossel (Ger) vineyard (Anb): Nahe. (Ber): Kreuznach. (Gro): Pfarrgarten. (Vil): Sommerloch.

Steinsatz (Aus) a vineyard site based on the banks of the River Kamp situated in the Kamptal region.

Steinsberg (Ger) vineyard (Anb): Baden. (Ber): Badische Bergstrasse/Kraichgau. (Gro): Stiftsberg. (Vil): Sinsheim (stadtteil Weiler).

Steinsberg (Ger) vineyard (Anb): Baden. (Ber): Badische Bergstrasse/Kraichgau. (Gro): Stiftsberg. (Vil): Steinsfurt.

Steinschiller (Rum) a white grape variety grown in the Banat Vineyard for the production of white wines in Teremia Mare and Tomnatec.

Stein Select (S.Afr) the label for a semi-sweet white wine (Palomino & Ugni blanc) produced by the Drostdy Wine Cellar winery, Tulbagh, Western Cape.

Stein Select (S.Afr) the label for a white wine (Chenin blanc) produced by the Old Vine Cellars winery, Cape Town, Western Cape.

Steinsfurt (Ger) village (Anb): Baden. (Ber): Badische Bergstrasse/Kraichgau. (Gro): Stiftsberg. (Vin): Steinsberg.

Steinsieker (Ger) a natural spring mineral water from Löhne. Mineral contents (milligrammes per litre): Sodium 19.6mg/l, Calcium 580mg/l, Magnesium 40mg/l, Potassium 2mg/l, Bicarbonates 270mg/l, Chlorides 90mg/l, Sulphates 1320mg/l, Fluorides 0.8mg/l.

Steinwand (Aus) a vineyard site on the banks of the River Danube situated in the Wachau region, Niederösterreich.

Steinwand (Aus) a vineyard site based on the banks of the River Kamp situated in the Kamptal region.

Steinweg (Ger) vineyard (Anb): Nahe. (Ber): Kreuznach. (Gro): Kronenberg. (Vil): Bad Kreuznach.

Steinweiler (Ger) village (Anb): Pfalz. (Ber): Südliche Weinstrasse. (Gro): Kloster Liebfrauenberg. (Vin): Rosenberg.

Steinwein (Ger) lit: 'stone wine', a term used to denote the wines of Franconia, which are white, dry and steely in flavour. Named after the vineyard.

Steinwein 1540 (Ger) the longest living wine recorded and is still drinkable! Discovered in Wurzberg in the t wentieth century.

Steinweizen (Ger) a rauch wheat beer from Rauchenfels. 3.5% alc by vol. See also Steinbier.

Steinwengert (Ger) vineyard (Anb): Baden. (Ber): Badische Bergstrasse/Kraichgau. (Gro): Hohenberg. (Vil): Wöschbach.

Steinwingert (Ger) vineyard (Anb): Nahe. (Ber): Schloss Böckelheim. (Gro): Burgweg. (Vil): Niederhausen an der Nahe.

Steinzeiler (Aus) the label for a red wine (Blaufränkisch, Cabernet sauvignon and Zweigelt blend) produced by the Römerhof Estate winery, Burgenland.

Steirisch Pils (Aus) a light, well-hopped pilsener lager brewed by the Gösser Brauerei at Leoben.

St. Eligius Heilwasser (Ger) a natural spring mineral water brand.

Stella Alpina (It) a natural spring mineral water from Fonte dell' Alta Valle Brembana, Moio de' Calvi. Mineral contents (milligrammes per litre): Sodium 0.97mg/l, Calcium 10mg/l, Magnesium 2.7mg/l, Potassium 0.74mg/l, Bicarbonates 36.6mg/l, Sulphates 4.6mg/l, Nitrates 3mg/l, Silicates 5.9mg/l. pH 7.46

Stella Alpina (S.Afr) a slightly acidic natural spring mineral water (established 2002) from Citrusdal. Mineral contents (milligrammes per litre): Sodium 13mg/l, Calcium 1.5mg/l, Magnesium 2mg/l, Potassium 1.8mg/l, Chlorides 23mg/l, Sulphates 1.4mg/l, Fluorides <0.1mg/l, Silicates 6.4mg/l. pH 5.6

Stella Artois (Bel) the largest brewery in Belgium. Its lager 1047 O.G. is brewed in Britain under licence by the Whitbread Brewery, London.

Stella Bella Wines (Austr) a winery based in the Margaret River district, Western Australia. Grape varieties include: Cabernet sauvignon, Merlot. Label: Suckfizzle. Website: http://www.stellabella.com.au

Stella Pils (Afr) a pilsener lager beer brewed by the Mauritius Brewery on the island of Mauritius.

Stellar Winery (S.Afr) a winery (established 1998) based in Olifants River, Western Cape. 100ha. Grape varieties: Cabernet sauvignon, Chenin blanc, Colombard, Merlot, Pinotage, Sauvignon blanc, Shiraz. Labels: Heaven on Earth, Live-A-Little, Rather Revealing, Really Ravishing, The Sensory Collection. Website: http://www.stellarorganics.com

Stellcape Vineyards (S.Afr) a winery (established 2003) based in Koelenhof, Stellenbosch, Western Cape. 200ha. Grape varieties: Cabernet sauvignon, Chenin blanc, Merlot, Pinotage, Sauvignon blanc, Shiraz. Labels: JJ Wines, Red Blend.

Stellekaya Winery (S.Afr) a winery (established 1999) based in Die Boord, Stellenbosch, Western Cape. Grape varieties: Cabernet franc, Cabernet sauvignon, Merlot, Pinotage, Sangiovese, Shiraz. Labels: Boschetto Rosso, Cape Cross, Orion. Website: http://www.stellekaya.co.za

Stellenbosch (S.Afr) a wine town and region of the

Western Cape in the Coastal Region (named in the seventeenth century after Simon van der Stel – the Governor). Produces most of the Cape's finest wines. Estates include Goede Houp, Jacobsdal, Meerlust, Middelvlei, Simonsig and Uitkyk.

Stellenbosch (S.Afr) the label for a range of red (Cabernet sauvignon/Cabernet sauvignon-Merlot/Pinotage) and white (Chardonnay) wines produced by the Neil Ellis Wines, Stellenbosch, Western Cape.

Stellenbosch Farmer's Winery (S.Afr) abbr: SFW. (Add): P.O. Box 46, Stellenbosch 7600. The largest wine wholesaler. Instituted the Nederburg Wine Auction. Labels include: Château Libertas, La Gratitude, Lanzerac, Oom Tas, Oude Libertas, Tasheimer, Taskelder and Zonnebloem.

Stellenbosch Hills (S.Afr) a winery (established 1945) based in Vlottenburg, Stellenbosch, Western Cape. 1000ha. Grape varieties: Cabernet sauvignon, Chardonnay, Chenin blanc, Merlot, Muscat de hamburg, Pinotage, Sauvignon blanc, Shiraz. Label: 1707 Reserve. Website: http://www.stellenbosch-hills.co.za

Stellenbosch Wine and Country Estate (S.Afr) a winery (established 2004) based in Stellenbosch, Western Cape. 29.8ha. Grape varieties: Chenin blanc, Pinotage, Shiraz. Produces varietal wines.

Stellendrift (S.Afr) a winery (established 1999) based in Stellenbosch, Western Cape. 12ha. Grape varieties: Cabernet sauvignon, Merlot, Pinotage. Labels: Cape White, Cilliers Cellars, Special Select.

StellenHills Wines (S.Afr) a winery (established 2001) based in Stellenbosch, Western Cape. Grape varieties: Cabernet sauvignon, Chardonnay, Shiraz. Labels: Barriques Nouveau, Charade. Website: http://www.stellenhills.co.za

Stellenrood (S.Afr) a light red wine produced from the Cabernet, Cinsault and Shiraz grapes by Bertrams Wines, Stellenbosch, Western Cape.

Stellenryck Collection (S.Afr) a range of varietal wines produced by the Die Bergkelder in the Coastal Region. Grape varieties include Cabernet sauvignon, Chardonnay.

Stellenzicht Vineyards (S.Afr) a winery based in Stellenbosch, Western Cape. 7ha. Grape varieties: Cabernet sauvignon, Chardonnay, Merlot, Pinotage, Sémillon, Shiraz, Syrah. Labels: Golden Triangle, Rhapsody. Website: http://www.stellenzicht.co.za

St. Elmo (Port) a brand of sweet white wine produced by SOGRAPE.

Steltzer Vineyard (USA) a vineyard based near Yountville, California. Grape varieties: Cabernet sauvignon and Johannisberg riesling. Produces varietal wines.

Stelvin (Eng) the technical name for a screw cap.

Ste. Marie (Fr) a rare white grape variety grown in Gascony.

Sté-Michelle Winery (Can) a vineyard based in Okanagin. Produces Labrusca-type and French hybrid wines.

St. Emiliana (Chile) the brand-name of a red wine produced by Concha y Toro.

St-Émilion (Fr) an A.C. wine region of eastern Bordeaux. Red wines only. First classified in 1955. Main Grape varieties: Cabernet franc, Merlot and Cabernet sauvignon. see Saint-Émilion and Saint-Émilion Classification.

Stemmed Glass (Eng) a glass with a long stem between the bowl and the foot. It enables the glass to be held without the drink being heated by the hand.

Stemming (Eng) the name given to the process of removing stalks from grapes using an Égrappoir or Foulograppe.

Stemmler (Ger) vineyard (Anb): Hessische Bergstrasse. (Ber): Starkenburg. (Gro): Schlossberg. (Vil): Heppenheim including Erbach and Hambach.

Stemmler Winery (USA) a winery based in the Dry Creek Valley, Sonoma County, California. Grape varieties: Cabernet sauvignon, Pinot noir, Chardonnay and Fumé blanc. Produces varietal wines without irrigation.

Stenkulla (Swe) a natural spring mineral water. Mineral contents (milligrammes per litre): Sodium 30mg/l, Calcium 58mg/l, Magnesium 3mg/l, Chlorides 33mg/l, Fluorides 1mg/l, Nitrates <0.2mg/l. pH 8.2

Stephanoderes hamjei (Lat) the Coffee Berry Borer, a parasite that attacks the berries of the coffee bush.

Stephansberg (Ger) vineyard (Anb): Baden. (Ber): Badische Bergstrasse/Kraichgau. (Gro): Rittersberg. (Vil): Hohensachsen.

Stephansberg (Ger) vineyard (Anb): Baden. (Ber): Badische Bergstrasse/Kraichgau. (Gro): Rittersberg. (Vil): Lützelsachsen.

Stephansberg (Ger) vineyard (Anb): Nahe. (Ber): Schloss Böckelheim. (Gro): Burgweg. (Vil): Bad Münster a. St-Ebernburg.

Stephanus-Rosengärtchen (Ger) vineyard (Anb): Mosel-Saar-Ruwer. (Ber): Bernkastel. (Gro): Kurfürstlay. (Vil): Bernkastel-Kues.

Stephenson Cellars (USA) a winery based near Walla Walla Valley, Washington. Grape varieties include: Merlot, Pinot noir.

Stephen Zellerbach Winery (USA) a winery based in the Napa Valley, northern California. Produces varietal wines.

Sterhuis (S.Afr) a winery (established 1980) based in Koelenhof, Stellenbosch, Western Cape. 48ha. Grape varieties: Chardonnay, Merlot, Sauvignon blanc.

Steril.O (Can) a purified and sterilized bottled water brand.

Sterke Drank (Hol) beverage/alcoholic liquor/spirits.

Sterken (Hol) to fortify with spirits.

Sterkens (Bel) a brewery (established 1650) based in Meer. Produces a range of beers that are sold in normal glass plus stone bottles. see Flanders Crock Ale, Hoogstraten Porter, St. Paul, St. Sebastiaan, Tremeloos Damiaanbier.

Sterling Vineyards (USA) a large winery in

Calistoga, Napa Valley, northern California. Grape varieties: Cabernet sauvignon, Chardonnay, Merlot, Pinot noir and Sauvignon blanc. Produces varietal wines. Owned by Seagram.

Sternberg (Ger) vineyard (Anb): Rheinhessen. (Ber): Bingen. (Gro): Rheingrafenstein. (Vil): Pleitersheim.

Sternbräu (Switz) a lager beer 1045 O.G. brewed by the Hurlimann Brauerei. Brewed under licence by the Shepherd Neame Brewery in Faversham, Kent.

Stern Dampfbier Brauerei (Ger) a brewery (established 1896) based at Essen-Borbeck. Brews: Borbecker Helles Dampfbier.

Sternenberg (Ger) vineyard (Anb): Baden. (Ber): Ortenau. (Gro): Schloss Rodeck. (Vil): Altschweier.

Sternenberg (Ger) vineyard (Anb): Baden. (Ber): Ortenau. (Gro): Schloss Rodeck. (Vil): Bühl (ortsteil Neusatz).

Sternenfels (Ger) village (Anb): Württemberg. (Ber): Württembergisch Unterland. (Gro): Stromberg. (Vin): König.

Stert Vineyard (Eng) a vineyard (established 1976) based at Barn Cottage, Stert, Devizes, Wiltshire. 0.5ha. Grape varieties: Müller-Thurgau and Wrotham pinot (Pinot meunier).

St-Estèphe (Fr) an A.C. wine commune within the Haut-Médoc. Has vineyards in the 1855 classification. Cabernet sauvignon, Cabernet franc and Merlot are the main grape varieties (red wines only) 1142ha (19% Cru Classé).

St. Etheldreda (Eng) a dry white, table wine produced by the Isle of Ely vineyard in Cambridgeshire.

St. Étienne-de-Baïgorry (Fr) a V.D.Q.S. district in south-western Irouléguy. Home to the only co-operative that controls all the Irouléguy wines.

Stetten (Ger) village (Anb): Baden. (Ber): Bodensee. (Gro): Sonnenufer. (Vins): Fohrenberg, Lerchenberg, Sängerhalde.

Stetten (Ger) village (Anb): Franken. (Ber): Maindreieck. (Gro): Rosstal. (Vin): Stein.

Stetten (Ger) village (Anb): Pfalz. (Ber): Mittelhaardt-Deutsche Weinstrasse. (Gro): Schnepfenflug vom Zellertal. (Vin): Heilighäuschen.

Stetten a. H (Ger) village (Anb): Württemberg. (Ber): Württembergisch Unterland. (Gro): Heuchelberg. (Vin): Sonnenberg.

Stetten i. R (Ger) village (Anb): Württemberg. (Ber): Remstal-Stuttgart. see Kernen.

Stetten i. R (Ger) village (Anb): Württemberg. (Ber): Remstal-Stuttgart. (Gro): Wartbühl. (Vins): Brotwasser, Häder, Lindhälder, Puvermächer.

Stettfeld (Ger) see Ubstadt-Weiher.

Stettyn Wynkelders Koöperatief (S.Afr) a co-operative (established 1964) winery based in Worcester, Western Cape. 300ha. (Add): Private Bag 3011, Worcester 6850. Grape varieties: Cabernet sauvignon, Chardonnay, Chenin blanc, Cinsaut, Colombard, Hanepoot, Merlot, Pinotage, Sauvignon blanc, Sémillon, Shiraz. Labels:

Baobob, Millstone, Signature Reserve, Tyne & Daly. Also produces varietal wines. Website: http://www.steyncellar.co.za

Steuk Wine Company (USA) a winery based near Cleveland, Ohio. Produces Concord, vinifera and French-American hybrid wines.

Stevenot Winery (USA) a winery based at Murphy's, Calaveras County, California. Grape varieties: Cabernet sauvignon, Chardonnay, Chenin blanc, White riesling and Zinfandel. Produces varietal and table wines.

Stewart and Son (Scot) a noted blender and exporter of Scotch whiskies based in Dundee and Glasgow. Noted for Stewarts Cream of the Barley and Royal Stewart. Now part of the Allied Group. Was formerly part of William Teacher and Sons.

Stewart Brewing (Scot) a brewery (established 2004). (Add): 33/2 Montague Street, Edinburgh, Midlothian EH8 9QS. Brews beers and lager. Website: http://www.stewartbrewing.co.uk 'E'mail: steve.stewart@stewartbrewing.co.uk

Stewarts Cream of the Barley (Scot) a blended Scotch whisky produced by Stewart and Son of Dundee, Glasgow. Has a high proportion of single malt whiskies (30) in the blend. Sold in a distinctive square-shaped bottle.

Stewed (Eng) a term used to denote a tea that has been brewed too long and has a bitter taste through too much tannin and caffeine.

Stewed (Eng) the term used to describe coffee brewed from freshly ground beans that has been kept hot for a long time. Has a bitter flat taste.

Stewed (Eng) a slang term for intoxicated (drunk).

Steyer (Ger) vineyard (Anb): Nahe. (Ber): Schloss Böckelheim. (Gro): Rosengarten. (Vil): Hüffelsheim.

Steyerberg (Ger) vineyard (Anb): Nahe. (Ber): Kreuznach. (Gro): Schlosskapelle. (Vil): Schweppenhausen.

St. Felician (Arg) a Cabernet-based wine produced by Esmeralda at Córdoba.

St. Feuillion (Bel) a 7.5% alc by vol. golden, top-fermented, bottle-conditioned abbaye triple beer brewed by Du Bocq in Purnode.

St. Fiacre (Fr) a village in the A.C. district of Muscadet Sèvre et Maine, Nantais, Loire. Produces some of the finest Muscadet Sur Lie.

St. Francis Abbey Brewery (Ire) oldest brewery (established 1710) in Ireland. Founded on a monastic site. Brews: Kilkenny.

St. Francis of Paula Brauerei (Ger) the first doppelbock created in Germany in Munich (in a monastery) named Salvator. Now known as the Paulaner-Thomas-Bräu Brauerei.

St. Francis Winery (USA) a winery based in Kenwood, Sonoma Valley, Sonoma County, California. 46ha. Grape varieties: Cabernet sauvignon, Chardonnay, Gewürztraminer, Johannisberg riesling, Merlot, Pinot noir, Zinfandel. Produces varietal and table wines. Labels include: Nun's Canyon Reserve.

St-Gall (Fr) the label used by the Champagne

Growers' Co-operative at Avize, Union-Champagne.

St. Galler Klosterbräu (Switz) a 5.2% alc by vol. klosterbräu brewed by Brauerei Schützengarten AG, St. Gallen.

St. Galler Landbier (Switz) a 5% alc by vol. landbier brewed by Brauerei Schützengarten AG, St. Gallen.

St. Galmier (Fr) *see* Saint Galmier.

St. Gambrinus (Czec) a pilsener lager beer 4.5% alc by vol. from St. Gambrinus in Pilsen.

St-Genès (Fr) a commune in the A.C. Côtes de Blaye, north-eastern Bordeaux.

St-Genès-de-Blaye (Fr) a commune in the A.C. Côtes de Blaye in north-eastern Bordeaux.

St. Genies-de-Comolas (Fr) a commune in the district of A.C. Lirac in the southern Rhône. Produces white, rosé and red wines.

St. George (Gre) a red grape variety. *see* Agiorgitiko.

St. George Brewery (Afr) a brewery based in Addis Ababa, Ethiopia. Brews a fine pilsener lager beer.

St. George Estate Winery (N.Z) a winery. (Add): PD St. Georges Road, South Hastings. 2.4ha. Grape varieties: Cabernet/Merlot, Petite sirah, Chardonnay, Gewürztraminer, Riesling and a medium-dry Chenin blanc.

St. Georgen (Aus) a wine-producing area in the Eisenstadt district.

St. Georgenberg (Ger) vineyard (Anb): Rheinhessen. (Ber): Bingen. (Gro): Kaiserpfalz. (Vil): Jugenheim.

St. Georgenberg (Ger) vineyard (Anb): Rheinhessen. (Ber): Wonnegau. (Gro): Liebfrauengarten. (Vil): Worms.

St. George's (Eng) a beer brewed by Deeping Ales micro-brewery, Kent.

St. Georges (Fr) a natural spring mineral water from Corsica. Mineral contents (milligrammes per litre): Sodium 14.05mg/l, Calcium 5.2mg/l, Magnesium 2.43mg/l, Potassium 1.15mg/l, Bicarbonates 30.5mg/l, Chlorides 25mg/l, Sulphates 6mg/l, Fluorides 0.06mg/l. pH 6.8

St. Georges Ale (Eng) a 4.3% alc by vol. draught ale (also bottled) brewed by the Daleside Brewery Ltd., North Yorkshire.

St. George's Ale (Eng) a 4.3% alc by vol. bottled ale brewed by Youngs Brewery, London.

St. George's Best (Eng) a 4.2% alc by vol. ale brewed with 100% Goldings hops by Tolly Cobbold, Ipswich, Suffolk.

St. Georges Bitter (Eng) a 4.3% alc by vol. bitter ale brewed by the Wye Valley Brewery Ltd., Herefordshire.

St. Georges Brewing C° Ltd (Eng) a brewery (established 2000). (Add): Bush Lane, Callow End, Worcester, Worcestershire WR2 4TF. Brews a range of beers.

St. Georges d'Orques (Fr) *see* Saint-Georges d'Orques.

St. Georges English Wines (Eng) *see* Waldron Vineyards.

St. Georges Saint-Émilion (Fr) an A.C. commune within the Saint-Émilion district in eastern Bordeaux.

St. Georges Vineyard (Austr) part of the Lindemans estate in New South Wales. 12ha. of mainly Cabernet sauvignon grapes.

St. George's Well (Eng) a natural spring mineral water. Mineral contents (milligrammes per litre): Sodium 4mg/l, Calcium 128mg/l, Magnesium 4.4mg/l, Potassium 8.9mg/l, Chlorides 24.4mg/l, Sulphates 13mg/l, Fluorides 4.05mg/l, Nitrates 18mg/l. pH 7.1

St. Georgshof (Ger) vineyard (Anb): Mosel-Saar-Ruwer. (Ber): Obermosel. (Gro): Gipfel. (Vil): Temmels.

St. Geran (S.Afr) a still natural spring mineral water (established 1981) from Natal. Mineral contents (milligrammes per litre): Sodium 5.9mg/l, Calcium 0.5mg/l, Magnesium 0.3mg/l, Potassium 0.7mg/l, Chlorides 8mg/l, Sulphates 0.6mg/l, Fluorides 0.1mg/l, Nitrates 0.1mg/l. pH 6.4

St. Germain (Cktl) ⅓ measure green Chartreuse, ⅓ measure grapefruit juice, ⅓ measure lemon juice, 1 egg white. Shake over ice and strain into a cocktail glass.

St. Germain d'Esteuil (Fr) a commune in the northern (Bas) Médoc, north-western Bordeaux.

St. Gero Heilwasser (Ger) a sparkling natural spring mineral water. Mineral contents (milligrammes per litre): Sodium 121mg/l, Calcium 331mg/l, Magnesium 109.4mg/l, Potassium 10.2mg/l, Bicarbonates 1775mg/l, Chlorides 39mg/l, Sulphates 34.8mg/l, Fluorides 0.15mg/l, Nitrates 8.28mg/l, Silicates 37.2mg/l, Strontium 2.45mg/l.

St-Gervais (Fr) part of the A.C. Côtes du Rhône-Villages, Gard département.

St. Gilbert (Austr) a blended red wine from the Botobolar vineyards in New South Wales (50% Cabernet sauvignon and 50% Shiraz grapes).

St-Girons (Fr) a commune in the A.C. Côtes de Blaye, north-eastern Bordeaux.

St. Goarshausen (Ger) village (Anb): Mittelrhein. (Ber): Rheinburgengau. (Gro): Loreleyfelsen. (Vins): Burg Katz, Burg Maus, Hessern, Loreley-Edel.

St. Goar-Werlau (Ger) village (Anb): Mittelrhein. (Ber): Rheinburgengau. (Gro): Burg Rheinfels. (Vins): Ameisenberg, Frohwingert, Kuhstall, Rosenberg.

St. Gualtier of Pontoise (Fr) the patron saint of vine-dressers.

St. Guilbert Brasserie (Bel) an abbaye brewery (established 1858) based at Mont-Saint-Guilbert. Also known as the Leffe Brasserie. Brews: Leffe Blond, Leffe Radieuse, Vieux Temps.

St. Hallett's Winery (Austr) a winery based near Tanunda in the Barossa Valley, South Australia. Produces varietal and table wines. Grape varieties: Cabernet sauvignon, Chardonnay, Merlot, Sauvignon blanc, Sémillon, Shiraz. Labels include: Gamekeeper's Reserve (Grenache, Shiraz and Touriga blend), Poacher's Blend (Riesling, Sauvignon and Sémillon blend)

St. Hallvard (Nor) a herb-flavoured liqueur. Has a base of spirit distilled from potatoes.

St. Helena (USA) an A.V.A. of Napa Valley, California since 1995. Grape varieties are mainly red Bordeaux.

St. Helena Wine Estate (N.Z) a winery based at Coutts Island Road, Christchurch, South Island. 20ha. Grape varieties: Cabernet sauvignon, Chardonnay, Gewürztraminer, Merlot, Müller-Thurgau, Pinot blanc, Pinot noir, Rhine riesling, Sauvignon blanc. Produces varietal and table wines.

St. Henri South Australian Cabernet (Austr) a red wine produced by the Penfolds Estate in South Australia from Shiraz grapes.

St. Hilarion (Cyp) a medium-dry white wine produced by Loël in Limassol.

St. Hilary (Austr) a label used by Orlando Wines for their white wine from Chardonnay grapes.

St. Hillary Winery (USA) a winery based in North Grosvenor, Connecticut. Produces mainly French hybrid wines.

St. Huberts Vineyard (Austr) a winery based near Lilydale in the Yarra Valley, Victoria. Produces still, sparkling and fortified wines. Grape varieties: Cabernet sauvignon, Chardonnay, Merlot, Pinot noir.

St. Hubertswein (Ger) the name for a wine produced from grapes harvested on 3rd November each year (a pre 1971 name).

St. Hubertus Vlassky Riesling (Czec) a dry Vlassky riesling wine produced near Bratislava in southern Czec.

St. Hugo (Austr) a label used by Orlando Wines for one of their Cabernet sauvignon wines.

Sticciano (It) a Chianti Putto producer based in Tuscany.

Stichcombe (Eng) a village in Wiltshire in which the Mildenhall Vineyard is situated.

Stich den Buben (Ger) vineyard (Anb): Baden. (Ber): Ortenau. (Gro): Schloss Rodeck. (Vil): Steinbach.

Stichtig (Ger) denotes a wine that is turning sour due to the presence of acetic acid.

Sticke Alt (Ger) the name given to a strong version of altbier from Düsseldorf. 7.5% alc by vol. Brewed in March or September, it is also known as Latzenbier.

Sticking Temperature (Eng) the point at which wine ceases to ferment either because the temperature is too low or too high.

St. Idesbald Blond (Bel) a 6.5% alc by vol. top-fermented, bottle-conditioned special beer brewed by the Huyghe Brouwerij, Melle.

Stiefel Bräu (Ger) produced by Brauerei G.A. Bruch in Saarbrücken. Hell and Dunkel Weizenbiers.

Stiege (Ger) vineyard (Anb): Baden. (Ber): Markgräflerland. (Gro): Vogtei Rötteln. (Vil): Weil am Rhein.

Stieglbrauerei zu Salzburg (Aus) a brewery. (Add): Kendlerstrabel, Salzburg A-5017. Noted for Columbus, Goldbräu and Paracelsus beers. Website: http://www.stiegl.at 'E'mail: office@stiegl.at

Stielweg (Ger) vineyard (Anb): Rheingau. (Ber): Johannisberg. (Gro): Daubhaus. (Vil): Hochheim.

Stierschneider [Karl] (Aus) a winery based in the Wachau. (Add): Kartäuserhof 6. Grape varieties: Grüner veltliner, Pinot blanc, Riesling. Produces a range of dry and sweet (botrytised) wines.

Stierschneider [Paul] (Aus) a winery based in the Wachau. (Add): 3601 Oberloiben 17. Grape varieties: Grüner veltliner, Pinot blanc, Riesling, Sauvignon blanc. Produces a range of dry and sweet wines.

Stiff Horse's Neck (Cktl) as for Horse's Neck but 90mls (¾ gill) of spirit instead of 60mls (½ gill).

Stift (Ger) vineyard (Anb): Pfalz. (Ber): Mittelhaardt-Deutsche Weinstrasse. (Gro): Schnepfenflug an der Weinstrasse. (Vil): Forst.

Stift Heiligenkreuz (Aus) a wine-producing monastery based at Thallern that produces some fine wines under the label of Thallern.

Stift Klosterneuburg (Aus) a winery and wine museum run by the Chorherren religious order in the town of Klosterneuburg, Thermenregion.

Stiftsberg (Ger) grosslage (Anb): Baden. (Ber): Badische Bergstrasse/Kraichgau. (Vils): Bauerbach, Binau, Diedesheim, Eberbach, Eichelberg, Eichtersheim, Elsenz, Eppingen, Eschelbach, Flehingen, Gemmingen, Hassmersheim, Heinsheim, Herbolzheim, Kirchardt (ortsteil Berwangen), Kraichtal (stadtteil Bahnbrücken, stadtteil Gochsheim, stadtteil Oberacker), Kraichtal (stadtteil Neuenbürg, stadtteil Menzingen, stadtteil Münzesheim), Kraichtal (stadtteil Landshausen, stadtteil Menzingen), Kürnbach, Michelfeld, Mühlbach, Neckarmühlbach, Neckarzimmern, Neudenau, Odenheim, Rohrbach a. G., Sinsheim (stadtteil Hilsbach), Sinsheim (stadtteil Weiler), Steinsfurt, Sulzfeld, Tiefenbach, Waldangelloch, Zaisenhausen.

Stiftsberg (Ger) vineyard (Anb): Ahr. (Ber): Walporzheim/Ahrtal. (Gro): Klosterberg. (Vil): Marienthal.

Stiftsberg (Ger) vineyard (Anb): Württemberg. (Ber): Württembergisch Unterland. (Gro): Staufenberg. (Vil): Heilbronn.

Stiftsberg (Ger) vineyard (Anb): Württemberg. (Ber): Württembergisch Unterland. (Gro): Staufenberg. (Vil): Horkheim.

Stiftsberg (Ger) vineyard (Anb): Württemberg. (Ber): Württembergisch Unterland. (Gro): Staufenberg. (Vil): Talheim.

Stiftsbräu (Aus)(Ger) a Trappiste-style beer, high in alcohol.

Stifts Export (Ger) a Dortmunder export beer brewed by the Dortmund Stifts Brauerei, Dortmund.

Stifts Pils (Ger) a 4.9% alc by vol. bottled pilsner brewed by the Dortmunder Stifts Brauerei, Dortmund.

Stiftsquelle (Ger) a natural spring mineral water.

S

Mineral contents (milligrammes per litre): Sodium 12mg/l, Calcium 214mg/l, Magnesium 33mg/l, Potassium 13mg/l, Bicarbonates 360mg/l, Chlorides 58.5mg/l, Sulphates 318mg/l.

Stilberg (S.Afr) a winery based in the Western Cape. Grape varieties include: Colombard.

Stiletto Cocktail (Cktl) ⅔ measure Bourbon whiskey, ⅓ measure amaretto, juice ½ lemon. Stir over ice in an old-fashioned glass.

Still (Eng) an apparatus either of the 'pot' or 'patent' variety where fermented beverages are distilled into spirits. (Fr) = alambic.

Stillage (Eng) also known as Thralls or Horsing, a wooden framework on which the beer casks are set up on in a public house cellar, held in position with scotches.

Stillage (USA) the name given to the residue after the alcohol has been distilled out of the beer in whiskey production. Is fed to cattle etc. Contains grain residue, yeasts and minerals.

Stillare (Lat) to distil.

Stille Nacht (Bel) a strong Christmas beer 8% alc by vol. from De Dolle Brouwers.

Stiller Quell (Ger) lit: 'spring water with no gas', denotes a bottle of still spring water.

Still Ice (Ire) a new potcheen, citrus and mineral water drink produced by Dillons Spirits sold in a new tamper-proof PET ™ bottle.

Still Man (Scot) the man who tends the stills and stokes the furnaces.

Stillman (Scot) a cask-conditioned ale from Tomintoul Brewery.

Still Metz (W.Ind) a non-carbonated version of Metz. Contains Bacardi, citrus essence and spring water. 5.4% alc by vol. Chill filtered. *See also* Black Metz.

Still Wine (Eng) a non-sparkling wine, has no trace of CO_2 present.

Sting (Ch.Isles) an alcoholic lemonade produced in Jersey.

Stinger (Cktl) 25mls (⅕ gill) Bourbon whiskey served over crushed ice with an equal quantity of soda.

Stinger Cocktail (Cktl) 20mls (¾ fl.oz) brandy, 20mls (¾ fl.oz) crème de menthe (white), Shake over ice, strain into a cocktail glass and add a twist of lemon peel juice on top.

Stingo (Eng) a highly hopped, semi-sweet, barley wine brewed in Yorkshire, was originally served when flat and stale after a long maturation period.

Stingo (Eng) a barley wine 1066 O.G. brewed and bottled by the Hall and Woodhouse Brewery in Blandford Forum, Dorset.

Stingo (Eng) a barley wine 1078 O.G. brewed and bottled by the Higsons Brewery in Liverpool, Lancashire.

Stingo (Eng) a barley wine 1076 O.G. brewed and bottled by the Watney Combe Reid Brewery in London.

Stinking Drunk (Eng) a slang term used to describe a very drunken person who is unpleasantly drunk.

Stinko (Eng) a slang term for an obnoxiously drunken person.

St. Innocent (USA) a winery based in Salem, Oregon. Grape varieties: Pinot noir, Chardonnay. Produces still and sparkling wines.

Stinray (Cktl) ⅓ measure pastis, ⅓ measure apricot brandy, ⅓ measure orange juice, dash egg white. Shake well with ice and strain into a cocktail glass.

Stip (Mac) a wine-producing area in Macedonia.

Stir (Eng) in cocktail making denotes to mix the ingredients together with ice until well chilled and blended. To stir in a mixing glass with the ice and then strain into the required glass.

Stir In (Eng) in cocktail making denotes the stirring in with a barspoon of the final ingredient.

Stirling Brig (Scot) the name for a beer brewed by the Bridge of Allan Brewery Ltd., Stirlingshire.

Stirn (Ger) vineyard (Anb): Mosel-Saar-Ruwer. (Ber): Saar-Ruwer. (Gro): Scharzberg. (Vil): Saarburg.

Stir Over Ice (Eng) in cocktail making denotes the stirring over ice, cubes in a mixing jug (or in the glass) with a barspoon, stirring rod etc.

Stirrers (Eng) assorted shaped spoons used to stir the drinks in either a glass or jug, can also have a muddler attachment. Often now made of disposable plastic.

Stirring Rod (USA) a glass rod used for mixing cocktails over ice in a mixing jug or glass. Is also used for making Pousse Cafés.

Stirrup Cup (Eng) the parting drink, the name comes from the custom in the olden days of having the last drink with the guests either to help him to his saddle or after he has mounted his horse before his journey. Now served to members of a hunting party before they set off. Served in a special glass without a base. Drink has to be finished as glass must be inverted to stand. *see* Sloe gin and Coup de l'Étrier. (Fr) = vin de l'étrier.

Stirrup Cup Cocktail (Cktl) ½ measure brandy, ½ measure cherry brandy, 2 dashes lemon juice, dash gomme syrup. Shake over ice and strain into an ice-filled old-fashioned glass.

Stir up a Drink (USA) making a mixed drink by using a mixing glass and barspoon. Stir over ice.

St. Ismier (Fr) a vineyard based in Vienne, Isère département. Produces red wines.

Stitsle Weller Distillery (USA) a distillery based in Louisville. Noted for the Kentucky Bourbon Rebel Yell.

St. Jakobsberg (Ger) vineyard (Anb): Rheinhessen. (Ber): Bingen. (Gro): Sankt Rochuskapelle. (Vil): Ockenheim.

St. James (Afr) a de-caffeinated tea.

St. James (W.Ind) a Martinique rum made by the pot-still method using sugar cane sap. Has a dry, burnt flavour and is very dark in colour.

St. Jame's Gate (Ire) the Guinness brewery based in Dublin.

St. James Winery (USA) a small winery based in St. James, Missouri. Produces Vinifera and French hybrid wines.

St. Jean Baptiste (Fr) a natural spring mineral water from Winny-St. Jean Baptiste. Mineral contents (milligrammes per litre): Sodium 8mg/l, Calcium 80mg/l, Magnesium 8mg/l, Potassium 2mg/l, Bicarbonates 263mg/l, Chlorides 12mg/l, Sulphates 13mg/l, Nitrates 0.6mg/l.

St-Jean-de-la-Porte (Fr) see Saint-Jean-de-la-Porte.

St. Jean-de-Minervois (Fr) an A.C. wine-producing district near Minervois in Languedoc-Roussillon, southern France.

St. Jean de Moirans (Fr) a vineyard based in Vienne, Isère département, central-western France.

St. Jean-de-Muzels (Fr) a commune in the A.C. district of Saint-Joseph in the northern Rhône.

St. Jeoire-Prieuré (Fr) an A.C. Cru village of Savoie, south-eastern France.

St. Jerome Wines (N.Z) a winery. (Add): 219 Metcalfe Road, Henderson. 8ha. Noted for Cabernet/Merlot blends.

St. Josef's Wine Cellar (USA) a winery based in Willamette Valley, Oregon. Produces 1005 varietal wines.

St-Joseph (Fr) see Saint-Joseph.

St. Jost (Ger) vineyard (Anb): Mittelrhein. (Ber): Bacharach. (Gro): Schloss Stahleck. (Vil): Bacharach/Steeg.

St. Julien (Fr) an A.C. wine commune in the Haut-Médoc in the western Bordeaux (red wines only), classified in the 1855 Médoc classification. 520ha (80% Cru Classé).

St. Julien Wine Company (USA) a winery based in Paw Paw, Michigan. Produces French/American hybrid wines.

St. Katharinen (Ger) village (Anb): Nahe. (Ber): Schloss Böckelheim. (Gro): Rosengarten. (Vins): Fels, Klostergarten, Steinkreuz.

St. Katharinenwein (Ger) the name for a wine made from grapes that are harvested on 25th November annually (a pre 1971 name).

St. Katherine (Cktl) 1 part Bacardi White Label, 1 part white crème de cacao. Mix well together over ice, strain into a cocktail glass, top with whipped cream and grated nutmeg.

St. Kilian (Ger) an Irish missionary, the patron saint of Vintagers in Franconia. Lived in the seventh century.

St. Klausen (Ger) vineyard (Anb): Franken. (Ber): Maindreieck. (Gro): Burg. (Vil): Ramsthal.

St-Laurent (Aus) a red grape variety, not permitted in the E.C (quality wines). (Cro) = Sentlovrenka, (Czec) = Svatovavrinecke/Vavrinecké, (Slo) = Sentlovrenka. Also known as the Pinot St. Laurent and Sankt Laurent.

St. Laurent (Fr) a commune within the A.C. Médoc district in western Bordeaux.

St. Laurent (Lux) a natural spring mineral water from Bron. Mineral contents (milligrammes per litre): Sodium 2.5mg/l, Calcium 90.2mg/l, Magnesium 1.2mg/l, Potassium 0.4mg/l, Bicarbonates 229mg/l, Chlorides 5.5mg/l, Sulphates 29.5mg/l, Nitrates 5.3mg/l.

St. Laurent-Ausstich (Aus) a red wine produced from the St-Laurent grape by the Augustine monks at Klosterneuburg, Vienna.

St. Laurent de Médoc (Fr) a commune in the A.C. Médoc. see St. Laurent.

St. Laurent des Arbes (Fr) a commune in the A.C. district of Lirac. Produces red, rosé and white wines.

St. Laurent des Combes (Fr) an A.C. commune in the Saint-Émilion district of eastern Bordeaux (red wines only).

St. Laurenzikapelle (Ger) vineyard (Anb): Rheinhessen. (Ber): Bingen. (Gro): Abtey. (Vil): Gau-Algesheim.

St. Leger (Eng) a brand-name drink, low in alcohol, made from mineral water, orange juice and white wine 3.5% alc by vol.

St. Leonard (Fr) a bière de garde from Boulogne.

St. Leonards Winery (Austr) a winery. (Add): St. Leonards Road, Wahgunyah, north-eastern Victoria. Produces varietal wines. Grape varieties: Cabernet franc, Cabernet sauvignon, Chardonnay, Chenin blanc, Gewürztraminer, Merlot, Riesling, Shiraz.

St. Leonhardsquelle (Ger) a still and sparkling natural spring mineral water from Bad Leonhardspfunzen, Rosenheim. (red label: sparkling/green label: light gas/yellow label: still). Mineral contents (milligrammes per litre): Sodium 5.4mg/l, Calcium 93mg/l, Magnesium 24mg/l, Potassium 1mg/l, Bicarbonates 393mg/l, Chlorides 13.1mg/l, Sulphates 9.4mg/l, Fluorides 0.05mg/l, Nitrates <0.05mg/l, Silicates 15mg/l, Iron 3.7mg/l. pH 7.68

St. Linus Heilwasser (Ger) a natural spring mineral water from Pechbrunn. Mineral contents (milligrammes per litre): Sodium 10.2mg/l, Calcium 12.9mg/l, Magnesium 6.4mg/l, Chlorides 3mg/l, Sulphates 14.8mg/l.

St. Louis Gueuze Lambic (Bel) a 4.5% alc by vol. spontaneous fermenting gueuze lambic beer brewed by Van Honsebrouck Brouwerij, Ingelmunster.

St. Louis Kriek Lambic (Bel) a 4.5% alc by vol. spontaneous fermenting gueuze kriek (cherry) beer brewed by Van Honsebrouck Brouwerij, Ingelmunster.

St. Lucia Distilleries Ltd. (W.Ind) a major rum distiller based on St. Lucia. Produces Bounty.

St. Macaire (USA) a red grape variety grown in California to make red table wines.

St. Magdalena-Gries (It) a rosé wine (Lagrein) produced by the Kellerei Bozen, Südtirol.

St. Magdalene (Scot) a single malt whisky distillery sited at Linlithgow. Owned by John Hopkins and C°. (whiskies bottled by Gordon MᶜPhail) a highland malt. Produces a vintage malt 1964, a 1980 Centenary and a 15 year old malt 45% alc by vol.

St. Magdalener (Ger) see Santa Maddalena.

St. Marco (Fr) see Saint Marco.

St. Margareten Heilwasser (Ger) a sparkling natural

spring mineral water (established 1850) from Steinsiek, Löhne. Mineral contents (milligrammes per litre): Sodium 19mg/l, Calcium 566mg/l, Magnesium 47mg/l, Potassium 1.8mg/l, Bicarbonates 250mg/l, Chlorides 63mg/l, Sulphates 1310mg/l, Fluorides 0.28mg/l, Strontium 6.87mg/l, Silicates 34.3mg/l.

St. Margarethan (Aus) a wine-producing area based in the lake district of Burgenland.

St. Mark Brandy (USA) the brand-name of a brandy bottled by the Guild of Wineries and Distillers at Lodi, California 40% alc by vol.

St. Martin (Fr) a fourth century monk who brought wine-making to the central Loire. Is reputed to have invented the art of pruning by cutting the vines low which produced better wines. Is also the patron saint of the Mosel vine growers. Also spelt Saint Martin. see St. Martin's Sickness.

St. Martin (Ger) a sparkling natural spring mineral water (established 1963). Mineral contents (milligrammes per litre): Sodium 123mg/l, Calcium 217mg/l, Magnesium 26.6mg/l, Potassium 8.6mg/l, Bicarbonates 545mg/l, Chlorides 104mg/l, Sulphates 342mg/l, Fluorides 0.2mg/l.

St. Martin (Ger) village (Anb): Pfalz. (Ber): Südliche Weinstrasse. (Gro): Schloss Ludwigshöhe. (Vins): Baron, Kirchberg, Zitadelle.

St. Martin (Ger) vineyard (Anb): Mosel-Saar-Ruwer. (Ber): Bernkastel. (Gro): Sankt Michael. (Vil): Ensch.

St. Martin (Ger) vineyard (Anb): Nahe. (Ber): Kreuznach. (Gro): Kronenberg. (Vil): Bad Kreuznach.

St. Martin (Ger) vineyard (Anb): Nahe. (Ber): Kreuznach. (Gro): Schlosskapelle. (Vil): Guldental.

St-Martin-Caussaude (Fr) a commune in the A.C. Côtes de Blaye in north-eastern Bordeaux.

St. Martin d'Abbat (Fr) a natural spring mineral water. (Add): Antartic S.A. B.P.83, 45110 St. Martin d'Abbat. Mineral contents (milligrammes per litre): Sodium 5.4mg/l, Calcium 49.7mg/l, Magnesium 5.6mg/l, Potassium 6.2mg/l, Bicarbonates 159.8mg/l, Chlorides 7mg/l, Sulphates 19mg/l, Nitrates <1mg/l. pH 7.6

St. Martiner Hofberg (Ger) vineyard (Anb): Mosel-Saar-Ruwer. (Ber): Saar-Ruwer. (Gro): Römerlay. (Vil): Trier.

St. Martinsberg (Ger) vineyard (Anb): Mittelrhein. (Ber): Rheinburgengau. (Gro): Schloss Schonburg. (Vil): Oberwessel.

St. Martinskreuz (Ger) vineyard (Anb): Pfalz. (Ber): Mittelhaardt-Deutsche Weinstrasse. (Gro): Höllenpfad. (Vil): Mertesheim.

St. Martin's Sickness (Fr) a term for intoxication in the Tours area (Touraine) of the Loire from a fourth century monk St. Martin who introduced wine making to the area.

St. Martinswein (Ger) a wine produced from grapes harvested on the 11th November annually (a pre 1971 name).

St. Matheiser (Ger) vineyard (Anb): Mosel-Saar-Ruwer. (Ber): Saar-Ruwer. (Gro): Römerlay. (Vil): Trier.

St. Matthias Quelle (Ger) a sparkling natural spring mineral water from Pilsting. (blue label: sparkling/green label: light gas). Mineral contents (milligrammes per litre): Sodium 6.9mg/l, Calcium 74mg/l, Magnesium 36mg/l, Potassium 1.1mg/l, Bicarbonates 410mg/l, Chlorides 2.5mg/l, Sulphates 10.2mg/l, Fluorides 0.18mg/l, Nitrates <0.3mg/l, Silicates 23.1mg/l.

St. Maurice-sur-Eygues (Fr) a village in the A.C. Côtes du Rhône-Villages. Produces mainly red wines (with a little rosé and white wine).

St. Maximiner Kreuzberg (Ger) vineyard (Anb): Mosel-Saar-Ruwer. (Ber): Saar-Ruwer. (Gro): Römerlay. (Vil): Trier.

St-Médard d'Eyrans (Fr) a commune in the A.C. Graves district in south-western Bordeaux.

St.-Merd-la-Breuille (Fr) a V.D.Q.S. wines from Creuse, south of the Loire from Pinot noir, Cabernet or Chardonnay grapes.

St. Michaelis (Ger) a sparkling natural spring mineral water from Trappenkamp bei Bad Segeberg. Mineral contents (milligrammes per litre): Sodium 29mg/l, Calcium 42.8mg/l, Magnesium 3.7mg/l, Potassium 3.5mg/l, Bicarbonates 180mg/l, Chlorides 10.7mg/l, Sulphates 12.1mg/l, Fluorides 0.21mg/l.

St. Michaelsberg (Ger) vineyard (Anb): Baden. (Ber): Kaiserstuhl-Tuniberg. (Gro): Vulkanfelsen. (Vil): Riegel.

St. Michael's Fino (Sp) the brand-name of a Fino Sherry produced by Fernando A. de Terry in Puerto de Santa Maria.

St-Michel (Fr) a commune in the A.C. Canon-Fronsac, eastern Bordeaux.

St. Morandus (Fr) the Alsatian patron saint of wine growers, a Bénédictine monk who lived in the twelfth century.

St. Morillon (Fr) a commune in the A.C. Graves district in south-western Bordeaux. Produces red and white wines.

St. Moritz (Cktl) ⅓ measure Marc du Valais, ⅓ measure Cointreau, ⅓ measure lemon juice, 5 dashes pastis. Shake over ice and strain into a cocktail glass.

St. Mungo's Spring (U.K) a natural spring mineral water brand.

St. Nazarius (Ger) see Codex Laureshamensis.

St. Nectaire (Fr) see Saint Nectaire.

St. Neots Bitter (Eng) a cask-conditioned (and keg) bitter 1041 O.G. brewed by the Paines Brewery in St. Neots, Cambridgeshire.

St. Nesbit (N.Z) a 5ha winery. (Add): Hingaia Road, Papakura, (P.O. Box 2647), Auckland. Produces red and rosé wines from Cabernet and Merlot grapes.

St-Nicaise Abbey (Fr) the cellars of Taittinger Champagne.

St. Nicholas's Christmas Ale (Eng) a 5% alc by vol. cask-conditioned ale produced by Vaux, Sunderland for the festive season.

S

St. Nicholas's Winter Tipple (Eng) a 6% alc by vol. dark hoppy ale tinged with spices and fruit from Vaux, Sunderland for the festive season.

St. Nicholas Vineyard (Eng) a vineyard (established 1979) based at Moat Lane, Canterbury, Kent. 1ha. Grape varieties: Müller-Thurgau and Schönburger.

St. Nicks (I.O.M) a 4.5% alc by vol. ale brewed by Okell & Sons Ltd., Isle of Man.

St. Nicolas-de-Bourgueil (Fr) an A.C. red wine in the Touraine district of the Loire, wines made from the Cabernet franc.

St. Nicolas Tawny Port (Austr) a wood-matured tawny Port-style wine produced by Sandalford in Western Australia.

St. Nikolaus (Ger) vineyard (Anb): Rheingau. (Ber): Johannisberg. (Gro): Erntebringer. (Vil): Mittelheim.

St. Nikolaus (Ger) vineyard (Anb): Rheingau. (Ber): Johannisberg. (Gro): Honigberg. (Vil): Mittelheim.

St. Nikolaus (Ger) a vineyard within the village of Mittelheim, 44.8ha (15%) of which is proposed to be classifed as Erstes Gewächs.

St. Nikolaus Wein (Ger) the pre 1971 name given to wine made from grapes harvested on 6th December (the Saint's day).

St. Nikolaus Wine (Ger) see St. Nikolaus Wein.

Stoat Beer (Eng) a cask-conditioned bitter 1036 O.G. brewed by the Ferret and Firkin home-brew public house in London.

Stock (It) a noted brandy, liqueur and vermouth producers based in Trieste, Piemonte, north-western Italy. see Bora Sambuca, Gala Caffé and Grappa Julia.

Stock Ale (Eng) a beer brewed over a long period, usually dark, well-hopped with a characteristic bitterness.

Stock Ale (Eng) a cask-conditioned ale 1085 O.G. brewed by the Godson Brewery in London. Also a bottled variety.

Stock Ale (Eng) an ale 1050 O.G. brewed and bottled by the Ridley Brewery in Chelmsford, Essex.

Stock Ale (Eng) a draught ale 1036 O.G. brewed by the Shepherd Neame Brewery in Faversham, Kent.

Stock Brandy (It) see Distilline Stock.

Stock Ferment (Eng) the name given to a yeast that has been activated in a starter solution.

Stockheim (Ger) village (Anb): Württemberg. (Ber): Württembergisch Unterland. (Gro): Heuchelberg. (Vin): Altenberg.

Stocking Filler (Eng) a 4.8% alc by vol. ale brewed by the York Brewery Company Ltd., North Yorkshire.

Stocks Brewery (Eng) a brewery based at the Hall Cross public house in Doncaster, Yorkshire. Noted for cask-conditioned Select 1044 O.G. and Old Horizontal 1054 O.G.

Stocks Vineyard (Eng) a vineyard (established 1972). (Add): Suckley, Worcestershire. 4ha. Grape varieties: Reichensteiner 80% and Riesling sylvaner 20%.

Stockton Distillers (USA) a winery based near Lodi, Central Valley, California.

Stod Brewery (Czec) a brewery based in western Czec.

St. Odile (Fr) the name given to Perle (cuve close) and Crémant F. Kobus (méthode traditionelle) sparkling wines fron Union Vinicole Divinal at Obernai, Alsace.

Stoep (S.Afr) the label for a range of wines produced by the Main Street Winery, Paarl, Western Cape.

Stoke Red (Eng) a variety of cider apple.

Stoke Red (Eng) a bottle fermented cider made from Stoke Red apples by a Somerset Farm. See also Kingston Black.

Stokers Stout (Eng) a 5% alc by vol. stout brewed by the Oakleaf Brewing C°. Ltd., Hampshire.

Stokoe's Trophy (Eng) a 3.8% alc by vol. bitter ale brewed by the Darwin Brewery, Tyne & Wear.

Stolichnaya (Rus) a vodka made from 100% grain spirits. 40% alc by vol. Produced in Leningrad. Also a Blue Label at 50% alc by vol., Crystal at 40% alc by vol. which is double distilled and quadruple filtered. Range now includes flavoured vodkas: Vanilla (infused with Madagascan and Indian vanilla), Razberi (fresh raspberries), Ohranj (essence and rind of fresh oranges).

Stollberg (Ger) vineyard (Anb): Franken. (Ber): Steigerwald. (Gro): Not yet assigned. (Vil): Handthal.

Stollenberg (Ger) vineyard (Anb): Nahe. (Ber): Schloss Böckelheim. (Gro): Burgweg. (Vil): Niederhausen an der Nahe.

Stolno Vino (Slo) table wine.

Stolovaya (Rus) a brand of vodka 48% alc by vol.

Stolovoe Vino (Rus) table wine.

Stolzenberg (Ger) vineyard (Anb): Mosel-Saar-Ruwer. (Ber): Zell/Mosel. (Gro): Weinhex. (Vil): Hatzenport.

Stolz Winery (USA) a large winery and vineyard based in St. James, Missouri. 52ha. Produces a large variety of wines.

Stomsdorfer (Ger) a herb-flavoured, digestive liqueur.

Stonebridge Mild (Eng) a 4% alc by vol. mild ale brewed by the Broadstone Brewing C°. Ltd., Nottinghamshire.

Stone Cellars (USA) the label for a red wine (Merlot) produced by the Beringer Vineyards winery, California.

Stonechurch Vineyards (Can) vineyards based at Niagara Peninsula, Ontario. Grape varieties include: Chardonnay, Vidal.

Stoneclear Springs (USA) a natural spring mineral water from Vanleer, Tennessee.

Stone Cocktail (Cktl) ¼ measure white rum, ¼ measure sweet vermouth, ½ measure sweet Sherry. Stir over ice and strain into a cocktail glass.

Stonecroft (N.Z) a 3ha winery. (Add): Mere Road, (RD 5), Hastings. Grape varieties: Cabernet sauvignon, Chardonnay, Gewürztraminer, Sauvignon blanc, Syrah.

Stonecrop Vineyards (USA) a vineyard based in Stonington, Connecticut. Produces mainly French hybrid wines.

1241

Stonecross (S.Afr) the label for a range of wines produced by the Deetlefs Estate winery, Rawsonville, Western Cape.

Stoned (Eng) a slang term for highly intoxicated. i.e. '*stoned out of his mind*'. (Fr) = soûl.

Stone Face (Cktl) 1 measure whisky, ice, 2 dashes Angostura. Stir in a highball glass and top up with dry cider. Also known as a Stone Fence Cocktail.

Stone Fence Cocktail (Cktl) *see* Stone Face.

Stonegate Winery (USA) a winery based near Calistoga, Napa Valley, California. Grape varieties: Cabernet sauvignon, Chardonnay, Pinot noir and Sauvignon blanc. Produces varietal wines.

Stonehaven (S.Afr) the label for white wine (Sauvignon blanc) produced by the Cape Point Vineyards winery, Cape Point, Western Cape.

Stonehenge Ales [Bunces Brewery] Ltd (Eng) a brewery (established 1984). (Add): The Old Mill, Mill Road, Netheravon, Salisbury, Wiltshire SP4 9QB. Brews: Bodyline 4.3% alc by vol., Danish Dynamite 5% alc by vol., Great Bustard 4.8% alc by vol., Great Dane 4.6% alc by vol., Heel Stone 4.3% alc by vol., Lunch Time Special 2.5% alc by vol., Old Smokey 5% alc by vol., Pigswill 4% alc by vol., Rudolph 5% alc by vol., Second to None 4.6% alc by vol., Sign Of Spring 4.6% alc by vol., Spire Ale 3.8% alc by vol. Website: http://www.stonehengeales.com 'E'mail: Stonehenge_ales@bigfoot.com

Stonehenge Bitter (Eng) a cask-conditioned bitter at 1041 O.G. brewed by Heritage Ales, Tisbury, Wiltshire. New name for Tisbury Brewery.

Stonehenge Real Ginger Beer (Eng) a cask-conditioned beer from the Wiltshire Brewery based at Tisbury, Wiltshire. Brewed by blending fresh ginger with malt 1070 O.G.

Stonehill Bristle (S.Afr) the label for a red wine (Cabernet sauvignon and Shiraz blend) produced by the Lorna Hughes winery, Stellenbosch, Western Cape.

Stone Hill Wine Company (USA) a small winery based in Hermann, Missouri. 16ha. Produces fruit, berry, generic and sparkling wines.

Stonehouse (Eng) a strong dry cider from Inch's Cider of Winkleigh, Devon.

Stonehurst (S.Afr) the label for a range of wines produced by the Excelsior Estate winery, Robertson, Western Cape.

Stoneleigh Vineyard (N.Z) a range of red, rosé and white wines (Cabernet sauvignon, Chardonnay, Pinot noir, Rhine riesling, Sauvignon blanc) from the Stoneleigh Estate in Marlborough on the north-east tip of the South Island. Label: Rapaura.

Stone Quarry Winery (USA) a winery with vineyards based in Waterford, Ohio. Produces American and French hybrid wines.

Stoneridge Winery (USA) a small winery based near Sutter Creek, Amador County, California. Grape varieties: Ruby cabernet and Zinfandel. Produces varietal wines.

Stones Best Bitter (Eng) a cask-conditioned bitter 1038 O.G. brewed by the Bass Worthington (Stones) Brewery in Sheffield, Yorkshire (originally 1039 O.G.).

Stones Creamflow (Eng) an ale brewed by the Cannon Brewery at Tadcaster, North Yorkshire.

Stone's Mac (Eng) a ginger wine and Scotch whisky drink produced by Whiskymac Ltd. of Moorland Street, London.

Stone's Original Green Ginger Wine (Eng) a wine made from dried grapes fermented then fined and fortified. Powdered pure root ginger is added and it is then matured for 9 months in oak vats. Produced in Leeds by J.E. Mather (a Matthew Clark subsidiary) 13.5% alc by vol.

Stones Original Pale Cream (Eng) a blend of Spanish Fino Sherry and British fortified wine from Matthew Clark at its Barchester Winery, Leeds.

Stone Square (Eng) another name for a square, the stone denoted the material from which it was made.

Stonestreet Winery (USA) a 28.25ha winery in Alexander Valley. Grape varieties: Cabernet sauvignon, Merlot.

Stonewall (N.Z) a winery based in Marlborough, South Island. Grape varieties include: Pinot noir, Sauvignon blanc.

Stonewall Bitter (Eng) a 3.7% alc by vol. bitter from York Brewery Company Limited, Toft Green, North Yorkshire.

Stonewall Jackson (Cktl) 1½ measures applejack brandy mixed with 300mls (½ pint) dry cider.

Stonewall Vineyard (USA) the label for a red wine (Pinot noir) produced by the Estancia winery, Santa Lucia Highlands, Monterey County, California.

Stonewall Wines (S.Afr) a winery (established 1828) based in Stellenbosch, Western Cape. 75ha. Grape varieties: Cabernet franc, Cabernet sauvignon, Chardonnay, Merlot, Pinotage, Sauvignon blanc, Shiraz. Label: Rubér.

Stone Wines (Ger) the old name that was given to the wines of Franconia (Stein wines) because they were placed in '*bocksbeutels*' stone bottles.

Stoney Croft (S.Afr) a winery (established 2000) based in Koelenhof, Stellenbosch, Western Cape. 3ha. Grape variety: Shiraz. Website: http://www.frontierlifestyle.co.za

Stoneyfell (Austr) an Adelaide wine company famous for Metala wines (Cabernet and Shiraz blend).

Stoney Ridge Cellars (Can) a winery. (Add): Winona, Niagara. Grape varieties: Merlot, Chardonnay and a Merlot/Cabernet franc blend called Millenium.

Stoney's (USA) a beer brewed by the Jones Brewery in Smithton, Pennsylvania.

Stonier's Merricks (Austr) a winery (established 1982). (Add): 362 Frankston-Flinders Road, Merricks, Victoria. Grape varieties: Chardonnay, Cabernet franc, Cabernet sauvignon, Pinot noir.

Stonsdorfer (Ger) a dark, bitter, herb liqueur 32% alc by vol.

S

Stonsdorferei [Die] (Ger) a distillery owned by Koerner that produces Enzian.

Stony Brook (S.Afr) a winery (established 1995) based in Franschhoek, Western Cape. 14ha. Grape varieties: Cabernet franc, Cabernet sauvignon, Malbec, Merlot, Petit verdot, Shiraz. Labels: Annie's Wine, Camissa, Ghost Gum, Reserve.

Stony Hill Vineyards (USA) a winery based in the St. Helena, Napa Valley, California. 16ha. Grape varieties: Chardonnay, Gewürztraminer and Riesling. Produces varietal wines.

Stonyridge Vineyard (N.Z.) a vineyard. (Add): 80 Onetangi Road, (P.O. Box 265), Ostend, Waiheke. 4ha. Produces Larose from Cabernet sauvignon, Cabernet franc, Merlot, Malbec, Petit verdot.

Stony Ridge Winery (USA) a winery based in Livermore Valley, Alameda, California. Grape varieties: Chardonnay, Petite syrah and Zinfandel. Produces varietal wines.

Stoop (Eng) an alternative spelling of Stoup (a cup/mug used in the religious ceremonies in the middle ages). *see* Stoup.

Stopper (Eng) a cork, plastic or cork and plastic bottle closure unit that excludes air, bacteria etc. from the contents of the bottle and also prevents the contents escaping.

Storchenbrünnle (Ger) vineyard (Anb): Franken. (Ber): Steigerwald. (Gro): Schlossberg. (Vil): Sickershausen.

Storers Strong (Eng) a barley wine brewed by the Reindeer, a home-brew public house in Dereham Road, Norwich.

Store Sandrib (Nor) a natural spring mineral water from Store Sandrib.

Stork Nest Estates (Bul) a winery with vineyards (428ha) around Bulgaria. Label: Black Stork.

Storm Brewing C° (Eng) a brewery (established 1998). (Add): 2 Waterside, Macclesfield, Cheshire SK11 7HJ. Brews: Ale Force 4.2% alc by vol., Beauforts Ale 3.8% alc by vol., Bitter Experience 4% alc by vol., Bosley Cloud 4.1% alc by vol., Dessert Storm 4% alc by vol., Typhoon 5% alc by vol. 'E'mail: thompsonhugh@talk21.com

Stormhoek (S.Afr) a winery (established 2003) based in the Western Cape (owned by Orbital Wines, London). Grape varieties: Cabernet sauvignon, Chenin blanc, Merlot, Pinot grigio, Sangiovese, Sauvignon blanc, Sémillon, Shiraz. Label: Reserve, The Storm plus varietal wines. Website: http://www.stormhoek.com

Stormonth Tait (Port) vintage Port shippers. Vintages: 1896, 1900, 1904, 1908, 1912, 1920, 1922, 1927.

Stormy Cape (S.Afr) the export label for wines produced by the Thelma Mountain Vineyards winery, Stellenbosch, Western Cape.

Storybook Mountain Winery (USA) a winery and vineyard based near Calistoga, Napa Valley, California. 17ha. Grape variety: Zinfandel.

Story Vineyards (USA) a winery based in the Sierra Foothills, Amador County, California. Grape varieties: Mission and Zinfandel. Produces table and varietal wines.

St. Oswald (Ger) vineyard (Anb): Mittelrhein. (Ber): Bacharach. (Gro): Schloss Stahleck. (Vil): Manubach.

Stotious (Ire) a term used to describe an intoxicated person.

Stoup (Eng) an old name used to describe a flagon, tankard, cup, mug or other drinking vessel. Usually used for religious ceremonies. Is also used to describe a draught of wine. *see* Stoop.

Stout (U.K.) a strong, rich style of porter. 2 styles: a dry, Irish version i.e. Guinness and Murphy's, a sweet English version i.e. Mackeson. The barley is roasted to a dark colour and it has a high proportion of malt and hops.

Stout 1816 (Eng) a 4.1% alc by vol. stout brewed by the Copper Dragon Skipton Brewery Ltd., North Yorkshire.

Stouter (Eng) a 5% alc by vol. ale brewed by the Edale Brewery C°., Derbyshire.

Stout Snout (Eng) a 4.4% alc by vol. stout brewed by the Slaughter House Brewery Ltd., Warwickshire.

Stoves (Eng) used to ward off late frosts in the vineyards in the spring and so protect the young shoots, placed between the vine rows. *see* Smudge Pots.

Stowells of Chelsea (Eng) famous wine merchants based in St. James, London. Noted for their range of bag-in-the-box wines from Australia, Bulgaria, Chile, France, Germany, Italy, New Zealand.

Stowford Export Cider (Eng) a premium dry cask cider 6% alc by vol. produced by Westons of Hereford.

Stowford Press (Eng) the brand-name of a bottled cider 6% alc by vol. produced by Westons of Hereford.

St. Pantaleimon (Gre) a monastery on Athos, a self-governing State. Tend the vines supplied by Tsantalis and harvest them under Tsantalis supervision.

St. Pantaléon-les-Vignes (Fr) a village in the A.C. Côtes du Rhône-Villages. Produces mainly red wines (with a little rosé and white wine).

St. Panteleimon (Cyp) a sweet white wine produced by the Keo Co. in Limassol.

St-Pardon-de-Conques (Fr) a commune of the A.C. Graves district, south-western Bordeaux.

St. Patrick's Day Cocktail (Cktl) ⅓ measure (white) crème de menthe, ⅓ measure Irish whiskey, ⅓ green Chartreuse, dash Angostura. Stir over ice and strain into a cocktail glass.

St-Paul (Fr) a commune in the A.C. Côtes de Blaye in north-eastern Bordeaux.

St. Paul Blond (Bel) a 5.3% alc by vol. top-fermented, bottled abbaye beer brewed by the Sterkens Brauerei, Meer.

St. Paul de Dominique (Fr) a Grand Cru Saint-Émilion vineyard.

St. Paul Double (Bel) a bottle-conditioned abbaye ale 6.9% alc by vol. from Sterkens Brauerei, Meer.

St. Pauli Girl (Ger) a bier produced by the Becks Brauerei in Bremen for the USA market.

St. Paul Special (Bel) a 5.5% alc by vol. amber coloured, top-fermented, bottled, abbaye ale brewed by Sterkens Brauerei, Meer.

St. Paul Triple (Bel) a bottle-conditioned strong abbaye ale 7.6% alc by vol. from Sterkens Brauerei, Meer.

St-Péray (Fr) *see* Saint-Péray.

St. Peter's Brewery Company (Eng) a brewery (established 1995). (Add): St. Peter's Hall, St. Peter South Elmham, Bungay, Suffolk NR35 1NQ. Brews: Golden Ale 4.7% alc by vol., St. Peter's Ale range, includes: Best Bitter 3.7% alc by vol., Cream Stout 6.5% alc by vol., Grapefruit Beer 4.7% alc by vol., Honey Porter 4.5% alc by vol., Lemon & Ginger Beer 4.7% alc by vol., Old Style Porter 5.1% alc by vol., Organic Ale (cask & bottled) 4.5% alc by vol., Organic Best Bitter (cask & bottled) 4.1% alc by vol., Spiced Ale 6.5% alc by vol., Strong Ale 5.1% alc by vol., Suffolk Gold 4.9% alc by vol., also King Cnut Ale, Session Ale, Winter Ale, Summer Ale, Fruit Beer and Wheat Beer. *see* Elderberry Fruit Beer. Website: http://www.stpetersbrewery.co.uk 'E'mail: beers@stpetersbrewery.co.uk

St. Peter's Well (Scot) a 4.2% alc by vol. ale brewed by the Houston Brewing C°., Renfrewshire.

St. Peters Winery (Austr) a winery based in Riverina, New South Wales. Produces varietal wines.

St. Petrusberg (Ger) vineyard (Anb): Mosel-Saar-Ruwer. (Ber): Saar-Ruwer. (Gro): Römerlay. (Vil): Trier.

St. Pierre (Fr) a natural spring mineral water from Vals les Bains, Ardèche. Mineral contents (milligrammes per litre): Sodium 460mg/l, Calcium 63mg/l, Magnesium 37mg/l, Potassium 35mg/l, Bicarbonates 1500mg/l, Chlorides 20mg/l, Sulphates 33mg/l.

St-Pierre-de-Mons (Fr) a commune in the A.C. Graves district of south-western Bordeaux. *See also* Saint-Pierre-de-Mons.

St. Pierre Smirnoff Fils (Fr) a Paris based firm, the original Smirnoff plant, now owned by Heublein of USA (the most popular vodka in the world).

St. Pirans Ale (Eng) a 4.5% alc by vol. ale brewed by the Skinner's Brewery C°. Ltd., Cornwall.

St. Pourçain-sur-Sioule (Fr) a V.D.Q.S. red, rosé and white wine-producing region in the Allier département in central France. Grape varieties: Chardonnay, Gamay, Pinot noir, Sauvignon blanc and Tressalier (Sacy). Also known as St. Pourçain.

Straal Queen Bronnen (Bel) a natural spring mineral water from Maarkedal.

Straccali (It) a Chianti Classico producer based in Tuscany.

Straccia Cambiale (It) an alternative name for the Bombino bianco.

Strade del Vino (It) lit: 'wine roads', sign-posted itineries through the vineyards.

Stradivarius (Fr) a prestige cuvée Champagne of De Cazanove in Épernay from 67% Chardonnay, 33% Pinot noir grapes. *See also* Brut Azur.

Stradivarius (It) a D.O.C. Barbera d'Asti wine aged for 1 year in new oak barriques by Bava (Roberto) in Piedmont.

Straffe Hendrik (Bel) a brewery (established 1989) based in Bruges. Brews: Brugse Straffe Hendrick.

Straight (Eng) a term used to imply that the customer wants a measure of spirits without the addition of other ingredients (usually whisky). (Den) = tør.

Straight Blonde (Cktl) fill a paris goblet with chilled Dubonnet Blonde, add a twist of lemon peel juice and a slice of lemon.

Straight Bourbon (USA) the produce of one distillery.

Straight 8 (Eng) an extra strong naturally sparkling perry from Showerings 8% alc by vol.

Straight Highball (USA) as for Highball (another name for).

Straight Law Cocktail (Cktl) ⅔ measure dry Sherry, ⅓ measure gin. Stir over ice and strain into a cocktail glass.

Straight Rye and Water Back (USA) a straight whiskey with a jug of water.

Straight-Siders (Eng) early name 1715–1730 given to the bladder bottle that had its sides flattened for storage. The forerunner of the bottle as we know it today.

Straight Up (Eng) a term used to denote a request for a drink with no ice.

Straight Whiskey (USA) an unblended whiskey aged for 2 years in new charred oak casks. Distilled at 80% alc by vol. corn whiskey may be aged in uncharred casks.

Straight Whisky (Scot) *see* Straight.

Strain a Drink (USA) to strain after mixing or shaking a drink, usually done through a hawthorne strainer.

Strainer (Eng) composed of a metal ring, covered with gauze and a handle attached. After the ingredients have been shaken or stirred the mixture is poured through it to strain out the pieces of ice, fruit pulp etc. *see* Hawthorne Strainer.

Straining (Eng) a term used for the removal of pulp from a fermenting liquid or must, removes large particles and pulp.

Strait (Eng) a low-alcohol draught beer from Burtonwood. Style is between lager and beer 1.1% alc by vol.

Straits Sling (Cktl) 60mls (½ gill) dry gin, 15mls (⅛ gill) dry cherry brandy, 20mls (¼ gill) Bénédictine, juice of ½ lemon, 2 dashes orange bitters, 2 dashes Angostura. Pour all the ingredients into a large highball with ice, top with soda water and add a slice of lemon.

Strakonice Brewery (Czec) an old established brewery (established circa 1659) based in south-western Czec.

St. Rambert (Fr) a vineyard based in the Grésivaudan Valley, Vienne département. Produces red wines.

Strangeways Brewery (Eng) a brewery based in Manchester. Brews: Fergie's Choice.

St. Raphaël (Fr) an apéritif wine made from wine,

S

quinine, bark and herbs 17% alc by vol. Red and white versions are produced in Sète, southern France.

St. Raphael (S.Afr) a dry red wine blended from Cabernet, Pinotage and Cinsault grapes made by the Douglas Green Group in Paarl, Western Cape.

St. Raphaël-Citron (Cktl) 60mls (½ gill) St. Raphaël, 60mls (½ gill) sirop de citron, soda water. Stir gently together in an ice-filled highball glass.

Strass (Aus) a wine-producing district based in the Kamp Valley, north-western Austria.

Strasswirtschaften (Ger) a house that is allowed to sell its wines at the roadside at certain times of the year.

Strata Series (S.Afr) the label for a range wines produced by the Flagstone Winery, Somerset West, Western Cape.

Stratégie Viticole (Fr) the planning and running of a vineyard (selection of grapes, method of vine-training, cultivation, etc.).

Stratford Glasses (Eng) the brand-name used by the Dema Glass for a range of glasses.

Stratford Winery (N.Z) a vineyard based in the Martinborough region of the North Island.

Strathalbyn Brewery (Scot) a brewery (established 1982) noted for cask-conditioned ales.

Strathallan Spring (Scot) a natural spring mineral water from Blackford, Perthshire.

Strathclyde (Scot) a grain whisky distillery based near the river Clyde.

Strathconon (Scot) a 12 year old vatted malt whisky produced by Buchanan and Company 57% alc by vol.

Strathearn (Scot) a natural spring mineral water from Blackford, Perthshire.

Strathglen Spring (Scot) a natural spring mineral water from Campsie Fells, Lennoxtown. Mineral contents (milligrammes per litre): Sodium 7.5mg/l, Calcium 23.7mg/l, Magnesium 5mg/l, Potassium 0.3mg/l, Bicarbonates 95mg/l, Chlorides 11mg/l, Sulphates 10mg/l, Fluorides 0.1mg/l, Nitrates 1.8mg/l. pH 7.3

Strathisla (Scot) a single malt whisky distillery (established 1786) in Keith, Banffshire (owned by Seagrams) a highland malt. Produces a 12 and 15 year old whisky. 43% alc by vol. and a 1980 vintage.

Strathisla-Glenlivet (Scot) see Strathisla.

Strathmill (Scot) a single malt whisky distillery based east of Keith, a highland malt whisky 43% alc by vol.

Strathmore Scottish Spring Water (Scot) a still and sparkling natural spring mineral water. (Add): Strathmore Mineral Water Company, West High Street, Forfar, Angus. DD8 1BP. Mineral contents (milligrammes per litre): Sodium 46mg/l, Calcium 60mg/l, Magnesium 15mg/l, Potassium 2.2mg/l, Bicarbonates 111–145mg/l, Chlorides 155mg/l, Sulphates 1mg/l, Nitrate 5 mg/l, Fluride 0.1mg/l. Also produces a range of flavoured mineral waters (including orange, mandarine and lemongrass/white grape and lychee/apple, jasmine and camomile).

Strathspey (Scot) a blended malt whisky from International Distillers and Vintners.

Stratmer Vineyards (Austr) a winery. (Add): Pimpala Road, Reynella, South Australia. Home to Mount Hurtle (a Geoff Merrill wine).

Stratos (Cktl) ¼ measure Cinzano dry vermouth, ¼ measure Drambuie, ⅜ measure dry gin, ⅛ measure crème de banane. Stir over ice, strain into a cocktail glass, add a cherry and a twist of lemon peel juice.

Stratospheric Tags (USA) a slang term for very high prices for rare wines.

Straub Brewery (USA) a brewery based in St Mary's, Pennsylvania. Noted for Straub beer.

Straussberg (Ger) vineyard (Anb): Nahe. (Ber): Kreuznach. (Gro): Kronenberg. (Vil): Hargesheim.

Stravecchia (It) a grappa that has had extra maturation.

Stravecchio (It) a term to denote very old, ripe or mellow wines. Usually applied to Marsala wines.

Stravecchio Branca (It) a brandy produced by Fratelli Branca of Milan.

Strawberry Blonde Cocktail (Cktl) 25mls (1fl.oz) Irish Mist, 3 fresh strawberries. Blend together with a scoop of crushed ice in a blender, pour into a flute glass, top with Champagne and dress with a strawberry.

Strawberry Brandy (Euro) a fruit brandy made from strawberries 44.5% alc by vol.

Strawberry Daiquiri (Cktl) 10mls (½ fl.oz) fraise liqueur, 35mls (1½ fl.oz) white rum, juice ½ lemon, 3 strawberries. Blend on high speed with 2 scoops crushed ice. Pour into a tall glass unblended, serve with short thick straws and a fresh strawberry.

Strawberry Dawn (Cktl) 2–3 fresh strawberries, 25mls (1fl.oz) gin, 25mls (1fl.oz) coconut cream, 2–3 scoops crushed ice. Blend well together, serve in a saucer type glass, decorate with a strawberry and short straws.

Strawberry Fields Bitter (Eng) a strawberry flavoured bitter from Bateman's in Lincolnshire. See also Yellow Belly.

Strawberry Liqueur (Fr) a liqueur made from strawberries steeped in spirit 30% alc by vol.

Strawberry Martini (Cktl) Chambraise and a fresh strawberry with a twist of lemon peel juice.

Strawberry Vermouth (Fr) a Chambéry vermouth flavoured with alpine strawberries, the brand-name in U.K. is Chambéryzette.

Straw Wines (Fr) sweet dessert wines (not botrytised) produced from grapes that have been dried on straw. (Aus) = strohwein/schilfwein, (Fr) = vin de paille, (Ger) = strohwein.

Straw Wine (S.Afr) the label for a sweet white wine (Chardonnay, Chenin blanc and Riesling blend) produced by the Signal Hill winery, Cape Town, Western Cape.

Strega (It) a spring herb liqueur, yellow in colour 40% alc by vol.

Strega Crossword (Cktl) 2 measures Strega, 2

measures white rum, 2 measures gin, 4 measures grapefruit juice. Shake over ice, strain into a highball glass with ice, decorate with mint and an orange slice.

Strega Flip (Cktl) ½ measure Strega, ½ measure Cognac, juice ¼ orange, 2 dashes lemon juice, 1 egg. Shake well over ice, strain into a cocktail glass and top with grated nutmeg.

Strega Shake (Cktl) 2 measures Strega, 3 measures orange juice, 1 measure vodka, 1 scoop vanilla ice cream. Stir all well together and serve in goblets with straws.

Strehn (Aus) a winery (43ha) based in Deutschkreutz, Mittel-Burgenland. (Add): Mittelgasse 9, 7301 Deutschkreuz. Grape varieties include: Blaufränkisch, Cabernet sauvignon, Merlot, Pinot noir, Zweigelt.

Strell [Josef] (Aus) a winery based in Radbrunn, Weinviertel. (Add): 3710 Radbrunn 138. Grape varieties: Cabernet sauvignon, Grüner veltliner, Riesling, Pinot blanc, Pinot noir, Sauvignon blanc, Zweigelt.

St. Remigiusberg (Ger) vineyard (Anb): Nahe. (Ber): Kreuznach. (Gro): Schlosskapelle. (Vil): Laubenheim.

Strength (Eng) strength (alcoholic content) is limited by regulations governing the wines and spirits by where they were made and by British Customs and Excise. *See also* Gay Lussac, Sykes, OIML and US Proof.

St-Reol (Fr) a Champagne producer. (Add): 2 Boulevard des Bermonts, 51150 Ambonnay. Co-opérative-manipulant. Produces vintage and non-vintage wines. Labels include: Préstige d'Argent.

Stretched (Eng) the term sometimes used to describe a good wine that has been increased by the addition of stronger, cheaper wines.

Stretched Wine (Eng) *see* Stretched.

Stretton Hills (Eng) a still and sparkling natural spring mineral water from Church Stretton, Shropshire. Mineral contents (milligrammes per litre): Sodium 15.2mg/l, Calcium 44mg/l, Magnesium 8.5mg/l, Potassium 1.2mg/l, Bicarbonates 146mg/l, Chlorides 17mg/l, Sulphates 31mg/l, Fluorides 0.1mg/l, Nitrates 13mg/l. pH 7.7

Striep (Bel) a Flemish drink composed of a glass of lager of which half is froth.

Strike (Cktl) ⅙ measure Cinzano dry vermouth, ⅙ measure Dubonnet, ⅙ measure Sève Fournier, ⅓ measure Canadian rye whisky. Stir over ice, strain into a cocktail glass, add a twist of orange peel and a cherry.

Strike Cola (Scot) the brand-name of a soft-drink produced by A.G. Barr. *See also* Irn-bru, Jusoda Orange, Tizer.

Strine Wine (Austr) a nickname for Australian wine.

Stringbag (Cktl) ⁷⁄₁₀ measure dry gin, ¹⁄₁₀ measure La Ina Sherry, dash Angostura, dash Roses lime juice, stir well together over ice and strain into an old-fashioned glass with ice.

String Neck Bottle (Eng) a seventeenth century bottle with a thick band of glass around the neck to stop the string loop which held the wooden cork or plug in place from slipping off.

String of Pearls (Ger) the brand-name for a range of sparkling ciders.

Strip and At It (Eng) a 4% alc by vol. ale brewed by the Freeminer Brewery Ltd., Gloucestershire.

Strip Back (Aus) the passing of grape must that has started to ferment before reaching the fermenting vats through charcoal to remove any oxidation.

Strobel (Aus) a vineyard site based on the banks of the River Kamp situated in the Kamptal region.

St. Roch (Ger) the patron saint of vine growers in the Rhine and Nahe regions, a Franciscan friar who lived in the fourteenth century.

Strofilia (Gre) a vineyard. (Add): Strofilia SA, 19013 Anavissos. Vineyards based around villages of Psari and Aspokambos. Grape varieties: Aghiorghitiko, Cabernet sauvignon.

Stroganoff (Ger) a brand of vodka produced by Schlichte Distillery of Steinhägen.

Stroh (Aus) a brand of rum produced by the Stroh Distillery based in Klagenfurt.

Stroh Beer (USA) *see* Stroh Brewery.

Stroh Brewery (USA) a very large brewery (established 1850) based in Detroit Michigan. Produces over 60 beers including Schlitz, Stroh's and Stroh's Light.

Stroh's (USA) a 5% alc by vol. light malty lager brewed by the Stroh Brewery, Detroit Michigan. Also a Stroh's Light version.

Strohwein (Aus) lit: 'straw wine', bunches of grapes are laid out on beds of straw during the winter and air-dried for a minimum of three months to take on extra sweetness (minimum 25° KMW). Wine must be bottled in Austria and not sold before 1st May of the following year. *see* Prädikatsweine. *See also* Schilfwein.

Strohwein (Ger) straw wine.

Stromberg (Ger) grosslage (Anb): Württemberg. (Ber): Württembergisch Unterland. (Vils): Bönnigheim, Diefenbach, Ensingen, Erligheim, Freudenstein, Freudental, Gründelbach, Häfnerhaslach, Hofen, Hohenhaslach, Hohenstein, Horrheim, Illingen, Kirchheim, Kleinsachsenheim, Knittlingen, Lienzingen, Maulbronn, Mühlhausen, Obererdingen, Ochsenbach, Ötisheim, Riet, Rosswag, Schützingen, Spielberg, Sternenfels, Vaihingen.

Stromberg (Ger) vineyard (Anb): Nahe. (Ber): Schloss Böckelheim. (Gro): Rosengarten. (Vil): Bockenau.

St. Ronan's Spring (U.K) a natural spring mineral water brand.

Strong Ale (Eng) an ale with an average O.G. of 1055 (6% alc by vol). can be dark or light in colour and sweet or dry. A common characteristic is the strength, which is higher than normal beers.

Strong Amber (Eng) *see* Alford Arms.

Strong And Dark (Eng) a 5.2% alc by vol. dark ale brewed by Twickenham Fine Ales, Middlesex.

Strong Arm (Eng) a ruby red bitter 1040 O.G.

brewed by the Camerons Brewery in Hartlepool. Also bottled 1046 O.G.

Strongbiers (Ger) a strong beer 18% plus O.G. Originally made to celebrate Christmas or Lent. Names usually end in -ator or in a Saints name.

Strongbow (Eng) the famous flagship cider of Bulmers, Hereford. Dry, strong and sparkling, sold as draught or in bottle. *See also* Sirrus.

Strongbow Ice (Eng) a 6% alc by vol. white bottled ice cider from Bulmers of Hereford. Originally 6.5% alc by vol.

Strongbow LA (Eng) a 0.9% alc by vol. cider from Bulmers of Hereford.

Strongbow Smooth (Eng) a 5% alc by vol. smoothflow cider from Bulmers of Hereford.

Strongbow Ten Eighty [1080] (Eng) a bottled cider, double-fermented 1080 O.G. produced by Bulmers of Hereford.

Strong Brew (Den) a strong lager beer 7.7% alc by vol. from Ceres Brewery at Aarhus.

Strong Brown (Eng) a brown ale 1045 O.G. brewed and bottled by the Samuel Smith Brewery in Tadcaster, Yorkshire.

Strong Country Bitter (Eng) a cask-conditioned bitter 1037 O.G. brewed by the Whitbread Brewery for the Essex region.

Strong Drink (Eng) the alternative name for alcoholic drink, applies especially to spirits.

Strongest Ale (Eng) *see* Wadsworth Strongest Ale.

Strongest Beer (World) many beers place claim to being the world's strongest ranging from 13% alc by vol (26° US proof) to 15% alc by vol (30° US proof).

Strong Export (Eng) a strong ale 6.4% alc by vol. from Young's Brewery, Wandsworth, London. *see* Old Nick.

Strong Golden (Eng) a barley wine 1100 O.G. brewed and bottled by the Samuel Smith Brewery in Tadcaster, Yorkshire.

Stronghart (Eng) a strong bottled ale 7% alc by vol. brewed for the winter season by McMullen and Son in Hertfordshire.

Stronghold (Eng) a 4.7% alc by vol. ale brewed by the Arundel Brewery Ltd., West Sussex.

Strong Pale Ale (Eng) a pale ale 1045 O.G. brewed and bottled by the Samuel Smith Brewery in Tadcaster, Yorkshire.

Strong Russet Ale (Eng) a 5.5% alc by vol. special reserve, limited edition seasonal beer from McMullen and Son, Hertford. The recipe includes honey from Hertford.

Strongs (Scot) the name given to the low wines at the Auchentoshan distillery in Dalmuir, Glasgow. *See also* Weaks.

Strongs Best Bitter (Eng) a 3.8% alc by vol. best bitter ale brewed by the Hampshire Brewery, Hampshire.

Strong Suffolk Ale (Eng) a bottled dark old ale 1056 O.G./6% alc by vol. brewed and bottled by the Greene King Brewery in East Anglia. Produced from a blend of Old 5X and BPA. Matured in sealed oak vats for 1 year.

Strong Waters (Eng) the mediaeval name for alcoholic beverages.

Stroppy Farmer [The] (Fr) a brand name for a French wine for the American market. The name designed to appeal to the Americans in place of the complicated French label names!

Stroumf (Cktl) ⅓ measure gin, ⅓ measure apricot brandy, ⅓ measure Amaretto di Saronno, dash lemon juice. Shake over ice, strain into an ice-filled highball glass and add a dash of orange juice.

Strubbe Brasserie (Bel) a brewery (established 1830). (Add): Markt 1, B-8480 Ichtegem. Brews: Dikke Mathilde. Website: http://www.brouwerij-strubbe.be

Strudel (Aus) a vineyard site on the banks of the River Danube situated in the Wachau region, Niederösterreich.

Strugure (Rum) grape.

Struis (Hol) a 9% alc by vol. strong, unfiltered, unpasteurised, top-fermented, bottled special brown beer brewed by 't IJ Brouwerij. Amsterdam.

Strümpfelbach (Ger) village (Anb): Württemberg. (Ber): Remstal-Stuttgart. (Gro): Wartbühl. (Vins): Gastenklinge, Nonnenberg.

Strümpfelbach (Ger) village (Anb): Württemberg. (Ber): Remstal-Stuttgart. *see* Weinstadt.

Strumpfwein (Ger) the name for any wine that is so sour (acidic) that it may rot your stockings.

St. Ruppertsberg (Ger) vineyard (Anb): Nahe. (Ber): Kreuznach. (Gro): Pfarrgarten. (Vil): Gutenberg.

St. Sampson (Eng) a vineyard in Golant, Cornwall.

St-Saphorin (Switz) a wine-producing region based near Lavaux in central Vaud. Produces dry white wines.

St. Saturnin (Fr) an A.C. red wine from the Grenache grape. Produced north of Montpellier in the Languedoc.

St-Sauveur (Fr) a commune in the A.C. Haut-Médoc, north-western Bordeaux.

St. Savin (Fr) a vineyard based in the Grésivaudan Valley, Vienne département. Produces red wines.

St. Sebastiaan Dark (Bel) a dark bottle-conditioned ale 6.9% alc by vol. from Sterkens Brauerei.

St. Sebastiaan Grand Cru (Bel) a bottle-conditioned bronze beer 7.6% alc by vol. from Sterkens Brauerei.

St-Selve (Fr) a commune in the A.C. Graves district of south-western Bordeaux.

St-Seurin-Bourg (Fr) a commune in the A.C. Côtes de Bourg, north-eastern Bordeaux.

St-Seurin-Cursac (Fr) a commune in the A.C. Côtes de Bourg, north-eastern Bordeaux.

St-Seurin-de-Cadourne (Fr) a commune in the A.C. Haut-Médoc, north-western Bordeaux.

St. Sixtus (Bel) a Westvleteren abbaye which produces abt beer 12% alc by vol. the strongest beer in Belgium. Also brews beers under the St. Bernadus label: Pater 6% alc by vol. Prior 8% alc by vol.

St. Stephan (Ger) vineyard (Anb): Pfalz. (Ber):

Mittelhaardt-Deutsche Weinstrasse. (Gro): Höllenpfad. (Vil): Grünstadt.

St. Sylvestre Brasserie (Fr) a brewery. (Add): F-59114 St. Sylvestre, Cappel. Brews beers and lager. Website: http://www.brasserie-st-sylvestre.com 'E'mail: contact@brasserie-st-sylvestre.com

St. Thomas Burgundy (Austr) a red wine from the Old Mill Winery in South Australia.

Stuart Highway (Austr) a part of the Bilyara Vineyards, Nurioopta, South Australia.

Stubby (Austr) a slang term for a small beer bottle.

Stück (Ger) a cask of the Rhineland holding 1200litres.

Stückfasser (Ger) see Stück.

Stuck Ferment (Eng) the name given to a fermenting must or wine in which the fermentation has prematurely stopped because it is too cold (or hot).

Stuck Wine (Eng) describes a wine that has stopped fermenting before all the sugar has been converted into alcohol.

Stud [The] (Cktl) 1 part vodka, 1 part Cinzano rosé. Stir together in an ice-filled highball glass.

Stud (Eng) a 4.3% alc by vol. ale brewed by Hambleton Ales, North Yorkshire.

Studena (Cro) a still natural spring mineral water from Lipik. Mineral contents (milligrammes per litre): Sodium 9.51mg/l, Calcium 62.25mg/l, Magnesium 20.67mg/l, Potassium 0.65mg/l, Bicarbonates 299.28mg/l, Chlorides 2.85mg/l, Sulphates 11.94mg/l, Fluorides 0.15mg/l, Silicates 27.04mg/l.

Studenac (Cro) a sparkling natural spring mineral water from Lipik. Mineral contents (milligrammes per litre): Sodium 803.2mg/l, Calcium 39.4mg/l, Magnesium 14.9mg/l, Potassium 87.4mg/l, Bicarbonates 1471.2mg/l, Chlorides 395.3mg/l, Sulphates 252.5mg/l, Fluorides 9.6mg/l.

Studenac Grofovo Vrelo (Cro) a natural spring mineral water. Mineral contents (milligrammes per litre): Sodium 809.6mg/l, Calcium 46.89mg/l, Magnesium 17.73mg/l, Potassium 87.9mg/l, Bicarbonates 1482.81mg/l, Chlorides 394.93mg/l, Sulphates 266.56mg/l, Nitrates 1.3mg/l.

Studen Brewery (Czec) an old established brewery based in central-southern Czec.

Stud Lite (Eng) a low-alcohol lager from Brent-Walker Breweries in Hartlepool (less than 1% alc by vol).

Stuffing (Eng) a wine drinkers term for meaty wines that have body and alcohol. i.e. Châteauneuf-du-Pape.

Stum (Eng) a partially-fermented grape must drink that was popular in the seventeenth century. Also drunk unfermented.

Stumpf (Ger) denotes a lifeless wine.

Stumpy's Brewery (Eng) a brewery (established 2004). (Add): 7 The Scimitars, Hill Head, Fareham, Hampshire PO14 3RW. Brews beers and lager. 'E'mail: lewisw556@aol.com

Stunn (Eng) alcoholic fruit-flavoured drinks from T. Mason in the Midlands (orange, lemon or blackcurrant).

Stunned Mullet Bitter (Eng) a 5% alc by vol. bitter beer brewed by the Garton Brewery, East Yorkshire.

Sturare (It) to uncork, or tap a cask.

St. Urbain (Switz) a white wine produced in Johannisberg in the Valais Canton.

St. Urban (Ger) the patron saint (a French monk) of the grape. 25th May is the Saints' day.

Sturm (Aus) a term that describes a wine (Bouvier grape) that is still fermenting and is drunk in the heurigen.

Sturn (Eng) a seventeenth century name for unfermented or partly fermented grape juice.

St. Ursula (Ger) a noted wine merchant based at Bingen. Grape varieties include Pinot blanc, Riesling.

Stuttgart (Ger) village (Anb): Württemberg. (Ber): Remstal-Stuttgart. (Gro): Weinsteige. (Vins): Kreigsberg, Mönchberg, Mönchhalde.

Stuttgart [ortsteil Bad Cannstatt] (Ger) village (Anb): Württemberg. (Ber): Remstal-Stuttgart. (Gro): Weinsteige. (Vins): Berg, Halde, Herzongenberg, Mönchberg, Mönchhalde, Steinhalde, Zuckerle.

Stuttgart [ortsteil Degerloch] (Ger) village (Anb): Württemberg. (Ber): Remstal-Stuttgart. (Gro): Weinsteige. (Vin): Scharrenberg.

Stuttgart [ortsteil Feuerbach] (Ger) village (Anb): Württemberg. (Ber): Remstal-Stuttgart. (Gro): Weinsteige. (Vin): Berg.

Stuttgart [ortsteil Gaisburg] (Ger) village (Anb): Württemberg. (Ber): Remstal-Stuttgart. (Gro): Weisteige. (Vin): Abelsberg.

Stuttgart [ortsteil Hedelfingen] (Ger) village (Anb): Württemberg. (Ber): Remstal-Stuttgart. (Gro): Weinsteige. (Vin): Lenzenberg.

Stuttgart [ortsteil Hofen] (Ger) village (Anb): Württemberg. (Ber): Remstal-Stuttgart. (Gro): Weinsteige. (Vin): Zuckerle.

Stuttgart [ortsteil Mühlhausen] (Ger) village (Anb): Württemberg. (Ber): Remstal-Stuttgart. (Gro): Weinsteige. (Vins): Steinhalde, Zuckerle.

Stuttgart [ortsteil Münster] (Ger) village (Anb): Württemberg. (Ber): Remstal-Stuttgart. (Gro): Weinsteige. (Vins): Berg, Steinhalde, Zuckerle.

Stuttgart [ortsteil Obertürkheim] (Ger) village (Anb): Württemberg. (Ber): Remstal-Stuttgart. (Gro): Weinsteige. (Vins): Ailenberg, Kirchberg.

Stuttgart [ortsteil Rohracker] (Ger) village (Anb): Württemberg. (Ber): Remstal-Stuttgart. (Gro): Weinsteige. (Vin): Lenzenberg.

Stuttgart [ortsteil Rotenberg] (Ger) village (Anb): Württemberg. (Ber): Remstal-Stuttgart. (Gro): Weinsteige. (Vin): Schlossberg.

Stuttgart [ortsteil Uhlbach] (Ger) village (Anb): Württemberg. (Ber): Remstal-Stuttgart. (Gro): Weinsteige. (Vins): Götzenberg, Schlossberg, Steingrube.

Stuttgart [ortsteil Untertürkheim] (Ger) village

(Anb): Württemberg. (Ber): Remstal-Stuttgart. (Gro): Weinsteige. (Vins): Altenberg, Gips, Herzogenberg, Mönchberg, Schlossberg, Wetzenstein.

Stuttgart [ortsteil Wangen] (Ger) village (Anb): Württemberg. (Ber): Remstal-Stuttgart. (Gro): Weinsteige. (Vin): Berg.

Stuttgart [ortsteil Zuffenhausen] (Ger) village (Anb): Württemberg. (Ber): Remstal-Stuttgart. (Gro): Weinsteige. (Vin): Berg.

St. Véran (Fr) an A.C. dry white wine from the Mâconnais.

St. Victor Lacoste (Fr) a commune of the Laudun district in the south-western Rhône. Produces red, rosé and white wines.

St. Vincent of Saragossa (S.Afr) a dry white wine from the Douglas Green Group in Paarl.

St. Vivien (Fr) a commune in Prignac in the Médoc, western Bordeaux.

St. Wernerberg (Ger) vineyard (Anb): Mittelrhein. (Ber): Rheinburgengau. (Gro): Schloss Schönburg. (Vil): Dellhofen.

St. Willehad (Ger) a natural spring mineral water from Weyhe bei Bremen. Mineral contents (milligrammes per litre): Sodium 230mg/l, Calcium 87mg/l, Magnesium 23mg/l, Bicarbonates 150mg/l, Chlorides 390mg/l.

Sty (Bel) a natural spring mineral water from Ottignies. Mineral contents (milligrammes per litre): Sodium 16mg/l, Calcium 109mg/l, Magnesium 12mg/l, Chlorides 53mg/l, Sulphates 82mg/l.

Style Cider 1080 (Eng) a special cider produced by Bulmers of Hereford.

Stylish (Eng) a term used to describe wines which possess charm, finesse and elegance.

Styll (Eng) the sixteenth century spelling of Still (distillation).

St. Yorre (Fr) a carbonated natural spring mineral water from the Bassin de Vichy, 03270 St. Yorre. Mineral contents (milligrammes per litre): Sodium 1708mg/l, Calcium 90mg/l, Magnesium 11mg/l, Potassium 132mg/l, Bicarbonates 4368mg/l, Chlorides 322mg/l, Sulphates 174mg/l, Fluorides 9mg/l. pH 6.6

Styria (Aus) a wine region, has volcanic soil. *see* Steiermark.

Styrian Gold (Eng) a 4.5% alc by vol. traditional English ale brewed in August and September by Cain Brewery, Stanhope Street, Liverpool using Styrian Golding and Fuggles hops.

Styrian Gold (Eng) a single varietal ale brewed by Wadworth & C°. Ltd., Northgate Brewery in Devizes, Wiltshire between May 31st and June 12th.

St-Yzans (Fr) a commune in the Bas Médoc, north-western Bordeaux. Wines have A.C. Médoc.

Su (Tur) fruit juice, can also denote water.

Suave (Port) sweet.

Subalterns' Soothing Syrup (Ind) the old name used for Madeira wine in India.

Sub-Balkan (Bul) 2 centres of viticulture: Rozova in west, Slaviantza, Sungulare in east. Mainly white wines produced. Grape varieties: Red misket, Rkatziteli.

Suber (Lat) cork.

Subercaseaux (Chile) the name given to brut and demi-sec sparkling wines produced by Concha y Toro (made by the traditional method).

Suberin (Eng) the waxy element in corks that makes it water impermeable and decay resistant.

Subirat-Parent (Sp) a white grape variety used in the making of cava wines. Also known as the Malvasia riojana and Rojal blanco.

Submarino (Mex) a 'shot' glass of tequila which is 'sunk' (immerged) in a glass of beer.

Subotica (Cro) *see* Suboticka (alternative spelling of).

Suboticka Pescara (Cro) a wine-producing area in Vojvodina. Produces red and white wines. Also spelt Subotica.

Subrouska (Pol) a green vodka. *see* Zubrowka.

Subrowka (Pol) *see* Zubrowka.

Subsoil (Eng) denotes the soil found under the top soil (3 metres in depth or more) rich in minerals.

Sub Zero (Eng) a 5.5% alc by vol. Soda from Scottish Courage. Flavoured with natural essences of citrus and spice.

Succinic Acid (Eng) HOCCH$_2$: CH$_2$COOH a wine acid produced through the result of fermentation. The principal acid in the form of esters. Gives the wine its flavour and aroma.

Succo (It) juice/sap.

Succo d'Arancia (It) orange juice.

Succo di Frutta (It) fruit juice.

Succo di Limone (It) lemon juice.

Succo di Mele (It) cider.

Succo di Pomodori (It) tomato juice.

Succo d'Uva (It) grape juice.

Succus (Lat) juice/sap.

Suc de Monbazillac (Fr) a green liqueur produced from wine and herbs. Produced in the Périgord region [also a yellow (sweet) version].

Sucesores de Alfonso Abellán (Sp) a winery based in Almanza. Produces wines mainly from the Monastrell grape.

Suchots [Les] (Fr) a Premier Cru vineyard in the A.C. commune of Vosne-Romanée, Côte de Nuits, Burgundy 13.1ha.

Sucio (Sp) a word used to describe an unclean Sherry.

Suckering (USA) the removal of all shoots that originate either below the ground or on the trunk of the vine if they are not fruit bearing.

Suckers (Eng) the excessive growth on the vine, removed so as to give the grapes increased nutrition.

Suckfizzle Augusta (Austr) a winery based in the Margaret River region of Western Australia. Grape varieties include: Cabernet sauvignon.

Suco (Port) juice.

Suco de Laranja (Port) orange juice.

Sucrage (Fr) a term used for the addition of sugar to the grape must during fermentation. *See also* Chaptalisation and Sugaring.

Sucré (It) usually denotes the addition of sugar to the must.

Sucrose (Eng) cane sugar used for Chaptalisation. Also the name of the sugar found in green coffee beans.

Sucrosite (Fr) a term to describe juicy sweetness of fruit flavours in a wine.

Sucu (Tur) water (drinking) seller.

Südbadischer Landwein (Ger) one of the 17 Deutsche Landwein zones. Must weight must be a minimum of 53°Oe.

Südbahn (Aus) lit: 'southern railway', an alternative name for the Thermenregion.

Süd-Burgenland (Aus) see South Burgenland.

Sudd (Wal) juice. See also Nodd.

Südlay (Ger) vineyard (Anb): Mosel-Saar-Ruwer. (Ber): Bernkastel. (Gro): Sankt Michael. (Vil): Pölich.

Südliche-Weinstrasse (Ger) the southern Wine Route.

Südliche Weinstrasse (Ger) bereich (Anb): Pfalz. (Gros): Bischofskreuz, Guttenberg, Herrlich, Kloster Liebfrauenberg, Königsgarten, Mandelhöhe, Ordensgut, Schloss Ludwigshöhe, Trappenberg.

Südost-Steiermark (Aus) lit: 'south-east Styria' (also spelt: Süd-Oststeiermark), a large 1200ha, sub-region of Styria (Steiermark). Soil: basalt, fossil chalk, loam, sand and volcanic. Main grape varieties: white (Chardonnay, Pinot blanc, Pinot gris, Riesling, Traminer, Welschriesling) red (Blauburger, Blauer wildbacher, St. Laurent, Zweigelt). Villages: Feldbach, Kapfenstein, Klöch, Leutschach, Straden, Tieschen.

Suds (USA) a slang term for the frothy head on a glass of beer.

Südsteiermark (Aus) the Austrian for South Styria, a wine district within the region of Steiermark. Produces mainly white wines.

Südtirol (It) South Tyrol, the German name for the Trentino-Alto-Adige region. Produces fine wines. Labels can be written in German or Italian or mixture of both. Often written Süd Tirol.

Süd Tirol (It) see Südtirol.

Südtiroler (It) an appellation on the label of South Tyrolean wines, appears in front of the grape variety.

Suelo (Sp) lit; 'the butt nearest the ground', term used in the Sherry region. see Solera.

Süesse (Ger) grape sugar. See also Süsse.

Süffig (Ger) denotes a light, young, supple wine.

Suffolk County Best Bitter (Eng) a 4% alc by vol. best bitter ale brewed by Nethergate Holdings Ltd., Suffolk.

Suffolk Gold (Eng) a 4.9% alc by vol. cask and bottled ale brewed by St. Peter's Brewery, St. Peter's Hall, South Elmham St. Peter, near Bungay, Suffolk.

Suffolk Pride (Eng) a 4.8% alc by vol. bitter ale brewed by Mauldon's Ltd., Suffolk.

Suffolk Shamrock (Eng) a beer brewed for St. Patrick's Day by Tollemache & Cobbold Brewery Ltd., Cliff Brewery, Ipswich, Suffolk

Sugar (Eng) $C_6H_{12}O_6$ the food that yeast needs to reproduce by binary fission. Is converted into alcohol and CO_2 i.e. grape sugar, maltose and sucrose. See also Chaptalisation.

Sugar Bush Ridge (S.Afr) the label for a red (Cabernet sauvignon & Merlot blend) and white (Sauvignon blanc) wines produced by the Dominion Wine Company winery, Stellenbosch, Western Cape.

Sugar Cane Juice (W.Ind) extracted by pressing sugar cane through successive roller mills. Contains 10%–12% sugar, rum is distilled from this fermented juice that results in a lightly flavoured rum.

Sugar Cane Syrup (W.Ind) produced by evaporating water from sugar cane juice in a vacuum distillation process, a brown viscous liquid. see Molasses.

Sugar Frosting (Eng) in cocktails the method of sugaring the rim of the glass by dipping the rim in egg white or fruit juice and then in sugar. see Frosted Glass.

Sugaring (Eng) the alternative name for Chaptalisation.

Sugarloaf Spring Rain (Can) a natural spring mineral water. Mineral contents (milligrammes per litre): Sodium 8.1mg/l, Calcium 23mg/l, Magnesium 1.6mg/l, Potassium 0.4mg/l, Chlorides 8.4mg/l, Sulphates 7.7mg/l, Fluorides 0.06mg/l, Nitrates 0.39mg/l. pH 7.78

Sugar Loaf Vineyard (Wal) a 2.3ha vineyard at Dummar Farm, Pentre Lane, Llwyndu, Abergavenny. Grape varieties: Madeleine angevine, Reichensteiner, Rondo, Seyval blanc, Siegerrebe, Triomphe d'alsace.

Sugar Mill (W.Ind) the brand-name of rum produced by the Rum Company (Jamaica) Ltd. on the island of Jamaica 43% alc by vol.

Sugar of Milk (Eng) lactose.

Sugar Ray (W.Ind) a light Jamaican rum punch from Wray and Nephew company using Jamaican rum.

Sugar Wine (Eng) produced by fermenting together water, sugar and grape husks.

Sughero (It) cork/corktree.

Suhindol (Bul) a D.G.O. wine-producing area in the northern region which is also the site of the first co-operative cellar for Cabernet, Gamza and Pamid grapes.

Suho (Bul) (Cro) dry.

Suider Terras (S.Afr) the label for a white wine (Sauvignon blanc & Sémillon) produced by the Bloemendal Estate winery, Durbanville, Western Cape.

Suikerbosch (S.Afr) a range of red (Rooi: 60% Shiraz plus Cabernet and Merlot) and white (Wit: Chenin blanc) wines under the Kaapse label produced by Zidela Wines, Stellenbosch.

Suio (It) a natural spring mineral water from Suio, Castelforte, Latina.

Suippes (Fr) a canton in the Châlons district in Champagne. Has the villages of Billy-le-Grand, Marne and Vaudemanges.

Suissesse (Cktl) ½ measure pastis, ½ measure lemon juice, 1 egg white. Shake well over ice, strain into a small tumbler and add a splash of soda water.

Suissesse Cocktail (Cktl) 25mls (1fl.oz) Pernod, 1 egg, dash anisette, dash (white) crème de menthe, dash orange flower water. Shake over ice and strain into a cocktail glass.

Suk (E.Asia) equivalent of saké, a type of rice beer made in Korea.

Sukhoe Vino (Rus) dry wine.

Sukkar (Arab) see Muscavado.

Sukur Ziada (Tur) sweet coffee, also known as Belon.

Sulak (Tur) a term to describe a watery, thin drink.

Sulbric (It) a D.O.C. Barbera d'Asti wine produced by Martinetti (Franco) in Piemonte. Contains some Cabernet to lower the acidity.

Sulfurous Acid (USA) see Sulphurous Acid.

Sulinko (Slo) a sparkling natural spring mineral water (established 1836) from Borehole MS-1 Johanus, Spring Sulinka, Lubovnianska Vrchovina, Presov. Mineral contents (milligrammes per litre): Sodium 1100.3mg/l, Calcium 271.6mg/l, Magnesium 344.3mg/l, Bicarbonates 555mg/l, Chlorides 75.3mg/l, Sulphates 1.1mg/l, Lithium 3.55mg/l.

Suljip (Kor) bar.

Sullivan County (USA) a wine region in the New York district, the Highland is the best.

Sullivan Vineyards (USA) a winery and vineyard based near Rutherford, Napa Valley, California. Grape varieties: Cabernet sauvignon, Chardonnay and Chenin blanc. Produces varietal wines.

Sulm [River] (Ger) a tributary of the river Neckar in Württemberg.

Sulmoniense (It) a red wine produced in central-eastern Italy during Roman times.

Sulphur (Eng) the principal use of sulphur in wine production is as a general preservative and safeguard against oxidation. This is especially true for white wines but also to a lesser extent for red wines. Sulphur is often added to the grape must to prevent aerobic yeasts from working before the anaerobic wine yeasts (the E.C. laid down strict set limits).

Sulphur Candles (Fr) used in Burgundy and other regions of Europe. They are burnt in the casks that new wine is to be racked into. Produces SO_2.

Sulphur-dioxide (Eng) abbr: SO_2. see Sulphur. (Fr) = anhydride sulfureux, (Ger) = schwefeldioxid.

Sulphurisation (Eng) excessive use of sulphur as a preservative, normally harmless but the smell is unpleasant, will disperse eventually if left to the air.

Sulphurous Acid (Eng) the result of SO_2 gas after being added to wine, reacts with water to form sulphurous acid. See also Sulphur.

Sulphurous Anhydride (Eng) a chemical added to the must of white wines and to red wine grapes. Destroys any biological disorders present but does not harm the wine yeasts.

Sulphurous Water (Eng) a mineral water impregnated with hydrogen. e.g. Challes, Harrogate and St. Boes.

Sultamine (Gre) a white grape variety grown mainly on the Isle of Crete and made mainly into raisins and dessert wines.

Sultana (Austr) a white grape variety grown in the Riverland, South Australia to make Australian brandy and sweet dessert wines. Also grown in Crete. see Sultanina.

Sultanina (USA) a white table grape variety which is grown in the Central Valley. Also known as the Kismis, Sultana, Sultanine, Thompson Seedless.

Sulwath Brewers Ltd (Scot) a brewery (established 1996). (Add): The Brewery, 209 King Street, Castle Douglas, Kirkcudbrightshire DG7 1DT. Brews: Criffel Ale 4.6% alc by vol., Cuil Hill 3.6% alc by vol., Galloway Gold 5% alc by vol., John Paul Jones 4% alc by vol., Knockendoch 5% alc by vol., Solway Mist 5.5% alc by vol., The Black Galloway 4.4% alc by vol. Website: http://www.sulwathbrewers.co.uk 'E'mail: info@sulwathbrewers.co.uk

Sulz (Ger) village (Anb): Baden. (Ber): Breisgau. (Gro): Schutterlindenberg. (Vin): Haselstaude.

Sulzbach (Ger) village (Anb): Baden. (Ber): Badische Bergstrasse/Kraichgau. (Gro): Rittersberg. (Vin): Herrnwingert.

Sülzbach (Ger) village (Anb): Württemberg. (Ber): Württembergisch Unterland. (Gro): Salzberg. (Vin): Altenberg.

Sulzbach (Fr) the German name for the village of Soultz-les-Bains in Alsace.

Sulzburg (Ger) village (Anb): Baden. (Ber): Markgräflerland. (Gro): Burg Neuenfels. (Vin): Altenberg.

Sulzegger (Aus) a natural spring mineral water from Sülzegg.

Sülzenberg (Ger) vineyard (Anb): Mittelrhein. (Ber): Johannisberg. (Gro): Petersberg. (Vil): Oberdollendorf.

Sulzfeld (Ger) village (Anb): Baden. (Ber): Badische Bergstrasse/Kraichgau. (Gro): Stiftsberg. (Vins): Burg Ravensburger Dicker Franz, Burg Ravensburger Husarenkappe, Burg Ravensburger Löchle, Lerchenberg.

Sulzfeld (Ger) village (Anb): Franken. (Ber): Maindreieck. (Gro): Hofrat. (Vins): Cyriakusberg, Maustal.

Sulzheim (Ger) village (Anb): Rheinhessen. (Ber): Bingen. (Gro): Adelberg. (Vins): Greifenberg, Honigberg, Schildberg.

Sumac Ridge Estate Winery (Can) a winery based in British Columbia. Grape varieties include Gewürztraminer, Pinot noir.

Sumaridge (S.Afr) a winery (established 2001) based in Hemel-en-Aarde Valley, Hermanus, Western Cape. 25ha. Grape varieties: Chardonnay, Merlot, Pinotage, Pinot noir, Sauvignon blanc, Syrah. Produces varietal wines. Website: http://www.sumaridge.co.za

Sumatra Coffee (E.Ind) an Indonesian coffee which produces a mellow flavour with a full musky aroma and full flavour.

Sumiller (Sp) sommelier.

S

Su-Mi-Re (Jap) a violet-coloured, spicy, liqueur cordial with a citric aroma, contains vanilla, almond, spices, fruit etc 30% alc by vol.

Summa Añares (Sp) *see* Bodegas Olarra.

Summa' That (Eng) a 5% alc by vol. summer ale from The Branscombe Vale Brewery Ltd., Devon.

Summer Ale (Eng) introduced in 1994 as an alternative to lager. 3.9% alc by vol. bottled or draught light golden beer. Brewed by Fuller, it is available from June to September.

Summer Ale (Eng) a 4.2% alc by vol. light-coloured seasonal summer ale from Arkells, Swindon, Wiltshire. Brewed using Styrian gold hops.

Summer Ale (Eng) a 4% alc by vol. seasonal ale from King WJ & C°., Horsham, West Sussex.

Summer Ale (Eng) a seasonal cask or bottled ale brewed by St. Peter's Brewery, St. Peter's Hall, South Elmham St. Peter, near Bungay, Suffolk.

Summer Ale (Wal) an ale brewed by S.A. Brain & C°. Ltd. in Cardiff.

Summer Cocktail (Cktl)(Non-alc) mash some blackcurrants, raspberries and strawberries with a muddler and sugar. Add juice of ½ a lemon and same quantity of water. Shake well over ice and strain into a 125mls (5fl.oz) wine glass.

Summer Cooler (Cktl)(Non-alc) 200mls (⅓ pint) orange juice, 10mls (½ fl.oz) Angostura, 25mls (1fl.oz) blackcurrant cordial, shake well over ice and strain into an ice-filled highball glass.

Summer Daze (Eng) a 4.1% alc by vol. ale brewed by the Millstone Brewery, Lancashire.

Summerdaze (Eng) a 3.9% alc by vol. ale brewed by the Slaughter House Brewery Ltd., Warwickshire.

Summer Dream (Cktl) 1 part Cherry 'B' and 1 part orange juice.

Summerfield Winery (Austr) a winery (established 1979) based in the Pyrenees, Victoria. Produces varietal wines from Cabernet sauvignon, Chardonnay, Shiraz, Trebbiano.

Summer Fun Cocktail (Cktl) ½ measure brandy, ½ measure crème de banane, 1½ measures orange juice, 1½ measures pineapple juice. Shake well over ice, strain into a highball glass and serve with straws.

Summer Golden Ale (Eng) an ale brewed by Samuel Allsopp Brewery in Burton using Mexican and Chinese honey (part of their Tapster's range).

Summerhill Estate Winery (Can) a winery based in British Columbia.

Summerhill Stout (Eng) a cask-conditioned stout 1044 O.G. brewed by the Big Lamp Brewery, Tyneside (established 1982).

Summer Knight (Eng) a 3.8% alc by vol. cask ale brewed by the Dorset Brewing Company, Dorset. *See also* Silent Knight.

Summer Lease (S.Afr) the label for a red wine (Shiraz, Mourvèdre and Pinotage blend) produced by the Diemersfontein Wines winery, Wellington, Western Cape.

Summer Lightning GFB (Eng) *abbr:* Gilbert's First Beer, a 5% alc by vol. strong hoppy ale from the Hop Back Brewery, Downtown, near Salisbury in Wiltshire, sold in 500mls bottles.

Summer Madness (Eng) a 4% alc by vol. fruity, floral, cask-conditioned wheat beer (using honey) brewed by Ushers of Trowbridge, Wiltshire (available June to September).

Summer Mint Cocktail (Cktl) ⅓ measure Galliano, ⅓ measure (green) crème de menthe, ⅓ measure Cointreau, ½ measure grapefruit juice, ½ measure lemon juice. Blend altogether with a scoop of crushed ice in a blender, pour into a flute glass, dress with mint and a cherry and serve with straws.

Summer Perle Golden Ale (Eng) a 3.8% alc by vol. golden ale brewed by the Westerham Brewery C°. Ltd., Kent.

Summer Pruning (Eng) the cutting back of the excess growth tendrils on the vine. This allows the energy of the vine to be concentrated on the grapes.

Summer Reverie Cocktail (Cktl) 25mls (1fl.oz) Beefeater gin, 10mls (½ fl.oz) Cointreau, 25mls (1fl.oz) French vermouth, 10mls (½ fl.oz) grapefruit juice, 10mls (½ fl.oz) apricot brandy. Mix well together over ice, strain into a cocktail glass, decorate with a half an apricot and a cherry.

Summersault (Eng) a 4% alc by vol. cask-conditioned summer ale from Wadworth Brewery, Devizes, Wiltshire. Brewed with light malt and 3 hops (fuggles, styrian, saaz) and then dry-hopped, available May – September (also a bottled version 4.5% alc by vol).

Summerskills Brewery (Eng) a brewery (established 1983). (Add): 15 Pomphlett Farm Ind Estate, Broxton Drive, Billacombe, Plymouth, Devon PL9 7BG. (first based in Kingsbridge, Devon then moved to Plymouth in 1985). Brews: (cask-conditioned) Bigbury Best Bitter 4.3% alc by vol (1044 O.G.), HopScotch 4.1% alc by vol., Indiana Bones, Menacing Dennis 4.5% alc by vol., Ninja Beer 5% alc by vol., Tamar 4.3% alc by vol., Whistle Belly Vengeance 4.7% alc by vol. Website: http://www.summerskills.co.uk 'E'mail: info@summerskills.co.uk

Summer Solstice (Eng) a dry, light-coloured 4.5% alc by vol. beer from the Charles Wells Brewery in Bedford, Bedfordshire.

Summer Sparkler (Cktl) 1 part Mardi Gras, 2 parts sparkling dry white wine. Stir gently over ice in a highball glass.

Summer Storm (I.O.M) a 4.2% alc by vol. ale brewed by Okell & Sons Ltd., Isle of Man.

Summer Swallow (Eng) a 3.9% alc by vol. seasonal ale brewed by George Bateman & Son Ltd., Lincolnshire. Available in August.

Summer Swallow (Eng) a 4.1% alc by vol. bitter brewed by Hardy and Hansons Brewery based in Kimberley, Nottinghamshire.

Summer That (Eng) a 3.9% alc by vol. light-coloured bitter from Wood's Brewery. A seasonal beer.

Summer This (Eng) a 4.2% alc by vol. ale brewed by the Hogs Back Brewery Ltd., Surrey.

Summertime (Cktl) in a tall glass with ice pour 25mls (1fl.oz) vodka, 25mls (1fl.oz) dry vermouth, juice ½ grapefruit, stir and top with tonic water.

Summertime Cocktail (Cktl) 1¼ measures Bacardi rum, ½ measure pineapple juice, ½ measure orange juice, 3 dashes golden rum, juice ¼ lemon. Stir over ice, strain into an ice-filled collins glass, dress with mint and an orange slice and serve with straws.

Summer Tyne (Eng) a 3.6% alc by vol. ale brewed by the Mordue Brewery Ltd., Tyne & Wear.

Summer Velvet (Eng) a 1040 O.G. pale bitter from the Reepham Brewery, Norfolk.

Summit (Austr) a natural spring mineral water brand. Mineral contents (milligrammes per litre): Sodium 16mg/l, Calcium 10mg/l, Magnesium 3mg/l, Potassium 1mg/l, Bicarbonates 40mg/l, Chlorides 12mg/l, Sulphates 3mg/l, Nitrates 1.5mg/l.

Summit (Phil) a natural spring mineral water brand. Mineral contents (milligrammes per litre): Calcium 20mg/l, Magnesium 10mg/l, Bicarbonates 150mg/l, Chlorides 10mg/l, Sulphates 5mg/l. pH 7.0

Summit (Ven) a still natural spring mineral water (established 1996) from San Diego de Los Altos. Mineral contents (milligrammes per litre): Sodium 4.49mg/l, Calcium 67.2mg/l, Magnesium 7.7mg/l, Potassium 2.1mg/l, Bicarbonates 181mg/l, Chlorides 17.3mg/l, Sulphates 49mg/l, Silicates 4.23mg/l, Barium 4.23mg/l. pH 7.48. Also known as Summit Springs.

Summit (USA) a label used by the Geyser Peak Winery in California for their generic and varietal wines.

Summit Ale (Eng) a 5.1% alc by vol. limited edition bottled beer brewed by Bass' Brewery, Cape Hill, Birmingham for Welsh Brewers, Cardiff to commemorate the meeting of the European Council.

Summit Brewing C° (USA) a brewery. (Add): 910 Montreal Circle, St Paul, MN55102. Brews beers and lager. Website: http://www.summitbrewing.com 'E'mail: info@summitbrewing.com

Summus (It) the label of a red wine produced by Castello Banfi, Montalcino, Siena.

Sumoll (Sp) a white grape variety grown in the Alella and Penedés regions. The main grape for Spanish Cava. *See also* Soumoll.

Sumoll Negro (Sp) a red grape variety grown in the Penedés region and Conca de Barber .

Sunbeam (Ch.Isles) traditional draught bitter 1045 O.G. (4.2% alc by vol.) from the Guernsey Brewery, St. Peter Port, Guernsey. *see* Braye, Captain, Champion, Pony Ale. Now brewed in Jersey.

Sun Best (Chi) a natural spring mineral water from Zhong Shan. Mineral contents (milligrammes per litre): Sodium 18.5mg/l, Calcium 48.9mg/l, Potassium 2.2mg/l, Bicarbonates 191mg/l. pH 7.3

Suncharm (Eng) a soft drinks manufacturer. (Add): Queen's Square, Honley, Huddersfield. Producer of Ting (a carbonated grapefruit crush) and Old Jamaica Ginger Beer.

Sunco (Bel) a natural spring mineral water from Sunco, Ninove.

Sun Country Refresher (USA) a proprietary drink of white wine, fruit juice and carbonated spring water. 5% alc by vol.

Sunderland Best (Eng) a 3.9% alc by vol. best bitter ale brewed by the Darwin Brewery, Tyne & Wear.

Sunderland Bitter (Eng) a cask-conditioned (and keg) bitter 1040 O.G. brewed by the Vaux Brewery in Sunderland.

Sun Dew Cocktail (Cktl)(Non-alc) 60mls (½ gill) orange juice, 30mls (¼ gill) grapefruit juice, 30mls (¼ gill) gomme syrup, dash Angostura. Stir well over ice, strain into an ice-filled highball glass, top with soda water and a slice of orange.

Sun Dial (Eng) a 4.7% alc by vol. ale brewed by the Boggart Hole Clough Brewery Ltd., Greater Manchester.

Sundial (USA) the name given to an unoaked Chardonnay produced by Fetzer Vineyards, Mendocino County (named after an 80ha vineyard).

Sundowner (Cktl) 25mls (1fl.oz) brandy, 5mls (¼ fl.oz) each of Van der Hum, lemon juice, orange juice. Shake over ice and strain into a cocktail glass.

Sundowner (S.Afr) a brand of rum produced in South Africa.

Sundowner Ale (Eng) a 5% alc by vol. seasonal ale brewed by Cain Brewery, Stanhope Street, Liverpool from Maris Otter hops (available June and July).

Sunfire (Eng) a 4.3% alc by vol. ale brewed by the Ventnor Brewery Ltd., Isle of Wight.

Sunflower (Chi) a brand-name used by the Shantung C.N.C.O.F.I.E.C. for their dry gin, whiskey and vodka.

Sungulare (Bul) a wine-producing area in east of Sub-Balkan region that produces a medium-dry white wine from Red misket grapes.

Sunjuice Ltd (Wal) fruit juice manufacturer (established 1986). (Add): Sun House, Llantrisant Business Park, Llantrisant, Rhondda Cynon Taf, Mid Glamorgan CF72 8LF. Produces a range of fruit and vegetable drinks. Website: http://www.sunjuice.co.uk

Sunkist (USA) a brand of carbonated orange drink with 5% orange juice. Produced by C.C.S.B. (saccharine-free).

Sun Lik (Chi) a lager beer 4.7% alc by vol. brewed by the San Miguel Brewery in Hong Kong.

Sunny Brook (USA) the brand-name of a blended whiskey 40% alc by vol.

Sunnycliff Winery (Austr) a winery based in the Murray River area, Victoria. Produces varietal and table wines.

Sunny Daze (Eng) a 4.2% alc by vol. ale brewed by the Wickwar Brewing C°. Ltd., Gloucestershire.

Sunny Dream (Cktl) 75mls (3 fl.ozs) orange juice, 25mls (1fl.oz) apricot brandy, 10mls (½ fl.oz) Cointreau, 1 scoop ice cream. Blend all together, serve in a goblet with straws and an orange slice.

Sunny Jim (Eng) a cask-conditioned summer ale 3.8% alc by vol. produced b y the Frederic Robinson Brewery, Stockport, Cheshire.

Sun Pride (Eng) the brand-name for a range of fruit juices produced by Gerber Foods International, sold in 2litres cartons.

Sunquick (Eng) the brand-name of a fruit concentrate which is drunk diluted. Also available in apple, grapefruit, orange and tangerine flavours.

Sunraku Ocean (Jap) a large winery based in Japan.

Sun Ridge (Can) a natural spring mineral water from Powassan Ontario.

Sunrise [1] (Cktl) ⅕ measure crème de banane, ⅕ measure Galliano, ⅖ measure tequila, ⅕ measure cream, dash grenadine, dash lemon juice. Shake over ice and strain into a cocktail glass.

Sunrise [2] (Cktl) ⅓ wine glass brandy, ¾ wine glass Port, 2 dashes Angostura, 25mls (1fl.oz) vanilla syrup. Shake well over ice, strain into a chilled tumbler and dress with lemon rind.

Sunrise Winery (USA) a winery based in Santa Cruz, California. Grape varieties: Cabernet sauvignon, Chardonnay and Pinot noir. Produces varietal wines.

Sunset (Cktl) 50mls (2fl.ozs) golden tequila, 25mls (1fl.oz) lemon juice, 10mls (½ fl.oz) light honey. Stir well together and serve in a cocktail glass with shaved ice.

Sunset (Eng) a 4% alc by vol. ale brewed by the Captain Cook Brewery Ltd., Cleveland.

Sunset (Leb) the label for a rosé wine produced by Château Ksara, Bekka Valley.

Sunset Club (Eng) a lightly sparkling British wine and citrus-fruit cooler (low in alcohol).

Sunset Glow (Cktl) 1 measure Cinzano Rosso, dash fresh lemon juice. Serve in an ice-filled highball and top with lemonade.

Sunset Hat (S.Afr) a rosé wine (Cabernet sauvignon 20%, Pinotage 80%) from the Concept Wines range produced by the Ashanti winery, Paarl, Western Cape.

Sunset Tea (Cktl) heat 50mls (2fl.ozs) orange juice, 25mls (1fl.oz) Curaçao and 10mls (½ fl.oz) light rum until nearly boiling. Pour into a heat-proof glass containing 200mls (⅓ pint) hot tea, decorate with cloves studded in a orange and a piece cinnamon stick.

Sunshine Beer (Eng) a 4.5% alc by vol. cask-conditioned golden ale (part of the Tapster's Choice range from Carlsberg-Tetley) available in August.

Sunshine Cocktail [1] (Cktl) 30mls (¼ gill) gin, 15mls (⅛ gill) Italian vermouth, 30mls (¼ gill) orange squash, 1 teaspoon orange bitters, 1 teaspoon grenadine. Stir over ice, strain into a small wine glass and serve with a cherry.

Sunshine Cocktail [2] (Cktl) 20mls (⅙ gill) each of Old Tom gin, French vermouth, Italian vermouth, 2 dashes orange bitters. Stir well over ice, strain into a cocktail glass and add lemon peel juice on top.

Sun Spring Eau de Glacier (Can) a natural spring mineral water from Agassize, British Columbia. Mineral contents (milligrammes per litre): Sodium 0.4mg/l, Potassium 0.8mg/l, Fluorides 0.2mg/l.

Sun Spring Eau de Source (Can) a natural spring mineral water from Agassize, British Columbia. Mineral contents (milligrammes per litre): Sodium 3.6mg/l, Potassium 0.4mg/l, Fluorides 1mg/l.

Sunstroke (Eng) a 3.6% alc by vol. ale brewed by The Durham Brewery Ltd., County Durham.

Suntipt Fruit Juices (Eng) the name given to frozen concentrated fruit juices. Distributed by Moccomat Beverage Systems.

Suntory (Jap) a large whiskey producer based at Hakushu. Use Scotch malt whisky in their blends. Produce a range of whiskies under the Suntory label. *see* Suntory Hibiki, Yamazaki. Also a large wine producer. Owns the Robert Weil Estate (Germany).

Suntory Brewery (Jap) a brewery based in Osaka which is noted for Suntory beer.

Suntory Chiyoda (Jap) a popular brand of saké produced by Suntory.

Suntory Hibiki (Jap) a de luxe blended whiskey 43% alc by vol. from Suntory.

Suntory Natural Mineral Water (Jap) a natural spring mineral water from Minami Alps. Mineral contents (milligrammes per litre): Sodium 4.9mg/l, Calcium 9.7mg/l, Magnesium 1.4mg/l, Potassium 2.8mg/l.

Suntory Whisky Custom (Jap) the brand-name of a light-style whiskey first produced in 1967 by the Suntory Distillery in Hakushu.

Suntory Whisky Excellence (Jap) the brand-name of a premium whiskey first produced in 1971 by the Suntory Distillery in Hakushu.

Suntory Whisky Gold Label (Jap) the brand-name of a light-styled whiskey first produced in 1965 by the Suntory Distillery in Hakushu.

Suntory Whisky Imperial (Jap) the brand-name of a premium whiskey first produced in 1964 by the Suntory Distillery in Hakushu.

Suntory Whisky Rawhide (Jap) the brand-name of a Bourbon-flavoured whiskey produced by the Suntory Distillery in Hakushu.

Suntory Whisky Red Label (Jap) the brand-name of a light-styled whiskey first produced by the Suntory Distillery in Hakushu.

Suntory Whisky Royal (Jap) the brand-name of a premium whiskey first produced in 1960 by the Suntory Distillery in Hakushu.

Suntory Whisky Special Reserve (Jap) the brand-name of a premium whiskey first produced in 1969 by the Suntory Distillery in Hakushu.

Sun Worship Cocktail (Cktl) 25mls (1fl.oz) Beefeater gin, 10mls (½ fl.oz) French vermouth,

5mls (¼ fl.oz) Campari, 5mls (¼ fl.oz) liqueur de framboise. Stir together over ice, strain into a cocktail glass and add a twist of orange.

Suomurrain (Fin) a liqueur made from cloudberries similar to Lakka produced by Lignell and Piispanen.

Supalitre (Eng) a pale ale 1031 O.G. brewed by the Gibbs Mews Brewery in Salisbury, Wiltshire, sold in litre bottles.

Super Ale (Eng) a brown ale 1032 O.G. brewed and bottled by the Burtonwood Brewery in Cheshire.

Super Bock (Port) a 5.8% alc by vol. pale straw, bottled, bock beer brewed by Unicer in Porto.

Super Brew (Eng) a cask-conditioned bitter ale 1047 O.G. brewed by the Baileys Brewery in Malvern, Worcestershire.

Super Ice (Scot) an 8.6% alc by vol. bottled strong lager from the Tennent Caledonian Brewery.

Superior (S.Afr) a wine classification. Must have at least 30g/l of residual grape sugar and be harvested at 28 or more degrees Baume of sugar.

Superiore (It) superior, to a wine means being from a clearly defined area and of defined quality. Usually it is aged for not less than 1–3 years and has a minimum alcoholic content.

Superiore di Cartizze (It) a D.O.C. white wine from the Veneto region. Made from the Prosecco and Verdiso grapes in the restricted area of Cartizze. Also produced by natural refermentation as Frizzante (semi-sparkling) and Spumante (sparkling).

Superiore Naturalmente Amabile (It) a term meaning a naturally semi-sweet wine. Must be aged minimum 2 years in oak/chestnut casks.

Superiore Naturalmente Dolce (It) a term meaning a naturally sweet wine. Must be aged minimum 2 years in oak/chestnut casks.

Superiore Naturalmente Secco (It) a term meaning a naturally dry wine. Must be aged minimum 2 years in oak/chestnut casks.

Superior Old Marsala (It) *see* S.O.M.

Superior Ruby (Port) a deep coloured Ruby Port produced by Ferreira Port shippers.

Super Lager (Scot) a lager beer 1081 O.G. brewed and bottled by the Tennent Caledonian Brewery.

Super Leeuw (Hol) a slightly bitter beer brewed by the De Leeuw Brouwerij based in Valkenburg, Limburg.

Supermalt (Den) the brand-name of a beer produced by Faxe Jyske Breweries.

Super Mild (Eng) a keg dark mild 1031 O.G. brewed by the Gibbs Mew Brewery in Salisbury, Wiltshire.

Supermont (Afr) a natural spring mineral water from Mount Cameroon, Cameroon. Mineral contents (milligrammes per litre): Sodium 12.7mg/l, Calcium 16mg/l, Magnesium 10.2mg/l, Potassium 5.2mg/l, Bicarbonates 128mg/l, Chlorides 2.1mg/l, Sulphates 1mg/l, Nitrates 4.1mg/l.

Super Nikka (Jap) a brand of whiskey produced by the Nikka Distilleries.

Superstition (Scot) a new malt whisky 2005

produced by the Isle of Jura distillery 40% alc by vol.

Super Tuscans (Eng) a slang term for the top wines of Tuscany in Italy. These include the wines that do not have D.O.C. or D.O.C.G's status (because they are produced from grapes or by methods that are forbidden under the D.O.C. and D.O.C.G. rules) e.g: Brancaia (IGT) and Sassicaia (now a D.O.C.).

Super White (S.Am) a light-styled rum, aged for 12 months and produced by Banks DIH in Guyana.

Supple (Eng) a term used to describe an easy-to-drink wine that with ageing the tannin becomes supple.

Supra-extraction (Eng) a term to describe where before pressing the grapes are frozen then defrosted. The grapes are gathered by hand, packed loosely in 10kgs cages and frozen. Structure of grape tissue is broken down by freezing and aromas are released. *See also* Cryo-extraction.

Supreme (Eng) a light tan-coloured beer from Abingdon Park Brewery.

Supreme (Eng) a 4% alc by vol. ale brewed by The Eccleshall Brewing Cº. Ltd., Staffordshire.

Supreme Bitter (Eng) a cask-conditioned bitter ale 1043 O.G. brewed by the Abbey Brewery in Retford, Nottinghamshire.

Supreme Bitter (Eng) a cask-conditioned bitter ale 1043 O.G. brewed by the Simpkiss Brewery in Brierley Hill, Staffordshire.

Supreme Coffee (S.Am) a grade of Colombian coffee. Produces a rich, smooth, strong brew.

Supremecorq (USA) the brand-name for coloured thermoplastic recyclable elastomer corks.

Sur (Den)(Wal) acidic/sour.

Sura (Ind) a spirit made from rice starch.

Sur Col (Fr) lit: 'on fining', denotes that the wine is receiving the fining process and will not taste true.

Surdo (Mad) a sweet wine fortified with grape alcohol after being fermented for only a short time.

Suresnes (Fr) ancient vineyards planted by priests in the tenth century.

Surfboard (Cktl) 2 measures Malibu poured over an ice cube in a large highball glass. Add 1 measure blue Curaçao and then fresh cream until the ice cube surfaces.

Surfers (W.Ind) a rum and coconut liqueur.

Surfer's Paradise (Cktl) build 3 dashes Angostura and 25mls (1fl.oz) lime juice in an ice-filled highball glass. Stir in lemonade and decorate with a slice of orange.

Surfing Cocktail (Cktl) ½ measure light rum, ½ measure apricot brandy, dash gomme syrup, 1 egg yolk. Shake well over ice, strain into a cocktail glass and top with grated nutmeg.

Surf Sailor Splash (Cktl) 25mls (⅛ gill) Cherry Heering placed in an ice-filled highball glass, top with 60mls (½ gill) orange juice and soda water.

Sur Gamay (Fr) a Premier Cru vineyard in the A.C. commune of Saint Aubin, Côte de Beaune, Burgundy 14ha.

Surger Unit (Eng) a device™ from Guinness for use at home to produce a 'traditional' glass of pub-style Guinness. Using ultra-sound to activate the settle of the Guinness in the glass to give the beer '*a rich, black body and smooth, creamy head*'.

Surgiva (It) a sparkling natural spring mineral water from Trento. Mineral contents (milligrammes per litre): Sodium 1.4mg/l, Calcium 8.2mg/l, Potassium 0.8mg/l, Bicarbonates 26.5mg/l, Chlorides 0.4mg/l, Sulphates 3.4mg/l, Nitrates 5.8mg/l, Silicates 9.9mg/l. pH 6.5

Surin (Fr) the alternative name used for the Sauvignon blanc grape in the Loire Valley.

Sur Lattes (Fr) lit: 'head in punt', the way bottles laid on wooden racks for maturation especially in Champagne. *see* Sur Pointe.

Sur Lavelle (Fr) a Premier Cru vineyard in the A.C. commune of Monthélie, Côte de Beaune, Burgundy 6.1ha.

Sur-le-Sentier-du-Clou (Fr) a Premier Cru vineyard in the A.C. commune of Saint Aubin, Côte de Beaune, Burgundy 12ha.

Sur-les-Grèves (Fr) a Premier Cru vineyard in the A.C. commune of Beaune, Côte de Beaune, Burgundy 4.02ha.

Sur Lie (Fr) lit: 'bottled off the lees'. i.e. Muscadet, the wine is transferred into the bottled without firstly racking.

Sur Maturité (Fr) over ripe/over maturity.

Surni (Wal) acidity.

Sur Plaque (Fr) the term to describe filtering, the wine is run through cellulose filters before being bottled.

Sur Pointe (Fr) lit: 'on its head', the name for Champagne bottles that are stored upside down with the head of one bottle in the punt of the one below after the second fermentation and before dégorgement. *see* Sur Lattes.

Surrender Sixteen Forty Six [1646] (Eng) a 3.6% alc by vol. beer brewed by the Springhead Brewery, Sutton-on-Trent.

Surrentinum (It) a red wine produced in central-western Italy in Roman times.

Surrey Bitter (Eng) a 3.7% alc by vol (1038 O.G) cask-conditioned bitter brewed by the Pilgrim Brewery in Woldingham, Surrey.

Surrey Down (Eng) a natural spring mineral water from Hawkshill, Leatherhead, Surrey.

Sur Souche (Fr) the term given when there is a great demand for wine and the merchants buy the wine when the grapes are still on the vine!

Sur Terre (Fr) the name for a type of filtration where the wine is passed through a powdered shell screen before going into casks. Used in Bordeaux.

Surup (Tur) fruit juice/cordial/syrup.

Susa Don Ramón (Sp) a noted wine-producer based in the Cariñena region.

Susana Balba (Arg) the label for a range of wines (Cabernet sauvignon/Malbec) produced by the Dominio del Plata winery in the Mendoza region. Also Brioso.

Susie Taylor Cocktail (Cktl) 25mls (⅙ gill) Bacardi White Label, juice ½ lime. Stir over ice in a highball glass and top with ginger ale.

Suso y Pérez [Vincente] (Sp) the largest wine producer in Cariñena, north-eastern Spain. *see* Don Ramon, Duque de Seville, Mosen Cleto and Old Duque de Sevilla Brandy.

Suspension (Cktl) ⅓ measure Scotch whisky, ⅓ measure orange juice, ⅓ measure ginger wine. Shake well together over ice and strain into a cocktail glass.

Süss [Süß] (Aus) lit: 'sweet', the classification of sweet wines which have over 45g/l of residual sugar. *See also* Lieblich.

Süss [Süß] (Ger) sweet.

Süssbenberg (Aus) the name of two vineyard sites on the banks of the River Danube situated in the Wachau region, Niederösterreich.

Süssdruck (Switz) a rosé (and light red wine) produced from the Pinot noir grape.

Süsse (Ger) grape sugar. *See also* Süesse.

Sussex Beers (Eng) the name of ales brewed by the Harvey Brewery in Lewes, Sussex.

Sussex Beers (Eng) the name of ales brewed by the King and Barnes Brewery in Horsham, Sussex.

Sussex Best (Eng) a 3.5% alc by vol. seasonal ale produced the by King and Barnes Brewery in Horsham, Sussex.

Sussex Light Ale (Eng) a 3.5% alc by vol. light ale brewed by Hepworth & C°. Brewers Ltd., West Sussex.

Sussex Mild (Eng) a 3.7% alc by vol. mild ale brewed by the Arundel Brewery Ltd., West Sussex.

Sussex Punch (Cktl) ⅛ measure dark rum, ⅜ measure elderberry wine, ⅛ measure dry cider, 1 dash lemon juice. Stir well over ice, strain into a cocktail glass and top with a spiral of lemon peel.

Sussex Sunset (Eng) the name of an English rosé table wine from Hildon Vineyards in Horam, East Sussex. Grape varieties include Pinot noir, Dunkenfelder.

Sussex Tap Water (Eng) a still-water, filtered or un-filtered, sparkling water is carbonated by Soda Stream.

Süsskopf (Ger) vineyard (Anb): Pfalz. (Ber): Mittelhaardt-Deutsche Weinstrasse. (Gro): Schepfenflug an der Weinstrasse. (Vil): Forst.

Sussling (Fr) an alternative name for the Chasselas grape in eastern France.

Süssmund (Ger) vineyard (Anb): Württemberg. (Ber): Württembergisch Unterland. (Gro): Wunnenstein. (Vil): Kleinbottwar.

Süssreserve (Ger) unfermented grape juice which has been centrifuged to remove all yeasts. Used to sweeten Tafel and QbA. wines.

Süssung (Ger) the name given to the process of adding süssreserve to wine prior to bottling. May only be practiced by growers and wholesalers.

Süsswasser (Ger) fresh water.

Süsswein (Ger) grape must where the yeasts are removed (filtered/centrifuged) or killed (pasteurised) without use of alcohol so further fermentation is possible.

Susu (Indo) milk.

Susumaiello (It) a red grape variety grown in southern Italy. Produces deep-coloured wines.

Sütçü (Tur) milkman.

Süthane (Tur) dairy.

Sutherland (S.Afr) the label for a dry white wine (Sauvignon blanc) produced by the Thelma Mountain Vineyards winery, Stellenbosch, Western Cape.

Sutherland Water (Scot) a natural spring water from the Scottish highlands.

Sutter Basin Vineyard (USA) a vineyard based in the Yolo County, California. Grape variety: Zinfandel. Vinified at the Carneros Creek Winery.

Sutterer (Ger) a noted eau-de-vie producer based in Mösbach, Schwarzwald.

Sutter Home (USA) a winery at 225 Helena Highway, Napa Valley in northern California. Grape varieties include Zinfandel (red and white), Cabernet sauvignon, Chardonnay, Chenin blanc, Muscat of alexandria, Sauvignon blanc. Owns Monteviña winery and vineyards in Amador County. Is famous for creating in 1972 the original White Zinfandel wine.

Sutton (Eng) a micro-brewery based in Plymouth, now known as the South Hams Brewery.

Sutton Comfort (Eng) a 4.5% alc by vol. ale brewed by the South Hams Brewery, Devon.

Suwannaphoome Distillery (Thai) a distillery that produces Regency VSOP brandy 38% alc by vol.

Suzao Teroldico (USA) a red grape variety grown in California to make dessert wines.

Suze (Fr) a bitter gentian-flavoured apéritif made by J.R. Parkinson (Pernod-Ricard) 17% alc by vol.

SV (Austr) abbr: Shiraz and Viognier, a blend of grape varieties in a particular wine.

Svagdricka (Swe) a dark, sweet beer that is low in alcohol 1.8% alc. by weight and with added yeast.

Svali (Ice) a natural spring mineral water brand.

Svart-Vinbärs (Swe) a blackcurrant-flavoured brannvin used to make kir.

Svatovavrinecke (Czec) a local name for the St. Laurent grape variety.

Svenzka (Eng) the brand-name of a vodka bottled by Thomas Shaw of London and Glasgow 37.2% alc by vol.

Sveta Nedelja (Euro) a wine-producing region in Dalmatia.

Sveti Roc (Cro) a still and sparkling natural spring mineral water from Sveti Roc, Lovinac. (green label: light gas/blue label: still). Mineral contents (milligrammes per litre): Sodium 1.2mg/l, Calcium 47.6mg/l, Magnesium 9.9mg/l, Potassium 0.3mg/l, Bicarbonates 189.1mg/l, Chlorides 1.7mg/l, Sulphates 2.3mg/l, Fluorides 0.02mg/l.

Svetlé (Czec) pale (beer).

Svetovar (Czec) a pilsener-type lager produced by the Gambrinus Brewery.

Sveva (It) a sparkling natural spring mineral water from Potenza. Mineral contents (milligrammes per litre): Calcium 74.2mg/l, Magnesium 24.8mg/l, Potassium 33.5mg/l, Bicarbonates 695mg/l, Fluorides 0.7mg/l. pH 6.5

Svijany Brewery (Czec) an old brewery (established 1546) based in north-western Czec.

S. Vincente (Port) a Dão wine produced by the Caves Borlida.

Svishtov (Bul) a noted D.G.O. wine area that produces Cabernet-based wines in a delimited area of the same name in the northern region.

S.V.I.T. (Fr) abbr: Syndicat Viticole de l'Appellation Tavel.

Svitavy Brewery (Czec) a brewery based in central Czec.

Swabian Wine Route (Ger) see Schwäbische Weinstrasse.

Swacked (Eng) a slang term for being in a very intoxicated state, very drunk.

Swale Brewery (Eng) a micro-brewery based in Sittingbourne. Brews: Copperwinkle 4% alc by vol. Indian Summer Pale Ale 4.2% alc by vol. Kentish Gold 5% alc by vol. Kentish Pride 3.8% alc by vol. Old Dick 5.2% alc by vol. and 75th anniversary Poppy Ale for Royal British Legion.

Swan Brewery (Austr) a large brewery based in Perth, Western Australia. Brews: Swan and Emu Lagers.

Swan Brewery (Eng) a brewery based at Aston Munslow. Noted for strong home-made ciders, each barrel is named after the farmer whose orchard provided the apples. see Little Nigel.

Swan Hill (Austr) a wine district of New South Wales. Produces good quality wines.

Swanky (Austr) a beer brewed by the Cooper's Brewery in South Australia.

Swan Premium Export Lager (Austr) a fine lager beer 5% alc by vol. brewed by the Swan Brewery in Perth. Distributed in the U.K. by Courage and Bass.

Swansea Brewing C° (Wal) a brewery (established 1996). (Add): Joiners Arms, 50 Bishopston Road, Bishopston, Swansea, Mid Glamorgan SA3 3EJ. Brews a variety of beers and stout. 'E'mail: rorygowland@fsbdial.co.uk

Swan's Neck (Eng) see Col du Cygne.

Swan Special Light (Austr) a low-alcohol lager 0.9% alc by vol. brewed in Western Australia.

Swan Special Lite Lager (Austr) see Swan Special Light.

Swan Throat (Fr) the curve of copper tubing which connects the still to a condenser in Cognac production.

Swan Valley (Austr) a hot wine region of Western Australia noted for dessert wines. Main winery is the Houghton Vineyard.

Swan Vineyards (USA) a winery based near Forestville, Russian River Valley, California. Grape varieties: Chardonnay, Pinot noir and Zinfandel. Produces varietal wines.

Swartberg Aristaat (S.Afr) a brand-name of the Ladismith Co-operative.

Swartland (S.Afr) a district on the west coast near the town of Malmesbury. Produces light wines.

Swartland (S.Afr) the label for a red wine (Shiraz) produced by the Tulbagh Mountain Vineyards winery, Tulbagh, Western Cape.

Swartland Koöperatiewe Wynmaatskappy [Die] (S.Afr) a co-operative winery (established 1945) based in Swartland, Western Cape. 3000ha. (Add): Box 95, Malmesbury 7299. Produces still and sparkling wines. Grape varieties: Bukettraube, Cabernet sauvignon, Chardonnay, Chenin blanc, Colombard, Ferñao pires, Hanepoot, Malbec, Merlot, Pinotage, Red jerepiko, Sauvignon blanc, Shiraz, Tinta barocca, Viognier. Labels: Bin 50, D'Vine, Eagle Crest, Indalo, Johannisberger. Also known as the Swartland Wine Cellar. Website: http://www.swwines.co.za

Swedish Punsch (Swe) based on Batavian arak, akvavit, spices, tea, lemon and sugar. Wine is added after a few months maturation 30% alc by vol.

Sweeney Estate (USA) a winery based in the Willamette Valley, Oregon. Grape variety: Pinot noir.

Sweet (Eng) fine wines obtain their sweetness from excess grape sugar after fermentation. (*See Botrytis cinerea*). Others are fortified with spirit to stop fermentation before all the sugar has been fermented out. Finally some wines have residual sweetness from unfermentable sugars remaining in the wine. (Den) = sød, (Port) = adomado. *See also* Vin Doux Naturel.

Sweet and Low (Cktl)(Non-alc) ⅓ measure grenadine, ⅓ measure lemon juice, ⅓ measure orange juice. Shake over ice and strain into a cocktail glass.

Sweet Beer (USA) a combination of beer with a fruit juice (lemon, lime or grape) to give a sweeter drink.

Sweet Blondy (Cktl) ⅓ measure sweet white vermouth, ⅓ measure Royal Mint Chocolate liqueur, ⅓ measure light rum, dash orange juice. Shake over ice, strain and add a slice of orange peel.

Sweet Cider (USA) unfermented apple juice. *See also* Hard Cider.

Sweet Desire (Cktl) ⅓ measure dry gin, ⅓ measure red Dubonnet, ⅙ measure kirsch, ⅙ measure Parfait Amour. Shake over ice and strain into a cocktail glass.

Sweet Dreams (Cktl) place 60mls (½ gill) crème de cacao into a highball glass, top with hot milk, stir and add grated nutmeg.

Sweetened Spirits (Eng) the H.M. Customs and Excise technical definition of Liqueurs.

Sweetheart (Scot) a bottled sweet stout 1035 O.G. brewed by the Tennent Caledonian Brewery.

Sweetlips (Eng) a 4.6% alc by vol. ale brewed by the Springhead Brewery, Nottinghamshire.

Sweet Maria Cocktail (Cktl) ½ measure vodka, ¼ measure amaretto, ¼ measure cream. Shake over ice and strain into a cocktail glass.

Sweet Martini Cocktail (Cktl) 30mls (¼ gill) gin, 30mls (¼ gill) Italian vermouth. Stir over ice, strain into a cocktail glass and add a squeeze of lemon peel juice on top.

Sweet Mash (USA) the yeasting process in the production of whiskey. Also known as the '*Yeast Mash Process*'. Is the adding of fresh yeast to the mash and no spent beer. *see* Sour Mash.

Sweet Memories (Cktl) ⅓ measure dry vermouth, ⅓ measure white rum, ⅓ measure orange Curaçao. Stir over ice and strain into a cocktail glass.

Sweet Millenary (Cktl) ⅓ measure rosé Cinzano, ⅓ measure Galliano, ⅓ measure Aperol Apértivo. Stir over ice, strain into a cocktail glass and add a twist of orange peel juice.

Sweet Nancy (USA) a sweet, botrytised white wine made from the Chenin blanc grape by Callaway Winery in Temecula, California.

Sweet Patootie (Cktl) ⅔ measure dry gin, ⅙ measure triple sec, ⅙ measure orange juice. Shake over ice and strain into a cocktail glass.

Sweet Permain (Eng) an old English cider-making apple.

Sweet Sauterne (USA) a Californian sweet white wine made from the Sauvignon blanc, Sémillon and Muscadelle grapes.

Sweet Springs Natural Mountain Water (USA) a natural spring mineral water from Gap Mills, West Virginia.

Sweet Stout (Eng) an English stout sometimes flavoured with oyster essence and oatmeal.

Sweet Stout (Eng) a processed stout 1043 O.G. brewed and bottled by the Federation Brewery in Dunston, Newcastle-upon-Tyne.

Sweet Surrender Pudding Wine (S.Afr) the label for a noble late harvest white wine (Bukettraube, Chenin blanc and Furmint blend) from the Isabela range produced by the Thirtytwo [32] South Ltd winery, Stellenbosch, Western Cape.

Sweetwater (Austr) an alternative name for the Palomino grape.

Sweetwell (S.Afr) the label for a red wine (Cabernet sauvignon) produced by the Terroir Wines of SA winery, Stellenbosch, Western Cape.

Sweet William Brewery (Eng) a brewery (established 2000). (Add): William IV, 816 High Road Leyton, London E10 6AE. Brews a range of beers and stout. 'E'mail: sweetwilliamivy.@aol.com

Sweet Wine(s) (Eng) the general term for wines which have retained some of their natural sugar after fermentation. *see* Ausbruch, Auslese, Barsac, Beerenauslese, Eiswein, Icewine, Picolit, Sauternes, Spätlese, Tokay Aszù, Trokenbeerenauslese, Vin de Paille. *See also* Vin Santo, Vins-doux-Naturels. (Fr) = vin doux, (Gre) = gleukos, (Ire) = fion milis.

Sweet Wort (Eng) the name given to the liquid run off from the mash tun to the copper.

Sweet Young Thing (Cktl) ½ measure Malibu, ½ measure crème de fraises, 2 dashes gomme syrup. Shake well over ice, strain into an ice-filled highball glass, top with iced Champagne and a fresh strawberry.

Swellendam (S.Afr) a district which stretches from the south coast inland to the town of Bonnievale.

Swift (Eng) a 4% alc by vol. ale brewed by the Butlers Brewery C°. Ltd., Berkshire.

Swift Half (Eng) a term to denote a quick drink, usually a half pint of beer and denotes that a person cannot stay long (drinking).

Swift Nick (Eng) a 3.8% alc by vol. ale brewed by the Barn Brewery, Derbyshire.

Swifty (Eng) a slang term for a quick drink.

Swig (Eng) a slang term for taking a large mouthful (draft) of drink usually from a bottle. (Fr) = lampée.

Swill (Eng) a slang term meaning to drink quickly/to guzzle.

Swilling (Eng) a slang term used to denote heavy, fast drinking.

Swillmore Original (Eng) a 4.2% alc by vol. bitter ale brewed by the Slaught House Brewery Ltd., Warwickshire.

Swindon Brewing C° Ltd (Eng) a brewery (established 1979). (Add): Penzance Drive, Swindon, Wiltshire SN5 7JL. Brews a variety of beers and lager including Swindon Pride. Also known as Archers Brewery. Website: http://www.archersbrewery.co.uk 'E'mail: sales@archersbrewery.co.uk

Swindon Pride (Eng) a beer brewed by Archers Brewery in Swindon, Wiltshire.

Swing (Scot) a de luxe blended Scotch whisky produced by John Walker and Sons Ltd. Sold in a dumpy bottle 40% alc by vol.

Swing (Eng) the name given to a blended aromatic coffee produced by Jacobs Suchard.

Swinger Cocktail [1] (Cktl) 1 part Glayva, 5 parts orange juice, shake well together over ice, strain into an ice-filled highball and decorate with a slice of lime.

Swinger Cocktail [2] (Cktl)(Non-alc) 25mls (1fl.oz) pineapple syrup, 10mls (½ fl.oz) gomme syrup, 200mls (⅓ pint) grapefruit juice. Shake over ice, strain into a highball glass, add a grapefruit segment and a cherry.

Swiss (Cktl) ½ measure pastis, ½ measure fresh cream, teaspoon grenadine. Shake over ice and strain into a cocktail glass.

Swiss Alpina (Switz) a natural spring mineral water from Fontana Rossa, Rothenbrunnen. (blue label: sparkling/green label: light gas/red label: still). Mineral contents (milligrammes per litre): Sodium 65mg/l, Calcium 153.9mg/l, Magnesium 48mg/l, Potassium 2.9mg/l, Bicarbonates 787.2mg/l, Chlorides 9.7mg/l, Sulphates 79.4mg/l, Fluorides 0.3mg/l, Nitrates <0.2mg/l, Silicates 32.6mg/l.

Swiss Colony (USA) see United Vintners.

Swiss Family (Cktl) ⅔ measure Bourbon whiskey, ⅓ measure French vermouth, 2 dashes pastis, 2 dashes Angostura. Stir over ice and strain into a cocktail glass.

Swiss Valley (USA) a small vineyard based in Vevay, Indiana. 1.25ha. Produces French hybrid wines.

Switz (Euro) abbr: **Switz**erland.

Switzerland (Switz) a small wine-producing country situated between the borders of France, Germany and Italy. Wines are influenced by the countries in their styles (vines and wines). Major regions are **French**: (Chablais, Geneva, La Côte, Lavaux, Neuchâtel, Northern Vaudois, Valais and Vaud). **German**: (Argovia, Basle, Schaffhausen, Thurgau and Zürich). **Italian**: (Ticino). Main grape variety is the Chasselas (Dorin, Fendant, Perlan), Merlot, Pinot noir, plus rosé from Gamay. Website: http://www.swisswine.ch

Swizzles (USA) a drink of spirits, sugar or other sweetening agent and soda. Made in pitchers with ice then served in ice-filled high-ball glasses.

Swizzle Stick (USA) a gadget used to remove the bubbles from sparkling wines. Popular in the 1930's.

Swizzle Stick (W.Ind) a device used to 'swizzle' ice and liquor together in a jug or glass to create a frost on the outside. Originally made from the dried stem of a tropical plant with a few small branches left on one end. Now often made of plastic. Up to two foot long.

Swn y Don (Wal) lit: 'sound of the waves', the rebirth of Welsh Whiskey. Made by Powys Promotions Ltd.

Swn y Mor (Wal) lit: 'sound of the sea', a whiskey produced in Mid-Wales from a Scottish malt grain blend, then steeped in local herbs. Produced by the Brecon Brewery Ltd. 40% alc by vol. see Chwisgi.

SW1 (Cktl) ⅓ measure Campari, ⅓ measure vodka, ⅓ measure orange juice, dash egg white. Shake over ice and strain into a cocktail glass.

SW1 (Eng) a cask-conditioned bitter ale brewed by the Clifton Inns home-brew public house in London.

Swordmaker (Eng) the name of an ale brewed by the Derwentrose Brewery in Consett, County Durham.

SW2 (Eng) a cask-conditioned bitter ale brewed by the Clifton Inns home-brew public house in London.

SX (Eng) a 4.2% alc by vol. ale brewed by Wilds Brewery Ltd., Herefordshire.

Sybillenstein (Ger) grosslage (Anb): Rheinhessen. (Ber): Wonnegau. (Vils): Alzey, Bechenheim, Dautenheim, Freimersheim, Heimersheim, Mauchenheim, Offenheim, Wahlheim, Weinheim.

SYC (N.Z) a producer of Sherry-style wines.

Sycamore Canyon (USA) the brand label for a red (Cabernet sauvignon) wine produced by Ernst & Julio Gallo.

Sycamore Creek Vineyards (USA) a winery based in Hecker Pass, Santa Clara, California. 6ha. Grape varieties: Cabernet sauvignon, Carignane, Chenin blanc, Johannisberg riesling and Zinfandel. Produces varietal wines.

Sycamore Vineyards (USA) a red wine (Cabernet Sauvignon) produced by the Freemark Abbey winery in the Napa Valley, California.

Sychedig (Wal) thirsty (sychedu = to thirst).

Sydney Aqua (Austr) a natural spring mineral water

Sydney. Mineral contents (milligrammes per litre): Sodium 9.1mg/l, Calcium 1mg/l, Magnesium 5.4mg/l.

Sydney Back (S.Afr) a 100% Chenin blanc-based, pot-stilled brandy aged in French Limousin oak casks for a minimum of 3 years. Produced by Backsberg Distillery, Paarl, West Cape.

Sydney Sunset (Cktl) 25mls (1fl.oz) Glayva, 50mls (2fl.oz) orange juice, 10mls (½ fl.oz) orange Curaçao, dash egg white. Shake well over ice, strain into a large cocktail glass. Decorate with a cherry, orange slice and serve with straws.

Sydoon-Gezer (Isr) the second largest wine-producing region. Noted for fine red and white wines.

Syd's Last Orders (Eng) a beer brewed by the Big Lamp Brewery, Tyneside, specially for a Northumberland free-trader.

Sykes Hydrometer (Eng) an instrument for measuring alcoholic strengths, named after the man who invented it (*see* Bartholomew Sykes).

Sylhet (Asia) a tea-producing area in Bangladesh.

Sylikou (Cyp) a wine village on the south eastern side of the island. Produces mainly red grapes for the making of Commandaria.

Syllabub (Eng) an old drink of fresh milk (full-cream), wine (or spirits) and spices. The milk should be as fresh as possible and warm. Whisk in the wine and spices and drink as soon as possible. Is also served as a dessert (modern).

Sylt Quelle (Ger) a natural spring mineral water (established 1993) from Sylt. Mineral contents (milligrammes per litre): Sodium 126mg/l, Calcium 21.8mg/l, Magnesium 22mg/l, Potassium 16.6mg/l, Bicarbonates 195mg/l, Chlorides 186mg/l, Sulphates 19mg/l, Fluorides 0.32mg/l.

Sylvaner (Fr) a superior white grape variety which gives fresh, fruity wines. Grown extensively in Austria, Germany, Switzerland and the USA. *See also* Silvaner (alternative spelling). Also known as the Gruber, Grünling, Gros rhin, Johannisberg and Öesterreicher.

Sylvaner Bechtau (Rus) a white grape variety used in the production of dry white wines in Stavropol.

Sylvaner Verde (It) a white grape variety planted in the Trentino-Alto-Adige.

SylvanVale Vineyards (S.Afr) a winery (established 1997) based in Stellenbosch, Western Cape. 10ha. Grape varieties: Cabernet sauvignon, Chenin blanc, Pinotage, Shiraz. Labels: Cape Blend-Devon Valley, Ghost Tree, Jewel of the Valley, Vine Dried Pinotage. Website: http://www.sylvanvale.co.za

Sylvatica (It) wild chestnut casks made from forest of same name and used in the Chianti region.

Sylvester Wine (Ger) a wine made on New Year's Eve. Usually of either trockenbeerenauslese or eiswein quality (illegal since 1971).

Sylvia Cocktail (Cktl) ⅓ measure Grand Marnier, ⅓ measure Bacardi White Label, ⅓ measure pineapple juice, 1 egg yolk, juice ¼ orange, 2 dashes grenadine. Shake over ice, strain into an ice-filled highball and serve with straws.

Sylvius (Hol) a doctor in Leyden who produced the first jenever in the sixteenth century. Also called De la Boe.

Symingtons Family Estates (Port) producers and owners of Port shippers: Dow, Gould Campbell, Graham, Quinta do Vesuvio, Quarles Harris, Smith Woodhouse and Warre.

Symonds (Eng) a noted cider-making company based in Hereford. Produces: Drystone (medium-sweet), Princess Pippin (a vintage cider) and Scrumpy Jack. (Add): Stoke Lacy, Bromyard, Hereford. Part of Greenhall Whitley.

Symons Spring (Wal) a natural spring mineral water from Churchstoke, Montgomery, Powys.

Symphony (USA) a white grape variety, a cross of Grenache gris x Muscat of alexandria.

Synchronicity (S.Afr) the label for a barrel-selected red wine (Cabernet sauvignon, Merlot and Pinotage blend) produced by the Meinert Wines winery, Stellenbosch, Western Cape.

Syndale Valley Vineyards (Eng) vineyards based at Newnham, near Faversham, Kent. Soil: chalk. Grape varieties: Müller-Thurgau, Reichensteiner, Seyval blanc, Ortega, Wurzer. Wines sold under the Newnham St. Peter label.

Syndicat (Fr) bodies formed in appellations for the control of wine production and quality within the appellation. The syndicates are under the overall control of the INAO.

Syndicat de Défense des Vins des Côtes de Provence (Fr) a body for the protection of the wines of the Côtes de Provence. Formed by a group of growers.

Syndicat des AOC Bordeaux et Bordeaux Supérieur (Fr) a wine co-operative based in Bordeaux. Produces Mouton Cadet and Malesan labels.

Syndicat des Crus Bourgeois du Médoc (Fr) the new controlling body for the Bordeaux Cru Bourgeois properties. Decides which group (Crus Bourgeois/Cru Bourgeois Supérieurs/Crus Bourgeois Exceptionnels) that the Cru Bougeois châteaux are places. The new classification will be issued in 2004-2005 (originally 2003) and revised every 12 years and will replace the existing classification listings.

Syndicat des Crus Classés du Médoc (Fr) a winery. (Add): 1, Cours du XXX Juliet, 33000 Bordeaux. A group that represents many of the great châteaux.

Syndicat des Producteurs de Vins Mousseux Méthode Traditionelle de Bourgogne (Fr) a body that represents over 30 firms in the Burgundy region regarding Crémant de Bourgogne and sparkling Burgundy.

Syndicat des Vignerons des Côtes du Couchois (Fr) a body (established 1957) to promote the wines of the A.C. Bougogne Côtes de Couchois. (Add): 71490 Couches.

Syndicat du Commerce des Vins de Champagne (Fr) a body founded in the late nineteenth century by

Paul Krug to help deal with phylloxera, consisted of a group of Champagne shippers.

Syndicat du Cru de Bonnezeaux (Fr) a body of the A.C. Bonnezeaux wine producers based in Thouarcé, Anjou-Saumur, Loire.

Syndicat National des Fabricants de Liqueurs (Fr) produce a selection of liqueurs from 90 members, has an inner court called the Groupement des Grandes Liqueurs de France.

Syndicat Viticole de Fronsac (Fr) les Gentilshommes de Fronsac. (Add): Maison des Vins, B.P. Nº7, 33126 Fronsac.

Syndicat Viticole de l'Appellation Tavel (Fr) a body for the promotion of A.C. Tavel wines. (Add): B.P.12. 30126 Tavel. *abbr*: SVAT. Website: http://www.tavel.tm.fr 'E'mail: aoctavel@mnet.fr

Synergy (S.Afr) the label for a red wine (Cabernet sauvignon and Merlot blend) produced by the Beyerskloof winery, Stellenbosch, Western Cape. Also Reserve (Cabernet sauvignon 55%, Merlot 8% and Pinotage 37%).

Synthetic Wine (Eng) a 'wine' made of glucose, glycerine, spirit, water and colouring, an artificial wine.

Syra (Fr) an alternative spelling of the Syrah grape.

Syrac (Fr) an alternative spelling of the Syrah grape.

Syracuse (It) a Muscat wine produced on the island of Sicily.

Syrah (Fr) a red grape variety, grown mainly in the Rhône (especially in the northern Rhône where it is the only red variety used). Gives deep colour, tannin and a distictive bouquet and flavour of blackberries together with black pepper, burnt rubber, liquorice,,spice, game, mint, tar, thyme, chocolate, clove and aniseed. Also known as the Chira, Entournerier, Hignan, Hignan noir, Petite sirah, Schiras, Sérine, Serrenne, Shiraz, Shyraz, Sirac, Sirah, Sirrah, Sirras, Syra, Syrac and Syras.

Syras (Euro) an alternative spelling of the Syrah grape in eastern Europe.

Syrberg (Lux) a vineyard site in the village of Nertert.

Syre (Den) acid.

Syrgis (Eng) an eighteenth century name for the Spanish wines of Sitges.

Syria (M.East) a lesser wine-producing country, vineyard areas are in the regions of Aleppo, Damascus and Homs.

Syrma (It) a sparkling natural spring mineral water from Boiola, Brescia. Mineral contents (milligrammes per litre): Sodium 1.1mg/l, Potassium 0.3mg/l, Chlorides 0.6mg/l, Sulphates 4.8mg/l. pH 7.9

Syrrah (Fr) another spelling of the Syrah.

Syrupy (Eng) a term used to describe wines that are excessively rich, i.e. Sauternes or very sweet Sherry, Madeira, Port.

System Twenty Four 24 (Eng) a patented unit produced by the Nestlé Cº. which dispenses their instant coffees. Is similar to the automatic drip filter method. Produces up to 22 x 3 pint carafes per filling.

Sytylos (Gre) a natural spring mineral water from Stylos Chania. Mineral contents (milligrammes per litre): Sodium 6.9mg/l, Calcium 32.1mg/l, Magnesium 11.2mg/l, Potassium 0.4mg/l, Bicarbonates 142.8mg/l, Chlorides 14.2mg/l, Sulphates 4.8mg/l, Fluorides 0.11mg/l, Nitrates 0.05mg/l. pH 7.4

Szamorodni (Hun) lit: 'as it comes', a Special-Quality Wine. Made from Furmint and Hárslevelü grapes. Associated with Tokaji wine. Denotes a dry (száraz) or sweet (édes) wine (depending on amount of noble rot present). Aged in Gönc. A flor forms on wine. *See also* Azsú.

Szampan (Pol) Champagne/sparkling wine.

Száraz (Hun) dry.

Száraz Szamorodni (Hun) a dry tasting Szamorodni wine from Tolna.

Szarvas Vineyard (Hun) formerly part of the Hapsberg Imperial Estate. Now a designated Great First Growth for Tokaji Aszú.

Sze Chuan Dah Poo Chiew (Chi) a medicinal wine said to help expectant mothers. From Hwarto.

Szekszàrd (Hun) a wine-producing district in southern Transdanubia, noted for red wines.

Szekszàrdi Kardarka (Hun) a full-bodied red wine produced in the Szekszàrd district.

Szekszàrdi Vörós (Hun) a strong, dark red wine from the Szekszàrd district.

Szemelt (Hun) selected berries. Similar to Auslese.

Szemes (Aus) a winery based in Pinkafeld, Süd-Burgenland. (Add): Weinhoferplatz 7, 7423 Pinkafeld. Grape varieties: Blaufränkisch, Cabernet sauvignon (bought in). Labels: Arachon, Imperial, Tradition.

Szilva (Hun) a spirit distilled from plums.

Szilvàni (Hun) an alternative name for the Sylvaner grape. *See also* Szilvanyi.

Szilvàni Zöld (Hun) *see* Szilvanyi Zöld.

Szilvany (Hun) sylvaner.

Szilvanyi Zöld (Hun) lit: 'green sylvaner', a medium-dry, white wine which has a soft bouquet and a green tinge. Made from the Sylvaner grape.

Szilva Pàlinka (Hun) a plum brandy produced in Szatmar County. Is also known as Szilvorium.

Szilvorium (Hun) *see* Szilva Pàlinka.

Szomerodny (Hun) a white table wine.

Szürkebarát (Hun) lit: 'grey friar', a white grape variety grown around Lake Balaton in the Badacsonyi area. Produces sweetish wines of the same name. Known as the Pinot gris in France.

T

T (S.Afr) the label for a noble late harvest white wine (Chenin blanc) produced by the Ken Forrester Wines winery, Stellenbosch, Western Cape.

T.A. (Gre) *abbr:* **T**raditional **A**ppellation.

Taba (Ind) a roadside café in the Punjab which sells hot and cold beverages and light snacks.

Tabali (Chile) a winery based in the Limarí region of northern Chile. Website: http://www.sanpedro.cl

Tabanon Distillery (W.Ind) a noted rum distillery based on the island of Guadeloupe.

Tabarrini Giampaolo (It) a winery in the DOCG Sagrantino di Montefalco, Umbria region.

Tabatha the Knackered (Eng) a 6% alc by vol. strong ale brewed by the Anglo Dutch Brewery, West Yorkshire.

Tab Clear (Eng) a brand-name of a sugar-free, clear diet cola from C.C.S.B.

Tabereiro (Port) publican/tavern-owner.

Taberna (Sp) tavern/inn/public house.

Tabisco (S.Afr) the label for a range of wines for the Danish market produced by the Nordale Winery, Robertson, Western Cape.

Tablas Creek (USA) a winery based in Paso Robles district, San Luis Obispo County, California. (Add): 9339 Adelaida Road, Paso Robles, CA 93446. Grape varieties: Counoise, Grenache noir, Mourvèdre, Petite syrah. Produces Rhône-style wines. Website: http://www.tablascreek.com

Table Beer (Eng) a term for a dinner ale/bottled beers.

Table de Trie (Fr) the name given to the table used to sort out the grapes when practising triage.

Tablespoon (USA) a bar-measure which equals ½ fl.oz (10mls). Imp: ⅜ fl.oz USA: 3 level teaspoons.

Table Water (Eng) natural or manufactured mineral waters, drunk on their own (or as mixers), usually low in minerals and alkaline. e.g. Aix-le-Chapelle, Apollinaris, Buxton, Malvern, Perrier and St. Galmier.

Table Wines (Eng) wines for everyday drinking, not for laying down, usually light and of no quality status, are suitable for drinking at the table with food. (Aus) = tafelwein, (Fr) = vin de table, (Ger) = tafelwein, (It) = vino da tavola, (Port) = vinho de mesa, (Sp) = vino de mesa, (Wal) = tafelwyn.

Tabontinaja (Chile) a winery based in the Loncomilla Valley (part of Maule Valley), noted for wines produced from Cabernet franc grapes.

Taboo (Eng) an exotic fruit, white wine and vodka-based drink 14% alc by vol. produced jointly by a William Grant subsidiary and Bulmers subsidiary.

Taboo Blue (Eng) a vodka, pineapple and tropical fruit juices 14.9% alc by vol. produced jointly by a William Grant subsidiary and Bulmers subsidiary

Tàbor Brewery (Czec) an old brewery (established 1612) based in western Czec.

Tabor Hill Vineyard (USA) a vineyard based in Berrien County, Michigan, produces: vinifera and hybrid wines.

Taburno (It) a D.O.C. red wine produced from Aglianico grapes in Southern Italy.

Tacama Gran Blanco (S.Am) a white wine from Ica Valley, Peru. Produced from Chenin blanc and Ugni blanc grapes.

Tacchetto (It) a vineyard (5ha) based in the D.O.C. Bardolino produced by Conti Guerrieri Rizzardi in Bardolino, Verona.

Tachar (Port) lit: 'to get drunk', to go on a binge.

Taché (Fr) lit: 'stained', a malady found in white wines when they obtain a slight rosé colour. Are treated with sulphuric acid.

Tâche [La] (Fr) a Grand Cru vineyard in the A.C. commune of Vosne-Romanée, Côte de Nuits, Burgundy 6ha.

Tâcheron (Fr) a piece worker, a term often used in the Côte d'Or for someone who is tending another persons vines.

Tachino (Bra) a cachaça drink produced from sugar-cane. Imported into the U.K. by Teacher.

Ta Chu (Chi) a grain spirit produced in Szechwan.

Tacoronte-Acentejo (Sp) a D.O. on the island of Tenerife, Canary Islands. Produces light, fruity red wines from Listán Negro, Negramoll. White from Malvasía, Listán blanco, Moscatel blanco. Rosado wines also produced.

Tacorontes (Sp) another name used for the 'mountain' wines.

Tadcaster Bitter (Eng) a cask-conditioned bitter beer 1035 O.G. brewed by the Samuel Smith Brewery in Tadcaster, Yorkshire.

Taddy Ales (Eng) a name used by the Samuel Smith Brewery in Tadcaster, Yorkshire for their beers.

Taddy Porter (Eng) a 5% alc by vol. porter from Samuel Smith Brewery, Tadcaster, Yorkshire. *See also* Imperial Stout.

Tadzhikistan (Rus) a wine-producing area in Armenia, noted for dessert wines, also the name for a red, Port-style wine.

Tae (Ire) tea (drink).

Taechiteal (Ire) tea kettle.

Taeniotic (Egy) an aromatic, sweet, greenish-white

wine produced in the second century A.D. near Alexandria. Was enjoyed by Athenaeus.

Taephota (Ire) tea pot.

Taetta (Scan) an alcoholic beverage fermented from milk (similar to Koumiss).

Tafarn (Wal) inn.

Tafarnwr (Wal) innkeeper.

Tafel Akvavit (Scan) a clean tasting caraway-flavoured akvavit 45% alc by vol.

Tafelaquavit (Scan) see Tafel Akvavit.

Tafelstein (Ger) vineyard (Anb): Rheinhessen. (Ber): Nierstein. (Gro): Güldenmorgen. (Vil): Dienheim.

Tafelwein (Aus) table wine, must have a minimum must weight of 10.6° KMW.

Tafelwein (Ger) a blend of wines from E.C. countries. see Aus Ländern der EWG. Deutscher Tafelwein is from German wines only.

Tafelweingebiete (Ger) consists of four designated table wine regions: Bayern, Neckar, Oberrhein, Rhein-Mosel. Minimum must weight is 50°Oe for Oberrhein, 44°Oe for others.

Tafelwyn (S.Afr) table wine.

Taffea (W.Ind) the alternative spelling of Tafia.

Taffia (W.Ind) the alternative spelling of Tafia.

Taffy Apple (Wal) a 6% alc by vol. strong Celtic cider from Hurns of Swansea. See also Hazy Dayz.

Tafia (Egy) a spirit distilled from sugar, usually high in alcohol (over 60% by vol).

Tafia (S.Am) the ancient negro word for rum, nowadays it is a dark spirit produced from inferior molasses (impure) in Guyana.

Tafia Habitant (W.Ind) a local fiery spirit made from sugar cane juice.

Tafia Industriel (W.Ind) a spirit obtained from molasses.

Tafski (Wal) a vodka produced by the Brecon Brewery, Powys, Mid-Wales, made with local spring water.

Tag Lag (Eng) a 4.4% alc by vol. ale brewed by the Barngates Brewery Ltd., Cumbria.

Tagler (Aus) a vineyard site based on the banks of the River Kamp situated in the Kamptal region.

Taglio (It) blended wine.

Tagus [River] (Port) see River Tejo.

Tahammür (Tur) fermentation.

Tahbilk (Austr) a wine estate based in Victoria, produces red and white wines. see Château Tahbilk.

Tahiti Club Cocktail (Cktl) ½ measure white rum, ⅙ measure lemon juice, ⅙ measure lime juice, ⅙ measure pineapple juice, 2 dashes maraschino. Shake well over ice, strain into an ice-filled old-fashioned glass and add a slice of lemon.

Tahsiang-Pin-Chiu (Chi) a sparkling wine.

Tai-Ara-Rau Wines (N.Z) a 2.5ha wine-making training institution (Add): Rural Studies Unit, Stout Street, (P.O. Box 640), Gisborne.

Taifi (Rus) a red grape variety grown in Tadzhikistan. Produces fine Port-style wines.

Taiga World (Can) a natural spring mineral water brand. Mineral contents (milligrammes per litre): Sodium 1.22mg/l, Chlorides 2.59mg/l, Sulphates 6.2mg/l, Nitrates 1.32mg/l. pH 7.74

Tail Box (USA) part of a gin still, retains the 'tails', the unwanted congeners from the spirit.

Tailings (Fr) the ends of the distillation which are removed after the 'heart' of the distillation has been taken. See also Heads.

Taillan [Le] (Fr) a commune in the A.C. Haut-Médoc, north-western Bordeaux.

Taille à Quarante (Fr) a style of vine training on the 'double guyot' line used in the Hérault département, is used to produce large crops of grapes.

Taille Chablis (Fr) a method of vine training in which 3, 4 or 5 main branches are trained parallel to the ground. Each is pruned to either 4 or 5 buds.

Taille en Archet (Fr) a style of vine training used in the northern Rhône where the vines are trained along sticks in a tepee shape.

Taillefine (Fr) a natural spring mineral water brand.

Taille-Genre Bordelaise (Fr) a method of vine training which consists of forming a stem with 2 main branches each bearing at least 2 short shoots (cocques courtes).

Taille Guyot (Fr) see Guyot.

Taille-Pieds (Fr) a Premier Cru vineyard in the A.C. commune of Volnay, Côte de Beaune, Burgundy.

Tailles (Fr) the remaining pressings in Champagne after the Tête de Cuvée has been removed.

Taillevent (Fr) a Champagne producer. (Add): Domaine des Conardins, 51530 Moussy 24ha.

Tails (Fr) see Tailings.

Tailspin (Cktl) ⅓ measure dry gin, ⅓ measure Italian vermouth, ⅓ measure green Chartreuse, 1 dash Campari. Stir over ice, strain into a cocktail glass, top with a twist of lemon peel juice and a cherry.

Tai Mai (Chi) a natural spring mineral water brand.

Taión (Sp) a style of Albariza soil in the Sherry region, has a high lime content.

Tairnbach (Ger) village (Anb): Baden. (Ber): Badische Bergstrasse/Kraichgau. (Gro): Mannaberg. (Vin): Rosenberg.

Taissy (Fr) a Premier Cru Champagne village in the Canton de Reims. District: Reims.

Taittinger (Fr) a Champagne producer. (Add): 9 Place Saint-Nicaise, B.P. 2741, 51100 Reims Cedex. 280ha. A Grande Marque. Produces vintage and non-vintage wines. Vintages: 1934, 1937, 1941, 1943, 1945, 1947, 1949, 1950, 1952, 1953, 1955, 1959, 1961, 1962, 1964, 1966, 1969, 1970, 1971, 1973, 1975, 1976, 1978, 1979, 1980, 1981, 1982, 1983, 1985, 1986, 1988, 1989, 1990, 1995, 1996, 1998, 1999, 2000. Produces: de luxe vintage cuvée Comte de Champagne (Blanc de Blancs and Rosé), Brut Réserve, Prestige Rosé and Prélude Grand Crus. Second label is Irroy. Owns Domaine Carneros in USA. Website: http://www.taittinger.com

Taiwan Brewery (Tai) a brewery based on the island of Taiwan that brews Taiwan beer.

Tàjbor (Hun) country wine.

Tajo [River] (Port) see River Tejo.

Tajón (Sp) a type of Albariza soil in Jerez, is high in

limestone. The soil is too hard for the vines which suffer from chlorosis if grown in it.

Tajut (It) an apéritif from Friuli.

Takara Shuzo (Jap) a company who, along with the Okura C°. have acquired the Tomatin Distillery in Scotland.

Takelsa (Afr) a co-operative winery based in Tunisia. Belongs to the UCCVT. Noted for rosé wines.

Taketia (Geo) a wine-producing region in Georgia that produces fine red and white wines.

Take to Drink (Eng) as for 'take to the bottle'.

Take to the Bottle (Eng) a term to denote a person who has resigned themselves to drinking alcoholic liquor to try and forget their problems.

Taki-Taki Spicy Tomato Cocktail (Mex) a brand of alcohol-free cocktail imported by Leisure Drinks in the U.K.

Talagante (Chile) a wine-producing area based near Santiago.

Talana Hill Vineyard (S.Afr) a vineyard based in Stellenbosch, Western Cape (part of the Vriesenhof Vineyards). Grape variety: Chardonnay.

Talbot [John] (Eng) the Earl of Shrewsbury. Commander of the English Expedition force who were defeated at the battle of Castillion in 1453 when the English lost Bordeaux.

Talbot Knightwick Ltd (Eng) the old name for the Teme Valley Brewery.

Talca (Chile) a province and wine-producing area in the Central Zone.

Talence (Fr) a commune within the A.C. Graves district of south-western Bordeaux.

Talento Metodo Classico (It) a bottle-fermented sparkling wine. See also Metodo Tradizionale, Classimò.

Talha (Port) a clay pot used to ferment wine in Alentejo.

Talheim (Ger) village (Anb): Württemberg. (Ber): Württembergisch Unterland. (Gro): Kirchenweinberg. (Vins): Hohe Eiche, Schlossberg, Sonnenberg.

Talheim (Ger) village (Anb): Württemberg. (Ber): Württembergisch Unterland. (Gro): Staufenberg. (Vin): Stiftsberg.

Talia (Port) a neutral flavoured white grape grown in the Ribatejo and Setúbal regions. Also spelt Thalia. (It) = Trebbiano.

Talians (Fr) a natural spring mineral water brand.

Talisker (Scot) a single highland malt whisky distillery (established 1830) in Carbost, Isle of Skye. Owned by John Walker and Sons (part of the DCL group). Produces an 8, 10, 12 and 15 year old malts 40%–45% alc by vol. also a 45.8% alc by vol. 175 year Anniversary malt (bottled 2005).

Talisman (Eng) a winter ale 5% alc by vol (1048 O.G) brewed by the Pilgrim Brewery in Woldingham, Surrey.

Talisman (Eng) a low-alcohol lager 0.9% alc by vol. brewed by the Charles Wells Brewery.

Talisman Cocktail (Cktl) ¼ measure white rum, ¼ measure golden rum, ¼ measure Grand Marnier, ¼ measure vodka, juice ¼ lime, 1 measure pear juice. Shake over ice, strain into a cocktail glass, dress with a cherry, slice of lime and mint sprig.

Taljanska Grasevina (Slo) a local name for the Welschriesling grape.

Talley Vineyards (USA) a 42.5ha winery based in the Arroyo Grande Valley (near Santa Barbara County). (Add): 3031 Lopez Drive, Arroyo Grande, CA 93420. Grape varieties: Chardonnay, Pinot noir. Website: http://www.talleyvineyards.com

Tall Fount (Scot) a tall pillar-tap situated on a bar counter which dispenses most traditional beers in Scotland. The beer is driven to the fount by either air pressure or electric pump.

Tall Sour (Cktl) as for a Sour but is served in a highball glass with ice and topped with soda water.

Tállya (Hun) a noted wine-producing village based in the southern foothills.

Tally Ho (Eng) a 5.5% alc by vol (1046 O.G) cask-conditioned summer ale brewed by the Palmer Brewery in Bridport, Dorset.

Tally Ho Barley Wine (Eng) a barley wine 1075 O.G. brewed and bottled by Adnams' Sole Bay Brewery in Southwold, Suffolk.

Talmettes [Les] (Fr) a Premier Cru vineyard in the A.C. commune of Savigny-lès-Beaune, Côte de Beaune, Burgundy.

Taltarni Vineyard (Austr) a winery. (Add): Moonambel, Victoria 3478. 110ha. Grape varieties: Cabernet franc, Cabernet sauvignon, Chardonnay, Chenin blanc, Malbec, Merlot, Rhine riesling and Shiraz. Produces both varietal and sparkling wines. Labels: Heathcote Vineyard and Pyrenees.

Talus-Saint-Prix (Fr) a Cru Champagne village in the Canton of Montmort. District: Épernay.

TAM (Eng) abbr: Tea After Meals.

Tamagozake (Cktl) 150mls (6fl.ozs) saké, 1 egg, 1 teaspoon sugar, boil the saké, ignite, remove from heat, stir in beaten egg and sugar and pour into a mug.

Tamar (Eng) a cask-conditioned ale 1039 O.G. brewed by home-brew public house The Royal Inn in Horsebridge, Devon.

Tamar (Eng) a 4.3% alc by vol. ale brewed by the Summerskills Brewery, Plymouth, Devon.

Tamara (Isr) a liqueur made from dates.

Tamarak (USA) a winery based in the Columbia Valley, Washington State. Grape varieties include: Syrah.

Tamarez (Port) a white grape variety grown in Lafões and Alentejo. Also known as the Trincadeira das Pratas.

Tarmar Ridge (Austr) a winery based in Tasmania. (Add): 653 Auburn Road, Kayena 7270 Tasmania. Grape varieties include: Chardonnay, Riesling, Sauvignon blanc. Label: Devils Corner. Website: http://www.tamarridgewines.com.au

Tamar Valley (Austr) one of five main wine producing areas in Tasmania, accounts for 25% of production.

Tamar Valley Vineyard (Austr) a winery. (Add): Foreshore Road, Deviot, Tasmania 7251. 35ha. Grape varieties: Cabernet sauvignon, Chardonnay, Müller-Thurgau and Pinot noir.

Tamay (S.Afr) the label for a sparkling white wine (Chardonnay, Hanepoot and Riesling blend) produced by the Rhebokskloof Private Cellar winery, Noorder-Paarl, Western Cape.

Tamboerskloof (S.Afr) the label for red wine (Shiraz) produced by the Kleinood winery, Stellenbosch, Western Cape.

Tamburlaine (Austr) a small vineyard based in New South Wales.

Tamdhu (Scot) a single highland malt whisky distillery based at Knockando, Banffshire (owned by the Highland Distilleries Cº. PLC). Produces a 10 year old malt 43% alc by vol.

Tamdhu-Glenlivet (Scot) *see* Tamdhu.

Tamebridge (Fr) a pale keg bitter from Allied Breweries.

Tamega (Port) a brand of full-flavoured Vinho Verde.

Tamerici (It) a natural spring mineral water from Pistoia.

Tamianka (Bul) a very sweet white wine.

Tamîioasa (Rum) a local name for the Muscat grape.

Tamîioasa Alba (Rum) a local name for the Muscat Blanc à Petits Grains grape.

Tamîioasa Hamburg (Rum) a local name for the Muscat Hamburg grape. *See also* Tamîioasa Neagra.

Tamîioasa Neagra (Rum) a local name for the Muscat Hamburg grape. *See also* Tamîioasa Hamburg.

Tamîioasa Ottonel (Rum) a local name for the Muscat Ottonel grape.

Tamîioasa Româneasca (Rum) a white grape variety also known as the Muscat of Hamburg. (Bul) = Tamianka, (Ger) = Weihrauchtraube.

Taminga (Aust) a white grape variety.

Taminick Cellars (Austr) a winery. (Add): Taminick via Glenrowan, Victoria 3675. 17ha. Grape varieties: Alicanté bouschet, Cabernet sauvignon, Shiraz and Trebbiano.

Tamnavulin-Glenlivet (Scot) a single highland malt whisky distillery based in Ballindalloch, Banffshire. Operated by Longman Distillers of Glasgow (part of Invergordon group). Produces an 8 year old 43% alc by vol. and a 10 year old 40% alc by vol.

Tamor (Asia) a natural spring mineral water from Nepal.

Tampico (Cktl) ½ measure Cointreau, ½ measure Campari, 2 dashes lemon juice. Stir over ice, strain into a Paris goblet, top with tonic water, a cherry and an orange slice.

Tamplins Bitter (Eng) a cask-conditioned bitter 1038 O.G. brewed by the Watney Mann, Truman Breweries.

Tamyanka (Rus) an alternative name for Muscat Blanc à Petits Grains grape.

Tanagra Private Cellar (S.Afr) a winery (established 2000) based in McGregor, Western Cape. 12ha. Grape varieties: Cabernet franc, Cabernet sauvignon, Chardonnay, Merlot, Pinotage, Shiraz. Labels: Carah, Felicity, Heavenly Chaos.

Tañama (Mex) a wine-producing region in the Baja California.

Tanat (Fr) an alternative spelling for the Tannat grape.

Tanbark Hill Vineyard (USA) a winery based in the Napa Valley, California. Grape varieties: Cabernet **sauvignon.**

Tanchão (Port) the name for a stake used to support a vine.

Tanduay (E.Ind) a leading brand of rum produced in the Philippine Islands.

Tang Emperor (Chi) a natural spring mineral water brand. Mineral contents (milligrammes per litre): Sodium 432mg/l, Calcium 87.3mg/l, Magnesium 14.6mg/l, Potassium 71.5mg/l, Bicarbonates 351.2mg/l, Silicates 107mg/l.

Tangerinette (Fr) a tangerine-flavoured liqueur, red in colour.

Tanglefoot Ale (Eng) a cask-conditioned strong ale 1048 O.G. brewed by the Hall and Woodhouse Brewery in Blandford Forum, Dorset.

Tanglewood Downs (Austr) a winery (established 1984). (Add): Bulldog Creek Road, Mornington Rural, Victoria. Grape varieties: Cabernet sauvignon, Chardonnay, Pinot noir, Riesling, Traminer.

Tango (Cktl). ½ measure gin, ¼ measure sweet vermouth, ¼ measure dry vermouth, 2 dashes orange Curaçao, dash orange juice. Shake over ice and strain into a cocktail glass.

Tango (Eng) a brand of carbonated soft drink produced by Britvic Corona. Flavours include: apple, blackcurrant, lemon, orange, tropical, grapefruit or pineapple.

Tangy (Eng) a descriptive term for wines with a zesty bouquet and an after-taste of an old Sherry or Madeira.

Tanisage (Fr) the practice of adding tannin to wines to increase the astringency.

Tankard (Eng) a jug or mug made out of glass, pewter or other material for beers (½ pint, 1pint, ½ litre or 1litre capacity).

Tankard Bitter (Austr) a high gravity lager 4.4% alc by vol. brewed by the Courage Brewery in Victoria.

Tankard Bitter (Eng) a keg bitter 1037 O.G. brewed by the Whitbread Breweries.

Tank Beer (Eng) brewery-conditioned beers delivered by road tanker to the public house and pumped into large disposable polythene bag-lined tanks in the cellar (90 or 180 gallon capacity), beer is dispensed to the bar pumps by air pressure.

Tankfull (Eng) a slang term for having had too much to drink/drunk/intoxicated.

Tannacker (Ger) vineyard (Anb): Baden. (Ber): Kaiserstuhl-Tuniberg. (Gro): Vulkanfelsen. (Vil): Endingen.

Tannat (Fr) a local red grape variety grown in the Madiran district of south-west France and Cahors that produces full-bodied wines. Known in Uruguay as the Harriague. *See also* Bordeleza, Belch, Moustrou and Tanat.

Tannate Film (Eng) finings and tannin which together form an insoluble film which slowly precipitates, acting as a filter which cleans the wine as it sinks to the bottom of the cask or vat.

Tannenberg (Ger) vineyard (Anb): Franken. (Ber): Steigerwald. (Gro): Schlosstück. (Vil): Hüttenheim.

Tannenkirch (Ger) village (Anb): Baden. (Ber): Markgräflerland. (Gro): Vogtei Rötteln. (Vin): Steingässle.

Tanner Bitter (Eng) a bitter ale brewed by Burts Brewery, Isle of Wight. Name derived from the six old pence (2.5 new pence) that the brewery paid for their water.

Tanner's Jack [The] (Eng) a 4.4% alc by vol. cask (and bottled) bitter brewed by Greene King. Formerly part of the Morland portfolio. Named after the tanners who supply the leathers for the ancient drinking vessels known as Jacks (known as Berkshire Best Bitter during its trial), a seasonal ale, it is available from January to April.

Tanners Wine Ltd. (Eng) a noted, old established, wine merchants based in Shrewsbury, Shropshire. Deal in fine wines, spirits and beers. *see* Mariscal.

Tannic (Eng) the term to describe a red wine that has excessive tannin.

Tànnico (It) tannic.

Tannin (Eng) $C_{76}H_{52}O_{46}$ tannic acid, an astringent acid in red wine found in the stalk, pips and skin of the grapes, also found in tea giving colour and bitterness. May be added to a wine to increase its structure. *See also* Cask Tannins and Grape Seed Tannins.

Tannisage (Fr) an alternative spelling of Tanisage.

Tanqueray (Eng) the brand-name of a dry gin produced by Charles Tanqueray and C°., Groswell Road, London. Part of the Distillers C°. Ltd.

Tanqueray London Dry (Eng) the brand-name of a dry gin produced by Charles Tanqueray and C°., Groswell Road, London 47.3% alc by vol.

Tansy (Eng) *see* Mugwort.

Tantale (Fr) tantalus.

Tantalus (Eng) a case for holding decanters, usually the decanters are visible but are locked so that the contents are secure (eighteenth and nineteenth century). (Fr) = tantale.

Tantalus Cocktail (Cktl) ⅓ measure brandy, ⅓ measure Forbidden fruit liqueur, ⅓ measure lemon juice. Shake over ice and strain into a cocktail glass.

Tanunda (Austr) a winery, part of the Masterton Estate in South Australia.

Tanus Mountains (Ger) a mountain range that protects the Rheinhessen and southern Rheingau from the northerly winds.

Tanzania (Afr) has a wine-producing region at Dodoma. Produces two vintages each year: August/September and December/January.

Tanzania Breweries (Afr) a brewery based in Tanzania, noted for Snow Cap Lager.

Tanzanian Coffee (Afr) produces a fruity-flavoured coffee from a mixture of Robustas and Arabicas. Most are coarse and low in acidity, used for blending (light bodied). *See also* Kibo Chagga.

Tanzanian Teas (Afr) African teas used mainly for blending.

Tap (Eng) found on beer casks, is driven into the keystone, made of wood or metal (*see* Beer-Tap). Also an expression used for connections to any form of beer container.

Tapadura (Sp) stopper.

Tap Ales (Eng) beers drawn from a cask or keg.

Tapanappa (Austr) a winery based in South Australia. Grape varieties: Cabernet sauvignon, Shiraz. Label: Whale Bone Vineyard.

Tap and Spile (Eng) a 4.3% alc by vol. cask-conditioned or bottled premium ale commissioned from Mansfield Brewery by Pubmaster.

Tapas (Sp) a lid of bread placed over a wine glass to keep out flies (also snacks served in bars).

Tapatio Blanco (Mex) the name of a tequila produced in a family run Mexican distillery.

Tap Beer (USA) draught beer.

Tap Bitter (Eng) a bitter ale brewed by the Truman's Brewery in Brick Lane (part of Watney Mann, Truman Brewers).

Tapestry Wines Ltd. (Eng) vineyards (established 1979) based at Wells Farm, Appurley, Gloucestershire and The Vineyard, Ampeney Crucis, Gloucestershire. 2.2ha. Grape varieties: Madeleine angevine, Müller-Thurgau, Reichensteiner and Seyval blanc.

Tap House (Eng) the name in the eighteenth and nineteenth centuries for an inn, bar or public house.

Tapio (Fin) a herb and juniper-flavoured liqueur 29% alc by vol. Produced by Lignell and Piispanen.

Tapón (Sp) cork/stopper.

Tapotage (Fr) the lifting of the bottle and allowing it to drop back into place again during the remuage process of Champagne, between tournage and remuage.

Tappaïe (Ch.Isles) a drinking bout.

Tappare (It) a cork or plug for a bottle or cask.

Tapping (Eng) *see* Broach.

Tappit-Hen (Scot) a bottle which holds 3 imperial quarts which is equivalent to 4½ reputed quarts. Used for whisky. Also an old Bordeaux bottle of same capacity.

Tappit Hen (Scot) the name for a pewter tankard in the nineteenth century which had a lid with a distinctive knob on top.

Tappo (It) cork/stopper.

Tap Room (Eng) a public bar where the customers were able to buy beers drawn from the cask stillaged behind the bar. (Fr) = salle à bière.

Tapster (Afr) a person who makes and sells Palm wine.

Tapster (Eng) the name for a barman in the nineteenth century.

T

Tapster's Choice (Eng) a range of cask-conditioned guest ales from Carlsberg-Tetley. Range includes: Black Baron, Bombardier, Footlights Ale, Gamekeeper's Autumn Ale, Houdini Ale.

Taps Too (Eng) *see* Tattoo.

Taptemelk (Hol) skimmed milk.

Taptoe (Hol) lit: 'shut taps' a seventeenth century military command to stop serving beer. *see* Tattoo.

Tapuy (E.Ind) a spirit distilled from rice and corn.

Tapuzza Coffee (W.Ind) a mild type of coffee produced in Costa Rica, popular at breakfast time.

Tap Water (Eng) denotes water from the domestic supply/drinking water. (Fr) = eau de robinet.

Tap Water Cocktail (Cktl) ½ measure dry din, ½ measure triple sec. Shake well over ice, strain into an ice-filled highball glass, top with lemonade and slice of lemon.

Tap Water Geneva – Eau du Lac (Switz) a bottled natural mineral water from Geneva. Mineral contents (milligrammes per litre): Sodium 7.7mg/l, Calcium 46.6mg/l, Magnesium 6.1mg/l, Potassium 1.4mg/l, Chlorides 9.5mg/l, Sulphates 46.6mg/l, Fluorides 0.16mg/l, Nitrates 2.6mg/l. pH 8.16

Tap Water Geneva – Réseau Arve (Switz) a bottled natural mineral water from Geneva. Mineral contents (milligrammes per litre): Sodium 6mg/l, Calcium 67.4mg/l, Magnesium 12.5mg/l, Potassium 1.5mg/l, Chlorides 16mg/l, Sulphates 53.9mg/l, Fluorides 0.16mg/l, Nitrates 4.9mg/l. pH 7.96

Tap Water Geneva – Réseau Nappe (Switz) a bottled natural mineral water from Geneva. Mineral contents (milligrammes per litre): Sodium 7.2mg/l, Calcium 91.9mg/l, Magnesium 19.4mg/l, Potassium 1.7mg/l, Chlorides 15.4mg/l, Sulphates 49.6mg/l, Fluorides 0.16mg/l, Nitrates 18.3mg/l. pH 7.7

Tap Water Munich (Ger) a bottled still mineral water from Munich. Mineral contents (milligrammes per litre): Sodium 3.6mg/l, Calcium 81.2mg/l, Magnesium 20mg/l, Potassium 1mg/l, Bicarbonates 298mg/l, Chlorides 5.9mg/l, Sulphates 28.9mg/l, Fluorides 0.1mg/l, Nitrates 8.1mg/l.

Tap Water Zurich (Switz) a bottled still natural water from Zurich. Mineral contents (milligrammes per litre): Sodium 5.2mg/l, Calcium 54mg/l, Magnesium 7.5mg/l, Bicarbonates 798.1mg/l, Sulphates 16mg/l, Fluorides 0.1mg/l, Nitrates 5mg/l.

Tap Wine (Austr) house wine, usually served from the cask.

Tap Wine (Eng) cask wines sold from the cask in cafés, inns etc.

Tar (Eng) used to preserve and hide 'off' flavours in wines in early times, also aroma that is found in some Barolo wines.

Tara (S.Afr) the label for a range of wines (Cabernet sauvignon/Sauvignon blanc) produced by the Southern Sky Wines winery, Paarl, Western Cape.

Taraesongkot (Kor) corkscrew.

Tarapacá Estate (Chile) a winery (established 1874) based in the Maipo Valley. Grape varieties: Merlot, Sauvignon blanc. Labels: Triunfo and Viña Taracapá.

Tarcal (Hun) a noted wine-producing village based in the southern foothills.

Tarcoola Winery (Austr) a winery (established 1971) based in Geelong, Victoria. Produces varietal and table wines from Cabernet sauvignon, Shiraz, Müller-Thurgau, Riesling.

Tarcoronte (Sp) the main wine-producing district on the island of Tenerife.

Tardania (Sp) an alternative name for the white Planta nova grape.

Tarefa de Barro (Port) a large earthenware container for fermenting wine.

Tarentinum (It) a red wine produced in south-eastern Italy in Roman times.

Targa Riserva 1840 (It) a superiore riserva Marsala produced by Cantine Fiorio, Sicily 19% alc by vol.

Targe (Fr) the brand-name for vinyl acetate corks.

Target (Eng) a disease resistant English hop variety high in acids.

Targon (Fr) a commune in Haut-Benauge, Entre-Deux-Mers, central Bordeaux.

Târgovichte (Bul) a wine-producing area in the eastern region, mainly white wines.

Tarik (Afr) a full-bodied red wine produced in the A.O.G. region of Beni M'Tir, Morocco. Made from Carignan, Cinsault and Grenache grapes. Bottled by CVM.

Tarka Ales Ltd (Eng) a brewery (established 2003). (Add): Yelland Manor Farm, Fremlington, Barnstable, Devon EX31 3DT. Brews: Challenge 4.2% alc by vol., Henry Williamson 4.8% alc by vol., Instow Gold 3.8% alc by vol., Premier Crew 4.3% alc by vol., Ruby Trale 3.9% alc by vol. 'E'mail: tarka-ales@instow.net

Tarlant (Fr) a Champagne producer (established 1687). (Add): 51480 Oeuilly. Vintage: 1996, 1997, 1999, 2000. Website: http://www.tarlant.com 'E'mail: champagne@tarlant.com

Tarnavale (Rum) a wine-producing region based in the Siebenbürgen district.

Tarnavelle (It) a wine commune of Chianti Classico Riserva.

Tarn-et-Garonne (Fr) a Vin de Pays area in the Tarn-et-Garonne département of south-western France. Includes the area of Saint-Sardos.

Tarniówka (Pol) a sloe-flavoured spirit.

Tarouca (Port) a white grape variety grown in the Dão region.

Tarquinio Lomelino (Mad) Madeira shippers that are noted for their antique wines. Use the label: Dom Henriques for their standard range of Madeiras.

Tarragona (Sp) a Denominación de Origen wine district of Cataluña, south-eastern Spain. 18422ha. Sub-zones: Tarragona Campo and Falset. Falset is further divided into Comarca de Falset and Ribera del Ebro. Grape varieties: Cariñena, Garnacha blanca, Garnacha tinta, Macabeo,

T

Parellada, Ull de llebre (Tempranillo), Xarel-lo, Cabernet sauvignon, Chardonnay, Merlot, Muscat. D.O. recognises 5 types of wine: Tarragona Campo White (dry white at 11%–13% alc by vol.) Tarragona Campo Rosado (dry rosé from Garnacha plus Cariñena/Ull de llebre at 11%–13% alc by vol.) Tarragona Campo Red (Red at 11%–13% alc by vol.) Falset Red (Garnacha and Cariñena, 11%–13% alc by vol.) Tarragona Clásico Licoroso (100% Garnacha at a minimum of 13.5% alc by vol.) Rancio wines (from Garnacha plus 10%–20% Cariñena at 14% alc by vol.)

Tarragona Campo (Sp) red, rosé and white table wines from the Tarragona district. Made by natural fermentation which differs to the Clásico Licoroso.

Tarragona Clásico Licoroso (Sp) a dessert white wine from Tarragona district. Made by subjecting the must to very high temperatures, this quickly oxidises it. The wine is then stored in glass vessels open to the air or oak vats of less than 2000litres for 12 years.

Tarragona Port (Sp) a fortified wine from the Tarragona district. Was sold as Tarragona Port in the USA but now the use of the word Port is banned by international law. In Spain is known as Priorato.

Tarragone (Fr) a name for green Chartreuse which the Carthusian monks used in Spain whilst in exile in 1903.

Tarrango (Austr) a light red (Tarrango) wine produced by the Brown Brothers Estate winery, Milawa, Victoria.

Tarrango (Austr) a red grape variety, a cross between Portuguese Touriga and Sultana grapes. Produces light dry red wines.

TarraWarra Estate (Austr) a winery at Healesville Road, Yarra Glen, Victoria 3775. Grape varieties: Chardonnay, Pinot noir. Label: Tin Cow. Website: http://www.tarrawarra.com.au

Tart (Eng) a term to describe sharp, acid wines.

Tartan Bitter (Scot) a keg/canned bitter beer 1036 O.G. brewed by the William Younger Brewery. (Part of Scottish and Newcastle).

Tartar (Eng) *Potassium hydrogen*, also known as argol, the deposit left behind during the fermentation of wine.

Tartaric Acid (Eng) COOH CHOH CHOH CHOH the main acid found in wine. Can be added to wine to adjust pH (acidity levels). see Tartrate Crystals. (Fr) = acide tartrique.

Tartarophtorum (Lat) a wine spoilage bacteria. see Toume.

Tartesio (Sp) a solera gran reserva brandy produced by José Esteve. See also Don Feliz, Tutor (El).

Tartrate Crystals (Eng) *Potassium hydrogen tartrate* found in wines that have been stored at very cold temperatures. The crystals are harmless and will usually disappear if the wine is brought to room temperature. Tend to soften the wine if removed by lowering the wine's acidity.

Tarula Farms (USA) a vineyard based in Clarksville, Ohio. Produces hybrid and varietal wines.

Tarw Du (Wal) a 4.5% alc by vol. bitter ale brewed by the Bragdy Ynys Mon, Gwynedd.

Tarwin Ridge (Austr) a winery. (Add): Wintle's Road, Leongatha, South Victoria. Grape varieties include: Cabernet, Pinot noir, Merlot, Fumé blanc.

Tasca (It) a rare grape found only on the Regaleali Winery, Sicily. Is thought to be a version of the Sauvignon, also known as the Tasca d'Almerita.

Tascas (Port)(Sp) bars where food and drink are sold in the Andalusian region of south-west Spain and in Portugal.

Tasche 1888 (Ger) a steinhäger produced by Tasche GmbH., Steinhägen.

Tasheimer Goldtröpfchen (S.Afr) a medium-sweet, fruity white wine made from a blend of the Clairette blanche and Steen grapes. Produced by the S.F.W.

Taskelder Wines (S.Afr) a range of varietal wines produced by the Stellenbosch Farmers' Winery.

Tasman Creek (N.Z) a winery based in Marlborough, South Island. Grape variety: Sauvignon blanc.

Tasmania (Austr) an island south of Australia. Split into the 5 main wine producing regions of: South-Hobart-Derwent Valley Area 5%, Coal River Area 8%, Tamar Valley 25%, East Coast 10%, Pipers Brook 52%. Vineyards include Pipers Brook, Moorilla Estate, Heemskerk. Noted for fine sparkling wine production.

Tasmanian Highland Spring Waters (Austr) a natural spring mineral water from Tasmania. Mineral contents (milligrammes per litre): Sodium 9.7mg/l, Calcium 13mg/l, Magnesium 8.7mg/l, Potassium 0.48mg/l, Chlorides 11mg/l, Sulphates 2.1mg/l, Nitrates <0.1mg/l, Silicates 40mg/l. pH 6.7

Tasse (Aus)(Fr)(Ger) cup.

Tasse à The (Fr) teacup.

Tasse à Vin (Fr) a Bordeaux tastevin, a plain cup with a bulge in the middle for the wine to run over to observe the colour.

Tassenberg (S.Afr) a very popular table wine made from a blend of Cinsault and Pinotage grapes. see Tassie.

Tassie (S.Afr) the nickname for Tassenberg.

Tassinaia (It) a red I.G.T. wine produced from Cabernet sauvignon, Merlot and Sangiovese grapes by Tenuta del Terriccio in Tuscany.

Taste (Eng) there are 4 taste sensations: bitter, sour, salt, sweet and umami (savoury).

Taste Buds (Eng) an area of the mouth that experiences taste.

Tasteverre (Fr) a wine glass created in 2003 by Jérôme Meunier of Dijon, Burgundy which is said to improve the bouquet of a wine by 20%. Has an uneven bottom.

Tastevin (Fr) a silver tasting cup that is common in the Burgundy region and other regions in France. Used mainly for checking the colour, clarity and taste of red wines.

Tastevinage (Fr) a wine tasting by the Confrérie des Chevaliers du Tastevin who judge and award a numbered seal to the top wines of Burgundy (established 1950). (Add): Tastevinage BP 12, 21701 Nuits-Saint-Georges. Website: http://www.tastevinage.com 'E'mail: tastevin@axnet.fr

Tasting (Eng) applied to the sampling of wines on offer for sale or to a pre-taste of the bottle of wine purchased by the customer in the restaurant to drink with the meal. *See* Sensoric Tasting.

Tasting Cup (Eng) tastevin, a utensil for tasting wine. *See also* Essais.

Tasting Glass (Eng) *see* I.S.O. Glass.

Tasting Notes (Eng) the record made of a tasting of wine, each is recorded and used as a reference to check on a wine's progress to maturity or quality.

Tatachilla Winery (Austr) a winery based in McLaren Vale, South Australia. Sell wines in the U.K. under the Keystone label. Website: http://www.tatachillawinery.com.au

Tate Brewery (Eng) a brewery (established 1985), brews four types of beer using natural spring water with no additives.

Tâte-Vin (Fr) an alternative name for Tastevin.

Tatizinho (Bra) lit: 'little armadillo', the brand-name of a cachaça.

Tatran (Czec) a lager beer brewed by the Poprad Brewery.

Tatra Vodka Tatrzanska (Pol) a light green-coloured, herb vodka produced by Polmos in the Kraków area 45% alc by vol.

Tatra Zwiec (Pol) a brand of a 1050 O.G. beer.

Tatria (USA) a red wine produced from 70% Cabernet sauvignon, 15% Cabernet franc and 15% Merlot produced by Stuart Cellars in Temecula, California.

Tatschler (Aus) the label for an oaked white wine (Chardonnay) produced by the Römerhof estate winery, Burgenland.

Tattie Howker (Eng) a 4.4% alc by vol. speciality ale (part of the Tapster's Choice range).

Tatton Ale (Eng) a 4.3% alc by vol. cask-conditioned ale brewed by Ridley for Greenall outlets.

Tattoo (Eng) from the old military bugle call of 'taps too'. Used to call soldiers back to barracks and tell the landlords to turn off the beer taps. *see* Taps Too and Taptoe.

Taubenberg (Ger) vineyard (Anb): Rheingau. (Ber): Johannisberg. (Gro): Steinmächer. (Vil): Eltville.

Taubenhaus (Ger) vineyard (Anb): Mosel-Saar-Ruwer. (Ber): Bernkastel. (Gro): Schwarzlay. (Vil): Traben-Trarbach.

Taubenschuss (Aus) a winery based in Poysdorf, Weinviertel. (Add): Körnergasse 2, 2170 Poysdorf. Grape varieties: Chardonnay, Grüner veltliner, Pinot blanc, Riesling, Zweigelt.

Tauber [River] (Ger) a tributary of the river Neckar in Württemberg. Has a soil of shell limestone.

Tauberberg (Ger) grosslage (Anb): Württemberg. (Ber): Kocher-Jagst-Tauber. (Vils): Elpersheim, Wermutshausen.

Tauberbischofsheim (Ger) village (Anb): Baden. (Ber): Badische Frankenland. (Gro): Tauberklinge. (Vin): Edelberg.

Tauberbischofsheim [ortsteil Impfingen] (Ger) village (Anb): Baden. (Ber): Badische Frankenland. (Gro): Tauberklinge. (Vin): Silberquell.

Tauberklinge (Ger) grosslage (Anb): Baden. (Ber): Badisches Frankenland. (Vils): Beckstein, Boxberg (stadtteil Unterschüpf), Dertingen, Gerlachsheim, Grossrinderfeld, Höhenfeld, Kembach, Königheim, Königshofen, Krautheim, Krautheim (stadtteil Klepsau), Külsheim, Lauda, Lindelbach, Marbach, Oberlauda, Oberschüpf, Reicholzheim, Sachsenflur, Tauberbischofsheim, Tauberbischofsheim (ortsteil Impfingen), Uissigheim, Werbach, Wertheim.

Tauberrettersheim (Ger) village (Anb): Franken. (Ber): Maindreieck. (Gro): Not yet assigned. (Vin): Königin.

Tauferer Badl-Quelle (It) a natural spring mineral water from Tscherms. Mineral contents (milligrammes per litre): Sodium 8.2mg/l, Calcium 54.1mg/l, Magnesium 18.5mg/l, Potassium 4.9mg/l, Bicarbonates 139mg/l, Chlorides 2mg/l, Sulphates 110mg/l, Fluorides 0.3mg/l, Iron 1.78mg/l, Silicates 9.7mg/l.

Tau Frisch (Ger) a sparkling natural spring mineral water from Leissling. Mineral contents (milligrammes per litre): Sodium 8.4mg/l, Calcium 91.7mg/l, Magnesium 25mg/l, Potassium 3.2mg/l, Bicarbonates 367mg/l, Fluorides 0.57mg/l.

Taunton Cider Company Limited (Eng) cider makers based in Norton Fitzwarren, Taunton, Somerset, TA2 6RD. Noted for Dry Blackthorn draught and bottled/canned cider. Taken over by Matthew Clark in November 1995. Now known as Matthew Clark Taunton Cider.

Taupette (Fr) *see* Preuve.

Taupine [La] (Fr) a Premier Cru vineyard in the A.C. commune of Monthélie, Côte de Beaune, Burgundy 4.3ha.

Taurasi (It) a D.O.C.G. red wine from the Campania region. Made from the Aglianico, Barbera, Piedirosso and Sangiovese grapes grown in the commune of Taurasi and others. Vinification can occur in province of Avellino. Must be aged 3 years (1 year in wood), if aged 4 years is classed Riserva (18 months in wood).

Tauriac (Fr) a commune in the A.C. Côtes de Bourg, north-eastern Bordeaux.

Taurina Spa (Austr) a natual spring mineral water brand.

Taurino (It) a pilsener lager made near Turin, in northern Italy.

Taurino [Cosimo] (It) a 130ha winery based at SS 605 Salice-Sandonaci, 73010 Guagnano (LE). Produces Chardonnay I.G.T. Salento, Notarpanaro Rosso del Salento, Salice Salentino D.O.C. Riserva, Il Patriglione, Stria Salento Bianco I.G.T. Scaloti Salento I.G.T. Rosato.

T

Tauro (Sp) a solera brandy produced by Garvey. *See also* Doña Ana, Esplendido, Valderrama.

Tauromenitanum (It) a red wine produced on Sicily during Roman times.

Täuscherspfad (Ger) vineyard (Anb): Rheinhessen. (Ber): Bingen. (Gro): Kaiserpfalz. (Vil): Ingelheim.

Tausendeimerberg (Aus) a vineyard site on the banks of the River Danube situated in the Wachau region, Niederösterreich.

Tauxières (Fr) a Premier Cru Champagne village in the Canton d'Aÿ. District: Reims.

Tavel (Fr) an A.C. (awarded in 1936) rosé wine from the southern Rhône, 960ha. Produced from the Bourboulenc, Calitor, Clairette and Grenache grapes. Soil: clay, sand and pudding stones. High in alcohol, minimum 11% by vol. (average 12%–13.5%), noted for its onion skin colour and sold in flute-shaped bottles.

Taveners Ale (Eng) a 5.3% alc by vol. ale brewed by Hanby Ales Ltd., Shropshire.

Tavern (Eng) a hostelry which caters for local custom (different to an Inn).

Tavern (Eng) the old name for keg beer from the Courage Brewery.

Taverna (It) pub/tavern.

Taverna (Port) an alternative spelling of Taberna.

Taverna (S.Afr) an everyday full red wine produced mainly from Pinotage grapes. Often oak aged.

Tavern Bottle (Eng) early bottles that had the seal of the Tavern embossed on them (circa 1657–1750).

Tavistock Beer (Eng) a cask-conditioned bitter 1036 O.G. brewed by a home-brew public house in London.

Tavola (USA) a label used by the Guild Wineries and Distilleries, California for table wines.

Tavora-Varosa (Port) a DOC wine area based in the Beiras region of northern Portugal.

Tavra (Port) a DOC wine area based in the Algarve region, southern Portugal.

Tawern (Ger) village (Anb): Mosel-Saar-Ruwer. (Ber): Obermosel. (Gro): Gipfel. (Vins): Sites not yet chosen.

Tawny (Port) the quality of paleness or golden tinge which Port wines acquire when matured in wood. *see* Tawny Port.

Tawny Ale (Eng) a bottled ale brewed by Usher of Trowbridge (part of the Vintage Ale Collection). *See also* Ruby Ale, White Ale.

Tawny Bitter (Eng) a 3.8% alc by vol (1040 O.G) cask-conditioned bitter brewed by the Cotleigh Brewery in Somerset.

Tawny Mild (Eng) a keg light mild 1032 O.G. brewed by the John Smith Brewery in Tadcaster, Yorkshire.

Tawny Port (Port) blended young Ports (non-vintage) that have been aged in casks for 6 years plus. Obtains a golden tinge as it ages. *see* Dated Ports.

Tay (Chi) the pronunciation of tea in China from which the word 'tea' derives. *see* T'é.

Taybeh Brewery (M.East) a brewery (established 1995) on the West Bank, Palestine. Brews beers of the same name (dark and golden at 5% alc by vol.).

Taylor (Port) vintage port shippers (established 1692). Vintages: 1870, 1872, 1873, 1875, 1878, 1881, 1884, 1887, 1890. 1892, 1896, 1900, 1904, 1906, 1908, 1912, 1917, 1920, 1924, 1927, 1935, 1940, 1942, 1945, 1948, 1955, 1960, 1963, 1966, 1970, 1975, 1977, 1980, 1982, 1983, 1985, 1992, 1994, 1995, 1997, 1998, 2000, 2003. Full name is Taylor, Fladgate and Yeatman. Single quinta is Quinta da Vargellas.

Taylor [Timothy] & C° Ltd (Eng) a brewery (established 1858). (Add): Knowle Spring Brewery, Keighley, West Yorkshire BD2 1AW. Noted for cask-conditioned Golden Best 1033 O.G. Bitter ale 1033 O.G. Landlord 1042 O.G. Ram Tam 1043 O.G. and bottled Northerner 1033 O.G. Blue Label 1043 O.G. Black Bess Stout 1043 O.G. Website: http://www.timtaylor.co.uk 'E'mail: andrewd@timtaylors.co.uk

Taylor California Cellars (USA) a winery owned by the Coca Cola C°.

Taylor, Fladgate and Yeatman (Port) *see* Taylor.

Taylor's VO (S.Afr) a brand of brandy produced by Sedgewick Taylor.

Taylors Wines (Austr) a winery based in Clare Valley, South Australia. Grape varieties: Cabernet sauvignon and Hermitage. Produces varietal wines.

Taylor-Walker (Eng) Ind Coope's London company beers are brewed at Burton and Romford. Brews most styles of beers.

Taylor Wine Company (USA) a leading wine-producer of the Finger Lakes region of the New York district (Lake Kenka), sells wines under Lake County and Great Western labels. Noted for pink (rosé) wines.

Taza (Sp) cup.

Taz Estate (USA) a winery based in the Santa Barbara County, California. Grape variety: Pinot Noir.

Tazza (It) cup.

Tazzelenghe (It) a red grape variety grown in Colli Orientali, north-east Italy.

Tba (Ger) *abbr*: Trockenbeerenauslese.

Tbilisi (Rus) is Russian 'Champagne', produced in Tbilisi between the regions of Anapa and Gelendshik in the Crimean Peninsular.

TCA (Lat) *abbr*: Tri-chloro-anisole.

Tcha (Chi) a Cantonese dialect word for tea from which Cha (English slang) is derived.

Tchibo Coffee International (Eng) formerly Jacobs Suchard.

Tchkhavéri (Geo) a white grape variety grown in Georgia that produces dessert wines.

Tchoung-Tchoung (E.Asia) a digestive liqueur made from fermented rice in Vietnam. *see* Choum.

Tchuve (Ch.Isles) vat.

T'é (Chi) tea.

Te (Den)(Isr)(Wal) tea.

Tè (It) tea.

Té (Sp) tea.

Tea (Eng) denotes a beverage made from the dried leaves of the tea bush grown between the latitudes of 42°N to 29°S. Main tea-producing countries are Africa, Caucasia (Russia, Turkey and Iran), China, India, Indonesia, Japan, Malaya, Pakistan, South America and Taiwan. *See also* Tisanes. (Arab) = shy, (Aus) = tee, (Chi) = t'é/cha, (Ch.Isles) = thée, (Den) = te, (Fr) = thé, (Ger) = tee, (Gre) = tsai, (Hol) = thee, (Indo) = the, (Ire) = tae, (Isr) = te, (It) = tè, (Jap) = ocha, (Kor) = cha, (Port) = chá, (Rus) = chay, (Sp) = té, (Thai) = namcha, (Wal) = te.

T.E.A. (Eng) *abbr:* Tongham English Ale 4.2% alc by vol. ale brewed using a single hop variety by the Hog Back Brewery, Tongham, near Guildford, Surrey.

Tea (Jap) green and black (fermented) varieties. *see* Bancha, Hojicha, Matcha, Mugicha and Ocha.

Téa (Sp) a wine-producing area on the river Miño in western Spain. Grape varieties: Caiño, Espadeiro and Tintarrón. Produces mainly red wines.

Tea Act (Eng) passed in 1773 allowed the East India Company to sell tea to the USA, caused the famous Boston Tea Party.

Tea After Meals (Eng) *abbr:* TAM an idea introduced by the Twining C°. a package containing two teabags. The idea being that the customer hands over teabags and host provides the water.

Tea Auctions (Eng) occur every Monday at Sir John Lyon House, London. Buying brokers bid for the tea available.

Tea Bag (Eng) a small perforated paper bag used to contain tea leaves. Boiling water is poured over and allowed to infuse. Very popular as they are easy to dispose of once used. Available in square, circular or pyramid shapes. (Fr) = sachet de thé.

Tea Ball (USA) a round, perforated metal infuser, filled with tea leaves for making tea. Is suspended in a jug, pot, etc. The forerunner of the tea bag, invented in the nineteenth century. (Fr) = boule à thé/infuseur à thé, (Ire) = insilteoir tae.

Tea Break (Eng) the name given to the rest period from working duties when workers would consume a cup/mug of tea in the morning and afternoon. *see* Tea Drinking. (Fr) = pause-thé.

Tea Breeze (Fr) a liqueur with a subtle taste of tea 25% alc. by. vol.

Tea Brick (Chi) an ancient way of transporting tea, compressed into bricks, it was also used as currency. Still made by the Tsaiao Liu China Tea Brick Factory.

Tea Bush (Asia) *Camellia sinensis* the plant from which the leaves (young leaf tips) are dried and used for making tea. There are 2 varieties: Cambodia and China with many hybrids and crosses. *See also* Black Tea, Green Tea, Gunpowder Tea. (Fr) = arbre à thé.

Tea Caddy (Eng) a container for keeping/storing tea, derived from the Chinese 'catty' which means weight. Was also used for mixing (blending) tea. Often locked, especially in the eighteenth century

when tea was a valuable commodity. (Fr) = boite à thé, (Ire) = boiscin tae.

Tea Camellia (Eng) tea bush. *see Camellia sinensis*.

Tea Cart (USA) tea trolley.

Tea Ceremonies (E.Asia) developed in 1124 by Hsu Ching, a Chinese envoy in Korea. Used teas from the Chiri mountains. *see* Tea of Bamboo Dew and Tea of Peacock's Tongue.

Tea Ceremony (Chi) evolved in the fourteenth century by a Buddhist priest called Shuko. Lasts up to two hours and uses green teas. *see* Cha No Yu.

Teacher [William and Sons] (Scot) a famous malt whisky distillery. Owns Ardmore and Glendronach distilleries in Aberdeenshire. Took over Stewart and Sons in Dundee. Now owned by Allied Domecq.

Teacher's Highland Cream (Scot) a blended Scotch whisky produced by William Teacher and Sons, (part of Allied Breweries). Has 45% malt whiskies in the blend 43% alc by vol.

Teacher's Sixty [60] (Scot) a de luxe blended Scotch whisky by William Teacher and Sons, (part of Allied Breweries). Has 60% malt whiskies in the blend 43% alc by vol.

Tea Chest (Eng) a box (wooden) for storing loose tea. (Fr) = caisse à thé, (Ire) = cófra tae.

Teach Gloine Finiúna (Ire) vinery.

Teach Leanna (Ire) ale house.

Tea Clipper (Eng) nineteenth century ships, 3 masted schooners that were used to transport tea from East to West (the Cutty Sark was the most famous).

Tea Clipper (Eng) a 4.2% alc by vol. ale brewed by the Itchen Valley Brewery, Hampshire.

Tea Cobbler (Cktl) 25mls (⅙ gill) Jamaican rum, few dashes sugar syrup and fresh brewed tea (cooled). Stir over ice, strain into an ice-filled highball glass, top with a little Port wine, serve with straws and fruit in season.

Tea Cosy (Eng) a cover for a teapot to keep the pot and its contents very hot, made of wool or other good insulating material. (Ire) = púic tae.

Teacup (Eng) a receptacle for drinking tea from, originally made from bone china, modern teacups are produced from a variety of flavourless heat resistant materials. (Fr) = tasse à the, (Ire) = cupán tae.

Tea Dance (Eng) an afternoon function practiced in the late nineteenth century where dancing took place during afternoon tea in hotels and restaurants. The idea was introduced and supported by the temperance movements of the day, has since been revived in the 1970's.

Tea Drinking (Eng) the ritual of tea drinking and to the process of placing the milk in the cup first derives from the time when milk (and sugar for energy) was added to the hot tea to give the mill workers nourishment during their working shift (tea break). The milk was added first because the clay 'mugs' tended to crack when the hot liquid was added, so the cold milk, added first, cooled the hot tea down.

Tea Egg (Eng) *see* Tea Maker.
Tea Flushes (Eng) *see* Flushes.
Tea for Two Cup (Cktl) 550mls (1pint) freshly brewed tea, 300mls (½ pint) Dubonnet, juice ½ lemon, 1½ tablespoons redcurrant jelly, 1 tablespoon soft brown sugar. Heat all together and serve with black grape halves which have been de-seeded.
Tea Gardens (Eng) mid eighteenth century gardens where people met to drink tea and be entertained with music and fireworks. The most popular was at Ranelagh near Chelsea, London.
Tea Kettle (Eng) *see* Kettle. (Ire) = taechiteal.
Tea Leaves (Eng) the name given to the dried cut tea leaf that is ready for brewing. (Fr) = feuilles de thé, (Ire) = duilleog tae.
Tea Liqueur (Jap) a liqueur made from 2 types of tea.
Tea Maker (Eng) a spoon (of teaspoon size) with a perforated top and bottom in which tea leaves are placed to infuse in a cup of boiling water to make 1 cup of tea. Also known as a Tea Egg or Infuser.
Tea Making (Eng) bring to the boil some freshly drawn cold water. Heat the teapot, place the correct measure of good quality tea (1 level teaspoonful per 150mls or ¼ pint of water) into the warmed teapot. When the water has come to a rapid boil, pour straight onto the tea leaves. Allow to infuse for 3–4 minutes (hard water requires a longer infusion time), stir and pour. Note: the strength of the brew depends on the quantity of tea used. Many advocate the addition of one extra measure of tea per pot (three cups of tea are obtainable from 1 pint of brewed tea). Brewed tea should never be allowed to '*stew*' as this will give the tea a bitter flavour.
Tea Mosquito (Eng) *see Helopeltis theivora.*
Teaninich (Scot) a single malt whisky distillery owned by R.W. Thompson and C°. in Ross-shire. A highland malt. Produces a 22 year old malt whisky at 45% alc by vol. and a 27 year old at 64.2% alc by vol.
Tea of Bamboo Dew (E.Asia) tea from the Chiri mountains in Korea, used in ancient tea ceremonies.
Tea of Peacock's Tongues (E.Asia) tea grown in the Chiri mountains, Korea. Used in ancient tea ceremonies.
Tea Parcel (Eng) a large quantity of tea usually associated with tea auctions.
Tea Plant (Eng) *see* Tea Bush. (Fr) = arbre à thé, (Ire) = planda tae.
Teapot (Eng) a heat-proof utensil used for the making (brewing) of tea, made of china, pottery or metal (silver, stainless steel or aluminium). (Den) = tepotte, (Fr) = theière, (Ire) = taephota.
Tea Poy (Eng)(Ind) a three-legged stand and tea caddy of the eighteenth and nineteenth centuries.
Tea Punch (Punch) ½ bottle Cognac, ½ bottle Jamaican rum, juice and rind of a lemon, 200grms (½ lb) sugar. Heat all together in a metal punch bowl, flame, add hot tea and serve.
Tears (Eng) a term used to describe the ethyl alcohol and glycerine lines which run down the glass when it is being drunk, also known as '*legs*'.
Tears of Joy (USA) *see* EOS Estate Winery.
Tea Scripture [The] (Chi) the '*Ch'a Ching of Lu Yu*', written in 800AD it was the book on how to make and serve tea.
Tea Service (Eng) teapot, hot water jug, teacup, saucer, teaspoon, strainer, slop-bowl, sugar bowl, sugar tongs and milk jug. (Fr) = service à thé, (Den) = testel.
Tea Set (Eng) an alternative name for a Tea Service. (Fr) = service à thé, (Den) = testel.
Teaspoon (Eng) an implement made of metal, china or plastic used for the stirring of tea that has had sugar/milk added (1 fluid dram). (Aus) = teelöffel, (Fr) = cuiller à thé/cuiller à café, (Ger) = teelöffel, (Sp) = cucharadita.
Teaspoon (USA) a bar measure that equals ⅛ fl.oz US. ⅙ fl.oz Imp.
Tea Strainer (Eng) a sieve or perforated dish to remove the spent tea leaves from brewed tea as it is poured into the teacup.
Tea Tipple (Cktl) 200mls (⅓ pint) freshly brewed tea, 25mls (⅕ gill) Cointreau. Add the liqueur to the tea and dress with a slice of orange.
Tea Towel (Eng) a cotton/linen cloth used for the drying of crockery, glassware, etc.
Tea Tray (Eng) a tray for holding the teapot, sugar bowl, milk jug and slops bowl when serving tea (especially afternoon tea). (Mor) = siniya.
Tea Tree (N.Z) **Leptospermum** a native tree of New Zealand and of Australia which is used as a tea substitute.
Tea Trolley (Eng) a trolley which is used to serve tea in factories, offices or in the home. Known as a Tea Cart or Tea Wagon in the USA. (Fr) = caisse à thé.
Tea Wagon (USA) *see* Tea Trolley.
Te Awa Winery (N.Z) a winery. (Add): Roys Hill Road, SH50, (RD 5), Hastings. 40ha. Grape varieties: Chardonnay, Cabernet sauvignon, Cabernet franc, Merlot, Pinotage, Shiraz.
Teberda (Rus) a natural spring mineral water from Stavropol Territory, Northern Caucasus. Mineral contents (milligrammes per litre): Sodium 1000–1600mg/l, Calcium 100–250mg/l, Magnesium 40–150mg/l, Potassium 1000–1600mg/l, Bicarbonates 2000–3500mg/l, Chlorides 700–1100mg/l, Sulphates <100mg/l.
Té Bheag Connoisseurs Blend (Scot) the label of a blended Scotch whisky 40% alc by vol.
Té Bheag Nan Eilean (Scot) the label of a blended Scotch whisky 40% alc by vol.
Tebot (Wal) teapot.
Tébourba (Afr) a noted wine-producing area in Tunisia.
Tecali [The] (Cktl) 3 parts silver tequila, 1 level teaspoon of coffee, 1 part lemon juice, 2 parts mineral water. Shake well with ice and strain into an ice-filled highball glass.
Tecate (S.Am) a 4.6% alc by vol. bottled pilsner

T

brewed by Cuauhtémoc Brewery, Monterrey, Mexico. Usually drunk in the USA with lemon wedges and salt.

Technical Hitch (Eng) a 5.3% alc by vol. ale brewed by the Barum Brewery, Devon.

Tech [River] (Fr) a river in the Pyrénées Orientales wine département of the Languedoc-Roussillon area.

Ted & Bens (Eng) a 4.7% alc by vol. organic cask ale brewed without finings by Brakspear at the Griffith Brewery, Chiswick in London Henley-on-Thames, Oxon. Part of the Brewers Selection range.

Teddy Bear (Eng) ⅛ measure stout, ⅛ measure Port wine, stirred gently to mix.

Teddy Hall Wines (S.Afr) an own-name label inexpensive white (Chenin blanc) wine produced in the Western Cape.

Tedeschi Vineyard (USA) a winery based on the island of Maui in Hawaii. 8ha. Produces grape and fruit wines (pineapple).

Tedge (Afr) an Ethiopean drink made from honey.

Tè di Camomilla (It) camomile tea.

Tee (Aus)(Ger) tea.

Teelöffel (Aus)(Ger) teaspoon.

Teeperdjookkuad (Thai) corkscrew.

Teetotal (USA) the name that derived from a meeting of the Temperance Society of Laingsbury, Michigan in the 1830's. Had 2 pledges. (1) for moderate drinking, O.P. [Old Pledge]. and (2) for complete abstinence. T. [Total Pledge]. People who took the Total pledge became known as 'T' totalers. (Fr) = antialcoolique/de tempérance.

Teetotaler (USA) see Teetotal.

Teflon (Eng) a 3.7% alc by vol. ale brewed by the Sawbridge North Brewery, Hertfordshire.

Tegea (Gre) a fragrant dry rosé wine.

Tegernseerhof (Aus) an estate and winery (25ha) based at Unterloiben in the Wachau. Grapes include: Grüner veltliner, Riesling.

Tegestologist (Eng) a collector of beer (drip) mats.

Teheran (Iran) a wine-producing province in northern Iran.

Tehigo (Sp) an area within Andalusia whose vineyards produce grapes for Sherry production.

Te Horo Estate (N.Z) a 5ha winery. (Add): State Hwy. 1, Te Horo (Main Rd. South, RD 1), Otaki. Grape varieties: Rhine riesling, Sauvignon blanc, Pinot noir, Sangiovese, Zinfandel, Montepulciano, Pinotage, Shiraz, Pinot gris, Pinot blanc.

Teichenné Schnapps (Sp) a wide range of quality schnapps from a family firm founded in 1956. Range includes ButterScotch, Kiwi, Lemon, White Melon. All either 20%, 21.5% or 22% alc by vol. See also Frangelico Hazelnut Liqueur, Opal Nera, Black Sambuca.

Teiera (It) teapot.

Teignworthy Brewery (Eng) a brewery (established 1994). (Add): The Maltings, Teign Road, Newton Abbot, Devon TQ12 4AA. Brews: Amys Ale 4.8% alc by vol., Beachcomber 4.5% alc by vol., Christmas Cracker 6% alc by vol., Old Moggie

4.4% alc by vol., Reel Ale 4% alc by vol., Spring Tide 4.3% alc by vol., also a cask-conditioned traditional ale 4% alc by vol., Malsters Ale 5% alc by vol., and Total Blackout 5.9% alc by vol. 'E'mail: john@teignworthy.freeserve.co.uk

Teinacher (Ger) a still and sparkling natural spring mineral water from Mineralbrunnen AG, 75385 Bad Teinach, Schwarzwald. (red label: sparkling/blue label: light gas/green label: still). Mineral contents (milligrammes per litre): Sodium 100mg/l, Calcium 100mg/l, Magnesium 20mg/l, Potassium 6.2mg/l, Bicarbonates 610mg/l, Chlorides 20mg/l, Sulphates 30mg/l, Fluorides 0.9mg/l, Nitrates 8.7mg/l.

Teinturiers (Fr) also known as 'dyers', black grapes with red juice, the only red grapes that cannot be used for white wines. i.e. Malbec.

Teissedre (Fr) a Bordeaux-based firm that produces fine fruit-based liqueurs.

Teissiéres-les-Bouliès (Fr) a natural spring mineral water (established 1821) from Auvergne. Mineral contents (milligrammes per litre): Sodium 9.4mg/l, Calcium 17.6mg/l, Magnesium 8.7mg/l, Potassium 1.2mg/l, Chlorides 3.2mg/l, Sulphates 12.7mg/l, Nitrates <1mg/l.

Teixeira [Tristao Vaz] (Mad) a Portuguese man who, together with João Goncalves Zarco, discovered Madeira in 1418.

Tej (N.Afr) a sweet honey mead made in Ethiopia.

Tejo [River] (Port) see Tajo River.

Te Kairanga Wines (N.Z) a winery. (Add): Martins Road, P.O. Box 52, Martinborough. 103ha. Grape varieties: Chardonnay, Cabernet sauvignon, Pinot noir, Sauvignon blanc. Label: Runholder. Website: http://www.tkwine.co.nz 'E'mail: ceo@tekairanga.co.nz

Te Kauwhata (N.Z) a wine area on the mid-west coast of the North Island.

Te Kauwhata Viticultural Research Station (N.Z) a research centre that has played an important role in the New Zealand commercial wine industry.

Tekel (Tur) on the neck label of a wine bottle guarantees quality, awarded by the state monopoly.

Tekel Brewery (Tur) a brewery based in Ankara. Produces pilsener and Münchener-style beers.

Tekirdag (Tur) a vineyard based in the region of Marmara and Thrace. Produces both red and white wines.

Tekirdag-Canakkale (Tur) a vineyard based in the Marmara and Thrace region. Produces red wines.

Teldeschi Vineyard (USA) a small vineyard based in Dry Creek, Sonoma County, California. Grape varieties: Cabernet sauvignon and Zinfandel.

Telenn Du (Fr) a 4.5% alc by vol. top-fermented, dark brewed, bottle-conditioned beer brewed by Bernard Lancelot in St. Servant-sur-Oust using buckwheat.

Telese (It) a sparling natural spring mineral water from Benevento. Mineral contents (milligrammes per litre): Sodium 135mg/l, Calcium 387mg/l, Magnesium 73mg/l, Potassium 21mg/l,

T

Bicarbonates 830mg/l, Chlorides 158mg/l, Sulphates 57mg/l, Silicates 16mg/l. pH 6.5

Television Cocktail (Cktl) ⅓ measure dry gin, ⅙ measure dry vermouth, ⅙ measure sweet vermouth, ⅙ measure crème de noyau. Shake over ice and strain into a cocktail glass.

Téliani (Geo) a red grape variety grown in Georgia, a variety of the Cabernet.

Téliani (Geo) a red wine produced by the Tsinandali Winery in the republic of Georgia (Kakheti region) from the grape of the same name.

Teller (Aus) a vineyard site based on the banks of the River Kamp situated in the Kamptal region.

Tellus (Swe) a sparkling natural spring mineral water (established 1996) from Helsingborg. Mineral contents (milligrammes per litre): Sodium 62mg/l, Calcium 60mg/l, Magnesium 6mg/l, Potassium 3.3mg/l, Bicarbonates 200mg/l, Chlorides 56mg/l, Sulphates 68mg/l, Nitrates <1mg/l.

Telteca Winery (Arg) a winery based in the Mendoza region, eastern Argentina. Website: http://www.teltecawinery.com 'E'mail: teltecawinery@vinasar.com

Telve (Tur) coffee grounds.

Tem (Gre) a natural spring mineral water from Perivolia, Crete. Mineral contents (milligrammes per litre): Sodium 15.4mg/l, Calcium 59.2mg/l, Magnesium 4.8mg/l, Potassium 1.4mg/l, Bicarbonates 184.2mg/l, Chlorides 30.4mg/l, Sulphates 8.6mg/l.

Te Mânia Estate (N.Z) a 8ha winery (established 1892) the oldest wine property in New Zealand. (Add): Pughs Road, RD 1 Richmond, Nelson. Grape varieties: Cabernet sauvignon, Merlot, Cabernet franc, Syrah, Chardonnay, Riesling, Sauvignon blanc and a late-harvest Riesling. Labels include Coleraine and Awatea.

Te Mata Winery (N.Z) a winery. (Add): P.O. Box. 8335, Havelock North, Hawkes Bay. 23ha. Grape varieties: Cabernet sauvignon, Chardonnay, Merlot, Shiraz and Sauvignon blanc. see Castle Hill, Elston, Coleraine.

Temecula (USA) a wine-producing district in southern California.

Te med Citron (Den) tea with lemon.

Te med Mælk (Den) tea with milk.

Tement (Aus) a winery (25ha) based in Berghausen, Styria. (Add): Zieregg 13, 8461 Berghausen. Grape varieties: Blaufränkisch, Cabernet sauvignon, Chardonnay, Pinot blanc, Sauvignon blanc, Traminer, Welschriesling, Zweigelt.

Teme Valley Brewery (Eng) a brewery (established 1997). (Add): The Talbot Inn, Bromyard Road, Knightwick, Worcester, Worcestershire WR6 5PH. Previously known as The Talbot Knightwick Ltd. Brews: Dark Stranger 4.4% alc by vol., Hearth Warmer 6% alc by vol., That 4.1% alc by vol., The Hops Nouvelle 4.1% alc by vol., This 3.7% alc by vol., T'other 3.5% alc by vol. Website: http://www.temevalley.co.uk 'E'mail: info@the-talbot.co.uk

Temmels (Ger) village (Anb): Mosel-Saar-Ruwer.

(Ber): Obermosel. (Gro): Gipfel. (Vins): Münsterstatt, St. Georgshof.

Te Moana (N.Z) the brand-name used by Vidal Wine Producers in Hawkes Bay for their white Riesling-Sylvaner wines.

Tempel (Slo) a sparkling natural spring mineral water from Rognaska Slatina. Mineral contents (milligrammes per litre): Sodium 118.6mg/l, Calcium 106.3mg/l, Magnesium 107.4mg/l, Bicarbonates 981.7mg/l, Chlorides 10.3mg/l, Sulphates 160.3mg/l.

Tempelchen (Ger) vineyard (Anb): Rheinhessen. (Ber): Nierstein. (Gro): Domherr. (Vil): Stadecken-Elsheim.

Temperance (USA) the abstinence from alcohol. see Teetotal.

Temperence Bars (Eng) bars opened in the 1870-1880's that sold no alcohol as a part of the temperance movement. Drinks such as sarsaparilla, black beer, dandelion and burdock were the bar's mainstay drinks! Now only one such bar remains: Fitzpatrick's of Rawtenstall, Manchester.

Temperance Mocktail (Cktl)(Non-alc) 75mls (3 fl.ozs) lemon juice, 25mls (1fl.oz) sugar syrup, 1 egg yolk, shake well over ice and strain into a large cocktail glass.

Temperance Society (N.Z) founded in 1853, tried to stop drinking and the establishment of breweries. Now part of New Zealand Breweries.

Temperance Special (Cktl)(Non-alc) 2 teaspoons grenadine, 1 egg yolk, 125mls (1gill) lemon juice. Shake well over ice and strain into a cocktail glass.

Temperate Zone (Eng) an area where vines that are best for wines are grown (latitudes 30°N–50°N and 30°S–50°S).

Temperature (Eng) important in wine and beer production, storage and service.

Tempest (Eng) a 4.2% alc by vol. stout from Mitchells Brewery in Lancaster.

Tempest (Scot) a 4.9% alc by vol. ale brewed by the Atlas Brewery, Argyll.

Templar [To Drink Like A] (Eng) a mediaeval saying which denotes a great thirst (the Knights of the Templar were noted drinkers of wines).

Templeton (USA) a wine town in the San Luis Obispo County, California. Home to many wineries.

Temple Wines (S.Afr) a winery (established 2000) based in the Nooder-Paarl, Western Cape. 3ha. Grape variety: Pinotage.

Templiers (Bel) an abbaye-produced beer.

Tempo Industries (Isr) the sole producer of beer in Israel. Produces: Maccabee 1045 O.G.

Temprana (Sp) the alternative name for the Palomino grape.

Tempranilla (Arg) an alternative name for the Tempranillo grape grown in Mendoza.

Tempranillo (Sp) the top red grape variety grown in the Rioja region that produces wines with an aroma and taste of violets, blackcurrants, tobacco,

1274

toffee-butter, spice, leather. Also known as the Ojo de Liebre, Ull de Llebre (in Cataluña), Cencibel (in La Mancha), Tinto Fino (in Ribera del Duero). Also Tinto de Toro, Tinto del Pais, Tinto Madrid, Tinto Roriz, Tempranillo de la Rioja, Tinto de la Rioja, Grenache de Logroño, Jacivera. Also spelt Tempranilla.

Tempranillo Bis (Sp) the name for the Cabernet sauvignon grape.

Tempranillo de la Rioja (Sp) an alternative name for the Tempranillo grape.

Temptation [1] (Cktl) 1 measure Nassau Orange Liqueur, 2 measures Scotch whisky, juice ½ lemon, dash grenadine. Shake well over ice, strain into an ice-filled highball glass. Top with chilled orange juice, add a slice of orange and a cherry.

Temptation [2] (Cktl) 7/10 measure rye whiskey, 1/10 measure Dubonnet, 1/10 measure pastis, 1/10 measure orange Curaçao. Shake over ice, strain into a cocktail glass, add a twist of orange and lemon peel juice.

Temptation (Eng) a 10% alc by vol. strong ale brewed by The Durham Brewery Ltd., County Durham.

Temptation Cocktail (Cktl) ¾ measure Bourbon whiskey, 2 dashes each of Cointreau, pastis and Dubonnet. Shake over ice, strain into a cocktail glass, top with a twist of orange and lemon peel juice.

Tempter (Cktl) ½ measure apricot liqueur, ½ measure Port wine. Stir over ice and strain into a cocktail glass.

Tempus Fugit (Scot) a 3.8% alc by vol. ale brewed by Caledonian Brewery based in Edinburgh.

Temulentus (Lat) drunken/intoxicated.

Tenab Shahmirzad (Iran) a natural spring mineral water (established 2001) from Shahmirzad. Mineral contents (milligrammes per litre): Sodium 4mg/l, Calcium 40mg/l, Magnesium 12.48mg/l, Potassium 0.3mg/l, Bicarbonates 150mg/l, Chlorides 7mg/l, Sulphates 15mg/l, Fluorides 0.3mg/l, Nitrates 2.9mg/l. pH 7.48

Tenant (Eng) a licensee of a brewery-owned public house, held under a tenancy agreement.

Tenant Streams (Eng) denotes the tenancies of one brewery.

Ténarèze (Fr) a town in the Gers département where Armagnac is made. Gives its name to one of the appellations of Armagnac.

Tenderfoot Mint Cocktail (Cktl)(Non-alc) 10mls (½ fl.oz) lemon juice, 25mls (1fl.oz) mint syrup, dash lime juice, 5mls (¼ fl.oz) gomme syrup. Shake over ice and strain into a Champagne saucer.

Tendone (It) a high method of vine training that gives a high grape yield.

Tendre (Fr) a rather light and delicate wine, usually a young wine.

Tendrils (Eng) the part of the vine which attaches it to the stakes, wires etc. for anchorage.

Tenementi (It) holding or estate. see Tenimenti.

Tenerife (Sp) one of the islands of Santa Cruz de Tenerife, part of the Canary Islands. See also La Gomera, El Hierro, La Palma. Spanish-owned islands off the coast of western Africa that produce average quality red and white wines. D.O.'s: Abona, El Hierro, La Palma, Tacoronte-Acentejo, Valle de Güimar, Valle de la Orotava, Ycoden-Daute-Isora. Also Vino de la Tierra area of La Gomera and Vino de Mesa area of Anaga.

Ten Fifty (Eng) a cask-conditioned strong ale brewed by the Grainstore Brewery, Rutland.

Ten High (USA) the brand-name of a Bourbon whiskey.

Tenimenti (It) denotes either a holding or estate. see Tenementi.

Tenke (Rum) a natural spring mineral water from Tenke (Tinca), Transylvania.

Tennen-sui (Jap) a natural spring mineral water brand. Mineral contents (milligrammes per litre): Sodium 49mg/l, Calcium 9.7mg/l, Magnesium 1.4mg/l.

Tennent Caledonian (Scot) Bass's Scottish Company, has breweries in Glasgow and Edinburgh. Has brewed lager beers since 1885, produces many fine beers under the Tennents label.

Tennents (Scot) the brand-name for a range of beers from Bass. Labels include: Tennents Extra (premium lager), Tennents L.A. (low-alcohol), Tennents Pilsner (draught lager), Tennents Super (superstrength lager).

Tennents L.A. (Scot) a low-alcohol lager 0.9% alc by vol. from Tennent Caledonian.

Tenner Brothers Winery (USA) a winery based in Patrick, South Carolina. Grape varieties: Catawba, Concord and Muscadine.

Tennessee Mountain (USA) a natural spring mineral water from Iron City, Tennessee.

Tennessee Sunrise (Cktl) 40mls (⅓ gill) rye whiskey, 4 dashes maraschino, 4 dashes lime juice. Shake over ice and strain into an ice-filled old-fashioned glass.

Tennessee Whiskey (USA) a straight whiskey distilled in Tennessee with no specific grain criteria 45% alc by vol.

Tennessee Wine (USA) a nickname for moonshine whiskey in the 1920's.

Teno (Chile) a wine-producing area in the Curicó region.

Ten o'Clock Swill (Eng) due to longer hours, more civilised drinking habits have occurred and this has now practically disappeared. Denoted the fact that the drinker tried to get as much drink as possible before the bar closed at 10 o'clock.

Ten Penny Stock Ale (Can) a dark ale 5.3% alc by vol. brewed by the Moosehead Brewery.

Ten Sixty Six [1066] (Eng) a draught winter ale 1066 O.G. brewed by the Goacher Brewery in Maidstone, Kent.

Ten Sixty Six [1066] (Eng) a keg beer 1064 O.G. brewed by the Alexander Brewery in Brighton.

Ten Sixty Six [1066] (Eng) a 6% alc by vol. ale from the Hampshire Brewery, Andover.

Ten Sixty Six [1066] Country Bitter (Eng) a 4% alc

by vol. bitter ale brewed by the Whirte Brewing C°., East Sussex.

Tent (Eng) an old Elizabethan corruption of the red wine Tinto produced in Spain and the Canaries.

Tent (Sp) a sweet wine red wine from Alicante.

Tent (Sp) *see* Tintilla de Rota.

Tenterden Vineyards (Eng) a vineyard (established 1993) based at Small Hythe, Kent. 4.25ha. Grape varieties: Bacchus, Gutenborner, Schönburger. Wine sold under the Spots Farm and Chapel Down labels.

Tenth (USA) bottle size 12.68 fl.ozs (⅖ quart) 375mls.

Tenue de Soirée (Fr) a Châteauneuf-du-Pape produced by Serre, Domaine de Saint Préfert, 84230 Châteauneuf-du-Pape, southern Rhône. Other labels include Cuvée Mélodie.

Tenuta (It) estate. *See also* Fattoria, Maso, Messeria.

Tenuta Amalia (It) a winery based in Emilia-Romagna. Produces sparkling wines by the cuve close method.

Tenuta Coppadoro (It) a wine estate based in Puglia. 120ha. Produces Radicosa.

Tenuta delle Terre Nere (It) a winery based on the island of Sicily. Label: Vigneto Guardiola.

Tenuta dell'Ornellaia (It) a 56ha estate that produces Ornellaia, Masseto, Le Volte, Pogia Alle Gazze, Pian dei Susini in Bolgheri, Tuscany.

Tenuta del Terricio (It) a 40ha winery. (Add): 56040 Castellina Marittima (PI). Produces Lupicaia, Tassinaia, Con Vento, Rondinaia, Saluccio.

Tenuta di Bibbiano (It) a 21ha winery. (Add): Via Bibbiano 76, 53011 Castellina in Chianti, Siena. Produces Tenuta di Bibbiano Montornello and Riserva Vigna del Cappannino, Grappa Chianti Classico.

Tenuta di Castiglione (It) a winery based on Mount Etna. Produces white wines from Carricante, red wines from Rovitello, Nerello Mascalese, Nerello Cappuccio.

Tenuta di Lilliano (It) a noted Chianti Classico winery. 45ha. (Add): Loc. Lilliano, 53011 Castellina in Chianti, Siena, Tuscany.

Tenuta di Pomino (It) the name for D.O.C. Pomino Rosso and Pomino Bianco wines in Tuscany. Produced by Marchesi de'Frescobaldi. Also a Vin Santo.

Tenuta di Vignole (It) a 20ha winery. (Add): Via Case Sparse 12, 50020 Panzano, Greve (FI). Noted for Chianti Classico Riserva, Vin Santo and Vignole Riserva.

Tenuta Il Poggione (It) a 100ha winery based in Montalcino, Siena. Produces D.O.C.G. Brunello di Montalcino, D.O.C. Rosso di Montalcino and San Leopoldo (a Super-Tuscan).

Tenuta La Tenaglia (It) a winery. (Add): Via Santuario di Crea 5, 15020 Serralunga di Crea (AL). 14ha. vineyard noted for Barbera d'Asti.

Tenuta Pegazzera (It) a winery based in Oltrepo Pavese, Lombardy.

Tenuta Rapitala (It) a winery based on the island of Sicily.

Tenuta Regaleali (It) a large winery based at Vallelunga, Sicily. 500ha. Wines sold under the Regaleali label.

Tenuta Scilio (It) a winery based on the island of Sicily. Label: Etna Rosato (rosé).

Tenuta Torciano (It) a winery. (Add): Via Crocetta 18, Loc. Ulignano, 53030 San Gimignano (SI), Tuscany. Produces Baldassare plus a range of D.O.C.G. and I.G.T. wines.

Tenuta Villanova (It) a winery (established 1499) based in Villanova di Farra in the Friuli-Venezia-Guilia region. Labels: Isonzo, Ronco Cucco. 105ha.

Tenute Le Quercie (It) a winery (established 1998) based in Barile, Basilicata region. Produces: D.O.C. Aglianico del Vulture.

Tenute Niccolai-Palagetto (It) a winery based in the DOCG Vernaccia di San Gimignano in the Tuscany region. Produces: Selezione Santa Chiara. Website: http://www.palagetto.it

Tenute Silvio Nardi (It) a winery based in the DOCG Brunello di Montalcino in the Tuscany region. (Add): Località Casale del Bosco, 53024 Montalcino, Siena. Website: http://www.tenutenardi.com 'E'mail: visite@tenutenardi.com

Ten [10] X (Eng) a strong ale 10% alc by vol. brewed by the Buffy's brewery, Norfolk.

Teobaldo Cappellano (It) a winery based in Serralunga d'Alba, Langhe, Piemonte. Noted for DOCG Barolo. *see* Otin Fiorin Piè Franco.

Teobar (Port) the brand-name of a red wine blended and bottled by Caves Dom Teodosio.

Téoulier (Fr) a rare white grape variety grown in the south-east.

Teplice Brewery (Czec) a brewery based in north-western Czec.

Tequador (Cktl) 35mls (1½ fl.ozs) tequila, 50mls (2 fl.ozs) pineapple juice, dash lime juice. Shake over ice, pour over ice into a large goblet, add a few drops grenadine and serve with short straws.

Tequila (Mex) a spirit made from distilled pulque (a beer made from fermented Agave Tequilana Weber Azul). Tequila is properly known as Mezcal, Tequila is the Mezcal from Tequila County and is only produced in the district of Jalisco and the surrounding area (Guanajuato, Michoacan, Nayarit plus Tamaulipas). Quality is mainly judged by the Agave content. Pure: 100% agave, Mixto (mixed): 51% agave & sugar distillate. Quality can also include age. Three styles. Blanco (Silver): lightly aged. Reposado: rested in oak for 2–11 months. Añejo (Golden): oak aged for more than one year. *see* Tequila [Straight Drink], Golden.

Tequila Añejo (Mex) the grading of golden tequila, is graded by the amount of time the spirit spends in wood.

Tequila Cocktail (Cktl) 25mls (1fl.oz) tequila, dash grenadine, dash gomme syrup, juice of a lime, blend with scoop of crushed ice in a blender. Strain into a cocktail glass and dress with a slice of lime.

Tequila Collins (Cktl) as for a Gin Collins using a measure of tequila in place of the gin.

Tequila Daisy (Cktl) 25mls (1fl.oz) tequila, juice ½ lime, 2 dashes grenadine. Shake over ice, strain into an ice-filled Paris goblet and top with soda water.

Tequila Especial (Mex) a brand of tequila produced by Gavilan of Jalisco 40% alc by vol.

Tequila Fizz (Cktl) 25mls (⅕gill) tequila, 25mls (⅕ gill) grenadine, juice ¼ lime, 1 egg white. Shake well over ice, strain into an ice-filled highball glass, top with ginger ale and stir.

Tequila Manhattan (Cktl) ⅔ measure tequila silver label, ⅓ measure Italian vermouth, dash lime juice. Shake over ice, strain into an ice-filled old-fashioned glass, top with an orange slice and a cherry.

Tequila Matador (Cktl) 1½ measures tequila, 75mls (3fl.ozs) pineapple juice, juice ½ lime. Shake over ice and strain into a flute glass.

Tequila Mockingbird (Cktl) ⅔ measure tequila, ⅓ measure (white) crème de menthe, juice of a lime. Shake over ice, strain into a cocktail glass and top with a slice of lime.

Tequila Old Fashioned (Cktl) 40mls (⅓ gill) tequila, 2 dashes gomme syrup, dash Angostura. Stir over ice in a highball glass, add a splash of soda and a pineapple cube.

Tequila Orange (Cktl) 40mls (⅓ gill) tequila placed over ice in a highball glass. Top with orange juice and a slice of orange.

Tequila Pink Cocktail (Cktl) ⅗ measure tequila, ⅖ measure French vermouth, dash grenadine. Shake over ice and strain into a cocktail glass.

Tequila Punch (Punch) 1 bottle tequila, 1 bottle Champagne, 3 bottles Sauternes, 1 melon cut into balls, mix altogether over ice and serve in flute glasses.

Tequila Rose (USA) a tequila and strawberry-flavoured cream liqueur 17% alc by vol. produced by the Tequila Rose Distilling company, Westom MO.

Tequila Sour (Cktl) 35mls (1½ fl.ozs) tequila, 20mls (¾ fl.oz) lemon or lime juice, 1 teaspoon powdered sugar. Shake over ice, strain into an old-fashioned glass, add a cherry and slice of orange.

Tequila [Straight Drink] (Cktl) 1 measure tequila, wedge lime (or of lemon), pinch of salt. Put the salt between the thumb and index finger on the back of the left hand, hold the glass of tequila in the right hand together with the lime wedge. Taste salt, drink tequila then suck the lime.

Tequila Sunrise (Cktl) 2 parts silver tequila, 6 parts orange juice, 2 parts grenadine. Place ice into a highball glass, add all the ingredients, stir gently.

Tequila Sunset [1] (Cktl) 4 parts golden tequila, 2 parts lemon juice, 1 part honey. Mix well until blended and serve in a highball glass over ice.

Tequila Sunset [2] (Cktl) into an ice-filled highball glass place 1 measure tequila, ½ measure lemon juice. Top with soda water, add 2 dashes crème de cassis and 2 dashes grenadine, do not stir. Place a slice of lemon on the glass rim and serve with straws.

Tequila Zapata (Sp) the brand-name used by Campeny in Barcelona for their tequila.

Tequini (Cktl) ¾ measure tequila, ¼ measure French vermouth, dash Angostura. Stir over ice, strain into a cocktail glass, top with a twist of lemon peel and an olive.

Tequonic (Cktl) 40mls (⅓ gill) tequila, juice ½ lime, stir over ice in a highball glass, top with tonic water and a squeeze of lemon peel juice.

Tepotte (Den) teapot.

Teran (Slo) the local name for the Italian red Refosco grape variety, produces a wine of same the name from Istria, Croatia. *See also* Rafosk.

Térbache (Rus) a white grape variety grown in Turkmenistan, produces dessert wines.

Terceira (Port) an I.P.R. wine, also labelled Biscoitos.

Tercher Año (Sp) a red wine produced by the Bodegas Carlos Serres, Rioja. Made from Garnacha, Tempranillo and Viura grapes. Matured in oak for 15 months and 1 year in bottle. Produced by carbonic maceration.

Tercia [La] (Sp) a noted vineyard based in the Montilla-Moriles region.

Tercier (Hol) the brand-name for a French cream liqueur made with Cognac and dry Curaçao. Produced by Cooymans, 14.9% alc by vol. also brand-name for fruit brandies from same company.

Tercios (Sp) a solera reserva brandy produced by Bodegas 501. *See also* Grana, 501 Etiqueta Negra.

Ter Dolen (Bel) a 6.1% alc by vol. top-fermented, bottled abbaye beer brewed by De Dool in Helchteren.

Teremia Mare (Rum) a wine-producing area, part of the Banat Vineyard. Grape varieties: Creata, Majarca and Steinschiller. Produces mainly white wines.

Terlaner (It) a white grape variety grown in the Trentino-Alto-Adige.

Terlaner Edel Muskateller (It) a sweet white wine from the Trentino-Alto-Adige.

Terlano (It) a D.O.C. white wine from Trentino-Alto-Adige. Made from the Pinot bianco, Riesling italico, Riesling renano, Sauvignon and Sylvaner grapes. Also Terlano Pinot Bianco, Terlano Riesling Italico, Terlano Riesling Renano and Terlano Sauvignon. All D.O.C.

Terme [Marquis de] (Fr) *see* Château Marquis de Terme.

Termeno Aromatico (It) a local name in Termeno for the Gewürztraminer grape.

Terminus (Fr) a noted absinthe producer.

Termo (Port) a white table wine.

Termo (Sp) Thermos flask™.

Termoflaske (Den) Thermos flask™.

Termos (Port) (Rus) Thermos flask™.

Termos Boca (Cro) Thermos flask™.

Ternay (Fr) a commune in the Vienne département.

Wines are produced under the A.C. Saumur, Anjou-Saumur, Loire.

Terne (Fr) a dull, ordinary wine that lacks quality.

Teroldego (It) a red grape variety grown in the Trentino-Alto-Adige.

Teroldego (It) a red wine from the Trentino-Alto-Adige. Made from a grape of the same name.

Teroldego Rotaliano (It) a D.O.C. red or rosé wine from the Trentino-Alto-Adige. Made from the Lagrein and Pinot grapes. Red can have Rubino (ruby) on the label.

Teroldego Rotaliano Superiore (It) a D.O.C. red wine from the Trentino-Alto-Adige. Made from the Lagrein and Pinot grapes. Minimum alcohol content 12% by vol.

Terpenes (Eng) chemicals (with strong floral compounds) that along with other substances make up tertiary constituents and add to the wine (Gewürztraminer/Muscat/Riesling) or spirit's character. They can develop a pungent resinous oiliness with age. Also called Terpenoid.

Terpenoid (Eng) see Terpenes.

Terra Alta (Sp) a Denominación de Origen region based west of Tarragona province, part of Cataluña. 10800ha. Produces red, rosé, white wines (dry to semi-sweet, plus mistelas). Grape varieties: 77% Garnacha blanca, 10% Macabeo plus Cabernet sauvignon, Cariñena, Chardonnay, Colombard, Garnacha tinta, Merlot, Moscatel Parellada, Peluda, Pinot meunier, Pinot noir, Tempranillo.

Terrabianca (It) a winery. Website: http://www.terrabianca.com

Terrace Bay (S.Afr) the label for a blended red wine produced by the Vergenoegd Estate winery, Stellenbosch, Western Cape.

Terrace Road (N.Z) a 15ha winery. (Add): Terrace Road, P.O. Box 33, Renwick, Marlborough. Grape varieties: Chardonnay, Sauvignon blanc, Merlot, Pinot noir. Produces still and sparkling (traditional method) wines.

Terraces (Port) a name given to the ledge-type vineyards of the Douro area, blasted out of the rocks in the upper Douro valley.

Terracina (It) a wine-producing city based south of Rome in the Latium region, noted for Muscat wines.

Terra del Capo (S.Afr) the label for a range of wines produced by the L'Ormarins Private Cellar winery, Franschhoek, Western Cape.

Terra Hutton (S.Afr) a red (Cabernet sauvignon) wine from the Darling Cellars, Coastal region.

Terran (Cro) a red grape variety grown in Istria, Croatia. See also Terrano.

Terranis (Fr) an alternative name for the Malbec grape.

Terrano (It) the local name for the Refosco or Teran grape.

Terrantez (Mad) a lesser known Madeira with a dry, bitter finish, also the name of a white grape variety. Known in the Douro as the Folgasão.

Terrantez Preto (Mad) a noble black grape variety.

Terra Promessa (It) a white grape grown in Verona for the production of Valpolicella.

Terra Rosa (Austr) a strip of red soil 1km wide by 9kms long in the Coonawarra district of South Australia. Produces Australia's premium red wines in good years.

Terras Altas (Port) the name given to the Dão wines produced by Fonseca in Bierra Alta.

Terras do Sado (Port) a new Vinho Regional for the DOC areas of Palmela and Setúbal.

Terrasola (Mex) the brand-name used by Productos Vinícola in Guadalupe, Baja California for a range of their wines.

Terrasses de Béziers (Fr) a new (2006) sub-region A.C. within the A.C. Coteaux du Languedoc based on its climate and soil.

Terrasses du Larzac (Fr) a new (2005) sub-region A.C. within the A.C. Coteaux du Languedoc based on its climate and soil (includes Montpeyroux and St-Saturnin).

Terra Valentine (USA) a winery based in the Spring Mountain District, Napa Valley, California. Grape varieties includes: Cabernet sauvignon, Merlot.

Terrazas de Los Andes Wines (Arg) a winery based in Perdriel, Mendoza. Produce a fine range of wines made from Chardonnay, Cabernet, Syrah and Malbec grapes (owned by Moët et Chandon). Website: http://www.terrazasdelosandes.com 'E'mail: info@terrazasdelosandes.com.ar

Terre Arse (It) a 10 year old Marsala Vergine from Cantine Florio, Sicily 19% alc by vol.

Terre Bouc (Fr) describes a sub-soil of alluvium and clay found in Bas Armagnac.

Terre Cortesi Moncaro (It) a winery in the D.O.C. Verdicchio dei Castelli di Jesi, Marches region. Label: Le Vele. Also produces I.G.T. Barocco wines.

Terre da Vino (It) a winery. (Add): Via Roma 50, 10020 Moriondo Torinese, Piemonte. Produces Barolo and Barbaresco wines.

Terre degli Svevi (It) a winery (established 1996) based in Venosa, Basilicata region. Produces: D.O.C. Aglianico del Vulture.

Terre dei Rotari (It) a well-known wine-producer of the Arneis grape in southern Piemonte.

Terre del Barolo (It) a growers' co-operative based in Barolo, Piemonte, north-western Italy.

Terre di Franciacorta (It) a D.O.C. in Lombardy for still red and white wines.

Terre di Genestra (It) a winery based in San Cipirello, Sicily. Produces red and white wines. Blended red wines are sold under the I Grilli di Villa label.

Terredora di Paolo (It) a vineyard based in Campania region. (Add): Via Serra 83030 Montefusco, Avellino. Produces: Fiano di Allellino, Greco di Tufo, Lacryma Christi del Vesuvio Bianco, Loggio della Serra, Taurasi Fatica Contadina. Website: http://www.terredora.com 'E'mail: info@terredora.com

Terreno [El] (Sp) a Sherry producer based in Jerez.

Terres Blanches (Fr) the Loire name for the

T

kimmeridge clay soil in and around Sancerre in the Central Vineyards.

Terres Blanches (Fr) an A.C. Coteaux des Baux-en-Provence, Saint-Rèmy-de-Provence.

Terres Brûlées (Fr) an A.C. Cornas Cru wine produced Colombo (Jean Luc), La Roche, Tain l'Hermitage. Also produces Les Ruchets and La Louvée (both A.C. Cornas). Plus Les Collines de Laure (Vin de Pays de Collines Rhodanniennes). Grape variety: Fiano di avellino.

Terres de Flein (Fr) a natural spring mineral water. Mineral contents (milligrammes per litre): Sodium 9mg/l, Calcium 116mg/l, Magnesium 4.4mg/l, Potassium 2.4mg/l, Bicarbonates 331mg/l, Chlorides 15.5mg/l, Sulphates 25.5mg/l, Nitrates <1mg/l. pH 7.2

Terres de Sommières (Fr) a new (2006) sub-region A.C. within the A.C. Coteaux du Languedoc based on its climate and soil.

Terres Fortes (Fr) heavy clay soil.

Terret-Bourret (Fr) a white grape variety grown in the Palette district of Provence.

Terret Gris (Fr) a white grape variety grown in the Languedoc.

Terret Noir (Fr) a red grape variety grown in the southern Rhône for Châteauneuf-du-Pape.

Terrici (It) an I.G.T. Chardonnay or I.G.T. red wine produced from 80% Sangiovese grosso, 15% Cabernet sauvignon and 5% Cabernet franc grapes by Azienda Agricola Lanciola, Imprunetana.

Terricio (It) a 40ha vineyard. Grape varieties: Sauvignon blanc, Chardonnay, Cabernet sauvignon, Merlot, Sangiovese, Petit verdot, Syrah, Tannat, Mourvèdre. Produces Saluccio, Tassinaia, Lupicaia.

Terricone s.p.a/Birra Morena (It) a brewery. (Add): Zona Industrialie di Baragiano, Balvano 85050. Brews beers and lagers. Website: http://www.blackroyal.com 'E'mail: birramorena@birramorena.com

Terrier (Eng) a 4.2% alc by vol. beer from the Darktribe Brewery, Gunness, near Scunthorpe, North Lincolnshire.

Terroir (Fr) a nature, structure and composition of the soil in a vineyard, the term is unique for France and identifies the individuality of vineyards and vineyard plots. *See also* Pangkarra. (Sp) = terruño.

Terroir de Caunes (Fr) an A.C. red wine from the Minervois district in the Midi.

Terroir Wines of SA (S.Afr) a winery (established 2002) based in Stellenbosch, Western Cape. Grape varieties: Cabernet sauvignon, Shiraz. Labels: JWL, Karmosyn, Sweetwell.

Terruño (Sp) terroir.

Terrunyo (Chile) a red wine produced from Carmenère grapes by Concha Y Toro in Casablanca Valley.

Terry (Sp) a brandy and Sherry producer. (Add): Fernando A. de Terry S.A. Santissima Trinidad, P.O. Box 30, Puerto de Santa Maria, Cadiz. Source of base wine is La Mancha. Solera brandies: Centenario V, Malla blanca. Solera Reserva

brandies: Competidor, Imperio, Malla Dorada, Solera Gran Reserva brandy: Terry Primero. Sherry brands include Solera 1900 and Maruja Fino.

Terry Primero (Sp) a solera gran reserva brandy produced by De Terry.

Terry's Chocolate Orange Cream (Eng) the brand-name of a dairy cream, chocolate and orange liqueur from Terry's Suchard 17% alc by vol.

Terskoye (Rus) a dessert wine produced near Machackala in eastern Russia.

Tertiary Constituents (Eng) *see* Tertiary Deposits.

Tertiary Deposits (Eng) the name used to cover substances such as terpenes, the essential oils which add to the character of the spirits. Also known as Tertiary Constituents.

Tertiary Fermentation (Eng) the third fermentation.

Tesalia (S.Am) a natural spring mineral water from Las Fuentes de Tesalia, Ecuador. Mineral contents (milligrammes per litre): Sodium 147mg/l, Calcium 46mg/l, Magnesium 148mg/l, Potassium 8mg/l, Bicarbonates 1120mg/l, Sulphates 23mg/l.

Tesanjski Dijamant (Bos) a slightly acidic natural spring mineral water from Tesanj, Bosnia and Herzegovina. Mineral contents (milligrammes per litre): Sodium 15mg/l, Calcium 64.92mg/l, Magnesium 47.62mg/l, Potassium 0.78mg/l, Bicarbonates 429.44mg/l, Chlorides 9mg/l, Sulphates 34mg/l, Fluorides 0.7mg/l, Nitrates 0.88mg/l, Oxygen 7.54mg/l. pH 5.5

Tesco Fountain Head Spring (Eng) a sparkling natural spring mineral water from Huddersfield, Yorkshire. Mineral contents (milligrammes per litre): Sodium 113mg/l, Calcium 27mg/l, Magnesium 10mg/l, Potassium 5mg/l, Bicarbonates 300mg/l, Chlorides 60mg/l, Sulphates 14mg/l, Fluorides 0.2mg/l, Nitrates 2mg/l. pH 7.5

Tesseron Lot 76 (Fr) the label of a 40% alc by vol Cognac.

Tesseydre (Fr) a noted grower based in the A.C. Cahors region who bottles his own wines.

Tessons [Les] (Fr) a vineyard in the A.C. commune of Meursault, Côte de Beaune, Burgundy.

Testa (Eng) *see* Silverskin.

Test Achats (Bel) a consumer journal that reports on types of commodities including beers. Organises tastings.

Testel (Den) tea service/tea set.

Testerbranntwein (Ger) marc brandy.

Testi (Tur) pitcher/urn.

Testut [Philippe] (Fr) a winery based in the A.C. Chablis, Burgundy. Produces a range of Chablis wines.

Testuz (Switz) noted négociant-éleveurs based at Dézaley, Lavaux.

Tête [Louis] (Fr) a noted négociant-éleveur based in the Beaujolais-Villages. (Add): 69430 Beaujeu, Lantigni.

Tête Blanche (S.Afr) the label for a white wine (Chenin blanc) produced by the Signal Hill winery, Cape Town, Western Cape.

T

Tête de Cuvée (Fr) the best growth, best wines from any vineyard.

Tetero (Cktl) 1 measure Ponche Crema, 1 teaspoon grenadine, place ice in an old-fashioned glass, add ingredients, do not mix and serve with straws.

Tetley Brewery (Eng) joined with Ansells and Ind Coope to form Allied Breweries in 1961. Public houses have the Huntsman sign. Noted for cask-conditioned Falstaff 1032 O.G. and keg Imperial 1042 O.G.

Tetley's Autumn Ale (Eng) a 4.4% alc by vol. cask-conditioned ale, brewed by Joshua Tetley in Leeds, Yorkshire to commemorate National Brewery Month in September.

Tetley's Bitter (Eng) a 3.8% alc by vol. draught canned bitter brewed by Joshua Tetley in Leeds, Yorkshire.

Tetley Tea (Eng) a famous brand-name for a range of teas produced by the Lyons Tetley C°.

Tetley Walker (Eng) a brewery based in Warrington, Lancashire, produces most styles of beers.

Tetovo (Mac) a wine-producing area based in Macedonia.

Tetra (Geo) a white grape variety grown in Georgia. Produces white dessert wines.

Tetra-Brik (Eng) small 125mls Tetrapacks™ used to sell fruit juices, easy to store, need minimum space. Also known as the Combi-Blok.

Tetraethylthiuram disulphide (Eng) *see* Antibuse.

Tetra Pack (Eng) cardboard package™ for wines, similar to fruit juice cartons, soft, 1litre or larger in capacity and usually foil lined.

Tettnang (Ger) a Bavarian hop variety and growing region used in continental beers.

Te Tui Vineyard (N.Z) the name of an old vineyard that now no longer exists.

Teubes Family Wines (S.Afr) a winery (established 2003) based in the Olifants River, Western Cape. 116ha. Grape varieties: Cabernet sauvignon, Chardonnay, Sauvignon blanc, Viognier. Produces varietal and organic wines.

Teufel (Ger) vineyard (Anb): Franken. (Ber): Steigerwald. (Gro): Not yet assigned. (Vil): Kammerforst.

Teufelsburg (Ger) vineyard (Anb): Baden. (Ber): Kaiserstuhl-Tuniberg. (Gro): Vulkanfelsen. (Vil): Kiechlinsbergen.

Teufelskeller (Ger) vineyard (Anb): Franken. (Ber): Maindreieck. (Gro): Ewig Leben. (Vil): Randersacker.

Teufelskopf (Ger) vineyard (Anb): Baden. (Ber): Badische Bergstrasse/Kraichgau. (Gro): Mannaberg. (Vil): Dielheim.

Teufelskopf (Ger) vineyard (Anb): Rheinhessen. (Ber): Nierstein. (Gro): Vogelsgärten. (Vil): Ludwigshöhe.

Teufelsküche (Ger) vineyard (Anb): Nahe. (Ber): Kreuznach. (Gro): Schlosskapelle. (Vil): Guldental.

Teufelspfad (Ger) vineyard (Anb): Rheinhessen. (Ber): Nierstein. (Gro): Domherr. (Vil): Essenheim.

Teufelstein (Ger) vineyard (Anb): Mittelrhein. (Ber): Rheinburgengau. (Gro): Loreleyfelsen. (Vil): Patersberg.

Teug (Hol) draught/drink.

Teuillac (Fr) a commune in the A.C. Côtes de Bourg in north-eastern Bordeaux.

Teurons [Les] (Fr) a Premier Cru vineyard [part] in the A.C. commune of Beaune, Côte de Beaune, Burgundy 7.32ha.

Teusser Medium (Ger) a sparkling natural spring mineral water from Löwenstein, Teusserbad. Mineral contents (milligrammes per litre): Sodium 38mg/l, Calcium 585mg/l, Magnesium 82mg/l, Potassium 8mg/l, Bicarbonates 350mg/l, Chlorides 43mg/l, Sulphates 1450mg/l, Nitrates <2mg/l, Silicates 14mg/l.

Teutonia (Ger) a natural spring mineral water from Teotoburger Waldquelle. Mineral contents (milligrammes per litre): Sodium 164mg/l, Calcium 265mg/l, Magnesium 59.1mg/l, Potassium 1.7mg/l, Bicarbonates 363mg/l, Chlorides 237mg/l, Sulphates 602mg/l.

Te Whare Ra (N.Z) a 4ha. winery. (Add): Anglesea Street, Renwick, Marlborough, South Island. Grape varieties: Cabernet franc, Cabernet sauvignon, Merlot, Chardonnay, Gewürztraminer, Riesling.

Te Whetu (N.Z) a winery. (Add): 5 Kirkbridge Road, Auckland.

Texas (Scot) a 4.5% alc by vol. ale brewed by the Houston Brewing C°., Renfrewshire.

Texas (USA) a southern state that has 30000 square miles of vineyards with 6 A.V.A. regions. *see* Hill Country Appellation (consists of 15000 square miles of vineyards) and Texas High Plain.

Texas Ale (Scot) a bottled ale 1056 O.G. brewed by the Belhaven Brewery in Dunbar. Brewed for export to Texas, USA.

Texas Fizz (Cktl) 125mls (1gill) gin, 25mls (1fl.oz) lemon juice, 25mls (1fl.oz) orange juice, ½ egg white, 4 dashes gomme syrup, shake over ice, strain into an ice-filled highball glass, top with soda water, serve with straws and a muddler.

Texas High plain (USA) one of six A.V.A. wine regions based in Texas.

Texas Tea (USA) a slang term for crude oil!

Texel Bier Brouwerij (Hol) a brewery (established 1994) based at Oudeschild. Brews: Licht van Troost.

Texture (Eng) the chemical reaction between proteins found in the mucous membrane in the mouth and the tannin in the wine.

Tezh Sar (Arm) a still natural spring mineral water. Mineral contents (milligrammes per litre): Sodium 6.8mg/l, Calcium 12.2mg/l, Magnesium 1.19mg/l, Potassium 1mg/l, Bicarbonates 71mg/l, Chlorides 0.67mg/l, Sulphates 4.6mg/l, Fluorides 0.65mg/l, Silicates 18.1mg/l. pH 7.7

T'Gallant (Austr) a winery (established in 1990) based at Red Hill Road, Red Hill, Victoria. Grape varieties: Chardonnay, Pinot noir.

T.G. Bright (Can) *see* Bright.

T

TGBOP (Eng) *abbr:* **T**ippy **G**olden **B**roken **O**range **P**ekoe, a grade of Broken Orange Pekoe black tea.

Thabani Wines (S.Afr) a winery based in the Stellenbosch, Western Cape. Grape varieties: Cabernet sauvignon, Merlot, Sauvignon blanc, Shiraz. Website: http://www.thabani.co.za

Thachbich (Viet) a natural spring mineral water. Mineral contents (milligrammes per litre): Sodium 115mg/l, Calcium 5.4mg/l, Magnesium 1.9mg/l, Potassium 1.3mg/l, Bicarbonates 132mg/l, Chlorides 9.7mg/l, Sulphates 8.2mg/l, Fluorides 0.7mg/l. pH 7.1

Thai Amarit Brewery (Thai) a brewery based in Bangkok, Thailand. Produces Amarit (a lager beer).

Thai Drinking Water (Thai) a bottled natural mineral water from Bangkok.

Thai Wine (Thai) red, rosé and white wines produced by United Products C°. Ltd. Nakornpathorn, Thailand.

Thalej (Arab) ice.

Thalia (Port) a neutral-flavoured white grape grown in the Setúbal and Ribatejo regions. Also spelt Talia. (Fr) = Ugni blanc, (It) = Trebbiano.

Thalland (Aus) a vineyard site on the banks of the River Danube in the Kremstal region.

Thallern (Aus) the brand-name used by Stift Heiligenkreuz for their range of wines. Is also the name of a village near Gumpoldskirchen.

Thames Distillers (Eng) distillers based in Clapham, South London. Produces: UK5 organic vodka, Juniper Green organic gin.

Thames Sticklbract (N.Z) *abbr:* TSB, a New Zealand hop variety.

Thames Valley Vineyard (Eng) a vineyard based in Stanlake Park, Twyford, Berkshire RG10 0BN. Produces Ascot. Also base for the Thames Valley and Chiltern Vineyard Association.

Thandi Vineyard (S.Afr) a winery (established 1996) based in Elgin. Grape varieties: Cabernet sauvignon, Chardonnay, Merlot, Pinot noir, Sauvignon blanc, Sémillon. Website: http://www.thandi.com

Thanh Tan (Viet) a natural spring mineral water from Hue. Mineral contents (milligrammes per litre): Sodium 48mg/l, Calcium 148mg/l, Magnesium 29.9mg/l, Bicarbonates 237.9mg/l, Chlorides 39mg/l, Sulphates 331.6mg/l, Fluorides 0.8mg/l, Silicates 53.8mg/l.

Thanksgiving Cocktail (Cktl) *see* Thanksgiving Special.

Thanksgiving Special (Cktl) ⅓ measure dry gin, ⅓ measure apricot brandy, ⅓ measure French vermouth, 2 dashes lemon juice. Shake over ice, strain into a cocktail glass and top with a cherry. Also known as a Thanksgiving Cocktail.

Thann (Fr) a town and wine commune in Alsace.

Thasian (Gre) a sweet wine produced in ancient Greece that was mixed with honeyed-dough. It was strained before it was served.

That (Eng) a 4.1% alc by vol. ale brewed by the Terne Valley Brewery, Knightwick, Worcestershire. *See also* This, T'Other, Wat Wassail.

Thatcher's Cider Company Ltd (Eng) a cider producer (established 1904). (Add): Myrtle Farm, Sandford, Winscombe, Avon BS25 5RA. Labels include Big Apple, Cheddar Valley, Cox's Katy, Christon, Dabinett, Dry Cider, Premium Press, Katy 7.4% alc. by vol, Mendip, Mendip Magic, Morgan, Old Rascal, Single Orchard (7.4% alc by vol.), Single Varietal ciders (Coxs & Katy), Somerset Red Streak, Tremlett's Bitter, White Magic. Website: http://www.thatcherscider.co.uk 'E'mail: info@thatcherscider.co.uk

Thatcher's Christon (Eng) a 7.4% alc by vol. premium dry (single orchard) cider produced by Thatcher's in Sandford, north Somerset.

Thatcher's Dry Cider (Eng) a 4.8% alc by vol. golden straw-coloured cider produced by Thatcher's in Sandford, north Somerset.

Thatcher's Ruin (Wal) a brand of cider produced by the Dragon Cider Company, Hirwaun, West Glamorgan.

Thatcher's Premium Press (Eng) a premium cider produced by Thatcher's in Somerset.

Thatcher's Sparkling Perry (Eng) a 7.4% alc by vol. perry from Thatcher's in Somerset. *See also* Katy, Somerset Red Streak, Tremlett's Bitter.

Thatcher's Third (Cktl) 1 measure blue Curaçao, stir over ice and strain into a cocktail glass. Float double cream on top and sprinkle with powdered chocolate.

That's Life (Eng) a 4.5% alc by vol. ale brewed by The Derby Brewing C°. Ltd., Derbyshire.

Thé (Fr) tea.

The (Indo) tea.

Thea (Lat) tea.

Theaflavins (Eng) chemicals which are an important part of tea, they give it life and are produced during the processing of the tea leaves.

Theakston [T & R] Brewery (Eng) a brewery (established 1827). (Add): The Brewery, Masham, Ripon, North Yorkshire HG4 4YD. Purchased the Carlisle State Brewery in 1974. Taken over itself in 1984 by Matthew Brown Brewery. Given independence in June 1988. In 1989 taken over by Scottish & Newcastle. Noted for Old Peculier 1057 O.G./5.7% alc by vol. (was 1058.5 O.G.), Black Bull 1035 O.G. XB 1044 O.G./4.5% alc by vol. Mild 1034.8 O.G./3.4% alc by vol. Best 1038 O.G./3.8% alc by vol. Masham Ale 6.5% alc by vol. Scotch Ale 1035 O.G. Lightfoot 3.7% and 5.2% alc by vol. also Cool Cask (cask-conditioned), Cool Beer (a nitrokeg). Website: http://www.theakstons.co.uk

Theakston's Cool Beer (Eng) a nitrokeg version of Theakston's Cool Cask.

Theakston's Cool Cask (Eng) a cask-conditioned ale served at 10°C (50°F) brewed at ScotCo's Tyneside subsidiary, aimed at cask beer drinkers who enjoy a cooler drink. Also a nitrokeg version called Theakston's Cool Beer.

The Andrew (S.Afr) the label for a red wine (Cabernet sauvignon, Cabernet franc and Merlot blend) produced by the Graham Beck Wines winery, Franschhoek, Western Cape.

Thearubigins (Eng) a group of chemicals which are an important part of tea, they give the tea briskness and brightness, are produced during the processing of the tea leaves.

Thea's Selection (USA) the label for a red wine (Pinot noir) produced by the Lemelson Vineyards winery, Willamette Valley, Oregon.

Theatre Dispense (Eng) the name given to bar top traditional ale dispence units where the customer can see the measure of beer in a glass cylinder in front of the pump prior to it being 'pulled'.

The Backchat Blend (S.Afr) the label for a red wine (Cabernet sauvignon, Merlot, Shiraz plus others blend) produced by the Flagstone Winery, Somerset West, Western Cape.

The Beer to Dine For (Eng) a beer specially brewed for the 'Beer with Food Week' held in the spring of 2005 using Tettnang hops.

The Bee's Knees (Austr) a red wine (Cabernet franc & Cabernet sauvignon, Merlot and Shiraz blend) produced by the Rymill estate, Coonawarra, South Australia.

The BenRiach (Scot) a single highland malt whisky distillery (established 1898) based in Morayshire. Produces a 10, 12 and 20 year old malts. Website: http://www.benraichdistillery.co.uk 'E'mail: info@benraichdistillery.co.uk

The Berrio (S.Afr) the label for a red (Cabernet sauvignon) and white (Sauvignon blanc) wine produced by the Flagstone Winery, Somerset West, Western Cape.

The Black Galloway (Scot) a 4.4% alc by vol. ale brewed by Sulwath Brewers Ltd., Kirkcudbrightshire.

The Blends (S.Afr) the label for a range of wines produced by the Bellingham winery, Wellington, Western Cape.

The Carbine (Austr) the label for a red wine (Cabernet sauvignon) from the Koltz Estate, McLaren Vale, South Australia.

The Chocolate Block (S.Afr) the label for a red wine (Cabernet sauvignon 17%, Cinsaut 11%, Grenache 25%, Syrah 45% and Viognier 2%) produced by the Boekenhoutskloof winery, Franschhoek, Western Cape.

The Dark and Stormy (Cktl) 50mls Captain Morgan rum in a highball glass over ice, top with ginger beer a juice of a quarter lime.

The Dark Side (Eng) a 4.4% alc by vol. dark ale brewed by the Boggart Hole Clough Brewery Ltd., Greater Manchester.

The Devastator (Eng) see Dévastateur [Le].

The Dogleg (S.Afr) the label for a red wine (Cabernet franc, Cabernet sauvignon, Merlot and Petit verdot blend) produced by the Laibach Vineyards winery, Stellenbosch, Western Cape.

The Drop of Live Water (Rus) a sparkling natural spring mineral water (established 1999). Mineral contents (milligrammes per litre): Sodium 1728.8mg/l, Calcium 215.8mg/l, Magnesium 149.6mg/l, Potassium 30.2mg/l, Bicarbonates 492.1mg/l, Chlorides 3097.1mg/l, Sulphates 173.2mg/l, Fluorides 2mg/l, Hydrobromide 11.5mg/l, Strontium 10.8mg/l, Silicates 29.8mg/l, Ammonium 3.4mg/l. pH 7.4

Thée (Ch.Isles) tea.

Thee (Hol) tea.

Theepot (Hol) teapot.

The Eventide (S.Afr) the label for a range of wines produced by the Mischa Estate winery, Wellington, Western Cape.

The Executioner (Eng) a 4.5% alc by vol. ale brewed by The Wharfedale Brewery, North Yorkshire.

The Eyrie Vineyards (USA) a winery based in the Willamette Valley, Oregon. Grape variety: Pinot Noir.

The Famous Gate (USA) the label for a red wine (Pinot noir) produced by Domaine Carneros, Carneros, California.

The Fifth Element (S.Afr) the label for a red wine (88% Shiraz 12% Viognier blend) produced by the Karusa Vineyards winery, Robertson, Western Cape.

The First Chukka (S.Afr) the label for a red wine (70% Shiraz plus Cabernet sauvignon and Pinotage blend) produced by the Gallop Hill winery, Stellenbosch, Western Cape.

The Foundry (S.Afr) a winery (established 2000) based in Die Board, Stellenbosch, Western Cape. Grape varieties: Syrah, Viognier. Website: http://www.thefoundry.co.za

The Futures Shiraz (Austr) a quality Shiraz wine from the Peter Lehmann winery, Barossa Valley.

The Garob (S.Afr) the label for a range of wines produced by the Kango Winery, Little Karoo (now no longer produced).

The Ghillie (Scot) a 4.5% alc by vol. bitter ale brewed by Broughton Ales Ltd., Lanarkshire.

The Glass Carriage (S.Afr) the label for a white wine (Sauvignon blanc) produced by the Flagstone Winery, Somerset West, Western Cape (now no longer produced).

The Glenlivet (Scot) a single highland malt whisky distillery in the Livet Valley, Banffshire. Operated by J.G. Smith Ltd. (Part of The Glenlivet Distilleries Ltd. [Seagram]). Range includes 12, 18 and 21 year old malts. 45% alc by vol. also produces The Glenlivet French Oak finish 1983. Website: http://www.theglenlivet.com

The Goats do Roam Wine Company (S.Afr) see Fairview.

The Good Earth (S.Afr) the label for a white wine (Sauvignon blanc) produced by the Goedverwacht Estate winery, Robertson, Western Cape.

The Guernsey Pub Company Ltd (Ch.Isles) a new company (established 2006) formed and operated by the Wychwood Brewery (Oxfordshire) that has taken over the Randall's Brewery on Guernsey.

The Hermit (USA) a red (Pinot noir) wine produced by the Francis Tannahill winery, Oregon.

The Hess Collection (USA) a winery based in the Mount Veeder, Napa Valley, California. Grape varieties: Cabernet sauvignon.

The Hops Nouvelle (Eng) a 4.1% alc by vol. ale brewed by the Teme Valley Brewery, Worcestershire.

Théière (Fr) teapot.

Theillier Brasserie (Fr) small family brewery based in Bavay. Brews: La Bavaisienne.

Theine (Eng) a name often used for the caffeine in tea.

The Joshua (S.Afr) the label for a red wine (Shiraz and Viognier blend) produced by the Graham Beck Wines winery, Franschhoek, Western Cape.

The Juno Wine Company (S.Afr) a winery (established 2004) based in Paarl, Western Cape. Grape varieties: Chardonnay, Shiraz (obtained from Bonnievale and Robertson). The labels are decorated with local artist's (Tertia du Toit) original oils on canvas. Website: http://www.junowines.com

The Keizer's Creek (S.Afr) the label for a range of wines (The White/The Red) produced by the Roodezandt Wines & Vineyards winery, Robertson, Western Cape.

The Ladybird (S.Afr) the label for a red wine (Cabernet franc 22%, Cabernet sauvignon 31% and Merlot 47% blend) produced by the Laibach Vineyards winery, Stellenbosch, Western Cape.

The Lane (Austr) a winery (established 1992) based near Hahndorf, Adelaide Hills. Grape varieties: Cabernet sauvignon, Chardonnay, Gewurztraminer, Pinot gris, Sauvignon blanc, Sémillon, Shiraz. Produces: Reunion Shiraz and 19th Meeting Cabernet Sauvignon. Website: http://www.thelane.com.au

The Last Word (S.Afr) the label for a Port-style wine produced by the Flagstone Winery, Somerset West, Western Cape.

The Last Straw (S.Afr) the label for a wine produced by the Hazendal winery, Stellenbosch, Western Cape.

Thelema Mountains Vineyards (S.Afr) a winery (established 1983) based in Stellenbosch. 50ha. (Add): Helshoogte Pass, P.O. Box 2234, Stellenbosch 7601. Grape varieties: Cabernet sauvignon, Chardonnay, Chenin blanc, Merlot, Muscat de frontignon, Pinotage, Rhine riesling, Sauvignon blanc, Shiraz. Labels: Arumdale, Ed's Reserve, Stormy Cape, Sutherland. Website: http://www.thelma.co.za

The Leveller (Eng) a 4.8% alc by vol. ale brewed by the Springhead Brewery, Nottinghamshire.

The Loch Fyne Liqueur (Scot) a Scotch whisky, tangerine, chocolate and orange liqueur 40% alc by vol. Website: http://www.lochfyneliqueur.com

The Lookout Cape Mountain (S.Afr) the label for a range of wines white (Chardonnay, Chenin blanc and Sauvignon blanc blend), red (Nebbilo blend) and rosé (Pinotage) produced by the Leopard's Leap Wines winery, Franschhoek, Western Cape.

The Macallam (Scot) see Macallan.

The Marais Family (S.Afr) a winery (established 1884) based in Robertson, Western Cape. 240ha. Grape varieties: Cabernet sauvignon, Chardonnay, Chenin blanc, Merlot, Pinotage, Ruby cabernet, Sauvignon blanc, Shiraz, Viognier. Labels include: La Bonne Vigne.

The Mason's Winery (S.Afr) a winery (established 2001) based in the Suider-Paarl, Western Cape. Grape variety: Shiraz.

The McKenzie (S.Afr) the label for a red wine (Cabernet sauvignon 70% Merlot 30%) produced by the Hartenberg Estate winery, Northern Cape.

The Milton Vineyard (N.Z) a vineyard. See also Family of Twelve.

The Music Room (S.Afr) the label for a red wine (Cabernet sauvignon) produced by the Flagstone Winery, Somerset West, Western Cape

The Naked Grape (Ger) the label for a dry Riesling wine from the Pfalz anbaugebiet produced by Dr. Loosen [Ernst].

The Ned (N.Z) the label for a red wine (Pinot noir) produced by the Wither Hills winery, Marlborough.

Theobroma cacao (Lat) the cocoa tree from which cocoa and chocolate is produced from its seeds.

Theobromine (Eng) a constituent of coffee, stimulates the heart, acts as a muscle relaxant and stimulates the nervous system, also helps to promote diuresis.

The Observatory Cellars (S.Afr) a winery (established 15ha) based in Swartland, Western Cape. Grape varieties: Carignan, Chardonnay, Chenin blanc, Pinotage, Shiraz, Syrah.

Theodora Quelle (Hun) a natural spring mineral water from Lake Balaton, Kekkut. Mineral contents (milligrammes per litre): Calcium 220mg/l, Magnesium 76mg/l, Bicarbonates 1050mg/l, Fluorides 0.8mg/l.

The Old Road (S.Afr) the label for a red wine (Pinotage) produced by the Graham Beck Wines winery, Franschhoek, Western Cape.

Theophylline (Eng) a constituent of coffee, stimulates the nervous system, acts as a muscle relaxant, promotes diuresis and stimulates the heart.

The Original Port Stout (Eng) a 4.8% alc by vol. stout brewed by O'Hanlon's Brewery C°. Ltd., Devon.

The Poetry Collection (S.Afr) the label for a red wine (Pinot noir) produced by the Flagstone Winery, Somerset West, Western Cape (now no longer produced).

The Portman Group (Eng) an organisation (established 1989) formed from drinks manufacturers and other bodies to advise on and promote sensible advertising, good conduct and operations within the drinks industry. (Add): 7–10 Chandos Street, Cavendish Square, London W1G 9DQ. Website: http://www.portmangroup.org.uk 'E'mail: info@portmangroup.org.uk

Thera (Gre) a wine-producing area on the island of Santorini, also the name of a white wine from the area.

The Reiver (Scot) a 3.8% alc by vol. ale brewed by Broughton Ales Ltd., Lanarkshire.

T

Theresienquelle Frankenbrunnen Natriumarm
(Ger) a natural spring mineral water. Mineral
contents (milligrammes per litre): Sodium
480mg/l, Calcium 100mg/l, Magnesium
30mg/l, Potassium 20mg/l, Bicarbonates
560mg/l, Chlorides 610mg/l, Sulphates
180mg/l.

The Ridge (S.Afr) the label for a red wine (Syrah)
produced by the Graham Beck Wines winery,
Franschhoek, Western Cape.

The Right Two (S.Afr) the label for a red (Cabernet
sauvignon and Merlot blend) and white
(Sauvignon blanc and Sémillon blend) produced
by the Nico Vermeulen Wines winery, Paarl,
Western Cape.

Therm au Rouge (Eng) a gel collar™ that can be
heated before placing around a bottle of red
wine. Used to bring the wine up to the required
temperature.

Thermenregion (Aus) lit: 'spa region', a wine-
producing region based in the centre of the wine-
growing eastern Austria. 2800ha. Soil: chalk, clay,
gravel and sand. The main grape varieties are:
white (Neuburger, Pinot blanc, Rotgipfler,
Zierfandler), red (Blauer portugieser, Cabernet
sauvignon, Pinot noir, Zweigelt). Also known as
the Südbahn. Main towns: Baden, Bad Vöslau,
Berndorf, Gumpoldskirchen, Günseldorf,
Leobersdorf, Mödling, Neunkirchen, Sooss,
Tattendorf, Traiskirchen and Wiener Neustadt.

Thermomètre à Vin (Fr) a wine thermometer. Is
used to test the temperature of wines to be drunk.

Thermos (Fr) Thermos flask™.

Thermosflasche (Aus)(Ger) Thermos flask™.

Thermos Flask (Eng) a glass flask™ having an inner
and outer section separated by a sealed vacuum.
The contents of the inner flask are kept either hot
(or cold) for long periods as the heat (or cold)
cannot pass through the vacuum section. (Aus) =
thermosflasche, (Cro) = termos boca, (Den) =
termoflaske, (Fr) = thermos, (Ger) =
thermosflasche, (Port) = garrafa termos/termos,
(Rus) = termos, (Sp) = termo.

Thermotic Bottling (Eng) a method of bottling
wine. Hot bottling at a temperature of 52°C–54°C
(125.6°F–129.2°F).

Thermovinification (Fr) the process of heating
grape musts to 60°C–70°C (140°F–158°F) for 12
hours, must is then cooled down and yeasts
added for fermentation. Process accentuates
colour and aroma.

The Rose (S.Afr) the label for a carbonated rosé wine
(Chardonnay, Chenin blanc, Pinot noir and Shiraz
blend) produced by the Twee Jongegezellen Estate
winery, Tulbagh, Western Cape.

Thés Blancs (Fr) lit: 'white teas', the name for China
teas that give very little colour when infused.

The Scotch Malt Whisky Society (Scot) an organization.
(Add): The Vaults, 87, Giles Street, Leith, Edinburgh,
Midlothian EH6 6BZ. Website: http://www.smws.com
'E'mail: enquiries@smws.com

The Sensory Collection (S.Afr) the label for a range

of red wines (Cabernet sauvignon/Merlot/
Pinotage/Shiraz) produced by the Stellar Winery,
Olifants River, Western Cape.

The Smooth Sweeter One (Scot) a blend of Irish and
Scottish malt whiskies by the Easy Drinking
Whisky Company 40% alc by vol.

The Spice Tree (Scot) a 46% alc by vol vatted malt
whisky blended by Compass Box company.
Website: http://www.compassboxwhisky.com

Thessaly (Gre) a wine region of central Greece.
Produces medium quality red and white table
wines from the Krassato, Stavroto and Xynomavro
grapes.

The Stables (S.Afr) a winery (established 2004)
based in KwaZuluNatal. 2ha. Grape varieties:
Cabernet sauvignon, Chardonnay, Merlot,
Nouvelle, Pinotage, Sauvignon blanc, Shiraz,
Viognier. Label: Blanc Fumé. Website:
http://www.rox-prop.co.za

The Stork (S.Afr) the label for a red wine (Shiraz)
produced by the Hartenberg Estate winery,
Northern Cape.

The Storm (S.Afr) the label for a red wine (Merlot
and Sangiovese blend) produced by the
Stormhoek winery, Western Cape.

Theta (S.Afr) the label for a red wine (Shiraz)
produced by the Tulbagh Mountain Vineyards
winery, Tulbagh, Western Cape.

The Tawny (Port) a special blended, non-dated Tawny
Port wine (blended from wines of 7 to 9 years of
age) produced by Graham's Port shippers.

Thetis (Gre) a sparkling natural spring mineral water
from Honeos, Thessaloniki. Mineral contents
(milligrammes per litre): Sodium 18.1mg/l,
Calcium 41.1mg/l, Magnesium 31.2mg/l,
Potassium 0.8mg/l, Bicarbonates 274.5mg/l,
Chlorides 16.7mg/l, Sulphates 14.1mg/l, Nitrates
9.5mg/l, Silicates 23.5mg/l. pH 7.6

The Travelling Stone (S.Afr) the label for a white wine
(Sauvignon blanc) produced by the Weltevrede
Estate winery, Robertson, Western Cape.

The Umpire Strikes Back (Eng) a 4% alc by vol. ale
brewed by The Brunswick Brewing C°.,
Leicestershire.

Theuniskraal Estate (S.Afr) a winery (established
1705) based in Tulbagh, Western Cape. 140ha.
(Add): Theuniskaal, Tulbagh 6820. Grape
varieties: Bukettraube, Cabernet sauvignon,
Chardonnay, Gewürztraminer, Riesling, Sémillon.
Label: Prestige, also produces varietal wines.
Website: http://www.theuniskraal.co.za

Thévenin [Roland] (Fr) a négociant-éleveur and
owner of Château Puligny-Montrachet, Côte de
Beaune, Burgundy. (Add): Domaine du Château,
Haut de Santenay, 21590 Santenay.

Thévenot (Fr) a Frenchman who opened the first
coffee house in Paris in 1647. Was known as the
Petit-Châtelet. *see* Cahouet.

The Village Bike (Eng) a 4.3% alc by vol. bitter ale
brewed by the Potton Brewery C°. Ltd.,
Bedfordshire.

The Wallflower (S.Afr) the label for a white wine

(Morio muscat & Sauvignon blanc blend) produced by the Flagstone Winery, Somerset West, Western Cape.

The Welsh Whisky Company (Wal) a distillery (established 1998). (Add): Penderyn, Brecon, Mid-Wales. A new distillery (Brains Brewery supplies the wash) whisky is matured in Bourbon casks and finished in Madeira casks. Produces Penderyn Single Malt Welsh Whisky. Website: http://www.welsh-whisky.co.uk

The William (S.Afr) the label for a red wine (Cabernet sauvignon 60% and Pinotage 40%) produced by the Graham Beck Wines winery, Franschhoek, Western Cape.

The Willows Vineyard (Austr) a vineyard based in the Barossa Valley, South Australia. Grape variety: Shiraz.

The Winery (S.Afr) a winery (established 1998) based in the Stellenbosch, Western Cape. 120ha. Grape varieties: Cabernet sauvignon, Carignan, Chardonnay, Chenin blanc, Grenache, Merlot, Sauvignon blanc, Sémillon, Shiraz, Viognier. Labels: Black Rock, Churchaven, New World, Radford Dale-Gravity, Three Gables, Winery of Good Hope. Website: http://www.thefunwinery.com

The Wolftrap (S.Afr) the label for a range of wines produced by the Boekenhoutskloof winery, Franschhoek, Western Cape.

The Work of Time (S.Afr) the label for a red wine (Cabernet franc 40%, Merlot 40% plus Cabernet sauvignon and Petit verdot blend) produced by the Springfield Estate winery, Robertson, Western Cape.

Thi [La] (Fr) a vineyard in the A.C. commune of Montagny, Côte Chalonnaise, Burgundy.

Thiaucourt (Fr) a red wine produced in Lorraine, north-eastern France.

Thibar (Afr) the brand-name for a wine produced by the Domaine de Thibar in Tunisia. 12% alc by vol (minimum).

Thibarine (Afr) a liqueur produced from a combination of liquorice and figs by Tunisian monks.

Thief Tube (Fr) the nickname for a pipette. *see* Valinch.

Thienot [Alain] (Fr) a Champagne producer. (Add): 14 Rue des Moissons, 51100 Reims. Négociant-manipulant. 13ha. Produces vintage and non-vintage wines.

Thier Export (Ger) a Dortmunder export lager produced by the Dortmunder Thier Brauerei in Dortmund, Westphalia.

Thiergarten Felsköpfchen (Ger) vineyard (Anb): Mosel-Saar-Ruwer. (Ber): Saar-Ruwer. (Gro): Römerlay. (Vil): Trier.

Thiergarten Unterm Kreuz (Ger) vineyard (Anb): Mosel-Saar-Ruwer. (Ber): Saar-Ruwer. (Gro): Römerlay. (Vil): Trier.

Thier Pils (Ger) a pilsner beer brewed by the Dortmunder Thier Brauerei in Dortmund, Westphalia.

Thiessen (Hol) a small winery based in the centre of Maastricht.

Thil (Fr) a Cru Champagne village in the Canton de Bourgogne. District: Reims.

Thilles [Les] (Fr) a vineyard in the A.C. commune of Montagny, Côte Chalonnaise, Burgundy.

Thillonnes [Les] (Fr) a vineyard in the A.C. commune of Montagny, Côte Chalonnaise, Burgundy.

Thimble (USA) an alternative name for a spirit measure.

Thin (Eng) a term used to describe a wine that lacks body and taste, almost wanting. (Ger) = duenn.

Thiniatiko (Gre) a red grape variety used to make Ktima Calliga (a dry wine).

Thin Ice (Eng) a 4.7% alc by vol. ale brewed by Elgood & Sons Ltd., Cambridgeshire.

Thins (Eng) a brewing term used by maltsters for rootlets and waste shed by barley during the malting process.

Thíra (Gre) an island in the Cyclades group of islands. Produces red and dessert wines, also a straw wine. *see* Santorini and Nycteri.

Third Degree (Cktl) a Martinez cocktail with a dash of absinthe and an olive, but with 40mls (⅓ gill) gin, 20mls (⅙ gill) French vermouth used instead.

Third Growths (Fr) the Bordeaux Haut-Médoc Grand Crus. *see* Troisiéme Crus.

Third [3ʳᵈ] Noel (Eng) a 4.9% alc by vol. ale brewed by the Acorn Brewery, South Yorkshire.

Third Rail (Cktl) ⅓ measure white rum, ⅓ measure applejack, ⅓ measure brandy, 2 dashes pastis. Shake over ice and strain into a cocktail glass.

Third Wine (S.Afr) the label for a red wine (Merlot 54% plus Cabernet sauvignon, Cabernet franc, and Petit verdot blend) produced by the Morgenster Estate winery, Stellenbosch, Western Cape.

Thirion [Archille] (Fr) an Alsace wine producer. (Add): 67 Route du Vin, 68580 St-Hippolite.

Thirst (Eng) to have a need for liquid refreshment.

Thirst-Pi (Asia) a natural spring mineral water from Nepal.

Thirsty (Eng) the term used to describe a person who needs liquid refreshment. (Aus) = durstig, (Cro) = Žedan, (Fr) = avoir soif, (Ger) = durstig, (Sp) = sediento, (Wal) = sychedig.

Thirsty Camel (Eng) the brand-name of a lightly carbonated spring water.

Thirsty Willy (Eng) a 3.7% alc by vol. ale from Bishop's Brewery, London.

Thirwell's Blue Cow Micro-Brewery (Eng) a brewery (established 1992). (Add): 29 High Street, South Witham, Grantham, Lincolnshire NG33 5QB. Brews beers and lager. Website: http://www.thebluecowinn.co.uk 'E'mail: Richard@thirwell.fslife.co.uk

Thirtyfive [35] South (Chile) the name of a Cabernet sauvignon wine produced by Viña San Pedro in the Central Valley (originally known as 35 Sur).

Thirtyfive [35] Sur (Chile) *see* 35 South.

Thirtynine [39] Steps (Eng) a 3.9% alc by vol. ale brewed by the Crouch Vale Brewery.

Thirtythree [33] Brasserie (Fr) a brewery based in Paris. Noted for Record and Porter 39 beers.

Thirtythree [33] Degrees South (S.Afr) the label for a red wine (Pinotage and Cinsaut blend) produced by the Wamakersvallei Winery, Wellington, Western Cape.

Thirtytwo [32] South Ltd (S.Afr) a winery (established 1998) based in the Stellenbosch, Western Cape. Grape varieties: Bukettraube, Cabernet sauvignon, Chenin blanc, Furmint, Pinotage, Shiraz. Labels: Bainskloof, Cape American Oak, Elephant Trail, Leopard Canyon (no longer produced), Limited Release, Sweet Surrender.

Thirwell's Best Bitter (Eng) a 3.8% alc by vol. session ale brewed by Thirwell micro-brewery in South Witham, near Grantham, Lincolnshire.

Thirwell's Witham Wobbler (Eng) a dark beer 4.2% alc by vol. ale brewed by Thirwell micro-brewery in South Witham, near Grantham, Lincolnshire.

This (Eng) a 3.7% alc by vol. ale brewed by the Terne Valley Brewery, Knightwick, Worcestershire. *see* That, T'Other, Wat Wassail.

Thisbe (Cyp) a medium-dry fruity white wine from Keo in Limassol.

Thisted Brewery (Den) a brewery based in North Jutland.

Thistle (Cktl) ½ measure Scotch whisky, ½ measure sweet vermouth, dash Angostura. Stir over ice and strain into a cocktail glass.

Thistle Brewery (Eng) part of the Maclay Brewery of Alloa. Brews Thrapple Warmer in December.

Thistle Glass (Eng) a specific shaped (thistle) glass used mainly for whisky-based liqueurs.

Thitarine (Afr) a sweet north African liqueur made from figs, herbs and liquorice.

Thomas Adams Distillers Ltd. (Can) a subsidiary of Seagram. Produces Antique, Homestead, Gold Stripe and Private Stock brands of Canadian whiskies.

Thomasberg (Ger) vineyard (Anb): Mosel-Saar-Ruwer. (Ber): Bernkastel. (Gro): Schwarzlay. (Vil): Burg.

Thomas Bewick Bitter (Eng) a 3.7% alc by vol. bitter ale brewed by the Dunn Plowman Brewery, Herefordshire.

Thomas Cooper's Finest Export (Austr) *see* Cooper's Finest Export [Thomas].

Thomas Fogarty (USA) a winery based in the Santa Cruz Mountains, San Francisco Bay, California. Grape variety: Pinot Noir. Label: Rapley Trail Vineyard.

Thomas Greenall's Original (Eng) a full-bodied cask-conditioned bitter 1045 O.G. brewed by Greenall in Warrington from Fuggles and Goldings hops.

Thomas Hardy (Eng) a 11.5% alc by vol. barley wine brewed by O'Hanlon's Brewery Cº. Ltd., Devon.

Thomas Hardy Ale (Eng) a naturally-conditioned, bottled beer, (barley wine). The strongest produced in Britain 1125 O.G./12% alc by vol. Brewed annually by the Eldridge Pope Brewery in Dorchester, Dorset since 1968. Needs to be matured in bottle for up to 4 years before it is at its peak, all bottles are individually numbered and dated.

Thomas Hardy Brewery [The] (Eng) a brewery (established 1997). (Add): Weymouth Avenue, Dorchester, Dorset DT1 1QT. Brews a range of beers. Website: http://www.thomashardybrewery.co.uk 'E'mail: david.holmes@thomashardybrewery.co.uk

Thomas Hardy Country Bitter (Eng) a bitter beer brewed by Eldridge Pope in Dorchester, Dorset as a tribute to 150th anniversary of Thomas Hardy's birth. *See also* Hardy Country Bitter.

Thomas Hardy Winery (Austr) a winery based in the Southern Vales, South Australia. Produces varietal and table wines.

Thomas Lund (Eng) a nineteenth century corkscrew producer who patented the Rack and Pinion corkscrew.

Thomas McGuinness Brewing Company (Eng) a brewery (established 1991). (Add): Cask & Feather Public House, 1 Oldham Road, Rochdale, Lancashire OL16 1UA. Brews: Junction Bitter 4.1% alc by vol., McGuinness Best Bitter 3.8% alc by vol., McGuinness Dark Mild 3.4% alc by vol., McGuinness SRB 4% alc by vol., Tommy Todd Porter 5% alc by vol., Utter Nutter 3.8% alc by vol. 'E'mail: tawnycask@hotmail.com

Thomas Slee's Academy Ale (Eng) an ale brewed by the Tirril Brewery, Cumbria.

Thomas Sykes Old Ale (Eng) a 10% alc by vol. cask-conditioned ale brewed by Burton Bridge Brewery in Burton-on-Trent.

Thomas Vineyards (USA) a winery based in Cucamonga, Southern California. Produces varietal, table, sparkling and dessert wines.

Thomas Winery (Austr) a winery based in the Margaret River area of Western Australia.

Thompson (USA) *see* Thompson Seedless.

Thompson Brewery (Eng) a brewery (established 1981) based in Ashburton, Devon. Brews: cask-conditioned Bitter 1040 O.G. Mild 1034 O.G. IPA 1045 O.G. keg Dartmoor Bitter 1037 O.G. Dartmoor Lager 1036 O.G. bottled Pale Ale 1045 O.G. IPA 1050 O.G. Yuletide Tipple.

Thompson Seedless (USA) a high yielding white grape variety used for blending with cheap table wines. *see* Wuhebai. Also known as Thompson.

Thompson Winery (USA) a winery based in Michigan. Produces sparkling wines under the labels of Père Hennepin and Père Marquete.

Thonon (Fr) a natural spring mineral water from Thonon-les-Bains, Versoie, Haute-Savoie. Mineral contents (milligrammes per litre): Sodium 5.1mg/l, Calcium 103mg/l, Magnesium 16.1mg/l, Potassium 1.4mg/l, Bicarbonates 332mg/l, Chlorides 8.2mg/l, Sulphates 14mg/l, Nitrates 14mg/l. pH 7.3

Thor Brewery (Den) a brewery based in Randers, North Jutland. Brews: Thunder beer (light-coloured lager beer) and Kastel Karl Lager 10.7% alc. vol.

Thor Dansk Vand (Den) a natural spring mineral water from Randers.

Thorin (Fr) a large noted négociant-éleveur based in the Beaujolais region in Burgundy at Pontaneveaux, 71570 La Chapelle-de-Guinchay. *see* Les Jarrons.

Thorins (Fr) the name given to wine from the Saône-et-Loire département in the Burgundy region.

Thornbury (Eng) vineyard (established 1972) based near Bristol. 0.5ha. Grape varieties include Müller-Thurgau. Produces Thornbury Castle wines.

Thornbury Castle (Eng) *see* Thornbury.

Thorne (Eng) a cask-conditioned bitter 1038 O.G. brewed by the Darley Brewery in Thorne, South Yorkshire.

Thornhill (S.Afr) the label for a red wine (Shiraz) produced by the Veenwouden Private Cellar winery, Paarl, Western Cape.

Thörnich (Ger) village (Anb): Mosel-Saar-Ruwer. (Ber): Bernkastel. (Gro): Sankt Michael. (Vins): Enggass, Ritsch.

Thorntree (S.Afr) the label for a range of wines produced by the Overhex Private Cellar winery, Worcester, Western Cape.

Thorntree Wines (S.Afr) a winery based in Constantia, Western Cape. Grape varieties: Cabernet sauvignon, Chardonnay, Chenin blanc, Merlot, Pinotage, Shiraz. Labels: Cape Mist, Thorntree, Witteboomen.

Thoroughbred (Wal) a 4.5% alc by vol. ale brewed by SA Brain & Cº. Ltd., South Glamorgan.

Thoroughbreds (Eng) a term used to describe wines which have turned out as expected of wines of their class.

Thoroughbred Special (Eng) a 5% alc by vol. beer from the Hambleton Brewery.

Thorp Cocktail (Cktl) 1 measure dry gin, ¼ measure maraschino, ½ measure gomme syrup, ½ measure Campari. Stir over ice in a highball glass and top with a dash lemon peel juice.

Thorspring (Ice) a natural spring mineral water from Reykjavik.

Thor's Thunder (Eng) a 4.4% alc by vol. ale from Viking Brewery, Thanet, Kent.

Thouarcé (Fr) a commune on the right bank of the river Layon in Coteaux du Layon, Anjou-Saumur district of the Loire. Produces Bonnezeaux.

Thousand Oaks Winery (USA) a vineyard and winery based in Starkville, Mississippi. 10ha. Produces French-American hybrids, Muscadine and vinifera wines.

Thrace (Gre) a wine region of north-eastern Greece.

Thralls (Eng) *see* Stillage.

Thrappledouser (Scot) a 4.3% alc by vol. bitter ale brewed by the Inveralmond Brewery Ltd., Perthshire.

Thrapple Warmer (Scot) a 5.2% alc by vol. rich, dark, winter cask ale brewed by the Maclay Brewery of Alloa in December.

Thrash (Eng) a slang term for a heavy drinking bout.

Three Anchor (S.Afr) the label for a range of wines (Cabernet sauvignon-Merlot and Chardonnay-Chenin blanc) produced by the Cape First Wines winery, Stellenbosch, Western Cape.

Three [3] B's (Eng) a 4% alc by vol. bitter brewed by Arkells Brewery in Swindon, Wiltshire.

Three Blind Mice (Eng) a 4.2% alc by vol. conditioned ale brewed by the Nursery Brewery, Keynsham, near Bristol.

Three Bridges (Austr) a label of the Westend Estate, Riverina.

Three Cape Ladies (S.Afr) the label for a red wine (Pinotage plus Cabernet sauvignon and Merlot blend) produced by the Warwick Estate winery, Stellenbosch, Western Cape.

Three Choirs Vineyard (Eng) a vineyard (established 1973). (Add): Newent, Gloucestershire GL18 1LS. 8.5ha. Grape varieties: Bacchus, Huxelrebe, Müller-Thurgau, Reichensteiner, Ortega, Riesling, Schönburger, Siegerrebe and Seyval blanc. Website: http://www.threechoirs.com 'E'mail: info@threechoirs.com

Three [3] Cliffs Gold (Wal) a 4.7% alc by vol. ale brewed by Hurns Brewing Cº., West Glamorgan.

Three Coins (Sri.L) a lager beer 12° Balling, brewed by the MᶜCallum Brewery in Colombo.

Three Corners Vineyard (Eng) a vineyard (established 1981) based at Beacon Lane, Woodnesborough, Kent. 0.5ha. Grape varieties: Madeleine angevine, Reichensteiner and Siegerrebe.

Three Counties Brewery (Eng) a brewery (established 1984) based in Gloucester. Produces cask-conditioned Three Counties Bitter 1040 O.G. Related to the Jolly Roger Brewery in Worcester. Covers the counties of Gloucester, Hereford and Worcester.

Three-Country-Corner (Euro) the area of France, Germany and Luxembourg which all have vineyards there.

Three Crowns (Eng) a home-brew public house based in Ashurstwood, Sussex. Noted for cask-conditioned session bitter 1038 O.G. strong ale 1050 O.G. A Phoenix Co. public house.

Three D Cocktail (Cktl) 1 part vodka, 1 part Dubonnet, 1 part orange juice. Shake over ice and strain into a cocktail glass.

Three Eight [8] (Eng) a 3.8% alc by vol. bitter ale brewed by the Three Tuns Brewery, Shropshire.

Three Feathers (Can) a Canadian rye whisky produced by Canadian Park and Tilford (a subsidiary of Canadian Schenley Distillers Ltd).

Three Gables (S.Afr) the label for a wine produced by The Winery, Stellenbosch, Western Cape.

Three Graces (S.Afr) the label for a red wine (Cabernet sauvignon 59%, Merlot and Shiraz blend) produced by the Graceland Vineyard winery, Stellenbosch, Western Cape.

Three Horses (Afr) a beer brewed in Madagascar using only natural constituents. *See also* Gold Star.

Three Horse Shoes Brewery (Afr) a brewery based in Cameroon that brews Breda Lager under licence.

Three Hundreds Old Ale (Eng) a 5% alc by vol. old

ale brewed by The Chiltern Brewery, Buckinghamshire.

Three Kings' Wine (Ger) an old designation for wines made from grapes gathered on the 6th January (Twelfth night), no longer used since 1971. *see* Drei Königs Wein.

Three Lancers (Can) the name for a Canadian whisky produced by Candian Park and Tilford (a subsidiary of Canadian Schenley Distillers Ltd).

Three Lions (Eng) a 5% alc by vol. bottled ale brewed by Wychwood, Oxfordshire.

Three Lions (Eng) a 4.8% alc by vol. cask-conditioned ale. Brewed by the Frog & Parrot brew-pub in 1998 Sheffield to celebrate the World Cup.

Three Miller (Cktl) ⅓ measure white rum, ⅔ measure brandy, 1 barspoon grenadine, dash of lemon juice. Shake over ice and strain into a cocktail glass.

Three O Three [303] AD (Eng) a 4% alc by vol. ale brewed by the Hook Norton Brewery, Oxfordshire.

Three Palms Vineyard (USA) part of Sterling Vineyards, Napa Valley, California. 41.5ha. Grape varieties: Cabernet sauvignon, Cabernet franc, Malbec, Merlot and Petit verdot. Sold under the Duckhorn and Sterling labels.

Three Peaks (S.Afr) the label for a range of wines (Pinotage Rosé) and (Chenin blanc) produced by the Mount Vernon Farm winery, Paarl, Western Cape.

Three Points (Eng) a 3.8% alc by vol. event ale brewed by Ridleys Hartford End Brewery, Chelmsford, Essex. Available in August.

Three Regions Shiraz (Austr) a rich red wine named after the three regions the grapes are harvested from (Adelaide Hills, Adelaide Plains and Langhorne Creek) produced by the Leabrook Estate, Adelaide Hills.

Three Rivers Brewing C° Ltd (Eng) a brewery (established 2003). (Add): Unit 18, Vauxhall Ind Estate, Greg Street, Stockport, Cheshire SK5 7BR. Brews: Black Moon Stout 4.8% alc by vol., Crystal Wheat Beer 5% alc by vol., Harry Jacks Ale 4.1% alc by vol., IPA 4.2% alc by vol., Pilgrims Progress 4.2% alc by vol., Simply Irish 5.6% alc by vol. 'E'mail: threerivers@acedial.co.uk

Three Sheets (Eng) a 5% alc by vol. Indian pale ale brewed by Brakspear, Henley-on-Thames, Oxon. Part of the Brewers Selection.

Three Sheets to the Wind (Eng) a slang term for being intoxicated. Is likened to the sails (sheets) of a ship that are flapping around in a variable wind.

Three Ships (S.Afr) a 10 year old Sherry-cask matured single malt whiskey (released 2003 only 6000 bottles) distilled by the James Sedgwick Distillery, Wellington, Western Cape.

Three Shires Bitter (Eng) a 4% alc by vol. bitter ale brewed by the Millstone Brewery, Lancashire.

Three Sisters (Scot) a 4.2% alc by vol. ale brewed by the Atlas Brewery, Argyll.

Three Stars Cognac [***] (Fr) a Cognac rating, under British law must be three years old. French law at least 18 months old.

Three Strikes (Eng) a 4.5% alc by vol. bitter ale brewed by Abbey Ales Brewery in support of the local Avon police force's anti-social drinking campaign of 'three strikes (convictions) and you will be barred from licensed premises in 2005.

Three Stripes Cocktail (Cktl) ⅔ measure gin, ⅓ measure French vermouth, juice ¼ orange. Shake over ice and strain into a cocktail glass.

Three Thirds (Eng) *see* Entire.

Three Threads (Eng) a mixture consisting of stale brown ale and pale ale.

Three [3] Threads (Eng) a 4.3% alc by vol. ale brewed by the 1648 Brewery Company, East Sussex.

Three Three Three [333] Cocktail (Cktl) ⅓ measure Cointreau, ⅓ measure calvados, ⅓ measure grapefruit juice, shake over ice, strain into a tulip glass, dress with a cherry and a slice of lemon.

Three Towns Export (Swe) a full-bodied beer 5.6% alc by vol. brewed by the Pripps Brewery.

Three Tuns Brewery (Eng) a brewery (established 2001). (Add): 16 Market Square, Bishop's Castle, Shropshire SY9 5BN. (An original home-brew public house of long standing). Brews: Clerics Cure 5% alc by vol., Golden Nut Mild 3.4% alc by vol., Old Screse 6% alc by vol., Solestice 4.7% alc by vol., Three 8 3.8% alc by vol., Triple XXX 4.3% alc by vol. used to brew cask-conditioned Castle Steamer 1045 O.G. Mild 1035 O.G. and XXX 1042 O.G. Website: http://www.thethreetunsbrewery.co.uk 'E'mail: tunsbrewery@aol.com

Three Vines (S.Afr) the label for a red wine (Merlot, Pinotage & Shiraz blend) produced by the Dellrust Wines winery, Stellenbosch, Western Cape.

Three [3] Vineyard (USA) the label for a red wine (Pinot noir) produced by the Chehalem winery, Willamette Valley, Oregon.

Threonine (Eng) an amino acid found in minute traces in wines formed by the yeasts.

Thresher (Eng) a large chain of wine shops owned by the Whitbread group.

Throne Ale (Eng) a special ale at 4.1% alc by vol. brewed by the Potton Brewing Company for the Golden Jubilee of Queen Elizabeth 2nd in 2002.

Throwley Vineyard (Eng) a vineyard based in Faversham, Kent. Produces still and sparkling wines. Grape varieties: Chardonnay, Ortega, Pinot noir.

Thumb (Sp) a short stub on the vine in the Sherry region which bears one or two buds, left after winter pruning. Also known as the Pulgar.

Thunder (S.Afr) the label for a red wine produced by the Hartswater Wine Cellar winery, Northern Cape (part of the Elements range).

Thunder and Lightning (Cktl) 25mls (⅕ gill) Cognac, 1 egg yolk, 2 dashes gomme syrup. Shake over ice and strain into a cocktail glass.

Thunderbird (USA) *see* Gallo's Thunderbird.

Thunderbolt Ale (Eng) a seasonal beer from Thwaites of Blackburn.

Thunderclap (Cktl) ⅓ measure dry gin, ⅓ measure Bourbon whiskey, ⅓ measure brandy. Shake over ice and strain into a cocktail glass.

Thunder Cocktail (Cktl) 25mls (⅛ gill) Cognac, 1 egg yolk, 1 teaspoon powdered sugar, dash Tobasco sauce. Shake well over ice and strain into a cocktail glass.

Thunder Holt (Eng) a bottled ale brewed by the Holts Brewery, Manchester.

Thunderstorm (Eng) a 5% alc by vol. ale brewed by the Hopback Brewery, Wiltshire using Progress hops.

Thüngersheim (Ger) village (Anb): Franken. (Ber): Maindreieck. (Gro): Ravensburg. (Vins): Johannisberg, Scharlachberg.

Thurgau (Switz) a key wine region. Produces red wines from Pinot noir, dry and medium white wines from German grapes.

Thüringen (Ger) see Saarle.

Thüringer Saal Quell (Ger) a sparkling natural spring mineral water from Thüringer Heidequelle. Mineral contents (milligrammes per litre): Sodium 5.4mg/l, Calcium 14.2mg/l, Bicarbonates 28.5mg/l, Chlorides 14.1mg/l, Sulphates 13mg/l.

Thüringer Waldquell (Ger) a still and sparkling natural spring mineral water from Thüringer Wald. Mineral contents (milligrammes per litre): Sodium 28mg/l, Calcium 106mg/l, Magnesium 50mg/l, Potassium 3mg/l, Bicarbonates 281mg/l, Chlorides 40mg/l, Sulphates 241mg/l.

Thurinum (It) a red wine produced in southern Italy in Roman times.

Thurn und Taxis Brauerei (Ger) a brewery based in Regensburg. Brews: Roggen, Weissbier.

Thurn und Taxis Roggen (Ger) a 4.7% alc by vol. dark, bottle-conditioned special beer brewed by Thurn und Taxis Brauerei, Regensburg using rye, barley and wheat malt.

Thurn und Taxis Weissbier (Ger) a 5.3% alc by vol. straw, bottle-conditioned wheat beer brewed by Thurn und Taxis Brauerei, Regensburg.

tHURSTy (Eng) a 4.1% alc by vol. event ale brewed by Ridleys Hartford End Brewery, Chelmsford, Essex (available in June).

Thwaites [Daniel] (Eng) a brewery (established 1807). (Add): P.O. Box 50, Star Brewery, Blackburn, Lancashire BB1 5BU. Noted for cask-conditioned bitter 1036 O.G. Best Mild 1034 O.G. Mild 1032 O.G. (also in keg). keg Stein Lager 1036 O.G. bottled Big Ben 1050 O.G. Daniel's Hammer, Danny Brown 1034 O.G., Kaltenberg Hell 4.1% alc by vol., East Lancs. 1036 O.G. Old Dan 1075 O.G. Craftsman, Thwaites Smooth Beer 3.4% alc by vol. (nitrokeg and widget can beer), Lancaster Bomber 4.4% alc by vol., König Ludwig Weissbier 5.5% alc by vol. Wine Merchants operation is James Pickup & Sons. Website: http://www.thwaites.co.uk 'E'mail: paulbaker@thwaites.co.uk

Thwaites Smooth (Eng) a 3.4% alc by vol. nitrokeg or widget can beer brewed by Thwaites at the Star Brewery, Blackburn, Lancashire.

Thyoneus (Lat) a word used for Bacchus. See also Bassareus, Bromius, Dionysus, Eleleus, Euhan, Euan, Euhius, Euius, Lacchus and Lyaeus.

Thyrsta (Eng) the mediaeval word for 'to thirst'.

Thyrsus (Gre) the staff (stick) of Dionysus (has a pine cone on top).

Tia Eggnogg (Cktl) 50mls (2fl.ozs.) Tia Maria, 25mls (1fl.oz) Cognac, 50mls (2fl.ozs) milk, 1 egg, 1 teaspoon sugar. Shake over ice, strain into a highball glass and top with nutmeg.

Tia Lola (Sp) the brand-name of a Fino Sherry produced by Findlater.

Tia Lusso (Eng) a Jamaican coffee, rum and fresh cream liqueur produced by Pernod-Ricard (ceased production in 2006).

Tia Maria (W.Ind) a coffee-flavoured liqueur from Jamaica. Rum-based with Blue Mountain coffee extract and spices 26.5% alc by vol.

Tian (S.Afr) the label for a red wine (Cabernet franc, Cabernet sauvignon, Malbec, Merlot and Petit verdot blend) produced by the Umkhulu Wines winery, Stellenbosch, Western Cape.

Tian Ci Zhuang (Chi) a natural spring mineral water from Xi-Shan, Beijing. Mineral contents (milligrammes per litre): Sodium 23.51mg/l, Calcium 60.01mg/l, Magnesium 22.91mg/l, Potassium 1.33mg/l, Bicarbonates 256.2mg/l, Sulphates 62.77mg/l. pH 7.55

Tiare du Pape [La] (Fr) the label of a Châteauneuf-du-Pape produced by Caves Saint-Pierre, Avenue Pierre de Luxembourg, 84230 Châteauneuf-du-Pape, southern Rhône. See also Clefs des Prelats.

Tiba (Egy) a still natural spring mineral water from El Sadat City. Mineral contents (milligrammes per litre): Sodium 33mg/l, Calcium 27.2mg/l, Magnesium 14.4mg/l, Potassium 3.5mg/l, Bicarbonates 195.2mg/l, Chlorides 16mg/l, Sulphates 14mg/l, Fluorides 0.15mg/l, Silicates 11mg/l. pH 7.2

Tibaani (Geo) a white grape variety grown in Georgia. Produces dry white wines.

Tibouren (Fr) a red grape variety grown in the Bandol district of Provence.

Tiburtinum (It) a red wine produced in central western Italy in Roman times.

Tiché (Lit) a sparkling natural spring mineral water from Klaipeda. Mineral contents (milligrammes per litre): Sodium 76mg/l, Calcium 220mg/l, Magnesium 73mg/l, Potassium 19mg/l, Bicarbonates 108mg/l, Chlorides 46mg/l, Sulphates 834mg/l, Fluorides 0.3mg/l.

Ticino (Switz) an Italian speaking wine region in the south-east. The Canton is famous for the production of Merlot wines. Grape varieties: Bondola, Merlot, Nebbiolo and Nostrano.

Tickety Boo (Eng) a 4.3% alc by vol. ale brewed by The Derby Brewing C°. Ltd., Derbyshire.

Tickety-boo (Eng) seasonal ale brewed by Hydes Brewery, Moss Side, Manchester.

Tickle Brain (Eng) an ale brewed at the Burton Bridge Brewery, Burton-on-Trent.

Tickled Pink (Ch.Isles) the name for a pink-tinged lager beer brewed by the Mary Ann Brewery, Jersey for the breast cancer awareness campaign (2005).

Tickled Pink (S.Afr) the label for a blanc de noir wine produced by the Domein Doornkraal winery, Little Karoo.

Tico (Sp) a light style of Sherry, produced by Harvey in Jerez de la Frontera (used mainly as a cocktail mixer).

Tidal Wave (Cktl) 1 measure Mandarine Napoléon, juice of a lemon. Shake over ice, strain into a cocktail glass, add a dash of bitter lemon and a slice of lemon.

Tidbit Cocktail (Cktl) 25mls (⅕ gill) dry gin, dash dry Sherry, scoop vanilla ice cream. Blend together in a blender and serve in a highball glass.

Tiddly (Eng) an eighteenth and nineteenth century term for a small drink (usually of gin).

Tiddly (Eng) a slang term for a person, usually female, under the influence of alcohol.

Tiddy (Can) a Canadian whisky-based liqueur.

Tie (Eng) a tied public-house where a brewery insists that they sell the brewery's wares either because the brewery owns the pub or has a contract with the pub. *See also* Guest Ales.

Tied House (Eng) *see* Tie.

Tiefenbach (Ger) village (Anb): Baden. (Ber): Badische Bergstrasse/Kraichgau. (Gro): Stiftsberg. (Vins): Schellenbrunnen, Spiegelberg.

Tiefenthal (Aus) a vineyard site on the banks of the River Danube in the Kremstal region.

Tiefenthal (Ger) village (Anb): Rheinhessen. (Ber): Bingen. (Gro): Rheingrafenstein. (Vin): Graukatz.

Tiegs Winery (USA) a winery based in Lenoir City, Tennessee. Produces French hybrid wines.

Tie Guanyin (Chi) lit: 'iron Buddha', a style of Chinese tea.

Tiélandry (Fr) a Premier Cru vineyard in the A.C. commune of Beaune, Côte de Beaune, Burgundy 1.98ha.

T'ien-Chin (Chi) a branch of the China National Cereals, Oils and Foodstuffs, Import and Export Corporation. Has a Golden Star branch.

Tiengen (Ger) village (Anb): Baden. (Ber): Kaiserstuhl-Tuniberg. (Gro): Attilafelsen. (Vin): Rebstal.

Tientan Beer (Chi) a beer brewed in T'ien Chin by C.N.C.O.F.I.E.C.

Tierce (Eng) a cask holding a ⅓ of a butt or pipe. *see* (Fr) = tierçon, (Ger) = tierze.

Tierçon (Fr) a cask holding ⅓ of a butt or pipe.

Tiergarten (Ger) village (Anb): Baden. (Ber): Ortenau. (Gro): Fürsteneck. (Vin): Renchtäler.

Tierhoek (S.Afr) a winery (established 2001) based in Citrusdal, Western Cape. 6ha. Grape varieties: Chenin blanc, Grenache, Sauvignon blanc. Produces varietal wines.

Tierra Blanca (Sp) Albariza soil. *See also* Tierra de Anafas.

Tierra de Anafas (Sp) Albariza soil. *See also* Tierra Blanca.

Tierra de Lebrija (Sp) diatomaceous earth used for fining wines. *see* Tierra de Vino.

Tierra de Vino (Sp) *see* Tierra de Lebrija.

Tierra Estella (Sp) one of five D.O. wine-producing districts in the Navarra, north-eastern, Spain.

Tierze (Ger) a cask holding ⅓ of a butt or pipe.

Tietericus (Lat) a word used to describe the festival of Bacchus.

Tiff (Eng) an eighteenth century word for a small drink. *See also* Tiffin.

Tiff (Eng) a mediaeval word for '*to sip*'. *see* Tiffing.

Tiffin (Eng) an eighteenth century name for a short (little) drink.

Tiffing (Eng) a mediaeval term meaning sipping (a drink).

Tiffon (Fr) a Cognac producer based in Jarnac. Produces *** (aged 7 years in cask) and V.S.O.P. (aged 12 years in cask).

Tiflis (Geo) a district of Georgia where strong red wines are made. *see* Saperavi and Mukuzani.

Tig (Eng) a wooden tankard used in Elizabethan times.

Tiger Ale (Eng) an ale 1038 O.G. brewed by the Brewing Up Shop in Leyland, Lancashire.

Tiger Beer (Sing) *see* Tiger Lager Beer.

Tiger Best Bitter (Eng) a full-flavoured bitter 1041 O.G. brewed by the Everards Brewery of Leicester. *See also* Tiger Triple Gold.

Tigerbone Wine (Chi) a wine sold in small earthenware jars.

Tiger Gold Medal Lager Beer (Sing) *see* Tiger Lager Beer.

Tiger Head (USA) a top-fermented ale 4.6% alc by vol. brewed by the Schmidt Brewery in Pennsylvania.

Tiger Lager Beer (Sing) a 5% alc by vol. straw coloured, bottled lager beer brewed by Asian Pacific Breweries. (Add): 459 Jalan Ahmad Ibrahim, Singapore. Also known as Tiger Beer, Tiger Gold Medal Lager Beer.

Tiger Lillet (Cktl) ⅓ measure Lillet, ⅓ measure Van der Hum, ⅙ measure maraschino, ⅙ measure dry vermouth. Stir over ice, strain into a cocktail glass and add a twist of orange peel.

Tiger Milk (Slo) a sweet white wine from the Radgona district of Slovenija. Made from the Ranina grape. Also known as Radgona Ranina. (Cro) = Tigrovo Mljeko

Tiger Rag (Punch) 1 bottle Tiger Milk, ½ bottle lemonade, 75mls (⅗ gill) dry gin, 40mls (⅓ gill) Port. Serve well-chilled with sliced fruit in season.

Tiger Red (Eng) a 5% alc by vol. alcopop drink from Federation Brewery, Tyneside.

Tiger Scotch (Fr) a well-known bière brewed by the BSN Bières.

Tiger's Eye Pinot Noir (Austr) a red Burgundy-style wine from the Château Barker Vineyards, Western Australia.

Tiger's Milk (Cktl) 1 egg, ½ measure crème de cacao, ½ measure cherry brandy, ½ measure Bénédictine,

1 measure Italian vermouth. Shake over ice, strain into a goblet and sprinkle with nutmeg.

Tiger's Tail (Cktl) ⅓ measure pastis, ⅔ measure fresh orange juice. Pour into an ice-filled old-fashioned glass and add a slice of orange.

Tiger Tops Brewery (Eng) a brewery (established 1995). (Add): 22 Oakes Street, Wakefield, West Yorkshire WF2 9LN. Brews: Axemans Block 3.6% alc by vol., Axemans Light 3.6% alc by vol., Blanche de Newland 4.5% alc by vol., Bock 6.4% alc by vol., Kinghorn Ale 5% alc by vol., Dark Wheat Mild 3.6% alc by vol. 'E'mail: tigertopsbrewery@hotmail.com

Tiger Triple Gold (Eng) a premium cask ale 5% alc by vol. brewed by Everards of Leicester. A commemorative version of Tiger Best Bitter. Brewed to celebrate 150th anniversary.

Tight (Eng) a slang term for drunk/intoxicated.

Tight Head (Eng) obtained by forcing beer through small holes in the sparkler on a beer pump, a stiff creamy foam appears.

Tiglat (Aus) the label for a white wine (Chardonnay) produced by the Velich winery, Burgenland.

Tigmandru (Rum) an important wine-producing area. Part of the Tîrnave Vineyard.

Tignanello (It) a Vino da Tavola red wine produced by Antinori in Tuscany from a blend of Cabernet sauvignon and Sangiovese grapes (aged in barriques).

Tignolo (It) an alternative name for the Sangiovese grape.

Tigrovo Mljeko (Cro) a sweet 'Tiger Milk' wine produced from the Ranina grape.

Tiha (Slo) a still natural spring mineral water from Tiha. Mineral contents (milligrammes per litre): Sodium 1.55mg/l, Calcium 74.7mg/l, Magnesium 35.9mg/l, Potassium 0.42mg/l, Bicarbonates 384.3mg/l, Chlorides 2.1mg/l, Sulphates 19mg/l, Nitrates 1.3mg/l.

't IJ Brouwerij (Hol) a brewery based in Amsterdam since 1984. Brews Columbus.

Tijuana Coffee Liqueur (Port) a coffee-based liqueur produced by Neto Costa.

Tikves (Mac) a wine-producing district in Macedonia.

Tilgesbrunnen (Ger) vineyard (Anb): Nahe. (Ber): Kreuznach. (Gro): Kronenberg. (Vil): Bad Kreuznach.

Tilia (Slo) a winery in Vipava Valley, Primorska, Slovenia.

Till Breweries (Swe) a large brewing company with breweries based in Bollnas, Gävle, Lulea, Ostersund and Umea. Produces Rodeorm mead and Spetsat herb beer.

Tilth (Eng) cultivated (tilled) land.

Tiltridge Vineyard (Eng) a vineyard based at Upper Hook Road, Upton-on-Severn, Worcestershire. Produces white and sparkling wine.

Tilts (USA) bars used for adjusting casks or scantlings to the desired position. Known in England as Scotches.

Tim Adams Winery (Austr) a winery based in the Clare Valley, South Australia. Grape varieties: Pinot gris, Riesling, Sémillon.

Timara (N.Z) the name of a white wine produced by Montana at 171 Pilkington Road, Glen Innes, Aukland. See also Poema.

Timbili (S.Afr) the label for a range of wines produced by the Ernst & CO Wines winery, Stellenbosch, Western Cape.

Time (Eng) see 'Call Time'.

Timisoara (Rum) a wine-producing area noted mainly for white wines with some red from the Cabernet sauvignon.

Timmermans Cassis (Bel) a 4% alc by vol. bottled, wheat lambic beer brewed by Timmermans Lambic Brasserie, Itterbeek.

Timmermans Framboise (Bel) a 4% alc by vol. bottled, raspberry lambic beer brewed by Timmermans Lambic Brasserie, Itterbeek.

Timmermans Gueuze (Bel) a 5% alc by vol. bottled, gueuze lambic beer brewed by Timmermans Lambic Brasserie, Itterbeek. Matured in oak casks.

Timmermans Kriek (Bel) a 5% alc by vol. bottled, red cherry lambic beer brewed by Timmermans Lambic Brasserie, Itterbeek. Matured in oak casks.

Timmermans Lambic Brasserie (Bel) brewers (established 1850) of wild lambic beers from Itterbeek, central Belgium. Their bottled Gueze is produced in naturelle and filtered forms. Also brew Lambic and Cherry beers. see Timmermans Cassis, Timmermans Framboise, Timmermans Gueuze, Timmermans Kriek, Timmermans Pêche.

Timmermans Pêche (Bel) a 4% alc by vol. bottled, peach lambic beer brewed by Timmermans Lambic Brasserie, Itterbeek.

Timorasso (It) a rare white grape variety grown in Piemonte.

Timor Coffee (E.Ind) an Indonesian coffee of the arabica type. Produces a good aroma and mellow flavour.

Timothy Taylor (Eng) see Taylor [Timothy] C° Ltd.

Timpert (Ger) vineyard (Anb): Mosel-Saar-Ruwer. (Ber): Saar-Ruwer. (Gro): Römerlay. (Vil): Kasel.

Tinaja (Sp) a large earthenware jar used in the Montilla-Moriles region in southern Spain to ferment wine. Buried up to the neck in earth helps to control the temperature of the fermenting must.

Tinas (Sp) earthenware containers used to hold Sherry must. Can also denote a large oak cask in the Rioja region.

Tin Cow (Austr) the label for a range of wines produced by the TarraWarra Estate, Yarra Valley, Victoria.

Tincture of Tiger Bone (Chi) a medicinal drink taken by people who have 'aches in their bones'.

Tinetas (Sp) baskets used for carrying the grapes from harvest to the vinery in the Sherry region.

Ting (Eng) the brand-name of a carbonated grapefruit crush made from real Jamaican grapefruit. (Add): Suncharm Ltd., Queens Square, Honley, Huddersfield, HD7 2QZ.

Tinglewood (Austr) a winemaker based in the Great Southern area of Western Australia.

T

Tin Mine (S.Afr) the label for a range of wines (white: Chardonnay 50%, Sauvignon blanc 40% and Viognier 10%), (red: Cabernet 23%, Merlot 26% and Shiraz 51%) from the Zevenwacht winery, Stellenbosch.

Tinnea (It) a natural spring mineral water from Ascoli. Mineral contents (milligrammes per litre): Sodium 3.7mg/l, Calcium 79mg/l, Magnesium 6.7mg/l, Potassium 0.9mg/l, Bicarbonates 260mg/l, Chlorides 5.9mg/l, Sulphates 12.3mg/l, Fluorides 0.16mg/l, Nitrates 5.1mg/l. pH 7.41

Tinners Ale (Eng) a 3.7% alc by vol (1038 O.G) cask-conditioned bitter ale brewed by the St. Austell Brewery in Cornwall. See also Wreckers.

Tinny (Austr) a slang term for a can of beer.

Tino (It) vat/tub.

Tino (Sp) a large oak vat that is used during the secondary fermentation process and racking of wine.

Tinta Amarela (Port) a red grape variety used in the production of Port. Gives colour to the wine. Also used in the Dão region. An alternative name for the Trincadeira.

Tinta Bairrada (Port) an alternative name for the Baga grape.

Tinta Barocca (S.Afr) a vintage red wine produced by the Landskroon Estate in Paarl and the Rust-en-Verde Wine Estates in the Stellenbosch.

Tinta Barroca (Port) a red grape variety grown in the Douro region.

Tinta Caida (Port) a grape variety grown in the Alentejo district.

Tinta Cão (Port) a red grape variety.

Tinta Carvalha (Port) a red grape variety grown in the Dão region to make red wines.

Tinta da Madeira (Mad) a red grape variety used in the production of Madeira. Is a vinifera cross variety.

Tinta das Baroccas (S.Afr) a red grape variety used in the making of Port-type fortified wines.

Tinta Fina (Sp) a red grape variety grown in Galicia.

Tinta Francesa (Port) a red grape variety used in the production of Port.

Tinta Francesca (Port) see Tinta Francisca.

Tinta Francisca (Port) a red grape variety used in the making of Port. Gives colour to the wine. Known in France as Teinturier.

Tintaine [La] (Fr) a herb and aniseed flavoured liqueur. Sold with a sprig of fennel inside the bottle.

Tinta Madeira (USA) a red grape variety grown in California to make dessert wines.

Tinta Miúda (Port) a red grape variety grown in the Torres Vedras district. See also Graciano.

Tinta Muera (Port) a black grape variety grown in the Alenquer district.

Tinta Nascida (Port) a red grape variety used in the production of Port to give colour to the wine.

Tinta Negra Mole (Mad) a black grape variety used in the production of Madeira. A vinifera cross between the Pinot noir and Grenache.

Tinta Negra Mole (Port) a major red grape variety grown in Madeira and the Algarve.

Tinta Pinheira (Port) a red grape variety grown near Viseu in the Dão region. Has Pinot noir connections.

Tinta Pomar (Port) a red grape variety used in the production of Port to give colour to the wine.

Tinta Port (USA) denotes a ruby Port made from Portuguese grapes instead of non-Portuguese varieties.

Tinta Portuguesa (Port) a red grape variety used in the production of Port to give colour to the wine.

Tintara (N.Z) the local name used for the Siebel 5437 red grape variety.

Tintara (Austr) the name given to a range of wines produced by Hardy's, McLaren Vale, South Australia from either Shiraz, Cabernet sauvignon or Chardonnay grapes.

Tintara Vineyard (Austr) a vineyard based in McLaren Vale, South Australia. Part of Hardys. Grape varieties include Chardonnay, Shiraz, Cabernet sauvignon.

Tinta Roriz (Port) a red grape variety used in the production of Port to give colour to the wine. Also known as the Aragonez. see Tempranillo.

Tintarrón (Sp) a red grape variety grown in Galicia.

Tintern Parva Farm Vineyard (Wal) a small vineyard based at Parva Farm, Tintern.

Tintilia (It) a red grape variety grown in Molise.

Tintilla (Sp) a deep-brown Sherry with a raisin aroma produced by Williams and Humbert.

Tintilla de Rota (Sp) a dark, red wine, often used for blending. Is also known as Tent.

Tintillo de Málaga (Sp) a red-style of Málaga.

Tinto (Port) red (wine).

Tinto (Sp) red (wine), also the name used for the red Mourvèdre grape.

Tinto Aragonés (Sp) the alternative name for the red Garnacho grape in the Rioja.

Tinto Cão (Port) a late ripening, mildew and rot-resistant red grape variety used in the production of Port to give colour to the wine. See also Tinta Cão.

Tinto Cazador (Sp) a red wine (aged 3 years in cask) produced by the Cavas del Ampurdán near Barcelona.

Tinto de la Rioja (Sp) an alternative name for the Tempranillo grape.

Tinto del País (Sp) a red grape variety grown in central Spain. see Tempranillo.

Tinto de Requena (Sp) an alternative name for the Bobal grape.

Tinto de Toro (Sp) a red grape variety grown in the Galicia region. Used in the production of D.O. Toro to produce full-bodied red wines, high in alcohol. Alternative name for the Tempranillo grape.

Tinto de Verano (Sp) a red wine spritzer.

Tinto Femia (Sp) a red grape variety grown in Galicia.

Tinto Fino (Sp) the alternative name for the Cencibel, Tempranillo or Ull de Llebre grape.

Tinto Francisca (Port) *see* Tinta Francisca.

Tinto Madrid (Sp) an alternative name for the Tempranillo grape.

Tinto Mazuela (Port) another name for the Carignan grape.

Tintometer (Port) an instrument for measuring the colour in wine.

Tintorera (Sp) a red grape variety grown in Galicia. Is also known as the Mencía.

Tinto Seco (Bra) dry red wine.

Tinto Suave (Bra) mellow red wine.

Tintourier (Port) a red grape variety used for colouring. Has colour right through to the pips.

Tio Diego (Sp) a brand of dry Amontillado Sherry produced by Valdespino at Jerez de la Frontera.

Tio Guillermo (Sp) a dry, full-bodied Amontillado Sherry produced by Garvey in Jerez de la Frontera.

Tio Mateo (Sp) a brand of Fino Sherry produced from the Palomino y vergara in Jerez de la Frontera.

Tio Pepe (Sp) a famous brand-name Fino Sherry from the house of Gonzalez Byass. Website: http://www.tiopepedryside.com

Tio Quinto (Arg) a Sherry produced for export by Peñaflor.

Tipa (Tur) to cork, seal or plug and cask or bottle.

Tipicità (It) denotes a wine that conforms to that expected from its origin and style.

Tipicity (Eng) a grading of how typical the wine is to the original style in wine tasting.

Tip Lady Cocktail (Cktl) 25mls (⅕ gill) Bacardi White Label, 20mls (⅙ gill) lemon juice, 15mls (⅛ gill) lime juice, 2 dashes gomme syrup. Shake over ice, strain into an ice-filled highball glass and dress with a cherry.

Tipo de la Bordeos (Sp) once found on the labels of Riojan wines to denote that the wine was of a Bordeaux-type.

Tipo de la Borgoña (Sp) once found on the labels of Riojan wines to denote that the wine was of a Burgundy-type.

Tippeny (Scot) a term for ale used by Robbie Burns.

Tipperary (Ire) a still and sparkling natural spring mineral water from Devil's Bit Mountain, Borrisoleigh, Tipperary. Mineral contents (milligrammes per litre): Sodium 25mg/l, Calcium 37mg/l, Magnesium 23mg/l, Potassium 17mg/l, Bicarbonates 282mg/l, Chlorides 15mg/l, Sulphates 10mg/l, Nitrates 0.5mg/l. pH 7.7

Tipperary Cocktail [1] (Cktl) 40mls (⅓ gill) gin, 20mls (⅙ gill) each of Italian vermouth, grenadine, orange juice, 2 sprigs mint, shake well over ice and strain into a cocktail glass.

Tipperary Cocktail [2] (Cktl) ⅓ measure irish whiskey, ⅓ measure green Chartreuse, ⅓ measure Italian vermouth, stir over ice and strain into cocktail glass.

Tipple (Ch.Isles) the brand-name of a Guernsey and Jersey cream liqueur sold in single cup-size individual vacuum packed portions. Served with coffee in lieu of milk or cream.

Tipple (Eng) a slang term for a drink. Usually denotes a person's favourite '*tipple*' (drink).

Tippled Newt (Eng) a 3.8% alc by vol. ale brewed by the Burrington Brewery, Devon.

Tipple LA (Eng) a low alcohol draught and bottled bitter brewed by Gibbs Mew, Salisbury, Wilts.

Tippler (Eng) a slang term for a consistent drinker, one who drinks small quantities of alcoholic beverage regularly.

Tippy Golden Broken Orange Pekoe (Eng) *abbr*: TGBOP a grape of Broken Orange Pekoe black tea from the golden tea buds which gives the finished tea golden tips.

Tipster (Eng) a summer ale brewed by the Mildmay Brewery, Holbeton, near Plymouth.

Tipsy (Eng) a slang term used to describe a person who is under the influence of alcohol.

Tipsy Guava (Cktl)(Non-alc) 200mls (⅓ pint) guava syrup, 10mls (½ fl.oz) lime juice, 5 dashes rum essence (non-alc), 2 dashes blackcurrant syrup. Blend together with scoop of crushed ice in a blender. Strain into a highball glass and dress with a slice of Guava.

Tipsy Toad Town House (Ch.Isles) a home-brew public house in St. Helier, Jersey. Owned by the Jersey Brewery. Brews Jimmy's Bitter, Cyrils, Horny Toad.

Tipsy Trotter (Eng) a 5.1% alc by vol. bitter ale brewed by the Ring 'O' Bells Brewery, Cornwall.

Tip Top Punch (Cktl) a brandy punch filled with Champagne instead of soda water.

Tiquira (S.Am) a white spirit made from fermented tapioca root 40%–45.5% alc by vol.

Tirabuzón (Sp) corkscrew.

Tirador (Sp) denotes the man who works the wooden screw used in the second pressing of the grapes.

Tirage (Fr) bottling/drawing wine from casks.

Tirajas (Sp) *see* Tinajas.

Tiraje (Sp) the addition of the yeast and sugar during cava production. French = liqueur de tirage.

Tirbousson (Gre) corkscrew.

Tirbuson (Tur) corkscrew.

Tiré au Tonneau (Fr) denotes wine that has been drawn from the wood (cask).

Tire-Bouchon (Ch.Isles) corkscrew.

Tire-Bouchon (Fr) corkscrew.

Tire-Bouchon à Champagne (Fr) a Champagne corkscrew. Used to extract corks from Champagne bottles (whose heads have broken off), fits over the top of the bottle neck to retain the cork.

Tire-Bouchon avec Plumeau (Fr) a corkscrew with a horsehair brush in the handle for the removal of verdigris from the top of the cork.

Tire Sur Lie au Château (Fr) bottled off its lees at the winery.

Tîrnave (Rum) a wine region in the heart of the Carpathian mountains. Named after the river that runs through the region. White wines are the best. Grape varieties include Welschriesling. *see* Perla, Tîrnave Riesling.

T

Tîrnaveni (Rum) quality vineyards situated in the Tîrnaveni in the central province of Transylvania.

Tîrnave Riesling (Rum) a medium sweet white wine from the Tîrnave region made with the Welschriesling grape.

Tirnovo (Bul) a very sweet red wine from south-western Bulgaria, a dessert wine.

Tirollinger (Aus) see Trollinger.

Tiros (Isr) an old Hebrew (Bible) word for strong medium-sweet wines. Also spelt Tirosh.

Tirosh (Isr) see Tiros.

Tirril Brewery (Eng) a brewery (established 1999). (Add): Tirril, Penrith, Cumbria CA10 2JF. Brews: Academy Ale 4.2% alc by vol., Best Bitter 4.3% alc by vol., John Bewsher's Bitter, Old Faithful 4% alc by vol., Thomas Slee's. Website: http://www.queensheadinn.co.uk 'E'mail: enquiries@queensheadinn.co.uk

Tisane (Fr) infusion.

Tisane de Champagne (Fr) a term that denotes a light-style Champagne.

Tisanes (Eng) a 'tea' that is not made from tea leaves. The general name for any hot herb infusions with boiling water such as chamomile, mint, maté, etc. Also spelt Tissanes. See also Infusions. (Ire) = leabhar tae.

Tisbury Brewery (Eng) a brewery (established 1980) based in Tisbury, Wiltshire by the Sussex Leisure C°. Known as Heritage Ales since February 2001. Noted for cask-conditioned Old Grumble 1060 O.G. Archibald Beckett 4.3% alc by vol. Old Wardour 4.3% alc by vol. Peter Austin's Original Formula 4% alc by vol. Stonehenge 4.3% alc by vol. Tisbury Best Bitter 3.8% alc by vol. Ale Fresco, Old Mulled Ale, Nadderjack.

Tischwein (Aus) table wine.

Tisdall (Austr) a winery (established 1979). (Add): Cornelia Creek Road, Echuca, Victoria 3625. 80ha. at Rosbercon. Grape varieties: Cabernet, Chardonnay, Chenin blanc, Colombard, Merlot and Sauvignon blanc. 50ha. at Mount Helen. Grape varieties: Cabernet, Chardonnay, Merlot, Pinot noir, Rhine riesling, Sauvignon blanc and Traminer.

Tissanes (Eng) an alternative spelling of Tisanes.

Titanic Brewery (Eng) a brewery (established 1985). (Add): Unit 5, Callender Place, Lingard Street, Burslem, Stoke-on-Trent, Staffordshire ST6 1JL. Brews the following under the Titanic label: Anchor 4.1% alc by vol., Best Bitter 3.5% alc by vol., Buck Ice 4.1% alc by vol., Captain Smiths 5.2% alc by vol., Iceberg 4.1% alc by vol., Last Porter Call 4.9% alc by vol., Life Boat 4% alc by vol., Mild 3.5% alc by vol., Nautical Mild 4.8% alc by vol., Premium 4% alc by vol., Revenge, Stout 4.5% alc by vol., Summer Wreckage 6.6% alc by vol., White Star 4.8% alc by vol., Valiant Stout, Wreckage 7.2% alc by vol. Website: http://www.titanicbrewery.co.uk 'E'mail: titanic@titanicbrewery.co.uk

Titje (Bel) a cloudy white wheat beer 5% alc by vol. from Silly. See also Saison de Silly, Silly Scotch, Double Enghien.

Titlis (Switz) a natural spring mineral water brand.

Titoki Liqueur (N.Z) a green-coloured liqueur made from the leaves and berries of the titoki bush and manuka honey. Produced by Balic in Henderson, North Island.

Titration (Eng) the total acid quantity of a wine is determined by titration.

Tittarelli S.A (Arg) a winery based in the Mendoza region, eastern Argentina. Website: http://www.bodegatittarelli.com.ar 'E'mail: akovacs@eatsa.com.ar

Titten Tei (Cktl) ⅔ measure Smirnoff Red Label vodka, ⅓ measure Bénédictine, dash orange juice, dash grenadine. Shake over ice, strain into a cocktail glass, fill with iced sparkling wine, dress with a slice of orange and a cherry.

Tivon (Isr) a tokay-style, sweet, dessert wine.

Tizer (Scot) the brand-name of a soft carbonated drink produced by A.G. Barr. See also Jusoda Orange, Strike Cola, Irn-Bru. Website: http://www.tizer.co.uk

Tiziano (Cktl) 25mls (1fl.oz) freshly squeezed grape juice topped with iced Asti Spumante, served in Champagne flutes.

Tizon Palo Cortado (Sp) the label of a medium Sherry produced by Wisdom & Warter.

Tizzano (It) a Chianti Classico producer based in Tuscany.

T.J. (S.Afr) abbr: Twee Jongegezellen Estate.

Tjan-Schan (Asia) a natural spring mineral water from Bulok, Kazakhstan. Mineral contents (milligrammes per litre): Sodium 3mg/l, Calcium 72mg/l, Magnesium 43mg/l, Bicarbonates 232mg/l, Chlorides 21mg/l, Sulphates 118.5mg/l.

TJ Light (S.Afr) the label for a light (8.5% alc by vol) white wine (Muscat-based) produced by the Twee Jongegezellen Estate winery, Tulbagh, Western Cape.

Tjoemenskaya-1 (Asia) a natural spring mineral water from Chumek, Kazakhstan. Mineral contents (milligrammes per litre): Sodium 1800mg/l, Calcium 100mg/l, Magnesium 50mg/l, Bicarbonates 300mg/l, Chlorides 2950mg/l, Sulphates 10mg/l.

Thirty Nine [39] (S.Afr) a dry white wine produced by the Twee Jongegezellen Estate, Stellenbosch from over 17 different grape varieties.

TJ's 5K (Eng) an ale brewed by the Barge & Barrel Brewing Company, Elland, near Halifax, West Yorkshire.

TKO (Scot) pure white spirit distilled from cereals by the Stewart Distillery in Glasgow. Matured for 3 years in oak 45% alc by vol.

Tlaxcala (Mex) a wine-producing area in southern Mexico.

Tlemcen (Alg) a noted V.D.Q.S. wine-producing area based near the Moroccan border.

't Lempke (Hol) a 6% alc by vol. amber-coloured, bottle-conditioned special beer brewed by De Drie Horne Bier Brouwerij, Kaatsheuvel. Top-fermented, it contains orange.

Tmavé (Czec) dark (beer).

Tmavé (Czec) a dark beer produced by the Branik Brewery in Prague.

TMV (S.Afr) the label for a range of wines produced by the Tulbagh Mountain Vineyards winery, Tulbagh, Western Cape.

T.N.T. [1] (Cktl) Montezuma Silver tequila over ice in a highball glass topped with iced tonic water.

T.N.T. [2] (Cktl) place the juice of ½ a lime together with the spent shell into an ice-filled highball glass. Add 25mls (⅛ gill) tequila, top with tonic water and stir well.

TNT [3] (Cktl) ⅔ measure brandy, ⅓ measure orange Curaçao, dash pastis, dash Angostura. Stir over ice and strain into a cocktail glass.

TNT Ale (Eng) a cask-conditioned ale 1050 O.G. brewed by the Simpkiss Brewery in Brierley Hill, Staffordshire.

T.N.T. Cocktail (Cktl) 1 measure Pernod, 1 measure rye whisky. Shake over ice and strain into a cocktail glass.

T.N.T. Liquid Dynamite (Eng) an alcoholic bottled drink produced by Round Imports, Abingdon, Oxfordshire.

T.O. (Gre) *abbr*: **T**ópikos **O**ínos.

Toad's Eyes (Fr) a term to denote sparkling wines that have large bubbles, often wines that have been charged with CO_2 gas.

Toar (It) a D.O.C. Valpolicella produced by Masi from Corvina, Rondinella, Molinara, Oseleta, Dindarella grapes.

Toast (Eng) the process of drinking to the health or future of a person. Usually made with Champagne or other sparkling wine especially at a wedding, christening, birthday etc. *See also* Cheers. (Aus) = trinkspruch, (Cro) = zdravica, (Fr) = porter un toast, (Ger) = trinkspruch, (It) = alla sua, (Sp) = brindis, (Wal) = llwncdestun.

Toast and Ale (Eng) ale and ginger root heated together, poured into a tankard and a piece of toasted bread floated on top.

Toasting [Casks] (Euro) the controlled process of heating the inside of wine casks so as to alter the chemical composition of the oak. The process allows wine makers to alter the final flavour of their wines.

Toasting Glass (Eng) a thin stemmed glass of the eighteenth century so called because after drinking the toast the stem was snapped to prevent anyone else's health being drunk from the same glass.

Toast Master (Eng) a person who proposes and announces after-dinner speakers and toasts at formal dinners (dressed in a red jacket). *See also* Toast Mistress.

Toast Mistress (Eng) a female Toast Master.

Toast Water (Eng) an old invalid remedy drink. Break a few slices of thin toast into a jug and cover with 550mls (1pint) boiling water. When cool, strain and sweeten, add a little grated nutmeg to taste.

Tobacco (Eng) a term applied to the wines of Bordeaux in wine tasting, for wines that have been oak matured.

Tobago Punch (Punch) 550mls (1pint) white rum, juice of a lemon, 150mls (¼ pint) sugar syrup, 150mls (¼ pint) pineapple juice, small can lychees. Stir over ice, decorate with 2 sliced bananas and serve.

Tobermory (Scot) a single highland malt whisky distillery on the Isle of Mull. Also called Ledaig. A 1974 vintage bottled in 1992, 43% alc by vol.

Tobía (Sp) the alternative name for the white grapes Blanca-Roja, Blanquirroja and Malvasia.

Tobin James Cellars (USA) a winery based in the Paso Robles, San Luis Obispo County, California. (Add): 8950 Union Road, Paso Robles. CA 93446. Grape varieties: Cabernet sauvignon, Zinfandel. Website: http://www.tobinjames.com

Toby (Eng) the name of Bass Charrington beers (has a Toby jug logo) keg Toby Light 1032 O.G.

Toby Light (Eng) *see* Toby.

Tocai (It) a white grape variety grown in the Friulia region. Also a wine of the same name.

Tocai (Slo) the alternative name for the Pinot gris grape in the Slovenia region.

Tocai di Lison (It) a D.O.C. white wine from Veneto. Made from 95% Tocai and 5% other grape varieties. If produced in a confined restricted area is entitled to the additional specification of Classico.

Tocai di San Martino Della Battaglia (It) a D.O.C. white wine from Lombardy. Made from the Tocai Friulano grapes.

Tocai Friulano (It) a white grape variety grown in Lombardy. Also known as the Trebbianello.

Tocai Rosso (It) the local name in Veneto for the Grenache (Granacha) grape.

Tocane (Fr) the name given to new Champagne that is produced from the first pressing of the grapes.

Tocjai Aszú (Hun) the alternative spelling of Tokaji Aszú.

Tocornal [José] (Chile) a noted exporter of wines to Canada and Venezuela.

Today (USA) a 4 year old Kentucky Bourbon whiskey. 40% alc by vol. Bottled by Modern Times Distillery, Bardstown, Kentucky.

Toddies (USA) a drink served either hot or cold of spirit, lemon slice, sugar, cloves and hot/cold water. Served in an old-fashioned glass (cold) or mug (hot).

Toddy (E.Ind) the sap of wine palms used as a non-alcoholic (or fermented) beverage.

Toddy (Eng) (Cktl) 1 measure spirit, 1 barspoon sugar. Dissolve sugar in a little water, add spirit, build in an old-fashioned glass, add a twist of lemon and serve with a stirrer.

Toddy (Eng) an old name for a measure (nip).

Toddy (Ind) a spirit that is obtained from the fermented jaggery. Also the alternative name for Raki and Arrack.

Toddy (Mal) an alcoholic drink made from coconut milk, has a sour after-taste. Produced in Malaya by the Indians.

Toddy (Sri.L) a spirit made from fermented palm sap.

T

Toddy (USA) originally the fermented sap of palm trees, now classed for a tot of spirit.

Toddy Ale (Eng) a 4.7% alc by vol. ale brewed without hops and fortified with Macleods Isle of Skye 8 year old blended whisky (2litres per barrel). Brewed by Highgate and Walsall Brewing Company (part of Bass Brewers' Caskmaster seasonal selection).

Toddy Glass (USA) a special handled glass or mug for serving hot Toddies in.

Toddy Lifter (Eng) an implement made of glass or metal consisting of a cup on a long handle used to draw a 'toddy' from a cask or barrel. Also a bottle-shaped glass with a hole at the base so that when placed in a cask of spirit the thumb is placed over the top to prevent the contents returning to the cask.

Toddy Mug (USA) see Toddy Glass.

Toddy Palm (E.Ind) see Wine Palm. (Fr) = abre à liqueur.

To Drink A Peg (Eng) an old English request in the Middle Ages for a measure of drink. see Peg.

Tod's Cooler (Cktl) place into a large tumbler 2 ice cubes, 60mls (½ gill) dry gin, 20mls (⅙ gill) cassis, juice of ½ lemon. Top up with soda water and stir well.

Toep (Bel) a natural spring mineral water from Toep, Brakel.

Toffoc (Wal) a toffee-flavoured vodka 27% alc by vol. produced on the island of Anglesey.

Togal (Sp) a red wine made from mainly Garnacha grapes by the Bodegas Bardón in Ribera Baja.

Tohani (Rum) a wine-producing area. Part of the Dealul-Mare Vineyard.

Tohu Wines (N.Z) a winery based in Marlborough. Noted for Chardonnay produced from grapes grown in Gisborne, plus a Sauvignon blanc wine produced from Marlborough grapes.

Toio (Cktl) ⅓ measure triple sec, ⅓ measure dry gin, ⅓ measure apricot brandy, 3 dashes lemon juice. Stir well over ice, strain into a cocktail glass and add a twist of lemon peel juice.

Toison de Oro (Sp) a gran reserva brandy produced by Agustín Blázquez.

Toka [1] (It) a natural spring mineral water from Capanna. Mineral contents (milligrammes per litre): Sodium 56.5mg/l, Calcium 248.5mg/l, Potassium 115.5mg/l, Bicarbonates 1850mg/l, Fluorides 0.6mg/l. pH 6.12

Toka [2] (It) a sparkling natural spring mineral water from Capanna. Mineral contents (milligrammes per litre): Sodium 420.1mg/l, Calcium 232mg/l, Magnesium 50.6mg/l, Potassium 107.5mg/l, Bicarbonates 1708mg/l, Fluorides 0.7mg/l, Nitrates 18.3mg/l. pH 6.2

Tokaier (Fr) an alternative name in eastern France for the Pinot gris.

Tokaj (Hun) n alternative spelling of Tokaji.

Tokaji Aszú (Hun) a Special-Quality Wine made in the Tokaji region from Furmint and Hárslevelü grapes that have been attacked by **Botrytis cinerea**. The attacked grapes are kept separate from the unaffected grapes. They were pounded into a paste which was then measured in Puttonyos. The number of Puttonyos added to the wine made from the non-affected grapes are recorded on the bottle neck-label. (3, 4, 5 or 6). This measurement now refers to the residual sugar. 3 = 60g/l., 4 = 90g/l., 5 = 120g/l., 6 = 150g/l. Matured in partly filled casks for 3–6 years. see Maté Lacko Sepsi.

Tokaji Aszú Essencia (Hun) an alternative spelling of Tokaji Aszú Eszencia.

Tokaji Aszú Eszencia (Hun) a Special-Quality Wine. Rarest of the Tokaji wines. The juice from botrytis-attacked grapes but only in the best years. Fermented with a special yeast (Tokay 22). Expensive, the sugar content is over 200g/l (over 6 puttonyos). Usually 14.5% alc by vol. Also spelt Tokaji Aszú Eszencia. See also Eszencia.

Tokaji Aztali (Hun) a wine made from the marc or lees of the Tokaji Aszú wines. Not usually shipped but consumed locally. See also Tokaji Forditàs and Tokaji Màslàs.

Tokaji Édes (Hun) describes the sweet Tokaji Szamorodni wine. See also Tokaji Szàraz.

Tokaji Essencia (Hun) see Tokaji Aszú Essencia.

Tokaji Forditàs (Hun) a wine made from the marc or lees of the pressing of Aszú. Usually consumed locally. See also Tokaji Aztali and Tokaji Màslàs.

Tokaji Furmint (Hun) a dry or medium-dry quality wine made from the Furmint grape in the Tokaji Hegyalja region.

Tokaji Hegyalja (Hun) a hilly wine-producing region in northern Hungary which produces fine Tokaji wines from the Furmint grape with Muskotály and Hárslevelü grapes used to a small degree.

Tokaji Hetsóló (Hun) a 47ha estate that produces Tokaji Aszú.

Tokaji Màslàs (Hun) a wine made from the marc or lees of the Aszú pressings that is consumed locally. see Tokaji Aztali and Tokaji Forditàs.

Tokaji Muskotályos (Hun) a dry Muscat wine made in the Tokaji region.

Tokaji Pecsenyebor (Hun) the lowest quality Tokaji wine that is available.

Tokaji Szamorodni (Hun) lit: "as it comes", a Special-Quality Wine. Two styles produced depending on the amount of noble rot present. Száraz (dry), Édes (sweet), aged in Gönc.

Tokaji Száraz (Hun) describes the dry Tokaji Szamorodni wine, little noble rot present, aged in Gönc. Flor forms on wine. See also Tokaji Édes.

To Kalon Vineyard Reserve (USA) a red wine (Cabernet sauvignon) produced by the Robert Mondavi winery, Napa Valley, California.

Tokara Winery (S.Afr) a winery (established 2000) based in Stellenbosch, Western Cape. 100ha. (Add): P.O. Box 662, Stellenbosch 7599. Grape varieties: Cabernet sauvignon, Chardonnay, Chenin blanc, Merlot, Petit verdot, Sauvignon blanc, Shiraz. Label: Zondernaam. Website: http://www.tokara.com

T

Tokay (Austr) the alternative name for the white Muscadelle grape.
Tokay Aszú (Hun) *see* Tokaji Aszú.
Tokay Aztali (Hun) *see* Tokaji Aztali.
Tokay d'Alsace (Fr) the Alsace name for the white Pinot gris grape (Tokay-Pinot Gris).
Tokayer (Ger) the name used in the Palatinate for the Ruländer or Grauer burgunder grape.
Tokay Essencia (Hun) *see* Tokaji Aszú Essencia.
Tokay Forditás (Hun) *see* Tokaji Forditás.
Tokay Furmint (Hun) *see* Tokaji Furmint.
Tokay Màslàs (Hun) *see* Tokaji Màslàs.
Tokay-Pinot Gris (Fr) a noble grape grown in Alsace, produces spicey wines, high in acidity, also known as Pinot Beurot in Burgundy. (Fr) = Pinot gris, (Ger) = Ruländer, (It) = Pinot grigio.
Tokay Szamorodni (Hun) *see* Tokaji Szamorodni.
Tokay 22 (Hun) a special strain of yeast used in the fermenting of Tokaji Aszú Essencia.
Tokeah (Isr) a sweet, tokay-style, dessert wine.
Tokier (Hun) *see* Tokaji Aszú.
Tokio Bloody Mark (Cktl) as for Bloody Mary using saké in place of vodka.
Tokkuri (Jap) small ceramic bottles (flasks) from which saké is traditionally served, it is served from these into sakazuki.
Tokyo Rose (Cktl) 1 measure raspberry saké, 1 measure vodka, shake over ice, strain into martini glass, top with lemonade, add 2–3 dashes crème de cassis and serve with straws.
Tolaga Bay (N.Z) part of Corbans.
Tolcsva (Hun) a noted wine-producing village based in the southern foothills.
Toledo (Sp) a wine-producing area in the La Mancha region.
Toledo Punch (Punch) in a large punch bowl place 2 lbs. sugar, 4 large bottles soda water, juice of 4 lemons, ¾ bottle brandy, 4 oranges, 1 pineapple cut up, 6 bottles Champagne, 2 bottles claret, 4 bottles Perrier water, mix well with ice and serve.
Tollana (Austr) a winery in the Barossa Valley, South Australia. Is noted for brandy.
Tolley's (Austr) a winery at 30 Barracks Road, Hope Valley, South Australia. Grape varieties: Cabernet sauvignon, Chardonnay, Gewürztraminer.
Tolley, Scott and Tolley's Winery (Austr) a winery based south of Nuriootpa in South Australia.
Tolleys Pedare (Austr) a winery in the Barossa Valley in South Australia. Produces varietal and table wines, also Tolleys TST Brandy.
Tolly Beano (Eng) a creamy stout 4.1% alc by vol. from Tolly Cobbold, Ipswich, Suffolk. *See also* Tolly's Strong Ale.
Tolly Cobbold (Eng) a brewery. (Add): Tollemache & Cobbold Brewery Ltd., Cliff Brewery, Ipswich, Suffolk. Noted for cask-conditioned bitter 1034 O.G. Cardinal 5.2% alc by vol. Mild 1032 O.G. Original 1036 O.G. Old Strong 1046 O.G. (also keg versions), Beano, bottled Light 1032 O.G. Dark 1032 O.G. Export 1036 O.G. 250 1073 O.G. Royal 1064 O.G. Daffodil Beer and Suffolk Shamrock. Is linked with the Camerons Brewery in Hartlepool (both owned by Ellerman Lines) which brews under licence DAB Lager 1046 O.G. and Hansa Keg Lager 1036 O.G.
Tolly Original (Eng) a 3.8% alc by vol. bitter ale brewed by TD Ridley & Sons Ltd., Essex.
Tolly's Strong Ale (Eng) a 4.6% alc by vol. ale brewed by Tolly Cobbold, Ipswich, Suffolk.
Tom and Jerry (USA) 20mls (⅙ gill) Jamaican rum, 20mls (⅙ gill) brandy, 1 beaten egg, hot water or milk and sugar. Serve in a Tom and Jerry mug or coffee cup.
Tom and Jerry Mug (USA) a special mug for serving Tom and Jerry cocktails in (tall and slim), a demi-tasse (coffee cup) can be used as a substitute.
Tomar (Port) an I.P.R. wine area within the I.P.R. region of Ribatejo.
Tomasello Winery (USA) a winery based in Hammonton, New Jersey 40ha. Produces hybrid wines.
Tomatin Distillery C° Ltd [The] (Scot) a single malt whisky distillery (established 1986). (Add): Tomatin, Inverness IV13 7YT. A highland malt. Taken over by 2 Japanese Companies (Okura and Takara Shuzo). Produces a 5 year old malt 43% alc by vol. and a 10 year old 40% alc by vol. Website: http://www.tomatin.com 'E'mail: info@tomatin.co.uk
Tomato Cocktail (Cktl) 25mls (⅕ gill) Pernod, 3 dashes grenadine. Pour into a small tumbler, top with iced water and a cherry.
Tomato Juice Cocktail (Cktl) 100mls (4 fl.ozs) tomato juice, 10mls (½ fl.oz) lemon juice, 2 dashes Worcestershire sauce, 2 dashes celery salt. Shake over ice and strain into 125mls (5fl.oz) goblet or an ice-filled highball glass.
Tomato Wine (Ch.Isles) *see* Aztecato.
Tomboladero (Port) a white enamel or porcelain saucer, similar to a tastevin, used in the Port trade to check the wine's colour.
Tomboy (Cktl) 1 part tomato juice, 1 part bitter beer.
Tom Collins (Cktl) 20mls (¾ fl.oz) lime or lemon juice, 1 teaspoon powdered sugar, 35mls (1½ fl.ozs) Old Tom dry gin. Shake over ice, strain into a highball glass, top with mineral water. Stir. Named after a nineteenth century bartender who worked in Limmer's Old House, London. Tom was famous for his gin sling cocktail.
Tomelloso (Sp) the centre of production of brandy and industrial alcohol in the La Mancha region of central Spain.
Tom Finney Ale (Eng) a 4.4% alc by vol. bottled ale brewed to honour one of Lancashire's best known football names (Sir Tom Finney).
Tom Hoskins Beaumanor Brewery (Eng) a brewery based in Leicester that once brewed Hoskins Bitter and Tom's Gold. Brewing now takes place in Swindon uner new owners Archers.
Tomintoul Brewery (Scot) brew cask-conditioned beers. Labels include Grampian's Nessie, Stag, Stillman, 80 Shilling.
Tomintoul-Glenlivet (Scot) a single malt whisky distillery based south of Ballindalloch, Banffshire.

Owned by Whyte and MᶜKay. A highland malt 40% alc by vol.

Tomlinson's Brewery (Eng) a micro-brewery in Pontefract. Brews: Double Helix Ale 5.3% alc by vol.

Tommasi Viticoltori (It) a winery. (Add): 37020 Pedemonte di Valpolicella. 100ha. Produces white wines in the D.O.C. regions: Soave, Lugana, Custoza. Also produces D.O.C. Valpolicella Classico, Amarone Classico, Valpolicella Classico Superiore, Ripasso, Recioto della Valpolicella. Website: http://www.tomasiwines.it 'E'mail: info@tommasiwines.it

Tømmermaend (Den) a slang term for a hangover.

Tommy Todd Porter (Eng) a 5% alc by vol. porter brewed by the Thomas MᶜGuinness Brewing Company, Lancashire.

Tomnatec (Rum) a wine-producing area, part of the Banat Vineyard. Noted for white wines produced from the Creata, Majarca and Steinschiller grapes.

Tomos Watkin Brewery (Wal) a brewery. (Add): Llandeilo, Dyfed, South Wales. A micro-brewery in the town's Castle Hotel.

Tom Paine (Eng) a 5.5% alc by vol. premium bottled ale from Harveys, Lewes, Sussex.

Tom Sayer (Cktl) 2 parts Southern Comfort, 1 part Galliano, dash orange bitters. Shake over ice, strain into an ice-filled highball glass. Top with lemonade, add an orange slice and serve with straws.

Tom's Best Bitter (Eng) a bitter brewed by Bateman's of Lincolnshire for The Retreat pub in Bocking, Braintree, Essex. Named after one of the pubs regular customers Tom Rose.

Tom's Coffee House (Eng) a coffee-house bought by Thomas Twining in 1706. Sold tea as well in an effort to attract customers, also sold dry tea for home use.

Tom's Gold (Eng) a beer brewed by Tom Hoskins Beaumanor Brewery, Leicester. Taken over by Archers of Swindon.

Tom Wood's Best Bitter (Eng) a 3.5% alc by vol. light coloured, dry bitter from the Highwood Brewery, Barnetby, Lincolnshire.

Tom Wood's Shepherd's Delight (Eng) a 4% alc by vol. beer produced from a single hop variety by the Highwood Brewery, Barnetby, Lincolnshire.

Ton (Hol) cask.

Tona (It) a fine wine-producer based in Lombardy. Produces D.O.C. Valtellina and Sforzato wines.

Tondeña [La] (E.Ind) a leading rum producer in the Philippines. Well-known brand is Manila.

Tondonia (Sp) a cask-aged white wine produced by López de Heredia.

Toneis (Port) a large maturing horizontal cask used in the Douro for maturing Port wine. See also Balseiros.

Tonel (Fr) an old French word for a cask.

Tonel (Port)(Sp) a large barrel/pipe/cask.

Tonelada (Sp) 10 hectolitres of wine.

Tonelero (Sp) cask maker/cooper.

Toneles (Port) vats.

Tongerlo (Bel) an 8% alc by vol. norbertine, top-fermented, bottle-conditioned triple abbaye beer brewed by Haacht Brouwerij in Boortmeerbeek. The abbaye of Tongerlo was founded in 1133.

Tongerlo Dubbel (Bel) a 6% alc by vol. norbertine, top-fermented, bottle-conditioned, brown double beer brewed by Haacht Brouwerij in Boortmeerbeek. The abbaye of Tongerlo was founded in 1133.

Tongham English Ale (Eng) a 4.2% alc by vol. ale brewed by the Hog's Back Brewery at Tongham, near Guilford, Surrey.

Tongue Twister (Eng) a 4.5% alc by vol. ale. brewed by the Ash Vine Brewery. Part of their Nightmare series.

Tonica (Mad) a bottom-fermented, sweet black beer.

Tonic Water (Eng) a carbonated water which contains a small amount of quinine. see Indian Tonic Water. Average calorific value per litre = 260kcals and carbohydrates 60 grammes. (Pol) = tonik.

Tonik (Pol) tonic water.

Toni Kola (Afr)(Fr) aromatic bitters made from the kola nut.

Tönissteiner (Ger) a sparkling natural spring mineral water (established 48BC) from Pönterquelle. Mineral contents (milligrammes per litre): Sodium 108mg/l, Calcium 164mg/l, Magnesium 130mg/l, Potassium 13.7mg/l, Bicarbonates 1351mg/l, Chlorides 31mg/l, Sulphates 30mg/l, Fluorides 0.23mg/l, Nitrates 1.5mg/l, Silicates 52mg/l. Website: http://www.toenissteiner.de

Tonmergel (Lux) type of soil.

Tonna (Lat) barrel/cask. see Tunna.

Tonne (Euro) 1000 kilogrammes (0.98 tons).

Tonneau (Fr) barrel/also a measurement of wine. Wines are bought by the Tonneau in Bordeaux. Equal to 4 hogsheads. 1 tonneau = 96 to 100 dozen bottles.

Tonnelier (Fr) cask maker/cooper.

Tonnellerie (Fr) cooperage.

Tonnerre (Fr) a wine town in the Yonne département in Burgundy. Produces fine red and white wines.

Tony's Trustworthy Tipple (Eng) one of a 3-pack of bottled beers brewed by the Great Stour Brewery in Canterbury in the mid 1990's. Named after politician Tony Blair (then leader of the main opposition party).

Tooheys (Austr) a 5% alc by vol. cold filtered, premium strength lager brewed by Tooheys Brewery, Sydney.

Tooheys Brewery (Austr) a brewery based in Sydney, New South Wales. Brews: Blue, Tooheys, Tooheys Extra dry, Tooheys Old Black Ale, Tooheys Red Bitter.

Tooheys Extra Dry (Austr) a 5% alc by vol. straw coloured, bottled lager brewed by Tooheys Brewery in Sydney.

Tooheys Old Black Ale (Austr) a 4.4% alc by vol. fruity, top-fermented, dark bottled ale brewed by

Tooheys Brewery in Sydney, New South Wales. Also known as Hunter Ale.

Tooheys Red Bitter (Austr) a 4.9% alc by vol. extra hopped, bottled lager brewed by Tooheys Brewery in Sydney.

Tooley Street Brewery (Eng) a brewery (established 1984) based in London. Serves the Dickens Inn, St. Katherine's Dock. Noted for cask-conditioned Dickens Own (or TSB) 1040 O.G. and Archway 1042 O.G.

Tooths Brewery (Austr) a brewery known for Resch's KB Lager.

Top (Afr) a lager beer brewed by the West African Breweries.

Top (Switz) a beer brewed by the Cardinal Brewery in Fribourg.

Topaz (Isr) a rich, sweet, golden wine produced for the USA market.

Topaz (W.Ind) the brand-name for a drink of white rum and passion fruit 28% alc by vol.

Topaz Wine (S.Afr) a winery (established 2000) based in the Stellenbosch, Western Cape. 0.04ha. Grape varieties (Pinot noir and Syrah) bought in from Bottelary Hills, Elgin and Pereberg.

Top Banana (Cktl) 20mls (⅙ gill) vodka, 20mls (⅙ gill) crème de banane, juice ½ orange. Shake over ice and strain into an ice-filled old-fashioned glass.

Top Brass Lager (Eng) a bottled/canned lager 1033 O.G. brewed by the Wilson Brewery in Manchester.

Top Brew Ale (Eng) a dark strong ale 1071 O.G. brewed and bottled by the Davenports Brewery in Birmingham.

Top Brew De Luxe (Eng) a dark extra strong ale 1075 O.G. brewed and bottled by the Davenports Brewery in Birmingham.

Top Dog Stout (Eng) a 5% alc by vol. stout brewed by the Burton Bridge Brewery, Staffordshire.

Topedo Cocktail (Cktl) ⅔ measure Calvados, ⅓ measure Cognac, dash dry gin. Shake over ice and strain into a cocktail glass.

Topette (Fr) lit: 'cheers', a toast in the Nantais region.

Topf (Aus) a winery (15ha) based in the Kampstal region. (Add): Herrengasse 6, 3491 Strass im Strassertal. Grape varieties: Cabernet sauvignon, Chardonnay, Grüner veltliner, Pinot blanc, Pinot noir, Riesling, Sauvignon blanc, Zweigelt. Produces dry and sweet wines.

Top Fermentation (Eng) in brewing, applied to ferments (yeasts) that stay on top of the brew (ales, porter and stout). ***Saccharomyces cerevisiae***.

Top Hat (Eng) half Guinness and half ginger beer mixed.

Top Hat Ale (Eng) a keg/bottled strong ale 4.8% alc by vol./1046 O.G. brewed by the Burtonwood Brewery in Warrington, Cheshire.

Tópikos Oínos (Gre) *abbr*: T.O. Country wine with the name of the region stated. (Fr) = vin de pays. *see* O.E., O.P.A.P., O.P.E.

Top Island Bitter (Ch.Isles) a keg best bitter 1042 O.G. brewed by the Randalls Vautier Brewery in St. Helier, Jersey.

Top-Kwaliteit (Hol) a natural spring mineral water from Baarle-Nassau. Mineral contents (milligrammes per litre): Sodium 8.5mg/l, Calcium 64mg/l, Magnesium 9.7mg/l, Bicarbonates 250mg/l, Chlorides 11mg/l, Sulphates 28mg/l.

Top Notch Cocktail (Cktl) 30mls (¼ gill) sloe gin, 30mls (¼ gill) French vermouth, 1 teaspoon raspberry syrup. Stir over ice, strain into a cocktail glass and serve with a cherry.

Topo Chico (Mex) a natural spring mineral water (established 1895) from Nueva Leon.

Top of the Hill (S.Afr) the label for a red wine (Pinotage) produced by the De Waal Wines winery, Stellenbosch, Western Cape.

Top of the World (Cktl) 25mls (1fl.oz) each of Mandarine Napoléon, tequila, grapefruit juice, orange juice, white of 1 egg. Shake over ice, strain into a highball glass, top with soda water, dress with mint, orange and lemon slices.

Topolcany Brewery (Czec) a brewery based in south-eastern Czec.

Topolos at Russian River Vineyards (USA) a winery based in Forestville, Sonoma County, California. Grape varieties: Cabernet sauvignon, Chardonnay, Petite syrah, Pinot noir and Zinfandel. Produces varietal wines.

Toppe-au-Vert [La] (Fr) a Premier Cru vineyard in the commune of Ladoix-Serrigny, A.C. Aloxe-Corton, Côte de Beaune, Burgundy.

Toppedt Szölöböl Keszült Bor (Hun) denotes a wine produced from ***Botrytis cinerea*** affected grapes (white).

Toppette (Afr) an alternative name for grog on Mauritius off the west African coast.

Topping Smile (Cktl) ⅗ measure Cognac, ⅕ measure Drambuie, dash anisette, dash cherry brandy, dash lemon and orange juice. Stir over ice and strain into a cocktail glass.

Topping-Up (Eng) the filling of casks or jars with wine in order to fill the air space to prevent contamination.

Top Pressure (Eng) a method of forcing beer up from the cellar to the bar tap using CO_2 gas under pressure.

Topsham & Exminster Brewery (Eng) a brewery (established 2003). (Add): Unit 5, Lions Rest, Station Road, Exeter, Devon EX6 8DZ. Brews beers and lager. Website: http://www.topexe.co.uk 'E'mail: beer@topexe.co.uk

Top Souveraine (Bel) a natural spring mineral water from Brakel. Mineral contents (milligrammes per litre): Sodium 170mg/l, Calcium 1.3mg/l, Magnesium 0.8mg/l, Potassium 12mg/l, Bicarbonates 300mg/l, Chlorides 71.5mg/l, Sulphates 60mg/l, Nitrates 0.9mg/l.

Topsy Turvy Ale (Eng) a 6% alc by vol (1055 O.G) strong ale brewed by the Berrow Brewery in Burnham-on-Sea, Somerset.

Top Tory (Cktl) ⅗ measure Scotch whisky, ⅕ measure

Peachtree liqueur, ⅕ measure (white) crème de menthe, dash egg white, ½ measure Schweppes Tropical Juice. Shake well over ice, strain into a goblet, add a dash of blue Curaçao and a cherry.

Top Totty (Eng) a 4% alc by vol. summer brew from Staffordshire Brewery, Ecceshall, Staffordshire.

Top-Up (Eng) a request for a glass of beer to be filled up after the head has settled and ended below the prescribed measure. e.g. "Top it up" or "Would you like a top up?".

Topvar (Slov) a brewery based in the Topolcany region, Slovakia. Brews a 4.5% alc by vol. premium lager and Brigita.

Toradh Tae (Ire) fruit tea.

Torbato (It) a white grape variety grown in Sardinia, (related to the Malvasia). Also known as Cannonau in Sardinia. (Fr) = Malvoisie de Roussillon/Tourbat.

Torcerse (Sp) sour wine.

Torchiati (It) vin de presse.

Torchio (It) a traditional method of grape pressing used in the Tuscany region (Brunello di Montalcino).

Torcolato (It) a D.O.C. passito wine from the Vespaiolo grape in Veneto from the D.O.C. region of Breganze.

Torconal (Chile) a wine-producing area of northern Chile near the Maipo river.

Tordiz (Port) a 40 year old Tawny Port produced by Burmester.

Toreador (Cktl) ⅔ measure brandy, ⅓ measure Kahlúa, dash egg white, shake over ice and serve 'on the rocks' in an old-fashioned glass.

Toreador Cocktail (Cktl) ¾ measure tequila, ¼ measure (white) crème de cacao, 1 measure cream. Shake over ice, strain into a cocktail glass, top with whipped cream and dust with cocoa powder.

Torera [La] (Sp) a brand of Manzanilla Sherry from the Diez Hermanos range produced by Diez Merito.

Torgaio (It) a young, fruity, light Chianti from Ruffino. D.O.C.G.

Torgiano (It) an area of Umbria in which the town of Assisi is found. Produces red and white wines.

Torgiano Bianco (It) a D.O.C. white wine from Umbria. Made from the Grechetto, Malvasia di candia, Malvasia toscano, Trebbiano toscano and Verdelho grapes in the commune of Torgiano.

Torgiano Rosso (It) a D.O.C. red wine from Umbria. Made from the Ciliegiolo, Montepulciano, Sangiovese and Trebbiano toscano grapes grown within the commune of Torgiano.

Torgiano Rosso Riserva (It) a D.O.C.G. red wine from Umbria. Made from 50%–70% Sangiovese, 15%–30% Canaiolo, 0%–10% Trebbiano toscano, 0%–10% Ciliegiolo/Montepulciano. Aged for 3 years.

Torgiano Torre di Giano (It) see Torgiano Bianco.

Torii Mor (USA) a winery in Dundee, Willamette Valley, Oregon. Grape varieties: Chardonnay, Pinot gris, Pinot noir.

Torlesse Wines (N.Z) a winery. (Add): Ferguson Avenue, P.O. Box 8237, Waipara. Grape varieties: Breidecker, Cabernet sauvignon, Chardonnay, Müller-Thurgau, Sauvignon blanc.

Tormaresca Estates (It) a wine estate in Southern Puglia. Owned by Antinori. Has 100ha. in D.O.C. Castel del Monte, 250ha. near Brindisi. Produces a 100% barrique-fermented Chardonnay, a red from 40% Aglianico, 30% Merlot and 30% Cabernet sauvignon grapes.

Tormes (Port) a winery based in the DOC Vinho Verde.

Tormore (Scot) a single highland malt whisky distillery at Advie, 7 miles north of Grantown-on-Spey, Morayshire. Produces a 10 year old malt 43% alc by vol.

Tornado (Eng) an 8.4% alc by vol. cider produced by Torre Cider, Washford, Somerset.

Tornado (Hol) a pineapple liqueur using Hawaiian fruit 43% alc by vol.

Tornado (Sp) the equivalent to the (Fr) = tourne.

Tornamagno (It) a red wine produced by Colonnara Marche Srl. from Sangioveto grosso, Sangiovese, Montanino and Montepulciano grapes. Matured in small oak casks.

Torna-Viagem (Port) lit: 'back from a journey', the name given to a Setúbal wine which has been shipped to and from the tropics like the old Madeiras. Was used as the ship's ballast.

Tornay [Bernard] (Fr) récoltants-manipulants in Champagne. (Add): 51150 Bouzy, Tours-sur-Marne. Produces vintage and non-vintage wines.

Tornio Brewery (Fin) the biggest brewery in Finland, situated on the River Tornio at the Finnish/Swedish border. Brews: Lapin Kulta. 3 versions: 1020 O.G. (home market), 1030 O.G. (Sweden), 1040 O.G. (U.K.).

Toro (Sp) a D.O. wine-producing area in northern Spain. 3000ha. Grape varieties: 58% Tinto de toro plus Garnacha tinta, Malvasía, Albillo, Aragonés, Jaén and Valencia, Verdejo. Produces mainly full-bodied, high in alcohol red wines plus some rosé and white.

Toro (Sp) a D.O. full-bodied red wine from La Nava, Castile.

Torontel (Chile) a white grape variety.

Torontés (Sp) see Torrontés.

Toronto Cocktail (Cktl) 15mls (⅛ gill) each of Scotch whisky, Dubonnet and gin. Stir over ice, strain into a cocktail glass, serve with a cherry and a dash of lemon peel juice.

Torrar (Port) denotes the roasting of the green coffee beans.

Torre à Decima (It) a Chianti Putto producer based in Tuscany.

Torre al Fante (It) a red I.G.T. wine produced from 100% Sangiovese grapes by Fassati in Tuscany.

Torre à Mosciano [Le] (It) a Chianti Putto producer based in Tuscany.

Torrebreba (Sp) an area within Andalusia whose grapes go to make Sherry.

Torre Cider (Eng) a cider producer at Washford, Somerset. Produces: Tornado.

Torre de Gall (Sp) cava producers. Grape varieties include Chardonnay, Maccabeu, Parellada. Moët et Chandon (France) have an interest here. *See also* Shadow Creek.

Torre Ercolana (It) a red wine produced by Bruno Colacicchi in Latium.

Torrefaction (Fr) a Champagne term to denote a taste of roasted nuts and/or coffee beans.

Torre Giulia (It) a full-bodied white wine produced by the Foggia Vineyards in Puglia.

Torrelongares (Sp) a winery based in Aragón. Grape varieties include: Cariñena, Tempranillo.

Torremilanos (Sp) a brand-name used by Bodegas Peñalba López in Ribera del Duero.

Torreón de Paredes (Chile) a winery in Cachapoal Valley, Central Chile. Grape varieties include: Fumé blanc (aged in French oak) and Cabernet sauvignon.

Torreperogil (Sp) a Vino de Mesa of Jaén, Andalucía.

Torres (Sp) a brandy producer. (Add): Bodegas Miguel Torres, Apartado 13- Commercio 22, Vilafranca del Penedés, Barcelona. Source of base wine is the second pressing of Parellada vines in Penedés.

Torres (Sp) a famous large wine producer and wine pioneer in the Penedés region of south-eastern Spain. (Add): Bodegas Miguel Torres, Apartado 13- Commercio 22, Vilafranca del Penedés, Barcelona. Produces fine wines: Viña Sol, Gran Viña Sol, Gran Sangre de Toro, San Valentin, Viña Magdala, Las Torres, Moscatel Oro, Fransola, Milmanda, Sangre de Toro, De Casta Rosado, San Valentin, Viña Esmeralda, Mas Borras, Coronas, Gran Coronas, Grans Muralles, Mas la Plana, Reserva Real. Also brandies. Has vineyards in Catalonia (Spain): (Grans Muralles), Curicó (Chile): (Manso de Velasco), Russian River Valley (USA): Sonoma County, California (Marimar). Website: http://www.torreswines.com

Torres [Las] (Sp) a 100% Merlot red wine produced by Torres in Penedés. Spends 2 months in oak.

Torres Claude (S.Afr) the label for a range of wines produced by the Crows Nest winery, Paarl, Western Cape.

Torres de Serrano (Sp) a range of wines produced by VINIVAL based in Valencia.

Torresella (It) a winery that produces Vino da Tavola wines. Noted for their labels depicting endangered bird species. Wines made from grapes grown in the Trentino-Alto-Adige and Friuli-Venezia Giulia regions of north-eastern Italy.

Torres Vedras (Port) a DOC wine area in the region of Estremadura on the plains of the river Tejo. Grape varieties: Alicanté, Fernão pires, Garnpal, Grand noir and João de santarém.

Torres [Miguel] Winery (Chile) a winery associated with Torres of Spain. Noted wines produced from Cabernet and Sauvignon grapes.

Torre Vecchia (It) a winery. (Add): Via dei Quertieri 23/a, 90146 Patermo. Sicily. Produces D.O.C. Cerasuolo di Vittoria, D.O.C. Bianco d'Alcamo, I.G.T. Insola, I.G.T. Nero d'Avola

Torrevento (It) a wine estate in D.O.C. Castel del Monte. Produces Vigna Pedale from 100% Nero di troia grapes.

Torre Vinaria (Sp) the name given to a modern gravity-fed tower that is used in wine production.

Torridge Best (Eng) a 4.4% alc by vol. best bitter ale brewed by the Clearwater Brewery, Devon.

Torridora (Cktl) ⅗ measure white rum, ⅕ measure Kahlúa, ⅕ measure cream. Shake over ice, strain into a cocktail glass and float 10mls (½ fl.oz) dark rum on top.

Torri Syched (Wal) to quench one's thirst.

Torrontés (Sp) a white grape variety grown in Galicia and Cordoba. Found also in Argentina. Also spelt Torontés.

Torrontés Mendozino (Arg) a white grape variety grown in the Rio Negro.

Torrontés Riojano (Arg) white grape variety grown in La Rioja.

Torrontés Sanjuanino (Arg) a white grape variety grown in San Juan. (Chile) = Moscatel de Austria.

Tortoise Hill (S.Afr) the label for a red wine (Cabernet sauvignon 50% plus Shiraz, Touriga and Zinfandel blend) and white (Sauvignon blanc 65% plus Chardonnay and Viognier blend) produced by the Glen Carlou winery, Paarl, Western Cape.

Tortosi (Sp) a white grape variety grown in Valencia. Also known as the Bobal blanco.

Tórula (Sp) an inactive yeast present on grape skins.

Torula compniacensis (Lat) a black fungus that lives off the alcohol fumes and grows on the roof and walls of spirit warehouses.

Torulaspora (Sp) *see* Tórula.

Torys (Jap) the brand-name of a whiskey produced by Suntory.

Tosca (Eng) a bitter-sweet apéritif (orange bitters) produced by Matthew Clark 17% alc by vol.

Toscana (It) the Italian spelling of Tuscany, a wine region of central Italy. Noted for Chianti.

Toscana Bianca (It) the Vino da Tavola of Tuscany, used to be known as white Chianti before red Chianti became well-known.

Toscanello (It) the 2 litre wicker-covered flask used for white wines of Orvieto.

Toso (Jap) a sweet, spicy style of saké that is usually drunk at the New Year.

Toso Pascual Winery (Arg) a winery based at San José, noted for Cabernet Toso, Riesling and sparkling wines.

Toss Off (Eng) a slang term to denote the drinking of a drink in one gulp.

Tosti (It) noted producers of a range of vermouths, Marsala and sparkling wines, based in Canelli.

Tot (Eng) a measure of no specific capacity, much depends on the region and laws, denotes a measure of spirits, fortified wines or cordial.

Total Acidity (Eng) the sum of fixed acids and volatile acids usually expressed in terms of grammes per litre (g/l).

Total Acids (Eng) the sum of all the acids found in grape must.

Total Alcohol (Eng) formed as a result of the addition of the residual sugar present (equals potential alcohol) to the amount of ethanol in the wine (equals actual alcohol).

Total Blackout (Eng) a 5.9% alc by vol. cask and bottled ale brewed by the Teignworthy Brewery at Tuckers Maltings, Newton Abbot, South Devon for the eclipse.

Total Extract (Eng) *see* Extract.

Totally Marbled (Eng) the name for a seasonal ale brewed by the Marble Brewery, Manchester.

Total Pledge (USA) *see* T. Pledge.

Totara Fu Gai (N.Z) a white wine blend of Chasselas, Chenin blanc, Müller-Thurgau and Muscat grapes produced by the Totara SYC.

Totara SYC (N.Z) a winery near Te Kauwhata. Unique in that it is owned by the Chinese.

Totara Vineyards (N.Z) a winery. (Add): Main Road, RD 1, Thames, North Island.

Tot of Rum (Eng) a daily tot of rum first given to British sailors in 1665 and abolished on 31st July 1970 (now known as Black Tot Day by British seamen).

T'Other (Eng) a 3.5% alc by vol. ale brewed by the Terne Valley Brewery, Knightwick, Worcestershire. *See also* This, That, Wat Wassail.

Tou Brewery (Nor) a brewery based in Stavanger, south-west Norway. Brews Tuborg Lager under licence.

Touchwood (Eng) a bottled ale brewed by the Holts Brewery, Manchester.

Toudja [1] (Alg) a still natural spring mineral water (blue label). Mineral contents (milligrammes per litre): Sodium 52.1mg/l, Calcium 60.92mg/l, Magnesium 13.44mg/l, Potassium 0.8mg/l, Bicarbonates 212.28mg/l, Chlorides 71.34mg/l, Sulphates 20.89mg/l.

Toudja [2] (Alg) a sparkling natural spring mineral water (green label). Mineral contents (milligrammes per litre): Sodium 35mg/l, Calcium 62.5mg/l, Magnesium 20.3mg/l, Potassium 1.4mg/l, Bicarbonates 167.4mg/l, Chlorides 55.6mg/l, Sulphates 13.7mg/l, Nitrates <0.02mg/l.

Toughman (Eng) a bottled energy drink produced by Yakult that contains ginseng extract and vitamins.

Toul (Fr) a vin gris (rosé wine) of Toul in Lorraine in eastern France.

Toulenne (Fr) a commune in the A.C. Graves district in south-western Bordeaux.

Toulon-la-Montagne (Fr) a Cru Champagne village in Canton de Verzy. District: Châlons.

Touniller (Ch.Isles) cooper.

Tour [La] (Fr) a wine-producing district of A.C. Bellet, Provence, southern France.

Touraillage (Fr) a term used for the drying and kilning of the malt during brewing.

Touraine (Fr) an A.C. wine district of the central Loire. Produces red, rosé, white (still and sparkling) wines. *see* Bourgueil, Cheverny, Chinon, Montlouis, St. Nicolas de Bourgueil, Vouvray.

Minimum alc by vol. (red) = 9% and (white) = 9.5%. Grape varieties: Arbois, Breton, Cabernet sauvignon, Chardonnay, Chenin blanc, Cot, Gamay, Groslôt, Pinot d'Aunis, Pinot meunier and Sauvignon blanc.

Touraine-Amboise (Fr) an A.C. area of the Touraine district in the Loire. Red, rosé and white wines are produced.

Touraine Azay-le-Rideau (Fr) an A.C. red, rosé and white wine area within the district of the Touraine in the central Loire.

Touraine-Mesland (Fr) an area of the Touraine in the central Loire. Produces red, rosé and white wines.

Touraine Mousseux (Fr) an old designation of the sparkling wines of the Touraine district in the central Loire.

Touraine Pétillant (Fr) an old designation of the slightly sparkling wines of the Touraine district in the central Loire.

Tourbat (Fr) an alternative name for the Malvoisie grape in the Roussillon. Also known as Torbato.

Tour Blanche [La] (Fr) a vineyard belonging to the French government at the commune of Bommes (Sauternes) making sweet white wines.

Tour Carnet [La] (Fr) a vineyard. (Add): Saint Laurent de Médoc, Médoc. A.C. Haut-Médoc. (Com): Saint Laurent. 31ha. Grape varieties: Cabernet franc, Cabernet sauvignon, Merlot, Petit verdot.

Tour de Mons [La] (Fr) a Cru Bourgeois. A.C. Margaux.

Tour des Combes (Fr) a Grand Cru Classé. A.C. Saint-Émilion. (Com): Saint Laurent des Combes. 17ha. Grape varieties: Cabernet franc, Cabernet sauvignon and Merlot.

Tour du Vatican (Fr) a red wine produced by Château Hanteillon in the commune of Cissac, Médoc, north-western Bordeaux.

Tourelles de Lamothe [Les] (Fr) the second wine of Château Lamothe, A.C. Sauternes, Bordeaux.

Tourelles de Longueville [Les] (Fr) the second wine of Château Pichon-Longueville Baron, A.C. Pauillac.

Touriga (Port) a red grape variety similar to the Cabernet franc of France used in the making of Port.

Touriga Franca (Port) an alternative name for the Touriga Francesca.

Touriga Francesa (Port) a red grape variety used in the production of Port. Also known as the Touriga Franca.

Touriga Nacional (Port) a red grape variety used in the production of Port and Dão wines to give body and fruit. Also know as the Preto Mortágua.

Tourigao (Port) a red grape variety used in the production of Port to give body.

Tourigo (Port) *see* Touriga.

Tourigo-do-Dão (Port) a red grape variety grown in the Dão region to make red wines.

Tourinio (Fr) a medium-dry white wine produced in Corsica.

Tourlopsis (Lat) a slime-forming spoilage yeast that

attacks low-acid musts and wines that have not been sulphated.

Tour Martillac [La] (Fr) a vineyard in the commune of Martillac. A.C. Graves, Bordeaux.

Tournage (Fr) a simple term for the heavy sediment when the remueur does not wish to shake the wine up too much during Champagne production.

Tourne (Fr) bacterial spoilage of wine by the bacteria **Tartarophtorum** (a rod bacteria). The wine loses colour and acidity. Tartaric acid and Glycerol being totally lost. (Sp) = tornado.

Tourne-Bride (Fr) referred to a country inn situated near a Château. Servants of visitors would be lodged here.

Tournée (Fr) a round (of drinks).

Tournon (Fr) a small district on the right bank of the Rhône. Produces red and white wines.

Tournus (Fr) a wine-producing area in the Saône-et-Loire département, central-eastern France.

Tours-sur-Marne (Fr) a Grand Cru Champagne village in the Canton d'Aÿ. District: Reims (red grapes).

Tours-sur-Marne (Fr) a Premier Cru Champagne village in the Canton d'Aÿ. District: Reims (white grapes).

Tourtel Malt (Bel) 0.1% alc by vol. straw coloured, alcohol-free bottled beer brewed by Alken-Maes Brasserie, Alken.

Toussaint Coffee Liqueur (Haiti) a 26.5% alc by vol. rich dry coffee liqueur. Named after General Toussaint–the architect of Haiti's independence.

Toussaints [Les] (Fr) a Premier Cru vineyard in the A.C. commune of Beaune, Côte de Beaune, Burgundy 6.43ha.

Tourtel (Fr) a bottled low alcohol lager 0.8% alc by vol. brewed by Kronenbourg Brasserie in Strasbourg, Alsace (not a dealcoholised lager).

Tout Court (Fr) simple wine.

Touzac (Fr) a commune in the Charente département whose grapes are classed Grande Champagne (Cognac).

Tovali Ltd (Wal) a mineral water producer (established 1937). (Add): Glanyrafon Road, Carmarthen, Carmarthenshire SA31 3AR. Produces carbonated drinks and mineral water. Website: http://www.tovali.co.uk 'E'mail: sales@tovali.co.uk

Tovarich Cocktail (Cktl) ⅔ measure vodka, ⅓ measure kümmel, juice ½ lime. Shake over ice and strain into a cocktail glass.

Tovtri (Ukr) a sparkling natural spring mineral water (established 2001) from Zaitchiki Village. Mineral contents (milligrammes per litre): Sodium 10-200mg/l, Calcium 40-80mg/l, Magnesium 30-60mg/l, Potassium 100-200mg/l, Bicarbonates 400-700mg/l, Chlorides 50-100mg/l, Sulphates <100mg/l.

Tow (Eng) wax used to plug the necks of wine bottles in the seventeenth century.

T'Owd Tup (Eng) a 6% alc by vol. dark, cask-conditioned stout brewed by the Dent Brewery, Cumbria. Also available bottled.

Tower Bitter (Eng) a cask-conditioned bitter 1036 O.G. brewed by the Bass Brewery. Formerly known as Brew Ten.

Tower Brewery (Eng) a nineteenth century style of brewery designed so that after the malt and water are raised to the top of the building, the materials flow downwards with gravity.

Tower Brewery (Eng) a brewery (established 2001). (Add): The Old Water Tower, Walstitch Maltings, Glensyl Way, Burton-on-Trent, Staffordshire DE14 1LX. Brews: Bitter 4.2% alc by vol., Malty Towers 4.4% alc by vol., Pale Ale 4.8% alc by vol., Tower of Strength 7.6% alc by vol., Walstitch Wobbler 5.2% alc by vol.

Tower Estate (Austr) a winery with vineyards based in the Barossa Valley, Coonawarra and Hunter Valley, South Australia.

Towerkop (S.Afr) the label for a fortified wine (Hanepoot) produced by the Ladysmith Koöperatiewe, Klein Karoo.

Tower of London (Sp) a brand of dry gin produced by Cocal in Telde, Canary Islands.

Tower of Strength (Eng) a 7.6% alc by vol. strong ale brewed by the Tower Brewery, Staffordshire.

Towersoet (S.Afr) the label for a range of wines produced by the Southern Cape Vineyards winery, Barrydale, Little Karoo

Town Crier (Eng) a 4.5% alc by vol. ale brewed by the Hobson's Brewery C°. Ltd., Worcestershire.

Townend (Eng) a producer of a large range of egg-based drinks based in Hull, Humberside.

Towngate Special (Eng) a cask-conditioned ale 1043 O.G. brewed by the Crouch Vale Brewery, Essex.

Toxic Waste (Eng) a limited edition beer brewed by Ash Vine Brewery in Trudoxhill, near Frome, Somerset to raise money for Surfers Against Sewage Pressure Group. See also Acid Rain.

T.P.E. (Austr) abbr: Thermoplastic Elastomer (see).

T. Pledge (USA) abbr: Total Pledge, taken in the nineteenth century by people who vowed to abstain from all types of alcohol. See Teetotal

Traballhadores (Port) the name given to the grape treaders.

Traben-Trarbach (Ger) village (Anb): Mosel-Saar-Ruwer. (Ber): Bernkastel. (Gro): Schwarzlay. (Vins): Burgweg, Gaispfad, Huhnerberg, Königsberg, Kräuterhaus, Kreuzberg, Schlossberg, Taubenhaus, Ungsberg, Würzgarten, Zollturm.

Traben-Trarbach [ortsteil Starkenburg] (Ger) village (Anb): Mosel-Saar-Ruwer. (Ber): Bernkastel. (Gro): Schwarzlay. (Vin): Rosengarten.

Traben-Trarbach [ortsteil Wolf] (Ger) village (Anb): Mosel-Saar-Ruwer. (Ber): Bernkastel. (Gro): Schwarzlay. (Vins): Auf der Heide, Goldgrube, Klosterberg, Schatzgarten, Sonnenlay.

Trace Elements (Eng) elements in the soil that go to produce fine wines. Iodine, Manganese, Molybedenum, Nickel, Vanadium, Zinc.

Trachyte (Hun) volcanic rock on which the grapes for Tokaji are grown.

Tracy (Fr) a commune in the Central Vineyards district of the Loire which produces A.C. Pouilly Fumé.

Trade Descriptions Act (Eng) an Act of Parliament passed in 1968 to protect the purchaser from inferior goods or goods that are sold different to the sales description. i.e. Scotch whisky being sold as Malt whisky, Vin de Pays wines being sold as A.C. wines, etc. (Fr) = réclame trompeuse. (Ger) = unlauterer wettbewerb. (Hol) = misleidende reklame.

Traders Coffee Ltd (Eng) a coffee manufacturer (established 1981). (Add): 274 Ewell Road, Surbiton, Surrey KT6 7AG. Produces a range of coffees. Website: http://www.coffeebay.co.uk 'E'mail: admin@coffeebay.co.uk

Trader Vic's Broadway Bar (Eng) the only L.V.A-owned public house in the U.K. Based in Huddersfield, Yorkshire.

Trader Vic's Punch (Cktl) 30mls (1¼ fl.ozs) each of light rum, Jamaican rum, ½ teaspoon orgeat syrup, teaspoon sugar, slice pineapple, juice of ½ orange and ½ lemon. Shake over ice and pour unstrained into a highball glass, add pineapple and straws.

Trade Winds (Scot) a 4.3% alc by vol. ale brewed by The Cairngorm Brewery C°. Ltd., Inverness.

Tradition (Austr) a red wine produced from a blend of Shiraz and Bordeaux grape varieties by Ryecroft in South Australia.

Traditional (Eng) a term applied to beer that has been brewed using a mash tun, open fermenters and no filtration, pasteurisation or re-carbonation.

Traditional Appellation (Gre) *abbr* T.A. used as a designation for Retsina, defines production technique.

Traditional Bush Vine (S.Afr) the label for a white wine (Sauvignon blanc) produced by the Villiera Wines winery, Stellenbosch, Western Cape.

Traditional English Ale (Eng) a 4.2% alc by vol. ale brewed by the Hogs Back Brewery Ltd., Surrey.

Traditional IPA (Eng) a 5% alc by vol. India pale ale from McMullens, Hertfordshire, produced using amber malt.

Traditional Standard (Eng) a dry session bitter 1035 O.G. brewed by Larkins Brewery at Larkins Farm, Chiddingstone, Kent. *See also* Sovereign, Larkins Best.

Traditionelle Flaschengärung (Ger) tradition bottle fermentation (sparkling wines).

Tradition Impériale (Fr) a 20–25 year old Cognac produced by Menard.

Trafalgar Ale (Eng) a 4.2% alc by vol. seasonal ale brewed by Gale's Brewery, Horndean, Hampshire.

Trafalgar IPA (Eng) a 6% alc by vol. India pale ale brewed by the Freeminer Brewery Ltd., Gloucestershire.

Trafalgar 200 (Eng) a barley wine to commemorate the 200th anniversary of the battle of Trafalgar by Gale's Brewery, Horndean. Each case of bottles will have a signed certificate (by head brewer Derek Lowe).

Traficante (It) a natural spring mineral water from Traficante.

Trago (S.Am) the local name in Colombia given to rum that is drunk neat in a single shot (measure).

Traisen (Ger) village (Anb): Nahe. (Ber): Schloss Böckelheim. (Gro): Burgweg. (Vins): Bastei, Kickelskopf, Nonnengarten, Rotenfels.

Traisental (Aus) a new designated wine region (established 1994) that adjoins Donauland 700ha. Soil: chalk, loam and loess. Main grape varieties: white (Chardonnay, Grüner veltliner, Müller-Thurgau, Neuburger, Pinot blanc, Riesling), red (Blauer portugieser, Blauburger, Zweigelt. Villages: Herzogenburg, Inzersdorf, Nussdorf, Traismauer and Wagram.

Traiskirchen (Aus) a wine village near Gumpoldskirchen, produces mainly medium-sweet and dry white wines.

Traismauer-Carnuntum (Aus) a wine-producing district in the Niederösterreich region.

Trait (Eng) describes a small quantity of liquor (approx 1 teaspoonful) used in cocktail preparations.

Trajadura (Port) a white grape variety used in the making of Vinhos Verdes. (Sp) = treixadura.

Trakia (Bul) a red wine produced from a blend of 60% Mavrud and 40% Pamid grapes.

Trakia (Rum) a well-balanced red and white wines shipped to the USA.

Trakya (Tur) the alternative name for Thrace in north-western Turkey, a major wine-producing region.

Trakya (Tur) red and white wines, the red light and dry, the white (from the Sémillon grape) dry and medium bodied.

Trale (Eng) a 3.9% alc by vol. ale brewed by Tarka Ales Ltd., Devon.

Tralles (It) a scale used for measuring the strength of alcohol in wines and spirits, similar to Gay Lussac.

Tramery (Fr) a Cru Champagne village in the Canton de Ville-en-Tardenois. District: Reims.

Tramin (It) a town situated in the Trentino-Alto-Adige (Süd-Tirol) from where the Traminer grape variety was named. *See also* Gewürztraminer.

Traminac (Slo) the local name for the Traminer grape grown in the Slovenia and Vojvodina regions.

Traminer (Euro) a white grape variety grown in eastern Europe, low in acidity, the best is the Gewürztraminer. Also known as the Gelber Traminer, Klevner d'Heiligenstein, Roter Traminer and Weisser Traminer.

Traminer Aromatico (It) a name for the white Gewürztraminer grape in the Trentino-Alto-Adige.

Traminer Musqué (Fr) an alternative name for the Gewürztraminer.

Traminette (USA) a hybrid grape variety developed in Kentucky from the Gewürztraminer and Joannes Seyve 23.416.

Tramini (Hun) a local name for the Traminer grape.

Tramontana (Fr)(Sp) the north wind that blows through the Penedés region in the winter months and the Languedoc-Rousillon.

T

Tranchette (Fr) a cone-shaped glass that evolved from French Inns. Travellers had to drink up before they could set the glass (inverted) on the table.

Trancy (Fr) a red wine area in Auxerre, Yonne département, Burgundy.

Tranksteuer (Aus) wine taxes introduced in 1780 by the Empress Maria Theresa.

Tranquility Tea (Cktl) 1 measure brandy, 550mls (1pint) hot tea, 1 teaspoon instant coffee, 1 teaspoon lemon juice, 1 tablespoon milk powder (mixed with a little water), dash vanilla essence, sugar syrup to taste. Whisk milk and lemon juice together, heat remaining ingredients, pour into glasses and add the topping in a swirl.

Transcaucasia (Asia) the place where the genius *Vitis* is thought to have originated.

Transdanubia (Hun) a wine-producing region that stretches between the rivers Danube and Drava.

Transetcom S.A. (Gre) a noted wine merchant based near Patras in the Peloponnese.

Transfer Method (Eng) a process of making sparkling wine where the second fermentation takes place in the bottle and then is filtered in a tank under pressure and re-bottled.

Transfusion (Eng) a slang term often used for the '*Hair of the dog*'.

Transka Bankya (Bul) a natural spring mineral water (established 2002) from Transka Bankya. Mineral contents (milligrammes per litre): Sodium 7.6mg/l, Calcium 72mg/l, Magnesium 16mg/l, Potassium 0.3mg/l, Bicarbonates 305mg/l, Chlorides 3.5mg/l, Sulphates 6.2mg/l, Fluorides 0.1mg/l, Nitrates 1mg/l, Silicates 9.7mg/l. pH 7.3

Transvasage (Fr) *see* Transvasion.

Transvasée (Fr) the method of transferring Champagne off its lees (sediment) into another bottle. Most of the bubbles were destroyed. This method was used before Dégorgement was introduced.

Transvasion (Fr) the second fermentation in bottle, then dégorgement under pressure into refrigerated tanks. Dosage added, clarified and filtered then re-bottled under pressure at 3°C (37.4°F). (Eng) = transfer method.

Trapiche (Arg) a winery based in the Mendoza region, eastern Argentina. Website: http://www.trapiche.com.ar 'E'mail: ccorina@trapiche.com.ar

Trapiche Syrup (Cktl) a cocktail ingredient: 200 grms (½ lb) cane sugar, ½ teaspoon ground cinnamon, ½ teaspoon ground cloves, 450mls (1pint) heated orange juice. Stir altogether, cool and strain into bottles.

Trappe [La] (Hol) the name given to a range of beers brewed by Schaapskooi Abbaye Brouwerij, Berkel-Enschot, Tilburg, Brabant. The only Trappiste brewery in Holland. Brews: La Trappe ale 5.5% alc by vol. plus Dubbel, Quadrupel.

Trappe [La] Dubbel (Hol) a 6.5% alc by vol. bottled Trappiste double beer brewed by Schaapskooi Abbaye Brouwerij, Berkel-Enschot, Tilburg, Brabant.

Trappe [La] Quadrupel (Hol) a 10% alc by vol. bottled autumn, strong, Trappiste beer brewed by Schaapskooi Abbaye Brouwerij, Berkel-Enschot, Tilburg, Brabant.

Trappenberg (Ger) grosslage (Anb): Pfalz. (Ber): Südliche Weinstrasse. (Vils): Altdorf, Bellheim, Böbingen, Bornheim, Essingen, Freimersheim, Gross u. Kleinfischlingen, Hochstadt, Knittelsheim, Lustadt, Ottersheim, Römerberg, Schwegenheim, Venningen, Weingarten, Zeiskam.

Trappiste Beers (Bel) are Belgian real draught beers, top fermented ales (not lagers), bottle conditioned, vary in strength from 5.7% to 12% alc by vol. from the Belgian Trappiste abbayes: Chimay, Orval, Rochefort, St. Sixtus, Westmalle, also from Schaapskooi in the Netherlands.

Trappistes Rochefort 8 (Bel) a 9.2% alc by vol. red-brown, top-fermented, bottle-conditioned Trappiste barley wine brewed by the Abbaye Notre Dame de St. Remy.

Trappistes Rochefort 10 (Bel) a 11.3% alc by vol. dark brown, top-fermented, bottle-conditioned Trappiste barley wine brewed by the Abbaye Notre Dame de St. Remy.

Trappistine (Fr) a herb liqueur with a base of Armagnac brandy, yellow green in colour, from the Abbaye de la Grâce de Dieu, Doubs.

Traquair House Brewery (Scot) a brewery (established 1965). (Add): Traquair House, Innerleithen, Peebles EH44 6PW. Noted for cask-conditioned Bear Ale 5% alc by vol (1050 O.G)., Traquair Jacobite Ale 8% alc by vol. Traquair House Ale 7.2% alc by vol (1075 O.G). Website: http://www.traquair.co.uk 'E'mail: enquiries@traquair.co.uk

Traquair House Ale (Scot) a 7.2% alc by vol. bottled dark ale brewed by the Traquair Brewery, Innerleithen, Peebleshire.

Traquair Jacobite Ale (Scot) an 8% alc by vol. strong, dark-brown ale brewed by the Traquair Brewery, Innerleithen, Peebleshire.

Trasanejas (Sp) the name given to a special Málaga which has been produced from solera wines that contain casks of over 200 years of age.

Trasfegar (Port) to decant, *Trasfega* = the decanting or racking of the wine off its lees.

Trasiego (Sp) decanting or racking of the wine off its lees.

Traslepuy (Fr) a rich, red Côtes-du-Rhône wine produced by F. Zobel, Rocquemaure.

Tras os Montes (Port) lit: 'across the mountains', a wine region north-east from river Douro. Has the DOC areas: Chaves, Planalto Mirandes, Porto/Douro and Valpaços. Produces red, rosé and pétillant wines. Is the base for Mateus Rosé.

Trattore (It) innkeeper/landlord.

Trattoria (It) inn.

Traube(n) (Aus)(Ger) grape(s).

Traubenmaische (Ger) unfermented grape mash containing less than 5 grammes of grape sugar.

Traubenmost (Aus)(Ger) grape must.

Traubenmost-Konzentrat (Ger) grape must concentrate (the dehydrated juice of Traubenmost or Traubenmaische).

Traubensaft (Ger) grape juice/must.

Traubensaftkonzentrat (Ger) concentrated grape must.

Traubisoda (Aus) a carbonated non-alcoholic grape juice drink for export to Muslim countries.

Trauersdorf (Aus) a wine-producing area in the Mattersburg district.

Trauntal (Aus) a vineyard site on the banks of the River Danube situated in the Wachau region, Niederösterreich.

Trautberg (Ger) vineyard (Anb): Franken. (Ber): Steigerwald. (Gro): Herrenberg. (Vil): Castell.

Trautlestal (Ger) vineyard (Anb): Franken. (Ber): Maindreieck. (Gro): Burg. (Vil): Hammelburg.

Travaglini (It) a top wine producer based in Piemonte. Produces D.O.C. Gattinara.

Travarice (Slo) a generic name for fruit brandies with herbs added.

Travellers Best (Eng) an ale brewed by the Wye Valley Brewery, 69 St. Owen Street, Herefordshire.

Trawal Wynkelders (S.Afr) a winery based in the Olifants River area. (Add): Box 2, Klawer 8145. Does not bottle, but sells wine to other co-operatives.

Trayer (Eng) a sixteenth century version of a barman who collected wines from the cellar casks and served to clients of inns.

Trbljan (Cro) a white grape variety on the Croatian coast. Also known as Kuc.

Treacle Stout (Eng) a 4.4% alc by vol. stout brewed by the Itchen Valley Brewery, Hampshire.

Treading (Eng) an old method of crushing grapes with the feet using spiked shoes or bare feet. Now little used except in Portugal and Madeira (very labour intensive).

Treana Winery (USA) a winery based in Paso Robles, San Luis Obispo County, California. (Add): P.O. Box 3260 Paso Robles, CA 93447. Website: http://www.treana.com

Treaty of Windsor (Port) a treaty signed in 1353, this established Portugal as England's oldest ally in war and trading partner in peace.

Trebbianello (It) a white grape variety grown in Lombardy. Also known as the Tocai friulano.

Trebbiano (It) a white grape variety which produces fine dry white wines. Many varieties. Known in France as the Ugni blanc.

Trebbiano d'Abruzzo (It) a white grape variety grown in Abruzzi. Also known as the Bombino bianco.

Trebbiano d'Abruzzo (It) a D.O.C. white wine from Abruzzi. Made from the Trebbiano d'Abruzzo, Trebbiano toscano, Coccocciola, Malvasia toscana and Passerina grapes. Produced throughout the Abruzzi region.

Trebbiano della Fiamma (It) a white grape variety.

Trebbiano di Aprilia (It) see Merlot di Aprilia.

Trebbiano di Lugana (It) a white grape variety grown in the Lombardy region.

Trebbiano di Romagna (It) a white grape variety grown in the Emilia-Romagna region.

Trebbiano di Romagna (It) a D.O.C. white wine from the Emilia-Romagna. Made from the Trebbiano di romagna grape. D.O.C. also applies to the Spumante wine (dry, semi-sweet and sweet) produced within a defined area in accordance to regulations.

Trebbiano di Soave (It) a white grape variety grown in the Lombardy region. Also known as the Trebbiano nostrano.

Trebbiano Giallo (It) a white grape variety grown in the Lazio region. Also known as the Castelli romani in Lombardy.

Trebbiano Nostrano (It) see Trebbiano di Soave.

Trebbiano Romagnolo (It) a white grape variety grown in the Emilia-Romagna. see Trebbiano di Romagna.

Trebbiano Toscano (It) a white grape variety grown in northern Italy. Also known as the Castelli romani.

Trebbiano Val Trebbia (It) a D.O.C. white wine from the Emilia-Romagna region. Made from the Trebbiano romagnolo, Malvasia di candia, Moscato bianco, Ortrugo and Sauvignon grapes. Vinification can take place throughout the 4 communes.

Trebbiano Verde (It) a white grape variety grown in the Latium region.

Trebellicanum (It) a red wine produced in central-western Italy in Roman times.

Trebern (Aus) a spirit distilled from apples.

Tre Bicchieri (It) a coveted wine award, awarded by the Gambero Rosso wine guide.

Trebien (Aus) a vineyard area based in the Kitzeck district of Süd-Steiermark.

Treble Gold Ale (Eng) a strong ale 1052 O.G. brewed and bottled by the Ind Coope Brewery in Burton-on-Trent for Friary Meux.

Treble Gold Cocktail (Cktl) 1 measure avocaat, ½ measure crème de banana, dash orange juice. Shake over ice, strain into an ice-filled highball glass and top with tonic water.

Treble Seven Mild (Eng) a keg dark mild 1034 O.G. brewed by the Gales Brewery in Horndean, Hampshire.

Trebon Brewery (Czec) an ancient brewery based in south-western Czec.

Trebujena (Sp) an area in the Jerez Supérieur district.

Treceño (Sp) a Vino de Mesa of Cantabria, north-central Spain.

Trechtingshausen (Ger) village (Anb): Mittelrhein. (Ber): Bacharach. (Gro): Schloss Reichenstein. (Vin): Morgenbachtaler.

Treeton (Austr) a district in the Margaret River region of Western Australia.

Trefethen Vineyards (USA) the brand-name for a Chardonnay and Cabernet range of wines produced by Trefethen Winery in California.

Trefethen Winery (USA) a winery based in the Napa Valley, northern California. 300ha. Grape varieties: Cabernet sauvignon, Chardonnay, Johannisberg riesling, Merlot and Pinot noir. Produces varietal and table wines.

Tre Filer (It) a sweet, 'botrytised' Vino da Tavola dessert vintage wine produced by the Azienda Agricola Cà dei Frati.

Tre Fontane (It) a liqueur produced by the Cistercian monks just outside Rome. Produce both a green and yellow variety, flavoured with Eucalyptus leaves.

Tre Fontane Xenia (It) a natural spring mineral water from Modena. Mineral contents (milligrammes per litre): Sodium 7.3mg/l, Calcium 61mg/l, Magnesium 9.47mg/l, Potassium 1.01mg/l, Chlorides 1.9mg/l, Nitrates 3.5mg/l. pH 7.45

Tregnum (Scot) a bottle of whisky containing 3 standard bottles (used by the Long John Whisky only).

Tregrehan Claret (Austr) a red wine from Angoves, South Australia. A blend of Cabernet and Shiraz grapes.

Treilles (Fr) a commune in the region of Fitou, southern France.

Treis-Karden (Ger) village (Anb): Mosel-Saar-Ruwer. (Ber): Zell/Mosel. (Gro): Goldbäumchen. (Vins): Dechantsberg, Juffermauer, Münsterberg.

Treiso (It) a commune in the D.O.C. Barbaresco, Piemonte.

Treixadura (Sp) a white grape variety grown in the Ribeiro area of north-western Spain. (Port) = Trajadura.

Trelawny's Pride (Eng) a cask-conditioned ale 4.4% alc by vol. from the St. Austell Brewery, Cornwall.

Trellis-Training (Fr) see Palissage.

Trelou-sur-Marne (Fr) a Cru Champagne village in the Canton de Condé-en-Brie. District: Château Thierry.

Tremeloos Damiaanbier (Bel) a 6.5% alc by vol. top-fermented, bottled special beer brewed by Sterkens in Antwerp.

Tremlett's Bitter (Eng) a 7.4% alc by vol. bottled dry cider from Thatcher's in Sandford, north Somerset. A single variety cider apple cider. See also Somerset Redstreak, Spartan, Cox's Katy.

Tremloos Damiaanbier (Bel) a 6.5% alc by vol. top-fermented, bottled special beer brewed by Sterkens, Antwerp.

Tre Monti (It) a winery based in the Tuscany region. Produces D.O.C. Sangiovese di Romagna. Label: Thea.

Tren (Sp) the name given to the bottling line where bottles are filled.

Trencianske Mitice (Slo) a natural spring mineral water from Carpathian Mountains. Mineral contents (milligrammes per litre): Sodium 42.5mg/l, Calcium 288.6mg/l, Magnesium 92.4mg/l, Potassium 3.5mg/l, Bicarbonates 1409.1mg/l, Chlorides 16.3mg/l, Sulphates 11.9mg/l, Nitrates 2.8mg/l.

Trenet (Fr) a 60% alc by vol absinthe.

Trenque (Arg) a still natural spring mineral water. Mineral contents (milligrammes per litre):

Sodium 12.2mg/l, Calcium 19.2mg/l, Magnesium 9.8mg/l, Chlorides 6.7mg/l, Sulphates 5mg/l, Fluorides 0.28mg/l, Nitrates <0.01mg/l. pH 7.75

Trentadue Winery (USA) a winery and vineyard based in the Alexander Valley, Sonoma County, California. 83ha. Grape varieties: Aleatico, Carignane, Early Burgundy, French colombard, Ruby cabernet, Sémillon, Zinfandel. Produces varietal and table wines.

Trent Bitter (Eng) a bottled/canned take-home bitter 1032 O.G. brewed by Allied Breweries.

Trentino-Alto-Adige (It) the northernmost region of Italy. Situated on the Austrian and Swiss border. Also known as the Südtirol in German. see Venezia Tridentina. Became Italian in 1919. See also Süd-Tirol. Also spelt Trentino-Alto Adige.

Trentino Cabernet (It) a D.O.C. red wine from the Trentino-Alto-Adige. Made from the Cabernet franc and Cabernet sauvignon grapes. Must be aged 2 years. (If 3 years classed Riserva).

Trentino Lagrein (It) a D.O.C. red wine from the Trentino-Alto-Adige. Made from the Lagrein grape. Must be aged 1 year. (If 2 years then classed Riserva).

Trentino Marzemino (It) a D.O.C. red wine from the Trentino-Alto-Adige. Made from the Marzemino grape. Must be aged 1 year minimum. (If 2 years then classed Riserva).

Trentino Merlot (It) a D.O.C. red wine from the Trentino-Alto-Adige. Made from the Merlot grape. Must be aged 1 year minimum. (If aged 2 years then classed Riserva).

Trentino Moscato (It) a D.O.C. white wine from the Trentino-Alto-Adige. Made from the Moscato giallo and Moscato rosa grapes. Must be aged 1 year minimum. (If aged 2 years then classed Riserva). D.O.C. also applies to fortified wines.

Trentino Pinot (It) a D.O.C. white wine from the Trentino-Alto-Adige. Made from the Pinot bianco and Pinot grigio grapes. Must be aged 1 year minimum (if 2 years then classed Riserva). D.O.C. also applies to the sparkling wines made from the Pinot bianco grapes.

Trentino Pinot Nero (It) a D.O.C. red wine from the Trentino-Alto-Adige. Made from the Pinot nero grape. Must be aged 1 year minimum. (If 2 years then classed Riserva).

Trentino Riesling (It) a D.O.C. red wine from the Trentino-Alto-Adige. Made from the Riesling italico, Riesling renano and Riesling sylvaner grapes.

Trentino Traminer Aromatico (It) a D.O.C. white wine from the Trentino-Alto-Adige. Made from the Gewürztraminer grape.

Trentino Vino Santo (It) a D.O.C. white wine from the Trentino-Alto-Adige. Made from the Pinot bianco grape (partly dried to raise the grape sugar level). D.O.C. also applies to fortified wines. Must be aged 1 year minimum (if 2 years then classed Riserva).

Trent Mild (Eng) a bottled 'take-home' mild beer 1033 O.G. brewed by Allied Breweries.

Trento (It) a D.O.C. white and rosé wines made by método tradizionale. Aged 24 months for vintage, 36 months for riserva. Grape varieties: Chardonnay, Pinot bianco, Pinot meunier, Pinot nero. 1200ha.

Trenzen (Aus) a vineyard site on the banks of the River Danube in the Kremstal region.

Trepat (Sp) a red grape variety grown in Conca de Barbera and Costers del Segre, north-eastern Spain.

Treppchen (Ger) vineyard (Anb): Mosel-Saar-Ruwer. (Ber): Bernkastel. (Gro): Michelsberg. (Vil): Piesport.

Treppchen (Ger) vineyard (Anb): Mosel-Saar-Ruwer. (Ber): Bernkastel. (Gro): Schwarzlay. (Vil): Erden.

Treppchen (Ger) vineyard (Anb): Mosel-Saar-Ruwer. (Ber): Zell/Mosel. (Gro): Rosenhang. (Vil): Treis-Karden.

Tresallier (Fr) a white grape variety grown in Allier département. Used in St. Pourçain production. Also spelt Tressallier.

Tre Santi (It) a sparkling natural spring mineral water from Macerata, Marche. Mineral contents (milligrammes per litre): Sodium 13mg/l, Calcium 139mg/l, Magnesium 10mg/l, Potassium 1.7mg/l, Chlorides 16.8mg/l, Sulphates 25.5mg/l, Silicates 14mg/l. pH 7.3

Tresbolillo (Sp) the name for the diagonal pattern used when planting vines.

Tres Castillos (W.Ind) a sweet, aniseed-flavoured liqueur produced in Puerto Rico.

Tres Cepas (Sp) a 2 year old solera brandy produced by Domecq.

Tres Ceros (Sp) a solera brandy produced by Osborne. See also Special Veterano.

Tres Coronas (Sp) a solera brandy produced by Real Tesoro.

Tres Espadas (Sp) a solera brandy produced by Sanchez Romate. See also Abolengo, Conquistador, Respetable.

Très Esquinas (S.Am) lit 'three corners', the brand-name of a rum produced by the state-owned Industria Licorera de Bolivar Distillery in Colombia. Made from molasses distilled twice. Is sold in a triangular bottle.

Treslon (Fr) a Cru Champagne village in the Canton de Ville-en-Tardenois. District: Reims.

Tres Magueyes (Mex) a noted tequila producer and brand-name of their tequila. Also produce Tres Magueyes Reserva de Don Julio made from 100% blue agave.

Tres Marias (Port) a brand of slightly sweet Vinho Verde produced in Vizela.

Tres Medallas (Sp) a solera brandy produced by Agustín Blázquez. See also Don Agustín, Felipe II.

Trésor (Fr) a prestige cuvée méthode traditionelle white wine produced by Bouvet-Ladubay, Saumur, Loire. Grape varieties: 80% Chenin blanc, 20% Chardonnay. Aged in oak. Also produce Trésor rosé.

Trésor de Famille (Fr) an Armagnac produced by La Croix de Salles.

Trésor du Poête (Fr) a red wine produced by Domaine la Tourmone from 85% Grenache and 15% Syrah.

Trésor Rosé (Fr) see Trésor.

Tres Palmas (Sp) a brand of Fino Sherry produced by La Riva.

Tresques (Fr) a commune of the region Laudun in the south-west Rhône. Produces red, rosé and white wines.

Très Rare Heritage (Fr) a 30–35 year old Cognac produced by Brillet 45% alc by vol.

Tres Rayas (Sp) lit: 'three strokes', used in Sherry production, the marks on a Sherry butt to denote that the wine is destined as ordinary wine to be used for cleaning and seasoning casks. see Raya.

Tressalier (Fr) the name given to the Sacy grape in Bourbonnais, eastern France. Used in the making of St. Pourçain. Also spelt Tresallier.

Tressat (Fr) see Tressot.

Très Sec (Fr) very dry.

Tressler Process (USA) the method of making Sherry-type wines. After fortification the wines are stored in special vats at temperatures of over 51.66°C (125°F) for several weeks during which time oxygen is bubbled through the wine. When the Sherry flavour is obtained they are aged in vats for set times.

Tressot (Fr) a red grape variety grown in the Yonne département to make Bourgogne rouge. Also known as Trousseau.

Tresterbranntwein (Ger) a brandy made from distilling the residue of grape pressings after wine-making. Also known as Trester-schnapps. (Fr) = marc.

Trestergeschmack (Aus) a term to describe a wine that tastes of grape cap (from being left to long in the mash or pressed too late). See also Tresterln.

Tresterhut (Ger) the name given to the cap of pulp, skins and pips.

Tresterln (Aus) see Tretergeschmack.

Tresterschnapps (Ger) a style of brandy distilled from grape skins, similar to French marc. see Tresterbranntwein.

Tres Torres Sangre de Toro (Sp) an oak (American) aged red wine produced by Torres in Penedés from 60% Garnacha and 40% Cariñena grapes.

Tresuva (S.Afr) the label for a red wine (50% Cabernet sauvignon, Merlot and Shiraz blend) produced by the Janéza Pivate Cellar winery, Robertson, Western Cape.

Très Vieille Grande Réserve (Fr) a 50 year old Cognac produced by Salignac.

Très Vieux Dillon (W.Ind) the brand-name of a dark rum produced by Bardinet in north-west Martinique.

Trettacher Gebirgswasser (Ger) a natural spring mineral water from Trettach.

Treuenfels (Ger) vineyard (Anb): Nahe. (Ber): Schloss Böckelheim. (Gro): Burgweg. (Vil): Altenbamberg.

Treviris Glass (Ger) a style of glass produced in Trier,

T

have shallow bowls with a particular pattern of cutting on them. Used to serve Mosel wines.

Treviso (It) a wine town north of Venice noted for Prosecco wine.

Tri (Fr) the '*sorting out*' of the grapes, selecting those that have **Botrytis cinerea**, occurs in Sauternes.

Tria Corda (S.Afr) a red Médoc-style wine made from Cabernet franc, Cabernet sauvignon and Merlot grapes by the Overgaauw Estate in Stellenbosch, Western Cape.

Triage (Eng) a grade of coffee bean, one that is broken or too short.

Triage (Fr) the separation of unsound grapes at harvest time. Used in the southern Rhône (Châteauneuf-du-Pape and Tavel).

Trialcohols (Eng) an alcohol that has 3 carbon atoms attached to the hydroxyl group.

Trial Finings (Eng) the name given to a quantity of fining agent used to ascertain the minimum amount of fining agent needed to clear a wine.

Triangle (S.Afr) the label for red wine (Cabernet sauvignon, Cinsaut and Merlot blend) produced by the Clovelly Wines winery, Stellenbosch, Western Cape.

Triangle (S.Afr) the label for a red wine (Cabernet franc, Cabernet sauvignon and Merlot blend) produced by the Goedverwacht Estate winery, Robertson, Western Cape.

Tribal Winemakers Collection (S.Afr) a label for a range of varietal wines produced by the African Terroir winery, Paarl, Western Cape.

Tribaut [G.] (Fr) a Champagne producer. (Add): 88 Rue d'Eguisheim, B.P. 5, 51160 Hautvillers. Propriétaire-Récoltant. Demi-sec, brut and rosé produced also ratafia. Website: http://www.champagne.g.tribaut.com 'E'mail: champagne.tribaut@wanadoo.fr

Tribute (Eng) a 4.2% alc by vol cask-conditioned ale produced by the St. Austell Brewery. Website: http://www.tributeale.co.uk

Tricastin (Fr) *see* Coteaux de Tricastin.

Tri-chloro-anisole (Lat) *abbr*: TCA. *see* Cork Taint.

Tricolore (S.Afr) the label for a range of wines (red, rosé and white) produced by the Weltevrede Estate winery, Robertson Western Cape.

Tricorne (Eng) a wine label used by the Three Corners Vineyard in Kent. Grape variety: Reichensteiner.

Tridente (S.Afr) the label for a red wine (Cabernet franc 10%, Cabernet sauvignon 40% and Merlot 50% blend) produced by the Vuurberg Vineyards winery, Stellenbosch, Western Cape.

Triebaumer [Ernst] (Aus) a winery (11ha) based in Rust, Neusiedlersee-Hügelland, Burgenland. (Add): Raiffeisenstrasse 9, 7071 Rust. Grape varieties: Blaufränkisch, Cabernet sauvignon, Chardonnay, Furmint, Merlot, Pinot blanc, Sauvignon blanc, Welschriesling. Label: Mariental.

Trier (Ger) village (Anb): Mosel-Saar-Ruwer. (Ber): Saar-Ruwer. (Gro): Römerlay. (Vins): Altenberg, Andreasberg, Augenscheiner, Benediktinerberg, Burgberg, Deutschherrenberg,

Deutschherrenköpfchen, Domherrenberg, Hammerstein, Herrenberg, Jesuitenwingert, Karthäuserhofberg Burgberg, Karthäuserhofberg Kronenberg, Karthäuserhofberg Orthsberg, Karthäuserhofberg Sang, Karthauserhofberg Stirn, Kupp, Kurfürstenhofberg, Leikaul, Marienholz, Maximiner, Rotlay, St. Martiner Hofberg, St. Matheiser, St. Maxitheiser, St. Maximiner Kreuzberg, St. Petrusberg, Sonnenberg, Thiergarten, Felsköpfchen, Thiergarten unterm Kreuz.

Trierbaumer [Paul] (Aus) a winery (8ha) based in Rust, Neusiedlersee-Hügelland, Burgenland. (Add): Neue Gasse 18, 7071 Rust. Grape varieties: Blaufränkisch, Cabernet sauvignon, Chardonnay, Furmint, Gelber muskateller, Grüner veltliner, Merlot, Nebbiolo, Pinot noir, Syrah, Traminer, Welschriesling, Zweigelt. Labels: Erster Nebel, Ried Gertberg.

Tries (Fr) lit: 'passes', the process in Sauternes of picking the individual botrytis-affected grapes off the bunches on the vine. The number of passes depends on the botrytis develpment and can take up to eight or more in difficult years. *see* Tri.

Tries-Karden (Ger) village (Anb): Mosel-Saar-Ruwer. (Ber): Zell/Mosel. (Gro): Rosenhang. (Vins): Greth, Kapellenberg, Treppchen.

Triesner (Euro) the name given to the wines produced from Triesen in Liechtenstein.

Trifalter (Aus) a light, spicy white wine from the Traminer grape, produced in the Wachau district.

Trifesti (Mol) a dessert wine made from the Pinot gris grape in the Moldavia.

Trigny (Fr) a Cru Champagne village in the Canton de Fismes. District: Reims.

Trilby Cocktail (Cktl) ⅔ measure bourbon whiskey, ⅓ measure Italian vermouth, 2 dashes Campari, stir over ice and strain into a cocktail glass.

Trilogy Estate Reserve (S.Afr) the label for a red wine (Cabernet sauvignon, Cabernet franc and Merlot blend) produced by the Warwick Estate winery, Stellenbosch, Western Cape.

Trimbach (Fr) an Alsace wine négociant-éleveur. (Add): 15 Route de Bergheim, 68150 Ribeauvillé, also produces eau-de-vie 28ha.

Trincadeira (Port) a red grape variety grown in Ribatejo. Also known as Castelão Francês, Espadeiro, Mortagua, Periquita and Tinta Amarela.

Trincadeira Branca (Port) a white grape variety grown near Bucelas.

Trincadeira das Pratas (Port) a white grape variety also known as the Tamarez.

Trincar (Sp) to drink a toast/to good health.

Trinchero Family (USA) a winery based in Rutherford, Napa Valley, California. Grape varieties: Cabernet sauvignon, Pinot Noir. Label: Chicken Ranch, Vista Montone.

Trinchieri (It) tonic wine.

Tring Brewery (Eng) a brewery (established 1992). (Add): 81-82 Akeman Street, Tring, Hertfordshire HP23 6AF. Brews: Colleys Black Dog 5.2% alc by vol., Jack O Legs 4.2% alc by vol., Side Pocket for a Toad 3.6% alc by vol., Ridgeway Bitter 4% alc by vol. plus Double Eagle, Leopards Head and Makers Mark under licence for The Vintage Hallmark Ale Company. Website: http://www.tringbrewery.com 'E'mail: info@tringbrewery.com

Trinidad Distillers Ltd. (W.Ind) a large rum distillery based at Lavenville, Trinidad. Produces Kairi, Limbo Drummer, Old Oak, Royal Oak Twelve and White Drummer rums.

Trinidad Punch (Cktl) 35mls (1½ fl.ozs) dark rum, 25mls (1fl.oz) lime juice, 2 dashes Angostura, teaspoon gomme syrup. Shake over ice, strain into an ice-filled goblet, top with grated nutmeg and a twist of lemon.

Trinidad Rum (W.Ind) a light, medium-coloured rum from Trinidad which is light in flavour with a slight sweet taste.

Trinity (Cktl) ⅓ measure gin, ⅓ measure French vermouth, ⅓ measure Italian vermouth. Stir over ice and strain into a cocktail glass.

Trinity Hill (N.Z) a wine-producing district in Hawkes Bay, North Island. Grape varieties: Cabernet sauvignon, Merlot, Syrah.

Trinity Springs (USA) a slightly alkaline still natural spring mineral water from Paradise, Idaho. Mineral contents (milligrammes per litre): Sodium 10mg/l, Calcium 1.4mg/l, Potassium 1.2mg/l, Bicarbonates 47.6mg/l, Chlorides 8mg/l, Fluorides 3.6mg/l, Silicates 74.6mg/l. pH 9.6

Trinity Vine (USA) an old vine grown in the western region in the eighteenth and nineteenth centuries.

Trinken (Aus)(Den) to drink.

Trinkspruch (Aus)(Ger) a toast.

Trinoro (It) a winery based in thne Tuscany region. Label: La Cupole.

Trinquer (Fr) to touch glasses in a toast.

Trio (Chile) the label of Concha y Toro Chardonnay, Cabernet sauvignon and Merlot range of varietal wines.

Triology (USA) the name of a wine produced by Flora Springs, St. Helena, California from a blend of Cabernet sauvignon, Cabernet franc and Merlot.

Triomphe (Fr) a 40 year old Cognac produced by Hine in Jarnac.

Triomphe d'Alsace (Fr) a red hybrid grape variety. Produced from Knipperlé and a Rupestris vine.

Trip Dog (Austr) a slang term for the imaginary dog that trips you up when you are drunk!

Tripel (Bel) a golden Trappiste ale 8% alc by vol. from the Abbaye of Westmalle Brasserie on the Dutch border.

Tripel Karmeliet (Bel) an 8% alc by vol. top-fermented, fruity, three grains, bottle-conditioned beer brewed by Bosteels, Buggenhout. Produced from wheat, oats and barley from a recipe dating from 1679.

Triple A (Aus) a natural spring mineral water from Quelle Thalheim. Mineral contents (milligrammes per litre): Sodium 2.9mg/l, Calcium 52.6mg/l,

Magnesium 6.4mg/l, Potassium 3.7mg/l, Chlorides 3.7mg/l, Sulphates 23.2mg/l, Nitrates 5.6mg/l. pH 7.5

Triple A (Eng) a cool, cask-conditioned beer brewed by Young's at the Ram Brewery, Wandsworth, London.

Triple Alliance (Cktl) ½ measure French vermouth, ¼ measure gin, ¼ measure Glayva. Stir over ice and strain into a 125mls (5fl.oz) cocktail glass.

Triple B (Eng) a 4.2% alc by vol. ale brewed by Davis'es Brewing C°. Ltd., Rutland.

Triple B-Boons Birthday Beer (Eng) produced by Clarks Brewery in Wakefield, Yorkshire to commemorate the birthday of their founder Henry Boon who was born in 1906.

Triple Creek (S.Afr) the label for a white wine (Chenin blanc, Chardonnay and Sémillon blend) from the Nelson's Creek range produced by the Nelson Estate winery, Paarl, Western Cape.

Triple Crown (Can) a Canadian rye whisky produced by Gilbey Canada Ltd.

Triple Crown (Port) the brand-name of a ruby Port produced by Croft.

Triple Crown Bitter (Eng) a keg bitter 1033 O.G. brewed by the Usher Brewery in Trowbridge, Wiltshire. Also sold under the Manns Brewery label.

Triple Distilled (U.K) refers to Irish whiskey which differs from the Scottish malt whisky which is only double distilled (except the Auchentoschen and Rosebank distilleries who triple distill).

Triple FFF Brewing C° (Eng) a brewery (established 1997). (Add): Unit 3, Magpie Works, Station Approach, Four Marks, Alton, Hampshire GU34 5HN. Brews: Altons Pride 3.8% alc by vol., Comfortably Numb 5% alc by vol., Dazed and Confused, I Can't remember 6.8% alc by vol., Moondance 4.2% alc by vol., Pressed Rat 3.8% alc by vol., Stairway 4.6% alc by vol., Water Hog 3.8% alc by vol., Witches Promise 6% alc by vol. Website: http://www.triplefff.com 'E'mail: triplefffbrewing@aol.com

Triple H (Eng) a 1048 O.G. ale produced by the Cameron Brewery to commemorate the retirement of their head brewer after 30 years service.

Triple Hop (Eng) a 4.1% alc by vol. bitter ale brewed by The Derby Brewing C°. Ltd., Derbyshire.

Triple Jump 500 (Eng) a 3.6% alc by vol. ale produced by the Mauldon Brewery, Sudbury, Suffolk.

Triple Moine (Bel) an 8% alc by vol. top-fermented, bottle-conditioned, pale ale with a hint of saison from Du Bocq Brasserie, Purnode. *See also* Blanche de Namur, St. Benoit Blonde, Gauloise (La), St. Benoit Brune.

Triple O (Eng) a 3.9% alc by vol. ale brewed by the Fernanders Brewery, West Yorkshire.

Triple Or (Fr) an orange and Cognac liqueur.

Triple Sec (Fr) a very sweet white Curaçao.

Triple Tun (Eng) a commemorative ale brewed by Archer's Brewery, Swindon, Wiltshire.

T

Triplex (Eng) a bitter ale 1044 O.G. brewed by the Hermitage Brewery in West Sussex.

Triple XXX (Eng) a 4.3% alc by vol. bitter ale brewed by the Three Tuns Brewery, Shropshire.

Trippelaer (Hol) an 8.5% alc by vol. top-fermented, bottle-conditioned triple beer brewed by De 3 Horme Brouwerij, Kaatsheuvel. Contains coriander and orange.

Tris (Fr) a term used to describe the continuous picking of the vineyard to obtain the ripest grapes.

Triton Purified Drinking Water (USA) a bottled drinking water brand.

Trittenheim (Ger) village (Anb): Mosel-Saar-Ruwer. (Ber): Bernkastel. (Gro): Michelsberg. (Vins): Altärchen, Apotheke, Felsenkopf, Leiterchen.

Triumph (Fr) a variety of barley malt which gives high sugar. Carmargue, Corgi, Doublet and Heriot are species.

Triumph Ale (Eng) a 4.3% alc by vol. golden summer ale, part of Tapster's Choice range from Carlsberg-Tetley (available May and June).

Triumphator (Ger) the name of the doppelbock beer brewed by the Löwenbräu Brauerei in Munich.

Triunfo (Chile) the label for the Tarapacá estate, Maipo Valley.

Triunfo (Mad) a black Vitis vinifera grape variety used in the production of Madeira.

Trivento Bodegas y Viñedos (Arg) a winery (established 1996) based in Mendoza. 980ha. Grape varieties include: Cabernet sauvignon, Chardonnay, Malbec, Merlot, Pinot noir, Syrah, Tempranillo, Viognier. Labels: Otra Vida (owned by Concha y Toro). Website: http://www.trivento.com 'E'mail: info@trivento.com

Trnava Brewery (Czec) a brewery based in south-eastern Czec.

Trnovo (Bul) a wine region of northern Bulgaria. Produces red, white, dessert and sparkling wines.

Trocadero Cocktail (Cktl) 30mls (¼ gill) Italian vermouth, 30mls (¼ gill) French vermouth, 1 dash orange bitters, 1 dash grenadine. Stir over ice, strain into a cocktail glass, add a cherry and a squeeze of lemon peel juice on top.

Trocken (Aus) dry, wines can have up to 9g/l of residual sugar when the total acidity is less than the residual sugar to a maximum of 2g/l.

Trocken (Ger) dry.

Trockenbeerenauslese (Aus) produced from overripe fully botrytis attacked and shriveled (in a rasin-like state) grapes. Must have a minimum must weight of 30° KMW. Wine must be bottled in Austria and cannot be sold before 1st May of year following the harvest. see Prädikatsweine.

Trockenbeerenauslese (Ger) a wine that has been made from edelfäule (noble rot) attacked grapes. 150° Oe–154° Oe.

Trockendiabetiker (Ger) a dry white wine produced by Bénédictine monks around Klosterberg in the Rheingau.

Trockenverbessert (Ger) equivalent to chaptalisation.

Trockenweine (Ger) dry wine.

Troesmes (Fr) a Premier Cru Chablis vineyard, often reclassified as the Premier Cru vineyard Beauroy.

Troika Cocktail (Cktl) ⅔ measure orange Chartreuse, ⅓ measure vodka, juice half a lime. Shake over ice and strain into a cocktail glass.

Trois Ceps [Les] (Fr) the local Chablis wine growers' fraternity founded in 1965. Meets in November and January.

Trois Glorieuses (Fr) the name given to the Hospices de Beaune sales held in November (third Sunday) in Beaune, Burgundy. see Paulée.

Troisgros (Fr) a Grande Champagne Cognac produced by Robin (Jules). Average age 25 years 43% alc by vol.

Troisième Cru (Fr) the third growths of the 1855 classification of the Médoc in western Bordeaux. 14 in total. Château Boyd-Cantenac, Château Calon-Ségur, Château Cantenac-Brown, Château Desmirial, Château d'Issan, Château Ferrière, Château Kirwan, Château Lagrange, Château la Lagune, Château Langoa-Barton, Château Malescot-St-Exupéry, Château Marquis d'Alesme-Becker, Château Palmer.

Troisième Taille (Fr) the fourth pressing of Champagne grapes: 266litres of grape must was produced (now no longer permitted in Champagne production).

Trois Monts (Fr) an 8.5% alc by vol bière de garde brewed by St. Sylvestre.

Trois-Puits (Fr) a Premier Cru Champagne village in the Canton de Reims. District: Reims.

Trois Rivières (Cktl) ⅔ measure Canadian rye whiskey, ⅙ measure red Dubonnet, ⅙ measure Cointreau. Shake over ice, strain into an ice-filled old-fashioned glass and top with a twist of orange peel juice.

Trois-Six (Fr) lit: 'three six', a term often used for alcohol at 85% by volume as 3 parts of this alcohol with 3 parts of pure water produces 6 parts of eau-de-vie.

Troissy-Bouquigny (Fr) a Cru Champagne village in the Canton de Dormans. District: Épernay.

Trojan Horse (Eng) a drink of half Guinness and half Cola.

Trollberg (Ger) vineyard (Anb): Nahe. (Ber): Kreuznach. (Gro): Schlosskapelle. (Vil): Dorsheim.

Trollberg (Ger) vineyard (Anb): Nahe. (Ber): Kreuznach. (Gro): Schlosskapelle. (Vil): Münster-Sarmsheim.

Trollinger (Ger) a red grape variety grown in the Württemberg anbaugebiet. Came originally from the Tirol, Austria. (Called the Tirollinger). Also known as the Black hamburg, Black muscat, Blauer malvasier, Frankenthaler, Schiava, Vernatsch.

Tromel (Arg) the brand-name of a wine produced by Bodegas Gonzáles Videla.

Tromphe La Morte (Ger) a brand of beer sold in a black bottle 1045 O.G.

Tronçais (Fr) an oak used for casks in the Cognac brandy maturation.

Tronche [La] (Fr) a vineyard based in Vienne, Isère département. Produces dry white wines.

Troödos (Cyp) a mountain range where grape vines are grown in Cyprus. Best regions Makheras, Marathassa and Pitsilia. The Kokkineli red wine from the Mavron grape is the most widely produced.

Trophy Bitter (Eng) a keg bitter 1035 O.G. brewed by the Whitbread Brewery. Brewed by Fremlins, Salford, Samlesbury and Sheffield Breweries. At the Cheltenham Brewery 1033 O.G. At Castle Eden Brewery a Special Trophy Bitter 1040 O.G. and in the north of England a cask Trophy Bitter 1037 O.G.

Tropical Chill (Sri.L) a bottled spring mineral water brand.

Tropical Cocktail (Cktl) ⅓ measure maraschino, ⅓ measure (white) crème de cacao, ⅓ measure Noilly Prat, dash Angostura. Stir over ice and strain into a cocktail glass.

Tropical Dawn (Cktl) ⅖ measure gin, ⅕ measure Campari, ⅖ measure orange juice. Shake orange and gin over ice, strain into a 250mls (8fl.oz) goblet containing a ball of crushed ice, add a dash of Campari and serve with straws.

Tropical Fruit Lotus Light (Eng) a blend of sparkling mineral water, British wine and tropical fruits 4.5% alc by vol.

Tropical Kiss Cocktail (Cktl) ⅕ measure maraschino, ⅕ measure white rum, ⅗ measure pineapple juice, dash grenadine. Shake well over ice, strain into a scooped-out pineapple shell, dress with a mint sprig and a cherry and serve with straws.

Tropical Mimosa Cocktail (Cktl) 25mls (⅕ gill) white rum, 75mls (⅗ gill) orange juice, dash grenadine. Stir over ice, strain into a flute glass, top with iced Champagne and a spiral of orange peel.

Tropical Spring (Eng) a sparkling, non-alcoholic soft drink produced by Schweppes. A blend of nine different fruits. Has 55% juice and 45% natural spring water with no sugar or preservatives.

Tropical Storm (Cktl) 35mls (1½ fl.oz) golden rum, 25mls (1fl.oz) orange juice, 10mls (½ fl.oz) each of vodka, lime juice, pineapple juice, dash Angostura, dash grenadine. Blend together with a scoop of crushed ice in a blender, pour into a highball glass, dress with an orange slice, cherry and banana slice and serve with straws.

Tropical Tonic Cocktail (Cktl) ⅔ measure Malibu, ⅓ measure Mandarine Napoléon. Stir over ice in a highball glass. Top with ginger ale, dress with a slice of orange and a cherry.

Tropicana (Cktl) ⅓ measure dry white wine, ⅔ measure grapefruit juice, 1 teaspoon Bénédictine, 1 teaspoon lemon juice. Shake over ice and strain into a goblet.

Tropicana (W.Ind) a white Caribbean rum.

Tropicana (S.Am) the brand-name of a rum produced in Guyana for Seagram 40% alc by vol.

Tropic of Capricorn (Cktl) 35mls (1½ fl.ozs) white rum, 20mls (¾ fl.oz) white crème de cacao, 100mls (4fl.ozs) orange juice, 1 egg white. Shake well over ice, strain into a highball glass, top with a dash of blue Curaçao, orange slice and a cherry.

Trotsky (Eng) the brand-name used by Davis and C°. for a range of their liqueurs.

Trottevieille (Fr) *see* Château Trottevieille.

Troubador (Sp) the brand-name of a Sherry range produced by Cuesta in Puerto de Santa Maria.

Troublé (Fr) lit: 'troubled', denotes a hazy, cloudy wine.

Trouffières [Les] (Fr) a vineyard in the A.C. commune of Montagny, Côte Chalonnaise, Burgundy.

Trou Gascon (Fr) a glass of chilled Armagnac served as a digestif mid-way between a large meal, also can be be served as an apéritif. *See also* Blanche d'Armagnac.

Trough Brewery (Eng) a brewery (established 1981) in Bradford, Lancashire. Noted for cask-conditioned Wild Boar 1039 O.G.

Trough Withering (Afr) a method of drying tea using a trough that has air forced through the tea leaf.

Trou Normand (Fr) lit: 'Norman hole', the name given to a glass of Calvados during a meal to stimulate the appetite and make more room for food.

Trou Normande [Un] (Fr) a brand of A.C. Calvados 40% alc by vol.

Trousseau (Fr) the local Jura name for the black Pinot grape. Used in the making of Vin gris.

Trousseau Grise (Fr) known as the Grey Riesling in California.

Trovador (Port) a brand of light rosé wine produced by Soc. Vinhos Borges & Irmao, Porto-Portugal.

Troyka (S.Afr) the label for red wine (Cabernet franc, Cabernet sauvignon and Merlot blend) produced by the Cape Chamonix Wine Farm winery, Franschhoek, Western Cape.

Troyka Black Bear Vodka (I.O.M) the brand-name of a vodka produced by Glen Kella Distilleries, Sulby. *See also* Lonsdale Northern Gin, Glen Kella.

Trub (Eng) during the brewing process a solid malt protein formed during the boiling of the wort, it is removed before fermentation.

Truchard Vineyard (USA) a vineyard based in the Carneros, Napa Valley, California. 6.5ha. Grape variety- Cabernet sauvignon. Wines are vinified at Carneros Creek. Website: http://www.truchardvineyards.com

True Blue Witches Brew (Cktl) 2 measures vodka, 1 measure Sambuca, 1 measure Bols Blue Curaçao. Stir over ice, strain into a cocktail glass with a twist of lemon. Stand the glass in a bowl of dry ice.

True Glory (Eng) a 4.3% alc by vol. 50th anniversary copper coloured ale brewed for V.E. day celebrations on 8th May, 1995 by Ringwood Brewery, Ringwood, Hampshire.

Trug Baskets (Fr) the name for the wooden baskets used by the grape pickers of Champagne to gather the grapes.

Truluck Winery (USA) a winery based in Lake City,

South Carolina. Produces French hybrid and vinifera wines.

Truman Brewery (Eng) a brewery based in Brick Lane, London (a partner of Watneys). Noted for cask-conditioned Sampson 1055 O.G. keg Ben Truman 1038 O.G. Prize Brew 1032 O.G. bottled Barley Wine 1086 O.G. and Brewer's Gold 1078 O.G.

Truman IPA (Eng) 3.5% alc by vol. session ale from Courage, Chelmsford, East Anglia.

Trumer Pils (Aus) a brewery. (Add): Brauhausgasse 2, 5162 Obertrum bei, Salzburg. Brews beers and lager. Website: http://www.trumer.at 'E'mail: jsigl@sigl.co.at

Truskavetska (Ukr) a natural spring mineral water from Truskavets. Mineral contents (milligrammes per litre): Sodium 70mg/l, Calcium 55mg/l, Magnesium 35mg/l, Bicarbonates 70mg/l, Sulphates 25mg/l.

Trustees Choice (Eng) a fine Tawny Port bottled by Howells of Bristol.

Trust Tavern (N.Z) a licensed bar/tavern owned by a community committee of trustees and where all the profits go to the benefit of the community.

Trutina (S.Afr) the label for a red wine (Cabernet sauvignon and Shiraz blend) produced by the De Meye Wines winery, Stellenbosch, Western Cape.

Trutnov Brewery (Czec) an old established brewery based in northern Czec.

Tryptophan (Eng) an amino acid found in small traces in wines formed by the yeasts.

Tsai (Gre) tea.

Tsantali Winery (Gre) a winery based in Agios Pavlos, Halkidiki. 90ha. Produces a wide range of table wines under the names of Aspéro, Blue Boy, Country Girl, Golden Delicious, Grecian Urn and Nemia. Grape varieties: Agiorgitiko, Cabernet sauvignon, Limnio, Xinomavro, Assyrtiko, Sauvignon blanc. Also produces Ouzo.

Tsaoussi (Gre) a white grape variety grown on island of Cephalonia.

Tsarina Cocktail (Cktl) ½ measure vodka, ¼ measure dry vermouth, ¼ measure apricot brandy, dash Angostura. Stir over ice and strain into a cocktail glass.

Tsar Mandarine (Cktl) 25mls (1fl.oz) Mandarine Napoléon, 20mls (¾ fl.oz) vodka, 1 tablespoon cream, dash grenadine. Shake over ice and strain into a cocktail glass.

TSB (Cktl) 25mls (⅕ gill) Golden Heart liqueur, juice ¼ lemon, 2 dashes pineapple juice. Stir over ice in a highball glass and dress with a spiral of lemon peel.

TSB (Eng) *abbr*: **T**ooley **S**treet **B**itter 1040 O.G. a cask-conditioned bitter brewed by the Tooley Street Brewery in London.

TSB (N.Z) *abbr*: *see* **T**hames **S**tickl**b**ract.

Tschaggele (It) a red grape variety grown in the Trentino-Alto-Adige. Known as the Tschaggelervernatsch in Germany.

Tschaggelervernatsch (Ger) a red grape variety from the Südtirol in Italy. Known as the Tschaggele in Italy.

Tscheppe [Eduard] (Aus) a winery (45ha) based in Leutschach, Styria. (Add): Pssnitz 168, 8463 Leutschach. Grape varieties: Blaufränkisch, Chardonnay, Muskateller, Pinot blanc, Zweigelt. Produces a range of red and white wines.

Tschermonegg (Aus) a winery based in Leutschach, Styria. (Add): Glanz an der Weinstrasse 50, 8463 Leutschach. Grape varieties: Gelber traminer, Sauvignon blanc, Traminer. Produces mainly white wines.

Tschida [Johann] (Aus) a vineyard (6ha) based in Illmitz, Burgenland. (Add): Angergasse 5, 7142 Illmitz. Grape varieties: Grüner veltliner, Muskat-ottonel, Pinot blanc, Scheurebe, Welschriesling, Zweigelt. Produces a range of sweet wines.

Tselepos Vineyards (Gre) vineyards based at Riza Tegeas, Arcadia. Produces red and white wines.

Tselinnoe (Rus) a white grape variety grown in Kazakhstan. Produces dessert and fortified wines.

Tsen Gon (Chi) a brand of rice wine from the Fukien branch of the C.N.C.O.F.I.E.C.

Tsimlianska (Rus) a wine-producing centre in the river Don area. Produces mainly white wines.

Tsimlyanskoye (Rus) a Champagne-type wine produced between the district of Anapa and Gelendshik in the Crimean Peninsular from a district of the same name. Also produces table wines.

Tsinandali (Geo) based in the Republic of Georgia. Red Teliani and white Hereti wines produced in Kakheti region from Cabernet sauvignon and Rkatsiteli grapes.

Tsindali N°1 (Geo) a dry white wine produced in the Alazan Valley in the Georgia region from the Mtsvane and Rkatsiteli grapes.

Tsingana (It) a Bordeaux (grape varieties) blend red wine produced by Monte Bernardi in Panzano, Tuscany.

Tsingtao (Chi) the name given to red or white wines produced by the Huadong Winery, Quingdao, Shandong, northern China. Grape varieties include Chardonnay, Riesling.

Tsingtao Brewery (Chi) a brewery based in Shandong, northern China that brews a pilsener-style beer of same name.

Tsipouri (Gre) a strong form of Ouzo.

Tsolikauri (Geo) an alternative spelling of Tsolikohouri.

Tsolikohouri (Geo) a white grape variety grown in Georgia to produce dry white wines. Also spelt Tsolikauri.

Tsuica (Rom) plum brandy, the national drink.

Tsun (Chi) a large old Chinese wine vessel (circa 1000BC) used as a chalice.

Tuaca (It) a 35% alc by vol, sweet, vanilla and orange essence-flavoured liqueur that has a brandy base. Produced in Tuscany, northern Italy.

Tualatin Vineyards (USA) a winery based in Tualatin, Oregon. 27.5ha. Produces varietal wines.

Tua Rita (It) wine estate based in Suvereto, Maremma, coastal region of Tuscany. Grape varieties: Merlot, Cabernet sauvignon, Cabernet franc, Sangiovese. Produces: Perlato del Bosco, Giustro di Notri, Redigaffi wines.

Tuay (Thai) cup.

Tuba (E.Ind) a wine produced in the Philippines from coconuts and nipa rice, when distilled is known as Lambanog.

Tube (Austr) the slang name for a can of beer.

Tübingen (Ger) village (Anb): Württemberg. (Ber): Kocher-Jagst-Tauber. (Gro): Not yet assigned. *see* Kressbronn am Bodensee Tübingen.

Tuborg (Den) a brewery in Copenhagen which together with the Carlsberg Brewery makes up the United Breweries. Noted for Tuborg Pilsener 1030 O.G. Tuborg Julebryg 5.5% alc by vol. and Tuborg Gold 1045 O.G. brewed in the U.K. at Carlsberg's Northampton Brewery.

Tuborg Blå Special (Den) a natural spring mineral water from Hellerup.

Tuborg Hvid Special (Den) a natural spring mineral water from Hellerup.

Tuchan (Fr) a commune in the A.C. Fitou region in southern France.

Tuchen (Fr) a noted wine-producing village based in Corbières in the Languedoc.

Tucher Bajuvator (Ger) a 7% alc by vol. bottled double bock beer brewed by Tucher Brauerei, Nuremberg.

Tucher Brauerei (Ger) a brewery (established 1692) based in Nuremberg. Produces a dry double-hopped beer of the same name, also Tucher Bajuvator, Tucher Helles Hefe Weizen.

Tucher Helles Hefe Weizen (Ger) a 5.3% alc by vol. bottle-conditioned wheat beer brewed by Tucher Brauerei, Nuremberg.

Tucquan Vineyards (USA) vineyards based in Holtwood, Pennsylvania. Produces hybrid wines.

Tudal Winery (USA) a winery based north of St. Helena, Napa Valley, California. Grape varieties: Cabernet sauvignon and Chardonnay. Produces varietal wines.

Tudela de Duero (Sp) a Vino de Mesa wine of the province Valladolid in Castilla-León.

Tudelilla (Sp) a Zona de Crianza in the Rioja Baja, north-western Spain.

Tudor Ale (Eng) a beer 1051 O.G. brewed and bottled by the Gales Brewery in Horndean, Hampshire. A bottled version of HSB is brewed for the French market.

Tudor Ale (Eng) a cask-conditioned bitter 1044 O.G. brewed by the Liddington Brewery in Rugby, Warwickshire.

Tudor Rose (Cktl) 3 parts Merrydown Mead, 1 part Bourbon whiskey, dash Angostura. Shake over crushed ice, strain, serve with lemon zest and splash of soda.

Tudor Rose (Eng) an oak-aged, dry, rosé wine produced by the St. George's Vineyard from Pinot noir grapes.

Tuella (Port) a red wine produced by Cockburn, D.O. Douro.

Tuerong Estate Vineyard (Austr) a winery (established 1984). (Add): Mornington-Flinders Road, Red Hill, Victoria. Grape variety: Chardonnay.

Tufa (Fr) a rock of vulcanized chalk (boiled limestone), easy to work for cellars, full of minerals, is porous and water retentive. Is found in the Touraine district of the Loire and in parts of Italy. *see* Calctufa and Calctuff.

Tufaie (It) a D.O.C. Soave Classico wine (part of the Gamma range) produced by Bolla from Garganega and Trebbiano di Soave grapes.

Tuff (Fr) volcanic (soil).

Tuffeau (Fr) a chalk-clay soil found in the Touraine district in the Loire region. Produces good red wines. Also found in Saumur.

Tuica (Rum) a plum brandy/plum liqueur, green-yellow in colour.

Tuilé (Fr) denotes a wine of brick-red colour that has lost its youthful purple.

Tuinwingerd (S.Afr) a white, dry wine from the Riesling grape made by the Montpellier Estate in Tulbagh.

Tuin Wyn (S.Afr) the label for a straw wine (Chenin blanc) produced by the Mellast winery, Paarl, Western Cape.

Tui Vale (N.Z) a range of varietal wines from Pask Winery, Hastings, Hawkes Bay. Grape varieties: Cabernet sauvignon, Chardonnay, Sauvignon blanc.

Tuke Holdsworth (Port) the original name used to ship Quinta de Eira Velha (prior to 1943).

Tuke Holdsworth Hunt, Roope and Cº. (Port) vintage port shippers. Vintages: 1870, 1873, 1874, 1875, 1881, 1884, 1887, 1890, 1892, 1894, 1896, 1900, 1904, 1908, 1912, 1917, 1920, 1922, 1924, 1927, 1934, 1935, 1943, 1945, 1947, 1950, 1955, 1960, 1963, 1966, 1987, 1991, 1994, 2003.

Tukulu (S.Afr) a winery (established 1998) based in Groenekloof, Stellenbosch, Western Cape. 245ha. Owned by Distell, Leopont 98 Properties and the Maluti Groenekloof Community Trust. Grape varieties: Cabernet sauvignon, Chardonnay, Chenin blanc, Pinotage, Sangiovese, Sauvignon blanc, Shiraz, Viognier. Website: http://www.tukulu.co.za

Tulare (USA) a wine district within the Great Central Valley in California. Produces sweet, dessert wines.

Tulatin Vineyards (USA) vineyards based in Forest Grove, Willamette Valley, Oregon. 85acres (38.5ha). Grape varieties: Pinot noir, Chardonnay, Gewürztraminer, Riesling.

Tulbagh (S.Afr) a still and sparkling natural spring mineral water. (green label: low gas/blue label: no gas). Mineral contents (milligrammes per litre): Sodium 35mg/l, Calcium 10.4mg/l, Magnesium 15.4mg/l, Potassium 1.6mg/l, Chlorides 68mg/l, Sulphates <5mg/l. pH 6.8

Tulbagh (S.Afr) a wine region which produces fine white wines and Sherry-style wines. Three estates: Montpellier, Theuniskraal and Twee Jongegezellen. Is the home of the Drostdy Co-operative and Tulbagh winery.

Tulbagh Mountain Vineyards (S.Afr) a winery (established 2000) based in Tulbagh, Western Cape. 16ha. Grape varieties: Cabernet sauvignon, Chenin blanc, Cinsaut, Merlot, Mourvèdre, Shiraz, Syrah. Labels: Swartland, TMV, Theta, Viktoria. Website: http://www.tmv.co.za

Tulbagh Winery (S.Afr) a co-operative winery (established 1906) based in Tulbagh, Western Cape. 550ha. (Add): P.O. Box 19, Tulbagh 6820. (The oldest co-operative winery in South Africa). Grape varieties: Cabernet sauvignon, Chardonnay, Chenin blanc, Colombard, Fernão pires, Hanepoot, Merlot, Pinotage, Pinot noir, Ruby cabernet, Sauvignon blanc, Shiraz, Zingier. Produces varietals and a range of wines. Website: http://www.tulbaghwine.co.za

Tulbingerkogel (Aus) a wine-producing district within the Donauland region that is noted for its eisweins.

Tulip Cocktail (Cktl) ⅓ measure applejack, ⅓ measure Italian vermouth, ⅙ measure lemon juice, ⅙ measure apricot brandy, shake over ice and strain into a cocktail glass.

Tulip Lager (Eng) a lager beer 1034 O.G. brewed and bottled by the Lees Brewery in Manchester.

Tulip Tumbler (Eng) a tulip-shaped beer glass produced by Dema Glass.

Tullamore Dew (Ire) a blended Irish whiskey from the Tullamore Dew Cº. Midleton, Dublin. Sold in a stone crock 40% alc by vol.

Tullibardine (Scot) a single highland malt whisky distillery in Blackford, Perthshire. Operated by Longman Distillers of Glasgow (part of the Invergordon group), produces 10 and 25 year old 43% alc by vol.

Tullins (Fr) a vineyard based in Vienne, Isère département. Produces white wines.

Tulloch Winery (Austr) a winery. (Add): Allied Vintners, De Beyers Road, Polkolbin, New South Wales 2321. Grape varieties: Cabernet sauvignon, Hermitage, Sémillon, Shiraz.

Tulocay Vineyards (USA) a winery based in Napa Valley, California. Grape varieties: Cabernet sauvignon, Pinot noir and Zinfandel. Produces varietal wines.

Tulun Valley (Arg) one of the countries main wine-producing areas.

Tumara (S.Afr) the label for a red wine blend (Cabernet sauvignon 69%) produced by the Bellevue Estate winery, Stellenbosch, Western Cape.

Tumbler (Eng) a straight-sided drinking glass of 150mls–300mls (6fl.ozs–12fl.ozs) capacity.

Tumbling Waters (Austr) a natural spring mineral water brand. Mineral contents (milligrammes per litre): Sodium 2mg/l, Calcium 40mg/l, Magnesium 29mg/l, Potassium 1mg/l, Bicarbonates 257mg/l, Chlorides 6mg/l, Sulphates 9mg/l, Nitrates 1mg/l.

Tumbril (Cktl) made from equal quantities of Guinness, Port, brandy and Champagne all in the same glass.

Tuminton (Scot) a brand of blended Scotch whisky 43% alc by vol.

Tumultuous Fermentation (Eng) the first violent fermentation usually from the wild yeasts.

Tun (Eng) a container for beer brewing. i.e. mash tun.

Tun (Eng) an old cask of 250 gallons.

Tun (Eng) a wine cask 9454litres/210 Imp.gallons/252 USgallons.

Tun Bitter (Eng) a cask-conditioned ale 1041 O.G. brewed by the Creedy Valley Brewery in Crediton, Devon.

Tungusian Arrack (Rus) an arrack, distilled from fermented mare's milk by the Tartars in Tungusia.

Tunisia (Afr) a North-African country that has made wine since before Roman times. Produces all types of wines especially Muscat. Red wines are the best styles for export.

Tunna (Lat) cask/tun. see Tonna.

Tunne (Eng) the mediaeval spelling of tun (cask).

Tunsel (Ger) village (Anb): Baden. (Ber): Markgräflerland. (Gro): Lorettoberg. (Vin): Maltesergarten.

Tunuyán (Arg) a wine-producing area in central Argentina.

Tuplàk (Czec) a boot-shaped glass used for festive occasions and drinking contests.

Tupungato (Arg) a wine-producing area based south of the Mendoza region.

Tura (It) a light, dry, sparkling white and rosé wine produced in the Veneto region.

Turacciolo (It) stopper/cork.

Turbar (Port) a cloudy wine, a wine that has turned cloudy through the bottle being shaken.

Turbid (Eng) denotes a cloudy (not clear) liquid, has suspended particles in it. i.e. a shaken old red wine.

Turbios (Sp) wine lees.

Turckheim (Fr) a commune in Alsace, north-eastern France.

Turf Cocktail (Cktl) 30mls (¼ gill) Plymouth Gin, 30mls (¼ gill) French vermouth, 2 dashes each of absinthe, orange bitters and maraschino. Stir over ice, strain into a cocktail glass and add an olive.

Turgeon and Lohr Winery (USA) a large winery based in San Jose, Salinas Valley, California. 116ha. Grape varieties: Cabernet sauvignon, Chardonnay, Johannisberg riesling, Petite syrah, Pinot blanc and Sauvignon blanc, produces varietal wines.

Turiga (Port) a red grape variety used in the making of Port.

Türk (Aus) a winery based in the Kremstal region. (Add): Kirchengasse 86, 3552 Stratzing. Grape varieties: Grüner veltliner, Riesling, Zweigelt. Produces a range of wine styles.

Turkey (Euro) a Muslim country with approximately 100 wine-producers that produces red, rosé and white wines mainly in Elazig, Yesilirmak Valley, very little is exported. Red grapes include Öküzgözü, Bogazkere. see Buzbag, Trakya.

Turkey's Last (Wal) a 4.4% alc by vol. festive ale brewed by Cambrian Brewery, Dolgellau,

T

Gwynedd using Marris Otter crystal and chocolate malts.

Turkish Blood (Eng) in a tankard mix ½ Burton XXX Ale and ½ red Burgundy.

Turkish Coffee (Tur) a coffee made from finely ground, dark roasted beans. Is boiled with sugar in small pans and served in small cups traditionally with iced water and a tot of Ouzo. *see* Ibrik and Zarf. Also known as Byzantine Coffee.

Turkish State Monopoly (Tur) has control of 17 wineries and has most exports of Turkish wines.

Turkmenistan (Rus) a noted wine-producing area.

Turkuaz (Tur) a natural spring mineral water brand.

Turley Cellars (USA) a winery based in Saint Helena, Napa Valley, California. Noted for red wines including Duarte Zinfandel produced from 100 year old ungrafted vines.

Turmberg (Ger) vineyard (Anb): Baden. (Ber): Badische Bergstrasse/Kraichgau. (Gro): Hohenberg. (Vil): Grötzingen.

Turmberg (Ger) vineyard (Anb): Baden. (Ber): Badische Bergstrasse/Kraichgau. (Gro): Hohenberg. (Vil): Karlsruhe-Durlach.

Turmberg (Ger) vineyard (Anb): Baden. (Ber): Badische Frankenland. (Gro): Tauberklinge. (Vil): Königshofen.

Turnbull (USA) a winery based in the Napa Valley, California. Grape varieties: Cabernet sauvignon.

Turned Over (W.Ind) a term used in rum production when the new rum is taken from a non-wood container to a wooden container to start its 3 years maturation (legal minimum). Most have more.

Turner (Can) a noted wine-producer based south of Toronto.

Turner Winery (USA) a winery based in San Joaquin and Lake County, California. 241ha. Grape varieties: Cabernet sauvignon, Chardonnay, Chenin blanc, Gamay, Johannisberg riesling and Zinfandel. Produces varietal wines.

Turning Leaf Vineyards (USA) a winery based in the Sonoma County, California. Grape varieties include: Pinot Noir. Part of Ernst & Julio Gallo.

Turning the Piece (Scot) the term used by the maltsters for the turning of the germinating barley corns to aeriate them.

Turnpike (Scot) a 4.1% alc by vol. ale brewed by the Harviestoun Brewery, Clackmannanshire.

Turquant (Fr) a commune in the Coteaux du Saumur, Anjou-Saumur, Loire.

Turque [La] (Fr) a noted A.C. Côte Rôtie wine produced by Guigal (using 7% Viognier) in the Côte Brune, northern Rhône. *See also* Mouline (La) and Lalandonne (La).

Turrentés (Sp) a black grape variety grown in the central regions of Spain.

Turriculae (Fr) a wine-based aperitif with added fenugreek and sea water from Mas de Tourelles. *see* Mulsum.

Tursan (Fr) a V.D.Q.S. region in south-western France. Produces red, rosé and white wines from a minimum of 50% Baroque plus Sauvignon,

Sémillon, Gros and Petit manseng grapes. Minimum alc. 10.5% by vol.

Turtucaia (Rum) a wine-producing region in the Dobruja district.

Tuscan (It) good quality red and white wines made in Tuscany. Have to be labelled 'Red Tuscan' or 'White Tuscan'.

Tuscany (It) a region south of Emilia-Romagna, it borders Liguria to the north-west, to the west is the Tyrrhenian Sea. Famous for red wines: Chianti, Brunello di Montalcino, Vino Nobile di Montepulciano (all D.O.C.G).

Tusker Bitter (Eng) a dry, special bitter 1046 O.G. brewed by the Whitbread brewery in London.

Tusker Lager (Afr) a premium, bottled lager beer brewed by the Kenyan Breweries in Nairobi, Kenya 4.8% alc by vol.

Tusker Lager (Afr) a lager beer (created 1922) 4.2% alc by vol (1038 O.G). brewed by the East African Breweries in Kenya.

Tusnad (Rum) a sparkling natural spring mineral water (established 1957) from Tusnad, Transylvania. Mineral contents (milligrammes per litre): Sodium 190.4mg/l, Calcium 129.06mg/l, Magnesium 71.7mg/l, Potassium 10mg/l, Bicarbonates 918mg/l.

Tut (Eng) the central part of the shive.

Tutankhamuns Ale (Eng) a limited edition ale brewed to a 3,250 year old Egyptian recipe by Scottish & Newcastle Breweries.

Tutela (It) guardian, the protective organisation for wines.

Tutor [El] (Sp) a solera gran reserva brandy produced by José Estevez in Jerez de la Frontera. *see* Don Feliz.

Tutschfelden (Ger) village (Anb): Baden. (Ber): Breisgau. (Gro): Burg Lichteneck. (Vin): Kaiserberg.

Tutti Cassis (Fr) a 17% alc by vol. cassis liqueur produced from cane sugar by the Lejay-Lagoute distillery.

Tutti Frutti (Fr) an alcool blanc made from a mixture of fruits.

Tutuven Valley (Chile) the most southerly part of the Maule Valley. Home to the co-operative Lornas de Cauquenes and the Martínez de Salinas winery.

Tütz (Fr) a 4.8% alc by vol. straw coloured, bottom-fermented, bottled ice beer brewed by Schutzenberger Brasserie, Schiltigheim.

Tuvilains [Les] (Fr) a Premier Cru vineyard in the A.C. commune of Beaune, Côte de Beaune, Burgundy 8.73ha.

Tuxedo Cocktail (Cktl) 30mls (¼ gill) each of Burnett Gin, French vermouth, (or Italian vermouth for a sweet version), 2 dashes maraschino, 2 dashes orange bitters, 1 dash absinthe. Stir over ice, strain into a cocktail glass and add a squeeze of lemon peel juice on top.

Tuzla Icmeleri (Tur) a natural spring mineral water (established 1927) from Tuzla, Istanbul. Mineral contents (milligrammes per litre): Sodium 610mg/l, Calcium 180.8mg/l, Magnesium

84.5mg/l, Potassium 30mg/l, Bicarbonates 428.5mg/l, Sulphates 153.7mg/l, Fluorides 0.1mg/l, Nitrates 3.87mg/l.

Tuzlanski Kiseljak (Bos) a sparkling natural spring mineral water from Ljubace, Bosnia and Herzegovina. Mineral contents (milligrammes per litre): Sodium 186.2mg/l, Calcium 56.05mg/l, Magnesium 650.3mg/l, Potassium 11.44mg/l, Bicarbonates 3706mg/l, Chlorides 411.8mg/l, Sulphates <0.1mg/l, Fluorides 0.1mg/l, Nitrates 0.08mg/l. pH 6.4

Tvichi (Geo) a white grape variety grown in Georgia. Produces dessert wines of same name. *See also* Tvishi.

Tvishi (Geo) an alternative spelling of Tvichi.

Twadell Scale (USA) a scale used to measure the gravity of liquids. 1° Twadell = 5° S.G. (on British scale).

Twankey (Eng) a grade of China tea.

Twann (Switz) a vineyard based in Berne, noted for deep, golden-coloured wines.

Twanner (Switz) the name given to a light Chasselas wine from Schafiser, Bern, also called Schafiser.

Tweed (Eng) a species of barley malt from the Golden Promise variety, gives medium sugar yields.

Twee Jonge Gezellen Estate (S.Afr) vineyards (established 1710) based in Tulbagh, Western Cape. 120ha. (Add): Krone Borealis, Box 16, Tulbagh 6820. Grape varieties: Chardonnay, Chenin blanc, Muscat de frontignan, Riesling, Sauvignon blanc, Shiraz, Viognier. Labels: Borealis Brut, Engeltjipipi, Krone-Balm of the Night, Night Nectar, Schanderl, The Rose, Thirty Nine [39], TJ Light. Also produces Sherries. Website: http://www.tjwines.co.za

Twelfth Night (Cktl) 1 apple, 1 bottle red wine. Stick the apple full of cloves and float in a bowl of the red wine (heated). Add hot water to dilute according to taste and add sugar syrup to taste.

Twelth Night (Eng) a 5% alc by vol. winter warmer brewed by Abbey Ales, Bath, Avon.

Twelve Clones (USA) the label for a red wine (Pinot noir) produced by the Morgan winery, Santa Lucia Highlands, Monterey County, California.

Twelve Days (Eng) a 5.5% alc by vol. dark-brown strong seasonal ale brewed by the Hook Norton Brewery, Banbury, Oxon.

Twelve Horse Ale (USA) a top-fermented ale 5% alc by vol. brewed by the Genesee Brewery of Rochester, New York.

Twentieth Century (Cktl) ⅕ measure Lillet, ⅖ measure gin, ⅕ measure crème de cacao, ⅕ measure lemon juice. Shake over ice and strain into a cocktail glass.

Twenty One [21] Not Out (Eng) a 4.5% alc by vol. ale brewed by the Ringwood Brewery, Ringwood, Hampshire.

Twenty Twenty [20/20] Wine C°. (USA) a company based at Westfield, New York that produces MD 20/20–a range of grape wine-based drinks at 13.5% alc by vol. peach or mango and lime versions.

Twickenham Fine Ales Ltd (Eng) a brewery (established 2004). (Add): The Crane Brewery, Ryecroft Works, Edwin Road, Twickenham, Middlesex TW2 6SP. Brews: Crane Sundancer 3.7% alc by vol., Strong and dark 5.2% alc by vol., Twickenham IPA 4.5% alc by vol., Twickenham Original 4.2% alc by vol. Website: http://www.twickenham-fine-ales.co.uk 'E'mail: stevebrown@twickenham-fine-ales.co.uk

Twiggy (Eng) a term which is similar to stalky.

Twin Hills Cocktail (Cktl) 25mls (⅕ gill) Bourbon whiskey, 10mls (½ fl.oz) each of lemon juice, lime juice, Bénédictine. Shake over ice, strain into a sour glass and add a slice of lime and lemon.

Twinings [R] & C° Ltd (Eng) an old, well-established tea and coffee company (established 1706) that produces many fine and famous tea blends. (Add): R. Twining & C°. South Way, Andover, Hampshire SP10 5AQ. *See also* Tom's Coffee House. http://www.twiningsfs.com http://www.twinings.co.uk

Twinings Tea Punch (Cktl) 5 measures Twinnings strong tea, 2 measures Sherry, 2 measures rum, 4 dashes lime juice cordial, juice ¼ lemon, sugar syrup to taste. Mix all together over ice, strain into a punch bowl and float orange slices on top.

Twinkle of the Polestar (Cktl) ⅓ measure dry gin, ⅙ measure dry vermouth, ⅙ measure Drambuie, ⅓ measure green Chartreuse, dash orange bitters. Stir over ice and strain into a cocktail glass.

Twin Peak (S.Afr) the label for a white wine (Sauvignon blanc) produced by the Lateganskop Winery, Worcester, Western Cape.

Twin Six (Cktl) ½ measure dry gin, ¼ measure Italian vermouth, ¼ measure orange juice, 1 egg white, 2 dashes grenadine. Shake over ice and strain into a cocktail glass.

Twist (Eng) a gin-based drink with citrus flavouring from Gordon's (Arthur Bell Distillers).

Twist [A] (Eng) in cocktails denotes a twist of citrus fruit zest.

Twisted Vine (Eng) a 5% alc by vol. fruit spritzer produced by Bass in Burton-on-Trent.

Twister (Cktl) a 35mls (1½ fl.ozs) vodka, teaspoon lime juice. Pour over ice into a highball glass and top with 7-Up.

Twists (USA) another name for a Collins.

Two Brewers Bitter (Eng) a 3.6% alc by vol. bitter ale brewed by the B & T Brewery Ltd., Bedfordshire.

Two Buck Chuck (USA) a wine range of cheap wines from Napa Valley grapes produced by Bronco Wines.

Two [2] B's (Eng) a 3.2% alc by vol. ale brewed by Arkell's Brewery Ltd., Wiltshire.

Two Cubs (S.Afr) the label for a Cape Red Blend wine (Merlot, Pinotage and Shiraz blend) and White Blend (50% Chenin blanc and others) produced by the Knorhoek winery, Stellenbosch, Western Cape.

Two Diamonds (Port) a fine Tawny Port produced by Pocas Junior Port shippers.

Two Dogs (Austr) a brand of an alcoholic lemonade drink. 4.2% alc by vol. Distributed in the U.K. by Merrydown.

Two Fingers Tequila (Mex) the brand-name of a bottled tequila 38% alc by vol. sold in a black bottle, white and gold versions available.

Two Hands (Austr) a winery with vineyards based in the Barossa Valley and Clare Valley, South Australia and Heathcote, Victoria. Labels: Max's Garden, Moscato Bianco, Samantha's Garden.

Two Henrys (Eng) a malty bitter 1040 O.G. brewed by the Nix Wincott Brewery based at Ye Three Fyshes, Turvey, near Bedford.

Two Hundred (Eng) a bottled beer 1055 O.G. brewed at the Berkshire Brewery, Reading, Berkshire to celebrate the 200th anniversary of Courage (1787–1987).

Two Hundred and Fifty [250] (Eng) a pale ale 1072 O.G. brewed and bottled by the Tolly Cobbold Brewery in Ipswich to celebrate 250 years of brewing in East Anglia.

Two Hundred & Twentyfive [225] Anniversary Cuvée (Fr) a vintage de luxe cuvée Champagne produced by Lanson (57% Chardonnay and 43% Pinot noir grapes).

Two in the Bush (Austr) a wine label of the Bird in Hand winery, Adelaide Hills.

Two Lane Blacktop (Eng) a drink of half Guinness and half dry ginger.

Two Oceans (S.Afr) the brand-name of a wine range from Drostdy Koöperatiewe. Grape varieties: Cabernet sauvignon, Merlot, Sauvignon blanc.

Two Pints Ale (Eng) a 4% alc by vol. ale brewed by the Cropton Brewery, Pickering, North Yorkshire..

Two Point Five [2.5] (Eng) a 2.5% alc by vol. bottled beer brewed by Brakspear, Henley-on-Thames, Oxon. Originally also available in draught form.

Two Roads (S.Afr) the label for a red wine (Pinot noir plus others blend) produced by the Flagstone Winery, Somerset West, Western Cape

Two Row Barley (Eng) the finest quality barley that is used in beer making. Refers to the 2 rows of grain on each ear of barley. *See also* Four Row, Six Row.

Two Shot (USA) a method of making gin.

Two Thousand [2000] Millennium Ale (Eng) a 5% alc by vol. limited edition, gift boxed, bottled ale brewed using Canterbury hops by Robert Cain, Liverpool.

Two [2] Vineyards Old Vines (USA) the label for a red wine (Pinot noir) produced by the Arlie winery, Willamette Valley, Oregon.

Two [2] XM (Eng) a 4.6% alc by vol. blonde ale brewed by Everards of Leicester using a combination of two different malts. Brewed to celebrate the year 2000.

Twyford Amber Ale (Eng) a bottled ale for export only brewed by the Guinness Park Royal Brewery in London.

Txakoli (Sp) an alternative spelling of Chacolí.

Txacoliñ Gorri (Sp) one of the two varieties of Chacolí wine produced from Ondarrubí beltza and Ondarrubí zuri grapes. *See also* Getariako Txakolina, Txacoliñ Zuri.

Txacoliñ Zurí (Sp) one of the two varieties of Chacolí wine produced from Ondarrubí beltza and Ondarrubí grapes. *See also* Getariako Txakolina, Txacoliñ Gorri.

Ty Brethyn Meadery (Wal) producers of mead. (Add): Llangollen, Clwyd, north Wales. Produces a range of Mead wines.

Tyee Wine Cellars (USA) a winery based in Corvallis, Willamette Valley Oregon. Grape varieties: Pinot noir, Chardonnay, Pinot gris, Pinot blanc, Gewürztraminer.

Tyke Bitter (Eng) a best bitter 1041 O.G. brewed by the West Riding Brewery in Huddersfield, Yorkshire.

Tykes Premier (Eng) an ale brewed by Ward's in Sheffield.

Tyland Vineyards (USA) a winery based in Mendocino County, California. 14.5ha. Grape varieties: Cabernet sauvignon, Chardonnay, Chenin blanc, Gamay, Johannisberg riesling and Zinfandel. Produces varietal wines.

Tyna (Afr) the brand-name of a wine produced in Tunisia.

Tyne and Daly (S.Afr) the export label for a range of wines produced by the Stettyn Winery, Worcester, Western Cape.

Ty Nant (Wal) a still and carbonated natural spring mineral (established 1989) water from the Cambrian Mountains, Mid-Wales. (Add): Bethania, Llanon, Ceredigion SY23 5LS. Is sold in a Bristol blue glass bottle for the sparkling (a red glass version created for the millennium and containing the still water). Mineral contents (milligrammes per litre): Sodium 22mg/l, Calcium 22.5mg/l, Magnesium 11.5mg/l, Potassium 1.2mg/l Chlorides 14mg/l, Sulphates 3.7mg/l, Fluoride 0.148mg/l, Nitrates <0.1mg/l, Iron 0.002mg/l. pH 6.8 Website: http://www.tynant.com 'E'mail: info@tynant.com

Typhoo (Eng) a famous brand of blended tea produced by Kenco-Typhoo Ltd.

Typhoon (Eng) a 5% alc by vol. ale brewed by the Storm Brewing C°., Cheshire.

Typhoon Cocktail (Cktl) ⅓ measure dry gin, ⅓ measure lime juice, ⅓ measure anisette. Shake over ice, strain into an ice-filled highball glass and top with Champagne.

Tyrconnell [The] (Ire) a 4 year old single malt whiskey from the Cooley Distillery in Dundalk. *See also* Kilbeggan.

Tyrells (Austr) a winery (established 1858). (Add): Broke Road, Pokolbin, New South Wales 2321. 83ha. owned (plus 83ha. leased). Grape varieties: Blanquette, Cabernet sauvignon, Chardonnay, Hermitage, Merlot, Pinot noir, Rhine riesling, Sauvignon blanc, Sémillon, Traminer and Trebbiano. Labels: Heathcote, Moore's Creek, Rufus Stone and Stevens. The winery is known as Ashman's Winery. Website: http://www.tyrrells.com.au

Tyrni (Fin) *see* Buckthorn Berry Liqueur, produced by Marli.

Tyrol (Aus) a vine-growing area of southern Austria.

Tyrosine (Eng) an amino acid found in small traces in wines, formed by the yeasts.

Tyskie Gronie (Pol) a 5.7% lager-style beer.

Tywallt (Wal) to decant/to pour.

Tzuica (Rum) a fruit brandy made from a distillate of plums and almonds.

U

U.A.C. (Sp) *abbr*: Unión Cooperativa Agria.

Uachaouuam [ad] (Aus) the name for the Wachau region in the time of Charlemagne (circa 800AD).

Uachtar (Ire) cream.

Uachtar Caife (Ire) coffee cream.

Uba (Bra) a slightly acidic natural spring mineral water from Fonte Wanda. Mineral contents (milligrammes per litre): Sodium 0.6mg/l, Calcium 1.2mg/l, Magnesium 0.36mg/l, Potassium 1.8mg/l, Bicarbonates 8.84mg/l, Fluorides 0.06mg/l, Nitrates 0.85mg/l. pH 5.3

Ubbriacare (It) to get drunk/tipsy.

Ubbriachezza (It) in an intoxicated state.

Übereltzer (Ger) vineyard (Anb): Mosel-Saar-Ruwer. (Ber): Zell/Mosel. (Gro): Goldbäumchen. (Vil): Moselkern.

Überlingen (Ger) village (Anb): Baden. (Ber): Bodensee. (Gro): Sonnenufer. (Vin): Felsengarten.

Überwasser (It) a natural spring mineral water from Überwasser, Ulten, Bozen. Mineral contents (milligrammes per litre): Sodium 4.25mg/l, Calcium 48.1mg/l, Magnesium 10.4mg/l, Potassium 3.95mg/l, Bicarbonates 74mg/l, Sulphates 102mg/l, Fluorides 0.2mg/l, Iron 4.3mg/l, Silicates 9.2mg/l.

Übigberg (Ger) vineyard (Anb): Ahr. (Ber): Walporzheim/Ahrtal. (Gro): Klosterberg. (Vil): Altenahr.

Ubriaco (It) drunk, excess of alcohol.

Ubriacone (It) drunkard.

Ubstadt (Ger) *see* Ubstadt-Weiher.

Ubstadt-Weiher [ortsteil Stettfeld] (Ger) village (Anb): Baden. (Ber): Badische Bergstrasse/ Kraichgau. (Gro): Mannaberg. (Vin): Himmelreich.

Ubstadt-Weiher [ortsteil Ubstadt] (Ger) village (Anb): Baden. (Ber): Badische Bergstrasse/ Kraichgau. (Gro): Mannaberg. (Vin): Weinhecke.

U.C.B. (Eng) *abbr*: Ultimate Curry Beer. 5.3% alc by vol. ale brewed by Wolverhampton and Dudley Breweries.

U.C.C.V.T. (Afr) *abbr*: Union des Caves Coopératives Vinicoles de Tunisie, a large wine co-operative in Tunisia. Has 14 individual co-operatives.

UC-Davis (USA) *abbr*: University of California at Davis, the base for the famous Department of Viticulture and Ecology which conducts research and teaching programmes. Created climatic classification system. *see* Degree Days.

Uchumi (Afr) a natural spring mineral water from Kenya.

Uco Valley (Arg) a wine-producing district of Mendoza (1400m above sea level) situated in the departments of: San Carlos, Tunuyán and Tupungato. Main grape varieties: Cabernet sauvignon, Chardonnay, Malbec, Merlot, Pinot noir, Sauvignon blanc and Tempranillo. *see* Clos de los Siete.

U.C.O.V.I.P. (Fr) *abbr*: Union des Coopératives Vinicoles du Pic Saint-Loup.

U.C.V.A. (Fr) *abbr*: Union des Caves de Vinification de l'Armagnac, a union of 10 Co-operatives from Gers for Armagnac.

Udan (Ind) an old Indian (Sanskrit) word for water.

Udenheim (Ger) village (Anb): Rheinhessen. (Ber): Nierstein. (Gro): Domherr. (Vins): Goldberg, Kirchberg, Sonnenberg.

Udens Kersenbier (Hol) a 5.5% alc by vol. top-fermented, bottle-conditioned cherry beer brewed by the Jantjes Brouwerij, Uden.

Udine (It) a district within the area of Friuli-Venezia-Giulia.

Ueberkinger (Ger) a sparkling natural spring mineral water from Bad Überkingen. (red label: sparkling/blue label: light gas). Mineral contents (milligrammes per litre): Sodium 1090mg/l, Calcium 20mg/l, Magnesium 15.8mg/l, Potassium 17.8mg/l, Bicarbonates 1480mg/l, Chlorides 100mg/l, Sulphates 1110mg/l, Fluorides 3mg/l, Nitrates <0.1mg/l.

Ueberschwefelt (Ger) a term used to describe a wine that contains too much sulphur.

Ueli Brauerei (Switz) a brewery based in Basel.

Uerige Alt (Ger) a 4.6% alc by vol. medium-brown, bottled altbier brewed by the Uerige Brauerei, Düsseldorf.

Uerige Brauerei (Ger) a brewery based in Düsseldorf that brews Uerige Alt.

Ufford Ales (Eng) a brewery (established 2004) based in Ufford, Peterborough, Cambridgeshire.

U Flèku Brewery (Czec) an old brewery in Prague north-western Czec. which brews beers for its own house. Produces a sweet, dark lager 5.4% alc by vol.

Ugandan Coffee (Afr) the best is from the Bugisu district. Mainly grow robusta beans that produce a mild, low grade coffee.

Ugandan Tea (Afr) African teas used mainly for blending.

Ughetta (It) a red grape variety.

Ugni Blanc (Fr) a white grape variety grown in the Cognac and Armagnac regions for making brandy,

U

giving low alcohol and acidic wines. Also known as the Clairette à grains ronde, Clairette de venice, Grasse roussanne, Queue de renard, Saint-Émilion and Trebbiano.

Ugni Blanc (USA) *see* California Ugni Blanc.

Uhambo (S.Afr) the label for a dry and a semi-sweet red wine (Cinsaut and Ruby cabernet blend) marketed by the Premium Cape Wines company, Stellenbosch, Western Cape.

Uhersky Brod (Czec) a brewery based in Eastern Czec.

Uhlbach (Ger) vineyard (Anb): Württemberg. (Ber): Remstal-Stuttgart. (Gro): Weinsteige. *see* Stuttgart.

Uhlen (Ger) vineyard (Anb): Mosel-Saar-Ruwer. (Ber): Zell/Mosel. (Gro): Weinhex. (Vil): Kobern-Gondorf.

Uhlen (Ger) vineyard (Anb): Mosel-Saar-Ruwer. (Ber): Zell/Mosel. (Gro): Weinhex. (Vil): Winningen.

U.H.T. (Eng) *abbr*: Ultra High Temperature, denotes milk or cream that has been heated to a high temperature 132°C (269.6°F) for 1 second to prolong its keeping qualities.

Uhu (Aus) lit: 'drunk like an owl', a slang term which refers to those who get drunk on uhudler wines.

Uhudler (Aus) a red grape variety and the name given to a rough wine produced from American vines species in Styria during the late nineteenth century. In 1992 the wine was given official recognition and around 23ha–25ha are still produced.

Uinta Brewing C° (USA) a brewery. (Add): 1722 South Fremont Drive, 2375 W, Salt Lake City, Utah 84104. Brews beers and lager. Website: http://www.uintabrewing.com 'E'mail: info@uintabrewing.com

Uisage Beatha (Ire) a Tullamore Dew whiskey that is bottled in a crock bottle.

Uisce (Ire) water.

Uisce Baugh (Eng) an old English for whisky (Usquebaugh).

Uisce Beatha (Ire) lit: 'water of life', the Irish (Gaelic) for whiskey, also spelt Uisge Baugh. *See also* Uisce Beathadh and Uisge Beatha.,

Uisce Beathadh (Ire) the sixteenth century spelling of water of life.

Uisce Beatha Malt Whisky Company (Scot) blenders that produce limited editions of Uisce Beatha Malt Whisky in specially designed flagons and containers. (Add): 33/34 Alfred Place, London WC1E 7DP.

Uisce Eorna (Ire) barley water.

Uisce Mianra (Ire) mineral water.

Uisce Oighrithe (Ire) iced water.

Uisge Baugh (Ire) an alternative spelling of Uisque Beatha.

Uisge Beatha (Ire) '*water of life*' the Celtic spelling (whisky).

Uisquebaugh (Scot) lit: 'the water of life', the gaelic word from which whisky derives.

Uissigheim (Ger) village (Anb): Baden. (Ber): Badische Frankenland. (Gro): Tauberklinge. (Vin): Stahlberg.

Uiterwyk Wine Estate (S.Afr) an alternative name for De Waal Wines.

Uiterwyk Young Vines (S.Afr) the label for a range of wines produced by the De Waal Wines winery, Stellenbosch, Western Cape.

Uitkyk Estate (S.Afr) 166ha of vineyards based in Stellenbosch, Western Cape. (Add): Box 3, Muldersvlei 7606. Grape varieties: Carlonet (Cabernet sauvignon), Chardonnay, Sauvignon blanc. Produces varietal wines. Website: http://www.uitkyk.co.za

Uitvlucht Co-operative Winery (S.Afr) a co-operative winery (established 1941) based in Montagu, Little Karoo, Western Cape. 325ha. Grape varieties: Cabernet sauvignon, Chardonnay, Chenin blanc, Merlot, Muscadel, Pinotage, Red muscadel, Shiraz. Label: Derde Heuval Rood.

Uitvlugt (S.Am) a noted rum distillery based in Guyana.

U.I.V.B. (Fr) *abbr*: Union Interprofessionnel des Vins du Beaujolais.

UK Bartenders Guild (Eng) an organisation. (Add): Duke of York, Dickons Road, Blackpool, Lancashire FY1 2AW. Website: http://www.ukbg.co.uk

UK Duty Stamps Scheme (Eng) a scheme (introduced 2006) designed to tackle alcohol fraud introduced by the UK government. Under the scheme, bottles of spirits, wine or made wine (over 30% alc by vol) destined for sale in the UK must carry a stamp to indicate that duty has been (or will be) paid. Website: http://www.hmrc.gov.uk

UK5 (Eng) an organic vodka produced at Thames Distillers in Clapham, South London.

Ukiah (USA) an A.V.A. wine-producing valley and town based in Mendocino County, California.

Ukraine (Ukr) a large vineyard area which includes the Crimea. The river Don is the centre for sparkling wine production.

Ukrainian (Ukr) a dark beer 13° Balling brewed by the Yantar Brewery.

U.K.R.I.G. (U.K) *abbr*: United Kingdom Rum Importers Group.

Ukusa (S.Afr) the export label for a range of wines from Oaklands Wine Exporters, Western Cape.

Ulanda Cocktail (Cktl) ⅔ measure dry gin, ⅓ measure Cointreau, 2 dashes pastis. Stir over ice and strain into a cocktail glass.

Ulander (Cktl) the same as for Ulanda Cocktail but 1 dash pastis only and is shaken not stirred.

Uleum (kor) ice.

Uley Brewery Ltd (Eng) an old brewery (re-established 1985). (Add): The Old Brewery, 31 The St. Uley, Dursley, Gloucestershire GL11 5TB. Brews: Uley Bitter and Old Spot Prize Ale. Website: http://www.uleybrewery.com

Ulfeldts Kildevæld (Den) a natural spring mineral water from Ulfeldts Kildevæld.

Ulir Monair (Indo) a natural spring mineral water from Bogor.

U

Uliveto (It) a sparkling natural spring mineral water (established 1868) from Uliveto, Pisa. Mineral contents (milligrammes per litre): Sodium 113.7mg/l, Calcium 202mg/l, Magnesium 29.8mg/l, Potassium 11.6mg/l, Bicarbonates 683.2mg/l, Chlorides 121.4mg/l, Sulphates 151mg/l, Fluorides 1.4mg/l, Nitrates 5.9mg/l, Silicates 7mg/l. pH 6.0

Ullage (Eng) the space between the liquid and the stopper in a bottle of wine, spirit or beer when improperly filled. Also when wine seeps through the cork to leave an air gap. Also a term given to beer that is drawn off from the cask during pipe cleaning or through bad service. *see* Ullage Allowance.

Ullage Allowance (Eng) the allowance a brewery gives to public houses for beer which is lost due to the finings contaminating the last of the liquid beer in a cask.

Ullastrell (Sp) a Vino de Mesa wine from the province of Barcelona in Cataluña.

Ull de Llebre (Sp) the alternative spelling of Ojo de Liebre.

Ullun Valley (Arg) a major wine-producing zone.

Ulm (Ger) village (Anb): Baden. (Ber): Ortenau. (Gro): Fürsteneck. (Vin): Renchtäler.

Ulmer (USA) a premium light beer brewed by the Schell Brewery in New Ulm, Minnesota.

Ulmeta (It) a sparkling natural spring mineral water from Ulmeta, Ormea. Mineral contents (milligrammes per litre): Sodium 0.7mg/l, Calcium 30mg/l, Magnesium 3.9mg/l, Potassium 0.5mg/l, Chlorides 1.4mg/l, Sulphates 4.3mg/l, Nitrates 1.4mg/l, Silicates 4.3mg/l. pH 7.5

Ulmtaler Klosterquelle (Ger) a natural spring mineral water from Löhnberg, HE. Mineral contents (milligrammes per litre): Sodium 228mg/l, Calcium 125mg/l, Magnesium 42.3mg/l, Potassium 11.9mg/l, Bicarbonates 705mg/l, Chlorides 257mg/l, Sulphates 33mg/l.

Ulrichsberg (Ger) vineyard (Anb): Baden. (Ber): Badische Bergstrasse/Kraichgau. (Gro): Mannaberg. (Vil): Östringen.

Ultimate Curry Beer (Eng) *see* U.C.B.

Ultimate Pub Nightmare (Eng) a series of beers brewed by the Ash Vine Brewery, Trudoxhill, Somerset. Labels include: Hell For Leather 5.2% alc by vol.

Ultima Thule (Austr) a late-picked Riesling from the Hickinbotham Family Vineyard in Victoria.

Ultraa (Rus) a vodka bottled in a modern cobalt blue bottle. Produced in St. Petersberg by Livis 37.5% alc by vol.

Ultra Premium Red (It) a joint venture between Robert Mondavi Winery and Marchesi de Frescobaldi. Range of 3 wines produced.

Ultrapura (Chile) a still and sparkling natural spring mineral water (established 1998) from Andes Mountains. Mineral contents (milligrammes per litre): Sodium 2.25mg/l, Calcium <0.01mg/l, Magnesium 0.03mg/l, Potassium <0.01mg/l, Bicarbonates 6.1mg/l, Chlorides 2.1mg/l, Sulphates <10mg/l, Fluorides <0.05mg/l, Nitrates 0.53mg/l. pH 6.4

Ultra Pure Water (Chi) a bottled spring mineral water brand.

Uludag (Tur) a sparkling natural spring mineral water (established 1874/1912) from Caybasi Koyu, Uludag, Bursa. Mineral contents (milligrammes per litre): Sodium 178.172mg/l, Calcium 168.336mg/l, Magnesium 59.231mg/l, Bicarbonates 1154.24mg/l, Chlorides 79.572mg/l, Sulphates 7.9mg/l. Website: http://www.uludaggazoz.com.tr

Ulumbaza (S.Afr) the label for a red wine (Shiraz) produced by the Springfontein winery, Walker Bay, Western Cape.

Ülversheim (Ger) village (Anb): Rheinhessen. (Ber): Nierstein. (Gro): Krötenbrunnen. (Vins): Aulenberg, Schloss.

Umalak (Rus) a white grape variety grown in Uzbekistan. Produces dessert wines.

Umani Ronchi [Azienda Agricola] (It) a noted Verdicchio and sparkling wine producer based in Osimo, the Marches. Produces: Plenio (Verdicchio di Jesi), San Lorenzo (Rosso Conero), Pelago (50% Cabernet sauvignon, 40% Montepulciano, 10% Merlot) and Casal di Serra wines. Website: http://www.umanironchi.it

Umathum [Josef] (Aus) a winery (12.5ha) based in Frauenkirchen, Burgenland. (Add): St. Andräer Strasse 7, 7132 Frauenkirchen. Grape varieties: Blaufränkisch, Cabernet sauvignon, Chardonnay, Pinot gris, Pinot noir, Sauvignon blanc, St. Laurent, Welschriesling, Zweigelt. Label: Hallebühl.

Umbel Ale (Eng) a 3.8% alc by vol (1039 O.G) ale brewed by Nethergate Holdings Ltd., Clare, Suffolk using coriander.

Umbel Magna (Eng) a 5% alc by vol. ale brewed by Nethergate Holdings Ltd., Clare, Suffolk.

Um Bongo (Eng) a brand-name for a style of fruit juices from Libby's.

Umbrella (Eng) in brewing it is a mushroom-like structure in the copper. The boiling wort rises up the central column and cascades over the domed top ensuring the contents are mixed well.

Umbria (It) a small internal region surrounded by Tuscany to the north, The Marches to the east, Latium to the south-west. Noted for Orvieto, Torgiano Rosso Riserva and Sagrantino di Montefalco. Produces both red and white wines.

Umculi (S.Afr) the export label for a range of wines produced by the Rooiberg Winery, Robertson, Western Cape.

Umechu (Jap) a medicinal wine.

Umeshu (Jap) a plum wine made by infusion.

Umfiki (S.Afr) the label for a red (Cinsaut, Merlot and Pinotage blend) and white (Clairette blanche blend) wine produced by the Goudini Wines winery, Worcester, Western Cape.

Umhali Water (Afr) a style of rum produced in the nineteenth century on the island of Madagascar.

Umkhulu Wines (S.Afr) a winery (established 2000)

U

based in Simondium, Stellenbosch, Western Cape. Grape varieties: Cabernet franc, Cabernet sauvignon, Malbec, Merlot, Petit verdot, Pinotage, Sauvignon blanc, Shiraz. Labels: Akira,Njalo, Tian. Website: http://www.umkhulu.com

Umor (Lat) liquid/fluid.

Umpqua Valley (USA) an area found in Oregon that has 217ha of vineyards

Umstadt (Ger) bereich (Anb): Hessische Bergstrasse. (Gro): Nil. (Vils): Dietzenbach, Gross Umstadt, Klein-Umstadt, Rossdorf.

Una Raya (Sp) lit: 'one stroke', a mark used in the Sherry region to denote the first classification of new wines.

Unbalanced (Eng) the term used to describe a wine that is either lacking in fruit or has too much tannin or acid.

Unbroken Tea (Eng) a grade of large tea, graded by passing through vibrating sieves. Such examples are Orange Pekoe, Flowering Orange Pekoe and Pekoe Souchong.

Unchair (Fr) a Premier Cru Champagne village in the Canton de Fismes. District: Reims.

Uncinula necator (Lat) a disease of the vine. *see* Oidium.

Uncinula spiralis (Lat) the former name for **Oidium** **tuckerii.**

Unclassified (Fr) not in the official wine classifications of the Médoc 1855, Saint-Émilion 1955 and Graves 1959.

Uncle Ben's Tartan Breweries (Can) noted breweries based in British Columbia. Taken over in 1976 by new owners.

Uncle Igor's Famous Falling over Water (Eng) a 21° Proof beer (originally was 17.3° Proof) from the Ross Brewing Company, Bristol (strongest beer in 1994). Also brew Hartcliffe Bitter, Ross's Pale Ale.

Uncle Sam (Cktl) ³/₁₀ measure Glayva, ⁵/₁₀ measure Bourbon whiskey, ¹/₁₀ measure lemon juice, ¹/₁₀ measure orange juice, ¹/₁₀ measure Martini (dry). Shake over ice and strain into a 150mls (6fl.oz) cocktail glass.

Uncle Sam (Eng) a mix of Cherry 'B' and American dry ginger ale.

Uncle Sam Cocktail (Cktl) 1 measure Peachtree liqueur, 1 measure Bourbon whiskey. Stir over ice in a highball glass, top with soda water and a spiral of lemon peel.

Uncle Sam's (Eng) a 4.4% alc by vol. ale brewed by the Cropton Brewery, Pickering, North Yorkshire.

Uncork (Eng) to remove the cork from a bottle of wine, beer, spirits, etc. (Fr) = déboucher.

Undenheim (Ger) village (Anb): Rheinhessen. (Ber): Nierstein. (Gro): Gutes Domtal. (Vin): Goldberg.

Under Age (Eng) denotes a juvenile who has not reached the age of eighteen years and who cannot, by law consume alcoholic liquor on licensed premises. They can though be on the premises if fourteen years of age.

Under-Age Drinking (U.K) the illegal drinking of alcoholic liquor by those under 18 years of age on licensed premises.

Underback (Eng) in brewing a vessel that does some filtering of the wort and is also used to dissolve invert (brewer's) sugar if it is to be added to the brew.

Underberg (Ger) a digestif™ of herbs and roots, hot macerated with distilled water and alcohol, then aged in oak casks. Invented in 1846 and sold in single portion bottles.

Undercliff Experience (Eng) a 4.1% alc by vol. ale brewed by the Yates Brewery, Isle of Wight.

Under Oaks (S.Afr) a winery (established 2003) based in Paarl, Western Cape. 30ha. Grape varieties: Cabernet sauvignon, Chardonnay, Chenin blanc, Crouchen, Sauvignon blanc.

Under Proof (Eng) a spirit whose alcoholic content is below proof. *see* Proof.

Under Strength (Eng) the term that applies mainly to spirits. If whisky, brandy, rum or vodka have a strength of below 40% alc by vol (vodka below 37.2% alc by vol.) must be described on the label as '*under strength*'.

Undertaker (Eng) a 9.5% alc by vol. ale brewed by the Fox and Newt in Leeds, West Yorkshire. *See also* Ghostbuster.

Undertone (Eng) a term used to describe wines that are subtle and supporting but not dominating.

Underwood (Eng) a chemist who discovered the 13 minerals present in wine necessary for life: calcium, chlorine, copper, cobalt, iron, iodine, magnesium, manganese, potassium, phosphorus, sodium, sulphur and zinc.

Un Deux Trois (S.Afr) a red wine (Cabernet sauvignon 58% plus Cabernet franc and Merlot blend) produced by the Seidelberg Estate, Paarl, Western Cape.

Undhof (Aus) a winery (20ha) based in the Kremstal region. (Add): Erich Salomon, Undstrasse 10, 3504 Krems-Stein. Grape varieties: Grüner veltliner, Pinot blanc, Riesling, Traminer, Zweigelt. Produces a range of wine styles.

Undurraga Winery (Chile) a family-owned winery. Produces Gran Vino Tinto, Viejo Roble and white wines.

Unfermented Grape Juice (Eng) the juice of freshly gathered grapes, known in France as Moët.

Unfermented Wine (Eng) a grape juice that has not been fermented.

Unfiltered Collection (S.Afr) the label for a range of wines produced by the Fleur du Cap winery, Stellenbosch, Western Cape.

U.N.G.C. (Fr) *abbr*: **U**nion **N**ormande des **G**rands **C**alvados, producers of Berneroy Calvados. (Add): 14130 Blangy le Château.

Ungegorener Traubenmost (Ger) unfermented grape must that has less than 5g/l of alcohol.

Ungeheuer (Ger) vineyard (Anb): Pfalz. (Ber): Mittelhaardt-Deutsche Weinstrasse. (Gro): Mariengarten. (Vil): Forst.

Ungezuckert (Ger) unsugared, pure wine.

Ungsberg (Ger) vineyard (Anb): Mosel-Saar-Ruwer. (Ber): Bernkastel. (Gro): Schwarzlay. (Vil): Traben-Trarbach.

Ungstein (Ger) village (Anb): Pfalz. (Ber): Mittelhaardt-Deutsche Weinstrasse. (Gro): Hochmess. (Vin): Michelsberg.

Ungstein (Ger) village (Anb): Pfalz. (Ber): Mittelhaardt-Deutsche Weinstrasse. (Gro): Honigsäckel. (Vins): Herrenberg, Nussriegel, Weilberg.

Ungstein (Ger) village (Anb): Pfalz. (Ber): Mittelhaardt-Deutsche Weinstrasse. (Gro): Kobnert. (Vins): Bettelhaus, Osterberg.

Unharmonisch (Ger) opposite to harmonious, an unbalanced wine.

União Comercial da Beira (Port) a noted Dão wine producer based in Oliveirinha.

União das Adegas Cooperativas do Dão (Port) a co-operative based in Dão. Produces wines under the Dão Adegas Cooperativas.

União Vinícola Regional de Bucelas (Port) a body now absorbed by the Junta Nacional do Vinho.

União Vinícola Regional de Carcavelos (Port) a body now absorbed by the Junta Nacional do Vinho.

União Vinícola Regional de Moscatel de Setúbal (Port) a body now absorbed by the Junta Nacional do Vinho.

Unibroue Brewery (Can) a brewery based in Chambly, Quebec. Brews: Maudite.

Unicellular (Eng) a single cell, applies to yeasts (and bacteria).

Unicer (Port) a brewery based in Porto. Brews Super Bock.

Unico (Sp) a term associated with Vega Sicilia in D.O. Ribera del Duero. The top red wine (made from vines of an average age of 45 years) traditionally aged for 6–10 years and only made in good years, produced from Bordeaux grapes (Cabernet sauvignon, Merlot and Malbec) plus Garnacha and Tinto fino. Vintages: 1924, 1936, 1940, 1941, 1951, 1953, 1955, 1956, 1957, 1959, 1960, 1961, 1962, 1964, 1965, 1966, 1967, 1968, 1970, 1972, 1973, 1974, 1975, 1976, 1978, 1980, 1981, 1982, 1983, 1985, 1986, 1989, 1990. *See also* Valbuena.

UniCognac (Fr) a Cognac co-operative. (Add): B.P. N°2, 17500, Jonzac. 5000 ha owned by 3500 growers. Distills, ages and blends Cognacs.

Unicorn (Eng) a best bitter 4.2% alc. by vol. and the brand sign for Robinsons Brewery in Stockport, Cheshire.

Unicum (It) aromatised herbal bitters made by the Zwack C°.

Unidor (Fr) a Dordogne-based union of co-operatives.

Uniewyn (S.Afr) a noted producer of a range of brandies.

Uni-Médoc (Fr) a co-operative based at Gaillan-en-Médoc, a group of four co-operatives in Bégadan, Ordonnac, Prignac and Queyrac.

Union (Slo) a beer brewed by the Ljubljana Brewery in Slovenia.

Union Agricole du Pays de Loire (Fr) a co-operative based in the Loire region. (Add): 49380 Brissac.

Union Brasserie (Bel) a brewery (established 1864) based in Jumet. Brews: Cuvée de Ciney Blond, Grimbergen Blond, Grimbergen Optimo Bruno, Grimbergen Triple.

Union Camerounaise de Brasseries (Afr) a brewery based in Cameroon which brews bock beers, a pilsener and a Breda beer.

Union Champagne (Fr) a Champagne producer. (Add): 7, Rue Pasteur – BP19, 51190 Avize. Labels: Champagne de Saint Gall (Premier Cru blanc de blancs) and Cuvée Orpale (blanc de blancs). Grape variety: Chardonnay.

Union Coffee Roasters (Eng) coffee manufacturers (established 2000). (Add): The New Roastery, Unit 2, 7a South Crescent, London E16 4TL. Produces a range of coffees, teas, cocoa and drinking chocolate. Website: http://www.unionroasters.com 'E'mail: roastmaster@unionroasters.com

Unión Cooperativa Agria (Sp) *abbr*: UCA. based in Tarragona, deals with the wines vinified by the co-operatives.

Union de Brasseries (Afr) a branch of the French brewery of same name that is active in north-west Africa.

Union de Brasseries (Fr) a brewery which has 6 plants, the largest near Paris at Drancy. Brews: Slavia and Porter 39 (a dark Stout-type beer).

Union des Caves Coopératives Vinicoles de Tunisie (Afr) *abbr*: U.C.C.V.T. Top wine exporter in Tunisia. Has 14 co-operatives as members: Bejaoua, Bou Arkoub, Borj El Armi, Ghezala, Grombalia, Bir Drassen, Kélibia, Khledia, Mornag, Mrira, Nahli, Sidi Tabet, Takelsa and Schuigui.

Union des Caves de Vinification de L'Armagnac (Fr) *see* U.C.V.A.

Union des Coopératives de l'Armagnac [Marquis de Caussade] (Fr) an Armagnac producer. (Add): Avenue de l'Armagnac, 32800 Eauze.

Union des Coopératives Vinicoles du Pic Saint-Loup (Fr) a body that markets the Le Pic range of red and white wines. *abbr*: UCOVIP.

Union des Grands Crus de Bordeaux (Fr) a body dedicated to maintain quality standards in Bordeaux. Member-properties may be from the whole of the Médoc.

Union des Producteurs de Saint-Émilion (Fr) a Grand Cru. A.C. Saint-Émilion co-operative winery. (Com): Saint-Émilion 851ha. Grape varieties: Cabernet franc, Cabernet sauvignon and Merlot. The largest co-operative in Saint-Émilion, has 350 members. (Add): B.P. 27, 33330 Saint-Émilion. Wines are sold under labels: Aurelius, Bois Royal, Côtes Rocheuses, Royal Saint-Émilion, Haut Quercus, Cuvée Galius and Saint-Émilion. Also vinifies many to Château wines.

Union des Propriétaires (Fr) co-operative.

Union des Propriétaires Récoltants Le Mesnil (Fr) a co-operative Champagne winery based in Le Mesnil. (Add): 19, Rue Charpentier Laurain, B.P. 17, 51190 Le Mesnil-sur-Oger. Produces vintage and non-vintage wines. Website: http://www.Union-Champagne.fr 'E'mail: lemesnil@wanadoo.fr

U

Union Interprofessionnelle des Vins du Beaujolais (Fr) abbr: U.I.V.B. a body based at 210, Boulevard Vermorel, 69400 Villefranche-sur-Saône, Beaujolais, Burgundy.

Union Jack (Cktl) ⅔ measure gin, ⅓ measure Crème Yvette, 2 dashes grenadine. Shake over ice and strain into a cocktail glass.

Union Jack Cocktail (Pousse Café) pour into a tall liqueur glass in order ⅓ measure green Chartreuse, ⅓ measure maraschino and ⅓ measure grenadine.

Union Mild (Eng) brewed by Marston's, Burton-on-Trent under the Head Brewers Choice Banner. See also Albion Porter, Regimental Ale.

Union Normande des Grands Calvados (Fr) see U.N.G.C.

Union of Rheingau Wine-Growers (Ger) a body which has 35 members.

Union Room (Eng) large fermenting halls that are part of the Burton Union System. See also Held in Union and Marston's Brewery.

Unión Territorial de Co-operativas del Campo (Sp) abbr: U.T.E.C.O. A body on the Register of Exporters. This permits the Bodegas to export directly if they wish to.

Union Vinicole Divinal (Fr) a co-operative based in Obernai, Alsace. Produces Crèmant d'Alsace and wines under the St. Odile label.

Union Vinicole du Liban (Leb) a newly formed association of 9 Lebanese wineries formed to promote the country's wines.

Union Vinicole Pour la Diffusion des Vins d'Alsace (Fr) a body formed by a merger of small proprietors, controls over 15% of the market.

Union Viti-Vinícola, S.A. (Sp) a co-operative winery. (Add): Ctra. de Logroño, s/n 26350 Cenicero, Rioja. 350ha. Wines include Marqués de Cáceres.

Union Voison (Bel) a bière brewed by the Dupont Brasserie in Tourpes.

Union Wine Limited (S.Afr) wine merchants based in Wellington. Wines sold under Bellingham, Culemborg and Val du Charron labels. (Add): P.O. Box 246 Wellington 7655.

Uniqato (Bul) a label for a red wine (Rubin) from the Damianitza winery.

Unison Vineyards (N.Z) a 6ha vineyard. Produce wines from Merlot, Cabernet sauvignon and Shiraz blends aged in French and American oak.

Unité (Fr) the label for a range of sparkling wines from the Cave de Lugny co-operative, Burgundy.

United Breweries (Den) a giant company that includes Carlsberg and Tuborg Breweries. Is linked with the Rupert group of South Africa.

United Breweries (Ind) a brewery (established 1857) based in Bangalore. Produces lagers and bitter stouts. see Kingfisher.

United Bulk (S.Afr) the label for a range of wines produced by the Seven Oaks winery, Worcester, Western Cape.

United Distilleries Company of Belfast and Londonderry (Ire) an old distilling company in Northern Ireland that closed down in 1929.

United Distillers (Austr) a subsidiary of the British-based DCL. Produces gin under the Vickers label.

United Kingdom Rum Importers Group (U.K) abbr: U.K.R.I.G. An important body that maintains close links with the W.I.R.S.P.A.

United Kingdom Vineyards' Association (Eng) superseded the English Vineyard Association on 1st April 1996. Award the Seal of Quality to English wines after tasting and analysis. (Add): Church Road, Bruisyard, Saxmundham, Suffolk IP17 2EF. 'E'mail: ian@ukva.fsnet.co.uk

United Rum Merchants (Eng) abbr: U.R.M, formed by the merger of 3 companies in 1946. Based in London. Brands include Black Heart Rum, Lamb's Navy Rum, Lemon Hart Rum, Red Heart Rum and Santiago White Rum.

United States of America (USA) see America.

United States of America Pint (USA) 16½ fl.ozs.

United Thai Distillery (Thai) a distillery based in Bangkok. Produces Cavalier 38% alc. by vol.

United Vintners (USA) abbr: U.V. Inglenook and Swiss Colony's operating company of distillers. Uses patent and pot-stills to produce a range of brandies under the labels of Petri, Lejon, Hartley and Jacques Bonet. Also produces wines (see Bali-Hai).

Universal-Aqua (Ind) a natural spring mineral water (established 2000) brand.

Universal Order of the Knights of the Vine of California (USA) a wine brotherhood based in California for the promotion of the region's wines.

Univitis (Fr) a co-operative based in Bordeaux. (Add): Société Coopérative, Les Leves, 33220, Sainte Foy la Grande. A large producer of A.C. Bordeaux white wine and V.D.Q.S. wines.

Unkel (Ger) village (Anb): Mittelrhein. (Ber): Rheinburgengau. (Gro): Burg Hammerstein. (Vins): Berg, Sonnenberg.

Unkenbach (Ger) village (Anb): Nahe. (Ber): Schloss Böckelheim. (Gro): Paradiesgarten. (Vins): Römerpfad, Würzhölle.

Unlauterer Wettbewerb (Ger) the German Trade Description Act. (Fr) = réclame trompeuse, (Hol) = misleidende reklame.

Unlicensed (Eng) denotes having no licence to sell alcoholic liquor.

Unrein (Ger) refers to an unclean wine.

Unsauber (Ger) denotes a defective, dirty tasting wine due to bad storage.

Unter Ausbrausen (Aus) lit: 'an effervescent manner', refers to the opening of a bottle of sparkling wine where the contents bubble up.

Unterbadischer Landwein (Ger) one of seventeen Deutsche Landwein zones. Minimum must weight is 53° Oe. Trocken or halb-trocken.

Unterberg (Ger) vineyard (Anb): Mosel-Saar-Ruwer. (Ber): Saar-Ruwer. (Gro): Scharzberg. (Vil): Filzen.

Untereisenheim (Ger) village (Anb): Franken. (Ber): Maindreieck. (Gro): Kirchberg. (Vin): Sonnenberg.

U

Untereisesheim (Ger) village (Anb): Württemberg. (Ber): Württembergisch Unterland. (Gro): Staufenberg. (Vin): Vogelsang.

Untere Ziestel (Aus) a vineyard site on the banks of the River Danube in the Kremstal region.

Untergebiete (Ger) table wine sub-areas, there are eight in total: Burgengau, Donau, Lindau in Bayern, Mosel, Rhein, Romertor in Oberrhein and Saar in Rhein and Mosel.

Untergruppenbach (Ger) village (Anb): Württemberg. (Ber): Württembergisch Unterland. (Gro): Kirchenweinberg. (Vin): Schlossberg.

Untergugen (Aus) a vineyard site based on the banks of the River Kamp situated in the Kamptal region.

Unterheimbach (Ger) village (Anb): Württemberg. (Ber): Württembergisch Unterland. (Gro): Lindelberg. (Vin): Schneckenhof.

Unterheinriet (Ger) village (Anb): Württemberg. (Ber): Württembergisch Unterland. (Gro): Schozachtal. (Vin): Sommerberg.

Unterjesingen (Ger) village (Anb): Württemberg. *see* Kressbronn am Bodensee Tübingen.

Unterlagen (Aus) root stock.

Unter Mitterhasel (Aus) a vineyard site based on the banks of the River Kamp situated in the Kamptal region.

Untermosel (Ger) another name for the Bereich Zell in the Mosel-Saar-Ruwer.

Unteröwisheim (Ger) *see* Kraichtal.

Untersätzen (Aus) a vineyard site on the banks of the River Danube situated in the Wachau region, Niederösterreich.

Untersteinbach (Ger) village (Anb): Württemberg. (Ber): Württembergisch Unterland. (Gro): Lindelberg. (Vin): Dachsteiger.

Untertürkheim (Ger) village (Anb): Württemberg. (Ber): Remstal-Stuttgart. (Gro): Weinsteige. *see* Stuttgart.

Unti Winery (USA) a winery based in the Dry Creek Valley, Sonoma County, California. Grape variety: Zinfandel.

Unusual Cocktail (Cktl) ⅓ measure gin, ⅓ measure Swedish punsch, ⅓ measure cherry brandy, dash lemon juice. Shake over ice and strain into a cocktail glass.

Unwins (Eng) a family-owned group of specialist wine shops that has 300 outlets in the south-east of England and East Anglia.

Up Front (Eng) a term applied to wines that have an attractive, simple quality which is easily recognisable.

U Pinkasu (Czec) an ale-house based in Prague.

Upland Estate (S.Afr) a winery (established 1998) based in Wellington, Western Cape. 12ha. Grape varieties: Cabernet sauvignon, Chardonnay, Chenin blanc, Crouchen, Merlot. Website: http://www.organicwine.co.za

Upper Ale (Eng) a 3.8% alc by vol. light, hoppy session bitter brewed by the Hale and Hearty Brewery in Surrey.

Upper Corgo (Port) the higher region of the river Douro where the grapes are grown for Port.

Upper Hunter (Austr) a wine region based in New South Wales. The vineyards are irrigated. Produces mainly white wines. Home to Rosemount.

Uppington (S.Afr) a wine region based north of Stellenbosch.

Upstairs (Cktl) ⅓ measure Port wine, ⅓ measure vodka, ⅙ measure Lakka liqueur, ⅙ measure lime juice. Shake over ice and strain into a cocktail glass.

Upstairs Cocktail (Cktl) 40 mls. (⅓ gill) Dubonnet, juice ½ lemon. Stir over ice in a highball glass, top with soda water and a slice of lemon.

Up-To-Date (Cktl) ⅓ measure dry vermouth, ⅓ measure rye whiskey, ⅙ measure Grand Marnier, dash Angostura. Stir over ice, strain into a cocktail glass and add a twist of lemon peel.

Upton Ranch (USA) a vineyard based in Amador County, California. Grape variety: Zinfandel. Vinified at the Lamb Winery.

Ur (Ger) lit: 'original', used by breweries that have adopted a beer-style such as Spaten Ur-Marzen, Pilsner Urquell. Also known as Urtyp.

Uraveli (Geo) a natural spring mineral water from Akhaltsikhe Village, Uraveli. Mineral contents (milligrammes per litre): Sodium 181mg/l, Calcium 224mg/l, Magnesium 220mg/l, Potassium 13mg/l, Bicarbonates 2147mg/l, Chlorides 114mg/l, Sulphates 16mg/l, Fluorides 0.44mg/l, Strontium 1mg/l, Silicates >50mg/l. pH 6.1

Urbacher (Ger) a natural spring mineral water brand.

Urbana Wine Company (USA) the former name for the Gold Seal Winery on Lake Keuka.

Urbanus Still (Ger) a still natural spring mineral water. Mineral contents (milligrammes per litre): Sodium 280mg/l, Calcium 100mg/l, Magnesium 60mg/l, Bicarbonates 1290mg/l.

Urbar (Ger) village (Anb): Mittelrhein. (Ber): Rheinburgengau. (Gro): Marksburg. (Vin): Rheinnieder.

Urbar [St. Goar] (Ger) village (Anb): Mittelrhein. (Ber): Rheinburgengau. (Gro): Schloss Schönburg. (Vin): Beulsberg.

Urbeis (Fr) the German name for the district of Orbey in Alsace.

Urbelt (Ger) vineyard (Anb): Mosel-Saar-Ruwer. (Ber): Saar-Ruwer. (Gro): Scharzberg. (Vil): Filzen.

Urbock 23° (Aus) a 9.9% alc by vol. full-bodied strong pils brewed by Eggenberger Schlossbrauerei in the Vorchdorf region, lagered for 9 months.

Urbräu (Ger) a lightly hopped Bavarian beer 5% alc by vol. from Hofbräu in Munich (also known as Helles Bier).

Urceus (Lat) pitcher/jug.

Urébères (Fr) a vine pest of early times now no longer found. Also spelt Uribères.

Uresso (It) a sparkling natural spring mineral water from Novara, Piemonte. Mineral contents (milligrammes per litre): Sodium 3.7mg/l,

U

Calcium 32.54mg/l, Magnesium 24.1mg/l, Potassium 5.2mg/l, Bicarbonates 75.64mg/l, Chlorides 1.7mg/l, Sulphates 832.8mg/l, Fluorides 0.11mg/l, Silicates 12mg/l, Oxygen 6.7mg/l. pH 7.6

Urfass (Ger) a premium lager 5.2% alc by vol. from Arcobräu Brauerei in Bavaria.

Urfé (Fr) a Vin de Pays area in the northern Loire. Produces red, rosé and dry white wines from the Aligoté, Chardonnay, Gamay, Pinot gris, Pinot noir and Viognier grapes.

Urfels (Ger) a bottled alt beer 4.8% alc by vol. and bottled pils 5% alc by vol. Both brewed in North Rhine Westphalia. Commissioned by Hofbräuhaus Urfels in Duisberg.

Uribères (Fr) see Urébères.

Uricani (Rum) a wine-producing area noted for red and white wines.

Urlati (Rum) a wine-producing area, a part of the Dealul-Mare Vineyard.

U.R.M (Eng) abbr: United Rum Merchants.

Urn (Eng) a large vase-like container of earthenware or metal used for holding liquids (hot and cold). Often is decorative with handles for carrying and a 'spout' for pouring. see Tea Urn. (Fr) = urne, (It) = urna.

Urna (It) urn.

Urne (Fr) urn.

Urstromtaler Mineralwasser (Ger) a sparkling natural spring mineral water. (green label: sparkling/blue label: light gas). Mineral contents (milligrammes per litre): Sodium 4.6mg/l, Calcium 59.4mg/l, Magnesium 5.8mg/l, Potassium 0.7mg/l, Bicarbonates 195mg/l, Chlorides 7.8mg/l, Fluorides 0.15mg/l, Silicates 23.2mg/l.

Ursulinengarten (Ger) vineyard (Anb): Ahr. (Ber): Walporzheim/Ahrtal. (Gro): Klosterberg. (Vil): Ahrweiler.

Urtyp (Ger) the name given to describe an ordinary beer of the Astra brand produced by the Bavaria-St. Pauli Brauerei in Hamburg.

Uruguay (S.Am) most of the vineyards are in the south. Vineyards areas include: Rivera (on the Brazilian border), Las Violetas (outside Montevido), Pisano (close to Rio de la Plata). Makes all styles of wine and spirits but for local consumption, small amount is exported. 10000ha. Grape varieties: **White**: Chardonnay, Gewurztraminer, Muscatel, Pinot gris, Riesling, Sauvignon blanc, Sylvaner, Torrontés, Viognier. **Red**: Cabernet franc, Cabernet sauvignon, Malbec, Merlot, Nebbiolo, Pinot noir, Shiraz, Sangiovese, Tannat.

Urweisse (Ger) a wheat beer 4.8% alc by vol. from Arcobräu Brauerei in Bavaria.

Ürzig (Ger) village (Anb): Mosel-Saar-Ruwer. (Ber): Bernkastel. (Gro): Schwarzlay. (Vin): Würgarten.

Usak (Tur) a wine-producing region in western Turkey, produces mainly white wines.

U Salzmanu (Czec) a famous beer tap-room in Pilsen.

Usana (S.Afr) a winery (established 2003) based in Stellenbosch, Western Cape. 8ha. Grape varieties: Cabernet sauvignon, Merlot, Sauvignon blanc, Shiraz. Website: http://www.usana.co.za

Usé (Fr) a wine past its best.

Us Heit Twels Pilsner (Hol) a 5% alc by vol. bottled pilsner brewed by the De Friese Brouwerij, Sneek.

Us Heit Twels Bokbier (Hol) a 6% alc by vol. dark-brown, top-fermented, bottle-conditioned bock beer brewed by the De Friese Brouwerij, Sneek.

Usher [Andrew] (Scot) a noted whisky distiller (part of DCL). Brands include Ushers Green Stripe.

Usher Brewery (Eng) Watneys West Country Brewery in Trowbridge. Noted for cask conditioned Founder's Ale 1045 O.G. keg Triple Crown 1033 O.G. Country Bitter 1036 O.G. canned Ploughman's Bitter 1032 O.G. Also Autumn Frenzy, Spring Fever, 1824 Particular, Dark Horse Porter, January Sale, Ruby Ale, Silbury Golden Organic Bitter, Summer Madness, Tawny Ale, White Ale, Winter Storm.

Usher's Green Stripe (Scot) a brand of blended Scotch whisky produced by Andrew Usher. 40% alc by vol (part of DCL).

Usher's O.V.G. (Scot) abbr: Old Vatted Glenlivet. One of the first blended malt whiskies introduced in 1853.

Usher's Special (Eng) a 3.8% alc by vol. keg bitter brewed by the Usher Brewery in Trowbridge. See also 1824 Particular.

U.S. Proof (USA) a measurement of alcoholic proof. Works as water equals 0° and pure alcohol 200°. See also Sykes.

Usquaebach, The Grand Whisky of the Highlands (Scot) a blended de luxe Scotch whisky, produced by Douglas Laing for the American C°. Twelve Stone Flagons, comes in stone flagon facsimile bottles with a cork stoppered closure.

Usquebaugh (Ire) a liqueur whiskey flavoured with coriander.

Usquebaugh (Scot) the Gaelic for 'water of life' from which the name whisky derives.

U.S.S.R. [The Soviet Union] was the largest producer of wines in the world. Produced most styles of beers, spirits (especially vodkas) and wines (mainly from hybrid vines). Is noted for traditional method sparkling wines. Main wine regions were: Armenia, Azerbaijan, Crimea, Georgia, Krasnodar, Moldavia, River Don, Stavropol and the Ukraine generally. Also produces some teas in the Southern Republics (now known as Russia and has been split into many separate countries).

Uster Brauerei (Switz) a brewery based in Uster. Part of the Interbeva group.

Ústí nad Labem Brewery (Czec). A brewery based in north-western Czec.

Usual (Eng) a crisp, dry 4.4% alc by vol. seasonal ale brewed by Hydes Brewery, 46 Moss Lane, West Manchester, Lancashire (available in June).

Ususha (Jap) the name given to a thin whipped tea made during the Chonoyu ceremony. The second stage of Chonoyu is held in another room.

U Svatého Tomáse (Czec) an ale house based in Prague.

U

Utan Bator Breweries Ltd. (Euro) a brewery based in Monrovia which brews Baadog a 4.6% alc by vol. ale.

U.T.E.C.O. (Sp) *abbr:* **U**nión **T**erritorial de **C**ooperativas del Campo.

Utero (Sp) red wines produced by the Bodegas José Palacios in Rioja. Made from the Garnacha, Mazuelo and Tempranillo grapes. Matured in cask and aged in bottle. Produces Reservas and Gran Reservas.

Utica Club Cream Ale (USA) a well-hopped, top-fermented beer brewed by the West End Brewing Co. in Utica.

Utica Club Pilsener (USA) a light, dry pilsener lager brewed by the West End Brewing Cº. in Utica.

Utiel-Requena (Sp) a Denominación de Origen region within the wine province of Valencia in southern Spain. Grape varieties: Bobal, Crujidera, Garnacha, Macabeo, Merseguera, Tempranillo. Produces red and rosé wines. *see* Doble Pasta.

Utkins UK5 (Eng) a 40% alc by vol. organic grain vodka.

Uto Mij (Hol) a noted distiller of jenever.

Utopia (USA) a natural spring mineral water from Utopia, Texas.

Utter Nutter (Eng) a 3.8% alc by vol. ale brewed by the Thomas McGuinness Brewing Company, Lancashire.

U.V. (USA) *abbr: see* United Vintners.

Uva (It) grape.

Uva (Lat) berry.

Uva (Port) berry (grape).

Uva (Sp) grape.

Uva Abruzzi (It) a name sometimes used for Montepulciano.

Uva Argentina (Arg) the local (cloned) name for the Malbec grape.

Uva Cão (Port) a grape variety grown in the Dão region.

Uva Cerreto (It) the Campania name for the white grape variety Malvasia di candia.

Uva de Mesa (Sp) a red dessert (table) grape of little use in wine making.

Uva di Spagna (Sp) an alternative name for the Garnacha grape.

Uva di Troia (It) a red grape variety which produces good colour in wines grown in the Puglia region, also known as the Nero di Troia. *see* D.O.C's Castel del Monte Rosso, Rosso Barletta, Rosso Canosa and Rosso de Cerignola.

Uva d'Oro (It) a red grape variety.

Uva Francesa (Arg) the local name for the Malbec grape.

Uva Francesca (It) the Tuscan name for the Cabernet grape.

Uvaggio (It) the name given to a wine made from a mixture of grape varieties.

Uval (Fr) pertaining to grapes.

Uva Mira (S.Afr) a winery (established 1997) based in Stellenbosch, Western Cape. 30ha. Grape varieties: Cabernet sauvignon, Merlot, Sauvignon blanc, Shiraz. Labels: Cellar Selection, Vintage Selection.

Uva Rara (Sp) a red grape variety known as the Bonarda novarese in Italy.

Uvas Pasa (Sp) raisin-like grapes.

Uveira (Port) tree vine.

UXB (Eng) a 3.8% alc by vol. bitter ale brewed by the White Star Brewery, Hampshire.

Uzbekistan (Rus) a wine-producing area based north of Turkmenistan in Armenia. Also the name for a red grape variety.

Uzège (Fr) a Vin de Pays area in the Gard département in south-western France. Produces red, rosé and dry white wines.

Üzüm (Tur) grape.

Üzüm Bagi (Tur) vineyard.

Üzüm Suyu (Tur) grape juice.

V

V.A. (Eng) *abbr*: **V**olatile **A**cidity.

V.A. (Fr) *abbr*: Vintage Appellation.

Vaalharts Co-operative (S.Afr) vineyards based at Vaalharts and Andalusia. (Add): Vaalharts Landboukoöperasie, Box 4, Hartswater 8750. Produces varietal wines under Overvaal Wines and Andalusia Wines labels.

Vaalharts Landboukoöperasie (S.Afr) *see* Vaalharts Co-operative.

Vaapukka (Fin) a raspberry liqueur.

Vaatje (Hol) keg.

Vaccarèse (Fr) a red grape variety grown in the southern Rhône. Often used in Châteauneuf-du-Pape and is one of the thirteen permitted varieties.

Vacio (Sp) a term used to describe a Sherry with a dumb bouquet.

Vacuum-Distilled Gin (USA) a gin distilled in a glass-lined vacuum still at a low temperature 32.2°C (90°F). Produces only a light gin with little bitterness and a light flavour.

Vacqueyras (Fr) an A.C. (awarded 1990) Côtes du Rhône-Villages. Produces full-bodied red wines.

Vacuum Method (Eng) a method of making coffee. Boiling water is drawn up through expansion from one container into another, holding the coffee grounds where infusion takes place. After the heat source has been removed from the bottom container, a vacuum is created which draws the infused coffee (liquid) back into the bottom container (the grounds are retained in the top unit by a special glass stopper valve). The Cona™ coffee system works on such a principle.

Vacuum Packed (Eng) ground or instant coffee that is packed in a vacuum package (tin, glass or cellophane) to retain freshness.

Vacuum Still (USA) a glass-lined still which distils at approx. 32.22°C (90°F). instead of 100°C (212°F), produces light flavoured spirits.

Vada (Rus) water.

Vadi (Tur) a medium-dry white wine produced by Diren at Tokat.

Vaduzer (Euro) the name given in Liechtenstein to two thirds of the red wine produced. It is light in colour and made with the Blauburgunder.

Vaegne (Ch.Isles) vine.

Vagnoni (It) a winery based in the DOCG Vernaccia di San Gimignano in the Tuscany region.

Vaia (It) a sparkling natural spring mineral water from Mignano, Bagolino, Brescia. Mineral contents (milligrammes per litre): Sodium 3.6mg/l, Calcium 24.7mg/l, Magnesium 4.4mg/l, Potassium 1mg/l, Bicarbonates 86mg/l, Chlorides 1.2mg/l, Sulphates 17.1mg/l, Fluorides 0.07mg/l, Silicates 6.6mg/l. pH 8.2

Vaihingen (Ger) village (Anb): Württemberg. (Ber): Württembergisch Unterland. (Gro): Stromberg. (Vin): Höllisch Feuer.

Vaillons (Fr) a Premier Cru Chablis vineyard, often has the Premier Cru vineyards of Beugnons, Châtains, Les Lys and Séché sold as its vintage.

Vaimato (S.Pac) a natural spring mineral water from Source de Papeari, French Polynesia. Mineral contents (milligrammes per litre): Sodium 15.4mg/l, Calcium 6.41mg/l, Magnesium 3.3mg/l, Potassium 2.15mg/l, Bicarbonates 73.2mg/l, Chlorides 12.1mg/l, Sulphates 1.3mg/l. pH 7.8

Vaimatp (S.Pac) a natural spring mineral water from Source de Papeari, French Polynesia. Mineral contents (milligrammes per litre): Sodium 11.32mg/l, Calcium 12.2mg/l, Magnesium 6.9mg/l, Potassium 2.35mg/l, Bicarbonates 85.4mg/l, Chlorides 11.35mg/l, Sulphates 0.95mg/l, Nitrates 0.2mg/l. pH 7.65

Vaison-la-Romaine (Fr) a commune of the Principauté d'Orange département in southern Rhône.

Vais Vista (USA) a vineyard based in the Alexander Valley, Sonoma County, California. 7.5ha. Grape varieties: Cabernet sauvignon and Chardonnay. Produces varietal wines.

Vajda, S.L. (Sp) a major wine-producer based in Rioja, north-western Spain.

Vajra (It) a winery based in the DOCG Barolo, Piemonte. Label: Bricco delle Viole.

Vakche (It) a red grape variety grown in Tadzhikistania. Produces dessert wines.

Val (Bel) a natural spring mineral water from Boortmeerbeek. Mineral contents (milligrammes per litre): Sodium 125mg/l, Calcium 2.5mg/l, Magnesium 1.8mg/l, Potassium 10mg/l, Bicarbonates 220mg/l, Chlorides 75mg/l, Sulphates 18mg/l.

Valagarina (It) a wine-producing area in the Trentino-Alto-Adige. Produces red wines.

Valais (Switz) a wine area producing dry white, dessert and red wines. Dôle is the most famous red wine. Grape varieties: Amigne, Arrine, Chasselas, Gamay, Humagne, Johannisberg riesling, Pinot noir.

Valaisanne (Switz) a brewery based in Sion. Part of the Feldschlösschen group.

Valbella (It) a natural spring mineral water from Valbella.

Valbina (It) a slightly acidic natural spring mineral water from Biella, Piemonte. Mineral contents (milligrammes per litre): Sodium 1.6mg/l, Calcium 7mg/l, Magnesium 2.06mg/l, Potassium 1.25mg/l, Bicarbonates 32.8mg/l, Chlorides 1.06mg/l, Sulphates 2.6mg/l, Silicates 9.1mg/l. pH 5.6

Valbuena (Sp) a D.O. red wine produced by Bodegas Vega Sicilia, Old Castille, Valladolid. Originally sold as 3 año or 5 año (years) old is now released after 30 months. Vega Sicilia Unico is the best quality and Valbuena is the second quality.

Valcalepio (It) a D.O.C. red wine from Pavia, Lombardy. Produced from the Cabernet sauvignon and Merlot grapes.

Valcalepio Bianco (It) a D.O.C. white wine from Bergamo, Lombardy. Produced from the Pinot bianco and Pinot grigio grapes.

Valcarcelia (Sp) a black grape variety grown in Rioja. Also known as the Mechín, Ministrel, Monastel, Monastrel, Moraster and Negralejo. Also grown in Aragón and Cataluña.

Valcele (Rum) a natural spring mineral water brand.

Val d'Adige Bianco (It) a D.O.C. white wine from the Trentino-Alto-Adige. Made from a wide variety of grapes including: Blanchetta trevigiana, Müller-Thurgau, Pinot bianco, Nosiola, Pinot grigio, Riesling italico, Sylvaner veltliner bianco, Trebbiano toscano and Vernacchia.

Val d'Adige Rosso (It) a D.O.C. red wine from the Trentino-Alte-Adige. Made from the Lagrein, Lambrusco, Merlot, Negrara, Pinot nero, Schiave and Teroldego.

Val d'Agly (Fr) a Vin de Pays area in the Côtes de Roussillon, Midi region. Produces red, rosé and dry white wines.

Val d'Aisne (Bel) a still natural spring mineral water. Mineral contents (milligrammes per litre): Sodium 6.4mg/l, Calcium 104mg/l, Magnesium 7.2mg/l, Potassium 1.8mg/l, Bicarbonates 308mg/l, Chlorides 19.7mg/l, Sulphates 27mg/l, Nitrates 17mg/l. pH 7.5

Val d'Aosta (It) the smallest wine region between Piemonte and the French/Swiss borders. 2 red D.O.C. wines produced: Donnaz and Enfer d'Arvier.

Val de Cesse (Fr) a Vin de Pays area in the Aude département in southern France.

Val de Chevreuse (Fr) a natural spring mineral water. Mineral contents (milligrammes per litre): Sodium 180mg/l, Calcium 7.5mg/l, Magnesium 1.2mg/l, Potassium 16.2mg/l, Bicarbonates 25mg/l, Sulphates 28mg/l.

Val de Dagne (Fr) a Vin de Pays area in the Aude département in southern France.

Valdejalón (Sp) a large producer of wines (15000ha of vines) situated west of the province of Zaragoza. A Vino de la Tierra Aragón. Grape varieties: Garnacha tinta, Garnacha blanca, Macabeo, Cabernet sauvignon. Red, rosé and white wines are produced. Noted for bulk wine production plus heavy, alcoholic, dark-coloured red wines.

Val de Loire (Fr) the Loire valley, the section of the river between Nantes and Bec d'Ambes. In this region all the important vineyards are found.

Valdemar (Sp) see Bodegas Martinez Bujanda.

Valdemontan Tinto Cosecha (Sp) wines produced by the Co-operative Vinícola de Cenicero, Bodegas Santa Daria, Rioja (Alta region).

Val de Monterrei (Sp) a small D.O. (600ha) district in the Galicia region.

Val de Montferrand (Fr) a Vin de Pays area in the Gard département in south-western France.

Valdeorras (Sp) a Denominación de Origen region in north-western Spain. 2300ha. Grape varieties: Godello, Garnacha tintorera (50%), Gran negro, Lado, María ardoña, Mencía, Merenzao, Palomino (27%) and Valenciana. Produces red, white and rosé wines.

Valdepeñas (Sp) a Denominación de Origen region (14973ha) of La Mancha, central-southern Spain. Grapes varieties: Aragón, Airén, Bobal, Castellana, Cencibel, Cirial, Garnacha, Godello, Jaén, Monastrel, Pardillo, Tinto basto plus Cabernet sauvignon and Chardonnay experimentally. Produces light red, red, rosé and white wines that are high in alcohol.

Valdepeñas (USA) a red grape variety used in the making of red and dessert wines in California.

Valdepusa (Sp) see Dominio de Valdepusa.

Val de Rance (Fr) a brut sparkling cider from Brittany.

Valderrama (Sp) a solera brandy produced by Garvey. See also Doña Ana, Esplendido, Tauro.

Val des Desmoiselles (Fr) a vintage rosé Champagne produced by André Drappier from Pinot noir grapes.

Valdespino (Sp) a Jerez de la Frontera Sherry and brandy bodega. Sherry labels include: Macharnudo Fino Inocente, Matador Manzanilla, Deliciosa Manzanilla.

Valdevimbre-Los Oteros (Sp) a Vino de la Tierra Castilla-León based in León/Valladolid. Home to two other wine areas: Vino de Mesa Ribera del Cea, Vino Comarcal Benevente. 3900ha. of vines along the banks of the river Esla. Main grape varieties are Prieto picudo (70%) plus Mencía and Granacha for red wines, Malvasía and Palomino for white wines.

Val di Cornia (It) an authorised D.O.C. used for those wines from estates around Severeto, Maremma in the Tuscan coastal region.

Val-Dieu (Bel) a brewery. (Add): Val-Dieu 225, Aubel B-4480. Brews a range of beers and lagers. Website: http://www.val-dieu.com

Valdiguié (Fr) an alternative name for Aramon, Gros Auxerrois grapes.

Val di Lentro (It) a sparkling natural spring mineral water from Genova. Mineral contents (milligrammes per litre): Sodium 4.8mg/l, Calcium 62mg/l, Magnesium 4.7mg/l, Potassium

0.53mg/l, Bicarbonates 201.8mg/l, Chlorides 5.8mg/l, Sulphates 10.8mg/l, Fluorides 0.012mg/l, Nitrates 0.38mg/l, Silicates 6.8mg/l, Oxygen 16.84mg/l. pH 7.65

Val di Lupo (It) a producer of red and white wines at Catania, Sicily.

Val di Meti (It) a sparkling natural spring mineral water from Val di Meti. Mineral contents (milligrammes per litre): Sodium 16mg/l, Calcium 72mg/l, Magnesium 24mg/l, Potassium 1.4mg/l, Bicarbonates 325mg/l, Chlorides 16mg/l, Sulphates 25mg/l, Fluorides 0.12mg/l, Nitrates 0.9mg/l, Silicates 7mg/l. pH 7.33

Val di Suga (It) a wine estate in Brunello di Montalcino, Tuscany. Produces the Cru wines: Vigna del Lago, Vigna Spuntali.

Valdivieso (Chile) a winery that produces barrel-fermented Chardonnay wines.

Valdizarbe (Sp) one of 5 D.O. wine-producing districts in the Navarra region of north-eastern Spain.

Valdobbiadene (It) a fine dry white wine from the province of Treviso in Venezia. Made from the Prosecco grape.

Valdo Cantina Sociale di Valdobbiadene (It) a producer of Prosecco di Conegliano-Valdobbiadene (a metodo classico produced sparkling wine), also a cuve close variety (based in the Veneto region).

Val do Minho (Sp) a Vino de la Tierra wine from the province Ourense in Galicia.

Val d'Or (W.Ind) a 'gold label' rum that has been aged for 10 years on the island of Martinique. Is derived from Rhum Dusquesne production.

Val d'Orbieu (Fr) a Vin de Pays area in the Languedoc-Roussillon, southern France. Produces: Chorus (Carignan, Cabernet franc), Cuvée Mythique [La] (Mourvèdre, Syrah, Carignan, Grenache, Cabernet sauvignon), Pas de Deux (Merlot/Syrah).

Valdoro (Sp) a 'cold-fermented' white wine produced by the Bodegas Felix Solis in the Valdepeñas region.

Val do Salnés (Sp) the largest of four sub-zones found in D.O. Rías Baixas, Galicia. 75% Albariño plus 25% of red varieties. See also Condado do Tea, O Rosal, Soutomaior.

Valdouro (Sp) a red wine produced from the Garnacha and Vencia grapes by the Cooperativa Jesus Nazareno.

Val du Charron Wines (S.Afr) a brand-name label for Union Wines Ltd.

Val du Torgan (Fr) a Vin de Pays area in the Aude département in southern France.

Valea Calugareasca (Rum) lit: 'valley of the monks', a wine region on the Black Sea. Part of the Dealul Mare Vineyard Produces fine sweet wines. see Muscat Ottonel and Segacea Cabernet.

Vale Ale (Wal) a 4.1% alc by vol. ale brewed by the Plassey Brewery, Clwyd.

Valea-Lunga (Rum) a wine-producing area, part of the Tîrnave Vineyard

Vale Brewery (Eng) a brewery (established 1994). (Add): Thame Road, Haddenham, Buckinghamshire HP17 8BY. Brews: Black Beauty 4.3% alc by vol., Black Swan Mild 3.3% alc by vol., Edgar's Golden Ale 4.3% alc by vol., Good King Senseless 5.2% alc by vol. Grumpling Old Ale 4.6% alc by vol., Hadders Headbanger 5% alc by vol., Notley Ale 3.3% alc by vol., Vale Best Bitter 3.7% alc by vol., Vale Special 4.5% alc by vol., Wychert Ale 3.9% alc by vol. Also markets seasonal beers under the Hadda umbrella, a winter warmer and bottled beers. Website: http://www.valebrewery.co.uk 'E'mail: valebrewery@yahoo.co.uk

Valeccito (Cktl) 35mls (1½ fl.ozs) pisco, 20mls (¾ fl.oz) Curaçao, 25mls (1fl.oz) dry vermouth, 25mls (1fl.oz) lemon juice. Shake over ice and strain into an ice-filled highball glass.

Vale do Bomfim (Port) a red D.O. Douro wine produced by Symington.

Vale do Rosas (Port) a dry white wine produced by DFJ Vinhos in the Ribatejo from Fernão pires grapes.

Vale do São Francisco (Bra) a wine-producing region in northern Brazil on the eighth parallel.

Vale dos Vinhedos (Bra) a wine-producing region based on the twenty-ninth parallel.

Valençay (Fr) a V.D.Q.S. area near Cheverny in the Indre département. Produces red, rosé and dry white wines. Minimum alc. 9% by vol. Grape varieties: Arbois, Cabernet franc, Cabernet sauvignon, Gamay and Pinot d'Aunis.

Valencia (Cktl) ⅔ measure apricot brandy, ⅓ measure orange juice, 4 dashes Angostura. Shake over ice and strain into a cocktail glass.

Valencia (Sp) a D.O. wine area of southern Spain. 15000ha. Home to the provinces of Alicante, Castellón de Plana, Valencia. Has the Denominación de Origen regions: Alicante, Cheste, Utiel-Requena and Valencia. Vino Comarcal areas of Benniarés, Lliber-Jávea (Alicante), San Mateo (Castellón). Vino de Mesa area of Benicasim (Castellón). Grape varieties: Bobal, Cabernet sauvignon, Cencibel (Tempranillo), Forcayat, Garnacha tinta, Garnacha tintorera, Macabeo, Malvasía, Merseguera, Monastrell, Moscatel romano, Pedro ximénez, Planta fina, Planta nova, Tintorera, Tortosí. The D.O. laws recognise Alto Turia Blanco Seco (100% Merseguera), Valentino Blancos (seco, semi-seco, dulce), Clariano blanco seco, plus a variety of dry/off-dry whites, rosado, red and vino de licor wines. Noted for the sweet white wine Moscatel de Valencia (fortified mistela or not).

Valencia Cocktail (Cktl) ⅔ measure apricot brandy, ⅓ measure orange juice, 4 dashes orange bitters. Shake over ice, strain into a flute glass and top with iced Champagne. Also known as a Valencia Smile.

Valencia de Alcántar (Sp) a Vino de Mesa wine from the province of Cáceres in the Extremadura.

Valenciana (Sp) a white grape variety grown in the Galicia region.

Valencia Smile (Cktl) see Valencia Cocktail.

V

. . . .

Valencia Winery (Austr) a winery based in the Swan Valley, Western Australia. Produces varietal wines.

Valentin Bianchi S.A.C.I.F (Arg) a winery based in the Mendoza region, eastern Argentina. Website: http://www.vbianchi.com 'E'mail: informes@vbianchi.com

Valentine (Eng) a 3.9% alc by vol. light, dry, cask-conditioned fruity ale brewed by Ridleys, Essex for Valetine's day.

Valentine (Fr) a natural spring mineral water. Mineral contents (milligrammes per litre): Sodium 3mg/l, Calcium 55mg/l, Magnesium 23mg/l, Potassium <1mg/l, Bicarbonates 271mg/l, Chlorides 4mg/l, Sulphates 7mg/l, Nitrates <1mg/l.

Valentine Ale (Eng) a 4% alc by vol. seasonal ale from King and Barnes Brewery, Horsham, West Sussex.

Valentine Ale (Eng) a 5% alc by vol. ale brewed by the Pitfield Brewery, Shoreditch, London using ginseng and ginger.

Valentine's Oat Malt (Eng) a 4.5% alc by vol. red-brown ale produced by Wadworth, Northgate Brewery in Devizes, Wiltshire for Valentine's Week. Has a high content of malted oats. Hops used are Fuggles and Progress.

Valentino (Sp) a wine produced in D.O. Valencia. Blanco may be seco, semi-seco or dulce, produced from Merseguera, Planta fina, Pedro ximénez and Malvasía grapes. Light red and tintos from Garnacha grapes. All must have a minimum of 11% alc by vol. Also Licoroso and Rancio wines with a minimum of 14% alc by vol. from Moscatel and Pedro ximénez grapes. see Moscatel de Valencia.

Valentino Brut (It) a metodo tradizionale sparkling wine produced by Podere Rocche dei Manzoni in the Piemonte region.

Valentins Helles (Ger) a 5.2% alc by vol. bottle-conditioned wheat beer brewed by Schlossquell Brauerei, Heidelberg.

Valécrin (Fr) a still natural spring mineral water (established 2002) from Parc National Les Ecrins, Valbonnais. Mineral contents (milligrammes per litre): Sodium 1.8mg/l, Calcium 61mg/l, Magnesium 17.5mg/l, Potassium 0.8mg/l, Bicarbonates 181.8mg/l, Chlorides 0.8mg/l, Sulphates 72mg/l, Nitrates 2.4mg/l.

Valeria (Switz) a red wine produced in Sion, Valais.

Valeric Acid (Eng) an ester that is present in wine in minute traces.

Valesa Târnavelor (Rum) a noted white wine-producing vineyard

Valeyrac (Fr) a commune in the Bas-Médoc, north-western Bordeaux. Has A.C. Médoc status.

Valfieri (It) a noted producer of Moscato d'Asti Spumante in the Piemonte region.

Valgella (It) a sub-district of the Lombardy in the foothills of the Alps in the Valtellina Valley. Produces red wines of the same name from the Nebbiolo grape.

Valhalla (Wal) the label of an original (3.8% alc by vol.) and premium (5% alc by vol.) beer produced by the Brecknock Brewery, Ystradgynlais, Swansea Valley.

Valhalla Brewery (Scot) a brewery. (Add): New House Mailland, Baltasound, Unst, Shetland, Shetland Islands ZE2 9DX. Brews a variety of beers and lager. Website: http://www.valhallabrewery.co.uk 'E'mail: sonnyandsylvia@valhallabrewery.co.uk

Valiant Bitter (Eng) a 4.2% alc by vol. bitter brewed by Bateman's Brewery, Lincolnshire. See also XXXB, Victory Ale, Ploughman's Ale, Nut Brown, Double Brown.

Valiant Stout (Eng) a stout brewed by the Titanic Brewery, Burslem, Stoke-on-Trent to commemorate local team Port Vale's football achievements in 1993. See also Lifeboat.

Valinch (Fr) pipette or 'thief tube' for drawing samples from a cask.

Valine (Eng) an amino acid found in small traces in wines formed by the yeasts.

Valladolid (Sp) a wine-producing area in the province of Castilla-León, north-western Spain. Home to the D.O. wines of Cigales and Rueda, Vino de la Tierra wine of Valdevimbre-Los Oteros, Vinos de Mesa wines of Tudela de Duero, La Ribera del Cea.

Vallana (It) a winery based in the Piemonte region. Produces: DOC Boca. Grape varieties include: Nebbiolo.

Vallechiara (It) a still natural spring mineral water from Vallechiara. Mineral contents (milligrammes per litre): Sodium 3.55mg/l, Calcium 3.3mg/l, Magnesium 2.1mg/l, Potassium 0.3mg/l, Bicarbonates 9.7mg/l, Chlorides 4.2mg/l, Sulphates 2.3mg/l, Nitrates 10.1mg/l, Silicates 4.5mg/l. pH 7.0

Valle d'Aosta (It) a small wine region of north-west Italy. Has 2 red D.O.C. wines. see Val d'Aosta

Valle de Colchagua (Chile) a D.O. region. One of ten sub-regions within the Rapel Valley.

Valle de Güimar (Sp) a D.O. wine zone on the island of Tenerife, Canarias.

Valle de la Orotava (Sp) a D.O. wine zone on the island of Tenerife, Canarias.

Valle de la Puerta S.A (Arg) a winery based in the La Rioja district, Cuyo region, central Argentina. Website: http://www.valledelapuerta.com 'E'mail: anoble@valledelapuerta.com

Valle del Miño-Ourense (Sp) a Vino de la Tierra of Galicia. Grape varieties: Teixadura, Torrontés, Godello, Albariño, Loureira, Palomino, Verdellorubio (white), Alicante, Mencía, Ferrón, Caiño, Pintilla (red). Originally known as Ribera del Sil.

Valle del Trono (It) an I.G.T. wine produced in Basilicata by the Basilicata co-operative.

Valle de Monterrei (Sp) a Denominación de Origen area based near the Portuguese border. 3000ha. Grape varieties: Alicante, Doña blanca, Godello, Garnacha, Gran negro, Mencía and Mouratón. Produces red and white wines.

Valle de Rosal (Sp) a noted rosé wine-producing

area in north-western Spain. Famous for Albariño grapes.

Valle de Vistalba (Arg) a wine district in the Mendoza region.

Valle d'Isarco (It) a valley north-east of Bolzano in the Trentino-Alte-Adige. Produces 5 white wines: Valle Isarco Müller-Thurgau, V.I. Pinot grigio, V.I. Silvaner, V.I. Traminer aromatico and V.I. Veltliner. If produced within part of the communes of Bressanone and Varna then has Bressanone on label. *see* Eisack Valley.

Valle d'Itria (It) a natural spring mineral water from the Valle d'Itria.

Valle d'Oro (It) a still and sparkling natural spring mineral water from the Fonti Crodo, Vena d'Oro. Mineral contents (milligrammes per litre): Sodium 2mg/l, Calcium 502mg/l, Magnesium 54mg/l, Potassium 5.5mg/l, Bicarbonates 77.5mg/l, Chlorides 0.6mg/l, Sulphates 1363mg/l, Nitrates 0.1mg/l, Silicates 6.7mg/l. pH 7.55

Valle d'Oro Winery (Austr) a winery based in McLaren Vale, Southern Vales, South Australia.

Vallée d'Auge (Cktl) heat 25mls (⅕ gill) Calvados and 200mls (⅓ pint) milk until almost boiling. Pour over 25grms (1oz) sugar that has been beaten with an egg yolk, stir until smooth, dress with a slice of apple and ground cinnamon.

Valle de Benasque (Sp) a natural spring mineral water from Manantial de Veri. Mineral contents (milligrammes per litre): Sodium 0.6mg/l, Calcium 74.4mg/l, Magnesium 1.4mg/l, Bicarbonates 207mg/l, Chlorides 1mg/l, Sulphates 13.9mg/l.

Vallée de la Loire (Fr) a Vin de Pays region in central France which contains the Vin de Pays districts: des Coteaux Charitois/des Coteaux de Tannay/des Coteaux du Cher et de l'Arnon/du Bourbonnais/ du Jardin de la France/du Jardin de la France 'Marches de Bretagne'/du Jardin de la France 'Pays de Retz'.

Vallée de la Marne (Fr) a vineyard area of Champagne around the town of Épernay. Grapes give fruit and body to the wines.

Vallée du Mistral [La] (Fr) the label of a Châteauneuf-du-Pape produced by Jarnet (Jean-Paul), Faubourg Saint-Georges, 84230 Courthézon, southern Rhône.

Vallée du Paradis (Fr) a Vin de Pays area in the Aude département in southern France.

Vallegarcía (Sp) a large winery with holdings in Ciudad Real, Castilla-La Mancha. Calzadilla, Sandoval, Manzaneque, Dehesa del Carrizal, Valdepusa, Aalto, Mauro, San Román. Likely to apply for Castilla-La Mancha private D.O. status.

Vallendar (Ger) village (Anb): Mittelrhein. (Ber): Rheinburgengau. (Gro): Marksburg. (Vin): Rheinnieder.

Vallée Noble (Fr) a still and sparkling natural spring mineral water from Soultzmatt. Mineral contents (milligrammes per litre): Sodium 109mg/l, Calcium 87mg/l, Magnesium 35mg/l,

Bicarbonates 120mg/l, Sulphates 38mg/l, Fluorides 0.45mg/l, Nitrates 2.6mg/l.

Valle Peligna (It) an I.G.T. of Abruzzo.

Valle Reale (It) a still natural spring mineral water from Popoli. Mineral contents (milligrammes per litre): Sodium 3.4mg/l, Calcium 90.46mg/l, Magnesium 16.53mg/l, Potassium 1.02mg/l, Bicarbonates 330mg/l, Chlorides 3.93mg/l, Sulphates 18.65mg/l, Fluorides 0.16mg/l, Nitrates 3.94mg/l, Silicates 4.13mg/l. pH 7.4

Valle Renondo (Mex) a wine-producing region based in the Baja California.

Vallerots [Les] (Fr) a Premier Cru vineyard [part] in the A.C. commune of Nuits-Saint-Georges, Côte de Beaune, Burgundy 9.7ha.

Valles del Famatina (Arg) a D.O. wine producing area that is noted for Torrontés.

Valle Stura (It) a sparkling natural spring mineral water from Cuneo, Piemonte. Mineral contents (milligrammes per litre): Sodium 1.2mg/l, Calcium 14mg/l, Bicarbonates 39mg/l, Sulphates 9mg/l, Oxygen 4.3mg/l, Silicates 2.5mg/l. pH 7.5

Vallet (Fr) a village in the Nantais district of the Loire, known as the '*Capital of Muscadet*'. From here some of the finest Muscadets are produced in the Sèvre et Maine A.C. Have excellent acidity and fruit.

Valley of the Moon (USA) a Californian valley between the Napa Valley and Sonoma Valley which produces fine table wines.

Valley of the Moon (USA) a natural spring mineral water from Philipsburg, Montana.

Valley of the Moon Winery (USA) a winery based in the valley of the same name in the Sonoma County, California. Grape varieties: Colombard, Pinot noir, Sémillon and Zinfandel. Produces varietal wines.

Valley View Vineyard (USA) a vineyard based in Applegate Valley, south-western Oregon. 12ha. Produces hybrid wines vinified in the Jacksonville Winery from Cabernet sauvignon, Merlot, Pinot noir, Pinot gris, Chardonnay grapes. Produces Anna Maria Old Stage Merlot, Anna Maria's Vintners Reserve.

Valley Vineyards (Eng) a vineyard based in Twyford, Berkshire. Website: http://www.valleyvineyards.co.uk

Valley Vineyards (USA) a vineyard based in Morrow, Ohio. 16ha. Produces hybrid and varietal wines.

Valley Vista (USA) the label used by Lytton Springs Winery's home vineyard in Alexander Valley, Sonoma County, California.

Valley Wines (S.Afr) a varietal brand-name wines from Gilbeys Limited.

Valley Wines (USA) wines from the valleys of California. Alexander, Napa, Naples, Russian River, Sonoma, etc.

Vallformosa (Sp) a cava wine produced by Masía Bach from 35% Parellada, 30% Xarel-lo, 35% Macabeo grapes. Spends 30 months on the lees.

Vallicelle (It) a natural spring mineral water from Vallicelle.

V

Valls de Riu Corb (Sp) *see* Costers del Segre.

Val Madre (It) a natural spring mineral water from Fusine.

Valmont (Fr) a natural spring mineral water. Mineral contents (milligrammes per litre): Sodium 7mg/l, Calcium 119mg/l, Magnesium 28mg/l, Potassium 2mg/l, Bicarbonates 430mg/l, Chlorides 18mg/l, Sulphates 52mg/l, Fluorides 0.75mg/l. pH 7.9

Valmora (It) a natural spring mineral water from Aburu. Mineral contents (milligrammes per litre): Sodium 1.5mg/l, Magnesium 2.9mg/l, Potassium 0.7mg/l, Chlorides 0.2mg/l, Sulphates 7.2mg/l. pH 8.4

Valmur (Fr) a Grand Cru vineyard in the A.C. Chablis, Burgundy.

Valmy (Cktl) 25mls (1fl.oz) Mandarine Napoléon, 25mls (1fl.oz) dark rum, 75mls (3 fl.ozs) orange juice, 1 teaspoon sugar. Shake over ice and strain into a cocktail glass.

Valon (Fr) a still and sparkling natural spring mineral water from Metzeral. Mineral contents (milligrammes per litre): Sodium 2.5mg/l, Calcium 6.2mg/l, Magnesium 1.8mg/l, Potassium 1mg/l, Bicarbonates 26mg/l, Chlorides 2mg/l, Sulphates 5mg/l, Nitrates 1mg/l. pH 6.5

Valorisation (Eng) a name given to the process by which countries try to regulate coffee prices (buying the crop and keeping it until the prices are favourable).

Valorisation (Eng) a term used to denote the elements of assessment in wine tasting. i.e. colour, aroma, flavour, etc with grades i.e. excellent, good, average, passable, poor, etc.

Valozières [Les] (Fr) a Premier Cru vineyard [part] in the A.C. commune of Aloxe-Corton, Côte de Beaune, Burgundy.

Valpaços (Port) a DOC wine area based in the Trás-Os-Montes region that produces a rich cherry red wine.

Valpantena (It) a dry red wine from the Veneto region. Also known as Valpolicella Valpantena.

Valpolicella (It) a D.O.C. red wine from the Veneto region. Made from the Barbera, Corvina veronese, Molinara, Negrara, Rondinella, Rossignola and Sangiovese grapes. Vinification can take place in Verona. If produced in Valpantena can add this name to the label. Also Valpolicella Classico (*see* Classico). If total alc. content is 12% by vol. and aged minimum 1 year then is classed Superiore.

Valpolicella Annata (It) a term used to identify a wine from the most recent vintage of D.O.C. Valpolicella that is a light, fresh and fruity wine for drinking. Annata is produced by many of the wineries in the region.

Valpolicella Classico (It) a D.O.C. sub-region of 'cru' vineyards around the village of Sant'Ambrogio and the valleys of Fumane, Marano and Negrar.

Valpolicella Recioto (It) a D.O.C. red wine from the Veneto region. Wine is made from the recie 'ears' or outer bunches of grapes that have had the most

sun. *See also* Amarone della Valpolicella, Recioto della Valpolicella.

Valpolicella Valpantena (It) *see* Valpantena.

Valporaiso (Chile) a province and wine-producing area in the Central Zone.

Valpré (S.Afr) a natural spring mineral water from Fricona Valley, Natal Highlands, Paulpietersburg. Mineral contents (milligrammes per litre): Sodium 9mg/l, Calcium 5mg/l, Magnesium 1mg/l, Potassium <1mg/l, Chlorides <5mg/l, Sulphates <5mg/l, Fluorides <0.2mg/l, Nitrates 1mg/l. pH 7.2 Owned by the Coca-Cola Company.

Valréas (Fr) a village in the A.C. Côtes du Rhône-Villages, Vaucluse. *see* Principauté d'Orange.

Valrey (Sp) a natural spring mineral water brand.

Vals (Fr) a sparkling natural spring mineral water (established 1983) from Vals-les-Bains. (Add): Société des Eaux Minérales de Vals, 33, Bd de Vernon, 07600 Vals-les-Bains. Mineral contents (milligrammes per litre): Sodium 453mg/l, Calcium 45.2mg/l, Magnesium 21.3mg/l, Potassium 32.8mg/l, Bicarbonates 1403mg/l, Chlorides 27.2mg/l, Sulphates 38.9mg/l, Nitrates <1mg/l. pH 6.2

Valsarte (Sp) the label of Rioja crianza and reserva wines produced by S.A.T. Arana, Abalos, Riioja.

Vals Baai (S.Afr) lit: 'false bay', the label for a range of wines produced by the False Bay Vineyards winery, Wellington, Western Cape.

Vals d'Agly (Fr) a Vin de Pays area in the Pyrénées Orièntales département in south-western France.

Valser (Switz) a naturally sparkling mineral water (established 1960) from Valser St. Petersquelle. (Add): Valser Mineralquellan AG. 7132 Vals/GR. 1257. Mineral contents (milligrammes per litre): Sodium 10.7mg/l, Calcium 436mg/l, Magnesium 54mg/l, Potassium 2mg/l, Bicarbonates 386mg/l, Chlorides 2.5mg/l, Sulphates 990mg/l, Fluorides 0.63mg/l, Nitrates <0.1mg/l. pH 6.5

Vals-St-Jean (Fr) a slightly pétillant natural spring mineral water brand.

Vals-Vivaraise (Fr) a sparkling natural spring mineral water from Vals-les-Bains. (Add): 33, Boulevard de Verron, 07600 Vals-les-Bains. Mineral contents (milligrammes per litre): Sodium 453mg/l, Calcium 45.2mg/l, Magnesium 21.3mg/l, Potassium 29.8mg/l, Bicarbonates 1403mg/l, Chlorides 27.2mg/l, Sulphates 38.9mg/l.

Valtellina (It) a wine area on the valley of the river Adda in northern Lombardy under the Alps. Produces mostly red wines from the Nebbiolo grape (known locally as the Chiavennasca).

Valtellina (It) a D.O.C. wine area within the Lombardy region. Has four superior zones: Grumello, Inferno, Sassella, Valgella. Red wines are made from the Chiavennasca (Nebbiolo) 70% and 30% Brugnola, Merlot, Pinot noir and Rossola grapes. Local speciality is Sfurzat or Sforzato (strained) from semi-dried grapes with a minimum alc. content of 14.5% by vol.

V

Valtellina Superiore (It) a D.O.C. red wine from Valtellina area within the Lombardy region. Made from the Chiavennasca (Nebbiolo) grape. If aged 4 years (1 year in wood) can be classed Riserva.

Valtiendas (Sp) a Vino Comarcal wine of the province Segovia in Castilla-León.

Valtorre (Sp) a still natural spring mineral water brand. Mineral contents (milligrammes per litre): Sodium 30.5mg/l, Calcium 25.6mg/l, Magnesium 23.6mg/l, Chlorides 39.7mg/l, Nitrates 4mg/l.

Valverde (It) a natural spring mineral water from Fonte S. Antonio, Valverde, Sicily. Mineral contents (milligrammes per litre): Sodium 2.98mg/l, Calcium 2.71mg/l, Magnesium 0.46mg/l, Potassium 0.39mg/l, Bicarbonates 8.72mg/l, Chlorides 1.1mg/l, Sulphates 2.88mg/l, Nitrates 4.64mg/l, Silicates 17.2mg/l. pH 6.1

Val Verde Winery (USA) a winery based south of Lubbock, Texas. Produces European and hybrid wines.

Valvert (Bel) a natural spring mineral water from Etalle, Ardennes. Mineral contents (milligrammes per litre): Sodium 1.9mg/l, Calcium 67.6mg/l, Magnesium 2mg/l, Potassium 0.2mg/l, Bicarbonates 204mg/l, Chlorides 4mg/l, Sulphates 18mg/l, Nitrates 3.5mg/l. pH 7.7

Valvita (S.Afr) a natural spring mineral water brand. Mineral contents (milligrammes per litre): Sodium 5mg/l, Calcium 41.9mg/l, Magnesium 23.5mg/l, Bicarbonates 202mg/l, Chlorides <5mg/l, Sulphates 6mg/l, Nitrates 1.4mg/l. pH 7.8

Val Viva (It) a sparkling natural spring mineral water from S. Giorgio in Bosco, Padova (PD). Mineral contents (milligrammes per litre): Sodium 35.2mg/l, Calcium 35.7mg/l, Magnesium 16.1mg/l, Potassium 2.2mg/l, Bicarbonates 270.7mg/l, Chlorides 9.2mg/l, Nitrates 6.5mg/l, Silicates 21mg/l. pH 7.6

Valwig (Ger) village (Anb): Mosel-Saar-Ruwer. (Ber): Zell/Mosel. (Gro): Rosenhag. (Vins): Herrenberg, Palmberg, Schwarzenberg.

Valzangona (It) a natural spring mineral water brand.

Vampire (Afr) the brand-name of a red wine sold in a black coffin-shaped box.

Vancouver Island (Can) a designated wine region in British Columbia.

Vand (Den) water.

Van Damme Distillerie (Bel) a farm-based distillery near Balagem that produces a range of jenevers.

Vanden Hautte (Bel) a brewery based in Groot Bijgaarden in northern Belgium.

Vanderbilt Cocktail (Cktl) 30mls (¼ gill) cherry brandy, 30mls (¼ gill) liqueur Cognac, 2 dashes Angostura, 3 dashes gomme syrup. Stir over ice, strain into a cocktail glass, add a cherry and a twist of lemon peel.

Van Der Hum (S.Afr) a liqueur made from mandarine oranges, brandy, plants, seeds and barks 30% alc by vol.

Van Der Hum Cocktail (Cktl) 1 measure brandy, 1 measure Van der Hum, 1 measure Port, ½ yolk of egg, ½ teaspoon sugar, ½ teaspoon whipped cream. Shake over ice (all except cream), strain into a 125mls (5fl.oz) goblet and top with the cream.

Vanderlinden Brasserie (Bel) a brewery based in Halle, central Belgium.

Vandermint (Hol) a mint chocolate liqueur. 30% alc by vol. Produced by Bols.

Vanderpan Vineyards (USA) a vineyard based near Greenfield, Salinas Valley, Monterey, California. Grape variety: Chardonnay.

Vanderspritz (Cktl) pour 50mls (2fl.ozs) Vandermint over ice in a highball glass and top with soda water.

Van der Stel [Simon] (S.Afr) a Dutchman who, together with Jan Van Riebeeck started the vineyards in South Africa in the late seventeenth century. see Stellenbosch.

Vandervelden Brasserie (Bel) a brewery based in Beersel, noted for dry, acidic, lambic beers.

Vandeuil (Fr) a Cru Champagne village in the Canton de Fismes. District: Reims.

Vandières (Fr) a Cru Champagne village in the Canton de Châtillon-sur-Marne. District: Reims.

Van Donck (S.Afr) the brand-name of an advockaat (advocaat).

Van Eecke Brasserie (Bel) a brewery (established 1852) based in Watou. Brews: Het Kapittel Abt, Het Kapittel Prior, Poperings Hommelbier.

Van Gent [Pieter] (Austr) a winery. (Add): Black Spring Road, P.O. Box 222, Mudgee, New South Wales 2850. Specialises in Chardonnay wines.

Van Honsebrouck Brouwerij sa (Bel) a brewery (established 1990). (Add): Oostrozebekestraat 43, Ingelmunster B-8770. Brews: Bacchus, Brigand, Kasteelbier Ingelmunster, Kasteelbier Ingelmunster Triple Gold, Poperings Hommelbier, St. Louis Gueuze Lambic, St. Louis Kriek Lambic, Vlaamsch Wit. Website: http://www.vanhonsebrouck.be 'E'mail: info@vanhonsebrouck.be

Vanilchina (It) a quinine and vanilla-flavoured vermouth produced by the Carpano company.

Vanilla (Eng) a term in wine tasting often used to describe the nose and palate of oak-aged wines. Originates from the aldehyde vanillin found in oak.

Vanilla de Mexico (Mex) a vanilla-flavoured liqueur produced by Vreez.

Vanilla Heist (Eng) a 5.3% alc by vol. flavoured alcoholic beverage from the Whitbread Beer C°. under the Shott's Alcoholic Seltzers label. Renamed Hoopers Hooch in 1997.

Vanillen-Geschmack (Ger) the vanilla taste found in many fine red wines.

Vanilla Ice (Eng) a 5% alc by vol. bottle conditioned wheat beer brewed by the St. Austell Brewery, Cornwall.

Vanillin (Eng) obtained from wooden casks and into the wine. see Aldehyde and Vanilla.

Van Loveren Vineyard (S.Afr) a winery (established

1335

V

1937) based at Robertson, Western Cape. 220ha. (Add): Box 97, Robertson 6705. Grape varieties: Cabernet sauvignon, Chardonnay, Chenin blanc, Colombard, Fernão pires, Hanepoot, Merlot, Muscat, Muscadel, Pinotage, Red muscadet, Riesling, Ruby cabernet, Sauvignon blanc, Shiraz, Tourigo. Labels: Four Cousins, Papillon, River White, Signature Series Reserve. Also produces a range of varietal wines. Website: http://www.vanloveren.co.za

Van Lubbeek (Bel) a sweet brown ale, low in alcohol, from the Leuven district.

Van Malder Brasserie (Bel) a brewery based in Anderlecht, Brussels.

Van Merritt (USA) a brand of beer brewed by the Peter Hand Brewery.

Van Offlen (Hol) a company that is owned by Heineken. Sells under the Zwarte Kip (black hen) label.

Van Ostade (Hol) a noted liqueur producer based in Zaandam.

Van Pur Browar (Pol) a brewery. (Add): 37-111 Rakaszawa 334. Brews beers and lager. Website: http://www.vanpur.com 'E'mail: vanpur@vanpur.com.pl

Van Riebeck Co-operative (S.Afr) a co-operative winery based at Riebeck, Kasteel, Malmesbury. Noted for white wines.

Van Riebeek [Jan] (S.Afr) a Dutchman who, together with Simon Van der Stel, started the first vineyards in South Africa in 1655. First wine was produced in 1659.

Van Ryn's Wine & Spirit C° Ltd (S.Afr) brandy producers based at Vlottenburg, Stellenbosch, Western Cape. Pot and patent still. Produce Rare Cabinet brandy (20 years of aging). Produces Viceroy. Website: http://www.vanryn.c.za

Van Schoor Wines (S.Afr) a winery (established 2001) based in Robertson, Western Cape. 83ha. Grape varieties: Cabernet sauvignon, Chardonnay, Merlot, Pinota, Shiraz. Label: Blacksmith. Website: http://www.vanschoorwines.co.za

Vansha (S.Afr) the label for a white wine (Chenin blanc and Sauvignon blanc) and Red wine (Cabernet franc, Cinsaut and Shiraz blend) produced by the Ridgeback Wines winery, Paarl, Western Cape.

Van Steenberge (Bel) a brewery (established 1785). (Add): Lindenlaan 25, Ertevelde B-9940. Brews: Gulden Draak, Keizersberg, Piraat. Website: http://www.vansteenberge.com 'E'mail: info@vansteenberge.com

Vantogrio (Czec) a non-alcoholic syrup.

Van Vleet Cocktail (Cktl) ⅗ measure Bacardi rum, ⅕ measure orange juice, ⅕ measure maple syrup. Shake well over ice and strain into an ice-filled old-fashioned glass.

Van Vollenhoven's Stout (Hol) a stout produced by bottom-fermentation from the Heineken Brouwerij 6.4% alc by vol.

Van Wyck Cocktail (Cktl) ½ measure dry gin, ½ measure sloe gin, dash orange bitters. Shake over ice and strain into a cocktail glass.

Van Zeller (Port) Vintage Port shippers. Vintages: 1878, 1881, 1884, 1887, 1890, 1892, 1896, 1904, 1908, 1912, 1917, 1922, 1924, 1927, 1935, 1983, 1985, 1991, 1994, 1997, 2003. Controlled by Quinta do Noval.

Van Zondt Cocktail (Cktl) ½ measure dry gin, ½ measure French vermouth, dash apricot brandy. Stir over ice and strain into a cocktail glass.

Van Zuylekom (Hol) a noted jenever (gin) producer.

Van Zylshof Estate (S.Afr) a winery (established 2003) based in Robertson, Western Cape. 32ha. (Add): P.O. Box 64, Bonnievale 6730. Grape varieties: Cabernet sauvignon, Chardonnay, Chenin blanc, Merlot, Sauvignon blanc. Label: Riverain.

V.A.O.G. (Afr) abbr: Vins d'Appellation d'Origine Garantie. A.C. conferred by Institut Algérien de la Vigne et du Vin.

Vappa (Lat) describes a wine that has gone flat, lifeless.

Var (Fr) a département in south-eastern France. Has the Provence wine-producing region within its boundaries.

Vara (Sp) a unit of measurement equivalent to 1.74 metres.

Varanda do Conde (Port) a D.O.C. Vinho Verde (Alvarhino & Trajadura blend) wine produced by the Provam co-operative.

Varanina (It) a sparkling natural spring mineral water from Varinana. Mineral contents (milligrammes per litre): Sodium 21.5mg/l, Calcium 119.4mg/l, Magnesium 31mg/l, Potassium 3.8mg/l, Bicarbonates 365mg/l, Chlorides 14.8mg/l, Sulphates 150mg/l, Fluorides 0.35mg/l, Nitrates 1.9mg/l, Silicates 20mg/l. pH 7.1

Vara y Pulgar (Sp) the traditional method of vine training and pruning in the Jerez region.

Varazdin (Cro) a wine-producing area in Croatia.

Varela (Sp) a Sherry and brandy producing bodega and shippers based in Puerto de Santa Maria.

Varichon et Clerc (Fr) a négociant-éleveur of sparkling wines based in Savoie.

Varietal (Eng) a grape which is slightly different to the main known varietal such as Welschriesling to the Riesling.

Varietal (Eng) a term applied to a wine which has a predominance of one grape variety and uses that grape's name for the name of the wine.

Varietal Bottling (USA) this indicates the grape from which the wine is produced, must be from at least 51% of single variety but local laws may require much higher proportions.

Varietal Labelling (E.C) any number of grape varieties may be indicated on the back label (in descending order) as part of a European light wines description. They must however, constitute a minimum of 85% of the blend. A maximum of three grape varieties may be indicated on the front label of sparkling wines.

Varignus [Le] (Fr) a vineyard in the A.C. commune of Montagny, Côte Chalonnaise, Burgundy.

Varil (Tur) a small cask/barrel.

Variopak (Hol) like a milk carton but for beer, produced in Holland. Sealed with a special clip.

Varm Mælk (Den) hot milk (drink).

Varna (Bul) a D.G.O. wine-producing area in the eastern region of Bulgaria that produces mainly white wines.

Varna Misket (Bul) a sub-variety of Red Misket. *See also* Sliven Misket.

Varnenski Misket (Bul) a white grape variety.

Varnhalt (Ger) village (Anb): Baden. (Ber): Ortenau. (Gro): Schloss Rodeck. (Vins): Klosterbergfelsen, Sonnenberg, Steingrübler.

Varogne [La] (Fr) a vineyard in the A.C. Hermitage, northern Rhône.

Varoilles [Les] (Fr) a Premier Cru vineyard [part] in the A.C. commune of Gevrey-Chambertin, Côte de Nuits, Burgundy 7.4ha. Belongs entirely to Domaine des Varoilles.

Varosa (Port) an I.P.R. region south of the river Douro.

Varrains (Fr) a commune in the A.C. Saumur district, Anjou-Saumur, Loire. Produces red and white wines.

Varshetz (Bul) a slightly alkaline still, natural spring mineral water from Spanchevtzi-Varshetz. Mineral contents (milligrammes per litre): Sodium 44.9mg/l, Calcium 7.2mg/l, Potassium 0.51mg/l, Bicarbonates 97.6mg/l, Chlorides 4.7mg/l, Sulphates 25.1mg/l, Fluorides 0.6mg/l, Nitrates 2mg/l. pH 8.8

Varsilaki (Tur) a red grape variety grown in the Thrace and Marmara region.

Varsity Bitter (Eng) a cask-conditioned bitter 4.3% alc by vol. brewed by the Morrells Brewery of Oxford.

Varsity Blues Cocktail (Cktl) ½ measure gin, ¼ measure vodka, ¼ measure blue Curaçao, dash maraschino. Stir over ice and strain into a cocktail glass.

Vasciano (It) a sparkling natural spring mineral water from Todi, Perugia. Mineral contents (milligrammes per litre): Sodium 47.5mg/l, Calcium 392.7mg/l, Magnesium 58mg/l, Potassium 25.7mg/l, Bicarbonates 1354.2mg/l, Chlorides 37.2mg/l, Sulphates 170.1mg/l, Nitrates 7.7mg/l, Silicates 21.4mg/l, Strontium 2.15mg/l, Oxygen 4.3mg/l. pH 6.15

Vasija R.F.N (Arg) a Bordeaux-style red wine made from the Sangiovetto piccolo and Merlot grapes in the Mendoza region.

Vasilha (Port) cask/barrel.

Vaslin Press (Sp) a horizontal, rotating press that enables the number of pressings and amount of pressure to be controlled.

Vaso (Sp) tumbler/glass.

Vaso de Agua (Sp) water glass.

Vaso [En] (Sp) the local name for the goblet method of vine-training.

Vasse Felix Winery (Austr) a winery based in the Margaret River Region, Western Australia. (Add): Cowaramup, 6284 Western Australia. 10ha. Grape varieties: Cabernet sauvignon, Chardonnay, Gewürztraminer, Hermitage, Malbec, Riesling, Sauvignon blanc, Sémillon, Shiraz. Labels: Adams Road, Heytesbury.

Vastatrix (Fr) one of the nicknames used in France for the **Phylloxera vastatrix** (the vine louse). *See also* Ravager.

V.A.T. (Cktl) *abbr*: for a Vodka And Tonic.

Vat (Eng) usually an open vessel used in the brewing process for beer fermentation.

Vat (Fr) large casks used for the blending and maturing of wines and spirits.

Vat (Hol) a container holding 100litres (22Imp.gallons), 26.4US gallons.

Vat 1884 (Egy) a brandy produced from local grapes by the Egyptian Vineyards and Distilleries Cº.

Vaticanum (It) a red wine produced in central-western Italy during Roman times.

Vat 69 (Scot) a famous blended Scotch whisky from William Sanderson and Son Ltd. Named after the original vat blend 40% alc by vol.

Vat 69 Reserve (Scot) a blended de luxe Scotch whisky 12 year old from William Sanderson and Son Ltd. at Queensferry 40% alc by vol.

Vatted Malt (Scot) a blend of pure malt (single) whiskies, up to 6 individual malts may be used. e.g. Speyside, Concannon, etc. Soon to be known (by law) as Blended Malt to prevent confusion (2005-06).

Vatting (Eng) mixing or blending in a vat.

Vat 20 (Egy) a brandy produced from local grapes by the Egyptian Vineyards and Distilleries Cº.

Vauban (Fr) a natural spring mineral water from the Source Vauban, 59230 St-Amand les Eaux. Mineral contents (milligrammes per litre): Sodium 40mg/l, Calcium 230mg/l, Magnesium 66mg/l, Potassium 8mg/l, Bicarbonates 280mg/l, Chlorides 58mg/l, Sulphates 620mg/l, Fluorides 1.3mg/l, Nitrates <1mg/l. pH 7.0

Vauchrétien (Fr) an A.C. commune in the Coteaux de l'Aubance in the Anjou-Saumur district of the Loire.

Vauciennes (Fr) a Cru Champagne village in the Canton d'Épernay. District: Épernay.

Vaucluse (Fr) a département in the north-eastern Rhône. *see* Roaix.

Vaucoupains (Fr) *see* Vaucoupan.

Vaucoupin (Fr) a Premier Cru vineyard in the A.C. Chablis, Burgundy. Also spelt Vaucoupains.

Vaucrains [Les] (Fr) a Premier Cru vineyard in the A.C. commune of Nuit-Saint-Georges, Côte de Nuits, Burgundy 6ha.

Vaud (Switz) a famous wine area with the sub-districts: Chablais, La Côte and Lavaux. Produces white wines from Chasselas and Riesling and red wines from Gamay and Pinot noir grapes. *see* Dorin, Perlan.

Vaudemanges (Fr) a Premier Cru Champagne village in the Canton de Suippes. District: Châlons.

Vaudésir (Fr) a Grand Cru Chablis vineyard

Vaudevey (Fr) a Premier Cru vineyard in the A.C. Chablis, Burgundy.

Vaudois Chablais (Switz) a strong, smooth white wines with a flavour of gunflint made at Aigle on Lake Leman in the canton of Vaud.

Vaudon [Pierre] (Fr) a Champagne co-operative. 1800 growers. (Add): 7 Rue Pasteur, 51190 Avize. Produce vintage and non-vintage wines. Vintages: 1985, 1988, 1989, 1990, 1993, 1995, 1997, 1998, 1999, 2000.

Vaugiraut (Fr) a Premier Cru vineyard in the A.C. Chablis, Burgundy. Is often reclassified as the Premier Cru vineyard Vosgros.

Vaulorent (Fr) a Premier Cru vineyard in the A.C. Chablis, Burgundy. Is often reclassified as the Premier Cru vineyard Fourchaume.

Vault (Eng) a cellar, originally a room where casks were stored especially in the north of England. Name is now used as an alternative to the public bar. (Ire) = siléar.

Vault (Eng) a 5.3% alc by vol. clear RTD soda drink from Carlsberg-Tetley. Sold in a clear bottle.

Vaunage (Fr) a Vin de Pays area in Provence, south-eastern France. Produces red, rosé and dry white wines.

Vaupulent (Fr) a Premier Cru vineyard in the A.C. Chablis, Burgundy. Is often reclassified as the Premier Cru vineyard Fourchaume.

Vauvert (Fr) an area of vinification for A.C. wines of Costières du Gard, Languedoc.

Vau Vintage (Port) a vintage Port produced to be drunk young by Sandeman.

Vauvry (Fr) a vineyard based in the A.C. commune of Rully, Côte Chalonnaise, Burgundy.

Vaux (Eng) a large brewing group with many public houses and breweries in Scotland, south Yorkshire, Sunderland and Belgium. Noted for cask-conditioned Sunderland Draught 1040 O.G. Samson 1042 O.G. plus many keg and bottled beers.

Vaux-en-Beaujolais (Fr) a commune in the Beaujolais district. Has A.C. Beaujolais-Villages or Beaujolais-Vaux-en-Beaujolais status.

Vauxhall Nectar (Eng) a mixture of rum, syrup and bitter almond, drunk diluted with water in the nineteenth century.

Vauxlaurens Brewery (Ch.Isles) a brewery based in St. Juliens Ave., St. Peter Port. One of two local breweries on the island of Guernsey. see Randalls Brewery.

Vauxrenard (Fr) a commune in the Beaujolais district. Has A.C. Beaujolais-Villages or Beaujolais-Vauxrenard status.

Vavasour Wines (N.Z) a 16ha vineyard and winery. (Add): Redwood Pass, Awatere Valley, Marlborough. Noted for Chardonnay and Sauvignon blanc wines. Labels include Dashwood.

Vavrinecké (Czec) a local name for the St. Laurent grape.

Vayres (Fr) a region of west Saint-Émilion in the Gironde on the river Dordogne. Produces red and white wines. Best known is the Graves de Vayres (white wine).

Vazart-Coquart (Fr) a Champagne producer

(established 1785). (Add): 6, Rue des Partelaines, 51530 Chouilly. 11ha. Produces vintage and non-vintage wines. Vintages: 1995, 1996, 1997, 1999. A member of the Club Tresors de Champagne. Labels: Cuvée Camille, Cuvée Grand Bouquet, Cuvée 'Spécial Club' Millésimée (Chardonnay 100%), Cuvée Spécial Foie Gras, Website: http://www.champagne-vazart-coquart.tm.fr 'E'mail: vazart@cder.fr

VB (Ch.Isles) *abbr:* **V**auxlaurens **B**rewery owned by R.W. Randall Ltd. of St. Peter Port, Guernsey. Initials are used on beer labels. i.e. VB Bitter (now no longer produced). See Randalls Brewery.

V.B. Bruzzone (It) a noted producer of sparkling wines produced by the traditional method based in the Piemonte region.

V.C. (Sp) *abbr:* **V**ino **C**omarcal.

VC (Wal) a 3.8% alc by vol. ale brewed by the Cwmbran Brewery, Gwent.

V.C.C. (Fr) *abbr:* **V**ins **O**rdinaires de **C**onsommation **C**ourante. These are wines for everyday drinking.

V.C.P.R.D. (Sp) *abbr:* **V**inos de **C**alidad **P**roducidos en **R**egiones **D**eterminadas.

V.d.L. (Fr) *abbr:* **V**in de **L**iqueur.

V.d.N. (Fr) *abbr:* **V**in **d**oux **N**aturel.

V.D.P. (Ger) *abbr:* **V**erband **D**eutscher **P**rädikats und Qualitätsweingüter

V.D.P.V. (Ger) *abbr:* **V**erband **D**eutscher **P**rädikatswein **V**ersteigerer.

V.D.Q.S. (Fr) *abbr:* **V**in **D**élimité de **Q**ualité **S**upérieure. Second from top classification of wines in France. Was introduced in 1949.

Vea (Eng) *see* Archer's Schnapps.

Veanor (Eng) a 5% alc by vol. ale brewed by the Greenwich Meantime Brewing C°. Ltd., London.

Vecchia Romagna (It) a riserva rare brandy made by the firm of Buton of Romagna. *see* Etichetta Nera, Etichetta Oro.

Vecchio (It) old, denotes a wine with cask age. i.e. Chianti must have minimum of 2 years in cask.

Vecchio Piemonte (It) a brandy produced by Martini and Rossi in Turin.

V.E. Commemorative Ale (Eng) brewed to commemorate D-day 50 year anniversary (in 1994). 4.7% alc by vol. from the Blackawton Brewery, Devon.

V.E. Day Ale (Eng) a 4.5% alc by vol. ale from Wye Valley Brewery in Hereford. See also V.J. Day Ale, Siege Ale.

Vedel System (S.Afr) a 'wine circle' tasting system of using asterisks instead of numbers to rate wines. ***** = excellent, **** = very good, *** = good, ** = acceptable and * = poor.

Vedett (Bel) an extra blond beer brewed by the Duvel Moorgat Brasserie.

Vedin (Arm) a wine-producing centre in Armenia.

Veedercrest Winery (USA) a winery based in Emeryville, Alameda, California. Grape varieties: Cabernet sauvignon, Chardonnay, Gewürztraminer, Johannisberg riesling and Merlot. Produces varietal wines. Also has a vineyard on Mount Veeder in the Napa Valley.

V

Veena (Ind) a light white wine from Laski Riesling grapes, blended with spices. Bottled in U.K. for United Breweries Ltd., London.

Veenagrat (Rus) grape.

Veeno (Rus) wine.

Veens Nat (Hol) a 5% alc by vol. top-fermented special beer brewed by De Drie Ringen Amersfoort Brouwerij, Amersfoort.

Veenwouden Private Cellar (S.Afr) a winery (established 1993) based in northern Paarl, Western Cape. 14ha. Grape varieties: Cabernet franc, Cabernet sauvignon, Chardonnay, Colombard, Malbec, Merlot, Pinot noir, Shiraz. Labels: Churton, Thornhill, Vivat Bacchus. Website: http://www.veenwouden.com

Veeport (Can) a red grape variety established by the Ontario Department of the Agricultural Experimental Station. Used in Port-style wine production.

Vega de Moriz (Sp) the label of a D.O. Cencibel wine from Casa de la Viña in Valdepeñas.

Vega Ibor (Sp) the label of a Crianza wine produced by Bodegas Real in Valdepeñas.

Vega Sicilia (Sp) a D.O. red wine from Old Castile established in 1864. Up to 16% alc by vol. Produced by the Bodegas Vega Sicilia. Unico is the top wine from Tinto fino, Cabernet sauvignon, Merlot, Malbec, Albiño. Valbuena 5 año is the second quality wine (receives less ageing and is sold 5 years after harvesting), Allión is the newest addition to the range. Wine is produced from a 250ha. area of the estate. D.O. Ribera del Duero. *see* Bodegas Pintia and Unico.

Vegaval Plata (Sp) the label of Reserva and Gran Reserva wines produced by Bodegas Miguel Calatayud in Valdepeñas.

Vega Winery (USA) a winery and vineyards based in the Santa Ynez Valley, Santa Barbara, California. Grape varieties: Gewürztraminer and White riesling. Produces varietal and table wines.

Vegetal (Eng) a wine-tasting term denoting a vegetable taste or aroma.

Veglio (It) a winery based in the DOCG Barolo, Piemonte. Label: Castelletto.

Vehissima (Port) when seen on a label denotes 'old'.

Veiga Franca and Cº. Ltd. (Mad) a noted Madeira wine shipper.

Veiling (Eng) a term used when one part of the wine masks or veils another part. i.e. the bouquet may veil part of the taste.

Veitshöchheim (Ger) village (Anb): Franken. (Ber): Maindreick. (Gro): Not yet assigned. (Vin): Sonnenschein.

Veitshöchheim (Ger) village (Anb): Franken. (Ber): Maindreieck. (Gro): Ravensburg. (Vin): Wölflein.

Velazquez (Sp) red wines produced by Bodegas Velazquez S.A. from 80% Tempranillo and 20% Garnacha grapes. All classes are produced.

Veldenz (Ger) village (Anb): Mosel-Saar-Ruwer. (Ber): Bernkastel. (Gro): Kurfürstlay. (Vins): Carlsberg, Elisenberg, Grafschafter Sonnenberg, Kirchberg, Mühlberg.

Veldt (Fr) a measure once used in the Cognac region.

27 veldts was equal to a 205litres cask. 35 veldts equals 60 Imp.gallons (72 US gallons).

Velenche (Sp) pipette or sonde used for drawing wine from the cask. Can be metal or glass, looks like a big syringe. Is plunged into the cask, filled, then the finger is placed over the top whilst it is lifted out. When the finger is removed the wine is released into the glass.

Velho (Port) old wine.

Velho Barreiro Cachaça (Bra) a 40% alc by vol. spirit with the flavour of sugar cane. Available as an unaged white spirit or an aged gold spirit.

Velich [Heinz & Roland] (Aus) a vineyard (3ha) based in Apetlon, Burgenland. (Add): Seeufergasse 12, 7143 Apetlon. Grape varieties: Chardonnay, Neuburger, Welschriesling. Label: Tiglat.

Velika Morava (Ser) a key region of Serbia. White wine: Laski rizling, red wine: Vranje.

Veliternum (It) a red wine produced in central-western Italy during Roman times.

Veliterra (Sp) a white wine produced from the Palomino, Verdejo and Viura grapes by Cooperativa La Seca in La Rueda.

Velké Brezno Brewery (Czec) an old brewery based in north-western Czec.

Velké Pavlovice (Czec) a wine district within the region of Bohemia. Produces some of the best wines of the region.

Velké Popovice Brewery (Czec) a large, noted brewery (established 1874) based in western Czec. Brews: Kozel Dark 10%, Kozel Straw 10%, Kozel Straw 12%.

Velké Saris Brewery (Czec) a brewery which is noted for a special pale ale of same name.

Velké Zernoseky (Czec) a wine-producing town based north of Prague.

Vellamo (Fin) a natural spring mineral water from Viikinäisten Syvälähde, Heinola.

Velletri Bianco (It) a D.O.C. white wine from the Latium region. Made from the Bellone, Bonvino, Malvasia and Trebbiano grapes grown in commune of Velletri and Lariano and part of commune of Cisterna di Latina.

Velletri Rosso (It) a D.O.C. red wine from the Latium region. Made from the Cesanese comune/di affile, Montepulciano and Sangiovese grapes grown in communes of Velletri and Lariano and part of the Cisterna di Latina commune.

Velloso & Tait (Port) a winery based in Oporto, produces an L.B.V. Port.

Vellutato (It) denotes wine with a velvety character.

Velluto Rosso (N.Z) a red table wine produced by Corbans in the Henderson Valley, North Island.

Velocity Cocktail (Cktl) 40mls (⅓ gill) gin, 20mls (⅙ gill) Italian vermouth. Shake well over ice, strain into a cocktail glass and add a slice of orange.

Velo de Flor (Sp) lit: 'veil of flor', the flor yeasts that float on the top of the new Sherry like a film (veil). *see* Flor.

Velo di Maya (It) a D.O.C. red barrique-aged Barbera wine produced by Alfiero Boffa, San Marzano Oliveto, Piemonte.

Velouté (Fr) used to describe a wine which has a soft, rich, mellow, '*velvety*' softness. A wine that has no roughness what-so-ever.

Veltelini (Hun) a white grape variety grown in north-western Hungary.

Veltins (Ger) a 4.8% alc by vol. bottled pilsner brewed by Veltins Brauerei, Meschede-Grevenstein.

Veltins Brauerei (Ger) a brewery (established 1824) based at Meschede-Grevenstein. Brews: Veltins, Veltins Leicht.

Veltins Leicht (Ger) a 2.4% alc by vol. bottled light pilsner brewed by Veltins Brauerei, Meschede-Grevenstein.

Veltliner (Aus) a white grape variety used in the production of Gumpoldskirchner. 3 variations: red (Roter), green (Grüner) and early red Veltliner. Also known as Veltlini, Veltlin Zelene, Veltlinske Zelené. *see* Brauner Veltliner, Frühtoter Veltliner.

Veltliner Bianco (It) a white grape variety grown in northern Italy.

Veltlini (Aus) *see* Veltliner.

Veltlinske Zelené (Aus) *see* Gruener Veltliner and Veltliner.

Veltlinsky (Aus) the label for a white wine (Grüner veltliner) produced by the Schlossweingut Graf Hardegg winery, Weinviertel.

Veltlin Zelene (Aus) *see* Gruener Veltliner and Veltliner.

Velut [Jean] (Fr) a Champagne producer. (Add): 9, Rue du Moulin, 10300 Montgueux. Grape varieties: Chardonnay 80% and Pinot noir 20%.

Velvet (Can) a name for the English drink Black Velvet. (half stout and half Champagne).

Velvet Cocktail (Cktl) ½ measure Scotch whisky, ⅓ measure dry vermouth, ⅙ measure parfait amour, dash absinthe, dash wormwood bitters. Shake over ice and strain into a cocktail glass.

Velvet Hammer [1] (Cktl) ⅓ measure Tia Maria, ⅓ measure Cointreau, ⅓ measure fresh cream. Shake over ice and strain into a cocktail glass.

Velvet Hammer [2] (Cktl) ⅗ measure Strega, ⅕ measure (white) crème de cacao, ⅕ measure cream. Shake over ice and strain into a cocktail glass.

Velvet Hammer Cocktail (Cktl) 25mls (⅕ gill) vodka, 15mls (⅛ gill) white crème de cacao, 15mls (⅛ gill) cream. Shake over ice and strain into a cocktail glass.

Velvet Hill (USA) the name used by the Llords and Elwood Winery in Livermore, California for a range of their wines.

Velvet Stout (Eng) a stout 1042 O.G. brewed and bottled by the Courage Brewery in London.

Velvet Stout (Eng) a stout brewed by the Reepham Brewery in Norfolk.

Velvet Stout (Eng) a stout 1042 O.G. brewed and bottled by the Webster Brewery in Halifax, Yorkshire.

Velvety (Eng) denotes a wine or beer that is very smooth and has no roughness.

Vemagering (Hol) maceration.

Vencac-Oplenac (Ser) a wine-producing region producing red and rosé wines from the Gamay, Pinot noir and Prokupac grape varieties.

Vencia (Sp) a red grape variety grown in Galicia.

Vendange (Fr) harvest/vintage.

Vendange Manuelle (Fr) harvested by hand.

Vendangeoirs (Fr) buildings in Champagne where the grapes are pressed also used to house the grape pickers.

Vendanges Manuelles (Fr) hand-picked grapes.

Vendange Tardive (Fr) a term to denote '*late harvested*', often used since 1983 in Alsace. Wines must be made from Gewurztraminer, Muscat, Pinot gris or Riesling grapes. Minimum natural must weight of 95°Oe for Muscat and Riesling, 105°Oe for others, chaptilisation forbidden. Wines are dry or medium-sweet, basic or Grand Cru status. *See also* Réserve Spéciale. (Aus) = spätlese, (Ger) = spätlese, (It) = vendemmia tardiva.

Vendangeur (Fr) grape picker/harvester/vintage worker.

Vendange Verte (Fr) summer pruning.

Vendemia (Sp) *see* Vendimia.

Vendémiarire (Fr) the month of the grape harvest. 23rd September–22nd October (the first month of the French Revolutionary Calendar).

Vendemmia (It) harvest/vintage.

Vendemmia Tardiva (It) late harvest. (Fr) = vendange tardive, (Ger) = spätlese.

Vendemmia Verde (It) method of reducing the crop by removing some of the berries whilst they are still green and hard.

Vendersheim (Ger) village (Anb): Rheinhessen. (Ber): Bingen. (Gro): Kurfürstenstück. (Vins): Goldberg, Sonnenberg.

Vendimia (Sp) vintage/harvest.

Vendimia Especial Reserve (Sp) wines produced by Bodegas Bilbainas, S.A. (Alta region) Rioja.

Vendôme (S.Afr) a winery (established 1999) based in Paarl, Western Cape. 70ha. Grape varieties: Cabernet franc, Cabernet sauvignon, Chardonnay, Chenin blanc, Colombard, Merlot, Shiraz. Labels: Classique, Le Roux. Website: http://www.vendome.co.za

Vendramino Vineyards (USA) a winery based in Paw Paw, Michigan noted for quality table wines.

Venecia (Sp) *see* Venencia.

Veneciador (Sp) *see* Venenciador.

Venegazzù Della Casa (It) an I.G.T. red wine produced from Cabernet franc, Cabernet sauvignon, Malbec and Merlot grapes by Azienda Agricola Conte Loredan Gasparini, Via Martignano Alto, 24/A, I-31040 Venegazzù di Volpago del Montello. Matured in French oak for 2 years.

Venencia (Sp) a metal cup which is on a long handle of bone or wood and is used to dip into Sherry casks to take out a sample of wine from the centre of the cask.

Venenciador (Sp) the man who uses a venencia to draw wine from the centre of the Sherry cask. Usually demonstrates his skill by pouring the wine into a number of copitas from a height at the same time without any spillage.

Venerable (Sp) an old Pedro Ximénez Sherry with an average age of 40 years old, produced by Domecq.

Venerable Bede (Eng) a 4.5% alc by vol. ale brewed by the Jarrow Brewery, Tyne & Wear.

Venetian Cream (It) a brandy-based cream liqueur 17% alc by vol.

Venetian Glass (It) early drinking glasses, soda glass, thin, light and fragile.

Venetian Sunset (Cktl) ⅖ measure dry gin, ⅕ measure Campari, ⅕ measure dry vermouth, ⅕ measure Grand Marnier. Stir over ice, strain into a cocktail glass and add a cherry on top.

Veneto (It) a region in north-eastern Italy. It borders Trentino-Alte-Adige, Venezia, Friulia, Emilia-Romagna, The Adriatic Sea, Lombardy and Austria. Lies between Lake Garda and River Po. Noted for Bardolino, Soave and Valpolicella wines. *See also* Venezia-Euganea.

Venezia-Euganea (It) the alternative name for the Veneto region.

Venezia Tridentina (It) the pre 1947 name for the Trentino-Alte-Adige (Süd Tirol) region.

Venezuelan Coffee (S.Am) a coffee used mainly for blending. Produces a light style of coffee with medium flavour and acidity. Has three main regions: Caracas, Maracibos and Meridas.

Venica e Venica (It) a winery based in Dolegna in the Friuli-Venezia-Guilia region.

Veniza (Gre) a natural spring mineral water from Vakontios.

Venloosch Alt (Hol) a 4.5% alc by vol. medium-brown, bottled alt beer brewed by De Leeuw Bier Brouwerij, Valkenburg aan de Geul.

Venningen (Ger) village (Anb): Pfalz. (Ber): Südliche Weinstrasse. (Gro): Trappenberg. (Vin): Doktor.

Vensac (Fr) a commune in the A.C. Médoc, north-western Bordeaux.

Vent (Eng) allowing the escape of a CO_2 gas build up in a beer cask owing to the secondary fermentation during conditioning (released through the soft spile).

Ventadour (Fr) a sparkling natural spring mineral water (established 1868) from Pestrin, Ardèche. (Add): Societé Ricard 4-6 Rue Berthelot, 13014 Marseilles. Mineral contents (milligrammes per litre): Sodium 13.4mg/l, Calcium 45mg/l, Magnesium 10.5mg/l, Potassium 2.1mg/l, Bicarbonates 223.3mg/l, Chlorides 2mg/l, Sulphates 6.3mg/l, Silicate 45.7mg/l.

Ventana Vineyards (USA) a winery based near Soledad, Monterey County, California. 125ha. Grape varieties: Chardonnay, Chenin blanc, Gamay, Johannisberg riesling, Muscat blanc, Petite sirah, Pinot noir, Sauvignon blanc and Zinfandel. Produces varietal, botrytised and table wines.

Ventasso (It) a sparkling natural spring mineral water from Monte Pizzarotta – Fonte S. Lucia. Mineral contents (milligrammes per litre): Sodium 11.5mg/l, Calcium 42.9mg/l, Magnesium 3.2mg/l, Potassium 0.25mg/l, Bicarbonates 134mg/l, Chlorides 3.3mg/l, Sulphates 23.5mg/l, Oxygen 4.5mg/l. pH 7.7

Vente Directe (Fr) on the outside of a château, domaine or winery. Denotes that wines can be bought from the winery.

Ventes sur Place (Fr) a term that denotes that the wines are sold on the premises.

Vente sur Souches (Fr) describes the sale of wines made prior to the harvest. Based on the amount of alcohol that should be produced, therefore the price may be fixed. It is altered if the amount of alcohol eventually produced is higher or lower.

Venteuil (Fr) a Cru Champagne village in the Canton d'Épernay. District: Épernay.

Ventnor Brewery (Eng) a brewery (established 1840). (Add): 119 High Street, Ventnor, Isle of Wight PO38 1LY. Brews: Admirals Ale 4% alc by vol., Hygeia 4.6% alc by vol., Old Ruby Bitter, Oyster Stout 5% alc by vol., Sand Rock 5.6% alc by vol., Sunfire 4.3% alc by vol., Wight Spirit 5% alc by vol. Website: http://www.ventnorbrewery.co.uk 'E'mail: sales@ventnorbrewery.co.uk

Venture (Eng) a 3.6% alc by vol. ale brewed by the Wentworth Brewery, South Yorkshire.

Venusbuckel (Ger) vineyard (Anb): Pfalz. (Ber): Südliche Weinstrasse. (Gro): Kloster Liebfrauenberg. (Vil): Billigheim-Ingenheim.

V.E.P (Fr) *abbr*: **V**ieillissement **E**xceptionnellement **P**rolonge, a liqueur brand.

Vera (It) a sparkling natural spring mineral water from San Giorio in Bosco. Mineral contents (milligrammes per litre): Sodium 2mg/l, Calcium 36mg/l, Magnesium 13mg/l, Potassium 0.6mg/l, Bicarbonates 154mg/l, Chlorides 2.1mg/l, Sulphates 18mg/l, Nitrates 3.6mg/l, Silicates 9mg/l, Oxygen 8mg/l. pH 8.03

Véraison (Fr) the ripening of the grapes/point where the grapes start to change colour.

Veramonte Estate (Chile) a winery based in Casablanca. Grape varieties include: Cabernet sauvignon, Carmenère, Merlot. Label: Primus.

Verband der Südtiroler Kellereigenossenschaften (It) the Union of Südtirol Co-operatives. A body that markets for 21 of the co-operatives in the Südtirol. Based at Crispistr.

Verband Deutscher Naturwein Versteigerer (Ger) the German natural wine auction-sellers association. *see* V.D.P.V. (new name).

Verband Deutscher Prädikats und Qualitätsweingüter (Ger) *abbr*: V.D.P. Association of leading German estates.

Verband Deutscher Prädikatswein Versteigerer (Ger) *abbr*: V.D.P.V. a wine-growers association. The new name given to the Verband Deutscher Naturwein Versteigerer. Works on the principle of grading vineyards according to quality of soil, micro-climate, etc. But has no legal standing (except to its members).

Verbena (Fr) a herb liqueur produced in south-western France. There are two styles: yellow (sweet) and green (dry).

Verbesco (It) a lightly sparkling white wine produced from Barbera, Freisa and Grignolino grapes by Gallo d'Oro.

V

Verbessert (Ger) the sugaring of the must in poor years to increase the alcohol content. *see* Anreicherung. (Fr) = chaptalisation.

Verbesserung (Ger) the process of adding sugar to the grape must. Now known as Anreicherung. *See also* Verbessert.

Verboten Cocktail (Cktl) 20mls (⅙ gill) dry gin, 5mls (¼ fl.oz) each of orange juice, lemon juice and forbidden fruit. Shake well over ice, strain into a cocktail glass and top with a cherry that has been soaked in old Cognac.

Vercoope (Port) a group of thirteen farmers who blend, bottle and market their wines. Produce Verdegar, a noted white Vinho Verde.

Verdana (It) the Pollino, Calabria name for the Malvasia bianca grape.

Verde (It) a natural spring mineral water from Fonte Verde.

Verde (Port) lit: 'green', used for Vinho Verde wines coming from the delimited area of Minho in northern Portugal. Wines are low in alcohol and are characterised by the slight prickle on the tongue (pétillance) traditionally from malo-lactic fermentation in the bottle. Green denotes age (young), not colour.

Verdea (Gre) a white pungent grape variety grown on the island of Zante in western Greece (Ionian Isles). Also grown in Colli Piacenti in Italy.

Verdeca (It) a white grape variety grown in the Puglia region.

Verdegar (Port) the brand-name of a Vinho Verde produced by Vercoope and an Aguardente produced in the Minho.

Verdejo (Sp) a white grape variety grown in Cigales, Rueda and Toro.

Verdejo Palido (Sp) a light, white wine produced by Sociedad Agrícola in La Seca, Rueda.

Verdelho (Mad) a white grape variety used in the production of a fortified wine of same name. Also used in the making of a white Port wine.

Verdelho (Mad) a medium dry fortified wine from the island of Madeira.

Verdelho Tinto (Mad) a black grape variety used in the production of Madeira wines.

Verdello (It) a white grape variety used in minor quantities to make Orvieto wine.

Verdenay (N.Z) a dry, bottle-fermented, sparkling wine produced from Chardonnay and Pinot noir grape varieties by Penfolds.

Verdencho (Sp) a white grape variety grown in the southern central regions.

Verdepino (Port) a noted Vinho Verde produced by C. Vinhas, S.A.R.L. P.O. Box 2422, Lisbon.

Verdesse (Fr) a white grape variety grown in Bugey, eastern France.

Verdet [Alain] (Fr) a noted producer of Crèmant de Bourgogne based in Arcrenat, Burgundy.

Verdi (Eng) a blend of spring water and fruit juices (including apple and kiwi fruit) with herbal extracts. Produced by Panda Drinks of Blandford Forum, Dorset.

Verdiana (It) a still and sparkling natural spring mineral water from Fonti di Ramiola S.p.A, Parma. Mineral contents (milligrammes per litre): Sodium 33mg/l, Calcium 88mg/l, Magnesium 24mg/l, Potassium 3.7mg/l, Bicarbonates 355mg/l. pH 7.5

Verdicchio (It) a white grape variety grown in the central regions of Italy. *see* Verdicchio dei Castelli di Jesi.

Verdicchio dei Castelli di Jesi (It) a D.O.C. (2000ha) white wine from The Marches region. Made from the Verdicchi (85% minimum), Malvasia and Trebbiano toscano grapes (maximum yield 100hl/ha). Sold in amphora-shaped bottles. Soil is of clay. D.O.C. also applies to naturally sparkling wines produced according to regulations. Also a Classico version.

Verdicchio dei Castelli di Jesi Classico (It) a D.O.C. Verdicchio dei Castelli di Jesi from the best vineyard zones within the D.O.C.

Verdicchio dei Castelli di Jesi Superiore (It) a D.O.C. Verdicchio dei Castelli di Jesi (maximum yield 75hl/ha). Riserva must have a minimum 13% alc by vol. And age for a minimum of two years (one year in bottle).

Verdicchio di Matelica (It) a D.O.C. (323ha) white wine from The Marches region Made from the Verdicchio (85% minimum), Malvasia and Trebbiano toscano grapes (maximum yield 95hl/ha). Soil: clay, chalk and silica. D.O.C. also applies to a sparkling wine made with musts or wines produced in accordance to regulations. A Riserva version is also produced.

Verdier (Fr) a French gentleman who, in 1850, perfected the Alambic Armagnaçais invented by Edouard Adam.

Verdil (Sp) a white grape variety grown in the Alicante, Valencia and Yecla regions. Also known as Merseguera, Verdosilla.

Verdiso (It) a white grape variety grown in the Veneto.

Verdiso (It) a white, dry wine of the Treviso province of Venetia made from a grape of the same name.

Verdlet (USA) a white hybrid grape variety also known as the Seibel 9110.

Verdoncho (Sp) a white grape variety grown in the La Mancha region. Is also known as the Verducho.

Verdosilla (Sp) an alternative name for the Merseguera grape.

Verdot (Fr) *see* Petit Verdot.

Verdot (USA) a red grape variety used for making red wines in California.

Verducho (Sp) a white grape variety grown in the La Mancha region. Is also known as the Verdoncho.

Verdun Estate (S.Afr) vineyards based in Stellenbosch. (Add): Verdun Kelders, Box 22, Vlottenburg 7604. Produces varietal wines.

Verdunnen (Hol) dilute.

Verduzzo (It) a white grape variety grown in the Veneto region.

Verduzzo Friulano (It) a variety of the white Verduzzo grape grown in the Friuli-Venezia-Giulia.

V

Verduzzo Trevigiano (It) a white grape variety grown in Veneto.

Vered (Isr) a Port-style, sweet dessert wine.

Vereinigte Hospitien (Ger) the German equivalent of the French Hospices de Beaune. Sited on the river Mosel at Trier.

Vereinigung der Charta Weingüter (Ger) an association of Charta wine estates. Founded in 1984 in Rheingau. Developed own regulations for producers. Bottle is recognised by 3 Roman arches on label. Must be 100% Riesling with sweetness levels between 9g/l and 13g/l and alcohol at least 0.5% by vol. higher than minimum outlined. Has drawn up list of Erstes Gewächs (first growths).

Verenberg (Ger) vineyard (Anb): Württemberg. (Ber): Württembergisch Unterland. (Gro): Lindelberg. (Vil): Verrenberg.

Vereots [Les] (Fr) a Premier Cru vineyard in the A.C. commune of Aloxe-Corton, Côte de Beaune, Burgundy.

Vergara (Sp) a Sherry and solera gran reserva brandy producer based in Jerez de la Frontera.

Vergelegen (S.Afr) a famous winery (established 1700) based in Stellenbosch, Western Cape. 1100ha. (Add): P.O. Box 17, Somerset West 7129, Stellenbosch. Grape varieties: Cabernet franc, Cabernet sauvignon, Chardonnay, Chenin blanc, Merlot, Muscat de frontignan, Sauvignon blanc, Sémillon, Shiraz. Labels: Mill Race Red, Schaapenberg, Vin de Florence. Website: http://www.vergelen.co.za

Vergelesses (Fr) an A.C. district of the Côte de Beaune which contains the Ile de Vergelesses and Les Basses-Vergelesses with an area of 9.75ha and 18.5ha respectively in the parish of Pernand. White wines are renowned for their finesse and distinction.

Verge Longue (Fr) the long shoot found on each arm of the guyot method of vine training.

Vergennes (USA) a lesser red grape variety of the *Vitis labrusca* used in the making of varietal wines.

Vergenoegd Estate (S.Afr) a winery (established 1773) based in Stellenbosch, Western Cape. 90ha. (Add): Vergenoegd Langoed (Faure and Faure) Box 1, Faure 7131. Grape varieties: Cabernet franc, Cabernet sauvignon, Merlot, Shiraz. Labels: Old Cape Colony, Terrace Bay. Website: http://www.vergenoegd.co.za

Vergenoegd Langoed (S.Afr) *see* Vergenoegd Estate.

Verger des Papes [Le] (Fr) the label of a Châteauneuf-du-Pape produced by Estevenin, Château des Papes, 84230 Châteauneuf-du-Pape, southern Rhône.

Vergers [Les] (Fr) a Premier Cru vineyard [part] in the commune of Chassagne-Montrachet, Côte de Beaune, Burgundy. 9.54 ha (white and red).

Vergine (It) a style of Marsala in Sicily, wine is kept 5 years in solera when it emerges lighter and drier.

Vergisson (Fr) a commune in the A.C. Pouilly-Fuissé, Mâconnais, Burgundy.

Vergnon [J.L.] (Fr) a Champagne producer. Vintage: 1995, 1996, 1998, 1999.

Vergoritis (Gre) a winery that is part of The General Wine Company. Grape varieties include: Rhoditis, Chardonnay, Sauvignon blanc, Gewürztraminer. *See also* Kyr-Yianni.

Verhaeghe Brouwerij (Bel) a brewery based in Vichte (established 1892). Brews: Kerstmis.

Verhoeven (Hol) a small jenever (gin) producing distillery.

Veri (Sp) a still natural spring mineral water from Bisaurri. Mineral contents (milligrammes per litre): Sodium 0.6mg/l, Calcium 65.9mg/l, Magnesium 2.4mg/l, Bicarbonates 190.3mg/l, Chlorides 0.6mg/l, Sulphates 13.3mg/l, Silicates 4.3mg/l.

Verín (Sp) a noted wine-producing town on the Portuguese border in Galicia. Produces high alcohol (14% by vol) red wines.

Verin Valley (Sp) a naturally sparkling mineral water from a valley of the same name in north-eastern Spain. Bottled by Fontenova.

Veri San Martin (Sp) a natural spring mineral water from San Martin de Veri. Mineral contents (milligrammes per litre): Sodium 0.6mg/l, Calcium 68.5mg/l, Magnesium 1.5mg/l, Potassium 0.3mg/l, Bicarbonates 200.1mg/l, Chlorides 1.1mg/l, Sulphates 12.5mg/l, Fluorides 0.1mg/l, Nitrates 1.5mg/l.

Veritas Winery (Austr) a winery based near Tanunda, Barossa Valley, South Australia. Produces varietal wines.

Verjuice (Eng) unripe grape juice.

Verjus (Fr) the juice from unripe grapes, usually the result of second or late flowering, very high in acidity.

Vermentino (It) a white grape variety grown in northern Italy and in Sardinia to produce light, dry wines. Known in Corsica as the Malvoisie de Corse and in Provence as Rolle.

Vermentino (It) a dry white wine from the Liguria region from a grape of same name.

Vermentino di Gallura (It) a D.O.C.G. white wine from north-central Sardinia. Made from the Vermentino grape. Area of production is Gallura and 17 communes in province of Sassari and 2 in the province of Nuoro. If minimum total alc. content is 14% by vol. then classed as Superiore.

Vermentino Ligure (It) a white wine made from Vermentino grape in the Liguna region. May be sparkling.

Vermont Pure (USA) a still natural spring mineral water from Vermont. Mineral contents (milligrammes per litre): Sodium 2mg/l, Calcium 41mg/l, Magnesium 4.2mg/l, Potassium 1.1mg/l, Chlorides 6.9mg/l, Sulphates 18mg/l, Nitrates 2.2mg/l. pH 7.2

Vermouté (Fr) vermouth.

Vermouth (Euro) a fortified wine flavoured with herbs, spices, barks and flowers by either infusion, maceration or distillation. Name derives from German 'wermut' (wormwood an ingredient of vermouth). Originally the French variety was white and dry, the Italian red and sweet. Now

V

firms from both countries as well as others produce all styles including sweet white, dry red and rosé. (Port) = vermut, (Sp) = vermut, (Tur) = vermut.

Vermouth Achampanado (Cktl) 40mls (⅓ gill) French vermouth placed over ice in a highball glass, 1 piece of lime peel, 1 teaspoon castor sugar, top with soda water and stir.

Vermouth Apéritif (Cktl) 40mls (⅓ gill) French vermouth, 40mls (⅓ gill) soda, 3 dashes brown Curaçao. Place the Curaçao in a wine goblet, add vermouth and soda and serve with a lump of ice.

Vermouth Cassis (Cktl) 35mls (1½ fl.ozs) dry vermouth, 5mls (¼ fl.oz) crème de cassis. Place in a 125mls (5fl.oz) goblet with 2 ice cubes, stir and top with mineral water.

Vermouth Cocktail (Cktl) ½ measure sweet vermouth, ½ measure French vermouth, dash Campari. Stir over ice, strain into a cocktail glass and top with a cherry.

Vermouth Curaçao (Cktl) 60mls (½ gill) French vermouth, 20mls (⅙ gill) Curaçao. Stir over ice, strain into an ice-filled highball glass and top with soda water.

Vermouth Highball (Cktl) as for Gin Highball using vermouth instead of gin. French = dry, Italian = sweet.

Vermouth Hour (Bra) *see* Copetin.

Vermut (Port)(Sp)(Tur) vermouth.

Verna (It) a sparkling natural spring mineral water from Chiusi della Verna. Mineral contents (milligrammes per litre): Sodium 6.5mg/l, Calcium 40.4mg/l, Magnesium 5.1mg/l, Potassium 1.1mg/l, Bicarbonates 133mg/l, Chlorides 6.4mg/l, Sulphates 18.5mg/l, Nitrates 0.5mg/l, Silicates 8.9mg/l. pH 7.7

Vernaccia (It) a white grape variety grown in Sardinia.

Vernaccia (It) a dry golden-yellow wine, high in alcohol with a Sherry taste. Unfortified, it has an almond blossom bouquet. Made from grapes of the same name. Drunk as an apéritif or digestive. Made in Sardinia.

Vernaccia del Campidano (It) *see* Vernaccia.

Vernaccia di Oristano (It) a white grape variety grown in Sardinia to make a wine of same name.

Vernaccia di Oristano (It) a D.O.C. white wine from Sardinia. Made from the Vernaccia di oristano grape. Aged for 2 years minimum in wood. If minimum alc. content is 15.5% by vol. and aged 3 years then classed Superiore. Liquoroso: fortified and aged 2 years in wood. Riserva: Superiore when wine has aged for minimum of 4 years in wood.

Vernaccia di San Gimignano (It) a white grape variety grown in the Tuscany region imported from Greece in the twelfth century.

Vernaccia di San Gimignano (It) a D.O.C.G. (from 1993 vintage/was created D.O.C. 1966) white wine from the Tuscany region. Made from the Vernaccia di san gimignano grapes (plus 10% maximum of Chardonnay, Malvasia and Trebbiano). Soil: clay, tufa and yellow sandstone. Vinification must occur within the production area (Siena). Wine is taken quickly off the skins. If aged minimum 1 year with 4 months in bottle then classed Riserva. D.O.C. applies to fortified wines according to specific regulation.

Vernaccia di Serrapetrona (It) a red grape variety grown in The Marches region. Also known as Vernaccia Nera.

Vernaccia di Serrapetrona (It) a D.O.C. red sparkling wine from the Marche. Production is limited to a few communes in the province of Macerata. Made from the Vernaccia di serrapetrona, Ciliegiolo, Montepulciano and Sangiovese grapes. Grapes are partially dried. Classed either as *amabile* (semi-sweet) or *dolce* (sweet).

Vernaccia Nera (It) an alternative name for Vernaccia di Serrapetrona.

Vernaccia Sarda (USA) a white grape variety grown in California to produce white wines.

Vernage (Eng) Chaucer's way of spelling Vernaccia wine from Tuscany in his 'Canterbury Tales'.

Vernatsch (It) a red grape variety grown in the Trentino-Alte-Adige region. Also known as the Schiave and the Trollinger in German.

Vernazza (It) one of the five towns in the Cinque Terre district of Liguna.

Vernet (Fr) a sparkling natural spring mineral water brand from the Ardèche. (Add): SGESM, Le Vernet 07380 Prades. Mineral contents (milligrammes per litre): Sodium 120mg/l, Calcium 29mg/l, Magnesium 17mg/l, Potassium 22mg/l, Bicarbonates 470mg/l, Chlorides 5.9mg/l, Sulphates 7mg/l, Fluorides 1.3mg/l, Nitrates <1mg/l.

Verneuil (Fr) a Cru Champagne village in the Canton de Dormans. District: Épernay.

Vernière (Fr) a sparkling natural spring mineral water from a source in Lanalou-lès-Bains. (Add): Source Vernière, Commune des Aires, 34240 Lamalou-les-Bains. Mineral contents (milligrammes per litre): Sodium 154mg/l, Calcium 190mg/l, Magnesium 72mg/l, Potassium 49mg/l, Bicarbonates 1170mg/l, Chlorides 18mg/l, Sulphates 158mg/l, Fluride <1mg/l. pH 6.0

Vernon [Admiral] (Eng) *see* Old Rummy.

Vernou (Fr) a commune in the Touraine district of the Loire. Produces A.C. Vouvray white and sparkling wines.

Véron (Fr) the local Loire name for the Breton (Cabernet franc) grape.

Véronique (Cktl) 1 measure Batida de Coco, 1 measure Cointreau, 1 measure Cognac, ½ measure vodka, ½ measure orange juice. Shake over ice, strain into a club goblet and dress with an orange slice.

Véronique Bottle (Fr) an elongated, flute bottle, usually clear in colour, with triple ring of ridges around the neck. Used for certain French white wines such as Tavel.

Verpelet (Hun) a noted wine-producing village in

Debrö that produces Hàrslevelü (a sweet white wine).

Verpoorten (Hol) producers of advocaat, made from free-range eggs.

Verre (Fr) glass/drinking glass.

Verre à Bordeaux (Fr) a bell-shaped glass for drinking red Bordeaux wines.

Verre à Eau (Fr) water glass.

Verre à INAO (Fr) the INAO glass, full-bowled with a tapered rim. Recommended as the most suitable glass for the tasting of wines.

Verre Ancien (Fr) antique drinking glass.

Vèrre à Pid (Ch.Isles) wine glass. *See also* Vèrre à Vin.

Vèrre à Vin (Ch.Isles) wine glass. *See also* Vèrre à Pid.

Verre à Vin (Fr) wine glass.

Verre à Vin du Moselle (Fr) the German mosel wine drinking glass.

Verre à Vin du Rhin (Fr) hock glass.

Verre Ballon (Fr) balloon glass/nosing glass.

Verre Couché (Fr) cut glass/crystal glass.

Verre de Cognac (Fr) a Cognac glass.

Verre Gravé (Fr) engraved drinking glass.

Verre Long (Fr) a speciality drink in the Cognac region of a highball-style glass filled with ice, measure of VSOP Cognac and topped with tonic water.

Verrenberg (Ger) village (Anb): Württemberg. (Ber): Württembergisch Unterland. (Gro): Lindelberg. (Vins): Goldberg, Verenberg.

Verre Ordinaire de Paris (Fr) the Paris goblet.

Verrerie (Fr) drinking glasses.

Verre Vaudois (Switz) a straight-sided drinking glass for wines.

Verrières (Fr) a commune in the Charente département whose grapes are classed Grande Champagne (Cognac).

Verruca (It) a natural spring mineral water brand.

Very Bitter (Eng) a term to describe a drink that is undrinkable because of the bitter eleents it contains (tannin, acid, etc.). (Port) = acérrimo.

Vers (Fr) a commune in the Mâconnais whose grapes may be used to produce Mâcon Supérieur.

Versa Cantina Sociale [La] S.p.A. (It) a producer of sparkling (metodo tradizionale) wines. (Add): Via Crispi 15, 27047 S. Maria della Versa, P.V.

Versailles Distillerie (S.Am) a noted rum distillery based in Guyana.

Versarmières (Fr) a vineyard in the commune of Fuissé, A.C. Pouilly-Fuissé, Mâconnais, Burgundy.

Verschnitt (Ger) the general term used for different spirits that are blended together, one spirit being dominant in flavour. *see* Rhum Verschnitt.

Verse 1 (Austr) a red (Cabernet sauvignon and Merlot blend) wine produced by the Brookland Valley Estate, Western Australia.

Verser (Fr) to pour.

Versetzte (Aus) a wine-based beverage. e.g. vermouths and aromatised wines.

Versetzte Wein (Aus) a fortified wine (one that has been manufactured).

Versieden (Aus) a term that describes the action of stopping a fermentation before all the sugar in the must has been converted into alcohol.

Versinthe (Fr) an absinthe-based liqueur from Provence.

Versterk (S.Afr) fortified (wine).

Vert (Fr) green/young wine.

Vert Doré (Fr) an alternative name used for the Pinot noir grape.

Vertex Reserve (S.Afr) the label for a red wine (Cabernet savignon, Shiraz) and white wine (Chardonnay) produced by the Bonnievale Cellar winery, Robertson, Western Cape.

Vertheuil (Fr) a wine-producing commune in the A.C. Haut-Médoc, Bordeaux.

Vertical Shoot Positioning (N.Z) *abbr*: VSP a method of vine training.

Vertical Tasting (Eng) a term to denote the tasting of wines of different vintages.

Vertical Vodka (Fr) a 40% alc by vol. vodka distilled by the Carthusian Brothers at Chartreuse.

Verticillium Wilt (Eng) a disease which affects hops, new wilt-resistant varieties have now almost eradicated it. i.e. Target.

Vertiente (S.Am) a natural spring mineral water from Bolivia. Mineral contents (milligrammes per litre): Calcium 24mg/l, Chlorides 77mg/l, Fluorides 1mg/l. pH 7.5

Vert Jus (Fr) lit: 'green juice', unripe grape juice, *see* Verjus.

Vert-la-Gravelle (Fr) a Cru Champagne village in the Canton de Vertus. District: Châlons.

Vertou (Fr) a noted wine village of Muscadet Sèvre et Maine, Loire.

Vertus (Fr) a canton in the district of Châlons in the Champagne region. Has the Premier Cru villages: Bergères-les-Vertus, Etrechy, Vertus and Villeneuve-Renneville.

Vertus (Fr) a Premier Cru Champagne village in the Canton de Vertus. District: Châlons.

Vertzami (Gre) a red grape variety grown mainly in central and western Greece.

Verulam Brewery (Eng) a brewery (established 1997). (Add): The Farmers Boy, 134 London Road, St. Albans, Hertfordshire AL1 1PQ. Brews: Special Bitter 3.8% alc by vol. I.P.A. 4% alc by vol. Farmer's Joy 4.5% alc by vol.

Verveine du Rouverge (Fr) a herb liqueur both green (dry) and yellow (sweet) based on the herb vervein, produced by Germain in southern France.

Verveine du Vélay (Fr) a digestive, herb liqueur made in both green and yellow versions. Based on the herb vervein, honey and brandy. Produced by Pages.

Verwaltung (Ger) administration (property).

Verwaltung der Staatsweinguter (Ger) a state wine domaine manager.

Veryan Vineyard (Eng) a vineyard based at Tregenna, Portloe, near Truro, Cornwall. Produes apple juice, mead and white wines.

Very Dry Gin (USA) the term on label to denote a gin that has a dry (botanical) taste.

Very Old (Fr) *abbr*: V.O. (Cognac), V.O. (Armagnac).

Very Old Tokay (Austr) a wine from the Brown

V

Brothers in Milawa, Victoria. A pale, tawny-coloured dessert wine.

Very Rare Age Inconnu (Fr) a fine Cognac brandy produced by Château Paulet.

Very Specially Recommended (Fr) *abbr*: V.S.R. awarded to certain merchants if the quality of their wines merits it.

Very Superior Extra Pale (Fr) *see* V.S.E.P.

Very Superior Old Pale (Fr) *see* V.S.O.P. (Cognac), V.S.O.P. (Armagnac).

Very Very Pale (Sp) *abbr*: V.V.P. colour grading for Manzanilla and Fino Sherries.

Verzenay (Fr) a Grand Cru Champagne village in the Canton de Verzy. District: Reims.

Verzy (Fr) a canton of the Reims district in the Champagne region. Has the Grand Cru villages: Beumont-sur-Vesle, Mailly-Champagne, Sillery, Verzenay and Verzy. Also the Premier Cru villages: Chigny-les-Roses, Ludes, Montbré, Puisieulx, Rilly-la-Montagne, Trépail, Villers-Aller and and Villers-Marmery.

Verzy (Fr) a Grand Cru Champagne village in the Canton de Verzy. District: Reims.

Vescovato (Fr) a noted red wine produced on the island of Corsica.

Vesevo (It) a winery based in the Avellino district in the Campania region. Produces: DOC Greco di Tufo.

Ves Heill (Scan) the old Norse toast for '*good health*'. *See also* Wassail.

Vesi Vatten (Fin) a natural spring mineral water. Mineral contents (milligrammes per litre): Sodium 1.8mg/l, Calcium 3mg/l, Potassium 0.32mg/l, Chlorides 1mg/l, Sulphates 3mg/l, Fluorides 0.1mg/l, Nitrates 0.8mg/l. pH 6.5

Vespaiola (It) a dry white wine from the Venetia region. Also known as Bresparolo.

Vespere (Fr) beetle. *see* Hanneton.

Vesper Martini (Cktl) 3 measures gin, 1 measure vodka, ½ measure French vermouth, shake over ice, strain into martini glass and decorate with a twist of lemon zest.

Vespétro (Fr) an ancient liqueur once produced in Grenoble from angelica, anise, coriander and fennel.

Vespitro (It) a herb flavoured liqueur made from sugar, brandy, aniseed, lemon, angelica, fennel and coriander.

Vespolina (It) a red grape variety.

Vesselle [Alain] (Fr) a Champagne producer. (Add): 8 Rue de Louvois, 51150 Bouzy, Tours-sur-Marne. Récoltants-manipulants. Produces non-vintage wines.

Vesselle [Georges] (Fr) a Champagne producer. 10ha. (Add): 4 Rue Victor-Hugo, B.P. 15, 51150 Bouzy, Tours-sur-Marne. Produces a Champagne from 100% Pinot noir- Brut, Rosé, Prestige rosé, demi-sec, also Bouzy rouge, La Juline (a blend of several vintage Champagnes). 100% Grand Cru.

Vestfyen Bryggeri (Den) a brewery. (Add): Fåborgvej 4, Assens, DK-5610. Brews a range of beers and lagers. Website: http://www.bryggerietvestfyen.dk

Vesuvio (Cktl) ⅔ measure Bacardi White Label, ⅓ measure lemon juice, ⅕ measure Italian vermouth, ½ egg white, 2 dashes gomme syrup. Shake well over ice and strain into an ice-filled old-fashioned glass.

Vesuvio (It) a dry red wine from the foot of Vesuvius in Campania. 11% alc by vol. it is normally sparkling. White version is also produced.

Vesuvio (It) a sparkling natural spring mineral water from Napoli. Mineral contents (milligrammes per litre): Sodium 172mg/l, Calcium 78.4mg/l, Magnesium 142.9mg/l, Potassium 300mg/l, Bicarbonates 952.8mg/l, Chlorides 369mg/l, Sulphates 220.2mg/l, Fluorides 6.4mg/l, Nitrates 9.5mg/l, Silicates 54.7mg/l, Oxygen 5.5mg/l. pH 6.7

Veterano (Sp) a 3 year old solera brandy produced by Osborne. 37% alc by vol. *See also* Tres Ceros.

Vetrice (It) a Chianti Putto producer based in Tuscany.

Vétroz (Switz) a wine-producing village based near Sion in the Valais. Produces Fendant wines.

Vetter (Ger) a noted liqueur and aquavit producer based in Wunsiedel.

Veuve Aimot Cuvée Haute Tradition (Fr) a brut méthode traditionelle A.C. sparkling wine from the Anjou-Saumur district of the Loire. Produced by Maison Elizabeth Amiot which is owned by Martini & Rossi.

Veuve Ambal (Fr) a wine-producer based in Burgundy. Noted for méthode traditionelle sparkling Burgundies.

Veuve Clicquot Ponsardin (Fr) a Champagne producer. 286ha. (Add): 12 Rue du Temple, 51100 Reims. A Grande Marque. Produces vintage and non-vintage wines. (La Grande Dame: de luxe vintage cuvée and Clicquot Rosé: vintage rosé, Rich Réserve. Vintages: 1904, 1906, 1911, 1915, 1919, 1920, 1921, 1923, 1926, 1928, 1929, 1937, 1942, 1943, 1945, 1947, 1949, 1952, 1953, 1955, 1959, 1961, 1962, 1964, 1966, 1969, 1970, 1973, 1975, 1976, 1979, 1980, 1982, 1983, 1985, 1988, 1989, 1990, 1995, 1996, 1998, 1999, 2000. *see* Grand Dame (La).

Veuve Clicquot Rich Réserve (Fr) a vintage Champagne produced from a blend of fifteen Premier Crus and Grand Crus from the Montagne de Reims, Vallée de la Marne, Côtes des Blancs. 64% Pinot noir, 33% Chardonnay, 3% Pinot meunier grapes.

Veuve Devaux (Fr) a Champagne producer. (Add): Domaine de Villeneuve, 10110 Bar-sur-Seine. Coopérative-manipulant. 800 growers own 1000ha. Produce vintage and non-vintage wines.

Veuve de Vernay (Fr) brut and demi-sec sparkling wines from the Bordeaux region. Produced by the tank method.

Veuve J. Goudoulin (Fr) an Armagnac producer. (Add): Domaine du Bigor, Courrensan, 32330 Gondrin. 20ha. in the Bas Armagnac.

Vevey Festival (Switz) a famous wine festival held in the town of Vevey near Montreaux since the seventeenth century. Occur every 25–30 years. The last was in 1977. *see* Fête des Vignerons.

Vézelay (Fr) a red and white wine area in Avallon, Yonne département.

Vézélise Brasserie (Fr) a brewery that is part of the Stella Artois Brasserie of Belgium.

Vezien [Marcel] (Fr) a Champagne producer. (Add): 68 Grande Rue, 10110 Celles-sur-Ource.

Vhrunsko (Slav) highest quality wine.

Viader Vineyards (USA) a 7.5ha bio-dynamic vineyard based at Howell Mountain in the Napa Valley, California. (Add): 1120 Deer Park Road, P.O.Box 280, Deer Park CA 94576-0280. Grape varieties: Cabernet sauvignon, Cabernet franc. Website: http://www.viader.com 'E'mail: delia@viader.com

Viagra (Eng) a 6.9% alc by vol. cask-conditioned ale brewed using malted rye by Poole Brewery, Poole.

Viagère [En] (Fr) a term to denote a system of acquiring vines, guaranteeing the owner rent for life.

Viana (Port) the original port from which Port wine was shipped to England. Is 60 miles north of Oporto.

Viano Winery (USA) a winery based in Martinez, Contra Costa County, California. Grape varieties: Barbera, Cabernet sauvignon and Zinfandel. Produces varietal wines.

Vibert Chasselas (Fr) a white grape variety which is suitable for wine production and eating.

Vibrisat (Sp) a term used to describe wines that are macerated on the skins. *See also* Vi verge: 'off the skins'.

Vibrona (Eng) an alcoholic British tonic wine 17% alc by vol. Produced by Vine Products Ltd., Kingston-Upon-Thames, London.

Vicar [The] (Austr) a red wine produced by Chapel Hill Winery, McLaren Vale, South Australia.

Vicar's Revenge (Eng) a 4.2% alc by vol. summer ale brewed by Burtonwood in Warrington as part of their Masterclass range.

Vicars Ruin (Eng) a 4.4% alc by vol. ale brewed by The Church End Brewery Ltd., Warwickshire.

V-Ice (Eng) *abbr*: **V**odka **I**ce from GBL, Chesterfield. A PPS.

Vicente (Sp) a bodega based near Sarragossa, Aragón. Noted for fine Cariñena wines.

Viceroy (S.Afr) the brand-name of a 10 y.o. liqueur 43% alc by vol. brandy produced by Castle Wine and Green.

Vichon Winery (Fr) the label for a range of Vin de Pays d'Oc wines produced by Mondavi of California. Grape varieties: Cabernet sauvignon, Merlot, Syrah, Sauvignon blanc and Viognier.

Vichy Boussange (Fr) a sparkling mineral water from Vichy.

Vichy Catalan (Sp) a sparkling natural spring mineral water from Caldes de Malavella, Girona. Mineral contents (milligrammes per litre): Sodium 1110mg/l, Calcium 54.1mg/l, Magnesium 9.2mg/l, Potassium 48mg/l, Bicarbonates 2135mg/l, Chlorides 601.5mg/l,

Sulphates 47.3mg/l, Fluorides 7.3mg/l, Nitrates <1mg/l, Silicates 76.8mg/l, Strontium 1.44mg/l, Lithium 1.3mg/l. pH 6.82

Vichy-Célestins (Fr) a sparkling natural spring mineral water (established 100AD) from Vichy. Eau Mineral Naturalle designation. (Add): Compagne Fermière de Vichy, 1-3, Avenue Eisenhower, 03200 Vichy. Mineral contents (milligrammes per litre): Sodium 1172mg/l, Calcium 103mg/l, Magnesium 10mg/l, Potassium 66mg/l, Bicarbonates 2989mg/l, Chlorides 235mg/l, Sulphates 138mg/l, Nitrates 2mg/l, Fluoride 5mg/l. pH 6.8 *see* Vichy Water.

Vichy Classique (Fr) a sparkling natural spring mineral water from Vichy. Mineral contents (milligrammes per litre): Sodium 30-70mg/l, Calcium 35-70mg/l, Magnesium 30-50mg/l, Potassium 90-120mg/l, Bicarbonates 200-400mg/l, Chlorides 120-250mg/l.

Vichy Grande Grille (Fr) a medicinal water from Vichy.

Vichy Hôpital (Fr) a medicinal water from Vichy.

Vichy Saint-Yorre (Fr) a naturally sparkling mineral water bottled at Saint-Yorre. Source: Royale Bassin de Vichy.

Vichy Water (Eng) the English name for Vichy-Célestins water.

Vickers (Austr) the brand-name for a gin produced by the United Distillers.

Vicomte Champagne Liqueur (Fr) a liqueur produced by the De Castellane Champagne house.

Vicomte d'Aumelas (Fr) a Vin de Pays area in the Hérault département, southern France.

Vicomte de Castellane (Fr) a Champagne producer based in Épernay. Produces vintage and non-vintage wines and liqueurs. *see* Vicomte Champagne Liqueur.

Vicomte Stephane de Castelbajac (Fr) a 12 year old Cognac produced by Logis de la Montagne.

Vic-sur-Seille (Fr) a wine-producing area in the Vins de la Moselle, Lorraine. Produces Vin gris.

Victor Cocktail (Cktl) ½ measure sweet vermouth, ¼ measure dry gin, ¼ measure Cognac. Shake over ice and strain into a cocktail glass.

Victor Hugo Brandy (USA) the brand-name of a brandy produced by the California Wine Association, Delano, California 40% alc by vol.

Victoria (Austr) a wine state in southern Australia. Areas include: Glenrowan/Milawa, Goulburn Valley, Great Western, Mildara, Rutherglen, Yarra Valley.

Victoria (Mex) a highly-carbonated 'clara' beer brewed by the Modelo Brewery in Mexico City.

Victoria Beer (Austr) a 4.9% alc by vol. light, straw coloured canned lager brewed by the Carlton and United Brewery in Melbourne.

Victoria Bitter (Eng) a 3.6% alc by vol. bitter ale brewed by the Earl Soham Brewery, Suffolk.

Victoria Brewery (Eng) a brewery (established 1981) based in Ware, Hertfordshire (closed 1990). Brewed cask-conditioned Special 1043 O.G. Bitter 1037 O.G. and Hellfire 1063 O.G.

Victoria Falls (Cktl) pour 1 measure orange juice over ice in highball glass. Add 1 measure lemonade, 1 squeeze of lemon juice, 3 drops Angostura and top with mineral water.

Victoria Heilwasser (Ger) a natural spring mineral water brand. Mineral contents (milligrammes per litre): Sodium 800mg/l, Calcium 70mg/l, Magnesium 40mg/l, Potassium 10mg/l, Bicarbonates 1610mg/l, Chlorides 360mg/l, Sulphates 290mg/l.

Victoria Regina (Sp) a brand of Oloroso Sherry produced by Diez Merito (part of their Diez Hermanos range).

Victoria Sour (Cktl) 30mls (¼ gill) whisky, 30mls (¼ gill) Sherry, dash rum, dash pineapple syrup, dash apricot syrup. Shake well over ice, strain into a wine glass and top with a dash of soda water.

Victory (Thai) a VSOP brandy 40% alc by vol. produced from Chenin blanc grapes grown at Château de Loei by CPK International.

Victory Ale (Eng) a rich ale 1070 O.G. brewed by the Paradise Brewery in Hayle, Cornwall.

Victory Ale (Eng) a 5.9% alc by vol. strong draught or bottled premium ale brewed by George Bateman & Son in Wainfleet, Lincolnhire to celebrate the defeat of two take-over bids.

Victory Ale (Wal) a seasonal ale brewed by S.A. Brain & Cº. Ltd. in Cardiff.

Victory Collins (Cktl) 25mls (1fl.oz) vodka, 50mls (2fl.ozs) grape juice, 50mls (2fl.ozs) lemon juice, 2 dashes gomme syrup. Shake over ice, strain into an ice-filled highball glass and dress with a slice of orange.

Victory Wines (N.Z) a small winery at 774 Main Road South, Stoke, Nelson, South Island. 1ha. Grape varieties: Cabernet sauvignon, Chasselas, Gamay.

Victualler (Eng) lit: 'purveyor of food', a licensed victualler is a purveyor of food and alcoholic beverages.

Vid (Sp) vine.

Vidal-Fleury (Fr) a négociant-éleveur based in the Rhône.

Vidal Ice Wine (Can) a dessert wine produced by Reif Estate, Niagara.

Vidal Winery (N.Z) a winery. (Add): 913 St. Aubyn Street, P.O. Box 48, Hastings, Hawkes Bay, North Island. 125ha. Grape varieties: Cabernet sauvignon, Chardonnay, Chenin blanc, Gewürztraminer, Merlot, Müller-Thurgau, Muscat, Pinot noir, Sémillon and Sauvignon blanc. Produces varietal wines and a unique 100% Cabernet sauvignon sparkling wine.

Vidange (Fr) the gap between the wine and the cask top. If allowed, can cause acescence (spoilage). See also Ullage.

Vida Nova (Port) a red wine (Aragonez, Mourvèdre, Syrah and Trajadura blend) produced by the Quinta do Moinho, Algarve.

Vide (Port) vine shoot.

Vidiella (S.Am) a red grape variety grown in Uruguay.

Vidigueira (Port) one of five D.O.C. wine districts in Alentejo, based south of Évora. Produces mainly white wines.

Vidonia (Sp) a popular eighteenth century, sweet dessert wine from the island of Tenerife (popular in England).

Vidueno (Sp) a white wine produced in the Canary Islands.

Vidure (Fr) an alternative name for the Cabernet franc grape.

Vie (Rum) vine.

Vie [La] (S.Afr) a low-alcohol, pétillant, Muscat wine made by the Stellenbosch Farmers' Winery. Label: Jules Grillet et Fils.

Vie de Romans (It) a winery based in Mariano del Friuli in the Friuli-Venezia-Guilia region. Grape varieties include: Chardonnay, Malvasia istriana, Pinot grigio, Sauvignon blanc, Tocai. Labels: Dessimis, Isonzo, Istriana dis Cumieris. Website: http://www.viederomans.it

Vieil (Fr) old. See also Vieille, Vieux.

Vieille (Fr) old. See also Vieil, Vieux.

Vieille Cure (Fr) a herb liqueur made at Cenon in the Gironde. Has a base of Armagnac and Cognac. Produced by Intermarque, Gironde 43% alc by vol.

Vieille Eau de Vie de Marc du Château Grancy (Fr) s fine Bourgogne marc made by Louis Latour which is matured for 4–5 years in oak casks.

Vieille Ferme [La] (Fr) a vineyard in the A.C. Côtes du Ventoux, southern France.

Vieille Récolte Fine (Egy) a brandy made from local grapes by the Egyptian Vineyards and Distilleries Cº.

Vieille Rélique (Fr) a 15 year old Armagnac produced by Samalens.

Vieille Réserve (Fr) a class of fine old Cognac or Armagnac with a minimum of 5 years of age.

Vieille Salme [La] (Bel) an 8.3% alc by vol. top-fermented, bottled special beer brewed by d'Achouffe in Achouffe-Wibrin.

Vieilles Vignes (Fr) old vines (which give the finest fruit). (Austr) = old block vines, (Ger) = alte reben, (Port) = vinhas velhas, (S.Afr) = old bush vines, (Sp) = viñas viejas.

Vieilles Vignes Françaises (Fr) a rare vintage 'blanc de noirs' Champagne made from ungrafted Pinot noir vines by Bollinger from two small vineyards in Aÿ and Bouzy. Is also a general term for un-grafted vines in the New World.

Vieilli au Tonneau (Fr) aged in wood (cask).

Vieillissement (Fr) an exclusive Corvoisier Cognac sold in a decanter, a rare blend of Cognacs (the oldest dates from 1892) only 300 produced.

Vieillissement Exceptionnellement Prolonge (Fr) abbr: V.E.P. superior green and yellow Chartreuse, 12 year old, only available in Voiron or Fauchon in Paris. Aged 8 years minimum in barrel.

Viejas Reservas (Sp) a grade of old fine matured wines of the Rioja region.

Viejisimo (Sp) very old.

Viejo (Sp) old.

Viejo Roble (Chile) a dry white wine produced by Undurraga.

Vien de Nus (It) a red grape variety grown in Valle d'Aosta.

Vienna (Aus) a city of Gumpoldskirchen, gives its name to a sweet white wine. *see* Wien.

Vienna (Aus) a full-bodied, malty, copper coloured lager, the style used at the Oktoberfest. Known as Marzen in Germany.

Vienna Lager (Aus) *see* Steffl.

Vienne (Fr) a noted wine-producing département which includes part of Saumur, Anjou-Saumur, Loire.

Vienne (Fr) a wine-producing city in Dauphiny, Isère département, south-eastern France. Produces red and white wines.

Viennese Apricot 'Old Glory' Liqueur (Aus) a liqueur made by the firm of J. Zwack using whole apricots, fermented and distilled 34% alc by vol.

Viennese Café (Aus) a coffee-flavoured liqueur made by the firm of J. Zwack.

Viennese Coffee (Aus) a blend of coffees which have had roasted figs added, gives the coffee a stronger, sweeter taste with a more bitter flavour.

Viennese Iced Coffee (Aus) iced coffee with a swirl of whipped cream on top or a topping of coffee ice cream.

Viennese Pear (Aus) a pear liqueur made by the firm of J. Zwack 34% alc by vol.

Viennese Velvet (Aus) into a highball glass place some vanilla ice cream. Pour on some double strength hot black coffee, top with whipped cream, grated chocolate and serve with straws.

Viénot [Charles] (Fr) a négociant-éleveur based at Nuits-Saint-Georges in the Burgundy region. (Add): 5 Quai Dumorey, 21700, Nuits-Saint-Georges. Owned by Boisset.

Vier (Ger) a 5% alc by vol bottled and 4% alc vy vol draught premium pilsener lager beer brewed by the Beck's Brauerei, Bremen.

Viertel (Ger) a special glass, shaped like a tulip with a handle like a punch glass. Quarter litre capacity. Used in Württemberg, west Germany.

Viertelstück (Ger) a round cask holding 300litres.

Viesch (Switz) a dry white wine produced in the upper Rhône Valley.

Vietti (It) a noted wine-producer based in the village of Castiglione Falletto, Piemonte.

Vieux (Fr) old. *See also* Vieil, Vieille.

Vieux Cahors (Fr) lit: 'old Cahors', a Cahors wine that has been kept to mature. Has no legal meaning but denotes aged in wood for 3 years.

Vieux-Château [Le] (Fr) a vineyard in the A.C. commune of Montagny, Côte Chalonnaise, Burgundy.

Vieux-Château-Boënot (Fr) a part of Château Bel-Air in the A.C. Pomerol, Bordeaux.

Vieux-Château-Bourgueneuf (Fr) a vineyard in the commune of Pomerol. A.C. Pomerol, Bordeaux.

Vieux-Château-Calon (Fr) a vineyard in the commune of Montagne-Saint-Émilion. A.C. Montagne-Saint-Émilion, Bordeaux 5ha.

Vieux Château-Certan (Fr) a vineyard in the commune of Pomerol. A.C. Pomerol. 13ha. Grape varieties: Cabernet franc, Cabernet sauvignon, Malbec.

Vieux-Château-Chauvin (Fr) a vineyard in the A.C. Saint-Émilion, Bordeaux 4ha.

Vieux-Château-Cloquet (Fr) a vineyard in the commune of Pomerol. A.C. Pomerol, Bordeaux 2ha.

Vieux-Château-Fortin (Fr) a vineyard in the A.C. Saint-Émilion, Bordeaux 6ha.

Vieux Château Gaubert (Fr) an A.C. Graves, Bordeaux. Grape varieties : Sauvignon blanc 25%, Sémillon 75%.

Vieux-Château-Goujon (Fr) a vineyard in the commune of Montagne-Saint-Émilion. A.C. Montagne-Saint-Émilion, Bordeaux 2ha.

Vieux-Château-la-Beyesse (Fr) a vineyard in the commune of Puisseguin-Saint-Émilion. A.C. Puisseguin-Saint-Émilion, Bordeaux 4ha.

Vieux Château Landon (Fr) vineyard in (Add): Bégadan 33340 Médoc. Cru Bourgeois A.C. Médoc. (Com): Bégadan. Grape varieties: Cabernet franc, Cabernet sauvignon, Malbec and Merlot.

Vieux-Château-l'Angélus (Fr) a vineyard in the commune of Pomerol. A.C. Pomerol, Bordeaux 1ha.

Vieux-Château-Mazerat (Fr) a part of Clos Haut-Mazerat in the A.C. Saint-Émilion, Bordeaux.

Vieux Château Negrit (Fr) a vineyard in the commune of Montagne-Saint-Émilion. A.C. Montagne-Saint-Émilion, Bordeaux 10ha.

Vieux-Château-Palon (Fr) a vineyard in the commune of Montagne-Saint-Émilion. A.C. Montagne-Saint-Émilion, Bordeaux 5ha.

Vieux-Château-Peymouton (Fr) a vineyard in the A.C. Saint-Émilion, Bordeaux 3ha.

Vieux-Château-Peyrou (Fr) a vineyard in the A.C. Saint-Émilion, Bordeaux 9ha.

Vieux-Château-Tropchaud (Fr) a vineyard in the commune of Pomerol. A.C. Pomerol, Bordeaux 2ha.

Vieux Chemin (Fr) the label used by Arnoux (Antonia et Fils), Quartier de Plaestor, 84100 Rhône for their Châteauneuf-du-Pape. *See also* Domaine de la Villeneuve.

Vieux Clos (Fr) a vineyard in the commune of Avensa. A.C. Médoc, Bordeaux. Bourgeois Supérieur.

Vieux-Domaine-Menuts (Fr) a vineyard in the A.C. Saint-Émilion, Bordeaux 3ha.

Vieux Donjon [Le] (Fr) the label of a Châteauneuf-du-Pape produced by Michel (Lucien), 9 Ave. St. Joseph, 84230 Châteauneuf-du-Pape, Rhône.

Vieux Mas de Papes (Fr) the label of a Châteauneuf-du-Pape produced by Brunier Frères, 2 Ave. Louis Pasteur, 84230 Châteauneuf-du-Pape, Rhône. *See also* Domaine de la Rocquette.

Vieux Pays (Switz) lit: 'old country', the other name for the Valais canton.

Vieux Rafiot (Cktl) ⅓ measure Mandarine Napoléon,

⅔ measure Cognac. Stir over ice, strain into a balloon glass and decorate with a slice of tangerine.

Vieux Réserve du Vigneron (Fr) a 30 year old plus Cognac produced by Destreilles.

Vieux Rouge du Valais (Switz) a red Vin de Pays wine from the Valais.

Vieux Rum (W.Ind) the term given to a rum that has been aged for more than 6 years. *see* Liqueur Rum.

Vieux Temps (Bel) a 5% alc by vol. amber-coloured, top-fermented, bottled Belgian ale brewed by St. Guilbert Brasserie, Mont-Saint-Guilbert.

Viewpoint of the German Wine-Route (Ger) *see* Aussichtsterrasse der Deutschen Weinstrasse.

Views Land Cº. (USA) a winery based in Sonoma County, California. Grape varieties: Cabernet sauvignon, Chardonnay and Gewürztraminer. Produces varietal wines.

Vif (Fr) a lively, brisk wine.

V Generation (S.Afr) the label for red (Cabernet sauvignon) and white (Chenin blanc) wine produced by the Cederberg Private Cellar winery, Olifants River, Western Cape.

Vigevanese (It) producers of Millefiori liqueur.

Vigezzo [1] (It) a still natural spring mineral water from Malesco (NO), Piemonte. Mineral contents (milligrammes per litre): Sodium 3.5mg/l, Calcium 5.7mg/l, Magnesium 3.4mg/l, Potassium 1.2mg/l, Bicarbonates 33.7mg/l, Chlorides 1.1mg/l, Sulphates 4.7mg/l, Fluorides 0.2mg/l, Nitrates 3.4mg/l, Silicates 16.7mg/l. pH 8.1

Vigezzo [2] (It) a still natural spring mineral water from Malesco (NO), Piemonte. Mineral contents (milligrammes per litre): Sodium 2.39mg/l, Calcium 3.11mg/l, Magnesium 0.72mg/l, Potassium 0.83mg/l, Bicarbonates 13.72mg/l, Chlorides 1.16mg/l, Sulphates 2.22mg/l, Fluorides 0.06mg/l, Nitrates 2.03mg/l, Silicates 12.84mg/l. pH 6.8

Vigiriega (Sp) a white grape variety grown in the Vino de la Tierra of Contraviesa-Alpujarra, Andalucía. Also known as Vijiriego.

Vigna (It) the Italian equivalent to the French Cru (vineyard).

Vigna Baccana (It) a vineyard based in the Friuli, nothern Italy that produces Sauvignon blanc wines.

Vigna Cicala (It) a Cru vineyard (3ha) based in the DOCG Barolo, Monforte d'Alba, Piemonte. Owned by Poderi Aldo Conterno. Soil: limestone and sand.

Vignacourt (Austr) a winery based in Swan Valley, Western Australia.

Vigna d'Alceo (It) a noted single red wine IGT vineyard based in Tuscany.

Vigna del Lago (It) *see* Zamò.

Vignaioli Piemontesi (It) producer of Moscato d'Asti Spumante in the Piemonte region.

Vignaiolo (It) wine grower. *See also* Viticolture.

Vignamaggio (It) a winery. (Add): Via Petriolo, 5 50022 Greve in Chianti (FI). Noted for D.O.C.G. Castello di Monna Lisa (Chianti Classico Riserva) and Vin Santo. Website: http://www.vignamaggio.com 'E'mail: info@vignamaggio.com

Vigna Pedale (It) a 100% Negro di Troia wine produced by Torrevento in Castel del Monte, Puglia.

Vigna Rionda (It) a cru vineyard (10ha) based in the DOCG Barolo near Serralunga, Piemonte. Grape variety: Nebbiolo. Owned by 6 growers and has limestone soil.

Vigna Spuntali (It) *see* Zamò.

Vigne (Fr) vine.

Vigneau et Chevreau (Fr) a noted sparkling Vouvray producer based at Chancay, Touraine, Loire.

Vigne de l'Enfant Jésus [La] (Fr) *see* Grèves (Les).

Vigne-Devant [La] (Fr) a vineyard in the A.C. commune of Montagny, Côte Chalonnaise, Burgundy.

Vigne di Zamò [Le] (It) a red wine produced in Friuli-Venezia-Giulia by Zamò from Pignolo grapes.

Vignée [La] (Fr) the brand-name for red and white wines from Bouchard Père et Fils in Burgundy.

Vigne en Fleur (Fr) lit: 'vine in flower', denotes new spirit after the wine has been distilled for Cognac. The spirit as it matures in cask.

Vigneron (Fr) a vine grower who may be working for himself or not.

Vigneron à Moitié (Fr) a vine grower who does not work for himself but receives part of the production for tending the vineyard.

Vigneronnage (Fr) in Burgundy is to a vineyard what a tenant farmer is to an agricultural estate. Used only in the Beaujolais.

Vignerons de Chusclan (Fr) a co-operative winery based in the village of Chusclan, Côtes-du-Rhône-Villages, Vaucluse. Labels include: Espirit du Rhône, Les Monticauts.

Vignerons de Franschhoek (S.Afr) a body based in the Franschhoek Valley east of Stellenbosch, Western Cape. Founded due to the Huguenot refugees who settled there to escape persecution in France. The vignerons planted vines there.

Vignerons de Oisly et Thesée (Fr) a noted co-operative based in the Touraine district of the Loire.

Vignerons de Saint Vincent (Fr) a wine fraternity started in 1950 for the Mâconnais and Chalonnaise. Meets at Château d'Aîné in the Mâcon.

Vignerons Reserve (S.Afr) the label for a white wine (Chardonnay) produced by the Glen Wood winery, Franschhoek, Western Cape.

Vignerons Réunis des Côtes de Buzet (Fr) a partnership (established 1955) of 150 vintners in Buzet. Co-operative which now has over 500 members.

Vignes Blanches [Les] (Fr) a vineyard in the A.C. commune of Montagny, Côte Chalonnaise, Burgundy.

Vignes Blanches [Les] (Fr) a wine-producing village in the commune of Fuissé, A.C. Pouilly-Fuissé, Mâcon, Burgundy.

V

Vignes-Couland [Les] (Fr) a vineyard in the A.C. commune of Montagny, Côte Chalonnaise, Burgundy.

Vignes-Derrières [Les] (Fr) a vineyard in the A.C. commune of Montagny, Côte Chalonnaise, Burgundy.

Vignes-Dessous [Les] (Fr) a vineyard in the A.C. commune of Montagny, Côte Chalonnaise, Burgundy.

Vignes-du-Puits [Les] (Fr) a vineyard in the A.C. commune of Montagny, Côte Chalonnaise, Burgundy.

Vignes-du-Soleil [Les] (Fr) a vineyard in the A.C. commune of Montagny, Côte Chalonnaise, Burgundy.

Vignes Franches [Les] (Fr) a Premier Cru vineyard in the A.C. commune of Beaune, Côte de Beaune, Burgundy 8.56ha.

Vignes Hautes (Fr) a method of vine training used in the Côte d'Or, Burgundy. Vines are widely spaced and are grown very high to obtain the maximum sunshine.

Vignes-Longues [Les] (Fr) a vineyard in the A.C. commune of Montagny, Côte Chalonnaise, Burgundy.

Vignes-Rondes [Les] (Fr) a Premier Cru vineyard in the A.C. commune of Monthélie, Côte de Beaune, Burgundy 2.7ha.

Vignes-Saint-Pierre [Les] (Fr) a vineyard in the A.C. commune of Montagny, Côte Chalonnaise, Burgundy.

Vignes-sur-le-Clou (Fr) a vineyard in the A.C. commune of Montagny, Côte Chalonnaise, Burgundy.

Vigneto (It) vineyard.

Vigneto Bucerchiale (It) a Cru vineyard (12ha) in the D.O.C.G. Chianti Rùfina, Tuscany. Owned by the Selvapiana winery.

Vigneto Corda della Briccolina (It) a D.O.C.G. Barolo from the commune of Serralunga d'Alba and produced by the Beni di Batasiolo winery.

Vigneto Rancia (It) a Cru vineyard (7ha) based in the D.O.C.G. Chianti Classico, Castelnuovo Beradenga, Tuscany. Owned by Felsina it has clay and sand soils.

Vignoble (Fr) vineyard.

Vignobles a Double Fin (Fr) the process by which producers of Cognac can decide what to do with their grapes after the harvest (selecting the best for Cognac and the remainder into a variety of products including: Vin de Pays/Pineau de Charentes/Vin de Table/Vin Mousseaux/Marc). System to cease in 2006 with new E.C. regulations.

Vìgnole Riserva (It) an oak aged Chianti Classico wine produced by Tenuta di Vignole, Via Case Sparse 12, 50020 Panzano, Greve (FI).

Vignolles (Fr) a commune in the Charente département whose grapes are used in Petite Champagne (Cognac).

Vigorello (It) a red I.G.T. wine produced from 70% Sangiovese and 30% Cabernet sauvignon grapes by San Felice in Tuscany.

Vigorous (Eng) the term used to describe wines with a lively, healthy, full flavour.

Viguerie du Madiran [La] (Fr) a wine society based in the Jurançon district, south-western France.

Viguerie Royale du Jurançon (Fr) a wine fraternity based in the Jurançon district, south-western France.

Viile (Rum) vineyard

Vijiriego (Sp) a white grape variety grown in the Vino de la Tierra of Contraviesa-Alpujarra, Andalucía. Also known as Vigiriega.

Viking (Cktl) 10mls (½fl.oz) aquavit, 10mls (½fl.oz) lime juice, 35mls (1½fl.ozs) Swedish Punsch. Shake over ice and strain into an old-fashioned glass 'on the rocks'.

Viking (Eng) a 3.8% alc by vol. ale brewed by the Rudgate Brewery Ltd., North Yorkshire.

Viking (S.Afr) the brand-name of a brandy produced by Huguenot Wine Farmers.

Viking Ale (Eng) an old name of a Devenish Brewery lager beer.

Viking Ale (Eng) a pale ale 1042 O.G. brewed and bottled by the Morland Brewery in Abingdon, Oxfordshire.

Viking Bitter (Eng) a cask-conditioned bitter 1043 O.G. brewed by the Rose and Crown home-brew public house in York. Owned by the Tetley Brewery.

Viking Brewery (Eng) a micro-brewery. (Add): Thanet, Kent. Brews: Thor's Thunder 4.4% alc by vol. Viking 3.9% alc by vol.

Vikos (Gre) a natural spring mineral water from Vikos. Mineral contents (milligrammes per litre): Sodium 2.1mg/l, Calcium 101.8mg/l, Magnesium 0.7mg/l, Potassium 0.8mg/l, Bicarbonates 297.6mg/l, Chlorides 8.9mg/l, Sulphates 2.4mg/l, Nitrates 2.5mg/l. pH 7.62

Viktoria (S.Afr) the label for a red wine (Cabernet franc, Cinsaut and Shiraz blend) produced by the Tulbagh Mountain Vineyards winery, Tulbagh, Western Cape.

Viktoriaberg (Ger) a famous vineyard of the village of Hochheim in the Rheingau. Named after Queen Victoria. see Königin Viktoriaberg and Hock.

Vila (Euro) a still natural spring mineral water from Vilica Bunaric, Bosnia and Herzegovina. Mineral contents (milligrammes per litre): Sodium 34.5mg/l, Calcium 153.91mg/l, Magnesium 22.84mg/l, Potassium 7.82mg/l, Bicarbonates 488mg/l, Chlorides 42.23mg/l, Sulphates 70mg/l, Strontium 2.02mg/l.

Viladrau (Sp) a natural spring mineral water from Viladrau, Girona. Mineral contents (milligrammes per litre): Sodium 9.6mg/l, Calcium 24.8mg/l, Magnesium 4.4mg/l, Potassium 1.4mg/l, Bicarbonates 97mg/l, Chlorides 4.9mg/l, Sulphates 10.7mg/l, Fluorides 0.5mg/l, Silicates 22.5mg/l. pH 7.4

Vilafonté (S.Afr) a winery (established 1996) based in Elsenburg, Paarl, Western Cape. 15ha. A joint venture between P. Freeze (S.Afr), Z. Long (USA),

Warwick Estate and B. Broadbent (U.K). Grape varieties: Cabernet franc, Cabernet sauvignon, Malbec, Merlot. Labels: Series C, Series M. Website: http://www.vilafonte.com

Vilafranca del Penedés (Sp) the name given to the mainly dry wines from Barcelona.

Vilàgos (Hun) an unpasteurised, mild lager beer.

Vilagrad Wines (N.Z) a winery. (Add): Rukuhia Road, Ohaupo, Waikato. 5ha. Grape varieties: Chardonnay, Gewürztraminer, Riesling, Cabernet, Pinot noir, Malbec, Merlot.

Vilajuiga (Sp) a still natural spring mineral water brand. Mineral contents (milligrammes per litre): Sodium 568mg/l, Calcium 83.4mg/l, Magnesium 46.7mg/l, Potassium 48mg/l, Bicarbonates 1561.6mg/l, Chlorides 236.9mg/l, Sulphates 54.4mg/l, Fluorides 2.5mg/l, Nitrates 0.5mg/l.

Vilamina (Swe) an alkaline natural spring mineral water brand. Mineral contents (milligrammes per litre): Sodium 7mg/l, Calcium 2mg/l, Magnesium 21mg/l, Potassium 3mg/l, Bicarbonates 110mg/l, Chlorides 3mg/l, Sulphates 9mg/l. pH 10.4

Vilamoura Marina (Cktl) ⁵⁄₁₀ measure Smirnoff vodka, ³⁄₁₀ measure yellow Chartreuse, ³⁄₁₀ measure blue Curaçao, ¹⁄₁₀ measure Galliano, 2 drops lemon juice. Shake over ice, strain into a cocktail glass and add 2 cherries.

Vilana (Gre) a white grape variety grown in Crete, especially in Peza. Produces straw-coloured wines with a grapey bouquet. Also spelt Villana.

Vila Nova de Gaia (Port) a town opposite Oporto on the river Douro estuary (southern bank) where the Port wine is stored in the lodges to mature.

Vila Nova de Gaia Pipe (Port) a cask of 547litres capacity. *see* Pipe.

Vilàny (Hun) a wine-producing city in Mecsek, southern Hungary. Is noted for Vilànyi Burgundi (a red wine produced from the Pinot noir grape).

Vilànyi Burgundi (Hun) *see* Vilàny.

Vila Real (Port) a Port town of the Alto Douro.

Vila Santa (Port) a red wine produced by J. Ramos. Website: http://www.jportugalramos.com

Vilas del Turbón (Sp) a still natural spring mineral water brand. Mineral contents (milligrammes per litre): Sodium 0.6mg/l, Calcium 47.7mg/l, Magnesium 1.5mg/l, Potassium 0.4mg/l, Bicarbonates 145.5mg/l, Chlorides 0.6mg/l, Sulphates 3.7mg/l, Fluorides 0.1mg/l, Nitrates 1.3mg/l.

Vilcagua (S.Am) a natural spring mineral water (established 1991) from Vilcabamba, Valle de Sagrado, Ecuador. Mineral contents (milligrammes per litre): Sodium 18mg/l, Calcium 40.8mg/l, Magnesium 9.3mg/l, Potassium 32mg/l, Bicarbonates 131mg/l, Chlorides 10.8mg/l, Sulphates 39mg/l, Nitrates 13mg/l. pH 7.4

VILE (Sp) a Léon group of merchants who form the Planta de Elaboración y Embotellado de Vinos S.A. *see* Catedral de León.

Viljoensdrift Wines (S.Afr) a winery (established 1998) based in Robertson, Western Cape. 120ha. Grape varieties: Cabernet sauvignon, Chardonnay, Chenin blanc, Colombard, Merlot, Pinotage, Sauvignon blanc, Shiraz. Labels: Die Breedekloof, Elandsberg, Keurfontein, River Grandeur, Serenity, Somerlust. Website: http://www.viljoensdrift.co.za

Villa Antinori (It) the trade-name of the Antinori family who produce fine D.O.C.G. Chianti and Chianti Classico. Also Tignanello and Solaia (100% Cabernet sauvignon wines) in Tuscany.

Villa Armando (USA) a winery based in the Livermore Valley, Alameda, California. 25ha. Grape varieties: Chardonnay and Pinot blanc. Produces varietal wines.

Villa Atuel (Arg) a wine-producing area in southern Argentina.

Villa Banfi (It) a noted producer of sweet, slightly sparkling Moscato wines.

Villa Bianchi (USA) a large winery based in Fresno, California. Grape varieties: French colombard and Zinfandel. Produces varietal and table wines.

Villa Branca (It) a 65ha. winery based at Villa Novoli 10, 50024 Mercatale Val di Pesa (FI). Grape varieties: Cabernet sauvignon, Canaiolo, Merlot, Petit verdot, Sangiovese. Produces D.O.C.G. Chianti Classico and Vin Santo wines. Website: http://www.villabranca.it 'E'mail: info@villabranca.it

Villa Bucci (It) a winery based in the Marche. Noted for D.O.C. Verdicchio di Jesi Classico Superiore.

Villabuena (Sp) a noted wine-producing village in the Rioja Alavesa.

Villa Cafaggio (It) a D.O.C.G. Chianti Classico producer based in Tuscany. Grape varieties include: Sangiovese. Labels: Cortaccio, San Martino.

Villa Calcinaia (It) a Chianti Classico producer based in Tuscany. Grape varieties include: Sangiovese.

Villa Cerna (It) a Chianti Classico producer based in Tuscany. Grape varieties include: Sangiovese.

Villa Costa (It) a sparkling wine producer based in Piemonte. Wines are made by metodo tradizionale.

Villa Crespia (It) a range of D.O.C.G. sparkling wines produced in Franciacorta, Lombardy 60ha. Grape varieties: Chardonnay and Pinot nero.

Villa del Sur (Arg) a natural spring mineral water from Buones Aires. Mineral contents (milligrammes per litre): Sodium 164mg/l, Calcium 19mg/l, Magnesium 21mg/l, Potassium 10mg/l, Bicarbonates 450mg/l, Chlorides 11mg/l, Sulphates 15mg/l, Fluorides 0.7mg/l, Nitrates 2mg/l.

Villa di Capezzana (It) a 100ha winery based in Carmignano, Tuscany.

Villa di Corte (It) a dry rosé wine produced by Frescobaldi. Has an '*onion skin*' colour.

Villa d'Ingianni Winery (USA) a winery based in Dundee, Finger Lakes, New York. 60ha. Produces American varietal wines.

Villa Dolores (Arg) a small wine region in the province of Córdoba which produces fine table wines.

Villa Doluca (Tur) a full-bodied, dry, red wine produced in Thrace.

Villa Flora (It) a winery based in the Lombardy region. Produces: D.O.C. Lugano.

Village [Le] (Fr) a Premier Cru vineyard in the A.C. commune of Saint-Aubin, Côte de Beaune, Burgundy.

Village Bitter (Eng) a cask-conditioned bitter 1035 O.G. brewed by the Archers Brewery in Swindon, Wiltshire.

Village Brewer (Eng) a brewery based in North Yorkshire. Brews: cask-conditioned Old Raby and White Boar.

Village-de-Volnay (Fr) a Premier Cru vineyard [part] in the A.C. commune of Volnay, Côte de Beaune, Burgundy.

Village Elder (Eng) a 3.8% alc by vol. ale brewed by The Cheriton Brewhouse, Hampshire.

Villa Gemma (It) the label for red and white wines from the Azienda Agricola Masciarelli based in the Abuzzo region.

Village Pride (Eng) a 3.7% alc by vol. ale brewed by the Clearwater Brewery, Devon.

Village Saint-Jacques (Fr) a Premier Cru vineyard in the A.C. commune of Gevrey-Chambertin, Côte de Nuits, Burgundy. Also sold as Clos Saint-Jacques 6.92ha.

Villa Giada (It) a winery. (Add): Reg. Ceirole 4, 14053 Canelli (Asti). 20 vineyards that produce: Barbera d'Asti, Moscato d'Asti, Dolcetto del Monferrato, Piemonte Chardonnay.

Villa Grande (It) a winery based near Etna in Sicily.

Villa Lobos (Mex) a pure grain vodka at 45% alc by vol. which contains a gusano (agave) worm (normaly associated with tequila).

Villa Maria Estate (N.Z) a winery. (Add): 5 Kirkbridge Road, Mangere, Auckland, North Island. 25ha. owned, 600ha. under contract. Grape varieties: Cabernet sauvignon, Chardonnay, Chenin blanc, Gewürztraminer, Merlot, Müller-Thurgau, Noble riesling, Pinot noir and Sauvignon blanc. Produces varietal and table wines. *See also* Family of Twelve. Website: http://www.villamaria.com.nz

Villa Matilde (It) a winery based in Campania, produces Falerno del Massico Bianco Vigna Caracci from 100% Falanghina grapes.

Villa Medeo Vineyards (USA) a vineyard based in Madison, Indiana. Grows French hybrid vines.

Villa Monte Rico (It) a wine estate based in Suvereto, Maremma, Tuscany. Produces I.G.T. Gabro, Nardo and Volpaiole wines.

Villa Mount Eden (USA) a vineyard estate in the Napa Valley, northern California. Grape varieties: Cabernet sauvignon, Chardonnay, Chenin blanc, Gewürztraminer and Pinot noir. Produces varietal wines.

Villana (Gre) an alternative spelling of Vilana.

Villànyer (Hun) the brand-name used by Villàny-Pécs (a wine-producing area) for its red and white wines.

Villàny-Pécs (Hun) a red and white wine-producing district in south-western Hungary. *see* Villànyer.

Villàny-Siklós (Hun) a wine-producing district based in southern Transdanubia. Produces top quality red wines.

Villa Pigna (It) a winery based in The Marche. 300ha. Produces D.O.C. wines. *see* Rosso Piceno.

Villa Poggio Salvi (It) a winery. (Add): Biondi Santi SpA, Via Panfilo dell'Oca 3, 53024 Montalcino (SI). Produces D.O.C.G. Brunello Montalcino, D.O.C. Rosso Montalcino, Moscadello di Montalcino 'Aurico', I.G.T. Lavischio (Merlot) Toscana, Grappa di Brunello.

Villard (Chile) a vineyard based in Casablanca Valley, Central Chile. Grape varieties: Chardonnay, Riesling, Sauvignon blanc, Merlot, Pinot noir.

Villard Blanc (Fr) a white hybrid grape variety. Also known as Seyve-Villard 12.375.

Villard Noir (Fr) a red hybrid grape variety. Also known as Seyve-Villard 18.315.

Villa Sachsen (Ger) a 28ha estate based in Bingen. Owned by St. Ursula.

Villa Sarvardo (It) the main wine label for the Cantina Beato Bartolomeo co-operative, Breganze, Veneto.

Villa Terciona (It) a Chianti Classico producer based in Tuscany.

Villatraful (Arg) a natural spring mineral water brand.

Villaudric (Fr) a small V.D.Q.S. wine-producing area in the Haut-Garonne, south-western France.

Villa Verde (S.Afr) the label for a range of wines produced by the Seven Oaks winery, Worcester, Western Cape.

Villavicencio [1] (Arg) a natural spring mineral water from the Andes. Mineral contents (milligrammes per litre): Calcium 25.9mg/l, Magnesium 23.6mg/l, Bicarbonates 403mg/l, Chlorides 42mg/l, Sulphates 220mg/l, Fluorides 1.6mg/l.

Villavicencio [2] (Arg) a still natural spring mineral water from the Andes. Mineral contents (milligrammes per litre): Sodium 272mg/l, Calcium 23.2mg/l, Magnesium 22.89mg/l, Potassium 7.2mg/l, Bicarbonates 478.7mg/l, Chlorides 46.8mg/l, Sulphates 180mg/l, Fluorides 1.84mg/l.

Villavicencio [3] (Arg) a sparkling natural spring mineral water from the Andes. Mineral contents (milligrammes per litre): Sodium 268mg/l, Calcium 23.2mg/l, Magnesium 23.46mg/l, Potassium 7.4mg/l, Bicarbonates 465.5mg/l, Chlorides 46.8mg/l, Sulphates 176.5mg/l, Fluorides 1.83mg/l.

Villaviciosa (Sp) a Vino Comarcal of Córdoba in Andalucía.

Villa Vignamaggio (It) a 48ha winery. (Add): Via Petriolo 5, 50022 Greve in Chianti, Tuscany (FI). Noted for Chianti Classico and Vini I.G.T. wines.

Villa Zarri (It) a pot-still brandy made from Trebbiano grapes grown in the Chianti zone of Tuscany. Aged 9 months in new French and Slovenian oak, then 21 months in small Limousin casks. Sold in 500mls bottles. Produced by Stock in Trieste.

V

Villedommange (Fr) a Premier Cru Champagne village in the Canton de Ville-en-Tardenois. District: Reims.

Ville-en-Tardenois (Fr) a Canton of the Reims district in the Champagne region. Has the Premier Cru villages: Écueil, Les Mesneux, Sacy and Villedommange. And Cru villages: Bligny, Bouilly, Bouleuse, Branscourt, Brouillet, Chambrecy, Chaumuzy, Coulommes-la-Montagne, Courcelles-Sapicourt, Courmas, Faverolles, Germigny, Gueux, Janvry, Jouy-les-Reims, Lagery, Marfaux, Paigny-les-Reims, Poilly, Rosnay, Sainte-Euphraise, Sarcy, Savigny-sur-Ardre, Serzy-et-Prin, Tramery, Treslon, Ville-en-Tardenois and Vrigny.

Ville-en-Tardenois (Fr) a Cru Champagne village in the Canton de Ville-en-Tardenois. District: Reims.

Villenave-d'Ornon (Fr) a commune within the A.C. district of Graves in south-western Bordeaux.

Villeneuve (Fr) a commune in the A.C. Côtes de Bourg, north-eastern Bordeaux.

Villeneuve de Cantemerle (Fr) the second wine of Château Cantemerle. A.C. Haut-Médoc.

Villeneuve-lès-Corbières (Fr) a commune in the A.C. Fitou district of southern France.

Villeneuve-Renneville (Fr) a Premier Cru Champagne village in the Canton de Vertus. District: Châlons.

Villenkeller (Ger) vineyard (Anb): Rheinhessen. (Ber): Nierstein. (Gro): Domherr. (Vil): Klein-Winternhaus.

Villers-Allerand (Fr) a Premier Cru Champagne village in the Canton de Verzy. District: Reims.

Villers Brasserie (Bel) a brewery (established 1996) based at Liezele-Puurs. Brews: Paranoia Green, Paranoia Pink.

Villers-Franqueux (Fr) a Cru Champagne village in the Canton de Bourgogne. District: Reims.

Villers-Marmery (Fr) a Premier Cru Champagne village in the Canton de Verzy. District: Reims.

Villers Monopole (Bel) a natural spring mineral water from Villers le Gambon. Mineral contents (milligrammes per litre): Sodium 8mg/l, Calcium 106mg/l, Magnesium 11mg/l, Potassium 2.4mg/l, Bicarbonates 340mg/l, Chlorides 19mg/l, Sulphates 48mg/l. pH 7.0

Villers-sous-Châtillon (Fr) a Cru Champagne village in the Canton de Châtillon-sur-Marne. District: Reims.

Villette (Switz) a noted vineyard based in Lavaux.

Villevenard (Fr) a Premier Cru Champagne village in the Canton de Montmort. District: Épernay.

Villié-Morgon (Fr) a commune in the Beaujolais district. Has A.C. Beaujolais-Villages or Beaujolais-Villié-Morgon status.

Villiera Wine Estate (S.Afr) a winery (established 1983) based in Stellenbosch, Western Cape. 260ha. (Add): P.O. Box 66, Koelenhof 7605, Paarl. Grape varieties: Cabernet sauvignon, Chardonnay, Chenin blanc, Gamay, Merlot, Muscat ottonel, Pinotage, Pinot meunier, Rhine riesling, Sauvignon blanc, Sémillon, Shiraz, Tinta, Touriga.

Labels: Cellar Door, Fired Earth, Gavotte, Minuet, Monro, Operette, Sonnet, Traditional Bush Vine. Website: http://www.villiera.com

Villiersdorp (S.Afr) a wine-producing region based east of Cape Town.

Villiersdorp-Koöperasie (S.Afr) a winery (established 1922) based in Overberg, Worcester, Western Cape. 500ha. (Add): Bpk., Box 14, Villiersdorp 7170. Grape varieties: Cabernet sauvignon, Chardonnay, Chenin blanc, Hanepoot, Jerepiko. Label: Bouquet Blanc and varietal wines. Website: http://www.vilko.co.za

Villman (Fin) raspberry-flavoured liqueurs produced by Chymos.

Villum (Lat) a drop of wine.

Villy (Fr) a commune in the A.C. Chablis, Burgundy.

Vilmart & Cie (Fr) a Champagne producer. (Add): Rue de la République, 51500 Rilly-la-Montagne. 12ha of Premier Cru vineyards. Produces vintage and non-vintage wines. Vintages: 1988, 1989, 1990, 1991, 1996, 1997, 1998, 1999, 2000, 2001. Special cuvées: Coeur de Cuvée, Cuvée Création, Cuvée Rubis.

Vilsa (Ger) a still and sparkling natural spring mineral water (established 1909) from Bremen. Mineral contents (milligrammes per litre): Sodium 18.6mg/l, Calcium 60.5mg/l, Magnesium 4.3mg/l, Potassium 2.4mg/l, Bicarbonates 196mg/l, Chlorides 22.3mg/l, Sulphates 22mg/l, Fluorides 0.18mg/l, Nitrates <0.3mg/l.

Vilsa Exclusiv (Ger) a natural spring mineral water from Bremen.

Vimeiro (Port) a still and sparkling natural spring mineral water from Vineiro 5, Lisbon. Mineral contents (milligrammes per litre): Sodium 178mg/l, Calcium 121mg/l, Bicarbonates 446mg/l, Chlorides 250mg/l. pH 7.13

Vimto (Eng) a branded sparkling soft drink. Produced by J.N. Nichols.

Vin (Den)(Fr) wine.

Viña (Sp) vine/vineyard

Viña [La] (USA) a vineyard based near Roswell, Mesilla Valley, New Mexico. 20ha. Produces vinifera wines.

Viña Albali (Sp) an oak-matured red wine produced by the Bodegas Felix Solis in the Valdepeñas district.

Viña Alberdi (Sp) a red wine from La Rioja Alta, S.A., Rioja. Made from the Garnacha, Graciano, Tempranillo and Viura grapes, matured in oak casks for 1½ years minimum and for 3 years in bottle.

Viña Albina (Sp) a red wine produced by the Bodegas Riojanas in the Rioja region.

Viña Alcorta (Sp) wine brand name owned by Allied Domecq.

Viña Altaïr (Chile) a winery based in the Cachapoal valley (works with Château Dassault of Saint-Émilion). Grape varieties: Cabernet sauvignon, Carmenère, Merlot. Website: http://www.vinaaltair.cl

Viña Amezola (Sp) a D.O.Ca. Rioja wine from

V

Bodegas Amezola de la Mora, Torremontralbo, Rioja. Grape varieties: Tempranillo, Mazuelo.

Viña Aquitania (Chile) a vineyard (18ha) based in the Quebrada de Maucul, Maipo in the foothills of the Andes by Santiago. Joint venture between Bruno Prats and Paul Pontallier. Wines are sold under the label of Domaine Paul Bruno. Grape varieties include Cabernet sauvignon, Cabernet franc, Merlot.

Viña Arana (Sp) a light-styled red wine from Rioja.

Viña Ardanza (Sp) a red wine from La Rioja Alta, Rioja. Made from the Tempranillo and Mazuelo grapes. Oak-matured for 3½ years and for 2 years in bottle.

Viña Berceo (Sp) red and white wines of various grades produced by the Bodegas Gurpegui, Rioja.

Viña Bosconia (Sp) a red wine produced by López de Heredia.

Viña Canepa (Chile) a winery (350ha) based in the Maipo. Grape varieties: Cabernet sauvignon, Malbec, Merlot, Pinot noir, Chardonnay, Gewürztraminer, Rhine riesling, Sauvignon blanc.

Viña Carmen (Chile) an organic vineyard (established 1994) and winery based at Buin in the Maipo Valley south of Santiago 25ha. Website: http://www.carmen.com

Viña Carossa (Sp) a white wine-producing vineyard based in the Penedés region.

Vinaccia (It) the name given to the residue grape pulp left after the pressing.

Vinaccio (It) grape brandy, the equivalent of French marc.

Vinacea (Lat) grape brandy, the equivalent of French marc.

Vinaceous (Eng) pertaining to wine.

Vinaceus (Lat) grape. *See also* Uva. Also denotes anything relating to wine.

Viña Cono Sur (Chile) a winery. Website: http://www.conosur.com

Viña Cubillo (Sp) a red wine produced by López de Heredia.

Viña Cumbrero (Sp) red and white wines produced by the Bodegas El Montecillo, Alto region, Rioja. Red wines from 100% Tempranillo and white wines from 100% Viura grapes.

Viña del Calar (Sp) a red wine produced by the Bodegas Princesa in the Valdepeñas region.

Viña del Perdón (Sp) a fruity red wine produced by Señorío de Sarría in the Navarra region.

Viña de Santa Ynez (USA) a vineyard based in Santa Ynez, Santa Barbara, California. Grape variety: Chardonnay.

Viña Doña Paula S.A. (Arg) a winery based in the Mendoza region, eastern Argentina. Website: http://www.donapaula.com.ar 'E'mail: info@donapaula.com.ar

Vinadri (It) wine merchants of Italy in the middle ages.

Viña Ederra (Sp) a red crianza Rioja produced by Bodegas Bilbanas S.A. in the Haro Rioja.

Viña Eguia (Sp) a wine produced by the Bodegas Domecq, S.A. Rioja. Red wine from the Tempranillo grape.

Viña el Pisón (Sp) a red wine produced by the Artadi vineyard in the D.O. Rioja Alavasa.

Viña Errazuriz (Chile) a famous winery (established 1870) based in the Aconcagua Valley that produces a wide range of wines.

Viña Esmeralda (Sp) a semi-dry white wine produced by Torres in the Penedés region from 40% Gewürztraminer and 60% Muscat d'Alsace grapes.

Viña Franca (Sp) a fruity white wine produced by Mascaró in Vilafranca del Penedés, Cataluña.

Viña Fresca (Sp) a light white wine from Mascaró in Vilafranca del Penedés, Cataluña.

Viña Fundación de Mendoza S.A. (Arg) a winery based in the Mendoza region, eastern Argentina. Website: http://www.fundaciondemendoza.com 'E'mail: info@fundaciondemendoza.com

Vinag (Slo) a large wine producing cellars in Maribor, Podravje, Slovenia. Noted for Renski Rizling (a Rhine riesling) wine.

Vinage (Fr) the term used for the addition of alcohol to wine in order to raise the alcoholic strength.

Vinagre (Port)(Sp) vinegar.

Viña Gracia (Chile) *see* Gracia.

Viña Gravonia (Sp) an extra dry, white wine produced by Lopez de Heredia.

Viña Herminia (Sp) a red wine produced by the Bodegas Lagunilla in Rioja. Made from the Tempranillo grape, oak-matured for 3 years and for 2 years in bottle.

Vinai dell'Abbate (It) a winery based in the D.O.C. Colli Orientali. Grape variety : Ribolla gialia.

Vinaigre (Fr) lit: 'sour wine', vinegar.

Viña Ijalba S.A. (Sp) a 60ha winery (established 1975) in Logroño, Rioja. Grape varieties: 90% Tempranillo, 5% Mazuelo, 5% Graciano. Label: Múrice.

Viña Lanciano (Sp) a red wine produced by the Bodegas Landalan in Rioja. Oak and bottle matured.

Viña Laranda Blanco (Sp) a white wine produced by Ferret y Mateu.

Vina la Rosa (Chile) a winery based in the Cachapoal Valley. Grape varieties include: Cabernet sauvignon, Carmenère, Chardonnay, Merlot. Labels: Don Reca and La Capitana. Website: http://www.larosa.cl

Vin Alb (Rum) white wine.

Viña Leyda (Chile) a winery based in the Lydia district of San Antonio. Website: http://www.leyda.cl

Vinalia (Lat) wine festival.

Viña Linderos (Chile) a winery based in the Maipo Valley. Noted for Cabernet-based wines.

Viñaluz Blanco (Sp) a white wine produced by Bodegas Real in Valdepeñas.

Viñalzada (Sp) the name of a Rioja wine produced by Maese Joan, Sdad. Coop. Ltda, Oyon, Alava.

Viña Madre (USA) a vineyard based near Roswell, Mesilla Valley, New Mexico. 16ha. Grape varieties:

Barbera, Cabernet sauvignon, Napa gamay, Ruby cabernet and Zinfandel. Produces varietal and table wines.

Viña Magdala (Sp) a fine red wine produced by Torres in the Penedés region from Tempranillo and Pinot noir grapes. Oak-aged for 2 years.

Viña Maria (Sp) a grand reserva Rioja from Bodegas Berberana.

Viña Mayor (Sp) a D.O. Ribera del Duero from Hijos de Antonio Barcelo, S.A. Quintanilla de Onésimo, Valladolid.

Viña Montana (Sp) the name given to the red and white wines from La Purisima in the Yecla region.

Viña Montes (Chile) a winery in the Colchaqua, Casablanca Valley that is noted for the flagship wine Montes M (launched 1988). Grape varieties: Cabernet sauvignon, Chardonnay, Merlot, Pinot noir.

Viña Monty (Sp) a red wine produced by the Bodegas El Montecillo in Rioja. Made from 90% Tempranillo and 10% Mazuelo grapes. Oak-matured then bottle-matured for 1½–2 years.

Viña Morande (Chile) a 430ha winery (established 1996) based in Casablanca, Maipo, Rapel Valley. Grape varieties include Riesling and Sauvignon blanc.

Viña Norte (Sp) a large co-operative winery based on the island of Tenerife. Labels include: Humbolt.

Viña Obvio (Arg) a winery based in the Mendoza region, eastern Argentina. Website: http://www.vinaobvio.com

Viña Paceta (Sp) the label of a white Rioja wine produced by Bodegas Bilbainas S.A. in Haro, Rioja.

Viña Pilar (Sp) a D.O. red wine from 90% Tinto del Pais (Tempranillo), 10% Cabernet sauvignon grapes. Produced by Bodegas Felix Callejo, S.A. in Ribera del Duero.

Viña Pomal (Sp) a red wine produced by the Bodegas Bilbainas S.A. in Haro, Rioja (Alta region). Produces Reserva and Gran Reserva wines.

Viña Porta (Chile) a winery based in Requino. Grape variety: Cabernet sauvignon.

Viña Q (Sp) a white wine produced by Bodegas Ayuso in La Mancha region.

Viña Real (Sp) a red wine produced by the C.V.N.E. in the Alta region of Rioja. Oak and bottle-matured. Also a Viña Real Reserve.

Viña Real Reserve (Sp) *see* Viña Real.

Viña Rebelde (Sp) a dry white wine produced by Alfonso Maldonaldo in the Rueda region.

Vinarius (Lat) vintner.

Vinaroz (Sp) a wine-producing area in the Levante near Tarragona. Produces mainly red wines.

Viña Salceda (Sp) a winery. (Add): Viña Salceda S.A. Carretera de Cenicero, km-3, Elciego, Alavesa, Rioja. 30ha. Grape variety: Tempranillo 100%. All wines oak and bottle-matured. Labels include: Conde de la Salceda.

Viña San Felipe Borgono Tinto (Arg) a Burgundy-style red wine made from the Cabernet sauvignon grape in the Mendoza region.

Viña San Pedro (Chile) the name of a noted winery that produces wines under the same name.

Viña Santa Digna (Chile) the name of a Cabernet-based wine produced by Torres.

Viña Santa Marta (Sp) a range of red and white wines produced by Bodegas J. Freixedas.

Viña Santa Rita (Chile) a large vineyard from Santiago in the Maipo district.

Vinas de Orfila (Arg) the brand-name of a white wine produced by Orfila in the Mendoza region.

Viña Sol (Sp) a dry white wine produced by Torres in the Penedés region from 100% Parellada grapes.

Viña Soledad (Sp) a white wine produced by the Bodegas Franco-Españolas, S.A. Alta region, Rioja. Made from 50% Malvasia and 50% Viura grapes.

Vinasse (Fr) the residue after distillation of wine into brandy.

Viñas Viejas (Sp) old vines. (Fr) = vieilles vignes, (Ger) = alte reben.

Viña Tamarí (Arg) a winery based in the Mendoza region, eastern Argentina. Website: http://www.tamari.com.ar 'E'mail: info@ southernsunwine.com

Viña Tarapacá (Chile) a winery based in La Florida, Central Valley, Santiago. Grape varieties include: Cabernet sauvignon, Chardonnay, Carmenère. Label: Gran Tarapacá.

Vinate (Sp) the label used in Spain for a range of wines from José López Bertran. *See also* Corrida.

Viña Tesos (Sp) a red wine produced by the Bodegas Lopez-Agos in Rioja. Made from 80% Tempranillo and 20% Garnacha grapes. Oak matured for 2 years and bottle matured for 4 years.

Viñatigo Malvasía Clásico (Sp) a sweet, late harvest dessert wine produced on the island of Tenerife.

Viña Tondonia (Sp) red and white oak and bottled matured wines produced by R. López de Heredia, Viña Tondonia S.A. Rioja.

Vinattieri (It) wine merchants of ancient Florence (1200 – 1282). The earliest controlling body for the production and sale of wine.

Viña Turzaballa (Sp) a red wine produced by the Bodegas Ramón Bilbao S.A. Rioja. Matured 2–4 years in oak and 10 years in bottle.

Viña Umbral (Sp) a red wine produced by the Bodegas Ramón Bilbao S.A. Rioja. Matured 2–4 years in oak and 1–10 years in bottle.

Viña Undurraga (Chile) the label used by a winery based in the Maipo Valley.

Vin au Tonneau (Fr) wine in the wood (cask).

Viña Valoria (Sp) a red wine produced by Gustillo, Alto region in Rioja. Made from 80% Tempranillo, 5% Garnacha and 15% Viura grapes. Oak matured for 3–6 months and 1 year in bottle.

Viña Vial (Sp) a red wine produced by Federico Paternina, Rioja. Oak and bottle matured.

Viña Vista (USA) a winery based in Sonoma County, California. Grape varieties: Cabernet sauvignon,

Chardonnay, Johannisberg riesling, Petite sirah and Zinfandel. Produces varietal wines.

Viña Vita (Sp) a wine produced by Bodegas Real in Valdepeñas.

Viña Von Siebenthal (Chile) a winery based in the Aconcagua valley. Grape varieties: Cabernet franc, Cabernet sauvignon, Carmenère, Merlot. Website: http://www.vinavonsiebenthal.cl

Vinay (Fr) a Cru Champagne village in the Canton d'Épernay. District: Épernay.

Vinay (S.Afr) the label for a range of wines produced by the Slanghoek Winery, Worcester, Western Cape.

Viña Zaco (Sp) a red wine produced by the Bodegas Bilbainas S.A. in the Alta region, Rioja. Produces Reserva and Gran Reserva wines.

Viña Zaconia (Sp) a white wine produced by R. López de Heredia, Viña Tondonia, S.A. Rioja. Made from 50% Malvasia and 50% Viura grapes. Oak matured for 5 years and 6 months in bottle.

Vin Blanc (Fr) white wine.

Vin Blanc Cassis (Fr) an apéritif made from white wine with Cassis. Not to be confused with the wine known as Vin Blanc de Cassis.

Vin Blanc de Cassis (Fr) an A.C. white wine from the Cassis district in the Côtes de Provence. Not to be confused with the apéritif known as Vin Blanc Cassis.

Vin Bourro (Fr) a term used for new wine, refers to the spicy nature of some new wines. *See also* Bourro (spiced wine).

Vin Bourru (Fr) the name used for wines which have just been drawn from the barrel or are still on the original lees.

Vin Brulaï (Ch.Isles) mulled wine/hot spiced wine.

Vin Brûlé (Fr) an alternative name for the Dutch term brandewijn.

Vin Cacher (Fr) lit: 'kosher wine', the kosher process of vinification, where the vinification equipment is sterilised in boiling water before use allowing for the production of a 'pure' wine which has no additives. All the processes are observed by the Rabbi (Shomrim). The wine is used for Jewish Kosher ceremonies. *See* Cachérisation and Shomrim.

Vin Capiteux (Fr) a spirity/heady wine.

Vincelles (Fr) a Cru Champagne village in the Canton de Dormans. District: Épernay.

Vincelli [Dom Bernado] (Fr) the name of the Bénédictine monk who invented the liqueur Bénédictine in 1510.

Vincente Sinó Santonja (Sp) a producer of fine wines from Valencia. Noted for Fondillón (a fine red wine).

Vincente Suso y Perez (Sp) the largest wine producer in Cariñena, north-eastern Spain. *see* Don Ramon, Duque de Sevilla, Mosen Cleto and Old Duque de Sevilla brandy.

Vincent Girardin (Fr) a négociant-producteur based in Santenay. Produces wines from own grapes and bought-in fruit.

Vincentka (Czec) a sparkling natural spring mineral water from Luhacovice. Mineral contents (milligrammes per litre): Sodium 2017mg/l, Calcium 245.29mg/l, Magnesium 18mg/l, Potassium 166mg/l, Bicarbonates 3989.4mg/l, Lithium 27.5mg/l, Sulphates 5.76mg/l, Fluorides 2.13mg/l, Nitrates 0.05mg/l, Silicates 21.12mg/l, Iron 6.99mg/l, Iodine 6.45mg/l, Hydrobromide 6.33mg/l, Aluminium 3.36mg/l. pH 6.1

Vin Chaud (Fr) mulled wine. (Ger) = glühwein.

Vin Ché (N.Z) a dry white wine produced by Balic, Sturges Road, Henderson, North Island.

Vin Choisi (Fr) simple wines. V.C.C. that are used for everyday drinking, ordinary drinking wines.

Vin Classé (Lux) classification of wines. *see* Marque Nationale.

Vincool Wine Pump System (Eng) a patented pump that pours out chilled wine at 25mls (1fl.oz) per second from a dispense. Marketed by Gilbeys.

Vin Cuit (Fr) a concentrated wine used to improve thin wines.

Vin d'Absinthe (Fr) a nineteenth century wine that was flavoured with wormwood.

Vin d'Alsace (Fr) a name given to wines that are not made from noble grape varieties in Alsace. i.e. Chasselas. If noble variety and gathered after certain date also called this.

Vin d'Alsace Zwicker (Fr) blended Alsace wine from noble grape varieties.

Vindara (Austr) a winery in the Swan Valley in Western Australia.

Vin de Blanquette (Fr) a still white wine from Limoux, south-western France. Made from 90% Mauzac and 10% Clairette blanche grapes. Also a sparkling version produced known as Limoux or Blanquette de Limoux. (Originally created by monks in 1531 at the abbey of St-Hilaire, produced by the 'rural-method' which results in a slight sediment occurring).

Vin de Bourgeoise (Fr) a wine offered during the middle ages to any citizen or mayor who was elected town Burgher.

Vin de Campagne (Fr) country wine/vin ordinaire of the Jura (Arbois).

Vin de Carafe (Fr) carafe wine/house wine.

Vin de Câtel (Ch.Isles) the new name for the tomato fruit wine Aztecato once produced in Guernsey (now no longer exists).

Vin de Consommation Courante (Fr) denotes 'everyday drinking'. Is often used to refer to the vin ordinaires or non-vintage and inexpensive wines. The term also applies to wines made from 'producteurs directs' (hybrid vines) and to the declassified wines in Bordeaux. *abbr*: V.C.C.

Vin de Constance (S.Afr) a noble late-harvest wine (Muscat de frontignan) produced by Klein Constantia winery Constantia, Western Cape..

Vin de Corse (Fr) the name used in Corsica for Tout Court. The areas Ajaccio and Patramino are both Cru wines.

Vin de Corse (Fr) an A.C. VdN red, rosé and white (semi-sweet or dry) wines. Produced in Corsica from Carignan, Cinsault, Mourvèdre, Niellucio,

Sciacarello, Syrah and Vermentino grapes. Minimum alc by vol. 11.5%.

Vin de Corse Calvi (Fr) an A.C. red, demi-sec and dry white wines produced in Corsica. Grape varieties: Niellucio, Sciacarello and Vermentino.

Vin de Côtes (Fr) a term used for wine obtained from vineyards sited on hillsides.

Vin de Coucher (Fr) lit: 'nuptial wine', wine offered by a newly married couple to their guests who attend the wedding feast just before they retire.

Vin de Coule (Fr) the name given to wine obtained from the first pressing of the grapes.

Vin de Cru (Fr) wine that is produced from grapes of a single vineyard.

Vin de Cuvée (Fr) in Champagne, the first juice of the marc (75litres from 160kgs).

Vin de Florence (S.Afr) the label for a white wine (Chenin blanc and Muscat de frontignan blend) produced by the Vergelegen winery, Stellenbosch, Western Cape.

Vin de Garde (Fr) wine for laying down to mature.

Vin de Gingembre (Fr) ginger wine.

Vin de Glacé (Fr) the German and Austrian Eiswein (Ice-wine).

Vin de Glacier (Switz) a speciality from Val d'Anniviers. Young wine from the valley vineyards taken to cellars of high altitude to finish its fermentation very slowly. Develops a hard, almost bitter taste. Matured in Larchwood casks for up to 15 years, topped up with new vintage when Alpine herdsmen return to mountains. Rarely found outside Switzerland. Made usually from the Rèze grape.

Vin de Glacière (S.Afr) the label for a white ice-wine (Muscat d'alexandrie) produced by the Signal Hill winery, Cape Town, Western Cape.

Vin de Goutte (Fr) poor quality wine from the last pressing of the grapes. Also denotes the first pressing of the grapes in the Cognac region.

Vin de la Moselle Luxembourgeoise (Lux) common wines. Put on the label together with the grape variety. i.e. Vin de la Moselle Luxembourgeoise Riesling.

Vin de l'Année (Fr) wine of the year, most recent vintage.

Vin de la Région (Fr) wine from a specific region. e.g. Champagne from the Champagne region.

Vin de Lavilledieu (Fr) a V.D.Q.S. wine-producing district in the Tarn-et-Garonne département. Main grape variety is Negrette.

Vin de l'Empereur (S.Afr) the label for a naturally sweet white wine (Muscat) produced by the Signal Hill winery, Cape Town, Western Cape.

Vin de l'Étrier (Fr) lit: 'stirrup cup', a drink offered to departing guests.

Vin Délimité de Qualité Supérieure (Fr) *see* V.D.Q.S.

Vin de Liqueur (Fr) *abbr*: V.d.L. a naturally sweet wine made by adding grape brandy to the unfermented must.

Vin de Lune (Fr) the name given to chaptalised wines.

Vin de Macadam (Fr) a term used to describe a sweet white wine that has been rushed to Paris straight from the fermenting vat.

Vin de Marc (Fr) grape brandy. *see* Marc.

Vin de Marcillac (Fr) a V.D.Q.S. wine-producing district in the Aveyron département.

Vin de Masa (Rum) table wine.

Vin de Messe (Fr) altar wine.

Vin de Meurveur (S.Afr) the label for a naturally sweet white wine (Colombard 100%) produced by the L'Avenir Estate winery, Stellenbosch, Western Cape.

Vindemia (Lat) vintage/grape harvest. *See also* Vindemiator.

Vindemiator (Lat) vintage/grape harvest. *See also* Vindemia.

Vindemiolo (Lat) small vintage.

Vin de Noix (Fr) a walnut-flavoured liqueur 14.8% alc by vol. often used as a base for cocktails.

Vin d'Entraygues et du Fel (Fr) a V.D.Q.S. wine-producing district in the Aveyron département and Cantal département.

Vin de Nuits (S.Afr) on a label denotes that the grapes were harvested during the night.

Vin de Paille (Fr) straw wine from the Jura. Named from the fact that Savagnin grapes are spread upon straw to dry for a period of time before they are pressed to concentrate the sugar (100kgs grapes = 10–25 litres of must). Usually sold in half litre bottles called 'clavelins'. *See also* Vin Jaune, Château Chalon and Château d'Arlay. (Sp) = vino dorado.

Vin de Pays (Fr) country wine, small local wine.

Vin de Paysan (Fr) the name used for poor quality Vin de Pays.

Vin de Pays Catalan (Fr) a Vins de Pays region in the Languedoc-Roussillon, south-western France.

Vin de Pays Charentais (Fr) a Vins de Pays region in the Sud-Ouest, south-western France.

Vin de Pays Charentais 'Île de Ré' (Fr) a Vins de Pays region in the Sud-Ouest, south-western France.

Vin de Pays Charentais 'Île d'Oléron' (Fr) a Vins de Pays region in the Sud-Ouest, south-western France.

Vin de Pays Charentais 'Saint-Sornin' (Fr) a Vins de Pays region in the Sud-Ouest, south-western France.

Vin de Pays d'Aigues (Fr) a Vins de Pays region in the Provence et Corse, south-eastern France.

Vin de Pays d'Allbrogie (Fr) a Vins de Pays region in the Rhône-Alpes, south-eastern France.

Vin de Pays d'Argens (Fr) a Vins de Pays region in the Provence et Corse, south-eastern France.

Vin de Pays de Bessan (Fr) a Vins de Pays region in the Languedoc-Roussillon, south-western France.

Vin de Pays de Bigorre (Fr) a Vins de Pays region in the Sud-Ouest, south-western France.

Vin de Pays de Cassan (Fr) a Vins de Pays region in the Languedoc-Roussillon, south-western France.

Vin de Pays de Caux (Fr) a Vins de Pays region in the Languedoc-Roussillon, south-western France.

Vin de Pays de Cessenon (Fr) a Vins de Pays region in the Languedoc-Roussillon, south-western France.

Vin de Pays de Cévennes (Fr) a Vins de Pays region in the Languedoc-Roussillon, south-western France.

Vin de Pays de Cévennes 'Mont-Bouquet' (Fr) a Vins de Pays region in the Languedoc-Roussillon, south-western France.

Vin de Pays de Cher (Fr) see Jardin de la France.

Vin de Pays de Corse (Fr) see L'Île de Beauté.

Vin de Pays de Cucugnan (Fr) a Vins de Pays region in the Languedoc-Roussillon, south-western France.

Vin de Pays de Drôme (Fr) see Coteaux de Baronnies.

Vin de Pays de Franche-Comté (Fr) a Vins de Pays region in the Bourgogne et Est, central-eastern France.

Vin de Pays de Franche-Comté 'Coteaux de Champlitte' (Fr) a Vins de Pays region in the Bourgogne et Est, central-eastern France.

Vin de Pays de Gers (Fr) includes areas of Côtes du Condomois, Côtes de Gascogne, Côtes de Montestruc and Côtes de Saint-Mont.

Vin de Pays de Jura (Fr) see Franche-Comté.

Vin de Pays de la Bénovie (Fr) a Vins de Pays region in the Languedoc-Roussillon, south-western France.

Vin de Pays de la Cité de Carcassonne (Fr) a Vins de Pays region in the Languedoc-Roussillon, south-western France.

Vin de Pays de la Côte Vermeille (Fr) a Vins de Pays region in the Languedoc-Roussillon, south-western France.

Vin de Pays de l'Agenais (Fr) a Vins de Pays region in the Sud-Ouest, south-western France.

Vin de Pays de la Haute-Vallée de l'Aude (Fr) a Vins de Pays region in the Languedoc-Roussillon, south-western France.

Vin de Pays de la Haute-Vallée de l'Orb (Fr) a Vins de Pays region in the Languedoc-Roussillon, south-western France.

Vin de Pays de l'Ain (Fr) a small Vin de Pays area in the Ain département, eastern France. Mainly dry white wines.

Vin de Pays de la Meuse (Fr) a white and Vin Gris wine-producing area in Lorraine, north-eastern France.

Vin de Pays de la Petite Crau (Fr) a Vins de Pays region in the Provence et Corse, south-eastern France.

Vin de Pays de la Principauté d'Orange (Fr) a Vins de Pays region in the Provence et Corse, south-eastern France.

Vin de Pays de l'Ardailhou (Fr) a Vins de Pays region in the Languedoc-Roussillon, south-western France.

Vin de Pays de l'Ardèche (Fr) see Coteaux de l'Ardèche.

Vin de Pays de l'Aude (Fr) a wine-producing area in the Aude département of southern France. Produces red, rosé and dry white wines. Main grapes are Carignan, Cinsault and Grenache.

Vin de Pays de la Vallée du Paradis (Fr) a Vins de Pays region in the Languedoc-Roussillon, south-western France.

Vin de Pays de la Vaunage (Fr) a Vins de Pays region in the Languedoc-Roussillon, south-western France.

Vin de Pays de la Vicomté d'Aumelas (Fr) a Vins de Pays region in the Languedoc-Roussillon, south-western France.

Vin de Pays de la Vistrenque (Fr) a Vins de Pays region in the Languedoc-Roussillon, south-western France.

Vin de Pays de l'Hérault (Fr) based in the Languedoc-Roussillon and includes the areas: Bessan, Caux, Cessenon, Collines de la Moure, Coteaux d'Enserune, Coteaux de Laurens, Coteaux de Libron, Coteaux de Murviel, Coteaux du Salagou, Côtes du Brian, Côtes de Thau, Côtes de Thongue, Gorges de l'Hérault, Haute Vallée de l'Orb, Vicomt, d'Aulmelas, Mont Baudile and Côtes de Céressou.

Vin de Pays de L'Île de Beauté (Fr) a Vins de Pays region in the Provence et Corse, south-eastern France. Denotes Corsican table wines.

Vin de Pays de l'Isère (Fr) see Balmes Dauphinoises and Coteaux du Grésivaudan.

Vin de Pays de Loire Atlantique (Fr) see Pays de Retz and Marches de Bretagne.

Vin de Pays de Lot (Fr) see Coteaux de Glanes and Coteaux de Quercy.

Vin de Pays de Lot-et-Garonne (Fr) see Agenais and Côte du Brulhois.

Vin de Pays de l'Yonne (Fr) describes the white wines from regions of Chablis, Coulange-la-Vineuse, Irancy and Saint-Bris in the Yonne département. Minimum alc by vol. 9%.

Vin de Pays d'Enserune (Fr) a Vins de Pays region in the Languedoc-Roussillon, south-western France.

Vin de Pays de Pézenas (Fr) a Vins de Pays region in the Languedoc-Roussillon, south-western France.

Vin de Pays de Pyrénées-Oriéntales (Fr) see Coteaux de Fenouillèdes, Pays Catalan, Vals d'Agley and Côte Catalane.

Vin de Pays de Sainte-Marie-la-Blanche (Fr) a Vins de Pays region in the Bourgogne et Est, central-eastern France.

Vin de Pays de Saint-Sardos (Fr) a Vins de Pays region in the Sud-Ouest, south-western France.

Vin de Pays des Alpes-de-Haute-Provence (Fr) a wine-producing area in the Haute Alpes département of south-eastern France. Produces red, rosé and dry white wines.

Vin de Pays des Alpes-Maritimes (Fr) a wine-producing area in the Alpes Maritimes département of south-eastern France. Produces red, rosé and white wines.

Vin de Pays de Savoie et Haut-Savoie (Fr) see Allogrogie.

Vin de Pays des Balmes Dauphinoises (Fr) a Vins de Pays region in the Rhône-Alpes, south-eastern France.

Vin de Pays des Bouches du Rhône (Fr) see Petite Crau and Sables du Golfe du Lion.

Vin de Pays des Collines de la Moure (Fr) a Vins de

Pays region in the Languedoc-Roussillon, south-western France.

Vin de Pays des Colines Rhodaniennes (Fr) a Vins de Pays region in the Rhône-Alpes, south-eastern France.

Vin de Pays des Comtés Rhodaniens (Fr) a Vins de Pays region in the Rhône-Alpes, south-eastern France.

Vin de Pays des Coteaux Cévenois (Fr) a Vins de Pays region in the Languedoc-Roussillon, south-western France.

Vin de Pays des Coteaux Charitois (Fr) a Vins de Pays region in the Vallée de la Loire, central France.

Vin de Pays des Coteaux de Bessilles (Fr) a Vins de Pays region in the Languedoc-Roussillon, south-western France.

Vin de Pays des Coteaux de Cèze (Fr) a Vins de Pays region in the Languedoc-Roussillon, south-western France.

Vin de Pays des Coteaux de Coiffy (Fr) a Vins de Pays region in the Bourgogne et Est, central-eastern France.

Vin de Pays des Coteaux de Fenouillèdes (Fr) a Vins de Pays region in the Languedoc-Roussillon, south-western France.

Vin de Pays des Coteaux de Fontcaude (Fr) a Vins de Pays region in the Languedoc-Roussillon, south-western France.

Vin de Pays des Coteaux de Glanes (Fr) a Vins de Pays region in the Sud-Ouest, south-western France.

Vin de Pays des Coteaux de la Cabrerisse (Fr) a Vins de Pays region in the Languedoc-Roussillon, south-western France.

Vin de Pays des Coteaux de l'Ardèche (Fr) a Vins de Pays region in the Rhône-Alpes, south-eastern France.

Vin de Pays des Coteaux de Laurens (Fr) a Vins de Pays region in the Languedoc-Roussillon, south-western France.

Vin de Pays des Coteaux de l'Auxois (Fr) a Vins de Pays region in the Bourgogne et Est, central-eastern France.

Vin de Pays des Coteaux de Miramont (Fr) a Vins de Pays region in the Languedoc-Roussillon, south-western France.

Vin de Pays des Coteaux de Murviel (Fr) a Vins de Pays region in the Languedoc-Roussillon, south-western France.

Vin de Pays des Coteaux de Narbonne (Fr) a Vins de Pays region in the Languedoc-Roussillon, south-western France.

Vin de Pays des Coteaux de Peyriac (Fr) a Vins de Pays region in the Languedoc-Roussillon, south-western France.

Vin de Pays des Coteaux des Baronnies (Fr) a Vins de Pays region in the Rhône-Alpes, south-eastern France.

Vin de Pays des Coteaux de Tannay (Fr) a Vins de Pays region in the Vallée de la Loire, central France.

Vin de Pays des Coteaux du Cher et de l'Arnon (Fr) a Vins de Pays region in the Vallée de la Loire, central France.

Vin de Pays des Coteaux du Grésivaudan (Fr) a Vins de Pays region in the Rhône-Alpes, south-eastern France.

Vin de Pays des Coteaux du Libron (Fr) a Vins de Pays region in the Languedoc-Roussillon, south-western France.

Vin de Pays des Coteaux du Littoral Audois (Fr) a Vins de Pays region in the Languedoc-Roussillon, south-western France.

Vin de Pays des Coteaux du Pont-du-Gard (Fr) a Vins de Pays region in the Languedoc-Roussillon, south-western France.

Vin de Pays des Coteaux du Salagou (Fr) a Vins de Pays region in the Languedoc-Roussillon, south-western France.

Vin de Pays des Coteaux du Verdon (Fr) area based in Provence. Covers red wines produced from Cabernet sauvignon.

Vin de Pays des Coteaux et Terrasses de Montauban (Fr) a Vins de Pays region in the Sud-Ouest, south-western France.

Vin de Pays des Côtes Catalanes (Fr) a Vins de Pays region in the Languedoc-Roussillon, south-western France.

Vin de Pays des Côtes de Gascogne (Fr) a Vins de Pays region in the Sud-Ouest, south-western France.

Vin de Pays des Côtes de Lastours (Fr) a Vins de Pays region in the Languedoc-Roussillon, south-western France.

Vin de Pays des Côtes de Montestruc (Fr) a Vins de Pays region in the Sud-Ouest, south-western France.

Vin de Pays des Côtes de Pérignan (Fr) a Vins de Pays region in the Languedoc-Roussillon, south-western France.

Vin de Pays des Côtes de Prouille (Fr) a Vins de Pays region in the Languedoc-Roussillon, south-western France.

Vin de Pays des Côtes de Thau (Fr) a Vins de Pays region in the Languedoc-Roussillon, south-western France.

Vin de Pays des Côtes de Thongue (Fr) a Vin de Pays in the Languedoc-Roussillon, south-western France. Grape varieties: Cabernet sauvignon, Merlot and Syrah.

Vin de Pays des Côtes du Brian (Fr) a Vins de Pays region in the Languedoc-Roussillon, south-western France.

Vin de Pays des Côtes du Céressou (Fr) a Vins de Pays region in the Languedoc-Roussillon, south-western France.

Vin de Pays des Côtes du Tarn (Fr) a Vins de Pays region in the Sud-Ouest, south-western France.

Vin de Pays des Côtes du Vidourle (Fr) a Vins de Pays region in the Languedoc-Roussillon, south-western France.

Vin de Pays des Gorges de l'Hérault Vin de Pays de Tarn (Fr) *see* Côtes du Tarn.

Vin de Pays des Hauts de Badens (Fr) a Vins de Pays region in the Languedoc-Roussillon, south-western France.

Vin de Pays des Maures (Fr) a Vins de Pays region in the Provence et Corse, south-eastern France.

Vin de Pays des Monts de la Grage (Fr) a Vins de Pays region in the Languedoc-Roussillon, south-western France.

Vin de Pays des Sables-du-Golfe-du-Lion (Fr) a Vins de Pays region in the Languedoc-Roussillon, south-western France.

Vin de Pays des Sables-du-Golfe-du-Lion (Fr) a Vins de Pays region in the Provence et Corse, south-eastern France.

Vin de Pays des Terroirs Landais (Fr) a Vins de Pays region in the Sud-Ouest, south-western France.

Vin de Pays des Terroirs Landais 'Coteaux du Chalosse' (Fr) a Vins de Pays region in the Sud-Ouest, south-western France.

Vin de Pays des Terroirs Landais 'Côtes de l'Adour' (Fr) a Vins de Pays region in the Sud-Ouest, south-western France.

Vin de Pays des Terroirs Landais 'Sables de l'Océan' (Fr) a Vins de Pays region in the Sud-Ouest, south-western France.

Vin de Pays des Terroirs Landais 'Sables Fauves' (Fr) a Vins de Pays region in the Sud-Ouest, south-western France.

Vin de Pays des Vals d'Agly (Fr) a Vins de Pays region in the Languedoc-Roussillon, south-western France.

Vin de Pays de Tarn-et-Garonne (Fr) *see* Saint-Sardos.

Vin de Pays de Thézac-Perricard (Fr) a Vins de Pays region in the Sud-Ouest, south-western France.

Vin de Pays de Var (Fr) *see* Les Maures, Coteaux Varois and Mont Caume.

Vin de Pays de Vendée (Fr) *see* Fiefs Vendéens.

Vin de Pays d'Hauterive (Fr) a Vins de Pays region in the Languedoc-Roussillon, south-western France.

Vin de Pays d'Hauterive 'Coteaux du Termémès' (Fr) a Vins de Pays region in the Languedoc-Roussillon, south-western France.

Vin de Pays d'Hauterive 'Côtes de Lézignan' (Fr) a Vins de Pays region in the Languedoc-Roussillon, south-western France.

Vin de Pays d'Hauterive 'Val d'Orbieu' (Fr) a Vins de Pays region in the Languedoc-Roussillon, south-western France.

Vin de Pays d'Oc (Fr) a group of eight Vin de Pays départements within the Languedoc-Roussillon: Ardèche, Aude, Bouches-du-Rhône, Drôme, Gard, Hérault, Var and Vaucluse in Southern France. A new designation of Grand d'Oc was introduced in 2001. To qualify the wines must be aged for a minimum of 12 months and bottled in the region. They are then taste tested.

Vin de Pays du Bérange (Fr) a Vins de Pays region in the Languedoc-Roussillon, south-western France.

Vin de Pays du Bourbonnais (Fr) a Vins de Pays region in the Vallée de la Loire, central France.

Vin de Pays du Comté de Grignan (Fr) a Vins de Pays region in the Rhône-Alpes, south-eastern France.

Vin de Pays du Comté Tolosan (Fr) a Vins de Pays region in the Sud-Ouest, south-western France.

Vin du Pays du Condomois (Fr) a Vins de Pays region in the Sud-Ouest, south-western France.

Vin de Pays du Duché d'Uzès (Fr) a Vins de Pays region in the Languedoc-Roussillon, south-western France.

Vin de Pays du Gard (Fr) includes areas: Coteaux Cévenols, Coteaux Flaviens, Coteaux du Pont du Gard, Coteaux du Salavès, Coteaux du Vidourle, Mont Bouquet, Serve de Coiran, Uzège, Val de Montferrand, Vistrenque, La Vaunage and Coteaux de Cèze.

Vin du Pays du Jardin de la France (Fr) a Vins de Pays region in the Vallée de la Loire, central France.

Vin de Pays du Jardin de la France 'Marches de Bretagne' (Fr) a Vins de Pays region in the Vallée de la Loire, central France.

Vin de Pays du Jardin de la France 'Pays de Retz' (Fr) a Vins de Pays region in the Vallée de la Loire, central France.

Vin de Pays du Mont-Baudile (Fr) a Vins de Pays region in the Languedoc-Roussillon, south-western France.

Vin de Pays du Mont-Caume (Fr) a Vins de Pays region in the Provence et Corse, south-eastern France.

Vin de Pays du Périgord (Fr) a Vins de Pays region in the Sud-Ouest, south-western France.

Vin de Pays du Périgord 'Vin de Domme' (Fr) a Vins de Pays region in the Sud-Ouest, south-western France.

Vin de Pays d'Urfé (Fr) a Vins de Pays region in the Rhône-Alpes, south-eastern France.

Vin de Pays du Torgan (Fr) a Vins de Pays region in the Languedoc-Roussillon, south-western France.

Vin de Pays du Val de Cesse (Fr) a Vins de Pays region in the Languedoc-Roussillon, south-western France.

Vin de Pays du Val de Dagne (Fr) a Vins de Pays region in the Languedoc-Roussillon, south-western France.

Vin de Pays du Val de Montferrand (Fr) a Vins de Pays region in the Languedoc-Roussillon, south-western France.

Vin de Pays du Vaucluse (Fr) a wine-producing area in the Vaucluse département of south-eastern France. Produces red, rosé and dry white wines. Grape varieties are mainly Cinsault and Grenache.

Vin de Pays Portes de Méditerranée (Fr) a Vins de Pays region in the Provence et Corse, south-eastern France.

Vin de Pays Regions (Fr) *see* Bourgogne et Est/Languedoc-Roussillon/Provence et Corse/Rhône-Alpes/Sud-Ouest/Vallée de la Loire.

Vin de Plaine (Fr) the name given to inferior wine from ordinary vineyards as opposed to wine from hillsides.

Vin de Porto (Fr) Port wine.

V

Vin de Première Presse (Fr) wine from the wet solids after the first écoulage (racking). If good, will be used for blending.

Vin de Presse (Fr) the wine made from the pressed marc (after fermentation). Used to give the workman as a daily ration.

Vin de Primeur (Fr) the name given to wine that is drunk the same year that it was made, usually 3 months after the harvest.

Vin de Queue (Fr) a poor quality, inferior wine made from the pressing of the stalks.

Vin de Réserve (Fr) fine old wine used in the dosage of Champagnes to sweeten them (the sugar is firstly dissolved in the old wine). Also applies to the old vintage Champagnes used in blending in poor years.

Vin d'Erstelle (S.Afr) the label for a medium sweet white wine (Colombard 53%, Riesling 39% plus Crouchen blend) produced by the L'Avenir Estate winery, Stellenbosch, Western Cape.

Vin de Sable (Fr) a Vin de Pays wine produced in the Midi region of southern France.

Vin de Saint-Pourçain-sur-Sioule (Fr) a V.D.Q.S. wine-producing district in the Allier département in central France.

Vin de Savoie (Fr) an A.C. red, rosé and dry white wines produced in Ain, Haute-Savoie, Isère and Savoie départements. Minimum alc by vol. 9%. Name can be followed by one of sixteen crus.

Vin de Savoie-Ayze Mousseux (Fr) see Mousseux de Savoie-Ayze.

Vin de Savoie-Ayze Pétillant (Fr) also known as Pétillant de Savoie-Ayze. A.C. sparkling wines produced by the méthode gaillaçoise.

Vin de Savoie Mousseux (Fr) see Mousseux de Savoie.

Vin de Savoie-Pétillant (Fr) also known as Pétillant de Savoie. A.C. sparkling wine produced by the méthode gaillaçoise.

Vin des Dieux (Fr) lit: 'wine of the Gods', a term used to describe sweet, botrytised wines.

Vin des Matines (Fr) a red wine from the A.C. Saumur, Anjou-Saumur, Loire.

Vin des Noces (Fr) lit: 'marriage wine', wine offered as a gift to the priest who performed the ceremony.

Vin d'Estaing (Fr) a V.D.Q.S. wine-producing district in the Aveyron département. Also known as Vins d'Estaing.

Vin de Table (Fr) the lowest classification of French table wine.

Vin de Taille (Fr) in Champagne after the Vin de Cuvée. The next 25litres of juice from the 160kgs of grapes.

Vin de Tête (Fr) an abbreviated form of Tête de Cuvée meaning best cuvée.

Vin de Veille (Fr) lit: 'vigilant wine' a night cap of wine placed beside the King's bed in case he required a drink during the night in the middle ages.

Vin de Vierge (Fr) lit: 'wine of the virgin', an old term for new wine.

Vin d'Honneur (Fr) signifies a drink on a moderately formal occasion to honour a guest.

Vin Diable (Fr) lit: 'devil wine', the name given to a bottle of Champagne which has burst through too much pressure.

Vindicta Bistrika (Cro) a sparkling natural spring mineral water from Bistrika. Mineral contents (milligrammes per litre): Sodium 1mg/l, Calcium 51mg/l, Magnesium 28mg/l, Potassium 1mg/l, Bicarbonates 280mg/l, Chlorides 2mg/l, Sulphates 9mg/l, Nitrates 1mg/l.

Vindima (Port) vintage/grape harvest.

Vindimador (Port) grape picker.

Vindimar (Port) the gathering (harvesting) of the grapes.

Vin d'Neuches (Ch.Isles) marriage wine.

Vin d'Orange (Fr) an orange-flavoured liqueur 14.8% alc by vol.

Vin Doré (USA) a sweet 'altar wine' produced by the Novitiate Vineyards of Los Gatos, California. Is a Sauternes-style wine.

Vin Doux (Fr) sweet wine.

Vin Doux Muté (Fr) a liqueur wine produced by adding alcohol to partially fermented grape must after extraction.

Vin Doux Naturel (Fr) a fortified wine produced in southern France where fermentation has been arrested by the addition of grape brandy to retain some of the natural sugar in the wine. Brandy can be added at an early stage of fermentation or later. Much depends on the style of wine. see Muscat de Beaumes de Venise, Banyuls, Muscat de Frontignan, Muscat de Rivesaltes.

Vin Doux Passerillé (Fr) liqueur wines produced from musts with high sugar contents and from raisin grapes. 13%–15% alc by vol (part of the sugar remains).

Vin Doux Semi-Muté (Fr) a liqueur wine produced by adding alcohol to the partially fermented musts to raise the alcohol to 15% by vol.

Vin du Bugey (Fr) a V.D.Q.S. district near Savoie. Produces white wine from the Roussette grape. Also light-styled, red, rosé and sparkling white wines. Includes A.C. Roussette de Bugey and Vin de Bugey (plus name of Cru) 9.5% alc by vol. minimum.

Vin du Bugey-Cerdon Mousseux (Fr) an A.C. sparkling wines produced in the Savoie region by the méthode traditionelle.

Vin du Bugey-Cerdon Pétillant (Fr) an A.C. sparkling wines produced in the Savoie region by the méthode gaillaçoise.

Vin du Bugey Mousseux (Fr) see Mousseux du Bugey.

Vin du Bugey Pétillant (Fr) also known as Pétillant du Bugey. A.C. sparkling wines produced by the méthode gaillaçoise in the Savoie region.

Vin du Clerc (Fr) a wine offered to the clerk of the court by the defendant if the verdict of the tribunal was found in his favour.

Vin du Coucher (Fr) night cap.

Vin du Curé (Fr) a wine offered after baptism to the priest who performed the service.

Vin du Glacier (Switz) see Vin de Glacier.

Vin du Haut-Poitou (Fr) a V.D.Q.S. wine-producing

district in the Vienne département. Produces red (minimum alc by vol. 9%), rosé and white wines (minimum alc by vol. 9.5%).

Vin du Marche (Fr) a wine originally given to someone as a gift for helping in a business transaction. Also known as Pot de Vin.

Vin du Mistral (USA) a white Viognier wine produced by Joseph Phelps, St. Helena, Napa Valley, California.

Vin d'Une Nuit (Fr) a St. Saturnin (rosé). So called because the grape skins were left in contact with the must for one night. Now are usually left in for longer periods.

Vin du Rhin Français (Fr) denotes Alsatian wines, wines from the French Rhine in Alsace. see Vins d'Alsace.

Vin du Thouarsais (Fr) a V.D.Q.S. wine-producing region in the Deux-Sèvres département, western France. Red, white and rosé from Cabernet franc, Cabernet sauvignon, Chenin blanc grapes.

Vin du Tursan (Fr) a V.D.Q.S. wine-producing region in the Landes département, south-western France.

Vin Dynamique (Fr) a herb-flavoured, tonic wine produced by the Bénédictine monks in the Middle Ages. see Buckfast (an off-spring of).

Vine (Eng) the plant on which grapes grow. see Vitis. (Ire) = finiuin.

Viné (Fr) the illegal practice of adding alcohol to wine to increase its alcoholic strength. Not to be confused with fortification.

Vinea (Eng) an old British name for monastery vineyards.

Vinea (Lat) vineyard, See also Vinetum.

Vinea Wachau Nobilis Districtus (Lat) created in 1985 it is the first Austrian designated wine region (from an orginal document circa 1285 by Leuthold I of Kuenring). The Steinfelder has a strict policy of not chaptalising their wines and a maximum alcohol content of 11% by volume. Over 85% of the region is covered by the policy.

Vine Cliff Winery (USA) a winery based in the Oakville, Napa Valley, California. Grape varieties include Chardonnay, Cabernet sauvignon, Merlot. Label: 16 Rows Private Stock.

Vinedale Brewery (Ind) a brewery based in Hyderabad. Produces: Black Beard 1044 O.G. Crazy 1064 O.G. and Regal 1042 O.G.

Vinedea (Gre) the Greek goddess of wine.

Vinedey (Fr) a Cru Champagne village in the Canton de Sézanne. District: Épernay.

Viñedo (Sp) vineyard

Viñedos del Contino (Sp) wines produced by the Sociedad Vinícola Laserna, Rioja. Oak matured.

Viñedos Emiliana (Chile) a winery based in Rapel. Grape varieties include: Cabernet sauvignon, Carmenère, Malbec.

Viñedos Organicos (Chile) an organic winery based in the Central Valley. Grape varieties include : Cabernet sauvignon, Carmenère, Merlot. Labels: Emiliana Adobe, Emiliana Novas.

Viñedos San Marcos (Mex) a noted vineyard based

in Aguascalientes. Owned by Don Nazario Ortiz Garza.

Viñedos y Bodegas de la Marquesa (Sp) a vineyard and winery. (Add): La Lleca s/n, 01307 Villabuena, Alava. Produces red Valserrano Rioja wine which is aged for 24 months in oak casks.

Viñedos y Bodegas Tempus Alba (Arg) a winery based in the Mendoza region, eastern Argentina. Website: http://www.tempusalba.com 'E'mail: info@tempusalba.com

Vine Dresser (Eng) a person who tends to the vines, a vineyard worker.

Vine Dried (Eng) the process of leaving the grapes to partially dry whilst still on the vine to concentrate the sugar content. The process can be used for both white and red grape varieties and is used extensively in California and South Africa. See also Late Harvest.

Vine Dresser (USA) old name for vineyard cultivators.

Vin Effervescent (Fr) sparkling wine, a term used in Vouvray in the Touraine district of the Loire.

Vine Flow (USA) the label used by the Bella Napoli Winery.

Vinegar (Eng) the result of the vinegar bacterium *Acetobacter* when it feeds upon the alcohol in wine or beer etc. The alcohol is converted into Acetic acid which turns the wine/beer etc. to vinegar. Prevented by excluding air. CH_3COOH. Acetic acid. (Arab) = khal, (Aus) = essig, (Chi) = cu, (Den) = eddike, (Fr) = acétique/vinaigre, (Ger) = essig, (Gre) = xithi, (Hol) = azijn, (Ind) = cuka, (Ire) = finéager, (Isr) = hometz, (It) = aceto, (Jap) = osu, (Kor) = sikcho, (Lat) = acetum, (Pol) = ocet, (Port) = vinagre, (Rus) = ooksoos, (Sp) = vinagre, (Thai) = namsomsaichoo, (Tur) = sirke.

Vinegar Eel (Eng) *Anguillula aceti* a nematode worm that feeds on the organisms that cause the fermentation in vinegar, etc. Also known as the vinegar worm.

Vinegar Fly (Eng) *Drosophila melanogaster* or fruit fly, attracted by the smell of fruit. Carries vinegar bacteria which in turn may infect the wine in the winery.

Vinegar Taint (Eng) the smell caused by lactic acid bacteria which produce acetic acid which gives wine a smell, also caused by wild yeasts. Wine **has not** turned to vinegar.

Vinegar Worm (Eng) see Vinegar Eel.

Vine Hill Vineyard (USA) a vineyard based in Santa Cruz, California. Grape varieties: Chardonnay and Johannisberg riesling. Owned by Smothers. See also Felton Empire.

Vineland Estates (Can) has the Saint Urban vineyard in Vineland, Ontario. 80ha. Wines produced include Riesling, barrel-fermented Chardonnay, Cabernet and ice wines.

Vine Leaf (Eng) the brand-name used by Lamb and Watt of Liverpool, Lancashire for Sherry.

Vinello (It) the Italian diminutive for wine, always poor, thin vin ordinaire. See also Vinetto and Vinettino.

Vine Louse (Eng) a slang term for the **Phylloxera vastatrix**.

Vine Mealybug (USA) **Planococcus ficus** a vine pest which resides under the vine bark and in the roots. Its presence damages the quality of the grapes. Trials of detection are being carried out with dogs (golden retrievers) to sniff out the mealybug.

Vinenca (Bul) a noted wine-producing area.

Vin en Vrac (Fr) *see* Vrac.

Vineous (Eng) wine-like/tastes of wine. (Ire) = finiúnach.

Vine Products Commission (Cyp) a body set up in 1968 to help maintain the quality and standard of wines.

Vine Products Cooperative Marketing Union Ltd. (Cyp) *see* SODAP.

Vine Products Ltd. (Eng) a winery. (Add): Kingston-Upon-Thames, London. Producers of British Wines including Hudson & Cooper Sherries, Lord Ducane, QC, RSVP, VP, Vibrona and Votrix. Now part of the Gaymer Group.

Viner (Fr) to add alcohol to a wine.

Vinería (Sp) winery.

Vinery (Eng) a place where grapes are grown. (Ire) = teach gloine finiúna.

Vine Tarius (Lat) wine merchant.

Vinetier (Fr) an old French word for a wine merchant.

Vinettino (It) poor, thin wine, vin ordinaire. *See also* Vinello and Vinetto.

Vinetto (It) poor, thin wine, vin ordinaire. *See also* Vinello and Vinettino.

Vinetum (Lat) vineyard *See also* Vinea.

Vineus (Lat) belonging to wine.

Vineux (Fr) vinosity.

Vine-Vivarium (It) a vine museum opened in the Asti district of Piemonte in the eighteenth and nineteenth centuries by the Rocchetta family at Rocchetta Tanaro. Had over 300 vine species growing.

Vinexport (Rum) a government-run body which controls wine production. Headquarters in Bucharest.

Vineyard (Eng) the name given to an area that is planted with vines. (Aus) = weingut, (Fr) = vignoble, (Ger) = weingut, (Ire) = fionghort, (It) = vigneto, (Lat) = vinetem/vinea, (Port) = vinha, (Rum) = viile, (Scan) = vingarthr, (Sp) = viñedo.

Vineyard Collection (S.Afr) the label for a range of wines produced by the Oranjerivier Wine Cellars winery, Lower Orange, Northern Cape.

Vineyard Collection (S.Afr) the label for a red wine (mainly Merlot) produced by the JP Bredell winery, Stellenbosch, Western Cape.

Vineyard Selection (S.Afr) the label for a range of wines produced by the Blaauwklippen Agricultural Estate winery, Stellenbosch, Western Cape.

Vineyard Selection (S.Afr) a label for a range of varietal wines produced by the Kleine Zalze Wines winery, Stellenbosch, Western Cape.

Vineyard 7 and 8 (USA) a winery based in the Spring Mountain District, Napa Valley, California. Grape varieties: Cabernet sauvignon. Website: http://www.vineyard7and8.com 'E'mail: fwi@vinrare.com

Vineyard Specific (S.Afr) the label for a range of wines (Chardonnay and Shiraz-Viognier) produced by the Cape Coastal Vintners winery, Paarl, Western Cape.

Vineyard 29 (USA) a winery based in the Napa Valley, California. Grape varieties include: Cabernet sauvignon.

Vineyards [The] (Eng) a vineyard (Add): Cricks Green, Felsted, Essex. 4.5ha. Soil: clay and loam. Grape varieties: Madeleine angevine, Sylvaner, Müller-Thurgau, Pinot chardonnay, Pinot noir, Scheurebe, Seyval blanc and Wrotham pinot.

Vin Fin (Fr) a loosely applied term meaning 'fine wine' or 'wine of quality'.

Vin Fin d'Alsace (Fr) a denomination that edelzwicker wines could use in Alsace.

Vin Fins des Hautes Côtes (Fr) the general term used for any wine that is from the specified area of western Burgundy.

Vin Flétri (Switz) the Swiss name for Vin de Paille (straw colour wine).

Vin Fou (Fr) the Jura name for the local sparkling wine.

Vin Fumé (S.Afr) a wood-matured, white wine produced by the Simonsig Estate Wines.

Vingaard (Den) winery.

Vingarthr (Scan) vineyard

Vingrau (Fr) denotes Côtes du Roussillon-Villages wines.

Vin Gris (Fr) a cheap wine made in the eastern part of France from a mixture of red and white grapes.

Vinha (Port) vineyard (also vine).

Vinha ao Alto (Port) describes vines planted in vertical lines running up and down a natural slope.

Vinha do Ponte (Port) a still red wine produced by Port shippers Quinta do Crasto.

Vinhão (Port) a black grape variety grown in the Entre Minho e Douro to produce deep red wines (has red flesh and juice). Also known as the Sousão.

Vinhas Velhas (Port) old vineyard (vines).

Vinhateiro (Port) wine-producer (vine-grower).

Vinhedo (Port) a large vineyard

Vinho (Port) wine.

Vinho à Granel (Mad) the name given to the bulk wine in Madeira production.

Vinho Branco (Port) white wine.

Vinho Claro (Mad) the name given to the new wine after fermentation and before fortification.

Vinho Consumo (Port) the term used to describe an ordinary everyday wine.

Vinho Criado (Port) wine waiter.

Vinho da Roda (Mad) lit: 'wine of the round voyage', the old nick-name for Madeira wines.

Vinho de Mesa (Port) table wine from no particular region.

V

Vinho de Mesa Regional (Port) denotes table wines from a specified region. One of five: Alentejo, Beiras, Estremadura, Ribatejo and Tràs-os-Montes.

Vinho de Pasto (Port) denotes quality table wine. *See also* Vinho de Mesa.

Vinho Doce (Port) sweet wine.

Vinho do Porto (Port) Port wine/Port.

Vinho do Rodo (Port) sparkling wine.

Vinho Espumante (Port) sparkling wine. *See also* Vinho Spumoso.

Vinho Estufado (Mad) the name given to Madeira wine after it leaves the estufada, after resting becomes Vinho Transfugado.

Vinho Garrafeira (Port) *see* Garrafeira.

Vinho Generoso (Mad) a Madeira wine that has been fortified and is ready to go into the solera system for blending.

Vinho Licoroso (Port) fortified wine. *See also* Vinho Liquoroso.

Vinho Liquoroso (Port) fortified wine. *See also* Vinho Licoroso.

Vinho Maduro (Port) wine which comes from the 4 regions: Bucelas, Colares, Dão and Douro. A normal mature table wine.

Vinho Qinado (Port) a tonic wine that contains quinine.

Vinho Regional (Port) a category of quality wines from one of five named (not demarcated) regions. These are: Região das Beiras, Região de Tràs-os-Montes, Região de Estremadura, Região do Ribatejo and Região do Alentejo.

Vinho Reserva (Port) an old wine from a good (vintage) year.

Vinho Rosado (Port) rosé wine.

Vinhos Barbeito (Mad) a noted Madeira wine shipper based in Funchal.

Vinhos de Monçao Lda (Port) one of 3 producers of Alvarinho. All the wine is fermented and matured in wood. Also produce Cepa Velha (a marc brandy).

Vinhos de Qualidade (Port) denotes quality wines from specified areas and produced from specified grapes.

Vinhos de Vinha (Port) single vineyard.

Vinho Seco (Port) dry wine.

Vinho Spumoso (Port) sparkling wine. *See also* Vinho Espumante.

Vinho Surdo (Mad) the name given to grape juice which is prevented from fermenting by the addition of alcohol, added to Madeira wine as a sweetening wine.

Vinho Surdo (Port) fortified wine, according to Portuguese law, Port wine must be a Vinho Surdo.

Vinho Tinto (Port) red wine.

Vinho Trasfegado (Mad) *see* Vinho Trasfugado.

Vinho Trasfugado (Mad) a Madeira wine that has been through the estufada system and then racked and ready to be fortified when it becomes Vinho Generoso.

Vinho Verde (Port) a D.O.C. region that produces light, young wine (white or red) in the Minho district. Is a pétillant wine originally produced by having the malo-lactic fermentation take place in the bottle. Nowadays more likely to be injected with CO_2. Verde denotes '*young*' and **not** '*green*'. Sub-regions: Barcelas, Moncão, Penafiel and Guimaraes. *see* APEVV. Website: http://www.vinhoverde.pt

Vini (It) wines.

Vini Bianchi (It) white wines.

Vinic (Eng) containing or relating to wine.

Vinica (Cro) a wine-producing area in Croatia.

Vinícola (Port) winery/wine-producing.

Vinicola Abbazia-Santero (It) a noted producer of Moscato Spumante in the Piemonte region.

Vinícola Andalucía (Sp) a producer and exporter of Málaga.

Vinícola de Castilla (Sp) a winery based in Manzanarès, La Mancha. Produces: Señorio de Guadianeja (a white perfumed wine). Also produce oak-aged red wines.

Vinícola del Marqués de Aguyo (Mex) a winery based at Parras de la Fuente, Coahuila. Produces table and sparkling wines.

Vinícola del Vergel (Mex) a winery and vineyard based west of Parras de la Fuente.

Vinícola de Nelas (Port) a producer of Dão wines based in Nelas.

Vinícola de Sangalhos (Port) a noted shipper of Dão wines.

Vinícola do Vale do Dão (Port) a modern winery producing Dão wines based near Viseu (owned by SOGRAPE).

Vinícola Hildago (Sp) a Sherry producer based at Sanlúcar de Barrameda. Labels include: Jerez Cortado Hildago and La Gitana.

Vinícola Ibérica (Sp) wineries (owns no vineyards) based in Utiel, Valencia and Tarragona.

Vinicola L.A. Cetto (Mex) a winery based in the Valle de Guadaloupe, Baja California. Grape varieties include: Nebbiolo.

Vinícola Navarra (Sp) a winery based Las Campanas in Navarra. Noted for Castillo de Tiebas (a full-bodied, red wine) and Las Campanas, partially owned by Savin.

Vinícola Ribalonga (Port) noted producers of red Dão wines based in the Bierra Alta.

Vinícola Vizcaina, Rojas y Cía (Sp) a noted wine-producer based in Rioja.

Vinicultor (Sp) wine grower.

Viniculture (Eng) the making and maturing of wine.

Vini da Bianco (It) table wine.

Vini da Tavola (It) table wines (plural), lowest classification of table wine. Vino da Tavola.

Vini dei Castelli (It) wines from the Alban hills near Rome. i.e. Est! Est!! Est!!! and Frascati.

Vini dei Castelli Romani (It) the name of the wine consumed by the Romans. Now known as Frascati.

Vini del Piave (It) *see* Piave.

Vini di Lusso (It) the term used for an expensive, fine, dessert wine (fortified).

Vinifera (Lat) part of the genus **Vitis**. Includes European vines which are cultivated all over the world. *see* **Vitis vinifera**.

Vinifera Vineyard (USA) a winery based near the west shore on Lake Keuka, Finger Lakes, New York. Grape varieties: Chardonnay, Pinot noir and Riesling. Produces varietal wines.

Vinifera Wine Grower's Association (USA) an experimental winery and vineyard based in Highbury, Virginia.

Vinification (Eng) the making of wine at all stages, fermentation, ageing, etc. (excluding vineyard work).

Vinification à Chaud (Fr) the fermentation method where a higher temperature than normal is used. Mainly used in the southern Rhône.

Vinificato Fuori Zona (It) a term denoting 'vinified outside the production area'.

Vinificato in Bianco (It) taken quickly off the skins, term used in the Tuscany region.

Vinificator (Eng) in distillation a condenser that collects escaping alcohol vapours.

Vinifié (Fr) vinified/made into wine.

Vinified (Eng) a term to denote that grape juice has been fermented into wine. (Fr) = vinifié.

Vinifier (Fr) the process where the grape juice is turned (fermented) into wine.

Viniloire Chasam (Fr) a winery. (Add): Boulevard de l'Industrie, Zide Nazelles Amboise, Touraine, Loire. A wine company that filters and bottles wines.

Vinimark (S.Afr) a winery based in Stellenbosch, Western Cape. Labels: Brad Gold, Jonkerskloof, Kleindal, Long Beach, Ravenswood, Silver Sands, Zomerlust. Website: http://www.vinimark.co.za

Vinimatic (USA) rotating horizontal stainless steel vat.

Vinimpex (Bul) the State Commercial Enterprise for Export and Import of Wines and Spirits. A monopoly that controlled all wine exports (ended in 1992).

Vini Rosati (It) rosé wine.

Vini Rossi (It) red wines.

Vinis Iambol (Bul) a private winery that buys in grapes from local producers.

Vinitaly (It) the world's largest, annual, specialty wine trade exhibition. Held in Verona during the first full week of April.

Vinitech (Euro) an annual international exhibition for vinification, oenology and cellar equipment.

Vini Tipici (It) a standard/ordinary wine.

Vinitor (Lat) vine dresser.

VINIVAL (Sp) a large winery based in Valencia, noted for Torres de Serrano (red and white wines).

Vini Veri (It) lit: 'real wines', a term used to describe naturally made wines without any artificial assistance.

Vinjak (Slo) brandy.

Vinjak Cezar (Slo) a brand of local grape brandy.

Vin Jaune (Fr) lit: 'yellow wine', a wine produced in the Jura region, eastern France where the wine is exposed to the air and flor is encouraged to grow. Produced from the Savagnin grape, aged in cask for 6 years. see Flor and Château Chalon.

Vinkrivier Wines (S.Afr) the label for the wines of the Rooiberg Koöperatiewe.

Vinland (N.Am) the Vikings name for the North Americas because of the vines there. Also known as Vinland the Good. see Vitis labrusca.

Vinmark (USA) a label used by the Markham Winery for wines produced from bought in grapes.

Vin Medecin (Fr) basic Bordeaux wine made a little more palatable by a small amount of wine from elsewhere other than Bordeaux.

Vinmonopolet (Nor) see A/S Vinmonopolet.

Vin Mousseux (Fr) sparkling wine.

Vin Mousseux Gazéifié (USA) sparkling wine carbonated artificially. Must have this term on the label.

Vinnaioli Jermann (It) a winery based in Farra d'Isonzo in the Friuli-Venezia-Guilia region.

Vin Nature (Fr) a natural, unsweetened (chaptalised) wine.

Vin Nature de Champagne (Fr) still wine made in the Champagne region. Also known as Coteaux Champenois.

Vin Nobile du Minervois (Fr) an A.C. sweet white wine produced in Minervois, southern France from Grenache, Maccabéo, Malvoisie and Muscat grapes. Minimum alc by vol. 13%.

Vin Non-Mousseus (Fr) the name given to still wine.

Vin Nouveau (Fr) new wine. see Beaujolais Nouveau.

Vino (Cro)(It)(Sp) wine.

Vino (S.Afr) the label for a non-vintage white wine (Chardonnay) produced by the Mons Ruber Estate winery, Little Karoo.

Vino Aloque (Sp) the name given to wine produced in Valdepeñas from a blend of red and white grapes.

Vino Bevanda (It) an ordinary beverage wine.

Vino Bianco (It) white wine.

Vino Blanco (Sp) white wine.

Vino Caldo (It) mulled Claret wine.

Vino Clarete (Sp) light red wine.

Vino Comarcal (Sp) abbr: V.C. a halfway house between between Vino de la Mesa and Vino de la Tierra. Full name: Vino de Otras Comarcas Con Derecho A La Utilización De Mención Geográfica En Vino De Mesa.

Vino Comun (Sp) an ordinary wine. See also Vino Corriente.

Vino Corriente (Sp) lit: 'current or running wine', vin ordinaire, usually red carafe wine. Also known as Vino Comun.

Vino Cotto (It) lit: 'cooked wine', made by boiling down grape must and adding brandy. i.e. in Marsala. For colouring and sweetening.

Vino Crudo (Sp) young/immature wine.

Vino da Arrosto (It) describes a fine wine with breeding.

Vino da Indicazione (It) replaces I.G.T. for the 1995/1996 harvest. Denotes a wine above the basic Vino da Tavola standard. Wines with this on the label must carry the name of geographical zone. Equivalent to the French Vin de Pays.

Vino da Meditazione (It) lit: 'for meditation', a great, fine wine which should be drunk with consideration, in peace and quiet and usually without food.

Vino da Pasto (It) denotes an everyday table wine.

Vino da Taglio (It) a wine used for blending.

Vino da Tavola (It) table wine.

Vino da Tavola con Indicazione Geografica Tipica (It) *abbr:* I.G.T. Denoted a table wine from a defined area. Introduced for 1995 harvest. Term was not recognised by E.C. For 1995/1996 harvest Vino da Indicazione had been approved.

Vino de Agujas (Sp) a pétillant, dry white wine produced in the Galicia region.

Vino de Añada (Sp) a young wine of one vintage ready for the criadera reservas.

Vino de Arrosto (It) *see* Vino da Arrosto.

Vino de Calidad (Sp) quality wines produced from free-run or lightly pressed juice which has undergone a controlled fermentation.

Vino de Color (Sp) denotes Pedro ximénez grape must boiled down and fortified with brandy to darken it. Used for enriching and adding colour to Sherries mainly for the British market. *see* Paxerete and Cuytes.

Vino de Corazón (Sp) the wine produced in Rioja after the vino de lágrima has been removed, the remaining grapes are aroused with a fork, fermented, and the resulting wine is then mixed with the vino de lágrima.

Vino de Cosecha Propria (Sp) a wine made by the owner of the vineyard.

Vino de Crianza (Sp) wines of the Rioja region which have been aged for a minimum of 2 complete years of which at least 1 year must be in oak cask with a capacity of 225 litres.

Vino de Crianza (Sp) a suitable wine destined to become Sherry.

Vino de Cuarte (Sp) the name given to a Valencian rosé wine.

Vino de Doble Pasta (Sp) a vino de lágrima that has had crushed grapes added. It ferments yielding a wine at 18% alc by vol.

Vino de Gran Reserva (Sp) red wines, aged for 2 years in oak, then 3 years in bottle. White and rosé wines aged for 4 years of which 6 months minimum should be in cask.

Vino de Jerez (Sp) Sherry, the wine from the Jerez district in Andalusia.

Vino de la Costa (Sp) a light, slightly sweet wine from the Andalucian hills in south-western Spain.

Vino de Lágrima (Sp) the wine after the first light pressing of the grapes. Produced in Rioja. Can also be made from the 'free-run juice'. *see* Vino de Corazón.

Vino de la Tierra (Sp) a Vin de Pays wine of the region. Just below D.O. Wines come from specially demarcated regions which do not have D.O. status but which are identifiably local wines with local character. Full name: Vino de Mesa Con Derecho Al Uso De Una Indicación Geográfica. (Fr) = vin de pays, (Ger) = landwein.

Vino della Riviera (It) describes a wine as having originated from the Lombardy region of Lake Garda.

Vino da Meditazione (It) lit: 'meditation wine' a slang term for any wine that is sipped and not quaffed.

Vino de Mesa (Sp) table wine.

Vino de Mesa Con Derecho Al Uso De Una Indicación Geográfica (Sp) better known as Vino de la Tierra.

Vino de Otras Comarcas Con Derecho A La Utilización De Mención Geográfica En Vino De Mesa (Sp) table wine from other districts with the right to the use of a regional mention. The equivalent to Vino Comarcal.

Vino de Pasto (Sp) table wine.

Vino de Prensa (Sp) a term used to refer to the wine that has been obtained by hydraulic pressing. Is rich in tannin, dark and undrinkable unless blended.

Vino de Reserva (Sp) red wines aged a minimum of 1 year in oak, then 2 years in bottle. White and rosé wines aged in cask and bottled for a minimum of 24 months including 6 months in oak.

Vino de Yema (Sp) lit: 'yolk of the wine', the name given to wine that is drawn off the vat first.

Vino de Zamora (Sp) a Vino de la Tierra Castilla-León situated between the towns of Toro and Zamora. 1500ha. Main grape varieties are Tinto del País, Garnacha tinta, Malvasía, Moscatel plus Cabernet sauvignon and Palomino. Wines are mainly red and rosé.

Vino di Famiglia (It) mellow wine, soft, with no acidity or tannin.

Vino di Lusso (It) fortified wine.

Vino Dolce Naturale (It) naturally sweet wine that has no added sugar.

Vinodolsko (Cro) a red wine produced off the north-western Croatian coast.

Vino Dorado (Sp) the equivalent to Vin de Paille.

Vino Dulce (Sp) sweet wine used for blending.

Vino Esperanto (Eng) a dry white wine produced by the St. Georges Vineyard to celebrate 100 years of the Esperanto language in 1984. The label written in Esperanto.

Vino Espumoso (Sp) sparkling wine, authorised vines are: Garnacha, Maccabéo, Malvasia, Monastrell, Parellada and Xarel-lo (cava wine). Only 100 litres of must may be extracted from 160kgs of grapes. Second fermentation is carried out in the bottle. Disgorging occurs by transferring to tank. Cork has a rectangle on base. If the second fermentation is carried out in sealed containers (tanks), the wine is known as Granvás. *See also* Vino Espumoso Método Tradicional.

Vino Espumoso Método Tradicional (Sp) equivalent production method as cava but outside the designated production area. Same maturation rules apply as for cava wines. Cork carries a four pointed star (as for cava) on base.

Vino Fiore (It) a red wine produced by Corvo in Sicily. *See also* Duca Enrico.

V

Vino Frizzante (It) a lightly sparkling-style of wine that is usually consumed locally.

Vino Gasificado (Sp) sparkling wine that has been produced by carbonation. Cork carries an equilateral triangle on the base.

Vino Generoso (Sp) fortified wine.

Vino Joven (Sp) lit: 'young wine', may or may not have spent time in cask, bottled year following vintage, equivalent to Sin Crianza.

Vinolentia (Lat) wine drinking.

Vinolentus (Lat) drunk/intoxicated. *See also* Potus.

Vino Liquoroso (It) fortified wine.

Vino-Lok (Ger) a new (2004) ™glass cork produced by the Alcoa company that can seal a wine bottle and be re-used to stopper the remaining contents of the bottle.

Vino Maestro (Sp) master wine, a sweet full wine used to lend character and body to a weaker, thin wine.

Vinometer (Eng) an implement used to test the alcohol content of a dry wine (not one with residual sugar).

Vino Naturalmente Dolce (It) a naturally sweet wine, has no added sugar.

Vino Nobile di Montepulciano (It) a D.O.C.G. red wine from the Tuscany region. Made from 50%–70% Prugnolo gentile plus Canaiolo, Malvasia del chianti, Mammolo, Pulcinculo and Trebbiano toscano grapes. Vinifiction and ageing must occur in Montepulciano. Must be aged 2 years in wood. If aged 3 years then classed Riserva. If 4 years then is classed Riserva Speciale.

Vino Novello (It) is Italy's answer to France's Beaujolais Nouveau. Released on November 14th.

Vino Ordinario (It) ordinary wine, not usually bottled.

Vino Passito (It) *see* Passito.

Vinophile (Eng) a wine lover.

Vinoproizvoditel (Bul) wine-producer.

Vino Qualité Produttorio Regione Delimité (It) *see* V.Q.P.R.D.

Vino Rancio (Sp) denotes a white wine that has maderised or has been fortified.

Vin Ordinaire (Fr) ordinary cheap wine for general consumption.

Vino Rosado (Sp) rosé wine.

Vino Rosso (It) red wine.

Vino Santo (It) lit: 'Saint's wine', a wine made from grapes dried indoors over the winter. Cantucci biscuits are usually served with the wine and are often dipped in the wine to soften them.

Vino Santo di Gambellara (It) *see* Vin Santo di Gambellara.

Vinos Blancos de Castilla (Sp) a noted winery based in Rueda.

Vinos Corrientes (Sp) the equivalent to the French Vin Ordinaires.

Vinos de Aguja (Sp) lit: 'needle wines', bone-dry and slightly pétillant, it is produced from Prieto picudo grapes.

Vinos de Año (Sp) red Rioja wines that are neither aged in cask or bottle.

Vinos de Calidad Producidos En Regiones Determinadas (Sp) *abbr*: V.C.P.R.D. equivalent to Q.W.P.S.R.

Vinos de Castilla (Sp) a large private bodega based in the La Mancha region. Produces Castillo de Manza wines.

Vinos de Chile (Chile) a noted winery and exporter of Chilean wines based in Santiago.

Vinos de Crianza (Sp) are Montilla-Moriles wines below 15% alc by vol. Matured through the solera system. *see* Afrutado, Vinos Generosos.

Vinos de Léon (Sp) the alternative name for VILE.

Vinos de Los Herederos del Marqués de Riscal (Sp) vineyards. (Add): Torrea, 1- Elciego (Alava) 300ha. Grape varieties: Cabernet 5%, Merlot 5%, Tempranillo 80% and Viura 10%. Produces 95% red wine and 5% rosé wine.

Vinos del Tea (Sp) wines produced in D.O. Palma. So called because they are aged in casks of pine wood (tea).

Vinos de Madrid (Sp) a Denominación de Origen area of Madrid of approximately 11758ha. Divided into 3 sub-zones: Arganda, Navalcarnero, San Martín de Valdeiglesias. Grape varieties: Garnacha, Tinto fino, Airén, Albillo, Malvar. Red, white and rosé wines are produced.

Vinos de Saca (Sp) export wines, from the word (sacar = to draw from). Sack may have derived from this word.

Vino Seco (S.Am) a mixture of red and white wines, fortified with alcohol which are allowed to maderise in the sun. Produced in Uruguay.

Vino Seco (Sp) dry wine.

Vinos Generosos (Sp) describes Montilla-Moriles wines that have reached above 15% alc by vol. They are lightly fortified and solera matured. *see* Afrutado, Vinos Generosos.

Vinosity (Eng) refers to the 'wine-like' smell and taste of the beverage.

Vinos Jovenes Afrutados (Sp) *see* Afrutado.

Vino Spumante (It) sparkling wine.

Vino Spumoso (Sp) the term for any sparkling wine. *See also* Cava and Granvas.

Vinos Quinados (Sp) the name given to tonic wines that contain quinine extract. e.g. Calisay.

Vinos Sanz (Sp) a winery based in La Seca and Medina del Campo, Rueda.

Vinosul S/A (Bra) *see* Central Vinícola do Sul.

Vinosus (Lat) wine-bibber, someone who is fond of wine.

Vinoteka (Slo) wine library.

Vinothek (Aus)(Ger) wine library.

Vinothéque (Fr) wine library.

Vino Tierno (Sp) a sweet wine made from dried out grapes. Used in the making of Málaga.

Vino Tintillo (Sp) pale red wine.

Vino Tinto (Sp) red wine.

Vinous (Eng) pertaining to wine.

Vinous Orders (Eng) denotes chapters and brotherhoods whose rules are for the promotion, quality maintainence etc. of wines. *See also* Chevaliers.

V

Vino Virgen (Sp) wine fermented from grapes without the skins or pips.

Vinozavod (Rus) wine factory.

Vin Piment (Fr) a red wine produced in early times usually flavoured with herbs.

Vin Pimentaï (Ch.Isles) mulled or spiced wine.

Vinprom (Bul) the state marketing organisation that owned 10% of vineyards, ran research institutes (disbanded in 1990).

Vinprom Pomorie (Bul) private winery, buys in grapes from local producers.

Vin Rafraîchisseur (Fr) wine cooler.

Vin Rosé (Fr) a pink coloured wine of varying shades made from red grapes, the wines being left on the skins for a short time only (from 2 hours to 2 days depending on the grape variety and climate). *See also* Blush Wines and White Zinfandel.

Vin Rose (Rum) rosé wine.

Vin Rosu (Rum) red wine.

Vin Rouge (Fr) red wine.

Vin Ruspo (It) *see* Rosato di Carmignano.

Vin Salso (It) a wine produced in Venice at the Cipriani Hotel. Grapes are transported to the Capanella vineyard in Gaiole, Tuscany. 1500 bottles produced. The oak matured wine is made from 80% Refosco plus Fragolino, Cabernet sauvignon and Merlot grapes.

Vins Amers (Fr) bitter wines. *see* Absinthe, Gentian and Quinquina.

Vinsanti (It) *see* Vino Santo.

Vin Santo (It) *see* Vino Santo.

Vin Santo del Chianti Classico (It) a D.O.C. wine. Grape varieties: min. 70% Trebbiano plus Malvasia. For Occhio di Pernice version a minimum of 50% Sangiovese. The grapes are not dried or pressed before December 1st or after March 31st. Must be vinified, kept and aged in caratelli with a capacity no greater than 5 hl. Not less than 3 years ageing. If aged 4 years = Riserva. At end of ageing must be 16% alc by vol.

Vin Santo di Carmignano (It) a D.O.C. wine. Grape varieties minimum: 75% Trebbiano/Malvasia with up to 25% other authorised, recognised white varieties such as San Colombano. Wine is aged in small caretelli for 3–4 years. Cannot be sold before November 1st of the fourth year after harvest.

Vin Santo di Gambellara (It) a D.O.C. white wine from the Veneto region. Made from partially dried Garganega, Nostrano and Trebbiano grapes. Must be aged for 2 years minimum.

Vin Sauvage (Fr) a sparkling white wine of the Gers region of south-east France. Has a powerful mousse and is very acidic, often used for the making of pousse rapière.

Vins Clairs (Fr) base wines (after the first fermentation in Champagne) before blending.

Vins d'Alsace (Fr) Alsatian wines, the wines of Alsace in north-eastern France. Also Vins du Rhin Français.

Vins d'Appellation d'Origine Garantie (Alg) *abbr:* V.A.O.G. an A.C. conferred by Institut Algérien de la Vigne et du Vin.

Vins de Base (Fr) base wines, a term used in sparkling wine production to denote what the base wine was.

Vins de Bugey (Fr) a V.D.Q.S. wine-producing district in Savoie, south-eastern France.

Vins de Café (Fr) everyday drinking wines often not bottled but served straight from the cask.

Vins de Comptoir (Fr) denotes everyday, pleasant drinking wines.

Vins de Consommation Courante (Fr) *abbr:* V.C.C. everyday drinking wines, also referred to as Vins Ordinaires de Consommation Courante.

Vins de Diable (Fr) lit: 'wines of the devil', an early term used to describe Champagnes that burst the bottles because of too much pressure.

Vins de Haut-Poitou (Fr) a V.D.Q.S. wine-producing district in the Vienne département in western France.

Vins de la Moselle (Fr) a V.D.Q.S. white wines produced in the valley of the river Moselle in Lorraine, north-eastern France. Three regions: Metz, Sierk and Vic-sur-Seille.

Vins de l'Étoile (Fr) dry white and sparkling wines of the Arbois area in the Jura region.

Vins Délimités de Qualité Supérieur (Fr) *see* V.D.Q.S. *See also* A.O.V.D.Q.S.

Vins de Liqueur (Fr) *see* Vin de Liqueur.

Vins de l'Orléanais (Fr) are V.D.Q.S. wines from the region around Orléans in the Touraine district of the Loire. Red, rosé and white wines.

Vins de Marcillac (Fr) a small V.D.Q.S. red wine-producing area in south-western France.

Vins de Marque (Fr) everyday wines, one up from V.C.C. wines though still for everyday drinking only.

Vins de Négoce (Fr) shippers' wines, wines, usually generic, that are blended by the négociant.

Vins d'Entraygues et du Fel (Fr) a small V.D.Q.S. light red and rosé wine-producing area in the Cantal and Aveyron départements in south-western France. Minimum alc by vol. red 9% and white 10%.

Vins de Paille (Fr) straw wines. *see* Vin de Paille.

Vins de Pays (Fr) country wines, the localised classification for table wines from defined areas.

Vins de Pays Départementaux (Fr) a classification for country wines that are produced from within a French administrative département (e.g. Pyrénées-Atlantique).

Vins de Pays Locaux (Fr) a classification for table wines from a defined local area (often within a Vins de Pays Régionaux) where the locallity is attached to the regional name (e.g. Vin de Pays de l'Aude-Coteaux de Narbonne).

Vins de Pays Régionaux (Fr) a classification for country wines from large regional areas.

Vins de Qualité Produits dans des Régions Déterminées (E.C.) *abbr:* V.Q.P.R.D. the grading for all quality wines in the E.C.

Vins de Renaison (Fr) the alternative name for Côtes Roannaises wines in the Loire.

Vins d'Estaing (Fr) a V.D.Q.S. wine-producing district

in the Aveyron département in central-southern France. Produces red and white wines.

Vins d'Orrance (S.Afr) a winery (established 2001) based in Constantia, Western Cape. Grape varieties include: Chardonnay. Labels: Cuvée Anaïs, Cuvée Ameena.

Vins Doux Mistelles (Fr) *see* Vins Doux Mûtes.

Vins Doux Mûte (Fr) fortified wines made by adding brandy to slightly fermented grape must. A Vin Doux Naturel, Vin Doux Liqueur. Is also known as Vins Doux Mistelles.

Vins Doux Passerillés (Fr) sweet fortified wines made from dried grapes 13%–15% alc by vol.

Vins Doux Semi-Mûte (Fr) a medium-sweet, fortified wine of around 15% alc by vol.

Vins du Lyonnais (Fr) a mainly red V.D.Q.S. wine-producing region based near Lyon in the Rhône. Wines produced from the Gamay and Syrah grape varieties.

Vins d'Une Nuit (Fr) *see* Vins Souples.

Vins du Thouarsis (Fr) a V.D.Q.S. sweet white, rosé and light red wine-producing region based south of the Loire region. Also spelt Thouarsais.

Vin Sec (Fr) dry wine.

Vins Effervescents (Fr) sparkling wines.

Vins Fins de la Côte de Nuits (Fr) the old appellation for the Côte de Nuits-Villages.

Vins Jaunes (Fr) yellow wines of the Jura. *see* Jura.

Vins Liquoreux (Fr) *see* Straw Wines.

Vinsmoselle (Lux) an association that consists of five of the six co-operatives in Luxembourg. (Grenenmacher, Greiveldange, Remerschen, Stadtbredimus and Wellenstein).

Vins Nouveaux (Fr) new wines. *see* Beaujolais Nouveau.

Vinsobres (Fr) a village in the A.C. Côtes du Rhône-Villages. Produces mainly red wines (with a little rosé and white wine).

Vinsol, S.A. (Sp) a noted producer of Montilla wines based in the Montilla-Moriles region.

Vins Ordinaires (Fr) simple ordinary wines for everyday drinking.

Vins Pétillants (Fr) slightly sparkling wines produced by allowing the malo-lactic fermentation to take place in the bottle instead of in the cask.

Vins Souples (Fr) wines made from free-run must with pressed grape must added. Also known as Vins d'Une Nuit.

Vins Tournés (Fr) lit: 'turned wines', a wine that has deteriorated in quality because of poor quality wine. The wine has usually been left on the lees too long, turns cloudy and has a rotten vegetable smell. Treated with citric acid and pasteurisation. Is **not** caused by acetobacter!

Vin Supérieur (Fr) wines for everyday drinking. They are controlled by regulations but not as strict as A.C.

Vin Superioare (Rum) superior top quality wine.

Vins Vieux (Fr) wines of the previous years.

Vintage (Eng) the gathering of the grapes, the harvest. (Fr) = vendange, (Hol) = jaargang, (Ire) = fómhar an fhiona, (It) = annata.

Vintage Ale (Eng) an 8.5% alc by vol. ale brewed by Fullers Brewery, London. Released each september, it is sold in individually signed and numbered bottles.

Vintage Appellation (Switz) *abbr:* V.A. subject to supervision by the authorities which grant or withhold entitlement to such appellations (Fendant and Dôle for the Valais, Dorin and Sauvignon for the Vaud).

Vintage Beers (Eng) a term used to denote a beer that needs bottle age, that is conditioned in the bottle. i.e. Bière de Garde, Chimay Trappiste and Bottle-Conditioned beers.

Vintage Character (Port) a term given to older blended good quality Ruby Ports that show Vintage Port characteristics.

Vintage Christmas Ale (Eng) a 6.7% alc by vol. premium christmas ale Brewed by Shepherd Neame. Sold in 500mls bottles.

Vintage Cider (Eng) a slightly sparkling cider produced by Merrydown in Essex. Also produce a vintage dry cider.

Vintage Darjeeling (Ind) a tea from Darjeeling, bordering the Himalayas. Blended from Darjeeling Flowery Orange Pekoe leaves. Has a superb aroma and flavour.

Vintage 1832 (Eng) a 4.6% alc by vol. seasonal ale brewed by Hardy and Hansons in Kimberley, Nottinghamshire. Available in April, it is brewed to celebrate the year production began at the Kimberley Brewery.

Vintage Hallmark Ale Company [The] (Eng) a brewery based in Norwich. Brews: cask-conditioned Double Eagle, Leopards Head, Makers Mark.

Vintage Henley (Eng) a 5.5% alc by vol. bottled beer brewed by Brakspear's Brewery.

Vintage Madeira (Mad) a Madeira produced from 100% noble grape varieties from a single year, kept in cask for a minimum of 20 years after estufagem and 2 years in bottle before sale.

Vintage Malt Whisky C° Ltd (Scot) blenders (established 1992). (Add): 2 Stewart Street, Milngavie, Glasgow, Lanarkshire G62 6BW. Produces a range of malts and Scotch whiskies. Website: http://www.vintagemaltwhisky.com 'E'mail: brian@vintagemaltwhisky.com

Vintage Port (Port) a Port wine from a single year. Blended and bottled in Portugal between the 2nd and 3rd year after the vintage. Not produced every year but is declared by some or all of the Port shippers on good years. Recent vintages are: 1960, 1963, 1966, 1970, 1975, 1977, 1980, 1982, 1983, 1985, 1987, 1991, 1992, 1994 1997, 2003. Originally bottled in the U.K. by the importer but now must now all be bottled in Oporto (since 1975).

Vintage Royale (Eng) a cider cocktail produced by Symonds of Hereford, Herefordshire. Contains cider, brandy and ginger wine.

V

Vintagers (Eng) workers of the harvest and winemaking.

Vintage Wine (Eng) a wine of a single year. (Ire) = fion den scoth.

Vintina Estate (Austr) a winery (established 1985). (Add): 1282 Nepean Highway, Mt. Eliza, Victoria. Grape varieties: Cabernet sauvignon, Pinot noir, Chardonnay, Sémillon, Sweet Muscat.

Vintitulist (Eng) a wine label collector.

Vintner (Fr) wine seller/merchant. (Ire) = fioncheannai.

Vintner [The] (Eng) the trading name for a specialist shop in Kensington Church Street, London. Belongs to Arthur Rackham. Home to the Vintners Wine Club.

Vintners' Choice (Wal) a predominantly Chardonnay-based traditional method sparkling wine produced by Andrac Vineyards, Llanvaches, Gwent.

Vintners' Choice (S.Afr) *see* Drop Inn Group.

Vintners' Quality Alliance (Can) *abbr*: V.Q.A. a quality label (established 1988) for those superior wines made from vitis vinifera and premium hybrids. Requires a blind tasting.

Vin Tranquille (Fr) still wine, the designation for the still wines of Vouvray in the Touraine district of the Loire.

Vinueño (Sp) a wine made from grapes grown on Albariza soil, not from Palomino grapes.

Vinum (Lat) wine. *See also* Merum.

Vinum Bonum Est (It) lit: 'the wine is good'. *see* Est! Est!! Est!!!

Vinum Claratum (Lat) clarified wine.

Vinum Clarum (Lat) light, clear wine.

Vinum Picatum (Fr) a Roman wine which was made from the black Picata grape which had a taste of pitch. Was produced in the Rhône region of southern France.

Vinum Theologicum (Lat) lit: 'the best wine'.

Vin-Union-Genève (Switz) a large growers' co-operative based at Satigny.

Vin Usoare (Rum) light wine.

Vin Veneto (Cktl) 1 measure grappa, ¼ measure Sambuca, ¼ measure gomme syrup, juice ¼ lemon, ½ egg white, shake over ice and strain into a cocktail glass.

Vin Vert (Fr) a young wine from the Roussillon made from the Maccabéo grape.

Vin Vieux (Fr) a wine of the previous year.

Vin Vif (Fr) the name used for sparkling wines in the Touraine district of the Loire.

Vin Viné (Fr) fortified wine.

Vin-X-Port (S.Afr) a winery (established 2001) based in Paarl, Western Cape. A large négociant that produces a large range of wines. Labels include: African Treasure, Bundu Star, Cape Circle. Website: http://www.x-port.co.za

Vinzel (Switz) a wine-producing village in La Côte, Vaud, western Switzerland.

Viognier (Fr) a white grape variety grown mainly in the northern Rhône that produces wines with aromas and flavours of apricots, peaches,

almonds, musk and orange blossom. Used for making Château Grillet, Condrieu and Hermitage. (USA) = vionnier.

Violet Fizz (Cktl) ⅓ measure dry gin, ⅓ measure Crème Yvette, 2 dashes gomme syrup, juice ¼ lemon. Shake over ice, strain into an ice-filled highball glass and top with soda water.

Violet Frères (Fr) a noted producer of Byrrh at Thuir, Pyrénées-Oriéntales.

Violette (Fr) a liqueur made by the infusion of violet roots and leaves. Produced by Serres in Toulouse.

Violland [Léon] (Fr) a Burgundy shipper based in Beaune.

Vion (Fr) a commune of the A.C. Saint-Joseph in the northern Rhône.

Vionnier (USA) the USA spelling of the Viognier grape.

Viosinho (Port) a white grape variety grown in the Douro region for Port production and in Trás-os-Montes.

VIP (Cktl) ⅓ measure Cointreau, ⅓ measure dry Cinzano, ⅓ measure rye whisky. Stir over ice, strain into a cocktail glass and add a twist of orange peel.

V.I.P. (Cktl) 35mls (1½ fl.ozs) gin, 25mls (1fl.oz) Pimms N°1, 50mls (2fl.ozs) passion fruit juice, 10mls (½ fl.oz) dry vermouth, 10mls (½ fl.oz) fresh lemon juice. Shake over ice, strain into 125mls (5fl.oz) glass and decorate with a white water lotus nut on a cocktail stick.

VIP Conception Brew (Eng) a cask ale brewed by the Castle Rock Brewery, Nottingham.

Vipava Valley (Slo) part of the coastal wine region in Primorska. 1943ha of vines. Upper Valley: Malvasia, Welschriesling, Sauvignon blanc, Pinela, Ribola. Lower Valley: Chardonnay, Barbera, Merlot, Cabernet sauvignon grapes. There are 17 Villages appellations. Home to the Vipava Valley co-operative.

Viré (Fr) *see* Viré-Clessé.

Viré-Clessé (Fr) an A.C. Mâconnais white wine from the Chardonnay grape. Originally prefixed Mâcon-Clessé, Mâcon-Viré. Established from the 1999 vintage.

Virelade (Fr) a commune in the A.C. Graves, central-western Bordeaux.

Virgas La Ideal II (Sp) a natural spring mineral water from Gran Canaria. Mineral contents (milligrammes per litre): Sodium 40.9mg/l, Calcium 59.3mg/l, Magnesium 32.6mg/l, Potassium 9.5mg/l, Chlorides 23.9mg/l, Sulphates 7.8mg/l, Fluorides 0.22mg/l, Nitrates 16.6mg/l.

Virgen [En] (Port) a term given to the Vinho Verde wine prior to fermentation when the skins, stalks and pips are removed. Bottled 3–4 months after fermentation and before the malo-lactic fermentation.

Virgin (Sp) a term to denote the driest of the Málagas.

Virgin Beaver (Eng) a cask-conditioned ale brewed by the Belvoir Brewery, Old Dalby, Leicestershire.

Virgin Brandy (Fr) a term applied to unblended Cognac brandies.

Virgin Cocktail (Cktl) ⅓ measure gin, ⅓ measure white crème de menthe, ⅓ measure Forbidden Fruit liqueur. Shake over ice and strain into a cocktail glass.

Virgin Cola (Eng) a brand of cola drink from Sir Richard Branson of Virgin Airlines.

Virgin Earth (S.Afr) a winery based in Little Karoo, Western Cape. Grape varieties: Cabernet franc, Cabernet sauvignon, Merlot, Petit verdot, Sauvignon blanc, Shiraz. Label: High 5ive.

Virgin Hills Winery (Austr) a winery (established 1969). (Add): Salisbury Road, Lauriston, West via Kyneton, Victoria. Produces varietal and table wines. Grape varieties include Cabernet sauvignon.

Virginia (It) a natural spring mineral water from Virginia, Prata Camportaccio, Sondrio.

Virginia (S.Afr) a medium sweet white wine from the SFW. Made from the Steen and Clairette blanche grapes.

Virginia (USA) has 6 A.V.A. areas. *see* Monticello.

Virginia Drams (USA) an early peach brandy that was probably the forerunner of Southern Comfort.

Virginia Gentleman (USA) the brand-name of a Bourbon whiskey at 45% alc by vol. Produced by the Smith Bowman Distillery in Sunset Hills, Fairfax County, Virginia.

Virgin Islands Rum (W.Ind) a light bodied rum, fairly dry and flavoured with a slightly sweet after-taste. Produced by the Virgin Islands Rum Industries Ltd.

Virgin Islands Rum Industries Ltd. (W.Ind) a noted rum producer based in the Virgin Islands. Sold under Old St-Croix and Cruzan labels.

Virgin Kiwi (N.Z) a still natural spring mineral water (established 1990) from Canterbury Plains, South Island. Mineral contents (milligrammes per litre): Sodium 6.9mg/l, Calcium 12mg/l, Magnesium 1.9mg/l, Potassium 0.7mg/l, Chlorides 3.9mg/l, Sulphates 3.6mg/l, Nitrates 0.26mg/l, Silicates 18mg/l. pH 7.9

Virgin Mary (Cktl) *see* Tomato Juice Cocktail.

Virgin Mary (Cktl) (Non-alc) stir 25mls lemon juice, 150mls tomato juice, 1 dash Tabasco sauce, 2 dashes Worcestershire sauce, salt and pepper over ice in a highball glass and serve with a celery stick and lemon slice with straws.

Virgin Spring Highland Water (Scot) a natural spring mineral water from Blarich, Rogart, Sutherland.

Virgin Vodka (Eng) triple distilled vodka from William Grant and Sons 37.5% alc by vol. Produced for the Sir Richard Branson Virgin Group.

Viriatus (Port) a Dão wine produced by Sociedade Com. Abel Pereira da Fonseca.

Virreyes (Mex) a well-known brand of tequila.

Vis (Euro) a pale white wine produced on the island of Vugava, off the Dalmatian coast.

Vis (It) a still natural spring mineral water from Sorgente del Ciliegio, Reggio Emilia. Mineral contents (milligrammes per litre): Sodium 50mg/l, Calcium 155mg/l, Magnesium 25mg/l, Potassium 2.9mg/l, Chlorides 8.9mg/l, Sulphates 185mg/l, Fluorides 0.5mg/l. pH 7.1

Visable Fermentation (Eng) the first sign of visable CO_2 gas during fermentation which bubbles to the surface.

Visage (S.Afr) the label for a red wine (Shiraz 42% plus Cabernet sauvignon, Grenache, Merlot and Pinotage blend) produced by the Porterville Cellars winery, Swartland, Western Cape.

Visan (Fr) a village in the A.C. Côtes du Rhône-Villages. Produces mainly red wines (with a little rosé and white wine).

Visanto (Gre) a sweet white wine produced from Aidani and Assyrtiko grapes, sun-dried for one to two weeks after picking. Rare speciality found on island of Santorini. Used as a communion wine in Greek Orthodox church.

Viscachani (S.Am) a natural spring mineral water from La Paz, Bolivia. Mineral contents (milligrammes per litre): Sodium 280mg/l, Calcium 19.6mg/l, Magnesium 20.6mg/l, Potassium 20.5mg/l, Bicarbonates 1192mg/l, Chlorides 64mg/l, Sulphates 60.2mg/l, Nitrates 3mg/l, Silicates 45mg/l. pH 6.9

Viscimetry (Eng) a term used to describe the mixing of two liquids with differing viscosities as they blend together e.g. water and whisky (especially when the two can be seen as separate '*strands*' in the glass).

Viscosity (Eng) a term used to describe, albeit loosely, the body of the wine through the alcohol and glycerine content. Is usually judged by the '*tears*' or '*legs*' left on the side of the glass after the wine has been swirled around the glass.

Visegr'di (Hun) a natural spring mineral water from Asvanyviz. Mineral contents (milligrammes per litre): Sodium 67mg/l, Calcium 163mg/l, Magnesium 62mg/l, Bicarbonates 820mg/l, Fluorides 1.6mg/l.

Viseu (Port) the principal wine town of the Dão region.

Vishnyovaya Nalivka (Rus) a cherry-flavoured liqueur.

Vision (Eng) a 4.2% alc by vol. ale brewed by the Merlin Brewery, Lancashire.

Vision (S.Afr) the label for a red wine (50% Cabernet sauvignon, 10% Merlot and 30% Pinotage blend) produced by the Kaapzicht Estate winery, Stellenbosch, Western Cape.

Visitor [The] (Cktl) ⅓ measure each of Cointreau, crème de banane and dry gin, dash orange juice, 1 egg white. Shake over ice and strain into a cocktail glass.

Viski (Tur) whiskey.

Vislijm (Hol) isinglass.

Visokokvalitetno (Slo) high quality wine.

Visperterminen (Switz) wines from the Valais canton, at 12000 feet above sea level are amongst the highest vineyards in the world.

Vista Montone (USA) the label for a red wine (Pinot noir) produced by the Trinchero winery, Napa Valley, California.

Vistrenque (Fr) a Vin de Pays area of the Gard département in south-western France.

Vit [Le] (Eng) an alcohol-free flavoured spring water containing 10 different flavours including lemon and passion fruit. From the Gaymer Group.

Vita (It) a red wine produced by Azienda La Mea di Marco Maci, Brindisi. *See also* Sire.

Vitaceae (Lat) a botanical family of which **Vitis** is part.

Vital [1] (Chile) a natural spring mineral water from Chanqueahue. Mineral contents (milligrammes per litre): Sodium 21.6mg/l, Magnesium 5.48mg/l, Potassium 0.39mg/l, Bicarbonates 13.72mg/l, Chlorides 33.25mg/l, Sulphates 20.12mg/l.

Vital [2] (Chile) a sparkling natural spring mineral water from Chanqueahue. Mineral contents (milligrammes per litre): Sodium 18.7mg/l, Calcium 17.9mg/l, Magnesium 2.5mg/l, Potassium 0.6mg/l, Chlorides 32.5mg/l, Sulphates 21.3mg/l, Silicates 22.6mg/l.

Vital (S.Hem) a natural spring mineral water from Mauritius. Mineral contents (milligrammes per litre): Sodium 18.6mg/l, Calcium 19.6mg/l, Magnesium 17.7mg/l, Potassium 1mg/l, Bicarbonates 95.3mg/l, Chlorides 32.4mg/l, Sulphates 15.5mg/l, Nitrates 17.6mg/l. pH 6.9

Vital (Port) a white grape variety grown in Torres Vedras. Also known as Malvasia Corado.

Vitale (Fr) a mineral water botled at the source of Plateau du Larzac, Montpeyroux.

Vitalis (Port) a slightly acidic natural spring mineral water from Vitalis 1, Castelo de Vide, Portoalegre. Mineral contents (milligrammes per litre): Sodium 6mg/l, Calcium 1.2mg/l, Magnesium 0.1mg/l, Potassium 2.1mg/l, Bicarbonates 7.3mg/l, Chlorides 7.4mg/l, Sulphates 1.9mg/l. pH 5.3

Vitality (Eng) the name given to a range of juices made from Florida Valencia oranges by Chevron Foods.

Vital Natural (Chile) a still natural spring mineral water from Chanqueahue. Mineral contents (milligrammes per litre): Sodium 22.5mg/l, Calcium 13.7mg/l, Magnesium 6mg/l, Potassium 0.4mg/l, Bicarbonates 13.7mg/l, Chlorides 31.2mg/l, Sulphates 20.5mg/l, Silicates 21.1mg/l.

Vitalwa (Fr) a natural spring mineral water brand. Mineral contents (milligrammes per litre): Sodium 12.3mg/l, Calcium 470mg/l, Magnesium 59mg/l, Chlorides 22mg/l.

Vitamalz (Ger) a malzbier.

Vitamins (Eng) essential to all life forms, many found in beers and wines. Vitamin B1 is needed by yeast during fermentation. Vitamin C used as the reducing agent (**Ascorbic acid**) which prevents oxidation (the browning of wines).

Vitas (It) a natural spring mineral water from Vitas.

Vitasnella (It) a sparkling natural spring mineral water from Boario Terme, Brescia. Mineral contents (milligrammes per litre): Sodium 3mg/l, Calcium 82mg/l, Magnesium 27mg/l, Bicarbonates 296mg/l, Sulphates 80mg/l, Fluorides 0.7mg/l, Nitrates 3mg/l. pH 7.3

Vita Star (Pol) a natural spring mineral water brand. Mineral contents (milligrammes per litre): Sodium 28mg/l, Calcium 17.64mg/l, Magnesium 8.27mg/l, Potassium 1.75mg/l, Bicarbonates 154.9mg/l, Chlorides 6.9mg/l, Fluorides 0.28mg/l.

Vita-Stout (N.Z) a stout brewed by the Dominion Brewery.

Vite (It) grape vine.

Viteau (Hol) a natural spring mineral water from Annen.

Viteus (Lat) denotes that it is 'of the vine'.

Viteus vitifolii (Lat) *Phylloxera vastatrix*.

Viti (Switz) a red wine produced in the Ticino canton from the Merlot grape.

Vitiano (It) the label of a red wine produced by the Falesco winery in Umbria.

Viticcio (It) a noted Chianti Classico producer based in Tuscany.

Viticolture (It) a grower. *See also* Vigniaolo.

Viticula (Lat) a small vine.

Viticulteur (Fr) a person who cultivates vineyards of which they are the owner.

Viticultura (It)(Port)(Sp) vine-growing/viticulture.

Viticultural and Oenological Research Advisory Council (N.Z) *abbr*: VORAC. comprises of a number of representatives from other associated bodies including the Wine Institute and Grape Growers' Council.

Viticultural and Oenological Research Institute (S.Afr) *abbr*: V.O.R.I. an institute for the improvement of vine species. Also known as Nievoorbij.

Viticultural Association of New Zealand (N.Z) an organisation formed by wine growers to respond to adversities facing the industry in the 1920's.

Viticultural Ecology (Eng) the study of the vine, soil and climate in which it grows. Examines the quality of fruit and wine produced.

Viticulture (Fr) the cultivation of the vine from the planting to the harvest. (Ire) = saothru.

Vitigenus (Lat) produced from the vine, originates from the vine.

Vitigno (It) vine/grape variety.

Vitinka (Bos) a sparkling natural spring mineral water (established 1880) from Kozluk, Bosnia and Herzegovina. Mineral contents (milligrammes per litre): Sodium 446.5mg/l, Magnesium 41mg/l, Potassium 23.5mg/l, Bicarbonates 3415mg/l, Chlorides 570mg/l, Sulphates 41mg/l, Fluorides 0.8mg/l, Strontium 3.2mg/l.

Vitinka (Ser) a natural spring mineral water from Serbia and Montenegro.

Vitis (Lat) vine genus.

Vitis aestivalis (USA) an American root stock grown

in the north-eastern states. Gives high acidity and a little foxiness.

Vitis amurensis (Asia) a vine root stock that originated from Japan, Mongolia and Sakhalin Islands.

Vitis argentifolia (USA) the alternative name for **Vitis bicolor** under the Bailey classification.

Vitis arizonica (USA) a vine root stock that originated from the western zone.

Vitis armata (Asia) a vine root stock that originated in China.

Vitisator (Lat) vine planter.

Vitis balansaeana (Asia) a vine root stock that originated in Tonkin.

Vitis berlandieri (USA) an American root stock. Native of the state of Texas.

Vitis bicolor (USA) a vine root stock that originated from the eastern zone. Also known as **Vitis argentifolia**.

Vitis bourgoeana (USA) a vine root stock that originated from the tropical zones.

Vitis california (USA) a vine root stock that originated from the western zone.

Vitis candicans (USA) a vine root stock that originated from the central zone.

Vitis cariboea (USA) a vine root stock that originated from the tropical zones. *see Vitis sola.*

Vitis chasselas (Lat) a vine root stock crossed with **Vitis berlandieri** to produce Millardet de Grasset.

Vitis cinerea (USA) a vine root stock that originated from the central zone.

Vitis coegnetiae (Euro) table grapes.

Vitis coignetiae (Asia) a vine root stock that originated from Japan, Korea and Sakhalin Islands.

Vitis cordifolia (USA) a vine root stock that originated from the central zone.

Vitis coriacea (USA) a vine root stock that originated from Florida and the Bahamas.

Vitis davidii (Asia) a vine root stock that originated from China.

Vitis elevenea (Ger) a vine similar to the Elbling. Was planted by the Romans in the Mosel.

Vitis flexuosa (Asia) a vine root stock that originated in Cochin-China, India, Japan, Korea and Nepal.

Vitis gigas (USA) a vine root stock that originated from Florida and the Bahamas.

Vitis labrusca (USA) an American vine species grown in the north-east states. A wild grape variety is used extensively for grafting in Europe because of its phylloxera resistance.

Vitis lanata (Asia) a vine root stock that originated from Burma, Dekkan, India, Nepal and southern China.

Vitis licecunici (USA) a vine root stock that originated from the eastern zone.

Vitis monticola (USA) a vine root stock that originated from the central zone.

Vitis munsoniana (USA) a vine root stock that originated from northern USA.

Vitis pagnucii (Asia) a vine root stock that originated in China.

Vitis pedicellata (Asia) a vine root stock that originated in the Himalayan mountains.

Vitis pentagona (Asia) a vine root stock that originated in China.

Vitis piasezkii (Asia) a vine root stock that originated in China.

Vitis popenoei (USA) a vine root stock that originated in northern USA.

Vitis retordi (Asia) a vine root stock that originated in Tonkin.

Vitis riparia (USA) an American vine species grown in the Riverbank area. Is used extensively for grafting in Europe because of its Phylloxera resistance. Is the grape species responsible for the 'foxy' smells and flavours in American wines. *see* Foxy and *Vitis vulpina*.

Vitis romaneti (Asia) a vine root stock that originated in China.

Vitis romanetia (Asia) *see Vitis romaneti*.

Vitis rotundifolia (USA) an early American grape variety of Florida in southern American.

Vitis rubra (USA) a vine stock that originated from the central zone.

Vitis rupestris (USA) an American vine species grown in the Rock region. Is used extensively in Europe for grafting because of its resistance to phylloxera.

Vitis rutilans (Asia) a vine root stock that originated in China.

Vitis silvestris (Euro) an old vine species from which it is thought the Riesling and Sylvaner grape varieties derived from.

Vitis sola (USA) along with **Vitis cariboea** the alternative name for **Vitis tilioefolia**. Under the Bailey classification the two species are recognised. *See also Vitis tilioefolia*.

Vitis thunbergii (Asia) a vine root stock that originated from Formosa, Japan, Korea and south-western China.

Vitis tilioefolia (USA) along with **Vitis sola** the alternative names for **Vitis cariboea**. Under the Bailey classification the two species are recognised.

Vitis vinifera (Euro) the European vine species (there are around 5000 varieties within the species and over 40000 local name variations) from which all of the European quality wines are made. After the phylloxera epidemic of the later nineteenth century with just a few exceptions, all the vines are grafted onto American vine root stocks. *see* Ampélographie.

Vitis vulpina (USA) the alternative name for the **Vitis riparia** under the Bailey classification.

Vitis wilsonae (Asia) a vine root stock that originated in China.

Vitiviniculture (Eng) the study of grape growing and wine-making.

Vitologatti (It) a sparkling natural spring mineral water from Vitologatti. Mineral contents (milligrammes per litre): Sodium 27.5mg/l, Calcium 462.9mg/l, Magnesium 137.3mg/l, Potassium 15.7mg/l, Bicarbonates 2116.7mg/l, Chlorides 18.4mg/l, Sulphates 30.7mg/l, Fluorides 0.2mg/l, Nitrates 1mg/l, Silicates 38.6mg/l, Strontium 3.9mg/l. pH 6.37

Vitovska (It) a perfumed white grape variety from the Friuli-Venezia-Guilia region.

Vitraille (Fr) an alternative name for the Merlot grape.

Vitrum (Lat) glass.

Vittel Grande Source (Fr) a still mineral water from Vittel in the Vosges mountains.

Vittel Grandes Tables (Fr) a still natural spring mineral water (established 1854) from Vittel, Vosges. Mineral contents (milligrammes per litre): Sodium 3.8mg/l, Calcium 202mg/l, Magnesium 36mg/l, Bicarbonates 402mg/l, Sulphates 306mg/l, Fluorides 0.28mg/l. pH 7.5

Vittel Hepar (Fr) a still natural spring mineral water (established 1854) from Vittel, Vosges. Mineral contents (milligrammes per litre): Sodium 7.3mg/l, Calcium 91mg/l, Magnesium 19.9mg/l, Potassium 4.9mg/l, Bicarbonates 258mg/l, Chlorides 3.7mg/l, Sulphates 105mg/l, Fluorides 0.6mg/l. pH 7.2

Vitteloise (Fr) a highly carbonated natural spring mineral water from Vittel, Vosges. Mineral contents (milligrammes per litre): Sodium 9mg/l, Calcium 100mg/l, Magnesium 23mg/l, Potassium 5mg/l, Bicarbonates 259mg/l, Chlorides 12mg/l, Sulphates 135mg/l.

Vitty (Viet) a natural spring mineral water brand. Mineral contents (milligrammes per litre): Sodium 16mg/l, Calcium 2mg/l, Magnesium 1mg/l, Potassium 2mg/l, Chlorides 17mg/l.

Viura (Sp) the principal white grape variety grown in the Rioja region. Also known as the Alcañol, Alcanón and the Macabeo.

Viuva Rosado Fernandes (Port) a small firm that produces full-bodied red wines in Alentejo.

Viva (Eng) the name of a beer brewed by King and Barnes in Horsham, Sussex that is approved by the Vegetarian Society.

Viva (It) a sparkling natural spring mineral water from Misia Bis. Mineral contents (milligrammes per litre): Sodium 3.6mg/l, Calcium 75mg/l, Magnesium 7.8mg/l, Potassium 0.88mg/l, Bicarbonates 213mg/l, Chlorides 6mg/l, Sulphates 42mg/l, Nitrates 2.5mg/l, Silicates 7mg/l.

Viva! (Phil) a still natural spring mineral water from Mount Makiling. Mineral contents (milligrammes per litre): Sodium 40mg/l, Calcium 48mg/l, Magnesium 14mg/l, Bicarbonates 259mg/l, Chlorides 15mg/l, Sulphates 17mg/l. pH 7.0

Vivace (Fr) the term used to denote a lively, fresh and slightly tart wine.

Vivace (It) slightly sparkling.

Viva Maria (Cktl) ¼ measure Tia Maria, ¼ measure Galliano, ¼ measure brandy, ¼ measure blackcurrant juice. Shake over ice, strain into a cocktail glass and top with a cherry.

Viva Rosport (Lux) a natural spring mineral water from Rosport. Mineral contents (milligrammes per litre): Sodium 34.6mg/l, Calcium 191mg/l, Magnesium 64.5mg/l, Potassium 15.8mg/l, Bicarbonates 461mg/l, Chlorides 26.6mg/l, Sulphates 398mg/l, Nitrates 0.5mg/l.

Vivasti (It) the name given to registered nurseries that sell vines.

Vivat Bacchus (S.Afr) the label for a red wine (Merlot 66% plus Cabernet franc, Cabernet sauvignon and Malbec blend) produced by the Veenwouden Private Cellar winery, Paarl, Western Cape.

Viva Villa Cocktail (Cktl) 25mls. (⅛ gill) tequila, juice of a lime, 3 dashes gomme syrup. Shake over ice and strain into a salt-rimmed, ice-filled old-fashioned glass.

Vive (W.Ind) the brand-name of a rum produced only from molasses by Bardinet on the island of Martinique.

Vivency (Fr) a wine-producer based at Saumur, Anjou-Saumur, Loire. Owned by Piper-Heidsieck. Noted for Saumur Mousseux.

Vi Verge (Sp) a term that describes wines that are macerated off the skins (vi brisat = 'on the skins').

Vivien (Hun) a still and sparkling natural spring mineral water (established 2000) from Gerecse Mountains. Mineral contents (milligrammes per litre): Sodium 4mg/l, Calcium 69mg/l, Magnesium 51mg/l, Potassium <0.5mg/l, Bicarbonates 464mg/l, Chlorides 4mg/l, Sulphates <10mg/l, Fluorides 0.13mg/l, Nitrates 3.7mg/l. pH 7.2

Viviers (Fr) a commune in the A.C. Chablis, Burgundy.

Viville (Fr) a commune in the Charente département whose grapes are classed Grande Champagne (Cognac).

Vivreau (Eng) a natural spring mineral water brand.

Vixen Beer (Eng) a cask-conditioned bitter 1036 O.G. brewed by the Fox and Firkin home-brew public house in London.

Viz Top Tipple (Eng) a 4.5% alc by vol. bottle-conditioned ale brewed by North Yorkshire Brewery at Middlesborough. Named after monthly magazine Viz.

V.J. Day Ale (Eng) a 4.5% alc by vol. ale from Wye Valley Brewery in Hereford. See also V.E. Day Ale, Siege Ale.

VK (Eng) abbr. Vodka Kick. an RTD bottled vodka-based energy drink. Website: http://www.clubvk.com

VK Iron Brew (Eng) a canned PPS drink. Range includes UK Blue. Also non-alcoholic VK Pure Energy.

VK Pure Energy (Eng) see VK Iron Brew.

Vlaamsch Wit (Bel) a 4.5% alc by vol. top-fermented, bottle-conditioned wheat beer brewed by Van Hounsebrouck Brouwerij.

Vladimarvellous (Cktl) 2 measures Vladivar vodka, 1 measure Pernod, juice of lemon, juice of orange. Shake over ice, strain into an ice-filled highball glass and dress with a sprig of mint.

Vladivar (Eng) a triple distilled vodka from Greenalls in Warrington, Cheshire 37.5% alc by vol.

Vladivar Gold (Eng) a high strength vodka from Whyte & Mackay Distillers 100° proof (57.15% alc by vol.).

Vladivar Imperial Gold (Eng) a brand of vodka

produced by Greenalls in Warrington, Cheshire 43% alc by vol.

Vladivar Veba (Eng) a 5.4% alc by vol. sweet and sour cherry flavoured vodka.

Vlasotinci (Ser) a wine-producing area based south of Serbia. Produces mainly rosé wines from the Plovdina and Prokupac grapes.

Vlassky Rizling (Czec) a local name for the Welschriesling grape.

Vloeistof (Hol) liquid.

Vlo Speciale (Hol) a 7% alc by vol. top-fermented, unpasteurised, bottle-conditioned special beer brewed by 't IJ Brouwerij, Amsterdam.

Vlottenburg Wynkelder Koöperatief (S.Afr) a co-operative winery based in Stellenbosch, Western Cape. (Add): Bpk., Box 40, Vlottenburg 7604. Has 29 members.

V.O. (Can) the top selling, straight rye whisky produced by Seagram.

V.O. (Fr) *abbr*: **V**ery **O**ld, a Cognac term found on a bottle label. Denotes that the brandy is very old having spent at least 10–12 years in cask. Must have a minimum age of 4½ years (4 years in U.K). For Armagnac 4 years minimum (also for Calvados).

Vocht (Hol) liquor/liquid.

Voda (Rus) water, the word from which vodka is a diminutive.

Voda Vrnjci (Ser) a natural spring mineral water from Serbia and Montenegro.

Vodka (E.Euro) a pure spirit (distilled from a variety of ingredients including potatoes, sugar beet, grain, etc.), charcoal-filtered which removes certain oils and congenerics. Various sorts. Name drives from (zhiznennia voda) = '*water of life*'. The word vodka or wodka means '*little water*'. The vodka is often flavoured. (Tur) = votka.

Vodka Collins (Cktl) as for Gin Collins but using vodka in place of the gin.

Vodka Cooler (Cktl) as for Gin Cooler but using vodka in place of the gin.

Vodka Daisy (Cktl) 40mls (⅓ gill) vodka, juice ½ lemon, 2 dashes gomme syrup, 4 dashes grenadine. Shake over ice, strain into an old-fashioned glass and dress with fruit in season.

Vodka Gibson (Cktl) 25mls (⅕ gill) vodka, dash dry vermouth. Stir over ice, strain into a cocktail glass and dress with an olive.

Vodka Gimlet (Cktl) as for Gin Gimlet but using vodka in place of the gin.

Vodka Grasshopper (Cktl) ⅔ measure vodka, ⅓ measure Bénédictine, dash Angostura. Stir over ice and strain into a cocktail glass.

Vodka Ice (Eng) a red star vodka and fruit juice bottled drink. Flavours include: Watermelon, Lime, Iron Brew, Original, Mega Mix (taurine & caffeine).

Vodka Kick (Eng) *see* VK.

Vodka Mac (Cktl) 25mls (1fl.oz) ginger wine, 25mls (1fl.oz) vodka. Shake over ice and strain into a 125mls (5fl.oz) goblet.

Vodka Martini (Cktl) ⅞ measure vodka, ⅛ measure dry Martini. Shake over ice, strain into a cocktail glass and top with a twist of lemon peel juice.

Vodka Mudshake (Eng) a 4% alc by vol. flavoured vodka RTD produced by Smirnoff. Flavours include chocolate, mint, strawberry and vanilla.

Vodka Pippin (Cktl) 25mls (⅕ gill) vodka on ice in a highball glass. Top with dry cider, stir and dress with an apple slice.

Vodka-Polar Cocktail (Cktl) ½ measure vodka, ½ measure Polar liqueur. Shake over ice and strain into a cocktail glass.

Vodka Reef (Eng) a vodka and exotic fruit juice mixed drink. 5% alc by vol. Range includes: mango & apple, orange & passion fruit, pineapple & citrus.

Vodka Salty Dog (Cktl) 20mls (⅙ gill) vodka, 125mls (1gill) grapefruit juice, ¼ teaspoon salt. Stir over ice in a highball glass.

Vodka Seven [7] (Cktl) 40mls (⅓ gill) vodka, juice ½ lime. Stir over ice in a highball glass, top with lemonade and the rind of lime.

Vodka Sling (Cktl) as for Gin Sling but using vodka in place of the gin.

Vodka Smoothie (Eng) a red star vodka and fruit juice bottled drink. 5.5% alc by vol. Flavours include: strawberry & banana, cranberry & apple, lemon.

Vodka Sour (Cktl) 1½ measures vodka, 20mls (¾ fl.oz) lemon or lime juice, 1 teaspoon powdered sugar. Shake over ice, strain into an old-fashioned glass, add a slice of orange and a cherry.

Vodka Source (Eng) a 5.3% alc by vol. sparkling fruit and vodka-based drink from Whitbread. Other flavours include: spiced apple, orange and cassis, lemon and lime, blackcurrant and pear. Also Kiwi Source, Passion Fruit Source.

Vodka Stinger (Cktl) ½ measure vodka, ½ measure white crème de menthe. Shake over ice and strain into a cocktail glass.

Vodkatini (Cktl) 40mls (⅓ gill) vodka, 20mls (⅙ gill) sweet Martini (or dry), mix together over ice, strain into a cocktail glass and dress with a twist of lemon peel juice.

Vodka Twistee Shots (Eng) a branded 30% alc by vol. fruit-flavoured schnapps and cream with vodka produced by Independent Distillers Ltd.

Vodka Venom (Eng) a 5% alc by vol. bottled pre-mixed vodka and fruit drink from the Federation Brewery, Dunston, Gateshead, Tyne and Wear. Flavours include: orange ice, tropical ice, cranberry ice and blueberry ice.

Vodka VR (Eng) *abbr*: **V**odka **R**eaction. 54% alc by vol. spirit that contains Vladivar Classic Vodka, glucose, taurine and caffeine.

V.O. Estilo Fine Marivaux (Sp) a brandy produced by Mascaró.

Vögelein (Ger) vineyard (Anb): Franken. (Ber): Maindreieck. (Gro): Kirchberg. (Vil): Nordheim.

Vogelleithen (Aus) a vineyard site on the banks of the River Danube situated in the Wachau region, Niederösterreich.

Vogelsang (Aus) a vineyard site on the banks of the

V

River Danube situated in the Wachau region, Niederösterreich.

Vogelsang (Ger) lit: 'birdsong', a popular name for German vineyards. 23 individual sites have this name.

Vogelsang (Ger) vineyard (Anb): Baden. (Ber): Badische Bergstrasse/Kraichgau. (Gro): Stiftsberg. (Vil): Gemmingen.

Vogelsang (Ger) vineyard (Anb): Baden. (Ber): Badische Bergstrasse/Kraichgau. (Gro): Stiftsberg. (Vil): Kirchhardt (ortsteil Berwangen).

Vogelsang (Ger) vineyard (Anb): Franken. (Ber): Steigerwald. (Gro): Burgweg. (Vil): Markt Einersheim.

Vogelsang (Ger) vineyard (Anb): Mosel-Saar-Ruwer. (Ber): Saar-Ruwer. (Gro): Scharzberg. (Vil): Irsch.

Vogelsang (Ger) vineyard (Anb): Mosel-Saar-Ruwer. (Ber): Saar-Ruwer. (Gro): Scharzberg. (Vil): Serrig.

Vogelsang (Ger) vineyard (Anb): Nahe. (Ber): Kreuznach. (Gro): Kronenberg. (Vil): Bad Kreuznach.

Vogelsang (Ger) vineyard (Anb): Nahe. (Ber): Kreuznach. (Gro): Kronenberg. (Vil): Bretzenheim.

Vogelsang (Ger) vineyard (Anb): Nahe. (Ber): Kreuznach. (Gro): Schlosskapelle. (Vil): Laubenheim.

Vogelsang (Ger) vineyard (Anb): Nahe. (Ber): Schloss Böckelheim. (Gro): Paradiesgarten. (Vil): Merxheim.

Vogelsang (Ger) vineyard (Anb): Rheingau. (Ber): Johannisberg. (Gro): Erntebringer. (Vil): Estate.

Vogelsang (Ger) vineyard (Anb): Rheinhessen. (Ber): Bingen. (Gro): Kurfürstenstück. (Vil): Wallertheim.

Vogelsang (Ger) vineyard (Anb): Rheinhessen. (Ber): Nierstein. (Gro): Gutes Domtal. (Vil): Zornheim.

Vogelsang (Ger) vineyard (Anb): Rheinhessen. (Ber): Nierstein. (Gro): Petersberg. (Vil): Gau-Odernheim.

Vogelsang (Ger) vineyard (Anb): Pfalz. (Ber): Mittelhaardt-Deutsche Weinstrasse. (Gro): Feuerberg. (Vil): Weisenheim am Berg.

Vogelsang (Ger) vineyard (Anb): Pfalz. (Ber): Mittelhaardt-Deutsche Weinstrasse. (Gro): Grafenstück. (Vil): Bockenheim.

Vogelsang (Ger) vineyard (Anb): Pfalz. (Ber): Mittelhaardt-Deutsche Weinstrasse. (Gro): Grafenstück. (Vil): Kindenheim.

Vogelsang (Ger) vineyard (Anb): Württemberg. (Ber): Württembergisch Unterland. (Gro): Heuchelberg. (Vil): Hausen/Z.

Vogelsang (Ger) vineyard (Anb): Württemberg. (Ber): Württembergisch Unterland. (Gro): Heuchelberg. (Vil): Kleingartach.

Vogelsang (Ger) vineyard (Anb): Württemberg. (Ber): Württembergisch Unterland. (Gro): Heuchelberg. (Vil): Leingarten.

Vogelsang (Ger) vineyard (Anb): Württemberg. (Ber): Württembergisch Unterland. (Gro): Heuchelberg. (Vil): Neipperg.

Vogelsang (Ger) vineyard (Anb): Württemberg.

Vogelsang (Ger) vineyard (Anb): Württemberg. (Ber): Württembergisch Unterland. (Gro): Heuchelberg. (Vil): Niederhofen.

Vogelsang (Ger) vineyard (Anb): Württemberg. (Ber): Württembergisch Unterland. (Gro): Heuchelberg. (Vil): Schwaigern.

Vogelsang (Ger) vineyard (Anb): Württemberg. (Ber): Württembergisch Unterland. (Gro): Staufenberg. (Vil): Untereisesheim.

Vogelsang (Lux) a vineyard site in the village of Ahn.

Vogelsberger (Ger) a natural spring mineral water brand. Mineral contents (milligrammes per litre): Sodium 6.7mg/l, Calcium 22mg/l, Magnesium 8.3mg/l, Potassium 5.5mg/l, Chlorides 2.9mg/l.

Vogelschlag (Ger) vineyard (Anb): Nahe. (Ber): Schloss Böckelheim. (Gro): Burgweg. (Vil): Duchroth.

Vogelsgärten (Ger) grosslage (Anb): Rheinhessen. (Ber): Nierstein. (Vils): Guntersblum, Ludwigshöhe.

Vogelsprung (Ger) vineyard (Anb): Pfalz. (Ber): Südliche Weinstrasse. (Gro): Bischofskreuz. (Vil): Flemlingen.

Vogensen's Vineyard (USA) a vineyard based in the Dry Creek Valley, Sonoma County, California. Grape variety: Zinfandel.

Vögerl Haseln (Aus) a vineyard site based on the banks of the River Kamp situated in the Kamptal region.

Vogiras (Fr) an alternative to Vosgros.

Vogteilberg (Ger) vineyard (Anb): Mosel-Saar-Ruwer. (Ber): Zell/Mosel. (Gro): Rosenhang. (Vil): Senheim.

Vogtei Rötteln (Ger) grosslage (Anb): Baden. (Ber): Markgräflerland. (Vils): Bamlach, Binzen, Blansingen, Efringen-Kirchen, Egringen, Eimeldingen, Feuerbach, Fischingen, Grenzach, Haltingen, Herten, Hertingen, Holzen, Huttingen, Istein, Kleinkems, Lörrach, Ötlingen, Rheinweiler, Riedlingen, Rümmingen, Schallbach, Tannenkirch, Weil am Rhein, Welmlingen, Wintersweiler, Wollbach.

Voile [Le] (Fr) the name used in the Jura region for flor, the fungus which form on the surface of certain wines. *see* **Mycodermae vini**, Vin Jaune.

Voiren-Jumel (Fr) a Champagne producer. Label: Cuvée 555 Vieilli en Fut de Chêne.

Voirin-Desmoulins (Fr) a Champagne producer (established 1960). (Add): 24, Rue des Partelaines, 51530 Chouilly. 9ha. Produces vintage and non-vintage wines. Vintages: 1995, 1996, 1997, 1999. A member of the Club Tresors de Champagne. Labels: Cuvée Retour de Chasse, Cuvée 'Spécial Club' Millésimée (Chardonnay 100%). Website: http://www.champagne-voirin-desmoulins.com

Voiura (Sp) *see* Viura.

Vojvodina (Ser) a wine region based in northern Serbia. Produces Plemenka and P.W. Berniet (a red vermouth). *see* Fruska Gora. Grape varieties: Gewürztraminer, Laski rizling, Neoplanta, Pinot blanc, Sauvignon blanc, Sylvaner.

Vok (Austr) a noted liqueur producer.

V

Volari (It) a brand-name red or white frizzante wine from the Emilia-Romagna region, north Italy.

Volatile (Eng) being able to change from liquid to vapour at low temperatures. i.e. acids, alcohol.

Volatile Acid (Eng) abbr: V.A. mainly acetic acid (vinegar) but also minute traces of other acids (butyric/formic/propionic), a normal by-product of alcoholic fermentation. Acceptable in wine up to 0.6 grammes–0.8 grammes. per litre. 600–800 parts per million.

Volatile Matter (Eng) in wine the acids, alcohol, aldehydes and esters.

Volcan (Fr) a natural spring mineral water from Aizac Ardèche. Mineral contents (milligrammes per litre): Sodium 13mg/l, Calcium 196.6mg/l, Magnesium 34.5mg/l, Potassium 1.3mg/l, Bicarbonates 420mg/l, Fluorides 0.23mg/l.

Volcania (Fr) a natural spring mineral water from Grand Barbier. Mineral contents (milligrammes per litre): Sodium 2.6mg/l, Calcium 4.6mg/l, Magnesium 1.2mg/l, Potassium 0.7mg/l, Bicarbonates 27mg/l, Chlorides 0.9mg/l, Sulphates 0.9mg/l, Nitrates 0.7mg/l, Silicates 30.8mg/l. pH 7.2

Volcanic Hill (USA) a red wine (Cabernet sauvignon) produced by the Diamond Creek winery, Napa Valley, California.

Volcan'o (Fr) a natural spring mineral water from Chapelle Ste. Marguerite, Auvergne. Mineral contents (milligrammes per litre): Sodium 400mg/l, Calcium 200mg/l, Magnesium 133mg/l, Potassium 41mg/l, Bicarbonates 1380mg/l, Chlorides 379mg/l, Sulphates 173mg/l, Nitrates 8mg/l. pH 5.8

Volcano Hill (USA) the brand-name used by the Diamond Creek Winery for one of their wines from a specific section of their property.

Volée [A la] (Fr) the old method of dégorgement in Champagne which uses the pressure in the bottle to push out the sediment from the second fermentation together with a small amount of the wine. See also Glace (A La).

Volenti (Eng) a 5.2% alc by vol. ale brewed by the Edale Brewery C°., Derbyshire.

Volidza (Gre) an ancient red grape variety.

Volkach (Ger) village (Anb): Franken. (Ber): Maindreieck. (Gro): Kirchberg. (Vin): Ratsherr.

Volker Eisele Vineyard (USA) see Eisele Vineyard

Volkmarer (Ger) a natural spring mineral water brand. Mineral contents (milligrammes per litre): Sodium 25mg/l, Calcium 133.2mg/l, Magnesium 43.6mg/l, Potassium 4.5mg/l, Chlorides 26.6mg/l.

Voll (Ger) full, denotes a wine that has a high percentage of alcohol.

Vollbieres (Ger) a term to describe beers with an O.G. of 11%–14%.

Vollburg (Ger) vineyard (Anb): Franken. (Ber): Steigerwald. (Gro): Not yet assigned. (Vil): Michelau i. Steigerwald.

Voll-Damm (Sp) the label of a strong lager brewed by Estrella-Damm in Barcelona.

Vollereaux (Fr) a Champagne producer. (Add): 48 Rue Léon-Bourgeois, B.P. 4, 51200 Pierry, Épernay. 40ha. Produces: Blanc de Blancs Brut, Brut S.A. (⅓ Chardonnay, ⅓ Pinot noir, ⅓ Pinot meunier), Cuvée Marguerite Brut Millésime, Cuvée Tradition Brut Vendange, Domaine de Corrigot Brut, Extra-Dry, Demi-Sec and Rosé Brut (Pinot noir 100%). Vintages: 1973, 1976, 1979, 1982, 1985, 1988, 1990, 1995, 1998. Website: http://www.Champagne-vollereaux.fr 'E'mail: Champagne.VollereauxSA@wanadoo.fr

Vollmersweiler (Ger) village (Anb): Pfalz. (Ber): Südliche Weinstrasse. (Gro): Guttemberg. (Vin): Krapfenberg.

Vollmond Bier (Switz) an organic lager-style beer 5% alc by vol brewed during a full-moon!

Volnay (Fr) an A.C. red wine commune (84.2ha) in the Côte de Beaune, Burgundy. The Premier Cru vineyards are: Clos des Ducs, La Barre, La Bousse d'Or, Le Clos des Chênes, Les Angles, Les Brouillards, Les Caillerets, Les Caillerets-Dessus, Les Champans, Les Chevrets, Les Fremiets, Les Mitans, Les Pointes d'Angles, L'Ormeau.

Volonté (Bel) the brand-name used for a range of fruit juices imported into U.K. by Leisure Drinks, Derby.

Volpaiole (It) an I.G.T. Cabernet and Merlot red wine produced by Villa Monte Rico, Maremma, Tuscany.

Völsk (Eng) a 5.3% alc by vol. vodka mixer with a koolberry flavour from Whitbread Beer C°.

Volsoet Rooi Muskadel (S.Afr) a red, rich, full dessert wine from the Boere Co-operative. Made with the Montagu muskadel grape.

Volstead (Cktl) 35mls (1½ fl.ozs) Swedish Punsch, 10mls (½ fl.oz) rye whiskey, 5mls (¼ fl.oz) each of raspberry syrup, orange juice. Shake over ice and serve 'on the rocks' in an old-fashioned glass.

Volstead Act (USA) 1919–1933 Senator Volstead prohibited wine-making altogether except for use in churches.

Volte [Le] (It) a blend of Sangiovese and Cabernet sauvignon grapes plus 10% Merlot and 5% Cannonau. Produced by Tenuta dell'Ornellaia, Bolgheri, Tuscany.

Voltipe (S.Afr) full-bodied.

Volunteer Bitter (Eng) a 4.2% alc by vol. bitter ale brewed by the Bank Top Brewery Ltd., Lancashire.

Voluptuous (Eng) in relation to wines, denotes one that gives feelings of luxurious pleasure and taste.

Volvic (Fr) a still natural spring mineral water from Le Clairvic Spring, 63530, Volvic, Puy de Dôme. Mineral contents (milligrammes per litre): Sodium 11.6mg/l, Calcium 11.5mg/l, Magnesium 8mg/l, Potassium 6.2mg/l, Bicarbonates 71mg/l, Chlorides 13.5mg/l, Sulphates 8.1mg/l, Nitrates 6.3mg/l, Silicates 31.7mg/l. pH 7.0

Volvilante (Fr) a natural spring mineral water brand. Mineral contents (milligrammes per litre): Sodium 9.4mg/l, Calcium 9.9mg/l, Magnesium 6.1mg/l, Potassium 5.7mg/l, Bicarbonates 65.3mg/l, Chlorides 8.4mg/l, Sulphates 6.9mg/l.

V

Volxheim (Ger) village (Anb): Rheinhessen. (Ber): Bingen. (Gro): Rheingrafenstein. (Vins): Alte Römerstrasse, Liebfrau, Mönchberg.

Vom Heissen Stein (Ger) grosslage (Anb): Mosel-Saar-Ruwer. (Ber): Bernkastel. (Vils): Briedel, Pünderich, Reil.

Vom Stein (Aus) a vineyard site on the banks of the River Danube situated in the Wachau region, Niederösterreich.

Vondel (Bel) an 8.5% alc by vol. brown, top-fermented, bottle-conditioned special double beer brewed by Riva in Dentergem.

Von der Hölle (Ger) vineyard (Anb): Nahe. (Ber): Schloss Böckelheim. (Gro): Paradiesgarten. (Vil): Desloch.

Vonkel (S.Afr) a medium-dry sparkling wine made by the Boplaas Estate from the Colombard grape using the cuve close method.

Vonkelwyn (S.Afr) sparkling wine.

Von Ortloff (S.Afr) a winery (established 1994) based in Franschhoek, Western Cape. 15ha. Grape varieties: Cabernet sauvignon, Chardonnay, Merlot, Sauvignon blanc. Labels: N°3 (un-oaked Chardonnay), N°5 (Sauvignon blanc), N°7 (Merlot).

Von Plettenberg (Ger) an estate in the Nahe at Bad Kreuznach.

Von Schubert (Ger) the owner of Maximin Grünhaus.

Von Simmern (Ger) a family estate at Hattenheim in the Rheingau.

Voodoo (Cktl) 1 measure rum, half measure Italian vermouth, half measure gomme syrup, shake over ice with apple juice and serve in an ice-filled highball glass.

Voorburg (Hol) a citrus-flavoured brandewijn.

Vooruitsig (S.Afr) a winery (established 1998) based in Paarl, Western Cape. 30ha. Grape varieties: Cabernet franc, Cabernet sauvignon, Malbec, Merlot, Shiraz. Produces varietal wines.

VORAC (N.Z) *abbr*: **V**iticultural and **O**enological **R**esearch **A**dvisory **C**ouncil.

Vorarlberg (Aus) a small wine-growing area on the Swiss border (17.5ha). Main grape varieties: Blauer portugieser, Bouvier, Müller-Thurgau, Riesling, Traminer, Zweigelt. Produces a range of wine styles.

Vorbachzimmern (Ger) village (Anb): Württemberg. (Ber): Kocher-Jagst-Tauber. (Gro): Tauberberg. (Vin): Schafsteige.

Vorbourg (Fr) a 72ha A.C. Alsace Grand Cru vineyard at Rouffach and Westhalten, Haut-Rhin.

Vorden Berg (Aus) a vineyard site on the banks of the River Danube in the Kremstal region.

Vorderberg (Ger) vineyard (Anb): Pfalz. (Ber): Mittelhaardt-Deutsche Weinstrasse. (Gro): Schwarzerde. (Vil): Kleinniedesheim.

Vorderseiber (Aus) a vineyard site on the banks of the River Danube situated in the Wachau region, Niederösterreich.

V.O.R.I. (S.Afr) *abbr*: South African **V**iticultural and **O**enological **R**esearch Institute (also known as Nievoorbij).

Vorlese (Ger) the early gathering of the grapes before the main harvest that takes place when adverse weather conditions occur.

Vornehm (Ger) exquisite, delightful wine.

Vörös (Hun) red.

Vörösbor (Hun) red wine.

Vorspannhof (Aus) a winery (10ha) based in the Kremstal region. (Add): Herrengasse 48, 3552 Dross bei Krems. Grape varieties: Chardonnay, Gelber muskateller, Grüner veltliner, Riesling, Sauvignon blanc. Produces a range of wine styles.

Vos (Hol) a 5% alc by vol. top-fermented, bottled special beer brewed by De Ridder City Brouwerij, Maastricht.

Vose Vineyards (USA) a winery based near Oakville, Napa Valley, California. 14.5ha. Grape varieties: Cabernet sauvignon, Chardonnay and Zinfandel. Produces varietal wines (Zinfandel wine is known as Zinblanca).

Vosges (Fr) a range of mountains that separate Lorraine from Alsace on which some of the famous Alsace vineyards are situated (also Vittel mineral waters).

Vosgia (Fr) a natural spring mineral water from Metzeral. Mineral contents (milligrammes per litre): Sodium 3mg/l, Calcium 6.4mg/l, Magnesium 1.2mg/l, Potassium 0.5mg/l, Bicarbonates 20mg/l, Chlorides 3mg/l, Sulphates 5mg/l, Nitrates 4mg/l. pH 6.5

Vosgros (Fr) a Premier Cru A.C. Chablis vineyard that often has the Premier Cru vineyard Vaugiraut used as a vintage wine under its name.

Vöslau (Aus) a district of the Niederösterreich south of Vienna that produces mainly red wines from the Blaufränkisch and Portugieser grapes.

Vöslau (Aus) the name given to a naturally sparkling mineral water from the Austrian Alps.

Vöslauer (Aus) a natural spring mineral water from Bad Vöslau, Harzberg. Mineral contents (milligrammes per litre): Sodium 13.71mg/l, Calcium 110.5mg/l, Magnesium 41.5mg/l, Potassium 1.68mg/l, Bicarbonates 254mg/l, Chlorides 19.8mg/l, Sulphates 229.3mg/l.

Vöslauer Rotwein (Aus) a fine red wine from the Vöslau district.

Vosne Romanée (Fr) an A.C. commune within the Côte de Nuits, Burgundy. Has the Grand Cru vineyards: La Richebourg, La Romanée, La Romanée-Conti, La Romanée Saint-Vivant and La Tâche. (25.13ha) The Premier Cru vineyards: Aux Brûlées, Aux Petits-Monts, Aux Reignots, Clos des Réas, La Chaume, La Grande Rue, Les Beaux-Monts, Les Malconsorts and Les Suchots. (47.5ha).

Vosne Romanée Premier Cru (Fr) the second wine of Domaine de la Romanée-Conti (a Premier Cru from Grand Cru vineyards). Produced from the second picking from the domaine's vineyards (except Romanéee-Conti) it is a revival of Cuvée Duvault-Blochet produced in the 1930's.

Voss (Nor) an ultra premium bottled water that is filtered in a virgin aquifier, low in sodium and almost free of minerals.

1379

V

Voss Artesian (Nor) a natural spring mineral water (established 1998) from the Voss Source, Iveland. Mineral contents (milligrammes per litre): Sodium 4mg/l, Calcium 3.8mg/l, Magnesium 0.78mg/l. pH 6.5

Voss Estate (N.Z) a 3ha winery. (Add): Puruatanga Road, P.O. Box 78, Martinborough. Produces a Bordeaux-style blend from Cabernet franc, Cabernet sauvignon and Merlot grapes.

Votka (Tur) vodka.

Votre Santé (Fr) lit:'your health', cheers!

Votrix (Eng) a British-made vermouth. Produced from concentrated grape juice fermented in England by Vine Products Ltd.

Vougeot (Fr) an A.C. commune of the Côte de Nuits. Has the Grand Cru Clos de Vougeot within the commune plus the Premier Crus: Clos Blanc de Vougeot, Les Cras and Les Petits-Vougeots 11.8ha.

Vouvray (Fr) an A.C. pétillant, sparkling or still white wine (sec to moelleux) from the Touraine district of the Loire. Made predominantly from Chenin blanc plus Arbois grapes. Produced on Tufa soil. Mimimum alc by vol. of 11%.

Vouvray Mousseux (Fr) an A.C. sparkling wine from the Touraine district of the Loire. Sweet, medium and dry varieties. Minimum alc by vol. of 9.5%.

Vouvray Pétillant (Fr) a dry, white wine with a slight prickle, made from the Chenin blanc grape in Touraine in the Loire.

Vov (It) a light 'egg-zabaglione' style of liqueur.

Vox (Eng) a colourless cider 8.4% alc by vol. from the Gaymer Group.

Voyager Estate (Austr) a winery based in the Margaret River region of Western Australia. Grape varieties include: Cabernet sauvignon, Chardonnay, Merlot, Sauvignon blanc, Shiraz.

Voyens [Les] (Fr) a vineyard in the A.C. commune of Mercurey, Côte Chalonnaise, Burgundy. Also known as Clos Voyen.

V.P. (Eng) abbr: Vine Products Ltd. Also the name of a popular brand of British Sherry produced by Vine Products Ltd.

V.P. (Eng) abbr: Vincent Powell a 4.1% alc by vol. ale brewed by Grain Brewery, Oakham, Rutland to commemorate the 1,000th guest ale served at the Queens Head, Sutton Bassett. Named after the licensee.

V.P.A. (Eng) abbr: Ventnor Pale Ale. a best bitter 1040 O.G. brewed by the Burt Brewery on the Isle of Wight.

V.Q.A. (Can) abbr: Vintners Quality Alliance.

V.Q.P.R.D. (E.C)(Fr) abbr: Vins de Qualité Produits dans des Régions Determinées.

V.Q.P.R.D. (E.C)(It) abbr: Vino Qualité Produttorio Regione Delimité.

VR (Eng) a 4.5% alc by vol. Vladivar vodka-based energy drink that also contains glucose, taurine and caffeine.

Vrac (Fr) lit: 'bulk', the wholesale price of wine sold. Includes the cork and bottle but not normally the label and capsule. Never includes the case price (also known as En Vrac and Vin en Vrac).

Vrachanski Misket (Bul) a white grape variety. Produces strong muscat-flavoured wines.

Vracs (Fr) plastic containers to hold 'draught' wine.

Vrai Auxerrois (Fr) an alternative name for the Pinot blanc grape.

Vranac (Euro) a red wine made from a local red grape variety in Montenegro on the Dalmatian coast.

Vrancea Vineyard (Rum) the largest area of vineyards. Contains areas of Cotesti, Nicoresti, Odobesti and Panciu. See also Focsani.

Vranje (Ser) a key red wine producing region in Serbia. Grape varieties include: Cabernet sauvignon, Merlot, Pinot noir.

Vranken Lafitte (Fr) a Champagne producer based at Vertus. Produces: Charles Lafitte, La Belle Idée de Champagne.

Vratislavice nad Nisou Brewery (Czec) a noted brewery based in northern Czec. Brews: Kapucín.

VRB (Eng) abbr: Vodka Revitalising Bevvy. 5.3% alc by vol. bottled vodka based drink containing taurine, glucose and caffeine.

Vrdnik (Slo) a wine-growing area in Fruska Gora, Vojvodina.

Vredendal (S.Afr) a brandy and dessert wine-producing area based north of Tulbagh.

Vredendal Co-op Winery (S.Afr) a winery. (Add): P.O. Box 75, Vredendal 8160, Olifants River. Labels include Maskam, Namaqua, Vredendal.

Vredenheim Estate Wines (S.Afr) a vineyard based in Stellenbosch, Western Cape. (Add): P.O. Box 7, Vlottenburg 7604. Produces varietal wines.

Vred en Lust Wine Farm (S.Afr) a winery (established 1996) based in Paarl, Western Cape. 42ha. Grape varieties: Cabernet sauvignon, Chardonnay, Chenin blanc, Cinsaut, Malbec, Merlot, Petit verdot, Sémillon, Shiraz. Labels: Barbère, Cara, Classic, Jacques de Savoy, Simond, Karien, Marguerite. Website: http://www.vnl.co.za

Vredenheim Wines (S.Afr) a winery (established 80ha) based in Stellenbosch, Western Cape. 30ha. Grape varieties: Cabernet sauvignon, Chardonnay, Chenin blanc, Merlot, Muscat, Pinotage, Shiraz. Labels: Reserve 214, Vrendenvonkel. Website: http://www.vrendenheim.co.za

Vreez (Mex) producers of liqueurs. Noted for Vanilla de Mexico (a vanilla-flavoured liqueur).

Vrendenvonkel (S.Afr) the label for a demi-sec sparkling wine (Chardonnay) produced by the Vrendenheim Wines winery, Stellenbosch, Western Cape.

Vrhunsko Vino (Cro) select wine: Q.W.P.S.R. see Cuveno Vino, Kvalitetno Vino.

Vriesenhof Vineyard (S.Afr) a winery (established 1980) based in Stellenbosch, Western Cape. 37ha. (Add): P.O. Stellenbosch 7600. Grape varieties: Cabernet franc, Cabernet sauvignon, Chardonnay, Merlot, Pinotage, Pinot noir, Shiraz. Labels: Enthopio, Kallister, Paradyskloof (second label), Royale, Talana Hills. Website: http://www.vriesenhof.co.za

Vrigny (Fr) a Cru Champagne village in the Canton de Ville-en-Tardenois. District: Reims.

Vrillon [Jean] (Fr) a producer of sparkling Touraine wines based at Faverolles-sur-Cher, Touraine, Loire.

Vrnicka Zlahtina (Cro) a white wine produced in north-western Croatia.

Vrnjacko Vrelo (Ser) a natural spring mineral water (established 2000) from Novo Selo, Vrnjacka Banja, Serbia and Montenegro. Mineral contents (milligrammes per litre): Sodium 26.1mg/l, Calcium 7.2mg/l, Magnesium 43.98mg/l, Potassium 1mg/l, Bicarbonates 287mg/l, Chlorides 4.82mg/l, Sulphates 5.63mg/l, Fluorides 0.19mg/l, Nitrates <0.05mg/l, Silicates 43.17mg/l, Oxygen 1.58mg/l. pH 7.97

Vrsac (Ser) a wine-producing centre in Banat. Produces mainly white wines.

Vruchtbaar Boutique Winery (S.Afr) a winery (established 2001) based in Robertson, Western Cape. 35ha. Grape varieties: Cabernet sauvignon, Chardonnay, Chenin blanc, Colombard, Merlot, Pinotage, Ruby cabernet, Sauvignon blanc.

V.S. (Eng) *abbr*: **V**ery **S**uperior. a designation on a Cognac brandy label.

V.S. (Rum) high quality wine produced in a specific region with a natural alcoholic strength of 10.5% alc by vol. or more. *see* V.S.O., V.S.O.C.

V.S.E.P. (Eng) *abbr*: **V**ery **S**uperior **E**xtra **P**ale. mainly for the USA market. Designation on a Cognac brandy label.

V.S.O. (Eng) *abbr*: **V**ery **S**uperior **O**ld. a designation on a Cognac brandy label. 12–17 years in cask.

V.S.O. (Rum) high quality wines with an A.O.C. Produced in strictly delimited regions from recommended grapes. No must enrichment. Must reach 11% alc by vol. *see* V.S., V.S.O.C.

V.S.O.C. (Rum) high quality wines with an A.O.C. and a quality grade. Divided into 3 grades: [1] Late harvest or late-picked grapes: 220g/l of sugar in must, min. alc. 10% by vol. [2] Noble maturity or selected harvest: late-picked grapes affected by noble rot 240g/l of sugar, min. alc. 10% by vol. [3] Late-picked grapes naturally raisined on vine by noble rot: 260g/l, min. alc. 11% by vol.

V.S.O.P. (Eng) *abbr*: **V**ery **S**uperior **O**ld **P**ale. Designation of a Cognac brandy label. The youngest Cognac must be 4 years old. New law. Old designations were for 20–30 years in cask (also for Armagnac which must have a minimum age of 4 years).

V.S.P. (Eng) a bitter brewed by the Original Brewing Company in Hertfordshire.

VSP (N.Z) *abbr*: **V**ertical **S**hoot **P**ositioning.

V.S.R. (Fr) *abbr*: **V**ery **S**pecially **R**ecommended.

V Two [2] (It) a 5.4% alc by vol. Russian vodka, Martini vermouth and mixer drink produced by Bacardi-Martini. Sold in a silver bottle.

Vuelta (Sp) an alternative word used for Tourne.

Vugava (Euro) a small wine-producing island on the Dalmatian coast. Produces high alcohol (Sherry-style) wines. Also noted for Vis wine.

Vugava (Euro) a white grape variety grown in the Dalmatian area.

Vuida de Romero (Mex) the brand-name of a popular local tequila.

Vujic (Euro) a still natural spring mineral water from Petnica, Serbia and Montenegro. Mineral contents (milligrammes per litre): Sodium 2.7mg/l, Calcium 105.3mg/l, Magnesium 21.6mg/l, Potassium 0.8mg/l, Bicarbonates 421mg/l, Chlorides 6mg/l, Sulphates 6.6mg/l, Nitrates 6.5mg/l, Silicates 11.97mg/l, Oxygen 7.6mg/l. pH 7.39

Vukovar (Cro) a noted wine-producing town in Croatia.

Vulcan [The] (Eng) a patented corkscrew based on the 1802 Thomason patent. Has a brush in the handle and cylinder that fits over the screw. Made by Westol Wine Consultants, 16 King Street, Bristol BS1 4EF.

Vulcano (Aus) the label for a red wine (Blaufränkisch and Cabernet sauvignon blend) produced by the Igler winery, Mittel-Burgenland.

Vulkanfelsen (Ger) grosslage (Anb): Baden. (Ber): Kaiserstuhl-Tuniberg. (Vils): Achkarren, Amoltern, Bahlingen, Bickensohl, Bischoffingen, Bötzingen, Breisach a. Rh., Burkheim, Eichstetten, Endingen, Ihringen, Ihringen (ortsteil Blankenhornsberg, Jechtingen, Kiechlinsbergen, Königschaffhausen, Leiselheim, Neuershausen, Nimburg, Oberbergen, Oberrotweil, Riegel, Sasbach, Schelingen, Wasenweiler.

Vulkania Heilwasser (Ger) a natural spring mineral water from Dreis, Vulkaneifel. Mineral contents (milligrammes per litre): Sodium 362.4mg/l, Calcium 277.4mg/l, Magnesium 380.9mg/l, Potassium 41.4mg/l, Bicarbonates 3754mg/l, Chlorides 23.9mg/l, Sulphates 23.1mg/l, Strontium 2.21mg/l, Ammonium 3.07mg/l, Iron 9.5mg/l, Barium 1.3mg/l.

Vulkanquelle (Ger) a natural spring mineral water from Dreis, Vulkaneifel. Mineral contents (milligrammes per litre): Sodium 115mg/l, Calcium 84mg/l, Magnesium 105mg/l, Potassium 18mg/l, Bicarbonates 1086mg/l, Chlorides 16mg/l, Sulphates 13mg/l, Nitrates 9mg/l.

Vully (Switz) a wine-producing area in northern Vaud. Produces white, pétillant wines.

Vulture (It) a D.O.C. wine produced in Basilicata from the Aglianico grape. *see* Aglianico del Vulture.

Vuurberg Vineyards (S.Afr) a winery (established 2000) based in Stellenbosch, Western Cape. 10ha. Grape varieties: Cabernet franc, Cabernet sauvignon, Grenache blanc, Malbec, Merlot, Petit verdot, Roussanne, Viognier. Label: Tridente. Website: http://www.vuurberg.com

V.V.P. (Sp) *abbr*: **V**ery **V**ery **P**ale. a colour grading of Sherries (Finos to the Manzanillas).

V.V.S.O.P. (Eng) *abbr*: **V**ery **V**ery **S**uperior **O**ld **P**ale. a designation of Cognac brandy. An old designation. Denotes that it has spent 40 years in cask.

VWB Winery C°. (USA) a winery based near St.

V

Helena, Napa Valley, California. Grape varieties: Cabernet sauvignon, Chardonnay and Sauvignon blanc. Produces varietal wines.

Vyborova (Pol) a brand of vodka (also spelt Wyborowa).

Vyhne Brewery (Czec) an old established brewery based in eastern Czec.

Vylan Vineyards (Hung) a winery and vineyards (Add): 7821, Kisharsany, Fekete-Hegy 092.hrsz. Produces Vilàny wines.

Vyskov Brewery (Czec) an old brewery based in central Czec.

Vysoky Chlumec Brewery (Czec) an old brewery based in western Czec.

W

Waboomsrivier Koöperatiewe Wynkelder (S.Afr) *abbr*: WKW a co-operative winery (established 1949) based at Worcester, Western Cape that has 40 members. (Add): Box 24, Breërivier 6858. Grape varieties: Cabernet sauvignon, Cinsaut, Colombard, Merlot, Pinotage, Ruby cabernet. Labels: Roodewagen, Rubellite and varietal wines under the Wageboom Wines label.

Wachau (Aus) a wine area (1450ha) of the Niederösterreich district, the best known of all Austrian wine areas. Soil: crystalline slate, gneiss, loess, rock, sand. Main grape varieties: white (Chardonnay, Grüner veltliner, Pinot blanc, Riesling), red (Cabernet sauvignon, Merlot, Pinot noir, Zweigelt). Villages: Arnsdorf, Bergen, Dürnstein, Jocking, Mautern, Mühlberg, Rossatz, Rossatzbach, Ruhrsdorf, Spitz, St. Michel, Weissenkirchen, Wösendorf. Vineyard sites: Achleiten, Achspoint, Altau, Alte Point, Angern, Atzberg, Auleithen, Bachsatz, Bärleiten, Biern, Bockfüssl, Brandstatt, Breitel, Bruck, Buchental, Burggarten, Burgstall, Buschenberg, Donauleiten, Donaupoint, Eichberg, Frauengärten, Frauenpoint, Frauenweingärten, Freal, Gründen, Hartberg, Heizenleithen, Herstell, Himmelreich, Hinter der Burg, Hinterkirchen, Hinterseiber, Hochrain (2), Hochstrasser, Höhereck, Hollerin, Holzapfel Feld, Jochinger, Johannserberg, Kaiserberg, Kalkofen, Kellerberg, Kellerweingärten, Kiernberg, Kirchweg, Kirschböck, Klaus, Kloster-Mitterfeldsaal, Kollmitz, Kollmütz, Kreutles, Kreuzberg, Küss den Pfennig, Langenzügen, Lichenstein, Lichtgartl, Liebenberg, Loibenberg, Marienfeld, Mühlberg, Mühlpoint, Oberhauser, Obersätzen, Offenberg, Pfaffenthal, Pichlpoint, Poigen, Pointe, Postaller, Pöttinger, Rauheneck, Ritzling, Rotes Tor, Rothenberg, Rothenhof, Scheibental, Schön, Schreiberberg, Schütt, Setzberg, Silberbühel, Singerriedel, Sonnleiten, Steiger, Stein am Rain, Steinborz, Steinertal, Steinriedl, Steinwand, Strudel, Süssbenberg (2), Tausendeimerberg, Trauntal, Untersätzen, Vogelleithen, Vogelsang, Vom Stein, Vorderseiber, Weingebirge, Zaum, Zornberg, Zweikreuzgarten, Zwerithaler. Produces fresh, light dry white wines, often pétillant, best known is Schluck. *See also* Federspiel, Smaragd, Steinfelder and Uachaouuam.

Wachauer Marillen (Aus) a liqueur made from apricots.

Wachelter Water (Bel) juniper water, produced in Hasselt in the province of Limburg in 1610.

Wachenheim (Ger) village (Anb): Pfalz. (Ber): Mittelhaardt-Deutsche Weinstrasse. (Gro): Mariengarten. (Vins): Altenburg, Belz, Böhlig, Gerümpel, Goldbächel, Rechbächel.

Wachenheim (Ger) village (Anb): Pfalz. (Ber): Mittelhaardt-Deutsche Weinstrasse. (Gro): Schenkenböhl. (Vins): Fuchsmantel, Königswingert, Mandelgarten, Odinstal, Schlossberg.

Wachenheim (Ger) village (Anb): Pfalz. (Ber): Mittelhaardt-Deutsche Weinstrasse. (Gro): Schnepfenflug an der Weinstrasse. (Vins): Bischofsgarten, Luginsland.

Wachenheim (Ger) village (Anb): Rheinhessen. (Ber): Wonnegau. (Gro): Domblick. (Vins): Horn, Rotenberg.

Wachholderkorn-Brannt (Ger) juniper-flavoured neutral spirit (similar to gin), the generic name for Steinhäger.

Wachhügel (Ger) vineyard (Anb): Franken. (Ber): Steigerwald. (Gros): Schlossberg, Wiesenbronn.

Wachstum (Ger) growth/grown by own vineyard.

Wachstum Söllner (Aus) a winery based in Gösing am Wagram, Donauland. (Add): Hauptstrasse 34, 3482 Gösing am Wagram. Grape varieties: Blauburger, Blauer portugieser, Cabernet sauvignon, Pinot noir, Riesling, Roter veltliner, Welschriesling, Zweigelt.

Wachtberg (Aus) a vineyard site on the banks of the River Danube in the Kremstal region.

Wächterbacher Doppel Bock (Ger) a 7.1% alc by vol. bottled double bock beer brewed by Hessens Brauerei, Wächterbach.

Wachtkopf (Ger) vineyard (Anb): Württemberg. (Ber): Württembergisch Unterland. (Gro): Stromberg. (Vil): Gründelbach.

Wackernheim (Ger) village (Anb): Rheinhessen. (Ber): Bingen. (Gro): Kaiserpfalz. (Vins): Rabenkopf, Schwalben, Steinberg.

Waddlers Mild (Eng) a cask-conditioned mild brewed by the Mallard Brewery, Carlton, Nottingham. *See also* Duckling Bitter.

Wa-de-Lock Vineyard (Austr) lit: 'wall of water' a vineyard (established 1987). (Add): Stratford Road, Maffra, Victoria. Grape varieties: Riesling, Sauvignon blanc, Pinot noir, Cabernet sauvignon, Merlot.

Wädenswil Brauerei (Switz) a brewery based in Wädenswil. Part of the Sibra Group (Cardinal) Breweries.

Wadworth Brewery (Eng) a brewery (established

1985) based at the Northgate Brewery in Devizes, Wiltshire. Noted for cask-conditioned Devizes Bitter 1030 O.G. XXXXXX 1040 O.G. Farmers Glory 1046 O.G. Old Timer 1055 O.G. keg Northgate Bitter 1036 O.G. Raker Bitter 1030 O.G. bottled Green Label 1040 O.G. Lovin' Sup, Valentine's Oat Malt Ale, The Bishop's Tipple 5.5% alc by vol. Also single varietal Hersbrucker Hallertau, Liberty, Mount Hood Mild, Pacific Gem, Styrian Gold. Website: http://www.wadworth.co.uk 'E'mail: sales@wadworth.co.uk

Wadworth Strongest Ale (Eng) an 11% alc by vol. bottle conditioned ale brewed by Wadsworth in Devizes, Wiltshire. Matured in oak with a limited edition (13000 bottles only).

Wageboom Wines (S.Afr) *see* Waboomsrivier Koöperatiewe Wynkelder.

Wagenstadt (Ger) village (Anb): Baden. (Ber): Breisgau. (Gro): Burg Lichteneck. (Vin): Hummelberg.

Wager Cup (Eng) an eighteenth century cup which consisted of a girl holding a cup in her arms (on a swivel) above her head. She was also full-skirted. The cup was filled with an alcoholic beverage and one had to drink from the cup whilst upending the girl. Her skirt would then be filled and this had to be drunk to win the wager (bet).

Waggle Dance (Eng) a 5% alc by vol. cask or bottled ale from Vaux, brewed from honey, had a trial under the name of Brew 101.

Waggle Spirit Canadian Spring Water (Can) a natural spring mineral water from Winnipeg, Manitoba.

Waggon [Off The] (Eng) denotes a person who has started drinking alcohol after a period of abstention. *see* Waggon (On The).

Waggon [On The] (Eng) denotes a person who has decided to abstain from alcohol, usually for health reasons. *See* Waggon [Off The].

Wagner Stein (Chile) a leading wine exporter based in Santiago.

Wagner Vineyards (USA) a winery (established 1979) based in Lodi in the Finger Lakes region of New York State (110ha).

Wagram (Aus) a wine-producing district within the Donauland region.

Wagramer Selektion (Aus) a group of producers from the Wagram district of the eastern Donauland who have joined together to improve and promote their wines and the region.

Wahaha (Chi) a natural spring mineral water brand. Mineral contents (milligrammes per litre): Sodium 10mg/l, Calcium 50mg/l, Magnesium 3.5mg/l, Potassium 1.3mg/l, Bicarbonates 200mg/l, Chlorides 3.5mg/l, Sulphates 2mg/l. pH 7.5

Wahlheim (Ger) village (Anb): Rheinhessen. (Ber): Wonnegau. (Gro): Sybillenstein. (Vin): Schelmen.

Wahrheit (Ger) vineyard (Anb): Mittelrhein. (Ber): Bacharach. (Gro): Schloss Reichenstein. (Vil): Oberheimbach.

Wahrsager (Ger) vineyard (Anb): Mosel-Saar-Ruwer. (Ber): Zell/Mosel. (Gro): Rosenhang. (Vil): Senheim.

Wah Water (Pak) an acidic natural spring mineral water from Wah Springs, Wah Cantt. Rawlalpindi. Mineral contents (milligrammes per litre): Sodium 22mg/l, Calcium 18mg/l, Magnesium 31mg/l, Potassium 2mg/l, Bicarbonates 350mg/l, Chlorides 35mg/l, Sulphates 50mg/l, Fluorides 1mg/l, Nitrates 0.5mg/l. pH 5.2

Waiblingen (Ger) village (Anb): Württemberg. (Ber): Remstal-Stuttgart. (Gro): Kopf. (Vin): Hörnle.

Waiblingen (Ger) village (Anb): Württemberg. (Ber): Remstal-Stuttgart. (Gro): Wartbühl. (Vin): Steingrüble.

Waiheke Vineyards (N.Z) a winery. (Add): 76 Onetangi Road, Onetangi, Waiheke Island. 10ha. Produces red wines.

Waihirere Winery (N.Z) the old name used for the Ormond Vineyards 40ha.

Waikato (N.Z) the brand-name given to beers brewed by New Zealand Breweries in Hamilton. Waikato Draught 1039 O.G. and Waikato XXXX 1036 O.G.

Waikato (N.Z) a wine-producing area in the northern part of the North Island.

Waikerie (Austr) a wine district along the river Murray in New South Wales. Produces fine quality wines.

Waikiki Beachcomer (Cktl) ½ measure dry gin, ½ measure Cointreau, ¼ measure pineapple juice. Shake over ice and strain into a cocktail glass.

Waikiki Cocktail (Cktl) 1 measure Bourbon whiskey, ¼ measure Curaçao, ½ measure lemon juice, 3 dashes grenadine. Blend altogether with a scoop of crushed ice in a blender and pour into a Champagne saucer.

Waimak (N.Z) a sparkling natural spring mineral water (established 1977) from Canterbury Plains, South Island. Mineral contents (milligrammes per litre): Sodium 6.9mg/l, Calcium 12mg/l, Magnesium 1.9mg/l, Potassium 0.7mg/l, Chlorides 3.9mg/l, Sulphates 3.6mg/l, Nitrates 0.26mg/l, Silicates 18mg/l, Hydrobromide 1.06mg/l. pH 7.9

Waimarama Estate (N.Z) a 4.3ha vineyard and winery. (Add): 31 Waimarama Road, Havelock North, Hawkes Bay. Grape varieties: Cabernet sauvignon, Merlot. Second label is Undercliffe.

Wain (Jap) wine.

Wainarii (Jap) winery.

Wainfleet Hedgerows (Eng) a 3.7% alc by vol. beer brewed with elderflowers by Bateman's Brewery, Wainfleet, Lincolnshire under the Mr. George's Unique Flavours range.

Waipara Downs (N.Z) a 4ha vineyard and winery based at Bains Road, Waipara. Grape varieties: Chardonnay, Cabernet sauvignon, Pinot noir.

Waipara Springs Wines (N.Z) a winery. (Add): SH1, P.O. Box 17, Waipara. 20ha. Grape varieties: Chardonnay, Pinot noir, Cabernet sauvignon, Riesling, Sémillon, Sauvignon blanc.

Waipara West (N.Z) a winery based in Waipara. Grape variety: Riesling.

Waipiro (N.Z) alcoholic liquor or spirits.

W

Wairau River Wines (N.Z) a winery. (Add): Cnr. Rapura Road & SH6 Giffords Road, RD3, Blenheim. 100ha. Grape varieties: Chardonnay, Sauvignon blanc.

Wairau Valley (N.Z) a wine area in the South Island, the Marlborough vineyards are planted here.

Waitemata (N.Z) a beer brewed by the Dominion Brewery under licence from the Scottish Brewery.

Waitrose Welsh Spring (Wal) a natural spring mineral water from Llandeilo, Carmarthenshire.

Waiwera (N.Z) a natural spring mineral water (established 1875) from the Waiwera Resort.

Wakamusha (Jap) a branded non-alcoholic cold green tea drink produced by Asahi.

Wakefield (Austr) a winery (established 1969) based in the Clare Valley, South Australia.

Wakefield Ale (Eng) see Henry Boon's Wakefield Ale.

Wakefield 100 Celebration Ale (Eng) a 1050 O.G. bottled beer brewed to celebrate Wakefield's 100 years as a city by the Clark Brewery, Wakefield, Yorkshire.

Wakefield Pride (Eng) a 4.5% alc by vol. ale brewed by the Fernanders Brewery, West Yorkshire.

Waldangelloch (Ger) village (Anb): Baden. (Ber): Badische Bergstrasse/Kraichgau. (Gro): Stiftsberg. (Vin): Sonnenberg.

Waldbach (Ger) village (Anb): Württemberg. (Ber): Württembergisch Unterland. (Gro): Lindelberg. (Vin): Schlossberg.

Waldböckelheim (Ger) village (Anb): Nahe. (Ber): Schloss Böckelheim. (Gro): Burgweg. (Vins): Drachenbrunnen, Hamm, Kirchberg, Kronenfels, Marienpforter Klosterberg, Muckerhölle, Muhlberg, Römerberg.

Waldböckelheim (Ger) village (Anb): Nahe. (Ber): Schloss Böckelheim. (Gro): Paradiesgarten. (Vins): Johannesberg, Kastell.

Waldecker (Ger) a sparkling natural spring mineral water from Volkmarsen. Mineral contents (milligrammes per litre): Sodium 18.6mg/l, Calcium 113mg/l, Magnesium 34.1mg/l, Potassium 3.5mg/l, Bicarbonates 345mg/l, Chlorides 35mg/l, Sulphates 104mg/l.

Waldlaubersheim (Ger) village (Anb): Nahe. (Ber): Kreuznach. (Gro): Schlosskapelle. (Vins): Alteburg, Bingerweg, Domberg, Hörnchen, Lieseberg, Otterberg.

Waldmeister (Ger) essence of woodruff which is sometimes added to Berliner weisse beer for flavour.

Waldmeisterlikoer (Ger) a pale green liqueur based on woodruff.

Waldquelle (Aus) a sparkling natural spring mineral water from Kobersdorf. Mineral contents (milligrammes per litre): Sodium 28.5mg/l, Calcium 88.2mg/l, Magnesium 14.9mg/l, Potassium 3.37mg/l, Bicarbonates 408.9mg/l, Chlorides 3.04mg/l, Sulphates 12.8mg/l, Silicates 42.6mg/l.

Wald-Quelle (Ger) a still natural mineral water from Kirkel. (Add): Nebgen-Mineralbrunnen, Waldstrasse 4, Kirkel. Mineral contents (milligrammes per litre): Sodium 2.8mg/l, Calcium 4.7mg/l, Magnesium 0.7mg/l, Potassium 2.2mg/l, Bicarbonates 15mg/l, Chlorides 7.9mg/l, Sulphates 3mg/l. pH 7.6

Waldrach (Ger) village (Anb): Mosel-Saar-Ruwer. (Ber): Saar-Ruwer. (Gro): Römerlay. (Vins): Doktorberg, Ehrenberg, Heiligenhauschen, Hubertusberg, Jesuitengarten, Jungfernberg, Krone, Kurfürstenberg, Laurentiusberg, Meisenberg, Sonnenberg.

Waldron Vineyards (Eng) a vineyard based in Waldron, Heathfield, East Sussex. 2ha. Grape varieties: Kerner, Müller-Thurgau, Ortega, Reichensteiner and Seyval blanc. Produces wines under the St. George's label. see Vino Esperanto.

Waldulm (Ger) village (Anb): Baden. (Ber): Ortenau. (Gro): Schloss Rodeck. (Vins): Kreuzberg, Pfarrberg.

Wales (U.K) a principality that produces only a little wine, is too far north for any major production. see Croffta, Llanerch, Llanrhystud, Monnow Valley and Offa's Vineyard.

Walheim (Ger) village (Anb): Württemberg. (Ber): Württembergisch Unterland. (Gro): Schalkstein. (Vins): Neckarberg, Wurmberg.

Walkabout (Austr) a natural spring mineral water brand.

Walkabout (Eng) a range of premium canned beers developed by a consortium. Walkabout 3 is a Belgian 3% alc by vol. lager. Walkabout 4 is an English 4% alc by vol. draught ale. Walkabout 5 is a Bavarian 5% alc by vol. Helles beer. Walkabout 7 is an Italian 7% alc by vol. dark lager.

Walkenberg (Ger) vineyard (Anb): Rheingau. (Ber): Johannisberg. (Gro): Steinmacher. (Vil): Niederwalluf.

Walkenberg (Ger) a vineyard within village of Walluf. 20ha. (50%) is proposed to be classified as Erstes Gewächs.

Walker [John & Sons] (Scot) a famous Scotch and malt whisky distillers (part of DCL) based at Kilmarnock, Ayrshire. Brands include: Cardhu, Johnnie Walker (red and black label), Swing, Talisker and Old Harmony (for Japanese market).

Walker [Peter] (Eng) a subsidiary brewery (established 1981) of the Tetley Walker group. Noted for cask-conditioned beers, keg Bergman's Lager 1033 O.G. bottled Brown Peter 1034 O.G.

Walker Bay (S.Afr) part of the Coastal wine region, south-east of Capetown, soil is sandstone to clay with rich shale. Grape varieties: Chardonnay, Pinot noir, Pinotage. Home to Hamilton-Russell.

Walker Brewery (Eng) a brewery based in Warrington, Cheshire. Subsidiary of Allied-Domecq. Produces Walker Winter Warmer.

Walker Estate (N.Z) a 3.7ha vineyard at Puruatanga Road, Martinborough, North Island. Grape varieties: Riesling, Syrah.

Walker Valley Vineyards (USA) a vineyard based in Hudson Valley, New York. 6ha. Produces white hybrid grapes.

Walker Winery (USA) a small winery based near

W

Santa Cruz mountains, Santa Clara, California. Grape varieties: Barbera, Chardonnay and Petite sirah.

Walker Winter Warmer (Eng) a dark, rich, extra-strong ale 1058–1062 O.G. brewed by the Walker Brewery in Warrington, Cheshire (a subsidiary of Allied-Domecq).

Wallace (Scot) the name of a single malt Scotch whisky liqueur distilled by Burn Stewart Distillers 35% alc by vol.

Walla Walla Valley (USA) an A.V.A. Falls within both Washington and Oregon. 400ha. Grape varieties include: Cabernet franc, Cabernet sauvignon, Merlot and Syrah. Soil: gravel, silt and clay. Climate is continental. See also Yakima Valley.

Walla Walla Vintners (USA) a winery based in Walla Walla Valley. Noted for Cabernet franc, Cabernet sauvignon and Merlot wines.

Wallburg (Ger) see Ettenheim.

Wallclife (Austr) a district in the Margaret River region of Western Australia.

Wallertheim (Ger) village (Anb): Rheinhessen. (Ber): Bingen. (Gro): Kurfürstenstück. (Vins): Heil, Vogelsang.

Wallhausen (Ger) village (Anb): Nahe. (Ber): Kreuznach. (Gro): Pfarrgarten. (Vins): Backöfchen, Felseneck, Hasensprung, Höllenpfad, Hörnchen, Johannisberg, Kirschheck, Laurentiusberg, Mühlenberg, Pastorenberg, Sonnenweg.

Wallick Cocktail (Cktl) ½ measure French vermouth, ½ measure dry gin, 4 dashes Grand Marnier. Stir over ice and strain into a cocktail glass.

Wallis Blue (Cktl) ½ measure Cointreau, ½ measure dry gin, juice of a lime. Shake over ice, strain into a sugar-rimmed (lime juice) and ice-filled old-fashioned glass.

Wallmauer (Ger) vineyard (Anb): Baden. (Ber): Badische Bergstrasse/Kraichgau. (Gro): Stiftsberg. (Vil): Neckarzimmern.

Wallop (Eng) an old slang term for beer.

Wallop (Eng) a winter ale 1056 O.G. brewed by the Bourne Valley Brewery, Andover, Hampshire.

Wallop (Eng) a 4.4% alc by vol. ale brewed by the Country Life Brewery, Devon.

Walluf (Ger) the oldest wine-producing town in Rheingau in the Steinmächer grosslagen (see Oberwalluf and Neiderwalluf).

Wallup (Eng) is a Cockney slang term for mild beer. See also Wallop.

Walnut Brown (Sp) an old Oloroso Sherry produced by Williams and Humbert.

Walnut Ridge (N.Z) a 2.5ha vineyard. (Add): 159 Regent Street, Martinborough. Grape variety: Pinot noir. 1994 was first vintage.

Walporzheim (Ger) village (Anb): Ahr. (Ber): Walporzheim/Ahrtal. (Gro): Klosterberg. (Vins): Alte Lay, Domlay, Gärkammer, Himmelchen, Krauterberg, Pfaffenberg.

Walporzheim/Ahrtal (Ger) bereich (Anb): Ahr. (Gro): Klosterberg.

Wälschriesling (Aus)(Ger) the alternative pronunciation of the Welschriesling grape. See also Grasevina, Laski Rizling, Olasz Rizling, Riesling Italico.

Walsheim (Ger) village (Anb): Pfalz. (Ber): Südliche Weinstrasse. (Gro): Bischofskreuz. (Vins): Forstweg, Silberberg.

Walsitch Wobbler (Eng) a 5.2% alc by vol. ale brewed by the Tower Brewery, Staffordshire.

Walter (Aus) a natural spring mineral water from Salzburg. Mineral contents (milligrammes per litre): Sodium 0.3mg/l, Calcium 39mg/l, Magnesium 2.9mg/l, Potassium 0.2mg/l, Bicarbonates 118mg/l, Chlorides 3.6mg/l, Sulphates 10.5mg/l, Nitrates 1.222mg/l.

Walter Brewery (USA) a brewery based in Eau Claire, Wisconsin.

Walter's Cocktail (Cktl) 25mls Scotch whisky, 15mls orange juice, 15mls lemon juice. Shake over ice and strain into a cocktail glass.

Waltershofen (Ger) village (Anb): Baden. (Ber): Kaiserstuhl-Tuniberg. (Gro): Attilafelsen. (Vin): Steinmauer.

Walterstal (Ger) vineyard (Anb): Baden. (Ber): Badische Frankenland. (Gro): Tauberklinge. (Vil): Königshofen.

Waltham Cross (Eng) an alternative name for Dattier.

Walton's Diamond (Cktl) 1 measure dry vermouth, 1 measure vodka, ⅓ measure Grand Marnier. Mix well over ice, strain 'on the rocks' in an old-fashioned glass and add a twist of orange.

Waltraud (Sp) a medium white wine made from the Riesling grape by Miguel Torres in Vilafranca del Penedés.

Walzbachtal [ortsteil Jöhlingen] (Ger) village (Anb): Baden. (Ber): Badische Bergstrasse/ Kraichgau. (Gro): Hohenberg. (Vin): Hasensprung.

Walzer [Ewald] (Aus) a winery based in the Kremstal region. (Add): Gneixendorfer Hauptstrasse 16, 3500 Krems. Grape varieties: Grüner veltliner, Müller-Thurgau, Pinot blanc, Riesling, Neuberger. Produces a range of dry and sweet (botrytised) wines.

Wamakersvallei Co-operative (S.Afr) a co-operative winery (1941) based at Wellington, Western Cape. 1400ha. (Add): Box 509, Wellington 7657. Grape varieties: Cabernet sauvignon, Chardonnay, Chenin blanc, Cinsaut, Hanepoot, Merlot, Pinotage, Sauvignon blanc, Shiraz. Labels: Bain's Way, Fisherman's, Jagters Port, La Cave, 33 Degrees South. Website: http://www.wamakersvallei.co.za

Wana Tallinn (Rus) a dark orange-brown, vanilla and cinnamon-flavoured spirit with a rum-like taste.

Wandalusia (Sp) the name given to the Sherry region in the eighth century A.D. by the Goths, from which the present day name Andalusia derived.

Wanderhaufen (Ger) an automatic malting process known as the 'moving couch'. The barley is turned automatically during germination and drying. Similar to the Saladin Box system.

Wanderhausen (Ger) an alternative spelling of Wanderhaufen.

W

Wandsbeck Wines (S.Afr) a co-operative winery (established 1965) based in Robertson, Western Cape. 448ha. Has 22 members. Grape varieties: Cabernet sauvignon, Chenin blanc, Cinsaut, Merlot, Muskadel, Pinotage, Ruby cabernet, Sémillon, Shiraz. Produces varietal wines.

Wangaratta (Austr) a wine-producing area in north-eastern Victoria.

Wangen (Ger) village (Anb): Württemberg. (Ber): Remstal-Stuttgart. (Gro): Weinsteige. *see* Stuttgart.

Wangford Arms (Eng) a home-brew public house (established 1985) based in Wangford, Suffolk. Noted for cask-conditioned Wangle 1040 O.G.

Wangle (Eng) *see* Wangford Arms.

Wanne (Ger) vineyard (Anb): Württemberg. (Ber): Remstal-Stuttgart. (Gro): Kopf. (Vil): Grossheppach.

Wan Quan Shen Shui (Chi) a natural spring mineral water brand. Mineral contents (milligrammes per litre): Sodium 25mg/l, Calcium 59.6mg/l, Magnesium 16.61mg/l, Potassium 1.1mg/l, Bicarbonates 261.2mg/l, Chlorides 15.91mg/l, Sulphates 22.67mg/l. pH 7.3

Wantirna Winery (Austr) a winery. (Add): Bushy Park Lane, Wantirna, South Victoria 3152. 4ha. Grape varieties: Cabernet sauvignon, Chardonnay, Merlot, Pinot noir.

Wappen (Ger) lit: 'coat of arms', found on a wine label.

Waratam Cocktail (Cktl) 1½ measures white rum, ¼ measure dry vermouth, ¼ measure grenadine. Stir over ice, strain into a tulip glass and dress with a slice of lemon.

Warburger Waldquell (Ger) a natural spring mineral water. Mineral contents (milligrammes per litre): Sodium 26mg/l, Calcium 240mg/l, Magnesium 49mg/l, Bicarbonates 366mg/l, Chlorides 9mg/l, Sulphates 555mg/l, Fluorides 1.04mg/l.

Warburn Estate (Austr) a winery based in New South Wales. Grape varieties: Cabernet sauvignon, Chardonnay, Merlot, Sirah.

Ward Best Bitter (Eng) the new name for Sheffield Best Bitter from the Vaux group.

Ward Brewery (Eng) a brewery based in Sheffield, Yorkshire, part of the Vaux Group, best noted for Sheffield Best Bitter 1038 O.G. *see* Ward Best Bitter.

Ward Eight (Cktl) 25mls whiskey, 25mls lemon juice, 1 teaspoon grenadine, shake over ice, strain into an ice-filled highball glass and top with soda.

Ward Eight Cocktail (Cktl) 25mls (1fl.oz) rye whiskey, 10mls (½ fl.oz) orange juice, 10mls (½ fl.oz) lemon juice, 4 dashes grenadine. Shake over ice and strain into a cocktail glass.

Ward's Frappé (Cktl) ½ measure brandy, ½ measure green Chartreuse, rind of lemon in a large cocktail glass, pour the brandy in last over crushed ice. Do not mix.

Waretaler (Ger) a natural spring mineral water. Mineral contents (milligrammes per litre): Sodium 25mg/l, Calcium 323mg/l, Magnesium 85mg/l, Chlorides 45mg/l.

Warhorse (Eng) a 4.8% alc by vol. ale brewed by the Broadstone Brewing C°. Ltd., Nottinghamshire.

Waris–Hubert (Fr) a Champagne producer. (Add): 227, Rue du Moutier, 51530 Cramant. Récoltant-Manipulant. Produces non-vintage wines. De Luxe label: Cuvée Equinoxe. 'E'mail: olivier.waris@wanadoo.fr

Waris–Larmandier (Fr) a Champagne producer. (Add): 608, Rempart du Nord, 51190 Avize. Produces vintage and non-vintage wines. Website: http://www.champagne-waris-larmandier.com 'E'mail: earlwarislarmandier@terre-net.fr

Warming Wintertime Ale (Eng) a 4.9% alc by vol. ale brewed by the Wye Valley Brewery, Herefordshire.

Warm Lake Estate (Can) a winery based on the Niagara Escarpment that produces a variety of wines. Label: Glacé Noir. Website: http://www.warmlakeestate.com 'E'mail: info@warmlakeestate.com

Warmth (Eng) a term used to describe southern-styled French wines. i.e. the Côtes du Rhône. These wines are high in alcohol and have a good full flavour.

Warner Vineyards (USA) a winery based in Michigan (formerly known as the Michigan Winery). Produces hybrid and sparkling wines.

Warneton Brasserie (Bel) an abbaye brewery based in West Flanders.

Warninks (Hol) a noted advocaat-producing company owned by Allied Breweries. Also peach, caramel and amaretto flavoured advocaats 17.2% alc by vol.

Warp (Aus) a non-alcoholic energy drink made from a blend of grapefruit and lemon. Contains the Vitamins B₂, B₆, B₁₂ and Niacin, plus Ca-Pantotheanate, Caffeine and Taurine.

Warramate Winery (Austr) a winery. (Add): Lot 4, Macklen's Lane, Gruyere, Victoria 3770. 2ha. Grape varieties: Cabernet sauvignon, Rhine riesling and Shiraz.

Warre (Port) vintage Port shippers. Vintages: 1870, 1872, 1875, 1878, 1881, 1884, 1887, 1890, 1894, 1896, 1899, 1900, 1904, 1908, 1912, 1917, 1920, 1922, 1924, 1927, 1931, 1934, 1945, 1947, 1950, 1955, 1958, 1960, 1963, 1966, 1970, 1975, 1977, 1980, 1982, 1983, 1991, 1994, 1995,1997, 1998, 2000, 2003. The oldest English Port Lodge (circa 1670) owned by Symingtons Family Estates.

Warre Cavadinha (Port) the top single quinta Port of Warre. Full name is Quinta de Cavadinha.

Warrenmang Vineyard (Austr) a winery. (Add): Mountain Creek Road, Moonambel, via Avoca, Victoria. 11ha. Grape varieties: Cabernet sauvignon, Chardonnay, Merlot, Shiraz.

Warren Sublette Winery (USA) a winery based in Cincinnati, Ohio. Produces French hybrid wines.

Warrington Brown (Eng) the export name for Old Chester 1067 O.G. A strong dark ale brewed by the Greenall Whitley Brewery in Warrington, Cheshire.

Warrior (Eng) a home-brew public house in Brixton, London. Noted for cask-conditioned Brixton Bitter 1036 O.G. and Warrior 1050 O.G.

W

Warrior Port (Port) the brand-name for a vintage character Port from the Port shippers Warre.

Warsaw Cocktail (Cktl) ⅓ measure vodka, ⅓ measure French vermouth, ⅓ measure blackberry brandy, 2 dashes lemon juice. Shake over ice and strain into a cocktail glass.

Warsteiner Brauerei (Ger) a brewery based in Warstein. Brews: Premium Verum 4.8% alc by vol. (contains no additives), Premium Light 2.4% alc by vol.

Warsteiner Fresh (Ger) a 0.5% alc by vol. low alcohol lager brewed by Warsteiner Brauerei, Warstein.

Warsteiner Premium Light (Ger) a 2.4% alc by vol. bottled light pilsner brewed by Warsteiner Brauerei, Warstein.

Warsteiiner Premium Verum (Ger) a 4.8% alc by vol. bottled pilsner brewed by Warsteiner Brauerei, Warstein.

Wartberg (Ger) vineyard (Anb): Rheinhessen. (Ber): Wonnegau. (Gro): Sybillenstein. (Vil): Alzey.

Wartberg (Ger) vineyard (Anb): Württemberg. (Ber): Württembergisch Unterland. (Gro): Staufenberg. (Vil): Heilbronn.

Wartberg (Ger) vineyard (Anb): Württemberg. (Ber): Württembergisch Unterland. (Gro): Wunnenstein. (Vil): Beilstein.

Wartbühl (Ger) grosslage (Anb): Württemberg. (Ber): Remstal-Stuttgart. (Vils): Aichelberg, Baach, Beutelsbach, Breuningsweiler, Endersbach, Geradstetten, Grossheppach, Grunbach, Hanweiler, Hebsack, Hertmannsweiler, Kleinheppach, Korb, Rommelshausen, Schnait i. R., Stetten i. R., Strümpfelbach, Waiblingen, Winnenden.

Warteck Brauerei (Switz) an independent brewery based in Basle.

Warteck Lager (Switz) a low-alcohol lager brewed by the Warteck Brauerei in Basle 0.5% alc by vol.

Warwick Estate (S.Afr) a winery (established 1964) based in Elsenburg, Stellenbosch, Western Cape. 65ha. (Add): P.O. Box 2, Muldersvlei 7606. Grape varieties: Cabernet franc, Cabernet sauvignon, Chardonnay, Merlot, Pinotage, Sauvignon blanc. Labels: Old Bush Vines, Professor Black, Stansfield, Three Cape Ladies, Trilogy Estate Reserve. Website: http://www.warwickwine.co.za

Wasenweiler (Ger) village (Anb): Baden. (Ber): Kaiserstuhl-Tuniberg. (Gro): Vulkanfelsen. (Vins): Kreuzhalde, Lotberg.

Wash (Scot) the name for the fermented liquor (between 4%–8% alc by vol) before it goes for distillation into whisky.

Wash (W.Ind) a mixture of molasses, water and fermenting agents ready for fermentation in rum production.

Wash Back (Scot) the fermenting vessel in the production of malt Scotch whisky.

Wash Down (Eng) a slang term for to take a drink after eating to help swallow the food.

Washed Coffee (Eng) another name for the coffee beans prepared by the wet method.

Washington (Cktl) ⅔ measure French vermouth, ⅓ measure brandy, 2 dashes Angostura, 2 dashes gomme syrup. Stir over ice and strain into a cocktail glass.

Washington (USA) a 10121ha. wine region in the Yakima Valley area around Puget Sound. Produces Labrusca, vinifera and hybrid wines. Noted for Merlot, Cabernet sauvignon, Pinot noir, Riesling and Syrah wines. Home to the A.V.A.'s of Columbia Valley, Red Mountain and Walla Walla. Wineries include Château Ste. Michelle, Hogue Cellars.

Washington [G.] (Eng) an Englishman who lived in Guatemala and invented instant coffee.

Washington Wine Quality Alliance (USA) *abbr*: W.W.Q.A. Endorses wineries within the region. Ensures that the wines are produced from state-approved appellations. The word '*reserve*' must only be used for small lot, limited release wines.

Wash Still (Scot) in malt whisky production the first copper still which distills the '*wash*' into low wines.

Waspsting (Eng) a mixture of equal quantities of Guinness and orange juice.

Wassail (Eng) derives from the Anglo-Saxon (wes hal = 'be of good health'), an old English seventeenth century drink of spiced beer.

Wassail (Eng) a seventeenth century festivity (party) where heavy drinking took place.

Wassail (Eng) a strong ale 1060 O.G. brewed by the Ballards Brewery in Sussex.

Wass Ale (Eng) a 4.5% alc by vol. ale brewed by the Bazens Brewery, Greater Manchester.

Wassail Bowl (Cktl) a hot punch containing many spices, eggs, Sherry or Madeira, garnished with whole cored and roasted apples. Is slightly frothy due to the beaten eggs.

Wasser (Aus) (Ger) water.

Wasser (Ger) a term which may be added to certain types of liqueurs made from fully-fermented fruits or berries (e.g. kirsch). Also known as geist if the relevant fruit is macerated in the pure distilled spirit.

Wasserbillig (Lux) a wine village on the river Moselle. Vineyard site is Bocksberg.

Wasserglas (Aus) (Ger) water glass.

Wasserliesch (Ger) village (Anb): Mosel-Saar-Ruwer. (Ber): Obermosel. (Gro): Gipfel. (Vins): Albachtaler, Reinig auf der Burg.

Wasserlos (Ger) village (Anb): Franken. (Ber): Maindreieck. (Gro): Not yet assigned. (Vin): Schlossberg.

Wasseros (Ger) vineyard (Anb): Rheingau. (Ber): Johannisberg. (Gro): Heiligenstock. (Vil): Kiedrich.

Wasseros (Ger) a vineyard within village of Kiedrich. 32.6ha. (12.3%) is proposed to be classified as Erstes Gewächs.

Wasson Brothers Winery (USA) a winery based in Sandy, Oregon. Produces still, sparkling and fruit wines. Grape varieties: Chardonnay, Gewürztraminer, Muscat, Pinot noir, White riesling.

W

Wasted (Eng) a slang term for getting very intoxicated and lose one's memory!

Water [H₂O] (Eng) the substance contained in *all* beverages. *See also* Distilled Water, Mineral Water, Natural Spring Water and Water Glass. (Arab) = ma'a, (Aus) = wasser, (Chi) = shui, (Cro) = voda, (Den) = vand, (Fr) = eau, (Ger) = wasser, (Gre) = nero, (Hol) = water, (Indo) = air, (Isr) = ma-eem, (It) = acqua, (Jap) = mizu, (Kor) = mool, (Lat) = acqua, (Pol) = woda, (Port) = água, (Rus) vada, (Sp) = agua, (Thai) = nam, (Tur) = sulamak, (Wal) = dwfr/dwr.

Water (Eng) an illegal additive to wine used to increase the volume (stretch) of the wine. Is also used to lower the alcoholic strength.

Waterberg Mineral water (S.Afr) a natural spring mineral water (established 1995) from Polokwane. Mineral contents (milligrammes per litre): Sodium 3mg/l, Calcium 1mg/l, Magnesium 1mg/l, Chlorides <5mg/l, Sulphates 5mg/l, Fluorides <0.2mg/l, Nitrates 1.3mg/l. pH 6.7

Water Boy (USA) a natural spring mineral brand.

Water Boys (Eng) a 4.1% alc by vol. ale brewed by the Blencowe Brewing C°. Ltd., Rutland.

Waterbrook (USA) a winery based at Walla Walla, Washington. Main grape variety is Cabernet.

Waterbury Cocktail (Cktl) 25mls (⅙ gill) brandy, juice ¼ lemon, ½ teaspoon sugar, 2 dashes grenadine, 1 egg white. Shake over ice and strain into a cocktail glass.

Water Cooler (USA) a unit which cools and dispenses drinking water, usually made of glass.

Water Engine (U.K.) an old method of dispensing beer using water pressure which is converted into air pressure. Now little used except in parts of Scotland.

Waterfill Frazier (USA) a Bourbon whiskey distillery based in south-western Frankfurt, Kentucky.

Waterford (Ire) an Irish whiskey and cream liqueur 17% alc by vol.

Waterford (Ire) the Irish glass-making centre. Famous for cut crystal glass especially for drinking glasses and decanters.

Waterford Estate (S.Afr) a winery (established 1998) based in Sellenbosch, Western Cape. 45ha. Grape varieties: Barbera, Cabernet sauvignon, Chardonnay, Chenin blanc, Malbec, Merlot, Mourvèdre, Muscat d'alexandrie, Petit verdot, Sauvignon blanc, Shiraz. Labels: Kevin Arnold, Heatherleigh Family Reserve, Pecan Stream. Website: http://www.warwickwine.co.za

Water Fountain (Fr) a nineteenth century glass bowl which is on a stand and has four taps from which can be drawn iced water. Was used for watering absinthe. Invented by Pernod.

Water Glass (Eng) a straight-sided glass of 250mls–300mls (½ pt) capacity used for serving iced water (still or carbonated). (Aus) = wasserglas, (Fr) = verre à eau, (Ger) = wasserglas, (Ire) = gloine, (Sp) = vaso de agua.

Waterhof (S.Afr) a winery (established 2003) based in Stellenbosch, Western Cape. 12ha. Grape variety: Shiraz. Website: http://www.waterhofestate.co.za

Water Hog (Eng) an ale brewed by Triple FFF Brewery, Four Marks, near Alton, Hampshire.

Watering Hole (Eng) a slang name for a public house, inn, hotel or licensed bar.

Waterkloof (S.Afr) the label for a range of wines produced by the False Bay Vineyards winery, Wellington, Western Cape.

Waterloo (Cktl) 25mls (1fl.oz) Mandarine Napoléon, 100mls (4fl.ozs) fresh orange juice. Build into an ice-filled highball glass.

Waterloo (Eng) a 4.5% alc by vol. ale brewed by the Freeminer Brewery Ltd., Gloucestershire.

Waterloo (Eng) a special cask ale 4% alc by vol. brewed by the Wentworth Brewery, South Yorkshire for the month of June 2005 to commemorate the 190th anniversary of the Battle of Waterloo.

Waterloo Cocktail (Cktl) 25mls (1fl.oz) white rum, 75mls (3fl.ozs) orange juice. Stir over ice in a highball glass and float 10mls (½ fl.oz) of Mandarine Napoléon on top.

Waterloo 1815 (Sp) a solera gran reserva brandy from Gil Luque.

Water of Life (Eng) the early name given to spirits. (Fr) = eau de vie, (Ire) = uisce beatha, (It) = acqua vitae, (Scot) = uisge beatha, (Wal) = dwr bywiol.

Waters and Robson (Eng) a soft drink producer from Essex who uses artesian well water. Head office is based at Sylvan Grove, London.

Waterstone (USA) a winery based in the Napa Valley, California. Grape varieties: Cabernet sauvignon.

Watervale (Austr) a wine region in the northern part of South Australia.

Watervale Shiraz-Cabernet (Austr) a red wine from Château Leonay in South Australia. Owned by Leo Buring C°.

Watervale Spätlese Rhine Riesling (Austr) a light, medium-sweet white wine from the Lindemans Winery in New South Wales.

Waterwheel Vineyards (Austr) a winery (established 1972). (Add): Bridgewater-on-Loddon, Victoria. Grape varieties: Chardonnay, Pinot noir, Riesling, Sauvignon blanc, Shiraz.

Watery (Eng) denotes a wine that lacks body/is thin.

Watkin's Whoosh (Wal) *see* Whoosh.

Watney Combe Reid (Eng) part of Grand Metropolitan, is a company that runs many public houses in the south-east of England. Owns the Stag Brewery in Mortlake. Brews many cask-conditioned, keg and bottled beers.

Watney Mann, Truman (Eng) a hotel and Leisure giant Grand Metropolitan's brewing division. Formed after 1972 when they took over Watneys. Owns 2 breweries abroad, the Maes Brasserie in Belgium and the Stern Brauerei in Germany.

WATP (USA) *abbr:* Wine And The People.

Watsons Water (Chi) a natural spring mineral water (established 1903) from Hong Kong.

Wattle Creek (USA) a winery based in the Alexander

Valley, Sonoma County, California. Grape varieties: Cabernet sauvignon.

Wattle Springs (Austr) a natural spring mineral water (established 2000) from Sutton Forest. Mineral contents (milligrammes per litre): Sodium 7mg/l, Calcium 1.2mg/l, Magnesium 1.1mg/l, Potassium 0.2mg/l, Bicarbonates 13.4mg/l, Chlorides 11mg/l, Nitrates 9mg/l. pH 7.1

Wattwiller (Fr) a sparkling natural spring mineral water from Jouvence 68700 Wattwiller, Alsace. Mineral contents (milligrammes per litre): Sodium 3mg/l, Calcium 126mg/l, Magnesium 15.9mg/l, Bicarbonates 167mg/l, Sulphates 223mg/l, Fluorides 1.97mg/l.

Wattwiller (Fr) a still natural spring mineral water from Lithinée Vosges. Mineral contents (milligrammes per litre): Sodium 300mg/l, Calcium 288mg/l, Magnesium 20.1mg/l, Potassium 1.4mg/l, Bicarbonates 142mg/l, Chlorides 3.9mg/l, Sulphates 678mg/l, Fluorides 2mg/l. pH 7.5

Wat Tyler (Eng) a 5% alc by vol. ale brewed by the Itchen Valley Brewery, Hampshire.

Wat Wassail (Eng) a 6% alc by vol. ale brewed by the Terne Valley Brewery, Knightwick, Worcestershire. *See also* This, That, T'Other.

Waugh (Eng) old English term for drinking beer or wine in large amounts (draughts).

Waukon Corporation (USA) a winery based in Waukon, Iowa. Produces mainly French hybrid wines.

Wawel (Pol) a mead made from honey and pasteurised fruit juices in the Royal Castle Wawel in Cracow. Sold in squat bottles 12%–14% alc by vol.

Wawern (Ger) village (Anb): Mosel-Saar-Ruwer. (Ber): Saar-Ruwer. (Gro): Scharzberg. (Vins): Goldberg, Herrenberger, Jesuitenberg, Ritterpfad.

Wax (Eng) used for the sealing of bottles in the eighteenth and nineteenth centuries. Bottle necks were dipped in molten wax after they had been corked to prevent air contamination. Used for vintage Ports until the 1970's.

Wax Cocktail [1] (Cktl) 60mls (½ gill) Plymouth gin, 3 dashes orange bitters. Stir over ice, strain into a cocktail glass, add a cherry and a squeeze of orange peel juice.

Wax Cocktail [2] (Cktl) ½ measure pastis, ½ measure gin, 1 egg white, 3 dashes gomme syrup. Shake over ice and strain into a cocktail glass.

Wayfarer (Scot) a 4.4% alc by vol. ale brewed by the Atlas Brewery, Argyll.

Wayland Smithy (Eng) a 4.4% alc by vol. ale brewed by the White Horse Brewery C°. Ltd., Oxfordshire.

WB (Eng) a cask-conditioned bitter 1037 O.G. brewed by the Cotleigh Brewery in Somerset. Brewed mainly for the New Inn public house in Waterley Bottom, Gloucestershire.

Weak (Eng) a term used to describe a wine or beer that has little alcohol or flavour.

Weaks (Scot) the name given to the 'feints' at the Auchentoshan Distillery in Dalmuir, Glasgow. *See also* Strongs.

Wealden Bitter (Eng) a 3.7% alc by vol. bitter ale brewed by the Rother Valley Brewing C°., East Sussex.

Wealden White (Eng) a medium dry white wine produced by Headcorn Vineyards in Kent from Reichensteiner, Seyval Blanc and Müller-Thurgau grapes.

Wear Best (Eng) a 3.9% alc by vol. cask ale from Vaux, Sunderland.

Weardale Bitter (Eng) a cask-conditioned bitter 1038 O.G. brewed by the King's Arms, a home-brew public house in Bishop Auckland, County Durham.

Weathering (USA) a method used in the making of vermouths to maderise the wine by exposing the casks to the sun.

Weather Weights (Eng) small brass washers used on early hydrometers to compensate for the weather conditions. Marked cold, hot and coldish.

Weavers Bitter (Eng) a cask-conditioned bitter 1037 O.G. brewed by the Bourne Valley Brewery, Andover, Hampshire.

Weavers Delight (Eng) a 4.8% alc by vol. ale brewed by the Goldcar Brewery, West Yorkshire.

Webersburg Wines (S.Afr) a winery (established 1996) based in Somerset West, Stellenbosch, Western Cape. 20ha. Grape varieties: Cabernet sauvignon, Merlot. Website: http://www.webersburg.co.za

Webster (Cktl) ½ measure dry gin, ¼ measure French vermouth, ⅛ measure apricot brandy, ⅛ measure lemon juice. Shake well over ice and strain into a cocktail glass.

Webster Brewery (Eng) Watney's brewery in Halifax, Yorkshire. Has a lager brewing plant for Budweiser, Carlsberg and Fosters. Also brews: cask-conditioned Yorkshire Bitter 1037.5 O.G. (also a keg version 1037.5 O.G.), bottled Sam Brown 1034 O.G. Green Label 1038 O.G. Velvet Stout 1042 O.G.

Webster XL (Eng) a 1.2% alc by vol. low alcohol beer from the Webster Brewery, Yorkshire.

Wechselberg (Aus) vineyard sites (2) based on the banks of the River Kamp situated in the Kamptal region.

Wedderburn (W.Ind) the local name in Jamaica for the dark traditional rums made from cane grown south on the island, also called Plummer.

Wedderwill Country Estate (S.Afr) a winery (established 1997) based in Stellenbosch, Western Cape. 24ha. Grape varieties: Sauvignon blanc, Shiraz. Website: http://www.wedderwill.co.za

Wedding Belle (Cktl) ⅓ measure dry gin, ⅓ measure Dubonnet, ⅙ measure orange juice, ⅙ measure cherry brandy. Shake over ice and strain into a cocktail glass.

Wedding Champagne (Eng) old disparaging name for B.O.B. Champagnes.

Wedding Vineyard (USA) a red wine (Cabernet sauvignon) produced by the Fisher Estate winery, Sonoma County, California.

Wedding Winner (Cktl) ⅕ measure Cointreau, ⅕ measure syrop de fraises, ⅒ measure Cognac, dash Calvados. Stir over ice, strain into a flute glass and top with iced Champagne.

Wederom (S.Afr) a winery (established 2002) based in Robertson, Western Cape. 20ha. Grape varieties: Chenin blanc, Merlot, Shiraz. Website: http://www.wederom.co.za

Weedkiller (Eng) a bitter beer brewed by the Wiltshire Brewery Company in Tisbury, Wiltshire.

Wee Heavy (Scot) a term for nip-sized bottles of strong ale. *see* Fowler's Wee Heavy.

Weening & Barge Winery (S.Afr) a winery (established 2003) based in Somerset West, Stellenbosch, Western Cape. 31ha. Grape varieties: Cabernet franc, Chenin blanc, Pinot noir, Sauvignon blanc, Shiraz. Labels: Cuvée Lynette, Cuvée Quint, Cuvée Terry Lynn. Website: http://www.weeningbarge.com

Weepers (Eng) the name for wine bottles that show leakage through the cork, applies mostly to Champagne and other sparkling wines.

Weeping (Eng) the loss of wine seeping out through a bottle of wine which has a poor cork that does not fit the bottle properly or is too small.

Weep-No-More (Cktl) ½ measure red Dubonnet, ½ measure Cognac, 2 dashes maraschino, juice ½ lime. Shake over ice and strain into a cocktail glass.

Wee Willie Ale (Scot) a brown and pale ale 1032 O.G. brewed and bottled by the William Younger Brewery in Edinburgh. Is sold mainly in Ulster.

Wegeler Erben (Ger) a 58ha estate owned by Deinhard in the Rheingau. Vineyards are Geisenheim, Mittelheim, Oestrich, Rüdesheim, Winkel.

Wehlen (Ger) village (Anb): Mosel-Saar-Ruwer. (Ber): Bernkastel. (Gro): Münzlay. (Vins): Klosterberg, Nonnenberg, Sonnenuhr.

Wehr (Ger) village (Anb): Mosel-Saar-Ruwer. (Ber): Obermosel. (Gro): Gipfel. (Vin): Rosenberg.

Weibel Champagne Vineyards (USA) a winery based in California. Grape varieties: Cabernet sauvignon, Chardonnay, Pinot noir and Zinfandel. Produces sparkling and table wines.

Weich (Ger) denotes soft, a wine that is low in acid and alcohol.

Weidlinger Predigtstuhl (Aus) a white wine made from the Muskat ottonel grape by the Augustine monks at Klosterneuburg, Vienna.

Weight (Eng) the term used to describe body in a wine.

Weihenstephan (Ger) a brewery (established 1040) based at Freising in Bavaria. owned by the Bavarian State. Brews: Weizen beers.

Weihenstephaner Hefe Weissbier (Ger) a 5.4% alc by vol. bottled wheat beer brewed by Weihenstephaner Brauerei, Freising.

Weihrauchtraube (Ger) an alternative name for the Tamîiosa Româneasca grape.

Weikersheim (Ger) village (Anb): Württemberg. (Ber): Kocher-Jagst-Tauber. (Gro): Tauberberg. (Vins): Hardt, Karlsberg, Schmecker.

Weil am Rhein (Ger) village (Anb): Baden. (Ber): Markgräflerland. (Gro): Vogtei Rötteln. (Vins): Schlipf, Stiege.

Weilberg (Ger) vineyard (Anb): Pfalz. (Ber): Mittelhaardt-Deutsche Weinstrasse. (Gro): Honigsäckel. (Vil): Ungstein.

Weiler (Ger) *see* Sinsheim.

Weiler (Ger) village (Anb): Nahe. (Ber): Kreuznach. (Gro): Schlosskapelle. (Vins): Abtei Ruppertsberg, Klostergarten, Römerberg.

Weiler (Ger) village (Anb): Württemberg. (Ber): Württembergisch Unterland. (Gro): Salzberg. (Vins): Handsberg, Schlierbach.

Weiler bei Monzingen (Ger) village (Anb): Nahe. (Ber): Schloss. Böckelheim. (Gro): Paradiesgarten. (Vins): Heiligenberg, Herrenzehntel.

Weiler/Z (Ger) village (Anb): Württemberg. (Ber): Württembergisch Unterland. (Gro): Heuchelberg. (Vin): Hohenberg.

Weilheim (Ger) village (Anb): Württemberg. (Ber): Remstal-Stuttgart. (Gro): Hohenneuffen. (Vin): Schlossteige.

Weimersheim (Ger) village (Anb): Franken. (Ber): Steigerwald. (Gro): Schlosstück. (Vin): Roter Berg.

Wein (Aus)(Ger) wine.

Weinachts Christmas Beer (Ger) a fine beer brewed by the Riegele Brauerei in Augsburg.

Weinähr (Ger) village (Anb): Mittelrhein. (Ber): Rheinburgengau. (Gro): Lahntal. (Vin): Giebelhöll.

Weinaufsicht (Aus) wine control. Inspectors who enter cellars, vineyards, press-houses, inspect books and ledgers, also takes samples of wines. Control the making and distribution of wines and vinous beverages.

Weinbau (Ger) the cultivation of the grapes.

Weinbauer (Ger) wine-grower.

Weinbaugebiet (Aus) wine area. *see* Weinbauregion.

Weinbaugebiet (Ger) a large area of production such as the Rhein, Mosel, Main, Neckar, Oberrhein.

Weinbaukataster (Ger) land register (established 1961) to help with the control of viticulture.

Weinbauort (Ger) wine village. *See also* Gemeinde, Gemarkung.

Weinbauregion (Aus) the name given to the four main wine-producing regions of Austria. Divided into sub-regions (Weinbaugebiete) and districts (Grosslage).

Weinbauschule (Aus)(Ger) wine college/wine school.

Weinbauverein (Aus) association of vine-growers.

Weinberg (Ger) hillside vineyard.

Weinbergrecht (Aus) vineyard law (viticultural law).

Weinbergslage (Ger) vineyard site.

Weinbergsrolle (Ger) the official register of vineyards as required by the 1971 German Wine Laws.

Weinbesserungs-Gesellschaft (Ger) a society for the improvement of wine. Founded in 1823 in Württemberg.

W

Weinblütenfest (Ger) a Mittelrhein wine festival held in Bacarach in June.

Weinbrand (Ger) brandy. Also spelt Weinbrannt.

Weinbrannt (Ger) see Weinbrand.

Weinert (Arg) a winery based in Mendoza. Full name is Bodega Y Caras de Weinert, noted for Merlot varietal wines. Grape varieties include: Cabernet sauvignon, Malbec, Merlot. Labels include: Carrascal.

Weinfass (Ger) wine cask.

Weinfelden Brauerei (Switz) a small brewery based in Weinfelden.

Weinfest (Ger) wine festival.

Weinfest [1] (Ger) a Mittelrhein wine festival held at Boppard in September.

Weinfest [2] (Ger) a Rheingau wine festival held at Rüdesheim in August.

Weinfest [3] (Ger) a Rheingau wine festival held at Hattenheim in August.

Weinfest der Mittelmosel (Ger) a Mosel-Saar-Ruwer wine festival held at Bernkastel in September.

Weinfest der Südlichen Weinstrasse (Ger) a Pfalz wine festival held at Edenkoben in September.

Weingarten (Ger) village (Anb): Baden. (Ber): Badische Bergstrasse/Kraichgau. (Gro): Hohenberg. (Vins): Katzenberg, Petersberg.

Weingarten (Ger) village (Anb): Pfalz. (Ber): Südliche Weinstrasse. (Gro): Trappenberg. (Vin): Schlossberg.

Weingebirge (Aus) a vineyard site on the banks of the River Danube situated in the Wachau region, Niederösterreich.

Weingeist (Ger) wine spirit (ghost).

Weinglas (Aus)(Ger) wine glass.

Weingrube (Ger) vineyard (Anb): Mittelrhein. (Ber): Rheinburgengau. (Gro): Gedeonseck. (Vil): Boppard.

Weingut (Ger) vineyard/winery.

Weingut A. Christmann (Ger) a winery based in Königsbach, Pfalz. Vineyard: Idig. Website: http://www.weingut-christmann.de 'E'mail: info@weingut-christmann.de

Weingut Allram (Aus) a winery based in the Kampstal region. (Add): Herrengasse 3, 3491 Strass. Grape varieties: Chardonnay, Grüner veltliner, Pinot blanc, Riesling, Zweigelt.

Weingut der Stadt Krems (Aus) a 32ha hospice estate and winery (established in the fourteenth century) based in Krems in the Kremstal region. (Add): Stadtgraben 11, 3500 Krems. Grape varieties: Cabernet sauvignon, Chardonnay, Grüner veltliner, Müller-Thurgau, Riesling, Neuberger, Pinot blanc, Pinot gris, Pinot noir, Zweigelt. Produces a range of wine styles. 'E'mail: stadtweingut@krems.gv.at

Weingut Dr. Bürklin-Wolf (Ger) a winery (84ha) based in Wachenheim, Pfalz. Vineyard: Gaisböhl Ruppertsberg.

Weingut Dr. von Bassermann-Jordan Kalkofen (Ger) a winery based in the Pfalz. Vineyard: Deidesheim.

Weingütesiegal (Aus) a seal of guarantee of the Austrian Wine Board. Wines of Spätlese quality and above must have the seal to be exported.

Weingut Freiherr Heyl zu Herrnsheim (Ger) a winery in the Nierstein Pettental, Rheinhessen. Label: Baron Heyl.

Weingut Georg Mosbacher (Ger) a winery (18.5ha) based in Forst, Phalz. Vineyard: Ungeheuer. Website: http://www.georg-mosbacher.de 'E'mail: info@georg-mosbacher.de

Weingut Hochheimer Königin Victoria Berg (Ger) a unique estate based in the Rheingau that has only one parcel of land unlike most other estates. Name is guaranteed by Queen Victoria.

Weingut Müller-Catoir Haardter (Ger) a winery based in the Phalz. Vineyard: Bürgergarten.

Weingut Ökonomierat Rebholz (Ger) a winery based in Siebeldingen, Phalz. Grape varieties: Chardonnay, Gewürztraminer, Pinot blanc, Pinot gris, Riesling. Vineyard: Kastanienbusch 14ha. Label: Rotliegenden. Website: http://www.oekonomierat-rebholz.de 'E'mail: wein@oekonomierat-rebholz.de

Weingut Reichsrat von Bühl (Ger) a winery based in the Phalz. Vineyard: Pechstein.

Weingut Siegfried (N.Z) a small winery near Blenheim, Upper Mourere, Nelson. 12ha. Produces table wines.

Weingut Zum Nationalpark (Aus) a wine estate in the Neusiedlesee. (Add): Josef Gangl, Schrändlgasse 50, 7142 Illmitz. Produces mainly white sweet and botrytised wines (including eiswein).

Weinhauer (Aus) vine grower.

Weinheber (Aus) an ornate wrought iron wine dispenser with a stainless steel dispense. Has a stand and cluster of grapes. Some have a candle and an ice-tube for cooling white wines.

Weinhecke (Ger) vineyard (Anb): Baden. (Ber): Badische Bergstrasse/Kraichgau. (Gro): Mannaberg. (Vil): Bruchsal (stadtteil Untergrombach).

Weinhecke (Ger) vineyard (Anb): Baden. (Ber): Badische Bergstrasse/Kraichgau. (Gro): Mannaberg. (Vil): Ubstadt-Weiher (ortsteil Ubstadt).

Weinheim (Ger) village (Anb): Baden. (Ber): Badische Bergstrasse/Kraichgau. (Gro): Rittersberg. (Vins): Hubberg, Wüstberg.

Weinheim (Ger) village (Anb): Rheinhessen. (Ber): Wonnegau. (Gro): Sybillenstein. (Vins): Heiliger Blutberg, Hölle, Kapellenberg, Kirchenstück, Mandelberg.

Weinhex (Ger) grosslage (Anb): Mosel-Saar-Ruwer. (Ber): Zell/Mosel. (Vils): Alken, Burgen, Dieblich, Güls, Hatzenport, Kattenes, Kobern-Gondorf, Koblenz (ortsteil Lay), Koblenz (ortsteil Moselweiss), Lehmen, Löf, Moselsürsch, Niederfell, Oberfell, Winningen.

Weinig (Ger) denotes high in alcohol.

Weiningenieur (Ger) lit: 'wine genius', the highest qualification for viticulture in Germany.

Weininstitut (Ger) oenological college.

Weinkammer (Ger) vineyard (Anb): Mosel-Saar-

Ruwer. (Ber): Bernkastel. (Gro): Schwarzlay. (Vil): Enkirch.

Weinkarte (Ger) wine list.

Weinkeller (Ger) vineyard (Anb): Rheinhessen. (Ber): Nierstein. (Gro): Sankt Alban. (Vil): Mainz.

Weinkellerei (Ger) wine cellars.

Weinkelter (Ger) the vintage.

Weinkühler (Ger) wine cooler.

Weinland Österreich (Aus) new wine region category comprising of the Lower Austria and Burgenland (but excluding Vienna).

Weinlaubenhof (Aus) a winery (7.5ha) based in the Neusiedlersee (Add): Alois Kracher, Apetloner Strasse 27, 7142 Illmitz. Grape varieties: Blaufränkisch, Bouvier, Chardonnay, Muskateller, Scherebe, Traminer, Welschriesling, Zweigelt. Produces white, sweet white and red wines.

Weinlehrpfad (Ger) a nature trail or wine education walk that usually ends at a wine cellar for tastings.

Weinlesefest (Ger) a Mittelrhein wine festival held at Bacharach in September.

Weinolsheim (Ger) village (Anb): Rheinhessen. (Ber): Nierstein. (Gro): Gutes Domtal. (Vins): Hohberg, Kehr.

Weinpfalz (Ger) a nickname for the Pfalz (Rheinpfalz).

Weinprobe (Ger) wine tasting.

Weinrebe (Ger) grape vine.

Weinrieder (Aus) a winery based in Birthal in the Weinviertel. (Add): 2170 Kleinhadersdorf 44. Grape varieties: Grüner veltliner, Riesling. Noted for its eiswein.

Weinsack (Ger) vineyard (Anb): Nahe. (Ber): Schloss Böckelheim. (Gro): Paradiesgarten. (Vil): Odernheim.

Weinsberg (Ger) village (Anb): Württemberg. (Ber): Württembergisch Unterland. (Gro): Salzberg. (Vins): Altenberg, Ranzenberg, Schemelsberg.

Weinsheim (Ger) village (Anb): Nahe. (Ber): Schloss Böckelheim. (Gro): Rosengarten. (Vins): Katergrube, Kellerberg, Steinkaut.

Weinstadt [ortsteil Beutelsbach] (Ger) village (Anb): Württemberg. (Ber): Remstal-Stuttgart. (Gro): Sonnenbühl. (Vin): Burghalde.

Weinstadt [ortsteil Endersbach] (Ger) village (Anb): Württemberg. (Ber): Remstal-Stuttgart. (Gro): Sonnenbühl. (Vin): Hintere Klinge.

Weinstadt [ortsteil Rommelshausen] (Ger) village (Anb): Württemberg. (Ber): Remstal-Stuttgart. (Gro): Sonnenbühl. (Vins): Mönchhalde, Mönchberg.

Weinstadt [ortsteil Schnait i. R] (Ger) village (Anb): Württemberg. (Ber): Remstal-Stuttgart. (Gro): Sonnenbühl. (Vin): Burghalde.

Weinstadt [ortsteil Strümpfelbach] (Ger) village (Anb): Württemberg. (Ber): Remstal-Stuttgart. (Gro): Sonnenbühl. (Vin): Altenberg.

Weinsteig (Ger) vineyard (Anb): Franken. (Ber): Maindreieck. (Gro): Ravensburg. (Vil): Erlabrunn.

Weinsteige (Ger) grosslage (Anb): Württemberg. (Ber): Remstal-Stuttgart. (Vils): Esslingen, Fellbach, Gerlingen, Stuttgart (ortsteil Gaisburg),

Stuttgart (ortsteil Untertürkheim), Stuttgart (ortsteil Uhlbach), Stuttgart (ortsteil Obertürkheim), Stuttgart (ortsteil Bad Cannstatt, Feuerbach, Münster, Wangen, Zuffenhausen), Stuttgart (ortsteil Bad Cannstatt), Stuttgart (ortsteil Bad Cannstatt, Untertürkheim), Stuttgart (ortsteil Obertürkheim), Stuttgart (ortsteil Hedelfingen, Rohracker), Stuttgart (ortsteil Bad Cannstatt, Untertürkheim), Stuttgart (ortsteil Degerloch), Stuttgart (ortsteil Rotenberg, Uhlbach, Untertürkheim), Stuttgart (ortsteil Uhlbach)', Stuttgart (ortsteil Bad Cannstatt, Mühlhausen, Münster), Stuttgart (ortsteil Untertürkheim), Stuttgart (ortsteil Bad Cannstatt, Hofen, Mühlhausen, Münster).

Weinstein (Ger) tartrate deposits.

Weinstrassen (Ger) wine roads for the touring motorist to follow.

Weinstübe (Ger) a wine bar in the Württemberg Anbaugebiet.

Weinstüble (Ger) see Weinstübe.

Weinträgerin (Aus) a vineyard site based on the banks of the River Kamp situated in the Kamptal region.

Weinverordung (Aus) wine decree, used to renew and enlarge on part of the Austrian wine law.

Weinviertel (Aus) one of the largest (18000ha) of the five wine-producing regions based in Niederösterreich on the Slovakia border. Divided into Falkenstein, Matzen and Retz. Soil: black earth, loam, loess, primary rock and sand. Main grape varieties: white 85% (Frühroter veltliner, Grüner veltliner, Muller-Thurgau, Neuburger, Pinot blanc, Roter veltliner, Ruländer, Welschriesling) red 15% (Blauer portugieser, Zweigelt). See also Donauland-Carnuntum, Kamptal-Donauland, Thermenregion, Wachau. See also Districtus Austriae Controllatus.

Weinvirtschaftsfond (Aus) wine industry institute.

Weinwirtschaftsgesetz (Ger) see Gesetz über Massnahmen auf dem Gebiete der Weinwirtschaft.

Weinwoche (Ger) a Mittelrhein wine festival held at St. Goarshausen in September.

Weinzierlberg (Aus) a vineyard site on the banks of the River Danube in the Kremstal region.

Weir House (Eng) a natural mineral water brand.

Weisbaden (Ger) a town on the north bank of the Rhine in the area of the Rheingau. Noted for such wines as Schloss Vollrads.

Weiss Buoy (Eng) a 4.5% alc by vol. beer brewed by Willy's Brewery, South Humberside.

Weischler GmbH (Aus) a noted producer of brandies and fruit spirits (part of Seagram).

Weisenbach (Ger) village (Anb): Baden. (Ber): Ortenau. (Gro): Schloss Rodeck. (Vin): Kestelberg.

Weisenheim am Berg (Ger) village (Anb): Pfalz. (Ber): Mittelhaardt-Deutsche Weinstrasse. (Gro): Feuerberg. (Vin): Vogelsang.

Weisenheim am Berg (Ger) village (Anb): Pfalz. (Ber): Mittelhaardt-Deutsche Weinstrasse. (Gro): Kobnert. (Vins): Mandelgarten, Sonnenberg.

Weisenheim/Sand (Ger) village (Anb): Pfalz. (Ber): Mittelhaardt-Deutsche Weinstrasse. (Gro): Rosenbühl. (Vins): Altenberg, Burgweg, Goldberg, Hahnen, Halde, Hasenzeile.

Weisinger's of Ashland (USA) a winery based in Ashland, Oregon. Grape varieties include Cabernet sauvignon, Chardonnay, Gewürztraminer.

Weiss (Bel) lit: 'white beer', a beer brewed from malted wheat 5% alc by vol. with a crisp, lemon-fruit flavour and being unfiltered has a cloudy appearance. Also known as Weizenbier and Witbier.

Weissarbstwein (Ger) the nineteenth century name for a rosé wine made mainly from the Spätburgunder grape. Is now known as Weissherbst.

Weissbach (Ger) village (Anb): Württemberg. (Ber): Kocher-Jagst-Tauber. (Gro): Kocherberg. (Vins): Altenberg, Engweg.

Weissbier (Ger) white beer, a weak, frothy beer served in Munich usually with a slice of lemon. A version of weizenbier.

Weissburgunder (Aus)(Ger) a white grape variety known as (Aus) = Weisser burgunder/Klevner, (Fr) = Pinot blanc/Clevner, (It) = Pinot bianco. Produces light neutral wines. Also known as the Muscadet in western France.

Weiss-Clevner (Ger) a local name for the Weissburgunder (Pinot blanc).

Weisse (Ger) a shortened term for Weissbier, refers mainly to the top-fermented pale brews of Berlin. *see* Berliner Weisse.

Weisse (Ger) filtered wheat beer 5.1% alc by vol. from Schöfferhofer Brauerei. *see* Hefeweizen.

Weisse Bier (Ger) *see* Weissbier.

Weisse Dunkel (Ger) a dark wheat beer 4.9% alc by vol. from Scherdel Brauerei. *See also* Doppelbock, Weisse Hell, Weizen.

Weisse Hell (Ger) a pale wheat beer 4.9% alc by vol. from the Scherdel Brauerei. *See also* Doppelbock, Weisse Dunkel, Weizen.

Weisse Muskateller (Ger) an alternative name for the Muscat blanc à petits grains.

Weissenberg (Ger) vineyard (Anb): Mosel-Saar-Ruwer. (Ber): Zell/Mosel. (Gro): Weinhex. (Vil): Kobern-Gondorf.

Weissenberger Quelle (Ger) a natural spring mineral water. Mineral contents (milligrammes per litre): Sodium 5mg/l, Calcium 151mg/l, Magnesium 41mg/l, Bicarbonates 371mg/l, Sulphates 229mg/l.

Weissenkirchen (Aus) a wine-producing area based in western Austria.

Weissenstein (Ger) vineyard (Anb): Mosel-Saar-Ruwer. (Ber): Bernkastel. (Gro): Kurfürstlay. (Vil): Bernkastel-Kues.

Weissenstein (Ger) vineyard (Anb): Nahe. (Ber): Schloss Böckelheim. (Gro): Paradiesgarten. (Vil): Mannweiler-Coelln.

Weissenstein (Ger) vineyard (Anb): Nahe. (Ber): Schloss Böckelheim. (Gro): Paradiesgarten. (Vil): Oberndorf.

Weisserberg (Ger) vineyard (Anb): Mosel-Saar-Ruwer. (Ber): Bernkastel. (Gro): Vom Heissen Stein. (Vil): Briedel.

Weisser Bruch (Ger) lit: 'white turbidity', describes wines with a cloudy, bluish-white appearance.

Weisser Burgunder (Aus) *see* Weissburgunder.

Weiss Erd (Ger) vineyard (Anb): Rheingau. (Ber): Johannisberg. (Gro): Daubhaus. (Vil): Kostheim.

Weisser Gutedel (Ger) a white grape variety grown mainly in the Baden region. Has high sugar and gives light, pleasant wines.

Weisser Hase (Ger) lit.: 'white hare' a 5.2% alc by vol. bottle-conditioned wheat beer brewed by Hasenbräu Brauerei, Augsburg.

Weisser Husa (Aus) a white wine produced from the Muscat grape by Sepp Höld in St. Georgen.

Weisser Klevner (Ger) a white grape variety, known as Pinot chardonnay in France.

Weisser Kreuz (Ger) vineyard (Anb): Mittelrhein. (Ber): Rheinburgengau. (Gro): Burg Hammerstein. (Vil): Leubsdorf.

Weisser Pressburger (Ger) a white grape variety.

Weisser Riesling (S.Afr) a white grape variety, known as Riesling in Germany.

Weisser Traminer (Aus) an alternative name for the rosé-coloured Traminer grape (known as the Savagnin in France).

Weisse Wein (Ger) white wine. Also Weisswein.

Weissherbst (Ger) a local rosé wine of Kaiserstuhl in Baden. Made from Blauer spätburgunder, Portugieser and Trollinger grapes. Grapes are pressed as for white wine. Name of the grape on the label must be the same size as Weissherbst. *See also* Weissarbstwein.

Weisslack (Ger) a QbA. wine from the Herrgottströpfchen range of wines from Jakob Gerhardt.

Weis Squad (Scot) a 4.5% alc by vol. brewed by the Fyfe Brewing C°., Fife.

Weiss Rössl Bräu (Ger) a brewery based in Eltmann. Brews: Weiss Rössl Leonhardi Bock.

Weiss Rössl Leonhardi Bock (Ger) a 6.6% alc by vol. dark. bottled wheat beer brewed by Weiss Rössl Bräu, Eltmann.

Weisswein (Ger) white wine. Also written Weisse Wein.

Weitgasse (Aus) a vineyard site on the banks of the River Danube in the Kremstal region.

Weitheimer (S.Afr) a label used by the Weltevrede Estate in Robertson for a range of their wines.

Weitraumkulturen (Aus) a term used to describe the wide-spaced training used in vine growing.

Weixelbaum (Aus) a winery based in the Kampstal region. (Add): Weinbergweg 196, 3491 Strass im Strassertal. Grape varieties: Grüner veltliner, Malvasia, Pinot blanc, Riesling, Roter veltliner, Zweigelt.

Weizen (Ger) a filtered wheat beer 4.9% alc by vol. from the Scherdel Brauerei. *see* Doppelbock, Weisse Dunkel, Weisse Hell.

Weizenbier (Bel) *see* Weiss.

Weizenbier (Ger) lit: 'wheat beer', made with a high

proportion of wheat, low in alcohol, light in colour and with a strong flavour. Served in tall narrow glasses.

Weizenbock (Ger) a strong version of weizenbier 6.25% alc by vol.

Weizenkorn (Ger) a whiskey made from a wheat base.

Weizenthaler (Ger) a low alcohol lager beer brewed in western Germany that is not allowed to ferment.

Welbedacht Wines (S.Afr) a winery (established 2003) based in Wellington, Western Cape. 130ha. Grape varieties: Cabernet sauvignon, Chardonnay, Chenin blanc, Merlot. Label: Cricket Pitch. Website: http://www.welbedacht.co.za

Weldra (S.Afr) a white grape variety, a cross of Chenin blanc x Trebbiano. Gives good acidity and bouquet.

Welgegund Farm (S.Afr) a winery (established circa 1800) based in Wellington, Western Cape. 30ha. Grape varieties: Cabernet sauvignon, Carignan, Merlot. Website: http://www.welgegund.co.za

Welgeleë Vineyards (S.Afr) a winery (established 1999) based in Klapmuts, Paarl, Western Cape. 3ha. Grape varieties: Cabernet sauvignon, Chardonnay, Shiraz.

Welgemeend Estate (S.Afr) a winery (established 1979) based in Suider-Paarl, Western Cape. (Add): P.O.Box 69, Klapmuts 7625. Grape varieties: Cabernet franc, Cabernet sauvignon, Grenache, Malbec, Merlot, Pinotage, Shiraz. Labels: Amadé, Douelle, Estate Reserve, Soopjeshoogte, Upelation (no longer produced). Website: http://www.welgemeend.co.za

Welgesheim (Ger) village (Anb): Rheinhessen. (Ber): Bingen. (Gro): Sankt Rochuskapelle. (Vin): Kirchgärtchen.

Well (Eng) a hole sunk into the ground so that water can be drawn from natural reservoirs under the surface.

Welland (Can) a wine region between Niagara and Crystal Beach.

Wellanschitz [Stefan] (Aus) a winery based in Neckenmarkt, Mittel-Burgenland. (Add): Lange Zeile 28, 7311 Neckenmarkt Grape varieties: Blaufränkisch, Cabernet sauvignon, Pinot noir, Zweigelt.

Well-Balanced (Eng) a term used to describe a harmonious wine.

Well Blathered (Eng) a 5% alc by vol. ale brewed by the Rudgate Brewery Ltd., North Yorkshire.

Wellen (Ger) village (Anb): Mosel-Saar-Ruwer. (Ber): Obermosel. (Gro): Gipfel. (Vin): Altenberg.

Wellenstein (Lux) a wine village on the river Moselle. Vineyard sites are Fulschette and Kourschels. Also the name of a co-operative that is part of Vinsmoselle.

Well Hung (Eng) a dark ale 4.4% alc by vol. brewed by the Wood Brewery, Winstanstow, Shropshire to honour Judge Jeffreys (Baron Jeffreys of Wem – the Hanging Judge).

Welling's Bitters (Hol) aromatic bitters.

Wellington (Austr) a winery based in Tasmania.

Grape varieties include: Riesling, Sauvignon blanc. Label: FGR.

Wellington (S.Afr) a wine-producing region based south of Tulbagh in Paarl. Produces table wines.

Wellington (N.Z) a small wine-producing area on the southern tip of the North Island.

Wellington Distilleries Ltd. (Afr) a noted distillery based in Sierra Leone, western Africa. Produces a range a spirits.

Wellington Glass (Eng) a beer glass of 300mls (12fl.oz) capacity, specially made for bottled top-fermented beers. Has a wide base, short stem and a bell-shaped bowl.

Wellington Wynboere Co-operative (S.Afr) a co-operative winery (established 1934) based in Wellington, Western Cape.1600ha. (Add): Die Wellington Wynboere Co-operative, P.O. Box 520, Wellington 7655. Grape varieties: Cabernet sauvignon, Chenin blanc, Cinsaut, Hanepoot jerepiko, Merlot, Pinotage, Ruby cabernet, Sauvignon blanc, Shiraz, Tinta. Produces varietal wines. Website: http://www.wellingtoncellar.co.za

Well-Knit (Eng) a wine term used to describe a strong, sturdy, firm wine (in body).

Well-Oiled (Eng) a slang term for intoxicated, usually applied to a person who talks a lot (with slurred speech) and is not fully comprehensible.

Wellow Vineyard (Eng) a 0.4ha vineyard (established 1989) based at Salisbury Road, West Wellow, Hampshire. Grape varieties include Bacchus and Reichensteiner. Also has a 0.4ha vineyard at Romsey, East Wellow, Hampshire. Grape varieties: Bacchus, Kerner, Müller-thurgau and Reichensteiner.

Wells [Charles] Brewery (Eng) a brewery. (Add): The Eagle Brewery, Havelock Street, Bedford, Bedfordshire MK40 4LU. Produces cask-conditioned Eagle Bitter 1035 O.G. Bombadier 1042 O.G. keg Silver Special 1030 O.G. Gold Eagle 1034 O.G. Noggin 1039 O.G. Red Stripe 1044 O.G. Red Stripe Jamaican Lager 4.7% alc by vol. Heart Breaker 4.1% alc by vol. Lock, Stock & Barrel, Josephine Grimbley, Noggin, Summer Solstice and a range of bottled beers. Website: http://www.charleswells.co.uk 'E'mail: sales@charleswells.co.uk

Wells Drinks (Eng) a soft drinks company based in Tenbury Wells, Worcestershire that produces a range of soft drinks under the Wells Wonderful World label.

Well-Succeeded (Eng) a term which denotes a wine that displays the best characteristics of its growth. (Fr) = très réussi.

Wells Wonderful World (Eng) see Wells Drinks.

Well Well Well (Eng) a natural mineral water brand.

Welmlingen (Ger) village (Anb): Baden. (Ber): Margräflerland. (Gro): Vogtei Rötteln. (Vin): Steingässle.

Welmoed Koöperatiewe Wynkelders (S.Afr) vineyards based in Stellenbosch. (Add): Box 23, Lynedock 7603. Produces varietal wines.

Welschriesling (Aus) lit: 'foreign Riesling' a white

grape variety, unrelated to Riesling (welsch means foreign in German). Used in most countries and for heurigen inn wines in Austria. Known in (Bul) = Welschrizling, (Cro) = Grasevina, (Hun) = Olasz rizling, (It) = Riesling italico, (Slo) = Laski risling, (Vojvodina) = Laski rizling.

Welsh Bitter (Wal) a keg bitter 1032 O.G. brewed by the Whitbread Brewery at Magor.

Welsh Brewers (Wal) a brewery belonging to Bass in Cardiff. Has some 500 public houses in the principality. Brews cask-conditioned Worthington Pale 1033 O.G. Hancock's PA 1033 O.G. Fussell's Best 1038 O.G. and keg Albright 1033 O.G.

Welsh Connection (Pousse Café) in an elgin liqueur glass pour in order half measure Midori, half measure red maraschino.

Welsh Connexion (Cktl) 25mls (1fl.oz) Malibu, 20mls (¾fl.oz) blue Curaçao, 50mls (2fl.ozs) orange juice, dash egg white. Shake well over ice, strain into a cocktail glass and top with a cherry.

Welsh Highland Bitter (Wal) a 5% alc by vol. bitter ale brewed by Snowdonia Park, Gwynedd.

Welsh Mist (Wal) a herb-flavoured liqueur, yellow-gold in colour 40% alc by vol.

Welsh Whiskey (Wal) a whiskey distilled near Frongoch, Bala, Powys. Made by Richard John Lloyd Price in 1898. *See* Fron Goch, Swn y Don and Swn y Mor. *See* Welsh Whisky Company [The]. *See also* Reaullt Hir.

Welsh Whisky Company Ltd [The] (Wal) a distillery (established 1999). (Add): Penderyn Distillery, Pontpren, Penderyn, Aberdare, Mid-Glamorgan CF44 0SX. Produces whisky and a variety of spirits and liqueurs. Website: http://www.welsh-whisky.co.uk 'E'mail: info@welsh-whisky.co.uk

Weltenburg Abbaye Brauerei (Ger) a brewery (established 1050) based in Kelheim. Brews: Weltenburger Kloster Asam-Bock.

Weltenburger Kloster Asam-Bock (Ger) a 6.5% alc by vol. dark, double bock bottled beer brewed by Weltenburg Abbaye Brauerei, Kelheim.

Weltevrede Wine Estate (S.Afr) a winery (established 1875) based at Robertson, Western Cape. 100ha. (Add): P.O. Box 6, Bonnievale 6730. Grape varieties: Cabernet sauvignon, Cinsaut, Colombard, Gewürztraminer, Merlot, Muscadel, Muscat de frontignan, Muscat de hambourg, Pinotage, Red muscadel, Rhine riesling, Sauvignon blanc, Sémillon, Syrah. Labels: Bedrock Black, Oude Weltevreden, Ouma se Wyn, Oupa se Wyn, Ovation, Philip Jonker Brut, Place of Rocks, Poet's Prayer, Privé du Bois (no longer produced), River's Edge, Rusted Soil, The Travelling Stone, Tricolore, Weitheimer. Website: http://www.weltevrede.com

Weltevrede Langoed (S.Afr) alternative name for the Weltevrede Estate.

Weltons Brewery (Eng) a brewery (established 2000). (Add): 1 Rangers Lodge, Oakhill Road, Horsham, West Sussex RH13 5LF. Brews: Horsham Old Ale 3.8% alc by vol., Kid & Bard 3.5% alc by vol., Old Cocky 4.3% alc by vol., Olde Swannie Best Bitter 4.3% alc by vol., Pride & Joy 2.8% alc by vol.

Website: http://www.weltons.co.uk 'E'mail: enquiries@weltons.co.uk

Welvanpas (S.Afr) a winery based in Wellington, Western Cape. Grape varieties: Cabernet sauvignon, Chenin blanc, Merlot. Produces 75% red wine and 25% white wine.

Wembley (Cktl) ⅓ measure Scotch whisky, ⅓ measure dry vermouth, ⅓ measure pineapple juice. Shake over ice and strain into a cocktail glass.

Wembley Ale (Eng) a pale ale 1036 O.G. brewed and bottled by the Wilson Brewery in Manchester.

Wembley Cocktail (Cktl) ⅔ measure dry gin, ⅓ measure French vermouth, 2 dashes apricot brandy, 2 dashes Calvados. Stir over ice and strain into a cocktail glass.

Wem Brewery (Eng) a Shropshire subsidiary of Greenall Whitley which produces cask-conditioned and other beers near Shrewsbury.

Wem Special (Eng) a 4.4% alc by vol. bitter ale brewed by Hanby Ales Ltd., Shropshire.

Wenceslas Winter Warmer (Eng) a 7.5% alc by vol. cask-conditioned winter warmer ale brewed by the Elgood & Sons, Northbrink Brewery, Wisbech, Cambridgeshire.

Wench's Quiver (Cktl) 25mls (1fl.oz) Mandarine Napoléon, 10mls (½ fl.oz) Galliano, 50mls (2fl.ozs) pineapple juice, 10mls (½ fl.oz) lemon juice, 1 egg white. Shake over ice, strain into a 300mls (10fl.oz) goblet with crushed ice and float 5mls (¼ fl.oz) blue Curaçao on top.

Wendelsheim (Ger) village (Anb): Rheinhessen. (Ber): Bingen. (Gro): Adelberg. (Vins): Heiligenpfad, Steigerberg.

Wendelstück (Ger) vineyard (Anb): Mosel-Saar-Ruwer. (Ber): Bernkastel. (Gro): Schwarzlay. (Vil): Burg.

Wenden (Eng) vineyard. (Add): Duddenhoe End, Near Saffron Walden, Essex. 1.25ha. Soil: clay loam on chalk. Grape variety is Müller-Thurgau. Vinification at Chilford Hundred Wine C°.

Wenden Quelle [1] (Ger) a sparkling natural spring mineral water from Dodow, Mecklenburg. Mineral contents (milligrammes per litre): Sodium 16.7mg/l, Calcium 64.1mg/l, Magnesium 4.5mg/l, Potassium 1.4mg/l, Bicarbonates 145mg/l, Chlorides 30.3mg/l, Sulphates 52mg/l, Fluorides 0.12mg/l, Nitrates 0.4mg/l.

Wenden Quelle [2] (Ger) a sparkling natural spring mineral water from Dodow, Mecklenburg. Mineral contents (milligrammes per litre): Sodium 18mg/l, Calcium 62mg/l, Bicarbonates 157mg/l, Chlorides 29.2mg/l, Nitrates <1mg/l.

Wenden Quelle [3] (Ger) a sparkling natural spring mineral water from Dodow, Mecklenburg. Mineral contents (milligrammes per litre): Sodium 19.6mg/l, Calcium 57.9mg/l, Bicarbonates 158mg/l, Chlorides 28.2mg/l, Nitrates <1mg/l.

Wendewein (Ger) a wine made in the Bodensee. It is so acidic that consumers have to keep turning over in bed at night so that it does not eat a hole through their stomachs!

W

Wendlstatt (Aus) a vineyard site on the banks of the River Danube in the Kremstal region.

Weninger (Aus) a winery based in Horitschon, Mittel-Burgenland. (Add): Florianigasse 11, 7312 Horitschon. Grape varieties: Blaufränkisch, Merlot, Pinot gris, Zweigelt.

Wenigumstadt (Ger) village (Anb): Franken. (Ber): Maindreieck. (Gro): Heiligenthal. (Vins): Assorted parts of vineyards.

Wenlock Spring Water Ltd (Eng) mineral and spring water producers (established 1989). (Add): Wolverton, Church Stretton, Shropshire SY6 6RR. Website: http://www.wenlockwater.com 'E'mail: info@wenlockwater.com

Wenneker (Hol) a distillery (established 1693) based in Roosendaal. (Add): P.O. Box 124, 4700 AC Roosendaal. Produces a range of spirits and liqueurs. Website: http://www.wenneker.nl 'E'mail: export@wenneker.nl

Wennol (Wal) a 4.1% alc by vol. ale brewed by the Bragdy Ynys Mon, Gwynedd.

Wente Bros Winery (USA) a winery based in Livermore Valley, Alameda, San Francisco Bay, California. Also has vineyards in Monterey County. Grape varieties: Cabernet sauvignon, Chardonnay, Chenin blanc, Sauvignon blanc, Sémillon, Ugni blanc. Produces varietal and table wines. Labels: Charles Wetmore Reserve, Reliz Creek Reserve. Website: http://www.wentevineyards.com

Wentworth Brewery (Eng) a brewery. (Add): The Power House, Gun Park, Wentworth, Rotherham, South Yorkshire S62 7TF. Brews: Best Bitter 4% alc by vol., Black Zac 4.6% alc by vol., Gryphon 5.1% alc by vol., Gun Park Dark 3.4% alc by vol., Needle's Eye 3.5% alc by vol., Oatmeal Stout 4.8% alc by vol., Rampant Gryphon 6.2% alc by vol., Venture 3.6% alc by vol., Wpa Woppa 4% alc by vol. *see* Worterloo. Website: http://www.wentworth-brewery.co.uk 'E'mail: info@wentworth-brewery.com

Wenzel (Aus) a winery (7ha) based in Rust, Neusiedlersee-Hügelland, Burgenland. (Add): Hauptstrasse 29, 7071 Rust. Grape varieties: Blaufränkisch, Cabernet sauvignon, Furmint, Gemischter satz, Muskateller, Pinot blanc, Pinot gris, Pinot noir, Sauvignon blanc, Welschriesling. Produces a range of wines.

Werbach (Ger) village (Anb): Baden. (Ber): Badische Frankenland. (Gro): Tauberklinge. (Vins): Beilberg, Hirschberg.

Wergild (Eng) a cask-conditioned lager brewed by Beowulf Brewery, Yardley, Birmingham.

Wermod (Eng) the Anglo-Saxon name for wormwood. *see* Wermut.

Wermut (Ger) wormwood, the name from which vermouth derives. *see* Wermod.

Wermutshausen (Ger) village (Anb): Württemberg. (Ber): Kocher-Jagst-Tauber. (Gro): Tauberberg. (Vin): Schafsteige.

Wernarzer Heilwasser (Ger) a natural spring mineral water from Bad Brücknau. Mineral contents (milligrammes per litre): Sodium 2.7mg/l, Calcium 30.4mg/l, Magnesium 13mg/l, Potassium 6.6mg/l, Chlorides 6.7mg/l, Sulphates 22.6mg/l, Fluorides 0.19mg/l. Website: http://www.badbrueckenauer.de

Wernersgrüner Brauerei (Ger) a brewery (established 1436) based in the Vogtland district in (eastern) Germany.

Wernersgrüner Pils Legende (Ger) a 4.9% alc by vol. pilsener lager beer brewed in the Wernersgrüner Brauerei in the Vogtland district of (eastern) Germany.

Wernig (Ger) vinious/vinosity.

Wernigeröder (Ger) a natural spring mineral water from Wernigerodel, Oberharz. Mineral contents (milligrammes per litre): Sodium 25mg/l, Calcium 93mg/l, Magnesium 27mg/l, Potassium 2mg/l, Bicarbonates 269mg/l, Chlorides 35mg/l, Sulphates 133mg/l.

Werretaler (Ger) a natural spring mineral water from Löhne. Mineral contents (milligrammes per litre): Sodium 21mg/l, Calcium 221mg/l, Magnesium 52mg/l, Potassium 2.4mg/l, Bicarbonates 232mg/l, Chlorides 55mg/l, Sulphates 532mg/l.

Wertheim (Ger) village (Anb): Baden. (Ber): Badische Frankenland. (Gro): Tauberklinge. (Vin): Schlossberg.

Wesh (Tur) lit: 'face', the name given to the foam on the top of a cup of Turkish coffee.

Wes Hal (Eng) an Anglo-Saxon word meaning 'be of good health'. *see* Wassail.

Wessex Best Bitter (Eng) a cask-conditioned best bitter 1042 O.G. brewed by the Cornish Brewery in Weymouth, Dorset. Also sold as bottled Wessex Pale Ale.

Wessex Pale Ale (Eng) *see* Wessex Best Bitter.

West African Breweries (Afr) a large brewery based in Nigeria. Produces Top Lager beer.

West Auckland Mild (Eng) a 3.3% alc by vol. mild ale from the Butterknowle Brewery, Lynesack, near Bishop Auckland.

West Berkshire Brewery C° Ltd (Eng) a brewery (established 1995). (Add): The Old Bakery, Yattendon, Thatcham, Berkshire RG18 0UE. Brews: Dr Hexters Healer 5% alc by vol., Full Circle 4.5% alc by vol., Good Old Boy 4% alc by vol., Maggs Mild 3.8% alc by vol., Mr Chubbs Lunchtime Bitter 3.7% alc by vol., New Special Monthly. Website: http://www.wbbrew.co.uk 'E'mail: davemaggs@wbbrew.co.uk

West Best Natural Spring Water (Can) a natural spring mineral water from Kent, British Columbia. Mineral contents (milligrammes per litre): Sodium 3.7mg/l, Calcium 13.5mg/l, Magnesium 4.2mg/l, Potassium 0.4mg/l, Bicarbonates 32.8mg/l, Chlorides 0.1mg/l, Sulphates 25.5mg/l, Fluorides 0.1mg/l.

Westbridge Vineyards (S.Afr) a winery (established 1998) based in Muldersvlei, Stellenbosch, Western Cape. 17ha. Grape varieties: Cabernet sauvignon, Chenin blanc, Merlot, Pinotage, Shiraz. Label: Juliette.

West Brook Winery (N.Z) a winery. (Add): 34

W

Awaroa Road, Henderson. 2ha. Premium label is Blue Ridge.

Westbury Farm Vineyard (Eng) a vineyard (established 1968). (Add): Purley, near Reading, Berkshire. 6.7ha. Grape varieties: Madeleine angevine, Müller-Thurgau, Pinot meunier, Pinot noir, Reichensteiner, Seibel, Siegerrebe and Seyval blanc.

West Cape Howe (Austr) a winery based in the Great Southern region of Western Australia. Grape varieties include: Cabernet sauvignon.

West Coast Brewery Company (Eng) brews a lager beer in the Kings Arms (a public house) in Brunswick, Manchester. *See also* North Country.

West Coast Cooler (Eng) a commercial blend of Pacific fruits and white wine 3.5% alc by vol.

WestCorp International (S.Afr) a large company (established 2002) and formed between Spruitdrift and Vredendal in Olifants River, Western Cape. 4990ha. Grape varieties: Cabernet sauvignon, Chardonnay, Chenin blanc, Colombard, Hanepoot jerepigo, Merlot, Pinotage, Ruby cabernet, Sauvignon blanc, Shiraz. Labels: B4 Spumante, D-Lite-Ful, Gôiya, Inanda Brut, Namaqua, Spruitdrift. Website: http://www.westcorp.co.za

West Country Ale (Eng) a cask-conditioned pale ale 1030 O.G. brewed by the Whitbread Brewery in Cheltenham, Gloscestershire.

West Country Cider (Eng) a fine cider produced by Landons at Hewish, Near Weston-Super-Mare, Avon.

West Country Gold (Eng) a 4.1% alc by vol. golden ale brewed by the Blackawton Brewery, Cornwall.

West Crown Brewery (Eng) a brewery based in Newark, Nottinghamshire. Brews: Regal Bitter, Greenwood's N°8 and Greenwood's N°10.

West End (Eng) a brand of coffee produced by Kenco-Typhoo Catering. A blend of arabica coffees.

West End and Southwark Brewery (Austr) a brewery based in Adelaide, South Australia.

West End Beer (Austr) a pasteurised, bottom-fermented bitter brewed by the Coopers Brewery in the West End district of South Australia.

West End Bitter (Austr) a lager beer brewed by the South Australian Brewing C°. in Adelaide.

West End Brewery (USA) a brewery based in Utica. *see* West End Brewing Company.

West End Brewing Company (USA) a brewery based at Utica. Brews: Maximus Super, Matt's Premium, Utica Club Cream Ale and Utica Club Pilsener.

Westend Estate (Austr) a winery based in the Riverina region. (Add): 1283 Brayne Road, Griffith, New South Wales 2680. 12.5ha. Grape varieties: Cabernet sauvignon, Chardonnay, Durif, Hermitage, Rhine riesling, Sauvignon blanc, Sémillon, Shiraz, Traminer. Labels: N°1, Old Vine and Three Bridges. One of the smaller wineries of the M.I.A.

Westerham Brewery C° Ltd (Eng) a brewery (established 2004). (Add): Grange Farm, Pootings Road, Edenbridge, Kent TN8 6SA. Brews: Black

Eagle Special Pale Ale 'SPA' 3.8% alc by vol., British Bulldog Best Bitter 4.3% alc by vol., General Wolfe 1759 Maple Ale 4.5% alc by vol., Gods Wallop Christmas Ale 4.3% alc by vol., Grasshopper Kentish Bitter 4.8% alc by vol., Little Scotney Ale 4% alc by vol., Puddledock Porter 4.5% alc by vol., Sevenoaks Bitter '7X' 4.8% alc by vol., Summer Perle Golden Ale 3.8% alc by vol., Westerham Special Bitter Ale '1965' 5% alc by vol. Website: http://www.westerhambrewery.co.uk 'E'mail: info@westerhambrewery.co.uk

Western Australia (Austr) a state with nearly 60 wineries whose 4500ha. of vineyards are concentrated in a 20kms strip. Divided into five zones: South West Australia is most important. Sub-divided into: Geographe, Great Southern, Margaret River, Blackwood Valley, Pemberton. *See also* Perth Hills, South West Coastal, Swan Valley.

Western Electric (Cktl) 25mls claret, 25mls Cointreau, 25mls Cognac. Shake over ice, strain into a highball glass and top with iced Champagne.

Western Monarch (Eng) a 4.3% alc by vol. ale brewed by the Buntingford Brewery, Hertfordshire.

Western Rose (Cktl) ½ measure dry gin, ¼ measure apricot brandy, ¼ measure dry vermouth, dash lemon juice. Shake over ice and strain into a cocktail glass.

Western Vineyards (N.Z) a former vineyard (now no longer in operation).

Western Wines South Africa/Kumala (S.Afr) a private company and winery (established 1981) based in Stellenbosch, Western Cape. 25ha. Owned by Vincor (Can). Grape varieties: Cabernet sauvignon, Chardonnay, Chenin blanc, Cinsaut, Colombard, Merlot, Pinotage, Ruby cabernet, Sauvignon blanc, Sémillon, Shiraz. Labels: Journey's End, Kumala. Website: http://www.kumala.com

Westerwald-Quelle (Ger) a sparkling natural spring mineral water from Biskirchen, Lahn. Mineral contents (milligrammes per litre): Sodium 237mg/l, Calcium 169mg/l, Magnesium 54.6mg/l, Potassium 8.4mg/l, Bicarbonates 866mg/l, Chlorides 334mg/l, Sulphates 31.2mg/l, Fluorides 0.5mg/l, Nitrates 0.4mg/l, Silicates 23.6mg/l.

Westfield (Austr) a winery based in the Swan Valley in Western Australia.

Westfield-Fredonia (USA) a wine district along Lake Erie in the New York region.

West Highland Malt Whisky (Scot) the old name for Islay Malt Whisky.

Westhofen (Ger) village (Anb): Rheinhessen. (Ber): Wonnegau. (Gro): Bergkloster. (Vins): Aulerde, Benn, Brunnenhäuschen, Kirchspiel, Morstein, Rotenstein, Steingrube.

West Indian Punch (Punch) into a large punch bowl place 500mls (1pint) each of Bacardi rum, pineapple juice, orange juice and lemon juice, 150mls (¼ pint) crème de banane, 100grms

W

(4ozs) castor sugar, grated nutmeg, cinnamon and cloves. Stir well, chill down in a refrigerator, dress with sliced bananas and serve.

West Indian Rum Refinery (W.Ind) a noted rum distillery based on the island of Barbados. Produces the Cockspur brand.

West Indies Distilleries Ltd. (W.Ind) a rum distillery based in the Virgin Islands.

West Indies Rum and Spirits Producers Association (W.Ind) *abbr*: WIRSPA. a group of West Indian islands: Antigua, Bahamas, Barbados, Guyana, Jamaica and Trinidad formed to promote and protect rum.

West Indies Swizzle (Cktl) ½ bottle Jamaican rum, 6 teaspoons sugar, 6 sprigs mint, 150mls (6fl.ozs) lime juice. Fill a jug with ice, add ingredients, place between feet and use a swizzle stick until the outside of the jug is frosted.

Westmalle (Bel) a Trappiste abbaye brewery (established 1836) based in Malle, Antwerp. Brews: Dubbel – 7% alc by vol. dark, top-fermented, bottle-conditioned Abbaye and Tripel–9% alc by vol. straw, top-fermented, bottle-conditioned abbaye beer.

Westmerian Ale (Eng) brewed by micro-brewery Cartmeal Brewery at Kendal, Cumbria to mark the second anniversary of the Westmorland beer festival.

Westminster (Cktl) ½ measure French vermouth, ½ measure Canadian rye whisky, 3 dashes arum, dash Angostura. Stir over ice and strain into a cocktail glass.

Westminster Pure Coffee (Eng) the brand-name of a ground coffee produced by Kenco-Typhoo Catering Services.

Westons (Eng) famous cider makers of Much Marcle in Herefordshire. Produces: Old Rosie Draught Scrumpy 7.3% alc by vol. Vintage Reserve Oak-conditioned Cider 8.2% alc by vol., 1st Quality Draught Cider 5% alc by vol. Herefordshire Country Perry 4.5% alc by vol., Stowford Export Premium Dry Cider 6% alc by vol., Stowford LC, Strong Organic Cider 6.5% alc by vol. Website: http://www.westons-cider.co.uk

Weston Winery (USA) a noted winery based in Idaho, Pacific North-West.

West Riding Brewery (Eng) a brewery (established 1980) based in Huddersfield, Yorkshire. Now based in Meltham, Yorkshire (due to a fire). Brews: cask-conditioned Tyke Bitter 1041 O.G.

Westrum (Ger) vineyard (Anb): Rheinhessen. (Ber): Nierstein. (Gro): Sankt Alban. (Vil): Bodenheim.

Weststeiermark (Aus) also known as West Styria, a wine district 480ha within the region of Steiermark. Soil: gneiss and slate. Main grape varieties: white (Pinot blanc, Welshriesling) red (Blauer wildbacher, Zweigelt). Villages: Deutschlandsberg, Frauental, Straden, St. Anna. Produces both red and white wines.

West Virginia's Pride of the Mountains (USA) a natural spring mineral from Laurel Mountains, Tucker County, west Virginia.

West Yorkshire Brewery (Eng) a micro-brewery based at Luddendenfoot. Brews Yorkshireman Best Bitter 4.1% alc by vol.

Wet (Eng) a slang term for a drink. "*to have a wet*".

Wet (USA) a person who advocates the free sale of alcoholic liquor.

Wet Cork (Eng) a taste in the wine often experienced when the cork has been in contact with the wine for many years (in storage). The cork's condition becomes saturated and gives the wine an unpleasant aroma and flavour of wet wood.

Wethered Brewery (Eng) the name for Whitbread's Brewery based in Marlow, Buckinghamshire. Noted for cask-conditioned beers (closed in 1989).

Wethereds (Eng) a guest ale (event ale) brewed by Ridleys Hartford End Brewery, Chelmsford, Essex.

Wet House (Eng) a slang term for a hostel for homeless alcoholics.

Wetlyanskaya (Rus) a sparkling natural spring mineral water (established 1998) from Samara. Mineral contents (milligrammes per litre): Sodium 36mg/l, Calcium 1800mg/l, Magnesium 52mg/l, Potassium 827mg/l, Oxygen 5.55mg/l.

Wet Method (Eng) the process of removing the coffee beans from the coffee cherries using water. Beans are soaked in tanks, fermented and the pulp washed away. *see* Washed Coffee and Dry Method.

Wet One's Whistle (Eng) a slang term for '*to have a drink*'. *see* Wet.

Wet Rent (Eng) the method of renting a public house to a tenant. The rent to the tenant was low and the brewery's income was from a surcharge on the wholesale price of the drink.

Wets Brasserie (Bel) a brewery based in St. Genisius-Rode, Central Belgium.

Wet Smell (Eng) the name given to the process of aroma testing (sniffing) of the coffee. Also known as the Crust Test.

Wet State (USA) the name for a State that permits the free sale of alcoholic liquor.

Wettelbrunn (Ger) village (Anb): Baden. *see* Staufen.

Wetterkreuz (Ger) vineyard (Anb): Nahe. (Ber): Schloss Böckelheim. (Gro): Rosengarten. (Vil): Braunweiler.

Wetzstein (Ger) vineyard (Anb): Württemberg. (Ber): Remstal-Stuttgart. (Gro): Wartbühl. (Vil): Endersbach.

Wetzstein (Ger) vineyard (Anb): Württemberg. (Ber): Remstal-Stuttgart. (Gro): Weinsteige. (Vil): Fellbach.

Wetzstein (Ger) vineyard (Anb): Württemberg. (Ber): Remstal-Stuttgart. (Gro): Weinsteige. (Vil): Stuttgart (ortsteil Untertürkheim).

Wexford Irish Cream Ale (Eng) a 4.6% alc by vol. beer from Greene King (a nitrokeg). An Irish beer produced using Irish ingredients to an original Irish recipe.

Weyher (Ger) village (Anb): Pfalz. (Ber): Südliche Weinstrasse. (Gro): Ordensgut. (Vins): Heide, Michelsberg.

Weymouth Best Bitter (Eng) a 4% alc by vol. best

bitter ale brewed by the Dorset Brewing Company Ltd., Dorset.

Weymouth Harbour Master (Eng) a 3.6% alc by vol. ale brewed by the Dorset Brewing Company Ltd., Dorset.

Weymouth JD 1742 (Eng) a 4.2% alc by vol. ale brewed by the Dorset Brewing Company Ltd., Dorset..

Weymouth Organic Gold (Eng) a 4.7% alc by vol. cask/bottle-conditioned organic ale brewed by the Quay Brewery, Hope Square, Weymouth.

Weymouth Special Pale Ale (Eng) an ale brewed by the Dorset Brewery Company Ltd., Dorset.

Weymouth Steam Bear (Eng) 4.5% alc by vol. ale brewed by the Dorset Brewing Company Ltd., Dorset.

WF6 Brewing C° (Eng) a brewery (established 2004). (Add): c/o Rose Farm Approach, Normanton, West Yorkshire WF6 2RZ. Brews the following under the Birkwoods label: Boulevard 3.8% alc by vol., Festive Fuel 4% alc by vol., January Ales 4.5% alc by vol., Original 4.5% alc by vol., St Georges Day 4% alc by vol., Time 3.8% alc by vol. Website: http://www.wf6brewingcompany.co.uk 'E'mail: info@wf6brewingcompany.co.uk

WGS (Aus) *abbr*: Öesterreichisches **W**eingute**s**iegel, the Austrian wine seal of quality.

Whale Ale (Eng) a cask-conditioned ale 1045 O.G. brewed by the home-brew public house Flounder and Firkin in London.

Whalehaven Wines (S.Afr) a winery (established 1995) based in Hemel-en-Aarde Valley, Hermanus, Western Cape. Grape varieties: Cabernet franc, Cabernet sauvignon, Chardonnay, Merlot, Pinotage, Pinot noir, Shiraz, Viognier. Labels: Bord de Mer, Old Harbour Red.

Whaps Weasel (Eng) a 4.8% alc by vol. ale brewed by the Hexhamshire Brewery, Northumberland.

Wharfedale (Eng) a 4.5% alc by vol (1045 O.G) cask-conditioned special ale brewed by the Goose Eye Brewery in Keighley, Yorkshire.

Wharfedale Brewery [The] (Eng) a brewery (established 2003). (Add): Coonlands Laithe, Rylestone, Skipton, North Yorkshire BD23 6LY. Brews: Folly Ale 5% alc by vol., Folly Gold 5% alc by vol., The Executioner 4.5% alc by vol. Website: http://www.follyale.com 'E'mail: david@follyale.com

Whatiri Wines (N.Z) a winery based in Poroti, west of Whangarei, Northland. 2ha (closed in 1983).

What's Yours? (Eng) an informal request to know what you would like to drink. An offer to buy a person a drink.

What The Fox Hat (Eng) a 4.2% alc by vol. ale brewed by The Church End Brewery Ltd., Warwickshire.

What the Hell (Cktl) ⅓ measure dry gin, ⅓ measure French vermouth, ⅓ measure apricot brandy, dash lemon juice. Stir over ice in an old-fashioned glass.

Wheat Beer (Eng) a beer brewed from malted wheat. *see* Weizenbier.

Wheat Beer (Eng) a 5% alc by vol. wheat beer brewed by the Greenwich Meantime Brewing C°. Ltd., London.

Wheat Beer (Eng) a 4% alc by vol. wheat beer brewed by O'Hanlon's Brewery C°. Ltd., Devon.

Wheat Mash (Eng) a 4.5% alc by vol. bottled seasonal ale produced by King and Barnes Brewery, Horsham, West Sussex.

Wheatsheaf (Eng) the name for a beer brewed by the Ballard's Brewery Ltd., Hampshire.

Wheat Whiskey (USA) a whiskey produced at not exceeding 160° US proof from not less than 51% of wheat mash and stored in charred oak casks at not more than 125° US proof.

Wheeler (USA) a winery with vineyards in Dry Creek Valley, Sonoma County, California. Noted for Merlot varietal wines.

Wheeltappers Ale (Eng) a 4% alc by vol. ale from Cottage Brewing Company, West Lydford, near Yeovil, Somerset.

Wheelwright (Eng) a low alcohol (less than 1% alc by vol.) draught or bottled bitter produced by the Robinson Brewery, Stockport, Greater Manchester.

Wherry Best Bitter (Eng) a best bitter 3.8% alc by vol (1039 O.G) brewed by the Woodforde Brewery Ltd., Norwich, Norfolkshire.

Whim Ales Ltd (Eng) a brewery (established 1993). (Add): Whim Farm, Hartington, Buxton, Derbyshire SK17 0AX. Brews: Arbour Light 3.6% alc by vol., Black Christmas, Hartington Bitter 4% alc by vol., Hartington IPA 4.5% alc by vol., High Street Porter, Magic Mushroom Mild 3.8% alc by vol., Old Izaak 4.8% alc by vol., Special 4.4% alc by vol.

Whip and Tongue (Eng) a method of grafting used in France that consists of cutting the scion and stock at the same angle and then splitting them so that they lock into each other.

Whip Cocktail (Cktl) 15mls Pernod, 15mls brandy, 15mls French vermouth, 15mls Curaçao, shake over ice and strain into a cocktail glass. Also known as a Kurbag Cocktail.

Whippling Golden Bitter (Eng) a 3.6% alc by vol. bitter ale brewed by the Belvoir Brewery, Leicestershire.

Whipskull (Scot) a mixed drink of egg yolks, sugar, cream, rum which is traditionally served in the Shetland Islands at Yuletide (January 6ᵗʰ), considered to be of Scandinavian origin.

Whirlpool (Eng) another name for the Centrifuge.

Whiskey (Eng) the spelling of whiskies other than Scotch whisky and the Canadian rye whisky.

Whiskey Cobbler (Cktl) place 40mls (⅓ gill) Bourbon whiskey into an old-fashioned glass over ice. Add 2 dashes of gomme syrup and a splash of soda, decorate with fruits in season and serve with straws.

Whiskey Cocktail (Cktl) 25mls (⅕ gill) Bourbon whiskey, 4 dashes gomme syrup, dash Angostura. Stir over ice, strain into a cocktail glass and add a cherry.

Whiskey Collins (Cktl) 50mls (2fl.ozs) Bourbon

whiskey, juice ½ lemon, 1 teaspoon powdered sugar. Shake over ice, strain into an ice-filled collins glass. Top with soda water, lemon slice, orange slice and a cherry and serve with straws.

Whiskey Daisy (Cktl) 50mls (2fl.ozs) Bourbon or rye whiskey, juice of ½ lemon or lime, 3 dashes gomme syrup. Shake over ice, strain into a small tumbler, top with soda water and a dash of grenadine.

Whiskey Eggnog (Cktl) 25mls (⅕ gill) Bourbon whiskey, 1 egg, 1 teaspoon powdered sugar. Shake well over ice, strain into a collins glass, top with milk, stir and add grated nutmeg.

Whiskey Fix (Cktl) dissolve 1 teaspoon of powdered sugar in the juice of ½ lemon in a highball glass. Add ice, 60mls (½ gill) Bourbon whiskey. Stir, top with a slice of lemon and serve with straws.

Whiskey Fizz (Cktl) 2 measures Bourbon whiskey, 1 teaspoon sugar, juice of a lemon. Shake over ice, strain into an ice-filled highball glass and top with soda water.

Whiskey Flip (Cktl) 25mls (⅕ gill) Bourbon whiskey, 1 egg, 15mls (⅛ gill) cream, 1 teaspoon powdered sugar. Shake well over ice, strain into a flip glass and top with grated nutmeg.

Whiskey Glass (USA) the alternative name for a nip glass. Holds a single measure.

Whiskey Highball (Cktl) as for Gin Highball but using whiskey instead of gin.

Whiskey Julep (Cktl) in a large glass dissolve 1 teaspoon of sugar in a little water. Fill with crushed ice. Top with Bourbon whiskey to within 10cms (½ in) of top and decorate with mint. The mint can be crushed with the sugar if desired.

Whiskey Milk Punch (Cktl) 40mls (⅓ gill) Bourbon whiskey, 185mls (1½ gills) milk, 1 teaspoon powdered sugar. Shake over ice, strain into a highball glass and top with grated nutmeg.

Whiskey Mist (Cktl) in an old-fashioned glass place some shaved ice, add 1 jigger of Bourbon or rye whisky and a twist of lemon peel juice.

Whiskey Orange (Cktl) 25mls (⅕ gill) Bourbon whiskey, juice ½ orange, 1 teaspoon powdered sugar, 2 dashes Pernod. Shake well over ice, strain into an ice-filled highball glass, top with a slice of lemon and orange.

Whiskey Rebellion (USA) took place on 15th September 1794. Distillers revolted against the Excise tax of 1791. Led to the first making of moonshine.

Whiskey Rickey (Cktl) 40mls (⅓ gill) Bourbon whiskey, juice ½ lime. Stir over ice, strain into a highball glass, top with soda water and a squeeze of lime peel juice.

Whiskey Sangaree (Cktl) dissolve ½ teaspoon of powdered sugar in a little water in a highball glass. Add ice and 25mls (⅕ gill) Bourbon whiskey. Top with 50mls (2fl.ozs) soda water, dash of Port and grated nutmeg.

Whiskey Skin (Cktl) into an old-fashioned glass place a sugar cube and 50mls (2fl.ozs) boiling water. Stir, add 25mls (⅕ gill) Bourbon whiskey and a twist of lemon peel and stir.

Whiskey Sling (Cktl) dissolve 1 teaspoon powdered sugar in the juice of half a lemon and 25mls (1fl.oz) water in an old-fashioned glass. Add 40mls (⅓ gill) rye whiskey, stir and add a twist of lemon peel.

Whiskey Smash (Cktl) muddle a cube of sugar with ½ jigger of water and some mint. Add ice, 1 jigger of whiskey, serve decorated with mint and top with club soda.

Whiskey Sour (Cktl) 20mls (¾ fl.oz) lemon or lime juice, 35mls (1½fl.ozs) Bourbon or rye whiskey, 1 teaspoon powdered sugar. Shake well over ice, strain into a cocktail glass, add a cherry and a slice of orange.

Whiskey Squirt (Cktl) 25mls (⅕ gill) Bourbon whiskey, 2 dashes grenadine. Shake over ice, strain into an ice-filled highball glass, top with a pineapple cube and fresh strawberry.

Whiskey Swizzle (Cktl) as for Gin Swizzle but using Bourbon whiskey in place of the gin.

Whiskey Toddy (Cktl) 40mls (⅓ gill) Bourbon (or rye) whiskey, ½ teaspoon powdered sugar, 20mls (⅙ gill) boiling water. Stir sugar in the water in an old-fashioned glass, add whiskey, stir and top with a twist of lemon peel.

Whisky (Eng) the spelling of whiskies that come from Scotland only with the exception of Canadian rye whisky. *see* Whiskey.

Whisky [The] (Jap) a special whiskey produced by Suntory. Only 6000 bottles are produced annually.

Whisky Ale (Eng) a real ale brewed by Smiles Brewery, Bristol. Partly made from whisky–1 bottle of 8 year old added to every barrel.

Whisky Cobbler (Cktl) 125mls (1gill) whisky, 30mls (¼ gill) brown Curaçao. Shake over ice, strain into an ice-filled highball glass. Serve with a dash of lemon peel juice, slices of fresh fruit, spoon and straws.

Whisky Cobbler (Cktl) 1 measure Scotch whisky, 1 teaspoon sugar, 4 dashes orange Curaçao. Fill a 125 ml. (5fl.oz) wine glass with ice. Add whisky, sugar and Curaçao, stir, decorate with fruit, mint sprig and serve with straws.

Whisky Cocktail [1] (Cktl) ⅘ measure Scotch whisky, ⅕ measure orange Curaçao, 2 dashes Angostura. Stir over ice, strain into a cocktail glass and add a cherry.

Whisky Cocktail [2] (Cktl) 40mls (⅓ gill) Scotch whisky, 2 dashes brown Curaçao, 1 dash Angostura, 1 lump sugar. Stir over ice, strain into a cocktail glass, serve with a cherry and a dash lemon peel juice on top.

Whisky Collins (Cktl) 90mls (¾ gill) Scotch whisky, dash lemon juice, sugar syrup to taste. Shake well over ice, strain into a highball glass and top with soda water.

Whisky Cooler (Cktl) 60mls (½ gill) Scotch whisky, 250mls (½ pint) soda water, 2 dashes orange bitters. Stir in a tall glass with an ice cube and serve with a slice of orange on top.

Whisky Crusta (Cktl) 40mls (⅓ gill) Scotch whisky, 20mls (⅙ gill) lemon juice, 1 teaspoon sugar syrup, 1 teaspoon maraschino, dash Angostura, dash orange bitters, ½ teaspoon powdered sugar. Moisten wine glass with lemon and add sugar, place in a spiral of lemon peel. Shake ingredients over ice, strain into a crusta glass and serve with slices of fruit.

Whisky Daisy (Cktl) 60mls (½ gill) Scotch whisky, 30mls (¼ gill) orange juice, 60mls (½ gill) lime juice, 60mls (½ gill) lemon juice, dash grenadine. Shake over ice, strain into a highball. Top with soda water. Serve with slices of fresh fruit and add 2 dashes brown Curaçao.

Whisky Egg Nogg (Cktl) 80mls (⅔ gill) Scotch whisky, 1 egg, dash rum, 1 teaspoon sugar, 90mls (¾ gill) milk. Shake over ice, strain into a tumbler and serve with a dash of nutmeg on top.

Whisky Elsie (Cktl) 1 teaspoon sugar, juice ½ lemon, 1 measure Scotch whisky, dash Angostura. Shake well over ice and strain into a wine glass.

Whisky Jug (Scot) an alternative name for old whisky bottles.

Whisky-Lime Grog (Cktl) 1 measure Scotch whisky, dash vanilla essence, 2 teaspoons sugar. Add to 300mls (½ pint) lime tea. Serve in a heatproof glass and decorate with a slice of lime.

Whisky Mac (Cktl). 35mls (1½ fl.ozs) Scotch whisky, 25mls (1fl.oz) Stone's Ginger wine. Build into an old-fashioned glass.

Whisky-Mint Cocktail (Cktl) 50mls (2fl.ozs) mint tea, 25mls (1fl.oz) Scotch whisky, juice of ½ lime, shake well over ice, strain into a cocktail glass and dress with mint leaves.

Whisky Punch (Cktl) 2 measures Scotch whisky, 1 measure Jamaican rum, ½ measure lemon juice, 1 teaspoon sugar, dash Angostura. Shake well over ice, strain into an ice-filled highball glass, dress with an orange slice soaked in Curaçao and a dash of soda water.

Whisky Safe (Scot) a glass case through which Scotch malt whisky runs during the second distillation. Is locked by the Customs and Excise. The distiller controls the flow (of foreshots and feints etc.) by remote control.

Whisky Sangaree (Cktl) dissolve 10grms (⅓ oz.) sugar in 125mls (5fl.ozs) water in a tumbler. Add 25mls (1fl.oz) Scotch whisky and 2 ice cubes and top with grated nutmeg.

Whisky Sling [Hot] (Cktl) 2 measures Scotch whisky in an old-fashioned glass, top with boiling water and grated nutmeg.

Whisky Smash (Cktl) as for Gin Smash but substituting Scotch whisky for the gin.

Whisky Toddy (Cktl) 50mls (2fl.ozs) Scotch whisky, 25mls (1fl.oz) water, 1 teaspoon sugar. Stir until sugar dissolves and serve in a 125mls (5fl.oz) wine glass.

Whisper (Cktl) equal measures of Scotch whisky, Italian and French vermouths served over cracked ice.

Whispering Springs Water (USA) a natural spring mineral water from Pierceton, Indiana.

Whispers-of-the-Past (Cktl) ⅓ measure Bourbon whiskey, ⅓ measure Port, ⅓ measure dry Sherry, 1 teaspoon powdered sugar. Stir over ice, strain into a cocktail glass, dress with a slice of lemon and orange.

Whist Cocktail (Cktl) ⅓ measure dark rum, ⅓ measure Italian vermouth, ⅓ measure Calvados. Shake over ice and strain into a cocktail glass.

Whistle Belly Vengance (Eng) a 4.7% alc by vol. beer brewed by Summerskills Brewery, Plymouth, Devon.

Whistler Water (Can) a still natural glacial spring mineral water from Burnaby, British Columbia. Mineral contents (milligrammes per litre): Sodium 2mg/l, Calcium 12mg/l, Magnesium 1mg/l, Potassium 1mg/l, Bicarbonates 20mg/l, Chlorides 3mg/l, Sulphates 8mg/l, Fluorides <0.1mg/l. pH 7.0–pH 7.3

Whistle Stop (Eng) a 4.4% alc by vol. ale brewed by the Wylam Brewery Ltd., Tyne & Wear.

Whistling Joe (Eng) a 3.6% alc by vol. ale brewed by the Brandy Cask Pub & Brewery, Worcestershire.

Whistling Will (Eng) a 4% alc by vol. seasonal ale brewed by Frederic Robinson Ltd., Unicorn Brewery, Stockport, Cheshire (available in July and August).

Whitbread (Eng) a famous national brewer with many public houses, breweries and 2 keg brewing plants in England and Wales. Noted for cask-conditioned Trophy Bitter 1035 O.G. (also keg). Tankard 1037 O.G. (also keg). Stella Artois 1047 O.G. bottled Forest Brown 1032 O.G. Mackeson 1042 O.G.

Whitbread Goldings (Eng) an English hop variety having a good aroma and flavour.

Whitbread Investments (Eng) the shares that Whitbread once had in some of the independent breweries. These were Border 17%, Boddington 22%, Brakspear 27%, Buckley 18%, Devenish 26%, Marston 35% and Morland 40%.

Whitbread Magor Celebration Ale (Wal) see Magor Brewery.

Whitbread Pale Ale (Eng) a 5.7% alc by vol. bottled ale brewed by the Whitbread Brewery, London.

Whitbread Shires (Eng) the shire horses originally used by the Whitbread Brewery in London to pull their dray (they were working shire horses).

Whitby's Own Brewery (Eng) a micro-brewery (established 1988) based in Whitby, North Yorkshire. Brews: Merry Man's Mild.

White [R.] (Eng) a noted producer of soft drinks based in Northamptonshire.

White Adder (Eng) a 5.3% alc by vol. ale brewed by Mauldon's Ltd., Suffolk.

White Ale (Eng) a bottled ale brewed by Usher of Trowbridge. Part of the Vintage Ale Collection. see Ruby Ale, Tawny Ale.

White Amarillo (Eng) a 4.1% alc by vol. ale brewed by The Durham Brewery Ltd., County Durham.

White and Mackay (Scot) a blended Scotch whisky 43% alc by vol.

White Angel (Eng) a 4.1% alc by vol. ale brewed by The Durham Brewery Ltd., County Durham.

W

White Bear (Eng) a 4.2% alc by vol. seasonal wheat beer brewed by J.W. Lees, Middleton, Manchester, Lancashire. Available May and June.

White Beer (Ger) see Weisse and Weizen.

White Bishop (Eng) a 4.8% alc by vol. ale brewed by The Durham Brewery Ltd., County Durham.

White Blend (Austr) a white wine made from the Chenin blanc and Sémillon grapes by the Freycinet Estate in Western Australia.

White Boar Bitter (Eng) a bitter 3.8% alc by vol. brewed by Hambleton Brewery, near Thirsk, Yorkshire. See also Bull, Old Raby Ale, Stallion.

White Brewing C° (Eng) a brewery (established 1995). (Add): The 1066 Country Brewery, Pebsham Farm Ind Estate, Pebsham Lane, Bexhill-on-Sea, East Sussex TN40 2RZ. Brews: 1066 Country Bitter 4% alc by vol., Dark Mild 4% alc by vol. 'E'mail: whitebrewing@fsbdial.co.uk

White Bullet (Eng) a 4.4% alc by vol. ale brewed by The Durham Brewery Ltd., County Durham.

White Cabernet (USA) a Cabernet sauvignon version of the famous White Zinfandel.

White Cap (W.Ind) a brand of white rum produced by the Hansen Caribbean Rum C°., Ariba 38% alc by vol.

White Cap Lager (Afr) a lager beer 1038 O.G. brewed by the East African Breweries in Tanzania.

White Cargo (Cktl) 25mls (⅛ gill) dry gin, scoop of vanilla ice cream. Blend together in a blender with 2 dashes Sauternes and pour into a flute glass.

White Chianti (USA) see California White Chianti.

White Cocktail (Cktl) 60mls (½ gill) dry gin, 15mls (⅛ gill) anisette, 2 dashes Orange bitters. Stir well over ice, strain into a cocktail glass, add an olive and a squeeze of lemon peel juice on top.

White Cooler (Cktl) 1 measure Scotch whisky, 250mls (½ pint) ginger ale, juice of ½ orange, dash Angostura. Stir over ice, strain into a large highball glass and dress with strips of orange zest.

White Coronas (Sp) a dry white wine produced by Torres from 75% Garnacha blanca and 25% Parellada grapes.

White Crystal (Eng) a 4.3% alc by vol. ale brewed by The Durham Brewery Ltd., County Durham.

White Delight Retsina (Gre) the name given to white Retsina produced by Tsantali.

White Diamond (S.Afr) a leading brand of double-distilled cane spirit.

White Dragon (Eng) an 8.2% alc by vol. white cider from Symonds of Hereford. See also Black Dragon, Gold Dragon, Silver Dragon.

White Drummer (W.Ind) a brand of rum produced on the island of Trinidad by the Trinidad Distillers Ltd.

White Dwarf (Eng) a 4.3% alc by vol. ale brewed by Oakham Ales, Cambridgeshire.

White Elephant Cocktail (Cktl) 40mls (⅓ gill) dry gin, 25mls (⅛ gill) French vermouth, 1 egg white. Shake over ice and strain into a cocktail glass.

White Flash (Port) the name given to the paint mark placed on vintage Port bottles to denote the position the bottles should be binned.

White French (S.Afr) an alternative name for the Palomino grape. see Frandsdruif.

White Friar (Eng) a 5% alc by vol. ale brewed by Abbey Ales Ltd., Avon.

White Friar (Eng) a 4.5% alc by vol. ale brewed by The Durham Brewery Ltd., County Durham.

White Frontignan (Eng) an alternative name for the Muscat blanc à petits grains.

White Gem (Eng) a 3.9% alc by vol. ale brewed by The Durham Brewery Ltd., County Durham.

White Gold (Eng) a 4% alc by vol. golden ale brewed by The Durham Brewery Ltd., County Durham.

White Grenache (USA) a Grenache version of the famous White Zinfandel.

Whitehall Lane Winery (USA) a winery based between Rutherford and St. Helena, Napa Valley, California. Grape varieties: Cabernet sauvignon, Chardonnay, Chenin blanc and Sauvignon blanc. Produces varietal wines.

White Hanepoot (S.Afr) an alternative name for the Muscat of Alexandria grape.

White Heather (Scot) an 8 year old blended Scotch whisky produced by Campbell's (Distillery) Ltd., part of Pernod-Ricard. Also produce a 15 year old whisky 43% alc by vol. The company also owns the Aberlour-Glenlivet Malt distillery.

White Heather Cocktail (Cktl) ½ measure gin, ¼ measure Curaçao, ⅛ measure dry vermouth, ¼ measure pineapple juice, dash Pernod. Shake over ice and strain into a cocktail glass.

White Herald (Eng) a 3.9% alc by vol. ale brewed by The Durham Brewery Ltd., County Durham.

White Horse (Scot) a famous blended Scotch whisky produced by the White Horse Distillers Ltd. in Glasgow 43% alc by vol.

White Horse America's Cup Limited Edition (Scot) a 12 year old blended Scotch whisky produced by White Horse Distillers for the 1987 America's Cup 43% alc by vol.

White Horse Brewery C° Ltd (Eng) a brewery (established 2004). (Add): Unit 3, White Horse Business Park, Ware Road, Stanford in the Vale, Faringdon, Oxfordshire SN7 8NY. Brews: Oxfordshire Bitter 3.7% alc by vol., Wayland Smithy 4.4% alc by vol. 'E'mail: andy@whitehorsebrewery.com

White Horse Daisy (Cktl) 60mls (½ gill) White Horse Scotch whisky, 1 teaspoon Pernod, 2 dashes grenadine, 60mls (½ gill) lemon juice, egg white. Shake over ice, strain into a highball glass, top with soda water, serve with slices fresh fruit and a spoon.

White Horse Distillers (Scot) owns 3 distilleries: Craigellachie, Glen Elgin and Lagavulin. Now part of DCL. Produces White Horse (a noted blended Scotch whisky).

White Knight (Eng) a 5.5% alc by vol. winter warmer ale brewed by Castle Eden Brewery, County Durham.

White Knight (Eng) a 4.7% alc by vol. well-hopped

bitter ale brewed by Goff's Brewery, Winchcombe, Gloucestershire.

White Label (Eng) a 1% alc by vol. (low alcohol) bitter ale brewed by Whitbread.

White Label Rum (W.Ind) a light-coloured neutral rum, dry in taste with a very slight molasses flavour.

White Lady (Austr) the Aborigine name for clear methylated spirits.

White Lady (Cyp) the brand-name of a dry white wine produced by Etko in Limassol.

White Lady (Cktl) 1 measure gin, ½ measure cointreau, ½ measure lemon juice, dash egg white. Shake well over ice and strain into a cocktail glass.

White Lady Cocktail (Cktl) 40mls (⅓ gill) gin, 10mls (½ fl.oz) cream, 1 egg white, 2 dashes gomme syrup. Shake over ice and strain into a cocktail glass.

White Lightning (Eng) 7.5% alc by vol. strong white cider produced by Inch's, Winkleigh, Devon.

White Lightning (USA) the nickname for moonshine liquor, also the name for the patent still for corn whiskey.

White Lily (Cktl) ⅓ measure gin, ⅓ measure white rum, ⅓ measure cointreau, dash pastis. Stir over ice and strain into a cocktail glass.

White Lion (Cktl) 75mls white rum, 25mls raspberry syrup, 25mls Curaçao, juice ½ lemon. Shake over ice, strain into an ice-filled highball glass and decorate with fruits in season.

White Lion (Eng) a 4.3% alc by vol. ale brewed by Bobs Brewing Company Ltd., West Yorkshire.

White Lion Bitter (Eng) a cask-conditioned bitter ale 1036 O.G. brewed by the Woodforde Brewery, Norfolk for the White Lion Inn in Norwich.

White Liquor (USA) another name for moonshine.

Whitely [William] (Scot) a Scotch whisky distillery based at Pitlochry. Produces House of Lords and Kings Ransom blended Scotch whiskies (owned by Pernod-Ricard).

White Magic (Eng) a 7% alc by vol. strong ale brewed by The Durham Brewery Ltd., County Durham.

White Magic (Eng) a cider produced by Thatcher's in Somerset.

White Magic Light (W.Ind) the brand-name of a light rum distilled, blended and bottled by Caroni in Trinidad.

White Merlot (USA) a Merlot version of the famous White Zinfandel.

White Mountain Vineyards (USA) a winery based in New Hampshire. Produces varietal and French hybrid wines.

White Muscadel (S.Afr) a local name for the Muscadelle.

White Nights (S.Afr) the label for a methode cap classique sparkling wine (60% Chardonnay and 40% Pinot noir) produced by the Hazendal winery, Stellenbosch, Western Cape.

White Orchid (Cktl) 1.5 measures Absolut Vanilla ½ measure Cointreau, ¼ measure Bols white crème de cacao, ½ measure lemon juice, tspn gomme syrup and ice, stir and strain into a chilled martini glass and decorate with an edible flower.

White Peach (It) an 18% alc by vol. peach liqueur produced by Vaccari.

White Pinot (Austr) a local name for the Pinot chardonnay grape of France.

White Pinot (S.Afr) a local name for the Chenin blanc. *See also* Steen.

White Plush Cocktail (Cktl) 40mls (⅓ gill) Bourbon whiskey, 125mls (1gill) milk, 2 dashes gomme syrup. Shake over ice and strain into a collins glass.

White Port (Port) a Port wine made from white grapes only. Always blended (non-vintage), sweet or dry varieties produced.

White Rabbit (Eng) a seasonal spring ale brewed by the Mansfield Brewery, Littleworth, Mansfield, Notts.

White Riesling (Euro) the name often given to the true Riesling grape to distinguish it from all other hybrids and varietals.

White Riesling (USA) the true Riesling grape. Also known as the Johannisberger riesling.

White Rose (Cktl) ½ measure gin, ½ measure kirsch, dash gomme syrup, white of egg. Shake well over ice and strain into a cocktail glass.

White Rose Cocktail (Cktl) 20mls (⅙ gill) dry gin, juice ½ lime, 15mls (⅛ gill) orange juice, 2 dashes maraschino, 1 egg white. Shake over ice and strain into a cocktail glass.

White Rot (Eng) a disease that affects the ripening berries by splitting them, is treated with a copper/sodium bisulphide solution. (Fr) = ***Pourriture blanc***.

White Rum (W.Ind) a colourless rum which is light in body, produced in patent stills. 40% alc by vol. Produced in Cuba, Puerto Rico and other islands.

White Russian (Cktl) 20mls (¾ fl.oz) Kahlúa, 10mls (½ fl.oz) vodka. Build into an ice-filled old-fashioned glass and float cream on top.

White Sapphire (Eng) a 4.5% alc by vol. ale brewed by The Durham Brewery Ltd., County Durham.

White Satin [1] (Cktl) ³⁄₁₀ measure gin, ⁶⁄₁₀ measure white Curaçao, ¹⁄₁₀ measure lemon juice. Shake over ice and strain into a cocktail glass.

White Satin [2] (Cktl) ⅓ measure Tia Maria, ⅓ measure Galliano, ⅓ measure cream. Shake over ice and strain into a cocktail glass.

White Satin (Eng) a popular dry gin produced by Burnett of London. 37.5% alc by vol (part of Seagram).

White Scotch [The] (Scot) a colourless Scotch whisky.

White Scroll (Eng) a 4.8% alc by vol. ale brewed by the Newby Wyke Brewery, Lincolnshire.

White Sea (Eng) a 5.2% alc by vol. ale brewed by the Newby Wyke Brewery, Lincolnshire.

White Shield (Eng) a famous bottle-conditioned ale 1051 O.G. brewed by the Bass Worthington Brewery (a sediment beer).

White Star (USA) a label for Moët et Chandon (extra brut Champagne) solely for the American market.

W

White Star Brewery (Eng) a brewery (established 2003). (Add): 5 Radcliffe Court, Radcliffe Road, Southampton, Hampshire SO14 0PH. Brews: Capstone 6% alc by vol., Dark Aishorer 4.7% alc by vol., Merjestic 4.2% alc by vol., Royal Standard 4.3% alc by vol., Star Light 5% alc by vol., UXB 3.8% alc by vol. Website: http://www.whitestarbrewery.com 'E'mail: info@whitestarbrewery.com

Whitestone Vineyards (Eng) a vineyard based in Bovey Tracey, near Newton Abbot, south Devon. 0.7ha. Grape varieties: Madeleine angevine 25% and Müller-Thurgau 75%.

White Swan (Can) a brand of dry gin produced by Hiram Walker 40% alc by vol.

White Swan (Fr) a well-known local brand of brandy.

White Tequila (Mex) a colourless tequila matured in wax-lined vats, it is also known as Silver Tequila.

White Valette (Switz) *see* Lausannois.

White Velvet (Cktl) ⅙ measure white Curaçao, ⅔ measure dry gin, ⅙ measure pineapple juice. Shake over ice and strain into a cocktail glass.

White Velvet (Eng) a 4.2% alc by vol. ale brewed by The Durham Brewery Ltd., County Durham.

Whitewash (Eng) the ideal covering for cellars, but will not inhibit the mould **Rhacodium celare**.

White Way Cocktail (Cktl) ⅔ measure dry gin, ⅓ measure (white) crème de menthe. Shake over ice and strain into a cocktail glass.

Whiteways (Eng) a subsidiary of Allied-Domecq based at The Wimple, Exeter, Devon. Had a wide range of apple-based drinks which included cider and also produce British Sherry (closed in July 1989).

White Wedding (Eng) the label of a wine 0.5% alc by vol. from Frank Wright Murphy.

White Wheat Whiskey (Can) a grain whiskey produced in Ontario by Seagram 40% alc by vol.

White Whiskey (USA) an uncoloured whiskey which still has a whiskey taste.

White Wine (Eng) wine which may be made from white or red grapes or a mixture of both (all grape juice is colourless). (Bul) = bjalo vino, (Den) = hvidvin, (Fr) = vin blanc, (Ger) = weisse wein, (Gre) = oenos, (Ire) = fion geal, (It) = vino bianco, (Port) = vinho branco, (Rum) = vin alb, (Rus) = belloe vino, (Sp) = vino blanco, (Wal) = gwyn gwin.

White Wine Cup (Cup) 3 bottles dry white wine, 1 bottle dry vermouth, 1 bottle lemonade, 1 orange and lemon (sliced), chill all ingredients, mix together, add fruit and mint.

White Wine Punch (Punch) 3 bottles dry white wine, ½ bottle brandy, 1 bottle dry Sherry, 400mls (¾ pint) lemon juice, 250mls (½ pint) gomme syrup, 250mls (½ pint) strong tea. Mix with ice in a large punch bowl, add a syphon of soda water and decorate with cucumber slices.

White Wing (W.Ind) a noted brand of rum produced in Jamaica by the Wray and Nephew Group.

White Witch (Cktl) (Non-alc) dissolve 1 teaspoon of honey in a little hot water, add ⅓ measure lemon juice, ⅓ measure grapefruit juice, ⅓ measure pineapple juice, ½ egg white. Shake well over ice, strain into a cocktail glass and top with a slice of lemon.

White Witch (Eng) a 4.5% alc by vol. ale brewed by the Wizard Brewery, Warwickshire.

White Witch Cocktail (Cktl) 25mls (1fl.oz) white rum, 10mls (½ fl.oz) white crème de cacao, 10mls (½ fl.oz) Cointreau, juice ½ lime. Shake over ice, strain into an ice-filled highball glass. Top with soda, stir, decorate with a slice of lime and mint sprig.

White Wych (Eng) a 4% alc by vol. golden cask ale brewed by Wychwood Brewery, at Eagle Maltings, Witney, Oxfordshire (available in July).

White Zinfandel (USA) a 'blanc de noirs', the name given to a varietal pink-coloured wine produced from the black Zinfandel grape by preventing skin contact with the juice. Created in 1972 by Bob Trinchero at Sutter Home.

Whitley Neill (Eng) a distillery based in London and noted for its London Dry Gin 42% alc by vol.

Whitstable Bay (Eng) a 4.1% alc by vol beer (draught and bottled) brewed from Golding hops a wineter pearl malting barley by the Shepherd Neame Brewery, Kent.

Whitstone Vineyards (Eng) a winery (established 1974) based at Bovey Tracey, near Newton Abbot, South Devon. (1.5acres) originally planted with 700 Müller-Thurgau and 300 Madeleine angevine vines.

Whitsunday (Austr) a natural spring mineral water brand. Mineral contents (milligrammes per litre): Sodium 17mg/l, Calcium 6mg/l, Magnesium 11mg/l, Potassium 1mg/l, Bicarbonates 49mg/l, Chlorides 29mg/l, Sulphates 2mg/l.

Whittards of Chelsea (Eng) an old tea firm. Produces a wide range of fine teas including Spice Imperial (clove, orange peel flavour), Lotus Flower (lotus blossom flavour) and Mango Indica (mango blossom flavour).

Whittington Brewery (Eng) a brewery (established 2003). (Add): Newent, Gloucestershire GL18 1LS. Brews: Cats Whiskers 4.2% alc by vol., Nine Lives 3.6% alc by vol. Website: http://www.whittingtonbrewery.co.uk 'E'mail: info@whittingtonbrewery.co.uk

Whizbang Cooler (Cktl) 60mls (½ gill) dry gin, 250mls (½ pint) ginger ale. Stir in a highball glass with lump of ice, top with a dash of peppermint and sprig of mint.

Whizz Bang Cocktail (Cktl) 40mls (⅓ gill) Scotch whisky, 20mls (⅙ gill) French vermouth, 2 dashes orange bitters, 2 dashes grenadine, 2 dashes Pernod. Stir well over ice, strain into a cocktail glass with a squeeze of lemon peel juice.

Whole Berry (S.Afr) a red wine (Cabernet sauvignon) produced by the Springfield Estate, Robertson, Western Cape.

Wholeberry (S.Afr) the label for a red wine (Cabernet sauvignon) produced by the BWC Wines winery, Stellenbosch, Western Cape.

Whole Milk (Eng) denotes milk which has had nothing removed. *See also* Skimmed Milk.

Wholesale Dealer's Licence (U.K.) a licence needed

to sell, at any time, wines or spirits in quantities of 9litres (2gallons) [1 case] or more, or beers in quantities of 20.25litres (4½ gallons) or more. Is supplied by H.M. Customs and Excise.

Wholesome Stout (Eng) a 1045 O.G./4.6% alc by vol. ale from the Wye Valley Brewery, Hereford. Available in March (part of the Dorothy Goodbody's Seasonal Ales).

Whoosh (Wal) a 3.7% alc by vol. session bitter brewed by The Castle Brewery, Carmarthen Breweries Limited, 40A Rhosmaen Street, Landeilo, Carmarthenshire.

Who Put The Lights Out? (Eng) a strong, single hopped cask-conditioned amber ale brewed by micro-brewer Skinner's of Truro, Cornwall to celebrate the 1999 eclipse of the sun on August 11th 1999.

Who's Shout (Eng) *see* Shout.

Whustlemas (Eng) a Christmas ale brewed by the Beer Engine brewery, Exeter.

Why Not Cocktail (Cktl) ⅓ measure dry gin, ⅓ measure apricot brandy, ⅓ measure French vermouth, dash lemon juice. Shake over ice and strain into a cocktail glass.

Whyte and Mackay Group (Scot) a blended Scotch whisky (established 1844) produced by a company of same name. (Add): Dalmore House, 310 St. Vincent Street, Glasgow, Lanarkshire G2 5RG. Also a 12 year old de luxe Scotch whisky version produced in a gold pot-still decanter, a 21 year old in a 'Harrods' whisky decanter 40% alc by vol. and Whyte and Mackay Supreme. 43% alc by vol. Website: http://www.whyteandmackay.co.uk

Whyte and Mackay Distillers Ltd (Scot) Scotch whisky producers. Own three distilleries: Fettercairn, Dalmore and Tournintoul. A subsidiary of the Whyte and Mackay Group. Website: http://www.whyteandmackay.co.uk

Whytingham (Port) a vintage Port shipper. Vintages: 2003.

Wicked Hathern Brewery (Eng) a micro-brewery based near Loughborough, Leicestershire.

Wicked Winter Ale (USA) the label of a beer with a raspberry aroma from Pete's Brewing Company.

Wicked Women (Eng) a 4.8% alc by vol. ale brewed by the Brewster Brewing C°. Ltd., Leicestershire.

Wickenden Vineyard (Eng) a 1.2ha vineyard based at Cliveden Road, Taplow, Buckinghamshire. Grape varieties: Müller-Thurgau 49%, Reichensteiner 39%, Sauvignon blanc 11% and Scheurebe 1%.

Wicker (Ger) village (Anb): Rheingau. (Ber): Johannisberg. (Gro): Daubhaus. (Vins): Goldene Luft, König Wilhelmsberg, Nonnberg, Stein.

Wicket & Willow (Eng) a 4.2% alc by vol. pale coloured cask-conditioned bitter ale brewed by Mansfield Brewery. Part of their Chadburns cask bitter range.

Wicket Bitter (Eng) a 4.3% alc by vol. strong dark malty bitter ale brewed by Hale and Hearty Brewery in Surrey.

Wickford Vineyards (USA) a winery based in North Kingstown. Produces French hybrid wines.

Wickham Vineyard (Eng) a vineyard in Sheffield, Hampshire that produces dry white wines.

Wicküler (Ger) a 4.9% alc by vol. bottled pilsner brewed by the Rheinisch-Bergische Brauerei, Cologne.

Wickwar Brewing C° Ltd (Eng) a brewery. (Add): The Old Brewery, Station Road, Wickwar, Wotton-under-Edge, Gloucestershire GL12 8NB. Brews: Autumnale (S) 4.6% alc by vol., Bob 4% alc by vol., Coopers 3.5% alc by vol., Cotswold Way 4.2% alc by vol., IKB 4.5% alc by vol., Mr Peretts 5.9% alc by vol., Rite Flanker 4.3% alc by vol., Spring Ale (S) 3.8% alc by vol., Station Porter 6.1% alc by vol., Sunny Daze 4.2% alc by vol. Website: http://www.wickwarbrewing.co.uk 'E'mail: bob@wickwarbrewing.co.uk

Widdern (Ger) village (Anb): Württemberg. (Ber): Kocher-Jagst-Tauber. (Gro): Kocherberg. (Vin): Hofberg.

Wide River Reserve (S.Afr) the label for noble late harvest wine produced by the Robertson Co-operative Winery, Robertson, Western Cape.

Widerkomm (Ger) a large glass used for ceremonial feasts in the middle ages.

Wide Yeast (S.Afr) the label for a white wine (Chardonnay) produced by the Springfield Estate winery, Robertson, Western Cape.

Widget (Eng) a small device (originally introduced in cans of Guinness) now in many canned beers to make them appear more like a pub '*draught beer*' when poured.

Widmer Amberbier (USA) a 5.2% alc by vol. deep amber coloured, aromatic, top-fermented, bottled amber beer brewed by Widmer Brothers, Portland, Oregon.

Widmer Blackbier (USA) a 6.5% alc by vol. top-fermented, bottled special beer brewed by Widmer Brothers Brewing C°., Portland, Oregon. Similar to a porter in style.

Widmer Brothers Brewing C°. (USA) a brewery (established 1984). (Add): 929 N Russell, Portland, Oregon OR97227. Brews: German style beers including Widmer Hefeweizen, Widmer Weizen, Widmer Alt, Widmer Amberbier, Widmer Blackbier, Widmer Widberry, plus a Bock beer and Oktoberfest. Website: http://www.widmer.com 'E'mail: webmail@widmer.com

Widmer Hefeweizen (USA) a 4.3% alc by vol. top-fermented, unfiltered, bottled wheat beer brewed by Widmer Brothers Brewing C°., Portland, Oregon.

Widmer's Wine Cellars (USA) leading wine producers (established 1883) of the Finger Lakes region of the New York State.

Widmer Widberry (USA) a 4.5% alc by vol. top-fermented, fruity bottled special beer brewed by Widmer Brothers Brewing C°., Portland, Oregon.

Widow Clicquot (Fr) a lady who invented the art of removing the sediment from a bottle of Champagne by remuage and dégorgement. *see* Veuve Clicquot.

Widow's Dream (Cktl) 25mls (⅛ gill) Bénédictine, 1

egg. Shake over ice, strain into a cocktail glass and float a little cream on top.

Widow's Kiss Cocktail (Cktl) ¼ measure Bénédictine, ¼ measure Chartreuse, ½ measure Calvados, dash Angostura. Shake over ice and strain into a cocktail glass.

Wid Wheat (Eng) a 4.1% alc by vol. beer brewed by the York Brewery Company Ltd., North Yorkshire.

Wiebelsberg (Fr) a 12ha. A.C. Alsace Grand Cru vineyard at Andlau, Bas-Rhin.

Wie Chuan Mineral Water (Chi) a natural spring mineral water brand.

Wieckse Witte (Hol) a 5% alc by vol. top-fermented, bottled, cloudy wheat beer brewed by De Ridder Brouwerij, Maastricht. Contains spices and citrus peel.

Wiedemann Brewery (USA) a brewery in Newport. Brews Royal Amber beer.

Wiedeman Vineyard (USA) a vineyard based west of Santa Clara County, California. Grape variety: Zinfandel.

Wieden (Aus) a vineyard site on the banks of the River Danube in the Kremstal region.

Wiederkehr Winery (USA) a winery based in Altus. Produces French hybrid wines.

Wiege (Aus) a vineyard site based on the banks of the River Kamp situated in the Kamptal region.

Wieland (Aus) a vineyard site on the banks of the River Danube in the Kremstal region.

Wielemans Brasserie (Bel) a brewery based in Brussels. Brews: Coronation Ale.

Weilkopolanka (Pol) a sparkling natural spring mineral water. Mineral contents (milligrammes per litre): Sodium 12mg/l, Calcium 110mg/l, Magnesium 16mg/l, Potassium 2.5mg/l, Chlorides 45mg/l, Sulphates 100mg/l.

Weilk Pieniawa (Pol) a sparkling natural spring mineral water. Mineral contents (milligrammes per litre): Sodium 73mg/l, Calcium 230.54mg/l, Magnesium 35mg/l, Potassium 43.3mg/l, Bicarbonates 1103.19mg/l, Chlorides 7.08mg/l, Sulphates 32mg/l, Fluorides 0.38mg/l.

Wiemer Winery (USA) a winery based in the Finger Lakes region. Grape varieties: Chardonnay and Riesling. Produces varietal wines.

Wien (Aus) the Austrian spelling of the Vienna wine region (731ha) lying on the banks of the river Danube. Soil: gravel, loam, loess, slate. Main grape varieties: white (Chardonnay, Gemischter satz, Grüner veltliner, Müller-Thurgau, Pinot blanc, Riesling, Welschriesling), red (Blauburger, Pinot noir, St. Laurent, Zweigelt). Villages: Alsegg, Bisamberg, Grinzing, Kahlenberg, Mauer, Neustift, Nussberg, Oberlaa, Sievering.

Wiener (Ger) a copper-coloured beer produced in Munich.

Wiener Ale (Den) a low alcohol, light beer brewed by the Wiibroe Brewery in Elsinore.

Wieninger (Aus) a winery (14ha) based in the Wien region. (Add): Stammersdorfer Strasse 80, 1210 Wien. Grape varieties: Bouvier, Cabernet sauvignon, Chardonnay, Grüner veltliner, Merlot, Müller-Thurgau, Pinot blanc, Pinot noir, Riesling, Sauvignon blanc, Welschriesling, Zweigelt. Produces a range of wine styles and noted Heurige.

Wiers Patent Lazy Tongs (Eng) a patent nineteenth century corkscrew that operated on the expanding arm method.

Wiesbaden (Ger) an old vineyard region around the town of the same name in the Rheingau.

Wiesberg (Ger) vineyard (Anb): Nahe. (Ber): Schloss Böckelheim. (Gro): Rosengarten. (Vil): Rüdesheim.

Wiese and Krohn (Port) vintage Port shippers. Vintages: 1927, 1934, 1935, 1947, 1950, 1952, 1960, 1967, 1970.

Wiesenbronn (Ger) village (Anb): Franken. (Ber): Steigerwald. (Gro): Schlossberg. (Vin): Wachhügel.

Wiesentaler (Ger) a sparkling natural spring mineral water from Waghäusel-Wiesental. Mineral contents (milligrammes per litre): Sodium 18.6mg/l, Calcium 180mg/l, Magnesium 35.2mg/l, Bicarbonates 451mg/l, Sulphates 162mg/l, Nitrates <0.3mg/l.

Wiesloch (Ger) village (Anb): Baden. (Ber): Badische Bergstrasse/Kraichgau. (Gro): Mannaberg. (Vins): Bergwäldle, Hagenich, Spitzenberg.

Wig & Pen (Austr) a brewery. (Add): Canberra House Arcade, Alinga Street, Canberra 2601. Brews a range of beers. Website: http://www.wigandpen.com.au

Wight Crystal (Eng) the name of a still and carbonated spring water bottled at source in Newport, Isle of Wight by Osel Enterprises.

Wight Spirit (Eng) a 5% alc by vol. ale brewed by the Ventnor Brewery Ltd., Isle of Wight.

Wight Winter Ale (Eng) a 5% alc by vol. winter ale brewed by the Yates Brewery, Isle of Wight.

Wight Winter Warmer (Eng) a 6.8% alc by vol. cask ale brewed by the Hartridge Island Brewery, Newport, Isle of Wight. see Nipper, Newport Best Bitter.

Wigwam (Fr) a method of planting vines in the Rhône to withstand the Mistral winds, also known as the gobelet system.

Wiibroe Brewery (Den) a brewery based in Elsinore. Owned by the United Breweries. Noted for Nanok 6.5% alc by vol. Wiener Ale and Dansk L.A. a full-bodied, low alcohol lager 0.9% alc by vol.

Wijn (Hol) wine.

Wijnfles (Hol) wine bottle.

Wijngaard (Hol) vineyard.

Wijngoed (Hol) winery.

Wijnhandel (Hol) wine shop.

Wijnkaart (Hol) wine list.

Wijnkoeler (Hol) wine cooler/Champagne bucket.

Wijnkooperij (Hol) wine merchants.

Wijnoogst (Hol) vintage. See also Jaargang.

Wijnstok (Hol) vine. See also Wingerd.

Wijnwater (Hol) holy water.

Wilbroe Bryggeri (Den) a brewery. (Add): HC Orstedsvej, Helsingor DK-3000. Brews a range of beers and lager. Website: http://www.wilbroe.dk 'E'mail: salg@wilbroe.dk

W

Wildalp (Aus) a still and sparkling natural spring mineral water from Seisensteinquelle. Mineral contents (milligrammes per litre): Sodium 1.97mg/l, Calcium 44.6mg/l, Magnesium 12.8mg/l, Potassium 0.3mg/l, Bicarbonates 181mg/l, Chlorides 2.87mg/l, Sulphates 14.7mg/l, Fluorides <0.1mg/l, Nitrates 3.63mg/l, Oxygen 9.6mg/l. pH 7.91

Wildbacher (Aus) a black grape variety, grown in Styria. Also known as Blauer Wildbacher.

Wildbadquelle (Ger) a natural spring mineral water from Wildbadquelle, Scwäbisch Hall. Mineral contents (milligrammes per litre): Sodium 40mg/l, Calcium 177mg/l, Magnesium 44mg/l, Potassium 2mg/l, Bicarbonates 197mg/l, Chlorides 110mg/l, Sulphates 214mg/l.

Wild Beer (Bel) see Lambic Beer.

Wild Beer (USA) a description of the condition when beer is served too warm and CO_2 gas escapes from the beer too quickly causing it to foam violently.

Wild Blonde (Eng) a 4.4% alc by vol. ale brewed by the South Hams Brewery, Devon.

Wild Blonde (Eng) a 4.5% alc by vol. ale from Wild's Brewery, Slaithwaite, Huddersfield, West Yorkshire.

Wild Boar (Eng) a 5.5% alc by vol. winter warmer ale brewed by the Mansfield Brewery, Nottingham.

Wild Boar (Eng) a 5.2% alc by vol. ale brewed by the Slaughter House Brewery Ltd., Warwickshire.

Wild Boar (S.Afr) a blended wine from a range of red grapes produced by the Akkerdal Estate, Franschhoek, Western Cape.

Wild Boar Bitter (Eng) a best bitter beer 1039 O.G. brewed by the Trough Brewery in Bradford, Yorkshire.

Wildboarcloagh (Eng) a natural spring mineral water from Wildboarcloagh. Mineral contents (milligrammes per litre): Sodium 8.8mg/l, Calcium 23.5mg/l, Magnesium 12.5mg/l, Potassium 1.1mg/l, Bicarbonates 227mg/l, Chlorides 26mg/l, Sulphates 13mg/l, Nitrates 3.2mg/l. pH 7.3

Wild Brew (Eng) a 4% alc by vol. drink produced by Whitbread from vodka, cranberry juice and caffeine.

Wild Cat (Scot) a 5.1% alc by vol. ale brewed by The Cairngorm Brewery C°. Ltd., Inverness.

Wild Chicory Coffee (Eng) the chicory roots are roasted in an oven, ground finely and then brewed for ten minutes.

Wild Dog Winery (Austr) a winery (established 1982). (Add): Warragul-Korumburra Road, Victoria. Grape varieties include Chardonnay, Shiraz.

Wild Duck Creek Estate (Austr) a winery based near Mount Ida, Heathcote, Victoria. Label: Duck Muck.

Wildekrans Estate (S.Afr) a winery (established 1993) based in Walker Bay, Western Cape. 40ha. Grape varieties: Cabernet sauvignon, Chardonnay, Chenin blanc, Merlot, Pinotage, Sauvignon blanc, Sémillon,

Shiraz. Label: Caresse Marine. Website: http://www.wildekranswines.co.za

Wildenberg (Ger) vineyard (Anb): Württemberg. (Ber): Württembergisch Unterland. (Gro): Salzberg. (Vil): Grantschen.

Wilderer's Distillery (S.Afr) a distillery based on the Franschhoek Road between Paarl and Simondium, Western Cape. Produces a range of grappas (Moscato and Pinotage) and eaux-de-vies.

Wild Ferment (Eng) is caused by a must with natural yeasts (no extra added) or other micro-organisms present either on the raw material present in the fermentation vessel or those that have landed on the must during fermentation.

Wild Fermentation (W.Ind) a very quick fermentation caused when dunder is added to the molasses, causes natural yeasts to multiply rapidly, also called spontaneous fermentation.

Wildfire (S.Afr) the label for a range of wines produced by the Cape Vineyards winery, Rawsonville, Western Cape.

Wildgrafenberg (Ger) vineyard (Anb): Nahe. (Ber): Schloss Böckelheim. (Gro): Paradiesgarten. (Vil): Kirschroth.

Wild Horse Winery (USA) a winery based in Paso Robles, San Luis Obispo, California. (Add): 1437 Wild Horse Winery Court, Templeton, CA 93465. Grape varieties: Cabernet sauvignon, Merlot, Petite syrah, Sangiovese, Syrah, Zinfandel. Website: http://www.wildhorsewinery.com

Wild Horse Valley (USA) an A.V.A. of Napa Valley since 1988. 40ha. Grape varieties include Pinot noir, Chardonnay, Riesling, Roussanne, Viognier.

Wild Irish Rose (USA) a 'pop wine' from the Canadaigua Wine Company in New York State.

Wildly Wicked (S.Afr) the label for a white wine (Chenin blanc 84% and Sauvignon blanc 16% blend) produced by the Stellar Winery, Olifants River, Western Cape.

Wild One (Eng) a 4.1% alc by vol. ale brewed by the Wilds Brewery Ltd., Herefordshire.

Wild Pig (USA) a brand name for a French wine produced by the Gabriel Meffre group for the American market. The name designed to appeal to the Americans in place of the complicated French label names!

Wild Redhead (Eng) a 4.5% alc by vol. ale from Wild's Brewery, Slaithwaite, Huddersfield, West Yorkshire.

Wild Rover (Eng) a 5.6% alc by vol. ale from Tetley-Walker, Warrington, Lancs.

Wildsau (Ger) vineyard (Anb): Rheingau. (Ber): Johannisberg. (Gro): Steinmacker. (Vil): Martinsthal.

Wildsau (Ger) a vineyard within the village Martinsthal. 34.9ha. (12.3%) is proposed to be classified as Erstes Gewächs.

Wildsberg (Ger) a natural spring mineral water brand.

Wild's Bitter (Eng) a 3.8% alc by vol. bitter ale from Wild's Brewery, Slaithwaite, Huddersfield, West Yorkshire.

Wild's Brewery (Eng) a brewery (established 1994). (Add): Slaithwaite, Huddersfield, West Yorkshire. Brewed: Wild Redhead, Wild's Bitter, Wild Blonde, Wild Thing, Wild Town, Wild West. Closed in 1996 and now known as Barnfield Brewery.

Wilds Brewery Ltd (Eng) a brewery (established 2005). (Add): Unit 6, Whitehall Park Ind Estate, Weobly, Hereford, Herefordshire HR4 8QE. Brews: Night 4.5% alc by vol., SX 4.2% alc by vol., Wild One 4.1% alc by vol.

Wild Strawberry Brandy (Euro) a French, German or Swiss fruit brandy made from wild mountain strawberries 44.5% alc by vol.

Wild Strawberry Liqueur (Fr) a liqueur made by steeping wild strawberries in brandy 30% alc by vol.

Wildtal (Ger) village (Anb): Baden. (Ber): Breisgau. (Gro): Burg Zähringen. (Vin): Sonnenberg.

Wild Thing (Eng) a 5% alc by vol. beer from Wild's Brewery, Slaithwaite, Huddersfield, West Yorkshire.

Wild Town (Eng) a 3.6% alc by vol. beer from Wild's Brewery, Slaithwaite, Huddersfield, West Yorkshire.

Wild Turkey (USA) the brand-name of an 8 year old straight Bourbon whiskey at 50.5% alc by vol. and a liqueur Bourbon whiskey at 40% alc by vol. produced by Austin Nichols, Lawrenceburg, Kentucky.

Wild West (Eng) a 4.1% mild ale from Wild's Brewery, Slaithwaite, Huddersfield, West Yorkshire.

Wildwood Vineyard (Austr) a winery (established 1983). (Add): St. John's Lane, Bulla, Victoria. Grape varieties: Chardonnay, Cabernet franc, Cabernet sauvignon, Pinot noir, Shiraz.

Wildwood Vineyard (USA) a winery (125ha) based near Kenwood, Sonoma Valley, California. Grape varieties: Cabernet sauvignon and Chardonnay. Produces varietal wines.

Wild Yeasts (Eng) *Kloeckera apiculata / Pichia membranaefaciens* the prolific micro-flora that are present in the bloom of the grape. They are aerobic and start the first violent fermentation. Destroyed by SO_2 or heat treatment.

Wiley Vineyard (USA) the label for a red wine (Pinot noir) produced by the Woodenhead winery, Anderson Valley, California.

Wilhelmsberg (Ger) vineyard (Anb): Baden. (Ber): Badische Bergstrasse/Kraichgau. (Gro): Mannaberg. (Vil): Nussloch.

Wilhelmsberg (Ger) vineyard (Anb): Franken. (Ber): Maindreieck. (Gro): Hofrat. (Vin): Kitzingen.

Wilhelmsquelle Heilwasser (Ger) a natural spring mineral water. Mineral contents (milligrammes per litre): Sodium 645mg/l, Calcium 645mg/l, Magnesium 82.7mg/l, Potassium 33mg/l, Chlorides 794mg/l, Sulphates 1820mg/l, Fluorides 0.84mg/l, Iron 1.52mg/l.

Wilhelmstaler Brunnen (Ger) a natural spring mineral water. Mineral contents (milligrammes per litre): Sodium 91.4mg/l, Calcium 310mg/l, Magnesium 111mg/l, Bicarbonates 1347mg/l, Chlorides 92.7mg/l, Sulphates 236mg/l. Website: http://www.hassia.com

Wilkins (Phil) a natural spring mineral water brand.

Willakenzie Estate (USA) a winery based in Yamhill, Willamette Valley, Oregon. Grape varieties: Pinot blanc, Pinot gris, Pinot noir. Labels: Kiana, Pierre Leon.

Willamette Valley (USA) a cool, hilly region in Oregon with 396ha of vineyards, has many fine wineries based there.

Willamette Valley Vineyards (USA) vineyards based in Turner, Willamette Valley, Oregon. Grape varieties: Chardonnay, Müller-Thurgau, Pinot gris, Pinot noir, Riesling.

Willespie (Austr) a winery based in the Margaret River region in Western Australia. Grape varieties include: Cabernet sauvignon.

Willet Distillery (USA) a Bourbon whiskey distillery based south-west of Frankfort, Kentucky.

William and Mary (Eng) a beer brewed by the Cornish Brewery Company for the Dutch market to commemorate the tercentenary of the Glorious Revolution.

William and Robin (Cktl) ⅓ measure William Christ, ⅓ measure orange Curaçao, ⅓ lemon juice, dash orange bitters. Shake over ice, strain into a cocktail glass, decorate with a slice of lemon and a cherry.

William Everson Wines (S.Afr) a winery (established 2001) based in Paarl, Western Cape. Grape varieties: Chardonnay, Pinotage, Shiraz. Produces varietal wines.

William Grant and Sons (Scot) a famous Scotch whisky distillery (established 1887) based at Dufftown, Banffshire. (Add): Strathclyde Business Park, Phoenix Crescent, Bellshill, Lanarkshire ML4 3AN. Produces Highland and Lowland Malt whiskies and blended Scotch whiskies. *see* Glenfiddich, Grants Royal, Hendrick's, Monkey Shoulder, Standfast, The Balvenie. *See also* Oak-Aged Ale, Quality Spirits UK Ltd. Website: http://www.glenfiddich.com 'E'mail: pr@wgrant.com

William Hill (N.Z) a 7ha winery. (Add): Dunstan Road, Alexandra, RD1, Central Otago. Grape varieties: Chardonnay, Gewürztraminer, Riesling, Sauvignon blanc, Pinot noir.

William Hill Winery (USA) *see* Hill Winery.

Williamine (Fr) (Switz) a pear-flavoured liqueur, usually an alcool blanc (eau-de-vie).

Williamine (Switz) 43% alc by vol. pear-flavoured liqueur from Distillerie Morand, Martigny, Valais. Also a Réserve at 48% alc by vol. Réserve Special and 100 year old at 45% alc by vol.

Williamine Morand (Switz) an eau-de-vie distillery (established 1889) based in Valais.

William Lawson's (Scot) a blended Scotch whisky produced by the Lawson [William] Distillery Ltd., Coatbridge and MacDuff.

William of Orange (Hol) the Dutch king who in 1688 became King of England and so made gin popular to the English.

William Saintot (Fr) a Champagne producer. (Add): 4, Rue Charles de Gaulle, 51160 Avenay val d'Or.

Récoltant-Manipulant. Produces non-vintage wines. Website: http://www.champagne-william-saintot.com

Williams and Humbert (Sp) a Sherry house that belongs to the Rumasa organisation. Bodega is at Nuno del Canas 1, Jerez de la Frontera. Sherry labels include: Canasta Cream, Dos Cortados, Dry Sack, Pando, Tintilla and Walnut Brown.

Williamsbirnen (Ger) a liqueur made from Poire Williams.

Williams Selyem (USA) a winery (established 1981) based in the Russian River Valley, Sonoma County, California. (Add): 6575 Westside Road, Healdsburg, California 95448. Also has vineyards in the Sonoma Coast. Grape varieties include: Pinot noir. Label: Allen Vineyard. Website: http://www.williamsseylem.com

Willmes Press (Euro) computerised press that works using an inflatable bag/balloon which presses the grapes against the slatted sides of the press (also rotates). *See also* Basket Press, Vaslin Press.

Willmes Schlauchpresse (Ger) *see* Willmes Press.

Willoughbys Ltd. (Eng) based in Manchester they produce Manchester Dry Gin 40% alc by vol.

Willow Bridge (Austr) a winery based in Western Australia. Grape varieties include: Cabernet sauvignon, Merlot. Label: Dragonfly.

Willowbrook (N.Z) the label used by Kindale Wines, Marlborough, South Island.

Willow Creek (Eng) a perry produced by CWF.

Willow Creek Vineyard (Austr) a winery (established 1989). (Add): 166 Balnarring Road, Merricks North, Victoria. Grape varieties: Cabernet sauvignon, Chardonnay.

Willow Creek Vineyard (USA) a vineyard based near Paso Robles, San Luis Obispo, California. Grape variety: Zinfandel. Vinified at the Monterey Peninsula Winery.

Willowside Vineyards (USA) a winery based in Santa Rosa, Sonoma County, California. Grape varieties: Chardonnay, Gewürztraminer, Pinot noir and Zinfandel. Produces varietal wines.

Will Rogers Cocktail (Cktl) 25mls (⅛ gill) dry gin, 3 dashes orange juice, 2 dashes French vermouth, dash Cointreau. Shake well over ice and strain into a cocktail glass.

Willsbach (Ger) village (Anb): Württemberg. (Ber): Württembergisch Unterland. (Gro): Salzberg. (Vins): Dieblesberg, Zeilberg.

Wills Resolve (Eng) a 4.6% alc by vol. ale brewed by the Sharps Brewery, Cornwall.

Willyabrup (Austr) a district in the Margaret River region of Western Australia.

Willyabrup Winery (Austr) a winery based in the Margaret River district of Western Australia.

Willy Gisselbrecht et Fils (Fr) an Alsace wine producer. (Add): 67650 Dambach-la-Ville. 15.5ha.

Willy's Brewery (Eng) a brewery (established 1989). (Add): 17 High Cliff Road, Cleethorpes, South Humberside DN35 8RQ. Brews: Burcom Bitter 4.2% alc by vol., Coxswains Special Bitter 4.9% alc by vol., Last Resort 4.3% alc by vol., Old Groyne 6.2% alc by vol., Original Bitter 3.9% alc by vol., Thoroughbred 4.5% alc by vol.

Willy's Revenge (Eng) a 4.7% alc by vol. ale brewed by Bishop's Brewery, London.

Willy's Wheat Beer (Eng) a 5.3% alc by vol. wheat beer brewed by the Springhead Brewery, Nottinghamshire.

Wilmont Wines (USA) a winery based in Schwenksville, Pennsylvania, produces hybrid wines.

Wilmot's Hop Cone (Eng) a cask-conditioned bitter ale 1042 O.G. brewed by the Godson-Chudley Brewery in London.

Wilsford Winery (Austr) a winery based in the Barossa Valley, South Australia, produces varietal wines.

Wilson Brewery (Eng) Watney's Manchester brewery. Has 720 public houses. Noted for cask-conditioned beers and keg Newton Bitter 1032 O.G. Grand Northern 1036 O.G. and bottled Wembley 1036 O.G. Top Brass Lager 1033 O.G.

Wilson Distillers (N.Z) a distillery based at Dunedin, produces 45 South and Wilsons Matured Blend whiskies.

Wilson's (Austr) a winery. (Add): Woods Hill Vineyard, Woods Hill Road, Summertown, South Australia. Produces Wilson's Brut sparkling wine.

Wilt (Eng) *see* **Verticillium wilt** (a fungal disease that attacks hops).

Wilting (Ind) a term used to describe the drying out of the tea leaf, also known as withering.

Wiltingen (Ger) village (Anb): Mosel-Saar-Ruwer. (Ber): Saar-Ruwer. (Gro): Scharzberg. (Vins): Braune Kupp, Braunfels, Gottesfuss, Hölle, Klosterberg, Kupp, Rosenberg, Sandberg.

Wiltshire Bitter (Eng) a cask-conditioned (and keg) special bitter 1036 O.G. brewed by the Gibbs Mew Brewery in Salisbury, Wiltshire.

Wiltshire Brewery Company (Eng) a brewery based in Tisbury, Wiltshire. Noted for Old Stonehenge Bitter 1041 O.G. Regency and Weedkiller beers.

Wilyabrup Winery (Austr) a winery based in Western Australia. Produces varietal and dessert wines.

Wimbledon (Cktl) 1 measure gin, ½ measure Bénédictine, 1 measure lemon juice, dash grenadine, dash Fraise, dash egg white. Shake over ice, strain into a cocktail glass, dress the rim of glass with sugar and a sugar-frosted strawberry.

Wimbledon Winner (Cktl)(Non-alc) 500mls (1pint) iced tea, juice ½ lemon, 50grms (2ozs) sliced strawberries. Leave to stand overnight, strain, decorate with strawberries rolled in castor sugar.

Wimmental (Ger) village (Anb): Württemberg. (Ber): Württembergisch Unterland. (Gro): Salzberg. (Vin): Altenberg.

Wimmer-Czerny (Aus) a winery based in Fels am Wagram, Donauland. (Add): Obere Marktstrasse 37, 3481 Fels am Wagram. Grape varieties: Chardonnay, Pinot blanc, Pinot noir, Riesling,

W

Roter veltliner, Traminer, Zweigelt. Produces a range of white and red wines.

Winalyzer (USA) a kit containing 9 small bottles of different characteristic essences found in wine tasting. Produced in North Carolina by Oenophilia.

Wincarnis Tonic Wine (Eng) the brand-name of a beef and malt-based tonic wine 14% alc by vol. Produced by R & C Vintners, Carrow, Norwich.

Winchelsea Estate (Austr) a winery. (Add): Lorne Deans, Marsh Road, Winchelsea, Victoria. Grape varieties include Chardonnay.

Wincheringen (Ger) village (Anb): Mosel-Saar-Ruwer. (Ber): Obermosel. (Gro): Gipfel. (Vins): Burg Warsberg, Fuchsloch.

Winchester Arms (Eng) a micro-brewery based in Buckland, Portsmouth. Brews: Buckland Best Bitter.

Winchester Quart (USA) an imperial quart measure used in the USA.

Wind Chimes Cocktail (Cktl) 35mls (1½ fl.ozs) Beefeater gin, 10mls (½ fl.oz) crème de menthe, 50mls (2fl.ozs) grapefruit juice. Mix well together over ice in a mixing glass, top with soda water, strain into a highball glass, decorate with segments of grapefruit and a cherry.

Winden (Ger) village (Anb): Pfalz. (Ber): Südliche Weinstrasse. (Gro): Kloster Liebfrauenberg. (Vin): Narrenberg.

Winderbar (Eng) the name given to low alcohol red and white wines 4% alc by vol. from the House of Hallgarten.

Windesheim (Ger) village (Anb): Nahe. (Ber): Kreuznach. (Gro): Schlosskapelle. (Vins): Breiselberg, Fels, Hausgiebel, Hölle, Römerberg, Rosenberg, Saukopf, Schäfchen, Sonnenmorgen.

Windfall (S.Afr) a winery (established 2000) based in Robertson, Western Cape. 14ha. Grape varieties: Merlot, Ruby cabernet. Produces varietal wines.

Windhoek Extra Stout (Afr) a bitter stout 1050 O.G. brewed and bottled by the South-West Breweries, Windhoek, Namibia.

Windhoek Mai-Bock (Afr) a bock beer 1072 O.G. brewed by the South-West Breweries in Windhoek, Namibia.

Windischenbach (Ger) village (Anb): Württemberg. (Ber): Württembergisch Unterland. (Gro): Lindelberg. (Vin): Goldberg.

Windjammer (Scot) the brand-name for a rum bottled by Scottish and Newcastle Breweries.

Windjammer (W.Ind) a dark Jamaican rum produced by MᶜKinlay and MᶜPherson 43% alc by vol.

Windleiten (Aus) a vineyard site on the banks of the River Danube in the Kremstal region.

Windmeul Koöperatiewe Wynkelders (S.Afr) a co-operative winery (established 1944) based in Paarl, Western Cape. Has 48 members. 1700ha. (Add): Box 2013, Windmeul 7630. Grape varieties: Cabernet franc, Cabernet sauvignon, Chenin blanc, Cinsaut, Merlot, Muscadel,

Pinotage, Ruby cabernet, Sauvignon blanc, Shiraz. Label: Mill Red, Mill White. Website: http://www.windmeulwinery.co.za

Winds (Eng) winds that affect grape production and need special protective precautions. Either warm or cold. *see* Bora, Katabatic Wind, Levante, Llebeig, Mistral, Poniente, Seré, Solanos, Tramontana.

Winds of Change (S.Afr) a range of red blended wines (Cabernet sauvignon and Pinotage/Merlot and Shiraz) produced by the African Terroir winery, Paarl, Western Cape.

Windsor (Austr) the brand-name used by Mildara Wines, Coonawarra, South Australia.

Windsor (Eng) a natural spring mineral water brand.

Windsor Castle Brewery (Eng) a brewery (established 2004). (Add): 7 Stourbridge Road, Lye, Stourbridge, West Midlands DY9 7DG. Brews: 1900 Original Bitter 4.5% alc by vol., IPA 4.8% alc by vol., Jack's Ale 3.8% alc by vol. Website: http://www.windsorcastlebrewery.com 'E'mail: enquiries@windsorcastlebrewery.com

Windsor Forest (Eng) a méthode traditionelle sparkling wine produced by D. & U. Wheeler, Lillibrooke Manor Vineyards.

Windsor Glasses (Eng) a brand-name used by the Dema Glass Cº. Ltd. for a range of shaped cocktail glasses and a Champagne saucer.

Windsor Vineyards (USA) the label used by the Sonoma Vineyards for their range of wines usually sold by mail order.

Windsurfer [The] (Cktl) 2 parts Johnny Walker Red Label, 2 parts blue Curaçao, 3 parts passion fruit, 3 parts orange juice, 1 egg white. Shake over ice, strain into an ice-filled highball glass and decorate with a slice of kiwi fruit.

Windward Vineyard (USA) a winery based in the Paso Robles, San Luis Obispo County, California. Grape varieties include: Pinot Noir.

Windy Corner Cocktail (Cktl) 40mls (⅓ gill) blackberry brandy stirred over ice. Strain into a cocktail glass and top with grated nutmeg.

Windy Hill (N.Z) a small vineyard based at Simpson Road, Henderson, North Island. 3ha. Grape varieties: Cabernet sauvignon, Gamay, Pinotage. Produces table wines and sherries.

Windy Miller (Eng) a 4.1% alc by vol. ale brewed by the Millstone Brewery, Lancashire.

Wine (Eng) definition: 'The juice of freshly gathered grapes vinified according to the customs and traditions from region to region'. See also British Wine and Fortified Wine. (Arab) = nabeeth, (Aus) = wein, (Chi) = putaojiu, (Cro) = vino, (Den) = vin, (Fr) = vin, (Ger) = wein, (Gre) = krasi, (Hol) = wijn, (Indo) = wine, (Ire) = fion, (Isr) = ya-een, (It) = vino, (Jap) = wain, (Kor) = sool, (Port) = vinho, (Rus) = veeno, (Sp) = vino, (Thai) = laowine, (Tur) = sarap, (Rus) = vino, (Wal) = gwin.

Wine Additives (Eng) it is very difficult to find a wine that is completely 'additive-free'. Most additives are added to adjust, clear, improve, stabilise, etc. the wine and are strictly regulated within the E.C. and some additives are illegal worldwide! *See:* Ascorbic Acid, Bentonite, Calcium Carbonate, Carbon Dioxide, Copper Sulphate, Diammonium Phosphate, Diethylene Glycol, Diethylpyrocarbonate, Egg White, Fruit Flavour Concentrates, Isinglass, Malolactic Bacteria, Oak Chips, Oak Extract, Ox-Blood, Oxygen, Pectinolytic Enzymes, Potassium Bicarbonate, Potassium Bitartrate, Sugar, Tannin, Tartaric Acid, Water, Yeast.

Wine Aid (Fr) a specific wine made in Burgundy (Beaujolais) and Bordeaux with a wine aid label, proceeds go to the starving African countries.

Wine and Food Society (Eng) a society founded by André L. Simon, *see* International Wine and Food Society.

Wine & Spirit (Eng) the new name for the Wine International magazine.

Wine and Spirit Association of Great Britain (Eng) *abbr:* W.S.A. (Add): Five Kings House, 1 Queen Street Place, London EC4R 1QS. Website: http://www.wsa.org.uk 'E'mail: info@wsa.org.uk

Wine and Spirit Board (S.Afr) *Wyn & Spiritusraad*, a government appointed body who award a seal about the size of a postage stamp which guarantees the authenticity of the wine in the bottle. The code was in the form of a series of coloured bands. **blue band** = origin, **red band** = vintage, **green band** = grape variety. If the seal was in gold then classed Superior. Replaced in 1993 with a numbered seal. *see* Bus Ticket, Wine of Origin Seal.

Wine and Spirit Education Trust (Eng). *abbr:* W.S.E.T. (established 1969). (Add): International Wine & Spirit Centre, 39-45 Bermondsey Street, London SE1 3XF. An independent, not-for-profit charity that provides training in wines and spirits for those in the trade and general public. Offers Q & C.A accredited wine courses: Certificate, Higher Certificate and Diploma grades. Examination side is controlled by The Wine and Spirit Education Trust School. Website: http://www.wset.co.uk 'E'mail: school@wset.co.uk

Wine and Spirit Education Trust School (Eng) a part of The Wine and Spirit Education Trust. Runs the W.S.E.T. examinations.

Wine And The People (USA) *abbr:* WATP. a winery based in Alameda, California. Grape varieties: Chardonnay, Merlot and Zinfandel. Produces varietal wines under the Berkeley Wine Cellars label.

Wine Bar (Eng) licensed premises where the main drink is wine. The licence may be a full On-Licence or have restrictions to the type of drink sold. Many are restaurant/wine bars.

Wine Basket (USA) a wine cradle.

Wine Bibber (Eng) the name for a person who drinks mostly wine in any quantity.

Wine Brokers (Fr) *see* Courtiers.

Wine Bucket (Eng) a container for holding ice and water into which wine bottles (especially sparkling wines) are placed to be cooled down. Also known as a wine cooler.

Wine Butler (Eng) a person who is in charge of everything involving a wine-cellar. It is usually he/she who decides the wines to be consumed with each course at a banquet. *See also* Cellar Master and Oinophoros. (Ire) = buitléir fiona.

Wine by Syphon (Eng) a silver pump syphon used in the nineteenth century to draw wine out of casks at the table. Has a key-type tap.

Wine Cellar (Eng) a room (usually underground for a constant temperature and humidity) for the exclusive storage of wines (cask or bottles). (Fr) = cave, (Ire) = sliéar fiona.

Wineck-Schlossberg (Fr) a 24ha A.C. Alsace Grand Cru vineyard at Katzenthal and Ammerschwihr, Haut-Rhin.

Wine Concepts (S.Afr) a wine shop group based in Cape Town, Western Cape that produces a red wine (Cabernet sauvignon) from grape grown in Wellington, Western Cape. Website: http://www.wineconcepts.co.za

Wine Cooler (Cktl) 1 measure red or white wine, 4 dashes grenadine. Add ice and grenadine to the wine in a highball glass and top with soda water.

Wine Cooler (Eng) *see* Wine Bucket.

Winecorp (S.Afr) a winery based in Stellenbosch, Western Cape. Wineries of Longridge and Spier form part of the company. Produces: Dumstani (a range of wines), Naledi (Cabernet sauvignon), Sejana (Merlot). Website: http://www.winecorp.co.za

Wine Country Farm Cellars (USA) a winery based in Dayton, Oregon. Grape varieties: Pinot noir, Chardonnay, Riesling, Müller-Thurgau.

Wine Cradle (Eng) a basket used to carry mature red wines that have thrown a sediment from the cellar so they can be decanted. Usually made from wicker, it enables the bottle to be carried horizontally and the sediment remain undisturbed. It is unsuitable as a pouring unit at the table since the sediment becomes mixed with the wine after approximately two thirds of the contents have been poured. Also known as a Wine Basket or Burgundy Basket.

Wine Diamonds (Austr) the local name given to tartrate crystals, seen in the bottles of some botrytised wines when stored at cool temperatures.

Wine Emperor (It) the Emperor Probus (A.D.260) who promoted German wines.

Wine Equity Act (USA) a law introduced in 1983 as a measure against wine trade barriers.

Wine Festivals (Euro) organised celebrations (with copious amounts of local wines) within a wine-producing region for such events as the patron Saint's day, ripening of the grapes, grape harvest, etc. that are usually held annually in the town or village.

Wine Fountains (Gre)(It) a fountain where wine flowed instead of water in ancient Greek and Roman times.

Wine 4U (S.Afr) the export label for wines produced by the Le Manoir de Brendal winery.

Wine Funnel (Eng) a device for decanting wines

from the bottle into a decanter, it has a curved tip to allow wine to run down the side of the decanter and not gather air.

Wine Gallon (Eng) an old English measure of 231 cubic inches.

Wine Glass (Eng) a glass especially designed for drinking (and tasting wine) having a narrower rim at the top than the body of the glass and with a stem for holding so that the warmth of the hands do not alter the temperature of the contents of the glass. (Aus) = weinglas, (Fr) = verre à vin, (Ger) = weinglas, (Ire) = fionghloine, (Sp) = copa para vino.

Wineglass (USA) a measure of 4fl.ozs (US).

Wine Gods (Euro) *see* Bacchus, Fufluns and Dionysus.

Wine Grower (Eng) a person who tends the vines in the vineyard. (Fr) = vigneron, (Ger) = winzer, (Ire) = fionghloine.

Wine Herb Cooler (Cktl) 125mls (1gill) rosé wine, 2 teaspoons tarragon vinegar, 2 sprigs fresh oregano, 250mls (2gills) apricot syrup. Make a syrup with wine, vinegar and herbs, bring to the boil, simmer 5 minutes, strain and cool. Add apricot syrup and ice, top with 500mls (4gills) iced rosé wine and decorate with fresh herbs.

Wine Institute (USA) a California-based voluntary trade association of wineries situated in San Francisco, researches wine and grape technology.

Wine Institute of California (Eng) information centre. (Add): Vigilant House, 120 Wilton Road, London SW1V 1JZ. Website: http://www.wineinstitute.org 'E'mail: California.wine@virgin.net

Wine International (Eng) *see* Wine Magazine.

Wine in the Wood (Eng) cask wine/bulk wine. (Fr) = vin au tonneau.

Wine Lake (Euro) a new term invented to describe the surplus cheap wine that E.C. countries have due to increased production. Most is made into industrial alcohol or vinegar. *See also* Bioethanol.

Wineland (Eng) a company belonging to Arthur Rackham and trading name for a retail outlet in Upper Richmond Road, Putney, London.

Wine Library (Eng) a library of bottles of wine for reference of colour, taste etc. Popular in Italy. *see* (Fr) = vinothéque, (It) = enoteca, (Sp) = biblioteca, (Slo) = vinoteka.

Wine List (Eng) the list of wines, offered by a restaurant for sale to their customers for consumption on the premises with a meal. Term also applies to the list of a wine merchant which is sent to customers at their homes for their perusal. (Fr) = carte de vin, (Ire) = liosta fionta.

Wine Magazine (Eng) an informative monthly wine and spirit magazine designed for the professional trade and public. (Add): Quest Media and Events, 6–14, Underwood Street, London. N1 7JQ. Became Wine International and now known as (2006) Wine & Spirit. Website: http://www.william-reed.co.uk

Winemaker's Collection (It) a rosé wine produced by Casa girelli in the Puglia region.

Winemaker's Reserve (S.Afr) the label for a range of wines produced by the McGregor Wines winery, Robertson, Western Cape.

Winemaker's Reserve (USA) the label for a red wine (Pinot noir) produced by the Amity Vineyards winery, Willamette Valley, Oregon.

Winemaker's Selection (S.Afr) the label for white (Chardonnay) and red (Shiraz) wine produced by the Cloverfield Private Cellar winery, Roberston, Western Cape.

Winemaster (USA) the label used by the Guild of Wineries and Distilleries in Lodi, California.

Winemaster's Guild Brandy (USA) the brand-name of a brandy bottled by the Guild of Wineries and Distillers at Lodi, California.

Wine Memory (Eng) the art of storing information from tastings of wines and recalling the sensations at future tastings.

Wine Menu (Eng) *see* Wine List.

Wine Merchant (Eng) a person who buys and sells wine. (Fr) = négociant, (Ire) = ceannai fiona.

Wine Museum (USA) a winery based in the Finger Lakes region.

Wine of Araby (Euro) the sixteenth century name for coffee. So called because the Muslims were forbidden to drink any wine or alcoholic beverage and so drank coffee as a substitute for stimulation.

Wine of Friendship (Eng) the term applied to Sherry because of its use as a meeting drink for centuries.

Wine of Origin (S.Afr) *abbr*: W.O. Seal of control board. *see* Wine and Spirit Board and Wine of Origin Superior.

Wine of Origin Superior (S.Afr) *abbr*: W.O.S. Seal of control board that guarantees the authenticity of the wine (region, grape variety, vintage, etc.) that replaced the old 'stamp system'. *see* Wine and Spirit Board.

Wine of the Month Club (S.Afr) a noted door-to door delivery of own-label wines and Select Winemakers Collection Limited Release. Website: http://www.wineofthemonth.co.za

Wine Outlet (USA) a wine shop/wine merchant.

Wine Pack (Austr) a container for selling wines in plastic bags within cardboard boxes. *see* Bag in the Box.

Wine Palm (Eng) also known as the Toddy Palm. Various species of palm trees whose sap is used as a drink. *see* Toddy.

Wine Press (Eng) an implement used to extract the juice from the grapes by crushing. Various types are used. *see* Basket Press, Vaslin Press, Willmes Press. (Cro) = preša za vino.

Winery (USA) the name given to the buildings used for making wine. (Aus) = weingut/winzerhaus, (Arab) = masna'a khumur, (Chi) = jiuchang, (Den) = vingaard, (Fr) = cave, (Ger) = weingut, (Gre) = inopiio, (Hol) = wijngoed, (Indo) = pabrik anggur, (Isr) = yekev, (It) = cantina vinicola, (Jap) = wainarii, (Kor) = podowon, (Port) = vinícola, (S.Afr) = wynmakery, (Sp) = vinería, (Thai) = raiarngoon.

Winery Lake Vineyard (USA) a winery based in Carneros, Napa Valley, California. 50ha. Grape varieties: Chardonnay, Johannisberg riesling, Merlot and Pinot noir. Produces varietal wines.

Winery of Good Hope (S.Afr) the label for a range of wines (Cabernet sauvignon-Merlot/Chardonnay/Chenin blanc) produced by The Winery, Stellenbosch, Western Cape.

Winery of the Abbey (USA) a winery based in Cuba, Missouri. Produces hybrid wines.

Winery Rushing (USA) a winery based in Merigold, Mississippi. 9ha. Produces Muscadine wines.

Wine Sangaree (Cktl) 1 teaspoon of powdered sugar into a highball glass, add chosen wine, 2 ice cubes, stir well and top with more of the same wine.

Wine Sellers (Eng) a retail chain of 140 shops belonging to the Bass group (who also own Augustus Barnett and Galleon Wine).

Wines from Spain (Eng) information centre. (Add): Spanish Institute for Foreign Trade, Spanish Embassy Economic & Comm Office, 66 Chiltern Street, London W1M 2LS. Website: http://www.mcx.es/londres 'E'mail: londres@mcx.es

Wine Skin (Eng) the skin of an animal (goats or sheep) which is cured, sewn up and used to hold wine.

Wineskin (Eng) an old skin bottle which monks hung from their girdle. The German Bocksbeutel is modelled on it.

Wine Society [The] (Eng) an social organisation. (Add): Gunnels Wood Road, Stevenage, Hertfordshire SG1 2BG. Website: http://www.thewinesociety.com .

Wines of Germany (Eng) information centre. (Add): 33, Long Acre, London WC2E 9LA. Website: http://www.winesofgermany.co.uk 'E'mail: german.wine@phippspr.co.uk

Wine Source South Africa (S.Afr) a winery (established 2002) based in Paarl, Western Cape. 95ha. Grape varieties: Cabernet sauvignon, Chardonnay, Chenin blanc, Merlot, Pinotage, Shiraz. Labels: Corundum, Daniel's Hat. Website: http://www.winesourcesouthafrica.com

Winespeak (Eng) a word to denote the terms used by wine drinkers to describe wines.

Wine Standards Board (Eng) a British body funded by the Worshipful Company of Vintners and run by them in conjunction with the Food Standards Agency. Act as an enforcing body at wholesale level, inspecting those products covered by E.C. regulations and also advising importers and potential importers on labelling. Website: http://www.wsb.org.uk 'E'mail: enquiries@wsb.org.uk

Wine State [The] (Austr) a designation given to the State of South Australia.

Wines [UK] Ltd. (Eng) an organisation formed by 4 English vineyards: Adgestone, Astley, Wickenden & Wooton and Pool. Resources to help develop markets at home and abroad.

Wine Village-Hermanus (S.Afr) a winery (established 1998) based in Hermanus, Walker Bay, Western Cape. Grape varieties: Cabernet sauvignon, Sémillon. Website: http://www.wine-village.co.za

Wine Waiter (Eng) a person who sells and serves wines in a restaurant. *see* Sommelier and Wine Butler. *See also* Oinochoikos.

Wingeard (Eng) the mediaeval name for a vineyard.

Wingeardnaem (Eng) lit: wine gathering', the Anglo-Saxon word used for the vintage (harvest time).

Wingerd (Hol) vine. *See also* Vijnstok.

Wingertsberg (Ger) vineyard (Anb): Hessische Bergstrasse. (Ber): Umstadt. (Gro): None assigned. (Vil): Dietzenbach.

Wingertsberg (Ger) vineyard (Anb): Rheinhessen. (Ber): Bingen. (Gro): Adelberg. (Vil): Nieder-Weisen.

Wingertstor (Ger) vineyard (Anb): Rheinhessen. (Ber): Nierstein. (Gro): Petersberg. (Vil): Bechtolsheim.

Winiak Luksusowy (Pol) matured brandy.

Winifred Springs (Austr) a natural spring mineral water (established 1989) from Rylstone. Mineral contents (milligrammes per litre): Sodium 6.7mg/l, Calcium <0.1mg/l, Magnesium 0.6mg/l, Potassium 0.6mg/l, Bicarbonates <1mg/l, Sulphates <1mg/l, Fluorides <0.1mg/l, Nitrates <1mg/l. pH 5.8

Winkel (Ger) village (Anb): Rheingau. (Ber): Johannisberg. (Gro): Erntebringer. (Vin): Dachsberg.

Winkel (Ger) village (Anb): Rheingau. (Ber): Johannisberg. (Gro): Honigberg. (Vins): Bienengarten, Gutenberg, Hasensprung, Jesuitengarten, Klaus, Schlossberg.

Winkelshoek Wine Cellar (S.Afr) a winery based in Swartland, Western Cape. Labels include: Cap Vino, Weskus.

Winkleigh Cider Company (Eng) a cider company based in north Devon. Originally the site of Inch's Cider.

Winkle on the Porter (Eng) a 4.7% alc by vol. ale brewed by the Goldcar Brewery, West Yorkshire.

Winklerberg (Ger) vineyard (Anb): Baden. (Ber): Kaiserstuhl-Tuniberg. (Gro): Vulkanfelsen. (Vil): Ihringen.

Winkler-Hermaden (Aus) a winery (16ha) based in Kapfenstein, Süd-Oststeiermark. (Add): Schloss Kapfenstein, 8353 Kapfenstein. Grape varieties: Cabernet sauvignon, Chardonnay, Gewürztraminer, Pinot gris, Pinot blanc, Pinot noir, Riesling, Sauvignon blanc, Welshriesling, Zweigelt. Produces a range of dry and sweet wines.

Winkles Brewery (Eng) a brewery (established 1979) based in Buxton, north Derbyshire. Brews: cask-conditioned BVA 1037 O.G. and Saxon Cross Mild 1037 O.G.

Winnenden (Ger) village (Anb): Württemberg. (Ber): Remstal-Stuttgart. (Gro): Kopf. (Vins): Berg, Holzenberg, Rossberg.

Winnenden (Ger) village (Anb): Württemberg.

(Ber): Remstal-Stuttgart. (Gro): Wartbühl. (Vin): Haselstein.

Winnie-the-Pooh (Cktl) ½ measure egg flip, ¼ measure fresh cream, ⅛ measure crème de cacao, ⅛ measure chocolate liqueur. Shake over ice and strain into a cocktail glass.

Winningen (Ger) village (Anb): Mosel-Saar-Ruwer. (Ber): Zell/Mosel. (Gro): Weinhex. (Vins): Brückstück, Domgarten, Hamm, Im Röttgen, Uhlen.

Winnowing (Eng) the method used in coffee production to remove dust, leaves, twigs from coffee cherries.

Winny-Roxanne Hovelange (Lux) a natural spring mineral water from Roxanne. Mineral contents (milligrammes per litre): Sodium 1.9mg/l, Calcium 67.6mg/l, Magnesium 2mg/l, Potassium 0.2mg/l, Bicarbonates 204mg/l, Chlorides 4mg/l, Sulphates 18mg/l, Nitrates 3.5mg/l.

Winny-Source Volette (Lux) a natural spring mineral water. Mineral contents (milligrammes per litre): Sodium 17mg/l, Calcium 1.3mg/l, Magnesium 0.8mg/l, Potassium 1.2mg/l, Bicarbonates 300mg/l, Chlorides 71.5mg/l, Sulphates 60mg/l, Nitrates 1mg/l.

Winny-St. Jean Baptiste (Lux) a natural spring mineral water. Mineral contents (milligrammes per litre): Sodium 8mg/l, Calcium 80mg/l, Magnesium 8mg/l, Potassium 2mg/l, Bicarbonates 263mg/l, Chlorides 12mg/l, Sulphates 13mg/l, Nitrates 0.6mg/l.

Wino (Eng)(USA) a slang term for an alcoholic who drinks mainly cheap wines.

Winogrono (Pol) grape.

Winslow Wines (N.Z.) a winery (established 1987). (Add): Princess Street, Martinborough. 2.2ha. Grape varieties: Cabernet franc, Cabernet sauvignon, Merlot, Sauvignon blanc.

Wins Sangría (Sp) the brand-name of a Sangría. 2 versions: an alcoholic one consisting of red wine and citrus juices and a non-alcoholic one (sparkling) made from pure red grape juice and citrus juices. Both are free of preservatives, sugar or colourings. Marketed by Helvita Sangría.

Winston (Bel) a bière 7.5% alc by vol. brewed by the Marbaix Brasserie.

Winston (Bel) a pale-style ale 7.5% alc by vol. brewed by the Du Bocq Brasserie Centrale.

Winston Pale Ale (Bel) a pale ale brewed by the Marbaix Brasserie.

Winston's Stout (Scot) a stout 1053 O.G. brewed and bottled for export to Italy by the Belhaven Brewery in Dunbar.

Winter Ale (Eng) ales produced and sold between November to February. Usually dark, rich, high-gravity draught ales.

Winter Ale (Eng) an extra strong ale 1060 O.G. from the Greene King Brewery. This winter warmer is a blend of BPA, St. Edmunds Ale and Five X. Originally known as Christmas Ale.

Winter Ale (Eng) a 5% alc by vol. ale from the Ridley Brewery, Chelmsford in Essex.

Winter Ale (Eng) a 6.5% alc by vol. winter warmer ale brewed by St. Peters Brewery, St. Peter's Hall, South Elmham St. Peter, near Bungay, Suffolk.

Winter Ale (Wal) a 5% alc by vol. seasonal ale from Crown Buckley Brewery, Llanelli.

Winter Andes (S.Am) a natural spring mineral water from Colombia. Mineral contents (milligrammes per litre): Sodium 0.23mg/l.

Winterbach (Ger) village (Anb): Württemberg. (Ber): Remstal-Stuttgart. (Gro): Kopf. (Vin): Hungerberg.

Winter Beacon (Wal) a 5.3% alc by vol. winter ale brewed by the Breconshire Brewery, Powys.

Winter Blues (Eng) a 5.2% alc by vol. seasonal ale brewed by Green Bottle Ltd., Worth Brewery, Keighley, Yorkshire.

Winterborn (Ger) village (Anb): Nahe. (Ber): Schloss Böckelheim. (Gro): Paradiesgarten. (Vin): Graukatz.

Winter Brew (Eng) a 4.2% alc by vol. cask ale brewed by Gales Brewery, Horndean, Hampshire.

Wintercoat Bryggeri (Den) a brewery. (Add): Gronvej 51, Sabro 8471. Brews beers and lagers. Website: http://www.wintercoat.dk

Winterfold (Eng) a 4.9% alc by vol. dark, sweet winter warmer brewed by Samuel Allsopp (part of the Tapster's Choice range).

Winter Fuel (Eng) a 5% alc by vol. ale brewed by the Blackawton Brewery, Cornwall.

Winter Glow (Eng) a 6% alc by vol. winter warmer ale brewed by the Exe Valley Brewery, Silverton, Devon. Brewed using Devon and chocolate malts.

Winter Gold (Eng) a 4.5% alc by vol. golden winter ale brewed by Mauldon's Ltd., Suffolk.

Winterhoek (S.Afr) a brand of wine produced in Tulbagh.

Winter Holiday (Eng) a 5% alc by vol. bottle-conditioned ale brewed by Lakeland Brewing Cº., Cartmel Fell, Cumbria.

Winter Knights (Eng) a seasonal beer brewed by Castle Eden Brewery, County Durham.

Winter Reserve (Ire) a winter ale 1044 O.G. brewed by the Hilden Brewery in Ulster.

Winter Royal (Eng) a winter ale 1056 O.G. brewed by the Wethered Brewery in Marlow, Buckinghamshire (until 1989).

Winter Royal (Eng) a light coloured beer 5.5% alc by vol. with a good strong hop to it. Brewed in County Durham at the Castle Eden Brewery.

Winter's Brewery (Eng) a brewery. (Add): 8 Keelan Close, Norwich, Norfolk NR6 6QZ. Brews a range of beers and lager. Website: http://www.wintersbrewery.com 'E'mail: sales@wintersbrewery.com

Wintersdorf (Ger) village (Anb): Mosel-Saar-Ruwer. (Ber): Obermosel. (Gro): Königsberg. (Vins): Sites not yet chosen.

Wintersheim (Ger) village (Anb): Rheinhessen. (Ber): Nierstein. (Gro): Krotenbrunnen. (Vin): Frauengarten.

Winter's Tale (Cktl) 2 parts Merrydown mead, 4 parts red Burgundy, cloves and cinnamon stick. Heat altogether, strain and serve.

Winter Storm (Eng) a 4.2% alc by vol. seasonal premium ale brewed by Ushers of Trowbridge using whisky malt (available December and January, cask-conditioned or bottled).

Winter Sun (Eng) a 4.2% alc by vol. ale brewed by the George Wright Brewing C°., Merseyside.

Wintersweiler (Ger) village (Anb): Baden. (Ber): Markgräflerland. (Gro): Vogtei Rötteln. (Vin): Steingässle.

Wintertime Ale (Eng) a 5.6% alc by vol (1055 O.G) seasonal ale from the Wye Valley Brewery, Herefordshire (part of Dorothy Goodbody's selection).

Winter Vorst (Hol) a 7.5% alc by vol. warming seasonal beer brewed with honey, cloves and orange peel by Grolsch at Enschede-Groenlo, Gelderland (available in the spring).

Winter Warmer (Cktl) heat 250mls (½ pint) of milk with 35mls (1½ fl.ozs) Scotch whisky until nearly boiling. Pour over 1 egg yolk beaten with 25grms (1oz) sugar, whisk until smooth and serve in a heat-proof glass.

Winter Warmer (Eng) a 5.2% alc by vol. ale brewed by the Fenland Brewery, Cambridgeshire.

Winter Warmer (Eng) a 5.2% alc by vol. ale from the Goddard Brewery, Ryde, Isle of Wight. *See also* Special Bitter.

Winter Warmer (Eng) a 6% alc by vol. winter ale brewed by the Old Luxters Brewery, Oxfordshire.

Winter Warmer (Eng) an old ale 1055 O.G. brewed by the Youngs Brewery, Wandsworth, London.

Winter Warmer (Punch) boil 400mls (¾ pint) of water with 10 cloves, 1 teaspoon mixed spice, 50grms (2ozs) sugar for 5 minutes. Strain, add 1 bottle malmsey Madeira wine, juice of a lemon and a whole lemon that has been studded with 12 cloves and roasted in the oven for 1 hour, reheat and serve in glasses.

Winter Warmer (USA) a dark, strong, brown ale 7.25% alc by vol. brewed by the Newman Brewery in Albany, New York.

Winter Welcome (Eng) a 4.7% alc by vol. seasonal ale brewed by Wye Valley Brewery, Herefordshire (available in December).

Winter Wellie (Eng) a seasonal ale brewed by Batemans Salem Bridge Brewery, Wainfleet, Skegness, Lincolnshire.

Winter Winner (Eng) a 5.5% alc by vol. strong seasonal winter warmer ale brewed by Ridleys, Essex.

Winter Wobbler (Eng) a 1090 O.G. beer brewed by the Jolly Roger Brewery in Worcester.

Wintrange (Lux) a wine village on the river Moselle. Vineyard sites are Felsberg and Hommelsberg.

Wintrich (Ger) village (Anb): Mosel-Saar-Ruwer. (Ber): Bernkastel. (Gro): Kurfürstlay. (Vins): Grosser Herrgott, Ohligsberg, Sonnenseite, Stefanslay.

Winy (Eng) denotes having a taste of wine or is intoxicating, heady.

Winzenberg (Fr) a 5ha A.C. Alsace Grand Cru vineyard at Blienschwiller, Bas-Rhin.

Winzenheim (Ger) an old wine parish in the Nahe.

Winzer (Ger) wine-grower.

Winzerfest [1] (Ger) a wine festival held in Dernau in the Ahr in September.

Winzerfest [2] (Ger) a wine festival held in Klingenberg in Franken in the middle of August.

Winzerfest [3] (Ger) a wine festival held in Nierstein in the Rheinhessen in August.

Winzerfest [4] (Ger) a wine festival held in Würzburg in Franken in September–October.

Winzergenossenschaft (Aus)(Ger) wine growers' co-operative.

Winzergenossenschaft Auggen (Ger) a large co-operative that services the whole of the Auggen vineyards (except one) and produces a vast range of wines and spirits. Grape varieties: Chardonnay, Gewürztraminer, Gutedel, Müller-Thurgau, Muskateller, Nobling, Regent, Riesling, Spätburgunder and Weisser burgunder. Website: http://www.auggener-wein.de 'E'mail: info@auggener-wein.de

Winzerhausen (Ger) village (Anb): Württemberg. (Ber): Württembergisch Unterland. (Gro): Wunnenstein. (Vins): Harzberg, Lichtenberg.

Winzerhaus (Aus) winery.

Winzerhaus Ott (Aus) a winery based in Feuersbrunn, Donauland. (Add): Neufang 36, 3483 Feuersbrunn. Grape varieties include: Grüner veltliner, Pinot blanc, Riesling, Sauvignon blanc, Zweigelt. 'E'mail: winzerhaus.ott@aon.at

Winzerkogel (Aus) a famous vineyard based in the south-east Styria. Noted for its red wines (Blauburger and Zweigelt) grown on the volcanic rock soil (olivin).

Winzer Krems (Aus) a co-operative winery (990ha) based in the Kremstal region. Has 1700 members (Add): Sandgrube 13, 3500 Krems. Grape varieties include: Cabernet sauvignon, Chardonnay, Grüner veltliner, Gewürztraminer, Müller-Thurgau, Neuburger, Pinot blanc, Pinot gris, Riesling, Neuberger, Welschriesling, Zweigelt. Produces a range of all wine styles.

Winzersekt (Ger) a recently formed association of over 500 growers who produce vintage traditional method Sekt.

Winzerverband (Aus) a regional co-operative.

Winzerverein (Ger) wine growers' co-operative.

Wipfeld (Ger) village (Anb): Franken. (Ber): Maindreieck. (Gro): Kirchberg. (Vin): Zehntgraf.

Wire Mesh (Sp) *see* Arame, Alambre and Alambrado.

Wirenka (Pol) a natural spring mineral water from Zrodla. Mineral contents (milligrammes per litre): Sodium 9.5mg/l, Calcium 74.5mg/l, Magnesium 11.3mg/l, Potassium 2mg/l, Bicarbonates 235mg/l, Chlorides 7mg/l, Sulphates 22mg/l.

Wirmsthal (Ger) village (Anb): Franken. (Ber): Maindreieck. (Gro): Burg. (Vin): Scheinberg.

Wirranirra Winery (Austr) a winery based in McLaren Vale, Southern Vales, South Australia. Produces varietal and table wines.

Wirra Wirra (Austr) a winery in the Clare-Watervale,

McLaren Vale and Southern Vales regions of South Australia. Label: Church Block, RSW. Grape varieties: Cabernet sauvignon, Merlot and Shiraz.

WIRSPA (W.Ind) *abbr*: **W**est **I**ndies **R**um and **S**pirits Producers Association.

Wirt (Ger) host/landlord/bartender.

Wirthaus (Ger) a drinking house/pub/inn.

Wirtin (Ger) bartender.

Wirtschaft (Ger) lit: 'drinking house' (inn).

Wisdom and Warter (Sp) a Sherry producer owned by Gonzalez Byass and based in Jerez de la Frontera. Labels include Cream of the Century, Feliciano, Olivar and Royal Palace.

Wish You Were Here (Eng) a seasonal ale brewed by Ridleys of Essex (available in July).

Wisniak (Pol) a cherry-flavoured liqueur 25% alc by vol.

Wisniówka (Pol) a cherry-flavoured vodka. 25%–40% alc by vol, made from wild cherries. Also produced in Russia and Czec.

Wissahickon Mountain Spring water (USA) a natural spring mineral water from Bangor, Pennsylvania.

Wissberg (Ger) vineyard (Anb): Rheinhessen. (Ber): Bingen. (Gro): Abtey. (Vil): Sprendlingen.

Wissberg (Ger) vineyard (Anb): Rheinhessen. (Ber): Bingen. (Gro): Kurfürstenstück. (Vil): Gau-Weinheim.

Wisselbrunnen (Ger) vineyard (Anb): Rheingau. (Ber): Johannisberg. (Gro): Deutelsberg. (Vil): Hattenheim.

Wisselbrunnen (Ger) vineyard within the village of Hattenheim of which 16.9ha (57.4%) is proposed to be classified as Erstes Gewächs.

Wissett (Eng) a vineyard based in Suffolk. Grape variety: Auxerrois.

Wit (S.Afr) white.

Witbier (Bel) *see* Weiss.

Witblits (S.Afr) lit: 'white lightning', the alternative name for poteen or moonshine.

Witches Cauldron (Eng) the name for a beer brewed by the Moorhouses Brewery (Burnley) Ltd., Lancashire.

Witches Promise (Eng) a 6% alc by vol. cask-conditioned ale brewed by the Triple FFF Brewery, Hampshire.

Witchfinder General (Eng) the name for a beer brewed by the Moorhouses Brewery (Burnley) Ltd., Lancashire.

Witchfinder General (Eng) a 4.3% alc by vol. porter launched for Hallowe'en in 1993. Brewed to a traditional recipe by the Ridley Brewery, Essex.

Withered (Ind) a term to denote the method of drying the tea leaves to reduce moisture and make them soft and flexible.

Wither Hills Vineyards (N.Z) a winery. (Add): 172 Hepburn Road, Henderson, Auckland. 16ha. Grape varieties: Chardonnay, Merlot, Pinot noir, Rhine riesling, Sauvignon blanc. Labels: Clocktower, The Ned.

Withering (Ind) the controlled method of drying tea. *See also* Wilting.

Withey's Warmer (Eng) a winter warmer from micro-brewer Rose and Crown, Stelling Minnis, near Canterbury. *See also* Minnis Ale, Legion.

Withies (Eng) the old name for willow trees that were used for binding the vines.

Withoek (S.Afr) a winery Zoha (Established 1996) based in Calitzdorp, Little Karoo. 20ha. Grape varieties: Cabernet sauvignon, Chenin blanc, Colombard, Hanepoot, Muscadel, Petit verdot, Ruby cabernet, Shiraz, Tinta, Toriga.

Withy Cutter (Eng) a 3.8% alc by vol. ale brewed by the Moor Beer Company, Somerset.

Witkampff (Hol) a moutwijnjenever from Schiedam.

Witkap Pater (Bel) a light-coloured, bottle-conditioned, top-fermented beer from the Brasschaat Brasserie.

Witkap Pater Dubbele Pater (Bel) a 7% alc by vol. top-fermented, bottle-conditioned dark brown double beer brewed by Slaghmuylder in Ninove.

Witkap Pater Stimulo (Bel) a 6% alc by vol. top-fermented, bottle-conditioned, straw coloured beer brewed by Slaghmuylder in Ninove.

Witkap Pater Tripel (Bel) a 7.5% alc by vol. top-fermented, bottle-conditioned, straw-coloured, triple beer brewed by Slaghmuylder in Ninove.

Witness Tree Vineyard (USA) located in the Eola Hills, Salem, Willamette Valley, Oregon. Grape varieties: Chardonnay, Pinot noir.

Witney Bitter (Eng) a cask-conditioned bitter ale 1037 O.G. brewed by the Glenny Brewery in Witney, Oxon.

Witteboomen (S.Afr) the export label for wines produced by the Thorntree Wines winery, Constantia, Western Cape.

Wittenseer Quelle (Ger) a still and sparkling natural spring mineral water (established 1896) from Wittenseer Quelle. Mineral contents (milligrammes per litre): Sodium 9.8mg/l, Calcium 83.8mg/l, Magnesium 5.7mg/l, Potassium 1.3mg/l, Bicarbonates 243mg/l, Chlorides 17.8mg/l, Sulphates 32mg/l, Fluorides 0.16mg/l, Silicates 30.4mg/l. pH 7.27

Witte Raf (Hol) a 5% alc by vol. top-fermented, bottle-conditioned cloudy wheat beer brewed by Arcen Bier Brouwerij, Arcen.

Witte Wieven Witbier (Hol) a 5.5% alc by vol. top-fermented, bottle-conditioned, unfiltered, cloudy wheat beer brewed by Maasland Brouwerij, Oss.

Wittlich (Ger) village (Anb): Mosel-Saar-Ruwer. (Ber): Bernkastel. (Gro): Schwarzlay. (Vins): Bottchen, Felsentreppche, Klosterweg, Kupp, Lay, Portnersberg, Rosenberg.

Wittmannsthal Quelle (Ger) a natural spring mineral water. Mineral contents (milligrammes per litre): Sodium 73mg/l, Calcium 174mg/l, Magnesium 50mg/l, Potassium 2mg/l, Bicarbonates 338mg/l, Sulphates 287mg/l.

Wittnau (Ger) village (Anb): Baden. (Ber): Markgräflerland. (Gro): Lorettoberg. (Vin): Kapuzinerbuck.

Wit Wyn (S.Afr) white wine.

Wizard Brewery (Eng) a brewery. (Add): The Hops, Whichford, Shipston-on-Stour, Warwickshire CV36 5PE. Brews: Apprentice 3.8% alc by vol., BAH Humbug 4.9% alc by vol., Black Magic 4.3% alc by vol., Bullfrog 4.8% alc by vol., Druid's Fluid 5% alc by vol., Mother in Law 4.2% alc by vol., One For The Toad 4% alc by vol., Sorcerer 4.3% alc by vol., White Witch 4.5% alc by vol. Website: http://www.thenormanknight.co.uk 'E'mail: brewery@thenormanknight.co.uk

WKD (Eng) label of a range of 5.5% alc by vol. RTD vodka-based bottled drinks from Beverage Brands. Range includes: Iron Brew, Original Vodka Blue, Kick, Blonde, Red, Black. *See also* WKD 40 and Woody's.

WKD 40 (Eng) the original WKD label vodka-based drinks but 40% alc by vol.

WKK (Aus) *abbr*: Amtliche Weinkostkommission.

WM Magner Ltd (Eng) a cider producer (established 1935). (Add): Trinity House, Cowley Road, Cambridge Business Park, Cambridge, Cambridgeshire CB4 0ZS. Produces a range of ciders. Website: http://www.magnerscider.com 'E'mail: magners.gb@contrell.ie

W.O. (S.Afr) *abbr*: Wine of Origin

Wobble in a Bottle (Eng) a 7.5% alc by vol. bottle-conditioned ale from the Hogs Back Brewery.

Wobbly Dog (Eng) an ale brewed by Skinners Brewery, Truro, Cornwall.

Wöber [Anton] (Aus) a winery based in Ziersdorf, Weinviertel. (Add): Hollabrunner Strasse 3, 3710 Ziersdorf. Grape varieties: Grüner veltliner, Riesling, Zweigelt.

Woda (Pol) water.

Woda do Picia (Pol) drinking water.

Woda Mineralna (Pol) mineral water.

Woda Sodowa (Pol) soda water.

Wodka (Rus) lit: 'little water', the original name for vodka.

Wodka Luksusowa (Pol) a luxury vodka brand produced from double-distilled potato spirits 45% alc by vol.

Wodka Mysliwska (Pol) *see* Hunter Vodka.

Woerdemann Winery (USA) a small winery based in Temecula, Southern California. Grape varieties: Cabernet sauvignon and Sauvignon blanc. Produces mainly varietal wines.

Wohlfahrtsberg (Ger) vineyard (Anb): Württemberg. (Ber): Württembergisch Unterland. (Gro): Salzberg. (Vil): Löwenstein.

Wohlmuth (Aus) a winery based in Kitzeck, Styria. (Add): Freising 24, 8441 Kitzeck. Grape varieties: Pinot blanc, Pinot gris, Riesling. Noted for its Kosher wines.

Wohra (Aus) a vineyard site based on the banks of the River Kamp situated in the Kamptal region.

Woild Moild (Eng) a 4.8% alc by vol. ale brewed by the Wolf Brewery Ltd., Norfolk.

Wojcieszowianka (Pol) a natural spring mineral water from Milek. Mineral contents (milligrammes per litre): Sodium 7mg/l, Calcium 78.5mg/l, Magnesium 16.5mg/l, Potassium 1mg/l, Bicarbonates 247.3mg/l, Sulphates 52.3mg/l.

Wokka Saké (Ja) a 40% alc by vol. branded spirit of a blend of Japanese saké and Russian triple-distilled vodka.

Woldsman Bitter (Eng) a 4.5% alc by vol. bitter ale brewed by the Garton Brewery, East Yorkshire.

Wold Top Brewery (Eng) a brewery (established 2003). (Add): Hunmanby Grange, Wold Newton, Driffield, East Yorkshire YO25 3HS. Brews: Falling Stone 4.2% alc by vol., Mars Magic 4.6% alc by vol., Wold Gold 4.8% alc by vol., Wold Top Bitter 3.7% alc by vol. Website: http://www.woldtopbrewery.co.uk 'E'mail: enquiries@woldtopbrewery.co.uk

Wolf Blass (Austr) a winery in the Barossa Valley, South Australia. Produces varietal and sparkling wines.

Wolf Brewery (Eng) a brewery (established 1996). (Add): 10 Maurice Gaymer Road, Attleborough, Norfolk NR17 2QZ. Brews: Big Red 4.5% alc by vol., Golden Jackal 3.7% alc by vol., Prairie 5% alc by vol., Stout 4.5% alc by vol., Woild Moild 4.8% alc by vol., Wolf Best Bitter 3.9% alc by vol. Website: http://www.wolf-brewery.ltd.uk 'E'mail: info@wolf-ales.co.uk

Wolfer (Ger) vineyard (Anb): Baden. (Ber): Markgräflerland. (Gro): Vogtei Rötteln. (Vil): Blansingen.

Wolfer (Ger) vineyard (Anb): Baden. (Ber): Markgräflerland. (Gro): Vogtei Rötteln. (Vil): Kleinkems.

Wolfhag (Ger) vineyard (Anb): Baden. (Ber): Ortenau. (Gro): Schloss Rodeck. (Vil): Bühl (ortsteil Neusatz).

Wolfhag (Ger) vineyard (Anb): Baden. (Ber): Ortenau. (Gro): Schloss Rodeck. (Vil): Ottersweier.

Wolfkloof (S.Afr) the label for a red wine (Shiraz) produced by the Robertson Co-operative Winery, Robertson, Western Cape.

Wölflein (Ger) vineyard (Anb): Franken. (Ber): Maindreieck. (Gro): Ravensburg. (Vil): Veitshöchheim.

Wolfsaugen (Ger) vineyard (Anb): Württemberg. (Ber): Württembergisch Unterland. (Gro): Heuchelberg. (Vil): Brackenheim.

Wolfsberg (Aus) a vineyard site on the banks of the River Danube in the Kremstal region.

Wolfsberg (Ger) vineyard (Anb): Pfalz. (Ber): Südliche Weinstrasse. (Gro): Guttenberg. (Vil): Schweighofen.

Wolfschmidt (Eng) a brand-name of a vodka. 40% alc by vol. Produced by Seagram.

Wolfschmidt (Den) the name for a kümmel 43% alc by vol. Produced in Copenhagen.

Wolfschmidt Royal (Cktl) 2 parts Wolfschmidt kümmel, 3 parts Scotch whisky. Shake over ice and strain into an old-fashioned glass 'on the rocks'.

Wolfsdarm (Ger) vineyard (Anb): Pfalz. (Ber): Mittelhaardt-Deutsche Weinstrasse. (Gro): Hofstück. (Vil): Meckenheim.

W

Wolfsgruben (Aus) vineyard sites (2) based on the banks of the River Kamp situated in the Kamptal region.

Wolfsheim (Ger) village (Anb): Rheinhessen. (Ber): Bingen. (Gro): Abtey. (Vins): Götzenborn, Osterberg, Sankt Kathrin.

Wolfshöhle (Ger) vineyard (Anb): Mittelrhein. (Ber): Bacharach. (Gro): Schloss Stahleck. (Vil): Bacharach.

Wolfsmagen (Ger) grosslage (Anb): Hessische Bergstrasse. (Ber): Starkenburg. (Vil): Bensheim.

Wolfsnack (Ger) vineyard (Anb): Mittelrhein. (Ber): Rheinburgengau. (Gro): Herrenberg. (Vil): Dörscheid.

Wolkersdorf (Aus) a district in the Weinviertel. Produces light-styled white wines.

Wollbach (Ger) village (Anb): Baden. (Ber): Markgräflerland. (Gro): Vogtei Rötteln. (Vin): Steingässle.

Wollersheim Winery (USA) a small winery based at Prairie du Sac, Wisconsin. 8ha. Produces vinifera and French hybrid wines.

Wollmesheim (Ger) village (Anb): Pfalz. (Ber): Südliche Weinstrasse. (Gro): Herrlich. (Vin): Mütterle.

Wollombi Brook Estate (Austr) a vineyard in the Hunter Valley in the South Australia. Owned by Leo Buring C°.

Wöllstein (Ger) village (Anb): Rheinhessen. (Ber): Bingen. (Gro): Rheingrafenstein. (Vins): Affchen, Haarberg-Katzensteg, Hölle, Ölberg.

Wolluk Nier (Hol) a 6.5% alc by vol. amber-coloured, top-fermented, bottle-conditioned wheat beer brewed by De 3 Horne Bier Brouwerij, Kaatsheuvel.

Wolmore Warmer (Eng) a 4.9% alc by vol. dark winter ale brewed by Banks Brewery.

Wolvendrift Private Cellars (S.Afr) a winery (established 1903) based in Robertson, Western Cape. 120ha. Grape varieties: Cabernet sauvignon, Chardonnay, Chenin blanc, Colombard, Merlot, Muscadel, Sauvignon blanc. Website: http://www.wolvendriftwines.co.za

Wolverhampton and Dudley Breweries plc [The] (Eng) *abbr*: W & D. (established 1890). (Add): P.O. Box 26, Park Brewery, Bath Road, Wolverhampton, West Midlands WV1 4NY. *see* Banks Brewery and Hansons Brewery. Website: http://www.wdb.co.uk

Wolvers Ale (Eng) a 4.1% alc by vol. ale brewed by the Newmans Brewery, Avon.

Women's Petition Against Coffee (Eng) a campaign started in 1674 as a revolt against coffee houses. Resulted in King Charles the Second passing an Act of Parliament banning coffee houses in 1675.

Wonder Bar Cocktail (Cktl) 40mls (⅓ gill) dry gin, 15mls (⅛ gill) French vermouth, 15mls (⅛ gill) Italian vermouth, dash absinthe, 3 dashes orange bitters, 3 dashes Angostura. Stir over ice, strain into a 125mls (5fl.oz) wine glass, serve with cherry and a dash of lemon peel juice.

Wonkey Donkey (Eng) a 4.3% alc by vol. ale brewed by the Goose Eye Brewery Ltd., West Yorkshire.

Wonneberg (Ger) vineyard (Anb): Pfalz. (Ber): Südliche Weinstrasse. (Gro): Guttenberg. (Vil): Bad Bergzabern.

Wonneberg (Ger) vineyard (Anb): Pfalz. (Ber): Südliche Weinstrasse. (Gro): Guttenberg. (Vil): Dörrenbach.

Wonnegau (Ger) bereich. (Anb): Rheinhessen. (Gros): Bergkloster, Burg Rodenstein, Domblick, Gotteshilfe, Liebfrauenmorgen, Pilgerpfad, Sybillenstein.

Wonsheim (Ger) village (Anb): Rheinhessen. (Ber): Bingen. (Gro): Rheingrafenstein. (Vins): Hölle, Sonnenberg.

Wood Aged (Austr) matured in cask.

Wood Aged Chenin Blanc (Austr) a dry white wine which has been aged in German oak puncheons, produced by the Jane Brook Estate in Western Australia.

Wood Aged Sémillon (Austr) a full-bodied, dry white wine from the Quelltaler Estate, South Australia.

Wood Alcohol (Eng) methanol.

Woodbourne Cabernet Sauvignon (N.Z) a red wine produced by Montana Wines Ltd., Marlborough.

Wood Brewery [The] (Eng) a brewery (established 1980). (Add): Winstanstow, Craven Arms, Shropshire SY7 8DG. Brews: Christmas Cracker 1060 O.G. Drovers (a 4.1% alc by vol. bitter), Marathon Challenger, 6.0, Hopping Mad, Wood's Bridge Builder, Sam Powell Original 3.7% alc by vol., Shropshire Lad 4.5% alc by vol., Wood's Parish 4% alc by vol (1040 O.G)., Wood's Special Bitter 4.2% alc by vol., Wood's Wallop 3.4% alc by vol., Wood's Wonderful 4.8% alc by vol. and Well Hung ale 4.4% alc by vol. Website: http://www.wookbrewery.co.uk 'E'mail: mail@woodbrewery.co.uk

Woodbridge (USA) a range of wines produced by Mondavi of California. Grape varieties: Cabernet sauvignon, Chardonnay, Merlot, Sauvignon blanc, Zinfandel and White Zinfandel.

Woodbury Brewery (Eng) a brewery based at Great Witley, Worcestershire. Brews: Green Goose Bitter.

Woodbury Vineyards (USA) a winery based in Chautauqua, New York. Noted for their Chardonnay and Riesling wines.

Woodbury Winery (USA) a winery based in San Rafael, Marin, California. Grape varieties: Cabernet sauvignon, Petite syrah and Zinfandel. Produces varietal wines.

Wood Chips (Ger) used for fining lager beers.

Woodcock (Eng) an old English cider-making apple.

Woodenhead (USA) a winery based in the Anderson Valley, California. Also has vineyards in the Russian River Valley. Grape varieties include: Pinot Noir. Label: Wiley Vineyard.

Woodforde's Brewery Ltd (Eng) a brewery (established 1981), moved to the Spread Eagle public house Erpingham since 1983. Now at: Broadland Brewery, Woodbastwick, Norwich, Norfolk NR13 6SW. Brews: Admiral's Reserve 5% alc by vol., Great Eastern 4.3% alc by vol., Head

Cracker 7% alc by vol., Kett's Rebellion 3.6% alc by vol., Mardler's 3.5% alc by vol., Nelson's Revenge 4.5% alc by vol., Norfolk Nip 8.5% alc by vol., Norfolk Nog, cask-conditioned Norfolk Pride 1036 O.G. Wherry 3.8% alc by vol (1039 O.G) and Phoenix XXX 1047 O.G. *See also* White Lion Bitter. Website: http://www.woodfordes.co.uk 'E'mail: info@woodfordes.co.uk

Woodford Reserve (USA) a pot distilled Bourbon whiskey produced by Labrot and Graham.

Woodham Bitter (Eng) a cask-conditioned bitter ale 1035.5 O.G. brewed by the Crouch Vale Brewery in Chelmsford, Essex.

Woodham's Old Chopper (Eng) first in a series of limited edition cask ales from Scottish Courage at the Bristol Brewery. 4.1% alc by vol. using amber malt and English target hops.

Woodhay (Eng) a label used by the Holt Vineyard for a range of their wines.

Woodhill (N.Z) the brand-name used by Penfolds for a selection of their wines.

Woodhouse [John] (Eng) a British importer of Marsala and Sicilian wines in the eighteenth century. Operated from Liverpool, Lancs.

Woodinvilla Brewery & Forecaster Public House (USA) a brewery. (Add): 14300 NE 145th Street, Woodinville WA98072. Brews beers and lager. Website: http://www.redhook.com 'E'mail: redhook@redhook.com

Woodland Claret (N.Z) a light, dry red wine from the Ormind Vineyard.

Woodlands Wines (Austr) a winery based in the Margaret River district, Western Australia. Grape varieties include: Cabernet sauvignon, Merlot. Labels: Emilie May, Margaret Reserve. (Add): P.O. Box 220, Cowaramup, Western Australia 6284. Website: http://www.woodlandswines.com

Woodleys (Austr) a winery in the Barossa Valley and Adelaide Hills, South Australia. Noted for Queen Adelaide label Claret.

Woodman Bitter (Eng) an own-label canned bitter beer from the Booker Cash and Carry. (Add): Malt House, P.O. Box 65, Field End Road, Eastcote, Ruislip, Middlesex HA4 9LA.

Wood Matured Chenin Blanc (Austr) a full-bodied, fruity wine, oak matured from the Peel Estate in Western Australia.

Woodpecker Cider (Eng) a leading brand-name cider from Bulmers of Hereford (dry or sweet).

Woodpecker Red (Eng) a high strength sweet cider produced by Bulmers of Hereford 7.4% alc by vol.

Wood Port (Port) denotes Port wines matured in cask. L.B.V. Tawny, Ruby and White Ports.

Wood's (W.Ind) producers of a fine old Navy Demerara Rum 57% alc by vol.

Wood's Bridge Builder (Eng) a 5% alc by vol. seasonal draught bitter ale brewed by Shropshire's Woods Brewery. Available February and March. Part of the Wood's Shropshire and Heroes Legends.

Woodside Valley Estate (Austr) a winery based in the Margaret River region, Western Australia. Grape varieties include: Cabernet sauvignon. Label: The Baudin Collection.

Woodside Vineyards (USA) a small winery based in San Mateo, California. 3.25ha. produces varietal wines.

Woodsman Mild (Eng) a keg dark mild ale 1034 O.G. brewed by the New Forest Brewery in Cadnam, Hampshire.

Wood's Old Navy Rum (W.Ind) *see* Wood's.

Wood Spirit (USA) wood alcohol, methanol.

Woodstock (Austr) a winery based in Clare-Watervale, South Australia.

Woodstock Cocktail (Cktl) ⅔ measure dry gin, ⅓ measure lemon juice, 25mls (1fl.oz) maple syrup, dash Cointreau. Shake well over ice and strain into a cocktail glass.

Woods Wallop (Eng) the new name for the 101 beer from Woods of Wistantow in Shropshire. Previously called Woods 99 (reflecting the cost price).

Woods Wedding Wallop (Eng) a beer brewed to celebrate the wedding of Edward Wood (brewer at Woods Brewery) in Wistantow.

Wood Tannins (Eng) tannins obtained from the wooden casks used to mature wines. Gives the wine flavour. Hydrolysable tannins, Gallic and Egallic acids, Aldehydes, Vanillin and Lignins.

Woodward Canyon Winery (USA) a winery. (Add): Route 1, Box 387, Lowden, Washington. Vineyards in Columbia Valley. Noted for Merlot.

Woodward Cocktail (Cktl) 25mls (⅕ gill) Scotch whisky, 15mls (⅛ gill) French vermouth, 15mls (⅛ gill) grapefruit juice. Shake over ice and strain into a cocktail glass.

Woody (Eng) a term used to describe a wine with a smell and taste of the cork or cask.

Woody Nook (Austr) a winery based in the Margaret River region in Western Australia. Grape varieties include: Cabernet sauvignon. Label: Gallagher's Choice.

Woody's (Eng) a label for a range of cocktails (5.3% alc by vol) and fruit flavoured drinks (4.7% alc by vol) sold in 330mls bottles by Beverage Brands. Cocktails: Bellini, Blue Lagoon, Cuba Libre, Pina Colada, Pineapple Daiquiri and Sea Breeze. Fruit flavours include: strawberry and lemon, orange, lemon, pink grapefruit, blood orange, Mexican lime, kiwi and lemon are at 5.3% alc by vol. *See also* WKD.

Woody's Ice (Eng) a range of bottled alcoholic fruit drinks. Flavours include: grapefruit, blueberry, orange, cranberry, all at 5.5% alc by vol.

Woogberg (Ger) vineyard (Anb): Mosel-Saar-Ruwer. (Ber): Zell/Mosel. (Gro): Rosenhang. (Vil): Ellenz-Poltersdorf.

Wooly Mammothweis (Eng) a 4.5% alc by vol. beer brewed by the Newmans Brewery, Avon.

Woolworths (S.Afr) market a range of wines under their own label including: Artisan, Art of Blending, Bag in Boxes, Flagship, Flexibles, Longmarket, Organic, The Wilds, What? and Zesties. Website: http://www.woolworths.co.za

Woolworths Spring Water (S.Afr) a still and sparkling spring water from the Drakenstein Mountains, Franschhoek, Western Cape. Mineral contents still (milligrammes per litre): Sodium 10mg/l, Calcium 0.3mg/l, Magnesium 1.1mg/l, Potassium 0.2mg/l, Chlorides 19mg/l, Sulphates 1.3mg/l, Nitrates 1mg/l. Also produce flavoured varieties. Website: http://www.woolworths.co.za

Wootton (Eng) a vineyard (established 1971). (Add): North Town House, North Wootton, Shepton Mallet, Somerset. 2.5ha. Soil: medium clay loam. Grape varieties: Auxerrois, Müller-Thurgau, Schönburger and Seyval blanc.

Wooyu (Kor) milk.

Worby Brewery (Swe) a co-operative brewery in Solleftea, central Sweden. Also a co-operative in Varby, eastern Sweden.

Worcester (S.Afr) a wine district around the town of Worcester in the Breede River Valley. Produces mainly dry and dessert wines.

Worcestershire Whym (Eng) a 4.2% alc by vol. ale brewed by the Malvern Hills Brewery, Worcestershire.

Workie Ticket (Eng) a 4.5% alc by vol. beer from the Mordue Brewery, North Shields, Tyne and Wear.

Working (Eng) a term used in brewing and wine production to describe an active fermentation.

Working Man's Drink (Eng) a nickname for beer.

Workie Ticket (Eng) a 4.5% alc by vol. ale brewed by the Mordue Brewery Ltd., Tyne & Wear.

Worldham Brewery (Eng) a micro-brewery in East Worldham, near Alton, Hampshire. Brews Barbarian 5.2% alc by vol. Old Dray 4.4% alc by vol. Session 3.6% alc by vol.

World's Largest Brewery (USA) see Anheuser-Busch Brewery, St. Louis, Missouri.

World's Top Wine Countries (World) the top five wine-producing countries (2006) in ascending order are: France/Italy/Spain/United States of America/Argentina.

Worm (Scot) the condensing copper tube which is used in the production of malt whisky.

Wormeldange (Lux) a wine village on the river Moselle, vineyard sites are: Elterberg, Koeppchen (Koepp) and Nussbaum. Also the name of a co-operative in the village.

Worms (Ger) village (Anb): Rheinhessen. (Ber): Wonnegau. (Gro): Liebfrauenmorgen. (Vins): Affenberg, Am Heiligen Häuschen, Bildstock, Burgweg, Goldberg, Goldpfad, Hochberg, Kapellenstück, Klausenberg, Kreuzblick, Lerchelsberg, Liebfrauenstift-Kirchenstück, Nonnenwingert, Remeyerhof, Rheinberg, Römersteg, Sankt Annaberg, St. Cyriakusstif, St. Georgenberg, Schneckenberg.

Wormseed (Mex)(USA) a style of tea produced from the ambroissier shrub.

Wormser Liebfrauenstifte (Ger) the original Liebfraumilch which now cannot be called Liebfraumilch without losing its original name.

Wormwood (Eng) *Artimisia absinthium* a herb used in absinthe and also in vermouth (from which it gets its name), wormwood contains thujone which has same chemical structure as THC (**Tetrahydrocannabinol**) psychoactive ingredient in cannabis. Name originates from its use as a treatment for intestinal worms. (Ger) = wermut, (Gre) = apsinthion, (Ire) = mormónta, (Sp) = ajento.

Wormwood Bitters (Eng) place 3–4 sprigs of wormwood into a container. Pour over a bottle of gin, cover, stand for 3 weeks, strain, bottle and use as required.

Wörrstadt (Ger) village (Anb): Rheinhessen. (Ber): Bingen. (Gro): Adelberg. (Vins): Kachelberg, Rheingrafenberg.

Wort (Eng) in brewing the name given to the liquid which holds the malt extract from the malted barley. In beer production hops are added. see Sweet Wort, Hopped Wort.

Worth Best Bitter (Eng) a 4.5% alc by vol. amber-coloured bottled bitter ale brewed by Green Bottle Ltd., Worth Brewery, Keighley.

Worth Brewery (Eng) see Green Bottle Ltd., Harvest Festival, Hi Summer, Owlcotes Special Ale, Queen of May, Ruggies' Russet Nectar, Santa Toss, Winter Blues, Worth Best Bitter.

Worthington BB (Wal) a best bitter 1037 O.G. brewed by the Welsh Brewers in Cardiff.

Worthington Brewery (Eng) a brewery that merged in 1927 with Bass. Brews cask-conditioned beers in South Wales. Keg 'E' 1041 O.G. See also Welsh Breweries.

Worthington Dark (Wal) a dark mild ale 1034 O.G. brewed by the Welsh Brewers, Cardiff.

Worthington Draught Bitter (Eng) a 3.6% bitter ale from a creamflow dispenser from the Worthington Brewery in Burton-on-Trent, Staffs.

Worthington E (Eng) a famous keg bitter ale 1041 O.G. brewed by the Worthington Brewery in Burton-on-Trent, Staffs.

Worthington Glass (Eng) another name used for the Wellington glass.

Worthington M (Wal) a light mild ale 1033 O.G. brewed by the Welsh Brewers in Cardiff.

Worthington White Shield (Eng) a bottle-conditioned ale 1051 O.G. brewed by the Worthington Brewery, Burton-on-Trent, Staffs.

Wortley Arms (Eng) a micro-brewery based at Wortley Arms, near Barnsley, South Yorkshire. Brews: Wortley Best Bitter 1036 O.G., Brewer's Best Bitter 1042 O.G., Old Porter 1040 O.G., Earls Bitter.

Wortley Best Bitter (Eng) a 1036 O.G. bitter ale brewed by Wortley Arms, Wortley in South Yorkshire. See also Earls Bitter, Brewer's Bitter, Old Porter.

W.O.S. (S.Afr) abbr: see Wines of Origin Superior.

Wöschbach (Ger) village (Anb): Baden. (Ber): Badische Bergstrasse/Kraichgau. (Gro): Hohenberg. (Vin): Steinwengert.

Wousselt (Lux) a vineyard site in the village of Ehnen.

Wowser (Austr) a slang term for a non-drinker, a fanatical teetotaler.

Wpa Woppa (Eng) a 4% alc by vol. ale brewed by the Wentworth Brewery, South Yorkshire.

Wraxall (Eng) a vineyard. (Add): Wraxall, Shepton Mallet, Somerset. 2.5ha. Grape varieties: Müller-Thurgau, Seyval blanc.

Wray and Nephew Group (W.Ind) a rum distiller based in St. Ann, Jamaica. Produces Black Seal, Green Seal, Red Rose and White Wing.

Wrecked (Eng) a slang term for being heavily intoxicated.

Wreckers (Eng) a strong beer 1050 O.G. from the St. Austell Brewery in Cornwall. See also Tinners.

Wreckin Bitter (Eng) a cask-conditioned beer formerly brewed at the Unicorn home-brew public house in Shropshire.

Wrexham Brewery (Wal) the oldest lager brewery in U.K. Brews: Skol and Wrexham Lager 1033 O.G. Taken over by Ind Coope in 1949. Brews keg, bottled and canned lagers under licence for Allied Breweries.

Wrexham Lager Brewery Company (Eng) formed by a merger between the Wrexham Lager Beer Company and Lloyd & Trouncer. Headquarters are in Wrexham with a depot in Llandudno.

Wrights (Austr) a winery in the Margaret River district of Western Australia.

Writer's Block (S.Afr) the label for a red wine (Pinotage) produced by the Flagstone Winery, Somerset West, Western Cape.

Wrotham Pinot (Eng) a black grape variety also known as the Pinot meunier.

W.S.A. (Eng) abbr: Wine and Spirit Association.

W.S.E.T. (Eng) abbr Wine and Spirit Education Trust.

Wuchtig (Ger) potent/high in alcohol.

Wuhebai (Chi) the ancient name for the Thompson seedless grape variety.

Wuhrer Group (It) a company that has 4 breweries in northern Italy.

Wülfel Brauerei (Ger) a co-operative owned brewery based in Hanover.

Wülfen (Ger) vineyard (Anb): Rheingau. (Ber): Johannisberg. (Gro): Steinmacker. (Vil): Rauenthal.

Wülfen (Ger) a vineyard in the village of Rauenthal of which 14ha (24.3%) is proposed to be classified as Erstes Gewächs.

Wulfgar (Eng) an ale brewed by Beowulf Brewery, Yardley, Birmingham.

Wu Liang Yu (Chi) a grain spirit produced in Szechuan.

Wu Lung (Chi) lit: 'black dragon', a semi-fermented large leaf tea with a flavour of ripe peaches.

Wunderbar (Ger) the brand-name of a de-alcoholised red wine.

Wunnenstein (Ger) grosslage (Anb): Württemberg. (Ber): Württembergisch Unterland. (Vils): Beilstein, Gronau, Grossbottwar, Hof und Lembach, Ilsfeld, Kleinbottwar, Ludwigsburg (ortsteil Hoheneck), Oberstenfeld, Steinheim, Winzerhausen.

Wünschelburger (Ger) a range of fruit liqueurs from Asmussen. Flavours include: plum, blackberry, cherry (all 25% alc by vol.), cream peach (17% alc by vol.).

Wurmberg (Ger) vineyard (Anb): Franken. (Ber): Maindreieck. (Gro): Not yet assigned. (Vil): Böttigheim.

Wurmberg (Ger) vineyard (Anb): Württemberg. (Ber): Württembergisch Unterland. (Gro): Schalkstein. (Vil): Besigheim.

Wurmberg (Ger) vineyard (Anb): Württemberg. (Ber): Württembergisch Unterland. (Gro): Schalkstein. (Vil): Gemmrigheim.

Wurmberg (Ger) vineyard (Anb): Württemberg. (Ber): Württembergisch Unterland. (Gro): Schalkstein. (Vil): Walheim.

Wurmhoeringer (Aus) a brewery. (Add): A-4950 Altheim, Stadtplatrz 10-11. Brews beers and lagers. Website: http://www.wurmhoeringer.at

Württemberg (Ger) a 9800ha anbaugebiet. (Bers): Kocher-Jagst-Tauber, Remstal-Stuttgart, Württembergisch Unterland. Main Grape varieties: Müllerrebe (Pinot meunier), Portugieser, Riesling, Silvaner and Trollinger.

Württemberg Information Service (Ger) an information centre. (Add): Werbegemeinschaft Württembergischer Weingärtnergenossenschaft. Heilbronnersstrasse 41, 7000 Stuttgart 1.

Württembergisch Unterland (Ger) bereich (Anb): Württemberg. (Gros): Heuchelberg, Kirchenweinberg, Lindelberg, Salzberg, Schalkstein, Schozachtal, Stauffenberg, Stromberg, Wunnenstein.

Württemberg Wine Festivals (Ger) see Heilbronner Herbst and Fellbacher Herbst.

Würtzberg (Ger) vineyard (Anb): Mosel-Saar-Ruwer. (Ber): Saar-Ruwer. (Gro): Scharzberg. (Vil): Serrig.

Wurzburg (Ger) village (Anb): Franken. (Ber): Maindreieck. (Gro): Not yet assigned. (Vins): Abtsleite, Innere Leiste, Kirchberg, Pfaffenberg, Schlossberg, Stein, Stein/Harfe.

Würzburger Hofbräu (Ger) a beer brewed in Würzberg.

Würzburger Perle (Ger) a white grape variety, a cross between Gewürztraminer and Müller-Thurgau. Is more resistant to frost.

Würzburger Stein (Ger) a famous vineyard in the Franconia region. Gave its name to the 'steinweine'.

Würzer (Ger) a white grape variety, a cross between Gewürztraminer and Müller-Thurgau that gives a strong bouquet.

Würzgarten (Ger) vineyard (Anb): Mosel-Saar-Ruwer. (Ber): Bernkastel. (Gro): Sankt Michel. (Vil): Detzem.

Würzgarten (Ger) vineyard (Anb): Mosel-Saar-Ruwer. (Ber): Bernkastel. (Gro): Schwarzlay. (Vil): Traben-Trarbach.

Würzgarten (Ger) vineyard (Anb): Mosel-Saar-Ruwer. (Ber): Bernkastel. (Gro): Schwarzlay. (Vil): Ürzig.

Würzgarten (Ger) vineyard (Anb): Rheingau. (Ber): Johannisberg. (Gro): Mehrholzchen. (Vil): Hallgarten.

Würzhölle (Ger) vineyard (Anb): Nahe. (Ber):

Schloss Böckelheim. (Gro): Paradiesgarten. (Vil): Unkenbach.

Würzig (Ger) spicy wine.

Würzlay (Ger) vineyard (Anb): Mosel-Saar-Ruwer. (Ber): Zell/Mosel. (Gro): Weinhex. (Vil): Lehmen.

Wüstberg (Ger) vineyard (Anb): Baden. (Ber): Badische Bergstrasse/Kraichgau. (Gro): Rittersberg. (Vil): Weinheim.

Wutschenberg (Ger) vineyard (Anb): Franken. (Ber): Steigerwald. (Gro): Not yet assigned. (Vil): Kleinlangheim.

W.W.Q.A. (USA) *abbr*: **W**ashington **W**ine **Q**uality **A**lliance.

Wyanga Park Winery (Austr) winery (established 1980). (Add): Baacles Road, Lakes Entrance, Victoria. Grape varieties: Cabernet sauvignon, Sauvignon blanc, Sémillon.

Wyborowa Wódka (Pol) a brand of vodka produced by the Polish State Polmos (Panstwowy Monopol Spirytusowy), distilled from pure grain (rye). Red Label 45% alc by vol., Blue label 40% alc by vol. and apple-flavoured version 40% alc by vol. also spelt Vyborowa.

Wychert Ale (Eng) a 3.9% alc by vol. ale brewed by the Vale Brewery C°., Buckinghamshire.

Wychwood Bitter (Eng) a cask-conditioned premium bitter 1044 O.G. brewed by the Glenny Brewery in Witney, Oxfordshire.

Wychwood Brewery (Eng) a brewery (established 1983). (Add): Eagle Maltings, The Crofts, Witney, Oxfordshire OX28 4DP. Brews: Wychwood Bitter, Alchemy Gold, Fiddler's Elbow, Corn Circle Organic Ale, Dogs Bollocks, Dreamcatcher, Goliath, Hobgoblin, Jingle Knockers, Romeo, Santa Claus, White Wych. *See also* Randall's Brewery, Refresh UK plc. and The Guernsey Pub Company Ltd. Website: http://www.refreshuk.com

Wycked (Ch.Isles) a 4.2% alc by vol. pale ale brewed by Randalls Brewery, St. Peter Port, Guernsey (originally known as Randalls Pale Ale).

Wyecliff Vineyard (Wal) a vineyard based at Wyecliff, Hay-on-Wye. Planted with Madeleine angevine grapes.

Wye Valley Bitter (Eng) a 1036 O.G./3.5% alc by vol. Bitter from Wye Valley Brewery, Herefordshire.

Wye Valley Brewery Ltd (Eng) a brewery (established 1985). (Add): Stoke Lacy, Herefordshire HR7 4HG. Noted for cask-conditioned beers. Brews: Butty Bach 4.5% alc by vol., under the Dorothy Goodbody seasonal ales label: Autumn Delight 4.4% alc by vol., Country Ale 6% alc by vol., Santa's Delight 4.2% alc by vol., Springtime Ale 4% alc by vol., Summertime Ale 4.2% alc by vol., Wholesome Stout 4.6% alc by vol., Golden Ale 4.2% alc by vol., plus Hereford Pale Ale 4% alc by vol., St. Georges Bitter 4.3% alc by vol., Wye Valley Bitter 3.7% alc by vol. also H.P.A., Classic, Supreme, Brew 69, Autumn Ale, Big Bang, Christmas Ale, Hereford Pale Ale, Skipper Ale, Travellers Best, Victory Ale, Winter Welcome. Website: http://www.wyevalleybrewery.co.uk 'E'mail: sales@wyevalleybrewery.co.uk

Wye Valley Classic (Eng) a 4.5% alc by vol. premium cask bitter ale from the Wye Valley Brewery in Herefordshire.

Wye Valley Supreme (Eng) a 1043 O.G./4.3% alc by vol. dark premium bitter ale from Wye Valley Brewery, Herefordshire.

Wykehams Glory (Eng) a 4.3% alc by vol. ale brewed by the Itchen Valley Brewery, Hampshire.

Wyken (Eng) a vineyard based in Suffolk. Grape variety: Madeleine angevine.

Wylam Brewery Ltd (Eng) a brewery (established 2000). (Add): South Houghton Farm, Heddon on the Wall, Newcastle-upon-Tyne, Tyne & Wear NE15 0EZ. Brews: Hedonist 3.8% alc by vol., Hoppin Mad 4.2% alc by vol., Landlords Choice 4.6% alc by vol., Whistle Stop 4.4% alc by vol., Wylam Bitter 3.8% alc by vol., Wylam Haugh 4.6% alc by vol. Website: http://www.wylambrewery.co.uk 'E'mail: john@wylambrewery.co.uk

Wylandgoed (S.Afr) wine estate.

Wyn & Spiritusraad (S.Afr) the Wine and Spirit Board.

Wynberg (S.Afr) a wine-producing region of the Cape Peninsula.

Wynboer (S.Afr) a bi-monthly wine paper produced in southern Paarl.

Wyndham Estate (Austr) a winery. (Add): Dalwood via Branxton, New South Wales 2335. 400ha. Grape varieties: Blanquette, Cabernet sauvignon, Chardonnay, Frontignac, Malbec, Merlot, Pinot noir, Rhine riesling, Ruby cabernet, Ruby red, Sauvignon blanc, Sémillon, Shiraz, Tokay, Traminer and Verdelho.

Wyndhams Bitter (Eng) a bitter beer made by the Sussex Brewery in Sussex.

Wyne (Eng) an old English word for wine in the sixteenth century.

Wyne Seck (Eng) the sixteenth century word for dry wine.

Wynkelders (S.Afr) wine cellars.

Wynmaker (S.Afr) wine producer, wine maker.

Wynmakery (S.Afr) winery.

Wyn Moneth (Eng) the old Anglo-Saxon name for October when the grapes were harvested in England.

Wynns (Austr) a winery in the Barossa Valley and Coonawarra in South Australia. (Add): Coonawarra, South Australia 5263. Produces red and white wines from Shiraz, Cabernet sauvignon, Chardonnay, Riesling.

Wyn Seck (Eng) the mediaeval name for the dry Spanish wine 'Vino Seco'.

Wynvale Winery (Austr) a winery. (Add): Miroul Avenue, Yenda, New South Wales 2681. No vineyards, grapes bought in from High Eden, Hunter Valley, McLaren Vale, M.I.A. and Padthaway.

Wyn Van Oorsprong (S.Afr) wine of origin.

Wyoming Swing (Cktl) ½ measure Italian vermouth, ½ measure French vermouth, juice ½ orange, dash gomme syrup. Stir over ice, strain into an ice-filled highball glass, top with soda and a slice of orange.

W

Wyre Piddle Brewery (Eng) a brewery (established 1992). (Add): Highgrove Farm, Pinvin, Pershore, Worcestershire WR10 2LF. Produces Piddle in the Hole and lager beer.

Wyvern L.A. (Eng) a 1% alc by vol. bitter beer sold in bottles and on draught. Produced by Gales Brewery, Horndean, Hampshire.

X

X (Eng) the old seventeenth century method of showing the strength of beer: X: standard, XX: double strength wort. Today the number of X's has no meaning and is only to the brewers' own classification.

Xampan (Sp) Champagne.

Xanache (S.Afr) the label for a red wine (Cabernet franc 10%, Cabernet sauvignon 50% and Merlot 40%) produced by the Lynx Wines winery, Franschhoek, Western Cape.

Xanadu Winery (Austr) a winery based in the Margaret River, Western Australia. (Add): Boodjidup Road, Margaret River, Western Australia. Grape varieties: Chardonnay, Cabernet sauvignon, Sauvignon blanc, Shiraz, Zinfandel. Website: http://www.xanaduwines.com.au 'E' mail: info@xanaduwines.com.au

Xanath (Mex) a cream of vanilla liqueur produced by Montini.

Xante (Austr) a black grape variety. Parent of Carina.

Xanthia (Cktl) ⅓ measure yellow Chartreuse, ⅓ measure cherry brandy, ⅓ measure gin. Stir over ice and strain into a cocktail glass.

Xarab al Maqui (Arab) an ancient Arabian sweet Málaga-style wine.

Xarello (Sp) see Xarel-lo.

Xarel-lo (Sp) a white grape variety grown in the Penedés and Alella regions. Also spelt Xarello, Xerello and Xerello. Also known as the Cartoixa and Pansa blanca.

XB (Eng) a 3.7% alc by vol (1036 O.G) bitter ale brewed by the George Bateman & Son Ltd., Lincolnshire.

XB (Eng) a best bitter 1040 O.G. brewed by the Hartley Brewery in Ulverston, Cumbria.

XB (Eng) a premium bitter 4.6% alc by vol. (1045 O.G.) brewed by the Theakston Brewery in Masham, Ripon, North Yorkshire. Also a 500mls bottled version produced.

XB (Scot) a heavy ale 1036 O.G. brewed by the Devanta Brewery in Aberdeen.

Xeito (Sp) the name given to white and red wines produced by Bodega Cooperativa de Ribeiro.

Xenia (It) a natural spring mineral water brand.

Xera (Sp the Phoenician/Greek name for Jerez.

Xerello (Sp) see Xarel-lo.

Xerel-lo (Sp) see Xarel-lo.

Xérès (Fr) Sherry.

Xeres (Hol) Sherry.

Xeres (USA) a white grape variety used in the making of dessert wines in California.

Xérès Cocktail [1] (Cktl) 40mls Fino Sherry, dash Campari. Stir over ice and strain into a cocktail glass.

Xérès Cocktail [2] (Cktl). 40mls. dry Sherry, dash peach bitters, dash orange bitters. Stir over ice and strain into a cocktail glass.

Xerez (Sp) Sherry.

Xeriñac (Sp) the alternative spelling of Jeriñac.

Xeros (Gre) dry. See also Xiros.

Xhibition Stout (Eng) a 4.5% alc by vol. stout brewed by the Hogs Back Brewery Ltd., Surrey.

Xiangbingjiu (Chi) Champagne/sparkling wine.

Xibeca (Sp) the label of a lager beer brewed by Estrella-Damm in Barcelona.

Xinomavro (Gre) a local red grape variety grown in the Salonica district. See also Xynomavro.

Xino Nero (Gre) a sparkling natural spring mineral water from Xino Nero. Mineral contents (milligrammes per litre): Sodium 4.8mg/l, Calcium 281mg/l, Magnesium 26.1mg/l, Potassium 1.3mg/l, Bicarbonates 969.9mg/l, Chlorides 5.8mg/l, Sulphates 5.7mg/l, Nitrates 8.3mg/l, Silicates 15.9mg/l. pH 5.9

Xiros (Gre) dry. See also Xeros.

Xishibao (Chi) a natural spring mineral water brand. Mineral contents (milligrammes per litre): Sodium 1.44mg/l, Calcium 75.6mg/l, Magnesium 7.78mg/l. pH 8.1

Xithi (Gre) vinegar.

Xithum (Egy) a drink produced in ancient Egypt, a cross between wine and beer produced from fermented barley.

XK50 (Eng) a 5% alc by vol. dark porter brewed by the City of Cambridge Brewing Company. Named after the 50th anniversary of the Jaguar XK marque.

XL (Eng) a low alcohol bitter beer 1.2% alc by vol. produced by Webster's (Samuel) using Penine water.

XL Bitter (Eng) a 4% alc by vol. bitter ale brewed by the Burton Bridge Brewery, Staffordshire.

Xmas Ale (Eng) a 4.8% alc by vol Christmas ale brewed by the Berrow Brewery, Somerset.

Xmas Herbert (Eng) a seasonal ale brewed by the North Yorkshire Brewery at Middlesborough.

XM Standard (S.Am) the name given to light and dark rums produced by Banks DIH in Guyana.

X.O. (Fr) when found on Cognac labels it indicates a minimum of 6 years of age.

X.O. (Fr) on Armagnac labels it indicates a minimum of 5 years of age.

X

X.O. (Fr) an old designation on Armagnac and Cognac labels, denoted that the brandy was Extra Old 45 years in cask.

Xochimilco (Pousse Café) pour 25mls (1fl.oz) of Kahlúa into a liqueur glass. Float 25mls (1fl.oz) cream on top.

Xocoatl (C.Am) an Aztec Indian beverage made from the Cacao plant. The modern chocolate beverage drink derived from this.

X.O. Impérial (Fr) a blend of very old Grande Champagne and Petite Champagne eaux-de-vies with mature 30 year old Borderies. Produced by Corvoisier.

Xorigeur (Sp) a gin produced from wine distillates on the island of Minorca in the Balearic Islands, owned by Diago.

X-Pert (Hol) an all-malt, unpasteurised beer 5% alc by vol. brewed by the Gulpen Brouwerij in Gulpen, Limburg.

XP Kaupangkilden (Nor) a sparkling natural spring mineral water from Kaupanger. Mineral contents (milligrammes per litre): Sodium 3.6mg/l, Calcium 12.8mg/l, Magnesium 0.6mg/l, Potassium 1.7mg/l, Chlorides 2.9mg/l, Sulphates 16.6mg/l.

XS (Eng) a winter ale 1052 O.G. brewed by the Clark Brewery in Wakefield, Yorkshire.

XSB (Eng) a 4.2% alc by vol. bitter ale brewed by the South Hams Brewery, Devon.

XSP (Eng) a hoppy ale brewed to celebrate the move from South Somerset to Webbs Heath, Kingwood of Bath Ales.

XTC (Eng) a 3.9% alc by vol. ale brewed by the Barum Brewery, Devon.

XX (Eng) a cask conditioned dark mild ale 1031 O.G. brewed by the Greene King Brewery in East Anglia.

XX (Eng) a cask conditioned mild ale 1030 O.G. brewed by the Harvey Brewery, Lewes, Sussex.

XX (Eng) a light keg mild ale1033 O.G. brewed by the Shepherd Neame Brewery, Faversham, Kent.

XXX (Eng) a cask conditioned mild ale 1030 O.G. brewed by the Brakspear Brewery in Henley-on-Thames, Oxfordshire.

XXX (Eng) a cask conditioned mild ale 1034 O.G. brewed by the Donnington Brewery in Stow-on-the-Wold.

XXX (Eng) a cask conditioned bitter ale 1036 O.G. brewed by the Paine Brewery in St. Neots, Cambridgeshire.

XXX (Eng) a cask conditioned mild ale 1034 O.G. brewed by the Ridley Brewery, Chelmsford, Essex.

XXX (Eng) a cask conditioned bitter ale 1042 O.G. brewed by the Three Tuns home-brew public house, Bishop's Castle, Shropshire.

XXX (Eng) a 6.3% alc by vol. winter ale from Bathamand Son, Delph Brewery, Brierley Hill, West Midlands.

XXX (Scot) a dark malty bitter ale 1042 O.G. brewed by the Devanha Brewery in Aberdeen.

XXXB (Eng) a 4.8% alc by vol. bitter ale brewed by George Bateman & Son Ltd., Lincolnshire.

XXXB (Eng) a cask conditioned malty bitter ale 1048 O.G. brewed by the Bateman's Brewery in Wainfleet, near Skegness, Lincolnshire. Also sold in bottles as Ploughman's Ale. See also Valiant Bitter, Victory Ale.

XXXD (Eng) a cask conditioned dark mild ale 1032 O.G. brewed by Gales Brewery in Horndean, Hampshire.

XXXL (Eng) a cask conditioned light mild ale 1030 O.G. brewed by Gales Brewery in Horndean, Hampshire.

XXXX (Eng) a cask conditioned mild ale 1031 O.G. brewed by the Bass Brewery in London.

XXXX (Eng) a cask conditioned ale 1043 O.G. brewed by Brakspear Brewery in Henley-on-Thames Oxfordshire.

XXXX (Eng) a cask conditioned old ale 1043 O.G. brewed by Harvey Brewery in Lewes, Sussex.

XXXX (Eng) a cask conditioned old ale 1046 O.G. brewed by the King and Barnes Brewery in Horsham, Sussex.

XXXX (Eng) a cask conditioned mild ale 1033 O.G. brewed by the Samuel Smith Brewery in Tadcaster, Yorkshire.

XXXX (Eng) a cask conditioned mild ale 1034 O.G. brewed by the St. Austell Brewery in Cornwall.

XXXX Porter (Eng) a 4.7% alc by vol. porter brewed by the Ringwood Brewery, Ringwood, Hampshire.

XXXXX (Eng) a winter ale 1044 O.G. brewed by Gales Brewery in Horndean, Hampshire.

XXXXXX (Eng) a barley wine 1064 O.G. brewed and bottled by the Holt Brewery in Manchester.

Xylose (Eng) a monosaccharide found in wine.

Xynisteri (Cyp) a white grape variety used in the production of dry white wines and Commandaria.

Xynomavro (Gre) a red grape variety grown in northern Greece, used in Macedonia to produce Naoussa: a rich heavy red wine and Amynteon.

X.Y.Z. (Cktl) ½ measure white rum, ½ measure Cointreau, ¼ measure lemon juice. Shake over ice and strain into a cocktail glass.

Y (S.Afr) the label for a range of wines produced by the Yonder Hill winery, Stellenbosch, Western Cape.

Yabba Dabba Doo (Eng) a 8.7% alc by vol. ale brewed by The Branscombe Vale Brewery Ltd., Devon.

Yacht Club (Cktl) ⅓ measure gin, ⅓ measure Italian vermouth, ⅓ measure orange juice, 2 dashes Campari, 2 dashes gomme syrup. Shake over ice and strain into a cocktail glass.

Yachtsman (Eng) a bitter ale brewed by Burt's Brewery on Isle of Wight. *See also* Lighthouse, Needles Bitter.

Ya-een (Isr) wine.

Yago Condal (Sp) a white wine produced by Bodegas Rioja Santiago in the Haro region.

Yago Sant'gria (USA) the brand-name of a Sangria, one of the largest selling brands. *see* Sangría, Rioja Santiago C°.

Yagsiz (Tur) skimmed milk.

Yakenet (Isr) the name given to a rich, red dessert wine produced by Carmel from the Alicante grape.

Yakima (USA) a variety of hop grown in Washington.

Yakima Pale Ale (Eng) a 4.5% alc by vol. pale ale brewed by Bobs Brewing Company Ltd., West Yorkshire.

Yakima River Winery (USA) a winery based in Prosser, Washington. Produces mainly white wines.

Yakima Valley (USA) one of two wine sub-appellations of Columbia Valley, Washington State. *See also* Walla Walla Valley.

Yakka Shiraz (Austr) a rich, red wine produced the Longview Vineyard, Adelaide Hills, South Australia.

Yaksan (S.Kor) a natural spring mineral water from Yaksoo-Peak, Mt. Kongjak. Mineral contents (milligrammes per litre): Fluorides 0.16mg/l, Nitrates 0.3mg/l, Silicates 4mg/l. pH 7.5

Yaldara Winery (Austr) a winery based in the Barossa Valley, South Australia. Produces varietal wines.

Yale Cocktail [1] (Cktl) ½ measure Italian vermouth, ½ measure dry gin. Shake over ice, strain into a highball glass. Top with soda water and a squeeze of lemon peel juice.

Yale Cocktail [2] (Cktl) ¾ measure dry gin, ¼ measure French vermouth, dash Angostura, 3 dashes Crème Yvette. Stir over ice and strain into a cocktail glass.

Yallingup (Austr) a district in the Margaret River region of Western Australia.

Yallum Ridge Estate (Austr) a winery based in south-eastern Australia. Grape variety: Shiraz.

Yalta (Rus) a wine district of the Crimea, produces good red, rosé and white wines.

Yalumba Vineyards (Austr) a winery. (Add): Eden Valley Road, Angaston, South Australia 5353. 400 ha. Grape varieties: Cabernet sauvignon, Chardonnay, Merlot, Riesling and Shiraz. Vineyards in the Barossa Valley. Website: http://www.yalumba.com

Yamagata (Jap) a small wine-producing province in southern Japan.

Yamanashi (Jap) a large wine-producing province based in Tokyo.

Yamazaki (Jap) a distillery built in the Vale of Yamazaki in 1923 by Shinjiro Torii (owned by Suntory). Produce a single malt whiskey of the same name. *See also* Hibiki.

Yamhill Valley Vineyards (USA) a 42ha vineyard in Willamette Valley, Oregon. Grape varieties: Chardonnay, Pinot gris, Pinot noir, Riesling.

Yammé (S.Afr) the export label for a range of wines produced by the Overhex Private Cellar winery, Worcester, Western Cape.

Yam Wine (Afr)(S.Am) a fermented beverage produced from the roots of the yam plant.

Yankee (Eng) a 4.3% alc by vol (1040 O.G) soft ale brewed at Roosters Brewery, Harrogate, North Yorkshire.

Yankee-Doodle Cocktail (Cktl) 20mls (⅙ gill) crème de banane, 20mls (⅙ gill) Cognac, 20mls (⅙ gill) Royal Mint Chocolate Liqueur. Shake well over ice and strain into a cocktail glass.

Yankee-Dutch (Cktl) ¼ measure Bourbon whiskey, ¼ measure cherry brandy, ¼ measure triple sec, ¼ measure vodka. Stir over ice, strain into a cocktail glass and add a twist of orange peel.

Yankee Invigorator (Cktl) add 400mls (¾ pint) cold strong coffee, 25mls (1fl.oz) brandy, ½ wine glass Port to a beaten egg and sugar to taste. Add ice, shake and strain into a tumbler.

Yannis Paraskevopolous (Gre) *see* Paraskevopolous (Yannis).

Yantar (Ukr) the name for the 'Amber' Brewery at Nikolayev. Brews: Zhiguli (unmalted barley and corn brew), Riga, Slavyanskoye, Moscow and Amber.

Yantra Valley (Bul) a vineyard area in the Northern Basic region.

Y

Yapincak (Tur) a derivative of the white Sémillon grape.

Yapp Brothers (Eng) a noted wine merchant based at The Old Brewery, Mere, Wiltshire. Specialise in the wines of the Loire, Rhône and Midi.

Yarck Winery (Austr) a winery in Central Victoria.

Yarden (Isr) the name given to a range of Israeli wines imported into the U.K. by the House of Hallgarten, London. Are Kosher wines produced from French vines on the Golan Height 160ha.

Yard of Ale (Eng) a long glass vessel used mainly for drinking contests. Holds between 1300mls and 2600mls (2¼ and 4½ pints) and has a bulbous end. The drinker must be careful as, if it is tipped too sharply, the beer may flow too quickly and drench the drinker.

Yard of Flannel (Eng) an old English drink of sugar, eggs and brandy heated, this is then added to hot ale and mixed until smooth then drunk hot.

Yard of Flannel (USA) traditionally a hot toddy of cider, cream and rum mixed with spices and beaten egg.

Yarlington Mill (Eng) a variety of cider apple.

Yarner (Eng) a natural spring mineral water brand.

Yarpie (Scot) the name used in the Orkneys to describe the second layer of peat. See also Frog, Moss.

Yarra Burn (Austr) a winery based at Settlement Road, Yarra Junction, Victoria. Grape varieties: Cabernet sauvignon, Chardonnay, Pinot noir, Sauvignon blanc, Sémillon.

Yarra Edge Vineyard (Austr) a winery (established 1982). (Add): Edward Road, Lilydale, Yarra Valley. Grape varieties: Cabernet franc, Cabernet sauvignon and Chardonnay.

Yarra Ridge Vineyard (Austr) a winery (established 1983). (Add): Glenview Road, Yarra Glen, Yarra Valley. Grape varieties: Chardonnay, Cabernet sauvignon, Pinot noir, Sémillon, Sauvignon blanc.

Yarra Valley (Austr) a key wine-producing region within Victoria. Home to Yarra Yering, Mount Mary, Coldstream Hills, Green Point. Grape varieties include: Cabernet sauvignon, Chardonnay, Pinot noir.

Yarra Valley Wines (Austr) a winery. Cabernet sauvignon, Rhine riesling and Shiraz wines from Fergussons, Yarra Glen, Victoria.

Yarra Yarra Vineyard (Austr) a winery (established 1979). (Add): Hunt's Lane, Steels Creek, Yarra Valley. Grape varieties: Cabernet franc, Cabernet sauvignon, Sauvignon blanc, Sémillon.

Yarra Yering Vineyard (Austr) a winery (established 1973). (Add): Briarty Road, via Coldstream, Victoria 3770. 12 ha. Grape varieties: Barbera, Cabernet sauvignon, Chardonnay, Malbec, Merlot, Pinot noir, Sangiovese and Shiraz. Labels: N°1 Dry Red (Cabernet-based), N°2 Dry red (Shiraz-based), N°3 Dry Red (Portuguese varieties). Website: http://www.yarrayering.com

Yashan Noshan (Isr) a sweet, dessert wine.

Yasman-Salik (Rus) a fortified wine produced in Turkmenistan.

Yasti (Ind) the old name for yeast.

Yates and Jackson (Eng) a brewery based in Lancaster. Brews a sharp, dark mild ale and a medium bitter.

Yates Bitter (Eng) a draught or bottled bitter 1035 O.G. brewed by Yates Brewery in West Cumbria.

Yates Brewery (Eng) a brewery (Add): Westnewtown, near Aspatria, West Cumbria. Brews: Yates Bitter 1035 O.G.

Yates Brewery (Eng) a brewery (established 2000). (Add): The Inn at St. Lawrence, The Undercliffe Drive, Ventnor, Isle of Wight PO38 1XG. Brews: Holy Joe 4.9% alc by vol., Undercliffe Experience 4.1% alc by vol., Wight Winter Ale 5% alc by vol., Yates Special draught (YSD) 5.5% alc by vol. Website: http://www.yates-brewery.co.uk 'E'mail: info@yates-brewery.co.uk

Yattarna (Austr) the label of a Chardonnay wine produced by Penfolds from grapes grown in Adelaide Hills and McLaren Vale. Has 10 months maturation in 60% new French oak barrels.

Yava (E.Ind). see Ava and Kava.

Yawa (Afr) a palm wine produced in west Africa.

Yayin (Isr) an old Hebrew (Bible) word for wine described as having originated from Noah's vineyard.

Yazoo (Eng) the name for a range of flavoured milk drinks from SDF Foods. Flavours include: strawberry, chocolate, banana.

Yburgberg (Ger) vineyard (Anb): Baden. (Ber): Ortenau. (Gro): Schloss Rodeck. (Vil): Steinbach.

Ycoden-Daute-Isora (Sp) a D.O. of Tenerife, Canary Islands. Noted for dry white wines. Grape varieties include: Bermejuela, Gual, Malvasía, Negramoll, Sabro. See also Tacoronte-Acentejo.

Yeadstone (Eng) a vineyard (established 1976). (Add): Bickleigh, Tiverton, Devon. 0.75 ha.

Yearlstone Vineyard (Eng) a vineyard based at Bickleigh, Tiverton, Devon. 1.5 ha. Grape varieties: Chardonnay, Madeleine angevine and Siegerrebe. Produce red, rosé and white wines.

Yeast (Eng) the organism Saccharomyces which converts sugars into alcohol and carbon-dioxide. Many strains (see Saccharomyces) of yeasts are used for various styles of alcoholic beverages. See also Cultured Yeasts and National Yeast Bank. (Fr) = levure, (Ger) = hefe, (Ind) = yasti.

Yeast Cultures (Eng) preparations made for adding to musts to encourage yeast growth, such as Potassium Phosphate, Ammonium Phosphate, Vitamin B1.

Yeasting (USA) the adding of pure yeast culture to the mash in the production of whiskey for fermentation.

Yeasty (Eng) describes a wine with a smell of yeast, possibly due to a secondary fermentation in the bottle.

Yebisu (Jap) an all-malt beer 4.5% alc by vol. brewed by the Sapporo Brewery Ltd. in Sapporo, Tokyo.

Yecla (Sp) a Denominación de Origen region of Murcia in south-eastern Spain. Grape varieties: 80% Monastrell, Garnacha, Macabeo, Merseguera and Verdil plus experimental varieties of Cabernet sauvignon, Merlot and Tempranillo. Produces red, white and rosé wines. D.O. recognises white wines at 11.5% alc by vol. Campo Arriba tintos and Doble Pastas at 16% alc by vol.

Yeisai (Jap) a Zen Buddhist abbot who promoted tea drinking in the thirteenth century in Japan.

Yekev (Isr) winery.

Yelgris (Ind) a natural spring mineral water from Gollapalli.

Yella Belly (Eng) a 4.2% alc by vol. certified organic pale ale brewed by Batemans at Salem Bridge Brewery, Wainfleet, Skegness, Lincolnshire. Brewed using organically grown hops and malted barley.

Yellow Belly (Eng) a 4% alc by vol. bitter beer flavoured with vanilla pods from Bateman's Brewery, Wainfleet, Lincolnshire.

Yellow Bird (Cktl) 35mls (1½ fl.ozs) white rum, 10mls (½ fl.oz) Cointreau, 10mls (½ fl.oz) Galliano, 10mls (½ fl.oz) lime juice. Shake well over ice, pour unstrained into a goblet and dress with a slice of lime.

Yellow Cellar (S.Afr) the label for a dry white wine (Chenin blanc) produced by the Helderkruin Wine Cellar winery, Stellenbosch, Western Cape.

Yellow Chartreuse (Fr) a slightly sweeter version of green Chartreuse produced 6 years later in 1838 56% alc by vol.

Yellow Daisy (Cktl) ⅖ measure dry gin, ⅖ measure dry vermouth, ⅕ measure Grand Marnier. Stir over ice and strain into a cocktail glass.

Yellow Dwarf (Cktl)(Non-alc) 1 egg yolk, ½ measure cream, ½ measure gomme syrup. Shake over ice, strain into an ice-filled highball glass and top with soda water.

Yellow Dwarf Cocktail (Cktl)(Non-alc) 75mls (3fl.ozs) cream, 1 egg yolk, dash almond essence, 25mls (1fl.oz) passion fruit syrup. Stir over ice, strain into a champagne saucer and add a splash of soda.

Yellow Fever (Cktl) Mix 10mls (½ fl.oz) vodka with ½ teaspoon of sugar in a highball glass until dissolved. Add 50mls (2fl.ozs) each of lemon juice and vodka and some ice, stir, top with soda water and a slice of orange.

Yellowglen Vineyard (Austr) a winery. (Add): White's Road, Smythesdale, Victoria 3351. 18 ha. Grape varieties: Cabernet sauvignon, Chardonnay and Pinot noir. Noted for sparkling wines.

Yellowhammer (Eng) a 4.2% alc by vol. ale brewed by O'Hanlon's Brewery C°. Ltd., Devon.

Yellow Label Red (Austr) a red wine blend of Cabernet sauvignon and Shiraz. Produced by the Bilyara Vineyards in South Australia.

Yellow Parrot Cocktail (Cktl) 20mls (⅙ gill) yellow Chartreuse, 20mls (⅙ gill) apricot brandy, 20mls (⅙ gill) Pernod. Shake well over ice and strain into a cocktail glass.

Yellow Rattler (Cktl) 15mls (⅛ gill) dry gin, 15mls (⅛ gill) French vermouth, 15mls (⅛ gill) Italian vermouth, 15mls (⅛ gill) fresh orange juice. Shake well over ice, strain into a cocktail glass and dress with a small crushed yellow pickled onion.

Yellow Sea (Cktl) ¼ measure light rum, ¼ measure Galliano, ⅛ measure maraschino, ⅜ measure vodka, juice of a lime, 1 teaspoon sugar. Shake over ice and strain into a cocktail glass.

Yellowstone (USA) a 6 year old Kentucky Bourbon whiskey produced by the Yellowstone Distilleries C°. in Owensboro and Louisville, Kentucky 43%, 45% and 50% alc by vol.

Yellowstone Headwaters (USA) a natural spring mineral water from Beartooth Range, Rocky Mountains. Mineral contents (milligrammes per litre): Calcium 66mg/l, Magnesium 17mg/l, Potassium 2mg/l.

Yema (Sp) the first pressing of the Sherry grapes to which gypsum is added.

Yemen Coffee (Arab) *see* Moka Coffee.

Yenda Winery (Austr) part of the McWilliams Estate, New South Wales.

Yen Hung (Chi) a noted brand of rice wine. *see* Shaoh-Sing Rice Wine.

Yenon (Isr) a sweet, dessert wine.

Ye Old Trip Ale (Eng) *see* Olde Trip.

Ye Old Trout (Eng) a 4.5% alc by vol. ale brewed by the Kemptown Brewery C°. Ltd., East Sussex.

Yeoman (Eng) a noted hop variety grown in the county of Kent.

Yeoman Bitter (Eng) a keg bitter 1038 O.G. brewed by the Greene King Brewery in East Anglia (named after a hop variety).

Yeradjes (Cyp) a wine village in the region of Marathassa in the north-west Troodos.

Yerasa (Cyp) *see* Yerassa.

Yerassa (Cyp) a wine village in the south-east of the island that grows the grapes used in Commandaria production. Also spelt Yerasa.

Yerba Maté (S.Am) a herbal tea from Paraguay, contains tannin and is good for slimmers. Traditionally drunk in hollowed out gourds known as culhas in Brazil or matés and sucked with straws known as bombillas. *see* Maté.

Yeringberg (Austr) a winery (established 1863) in the Yarra Valley, Victoria. Grape varieties include: Cabernet sauvignon, Chardonnay, Marsanne, Merlot, Pinot noir, Roussanne, Shiraz. Website: http://www.yering.com

Yering Farm (Austr) a winery based in the Yarra Valley, Central Victoria. (Add): St. Hubert's Road, Yerring, Victoria. Website: http://www.yeringfarmwines.com

Yering Station (Austr) a winery (established 1838) based in the Yarra Valley, Victoria. Grape varieties include: Cabernet sauvignon, Marsanne, Pinot noir, Roussanne, Viognier, Shiraz.

Yes (Tai) a natural spring mineral water brand.

Yesca (Sp) a fungus which attacks faulty vine prunings in the Málaga region.

Yeso (Sp) ***Calcium sulphate*** (gypsum) which was traditionally sprinkled on the grapes during the first pressing (yema) to slow down fermentation and increase acidity. Now tartaric acid is more commonly used. *See also* Plastering.

Y

Ye'-Ye' (Cktl) 25mls (1fl.oz) Mandarine Napoléon, 40mls (1¾ fl.ozs) grapefruit juice, 20mls (¾ fl.oz) rum. Shake over ice, strain into a highball glass, top with bitter lemon, decorate with 2 cherries, a slice each of lemon and cucumber.

Yfed (Wal) to quaff/drink easily.

Y Grec (Fr) the brand-name of the dry wine from Château d'Yquem (very rare).

Yianakohori (Gre) a Vin de Pays de Imathia from Xinomavro and Merlot grapes. Produced from grapes grown at Ktimi Kir-Yianni, the (50ha) private estate of Yiannis Boutari, northern Greece.

Yinliao (Chi) beverage/drink.

Yixing Brewery (Chi) a brewery based in the Jiangsu Province. Brews: Yixing beer.

Ynocente (Sp) a brand of Fino Sherry produced by Valdespino.

Yo Ho Ho (Eng) a winter beer brewed by Branscombe Vale Brewery, Devon.

Yokohama Cocktail (Cktl) 20mls (⅙ gill) crème de menthe, 20mls (⅙ gill) dry gin, 20mls (⅙ gill) Italian vermouth. Shake over ice, strain into a cocktail glass, serve with an olive and dash of lemon peel juice.

Yoksum Brewery (Ind) a brewery based in Yoksum. Brews: bottled Dansberg, Hit, He Man 9000 Ultra Super Strong.

Yolanda (Cktl) ⅓ measure Cognac, ⅓ measure dry gin, ⅓ measure anisette, 25mls (1fl.oz) Italian vermouth, dash grenadine. Shake well over ice, strain into a cocktail glass and top with a twist of orange peel juice.

Yolo (USA) a small wine-producing district and county in Sacramento Valley, California.

Yonder Hill (S.Afr) a winery (established 1989) based in the Stellenbosch, Western Cape. 10ha. Grape varieties: Cabernet franc, Cabernet sauvignon, Chardonnay, Merlot, Muscadel, Shiraz. Labels: Inanda, Y. Website: http://www.yonderhill.co.za

Yonne (Fr) a wine-producing département in central France (was originally part of Burgundy).

Yop (Fr) a yoghurt fruit-flavoured drink from Yoplait.

York Brewery Company Ltd. (Eng) a brewery (established 1996). (Add): 12 Toft Green, Micklegate, York, North Yorkshire YO1 6JT. Brews: Ashes Ale 4.3% alc by vol., Brideshead Bitter 4% alc by vol., Cascade 4% alc by vol., Centurion's Ghost Ale 5.4% alc by vol., Guzzler 3.6% alc by vol., Hallertauer 4% alc by vol., Last Drop Bitter 4.5% alc by vol., Mt. Hood 4% alc by vol., Progress 4% alc by vol., Royal York 4% alc by vol., Stocking Filler 4.8% alc by vol., Stonewall Bitter 3.7% alc by vol., Wild Wheat 4.1% alc by vol., York Bitter 4% alc by vol., York IPA 5% alc by vol., Yorkshire Bitter 4.2% alc by vol., Yorkshire Terrier 4.2% alc by vol. also Final Whistle 3.9% alc by vol. to celebrate the 1998 World Cup. Website: http://www.yorkbrew.co.uk 'E'mail: at@yorkbrew.co.uk

York Cocktail (Cktl) another name for the Thistle Cocktail.

York Creek (USA) a vineyard based near St. Helena, Napa Valley, California. 41.5ha. Grape varieties: Cabernet sauvignon, Petite sirah and Zinfandel. Produces varietal wines.

York Mountain Winery (USA) a winery based near Templeton, Edna Valley, San Luis Obispo County, California. Grape varieties: Cabernet sauvignon, Chardonnay, Merlot, Pinot noir and Zinfandel. Produces varietal, dessert and sparkling wines.

Yorkshire Ale (Eng) a 5% alc by vol. premium bottled bitter beer from Ward's (a subsidiary of Vaux), Sheffield.

Yorkshire Bitter (Eng) a cask conditioned bitter ale 1036 O.G. brewed by the John Smith Brewery in Tadcaster, Yorkshire (also a keg version produced).

Yorkshire Bitter (Eng) a cask conditioned bitter ale 1037.5 O.G. brewed by the Webster Brewery in Halifax, Yorkshire (a keg version also produced), sold in the south of England.

Yorkshire Bitter (Eng) a 4.2% alc by vol. bitter ale from the York Brewery Company Ltd., Toft Green, North Yorkshire.

Yorkshire Grey (Eng) a Clifton home-brew public house owned by Clifton Inns. Noted for cask conditioned Headline Bitter 1037 O.G. and Holborn Best 1047 O.G.

Yorkshireman Best Bitter (Eng) a 4.1% alc by vol. bitter beer brewed by the West Yorkshire Brewery, Luddendenfoot.

Yorkshire Moors (Eng) a 4.6% alc by vol. ale brewed by the Cropton Brewery, North Yorkshire.

Yorkshire Spring (Eng) a natural spring mineral water from Yorkshire.

Yorkshire Square (Eng) a term used in the north for fermenting vessels used in the brewing process. *see* Square.

Yorkshire Square Ale (Eng) a 5% alc by vol. single hop bottled ale brewed by the Black Sheep Brewery, Masham, North Yorkshire.

Yorkshire Terrier (Eng) a 4.2% alc by vol. ale brewed by the York Brewery, Toft Green, North Yorkshire.

York Springs Winery (USA) a winery based in York Springs, Pennsylvania. Produces hybrid wines.

Yorkville Highlands (USA) a 40ha vine area east of Anderson Valley (established 1995), home to four small wineries.

You (Fr) a brand name for a French wine produced for the American market. The name designed to appeal to the Americans in place of the complicated French label names!

Youkous (Alg) a still and sparkling natural spring mineral water. Mineral contents (milligrammes per litre): Sodium 11.96mg/l, Calcium 67.32mg/l, Magnesium 10.08mg/l, Potassium 4.82mg/l, Bicarbonates 216.07mg/l, Chlorides 20.82mg/l, Sulphates 27.36mg/l, Nitrates 2.5mg/l, Silicates 2.33mg/l. pH 7.4

Young (Eng) a term used to denote a wine which is not fully matured or one which remains fruity and lively despite its age. (Fr) = jeune, (Sp) = joven.

Young Blade (Cktl) 1 measure cherry brandy, juice of

Y

an orange, cube of sugar. Shake well over ice, strain into a flute glass and top with iced champagne.

Young Boys Bitter (Eng) a 4.1% alc by vol. bitter ale brewed by the Blencowe Brewing C°., Rutland.

Younger (Scot) the brand-name used by the Fountain Brewery in Edinburgh (part of the Scottish and Newcastle Breweries).

Younger [William] (Eng) is Scottish and Newcastle's southern England and South Wales marketing company.

Younger's Shilling Bitter (Eng) draught and bottled half alcohol bitter beer 1.6% alc by vol. (1036 O.G) from the Home Brewery, Nottingham.

Young Hyson (Chi) a type of unfermented green tea from China.

Young Man Cocktail (Cktl) see Diabolo Cocktail.

Young's Brewery (Eng) a famous brewery (established 1831) and wines and spirits merchant. (Add): The Ram Brewery, Wandsworth, London SW18 4JD. Noted for cask conditioned and keg ales, also bottled London Lager 1037 O.G. Old Nick Barley wine 1084 O.G. RamRod 1046 O.G. Chocolate Stout, Damselfly, Luxury Double, Oregon Amber, Special Bitter 3.7% alc by vol., Special London Ale, St. George's Ale 4.3% alc by vol., Triple A. Website: http://www.youngs.co.uk 'E'mail: sales@youngs.co.uk

Young's Extra Light (Eng) a low alcohol beer 1% alc by vol. brewed by Young's Ram Brewery, Wandsworth, London.

Young's Special (Eng) a 4.6% alc by vol. (1043–1049 O.G.) beer from Young's Ram Brewery, Wandsworth, London.

Young's Special Bitter (Eng) a 4.6% alc by vol. premium strength bitter brewed by Young's Ram Brewery, Wandsworth, London.

Young Tom (Eng) a 4% alc by vol. seasonal cask ale brewed by the Robinson Brewery, Stockport.

Young Vineyards (USA) a large winery based in the Alexander Valley, Sonoma County, California. 114ha. Grape varieties: Chardonnay, Gewürztraminer, Johannisberg riesling and White riesling. Produces varietal and table wines.

Yountville (USA) an A.V.A. in the Napa Valley, California. 3442ha. Home to many wineries.

Your Bard (Eng) a 4% alc by vol. seasonal ale brewed by Hydes at 46 Moss Lane, West Manchester, Lancashire (available July and August a part of their Craft Ale range).

Your Shout (Eng) see Shout.

Youthful (Eng) a term used to describe a wine with a fresh acidity.

Youzhitianranbaojiankuangquanshui (Chi) a natural spring mineral water brand. Mineral contents (milligrammes per litre): Sodium 42mg/l, Calcium 247mg/l, Magnesium 51.3mg/l, Potassium 6mg/l.

Yovac (Slo) a wine district.

YPA (Eng) abbr: Yankee Pale Ale a 4.3% alc by vol. pale ale brewed by the Roosters Brewing C°. Ltd., North Yorkshire.

Ypioca (Bra) see Ypiocha.

Ypiocha (Bra) the brand-name of a cachaça that has a slight yellow colour due to wood ageing. Also spelt Ypioca.

YSD (Eng) abbr: Yates Special Draught a 5.5% alc by vol. draught bitter beer brewed by the Yates Brewery, Isle of Wight.

Y2K (Eng) a bottled and cask ale brewed for the millennium by Ridleys of Essex.

Yuba (USA) a small wine-producing county based in the Sacramento Valley, California.

Yubileyneya Osobaya (Pol) a vodka also known as Jubilee Vodka (contains honey, brandy and botanicals).

Yucateca Brewery (Mex) an independent brewery which produces Montejo and Leon Negra beers.

Yudumlamak (Tur) to sip a drink.

Yuengling Brewery (USA) the oldest brewery (established 1829) in the America, based in Pottsville, Pennsylvania.

Yugoslav Amselfelder Spätburgunder (Ser) a red wine from the Kosovo Pilje vineyards which is also sold under the same name. See also Burgomer Burgundec.

Yugoslavia (Euro) a wine-producing country that is at present re-named Slavina (or Southern Slav) and includes the six republics of Bosnia-Herzegovina, Croatia, Macedonia, Montenegro, Serbia and Slovenia. see Kvalitetno Vino, Cuveno Vino, Slav. Has now broken up into into independent states (circa 1995).

Yukon Brewing Company (Can) a brewery. (Add): 102A Cooper Road, Whitehouse Y1A 2Z6. Brews a range of beers and lager. Website: http://www.yukonbeer.com 'E'mail: greatbeer@yukonbeer.com

Yukon Gold (Can) a pilsener-style beer brewed by the Old Fort Brewery, British Columbia.

Yukon Spring (Can) a natural spring mineral water. Mineral contents (milligrammes per litre): Sodium 6.13mg/l, Calcium 84.7mg/l, Magnesium 13.9mg/l, Potassium 1.71mg/l, Bicarbonates 305mg/l, Chlorides 29.1mg/l, Sulphates 46.9mg/l, Fluorides 0.07mg/l, Nitrates 0.34mg/l, Silicates 9.88mg/l. pH 7.29

Yule Fuel (Eng) a Christmas ale brewed by Hadrain Brewery, Tyneside. See also Centurion Best Bitter, Emperor Ale.

Yuletide Ale (Eng) a 4.7% alc by vol. amber coloured draught ale brewed by Marstons, Shobnall Road, Burton-on-Trent, Staffordshire.

Yuletide Tipple (Eng) a winter warmer ale brewed by the Thompson Brewery, Ashburton, Devon.

Yuma Jana Cocktail (Pousse Café) ⅕ measure each of the following in order in a elgin glass: crème de cacao, apricot brandy, Prunée cordial, Regina cordial, cream.

Yunnan (Chi) a delicate, flavoured tea produced in western China.

Yuntero (Sp) a full, dry, white wine produced by Nuestro Padre Jesus del Perdon in La Mancha.

Yu-Vi (Indo) a natural spring mineral water from Slawi.

Y

Yvecourt (Fr) the label for a red A.C. Bordeaux. Grape varieties: Cabernet franc 20%, Cabernet sauvignon 20%, Merlot 60% and A.C. Bordeaux Blanc Sec. Grape variety: Sauvignon blanc 100%.

Yverdon Vineyards (USA) a winery based near St. Helena, Napa Valley, California. Grape varieties: Cabernet sauvignon, Chenin blanc, Johannisberg riesling and Gamay. Produces varietal and table wines.

Yvon [M.] (Fr) a famous Frenchman who managed to make Cognac during the phylloxera epidemic in the nineteenth century by finding a way of beating the louse (the company is now owned by Hennessy).

Yvon Mau et Fils (Fr) a noted négociant based in south-western France. (Add): Rue de la Gare, 33190 Gironde-sur-Dropt.

Yvorne (Switz) a dry white wine from the Vaud canton.

Z

Z (Eng) the new name for Dr. Thirsty's Beetlejuice produced by the Wychwood Brewery C°. Ltd.

Zaber [River] (Ger) a tributary of the river Neckar in Württemberg.

Zaberfeld (Ger) village (Anb): Württemberg. (Ber): Württembergisch Unterland. (Gro): Heuchelberg. (Vin): Hohenberg.

Zaca Mesa Winery (USA) a large winery based in Santa Barbara, California. Grape varieties: Cabernet sauvignon, Chardonnay, Johannisberg riesling, Pinot noir and Zinfandel. Produces varietal and table wines.

Zacatecas (Mex) an area where grapes are grown.

Zaca Vineyard [La] (USA) a large vineyard on Zaca Mesa, Santa Barbara, California. 42ha. Grape varieties: Cabernet sauvignon, Chardonnay, Johannisberg Riesling.

Zaccagnini (It) (It) a winery in the D.O.C. Verdicchio dei Castelli di Jesi, Marches region. Label: Salmagina. Also a noted producer of cuve close sparkling wines.

Zacinka (Ser) a red wine produced in eastern Serbia.

Zaco (Sp) a light, dry, red and white wines produced by Bodegas Bilbainas in Haro, Rioja Alta, north-western Spain.

Zaeh (Ger) denotes a ropy, oily, thick wine.

Zaer (Afr) an A.O.G. area in Morocco in the wine-producing region of Gharb.

Zagarese (It) a ruby-red sweet wine from the Apulia region 17%–18% alc by vol.

Zagarolo (It) a D.O.C. white wine from the Latium region. Made from the Malvasia and Trebbiano grapes in the communes of Gallicano and Zagarolo. Vinification has to occur within the delimited territory. If total alc. content is 12.5% by vol. then classed Superiore.

Zagarrón (Sp) a label used by Cooperativa de Manjavacas in the La Mancha region.

Zagori (Gre) a natural mineral water based in Ioannina. Mineral contents (milligrammes per litre): Sodium 2.4mg/l, Calcium 69.9mg/l, Magnesium 4.9mg/l, Potassium 1mg/l, Bicarbonates 206.8mg/l, Chlorides 10.6mg/l, Sulphates 11.2mg/l, Nitrates 7.3mg/l. pH 7.7 Website: http://www.zagoriwater.gr

Zagreb (Cro) a wine-producing area in northern Slavina that produces mainly white wines.

Zähe (Aus) denotes a wine that is thick and full-bodied.

Zahtila Vineyards (USA) a winery based in Rutherford, Napa Valley, California. Grape variety: Cabernet sauvignon. Label: Beckstoffer Vineyards Georges III.

Zaire (Afr) a major coffee-producing country in southern Africa. Produces high acidity coffees which are used mainly in blending. Ituri and Kivi are the main producing areas.

Zaisenhausen (Ger) village (Anb): Baden. (Ber): Badische Bergstrasse/Kraichgau. (Gro): Stiftsberg. (Vin): Lerchenberg.

Zakkelweiss (Rum) a white grape variety also known as the Banater riesling, Kriacza, Kreaca and Creaca.

Zaklady Piwowarskie Glubczyce SA (Pol) a brewery. (Add): Ul 1 Armil WP-16-18, 48-100 Glubczyce. Brews a range of beers and lager. 'E'mail: brax@glubczyce.pl

Zakon Za Vinto (Bul) the Wine Law, governs the wine production and classification.

Zala (Slo) a still natural spring mineral water. Mineral contents (milligrammes per litre): Sodium 9.5mg/l, Calcium 59.5mg/l, Magnesium 15.5mg/l, Potassium 1.2mg/l, Bicarbonates 259.2mg/l, Chlorides 12.8mg/l, Sulphates 17.9mg/l, Fluoride 0.02mg/l, Nitrates 9.7mg/l. pH 7.4

Zala Gyöngye (Hun) a white table grape, a cross between an Eger grape and Pearl of Csaba.

Zalema (Sp) a white grape variety grown in Condado de Huelva.

Zam (Indo) a natural spring mineral water based in Slawi. Mineral contents (milligrammes per litre): Sodium 12mg/l, Calcium 31.7mg/l, Magnesium 7.3mg/l, Bicarbonates 130mg/l, Chlorides 12.5mg/l, Sulphates 10mg/l. pH 7.1

Zambezi (S.Afr) a bottled lager 4.5% alc by vol. brewed by the National Breweries in Harare, Zimbabwe.

Zambra (Sp) the name given to a range of mature wines produced by San Isidro in Jumilla, Levante.

Zambra (Sp) a natural mineral water based in the Parque Naturale Zambra. Mineral contents (milligrammes per litre): Sodium 21.3mg/l, Calcium 93.8mg/l, Magnesium 25.3mg/l, Bicarbonates 245.6mg/l.

Zàmek (Czec) a premium lager 4.5% alc by vol. from Samson Brewery in Ceské Budejovice.

Zamkowa Zora (Ukr) a natural mineral water. Mineral contents (milligrammes per litre): Sodium 50mg/l, Calcium 105mg/l, Magnesium 25mg/l, Bicarbonates 350mg/l, Chlorides 25mg/l, Sulphates 40mg/l.

Zamkowe Jasne (Pol) a 5.5% alc by vol. lager beer brewed by the Namyslow Brewery.

Zamò (It) a winery based in Friuli-Venezia-Giulia. Produces Vigne di Zamò, Ronco dei Rosetti.

Zamora (Sp) a wine-producing province based near Salamanca. Noted for dark Toro wines.

Zamoyski (Pol) a brand of vodka distilled from pure grain by Polmos.

Zam Zam (Fr)(Scot) a Mona Lisa brand of water bottled at source in Scottish Highlands and France. Enables Asian and ethnic style restaurants to serve bottled water to compliment their cuisine.

Zandberg Farm (S.Afr) a winery (12ha) based in Stellenbosch, Western Cape. Grape varieties: Cabernet sauvignon, Merlot. Website: http: www.zandberg.co.za

Zanddrift Vineyards (S.Afr) a winery based in Suider-Paarl, Western Cape.

Zandvliet Estate (S.Afr) a 200ha vineyard based in Robertson. (Add): P.O. Box 55, Aston 6715. Produces varietal wines from Chardonnay, Cabernet sauvignon, Colombard, Merlot, Pinotage, Shiraz. Labels: Kalkveld Shiraz and Kalkveld Hill of Eon. Website: http://www.zandvliet.co.za

Zanjan (Iran) a wine-producing province in northern Iran.

Zante (Gre) an Ionian island in western Greece that produces wines mainly for local consumption.

Zantsi Natural Sweet (S.Afr) the label for a range of sweet white wines produced by the Darling Cellars, Swartland.

Zapatos de Pisar (Sp) special boots used for treading the grapes in the Sherry region.

Zapekanka (Rus) a cherry-based spirit 40% alc by vol.

Zapfeter (Aus) an alternative name for the Furmint grape.

Zapfner (Aus) an alternative name for the Furmint grape.

Zapoi (Rus) drunkard.

Zapple (Eng) a non-alcoholic sparkling apple juice drink produced by Showerings that contains no artificial colouring or preservatives.

Zara Cocktail (Cktl) the alternative name for the Zaza Cocktail.

Zaràfa (S.Afr) the label for a range of wines produced by the Mountain River Wines winery, Paarl, Western Cape.

Zaragoza (Sp) a province of Aragón. Has the D.O. wines: Calatayud, Campo de Borja, Cariñena. Vinos de la Tierras of Tierra Bajas de Aragón, Valdejalón. Vinos Comarcales of Belchite and Daroca.

Zarco [João Gonçalves] (Mad) re-discovered the island of Madeira in 1418.

Zardetto (It) a noted producer of Prosecco di Conegliano-Valdobbiadene in Veneto.

Zarf (Arab) a glass where the bowl fits into an ornate holder made of precious metal. Used for drinking Turkish-style coffee, was also made of porcelain.

Zaros (Gre) a natural spring mineral water based in Zaros, Kreta. Mineral contents (milligrammes per litre): Sodium 7.8mg/l, Calcium 35.3mg/l, Magnesium 13.1mg/l, Potassium 0.4mg/l, Bicarbonates 161.1mg/l, Chlorides 16mg/l, Sulphates 4.3mg/l, Fluoride 0.04mg/l, Silicates 6.8mg/l. pH 67.4

Zarragon (Sp) a dry white wine produced by the Bodega Cooperative del Campo Nuestra Señora in La Mancha.

Zarrin (Iran) a natural spring mineral water. Mineral contents (milligrammes per litre): Sodium 6mg/l, Calcium 12.8mg/l, Magnesium 6.72mg/l, Chlorides 15mg/l, Sulphates 10mg/l, Fluoride 0.4mg/l. pH 7.22

Zartchin (Bul) a wine-producing area noted for red wines.

Zasen (Aus) a vineyard site on the banks of the River Danube in the Kremstal region.

Zat (Hol) drunk/inebriated.

Zatec Brewery (Czec) a brewery (established 1801) based in north west Czec.

Zatec Red (Czec) a variety of Bohemian hop that derives from an 1865 strain.

Zatte (Hol) an 8% alc by vol. top-fermented, bottle-conditioned triple beer brewed by 't IJ Brouwerij, Amsterdam.

Zatte Bie (Bel) a 9% alc by vol. top-fermented, bottled special dark beer brewed by De Bie Brouwerij, Watou (contains spices).

Zaum (Aus) a vineyard site on the banks of the River Danube in the Kremstal region.

Zaum (Aus) a vineyard site on the banks of the River Danube situated in the Wachau region, Niederösterreich.

Zauner (Aus) a famous coffee house in Bad Ischl.

Zaximus (S.Afr) the brand label for a range of wines (for the U.K. and Italy) produced by the Citrusdal Cellars winery, Swartland, Western Cape.

Zaza [1] (Cktl) 1 measure dry gin, 1 measure Dubonnet, dash Angostura, stir over ice and strain into a cocktail glass.

Zaza [2] (Cktl) ⅔ measure Old Tom gin, ⅓ measure Dubonnet, dash orange bitters. Stir over ice and strain into a cocktail glass. Also known as a Zara Cocktail.

Zazie (Cktl) ⅓ measure Curaçao, ⅓ measure gin, ⅓ measure Stock apéritif. Stir over ice, strain into a cocktail glass and add a twist of orange peel.

Zazou (Eng) an RTD available in 2 styles: Cor de Amora (perry & raspberry) and Douardo (perry & tropical fruit) 5.4% alc by vol. from Showerings.

Z.B.W (Ger) *abbr*: **Z**entralkelleri **B**adischer **W**inztergenossenschaften. E.G. Breisach, Kaiserstuhl. *see* ZKW.

Z*D (Austr) *abbr*: **Z**ero **D**osage, vintage blanc de blancs sparkling wine from Domaine Chandon, Yarra Valley, Victoria.

Zdravica (Cro) a toast.

Z-D Wines (USA) a winery based near Rutherford, Napa Valley, California. Grape varieties: Chardonnay, Gewürztraminer, Pinot noir, White riesling and Zinfandel. Produces varietal and table wines.

Zebibi (Arab) an ancient Arabian, sweet, Málaga-style wine produced from grapes that have been partially dried in the sun.

Zebra Best Bitter (Eng) a 4.3% alc by vol. best bitter ale brewed by the Bazens Brewery, Greater Manchester.

Zebra Collection (S.Afr) the export label for a range of wines produced by the Rooiberg Winery, Robertson, Western Cape.

Zechberg (Ger) vineyard (Anb): Rheinhessen. (Ber): Nierstein. (Gro): Petersberg. (Vil): Framersheim.

Zechpeter (Ger) vineyard (Anb): Pfalz. (Ber): Südliche Weinstrasse. (Gro): Bischofskreuz. (Vil): Flemlingen.

Zechwein (Ger) lit: 'the drinker's wine', a fruity, light, ruby red wine made from the Trollinger grape in Württemberg.

Zedan (Cro) thirsty.

Zeer Oude (Hol) abbr: Z.O. very old (refers to old jenever).

Zefir (Hun) a cross of two native grapes: Léankya and Hárslevelü.

Zehetnerin (Aus) a vineyard site on the banks of the River Danube in the Kremstal region.

Zehnmorgen (Ger) vineyard (Anb): Rheinhessen. (Ber): Nierstein. (Gro): Auflangen. (Vil): Nierstein.

Zehntgraf (Ger) vineyard (Anb): Franken. (Ber): Maindreieck. (Gro): Kirchberg. (Vil): Wipfeld.

Zehnt-Wein (Ger) a charge paid by a tenant to a landlord (a tenth of his grape harvest or must). The time to pick the grapes is decided by the landlord.

Zeil (Ger) village (Anb): Franken. (Ber): Steigerwald. (Gro): Kapellenberg. (Vin): Kronberg.

Zeil a. Main (Ger) village (Anb): Franken. (Ber): Steigerwald. (Gro): Not yet assigned. (Vin): Mönchshang.

Zeilberg (Ger) vineyard (Anb): Württemberg. (Ber): Württembergisch Unterland. (Gro): Salzberg. (Vil): Affaltrach.

Zeilberg (Ger) vineyard (Anb): Württemberg. (Ber): Württembergisch Unterland. (Gro): Salzberg. (Vil): Löwenstein (ortsteil Hösslinsülz).

Zeilberg (Ger) vineyard (Anb): Württemberg. (Ber): Württembergisch Unterland. (Gro): Salzberg. (Vil): Willsberg.

Zeisel (Ger) vineyard (Anb): Mosel-Saar-Ruwer. (Ber): Zell/Mosel. (Gro): Goldbäumchen. (Vil): Pommern.

Zeiselberg (Aus) a vineyard site based on the banks of the River Kamp situated in the Kamptal region.

Zeiskam (Ger) village (Anb): Pfalz. (Ber): Südliche Weinstrasse. (Gro): Trappenberg. (Vin): Klostergarten.

Zeiss Bier (Ger) a strong premium lager beer.

Zelal (Ger) a natural spring mineral water based in Aquarossa, Thalfang. Mineral contents (milligrammes per litre): Sodium 3.82mg/l, Calcium 7.83mg/l, Magnesium 4.19mg/l, Potassium 0.81mg/l, Bicarbonates 49mg/l, Chlorides 2.78mg/l, Sulphates 2.56mg/l, Fluoride 0.35mg/l.

Zell (Ger) village (Anb): Mosel-Saar-Ruwer. (Ber): Zell/Mosel. (Gro): Schwarze Katz. (Vins): Burglay-Felsen, Domherrenberg, Geisberg, Kreuzlay, Nussberg, Petersborn-Kabertchen, Pommerell.

Zell (Ger) village (Anb): Pfalz. (Ber): Mittelhaardt-Deutsche Weinstrasse. (Gro): Schnepfenflug vom Zellertal. (Vins): Königsweg, Kreuzberg, Klosterstück, Schwarzer Herrgott.

Zellerberg (Ger) vineyard (Anb): Mosel-Saar-Ruwer. (Ber): Bernkastel. (Gro): Sankt Michael. (Vil): Longen.

Zellerberg (Ger) vineyard (Anb): Mosel-Saar-Ruwer. (Ber): Bernkastel. (Gro): Sankt Michael. (Vil): Lörsch.

Zellerberg (Ger) vineyard (Anb): Mosel-Saar-Ruwer. (Ber): Bernkastel. (Gro): Sankt Michael. (Vil): Mehring.

Zeller Schwarze Katz (Ger) a wine from the Mosel-Saar-Ruwer (of which 75% of the grapes must come from the village of Zell). see Schwarze Katz.

Zellerweg am Schwarzen Herrgott (Ger) vineyard (Anb): Rheinhessen. (Ber): Wonnegau. (Gro): Domblick. (Vil): Mölsheim.

Zell-Kaimt (Ger) village (Anb): Mosel-Saar-Ruwer. (Ber): Zell/Mosel. (Gro): Schwarze Katz. (Vins): Marienburger, Römerquelle, Rosenborn.

Zell-Merl (Ger) village (Anb): Mosel-Saar-Ruwer. (Ber): Zell/Mosel. (Gro): Grafshaft. (Vins): Sites not yet chosen.

Zell-Merl (Ger) village (Anb): Mosel-Saar-Ruwer. (Ber): Zell/Mosel. (Gro): Schwarze Katz. (Vins): Adler, Fettgarten, Klosterberg, Königslay-Terrassen, Stefansberg, Sonneck.

Zell/Mosel (Ger) bereich (Anb): Mosel-Saar-Ruwer. (Gros): Goldbäumchen, Grafshaft, Rosenhang, Schwarze Katz, Weinhex.

Zell-Weierbach (Ger) village (Anb): Baden. see Offenburg.

Zeltingen-Rachtig (Ger) village (Anb): Mosel-Saar-Ruwer. (Ber): Bernkastel. (Gro): Münzlay. (Vins): Deutscherrenberg, Himmelreich, Schlossberg, Sonnenuhr.

Zemmour (Afr) an A.O.G. area in Morocco in the wine-producing region of Gharb.

Zenata (Afr) an A.O.G. area in Morocco in the wine-producing region of Casablanca.

Zenato (It) a winery. (Add): Via San Benedetto 8-37010 San Benedetto di Lugana, Peschiera, Verona. Produces: Amarone Classico della Valpolicella. Has 60ha of vineyards. Label: Vigneto Massoni. Website: http://www.zenato.it 'E'mail: info@zenato.it

Zeni [Roberto] (It) a small winery based in Grumo near San Michele all'Adige in Trentino-Alto Adige 7ha.

Zenit (Hun) a cross grape developed from the indigenous varietal Ezerjó and the Slovenian hybrid Bouvier.

Zenith Cooler (Cktl) crush a slice of fresh pineapple into a shaker, add ice, 90mls (¾ gill) gin, dash sugar syrup. Shake well, strain into a tumbler with ice, top with soda water and decorate with pieces of pineapple.

Zenner Estate (It) a winery based on the island of Sicily. Grape variety: Nero d'Avola. 3ha. Label: Terra delle Sirene.

Zens [Josef] (Aus) a winery based in Mailberg, Weinviertel. (Add): Holzgasse 66, 2024 Mailberg. Grape varieties: Chardonnay, Grüner veltliner, Riesling, Zweigelt.

Zentgericht (Ger) vineyard (Anb): Hessische Bergstrasse. (Ber): Starkenberg. (Gro): Schlossberg. (Vil): Heppenheim (including Erbach and Hambach). Also spelt Centgericht.

Zentralkellerei Badischer Winzergenossenschaften (Ger) *abbr*: Z.B.W. the central winery of Baden wine-growers co-operatives, the largest wine co-operative in Europe.

Zephyrhills (USA) a natural spring mineral water based in Zephyr Hills, Florida. Mineral contents (milligrammes per litre): Sodium 5.1mg/l, Calcium 58mg/l, Magnesium 3.9mg/l, Potassium 0.2mg/l, Bicarbonates 140mg/l, Chlorides 11mg/l, Sulphates 8mg/l, Fluoride 0.2mg/l. pH 7.7

Zeppwingert (Ger) vineyard (Anb): Mosel-Saar-Ruwer. (Ber): Bernkastel. (Gro): Schwarzlay. (Vil): Enkirch.

Zerhoun (Afr) an A.O.G. area in Morocco in the wine-producing region of Meknès-Fez.

Zero (Nor) a non-alcoholic beer.

Zero Degrees Blackheath (Eng) a brewery. (Add): 29-31 Montpellier Vale, Blackheath, London SE3 0TJ. Brews: under the Zero Degrees label: Black Lager 4.8% alc by vol., Pale Ale 4.6% alc by vol., Pilsner 4.8% alc by vol., Wheat Ale 4.6% alc by vol. Website: http://www.zerodegrees.co.uk 'E'mail: info@zerodegrees.co.uk

Zerodegrees Bristol (Eng) a brewery (established 2004). (Add): 53 Colston Street, Bristol, Avon BS1 5BA. Brews a range of beers and lager. Website: http://www.zerodegrees.co.uk 'E'mail: info@zerodegrees.co.uk

Zero Hour Cocktail (Cktl) 30mls (¼ gill) brandy, 15mls (⅛ gill) apricot brandy, 3 dashes crème de menthe, 2 dashes absinthe. Shake over ice, strain into a cocktail glass, serve with an olive and 2 dashes absinthe on top.

Zero Lager (Ger) a brand of low alcohol lager beer.

Zero Mint Cocktail (Cktl) blend 40mls (⅓ gill) of green crème de menthe which has been stirred over ice with 20mls (⅙ gill) of iced water and serve in a cocktail glass.

Zest (Eng) for cocktails, thin pieces of citrus peel (the white pith excluded), the essential oil is squeezed on top of a drink.

Zeta River Valley (Ser) a noted wine-producing area in Montenegro, south-eastern Slav. Produces red wines mainly from the Vranac grape.

Zetland Bitter (Eng) a bitter ale brewed by the Hadrian Brewery on Tyneside. *See also* Emperor Ale, Centurion Best Bitter.

Zeus (It) a natural mineral water based in the Abruzzo.

Zeutern (Ger) village (Anb): Baden. (Ber): Badische Bergstrasse/Kraichgau. (Gro): Mannaberg. (Vin): Himmelreich.

Zevenrood (S.Afr) the label for a red wine produced by the Zevenwacht Vineyard, Stellenbosch.

Zevenwacht (S.Afr) an acidic still natural spring mineral water. Mineral contents (milligrammes per litre): Sodium 5mg/l, Calcium 1.3mg/l, Magnesium 0.71mg/l, Potassium <1mg/l, Chlorides 10mg/l, Sulphates 5mg/l, Fluoride <0.05mg/l, Nitrates <0.3mg/l. pH 5.7

Zevenwacht Vineyard (S.Afr) a 200ha winery and vineyards based in Kuils river, Stellenbosch. (Add): P.O. Box 387, Kuilsrivier 7580 Western Cape. Produces varietal wines from Cabernet sauvignon, Chardonnay, Chenin blanc, Gewurztraminer, Merlot, Pinotage, Pinot noir, Sauvignon blanc, Shiraz and Viognier grapes. Labels: Primitivo, Tin Mine and Zevenrood.

Zgarolo (It) a D.O.C. white wine from the Lazio region.

Zhao Qing Brewery (Chi) producers of ginseng beer based in Guangdong province.

Zhiguli (Ukr) a light beer 4.2% alc by vol. brewed using un-malted barley and cornflour by the Yantar Brewery.

Zhitomiraskaya Vodka (Ukr) the main vodka-style produced in Zhitomir.

Zhu Jiang (Chi) a 5.2% alc by vol. straw coloured, bottled lager brewed by Interbrew on behalf of the Zhu Jiang Beer Group.

Zibeben (Aus) the name given to sun-dried grapes used in wine production, derives from the Arabic: Zabib (dried raisin).

Zibib (Egy) a fiery spirit distilled from dates.

Zibibbo Moscato (It) a white grape variety grown in southern Italy. Used in the production of Moscato Passito di Pantelleria. Also known as the Muscat of Alexandria.

Zichron-Jacob (Isr) the Israeli viticultural centre which produces most styles of wines from French grape varieties.

Zickelgarten (Ger) vineyard (Anb): Mosel-Saar-Ruwer. (Ber): Saar-Ruwer. (Gro): Scharzberg. (Vil): Ockfen.

Zickend (Aus) a term that describes a wine with a taste of rancid butter.

Zidela Wines (S.Afr) a winery based in the Stellenbosch, Western Cape. Grape varieties: Cabernet sauvignon, Chardonnay, Chenin blanc (Steen), Merlot, Sauvignon blanc, Shiraz. Labels: Suikerbosch (Kaapse.Rooi, Kaapse Wit), Perlé Rosé. Website: http://www.zidelawines.co.za

Ziegelanger (Ger) village (Anb): Franken. (Ber): Steigerwald. (Gro): Kapellenberg. (Vin): Ölschnabel.

Ziegelhof Brauerei (Switz) an independent brewery based in Liestal.

Ziegler Winery (USA) a winery based in Cuba, Missouri. Produces Concord grape wines.

Ziem Vineyards (USA) a small winery based in Fairplay, Maryland. Produces hybrid wines.

Z

Zieregg (Aus) a 12ha Cru vineyard area on the Slovenian border.

Zierer [Harold] (Aus) a winery based in Gumpoldskirchen, Thermenregion. (Add): Badener Strasse 36, 2352 Gumpoldskirchen. Grape varieties: Chardonnay, Gewürztraminer, Rotgipfler, Traminer, Zweigelt. Produces dry and sweet (botrytised) wines.

Ziggurat Vineyards (S.Afr) a winery (established 1962) based in Paarl, Western Cape. 174ha. Grape varieties: Cabernet sauvignon, Merlot, Pinotage, Shiraz. Website: http://www.ziggguratwines.co.za

Zierfändler (Aus) a white grape variety used in Gumpoldskirchen production along with Rotgipfler. See also Spätrot-Rotgipfler.

Zig Zag Stout (Eng) a 4.5% alc by vol. stout brewed by the Mill Street Brewery, Somerset.

Zikhron-Yaacov (Isr) the largest wine-producing region based around the slopes of Mount Carmel. Produces most styles of wines.

Zilavka (Cro) a white grape variety grown in Croatia to make Mostarska Zilavka, a dry, white, fruity, perfumed wine.

Zilia (Fr) a natural spring mineral water from Corsica. Mineral contents (milligrammes per litre): Sodium 15mg/l, Calcium 11mg/l, Magnesium 5.1mg/l, Potassium 1.3mg/l, Bicarbonates 67.7mg/l, Chlorides 15mg/l, Sulphates 5mg/l, Nitrates 1.6mg/l. pH 7.5

Zimbabwe (Afr) a coffee tea and wine-producing country of central-eastern Africa. see Mateppe.

Zimmermann (Aus) a winery based in the Kremstal region. (Add): Hauptstrasse 20, 3494 Theiss. Grape varieties: Grüner veltliner, Riesling. Produces a range of wine styles.

Zin (USA) abbr: Zinfandel.

Zinblanca (USA) the name given to the white Zinfandel-based wine produced by Vose Vineyards, California.

Zind-Humbrecht (Fr) a fine wine producer of Alsace. (Add): 34 Rue du Maréchal-Joffre, Wintzenheim, 68000 Colmar.

Zinfandel (It) a purple-red grape variety grown in Bari, also known as Primitivo from Apulia.

Zinfandel (USA) a black grape variety popular to California that produces wines with a ripe cherry, black pepper, stalky, elderberries, ripe blackberries fruits and spice aroma and flavour. Was also known as Primitivo and thought to be the clone of. However in 2002 it had been genetically identified (DNA) with the Crljenak by the University of California. See also California Zinfandel.

Zinfandel Essence (USA) a wine made from botrytised grapes in San Benito, California by the Calera Wine Cº.

Zinfandel Rosé (USA) a rosé wine made from the Zinfandel grape in California.

Zingy (Eng) a term applied to wines that are refreshing, vital and lively, resulting from a high balance of acidity, fruit or pétillance. See also Zippy.

Zinnkoepfle (Fr) a 62ha A.C. Alsace Grand Cru vineyard at Westhalten and Soultzmatt, Haut-Rhin.

Ziolowy (Pol) a herb-flavoured liqueur produced by Polmos.

Zipfer Brauerei (Aus) a brewery (established 1858) based in Linz, is a subsidiary of Bräu AG.

Zipfer Original (Aus) a 5.4% alc by vol. straw coloured, bottled lager brewed by Zipfer Brauerei, Linz.

Zipfer Stefanibock (Aus) a pale bock beer 6.75% alc by vol. brewed by the Zipfer Brauerei.

Zipfer Urtyp (Aus) a dry, pale premium lager brewed by the Zipfer Brauerei, Linz

Zippy (Eng) an alternative word for Zingy.

Zirpass Brewery (Switz) an independent brewery based in Buchs.

Zistersdorf (Aus) a wine-producing district in the Weinviertel region. Produces light, white wines.

Zitadelle (Ger) vineyard (Anb): Pfalz. (Ber): Südliche Weinstrasse. (Gro): Schloss Ludwigshöhe. (Vil): St. Martin.

Zitsa (Gre) an A.O.Q.S. dry or medium-dry white, pétillant wine from the Debina grape produced in the region of Epirus.

Zivania (Cyp) the name used for grape alcohol.

ZKW (Ger) abbr: the former initials of the ZBW formed in 1952 that changed to present name in 1954.

Zlata Kaplja (Slo) a still natural spring mineral water based in Sveta Katarina. Mineral contents (milligrammes per litre): Sodium 3.9mg/l, Calcium 30.75mg/l, Magnesium 13.75mg/l, Potassium 0.4mg/l, Bicarbonates 166.2mg/l, Chlorides 4mg/l, Sulphates 2.6mg/l, Nitrates 1.8mg/l.

Zlatoroc Pivo (Slo) a pale lager 12% alc by vol. brewed at Lasko in Slovenia.

Zlatý Bazant (Czec) a stout made near the Hungarian border.

Zlatý Kun (Czec) lit: 'golden horse', a lager beer from Beroun.

Zlatý Trumf 10% (Czec) a 4.3% alc by vol. straw coloured, bottled lager brewed by Starobrno in Brno.

Zleni Veltlinac (Ser) a white grape variety grown in Serbia, is also known as Grüner veltliner.

Zlota Woda (Pol) a style of goldwasser.

Znojmo Brewery (Czec) a brewery (established 1720) based in southern Czec.

Z.O. (Hol) abbr: Zeer Oude.

Zobelsberg (Ger) vineyard (Anb): Franken. (Ber): Maindreieck. (Gro): Hofrat. (Vil): Segnitz.

Zöbing (Aus) a wine-producing area noted for Riesling wines.

Zoco (Sp) a 28% alc by vol. red-coloured blackcurrant drink made by Ambrosio Velasco, S.A. in Pamplona, Navarra.

Zodiac (Eng) a 7.5% alc by vol. white cider from Lanchester of Durham.

Zodiac Mystic Brew (Eng) see Mystic Brew.

Zoetendal Wines (S.Afr) a winery (8ha) based in Elim, Southern Cape. Grape varieties: Sauvignon blanc, Shiraz.

Zoilo Ruiz-Mateos (Sp) a Sherry bodega and producer based in Jerez de la Frontera.

Zolal (Iran) a still natural spring mineral water from Jijroft Chaman. Mineral contents (milligrammes per litre): Calcium 45mg/l, Magnesium 7mg/l, Potassium 2mg/l, Bicarbonates 128mg/l, Nitrates 7mg/l. pH 7.0

Zöld (Hun) green.

Zöldszilvàni (Hun) a variety of Sylvaner grape with a green skin grown near lake Balatòn.

Zöldveltelini (Hun) a local name for the Grüner veltliner grape.

Zólensky (Rus) a lemon-flavoured vodka mixed drink 5% alc by vol.

Zollturm (Ger) vineyard (Anb): Mosel-Saar-Ruwer. (Ber): Bernkastel. (Gro): Schwarzlay. (Vil): Traben-Trarbach.

Zollverein (Ger) the nineteenth century customs union organised to raise and standardise the German wines including a register of the vineyards.

Zolotaya Osen (Rus) lit: 'golden autumn', a liqueur made from quinces, apples and Caucasian damsons.

Zombie (Cktl) 20mls (¾ fl.oz) lime juice, 20mls (¾ fl.oz) pineapple juice, 1 teaspoon Falernum (or sugar syrup), 25mls (1fl.oz) White Label rum, 50mls (2fl.ozs) Gold Label rum, 25mls (1fl.oz) Jamaican rum, 10mls (½ fl.oz) 100° US proof rum, 10mls (½ fl.oz) apricot liqueur. Shake well over ice, strain into a zombie glass with ice, garnish with an orange slice and mint sprig and serve with straws.

Zombie Cocktail (Cktl) ¾ measure golden rum, ¾ measure lemon juice, ½ measure white rum, 1 measure orange juice, dash grenadine, dash lime juice, 2 dashes Grand Marnier, 2 dashes crème de noyeau. Stir over crushed ice, pour into a zombie glass, dress with an orange slice, mint leaves and serve with straws.

Zombie Glass (USA) an especially large glass 400mls (14fl.ozs) used for the serving of Zombie cocktails.

Zomer Bokbier (Hol) a 7% alc by vol. top-fermented, bottle-conditioned, seasonal beer brewed by De Gans Bier Brouwerij, Goes.

Zomergoud (Hol) a 4.5% alc by vol. zesty, seasonal beer brewed by Grolsch at Enschede-Groenlo, Gelderland, available in summer.

Zomerlust (S.Afr) the label for a wine range originally produced by the Robertson Winery, Robertson, Western Cape (now no longer produced).

Zona de Crianza (Sp) an area within which the Denominación de Origen where quality wines may be matured and blended.

Zona de Jerez Superior (Sp) a zone of superior Sherry vineyards, lies between the towns of Puerto de Santa Maria, Jerez de la Frontera and Sanlúcar de Barrameda. Soil is of chalk. see Albariza.

Zona del Albariño (Sp) a noted Vinos Verdes wine producer based in Galicia.

Zona del Albero (Sp) the name given to Moriles Altos in southern Spain.

Zona d'Origine (It) lit: 'in the growing area'.

Zonage (Fr) a term used by C.I.V.C. to recognise the importance of the soil for the production of quality Champagnes.

Zonda Valley (Arg) a major wine-producing area in central Argentina.

Zondernaam Estate (S.Afr) a winery based in the Stellenbosch, Western Cape. Grape varieties include: Cabernet sauvignon. see Tokara.

Zones (Ger) the 'table wine' zones of Germany: Ahrtaler Landwein, Rheinburger Landwein, Altrheingauer Landwein, Nahegauer Landwein, Rheinischer Landwein, Starkenburger Landwein, Pfalzer Landwein, Landwein der Mosel, Landwein der Saar, Unterbadischer Landwein, Südbadischer Landwein, Schwäbischer Landwein, Frankischer Landwein, Regensburger Landwein and Bayerischer Boden see Landwein.

Zonked (Eng) a slang term for highly intoxicated/very drunk.

Zonnebloem (S.Afr) large estates in Simondium, Driesprong, Muratie and Rustenburg in Stellenbosch. Grape varieties: Cabernet sauvignon, Chardonnay, Colombard, Merlot, Pinotage, Sauvignon blanc, Shiraz. Label: Lauréat. Also produces a Premier Grand Cru (Chenin blanc & Colombard blend).

Zonnebloem Wines (S.Afr) varietal wines made by the S.F.W.

Zonneweelde (S.Afr) the export label for a range of wines produced by the Slanghoek Winery, Worcester, Western Cape.

Zonnheimer (S.Afr) a white wine made from Steen, Hanepoot and Clairette blanche grapes.

Zoom (USA) a measure of any spirit, honey dissolved in boiling water and fresh cream. Shaken over ice, strained and served in a wine glass.

Zoopiyi (Cyp) a wine village in the south-east of the island. Produces the grapes used in the making of Commandaria.

Zorgvliet (S.Afr) a winery (70ha) based at Banhoek Valley (near the Helshoogte Mountain) in Stellenbosch. Grape varieties include: Cabernet franc, Cabernet sauvignon, Chardonnay, Merlot, Petit verdot, Sauvignon blanc, Shiraz. Labels: Silver Myn, Spring Grove. (Own Le Pommer Fine Wines). Website: http://www.zorgvlietwines.co.za

Zornberg (Aus) a vineyard site on the banks of the River Danube situated in the Wachau region, Niederösterrich.

Zornheim (Ger) village (Anb): Rheinhessen. (Ber): Nierstein. (Gro): Gutes Domtal. (Vins): Dachgewann, Güldenmorgen, Mönchbäumchen, Pilgerweg, Vogelsang.

Zot Manneke (Hol) a 10% alc by vol. top-fermented, bottle-conditioned special beer brewed by De Gans Bier Brouwerij, Goes.

Zottegemse Grand Cru (Bel) an 8.4% alc by vol. top-fermented, bottled special beer brewed by the Crombé Brasserie, Zottegem.

Zottlöderer (Aus) a winery based in the Kampstal region. (Add): Sauerbrunngasse 49, 3491 Strass im Strassertal. Grape varieties: Chardonnay, Grüner veltliner, Pinot blanc, Riesling, Sauvignon blanc, Welschriesling. Produces a range of dry and sweet wines.

Zotzenberg (Fr) a 34ha A.C. Alsace Grand Cru vineyard at Mittelbergheim, Bas-Rhin.

Zotzenheim (Ger) village (Anb): Rheinhessen. (Ber): Bingen. (Gro): Sankt Rochuskapelle. (Vins): Johannisberg, Klostergarten, Sackträger, Schützenhütte, Zuckerberg.

Zoute [Le] (Cktl) 35mls (1½ fl.ozs) vodka, 10mls (½ fl.oz) Mandarine Napoléon, 75mls (3fl.ozs) grapefruit juice, mix with ice and strain into a 125mls (5fl.oz) glass.

Zrno Kave (Cro) coffee bean.

Źródóana (Pol) a natural spring mineral water. Mineral contents (milligrammes per litre): Sodium 12.8mg/l, Calcium 77.47mg/l, Magnesium 11.81mg/l, Potassium 1.4mg/l, Bicarbonates 308.5mg/l, Chlorides 6.44mg/l, Sulphates 8.64mg/l, Fluoride 0.3mg/l.

Źródło (Pol) spring (water).

Zsiráf (Hun) an export beer marketed in Africa.

Zuani (It) a vineyard (7ha) based in the Friuli-Venezia Giulia. Grape varieties: Chardonnay, Pinot grigio, Sauvignon blanc, Tocai friulano.

Zuber (Pol) a natural spring mineral water. Mineral contents (milligrammes per litre): Sodium 5600.5mg/l, Calcium 184.7mg/l, Magnesium 464.2mg/l, Potassium 200.3mg/l, Bicarbonates 17240.6mg/l, Chlorides 616.5mg/l, Sulphates 54.7mg/l, Iron 3.4mg/l, Iodine 1.4mg/l.

Zuber (Switz) an eau-de-vie distillery based in Arisdorf, Basel.

Zuber Estate (Austr) a winery (established 1971) based in Victoria. Grape varieties: Cabernet sauvignon, Pinot noir, Shiraz, Chardonnay.

Zubrovka (Rus) see Zubrówka.

Zubrówka (Pol) a bison grass vodka, each bottle has a blade of bison grass (**Hierochloe odorata**) in it, is lemon coloured and has a grassy taste. Also spelt Subrouska. Produced by Polmos.

Zubrówka Grass (Hun) **Hierochloe odorata** also known as bison grass. see Zubrówka.

Zuccardi (Arg) a winery based in Mendoza. Grape varieties include: Cabernet sauvignon, Carmenère, Charbono, Malbec. Label: Q.

Zucco (It) a noted dessert wine produced in Sicily.

Zuckerberg (Ger) vineyard (Anb): Rheinhessen. (Ber): Bingen. (Gro): Sankt Rochuskapelle. (Vil): Zotzenheim.

Zuckerhütl (Aus) a wine that has a slight amount of residual sugar left after fermentation.

Zuckerkulor (Ger) on a label denotes that a spirit has been sweetened and coloured with colouring sugar (caramel).

Zucherle (Ger) vineyard (Anb): Württemberg. (Ber): Remstal-Stuttgart. (Gro): Weinsteige. (Vil): Stuttgart (ortsteil Cannstatt).

Zuckerle (Ger) vineyard (Anb): Württemberg. (Ber): Remstal-Stuttgart. (Gro): Weinsteige. (Vil): Stuttgart (ortsteil Hofen).

Zuckerle (Ger) vineyard (Anb): Württemberg. (Ber): Remstal-Stuttgart. (Gro): Weinsteige. (Vil): Stuttgart (ortsteil Mühlhausen).

Zuckerle (Ger) vineyard (Anb): Württemberg. (Ber): Remstal-Stuttgart. (Gro): Weinsteige. (Vil): Stuttgart (ortsteil Münster).

Zuckerung (Ger) the old name for Anreicherung or Verbesserung.

Zuffenhausen (Ger) village (Anb): Württemberg. (Ber): Remstal-Stuttgart. (Gro): Weinsteige. see Stuttgart.

Zügernberg (Ger) vineyard (Anb): Württemberg. (Ber): Remstal-Stuttgart. (Gro): Wartbühl. (Vil): Grossheppach.

Zugober S.A. (Sp) a 22ha winery. (Add): Tejeris, s/n 01306 Labpuebla de Labarca, Alava. Labels include: Belzos.

Zuijlekom (Hol) a small distillery based in Amsterdam.

Zukunft (Ger) lit: 'for the future', a wine that will lay down for keeping.

Zull [Werner] (Aus) a winery based in Schrattenthal, Weinviertel. (Add): 2073 Schrattenthal 9. Grape varieties: Cabernet sauvignon, Grüner veltliner, Merlot, Riesling, Zweigelt.

Zulu 42 (Ger) a bottled vodka and lemon drink 18% alc by vol. Imported into the U.K. by Spirit 2000.

Zumbo Cocktail (Cktl) ½ measure dry gin, ⅙ measure Grand Marnier, ⅙ measure Italian vermouth, ⅙ measure French vermouth, 2 dashes Fernet Branca. Shake over ice and strain into a cocktail glass.

Zummy Cocktail (Cktl) ⅓ measure gin, ½ measure Bénédictine, ¼ measure French vermouth, ¼ measure Italian vermouth, dash Campari. Shake over ice and strain into a cocktail glass.

Zum Schlüssel (Ger) a noted brewery of Bolkerstrasse in Düsseldorf that produces fine altbiers. see Zum Schlüssel Alt and Gatzweiler Alt.

Zum Schlüssel Alt (Ger) an altbier produced by the Zum Schlüssel Brauerei, Düsseldorf, is bitter and slightly acidic.

Zum Uerige (Ger) a brewery in the Bergerstrasse in Düsseldorf. Noted for altbier. see Zum Uerige Altbier.

Zum Uerige Altbier (Ger) a fine, full hop-flavoured bitter altbier brewed by the Zum Uerige Brauerei in Düsseldorf.

Zunsweier (Ger) village (Anb): Baden. (Ber): Ortenau. (Gro): Fürsteneck. (Vin): Kinzingtäler.

Zunzingen (Ger) village (Anb): Baden. (Ber): Markgräflerland. (Gro): Burg Neuenfels. (Vin): Rosenhang.

Zupa (Ser) a wine-producing district based in Central Serbia. Noted for red and rosé wines produced from the Plovdina and Prokupac grapes.

Zupsko Crno (Ser) a red wine produced in the Zupa district of central Serbia from a blend of Plovdina and Prokupac grapes.

Zupsko Ruzica (Ser) a rosé wine produced in the Zupa district of central Serbia from a blend of Plovdina and Prokupac grapes.

Zürich (Switz) a wine-producing region in north-eastern Switzerland. Produces sweet red and dry white wines.

Zurrapa (Port) a rough, poor wine.

Zusammenschluss (Ger) describes an association or co-operative that produces wines from their own members' grapes.

Zutimuscat (Slo) an alternative name for Muscat blanc à petits grains.

Zuur (Hol) acid.

Zuurheid (Hol) acidity (zuur = acid).

Zwack (Aus) a noted liqueur producer. Produces a fine range of liqueurs including Viennese Café, Viennese Pear and Barack Pálinka.

Zwack Unicum (It) an eau-de-vie based, bitter-flavoured liqueur produced from 40 herbs and roots. 40% alc by vol. Produced in Milan and Genoa. An orange and mint-flavoured variety also produced.

Zwala (S.Afr) the label for a red wine (Cabernet sauvignon) produced by the Neil Ellis Meyer-Näkel winery, Stellenbosch, Western Cape.

Zwartbier (Hol) stout (beer).

Zwarte Kip (Hol) lit: 'black hen', a label used by the Heineken-owned Van Offlen Company.

Zweifelberg (Ger) vineyard (Anb): Württemberg. (Ber): Württembergisch Unterland. (Gro): Heuchelberg. (Vil): Brackenheim.

Zweigelt [Professor] (Aus) a famous vine breeder (crosses and clones) of the early twentieth century.

Zweigelt (Aus) see Zweigeltrebe.

Zweigeltrebe (Aus) a red grape variety, a cross between the St. Laurent and Blaufränkischer varieties, can withstand frosts, also known as Zweigelt, Blauer Zweigelt and Rotburger.

Zweikreuzgarten (Aus) a vineyard site on the banks of the River Danube situated in the Wachau region, Niederösterreich.

Zwerithaler (Aus) a vineyard site on the banks of the River Danube situated in the Wachau region, Niederösterreich.

Zwestener Löwensprudel (Ger) a natural spring mineral water. Mineral contents (milligrammes per litre): Sodium 420mg/l, Calcium 180mg/l, Magnesium 83mg/l, Potassium 8mg/l, Bicarbonates 629mg/l, Chlorides 685mg/l, Sulphates 325mg/l, Fluoride 1.5mg/l.

Zwestener Löwensprudel Heilwasser (Ger) a natural mineral water. Mineral contents (milligrammes per litre): Sodium 630mg/l, Calcium 225mg/l, Magnesium 90mg/l, Potassium 8mg/l, Bicarbonates 761mg/l, Chlorides 910mg/l, Sulphates 400mg/l, Fluoride 1.5mg/l.

Zwetgenwasser (Ger) a fruit brandy made from switzen plums 44.5% alc by vol. also known as zwetschenwasser.

Zwetgenwasser (Switz) a fruit brandy made from quetsch plums 45% alc by vol.

Zwetschenwasser (Ger) see Zwetgenwasser.

Zwetschenwasser (Switz) a zwetgenwasser made from mirabelle plums.

Zwickelbier (Ger) the term for an unfiltered beer.

Zwicker (Fr) an Alsatian word which denotes a blend. see Edelzwicker.

Zwingenberg (Ger) village (Anb): Hessische Bergstrasse. (Ber): Starkenburg. (Gro): Rott. (Vins): Steingeröll, Alte Burg.

Zymamonas (Lat) see Rope.

Zymase (Eng) the specific enzyme in yeast cells which causes vinous fermentation and whose catalytic action converts sugars into alcohol and CO_2.

Zymotechnology (Eng) the technology of yeast fermentation.

Zymurgy (USA) the name of an American home-brewers' magazine (art and science of brewing).

Zytnia (Pol) a clear, dry, flavoured vodka 40% alc by vol. produced by Polmos using rye. Has an aromatic, fruit (apple and cherry added to give it a yellowish tint) flavour.

Zywiec Brewery (Pol) a brewery based south of Cracow. Brews Krakus.

Zywiec Zdroj (Pol) a sparkling natural spring mineral water from Wegierska. Mineral contents (milligrammes per litre): Sodium 4.5mg/l, Calcium 55.31mg/l, Magnesium 11.19mg/l, Bicarbonates 192.6mg/l, Chlorides 8.6mg/l.

Zywiec Zdroj 2 (Pol) a lightly sparkling mineral water from Wegierska. Mineral contents (milligrammes per litre): Sodium 2mg/l, Calcium 23.1mg/l, Magnesium 3.3mg/l, Potassium 0.9mg/l, Bicarbonates 76.3mg/l, Chlorides 13.6mg/l, Sulphates 1.8mg/l, Fluoride 0.1mg/l. pH 7.2

Zywiec Zdroj Still (Pol) a still, natural spring mineral water from Wegierska. Mineral contents (milligrammes per litre): Sodium 20mg/l, Calcium 26.89mg/l, Magnesium 7.97mg/l, Bicarbonates 130.7mg/l, Chlorides 6.9mg/l.

Z.Y.X. (Cktl) 1 measure Sambuca, 1 measure orange juice, dash lemon juice, shake over ice, strain into an ice-filled highball glass and top with bitter lemon.